D1597514

THE ULTIMATE SPANISH PHRASE FINDER

FRASES EQUIVALENTES:

inglés-español, español-inglés

WHIT WIRSING

New York Chicago San Francisco Lisbon London Madrid Mexico City
Milan New Delhi San Juan Seoul Singapore Sydney Toronto

The McGraw-Hill Companies

Library of Congress Cataloging-in-Publication Data

Wirsing, Whit.
The ultimate Spanish phrase finder : frases equivalentes : inglés–español, español–inglés / Whit Wirsing.
p. cm.
ISBN 0-07-143303-1

PC4121.W57 2008
468.3'/421—dc22 2008012722

1 2 3 4 5 6 7 8 9 10 11 12 13 14 15 16 17 18 19 20 21 22 QPD/QPD 0 9

ISBN 978-0-07-143303-7
MHID 0-07-143303-1

Interior design: Pamela Juárez

This book is printed on acid-free paper.

Contents

Índice

Acknowledgments

Agradecimientos

Without the help of the many excellent translators who worked with me, I could not have researched and compiled this valuable reference book. I wish to thank Cecilia de la Viesca Santa Fe, M.A., of Madrid, a civil engineer and able linguist who worked with me for five years; Iván Rodríguez Quintana, Ph.D., of Necochea, Argentina, a physicist and lexicographer par excellence, who assisted me for two; and Eduardo F. Elias, Ph.D., Spanish professor at the University of Utah, who possesses a journalist's ear for both Spanish and English. His help in fine-tuning the manuscript in the final weeks before publication was invaluable. Others who translated thousands of phrases include: María Cabezas de Herrera Cuéllar, Rosario López de Tejada, Rocío Gayarre, Javier Sánchez de la Nieta Rico, Carlos Podadera Cobos, Alberto Rayón Fernández, Elizabeth J. Smith, and Diana Grayland, all of Madrid; E. Susana González Palenzuela of Havana; Susana Carvajal Rousseau of Quito; Marta Merino of Lima; Esteban La Paz of Montevideo; Andrés Osorio Alcántara of Caracas; Leticia Klemetz of Las Palmas, Mallorca; Marcela Solís of Valladolid, Spain; Antonia Henrie of Toluca, Mexico; María de la Cruz Fimbres of Hermosillo, Mexico; and Parker Dylan Shaw, Ph.D., of Pittsburgh, Pennsylvania. Together they put approximately three thousand hours into the manuscript.

Many other translators contributed valuable work as their schedules permitted: Gema Ortiz Vicente de Gurrola, Paz Ferrer, David García, Helen Leese, Felipe Queipo, Ana Carballal Broome, Zuleika Dealba Leri, Belén Vasallo, Jane Kalim, Ward Wallace, and Nathaniel Chaney of Madrid; Víctor Viñuela and Jennifer Farrington of Sevilla; Alejandro Romero of Murcia; Amparo Fuentes de Johnson of Arequipa, Peru; Juan Carlos López Carrera of Guatemala City; Mariangélica Samper de Groves of Bogotá; Virginia B. Bayani of Manila; Paz Alonso López of Valladolid; Carlos Alberto Castellanos Coutiño of Tuxtla Gutiérrez, Mexico; Ángela Jo Medina of Austin, Texas; Ariana Mangual of New York City; and Aaron Snyder of San Jose, California.

I wish to thank the professors who have enriched my appreciation of Hispanic literature and culture. At Virginia Polytechnic Institute and State University, I owe a special debt to the late James Lemuel Wells West, under whom I first read *Don Quixote*. At the University of Utah, my knowledge of the literature and culture of Spain has been broadened by Carolyn R. Morrow, chairperson of the department of languages, and Luis Lorenzo Rivero, and my knowledge of Latin American literature and culture has been enriched by Joel C. Hancock, Eduardo F. Elías, Edward H. Mayer, William H. González, Carlos Polit, and Oriana Reyes. At the University of Valladolid, I wish to thank especially María Ángeles Sastre Ruano, grammarian extraordinaire, and Elisa Domínguez de Paz, who deepened my understanding of San Juan de la

Cruz, Quevedo, Góngora, and others; and at Saint Louis University's Madrid campus I wish especially to thank Alicia Ramos, Anne McCabe, Anne Dewey, Verónica Azcue, and Aitor Bikandi for extending my knowledge of Hispanic literature, linguistics, poetry, and culture.

An essential and unique contribution to the *Phrase Finder* was made by my students at the Instituto de Ingeniería del Conocimiento at the Autonomous University of Madrid, including Idoia Alarcón Rodríguez, Mario Álvarez Martín, Ramón Casajuana, Marta Colomino, Julia Díaz García, Fernando Domínguez Celorrio, Nacho García del Amo, José María Gil Sánchez, Diego Gómez Prat, Esther Heredia Doval, Jaime López Jiménez, Roberto Latorre Camino, Alejandro Martínez, Andrés Muñoz Bachiller, Lola Muñoz Cáceres, Carolina Nieva Monserrat, Pedro S. Pascual Broncano, Oscar Pérez Lozano, Trinidad Pertusa Seva, Almudena Rodríguez Cordero, Marisol Romero Mani, Carlos Santa Cruz Fernández, Manuel del Valle Martínez, and Ángel Francisco Zato del Corral. The students contributed countless phrases related to sports, bullfighting, automobiles, music, and culture in general. They critiqued and corrected parts of the text, and their questions about English inspired several aspects of the format, notably the treatment of phrasal verbs.

Friends made a significant contribution, and several deserve special mention. Carlos Centeno Cortés, M.D., of Pamplona, Spain, contributed more than a thousand phrases. Others made hundreds of contributions, among them: René Álvarez Martínez, Susana Marmolejo de Álvarez, and Emmanuel Álvarez Marmolejo of Delicias, Chihuahua, Mexico; Sam Picard and Javier Yustos Ureña of Valladolid; Luisa Barrio Carracedo, Santiago Ezkerra Fernández, Santiago Ezkerra Beltza, Eduardo and Lola Castellanos, Adolfo Llavona, Carlos Vázquez Herrero, and the late Paula Paino, all of Madrid; Betsy Ávila Lúcar of Lima; Manuel Gallardo of Córdoba, Argentina; Joseph T. Snow, Ph.D., of Michigan State University; María Teresa Carrillo de Mixco of Las Cruces, New Mexico; and Glenn McNulty Barefoot of Wilmington, North Carolina. Arturo Alejandro Murrieta Lobato of Xalapa, Veracruz, added Mexican equivalents to many of the Iberian peninsular phrases. Andrea Falcón, visiting assistant professor of philosophy at Virginia Polytechnic Institute and State University, assisted with the translation of philosophical terms. Lanier Frantz of Salem, Virginia, helped translate phrases related to aviation. I wish to thank my computer technicians, E. Susana González Palenzuela, Carlos de la Viesca, and Joshua M. Holt, who shepherded the book's development for more than eleven years. I am indebted to my editor at McGraw-Hill, Christopher Brown, for the excellent format he designed, and to Susan Moore, the editing, design, and production supervisor at McGraw-Hill who oversaw the production of the complete manuscript.

And particularly, I wish to acknowledge my Spanish teacher at Jefferson and Patrick Henry High Schools in Roanoke, Virginia, the late Martha Miriam Bowman, from whom I acquired my foundation in Spanish. She was a perfect teacher.

Preface

The *Ultimate Spanish Phrase Finder* is the book I had looked for in vain all my professional life, so I created it myself! I wanted to look up set phrases quickly, without having to construct them word for word or waste time trying to find them in non-alphabetized listings under the key words. I wanted to see synonymous phrases and expressions from literature and common word pairings, and I wanted the phrases, where needed, to be illustrated with examples clarifying whether to use the verb *ser* or *estar*, the simple past or past continuous tense, and *le*, *lo*, or *la* as object pronouns.

A phrase that can confound an English speaker translating into Spanish is, "That was delicious!" Do you use *ser* or *estar*, the preterite or imperfect? A Hispanic is most likely to say *estaba* followed by *buenísimo, riquísimo, delicioso*, or *sabroso*. I also wanted a dictionary which would highlight differences in English and Spanish phraseology. For instance, "the winds of change" is rendered in Spanish "the winds of *the* change," *los vientos del cambio*. I also wanted to find the range of phrases possible in a situation. "And here I am today" is *y hasta hoy* or *y aquí estoy yo*. By looking up either, you will find the other.

To illustrate the usefulness of the *Phrase Finder*, the following are a few examples of phrases that are difficult to construct using a conventional dictionary: "for the sole purpose of" *con el único propósito de*, "take as much time as you need" *tómate todo el tiempo que necesites*, "she told me what to do" *ella me dijo qué hacer* or *ella me dijo lo que (yo) tenía que hacer*, "she's casting sidelong glances at me" or "she keeps looking at me out of the corner of her eye" *me está echando miradas de reojo*, "may I have a drink of water?" *¿me das agua?* or *¿me regalas agua?*, "to walk back" (return on foot) *regresar(se) caminando* or, in Spain, *volver(se) andando*, "I'll walk back home" *me regreso a casa caminando* or *me vuelvo a casa andando*. The Mexican students ask the North American teacher where he is from. Innocently he replies, "I have two homes. I'm from California but I've lived for many years in New York." The class chuckles because the students have interpreted "I have two homes" as *tengo dos casas*, which implies that the teacher has both a wife and a mistress. A phrase dictionary is the ideal vehicle for clarifying these ambiguities.

I also wanted a dictionary that permitted me to subvocalize a phrase (hear it in the mind) because I believe that our mental dictionaries are "alphabetized" by sound and that, as a result, we spontaneously subvocalize phrases when acquiring them. Hence I avoided abbreviations. And I wanted a *dictionary*, not a smattering of idioms.

The concept of *The Ultimate Spanish Phrase Finder* first came to me many years ago when I was taking third-year Spanish at Patrick Henry High School in Roanoke, Virginia, studying under an excellent teacher, Martha Miriam Bowman. We read, among other things, *José* by Armando Palacio Valdés. I found that my dictionaries did not clarify many of the difficult phrases in this work. Word dictionaries offer almost no phrase coverage for the works of Jorge Luis Borges, Horacio Quiroga, Benito Pérez Galdós, and scores of other important authors that college students must read. I wanted the *Phrase Finder* to be a supporting text for the reading of literature. Some word dictionaries have complex systems of notations such as asterisks and clusters of asterisks, daggers, and other symbols to indicate that a phrase might be used by a family at the dinner table but not in more formal speech, that the word is mildly or grossly off-color, and so on. The *Phrase Finder* avoids excessive notation because if the phrases are parallel, most notations are superfluous. "To have a growth spurt" is *crecer rápidamente* or *aumentar de estatura*, but "to shoot up like a weed" is *dar un estirón* or, in Spain, *pegar un estirón*. A student hearing *si en el caso de que* will connect it to "(if) in the event that" but might miss another important equivalence, "whether, if," as in "The interviewer asked the applicant whether, if they offered her the job, she would be willing to relocate."

Linguists distinguish between descriptive and prescriptive grammar. Descriptive grammar accepts as correct any understandable utterance, including words like "gotta," "wanna," and "ain't." In descriptive grammar, "loan" can be a noun or a verb. To a prescriptive grammarian, however, "would you loan me a dollar?" is bad grammar. "Would you *lend* me a dollar?" is the correct form. Although I side with the descriptive grammarians in principle, the *Phrase Finder* is prescriptive. Many people nowadays say, "If I would have had time, I would have gone." This sentence loses the important distinction between the conditional and the subjunctive. The more logical expression is, "if I had had time, I would have gone" or even "had I had time, I would have gone." Spanish speakers make a similar mistake when they say, *si lo probabas te gustaría* instead of the more logical *si lo probaras te gustaría*. I believe that Hispanic universities want their English professors to teach the best English usage and stylistics, and universities in English-speaking countries want their Spanish professors to do likewise. The *Phrase Finder* provides the best usage and stylistics in both languages.

Prólogo

The Ultimate Spanish Phrase Finder (Frases Equivalentes) es el libro que había buscado en vano en mi vida profesional, así que decidí escribirlo. Era mi intención buscar frases ya configuradas, sin tener que construirlas palabra por palabra o perder tiempo intentando encontrarlas en listas no alfabetizadas bajo palabras claves. Yo quería ver las frases sinónimas, expresiones de la literatura y palabras que comúnmente van juntas. Quería que las frases donde fuera necesario aparecieran con ejemplos aclarando si requerían el verbo *ser* o *estar*, el tiempo pretérito o el imperfecto, y *le*, *lo* o *la* como pronombres objetivos.

Una frase que puede confundir a un hispanohablante al comunicarse en inglés, es "si alguna vez encuentras un tapete de Temoaya, me lo compras" *if you ever find a Temoya rug, buy it for me* o aun mejor *if you should come across a Temoaya rug, buy it for me* o *if you happen to see a Temoaya rug, buy it for me*. Yo quería un diccionario que resaltara o marcara las diferencias entre la fraseología de cada idioma. Por ejemplo "los vientos del cambio" es *the winds of change* en inglés, frase en la cual no se usa el artículo determinado *the* antes de *change*. Yo quería encontrar una gama de frases posibles. Por ejemplo, "y hasta hoy" o "y aquí estoy yo," debería buscarse bajo la palabra clave "hoy," pero no se encuentra en la mayoría de los diccionarios. "Y hasta hoy" o "y aquí estoy yo" es *and here I am today*.

Para ilustrar la utilidad del *Phrase Finder*, he aquí algunos ejemplos de frases que son difíciles de construir usando un diccionario convencional: "con el único propósito de" es *for the sole purpose of*. "Tómate todo el tiempo que necesites" es *take all the time you need*, pero igualmente es *take as much time as you need*. "Ella me dijo lo que (yo) tenía que hacer" es *she told me what (I had) to do*. "Me está echando miradas de reojo" es *she's casting sidelong glances at me* o *she keeps looking at me out of the corner of her eye*. "¿Me das agua?" o "¿me regalas agua?" es *may I have a drink of water?* o *could I have a drink of water?* "Regresar(se) caminando" o en España "volver(se) andando" es *to walk back*. "Me regreso a casa caminando" es *I'll walk back home*. Los estudiantes mexicanos preguntan al professor norteamericano de dónde es. Inocentemente responde, *I have two homes. I'm from California but I've lived for many years in New York*. La clase se ríe entre dientes porque los estudiantes han interpretado *I have two homes* como "tengo dos casas," lo cual implica que tiene doble vida marital. Un diccionario de frases es el vehículo para aclarar estas ambigüedades.

También yo quería un diccionario que me permitiera vocalizar una frase (oírla en la mente) porque creo que nuestros diccionarios mentales están "alfabetizados" por sonido y que, en consecuencia, espontáneamente vocalizamos las frases al incorporarlas en nuestro léxico. Por eso, evité abreviaturas. Deseaba un diccionario completo, no una selección limitada de expresiones.

El concepto del *Phrase Finder* se me ocurrió cuando cursaba el tercer año de español en la preparatoria Patrick Henry en

Roanoke, Virginia, con una excelente profesora, Martha Miriam Bowman. Leímos entre otras cosas *José* de Armando Palacio Valdés y descubrí que mis diccionarios no aclaraban muchos términos difíciles contenidos en esta obra. Los diccionarios de palabras no ofrecen por ejemplo suficiente información en la comprensión de autores como Jorge Luis Borges, Horacio Quiroga, Benito Pérez Galdós y docenas de otros autores importantes que los estudiantes universitarios tienen que leer. Quería que el *Phrase Finder* fuera un texto que ayudara en el estudio de la literatura hispana. Algunos diccionarios tienen sistemas complejos de anotaciones tales como asteriscos, cruces y otros símbolos para indicar que una frase podría usarse en una situación casual pero no se aplica en una situación donde se usa lenguaje formal, que una palabra es un poco o muy subida de tono, y así sucesivamente. El *Phrase Finder* evita la anotación excesiva porque si las frases son paralelas, la mayoría de las anotaciones son superfluas. "Crecer rápidamente" o "aumentar de estatura" es *to have a growth spurt.* "Dar un estirón" es *to shoot up like a weed.* "Si en el caso de que" no es sólo *(if) in the event that* sino también *whether, if* como en "El entrevistador le preguntó a la candidata si en el caso de que le ofrecieran el trabajo, estaría dispuesta a cambiar de localidad" *The interviewer asked the applicant whether, if they offered her the job, she would be willing to relocate.*

Los lingüistas distinguen entre la gramática descriptiva y la normativa. La gramática descriptiva acepta como correcta cualquier unidad de habla comprensible como *las gentes* y *nadien.* Para el gramático normativo, *las gentes* y *nadien* son incorrectas. Aunque en teoría me pongo de parte de los gramáticos descriptivos, el *Phrase Finder* es normativo. Algunas personas hoy en día dicen "si lo probabas te gustaría" en vez del más lógico "si lo probaras te gustaría" o "si lo pruebas te va a gustar" *if you tried it, you'd like it.* Los anglohablantes cometen un error parecido cuando dicen *if I would have had time, I would have gone* en vez de la expresión más lógica *if I had had time, I would have gone* o *had I had time, I would have gone.* Creo que las universidades hispanas quieren que los profesores de filología inglesa enseñen lo mejor del uso y del estilo, y las universidades en los países de habla inglesa quieren que sus catedráticos de filología hispana hagan lo mismo. El *Phrase Finder* es una herramienta de trabajo que provee la oportunidad de aplicar el mejor uso y estilo de la palabra en ambos idiomas.

Commonly used field labels and abbreviations

Indicaciones semánticas y estilísticas y abreviaturas más usados

arcaico	archaic
Arg.	Argentina
Chi.	Chile
coloquial	coll., colloquial
culto	educated
despectivo	disparaging
deportes	sport
él	*he*
ella	*she*
ello	*it*
Esp., España	Sp., Spain
figurativo	figurative
futuro	future
informática	computers
jerga	jargon
juvenil	juvenile
L.am., Latinoamérica	L. Am., Latin America
leísmo	use of *le*
literal	literal
literario	literary
Méx., México	Mex., Mexico
militar	military
pasado	past
película	movie, film
plural	plural
presente	present
singular	singular
Sudamérica	S. Am.
tiempo pasado	past time
titular	headline
tú	(*you* informal singular)
usted	(*you* formal singular)
ustedes	(*you* plural)
vosotros	(*you* plural, esp. Spain)

SPANISH – ENGLISH

ESPAÑOL – INGLÉS

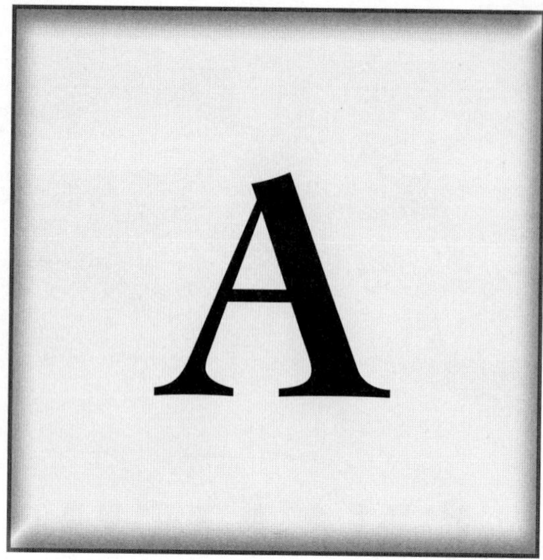

@ ■ arroba *(informática)* at ■ at sign ■ @

a altas horas de la noche ■ a altas horas de la madrugada in the wee hours of the night ■ at all hours (of the night)

estar **a años luz** ■ quedar a años luz to be light-years away ■ to be light-years distant ➤ La Estrella Polar está aproximadamente a 430 años luz, con un error posible de más o menos cien años luz. ■ La Estrella Polar queda a 430 años luz, con un error posible de más o menos cien años luz. The Pole Star is 430 light years away, plus or minus a hundred light years. ■ The Pole Star is 430 light years distant, plus or minus a hundred light years.

estar **a años luz de lo que...** to be light-years ahead of where... ➤ La tecnología médica está a años luz de lo que estaba una generación atrás. Medical technology is light-years ahead of where it was a generation ago.

estar **a años luz en un asunto** ■ estar separados años luz ■ ser diametralmente opuesto en un asunto to be light-years apart on an issue ■ to be diametrically opposed on an issue

a babor: virar ~ to turn to port

¡**a bailar!** everyone on the dance floor!

a barullo *(Esp.)* ■ en gran cantidad lots of ■ galore

a base de **1.** por medio de ■ gracias a by ■ by means of **2.** basado en -based ➤ A base de mucho trabajo By hard work ■ By means of hard work ➤ Un régimen a base de proteínas A protein-based diet ■ A protein diet

a base de: estar hecho ~ to have as its essential ingredient ➤ Este plato está hecho a base de chocolate. This is a chocolate dish. ■ The essential ingredient in this dish is chocolate.

a base de bien *(Esp.)* ■ en abundancia ■ desaforadamente in abundance

a base de bien: comer ~ *(Esp.)* to eat very well ■ to have plenty to eat ■ *(literario)* to have a sumptuous repast

a base de bien: hacer el amor ~ *(Esp.)* to have an intense session of lovemaking ■ to really go at it

a base de bien: pillar a alguien ~ to get someone good ➤ Esa maldita ave nos pilló a base de bien. That damned bird got us good.

a base de bien: regañarle ~ *(Esp.)* to chew someone out ■ to give someone a dressing down ■ to really let someone have it ➤ Su madre le regañó a base de bien. His mother really let him have it.

ser **a beneficio de** to be for the benefit of ■ to go for benefits ➤ El concierto es a beneficio de los niños. The concert is for the benefit of children. ■ The concert's proceeds go for children's benefits.

estar **a bien con alguien** ■ estar a buenas con alguien to be on good terms with someone ■ to get along well with someone ➤ Estoy a bien con todos. I'm on good terms with everyone. ■ I get along with everyone.

a bien: tenga usted ~ *(Esp., muy formal)* ■ sería tan amable de ■ tendría la bondad de would you be so kind as ➤ Tenga usted a bien decirme... Would you be so kind as to tell me...

a boca by word of mouth ■ by mouth ■ verbally

estar **a boca de cañón** ■ estar a punto ■ estar a tiro to be close to ■ to be within reach of ➤ El Real Madrid está a boca de cañon de conseguir el título de la liga. ■ El Real Madrid está a punto de conseguir el título de la liga. ■ El Real Madrid está a tiro de conseguir el título de la liga. Real Madrid is within reach of getting the league title. ■ Real Madrid is close to getting the league title.

a boca de jarro: decirle algo a alguien ~ *(especialmente malas noticias)* to tell someone something straight out ■ to tell someone something flat out

a bocajarro: decírselo ~ ■ soltárselo a bocajarro ■ decírselo a la cara ■ decírselo de frente to tell someone flat out ■ to tell someone straight out ■ to tell someone flatly ➤ Se lo dijo a bocajarro. ■ Se lo soltó a bocajarro. He told him flat out. ■ He told him straight out.

a bocajarro: disparar a alguien ~ ■ pegar un tiro a alguien a bocajarro to shoot someone at pointblank range

a bocajarro: venir ~ ■ venir embolado to come barreling down ➤ Los coches vienen a bocajarro por Avda. Don Sancho. ■ Los coches vienen embolados por Avda. Don Sancho. The cars really come barreling down Don Sancho Ave.

a boleo ■ al tanteo ■ al tuntún ■ aleatoriamente at random ■ out of the blue ■ *(jerga)* sort of half-assed ➤ Adiviné las respuestas del examen a boleo. ■ Adiviné las respuestas del examen al tanteo. I guessed at the answers on the test. ■ *(jerga)* I did the test sort of half-assed.

a boleo: eligir a alguien o algo ~ ■ eligir a alguien o algo al azar to pick someone or something out of the blue ■ to pick someone or something at random

a bombo y platillo: hacer algo ~ to do something with great fanfare ■ to do something with a lot of hype

a borbotones: salir ~ *(líquido)* ■ salir a chorros to gush out

a borbotones: sangrar ~ to spurt blood ■ to bleed spurts of blood ■ to bleed in spurts of blood ■ to bleed profusely ➤ El animal sangraba a borbotones. The animal was spurting blood. ■ The animal was bleeding spurts of blood. ■ The animal was bleeding profusely.

estar **a bordo** ■ estar embarcado to be on board

a bordo: ir ~ to board ■ to go aboard ■ to go on board ■ to get on (board) ➤ Los pasajeros van a bordo del avión. The passengers are boarding the plane.

a bote pronto: calcular ~ ■ calcular mentalmente to calculate off the top of one's head

a bote pronto: decidir ~ ■ decidir de pronto to decide on the spur of the moment

a bote pronto: decir ~ ■ decir de pronto ■ decir de repente to say off the top of one's head

a bote pronto: recordar algo ~ ■ acordarse a bote pronto de algo ■ acordarse de pronto algo ■ recordarse de pronto algo to remember something off the top of one's head

a brazo partido: el combate ~ hand-to-hand combat

a brazo partido: luchar ~ **1.** luchar cuerpo a cuerpo ■ combatir cuerpo a cuerpo to engage in hand-to-hand combat **2.** luchar con uñas y dientes to fight tooth and nail **3.** luchar mucho (por lograr algo) to struggle hard to achieve something **4.** defender a alguien ■ sacar la cara por alguien to stick up for somebody

a brazo partido: trabajar ~ ■ deslomarse ■ trabajar como un burro ■ romperse la espalda trabajando to break one's back working ■ to do back-breaking work ■ to work one's fingers to the bone ■ *(coloquial)* to work one's butt off ■ to bust one's butt

a buen entendedor pocas palabras a word to the wise is sufficient

a buen hambre no hay mal pan ■ a falta de pan, tortillas ■ a buen hambre no hay pan duro ■ a falta de pan buenas son tortas hunger is the best sauce

a buen paso: avanzar ~ to advance at a good pace ■ to advance apace ■ to proceed at a good pace ■ to proceed apace ➤ La construcción está avanzando a buen paso. The construction is proceeding at a good pace. ■ The contruction is proceeding apace.

a buen recaudo: guardar ~ ■ guardar bajo llave ■ guardar en un lugar seguro to keep under lock and key ■ to keep in a safe place ➤ Guárdarlo a buen recaudo. Keep it under lock and key. ▪ Keep it in a safe place.

a buen recaudo: tener algo ~ 1. *(literal)* to have something in a safe place ▪ to have something in a secure place **2.** *(figurative)* keep something to oneself ▪ to keep one's counsel

a buen seguro ▪ **1.** con certeza for sure **2.** bajo seguro in a safe place ➤ A buen seguro María Ángeles conoce unos platos auténticos madrileños. For sure María Angeles will know some authentic Madrid dishes. ➤ Pondremos las joyas a buen seguro. Let's keep the jewelry under lock and key. ▪ Let's keep the jewelry in a safe place.

estar **a buenas con alguien** ▪ estar a bien con alguien to be on good terms with someone ▪ to get along well with someone

¡a buenas horas, mangas verdes! ▪ ¡a buena hora (te acomides)! ▪ ¡a buenas horas! ▪ ¡a burro muerto, la cebada al rabo! **1.** *(cuando se llega demasiado tarde) now* you show up! **2.** *(cuando se dice algo demasiado tarde) now* you tell me!

a bulto: echarlo ~ to make a rough guess

a burro muerto, cebada al rabo ▪ a buenas horas, mangas verdes **1.** *(cuando se llega demasiado tarde) now* you show up! ▪ **2.** *(cuando se dice algo demasiado tarde) now* you tell me! ▪ it's too late now! ▪ your timing's not too great!

a caballo: ir ~ to go on horseback

a caballo: ir a montar ~ ▪ ir a andar a caballo to go horseback riding

a caballo: montar ~ ▪ andar a caballo to ride horseback ▪ to horseback ride

estar **a caballo de alguien** to be close behind someone ▪ to be right behind someone ▪ to be on someone's heels ▪ to be breathing down someone's neck

a caballo entre dos lugares: vivir ~ *(Esp.)* ▪ vivir un tiempo un sitio y otro tiempo en otro to live part of the time in one place and part in another

a caballo regalado no se le mira el colmillo ▪ a caballo regalado no le mires el dentado ▪ a caballo regalado no le mires el diente don't look a gift horse in the mouth

a cachondeo: decir algo ▪ decir algo en broma to say something as a joke ▪ to say something jokingly ▪ to say something in jest

a cada cerdo le llega su San Martín ▪ a cada marrano le llega su Noche Buena ▪ a cada quien le llega su hora *(a él)* his time is coming! ▪ his turn is coming! ▪ *(a ti)* your time is coming! ▪ your turn is coming!

a cada cierta distancia por el camino at regular intervals along the way

a cada cual lo suyo ▪ a cada quien lo suyo to each his own

a cada cual según su capacidad ▪ cada persona depende de su capacidad each according to his capacity

a cada día le corresponde... each day brings... ➤ A cada día le corresponde un reto nuevo. ▪ Cada día ofrece un nuevo reto. Each day brings a new challenge.

a cada hora ▪ a cada instante ▪ a cada momento ▪ a cada paso all the time ▪ continuously ▪ constantly ➤ Me están llamando a cada hora. I get calls all the time. ▪ I get calls constantly. ▪ I get calls continuously.

a cada instante ▪ a cada momento ▪ a cada hora ▪ a cada paso all the time ▪ continuously ▪ constantly

a cada marrano le llega su Noche Buena ▪ a cada cerdo le llega su San Martín *(a él)* his time is coming! ▪ his turn is coming! ▪ *(a ti)* your time is coming! ▪ your turn is coming!

a cada momento ▪ continuamente ▪ siempre all the time ▪ every instant ▪ continuously

a cada parte hay tres leguas de mal camino nothing is perfect

a cada paso 1. a cada instante at each step ▪ at every step **2.** a cada rato ▪ todo el tiempo all the time ▪ continuously ▪ constantly ➤ El anciano se paraba a cada paso para recuperar el aliento. The old man would stop at each step to catch his breath.

a cada quien lo suyo ▪ a cada cual lo suyo to each his own

a cada rato every so often

a cada uno le duele lo suyo everyone has his troubles ▪ everyone has his problems

a cada uno lo suyo ▪ al César lo que es del César ▪ a cada cual lo suyo ▪ cada cual a su aire ▪ cada uno a su antojo to each his own

a cada *x* kilómetros por el camino (at) each *x* kilometers along the way

a cal y canto: cerrar algo ~ to close something tight(ly) ▪ to close something securely ▪ to lock something (up)

a cal y canto: guardar algo ~ ▪ guardar algo a piedra y lodo ▪ guardar algo bajo llave to keep something under lock and key

a cala y a cata: vender un melón ~ to sell a melon after giving the customer the right to sample it first

(a) cámara lenta ▪ en cámara lenta in slow motion

a cambio de algo ▪ trueque de algo ▪ en lugar in exchange for something

a cántaros: llover ~ ▪ caer chuzos de punta to rain cats and dogs ▪ to rain in buckets ▪ to rain in sheets ➤ Está lloviendo a cántaros. ▪ Están cayendo chuzos de punta. It's raining cats and dogs. ▪ It's raining in buckets. ▪ It's raining in sheets.

a capa y espada: defender a alguien ~ to defend someone with all one's might ▪ to defend oneself with everything one has got ▪ to defend someone tooth and nail ▪ to defend someone to the death

a capa y espada: defenderse ~ to defend oneself with all one's might ▪ to defend oneself with everything one has got

a cara descubierta ▪ sin tapujos ▪ sin esconder nada completely honestly ▪ without holding anything back

a cara descubierta: confesarse ~ to confess without holding anything back

a cara descubierta: hablar ~ ▪ hablar sin tapujos ▪ hablar sin esconder nada ▪ hablar sin careta to speak completely honestly

(a) cara o cruz: jugar algo ~ to call heads or tails ▪ to flip (a coin) over ➤ Jugamos cara o cruz para decidir quién iba primero. We flipped to see who would go first. ▪ We flipped over who'd go first. ➤ Jugaremos cara o cruz para decidir quién irá primero. We'll flip to see who goes first. ▪ We'll flip to see who'll go first. ▪ We'll flip over who'll go first.

estar **a cargo (de)** to be in charge (of) ➤ Estoy a cargo de la cocina. I'm in charge of the kitchen.

a carta cabal: hacer algo ~ ▪ realizar algo a carta cabal to accomplish something fully and well ▪ to accomplish something with flying colors ➤ Terminó sus estudios a carta cabal. He finished with flying colors.

a casa: ir ~ to go home

a casa de alguien: ir ~ to go to someone's house

a causa de *(más común)* por causa de ▪ por motivo de ▪ por razón de because of

a centenares *(más común)* por centenares ▪ a cientos ▪ a centenadas by the hundreds ➤ Las hormigas vinieron a centenares. The ants came by the hundreds.

a cepillo: cortarle el pelo a alguien ~ to give someone a crew cut ▪ to give someone a military haircut

a cepillo: cortarse el pelo ~ to get a crew cut ▪ to get a military haircut

estar **a cero** *(Esp.)* ▪ estar en cero **1.** *(déposito)* to be on empty ▪ to be empty **2.** *(cuenta)* to have no money in the account ▪ to have nothing in the account

a chorros in spurts ▪ in jets ▪ in abundance

a chorros: correrse ~ *(subido de tono)* to come in spurts ▪ to come hard ▪ to ejaculate

a chorros: llover ~ ▪ llover a cántaros to rain in buckets ▪ to rain in sheets

a chorros: salir ~ ▪ salir a borbotones to gush out

a chorros: sangrar ~ to bleed profusely ▪ *(coloquial)* to bleed all over the place ➤ El animal sangraba a chorros. The animal was bleeding profusely.

a ciegas: hacer algo ~ ▪ hacer algo ciegamente ▪ hacer algo a tientas to do something blindly ▪ to feel one's way (along)

a cielo descubierto ▪ al descubierto **1.** (out) in the open ▪ under the open sky **2.** in open country ▪ away from civilization

a cien: ponerle ~ 1. to get on someone's nerves ▪ *(con humor, en Mark Twain)* to give someone the fantods **2.** turn someone on (sexually) ➤ Me pone a cien. He gets on my nerves. ▪ He gives me the fantods. ➤ (Él) le pone a cien (a ella). He turns her on. ➤ (Ella) le pone a cien (a él). She turns him on.

a cien leguas ▪ a la legua a mile away ▪ a mile off ➤ Se le podía oler la mentira a cien leguas. You could smell his lie a mile away. ▪ You could smell his lie a mile off.

a ciencia cierta: saber ~ to know for certain ▪ to know for sure

a cientos ▪ a centenares by the hundreds ➤ Cuando Lindbergh aterrizó en Paris, la gente corría hacia su avioneta a cientos. ▪ Cuando Lindbergh aterrizó en Paris, la gente corría hacia su avioneta a centenares. When Lindbergh landed in Paris, people ran toward his plane by the hundreds.

a cobrar: la cantidad ~ amount owed ▪ amount (still) to be collected from the debtor

a cobro revertido: llamar a alguien ~ ▪ llamar a alguien por cobrar to call someone collect

estar **a cojón de mico** to be very expensive ▪ to cost a pretty penny

¡**a comer!** dinner time! ▪ dinner's ready! ▪ come to dinner!

a comienzos de ▪ a principios de at the beginning of ▪ in early ➤ Este año voy a terminar mis compras navideñas a comienzos de diciembre. ▪ Este año voy a terminar mis compras navideñas a principios de diciembre. This year, I'm going to finish my Christmas shopping in early December.

a comisión: trabajar ~ *(Esp.)* ▪ trabajar por comisión to work on commission ▪ to work for a commission

¿**a cómo está?** *(Esp., coloquial)* ▪ ¿a qué precio está? ▪ ¿qué vale? ▪ ¿cuánto cuesta? how much is it? ➤ ¿A cómo están las lechugas? How much are the heads of lettuce?

¿**a cómo lo compraste?** *(Esp.)* ▪ ¿en cuánto lo compraste? how much did you pay for it?

a conciencia: hacer algo ~ ▪ hacer algo con rigor ▪ hacer algo en profundidad to do something conscientiously ▪ to do something thoroughly ▪ to do something in depth

a conciencia: limpiar algo ~ to clean something thoroughly ▪ to give something a thorough cleaning

a conciencia: tomar una decisión ~ to make a decision carefully ▪ to make a decision with careful deliberation

a condición de que ▪ con la condición de que on the condition that

a consecuencia de ▪ como consecuencia de ▪ en consecuencia de ▪ por consecuencia de ▪ como fruto de ▪ por as a consequence of ▪ as a result of ▪ because of

a continuación (and) next ▪ (and) now ➤ *(guía de museo)* A continuación vamos a la pieza inmediata. And now we will go to the adjoining room.

a continuación a next to ▪ alongside ➤ El parque está a continuación a la biblioteca. The park is (right) next to the library. ➤ Condujeron a continuación a él. They drove up next to him. ▪ They drove up alongside him.

a continuación de immediately after ▪ immediately following ➤ A continuación de la charla se ofrecerá un aperitivo. Immediately after the talk, refreshments will be served ▪ Immediately following the talk, refreshments will be served.

a contracorriente: ir ~ ▪ ir contra la corriente ▪ ir contra corriente to go against the grain ▪ to go against the tide ▪ to be out of step

a contramano: ir ~ *(Arg.)* ▪ ir a contrasentido to go the wrong way (in traffic) ➤ Vas a contramano por esta calle. You're going the wrong way on this street.

a contrapelo: ir ~ to go against the grain

a contrasentido: ir ~ *(Arg.)* ▪ ir a contramano to go the wrong way (in traffic)

a contratiempo: tocar música ~ to play music with a syncopated beat ▪ to play counterpoint ▪ to play music offbeat

a corazón abierto: cirugía ~ open heart surgery

a cordel in a straight line ▪ straight

a coro ▪ al unisono in unison

a coro: contestar ~ ▪ contestar al unísono to answer in unison ➤ Contestaron a coro. They answered in unison.

a corto plazo over the short term ▪ in the short term

a corto plazo: objetivo ~ short-term objective ▪ short-term goal

a cosa hecha nada se puede hacer ▪ lo hecho hecho está what's done is done ▪ there's nothing you can do about it

a costa ajena: vivir ~ *(se refiere sólo a personas)* ▪ vivir a costa de otros to live off other people ▪ to live at the expense of others ▪ to live at others' expense ➤ El gorrón vive a costa ajena. Sponges live off other people. ▪ Leeches live off other people.

a costa de : vivir ~ *(se refiere a cosas o personas)* to live at the expense of ▪ to live off (of) ➤ Los hijos de treinta años siguen viviendo a costa de sus padres. Their children, now in their thirties, still live off their parents. ➤ El Manolo vive a costa de churros todos los días. Manolo lives off churros day in and day out.

ser **a costa mía** ▪ ser a mi costa to be at my expense ➤ El chiste fue a costa mía. ▪ El chiste fue a mi costa. The joke was at my expense.

a costa suya ▪ a su costa at one's expense ➤ Se rieron a mi costa. They laughed at my expense.

a crédito: comprar algo ~ to buy something on credit

a crédito: pagar una deuda ~ ▪ pagar una deuda a plazos to pay a debt in installments

ser **a cuál más...** to be all equally...

ser **a cuál más rápido que alguien en algo** to be faster than someone at something ▪ to be faster at something than someone else

a cualquier precio at any price

¡**a cualquiera que se le diga!** ▪ ¡a cualquiera que se lo cuente! no one will (ever) believe me

¡**a cualquiera que se lo cuente!** ▪ ¡a cualquiera que se le diga! no one will (ever) believe me

¿**a cuántas horas estamos de diferencia?** ▪ ¿cuántas horas nos apartan? how many hours' difference are there between here and there? ▪ how many hours apart are we?

¿**a cuánto?** ▪ ¿a qué precio? how much?

¿**a cuánto asciende?** ▪ ¿a cuánto está? how much does it come to? ▪ what does it come to? ▪ what does it come out to? ▪ what's the total?

¿**a cuánto está...?** ▪ ¿a cómo está? how much is...?

¿**a cuánto estamos?** ▪ ¿a qué día estamos hoy? ▪ ¿qué día es hoy, me refiero al número de día? ▪ ¿qué fecha es hoy? what is today's date? ▪ what's today's date? ▪ what's the date today? ▪ what is the date of today?

¿**a cuánto están...?** how much are...?

estar **a cuatro pasos** ▪ estar muy cerca to be close by ▪ to be very close to (a place)

a cubierto: ponerse ~ to take cover ▪ to take shelter

estar **a cubierto de** to be protected from ▪ to be shielded from

a cuenta on the bill ▪ on one's charge account ▪ on one's account

a cuenta: te lo dejo ~ *(en comercios pequeños entre conocidos)* I'll owe you ▪ I'll pay you back

ser **a cuenta de la casa** ▪ correr a cuenta de la casa to be on the house ➤ Las bebidas son a cuenta de la casa. ▪ La bebidas corren a cuenta de la casa. Drinks are on the house.

a cuenta de que ▪ a propósito de que on account of ▪ because

a cuento: no venir ~ ▪ no venir al tema ▪ ser irrelevante to be irrelevant

a cuento: venir ~ ▪ venir al tema ▪ ser relevante to be relevant

a cuerpo de rey: vivir ~ ▪ vivir como un rajá to live like a king

estar **a cuerpo gentil** to be without a coat

a cuerpo gentil: salir ~ to go out without a coat

a cuestas on one's back ➤ Con la mochila a cuestas, emprendí la caminata de dos horas a la cima. With my knapsack on my back, I set off on the two-hour hike to the summit.

a cuestas: cargar con alguien ~ 1. *(literal)* to carry someone on one's back **2.** *(figurativo)* to put up with someone ➤ Tengo que cargar con mi suegra a cuestas este verano. I have to put up with my mother-in-law this summer.

¡**a cumplir!** keep your promise! ▪ don't let me down! ▪ get to it! ▪ chop, chop!

¿**"A" de Alberto?** ▪ ¿"A" como en Alberto? ▪ ¿"A" igual que en Alberto? "A" as in Albert?

estar **a débito** ▪ estar en números rojos to be in the red

a decir verdad to tell you the truth

a dedo: ir a algun lugar ~ to hitch a ride to a place ▪ to hitchhike to a place ▪ to thumb one's way to a place

estar **a dedos de** ▪ estar a pique de to be at the point of

a derechas: hacer algo ~ to do something correctly ■ to do something right ■ to do something the right way

a deshora(s) ■ fuera de tiempo ■ a destiempo **1.** at a bad time ■ at the wrong time **2.** at off times ➤ Los diabéticos tienen que comer a deshora. Diabetics have to eat at off times.

a destajo: trabajar ~ ■ trabajar sin descansar ■ trabajar sin parar to work without a break ■ to work without stopping ➤ *(noticia)* La lluvia hizo trabajar a los bomberos a destajo. The rain forced the firemen to work without a break. ■ The rain forced the firemen to work without stopping.

a destiempo: cantar ~ to sing off beat ■ to be out of sync with the music

a destiempo: entrar ~ to enter at the wrong time ■ to enter off cue

a destiempo: hablar ~ to speak out of turn

a destiempo: marchar ~ to march out of step

a destiempo: opinar ~ to give one's opinion at the wrong moment

a destiempo: viajar ~ to travel at the wrong the time ■ to travel at a bad time

a día de hoy as of today

a diario ■ todos los días ■ diariamente ■ por día ■ cada día a day ■ daily ■ every day ➤ Tomar aspirina a diario tiene muchos beneficios para la salud. Taking an aspirin a day has many health benefits.

a días 1. de cuando en cuando ■ de vez en cuando ■ algunas veces at times ■ from time to time **2.** así así up and down ➤ ¿Cómo estás?-A días How are you?-It's up and down. ■ How are you?-Some days are better than others.

a diestra y siniestra *(L.am.)* ■ sin ton ni son left and right ■ all over the place ■ willy-nilly ➤ Dio tortas a diestra y siniestra. He hit all over the place. ➤ Las bombas caían a diestra y siniestra. The bombs were falling all over the place. ■ The bombs were falling left and right.

a diestro y siniestro *(Esp.)* ■ sin ton ni son left and right ■ all over the place ➤ Dio tortas a diestro y siniestro. He hit all over the place. ➤ Las bombas caían a diestra y siniestra. The bombs were falling all over the place. ■ The bombs were falling left and right.

estar **a dieta** ■ estar a régimen to be on a diet

a diferencia de ■ en contraposición a ■ frente a unlike ■ as opposed to ■ in contrast to ➤ A diferencia de la Inquisición en Italia, la Inquisición española fue dirigida a los judíos. Unlike the Inquisition in Italy, the Spanish Inquisition was directed at the Jews. ➤ *(noticia)* Las elecciones allí han sido limpias y transparentes a diferencia de la mayoría de los países de la región. The elections there were clean and transparent, unlike (in) the majority of countries in the region. ➤ Agua dulce a diferencia de agua salada ■ Agua dulce frente al agua salada Fresh water as opposed to salt water ➤ Un inquilino *de facto* no figura en el contrato, frente al inquilino *de jure* que sí. A *de facto* tenant is one who is not on the lease, as opposed to a *de jure* tenant, who is. ➤ Los teóricos del dinamismo, a diferencia de los conductistas, creen que es posible analizar los procesos mentales. ■ Los teóricos del dinamismo, en contraposición a los conductistas, creen que es posible analizar los procesos mentales. The dynamic theorists, as opposed to the behaviorists, believe it is possible to analyze mental processes.

a Dios gracias ■ gracias a Dios thank God

a Dios pongo por testigo as God is my witness ➤ *(Scarlet O'Hara)* A Dios pongo por testigo que nunca volveré a pasar hambre. As God is my witness, I'll never go hungry again.

a Dios rogando y con el mazo dando pray as if everything depended on God, and work as if everything depended on you ■ praise God and pass the ammunition

a discreción ■ a voluntad at one's discretion

a disgusto: hacer algo ~ to do something unwillingly ■ to something against one's will

estar **a disposición de hacer algo** to be willing to do something

estar **a disposición de hacer algo para alguien** to be willing to do something for someone

a disposición del cliente at the customer's request ■ at the customer's disposal ➤ *(cartel en un restaurante)* Existen hojas de reclamaciones a disposición del cliente. Complaints forms are available at the customer's request. ■ Complaints forms are available at the customer's disposal. ➤ Tenemos un amplio surtido de guarniciones a disposición del cliente. We have a large variety of condiments at the customer's request.

a distancia at a distance

a distancia: curso ~ correspondence course

a distancia: mantenerse ~ to stay at arm's length

a distintas horas at different times

¡a divertirnos! let the good times roll! ■ let's have a good time! ■ let's have fun!

a doble espacio: ser redactado ~ to be double spaced ➤ El documento ha sido redactado a doble espacio. The document is double spaced.

a domicilio: repartir ~ to have home delivery ■ to deliver ➤ ¿Reparte usted a domicilio? ■ ¿Reparten ustedes a domicilio? Do you deliver?

a domicilio: servicio ~ home delivery service

a dónde acudir: no tener ~ not to have anywhere to turn ■ to have nowhere to turn ➤ (Yo) no tenía a dónde acudir. I didn't have anywhere to turn.

a donde el corazón se inclina, el pie camina follow your heart's promptings ■ do what you love

¿a dónde nos conduce eso? ■ ¿a dónde nos lleva eso? where's that going to get us?

¿a dónde quieres llegar (con eso)? ■ ¿qué se supone que buscas con eso? ■ ¿a dónde vas a parar con eso? what are you getting at? ■ what are you driving at?

¡a dormir! ■ ¡hora de acostarse! bedtime! ■ time for bed!

a dos manos: hacer algo ~ to do something with both hands

a dos manos: jugar ~ to play with both hands ■ to play using both hands

estar **a dos pasos** ■ estar a cuatro pasos ■ estar muy cerca (de) to be just steps away ■ to be close by ■ to be right near ➤ Está a dos pasos de donde vivo. ■ Está muy cerca de donde vivo. It's just steps away from where I live. ■ It's right by where I live. ■ It's right near where I live.

a dos velas: quedarse ~ ■ estar a dos velas ■ estar seco ■ estar sin blanca ■ estar sincero ■ estar planchado to be broke

a duras penas ■ a graves penas ■ a malas penas just barely ■ barely ■ hardly ■ with great difficulty ➤ A duras penas (yo) podía seguirle. I could hardly keep up with him. ■ I could (just) barely keep up with him. ➤ Se levanta a duras penas de la cama por la mañana. He can hardly get out of bed in the morning. ■ He can (just) barely get out of bed in the morning. ➤ Te oigo a duras penas. I can (just) barely hear you. ■ I can hardly hear you. ➤ Puedo verlo a duras pensas. I can just barely see it.

a duras penas no hablar un idioma ■ no hablar un idioma a duras penas ■ apenas hablar un idioma ■ no hablar un idioma apenas ■ prácticamente no hablar un idioma ■ no hablar un idioma prácticamente ■ casi no hablar un idioma ■ no hablar un idioma casi ■ a duras penas hablar un idioma ■ hablar un idioma a duras penas to barely speak a language ■ to hardly speak a language ➤ A duras penas no hablaba español cuando llegó a Buenos Aires. She barely spoke Spanish when she arrived in Buenos Aires. ■ She hardly spoke Spanish when she arrived in Buenos Aires.

a duras penas (yo) podía... I could barely...

a efectos de for the purposes of ■ with a view to ■ with the object of ➤ A efectos de la investigación se les dio a todos las poblaciones el mismo peso. For the purposes of the study, all the populations were given the same weight.

a él le corresponde... it is he who has to... ■ it is he who must...

a él no le basta that's not good enough for him ■ that doesn't satisfy him

a ella no le basta that's not good enough for her ■ that doesn't satisfy her

a elegir *(Esp.)* your choice of ➤ Tortillas a elegir Your choice of omelets

a empellones: abrir paso ~ ■ abrir paso a empujones to push one's way through ■ to shove one's way through

a empujones: meterse ~ to push one's way in

a enemigo que huye, puente de plata good-bye and good riddance!

a esa edad at that age

a ésa no te la papeas ni de coña *(jerga, subido de tono)* you're never gonna to make it with her

a esas alturas de su vida at this stage of one's life ▪ at this stage of your life

a escala: dibujar ~ to draw to scale ➤ I want to draw this floor plan to scale on my computer. Quiero dibujar este plano del piso a escala en mi computadora.

a escape: ir ~ ▪ ir a todo correr to go at top speed ▪ to go at breakneck speed

a escasa distancia: disparar ~ ▪ disparar desde muy cerca to fire at close range ▪ to fire from a short distance

a escasos *x* metros de barely *x* meters from

¡a esconderse que viene la basura! *(humor cubano)* hide, because here comes the garbage man!

a escondidas ▪ a escondidillas ▪ a espaldas de alguien ▪ a hurtadillas behind someone's back ▪ behind one's back ➤ (Se) lo hizo a escondidas. He did it behind her back. ➤ (Se) lo hizo a escondidas. She did it behind his back.

a escondidas de todos: hacer algo ~ 1. to do something when no one is looking ▪ to do something while nobody is looking ▪ to do something hidden from view ▪ to do something out of sight ▪ to do something out of the view of others ▪ to do something furtively **2.** to do something in secret ▪ to do something secretly **3.** to do something indecent ➤ El niño se comió los chocolates a escondidas de todos. The child ate the chocolates while nobody was looking. ➤ Se casaron a escondidas de todos. They got married secretly.

a escote: ir ~ to go Dutch

a escote no hay pegote *(jerga)* you're never gonna make it with her

estar **a escuadra** ▪ estar en ángulo recto ▪ formar un ángulo recto to be at right angles ▪ *(carpintería)* to be true

a ese paso ▪ de esa forma ▪ a este paso ▪ de esta forma at that rate ▪ at this rate ➤ A ese paso no vamos a comer sobre las tres. ▪ De esa forma no vamos a comer sobre las tres. At that rate we won't (be ready to) eat by three o'clock.

a eso de ▪ alrededor de ▪ sobre ▪ a más o menos at about ▪ at around ▪ about ▪ around ➤ A eso de las dos de la tarde. At about two in the afternoon. ▪ About two in the afternoon ▪ Around two in the afternoon

a eso no le saca ni con agua caliente ▪ a eso no le saca ni con sacacorchos you'll never get anywhere with him ▪ there's no convincing him

a eso no le saca ni con sacacorchos ▪ a eso no le saca ni con agua caliente you'll never get anywhere with him ▪ there's no convincing him

a eso voy I'm coming to that ▪ I'm getting to that

a espaldas ▪ a sus espaldas behind one's back ➤ Ella lo hizo a sus espaldas. She did it behind his back.

a espaldas de alguien: hacer algo ~ to do something behind someone's back ➤ Lo hizo a espaldas de su esposa. He did it behind his wife's back.

a espetaperro ▪ que pierde el culo at breakneck speed ➤ El coche iba a espetaperro. The car was going at breakneck speed.

a espuertas ▪ a puñados coming out one's ears ▪ hand over fist ▪ a lot of ▪ by the ton ➤ Gana dinero a espuertas. He makes money hand over fist. ▪ He makes a lot of money.

a esta hora at this time ▪ at this hour ➤ El domingo a esta hora te estaré esperando. I'll be waiting for you at this time on Sunday.

a estas alturas at this point ▪ by now ▪ by this time ▪ any more ▪ at this point ▪ at my age ▪ having come this far ➤ Esperaba haber sabido de ti a estas alturas. I had expected to hear from you by now. ➤ Creo que ya tengo suficiente dominio a estas alturas. I think I have sufficient mastery at this point. ➤ A estas alturas... At my age... ➤ Es poca cosa lo que pueda hacer el gobierno a estas alturas. There's not much the government can do at this point.

a estas alturas del año at this time of year ▪ at this point in the year

a estas horas ▪ en este momento at this hour ➤ ¿Qué haces despierto(-a) a estas horas? ▪ ¿Qué haces levantado(-a) a estas horas? What are you doing up at this hour?

a este paso ▪ a este ritmo at this rate ➤ A este paso nunca llegaremos. ▪ A este ritmo nunca llegaremos. At this rate we'll never get there.

a este punto at this point

a este ritmo ▪ a este paso at this rate ➤ A este ritmo nunca llegaremos. ▪ A este paso nunca llegaremos. At this rate we'll never get there.

a este tenor ▪ de esta manera like this one ▪ in the same fashion as this one ➤ Quiero que me presentes tu trabajo a este tenor. I want you to present me your work in the same fashion (as this one is done). ▪ I want you to present me your work like this (one).

a este tono ▪ a este tenor in the same vein

a esto siguió... there followed...

a estribor: virar ~ ▪ girar a estribor to turn to starboard

a excepción de except for ▪ with the exception of

a exceso de velocidad: ir ~ ▪ conducir a exceso de velocidad to speed ▪ to go at excessive speed

a exceso de velocidad: parar a alguien por conducir ~ ▪ detener a alguien por conducir a exceso de velocidad ▪ parar a alguien por ir a exceso de velocidad ▪ detener a alguien por ir a exceso de velocidad to stop someone for speeding ➤ El policía lo hizo parar por conducir a exceso de velocidad. ▪ El policía lo paró por conducir con exceso de velocidad. ▪ *(Esp. y partes de la América del Sur, leísmo)* El policía le hizo parar por conducir a exceso de velocidad. ▪ El policía le paró por conducir a exceso de velocidad. The policeman stopped him for speeding. ➤ El policía la hizo parar por conducir a exceso de velocidad. ▪ El policía la paró por conducir con exceso de velocidad. ▪ *(Esp. y partes de la América del Sur, leísmo)* El policia le hizo parar por conducir a exceso de velocidad. ▪ El policía le paró por conducir con exceso de velocidad. The policeman stopped her for speeding.

a expensas de alguien: ir ~ ▪ ir por cuenta de alguien ▪ ir a costo de alguien to go at the expense of someone ▪ at someone's expense

a falta de for lack of ▪ in the absence of ▪ because of not having any ➤ A falta de electricidad, no pudimos trabajar con la computadora. For lack of electricity, we couldn't work at the computer. ➤ Fuimos al cine el sábado a falta de nada mejor (que hacer.) We went to the movies on Saturday for lack of anything better to do. ▪ We went to the movies on Saturday in the absence of anything better to do. ➤ A falta de algo mejor, nos conformaremos con las sobras de ayer. For lack of anything better (to eat), we'll settle for yesterday's leftovers.

a falta de pan, buenas son tortas 1. tenemos que conformarnos con lo que tenemos we'll make do with what we have ▪ we'll make the most of what we have **2.** a buen hambre no hay mal pan hunger is the best sauce

a falta de una semana para... with less than a week until... ▪ with less than a week before... ➤ A falta de una semana para las elecciones autonómicas, los candidatos se enzarzaron ayer en un nuevo capítulo de descalificación. With less than a week until the local elections, the candidates locked horns yesterday in a new round of condemnations.

estar **a favor 1.** to be in favor of **2.** *(cuenta bancaria)* to have a positive balance ▪ to have a balance in one's favor ➤ Nadie está a favor de la pobreza. No one is in favor of poverty. ➤ El saldo de su cuenta bancaria está a su favor. Your bank account has a positive balance. ▪ Your bank account has a balance in your favor.

estar **a favor (de algo)** ▪ estar en aplauso de ▪ estar en pro de to be in favor (of something) ▪ to be for something

a favor de algo: mostrarse ~ to come out in favor of something

estar **a favor de algo al cien por cien** ▪ estar totalmente a favor de algo ▪ aprobar algo al cien por cien ▪ aprobar al cien por cien algo to be completely in favor of something ▪ to be all for something ➤ Estoy a favor al cien por cien. ▪ Estoy totalmente a favor. ▪ Lo apruebo al cien por cien. I am completely in favor of it. ▪ I'm all for it.

a filo de las *x* ▪ a las *x* en punto at *x* o'clock sharp ▪ at *x* on the dot ➤ Al filo de las doce At twelve o'clock sharp ▪ At twelve o'clock on the dot

a fin de ▪ con objeto de ▪ para to ▪ for the purpose of ▪ with the aim of ▪ with the intention of ▪ with the objective of ➤ Voy a Valladolid a fin de visitar el Museo Colón. I'm going to Valladolid to visit the Columbus Museum. ■ I'm going to Valladolid for the purpose of visiting the Columbus Museum.

a fin de cuentas ■ en resumen in the end ■ in the final analysis ■ when all is said and done ■ ultimately ■ *(coloquial)* at the end of the day

a fin de mes ■ al final del mes at the end of the month

a fin de mes: llegar ~ to make ends meet ■ to make it through the month (financially) ■ to make it to the end of the month (financially)

a fin del día ■ al final del día late in the day ■ toward the end of the day ■ at the end of the day

a finales de abril in late April ■ toward the end of April ■ at the end of April ■ near the end of April

a finales de año ■ para finales de año by the end of the year

a finales de mes late in the month ■ toward the end of the month ■ near the end of the month ■ at the end of the month

a finales del año toward the end of the year ■ near the end of the year ■ late in the year

a finales del mes toward the end of the month ■ late in the month

a finales del mes que viene toward the end of next month ■ late next month

a finales del verano de late in the summer of

a fines del año at the end of the year

a flor de piel: estar los nervios ~ ■ tener los nervios de punta to be on edge ■ to be edgy ■ to feel edgy ➤ Mis nervios están a flor de piel. ■ Tengo los nervios de punta. My nerves are on edge. ■ I'm edgy. ■ I feel edgy.

a flor de piel: tener los nervios ~ to be jumpy (as a goat) ■ to be jittery

a flote: sacar algo ~ 1. to raise something to the surface of the water 2. *(un negocio)* to get a business afloat ■ to make (a business) profitable

a flote: salir ~ to land on one's feet

a fondo: investigar algo ~ to investigate something thoroughly

a fondo: limpiar algo ~ to clean something thoroughly

a fondo: pisarlo ~ *(acelerador)* 1. to floor it 2. *(figurativo)* to give it all you got ➤ ¡Písalo a fondo! Floor it! ■ Give it all you've got!

¡a freír espárragos! ■ a freír monas ■ vete a freír espárragos go jump in a lake! ■ (go) take a hike! ➤ Le mandé a freír espárragos. I told him to go jump in a lake. ■ I told him to take a hike. ➤ Vete a freír espárragos. Go jump in a lake! ■ Go take a hike!

¡a freír monas! ■ ¡a freír espárragos! go jump in a lake! ■ (go) take a hike!

a fuego lento: cocer ~ ■ calentar a fuego lento to cook over low heat

a fuego medio: cocer ~ to cook over medium heat

a fuerza de...: conseguir algo ~ to get something by... ■ to obtain something by...

a fuerza de...: hacer algo ~ ■ de tanto hacer... to do something by... ➤ A fuerza de vivir en los bosques... As a result of living in the woods... ■ By having lived in the woods... ■ By force of having lived in the woods...

a galope tendido: partir ~ to take off at full gallop

a gatas: ir ~ ■ caminar a gatas to go on all fours ■ to crawl on all fours

a golpe de cañón: ir ~ to hightail it ➤ Me dirigí hacia el centro a golpe de cañón. I hightailed it downtown.

a golpe de algo: hacer algo ~ to do something by dint of something ■ to use something to do something

a golpe de crisis as a result of the crisis ➤ *(titular)* El poderío de EE UU en el mundo ha ido avanzando a golpe de crisis. The power of the U.S. in the world has advanced in step with the crisis.

a golpe de ratón: dibujo ~ drawing (on the computer) by using the mouse

a golpe de talonario by writing checks to people (to secure their cooperation)

a gran escala ■ en gran escala large scale

a gran prisa, gran vagar haste makes waste ■ *(gracioso)* the hurrier I go, the behinder I get

a gran salto, gran quebranto nothing ventured, nothing gained

a gran seca, gran mojada *(L.am.)* nothing ventured, nothing gained

a gran velocidad at high speed

a grandes males, grandes remedios great problems demand great solutions

a grandes rasgos in general terms ■ generally (speaking)

a grandes zancadas in big strides

a granel in bulk ➤ ¿Se venden frutos secos a granel? Do you sell nuts in bulk?

a grito herido: llorar ~ 1. *(dolor físico)* to cry out in pain 2. *(dolor físico o emocional)* to cry out in agony ➤ Él lloró a grito herido. He cried out in agony.

a grito limpio ■ a grito pelado at the top of one's voice ■ at the top of one's lungs ➤ El niño lloraba a grito limpio. ■ El niño lloraba a grito pelado. The child was crying at the top of his voice. ■ The child was crying at the top of his lungs.

a grito pelado ■ a grito limpio at the top of one's lungs ➤ El niño lloraba a grito pelado. ■ El niño lloraba a grito limpio. The child was crying at the top of his voice. ■ The child was crying at the top of his lungs.

a gritos: pedir algo ~ to clamor for something ➤ El bebé pidió a gritos la comida. The baby was clamoring for his food.

(a) grosso modo roughly ■ in the ballpark

a guantazo limpio barehandedly ■ with one's bare hands

a guisa de ejemplo ■ por ejemplo by way of example ■ as an example ■ (just) to give you an example

estar **a gusto** 1. to be comfortable 2. to be content ■ to be fine ➤ Estoy a gusto sentado aquí. I'm comfortable sitting here. ➤ Estoy a gusto viendo la tele. I'm content watching TV. ■ I'm fine watching TV.

a gusto: ponerse ~ to make oneself comfortable ■ to make oneself at home ➤ Ponte a gusto. Make yourself comfortable. ■ Make yourself at home.

estar **a gusto con** to be satisfied with ■ to be content with ➤ Estoy a gusto con mi trabajo. I'm satisfied with my job. ■ I'm content with my job.

estar **a gusto en una situación (nueva)** to be comfortable in a (new) situation

¡a hacer puñetas! ■ ¡vete a hacer puñetas! get lost! ■ beat it!

a hombros: llevar algo ~ ■ cargar algo a hombros to carry something on one's shoulders

a horas intempestivas at an ungodly hour

a horcajadas: sentarse en una silla a ~ to straddle a chair

a huevo: comprar algo ~ *(Esp., subido de tono)*to buy something on impulse

a huevo: decirle ~ *(Esp., subido de tono)* to say something off the top of one's head

a huevo para algo: ponerlo ~ *(Esp., subido de tono)* to set something up ■ to lay the groundwork for something ➤ Te lo he puesto a huevo. I've laid the groundwork for you. ➤ Te lo he puesto a huevo para que salgas con Verónica. I've set it up for you to go out with Verónica.

a huevo para que alguien haga algo: ponerlo ~ *(Esp.)* to set it up for someone to do something ■ to lay the groundwork for someone to do something

a huevo: responder a una pregunta ~ *(Esp., subido de tono)* to answer off the top of one's head ➤ ¿Dónde está Ipanema? -A huevo, creo que Río de Janeiro. Where's Ipanema?-(Just) off the top of my head, I'd say Río de Janeiro.

a huevo: vender algo ~ *(Esp., subido de tono)* to sell something for peanuts

a hurtadillas ■ a escondidas on the sly ■ stealthily

a hurtadillas: salir ~ to sneak out ■ to sneak away ■ to slink away ➤ El joven salió a hurtadillas de la casa. The youth snuck out of the house.

a instancia(s) de alguien 1. a petición de ■ a ruegos de at the request of ■ at someone's request 2. por orden de alguien at the order of someone ■ at someone's order 2. a insistencia de alguien at someone's insistence ■ at someone's behest

a instancias suyas at someone's insistance ■ at someone's urging ■ at someone's request

a intervalos regulares ■ en intervalos regulares at regular intervals

a invierno lluvioso, verano abundoso April showers bring May flowers

a izquierdas: ir ~ ▪ ir al revés ▪ apretarse a la izquierda to have a left-handed thread ▪ to tighten counterclockwise ➤ ¡Ojo, que ese tornillo va a izquierdas! Careful, that screw has a left-handed thread! ▪ Careful, you tighten that screw counterclockwise.

¡**a joderse tocan!** *(subido de tono)* now it's your turn to get screwed ▪ turnabout is fair play

a jornada completa ▪ tiempo completo full-time

a jornal: trabajar ~ to be paid by the day

a juego: colores ~ matching colors

a juego con: ir ~ 1. combinar bien con ▪ hacer juego con ▪ pegar con to match ▪ to go with 2. vestirse parecido to be dressed alike ▪ to be dressed in matching clothes ➤ La corbata va a juego con la camisa. ▪ La corbata combina con la camisa. ▪ La corbata pega con la camisa. The tie matches the shirt. ➤ Las gemelas siempre van a juego. The twins are always dressed alike. ▪ The twins are always dressed in matching clothes.

a juego: ropa ~ matching clothes

a juzgar cómo judging by how

a juzgar por judging by

a la alpargata on the cheap ▪ on a shoestring budget

estar **a la altura** to be up to the occasion ➤ Hay que estar a la altura.You have to be up to the occasion. ▪ You've got to be up to the occasion.

estar **a la altura de algún lugar** 1. at the height of 2. to be right by a place ▪ to be in front of a place ➤ La tienda está a la altura del metro de Alvarado. The store is right by the Alvarado metro station.

estar **a la altura de las circunstancias** to be equal to the situation ▪ to be up to the situation ▪ to rise to the occasion

a la altura de la situación: portarse ~ to rise to the occasion

estar **a la altura de su reputación** to live up to one's reputation

estar **a la altura del betún** *(pintoresco)* to be embarrassed

a la antigua the old-fashioned way ▪ the way they did it in the old days

a la atención de care of

a la bajada del sol ▪ al sol puesto at sundown

estar **a la bartola** to be laid back ➤ Los domingos estoy a la bartola. On Sundays I'm (very) laid back.

a la bartola: tumbarse ~ ▪ echarse a la bartola ▪ tirarse a la bartola to flop down ➤ Se tumbó a la bartola en el sofá. He flopped down on the couch.

a la boca de la calle ▪ en la bocacalle ▪ en la boca de la calle ▪ al principio de la calle ▪ al comienzo de la calle at the beginning of the street

a la brasa: cocinar ~ ▪ hacer a la brasa to grill over charcoal ▪ to charcoal ➤ Pechuga de pollo a la brasa Charcoaled chicken breast ▪ Chicken breast grilled over charcoal

a la brava ▪ por la fuerza whether you like it or not ▪ whether you want to or not

estar **a la buena de Dios** to be in God's hands ▪ to be at the mercy of fate ➤ Se fue sin dinero a la buena de Dios. He left penniless and at the mercy of fate.

a la buena de Dios: dejarlo ~ to leave it to God ▪ to leave it in God's hands ▪ to leave it to providence

a la buena de Dios: hacer algo ~ to do something trusting in fortune ▪ to do something trusting in fate

a la buena ventura de alguien: hacer un brindis ~ to toast to someone's good fortune

a la búsqueda de *(poco común)* ▪ en busca de in search of ➤ El presidente, en busca de su lugar en la historia The president, in search of his place in history ➤ *(título de libro)* A la búsqueda de sí mismo In Search of Oneself

estar **a la cabeza** to be in front ▪ to be at the head

a la cabeza de la búsqueda de... leading the search for...

estar **a la cabeza de la cola** ▪ estar el primero de la fila to be first in line ▪ to be at the head of the line ▪ to be at the front of the line ▪ to be at the beginning of the line

estar **a la cabeza del pelotón** to be at the head of the pack

a la cabeza del pelotón: ir ~ to be the leader of the pack

a la caída de la noche ▪ al anochecer at nightfall ▪ at dusk ▪ at twilight

a la cama no te irás sin saber una cosa más you learn something new every day

a la cara: decírselo ~ ▪ decírselo en su cara ▪ decírselo de frente to tell (it to) someone to his face ▪ to say it to someone to his face ➤ Ella se lo dijo a la cara. She told him (directly) to his face. ▪ She said it to him (right) to his face.

¡**a la carga!** charge!

a la carga: volver ~ to get back to work

a la carrera on the run ➤ Cogí el autobús a la carrera. I caught the bus on the run.

a la caza de un empleo: ir ~ to go job hunting

a la caza de una mujer: ir ~ to go looking for female companionship

a la chita callando: hacer algo ~ ▪ hacer algo en secreto, sin llamar la atención to do something on the quiet ▪ to do something on the sly ▪ to do something stealthily

a la corta o a la larga ▪ tarde o temprano ▪ a la larga o a la corta ▪ antes o después sooner or later

estar **a la cuarta pregunta** ▪ andar a la cuarta pregunta ▪ estar sin blanca to be broke

a la (cuenta de) tres on the count of three ▪ at the count of three ▪ a la tercera, va la vencida persistence pays (off) ▪ third time lucky

estar **a la defensiva** to be on the defensive

estar **a la derecha** 1. to be on the right ▪ to be to the right ▪ to be at the right 2. en el sentido de las agujas del reloj clockwise ➤ Al entrar, está situado a la derecha. It's on the right as you go in. ▪ It's to the right as you go in.

a la derecha: girar ~ ▪ doblar a la derecha ▪ *(Latinamérica)* ▪ virar a la derecha 1. to turn right ▪ to turn to the right 2. en el sentido de las agujas del reloj to turn clockwise ➤ Gira a la derecha. Turn right. ▪ Turn to the right.

estar **a la deriva** to be adrift ▪ *(figurativo)* to flounder ➤ El náufrago estuvo diez días a la deriva en una balsa. The shipwrecked sailor was adrift on a raft for ten days. ➤ Yo estaba a la deriva durante esa época de mi vida. I floundered during that period of my life.

a la desesperada: hacer algo ~ to do something in desperation ▪ to act out of desperation ▪ to act in desperation

estar **a la disposición de alguien** to be at someone's disposal

estar **a la disposición de uno** to be at one's disposal

estar **a la escucha de** to listen out for

estar **a la espera de** to be waiting for ➤ Estoy a la espera de tiempos mejores. I'm waiting for better times. ➤ Estoy a la espera del vuelo que llega de Manchester. I'm waiting for the flight from Manchester.

estar **a la expectativa** to be waiting to see ▪ to wait and see

estar **a la expectativa de que ocurra algo** to be waiting for something to happen ▪ to be waiting for something to take place ➤ Estamos a la expectativa del final de la huelga de los controladores aéreos para irnos de viaje. We're waiting for the air traffic controllers' strike to end before we take our trip.

estar **a la expectativa de que pase algo** 1. to be expecting that something will happen 2. to be waiting for something to happen ➤ Estoy a la expectativa de que me ofrezcan un trabajo. I'm expecting them to offer me a job. ▪ I expect that they will offer me the job. ➤ Estoy a la expectativa de que suba el dólar antes de comprar el piso. I'm waiting for the dollar to go up before buying a condominum.

¡**a la formación!** *(militar)* fall in!

a la fuerza: hacer algo ~ 1. hacer algo por necesidad to do something out of necessity 2. hacer algo por obligación to do something out of obligation 3. hacer algo por coacción to do something under duress

a la fuerza: hacerle hacer algo ~ to make someone do something (against his will) ▪ to force someone to do something (against his will) ➤ Le hicieron dimitir a la fuerza. He was forced to resign. ▪ They forced him to resign. ▪ They made him resign.

a la fuerza: tener que hacer algo ~ ▪ tener que hacer algo por fuerza to have to have done something (inevitably) ▪ to be bound to have done something ➤ Estaban en el piso de al lado, y a la fuerza tuvieron que oírnos. ▪ Estaban en el piso de al lado, y por fuerza tuvieron que oírnos. They must have heard us. They were in the next apartment. ▪ They were bound to have heard us. They were in the next apartment. ■ They had to have heard us. They were in the next apartment.

a la fuga: darse ~ ■ huir to flee ➤ Los atracadores se dieron a la fuga a pie. ■ Los atracadores huyeron a pie. The assailants fled on foot.

¡**a la grande!** *(del juego de naipes "mus")* splendid! ■ great!

estar **a la greña con alguien** ■ andar a la greña con alguien ■ andar a palos con alguien to be at loggerheads with someone ➤ *(noticia)* El presidente Bush y el presidente de la Reserva Federal, Alan Greenspan, están a la greña por la cuantía de la rebaja fiscal. President Bush and Federal Reserve chairman Alan Greenspan are at loggerheads over the size of the tax cut.

a la heroica: actuar ~ to act brashly

a la hora ■ puntualmente at the same hour ■ at the same time ➤ Mañana, si no estoy a la hora, es que no vengo, ¿vale? If I'm not here tomorrow at the same time, it means I'm not coming, okay?

a la hora convenida ■ a la hora establecida at the appointed time

a la hora de 1. at the time of ■ 2. when it comes to

a la hora de comer at dinner time *(Nota: en los Estados Unidos "dinner" se refiere a la comida principal y no a la hora, así que la comida se puede servir de día o de noche, y más comúnmente se sirve entre las 18 y 1930 horas.)*

a la hora de la cena at supper time ■ at dinner time *(Nota: En los Estados Unidos "dinner", la comida principal del día, se sirve entre las 6 y 8 p.m. y coincide aproximadamente con la merienda.)*

a la hora de la verdad 1. at the moment of truth 2. cuando realmente importa when it really matters ➤ Ha llegado a la hora de la verdad. The moment of truth has arrived.

a la hora de pagar when it's time to pay ■ when it comes time to pay

a la hora especificada ■ a la hora indicada at the specified time

a la hora justa (just) in the nick of time

a la hora prevista at the appointed hour ■ at the appointed time ➤ Nos cita y luego a la hora prevista no se presenta. He makes an appointment, and then at the appointed time he doesn't show up.

a la hora que uno quiera ■ cuando (así lo) quiera any time one wants (to) ■ whenever one wants (to) ➤ Podemos irnos a la hora que quieras. ■ Podemos irnos cuando (así lo) quieras. We can leave any time you want (to). ■ We can leave whenever you want (to).

a la inglesa *(frase preposicional)* in the English style ■ *(adjetivo)* English-style

estar **a la intemperie** ■ estar a la merced de los elementos to be at the mercy of the elements ■ to be at the mercy of the weather

a la intemperie: quedarse ~ to be (left) at the mercy of the elements

a la inversa: escribir algo ~ ■ escribir algo al revés to write something backwards ➤ La palabra "ambulancia" está escrita a la inversa en el frontal de la ambulancia para que parezca al derecho cuando se vea por el espejo retrovisor. ■ La palabra "ambulancia" está escrita al revés en el frontal de la ambulancia para que parezca al derecho cuando se vea por el espejo retrovisor. The word "ambulance" is written backwards on the front of the ambulance so that it will appear frontwards when seen through a rearview mirror. ➤ La palabra "radar" se escribe igual al derecho y a la inversa. ■ La palabra "radar" se escribe igual al derecho y al revés. The word "radar" is written the same frontwards and backwards. ■ The word "radar" is the same, written frontwards or backwards.

a la inversa: hacer algo ~ ■ hacer algo al revés to do something backwards ➤ *(Bob Theves)* Ginger Rogers hacía todo lo que hacía Fred Astaire pero a la inversa y con tacones altos. ■ Ginger Rogers hacía todo lo que hacía Fred Astaire pero al revés y con tacones altos. Ginger Rogers did everything Fred Astaire did, but backwards, and in high heels. ➤ Se desata el nudo igual que lo ataste, sólo que a la inversa. ■ Se desata el nudo igual que lo ataste, sólo que al revés. You untie the knot the same way you tied it, only backwards. ➤ Vamos a repetir la coreografía empezando desde el final, esto es, desde atrás hacia delante. Let's repeat the dance steps starting at the end, that is, backwards.

a la inversa: imprimir algo ~ ■ imprimir algo al revés to print something backwards ➤ La foto está impresa a la inversa. Le han dado la vuelta al negativo. ■ La foto está impresa al revés. Le han dado la vuelta al negativo. This picture is printed backwards. They reversed the negative.

ser **a la inversa** ■ ser al contrario ■ ser al revés to be backwards ➤ ¿Plaza Cuzco queda después de Plaza de Castilla o es a la inversa? ■ ¿Plaza Cuzco queda después de Plaza de Castilla o es al contrario? Is Cuzco Plaza after Plaza de Castilla or is it the other way around? ■ Is Cuzco Plaza after Plaza de Castilla, or have I got it backwards?

a la italiana *(frase preposicional)* in the Italian style ■ *(adjetivo)* Italian-style

a la izquierda 1. on the left ■ to the left ■ at the left 2. contra el sentido de las agujas del reloj counterclockwise ➤ Está, entrando, a la izquierda. It's on the left as you go in. ■ It's to the left as you go in. ➤ Gira a la izquierda. Turn to the left. ➤ Se aprieta la rosca al revés a la izquierda. You tighten a reverse thread counterclockwise. ■ You tighten a left-handed thread counterclockwise.

a la jardinera: preparar comida ~ to garnish a dish with diced or cooked vegetables ■ à la jardinère

a la larga in the long run ➤ A la larga, el Consejo de la Propiedad está preocupado por la posibilidad de que se produzca un éxodo de empresas hacia el extrarradio. In the long run, the Real Estate Equalization Board is worried about the possibility of a possible exodus of business beyond the perimeter (of the city).

a la larga o a la corta *(poco común)* ■ a la corta o a la larga ■ *(más común)* ■ tarde o temprano ■ antes o después sooner or later

a la legua a mile off ■ a mile away ➤ Se le ve venir a la legua. You can see him coming a mile off. ■ You can see him coming a mile away.

a la ley: conforme ~ in accordance with the law ■ according to the law ➤ Debes registrar tu empresa conforme a la ley. You should register your business in accordance with the law.

a la ligera: juzgar algo ~ to judge something superficially ■ to pass judgment on something

a la ligera: tomar algo ~ to take something lightly ■ not to take something seriously

a la loquesca *(arcaico)* ■ a lo loco like crazy ■ haphazardly ■ *(subido de tono)* half-assed

estar **a la luna** ■ a la luna de Valencia ■ en la luna to be (left) out in the cold

a la luna de Valencia: dejarse to be left out in the cold

a la luz: sujetar algo ~ ■ poner algo contra la luz to hold something up to the light ■ to hold something up in the light ➤ Sujétalo a la luz para que pueda verlo con claridad. Hold it (up) to the light so I can see it clearly. ■ Hold it (up) in the light so I can see it clearly.

a la luz de acontecimientos recientes in light of recent events

a la luz de la luna by moonlight ■ by the light of the moon ■ in the moonlight

a la luz de las velas by candlelight

a la llana: decir ~ to say flatly ■ *(coloquial)* to say flat out

a la mañana siguiente the next morning ■ (on) the following morning

a la mañana siguiente muy temprano early the next morning ■ early (on) the following morning

a la marinera: arroz ~ rice cooked in fish broth ■ seafood-flavored rice

a la matiega in the style of the composer Joseph Matiega

a la mayor brevedad posible ■ con la mayor brevedad posible ■ en cuanto le sea posible ■ lo más pronto posible ■ lo antes posible ■ tan pronto como sea posible as soon as possible ■ as quickly as possible ■ *(en los negocios)* at one's earliest convenience

a (la) medida: estar construido ~ to be custom built ■ to be built to specifications

a la medida: estar hecho ~ to be custom made ■ to be made to measure

a la medida de mi deseo to my heart's desire

a la medida del deseo de uno to one's heart's desire

a la memoria de ■ en recuerdo de in memory of

estar **a la merced de los elementos** ■ estar a la intemperie to be at the mercy of the elements

a la mesa del comedor at the dinner table ➤ Estabamos sentados a la mesa del comedor cuando sonó el timbre. We were sitting at the dinner table when the doorbell rang. ■ We were seated at the dinner table when the doorbell rang.

¡a la mierda! *(subido de tono)* go to hell! ➤ ¡Vete a la mierda!-En ella estoy. Go to hell!-That's where I am.

a la milanesa: freír ~ to fry in batter

a la mínima salta the least little thing gets him going ➤ A la mínima salta ese perro. The least little thing gets that dog going.

estar **a la mirada de** to be on the lookout for

estar **a la moda** to be in style ■ to be in fashion

a la moda: ir ~ to be dressed in the latest fashion ■ to wear the latest fashion

a la noche 1. at night 2. *(tiempo pasado)* that night

a la ocasión la pintan calva ■ la ocasión la pintan calva strike while the iron is hot

¡a la orden! ■ ¡a sus ordenes! *(Esp., militar)* yes, sir! ■ *(Méx., camareros)* at your service!

a la orilla de ■ muy cerca de near ■ not far from ■ right by ➤ Hay un buen restaurante mexicana a la orilla de mi casa. There's a good Mexican restaurant near my house.

estar **a la par** 1. to be at par 2. to be at the same level (of proficiency) ➤ Los alumnos están a la par. The students are at the same level.

estar **a la par de** at the same time as ■ at the same level as ■ level with ■ at par with ■ along with

a la par de: ir ~ to go at the same pace as

a la par que as well as ➤ Es inteligente a la par que guapa. She's smart as well as pretty. ■ She's as smart as she is pretty.

a la par que: mejorar ~ to improve at the same pace as ■ to improve at the same rate as

a la parrilla cooked on a grill ■ grilled

a la parrilla: bisté ~ grilled steak

a la parrilla: pechuga de pollo ~ grilled chicken breast

a la pata coja: ir ~ ■ saltar a la pata coja to hop along ■ to hop (on one foot)

a la perfección to perfection

a la plancha cooked on a griddle ■ cooked on a flat surface ➤ Pechuga de pollo a la plancha Chicken breast cooked on a griddle

a la porra: mandar a alguien ~ to tell someone to get lost

a la postre in the end ➤ A la postre, fue un fracaso la reunión. In the end, the meeting was a failure.

a la primera 1. at first 2. on the first try ➤ No contestó a la primera. He didn't answer at first.

a la primera de cambio 1. right off the bat 2. con la más mínima excusa at the drop of a hat ➤ Si le contratamos, él dejará el trabajo a la primera de cambio. If we hire him he'll quit right off the bat. ➤ Si eligimos a ese pólitico, nos abandonará a la primera de cambio. If we elect that politician, he'll abandon us at the drop of a hat.

a la primera descarga at the first shot

a la primera oportunidad at the first opportunity

a la prueba me remito a las pruebas me remito I rest my case

estar **a la puerta** ■ estar en la puerta to be at the door ➤ Hay alguien a la puerta. ■ Hay alguien en la puerta. Someone's at the door. ■ There's someone at the door. ➤ Ve a ver quién está a la puerta. ■ Mira a ver quién está a la puerta. Ve a ver quién está en la puerta. ■ Mira a ver quién está en la puerta. Go see who's at the door.

a la que 1. to which 2. to whom 3. whose ➤ La generación a la que le tocó vivir la guerra civil en España... The generation whose fortune it was to live through the civil war in Spain... ■ The generation whose fate it was to live through the civil war in Spain... ■ The generation whose lot it was to live through the civil war in Spain... ➤ "To crash a party" significa asistir a una fiesta a la que no has sido invitado. "To crash a party" means to attend a party you haven't been invited to.

a la rama de: pertenecer ~ to belong to the category of ■ to fall into the category of ■ to belong to the field of ■ to fall into the domain of ➤ Sus productos pertenecen a la rama de calzado. Their products fall into the category of footwear. ➤ El estudio de los reflejos pertenece a la rama de la neurología. The study of reflexes belongs to the field of neurology. ■ The study of reflexes falls within the domain of neurology.

a la redonda in any direction ➤ No hay farmacias cinco calles a la redonda. There is no pharmacy for five blocks in any direction.

a la romana coated with flour and egg

a la rutina as usual

a la rutina: acostumbrarse ~ to adapt to the routine ■ to get used to the routine

a la salida de at the end of ➤ A la salida de la misa se anunció que... At the end of mass it was announced that...

a la salida del sol ■ al salir el sol at sunrise ■ at sunup ■ *(pasado)* when the sun rose ■ when the sun came up ■ *(futuro)* when the sun rises ■ when the sun comes up

a la sazón *(literario)* ■ en aquel entonces ■ por entonces ■ por aquel entonces ■ por esa época at that time

a la semana 1. por semana a week ■ per week 2. una semana más tarde a week later ➤ Levanta pesos tres veces a la semana. ■ Levanta pesos tres veces por semana. He lifts weights three times a week.

estar **a la sombra** 1. estar en la sombra to be in the shade 2. estar en la cárcel to be in jail

estar **a la sombra de alguien** ■ estar al cobijo de alguien seguro ■ estar al respaldo de algo ■ estar cubierto por algo ■ estar asegurado de algo to be under the protection of someone ■ under someone's protection

a la sombra de alguien: vivir ~ ■ vivir bajo la protección de to live in the shadow of someone ➤ Vive a la sombra de su cuñado famoso He lives in the shadow of his famous brother-in-law.

estar **a la sombra de un lugar** to be (right) near a place ■ to be (right) nearby a place ■ to be (right) close by a place ■ to be (right) close to a place

a la sopa boba 1. ser un viva la virgen to live off other people ■ to scrounge off other people 2. no estar pendiente (en clase) not to be paying attention (in class)

a la suerte ■ al azar ■ aletoriamente at random

a la tercera, va la vencida third time lucky ■ the third time is a charm

estar **a la última** to be up on the latest ■ *(refiriéndose a la moda)* to be up on the latest fashion ■ to be down to one's last...

estar **a la última moda** to be the latest fashion

a la última (moda): ir ~ ■ ir a la moda to be dressed in the latest fashion ■ always to wear the latest fashion

estar **a la ultimísima** to be up on the very latest

a la ultimísima: ir ~ to be dressed in the very latest fashion ■ to wear the very latest

a la una, a las dos, (y) a las tres ready, (get) set, go!

estar **a la vanguardia** to be on the cutting edge ➤ El jazz cubano contemporáneo está a la vanguardia. Contemporary Cuban jazz is on the cutting edge.

a la vanguardia de: ir ~ estar en primera línea de to be at the forefront of ■ to be on the cutting edge of

¡a la vejez, viruelas! a pox on old age!

a la venta ■ se vende for sale ➤ Ya a la venta Now for sale ■ Now on sale ➤ Se vende el chalet. The house is for sale.

a la ventura: irse ~ to go without a fixed plan ■ to rough it

a la vera del río *(poético)* by the river ■ beside the river ■ next to the river

a la vera mía *(poético)* by my side ■ at my side ■ beside me

a la verdad ■ a decir verdad to tell you the truth ■ to be quite honest ■ to be truthful

a la vez ■ al mismo tiempo ■ al tiempo ■ a un tiempo ■ paralelamente at the same time

estar **a la vista** 1. to be in sight 2. to be within sight ➤ Casi llegamos a Segovia. La torre de la catedral está a la vista. We're almost in Segovia. The tower of the cathedral is in sight. ➤ El fin de la guerra está a la vista. The end of the war is in sight. ■ The end of the war is within sight.

estar **a la vista** to be in view ■ to be in sight

a la vista: ocultarse ~ to be hidden from view

estar **a la vista de** within view of ■ visible from ■ *(figurativo)* in view of

a la vista de: decidir ~ to decide in view of

a la vista de: hacer algo ~ to do something in view of

a la vista de: tomar una acción ~ to take an action in view of

estar **a la vista que...** to be obvious that... ➤ Está a la vista que... It is obvious that... ■ You can see that... ■ One can see that...

estar **a la vuelta** 1. *(de la esquina)* to be around the corner 2. *(al regreso)* to be on the way back

a la vuelta de ■ al volver de on the way back from ■ on returning from ■ *(literario)* upon returning from ■ *(yo, futuro)* when I get back from ■ *(yo, pasado)* when I got back from ➤ A la vuelta de Barcelona, te llamaré. When I get back from Barcelona, I'll call you. ➤ A la vuelta de Barcelona, tu carta estaba en el buzón. When I got back from Barcelona, your letter was in the mailbox.

a la vuelta de la esquina 1. around the corner 2. *(figurativo)* right out the door from here ➤ La zapatería está a la vuelta de la esquina de mi piso. The shoe repair shop is right around the corner from my apartment.

a la vuelta de la página on the back of the page ■ on the reverse side of the page ■ on the flip side of the page

a la vuelta de mi viaje ■ al volver de mi viaje *(pasado)* when I got back from my trip ■ on returning from my trip ■ *(futuro)* when I get back from my trip ■ on returning from my trip

a la zaga at the back ■ at the rear ■ behind ■ in last place ➤ *(titular)* Madrid, a la zaga en contratos indefinidos. Madrid is in last place in permanent contracts.

a larga distancia ■ a lo lejos ■ de lejos ■ desde lejos in the distance

a largo plazo in the long run

a largo plazo: objetivo ~ long-term objective ■ long-term goal

a las altas horas de la madrugada in the early hours of the morning

a las altas horas de la noche in the wee hours of the night ■ in the dead of night

a las ancas: cargar a alguien ~ to carry someone on one's back ■ to carry someone piggyback

a las bravas ■ por las bravas 1. brazenly ■ adamantly ■ without regard for the consequences 2. unprotected ➤ Se presentó en mi fiesta a las bravas. He brazenly crashed my party. ➤ El cliente vino reclamando la devolución del importe a las bravas. The customer adamantly demanded a refund. ➤ Los albañiles que trabajan en los rascacielos cruzan la vigas suspendidas en el aire a las bravas: sin arnés ni ningún tipo de seguridad. The construction workers who build skyscrapers walk across the beams in the open air unprotected: no harness, or other kinds of security.

a las bravas: conseguir algo ~ to get something easily ■ to get something by evading the bureaucracy ➤ No se puede conseguir un permiso de armas a las bravas. Hay que solicitarlo y satisfacer unos requisitos. You can't just walk in off the street and get and weapons permit. You have to apply and undergo a screening.

a las buenas willingly ➤ ¿Me vas a obedecer a las buenas o a las malas? Are you going to obey me, or do I have to get tough with you?

estar **a las buenas** to be doing fine ➤ Estás a las buenas. You're doing fine.

estar **a las buenas con alguien** to be on good terms with someone ■ to get along well with someone ➤ Quiero estar a las buenas con mis compañeros de trabajo. I want to be on good terms with my co-workers.

a las calladas on the quiet ■ stealthily ■ in secret

a las cinco de la tarde at five in the afternoon ■ *(refiriéndose al poema de García Lorca)* the moment when one's death is about to occur

a las claras: decir ~ to say openly ■ to say up front

a las claras: decirle a alguien ~ to tell someone openly ■ to tell someone up front

a las claras: hablar ~ to speak openly ■ to speak sincerely ■ to speak directly to the issue ■ to go straight to the point

¡a las doce, el que no tenga pan, que retoce! if you haven't gotten up for breakfast by noon, tough luck!

a las duras y a las maduras ■ para bien o para mal no matter what (happens) ➤ Sé que puedo contar contigo a las duras y a las maduras. I know that I can count on you no matter what.

a las espaldas de 1. behind one's back 2. detrás de in back of ■ behind ➤ La clínica está a las espaldas del banco. ■ La clínica queda a las espaldas del banco. The hospital is in back of the bank. ■ The hospital is behind the bank

a las mil maravillas: hacer algo ~ to do something perfectly

a las mil maravillas: ir ~ to go perfectly ■ to run perfectly ■ to function perfectly ■ to go smoothly ■ to run smoothly ➤ El motor va a las mil maravillas. The motor is running perfectly. ■ The motor is running smooth as silk.

a las mil maravillas: irle ~ to go great ➤ Todo me fue a las mil maravillas. Everything went great.

a las obras con las sobras make do with what you have

a las órdenes ■ a la orden at your service

estar **a las órdenes de alguien** 1. to be under someone's command 2. *(película)* to be directed by someone ■ under the direction of someone

a las primeras de cambio *(Esp.)* ■ de buenas a primeras ■ de entrada 1. right off the bat ■ all at once ■ all of a sudden ■ at first sight ■ point blank 2. a la primera oportunidad at the first opportunity

a las pruebas me remito a la prueba me remito I rest my case ➤ Este producto no se vende. La cifras de ventas lo demuestran. A las pruebas me remito. This product doesn't fly. The sales figures show it. I rest my case.

estar **a las puertas** to be close by

estar **a las puertas de la muerte** to be at death's door

a las quinientas: una vez ~ very rarely ➤ Yo viajo en avión una vez a las quinientas. I travel by plane very rarely. ■ I rarely travel by plane.

a las tantas: llegar ~ ■ llegar muy tarde 1. to arrive very late 2. *(a casa)* to get home very late

a las veces a veces at times

a la(s) *x* abrimos we open at *x* ➤ A las diez abrimos. We open at ten. ➤ A la una abrimos. We open at one.

a libre albedrío of one's own free will

a listo no hay quien le gane *(a él)* no one can beat him at being smart ■ *(a ella)* no one can beat her at being smart

a lo alto at the top ■ (way) up high ■ high up ➤ ¿Ves la casa en la sierra, a lo alto? Do you see the house (way) up high on the side of the mountain? ■ Do you see the house high up on the side of the mountain?

a lo alto: tirar ~ to be on the high side ■ to be on the high end ■ to estimate on the high side ➤ Tirando a lo alto, puede valer doce mil euros. (Estimating) on the high side, it could be worth twelve thousand euros.

a lo bestia: beber ~ to drink oneself under the table

a lo bestia: comer ~ to pig out ■ to eat like a hog

a lo bobo stupidly ■ foolishly

a lo concreto getting right down to it ■ getting down to brass tacks ➤ Si vamos a lo concreto, el problema es el precio. Getting right down to it, the problem is the price. ■ Getting down to brass tacks, the problem is the price.

¡a lo concreto! ■ habla sin ambages ■ ve al grano get to the point!

a lo escrito me remito I will honor what's in writing

a lo grande ■ por todo lo alto on a grand scale ■ on the grand scale ➤ En ocasión de la boda del príncipe los reyes dieron un banquete a lo grande. ■ En ocasión de la boda del príncipe los reyes dieron un banquete por todo lo alto. The king and queen threw a banquet on a grand scale on the occasion of the crown prince's wedding.

a lo hecho no hay remedio, y a lo por hacer, consejo what's done is done, but next time, listen to people's advice ■ let that be a lesson to you

a lo hecho, pecho there's no use crying over spilled milk ■ grin and bear it

a lo largo throughout ■ along the length ■ along

a lo largo de generaciones for generations

a lo largo de la historia throughout history

(a lo largo de) toda la noche all night long ■ (all) through the night

a lo largo del día throughout the day

a lo largo del tiempo over time ■ with time ■ with the passage of time ■ in the course of time

a lo largo y (a lo) ancho de la ciudad: buscar algo ~ to look all over town for something

a lo largo y (a lo) ancho de la habitación: buscar algo ~ to search the room high and low for something

a lo largo y (a lo) ancho del país: viajar ~ to travel throughout the country ▪ to travel all over the country ▪ to travel nationwide ▪ to travel far and wide

a lo largo y (a lo) ancho del planeta: viajar ~ to travel far and wide ▪ to travel all over the world

a lo lejos ▪ a larga distancia in the distance

a lo loco like crazy ▪ haphazardly ▪ *(subido de tono)* half-assed ➤ Se pusieron a bailar a lo loco. They started dancing like crazy. ➤ *(película de Billy Wilder) Con faldas y a lo loco Some Like It Hot* ➤ Hace su trabajo a lo loco. He does his work haphazardly. ▪ He does his work half-assed.

a lo más injusto, justicia luego for the unjust, justice will come ▪ *(sarcasmo)* for the unjust, justice some day ▪ for the unjust, justice later ▪ for the unjust, justice some other time

a lo más rodado, más zorro the older, the slyer

a lo más largo ▪ a lo sumo ▪ como máximo ▪ como mucho at most ▪ maximum ➤ Te doy cinco horas a lo más largo. I'll give you five hours maximum.

a lo mejor probably

a lo mejor me gustará I'll probably like it

a lo mejor me gustaría I'd probably like it

a lo menos at least ➤ El perro a lo menos te obedece a ti, pero no a mí. At least the dog obeys you, but not me.

a lo mero macho in a display of manliness ➤ A lo mero macho él apagó el cigarillo con el dedo gordo del pie descalzo. In a display of manliness, he put out the cigarette with his bare big toe.

a lo que to which

a lo que iba as I was saying ▪ then again

a lo que llamaba uno... to what one called... ➤ Fui el primero en probar lo que el chef llamaba su obra cumbre. I was the first (one) to taste what the chef called his greatest creation.

a lo que no te agrada, haz como que no oyes nada turn a deaf ear to unpleasant comments

a lo que no tiene remedio, cuartillo y medio don't tackle what can't be solved

a lo que salga ▪ salga lo que salga ~ regardless of the consequences ▪ no matter what the outcome ▪ no matter how it turns out

a lo que se dice... rumor has it that... ▪ it's been going around that... ▪ the scuttlebutt is that...

a lo que se ve ▪ *(más común)* ▪ por lo que se ve ▪ aparentemente apparently

a lo que te iba what I was going to tell you ▪ what I was going to say

a lo salvaje in the wild

a lo sumo ▪ como máximo ▪ como mucho ▪ a todo tirar ▪ a lo más largo ▪ cuando más at most ➤ Tres a lo sumo Three at most

estar **a lo suyo** ▪ estar centrado en lo suyo to be minding one's own business ➤ Yo estaba a lo mío cuando él me interrumpió. I was minding my own business when he interrupted me.

a lo tonto: actuar ~ to do something (really) dumb

a lo tonto: dar vueltas ~ 1. *(taxista)* to make unnecessary turns **2.** *(hablador)* to avoid the subject ▪ to evade the issue ▪ to hem and haw ➤ Para alargar el viaje, el taxista dio vueltas a lo tonto. To inflate the trip, the taxi driver made turns unnecessarily.

a lo tonto: hacer algo ~ ▪ hacer algo sin querer to do something without meaning to ▪ to do something unintentionally ➤ Pasé por el torno de salida a lo tonto. Ahora tengo que volver a pagar. I went through the exit turnstile without meaning to. Now I have to pay again.

a lo tonto: hacer el viaje ~ 1. hacer el viaje para nada to make the trip for nothing **2.** hacer el viaje en un impulso to make the trip on impulse ➤ Hice el viaje a lo tonto. I made the trip for nothing. ▪ I made the trip on impulse.

estar **a lo último de algo** to be nearly at the end of something ▪ to nearly have finished something ➤ Estoy a lo último. I've almost finished. ▪ I'm almost done.

a lomo: llevar algo ~ ▪ cargar algo a lomo to carry something on one's back

a lomos de un animal: cargar algo ~ to carry something by pack animal

a lomos de un caballo: montar ~ to go on horseback ▪ to ride horseback

a lomos de un caballo: ver ~ to see from horse back ▪ to view from horseback

a los cuatro vientos: gritar algo ~ to broadcast something all over the place ▪ to tell the whole world something ▪ to tell something to the whole world ▪ to tell everybody and his brother ➤ Lo gritó a los cuatro vientos. He told everybody and his brother. ➤ ¿Tuviste que decirlo a los cuatro vientos? Did you have to go and tell the whole world about it? ▪ Did you have to go and broadcast it all over the place? ▪ Did you have to (go) tell everybody and his brother?

a los lados 1. on the sides **2.** *(de un cerro)* on the slopes **3.** around the perimeter ▪ to either side ➤ A los lados de la Sierra de Madrid, hay muchas haciendas. On the slopes of the Madrid Sierra, there are a lot of ranches. ➤ A los lados de la Plaza Mayor hay muchos músicos peregrinos. Around the perimeter of the Plaza Mayor, there are a lot of street musicians.

a los ojos de in the eyes of ➤ A los ojos del estado... In the eyes of the state...

a los pies de alguien to be at someone's service

a los pies de usted at your service

a los pocos años de a few years after ▪ within a few years of

a los pocos días ▪ pocos días después ▪ unos días después a few days later ▪ a few days afterwards ▪ after a few days

a los pocos días de... a few days after... ▪ within a few days of

a los pocos minutos ▪ pasados unos minutos a few minutes later ▪ minutes later ▪ after a few minutes ▪ within minutes ➤ La ambulancia llegó a los pocos minutos. The ambulance arrived within minutes.

a los pocos momentos ▪ pasados unos momentos moments later ▪ after a few moments

a los principios *(poco común)* ▪ al principio at the beginning ▪ in the beginning

a los suyos to his men

a los *x* at (the age of) *x* ▪ at age *x* ➤ A los catorce (años) At the age of fourteen ▪ At age fourteen

a los *x* años ▪ con los *x* ▪ años at age *x* ▪ at the age of *x* ▪ after *x* years ▪ *x* years later ▪ within *x* years ➤ A los catorce años At age fourteen ▪ At the age of fourteen

a los *x* semanas within *x* weeks ➤ A los dos semanas Within two weeks

a mal paso: ir ~ ▪ ir a mal ritmo to go too slowly ▪ to go at too slow a pace

estar **a mal recaudo** to be stored in an unsafe place ▪ not to be stored in a safe place

a mal ritmo: ir ~ ▪ ir a mal paso to go too slowly ▪ to go at too slow a pace

a mala idea with premeditated malice

a mandíbula batiente: reírse ~ to laugh one's head off

a manera de in the style of ▪ like

estar **a mano 1.** to be (close) at hand ▪ to be handy ▪ to be nearby ▪ to be right where one needs it **2.** estar en paz to be even Steven ▪ to be square ➤ En mi oficina, todo está a mano. In my office, everything is (close) at hand. ▪ In my office, everything is handy. ▪ In my office, everything is nearby. ▪ In my office, everything is right where I need it. ➤ Estamos a mano. ▪ Estamos en paz. We're even (Steven). You don't owe me anything. ▪ We're square. You don't owe me anything.

a mano: hacer algo ~ to make something by hand

a mano: tener algo ~ to have something at hand

a mano alzada by a show of hands

a mano derecha on the right ▪ to the right

a mano izquierda on the left ▪ to the left

a mano limpia: hacer algo ~ to do something with one's bare hands

a manos de at the hands of ➤ La caída de Constantinopla a manos de los musulmanes marcó el final de la Edad Media. The fall of Constantinople at the hands of the Muslims marked the end of the Middle Ages.

a manos llenas liberally ▪ generously ▪ abundantly

a mansalva in large numbers

a mansalva: acercarse ~ to crowd around ➤ Los paparazzis se acercaron a mansalva a la superestrella. The paparazzi crowded around the superstar.

a mansalva: caer ~ to fall all over the place ➤ Las peras caían a mansalva del árbol. The pears were falling all over the place (from the tree).

a mansalva: disparar a alguien ~ to shoot someone at close range

a marchas forzadas: hacer algo ~ ■ hacer algo a trancas y barrancas to do something with great difficulty

a más andar ■ a todo andar as fast as possible ■ at full speed

a más... the more... ➤ A más trabajo, más dinero... The more work, the more money...

a más mar, más vela when the going gets tough, the tough get going

a más no poder for all one is worth ■ as hard as possible ■ to the utmost

a más no poder: bailar ~ to dance one's heart out

a más no poder: comer ~ to stuff oneself to the gills

a más no poder: correr ~ to run as fast as one can ➤ Corrió a más no poder. He ran as fast as he could.

a más no poder: hablar ~ to talk one's head off ■ to talk one's fool head off

a más tardar ■ como muy tarde at the latest

a más tardar *x* días después *x* days from now at the latest

a matacaballo: ir ~ to go at breakneck speed

estar **a matar con alguien** ■ llevarse a matar con alguien to be mad enough to scalp someone

estar **a matarse** to be at the point of ending it all

a mayor altura que higher up than ■ positioned above

a mayoreo wholesale

a media asta ■ a medio izar at half mast ■ at half staff

a media hora de vuelo half an hour into the flight ■ a half hour into the flight

a media mañana in mid morning ■ at mid morning

a media tarde in mid afternoon ■ at mid morning

a media voz ■ con voz baja ■ por lo bajo in a soft voice ■ softly ■ quietly ■ in a low voice ■ sotto voce

a mediados de in mid ■ in the mid ■ half way through ■ in the middle of ➤ Ella sale a mediados de Diciembre. She's leaving in mid December. ■ She leaves in mid December. ➤ A mediados del siglo XIX In the mid 19th Century

a mediados de año at mid year

a mediados de la semana at midweek

a mediados de mes at mid month

a mediados de semana at midweek ■ in the middle of the week

a mediados de siglo at mid century

a medianoche at midnight

a medias: ir ~ ■ ir a pachas to go halves ■ to go fifty-fifty ➤ Vamos a medias. ■ Vamos a pachas. Let's go halves. ■ Let's go fifty-fifty.

a medias palabras: decir algo ~ ■ decir algo con insinuaciones to say something in so many words

a medida que as ■ in proportion as ➤ A medida que nos acercamos al invierno, hace más frio. As winter approaches, it gets colder. ➤ A medida que baja la temperatura, el aceite se vuelve más espeso. As the temperature drops, the oil thickens. ■ As the temperature drops, the oil gets thicker.

a medida que iban pasando los años ■ según iban pasando los años ■ conforme iban pasando los años as the years went by ■ as the years passed by

a medida que fueron pasando los años ■ conforme fueron pasando los años as the years went passing by ■ as the years passed by ■ as the years went by

a medida que los años pasan ■ a medida que pasan los años ■ como pasan los años ■ según pasan los años ■ conforme pasan los años as the years go by ■ as the years pass (by)

a medida que pasa el tiempo ■ según pasa el tiempo ■ conforme pasa el tiempo ■ con el paso de tiempo as time goes by ■ as time passes ■ with (the passage of) time ➤ A medida que pasa el tiempo, me voy olvidando de él. As time goes by, I'm forgetting him.

a medida que pasan los años ■ a medida que los años pasan ■ a medida que van pasando los años ■ a medida que los años van pasando ■ a medida que pasan los años ■ según pasan los años ■ según van pasando los años ■ conforme pasan los años ■ conforme van pasando los años as the years go by ■ as the years pass (by)

a medida que van pasando los años ■ según van pasando los años ■ conforme van pasando los años as the years go passing by ■ as the years pass (by)

a medio camino half way ■ at the half-way point

estar **a medio camino entre** to be half way between

a medio gas: ir ~ to poke along ■ to go poking along

estar **a medio hacer** to be half done

a medio plazo de half way through the term ■ in the medium term

a medio plazo: objetivo ~ interim objective ■ interim goal

a mediodía *(L.am.)* at (twelve) noon ■ *(Esp.)* at 2 p.m.

estar **a medios pelos** *(Esp.)* ■ estar achispado to be tipsy ■ to be feeling no pain

a menos: ir ~ to go to seed ➤ El barrio ha ido a menos. The neighborhood has gone to seed.

a menos: venir ~ to come down in the world

a menos de cierta distancia de within a certain distance of

a menos palabras, menos pleitos the less said, the better

a menos que ■ a no ser que unless ➤ No pare a menos que se lo diga (a usted...) ■ No pare a no ser que se lo diga (a usted...) Don't stop unless I tell you...

a menudeo *(Méx.)* retail

a menudo ■ con frecuencia ■ frecuentemente often ■ frequently

a merced ■ a mercedes ■ sin salario without pay ■ without remuneration ■ voluntarily

estar **a merced de algo** to be at the mercy of something

estar **a merced de alguien** to be at the mercy of someone ■ to be at someone's mercy

estar **a mesa puesta** ■ venir a mesa puesta ■ vivir a mesa puesta not to have to work for a living ■ not have any financial worries ■ to be fixed for life

estar **a mesa y mantel** to be supported by someone

a mesa y mantel: tener a alguien ~ ■ mantener a alguien to support someone

a mi aire in my own way ■ my way ■ on my own

¿a mí con cañas, que soy el padre de las castañas? are you making fun of me? ■ are you poking fun at me?

a mi costa at my expense

a mi edad ■ a estas alturas at my age

a mi entender the way I see it ■ to my way of thinking

a mi juicio in my judgment

a mi manera my way ■ (in) my own way

a mi manera de ver the way I look at it ■ the way I see it

a mí me deja frío it leaves me cold ■ it doesn't do anything for me

¿a mí me lo vas a decir? you're telling *me*?

a mí me toca ■ me toca a mí it's my turn

a mi modo de ver to my way of thinking ■ the way I look at it

(a mí) no hay nada que me guste más (que...) there's nothing I like better (than...) ■ I like nothing better (than...)

¡a mí no me la cuelas! don't give me that! ■ I don't buy it!

a mí no me mires 1. *(porque no lo hice)* don't look at *me* **2.** *(porque no puedo ayudarte)* don't look to me ■ don't come to me ■ *(más despectivo)* don't come crying to me

a mí no me mires para... don't look to me for... ■ don't come crying to me for...

¡a mí, plin! ■ ¡a mí qué! ■ a mí que me importa ■ allá cuidados I couldn't care less ■ I don't give a flying damn

¿a mí, que las vendo? are you trying to tell me something I don't know?

¡a mí que me registren! you can search me! I've got nothing to hide ■ you got *me*! ■ I haven't got a clue ■ search me!

a mí siempre me liga... I'm always the one who gets stuck with...

a mí tampoco me gusta ■ tampoco me gusta ■ no me gusta tampoco I don't like it, either

a mi ver to me ■ the way I see it

a mil leguas a mile off ➤ Se podría ver su deshonestidad a mil leguas (de distancia). You could spot his crookedness a mile off.

a mis adentros: llegar ~ to touch me deeply ➤ Me ha llegado a mis adentros. It has touched me deeply.

a mis espaldas to my back ■ behind me ➤ *(reportero de noticias de televisión)* La Torre Windsor, que puedes ver a mis espaldas... The Windsor tower, which you can see behind me...

a mitad de halfway through ■ midway through ➤ Normalmente, hay un examen parcial a mitad de la asignatura. Normally, there is a midterm exam halfway through the course. ■ Normally, there is a midterm exam midway through the course.

estar **a mitad de camino** to be half way

a mitad de vuelo halfway through the flight ■ midway through the flight

estar **a mitad del camino** to be halfway (through the trip) ■ to be at midpoint (in the trip) ■ *(literario)* to be at midpoint in the journey

a modo de in the form of a ■ like ■ as ➤ *(Unamuno)* Quiero dejar consignado a modo de confesión... I want to record for posterity in the form of a confession

a mogollón: tener algo ~ *(más común)* ■ tener mogollón de algo to have loads of something ■ to have a ton of something ■ to have tons of something ➤ El brownie con helado, sirope y nata tiene calorias a mogollón. ■ El brownie con helado, sirope y nata, tiene mogollón de calorías. A brownie with ice cream, syrup and whipped cream has loads of calories.

a montones in abundance ■ tons of

a morro: beber ~ **1.** beber de la botella to drink from the bottle ■ to drink out of the bottle **2.** beber de la lata to drink from the can ■ to drink out of the can

a motor motorized ➤ Lancha neumática a motor Motorized rubber raft

a mucha cortesía, mayor cuidado beware of excessive courtesy ■ *(idea relacionada, en* Hamlet*)* methinks thou dost protest too much

a mucho hablar, poco acertar to be all talk (without really knowing)

¡a muerte! to the death!

a muerte: ser una lucha 1. ser un duelo a muerte to be a fight to the death **2.** ser una pelea contra la corriente to be an uphill battle

a mujeriegas: montar ~ ■ montar a la mujeriega to ride side saddle

a nadie le amarga un dulce don't refuse a gift

a nadie más a quien acudir: no tener ~ to have no one else to turn to ■ not to have anyone else to turn to ➤ No tenía a nadie más a quien acudir. I didn't have anyone else to turn to. ■ I had no one else to turn to.

a nado ■ nadando by swimming ➤ Cruzó el río a nado ■ Cruzó el río nadando. He swam across the river. ■ He swam the river. ■ He crossed the river by swimming (it).

a ningún sitio nowhere

a ninguna parte nowhere

estar **a nivel** ■ estar horizontal *(superficie)* to be level ➤ The table is not level. La mesa no está a nivel. ■ La mesa no está horizontal.

a nivel de *(incorrecto, pero común)* ■ en cuanto a as for ■ with respect to ■ when it comes to ■ -wise ■ as regards ➤ A nivel de clima, ganamos. Weather-wise, we've got you beat

a nivel freático at the level of the water table ■ at water-table level

¡a no dejarlo! go ahead! ■ you do that! ■ don't give up!

a no dudar(lo) ■ sin duda no doubt ■ undoubtedly

a no ser por el hecho de que... ■ *(más común)* de no ser por el hecho de que... if it were not for the fact that... ■ if it weren't for the fact that... ■ were it not for the fact that...

a no ser por ti ■ si no fuera por ti ■ de no ser por ti if it were not for you ■ if it weren't for you ■ were it not for you

a no ser por usted ■ si no fuera por usted ■ de no ser por usted if it were not for you ■ if it weren't for you ■ were it not for you ■ *(frase usable en el mismo contexto)* if it had not been for you ■ if it hadn't been for you ■ had it not been for you

a no ser que unless ➤ A no ser que me surja algo ineludible en el congreso, iré con toda seguridad. Unless something comes up at the meeting that I can't get out of, I'll definitely go. ➤ A no ser que lo que quieras sea simplemente un intercambio de ideas... Unless you just want simply an interchange of ideas...

estar **a nombre de alguien 1.** to be under the name (of) someone ■ to be in the name of someone **2.** ir dirigido a alguien ■ venir dirigido a alguien to be addressed to someone ➤ Han (ustedes) apartado un libro para mí a nombre de García Pérez. You're holding a book for me under the name (of) García Pérez. ■ You're holding a book for me in the name of García Pérez.

¿a nombre de quien? what name is it in? ■ what name is it under? ■ under whose name?

a ojímetro ■ al ojo de buen cubero ■ a ojo de buen cubero offhand ■ at a glance ■ by the seat of one's pants ■ making a rough guess ■ *(coloquial)* a guesstimate would be...

a ojo ■ a ojo de buen cubero ■ al ojo de buen cubero ■ *(pintoresco)* ■ a ojímetro **1.** by eye ■ judging by eye ■ just looking at it ■ by the look of it **2.** *(sin medir)* without measuring **3.** *(ropa)* without trying on ➤ Así a ojo calculo que aún nos faltan doscientos metros para la cumbre. By the look of it, I'd say we have about two hundred meters to go before reaching the summit. ➤ He comprado la tela de las cortinas a ojo; espero no haberme pasado mucho. I bought a generous amount of cloth for the curtains because I was judging by the eye. ➤ Escogí la camisa a ojo. I chose the shirt without trying it on. ■ I picked out the shirt without trying it on. ■ I picked the shirt out without trying it on.

a ojos cerrados with one's eyes closed

a ojos vistas noticeably ■ perceptibly ■ visibly

a orillas de on the banks of ➤ Ciudad Bolivar, fundada en 1595, está situada a orillas del Río Orinoco en Venezuela. Ciudad Bolivar, founded in 1595, lies on the banks of Venezuela's Orinoco River.

estar **a oscuras** to be dark (in here) ➤ Enciende la luz, que estamos a oscuras. Turn on the light, it's dark in here. ➤ No se puede leer a oscuras. You can't read in the dark. ➤ Estoy completamente a oscuras. Dime lo que está pasando. I'm completely in the dark. Tell me what's going on.

a oscuras: quedarse ~ to be left in the dark ➤ Se fue la luz de mi casa, y nos quedamos a oscuras. The lights went off at home, and we were left in the dark.

a otra cosa, mariposa ■ a otra rosa, mariposa let's talk about something else ■ let's change the subject ■ moving right along...!

a otra rosa, mariposa ■ a otra cosa, mariposa let's talk about something else ■ let's change the subject ■ moving right along...!

¡a otro perro con ese hueso! ■ ¡cuéntatelo a tu abuelita! go tell it to the Marines!

a pachas: ir ~ ■ ir a medias to go halves ■ to go fifty-fifty ➤ Vamos a pachas. Let's go halves. ■ Let's go fifty-fifty.

a pagar ■ cantidad a pagar amount owed ■ amount still to be paid

¡a pagar tocan! money talks

a palabras necias, oídos sordos turn a deaf ear to nonsense ■ don't argue with ignorance

a palo seco 1. *(whisky)* straight **2.** *(comida)* by itself ■ without anything to drink (with it)

a palo seco: beber vino ~ to drink wine without food

a palo seco: comer ~ to have something to eat without anything to drink with it ■ to eat without having anything to drink with it

a palos (con alguien): caerse ~ *(Ven.)* to get to drinking (with someone) ➤ Me caí a palos de whiskey con mis amigos. My friends and I got to drinking whiskey.

a palos con alguien: entrarse ~ ■ agarrarse a palos con alguien ■ meterse a palos con alguien ■ irse a las manos con alguien to come to blows with someone

a pan de quince días, hambre de tres semanas hunger is the best sauce

a pan duro diente agudo when the going gets tough, the tough get going

a pan y agua on bread and water

a pares in pairs ■ by twos ■ two by two

a pares y nones perdí mis calzones I lost my shirt gambling ■ *(literalmente)* I lost my undershorts gambling

a partir de 1. *(un suceso)* after **2.** *(precio)* desde starting at **3.** *(fecha)* starting on ■ beginning on ■ as of ■ after ➤ A partir de la pelea, nunca se volvieron a hablar. After the fight, they never spoke to each other again. ➤ A partir de 369 euros Starting at 369 euros ➤ A partir del quince del mes Starting on the fifteenth of this month ▪ Beginning on the fifteenth of this month ▪ As of the fifteenth of this month ▪ After the fifteenth of this month

a partir de ahí ▪ desde ahí 1. de ahora en adelante from now on 2. de aquí en adelante from here on

a partir de allí ▪ desde allí 1. de entonces en adelante from then on ▪ from that time on 2. de allí en adelante from there on

a partir de ahora starting now ▪ beginning now ▪ from this point on ▪ from now on

a partir de entonces from then on

a partir de ese momento 1. from that time on ▪ from then on 2. after that ▪ beyond that (time) ➤ Estaré aquí en Madrid hasta el final del año. A partir de ese momento, no tengo ni idea de lo que va a pasar. I'll be here in Madrid until the end of the year. Beyond that, I have no idea what's going to happen.

a partir de este momento from this moment on ▪ beginning right now ▪ starting right now

a partir de hoy starting today ▪ beginning today ▪ as of today

a partir de mañana starting tomorrow ▪ beginning tomorrow

estar **a partir un piñón (con alguien)** to be thick as thieves ▪ to be bosom pals ▪ to be bosom buddies

a paseo: andar ~ ▪ irse a paseo to go jump in a lake ▪ to go fly a kite ▪ to go take a hike ➤ ¡Anda a paseo! Go jump in a lake! ▪ Go fly a kite! ▪ Go take a hike!

a paseo: irse ~ ▪ andar a paseo to go take a hike ▪ to go jump in a lake ▪ to go fly a kite ➤ ¡Vete a paseo! Go take a hike! ▪ Go jump in a lake! ▪ Go fly a kite!

a paseo: mandar a alguien ~ to tell someone to go take a hike ▪ to send someone packing ▪ to send somone about his business

a paso de 1. a step away from 2. on the verge of ▪ at the point of ➤ A un paso del acuerdo sobre... A step away from agreement on... ➤ La pésima gestión ha puesto a la compañía a un paso de la bancarrota. Poor management has put the company on the verge of bankruptcy. ▪ Poor management has taken the company to the verge of bankruptcy. ▪ Poor management has brought the company to the verge of bankruptcy. ▪ Poor management has taken the company to the point of bankruptcy. ▪ Poor management has brought the company to the point of bankruptcy.

a paso de cangrejo ▪ a paso de tortuga at a snail's pace

a paso de liebre: correr ~ to run like a rabbit

a paso de tortuga ▪ a paso de cangrejo at a snail's pace

a paso firme: avanzar ~ to advance steadily ➤ La tecnología de los teléfonos celulares avanza a paso firme. Cell phone technology is advancing steadily. ➤ El fuego forestal avanza a paso firme hacia una zona de viviendas. The forest fire is steadily advancing toward a residential neighborhood.

a paso largo ▪ de prisa rapidly ▪ quickly

a paso ligero: caminar ~ to walk fast ▪ to walk at a fast pace ▪ to walk at a clip

a paso redoblado: marchar ~ to march in double time ▪

a pasos agigantados: avanzar ~ to make giant stides ▪ to make huge strides ➤ La tecnología avanza a pasos agigantados. Technology is making giant strides.

a pasto in unlimited quantities

a pata ▪ a pie ▪ andando on foot

a patadas galore ▪ a lot of ▪ lots of ➤ Mi español tiene lagunas a patadas. My Spanish has a lot of gaps.

a pecho: tomar algo ~ to take something to heart

estar **a pecho descubierto** to be unarmed ▪ to be defenseless

a pedazos ▪ en porciones ▪ por partes piecemeal ▪ in bits and pieces ▪ step by step ➤ La historia ha sido contada a pedazos, pero nunca en una presentación sistemática. The history has been told piecemeal, but never in a sytematic presentation.

a pedir de boca to one's heart's content ▪ to one's heart's desire

a pedir de boca: salir ~ to turn out perfectly

a pelo 1. *(cabalgar)* bareback ▪ without a saddle 2. *(trabajar)* without protective gloves 3. *(hacerlo)* in the raw ▪ without using a condom

a pelo y a pluma: hacerlo ~ ▪ ser bisexual to go both ways ▪ to be AC/DC ▪ to be bisexual

a perpetuidad in perpetuity ▪ forever

a perro flaco, todas son pulgas when it rains it pours

a perro viejo, no hay cus cus with experience comes caution

a persona lisonjera no le des oreja don't be seduced by flattery

a pesar de in spite of ▪ despite

a pesar de lo que haya podido pensarse contrary to what one might think ▪ contrary to what you might think

a pesar de los pesares in spite of everything

a pesar de que despite the fact that ▪ although ▪ even though

a pesar de todo in spite of everything ▪ for all that

a pesar mío in spite of myself ▪ against my better judgment

a peso de oro: vender algo ~ to sell something at an exorbitant price ▪ to sell something for an exorbitant price

a petición de alguien a instancia(s) de alguien at the request of someone ▪ at someone's request ➤ Rastas fue al peluquero a petición de su jefe. Dreadlocks went to the barber at his boss' request. ➤ El pianista tocó Cumpleaños Feliz a petición del cliente. The pianist played Happy Birthday at the customer's request.

a petición propia at one's own request ▪ *(de él)* at his own request ▪ *(de ella)* at her own request ➤ El presidente comparecerá en el Congreso, a petición propia. The president will appear before (the) Congress at his own request.

a petición suya at the request of one ▪ at one's request ➤ La reunión fue convocada a petición suya. The meeting was called at her request. ➤ Vino a petición mía. She came at my request.

a pie: ir ~ ▪ ir andando ▪ ir a pata to go on foot ▪ to walk ➤ Fuimos a pie. We went on foot. ▪ We walked. ➤ ¿Es bastante cerca para ir a pie? Is it close enough to walk to? ▪ Is it close enough to go on foot?

a pie de avión at planeside ➤ ¿Podemos recoger el equipaje a pie de avión? Can we get our bags at planeside?

a pie de obra *(Esp.)* on the spot

estar **a pie de fábrica** *(Esp.)* ▪ estar muy cerca to be close by ▪ to be near (here) ➤ Mi apartamento está a pie de fábrica. My apartment is close by. ▪ My apartment is near here.

a pie firme without moving ▪ standing fast

a pie juntillas to the letter ▪ in every particular ▪ to the last particular ➤ Pocas personas hoy en día aceptan a pie juntillas las teorías de Freud. Few people today accept Freud's theories to the letter.

a pie llano: andar ~ *(Esp.)* ▪ caminar a pie llano to have a flat-footed walk ▪ to walk flat-footed

a pierna suelta: dormir ~ ▪ dormir a pierna tendida to sleep like a log ▪ to sleep soundly

a pierna suelta: roncar ~ to snore loudly ▪ *(coloquial)* to saw logs

a pique: irse ~ 1. hundirse to sink 2. venirse abajo to be ruined

estar **a pique de** ▪ estar a dedos de to be at the point of ▪ to be in danger of

a plazo fijo: depositar dinero ~ to deposit money for a fixed term ▪ to open a money market account

a plazo fijo: tener una cuenta ~ to have a money market account ▪ to have a fixed-term account ➤ Tenemos dinero en el banco a plazo fijo. We have a money market account.

a plazos on credit ▪ in installments ▪ in installment payments

a plena luz del sol ▪ a pleno sol ▪ en pleno día in broad daylight

a pleno día ▪ en pleno día ▪ a pleno sol in broad daylight

a pleno pulmón: gritar ~ to shout at the top of one's lungs

a pleno rendimiento: funcionar ~ to function optimally

a pleno sol ▪ en pleno día ▪ a plena luz del sol in broad daylight

a poca barba, poca vergüenza youth is impetuous

a poca distancia a short distance away ▪ at a short distance

a poco de shortly after ➤ A poco de irse el profesor los niños se desmadraron. Shortly after the teacher left, the kids went wild.

a poco viento remos sin cuento if it's difficult, work hard

a pocos lances in a very short time

estar **a pocos pasos** to be (just) steps away ▪ to be a few steps away ▪ a short distance away

a por a y b por b in depth ▪ thoroughly ▪ systematically

¡a por ello! *(Esp.)* ¡ve por ello! go for it!

¡a por ellos! *(Esp.)* go get 'em!

¡a por ése! stop that man!

estar **a por uvas** to be clueless ■ not to have a clue

a porrazo limpio: coger a alguien ~ ■ pillar a alguien a porrazo limpio to clean someone's clock ■ to beat someone to a pulp ➤ A ese pájaro le voy a coger a porrazo limpio. I'm gonna clean that guy's clock. ■ I'm gonna beat that guy to a pulp.

a porrazo limpio: dar a alguien ~ 1. to give someone a beating 2. *(padres a sus hijos, en tono ligero)* to give someone a thrashing ➤ *(madre a hijo)* Te voy a dar a porrazo limpio si no me haces caso. ■ Te voy a dar a porrazo limpio si no me echas cuenta. If you don't mind me, I'm going to give you a thrashing.

a porrazo limpio: hacer algo ~ to do something the hard way

a porrazo limpio: pillar ~ ■ coger a alguien a porrazo limpio to clean someone's clock ■ to beat someone up ➤ A ese pájaro le voy a pillar a porrazo limpio. I'm gonna clean that guy's clock.

a porrazos a alguien: disfigurarle la cara ~ ■ partirle la cara a alguien to beat someone's face to a pulp ■ to smash someone's face

a porrillos ■ en abundancia galore ■ in abundance

a posteriori a posteriori ■ inductive ■ empirical

a precio de fábrica at the factory price ■ at the manufacturer's price ■ at the wholesale price ■ wholesale

a precio de costo: comprar algo ~ ■ comprar al costo ■ conseguir al costo to buy something at cost ■ to get something at cost

a precio de saldo at clearance sale price ■ at liquidation price

a presión: estar almacenado ~ to be stored under pressure ➤ El gas está almacenado a presión en tanques cilíndricos. The gas is stored under pressure in cylindrical tanks.

a primera hora de la mañana 1. first thing in the morning ■ first thing tomorrow (morning) ■ *(coloquial)* at the crack of dawn ➤ Ya está listo a primera hora de la mañana. He's up every morning at the crack of dawn.

a primera hora esta mañana first thing this morning

a primera vista at first sight ■ at a glance

a primeras horas de la noche early in the evening ■ in the early evening

a primeros (de mes) at the beginning of the month

a principios de ■ al comienzo de at the beginning of ■ early in ■ in the early ➤ A principios de siglo At the beginning of the century ■ Early in the century ➤ A principios del Siglo XX At the beginning of the 20th Century ■ In the early 20th Century

a principios de abril in early April ■ at the beginning of April

a principios de la primavera in early spring ■ early in the spring ■ at the beginning of (the) spring

a principios de la primavera pasada early last spring

a principios de la semana que viene early next week

a principios de siglo at the beginning of the century

a principios del invierno in early winter ■ early in the winter ■ at the beginning of (the) winter

a principios del invierno pasado early last winter

a principios del mes at the beginning of the month ■ early in the month

a principios del otoño in early fall ■ at the beginning of the fall

a principios del otoño pasado early last fall ■ early last autumn

a principios del Siglo XX at the beginning of the Twentieth Century ■ at the beginning of the 20th Century

a principios del verano in early summer ■ at the beginning of the summer

a principios del verano pasado early last summer

a priori a priori ■ deductive ■ prior to experience

a prisa: hacer algo ~ to do something hurriedly ■ to do something hastily

a prisa: ir ~ to go hurriedly ■ to go hastily

a propósito 1. by the way 2. a posta ■ adrede ■ con intención on purpose ■ deliberately ■ intentionally ➤ A propósito, ¿de que va la película? By the way, what's the movie about?

a propósito de ■ con respecto a 1. speaking of 2. regarding ■ with respect to ■ *(culto)* apropos of ➤ A propósito del Museo del Prado, ¿has visto la exhibición de mesas en el último piso? Speaking of the Prado Museum, did you see the exhibit of tables on the top floor? ➤ *(título de película)* A propósito de Enrique Regarding Henry ➤ A propósito de tu sugerencia... Regarding your suggestion... ■ Apropos of your suggestion...

a propósito de que speaking of which

ser **a propósito para** to be appropriate for

ser **a propósito para el tiempo** to be appropriate for the weather ➤ Ponte esta chaqueta. Es muy a propósito para este tiempo. Wear this jacket. It very appropriate for the weather.

a prueba on approval ■ on a trial basis

ser **a prueba de bomba** 1. to be bomb proof 2. *(figurativo)* to be very sturdy ■ to be indestructible ➤ Ese niño es a prueba de bomba. That child is indestructible.

ser **a prueba de fallos** to be fail-safe

ser **a prueba de todo** ■ a toda prueba to be unbreakable

ser **a prueba que no se destiñe** ■ ser prueba que no destiña to be colorfast

a prueba y error ■ por prueba y error by trial and error

ser **a puerta cerrada** to be held behind closed doors ■ to be conducted behind closed doors ■ to be closed door... ➤ Fue una reunión a puerta cerrada. ■ La reunión fue a puerta cerrada. The meeting was held behind closed doors. ■ The meeting was conducted behind closed doors. ■ It was a closed-door meeting.

a pulso: dibujo ~ freehand drawing

a pulso: ganárselo ~ to earn something by hard work ■ to earn something by working hard

a pulso sudando: ganárselo ~ ■ ganárselo con el sudor de la frente to earn it by the sweat of one's brow ■ to get it by the sweat of one's brow

a punta de pistola at gunpoint

a punta pala: tener algo ~ to have tons of something ■ to have scads of something ■ *(literally)* to have a shovel full of something ➤ Tiene discos a punta pala. He has scads of CDs. ■ He's got scads of CDs. ➤ Tiene dinero a punta pala. He has tons of money. ■ He's got megabucks.

a puntapiés: tratar a alguien ~ to treat someone badly ■ to treat someone shabbily

estar **a punto** *(cocina, reacciones químicas, etc.)* to be exactly right ■ to be at exactly the right point ➤ La salsa está a punto. The salsa is exactly right. ➤ El líquido está a punto para formar un sirope. Más caliente y se cuajará. The liquid is at exactly the right point to form a syrup. Any hotter and it will curdle.

estar **a punto de** to be at the point of ■ to be about to ➤ El agua está a punto de hervir. The water is about to boil. ■ The water is at the boiling point. ■ The water is at the point of boiling.

estar **a punto de anunciar** to announce shortly ■ to be about to announce ➤ El presidente está a punto de anunciar... The president will announce shortly...

estar **a punto de cambiar** to be about to change ➤ Nuestras vidas estaban a punto de cambiar para siempre. Our lives were about to change forever.

estar **a punto de caramelo** ■ estar en su punto 1. *(comida)* to be just right 2. *(situación)* to be about to come together

a punto de caramelo: tenerlo ~ *(matiz sexual)* to have him right where you want him

a punto de caramelo: tenerla ~ *(matiz sexual)* to have her right where you want her

estar **a punto de cumplir** to near completion of ➤ Cuando Bush está a punto de cumplir cinco años en el cargo As Bush nears completion of his fifth year in office

estar **a punto de morir** ■ estar en trance de muerte to be at the point of death

a punto de nieve: batir las claras ~ to beat the egg whites until the peaks are stiff ➤ Bata las claras a punto de nieve. Beat the egg whites until the peaks are stiff.

estar **a punto de no poder volver atrás** to be at the point of no return

a punto fijo: saber ~ to know for sure ■ to know with certainty ■ to know for a fact

a puñados: ganar dinero ~ ■ ganar dinero a espuertas to make money hand over fist ➤ Gana dinero a puñados. He makes money hand over fist.

a puñetazo limpio: pegar a alguien ~ to clean someone's clock ▪ to beat someone to a pulp ▪ to give someone a beating ➤ Le han pegado a puñetazo limpio. They cleaned his clock. ▪ They beat him to a pulp. ▪ They gave him a beating.

a puño cerrado with one's fist clinched ▪ with one's fist clenched

a puro ▪ a fuerza de by dint of

a que 1. to the fact that 2. *(Méx., coloquial)* (in order) to ➤ El conferenciante aludió a que... ▪ El orador aludió a que... The speaker aluded to the fact that... ➤ Le operaron a que le sacaran un segmento del intestino grueso. They operated on him (in order) to remove a segment of the large intestine.

¡a que...!: (qué te apuestas) ~ (I) bet...

¿a qué? ▪ ¿para qué? what for?

¡¿a que ahora resulta que la culpa la tengo yo?! ▪ ahora resulta que yo tengo la culpa ▪ o sea que ahora yo tengo la culpa so now it's *my* fault?!

a qué atenerse: no saber ~ *(normalmente negativo)* not to know which end is up ▪ not to know who's right ▪ not to have a clue as to what's going on ➤ No sé a qué atenerme. I don't have a clue about what's going on.

¿a qué día estamos (hoy)? ▪ ¿a cuánto estamos? ▪ ¿qué día es hoy? ▪ ¿qué día es hoy, me refiero al número de día? what's today's date? ▪ what's the date today? ▪ what is the date of today?

¿a qué distancia está...? how far (away) is...? ➤ ¿Desde un avión volando a los 35.000 pies, a qué distancia está el horizonte?-Doscientos veintinueve millas. From an airliner lying at 35,000 feet, how far (away) is the horizon?-Two hundred twenty-nine miles.

¿a que es bonita? she's good looking, huh?

¿a qué estamos esperando? what are we waiting for?

¿a qué ha venido eso? what was *that* about?

¿a qué habrá venido? *(él)* what's he doing here? ▪ I wonder what (in the world) he's doing here? ▪ *(ella)* what's she doing here? ▪ I wonder what (in the world) she's doing here?

¿a qué habrás venido? what are *you* doing here?

¿a qué has venido? ▪ ¡tú por aquí! what are *you* doing here?

¿a qué hora? what time? ▪ at what time?

¿a qué hora debería pasar el autobús? what time is the bus supposed to come by?

¿a qué le tienes miedo? what are you afraid of?

¡a que te gustaría saberlo! wouldn't you like to know!

¡a que no! no, you aren't ▪ no, you don't! ▪ no, you won't! ▪ no, you can't! ▪ no, you didn't! *(Nota: o cualquier otro verbo auxiliar)*

¡a que no eres capaz! bet you can't!

¡a que no me coges! *(Esp.)* ▪ ¡a que no me pillas! bet you can't catch me!

¡a que no me encuentras!-¡a que no te busco! bet you can't find me!-bet I won't look for you!

¡a que no me pillas! ▪ ¡a que no me coges! bet you can't catch me!

¡a que no puedes...! bet you can't...!

¡a que no sabes...! bet you can't guess... ▪ you'll never guess...

¡a que no sabes quién soy! ▪ te apuesto que no adivinas quién soy ▪ ¡a que no puedes adivinar quién soy! 1. *(niño trayendo disfráz)* (I) bet you can't guess who I am! ▪ you'll never guess who I am 2. *(persona que llama por teléfono)* (I) bet you can't guess who this is ▪ I'll bet you can't guess who this is

¿a qué precio? 1. ¿a cuánto? how much (is it)? 2. *(literal y figurativo)* at what price ▪ at what cost ▪ at what sacrifice? ➤ Tiene una carrera profesional muy interesante.-Sí, pero ¿a qué precio? Ha sacrificado su vida personal. He has a very interesting career.-Yes, but at what price? He's sacrificed his personal life.

¿a qué sabe? what does it taste like? ➤ ¿A qué sabe la leche en una caja? What does milk from a box taste like?

¿a qué se debe que...? why is it that...? ▪ what accounts for the fact that...? ▪ to what do we owe the fact that...?

¿a qué se dedica (usted)? ▪ ¿cómo se gana (usted) la vida? what do you do (for a living?) ▪ what is your line of work?

¿a qué se parece? what does it look like?

¿a qúe se refiere (usted)? what are you referring to? ▪ what are you talking about?

a qué se siente what it feels like ▪ what it's like ➤ ¿A qué se siente? What does it feel like? ▪ What's it like?

a que sí bet I can! ▪ yes, I can! ▪ yes, you are! ▪ yes, you do! ▪ yes, you will! ▪ yes, you can! ▪ yes, you did! *(o cualquier otro verbo auxiliar)*

¿a que sí? is it? ▪ are they?

¡a que sí puedes! (I) bet you can!

¡a que sí puedo! (I) bet I can!

¿a qué tantas...? why so many...? ➤ ¿A qué tantas preguntas? Why so many questions? ▪ *(a un niño)* You're full of questions.

¿a qué tanto...? why (is there) so much...? ▪ what's all...? ➤ ¿A qué tanto jaleo? What's all the ruckus? ➤ ¿A qué tanto odio en el mundo? Why is there so much hatred in the world?

¿a qué tantos...? why so many...? ▪ *(coloquial)* how come there are...? ➤ ¿A qué tantos problemas? How come there are so many problems?

¿a qué te dedicas? ▪ ¿cómo te ganas la vida? what do you do (for a living)? ▪ what is your line of work?

¡a que te pego! *(coloquial)* I'm gonna bop you one ▪ I'm gonna bean you one! ▪ you're gonna get it! ➤ ¡A que te pego si sigues así! (If) you keep that up, I'm gonna bop you one. ▪ (If) you keep that up, I'm gonna bean you one. ▪ (If) you keep that up, you're gonna get it.

¿a qué te refieres? what are you referring to? ▪ what do you mean? ▪ what are you talking about?

¿a qué velocidad? how fast? ▪ at what speed? ➤ ¿A qué velocidad vas? How fast are you going?

¿a qué viene eso? 1. what's the point? 2. what's that got to do with it?

¿a qué viene (todo) esto? what's that supposed to mean? ▪ what's that all about?

a quemarropa: disparar a alguien ~ to shoot someone at point-blank range ▪ to shoot someone point-blank

a quemarropa: pegar un tiro ~ to fire (a shot) at point-blank range

¿a quién? to whom? ▪ *(coloquial)* who to?

a quién acudir: no tener ~ not to have anyone to turn to ➤ No tenía a quién acudir. I didn't have anyone to turn to.

¿a quién apoyas? ▪ ¿de parte de quién estás? who are you for?

a quien conteste 1. to whomever answers ▪ *(coloquial)* to whoever answers 2. station to station ➤ Sólo da el mensaje a quien conteste. Just give the message to whoever answers.

¿a quién corresponde la factura? whose name is the bill in? ▪ whose name is on the bill?

a quien dan no escoge beggars can't be choosers

a quien le dan el pie, se toma la mano ▪ dar a alguien el pie y se toma la mano give someone an inch and they take a mile

¿a quién le toca? ▪ ¿quién va? whose turn is it?

a quien madruga, Dios le ayuda God helps those who help themselves ▪ the early bird gets the worm

¿a quién pertenece esto? ▪ ¿de quién es? who does this belong to? ▪ whose is this? ▪ *(formal)* to whom does this belong?

a quien recurrir ▪ a quien acudir who to turn to ➤ No sé a quién recurrir. ▪ No sé a quién puedo recurrir. I don't know who to turn to.

a quien se ayuda, Dios le ayuda God helps those who help themselves

¡a quién se le ocurre...! who would ever think...! ➤ ¡A quién se le ocurre decir tantas tonterías...! Who would ever think of saying such stupid things!

¡a quien se lo cuentas! you're telling me!

a quien votaré ▪ por quien votaré who I'm going to vote for

a rabiar tremendously ▪ enormously ➤ Es guapa a rabiar. She's gorgeous. ➤ Es malo a rabiar. He's vicious.

a rachas: estudiar ~ to study intermittently ▪ to study off and on ▪ to study in spells

a rachas: llover ~ to rain on and off ▪ to rain off and on ➤ Llueve a rachas. It rains on and off.

a raíz de ▪ como consecuencia de ▪ a causa de because of ▪ as a result of ▪ *(coloquial)* due to ➤ A raíz del accidente, nunca volvió a andar. As a result of the accident, he never walked again.

a rajatabla ▪ estrictamente strictly ▪ to the letter

a rajatabla: seguir las instrucciones ~ to follow the instructions to the letter

estar **a ras de** to be level with ▪ to be flush with

a ras del agua at water level

a ras del agua: volar ~ to fly just above (the level of) the water ▪ to fly (at) close to water level ▪ to fly close to the water ▪ to fly just off the water ➤ Lindbergh flew close to the water during the day. Lindbergh voló a ras del agua durante el día.

a ras del suelo at ground level

a rastras: llegar a casa ~ ▪ llegar a casa arrastrándose to come home dragging ▪ to come home beat ▪ to come home completely whipped

a rastras: andar ~ ▪ andar arrastrando los pies ▪ caminar arrastrando los pies to drag one's feet (as one walks) ▪ to shuffle one's feet (as one walks) ▪ to shuffle one's feet (when one walks) ➤ Anda a rastras. He shuffles his feet (when he walks).

a ratos ▪ de cuando en cuando ▪ de vez en cuando on and off ▪ at times ▪ sometimes ▪ from time to time

a ratos perdidos: hacer algo ~ to do something in one's spare time

a raudales: haber algo ~ (for) there to be something in abundance ➤ Había luz a raudales. It was flooded with light. ▪ It was bathed in light.

a raudales: agua ~ torrents of water

a raudales: dinero ~ tons of money ▪ money coming out one's ears ▪ *(cómico)* megabucks

a raudales: sangrar ~ to bleed profusely

a raya: poner a alguien ~ ▪ tener a alguien a raya ▪ mantener a alguien a raya to hold someone at bay ▪ to keep someone at bay

a rayas: camisa ~ ▪ camisa de rayas striped shirt

a rayos: oler ~ ▪ oler mal ▪ apestar to reek ▪ to stink (to high heaven) ➤ Huele a rayos. It reeks. ▪ It stinks.

a razón de 1. at the rate of **2.** at the price of ▪ for ➤ El avión descargaba el combustible a la razón de cien litros por hora. The airplane consumed fuel at a rate of a hundred litres per hour. ➤ El trabajo se contabilizó a razón de quince dólares la hora. Labor was computed at the rate of fifteen dollars per hour. ➤ Compré los tomates a razón de dos dólares la libra. I bought the tomatoes for two dollars a pound.

a regañadientes: hacer algo ~ to do something grudgingly ▪ to do something begrudgingly ▪ to do something unwillingly

a remojo: poner ~ ▪ poner en remojo to soak ➤ Pon los frijoles a remojo durante la noche. ▪ Pon los frijoles a remojo toda la noche. Soak the beans overnight.

a remolque: hacer algo ~ to do something unwillingly ▪ to be cajoled into doing something

a remolque de in tow ➤ El chico de los periódicos lleva a remolque a todos los perros y niños del barrio. The paper boy has all the dogs and children in the neighborhood in tow.

a remolque de alguien: andar ~ ▪ ir tras alguien ▪ depender de alguien to follow someone around ▪ to be dependent on someone ➤ Los hijos dependen de los padres. Children are dependent on their parents.

a remolque de alguien: ir ~ 1. to be in tow **2.** to lag behind someone

a renglón seguido 1. justo después immediately afterwards ▪ right afterwards **2.** justo después de eso immediately after that ▪ right after that

estar **a resguardo de** to be protected from ▪ to be sheltered from

a retaguardia in the rear

estar **a reventar** to be bursting at the seams ▪ to be crowded ➤ La oficina está a reventar. The office is bursting at the seams.

a rey muerto, rey puesto easy come, easy go ▪ there's another bus (along) every ten minutes

a rienda suelta freely ▪ unrestrained ▪ without restraint

a riesgo suyo ▪ por cuenta y riesgo ▪ de cuenta y riesgo at one's own risk ▪ *(de él)* at his own risk ▪ *(de ella)* at her own risk

a río revuelto, ganancia de pescadores troubled waters invite opportunists

a saber 1. namely ▪ *(literario)* to wit **2.** me pregunto I wonder ➤ A saber a dónde ha ido el perro. I wonder where the dog has gone.

a saber si I wonder if... ▪ I wonder whether...

¡**a saber lo que estarán tramando!** I wonder what they're up to ▪ it's no telling what they're up to ▪ there's no telling what they're up to

a sabiendas knowingly

a sabiendas de que... knowing that... ▪ with full knowledge that... ▪ aware that...

a salto de mata: vivir ~ to eke out a living

a saltos: funcionar ~ to skip ➤ El tocadiscos funciona a saltos. The record player skips.

a saltos y corvos ▪ a trompicones ▪ a empujones ▪ a tontas y locas by fits and starts ▪ in fits and starts

a salvo: no dejar (ni) ~ not to spare (even)

a salvo: poner algo ~ to put something in a safe place

estar **a salvo (de)** to be safe (from) ▪ to be out of danger ➤ Gracias a una reforma, el desnivel de la torre inclinada de Pisa ha pasado de 6 a 5,5 grados y ya está a salvo. Thanks to an adjustment, the tilt of the Leaning Tower of Pisa has gone from 6 to 5.5 degrees, and it is now out of danger.

a salvo: ponerse ~ to reach safety ▪ to get to a safe place ▪ to get to safety

a sangre fría in cold blood

¿**a santo de qué...?** ▪ ¿por qué regla de tres...? ▪ ¿con qué motivo? ▪ ¿a fin de qué? ▪ ¿con qué pretexto? why on earth...? ▪ why in the world...? ▪ for what earthly reason...?

a secas just plain ▪ just ▪ plainly ▪ simply

a simple vista: ver ~ 1. to see at a glance **2.** to see with the naked eye ▪ to see with the unaided eye

a simple vista: ser visible ~ to be visible to the naked eye ▪ to be visible with the unaided eye ▪ to be visible without a telescope ▪ to be visible without binoculars

a simple vista: ver ~ 1. to see with the naked eye ▪ to see with the unaided eye **2.** to see at a glance

a solapo ▪ de ocultis on the sly

a solas con alguien: verse ~ ▪ estar a solas con alguien to be alone with someone ▪ to be alone together

a sólo una semana de... only a week before...

a su aire: hacer algo ~ to do something one's own way

a su aire: vivir ~ to do whatever one likes ▪ to do whatever one wants

a su antojo 1. *(presente)* as one pleases **2.** *(pasado)* as one pleased

a su bola: hacer algo ~ *(subido de tono)* ▪ hacer algo a su aire to do something one's own way

a su bola: ir ~ *(coloquial)* to do one's own thing ▪ to go off on one's own ➤ No trabaja en equipo. Va a su bola. He doesn't work well on a team. He does his own thing. ➤ Va a su bola. Pasa de todo el mundo. He goes off on his own. He ignores everyone else.

a su costa: reírse ~ to laugh at one's expense ➤ Se rieron a mi costa. They laughed at my expense.

a su costa: vivir ~ ▪ vivir a costa ajena to live at someone else's expense ▪ to be supported by someone else ➤ La mayoría de los jovenes en España viven a costa de sus padres hasta los treinta años. Most Spanish young people live at the expense of their parents until they're in their thirties.

a su debido momento ▪ a su debido tiempo ▪ a su tiempo in due course ▪ when the time is right

a su debido tiempo ▪ a su debido momento ▪ a su tiempo in due course ▪ when the time is right

a su disposición at your service ▪ at your disposal

a su favor (de uno) in one's favor ➤ La votación resultó en tres a su favor y dos en contra. The vote was three to two, in favor. ▪ The vote was three in favor, two against.

a su libre albedrío (de uno) of one's own free will

a su modo (de uno) in one's own way ➤ Me gusta hacer las cosas a mi modo. I like to do things in my own way.

a su muerte on one's death ▪ at one's death ▪ when one dies

a su paso por as it runs through ▪ as it flows through ▪ as it goes through

a su propio ritmo: trabajar ~ to work at one's own pace

a su tiempo se sabrá ▪ el tiempo lo dirá time will tell

a su vez in turn

a (su) voluntad at will ➤ Cien años atrás, las personas no podían escuchar un concierto de piano de Beethoven a su voluntad, pero hubiesen tenido que esperar años para ello. A century ago, people couldn't listen to a Beethoven concerto at will, but might have to wait years to hear it.

a sueldo on a salary

a suertes: jugárselo ~ ▪ jugárselo al azar to leave it to chance

a suertes: echarlo ~ to draw straws ➤ Echémoslo a suerte quién trabaja en Navidad. Let's draw straws to see who works on Christmas.

a súplica de ~ *(legal)* ▪ at the request of ➤ A súplica del abogado, el juez dictó una reducción de la condena impuesta al condenado. At the lawyer's request, the judge reduced the convicted man's sentence.

estar **a sus anchas** ▪ estar en su (propia) salsa to be in one's element ▪ to feel at home ▪ to feel at ease

a sus espaldas: hacer algo ~ ▪ hacer algo a espaldas to do something behind one's back ➤ Lo hizo a sus espaldas. She did it behind his back.

a sus ordenes at your service

a sus *x* años at age *x* ➤ A sus seis años Mozart ya era un niño prodigio. At age six, Mozart was already a child prodigy.

a tal grado que ▪ a tal punto que so much so that ▪ to such an extent that

a tal punto que ▪ a tal grado que so much so that ▪ to such an extent that

a tambor batiente: anunciar ~ *(más común)* ▪ anunciar a bombo y platillo to announce with great fanfare ▪ to announce with a lot of hype

a tantos días vista from the date of receipt ➤ La factura es a pagar a treinta días vista. The bill is due thirty days from the date of receipt.

a tantos euros por hora at so many euros per hour

a temperatura ambiente at room temperature ▪ at ambient termperature

a tenor de ▪ de acuerdo con according to ▪ in accordance with

a terceros: seguro ~ ▪ seguro por daños a terceros ▪ seguro a terceras personas liability insurance

¿a ti qué te parece? ▪ ¿y tú, qué crees? ▪ ¿y tú, qué piensas? do bears live in the woods? ▪ is the pope Catholic? ▪ is a four-pound robin fat? ▪ what do you *think*?

¿a ti quién te ha dado vela en este entierro? what business is it of *yours*? ▪ who asked *you*?

a ti te conviene it would be well for you to ▪ it would be a good idea if you

a tiempo: llegar ~ to arrive on time ➤ El avión llegó a tiempo. The plane arrived on time.

a tiempo completo *(adverbio)* full time ▪ *(adjetivo)* full-time

a tiempo de hacer algo ▪ a tiempo para hacer algo in time to do something ➤ Llegamos a tiempo de cenar. We arrived in time to have dinner. ➤ El general llegó a tiempo de recomponer la fuerzas. The general arrived in time to reform the forces.

a tiempo para algo in time for something ➤ Llegamos a tiempo para el concierto. We arrive in time for the concert. ➤ Llegamos a tiempo para la obra. We arrived in time for the play.

a tiempo para hacer algo in time to do something ➤ Llegamos a tiempo para comer. We arrived in time for dinner. ▪ We arrived in time to have dinner. ▪ We arrived in time to eat dinner. ▪ *(formal)* We arrived in time to dine.

a tiempo parcial: trabajar ~ ▪ trabajar medio turno to work part time

a tiempo parcial: trabajo ~ part-time job

a tiempos ▪ de vez en cuando at times ▪ occasionally ➤ Voy de caminata a tiempos. ▪ Voy de caminata de vez en cuando. I go hiking occasionally.

a tientas by feeling one's way along ▪ gropingly

estar **a tiro** to be within range ▪ to be within reach

estar **a tiro de piedra (de un sitio)** a stone's throw (from a place) ▪ a stone's throw away ▪ within spitting distance

a tiro hecho: pronosticar el tiempo ~ to predict the weather with perfect accuracy

a tiro limpio: lanzar una pelota ~ to make to perfect shot with the ball

a título de ▪ en calidad de as a ▪ as an ▪ by way of

a título de amigo: actuar ~ ▪ actuar como amigo ▪ actuar en calidad de amigo to act as a friend ▪ to act out of friendship

a título de información for your information ▪ as a piece of information

a título de introducción by way of introduction

¿a título de qué? ▪ ¿en calidad de qué? in what capacity?

a título personal: decir ~ to speak for oneself only ➤ Esto lo digo a título personal. I'm speaking for myself only.

a tocateja: pagar ~ ▪ pagar en efectivo to pay in cash ▪ to pay cash

a toda costa at all cost ▪ at any cost ▪ at whatever cost ▪ whatever it takes

a toda luz ▪ a todas luces any way you look at it ▪ all things considered ▪ no matter how you look at it

a toda máquina (at) full speed ▪ full blast

a toda marcha (at) full speed ▪ full blast

a toda mecha (at) full speed ▪ full blast

a toda pastilla: ir ~ to go full blast ▪ to go at top speed

a toda pastilla: subir ~ ▪ subir a todo volumen to turn up full blast ▪ to turn up as high as it'll go ▪ to turn up as loud as it'll go ▪ to put at top volume

a toda plana: anuncio ~ full-page ad

a toda prisa 1. (at) full speed 2. very quickly 3. right away ➤ Llámale a toda prisa. Call him right away.

a toda prueba ▪ a prueba de todo unbreakable

a toda razón y efecto for all intents and purposes ➤ Si la Corte Suprema Española rechaza el Plan Ibarretxe, éste será a toda razón y efecto muerto. If the Spanish Supreme Court rejects the Ibarretxe Plan, it is for all intents and purposes, dead.

a toda vela: ir ~ to go full sail ▪ to go at top speed

a toda velocidad: ir ~ to go (at) full speed

a todas horas ▪ a cada hora at all hours

a todas luces ▪ a toda luz any way you look at it ▪ all things considered ▪ no matter how you look at it

a todas partes everywhere

estar **a todo** ▪ estar muy al tanto de todo ▪ estar muy dependiente de todo 1. to be into everything 2. to be up on everything

a todo andar ▪ a más andar at full speed

a todo cerdo le llega su San Martín ▪ a cada marrano le llega su Noche Buena ▪ a cada quien le llega su hora the day of reckoning comes to everyone ▪ everyone has his day of reckoning ▪ one's time is coming

a todo correr at full speed

a todo esto ▪ mientras tanto ▪ entre tanto meanwhile ▪ while all this was going on

a todo gas 1. *(carro)* with the accelerator floored 2. *(avión, avioneta)* at full throttle ➤ ¡A todo gas! Floor it!

a todo hay remedio, sino a la muerte only death is unavoidable

a todo meter: conducir ~ to drive at full speed

a todo meter: hacer algo ~ to immerse oneself in something

a todo meter: ir ~ to go full speed

a todo motor: ir ~ to go (at) full throttle

a todo tirar ▪ como máximo ▪ a lo sumo ▪ como mucho ▪ cuando más at most

a todo trapo: ir ~ ▪ ir a toda vela to go at full sail ▪ to go at full speed ▪ to go at top speed

a todo tren: ir ~ to go (at) full speed

a todo vapor to go (at) full steam ▪ full steam

a todo volumen ▪ a toda pastilla on full volume ▪ full blast ▪ 1. *(presente, futuro)* as high as it'll go 2. *(pasado)* as high as it would go

a todos to all ▪ to everyone ▪ to everybody ➤ *(Santa Claus en el poema de C.C. Moore)* ¡Feliz Navidad a todos y a todos buenas noches! Happy Christmas to all and to all a good night!

a tomar el fresco: salir ~ to go out for some fresh air

a tomar el fresco: mandar ~ to send someone packing ▪ to tell someone where to get off

a tomar por el culo *(subido de tono)* to fuck off

a tomar por el saco: vivir ~ ▪ vivir muy lejos to live in a remote place

estar **a tono** ▪ estar al unísono ▪ estar de acuerdo to be on key ▪ to conform to acccepted standards estar **a tono con** to be in keeping with

a tono: no venir ~ to be out of place ■ to be inappropriate

a tono: ponerse ~ to get in the mood

a tontas y a locas ■ sin pensar every which way ■ any which way ■ haphazardly

a tope: jugar ~ to gamble non-stop

a tope: subir ~ to turn all the way up

estar **a tope sin drogas** to be high without drugs ■ to be fulfilled without drugs

a tragos: pasar la vida ~ ■ pasar un mal trago to live a dog's life ■ to have a rough time of it

a traición with treachery ■ treacherously

a trancas y barrancas by the hardest ■ with great difficulty

a trasluz: copiar algo ~ to trace (over) something

a trasluz: verlo ~ to see it against the light ■ to hold it against the light ■ to hold it up to the light

estar **a trasmano** to be inaccessible ■ to be inconveniently located ■ to be out of one's way ■ to be out of the way

a través crosswise ➤ Pon el mantel a través. Place the tablecloth crosswise. ■ Lay the tablecloth crosswise.

a través de through ■ across ➤ Tengo mi cuenta de correo electrónico a través de la universidad. I have my e-mail account through the university.

a través de la habitación across the room

a través del tiempo through time

a trechos in stretches ■ in places ■ in spots

a troche y moche ■ a trochemoche haphazardly ■ helter-skelter

a trocitos ■ a saltos intermittently ➤ El bebé duerme a trocitos. The baby sleeps intermittently.

a trompicones ■ a tontas y locas ■ a saltos y corvos ■ a empujones in fits and starts ■ by fits and starts

a tu gusto as you like ■ the way you want to ■ according to your own tastes

¡**a tu salud!** to your health! ■ cheers!

a tutiplén *(Esp.)* ■ en cantidad **1.** in abundance **2.** to excess **3.** freely **4.** aplenty

a última hora 1. late in the afternoon ■ late in the evening **2.** at the last minute

a última hora de ayer late yesterday

a ultranza: defender a alguien ~ to defend someone tooth and nail

¡**a un lado!** ■ ¡atrás! make way! ■ stand back!

a un mal, otro igual when it rains, it pours

a un momento dado at a given moment

estar **a un paso** to be a step away

estar **a un poco menos de** ■ quedar a un poco menos de to be not quite as far as ■ to be a little less distant than ➤ Aplicando la ley de senos a sus observaciones visuales, Copérnico determinó que Venus está a un poco menos de tres cuartos de la distancia que hay entre el Sol y la Tierra. ■ Aplicando la ley de senos a sus observaciones visuales, Copérnico determinó que Venus queda a un poco menos de tres cuartos de la distancia que hay entre el Sol y la Tierra. By applying the law of sines to his visual observations, Copernicus determined that Venus is not quite three-fourths as far from the sun as the Earth is.

a un ritmo de at a rate of ■ at the rate of

a un tiempo ■ a la vez ■ al mismo tiempo ■ al tiempo ■ paralelamente at the same time ■ simultaneously ■ in unison ➤ Los niños cantaron a un tiempo. The children sang in unison.

estar **a un tris de** ■ estar en un tris de to be within a hair's breadth of ■ to come very close to

estar **a una calle** *(implica una calle paralela)* ■ quedar a una calle **1.** to be one street over (parallel) **2.** to be one block away (in any direction) ■ to be a block away (in any direction)

estar **a una cuadra** *(L.am.)* ■ estar a una manzana to be a block away

estar **a una cuarta** ■ estar a una octava ■ estar a unas pulgadas to be a few inches away

a una hora an hour later ■ an hour afterwards ■ in an hour

a una hora de... an hour after...

estar **a una manzana** *(Esp.)* ■ estar a una cuadra to be a block away

a una octava ■ a una cuarta ■ a unas pulgadas a few inches away

a una tasa anual del *x* por ciento at an annual rate of *x* percent ■ at the rate of *x* percent annually

a una voz 1. unanimously ■ **2.** in unison

a unas horas determinadas ■ a unas determinadas horas ■ a unas horas fijas at set times ■ at fixed times

a unas determinadas horas ■ a unas horas determinadas ■ a unas horas fijas at set times ■ at fixed times

a unas horas fijas ■ a unas determinadas horas ■ a unas horas determinadas at set times ■ at fixed times

estar **a unas pulgadas** ■ a una octava ■ a una cuarta to be a few inches away

a unos minutos within minutes

a usted le conviene it would be well for you to ■ it would be a good idea if you

estar **a vanguardia** ■ ir a la vanguardia to be on the cutting edge ■ to be in the vanguard

a veces ■ de vez en cuando ■ algunas veces ■ de cuando en cuando ■ cien de vez en vez at times ■ sometimes ■ occasionally ■ at intervals

a veces los arboles no dejan ver el bosque sometimes you can't see the forest for the trees

a veces sí, a veces no sometimes I do, (and) sometimes I don't *(Nota: O cualquier otro sujeto o verbo auxiliar, p.ej.: sometimes we can, (and) sometimes we can't, etc.)*

¡**a ver!** let's see!

a ver qué pasa let's see what happens

a ver si... watch...

a ver si cuela let's see if they'll go for it ■ let's see if it'll fly ■ let's see if we can pull it off ■ let's see if they'll fall for it ■ let's see if we can get away with it

a ver si te estás quieto (-a) *(a los niños)* be still ■ sit still

a vida o muerte to the death

a vista de in front of ■ in the presence of

a vista de pájaro: revisar ~ ■ echar un vistazo to review rapidly ■ to check (over) rapidly ■ to skim ➤ He revisado el borrador del tema a vista de pájaro. I checked over the draft of the theme quickly.

a vista de pájaro: ver ~ to see from a bird's eye view ■ to see from the air

a viva voz: decir algo ~ to say something in a loud voice

a vivir, que son dos días life is short, so make the most of it

a voces: decir algo ~ to say something in a loud voice

a voleo at random ■ any old way

a voleo: contestar ~ to answer the first thing that comes to mind ■ to answer off the top of one's head

a voluntad ■ a su voluntad at will ➤ Cien años atrás, las personas no podían escuchar un concierto de piano de Beethoven a voluntad, pero hubiesen tenido que esperar años para ello. A century ago, people couldn't listen to a Beethoven concerto at will, but might have to wait years to hear it.

a voluntad: servirse ~ to have as much as one wants ■ to have as much as one likes ■ to take as much as one wants ➤ *(tú)* Sírvete a voluntad. ■ *(usted)* Sírvase a voluntad. Have as much as you like. ■ Take as much as you like. ■ Have as much as you want. ■ Take as much as you want.

a voz en cuello: gritar ~ ■ gritar a voz en grito to shout at the top of one's lungs ■ to shout at the top of one's voice

a voz en grito: hablar ~ ■ hablar a voz en cuello to talk loud ■ to talk in a loud voice

a vuela pluma: escribir ~ ■ *(carta, poema, ensayo, etc.)* componer a vuela pluma ■ escribir al correr de la pluma ■ componer al correr de la pluma to dash off

a vuelta de correo by return mail

estar **a *x* años luz** ■ quedar a *x* años **1.** to be *x* light-years away ■ to be *x* light-years distant **2.** *(figurativo)* ser diametralmente opuestos (en un asunto) to be light years apart (on an issue) ■ to be diametrically opposed (on an issue) ➤ La Estrella Polar está a 430 años luz, con una incertidumbre del más o menos cien años luz. ■ La Estrella Polar queda a 430 años luz, con una incertidumbre del más o menos cien años luz. The Pole Star is 430 light years away, plus or minus a hundred light years. ■ The Pole Star is 430 light years away, give or take a hundred light years.

a *x* columnas *(titular)* *x* columns wide ▪ *x* columns across

a *x* días vista ▪ dentro de *x* ▪ días in *x* days

estar **a *x* kilómetros** ▪ quedar a *x* kilómetros to be *x* kilometers from here ▪ to be *x* kilometers away ➤ A diez kilómetros Ten kilometers away ➤ Está a un kilómetro. ▪ Queda a un kilómetro. It's a kilometer from here. ▪ It's a kilometer away.

a *x* minutos de *x* minutes before ➤ Falló un motor a tres minutos de aterrizar. An engine quit three minutes before landing.

a *x* minutos del vuelo *x* minutes into the flight ➤ A treinta minutos del vuelo ▪ A media hora del vuelo Thirty minutes into the flight ▪ Half an hour into the flight ▪ A half hour into the flight

estar **(a) *x* puntos por delante del otro equipo** ▪ llevar *x* puntos de ventaja sobre el otro equipo ▪ ir (a) *x* puntos por delante del otro equipo to be *x* points ahead of the other team ▪ to be ahead of the other team by *x* points

a *x* segundos de within *x* seconds of ➤ Los aviones pasan a veinte segundos de la Casa Blanca, el Capitolio y el Pentágono. Airplanes pass within twenty seconds of the White House, Capitol and Pentagon.

a *x* semanas *x* weeks away ➤ A seis semanas Six weeks away

¡**abajo...!** down with...!

¡**abajo el telón!** curtain!

abalanzarse a alguien to rush at someone

abalanzarse hacia algo to rush toward something

abalanzarse hacia alguien to rush toward someone

abalanzarse sobre algo to jump on something ▪ to throw oneself on something ▪ to leap on something

abalanzarse sobre alguien to fall toward someone ▪ to fall on someone

abandonar a alguien a su suerte ▪ dejar a alguien de la mano de Dios to abandon someone to his fate

abandonar algo **1.** to abandon something **2.** to quit doing something ▪ to stop doing something ➤ Alguien abandonó a un bebé en la entrada de la iglesia. Someone abandoned a baby at the entrance to the church. ➤ Abandonó las lecciones de piano. She quit taking piano lessons. ▪ She stopped taking piano lessons.

abandonar algo por ser una causa perdida to give up something as a lost cause ▪ to give something up as a lost cause

abandonar el local to leave the premises

abandonar el poder to give up power ▪ to relinquish power ▪ to step aside ➤ No quiere abandonar el poder. He doesn't want to give up power. ▪ He doesn't want to relinquish power. ▪ He doesn't want to step aside.

abandonar la idea de to give up the idea of ▪ to abandon the idea of

abandonar la última plaza to get out of last place ➤ Va a ser difícil abandonar la última plaza. It's going to be difficult to get out of last place.

abandonar la vigilancia to let down one's guard

abanico de opciones range of options

abaratar el despido de to reduce the dismissal compensation for ▪ to lower the dismissal compensation for ➤ *(noticia)* El ministerio de trabajo quiere abaratar el despido para todos los contratos nuevos. The labor ministry wants to lower dismissal compensation for all new hires.

abaratar el precio de to reduce the price of ▪ to lower the price of

abarcar desde...hasta to extend from...to

abarcar muchas cosas to encompass many things

estar **abarrotado de gente** to be (jam) packed with people ▪ to be crammed with people

abarrotar un sitio to pack a place ▪ to crowd into a place

abastecerse de ▪ abastecerse con to stock up on

estar **abatido por algo** ▪ sentirse abatido por algo to be depressed about something

estar **abochornado(-a)** to be embarrassed

abatir a tiros **1.** *(avión)* derribar to shoot down **2.** *(animal)* to shoot

abatir el objetivo to pound the target

abatirse por algo to become dejected because of something ▪ to become dispirited because of something ▪ to become disheartened because of something

abatirse sobre algo **1.** to swoop down on something **2.** to descend on something ➤ El pelícano se abatió sobre el pez y lo cogió en su pico. The pelican swooped down on the fish and caught it in its beak. ➤ Cuando las nieves se abatían sobre los bosques... When the snows descended on the forests...

abdicar el reino to abdicate the throne

estar **abierto(-a) a sugerencias** to be open to suggestions

abismos insondables unfathomable depths

estar **abochornado de algo** *(Esp.)* ▪ estar apenado de algo ▪ estar avergonzado de algo to be embarrassed about something

ser **abochornado por algo** *(Esp.)* ▪ ser apenado por algo ▪ ser avergonzado por algo to be embarrassed by something

abochornar a alguien ▪ avergonzar a alguien ▪ dar vergüenza a alguien to embarrass someone ➤ It embarrasses me. Me abochorna. ▪ Me avergüenza. ▪ Me da vergüenza. It embarrasses me. ➤ It embarrasses me when you kiss me in public. Me avergüenza que me beses en público. ➤ Abochorna a su mujer. He embarrasses his wife. ➤ He embarrasses her. Él la abochorna.

abochornarse de algo to be embarrassed by something ▪ to feel embarrassed by something ➤ Me abochorné de lo que dijo. I was embarrassed by what he said.

abogado de oficio court-appointed attorney

abogado defensor defense attorney

abogado del diablo: hacer de ~ to play the devil's advocate ➤ Déjame que haga un poco de abogado del diablo porque tu plan no me convence del todo. Let me play devil's advocate for a minute because I have some doubts about your plan.

abogar por to call for ➤ El presidente abogó por el inicio de un diálogo entre ambos gobiernos. The president called for the beginning of a dialogue between the two governments.

abogar por alguien to speak for someone ▪ to speak in behalf of someone ▪ to speak in favor of someone

abonar dinero en la cuenta de uno to credit to one's account

abonarse a to buy a season ticket for ▪ to buy a season's ticket to ▪ to subscribe to ➤ Me aboné a la temporada de conciertos de la sinfonía. I bought a season ticket to the symphony.

abonarse a una publicación to subscribe to a publication

ser **abordado por** to be approached by ➤ Abordado en plena rueda de prensa por el dueño de un pianobar de Marbella que quería su foto "para el negocio", el actor (Kevin Costner) hizo gala de su paciencia, de sus gafas de miope y de su coquetería. Approached in the middle of the press conference by the owner of a piano bar who wanted his photograph for his business, the actor made a full display of his patience, thick glasses, and flirting charm.

abordar a alguien to deal with someone ▪ to approach someone ▪ to go up to someone ➤ Kennedy encontró a Khrushchev difícil de abordar. Kennedy found Khrushchev difficult to deal with. ➤ Un grupo de periodistas aborda a un funcionario taliban a su salida de la embajada en Islamabad. A group of journalists approach a Taliban official as he was coming out of the embassy in Islamabad.

abordar a alguien con un asunto to approach someone about a matter ▪ to approach someone with a matter

abordar de lleno el desafío to meet the challenge head on ➤ La cumbre europea aprobó ayer un programa de reformas para abordar de lleno el desafío... The European summit yesterday approved a series of reforms to meet head on the technological challenge. . .

abordar el asunto to deal with the matter

abordar el tema to deal with the subject

abordar una situación to deal with a situation ▪ to come to grips with a situation

abortar el plan ▪ hacer fracasar el plan ▪ *(a menudo plural)* ▪ abortar los planes ▪ hacer fracasar los planes to foil a plot

abortar la maniobra de despegue to abort a takeoff

abortar los planes de alguien ▪ hacer fracasar los planes ▪ abortar el plan ▪ hacer fracasar el plan to frustrate someone's plans

abortar un desastre to avert a disaster ▪ to prevent a disaster

¡**(abran) paso a la juventud!** make way for youth ▪ make way for the younger generation!

abrasarse de calor ▪ morirse de calor to be sweltering

abrasarse vivo to be burning up ▪ to be roasting (alive) ➤ Me abraso vivo aquí. *(dentro de la casa)* I'm buring up (in here). ▪ *(afuera)* I'm burning up (out here).

¡ábrete Sésamo! Open Sesame!
ser una **abreviatura de** to be short for ➤ CentCom es una abreviatura de Central Command. CentCom is short for Central Command.
estar **abriéndose el apetito** to work up an appetite ▪ to get hungry ➤ Estuvimos abriéndonos el apetito haciendo excursionismo. We worked up an appetite by going hiking. ▪ We worked up an appetite as we hiked.
abrigar de to provide protection from ▪ to shield from ▪ to protect from ▪ to form a protective barrier against
abrigar esperanzas de... to cherish the hope of...
abrigar esperanzas de que... to cherish the hope that...
abrigar más que... ▪ ser más calido que... ▪ ser más abrigado que... ▪ calentar más que... to be warmer than... ▪ to provide more warmth than... ➤ Las nuevas botas espaciales abrigan más que las antiguas (botas) de cuero. ▪ Las nuevas botas espaciales son más cálidas que las antiguas (botas) de cuero. ▪ Las nuevas botas espaciales son más abrigadas que las antiguas (botas) de cuero. ▪ Las nuevas botas espaciales calientan más que las antiguas (botas) de cuero. The new "moon" boots are warmer than the old leather ones.
abrigar mucho *(ropa)* ▪ dar mucho calor to be warm
abrigar resentimientos ▪ guardar resentimiento ▪ guardar rencor to harbor resentment ▪ to bear a grudge ▪ to have a grudge ▪ to hold a grudge
abrigo caliente warm coat
abrigo de visón mink coat
¡abrimos hoy! opening today!
¡abrimos próximamente! opening soon!
abrir boca ▪ hacer boca ▪ despertar el apetito to whet one's apetite
abrir brecha entre 1. to break through 2. to make an opening in ➤ El sol abrió brecha entre las nubes. The sun broke through the clouds. ➤ La policia abrió brecha entre la multitud. The police made an opening in the crowd.
abrir bufete ▪ abrir un bufete to open a law practice ▪ to begin practicing law
abrir camino to pave the way ▪ to pioneer
abrir cancha ▪ dar cancha ▪ hacer cancha 1. *(para algo)* to make way ▪ *(a alguien)* to accommodate someone ➤ *(The Magnificent Men and Their Flying Machines)* ¡Abran cancha! Make way (below)!
abrir de par en par to open wide
abrir el alma ▪ abrir el corazón to open one's heart
abrir el apetito ▪ despertar el apetito to whet one's appetite ▪ to work up an appetite
abrir el camino para to open the way for
abrir el corazón ▪ abrir el alma to open one's heart
abrir el desfile ▪ encabezar el desfile to lead the parade ▪ to head the parade
abrir el grifo *(Esp.)* to turn on the tap ▪ to turn the tap on
abrir el juego ▪ abrir juego to start the game ▪ to start the match ▪ to make the opening bet
abrir el juicio to open the trial ▪ to start the trial ▪ to start the hearing
abrir en canal *(Esp.)* to split open
abrir expediente to open a criminal investigation ▪ to begin a criminal investigation ▪ to start a criminal investigation
abrir fuego a to open fire on
abrir juego ▪ abrir el juego to start the game ▪ to start the match ▪ to make the opening bet
abrir la boca 1. to open one's mouth ▪ 2. to talk too much ▪ to reveal too much
abrir la carrera por la presidencia to begin the presidential race ▪ to kick off the presidential campaign
abrir la marcha ▪ encabezar la procesión to head the procession
abrir la negociación ▪ arrancar la negociación ▪ empezar la negociación to begin negotiations
abrir la puerta ▪ atender la puerta ▪ ver quién hay en la puerta to answer the door ▪ to see who's at the door ➤ Vete a atender la puerta. ▪ Vete a abrir la puerta. ▪ Vete a ver quién hay en la puerta. Go answer the door. ▪ Go see who's at the door.
abrir la puerta empujándola to open the door outward(s) ▪ to open the door away from you
abrir la puerta para ▪ abrir las puertas para to open doors for ▪ to open doors to ▪ to pave the way for
abrir la puerta tirando to open the door inward ▪ to open the door toward(s) you
abrir la sesión to open the session ▪ to open the meeting
abrir las cortinas to open the curtains ▪ to draw back the curtains
abrir las piernas to spread one's legs
abrir las puertas para ▪ abrir la puerta para to pave the way for
abrir los oídos to listen up
abrir los ojos (a uno) to open one's eyes
abrir paso a to open the way to
abrir su corazón to open one's heart
abrir trinchera *(militar)* to open the trenches
abrir (un) bufete to open a law practice ▪ to open a law firm
abrir un foso to create a rift ▪ to cause a rift ➤ EE UU descubre que la pena de muerte abre un foso con sus aliados europeos. USA discovers that the death penalty creates a rift with its European allies.
abrir un hueco en algo (por explosión) to blow a hole in something ➤ La explosión del mortero abrió un agujero en un lado del edificio. The mortar shell blew a hole in the side of the building. *(Nota: El inglés prefiere el artículo definido "the side" en vez de "a side".)*
abrir un sumario contra alguien ▪ instruir un sumario contra alguien to indict someone ▪ to issue an indictment against someone ▪ to issue an indictment of someone ▪ to file legal proceedings against someone
abrir una brecha entre las nubes to break through the clouds
abrir una crisis to touch off a crisis ▪ to precipitate a crisis
abrir una investigación ▪ iniciar una investigación to open an investigation ▪ to begin an investigation
abrirle algo a alguien 1. to open something for someone ▪ to let someone in 2. to split open something ▪ to split something open ➤ Me abrió la puerta. She opened the door for me. ▪ She let me in. ➤ El impacto de la roca le abrió la cabeza. The impact of the rock split his head open. ▪ The impact of the rock split open his head. ➤ El impacto de la roca se la abrió. The impact of the rock split it open.
abrirle el apetito to whet one's appetite
abrirle los ojos to open one's eyes
abrirse a to open oneself to
abrirse a alguien ▪ abrirse con alguien to open up to someone
abrirse ante uno to open up in front of one ▪ to open up before one
abrirse camino 1. abrirse paso to make one's way 2. desenvolverse to get one's foot in the door
abrirse camino a to make one's way to
abrirse camino a través de la multitud to make one's way through the crowd
abrirse camino en el mundo to make one's way in the world
abrirse camino hacia to make one's way toward ▪ to make one's way to
abrirse camino a través de la multitud ▪ abrirse paso a través de la multitud to make one's way through the crowd
abrirse con alguien ▪ abrirse a alguien to open up to someone
abrirse el día ▪ despejarse to clear up ▪ (for) the sun to come out
abrirse hacia adentro to open inward(s) ▪ to open toward(s) you ▪ to open in
abrirse hacia fuera to open outward(s) ▪ to open away from you ▪ to open out
abrirse paso 1. to get a foot in the door 2. to get through ➤ Tuve que esforzarme para abrirme paso. I had to struggle to get a foot in the door. ➤ Conseguimos abrirnos paso. We managed to get through.
abrirse paso a través de la multitud ▪ abrirse camino a través de la multitud to make one's way through the crowd
abrirse una hernia ▪ saltarse una hernia (for) a hernia to balloon out
abrirse una puerta to get one's foot in the door

abrírsele una fuga to spring a leak

abrírsele una vía de agua ▪ comenzar una fuga de agua to spring a leak *(Nota: dícese de barcos)*

abrírsele el apetito to work up an appetite ▪ to get an appetite

abrírsele una hernia ▪ salírsele una hernia ▪ saltársele una hernia (for) a hernia to balloon out ➤ Se le abrió la hernia. ▪ Se le salió la hernia. ▪ Se le saltó la hernia. The hernia ballooned out. ▪ *(a él)* His hernia ballooned out. ▪ *(a ella)* Her hernia ballooned out.

abrochar un botón to button a button

abrocharse con alguien *(Mex., jerga)* to lay someone ▪ to have sex with someone

¡abróchense los cinturones! fasten your seatbelts!

abroquelarse contra to shield oneself against

estar **abrumado(-a) con trabajo** to overwhelmed with work

abrumadoramente positivo(-a) overwhelmingly positive

absentismo laboral ▪ ausentismo laboral absenteeism from work

absolver a uno de su promesa to release one from one's promise

absolver la instancia to dismiss the case

abstenerse de hacer algo to abstain from doing something ▪ to refrain from doing something

abstenerse de votar to abstain from voting

abstención parlamentaria parliamentary abstention ▪ pass

abultar el kilometraje ▪ inflar el kilometraje to inflate the mileage

estar **aburrido(-a) como una ostra** to be bored stiff ▪ to be bored to death ▪ to be bored silly

estar **aburrido(-a) de** ▪ sentirse aburrido de to be bored by ▪ to feel bored by ➤ El poeta John Ciardi dijo que se sentía aburrido de sus estudiantes. The poet John Ciardi said he was bored by his students. ▪ The poet John Ciardi said he felt bored by his students.

aburrirse como una ostra ▪ aburrirse soberanamente to be bored stiff ▪ to be bored to death

abusar de alguien ▪ propasarse con alguien **1.** to abuse someone ▪ to mistreat someone ▪ **2.** to take (unfair) advantage of someone

abusar de la bebida to drink too much ▪ to abuse alcohol ▪ to drink heavily

abusar de la hospitalidad de alguien to wear out one's welcome (with someone) ▪ to abuse someone's hospitality

abusar de las drogas to abuse drugs ▪ to be a drug abuser ▪ to be heavy into drugs

abusar del trabajo to overwork

abuso de confianza breach of confidence

abuso de poder abuse of power

abuso de autoridad abuse of authority

abyecta sordidez: vivir en ~ ▪ vivir en pésimas condiciones to live in abject squalor ▪ to live in abject poverty

¡acaba con esto rápido! get it over with, quick!

acabada la reunión when the meeting was over

acabado: revisar el ~ to look over the finished product ▪ to check (over) the finished product

acabar algo 1. to end something **2.** terminar algo to finish something **3.** agotar algo to use up something

acabar ante el tribunal to end up in court ➤ Los vecinos acabaron ante el tribunal. The neighbors ended up in court.

acabar bien ▪ tener un feliz desenlace ▪ tener un final feliz to have a happy ending

acabar como el rosario de la aurora to end up on bad terms ▪ to break up in confusion ▪ to break up in disarray

acabar con algo 1. to put an end to something ▪ to get something over with **2.** *(comida, vino)* to finish off ▪ to polish off ➤ Será mejor que acabe con ello. ▪ Mejor será que acabe con ello. ▪ Sería mejor que acabara con ello. ▪ Mejor sería que acabara con ello. ▪ I might as well get it over with. ➤ Habré terminado (para) la semana que viene. ▪ Habré acabado (para) la semana que viene. I'll be done sometime next week.

acabar con alguien 1. romper con alguien to break up with someone **2.** deshacerse de alguien to finish someone off ▪ to get rid of someone

acabar con la paciencia de alguien ▪ agotar la paciencia de alguien to exhaust one's patience

acabar con los exámenes to finish (taking) exams

acabar con un final feliz to end on a happy note

estar **acabado de hacer** to be freshly made

acabar de hacer algo ▪ terminar de hacer algo to just do something ▪ to just finish (doing) something ➤ Acabamos de cenar hace un momento. We just finished supper a few minutes ago. ➤ Acaban de salir. They just left.

acabar de raíz con algo to nip something in the bud ▪ to cut something out at the root

acabar el diploma de estudios avanzados (DEA) 1. terminar el diploma de estudios avanzados ▪ acabar el master ▪ terminar el master to complete a master's (degree) ▪ to finish a master's (degree) **2.** diplomarse en estudios avanzados to get a master's (degree)

acabar el doctorado ▪ terminar el doctorado ▪ doctorarse to complete one's doctorate ▪ to finish one's doctorate ▪ to complete one's doctoral degree ▪ to finish one's doctoral degree

acabar el master ▪ acabar el diploma de estudios avanzados (DEA) ▪ diplomarse en estudios avanzados ▪ terminar el master ▪ terminar el diploma de estudios avanzados (DEA) to complete one's master's (degree) ▪ to finish one's master's (degree)

acabar en ▪ acabar por to end in

acabar en mal ▪ parar en mal to come to a bad end ▪ to meet an ill fate

acabar en punta to have a pointed end

acabar en tablas ▪ quedar en tablas ▪ hacer tablas to end in a stalemate

acabar en urgencias to end up in the emergency room

acabar hablando de un tema to end up on a subject ▪ to get off on a subject ➤ ¿Cómo acabé hablando de esto? How did I end up on that subject? ▪ How did I get off on that subject?

acabar haciendo una cosa ▪ acabar por hacer una cosa to end up doing something ➤ Fue a España a estudiar y acabó quedándose a vivir. He went to Spain to go to school and ended up living there. ➤ Me pongo la cazadora por la mañana, pero para las diez, hace tanto calor que acabo quitándomela. I wear my jacket in the morning, but by 10 a.m. it's so warm, I end up taking it off.

acabar la licenciatura ▪ terminar la licenciatura ▪ licenciarse to complete one's bachelor's (degree) ▪ to finish one's bachelor's (degree)

acabar las clases ▪ salir de clase to get out of classes (for the day) ▪ to get out of school (for the day) ➤ ¿A qué hora acabas las clases? What time do classes get out? ▪ What time are classes over? ▪ What time do you get out of class? ▪ What time do you get out of school?

acabar los estudios ▪ terminar los estudios to complete one's degree ▪ to finish one's degree

acabar mal 1. to end badly **2.** *(una relación)* to end up on bad terms

acabar por hacer una cosa ▪ acabar haciendo una cosa ▪ concluir por hacer una cosa to end up doing something ➤ En la novela de Unamuno, el agnóstico, Lázaro, acabó por ir a misa todos los domingos. In Unamuno's novel, the agnostic Lazaro ends up going to mass every Sunday.

acabar por tener que hacer algo ▪ acabar teniendo que hacer algo to end up having to do something ➤ Acabé por tener que hacerlo. ▪ Acabé teniéndolo que hacer. I ended up having to do it.

acabar teniendo que hacer algo ▪ acabar por tener que hacer algo to end up having to do something ➤ Acabé teniéndolo que hacer. ▪ Acabé por tener que hacerlo. I ended up having to do it.

acabar sus días to end one's days

¡acabara ya! let's be done with it! ▪ I'm sick of it!

¡acabáramos! now I get it! ▪ got it! ▪ I've finally figured it out! ▪ finally! ▪ at last!

acabarle la paciencia a alguien ▪ colmarle la paciencia a alguien ▪ fregarle la paciencia a alguien ▪ gastarle la paciencia a alguien to try someone's patience ▪ to exhaust someone's patience

acabarse su tiempo ▪ agotarse su tiempo to run out of time ▪ *(poético)* for one's time to grow short ➤ Mi tiempo se acaba. I'm running out of time. ▪ *(poético)* My time grows short.

acabársele el tiempo ▪ agotársele el tiempo to be out of time ➤ Se me acaba el tiempo. ▪ Se me agota el tiempo. I'm out of time.

acabársele el tiempo para ▪ quedarse sin tiempo para ▪ agotarse su tiempo para to run out of time to ➤ Se le acaba el tiempo fijo para completar el proyecto. He was running out of the time allotted to finish the project.

acabársele la paciencia a alguien ▪ agotársele la paciencia a alguien to run out out of patience ▪ (for) one's patience to be exhausted ➤ Se me está acabando la paciencia. I'm running out of patience.

acabársele los abastecemientos ▪ acabársele las provisiones to run out of provisions ▪ to run out of supplies ➤ Se nos acabaron los abastecemientos. We ran out of provisiones. ▪ Our provisiones ran out.

acabo de acordarme ▪ acabo de recordarlo I just remembered

acabo de enterarme de eso I just found that out

acabo de enterarme (de que...) ▪ me acabo de enterar (de que...) I just found out that...

acabo de llegar I just got here ▪ I just arrived

acabo de llegar en este momento ▪ acabo de llegar ahora mismo I just this second got here ▪ I just this second walked in the door

acabo de perder el autobús I just missed the bus ➤ Acabo de perderlo. I just missed it.

¡**acabóse!** ▪ ¡se acabó! period! ▪ that's the end of it! ▪ that's that! ➤ Y acabóse. And that's that!

ser el **acabóse** ▪ ser el colmo to be the limit ➤ ¡Es el acabóse! That's the limit! ▪ That's the last straw! ▪ I've had all I can take! ▪ That's all I can take!

acalorada discusión: suscitar una ~ to provoke a heated argument ▪ to spark a heated argument ➤ Ha suscitado una acalorada discusión. It (has) provoked a heated argument. ▪ It (has) sparked a heated argument.

acalorado debate: encadenar ~ to spark a heated debate

acampada: ir de ~ to go camping

acamparse como uno quiera ▪ hacer lo que uno quiera ▪ seguir uno mismo to do as one pleases ▪ to do as one likes ➤ *(tú)* Acámpate como quieras. ▪ Haz lo que quieras. ▪ Sigue tú mismo(-a). *(usted)* Acámpese usted como quiera. ▪ Haga usted lo que quiera. ▪ Acámpese como quiera. ▪ Siga usted mismo(-a). Do as you please. ▪ Do as you like.

acaparador(-a) de votos vote getter

acaparar comida to hoard food ➤ *(titular)* Judíos y palestinos acaparan comida por miedo a la guerra. Jews and Palestinians hoard food for fear of war.

acaparar la atención to attract attention ▪ to command attention ➤ Acaparó la atención de los medios. It attracted media attention.

acaramelar a alguien ▪ engatusar a alguien ▪ hacerle juego a alguien to sweet-talk someone

acariciar a un animal to pet an animal

acariciar la idea to embrace the idea

acarrear algo to lead to something ▪ to give rise to something

acarrear a alguien una oposición to give rise to opposition to someone ▪ to provoke opposition to someone

acarrear dificultades to lead to difficulties

acarrear efectos adversos to lead to adverse effects ▪ to cause adverse effects

acarrear problemas ▪ acarrear disgustos to lead to problems ▪ to cause trouble

acaso es lo mejor perhaps it's the best thing ▪ perhaps it's for the best

¿**acaso es lo mejor?** 1. *(lo que hago)* am I doing the right thing? 2. *(lo que hacemos)* are we doing the right thing?

¿**acaso la viste?** ▪ ¿por casualidad la viste? 1. *(persona)* did you see her, by any chance? 2. *(cosa, de género femenino)* did you see it, by any chance?

¿**acaso le viste?** *(Esp., leísmo)* ▪ ¿acaso lo viste? did you see him, by any chance?

¿**acaso lo viste?** ▪ ¡por casualidad lo viste? 1. *(a él)* did you see him, by any chance? 2. *(ello)* did you see it, by any chance?

¿**acaso no es maravilloso?** 1. isn't it marvelous? ▪ isn't it wonderful? ▪ isn't that marvelous? ▪ isn't that wonderful? 2. *(él)* isn't he marvelous? ▪ isn't he wonderful? 3. *(ella)* ▪ ¿acaso no es maravillosa isn't she marvelous? ▪ isn't she wonderful? ➤ *(al oír la música de un piano, por ejemplo)* ¿Acaso no es maravilloso? Isn't it marvelous? ▪ Isn't it wonderful. ▪ Isn't that marvelous? ▪ Isn't that wonderful? ➤ *(de una pianista, por ejemplo)* Isn't she marvelous? ▪ Isn't she wonderful?

¡¿**acaso te parece imparcial?!** you call that fair?!

acatar el pacto ▪ cumplir con el acuerdo ▪ atenerse al convenio to abide by the agreement ▪ to conform to the agreement ▪ to conform with the agreement

acatar la decisión ▪ atenerse a la decisión to abide by the decision

acatar la ley ▪ obedecer la ley to abide by the law ▪ to obey the law

acatar la orden to obey the order ▪ to comply with the order

acatar la resolución to comply with the resolution

acatar la responsabilidad de to be responsible for ▪ to take responsibility for

acaudalado(-a) cliente wealthy client ▪ well-to-do client

acaudalado(-a) morador(-a) *(de una casa)* well-heeled occupant ▪ rich resident

acceder a *(informática)* to access ➤ Es difícil acceder al servidor universitario desde afuera del campus. It is difficult to access the university server from off campus.

acceder a algo ▪ acordar algo to agree to something ➤ Accedió a ello por su propia cuenta. ▪ Lo acordó por su propia cuenta. He agreed to it on his own.

acceder a hacer algo to agree to do something ➤ Accedió a ello por su propia cuenta. He agreed to it on his own.

acceder a la presidencia to attain the presidency ▪ to come to the presidency

acceder al trono to succeed to the throne ▪ to come to the throne

acceder el patio to open out onto the patio

acceso de rush of

acceso de celos fit of jealousy

acceso de cólera fit of anger

acceso de neumonía: tener un ~ to have a bout of pneumonia

acceso prohibido no admittance ▪ no trespassing

acceso sin restricción unrestricted access

accesos de fiebre bouts of fever

el **accidente de aviación** airplane crash

el **accidente de caballo** horseback riding accident ➤ Su bisabuela murió en un accidente de caballo. His great grandmother was died in a horseback riding accident.

el **accidente en cadena** chain reaction collision

el **accidente laboral** accident at work ▪ accident on the job ▪ on-the-job accident ▪ accident while at work

accidente raro freak accident

accidentes costeros rugged coastline ▪ ruggedness of the coastline

los **accidentes del relieve** ruggedness of the terrain ▪ roughness of the terrain ▪ unevenness of the terrain

los **accidentes del terreno** lay of the land ▪ unevenness of the terrain ▪ ruggedness of the terrain ▪ roughness of the terrain

accidentes geográficos geographical features

acciones cuyas fluctuaciones dan la tónica del mercado bellwether stock

la **acción pasa** ▪ la acción está ambientada the story takes place ▪ the story is set in ➤ La acción pasa en Rota. The story takes place in Rota.

la **acción reprobable** reprehensible act

la **acción sobre la gente** *(literario)* ▪ efecto sobre la gente effect on people ➤ *(Unamuno)* Su acción sobre la gente era tal que nadie se atrevía mentir ante él. His effect on people was such that no one dared lie to him.

acción u omisión commission or omission

accionar la llave ■ girar la llave to turn the key ➤ Accionar la llave según la dirección de la flecha. Turn the key in the direction of the arrow.

accionar la puerta automática to activate the automatic door

las **acciones hablan más que las palabras** ■ las acciones dicen más que palabras actions speak louder than words

acechar como el gato al ratón like a cat stalking a mouse ■ to lie in wait like a cat for a mouse

aceite de hígado de bacalao codliver oil ➤ El aceite de hígado de bacalao es una fuente primaria de vitaminas A y D. Codliver oil is a primary source of Vitamins A and D.

aceite de las semillas de lino lindseed oil

acentuar la presión para que to step up the pressure (in order) to ➤ *(titular)* EE UU acentúa la presión para que la OTAN apoye sus planes de guerra. U.S. steps up the pressure to get NATO to support its war plans. ■ U.S. steps up the pressure on NATO to support its war plans.

acentuar los ataques contra to step up the attacks on

aceptación paterna parental acceptance

aceptar a buen grado *(Esp.)* ■ aceptar de buen grado to accept willingly ■ to willingly accept ■ willingly to accept

aceptar a las personas tal (y) como son to accept people the way they are ■ to accept people as they are

aceptar a pie juntillas ■ creer a pie juntillas to believe blindly ■ to believe without questioning

aceptar algo to accept something ➤ Acepto tu oferta. I accept your offer.

aceptar algo con filosofía ■ aceptar algo filosóficamente ■ resignarse a algo ■ tomarse algo con filosofía to accept something philosophically ■ to come to terms with something ➤ Ha aceptado con filosofía (el) estar confinado a una silla de ruedas. ■ Ha aceptado filosóficamente (el) estar confinado a una silla de ruedas. ■ Se ha resignado a estar confinado a una silla de ruedas. ■ Se ha tomado con filosofía el estar confinado a una silla de ruedas. He has accepted philosophically being confined to a wheelchair. ■ He has come to terms with his being confined to a wheel chair.

aceptar de buen grado ■ aceptar a buen grado to accept willingly ■ to willingly accept ■ willingly to accept

aceptar negociar ■ acordar negociar to agree to negotiate ➤ Las dos partes aceptaron negociar. ■ Las dos partes acordaron negociar. The two sides agreed to negotiate.

aceptar la responsabilidad to accept the responsibility ■ to accept the consequences

aceptar la responsabilidad de hacer algo ■ asumir la responsabilidad de hacer algo ■ acatar la responsabilidad de hacer algo **1.** to accept the responsibility to do something ■ to take on the responsibility to do something ■ **2.** to take responsibility for doing something ➤ Si consiguimos un perro, los niños deben aceptar la responsabilidad de darle de comer. If we get a dog, the children must accept the responsibility for feeding it.

aceptar que to accept ■ to approve ■ to agree to ■ to give one's approval to ■ to okay ➤ *(noticia)* La Iglesia griega acepta que el Papa visite Atenas. The Greek church gives its approval to a papal visit to Athens. ■ The Greek church okays a papal visit to Athens. ■ The Greek church okays the Pope's visit to Athens.

aceptar responsabilidad to accept responsibility

aceptar una invitación to accept an invitation

aceptar una propuesta de alguien ■ aceptar la oferta de alguien to accept someone's offer ■ to accept an offer from someone ■ to take someone up on an offer

acerca de ■ sobre about ■ concerning ■ on ➤ Un libro acerca de la física. ■ Un libro sobre la física A book on physics ■ A book about physics

acerca de si ■ en relación a si about whether ■ over whether ■ on

acera de la sombra shady side of the street

acera del sol sunny side of the street

estar **acercándose** to move (in) closer ➤ Las tropas del enemigo se están acercando. The enemy troops are moving (in) closer to us.

acercar algo a alguien to bring someone something ➤ Acércame la medicina, por favor. Bring me the medicine, please.

acercar posturas to resolve ones' differences ➤ El presidente y primer ministro intentarán acercar posturas. The president and the prime minister will try to resolve their differences.

acercar posturas con alguien to resolve one's differences with someone.

acercarse a algo ■ aproximarse a algo **1.** to approach something ■ to come close to something ■ to get close to something ■ to come near something ■ *(literario)* to near something **2.** to come to something ➤ Hay un excelente concierto de piano norteamericano, la *Rapsodia en azul* de Gershwin, y un par de otros que se le acercan. ■ Hay un excelente concierto de piano norteamericano, la *Rapsodia en azul* de Gershwin, y un par que se le aproximan. There is one excellent American piano concerto, Gershwin's *Rhapsody in Blue* and a couple others that come close (to it). ■ There is one excellent American piano concerto, Gershwin's *Rhapsody in Blue*, and a couple others that approach it. ➤ *(anuncio)* El teatro se acerca a las aulas: la comedia, la farsa, la poesía y la sátira al encuentro del alumno. The theater comes to the classroom: comedy, farce, poetry, and satire come to the student.

acercarse a alguien (sobre algo) to approach someone (about something) ➤ El jugador sudamericano se acercó a Real Madrid sobre formar parte del equipo. The South American player approached Real Madrid about being on the team.

acercarse a su fin ■ acercarse al final ■ terminar to draw to a close ■ to come to an end ➤ Conforme el año se acerca a su fin, he empezado a pensar en mis planes y propósitos para el año nuevo. ■ Conforme el año se acerca al final, he empezado a pensar en mis planes y propósitos para el año nuevo. As the year draws to a close, I have begun to think about my plans and resolutions for the new year.

acercarse a una fecha tope ■ aproximarse a una fecha límite to approach a deadline ➤ Se (nos) acerca rapidamente la fecha límite para presentar los impuestos el quince de abril. ■ Nos aproximamos rápidamente a la fecha límite del quince de abril. The April fifteen tax deadline is rapidly approaching. ■ We are rapidly approaching the April 15 deadline.

acercarse al final ■ acercarse a su fin ■ terminar to draw to a close ■ to come to an end

acercarse al horizonte ■ irse aproximando al horizonte to approach the horizon ■ to move closer to the horizon ■ to get lower in the sky ➤ Conforme un barco viaja al sur, la estrella polar se acera más al horizonte. ■ Conforme un barco viaja al sur, la estrella polar se va aproximando al horizonte. As a ship travels south, the (northern) pole star gets lower in the sky. ■ As a ship travels south, the (northern) pole star moves closer to the horizon.

acercarse hasta to go to ➤ Pensaba acercarme hasta la playa. I was thinking of going to the beach ■ I was planning to go to the beach.

acercarse más ■ aproximarse más to come closer ➤ "Acércate más, pequeña," le dijo el lobo a Caperucita Roja. ■ "Aproxímate más, pequeña," le dijo el lobo a Caperucita Roja. "Come closer, my dear," said the wolf to Little Red Riding Hood.

acercársele a alguien to go up to someone

el, la **acertante de...** *(lotería, concurso)* ■ ganador(-a) de... winner of...

acertar a la primera to guess right on the first try

acertar a llegar to arrive okay ■ 1. *(aquí)* to get here okay **2.** *(allí)* to get there okay

acertar al blanco to hit the target

acertar con to find the right one ➤ Acerté con la calle. I found the right street.

acertar en el blanco to hit the target

acertar errando ■ acertar al tanteo to get the answer by trial and error ■ to get the answer through trial and error

acertar por chambra *(Esp.)* ■ acertar por suerte to make a lucky guess ■ to hit on it

acertar por suerte to make a lucky guess ■ to hit on it

acervo de conocimientos store of knowledge

achacar a alguien la responsabilidad to hold someone responsible for something

achaques de (enfermedad): tener ~ to have spells of (illness) ➤ Tiene achaques de reuma con el frío. She has spells of rheumatism in the cold weather.

aciago día ■ día aciago fateful day

acicatear la curiosidad ▪ picar la curiosidad ▪ llamarle la atención to arouse curiosity
ácido ribonucléico ▪ ARN ribonucleic acid ▪ RNA
ser el **acierto** *(en un examen, por ejemplo)* to be the correct answer ▪ to be the right answer
ser un **acierto** to be a good decision ▪ to be a wise move
aclarar el día 1. despejarse to clear up ▪ 2. amanecer *(sólo con el subjuntivo)* to dawn ➤ Cuando aclare el día When it clears up ▪ When it clears off ▪ When day breaks ▪ When it gets light ▪ When it dawns
aclarar la voz ▪ carraspear to clear one's throat
¡aclaráos vosotros! you all work it out among yourselves! ▪ you all resolve it among yourselves!
estar **acodado en la ventana** to sit (looking out the window) with one's elbows on the window sill
acodarse sobre la mesa to put one's elbows on the table ➤ Se acodó sobre la mesa He put his elbows on the table.
acoger a alguien en su seno to take in someone ▪ to take someone in ▪ to give someone shelter ▪ to give shelter to someone
acoger a un niño huérfano ▪ recoger a un niño huérfano ▪ albergar a un niño huérfano to take in an orphan ▪ to shelter an orphan
acoger algo con escepticismo ▪ recibir algo con escepticismo to greet something with skepticism
acoger una colección ▪ albergar una colección to house a collection
acogerse a sagrado to take sanctuary
acogerse mutuamente to protect each other ▪ to look out for each other ▪ to welcome each other
acogí al ratón en mi agujero, y volvióse mi heredero I took in the mouse, and it became my heir ▪ I took the mouse in, and it became my heir
ser **acogido con escepticismo** to be greeted with skepticism
ser **acogido con una gran carcajada** to be greeted with an outburst of laughter ▪ to be greeted by peals of laughter ➤ Sus palabras fueron acogidas con una gran carcajada. His words were greeted with an outburst of laughter. ▪ His words were greeted with peals of laughter.
ser **acogido por alguien** to be taken in by someone ▪ to be given shelter by someone ▪ to be given a home by someone
acojonado: quedarse ~ ▪ quedarse petrificado to be scared stiff
acometer hace vencer ▪ la mejor defensa es una buena ofensa the best defense is a good offense ▪ a good offense is the best defense
acometerle dudas *(formal)* ▪ meterle dudas ▪ asaltarle (las) dudas to be assailed by doubts ▪ to be plagued with doubts ➤ A ella le acometieron dudas. ▪ A ella le metieron la(s) duda(s). She was assailed by doubts.
acomodarse a los tiempos to adapt to the times
estar **acompañado de** to be accompanied by
acompañar a alguien ▪ ir con alguien to go with someone ▪ to accompany someone ➤ Quiero acompañarlo. ▪ *(Esp.)* Quiero acompañarle. I want to go with him.
acompañar a alguien en el sentimiento to be with someone in one's grief ▪ to be with someone in one's pain ➤ Te acompaño en el sentimiento. I'm with you in your grief. ▪ I'm with you in your pain.
acompañar a alguien a la puerta ▪ llevar a alguien a la puerta to show someone to the door ▪ to see someone to the door ▪ to go with someone to the door ➤ Cuando María me lo pidió, la acompañé a la puerta, y allí me dio un beso. When Mary asked me, I showed her to the door, and there she gave me a kiss. ➤ Los acompañó a la puerta. ▪ Los llevó a la puerta ▪ *(Esp. leísmo)* Les acompañó a la puerta. ▪ Les llevó a la puerta. He showed them to the door. ▪ He saw them to the door. ▪ He went with them to the door. ▪ He accompanied them to the door.
acompasar el calendario con el movimiento del sol ▪ sincronizar el calendario con el movimiento del sol to synchronize the calendar with the movement of the sun
aconteceres históricos historical events
acontecimiento bisagra decisive event ▪ watershed event
acontecimiento científico trascendental scientific breakthrough
acontecimiento trascendental 1. revolutionary development ▪ turning point ▪ breakthrough 2. *(en la vida de una persona)* important event (in a person's life)
acordar algo ▪ acceder a algo to agree to something ➤ Lo acordó por su propia cuenta. ▪ Accedió a ello por su propia cuenta. He agreed to it on his own.
acordar hacer algo to agree to do something ➤ Los candidatos acuerdan celebrar tres debates. The candidates agree to hold three debates.
acordar la paz to conclude a peace agreement ▪ to draw up and sign a peace agreement ➤ Los presidentes acordaron la paz. The presidents concluded a peace agreement.
acordar negociar ▪ aceptar negociar to agree to negotiate ➤ Las dos partes acordaron negociar. ▪ Las dos partes aceptaron negociar. The two sides agreed to negotiate.
acordar oír el caso to agree to hear the case
acordar una cita para recoger algo con alguien to arrange a pickup with someone
acordar una entrega to schedule a delivery ▪ to arrange (for) a delivery
acordarse de algo to remember something
acordarse de alguien con cariño ▪ recordar a alguien con cariño to remember someone fondly ▪ to remember someone with affection
acordarse de hacer algo to remember to do something ➤ ¡Acuérdate de...! Remember to...!
acordarse de Santa Bárbara cuando truena ▪ recordar cuando es demasiado tarde to remember when it's too late
acordarse de la familia de alguien ▪ recordarle la familia de alguien to insult someone's ancestors ▪ to call someone a bastard ▪ to call someone a son-of-a-bitch
acordarse de la madre de alguien ▪ recordarle la madre de alguien to insult someone's mother ▪ to call someone a bastard ▪ to call someone a son-of-a-bitch
acorralado: tenerle a alguien ~ to have someone cornered ▪ to hold something at bay ➤ ¡Ya te tengo acorralado! I've got you cornered!
acorralar a alguien to corner someone
acortar distancias con alguien to be catching up with someone ➤ Acortamos distancias con ellos. We're catching up with them.
acortar la ventaja de to cut into someone's lead ▪ to cut into someone's advantage
acortar el paso to shorten one's stride ▪ to take smaller steps
acosar a alguien to harass someone
acosar a alguien a preguntas to hound someone with questions ▪ to pester someone with questions
acosar a alguien con críticas to barrage someone with criticism
acoso sexual sexual harassment
acoso sin tregua relentless pursuit
acoso y derribo: operación de ~ search and destroy mission ▪ search and destroy operation
acostarse a la hora de las gallinas to go to bed with the chickens ▪ to go to bed early
acostarse con alguien to go to bed with someone
acostarse con hambre to go to bed hungry ➤ Mil milliones de personas se acuestan todas las noches con hambre. A billion people go to bed hungry every night.
acostarse juntos to go to bed together
estar **acribillado a balazos** to be riddled with bullets
acribillar a alguien a balazos ▪ coser a alguien a balazos to riddle someone with bullets
acribillar a preguntas to fire off questions ▪ to bombard with questions
el **acta de nacimiento** birth certificate
actas de una reunión minutes of a meeting ▪ conference proceedings ▪ proceedings of a conference
la **actitud condescendiente** condescending attitude ▪ patronizing attitude
la **actitud hacia** ▪ actitud para con attitude toward ▪ attitude towards

actitud informal ■ actitud floja ■ actitud perezosa lackadaisical attitude ■ lazy attitude ■ indolent attitude

la **actitud profesional** business-like attitude

activar la economía to stimulate the economy

activar un explosivo to detonate an explosive ■ to set off an explosive

activar un programa *(informática)* to enable a program ■ to activate a program ➤ Hay que activar Javascript para utilizar este navegador. You must enable Javascript before using this browser.

activar una alarma to activate an alarm

acto conmemorativo comemorative event

acto continuo ■ acto seguido immediately afterwards

acto de apertura opening ceremony ■ opening ceremonies ■ opening act

acto de campaña campaign appearance ■ campaign stop

ser un **acto de equilibrio** to be a balancing act

acto de valentía courageous act ■ act of courage

acto seguido ■ acto continuo **1.** immediately afterwards **2.** at that ➤ La tía Polly se dio la vuelta, y acto seguido, Tom salió pitando por la puerta de la cocina. Aunt Polly turned her back, and at that, Tom fled out the kitchen door.

acto sexual sex act

acto vandálico ■ acto de vandalismo act of vandalism

actos sociales social events

actuación de flamenco flamenco performance ■ performance of flamenco ➤ Hay una actuación de flamenco esta noche. There is a flamenco performance tonight.

actualización sobre the latest on ■ update on

actualizar un talonario ■ cotejar un talonario (con el extracto de cuenta) to balance a checkbook

actuar así ■ obrar como uno obra to act as one does ➤ Actué así porque... I acted as I did because...

actuar bajo las instrucciones ■ actuar con las instrucciones de alguien to act in accordance with someone's instructions ■ to act according to someone's instructions

actuar con decisión to act decisively

actuar con justicia ■ actuar con equidad to act fairly

actuar conjuntamente con alguien to act in conjunction with someone

actuar de acuerdo con to act in accordance with ■ to act according to

actuar de acuerdo con las instrucciones de alguien ■ actuar bajo las instrucciones de alguien to act in accordance with someone's instructions ■ to act according to someone's instructions

actuar de buena fe ■ actuar en buena fe ■ actuar por buena fe to act in good faith

actuar de maestro de ceremonias ■ actuar como maestro de ceremonias to act as master of ceremonies

actuar de manera interesada ■ tener un interés personal to have an ax to grind

actuar en buena fe ■ actuar de buena fe ■ actuar por buena fe to act in good faith

actuar en contra de uno to work against one ➤ Su impetuosidad a veces actúa en su contra. His brashness sometimes works against him. ■ His impetuosity sometimes works against him.

actuar en nombre de alguien ■ representar a alguien ■ actuar en representación de alguien to act on someone's behalf ■ to act in someone's behalf ■ to act on behalf of someone ■ to act in behalf of someone

actuar por buena fe ■ actuar de buena fe ■ actuar en buena fe to act in good faith ➤ El médico que ayudó a la víctima no debería haber sido castigado por su buena fe. The doctor who helped the victim should not have been punished for acting in good faith.

actuar por impulso to act on impulse

actuar por un sentido de deber ■ actuar por su sentido de deber to act out of a sense of duty ■ to act out of one's sense of duty

actuar sin reflexión to act without thinking

actuar sobre algo 1. to act on something **2.** to take action on something ➤ El agente químico de limpieza actúa sobre la mancha. The cleaning agent acts on the stain.

actuar sobre una fuerza *(física)* to act on a force

acuchillar a alguien to stab someone ■ to knife someone

acuchillar el suelo *(Esp.)* ■ acuchillar el parquet to sand the floor

acuchillar un mueble to scrape furniture

ser **acuciado por problemas** *(literario)* ■ ser asediado por problemas to be beset by problems

acudir a alguien to turn to someone ■ to go to someone

acudir a la llamada para to answer the call for

acudir a las urnas to go to the polls

acudir a los tribunales to go to court ➤ *(noticia)* Bush acude a los tribunales para impedir un nuevo recuento a mano. Bush goes to court to prevent another recount by hand.

acudir a la ayuda de alguien to come to someone's aid ■ to go to someone's aid

acudir presuroso a to hurry over to ➤ El jefe acudió presuroso a mi escritorio. The boss hurried over to my desk.

acudirle a la memoria ■ venirle a la mente to come to mind

acudir a un reclamo *(derecho)*to counter a claim ■ to rebut a claim

¡**acuérdate de...!** remember to...! ■ don't forget to...!

acuérdate de ti y olvídate de mí look after yourself and forget about me ■ mind yourself and never mind me

acuerdo bilateral ■ convenio bilateral bilateral accord ■ bilateral agreement

acuerdo comercial con otro país trade agreement ➤ *(titular)* El presidente consigue poderes especiales para negociar acuerdos comerciales con otros países. The president gets special powers to negotiate trade agreements.

acuerdo de divorcio divorce settlement

acuerdo de gran alcance far-reaching agreement

acuerdo entre caballeros gentlemen's agreement ■ trust agreement

acuerdo global overall agreement ■ general agreement

acuerdo nítido clear agreement ➤ El primer ministro recordó al rey que el acuerdo es "nítido" y sólo debe cumplirse. The prime minister reminded the king that the agreement is clear and needs only to be honored.

el **acuerdo quedó cerrado** ■ el trato quedó cerrado the bargain was struck ■ the deal was struck

acuerdo tácito tacit agreement ■ unspoken agreement ■ unwritten agreement

acuerdo vinculante binding agreement

acumular pérdidas to accumulate losses ■ *(informal)* to rack up losses

acumular polvo ■ juntar polvo to collect dust

acumular vapor to get up steam

acumular victorias to accumulate victories ■ *(informal)* to rack up victories ■ to rack up wins

acuñar dinero *(de papel y metal)* to mint money ■ *(monedas metálicas)* to coin money

acuñar una frase to coin a phrase

acuñar una palabra to coin a word

acusar recibo de to acknowledge receipt of

acuse de recibo acknowledgment of receipt ■ letter received

adaptarse a las circunstancias ■ bailar al son que le tocan ■ ir normalito y bien ■ andar al uso ■ ir con la corriente to adapt to the circumstances ■ *(informal)* to go with the flow

adecuadamente: cerrar el programa ~ ■ cerrar el programa correctamente ■ cerrar el programa apropiadamente to exit (from) the program correctly ➤ Cuando cierras adecuadamente el programa... When you exit from the program correctly...

ser **adecuado para un rey** to be fit for a king

estar **adelantado a su tiempo** ahead of its time ■ ahead of one's time ➤ La casa de Thomas Jefferson, Monticello, estaba cien años adelantado a su tiempo. Thomas Jefferson's house, Monticello, was a hundred years ahead of its time.

adelantar a un carro en la carretera ■ adelantar un carro en la carretera ■ rebasar un carro un la carretera ■ ponerse por delante de un carro ■ to pass a car on the highway ■ to get ahead of a car on the highway ■ to overtake a car on the highway

adelantarse a alguien ■ anticiparse a alguien **1.** to get ahead of someone **2.** to beat someone to it ➤ Ella sigue tratando de adelantárseme en la fila. ▪ Ella sigue tratando de adelantárseme en la cola. She keeps trying to get ahead of me in line. ➤ *(al coger la última galleta)* ¡Te me has adelantado! ▪ ¡Te me anticipaste! You beat me to it! ➤ Te me adelantaste la última vez por última vez. Ahora me anticiparé a tí. You beat me to it last time, and that was the last time. I'm going to beat you to it this time!

adelantarse a la multitud to beat the rush

adelante, la escucho (a usted) go on, I'm listening

adelante, le escucho (a usted) *(Esp., leísmo)* go on, I'm listening

adelante, lo escucho (a usted) go on, I'm listening

adelante, te escucho go on, I'm listening

ser un **adelanto de lo que venía** to be a taste of what was coming

ser un **adelanto de lo que viene** to be a taste of what is coming ▪ to be a taste of what's coming

adelantos de la ciencia ▪ adelantos científicos scientific advances

adelgazar *x* kilos to lose *x* kilos

adelgazar *x* libras to lose *x* pounds

además de in addition to ▪ besides

además de cornudo, apaleado it was the insult added to the injury

además de eso ▪ por lo demás apart from that ▪ other than that ▪ aside from that ▪ except for that ▪ otherwise ▪ besides that

además de que ▪ aparte de que ▪ fuera de que 1. besides which 2. besides the fact that ▪ apart from the fact that

adentrarse en el sendero to set off along the path ▪ to set off down the path ▪ to start down the path

adentrarse en la política ▪ meterse en política ▪ entrar en política to get into politics ▪ to enter politics

¡**adentro!** ▪ adelante ▪ *(Méx., coloquial)* pásale come in!

adherirse a la línea del partido to adhere to the party line

adherirse a la opinion de que... to be of the opinion that... ▪ to hold the opinion that...

adherirse a un club ▪ hacerse miembro de un club to join a club

adherirse a un partido ▪ hacerse miembro de un partido to join a party

adherirse a un punto de vista to subscribe to a point to view ▪ to hold a point of view ▪ to adhere to a point of view

adherirse a una asociación ▪ hacerse miembro de un partido to join an association

adherirse a una idea to subscribe to the idea

adherirse al ejercito *(poco común)* ▪ unirse al ejercito ▪ alistarse en el ejercito to join the army

adherirse al paro to join the strike

la **adicción a las drogas** drug addiction

¡**adiós, mi vergüenza!** good-bye, my self-respect! ▪ and so much for my dignity!

¡**adiós, muy buenas!** so much for that!

¡**adivina qué!** guess what!

¡**adjudicado!** sold! ▪ *(en una subasta)* gone!

adjudicarle un contrato a alguien to award a contract to someone

la **administración y dirección de empresas** *(carrera académica)* business administration

administrar dinero to manage money

administrar la justicia to administer justice

administrar tiempo to manage time

administrativo intermedio ▪ cargos medios middle management

la **admiración de la ignorancia nació** *(la admiración nace de la ignorancia)* admiration stems from ignorance

admirarse de to wonder at ▪ to marvel at ▪ to be surprised by ➤ Me admiré de la belleza del Salto del Ángel en Venezuela. I marveled at the beauty of Angel Falls in Venezuela.

admitamos que... let's suppose that... ▪ suppose that...

admitir a un estudiante no matriculado to admit a student on a non-matriculated basis ▪ to admit a student (as) non-matriculated

admitir que uno tiene razón ▪ darle la razón a uno to admit that one is right ➤ Tienes que admitir que tengo razón. ▪ Me tienes que dar la razón. You have to admit that I'm right. ▪ You've got to admit that I'm right. ▪ *(colloquial)* You gotta admit that I'm right.

admitir sin rodeos que... ▪ admitir sin vueltas que... to admit straight out that... ▪ to admit without beating around the bush that... ▪ to admit without reservation that... ▪ to admit unabashedly that...

admitir sin vueltas que... ▪ admitir sin rodeos que... to admit straight out that... ▪ to admit without beating around the bush that... ▪ to admit without reservation that... ▪ to admit unabashedly that...

admitir un juicio a trámite (contra alguien) ▪ presentar un juicio (contra alguien) ▪ presentar una demanda judicial (contra alguien) ➤ Una vez admitido a trámite, el juicio debe ser celebrado a menos que el demandante desista. Once filed, the lawsuit must be heard unless the plaintiff drops it.

adolecer de una enfermedad ▪ sufrir de una enfermedad ▪ padecer de una enfermedad to suffer from an illness

adónde acudir where to turn ➤ No sé adónde acudir. ▪ Ya no sé qué hacer. I don't know where to turn.

adónde ir: no saber ~ not to know where to go

adónde ir: no tener ~ not to have anywhere to go

adónde volver: no tener ~ not to have anywhere to return to ▪ not to have anywhere to go back to ➤ Ya no tengo domicilio allí adonde volver. I no longer have a domicile there to return to.

adoptar medidas para ▪ tomar medidas para to take steps to

adoptar una postura sobre un asunto to take a position on an issue

adorar el becerro de oro to worship the golden calf ▪ to worship material things

adorar el béisbol to love baseball

adoraría saber si...: (yo) ~ *(poco común)* ▪ me encantaría saber si... I would love to know if... ▪ *(si o no)* I would love to know whether (or not)...

adormecer los sentidos de uno to give one a false sense of security

adornarle mil virtudes to be crowned with virtues

estar **adosado a algo** ▪ estar pegado a algo to be attached to something ▪ to be stuck onto something ▪ to be stuck to something ▪ to be stuck on something ➤ En ese momento, una bomba lapa adosada a los bajos de su coche hizo explosión. At that moment, a limpet (stick-on) bomb attached to the underside of his car exploded. ➤ No había ningún recibo adosado a la caja. ▪ No había ningún recibo pegado a la caja. There was no receipt attached to the box. ▪ There was no receipt stuck onto the box. ▪ There was no receipt stuck on the box. ▪ There was no receipt stuck to the box.

adosar algo a algo ▪ pegar algo a algo ▪ adjuntar algo a algo to stick something (on)to something ▪ to attach something to something ➤ Una bomba lapa adosada a los bajos de su coche hizo explosión. A limpet (stick-on) bomb stuck to the underside of the car exploded.

adquirir éxito to achieve success

adquirir importancia to take on importance

adquirir un compromiso to get (oneself) into a bind ▪ to get into something (unwillingly) ➤ Mi nueva secretaria me adquirió este compromiso. My new secretary got me into this.

adquirir un hábito ▪ adquirir una costumbre to get into a routine ▪ to adopt a routine *(Nota: en un sentido positivo ▪ in a postive sense)*

adquirir una costumbre ▪ adquirir un hábito to get into a routine ▪ to adopt a routine *(Nota: en un sentido positivo ▪ in a postive sense)*

adquirir una nueva dimensión to take on a new dimension

adrede: hacer algo ~ *(implica malicia)* ▪ hacer algo con mala intención to do something deliberately ▪ to do something on purpose

aducir pruebas to furnish proof ▪ to give as evidence

aducir falta de pruebas to claim lack of proof

aducir no saber to claim not to know

aducir que... to claim that... ➤ *(titular)* Rabat aduce que un helicóptero español viola su espacio aereo. Rabat claims that a Spanish helicopter violated its air space.

aducir razones de que to give reasons for ■ to give reasons why ■ to put forward reasons for

aducir un argumento a favor de to put forward an argument for ■ to advance an argument for

adueñarse de to take hold of ■ to take possession of ■ to take over (without permission or invitation) ➤ La gata entró cierto día y se adueñó de la casa. No había nada que pudiese hacer. The cat just walked in one day and took over. There was nothing I could do.

adueñarse del mundo to take over the world

advertir a alguien de algo to warn someone of something

advertir (a alguien) de que... to warn (someone) that...

advertir el cambio más imperceptible en ■ notar el cambio más imperceptible en to notice the slightest change in

advertirle a alguien que no haga algo to warn someone not to do something ➤ *(Bernal Díaz)* Nos habían advertido que no entrásemos en la cuidad. They had warned us not to enter the city.

el **afán de agradar** eagerness to please

el **afán de aventuras** thirst for adventure

el **afán de dominio** lust for power ■ thirst for power

el **afán de revancha** ■ deseo de venganza desire for revenge ■ thirst for revenge

la **afección común** common ailment

afecciones cardiacas: contraer ~ to develop heart problems

afecciones cardiacas: estar aquejado de ~ to have heart problems ■ to suffer from heart problems

estar **afectado por algo** verse afectado por algo to be affected by something

estar **aferrado a la vida** to be clinging to life

aferrarse a la esperanza de que... to cling to the hope that...

la **afición ciega la razón** fondness blinds objectivity

ser **aficionado al baloncesto** ■ ser fan del baloncesto to be a basketball fan

ser **aficionado al béisbol** ■ ser fan del béisbol to be a baseball fan

ser **aficionado al fútbol** ■ ser fan del fútbol 1. *(fútbol americano)* to be a football fan 2. *(fútbol europa)* to be a soccer fan

afilar el diente to whet one's appetite

afilar el ingenio to sharpen one's wits

afilar el puñal to sharpen one's dagger

afilar la calumnia to make the slander even more vicious

afilar la lengua to sharpen one's tongue ■ to be ready with a snide comeback

afilarse las garras para alguien to get one's knives out for someone ■ to have it in for someone

ser **afín a algo** to be related to something ■ to be akin to something

ser **afín a alguien** to be related to someone

afinar el oído to heighten one's music appreciation

afinar la oreja to prick up one's ears

afinar la puntería a to take aim at ■ to aim carefully at ■ to hone in on

afinar un instrumento ■ concertar un instrumento to tune an instrument ■ to tune up an instrument ■ to tune an instrument up

apretar (fuerte) ■ marcar (bien) ■ remarcar bien to bear down (hard) ■ to press hard ➤ Aprieta fuerte para que las copias sean legibles. ■ Marca bien para que las copias sean legibles. Remarca fuerte para que las copias sean legibles. Bear down hard so that the copies will be legible. ■ Press hard so that the copies will be legible.

afinidad natural para ■ simpatía natural natural affinity for ■ natural sympathy for

afirmar con la cabeza 1. to nod in the affirmative ■ to nod 2. to nod one's approval

afirmarse en los estribos to stick to one's guns

afirmarse en su decisión to stick to one's decision ■ to dig in one's heels

aflojar el bolsillo to pay up ■ to cough it up

aflojar la bolsa to pay up ■ to cough it up

aflojar la bolsilla to pay up ■ to cough it up

aflojar la cintura un agujero to loosen one's belt a notch

aflojar la lana *(Méx.)* to cough it up ■ to pay up

aflojar un tornillo to loosen a screw

afluencia de gente influx of people ■ crowd of people

afluencia de turistas influx of tourists

ser un **afluente de** ■ fluir a to be a tributary of ■ to flow into ➤ El Río Cifuentes es un afluente del Tajo. ■ El Río Cifuentes fluye al Tajo. The Cifuentes River is a tributary of the Tagus. ■ The Cifuentes River flows into the Tagus.

afortunado en el juego, desafortunado en amores ■ afortunado en el juego, desgraciado en amores lucky at cards, unlucky in love

Africa empieza en los Pirineos *(tontería española)* Africa begins at the Pyrenees

afrontar la adversidad to face adversity

afrontar el reto to face the challenge

afrontar los costos 1. to defray the costs 2. to afford the costs ➤ No puedo afrontarlo. ■ No me lo puedo permitir. ■ No puedo permitírmelo. I can't afford it.

afrontar un dilema to face a dilemma

afrontar un nuevo reto ■ enfrentarse a un nuevo reto ■ hacer algo que no se ha hecho antes ■ haber superado una etapa profesional to accept a new challenge ■ to take on a new challenge ■ to face a new challenge ■ *(coloquial)* to be a case of been there, done that ➤ El guionista se hizo director. Dijo que sencillamente era una cuestión de afrontar un nuevo reto. The screenplay writer became a director. He said it was just a case of been there, done that.

afrontar una emergencia to deal with an emergency

el **after hours** *(Esp.)* discotheque that opens at 5 a.m.

estar **afuera** ■ estar al raso to be in the open air ■ to be outside

afueras de la ciudad outskirts of the city

agachar la cabeza ■ bajar la cabeza to bow one's head ■ to lower one's head ■ *(figurativa)* to hang one's head ■ to be ashamed ➤ No tienes por qué agachar la cabeza delante de nadie. ■ No tienes por qué bajar la cabeza delante de nadie. You don't have anything to be ashamed of.

agachar las orejas to hang one's head

¡**agáchate!** *(tú)* duck!

¡**agáchese!** *(usted)* duck!

agarrar a alguien como rehén ■ tomar a alguien como rehén to take someone hostage

agarrar a alguien de buenas ■ *(Esp.)* coger a alguien de buenas to catch someone in a good mood

agarrar a alguien desprevenido to catch someone off guard

agarrar a alguien in fraganti ■ pillar a alguien in fraganti ■ pescar a alguien in fraganti ■ *(Esp.)* coger a alguien in fraganti ■ agarrar a alguien en flagrante delito ■ pillar a alguien en flagrante delito ■ *(Esp.)* coger a alguien en flagrante delito to catch someone in the act ■ to catch someone red handed

agarrar a alguien con las manos en la masa ■ pillar a alguien con las manos en la masa ■ *(Esp.)* ■ coger a alguien con las manos en la masa to catch someone red handed ➤ Te agarramos con las manos en la masa. We caught you red handed.

agarrar a alguien en flagrante delito ■ pillar a alguien en flagrante delito ■ *(Esp.)* coger a alguien en flagrante delito to catch someone in the act

agarrar a alguien mintiendo *(Méx.)* ■ pillar a alguien mintiendo ■ *(Esp.)* coger a alguien mintiendo to catch someone lying ■ to catch someone in a lie ➤ Lo agarré mintiendo. *(a él)* I caught him lying. ■ I caught him in a lie. ■ *(a usted* I caught you lying. ■ I caught you in a lie. ➤ La agarré mintiendo. I caught her lying. ■ I caught her in a lie.

agarrar a alguien por el brazo to grab someone by the arm ■ to seize someone by the arm

agarrar algo al vuelo to catch something on the fly

agarrar de los pelos ■ asir de los pelos to grab by the hair ➤ Ella le agarró de los pelos. She grabbed him by the hair.

agarrar el ramo de novia ■ *(Esp.)* ■ coger el ramo de novia to catch the bouquet

agarrar el toro por los cuernos ■ *(Esp.)* ■ coger al toro por los cuernos to grab the bull by the horns ■ to take the bull by the horns

agarrar un cabreo ■ coger un cabreo ■ pillar un cabreo to fly off the handle

agarrar un catarro fuerte *(L.am.)* ▪ agarrar un catarro grave ▪ agarrar un catarro serio ▪ agarrar un resfriado fuerte ▪ agarrar un resfriado grave ▪ agarrar un resfriado serio to get a bad cold ▪ to catch a bad cold ▪ to come down with a bad cold

agarrar una gripe muy fuerte ▪ enfermarse de una gripe muy fuerte ▪ *(Esp.)* ▪ coger una gripe muy fuerte to come down with a bad case of the flu ▪ to develop a bad case of the flu

agarrarle desprevenido a alguien 1. to take someone (completely) by surprise 2. to be taken (completely) by surprise ➤ Le agarraron desprevenido. They took him by surprise. ▪ He was taken by surprise. ➤ Me agarró desprevenido. It took me by surprise. ▪ I was taken (completely) by surprise.

agarrarle la mano a algo ▪ tomarle la mano a algo ▪ *(Esp.)* cogerle el aire a algo to get the hang of something

agarrarlo a alguien en una mentira ▪ cogerlo en una mentira to catch someone lying ▪ to catch someone in a lie

agarrarse a un clavo ardiendo to grasp at straws

agarrarse a una mierda to get plastered ▪ to get wasted

agarrarse una rabieta ▪ agarrarse un berrinche ▪ *(Esp.)* cogerse una rabieta ▪ coger un berrinche to throw a tantrum ▪ to have a tantrum

agarrarse una rabieta que le sube la presión to have a purple fit ▪ to fly into a rage

¿agarras mi onda? ▪ ¿entiendes lo que te digo? do you catch my drift? ▪ do you understand what I'm saying?

¡agárrate! *(tú)* 1. *(para una sorpresa)* brace yourself! 2. *(para un impacto)* hold on!

¡agárrese! (usted) *(usted)* 1. *(para una sorpresa)* brace yourself! 2. *(para un impacto)* hold on!

agencia de abogados law firm

agencia de alquiler de coches car rental agency ▪ rental car agency

agencia de noticias wire service

agenciárselas para to manage somehow to ➤ Me las agenciaré para... I'll manage somehow to...

el, la **agente de circulación** traffic officer

el, la **agente de incógnito** agente encubierto(-a) undercover agent

el, la **agente de negocios** broker

el, la **agente de policía** police officer

agente encubierto(-a) ▪ agente de incógnito undercover agent ➤ *(titular)* Aerolíneas europeas introducen agentes encubiertos en algunos vuelos. ▪ Aerolíneas europeas introducen agentes de incógnito en algunos vuelos. European airlines introduce undercover agents on some flights.

agilizar el aprendizaje to facilitate learning ▪ to speed up the learning process

agitar la mano a alguien 1. to wave at someone (to get their attention) ▪ 2. saludar a alguien to wave to someone

agitar un pañuelo to wave a handkerchief

aglutinar (al cocinar) to lump up ▪ to form lumps

aglutinar grupos diversos to bring together diverse groups ▪ to draw together diverse groups

estar **agobiado de trabajo** to be snowed under with work

agonizar en el hospital to be dying in the hospital ▪ to be near death in the hospital

agotar a alguien to wear someone out ▪ to wear out someone ➤ Un par de gemelos de cuatro años pueden agotar a una madre en unas dos horas. A pair of four-year-old twins can wear a mother out in about two hours. ➤ La agotaron en unas dos horas. They wore her out in about two hours.

agotar al más fuerte to be hard on even the most hardy ▪ to take a lot out of you ➤ Las once horas y media de viaje agotan al más fuerte. The eleven-and-a-half hour trip takes a lot out of you.

agotar la paciencia de alguien ▪ acabar con la paciencia de alguien to exhaust someone's patience

agotarse la tinta ▪ estar agotada la tinta ▪ estar por terminarse la tinta ▪ terminársele la tinta to run out of ink ➤ El cartucho de tinta se está agotando. ▪ El cartucho de tinta está practicamente agotado. ▪ El cartucho de tinta está por terminarse. ▪ El cartucho de tinta se (me) ha terminado. The printer cartridge is running out of ink.

agotarse las entradas ▪ estar todas vendidas to be sold out ➤ El concierto, en el que se agotaron las entradas... ▪ El concierto, en el que todas las localidades están vendidas... The concert, which was sold out...

agotársele el tiempo ▪ acabársele el tiempo to be out of time ➤ Se me agota el tiempo. ▪ Se me acaba el tiempo. I'm out of time.

agotársele la paciencia a alguien ▪ acabársele la paciencia a alguien to exhaust someone's patience ▪ to run out of patience ➤ Se le está agotando la paciencia. *(a él)* He's running out of patience. ▪ *(a ella)* She's running out of patience. ➤ Se me está agotando la paciencia. I'm running out of patience. ▪ My patience is running out.

agradecerle a alguien con el alma ▪ agradecer a alguien en el alma to thank someone from the bottom of one's heart

agradecerle a alguien de que hayan hecho algo to thank someone for doing something

agradecerle a alguien en el alma ▪ agradecer a alguien con el alma to thank someone from the bottom of one's heart

agradecerle a alguien por (hacer) algo to thank someone for (doing) something

agradecerle a alguien vivamente ▪ agradecer a alguien copiosamente to thank profusely

agradecido del corazón with heartfelt gratitude

agradecido, no olvida el bien recibido the truly grateful one does not forget a favor

agradezco su ayuda (a usted) ▪ le agradezco su ayuda (a usted) I appreciate your help

agradezco su llamada (a usted) ▪ le agradezco su llamada (a usted) I appreciate your call

agradezco tu ayuda ▪ te agradezco tu ayuda I appreciate your help

agradezco tu llamada ▪ te agradezco tu llamada I appreciate your call

agrado de: tener el ~ to be pleased to ➤ Tenemos el agrado de anunciar... We are pleased to announce...

agrandamiento de corazón enlargement of the heart

agravar la crisis to deepen the crisis ▪ to worsen the crisis ▪ to intensify the crisis

agravar la dificultad to compound the difficulty

agravio comparativo resentment arising from unequal treatment

agredir a alguien ▪ atracar a alguien to mug someone ▪ to attack someone ▪ to assault someone

agregado (diplomático) attaché

agrietar la coalición to split the coalition

la **agrupación coral** choral society ▪ glee club

agruparse en torno a to gather around

el **agua a raudales** torrents of water

el **agua bendita** holy water

el **agua con gas** carbonated water ▪ sparkling water

el **agua corriente** running water

ser **agua de borrajas** to hardly matter ➤ A este punto cómo el jefe ligó su trabajo es agua de borrajas. How the boss fineggled his job hardly matters at this point.

el **agua de colonia** eau de cologne ▪ cologne ▪ perfume

el **agua de lluvia** rainwater

ser **agua de mayo** to be a Godsend ▪ to be a political windfall ▪ to be a political bonanza

el **agua de mayo: venirle como** ~ ▪ venirle como caído del cielo to be a Godsend

el **agua del bautismo** baptismal water ▪ waters of baptism

el **agua del grifo** *(Esp.)* tap water

el **agua dulce** fresh water

el **agua hervida** boiled water ▪ water which has been boiled

el **agua hirviendo** boiling water

el **agua milagrosa** ▪ agua que cura miracle water ▪ water with miraculous powers ▪ water with healing powers

ser **agua pasada** ▪ estar ya olvidado it's water under the bridge ▪ it's forgotten

ser **agua pasada** to be water under the bridge

agua pasada no mueve molino it's water under the bridge

el **agua potable** drinking water

agua que no has de beber, déjala correr get over it and move on
el **agua residual** waste water
el **agua salada** salt water
el **agua sin gas** plain water ▪ uncarbonated water
el **agua templada** lukewarm water
el **agua tónica** tonic water
el **agua turbia** cloudy water
¡agua va! look out! ▪ look out below ▪ *(subido de tono)* the shit's gonna hit the fan *(Nota: De los siglos de antaño cuando se vaciaban los orinales en la calle.)*
agua va: sin decir ~ suddenly ▪ without warning ▪ out of the blue
el **agua corriente** running water
aguaitar por la ventana *(L.am.)* ▪ chusmear por la ventana ▪ chismear por la ventana to spy on the neighbors out the window
aguanta un pelo ▪ aguanta un pelín wait a second ▪ hold on a second ▪ hold on (just) a minute
aguanta un pelín ▪ aguanta un pelo wait a second ▪ hold on a second ▪ hold on (just) a minute
aguantar bajo la presión ▪ aguantar bajo las circunstancias to bear up under the strain ▪ to stand up under the strain ▪ to stand the strain ▪ to withstand the strain ➤ El primer ministro ha aguantado muy bien bajo la presión del cargo. The prime minister has borne up very well under the strain of his office.
aguantar carros y carretas ▪ tragar carros y carretas to put up with murder
aguantar el chaparrón to hold up under pressure ▪ to bear up under pressure
aguantar el chubasco ▪ aguantar el temporal ▪ capear la tormenta ▪ capear el temporal to weather the storm ▪ to ride out the storm
aguantar el dolor to stand the pain ▪ to endure the pain ▪ to withstand the pain
aguantar el temporal ▪ capear la tormenta ▪ capear el temporal ▪ aguantar el chubasco to weather the storm ▪ to ride out the storm
aguantar el tipo ▪ mantener el tipo to keep one's cool ▪ to put on a brave face
aguantar hasta comer algo ▪ *(Esp.)* matar el gusanillo hasta comer algo to tide one over ➤ *(L.am.)* ¿Quieres una botana para aguantar hasta la cena? ▪ *(Esp.)* ¿Quieres picar algo para aguantar hasta la cena? ▪ ¿Quieres picar algo para matar el gusanillo hasta la cena? Do you want a little snack to tide you over until supper?
aguantar hasta el día de pago to tide one over until payday ➤ ¿Podrías prestarme veinte dólares para aguantar hasta el día de pago? Could you lend me twenty dollars to tide me over until payday?
aguantar la carga de algo ▪ soportar la carga de algo ▪ llevar a cuestas la carga de algo to bear the burden of something
aguantar la lucha ▪ esperar el momento oportuno to bide one's time
aguantar la respiración ▪ contener la respiración ▪ contener el aliento to hold one's breath
aguantar la vela ▪ atenerse a las consecuencias ▪ enfrentar las consecuencias to face the music ▪ to face the consequences
aguantar lo que te echen to take the flack ▪ to take whatever they throw at you
aguantar lo suyo to put up with an awful lot
aguantar muy bien to bear up very well ➤ Los niños han aguantado muy bien. The children have borne up very well.
aguantar tanto tiempo sin... to go so long without...
aguar la fiesta to be a party pooper ▪ to be a wet blanket
aguar las ideas de alguien to throw cold water on someone's ideas
aguar los planes de alguien to throw cold water on someone's plans
aguardar la fiesta to be looking forward to the party
aguardarle en el futuro ▪ depararle el futuro to have in store for someone ▪ for the future to hold for someone ➤ No sé lo que me aguarda en el futuro. I don't know what the future has in store for me. ▪ I don't know what the future holds for me.
aguarse la fiesta (for) the party to be ruined
aguas abajo: ir ~ ▪ ir con la corriente to go with the current
aguas arriba: ir ~ ▪ ir contra la corriente ▪ ir a contrapelo to go against the current
las **aguas jurisdiccionales** territorial waters
agudeza visual visual acuity
el **aguijón de los celos** pang of jealousy
aguijonearle en la sospecha to raise one's suspicions ▪ to provoke one's suspicions ▪ to heighten one's suspicions ▪ to intensify one's suspicions
agüita amarilla pee pee
aguja de calibre *x* *x*-gauge needle ➤ La aguja de calibre veintineve es tan pequeña de diámetro que el gato ni siquiera reacciona cuando le damos su inyección de insulina. The twenty-nine-gauge needle is so tiny in diameter that the cat doesn't even react when we give him his insulin shot.
agujero negro *(astronomía)* black hole
aguzar el ingenio ▪ alfilar el ingenio to sharpen one's wits
aguzar la vista to keep one's eyes peeled ▪ to be on the lookout ▪ to look closely
aguzar los oídos ▪ aguzar el oído to prick up one's ears ▪ to listen out for
ah, bueno, menos mal oh, well, that's good ▪ oh, well, it's a good thing
¿ah, sí? oh, yeah? ▪ would it? ▪ really?
ahí abajo down there
estar **ahí con alguien** ▪ apoyar a alguien en un mal momento to be there for someone
ahí está ▪ ahí lo tienes **1.** there it is ▪ **2.** that's just it
ahí está el quid that's the heart of it
ahí está la cosa that's just it ▪ that's it ▪ that's what I mean ▪ that's what I'm getting at ▪ you hit on it
ahí está la madre del cordero that's just it ▪ that's just the point
ahí lo encontrarás *(coloquial)* that's where you'll find it ▪ that's where it is
¿ahí le duele a usted? is this where it hurts? ▪ it hurts (you) right there? ▪ do you feel a pain right there?
ahí le has dado you have a point (there) ▪ you've got a point (there)
ahí me aprieta el zapato that's where the shoe pinches (me) ▪ that's where it's too tight (on me)
ahí queda eso that's where it goes ▪ that's where you put it ▪ that's where it stays
ahí queda eso con cáscara y hueso that's how it stands ▪ that's how things stand ▪ that's where things stand
¿ahí te duele? it hurts (you) right there? ▪ this is where it hurts? ▪ do you feel a pain right there?
ahí te quedas suit yourself ▪ we'll leave it at that
¡ahí tienes! there you go!
¡ahí va! 1. here goes! **2.** oh, no! **3.** there it goes
estar **ahogado de trabajo** ▪ verse ahogado de trabajo to be swamped with work
ahogar el sonido to drown out the sound ▪ to drown the sound out ➤ El órgano en la estrofa final necesita estar fuerte sin ahogar al coro. The organ on the final verse needs to be loud without drowning out the choir. ➤ El ruido el helicóptero ahogó el sonido de la televisión. The sound of the helicopter drowned out the TV.
ahogar las penas en la bebida ▪ ahogar las penas en el alcohol to drown one's sorrows in drink ▪ to drown one's troubles in drink
ahogarse con algo to choke on something
ahogarse en poca agua ▪ ahogarse en un vaso de agua to get all bent out of shape over nothing ▪ to make a mountain out of a mole hill
ahogarse en un vaso de agua ▪ ahogarse en poca agua to get all bent out of shape over nothing ▪ to get all worked up over nothing ▪ to make a mountain out of a mole hill
ahondar la división entre to deepen the division between
¡ahora bien! now then!
ahora entro yo it's my turn to come in ▪ that's where I come in
ahora es el momento en el que... now is the time to...

ahora es la mía ▪ ahora me toca a mí ▪ voy yo now it's my turn
¡**ahora (lo) entiendo!** ▪ ¡ya entiendo! ▪ *(Esp.)* ¡(ah,) ya lo cojo! now I get it! ▪ (oh,) I get it!
ahora lo veredes *(Amadís de Gaula, arcaico)* you'll see now
ahora lo ves, ahora no ▪ visto y no visto now you see it, now you don't
ahora más que nunca now more than ever
ahora me he quedado dudando now I'm not sure
ahora mismo *(presente)* right now ▪ *(pasado)* just now ▪ a moment ago ▪ *(futuro)* in just a second ▪ shortly ➤ Lo acabo de oír, ahora mismo. I heard it, just now. ➤ *(teléfono)* Ahora mismo se pone. He'll be here in just a second. ▪ He'll pick (it) up in just a second. ▪ He'll be here shortly. ▪ He'll pick it up shortly.
ahora mismo salgo I'm leaving right now ▪ *(a alguien que espera afuera)* I'll be right out
ahora nos vemos *(presentador de programa de televisión)* we'll be right back
ahora que... now that...
ahora que lo dices... now that you mention it...
ahora que lo pienso come to think of it ▪ now that I think of it
¡**ahora que se las apañe!** ▪ ¡que se las aguante! ▪ ¡que se las banque! **1.** *(él)* and now he can get himself out of it! **2.** *(ella)* and now she can get herself out of it!
¡**ahora resulta que yo tengo la culpa!** ▪ ¡a que ahora resulta que la culpa la tengo yo! ▪ ¡o sea que ahora yo tengo la culpa! so now it's *my* fault!
ahora sólo se habla de all you ever hear about now is ▪ now all you ever hear about is ▪ now all anybody ever talks about is
ahora viene lo difícil now comes the hard part
¡**ahora vienen los problemas!** here comes trouble!
ahora vuelvo ▪ ya regreso ▪ espera que ya vuelvo ▪ espera que ya vengo ▪ espera que ahora vengo I'll be right back
estar **ahorcado de dinero** to be hard up financially ▪ to be short of funds
ahorcar los hábitos ▪ colgar los hábitos to leave the priesthood
ahorcar los libros ▪ colgar los libros to drop out of school ▪ to abandon one's studies
ahora mismo salgo I'm leaving right now ▪ *(a alguien que espera afuera)* I'll be right out
ahorita salgo *(Méx.)* ▪ ahora mismo salgo I'm leaving right now ▪ *(a alguien que espera afuera)* I'll be right out
ahorrar camino *(Esp.)* ▪ cortar camino ▪ ir por el atajo ▪ cortar por el atajo ▪ acortar camino to take a shortcut
ahorrar críticas to hold one's tongue ▪ to save one's breath
ahorrarle los detalles a alguien to spare someone the details
ahorrarse el viaje to save oneself the trip
ahorrarse problemas... to save oneself a lot of trouble...
ahorros de toda una vida life savings
ahuecar el ala ▪ marcharse to take off ▪ to leave
ahuecar la mano detrás del oído to cup one's hand behind one's ear
ahuecar las manos to cup one's hands
ahuyentar (a golpes) un animal to ward off an animal ▪ to ward an animal off ▪ to chase an animal off ▪ to beat back an animal
ahuyentarle a alguien to scare someone off ▪ to run someone off
ahuyentarlo a alguien to chase someone off ➤ Mi hermano mayor los ahuyentó. My big brother chased them off.
el **aire caliente sube** hot air rises
aire comprimido compressed air
el **aire de arrogancia** air of arrogance ▪ arrogant air (about one)
el **aire de familia** ▪ parentezco family resemblance ➤ Veo un aire de familia. ▪ Veo un parentezco. I can see a family resemblance.
el **aire de suficiencia** air of self-assuredness ▪ air of superiority
aire fresco fresh air ➤ Abre la ventana para que entre un poco de aire fresco en la habitación. Open the window to let some fresh air into the room.
el **aire triunfalista** triumphant air
ser **aire (una cosa)** ▪ ¡patrañas! to be a bunch of hot air ➤ Lo que dice es aire. What he says is a bunch of hot air.
airear los trapos sucios en público to wash one's dirty linen in public
estar **aislado a consecuencias del temporal** to be stranded by the storm ▪ to be stranded as a result of the storm ➤ Cientas de personas estaban aisladas a consecuencias del temporal. Hundreds of people were stranded by the storm ▪ hundreds of people were stranded as a result of the storm.
aires de grandeza: tener ~ to have an air of self-importance ▪ to have airs of self-importance
ajado mobiliario ▪ muebles ajados beat-up furniture
ajar las ruinas to take its toll on the ruins ➤ El tiempo ha ajado las ruinas antiguas. Time has taken its toll on the ancient ruins.
ajarle a alguien la vanidad to wound someone's pride
ajarle las manos to make one's hands rough
ser **ajeno a la historia** to have nothing to do with the actual history ▪ not to be based on the actual history
ser **ajeno a la verdad 1.** *(persona)* to be ignorant of the truth **2.** *(obra teatral, obra de ficción)* to have nothing to do with the truth ▪ not to be based on the truth
¡**ajo y agua!** too bad!
el **ajuar de novia** trousseau
ajustado triunfo narrow victory ➤ *(noticia)* Los votantes portugueses han dado por concluido un ciclo socialista con el ajustado triunfo de los socialdemócratas. Portuguese voters have ended the socialist period with the narrow victory of the social democrats.
ajustar algo to adjust something ▪ to get something (adjusted) right ➤ No puedo ajustar la calefacción aquí. O me paso o no llego. I can't get the heat (adjusted) right in here. It's either too much or too little. ➤ No puedo ajustar la luz bien. I can't get the light (adjusted) right. ➤ Cuando apareció la televisión en color por primera vez, era difícil ajustar el color. When color TV first came out, it was hard to get the color right.
ajustar cuentas ▪ arreglar cuentas **1.** pagar una deuda to settle accounts ▪ to settle up **2.** saldar cuentas to get even ▪ to get revenge ▪ to settle accounts
ajustar una cuenta to settle an account
ajustarle las cuentas a alguien to give someone a piece of one's mind ▪ to tell someone off ▪ to settle accounts with someone
ajustarse a to accord ▪ to be in accordance with
el **ajuste de cuentas** ▪ arreglo de cuentas settling of accounts ▪ act of revenge ▪ reprisal ▪ act of vengeance ➤ *(noticia)* Dos narcotraficantes fueron asesinados a tiros en un ajuste de cuentas. Two drug traffickers were shot to death in a settling of accounts.
¡**al abordaje!** *(orden militar)* go aboad! ▪ board the ship!
al abrigo de under cover of
estar **al abrigo de la lluvia** to be out of the rain ▪ to be protected from the rain
al abrigo de la noche ▪ al amparo de la noche **1.** bajo el manto de la oscuridad under cover of darkness **2.** protected from the night ➤ Los insurgentes se acercaron al campamento al abrigo de la noche. The insurgents approached the camp under cover of darkness. ➤ Los nómadas buscaron una cueva para ponerse al abrigo de la noche. ▪ Los nómadas buscaron una cueva para estar al abrigo de la noche. The nomads looked for a cave in which they would be protected from the night. ▪ The nomads looked for a cave which would serve as protection from the night.
estar **al acecho de** ▪ estar en acecho de ▪ estar de acecho de ▪ estar a la espera de to lie in wait
al agradecido, más de lo pedido the grateful get more than they expected ▪ the grateful receive more than they expected
¡**al agua, patos!** *(a los niños en la hora de bañarse)* okay, ducks, hit the water!
al aire libre ▪ a la intemperie ▪ al raso ▪ a cielo abierto in the open air
al ajillo in garlic sauce
al alba at dawn ▪ at (morning) twilight ▪ *(coloquial)* at the crack of dawn ➤ Cada día se levanta al alba. ▪ Ya está listo al alba todas las mañanas. He's up and at it every morning at the crack of dawn. ▪ He's rarin' go to every morning at (the crack of) dawn.

al alcance within reach

al alcance de within reach of

al alcance de la mano ▪ al alcance de su mano within reach ▪ at one's fingertips ➤ La paz está al alcance de la mano. Peace is at hand.

al alcance de la vista within sight

estar **al alcance de la voz** to be within calling distance

al alcance de su mano ▪ al alcance de la mano at one's fingertips

estar **al alcance de todos** to be within reach of everyone

estar **al alcance de todos los bolsillos** to be affordable by everyone

al alimón in collaboration ▪ together ▪ jointly ▪ simultaneously

al alimón: capea ~ *(tauromaquia)* pass made as the cape is held by two bullfighters

al almendro y al villano, con el palo en la mano for the almond tree to yield nuts, you have to hit it with a stick, like you would a villain

al amanecer at dawn ▪ at sunrise ▪ *(presente o futuro)* when the sun comes ▪ *(pasado)* when the sun came up ▪ at sunup

al amor de la lumbre ▪ al amor del fuego by the fire ▪ at the fireside

al amor del agua near the water ▪ by the river

al amor del fuego ▪ al amor de la lumbre ▪ arrimado al fuego ▪ arrimado al fogón by the fire ▪ at fireside

al amor lo pintan ciego love is blind

al amparo de ▪ al arrimo de ▪ bajo la protección de under the protection of

al amparo de la noche ▪ al abrigo de la noche ▪ bajo el manto de la oscuridad ▪ con nocturnidad under cover of darkness

al anochecer ▪ a la caída de la noche at nightfall ▪ *(presente o futuro)* when it gets dark ▪ when night falls ▪ *(pasado)* when it got dark ▪ when night fell

al año 1. un año después a year later **2.** anuales ▪ por año per year ▪ in a year ➤ *(noticia)* El agente doble, cuyo sueldo en el FBI era de $100.000 dólares anuales... The double agent, whose salary at the FBI was $100,000 a year...

al año: ganar ~ to earn per year ▪ to earn in a year ▪ to earn yearly

al año de vida in the first year of life ▪ before the end of the first year of life

al año exactamente a year ago today ▪ exactly one year ago

al año siguiente the following year ▪ the next year

¡al aparato! get the phone! ▪ pick up the phone!

estar **al aparato** to be on the phone

al aparato: ponerse ~ to get the phone ▪ to pick up the phone

al arrimo de ▪ al amparo de ▪ bajo la protección de under the protection of

al atardecer ▪ a la caída del sol ▪ al atardecer at sunset ▪ at dusk ▪ at nightfull ▪ as the sun was going down ▪ as it was getting dark

al avemaría at dusk ▪ at sundown ▪ at nightfall

¡al avemaría! good heavens!

¡al avío! let's get going! ▪ let's get started!

al azar ▪ aleatoriamente at random ▪ randomly

al azar: dejarlo ~ to leave it to chance

al baño María in a double boiler

al bies ▪ sesgado diagonally

estar **al borde de** to be on the verge of ▪ to be about to ➤ *(titular)* El partido comunista al borde de una escisión Communist Party on the verge of a split ➤ *(título de película)* *Mujeres al borde de un ataque de nervios* *Women on the Verge of a Nervous Breakdown*

estar **al borde de la guerra** to be on the verge of war

estar **al borde de la paciencia** ▪ estársele agotando la paciencia ▪ estársele acabando la paciencia to be at the end of one's patience ▪ to be running out of patience

al borde de la quiebra on the verge of bankruptcy

estar **al borde (del abismo)** ▪ estar al borde del precipicio to be on the edge of the abyss ▪ to be at the edge of the abyss

al borde del colapso on the verge of collapse

al borde del precipicio ▪ al borde del abismo at the edge of the abyss

al cabo ▪ por último ▪ al fin in the end ▪ after all ▪ finally

al cabo de ▪ de al fin de at the end of

estar **al cabo de la calle 1.** ser conocido to be very well known **2.** estar en boca de todos to be the talk of the town **3.** estar bien informado to know the score ▪ to be well informed ▪ to have good information

al cabo de la jornada at the end of the day

al cabo de un año after a year ▪ in a year

al cabo de un mes in a month ▪ after a month ▪ a month later

al cabo de un momento ▪ después de un momento ▪ tras un momento a moment later ▪ after a moment

al cabo de un rato ▪ al poco rato after a while

al cabo de unos segundos ▪ después de unos segundos ▪ tras unos segundos after a few seconds

al cabo de *x* años at the end of *x* years ▪ after *x* years

al cabo de *x* meses at the end of *x* months

al cabo de *x* minutos when *x* minutes are up ▪ when *x* minutes were up

estar **al caer** ▪ estar por caer to be here any minute (now) ▪ to be about to happen ➤ Están al caer. ▪ Están por caer ▪ En cualquier momento caen. They'll be here any minute (now).

al caer el día ▪ al final del día at the end of the day

al caer el sol ▪ al atardecer ▪ en la puesta del sol at sunset ▪ at dusk ▪ as the sun was going down ▪ as the sun was setting

al caer la noche ▪ al anochecer at nightfall

al calor de by the warmth of ➤ Al calor del fuego By the warmth of the fire

al caso: hablar ~ to speak to the issue

al caso: no venir ~ to be beside the point

al cero: cortar el pelo ~ to shave one's head ▪ to cut all one's hair off

al César lo que es del César, y a Dios lo que es de Dios render unto Caesar that which is Caesar's, and unto God what is God's

estar **al cien por cien** ▪ dar lo mejor de sí mismo ▪ dar lo mejor de uno mismo to be at one's best

al ciento por ciento a hundred percent ▪ one hundred percent

al cierre de la edición ▪ al cierre de esta edición at press time

estar **al comando de alguien** at one's command ▪ at one's service

al comienzo de la calle ▪ al principio de la calle ▪ en la bocacalle ▪ a la boca de la calle at the beginning of the street

al comienzo de la hora ▪ al principio de la hora ▪ al empezar la hora at the beginning of the hour ▪ at the top of the hour

al comienzo de la película ▪ al principio de la película at the beginning of the movie

al comienzo del año ▪ al inicio del año at the beginning of the year

al comienzo del otoño (de) early in the fall (of) ▪ early in the autumn (of) ▪ in the early fall (of) ▪ in the early autumn (of)

al compás de la música in time to the music ▪ in time with the music ▪ to the beat of the music

estar **al completo** to be filled to capacity ➤ El autobús está al completo. The bus is filled to capacity. ▪ The bus is full. ➤ Las clases están al completas. The classes are full.

al comprobar que... ▪ al ver que... on seeing that... ▪ *(futuro)* when one sees that ▪ *(pasado)* when one saw that

al confesar after confessing ▪ on confessing ▪ *(yo)* when I confessed ▪ *(él)* when he confessed ▪ *(ella)* when she confessed

al conocerse que... ▪ al saberse que... **1.** *(pasado)* when it became known that... **2.** *(futuro)* when it becomes known that...

al contado: comprar ~ ▪ comprar en efectivo to buy for cash

al contado: pagar ~ ▪ pagar en efectivo to pay (in) cash

al contar hasta diez on the count of ten ➤ Al contar hasta diez, abre los ojos. On the count of ten, open your eyes.

al contrario on the contrary

al contrario de contrary to ➤ Al contrario de lo que piensa la mayoría... Contrary to what most people think...

al correr de la pluma: escribir algo ~ *(carta, poema, ensayo, etc.)* ▪ componer al correr de la pluma ▪ escribir a vuela pluma

▪ componer a vuela pluma to dash off something ▪ to dash something off

al correr del tiempo in the course of time ▪ *(presente and futuro)* as time goes by ▪ *(pasado)* as time went by

estar **al corriente de** to be up to date on ▪ to be fully informed about

al costado de algo: caminar ▪ andar al costado de to walk along the side of ➤ Caminamos a lo largo del costado del Escorial. We walked along the side of the Escorial.

estar **al costado de** to be at the edge of ➤ Estoy al costado de la plaza mayor. I'm (standing) at the edge of the main square.

al crepúsculo at (morning) twilight

¡**al cuerno: vete ~!** go to hell!

estar **al cuidado de** to be responsible for ▪ to be in charge of

al dar la hora on striking the hour

al dedillo: saberse algo ~ to have something down pat ▪ to know something upside down and backwards

al descubierto in the open ▪ exposed

al descuido accidentally

al despuntar el día ▪ al romper el día ▪ al amanecer at daybreak ▪ at dawn ▪ at the break of dawn ▪ at the morning twilight

al detalle ▪ detalladamente in detail

al día 1. por día a day ▪ per day 2. de uso actual to be up to date ▪ to be the latest (fashion) ▪ to be trendy ➤ Este archivo crece al ritmo de una página al día. ▪ Este archivo crece al ritmo de una página al día. This file grows at the rate of a page a day. ➤ *(título del texto clásico de Turk y Allen)* El español al día Spanish up to date ▪ Up-to-date Spanish

estar **al día** to be up to date ▪ to be the latest (fashion) ▪ to be trendy ➤ *(título del texto clásico de Turk y Allen)* El español al día Spanish up to date ▪ Up-to-date Spanish ➤ Con lo que al día a día se refiere On a day-to-day basis

al día siguiente ▪ al otro día the next day ▪ (on) the following day

al empezar la hora ▪ al comienzo de la hora ▪ al principio de la hora at the beginning of the hour ▪ at the top of the hour

al encuentro de alguien: ir ~ to go meet someone ▪ to go to meet someone

al enemigo, ni agua show no mercy to the enemy

al enhornar se tuerce el pan there's many a slip 'twixt cup and lip

al enterarse de que ▪ al saberse que ▪ al conocerse que on finding out that ▪ on learning that ▪ *(futuro)* when one finds out that ▪ *(pasado)* when one found out that

al escampar 1. *(futuro)* when it stops raining 2. *(pasado)* when it stopped raining

al fiado on credit ▪ on trust

estar **al filo de** to be at the edge of ➤ Estaba de pie al filo del precipicio. He was standing at the edge of the cliff.

al filo de la medianoche at the stroke of midnight

estar **al filo de la muerte** to be on the edge of death ▪ to be at the edge of death ▪ to be at death's door

al filo de las doce at the stroke of twelve

estar **al filo de lo imposible** to be next to impossible ▪ to be almost impossible ▪ to be nearly impossible ▪ to verge on the impossible

al fin ▪ por fin ▪ en fin at last ▪ finally ▪ at the end ▪ after all ➤ Al fin todo estaba preparado para el largo viaje. At last preparations for the trip were complete.

al fin de la jornada at the end of the day ▪ at the end of the journey

al fin de la línea *(metro, tren, autobús)* end of the line

al fin del mundo at the end of the world ▪ till the end of the world

al fin y al cabo 1. at last 2. after all 3. when all is said and done

al final in the end ▪ at the end ▪ when all is said and done ▪ the bottom line is ➤ Al final, no sé. The bottom line is, I don't know.

al final de la calle ▪ al fondo de la calle at the end of the street

al final de la cola at the end of the line

al final de la hora at the end of the hour ▪ at the bottom of the hour

al final de la página ▪ al pie de la página at the bottom of the page ▪ at the foot of the page

al final del año at the end of the year

al final del concierto at the end of the concert ➤ Al final del concierto, el público pidió un bis. At the end of the concert, the audience demanded an encore.

estar **al final del corredor** ▪ estar en el fondo del corredor ▪ estar en el extremo del corredor to be at the end of the hall ▪ to be at the end of the hallway ▪ to be at the end of the corridor

al final del día ▪ a fin del día late in the day ▪ toward the end of the day ▪ at the end of the day ▪ *(figurativo)* toward the end of one's life

al final del noveno tiempo *(béisbol)* at the bottom of the ninth (inning) ▪ at the end of the ninth (inning)

estar **al final del pasillo** ▪ estar en el fondo del pasillo ▪ estar en el extremo del pasillo to be at the end of the aisle

al final del verano at the end of the summer

al final todo se sabe it will all come out in the wash ▪ it will all come out eventually

al fondo all the way down (to the end) ▪ (all the way) down to the end ▪ at the back ➤ Al fondo y a la derecha All the way down and to the right ▪ Down to the end and to the right

al fondo de at the back of ▪ at the bottom of

al fondo de la calle ▪ al final de la calle at the end of the street

al fondo del corredor ▪ en el extremo del corredor ▪ al final del corredor ▪ al fondo del corredor en el extremo del corredor ▪ al final del corredor at the end of the hall ▪ at the end of the hallway ▪ at the end of the corridor

al freír será el reír he who laughs last laughs best

estar **al frente** to be in charge ▪ to be in command

estar **al frente de** 1. to be the head of 2. to be at the front of ➤ La Dra. Morrow está al frente del departmento de idiomas. Dr. Morrow is head of the department of languages. ➤ El capitán estaba al frente del escuadrón. The captain was at the front of the squadron.

al fresco in the open air ▪ in the fresh air

al fresco: pintar ~ to paint using the fresco technique ▪ to paint frescos

al galope: ir ~ to go at a gallop ▪ to gallop

al gusto to taste ➤ Sal y pimienta al gusto Salt and pepper to taste

¡**al habla!** *(contestando el teléfono)* speaking!

estar **al habla con alguien** to be on the phone with someone ▪ to be talking to someone on the phone ▪ to have someone on the line ➤ Está al habla. *(él)* He's on the phone. ▪ *(ella)* She's on the phone.

al hilo one after the other ▪ in a row

al hilo: ganar *x* partidos ~ to win *x* games in a row

al horno baked ➤ *(L.am.)* Papas al horno ▪ *(Esp.)* Patatas al horno Baked potatoes

al igual que like ▪ just as ➤ Al igual que muchas otras personas... Like a lot of other people...

al ingerirse ▪ al ingerirlo when it is ingested ▪ on being ingested ▪ when you ingest it ➤ Beta caroteno se convierte en vitamina A al ingerirse. ▪ El beta caroteno se convierte en vitamina A al ingerirlo. Beta carotene turns into vitamin A when it is ingested.

al instante ▪ al punto ▪ inmediatamente instantly ▪ immediately

al irlo a mirar ▪ al ir a mirarlo ▪ al ir a verlo *(yo)* when I went to look at it ▪ *(él)* when he went to look at it ▪ *(ella)* when she went to look at it

estar **al lado** ▪ estar pegadito to be next door

estar **al lado de** ▪ estar junto a ▪ estar a la vera de 1. to be beside ▪ to be next to 2. to be next door to

estar **al límite** to be in a critical situation ▪ to be critical

al llegar a on arriving in ▪ *(más formal)* upon arriving in ▪ *(con cualquier sujeto o tiempo)* when one gets to ➤ Al llegar a Necochea On arriving in Necochea ▪ Upon arriving in Necochea ▪ *(yo, pasado)* When I got to Necochea ▪ *(yo, futuro)* When I get to Necochea

estar **al llegar** to be about to arrive ▪ to be imminent ➤ La decisión está al llegar. The decision is imminent.

estar **al límite de su resistencia** ■ estar al límite de sus fuerzas to be completely exhausted ■ to be at the limits of one's endurance ■ *(coloquial)* to be at the end of one's rope ■ to be at the end of one's tether

estar **al límite de sus fuerzas** 1. estar al límite de su resistencia to be at the limits of one's endurance 2. to be at the end of one's rope ■ to be at the end of one's tether ■ to be at one's wits' end

¡**al loro!** look out! ■ watch out!

estar **al loro** *(coloquial)* ■ mantener los ojos abiertos to keep one's eyes open ■ to keep an eye out ■ to be on the lookout

estar **al loro de algo** ■ estar al día to be up on ➤ Está al loro de los últimos acontecimientos. He's up on current events.

al mal tiempo, buena cara grin and bear it

estar **al mando** to be at the controls

estar **al mando de alguien** to be under the command of someone ■ to be under someone's command

estar **al margen (de)** ■ estar fuera (de) 1. to be outside (of) ■ to be on the fringes (of) 2. to be about to

al margen de algo: mantenerse ~ ■ quedarse al margen de algo to stay out of something ■ to keep out of something

al más alto nivel: conversaciones ~ top-level talks

al máximo histórico to the highest level in history ■ to its highest level in history ■ to historic highs ➤ *(titular)* La ola de calor dispara en España el consumo de la energía eléctrica al máximo histórico. The heat wave in Spain rockets electricity consumption to its highest level in history.

al máximo nivel at the highest level

al menos ■ por lo menos at least ➤ El ataque ha causado al menos trece muertes. ■ El ataque ha causado por lo menos trece muertos. The attack caused at least thirteen deaths. ➤ Al menos esa moto tiene un silenciador. At least that motorcycle has a muffler.

al menos así lo he creído *(Esp.)* ■ por lo menos así lo creí at least that's what I thought

al menos en cierto modo ■ al menos en cierta parte at least to some extent

al menos un poco at least a little ■ at least to some extent

al mes a month later ■ in a month

al mirar atrás on looking back ■ *(con "yo")* when I looked back

al mismo tiempo ■ a la vez ■ al tiempo ■ a un tiempo ■ paralelamente at the same time ■ at once ■ at a time ➤ Es al mismo tiempo una reafirmación de lo antiguo y una celebración de lo nuevo. It is at the same time an affirmation of the old and a celebration of the new. ■ It is at once an affirmation of the old and a celebration of the new. ➤ Solía pintar dos cuadros a la vez, alternando uno y otro. She would paint two pictures at once, alternating between the two. ■ She would paint two pictures at the same time, alternating between the two. ■ She would paint two pictures at a time, alternating between the two.

al mismo tiempo que... ■ a la vez que... at the same time that...

al momento de when it came time to ➤ Al momento de levantar la mesa, los invitados se borraron. When it came time to clean the table, the guests beat a trail out of Dodge.

al nacer at birth ➤ El hospital materno-infantil de Vall d'Hebron en Barcelona ha logrado que un bebé que pesó al nacer tan sólo 390 gramos sobreviva. Vall d'Hebron Maternity Hospital in Barcelona has kept alive a baby weighing only 390 grams at birth.

al natural (packed) in water ➤ Atún al natural Tuna (packed) in water

estar **al nivel de las circunstancias** to rise to the occasion ■ to save the day

al nivel del mar at sea level

al no tener que... ■ por no tener que... by not having to... ■ by not being required to...

al oído: decirle algo a alguien ~ to whisper something in someone's ear

al oírse la señal (acústica) at the sound of the beep

al oírselo on hearing one speak that way

al óleo (in) oil ➤ Pintura al óleo Oil painting ■ Painting in oil ➤ Retrato al óleo Oil portrait ■ Portrait in oil

al otro día ■ al día siguiente the next day ■ (on) the following day

al otro lado on the other side

al otro lado de la línea *(línea telefónica)* on the other end of the line ➤ ¿Quién está en el otro lado de la línea? Who's on the other end of the line?

al pan, pan, y al vino, vino: llamarle ~ to be upfront ■ to be straightforward

al parecer ■ por lo visto apparently

al paso: ir ~ to go at a canter ■ to canter

al paso de in proportion to

al paso que... at the rate (that...) ■ at the rate (at which...)

al paso que uno va at the rate one is going ➤ Al paso que vamos, nunca llegaremos. At the rate we're going, we'll never get there.

al pedirle a alguien que haga algo on asking someone to do something ■ when you ask someone to do something

al pelo: venirle ~ ■ caerle al pelo to suit one to a T ■ to be perfectly suited to one ■ to be perfect for one ➤ Me viene al pelo. It suits me to a T. ➤ Este trabajo me cae al pelo. This job is perfectly suited to me. ■ This job is perfect for me. ■ This job suits me to a T. ■ This job is perfectly suited to me, and I am perfectly suited to it.

al permitir a los médicos ver... by allowing doctors to see...

al perro flaco, todo son pulgas ■ al perro flaco, todo se le vuelven pulgas when it rains, it pours

al pie de la letra: seguir ~ ■ a rajatabla to follow to the letter ■ to follow strictly ■ to follow exactly

al pie de la página ■ al final de la página at the foot of the page ■ at the bottom of the page

estar **al pie del cañón** to hold down the fort ➤ Hoy estoy al pie del cañón. I'm holding down the fort today.

al poco rato ■ al cabo de un rato after a while ■ in a little while ■ a little later (on)

al poco tiempo ■ poco tiempo después ■ dentro de poco ■ en breve a short time later ■ a little later (on) ■ shortly afterwards ■ soon (afterwards) ■ in a little while ■ a short time after that ■ shortly after that ■ soon after that ■ a short time after that ■ before long

al poco tiempo de llegar a soon after arriving in

al ponerse el sol ■ al caer el sol ■ al atardecer at sunset ■ at sundown

al por mayor *(Esp.)* ■ *(Méx.)* a mayoreo wholesale

al por menor *(Esp.)* ■ *(Méx.)* a menudeo retail

al precio de costo at cost

al primer envite right off ■ at once

al primer indicio de problemas at the first sign of trouble

estar **el primero de la lista** ■ encabezar la lista to be at the top of the list ■ to head the list ■ to top the list

al principio at first ➤ Al principio no la vi. At first I didn't see her. ■ I didn't see her at first. ➤ Al principio resultó gracioso. At first it was funny. ■ In the beginning it was funny.

al principio de ■ al comienzo de at the beginning of ➤ Al principio de la película... ■ Al comienzo de la película... At the beginning of the movie... ■ At the beginning of the film...

al principio de la calle ■ al comienzo de la calle ■ en la bocacalle ■ a la boca de la calle at the beginning of the street

al principio de la hora ■ al comienzo de la hora ■ al empezar la hora at the beginning of the hour ■ at the top of the hour

al principio de la película ■ al comienzo de la película at the beginning of the movie

al principio era gracioso ■ al principio era cómico ■ al principio era chistoso at first it was funny

al punto ■ a la hora ■ al instante ■ inmediatamente instantly

al punto de que... it got so bad that...

al punto instantly ■ at once

al que to which

al que le caiga el sayo que se lo ponga ■ al que le venga el sayo que se lo ponga if the shoe fits, wear it

al que le venga el sayo que se lo ponga ■ al que le caiga el sayo que se lo ponga if the shoe fits, wear it

al que lo ha llevado a que lo vea es al niño *(Unamuno)* it was the child (whom) she took to see him

al que madruga, Dios le ayuda the early bird gets the worm

estar **al quite** *(taurino)* to keep one's eyes open ■ to keep one's ears open estar **al ralentí** 1. *(motor)* to idle ■ to be idling ■ to be in idle 2. *(cine)* to be in slow motion

al raso: pasar la noche ~ to spend the night outdoors ■ to spend the night outside ➤ Los muchachos pasaron la noche al raso en una carpa. The boys spent the night outside in a tent.

al rebufo (de): ir ~ to travel in the wake (of) ■ *(en carreras de coches)* to slipstream

al regresar de ■ cuando regresaba de ■ mientras regresaba de ■ *(Esp.)* al volver de ■ cuando volvía de ■ mientras volvía de on the way back from ■ (on) coming back from ■ on returning from ➤ Al regresar del aeropuerto, paramos para comprar película. ■ Al volver del aeropuerto, paramos para comprar película. ■ Al retornar del aeropuerto, paramos para comprar película. On the way back from the airport, we stopped to buy some film. ■ Coming back from the airport, we stopped to buy some film. ■ On returning from the airport, we stopped to buy some film.

al regreso on the way back ■ on returning

al rescate to the rescue

al respecto 1. about it 2. in that respect ■ in that connection ➤ No sé nada al respecto. I don't know anything about it. ➤ No puedo hacer nada al respecto. I can't do anything about it.

al resplandor del fuego by the firelight ■ by the light of the fire

al revés 1. al contrario other way around ■ on the contrary 2. patas arriba ■ invertido ■ cabeza abajo upside down ➤ Pensaba que era al revés. I thought it was the other way around.

al revés: estar escrito ~ ■ estar escrito a la inversa to be written backwards ➤ La palabra "ambulancia" está escrita al revés en el frontal de la ambulancia para que parezca al derecho cuando se vea por el espejo retrovisor. ■ La palabra "ambulancia" está escrita al revés en el frontal de la ambulancia para que parezca al derecho cuando se vea por el espejo retrovisor. The word "ambulance" is written backwards on the front of the ambulance so that it will appear frontwards when seen through a rearview mirror.

al revés: estar impreso ~ ■ estar impreso a la inversa to be printed backwards ➤ La foto está impresa al revés. Le han dado la vuelta al negativo. ■ La foto está impresa a la inversa. Le han dado la vuelta al negativo. This picture is printed backwards. They reversed the negative.

al revés que alguien ■ a diferencia de alguien unlike someone ➤ Mi madre, al revés que mi padre... My mother, unlike my father...

al ritmo de ■ a un ritmo de ■ a razón de at the rate of ➤ Este fichero crece al ritmo de una página diaria. This file grows at the rate of a page a day.

estar **al rojo vivo** to be red hot ■ *(título de película) Mercury Rising*

al saber que... 1. on finding out that... ■ on learning that... 2. al enterarse de que... *(pasado)* when one found out that... ■ when one learned that... ■ *(futuro)* when one finds out that... ■ when one learns that...

al saberse que... ■ al conocerse que... 1. *(pasado)* when it became known that... 2. *(futuro)* when it becomes known that...

al salir el sol ■ a la salida del sol at sunrise ■ at sunup ■ *(pasado)* when the sun rose ■ when the sun came up ■ *(futuro)* when the sun rises ■ when the sun comes up

al ser preguntada sobre ello when she was asked about it

al ser preguntado sobre ello when he was asked about it

estar **al sol** to be in the sun

al sol: trabajar ~ to work in the sun

al sol del éxito in the sunshine of success

al sol puesto at sundown

estar **al tanto de algo** 1. to be up (to date) on something 2. to be aware of something ■ to know about something ➤ Está al tanto de lo último en sonido. He's (really) up on stereo equipment. ➤ Deberías estar más al tanto de lo que hace tu hijo. You should be more aware of what your son is doing.

al tanto de algo: mantenerse ~ to keep abreast of something ■ to keep up to the minute on something

estar **al tanto de las últimas tendendencias** to be up all the latest

estar **al tanto en un tema** ■ estar puesto en un tema to be up (to date) on a subject

al tiempo ■ al mismo tiempo ■ a la vez ■ a un tiempo ■ paralelamente at the same time

al tiempo que ■ a la vez que ■ al mismo tiempo que at the time that ■ simultaneously as

¡al tren! all aboard!

al trote at a trot ➤ La vaca venía hacia mí al trote, mugiendo. The cow was coming at me at a trot, mooing.

al tuntún: hacer algo ~ ■ hacer algo al buen tuntún to do something haphazardly

al último momento at the last minute ■ on short notice

al vacío: caer ~ 1. to fall in a vacuum 2. to freefall 3. to jump to one's death ➤ Una pluma cae al vacío igual de rápido que una pieda. ■ En el vacío una pluma cae igual de rápido que una piedra. In a vacuum, a feather falls just as fast as a rock.

al vapor steamed

al ver que... ■ al comprobar que... on seeing that... ■ *(futuro)* when one sees that ■ *(pasado)* when one saw that

al volver de *(Esp.)* ■ cuando volvía de ■ mientras volvía de ■ al regresar de ■ cuando regresaba de ■ mientras regresaba de ■ *(literario)* al retornar de ■ cuando retornaba de ■ mientras retornaba de on the way back from ■ (on) returning from ■ coming back from ➤ Al volver del aeropuerto, paramos para comprar película. ■ Cuando volvíamos del aeropuerto, paramos para comprar película. ■ Mientras volvíamos del aeropuerto, paramos para comprar película. On the way back from the airport, we stopped to buy (some) film. ■ (On) returning from the airport, we stopped to buy (some) film. ■ Coming back from the airport, we stopped to buy (some) film.

al *x* le tocó on the count of *x*, you're "it" ➤ Al cuatro te tocó. On the count of four, you're it.

al *x* por ciento at *x* percent

ala delta hang glider

el **alba rayaba** *(poético)* ■ amanecía the dawn was breaking

¡alabado sea Dios! praise God! ■ praised be God!

alabar algo o a alguien to applaud something or someone ➤ *(noticia)* El presidente español dijo que existe una voluntad positiva por parte de los británicos que alaba, y también del gobierno español. The Spanish president said there a positive intention on the part of the British that he applauds, as well as on the part of the Spanish.

alarido(s) de agonía scream(s) of agony

alarido(s) de placer screams(s) of pleasure

alarma de velocidad insuficiente *(de un avión o avioneta)* stall warning

albergar a alguien ■ acoger a alguien ■ cobijar a alguien ■ dar asilo a alguien to take in someone ■ to take someone in ■ to give shelter to someone ➤ Cada familia alberga a otra que ha quedado sin vivienda. Each family is taking in another that has been left homeless.

albergar a un niño huérfano ■ acoger a niño huérfano ■ recoger a un niño huérfano to take in an orphan ■ to give shelter to an orphan ■ to shelter an orphan

albergar amor to have love ■ to be loving ➤ Su corazón alberga mucho amor. She is very loving.

albergar la esperanza de... to nurture the hope of... ■ to cherish the hope of...

albergar la esperanza de que... to nourish the hope that... ■ to nurture the hope that... ■ to cherish the hope that... ■ to still have the hope that... ■ to maintain the hope that...

albergar la vida ■ haber vida to have life ■ to contain life ■ (for) there to be life ➤ ¿Alberga Marte la vida? ■ ¿Hay vida en Marte? Does Mars have life? ■ Does Mars contain life? ■ Is there life on Mars?

el **albergue ecológico** wildlife refuge

el **albergue juvenil** youth hostal

el **albergue para animales** animal shelter

los **albores de la aviación** dawn of aviation ■ early days of aviation ■ beginning(s) of aviation

los **albores de la civilización** dawn of civilization

alborotar un avispero ■ revolver un avispero to stir up a hornets' nest

el **alcance de la crisis** ■ (la) profundidad de la crisis extent of the crisis ■ the depth of the crisis

el **alcance de las averías** extent of the damage

el **alcance del peligro** extent of the danger

los **alcances de la ignorancia de uno** depths of one's ignorance

alcanza para vivir it's enough to live on

ser **alcanzado por algo** to be hit by something ■ to be struck by something ➤ *(noticia)* Fallece un niño tras ser alcanzado por la carcasa de unos fuegos artificiales Boy dies after being hit by a fireworks shell ■ Boy dies after being struck by a fireworks shell

ser **alcanzado por una bala** ■ ser atracado por una bala to be struck by a bullet ■ to be hit by a bullet ➤ *(noticia)* La víctima ha sido alcanzada en el pecho cuando estacionaba el vehículo. The victim was struck in the chest as he was parking his vehicle.

alcanzar a alguien to catch up with someone ■ to be along ➤ Vayan ustedes delante, que los alcanzaré más tarde. ■ Vayan ustedes delante, que los alcanzaré luego. ■ *(Esp., vosotros)* Idos delante, que os alcanzaré más tarde. ■ Idos delante, que os alcanzaré luego. ■ *(Esp. leísmo)* Vayan ustedes delante, que luego les alcanzaré. ■ Vayan ustedes delante, que luego les cojo. You all go (on) ahead, and I'll catch up (with you) later. ■ You all go (on) ahead, and I'll be along later. ➤ Nos alcanzará más tarde. He's going to catch up with us later. ➤ Vayan saliendo. Los alcanzo en unos pocos minutos. ■ *(Esp., vosotros)* Id saliendo. Os alcanzo en unos pocos minutos. ■ You all go ahead. I'll catch up with you in a few minutes. ■ You all go ahead. I'll be along in a few minutes. ■ You all go on and go. I'll catch up with you in a few minutes. ➤ Lo alcanzamos en el vestíbulo. ■ *(Esp. leísmo)* Le alcanzamos en el vestíbulo. We caught up with him in the lobby.

alcanzar a alguien de lleno en... ■ dar a alguien de lleno en... to hit someone right smack in... ■ to hit someone square in... ➤ El pastel lo alcanzó de lleno en la cara. ■ *(Esp. leísmo)* El pastel le alcanzó de lleno en la cara. The pie hit him right smack in the face. ■ The pie hit him square in the face.

alcanzar a oír a alguien decir to overhear someone say ■ to overhear someone saying

alcanzar a ver to be able to see ■ to have an unobstructed view ■ to make out ➤ No alcanza a ver los números de la báscula por su estomago. He can't see the numbers on the bathroom scale because of his stomach ➤ No alcanzo a leer el nombre en el buzón. I can't make out the name on the mail box.

alcanzar la lluvia a alguien ■ coger la lluvia a alguien ■ agarrarle el agua to get caught in the rain ➤ No quiero que me alcance la lluvia. ■ No quiero que me coja la lluvia. ■ No quiero que me agarre el agua. I don't want to get caught in the rain. ➤ Me alcanzó la lluvia. ■ Me cogió la lluvia. I got caught in the rain.

alcanzar la madurez 1. to reach maturity 2. alcanzar el dominio de algo ■ ejercer el magisterio de algo to come into one's own ➤ La mayoría de los seres humanos alcanzan la madurez física a los doce años. Most humans reach physical maturity by age twelve. ➤ Einstein alcanzó su madurez como físico a la edad de dieciséis años. Einstein had reached maturity as a physicist by the time he was sixteen. ■ Einstein had come into his own as a physicist by the time he was sixteen.

alcanzar las más altas cotas del éxito ■ alcanzar la cima del éxito ■ alcanzar el pináculo del éxito to reach the pinnacle of success

alcanzar para vivir ■ ser suficiente para vivir to be enough to live on ➤ No es un gran salario, pero alcanza para vivir. ■ No es un gran salario, pero es suficiente para vivir. It's not a big salary, but it's enough to live on.

alcanzar su deseo to get one's wish ■ to realize one's dream ■ to achieve one's dream

alcanzar un acuerdo to reach an agreement

alcanzar un veredicto ■ llegar a un veredicto to reach a verdict ➤ El jurado ha alcanzado un veredicto. The jury has reached a verdict.

alcanzar una pronta fama ■ hacerse famoso instantáneamente to become instantly famous ■ to achieve instant fame ■ to become famous instantly

alcanzar uno el dominio de algo ■ ejercer uno el magisterio de algo to come into one's own as

¡alégrame el día! *(Clint Eastwood como Harry Callahan)* go ahead, make my day! ■ come on, make my day!

alegar no to claim not to ■ to claim one does not

alegar razones para to give reasons for

alegrarle oír decírselo to be glad to hear it ➤ Me alegra oír decírselo. ■ Me alegra saberlo. I'm glad to hear it. ■ I'm glad to know it.

alegrarse de... to be glad to...

alegrarse de que to be glad that...

estar **alegre como unas castañuelas** to be happy as a lark ■ to be happy as a clam ■ to be happy as can be

ser **alegre de cascos** *(Esp.)* ■ ser ligero de cascos 1. *(informal)* to be reckless ■ to be scatterbrained 2. *(frívolo)* to be flighty

estar **alejado de la verdad** to be far from the truth

estar **alejado del camino** to be off the track ■ to be on the wrong road

ser un **alejamiento de (la) tradición** to be a departure from tradition

Alejandro Magno Alexander the Great

alejarse de algo to get away from something ■ *(coloquial)* to steer clear of ➤ Aléjate de la pared. Podría derrumbarse. Get away from the wall. It could collapse.

alejarse enfurruñado to go away sulking

alertar a alguien de algo ■ alertar a alguien sobre algo to warn someone of something ■ to warn someone about something ➤ La Cruz Roja alerta sobre una catástrofe humanitaria. The Red Cross warns of a humanitarian catastrophe.

el **alféizar de la ventana** window sill

alfilar el ingenio ■ aguzar el ingenio to sharpen one's wits

algo anda mal something's wrong ■ something's not right

algo brotó ■ algo sucedió something just clicked ■ it just clicked

algo bueno puede salir de ello ■ algo de bueno puede salir de ello ■ algo (de) bueno puede resultar de ello some good can come out of it ■ some good can come from it ■ something good can come out of it ■ something good can come from it

algo de pretty ■ fairly ■ somewhat ➤ Hace algo de frío aquí todavía. It's still pretty cold here. ■ It's still fairly cold here.

algo de beber ■ algo para beber ■ algo de tomar ■ algo para tomar something to drink

algo (de) bueno puede salir de ello ■ algo (de) bueno puede resultar de ello something good might come out of it ■ some good might come out of it

algo de comer ■ algo para comer something to eat

algo de nieve ■ un poquito de nieve ■ *(Esp.)* un pelín de nieve a trace of snow

algo debo de estar haciendo bien I must be doing *something* right

algo es algo at least it's something

algo es mejor que nada something is better than nothing (at all) ■ a little is better than nothing (at all) ■ a little is better than none (at all)

algo está maquinando ■ algo está tramando ■ algo se trae entre manos something is up ■ something's up

algo está tramando ■ algo está maquinando ■ algo se trae entre manos something is up ■ something's up

algo falló ■ algo salió mal ■ algo anduvo mal something went wrong

algo no va bien ■ algo no está bien something's not right

algo parecido something like that ■ sort of

algo por debajo de la cuerda strings ■ hidden conditions

algo por el estilo something like that ■ something to that effect ■ something along those lines ➤ O algo por el estilo Or something like that ■ Or something to that effect

algo que no ha quedado claro: haber ~ ■ haber alguna pregunta restante ■ haber alguna duda restante ■ haber cualquier pregunta restante (for) there to be any remaining questions ➤ ¿Hay algo que no haya quedado claro? ■ ¿Hay algo que no ha quedado claro? ■ ¿Hay alguna pregunta restante? ■ Hay alguna duda restante? ■ Hay cualquier pregunta restante? Are there any remaining questions? ■ Are there any other questions? ➤ If there are any remaining questions, you can come by my office after class. Si hay cualquier pregunta restante, podéis pasar por mi oficina luego de la clase.

algo que ponerse anything to wear ➤ ¿Tienes algo que ponerte para la boda? Do you have anything to wear to the wedding?

algo se está tramando ■ algo se está maquinando ■ algo está tramando ■ algo está maquinando ■ algo se trae entre manos something's up ■ something's going on

algo se trae entre manos ■ algo se está maquinando ■ algo está maquinando ■ algo se está tramando ■ algo está tramando something's up ■ something is up

algo semejante something of the sort ■ something like that ■ something similar

algo sucedió ■ algo brotó something just clicked ■ it just clicked

algo va mal something's wrong

¿algo va mal? ■ ¿ocurrió algo? is something wrong? ■ is anything wrong? ■ is anything the matter?

el **algodón (dulce)** cotton candy

alguien conocido 1. alguien que conozco someone I know ■ somebody I know 2. alguien que conoces ■ alguien que conoce usted someone you know ■ somebody you know ➤ ¿Alguien conocido? ■ ¿Alguien que conozca? Anyone I know? ■ Anybody I know? ➤ ¿Alguien que conoces? ■ Alguien que conoce usted? Anyone you know? ■ Somebody you know?

alguien en algún lugar someone, somewhere ➤ H.L. Mencken dijo que el puritanismo es el miedo angustiado de que alguien en algún lugar pueda ser feliz. H.L. Mencken said that puritanism is the haunting fear that someone, somewhere may be happy.

alguien en quien no se confía someone you don't trust ➤ Es muy difícil trabajar con alguien en quien no se confía. It's very difficult to work with someone you don't trust.

alguien de quien se fíe la gente someone people trust

alguien de quien se pueda fiar la gente someone people can trust

¿alguien que conozca? ■ ¿alguien conocido? anyone I know? ■ anybody I know?

alguien resfriado someone with a cold

algún día ■ el día de mañana some day

algún día de abril some time in April

alguna cosa de ■ algo de anything about ■ something about

¿alguna cosa más? ■ ¿algo más? ■ ¿más cosas? anything else?

¿alguna duda? any questions?

alguna otra cosa something else

alguna que otra vez occasionally ■ here and there ■ once in a while

alguna vez 1. una vez once ■ one time ■ at some time ■ at any time ■ ever 2. jamás ever ➤ *(Unamuno)* Alguna vez una madre le pidió a Don Manuel que le curara a su hijo. Once a mother asked Don Manuel to heal her son. ■ One time a mother asked Don Manuel to heal her son. ➤ ¿Has estado alguna vez en la ciudad de México? Have you ever been to Mexico City? ➤ Es lo más absurdo que jamás he oído. That's the must absurd thing I've ever heard. ➤ Es dudoso que el presidente haya leído alguna vez el documento. It's doubtful that the president has ever read the document. ➤ *(tú)* ¿Te han dicho alguna vez que te pareces a un famoso? ■ *(usted)* ¿Le han dicho a usted alguna vez que se parece a un famoso? Has anyone ever told you that you look like someone famous?

¿alguna vez se imaginó (usted) que...? did you ever imagine that...?

¿alguna vez te has preguntado cómo...? have you ever wondered how...?

¿alguna vez te has preguntado lo que...? ■ ¿alguna vez te has preguntado qué...? have you ever wondered what...?

¿alguna vez te imaginaste que...? did you ever imagine that...?

alguna vez tuve... I once had...

algunas diligencias restantes ■ algunos asuntos (de negocios) restantes any remaining items of business

algunas personas some people

algunas veces ■ a veces ■ de vez en cuando sometimes

¿alguno de ustedes? anyone?

alguno de vosotros *(Esp.)* some of you ➤ Como alguno de vosotros ya sabe As some of you already know

¿alguno de vosotros? ■ ¿alguno de ustedes? anyone?

alguno que otro an occasional ➤ Me gusta comer alguno que otro chocolate. I like to eat an occasional chocolate.

algunos asuntos (de negocios) restantes ■ algunas diligencias restantes any remaining items of business

algunos de ustedes some of you ➤ Como alguno de ustedes ya sabe As some of you already know

aliado preferente closest ally

aliarse contra alguien ■ unirse contra alguien to gang up on someone

los **alicates de punta** ■ pinzas de punta needlenose pliers

el **aliciente para** incentive to ■ enticement to ■ come-on (to get someone to)

aligerar el paso to quicken one's pace ■ to quicken one's step ■ to quicken the pace

alijo de armamentos weapons cache ■ cache of weapons

alijo de drogas cache of drugs ➤ *(titular)* Intervenido en Ibiza el mayor alijo de éxtasis de este año. Year's largest cache of extasy seized in Ibiza.

alimentar el deseo to fuel desire

alimentar las sospechas de que... to heighten the suspicions that... ■ to heighten one's suspicions that...

alimentarse de to feed on

alimentarse de esperanzas to live on hope

alimento perecedero perishable food

alimentos elaborados processed foods ➤ *(titular)* Grasas insanas en tres de cada cuatro alimentos elaborados. Unhealthy fats in three out of four processed foods.

aliñar una ensalada ■ arreglar una ensalada ■ aderezar una ensalada to put oil and vinegar on a salad ■ to put dressing on a salad ■ to dress a salad ➤ ¿Está aliñada la ensalada? ■ ¿Está arreglada la ensalada? Does the salad already have dressing on it?

alistarse en el ejército ■ unirse al ejército ■ enlistarse en el ejercito to enlist in the army ■ to join the army

aliviar la vejiga to empty the bladder ■ to empty one's bladder

¡allá él! so much for him!

¡allá ellos! so much for them

allá en back in ■ back when ■ back in the days when ➤ Allá en Necochea Back in Necochea

allá en el tiempo de las carretas way back in the days of covered wagons

allá en el tiempo de las cavernas way back when dinosaurs roamed the earth

allá en los cincuenta, sesenta, setenta, etc. back in the fifties, sixties, seventies, etc.

allá en mi pueblo back home ➤ Allá en mi pueblo tenemos un dicho. Back home we have a saying.

allá entre él y Dios that's between him and God ■ that's between him and his conscience

allá eso so much for that

allá me las arreglo (yo) that's my problem

¡allá películas! that's nonsense! ■ that's a bunch of crap!

¡allá penas! so much for that!

allá por la prehistoria back in the dark ages

allá que se las arregle *(él)* that's his problem ■ *(ella)* that's her problem ■ *(usted)* that's your problem

allá que se las arreglen *(ellos)* that's their problem ■ *(ustedes)* that's your problem

allá que se las componga *(él)* that's his problem ■ *(ella)* that's her problem ■ *(usted)* that's your problem

allá que se las compongan *(ellos)* that's their problem ■ *(ustedes)* that's your problem

allá que se las haya *(él)* that's his problem ■ *(ella)* that's her problem ■ *(usted)* that's your problem

allá te las arregles ■ arréglatelas that's your problem

allá te las compongas that's your problem

¡allá tú! 1. to heck with you! ■ 2. it's your call

allá va there goes ➤ Allá va Marta. There goes Marta.

¡allá vamos! here we go!

¡allá voy! here I come! ■ here I go!

¡allá voy otra vez! *(Ronald Reagan)* there I go again!

allanar el camino para ■ allanar el terreno para to pave the way for ■ to prepare the way for ■ to smooth the way for

allí a lo lejos off in the distance

allí abajo down there

allí arriba up there

allí dentro in there

¡**allí estaré!** I'll *be* there!

allí le has dado ▪ tienes un buen punto ▪ tienes un buen argumento you have a point ▪ you've got a point

allí mismo right there ▪ on the spot ➤ La víctima acabó con la pierna derecha tan dañada que los socorristas tuvieron que amputársela allí mismo. The victim's leg was so badly injured that the recuers had to amputate it on the spot.

allí también hay you can get them there, too ▪ they have them, too ▪ they carry them, too

el **alma gemela** soul mate

alma perdida lost soul

estar **almacenado a presión** to be stored under pressure ➤ El gas está almacenado a presión en tanques cilíndricos. The gas is stored under pressure in cylindrical tanks.

almacenar la memoria to store memory ➤ ¿En qué parte de la computadora se almacena la memoria? Where does the computer store memory? ▪ Where in the computer is (the) memory stored? ▪ In what part of the computer is (the) memory stored?

almacenar los recuerdos to store memory ➤ ¿Dónde en el cerebro se almacenan los recuerdos? Where in the brain is memory stored?

almendras machacadas ground almonds

almuerzo de trabajo working lunch

alojarse en la casa de alguien ▪ quedarse en la casa de alguien ▪ hospedarse en la casa de alguien to stay at someone's house

alquilo habitación ▪ se alquila habitación room for rent

alrededor de around

alrededor de él ▪ en torno a él ▪ en torno suyo ▪ alrededor suyo around him

alrededor de ella ▪ en torno a ella ▪ en torno suyo ▪ alrededor suyo around her

alrededor de esa fecha around that time ▪ around that date

alrededor de esa hora around that time ▪ at about that hour

alrededor de esta fecha around this time ▪ around this date

alrededor de esta hora ▪ sobre esta hora around this time ▪ about this time ▪ right about now

alrededor de la casa *(interior y exterior)* around the house

alrededor de la época de hacia la época de ▪ por la época de ▪ sobre la época de around the time of ▪ at about the time of

alrededor de un *x* por ciento around *x* percent ▪ some *x* percent

alrededor suyo ▪ en torno suyo **1.** alrededor de él ▪ en torno a él around him **2.** alrededor de ella ▪ en torno a ella around her

alta abstención (de votantes) ▪ baja participación (de votantes) ▪ menguada asistencia (de votantes) low (voter) turnout

alta participación (de votantes) high (voter) turnout

alta traición high treason

alterado(-a): estar (muy) ~ to be upset ➤ Estaba muy alterado. He was very upset.

altercar razones to converse

altibajos de la bolsa ▪ altibajos en la bolsa fluctuations in the stock market ▪ stock-market fluctuations

altibajos de la fortuna vagaries of fortune

altibajos de la vida ▪ (los) azares de la vida life's ups and downs ▪ ups and downs of life ▪ ups and downs in life

altibajos de una fiebre fluctuations in a fever

altibajos del terreno ▪ altibajos en el terreno undulations in the terrain ▪ depressions and elevations of the terrain

la **altitud de un avión** altitude of an airplane

la **altitud sobre el nivel del mar** ▪ (la) altitud sobre el nivel del mar altitude above sea level ▪ elevation above sea level ▪ height above sea level

alto cargo del gobierno ▪ alto funcionario del gobierno high government official

alto porcentaje de electores ▪ elevada concurrencia de votantes ▪ gran número de votantes high voter turnout ▪ large voter turnout ▪ heavy voter turnout

altura sobre el nivel del mar ▪ (la) altitud sobre el nivel del mar elevation above sea level ▪ height above sea level ▪ altitude above sea level

el **alud de llamadas** flood of calls ▪ avalanche of calls

el **alud de tierra** avalanche

alumbrar el camino ▪ iluminar el camino to light the way

alumno(-a) del primer año *(de la preparatoria o de la universidad)* freshman

aluvión de flood of ▪ barrage of

el **aluvión de cartas** ▪ aluvión de correo ▪ avalancha de cartas ▪ avalancha de correo blizzard of letters ▪ blizzard of mail

alveolos en diagonal *(Esp.)* diagonal sockets ➤ Una base con alveolos en diagonal A multiple-outlet base with diagonal sockets

el **alza de la inflación** ▪ subida de la inflación rise in inflation

alzar la mano ▪ levantar la mano to raise one's hand

alzar la voz ▪ levantar la voz to raise one's voice ➤ No alces tu voz. Don't raise your voice.

alzarse contra ▪ alzarse en contra de ▪ levantarse en contra de ▪ levantarse contra to rise up against ➤ *(titular)* Las tribus pastunes se alzan contra los talibanes. The Pashtun tribes rise up against the Taliban.

alzarse de una silla ▪ levantarse de una silla to get up out of a chair

alzarse en armas ▪ levantarse en armas to rise up in arms

alzarse en rebelión ▪ levantarse en rebelión to rise up in rebellion ▪ to rebel

alzarse por la fama ▪ subirle la fama a la cabeza to let fame go to one's head ➤ Le subió la fama a la cabeza. She let fame go to her head. ▪ Fame went to her head.

alzarse sobre las puntas de los pies ▪ levantarse sobre las puntas de los pies to stand on tiptoes

el **ama de casa** *(siempre se refiere a una mujer)* head of the house ▪ housewife

el **ama de cría** *(aunque se refiere siempre a una mujer, lleva el artículo masculino)* ▪ nodriza ▪ ama de leche ▪ madre de pecho wet nurse

amaestrar un animal ▪ enseñar un animal ▪ entrenar un animal to train an animal

amago de infarto: tener ~ to have a mild heart attack

amago de sonrisa hint of a smile

amanecía ▪ el alba rayaba the dawn was breaking

amansar un par de zapatos ▪ estirar un par de zapatos to break in a pair of shoes

el, la **amante de arte** art lover

amaos los unos a los otros como yo os he amado *(mandamiento bíblico)* love one another as I have loved you

amar al prójimo como a sí mismo *(mandamiento bíblico)* love thy neighbor as thyself

amarga disputa bitter dispute

amargar la existencia de uno ▪ amargar la vida de alguien ▪ ser la cruz de uno ▪ ser la pesadilla de uno to be the bane of one's existence ▪ to make someone's life hell ▪ to be the cross one has to bear ➤ Las lecciones de violín amargaban la existencia del niño. Violin lessons were the bane of the boy's existence.

amargar las relaciones entre to sour relations between

amarrar fuertemente ▪ atar fuertemente to tie securely

amartillar un rifle ▪ amartillar un fusil to cock a rifle

amartillar un revólver to cock a revolver ▪ to cock a pistol

amartillar una pistola to cock a pistol

ambas caras ▪ ambos lados both sides ▪ front and back (sides) ➤ ¿Me copiaría esta hoja, ambas caras? Would you copy this for me, front and back? ▪ Would you make me a copy of this, front and back? ▪ Would you make a copy of both sides (of this) for me? ▪ Would you Xerox this for me, front and back?

ambas partes de un asunto ▪ ambos lados de un asunto both sides of an issue ➤ Escuché a ambas partes del asunto. I listened to both sides of the issue.

la **ambición de ser alguien** ambition to be somebody ▪ ambition to be someone

ambiciones celestiales: tener ~ to have high hopes

estar **ambientado en** to be set in ▪ to take place in ➤ El cuento está ambientado en Barcelona. The story is set in Barcelona. ▪ The story takes place in Barcelona.

el **ambiente acogedor** ▪ ambiente cálido warm atmosphere ▪ cozy atmosphere ▪ inviting atmosphere

ambiente cálido ▪ ambiente acogedor warm atmosphere ▪ inviting atmosphere ▪ cozy atmosphere ➤ Tu piso tiene un ambiente cálido. ▪ Tu piso tiene un ambiente muy acogedor. Your apartment has a warm atmosphere. ▪ Your apartment has an inviting atmosphere. ▪ Your apartment has a cozy atmosphere.

el **ambiente de bares** ▪ *(coloquial)* ambiente tipo bares ▪ ambiente en plan bares bar scene ➤ Si te gusta el ambiente de bares, te va a encantar esta ciudad. ▪ Si te va el ambiente de bares, te va a encantar esta ciudad. If you like the bar scene you'll love this city.

el **ambiente de desconfianza** ▪ ambiente de recelo atmosphere of distrust

el **ambiente de recelo** ▪ ambiente de desconfianza atmosphere of distrust

el **ambiente lleno de tensión** tension-filled atmosphere

el **ambiente propicio para el diálogo** atmosphere conducive to talks ▪ atmosphere conducive to discussion

ámbito académico 1. medio académico academic environment 2. campo académico academic field

ámbito laboral work environment

ámbito político political environment

ámbito profesional profession ▪ line of work ➤ ¿Cuál es tu ámbito profesional? What's your profession? ▪ What's your line of work?

ámbito social ▪ entramado social social fabric ➤ En el pasado, la diferencias políticas enrarecieron el ámbito social español. In the past, political differences strained the Spanish social fabric.

ambos hombres y mujeres ▪ tanto hombres como mujeres ▪ lo mismo hombres que mujeres both men and women ▪ men as well as women ▪ men and women alike

ambos padres ▪ sus dos padres ▪ los dos padres de uno both (one's) parents

amén de ser algo, es... as well as being something, it's... ▪ in addition to being something, it's... ➤ Amén de ser hermoso, es barato. As well as being pretty, it's also cheap.

amena charla con alguien: tener una ~ to have an enjoyable chat with someone ▪ to have a pleasant chat with someone ▪ to have a nice chat with someone

amenaza creíble credible threat

amenaza lluvia it's threatening to rain ▪ it looks like rain

amenazar con hacer algo to threaten to do something ➤ El gobierno amenaza con recurrir a la fuerza. The government threatens to resort to force.

América Central ▪ Centroamérica Central America

América del Norte North America *(Nota: "Norteamérica" se refiere especificamente a los Estados Unidos.)*

América del Sur ▪ Sudamérica South America

América Latina ▪ Latinoamérica Latin America

amigo(-a) de lo ajeno *(coloquial)* ▪ rápido para las uñas shoplifter

amigo(-a) auténtico(-a) ▪ amigo verdadero true friend ▪ genuine friend

ser **amigo(-a) de** to be fond of ▪ to be a great one for ▪ to get a charge out of

ser **amigo(-a) de alguien** to be someone's friend ▪ to be a friend of someone

amigo(-a) de siempre old friend ▪ lifelong friend ▪ friend forever

amigo(-a) del alma beloved friend

amigo(-a) del trabajo friend from work

amigo(-a) en común ▪ amigo mutuo mutual friend

amigo(-a) íntimo(-a) close friend ▪ great friend

amigo(-a) invisible ▪ amigo secreto Secret Santa *(Nota: juego especialmente en Navidad que consiste en hacer un regalo a un miembro de la familia o a un compañero de trabajo en el que uno toma al azar el nombre del receptor y le hace llegar el regalo de forma anónima ▪ a game especially at Christmas that consists of giving a present to a family member or work colleague in which one draws the name of the prospective recipient at random and gives him or her the gift anonymously)*

amigo(-a) mayor elderly friend ▪ aging friend ▪ friend who's up in years

amigo(-a) por correspondencia pen pal

amigo(-a) querido(-a) beloved friend

amigo(-a) verdadero(-a) ▪ amigo auténtico true friend ▪ genuine friend

amigos de mis amigos son mis amigos any friends of yours is a friend of mine

amigos entrañables close friends

aminorar el paso ▪ reducir la velocidad to slow down

aminorar la marcha to slow down

amistad no correspondida one-sided friendship

El **amor brujo** *(obra de Manuel de Falla)* Love, the Magician

el **amor del bueno** ▪ amor verdadero true love

el **amor es ciego** love is blind

el **amor fraternal** brotherly love

el **amor libre** free love

amor mío my dear

el **amor nunca deja de ser** ▪ el amor es eterno love is eternal

amor platónico platonic love ▪ unselfish love ▪ nonsexual love

amor por love for

amor propio 1. self love ▪ love of oneself 2. vanity

amor propio: tener ~ to have dignity ▪ to have self-respect ➤ Tengo demasiado amor propio para correr desnudo por el campo de fútbol. I have too much dignity to streak across a soccer field.

el **amor todo lo puede** love conquers all things

amor verdadero ▪ amor del bueno true love

amoratarse el ojo to get a black eye ➤ Me amoraté el ojo jugando al béisbol. I got a black eye (when I was) playing baseball.

amordazar la prensa to muzzle the press

amortiguar la caída de alguien to cushion someone's fall ▪ to break someone's fall

amortiguar un golpe to cushion a blow

estar **amparado en** to be backed by ▪ to be backed up by ▪ to be supported by

ampararse en que... to defend one's action by saying that... ▪ to defend one's action by maintaining that...

amplia cobertura wide coverage ➤ Los medios de comunicación habían dedicado amplia cobertura a la historia. The media had given the story wide coverage.

ampliar la memoria *(informática)* to expand the memory

ampliar los horizontes de uno ▪ ensanchar los horizontes de uno to broaden one's horizons ▪ to expand one's horizons

el **amplificador de sonido** ▪ sistema de altavoces P.A. system ➤ Is that someone's radio, or is that coming over the bus' P. A. system? ¿Eso que suena es la radio de alguien, o procede de los altavoces del autobus?

amplio consenso en wide consensus of ▪ broad consensus of

la **amplitud de la franja** bandwidth

la **amplitud de la victoria** ▪ (el) margen de la victoria margin of victory ➤ La amplitud de la victoria de Blair será un termómetro de hasta qué punto... The margin of Blair's victory will be a barometer of the extent to which...

amuleto de (buena) suerte good-luck charm

analfabeto(-a) funcional functional illiterate

el **análisis en profundidad** in-depth analysis

análisis matemático real analysis

analizar la posibilidad de hacer algo to study the possibility of doing something

analizar detalladamente ▪ analizar pormenorizadamente to analyze in detail

ancho de banda 1. *(telecomunicaciones)* bandwidth 2. *(jerga informática)* ▪ que posee un gran talento computer whiz

ser **ancho de espaldas** ▪ tener espaldas anchas to be broad shouldered ▪ to have broad shoulders

¡anda a saber! ▪ ¡vete a saber! 1. ¿quién sabe? who knows? ▪ who's to say? ▪ there's no telling ▪ it's anyone's guess ▪ God knows! ▪ goodness knows! 2. *(cuando la situación es absurda)* go figure! ▪ you figure it out!

¡anda al infierno! *(subido de tono)* ▪ vete al infierno ▪ vete a la mierda go to hell!

¡anda mi madre! ▪ ¡a la pucha! holy cow!

¡anda ya! *(jerga)* nah! ▪ get outta here! ▪ don't gimme that! ▪ you gotta be kidding me!

ándale pues 1. okay then 2. you go right ahead

¡andando, que es un gerundio! ■ ¡ándale! get moving! ■ get going! ■ *(ligeramente subido de tono)* get the lead out of your butt!

andar a capa caída *(Esp.)* ■ ir a capa caída ■ andar de capa caída ■ ir de capa caída to be crestfallen ■ to be downcast

andar a cuatro patas **1.** caminar a gatas to walk on all fours **2.** *(bebés)* gatear to crawl

andar a la caza de gangas ■ ir a la caza de gangas to go bargain hunting

andar a la caza de grillos to go on a wild goose chase

andar a la cuarta pregunta to be broke

andar a la greña con alguien *(Esp.)* ■ estar a la greña con alguien ■ andar a palos con alguien to be at loggerheads with someone ➤ El presidente Bush y el presidente de la Reserva Federal, Alan Greenspan, andan a la greña por la cuantía de la rebaja fiscal. President Bush and Federal Reserve Chairman Alan Greenspan are at loggerheads over the size of the tax cut.

andar a malas (con alguien) to be on bad terms (with someone)

andar a medias tintas ■ andarse con rodeos to beat around the bush ■ to hem and haw ■ to avoid giving a direct answer

andar a palos (con alguien) **1.** to come to blows (with someone) **2.** estar en desacuerdo con alguien ■ estar en conflicto con alguien to be at loggerheads (with someone)

andar a paso de tortuga to go at a snail's pace ■ to proceed at a snail's pace

andar a paso ligero to walk fast

andar a paso liviano to walk lightly

andar a tientas to feel one's way along ■ to grope one's way along

andar al uso ■ ir con la corriente ■ adaptarse a las circunstancias ■ bailar al son que le tocan to go with the flow ■ to adapt to the circumstances

andar alguien por su mala cabeza ■ verse alguien por su mala cabeza **1.** to obey one's worst instincts ■ to follow one's worst instincts ■ to be ruled by one's worst instincts **2.** to have no common sense

andar arrastrado to lead a wretched existence ■ to lead a wretched life

andar arrastrando los pies ■ andar a rastras ■ caminar arrastrando los pies to drag one's feet (when one walks) ■ to shuffle one's feet (when one walks) ➤ Anda arrastrando los pies. He shuffles his feet (when he walks).

andar barriendo las cosas ■ hacer movimiento de barrido ■ hacer un barrido to shove things aside ■ to bat things around ➤ A los gatos les gusta andar barriendo las cosas. Cats like to bat things around.

andar bien *(reloj)* to go smoothly ■ to keep good time

andar buscando algo to go looking for something

andar como calzón de puta, (para arriba y abajo) *(subido de tono)* ■ andar como maleta de loco to run around like a chicken with its head cut off

andar como Dios le trajo al mundo to be in one's birthday suit ■ to be stark naked

andar como la seda to run smooth as silk ■ to go smoothly ■ to hum along

andar como Pedro por su casa to act as if one owns the place

andar como una tortuga ■ ir como una tortuga to go at a snail's pace

andar con la barba por el suelo to be old and decrepit

andar con la cabeza muy alta to hold one's head high ■ to have a sense of pride ■ to have a sense of self worth

andar con los patos volados to be in a dither ■ to be frazzled ■ to be all upset

andar con mala gente ■ rondar con mala gente ■ merodear con mala gente ■ holgazanear con mala gente ■ haraganear con mala gente ■ reunirse con mala gente to run around with a bad crowd ■ to hang around with a bad crowd ■ to hang out with a bad crowd ■ to run around with the wrong crowd

andar con melindres ■ ser tiquismiquis to be fussy

andar de acá para allá *(Esp.)* ■ andar de arriba para abajo to be on the move

andar de adelante a atrás ■ andar de un lado a otro to pace back and forth ➤ El novio andaba de adelante a atrás esperando a la novia. The groom was pacing back and forth waiting for the bride.

andar de boca en boca ■ ir de boca en boca ■ andar en boca de todos to be the talk of the town

andar de cabeza ■ hacer de la noche día to burn the candle at both ends

andar de caída to be on the decline

andar de capa caída ■ ir de capa caída ■ andar a capa caída ■ ir a capa caída to be downcast ■ to be demoralized ■ *(literario)* to be crestfallen

andar de casa en casa ■ andar de puerta en puerta to go from house to house ■ to go from door to door

andar de espaldas *(Esp.)* ■ caminar de espaldas to walk backwards ➤ Cuando marchó por última vez del hogar de su niñez, andaba de espaldas por el camino con lágrimas en los ojos. As he left his boyhood for the last time, he walked backwards down the road with tears in his eyes.

andar de la Ceca a la Meca ■ ir de la Ceca a la Meca to run from pillar to post

andar de novios to go steady ➤ Enrique y María andan de novios. Enrique and Maria are going steady.

andar de picos pardos ■ ir de picos pardos to cat around ■ to go looking for whatever

andar de prisa to be in a hurry

andar de puntillas to tiptoe ■ to walk on tiptoes

andar de ronda to wander around

andar de un lado a otro ■ andar de adelante a atrás to pace back and forth ➤ Anda de un lado a otro como un león enjaulado. He paces back and forth like a caged lion.

andar descamisado ■ ir descamisado to go shirtless ■ to go without a shirt

andar desnudo ■ andar en cueros ■ andar en pelotas to go around naked ■ to parade around in the buff ■ to parade around in the nude

andar destemplado ■ estar destemplado ■ andar con fiebre moderada ■ tener un poco de fiebre to have a mild fever ■ to have a low fever ■ to have a slight fever

andar detrás del dinero de alguien to be after someone's money ➤ Ella sólo anda detrás de su dinero. She's just after his money.

andar empantanado con ■ empantanarse en ■ atascarse en ■ estar liado con to get bogged down in ➤ Andamos empantanados con los detalles. We get bogged down in (the) details. ■ We're getting bogged down in (the) details.

andar en boca de la gente ■ andar en boca de todos ■ andar de boca en boca ■ ir de boca en boca to be the talk of the town

andar en boca de todos ■ andar en boca de la gente ■ andar de boca en boca ■ ir de boca en boca to be the talk of the town

andar en coche de San Fernando, (un rato a pie y otro andando) *(cómico)* caminar en coche de San Fernando, (un rato a pie y otro caminando ■ ir a pie to go on shank's mare ■ to go on foot ■ not to have a ride

andar en cueros ■ andar en pelotas ■ andar desnudo parade around in the buff ■ to parade around in the nude ■ to go around in the buff ■ to go around in the nude

andar en dares y tomares to engage in give and take ■ to go back and forth ■ to spar

andar en la cuerda floja ■ caminar sobre la cuerda floja to walk a tightrope

andar en paños menores to go around in one's underpants ■ to parade around in one's undies ■ to parade around in one's skivvies

andar en pelotas ■ andar en cueros ■ andar desnudo to go around in the buff ■ to go around in the nude ■ to parade around in the buff ■ to parade around in the nude

andar en su onda ■ hacer la suya ■ ir a su bola ■ ir a su rollo to do one's own thing

andar encuerado to go naked

andar erguido *(Esp.)* ■ caminar derecho **1.** to walk upright **2.** to walk straight ahead

andar escaso de dinero ■ andar corto de dinero ■ andar mal de dinero to be strapped for cash

andar escaso de tiempo ▪ ir fatal de tiempo to be pressed for time

andar hecho un pingo ▪ ir hecho un pingo ▪ ir muy mal vestido to look a sight ▪ to be shabbily dressed ▪ to look like a wreck ▪ to be badly dressed

andar lento 1. andar despacio ▪ caminar lento ▪ caminar despacio to walk slow(ly) 2. *(máquina)* andar despacio to run slowly ➤ La computadora anda lenta. ▪ La computadora anda despacio. ▪ *(Esp.)* El ordenador anda lento. ▪ El ordenador anda despacio. The computer runs slow.

andar mal not to be doing very well ▪ not to be doing so well ▪ not to be doing too well

andar mal de dinero to be short of money ▪ to be short of cash ▪ to be short on cash ▪ to be short of funds

andar manga por hombro ▪ estar manga por hombro to be in a state of chaos ▪ to be topsy-turvy

andar por *x* ▪ rodar los *x* to be about *x* ➤ (Ella) anda por los cuarenta. ▪ Ronda los cuarenta. She's about forty. ➤ (Ella) andaba por los cuarenta. ▪ Rondaba los cuarenta. She was about forty.

andar para atrás ▪ ir para atrás to go backwards

andar perdido not to have one's bearings ▪ to be finding one's way around

andar solos *(calcetines y pantolones sucios)* to stand up by themselves

andar suelto *(Esp.)* ▪ seguir en libertad to remain at large ▪ to be on the loose ▪ to be loose

andar una barbaridad to do a lot of walking

andarse con ojo to watch out ▪ to be careful

andarse con rodeos *(Esp.)* ▪ andarse por las ramas ▪ irse por las ramas ▪ irse por los cerros de Úbeda ▪ marear la perdiz ▪ andarse con medias tintas ▪ andar con vueltas to beat around the bush

andar(se) por las ramas ▪ andarse con rodeos ▪ irse por las ramas ▪ irse por los cerros de Úbeda ▪ marear la perdiz ▪ andarse con medias tintas ▪ andar con vueltas to beat around the bush

andarse por los cerros de Úbeda *(Esp., coloquial)* to beat around the bush ▪ to hem and haw

ande yo caliente y ríase la gente who cares what people think if I feel comfortable with who I am ▪ I don't care what people think ▪ I don't care what anyone thinks

anegar el carburador ▪ calar el carburador to flood the curburetor ▪ to flood the engine

anegar el sótano to flood the basement

anexo a un correo electrónico attachment to an E-mail ▪ E-mail attachment

el **ángel de la guarda** guardian angel

angosta escalera narrow stairway ▪ narrow stair(s)

ángulo de ataque *(aerodinámica)* angle of attack

ángulo de incidencia *(aerodinámica)* angle of incidence

ángulo muerto (en el espejo retrovisor de un carro) ▪ punto ciego ▪ espacio no visible blind spot (in a car's rear-view mirror)

ángulo recto right angle

anhelo frustrado frustrated longing

anidar en el corazón de uno to dwell in one's heart

anillo de boda ▪ anillo nupcial ▪ anillo de matrimonio ▪ alianza wedding ring ▪ wedding band

anillo de compromiso ▪ anillo de prometida ▪ sortija engagement ring

anillo de matrimonio ▪ anillo de boda ▪ anillo nupcial ▪ alianza wedding ring ▪ wedding band

anillo nupcial ▪ anillo de boda ▪ anillo de matrimonio ▪ alianza wedding ring ▪ wedding band

anillos de Saturno rings of Saturn

estar **animado por hacer algo** to be anxious to do something ▪ to be excited about doing something ➤ Estoy muy animado por empezar. I'm really anxious to get started.

el **animal de sangre caliente** warm-blooded animal

el **animal de sangre fría** cold-blooded animal

animal diurno diurnal animal ▪ animal active during the day

animar a alguien para que haga algo to encourage someone to do something

animarse a hacer algo to make up one's mind to do something ▪ to get up the courage to do something ▪ to muster the courage to do something ▪ to summon the courage to do something ▪ to gather the courage to do something

los **ánimos se caldearon** tempers flared ▪ tempers rose

aniquilar una población ▪ exterminar una población ▪ diezmar una población to annihilate a population ▪ to wipe out a population ▪ to obliterate a population ➤ El sarampión diezmó la mitad de la población de Hawaii. Measles wiped out half the population of Hawaii.

aniversario de su matrimonio wedding anniversary ▪ anniversary ➤ Estaban celebrando el cincuagésimo aniversario de su matrimonio. They were celebrating their fiftieth wedding anniversary. ▪ They were celebrating their fiftieth anniversary.

anotar la matrícula ▪ coger la matrícula ▪ ver la matrícula to get the license (plate) number

anotar un punto ▪ marcar un gol to score a point ▪ to score a goal

anotar un tanto *(baloncesto)* to score (a basket)

anotarse para el exam TOEFL ▪ suscribirse para el examen TOEFL ▪ comprometerse para el examen TOEFL to sign up for the TOEFL test ▪ to sign up for the TOEFL exam

ansia de dinero ▪ (la) sed de dinero lust for money ▪ thirst for money

ansia de poder ▪ (la) sed de poder lust for power ▪ thirst for power

estar **ansioso(-a) por** ▪ estar deseoso de ▪ tener ganas de to be anxious to ▪ to be eager to ➤ Estoy ansioso por llegar. I'm anxious to get there. ▪ I'm anxious to arrive.

estar **ansioso(-a) por ver a alguien** ▪ tener ansias de ver a alguien to be anxious to see someone

ante algo así (when) faced with something like that ▪ on hearing something like that ▪ when one hears something like that ▪ on seeing something like that ▪ when one sees something like that

estar **ante el altar** ▪ estar frente al altar ▪ estar delante del altar to stand before the altar ▪ to stand at the altar ▪ to stand in front of the altar

ante el riesgo de faced with the risk of

ante la insistencia de at the insistence of ▪ at the urging of ▪ at the instigation of ▪ at the suggestion of ➤ Fui a la exposición ante la insistencia de un par de mis amigos. I went to the art exhibit at the insistence of a couple of my friends. ▪ I went to the art exhibit at the urging of a couple of my friends. ▪ I went to the art exhibit at the instigation of a couple of my friends. ▪ I went to the art exhibit at the suggestion of a couple of my friends.

ante la posibilidad de que in view of the possibility that

ante las (mismas) narices de uno under one's nose ➤ ¿Pueden los terroristas haberse reagrupado ante nuestras (mismas) narices? Could the terrorists have regrouped under our noses?

ante las narices de uno ▪ ante las mismas narices de uno under one's nose

ante meridiem ▪ ante meridiano antemeridian ▪ ante meridiem

ante todo first and foremost ▪ first of all

ante una emergencia ▪ en una emergencia in an emergency

los **antecedentes penales** criminal record

la **antena parabólica** satellite dish

anteproyecto de ley draft of a bill

antes de anoche ▪ anteanoche night before last

antes de ayer ▪ anteayer day before yesterday

antes de Cristo ▪ a.C. before Christ ▪ B.C.

antes de eso 1. más pronto before that ▪ sooner than that 2. anteriormente before that ▪ prior to that (time) ➤ Aunque no estaré en la facultad hasta el miércoles, de todas formas podemos encontrarnos antes (de eso) si necesitas ayuda con tu trabajo. ▪ Aunque no estaré en la facultad hasta el miércoles, de todas formas podemos encontrarnos más pronto si necesitas ayuda con tu trabajo. ▪ *(Esp.)* Aunque no estaré en la facultad hasta el miércoles, de todas formas podemos quedar antes si necesitas ayuda con tu trabajo. Even though I won't be on campus til Wednesday, we can still meet if you need help on your paper before that. ▪ Even though I won't be on campus til Wednesday, we can still meet if you need help on your paper sooner (than that). ➤ Antes de eso, trabajaba en Washington. ▪ Anteriormente, trabajaba en Washington. Before that, he worked in Washington. ▪ Prior to that (time) he worked in Washington.

antes de fecha early ▪ ahead of schedule ▪ before something is due

antes de hacer nada, consúltalo con la almohada before you do anything, sleep on it ▪ before going ahead, sleep on it ▪ before you do anything, consult your pillow

antes de la Navidad before Christmas

antes de (llegar a) la cuenta de diez ▪ antes de llegar al conteo de diez ▪ antes del conteo de diez before the count of ten ➤ El boxeador volvió en sí antes de llegar a la cuenta de diez. The boxer came to before the count of ten.

antes de lo programado: andar ~ *(dícese de relojes, eventos, proyectos)* to run ahead of schedule

antes de lo programado: llegar ~ to arrive ahead of schedule

antes de lo programado: recorrer ~ *(dícese de medios de transporte)* to run ahead of schedule

antes de lo que (yo) esperaba sooner than I expected (to)

antes de media hora in less than half an hour ▪ within half an hour ▪ in less than a half hour ▪ within a half hour

estar **antes de mí en la cola** ▪ estar antes que yo en la cola ▪ ir antes de mí en la cola ▪ ir antes que yo en la cola ▪ ir delante de mí en la cola ▪ estar delante de mí en la cola ▪ ir delante mío en la cola ▪ estar delante mío en la cola to be before me in line ▪ to be in front of me in line

antes de nacer before one was born

antes de que before which

antes de que acabe el año ▪ antes del fin del año before the end of the year

antes de que amanezca ▪ antes de que se haga de día ▪ antes de que salga el sol ▪ antes del amanecer ▪ antes del día ▪ antes del alba ▪ antes de la aurora before the sun comes up ▪ before sunrise ▪ before daybreak ▪ before dawn ▪ before the sun rises ▪ before (morning) twilight

antes de que me diera cuenta de lo que pasó before I knew what had happened ▪ before I realized what had happened

antes de que naciera ▪ antes de que naciese *(yo)* before I was born ▪ *(usted)* before you were born ▪ *(él)* before he was born ▪ *(ella)* before she was born

antes de que naciese ▪ antes de que naciera **1.** *(yo)* before I was born **2.** *(usted)* before you were born **3.** *(él)* before he was born **4.** *(ella)* before she was born

antes de que pudiera... *(yo)* before I could... ▪ *(él)* before he could... ▪ *(ella)* before she could...

antes de que pudiera pararle ▪ antes de que pudiese pararle **1.** *(yo)* before I could stop him **2.** *(él)* before he could stop him **3.** *(ella)* before she could stop him

antes de que pudiese... *(yo)* before I could... ▪ *(él)* before he could... ▪ *(ella)* before she could...

antes de que salga el sol before the sun comes up ▪ before the sun rises ▪ before sunrise ▪ before sunup

antes de que se dé cuenta ▪ antes de que lo sepa uno ▪ antes de que se tenga en cuenta before you know it

antes de que se haga de día ▪ antes de que amanezca ▪ antes de que salga el sol ▪ antes del amanecer ▪ antes del día ▪ antes del alba ▪ antes de la aurora before the sun comes up ▪ before sunrise ▪ before daybreak ▪ before dawn ▪ before the sun rises ▪ before (morning) twilight

antes de que se haga de noche ▪ antes de que anochezca ▪ antes del crepúsculo (de la noche) before it gets dark ▪ before dark ▪ before nightfall ▪ before dusk ▪ before twilight

antes de que se ponga el sol ▪ antes del ocaso ▪ antes de la puesta del sol before the sun goes down ▪ before sunset ▪ before sundown

antes de que se tenga en cuenta ▪ antes de que se dé cuenta ▪ antes de que se dé en cuenta ▪ antes de que uno se dé cuenta de nada before you know it

antes de que siquiera pudiera... ▪ antes de que siquiera pudiese... **1.** *(yo)* before I could even **2.** *(él)* before he could even **3.** *(ella)* before she could even

antes de que te des cuenta ▪ antes de que te enteres ▪ sin que te des cuenta before you know it ➤ La Navidad llegará antes de que te des cuenta. ▪ La Navidad llegará sin que te des cuenta. ▪ La Navidad llegará sin que te enteres. Christmas will be here before you know it.

antes de que te enteres ▪ antes de que te des cuenta ▪ sin que te enteres ▪ sin que te des cuenta before you know what has hit you ▪ so fast it'll make your head spin ▪ before you have realized what's going on ➤ Antes de que te enteres, ellos te sacarán todo tu dinero. They'll have all your money before you know what's hit you. ▪ They'll have all your money so fast it'll make your head spin.

antes de que uno cuente hasta diez before the count of ten ▪ before one counts to ten ▪ before one reaches the count of ten ➤ El boxeador volvió en sí antes de que el árbitro contara hasta diez. The boxer came to before the referee reached the count of ten.

antes de que uno se dé cuenta de nada ▪ antes de que uno se entere before one knows it

antes de que (yo) naciera ▪ antes de que (yo) naciese before I was born

antes de que (yo) naciese ▪ antes de que (yo) naciera before I was born

antes de que (yo) pudiera... ▪ antes de (yo) pudiera before I could... ➤ Antes de que pudiera salir de mi asombro... Before I could recover from my astonishment... ▪ Before I could recover my composure...

antes de que (yo) pudiera pararle (de hacer algo) ▪ antes de que (yo) pudiera impedirle (que hiciera algo) ▪ antes de que (yo) pudiera impedírselo before I could stop him (from doing something)

antes de que (yo) pudiera responder... before I could answer...

antes de que (yo) pudiera siquiera... before I could even...

antes de que (yo) pudiese pararle (de hacer algo) ▪ antes de que (yo) pudiese impedirle (que hiciera algo) ▪ antes de que (yo) pudiese impedírselo before I could stop him...

antes de que (yo) pudiese responder... before I could answer...

antes de que (yo) pudiese siquiera... before I could even...

antes de *x* años ▪ dentro de *x* años within *x* years ➤ Si no hacemos nada, el oso polar será extinto dentro de cincuenta años. If we don't do something, the polar bear will be extinct within fifty years.

antes del alba ▪ antes de la aurora ▪ antes de que caiga el día ▪ antes del amanecer ▪ antes de que se haga de día ▪ antes de que amanezca before daybreak ▪ before dawn ▪ before twilight

antes del amanecer ▪ antes de que amanezca ▪ antes del alba ▪ antes de la aurora ▪ antes del día before the sun comes up ▪ before sunrise ▪ before daybreak ▪ before dawn ▪ before the sun rises ▪ before (morning) twilight

antes del aurora ▪ antes del alba ▪ antes del día ▪ antes del amanecer ▪ antes de que amanezca before dawn ▪ before daybreak ▪ before (morning) twilight

antes del conteo de diez *(Sudamérica)* ▪ antes de llegar al conteo de diez ▪ antes de (llegar a) la cuenta de diez before the count of ten ➤ El boxeador volvió en sí antes del conteo de diez. The boxer came to before the count of ten.

antes del crepúsculo **1.** *(de la mañana)* before dawn **2.** *(de la tarde)* before dusk

antes del día ▪ antes del amanecer ▪ antes de que salga el sol ▪ antes de que se haga de día ▪ antes de que amanezca ▪ antes del alba ▪ antes de la aurora before daybreak ▪ before dawn ▪ before the sun comes up ▪ sun rises ▪ before (morning) twilight

antes del final del año ▪ antes de fin de año ▪ antes de que acabe el año before the end of the year

antes del ocaso ▪ antes de que se ponga el sol ▪ antes de que se meta el sol ▪ antes de la caída del sol before sundown ▪ before the sun goes down ▪ before sunset

antes era... *(yo)* I used to be... ▪ *(él)* he used to be... ▪ *(ella)* she used to be... ➤ Antes yo era un sabihondo. I used to be a know-it-all.

antes hoy que mañana ▪ cuanto antes mejor the sooner the better

antes no me gustaba... I didn't use to like... ➤ Antes no me gustaba la música clásica, pero ahora sí. I didn't use to like classical music, but I do now.

antes o después ■ tarde o temprano ■ a la larga o a la corta ■ a la corta o a la larga sooner or later

antes que anochezca ■ antes de que se haga noche ■ antes de que se ponga el sol ■ *(literario)* antes del crepúsculo ■ antes del ocaso before it gets dark ■ before dark ■ before nightfall ■ before dusk ■ before twilight

estar **antes que** to be before ■ to be in front of ➤ Ella está antes que yo. She's before me. ■ She's in front of me.

antes que nada ■ antes que todo ■ antes de todo first of all

antes que nadie before anyone else ➤ Me enteré de las noticias antes que nadie. I heard the news before anyone else. ■ I was the first to hear the news.

antes que todo ■ antes que nada ■ antes de todo first of all

antes que uno (hiciera algo) before one did (something) ➤ They got there before I did. Llegaron antes que yo.

estar **antes que yo en la cola** ■ estar antes de mí en la cola ■ ir antes de mí en la cola ■ ir antes que yo en la cola ■ ir delante de mí en la cola ■ estar delante de mí en la cola to be before me in line ■ to be in front of me in line

antes que yo (lo hago) before I do ➤ Mi madre se levanta una hora antes que yo. My mother gets up an hour before I do.

anticiparse a alguien ■ adelantarse a alguien to beat someone to it ➤ ¡Te me anticipaste! ■ ¡Te me adelantaste! You beat me to it! ➤ (Él) se me anticipó. ■ (Él) se me adelantó. He beat me to it.

antigua balada old ballad

antigua estirpe de a long (ancestral) line of

antípodas de ■ cara opuesta de opposite side of ■ other side of ➤ *(noticia)* El robot de NASA aterriza con éxito en las antípodas de Marte donde está su gemelo "Spirit". ■ El robot de NASA aterriza con éxito en la cara opuesta de Marte donde está su gemelo "Spirit". The NASA robot lands successfully on the opposite side of Mars from its twin "Spirit." ■ The NASA robot lands successfully on the other side of Mars from its twin "Spirit."

antojársele algo ■ darle antojo de hacer algo ■ darle la vena por hacer algo to have the urge to do something ■ to strike one's fancy to do something ➤ Se le antojó a ella tocar las nalgas del David de Miguel Ángel. She had the urge to touch the buttocks of Michelangelo's David.

antro de mala muerte ■ antro de perdición den of iniquity

antro de perdición ■ antro de mala muerte den of iniquity

anudarse la voz ■ hacérsele a uno un nudo en la garganta to get a lump in one's throat

anunciar a bombo y platillo ■ pregonar a bombo y platillo to announce with great fanfare ■ to announce with a lot of hype ■ to hype

anunciar su compromiso matrimonial to announce one's engagement ■ to announce their engagement

anuncios breves classified ads

anular las configuraciones por defecto *(informática)* ■ suprimir las configuraciones por defecto to turn off the defaults ■ to remove the defaults ■ to eliminate the defaults ■ to delete the defaults

anular una reserva ■ cancelar una reserva to cancel a reservation ➤ No la anules. Don't cancel it.

añadir leña al fuego ■ echar leña al fuego to add fuel to the flames ■ to add fuel to the fire

añejar vino to age wine ➤ ¿Cuántos años ha estado añejado el vino? How many years has it been aged?

año académico academic year

el **año anterior** the year before ■ the previous year ■ the preceding year

año bisiesto leap year

año eclesiástico *(catolicismo)* church year *(Nota: el cual empieza con el primer domingo de Adviento, cuatro domingos antes de la Navidad ■ which begins on the first Sunday of Advent, four Sundays before Christmas)*

año económico fiscal year

año lectivo *(en el hemisferio norte, de septiembre a junio; en el hemisferio sur, de marzo a diciembre)* ■ año escolar ■ año académico school year ■ academic year

año luz light year

el **año pasado** last year

el **año pasado por estas fechas** around this time last year

el **año próximo** ■ el próximo año ■ el año que viene next year

el **año que (se) avecina** ■ el año que viene ■ el año venidero the coming year

el **año que viene** **1.** el próximo año ■ el año próximo ■ el año venidero ■ el año que se avecina ■ el año que viene next year **2.** el año venidero ■ el año que (se) avecina the coming year

año sideral *(determinado por las estrellas)* ■ año sidéreo sidereal year

año sinódico *(determinado por la conjunción de dos cuerpos astronómicos)* synodic year

año tras año year after year

el **año venidero** ■ el año que viene ■ el año que (se) avecina the coming year

años de escuela ■ school years

años de formación académica one's college years ■ one's university years

años de las vacas flacas lean years

años formativos formative years

años ha que... *(poético)* ■ años hace que... ■ han pasado años que... it's been years since...

años intermedios: en los ~ in the intervening years ■ in the years in between

apabullar a alguien to squelch someone ➤ No quiero tomar una clase de ese maestro porque apabulla a los que hacen preguntas. I don't want to take a class from that teacher because he squelches questions. ■ I don't want to take a class from that teacher because he squelches whoever asks a question.

apaga y vámonos ■ corramos un tupido velo ■ pasa de eso let's just drop it ■ moving right along!

apagar el fuego ■ extinguir el fuego to put out the fire ■ to extinguish the fire

apagar la luz to turn off the light ■ to turn the light off ■ to turn out the light ■ to turn the light out ➤ Don't forget to turn out the lights when you leave. ■ Don't forget to turn off the lights when you leave. No te olvides de apagar las luces cuando salgas.

apagar la sed to quench one's thirst

apagar un cigarro to put out a cigarette

apagar un fuego ■ apagar un incendio ■ extinguir el fuego to put out a fire ■ to extinguish a fire

apagar un incendio ■ apagar un fuego ■ extinguir el incendio to put out a fire ■ to extinguish a fire

apagarse el motor (for) the engine to stall ■ (for) the engine to quit ■ (for) the motor to stall ■ for the motor to quit ➤ Trata que no se te apague el motor. Try not to let the engine quit.

apagones programados rolling blackouts

apalear a alguien hasta la muerte ■ asesinar a golpes a alguien to beat someone to death

apalancarse en un sillón ■ acomodarse en un sillón ■ desparramarse en un sillón to sink into an armchair ■ to settle into an armchair

estar **apañado** **1.** estar forrado to be loaded (with dough) **2.** *(irónico)* ■ estar arreglado to be done for ■ to have had it

apañar el costo to foot the bill ■ to pay the cost

apañar a un niño *(Sudamérica)* ■ mimar a un niño ■ consentir a un niño ■ sobreproteger a un niño to spoil a child ■ to be overprotective of a child

apañar las elecciones ■ dar el pucherazo to rig an election ■ to stuff ballot boxes

apañarse con ■ apañarselas con ■ arreglarse con ■ arreglárselas con **1.** *(referido a dinero)* to manage on ■ to get by on ■ to make do on ■ to survive on **2.** *(referido a cosas)* to manage with ■ to get by with ■ to make do with ➤ Con el dólar a la baja, tengo que apañármelas con ochocientos euros al mes. With the weak dollar, I have to manage on eight hundred euros a month. ■ With the weak dollar, I have to get by on eight hundred euros a month. ■ With the weak dollar, I have to make do on eight hundred euros a month. ➤ Me he quedado sin harina, pero me apañaré con fécula de maíz para espesar la salsa (de carne). I'm out of flour, but I'll manage with corn starch to thicken the gravy. ■ I'm out of flour, but I'll make do with corn starch to thicken the gravy. ■ I'm out of flour, but I'll get by with corn starch to thicken to gravy.

apañárselas con algo to manage with something ■ to make do with something ➤ No tenemos una ensaladera lo suficientemente grande, así que nos las tendremos que apañar con dos más pequeñas. ■ No tenemos una ensaladera lo suficientemente grande, así que tendremos que apañárnoslas con dos más pequeñas. We don't have a big enough salad bowl, so we'll have to manage with two smaller ones. ■ We don't have a big enough salad bowl, so we'll have to make do with two smaller ones.

apañarselas solo to manage on one's own ■ to manage alone ■ to get along by oneself

apañárselas uno (para hacer algo) arreglárselas uno (para hacer algo) to manage to do something ➤ No sé cómo, pero se las apañó para salir del accidente sin un rasguño. I don't know how, but he managed to come out of the accident without a scratch.

apañárselas uno sin... *(Esp.)* ■ arreglárselas uno sin... to manage without... ■ to get along without... ■ to get by without... ■ to make do without... ■ to do without... ➤ El pintor se ha enfermado así que tendremos que apañárnoslas sin él (para acabar la remodelación). The painter has gotten sick, so we'll have to manage (to finish the remodeling) without him. ■ The painter has gotten sick, so we'll have to get along without him (in order to finish the remodeling). ■ The painter has gotten sick, so we'll have to get by without him (to finish the modeling). ■ The painter has gotten sick, so we'll have to make do without him (to finish the modeling).

ser un **aparato bárbaro** *(Arg.)* to be a big phony ■ to be a put-on

aparato de captación recruiting arm

aparato de música (combination) CD and tape player

aparatosa caída por la escalera spectacular stairway fall ■ spectacular fall down a stairway

aparatosa cornada ■ cornada muy espectacular spectacular goring

aparatoso accidente ■ accidente muy espectacular spectacular accident

estar **aparcado en batería** *(Esp.)* ■ estar estacionado contra la curva to be parked at an angle to the curb ➤ El carro está aparacado en batería. The car is parked at an angle to the curb.

aparcar de oído *(cómico)* to park "by ear"

aparcar el asunto ■ dejar de lado el asunto to put the matter on the back burner ■ to shelve the matter

aparcar el coche *(Esp.)* ■ estacionar el carro ■ estacionar el auto to park the car

aparcar en batería *(Esp.)* ■ estacionar en diagonal **1.** *(aparcar en oblicuo)* to park at an angle to the curb ■ to park diagonally **2.** *(aparcar en forma perpendicular)* to park perpendicular to the curb ■ to pull straight in

aparcar en doble fila *(Esp.)* ■ estacionar en doble fila to double park

aparcar los planes *(coloquial)* to put the plans on the back burner

aparcar un proyecto de ley to shelve a bill

aparcar una idea *(coloquial)* to put an idea on the back burner

aparecer ahorcado to be found hanged ➤ El prisionero ha aparecido ahorcado en su celda. The prisoner was found hanged in his cell.

aparecer como bajado del cielo ■ llegar como bajado del cielo ■ venirle como agua de mayo ■ venirle como caído del cielo ■ ser agua de mayo to be a Godsend

aparecer en to show up on ➤ No apareció en el scanner. ■ No apareció en la resonancia. It didn't show up on the CAT scan.

aparecer en el lugar ■ aparecer en la escena to appear at the scene ➤ Muchos curiosos aparecieron en el lugar del accidente. Many onlookers appeared at the scene of the accident. ➤ El delincuente apareció después en la escena del crimen. The criminal later appeared at the scene of his crime.

aparecer en escena ■ entrar en escena ■ tener sus orígines to appear on the scene ➤ El órgano de cañones apareció en escena en la Roma del siglo quinto para atraer a la gente al circo. The pipe organ appeared on the scene in fifth-century Rome to attract people to the circus.

aparecer en un mal momento to show up at the wrong time ➤ Apareció en un mal momento. He showed up at the wrong time.

aparecer en una escena ■ salir en una escena to appear in a scene ➤ Falstaff sale en la primera escena del primer acto. ■ Falstaff aparece en la primera escena del primer acto. Falstaff appears in the first scene of the first act.

aparecer con vida to be found alive

aparecer muerto to be found dead

aparecérsele la Virgen 1. to have a vision of the Virgin Mary **2.** for one's ship to come in ■ to hit it big

la **aparición de los síntomas** ■ evidencia de síntomas onset of symptoms ■ appearance of symptoms

apariencia externa outward appearance

las **apariencias engañan** ■ no todo lo que brilla es oro ■ aunque la mona se vista de seda, mona se queda appearances are deceiving

estar **apartado de 1.** *(geográficamente)* to be far (away) from **2.** *(emocionalmente)* to be aloof from ■ to be distant from

apartado de correo ■ correo postal post office box ■ P.O. box

un **apartado (que ponía...)** *(periodísmo)* a subhead (saying...)

apartar a alguien a empujones to push someone aside ■ to push someone out of the way

apartar algo de la mente to get something out of one's mind ■ to put something out of one's mind

apartar la cara to turn away

apartar la idea de sí ■ rechazar la idea de sí ■ sacarse la idea de encima to get the idea out of one's head ■ to dismiss the idea (out of hand) ■ to reject the idea (out of hand) ■ ➤ Aparté la idea de mí. ■ Rechacé la idea de mí. I dismissed the idea out of hand. ■ I rejected the idea out of hand.

apartar la vista to look away ■ to avert one's gaze ■ to avert one's eyes

apartarse de alguien 1. to get away from someone ■ to move away from someone ■ **2.** deshacerse de alguien to ditch someone ■ to get rid of someone ■ to lose someone ■ to drop someone ➤ *(mujer a su amiga)* Apártarte de ese tipo. Tiene dos ex-mujeres, siete peques, y colección de tarántulas vivas en el sótano. Ditch that guy. He has two ex-wives, seven kids, and a tarantula collection in the basement.

apartarse de la tradición ■ romper con la tradición to depart from tradition ■ to break with tradition

apartarse del tema ■ desviarse del tema ■ irse por las ramas to get off the subject ■ to get sidetracked ➤ Me estoy apartando del tema. ■ Me estoy desviando del tema. I'm getting off the subject. ➤ No es por apartarme del tema, pero... ■ No es por desviarme del tema, pero... Not to get off the subject, but... ➤ No quiero apartarme mucho del tema. ■ No quiero desviarme mucho del tema. I don't want to get too far off the subject. ■ I don't want to get sidetracked

apartarse como un rayo ■ salirse como un rayo to be off like a shot ➤ Se apartó como un rayo. ■ Se salió como un rayo. He was off like a shot.

apártate que me tiznas ■ apártate que me contagias you're tainting me by association ■ I'm with stupid here

"apártate que me tiznas," dijo la sartén al cazo the pot's calling the kettle black

aparte, como estaba diciendo ■ aparte, como iba diciendo anyway, as I was saying

aparte, como te estaba diciendo ■ aparte, como te iba diciendo anyway, as I was telling you

aparte de besides ■ aside from ■ apart from ■ other than

aparte de eso apart from that ■ aside from that ■ besides that ■ other than that

aparte de que... ■ además de que... ■ fuera de que... **1.** besides which... **2.** apart from the fact that... ■ besides the fact that...

aparte quizá de *(literario)* ■ con la excepción posible de with the possible exception of

aparte, volviendo a lo que estaba diciendo anyway, getting back to what I was saying

aparte, volviendo a lo que te estaba diciendo anyway, getting back to what I was telling you

apear un río ■ vadear un río (a pie) ■ cruzar un río vadeando ■ franquear un río to ford a river ■ to ford a stream

apearse de to dismount from ■ to get down from ■ to get off ■ to alight from

apearse del autobús ■ bajar(se) del autobús to get off the bus

apearse del burro *(pintoresco)* ■ bajarse del burro to give up power ■ to relinquish power ■ to step aside ■ to get off one's high horse ■ to come down from one's high horse ➤ No quiere apearse del burro. He doesn't want to give up power. ■ He doesn't want to get off his high horse.

apearse del carro *(coloquial)* ▪ bajarse del carro ▪ retirarse to call it quits ▪ to bow out ▪ to abandon ship

apearse del tren ▪ bajar(se) del tren to get off the train

apechar con algo to put up with something ▪ to cope with something

apechugar con alguien *(coloquial)* ▪ aguantar a alguien to put up with someone ▪ to endure someone

apelar a las emociones to appeal to the emotions

apelar una decisión a un tribunal superior ▪ apelar una decisión a un tribunal de (una) instancia más alta to appeal a decision to a higher court ➤ Los abogados apelaron la decisión del caso a un tribunal superior. ▪ Los abogados apelaron la decisión del caso a un tribunal de (una) instancia más alta. The lawyers appealed the decision in the case to a higher court.

apelativo cariñoso endearment ▪ affectionate nickname

apellido de casada ▪ nombre de casada married name

apellido de soltera maiden name

estar **apelotonados en la entrada** to be crowded around the entrance

apelotonarse en un sitio to be crowded together in a place ▪ to be crammed together in a place

apenas cabe esperar que... it can hardly be expected that...

apenas éramos cuatrocientos soldados *(Bernal Díaz)* there were barely four hundred of us soldiers

apenas había salido cuando... ▪ ni bien había salido cuando... **1.** *(él)* no sooner had he left than... **2.** *(ella)* no sooner had she left than... ➤ Apenas había salido el médico que el paciente sufrió un desmayó. ▪ Ni bien el doctor había salido el paciente sufrió un desmayo. No sooner had the doctor left than the patient passed out. ➤ Apenas había salido para la clase cuando llamaron y la cancelaron. No sooner had she left for class than they called and cancelled it.

apenas hablar un idioma ▪ casi no hablar un idioma ▪ prácticamente no hablar un idioma to barely speak a language ▪ to hardly speak a language ➤ Apenas hablaba español cuando llegó a Buenos Aires. ▪ Casi no hablaba español cuando llegó a Buenos Aires. ▪ Prácticamente no hablaba español cuando llegó a Buenos Aires. She barely spoke Spanish when she arrived in Buenos Aires. ▪ She hardly spoke Spanish when she arrived in Buenos Aires.

apenas hubo... *(él)* no sooner had he... ▪ *(ella)* no sooner had she... ➤ Apenas él hubo llegado que... No sooner had he arrived than...

apenas le oigo ▪ casi no le oigo *(a usted)* I can hardly hear you ▪ I can barely hear you ▪ *(a él)* I can hardly hear him ▪ I can barely hear him ▪ *(a ella)* I can hardly hear her ▪ I can barely hear her

apenas lo justo para just enough to ▪ barely enough to

apenas lo justo para no just enough not to

apenas me encontré solo(-a)... ▪ ni bien me quedé solo... no sooner was I alone than... ➤ Apenas me encontré solo comencé a oír ruidos extraños provenientes del piso de al lado. No sooner was I alone than I began to hear strange noises coming from the apartment next door.

apenas nadie ▪ casi nadie hardly anyone ▪ almost no one

apenas no la compro *(con un antecedente femenino)* ▪ casi no la compro I hardly ever buy it

apenas no lo compro *(con un antecedente masculino)* ▪ casi no lo compro I hardly ever buy it

apenas poder levantarse de la cama ▪ levantarse a duras penas de la cama ▪ casi no poder levantarse de la cama ▪ prácticamente no poder levantarse de la cama to barely be able to get out of bed ▪ to hardly be able to get out of bed ➤ Apenas puede levantarse de la cama por la mañana. ▪ Se levanta a duras penas de la cama por la mañana. ▪ Casi no puede levantarse de la cama por la mañana. ▪ Prácticamente no puede levantarse de la cama por la mañana. He can barely get out of bed in the morning. ▪ He can hardly get out of bed in the morning.

apenas podía hablar *(yo)* I could hardly speak *(él)* he could hardly speak ▪ he could barely speak ▪ *(ella)* she could hardly speak ▪ she could barely speak

apenas podría creerse que... ▪ es casi increíble que... ▪ ni siquiera se le pasaría por la cabeza que... it's almost unbelievable that...

apenas puedo distinguirlo ▪ casi no puedo distinguirlo I can barely make it out ▪ I can hardly make it out

apenas quedar margen para not to have much leeway to ▪ not to give one much wiggle room to

apenas puedo esperar ▪ casi no puedo esperar I can hardly wait

apenas te oigo ▪ casi no te oigo ▪ te oigo a duras penas I can hardly hear you ▪ I can barely hear you

apenas tengo tiempo de... I hardly have time to... ➤ Apenas tengo tiempo de comer. I have hardly have time to eat (dinner).

apenas tocar ▪ casi no tocar ▪ prácticamente no tocar to barely touch ▪ to hardly touch ➤ Apenas tocó su cena. ▪ Casi no tocó su cena. ▪ Prácticamente no tocó su cena. He barely touched his supper. ▪ He hardly touched his supper.

apenas unas horas después de ▪ sólo unas horas después de only a few hours after ▪ just hours after

ser **apenas velado como** to be thinly disguised as ➤ Fue una crítica apenas velada como un cumplido. It was a criticism thinly disguised as a compliment.

apencar con algo *(coloquial)* ▪ apechar con algo ▪ apechugar con algo to put up with something

apencar con la factura ▪ cargar con la factura to foot the bill

apencar con las consecuencias to live with the consequences ▪ to suffer the consequences ▪ to bear the consequences

apencar con una responsabilidad to shoulder a responsibility ▪ to bear responsibility (for) ▪ to assume responsibility ▪ to take on responsibility

aperitivo: hora del ~ cocktail hour

aperitivos: servir ~ to serve drinks and hors d'oeuvres ▪ to serve refreshments ➤ A continuación de la charla, se ofrecerá un aperitivo. Following the talk, refreshments will be served.

apesadumbrarle la idea de que... to be saddened by the idea that...

estar **apestado de algo** to be infested with something ➤ El edificio está apestado de cucarachas. The building is infested with cockroaches.

apetecerle algo to fancy something ▪ to want someone ▪ to desire something ➤ I fancy that Corvette. Me apetece ese Corvette.

apetecerle (para) cenar ▪ querer (para) cenar ▪ desear (para) cenar to want for supper ➤ ¿Qué te apetece (para) cenar? ▪ ¿Qué quieres (para) cenar? ▪ ¿Qué deseas (para) cenar? What do you want for supper?

aplazar el debate to postpone the debate

aplazar una ejecución to delay an execution

aplicar frotando to rub in ▪ to massage in

aplicar la ley ▪ llevar a cabo la ley to enforce the law

aplicar la normativa en contra de fumar ▪ hacer cumplir la normativa en contra de fumar to enforce the no smoking rule

aplicar la pintura, laca, etc. to apply paint, lacquer, etc. ➤ La mejor manera de aplicar la laca es diluirla y aplicar varias capas finas. The best method is to thin the lacquer and apply several light coats. ▪ The best method is to thin the lacquer and apply several thin coats.

aplicar presión a algo to apply pressure to something ➤ La presión aplicada por las abrazaderas a las piezas encoladas las reforzará una vez secas. The pressure applied by the clamps to the glued pieces will make them stronger once (they are) dry.

aplicar sanciones to impose sanctions

aplicar un impuesto to levy a tax

aplicarle un correctivo ▪ darle una lección to take disciplinary action against someone

aplicarle una inyección ▪ ponerle una inyección to give someone a shot ▪ to give someone an injection

ser **apócope de** to be short for ➤ Prop es apócope de propeller. Prop is short for propeller.

apoderarse de to take control of ▪ to take possession of ▪ to seize

apoderarse del poder to seize power ▪ to take power

apología de support for ▪ supporting ➤ *(titular)* Detenido por apología del terrorismo Arrested for supporting terrorism

apoquinar lo suyo ▪ pagar lo suyo to pay one's own way ➤ Cada uno apoquina lo suyo. Each (person) pays his own way. ➤ ¡Apoquina! Pay up! ▪ Fork it over!

aportar el capital to put up the capital ▪ to provide the capital

aportar fondos to provide funds

aportar la pruebas es la responsabilidad del acusador the burden of proof is on the accuser

aportar uno su granito de arena ▪ poner uno su granito de arena to get in one's two cents' worth ▪ to put in one's two cents' worth

aportar *x* dólares para to contribute *x* dollars for ▪ to provide *x* dollars for ▪ *(informal)* to chip in *x* dollars for

aposta: hacer algo ~ ▪ hacer algo a propósito ▪ hacer algo adrede to do something on purpose ▪ to do something deliberately ▪ to do something intentionally

apostar a un caballo ▪ apostar por un caballo to bet on a horse ➤ ¿A qué caballo vas a apostar? ▪ ¿Por qué caballo vas a apostar? Which horse are you going to bet on?

apostar fuerte a ▪ apostar fuerte por to bet heavily on ▪ to bet high on

apostar fuerte por ▪ apostar fuerte a to bet heavily on ▪ to bet high on

apostar por un caballo ▪ apostar a un caballo to bet on a horse ➤ ¿Por qúe caballo vas a apostar? ▪ ¿A qué caballo vas a apostar? Which horse are you going to bet on?

apostaría la cabeza que... I'll bet you anything (that)... ▪ I bet you anything (that)... ▪ I'd bet you anything (that)...

apostarle a un caballo to bet on a horse

apoyado en el marco de la puerta leaning against the door frame

apoyar a alguien ▪ sacar la cara por alguien to back someone (up) ➤ Si el jefe te reta, yo te apoyaré. ▪ Si el jefe te reta, sacaré la cara por ti. If the boss challenges you, I'll back you up.

apoyar a alguien para un puesto to back someone for a post ▪ to back someone for a position

apoyar algo de boca para afuera to pay lip service to something

apoyar el testimonio de alguien ▪ corroborar el testimonio de alguien to back up someone's testimony ▪ to support someone's testimony ▪ to affirm someone's testimony ▪ to corroborate someone's testimony

apoyar la espalda contra algo to lean against something

apoyarse en los pies *(después de un periodo de recuperación)* to get up on one's feet ➤ Se apoyó en los pies. He got up on his feet.

apoyo a alguien support for someone

apoyo sentimental ▪ apoyo emocional emotional support ▪ moral support

ser **apreciado por alguien como** to be valued by someone as

apreciar a alguien ▪ estimar a alguien to hold someone in high regard ▪ to esteem someone ▪ to appreciate someone

aprehender a un sospechoso ▪ detener a un sospechoso ▪ poner a un sospecho bajo custodia justicial to apprehend a suspect ▪ to detain a suspect ▪ to take a suspect into custody ➤ Algunos potenciales sospechosos fueron aprehendidos para ser interrogados. ▪ Algunos potenciales sospechosos fueron detenidos para ser interrogados. ▪ Algunos potenciales sospechosos fueron puestos bajo custodia judicial para ser interrogados. Some potential suspects were apprehended for questioning. ▪ Some potential suspects were detained for questioning. ▪ Some potential suspects were taken into custody for questioning.

aprender de las experiencias to learn from experience

aprender por las malas to learn something the hard way

aprender sobre... to learn about...

aprender sobre la marcha to learn as one goes (along) ➤ Aprendo sobre la marcha. I learn as I go along. ▪ I learn as I go.

aprendiz de mucho, maestro de nada jack of all trades and master of none ▪ he who tries to become expert in all fields, masters none

aprestarse a to get ready to

apresurar el paso to quicken one's pace ▪ to quicken one's step

apretada semana busy week

apretadísima agenda very long agenda

apretados alrededor clustered around

apretar el botón (del inodoro) ▪ tirar la cadena (del inodoro) ▪ jalar la bomba (del inodoro) ▪ tirar la cisterna to flush the toilet

apretar el gatillo to pull the trigger

apretar el gaznate to tighten the noose

apretar el paso ▪ avivar el paso to walk faster ▪ to accelerate one's pace

apretar el puño ▪ cerrar el puño to clench one's fist ▪ to make a fist

apretar la cintura un agujero to tighten one's belt a notch

apretar las tuercas a alguien to put the screws to someone

apretar los puños to clench one's fists

apretar los talones to take to one's heels

apretar un tornillo to tighten a screw

apretarle la mano a alguien to squeeze someone's hand

apretarse el cinturón to tighten one's belt ▪ to reduce expenditures ▪ to cut costs ▪ to live on less

el **apretón de manos** handshake

apretón de manos: darle a alguien un ~ 1. *(para animar)* to give someone a sqeeze of the hand 2. *(para saludar)* dar la mano to shake someone's hand

apretujarse (un poco) to double up ▪ to squeeze in (together) ▪ to squeeze (in) together ▪ *(informal)* to squinch up ➤ Si nos apretujamos (un poco), cabremos todos. If we double up, we can all fit. ▪ If we squeeze in together, we can all fit. ▪ If we squinch up, we can all fit.

la **aprobación del jefe** ▪ visto bueno del jefe approval of the boss ▪ good graces of the boss ➤ Necesitas la aprobación del jefe. ▪ Necesitas el visto bueno del jefe. You need the good graces of the boss.

aprobación tácita tacit approval

ser **aprobado por unanimidad** to pass unanimously ▪ to be passed unanimously

aprobar algo al cien por cien ▪ aprobar al cien por cien algo ▪ estar a favor de algo al cien por cien ▪ estar totalmente a favor de algo to approve of something a hundred percent ▪ to approve of something completely ▪ to be a hundred percent in favor of something ▪ to be all for something ➤ Lo apruebo al cien por cien. I approve of it a hundred percent. ▪ I completely approve of it. ▪ I'm all for it.

aprobar con la cabeza to nod agreement ▪ to nod in agreement ▪ to nod one's agreement

aprobar la prueba ▪ superar la prueba ▪ aprobar el examen to pass the test ▪ to meet the challenge ▪ to make the grade

aprobar por los pelos ▪ aprobar justo en el límite to be a borderline student ➤ Yo aprobaba por los pelos. I used to be a borderline student.

aprobar por unanimidad ▪ ser aprobado por unanimidad ▪ aprobarse por unanimidad ▪ aprobar por unanimidad to pass unanimously ▪ to be passed unanimously ➤ El Senado aprobó el proyecto de ley por unanimidad. El proyecto de ley fue aprobado por unanimidad. ▪ El proyecto de ley se aprobó por unanimidad. ▪ Aprobaron el proyecto de ley por unanimidad. The Senate passed the bill unanimously. ▪ The bill (was) passed by the Senate unanimously.

aprobar sin reservas to approve of wholeheartedly ▪ to approve wholeheartedly of

aprobar un examen to pass a test

aprobar una ley ▪ promulgar una ley to pass a law ▪ to enact a law

aprovecha que... 1. take advantage of... ▪ make the most of... 2. take advantage of the fact that... ▪ as long as... ➤ Aprovecha que eres joven. Take advantage of your youth. ▪ Make the most of your youth. ➤ Aprovecha que no está tu papá. Take advantage of the fact that your Dad isn't here. ➤ Aprovecha que vas al banco y pásate por la farmacia. Take advantage of the fact that you're going to the bank and go by the drug store. ▪ As long as you're going to the bank, go by the drug store. ▪ Since you're going to the bank, go by the drug store. ➤ Corre, aprovecha que no te han visto. Run, take advantage of the fact that no one has seen you. ➤ No seas tonto, aprovéchate y coge un bollo. Don't be a dummy, go for it and grab a bun.

aprovechar la coyuntura to take advantage of the opportunity ▪ to seize the moment ▪ to take advantage of the opening

aprovechar mucho el tiempo to get a lot done ➤ Aprovechamos mucho el tiempo. We got a lot done. ➤ El viernes, sábado y domingo son los días en los que aprovecho mucho el tiempo. Friday, Saturday and Sunday are the days (when) I get the most done. ▪ Friday, Saturday and Sundays are the days on which I get the most done.

aprovecharse de to take advantage of an opportunity

aprovecharse injustamente de una situación to take unfair advantage of a situation

aproximarse a algo ▪ acercarse a algo to approach something ▪ to come close to something ➤ Hay un excelente concierto piano norteamericano, la *Rapsodia en azul* de Gershwin, y un par de otros que se le acercan. ▪ Hay un excelente concierto piano norteamericano, la *Rapsodia en azul* de Gershwin, y un par que se le aproximan. There is one excellent American piano concerto, Gershwin's *Rhapsody in Blue*, and a couple others that come close (to it). ▪ There is one excellent American piano concerto, Gershwin's *Rhapsody in Blue*, and a couple others that approach it.

aproximarse a una fecha tope ▪ acercarse a una fecha tope to approach a deadline ➤ Nos aproximamos rápidamente a la fecha límite del quince de abril. ▪ Nos acercamos rápidamente a la fecha límite del quince de abril. We are rapidly approaching the April 15 deadline. ▪ The April 15 deadline is rapidly approaching.

aproximarse más ▪ acercarse más to come closer ➤ "Aproxímate más, pequeña," le dijo el lobo a Caperucita Roja. ▪ "Acércate más, pequeña," le dijo el lobo a Caperucita Roja. "Come closer, my dear," said the wolf to Little Red Riding Hood.

aptitud(es) para los idiomas: tener ~ ▪ tener facilidad de idiomas ▪ tener habilidad para los idiomas to have an aptitude for languages ▪ to have an ear for languages

ser **apto para** to be suitable for ➤ Playas no aptas para el baño. Beaches not suitable for bathing. ▪ Beaches unsuitable for bathing. ➤ La película es apta para menores. The movie is suitable for minors. ➤ Esta cacerola es apta para carne, pescado y verduras. This pan is suitable for meat, fish and vegetables.

apuesto a que... I bet... ▪ I'll bet... ➤ Apuesto a que no te lo puedas comer todo. I bet you can't eat the whole thing.

¡apuesto a que no! ▪ ¡que no eres capaz! bet you can't!

¡apuesto a que sí! I bet! ▪ I'll bet! ▪ I bet you can!

apuesto por ti I'm betting on you

apuesto que te alegras I bet you're glad

apuntar a alguien to put someone down (in writing) ➤ Apúntenos para cuatro personas. Put us down for four people.

apuntar algo to write down something ▪ to write something down ➤ ¿Apuntaste la matrícula? Did you write down the license number? ▪ Did you write the license number down? ➤ ¿La apuntaste? Did you write it down?

apuntar con un arma a un objetivo ▪ apuntar con un arma a un blanco to aim a weapon at a target

apuntar en el papel to put down on paper ▪ to put pen to paper

apuntar que... to point out that...

apuntarse a un curso ▪ apuntarse en un curso to sign up for a course

apuntarse a una clase ▪ apuntarse en una clase to sign up for a class

apuntarse a las clases ▪ inscribirse a las clases to register for class(es) ➤ ¿Te has apuntado a las clases ya? Have you registered for class yet? ▪ Have you registered for classes yet? ▪ Have you registered yet? ▪ Have you signed up for your classes yet?

apuntárselo a alguien ▪ hacérselo notar a alguien to point it out to someone

apuntillar a alguien to finish off someone ▪ to finish someone off ➤ *The Times* de Londres apuntilló al líder conservador al apoyar el voto laborista por primera vez en su historia. *The London Times* finished off the conservative leader, supporting the labor vote for the first time in its history.

apuntillar al toro to finish off the bull (in a bullfight) ▪ to finish the bull off

estar **apurado de dinero** to be hard up for money ▪ to be hard up financially

estar **apurado de tiempo** ▪ estar apresurado de tiempo ▪ estar fatal de tiempo ▪ andar corto de tiempo to be pressed for time

¡apúrate! ▪ ¡ándale! ▪ ¡venga! hurry! ▪ hurry up!

estar **aquejado de** ▪ aquejarse de to be afflicted with ▪ to be suffering from ➤ Estaba aquejada de cáncer. ▪ Se aquejaba de cáncer. She was suffering from cancer.

aquella noche that night

estar **aquí arriba** to be up here ➤ Estoy aquí arriba. I'm up here.

estar **aquí desde hace...** ▪ llevar aquí... to have been here for... ➤ Estoy aquí desde hace cuatro meses. ▪ Llevo cuatro meses aquí. I've been here for four months.

aquí hay gato encerrado ▪ aquí hay algo oculto I smell a rat ➤ Aquí hay gato encerrado.-Pues, ya se escapará el gato. I smell a rat.-Well, it's going to come out in the open.

aquí lo tiene (usted) here you are ▪ here you go ▪ here!

aquí lo tienes here you are ▪ here you go ▪ here!

estar **aquí mismo** ▪ estar justo aquí to be right here ➤ En el diagrama estamos aquí mismo. ▪ En el diagrama, estamos aquí mismo. In the diagram we're right here.

aquí no hay quien viva nobody can stand to live here ▪ nobody can tolerate this place

aquí no hay tu tía give it up ▪ not a chance ▪ no way

aquí nos vamos a quedar hoy ▪ es todo esto por hoy that's all for today ▪ that's it for today

estar **aquí para quedarse** ▪ llegar para quedarse to be here to stay ➤ Por mediocres que sean, las comedias de la televisión están aquí para quedarse. Mediocre though they are, TV sitcoms are here to stay.

¡aquí viene Paco con las rebajas! *(Esp.)* ▪ ¡aquí viene armando roscas! here comes trouble!

aquí y allá here and there

aquí yacen los restos de here lies

arañar el suelo to scratch the floor

arar en el mar **1.** machacar en hierro frío to beat a dead horse **2.** gastar esfuerzo sin avanzar to spin one's wheels

¡árbol va! ▪ ¡tronco va! timber!

los **árboles no le dejan ver el bosque** *(él)* he can't see the forest for the trees ▪ *(ella)* she can't see the forest for the trees ▪ *(usted)* you can't see the forest for the trees

los **árboles no te dejan ver el bosque** you can't see the forest for the trees

arca de la alianza Ark of the Covenant

arco de tejo *(de Robin Hood)* yew bow

arco y flechas bow and arrows

arena absorbente (para gatos) kitty litter

arena menuda fine sand

arena movediza quicksand

el **argot juvenil** teenage slang

argumento contra argument against

ser el **argumento de un libro** ▪ ser el tema de un libro to be the subject of a book

argumento está lleno de agujeros argument is full of holes

argumento erróneo ▪ argumento defectuoso flawed argument ▪ defective argument

argumento defectuoso ▪ argumento erróneo flawed argument ▪ defective argument

argumento tiene agujeros argument has holes in it

arma de doble filo double-edged sword

arma empleada en el asesinato murder weapon ▪ weapon used in the murder

Armada Española: derrota de la ~ *(1588)* defeat of the Spanish Armada

armado hasta los dientes armed to the teeth

armadura de clave *(música)* key signature ➤ La clave de fa mayor tiene la misma armadura que la tonalidad de re menor: hay que bemolar todo B. The key of F major has the same signature as the key of D minor: all B's are played flat.

armar barullo ▪ hacer barullo to raise a ruckus ▪ to make a racket

armar caballero a alguien to knight someone ▪ to dub someone a knight

armar ruido to make noise

armar un berrinche *(dícese de los niños)* to make a scene ▪ to have a tantrum

armar un escándolo **1.** to make a lot of noise **2.** hacer un desplante to make a scene ▪ to have a tantrum

armar un lío **1.** armar barullo to raise a ruckus **2.** hacer un desbarajuste to make a mess

armar una maqueta ■ ensamblar una maqueta ■ montar una maqueta ■ hacer una maqueta to assemble a kit ■ to put together a kit ■ to put a kit together

armar una carpa ■ armar una tienda (de campaña) ■ montar una tienda (de campaña) to pitch a tent ■ to put up a tent ■ to erect a tent

armar una tienda (de campaña) ■ montar una tienda (de campaña) to pitch a tent ■ to put up a tent ■ to erect a tent

armarios de cocina kitchen cabinets

armarse de paciencia to resolve to be patient ■ to be patient

armarse de valor to get up one's courage ■ *(coloquial)* to screw up one's courage

armarse de valor para... to get up the nerve to... ■ to get up the courage to... ■ to gather the courage to... ■ to pluck up the courage to...

armarse hasta los dientes to arm oneself to the teeth

armarse una gran barahunda ■ armarse un gran cacao (for) all hell to break loose ➤ Se armó una gran barahunda. All hell broke loose.

¡armas al hombro! shoulder arms!

armas cortas side arms

armas de destrucción masiva weapons of mass destruction ➤ *(noticia)* Irak niega poseer armas de destrucción masiva. Iraq denies it possesses weapons of mass destruction.

armazón de las costillas rib cage

aros de cebolla onion rings

arquear las cejas to raise one's eyebrows

arraigar a alguien to place a restraining order on someone

arraigarse en to take root in

arrancar a cantar to break into a song ■ to burst into song

arrancar a correr to break into a run ■ to take off running

arrancar algo de cuajo ■ arrancar algo de raíz ■ extirpar algo to pull up something by the roots ■ to pull something up by the roots

arrancar algo de raíz ■ arrancar algo de cuajo ■ extirpar algo to pull up something by the roots ■ to pull something up by the roots

arrancar aplausos to draw applause ■ to bring applause

arrancar el alma de alguien ■ herir los sentimientos de alguien to hurt someone's feelings ➤ Creo que le has arrancado el alma. *(de él)* I think you hurt his feelings. ■ *(de ella)* I think you hurt her feelings.

arrancar el carro con cocodrilos ■ arrancar el carro con pinzas to start the car with jumper cables ■ to jump start the car using jumper cables

arrancar el carro dejándolo deslizarse to jump-start the car by coasting it (and popping the clutch) ■ to jump-start a car by letting it coast (and popping the clutch) ➤ Para arrancar el carro dejándolo deslizarse, gira la llave, mete segunda, déjalo deslizarse unos metros por la pendiente y suelta el embrague de golpe. To jump-start the car, turn on the ignition, put it in second, coast it a few yards, and pop the clutch. ■ To jump-start the car, turn on the ignition, put it in second, let it coast a few yards, and pop the clutch.

arrancar el carro empujándolo to jump-start the car by pushing it (and popping the clutch) ➤ Para arrancar el carro empujándolo, gira la llave, mete segunda, empujalo unos metros y suelta el embrague de golpe. To jump-start the car by pushing it, turn on the ignition, put it in second, push it a few yards, and pop the clutch.

arrancar el motor to start the engine ■ to start the motor

arrancar la flema ■ sacar la flema tosiendo ■ echar la flema ■ arrojar la flema ■ expulsar la flema ■ despedir la flema tosiendo to loosen the phlegm ■ to cough up phlegm ➤ El médico le prescribió un expectorante para arrancar la flema. The doctor prescribed him an expectorant to loosen the phlegm.

arrancar las malas hierbas to pull weeds

arrancar la negociación ■ empezar la negociación ■ abrir la negociación to begin negotiations

arrancar páginas de to tear pages out of ■ to rip pages out of ➤ Algunas páginas habían sido arrancadas del libro. Some of the pages had been torn out of the book. ■ Some of the pages had been ripped out of the book.

arrancar risa to bring laughter ■ to provoke laughter ■ to draw laughter ■ to cause laughter

arrancar un acuerdo to hammer out an agreement ➤ *(titular)* Clinton arranca un frágil acuerdo de paz en Oriente Medio. Clinton hammers out a fragile Middle East peace agreement.

arrancar un trozo de un mordisco ■ arrancar un trozo con los dientes to bite off a piece ➤ Arrancó un trozo de la chocolatina de un mordisco. ■ Arrancó un trozo de la chocolatina con los dientes. He bit off a piece of the candy bar. ■ He bit a piece off (of) the candy bar. ➤ Lo arrancó de un mordisco. ■ Lo arrancó con los dientes. He bit it off. ➤ Arrancó de cuajo el retoño. He pulled up the sprout by the roots.

arrancarle la cabeza a alguien to cut someone's head off

el **arranque de celos** fit of jealousy

el **arranque de emoción** fit of emotion

el **arranque de furia** ■ (el) ataque de rabia ■ ataque de ira fit of rage

el **arranque de genialidad** stroke of genius

arrasar con algo to make a clean sweep of something ➤ La película arrasó con todos los Oscars, ganando en todas las categorías. The film made a clean sweep of the Oscars, winning in all categories. ➤ Los candidatos moderados arrasaron con las elecciones, ganando todos los diez distritos. The moderate candidates made a clean sweep of the elections, winning in all ten districts.

arrasar en las urnas to win by a landslide

arrasársele los ojos de lágrimas ■ arrasársele los ojos en lágrimas (for) one's eyes to fill with tears ➤ Al niño se le arrasaron los ojos de lágrimas. ■ Al niño se le arrasaron los ojos en lágrimas. The boy's eyes filled with tears.

arrastrar a alguien (cogido) por los pelos ■ arrastrar a alguien (cogido) de los pelos ■ llevar a alguien a rastras to drag someone by the heels ➤ Prácticamente tuvimos que arrastrar a mi tía por los pelos para hacer que vaya al médico. ■ Prácticamente tuvimos que arrastrar a mi tía de los pelos para hacer que vaya al médico. ■ Practicamente tuvimos que llevar a mi tía a rastras para hacer que vaya al médico. We practically had to drag my aunt by the heels to get her to go to the doctor.

arrastrar algo por el suelo to drag something across the floor ➤ ¿Me ayudarías a mover esta mesa? No quiero arrastrarla por el suelo. Would you help me move this table? I don't want to drag it across the floor.

arrastrar el ala a alguien ■ menearle el ala a alguien ■ tirar el tejo a alguien to make a pass at someone ■ to come on to someone

arrastrar el suelo *(colcha o edredón)* to touch the floor

arrastrar los pies to drag one's feet ■ to shuffle one's feet ➤ Mi hijo adolescente va arrastrando los pies. My teenage son drags his feet when he walks. ■ My teenage son shuffles his feet when he walks.

arrastrar y soltar *(informática)* to drag and drop

arrastrarse de cansancio to drag a little (from weariness) ➤ Se arrastra de cansancio. She's dragging a little.

¡arre, arre! giddyup! ■ *(a los niños)* hurry up! ■ let's get going! ■ let's get a move on!

arre que arre: darle ~ to go great guns ➤ Le dan arre que arre para terminar la estación de metro a primeros de marzo. They're going great guns to get the subway station finished by the first of March.

estar **arre que arre con** ■ seguir arre que arre con to be a fanatic ■ to be a freak ➤ Ese chico está arre que arre con el yo-yo. That kid's a yo-yo freak. ■ That kid's a yo-yo fanatic.

estar **arre que arre para** to be going bonkers to ■ to be bonkers to ➤ Josito está arre que arre para ir al circo. Joey is going bonkers to go to the circus.

arre que arre: seguir ~ ■ estar arre que arre **1.** to be a fanatic ■ to be a freak **2.** to continue doggedly ■ to be bound and determined to keep... ➤ Ese chico sigue arre que arre con el yo-yo. That kid's a yo-yo freak. ■ That kid's a yo-yo fanatic. ➤ Él sigue arre que arre con el crucigrama. He doesn't put down the crossword puzzle until it's completely worked. ➤ Josito sigue arre que arre para ir al circo. Joey is going bonkers to go to the circus.

arrebatárselo a alguien to snatch it from from someone ■ to grab it (away) from someone ■ to wrest it from someone ➤ Se lo arrebató a ella. He snatched it from her. ■ He grabbed it from her.

arrebato de cólera fit of anger ▪ outburst (of anger)
arrebato de entusiasmo burst of enthusiasm
arrebato de furia purple fit ▪ blind rage
arrebato de pasión fit of passion
arreglar cuentas to settle accounts ▪ to settle up
arreglar el jardín to work in the yard
arreglar la cama ▪ hacer la cama to make the bed
arreglar un mal entendido to clear up a misunderstanding
arreglar una cita ▪ hacer una cita to set up an appointment ▪ to arrange an appointment
arreglar una ensalada ▪ aliñar una ensalada ▪ aderezar una ensalada **1.** to put oil and vinegar on a salad ▪ **2.** to put dressing on a salad ▪ to dress a salad ➤ ¿Está arreglada la ensalada? ▪ ¿Está aliñada la ensalada? Does the salad already have dressing on it?
arreglarse para compaginar dos actividades to manage to do two things at once ▪ to manage to combine two activities
arreglarse para hacer algo to manage to do something ➤ La familia se las arreglaba para vivir con muy pocos recursos. The family managed to live on very little.
arreglárselas to shift for oneself
arreglárselas con algo ▪ arreglarse con algo ▪ apañarse con algo ▪ apañárselas con algo **1.** *(cosa)* to manage with something ▪ to get by with something ▪ to get along with something ▪ to make do with something **2.** *(dinero)* to manage on an amount of money ▪ to get by on an amount of money ▪ to get along on an amount of money ▪ to make do with an amount of money ➤ No tenemos una ensaladera grande así que tendremos que arreglárnoslas con algo más pequeño. We don't have a big salad bowl, so we'll have to manage with something smaller. ▪ We don't have a big salad bowl, so we'll have to get by with something smaller. ▪ We don't have a big salad bowl, so we'll have to get along with something smaller. ▪ We don't have a big salad bowl, so we'll have to make do with something smaller. ➤ La caída del dólar respecto al euro ha hecho que este mes tenga que arreglármelas con setecientos euros. The fall of the dollar against the euro has forced me to manage on seven hundred euros a month. ▪ The fall of the dollar against the euro has forced me to get by on seven hundred euros a month. ▪ The fall of the dollar against the euro has forced me to get along on seven hundred euros a month. ▪ The fall of the dollar against the euro has forced me to make do with seven hundred euros a month.
estar **arrejuntados** ▪ estar juntados to live together ▪ to cohabit ▪ *(argot)* to shack up (together)
arremeterse contra alguien **1.** *(físicamente)* to charge at someone ▪ to hit at someone ▪ to strike (out) at someone **2.** *(verbalmente)* to lash out at someone
arremolinar alrededor to crowd around
estar **arrepentido** to be sorry ▪ to regret it ▪ to be repentant ➤ ¡Estarás arrepentido! You'll be sorry! ▪ You'll regret it!
arrepentirse de haber hecho algo ▪ pesarle a uno haber hecho algo to regret doing something ▪ to regret have done something ▪ to be sorry one did something ➤ Me arrepiento de haberlo hecho. ▪ Me pesa haberlo hecho. I regret doing it. ▪ I regret having done it. ▪ I'm sorry I did it.
arresto domiciliario: estar en (situación de) ~ to be under house arrest
arresto domiciliario: ser puesto en ~ ▪ quedar en (situación de) arresto domiciliario to be placed under house arrest ▪ to be put under house arrest ➤ Galileo fue puesto en arresto domiciliario. Galileo was placed under house arrest. ▪ Galileo was put under house arrest. ➤ *(noticia)* El ex-presidente de Yugoslavia, Slobodan Milosevic, quedó a la 1.30 hoy en situación de arresto domiciliario. Former Yugoslav president Slobodan Milosevic was placed under house arrest at 1:30 a.m. today.
arriar la bandera to lower the flag ➤ Arriar la bandera hasta media asta. To lower the flag to half mast. ▪ To lower the flag to half staff.
estar **arriba de** ▪ estar sobre to be on ➤ Los papeles que buscas están arriba de mi escritorio. ▪ Los papeles que buscas están sobre mi escritorio. The papers you are looking for are on my desk.
¡arriba el telón! curtain up!
arriesgarse con algo to take a chance on something
arrimar el hombro to put one's shoulder to the wheel
arrimar una silla ▪ cogerse una silla to pull up a chair ➤ ¡Arrima una silla! ▪ ¡Cógete una silla! Pull up a chair! ▪ Grab a chair!
arrimarse *(normalmente acompañado con un gesto de mano)* to come closer ▪ to come over here ▪ to come this way ▪ to move in closer ▪ to get closer ➤ *(tú)* ¡Arrímate! ▪ *(usted)* ¡Arrímese! ▪ *(vosotros)* ¡Arrimaos! ▪ *(ustedes)* ¡Arrímense! Come closer! ▪ Come this way! ▪ Come over here! ▪ Move in closer! ▪ Get closer!
arrimarse a alguien **1.** caerle simpático a alguien to ingratiate oneself with someone ▪ to win someone over **2.** acurrucarse con alguien to snuggle up to someone **3.** acercarse a alguien to go up to someone ▪ to lean on someone (for support) ▪ to scrounge off someone
arrimarse al sol que más calienta ▪ ser oportunista to be an opportunist ▪ to change with the political winds
arrimársele a alguien to edge closer to someone
arrodillarse ante el altar ▪ arrodillarse frente al altar ▪ arrodillarse delante del altar ▪ ponerse de rodillas ante el altar ▪ ponerse de rodillas frente al altar ▪ ponerse de rodillas delante del altar to kneel before the altar
arrodillarse ante el obispo ▪ ponerse de rodillas ante el obispo to kneel before the bishop
arrojar a alguien a los lobos to throw someone to the wolves
arrojar a los moros de España to drive the Moors out of Spain ▪ to drive the Moors from Spain
arrojar de sí a alguien ▪ librarse de alguien ▪ quitarse a alguien de encima to get rid of someone
arrojar de sí algo ▪ librarse de algo ▪ quitarse algo de encima to get rid of something
arrojar algo desde... to throw something from... ➤ *(noticia)* La niña fue arrojada desde una cuarta planta. The child was thrown from the fourth floor.
arrojar combustible ▪ evacuar combustible to dump fuel ▪ to jettison fuel ➤ El avión arrojaba queroseno antes del siniestro. The airplane was dumping kerosene before the crash.
arrojar el guante to throw down the gauntlet ▪ to challenge someone to fight
arrojar la esponja ▪ arrojar la toalla ▪ tirar la toalla to throw in the towel
arrojar la pelota ▪ lanzar la pelota ▪ tirar la pelota to pitch the ball
arrojar la primera piedra tirar la primera piedra to cast the first stone
arrojar la toalla ▪ tirar la toalla ▪ arrojar la esponja to throw in the towel
arrojar luz sobre un tema to throw light on a subject
arrojar piedras contra su (propio) tejado ▪ tirar piedras contra su (propio) tejado ▪ morder la mano que te da de comer to bite the hand that feeds you
arrojar un balance de to leave a total of ➤ El choque ha arrojado un balance de ocho personas heridas. The collision left a total of eight people injured.
arrojar un chorro de propaganda ▪ arrojar chorros de propaganda ▪ arrojar nubes de propaganda to spout off propaganda
arrojar un resultado to show a result
arrojar un saldo de to show a balance of ➤ La cuenta arroja un saldo actual de ochocientos dólares. The account shows a current balance of eight hundred dollars.
arrojar una bomba ▪ lanzar una bomba to drop a bomb
arrojarse a nadar to dive in
ser **arrollado por algo** ▪ ser destruido por algo ▪ ser desolado por algo to be devastated by something
estar **arrollado sobre sí para atacar** ▪ estar enroscado para atacar to be coiled to strike
el **arroz con pollo** rice with chicken
el **arroz integral** brown rice
el **arroz rápido** minute rice
estar **arrugado como una ciruela pasa** ▪ estar arrugado como una pasa de uva to be old and wrinkled
arrugar el gesto ▪ torcer el gesto to make an angry face ▪ to make a disapproving face
arrugar el hocico ▪ arrugar el morro to make an angry face ▪ to wrinkle one's snout

arte nuevo art nouveau
el **arte por (amor al) arte** ▪ l'art pour l'art art for art's sake
artefactos de iluminación light fixtures ▪ lighting fixtures
las **artes marciales** martial arts
artes plásticas plastic arts
las **artes y oficios** arts and crafts
artículo de colección collector's item
artículo de fe article of faith
artículo de lujo luxury item
artículo determinado ▪ artículo definido definite article
artículo indeterminado ▪ artículo indefinido indefinite article
artículos deportivos sporting goods
artículos en oferta items on sale ▪ sale items
el **artífice de la política** the architect of the policy
el, la **artista de la cocina** gourmet cook
los **artistas del mundo nunca son (unos) puritanos, y rara vez resultan siquiera medianamente respetables** *(H.L. Mencken)* the artists of the world are never puritans, and seldom even ordinarily respectable
los, las **artistas noveles** new artists
asaltarle una idea to be struck by an idea
asarse de calor to burn up ▪ to roast
asarse vivo ▪ estar asándose to be burning up ➤ Me aso vivo. I'm burning up.
asa aislada insulated handle ➤ Quiero una sarten con una asa aislada. I want a frying pan with an insulated handle. ➤ Quiero un baño de María con asas aisladas. I want a double boiler with insulated handles.
ascender a (una cantidad) ▪ sumarse en una cantidad to amount to a quantity ▪ to add up to a quantity ➤ Los intereses de cincuenta dólares a la semana ascienden en cuarenta años a muchísimo dinero. ▪ Los intereses de cincuenta dólares a la semana se suman en cuarenta años a muchísimo dinero. Fifty dollars a week compounded over forty years amounts to a great deal of money. ▪ Interest on fifty dollars a week compounded over forty years amounts to a great deal of money.
ascensión recta *(astronomía)* right ascension
ascenso medio ▪ aumento medio average increase
el **ascensor (se) para** the elevator stops ➤ Este ascensor no para hasta el piso veinte. This elevator doesn't stop until it reaches the twentieth (20th) floor. *(Nota: Fíjese que en los países hispánicos, a la planta baja se le considera cero, así que el piso diecinueve sería el piso veinte en los Estados Unidos.)* ➤ El ascensor no se para en ese piso. The elevator doesn't stop on that floor. ▪ There is no elevator stop on that floor.
asediar a preguntas a alguien to barrage someone with questions
asegurarle a alguien que está perfectamente sano ▪ asegurarle a alguien que está perfectamente saludable to give someone a clean bill of health ➤ El médico le aseguró (a ella) que estaba perfectamente sana. The doctor gave her a clean bill of health.
asegurarse de hacer algo ▪ cerciorarse de hacer algo to be sure to do something ▪ to be sure and do something ➤ Asegúrate de devolverlo. ▪ Asegúrate de que lo devuelvas. Be sure to take it back. ▪ Be sure and take it back. ▪ Be sure to return it. ▪ Be sure and return it. ➤ Asegúrate de devolvérmelo. Be sure and return it to me. ▪ Be sure and bring it back. ➤ Asegúrate de llamarme. ▪ Asegúrate de que me llamas. Be sure to call me. ▪ Be sure and call me. ➤ Asegúrate de decirle que su regalo fue un gran éxito. Be sure and tell him what a great hit his present was. ▪ Be sure to tell him what a great hit his present was. ▪ Be sure and tell him his present was a great hit ▪ Be sure to tell him his present was a great hit.
asegurarse de que uno haga algo ▪ cerciorarse de que uno haga algo to be sure do something ▪ to be sure and do something ➤ Asegúrate de que me llames. ▪ Asegúrate de llamarme. Be sure and call me. ▪ Be sure to call me. ➤ Asegúrate de que lo devuelvas. ▪ Asegúrate de devolverlo. Be sure and take it back. ▪ Be sure to take it back. ▪ Be sure and return it. ▪ Be sure to return it.
asentar la cabeza ▪ madurar to get one's head on straight ▪ to get one's head together
asentarse en los pulmones ▪ situarse en los pulmones ▪ colocarse en los pulmones to settle in one's lungs ➤ La infección se ha asentado en los pulmones. ▪ La infección se ha situado en los pulmones. ▪ La infección se ha colocado en los pulmones. The infection has settled in his lungs.
asentarse en un lugar ▪ instalarse en un lugar to get settled in a place ➤ Todavía estoy asentándome aquí en Valladolid. I'm still getting settled here in Valladolid.
asentimiento común common consent
asentir con la cabeza to nod one's agreement ▪ to nod (one's head) in agreement
aseos personales personal items ▪ toiletries ▪ personal belongings
asequible: manual manual that is easy to understand ▪ clear manual ➤ Este manual de informática es asequible. This computer manual is easy to understand.
asequible: persona ~ approachable person ▪ person who is easy to get to know ➤ Es muy asequible. He is very approachable. ▪ He is very easy to get to know.
asesinar a golpes a alguien ▪ apalear hasta la muerte a alguien ▪ matar a golpes a alguien to beat someone to death
asesinar a tiros a alguien ▪ tirotear hasta la muerte a alguien ▪ matar a tiros a alguien to shoot someone to death
asesinato en serie serial killing ▪ serial murder
asesino a sueldo hit man ▪ hired killer
asesino confeso confessed murderer ▪ confessed killer
asesino en serie serial killer ▪ serial murderer
asesino frío cold-blooded killer
asesorando con alguien: estarse ~ ▪ estar consultando con alguien to be in consultation with someone ▪ to be consulting someone ➤ El gobierno español se está asesorando con otros gobiernos europeos. ▪ El gobierno español está consultando con otros gobiernos europeos. The Spanish government is in consultation with other European governments. ▪ The Spanish government is consulting with other European governments.
asesorarse con alguien to consult with someone
así así so so ▪ okay
así bien well ➤ Así bien, senador Well, senator
así como as well as ▪ like ▪ along with ➤ Geográficamente, Virginia es un estado del centro de la costa atlántica, así como Maryland y Delaware. Geographically, Virginia is a Central Atlantic state, along with Maryland and Delaware.
así como así ▪ de cualquiera manera ▪ así que así any which way ▪ every which way
así como lo oyes just like you heard it ▪ it's true
así como tú..., yo just as you..., I ▪ in the same way that you..., I
así cualquiera just anybody
así de este tamaño about this size
así de fácil that's all there is to it ▪ it's that easy ▪ it's as easy as that
así de golpe just like that
así de grande this big
así de grande que... so big that...
así de pequeño this little ▪ this small
así de pequeño que... so small that... ▪ so little that...
así debería ser that's how it ought to be▪ that's how it should be
así él como ella he as well as she ▪ both he and she
así era hasta en mi casa at least that's how it was at my house
así es that's right ▪ that's the way it is ▪ that's how it is
así es como that is how ▪ that's how ➤ Así es como yo la traducería. That's how I would translate it. *(Nota: "La" se refiere a "la frase".)*
así es la vida that's life ▪ c'est la vie ▪ *(jerga)* that's the way the cookie crumbles
así es que so ▪ so that ▪ and so ▪ so this
así es que es aquí donde trabajas so this is where you work
así es que es aquí donde vives so this is where you live
así están las cosas that's the way it is ▪ that's how it is
así haber quedado de to be all that's left of ➤ Así ha quedado el aeropuerto de Kabul tras el bombardeo. That's all that's left of the Kabul airport after the bombing.
así habrá sido it must have been like that
así las cosas given the situation
así lo consigo that works for me ▪ that does it for me

así lo espero I hope so

así lo hace cualquiera anybody can do it ■ it's easy

así lo haré that's what I'll do ■ I'll do that

así lo hice that's what I did

así me aspen *(Esp., coloquial)* ■ aunque me aspen even if they string me up ■ no matter what

así me gusta (a mí) **1.** that's how I like it ■ that's the way I like it **2.** good for you!

así me llaman that's what they call me ■ that's what everyone calls me

así no voy a llegar a ninguna parte I'm not getting anywhere (with this) ■ this isn't getting me anywhere

así o asá however you want to ■ however you like ■ any way you want to ■ any way you like

así para oír como para ver (in order) to hear as well as see ■ so that one can hear as well as see ■ (in order) to both hear and see ➤ Enciende el sonido así para oír como para ver la tarjeta Navideña electrónica. Turn on the sound in order to hear as well as see the electronic Christmas card. ■ Turn on the sound so that you can hear as well as see the electronic Christmas card. ■ Turn on the sound in order to both hear and see the electronic Christmas card.

así pasó ■ así se hizo that's what happened

así pues that way ■ by doing that ■ now ■ so

así que so that ■ therefore

así que así ■ de cualquiera manera ■ así como así any which way ■ every which way

así que llegue allá *(yo)* then when I get there ■ *(él)* then when he gets there ■ *(ella)* then when she gets there

así que os casáis *(Esp., vosotros)* so you're getting married ■ so you all are getting married

así que te casas so you're getting married

¡así que te chinchas! *(Esp.)* ■ ¡así que te jorobas! ■ ¡chínchate! so there! ■ take that! ➤ Sally Brown le dijo a Linus, "Supongo que pensabas que me iba a creer que me estabas llamando para invitarme a ir al cine. Bueno, no lo pensé, y no iría contigo ahora aunque me invitaras, ¡así que te chinchas!" ■ Sally Brown le dijo a Linus, "Supongo que pensabas que me iba a creer que me estabas llamando para invitarme a ir al cine. Bueno, no lo pensé, y no iría contigo ahora aunque me invitaras, ¡así que te jorobas!" Sally Brown said to Linus, "I suppose you thought I'd think you were calling to ask me to go to the movies. Well, I didn't, and I wouldn't go with you now even if you asked me, so there!"

así que (yo) llegue ■ en cuanto (yo) llegue ■ ni bien llegue (yo) as soon as I get there

así se esconda en el fin del mundo... no matter where he tries to hide

así se hace that's how you do it ■ that's the way you do it ■ *(en una receta)* method of preparation

¡así se hace! way to go!

así se hacía antes that's how they used to do it ■ that's the way they used to do it ■ that's how it used to be done ■ that's the way it used to be done ■ that's how it was previously done ■ that's the way it was previously done ■ that's how they used to make it ■ that's the way they used to make it ■ that's how it was previously made ■ that's the way it was previously made ■ that's how it used to be made ■ that's the way it used to be made *(Nota: "Formerly" puede usarse en vez de "previously".)*

así se hizo ■ así pasó that's what happened

así sea ■ amén **1.** amen **2.** ¡estoy contigo! amen (to that)! ■ I'm with *you*

así sin más just like *that*

así son that's the way they are

así soy ■ yo soy así that's (just) the way I am ■ that's just how I am

así tal cual just like that ■ just like you have it

así va de cuento so the story goes

así y todo ■ a pesar de eso ■ pese a todo ■ aun siendo así in spite of everything ■ even so

asiduo lector regular reader

asiento de atrás ■ asiento trasero back seat ➤ (Yo) viajaba en el asiento de atrás. ■ (Yo) viajaba en el asiento trasero. I was riding in the back seat.

asiento designado assigned seat ➤ ¿Están designados los asientos? Are the seats assigned?

asiento trasero ■ asiento de atrás back seat

asiento vacío que había junto al de nosotros empty seat next to ours

asiento vacío que había entre nosotros empty seat between us ■ empty seat between our two seats

asignar atributos humanos a los animales ■ otorgar atributos humanos a los animales to attribute human qualities to animales

asignarle a alguien de compañero ■ ponerle a alguien de compañero to assign someone as a companion ➤ Me asignaron de compañero al nuevo. ■ Me pusieron de compañero al nuevo. I was assigned to the newcomer as a companion.

asignarle a alguien el cometido de hacer algo ■ asignarle a alguien la tarea de hacer algo ■ encargarle a alguien hacer algo ■ encargarle a alguien que haga algo to assign someone the task of doing something ■ to charge someone with the task of doing something

asignarle a alguien la tarea de hacer algo ■ asignarle a alguien el cometido de hacer algo ■ encargarle a alguien hacer algo ■ encargarle a alguien que haga algo to assign someone the task of doing something ■ to charge someone with the task of doing something

asignarle a alguien un compañero ■ ponerle un compañero a alguien to assign someone a companion ➤ Le asignaron un compañero al policía. ■ Le pusieron un compañero al policía. They assigned the police officer a companion.

asignatura: hacer una ~ to take a course ■ take a subject ➤ María hace una asignatura de matemáticas. María is taking a math course. ➤ ¿Qué asignaturas haces? What subjects are you taking?

asignatura favorita favorite subject

asilo para huérfanos ■ orfanato ■ orfanatorio orphanage

asilo político political asylum

asir de los pelos ■ agarrar de los pelos to grab by the hair ➤ Ella le asió de los pelos. She grabbed him by the hair.

el, la **asistente de vuelo** flight attendant

asistir en carácter de invitado to go as a guest

asociación no lucrativa non-profit association ■ non-profit organization

estar **asociado a** to be associated with ➤ Teodora contribuyó a la grandeza del reinado de Justiniano, al que siempre estuvo asociada. Theodora contributed to the greatness of the reign of Justinian, with which she was always associated.

asociarse a una organización to become a member of an organization ■ to join an organization

asomar la cabeza por la ventana to stick one's head out the window

asomarse a la puerta to stand in the doorway ■ to look out the door

asomarse a la ventana to come to the window ■ to look out the window

asomarse por el balcón to lean over the balcony

asombrado cuando...: quedarse ~ ■ estar asombrado cuando... ■ estar asombrado cuando... to be astonished when... ■ to be astonished that... ➤ Se quedó asombrado cuando le subieron el sueldo después de un mes trabajando. He was astonished when they gave him a raise after a month on the job. ➤ Estábamos asombrados cuando nos invitaron a cenar. We were astonished when they invited us to (have) supper.

asombrosa exactitud uncanny accuracy

aspas de un abanico *(Méx.)* ■ aspas de un ventilador blades of a fan ■ fan blades

aspas de un molino (de viento) arms of a windmill

aspas de un ventilador blades of a fan ■ fan blades

aspas de una hélice (wide) blades of a propeller ■ (wide) propeller blades

astuto engaño clever deception

asumir algo bien to take something in stride ➤ Lo asumió bien. He took it in stride.

asumir con todas las consecuencias to take full responsibility for ■ to accept full responsibility for ■ to assume full responsibility for

asumir el costo de algo ■ asumir el gasto de algo to bear the cost of something ■ to bear the expense of something

asumir el gasto de algo ▪ asumir el costo de algo to bear the expense of something ▪ to bear the cost of something
asumir la responsabilidad de hacer algo ▪ tomar sobre sí la responsabilidad de hacer algo to assume responsibility to do something ▪ to take on responsibility to do something
asumir la responsabilidad por algo (que ha sucedido) to assume responsibility for something (that has happened)
asumir que... to assume that...
asumir riesgos to take risks
asumir una actitud de to adopt an attitude of
asumir una tarea to take on a task
el **asunto aún colea** (one) has not heard the last of it *(Nota: Lleva cualquier pronombre ▪ Takes any pronoun)*
asunto baladí trivial matter
asunto concreto: en un ~ on a particular matter
el **asunto en cuestión es...** at issue is... ▪ the issue in question is...
asunto espinoso 1. thorny issue 2. difficult subject (to understand)
asunto intrincado complicated matter
asunto sencillo simple matter ▪ simple affair
asuntos de gobierno matters of government ▪ governmental matters
asuntos internacionales foreign affairs
estar **asustado hasta de su propia sombra** ▪ tener miedo hasta de su sombra to be afraid of one's (own) shadow ➤ Tiene miedo hasta de su sombra. He's afraid of his (own) shadow.
ser **atacado por un animal** to be attacked by an animal
ser **atacado sin tregua** to be relentlessly attacked
atacar sin tregua to attack relentlessly ▪ relentlessly to attack
atacarle a los pulmones to settle in one's lungs
estar **atado de pies y manos** to be bound hands and feet ▪ (for) one's hands and feet to be bound ▪ (for) one's hands and feet to be tied
atajar la hemorragia ▪ parar la hemorragia to stop the bleeding ▪ to stop the hemorrhage
atajar la violencia doméstica to check the spread of domestic violence ▪ to curb domestic violence ➤ Juristas europeas exigen el uno porciento de los presupuestos para atajar la violencia doméstica. European jurists demand one percent of tax revenues to check the spread of domestic violence.
atajar por ▪ atajar a través de ▪ cortar el camino por to take a shortcut through
atajar un fuego to contain a fire
atañerle a uno to concern one ▪ to be one's concern ➤ Eso no me atañe. That doesn't concern me. ▪ It doesn't concern me. ▪ It's not my concern. ➤ Le atañe profundamente. *(a él)* It concerns him deeply. ▪ *(a ella)* It concerns her deeply. ➤ Por lo que a mí me atañe As far as I'm concerned
ataque a: desplegar un ~ to launch an attack on
el **ataque a un objetivo** ▪ atentado contra un objetivo attack on a target ➤ Ataque a un destructor EE UU en Yemen Attack on a U.S. destroyer in Yemen ➤ En la alianza atacar a uno solo se considera como un ataque al resto. In the alliance, an attack on one is considered an attack on all.
el **ataque al corazón** heart attack
el **ataque contundente** shock and awe attack
ataque de apoplejía: sufrir un ~ 1. to have a seizure 2. sufrir un derrame cerebral to have a stroke
el **ataque de ira** ▪ ataque de enfado fit of anger
el **ataque de rabia** fit of rage
el **ataque de risa** fit of laughter
ataque mortífero deadly attack
el **ataque relámpago** lightning attack
ataques aéreos air strikes ▪ air attacks
atar cabos ▪ unir cabos to put two and two together
atar en corto a alguien ▪ mantener a alguien atado en corto ▪ mantener a alguien con una correa corta to keep someone on a short leash ▪ to keep someone under tight control
atar la cuerda a 1. to tie the rope to 2. to tie the rope around ➤ Ató la cuerda al árbol. He tied the rope around the tree.
atar las manos a la espalda to tie someone's hands behind his back
atar los cabos sueltos to tie up (the) loose ends
atar y amordazar a alguien to bind and gag someone
atarle las manos a la espalda to tie someone's hands behind his back
atarse los cordones to tie one's shoes
estar **atascado en la impresora** to be jammed in the printer ▪ to be stuck in the printer ➤ El papel está atascado en la impresora. The paper is jammed in the printer. ▪ The paper is stuck in the printer.
estar **atascado en la nieve** to be stuck in the snow ➤ El coche está atascado en la nieve. The car is stuck in the snow.
atascarse en 1. to get jammed in 2. to get stuck in ➤ El papel se atasca en la impresora. The paper gets jammed in the printer. ➤ *(ustedes)* ¡Que no se atasquen en la nieve! ▪ *(Esp., vosotros)* ¡Que no os atasquéis en la nieve! Don't get stuck in the snow.
atasco (de tráfico) ▪ (la) retención ▪ embotellamiento traffic jam
estar **ataviado de** to be decked out in
la **atención a las necesidades de otra gente** responsiveness to the needs of others ▪ responsiveness to other people's needs
atención al cliente ▪ atención a clientes ▪ servicio al cliente customer service
atended mis cosas un momento somebody watch my things for a minute
atender la puerta ▪ abrir la puerta ▪ ver quién hay en la puerta to answer the door ▪ to see who's at the door ➤ Vete a atender la puerta. ▪ Vete a abrir la puerta. ▪ Vete a ver quién hay en la puerta. Go answer the door. ▪ Go see who's at the door.
atender mesas en un restaurante to wait tables in a restaurant
atenerse a las consecuencias ▪ enfrentar las consecuencias to face the consequences ▪ to face the music
atenerse al convenio ▪ cumplir con el acuerdo ▪ acatar el pacto to abide by the agreement
atenerse al resultado ▪ atenerse a los resultados ▪ respetar el resultado to abide by the result ➤ Los candidatos dijeron que si el proceso electoral fuera observado por Jimmy Carter, que ellos se atendrían a los resultados. The candidates said if the election were monitored by Jimmy Carter, they would abide by the result.
atenerse al tema to keep to the point
atentados contra civiles: llevar a cabo ~ to carry out attacks on civilians
estar **atento a algo** to monitor something ▪ to follow something closely ▪ to watch something closely ➤ Durante los próximos meses estaremos muy atentos a las fluctuaciones del dólar. In the coming months we will closely monitor the fluctuations in the dollar.
estar **atento a alguien** 1. estar pendiente de alguien to await word from someone 2. to watch for someone 3. to listen (out) for someone ➤ Estoy atento a otra persona que vendrá a verme el lunes o martes. I'm awaiting word from someone else who will come see me either Monday or Tuesday.
estar **atento a que...** 1. to be waiting for word from ▪ to be awaiting word from 2. to be watching (out) for ➤ Estamos atentos a que el viñedo español confirme nuestro pedido de mil botellas de amontillado. We're waiting (for word) from the Spanish winery to confirm our order of a thousand bottles of Montilla sherry. ➤ No puedo salir porque estoy atento a que el repartidor me traiga la secadora. I can't leave because I'm watching (out) for the delivery man to bring the dryer.
estar **atento a la radio** to keep an ear to the radio ➤ Estoy atento a la radio porque van a decir quiénes son los diez superventas. I have to keep an ear to the radio because they're going to tell who the top ten (selling records) are. ▪ I have to keep an ear to the radio because they're going to announce the top ten.
estar **atento a la sopa** to keep an eye on the soup ▪ to watch the soup ➤ Tengo que estar atenta a la sopa para que no se salga. I have to watch the soup so (that) it won't boil over. ▪ I have to keep an eye on the soup so (that) it won't boil over.
ser **atento a las necesidades de otros** to be responsive to the needs of others ▪ to be responsive to other people's needs
estar **atento al bebé** to watch the baby ▪ to keep an eye on the baby ➤ Estáte atento a la bebé mientras bajo a hacer la compra.

Watch the baby while I go to the grocery store. ▪ Keep an eye on the baby while I go to the grocery store.

estar **atento de alguien** to focus one's attention on someone ▪ to cater to someone ➤ A los bebés les gusta que uno esté atento de ellos. Babies like to be paid (a lot of) attention to. ▪ Babies like to be babied. ➤ Algunos hombres son como niños. Les encanta que las mujeres estén atentas de ellos. Some men are like children. They love for women to cater to their every whim.

ateo declarado avowed athiest

aterrizaje forzoso forced landing

aterrizaje frustrado aborted landing

el **aterrizaje fuerte** ▪ aterrizaje duro hard landing

el **aterrizaje sin tren** belly landing

atiborrarse (de alimento) to stuff oneself (with food)

atinar a hacer algo to succeed in doing something

atinar con la solución to hit on the solution

atisbar un rayo de esperanza to (be able to) see a ray of hope ▪ to (be able to see) a glimmer of hope

atisbar una figura to make out a figure ▪ to discern a figure

atizar a alguien to stir up someone ▪ to stir someone up ▪ to incite someone ▪ to inflame someone ➤ *(titular)* El partido socialista atiza a los inmigrantes para debilitar al gobierno. The socialist party stirs up immigrants to weaken the government.

atizar el fuego ▪ avivar el fuego to stoke the fire

atizar la polémica de to stir up controversy over

atleta nato(-a) born athlete

la **atomización familiar** ▪ disgregación familiar breakdown of the family

estar **atónito al...** to be astonished to... ➤ El nominado al Tribunal Supremo dijo que estaba atónito al recibir la nominación. The Supreme Court nominee said he was astonished to receive the nomination.

atónito al descubrir que: quedarse ~ to be astonished to discover that...

atónito cuando...: quedarse alguien ~ to be astonished when... ▪ to be astonished that... ➤ Quedó atónito cuando le subieron el sueldo después de un mes trabajando. He was astonished when they gave him a raise after one month on the job. ▪ He was astonished that they gave him a raise after one month on the job.

atracador de bancos bank robber

atracar un banco ▪ robar un banco to rob a bank ▪ to hold up a bank ▪ to hold a bank up ➤ Un trío de ladrones atracaron el banco. A trio of robbers help up the bank. ▪ A trio of robbers held the bank up. ▪ A trio robbed the bank. ▪ Three people robbed the bank. ➤ Un trío de atracadores lo robaron. ▪ Un trío de ladrónes lo atracaron. A trio of robbers held it up.

atractivo sexual sex appeal

atraer hacia sí la atención de to draw attention to oneself

atraer la atención de alguien ▪ llamar la atención de alguien to catch someone's attention ▪ to get someone's attention ▪ to attract someone's attention ➤ Una noticia en el periódico atrajo mi atención. ▪ Una noticia en el periódico llamó mi atención. ▪ Una noticia en el periódico me llamó la atención. An item in the newspaper caught my attention. ▪ An item in the newspaper got my attention. ➤ Mira si puedes atraer la atención de ese mesero. ▪ Mira si puedes llamar la atención de ese mesero. ▪ *(Esp.)* Mira si puedes llamar la atención de ese camarero. See if you can catch that waiter's attention. ▪ See if you can get that waiter's attention.

atraer la mirada to draw the eye ▪ to catch the eye ▪ to attract the eye ➤ Atrajo mi mirada. He caught my eye. ▪ He drew my eye. ▪ He attracted my eye. ▪ It caught my eye. ▪ It drew my eye.

atraer una multitud draw a crowd ➤ La película sobre los dinosaurios atrajo una mayor multitud. The dinosaur movie drew a bigger crowd. ➤ La película sobre los dinosaurios atrajo la mayor multitud. The dinosaur movie drew the bigger crowd (of the two). ➤ La película sobre los dinosaurios atrajo la mayor multitud. The dinosaur movie drew the biggest crowed. ➤ La muestra de motos antiguas atrajo a una multitud interesada. ▪ La muestra de motos antiguas atrajo una considerada multitud. The antique motorcycle display was drawing an appreciative crowd.

atraerlo(-a) a alguien hacia sí to pull someone toward you

atragantarse con algo to choke on something

atraído por alguien: sentirse ~ to feel attracted to someone ▪ to be attracted to someone

atrancar el tráfico to block off traffic ▪ to erect a barricade to block off traffic

atrancar la puerta to bar the door ▪ to barracade the door

estar **atrapado en el tráfico** to be stuck in traffic

estar **atrapado en una inundación** to be stranded in a flood ➤ Muchas personas estuvieron atrapadas por varios días después de que el huracán alcanzara Nueva Orleans. Many people were stranded for days after the hurricane struck New Orleans.

Atrápame si puedes *(título de película) Catch Me If You Can*

estar **atrasado de noticias** to be behind the times ▪ to be out of touch with what is going on

estar **atrasado con el trabajo** ▪ llevar retraso con el trabajo ▪ ir retrasado en el trabajo to be behind in one's work ▪ to be behind with one's work ➤ Estoy atrasado con el trabajo. ▪ Estoy atrasado con mi trabajo. ▪ Llevo retraso con mi trabajo. I'm behind in my work. ▪ I'm behind with my work.

atrasarse con su trabajo ▪ retrasarse con el trabajo to get behind in one's work

estar **atravesado en la garganta** to be caught in the throat

atravesar a nado to swim across ➤ Atravesó el lago a nado. He swam across the lake.

atravesar algo en su mayor anchura to cross the entire width of something

atravesar el océano Atlántico to cross the Atlantic Ocean

¡atrévete y verás! I dare you!

ser **atrevido con alguien** to be bold with someone ▪ to be brazen with someone

atrevimiento de sus acciones *(de él)* boldness of his actions ▪ *(de ella)* boldness of her actions

atribuirse la victoria to claim victory

atribuirse un ataque ▪ reivindicar (la autoría de) un ataque to claim responsibility for an attack

estar **atrincherado en** 1. *(un edificio)* to be holed up in 2. *(militar)* to be entrenched in ▪ to be dug in at

audiencia de un periódico readership of a newspaper

aumentar al triple to triple ▪ to treble ▪ to increase threefold

aumentar el autoestima to raise one's self-esteem

aumentar el flujo sanguíneo to increase blood flow ▪ to increase the flow of blood

aumentar el riesgo to increase the risk ▪ to heighten the risk

aumentar la moral to build morale

aumento de peso weight gain ▪ increase in weight ▪ gain in weight

aumento de velocidad increase in speed

aumento del alquiler ▪ subida del alquiler rent increase ▪ increase in the rent

aumento medio ▪ ascenso medio average increase

aun así even so

aún estar por ver ▪ quedar por ver to remain to be seen

aún faltarle a uno lo peor the worst is yet to come ➤ Aún me faltaba lo peor. The worst (for me) was yet to come.

aún hoy en día ▪ hasta hoy ▪ hasta este momento to this day

aún más 1. even more ▪ even further 2. furthermore ➤ Para enturbiar aún más las cosas To complicate matters even more ▪ To complicate matters even further

aún no lo sé ▪ todavía no lo sé ▪ no lo sé aún ▪ no lo sé todavía I don't know yet ▪ I still don't know

aún no ha llegado ▪ todavía no ha llegado 1. llegado aquí *(él)* he's not here yet ▪ he still hasn't gotten here ▪ *(ella)* she's not here yet ▪ she still hasn't gotten here 2. llegado allí *(él)* he's not there yet ▪ he still hasn't gotten there ▪ *(ella)* she's not there yet ▪ she still hasn't gotten there

aún peor que even worse than

aún por determinarse yet to be determined ▪ still to be determined ▪ as yet undetermined

ser **aún pronto para** to be too early to ➤ Las autoridades indicaron que era aún pronto para averiguar las causas del siniestro. The authorities indicated it was too early to determine the causes of the (airplane) crash.

aún seguir vivo(-a) still to be alive ➤ Aún sigue vivo. He's still alive.

aún tengo hambre ▪ todavía tengo hambre I'm still hungry
aunar esfuerzos para... to join forces to...
aunque cueste a uno at the price of ➤ Certeza aunque nos cueste la honestidad Certainty at the price of honesty
aunque fuera leve however remote
aunque haya... even if there is... ▪ even if there should be...
aunque me aspen ▪ así me aspen even if they string me up ▪ no matter what
aunque no lo creas ▪ aunque parezca mentira ▪ aunque no lo parezca believe it or not ▪ although you might find it hard to believe ▪ although you may find it hard to believe ▪ although it might not seem like it ▪ although it may not seem like it
aunque no lo parezca ▪ aunque parezca mentira ▪ aunque no lo creas believe it or not ▪ althought it might not seem like it ▪ although it may not seem like it ▪ although you might find it hard to believe ▪ although you may find it hard to believe
aunque parece mentira ▪ aunque no lo parece believe it or not ▪ althought it doesn't seem like it
aunque parezca lo contrario although it might seem otherwise ▪ although it may seem otherwise
aunque parezca mentira ▪ aunque no lo creas ▪ aunque no lo parezca believe it or not ▪ although you might find it hard to believe ▪ although you may find it hard to believe
aunque sea por if only by ➤ James Bond siempre le gana la partida al tiempo, aunque sea por un segundo. James Bond always beats the clock, if only by a second.
aunque sea sólo un momento if only for a moment
aunque sólo sea por if for no other reason than
aurora boreal(is) northern lights ▪ aurora borealis ▪ aurora polaris
ausencia de cooperación lack of cooperation ▪ absence of cooperation
ausentismo laboral ▪ absentismo laboral absenteeism (from work) ➤ El alcoholismo es una de las principales causas de ausentismo laboral. Alcoholism is one of the principal causes of absenteeism (from work).
ser un **(auténtico) universo en sí mismo** ▪ ser una persona trascendental to be a world in oneself ▪ to be bigger than life ➤ San Francisco, Juana de Arco, Cervantes, el filósofo Immanuel Kant y Lincoln son auténticos universos en sí mismos. Están entre las grandes personalidades de todos los tiempos. St. Francis, Joan of Arc, Cervantes, the philosopher Immanuel Kant, and Lincoln are bigger than life. They are among the great personalities of the ages.
auténtico y genuino ▪ de pura cepa authentic and genuine
autor de obras entre las que destacan author of such notable works as
autor de sus días one's father
autora de sus días one's mother
la **autoridad en materia de seguridad** security expert
las **autoridades pertinentes** the appropriate authorities ▪ the relevant authorities
el **autobús de** ▪ autobús proveniente de bus from ▪ bus coming from
el **autobús de dos pisos** double-decker bus
el **autobús para** ▪ autobús a ▪ autobús hacia ▪ autobús que va para bus to ▪ bus for
el **autobús turístico** tour bus
automático general ▪ disyuntor circuit breaker ➤ Saltó el automático general por una corto(circuito) en el termo de agua caliente. ▪ Saltó el disyuntor por una corto(circuito) en el termo de agua caliente. A short(-circuit) in the hot water heater tripped the circuit breaker.
auto-indicativo ▪ auto-instructivo self-prompting
auto-instructivo ▪ auto-indicativo self-prompting
el **autobús escolar** school bus
el **automóvil de alquiler** rented car ▪ rental car
autor del delito perpetrator of a crime ▪ assailant
ser **autor intelectual de** to be the mastermind of ▪ to be the mastermind behind ▪ to mastermind ➤ El ex dictador (Pinochet) acusado de ser autor intelectual de los crímenes de la "caravana de la muerte" The former dictator (Pinochet) accused of being the mastermind of the "caravan of death" crimes ▪ The former dictator (Pinochet) accused of masterminding the "caravan of death" crimes
autoridad portuaria port authority
autorizado por authorized by ▪ with the consent of
ser **autorizado por** to be authorized by
auxiliar de vuelo ▪ azafato(-a) flight attendant
avalancha de críticas barrage of criticism ➤ Una avalancha de críticas está cayendo sobre el gobierno por... A barrage of criticism is being leveled at the government for...
avalanche de insultos ▪ rosario de insultos ▪ flujo de insultos ▪ plétora de insultos ▪ cantidad de improperios barrage of insults ▪ stream of insults
avalar un préstamo to guarantee a loan ▪ to be the guarantor of a loan
estar **avanzado para su momento** ▪ estar avanzado para su tiempo to be ahead of its time
estar **avanzado para su tiempo** ▪ estar avanzado para su momento to be ahead of its time
avanzar más de lo que to advance farther than ➤ A sus marineros Colón les dijo que habían avanzado más de lo que realmente habían hecho. Columbus told his sailors they had advanced farther than they really had.
ser una **ave de mal agüero** ▪ ser un pájaro de mal agüero to be a bird of ill omen ▪ to be bad news ▪ to be a bad-news bearer
el **ave de paso** migratory bird ▪ *(figurativo)* transient ▪ someone just passing through
el **ave de presa** ▪ ave de rapiña bird of prey
el **ave de rapiña** ▪ ave de presa bird of prey
Ave María Purísima 1. Hail Mary full of grace 2. *(coloquial)* for heaven's sake! ▪ good heavens!
la **ave rapaz** bird of prey
avenirse a hacer algo to agree to do something ▪ to agree on something ➤ No se avinieron a elegir la sede para los Juegos Olímpicos. They couldn't agree on a place for the Olympic Games.
aventura amorosa love affair
aventura cargada de acción action-packed adventure
aventurar una respuesta to hazard a guess
avergonzar a uno ▪ abornochar a uno ▪ apenar a uno ▪ dar vergüenza a uno to embarrass one ➤ Me avergüenza. ▪ Me abochorna. ▪ Me da verguënza. It embarrasses me. ➤ Me avergüenza que me beses en público. It embarrasses me when you kiss me in public. ➤ Avergüenza a su mujer. ▪ Abochorna a su mujer. He embarrasses his wife.
avergonzarse de to be ashamed of
avergüenza decirlo, pero... I'm ashamed to say it, but...
avería mecánica mechanical breakdown ▪ breakdown of mechanical equipment ▪ breakdown in mechanical equipment
averiguaciones sobre ▪ hallazgos sobre findings about
averiguar algo 1. to find out something 2. to check something ➤ ¿Lo averiguarías por mí? Would you find out about it for me? ▪ Would you check on it for me?
averiguárselas para hacer algo *(Méx.)* ▪ arreglárselas para hacer algo to manage to do something
aviesas intenciones ▪ malas intenciones evil intentions
el **avión aterrizó de panza** the airplane pancaked ▪ the airplane belly landed
el **avión bimotor** twin-engine airplane
el **avión de reconocimiento** reconnaisance plane ▪ reconnaissance aircraft
el **avión desnivelado** untrimmed airplane ▪ airplane without the trim tabs adjusted
el **avión no tripulado** unmanned airplane
el **avión se desplomó** the airplane went down ▪ the airplane plummeted to the ground ➤ Nada más despegar, el avión se desplomó tras perder un motor. Shortly after takeoff, the airplane lost an engine and plummeted to the ground.
el **avión siniestrado** wreckage of an airplane
los **aviones de reconocimiento** reconnaissance aircraft
avisar a alguien con antelación ▪ entregar a alguien el aviso con antelación ▪ dar a alguien el aviso con antelación to give someone advance notice ➤ Avisó de su mudanza a su casero con un mes de antelación. She gave her landlord a month's advance notice of her intention to move. ➤ Avisé a la compañía eléctrica con un mes de antelación del cambio de dirección. ▪ Avisé del cambio de dirección al a compañía eléctrica con un

mes de antelación. ▪ Avisé a la compañía eléctrica del cambio de dirección con un mes de antelación. I gave the power company a month's (advance) notice of our change of address.

avisar a alguien de algo 1. to warn someone of something 2. to let someone know something

avisar de que to warn that ➤ El presidente de la Comisión Europea avisa de que la cumbre de Niza va hacia el fracaso. The president of the European Commission warns that the Nice summit is headed for failure. ➤ El primero, que avisó de que uno de los trenes marchaba en dirección errónea, hablaba en francés, pero el otro le respondía en flamenco. The first (man), who warned that one of the trains was going in the wrong direction, was speaking (in) French, but the other answered him in Flemish.

avisar un taxi ▪ llamar un taxi to call a taxi ▪ to call a cab

avisarle a alguien con tiempo to let someone know ahead of time

aviso de embargo eviction notice

avistar la tierra to sight land ➤ De la vigía de la Pinta, Rodrigo de Triana avistó la tierra. From the crow's nest of the Pinta, Rodrigo de Triana sighted land.

avivar el fuego ▪ atizar el fuego to stoke the fire

avivar una crisis to deepen a crisis ▪ to intensify a crisis

¡**ayayay!** ooh!

ayer hizo un año a year ago yesterday

ayer mismo just yesterday ▪ only yesterday

ayer por la mañana yesterday morning

ayer por la noche ▪ anoche last night

ayer por la tarde yesterday afternoon

ayuda foránea foreign aid

ayudar a alguien con sólo escucharlo(-a) to help someone just by listening

ayudar a alguien a que fuera más... to help someone (to) be more...

ayudar a alguien a que sea más... to help someone (to) be more...

ayudar con los labores to help out with the chores

el **azar quiso que...** ▪ el destino decretó que... fate decreed that...

los **azares de la vida** ▪ altibajos de la vida life's ups and downs ▪ ups and downs of life ▪ ups and downs in life

el **azúcar sin refinar** unrefined sugar

baca de coche *(Esp.)* ▪ baca de vehículo ▪ (el) portaequipajes luggage rack
bacterias causantes de... bacteria causing... ▪ bacteria which causes...
Bahía Cochinos *(denominación más extendida de Playa Girón)* Bay of Pigs
bailar a cualquier son ▪ seguir la manada ▪ hacer siempre lo que hacen los demás to follow the crowd ▪ to follow the herd
bailar al son que le tocan ▪ ir con la corriente to go with the flow
bailar con la más fea to get the short end of the stick
bailar el agua a alguien *(Esp.)* **1.** hacerle la pelota to suck up to someone **2.** beber los vientos por alguien to admire someone
bailar en la cuerda floja to live dangerously ▪ to test the limits ▪ to push the envelope
baile de cortejo *(animales)* mating dance
baile de salón ballroom dance ➤ El tango es un baile de salón. The tango is a ballroom dance.
el **baile de San Vito** ▪ baile de sanbito St. Vitus' dance
los **bailes de salón** **1.** ballroom dancing **2.** ballroom dances
baja concurrencia de votantes ▪ escasa participación de electores ▪ elevada abstención (de votantes) low voter turnout ▪ light voter turnout ▪ high voter abstention
baja Edad Media late Middle Ages
¡**baja el arma!** drop the gun! ▪ drop your gun!
baja frecuencia low frequency
baja participación (de votantes) ▪ menguada asistencia (de votantes) ▪ alta abstención (de votantes) low (voter) turnout
bajada de bandera *(en un taxi)* start of the meter
bajada de los tipos de interés drop in interest rates ▪ lowering of interest rates
bajada de tensión: tener una ~ ▪ sufrir una bajada de tensión ▪ bajarle la tensión a alguien to have a drop in blood pressure ▪ to experience a drop in blood pressure ▪ to suffer a drop in blood pressure
bajado del cielo: llegar como ~ ▪ aparecer como bajado del cielo ▪ llegar como caído del cielo ▪ ser un regalo del cielo ▪ ser un regalo de Dios to be a Godsend
estar **bajando *x* planta(s)** (to be) *x* floors down ➤ ¡Bajando una planta! (It's) one floor down. ➤ ¡Bajando dos plantas! (It's) two floors down.
bajar a hacer algo ▪ bajar para hacer algo to go down(stairs) to do something ➤ Ella bajó a coger el correo. ▪ Ella bajó para coger el correo. ▪ Ella bajó a buscar el correo. ▪ Ella bajó para buscar el correo. She went down(stairs) to get the mail.
bajar a la calle to go out
bajar a la realidad ▪ bajar de las nubes to wake up to reality ▪ to face reality ▪ to come down out of the clouds
bajar corriendo to run downstairs
bajar de cero *(temperatura)* to drop below zero
bajar de las nubes ▪ bajar a la realidad ▪ despertar a la realidad to come down out of the clouds ▪ to wake up to reality
bajar de peso to lose weight
bajar de un salto de to jump down from
bajar del árbol to climb down out of the tree ▪ to climb down from the tree ▪ to come down out of the tree
bajar del autobús ▪ bajarse del autobús to get off the bus ➤ ¿En qué parada (te) bajas? What stop do you get off at? ➤ ¿Dónde (te) bajas? Where do you get off? ➤ Quiero bajarme en la próxima parada. I'd like to get off at the next stop. ➤ Me bajo en Chapultepec. I get off at Chapultepec.
bajar del avión ▪ bajarse del avión to get off the airplane ▪ to get off the plane
bajar del tren ▪ bajarse del tren to get off the train ➤ Bajamos del tren en Chamartín. We get off the train at Chamartín.
bajar el dobladillo to let down the hem ▪ to let out the hem ▪ to take down the hem ➤ La costurera le bajó el dobladillo al vestido de novia. The seamstress lowered the hem of her bridal gown. ▪ The seamstress let out the hem of her bridal gown.
bajar el dobladillo *x* centímetros to lower the hem (by) *x* centimeters
bajar el flujo sanguíneo ▪ reducir el flujo sanguíneo to decrease the flow of blood ▪ to reduce the flow of blood ▪ to decrease (the) blood flow ▪ to reduce (the) blood flow

bajar el tono de voz **1.** to lower one's voice ▪ to speak softly ▪ to speak quietly **2.** to quiet down ▪ to pipe down
bajar la bandera *(en un taxi)* to start the meter ▪ to turn on the meter
bajar la Bolsa (for) the stock market to drop ➤ Bajó la Bolsa durante la sesión de hoy. The stock market dropped in today's session.
bajar la cabeza **1.** agachar la cabeza ▪ agacharse to lower one's head ▪ to duck **2.** avergonzarse to hang one's head (in shame) **3.** to bow one's head (in reverence) ➤ No tienes por qué bajar la cabeza delante de nadie. You don't have anything to be ashamed of. ➤ Bajó la cabeza mientras oraba. He bowed his head while he was praying.
bajar la calefacción to turn down the heat
bajar la comida to work off one's dinner ➤ Demos un paseo para bajar la comida. Let's take a walk to work off our dinner.
bajar la escalera to go downstairs ▪ to go down the steps ▪ *(literario)* to descend the stairs
bajar la guardia to let down one's guard
bajar la mano to lower one's hand
bajar la medicina ▪ tragar el medicamento to swallow the medicine ▪ to get the medicine down
bajar la tripa ▪ adelgazar ▪ perder peso to slim down ▪ to lose weight
bajar la vista to look down
bajar los humos a alguien ▪ bajarle los humos a alguien to shoot someone down ▪ to take someone down a notch
bajar los impuestos a ▪ bajar los impuestos sobre to lower taxes on ➤ El Congreso ha bajado los impuestos a las empresas. Congress has lowered taxes on businesses.
bajar por la barandilla ▪ dejarse resbalar por la barandilla ▪ deslizarse por la barandilla to slide down the bannister
bajar un archivo ▪ descargar un archivo to download a file ➤ Bajé el archivo de Internet. I downloaded the file from the Internet. ▪ I downloaded the Internet file.
bajaré y lo buscaré I'll go down and get it
bajarle el copete a alguien ▪ bajarle los humos a alguien ▪ poner a alguien en su lugar to put someone in his place ▪ to take someone down a peg
bajarle la tensión a alguien to reduce the blood pressure ▪ to bring down the blood pressure
bajarle los humos a alguien ▪ bajarle el copete a alguien ▪ poner a alguien en su lugar to put someone in his place ▪ to take someone down a peg
bajarse de la escalera to get down off the ladder ▪ to get down from the ladder
bajar(se) del autobús to get off the bus ➤ ¿Dónde bajamos? Where do we get off? ▪ What stop do we get off at?

bajar(se) del avión to get off the airplane ▪ to get off the plane

bajarse del caballo to get off the horse ▪ to get down from the horse

bajar(se) del carro *(L.am.)* ▪ salir del carro to get out of the car

bajar(se) del coche *(Esp.)* ▪ salir del coche to get out of the car

bajar(se) del metro to get off the metro ▪ to get off the subway ➤ (Nos) bajamos del metro en División del Norte. We get off the metro at División del Norte. ▪ We get off the subway at División del Norte.

bajarse el dobladillo (for) the hem to be lowered

bajarse las gafas to lower one's glasses ➤ Se bajó las gafas y miró por encima. He lowered his glasses and peered out over his nose.

bajarse los pantalones to drop one's pants ▪ to lower one's pants ▪ to drop one's trousers ▪ to lower one's trousers

bajársele los humos a alguien to bring someone down a notch

bájate de ahí *(a un perro)* (get) down!

¡**bájate del carro!** ▪ ¡bájate de la moto! get real! ▪ c'mon, get real!

bajeza moral moral turpitude

bajo altas medidas de seguridad ▪ entre fuertes medidas de seguridad under tight security

estar **bajo arresto** ▪ estar bajo detención ▪ estar detenido to be under arrest ▪ to be in detention

bajo cero: la temperatura es de *x* (grados Celsius) ~ ➤ La temperatura es de diez (grados Celsius) bajo cero. The temperature is minus ten, Celsius. ▪ The temperature is ten below zero, Celsius. *(Nota: Catorce grados Fahrenheit.)*

estar **bajo control** to be under control

estar **bajo control médico** to be medically supervised ▪ to be under medical supervision ➤ Su dieta está bajo control médico. His diet is medically supervised.

bajo cuerda: trabajar ~ ▪ trabajar en negro ▪ trabajar bajo la mesa ▪ trabajar fuera de los libros to work under the table ▪ to work invisibly to the government

estar **bajo de ánimo** to be in poor spirits ▪ to be depressed

estar **bajo de fondos** to be low on funds

bajo de la camisa ▪ los bordes de la camisa shirttail(s)

bajo de un pantalón cuff of the pant(s) ▪ pants cuff

bajo de una falda the hem of the skirt

estar **bajo detención** ▪ estar bajo arresto ▪ estar detenido to be under arrest ▪ to be in detention

bajo el mandato del presidente... ▪ bajo el presidente... under the president ▪ during the term of the president ➤ Dean Rusk fue ministro de asuntos exteriores bajo los mandatos de los presidentes Kennedy y Johnson. Dean Rusk was secretary of state during the terms of Presidents Kennedy and Johnson. ▪ Dean Rusk was secretary of state under Presidents Kennedy and Johnson.

bajo el mando de under the command of

bajo el manto de la noche: huir ~ ▪ huir bajo el manto de la oscuridad ▪ huir al abrigo de la noche ▪ huir al amparo de la noche to flee under cover of darkness

bajo el manto de la oscuridad ▪ al abrigo de la noche ▪ al amparo de la noche under cover of darkness

bajo el pabellón de ▪ bajo la bandera de under the flag of ➤ El barco opera bajo el pabellón de Panamá. The ship operates under the Panamanian flag. ▪ The ship operates under the flag of Panama.

bajo el presidente... ▪ bajo el mandato del presidente... under the president... ▪ during the term of president...

bajo el punto de vista de ▪ desde el punto de vista de from the point of view of

bajo juramento: declarar ~ to testify under oath

estar **bajo la enseñanza de** to be under the tutelage of ▪ to be tutored by

bajo la fachada de ▪ debajo la fachada de ▪ bajo la aparencia de beneath the façade of ➤ Bajo la fachada clasicista latía el corazón de un romántico encerrado. Beneath the classicist façade, the heart of a closet romantic was beating.

bajo la ley under the law

bajo la mesa: trabajar ~ ▪ trabajar fuera de los libros ▪ trabajar bajo cuerda ▪ trabajar en negro to work under the table ▪ to work invisibly to the government

bajo la mirada de alguien: ser vigilado ~ to be watched by someone

bajo la mirada del público: encontrarse ~ to be in the public spotlight ▪ to be in the public eye

bajo la protección de ▪ al amparo de ▪ al arrimo de under the protection of

bajo la protección policial under police protection

bajo la rúbrica de under the rubric of

bajo la superficie ▪ debajo de la superficie beneath the surface

bajo la tutela de ▪ bajo los auspicios de under the auspices of ▪ under the aegis of ▪ under the egis of

estar **bajo las faldas de su madre** ▪ estar en las faldas de su madre to be tied to one's mother's apron strings

estar **bajo llave** ▪ estar bajo siete llaves to be under lock and key

bajo los auspicios de ▪ bajo la tutela de under the auspices of ▪ under the aegis of ▪ under the egis of

estar **bajo los focos** *(en un escenario)* to be under the lights

bajo mano underhandedly

bajo mi punto de vista ▪ desde mi punto de vista from my point of view

estar **bajo mucha presión** to be under a lot of pressure ▪ *(coloquial)* to be under the gun

bajo ningún concepto ▪ por ningún concepto ▪ bajo ninguna circunstancia ▪ en ningún caso under no circumstances

bajo ninguna circunstancia ▪ bajo ningún concepto ▪ en ningún caso under no circumstances

bajo nueva administración under new management

bajo plica: mandar un manuscrito ~ ▪ mandar un manuscrito bajo sistema de plica to submit a manuscript with the name covered (as in a literary competition) ➤ Nicanor Parra, el autodenominado "antipoeta" chileno, al mandar tres manuscritos bajo plica, ganó el primero, segundo y tercer puestos de un concurso literario. Nicanor Parra, the self-styled Chilean "antipoet," on submitting three manuscripts anonymously to a literary competition, won first, second, and third prize.

bajo petición ▪ a súplica by request

bajo receta (médica): conseguirse únicamente ~ to be available by prescription only

estar **bajo presión** to be under pressure ➤ El primer ministro está bajo mucha presión del partido de la oposición. The prime minister is under great pressure from the opposition party.

bajo receta archivada: conseguirse ~ to be available by prescription in triplicate (a record of which is kept by the physician, the pharmacy and the insurance company) ➤ La morfina se consigue únicamente bajo receta archivada. Morphine is available only by prescription in triplicate.

estar **bajo siete llaves** ▪ estar bajo llave to be under lock and key

estar **bajo tierra** to be underground

estar **bajo tutela jurídica** to be under legal guardianship

bajo su palabra on one's word

bajo un frío polar engulfed in a polar freeze

bajo un sol de justicia under a punishing sun ▪ with a punishing sun beating down (on one)

bajo un sol terrible with the sun beating down (on one)

bala de fogueo ▪ cartucho de fogueo blank (bullet)

bala de heno bale of hay

bala que le atraviesa el pecho bullet through the chest ➤ El avión del Barón Rojo se estrelló tras recibir el piloto una única bala que le atravesó el pecho. The Red Baron's plane crashed after the pilot was struck by a single bullet through the chest.

bala gastada spent bullet

bala perdida stray bullet

ser una **bala perdida** to be good for nothing ▪ to be a hopeless case ▪ to be a lost cause ▪ to be beyond hope ▪ to be unreachable ▪ to be unrehabilitatable

bala rasa musket ball ▪ round shot

el **balance de la situación** balance sheet

balancearse con el viento to sway in the wind ▪ to rock in the wind
balancearse de un extremo a otro to swing back and forth ▪ to swing to and fro ▪ to sway
balanza de pagos balance of payments
balanza de precisión ▪ báscula de precisión precision scale
balanza precisa ▪ balanza exacta ▪ báscula precisa ▪ báscula exacta accurate scale
ser un **balón de oxígeno** ▪ suponer un balón de oxígeno to be a lifesaver ▪ to be a shot in the arm
ser una **balsa de aceite** to be placid ▪ to be peaceful
estar **bañado en glaseado** to be coated with glaze ▪ to be glazed ➤ ¿Qué te gusta más? ¿Las manzanas bañadas en caramelo o glaseado rojo? Which do you like better, apples coated with caramel or with red glaze? ➤ El jamón está bañado en glaseado. The ham is coated with a glaze. ▪ The ham is glazed. ➤ Desayuné un café y un donut glaseada. For breakfast I had coffee and a glazed doughnut.
bañarse en la piscina to go for a swim
banco de datos ▪ (la) base de datos data bank ▪ data base
banco de fomento development bank
banco de niebla fog bank
banco de peces school of fish
banco de pruebas quality control laboratory ▪ testing laboratory ▪ beta test laboratory
banda de frecuencia ▪ faja de frecuencia wave band
banda de ladrones band of thieves ▪ gang of thieves
banda de tierra strip of land
banda del espectro político ▪ franja del espectro político band of the political spectrum ➤ El presidente y el primer ministro ocupan la misma banda del espectro político. ▪ El presidente y el primer ministro ocupan la misma franja del espectro político. The president and the prime minister occupy the same band of the political spectrum.
banda sonora sound track
banda terrorista terrorist group
bandada de pájaros flock of birds
bandeja de galletas ▪ horneada de galletas ▪ hornada de galletas batch of cookies
baño de sangre blood bath
baño María ▪ baño de María double boiler ▪ bain marie
baraja de cartas deck of cards
baraja (de cartas) española Spanish-style deck of cards
baraja de cartas (para jugar al póker) deck of cards (suitable for poker)
baraja de naipes española *(exclusivamente en España)* deck of cards
baraja de naipes francés *(usada en Francia y Estados Unidos)* deck of cards
barajar algo en el aire *(Arg., Chi., Uru.)* to see the point of something
barajar diversos escenarios ▪ barajar diversos posibilidades ▪ barajar varios escenarios ▪ explorar varias opciones to consider various scenarios ▪ to consider a number of scenarios ▪ to explore various scenarios ▪ to explore a number of scenarios ▪ to weigh various scenarios ➤ Los analistas barajan diversos escenarios. Analysts consider various scenarios. ▪ Analysts are considering various scenarios.
barajar la posibilidad to consider the possibility
barajar una pretensión de to like to think of oneself as
barajarse sobre to be considered regarding ➤ La única hipótesis que se baraja sobre las razones que pudieron impulsarlos a cometer el crimen... The only hypothesis being considered regarding the reasons that could have driven them to commit the crime...
barba cerrada thick beard
barba de dos días two days' (growth of) beard
una **barbaridad de** an awful lot of ➤ Te has comido una barbaridad de helado. You've eaten an awful lot of ice cream.
barbitúrico de acción rápida fast-acting barbiturate
barco pesquero fishing boat
barra de cereal granola bar
barra de desplazamiento scroll bar
barra de pan loaf of bread
barra del coche steering wheel locking bar
barra espaciadora *(en un teclado)* space bar
barra libre open bar ▪ on the house
barra para adelante forward slash
barra para atrás back slash
barraca de feria booth (at a fair) ▪ fair booth
las **barras y estrellas** *(bandera estadounidense)* the stars and stripes
barrer a alguien en las urnas to ravage someone at the polls ▪ to trounce someone in the polls
barrer con algo to finish off something ▪ to finish something off ▪ to make short work of something
barrer hacia dentro ▪ barrer para adentro ▪ barrer para casa ▪ barrer para sí mismo to look out for number one ▪ to put oneself first
barrer la mente a alguien to brainwash someone ➤ Le han barrido la mente. *(a él)* He's been brainwashed. ▪ They brainwashed him. ▪ *(a ella)* She's been brainwashed. ▪ They brainwashed her.
barrer para adentro ▪ barrer para dentro to look out for number one ▪ to put oneself first
barrer para casa ▪ barrer para sí mismo ▪ barrer hacia dentro ▪ barrer para adentro to look out for number one ▪ to put oneself first ▪ to head home ▪ to head for home
barrer para sí mismo ▪ barrer hacia dentro ▪ barrer para adentro ▪ barrer para casa to look out for number one ▪ to put oneself first
barrera del sonido sound barrier
barrera infranqueable impenetrable barrier
barrica de roble de vino oak wine cask ▪ oak wine barrel
Barridos por la marea *(título de película) Swept Away*
el **barril de petróleo** barrel of oil ▪ drum of oil
el **barril de pólvora** keg of powder ▪ powder keg
ser un **barril de pólvora** ▪ ser una caja de bombas ▪ ser una bomba a punto de estallar to be an extremely dangerous person ▪ to be (like) a bomb about to go off
el **barril de ron** barrel of rum
ser un **barril sin fondo** ▪ ser un pozo sin fondo to be a bottomless pit ▪ to have an insatiable appetite
barrio bien well-to-do neighborhood ▪ upper-class neighborhood
barrio chino Chinatown
barrio cómodo (para vivir) ▪ vecindario cómodo (para vivir) convenient neighborhood ➤ Este es un barrio muy cómodo (para vivir). This is a very convenient neighborhood.
barrio peligroso ▪ mal barrio dangerous neighborhood ▪ bad neighborhood
barruntar algo to sense something ▪ to suspect something ▪ to have a foreboding of something
barruntar que... to have a feeling that... ▪ to suspect that... ▪ to sense that... ▪ to have a feeling that...
bártulos: recoger los ~ to gather up one's things
estar **basado en** ▪ estar fundamentado en ▪ tener su base en ▪ tener su fundamento en to be based on
estar **basado en hechos reales** to be based on fact ▪ to be based on actual events ▪ to be based on a true story
basado en lo que he leído based on what I've read
basado en lo que he visto based on what I've seen
basado en lo que he vivido ▪ basado en mi experiencia based on my experience
basado en mi experiencia ▪ basado en lo que he vivido based on my experience
estar **basado en una historia verdadera** ▪ estar basado en una historia real ▪ estar basado en una historia verídica to be based on a true story
basándose en ▪ en base a ▪ con base a based on ▪ on the basis of ➤ Que los medios de comunicación apunten a un candidato como vencedor en un estado basándose en las encuestas a pie de urna es absurdo. ▪ Que los medios de comunicación apunten a un candidato como vencedor en base a las encuestas a pie de urna es absurdo. ▪ Que los medios de comunicación apunten a un candidato como vencedor en un estado con base a las encuestas a pie de urna es absurdo. For the media to call a state for a candidate based on exit polls is asinine. ▪ For the media to call a state for a candidate on the basis of exit polls is asinine.

báscula de precisión ▪ balanza de precisión precision scale ▪ finely calibrated scale

báscula precisa ▪ báscula exacta ▪ balanza precisa ▪ balanza exacta accurate scale

la **base con protección** surge protector ➤ Necesito una base con protección con seis tomas y toma de tierra. I need a surge protector with six outlets and a ground.

la **base de datos** ▪ banco de datos data base ▪ data bank

la **base de galleta integral** graham cracker crust

la **base de la comparación** basis for comparison

la **base factible** factual basis

la **base imponible** tax base

¡**basta!** stop it!

¡**basta de...!** ▪ ¡para de...! ▪ ¡deja de...! enough of...! ▪ that's enough... ▪ stop...!

basta de (hacer) tonterías that's enough nonsense ▪ cut out the nonsense ▪ cool it!

¡**basta de hacerte el interesante!** 1. basta de intentar ser el centro de atención stop trying to be the center of attention! 2. stop trying to be so mysterious!

¡**basta de tonterías!** that's enough nonsense! ▪ cut out the nonsense! ▪ cool it!

basta decir que... suffice it to say that...

basta con simply ▪ just ▪ all you have to do is ➤ Basta con enchufar el cable adaptador al mechero del vehículo. Simply plug the adapter cable into the car's cigaret lighter. ▪ Just plug the adapter cable into the car's cigaret lighter. ▪ All you have to do is plug the adapter cable into the car's cigaret lighter.

¡**basta enchufarlo!** ▪ ¡sólo tienes que enchufarlo! just plug it in! ▪ all you have to do is plug it in!

basta y sobra con all you have to do is ▪ all one has to do is ➤ Basta y sobra con calentar mucho el aceite para que la carne quede en su punto. All you have to do is get the oil really hot for the meat to turn out perfect.

¡**basta ya!** enough!

bastante a menudo quite often ▪ very often

ser **bastante agradable** to be really nice

ser **bastante grande para que quepa** to be plenty big for it to fit

bastante hemos hablado (ya) ▪ todo está hablado we've talked enough ▪ we've covered the subject ▪ everything's been said

ser **bastante leído** to be (very) well read

ser **bastante simpático(-a)** to be very likeable

bastantes veces 1. numerosas veces quite a few times 2. en varias ocasiones on a number of occasions ▪ on quite a few occasions

bastar para que... to be enough to ▪ to manage to ➤ No bastó para que dejaran de creerlo. It wasn't enough to make them stop believing it. ▪ It wasn't enough to convince them.

bastarse y sobrarse para to be more than capable of ▪ to be perfectly capable of ➤ La estudiante se sabe la asignatura tan bien que se basta y se sobra para dar ella la clase. The student knows the subject so well that she is perfectably capable of teaching the class herself.

ser un **bastión de** ▪ ser un reducto de to be a bastion of ▪ to be a stronghold of ➤ Durante la Guerra Civil Americana, la parte este de Tennessee fue un bastión de sentimiento unionista dentro de la Confederación. ▪ Durante la Guerra Civil Americana, la parte este de Tennessee fue un reducto de sentimiento unionista dentro de la Confederación. During the U.S. Civil War, East Tennessee was a bastion of Unionist sentiment within the Confederacy. ▪ During the U.S. Civil War, East Tennessee was a stronghold of Unionist sentiment within the Confederacy.

basura radioactiva ▪ detrito radioactivo radioactive waste

bata guateada padded robe with a lining

ser una **batalla abierta** to be an ongoing battle ➤ La relación entre José y María es una batalla abierta. The relationship between José and María is an ongoing battle.

batalla campal: estallar una ~ to erupt into a pitched battle ▪ to break (out) into a pitched battle

la **batalla está en su punto álgido** the battle is raging

batalla de Inglaterra *(Segunda Guerra Mundial)* the Battle of Britain

ser una **batalla perdida (antes de empezar)** ▪ ser una causa perdida to be a lost cause

batalla por battle for ➤ *(noticia)* La batalla por la Casa Blanca se libra mañana en el Tribunal Supremo de Florida. The battle for the White House ends tomorrow in the Florida Supreme Court.

la **batalla seguía en su punto álgido** the battle raged on

batería de preguntas barrage of questions

batería de pruebas battery of tests

batería de pruebas a algo: hacer ~ to perform a battery of tests on something ▪ to do a battery of tests on something

batería de tests psicológicos: hacerle a alguien una ~ to give someone a battery of psychological tests

batería de tests psicológicos: hacerse una ~ to undergo a battery of psychological tests ▪ to take a series of psychological tests

batería de tests psicotécnicos: hacerle a alguien una ~ to give someone a battery of psychometric tests

batería de tests psicotécnicos: hacerse una ~ to undergo a battery of psychometric tests ▪ to take a series of psychometric tests

la **batería está descargada** ▪ se ha quedado sin batería ▪ la batería ha muerto the battery is dead ▪ the battery has lost its charge

batería superconductora *(batería construida con materiales superconductores)* superconducting battery ➤ Las baterías superconductoras almacenan la electricidad a muy bajas temperaturas. Superconducting batteries store electricity at extremely low temperatures.

batida de banderas flag waving

batida de la policía ▪ batida policial police raid ▪ raid by the police

batida de llamadas ▪ redada de llamadas search of telephone records

batida policial ▪ batida de la policía police raid ▪ raid by the police

batir algo con un batidor ▪ batir algo con una batidora eléctrica to beat something with a mixer ▪ to beat something with an electric mixer ➤ Batir las claras a punto de nieve. Beat the egg whites until the peaks are stiff.

batir banderas to wave flags

batir el campo ▪ peinar el campo ▪ mirar el campo palmo a palmo to comb the area

batir el vuelo to take flight ▪ to fly away ▪ to fly off

batir la mantequilla to whip the butter ▪ to cream the butter

batir la zona to search the area

batir las alas ▪ aletear to beat their wings ▪ to flap their wings ➤ Leonardo da Vinci se dio cuenta de que, excepto durante el despegue, las aves baten las alas para propulsarse, no para mantenerse en el aire. ▪ Leonardo da Vinci se dio cuenta de que, excepto durante el despegue, las aves aletean para propulsarse, no para mantenerse en el aire. Leonardo da Vinci realized that, except during take-off, birds beat their wings for propulsion, not lift. ▪ Leonardo da Vinci realized that, except during take-off, birds flap their wings for propulsion, not lift.

batir palmas ▪ dar unas palmadas to clap one's hands

batir un huevo to beat an egg

batir un récord to break a record

batir una bandera to wave a flag

batir una marca to break a record

batirse el cobre por algo ▪ batirse en duelo por algo ▪ ir a por todas por algo to go all out for something

batirse en duelo por algo ▪ batirse en cobre por algo ▪ ir a por todas por algo to go all out for something

batirse en retirada to beat a (hasty) retreat

bautismo de fuego baptism by fire ▪ baptism of fire

baza contra algo ▪ argumento contra algo argument against something

baza de órdago *(Valle-Inclán)* spectacular trick

bebé a bordo baby on board

el **bebé de probeta** test-tube baby

el **bebé está a punto de nacer** ▪ el bebé va a nacer ahora ▪ ya llega el bebé the baby is due (now) ▪ the baby is due any time now

el **bebé nacerá** ■ (la madre) sale de cuentas the baby is due ➤ (La madre) sale de cuentas la semana que viene. The baby is due next week. ➤ El bebé nacerá en noviembre. ■ (La madre) sale de cuentas en noviembre. The baby is due in November.

beber a la salud de alguien to drink to someone's health

beber a morro 1. beber de la botella to drink from the bottle ■ to drink out of the bottle **2.** beber de la lata to drink from the can ■ to drink out of the can

beber agua to drink water ➤ Voy a beber agua. I'm going to get a drink of water.

beber como una esponja to drink like a fish

beber en buenas fuentes ■ tener noticias fiables ■ tener noticias certeras to have it on good authority

beber en los grandes maestros to learn from the great masters

beber los vientos por alguien ■ suspirar por alguien to pine for someone ■ to long for someone ■ to feel lonesome for someone

beberse el libro ■ leerse el libro muy rápido to read a book very quickly ■ *(coloquial)* to read a book really fast ➤ Este libro se bebe. You can read this book very quickly. ➤ Ella se bebió el libro. She read the book really fast.

bebida estimulante stimulating drink

bebida isotónica ■ bebida energética energy drink

bebidas fuertes hard drinks ■ drinks made with liquor

bel canto bel canto

bella casa ■ casa hermosa ■ casa preciosa beautiful house

bellas artes fine arts

la **belleza está en los ojos del que mira** beauty is in the eyes of the beholder

bello hogar beautiful home

bemol mayor flat major ➤ Trio para piano en Mi bemol mayor de Schubert. Schubert's piano trio in E flat major.

ser una **bendición (de Dios)** ■ ser un regalo de Dios to be a blessing ■ to be a Godsend

ser una **bendición diluida** to be a mixed blessing

¡**bendito sea Dios!** thank goodness!

beneficiario de una poliza de seguros, fondo, testamento, etc. beneficiary of an insurance policy, trust, will, etc.

beneficiarse con ■ beneficiarse de ■ sacar provecho de to benefit from

beneficiarse de ■ beneficiarse con ■ sacar provecho de ■ *(coloquial)* sacar tajada de to benefit from ■ to profit from

beneficiársela a ella *(argot, subido de tono)* to take advantage of her ■ to put it to her ■ to have sex with her

ser el **benjamín de la familia** ■ ser el benjamín de la casa to be the baby of the family ■ to be the youngest in the family

ser la **benjamina de la familia** ■ ser la benjamina de la casa to be the baby of the family ■ to be the youngest in the family

besar el suelo ■ caerse de bruces to fall flat on one's face

besar el suelo por donde pisa alguien to worship the ground someone walks on

besar la jarra (hasta verle el culo) to bottoms up a mug

beso a usted la mano *(arcaico y muy cortés)* good-bye

beso de Judas kiss of Judas ■ (act of) betrayal

beso de tornillo ■ beso francés French kiss

beso francés ■ beso de tornillo French kiss

beso fuerte big kiss ➤ Dame un beso fuerte. Give me a big kiss.

best séller best seller ■ that sells the best

bestia de carga ■ bestia de tiro beast of burden

bestia de tiro ■ bestia de carga beast of burden

bestia parda 1. *(tigre)* tiger **2.** *(puma)* ocelot **3.** *(leopardo)* gato pardo leopard

bestia porcina *(jabalí)* wild boar

bestialidad de comida ■ toneladas de comida ■ burrada de comida tons of food

bestialidad de ejército ■ burrada de ejército huge army ■ *(argot)* humongous army

ser la **Biblia en verso** ■ ser muy completo to be very thorough ■ to be very complete ➤ Es la Biblia en verso. It's very thorough.

biblioteca virtual *(informática)* ■ biblioteca on-line on-line library ■ virtual library

bicho malo bad guy

bicho malo nunca muere mean people never die

bicho raro strange bird ■ odd duck

bicho viviente ■ (el) alma viviente living soul ➤ Cuando llegamos no había bicho viviente en el pueblo. There was not a living soul in the town when we got there.

estar **bien abrigado con** ■ estar arrebujado en to be all bundled up in

estar **bien adentrado en** to be well into ➤ Está bien adentrado en los sesenta. He's well into his sixties.

estar **bien ajustado** ■ estar bien regulado ■ estar bien en su sitio ■ estar bien en su posición **1.** to be properly adjusted ■ to be correctly adjusted ■ to be in proper adjustment **2.** *(ropa)* estar ajustado ■ estar ceñido to be tight-fitting ■ to be body tight

estar **bien avenidos** *(pareja)* ■ ser una pareja bien avenida to be very compatible ■ to be a very compatible couple

bien bien for sure ➤ No me acuerdo bien bien. I don't remember for sure.

bien caliente *(comida)* nice and hot ■ good and hot

estar **bien centrado** ■ estar bien equilibrado ■ estar bien adaptado to be well rounded ■ to be well adjusted ■ to be well balanced

bien cierto es ■ bien es cierto to be sure

estar **bien con alguien** ■ estar a bien con alguien ■ estar a buenas con alguien to get along well with someone ■ to be on good terms with someone

bien conformado(-a) long-suffering

¡**bien conservado!** like new!

estar **bien considerado** ■ estar bien visto ■ estar bien recibido to be well seen ■ to be well regarded ■ to be approved of

bien creí que... I thought for sure that... ■ I thought surely that...

estar **bien de salud** to be in good health

bien delimitado clear cut

bien delimitados los bordes clear cut

bien, ¿dónde estaba? ■ bueno, ¿por dónde iba? now, where was I?

estar **bien dotado** to be well endowed

estar **(bien) educado(-a)** to be well behaved

estar **bien emparentado(-a)** to be well bred

bien empleado: estarle ~ ■ estarle bien merecido to have it coming ■ to be well deserved ■ to get what one deserves ■ to serve someone right

bien empleado le está *(a él)* that'll teach him ■ it serves him right *(a ella)* that'll teach her ■ it serves her right

estar **bien en su posición** ■ estar bien en su sitio ■ estar bien ajustado ■ estar bien regulado to be properly adjusted ■ to be correctly adjusted ■ to be in proper adjustment

estar **bien encaminado** ■ ir por buen camino to be on the right track

bien entrado en el próximo año ■ bien entrado en el año que viene well into next year

bien equilibrado(-a) ■ bien centrado well balanced ■ well rounded ■ well adjusted

bien es cierto ■ bien cierto es to be sure

bien escaso scarce commodity

bien frío ice cold ■ good and cold

bien fundado well founded

bien hablado well spoken

bien hecho well done ➤ Me gustaría el filete bien hecho. I'd like the steak well done.

¡**bien hecho!** well done! ■ right on!

ser **bien llevado a la práctica** to come out well ■ to come off well ➤ El plan fue bien llevado a la práctica. The plan came out well. ■ The plan came off well.

bien merecido: estarle ~ ■ estarle bien empleado to have it coming ■ to be well deserved ■ to get what one's deserves

bien merecido lo tienes it serves you right

ser **bien nacido(-a)** ■ ser de buen nacer to be well born

estar **bien parecido(-a)** ■ ser bien parecido to be good looking

¡**bien pensado!** good thinking!

estar **bien pensado** to be well thought of

ser **bien parecido(-a)** ▪ ser bien plantado(-a) ▪ ser guapo(-a) ▪ estar bien plantado ▪ tener buena planta to be good looking ▪ *(hombre)* to be handsome ▪ *(mujer)* to be beautiful

ser **bien plantado(-a)** ▪ ser bien parecido(-a) ▪ ser guapo(-a) to be good looking ▪ *(hombre)* to be handsome ▪ *(mujer)* to be beautiful

bien podías haberme llamado ▪ ya me podías haber llamado you could very well have called me

bien podría ser así it could well be ▪ it could well be that way

bien podría ser que... it could well be that...

bien podría haber sido así it could well have been ▪ it could well have been that way

bien podría haber sido que... it could well have been that...

bien por... o bien por either by... or by ▪ either from... or from ➤ La víctima podría haber muerto bien por los golpes sufridos o bien por parada cardiorespiratoria. The victim could have died either from the blows suffered or from heart failure. ➤ Bien por el esfuerzo diplomático o bien por la fuerza ▪ O por el esfuerzo diplomático o por la fuerza Either by diplomacy or by force

bien preciado prized possession ➤ El gallo era el bien más preciado del coronel. The rooster was the colonel's most prized possession.

bien pronto pretty soon ▪ very soon ▪ quite soon

bien pudiera ser que... it could well be that...

bien pudo ser que... it could well have been that...

bien pudo ser así it could well have been ▪ it could well have been like that

bien pudo ser que... it could well have been that...

bien que mal 1. good or bad 2. para bien o para mal for good or ill

ser **bien recibido por alguien** to be well received by someone

estar **bien regulado** ▪ estar bien ajustado to be properly adjusted ▪ to be correctly adjusted

bien respetado(-a) de well respected by

bien saber que... ▪ saber perfectamente que... to know perfectly well that... ▪ to know full well that... ▪ to know very well that... ➤ *(editorial)* Sabe perfectamente que perdería una elección abierta, con voto secreto. ▪ Bien sabe que perdería una elección abierta, con voto secreto. He knows perfectly well that he would lose an open election by secret ballot.

ser **bien sabido que...** to be common knowledge that...

bien se dice que... ▪ no se dice por nada que... it's for good reason that they say (that)... ▪ not for nothing do they say (that)...

estar **bien seguro(-a)** to be certain ▪ to be positive ▪ to be sure ➤ Estoy bien seguro. I'm positive. ▪ I'm certain (of it). ▪ I'm sure of it.

bien seguro se halla *(Valle-Inclán)* he's safe

estar **bien templado** to be well tuned ➤ La guitarra está bien templada. The guitar is well tuned.

estar **bien tensado** to be taut (Historias del Kronen *de José Ángel Mañas)* ➤ Manolo me pasa un talego con el que me hago un canutillo bien tensado y me meto la primera raya (de coca). Manolo hands me a big bill and with that I make myself a nice, taut little tube and snort the first line (of cocaine).

bien vale el dinero it's well worth the money

bien vale la pena it's well worth the trouble

ser **bien venido, como el agua de mayo** to be a Godsend

estar **bien visto** ▪ estar bien considerado to be well considered ▪ to be approved of

el **bien y el mal** good and evil

bien yo querría, pero I'd really like to, but

bienaventurados sean los mansos, porque ellos heredarán la Tierra blessed are the meek, for they shall inherit the Earth

los **bienes de capital** capital goods

los **bienes de consumo** consumer goods

los **bienes de equipo** company property

bienes duraderos durable goods ➤ *(noticia)* El departamento de comercio da a conocer las cifras de bienes duraderos de diciembre The Department of Commerce releases the figures on durable goods for December

los **bienes gananciales** property jointly owned by a married couple

los **bienes inmuebles** *(Esp.)* ▪ propiedad inmobiliaria real estate

los **bienes raíces** *(Méx.)* real estate

los **bienes terrenales** worldly goods ▪ earthly possessions

bienes valiosos valuables

bienvenida calurosa ▪ bienvenida cálida ▪ acogida calurosa ▪ acogida cálida warm welcome

bienvenido(-a) al hogar ▪ bienvenido(-a) a casa welcome home

bienvenido(-a) de nuevo ▪ bienvenido(-a) de nuevo a casa welcome back

bienvenidos a los Estados Unidos welcome to the United States

los **bigotes de un gato** whiskers of a cat

los **bigotes de un langostino** antennae of a crayfish ▪ feelers of a crayfish

ser un **billete a ninguna parte** ▪ no llevar a alguien a ninguna parte to be a ticket to nowhere ➤ Su actitud no le lleva a ninguna parte. ▪ Su actitud es un billete a ninguna parte. His attitude is a ticket to nowhere.

el **billete de avión** ▪ billete de vuelo ▪ (el) pasaje de avión airplane ticket ▪ plane ticket

el **billete de ida y vuelta** round-trip ticket

el **billete de juguete** ▪ billete de pega ▪ billete de mentirilla bogus bill ▪ counterfeit bill

el **billete de mentira** ▪ billete de juguete ▪ billete de pega play money

el **billete de pega** ▪ billete de juguete ▪ billete de mentira play money

el **billete no reembolsable** non-refundable ticket

(billete) sencillo one-way ticket

el **billete trucho** *(Arg.)* ▪ billete falso counterfeit bill ▪ bogus bill

el **billete verde** *(Esp., arcaico)* ▪ mil pesetas a thousand pesetas ▪ thousand-peseta bill

un **billón de años** ▪ un millón de millones de años a million million years

birlarle algo a alguien ▪ raparle algo a alguien ▪ sustraerle algo a alguien to swipe something from someone

birlarle un punto *(deportes)* to steal a point

biselar el borde to bevel the edge ➤ No quería que biselara el borde de la mesa, lo quería plano. I didn't want you to bevel the edge of the table. I wanted it flat.

bizcocho borracho *(Esp.)* cake soaked in alcohol

blanca flor de chimenea floozy

blanca y en botella, (leche): es ~ there's no question about it ▪ there's no contest ▪ hands down ➤ ¿Quién es el terrorista más buscado del mundo?-¡Quién va a ser! Blanca y en botella, (leche): Bin Laden! Who's the most wanted terrorist in the world?-Who do you think? There's no question about it: Bin Laden. ▪ Who's the most wanted terrorist in the world?-Who do you think? There's no question about it: Bin Laden, hands down.

estar **blanco como el papel** ▪ estar blanco como la cera ▪ estar blanco como la pared to be white as a sheet

estar **blanco como la cera** ▪ estar blanco como el papel to be white as a sheet ➤ Al oír la noticia mi marido se puso blanco como la cera. When my husband heard the news, he turned white as a sheet.

ser el **blanco de ataques terroristas** to be the target of terrorist attacks

ser el **blanco de la puya** to be the butt of the joke

ser el **blanco de todas las miradas** to take all eyes

ser el **blanco de sus críticos** to be the butt of one's critics ▪ to be fodder for one's critics

blandir un puñal to brandish a dagger

blandir una espada ▪ blandir un sable to brandish a sword

blandir una pistola to brandish a pistol

ser **blando(-a) de corazón** ▪ tener un corazón blando to be tender hearted ▪ to be soft hearted

ser **blando(-a) de voz** to be soft spoken

blando para el crimen: ser (muy) ~ to be soft on crime

blanquear dinero ▪ lavar dinero to launder money

blanqueo de dinero ▪ lavado de dinero money laundering

blindarse ante algo to move to protect oneself from something ▪ to brace oneself for something ➤ *(titular)* Los bancos se blindan ante la crisis. The banks move to protect themselves from the crisis. ▪ The banks brace themselves for the crisis.

blindarse por algo to move to protect oneself from something ▪ to brace oneself for

el **bloc de papel** pad of paper

el **bloque de apartamentos** ▪ edificio de apartamentos apartment building

el **bloque de electores** ▪ bloque electoral block of voters ▪ voting block

el **bloque de pisos** apartment building

bloquear a alguien 1. to block someone 2. to block someone in

bloquear el tráfico to block traffic

bobina de inducción induction coil ▪ inductor

boca a boca: resuscitatión ~ ▪ reanimación boca a boca mouth-to-mouth resuscitation

boca abajo: acostarse ~ ▪ tumbarse boca abajo to lie on one's stomach ▪ to lie face down ▪ to lie prone

boca abajo: yacer ~ to lie face down ▪ to lie prone

boca arriba: acostarse ~ ▪ tumbarse boca arriba to lie on one's back ▪ to lie face up ▪ to lie supine

boca de escorpión evil tongue

ser un **boca de lobo** 1. to be pitch black dark 2. to be a spooky place 3. to be a dangerous situation

boca del lobo: meterse en la ~ to expose oneself to grave danger

boca de metro subway entrance ▪ metro entrance

boca de riego (outdoor) water spigot

boca del estómago pit of one's stomach ➤ El médico le dijo que el ardor en la boca del estómago era por una úlcera. The doctor told him the burning (sensation) in the pit of the stomach was from an ulcer. ➤ Cuando escuché la noticia, sentí un dolor agudo en la boca del estómago. When I heard the news, I had a sick feeling in the pit of my stomach.

estar la **boca que arde** *(de comer pimientos picantes)* to be on fire ▪ to be burning ➤ Mi boca está que arde. My mouth is on fire. ▪ My mouth is burning

bocadillo de una viñeta (comic strip) balloon

bocado de Adán ▪ (la) nuez de Adán Adam's apple

bocado del león lion's share

ser un **bocazas** ▪ ser un boceras to be a big mouth

bochornoso: ser un día ~ ▪ ser un día caluroso y húmedo to be a muggy day ▪ to be muggy ▪ to be a hot and humid day ▪ to be hot and humid

bochornoso: ser un tema ~ 1. ser un tema vergonzoso to be an embarrassing subject 2. ser un tema pesado to be a boring subject

boda de penalty shotgun wedding

boda saca boda one wedding leads to another

bodas de diamante: celebrar las ~ ▪ celebrar el sexagésimo aniversario to celebrate one's seventy-fifth anniversary ▪ to observe one's seventy-fifth anniversary

bodas de oro: celebrar las ~ ▪ celebrar el quincuagésimo aniversario to celebrate one's fiftieth anniversary ▪ to observe ones' fiftieth anniversary

bodas de plata: celebrar las ~ to celebrate one's twenty-fifth wedding anniversary ▪ to observe one's twenty-fifth anniversary

los **Boinas Verdes** the Green Berets

ser una **bola de billar** to be bald like Yul Brenner ▪ *(jerga)* to be a chrome dome

bola de helado scoop of ice cream

bola de goma de mascar wad of chewing gum

bola de masa ball of dough ▪ lump of dough ▪ wad of dough

bola negra: estar detrás de la ~ to be behind the eightball ▪ to be in a tough spot ▪ to be in a difficult predicament

bolas de naftalina ▪ bolitas de naftalina ▪ naftalina moth balls

bolsa con asas bag with handles

bolsa de aire ▪ vacío de aire ▪ (el) bache air pocket

bolsa de resistencia pocket of resistance

bolsa de trabajo job market

la **bolsa o la vida** your pocketbook or your life

bolsillo de adelante ▪ bolsillo delantero front pocket

bolsillo de atrás ▪ bolsillo trasero back pocket

bolsillo delantero ▪ bolsillo de adelante front pocket

bolsillo interior inside pocket

bolsillo trasero ▪ bolsillo de atrás back pocket

ser la **bomba** to be riding high ➤ ¡Somos la bomba! We're riding high!

bomba de dirección hidráulica power-steering pump

bomba de relojería ▪ bomba de tiempo time bomb

bomba de tiempo ▪ bomba de relojería time bomb

bomba lapa stick-on bomb

bomba perdida stray bomb

bombear los frenos to pump the brakes

las **bondades del sueño** benefits of sleep

ser **bondadoso con alguien** to be kind to someone

bonito de verdad really pretty

ser un **bonito reto** ▪ ser todo un reto to be an interesting challenge ▪ to be challenging ▪ to be quite a challenge

bono cuyas fluctuaciones dan la tónica del mercado ▪ obligación cuyas fluctuaciones dan la tónica del mercado bellwether bond

boquita de piñon: tener una ~ to have a pretty little mouth

borde biselado beveled edge

el **borde del abismo** edge of the abyss

el **borde delantero del ala** leading edge of the wing

borde mellado ragged edge ▪ nicked edge

bordear en lo ridículo ▪ rayar en lo ridículo ▪ rozar lo ridículo ▪ estar en los umbrales de lo ridículo ▪ frisar en lo ridículo to border on the ridiculous ➤ Eso bordea lo ridículo ▪ Eso raya en lo ridículo. ▪ Eso roza lo ridículo. ▪ Eso está en los umbrales de lo ridículo. That borders on the ridiculous.

bordearse una catástrofe to (just barely) avoid a catastrophe ▪ to skirt a catastrophe ➤ *(titular)* Tres muertos en una refinería en la que se bordeó una gran catástrofe Three dead in a refinery where a catastrophe was just barely avoided

borrar algo del mapa to wipe something off the map ▪ to blow something off the map

borrar la pizarra to erase the (black)board

borrón y cuenta nueva: hacer ~ to wipe the slate clean ▪ to start afresh ▪ to begin a new page

bosques lluviosos rain forests

bota de vino wineskin

botas camperas: llevar puestas ~ to wear cowboy boots ➤ Llevaba puestas botas camperas. He was wearing cowboy boots.

botas de montar: llevar puestas ~ to wear riding boots

el **bote de pintura** ▪ tarro de pintura bucket of paint

el **botín de guerra** the spoils of war

el **botiquín de primeros auxilios** ▪ equipo de primeros auxilios first-aid kit

el **botiquín (de un sitio)** infirmary

el **botiquín para medicamentos** ▪ botiquín de medicamentos medicine cabinet ▪ medicine chest

botón candente: pulsar el ~ to push one's hot button

el **botón de encendido** on-off switch

el **botón de muestra** sample ▪ prototype ▪ illustration

el **botón del cuello (de una camisa)** collar button (of a shirt) ➤ ¿Podrías coserme este bóton del cuello? ▪ ¿Podrías pegarme este bóton del cuello? Would you sew on this collar button for me? ▪ Would you sew this collar button on for me?

brazo a brazo: ir ~ ▪ andar brazo a brazo ▪ pasear brazo a brazo to go arm-in-arm ▪ to walk arm in arm

brazo de gitano *(Esp.)* ▪ brazo gitano Swiss roll ▪ custard-filled pastry

brazo de la justicia es muy largo the arm of justice is (very) long

brazo de mar: estar hecho ~ to be dressed to the nines ▪ to be dressed to kill

ser el **brazo derecho de alguien** to be someone's right-hand man/woman ▪ to be someone's right arm

brecha generacional generation gap

breve plazo brief period ➤ El tribunal dio un breve plazo, catorce días, para que apelen la sentencia. The court provided a brief period, fourteen days, to appeal the decision.

brigada de desactivación de bombas bomb squad
brillar por su ausencia to be conspicuous by one's absence
brincar de alegría ▪ saltar de alegría ▪ dar un salto de alegría to jump for joy
brincar el charco *(coloquial)* ▪ cruzar el charco to fly across the Atlantic Ocean
brindar a la salud de alguien ▪ beber a la salud de alguien to toast someone's health ▪ to drink to someone's health ➤ ¡Brindemos a tu salud! Here's a toast to your health.
brindar por algo to toast something ▪ to drink to something
brindar por alguien ▪ beber por alguien to toast someone ▪ to drink to someone
brindar promesa to hold promise
brindar un aplauso a alguien to applaud someone enthusiastically ▪ to give someone an ovation
brindar un significado especial a algo to lend a special significance to something
brindarle la oportunidad de hacer algo a alguien to give someone the opportunity to do something
brindarse a dar información to volunteer information
brindarse a hacer algo to volunteer to do something ▪ to offer to do something ➤ Ella se brindó a ir conmigo. She volunteered to go with me. ▪ She offered to go with me.
brindis a la salud de alguien toast to someone's health ➤ ¡Un brindis a tu salud! A toast to your health!
brindo por eso I'll drink to that
brisa marina sea breeze
brizna de hierba blade of grass
el **broche de oro** ▪ el broche final finishing touches
el **broche final** ▪ el broche de oro finishing touches
bromas aparte ▪ fuera de broma (all) kidding aside ▪ seriously, though
bromear al respecto to joke about it
bronca formada: tener una ~ to make a fuss ▪ to throw a fit
brotar como los hongos ▪ nacer como los hongos to sprout (up) like mushrooms ▪ to sprout up like weeds
brotar sangre de una herida 1. *(de un accidente)* to bleed profusely from a injury 2. *(de un arma)* to bleed profusely from a wound
el **brote de agua** 1. *(de un manantial)* spring 2. *(de una válvula rota)* surge of water
el **brote de la peste** outbreak of the plague
el **brote ha surgido** the shoot has sprouted ▪ *(pintoresco)* the volunteer has sprouted
los **brotes de soja** beansprouts
brújula ética moral compass
brusca caída sharp drop
bucear en busca de to dive for ➤ Bucearon en busca de perlas y tesoro. They dived for pearls and treasure.
buche de: tomar un ~ to take a mouthful of ➤ Tomé un buche de esa cosa y lo escupí. I took a mouthful of that stuff and spit it (back) out.
buen barrio good neighborhood
buen bocado ▪ buena cantidad de dinero pretty good chunk of dough
buen camino: ir por el ~ to be on the right track
buen confidente: tener un ~ to have a confidante
ser de **buen conformar** ▪ *(más común)* tener buen conformar to be easy (to please) ▪ to be easy to be around
buen cuerpo: tener un ~ to have a good body
un **buen día** ▪ cierto día one day
buen entendimiento con alguien: tener un ~ ▪ llevarse bien con alguien to have a good rapport with someone
buen funcionamiento proper functioning ▪ correct functioning
el **buen hacer** expertise ➤ Los años le han dado serenidad, tablas y buen hacer. The years have given him serenity, experience, and expertise.
buen humor: estar de ~ ▪ tener buen humor to be in a good mood
¡**buen intento!** nice try!
ser un **buen lenitivo para** to be good for alleviating ▪ to be good for curing ➤ Dos aspirinas disueltas en una limonada caliente es un buen lenitivo para los catarros y la bronquitis. Two aspirins dissolved in a hot lemonade is good for alleviating colds and bronchitis.
buen pájaro está hecho he's really sharp
buen palmito: tener un ~ to have a nice little butt ▪ to have a beautiful tail
ser un **buen partido** to be a good catch ➤ (Él) es un buen partido. He's a good catch. ➤ (Ella) es un buen partido. She's a good catch.
buen paso: andar a ~ ▪ andar aprisa to walk fast ▪ to walk briskly ▪ to walk at a good pace
buen pastor good sheperd
el **buen pastor da la vida por sus ovejas** the good shepherd gives his life for his sheep
el **buen patrón hace buen soldado, y el buen soldado hace buen patrón** a good boss makes a good soldier, and a good soldier makes a good boss
un **buen presagio** ▪ una buena señal a good sign
¡**buen provecho!** ▪ ¡que aproveche! bon apetit! ▪ enjoy your dinner!
el **buen salvaje** *(en la filosofía de Rousseau)* the noble savage
buen tiempo 1. good weather 2. *(tiempo cálido)* warm weather
buen tipo good guy
buen tono social: tener un ~ ▪ tener una buena presencia to have a good presence
¡**buen trabajo!** good job!
¡**buen viaje!** bon voyage!
¡**buena alhaja!** ▪ ¡buena pieza! what a piece of work!
buena dosis de suerte: tener una ~ to have a dose of good luck
buena estampa: ser de ~ to be fine looking ▪ to be of excellent bearing
buena estampa: tener ~ to have a good presence ▪ *(literario)* to cut a (good) figure
buena falta me hace I really need it ▪ it would do me good
buena figura: tener una ~ to have a good figure
¡**buena la has hecho!** look what you've done!
buena mano: hacer algo con ~ to be good at doing something ▪ to do something well
ser una **buena moza** 1. es tía buena to be a nice-looking girl 2. es una buena chica to be a nice girl
buena obra charitable deed ▪ *(suele usarse en plural)* good works
¡**buena pieza!** ▪ ¡buena alhaja! piece of work ➤ ¡Buena pieza estás tú hecho! What a piece of work you are!
buena planta: tener ~ to hava a good build ▪ to have a good physique
ser una **buena señal** ▪ ser un buen presagio to be a good sign
buena sociedad ▪ el gran mundo high society
¡**buena suerte!** ▪ ¡que te vaya bonito! good luck!
buena ventura a alguien: leerle la ~ to read someone's palm
buenas manos: tener ~ to have good manual dexterity ▪ to be good with one's hands
¡**buenas noches!** 1. ¡hola! good evening! 2. ¡adiós! good night!
buenas palabras kind words ➤ Gracias por sus buenas palabras. Thank you for your kind words.
buenas tardes good afternoon
¡**está buenísimo(-a)!** ▪ ¡es buenísimo! ▪ ¡está genial! ▪ ¡es genial! ▪ ¡(está) estupendo! ▪ ¡(es) estupendo! 1. that's great! 2. *(comida)* that's delicious ▪ it's delicious 3. está como para parar un tren *(ella)* she's a hottie ▪ *(él)* he's a hottie
ser **bueno para (hacer) algo** ▪ dársele bien algo to be good at (doing) something ➤ No soy bueno para eso. ▪ No se me da muy bien. I'm not very good at it.
bueno, ¿por dónde iba? ▪ bien, ¿dónde estaba? now, where was I?
¡**bueno, regio!** okay, great!
bueno, vale well, okay ▪ okay, then
bueno, vamos con and now for
buenos días *(hasta las 3 p.m.)* good morning
buenos modales ▪ modales buenos good manners
buenos oficios de uno, ofrecer a alguien los to offer someone one's good offices

buenos oficios de uno: recompensar a alguien los ~ to reward someone for his good offices

el **buey (de mar)** *(Esp.)* ■ cangrejo crab

buey suelto free agent

el **buey suelto bien se lame** ■ el buey solo bien se lame freedom is great

bufar por algo 1. to fume with anger about something 2. *(gato)* to hiss (at something)

bufete: establecir un ~ to set up a law practice ■ to establish a law practice

bufete privado private (legal) practice

bulliciosa calle bustling street

bullir de actividad to bustle with activity

bullir de gente to be swarming with people ■ to be bustling

bullirle ideas en la cabeza a alguien (for one's) head to buzz with ideas ➤ Al salir de la clase, le bullían mil ideas en la cabeza sobre cómo solucionar el problema. When he left class, his head was buzzing with ideas about how to solve the problem.

bullirle a alguien la sangre ■ hervirle a alguien la sangre to make someone's blood boil

bullirle posibilidades en a cabeza a alguien (for) one's head to buzz with possibilities

el **buque insignia** flagship work ■ magnum opus

burbuja inmobiliaria real estate bubble ➤ *(titular)* La burbuja inmobiliaria amenaza a deshincharse The real estate bubble threatens to burst

burda imitación cheap imitation

burla burlando ■ sin darse cuenta unawares ■ without realizing it

burlar algo to avoid something ■ to mock something

burlar la censura to evade the censor ■ to get around the censor

burlar la justicia to avoid justice ■ to mock justice

burlarse de algo 1. mofarse de algo to make fun of something 2. evitar algo to get out of something

burlarse de su propia sombra ■ no tener miedo de nada 1. to mock one's shadow ■ to fear nothing ■ not to fear anything ■ not to be afraid of anything ■ to be afraid of nothing 2. to take nothing seriously ■ not to take anything seriously

una **burrada de gente** ■ gentío (whole) bunch of people ■ mob of people

burrada de trabajo ton of work

burro de arranque ■ (el) motor de arranque starter motor ■ starter

burro de carga: tratar a los obreros como ~ to treat the workers like slaves

burro de costumbre ■ animal de costumbre creature of habit ➤ El hombre es un burro de costumbre. Man is a creature of habit.

burro de San Vicente, que lleva la carga y no la siente he's wearing a "kick me" sign (and doesn't know it)

burro grande, ande o no ande when in doubt, take the big one ■ when you get to choose, take the biggest (one)

burro mal esquilado, cuatro días igualado you'll snap right back ■ you'll be well in no time

buscad y hallaréis, pedid y se os dará, llamad y se os abrirá seek and ye shall find, ask and it shall be given to you, knock and it shall be opened to you

buscando guayabas ando yo *(L.am., coloquial)* I'm trying to find some

buscar a alguien el bulto to nitpick

buscar a alguien una casa to find someone a house

buscar a lo largo y (a lo) ancho ■ buscar por todas partes to look far and wide ■ to look everywhere ➤ Hemos buscado un mantel de encaje español que le quede bien a esta mesa a lo largo y (a lo) ancho. We've looked far and wide for a Spanish lace tablecloth that would fit this table. ■ We've looked everywhere for a Spanish lace table cloth that would fit this table.

buscar a tientas to feel around for ■ to grope around for ■ to fumble around for

buscar al camarero to look for the waiter

buscar algo contrarreloj to work against the clock to bring something about ➤ La alianza busca contrareloj un gobierno provisional. The alliance works against the clock to bring about a provisional government.

buscar atención pública para algo to seek public exposure for something

buscar camarero to look for a waiter (to hire)

buscar casa to look for a place to live ■ *(buscar un chalet)* to house hunt

buscar camorra to look for trouble ■ to go looking for trouble ➤ No busques camorra. Don't go looking for trouble.

buscar el pelo al huevo to look for grievances ■ to seek grievances

buscar el periódico to go find a newspaper ■ to go out and get a newspaper

buscar el máximo escaparate to reach the widest possible audience ■ to seek the maximum exposure

buscar incansablemente to seek tirelessly

buscar la boca a alguien 1. (to try) to draw someone out ■ (to try) to get someone going 2. to aggravate someone

buscar las cosquillas a alguien ■ buscar las vueltas a alguien ■ buscar la pulgas a alguien to get someone going ■ to rile someone up ■ to get someone riled up ■ to stir things up

buscar las pulgas a alguien ■ buscar las vueltas ■ buscar las cosquillas to get someone going ■ to rile someone up ■ to get someone riled up ■ to stir things up

buscar las vueltas ■ buscar las cosquillas ■ buscar las pulgas a alguien to get someone going ■ to rile someone up ■ to get someone riled up ■ to stir things up

buscar los cinco pies al gato to overanalyze ■ to split hairs

buscar oriente ■ orientarse ■ buscar el norte to get one's bearings ■ to orient oneself

buscar pelea to spoil for a fight ■ to look for a fight ➤ El matón de la escuela buscaba pelea. ■ El matón de la escuela estaba buscando pelea. The school bully was spoiling for a fight.

buscar por todas partes ■ buscar a lo largo y (a lo) ancho to look everywhere ■ to look far and wide ➤ Hemos buscado un mantel de encaje español que le quede bien a esta mesa por todas partes. We've looked everywhere for a Spanish lace tablecloth that would fit this table. ■ We've looked far and wide for a Spanish lace tablecloth that would fit this table.

buscar refugio en to seek refuge in

buscar tiempo para hacer algo ■ intentar encontrar tiempo para hacer algo to try to find time (to do something)

buscar un punto en común to seek common ground

buscar un remedio bajo receta to get a prescription filled ■ to have a prescription filled ➤ Tengo que buscar este remedio (bajo receta). I have to get this prescription filled.

buscar una aguja en un pajar to look for a needle in a haystack ➤ La secuenciación del genoma humano es como buscar agujas en un pajar. Mapping the human genome is like trying to find needles in a haystack.

buscar una palabra en el diccionario to look up a word in the dictionary

buscarle la quinta pata al gato ■ buscarle tres pies al gato to split hairs

buscarle las vueltas a alguien ■ intentar encontrar el punto débil a alguien to look for someone's weak point

buscarle tres pies al gato ■ buscarle la quinta pata al gato ■ buscarle complicaciones a algo to split hairs

buscarse la ruina ■ cavarse su propia tumba ■ echarse la soga al cuello to dig one's own grave

buscarse la vida ■ buscarse los garbanzos ■ buscarse los porotos to earn one's living

buscarse las habichuelas ■ buscarse los garbanzos to bring home the bacon

buscarse los garbanzos ■ buscarse la vida ■ to bring home the bacon

buscarse problemas to look for trouble ■ to go looking for trouble

buscársela to be asking for it ■ to be asking for trouble

¡**búscate la vida!** get a life!

ser un, una **buscavidas** to be a busybody

búsqueda de algo search for something ➤ La búsqueda de los reporteros desaparecidos The search for the missing reporters

C.A.E. ▪ cobra al entregar ▪ cobrar a la entrega C.O.D. ▪ Collect on Delivery

cabalgar a mujeriegas to ride sidesaddle

cabalgar contra viento y marea to struggle against obstacles

La **cabalgata de las Walkyrias** *(composición de Wagner)* The Ride of the Valkyries

caballero andante knight errant

caballero de la triste figura *(Don Quijote)* knight of the woeful countenance

el **caballete de la nariz** bridge of the nose

caballo asustadizo skittish horse

caballo con nervio spirited horse

caballo de batalla bone of contention

caballo de carga work horse

caballo de carreras race horse

caballo de mucho nervio ▪ caballo fogoso spirited horse

caballo de vapor horse power

caballo desbocado runaway horse

caballo fogoso ▪ caballo de mucho nervio ▪ caballo chúcaro ▪ caballo furioso spirited horse

caballo grande, ande o no ande ▪ cuánto más grande mejor the bigger, the better

caballos de vapor horsepower

cabe alcanzar que... it's quite possible that... ▪ it's within the realm of possibility that...

cabe en la mano it fits in your hand ▪ it fits in the hand

cabe esperar it is to be expected ▪ it's to be expected ➤ Cabía esperar que Javier aprobara selectividad. It was (to be) expected that Javier would pass his qualifying exam.

cabe imaginar que it's within the realm of possibility that ➤ Cabe imaginar que una mujer sea presidenta de los Estados Unidos. It's within the realm of possibility that a woman could become president of the United States.

cabe la posibilidad de hacer algo there's a possiblity of doing something ➤ Cabe la posibilidad de ir a Sevilla este fin de semana. There's a possibility of going to Sevilla this weekend.

cabe la posibilidad de que... there's a possiblity that... ▪ there's the possibility that... ➤ Cabe la posibilidad de que vayamos a Sevilla este fin de semana. There's a possibility that we might go to Seville this weekend. ▪ There's a possibility that we'll go to Seville this weekend. ▪ There's a possibility that we're going to Seville this weekend.

cabe mencionar que... it should be mentioned that... ▪ it is worth mentioning that...

cabe pensar que... ▪ cabría pensar que... ▪ uno podría pensar que... ▪ se podría pensar que... one would think that... ▪ you would think that...

cabe precisar ▪ deberíamos fijar we should set... ▪ we should determine... ▪ we should specify... ➤ Cabe precisar la hora del encuentro. We should set the time of the meeting

cabe señalar que... it should be pointed out that... ▪ it should be noted that...

cabecillas de la insurgencia leaders of the insurgency

cabello crespo frizzy hair

cabello de ángel **1.** angel hair pasta **2.** sweet egg strands cooked in syrup

cabello desgreñado disheveled hair

cabello rizado curly hair

caben *x* personas there is room for *x* people ▪ there's room for *x* people

caber de pie **1.** to fit standing up ▪ to fit when turned upright **2.** to have room to stand only ▪ (for) there to be standing room ➤ Cabe de pie. It will fit if we turn it upright. ➤ Cabemos de pie. There is standing room only (for us). ▪ There is room for us if we stand.

caber en ▪ entrar (en) to fit ▪ to get into ▪ to get (an article of clothing) on ➤ No quepo en estas botas. ▪ No entro en estas botas. These boots don't fit (me). ▪ I can't get into these boots. ▪ I can't get these boots on.

caber juntos (for) there to be room for both ➤ *(titular)* Beckham y Figo caben juntos. There's room for (both) Beckham and Figo.

caber la posibilidad de que algo haga algo ▪ caber la posibilidad de hacer algo (for) it to be possible to do something ▪ (for) there to be a possibility of doing something ➤ Los expertos creen que cabe la posibilidad de que las aves migratorias extiendan la gripe aviar. Experts believe that it is possible that migratory birds could spread bird flu. ▪ Experts believe there is a possibility that migratory birds could spread bird flu.

caber la posibilidad de que... it's possible that... ▪ the possibility exists that...

caber por to fit through

caber sentados en to seat ▪ to fit sitting ➤ ¿Cuántos espectadores caben sentados en el teatro? How many people does the theater seat?

caberle el dudoso honor de ser... to have the dubious honor of being...

caberle un pan en la boca ▪ reírse a mandíbula batiente to laugh one's head off

cabeza abajo ▪ al revés ▪ vuelto lo de arriba abajo upside down

cabeza arriba right side up

cabeza de alcornoque pea brain ▪ pea-brained person

cabeza de chorlito: tener una ~ ▪ tener una cabeza hueca ▪ tener la cabeza para llevar los pelos to be an air head

cabeza de familia head of the family

ser el **cabeza de serie** leader of the series ▪ contestants who will not confront each other in the early rounds

ser la **cabeza de turco** ▪ pagar el pato ▪ ser el chivo expiatorio to be the scapegoat

ser la **cabeza del pelotón** to be the head of the pack ▪ to be the leader of the pack

cabeza hueca: tener una ~ ▪ tener una cabeza de chorlito to be an air head

cabeza llena de pájaros: tener la ~ **1.** ser poco realista to have one's head in the clouds **2.** ser poco enfocado to be scatterbrained

ser un, una **cabeza loca** ▪ ser un(-a) bala perdida **1.** to be on the wild side **2.** to be a loose cannon

cabeza nuclear nuclear warhead

cabeza rapada skinhead

cabezear la pelota *(fútbol)* ▪ dar de cabeza la pelota to hit the ball with one's head

cabina de información information booth

cabina de un camión cab of a truck

cabina de votación voting booth

cabina del ascensor ▪ caja del ascensor elevator car

cabina (del avión) *(avión de pasajeros)* flight deck

el **cable (con tensión) pelado** ▪ cable electrificado pelado ▪ cable con corriente pelado live wire

el **cable de batería** battery cable

cable derribado downed line ▪ line down

cable pelado frayed cord ▪ frayed wire ▪ *(cable grueso)* frayed cable
cable pelado: tener un ~ ▪ faltarle un tornillo to have a screw loose ▪ to have a few loose screws ▪ to have a few screws loose
los **cables de alta tensión** high tension (power) lines
los **cables para pasar corriente** ▪ cocodrilos jumper cables ▪ booster cables
cabo de vela rigging (of a sail) ▪ ropes for controlling the sail
cabo primero *(militar)* lance corporal
cabo segundo *(militar)* corporal
cabo suelto 1. *(náutica)* untied rope **2.** *(figurativo)* loose end
cabra que tira al monte, no hay cabrero que la guarde a leopard cannot change its spots
la **cabra (siempre) tira al monte** a leopard cannot change its spots ▪ the leopard cannot change its spots
estar **cabreado(-a) como una mona** to be mad as a wet hen
cabría pensar que... ▪ cabe pensar que... ▪ uno podría pensar que... ▪ se podría pensar que... one would think that... ▪ you would think that...
¡caca de (la) vaca! ▪ ¡bosta! bullshit!
caca de vaca: es ~ 1. *(opinión)* that's (a bunch of) crap ▪ that's bullshit ▪ **2.** *(libro, p.ej.)* it's (a piece of) crap ▪ it's crappy
cacao mental: tener un ~ ▪ estar en un cacao mental to be in a muddle ▪ to be in a fog ▪ not to know whether one is coming or going
cacarear acerca de una cosa 1. fanfarronear sobre algo to crow about something **2.** promocionar algo to tout something
cachar a alguien en el acto *(L.am.)* ▪ pillar a alguien con las manos en la masa to catch someone in the act ▪ to catch someone doing something ▪ to catch someone red-handed
ser un **cacho de pan 1.** ser un pedazo de pan ▪ ser un buenazo ▪ ser un cielo to be easygoing ▪ to be a peach **2.** ser inofensivo to be harmless
ser un **cachondo mental** to be a scream ▪ to be a riot ▪ to be hilarious
caciquear a alguien to boss someone around
cada casa es un caso every case is different
cada casa es un mundo every house is a world
cada cierto tiempo every so often
cada cosa a su tiempo give it some time; don't rush it
cada cosa por su lado ▪ cada cosa va por su lado everything goes in its (own) place
cada cual each person ▪ everyone ▪ each and every person
cada cual tiene sus problemas we all have our problems
cada cual a su aire to each his own
cada cual con su cada cual ▪ cada oveja con su pareja ▪ cada oveja tiene su pareja birds of a feather flock together
cada cual en su sitio ▪ cada cual tiene su sitio everything has its place
cada cual habla de la feria según le va en ella each one calls it the way he sees it ▪ we call it like we see it
cada cual lleva su cruz everyone has a cross to bear
cada cual por su lado: ir ~ ▪ ir cada uno por su lado to go one's separate ways
cada cual se arrima a su cada cual birds of a feather flock together
cada cual tiene lo que se merece you get what you deserve
¿cada cuánto? how often?
¿cada cuánto tiempo? ▪ ¿cada cuánto? ▪ ¿con qué frequencia? how often? ➤ ¿Cada cuánto tiempo pasa al autobús aquí? How often does the bus come by here?
cada día each day ▪ every day
cada día que pasa each day that passes ▪ each passing day
cada día que pasaba each day that passed ▪ each passing day
cada dos every other ▪ every two
cada dos años ▪ un año sí y otro no every other year ▪ every two years ▪ once every two years
cada dos por tres continually ▪ regularly ▪ every time you turn around
cada dos por tres: funcionar mal ~ ▪ funcionar mal alternadamente to malfunction regularly ▪ *(coloquial)* to go out of whack every time you turn around ▪ to be on the blink constantly ➤ Cada dos por tres, funciona mal. It's constantly on the blink.
cada dos por tres: venir ~ ▪ ir a la casa cada dos por tres to come over all the time ▪ to be a regular fixture ▪ to be a regular fixture around here ▪ to come over every time you turn around ➤ ¿Viene mucho a tu casa?-Sí, cada dos por tres Does he come over a lot?-Yeah, all the time. ▪ Does he come over a lot?-Yeah, he's a regular fixture around here. ▪ Does he come over a lot?-Yeah, every time I turn around.
cada equis tiempo at such and such times
cada gallo canta en su gallinero every man is (the) king of his castle
cada hijo al nacer trae un pan debajo del brazo every child brings a blessing
cada hijo de vecino ▪ cualquier hijo de vecino ▪ todo hijo de vecino every Tom, Dick and Harry
cada hijo de vecino: como ~ like everbody else ▪ like everyone else
cada historia: oir ~ to hear unbelievable things
cada hora ▪ a toda hora ▪ continuamente all the time ▪ nonstop
cada idea: tener ~ to have funny ideas ▪ to have strange ideas ➤ ¡Tienes cada idea! ▪ *(literario)* ¡Cada idea tienes! The things you think of!
cada instante ▪ a cada instante ▪ a cada paso ▪ a cada momento continually ▪ repeatedly
cada loco con su tema different strokes for different folks ▪ to each his own
cada maestrillo tiene su librillo everyone has his own way of doing things
cada martes tiene su domingo every cloud has a silver lining
cada mochuelo a su olivo party's over! ▪ time to go! ▪ everyone out!
cada muerte de obispo once in a blue moon
cada oveja con su pareja ▪ cada cual con su cada cual ▪ Dios los cría y ellos se juntan birds of feather flock together
cada palo aguante su vela 1. each person must bear the consequences of his actions **2.** each person must carry his own weight
cada paso es un tropiezo life is a struggle ▪ life is not a bed of roses ▪ life is not a bowl of cherries
cada pocas líneas every few lines
cada poco at every juncture ▪ continually ➤ Se siguien descubriendo nuevas lunas de Júpiter cada poco. They are continually discovering new moons around Jupiter.
cada pocos kilómetros every few kilometers
cada pocos minutos every few minutes
cada pro tiene su contra every pro has its con
cada segundo cuenta every second counts
cada trayecto each way ➤ El viaje lleva dos horas (para) cada trayecto. The trip takes two hours each way.
cada uno each one
cada uno a su antojo to each his own
cada uno a su gusto each according to his (or her) own taste ▪ each according to his (or her) own liking
cada uno a su propia manera each in his (or her) own way
cada uno cuenta la feria según le va en ella everyone has a bias ▪ everyone's opinions are based ▪ each judges based on his own experience
cada uno de ellos each (one) of them ▪ they each
cada uno de nosotros each (one) of us ▪ we each
cada uno es cada uno people are the way they are
cada uno es hijo de su padre y de su madre we are molded by our parents
cada uno es hijo de sus obras we reap what we sow
cada uno es maestro en su oficio 1. each is the master of his own task **2.** each is the master of his own trade
cada uno pasa lo suyo everyone has a cross to bear ▪ each of us has his own cross to bear
cada uno por su lado: ir ~ ▪ ir cada cual por su lado to go ones' separate ways
cada uno sabe dónde le aprieta el zapato ▪ cada uno se rasca donde le pica everyone knows what's best for oneself

cada uno se rasca donde le pica ■ cada uno sabe dónde le aprieta el zapato everyone knows what's best for oneself

cada uno tiene su plaza everyone has a place

cada uno va por su lado 1. each one is doing his own thing 2. each one chooses his own path

cada vez each time ■ every time

cada vez más more and more

cada vez más arriba higher and higher

cada vez más grande: volverse ~ to get bigger and bigger

cada vez más real more and more likely ■ more and more real ➤ *(noticia)* La posibilidad de que Al Qaida esté operando en Irak parece cada vez más real. The possiblity that Al Qaeda is operating in Iraq seems more and more likely.

ser **cada vez mejor** ■ estar cada vez major ■ ser mejor que mejor ■ ponerse cada vez mejor ■ ir a mejor to get better and better

estar **cada vez peor** to be losing it ➤ Cada vez estoy peor. Me dejé las gafas en el tren y el libro en el restaurante. I must be losing it. I left my glasses on the train and my book in the restaurant.

cada vez peor: ponerse ~ to get worse and worse

cada vez que ■ siempre que ■ cuandoquiera que 1. whenever 2. every time ➤ Cada vez que tengo ropa que lavar, vengo a esta lavandería. Whenever I have clothes to wash, I come to this laundromat. ➤ Cada vez que tenga ropa que lavar, vendré a esta lavandería. ■ Siempre que tenga ropa que lavar, vendré a esta lavandería. Whenever I have clothes to wash, I'm coming to this laundromat. ■ Whenever I have clothes to wash, I'll come to this laundromat.

cada vez que abre la boca ■ siempre que abre la boca *(yo)* whenever I open my mouth ■ every time I open my mouth ■ *(él)* whenever he opens his mouth ■ every time he opens his mouth ■ *(ella)* whenever she opens her mouth ■ every time she opens her mouth

cada vez que ocurre algo every time something happens ➤ Cada vez que ella llama... Every time she calls...

cada vez que visita ■ en cada visita *(él)* each time he visits ■ *(ella)* each time she visits ■ on each visit

cada vez que visitaba on each visit ■ *(él)* each time he visited ■ each time he would visit ■ *(ella)* each time she visited ■ each time she would visit

cada vez uno(-a) each (person) do one ■ to alternate ■ to take turns

cada *x* tiempo at such and such times

cada y cuando ■ cada cuando every once in a while

cada y siempre que as soon as

cadena de series of ➤ *(titular)* Cadena de atentados se cobran la vida de quince personas. Series of terrorist attacks claim fifteen lives.

cadena de montaje ■ línea de montaje assembly line

cadena de montañas mountain range

cadena perpetua: condenar a alguien a ~ to sentence someone to life imprisonment

cadena perpetua sin la posibilidad de salir en libertad condicional life imprisonment without parole

caer a la tentación to fall into temptation

caer a plomo en to beat down on ➤ Sufrió el vahído al mediodía cuando el sol caía a plomo en la plaza. He fainted at midday as the sun was beating down on the plaza. ■ He fainted while standing under the intense midday sun.

caer a torrentes ■ venirse el cielo abajo to pour down rain ➤ La lluvia caía a torrentes. The rain was pouring down. ■ It was pouring down rain.

caer a trozos ■ caerse a pedazos to fall to pieces ■ to fall apart ➤ *(Méx.)* El suéter apolillado se cae a trozos. ■ *(Esp.)* El jersey apolillado se cae a trozos. The moth-eaten sweater is falling to pieces. ➤ Durante el terremoto algunos de los edificios se caían a trozos. During the earthquake, some buildings fell to pieces. ■ During the earthquake, some buildings fell apart. ■ During the earthquake, some buildings broke into pieces.

caer aguanieve to rain and snow simultaneously

caer al este ■ caer hacia el este to lie to the east

caer al norte ■ caer hacia el norte to lie to the north

caer al oeste ■ caer hacia el oeste to lie to the west

caer al sur ■ caer hacia el sur to lie to the south

caer al vacío ■ caerse al vacío 1. to fall into a vacuum ➤ Una pluma cae al vacío igual de rápido que una pieda. ■ En el vacío una pluma cae igual de rápido que una piedra. In a vacuum, a feather falls just as fast as a rock.

caer bajo to stoop low ➤ Caíste muy bajo cuando traicionaste lo que te confió tu amigo. You stooped really low when you breached your friend's confidence.

caer bien a alguien 1. to like someone 2. to be liked by someone ➤ Me cae bien. *(él)* I like him. ■ *(ella)* I like her. ➤ Ella cae muy bien a sus compañeros de trabajo. ■ Ella es muy apreciada por sus compañeros. ■ Ella es muy querida por sus compañeros. She is well-liked by her co-workers.

caer chuzos de punta ■ llover a cántaros to rain cats and dogs ➤ Caen chuzos de punta. It's raining cats and dogs.

caer como chinches ■ morir como chinches to drop like flies

caer como las moscas ■ caer como chinches to drop like flies

caer como moscas ■ morir como moscas to drop like flies ■ to die like flies

caer cuatro gotas ■ llover muy poco (for there) to be a trace of rain ■ to sprinkle

caer de bruces to fall forward ■ to fall on one's face

caer de cabeza to fall head first

caer de cajón ■ caer de maduro ■ ser de cajón ■ ser de perogrullo ■ ser como el huevo de Colón to be obvious ■ to be plain as day ■ to go without saying ■ to be what you'd expect

caer de espaldas sobre to fall backwards onto

caer de la burra ■ caer del burro ■ caer en la cuenta (for) something to hit one ■ (for) something to come to one ■ to suddenly occur to one ➤ Y de repente caí de la burra. And all at once it hit me.

caer de lomo to fall on one's back

caer de pie ■ aterrizar de pie to land on one's feet

caer de plano to fall flat

caer de plomo 1. to fall hard 2. *(el sol)* to beat down (hard)

caer de rodillas to fall on one's knees

caer de su asno *(coloquial)* ■ darse cuenta de su error to realize one's mistake

caer del burro ■ caerse del burro ■ caer de la burra ■ caer en la cuenta to realize one's mistake ➤ Y de repente caí del burro. And all at once I realized my mistake.

caer desde lo alto to fall from a height

caer desvanecido(-a) 1. to pass out 2. *(literario, o por causas emocionales)* to fall into a swoon ■ to swoon

caer dormido ■ dormirse ■ quedarse dormido to fall asleep

caer el día (for) the sun to set

caer el sol 1. ponerse el sol (for) the sun to set 2. (for) the sun to beat down

caer el *x* por ciento to drop *x* percent

caer en barrena *(avioneta)* to go into a spin

caer en desgracia 1. to have some bad luck ■ (for) one's luck to fail one ■ *(literario)* (for) bad luck to befall one 2. to be disgraced ■ to fall into disgrace

caer en desolación to come to grief ■ to end in misfortune

caer en el chiste to catch onto the joke ■ to catch on

caer en el lazo ■ picar el anzuelo ■ caer en la trampa ■ caer en la trama to fall into the trap ■ to swallow the bait ■ to take the bait ■ to be hoodwinked

caer en ello ■ comprenderlo to get it ■ to catch on

caer en falta to fall into need ■ to become needy ■ to fall into want

caer en el mal to fall into bad ways

caer en el olvido ■ olvidarse de to fall into oblivion

caer en gracia a alguien ■ caerle en gracia a alguien to make a good impression on someone ■ to impress someone ➤ Tu amiga me cayó en gracia. I thought your friend was really nice. ■ Your friend really impressed me.

caer en la cuenta ■ caer del burro ■ caer de la burra to gradually become aware of something ■ for something to hit you ■ for something to come to you ➤ Y de repente caí en la cuenta. And all at once it hit me.

caer en estos infantilismos to start acting like a child ■ to be childish

caer en gracia ■ caerle en gracia algo a alguien **1.** to hit one as funny ■ to strike one as amusing **2.** to like someone ➤ La protagonista de la comedia me cayó en gracia. The star of the comedy struck me as funny. ➤ Me alegro de haber conocido a tu hermana. Me cayó en gracia. I enjoyed meeting your sister. I liked her.

caer en gracia a alguien to take a liking to someone ➤ Parece que le ha caído en gracia al jefe. Apparently the boss has taken a liking to him.

caer en la cuenta de que... ■ caer del burro to hit one that ■ to come to one that ➤ Y de repente caí en la cuenta de que... And all at once it hit me that...

caer en la trampa ■ caer en el lazo ■ caer en las redes ■ ser engañado to take the bait ■ to swallow the bait ■ to fall for it ■ to fall into the trap

caer en las garras de alguien to fall into someone's clutches

caer en manos de alguien to fall into the clutches of somone

caer en picada *(Arg.)* ■ caer en picado to drop sharply ■ to (take a) nose-dive ■ to plunge ■ to plummet

caer en picado to drop sharply ■ to (take a) nose-dive ■ to plunge ■ to plummet ➤ *(titular)* Cae en picado el número de seminaristas. The number of seminarians drops sharply.

caer en saco roto to fall on deaf ears ■ to go in one ear and out the other

caer en su lugar ■ salir a pedir de boca to fall into place ➤ Primero fija una meta posible, persiguela con toda tu mente, y tu vida caerá en su lugar. First choose a realistic goal, pursue it singlemindedly, and your life will fall into place.

caer en una trama ■ caer en una trampa to fall into a trap ■ to be the victim of a scam

caer en vacío to fall on deaf ears ➤ Mi explicación ha caído en vacío. My explanation fell on deaf ears.

caer enfermo ■ caer malo to become ill

caer extenuado to fall exhausted ➤ Cayó extenuada en el sofa. She fell exhausted on the sofa.

caer hacia el este ■ caer al este to lie to the east

caer hacia el norte ■ caer al norte to lie to the north

caer hacia el oeste ■ caer al oeste to lie to the west

caer hacia el sur ■ caer al sur to lie to the south

caer herido mortalmente to fall mortally wounded

caer la lluvia a torrentes ■ venirse el cielo abajo to pour down rain ➤ La lluvia caía a torrentes. The rain was pouring down. ■ It was pouring down rain.

caer la maldición a algo to be cursed

caer la maldición a alguien to be cursed

caer la tarde for the sun to go down

caer mal ■ caer gordo not to like someone ■ to dislike someone ■ to be disliked by someone ➤ Me cae mal. ■ Me cae gordo. I don't like him. ■ I dislike him ➤ Le caí gordo. He didn't like me. ■ He disliked me. ➤ Él le cae mal (a ella). ■ Él le cae gordo (a ella) ■ Ella le tiene manía (a él). ■ Ella lo tiene entre ceja y ceja. She dislikes him. ■ She doesn't like him. ➤ Le caigo mal. ■ Le caigo gordo. ■ No le caigo bien. ■ Me tiene manía. ■ Me tiene entre ceja y ceja. He dislikes me. ■ He doesn't like me. ➤ Les cae mal a sus compañeros. ■ Les cae gordo a sus compañeros. He's disliked by his peers.

caer malo ■ caer enfermo to become ill

caer patas arriba *(animal)* to fall and turn over ■ to fall (over) on its back ➤ El león cayó patas arriba cuando recibió el disparo. The lión fell and turned over when it was shot. ■ The lion fell (over) on its back when it was shot.

caer por debajo de to fall below ➤ El Dow Jones cayó por debajo de 10.000 por primera vez desde marzo. The Dow Jones fell below 10,000 for the first time since March.

caer por su base ■ no tener fundamento to have no basis ■ to be baseless ■ not to have any basis ■ to be without basis ■ not to have a solid basis ➤ Tu argumento cae por su base. Your argument has no basis. ■ Your argument is baseless.

caer por un terraplén to go over a steep embankment ■ to careen down a steep embankment

caer redondo ■ caerse redondo to collapse in a heap (from intoxication or injury)

caer rendido a los pies de alguien to prostrate oneself at someone's feet

caer rendido de cansancio to collapse from exhaustion

caer rendido de sueño to fall fast asleep

caer siempre de pie, como los gatos ■ tener gran suerte always to land on one's feet ■ always to pull it off

caer sobre alguien todo el peso de la ley ■ caerle a alguien todo el peso de la ley to have the book thrown at one

caer una cosa como llovida del cielo to fall like manna from heaven ■ to be a Godsend ➤ El cheque cayó como llovido del cielo. The check was a Godsend.

caer una helada to have a frost ■ (for) there to be a frost ➤ Cayó una helada anoche. There was a frost last night. ■ We had a frost last night.

caerle a alguien de sorpresa to drop in on someone by surprise

caerle bien a alguien to be liked by someone ■ (for) someone to like you ➤ Me cae bien. *(él)* I like him. ■ *(ella)* I like her.

caerle como una bomba to hit one like a ton of bricks ➤ La noticia le cayó como una bomba. The news hit him like a ton of bricks.

caerle de sorpresa a alguien to drop in on someone by surprise ➤ Quería caerte de sorpresa y felicitarte en tu cumpleaños. I wanted to drop in on you by surprise and wish you a happy birthday.

caerle gordo a alguien ■ tenerle manía a alguien ■ tenerle a alguien entre ceja y ceja ■ caerle mal a alguien ■ no caerle bien a alguien not to like someone ■ to dislike someone ➤ Le caigo gordo (a él). ■ Le caigo mal. ■ No le caigo bien. ■ Me tiene manía. ■ Me tiene entre ceja y ceja. He doesn't like me. ■ He dislikes me.

caerle mal a alguien ■ no caerle bien a alguien ■ caerle gordo a alguien ■ tenerle manía a alguien ■ tenerle a alguien entre ceja y ceja to dislike someone ■ not to like someone ➤ Él le cae mal a ella. ■ Él no le cae bien a ella. ■ Él le cae gordo a ella. ■ Ella le tiene manía a él. ■ Ella le tiene entre ceja y ceja. She doesn't like him. ■ She dislikes him.

caerle simpático a alguien ■ arrimarse a alguien to win someone over ■ to ingratiate oneself with someone

caerse a pedazos a trozos ■ caer a trozos to fall to pieces ■ to fall apart

caerse al agua to fall into the water

caerse al vacío to fall into the void

caerse con todo el equipo ■ fracasar rotundamente to fail completely

caerse de ánimo ■ tener el ánimo caído to be dispirited ■ to be crestfallen

caer(se) de bruces ■ caer(se) de morros ■ caer(se) de narices to fall (flat) on one's face

caerse de bueno to be very kind ➤ Se cae de bueno. *(él)* He's very kind. ■ *(ella)* She's very kind.

caerse de culo *(fuerte)* to fall on one's ass

caerse de espaldas to fall on one's back ■ to fall down backwards (to the ground) ➤ Ella se cayó de espaldas. She fell on her back. ■ She down backwards.

caerse de hinojos ■ postrarse de hinojos to fall on one's knees ■ to go down on one's knees

caerse de la cama to fall out of bed ➤ ¿Te caíste de la cama? Did you fall out of bed?

caerse de maduro: estar para ~ *(jerga)* ■ ir a caerse de maduro to be about to drop (dead) ■ to be on one's last legs ■ *(Arg.)* to be obvious

caerse de morros ■ caerse de narices ■ caerse de bruces to fall (flat) on one's face

caerse de narices ■ caerse de morros ■ caerse de bruces to fall (flat) on one's face

caerse de risa ■ partirse de risa ■ desternillarse de risa ■ descoyuntarse de risa to roll on the floor laughing ■ to laugh one's head off ■ to split one's sides laughing

caerse de su peso to collapse under its own weight

caerse de sueño to be about to drop (off to sleep)

caerse de un guindo 1. caerse del guindo ■ hacerse de nuevas to finally get it (after everyone else has) ■ to finally figure out something ■ to finally realize what's going on **2.** to figure out how to work a problem **3.** avivarse de algo ■ despabilarse to wise up (to something) ■ to get wise (to something) ■ to cotton on ▪ to realize that one is being deceived **4.** *(precedido por "no")* no nacer ayer not be be born yesterday ➤ Oye, que no me he caído de un guindo. ▪ Oye, no nací ayer. Look, I wasn't born yesterday. ➤ Parece que él se ha caído del guindo. It looks like he's finally figured it out.

caerse del susto to reel from fright

caerse el moco ▪ ser infantil ▪ ser simple to be a kid ➤ Si todavía se le cae el moco. He's still a kid.

caerse muerto ▪ morirse to drop dead

caerse muerto de miedo to be scared to death

caerse muerto de risa to die laughing

caerse muerto del susto to be scared nearly to death ▪ (for) the daylights to be scared out of one ➤ Casi me caí muerto del susto. It scared the daylights out of me.

caerse por su (propio) peso 1. to collapse under its own weight **2.** to be obvious

caerse por tierra to fall through ➤ Mis planes se cayeron por tierra. My plans fell through.

caérsele to drop (accidentally) ➤ ¡Ay, se me cayó! Oops, I dropped it!

caérsele algo en el ojo to get something in one's eye ➤ Se me cayó algo en el ojo. I got something in my eye.

caérsele (de la cabeza) to fall off (one's head) ➤ La gorra se le cayó (de la cabeza) His cap fell off. ▪ The cap fell off his head.

caérsele de las manos 1. to drop accidentally **2.** to lose one's audience (by boring them)

caérsele el alma a los pies ▪ desanimarse ▪ abatirse (for) one's heart to sink ➤ Se me cayó el alma en los pies. My heart sank.

caérsele el empaste ▪ desprendérsele el empaste for one's filling to come out ▪ for one's filling to fall out ▪ for one's filling to come loose

caérsele el moco 1. ser inmaduro to be inexperienced ▪ to be green behind the ears **2.** estar resfriado to have a runny nose ▪ to have the sniffles

caérsele el mundo encima (for) the world to fall in on one

caérsele el pelo to get into trouble ▪ *(coloquial)* to get in trouble

caérsele la baba 1. to drool **2.** babear por alguien to drool over someone ➤ Al bebé se le cae mucho la baba porque le están saliendo los dientes. The baby drools a lot because he's teething. ➤ A las chicas se les cae la baba por Ricky Martin. ▪ Las chicas babean por Ricky Martin. The women are drooling over Ricky Martin.

caérsele la baba con alguien ▪ caérsele la baba por alguien to dote on someone ▪ *(coloquial)* to ooh and aah over someone

caerse la cara de vergüenza ▪ caérsele la cara de vergüenza to be overwhelmed with shame ▪ to feel acutely embarrassed ▪ to be acutely embarrassed

caérsele la casa encima de uno 1. (for) the house to fall in on one ▪ for the house to collapse on one **2.** for one's world to collapse ➤ Durante el terremoto, se le cayó la casa encima a la familia. The house collapsed on the family during the earthquake. ➤ Cuando suspendió las oposiciones, se le cayó la casa encima. When he failed the civil service examination, his world collapsed.

caérsele la venda de los ojos to see the light ▪ to wake up and smell the coffee ▪ to have a rude awakening

caérsele los anillos por hacer algo ▪ caérsele los anillos al hacer algo to be beneath someone to do something ➤ A Jimmy Carter, a pesar de ser un ex-presidente, no se le caían los anillos trabajando de carpintero. It was not beneath Jimmy Carter, though a former president, to work as a carpenter.

caérsele los huevos *(argot juvenil)* to have one by the balls ➤ Se nos caen los huevos. They've got us by the balls.

caérsele un diente to lose a tooth ▪ (for) a tooth to fall out

caérsele un empaste to lose a filling ▪ (for) a filling to fall out ▪ (for) a filling to come out ➤ Se le cayó un empaste. *(a él)* He lost a filling. ▪ His filling came out ▪ *(a ella)* She lost a filling. ▪ Her filling came out.

el **café al aire libre** open-air cafe ▪ outdoor café

el **café fuerte** ▪ café muy cargado strong coffee

café largo ▪ parecido al café americano coffee with extra water

café mañanero morning coffee

café muy cargado ▪ café fuerte strong coffee

café solo black coffee

cafetería de émbolo coffee percolator (containing a piston which is pushed down)

estar **cagado de miedo** *(subido de tono)* to be scared shitless ▪ *(alternativa inofensiva)* to be scared out of one's wits

cagando leches: ir ~ *(subido de tono)* ▪ ir a toda hostia to haul ass

cagarla de mala manera *(subido de tono)* ▪ meter la pata to fuck it up big time ▪ to blow it big time

cagarse de miedo *(subido de tono)* ▪ ciscarse de miedo to be scared shitless

cagarse en diez *(subido de tono, eufemismo para "me cago en Dios", obsoleto)* ▪ cagarse en todo (lo que se menea) ▪ cagarse en la mar to get really pissed off ▪ to get super pissed off ▪ to get royally pissed off ➤ ¡Me cago en diez! ▪ ¡Me cago en lo que se menea! ▪ ¡Me cago en la mar! God damn it!

cagarse la pata abajo *(subido de tono)* to shit in one's pants (from fear) ▪ to scare the shit out of one

caída de la tarde nightfall

caída del cabello hair loss

caída del hombre fall of man

caída libre: en ~ in free fall ➤ *(noticia)* ▪ En caída libre, el paracaidista romperá la barrera de sonido. In free fall, the parachutist will break the sound barrier.

caída libre de la renta variable free fall in variable interest rates

estar **caído de hombros** to be stoop-shouldered

caído de las nubes: como ~ ▪ como caído del cielo like manna from heaven

caído del cielo: como ~ ▪ como caído de las nubes **1.** out of the blue **2.** like manna from heaven

estar **caído en combate** to be fallen in combat

ser **caído en combate** to be wounded in combat ▪ to be put out of commission in combat

caiga quien caiga no matter who gets hurt ▪ let the chips fall where they may

caigo en la cuenta de preguntártelo ▪ caigo en la cuenta de preguntarte ▪ caigo en la cuenta de hacerte la pregunta I remember asking you (the question)

caigo en la cuenta de pedírtelo I remember asking you

caigo en la cuenta de pedirte que lo hagas ▪ recuerdo que te pedí I remember asking you to do it

caja de arena *(para gatos)* litter box

ser una **caja de bombas** ▪ ser un barril de pólvora someone to stay away from ▪ someone to be wary of

caja de cambios gear box

caja de cartón cardboard box

caja de caudales safe ▪ strong box

caja de música music box

caja de Pandora Pandora's box

caja de Petri petri dish ▪ Petri dish

ser una **caja de sorpresas** to be a bundle of surprises

caja del ascensor ▪ cabina del ascensor elevator car

caja fuerte safe ▪ strong box

caja para envíos box for mailing ▪ box to send it in

caja rápida express checkout ▪ express lane ▪ express line ➤ Caja rápida: máximo diez artículos. Express checkout: maximum ten items.

caja registradora cash register

caja tonta boob tube ▪ idiot box

caja torácica rib cagc

cajas destempladas: echar a alguien con ~ to give someone the boot ➤ Lo han echado con cajas destempladas. They gave him the boot.

cajero automático automated teller machine ▪ ATM

un **cajón de sastre** a jumble ▪ a mess

estar **calado hasta los huesos** ▪ estar hecho una sopa to be soaked to the bone ▪ to be soaked to the skin

cálamo currente: escribir algo a ~ *(de Don Quijote)* ▪ escribir algo a vuelo de pluma to write something in haste ▪ to write something hastily

calaña de uno: de la ~ *(peyorativo)* of one's stripe ▪ of one's ilk ➤ La gente de su calaña People of his stripe ▪ People of his ilk

calar a alguien ■ tener a alguien calado to peg someone ■ to have someone pegged

calar el carburador ■ ahogar el carburador ■ calar el motor ■ ahogar el motor to flood the carburetor ■ to flood the engine

calar el motor 1. to stall the motor ■ to kill the motor ■ to stall the engine ■ to kill the engine **2.** *(ahogando el carburador)* to stall the motor (by flooding the carburetor) ■ to stall the engine (by flooding the carburetor) ■ to flood the motor ■ to flood the engine ➤ El estudiante de conducción caló el motor al soltar el pedal del embrague demasiado de prisa. The student driver stalled the motor by releasing the clutch too quickly. ■ The student driver killed the motor by releasing the clutch (pedal) too quickly.

calarse el motor ■ apagarse el motor (for the) engine to stall ■ (for the) motor to stall ➤ Intenta que no se te cale. ■ Intenta que no se te apague. Try not to let the engine stall (on you). ■ Try not to let the motor stall (on you).

calarse en la lluvia ■ empaparse en la lluvia to get drenched in the rain ■ to get soaked in the rain ■ to get drenched by the rain ■ to get soaked by the rain

calarse hasta los huesos ■ ponerse como una sopa ■ ponerse hecho una sopa ■ empaparse to get soaked to the bone ■ to get drenched

ser el **calco de alguien** to look exactly like someone ■ to be the spitting image of someone

calcular algo a bulto to estimate something roughly

calcular algo a ojo ■ calcular algo a simple vista ■ (calcular) a ojo de buen cubero to judge something by eye ■ (to judge) by looking at something ■ to estimate by eye ➤ (Calculando) a ojo, diría que mide unos dos metros. Judging (him) by eye, I'd say he's about two meters tall. ■ (Judging by looking at him, I'd say he's about two meters tall. ■ Estimating by eye, I'd say he's about two meters tall.

calcular por lo bajo to estimate conservatively ■ to calculate the minimum (of something)

calcular que... to guess that... ■ (for) one's best guess to be that... ➤ Calculo que... My (best) guess is that...

calcularse en to be computed at (a rate of) ➤ El consumo de combustibles se calculó en 50 millas por galón. Fuel consumption was computed at the rate of 50 miles per gallon.

cálculo diferencial *(matemáticas)* differential calculus

cálculo infinitesimal *(matemáticas)* infinitesimal calculus

cálculo mental mental arithmetic

calculo que tendrá unos (cuarenta años) I'd guess he's about (forty)

caldera individual *(anuncio de inmobiliario)* its own water heater

calderas de Pedro Botero hell

calderilla: tener ~ ■ tener feria to have (some) small change

caldo de cultivo (para) 1. culture medium **2.** breeding ground (for) ➤ Caldo de cultivo para los microbios Culture medium for microbes ➤ Caldo de cultivo para terroristas Breeding ground for terrorists

caldo de pollo chicken broth ■ chicken bouillon

caldos jerezanos sherry wines of Jérez, Spain

calentamiento global global warming

calentar de más to overheat

calentar el banco *(deportivo)* to warm the bench

calentar el culo a alguien *(coloquial)* ■ poner el culo como un tomate a alguien ■ dar unos azotes (en el culo) a alguien ■ dar a alguien en el culo ■ azotar a alguien (en el trasero) ■ zurrar a alguien to tan someone's hide ■ to give someone a spanking ■ to spank someone

calentar la badana a alguien ■ darle un azote a alguien ■ zurrar la badana a alguien ■ sobar la badana a alguien to tan someone's hide ■ to give someone a spanking

calentar la cabeza para hacer algo ■ calentar la cabeza para que haga algo to talk someone into doing something ➤ Me estuvo calentando la cabeza para que fuese al cine. He was trying to talk me into going to the movies.

calentar más que... ■ abrigar más que... ■ ser más calido que... ■ ser más abrigado que... to be warmer than ■ to provide more warmth than ➤ Las nuevas botas espaciales calientan más que las antiguas (botas) de cuero. ■ Las nuevas botas espaciales son más cálidas que las antiguas (botas) de cuero. ■ Las nuevas botas espaciales son más abrigadas que las antiguas (botas) de cuero. ■ Las nuevas botas espaciales abrigan más que las antiguas (botas) de cuero. The new "moon" boots are warmer than the old leather ones.

calentarle a alguien la cabeza ■ molestarle to burn someone up ■ to make someone mad

calentarse el tarro por algo ■ barrenar sobre algo to rack one's brain over something ■ to rack one's brain over something

calentarse la cabeza to suffer burnout

calentarse la sangre to make one's blood boil ■ to make one boiling mad

calentársele la boca a alguien to get worked up ■ to get exercised ➤ No te calientes la boca. Don't get worked up. ■ Don't get exercised. ■ Don't get your shirt in a knot. ■ Don't get your nose out of joint.

estar **calentita en el invierno** *(casa)* to be warm (as toast) in the winter

cálida bienvenida: dar a alguien una ~ ■ dar a alguien una calurosa bienvenida to give someone a warm welcome

calidad de enseñanza quality of instruction

calidad de vida quality of life

cálidas aguas: puerto de ~ warm water port

calidez humana ■ calor humano human warmth

estar **caliente 1.** *(temperatura)* to be hot **2.** estar a punto de pelear to be ready to fight **3.** to be turned on (sexually) ■ to have the hots ■ to be hot (as a firecracker)

¡caliente, caliente! you're getting warm! ■ you're getting close! ■ you're about to guess it!

ser **calificado(-a) de** to be labeled as ■ to be described as ■ to be characterized as

calificar a alguien de algo 1. to describe someone as something **2.** *(peyorativo)* ■ tildar a alguien de algo to label someone as something ■ to brand someone as something

calificar algo de algo 1. to describe something as something **2.** *(peyorativo)* ■ tildar a alguien de algo to label something as something ■ to brand something as something

calificar a alguien como to describe someone as ■ to characterize someone as ➤ A la que calificó como una buena amiga Whom he described as a good friend

calificar algo de to characterize something as ■ to describe something as ➤ El presidente ha calificado las elecciones en Irak como un éxito. The president has characterized the elections in Iraq as a success. ■ The president has described the elections in Iraq as a success.

calificar los exámenes ■ corregir los exámenes to grade the tests ■ to correct the tests

calificativo de alguien como algo: dar el ~ ■ describir a alguien como algo to describe someone as (being) something

¡calla! ■ ¡cállate! be quiet! ■ keep quiet!

calla callando shhhhh! (be) quiet. ➤ Calla callando que viene la profe. Shhhh! Quiet. The teacher's coming.

calla callando: venir ~ to come quietly

¡calla la boca! ■ ¡cállate la boca! shut up!

calla y come don't eat with your mouth open

¡callaos! *(Esp., vosotros)* (you all) be quiet!

callar como un muerto to be dead silent

callar como un poste to be dead silent

callar el pico to shut one's trap

callar la boca to shut one's mouth ■ to keep one's mouth shut

callar es otorgar ■ quien calla otorga silence implies consent

callar su opinión to keep one's opinions to oneself

callarse sobre algo to keep quiet about something ➤ Tener que callarnos sobre ello nos hizo sentir culpables. Having to keep quiet about it made us feel quilty.

¡cállate de una puta vez! *(subido de tono y degradante)* shut up!

¡cállate (la boca)! ■ ¡calla la boca! ■ ¡a callar! be quiet!

calle abajo down the street

calle adelante along the street

calle angosta y tortuosa ■ calle estrecha y sinuosa ■ calle angosta y torcida narrow winding street

calle arriba up the street

calle concurrida ■ calle muy transitada busy street ➤ Una de las calles más concurridas de la ciudad One of the busiest streets in the city

la **calle de dirección única** ▪ calle de una sola vía ▪ calle de un solo sentido ▪ calle de una sola mano one-way street

la **calle de doble sentido** ▪ calle de doble vía ▪ calle de dos manos ▪ calle de doble mano two-way street ➤ La calle Orense se hace de doble sentido cuando llegas al Santiago Bernabeu. Calle Orense becomes a two-way street when you reach Santiago Bernabeu.

la **calle de un sentido** ▪ calle de dirección única ▪ called de un solo sentido ▪ calle de una sola vía one-way street

la **calle de una sola vía** ▪ calle de dirección única ▪ calle de un solo sentido ▪ calle de una sola mano one-way street

calle empedrada cobblestone street

calle empinada (steeply) sloping street ▪ uphill street ▪ downhill street ➤ Calles estrechas y empinadas Narrow (steeply) sloping steets

la **calle en que hay mucho ruido** noisy street

calle estrecha y tortuosa ▪ calle angosta y sinuosa ▪ calle estrecha y torcida winding narrow street

calle muy transitada ▪ calle concurrida busy street

calle pavimentada paved street

la **calle que no tiene salida** dead end street

la **calle se bifurca** ▪ el camino se bifurca ▪ se bifurca la calle ▪ se bifurca el camino the road forks ➤ Donde el camino se bifurca, una ramificación lleva a Salamanca y la otra a Valladolid. Where the road forks, one fork leads to Salamanca, and the other (fork leads) to Valladolid.

la **calle sin salida** ▪ calle que no tiene salida dead end street

calle solitaria deserted street ▪ abandoned street

callejas (pequeñas y poco frecuentadas) back streets

el **callejón oscuro** blind alley ➤ La política ha llevado al país por un callejón oscuro. The policy has led the country down a blind alley.

callejón sin salida 1. blind alley 2. dead end alley ▪ dead end street ➤ La política ha llevado al país por un callejón sin salida. The policy has led the country down a blind alley.

¡**cállense (la boca)** (you all) be quiet!

las **calles a la redonda** surrounding streets ▪ calles circundantes

las **calles interiores** back streets

las **calles olvidadas** abandoned streets

calma chicha dead calm

el **calor de muerte** ▪ calor infernal suffocating heat

el **calor de pecho ajeno** 1. tender loving care 2. shoulder to cry on ▪ someone to commiserate with

calor humano ▪ calidez humana (human) warmth

el **calor infernal** ▪ calor de muerte suffocating heat

calor negro heat not hot enough to generate light

calor popular: perder el ~ to lose the affection of the masses ▪ to lose the affection of the people ➤ *(titular)* El primer ministro pierde el calor popular. The prime minister loses the affection of the people.

calumnia, que algo queda false witness can never be completely erased ▪ damage to a person's reputation can never be completely undone

calumniar a alguien ▪ levantar falso testimonio sobre alguien to bear false witness against someone

calurosa acogida: dar a alguien una ~ to make someone feel at home ▪ to make someone feel comfortable

calva: tener una ~ to have a bald spot

calvario de la recuperación ordeal of the recovery

calzar ancho to have a lax conscience

calzar estrecho to have a strict conscience

calzarse los calcetines *(arcaico)* ▪ ponerse los calcetines to put on one's socks

calzarse los guantes *(arcaico)* ▪ ponerse los guantes to put on one's gloves

calzarse los zapatos *(arcaico)* ▪ ponerse los zapatos to put on one's shoes

cama deshecha unmade bed

cama donde dormir ▪ cama para dormir bed to sleep in

cama para dormir ▪ cama donde dormir bed to sleep in

cama plegable folding bed

cama redonda group sex

cámara alta upper house of a legislature ▪ senate

cámara baja lower house (of a legislature) ➤ En España, el Congreso de los Diputados es la cámara baja de la asamblea legislativa nacional. In Spain, the Congress of Deputies in the lower house of the national legislature.

cámara cargada loaded camera ▪ camera loaded with film

cámara de cine movie camera

cámara (de neumático) inner tube ➤ La cámara se está saliendo a través de la llanta formando un globo. ▪ La cámara se está saliendo a través de la llanta formando un huevo. The inner tube is ballooning through the outer layer of the tire.

cámara de representantes *(estadounidense)* House of Representatives

cámara frigorífica *(en un mercado)* cold case ▪ cooler

al **camarón que no se mueve se lo lleva la corriente** time waits for no man

camastro de lona hard canvas bed

cambiar de aires ▪ mudar de aires to get a change of scenery ▪ to have a change of scenery

cambiar de argumentos to change one's argument

cambiar de camisa ▪ cambiar de chaqueta ▪ cambiar de lado to switch sides ▪ to switch loyalties ▪ to switch allegiances

cambiar de casa ▪ mudarse de casa ▪ trasladarse to move

cambiar de categoría to change one's socioeconomic status

cambiar de chaqueta ▪ cambiar de camisa ▪ cambiar de lado to switch sides ▪ to switch loyalities ▪ to switch allegiances

cambiar de color to change color

cambiar de disco 1. cambiar el disco to change the CD 2. cambiar de rollo to change the subject

cambiar de dueño to change hands

cambiar de idea to change one's mind

cambiar de lado ▪ cambiar de camisa ▪ cambiar de chaqueta to switch sides ▪ to switch loyalties ▪ to switch allegiances

cambiar de manos ▪ cambiar de dueño ▪ cambiar de amo to change hands ▪ to change ownership ▪ to be under new ownership

cambiar de marcha to shift gears ▪ to change gears

cambiar de parecer to change one's mind

cambiar de postura 1. mover la posición to change one's position 2. cambiar de idea to change one's opinion ▪ to change one's position (on an issue) ▪ to change one's mind (on an issue)

cambiar de rollo ▪ 1. cambiar de disco to change the subject 2. cambiar la película en una cámara to change film ▪ to put in a new roll of film

cambiar de sentido to change directions ▪ to turn around and go the other way

cambiar de sitio con alguien to change places with someone ▪ to trade places with someone

cambiar de tema to change the subject

cambiar de tercio *(taurino)* ▪ cambiar el tercio 1. to enter the next stage of the bullfight 2. cambiar de tema to change the subject 3. cambiar de actividad to do something else

cambiar de tono ▪ cambiar el tono to change one's tone (of voice) ➤ You change your tone, young man, or you're not going to the park. Cambia de tono, jovencito, o no vas a ir al parque. ▪ Cambia ese tono, jovencito, o no vas a ir al parque.

cambiar de tornas 1. to turn the tables 2. to have a sudden change of plans ➤ Cambiamos de tornas cuando coincidimos con mis amigos. We changed our plans when we met up with our friends.

cambiar de tren to change trains

cambiar diametralmente ▪ dar media vuelta to change one's mind ▪ to do an about face

cambiar dólares por pesos to change dollars into pesos ▪ to exchange dollars for pesos

cambiar el agua a los garbanzos ▪ cambiar el agua a las aceitunas ▪ echar una meada ▪ echar un cloro ▪ cambiar el aceite to take a leak ▪ to take a pee ▪ *(más fuerte)* to take a piss ➤ Tengo que cambiar el agua a los garbanzos. ▪ Tengo que cambiar el agua a las aceitunas. I have to take a leak. ▪ I've got to take a leak. ▪ I have to take a pee. ▪ *(jerga fuerte)* I gotta take a piss.

cambiar el ángulo de incidencia de las palas de la hélice to change the pitch of the propeller ▪ to vary the pitch of the propeller

cambiar el asunto to change the subject

cambiar el tercio ▪ cambiar de tercio 1. *(taurino)* to enter the next stage of the bullfight 2. *(figurativo)* to change the subject ▪ to go on to something else

cambiar el tono (de voz) to change one's (tone of) voice ▪ to alter one's (tone of) voice ▪ to change the tone of one's voice ▪ to alter the tone of one's voice ➤ He changed his tone of voice to disguise who he was. Cambió su tono de voz para disfrazarse.

cambiar en to change into ▪ to be changed into

cambiar experiencias ▪ intercambiar experiencias to catch up with each other ▪ to catch up on each other's news

cambiar impresiones to compare opinions or impressions ▪ to exchange opinions or impressions

cambiar la tendencia 1. *(la bolsa)* to change direction 2. *(la moda)* (for) the trends to shift

cambiar las tornas en to turn the tables on ▪ to reverse the course of ▪ to break the back of ➤ Mark Twain señala que Juana de Arco logró la memorable victoria de Patay sobre lo ingleses, cambiando las tornas en la Guerra de los Cien Años. Mark Twain notes that Joan of Arc won the memorable victory of Patay over the English and broke the back of the Hundred Years' War. ▪ Mark Twain notes that Joan of Arc won the memorable victory of Patay over the English and reversed the course of the Hundred Years' War.

cambiar los muebles de sitio to change the furniture around ▪ to change around the furniture

cambiar para bien to change for the better

cambiar para mal to change for the worse

cambiar radicalmente las cosas to change things radically ▪ to change everything

cambiar sus favores por dinero to offer one's favors in exchange for money ▪ to trade one's favors for money

cambiar una rueda to change a tire

cambiar unas palabras con alguien to exchange a few words with someone

cambiarle la vida a uno to change one's life ➤ Te cambiará la vida. It will change your life. ▪ It'll change your life.

cambiarle un billete a alguien to change a bill (for someone) ➤ ¿Me puedes cambiar uno de cincuenta? Can you change a fifty (for me)?

cambiarle una ficha (a alguien) 1. to cash in a gambling chip (for someone) 2. to exchange a gambling chip for cash ➤ Al final del juego, el jugador cambió sus fichas y se fue. At the end of the game, the gambler cashed in his chips and left. ➤ El cajero le cambió las fichas al jugador por efectivo. The cashier exchanged the gambler's chips for cash.

cambiarlo de lugar change its place ▪ to move it

cambiarse de casa ▪ mudarse de casa ▪ cambiar de domicilio to move ▪ *(literario)* to change domiciles

cambiársele la hora to change the time (for someone) ➤ Los estudiantes han pedido que se les cambie la hora de la clase. The students have requested that the time of the class be changed. ▪ The students have requested that we change the time of the class.

cambio anímico ▪ cambio de humor mood swing

cambio brusco sudden change

cambio de aires change of scenery ▪ change of scene

cambio de categoría change in socioeconomic status

cambio de humor ▪ cambios anímicos mood swings

cambio de jurisdicción change of venue

cambio de los tiempos ▪ tiempos cambiantes changing times ➤ En una muestra evidente del cambio de los tiempos, las cadenas de televisión han sustituido a los diarios escritos en el protagonismo de pifias monumentales. In a clear example of the changing times, the TV networks have replaced daily newspapers in the commission of glaring mistakes.

cambio de medio ▪ cambio de aires change of scenery ▪ change of scene

cambio de paradigma paradigm shift

cambio de rasante 1. cambio de grado change of grade ▪ change of gradient 2. cresta de una colina crest of a hill ▪ top of a hill ▪ *(literario)* brow of a hill 3. pie de una colina bottom of a hill ▪ foot of a hill

cambio de sentido turnaround ➤ Último cambio de sentido los 20 próximos kilómetros Last turnaround next 20 kilometers

cambio de tendencias 1. *(la bolsa)* change in direction ▪ change in the trends 2. *(la moda)* change in fashions ▪ change in the style ▪ change in styles ➤ Ha habido un cambio de tendencias en la bolsa. There's been a change in direction in the stock market. ➤ Ha habido un cambio de tendencias respecto a la temporada anterior. There has been a change in the style since last season.

cambio de tornas turning of the tables ▪ reversal of course

cambio generacional generation change

cambio manual straight shift ▪ *(coloquial)* stick shift

cambio sentido ▪ *(mejor dicho)* cambio de sentido turnaround ➤ Último cambio sentido los 20 próximos kilómetros. Last turnaround next 20 kilometers.

¡cambia y cierro! *(comunicación por radio)* ▪ ¡cambio y fuera! over and out!

¡cambio y corto! *(comunicación por radio)* over!

¡cambio y fuera! *(comunicación por radio)* ▪ ¡cambio y cierro! over and out!

camelar a alguien to butter somebody up

caminaba desde hacía... *(Méx.)* ▪ andaba desde hacía... *(Esp.)* 1. *(yo)* I had been walking for... ▪ I'd been walking for... 2. *(él)* he had been walking for... ▪ he'd been walking for... 3. *(ella)* she had been walking for... ➤ (Yo) caminaba desde hacía cuatro horas. I had been walking for four hours. ▪ I'd been walking for four hours.

caminar a cuatro patas 1. *(seres humanos)* to walk on all fours ▪ to crawl 2. *(cuadrúpedos)* to walk on four feet

caminar a gatas ▪ andar a cuatro gatas ▪ andar a cuatro pies ▪ gatear to walk on all fours ▪ to crawl

caminar a vanguardia ▪ estar a vanguardia ▪ estar a la delantera to be on the cutting edge

caminar de un lado a otro ▪ recorrer la habitación ▪ dar zancadas to pace the floor ➤ ¿Quieres dejar de ir de un lado a otro como león enjaulado? Would you quit pacing the floor like a caged lion?

caminar derecho 1. *(todo recto)* to walk straight ahead 2. *(con postura recta)* to walk upright 3. *(figurativo)* ▪ caminar derecho (en la vida) to walk upright(ly) ➤ Camina dos cuadras todo derecho. ▪ Camina dos cuadras recto. *(Esp.)* Anda dos manzanas todo recto. Walk two blocks straight ahead.

caminar en coche de San Fernando, (un rato a pie y otro caminando) *(cómico)* andar en coche de San Fernando, (un rato a pie y otro andando ▪ ir a pie to go on shank's mare ▪ to go on foot ▪ not to have a ride

caminar en sueños ▪ ser sonámbulo to walk in one's sleep ▪ to sleepwalk ▪ to somnambulate ▪ to be a sleepwalker

caminar entre el barro to walk through deep mud

caminar la cuerda floja *(literal y figurativo)* to walk a tightrope

caminata: ir de ~ ▪ hacer senderismo to go on a hike ▪ to go hiking ➤ Fuimos de caminata de Catawba a Cloverdale. On our hike we went from Catawba to Cloverdale.

el **camino a seguir** 1. to road to take 2. *(figurativo)* the road to follow ➤ El camino a seguir es la Autopista de Burgos. The road to take is the Burgos Highway. ➤ El camino a seguir para triunfar es el de la disciplina y el trabajo riguroso. The road to follow is that of discipline and hard work.

camino acertado: ir por el ~ 1. ir por el camino correcto to go the right way ▪ to be on the correct route 2. tomar las decisiones correctas to make the right choices ▪ to do the right thing

ser el **camino acertado** 1. ser el camino correcto to be the right way ▪ to be the right route 2. ser la elección correcta to be the right choice ➤ This is the right way. ▪ This is the right route. Este es el camino acertado.

camino adelante farther up the road ▪ farther down the road ▪ farther along the road

camino certero sure way ▪ surest way ➤ El camino certero para llegar ahí es tomando el (tren de) cercanías a Canto Blanco. ▪ El camino certero para llegar ahí es tomar el (tren de) cercanías a Canto Blanco. The surest way to get there is to take the commuter train to Canto Blanco. ▪ A sure way to get there is to take the commuter train to Canto Blanco.

camino comarcal ▪ carretera comarcal country road ➤ Los caminos comarcales serpentean incesantemente por las montañas de esa región. ▪ Las carreteras comarcales serpentean incesantemente por las montañas de esa región. The country roads wind endlessly through the mountains of that region.
camino de ▪ hacia ▪ en dirección a on the way to
camino de cabras goat trail ▪ *(figurativo)* ▪ camino pedregoso bumpy road ▪ difficult time
camino de en medio: coger ~ *(Esp.)* ▪ tomar el camino de en medio **1.** to take the middle road **2.** *(figurativo)* to compromise ▪ to take the way of compromise ▪ to take a compromise position ▪ to take a middle of the road position
camino de en medio: tomar el ~ **1.** to take the middle road **2.** *(figurativo)* to compromise ▪ to take the way of compromise ▪ to take a compromise position ▪ to take a middle of the road position
camino de fuego **1.** revolutionary path ▪ path of revolution **2.** fire barrier ▪ barrier of fire ➤ Construyeron un camino de fuergo para protegerse de una invasión de hormigas de combate. They built a fire barrier to ward off an invasion of army ants.
camino de menos resistencia ▪ sendero de menos resistencia path of least resistance
camino de Santiago pilgrimage route to Santiago de Compostela
camino derecho ▪ camino recto **1.** straight road **2.** (ethically) right way ▪ straight and narrow
camino fragoso bumpy road ▪ rough road
camino más fácil: tomar el ~ to take the easiest way ▪ take the path of least resistance
camino pedregoso rocky road ▪ bumpy road
el **camino que los acontecimientos han tomado en los últimos días** ▪ el rumbo que los acontecimientos han tomado en los últimos días ▪ el cauce que los acontecimientos han tomado en los últimos días the turn of events in the last few days ▪ the course events have taken in the last few days
camino real royal road
camino recto ▪ camino derecho **1.** straight road **2.** (ethically) right way ▪ straight and narrow
camino resbaladizo slick road ▪ slippery road
el **camino se bifurca** ▪ la calle se bifurca ▪ se bifurca la calle ▪ se bifurca el camino road forks ➤ Donde el camino se bifurca, una ramificación lleva a Roma, y la otra a Roma también. Where the road forks, one fork leads to Rome, and the other fork leads to Rome, too. ➤ The line forks immediately after you pass Canto Blanco. La vía se bifurca inmediatamente después de pasar Canto Blanco.
camino torcido winding road
camino trillado beaten path ➤ El genio desdeña el camino trillado. Genius disdains a beaten path.
camión cisterna tanker truck
el **camión de menor tara** light-weight truck ▪ low-weight truck
el **camión de remolque** tow truck
el **camión de reparto** delivery truck
el **camión de *x* toneladas** *x*-ton truck
el **camión hormigonera** concrete mixer ▪ concrete-mixing truck
el **camión sin control** ▪ camión sin frenos runaway truck ▪ truck with failed brakes ▪ out-of-control truck
camisa cuadrada plaid shirt ▪ checked shirt
camisa de once varas: meterse en ~ ▪ meterse en asuntos que uno no domina ▪ venirle grande to be out of one's depths
camisa de sport sport shirt
campamento base base camp
campamento: ir de ~ to go camping
campamento de verano (summer) camp ➤ Va a un campamento de verano todos los veranos. ▪ Va de campamento todos los veranos. He goes to camp every summer.
campana extractora de humos ▪ campana extractora stove hood
campaña de difamación smear campaign
campaña electoral election campaign ➤ Los candidatos enfilan la recta final de una campaña electoral. The candidates head for the home stretch in the election campaign.
campar por su cuenta to do as one pleases
campar a sus anchas ▪ campear a sus anchas ▪ estar a sus anchas to do things one's own way
campar por sus respetos to do things one's own way ▪ to do things according to one's own lights
campear a sus anchas ▪ campar a sus anchas ▪ estar a sus anchas to do things one's own way
campear de sol a sol ▪ campear a sombra to work in the fields from dawn to dusk
campear en el ambiente to pervade the atmosphere
ser **campechano** to be unpretentious
campo abierto ▪ campo raso ▪ campiña open country ▪ open countryside
campo abonado fertilized field
campo asunto *(correo electrónico)* subject line
campo a través cross country
campo de aplicación (de una teoría) field of application (of a theory)
campo de béisbol baseball diamond ▪ baseball field
campo de cultivo field for growing crops
campo de entrenamiento training camp
campo de fuerza *(física)* force field
campo de golf golf course
campo de honor battle ground
campo de batalla **1.** battlefield **2.** desbarajuste mess ➤ Mi piso es un campo de batalla. ▪ Mi piso es un desbarajuste. My apartment is a mess.
campo de pruebas testing ground ▪ proving ground
campo de tiro rifle range ▪ shooting range
campo gravitatorio gravitation field
campo magnético magnetic field
campo minado mine field
campo petrolífero ▪ yacimiento petrolífero oil field
campo raso ▪ lo raso open country ▪ the open
campo santo ▪ camposanto Catholic cemetery
campo través ▪ campo traviesa cross country
campo visual field of vision
canales internos back channels
cancha de baloncesto basketball court
canción de cuna cradle song ▪ lullaby
canción de moda popular song
ser **candidato a** to be a candidate for ➤ *(titular)* Aznar pide a Gallardón que sea candidato a la acaldía de Madrid Aznar asks Gallardón to be a candidate for mayor of Madrid.
el **canje de prisioneros** exchange of prisoners ▪ prisoner exchange
cansarse de algo to get tired of something ▪ to grow tired of something
cansino(-a) con alguien: ser muy ~ ▪ ser muy pesado(-a) con alguien ▪ ser muy plasta con alguien to be wearing on someone
estar **cantado que...** ▪ ser obvio que to be obvious that...
ser un, una **cantamañanas** ▪ ser de mucho decir y luego nada ▪ ser de mucho hablar y poco actuar ▪ tanto hablar, seca la boca ▪ mucho lirili y poco lerele ▪ ser mucho ruido y pocas nueces to be all talk and no action
cantar a uno la cartilla ▪ leer a uno la cartilla to read someone the riot act
cantar claro to speak one's mind
cantar como un ruiseñor to sing beautifully
cantar como una chicharra to have a lousy (singing) voice
cantar de bajo to sing bass
cantar de oído to sing by ear
cantar de plano to make a full confession
cantar el alirón to sing the victory song (after winning the league pennant)
cantar las alabanzas de alguien ▪ ensalzar a alguien to sing someone's praises ▪ to extol someone's virtues ▪ to extol the virtues of someone
cantar las cuarenta a alguien ▪ leer la cartilla a alguien to read somebody the riot act
cantar las cuatro verdades to read someone the riot act

cantar misa to sing mass

cantarle a alguien la cartilla ■ leerle a alguien la cartilla to read someone the riot act

cantarle las cuarenta a alguien to read someone the riot act

cantarle los pinreles ■ tufarle los pies ■ olerle los pies to have stinky feet ■ (for) one's feet to stink ■ (for) one's feet to reek ■ (for) one's feet to smell ➤ Le cantan los pinreles. ■ Le tufan los pies. ■ Le huelen los pies. His feet stink. ■ His feet reek ■ His feet smell.

cántaro que no está lleno, suena a hueco someone that dumb can't hide it

cante jondo (deep-voiced) flamenco singing

cantera de jugadores pool of players

cantera de valores *(deportivo)* pool of talent ■ talent pool

la **cantidad a cobrar** amount owed (to someone)

la **cantidad a pagar** amount owed (by someone)

la **cantidad adecuada de** right amount of

la **cantidad de...** the number of...

cantidad de comida ■ mucha comida ■ una bestialidad de comida a lot of food ■ tons of food

cantidad de improperios ■ flujo de insultos ■ rosario de insultos ■ avalancha de insultos ■ plétora de insultos barrage of insults ■ stream of insults

cantidades ilimitadas unlimited quantities ➤ El agua del mar y la arena, los dos recursos naturales que se necesitan para aprovechar la energía solar, están disponibles en cantidades ilimitadas. Sea water and silicon, the two natural resources needed to harness solar energy, are available in unlimited quantities.

canto de un duro: estar como el ~ to be (skinny as) a bean pole ■ to be skinny as a rail ■ to be skinny as a toothpick

canto de un duro para que...: faltarle el ~ to come within a hair's breadth of ■ to come very close to

canto de un libro ■ lomo de un libro spine of a book

canto de una moneda edge of a coin ■ rim of a coin

canto de cisne swan song ■ final performance (of one's career)

canto participativo participatory singing

canto rodado smooth pebble

caña de pescar fishing rod

¿caña o botellín? *(Esp.)* draft or bottle? *(Nota: Ambos "caña" y "botellín" se refieren a las cantidades más pequeñas. ■ Both "caña" and "botellín" refer to the smallest units.)*

las **cañas se vuelven lanzas** a few beers can do you in ■ a few beers can knock you for a loop

el **cañón de una pistola** barrel of a pistol

cañonera fluvial (municipal) drainage system

caos más absoluto: sumirse en el ~ to be plunged into total chaos

capa antiadherente non-stick coating

capa de hielo *(grueso)* layer of ice ■ *(delgado)* sheet of ice ■ *(polar)* ice cap

capa de nieve ■ manto de nieve layer of snow ■ blanket of snow

capa de ozono ■ ozonosfera ozone layer ■ ozonosphere

capa de pintura ■ una mano de pintura a coat of paint

capa fina *(pintura, laca, etc.)* **1.** thin coat ■ light coat **2.** thin layer ➤ La mejor manera de aplicar la laca es diluirla y aplicar varias capas finas. The best method is to thin the lacquer and apply several light coats. ■ The best method is to thin the lacquer and apply several thin coats. ➤ Hay una capa fina de hielo en la carretera. There's a thin layer of ice on the road. ➤ Hay una capa fina de hielo en la laguna. There's a thin layer of ice on the pond.

capa freática water table

capa límite *(física)* boundary layer ➤ Uno de los grandes avances en la dinámica de fluidos fue el descubrimiento de Ludwig Prandtl de la capa límite. One of the great advances in fluid dynamics was Ludwig Prandtl's discovery of the boundary layer.

capa rústica paperback

capacidad de: tener la ~ to have the ability to

capacidad de aguante ■ capacidad de aguantar endurance

capacidad de recuperación ability to bounce back

el, la **capataz de obras de construcción** construction foreman

ser **capaz de** to be capable of ■ to be able to ➤ No hay tecnología capaz de resolver ese problema. There is no technology capable of solving that problem. ■ There is no technology that can solve that problem. ➤ Si el entrevistado dice, después de una interrupción, "Por dónde iba?" el reportero debe ser siempre capaz de decírselo. If the interview subject says, after an interruption, "Where was I?," the reporter should always be able to tell him.

ser **capaz de resucitar a un muerto** to be someone who can fix anything

capear al toro *(tauromaquia)* **1.** to wave the cape at the bull ■ to incite the bull to charge by waving the cape **2.** to deal with a situation

capear con rebozado ■ cubrir con rebozado to coat with batter

capear el temporal ■ capear la tormenta ■ aguantar el temporal to weather the storm ■ to ride out the storm ➤ Es un político que ha sabido capear los temporales. He's a politician who has managed to weather the storms.

capear la crisis to weather the crisis

capear la tormenta ■ capear el temporal ■ aguantar el temporal to weather the storm ■ to ride out the storm

Caperucita Roja Little Red Riding Hood

capilla ardiente funeral chapel ■ wake

el **capital inmueble** fixed capital

el **capital mueble** movable capital

Capitanes intrépidos *(novela de Rudyard Kipling)* Captains Courageous

ser **capítulo aparte** to be another thing altogether ■ to be something else again ■ to be a different question altogether ■ to be another question altogether ■ to be a completely different question ➤ Es un capítulo aparte. That's anothing thing altogether. ■ That's something else again. ■ That's a different question altogether.

capricho del destino quirk of fate

captar al vuelo to catch on the fly ➤ Su profesora de español le dijo que le gustaba la manera en que captaba las cosas al vuelo. His Spanish teacher told him she likes the way he catches things on a fly.

captar el sentido de to capture the sense of

captar la indirecta ■ pescar la indirecta to catch the hint ■ to get the hint

captar la onda *(L.am.)* ■ coger la onda to catch the drift ■ to catch the hint ■ to get the hint

captar que... ■ to grasp that... ■ to realize that...

ser **capturado con vida** to be captured alive ■ to be taken alive

capturar a alguien vivo(-a) to take someone alive

capturar con vida a alguien to capture someone alive

capturar con vida a un animal to capture an animal alive

capullo de rosa rosebud

cara a cara ■ frente a frente face to face

cara a cara: aparearse ~ to mate face to face ➤ Los orangutáns se aparean cara a cara. Orangutan(g)s mate face to face.

cara a cara: encontrarse ~ to come face to face ➤ Nos encontramos cara a cara. We came face to face. ➤ No querría encontrarme cara a cara con ese tipo. I wouldn't want to come face to face with that character.

cara conocida familiar face

cara de acelga: tener ~ to be pale faced ■ to look pale

cara de asombro: observar su ~ to see the astonished look (on someone's face) ■ to see the look of amazement on someone's face

cara de cemento: tener una ~ ■ ser un caradura ■ tener cara de cemento armado to have gall

cara de chiste: tener una ~ to have a comical face

cara de circunstancias: tener ~ to look serious

cara de cordero degollado to have a sad face ■ to have a melancholic face ➤ No me mires con cara de cordero degollado. Don't give me that sad look.

cara de crío baby face

cara de hambre hungry look

cara de niño fresh face ■ young face

cara de mala leche angry face ■ angry look

cara de palo blank face ■ unexpressive face

cara de perro: tener ~ 1. to have mean face 2. to have an angry look (on one's face)

cara de pan: tener ~ to be moon faced ▪ to have a round face

cara de pocos amigos: tener ~ to have an angry face

cara de póquer: tener ~ to be poker faced

cara de sargento: tener ~ to have a hard face ▪ to have a severe face ▪ to have an unfeeling face

cara de vinagre: tener ~ to have a sour (looking) face

cara es conocida face is familiar ➤ Su cara es conocida. *(de él)* His face is familiar. ▪ *(de ella)* Her face is familiar.

la **cara es el espejo del alma** the face is the mirror of the soul ▪ *(se dice en el mismo contexto)* the eyes are the mirror of the soul

cara hermosa: tener una ~ ▪ tener una cara preciosa to have a beautiful face ➤ Esa niña tiene una cara hermosa. ▪ Esa niña tiene una cara preciosa. That little girl has a beautiful face.

cara larga: poner (una) ~ ▪ ponerse una cara larga to put on a long face

¿cara o cruz? *(Esp.)* heads or tails?

cara opuesta de ▪ antípodas de opposite side of ▪ other side of ➤ *(noticia)* El robot de NASA aterriza con éxito en la cara opuesta de Marte donde está su gemelo "Spirit". ▪ El robot de NASA aterriza con éxito en las antípodas de Marte donde está su gemelo "Spirit". The NASA robot lands successfully on the opposite side of Mars from its twin "Spirit." ▪ The NASA robot lands successfully on the other side of Mars from its twin "Spirit."

cara posterior del muslo back (side) of the thigh ➤ *(noticia)* El quinto toro le pegó al torero una cornada en la cara posterior del muslo derecho. The fifth bull gored the bullfighter in the back (side) of the right thigh.

cara preciosa: tener una ~ ▪ tener una cara hermosa to have a beautiful face ➤ Esa chica tiene una cara preciosa. ▪ Esa chica tiene una cara hermosa. That girl has a beautiful face.

carácter adusto stern nature ▪ harsh nature ▪ unfeeling nature ▪ austere nature

características de maniobrabilidad *(de un vehículo)* ▪ características de conducción ▪ propias características handling characteristics

ser **caracterizado por** ▪ caracterizarse por to be characterized by

caracterizarse por ▪ ser caracterizado por to be characterized by

¡carajo: y un! ~ *(subido de tono)* 1. bullshit! 2. *(sarcástico)* yeah, right! 3. ni de coña no fuckin' way!

¡caramba, carambita, carambola! yay, yay, yay!

caramba con... ▪ caray con 1. *(positive)* good for... ▪ way to go... 2. *(negative)* damned... ▪ blasted... ➤ ¡Caramba con Marta, aprobó todos los examenes! ¡Qué alegría! ▪ ¡Caray con Marta, aprobó todos los examenes! ¡Qué alegría! Good for Marta. She passed all her exams. That's great! ▪ Way to go, Marta. She passed all her exams. ➤ Caramba con el (tren de) cercanías. Todos los sábados están de huelga. ▪ Caray con el (tren de) cercanías. Todos los sábados están de huelga. Damned commuter trains. Every Saturday, they're on strike. ▪ Blasted commuter trains. Every Saturday, they're on strike.

carambola legal *(coloquial)* legal technicality ▪ legal fluke ▪ legal loophole ➤ *(noticia)* Como resultado de carambolas legales, el violador salió en libertad. As a result of legal technicalities, the rapist went free. ▪ As a result of legal flukes, the rapist went free.

caramelo de azúcar de arce maple sugar candy

ser **caras de la misma moneda** to be two sides of the same coin

caray con ▪ caramba con 1. *(positive)* good for... ▪ way to go... 2. *(negative)* damned... ▪ blasted...

carbohidratos sin refinar unrefined carbohydrates

carcomer algo ▪ desgastar algo ▪ corroer algo to eat away at something

carcomer la salud to undermine one's health

cardar la lana to card wool ▪ to comb wool (for spinning)

cardo borriquero ~ 1. feo extremely ugly person ▪ hideous person 2. antipático prickly person ▪ cold person

careciendo de fundamento ▪ carente de fundamento unfounded ▪ baseless ▪ without basis

carecer de encanto ▪ estar desprovisto de encanto to be devoid of charm ➤ H.L. Mencken, el columnista sindical de los años 20, remarcó que los pueblos de acero del oeste de Pensilvania carecían totalmente de encanto. H.L. Mencken, the syndicated columnist of the 1920s, noted that the steel towns of western Pennsylvania were devoid of charm.

carecer de emoción ▪ estar desprovisto de emoción to be devoid of emotion

carecer de sentido to be senseless ▪ to be lacking in sense

estar **carente de algo** to be lacking (in) something

estar **carente de fundamento** ▪ estar careciendo de fundamento to be unfounded ▪ to be baseless

carente de motor *(avioneta, planeador, etc.)* unpowered ▪ motorless ▪ engineless

carga de la prueba ▪ peso de la prueba burden of proof ➤ Quien acusa lleva la carga de la prueba. The burden of proof lies with the accuser.

carga de los años weight of the years

carga de profundidad *(militar)* depth charge

carga de un camión truckload

carga de un tren trainload

carga eléctrica electrical charge ▪ electric charge

ser una **carga para el gobierno** ▪ ser un peso para el gobierno ▪ ser un lastre para el gobierno to be a burden on society ▪ to be a weight on society ▪ to be a dead weight on society

ser una **carga para la sociedad** ▪ ser un peso para la sociedad ▪ ser un lastre para la sociedad to be a burden on society ▪ to be a weight on society ▪ to be a dead weight on society

estar **cargado de** to be loaded with

estar **cargado de amor** ▪ estar lleno de amor to be filled with love ▪ to be full of love

estar **cargado de desafíos** ▪ estar lleno de desafíos to be filled with challenges ▪ to be full of challenges

cargado de espaldas: ir ~ ▪ ir cargado de hombros to carry something on one's back ▪ to be carrying something on one's back

cargado de hombros: ir ~ ▪ ir cargado de espaldas to be carrying something on one's back

estar **cargado de sorpresas** ▪ estar lleno de sorpresa to be filled with surprises ▪ to be full of surprises

cargar a alguien con la culpa de algo ▪ echarle la culpa a alguien ▪ inculpar a alguien por algo to blame someone for something

cargar a alguien la culpa de algo ▪ echar la culpa a alguien por algo ▪ colgar a alguien el sambenito to lay the blame on someone for something ▪ to lay the blame for something on someone ▪ to put the blame for something on someone ▪ to blame someone for something

cargar a alguien la culpa de lo que pasó to lay the blame on someone for what happened ▪ to lay the blame for what happened on someone ▪ to put the blame for what happened on someone ▪ to blame someone for what happened

cargar a un estudiante en una asignatura ▪ suspender a un estudiante en una asignatura ▪ tirar a un estudiante to fail a student in a subject

cargar algo a un lado ▪ cargar algo en un lado ▪ cargar algo sobre un lado to carry something on one side ➤ Yo cargaba la mochila al lado derecho. ▪ Cargaba la mochila en el lado derecho. ▪ Cargaba la mochila sobre el lado derecho. I was carrying the knapsack on my right side. ▪ I was carrying the backpack on my right side.

cargar algo sobre los hombros to carry something on one's shoulders

cargar con combustible to fuel up ▪ to fill up with fuel

cargar con algo ▪ llevárselo 1. to carry something (in one's hands) 2. to carry something (on one's back) ▪ to carry physically ➤ Tenían que cargar con sus provisiones y alimentos. They had to physically carry their food and supplies.

cargar con la cruz ▪ llevar la cruz a cuestas 1. to carry the cross 2. *(figurativo)* to carry the burden (on one shoulders)

cargar con la culpa to assume the blame ▪ to bear the consequences

cargar con las consecuencias to suffer the consequences

cargar contra alguien por algo 1. to charge (at) someone 2. to take on someone for something ▪ to take someone on for something ▪ to challenge someone about something ▪ to challenged someone over something **3.** to criticize someone for something ▪ *(coloquial)* to get on someone's case about something ➤ La caballería cargó contra el enemigo. The cavalry charged the enemy. ➤ Los jugadores del equipo cargaron contra el árbitro por haber favorecido descaradamente a sus rivales. The team members got on the referee's case for having shamelessly favored the rival team. ➤ Los jugadores cargaron contra él. The players got on his case. ▪ The players took him on. ▪ The players challenged him. ➤ Mi madre cargó contra mi por el desorden en la cocina. My mother criticized me for the messy kitchen. ➤ Carga contra mí sólo porque no le gusta mi forma de vestir. He gets on my case because he doesn't like the way I dress.

cargar de cadenas a alguien to weight someone down with chains

cargar el mochuelo a alguien ▪ cargar el muerto a alguien to point the finger at someone ➤ Los niños de la guardería montaron un estropicio pero cargaron con el mochuelo a la otra clase. The kindergarden children made a colossal mess but pointed the finger at the other class.

cargar el muerto a alguien ▪ cargar el mochuelo a alguien to point the finger at someone ➤ Los niños de la guardería montaron un estropicio pero cargaron el muerto a la otra clase. The kindergarden children made a colossal mess but pointed the finger at the other class.

cargar el pato a alguien to make someone the scapegoat ▪ to make someone the fall guy

cargar el sambenito a alguien ▪ colgar el sambenito a alguien ▪ poner el sambenito a alguien to blame someone ▪ to put the blame on someone ▪ to lay the blame on someone ▪ to hang the blame on someone ▪ to pin the blame on someone

cargar el tanque de gasolina to fill the tank with gas(oline)

cargar la batería *(automóvil, motocicleta, etc.)* to charge the battery

cargar la pila *(teléfono móvil, etc.)* to charge the battery

cargar la responsabilidad de algo sobre alguien *(antes del hecho)* to give someone the responsibility to do something ▪ to charge someone with the responsibility of doing something ▪

cargar la responsabilidad por algo sobre alguien *(después del hecho)* to hold someone responsible for doing something ▪ to hold someone responsible for having done something ▪ to hold someone liable for doing something ▪ to hold someone liable for having done something

cargar las pilas *(telefóno móvil, radio, etc.)* ▪ recargar pilas **1.** to charge the batteries **2.** to recharge one's batteries ➤ Necesito cargar las pilas de mi móvil. I need to recharge my cell phone battery. ➤ Cargué las pilas pasando una semana en Acapulco. I recharged my batteries by spending a week in Acapulco.

cargar las tintas to exaggerate ▪ to go too far (in one's assumptions) ▪ to embellish a story ➤ Cada vez que cuenta esa historia, carga más y más las tintas. Each time he tells that story, it becomes more and more embellished.

cargar los dados to load the dice

cargar sobre alguien to weigh on someone

cargarse un curso to fail a course ▪ *(informal)* to flunk a course ➤ Se ha cargado (las) matemáticas. He failed math. ➤ Se está cargando (las) matemáticas. He's failing math.

cargar un arma to load a weapon ➤ El soldado cargó el arma. The soldier loaded the weapon. ➤ El soldado cargó las armas. The soldier loaded the weapons.

cargar un arma de fuego to load a firearm ▪ to load a gun ➤ El soldado cargó el arma de fuego. The soldier loaded the firearm. ➤ El soldado cargó las armas de fuego. The soldier loaded the firearms.

cargar un programa a la computadora *(L.am.)* ▪ cargar un programa en el ordenador to load a program onto the computer ▪ to install a program in the computer ▪ to install a program on the computer

cargar un programa al ordenador *(Esp.)* ▪ cargar un programa a la computadora to load a program onto the computer ▪ to install a program in the computer ▪ to install a program on the computer

cargar una estilográfica to fill a (fountain) pen

cargar una factura con cobras adicionales to pad the bill with extra charges

cargarle a alguien en su mente *(L.am.)* to have someone in one's thoughts

cargarle el mochuelo a alguien to point the finger at someone else ▪ to put the blame on someone else ➤ Los niños de la guardería dejaron la clase hecha una leonera pero le cargaron el mochuelo a la otra clase. The kindergarten children made a colossal mess but pointed the finger at the other class. ▪ The kindergarten children turned the place into a pigpen but pointed the finger at the other class.

cargarle con el muerto a alguien to be left holding the bag ▪ to get left holding the bag ▪ to get blamed for something ▪ to catch the blame for something

cargarle una asignatura a alguien to fail someone in a subject ▪ to give someone a failing grade in a subject ➤ Le han cargado el cálculo. *(a él)* They gave him an F in calculus. ▪ He got an F in calculus. ▪ *(a ella)* They gave her an F in calculus. ▪ She got an F in calculus.

cargarse a alguien 1. matar a alguien ▪ asesinar a alguien to kill someone **2.** *(como cliente)* to kill off **3.** suspender to fail ▪ to flunk ➤ Te lo cargaste como cliente por cobrarle seiscientas pesetas para ver su correo electrónico. You killed him off as a customer by charging him six hundred pesetas to check his E-mail.

cargarse algo ▪ romper algo to break something ➤ Me he cargado la lavadora. I broke the washing machine. ▪ I've broken the washing machine.

cargarse de deudas (hasta el cuello) to go deep into debt ▪ to become saddled with debt ▪ to saddle oneself with debt

cargarse de pilas to recharge one's batteries

cargarse de preocupaciones to be filled with worries ▪ to be burdened (down) with worries

cargarse de razón 1. to approach things rationally

cargarse el cielo ▪ nublarse to become overcast

cargarse una asignatura ▪ cargarse una materia ▪ reprobar una asignatura ▪ reprobar una materia *(coloquial)*to flunk a subject ▪ to fail a subject ➤ Se ha cargado (las) matemáticas. He flunked math. ▪ He failed math.

cargarse en marcha to become recharged in use ➤ Las baterías se cargan en marcha. The batteries recharge themselves as the car runs.

cargarse la cabeza ▪ cargársele a alguien la cabeza **1.** to have a lot on one's mind **2.** to rack one's brains ➤ Me cargo la cabeza demasiado entre trabajo y estudios. ▪ Se me carga la cabeza demasiado entre trabajo y estudios. Between work and school, I've got too much on my mind. ➤ Me he cargado la cabeza intentando resolver este problema de cálculo. ▪ Se me cargó la cabeza intentando resolver este problema de cálculo. I've racked my brain trying to solve this calculus problem.

cargarse la lengua ▪ destrozar la lengua to butcher the language

cargarse para alguien to favor someone

cargársele a alguien la cabeza ▪ cargarse la cabeza **1.** to have a lot on one's mind **2.** to rack one's brains ➤ Se me carga la cabeza demasiado entre trabajo y estudios. ▪ Me cargo la cabeza demasiado entre trabajo y estudios. Between work and school, I've got too much on my mind. ➤ Se me cargó la cabeza intentando resolver este problema de cálculo. ▪ Me he cargado la cabeza intentando resolver este problema de cálculo. I've racked my brain trying to solve this calculus problem.

cargársela 1. romperla ▪ quebrarla to break it **2.** to be in for it ➤ *(una copa, por ejemplo)* Me la cargué. I broke it. ➤ Te la vas a cargar. You're going to break it. ➤ ¡Te la vas a cargar! ¡You're in for it (now)!

cargárselas 1. to be in for it **2.** to break them ➤ ¡Te las vas a cargar! You're in for it (now). ➤ Te las vas a cargar si no tienes cuidado. You're going to break them if you're not careful.

cargárselo ▪ romperlo ▪ quebrarlo to break it ➤ *(un lápiz, por ejemplo)* Me lo cargué. ▪ Lo rompí. ▪ Lo quebré. I broke it.

cargárselo a alguien to do someone in ➤ Se lo cargaron. They did him in.

cargárselo (a hombros) to carry it on one's back ▪ to carry him on one's back ➤ *(mochila)* Se la cargó a hombros. *(él)* He carried it on his back. ▪ *(ella)* She carried it on her back. ➤ *(niño)* Se lo cargó a hombros. *(él)* He carried him on his back. ▪ *(ella)* She carried him on her back. ➤ *(niña)* Se la cargó a hombros. *(él)* He carried her on his back. ▪ *(ella)* She carried her on her back.

cargárselo como cliente to kill off someone as a customer ➤ Te lo cargaste como cliente por cobrarle seiscientas pesetas para ver su correo electrónico. You killed him off as a customer by charging him six hundred pesetas to check his E-mail.

¿cargas dinero? 1. do you have any money on you? ▪ do you have any money with you? ▪ have you got any money on you? ▪ have you got any money with you? 2. to charge (money)

¿cargas (dinero) por el pan? ▪ ¿cargas extra por el pan? do you charge for the bread?

cargo de conciencia a alguien: darle ~ ▪ hacer sentir culpable a alguien to make someone feel guilty

cargo de conciencia por algo: tener (un) ~ to feel guilty about something

cargo protocolario ceremonial role ▪ ceremonial position

cargos a cuenta service charges

cargos intermedios ▪ cargos medios ▪ administrativo intermedio middle management

caricatura política political cartoon

la **caridad bien entendida empieza por uno mismo** charity begins at home

cariz dantesco: tomar un ~ ▪ tomar un cariz esperpéntico ▪ tomar un cariz grotesco ▪ tomar un giro dantesco ▪ tomar un giro esperpéntico ▪ tomar un giro grotesco to take a bizarre twist ▪ to take a bizarre turn

cariz esperpéntico: tomar un ~ ▪ tomar un cariz dantesco ▪ tomar un cariz grotesco ▪ tomar un giro esperpéntico ▪ tomar un giro dantesco ▪ tomar un giro grotesco to take a bizarre twist ▪ to take a bizarre turn

cariz grotesco: tomar un ~ ▪ tomar un cariz dantesco ▪ tomar un cariz esperpéntico ▪ tomar un giro grotesco ▪ tomar un giro dantesco ▪ tomar un giro esperpéntico to take a bizarre twist ▪ to take a bizarre turn

carne asada 1. roast beef 2. *(Méx.)* cookout ➤ A veces nos reunimos las familias para hacer una carne asada o a una comida sencilla con antojitos mexicanos. At times our families get together for a cookout or simple meal of Mexican appetizers.

ser **carne de** to be fuel for ➤ Es carne de un segundo libro. It's fuel for a second book.

la **carne de burro no se transparenta** down in front, (I can't see through you)!

ser **carne de cañón** *(persona) que no puede ser rehabilitada* ▪ ser una bala perdida to be hopeless ▪ to be beyond hope ▪ to be a lost cause ▪ to be a hopeless case

carne de cerdo picada ground pork

el **carné de conducir** ▪ (el) carnet de conducir ▪ permiso de conducir driver's license

carne de gallina: ponérsele ~ to give one goose bumps ▪ to give one goose flesh ▪ to get goose bumps ▪ *(de emoción)* to make chills run up and down one's spine ➤ Se me pone carne de gallina. It gives me goose bumps. ▪ It makes chills run up and down my spine.

el **carné de identidad** ▪ (el) carnet de identidad I.D. card ▪ identity card

la **carne de membrillo** flesh of the quince fruit

la **carne de playa** beach scenery ▪ bodies at the beach

la **carne es débil** the flesh is weak

carne molida ▪ carne picada ground beef

carne picada ▪ carne molida ground beef

carne ripiada shredded beef

carne roja red meat

carne seca beef jerky

carne viva: estar en ~ 1. (for) one's flesh to be rubbed raw ▪ (for) one's flesh to be rubbed bare 2. (for) a wound to be open

(la) **carne y hueso** flesh and bone

(la) **carne y sebo, todo cuesta dinero** nothing (in life) is free

carrera armamentista ▪ carrera armamentística arms race

carrera contra el tiempo race against time ▪ race with time

carrera contra reloj race against the clock

carrera de las elecciones (electoral) races ▪ (political) races

carrera de obstáculos obstacle course

carrera en la media: tener una ~ to have a run in one's stocking

el **carrete de hilo** spool of thread

el **carrete de película** roll of film

carretilla elevadora ▪ toro fork lift

carril lento slow lane ➤ Rehuimos los carriles lentos. We avoid the slow lanes.

carril vaho diamond lane ▪ car pool(ing) lane ▪ express lane

carrito de comida *(en un avión)* food cart

carro de caballos ▪ carro tirado por caballos horse-drawn wagon

carro de combate tank

carro de compra ▪ carrito 1. shopping cart 2. *(tienda de comestibles)* grocery cart

carro deportivo ▪ coche deportivo ▪ auto deportivo sports car

carro que los llevaría ▪ carro que los iba a llevar ▪ *(Spain)* el coche que los llevaría ▪ coche que los iba a llevar ▪ *(Spain, leísmo)* coche que les llevaría ▪ coche que les iba a llevar car that would take them ▪ car that was to take them

carros y carretas bumps in the road ▪ problems along the way

carroza (de caballos) 1. carroza (tirada por caballos) horse-drawn carriage 2. diligencia stagecoach

carta abierta open letter

carta blanca carte blanche

carta de acosación dunning letter

carta de ajuste test pattern

carta de pago: dar una ~ ▪ librar una carta de pago letter acknowledging receipt of payment

carta de presentación cover letter

carta de recomendación letter of recommendation

carta en la mesa está *(Esp.)* ▪ lo hecho hecho está what's done is done

carta magna bill of rights

carta sin destinatario explícito (que empieza por "A quien pueda interesar" o "A quien pueda resulta de interés") blind letter (which begins with "Dear Sir" or "To Whom It May Concern")

cartas al director (de un periódico) letters to the editor

cartas credenciales: presentar las ▪ entregar las cartas credenciales to present one's credentials

cartas están sobre la mesa one's cards are on the table

cartas sobre la mesa: poner las ~ to put one's cards on the table

cartearse con alguien to correspond (regularly) with each other ▪ to write to each other ▪ to have a correspondence with someone ▪ to exchange letters (regularly)

cartel de la calle street sign ➤ *(pie de foto)* Bill Clinton saluda ante el cartel de la calle de Little Rock que ha sido bautizada con su nombre. Bill Clinton waves in front of the street sign of a street in Little Rock that has been named for him.

cartera de valores stock portfolio

cartílago roto torn cartilege

casa consistorial city hall

casa cuna ▪ orfanato orphanage

casa de house in ➤ Todos dicen haber visitado su casa de Buenos Aires. They all claim to have visited your house in Buenos Aires.

casa de baños bath house

casa de beneficiencia poor house

casa de campo country house

casa de citas ▪ casa de putas ▪ prostíbulo ▪ (el) burdel ▪ casa de prostitutas whore house ▪ brothel ▪ red-light house ▪ house of prostitution

casa de correos ▪ oficina de correos post office ➤ Irá más rápido si lo mandas a la casa de correos. It goes faster if you mail it at the post office.

casa de Dios house of God ▪ church ▪ temple

casa de empeños pawn shop

casa de ensueño dream house

casa de huéspedes ▪ pensión boarding house

casa de la moneda (currency) mint

casa de locos 1. manicomio ▪ loquero crazy house ▪ loony bin 2. *(lugar muy desorganizado)* madhouse

casa de mucha altura upscale house ▪ very nice house

casa de muñecas doll house

casa de oración house of prayer ▪ house of worship
casa de putas ▪ casa de citas ▪ prostíbulo ▪ (el) burdel ▪ casa de prostitutas whore house ▪ brothel ▪ red-light house ▪ house of prostitution
ser la **casa de tócame Roque** to be a madhouse
casa del Padre heaven
casa del Señor house of the Lord
la **casa donde me crié** ▪ la casa donde crecí the house I grew up in ▪ house where I grew up
casa hermosa ▪ casa preciosa ▪ bella casa beautiful house
casa normal ▪ casa típica a typical house ➤ Es una casa normal para esa región. It's a typical house for that region.
casa preciosa casa hermosa ▪ casa bella beautiful house
casado casa quiere when you're married you want a house of your own
casado pero no capado *(en los anuncios personales)* married but wanting to stray
casamiento por lo civil civil marriage
casar bien con algo to go well with something ▪ to go well together ➤ La alfombra oriental casa bien con el sofa. The oriental rug goes well with the sofa. ▪ The oriental rug and the sofa go well together.
casas apelotonadas houses crowded together
casarse bien con alguien to marry well ▪ to marry someone with money
casarse de penalti ▪ casarse por el sindicato ▪ casarse en estado to have to get married ▪ to have a shotgun wedding
casarse con la suerte to have good fortune in life
casarse con su dictamen ▪ casarse con su opinión ▪ casarse con su parecer to hold fast to one's point of view
casarse en estado ▪ casarse de penalti ▪ casarse por el sindicato de las prisas to have to get married ▪ to have a shotgun wedding
casarse por detrás de la iglesia ▪ amancebarse ▪ concubinarse ▪ amontonarse to live together (without being married) ▪ to be in a common-law marriage ▪ to have a common-law marriage
casarse por el sindicato (de las prisas) ▪ casarse de penalti ▪ casarse en estado to have to get married ▪ to have a shotgun wedding
casarse por lo civil to marry in a civil ceremony ▪ to get married in a civil ceremony
casas adosadas row houses
cascar a alguien 1. dar una paliza a alguien ▪ zurrar a alguien to beat someone up **2.** dar un azote a alguien to spank someone
cascar un huevo to crack (open) an egg
¡cáscaras! 1. ¡vaya! wow! **2.** ¡mecachis! darn it!
cascársela *(subido de tono)* ▪ hacerse una paja ▪ pelársela to jack off ▪ to beat one's meat ▪ to jerk off
casco antiguo old (part of a) city
casco de la ciudad city limits
caseta de peaje toll booth
casi con certeza: decir algo ~ to say something with near certainty
estar **casi desconocido** to be almost unrecognizable ▪ to be barely recognizable
casi desde que... almost from the time that...
casi haberse olvidado ▪ tener casi olvidado ▪ ya casi no acordarse to have almost forgotten ▪ barely to remember ➤ Casi me he olvidado de cómo suena el inglés por haber estado fuera tanto tiempo. ▪ Tengo casi olvidado cómo suena el inglés por haber estado fuera tanto tiempo. ▪ Ya casi no me acuerdo de cómo suena el inglés por haber estado fuera tanto tiempo. I've almost forgotten what English sounds like, I've been away so long. ▪ I barely remember what English sounds like, I've been away so long.
casi lo olvido *(L.am.)* ▪ casi se me olvida *(Esp.)* **1.** I almost forgot **2.** I almost forgot it
casi me da un ataque al corazón I nearly had a heart attack ▪ I almost had a heart attack ▪ I practically had a heart attack
casi nada se sabe de almost nothing is known of
casi nadie ▪ apenas nadie almost no one ▪ hardly anyone
casi no dar to give hardly any
(casi) no dar más de sí ▪ estar que no dar más de sí not to be able to go on any more ▪ to reach one's limit ➤ Casi no doy más de mí. ▪ Estoy que no doy más de mí. I can't go on any more. ▪ I've reached the limit (of my endurance).
casi no hablar un idioma ▪ no hablar un idioma casi ▪ apenas hablar un idioma ▪ no hablar un idioma apenas ▪ prácticamente no hablar un idioma ▪ a duras penas hablar un idioma ▪ prácticamente no hablar un idioma ▪ no hablar un idioma prácticamente ▪ a duras penas hablar un idioma ▪ hablar un idioma a duras penas to barely speak a language ▪ to hardly speak a language ➤ Ella casi no hablaba español cuando llegó a Buenos Aires. ▪ Ella no hablaba español casi cuando llegó a Buenos Aires. ▪ Ella apenas hablaba español cuando llegó a Buenos Aires. ▪ Ella hablaba español apenas cuando llegó a Buenos Aires. ▪ Prácticamente no hablaba español cuando llegó a Buenos Aires. ▪ No hablaba español prácticamente cuando llegó a Buenos Aires. ▪ A duras penas hablaba español cuando llegó a Buenos Aires. ▪ Hablaba español a duras penas cuando llegó a Buenos Aires. She barely spoke Spanish when she arrived in Buenos Aires. ▪ She hardly spoke Spanish when she arrived in Buenos Aires.
casi no lo escucho ▪ casi no lo oigo *(a usted)* I can barely hear you ▪ I can hardly hear you ▪ *(a él)* I can barely hear him ▪ I can hardly hear him ▪ *(a ella)* I can barely hear her ▪ I can hardly hear her
casi no lo oigo ▪ casi no lo escucho *(a usted)* I can barely hear you ▪ I can hardly hear you ▪ *(a él)* I can barely hear him ▪ I can hardly hear him ▪ *(a ella)* I can barely hear her ▪ I can hardly hear her
casi no poder levantarse de la cama ▪ prácticamente no poder levantarse de la cama ▪ apenas poder levantarse de la cama ▪ levantarse a duras penas de la cama to barely be able to get out of bed ▪ to hardly be able to get out of bed ➤ Casi no puede levantarse de la cama por la mañana. ▪ Prácticamente no puede levantarse de la cama por la mañana. ▪ Apenas puede levantarse de la cama por la mañana. ▪ Se levanta a duras penas de la cama por la mañana. He can barely get out of bed in the morning. ▪ He can hardly get out of bed in the morning.
casi no podía creerlo *(yo)* I could hardly believe it ▪ *(él)* he could hardly believe it ▪ *(ella)* she could hardly believe it
casi no podía mantener los ojos abiertos I could hardly keep my eyes open ▪ I could barely keep my eyes open
casi no puedo distinguirlo ▪ apenas puedo distinguirlo I can barely make it out ▪ I can hardly make it out
casi no puedo esperar ▪ apenas si puedo esperar I can hardly wait
casi no puedo ni oírte I can just barely hear you ▪ I can hardly hear you
casi no te escucho I can barely hear you ▪ I can hardly hear you
casi no te oigo ▪ apenas te oigo ▪ te oigo a duras penas I can hardly hear you ▪ I can (just) barely hear you
casi no tocar ▪ prácticamente no tocar ▪ apenas tocar to barely touch ▪ to hardly touch ➤ Casi no tocó su cena. ▪ Prácticamente no tocó su cena. ▪ Apenas tocó su cena. He barely touched his supper.
casi pierdo el autobús ▪ estuve a punto de perder el autobús ▪ *pintoresco* agarré el autobús barriéndome ▪ *(Esp.)* cogí el (auto)bús por los pelos ▪ casi se me va el (auto)bús I almost missed the bus ▪ I nearly missed the bus ▪ I just barely made it to the bus
casi pierdo el avión ▪ por poco pierdo el avión ▪ estuve a punto de perder el avión **1.** I almost missed the plane **2.** *(el mismo día, semana o mes)* ▪ he estado a punto de perder el avión I almost missed the plane ➤ Cuando fui a Barcelona el verano pasado, casi pierdo el avión. ▪ Cuando fui a Barcelona el verano pasado, por poco pierdo el avión. ▪ Cuando fui a Barcelona el verano pasado, estuve a punto de perder el avión. When I went to Barcelona last summer, I almost missed the plane. ➤ Hoy he estado a punto de perder el avión. I almost missed the plane today.
casi se me olvida *(Esp.)* ▪ casi lo olvido *(L.am.)* **1.** I almost forgot **2.** I almost forgot it
casi sin darme cuenta almost without realizing it
casi sin tocar barely having touched ▪ having barely touched ▪ hardly having touched ▪ having hardly touched ➤ Se levantó de la mesa casi sin tocar su cena. ▪ Se levantó de la mesa prácticamente sin tocar su cena. He left the table having barely touched

his supper. ■ He left the table barely having touched his supper. ■ He got up from the table hardly having touched his supper. ■ He got up from the table having hardly touched his supper.

estar **casi todo igual** (for) everything to be almost the same

casi todo igual: seguir ~ (for) nothing to change ■ (for) everything to remain almost the same ➤ Sigue casí todo igual. Nothing has changed.

ser **casi un desconocido(-a)** to be almost a stranger

casita de juguete doll house ■ toy house

ser un **caso de** to be an instance of ■ to be a case of ➤ El teorema de Pitágoras es un caso del teorema binomial. The Pythagorean theorem is an instance of the binomial theorem.

ser un **caso de lealtades divididas** ■ ser un caso de lealtades repartidas to be a case of divided loyalties ➤ It was a case of divided loyalties. Fue un caso de lealtades divididas.

el **caso es que...** the point is that...

caso grave de...: tener ~ to have a bad case of... ➤ Tiene un caso grave de gripe. He has a bad case of the flu. ➤ Ese editorialista sufre un caso grave de falta de atención selectiva. That editorial writer has a bad case of selective inattention.

ser un **caso límite 1.** to be a borderline case **2.** to be an extreme case

el **caso más llamativo** the case commanding the most attention

ser un **caso perdido** to be a hopeless case

¡cáspita! *(Esp.)* ■ ¡caramba! ■ ¡caray! wow!

castigar con todo rigor a alguien to impose the maximum sentence on someone ■ to throw the book at someone

castigarse con la muerte to be punishable by death ➤ El delito se castiga con la muerte. The crime is punishable by death.

¡cataplum! ■ ¡cataplun! **1.** crash! ■ bang! **2.** and lo!

catar (la) comida to sample (the) food

catar vino to taste wine

catarata de escándalos scandal after scandal ■ one scandal after another ■ stream of scandals

cataratas incipientes ■ cataratas nacientes **incipient cataracts** ■ **cataracts in the early stages (of development)**

ser **categóricamente extraño** ■ ser realmente extraño to be downright strange ➤ El médico me puso una prueba de fibra óptica muy profunda en las fosas nasales que me hizo sentir categóricamente extraño. The doctor put a fiberoptic probe way up into my nasal passage that felt downright strange.

católico: no estar ~ ■ no sentirse bien not to feel well ➤ No estoy católico. ■ No me siento bien. I don't feel well.

ser **católico (romano)** to be (Roman) Catholic

católico consecuente exemplary Catholic

católico practicante practicing Catholic

cauce para la expresión de algo: tener (una) ~ ■ dar cauce a la expresión de algo ■ dar cauce a la imaginación de uno to have an avenue for the expression of something ➤ Sin tener cauce para su expresión Without having any avenue for its expression ➤ Sin poder dar cauce a su imaginación Without having an avenue to express one's imagination

el **cauce que los acontecimientos han tomado en los últimos días** ■ el rumbo que los acontecimientos han tomado en los últimos días ■ el camino que los acontecimientos han tomado en los últimos días the turn of events in the last few days ■ the course events have taken in the last few days

cauce seco dry river bed

causa abierta *(derecho)* ■ caso abierto lawsuit ➤ *(noticia)* El ayuntamiento comparece en la causa abierta contra los contables por... The city government joins the lawsuit against its accountants for...

ser la **causa de los celos de alguien** ■ ser el origen de los celos de alguien ■ ser el motivo de los celos de alguien ■ tener la culpa de los celos de alguien to be the cause of someone's jealousy ➤ Él es la causa de los celos de mi marido. ■ Él es el motivo de los celos de mi marido. ■ Él es el origen de los celos de mi marido. ■ Él tiene la culpa de los celos de mi marido. He is the cause of my husband's jealousy. ■ He is the reason for my husband's jealousy.

la **causa del problema** ■ (el) origen del problema cause of the problem ➤ La causa del desastre del transbordador fue una hendidura en una de las láminas resistentes al calor. ■ El origen del desastre del transbordador fue una hendidura en una de las láminas resistentes al calor. The cause of the shuttle disaster was a nick in one of the heat-resistant tiles.

causa justificada just cause

ser una **causa perdida** to be a lost cause

causa subyacente underlying cause

causar alta en una organización ■ dar de alta en una organización ■ ingresar en una organización to enroll in an organization ■ to become a member of an organization

causar asombro to cause amazement

causar baja 1. darse de baja to drop out **2.** *(en una guerra)* to be killed ➤ Él causó baja en la universidad por falta de fondos. He dropped out of the university for lack of funds. ➤ Ayer tres soldados causaron baja en la guerra de Irak. Three soldiers were killed in Iraq yesterday.

causar daños en algo to cause damage to something ■ to damage something ➤ La sequía ha causado daños en los olivos. The draught has caused damage to the olive trees. ■ The draught has damaged the olive trees.

causar desperfectos en to cause damage to

causar dolor (físico) ■ provocar dolor (físico) to cause (physical) pain

causar efectos negativos en to have an adverse affect on ■ to adversely affect ➤ *(noticia)* El concejal hizo especial hincapié en (el tema de) las palomas que causan efectos negativos en la salud y en los edificios de la capital. The councilman drew special attention to the pigeons in the capital that adversely affect public health and public buildings.

causar estragos (con) ■ hacer estragos (con) ■ crear un caos (con) to wreak havoc (with)

causar heridas causar lesiones ■ producir daños to cause injury ■ to cause injuries

causar jaqueca ■ causar un dolor de cabeza to give one a headache ➤ El ruido en el apartmento de mi vecino me está causando jaqueca. The noise in the neighbor's apartment is giving me a headache.

causar lesiones ■ causar heridas ■ producir daños to cause injury ■ to cause injuries

causar quebraderos de cabeza to cause an upset ■ to cause a major headache

causar un gran desconcierto 1. to cause great confusion **2.** to make a big mess **3.** to upset (someone)

causar una buena impresión en un grupo de gente to make a good impression on a group of people

causarle una buena impresión a alguien to make a good impression on someone

causarle quebraderos de cabeza a alguien to cause a major headache for someone

causa(s) de ■ motivo(s) de cause of ➤ Los investigadores trataban de averiguar anoche las causas del derrumbe. ■ Los investigadores trataban de averiguar anoche los motivos del derrumbe. Investigators last night were trying to determine the cause of the collapse.

cavar(se) su propia fosa ■ cavar(se) su propia tumba ■ cavar(se) su propia sepultura to dig one's own grave

caza a reacción ■ caza de reacción fighter jet ■ jet fighter

cazador furtivo poacher

cazadores errantes wandering hunters ■ nomadic hunters ■ itinerant hunters

estar **cazando moscas** ■ estar en la luna ■ estar en las nubes ■ estar en babia to be off in the ozone

cazar a un animal ■ prender a un animal to catch an animal

cazar animales en vedado to poach animals

cazar moscas 1. to catch flies **2.** perder el tiempo to waste time

cazar ratones to catch mice

cazarlas al vuelo to catch things on the fly

ce por ce: describir algo ~ ■ describir algo ce por be ■ describir algo con lujo de detalles to describe something in great detail ■ to describe something in complete detail

cebar el anzuelo ■ poner el cebo en el anzuelo to bait the hook

cebarse con alguien ■ cebarse en alguien **1.** to take it out on someone **2.** to vent one's anger at someone **3.** to ravage someone ➤ *(noticia)* Hambruna y sida se ceban con los más débiles de Zambia. Starvation and AIDS ravage the poor in Zambia

cebarse en alguien ▪ cebarse con alguien **1.** to take one's anger out on someone **2.** to vent one's anger at someone

cebarse la mala suerte con alguien (for) tragedy to strike someone ➤ *(noticia)* La mala suerte se cebó ayer con dos trabajadores que murieron sepultados al derrumbarse un edificio en Valencia. Tragedy struck two workers who died when a building collapsed on them in Valencia.

cebolla picada finely chopped onion

cebolla troceada chopped onion ▪ *(en forma seca)* minced onion

ceder (a algo) to give in (to something)

ceder (a alguien) to give in (to someone)

ceder a la llamada del placer to give in to temptation

ceder a la tentación to give in to temptation

ceder ante la presión ▪ plegarse a la presión to bow to pressure ▪ to give in to pressure ▪ to buckle under pressure

ceder el paso a to yield to ▪ to give way to

ceder el paso a alguien to yield the right of way to someone ▪ to step aside for someone ▪ to make way for someone ➤ *(Selecciones de Reader's Digest)* No cedo el paso a ningún imbécil. -Pues yo, sí, ¡pase! I don't step aside for embeciles!-Well, I do. Go ahead.

ceder el uso de la palabra a alguien to yield the floor to someone

ceder terreno *(en debate, discusión)* to give ground

ceder un poco ▪ ceder ligeramente to give a little ▪ to give slightly ➤ El puente colgante cedió un poco bajo el peso de la muchedumbre. ▪ El puente colgante cedió ligeramente por el peso de la muchedumbre. The suspension bridge gave a little under the weight of the crowd. ▪ The suspension bridge gave slightly under the weight of the crowd.

ser **cegado por la luz** ▪ ser deslumbrado por la luz to be blinded by the light

cegar un motor to clog an engine ➤ Han descartado que una bandada de pájaros cegara el motor. They have ruled out that a flock of birds clogged the engine.

ceguera de río ▪ enfermedad dada en países subdesarrollados river blindness

cejar en un empeño to give up an undertaking ▪ to give up an effort

celar por algo ▪ celar sobre algo ▪ velar por algo to watch over something ➤ Los pastores celaban por sus rebaños. ▪ Los pastores celaban sobre sus rebaños. ▪ Los pastores velaban por sus rebaños. The shepherds watched over their flocks.

celar(se) de alguien to get jealous of someone

celarse de que... to be watchful lest... ▪ to be suspicious lest... ▪ to be watchful in case... ▪ to be suspicious in case...

celda de castigo solitary confinement

celebrar a puerta cerrada to hold behind closed doors ➤ El Supremo aceptó que los juicios se celebren a puerta cerrada. The Supreme Court permitted the trials to be held behind closed doors.

celebrar la vista oral to hold the oral hearing ➤ Ayer los abogados pidieron más tiempo de preparación durante la vista oral celebrada en la audiencia provincial. In yesterday's oral hearing in county court, the attorneys requested more preparation time.

celebrar la cena navideña *(después de anochecer)* to have Christmas (Eve) dinner ▪ to have Christmas (Eve) supper

celebrar la comida navideña *(antes de anochecer)* to have Christmas dinner

celebrar las fiestas ▪ guardar las fiestas to celebrate the feasts ▪ to observe the holy days of obligation

celebrar misa ▪ decir misa ▪ oficiar misa to celebrate mass ▪ to say mass

celebrar muchísimo to be very glad

celebrar un juicio to hold a trial ▪ to conduct a trial

celebrar una conferencia to hold a meeting ▪ to hold a conference

celebrarse en ▪ tener lugar en to take place in ▪ to be held in ▪ to take place at ▪ to be held at ➤ La reunión se celebrará en Madrid. The meeting will take place in Madrid. ➤ La reunión se celebrará en el Hotel Meliá Castilla. The meeting will take place at the Meliá Castilla Hotel.

celebrarse en grande to be celebrated in a big way ➤ En Ecuador se celebra en grande la fiesta de Cristo Rey. In Ecuador they celebrate the feast of Christ the King in a big way.

celebro que... I'm delighted that... ➤ Celebro que te sea de ayuda. I'm delighted that it helps you. ▪ I'm delighted that it's helpful to you.

células durmientes sleeper cells

células embrionarias embryonic cells

células madre mother cells

cena ligera ▪ cena menuda light supper

cenar fuera ▪ salir a cenar to go out for supper ▪ to go out for dinner

cenizas no levantan llamas what's past is over ▪ what's past is past

un **centenar de metros** ▪ unos cien metros some hundred meters ▪ some one hundred meters

centenar de personas: alrededor de un ~ about a hundred people ▪ about one hundred people

centenares de personas: *x* ~ *x* hundred people ➤ Seis centenares de personas acudieron a la conferencia. Six hundred people attended the lecture.

centenares de años *(poco común)* ▪ cientos de años hundreds of years

centenares de animales ▪ cientos de animales hundreds of animals

centenares de personas ▪ cientos de personas hundreds of people

centímetro a centímetro ▪ palmo a palmo inch by inch

céntimo a céntimo se hace una peseta 1. it eventually adds up **2.** many small steps will take you far

la **central eléctrica** electric power plant

la **central nuclear** nuclear power plant

centrarse en to focus on ▪ to highlight ▪ to be centered around ➤ El día de San Valentín se centra en el romance. Valentine's Day is centered around romance.

centrarse en un asunto naturalmente to take to something naturally ➤ Se centra en la informática naturalmente. He takes to computers naturally.

centro comercial shopping center

ser el **centro de atención** to be the center of attention ➤ A los niños les encanta ser el centro de atención. Children love to be the center of attention.

centro de atención al cliente customer service

centro de gravedad center of gravity

centro de trabajo: en el ~ in the workplace

ceñida: ropa ~ ▪ ropa ajustada body-tight clothes ▪ tight-fitting clothes ➤ Llevaba una camiseta ceñida. She wore a body-tight T-shirt.

ceñir a alguien la espada to knight someone

ceñirse a la letra 1. to go by the book ▪ to adhere to the letter **2.** to interpret the scripture literally ➤ No podrás convencer al juez. Siempre se ciñe a la letra. You'll never be able to persuade the judge. He always goes by the book.

ceñirse a la ley to adhere strictly to the law ▪ *(coloquial)* to stick to the law

ceñirse a un tema to concentrate on one thing ▪ to focus on one thing ▪ to limit oneself to one main focus

ceñirse al texto to stick to the text

ceñirse la corona to begin one's reign (as a monarch)

cepillarse a alguien *(subido de tono)* **1.** tirarse a alguien to screw someone **2.** cargarse a alguien to bump someone off ▪ to murder someone

cepillarse el pelo to brush one's hair

cepillarse los dientes to brush one's teeth

cepillárselo ▪ dejar fuera de fuego to take out a military target ▪ to eliminate a military target ➤ Cuando detectan un radar encendido, van y se lo cepillan. When they detect a radar turned on, they go and take it out.

cerca de near

cerca de aquí near here ▪ nearby

estar **cerca de la completación** ▪ estar cerca de la terminación to be near completion ▪ to be close to completion

cerca de la mitad de los... nearly half of all... ■ close to half of all... ➤ Cerca de la mitad de los estudiantes... Nearly half of all students...

cercana ciudad nearby city

estar **cercano(-a) ya** to be nearing ■ to be approaching ➤ El presidente, cercano ya el final de su liderazgo... The president, (now) approaching the end of his term...

cercar una parcela to fence off a plot (of ground) ■ to fence off a lot ➤ Compramos una parcela y la cercamos. We bought a lot and fenced it off.

cercenar la autoridad de alguien to limit someone's authority

cercenar la libertad de alguien to curtail someone's freedom ■ to limit someone's freedom ■ to impose limits on someone's freedom ➤ El nuevo gobierno militar cercenó las libertades de los ciudadanos. The new military government placed restrictions on the citizens' freedom.

cercenar las atribuciones de to limit someone's power to

cercenar los derechos to curtail one's rights

cercenar los vínculos con alguien to distance oneself from someone

cerciorarse de ■ asegurarse de to make sure of

cerciorarse de que... ■ asegurarse de que... to make sure that... ■ to make sure...

el **cerco contra él se va cerrando** ■ el caso contra él se va cerrando the case against him is about to be proved ■ the case against him is about to be established ■ *(coloquial)* they're about to nail him ➤ El cerco contra los responsables del mayor atentado de la historia se va cerrando. The case against those responsible for the greatest terror attack in history is about to be proved. ■ The case against those responsible for the greatest terror attack in history is about to be nailed down.

cerco policial police dragnet

cerebro de mosquito: tener ~ to be pea brained

cernerse las sombras de la noche sobre el jardín ■ cernirse las sombras de la noche sobre el jardín evening shadows were enveloping the garden

cernerse sobre ■ cernirse sobre **1.** to hang over **2.** *(helicóptero)* to hover over ➤ La amenaza del invierno se cierne sobre los refugiados afganos. The threat of winter hangs over the Afghan refugees.

ser un **cero a la izquierda** to be totally useless

cero patatero: sacar un ~ to get a flat F

cero puntos: ganar ~ to win no points ■ to get no points

cerradas ovaciones thunderous ovation

estar **cerrado a cal y canto** **1.** *(cosa)* to be locked up tight **2.** *(persona)* to be really uptight ■ to be extremely guarded ■ to be extremely withdrawn ➤ La puerta del museo está cerrada cada noche a cal y canto. The museum is locked up tight at night.

cerrado aplauso: dar a alguien ~ to give someone a warm round of applause

cerrado(-a) aplauso: recibir un ~ to receive a warm round of applause

ser **cerrado de mollera** ■ ser duro de mollera to be thick-headed ■ to be pig-headed

estar **cerrado por obras** to be closed for repairs ■ to be closed for remodeling

estar **cerrado por reformas** **1.** to be closed for remodeling **2.** to be closed for repairs

cerrar con broche de oro ■ cerrar con un broche de oro to close with a spectacular ending

cerrar con caídas ligeras *(bolsa)* to close slightly lower

cerrar con ligeras alzas *(bolsa)* to close slightly higher

cerrar con ligeras caídas *(bolsa)* to close slightly lower

cerrar con (un) broche de oro to close with a spectacular ending

cerrar el año con un superávit to end the year with a (budget) surplus

cerrar el grifo to turn off the tap ■ to turn off the faucet

cerrar el juego *(naipes)* to make the closing play of the game

cerrar el paso to block the way

cerrar el periodo de sesiones to adjourn ■ to recess ➤ El Supremo, en su última decisión antes de cerrar el periodo de sesiones de esta temporada... The Supreme Court, in its last decision before recessing for the season...

cerrar el pico ■ quedarse callado to keep one's trap shut ■ to keep mum ■ to keep it to oneself ■ to keep quiet

cerrar el programa adecuadamente *(informática)* to exit (from) the program correctly ➤ Cuando cierras adecuadamente el programa... When you exit from the program correctly...

cerrar el puño to make a fist

cerrar filas ■ cerrar las filas to close ranks

cerrar filas en torno a alguien to close ranks around someone

cerrar la boca a alguien ■ hacer callar a alguien **1.** tapar la boca a alguien to put one's hand over someone's mouth **2.** cerrar el pico a alguien to shut someone up

cerrar la mano to tighten one's belt ■ to live on less

cerrar la mollera ■ cerrarse la mollera ■ tener cerrada la mollera to close one's mind

cerrar la puerta a algo to close the door on something ■ to end something

cerrar la puerta a alguien to close the door on someone ■ to deny someone an opportunity

cerrar las cortinas to close the curtains ■ to draw the curtains

cerrar (las) filas to close ranks

cerrar los labios ■ sellar los labios to close one's lips ■ to seal one's lips

cerrar los ojos to close one's eyes ■ to shut one's eyes

cerrar plaza *(tauromaquia)* to vacate the bullring

cerrar un acuerdo to close a deal

cerrar un pacto to make a pact ■ to close a deal

cerrar un trato to close a deal

cerrar una herida *(a menudo figurativo)* to close a wound ■ to bind up a wound ➤ *(Lincoln)* Cerrar las heridas de la nación To bind up the nation's wounds.

cerrar una venta to close a sale

cerrar viejas heridas to heal old wounds

cerrarse a la banda ■ cerrarse en banda to dig in one's heels

cerrarse con to end with ➤ *(titular)* El conflicto del gasóleo se cierra con 120.000 milliones en ayudas. The gasoline controversy ended with 120,000 million in aid.

cerrarse el acuerdo **1.** *(de negocios)* to close the deal **2.** *(político)* to sign the accord ■ to sign the agreement

cerrarse el cielo ■ nublarse ■ cargarse ■ cubrirse de nubes to become overcast

cerrarse el día (for) the work day to end

cerrar(se) el plazo de solicitud de matricula en la universidad (for) the university application deadline to pass

cerrarse en banda ■ cerrarse a la banda to be resistant ■ to dig in one's heels

cerrarse la noche *(literario)* (for) night to close in

cerrarse todas las puertas ■ cerrarse todas las oportunidades (for) doors to be closed to one ➤ Se me cierran todas las puertas por no tener un título universitario. All the doors are closed to me because I don't have a degree.

cerrarse ya finally to close ■ to close finally ➤ Después de muchos meses anunciándolo, mañana se cierra ya el antiguo instituto. After announcing it for months, tomorrow the old high school will finally close. ➤ Por fin se cierra ya ese maloliente vertedero. They're finally going to close that smelly garbage dump.

cerro de gente ■ (un) montón de gente ■ *coloquial* ■ (un) puña'o de personas a bunch of people

cerro de papeles ■ montaña de papeles ■ pila de papeles ■ (un) montón de papeles ■ *(coloquial)* ■ (un) puña'o de papeles stack of papers ■ pile on papers

cerro de personas ■ (un) montón de personas ■ montaña de personas ■ *(Esp., coloquial)* ■ (un) puña'o de personas bunch of people

certificado de notas ■ historial académico transcript(s)

cerveza oscura dark beer

cerveza rubia light beer

el **cese al fuego** *(negociado por acuerdo)* ■ cese de hostilidades cease fire ■ cessation of hostilities

el **cese de fuego** ■ alto de fuego cessation of fire

el **cese de violencia** cessation of the violence ▪ halt to the violence ▪ halt in the violence

el **césped vallado** fenced lawn ▪ fenced yard

la **cesta de la compra** shopping basket (with handles)

chachi (piruli) super (duper) ▪ awesome ➤ Los peques pensaron que la visita al zoo fue chachi piruli. The kids thought the visit to the zoo was super duper.

chafar a alguien ▪ dejar chafado a alguien to take the wind out of someone's sails

chafar la guitarra a alguien to take the wind out of someone's sails ➤ Le chafó la guitarra al decirle que el plazo de inscripción se había cerrado hacía un mes. It took the wind out of his sails to be told that the registration period had ended a month before.

chafársele to go up in smoke ➤ Se le han chafado todos sus planes. All his plans have gone up in smoke.

estar **chalado(-a) por algo** to be crazy about something

estar **chalado(-a) por alguien** to be crazy about someone

chaleco antibalas bulletproof vest

chanela como nadie *(Valle-Inclán)* he understands better than anybody else

chapado a la antigua old-fashioned

estar **chapado a la antigua** to be old fashioned

estar **chapado en oro** to be gold-plated

estar **chapado en latón** to be brass-plated

estar **chapado en plata** to be silver-plated

chasquear los dedos to snap one's fingers ➤ Él es popular con los niños porque puede chasquear dos dedos a la vez. He's popular with the kids because he can snap two fingers at a time.

chasquear un látigo to crack a whip

el **cheque en blanco** blank check

chequear el correo electrónico *(Esp.)* ▪ mirar el correo electrónico ▪ mirar si uno tiene correo electrónico ▪ ver el correo electrónico ▪ checar el correo electrónico to check one's E-mail

chica de alterne prostitute

el **chichón en la cabeza** knot on one's head ▪ bump on one's head

el **chicle de pompa** *(Esp.)* bubble gum

chiflarse por completo por alguien to fall for someone ▪ to flip over someone

chillar más que una rata to squeal like a stuck pig ▪ to overreact

chinchín *(cuando se brinda)* ▪ ¡salud! to your health

chincha rabiña, que tengo una piña con muchos piñones y tú no los comes na, na, na, na, *na*, na

chinchar a alguien to get someone going

¡**chínchate!** ▪ ¡lástima! ▪ ajo y agua ▪ mala suerte ▪ te fastidias so there! ▪ take that! ▪ tough luck! ▪ too bad!

chipendi lerendi *(Esp., coloquial)* chupi lerengui ▪ chachi piruli super duper

chirrido de frenos squealing of brakes ▪ screeching of brakes

chirrido de la puerta creaking of the door ▪ squeaking of the door ➤ Esa puerta tiene un chirrido espantoso. The door creaks badly. ▪ The door squeaks badly.

¡**chis!** hey, you! ➤ ¡Chis!-¡No soy una lechuza! Hey, you!-Straw's cheaper, and grass is free.

chisme: pasar un ~ ▪ pasar un cotilleo to spread gossip

ser **chismes de vecindad** ▪ ser la comidilla del vecindario to be the butt of neighborhood gossip ▪ to be the victim of neighborhood gossip

chispear to sprinkle lightly ▪ to drizzle lightly ▪ to spit rain

chiste impropio ▪ chiste verde ▪ chiste de color subido ▪ chiste fuera del tiesto off-color joke

el **chiste verde** off-color joke

chivársele a alguien to tell on someone ▪ to squeal on someone ▪ to tell ➤ No te me chives. Don't tell on me. ➤ No chives a mi madre. Don't tell my mom.

ser el **chivo expiatorio** ▪ pagar el pato to be the scapegoat

¡**choca esos cinco!** give me five! ▪ give me a high five!

¡**chócala!** give me a high five!

¡**chócalas!** *(con ambas manos)* give me ten!

chocar y huir hit and run ➤ Le acusaron de chocar y huir después de que dejó la escena del hecho. He was charged with hit and run after the leaving the scene of the accident.

chócate esa ▪ chócatela shake my hand! ▪ give me handshake!

chocar de frente contra to collide head-on with

chocar los cinco to give someone a high five

estar **chocho(-a) de que...** to be tickled pink that... ▪ to be just delighted that...

el **choque de frente** ▪ choque frontal head-on collision

el **choque frontal** ▪ choque de frente head-on collision

¡**chorradas!** nonsense! ▪ horse feathers!

chorreo mental brain storm ▪ outpouring of ideas

chorrito de aceite de oliva a dash of olive oil ▪ a splash of olive oil

chorrito de líquido splash of liquid ▪ dash of liquid ➤ Se añade seis cucharadas de harina y por último un chorrito de leche. Add six tablespoons of flour, and last, a splash of milk. ▪ Add six tablespoons of flour, and last, a dash of milk.

chorro de whiskey a shot of whiskey ➤ ¿Podrías echarle un chorro de whiskey? Could you put a shot of whiskey in it?

chorros de luz streams of light

ser un **chupacámara** to be a camera hog

chupar banquillo calentar banquillo to warm the bench

chupar cámara to hog the camera

chupar como una esponja to absorb knowledge like a sponge

chupar del bote to be a boot licker ▪ to curry favor with someone

chupar la sangre a alguien to be a leech ➤ Ese tipo les está chupando la sangre a sus amigos. Siempre les pide dinero. That guy's a leech. He's always trying to borrow money from his friends.

chupar rueda (de un coche) ▪ ir a la rueda (de un coche) **1.** to tailgate (a car) **2.** *(coches de carrera)* to slipstream *(Nota: también se aplica al ciclismo)*

chuparse el dedo 1. to suck one's thumb **2.** ser ingenuo to be a babe in the woods ▪ to be naïve ▪ to be unsuspecting ➤ Que no creas que me chupo el dedo. Don't think I'm that naïve.

chuparse los dedos: estar para ~ to be scrumptuous ▪ to be finger-licking good

¡**chúpate esa!** ▪ aguántate con eso put that in your pipe and smoke it!

chutar (el balón) ▪ darle al balón ▪ tirar el balón to kick the ball

cibernética matemática informática computer science

ciclo socialista socialist period ➤ Los votantes portugueses han dado por concluido el ciclo socialista con el ajustado triunfo de los socialdemócratas. Portuguese voters have drawn to a close the socialist period with the narrow victory of the social democrats.

estar **ciego(-a) a los defectos de alguien** to be blind to someone's faults

estar **ciego(-a) con algo** to be wild about something

estar **ciego(-a) con alguien** to be wild about someone

ciego(-a) de comida: ponerse ~ to eat oneself blind

ciego(-a) de alcohol: ponerse ~ to drink oneself under the table

Cielito Lindo *(canción tradicional de México)* Heavenly One

cielo despejado ▪ cielo diáfano clear sky ▪ wall-to-wall sunshine

cielo diáfano ▪ cielo despejado clear sky ▪ wall-to-wall sunshine

cielo encapotado overcast sky

cielos despejados clear skies ▪ *(informal)* wall-to-wall sunshine

cien metros lisos (one) hundred-meter dash ▪ (one) hundred-yard dash

cien metros vallas (one) hundred-meter hurdles ▪ (one) hundred-yard hurdles

cien por cien ▪ ciento por ciento a hundred percent ▪ one hundred percent ▪ completely ▪ fully ➤ No funciona al cien por cien. It's not working a hundred percent. ▪ It's not working completely. ▪ It's not fully functional. ▪ It's not fully functioning. ➤ Estoy cien por cien preparado para el examen. I'm fully prepared for the exam. ➤ Es cien por cien lo que estaba buscando. That's exactly what I was looking for. ➤ Estoy cien por cien seguro de ello. I'm absolutely positive (of it). ▪ I'm absolutely sure.

cien por cien: estar al ~ ▪ funcionar a pleno rendimiento to be at one's best ➤ Los candidatos estuvieron al cien por cien durante el debate. The candidates were at their best during the debate.

cien por cien a la disposición de alguien: estar al ~ to be completely at someone's disposal ▪ to be entirely at someone's disposal

estar **cien por cien de acuerdo (con...)** to be in complete agreement (with...)

ciencias de la naturaleza natural sciences

ciento por ciento ▪ cien por cien a hundred percent ▪ one hundred percent ▪ completely ▪ fully

ciento y la madre *(Esp.)* everybody under the sun ▪ everybody and his brother ➤ Eramos ciento y la madre. **1.** Everybody and his brother were there. ▪ Everybody under the sun was there. **2.** Everybody and his brother were here. ▪ Everybody under the sun was here.

cientos de años hundreds of years

cientos de llamadas ▪ centenares de llamadas hundreds of calls

cientos de personas ▪ centenares de personas hundreds of people

cierra tu puerta y la de tus vecinos guard your own privacy, honor that of your neighbors

el **cierre de filas de** closing of ranks by ▪ closing of ranks on the part of

cierta duda sobre some doubt about ➤ Existía cierta duda sobre... There was some doubt about...

cierta mañana one morning

cierto día ▪ un buen día one day ➤ Cierto día el padre de Schubert acudió a la escuela de su hijo para ver su historial. One day, Schubert's father went to his son's school to look at his school record.

cifra de fallecidos ▪ cifra de los muertos death toll

cifra de muertos ▪ cifra de fallecidos death toll

cifras récord all-time record

cima de una montaña summit of a mountain ▪ the highest point on a mountain ▪ the highest point of a mountain ▪ top of a mountain

ser la **cima del iceberg** ▪ ser la punta del iceberg that's (just) the tip of the iceberg ➤ That's just the tip of the iceberg. Sólo es la cima del iceberg.

cima nevada snow-covered peak

cine mudo silent movies ▪ silent film(s)

cinta aislante duct tape

cinta de equipajes baggage carousel

cinta de lomo adobada marinated pork loin

cinta métrica metric tape measure ▪ measuring tape

cintura de avispa hour-glass figure

cintura de un pantalón waist of a pair of pants ▪ pant waist

cinturón de castidad chastity belt

circo mediático ▪ circo de los medios de difusión media circus

circuito automovilístico race track

circuito cerrado: emitirse por ~ to be broadcast over closed circuit ▪ to be broadcast via closed circuit

circuito de espera *(aeronáutica)* holding pattern

circular a alta velocidad to travel at high speed ▪ to go at high speed ▪ to move at a high speed ➤ El Ave circula a 300 kilómetros por hora. The Ave travels at 300 kilometers per hour. ➤ El coche circulaba a noventa millas por hora. The car was traveling at ninety miles per hour. ▪ The car was going 90 miles per hour.

circular a *x* kilómetros por hora ▪ ir a *x* kilómetros por hora to travel at *x* kilometers per hour ▪ to go *x* kilometers per hour

circular por el sentido contrario to travel in the opposite direction ▪ to move in the opposite direction ▪ to go in the opposite direction ▪ to go in the other direction ▪ *(más coloquial)* to go the other way ▪ to go the opposite way ➤ En ese momento, la hormigonera circulaba por el sentido contrario. At that moment, the cement mixer was travelling in the opposite direction. ▪ At that moment, the cement mixer was moving in the opposite direction. ▪ At that moment, the cement mixer was going in the opposite direction. ▪ At that moment, the cement mixer was going the other way.

círculo más allegado inner circle

círculo de la pobreza: salir del ~ to break out of the poverty cycle

círculo vicioso: formarse un ~ to become a vicious circle ➤ Se forma un círculo vicioso. It becomes a vicious circle.

circundar algo to surround something ➤ La policía circundó el edificio. The police surrounded the building.

circundar a alguien una aureola de respeto to be surrounded by an aura of respect ▪ to be highly respected

circunnavegar al globo ▪ dar la vuelta al globo to circumnavigate the globe

circunstancias atenuantes attenuating circumstances ▪ mitigating circumstances

circunstancias en que le toca a uno vivir circumstances that it is one's fate to endure

circunstancias sin aclarar unclear circumstances

cirio pascual *(catolicismo)* paschal candle

ciruela escarchada candied plum

cirugía a corazón abierto ▪ operación a corazón abierto open-heart surgery

cirugía de derivación coronaria coronary bypass surgery

ciscarse de miedo ▪ cagarse de miedo to be scared shitless

cita a ciegas blind date

cita de negocios business appointment

cita electoral election day

cita ficticia phony quotation

cita literal direct quotation

cita soñada dream date

ser **citado(-a) a través de otro médico** to be referred by another doctor

citar a alguien textualmente to quote someone word for word

citar a un animal to bait an animal

citar a un toro to incite a bull ▪ to bait a bull ▪ to wave the cape at a bull

citar un reparto ▪ citar una entrega to schedule a delivery

citar una entrega ▪ citar un reparto to schedule a delivery

citar una recogida to schedule a pickup

citarse con alguien ▪ concretar una cita con alguien ▪ quedar con alguien ▪ hacer una cita con alguien **1.** to make a date with someone **2.** to make an appointment with someone

citius, altius, fortius faster, higher, stronger

ciudad adoptiva adopted city

cuidad agobiada stressful city

ciudad de los reyes ▪ Lima, Perú city of the kings ▪ city of the maji *(Nota: Nombrado así por Pizarro porque fue fundado en Epifanía (duodécimo día de Navidad). ▪ So named by Pizarro because it was founded on Epiphany (the Twelfth Day of Christmas).)*

la **Ciudad del Vaticano** Vatican City

ciudad dormitorio bedroom community

ciudad hermana sister city

ciudad jardín *(apodo de Madrid)* the garden city ▪ Madrid

la **ciudad natal** ▪ patria chica hometown

ciudad satélite satellite city ▪ satellite community ▪ outlying city ▪ *(plural)* satellite cities ▪ satellite communities ▪ outlying cities ▪ surrounding cities

ciudad satélite (de) surrounding cities ▪ outlying cities ▪ satellite cities

ciudadano de la tercera edad ▪ persona de la tercera edad senior citizen

ciudadano de segunda second-class citizen

ciudadano modelo ▪ ciudadano ejemplar model citizen ▪ exemplary citizen

ciudadanos corrientes ordinary citizens

civilizaciones antiguas ancient civilizations

clamar al cielo to cry (out) for attention ➤ El estado de las calles de Vallecas clama al cielo. The state of the streets in Vallecas cries out for attention.

clamar en el desierto to cry out in vain

clamar por justicia to cry out for justice ▪ to appeal for justice

el **clamor de la multitud** the roar of the crowd

el **clamor de los aplausos** thunderous applause ▪ thunderous ovation ➤ Todo político busca el clamor de los aplausos. All politicians thirst after the sound of applause. ▪ All politicians thirst after popular acclaim.

el **clan inmobiliario** real estate clans ■ real estate cliques ■ real estate mafias ➤ *(noticia)* El líder del partido socialista tomará medidas para acabar con los clanes inmobiliarios en el partido. The socialist party leader will take measures to do away with real estate mafias within the party.

ser una **clara señal de que...** to be a clear indication that...

¡**claro!** ■ sí, sí 1. yeah! ■ uh-huh 2. of course ■ sure 3. got it!

¡**claro, adelante!** sure, go ahead!

estar **claro como el agua** to be crystal clear ■ to be clear as a bell

claro de luna ■ (la) luz de la luna moonlight

claro del bosque ■ esplanada del bosque clearing in the woods ■ clearing in the forest

¡**claro está!** that's obvious! ■ that's clear!

claro que naturally ■ of course

claro que lo hace 1. *(él)* yes, he does ■ he does, indeed 2. *(ella)* yes, she does ■ she does, indeed

claro que lo hacen yes, they do

claro que lo haré ■ por supuesto que lo haré of course I will (do it) ■ of course I'll do it

¡**claro que no!** of course not! ■ certainly not!

claro que puedo ■ por supuesto que puedo of course I can

¡**claro que sí!** ■ ¡efectivamente! ■ ¡eso es! ■ ¡por supuesto! ■ ¡cómo no! of course! ■ right! ■ it sure does! ■ it certainly does! ➤ ¿Llueve mucho en Costa Rica?-Claro que sí. Does it rain a lot in Costa Rica?-It sure does. ■ Does it rain a lot in Costa Rica?-It certainly does.

clase alta upper class

clase baja lower class

clase media ■ burguesía middle class

clase dirigente ■ clase dominante ruling class

clase dominante ■ clase dirigente ruling class

clase particular tutoring session

la **clase se ha terminado** ■ la clase se ha acabado ■ la clase se terminó ■ la clase se acabó class is over

clases de vuelo: recibir ~ to take flying lessons

claudicar ante la presión to give in to pressure ■ to buckle under pressure ■ to cave in to pressure

ser el **clavadito de alguien** ■ ser la viva imagen de alguien ■ ser la estampa de alguien to be the spitting image of someone ■ to look exactly like someone

ser **clavado a alguien** to be the spitting image of someone ■ to look just like someone ■ to look exactly like someone

clavar a alguien to gouge someone ■ to overcharge someone ➤ Nos clavaron. They gouged us. ■ They overcharged us. ■ We paid through the nose.

clavar la vista en alguien to stare at someone ■ to glare at someone

clavar los ojos en algo to fix one's eyes on something ■ to fix one's gaze on something

clavar los ojos en alguien to fix one's eyes on someone ■ to fix one's gaze on someone ➤ Es tan burro que clavaría un clavo con la cabeza. He's so stupid he'd pound in a nail with his head.

clavarle espuelas al caballo ■ meterle espuelas al caballo ■ espolear al caballo ■ picar al caballo to spur (on) the horse

clavarse la mirada en alguien ■ mirar fijamente a alguien ■ mirar con fijeza a alguien to stare at someone ➤ Ella se clavó la mirada en mí. She stared at me.

clavársele en el corazón to cut someone to the quick ■ to hurt someone deeply

clavársele una astilla to get a splinter ➤ Se me clavó una astilla. I got a splinter.

clavija telefónica telephone jack ■ phone jack

clavo duro de morder *(L.am.)* ■ un hueso duro de roer a tough nut to crack

el, la **cliente habitual** ■ (el, la) habitual del local regular customer

el **cliente siempre tiene la razón** the customer is always right

clima amable agreeable climate

clima árido arid climate ■ dry climate

clima húmedo humid climate

clima maravilloso ■ tiempo radiante beautiful weather ■ magnificent weather ■ wall-to-wall sunshine ➤ El clima está maravilloso hoy. ■ El tiempo está radiante hoy. The weather is beautiful today. ■ The weather is magnificent today. ■ It's wall-to-wall sunshine today.

clima templado ■ clima cálido temperate climate ➤ El clima de la Ciudad de México no es muy templado por su altitud sobre el nivel del mar. The climate of Mexico City is not very warm because of its elevation above sea level.

clínicamente probado clinically tested

cloroformo impreso *(Mark Twain)* chloroform in print

coágulo de sangre blood clot

coartar las libertades de alguien to limit someone's freedom ■ to curtain someone's freedom

cobertura informativa ■ cobertura de una información news coverage ■ coverage of the news

ser **cobijado por alguien** to be given safe haven by someone ■ to be protected by someone

cobra buena fama y échate a dormir get into the right people's good graces, you needn't worry about your future

cobrar derechos de autor to get royalties ■ to be paid royalties

cobrar fama ■ ganarse el favor de la gente to get in people's good graces

cobrar fuerza to gather force ➤ El huracán cobró fuerza con el cálido aire proveniente del este. The hurricane gathered force with the warm air coming from the east.

cobrar fuerzas ■ cargar pilas to recharge one's batteries ➤ Necesito cobrar fuerzas. ■ Necesito cargar pilas. I need to recharge my batteries. ■ I need to rest and regain my energy.

cobrar el alquiler a los inquilinos ■ cobrar los alquileres a los inquilinos to collect the rent from the tenants ➤ El dueño pasa por aquí una vez al mes para cobrar el alquiler a los inquilinos. The landlord comes around once a month to collect the rent from the tenants.

cobrar pagos a plazos to collect payments in installments

cobrar perspectiva to come into focus ■ to take on perspective ■ to resolve

cobrar por el pan to charge for the bread ➤ ¿Cobra usted por el pan? Do you charge for the bread?

cobrar sentido to take on meaning ➤ Desde su muerte sus palabras han cobrado un sentido especial. Since his death, his words have taken on special meaning.

cobrar una indemnización to collect an insurance compensation payment ■ to receive an insurance compensation payment

cobrar valentía ■ tomar aliento ■ animarse to take heart

cobrar vida to come to life

cobrar vidas to cost lives ■ to claim lives

cobrar *x* dólares de más a alguien por algo to overcharge someone (by) *x* dollars for something

cobrarle el pago domiciliado tener el pago domiciliado to draft one's bank account ■ to do a draft of one's bank account

cobrarse su víctima mortal to claim its victim ■ to claim its fatality ➤ El brote de legionella se ha cobrado su quinta víctima mortal. The outbreak of Legionnaire's disease had claimed its fifth victim ■ The outbreak of Legionnaire's disease has claimed its fifth fatality.

cobrárselo en carne *(subido de tono)* ■ cobrárselo en especies to take it in flesh ■ to collect in flesh ➤ *(dícese en broma)* No te preocupes por devolverme el dinero. Te lo cobraré en carne. Don't worry about paying me back. I'll take it in flesh.

cobros impagados ■ cobros morosos payments in arrears ■ late payments

el **coche bomba** ■ *(plural)* ■ coches bomba car bomb

el **coche cama** Pullman (car)

coche compacto ■ auto compacto compact car

el **coche con mucha aceleración** *(Esp.)* ■ carro con mucha aceleración car with good pickup

el **coche controlado a distancia por la red** car remotely controlled by computer

el **coche de carreras** race car

el **coche de marchas** a (car with a) stick shift ➤ ¿Es de marchas o automático? Is it a stick or (an) automatic?
el **coche de prueba** demonstrator car
coche deportivo ▪ carro deportivo ▪ auto deportivo sports car
el **coche es un siniestro total** car was totalled ➤ El coche ha sido declarado un siniestro total. The car was declared totalled.
ser el **coche escoba (en una carrera)** last car (in a race)
el **coche patrulla** ▪ coche patrullero patrol car
el **coche que les llevaría** *(Esp., leísmo)* ▪ coche que los llevaría **1.** *(a ellos)* the car that was to take them **2.** *(a ustedes)* the car that was to take you
el **coche que los llevaría 1.** *(a ellos)* the car that was to take them **2.** *(a ustedes)* the car that was to take you
los **coches de choque** ▪ autitos chocadores bumper cars
los **coches veloces** ▪ carros veloces fast cars
cochina envidia que le corroe that's envy talking ▪ *(tú)* you're just jealous ▪ *(él)* he's just jealous ▪ *(ella)* she's just jealous
cocina casera home cooking
cocina independiente con tendedero *(anuncio de inmobiliario)* ▪ cocina independiente con lavadero separate kitchen with utility porch
estar **cocinando** to be cooking ▪ to do some cooking ➤ Estuve cocinando este fin de semana. I did some cooking this weekend.
cocinar a fuego fuerte ▪ cocinar a fuego alto to cook on high heat ▪ to cook over high heat
cocinar a fuego lento ▪ cocinar a llama baja to cook on low heat ▪ to cook over low heat
codearse con gente rica y famosa to rub shoulders with the rich and famous
codificado por colores *(adjetivo)* color-coded
código de barras bar code
código de circulación driver's license manual
código de vestimenta dress code
código fuente *(informática)* source code
código postal zip code ▪ postal code
codo con codo: trabajar ~ to work side by side ▪ to work elbow to elbow ▪ to work together
coeficiente intelectual intelligence quotient ➤ Coeficiente intelectual superior a lo normal Higher than average I.Q.
coeficientes de sustentación y arrastre *(aerodinámica)* lift and drag coefficients ➤ Los coeficientes de sustentación y arrastre, prediciendo el comportamiento de las alas de un avión, fueron desarrollados por Ludwig Prandtl en la Universidad de Göttingen. The lift and drag coefficients, predicting airplane wing performance, were developed by Ludwig Prandtl at the University of Göttingen.
cofa de vigía ▪ (la) torre de vigía crow's nest (of a ship)
cógeme eso ▪ pásame eso pass me that ▪ pass that to me
coger a alguien con las manos en la masa *(Esp.)* ▪ pillar a alguien con las manos en la masa ▪ pillar a alguien in fraganti ▪ agarrar a alguien con las manos en la masa ▪ agarrar a alguien in fraganti to catch someone red-handed ▪ to catch someone in the act
coger a alguien desprevenido ▪ coger a alguien en bragas to catch someone unprepared
coger a alguien en la acción de hacer algo *(Esp.)* ▪ agarrar a alguien en la acción de hacer algo ▪ pillar a alguien en la acción de hacer algo to catch someone in the act of doing something
coger a alguien en bragas *(Esp.)* ▪ pillar a alguien en bragas to catch someone with his pants down ▪ to catch someone unprepared
coger a alguien en el acto ▪ pillar a alguien en el acto to catch someone in the act
coger a alguien en mal latín to catch someone pulling the wool over someone's eyes ▪ to catch someone in a deception
coger a alguien en mal momento *(Esp.)* ▪ pillar a alguien en mal momento ▪ enganchar a alguien en mal momento to catch someone at a bad time
coger a alguien en medio de algo *(Esp.)* ▪ tomar de en medio ▪ agarrar a alguien de en medio de algo to catch someone in the middle of something ▪ to interrupt someone in the middle of something
coger a alguien en pelotas to catch someone with his pants down ▪ to catch someone unprepared
coger a alguien en un renuncio *(Esp.)* ▪ pillar a alguien en un renuncio to catch someone in a lie
coger a alguien fuera de juego *(Esp.)* ▪ pillar a alguien fuera de juego to catch someone off guard ▪ to have got me on that one ➤ Me has cogido fuera de juego. You've got me on that one. ▪ You've got me on that one.
coger a alguien improvisto to catch someone unawares
coger a alguien mintiendo *(Esp.)* ▪ pillar a alguien mintiendo ▪ agarrar a alguien mintiendo to catch someone lying ▪ to catch someone in a lie ➤ (Esp., leísmo) Le cogí mintiendo. I caught him lying. ▪ I caught him in a lie. ▪ *(a ella)* I caught her lying ➤ La cogí mintiendo. I caught her lying. ▪ I caught her in a lie.
coger a alguien por banda to get even with someone
coger agua con cubeta to draw water with a bucket
coger agua en cesto ▪ coger agua en canasta ▪ coger agua en harnero not to have things under control ▪ (for) things to get out of hand ▪ to try to juggle too many things at once
coger al dedillo ▪ coger a dedo to get something down pat ▪ to get something (down) perfectly ▪ to learn something perfectly ➤ Has cogido ese problema de cálculo al dedillo. You've got that calculus problem down pat.
coger al toro por los cuernos ▪ agarrar el toro por los cuernos to take the bull by the horns
coger algo al dedillo to get something (down) perfectly ▪ to get something down pat ▪ to learn something perfectly
coger algo al instante 1. to catch on (to something) instantly **2.** *(beisbol, idea)* ▪ coger algo al vuelo to catch something on the fly
coger algo al oído ▪ coger algo al vuelo ▪ tomar algo al oído to catch something on the fly ▪ to learn something instantly (without writing it down)
coger algo al vuelo *(Esp.)* ▪ agarrar al vuelo **1.** to catch something on the fly ▪ to catch something in mid air **2.** *(figurativo)* to catch something on the fly ▪ to learn something instantly (without even writing it down)
coger algo de oído *(como el compositor Saint-Saëns)* to hear music and be able to play it ▪ to get something by ear
coger algo con papel de fumar to handle something with kid gloves
coger algo de paso *(Esp.)* ▪ pillar algo de paso to catch something in passing
coger apuntes *(Esp.)* ▪ tomar apuntes to take notes ➤ Tengo que faltar a clase mañana. ¿Podrías cogerme los apuntes? I have to miss class tomorrow. Will you take notes for me?
coger buen sitio *(Esp.)* ▪ agarrar un buen sitio to get a good seat
coger confianza (con alguien) 1. *(positivo)* to develop a (good) rapport with someone **2.** *(negativo)* to be taken advantage of by someone ➤ A lo largo de dos años trabajando juntos, hemos cogido confianza mutua. In the course of working together for two years, we've developed a good rapport. ➤ Es casi una emboscada, cogieron confianza y me esperan cada mañana para que los lleve en mi carro. ▪ *(Esp. leísmo)* Es casi una emboscada, cogieron confianza y me esperan cada mañana para que los lleve en mi coche.
coger cuerda to get the knack (of it)
coger de buenas a alguien *(Esp.)* ▪ agarrar a alguien de buenas to catch someone in a good mood
coger de improviso a alguien *(Esp. y L.am.)* to catch someone by surprise
coger de novato a alguien *(Esp.)* ▪ tomar de novato a alguien to take someone on as a novice, with no experience
coger el auricular *(Esp.)* ▪ levantar la bocina ▪ agarrar el teléfono ▪ levantar el tubo to pick up the receiver
coger el autobús por los pelos *(Esp.)* ▪ agarrar el camión por los pelos to catch the bus just in time ▪ to (just) barely make it to the bus ▪ to barely make it the bus ➤ Cogí el autobús por los pelos. I caught the bus just in time. ▪ I just barely made it to the bus. ▪ I almost missed the bus.
coger el dobladillo to take up the hem ▪ to take in the hem ➤ Me cogieron el dobladillo. I had the hem taken up. ▪ I had the hem taken in.
coger el guante ▪ aceptar el guante to take up the gauntlet ▪ to accept a challenge to fight

coger el hábito de hacer una cosa ■ coger la costumbre de hacer una cosa ■ acostumbrarse a hacer una cosa ■ habituarse a algo to get into the habit of doing something
coger el hilo de la clase ■ ponerse al día con la clase to catch up with the rest of the class
coger el hilo de la conversación ■ toman el hilo de la conversación to pick up on the conversation
coger el montante *(Esp.)* to walk out (in a huff) ■ to leave abruptly
coger el paso con alguien to catch up with someone (on foot)
coger el portante *(Esp., coloquial)* ■ tomar el portante to head for the door ■ to get out of there ➤ Cogimos el portante. We got out of there.
coger el puntillo to be feeling no pain ■ to be slightly high from wine
coger el ramo de novia *(Esp.)* ■ agarrar el ramo de novia to catch the bouquet
coger el ritmillo ■ coger el ritmo to get into the swing of things ■ to get into the groove
coger el ritmo ■ coger el ritmillo to get into the swing of things ■ to get in the groove
coger el toro por los cuernos ■ agarrar el toro por los cuernos to take the bull by the horns ■ to grab the bull by the horns
coger el tranquillo ■ coger el truco ■ agarrarle la mano a algo to get the knack of it
coger el sueño ■ dormirse ■ conciliar el sueño to fall asleep ■ to go to sleep
coger fiebre ■ enfermarse de fiebre to come down with ➤ Cogió fiebre. She came down with a fever.
coger frío ■ enfriarse ■ acatarrarse to catch cold
coger impulso to get up speed
coger la calle to take to the street
coger la costumbre de hacer una cosa ■ coger el hábito de hacer una cosa ■ acostumbrarse a hacer una cosa to get into the habit of doing something
coger la delantera *(Esp.)* ■ tomar la delantera to take the lead
coger la manía *(Esp.)* ■ coger la maña ■ agarrar la maña to develop the habit ■ to get into the habit
coger la maña *(Esp.)* ■ coger la manía ■ agarrar la maña to develop the habit ■ to get into the habit
coger la onda ■ captar la onda ■ coger el hilo ■ agarrar la onda to catch the drift ■ to catch the hint ■ to get the hint
coger la horizontal *(Esp.)* ■ tomar la horizontal ■ cacharlo jetón ■ agarrar jetón ■ agarrarlo dormido to catch some Z's ■ to take a snooze ■ to take a nap
coger la lluvia a uno ■ alcanzar la lluvia a alguien to get caught in the rain ➤ No quiero que me coja la lluvia. ■ No quiero que me alcance la lluvia. I don't want to get caught in the rain. ➤ Me cogió la lluvia. ■ Me alcanzó la lluvia. I got caught in the rain.
coger la matrícula ■ anotar la matrícula to get the license number ➤ ¿Cogiste la matrícula? Did you get the license number?
coger la onda *(Esp.)* ■ agarrar la onda **1.** to catch the drift ■ to catch one's drift **2.** to get the hint
coger la palabra *(Esp.)* ■ coger las palabras ■ tomar la palabra to take the floor
coger la palabra a alguien *(Esp.)* ■ tomar la palabra a alguien to take someone's word for something ➤ Me has dicho que terminarías el trabajo el viernes. Te cojo la palabra. You said you'd finish by Friday, and I'm going to hold you to it.
coger la puerta ■ azotar la puerta ■ detener la puerta to storm out ■ to stalk out ■ to leave in a huff
coger la sartén por el mango *(Esp.)* ■ tomar la sartén por el mango ■ tener la sartén por el mango to call the shots
coger las de Villadiego *(Esp.)* ■ tomar las de Villadiego **1.** marcharse precipitadamente to up and leave **2.** huir to beat a trail out of Dodge
coger las palabras ■ coger la palabra to take the floor
coger las riendas ■ tomar las riendas to take the reins
coger onda to catch the hint
coger peso *(Esp.)* ■ engordar ■ ganar peso to put on weight ■ to gain weight
coger por banda a alguien ■ coger de lado a alguien ■ tomar de lado a alguien ■ tomar de banda a alguien to buttonhole someone
coger por sorpresa a alguien to catch someone by surprise ■ to take someone by surprise
coger su tiempo *(Esp.)* ■ tomar su tiempo to take one's time
coger un catarro *(Esp.)* ■ coger un resfriado ■ agarrar un catarro ■ agarrar un resfriado to catch (a) cold ■ to come down with a cold ■ to get a cold
coger un resfriado *(Esp.)* ■ coger un catarro ■ agarrar un resfriado to catch (a) cold ■ to come down with a cold ■ to get a cold
coger un tablón *(Esp. y L.am.)* ■ emborracharse to get smashed ■ to get plastered ■ to get drunk
coger una cogorza *(Esp.)* ■ coger una buena cogorza ■ agarrar una cogorza ■ pillar una tajada to get smashed ■ to get looped ■ to get soused ■ to get drunk as a skunk
coger una gripe muy fuerte *(Esp.)* ■ agarrar una gripe muy fuerte ■ enfermarse de una gripe muy fuerte to come down with a bad case of the flu ■ to get a bad case of the flu
coger una mierda *(subido de tono)* ■ coger un pedal ■ coger una mona ■ agarrar un pedo to get plastered ■ to get drunk
coger una mona *(Esp.)* ■ agarrar una mona *(jerga)* to get plastered ■ to get drunk
coger una perra *(Esp., subido de tono)* ■ coger un cabreo to get pissed off
cogerla con alguien ■ tomarla con alguien to get made
cogerle a uno la palabra to hold someone to one's word ■ to hold someone to what one has said
cogerle aversión a algo *(Esp.)* ■ tomarle aversión a algo to become averse to something ■ to develop an aversion to something ➤ En su vejez le cogió aversión al peine. ■ En su vejez le tomó aversión al peine. In his old age he has become very averse to a comb.
cogerle cariño a alguien *(Esp.)* ■ encariñarse con alguien to take a liking to someone ■ to get attached to someone
cogerle el aire a algo *(Esp.)* ■ tomarle la mano a algo ■ agarrarle la mano a algo to get the hang of something
cogerle el dobladillo *(Esp.)* ■ tomar el dobladillo to be taken up ■ to be taken in ➤ Me cogieron el dobladillo. I had the hem taken up. ■ I had the hem taken in.
cogerle gusto a algo *(Esp.)* ■ tomarle el gusto a algo to take a liking to something
cogerle la delantera *(Esp.)* ■ tomarle la delantera to take the lead
cogerle simpatía a alguien to take a liking to someone
cogerse de la mano *(Esp.)* ■ tomarse de la mano to hold hands
cogerse la cabeza *(Esp.)* ■ tomarse de la cabeza to hold one's head
cogerse los dedos *(Esp.)* ■ quemarse los dedos ■ pillarse los dedos to get your fingers burned
cogí el autobús por los pelos *(Esp.)* ■ agarré el autobús barriéndome ■ a penas agarré el autobús ■ casi se me va el güey I just barely made it to the bus ■ I almost missed the bus
estar **cogido con alfileres** *(Esp.)* ■ estar cogido con pinzas ■ estar agarrado con pinzas ■ estar pendiente de un hilo ■ estar pendiente de un cabello to be hanging by a thread
ser **cogido por la policía** *(Esp.)* ■ ser pillado por la policía ■ ser trincado por la policía ■ ser agarrado por la policía to be caught by the police ■ *(coloquial) to get busted by the police*
ser **cogido por sorpresa (por)** *(Esp.)* ■ ser cogido desprevenido (por) ■ ser tomado por sorpresa (por) ■ tomarlo a uno desprevenido ■ agarrarlo a uno por sorpresa ■ agarrarlo desprevenido ■ *(Esp., leísmo)* cogerle a uno desprevenido ■ tomarle a uno desprevenido ■ agarrarle por sorpresa to be taken (completely) by surprise ■ to be caught by surprise
cogidos del brazo: andar ~ ■ ir cogidos del brazo *(Esp.)* ■ andar tomados del brazo ■ ir tomados del brazo to walk arm in arm ■ to go arm in arm
cogollo de la sociedad ■ crème de la crème cream of society ■ upper crust
cogollo de una lechuga heart of a lettuce
cogollo del árbol ■ campana del árbol tree top ■ top (part) of the tree
cogollo del asunto ■ centro del problema heart of the matter
ser **coherente en su totalidad** to be consistent throughout

coincidencias con un nombre matches to a name ➤ Hay cientos de coincidencias con el nombre John Smith. There are hundreds of matches to the name John Smith.

coincidir con alguien to agree with someone ▪ to be of the same opinion as somone ➤ Coincido con Leticia. I agree with Leticia. ▪ I'm in agreement with Leticia. ▪ I'm of the same opinion as Leticia.

coincidir en el mismo lugar to be in the same place at the same time ➤ *(noticia)* Woody Allen y Bruce Springsteen coincidieron ayer en Madrid. Woody Allen and Bruce Springsteen were both in Madrid yesterday.

coincidir en hacer algo to agree to do something ➤ La junta directiva coincidió en introducir al mercado un carro que funciona con combustible orgánico. The board of directors agreed to introduce onto the market a car that runs on organic fuel.

coincidir en que to agree that ▪ to be in agreement that ➤ Los científicos coinciden en que... (The) scientists agree that... ▪ (The) scientists are in agreement that...

coincido contigo ▪ estoy de acuerdo contigo I agree with you ▪ I'm of the same opinion as you

colaborador estrecho close collaborator

ser **colaboradores de** to be affiliated with

colapsar el tráfico ▪ provocar un entorpecimiento del tráfico to halt traffic ▪ to snarl traffic ▪ to bring (the) traffic to a halt

colapso de la economía ▪ (el) derrumbe de la economía ▪ hundimiento de la economía collapse of the economy ▪ sinking of the economy

colapso del suministro eléctrico ▪ colapso del suministro de la electricidad disruption of the electrical power supply ▪ disruption in the supply of electrical power ➤ Estado de emergencia en California por el colapso del suministro eléctrico. State of emergency in California over the disruption of the electrical power supply.

colar el café to percolate the coffee

colarse (en la cola) to butt in line ▪ to cut in line ➤ No se cuelen, por favor. ▪ *(Esp., vosotros)* No os coléis, por favor. Please don't (you all) butt in line.

colarse al otro lado de una valla to go over a fence (to avoid paying)

colarse de rondón en una fiesta ▪ colarse de invitado en una fiesta to crash a party ➤ Nos colocamos de rondón en la fiesta. We crashed the party.

colarse en to sneak into ➤ El ladrón se coló en la habitación de la víctima. The thief snuck into the victim's room.

colchón neumático air mattress

coleccionismo filatélico stamp collecting

coleccionismo privado private collecting

Colegio cardenalicio *(catolicismo)* College of Cardinals

Colegio de abogados de los Estados Unidos American Bar Association

colegio del barrio neighborhood school

colegio interno boarding school

colegio mayor college dormitory ▪ university dormitory

colesterol bueno ▪ lipoproteínas de alta densidad ▪ LAD good cholesterol ▪ high-density lipoproteins ▪ HDL

colesterol malo ▪ lipoproteínas de baja densidad ▪ LBD bad cholesterol ▪ low-density lipoproteins ▪ LDL

estar **colgado por** to be stuck on

estar **colgado de un hilo** ▪ estar pendiente de un hilo to be hanging by a thread

colgar algo en la red to post something on the web

colgar de un hilo ▪ pender de un hilo to hang by a thread

colgar el abrigo ▪ dejar el abrigo (en la percha) to hang up one's coat

colgar el sambenito de... a alguien *(Esp.)* ~to hang the label of... on someone ▪ to label someone as...

colgar las botas to retire from football

colgar los guantes to hang up the (boxing) gloves ▪ to retire from boxing

colgar los hábitos ▪ ahorcar los hábitos to leave the priesthood

colgarse el ordenador *(Esp.)* ▪ quedarse colgado el ordenador to hang up the computer ▪ to hang the computer up ➤ Algo ha hecho que se quede colgado el ordenador. Tal vez tengamos que reiniciarlo. ▪ Algo ha hecho que se cuelgue el ordenador. Tal vez tengamos que reiniciarlo. Something has hung up the computer. We might have to restart it. ▪ Something has hung the computer up. We might have to restart it. ➤ Algo lo ha colgado. Something has hung it up.

colgarse la computadora *(L.am.)* ▪ quedarse colgada la computadora to hang up the computer ▪ to hang the computer up ➤ Algo ha hecho que se quede colgada la computadora. Tal vez tengamos que reiniciarla. ▪ Algo ha hecho que se cuelgue la computadora. Tal vez tengamos que reiniciarla. Something has hung up the computer. We might have to restart it. ▪ Something has hung the computer up. We might have to restart it. ➤ Algo la ha colgado. Something has hung it up.

colindar con ▪ lindar con to adjoin ▪ to border on ▪ to be adjacent to ▪ to have a (common) border with ▪ *(en el caso de la parte de atrás de una parcela)* to face ▪ to back onto ➤ La parte de atrás de la propiedad colinda con un lago. ▪ La parte de atrás de la propiedad linda con un lago. ▪ La parte de atrás de la propiedad da a un lago. The back part of the property borders on a lake. ▪ The back part of the property faces a lake. ▪ The limit of the back part of the property is a lake. ▪ The back (part) of the property faces a lake. ▪ The property backs onto a lake.

la **colisión por alcance** rear-end collision

colisionar con ▪ chocar con to collide with ➤ El coche colisionó de frente con un camión. The car collided head-on with a truck.

colita del bebé: estar suave como la ~ to be smooth as a baby's bottom ▪ to be smooth as a baby's butt

colmarle de besos a alguien to smother someone with kisses

colmarle la paciencia a alguien ▪ acabarle la paciencia a alguien ▪ fregarle la paciencia a alguien ▪ gastarle la paciencia a alguien to try someone's patience ▪ to exhaust someone's patience

ser el **colmo** to be the limit

ser el **colmo de lo ridículo** to be the height of the ridiculous

colocación de los pies *(buceo)* the position of the feet ▪ the positioning of the feet

colocar a alguien contra las cuerdas to put someone on the ropes

colocar al borde del colapso to place on the verge of collapse

colocar algo en orden ▪ ubicar algo to place something in (its proper) order

colocar algo de lado to lay something sideways

colocar explosivos to plant explosives

colocar la compra ▪ ordenar la compra ▪ almacenar la compra ▪ guardar la compra ▪ to put away the groceries ▪ to put the groceries away ▪ to put up the groceries ▪ to put the groceries up ➤ I can start dinner as soon as I put away the groceries. ▪ I can start dinner as soon as I put the groceries away. Puedo empezar a preparar la comida tan pronto como coloque la compra. ▪ Puedo empezar a preparar la comida tan pronto como ordene la compra. ➤ Puedo empezar la comida tan pronto como la coloque. I can start dinner as soon as I put them away.

colocar ladrillos to lay bricks

colocar libros (en las estanterías) to shelve books

colocar los pies en alto ▪ poner los pies en alto to put one's feet up

colocar un anuncio to place an ad

colocar un marcapasos a alguien to install a pacemaker in someone ➤ Los médicos colocaron un marcapasas al vicepresidente Cheney. Doctors installed a pacemaker in vice president Cheney.

colocarse en los pulmones ▪ asentarse en los pulmones ▪ situarse en los pulmones to settle in one's lungs ➤ La infección se ha colocado en los pulmones. ▪ La infección se ha asentado en los pulmones. ▪ La infección se ha situado en los pulmones. The infection has settled in his lungs.

color de rosa pálido rose color ▪ light pink

estar **colorado de ira** ▪ estar colorado de enfado to be flushed with anger

colorante alimenticio food coloring

color cálido warm color

color fuego fiery red

colores vistosos bright colors

columna de números ▪ lista de números ▪ suma column of figures ▪ column of numbers ➤ Esta columna de números suma seiscientos cuarenta y cinco. This column of figures adds up to six hundred forty-five.

el **comandante en jefe** commander in chief

el **comandante militar** military commander

comandos especiales special forces

combar metal ▪ encorvar metal ▪ doblar metal to bend metal

el **combate a brazo partido** ▪ el combate cuerpo a cuerpo hand-to-hand combat

el **combate cuerpo a cuerpo** ▪ el combate a brazo partido hand-to-hand combat

combatiente enemigo enemy combatant

ser una **combinación invencible** to be an unbeatable combination ➤ No está casado porque corre deprisa y nadie le persigue. Es una combinación invencible. He's not married because he runs fast, and no one's chasing him. It's an unbeatable combination.

combinar con to go with ▪ to complement each other ➤ Los colores de la corbata no combinan con los de la chaqueta. The colors in the tie don't go with the jacket.

combinarse para hacer algo to join forces to do something ▪ to team up to do something

comedia de enredo(s) comedy of intrigue

ser **comedidamente optimista** ▪ ser moderadamente optimista ▪ ser optimista de forma moderada ▪ sentirse moderadamente optimista to be guardedly optimistic ▪ to be cautiously optimistic

ser **comedura del tarro** to be food for thought

comentar la jugada de algo to tell someone about something ➤ Coméntame la jugada de tu cita con cómo se llame. Tell me about your date with what's-her-name.

comentar los detalles to discuss the details ➤ Necesitamos comentar los detalles del plan. We need to discuss the details of the plan.

comentario mordaz 1. biting remark ▪ caustic remark **2.** caustic commentary ▪ caustic essay

el, la **comentarista de televisión** television commentator ▪ TV commentator

comentario ofensivo offensive remark

comenzando en la página *x* ▪ comenzando por la página *x* ▪ empezando en la página *x* ▪ empezando por la página *x* beginning on page *x* ▪ starting on page *x*

comenzando por la página *x* ▪ comenzando en la página *x* ▪ empezando por la página *x* ▪ empezando en la página *x* beginning on page *x* ▪ starting on page *x*

comenzar a hacer algo ▪ empezar a hacer algo to start to do something ▪ to begin to do something

comenzar a sospechar de alguien to become suspicious of someone ▪ to begin to suspect someone ▪ to start to suspect someone ▪ to become suspicious of someone

comenzar avanzado ▪ tener un comienzo avanzado ▪ salir con ventaja (en una carrera) to get a head start ▪ to have a head start

comer algo a dos carrillos to wolf down food ▪ to wolf food down ➤ Lo comí a dos carrillos. I wolfed it down.

comer algo a palo seco to eat something without drinking anything with it ▪ to eat something without drinking anything alongside it

comer algo tal cual 1. comer algo como te lo sirven to eat something as it is ▪ to eat something as (it is) served **2.** comer algo crudo to eat something raw ▪ to eat something uncooked ➤ Se come tal cual. No se añade sal. You eat it as it is. You don't add salt. ➤ Las zanahorias te las puedes comer tal cual. You can eat carrots raw. ▪ You can eat carrots uncooked.

comer como un cerdo ▪ empacharse ▪ glotonear to eat like a pig ▪ to pig out

comer como un descosido ▪ hartarse de comer ▪ ponerse el Quico ▪ ponerse las botas to eat like a horse

comer como una lima (nueva) ▪ hartarse de comer ▪ ponerse el Quico ▪ ponerse las botas ▪ comer como un descosido to eat like a horse

comer en la mano de alguien to eat out of someone's hand ▪ to eat out of the palm of someone's hand

comer en solitario to eat alone ▪ to eat by oneself ▪ to dine alone

comer en un mismo plato to be close friends

comer entre horas to eat between meals

comer fuera ▪ salir a comer to go out for dinner ▪ to dine out ▪ to eat out ➤ Vamos a comer fuera. **1.** Let's go out for dinner. ▪ Let's eat out. 2. We're going out for dinner. ▪ We're going to eat out.

comer hasta reventar to eat until one's about to explode ▪ to eat until one's about to pop

comer lo que hay en casa de alguien to eat someone out of house and home

el, la **comerciante de antigüedades** antiques dealer

comerciar con to deal in ➤ Comercia con libros fuera de catálogo. He deals in out-of-print books.

comerle a alguien los hígados *(Esp.)* ▪ comer a alguien crudo to wring someone's neck ➤ Si veo a ese tipo, voy a comerle los hígados. ▪ Si veo a ese tipo, me lo como crudo. If I see that guy I'm going to wring his neck.

comerlo a palo seco to eat it without drinking anything with it ▪ to eat it without drinking anything alongside it

comerlo tal cual 1. comerlo como te lo sirven to eat it as it is ▪ to eat it as served **2.** comerlo crudo to eat it raw

comerse a besos a alguien to smother someone with kisses

comerse algo to eat something up ➤ Los perros se lo comerán. The dogs will eat it up.

comerse el coco ▪ devanarse los sesos ▪ cargarse la cabeza ▪ comerse el tarro to rack one's brains

comerse el semáforo *(coloquial)* ▪ saltarse el semáforo to crash into the traffic light post

comerse el tarro ▪ devanarse los sesos ▪ cargarse la cabeza ▪ comerse el coco to rack one's brains

comerse los dedos to be edgy ▪ to be on edge

comerse una rebanada de humildad to eat humble pie

comerse una rosca con alguien *(Esp.)* to make it with someone (sexually)

comérselo la envidia ▪ comerse de envidia to be consumed with envy

comérselo todo 1. to eat it (all) up **2.** to get eaten (up) ➤ Los perros se lo comerán. The dogs will eat it up. ➤ Era un pastel tan bueno que sabía que se lo comerían todo. It was such a good cake I knew it would get eaten (up).

cometa extinguido dead comet ▪ spent comet

cometer perjurio ▪ perjurarse ▪ mentir bajo juramento ▪ jurar en falso to commit perjury ▪ to perjure oneself ▪ to lie under oath

cometer un error to make a mistake

cometer un solemne disparate ▪ hacer un tremendo disparate to do something really outlandish ▪ to do something really crazy ➤ He cometido un solemne disparate. I've done something really outlandish. ▪ I've done something really crazy.

comicios generales general elections

comida a patadas tons of food ▪ loads of food

comida anodina bland food

comida basura junk food

comida chatarra *(Méx.)* ▪ comida basura junk food

ser **comida de niños** ▪ ser un juego de niños to be child's play

comida equilibrada balanced meal ➤ Quiero una comida equilibrada con verduras, hidratos de carbono y carne. I want a balanced meal of vegetables, starches and meat.

comida fuerte rich food ➤ Estos postres son muy fuertes para mi régimen. These desserts are too rich for my diet.

comienzo del documento beginning of the document

Comisión del Mercado de Valores *(EE UU)* Securities and Exchange Commission

comisuras (de los labios) corners of the mouth

comité ejecutivo ▪ consejo de administración board of directors ▪ executive committee

comitiva de bodas wedding party ➤ La novia, el novio, la madrina, el portaanillos,... the bride, the groom, the matron of honor, the ringbearer...

como (a él) le gusta que le llamen as he likes to be called

como (a ella) le gusta que le llamen as she likes to be called estar **como abeja en flor** to be happy as a lark ■ to be happy as a clam

como agua de mayo: venir ~ to be a Godsend

como alguno de ustedes ya sabe as some of you already know

como alguno de vosotros ya sabe *(Esp.)* as some of you already know

como alma que lleva el diablo: huir ~ to run like a bat outta hell *(Nota: "Outta" es la contracción coloquial de "out of".)*

¿como andamos? ¿how are you doing?

como anillo al dedo: venirle a alguien ~ ■ venirle a alguien al pelo to suit one to a T ■ to suit one perfectly

como aparenta as it appears ■ as it appears to be

estar **como ausente** to be off in the ozone

como balance provisional *(periodismo)* according to the initial estimates ■ according to the most recent estimates ➤ La niebla, unida al exceso de velocidad y a la falta de distancias de seguridad causó catorce muertos y setenta heridos como balance provisional. Fog, together with excessive speed and lack of safe distances between cars, caused fourteen deaths and seventy injuries, according to the initial estimates.

estar **como boca de lobo** to be pitch (black) dark

como caballo desbocado: ir ~ to go like a bat out of hell ■ *(coloquial)* to go like a bat outta hell

como cabe esperar ■ como cabría esperar ■ como sería de esperar as you would expect ■ as you'd expect ■ as one would expect

como cabe suponer ■ como cabría suponer ■ como sería de suponer as you might suppose ■ as one might suppose ■ as you might guess ■ as you might have guessed

como cabría esperar ■ como cabe esperar ■ como sería de esperar as you would expect ■ as one would expect ■ as you'd expect

como cabría suponer ■ como cabe suponer ■ como sería de suponer as you might suppose ■ as one might suppose

como cada quisque ■ como todo quisque like everyone else

como caído del cielo: venir ~ to be a Godsend ■ *(menos común)* to be like manna from heaven

estar **como chico con zapatos nuevos** to be like a kid with new shoes

¡cómo cocina! ■ ¡sí que cocina! *(ella)* can she ever cook! ■ *(él)* can he ever cook!

como consecuencia de ■ en consecuencia de ■ a consecuencia de ■ como fruto de ■ por consecuencia de ■ por as a result of ■ as a consequence of

como consta en... as stated in... ■ as it states in... ■ as recorded in...

¡como corre el tiempo! how time flies!

como cosa corriente y normal as a matter of course ■ routinely

como dice uno as one puts it ➤ La hermosa instructora de vuelo usó un anillo de compromiso durante toda la guerra para "ahuyentar a los lobos," como dice mi tía. The beautiful flight instructor wore an engagement ring all during the war "to chase away the wolves," as my aunt puts it.

como de as if from ➤ El país se despertó de la revolución como de una pesadilla. The country awoke from the revolution as if from a nightmare.

cómo de a menudo ■ con qué frecuencia ■ con cuánta frecuencia ■ cada cuándo how often

como de costumbre as usual

como de encargo: parecer ~ to be as though it was made to order ■ to be as if it were made to order

ser **como de la familia** to be like one of the family ■ to be like a member of the family

como de la noche al día: ser diferentes ~ to be as different as night and day ➤ Puede que sean gemelas idénticas, pero son diferentes como de la noche al día. They may be identical twins, but they're as different as night and day.

como de la peste: huirle a alguien ~ to avoid someone like the plague ➤ (Ella) le huye (a él) come de la peste. She avoids him like the plague.

como debe ser the way it has to be ■ the way it's got to be ■ as it has to be

como debería ser as it should be ■ the way it should be

como decíamos ayer *(Fray Luis de León)* as we were saying yesterday

¿cómo demonios...? how in the dickens...? ➤ ¿Cómo demonios voy a lograr eso? How in the dickens am I going to manage that?

como dice el refrán as the saying goes

como digas whatever you say

como Dios: salirle algo a alguien ~ *(coloquial)* ■ salirle algo a alguien de lujo to turn out great ➤ Me ha salido una paella como Dios. ■ Me ha salido una paella de lujo. The paella turned out great.

estar **como Dios, en todas partes** to be everywhere ■ to be all over the place

como Dios le da a entender according to one's whim

como Dios manda according to the book

estar **como Dios trajo a uno al mundo** ■ desnudo(-a) to be in one's birthday suit ■ (stark) naked

como dos gotas de agua: parecerse ~ to be like two peas in a pod

como el burro que tocó la flauta ■ de chiripa as a fluke ➤ Aprobé el examen como el burro que tocó la flauta. ■ Aprobé el examen de chiripa. I was just a fluke that I passed the exam.

ser **como el camino que no lleva a ninguna parte** to be a ticket to nowhere

estar **como el canto de un duro** ■ estar como un silbido ■ estar flaquísimo to be skinny as a rail ■ to be (skinny as) a bean pole

como el convidado de piedra without saying a word

ser **como el huevo de Colón** *(Esp., coloquial)* ■ ser de perogrullo ■ ser de cajón ■ caer de cajón ■ caer de maduro to be plain as day ■ to go without saying ■ to be what you'd expect ➤ Si rayas el CD no se va a oir bien luego, eso es como el huevo de Colón ■ Si rayas el CD no se va a oir bien luego, eso es de perogrullo. If you scratch the CD, it's obviously not going to sound right. It's plain as day. ■ If you scratch the CD, it's obviously not going to sound right. It goes without saying. ■ If you scratch the CD, naturally it's not going to sound right. It's what you'd expect.

ser **como el perro del hortelano (que ni come las berzas ni las deja comer)** to be like the dog in the manger

como el perro y el gato: llevarse ~ ■ llevarse mal to get along like cats and dogs

como el que más: ser honrado ~ to be competely honest ■ to be honest as the most honest

como el que más: ser trabajador ~ to work as hard as the best of them ■ to work as hard as anyone else ■ to be as hardworking as anyone

como el que más: ser valiente ~ to be as brave as the bravest

como el que no quiere la cosa: hacer algo ~ to do something as if it were nothing ■ to do something as if there were nothing to it ■ to do something as if there were nothing unusual about it

como el reloj like clockwork ■ exactly on schedule ■ right on time ➤ In Spain the trains run like clockwork. En España los trenes corren como el reloj.

como el viento: correr ~ to run like the wind

como en ■ igual que en ■ de as in ➤ ¿"A" como en Alberto? ■ ¿"A" igual que en Alberto? ■ ¿"A" de Alberto? "A" as in Albert?

como en la etiqueta as marked ➤ Están los precios como en la etiqueta, o un diez por ciento menos? En otras palabras, ¿la etiqueta incluye el descuento? Are the prices as marked, or ten percent off that? In other words, does the marked price include the discount?

como en los viejos tiempos like old times

como en misa: estar callado ~ to be quiet as a mouse

¿cómo era? **1.** what was it like? **2.** *(canción, poema)* how did it go?

como era de esperar as was expected ■ as you'd expect

cómo eran las cosas cuando... what it was like when...

¿cómo eran las cosas cuando...? what was it like when...?

como es de esperar as is expected

cómo es de fácil how easy it is

cómo es de potente how powerful it is ➤ Cómo fue de potente. How powerful it was *(Nota: refiriéndose a la explosión a bordo el submarino ruso "Kursk" ■ referring to the explosion on board the Russian submarine "Kursk")*

cómo es de sencillo how simple it is

como es de suponer as you would expect ▪ as you'd expect ➤ Como es de suponer con este mal tiempo poca gente ha ido a la playa. As you would expect in the cold weather, (very) few people have gone to the beach.

como es debido: hacer algo ~ to do something without taking shortcuts ▪ to do something without compromising quality ▪ to do something thoroughly ▪ to do something properly ▪ to do something right ➤ *(madre al hijo)* Haz los deberes como es debido. Do your homework thoroughly. ▪ Do your homework without taking shortcuts. ▪ Do your homework right!

ser **como esperar a que las ranas críen pelos** to be like waiting for Godot ▪ to be like waiting for hell to freeze over ➤ Es como esperar a que las ranas críen pelos. It's like waiting for Godot.

cómo está de cerca ▪ qué tan cerca está how close it is ▪ how near it is

¡cómo está el patio! what's the world coming to?

¿cómo estamos de cerca a...? how near are we to...? ➤ ¿Cómo estamos de cerca aquí a Nuevos Ministerios? How near are we here to Nuevos Ministerios?

¿cómo estoy? how do I look?

como fruto de ▪ cómo consecuencia de ▪ en consecuencia de ▪ por as a result of ▪ as a consequence of ▪ for

estar **como gallina en corral ajeno** ▪ estar como gallo en corral ajeno to be like a fish out of water ▪ to feel out of place

estar **como gallo en corral ajeno** ▪ estar como gallina en corral ajeno to be like a fish out of water ▪ to feel out of place

estar **como garbanzo en olla grande** to be a little fish in a big pond

como gato panza arriba: defenderse ~ 1. *(en una pelea)* to defend oneself fiercely 2. *(en general)* to handle something very well

como gesto de buena voluntad ▪ en ademán de buena voluntad ▪ en señal de buena voluntad as a gesture of goodwill ▪ as a goodwill gesture

como grupo as a group

como guste usted ▪ como usted guste as you wish ▪ as you like

como gusten ustedes ▪ como ustedes gusten as you wish ▪ as you like

como gustes as you wish ▪ as you like

como habíamos hablado ▪ como habíamos quedado as we had discussed

como habíamos quedado ▪ como habíamos hablado as we had discussed

como ya habrás supuesto ▪ como te habrás imaginado as you probably guessed

como hacía todos los días as he did every day ▪ the way he did every day ▪ *(coloquial)* like he did every day

¿cómo has estado? how have you been?

¿cómo has podido fallar? how could you miss (the target)?

¿cómo has podido mentirme? how could you lie to me?

como hay pocos: ser alguien ~ ▪ ser alguien donde los haya to be one of the best ➤ Es un jugador como hay pocos. ▪ Es un jugador donde los haya. He's one of the best players. ▪ He's a player's player.

como he dicho as I have said ▪ as I've said ▪ as I say

como he dicho en reiteradas ocasiones as I have said on numerous occasions

como he dicho muchas veces as I have said many times

como he dicho repetidas veces ▪ as I have said repeatedly

como hemos ido viendo as we have seen

como hobby: hacer algo ~ ▪ hacer algo como afición to do something as a hobby

¿cómo iba a saberlo? ▪ ¿cómo iba yo a saberlo? how was I to know? ▪ how was I supposed to know?

como iba diciendo ▪ como decía as I was saying

ser **como la copa de un pino** to be something of the first rank ➤ Es un jugador como la copa de un pino. He's a player of the first rank. ➤ Dio un concierto como la copa de un pino. She gave a concert of the first rank. ➤ Ha escrito una novela como la copa de un pino. She wrote a novel of the first rank.

como la haya ▪ como la ve ▪ tal y como la ve ▪ tal como la ve ▪ según la ve ▪ así como la ve as is ➤ Esta porcelana se vende como la haya. This china is sold as is.

estar **como la madre le trajo al mundo** *(Esp., leísmo)* ▪ estar como la madre lo trajo al mundo to be wearing one's birthday suit

estar **como la madre lo trajo al mundo** to be in one's birthday suit ▪ to be wearing one's birthday suit

como la palma de la mano: conocer algo ~ to know something like the back of one's hand

estar **como la patena** ▪ estar tan limpio como la patena ▪ estar (tan limpio) como los chorros del oro to be clean as a whistle ▪ to be spick-and-span ▪ to be spotless

ser **como la pescadilla que se muerde la cola** ▪ ser un círculo vicioso to be a vicious circle ▪ to be a Catch twenty-two ▪ to be a no-win situation

como la seda: estar (suave) ~ smooth as silk ➤ Su piel está suave como la seda. Her skin is smooth as silk

como la seda: ir ~ to run smooth as silk ➤ El motor va como la seda. The engine is running smooth as silk. ➤ El negocio va como la seda. ▪ La empresa va como la seda. The business is running smooth as silk.

como la seda: ser (suave) ~ to be smooth as silk ➤ Su piel es suave como la seda. Her skin is smooth as silk.

estar **como la suela de un zapato** *(filete)* to be tough as shoe leather

como la vez anterior as before

como las haya ▪ como las ve ▪ tal y como las ve ▪ tal como las ve ▪ según las ve ▪ así como las ve as is ➤ Estas estanterías se venden como las haya. This shelving is sold as is.

estar **como las maracas de Machín** *(Esp.)* ▪ estar como un cencerro ▪ estar como una cabra to be a nut case ▪ to be nutty as a fruitcake

como le dé la gana (a usted) whatever you like ▪ whatever you feel like doing ▪ as you like ▪ as you wish ▪ *(pintoresco)* whatever turns you on ▪ whatever spins your beanie

como le guste que le llamen 1. *(a él)* as he likes to be called 2. *(a ella)* as she likes to be called

como le pille... *(Esp.)* ▪ como lo pille if I catch him... ▪ if I catch that guy...

como llevar leña al monte ▪ como llevar agua al mar like carrying coals to Newcastle

ser **como llovido del cielo** to be a Godsend

¿cómo lo contrajo? *(meningitis; él)* how did he get it? ▪ how did he catch it? ▪ how did he contract it? ▪ *(ella)* how did she get it? ▪ how did she catch it? ▪ how did she contract it?

¿cómo lo explicas entonces? then how do you explain it?

como lo fui yo as was I ▪ as I was ▪ as I had been

como lo había prometido as one had promised ➤ Como lo habíamos prometido... As we had promised...

como lo habrás advertido as you probably realize

como lo haya ▪ como lo ve ▪ tal y como lo ve ▪ tal como lo ve ▪ según lo ve ▪ así como lo ve as is ➤ Este coleccionable se vende como lo haya. This collectible is sold as is.

como lo hemos hecho siempre as we always have

¿cómo lo llevas? how are you getting along?

¡como lo oyes! ▪ ¡como lo que oyes! I'm telling you, it's true!

¡como lo (que) oyes! I'm telling you, it's true!

¿cómo lo sabes? how do you know?

¿cómo lo voy a saber? how would I know? ▪ how am I supposed to know?

como los ángeles: cantar ~ to sing like an angel

como los chorros del oro ▪ tan limpio como los chorros del oro ▪ (tan limpio) como la patena clean as a whistle ▪ spick-and-span ▪ spotless

como los de Fuenteovejuna, todos a una ▪ todos a la vez all together (now)!

como los haya ▪ como los ve ▪ tal y como los ve ▪ tal como los ve ▪ según los ve ▪ así como los ve as is ➤ Estos muebles se venden como los haya. This furniture is sold as is.

como máximo ▪ a lo sumo ▪ a todo tirar ▪ como mucho at most

¡cómo me alegro de verte! ▪ ¡cuánto me alegro de verte! I'm so glad to see you!

¡como me llamo..., que... sure as my name's...

como media on (the) average ➤ En China tienen un hijo por familia como media. In China couples have one child on average. ▪ The average number of children per family in China is one.

como mejor (at) best ➤ Como mejor se puede describir el éxito de las misiones de exploración de Marte es como parcial. The success of the Mars exploration missions to date can (at) best be described as mixed.

cómo moverse en Madrid how to get around in Madrid

como mucho ▪ como máximo ▪ a lo sumo ▪ a todo tirar at most ▪ at maximum ▪ *(coloquial)* at the outside ➤ Hay un tren cada cinco minutos como mucho, y normalmente pasa entre uno y tres minutos. There's a train every five minutes at the outside, and usually (one) every one to three minutes.

como muestra la foto ▪ como se ve en la foto as shown in the photo ▪ as seen in the photo

como muy pronto ▪ como muy temprano ▪ lo más pronto at the earliest

como muy tarde ▪ a más tardar ▪ como máximo at the latest

como muy temprano ▪ como muy pronto ▪ lo más pronto at the earliest

ser **como nave sin timón** ▪ ir a la deriva to drift ▪ to be adrift ▪ to flounder

estar **como niño con zapatos nuevos** to be like a kid with new shoes

como nunca as never before ▪ more than ever before ➤ Nos hemos divertido como nunca esta Navidad. We've enjoyed this Christmas more than ever.

¿cómo no? of course!

¿cómo no iba a estar contigo? why wouldn't I be with you? ▪ why would I *not* be with you?

¿cómo no lo ha de estar? how could it not be?

¿cómo no lo he de saber? how could I not know?

como no te apures ▪ como no te des prisa ▪ como no te menees if you don't hurry up...

como no te menees ▪ como que no te apures ▪ como que no te des prisa if you don't hurry up...

¿cómo no voy a recordarlo? how can I forget? ▪ how could I forget?

como nube de verano fleeting ▪ transitory ▪ ephemeral

¡como nunca! better than ever! ➤ ¿Estás bien?–¡Como nunca! Are you (doing) okay?-Better than ever!

como para as if to

ser **como para caerse de espaldas** ▪ ser como para caerse de culo to be stunning ▪ to make one reel back in awe ➤ El Escorial es como para caerse de espaldas. The Escorial is stunning. ▪ The Escorial is a stunning building. ▪ The Escorial just makes you reel back in awe.

ser **como para chuparse los dedos** to be finger-licking good

como para saber con certeza to know with certainty ▪ to know for sure ➤ La información es muy fragmentada como para saber con certeza. The information is too fragmented to know with certainty

estar **como para parar un tren** to be extremely good-looking

como para que algo ocurra for something to happen ➤ Las grandes estrellas están demasiado calientes y se consumen demasiado rápido como para que la vida evolucionada prospere en los planetas de alrededor. Big stars are too hot and burn out too quickly for advanced life to evolve on the planets around them.

como para que fuera so as to be ▪ so that it is ➤ Con ese apellido, le dije que debíamos de ser primos, con suerte no tan lejanos como para que fuera irrelevante. With the same rare last name, I told him we had to be cousins, and hopefully not so far back as to be academic. ➤ Su casa estaba suficientemente lejos como para que fuera un problema llevarle. He lived far enough away that it was a problem to give him a ride home.

como para ser so as to be ▪ so that it is

como Pedro por su casa *(él)* as if he owned the place ▪ *(ella)* as if she owned the place ▪ *(ellos)* as if they owned the place

como perros y gatos: andar ~ to get along like dogs and cats

estar **como pez en el agua** to be in one's element

estar **como pez fuera del agua** to be like a fish out of water ▪ to feel out of place ▪ to be out of one's element

estar **como piojos en costura** ▪ estar como sardinas en lata ▪ estar como una piña to be packed like sardines ▪ to be packed in like sardines

como poco at a minium ▪ at least

como pocos as few people have ➤ Ella tiene un pasado cultural rico como pocos. She has a rich cultural background as few people have.

como podía esperarse as was to be expected ▪ as could be expected ▪ as could have been expected

¿cómo podría hacerse? how might it be done? ▪ in what way could it be done? ▪ in what way could you do it? ▪ how could you do it? ▪ how could it be done? ▪ how could one do it? ▪

¿cómo podría haber? how could there be?

como por arte de birlibirloque *(Esp.)* ▪ como por arte de magia as if by magic

como por arte de magia ▪ como por ensalmo ▪ como por arte de birlibirloque as if by magic

como por encantamiento ▪ como por encanto as if by enchantment

como por encanto ▪ como por encantamiento as if by enchantment

como por ensalmo ▪ como por arte de magia as if by magic

como premio por su bondad 1. *(de él)* as a reward for his kindness ▪ 2. *(de ella)* as a reward for her kindness

como promedio on the average

como puta por rastrojos: andar ~ *(subido de tono)* to be in the gutter ▪ to be destitute

como que as if ▪ inasmuch as ▪ because

¿cómo qué? like what? ▪ why?

¿cómo que bueno? what do you mean, good...?

¿cómo que no? what do you mean, no?

¿cómo que no puedes? what do you mean, you can't?

¿cómo que sí? what do you mean, yes?

cómo quedan las cosas where things stand ➤ Cuando el río vuelva a su cauce, veremos cómo quedan las cosas. ▪ Cuando las aguas se decanten, veremos cómo quedan las cosas. When the dust settles, let's see where things stand.

como queriendo... as if one were trying to... ➤ Reemprendió su camino, como queriendo recuperar el tiempo perdido. He got back on the road, as if trying to make up for lost time.

como quien dice ▪ podríamos decir ▪ por decir(lo) así ▪ así por decir(lo) so to speak

como quien no dice nada: hacer algo ~ ▪ hacer algo a la chita callando to do something very quietly ▪ to do something very inconspicuously

como quien no quiere la cosa as if it were nothing ➤ Fue a Tiffanys y se compró la vajilla de plata más cara de toda la tienda como quien no quiere la cosa. He went into Tiffany's and bought the most expensive silver service in the place as if it were nothing.

estar **como quiere** to be one's own person

¿cómo rayos...? how on earth...? ▪ how in the world...?

como sabrás as you probably know

¿cómo sacaste esa conclusión? how did you arrive at that conclusion?

estar **como sardinas en lata** ▪ estar como piojos en costura ▪ estar como una piña to be packed like sardines ▪ to be packed in like sardines

como se acostumbra according to habit ▪ *(él)* as is his custom ▪ *(ella)* as is her custom

¿cómo se atreve? how dare you?

¿cómo se deja notar? how can you tell?

¿cómo se diferencian...? how do you tell the difference between...? ▪ how do you differentiate...?

¿cómo se entiende? what is the meaning of this? ▪ what's the meaning of this?

¿cómo se gana (usted) la vida? ▪ ¿a qué se dedica (usted) what do you do for a living?

¿cómo se hace el helado? how do you make ice cream? ▪ how is ice cream made?

como se haya (usted) if you've...

¿cómo se le ha ocurrido eso (a usted)? how did you get that idea? ▪ what gave you that idea? ▪ where did you get that idea? ▪ how'd you get that idea? ▪ where'd you get that idea?

como se llama a sí misma as she refers to herself
como se llama a sí mismo as he refers to himself
¿cómo se llama usted? what's your name?
como se podría esperar as could be expected ▪ as you would expect ▪ as one would expect ▪ as you could expect ▪ as one could expect
como se podría imaginar ▪ como se podría pensar ▪ como sería de imaginar ▪ como sería de pensar as you might think ▪ as one might think ▪ as you would think ▪ as one would think
como se podría pensar ▪ como se podría imaginar ▪ como sería de pensar ▪ como sería de imaginar as you might think ▪ as one might think ▪ as you would think ▪ as one would think ➤ Aprender a pilotar aviones no es tan difícil como se podría pensar. Learning to fly airplanes is not so difficult as one might think. ▪ Learning to fly airplanes is not as difficult as one might think.
como se podria suponer as could be expected ▪ as you would expect ▪ as one would expect ▪ as you could expect ▪ as one would expect
como se suponía as was thought ▪ as had been thought ▪ as was supposed
¿cómo se te ha ocurrido eso? how did you get that idea? ▪ what gave you that idea? ▪ where did you get that idea? ▪ how'd you get that idea? ▪ where'd you get that idea?
¿cómo se te ocurrió eso? ~ 1. what gave you that idea? ▪ what made you think that? 2. *(al solucionar un problema)* how did you come up with that? ▪ how did you get that? ▪ how did you derive that?
cómo se ve desde el exterior how it looks from the outside
como se ve en la foto ▪ como muestra la foto as seen in the photo ▪ as shown in the photo
cómo será el tiempo what the weather will be like
como sería de esperar ▪ como cabe esperar ▪ como cabría esperar as you would expect ▪ as you'd expect ▪ as one would expect ▪ as expected
como sería de imaginar ▪ como sería de pensar ▪ como se podría imaginar ▪ como se podría pensar as you would think ▪ as one would think ▪ as you might think ▪ as one might think ▪ as you would imagine ▪ as one would imagine ▪ as you might imagine ▪ as one might imagine
como sería de suponer ▪ como cabe suponer ▪ como cabría suponer as you might guess ▪ as one might guess ▪ as you would suppose ▪ as one might suppose ▪ as might be supposed
como sería de pensar ▪ como sería de imaginar ▪ como se podría pensar ▪ como se podría imaginar as you would think ▪ as one would think ▪ as you might think ▪ as one might think ➤ Aprendar español no es tan difícil como sería de pensar. ▪ Aprender español no es tan difícil como sería de imaginar. Learning English is not so difficult as you would think. Learning English is not as difficult as you would think. ▪ Learning English is not so difficult as you might think. Learning English is not as difficult as you might think.
como si as if ▪ as though ➤ Estudió como si todo su futuro dependiera de ello. He studied as if his whole future depended on it. ▪ He studied as though his whole future depended on it. ➤ ¡Como si me importara lo que piensa él! As if I cared what he thinks!
como si dijéramos ▪ podríamos decir ▪ por así decir ▪ por decirlo así so to speak ▪ as it were
como si fuera cosa de ayer ▪ como si fuera ayer as if it were yesterday
como si lo viera I can almost see it ▪ it's as if I were seeing it
como si nada just like that ▪ as if nothing had happened ▪ just like it was before
como si nada haya pasado: actuar ~ to act as if nothing has happened ▪ to act as though nothing has happened
como si nada hubiera sucedido as if nothing had happened ▪ as though nothing had happened
como si nada pasara as if nothing happened ▪ as though nothing happened
como si no hubiera dicho nada as if one hadn't said anything
como si no hubiera pasado nada ▪ como si nada (hubiera pasado) ▪ como si no hubiese pasado nada ▪ como si nada hubiese pasado as if nothing had happened
como si nos hubiésemos conocido toda la vida as if we had known each other all our lives
como si se hablara con la pared like talking to a brick wall ▪ as if one were talking to a brick wall
estar **como si tal cosa** ▪ estar como si no hubiera pasado nada 1. *(presente)* to act as if nothing has happened 2. *(pasado)* to act as if nothing had happened
como si no tuviera otra cosa que hacer 1. *(yo)* as if I didn't have anything else to do 2. *(él)* as if he didn't have anything else to do 3. *(ella)* as if she didn't have anything else to do
estar **como su madre le trajo al mundo** to be in one's birthday suit ▪ to be wearing one's birthday suit
como suele decirse as the saying goes
como suena as it sounds ▪ *(coloquial pero incorrecto)* like it sounds
como tal as such
¿cómo te atreves? how dare you?
como te dé la gana (a ti) whatever you like ▪ whatever you feel like doing ▪ as you like ▪ as you wish ▪ *(coloquial)* whatever turns you on ▪ whatever spins your beanie
¿cómo te explicas esto? ▪ ¿cómo te lo explicas? ▪ ¿qué te parece esto? ▪ ¿y eso cómo se come? what do you make of it? ➤ *(Lindbergh)* El motor está a treinta revoluciones por debajo. ¿Cómo te lo explicas? ¿Aire húmedo? ▪ El motor está a treinta revoluciones por debajo. ¿Cómo te explicas esto? ¿Aire húmedo? The engine's thirty revolutions low. What do you make of it? Damp air?
cómo te fue how it went ▪ how it was ➤ Me muero por saber cómo te fue tu cita a ciegas. I'm dying to find out how your blind date went. ▪ I'm dying to find out how your blind date was.
¿cómo te fue? how did it go? ▪ how was it?
¿cómo te ganas la vida? ▪ ¿a qué te dedicas? what do you do for a living?
como te habrás imaginado ▪ como ya habrás supuesto as you probably have guessed
como te hayas... if you've...
¿cómo te llamas? what's your name?
¡cómo te lo agradezco! I appreciate it so much! ▪ thank you so much!
¿cómo te lo digo? ▪ ¿cómo te lo explico? ▪ ¿cómo te lo expreso? how shall I say?
¿cómo te lo explicas? ▪ ¿cómo te explicas esto? ▪ ¿qué te parece esto? ▪ *(pintoresco)* ▪ ¿y eso cómo se come? what do you make of it?
como te lo prometí as I promised ▪ as I promised you
¿cómo te sentiste? 1. how did it feel? ▪ what did it feel like? 2. what was it like?
¿cómo te sentiste al...? 1. how did it feel to...? ▪ what did it feel like to...? 2. what was it like to...?
¿cómo te sentiste cuando...? how did it feel when...? ▪ what did it feel like when...?
¿cómo te trata la vida? ▪ ¿cómo te va? how's life treating you? ▪ how are things going?
¿cómo te va? how are you doing? ▪ how's it going? ▪ how are things going?
¿cómo te va el trabajo? how's the work going? ▪ how are you getting along at work?
¿cómo te va en tu trabajo? how are things going at work? ▪ how is work?
¿cómo terminó el marcador? ▪ ¿cuál fue la puntuación final? ▪ ¿cuál fue el tanteador? what was the (final) score?
como sabe todo el mundo as everyone knows
como todo hijo de vecino like everybody else ➤ Usted tiene que guardar cola como todo hijo de vecino. You have to stand in line like everybody else.
como todos sabemos as we all know ▪ as all of us know
como tú bien sabes as you well know
como última opción ▪ como último remedio ▪ como último recurso ▪ en última instancia ▪ cuando la otra opción es mucho peor as a last resort
como último recurso ▪ como último remedio ▪ como última opción ▪ en última instancia ▪ cuando la otra opción es mucho peor as a last resort

como último remedio ■ como último recurso ■ como última opción ■ en última instancia ■ cuando la otra opción es mucho peor as a last resort
ser **(como) un ángel** to be an angel
como un bólido like a flash
estar **como un bombón** to be good-looking
como un burro: trabajar ~ to work like a dog
ser **como un camaleón** to be a chameleon ■ to have many faces
estar **como un camión** ■ ser como un tren to be a knockout ■ to be really good looking
estar **como un cangrejo** to be as red as a lobster (from sunburn)
estar **como un cencerro** ■ estar como una cabra ■ andar con los patos volados ■ estar como las maracas de Machín to be a nut case
estar **como un clavo** ■ estar a la hora exacta ■ siempre venir a la hora exacta ■ ser muy preciso en la hora ■ ser muy puntual to be punctual ■ to always be on time
como un condenado: trabajar ~ to work like a dog ■ to slave away
ser **como un dolor de muelas** to be a pain in the neck
estar **como un fideo** ■ ser flaco como un palillo ■ estar como un palo de escoba to be skinny as a rail ■ to be a bean pole
estar **como un flan** to shake like a leaf ➤ Estás como un flan. You're shaking like a leaf.
ser **como un imán** to be a magnetic person ■ to have personal magnetism
ser **como un lagarto** to be a sun worshipper
ser **(como) un libro abierto** to be an open book
estar **como un palo de escoba** ■ estar como un fideo ■ ser flaco como un palillo to be skinny as a rail ■ to be a bean pole
estar **como un pasmarote** to be a snoop
estar **como un pez en el agua** to be in one's element
como un pollo sin cabeza: correr ~ to run around like a chicken with its head cut off
estar **como un queso** *(mujer guapa)* to be a dish
estar **como un roble** to be robust
estar **como un silbido** ■ estar como el canto de un duro ■ estar flaquísimo to be skinny as a rail ■ to be (skinny as) a bean pole
como un todo 1. as a whole 2. as a set ➤ "Hacer conjunto con" puede ser interpretado de dos formas, en primer lugar que las prendas en cuestión combinan bien entre sí y en segundo lugar que las ropas han sido concebidas para ser llevadas juntas, esto es, como un todo. "Hacer conjunto con" has two senses, first that the clothes complement each other, and second that the pieces of clothing were designed to be worn together as a set.
estar **como un tonel** to be really fat
estar **como un tren** ■ estar como un camión to be a knockout ■ to be really good-looking
estar **como un zombi** to be a zombie
como una atención (por) as a favor (for)
como una bala: salir ~ ■ salir como una flecha ■ salir disparado to be off like a shot
estar **como una balsa (de aceite)** *(el mar)* to be (dead) calm ■ to be smooth as glass
como una balsa de aceite: ir ~ ■ ir viento en popa to go smoothly ■ to be sailing along
estar **como una cabra** ■ estar un poco loco ■ estar como un cencerro ■ estar como una regadera ■ estar chiflado to be cracked ■ to be crazy as a bedbug ■ to be crazy as a loon
estar **como una chota** to be crazy
como una cuba: estar (borracho) ~ to be smashed ■ to be drunk as a skunk
como una flecha: salir ~ ■ salir como una bala ■ salir disparado to be off like a shot
estar **como una moto** ■ estar acelerado to be hyper
estar **como una pasa** to be wrinkled (from being in water) ■ to be shriveled (from being in water)
estar **como una piña** ■ estar como sardinas en lata ■ estar como piojos en costura to be packed like sardines
estar **(como) una regadera** to be crazy as a bed bug ■ to be nutty as a fruit cake ■ to be mad as a hatter
estar **como una rosa** to feel great
estar **como una tabla** to be flat-chested
estar **como una tapia** to be crazy
estar **como una vaca** to be fat
ser **como una veleta** to shift with the (political) winds
estar **como unas castañuelas** to be happy as can be
estar **como unas pascuas** to be happy as a lark ■ to be happy as can be
como uno acostumbra ■ como uno suele estar as one usually is ➤ Hoy no estoy tan apurado como acostumbro. ■ Hoy no estoy tan apurado como suelo estar. Today I am not as rushed as I usually am. ■ Today I'm not as rushed as I usually am.
como uno solo as one can be ➤ Es simpática como ella sola. ■ Es agradable como ella sola. She's as nice as she can be. ➤ Freddy Krueger es feo como él solo. Freddy Krueger is as ugly as he can be.
como uno suele estar ■ como uno acostumbra as one usually is ➤ Hoy no estoy tan apurado como suelo estar. ■ Hoy no estoy tan apurado como acostumbro. Today I am not as rushed as I usually am.
como uno suele ser as one usually is
como uno suele tener as one usually has ■ as one usually is ➤ No tengo tanta hambre esta noche como suelo tener. I'm not as hungry tonight as I usually am.
ser **(como) uña y carne** ■ ser como uña y carne to be thick as thieves ■ to be inseparable
como usted bien sabe as you well know
como usted sabrá as you probably know
¿cómo va el marcador? ■ ¿cómo van? ■ ¿cuál es la puntuación? what is the score? ■ what's the score?
¿cómo vamos de tiempo? ■ ¿qué tal vamos de tiempo? how are we doing on the time?
¿cómo van? ■ ¿cuál es el marcador? what's the score? ➤ Van tres a uno. It's three to one.
¿cómo voy de tiempo? ■ ¿qué tal voy de tiempo? how am I doing on the time?
como yo ■ igual que yo like me ➤ Hay un ejercito creciente de personas que, como yo, trabaja en casa. ■ Hay un ejercito creciente de personas que igual que yo, trabaja en casa. There is a growing army of people who, like me, work at home.
¿cómo (yo) iba a saberlo? how was I supposed to know?
como yo soy así since that's the way I am
el **cómo y el porqué** the whys and wherefores
comoquiera que... since ■ considering the fact that...
comoquiera que sea eso... however that may be ■ though that may be
compadecer a alguien ■ tener compasión de alguien to feel sorry for someone
compadecerse de alguien take pity on someone
compadecerse de sí mismo ■ lamentarse uno de su suerte to feel sorry for oneself
compaginar con to combine with ■ to go together with ■ to fit with
compaginarse bien to fit together well ■ to fit together nicely ■ to dovetail
compaginarse con to be on the same page with ■ to agree with
compañero(-a) de curso classmate
compañero(-a) de viaje traveling companion
compañero(-a) sentimental gay lover
compañeros de crimen partners in crime
compañeros de fechorías *(dicho en broma)* partners in crime
comparecer ante el tribunal ■ presentarse ante el juez to appear in court
comparecencia de uno ante el tribunal one's appearance before the court
compartimiento superior *(en un avión)* overhead bin ■ overhead compartment
compartir algo con alguien to share something with someone ➤ Schopenhauer comparte con Freud la creencia de que el comportamiento de los seres humanos se reduce a unos pocos

instintos básicos. Schopenhauer shares with Freud the belief that human behavior can be reduced to a few basic drives. ➤ Compartimos un piso cuando éramos estudiantes. We shared an apartment when we were students.

compartir el papel protagonista con alguien ▪ compartir el papel estelar con alguien to co-star with someone ▪ to star with someone

compartir la tarea de to share the task of

compartir las mismas raíces to spring from the same roots ▪ to share the same roots ➤ El tango y la milonga son, como quien dice, bailes primos hermanos, en tanto en cuanto comparten los las mismas raices. The tango and the milonga are, so to speak, first cousins, in that they spring from the same roots.

compartir mesa y mantel con alguien 1. *(comida)* to have dinner with someone 2. *(cena)* to have supper with someone

compartir sus secretos con alguien ▪ compartir sus intimidades con alguien to confide one's secrets to someone ▪ to tell one's secrets to someone

compartir un piso con alguien to share an apartment with someone ▪ to share a flat with someone

compás de espera ▪ la espera waiting time ▪ the wait

compás de espera: estar en to be waiting to hear ▪ to be awaiting word

compensa comprar *(Esp.)* ▪ vale la pena comprar ▪ te merece la pena comprar it's worth it (to buy...) ➤ Si tomas el metro cuatro veces al día, compensa comprar un abono transporte. If you take the metro four times a day, it's worth it to buy a pass. ➤ Compensa comprarlo. It's worth it to buy one.

compensar el efecto de to correct for ➤ El compensador del timón compensa el efecto del viento cruzado. The rudder trim tab corrects for the cross wind.

competición (muy) reñida hard-fought competition

competir el uno contra el otro to compete with each other

complacerse con to delight in ▪ to take pleasure in ▪ to really enjoy ▪ to very much enjoy

complacerse de to delight in ▪ to take pleasure in ▪ to really enjoy ▪ to very much enjoy

complacerse en to delight in ▪ to take pleasure in ▪ to really enjoy ▪ to very much enjoy

complejo de mando *(militar)* command center

complejo industrial-militar military-industrial complex

complementos alimenticios ▪ suplementos vitamínicos ▪ complementos vitamínicos food supplements ▪ vitamin supplements

complementos vitamínicos ▪ suplementos vitamínicos ▪ complementos alimenticios vitamin supplements ▪ food supplements

ser **completamente imposible** to be completely impossible ▪ to be utterly impossible ▪ to be altogether impossible

estar **completo** 1. *(concierto, etc.)* to be booked solid 2. *(clase)* to be full ➤ El concierto está completo. The concert is booked solid. ➤ Las clases están completas. The classes are full.

completo: ser muy ~ to be well rounded ➤ Es muy completa: buena estudiante, atleta, le gusta todo tipo de música. She's well rounded: good student, athletic, likes all kinds of music.

complexión media: ser de ~ to be of average build ▪ to have an average build

complicar las cosas to complicate matters ▪ to complicate things

componer al correr de la pluma ▪ escribir al correr de la pluma ▪ componer o escribir a vuela pluma to dash off *(Nota: carta, poema, ensayo, etc.)*

componer el semblante to compose oneself

componer música to compose music

componerse de to be made up of ▪ to be composed of ➤ *(Ortega y Gasset)* El ejército humano se compone ya de capitanes. The human army is now made up of officers.

comportarse como tal to act like one

compartarse (tan) mal to behave badly ▪ to act up ➤ Deja de comportarte tan mal o te quito la paga. Quit acting up, or I'm going to suspend your allowance.

composición de lugar: hacerse una ~ ▪ hacerse una idea de la situación just to give you an idea

comprar algo a barullo ▪ comprar sin ton ni son ▪ comprar sin reflexión to buy on impulse

comprar algo a plazos to buy in installments

comprar algo al fiado to buy something on credit

comprar algo para alguien ▪ comprarle algo a alguien to buy something for someone ➤ Compré el coche para mi hijo. I bought the car for my son. ➤ Le compré un coche. I bought him a car. ▪ I bought a car from him.

comprar algo sin reflexión ▪ comprar a barullo ▪ comprar sin ton ni son to buy something on impulse

comprar algo sin ton ni son ▪ comprar a barullo ▪ comprar sin reflexión to buy something on impulse

comprar un billete to buy a ticket ▪ to get a ticket ➤ No pude comprar un billete para el tren de primera hora. Estaban todos vendidos. I couldn't get a ticket for the early train. They were (all) sold out.

comprar una apuesta de la lotería to buy a chance to win the lottery

comprar una entrada to buy a ticket ▪ to buy an admission ticket ➤ (Nos) he comprado entradas para el concierto. I bought (us) tickets to the conert.

comprarle algo a alguien 1. ▪ comprar algo para alguien to buy something for someone 2. ▪ comprar lo vendido por alguien to buy something from someone ➤ Le compré un collar a mi novia. I bought a necklace for my girlfriend. ➤ Le compré a un joyero un collar para mi novia. I bought the necklace for my girlfriend from a jeweler. ➤ Le compré un coche a mi hijo. I bought a car for my son. *(In Spanish, "comprar algo a alguien" is ambiguous, meaning both "to buy something for someone" and "to buy something from someone," so Hispanics add "le" to indicate "for," as shown in the foregoing example. To indicate "from," they use "de" or avoid the verb "comprar" altogether: "Lo compré de mi hijo" or "Mi hijo me lo vendió.")*

comprobar a su alrededor ▪ mirar alrededor to look around ▪ to survey the surroundings ➤ Comprobaron a su alrededor para asegurarse de que estaban solos. They looked around to make sure they were alone.

comprobar algo ▪ confirmar algo ▪ corroborar algo to bear out something ▪ to bear something out ▪ to confirm something ▪ to corroborate something ➤ El experimento comprobó lo que Einstein sabía desde un principio-que la gravedad tuerce la trayectoria de la luz. ▪ El experimento confirmó lo que Einstein sabía desde un principio-que la gravedad tuerce la trayectoria de la luz. ▪ El experimento corroboró lo que Einstein sabía desde un principio-que la gravedad tuerce la trayectoria de la luz. The experiment bore out what Einstein knew all along-that gravity bends light. ▪ The experiment confirmed what Einstein knew all along-that gravity bends light. ▪ The experiment corroborated what Einstein knew all along-that gravity bends light. ➤ El experimento lo comprobó. ▪ El experimento lo confirmó. ▪ El experimento lo corroboró. The experiment bore it out. ▪ The experiment confirmed it. ▪ The experiment corroborated it.

comprobar cómo... to see how...

comprobar el buzón de voz ▪ comprobar los mensajes de voz ▪ comprobar si se tienen mensajes de voz to check one's voice mail ▪ to check one's (telephone) messages

comprobar la hora to check the time

comprobar que... 1. to check to see that... 2. ver que... to see that... ▪ to find that... 3. asegurarse de que... to make sure that... ➤ El estudiante comprobó que el profesor lo miraba. ▪ *(Esp. leísmo)* El estudiante comprobó que el profesor le miraba. The student saw that the teacher was looking at him.

comprobar la disponibilidad de los billetes to check on the availability of tickets

comprobar los mensajes de voz ▪ comprobar el buzón de voz ▪ comprobar si se tienen mensajes de voz ▪ revisar los mensajes telefónicos to check one's voice mail ▪ to check one's (tele) phone messages

comprobar si se tiene algo to check on the availability of something

comprobar uno mismo to see for oneself ➤ Compruébalo tú mismo. See for yourself.

comprometerle a alguien a hacer algo to hold someone to doing something ➤ Voy a comprometerte a que lo hagas. I'm going to hold you to it.

comprometerse a llamarle a alguien (por teléfono) to promise to call someone

comprometerse a todo to say yes to everything ▪ to say yes to anything ▪ to agree to everything ▪ to agree to anything

estar **comprometido con** to be committed to

estar **comprometido con alguien** to be engaged to someone ➤ Están comprometidos. They're engaged (to be married).

compromiso con commitment to

compromiso ineludible firm commitment ▪ binding commitment ▪ commitment that one cannot get out of

compromiso presupuestario budget compromise

compruébalo tú mismo see for yourself

compuesta y sin novio ▪ soltera y entera happily single woman

las **computadoras están fuera de servicio** ▪ las computadoras están bloqueadas the computers are down

comulgar con ruedas de molino to swallow nonsense ➤ No voy a comulgar con ruedas de molino. I'm not going to swallow that nonsense.

común denominador common denominator

común y corriente run of the mill

comunicar con to lead to ▪ to go into ▪ *(el exterior)* to open onto ➤ Esta puerta comunica con la cocina. This door leads to the kitchen. ▪ This door goes into the kitchen.

comunicar que... to report that... ➤ El piloto comunica que el avión ha golpeado un objeto. The pilot reports that the airplane has hit something.

comunicar algo con algo to connect something with something ➤ La puerta que comunicaba la oficina con el resto de la casa. The door that connected the office with the rest of the house.

comunicarse con alguien *(Méx.)* to speak with someone (on the phone) ▪ *(Esp.)* to manage to get in touch with someone ➤ ¿Me podría comunicar con Elena? May I please speak with Elena? ➤ Después de toda la mañana intentándolo por fin me comuniqué con el jefe. After trying all morning, I finally managed to get in touch with the boss. ▪ After trying all morning, I finally managed to reach the boss.

comunicarse con el patio to lead to the patio ➤ El pasillo se comunica con el patio. The hall(way) leads to the patio. ▪ The corridor leads to the patio.

comunicarse una habitación con otra to adjoin ▪ to connect to ▪ to connect with each other ➤ El comedor se comunica con la cocina. The dining room adjoins the kitchen. ▪ The dining room connects to the kitchen.

comunicarse dos habitaciones to adjoin ▪ to connect

comunión de los Santos *(catolicismo)* communion of saints

con acierto with precision ▪ well done *(Nota: Olympic commentator on a diver's execution of a dive)*

con adornos azules with blue trim

estar **con algo** ▪ estar a favor de algo to favor something ▪ to be in favor of something ▪ to be for something

con antecedentes de with a history of

con antecedentes por with a history of ▪ with a prior history of ➤ La policía detuvo al presunto, con antecedentes por robo con violencia. Police detained a suspect with a prior history of armed theft.

con antelación ▪ por anticipado ▪ de antemano ▪ con tiempo in advance ▪ ahead of time

con banderas desplegadas with flying colors

con base a ▪ basándose en ▪ en base a based on ▪ on the basis of ➤ Que los medios de comunicación apunten a un candidato como vencedor en un estado con base a las encuestas a pie de urna es absurdo. ▪ Que los medios de comunicación apunten a un candidato como vencedor en base a las encuestas a pie de urna es absurdo. ▪ Que los medios de comunicación apunten a un candidato como vencedor en un estado basándose en las encuestas a pie de urna es absurdo. For the media to call a state for a candidate based on exit polls is asinine. ▪ For the media to call a state for a candidate on the basis of exit polls is asinine.

con bombo y platillos with a lot of hype

con buen arte cleverly

con buen fin ▪ con buenas intenciones with good intentions

con buenas intenciones ▪ con buen fin with good intentions

con buenas palabras nadie come words are cheap

con cabida para big enough for ▪ with room enough for ▪ to fit

con cada día que pasa with each day that passes ▪ with each passing day

con cada día que pasaba with each day that passed ▪ with each passing day

con calma calmly ▪ at one's leisure ▪ without pressure ▪ without being pressured

con cargo a la empresa at the company's expense ▪ at company expense ➤ Compré la computadora con cargo a mi empresa. I bought the computer at the company's expense. ▪ I bought the computer at company expense. ▪ The company paid for the computer.

con cargo a mi cuenta: comprar algo ~ to put something on my account ▪ to put something on my bill

con cargo a mi tarjeta: comprar algo ~ to buy something on my credit card ▪ to put something on my credit card

con conocimiento de causa based on the facts

con conocimiento de causa: hablar ~ to speak with full knowledge of the facts

con creces more than amply ▪ and then some

con cualquier motivo over the least little thing ▪ over any little thing

con cuánta frecuencia ▪ con qué frecuencia ▪ cada cuándo ▪ cómo de a menudo how often

con desesperación in desperation

con desgana: hacer algo ~ **1.** to do something without enthusiasm ▪ to do something unenthusiastically **2.** to do something reluctantly

con destino a bound for ▪ headed for ▪ heading for ▪ for

con diferencia ▪ con mucho by far

con disimulo furtively

estar **con dolores** to be in labor

con dos cojones: hacer algo ~ *(subido de tono)* to do something that takes balls

con dos narices to do something that takes guts ▪ to do something gutsy

con edades comprendidas entre *x* y *y* años ranging in age from *x* to *y* ➤ *(noticia)* Dos espectaculares accidentes de tráfico ocurridos en un intervalo de apenas veinte minutos acabaron con la vida de cuatro jóvenes con edades comprendidas entre diecinueve y veintidós años. Two serious automobile accidents within twenty minutes of each other took the lives of four youths ranging in age from ninteen to twenty-two.

estar **con el agua a la boca** ▪ estar con el agua hasta la boca **1.** to be in the water up to one's chin **2.** to be swamped with work

estar **con el agua al cuello** to be in debt over one's head ▪ to be over one's head in debt ▪ to be in (debt) over one's head ▪ to be up against a wall ▪ to be in a tight spot

estar **con el alma en vilo** to be on pins and needles

con el ánimo de with the intention of ▪ intending to

con el ánimo de charlar trying to make conversation ▪ with the intention of making conversation

con el beneplácito de with the consent of

con el corazón en la mano: decir algo ~ to say something with complete sincerety (holding back nothing)

con el correr de los años over the years

con el cual at which point ▪ whereupon ▪ with which

estar **con el culo en el aire** *(Esp.,)* to be exposed ▪ to be vulnerable ▪ to be unprotected

con el debido respeto with all due respect

con el estómago vacío on an empty stomach

con el fin de for the purpose of ▪ in order to ▪ to

con el hielo on the ice ➤ Ten cuidado con el hielo. Be careful on the ice. ➤ Es difícil dar la vuelta con el hielo. It's difficult to turn on the ice.

estar **con el mes** ▪ tener la regla to be that time of the month ▪ to have one's menstrual period

estar **con el mono** *(de adicción narcótica)* to be going through withdrawal ▪ to be in withdrawal

con el pecho oprimido ▪ apesadumbradamente ▪ acongojado with a heavy heart

con el pie que tengo with my foot the way it is

con el pretexto de ▪ so capa de ▪ bajo capa de on the pretext of ▪ under the pretext of ▪ on the pretense of ▪ under the pretense of
con el propósito de 1. for the purpose of 2. with the intention of ▪ intending to
con el que with which ▪ with what
con el rabillo del ojo out of the corner of one's eye
estar **con el semáforo rojo** *(Esp., subido de tono)* to be on the rag
con el sudor de la frente: ganárselo ~ ▪ ganárselo a pulso sudando to earn it by the sweat of one's brow ▪ to get it by the sweat of one's brow
con el tiempo with time ▪ over time ▪ in the course of time ▪ with the passage of time ▪ in time ▪ eventually ➤ Los tumores pueden volverse malignos con el tiempo. The tumors can become malignant with time.
con el tiempo pegado al culo *(Esp., pintoresco)* ▪ con la hora pegada al culo ▪ a última hora at the very last minute ▪ right at the last minute ▪ in the nick of time ▪ none too soon
con el único propósito de for the sole purpose of
con esa clase de amigos no hacen falta enemigos with friends like them, who needs enemies?
con escala en with a stopover in
con eso no contaba I hadn't figured on that ▪ I had taken that into account ▪ I hadn't counted on that
con eso quiero decir que... ▪ quiero decir con estas palabras que... by that I mean (that)...
con este tiempo in this weather
con esto hereby ➤ Con esto todos los estudiantes hacen las siguientes promesas... All students hereby make the following promises...
con esto de que this being ▪ with something's being ➤ Te contesto rápidamente porque con esto de que la semana es corta, ando con mucha prisa. I'm answering quickly because, this being a short week, I'm in a hurry. ➤ Con esto de la tecnología, es muy fácil mantenerse en contacto con la familia. With technology's being the way it is, it is easy to keep in touch with the family.
con este en mente ▪ pensando en eso with that in mind
con esto no contaba I hadn't figured on that ▪ I didn't figure on that ▪ I hadn't taken that into account
con excesiva lentitud extremely slowly
con falsas pretensiones under false pretenses
con fines médicos for medical purposes
con firmeza firmly
con forma de in the form of
con frecuencia ▪ frecuentemente frequently ▪ often
con fuerza violently ▪ by force ▪ forcefully
con gallardía gallantly
con gastos considerables at considerable cost
con gotas: café ~ *(Valle-Inclán)* ▪ carajillo laced coffee ▪ coffee with a shot of liquor
con gran esmero with great pains ▪ with great care
con gran sentimiento to one's great sorrow
con harta frecuencia with dismal regularity
con ilustraciones illustrated ➤ En la asignatura de arte, necesitamos un libro de texto con ilustraciones. In the art course, we need an illustrated text.
con intención ▪ aposta ▪ adrede ▪ a propósito on purpose ▪ deliberately ▪ intentionally
con intención o sin ella whether one meant to or not ▪ by intent or by default
con justicia ▪ con equidad fairly
estar **con la antena puesta** to listen in ▪ to eavesdrop
con la boca pequeña (with) tongue in cheek ▪ tongue-in-cheek
con la cabeza calva: el hombre ~ the man with the bald head
con la condición de que... ▪ a condición de que... on the condition that...
estar **con la cosa** ▪ tener la regla to having one's menstrual period
con la cual at which point ▪ whereupon ▪ with which
con la frente bien alta ▪ con la frente en alto ▪ con la frente muy alta with one's head (held) high ▪ holding one's head high
con la frente en alto ▪ con la frente muy alta ▪ con la frente bien alta with one's head held high ▪ holding one's head high
con la frente muy alta ▪ con la frente en alto ▪ con la frente bien alta with one's head held high ▪ holding one's head high
con la hora pegada al culo *(pintoresco)* ▪ con el tiempo pegado al culo at the very last minute ▪ right at the last minute ▪ in the nick of time ▪ none too soon
con la lengua fuera ▪ con la lengua afuera ▪ agotado weary ▪ beat
con la más mínima excusa at the least excuse ▪ at the drop of a hat
con la mayor brevedad posible ▪ a la mayor brevedad posible ▪ en cuanto le sea posible at one's earliest convenience
estar **con la mente en blanco** to be drawing a blank ➤ Estoy con la mente en blanco. I'm drawing a blank.
con la misma facilidad que just as easily as ➤ Desde la Plaza de Castilla se puede llegar hasta Tribunal por la línea diez con la misma facilidad que por la uno. From the Plaza de Castilla, you can get to Tribunal just as easily on line ten as on line one.
estar **con la mosca en la oreja** ▪ estar con la mosca detrás de la oreja ▪ tener la mosca en la oreja (for) something to be bugging one
con la que with which ▪ with what
estar **con la soga en el cuello** ▪ estar con la soga al cuello to have a noose around one's neck ▪ to be up against it
con la vista puesta en with one's sights set on
con lápiz with a pencil
con las encuestas en su contra lagging in the polls ▪ with the pollings running against one
con las manos en la masa: pillar a alguien ~ ▪ pillar a alguien in fragantí ▪ pillar a alguien en flagrante delito to catch someone red-handed ▪ to catch someone in the act ▪ *(literario)* to catch someone en medias res
con las manos vacías: marcharse ~ to go away empty-handed ▪ to come away empty-handed
estar **con las orejas gachas** ▪ andar a capa caída to have one's tail between one´s legs ▪ to be crestfallen
con libertad freely
con lo clásico que es being the traditionalist that he is ▪ traditionalist that he is
con lo cual at which point ▪ whereupon
con lo de with respect to
con lo que with which ▪ with what
con lo que no consigo dar ▪ con lo que no puedo dar that I cannot (quite) put my finger on ▪ that I can't (quite) put my finger on ➤ Ella tiene algo con lo que no consigo dar. ▪ Ella tiene algo con lo que no puedo dar. She has a certain something that I can't quite put my finger on.
con lo que no puedo dar ▪ con lo que no consigo dar that I cannot (quite) put my finger on ▪ that I can't (quite) put my finger on ➤ Ella tiene algo con lo que no puedo dar. ▪ Ella tiene algo con lo que no consigo dar. She has a certain something that I can't quite put my finger on.
con lo recaudado with the proceeds ▪ with the money raised
estar **con los amigos** to be with one's friends
estar **con los angelitos** *(dícese de niños)* ▪ estar en los brazos de Morfeo to be asleep
con los brazos abiertos: recibir a alguien ~ to receive someone with open arms
con los días in the coming days ▪ in the next few days ➤ Te iré mandando más fotos con los días. I'll be sending you (some) more photos in the coming days. ▪ I'll be sending you (some) more photos in the next few days.
con los ojos cerrados *(coloquial)* blindfolded ▪ with one's eyes closed
con los que that ▪ with which ▪ which ▪ which...with ➤ En las cajas se encontraron los instrumentos con los que había eliminado y fasificado los sellos de identidad de las bibliotecas. In the boxes (police found) the instruments with which he had eliminated and falsified the libraries' identification seals.
con los *x* (años) ▪ a los *x* ▪ (años) at (age) *x* ▪ at the age of *x* ➤ Con los catorce (años) At (age) fourteen ▪ at the age of fourteen
con lupa 1. with a magnifying glass 2. *(figurativo)* with a fine-tooth comb

con más motivo all the more reason
con mesura in moderation
con miras a ■ con propósito de with a view to ■ with the intention of
con mucho ■ con diferencia by far
con mucho cuidado very carefully
¡con mucho gusto! I'd be delighted! ■ I'd be glad to ■ with pleasure!
con mucho lujo very elegantly
con muchos giros: hablar un idioma ~ to speak a language using lots of expressions
con nocturnidad ■ al abrigo de la noche ■ al amparo de la noche ■ bajo el manto de la oscuridad under cover of darkness
¡con ojo! look out! ■ watch out!
estar **(con) ojo avizor** to be super alert
con partes equivalentes de with equal parts of
con pelos y señales: contarle algo a alguien ~ to give someone a blow-by-blow account of something
con permiso 1. excuse me, (may I get by?) **2.** *(al excusarse de una conversación)* 2. pardon me ■ excuse me
con plenos poderes with full authority ■ with full power(s)
con pocas horas de diferencia within a few hours (of each other)
con poco tiempo on short notice ➤ A veces me llaman para substituir con poco tiempo. Sometimes they call me to substitute on short notice.
con precisión accurately
con premeditación y alevosía with premeditated malice
con pretensiones glorified ■ pretentious
con profunda conformidad: leer algo ~ to read something with wholehearted agreement ■ to agree wholeheartedly with something one has read
con prudencia in moderation
con que as long as
¿con qué dinero se lo consigue? where's the money coming from? ■ where's the money going to come from?
con que estés as long as you're here
¿con qué frecuencia? ■ ¿con cuánta frecuencia? ■ ¿cómo de a menudo? ■ ¿cada cuánto tiempo? ■ ¿cada cuánto? how often...? ■ how frequently...? ➤ ¿Con qué frecuencia pasa el autobús? How often does the bus come by?
¿con qué intención...? why...?
¿con qué título? by what right?
con que uno haga algo with one's doing something ➤ No hay problema con que me devuelvas el dinero cuando te paguen. There's no problem with your paying me back when you get paid.
¿con quién? with whom? ■ *(coloquial)* who with?
¿con quién tengo el gusto de hablar? ¿with whom do I have the pleasure of speaking?
con razón ■ con toda razón rightly so ■ with good reason
¡con razón! no wonder!
con razón o sin ella right or wrong
con recelo: mirarle a alguien ~ to look at someone suspiciously
con relación a su tamaño in relation to its size
con respecto a ■ en torno a ■ a propósito de ■ en cuanto a with respect to
con retraso 1. tardíamente belatedly **2.** tarde late
con sede en based in ■ with headquarters in ➤ La empresa, con sede en Seattle...) The company, based in Seattle... ■ The company, with headquarters in Seattle...
con segundas (intenciones) with a hidden agenda
con sendos... each with ■ with individual... ■ with corresponding...
con ser for being ➤ Con ser pobres, logran llegar a fin de mes. For being poor, they manage to make ends meet.
con solera: una calle ~ street with a lot of character ■ a street with traditional architecture
con solera: una ciudad ~ a historic city
con solera: zona ~ historic area ■ historic district ■ historic zone
con sólo just by ■ by just ■ simply by ■ by simply
con sólo escucharlo(-a): ayudar a alguien ~ to help someone just by listening ■ to help someone by just listening
con su pan se lo coma ■ que le aproveche *(él)* he made his bed, now he can sleep in it ■ *(ella)* she made her bed, now she can sleep in it ■ *(usted)* you made your bed, now you can sleep in it
con su permiso 1. *(de usted)* with your permission **2.** *(de él)* with his permission **3.** *(de ella)* with her permission
con suficiente antelación well ahead of time
con tal de in order to ■ so long as ■ provided (that)
con tal de comprender mejor in order to better understand ➤ Con tal de comprender mejor las llamas, los investigadores las filmaron a cámara lenta. In order to understand flames better, the investigators filmed them in slow motion.
con tal de que ■ con tanto que ■ en tanto que so long as ■ provided that ➤ Puedes doblar las cortinas con tal de que no se arruguen. You can fold the curtains so long as they don't get wrinkled.
con tanta prisa: ir ~ ■ tener tanta prisa ■ ir con tanto apuro to be in such a hurry ➤ ¿Por qué vas con tanta prisa? ■ ¿Por qué tienes tanta prisa? Why are you in such a hurry?
con tanto afán with so much enthusiasm
con tanto que ■ con tal de que so long as ■ provided that
con tiempo ahead of time ■ in good time ■ with time to spare ➤ Le aviso con tiempo. I'll let you know ahead of time.
con tintes de with overtones of
con toda el alma ■ con todas las entrañas with all one's heart
con toda la barba, un hombre a real man
con toda sinceridad in all honesty
con todas las de la ley: ganar ~ to win fair and square ■ to win fairly
con todas las de la ley: ganar a alguien ~ to beat someone fair and square ■ to beat someone fairly ■ to win over someone fair and square ■ to win over someone fairly
con todas las entrañas ■ con todo el alma with all my heart
con todo however ■ still ■ despite
con todo el cuidado posible as carefully as possible
con todo el tiempo for all the time ➤ Con todo el tiempo que ha pasado en España, todavía no ha visto una corrida de toros. For all the time she's spent in Spain, she has yet to see a bull fight.
con todo lujo de detalles in complete detail
con todo y and all
con todos los gastos pagados (with) all expenses paid
con tu pan te lo comas ■ que te aproveche you made your bed, now you can sleep in it
con un año de adelanto a year early
con un año de adelanto de horario a year ahead of schedule
con un error posible de más o menos with a possible error of plus or minus ■ plus or minus ■ give or take ➤ La Estrella Polar está aproximadamente a 430 años luz, con un error posible de más o menos cien años luz. ■ La Estrella Polar queda a 430 años luz, con un error posible de más o menos cien años luz. The Pole Star is 430 light years away, plus or minus a hundred light years. ■ The Pole Star is 430 light years distant, plus or minus a hundred light years.
con un final feliz: acabar ~ to end on a happy note
con un llamamiento de que with a call for
con un lujo de detalles: describir algo ~ ■ describir algo ce por ce ■ describir algo ce por be to describe something in great detail ■ to describe something in complete detail
estar **con un pie en la puerta** to have one's foot in the door
estar **con un pie en la sepultura** ■ estar con un pie en la tumba ■ estar con un pie en el hoyo to have one foot in the grave
con un poco de adelanto a little early
con un poco de adelanto: llegar ~ ■ llegar un poco antes de tiempo ■ llegar un poco adelantado ■ llegar un poquito adelantado ■ llegar un poco pronto ■ llegar un poquito pronto to arrive a little (bit) early
con un poco de labia with a little cajoling ➤ Con un poco de labia, me podrías persuadir. With a little cajoling, I could be persuaded.
con un solo... with a single... ■ with just one... ➤ Es cierto que se puede vivir con un solo riñón. It's true that one can live with a single kidney. ■ It's true that one can live with just one kidney.

con una previsión de *x* visitantes with an expected turnout of *x* visitors

con vista al mar: una casa ~ a house overlooking the sea ▪ a house overlooking the ocean

con voto secreto: elegir ~ to elect by secret ballot ➤ *(editorial)* Sabe perfectamente que perdería una elección abierta, con voto secreto. He knows perfectly well that he would lose an open election by secret ballot.

con *x* años at age *x* ➤ *(titular)* Los escolares empiezan a fumar con 13 años. School children begin smoking at age 13.

con *x* años recién cumplidos just turned *x* ➤ Camilo José Cela, con ochenta y cinco años recién cumplidos Camilo José Cela, just turned eighty-five

con *x* días de vida ▪ *x* days old

con *x* horas de antelación ▪ con *x* horas de anticipación ▪ *x* horas antes *x* hours early ▪ *x* hours ahead of time ➤ Estáte en el aeropuerto con dos horas de antelación. Be at the airport two hours early. ➤ Vete al aeropuerto con dos horas de anticipación. Get to the airport two hours early.

con *x* horas de anticipación ▪ con *x* horas de antelación ▪ *x* horas antes *x* hours early ▪ *x* hours ahead of time ➤ Estáte en el aeropuerto con dos horas de antelación. Be at the airport two hours early. ➤ Vete al aeropuerto con dos horas de anticipación. Get to the airport two hours early.

concatenar los hechos to connect the dots ▪ to see the overall picture

estar **concebido para** to be designed to be ▪ to be intended for

conceder a alguien el beneficio de la duda to give someone the benefit of the doubt

concederle a alguien el beneficio de la duda to give someone the benefit of the doubt

concederle a alguien un préstamo to get a loan ▪ to take out a loan ▪ to secure a loan ▪ to be granted a loan ➤ Le concedieron un préstamo. He got a loan. ▪ He took out a loan. ▪ He secured a loan. ▪ He was granted the loan.

concerniente a relating to ▪ concerning

concebir esperanzas to nourish the hope

conceder audiencia a alguien to grant someone a hearing ▪ to grant a hearing to someone

conceder una entrevista a alguien to grant an interview to someone

conceder una tregua to grant a truce

conceder valor a la opinión de alguien to lend weight to someone's opinion ▪ to give weight to someone's opinion

concederle a alguien el beneficio de la duda to give someone the benefit of the doubt

concederle el indulto a alguien to grant a pardon to someone ▪ to pardon someone ➤ Lincoln le dijo al soldado Scott, "Le voy a conceder el indulto." Lincoln told Pvt. Scott, "I'm going to pardon you."

concederle un deseo a alguien ▪ satisfacerle un deseo to grant someone a wish

concederle un premio a alguien ▪ serle concedido un premio ▪ ser galardonado con un premio **1.** to award a prize to someone ▪ to award someone a prize **2.** to be awarded a prize ➤ A John F. Kennedy le concedieron el Premio Pulitzer de literatura por su libro *Perfiles en Valor.* ▪ A John F. Kennedy le fue concedido el Premio Pulitzer de literatura por su libro *Perfiles en Valor.* ▪ John F. Kennedy fue galardonado con el Premio Pulitzer de literatura por su libro *Perfiles en Valor.* John F. Kennedy was awarded the Pulitzer Prize for literature for his book *Profiles in Courage.* ➤ En 1977 se le concedió el premio Nobel al poeta español Vicente Aleixandre. In 1977 the Spanish poet Vicente Aleixandre was awarded the Nobel prize. ▪ In 1977 the Nobel prize was awarded to the Spanish poet Vicente Aleixandre.

concederle una medalla a alguien ▪ entregarle una medalla a alguien ▪ imponerle una medalla a alguien to award someone a medal ▪ to award a medal to someone

concedérsele un deseo to be granted a wish

cancelación de una deuda ▪ condonación de una deuda cancellation of a debt ▪ forgiveness of a debt

concernir a to concern ➤ Mi pregunta de hoy concierne a... My question today concerns...

concertar con to be consistent with ▪ *(informal)* to jive with

concertar en persona, número y género con ▪ concertar en persona, número y género entre to agree in person, number and gender with

concertar un instrumento ▪ afinar un instrumento to tune an instrument ▪ to tune up an instrument ▪ to tune an instrument up

concesionario de coches car dealership

estar **conchabado con alguien** to be in cahoots with someone

conchabarse contra alguien to gang up on someone

conchabarse para to hatch a scheme to

conciencia de: tener ~ ▪ estar consciente de... to be conscious of something

conciencia de que...: tener ~ ▪ estar conciente de que... to have knowledge of ▪ to be aware of

conciencia limpia: tener la ~ ▪ tener la conciencia tranquila to have a clear conscience

conciencia tranquila: tener la ~ ▪ tener la conciencia limpia to have a clear conscience

estar **concienciado con** to be aware of ➤ Los alumnos están concienciados con la necesidad de estudiar. The students are aware of the need to study.

conciliar el sueño ▪ dormirse ▪ quedarse dormido to get to sleep ▪ to fall asleep

conciliar el sueño (de nuevo) ▪ volver a dormirse ▪ dormirse otra vez to get back to sleep ▪ to go back to sleep ▪ to fall back to sleep ➤ Después de que la sirena la despertara, no pudo conciliar el sueño (de nuevo). ▪ Después de que la sirena la despertara, no pudo volver a dormirse. ▪ Después de que la sirena la despertara, no pudo dormirse otra vez. After the siren woke her up, she couldn't get back to sleep.

Concilio de Nicea *(325 d.C.)* Council of Nicea ➤ El Concilio de Nicea estableció que La Pascua de la Resurrección es el domingo siguiente a la primera luna llena después del equinoccio de primavera (fecha establecida como el veinte o veintiuno de marzo), así que la Pascua de la Resurrección cae entre el 22 de marzo y el 25 de abril. The Council of Nicea established the date of Easter as the first Sunday after the first full moon after the vernal equinox (which falls on the twentieth or twenty-first of March), so that Easter falls between March 22 and April 25.

Concilio de Trento *(1545-1563)* Council of Trent

Concilio universal *(del Papa Juan XXIII)* ▪ Concilio ecuménico Ecumenical Council

concluir algo de una vez (por todas) ▪ hacer algo para salir de eso to get something over with ➤ El dentista me dijo que tenía que sacarme las muelas del juicio en algún momento, así que más me valdría concluirlo de una vez. ▪ El dentista me dijo que tenía que sacarme las muelas del juicio en algún momento, así que más me valdría hacerlo para salir de eso. The dentist said I had to have my wisdom teeth out at some point, so I might as well get it over with.

concluir una reunión ▪ finalizar una reunión to wind up a meeting ▪ to bring a meeting to an end ▪ to conclude a meeting ▪ to end a meeting ➤ Llevamos aquí cuatro horas y no hemos resuelto ni una maldita cuestión. Necesitamos concluir esto e irnos a casa. We've been here four hours, and we haven't solved a damned thing. We need to wind this up and go home.

concluyo mi alegato I rest my case

concordar con to agree with ▪ to be in keeping with ➤ "No hay" no concuerda con "disculparte". Tienes dos opciones igualmente válidas: "no hay que disculparse" o "no tienes que disculparte". "No hay" doesn't agree with "disculparte." You have two equally valid options: "no hay que disculparse" o "no tienes que disculparte." (There's no need to apologize.)

concretar la hora para to set a (definite) time for ▪ to set a (definite) time to ▪ *(coloquial)* to firm up a time for ▪ to firm up a time to ➤ Necesitamos concretar una hora para la reunión. We need to firm up a time for the meeting. ➤ Necesitamos concretar una hora para que nos traigan los suministros. We need to set a time to have the supplies delivered.

concretar una cita con alguien ▪ quedar con alguien ▪ hacer una cita con alguien **1.** *(social)* to make a date with someone **2.** *(negocio)* to make an appointment with someone

concretar una hora para... ▪ fijar una hora para... ▪ establecer una hora para... ▪ *(L.am., coloquial)* ▪ cuadrar una hora para... **1.** to set a time for... ▪ to schedule a time for... **2.** to set a time to...

■ to schedule a time to... ➤ Necesitamos concretar una hora para la reunión. We need to set a time for the meeting. ■ We need to schedule a time for the meeting. ➤ Necesitamos concretar una hora para que nos hagan llegar los suministros. ■ Necesitamos fijar una hora para que nos hagan llegar los suministros. ■ Necesitamos establecer una hora para que nos hagan llegar los suministros. ■ Necesitamos cuadrar una hora para que nos hagan llegar los suministros. We need to set a time to have the supplies delivered. ■ We need to schedule a time to have the supplies delivered.

concurrencia de votantes voter turnout

concurrir a los comicios to go to the polls

concurrir al premio to compete for the prize ■ to contend for the prize

concurso académico quiz show

concurso de belleza beauty pageant

ser **condenado por un crimen** ■ ser declarado culpable de un crimen to be convicted of a crime ■ to be found guilty of a crime

condenar a alguien a algo to sentence someone to something ➤ El tribunal condenó al acusado a penas de entre dos y cuatro años de cárcel. The court sentenced the accused to (punishments of) two to four years in jail.

condenar a alguien con elogios tibios ■ condenar a alguien con tibios elogios to damn someone with faint praise

condiciones atmosféricas atmospheric conditions

condimento de la sopa ■ salsa de la sopa the liquid part of the soup ■ the broth of the soup

condonación de una deuda ■ cancelación de una deuda cancellation of a debt ■ forgiveness of a debt

condonar una deuda ■ cancelar una deuda ■ perdonar una deuda to cancel a debt ■ to forgive a debt

ser **conducido a** 1. to be led to 2. to be led off to

conducir a to lead to ➤ Todos los caminos conducen a Roma. All roads lead to Rome.

conducir a continuación a to drive up next to ➤ Condujeron a continuación a él. They drove up next to him.

conducir a la captura de alguien to lead to the capture of someone ■ to lead to someone's capture

conducir a un lugar 1. manejar a un lugar to drive to a place 2. llevar a un lugar ■ dirigirse a un lugar ■ salir a un lugar to lead to a place ■ to go to a place ■ to take you to a place ➤ Esta carretera conduce a San Salvador. ■ Esta carretera lleva a San Salvador. ■ Esta carretera se dirige a San Salvador. ■ Esta carretera sale a San Salvador. This road leads to San Salvador. ■ This road goes to San Salvador. ■ This road takes you to San Salvador.

conducir al trabajo to drive to work

conducir de forma temeraria to drive recklessly

conducir de vuelta a to drive back to ➤ Mientras iba de vuelta a casa... As I was driving back home... ■ As I was driving back to my house...

conducir el calor to conduct (the) heat

conducir hasta alguien to lead to someone ➤ *(noticia)* Las investigaciones condujeron hasta el sospechoso. The investigation led to the suspect.

conducir por la izquierda to drive on the left

conducir sobre la nieve to drive in the snow ➤ La nieve es hermosa, pero no me gusta conducir sobre ella. The snow is beautiful, but I don't like to drive in it.

conducir un coche ■ manejar un coche to drive a car

conducirle a alguien engañado to entice someone

conducirle a uno a creer ■ llevarle a uno a creer to lead one to believe

conducta antideportiva unsportsmanlike conduct

conductor cuidadoso ■ conductor prudente careful driver ■ good driver

conductor de hombres leader of men

conductor ebrio drunk driver ■ intoxicated driver

conductor prudente ■ conductor cuidadoso careful driver ■ good driver

conectar algo sobre to connect something to ➤ *(instrucciones para prolongador)* Conecte su prolongador sobre un enchufe con toma de tierra. Connect your extension cord to an outlet with ground.

conejillo de Indias: usar a alguien de ~ to use someone as a guinea pig ■ to use as the subject for experimentation

conexión efectuada actual connection ■ *(coloquial)* actual connect ➤ La compañía telefónica te cobra tanto los intentos de conexión con el servidor como la conexión efectuada. The phone company here charges for the attempts to connect to the server as well as for the actual connection.

estar **confabulado con alguien** to be in conspiracy with someone ■ to be in cahoots with someone

confabularse con alguien to conspire with someone

confección de punto needlework ➤ Mi hermana tenía una tienda de confección de punto. My sister had a needlework shop.

confeccionar un escrito to draft a document

confeccionar un traje to tailor-make a suit ■ to make a suit ➤ Es un traje muy bien confeccionado. It's a very well made suit. ■ It's a very well-tailored suit.

confeccionar una carta to draft a letter

confeccionar una lista to make up a list ■ to draw up a list ➤ Confecciona una lista de las cosas que tenemos que comprar en el mercado. Make up a list of things we need to get at the store.

conferencia de prensa ■ rueda de prensa ■ rueda de periodistas press conference ■ news conference

confesarse culpable del delito to plead guilty to the crime

confianza en uno mismo ■ confianza en sí mismo self-confidence ■ confidence in oneself ➤ (Ella) tiene mucha confianza en sí mismo. He has a lot of self-confidence. ■ She has a lot of confidence in herself. ➤ Tienes mucha confianza en ti mismo. You have a lot of self-confidence. ■ You have a lot of confidence in yourself.

confianza mutua mutual trust

confiar en alguien 1. to rely on someone 2. *(fiarse de alguien)* to trust someone

confiar en sus habilidades to have confidence in one's abilities

confiar una responsabilidad a alguien to place a responsibility on someone ■ to bestow a responsibility on someone

confieso mi pecado 1. I acknowledge my sin 2. I acknowledge my error ■ I acknowledge my fault

la **configuración por defecto** *(informática)* ■ configuración predeterminada default setting

confirmar algo ■ comprobar algo ■ corroborar algo to bear out something ■ to bear something out ■ to confirm something ■ to corroborate something ➤ El experimento confirmó lo que Einstein sabía desde un principio-que la gravedad tuerce la trayectoria de la luz. ■ El experimento comprobó lo que Einstein sabía desde un principio-que la gravedad tuerce la trayectoria de la luz. ■ El experimento corroboró lo que Einstein sabía desde un principio-que la gravedad tuerce la trayectoria de la luz. The experiment bore out what Einstein knew all along-that gravity bends light. ■ The experiment confirmed what Einstein knew all along-that gravity bends light. ■ The experiment corroborated what Einstein knew all along-that gravity bends light. ➤ El experimento lo confirmó. ■ El experimento lo comprobó. ■ El experimento lo corroboró. The experiment bore it out. ■ The experiment confirmed it. ■ The experiment corroborated it.

confirmar si... to confirm that... ➤ Por favor confirma si recibiste este correo electrónico. Please confirm that you got this E-mail.

conformarse con algo 1. to settle for something ■ to be okay with something ■ to be satisfied with something 2. to be content to ➤ Me conformo con esa cantidad. I'll settle for that amount. ■ I'm okay with that amount. ■ I'm satisfied with that amount. ➤ Me conformo con estar de pie, gracias. I'm content to stand, thanks.

conformarse con cualquier cosa to go along with anything

conforme a in compliance with

conforme a la ley in accordance with the law

conforme a tu palabra *(misa)* in accordance with thy word

estar **conforme con algo** to be content with something

conforme uno hace algo ■ mientras uno hace algo as one does something ■ while one does something ➤ Conforme pasa las hojas, mi hijita menciona los objetos ausentes de los dibujos. As my little girl turns the pages, she identifies the objects missing from the pictures.

conforme envejecemos as we get older ■ as we grow older

conforme estamos hablando (en estos precisos momentos) ■ conforme hablamos ■ según estamos hablando (en estos precisos momentos) as we speak ➤ Estoy trabajando en ello conforme estamos hablando (en estos precisos momentos). I'm working on it as we speak.

conforme fueron pasando los años ■ a medida que fueron pasando los años ■ según fueron pasando los años as the years went (passing) by

conforme iban pasando los años a medida que iban pasando los años ■ según fueron iban los años as the years went (passing) by

conforme pasaban los años a medida que pasaban los años ■ según pasaban los años as the years passed (by) ■ as the years went by

conforme pasan los años a medida que pasan los años ■ según pasan los años as the years pass (by) ■ as the years go by

conforme pase el tiempo *(futuro)* as time goes by ➤ Te sentirás mejor conforme pase el tiempo. You'll feel better as time goes by. ➤ Se te dará mejor conforme pase el tiempo. You'll get better at it as time goes by.

conforme van pasando los años ■ a medida que van pasando los años ■ según van pasando los años as the years go passing by

estar **confundido(-a) por** ■ estar confundido sobre ■ estar confundido de to be confused about ■ to be all mixed up about ➤ Estoy confundido por este horario de trenes. I'm confused by this train schedule. ➤ Estoy confundido de trenes. I'm confused about the trains.

confundir algo to get something mixed up ■ to have something mixed up ■ to mix up something ■ to mix something up ➤ Confundí los días. I got the days mixed up. ■ I had the days mixed up. ■ I mixed up the days. ■ I mixed the days up.

confundir el asunto ■ confundir la cuestión to confuse the issue

confundir la cuestión ■ confundir el asunto to confuse the issue

confundir la velocidad con el tocino *(Esp.)* not to know one's ass from a hole in the ground ■ not to know shit from shinola *(subido de tono en inglés)*

ser una **confusión total** ■ ser un borrón to be all a blur ➤ Sus clases son una confusión total. ■ Sus clases son un borrón. His lectures are all a blur.

congelamiento de precios y salarios wage and price freeze

congeniar con alguien to enjoy someone's company ■ to hit it off with someone

congestión cerebral ■ infarto cerebral ■ derrame cerebral ■ trombosis cerebral stroke ■ cerebral hemorrhage

congraciar a alguien ■ to win someone over ■ to win over someone *(Nota: "To win over someone" es menos claro porque también significa "ganar a alguien". ■ "To win over someone" is less clear because it also means "to defeat someone" or "to beat someone.")*

congraciarse con alguien to ingratiate oneself to someone ■ to win over someone over ■ to win over someone

conjugarse en armonia con to fit together harmoniously with ■ to combine harmoniously with

conjunto de auricular y micro(fono) (telephone) headset

conjunto de estrellas ■ constelación constellation ■ star cluster

conjurar una crisis to avert a crisis

conllevar riesgo ■ involucar un riesgo to involve risk ■ to involve taking (a) risk

conllevar tiempo ■ llevar tiempo to take time

conmoción cerebral ■ concusión (cerebral) (brain) concussion

estar **conmocionado** to be badly shaken

conocer a alguien 1. *(por primera vez)* to meet someone 2. *(desde hace tiempo)* to know someone ➤ ¿Lo has conocido? Have you met him? ➤ ¿La has conocido? Have you met her? ➤ *(Esp. leísmo)* ¿Le has conocido? Have you met him? ➤ ¿Cuánto tiempo la has conocido? How long have you known her?

conocer a alguien a simple vista to recognize someone right off ■ to know who it is right off

conocer a alguien como la madre que lo parió to know someone like a book

conocer a alguien desde la cuna ■ conocer a alguien desde siempre to have known someone all his life

conocer a alguien desde siempre ■ conocer a alguien desde la cuna to have known someone all his life

conocer a fondo to know in depth ■ to know thoroughly ■ to know inside out

conocer algo a palma de la mano to know something like the back of one's hand ➤ Conoce Madrid a palma de la mano. She knows Madrid like the back of her hand.

conocer algo como el abecé to know something upside down and backwards

conocer algo como la palma de la mano ■ conocer algo palmo a palmo ■ saber algo como la palma de la mano to know something like the back of one's hand ➤ Conoce Madrid como la palma de la mano. He knows Madrid like the back of his hand.

conocer el percal to know the score ■ to know what one is doing

conocer la diferencia entre ■ saber cuál es la diferencia entre to know the difference between ➤ ¿Conoces la diferencia entre "en decúbito prono" y "en decúbito supino"? Estar en decúbito prono es estar boca abajo. Estar en decúbito supino es estar boca arriba. ■ ¿Sabes cuál es la diferencia entre "en decúbito prono" y "en decúbito supino"? Estar en decúbito prono es estar boca abajo. Estar en decúbito supino es estar boca arriba. Do you know the difference between "prone" and "supine"? To lie prone is to lie face down. To lie supine is face up.

conocer los sitios de comer ■ controlar los sitios de comer to know all the good places to eat

conocer mal a alguien ■ tener mala opinión de alguien to think badly of someone ■ *(literario)* to think ill of someone ➤ *(Unamuno)* Un juez que conocía mal a Don Manuel A judge who thought badly of Don Manuel

conocer sus limitaciones y fortalezas to know one's strengths and weaknesses

conocerle el juego a alguien ■ verle el juego a alguien to be onto someone

conocerse el percal *(Esp.)* ■ saber lo que está pasando ■ estar enterado de lo que está pasando to know the score ■ to know what's going on ➤ Me conozco el percal. I know what's going on. ■ I know the score.

conocerse la noticia de que to bring the news that

conocerse todos los trucos habidos y por haber to know every trick in the book

conócete a ti mismo ■ conócete tú mismo *(Socrates)* know thyself

conocida la noticia *(literario, en periodismo)* ■ cuando se supo la noticia ■ cuando conoció la noticia when the news broke

ser **conocido por tener** 1. to be known to have ■ 2. to be known for having

conociéndote ■ sabiendo cómo eres ■ conociéndote como te conozco knowing *you* ➤ Conociéndote, no te lo vas a beber todo. ■ Conociéndote, no te vas beber todo eso. Knowing *(you)*, you won't drink the whole thing.

conocimiento de embarque bill of lading

conocimiento del medio social and environmental studies

conocimiento público public knowledge ➤ Debe ser de conocimiento público que... It needs to be public knowledge that... ■ It needs to be publicly known that... ■ The public needs to be aware that...

conocimientos actuales: según los ~ according to present-day knowledge

conocimientos residuales residual knowledge

conquistar el poder to take power

consagración de una carrera the high point of a career ■ the crowning of a career

consagrar la vida a to dedicate one's life to ■ to devote one's life to

consagrar el tiempo a to dedicate time to ■ to devote time to

ser **consciente de algo** to be aware of something ➤ ¿Eres consciente de lo que has hecho? Are you aware of what you did?

ser **consciente de que...** to be aware that... ➤ ¿Eras consciente de que su hermano está enfermo? ■ ¿Sabías que su hermano estaba enfermo? Were you aware that her brother is ill? ■ Did you know that her brother is ill? ➤ Consciente de que lo seguían, el agente secreto giró bruscamente y se dirigió a la comisaría. ▪ *(Esp. leísmo)* Consciente de que le seguían, el agente secreto giró bruscamente y se dirigió a la comisaría. Aware that he was being followed, the secret agent turned abruptly and headed for the police station.

consecuencias de ▪ el impacto en impact on

consecuencias imprevisibles unforeseeable consequences

consecuencias sombrías dire consequences

consecuente: católico ~ exemplary Catholic

conseguir a un médico ▪ llamar a un médico to get a doctor ▪ to call a doctor

conseguir abrirse camino 1. to manage to get through 2. to manage to get a foot in the door ➤ Conseguimos abrirnos paso. We managed to get through.

conseguir acceso a ▪ lograr acceso a to get access to ▪ to gain access ➤ ¿Hay una pista sobre cómo consiguieron acceso a toda esa munición? ▪ ¿Hay una pista sobre cómo lograron acceso a toda esa munición? Is there any indication (as to) how they got access to all that ammunition? ▪ Is there any indication (as to) how they gained access to all that ammunition?

conseguir algo por las bravas to get something easily ▪ to get something by going around the bureaucracy ➤ No se puede conseguir un permiso de armas por las bravas. Hay que solicitarlo y satisfacer unos requisitos. You can't just walk in off the street and get a weapons permit. You have to apply and undergo a screening.

conseguir algo por su cara bonita 1. conseguir algo gratis to get something for free 2. sin esfuerzo to get something by smooth talking ➤ Me regalaron este reloj por mi cara bonita, no tuve que hacer nada (para conseguirlo). They give me this watch for free. I didn't have to do anything (to get it). ➤ ¿Te crees que te van a aprobar por tu cara bonita? Do you just think you're going pass the test just on your looks? ▪ Do you just think you're going pass the test just for your looks?

conseguir evitarle a alguien to manage to avoid someone

conseguir hacer algo to manage to do something ➤ John Logie Baird realizó las primeras pruebas de televisión en 1928 y ocho años después consigió emitir en color y con una definición más alta. John Logie Baird carried out the first trials of television in 1928 and eight years later got it to broadcast in color and with higher definition.

conseguir información to get information

conseguir la máxima puntuación ▪ obtener la máxima puntuación to get the highest score

conseguir levantar el país to get the country back on its feet

conseguir lo máximo en la vida to get the most out of life

conseguir el permiso de alguien para hacer algo to get permission from someone to do something

conseguir entrar en to gain entry into

conseguir hacer algo ▪ conseguir que algo haga algo to get something to do something ➤ John Logie Baird realizó las primeras pruebas de televisión en 1928 y ocho años después consigió emitir en color y con una definición más alta. John Logie Baird carried out the first trials of television in 1928 and eight years later got it to broadcast in color and with higher definition.

conseguir hacer funcionar el coche to get the car running

conseguir huir to manage to get away ➤ Los atracadores consiguieron huir. The assailants managed to get away.

conseguir información sobre algo ▪ buscar información sobre algo to get information on something ➤ El editor le dijo al reportero, ve a ver si puedes conseguir algo sobre el nuevo director de la secundaria. The editor said to the reporter, see if you can get something on the new high school principal.

conseguir permiso para to get permission to

conseguir que algo funcione ▪ hacer que algo funcione ▪ hacer funcionar algo to get something to work ▪ to get something to function

conseguir que algo salga adelante to be able to get something off the ground ➤ No conseguimos que el proyecto saliera adelante. We couldn't get the project off the ground.

conseguir que la gente se ría de... ▪ conseguir que se ría la gente de... to make people laugh at...

conseguir que no sospeche alguien to manage to avoid suspicion by

conseguir que se hagan las cosas to get things done ➤ El presidente Polk, dijo el historiador Bernard DeVoto, supo cómo conseguir que se hicieran las cosas. President Polk, said historian Bernard DeVoto, knew how to get things done.

conseguir que se ría la gente de... ▪ conseguir que la gente se ría de... to make people laugh at...

conseguir recobrar fuerzas to get a second wind

conseguir trabajo to find work ▪ to get a job

conseguir un puesto to get a job

conseguiré el dinero de alguna forma I'll come up with the money somehow ▪ I'll get the money somehow

conseguirse mediante to be achieved through ▪ to be achieved by means of

conseguirse por menos de to get something for less than ➤ Se consiguen por menos de diez dólares. You can get them for less than ten dollars.

consejero académico academic adviser

consejo de administración ▪ consejo administrativo ▪ junta directiva board of directors

consejo de guerra military tribunal ▪ military court

Consejo de Seguridad Nacional *(EE UU)* National Security Council

consejo del reino privy council

consejo escolar school board

consejo rector ▪ *(Esp.)* ▪ junta rectora doctoral committee

consejos de cómo... tips on how to...

consejos prácticos tips

consenso internacional world opinion

¡consérvalo así! ▪ ¡sigue así! keep it up!

conservar el control de to maintain control of

conservar en el frigorífico *(Esp.)* ▪ conservar en la nevera ▪ conservar en el refrigerador ▪ conservar en la heladera 1. *(infinitivo)* to keep refrigerated ▪ 2. *(como un mandato)* keep refrigerated

conservar la amistad de to hold onto someone's friendship

conservar la memoria de una cosa to preserve the memory of something

conservas alimenticias canned goods

considerar a alguien como to regard somone as ▪ to consider someone to be ➤ La mayoría de los historiadores consideran a Lincoln como el más grande de los presidentes de Estados Unidos. Most historians regard Lincoln as the United States' greatest president.

considerar que había sido desairado to feel slighted

considerársele to be considered ➤ A Madrid se le considera una de las ciudades más interesantes de Europa. Madrid is considered one of the most interesting cities in Europe.

considero que... I find that...

considero que, por mi parte... personally, my opinion is that... ▪ personally, I'm of the opinion that...

consignación de mercancías ▪ partida de bienes consignment of goods

consignar algo para la posteridad to record something for posterity ▪ to note down something for posterity ▪ to note something down for posterity

consigo mi parte I get my share

consonante sonora voiced consonant ▪ voiced stop

consonante sorda unvoiced consonant ▪ unvoiced stop ▪ voiceless stop ➤ En inglés, la letra T es una D sorda, y P una B sorda, mientras que la K es una G (como en "go") sorda. In English, the letter T is a voiceless D, and P an unvoiced B, while K is an unvoiced G (as in "go").

consta que... just so you know (that)... ▪ I'm gonna tell you... ▪ let me tell you!...

constancia da sus frutos ▪ la perseverencia da sus frutos persistence pays off

la **constante de la gravitación** *(física)* gravitational constant

las **constantes vitales** ▪ indicios vitales vital signs ▪ signs of life ➤ Mantener las constantes vitales de alguien... To keep someone alive...

constar de ▪ estar compuesto de to consist of ▪ to be composed of

constarle algo a alguien ▪ estar enterado de algo ▪ ser consciente de algo ▪ tener conocimiento de algo to be aware of something ■ to know about something ➤ Quería decirte algo que a ti probablemente no te conste. ■ Quería decirte algo de lo que probablemente no estés enterado. ■ Quería decirte algo de lo que puede que no seas consciente. ■ Quería decirte algo de lo que probablemente no tengas conocimiento. I wanted to tell you something you may not be aware of. ■ I wanted to tell you something you might not be aware of. ■ I wanted to tell you something you're possibly not aware of. ■ I wanted to tell you something that you may not know about.

constatar el hecho por sí mismo to see for oneself ➤ Puedes constatar el hecho por ti mismo. You can see for yourself.

constatar que... to verify that...

estar **constipado** to have a stopped-up nose ■ (for) one's nose to be stopped up

constiparse el vientre ■ estreñirse to be constipated ■ to become constipated

la **constitución del tribunal** the makeup of the court ■ the composition of the court

constituir una hipoteca to create a mortgage

constituirse en to be made into

constreñir a alguien a hacer algo to force someone to do something

construir castillos en el aire ■ hacerse ilusiones to engage in wishful thinking

construir una frase to assemble a phrase

estar **consultando con alguien** ■ estarse asesorando con alguien to be in consultation with someone ■ to be consulting someone ➤ El gobierno español está consultando con otros gobiernos europeos. ■ El gobierno español se está asesorando con otros gobiernos europeos. The Spanish government is in consultation with other European governments. ■ The Spanish government is consulting with other European governments. ➤ Consulta con el jefe antes de ordenar cualquier nueva existencia. Check with the boss before you order any new stock.

consultar con la almohada to sleep on it ➤ Es mejor consultar las cosas con la almohada a tiempo que perder el sueño por su causa después. It's better to sleep on it than (to) lose sleep because of it.

consultar con el bolsillo to see how much money (I've) got ■ *(culto)* to consult with one's exchequer

consultorio sentimental advice column

consumar el matrimonio to consummate the marriage

consumir como un mechero *(coloquial)* ■ tener bajo consumo ■ tener un buen consumo to get good mileage ■ to have good fuel efficiency ■ to be (very) fuel efficient

consumir *x* litros de combustible al kilómetro ■ consumir *x* litros de carburante al kilómetro to consume *x* liters of fuel per kilometer ■ to burn *x* liters of fuel per kilometer

consumo energético energy consumption ■ consumption of energy

consumo medio mensual de electricidad average annual monthly consumption of electricity

contabilizarse a razón de to be computed at a rate of ■ to be computed at ➤ Labor was computed at the rate of fifteen dollars per hour. El trabajo se contabilizaba a razón de quince dólares por hora.

ser **contactado telefónicamente** to be contacted by telephone ■ to be contacted by phone

contactar a alguien ■ contactarse con alguien to contact someone

contactarse con alguien ■ contactar a alguien to contact someone

contacto de piel a piel direct physical contact

contadas las tardes que falta he rarely misses an evening ■ there's rarely an evening when he doesn't come over

ser **contagiado por** to be influenced by ■ to be prompted by

la **contaminación acústica** noise pollution

la **contaminación del aire** ■ contaminación ambiental air pollution

contándolos todos bar none ■ without exception ■ taking all into account ➤ Contándolos todos, este es el mejor restaurante mexicano de Madrid. This is the best Mexican restaurant in Madrid, bar none. ■ This is, without exception, the best Mexican restaurant in Madrid. ■ This is the best Mexican restaurant in Madrid, taking all into account.

contante y sonante ■ dinero en efectivo cash

contar batallitas ■ contar historias de la guerra to tell war stories ■ to reminisce (about old times)

contar con algo 1. to count on something ■ to bank on something ■ to figure on something ■ to anticipate something 2. atenerse a algo to rely on something ■ to have something ➤ No contaba con eso. I hadn't figured on that. ■ I hadn't anticipated that. ■ I hadn't counted on that. ➤ (Yo) no contaría con con ello. ■ (Yo) no contaría con eso. I wouldn't bank on it. ■ I wouldn't count on it. ➤ Madrid cuenta con un buen sistema de transporte público. Madrid has a good public transportation system.

contar con alguien to count on someone ■ to bank on someone

contar con alguien para algo to depend on someone for something ■ to count on someone for something ➤ ¿Cuento contigo para la mudanza el sábado? Can I count on you to help me move this Saturday?

contar con su palabra to take one's word for it ➤ Cuenta con mi palabra. Take my word for it.

contar de *x* (en *x*) hasta *y* to count by *x*'s to *y* ➤ Contar de cinco en cinco hasta cien To count by fives to a hundred ■ To count by fives to one hundred

contar el tiempo de algo ■ medir el tiempo de algo ■ cronometrar algo to time something ➤ Él contó el tiempo que tardó en ir a la universidad. He timed how long it took him to get to the university.

contar por los dedos to count on one's fingers

contar siempre la misma canción to be a broken record

contar un chiste to tell a joke

contar *x* años ■ tener *x* ■ años to be *x* years old

contarle al oído ■ decirle al oído to whisper in one's ear ➤ Cuéntame al oído. ■ Dime al oído. Whisper it in my ear.

contarle algo a alguien con pelos y señales to give someone a blow-by-blow account of something

contarse con los dedos de la mano to be able to count something on one's fingers ■ to be few in number

contárselo a alguien to tell someone about it

contárselo en dos palabras to tell it in a few words ■ to give a thumbnail sketch

contemplar a alguien to study someone ■ to gaze at someone ➤ Felipe lo contempló con una mirada inquisitiva. Felipe studied him with an inquisitive look.

contemplar a los niños to indulge the children

contemplar algo 1. to contemplate something 2. to gaze at something 3. to study something

contemplar un asunto to consider a matter

contemplar un aumento de sueldo to provide for a salary increase ■ to call for a salary increase ■ to stipulate a salary increase

contener el aliento ■ contener la respiración ■ aguantar la respiración to hold one's breath

contener la respiración ■ contener el aliento ■ aguantar la respiración ■ aguantar el aliento to hold one's breath

contestador automático voice messaging

contestar a coro ■ contestar al unísono to answer in unison

contestar al unísono ■ contestar a coro to answer in unison

contestar con desgana to answer unwillingly ■ to answer reluctantly

contestar con una evasiva ■ esquivar una pregunta to dodge a question ■ to evade a question

contestar sin titubear to answer without hesitation

contienda histórica historic struggle

contigo ni a misa ■ contigo ni en la foto I wouldn't be caught dead with you

estar **contiguo a** ■ estar justo al lado de ■ estar pegado a ■ estar a continuación de to be adjacent to ■ to be right next to ■ to be right by ■ to be (right) beside ➤ The park is adjacent to the library. ■ The park is (right) next to the library. ■ The park is (right) beside the library. ■ The park is (right) by the library. El parque está contiguo a la biblioteca. ■ El parqué está justo al lado de la biblioteca. ■ El parque está pegado a la biblioteca. ■ El parque está a continuación de la biblioteca.

continuamente: hacer algo ~ to do something all the time ■ a todas horas around the clock ➤ Me corrigen continuamente. They correct me all the time. ■ They correct me continuously. ■ They correct me nonstop.

continuo rodar de coches continuous stream of cars

contra el sentido de las agujas del reloj ■ a la izquierda counterclockwise

contra el vicio de pedir, la virtud de no dar just say no

contra la corriente: ir ~ ■ ir a contracorriente ■ ir contra corriente to go against the grain ■ to go against the tide ■ to be out of step

estar **contra las cuerdas** to be on the ropes ■ to be about to be overthrown

contra viento y marea: hacer algo ~ ■ hacer algo a toda costa ■ hacer algo cueste lo que cueste to do something come hell or high water ■ to do something no matter what it takes ■ to do something whatever it takes ■ to do something no matter what the cost ■ to do something whatever the cost

ser una **contradicción de términos** to be a contradiction in terms

contraer afecciones cardiacas ■ desarrollar problemas cardiacos to develop heart problems

contraer deudas to get into debt

contraer matrimonio ■ casarse to get married

contraer una deuda to go into debt

contraportada de una revista back cover of a magazine

contrarrestar la fuerza de torsión to counter the torque ■ to offset the torque ■ to compensate for the torque ➤ Los tornillos de ruedas tienen las roscas al revés para contrarrestar la fuerza de torsión. Wheel bolts have reversed threads to counter the torque.

contratar a alguien para hacer algo to hire someone to do something ■ to enter into a contract with someone to do something ■ to contract with someone to do something

contratar para to sign up for ➤ ¿Has contratado para el examen TOEFL? Have you signed up for the TOEFL test?

contrato blindado airtight contract

contrato millonario 1. multi-million-dollar contract 2. multi-million-euro contract

contrato vinculante binding contract

contribuir los impuestos to pay taxes

el **control de precios y salarios** wage and price controls

el **control de tráfico** checkpoint

control médico medical supervision

control médico: bajo ~ medically supervised ■ under medical supervision

controlador aéreo air traffic controller

controlar los movimientos de alguien ■ monitorear los movimientos de alguien to tail someone ■ to monitor someone ➤ Los terroristas siguen controlando nuestros movimientos. The terrorists are continuing to tail us.

controlar los sitios de comer ■ conocer los sitios de comer to know all the good places to eat

controlar su genio to control one's temper ■ *(coloquial)* to cool it ➤ ¡Controla tu genio! Control your temper! ■ Cool it!

controlar su tiempo ■ hacerse control de su tiempo to get control of one's time

controlarse con la bebida to watch one's alcohol consumption

controversia en torno a controversy surrounding

convalecer de una lesión to recover from an injury

estar **convencido de que...** to be convinced that...

convencer a alguien para que haga algo to persuade someone to do something

estar **convencido de que...** to be convinced that...

Convenciones de Ginebra Geneva Conventions

convendría recordar que... it should be remembered that...

¿convendrías conmigo que...? would you agree with me that...?

convenio bilateral ■ acuerdo bilateral bilateral agreement ■ bilateral accord

convenir en que... to be of the same opinion that... ■ to agree that...

convenirle a sus intereses to serve one's (own) interests

la **conversación coloquial** ■ (el) lenguaje coloquial colloquial speech

convertir algo en algo to turn something into something ➤ Han convertido la búsqueda de un nuevo papa en un circo mediático. They've turned the search for a new pope into a media circus.

convertir algo en algo ventajoso para sí mismo ■ convertir algo en algo ventajoso para uno mismo to turn something to one's advantage

convertir en cenizas to reduce to ashes

convertirse en el foco to become the focal point

convertirse en el foco de atención ■ convertirse en el centro de atención to become the focal point of attention ■ to become the center of attention

convertirse en el foco de la atención de uno ■ convertirse en el centro de atención de uno to become the focal point of one's attention ■ to become the focus of one's attention

convertirse en el foco de la charla to become the focal point of the discussion

convertirse en el foco del debate to become the focal point of the debate

convertirse en instintivo ■ volverse instintivo to become second nature ■ to become instinctive ➤ Para un piloto aterrizar se convierte en algo instintivo. ■ Para un piloto aterrizar se vuelve instintivo. To a pilot, landing becomes second nature. ■ To a pilot, landing becomes instinctive.

convertirse en presidente to become president

convertirse en un bien escaso to become a scarce commodity

convertirse en un éxito en ventas to become a bestseller

convertirse en una víctima mortal ■ convertirse en una víctima fatal to become a fatality ➤ *(noticia)* Un niño de diez años se convirtió en la primera víctima mortal de un tiburón en Estados Unidos este verano. A ten-year-old boy became this summer's first shark fatality in the United States.

conviene recordar que... it should be remembered that...

convivir con alguien to live with someone (as a couple) ■ to live together ■ to cohabit

convocar elecciones to call elections

convocar un pleno to call a joint session

convocar una sesión to call a meeting

cooperación intensa close cooperation

copar el mercado to corner the market

copia al carbón carbon copy

copia de respaldo ■ copia de seguridad backup copy ■ security copy ■ copy for security purposes

copia de seguridad ■ copia de respaldo security copy ■ backup copy ■ copy for security purposes

copia impresa hard copy ■ printed copy

¡copiado! copy!

copiar y pegar to copy and paste

copo de algodón ball of cotton ■ cottonball

copo de lana ■ ovillo de lana ■ madeja de lana ball of yarn

copo de nieve snowflake

corazonada: tener una ~ ■ tener un presentimiento to have a hunch

cordero pascual *(judaísmo y catolicismo)* paschal lamb

cordero recental suckling lamb

corroborar el testimonio de alguien ■ refrendar el testimonio de alguien ■ apoyar el testimonio de alguien to corroborate someone's testimony ■ to affirm someone's testimony ■ to support someone's testimony ■ to back up someone's testimony

corralito financiero *(pintoresco)* financial bind

¡corre! hurry! ■ quick!

corre la voz de que there's a rumor going around that

corredor de la muerte: estar en ~ to be on death row ■ to be awaiting execution

corregir lo dicho to set the record straight

correligionario 1. political ally 2. *(communist sympathizer)* fellow traveler

correo electrónico *(coloquial)* ■ emilio electronic mail ■ e-mail ■ E-mail ➤ Me han devuelto todos los correos que te he enviado. All my e-mails to you have bounced.

correr a cuenta de la casa ■ ser a cuenta de la casa to be on the house ➤ Las bebidas corren a cuenta de la casa. ■ La bebidas son a cuenta de la casa. Drinks are on the house.

correr a la tienda ■ irse a la tienda to run to the store ■ to run over to the store ➤ Corre a la tienda y trae un pan. ■ Vete a la tienda y trae un pan. Run over to the store and get a loaf of bread.

correr a *x* kilómetros por hora to go *x* kilometers per hour

correr como el viento to run like the wind

correr como la pólvora ■ correr como un reguero de pólvora ■ propagarse como la pólvora to spread like wildfire ➤ La noticia corrió como la pólvora. The news spread like wildfire.

correr como un galgo to run like a greyhound ■ to run like a hare

correr como un pollo sin cabeza to run around like a chicken with its head cut off

correr como un reguero de pólvora ■ correr como la pólvora ■ propagarse como la pólvora to spread like wildfire

correr como una liebre to run like a rabbit

correr con 1. to run with **2.** be responsible for

correr con los gastos de to pay the expenses of

correr con sus gastos trabajando durante su etapa estudiantil ■ costearse sus gastos trabajando durante su etapa estudiantil to work one's way through college ■ to pay one's way through college by working

correr contra el tiempo ■ ganar tiempo al tiempo to race against time ■ to try to beat time

correr de boca en boca to spread by word of mouth

correr de espaldas run backwards ➤ Los jugadores de béisbol a veces tienen que correr de espaldas para coger la bola en el campo exterior. Baseball players sometimes have to run backwards to catch the ball in the outfield.

correr de la Ceca a la Meca to run from pillar to post ■ to run from Herod to Pilate

correr de un lado a otro correr de un lado para otro ■ correr por todos lados ■ correr por todas partes to run all over the place

correr detrás de alguien to run after someone

correr el riesgo de (que) ■ exponerse a (que) to run the risk of ■ to take the risk of ■ to take the chance of

correr el tiempo (for) time to fly ➤ ¡Cómo corre el tiempo! How time flies!

correr en pos de algo to run after something ■ to chase after something

correr en pos de alguien to run after someone ■ to chase (after) someone

correr escaleras abajo to run downstairs

correr escaleras arriba to run upstairs

correr hacia algo ■ estrellarse contra algo ■ darse contra algo to run into something ➤ *(Wile E. Coyote)* Se pegarán si es que corren hacia él. They'll stick to it if they run into it.

correr la voz to spread the word

correr lo más de prisa que uno pueda to run as fast as one can

correr para ponerse a salvo to run for one's life ■ to run to safety

correr peligro ■ correr un peligro to run a risk ■ to be in danger

correr por costa mía to be at my expense ➤ La cena corrió por costa mía. The dinner was at my expense. ■ The supper was at my expense.

correr por todas partes ■ correr por todos lados ■ correr de un lado para otro ■ correr de un lado a otro to run all over the place ■ to go all over the place

correr prisa to be urgent

correr riesgo to run a risk ■ to take a risk

correr ríos de tinta sobre un asunto to spill rivers of ink on a subject

correr rumores de que for rumors to run rampant

correr sin freno to run free ■ *(figurado)* to do one's own thing

correr un peligro ■ correr peligro to run a risk ■ to be in danger

correr un riesgo de to run a risk of

correr un tupido velo ■ dejar el asunto to drop the subject ➤ Corramos un tupido velo. ■ Dejemos ese asunto. Let's drop the subject.

correr vueltas to run laps ➤ Tenemos que correr dos vueltas alrededor de la pista. We have to run two laps around the track.

correr *x* kilómetros por hora to go *x* **kilómetros por hora**

correrse (de vergüenza) *(L.am.)* to be ashamed ■ *(literario)* ■ to be filled with shame ➤ *(César Vallejo)* Me moriré en Paris y no me corro. I will die in Paris, and I am not ashamed (to admit it).

correrse una juerga *(coloquial)* to paint the town red

corresponder a un favor to return a favor

corresponder a un saludo to return a greeting ■ to speak back

corresponder a una invitación to reciprocate an invitation ■ to return an invitation

corresponder al estereotipo de to fit the stereotype of

corresponder con ■ ser el mismo que to be the same as ■ to correspond to ➤ Antes de conectar el aparato, compruebe que la tensión corresponde con la indicada en la placa de características. Before connecting the appliance, check to see that the voltage is the same as that indicated on the characteristics plate.

corresponder un detalle to reciprocate a gift

corresponder un favor to return a favor ■ to reciprocate a favor

corresponder una invitación to return an invitation ■ to reciprocate an invitation

corresponderle a uno *(derecho)* ■ pertenecer a alguien ■ ser de alguien to belong to one

corría el año *x* cuando... it was in (the year) *x* that...

corriente alterna alternating current

corriente continua direct current

la **corriente de pensamiento** school of thought ■ current of thought

corriente principal: estar en la ~ to be in the mainstream

corriente y moliente run of the mill

corrígeme si me equivoco ■ rectifícame si me equivoco correct me if I'm wrong

corrimiento de tierra(s) ■ derrumbamiento de tierras ■ derrumbe de tierras ■ desprendimiento (de tierras) landslide

la **corroboración de un testimonio** ■ refrendo de un testimonio corroboration of testimony ■ affirmation of testimony

corroborar algo ■ confirmar algo ■ comprobar algo to bear out something ■ to bear something out ■ to confirm something ■ to corroborate something ➤ El experimento corroboró lo que Einstein sabía desde un principio-que la gravedad tuerce la trayectoria de la luz. ■ El experimento confirmó lo que Einstein sabía desde un principio-que la gravedad tuerce la trayectoria de la luz. ■ El experimento comprobó lo que Einstein sabía desde un principio-que la gravedad tuerce la trayectoria de la luz. The experiment bore out what Einstein knew all along-that gravity bends light. ■ The experiment confirmed what Einstein knew all along-that gravity bends light. ■ The experiment corroborated what Einstein knew all along-that gravity bends light. ➤ El experimento lo corroboró. ■ El experimento lo confirmó. ■ El experimento lo comprobó. The experiment corroborated it. ■ The experiment confirmed it. ■ The experiment bore it out.

¡corta! *(cartas, naipes)* cut!

estar **cortado por el mismo patrón** ■ estar cortado por el mismo molde to be cut from the same cloth ■ to be cast in the same mold ■ to be cast from the same mold ■ to be like that ➤ Toda la familia está cortada por el mismo patrón de conducta. The whole family is like that.

ser **cortado por el mismo patrón** ■ ser cortado por el mismo molde to be cut from the same cloth ■ to be cast in the same mold ■ to be cast from the same mold ■ to be like... ➤ Ha sido cortado por el mismo patrón de conducta familiar. He's like the rest of his family. ■ His behavior pattern runs in his family.

cortar a alguien ■ dar un corte a alguien ■ dejar a alguien fuera de juego to blank someone out ➤ Cuando reaccionó diciéndote "pobrecito", él te estaba cortando. ■ Cuando reaccionó diciéndote "pobrecito", él te estaba dando un corte. ■ Cuando reaccionó diciéndote "pobrecito", él te estaba dejando fuera de juego. When he reacted by saying "poor baby," he was blanking you out.

cortar a alguien las alas to clip someone's wings

cortar algo a rodajas ■ cortar en rodajas to slice (radially)

cortar algo en diagonal to cross something at an angle ■ to cross something diagonally ■ to intersect something at an angle ■ to intersect something diagonally ➤ El Paseo de la Reforma corta la Avenida Hidalgo en diagonal. The Paseo de la Reforma crosses Hidalgo Avenue at an angle. ■ The Paseo de la Reforma crosses Hidalgo Avenue diagonally. ■ The Paseo de la Reforma intersects Hidalgo Avenue at an angle. ■ The Paseo de la Reforma intersects Hidalgo Avenue diagonally.

cortar algo en dos mitades to cut something in half

cortar algo en rodajas ■ cortar a rodajas to slice (radially)

cortar algo en trozos to cut something into pieces

cortar algo a lo largo ■ cortar algo transversalmente ■ partir algo por el medio to cut something in two lengthwise ■ *(más técnico)* to cut something in two transversally ➤ Para preparar un banana split, se corta el plátano a lo largo. To make a banana split, you cut the banana in half lengthwise.

cortar algo de raíz 1. to root out something ■ to root something out 2. to stop something before it becomes a habit ■ to nip something in the bud

cortar cabezas to make heads roll

cortar camino ■ ir por el atajo ■ cortar por el atajo to take a shortcut

cortar con alguien ■ romper con alguien ■ terminar con alguien to break up (with someone) ■ to split up ➤ She broke up with him. Ella cortó con él. ➤ Han cortado. ■ Han roto. ■ Han terminado. They broke up. ■ They split up.

cortar con su novia to break up with one's girlfriend

cortar con su novio to break up with one's boyfriend

cortar el bacalao to call the shots ■ to run the show

cortar el césped ■ segar el césped to cut the grass ■ to mow the lawn

cortar el gas ■ cerrar el gas to turn off the gas ■ to turn the gas off

cortar el pan to slice the bread

cortar el paso to interrupt ■ to block

cortar el pelo al cero a alguien ■ cortar el pelo a cero a alguien ■ rapar a alguien a cero ■ rapar el pelo a alguien al cero to shave someone's head (bare)

cortar en juliana to julienne ■ to cut in long, thin strips

cortar hacia fuera to cut away from you ➤ Al usar el cuchillo, corta hacia fuera. When carving with a knife, cut away from you.

cortar (la) comida en bocaditos ■ cortar (la) comida en trocitos to cut the food into bite-size piece ■ *(coloquial)* to cut the food in bite-size pieces

cortar la línea telefónica ■ cortar la línea to cut off the telephone ■ to cut the telephone off

cortar un trozo de pizza a alguien ■ cortar un poco de pizza a alguien ■ cortar algo de pizza a alguien to cut a piece of pizza for someone ■ to cut someone a piece of pizza ➤ ¿Me cortarías un trozo de pizza? ■ ¿Me cortarías un poco de pizza? ■ ¿Me cortarías algo de pizza? Would you cut me a piece of pizza?

cortar las alas a alguien ■ quebrar las alas a alguien to clip someone's wings

cortar las cartas ■ cortar los naipes ■ cortar la baraja ■ cortar el mazo to cut the cards ■ to cut the deck

cortar las ligaduras to cut the bonds

cortar los naipes ■ cortar las cartas ■ cortar la baraja ■ cortar el mazo to cut the cards ■ to cut the deck

cortar por la línea de puntos to cut along the dotted line

cortar y pegar to cut and paste

cortar un jamón to carve a ham

cortar una pierna de cordero ■ trinchar una pierna de cordero to carve a leg of lamb

cortarle el aliento a uno ■ quitarle el aliento to take one's breath away ■ to be breathtaking ➤ El interior de la catedral me cortó el aliento. ■ El interior de la catedral me quitó el aliento. The interior of the cathedral took my breath away. ■ The interior of the cathedral was breathtaking.

cortarle la línea a alguien to disconnect someone's telephone ■ to cut off someone's telephone ➤ Me han cortado la línea. They cut off my telephone. ■ I got disconnected. ■ My telephone was cut off. ■ My telephone was disconnected.

cortarle la respiración a uno to knock the breath out of one ➤ El impacto le cortó la respiración. The impact knocked the breath out of him.

cortarlo antes de tiempo to nip it in the bud

cortarlo por lo sano to take drastic action

cortarse el pelo to get a haircut ➤ Tengo que cortarme el pelo hoy. I have to get a haircut today. ■ I've got to get a haircut today.

cortarse el pelo a cero ■ cortarse el pelo al cero ■ raparse el pelo a cero ■ raparse el pelo al cero to shave one's head (bare)

cortarse la leche (for) the milk to go sour ■ (for) the milk to turn sour

cortarse la línea to get disconnected ➤ Se ha cortado la línea. I got disconnected. ➤ Se nos ha cortado la línea. We got disconnected.

cortársele el aliento to take one's breath away ■ to be breathtaking ➤ El interior de la catedral me cortó el aliento. The interior of the cathedral took my breath away. ■ The interior of the cathedral was breathtaking.

cortársele la respiración 1. dejar de respirar to stop breathing 2. *(como resultado de un impacto)* to get one's breath knocked out ■ to have one's breath knocked out ➤ En el medio de la cirugía al paciente se le cortó la respiración. In the middle of the operation the patient stopped breathing. ➤ Se me cortó la respiración cuando caí del árbol. I got my breath knocked out when I fell out of the tree.

el **corte de digestión** stomach cramp ➤ El deportista es atendido tras desplomarse por un corte de digestión. The athlete is attended after being felled by a stomach cramp.

el **corte de luz** ■ (el) apagón power outage ➤ Necesito un reloj a pilas para los viajes y para los cortes de luz. I need a battery-powered clock for traveling and power outages.

el **corte de pelo irregular** ragged haircut

los **cortes y moratones de poca importancia** minor cuts and bruises ➤ La víctima sufrió cortes y moratones de poca importancia. The victim suffered minor cuts and bruises in the accident.

corteza terrestre Earth's crust

cortina de hierro iron curtain

cortina de humo: echar una ~ ■ echar una pantalla de humo to put up a smoke screen

cortina de niebla ■ velo de niebla fog bank ■ layer of fog

corto de miras short-sighted

corto(-a) de vista ■ miope near-sighted ■ short-sighted

¡corto y cierro! over and out!

la **cosa así queda** ■ el asunto así queda and that's how it stands ■ and that's where it stands ■ and that's how the matter stands ■ and that's where the matter stands

ser una **cosa cierta** to be a certainty ■ to be a sure thing

ser **cosa de chicha y nabo** to be insignificant

ser **cosa de hombres** to be a guy thing ➤ Es cosa de hombres. It's a guy thing.

ser **cosa de reír** ■ ser cosa de risa to be laughable ➤ *(Bernal Díaz)* Es cosa de reír que los de una provincia o ciudad no ayudaban a los otros. It's laughable that the people of one province or town would not help the (people from the) others.

ser **cosa de risa** ■ ser cosa de reír to be laughable

cosa del otro jueves: no ser ~ to be nothing to write home about ■ to be no big thing ➤ No es cosa del otro jueves. It's nothing to write home about. ■ It's no big thing.

la **cosa es que** the thing of it is that ■ the thing is that

ser **cosa hecha** to be a done deal ■ to be in the bag ■ to have it in the bag

ser una **cosa mala perder** ■ ser una mala cosa perder to be a bad thing to lose ➤ Es una cosa mala perder el pasaporte. ■ Es una mala cosa perder el pasaporte. A passport is a bad thing to lose.

cosa más parecida closest thing (one has) to

estar la **cosa que arde** to be at the bursting point ■ to be at the boiling point

cosas de esas ■ cosas así ■ cosas por el estilo things like that

las **cosas de palacio van despacio** 1. these things take time ■ 2. the bureaucratic mill is slow

cosas estorbando el paso ▪ cosas por medio things in the way
las **cosas pasan por algo** things happen for a reason
las **cosas marchan sobre ruedas** things are rolling
las **cosas no podrían estar peor** things couldn't be worse
las **cosas no podrían ir peor** things couldn't get any worse
cosas por el estilo that kind of thing ▪ that sort of thing ▪ things of that kind
cosas por medio ▪ cosas estorbando el paso things in the way
cosas que picar ▪ (los) entremeses hors d'ouvres
cosas tales things of that sort ▪ things of that kind
¡las **cosas tuyas!** the things you come up with!
coser a balazos ▪ acribillar a balazos to riddle with bullets
coser un botón ▪ pegar un botón to sew on a button ➤ ¿Me coserías el bóton del cuello (de la camisa)? Would you sew on this collar button for me?
ser **coser y cantar** ▪ ser pan comido to be easy as pie ▪ to be a piece of cake
coserse la boca to keep one's lips zipped ▪ to zip one's lips ▪ to keep quiet ▪ to keep mum
ser **cosita de gusto** to be nothing to rave about ▪ to be nothing to write home about
costa de barlovento windward coast ▪ windward side (of an island)
costa de sotavento leeward coast ▪ leeward side (of an island)
costado de una silla ▪ (el, los) apoyabrazos arm of a chair
costar caro to cost a lot ▪ to be expensive
costar la vida a alguien to take the life of someone ▪ to take someone's life ▪ to cost the life of someone
costar más el remedio que la enfermedad the cure is worse than the disease
costar trabajo to be hard ▪ to be difficult
costar un huevo *(subido de tono)* ▪ costar un ojo de la cara ▪ costar un riñón to cost an arm and a leg
costar un ojo de la cara ▪ costar un riñón ▪ *(subido de tono)* costar un huevo to cost an arm and a leg
costar un riñón ▪ costar un ojo de la cara ▪ *(subido de tono)* costar un huevo to cost an arm and a leg
costar una porrada to cost a bundle
costarle caro to get one into a lot of trouble ▪ to cost one ➤ Mentir bajo juramento puede costarle caro. Lying under oath can get you in(to) a lot of trouble. ▪ Lying under oath can cost you.
costarle hacer una cosa to have a hard time doing something ➤ Me cuesta encontrar lo peor de esta asignatura. I have a hard time thinking of anything I don't like about the course.
costarle la vida to cost one one's life
costarle trabajo hacer algo 1. to have a hard time doing something 2. to go to a lot of trouble to do something ➤ Le costó trabajo persuadirle. He had a hard time persuading him. ▪ He went to a lot of trouble to persuade him.
costarle un buen dinero to cost one a lot ▪ to cost one plenty ➤ Me costó un buen dinero. It cost me a lot. ▪ It cost me plenty.
costarle una pasta gansa to cost one a pretty penny
costear algo ▪ pagar algo to cover the cost of something ▪ to pay for something
costearse sus gastos trabajando durante su etapa estudiantil ▪ correr con sus gastos trabajando durante su etapa estudiantil to work one's way through college ▪ to pay one's (own) way through college by working ➤ Él se costeó sus gastos pintando durante su etapa estudiantil. ▪ Él corrió con sus gastos pintando durante su etapa estudiantil. He worked his way through college by painting.
costilla de Adán ▪ esposa wife
costo de algo cost of something
costo de la vida cost of living
costo de producción production cost
ser una **costumbre muy común** to be a common practice
costumbres persistentes: ser un hombre de ~ to be a man of regular habits
costumbres persistentes: tener ~ to have regular habits
cota de un mapa numbers (on a map) indicating the height above sea level
cotas bajas: en (las) ~ in the lower elevations ➤ Va a nevar mañana en cotas bajas. It will snow tomorrow in the lower elevations. ▪ It is going to snow tomorrow in the lower elevations.
cotejar un talonario (con el extracto de cuenta) ▪ actualizar un talonario to balance a checkbook
coyuntura política political situation
crear falsas expectativas en to raise false hopes in ▪ *(entre un grupo de personas)* to raise false hopes among ▪ to raise false hopes in
crear un caos (con) ▪ hacer estragos (con) ▪ causar estragos (con) to wreak havoc (with)
crear un precedente ▪ sentar un precedente to set a precedent
crear una amistad con alguien to develop a good friendship with someone ➤ Hemos creado una buena amistad. ▪ Hemos creado una fuerte amistad. We have developed a good friendship.
ser **creativo con** ▪ resultar creativo con to get creative with ▪ to get creative on ➤ Fui muy creativo con los colores. ▪ Resulté muy creativo con los colores. I got creative with the colors. ▪ I got creative on the colors.
crecer a pasos gigantescos to grow in leaps and bounds ➤ Su negocio crece a pasos gigantescos. ▪ Su negocio está creciendo a pasos gigantescos. His business is growing in leaps and bounds.
crecer como la mala hierba ▪ pegar un estirón to grow like a weed ▪ to shoot up like a weed ▪ to have a growth spurt
crecer un pastel (for) a cake to rise ➤ El pastel no crecerá si abres el horno durante la cocción. The cake won't rise if you open the oven during baking.
crecer una media de to grow an average of
crecerse con las circunstancias to rise to the occasion
crecida de un arroyo rising of a stream ▪ swelling of a stream
crecida de un río rising of the river ▪ swelling of the river
crecimiento alcanzable ▪ crecimiento posible ▪ crecimiento realista attainable growth
crecimiento sostenible sustainable growth
crecimiento sostenido sustained growth
crecimiento cero zero growth
crédito en la cuenta credit on the account ➤ Tengo crédito en mi cuenta. I have a credit on my account.
creer que no not to think so ▪ not to believe so ▪ *(más culto)* to think not ▪ to believe not ➤ Creo que no. I don't think so. ▪ I don't believe so. ▪ I think not. ▪ I believe not.
creer que sí to think so ▪ to believe so ➤ Creo que sí. I think so. ▪ I believe so.
creer saber to believe one knows ▪ to think one knows ➤ Creemos saber donde... We believe we know where... ▪ We think we know where...
creerse Dios ▪ creer que uno es Dios to thinks one is God ▪ to have an exaggerated opinion of oneself ➤ Se cree Dios. ▪Cree que es Dios. 1. He thinks he's God. 2. She thinks she's God.
creerse el ombligo del mundo ▪ creer que uno es el ombligo del mundo to think the world revolves around one
creerse más que nadie to have a superiority complex
creérselo(-a) to fall for it ▪ to be taken in by it ▪ to be duped ➤ *(Wile E. Coyote)* The trick is working; they're falling for it El truco sirve-¡se lo están creyendo!
crema agria ▪ nata agria sour cream
crema batida ▪ nata batida whipped cream
crema chantillí *(Arg.)* whipped cream
crema de cacahuate *(Méx.)* ▪ crema de cacahuete peanut butter
crema de cacahuete *(Esp.)* peanut butter
crema de maní *(Arg.)* ▪ crema de cacahuete peanut butter
cremallera se engancha ▪ cremallera se queda zipper catches ▪ zipper sticks ➤ Los dientes de esta cremallera no coinciden, y se engancha. ▪ ...y se queda. This zipper's teeth are not lined up correctly, and it catches. ▪ ...and it sticks.
creo que lo tengo I think I've got it ▪ I think I have it
creo que no importa I don't think it matters
creo que no puedes mejorarlo I don't think you can improve on it
creo que no se puede mejorar I don't think you can improve on it ▪ I don't think it can be improved on

creo que no se puede superar ▪ creo que no se puede mejorar ▪ creo que no haya mejor ▪ creo que es lo mejor que hay I don't think you can beat it ➤ Con respecto a la comida mexicana en Madrid, creo que no se puede superar. For Mexican food in Madrid, I don't think you can beat it.

creo que sea grave it sounds urgent (to me) ▪ it sounds to me like it's urgent

creo recordar I seem to recall ▪ as I recall

creo recordar que... I seem to recall that...

crepúsculo matutino morning twilight

cresta de una ola crest of a wave ▪ wave crest

cría de ballena baby whale ▪ calf

cría de foca baby seal ▪ pup

cría de murciélago bitten ▪ baby bat

cría de oso bear cub

estar **criado entre algodones** to be brought up in luxury ▪ to have a sheltered upbringing

criador(-a) de perros dog breeder

estar **criando malvas** *(Esp.)* ▪ ver crecer las flores de abajo para arriba to be pushing up daisies ▪ to be six feet under

criar callos 1. to develop calluses **2.** to become hardened ▪ to become inured

criar el vino ▪ añejar el vino to age wine ➤ ¿Cuántos años ha estado criado el vino? ▪ Cuántos años ha criado el vino? ▪ ¿Cuánto años ha estado añejado el vino? ▪ ¿Cuántos años ha añejado el vino? How many years has it been aged?

criarse con to be raised on ➤ Marcelino se crió con la leche de cabra. Marcelino was raised on goat's milk.

criarse en un sitio to grow up in a place ▪ to be raised in a place ➤ Es la casa donde me crié. That's the house I grew up in.

criarse en un sitio to grow up in a place ▪ to be raised in a place ➤ Es la casa donde me crié. That's the house I grew up in. ▪ That's the house where I grew up. ▪ That's the house I was raised in.

criarse católico to be raised Catholic

criarse en la misma escuela to be cut from the same cloth ➤ Nos criamos en la misma escuela. We were cut from the same cloth.

el **crimen de alta alcurnia** white-collar crime

el, la **criminal en serie** serial killer

criminal nato(-a) born criminal

la **crisis de asma** asthma attack ➤ Sufrió una crisis de asma. She had an asthma attack. ▪ She suffered an asthma attack.

una **crisis se está cociendo** ▪ una crisis se está tramando ▪ se teje una crisis a crisis is brewing

la **crisis ya es historia** the crisis is over

la **crispación de los nervios: sentir ~** to feel on edge

la **crispación política** political unrest

la **crispación social** social unrest

cristal cascado ▪ cristal picado ▪ cristal mellado ▪ cristal saltado chipped glass

críticas constructivas constructive criticism

cromatografía gaseosa gas chromatography

cronometrar algo ▪ medir el tiempo de algo ▪ contar el tiempo de algo to time something

cruce de cross between ➤ La mula es un cruce de un caballo y un burro. The mule is a cross between a horse and a donkey.

crucero de lujo luxury cruise ➤ Crucero de lujo por el Mediterráneo. Luxury Mediterranean cruise ▪ Luxury cruise of the Mediterranean

cruda realidad ▪ dura realidad harsh reality

ser la **cruz de uno** ▪ amargar la existencia de uno ▪ ser la pesadilla de uno to be the cross one has to bear ▪ to be the bane of one's existence

cruzar a nado ▪ cruzar nadando ▪ atravesar a nado ▪ atravesar nadando to swim across

cruzar a pie 1. *(linear)* to walk across **2.** *(dos o tres dimensiones)* to walk through ➤ Cruzó el puente a pie. He walked across the bridge. ➤ Cruzó el parque a pie. He walked through the park. ▪ He walked across the park.

cruzarse con alguien (muy de cerca) to walk (right) in front of someone ▪ to walk into someone ▪ to walk right into one's path

cruzar el charco *(coloquial)* to cross the Atlantic Ocean

cruzar la aduana ▪ pasar por aduanas to go through customs

cruzar la cara ▪ mirar uno a otro to look at each other

cruzar la espada con alguien to cross swords with someone

cruzar la línea fronteriza to cross the border

cruzar la meta final to cross the finish line

cruzar un río a nado ▪ cruzar un río nadando ▪ atravesar un río a nado ▪ atravesar un río nadando to swim across a river ▪ to swim a river

cruzar un río vadeando ▪ vadear un río a pie ▪ apear un río ▪ franquear un río to ford a river ▪ to wade across a river

cruzarle la cara alguien to slap someone in the face

cruzarse de brazos ▪ estar de brazos cruzados **1.** to cross one's arms **2.** to sit on one's ass

cruzarse en la vida ▪ entrar en la vida to come into someone's life

cruzársele a uno los cables 1. *(comportamiento extravagante)* to get a little wacky **2.** *(comportamiento peligroso)* to go berserk ➤ Al tío se le cruzaron los cables y empezó a disparar a la gente. The guy went berzerk and started shooting at people.

cuaderno de apuntes ▪ libro de apuntes notebook

cuadrar el inventorio to take inventory

cuadrar una hora para *(L.am., coloquial)* ▪ fijar una hora para ▪ establecer una hora para ▪ concretar la hora para **1.** to set a time for ▪ to schedule a time for **2.** to set a time to ▪ to schedule a time to ➤ Necesitamos cuadrar una hora para la reunión. We need to set a time for the meeting. ➤ Necesitamos cuadrar una hora para que nos traigan los suministros. We need to set a time to have the supplies delivered. ▪ We need to schedule a time to have the supplies delivered.

cuadrarle bien a alguien to fit someone well ▪ to suit somone well ➤ El nombre le cuadra bien. The name fits him well. ▪ The name suits him well.

cuadro de diálogo *(informática)* dialogue box

cuadro de síntomas set of symptoms

cuadro mental ▪ dibujo mental mental picture

estar **cuajado de** to be full of ▪ to be covered with ▪ to be riddled with ▪ to be studded with

cuajar to take hold ▪ to jell ▪ to catch on

¿cuál dices? which one do you mean?

cuál es cuál *(presente)* which is which ▪ *(pasado)* which was which ➤ Él no sabía cuál era cuál. He didn't know which was which.

¿cuál es el apuro de...? what's your hurry to...?

¿cuál es el marcador? ▪ *(más común)* ▪ ¿cómo van? what's the score? ➤ Van tres a uno. It's three to one.

¿cuál es el pronóstico del tiempo para mañana? what is the weather forecast for tomorrow?

¿cuál es la diferencia? what is the difference? ▪ what's the difference?

¿cuál es la diferencia entre...? what is the difference between...? ▪ what's the difference between...?

¿cuál es la explicación? what is the explanation ▪ what's the explanation?

¿cuál es la fecha de hoy? ▪ ¿qué fecha es hoy? ▪ ¿a cuántos estamos? what's today's date? ▪ what's the date today? ▪ what is the date of today?

¿cuál es la hora más pronto que puedo llamarte? what's the earliest I can call you?

¿cuál es la hora más tarde que puedo llamarte? what's the latest I can call you?

¿cuál es la última novedad? what's the latest?

¿cuál es tu teléfono? what's your phone number?

¿cuál es su beneficio? ▪ ¿cuál es su utilidad? *(de él)* what is his profit? ▪ how much is his profit? ▪ *(de usted)* what's your profit ▪ how much is your profit?

¿cuál es el significado de...? what is the meaning of...?

¿cuál fue la puntuación (final)? ▪ ¿cómo terminó el marcador? ▪ ¿cuál fue el tanteador? what was the (final) score?

cual más cual menos some more than others

cual si ▪ como si as if ➤ Actuó cual si ya entendiese. ▪ Actuó como si hubiese entendido. He acted as if he understood. ▪ He acted as if he had understood.

cual si (yo) fuera... ▪ como si (yo) fuera as if I were...

cual si (yo) tuviera... ▪ como si (yo) tuviera as if I had...

cualquier cosa anything

cualquier cosa entre everything from ➤ Ah, te llamas Helle. Te he llamado cualquier cosa entre Elena y Ellen y Helen. Oh, your name is Helle. I was calling you everything from Helen to Ellen to Elena.

cualquier cosa, llámame if you need anything, call me ▪ if anything comes up, call me

¡cualquier día! ▪ ¡ni por ensueño! ▪ ¡no! ni ahí not on your life!

cualquier día de éstos any day now

cualquier hijo de vecino ▪ cada hijo de vecino every Tom, Dick and Harry

cualquier otro any other ➤ ¿Responde (ella) a cualquier otro nombre? Does she go by any other name? ➤ Una rosa con cualquier otro nombre olería igual de dulce. A rose by any other name would smell as sweet.

(cualquier punto) entre *x* e *y* ▪ de *x* a *y* anywhere from *x* to *y* ➤ (Cualquier punto) entre diez y veinte ▪ De diez a veinte Anywhere from ten to twenty

cualquier sueño me valdrá *(letra de Andrew Lloyd-Webber)* any dream will do

cualquier trío: elige ~ ▪ elige cualquier grupo de tres choose any three

cualquiera diría que... you'd think...

cualquiera sabe ▪ vete a saber ▪ vaya a saber ▪ ¿quién sabe Ande? who knows? ▪ God only knows

cuan largo es: tender ~ to extend as far as it will go

¡cuán largo me lo fiáis! ▪ ¡tan largo me lo fiáis! ▪ ¡qué largo me lo fiáis! ▪ lo creeré cuando lo vea I'll believe it when I see it

cuán lejos está de pensar que... **1.** *(él)* little does he think that... **2.** *(ella)* little does she think that...

cuán lejos estaba de pensar que... little did he think that...

cuando a mí, sí *(Méx.)* but it is to me ▪ *(después de no gustarle)* but I do

cuando a uno le dé la gana ▪ cuando a uno le guste ▪ cuando a uno le apetezca whenever you feel like (it) ▪ (just) any old time ➤ Crees que puedes entregar los deberes cuando te dé la gana. Bueno, pues no (puedes). ¡Es para hoy! You think you can turn in your homework whenever you feel like it? Well, you can't. It's due today! ▪ You think you can turn in your homework (just) any old time. Well, you can't. It's due today!

cuando (así lo) quiera ▪ a la hora que uno quiera any time one wants (to) ▪ whenever one wants (to) ➤ Podemos irnos a la hora que quieras. ▪ Podemos irnos cuando (así lo) quieras. We can leave any time you want (to). ▪ We can leave whenever you want (to).

cuando conoció la noticia ▪ cuando se supo la noticia ▪ conocida la noticia when the news broke

cuando crecía **1.** *(yo)* when I was growing up **2.** *(él)* when he was growing up **3.** *(ella)* when she was growing up **4.** *(usted)* when you were growing up

cuando crezca **1.** *(yo)* when I grow up **2.** *(él)* when he grows up **3.** *(ella)* when she grows up

cuando el reloj marca... when one's watch says... ▪ when the clock strikes...

cuando el río suena, agua lleva ▪ cuando el río suena, piedras lleva where there's smoke there's fire

cuando el río vuelva a su cauce ▪ cuando las aguas se decanten ▪ cuando todo vuelva a la normalidad when things get back to normal ▪ when things return to normal when things settle down

cuando estaba haciendo la mili when I was in the military ▪ when I was in the service

¿cuándo fue la última vez que viste a un médico? ▪ ¿cuándo viste un médico por última vez? when was the last time you saw a doctor? ▪ how long has it been since you last saw a doctor? ▪ when did you last see a doctor? ▪ how long has it been since you saw a doctor? ▪ when was the last time you saw a doctor?

cuando fueres a Roma vive como romano ▪ donde estuviere haz lo que viere when in Rome do as the Romans do

¿cuándo ha llegado? **1.** *(él)* when did he get here? **2.** *(ella)* when did she get here? **3.** *(ello, ella)* when did it get here?

cuando hube leído el artículo when I had read the article ▪ once I had read the article ▪ after I had read the article *(Nota: Se pronuncia "read" como la primera "e" en desde)*

cuando hubo... ▪ no bien hubo... **1.** *(él)* as soon as he had... **2.** *(ella)* as soon as she had...

cuando hubo concluido when it was over

cuando la rana tenga pelos ▪ cuando los pericos mamen ▪ cuando las ranas críen pelo ▪ cuando los chanchos vuelen when hell freezes over

cuando la otra opción es mucho peor ▪ como último recurso ▪ como último remedio ▪ como última opción ▪ en última instancia as a last resort

cuando las aguas vuelvan a su cauce ▪ cuando el río vuelva a su cauce ▪ cuando las aguas se decanten ▪ cuando todo vuelva a la normalidad when things get back to normal ▪ when things return to normal ▪ when things settle down

cuando las ranas críen pelos ▪ cuando la rana tenga pelos ▪ cuando los pericos mamen when hell freezes over

cuando le place a uno *(formal)* ▪ cuando (uno) quiere whenever one wants ▪ at will

cuando le placía a uno *(formal)* ▪ cuando (uno) quería whenever one wanted ▪ at will

cuando llegue el momento when the time comes

cuando llegue ese día when that day comes

cuando lo desees whenever you wish ▪ whenever you like ▪ whenever you want (to)

cuando lo hago when I do (it) ➤ Voy a surfear, y cuando lo hago, me siento el tío más feliz de la tierra. I go surfing, and when I do, I feel like the happiest guy on Earth.

cuando lo lea when I read it *(Nota: Se pronuncia "read" como "rid")*

cuando lo leí when I read it *(Nota: Se pronuncia la "e" en "read" como la primera "e" en " desde")*

cuando lo leía when I was reading it *(Nota: Se pronuncia "reading" como "riding")*

cuando lo leo when I read it *(Nota: Se pronuncia "read" como "rid")*

cuando los pericos mamen ▪ cuando la rana tenga pelos ▪ cuando las ranas críen pelos when hell freezes over

cuando marzo mayea, mayo marzea when March is like May, May is like March

cuando más ▪ como máximo ▪ a lo sumo ▪ como mucho ▪ a todo tirar at most

cuando más lo necesita (usted) when you need it most ▪ when you most need it

cuando más lo necesitas when you need it most ▪ when you most need it

cuando me di cuenta de lo que me había pasado ▪ para cuando me di cuenta de lo que me había pasado ▪ (para) cuando quise darme cuenta de lo que me había pasado before I knew what (had) hit me

cuando me haya ido ▪ cuando yo me haya ido when I'm gone

cuando me pasa (eso) when that happens (to me) ▪ when I do ➤ I get sunburned on the top of my head sometimes, and when I do, I rub in some aloe vera gel, and it really helps (it). Me quemo la calva de vez en cuando, y cuando me pasa, me froto algún gel de aloe vera y realmente ayuda. I get sunburned on the top of my head sometimes, and when that happens, I rub in some aloe vera gel, and it really helps it. ▪ I get sunburned on the top of my head sometimes, and when I do, I rub in some aloe vera gel, and it really helps (it).

cuando me quise dar cuenta before I knew it

ser **cuando me viene mejor** ▪ ser la hora que me viene mejor to be best time for me ▪ to be the time that suits (me) best ▪ to be the most convenient time for me ▪ to be time that's most convenient for me

cuando menos se lo espera when (it is) least expected

cuando menos se lo esperaba when (it was) least expected

cuando menos lo pienses ▪ cuando menos se piense when you least expect ▪ when least expected

cuando menos se piense ▪ cuando menos lo pienses when you least expect

cuando menos te lo esperas when you least expect (it)

cuando niño(-a) ▪ de niño(-a) as a child ▪ *(yo)* when I was a child

cuando podía haber habido alguien when there could have been someone ▪ when there might have been someone

¿cuándo puedes llegar? how soon can you get here? ▪ when can you get here?
cuando quiera whenever you want (to)
cuando quise darme cuenta de lo que me había pasado ▪ (para) cuando quise darme cuenta de lo que me había pasado ▪ (para) cuando me di cuenta de lo que me había pasado before I knew what (had) hit me
cuando salga 1. *(yo)* when I leave 2. *(él)* when he leaves 3. *(ella)* when she leaves 4. *(usted)* when you leave
cuando salgas when you leave
¿cuándo se acaba? when is it over?
¿cuándo se reanudan las clases? when do classes resume? ▪ when do classes start back (up)
¿cuándo se tiene previsto que llegue? 1. *(él)* when is he expected to arrive? 2. *(ella)* when is she expected to arrive? 3. *(ello, ella)* when is it expected to arrive?
cuando se supo la noticia ▪ cuando conoció la noticia ▪ conocida la noticia when the news broke ▪ when it came out
cuando se trata de when it comes to
cuando todo esto pase when this is all over ▪ when it's all over
cuando todo se haya tranquilizado when things settle down
cuando todo vuelva a la normalidad ▪ cuando las aguas vuelvan a su cauce when things get back to normal ▪ when things return to normal
cuando una puerta se cierra, se abre una ventana ▪ donde una puerta se cierra, se abre una ventana when one door closes, another opens
cuando uno está a punto de as one nears ▪ as one approaches ▪ as one reaches ➤ Cuando el presidente está a punto de cumplir cinco meses en el cargo. As the president nears completion of his fifth month in office.
cuando (uno) quería whenever one wanted ▪ at will
cuando (uno) quiere whenever one wants ▪ at will
¿cuándo va a venir el buen tiempo? when is the weather going to warm up? ▪ when's the weather going to warm up?
¿cuándo vas a venir a México? ▪ ¿cuándo vienes a México? ▪ ¿cuándo vendrás a México? when are you coming to Mexico? ▪ when will you be coming to Mexico?
cuando vaya a hervir ▪ en cuanto hierva when it comes to a boil ▪ when it starts to boil ▪ when it begins to boil ➤ Cuando vaya a hervir, añadir la harina batiendo fuertemente la mezcla. When it comes to a boil, add the flour while beating the mixture vigorously.
¿cuándo vendrás a México? ▪ ¿cuándo vas a venir a México? ▪ ¿cuándo vienes a México? when will you be coming to Mexico? ▪ when are you coming to Mexico?
¿cuándo vienes a México? ▪ ¿cuándo vas a venir a México? ▪ ¿cuándo vendrás a México? when are you coming to Mexico?
¿cuándo viste un médico por última vez? ▪ ¿cuándo fue la última vez que viste un médico? when did you last see a doctor? ▪ when was the last time you saw a doctor? ▪ how long has it been since you've seen a doctor? ▪ how long has it been since you last saw a doctor?
cuando ya era hora when it was time
cuando (yo) haya leído el artículo when I have read the article ▪ once I have read the article ▪ after I have read the article *(Nota: Se pronuncia "read" como la primera "e" en "desde".)*
cuando (yo) lea el artículo when I read the article ▪ once I read the article ▪ after I read the article *(Nota: Se pronuncia "read" como "rid".)*
cuando (yo) leí el artículo when I read the article ▪ once I read the article ▪ after I read the article *(Nota: Se pronuncia "read" como la primera "e" en "desde".)*
cuando (yo) me haya ido when I'm gone
cuanta más gente the more people
¿cuántas habitantes tiene...? what's the population of...?
¿cuántas horas nos apartan? ▪ ¿a cuántas horas estamos de diferencia? how many hours apart are we? ▪ how many hours' difference are there between here and there?
cuantiosas pérdidas heavy losses
cuanto antes ▪ lo más pronto posible ▪ lo antes posible ▪ tan pronto como sea posible ▪ a la mayor brevedad posible as soon as possible ▪ as quickly as possible
cuanto antes mejor the sooner the better
cuanto antes se olvide es mejor the sooner it is forgotten the better ▪ the sooner it's forgotten, the better
cuanto antes se olvidara era mejor ▪ cuanto antes se olvidase era mejor the sooner it was forgotten the better
cuanto cabe alcanzar to the extent that it is possible ▪ as far as is achievable ▪ as far as is attainable
¿cuánto camino hay de aquí a...? how far is it from here to...?
¿cuánto cuesta entrar? how much does it cost to get in?
cuánto de real había en el sueño: para saber ~ to know if it was really a dream
¿cuánto dura el viaje? how long is the trip?
¿cuánto hace que...? ▪ ¿cuánto tiempo hace que...? how long has it been since...? ➤ ¿Cuánto hace que no vas al médico? ▪ ¿Cuánto hace que no vas al doctor? How long has it been since you went to the doctor?
¿cuánto lleva? ▪ ¿cuánto tiempo lleva? ▪ ¿cuánto se tarda? how long does it take?
cuánto lo siento ▪ lo lamento I'm awfully sorry
cuanto más the more ➤ Cuanto más hago los ejecercios, mejor me siento. The more I exercise, the better I feel.
cuanto más grande, mejor ▪ caballo grande, ande o no ande the bigger, the better
cuanto más lejos el santo, más cerca la devoción absence makes the heart grow fonder
cuanto más miedo mejor the scarier the better
cuanto más tiempo hago esto, más... the longer I do this, the more...
¡cuánto me alegro de verte! ▪ ¡qué bueno verte! ▪ ¡cómo me alegro de verte! I'm so glad to see you!
¿cuánto me saldrá esto? how much will it be? ▪ how much will it come to? ▪ how much is it going to come to?
cuanto menos, mejor the less, the better
cuanto menos se diga mejor the less said, the better
¿cuánto mides? ▪ ¿de qué altura eres? how tall are you? ▪ what is your height?
¿cuánto pides? ▪ ¿qué pides? how much do you want for it? ▪ how much are you asking for it? ▪ what do you want for it? ▪ what are you asking for it?
¿cuánto pides por...? ▪ qué pides por...? how much do you want for...? ▪ how much are you asking for...? ▪ what do you want for...? ▪ what are you asking for...?
¿cuánto queda? how much is left?
¿cuánto quieres? how much do you want? ▪ how much would you like?
cuánto quiero... how I wish... ▪ I sure wish...
cuanto quiso 1. all one wanted ▪ all one liked 2. mientras uno quiso as long as one liked ➤ Comió cuantas galletas quiso. He ate all the cookies he wanted. ▪ He ate all the cookies he liked. ➤ El elefante bebió del charco cuanto quiso y luego barritó su satisfacción con su trompa. The elephant drank from the pond as long as he liked, and then trumpeted his satisfaction with his trunk.
¿cuánto se tarda? ▪ ¿cuánto (tiempo) lleva? how long does it take?
¿cuánto (tiempo) hace de tus últimas vacaciones? ▪ ¿cuánto (tiempo) hace desde tus últimas vacaciones? how long has it been since your last vacation? ▪ how long has it been since you (last) took a vacation?
¿cuánto tiempo estáis casados? ▪ ¿cuánto tiempo hace que estáis casados? how long have you (all) been married?
¿cuánto tiempo (hace que) estáis casados? how long have you (all) been married?
¿cuánto tiempo hace que nieva? how long has it been snowing?
¿cuánto tiempo (hace que) tienes ese coche? how long have you had that car?
¿cuánto (tiempo) hace que viste a un médico? ▪ ¿cuánto (tiempo) hace desde que viste a un médico? how long has it been since you (last) saw a doctor?
¿cuánto tiempo has estado esperando? how long have you been waiting? ➤ ¿Cuánto tiempo has estado esperando?-No mucho. How long have you been waiting?-Not long.

cuánto tiempo iba a tardar en hacer algo how long it would take to do something ▪ how long it was going to take to do something ➤ Salí pronto porque no sabía cuánto tiempo iba a tardar en llegar. I left early because I didn't know how long it would take (me) to get here. ➤ Salimos pronto porque no sabíamos cuánto tiempo íbamos a tardar en llegar. We left early because we didn't know how long it would take (us) to get here.

¿cuánto (tiempo) lleva? ▪ ¿cuánto se tarda? how long does it take?

¿cuánto tiempo llevas esperando? ▪ ¿cuánto tiempo has estado esperando? how long have you been waiting? ➤ ¿Cuánto tiempo llevas esperando?-No mucho. How long have you been waiting?-Not long.

¿cuánto tiempo llevas trabajando aquí? how long have you been working here?

¡cuánto tiempo sin verte! it's been a long time (since I've seen you) ▪ it's been so long since I've seen you ▪ I haven't seen you in ages! ▪ I haven't seen you for ages! ▪ I haven't seen you forever! ▪ *(argot juvenil)* long time, no see!

¿cuánto tiene de circunferencia? *(círculo, rectángulo)* how big around is it? ▪ *(más técnico)* what's the circumference?

¿cuánto vale el cubierto? how much is the cover charge?

¿cuánto vas a demorar? how long are you going to be?

¿cuántos años le das? *(a él)* how old do you think he is? ▪ *(a ella)* how old do you think she is? ▪ *(a algo)* how old do you think it is?

¿cuántos años le echas? how old do you think he is? ▪ how old do you reckon he is? ▪ how old would you guess he is? ▪ how old would you say he is?

¿cuántos años podía tener...? how old could he have been...? ▪ how old do you think he was...?

cuantos más the more

cuántos más, mejor the more, the merrier

¿cuántos quedan? how many are left?

cuarteado por broken by ▪ interrupted by ➤ En una oscuridad cuarteada por los relámpagos In a darkness broken by flashes of lightning ▪ In a darkness interrupted by flashes of lightning

el **cuartel general** headquarters

cuarto creciente *(fase lunar)* first quarter

cuarto de baño bathroom

cuarto de estar 1. *(cuando la cocina es parte)* recreation room ▪ great room 2. *(cuando la cocina no es parte)* living room

cuarto de luna lunar quarter

cuarto menguante *(fase lunar)* third quarter

cuarto poder: elevar al ~ to raise to the fourth power

(cuarto) trastero storage locker ▪ storage unit

cuatro ojos ven más que dos two heads are better than one

cuatro quintos four fifths

cuba de vino *(colocada verticalmente)* barrel of wine

Cuba libre ▪ *(Esp.)* ▪ cubata rum, Coca-Cola and lime juice

cubanear en Miami ▪ ir de cubaneo en Miami to have a night on the town in Miami's Cuban barrio

cubertería de acero inoxidable stainless steel flatware

cubertería de plata silverware

cubierto de mala hierba overgrown with weeds

cubierto de nieve covered with snow

cubito de caldo bouillon cube

cubito de hielo ice cube

cubo de basura trash can ▪ garbage can

cubo de hielo block of ice

cubrir a alguien de fango to smear someone ▪ to sling mud

cubrir con rebozado ▪ capear con rebozado to coat with batter

cubrir la demanda ▪ responder a la demanda to meet the demand ▪ to cover the demand ▪ to answer the demand ➤ No hay suficiente petróleo en el mundo para cubrir la demanda. ▪ No hay suficiente petróleo en el mundo para responder a la demanda. There is not enough petroleum in the world to meet the demand.

cubrir las necesidades de alguien to meet the needs of someone ▪ to meet someone's needs ➤ Este software no cubre las necesdidades del usuario. This software doesn't meet the needs of the user. ▪ This software doesn't meet user's needs.

cubrir los frentes ▪ tomar en consideración todas las posibilidades to cover the waterfront ▪ to take into account all the possibilities ▪ to take all the possibilities into account

cubrir (los) gastos ▪ recuperar los gastos ▪ no tener pérdidas ni beneficios to break even ▪ to recover expenses

cubrir los gastos de uno to meet one's expenses ▪ to cover one's expenses

cubrir una noticia ▪ cubrir una información ▪ cubrir un acontecimiento *(periodismo)* to cover a story ▪ to cover an event

cubrir una sección *(periodismo)* to cover a beat

cubrir una vacante to fill a vacancy

cubrirse de alegría to express joy ▪ to express great happiness

cubrirse de pintura (hasta las cejas) ▪ ponerse perdido de pintura ▪ llenarse de pintura (hasta las cejas) to get paint all over oneself ➤ Me puse perdido de pintura. ▪ Me cubrí de pintura (hasta las cejas). ▪ Me llené de pintura (hasta las cejas). I got paint all over myself.

cucharada bien colmada heaping tablespoon

cucharada colmada rounded tablespoon

cucharada sopera rasada de... level soup spoon of... ▪ level tablespoon of...

cucharadita bien colmada heaping teaspoon

cucharadita colmada rounded teaspoon

cuelgue y vuelva a marcar hang up and re-dial

cuenca del Amazonas Amazon basin

cuenca del Caribe *(la zona del Mar Caribe y de la costa Caribe desde el Istmo de Panamá hasta el Río Orinoco de Venezuela)* Spanish Main ➤ Los legendarios piratas de la cuenca del Caribe inspiraron la película Disney y la atracción de Disneylandia "Los piratas del Caribe". The legendary pirates of the Spanish Main inspired the Disney movie and Disneyland ride "Pirates of the Caribbean."

cuenta bancaria bank account

cuenta bancaria conjunta joint bank account

cuenta con mis palabras take my word for it

cuenta corriente operating account ▪ checking account

cuenta está al día account is up to date ▪ account is current

cuenta propia ▪ trabajar poz ▪ trabajar para uno mismo ▪ ser autómono(-a) to be self-employed ▪ to work for oneself

¡cuenta que...! remember! ▪ bear in mind ▪ keep in mind ▪ don't forget!

cuéntame (tú) tell me about it

cuentas morosas delinquent accounts

cuéntaselo a tu abuelita ▪ ¡a otro perro con ese hueso! go tell it to the Marines!

cuénteme (usted) tell me about it

cuento antes de dormir bedtime story

cuento chino tall tale

cuento de hadas fairy tale ▪ fairy story

ser el **cuento de nunca acabar** to be the never-ending story

cuento de siempre ▪ cuento intemporal timeless story

ser el **cuento de siempre** ▪ ser el mismo cuento de siempre to be the same old story ▪ to be the same old excuse

ser **cuento de viejas** to be an old wives' tale

cuento intemporal ▪ cuento de siempre timeless story

cuerda de apertura *(de un paracaídas)* rip cord

cuerda de arco bowstring

cuerda de la montaña ▪ (la) dorsal de la montaña mountain ridge ▪ ridge of the mountain ▪ crest of the mountain

cuerpo a cuerpo ▪ a brazo partido hand-to-hand ➤ El combate cuerpo a cuerpo Hand-to-hand combat

cuerpo a punto body in shape

cuerpo celeste heavenly body

cuerpo de policía police force

cuerpo del tamaño de Marte object the size of Mars

cuerpo fornido *(culto)* well-built body ▪ well-built frame

cuerpo serrano beautiful body

cuesta abajo downhill

cuesta arriba uphill

cuesta creerlo that's hard to believe ▪ it's hard to believe ▪ that's hard to imagine

cuesta de enero January slump ▪ post-Christmas business slump

cuesta de una colina (steep) slope of a hill ■ incline of a hill
cuesta de una montaña (steep) slope of a mountain ■ incline of a mountain
cuesta más el remedio que la enfermedad ■ el remedio es peor que la enfermedad the cure is worse than the disease
cueste lo que cueste 1. sin reparar en gastos whatever the cost ■ regardless of the cost ■ no matter how much it costs 2. sin tomar en cuenta el esfuerzo regardless of the difficulty ■ no matter how difficult it is ■ no matter how hard it is
la **cuestión candente** pressing issue ■ hot issue ■ political hot potato
cuestión de opiniones matter of opinion ➤ Es una cuestión de opiniones. That's a matter of opinion.
cuestión de si question whether ➤ Dejando de lado la cuestión de si... Leaving aside the question whether... ■ Setting aside the question whether...
cuestionar la autoridad to question authority
cuestiones más importantes key issues
cueva de ladrones den of thieves
cuida tus modales mind your manners
¡**cuidado!** ■ ¡ten cuidado! ■ ¡ojo! (be) careful! ➤ ¡Ten cuidado con el hielo! (Be) careful on the ice!
¡**cuidado con el perro!** beware of the dog!
¡**cuidado la cabeza!** watch your head!
cuidar de alguien to take care of someone ■ to look after someone
cuidar las manos y las uñas to give a manicure
cuidar sus modales to mind one's manners
cuidarse de todo ■ preocuparse de todo to take care of everything ➤ Me cuido de todo. ■ Me preocupo de todo. I'll take care of everything.
cuidarse las espaldas to watch your back side
culito de un niño: estar suave como el ~ to be smooth as a baby's butt
culito del bebé *(Esp.)* ■ colita del bebé baby's bottom ■ baby's butt
culminar en algo ■ culminar con algo to culminate in something
culminar un acuerdo to conclude an agreement
culminar un objetivo to attain an objective ■ to reach an objective ■ to attain a goal ■ to reach a goal
culminar una hazaña to accomplish a feat
culo del mundo armpit of the world
culpable o inocente guilty or innocent
ser **culpado de** to get blamed for ■ to be blamed for
culpar a alguien de algo ■ culpar a alguien por algo ■ echar la culpa a alguien de algo ■ echar la culpa a alguien por algo to blame someone for something ■ to blame something on someone ➤ *(titular)* Putin culpa al terrorismo checheno de la matanza en el metro de Moscú. Putin blames Chechin terrorism for the carnage in the Moscow subway.
culpar a alguien por algo ■ culpar a alguien de algo ■ echar la culpa a alguien por algo ■ echar la culpa a alguien de algo to blame someone for something ■ to blame something on someone ➤ (Él) la culpa por todo. ■ (Él) la culpa de todo. ■ (Él) le echa la culpa (a ella) por todo. ■ (Él) le echa la culpa (a ella) de todo. He blames her for everything. ➤ (Ella) lo culpa de todo. ■ (Ella) lo culpa por todo. *(Spain, leísmo)* ■ (Ella) le culpa de todo. ■ (Ella) le culpa por todo. She blames him for everything.
culto: ser muy ~ ■ tener una buena educación to be well educated ■ to have a good education ■ to have a well rounded education
culto a los antepasados ancestor worship
cumplido ambiguo ■ cumplido envenenado ■ cumplido malintencionado back-handed compliment
cumplido oportuno good compliment
cumplimiento de un contrato completion of a contract
cumplir con el acuerdo ■ atenerse al convenio ■ acatar el pacto to abide by the agreement ■ to conform to the agreement ■ to conform with the agreement
cumplir con su deber to do one's duty
cumplir con sus obligaciones to fulfill one's obligations ■ to comply with one's obligations
cumplir con el cometido to do what one is told
cumplir con su palabra ■ ser fiel a su palabra to be true to one's word ■ to keep one's word
cumplir con su promesa ■ ser fiel a su promesa to be true to one's promise ■ to keep one's promise
cumplir con su trabajo to do one's job
cumplir con una petición to fulfill a request ■ to honor a request
cumplir los requisitos to meet the requirements ■ to satisfy the requirements
cumplir los *x* años to turn *x* ■ to reach age *x* ■ to reach *x* ➤ Acaba de cumplir los cuarenta años. He just turned forty. ➤ *(anuncio)* ¿Sabe lo que pasa cuando un buen conductor cumple los cuarenta años? Know what happens when a good driver turns forty? ■ Know what happens when a good driver reaches (age) forty?
cumplir su palabra ■ mantener su palabra to keep one's word
cumplir tiempo de cárcel to serve time in jail ➤ Uno de los capturados había cumplido dieciocho años de cárcel. One of those captured had served eighteen years in jail.
cumplir una condena to serve a sentence
cumplir una hipoteca ■ redimir una hipoteca to pay off a mortgage
cumplir una promesa to keep a promise
cumplirse un sueño (for) a dream to come true ➤ Se nos ha cumplido un sueño. Our dream has come true.
cúmulo de estrellas ■ cúmulo estelar star cluster
cunde mucho ■ da para mucho it goes a long way
cunde *x* platos ■ da para *x* platos yields *x* servings
cundió el pánico en la aldea panic spread through the village ■ panic engulfed the village
cundirle el tiempo ■ rendirle mucho el tiempo to make the most of one's time ■ to get a lot done ➤ ¡Que te cunda el tiempo! Make the most of your time. ➤ Nos cundió mucho el tiempo. We got a lot done.
cundirle mucho el trabajo to get a lot (of work) done
cuota de abono base rate ➤ Repartimos la cuota de abono entre los compañeros del apartamento. We split the base rate among the apartment mates. ➤ ¿Cuál es la cuota de abono si no hago llamadas a larga distancia? What is the base rate if I don't make any long distance phone calls?
cuota de mercado market share
el **cupón de la lotería** lottery ticket
cúpula del gobierno leadership of the government ■ upper echelons of the government
cúpula militar top brass ■ *(EEUU)* joint chiefs (of staff)
cúpula de la empresa top management of the firm
cura contra ■ remedio contra cure for
curiosear en un cajón to rummage through a drawer
curiosidad continua endless curiosity
curioso que... curious that... ■ strange that... ➤ Curioso que lo pensara entonces. Curious that he should think of it just then. ■ Strange that he should think of it just then.
el **currículum vitae** resumé
cursar primero to be in the first grade ➤ Cuando cursaba primero... 1. *(yo* When I was in the first grade... 2. *(él)* When he was in the first grade... 3. *(ella)* When she was in the first grade...
curso a distancia correspondence course
curso acelerado crash course
curso de formación: hacer un ~ to take a training course
curso de los acontecimientos ■ marcha de los acontecimientos course of events
curva cerrada (en la carretera) hairpin curve ■ hairpin turn
curva de felicidad middle-age spread
la **cúspide de un triángulo** apex of a triangle
la **cúspide de una carrera** the high point of a career
cuya copia conservo which I have a copy of ■ which I have kept a copy of ■ which I have retained a copy of
cuya salida whose outcome ■ the outcome of which

da a quien dio, pero no pidas a quien pidió give to the one who has given, but do not ask of one who has asked ■ give to the one who has given, but do not ask the one who asked

da abasto para... ■ rinde para it's enough for... ➤ La comida da abasto para seis personas. There's enough food for six people. ■ There's enough to feed six.

da igual it doesn't make any difference ■ it doesn't matter ■ it makes no difference

da la casualidad que it just so happens that

da lo mismo ■ es lo mismo it doesn't make any difference ■ it makes no difference

da lo mismo ocho que ochenta if you've seen one, you've seen them all

da para mucho ■ cunde mucho it goes a long way

da para *x* platos ■ cunde *x* platos yields *x* servings

¡da resultado! it works! ➤ ¿Lo ves? ¡Da resultado! (You) see? It works!

dad al César lo que es del César, y a Dios lo que es de Dios *(bíblico)* render unto Caesar that which is Caesar's, and unto God that which is God's

dad y recibiréis give and you shall receive ■ *(bíblico)* give and thou shalt receive

dadas las circunstancias ■ dado el caso ■ dentro de lo que cabe given the circumstances ■ under the circumstances ■ considering the circumstances ■ in that case ■ in this case ➤ Creo que es una petición justa dadas las circunstancias. I think it's a fair request under the circumstances. ■ I think it's a fair request given the circumstances. ■ I think it's a fair request considering the circumstances. ■ I think it's a fair request in this case.

¡dadles fuerte! let them have it! ■ *(coloquial)* let 'em have it! ■ give it to 'em good and hard!

ser **dado a algo** ■ ser propenso a to be given to something ■ to tend toward something ■ to have a propensity to something

ser **dado a hacer algo** to be given to doing something ■ to be in one's nature to do something ➤ En México somos muy dados a hacer frases nuevas. In Mexico we are very given to making (up) new phrases. ■ In Mexico it's in our nature to make (up) new phrases.

ser **dado de alta del hospital** ■ darle de alta del hospital to be released from the hospital

dado el caso dadas las circunstancias in that case ■ in this case ■ given the circumstances ■ under the circumstances ■ considering the circumstances

estar **dado por sentado que...** ■ sobrentenderse que... to be understood that...

dado que... ■ siendo que... given (the fact) that... ➤ Dado que este tema es muy complejo ■ Siendo que este tema es muy complejo... Given (the fact) that this matter is very complex... ■ Given the complexity of this matter...

¡dale! go, man, go! ■ go, go, go!

¡dale bola! *(él)* don't pay him any mind ■ *(ella)* don't pay her any mind

¡dale, macho! go, man, go!

dale mis mejores recuerdos 1. *(a él)* give him my best ■ tell him I said hello 2. *(a ella)* give her my best ■ tell her I said hello

estar **dale que dale** over and over (again) ➤ Mi mujer está dale que dale con que haga la declaración de la renta. My wife is hounding me to do the income tax.

estar **dale que dale** to be at it (again) ■ to be going to town ■ to be going at it ■ to be hard at it ➤ Ya está mi abuelo, dale que dale, con la Guerra Civil Española. My grandfather's at it again, reliving the Spanish Civil War. ➤ Está dale que dale con el ordenador. ■ Está dale que te pego con el ordenador. He's really going to town at the computer. ➤ Los vecinos están dale que dale. The neighbors are going at it.

estar **dale que te pego** ■ estar corre que te alcanzo to be going to town ■ to be hard at it ➤ *(L.am.)* Está dale que te pego en la computadora. ■ Está corre que te alcanzo en la computadora. *(Esp.)* Está dale que te pego en el ordenador. He's going to town at the computer. ■ He's really (going) hard at the computer.

dale tiempo al tiempo ■ el tiempo lo dirá time will tell

¡dalo por hecho! consider it done!

dama de honor maid of honor ■ matron of honor

damas chinas Chinese checkers

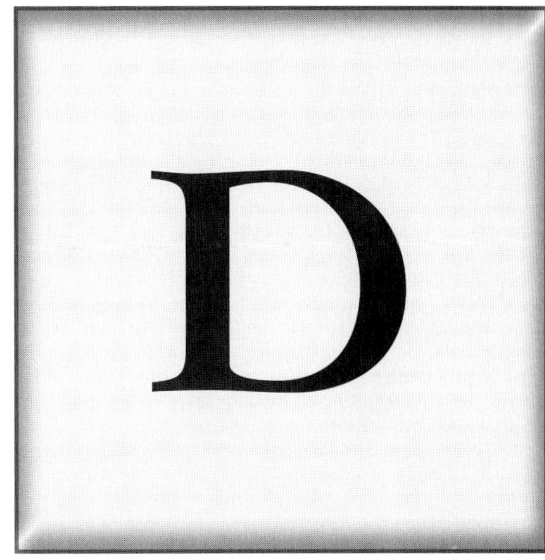

dame un timbrazo ■ llámame (por teléfono) give me a ring ■ call me

dame una calada (de tu cigarrillo) give me a drag (off your cigarette)

dan ganas de morirse it's to die for

estar **dando las boqueadas** ■ dar las boqueadas to breathe one's last breaths ■ to give one's last gasps ■ to be gasping one's last breaths

dando tumbos: ir ~ 1. to wander around lost 2. *(de embriaguez)* to stagger (around) ■ to lurch

estar **dándose la gran vida** to be living it up

danos de beber 1. quench our thirst 2. *(figurativo)* quench our thirst for knowledge 3. *(figurativo)* feed our spiritual longings

danza de vientre belly dance

danzar sobre un volcán to tread on thin ice

daño cerebral brain damage

daños catastróficos catastrophic damage

daños colaterales collateral damage

daños de importancia: producir ~ to cause major damage

daños físicos: producir ~ to cause damage

daños (personales): producir ~ to cause injury ■ to cause injuries

daños psicológicos: producir ~ to cause psychological damage ■ to traumatize

daos prisa, que llegamos tarde *(Esp.)* ■ dense prisa que llegamos tarde (you all) hurry or we'll be late

dar a to face ■ to overlook ■ to look out on ■ to open onto ➤ El piso da a Sor Angela de la Cruz. The apartment faces Sor Angela de la Cruz.

dar a alguien de lleno en la cara ■ alcanzar a alguien de lleno en la cara to hit someone right smack in the face ■ to hit someone square in the face ➤ El pastel lo dio de lleno en la cara. ■ *(Esp. leísmo)* El pastel le dio de lleno en la cara. The pie hit him right smack in the face. ■ The pie hit him square in the face.

dar a alguien el aviso con antelación ■ avisar a alguien con antelación ■ entregar a alguien el aviso con antelación to give someone advance notice ➤ Le dio el aviso de (su) renuncia a su jefe con dos semanas de antelación. He gave his employer two weeks' advance notice that he was going to quit. ■ He gave his employer two weeks' advance notice of his resignation.

dar a alguien el día to ruin one's whole day ■ to cast a cloud on one's day

dar a alguien el papel de alguien to cast someone as someone ➤ Steven Spielberg dio a Liam Neeson el papel de Abraham Lincoln. Steven Spielberg cast Liam Neeson as Abraham Lincoln.

dar a alguien el pie y se toma la mano ■ dar a alguien la mano y se toma el codo to give someone and inch and he takes a mile

dar a alguien el silencio por respuesta to give someone silence for an answer ▪ to answer someone with silence ▪ to give someone the silent treatment

dar a alguien en el hombro 1. *(suavemente)* to pat someone on the shoulder **2.** *(con fuerza)* to slap someone on the shoulder

dar a alguien en la cabeza 1. *(en lo alto de la cabeza)* to hit someone on the head **2.** alcanzarle en la cabeza to hit someone in the head ▪ to strike someone in the head ➤ La manzana realmente no le dio a Newton en la cabeza. The apple didn't really hit Newton on the head. ➤ La bala le dio en la cabeza. ▪ La bala le alcanzó en la cabeza. The bullet struck him in the head. ▪ The bullet hit him in the head.

dar a alguien en las narices 1. to hit someone in the nose **2.** *(con el puño)* to punch someone in the nose ▪ to hit someone in the nose

dar a alguien entre ceja y ceja to hit someone between the eyes ▪ to strike someone between the eyes

dar a alguien por muerto 1. to give someone up for dead ➤ The police have given up the boy for dead and abandoned their search. La policia ha abandonado la búsqueda del muchacho, dándole por muerto.

dar a alguien un azote to give someone a spanking ▪ *(coloquial)* to tan someone's hide

dar a alguien un suave capirotazo (en la cabeza) ▪ dar a alguien un golpe suave en la cabeza to bat someone on the head ▪ to give someone a bat on the head ➤ Mi gata le da un suave capirotazo en la cabeza al otro gato sólo para provocarle. ▪ Mi gata le da un golpe suave en la cabeza al otro gato sólo para provocarle. My cat bats the other cat on the head just to get him going. ▪ My cat gives the other cat a bat on the head just to get him going.

dar a cada uno su merecido 1. *(positivo)* to give one credit where credit is due **2.** *(positivo o negativo)* to give one his just desserts

dar a comer a la familia ▪ dar de comer a la familia to feed the family

dar a comer al perro ▪ dar de comer al perro to feed the dog

dar a conocer algo to get the word (of something) out

dar a conocer datos to release data ▪ to disclose data ▪ to make data public

dar a conocer hallazgos to release findings ▪ to disclose findings ▪ to make findings public

dar a entender (que) ▪ insinuar (que) to give the impression (that) ▪ to imply (that) ▪ to say in so many words (that) ▪ to show (that) ➤ No fue directamente al grano, pero lo dio a entender. She didn't come right out and say it, but she said it in so many words.

dar a la imprenta un manuscrito 1. to send a manuscript to the publisher **2.** to send a manuscript to the printer

dar a la luz ▪ sacar a la luz to bring to light ➤ El periódico dio a la luz el robo de millones de euros en la sede del partido. ▪ El periódico sacó a la luz el robo de millones de euros en la sede del partido. The newspaper brought to light the theft of millions of euros at the party's headquarters.

dar a la pelota ▪ patear la pelota ▪ tirar la pelota ▪ chutar a la pelota to kick the ball

dar a lavar y planchar las ropas ▪ poner la ropa a hacer ▪ dar a hacer la colada to send out the laundry ▪ to send the laundry out ▪ to have the laundry done

dar a luz a un niño ▪ dar a luz a un varón to give birth to a (little) boy ▪ to give birth to a (baby) boy ➤ Dio a luz a un niño saludable que pesa nueve libras y once onzas con tres cuartos, y mide veintiuna pulgadas y media. She gave birth to a healthy little boy, weighing nine pounds, eleven and three-quarter ounces and measuring twenty-one and a half inches.

dar a luz a una hembra *(Esp.)* ▪ dar a luz a una niña to give birth to a (little) girl ▪ to give birth to a (baby) girl

dar a luz a una niña to give birth to a (little) girl ▪ to give birth to a (baby) girl ➤ Dio a luz a una niña saludable que pesa ocho libras y diez onzas, y mide veinte pulgadas y media. She gave birth to a healthy little girl, weighing eight pounds, ten ounces and measuring twenty and a half inches.

dar a mamar a la bebé ▪ dar la teta a la bebé to breastfeed an infant (girl) ▪ to nurse an infant (girl) ▪ to suckle an infant (girl)

dar a mamar al bebé ▪ dar la teta al bebé to breastfeed an infant ▪ to nurse an infant ▪ *(literario)* to suckle an infant *(Nota: "El bebé" se refiere así a hembras como a varones. ▪ "El bebé" refers to both male and female infants.)*

dar abasto a un pedido ▪ surtir un pedido to fill an order

dar abasto con todo to (be able to) do it all ➤ Ella da abasto con todo (el trabajo). She can do it all.

dar abasto para todos to be enough to go around ▪ to be plenty to go around ▪ to be plenty for everyone ➤ Da abasto para todos. There's enough to go around. ▪ There's plenty to go around. ▪ There's plenty for everyone.

dar abasto para *x* personas ▪ dar para *x* platos to serve *x* people ▪ to yield *x* servings

dar acogida a alguien 1. to take someone in ▪ to take in someone ▪ to give someone a place a place to stay ▪ to give someone shelter **2.** to give someone a welcome ▪ to give someone a reception ➤ Di acogida a mi hermano cuando vino a España. I took in my brother when he came to Spain. ▪ I took my brother in when he came to Spain. ➤ Le di acogida cuando vino a España. I took him in when he came to Spain. ➤ El presidente dio una acogida tibia al líder separatista. The president gave the separatist leader a lukewarm welcome. ▪ The president gave the separatist leader a lukewarm reception.

dar achares a alguien *(Esp.)* ▪ dar celos a alguien ▪ poner celoso a alguien to make someone jealous

dar aire a algo 1. to air out something **2.** to bring something out into the open

dar al manubrio 1. to crank the handle **2.** to go on and on **3.** *(jerga)* to masturbate

dar al traste con algo to ruin something

dar al traste con su vida to ruin one's life

dar alas a algo to give something wings ▪ to launch something ▪ to give impetus to something

dar alas a alguien to give someone wings ▪ to give impetus to someone

dar alcance a alguien ▪ alcanzar a alguien to catch up with someone

dar algo a conocer a alguien to introduce someone to something ➤ Carlos me dio a conocer la música folk y yo a él le di a conocer la música clásica. Carlos introduced me to folk music, and I introduced him to classical music.

dar algo a crédito ▪ ofrecer algo a crédito to offer something on credit

dar algo a hacer to have something done ▪ to have something sent out to be done

dar algo al público to make something public

dar algo por descontado to just assume ▪ to take for granted ➤ Daba por descontado que el piso tendría una conexión para el teléfono. I just assumed the apartment would have a telephone jack.

dar algo por la tremenda ▪ tomar algo por la tremenda to make a big fuss about something ▪ to raise a big stink about something

dar algo por sabido to consider it sufficiently explained ▪ to consider it sufficiently known

dar algo por sentado ▪ dar algo por supuesto to take something for granted

dar algo por supuesto ▪ dar algo por sentado to take something for granted

dar algo un hervor to bring something to a boil ➤ Limpie las zanahorias y los calabacines y déles un hervor junto a los dientes de ajo. Wash the carrots and zucchini, and bring them to a boil together with the garlic cloves.

dar ánimos a alguien to cheer someone up ▪ to cheer up someone

dar arcadas 1. to get nauseated ▪ to get sick to one's stomach **2.** *(por embarazo)* to have morning sickness ▪ to suffer from morning sickness **3.** to retch ➤ A mi hijo siempre le dan arcadas cuando viajamos en avión. My son always gets nauseated when we travel by air. ▪ My son always gets sick to his stomach when we travel by air. ➤ Mi esposa está embarazada y le dan arcadas por las mañanas. ▪ Mi esposa está embarazada y tiene arcadas por las mañanas. My wife is pregnant and has morning sickness. ▪ My wife is pregnant and suffers from morning sickness.

dar azotes a alguien 1. to give someone a spanking ▪ to spank someone 2. *(castigo, tortura)* to whip someone ▪ to give someone lashes
dar barniz a un mueble to varnish a piece of furniture
dar barreno a un barco ▪ echar un barco al fondo to scuttle a ship
dar batalla... to put up a fight against...
dar betún a alguien to butter someone up ▪ to flatter someone
dar boca to gab ▪ to yak ▪ to chat
dar bombo a algo to puff something ▪ to tout something
dar brillo a algo to polish something ▪ to shine something
dar brincos cortos to hop and skip
dar brincos de alegría ▪ pegar brincos de alegría to jump for joy
dar buena espina a uno to give one a good feeling ➤ La forma en que me habló me dio buena espina. The way he spoke to me gave me a good feeling.
dar buena imagen to make a good impression ▪ to give a good impression ▪ to project a good image ▪ to come across well
dar cabezadas ▪ cabecear to nod off
dar cabida a ▪ hacer sitio para ▪ hacer lugar para ▪ hacer corro para ▪ hacer espacio para to make room for
dar calor to give off heat ▪ to be too hot ➤ Este abrigo me da calor. This coat's too hot.
dar campo a to give free rein to
dar cancha to make space
dar caña ▪ meter caña ▪ ir a toda pastilla to go full speed
dar caña a alguien to ride herd on someone ➤ El nuevo jefe del departamento está dando caña a los becarios. The new department head is really riding herd on the teaching assistants.
dar carpetazo a una moción to shelve a motion
dar carrera libre a to give free rein to
dar carrete a alguien to keep someone in suspense
dar caza to give chase
dar celos a alguien ▪ dar achares a alguien ▪ poner celoso a alguien to make someone jealous
dar cerrojazo a un asunto ▪ dar el cerrojazo a un asunto to put an abrupt end to a matter ▪ to end a matter abruptly
dar cien vueltas a alguien to run rings around someone
dar clases to teach classes ▪ to give classes
dar coba a alguien to butter someone up ▪ to play up to someone ▪ to suck up to someone
dar cobijo a los terroristas to give safe haven to terrorists ▪ to harbor terrorists
dar cobijo a un extraño to take in a stranger
dar coces ▪ dar patadas to kick things (around) ➤ El niño estuvo dando coces toda la mañana. The boy has been kicking things (around) all morning.
dar color to give color
dar como ganador to declare as the winner
dar como perdedor to declare as the loser
dar con 1. to meet 2. to get to ▪ to come to 3. to find ➤ Ha dado con la horma de su zapato. He's met his match. ➤ Estábamos haciendo turismo en Segovia, y cuando dimos con el Alcázar... We were sightseeing in Segovia, and when we got to the Alcázar... ▪ We were sightseeing in Segovia, and when we came to the Alcázar... ➤ Pusimos la casa patas arriba hasta que dimos con el comprobante. We turned the house upside down until we found the receipt.
dar con el codo a alguien to nudge someone (with one's elbow) ▪ to jab someone ▪ to dig someone in the ribs ▪ to give someone a dig in the ribs ▪ to elbow someone
dar con el quid de la cuestión to get to the heart of the matter
dar con el suelo to hit the floor
dar con la cabeza en las paredes to bang one's head against a (brick) wall
dar con la clave to hit on it ▪ to hit the nail on the head
dar con la horma de su zapato to meet one's match
dar con la puerta en la cara to slam the door in someone's face
dar con la puerta en las narices to slam the door in someone's face
dar con los huesos en la cárcel to land in jail ▪ to end up in jail
dar con los huesos en la tierra to land on the ground
dar con un escollo ▪ tropezar con una dificultad ▪ dar con una dificultad to hit a snag
dar con una dificultad ▪ dar con un escollo ▪ tropezar con una dificultad to hit a snag
dar con una idea to hit on an idea ▪ to come up with an idea
dar consejos ▪ dar un consejo ▪ aconsejar to give advice ▪ to advise
dar consigo en to end up in
dar contra ▪ golpear contra to beat against ➤ La lluvia daba contra el parabrisas. ▪ La lluvia golpeaba contra el parabrisas. The rain was beating against the windshield.
dar cuartel a alguien ▪ dar cuartellilo a alguien 1. to act with leniency toward someone 2. to give someone a little more leeway ▪ to take the pressure off someone
dar cuartelillo a alguien ▪ dar cuartel a alguien to give someone a little more leeway ▪ to take the pressure off someone
dar cuenta de algo a alguien to report something to someone
dar cuerda a un caballo to lunge a horse
dar cuerda a un reloj to wind a clock ▪ *(de pulsera)* to wind a watch
dar de alta el contrato ▪ firmar el contrato to sign the contract ▪ to conclude the agreement ➤ Ayer quedé con la casera para dar de alta el contrato de arrendamiento. Yesterday I met with the landlady to sign the rental contract. ▪ Yesterday I met with the landlady to conclude the rental agreement.
dar de alta el gas ▪ poner el gas to have the gas turned on
dar de alta el teléfono ▪ conectar el teléfono ▪ poner el teléfono to have the telephone turned on ▪ to have the telephone connected
dar de alta la luz ▪ poner la luz to have the electricity turned on
dar de alta la televisión por cable ▪ poner la televisión por cable to have TV cable turned on ▪ to have the TV cable connected
dar de alta una cuenta to open an account
dar de baja el gas ▪ quitar el gas to have the gas turned off ➤ Ya he quedado en que el lunes que viene dan de baja el gas. I've arranged for the gas to be turned off next Monday.
dar de baja el teléfono ▪ quitar el teléfono ▪ desconectar el teléfono to have the telephone turned off ▪ to have the telephone disconnected
dar de baja la luz ▪ quitar la luz to have the electricity turned off
dar de baja la televisión por cable ▪ quitar la televisión por cable to have the cable TV turned off ▪ to have the cable service disconnected
dar de bofetadas a alguien to slap someone
dar de bruces con ▪ ir de bruces a to run headlong into ➤ Dio de bruces con una colmena de abejas. He ran headlong into a nest of bees.
dar de cabeza la pelota *(fútbol)* ▪ cabezear la pelota to hit the ball with one's head
dar de comer a alguien ▪ dar a comer a alguien to feed someone ▪ to give someone something to eat
dar de comer al perro ▪ alimentar al perro to feed the dog ▪ to give the dog something to eat ➤ Se les da de comer a los perros dos veces al día. The dogs are fed twice a day.
dar de culo a alguien *(Esp.)* to throw someone out on his ass ▪ to kick someone out on his ass
dar de leches a alguien *(jerga)* to beat someone up
dar de lleno (en algo) ▪ dar de pleno (en algo) ▪ acertar ▪ atinar to hit the nail on the head
dar de menos en el cambio to shortchange
dar de narices contra la pared to bang one's head against the wall
dar de pleno (en algo) ▪ dar de lleno (en algo) ▪ acertar ▪ atinar to hit the nail on the head

dar de sí 1. ■ extirar to stretch 2. ■ hacer más grande to have something stretched ■ to get something stretched 3. ■ cundir to go a long way ➤ Quisiera dar de sí este suéter. I'd like to have this sweater stretched. ■ I'd like to get this sweater stretched.

dar de sí los zapatos ■ meter los zapatos en la horma to stretch (a pair of) shoes

dar dentera a uno ■ dar grima a uno ■ dar repeluzno a uno ■ dar repelús a uno to make one cringe ■ to make one's flesh crawl ➤ Cuando araña la pizarra, me da dentera. When he runs his fingernails down the blackboard, it makes me cringe.

dar destino a algo to find a good use for something

dar dolor de tripas a alguien to give someone a stomachache

dar ejemplo ■ marcar las pautas to set an example ■ to set the example

dar el alta a to discharge ■ to release ➤ El lunes me dan el alta, y el martes vuelvo al trabajo. The doctor has cleared me as of Monday, so Tuesday I'll be back at work.

dar el asunto por concluido ■ dar el asunto por zanjado ■ dar el asunto por finalizado ■ dar el asunto por resuelto ■ considerar el capítulo como cerrado to consider the matter settled ■ to consider the matter closed

dar el asunto por finalizado dar el asunto por zanjado ■ dar el asunto por concluido ■ dar el asunto por resuelto ■ considerar el capítulo cerrado to consider the matter settled ■ to consider the chapter closed

dar el asunto por zanjado ■ dar el asunto por concluido ■ dar el asunto por finalizado ■ dar el asunto por resuelto ■ considerar el capítulo como cerrado to consider the matter settled

dar el bote a alguien ■ echarle to give someone the boot ■ to can someone ■ to fire someone ■ to sack someone

dar el braguetazo to marry someone for money

dar el brazo a torcer to let someone twist your arm ■ to let your arm be twisted

dar el callo ■ *(Esp.)* currar to bust one's butt ■ to work one's butt off ■ to slog away ■ to slave away

dar el cambiazo to switch exams ■ to switch papers *(Nota: una forma de hacer trampas en un examen, que consiste en cambiar el original por uno preparado anteriormente ■ a form of cheating on an exam in which the original is exchanged for one prepared in advance)*

dar camelo a alguien 1. burlarse de alguien to make fun of someone 2. engañar a alguien to tell a big fat lie ■ to tell a whopper

dar el cante to stick out

dar el chivatazo a alguien to expose someone ■ to blow someone's cover ■ to tip someone off

dar el coñazo a alguien *(Esp., subido de tono)* ■ joderle la marrana ■ darle la brasa a alguien to be a damned nuisance to someone ■ to make a nuisance of oneself

dar el corazón que to predict that ■ one's feeling is that ■ one's sense of it is that ➤ Me da el corazón que... I predict that... ■ My feeling is that... ■ My sense of it is that...

dar el do de pecho to do one's utmost

dar el golpe to deal the blow

dar el golpe de gracia to deal the coup de grace ■ to deal the finishing blow

dar el frenazo to slam on the brakes

dar el pasaporte a alguien 1. despedirle a alguien to give someone his walking papers ■ to give someone the boot ■ to give someone his marching orders 2. matar a alguien to bump someone off

dar el pecho al bebé to breastfeed the baby

dar el pésame a to give one's condolences to

dar el pistoletazo de salida a la campaña presidencial ■ abrir la carrera por la presidencia to kick off the presidential campaign ■ to kick off the campaign for the presidency ■ to open the presidential campaign

dar (el) quién vive a alguien *(soldado de guardia)* to ask "who goes there?" ➤ Si el guardia te da quién vive, y no le contestas, hará fuego. If the guard asks "who goes there?" and you don't answer, he'll open fire.

dar el salto to take the plunge

dar el salto a la fama to be catapulted to fame

dar el salto de empresa *(coloquial)* to change jobs

dar el santo y seña to say the password ■ to say the secret word

dar el sí 1. to agree ■ to consent 2. casarse to say "I do" ■ to get hitched ■ to tie the knot

dar el tono to set the tone

dar el toque hispano to give a Hispanic touch ■ to add a Hispanic touch ■ to give the Hispanic touch ■ to add the Hispanic touch ➤ La presencia de Javier Bardem, Jennifer López, Penélope Cruz y Benicio del Toro en los Oscar dio el toque hispano. The presence of Javier Bardem, Jennifer Lopez, Penelope Cruz and Benicio del Toro gave the Oscars a hispanic touch. ■ The presence of Javier Bardem, Jennifer Lopez, Penelope Cruz and Benicio del Toro lent the Oscars a hispanic touch. ■ The presence of Javier Bardem, Jennifer Lopez, Penelope Cruz and Benicio del Toro provided for the Oscars a hispanic touch.

dar el último suspiro to breathe one's last (breath)

dar el visto bueno a to give one's approval

dar el voto a to cast one's vote for

dar en el blanco ■ dar en la diana to hit the bull's eye

dar en el clavo to hit nail on the head

dar en el clavo otra vez to strike again ➤ ¡Wile E. Coyote da en el clavo otra vez! Wile E. Coyote strikes again!

dar en la diana ■ dar en el blanco ■ dar en el clavo ■ hacer blanco to hit the bull's eye

dar en llamar a to christen ■ to name ■ to start calling someone something

dar en qué pensar to be something to think about ■ to give one something to think about

dar en tierra con 1. to drop (accidentally) 2. to drop (on purpose) ■ to throw down 3. to knock over

dar en vano to be useless ■ to be of no avail ➤ En un restaurante chino, darme los palillos es dar en vano. Tengo que tener un tenedor. In a Chinese restaurant, giving me chop sticks is useless. I have to have a fork. ■ In a Chinese restaurant, giving me chop sticks is of no avail. I have to have a fork.

dar entre ceja y ceja a alguien ■ tener entre ceja y ceja a alguien to take a dislike to someone

dar esperanzas a to give hope to

dar esquinazo a alguien to duck out of sight

dar estudios a alguien to pay for someone's education

dar excesiva relevancia a to overplay the importance of ■ to give too much importance to

dar facilidades de pago to have an easy-payment plan ■ to offer an easy-payment plan

dar fama a alguien to make someone famous

dar fe a una firma ■ legitimar una firma to notarize a signature

dar fe de to vouch for

dar fe de que to verify that ■ to vouch for (the fact that) ➤ Doy fe de que este hombre es quien dice ser. I can verify that he is who he says he is. ➤ Doy fe de ello. I can vouch for it.

dar fin to end

dar fin a ■ poner fin a ■ acabar to put an end to

dar finiquito to close out one's employment contract

dar firma en blanco a to give blanket approval to

dar forma a to give shape to

dar frutos ■ rendir frutos to bear fruit

dar ganas de to make one feel like ➤ Da ganas de llorar. It makes you want to cry. ■ It makes you feel like crying. ■ It brings tears to the eyes. ➤ Me da ganas de llorar. It makes me want to cry. ■ It makes me feel like crying. ■ It brings tears to my eyes.

dar gato por liebre to pull the wool over someone's eyes ➤ Me han dado gato por liebre. They pulled the wool over my eyes.

dar gozo de verlo to be pleasing to the eye

dar gracias por to give thanks for

dar grima a uno ■ dar dentera a alguien ■ dar repeluzno a alguien ■ dar repelús a alguien to make one cringe ■ to make one's flesh crawl ➤ Cuando araña la pizarra, me da grima. When he runs his fingernails down the blackboard, it makes me cringe. ■ When he runs his fingernails down the blackboard, it makes my flesh crawl.

dar gritos ■ gritar to shout

dar guerra to cause trouble ■ *(niño)* to be naughty ■ to be bad

dar gusto to please
dar hambre a uno to make one hungry ➤ La aroma de la panadería me da hambre. The smell of the bakery makes me hungry.
dar hasta la camisa a alguien to give someone everything one has (even the shirt off one's back)
dar hora to schedule the time (of an appointment) ■ to schedule an appointment for (a certain time) ➤ Me han dado hora para las seis. They scheduled me for six o'clock.
dar igual for one not to care ➤ Me da igual. I don't care. ■ I don't mind.
dar jaqueca a alguien ■ ser un pelma to be a pain in the neck ■ to bore someone to distraction
dar la alarma to sound the alarm ■ to give the alarm
dar la batalla to put up a fight
dar la brasa a alguien ■ dar la vara a alguien ■ dar la lata a alguien to bother someone ■ to pester someone ➤ Deja ya de dar la brasa. Stop bothering me.
dar la cabezada to bow one's head in respect
dar la callada por respuesta to answer with silence
dar la campanada 1. *(positivo)* to cause a sensation **2.** *(negativo y coloquial)* to cause a stink ■ to raise a stink **3.** *(positivo o negativo)* to cause a stir
dar la cara a alguien ■ enfrentarse a las consecuencias to face up to someone ■ to show the courage of one's convictions
dar la cara (a una situación) to stand up and be counted ■ to face (up to) a situation
dar la cara por lo que ha hecho alguien to take the rap (on purpose) for something someone else has done ■ to take the blame (on purpose) for something someone has done ➤ Di la cara por lo que había hecho mi hermano. I took the rap (on purpose) for what my brother had done. ■ I took the blame (deliberately) for what my brother had done.
dar la cara por alguien to stick up for someone ■ to go to bat for someone
dar la espalda ■ volver la espalda to turn one's back
dar la espalda a algo to turn one's back on something
dar la espalda a alguien ■ volver la espalda a alguien to turn one's back on someone
dar la firma a otro to authorize someone else to sign for one
dar la hora to strike the hour ■ to tell someone what time it is ➤ El reloj dio la medianoche. The clock struck midnight.
dar la imagen to give the impression
dar la imagen de... to give the impression of
dar la imagen de que... to give the impression that...
dar la lata a alguien ■ dar la brasa a alguien ■ dar la vara a alguien to pester someone ■ to bother someone ➤ Deja ya de dar la lata. ■ Deja ya de dar la vara. Stop bothering me. ■ Quit bothering me
dar la lección to give the lesson
dar la ley to lay down the law
dar la luz ■ *(L.am.)* ■ prender la luz ■ *(Esp.)* ■ encender la luz to turn on the light ■ to turn the light on
dar la luz de arriba ■ dar la luz del techo ■ *(L.am.)* ■ prender la luz de arriba ■ prender la luz del techo ■ *(Esp.)* ■ encender la luz del techo ■ encender la luz de arriba to turn on the ceiling light(s) ■ to turn on the overhead light(s)
dar la mano extend one's hand ■ to outstretch one's hand
dar la mano a alguien to shake someone's hand ➤ Una vez le di la mano al presidente. I shook the president's hand once. ■ I shook hands with the president once.
dar la matraca ■ dar la paliza ■ dar la murga **1.** to bore someone silly **2.** to be a royal pain
dar la medicina que figura en una receta to fill a prescription
dar la noche a alguien to keep someone up all night ➤ El bebé se puso malo y nos dio la noche. The baby came down with something and kept us up all night.
dar la nota to call attention to oneself ■ to stand out like a sore thumb ■ to make an ass of oneself
dar la noticia to break the news
dar la palabra a alguien *(procedimiento parlamentario, debate formal)* ■ ceder la palabra a alguien ■ otorgar la palabra a alguien ■ ceder el turno de palabra a alguien to yield the floor to someone ■ to give someone the floor ➤ Le doy la palabra a... I give the floor to... ■ I yield the floor to...
dar la paliza a alguien to beat someone ■ to give someone a beating
dar la patada to kick someone ■ to give someone a kick
dar la paz *(catolicismo y anglicanismo)* to wish someone peace
dar la pelota ■ chutar la pelota ■ tirar la pelota to kick the ball
dar la primera pala to break ground
dar la puntilla to perform a coup de grâce ■ to do a coup de grâce
dar la puntuación *(deportes)* ■ dar el marcador to give the score
dar la razón a alguien to rule in favor of someone ■ to rule in someone's favor
dar la receta para to be the model for
dar la ropa a lavar to send out the clothes to be washed
dar la señal de partida ■ to give the starting signal
dar la tabarra a alguien to pester someone ■ to bother someone ■ to be a pain in the neck ■ to be a nuisance
dar la talla para to set the standard for
dar la teta a un bebé to breastfeed a baby ■ to nurse a baby ■ *(literario)* to suckle an infant
dar la última mano 1. to give (something) the final coat of paint **2.** to deal the final hand of cards
dar la última pincelada a ■ dar las últimas pinceladas a to give the finishing touches to
dar la vara a alguien *(Esp.)* ■ dar la brasa a alguien ■ dar la lata a alguien to bother someone ➤ Deja ya de dar la vara. Stop bothering me. ■ Quit bothering me.
dar la vida por to give one's life for
dar la voz de alerta to sound the alarm
dar la vuelta to turn around
dar la vuelta a to go around ■ to circle
dar la vuelta a la manzana to go around the block
dar la vuelta a la tortilla to turn the tables
dar la vuelta al globo ■ circunnavegar el globo to circumnavigate the globe
dar la vuelta al mundo to go around the world
dar largas a algo to put something off
dar largas a alguien to put someone off
dar las cartas ■ dar los naipes to deal the cards
dar (las) gracias a alguien por algo to thank someone for something
dar las luces ■ dar ráfagas to flash one's headlights ■ to flash one's lights ➤ El coche que iba detrás de mí dio las luces para que le dejara pasar. ■ El coche que iba detrás de mí dio ráfagas para que le dejara pasar. The car behind me flashed its lights so that I would let it pass. ■ The driver behind me flashed his lights (at me) so I would let him pass.
dar las señas de alguien to give someone's address
dar lástima to make one feel sad ■ to make one feel pity ➤ Eso da lástima. That's sad. ➤ Eso me da lástima. That makes me feel sad.
dar leche to give milk
dar leches to hit (with one's fist) ■ to punch
dar lluvia to rain ➤ Mi instructor de vuelo me enseñó que las nubes altas no dan lluvia, por más amenazadoras que parezcan. My flight instructor taught me that high clouds won't rain, no matter how threatening they look.
dar lo mejor de sí (mismo) ■ dar lo mejor de uno mismo to give one's best ■ to give the best of oneself ➤ Los candidatos dieron lo mejor de sí mismos durante el debate. The candidates gave their best during the debate. ■ The candidates gave the best of themselves during the debate.
dar lo mismo ■ ser lo mismo not to make any difference ■ to make no difference ➤ Da lo mismo. ■ Es lo mismo. It doesn't make any difference. ■ It makes no difference. ➤ Me da lo mismo. ■ Para mí es lo mismo. It doesn't make any difference to me. ■ It makes no difference to me.
dar los naipes ■ dar las cartas to deal the cards
dar los últimos retoques a to put the finishing touches on
dar lugar a algo ■ dar origen a algo ■ provocar algo ■ ocasionar algo to give rise to something

dar luz verde a algo to give the green light ▪ to give the go-ahead ➤ El jefe dio luz verde al proyecto. The boss gave the project the green light. ▪ The boss gave the project the go-ahead.

dar luz verde a alguien para hacer algo to give someone the green light to do something ▪ to give someone the go-ahead to do something

dar luz verde para hacer algo to give the green light to do something ▪ to give the go-ahead to do something ➤ El jefe dio luz verde a los empleados para empezar el proyecto. The boss gave the green light to the employees to begin the project. ▪ The boss gave the go-ahead to the employees to begin the project. ➤ El jefe dio luz verde a los empleados para que empezaran el proyecto. The boss gave the green light to the employees to begin the project. ▪ The boss gave the go-ahead to the employees to begin the project.

dar mal los naipes to misdeal the cards

dar mala espina a uno to give one a bad feeling ➤ La forma en que me miró me dio mala espina. The way he looked at me gave me a bad feeling.

dar mala imagen to make a bad impression ▪ to give a bad impression ▪ to make someone look bad ▪ to project a bad image ▪ not to come across well

dar marcha atrás 1. recoger velas ▪ echarse atrás to back down 2. ir marcha atrás ▪ retroceder ▪ recular to back up 3. cambiar de idea to change one's mind 4. perder entusiasmo para la idea to cool to the idea ➤ El pastor alemán del hombre de mantenimiento dio marcha atrás cuando mi gata se le enfrentó. The maintenance man's German Shepherd backed down when (he was) confronted by my cat. ➤ Da marcha atrás un poco. ▪ Ve marcha atrás un poco. ▪ Retrocede un poco. ▪ Recula un poco. Back up a little (bit). ➤ Pensaba ir al cine este fin de semana, pero di marcha atrás. I was planning to go to the movies this weekend, but I changed my mind. ▪ I was planning on going to the movies this weekend, but I changed my mind. ➤ Iba a trasladarme al norte de Alberta, pero voy dándome marcha atrás con la idea. I was going to move to northern Alberta, but I'm cooling to the idea.

dar marcha atrás a to back onto ➤ Da marcha atrás al remolque con el barco por la rampa. Back the boat trailer onto the ramp.

dar marcha atrás a una medida to repeal a measure

dar marcha atrás al coche en la entrada ▪ dar marcha atrás al coche por la entrada ▪ meter marcha atrás al coche to back the car out of the driveway ➤ El coche dio marcha atrás en la entrada. ▪ El coche dio marcha atrás por la entrada. The car backed out of the driveway.

dar marcha atrás al carro por la entrada ▪ dar marcha atrás al carro en la entrada ▪ meter marcha atrás al carro to back the car out of the driveway ➤ Di marcha atrás al carro por la entrada. ▪ Di marcha atrás al carro en la entrada. ▪ Metí marcha atrás al carro en la entrada. I backed the car out of the driveway.

dar marcha atrás en una entrada ▪ dar marcha atrás por una entrada ▪ salir reculando de una entrada to back out of a driveway

dar marcha atrás hasta la calzada ▪ sacar el carro de culo hasta la calzada to back (out) onto the street ➤ Da marcha atrás hasta la calzada. Back out onto the street. ➤ Da marcha atrás hasta la calzada para que pueda sacar mi carro. Back out onto the street so (that) I can get my car out.

dar marcha atrás por una entrada ▪ dar marcha atrás en una entrada ▪ salir reculando de una entrada to back out of a driveway

dar marcha atrás a una propuesta ▪ echar marcha atrás una propuesta ▪ recapacitar sobre una propuesta retroceder en una propuesta ▪ replantearse una propuesta 1. to back away from a proposal 2. to withdraw a proposal

dar mascado un tema to explain a subject in simple terms

dar mucha rabia a alguien to make someone really angry ▪ *(coloquial)* to make someone really mad

dar mucho de que hablar to cause a lot of comment ▪ to generate a lot of interest

dar muerte to put to death ▪ to kill ▪ to execute

dar nombres ▪ decir nombres to name names ➤ No voy a dar nombres. ▪ No voy a decir nombres. I'm not going to name names.

dar órdenes to give orders

dar origen a un movimiento to give rise to a movement ▪ to give birth to a movement

dar origen a una idea to give birth to an idea ▪ to be the source of an idea

dar palmada ▪ aplaudir to clap ▪ to applaud

dar palmaditas en la espalda a alguien to give someone a pat on the back ▪ to pat someone on the back

dar palmas to clap rhythmically

dar palos de ciego 1. to grope for answers ▪ to grope for solutions 2. *(al criticar)* to lash out

dar palos de ciego para las respuestas to grope for answers

dar palos de ciego para las soluciones to grope for solutions

dar parte to inform the police ▪ to inform the authorities

dar parte a alguien de algo to report something to someone

dar pasaporte a alguien (para el otro barrio) *(jerga)* to bump someone off ▪ to bump off someone ▪ to kill someone ▪ to murder someone ➤ *(Valle-Inclán)* Darle pasaporte a don Joselito To bump off don Joselito

dar paso a 1. abrir camino a ▪ conducir a to lead to ▪ to give rise to ▪ to make way for 2. ceder ante ▪ ceder al empuje de to give way to 3. ceder el paso a ▪ permitir el paso a to step aside for ➤ La secuenciación del genoma humano dará paso a nuevos tratamientos médicos. ▪ La secuenciación del genoma humano abrirá camino a nuevos tratamientos médicos. ▪ La secuenciación del genoma humano conducirá a nuevos tratamientos médicos. The mapping of the human genome will lead to new medical treatments ▪ The mapping of the human genome will give rise to new medical treatments ▪ The mapping of the human genome will make way for new medical treatments. ➤ En 1854, el Compromiso de Misuri dio paso a la doctrina de la soberanía popular que hizo de la esclavitud una opción local. ▪ En 1854, el Compromiso de Misuri cedió al empuje de la doctrina de la soberanía popular que hacía de la esclavitud una opción local. In 1854, the Missouri Compromise gave way to the doctrine of popular sovereignty, which made slavery a local option. ➤ No doy paso a ningún cateto.-Pues, yo sí. Pase. ▪ No le cedo el paso a ningún cateto.-Pues, yo sí. Pase. ▪ No le permito el paso a ningún cateto.-Pues, yo sí. Pase. I don't step aside for hicks.-Well, I do. Go ahead.

dar paso a la posibilidad to give rise to the possibility

dar pasos hacia atrás ▪ retroceder to step back ▪ to back away

dar pena a alguien to make someone sad ▪ to upset someone ▪ to make someone feel sorry

dar plantón a alguien ▪ dejar plantado(-a) a alguien to stand someone up

dar poca importancia al asunto to treat the whole thing lightly ▪ to treat the matter lightly

dar por acabado algo to consider something finished

dar por cerrado un asunto to consider a matter closed

dar por concluido un asunto to consider a matter closed ▪ to dismiss a matter ▪ to bring a matter to a close ▪ to bring a matter to an end

dar por concluido un ciclo to bring a period to a close ➤ Los votantes portugueses han dado por concluido un ciclo socialista con el ajustado triunfo de los socialdemócratas. Portuguese voters have ended the socialist period with the narrow victory of the Social Democrats. ▪ Portuguese voters have brought the socialist period to a close with the narrow victory of the Social Democrats.

dar por desarticulado to consider dismantled ▪ to consider taken out of action

dar por finalizado un asunto to consider a matter closed

dar por hecho que... ▪ dar por sentado que... ▪ dar por sabido que... ▪ dar por supuesto que... to take it for a fact that... ▪ to consider it an established fact that... ▪ to take for granted that...

dar por muerto to presume dead ▪ to give up for dead ➤ *(noticia)* Rusia da por muertos a los 118 tripulantes del submarino ▪ Rusia da por muerta a toda la tripulación Rusia presumes dead the 118 submarine crewmen

dar por perdido algo to give something up for lost

dar por sentado ▪ dar por supuesto to take for granted

dar por supuesto ▪ dar por sentado to take it for granted ▪ to take it as read

dar por terminado el asunto to consider the matter closed

dar positivo en la prueba de (alcoholemia) to test positive for alcohol consumption

dar pucherazo ■ apañar unas elecciones to rig an election

dar que hacer to be a handful ➤ Esa niña les dará que hacer. That little girl is a handful.

dar que pensar que... ■ hacer pensar que... to give the impression that...

dar ráfagas ■ dar las luces to flash one's headlights ■ to flash one's lights ➤ El coche que iba detrás de mí dio ráfagas para que le dejara pasar. ■ El coche que iba detrás de mí dio ráfagas para que le dejara pasar. The car behind me flashed its lights so that I would let it pass. ■ The driver behind me flashed his lights (at me) so I would let him pass.

dar razón to give information

dar realce a la imagen ■ realzar la imagen to enhance the image ■ to enhance one's image

dar repelús a alguien ■ dar repeluzno a alguien ■ dar dentera a alguien ■ dar grima a alguien to make someone cringe ➤ Cuando araña la pizarra, me da repelús. When he runs his fingers down the blackboard, it makes me cringe.

dar repeluzno a alguien ■ dar repelús a alguien ■ dar dentera a alguien ■ dar grima a alguien to make someone cringe ■ to make someone shudder ➤ Cuando araña la pizarra, me da repeluzno. When he runs his fingers down the blackboard, it makes me cringe.

dar rienda suelta a los impulsos to give free rein to one's impulses

dar saltos ~ **1.** saltar to jump up and down **2.** *(corazón)* to pound **3.** *(avión)* to bounce around ■ to hit air pockets ■ to encounter turbulence

dar saltos de alegría ■ saltar de alegría ■ brincar de alegría ■ brincar de júbilo ■ dar botes de alegría to jump for joy

dar señales de vida to show signs of life

dar señas de to show signs of ■ to give indications of

dar señas de enfado *(Esp.)* to betray one's anger

dar señas de enojo *(L.am.)* to betray one's anger

dar su aprobación to give one's approval

dar su conformidad to give one's consent

dar su mano to give one's hand in marriage ■ to give one's hand

dar su merecido a alguien to give someone his just desserts

dar su palabra (de honor) a alguien to give someone one's word (of honor) ➤ Te doy mi palabra. I give you my word.

dar su voto a alguien ■ votar por alguien to cast one's vote for someone ■ to vote for someone

dar testimonio de que to testify that... ■ to give evidence that... ■ to bear testimony that...

(dar) tiempo al tiempo to give something (some) time ➤ Tiempo al tiempo. Give it some time. ■ Give it time.

dar traste con to throw a monkey wrench into ■ to wreak havoc with ■ to wreak havoc on

dar tratamiento (médico) a alguien to give someone medical treatment ■ to give medical treatment to someone ■ to treat someone

dar trompicones to stagger (around)

dar un alarido *(de placer o dolor)* to scream ■ to shriek ■ to howl

dar un azote a alguien 1. *(Esp.)* to give someone a spanking ■ to spank someone **2.** *(L.am.)* to whip someone

dar un bandazo ■ dar un volantazo to swerve sharply ■ to swerve abruptly ■ to swerve violently

dar un brinco ■ pegar un brinco ■ dar un salto to jump

dar un brinco de alegría ■ brincar de alegría ■ dar un salto de alegría ■ saltar de alegría to jump for joy

dar un buen meneo a un niño *(Esp.)* ■ zarandear a un niño to scold a child severely (by shaking his shoulders)

dar un buen repaso to go over it well ■ to give it a good going over

dar un chasco a alguien to play a trick on someone

dar un corte a alguien ■ cortar a alguien ■ dejar a alguien fuera de juego to blank someone out ➤ Cuando reaccionó diciéndote "pobrecito", él te estaba dando un corte. ■ Cuando reaccionó diciéndote "pobrecito", él te estaba cortando. ■ Cuando reaccionó diciéndote "pobrecito", él te estaba dejando fuera de juego. When he reacted by saying "poor baby," he was blanking you out.

dar un discurso ■ pronunciar un discurso to give a speech ■ to make a speech ■ to deliver a speech

dar un empellón a alguien ■ dar un empujón a alguien to give someone a shove ■ to shove someone

dar un empujón a alguien ■ dar un empellón a alguien to give someone a shove ■ to shove someone

dar un estirón ■ pegar un estirón to shoot up like a weed ■ to have a growth spurt

dar un frenazo (brusco) to slam on the brakes ■ to hit the brakes

dar un gran rodeo to go way out of the way ■ to go around Robin Hood's barn ➤ Para conducir desde Roanoke, Virginia, hasta Pittsburgh, Pensilvania, hay que dar un gran rodeo. To drive from Roanoke, Virginia, to Pittsburgh, Pennsylvania, you have to go way out of the way ■ To drive from Roanoke, Virginia, to Pittsburgh, Pennsylvania, you have to go around Robin Hood's barn.

dar un giro a su posición (sobre) ■ dar un giro en su postura (sobre) to change one's position (on) ■ to shift one's position ➤ El gobierno dio un giro a su posición. The government changed its position.

dar un giro brusco to swerve sharply ■ to swerve suddenly

dar un giro equivocado to take a wrong turn

dar un giro inesperado to take an unexpected turn ➤ *(noticia)* El caso del *asesino del naipe* dio ayer un nuevo giro inesperado. El case of the *card killer* took another unexpected turn yesterday. *(Nota: El asesino plantaba un naipe en la escena de cada asesinato.)*

dar un golpe de efecto to have a dramatic effect

dar un gran salto to take a giant leap

dar un grito ■ lanzar un grito ■ gritar to shout ■ to give a shout

dar un grito de alegría to shout for joy

dar un jabón a alguien to give someone a lathering ■ to give someone a dressing down

dar un ojo de la cara por to give one's eye teeth for

dar un manotazo a alguien ■ dar una cachetada a alguien to slap someone

dar un meneo a alguien ■ zarandear a alguien **1.** to shake someone by the shoulders in anger **2.** to chew someone out ■ to give someone a dressing down ■ to let someone have it ■ to read someone the riot act ■ to give someone a talking to

dar un mordisco a algo ■ morder algo to bite into something ➤ Dio un mordisco a la manzana. He bit into the apple. ➤ Acabo de dar un mordisco a un trozo de cebolla que no había sido cocinado. I just bit into a piece of onion that didn't get cooked.

dar un par de hostias a alguien to beat the crap out of someone ■ *(subido de tono)* to beat the shit out of someone

dar un paseo to go for a walk ■ to take a walk

dar un paseo en coche to go for a drive

dar un paseo en avioneta to go for an airplane ride

dar un paso to take a step

dar un paso adelante to take a step forward

dar un paso al frente *(militar)* ■ dar la cara to step forward ■ to take responsibility ■ to own up ■ to show oneself

dar un paso en falso to make a false move ■ to make one false move ■ to take a false step

dar un paso más to go one step further

dar un paso más por adelante de alguien to go one step further than someone

dar un paso para atrás ■ dar un paso por detrás to take a step backwards ■ to take a step back

dar un paso por detrás ■ dar un paso para atrás to take a step backwards ■ to take a step back

dar un patinazo to skid ➤ El coche dio un patinazo sobre el hielo. The car skidded on the ice.

dar un plantón a alguien ■ dejar plantado a alguien to stand someone up

dar un portazo ■ tirar la puerta ■ azotar la puerta to slam the door

dar un puñetazo en la mesa to bang one's fist on the table

dar un rebote en to bounce off (of) ■ to rebound off (of)

dar un repaso a algo ~ **1.** to go over something ■ to give a review **2.** to take a look at something **3.** to tidy up something ■ to spruce up something ➤ El libro da un repaso al catolicismo en la España contemporanea. The book takes a look at Catholicism in contemporary Spain. ➤ Voy a darles a ustedes un repaso de la primera lección. I'm going to give you (all) a review of the first lesson. ➤ Tendremos invitados para la cena, así que hay que dar un repaso a la casa. Company's coming for dinner, so we need to tidy up the house.

dar un rodeo to go (way) out of the way ▪ *(pintoresco)* to go around Robin Hood's barn ▪ *(ligeramente subido de tono)* to go way the hell out of the way ▪ to go way the hell around Robin Hood's barn

dar un rugido ▪ lanzar un rugido ▪ proferir un rugido to let out a roar

dar un sablazo to give a sword thrust ▪ to thrust a sword

dar un sablazo a alguien 1. to ask someone for a loan ▪ to ask someone to lend you money **2.** to run someone through with a sword

dar un salto de alegría to jump for joy

dar un soponcio 1. to faint ▪ to swoon **2.** *(exageración)*to nearly die ➤ Cuando ella entró al cuarto, casi me dio un soponcio. When she came into the room, I nearly died.

dar un suspiro ▪ soltar un suspiro to heave a sigh ▪ to sigh ➤ Ella dio un profundo suspiro. She heaved a deep sigh. ▪ She sighed deeply. ▪ She sighed heavily.

dar un telefonazo a alguien to give someone a ring ▪ to give someone a call

dar un tiempo muerto to stop the clock

dar un tiento a la botella to take swig from the bottle

dar un timo a alguien to swindle someone ▪ to con someone ▪ to rip someone off

dar un tono de fondo a madera to stain wood ➤ Me gustaría dar un tono de fondo y barnizar esta mesa. I'd like to stain and varnish this table.

dar un toque a alguien to call someone on the carpet

dar un toque en el hombro a alguien to tap someone on the shoulder

dar un vistazo ▪ echar un vistazo to have a look

dar un volantazo ▪ dar un bandazo to swerve sharply ▪ to swerve abruptly ▪ to swerve violently

dar un vuelco to be turned upside down ➤ Con la muerte de su esposa, su vida dio un vuelco. The death of his wife turned his life upside down.

dar un vuelco el corazón to touch one's heart ▪ to give someone a buzz

dar una bofetada to hit someone ▪ to land a blow on someone

dar una buena impresión to make a good impression

dar una buena lección to teach someone a lesson

dar una cabezada ▪ echar una cabezada ▪ dar una cabezadita ▪ echar una cabezadita to doze off ▪ to nod off ➤ Intenta no dar una cabezada después de comer. ▪ Intenta no echar una cabezada después de comer. ▪ Intenta no dar una cabezadita después de comer. ▪ Intenta no echar una cabezadita después de comer. Try not to doze off after dinner. ▪ Try to keep from dozing off after dinner. ▪ Try not to nod off after dinner. ▪ Try to keep from nodding off after dinner.

dar una calada (a alguien) to give someone a drag off one's cigarette ➤ Dame una calada (de tu cigarrillo). Give me a drag (off your cigarette).

dar una charla to give a talk

dar una citación a alguien ▪ extender una citación a alguien ▪ multar a alguien to give someone a ticket ▪ to give someone a citation

dar una conferencia to give a lecture

dar una de cal y otra de arena 1. to blow hot and cold ▪ to run hot and cold ▪ to both praise and criticize **2.** to apply a policy of carrot and stick

dar una hostia *(fuerte)* ▪ partir la cara ▪ partir la boca to hit in the face ▪ to bust in the mouth

dar una interpretación to interpret ▪ to perform music

dar una lección a alguien ▪ dar una lección to teach someone a lesson ➤ *(titular en la sección de deportes)* España dio una lección. Spain taught them a lesson.

dar una leche a alguien *(Esp.)* ▪ dar un puñetazo a alguien ▪ dar un tortazo a alguien ▪ dar una hostia a alguien to punch someone ▪ to hit someone

dar una mano a alguien to give someone a hand ▪ to lend a hand

dar una paliza a alguien to beat someone up ▪ to hit someone hard

dar una palmada (en la espalda de alguien) to give someone a pat on the back ▪ to pat someone on the back

dar una pasada a alguien ▪ reprender a alguien to tell someone off

dar una patada to kick

dar una patada a la lengua ▪ dar una patada al idioma to butcher the language

dar una pitada to boo ▪ to give a Bronx cheer

dar una puntuación a alguien to explain a point of grammar to someone

dar una vuelta to go for a walk ▪ to go for a stroll ▪ to take a walk ▪ to take a stroll

dar una vuelta de campana to flip over ▪ to roll over ➤ El avión se salió del extremo de la pista, chocó con una valla y dio una vuelta de campana. The airplane ran off the end of the runway, hit a fence and flipped over. ➤ El coche dio una vuelta de campana. The car rolled over.

dar una vuelta positiva a to put a positive spin on ➤ La Casa Blanca dio una vuelta positiva a la misión diplomática de Powell. The White House put a positive spin on Powell's diplomatic mission.

dar unas palmadas ▪ batir palmas to clap one's hands

dar uno de cal y otro de arena to blow hot and cold ▪ to run hot and cold ▪ to praise one minute and criticize the next

dar uno la cara por otro to take the rap for someone else

dar unos azotes en el culo a alguien ▪ dar a alguien en el culo ▪ azotar a alguien (en el trasero) ▪ zurrar a alguien ▪ *(coloquial)* ▪ calentar el culo a alguien ▪ poner el culo como un tomate a alguien to give someone a spanking ▪ to spank someone ▪ *(coloquial)* to tan someone's hide

dar vaya a ▪ burlarse de to make fun of

dar vergüenza to embarrass ▪ to be shameful ➤ Eso da vergüenza. That's shameful.

dar vida a un personaje to play someone ➤ *(noticia)* Matt Damon da vida a un espía. Matt Damon plays a spy.

dar vivas a algo to abet something

dar vivas a alguien to give encouragement to someone

dar voces to raise one's voice ▪ to shout ➤ No hay que dar voces. There's no need to raise your voice. ▪ There's no need to shout. ▪ You don't need to shout. ▪ You don't have to shout.

dar voces al viento to spin one's wheels

dar volteretas laterales ▪ *(Arg.)* hacer medialunas to do cartwheels

dar vueltas ▪ dar vueltas al coco to keep thinking about it ➤ No le des más vueltas. Don't think any more about it. ▪ Don't keep thinking about it. ▪ Let it go.

dar vueltas a lo tonto to make unnecessary turns ▪ to inflate the trip ▪ take a longer route than necessary

dar vueltas al coco to keep thinking about it ➤ No le des más vueltas al coco. Don't think any more about it. ▪ Don't keep thinking about it. ▪ Let it go.

dar vueltas de campana *(de un vehículo)* to roll over repeatedly ▪ to roll over and over

dar vueltas por lo alto ▪ dar vueltas en lo alto ▪ dar vueltas a lo alto ▪ dar vueltas por arriba to circle overhead ➤ El avión daba vueltas por lo alto. ▪ El avión daba vueltas en lo alto. ▪ El avión daba vueltas a lo alto. ▪ El avión daba vueltas por arriba. The airplane was circling overhead.

dar vueltas (y vueltas) to toss and turn ➤ Di vueltas (y vueltas) toda la noche. I tossed and turned all night.

dar *x* to add up to *x* ▪ to total *x* ➤ Esta suma da seiscientos cuarenta y cinco. This column of figures adds up to six hundred forty-five.

dar *x* puntos de ventaja a alguien sobre *y* to show an *x* point-lead over *y* ➤ El último sondeo da diecisiete puntos de ventaja a Bush sobre Gore. The latest poll shows Bush leading Gore by seventeen points.

dares y tomares con alguien: andar en ~ to bicker with someone ▪ to argue with someone

daría cualquier cosa por saber qué... I'd give anything to know what...

daría un ojo de la cara por... I'd give my eye teeth for... ▪ I'd give my eye teeth to...

darle a alguien a beber hieles *(literario)* ▪ fastidiar a alguien to give someone a hard time

darle a alguien con la puerta en las narices to slam the door in someone's face

darle a alguien crédito por una asignatura to give someone credit for a course ➤ Me dieron crédito posgrado por la asignatura. They gave me graduate credit for the course.

darle a alguien el control to give someone control ▪ to put someone in control ➤ Me da el control. It puts me in control.

darle a alguien el tiempo para hacer algo to give someone time to do something

darle a alguien el tiempo que... to give someone the time that...

darle a alguien en plena cara to hit someone right in the face

darle a alguien la bienvenida (a) to welcome someone (to)

darle a alguien la ley de hielo ▪ darle a alguien la espalda to give someone the silent treatment

darle a alguien lo que es de justicia ▪ darle a alguien lo que le corresponde to give someone his due

darle a alguien lo que le corresponde ▪ darle a alguien lo que es de justicia to give someone his due

darle a alguien mucho en que cavilar ▪ darle a alguien mucho que pensar to give someone a lot to think about

darle a alguien (mucho) que pensar ▪ darle a alguien mucho en que cavilar to give someone a lot to think about

darle a alguien un buen baño to give someone a bath

darle a alguien un coscorrón to give someone a bump on the head

darle a alguien un sablazo *(coloquial)* to hit someone up for (some) money ▪ to hit someone up for some bucks ➤ Cada vez que su cuñado se le acerca se pone en guardia. Normalmente sólo se dirige a él para darle sablazos. Every time his brother-in-law comes around, he puts up his guard. Usually he only goes to him to hit him up for some bucks.

darle a alguien una dosis de su propia medicina to give someone a dose of his own medicine

darle a alguien una jabonadura to tell someone off

darle a la botella to hit the bottle

darle a la lengua 1. to shoot the bull ▪ to shoot the breeze ▪ to chew the fat **2.** to run one's mouth ▪ to talk and talk ▪ to tongue wag ➤ Es una pesada; está siempre dándole a la lengua. She's a pain, always running her mouth. ➤ Es un pesado; nunca para de darle a la lengua. He's a pain. He never stops running his mouth.

darle a un mueble un nuevo acabado to refinish a piece of furniture ➤ Le di a esta mesa un nuevo acabado. I refinished this table.

darle a uno clase to have for a class ➤ Ella no me da clase este trimestre. I don't have her for a class this quarter.

darle a uno de alta to be released from the hospital ➤ A ella le dieron de alta ayer. She was released from the hospital yesterday. ▪ She was released yesterday.

darle a uno la noche to have (quite) a night of it ➤ Parece que te ha dado la noche. It looks like you've had quite a night of it.

darle al diente to sink one's teeth into it ▪ to dig in ➤ ¡Denle al diente! ▪ *(Esp.)* ¡Dadle al diente! Dig in!

darle al diente sin miedo to eat like a horse

darle ánimo a alguien ▪ animar a alguien **1.** alentar a alguien to give someone encouragement ▪ to encourage someone **2.** levantarle los ánimos a alguien to cheer someone up ▪ to lift someone's spirits ▪ to raise someone's spirits

darle antojo de hacer algo ▪ darle la vena por hacer algo ▪ antojársele hacer algo to take a notion to do something ▪ to up and do something

darle arcadas 1. *(literal)* to make one gag ▪ to make one retch **2.** *(figurativo)* to be revolting

darle arre que arre *(Esp., coloquial)* to go great guns

darle asco 1. causar mal estomacal to make one nauseated ▪ to make one sick **2.** dar impresión to be revolting

darle bombo for it to be all one can talk about ▪ to talk up ▪ to talk it up ▪ *(culto)* to be teeming with news about ➤ Le ha dado un bombo a su casa nueva. All she can talk about is her new house.

darle calabazas a alguien to jilt someone ▪ to give someone the cold shoulder

darle cancha 1. *(a alguien)* to give someone a chance **2.** *(a algo)* to give something a chance

darle caña a alguien *(Esp.)* to pressure someone to work hard ▪ to ride herd on someone ➤ ¡Date caña! Get moving! ▪ Get a move on! ▪ Get going! ▪ Step on it!

darle cargo de conciencia to feel bad about

darle cargo de conciencia que to feel bad that

darle cera al suelo ▪ darle cera al piso ▪ encerar el suelo ▪ encerar el piso to wax the floor ➤ Hay que pasar la fregona y darle cera al suelo. ▪ Hay que pasar la fregona y encerar el suelo. We need to mop and wax the floor.

darle con la puerta en las narices to slam the door in someone's face

darle consuelo a alguien ▪ consolar a alguien ▪ reconfortar a alguien to console someone ▪ to comfort someone

darle coraje a alguien *(Méx.)* ▪ darle bronca a alguien to make someone furious ➤ Me dio mucho coraje. It made me furious.

darle corte a alguien *(coloquial)* ▪ darle vergüenza a alguien not to have the nerve ▪ to be too shy ▪ to embarrass someone ▪ to be (too) embarrassed ➤ Me gustaría pedirle que venga al baile conmigo, pero me da corte. I'd like to ask her to go to the dance with me, but I don't have the nerve. ▪ I'd like to ask her to the dance, but I don't have the nerve.

darle cuerda a alguien to wind someone up ▪ to get someone going

darle cuerda a una caja de música to wind up a music box ▪ to wind a music box up ➤ Se necesita una manivela para darle cuerda a esas grandes cajas de música suizas. It takes a crank to wind up those big Swiss music boxes. ▪ It takes a crank to wind those big Swiss music boxes up. ➤ Se necesita una manivela para darles cuerda. It takes a crank to wind them up. ➤ Le di cuerda a la caja de música. I wound up the music box. ▪ I wound the music box up.

darle al balón to kick the ball

darle algo a alguien a regañadientes to be done out of something ➤ Le di uno de veinte a regañadientes. He did me out of a twenty.

darle de alta 1. salir del hospital to discharge someone from the hospital **2.** estar listo para volver al trabajo to discharge someone from sick leave ➤ Le dieron de alta. *(él)* They released him from the hospital ▪ *(ella)* They released her from the hospital. ➤ El lunes me dan el alta. They're going to let me go back to work (on) Monday.

darle de alta en la Seguridad Social to sign someone up for Social Security

darle de alta en un servicio to sign someone up for a service

darle de alta en un servidor to sign someone up with a server

darle de baja to put someone on sick leave ▪ *(servicio militar)* to discharge someone

darle de menos to short someone ▪ to give someone less than one should have ➤ Me dieron uno de menos. They shorted me one. ▪ They gave me one less than they should have. ▪ I was shorted one. ▪ I got shorted one.

darle el aviso a alguien ▪ darle el preaviso a alguien to turn in one's notice ▪ to give notice

darle el beneficio de la duda a alguien ▪ concederle el beneficio de la duda a alguien to give someone the benefit of the doubt

darle el coñazo *(Esp., subido de tono)* ▪ insistir de forma reiterada y pesada to pester someone ▪ to hound someone ➤ Me da el coñazo todo el tiempo. He pesters me constantly. ▪ He hounds me all the time.

darle el coraje a alguien (para hacer algo) to give someone the courage (to do something) ➤ Sus consejos me dieron el coraje para seguir. Her advice gave me the courage to go on.

darle el corazón que to predict that ▪ one's feeling is that ▪ one's sense of it is that ➤ Me da el corazón que I predict that... ▪ My feeling is that... ▪ My sense of it is that...

darle el cuarto de hora to throw a fit ▪ to have one's fifteen minutes of fame ➤ (Ella) le dio (a él) el cuarto de hora She threw a fit. ▪ She had her fifteen minutes of fame.

darle el preaviso a alguien ▪ darle el aviso a alguien to turn in one's notice ▪ to give notice

darle el tema mascado to be a good explainer

darle el visto bueno to give one's approval to someone ▪ to give one's approval to something

darle en el corazón to touch one's heart

darle en los morros a alguien to slap someone lightly in the mouth

darle fiebre *(Esp.)* ▪ coger fiebre to come down with a fever ▪ to develop a fever ➤ Le dio fiebre *(ella)* She came down with a fever. ▪ She developed a fever. ▪ *(él)* He came down with a fever. ▪ He developed a fever.

darle golpes el corazón to make one's heart pound ▪ (for) one's heart to pound ➤ Le da golpes el corazón *(a él)* His heart is pounding ▪ *(a ella)* Her heart is pounding ➤ Le dio golpes el corazón *(a él)* His heart pounded ▪ *(a ella)* Her heart pounded ➤ Le daba golpes el corazón. *(a él)* His heart was pounding. ▪ His heart pounded. ▪ *(a ella)* Her heart was pounding. ▪ Her heart pounded.

darle guerra to give someone a lot of trouble ▪ *(niño)* to be naughty ➤ Este coche me ha dado guerra. This car has given me a lot of trouble. ➤ Uno de los estudiantes me da mucha guerra en la clase. One of the students causes (me) a lot of trouble in class

darle hora para... to scheduled one for... ▪ to schedule one's appointment for... ▪ to set one's appointment for... ➤ Me ha dado hora para lunes. He scheduled me for Monday. ▪ He scheduled my appointment for Monday. ▪ He set my appointment for Monday.

darle cera al piso ▪ darle cera al suelo to wax the floor

darle la cara a alguien ▪ mirar en la cara de alguien to look (directly) at someone ➤ "Dame la cara," le dijo al niño. "Look at me," she said to the child.

darle la idea para... to give one the idea for...

darle la lata a alguien ▪ fastidiarlo ▪ molestarlo ▪ irritarlo ▪ preocuparlo to bother someone ▪ to pester someone

darle la modorra a uno *(Esp.)* ▪ amodorrarle a uno ▪ darle sueño a uno ▪ adormilarle a uno to make one drowsy ➤ La comida siempre me da la modorra. Dinner always makes me drowsy.

darle la razón a alguien 1. *(sentido positivo)* admitir que alguien tiene razón to admit that someone is right **2.** *(sentido negativo)* to concede the point (so that the person will shut up) ➤ No me des la razón como a los locos. Don't concede the point just to humor me.

darle la real gana de to have a hankering to ▪ to have a yen to

darle la velada a alguien ▪ arruinar la noche a alguien to ruin someone's evening

darle la vena por hacer algo ▪ darle antojo de hacer algo ▪ antojársele hacer algo to take a notion to do something ▪ to up and do something

darle la vena y hacer algo to (just) up and do something ▪ to take a notion to do something ➤ Patrick se dio la vena y se tiñó el pelo de verde. Patrick (just) up and dyed his hair green.

darle la venada y hacer algo to (just) up and do something ➤ Le dio la venada y se tiñó el pelo. He (just) up and dyed his hair.

darle la vuelta a algo 1. volcar algo to turn something upside down **2.** orbitar algo to revolve around something ▪ to orbit something ➤ Dale la vuelta a la caja y ábrela por abajo. Turn the box upside down and open it from the bottom.

darle la vuelta a la tortilla (for) big changes to be in the works

darle la vuelta a una tortita to flip a pancake

darle las uvas *(Esp., coloquial)* ▪ llevarle a alguien todo el año to take all year ➤ A ese ritmo a Chema le van a dar las uvas antes de que termine su trabajo de biología. ▪ A ese ritmo a Chema le va a llevar todo el año terminar su trabajo de biología. At this rate Chema is going to take all year to get his biology paper done. ▪ At this rate Chema is going to take all year doing his biology paper.

darle lumbre a alguien to give someone a light

darle lo suyo to teach someone a lesson

darle los buenos días a alguien to say good morning to someone

darle mala espina to have a bad feeling about something ▪ to have an uneasy feeling about something ➤ Me da mala espina. I have a bad feeling about it. ▪ I have an uneasy feeling about it.

darle mala vida a alguien to make someone's life miserable

darle más gas al motor to gun the engine ▪ to rev (up) the engine

darle más vueltas que una llave to turn it over and over in one's mind ▪ to be stuck in one's craw

darle miedo a uno to make one feel afraid ▪ to scare one ▪ to feel afraid

darle mil vueltas a alguien to run rings around someone

darle muerte a alguien to kill someone ➤ El tanque disparó dándole muerte al fotógrafo. The tank fired, killing the photographer.

darle la noche a alguien to keep someone up all night ➤ El bebé se puso malo y nos dio la noche. The baby came down with something and kept us up all night.

darle nostalgia ▪ darle morriña **1.** to feel lonesome for someone **2.** to feel homesick for a place **3.** to feel nostalgia

darle pena a uno to make one sad ▪ to upset one

darle permiso a alguien *(Esp.)* to give someone time off ➤ Me han dado permiso en el trabajo. They gave me (some) time off at work.

darle permiso a alguien para hacer algo to give someone permission to do something

darle por ganador a alguien to expect someone to be the winner ▪ to call the election for someone

darle por perdido to give someone up ➤ Te había dado por perdido. I had given you up.

darle repelús a alguien to give someone the creeps

darle sueño a uno to make one sleepy ➤ El vino me ha dado sueño. The wine has made me sleepy.

darle tiempo to have time ➤ Iré si me da tiempo. I'll go if I have time. ➤ Iría si me diera tiempo. I'd go if I had time. ➤ Habría ido si me hubiera dado tiempo. I would have gone if I had had time. ➤ Me habría dado tiempo a terminar mis deberes si no hubiera ido al cine. I have would have had time to finish my homework if I hadn't gone to the movies.

darle todo igual a uno to be all the same to one ➤ Si todo te da igual, prefiero quedarme en casa y ver la tele. If it's all the same to you, I'd rather stay home and watch TV.

darle un ahogo to get short of breath ▪ to run out of breath ➤ *(Unamuno)* Le dio un ahogo y, respuesto de él, prosiguió. He got short of breath and, once recovered, went on.

darle un arrebato to fly into a rage ▪ to have a purple fit ➤ Le dio un arrebato. He flew into a rage. ▪ He had a purple fit.

darle un azote a alguien ~ 1. *(Esp.)* to spank someone ▪ to give someone a spanking **2.** *(Arg.)* to lash someone ▪ to whip someone

darle un consejo a alguien to give someone some advice

darle un palo por to give someone a spanking for ➤ Te voy a dar un palo por I'm going to give you a spanking for

darle un presupuesto a alguien to give someone a bid ▪ to give someone an estimate

darle un servicio a alguien to provide someone a service ▪ to furnish someone a service

darle un soponcio ~ 1. to faint ▪ to swoon **2.** to nearly die (of embarrassment or surprise)

darle un susto a uno to give one a scare ▪ to scare one ➤ Me dio un susto bastante grande. It scared me a lot. ▪ *(informal)* It scared the daylights out of me.

darle un susto de muerte a alguien to scare someone to death

darle un tiro a alguien *(se usa sólo en el pretérito)* to shoot someone ➤ Le dio un tiro en la pierna. He shot him in the leg.

darle un tirón de orejas to pull lightly someone's ear lobes *(Nota: Realizado en los cumpleaños en España y Argentina ▪ Done on birthdays in Spain and Argentina.)*

darle un vapuleo a alguien to give someone a beating ▪ to give someone a thrashing

darle un vuelco al corazón to make one's heart ache

darle una azotaina a alguien *(Esp.)* ▪ darle una palmada a alguien to give someone a spanking

darle una bofetada a alguien ■ abofetear a alguien ■ darle una cachetada a alguien ■ cruzarle la cara a alguien to slap someone

darle una buena impresión a alguien ■ causarle una buena impresión a alguien to make a good impression on someone ➤ Me dio una buena impresión. ■ Me causó una buena impresión. He made a good impression on me. ➤ Mi novia le dio una buena impresión a mi madre. ■ Mi novia le causó una buena impresión a mi madre. My girlfriend made a good impression on my mother.

darle una hostia a alguien *(subido de tono)* to beat the crap out of someone

darle una nota 1. to give a grade 2. *(música)* to hit a note ■ to give a note ➤ Le di a Cristina un sobresaliente por su trabajo. I gave Cristina an A on her paper. ➤ Dame un do. Hit a C. ■ Give me a C.

darle una orden a alguien para hacer algo ■ darle una orden a alguien para que haga algo ■ mandar a alguien a hacer algo to give someone an order to do something ■ to order someone to do something

darle una nalgada a alguien *(Méx.)* to give someone a spanking

darle una paliza a alguien to beat someone up ■ to beat up someone ➤ Le dieron una paliza. They beat him up.

darle una pasada de pintura to give it a coat of paint

darle una puntada to stitch

darle vergüenza a alguien *(coloquial)* ■ darle corte a alguien not to have the nerve ■ to be too shy ■ to be too embarrassed ➤ Me gustaría pedirle que venga al baile conmigo, pero me da corte. I'd like to ask her to go to the dance with me, but I don't have the nerve. ■ I'd like to ask her to the dance, but I don't have the nerve.

darle vuelta la cabeza for one's head to spin

darle vueltas a asuntos que se tienen pendientes to worry about upcoming events ■ to have a lot on one's mind

darle vueltas a la cabeza to dwell on something ■ to have something going around in one's head

darle vueltas a una idea to tinker with an idea ■ to turn an idea over in one's mind

darle vueltas al asunto to turn the matter over in one's mind

darlo por sabido to consider it common knowledge

darse a ■ relacionarse to associate with ➤ No se daba a nadie. He didn't associate with anybody.

darse a conocer to come out ■ to become public ■ to become known ➤ Se ha dado a conocer. It's already come out.

darse a entender to be given to understand ■ to have it on good authority

darse a la fuga ■ escapar 1. to flee 2. to get away ■ to escape ➤ Los atracadores se dieron a la fuga a pie. The assailants fled on foot. ➤ Los atacantes lograron darse a la fuga. The attackers managed to to get away. ■ The attackers managed to escape.

darse a la vida sin alguien to face life without someone

darse aire to fan oneself

darse aires de to think of oneself as ➤ Me gusta darme aires de... I like to think of myself as...

darse aires de grandeza to give oneself airs of grandeur

darse besos en las mejillas ■ darse un beso en la mejilla to kiss each other on the cheek

darse bombo to blow one's own horn ■ to blow one's own trumpet

darse casos de (for) there to be cases of ➤ *(informe)* Con frecuencia se dan casos de mujeres maltratadas... There are frequent cases of spousal abuse.

darse cita to meet up

darse coba de que... to be boastful about... ➤ Se daba mucha coba. She was very boastful.

darse con algo ■ correr hacia algo ■ estrellarse contra algo to hit something ■ to run into something

darse con el martillo en el dedo to hit one's finger with the hammer

darse con un canto en los dientes ■ considerarse con suerte ■ considerarse afortunado ■ considerarse con buena fortuna to consider oneself lucky ■ to count oneself lucky

darse contra las paredes to bang one's head against a wall ■ to bang one's head against a brick wall

darse cuenta de algo to realize something ■ to notice something ■ to pick up on something ■ to be able to tell (something) ■ to be able to tell it

darse cuenta de que... to realize that... ■ to recognize that... ■ notarse to be able to tell that... ■ to pick up on someone's... ➤ No puedo darme cuenta de que el inglés no es tu lengua materna. I can't tell that English is not your native language. ➤ Yo empezaba a darme cuenta de que... I was beginning to realize that... ➤ Leonardo da Vinci se dio cuenta de que, excepto durante el despegue, las aves aletean para propulsarse, no para mantenerse en el aire. Leonardo da Vinci recognized that, except during take-off, birds flap their wings for propulsion, not lift. ■ Leonardo da Vinci realized that, except during take-off, birds beat their wings for propulsion, not lift.

darse de alta to be released from the hospital ■ to leave the hospital ■ to get out of the hospital

darse de alta en un club ■ apuntarse a un club to join a club ■ to sign up as a member of a club

darse de alta en un servicio ■ contratar un servicio ■ apuntarse a un servicio to contract for a service ■ to sign up for a service

darse de alta en un servidor to sign up with a server

darse de alta en una academia ■ apuntarse a una academia to enroll in an academy

darse de alta en una empresa to join a firm ■ to join a company

darse de baja to go on sick leave

darse de baja de los estudios ■ abandonar los estudios ■ dejar los estudios to drop out of school

darse de baja del ejército ■ abandonar el ejército ■ salirse del ejército to be discharged from military service ■ to leave military service ■ to get out of the service

darse de baja de un abono to drop a subscription ■ to let a subscription expire ■ to cancel a subscription

darse de baja de un empleo to quit a job

darse de baja de un servicio to discontinue a service ■ to drop a service ■ to cancel a service ■ to have a service discontinued

darse de bofetadas to come to blows

darse de bofetadas una cosa con otra to clash

darse de bruces con algo to run headlong into something

darse de cabeza contra un muro to beat one's head against a wall

darse de cuerpo y alma a ■ entregarse en cuerpo y alma a to give oneself wholeheartedly to ■ to give oneself completely to

darse el lote con alguien ■ pegarse el lote con alguien to get it on with someone

darse el trabajo de to take it upon oneself to

darse en 1. to be held at 2. to be held in ➤ La recepción se dará en casa de los abuelos de la novia. The reception will be held at the home of the bride's grandparents. ■ The reception will be held at the bride's grandparents' house.

darse golpes de pecho to beat one's chest

darse importancia ■ darse tono ■ darse aires ■ afectar superioridad to give oneself airs

darse ínfulas to give oneself airs

darse la gran vida ■ vivir a lo grande to live it up

darse la mano ■ estrechar la mano to shake hands ➤ Nos dimos la mano. We shook hands. ➤ Nos dimos la mano para cerrar el trato. We shook on the deal. ➤ Le di la mano al presidente de España. I shook hands with the president of Spain.

darse la paliza haciendo algo ■ matarse a hacer algo to knock oneself out doing something ■ to work oneself to the bone doing something ➤ María se dio una paliza limpiando la casa. María knocked herself out cleaning the house. ■ María worked herself to the bone cleaning the house.

darse maña para hacer algo to be good at doing something ■ to be skillful at doing something

darse miedo to get scared

darse miedo de que... *(coloquial)* to be afraid that... ■ *(literario)* to be fearful that...

darse muerte ▪ suicidarse ▪ quitarse la vida to kill oneself ▪ to commit suicide ▪ to take one's (own) life

darse para to be right for ➤ *(noticia)* Sharon dice que se dan las condiciones para llegar a su "acuerdo histórico" con los palestinos. Sharon says conditions are right for coming to a historic agreement with the Palestinians.

darse por aludido ▪ cazar el diptongo **1.** to take the hint ▪ to get the hint ▪ to catch the hint **2.** *(en la negación)* to tune out ▪ not to internalize ▪ not to be engaged by ➤ Los hispanos dicen "¡allá penas!" para no darse por aludido de lo que la otra persona está diciendo. Hispanics say "allá penas" (it's not my problem) in order to tune out what the other person is saying.

darse por contento con algo to be satisfied with something

darse por derrotado to concede defeat

darse por hacer to be up to

darse por hacer algo ▪ decidir hacer algo to decide to do something

darse por satisfecho con to be satisfied with ➤ El senador no se daba por satisfecho con las garantías del candidato. The senator was not satisfied with the nominee's reassurances.

darse por vencido ▪ rendirse to give up

darse prisa to hurry ▪ to hurry up ➤ Tenemos que darnos prisa. We have to hurry. ▪ We've got to hurry. ➤ ¡Date prisa! Hurry! ▪ Hurry up!

darse tiempo para to leave oneself time for

darse tiempo para que... to leave oneself time to...

darse tono to put on airs

darse un aire to have an air about one ➤ Se da un aire. There's an air about him.

darse un aire a alguien ▪ parecerse to resemble someone ▪ to look like someone

darse un atracón de helado to pig out on ice-cream

darse un beso en la mejilla ▪ darse besos en las mejillas to kiss each other on the cheek

darse un capricho de ▪ capricharse to throw caution to the wind(s) and... ➤ Me di el capricho de un cucurucho de helado. ▪ Me di un capricho y me comí un cucurucho de helado. ▪ I threw caution to the wind and had an ice-cream cone.

darse un coscorrón to bump one's head ▪ to hit one's head ➤ Me he dado un coscorrón en el marco de la puerta. I bumped my head on the door frame. ▪ I hit my head on the door frame.

darse un empacho de ▪ darse un hartazgo de ▪ tener un empacho de **1.** to have one's fill of **2.** to overdose on

darse un garbeo ▪ darse una vuelta ▪ ir de paseo ▪ dar un paseo ▪ dar una vuelta ▪ darse un voltio **1.** *(en carro o motocicleta)* to go for a ride ▪ to go for a spin ▪ to go for a joy ride **2.** *(a pie)* to go for a stroll ▪ to go for a walk

darse un hartazgo de algo ▪ darse un empacho de algo to have one's fill of something

darse un hartón de llorar ▪ llorar a moco tendido to cry one's eyes out

darse un respiro ▪ darse una tregua to give oneself a breather ▪ to give oneself a break

darse un revolcón to have a roll in the hay

darse un rulo *(coloquial)* ▪ darse un paseo to go for a stroll

darse un tajo ▪ hacerse un tajo to cut oneself ➤ Me di un tajo en la pierna. I cut my leg. ▪ I cut myself in the leg

darse un testarazo ▪ darse un coscorrón to bump one's head

darse un voltio ▪ darse un garbeo ▪ darse una vuelta ▪ dar un paseo ▪ dar una vuelta ▪ ir de paseo **1.** *(en coche o motocicleta)* to go for a ride ▪ to go for a spin **2.** *(a pie)* to go for a stroll ▪ to go for a walk

darse una hostia *(jerga)* ▪ dañarse to hurt oneself ➤ Me he dado una hostia. ▪ Me he dañado. I hurt myself.

darse una palmada en la rodilla to slap one's knee

darse una testarada to bump one's head

darse una tregua ▪ darse un respiro to give oneself a break ▪ to give oneself a breather

dársela (con queso) a alguien ▪ pegársela con queso a alguien to pull the wool (over someone's eyes)

dársela (con queso) a su esposa to cheat on one's wife ▪ to be unfaithful to one's wife

dársela (con queso) a su marido to cheat on one's husband ▪ to be unfaithful to one's husband

dársela puerta ▪ salir a la francesa to fly the coop ▪ to quit without giving notice ▪ to leave without saying good-bye

dárselas de listo to act like a know-it-all ➤ Siempre se las da de listo. He always acts like a know-it-all.

dársele bien ▪ desenvolverse bien to be good at something ➤ Se le da muy bien. ▪ Se desenvuelve bien. He's good at it.

dársele fácil a uno to come easy for one ▪ to come easy to one ▪ to come without effort for one ➤ A Andrés se le dan fácil los idiomas. Languages come easy for Andrés. ▪ Languages come easy to Andrés. ▪ Languages come without effort for Andrés.

dárselo a alguien ▪ regalárselo a alguien to give it to someone

la **datación de acontecimientos antiguos** dating of ancient events

la **datación de objetos antiguos** dating of ancient objects ➤ La datación precisa de acontecimientos antiguos a menudo es posible cuando coinciden con eclipses y con la aparición de algún cometa. Precise dating of ancient historical events is often possible when they coincide with eclipses or appearances of comets. ➤ La datación con carbono es una manera de datar los fósiles y las formaciónes de roca. Carbon dating is a way of dating fossils and rock formations.

¡date cuenta! imagine that!

date cuenta de cómo... ▪ que te des cuenta de cómo... (just) be aware of how...

date cuenta de que... ▪ que te des cuenta de que... (just) be aware that...

¡date la vuelta! **1.** *(al estar de pie)* turn around! **2.** *(al estar tumbado)* turn over!

date la vuelta y no mires hacia atrás make up your mind, and don't look back

¡date prisa! hurry!

¡date prisa, que llegamos tarde! hurry or we'll be late

datos en crudo raw data

de acá para allá ▪ de aquí para allá to and fro

¡de acuerdo! okay! ▪ agreed!

estar **de acuerdo** to agree ▪ to be in agreement

de acuerdo con ▪ conforme ▪ según in agreement with ▪ in accord with ▪ in step together ▪ consistent with

estar **de acuerdo con** **1.** to agree with ▪ to be in agreement with **2.** aprobar to approve of

estar **de acuerdo en algo** to agree on something ▪ to be in agreement on something ▪ to be in agreement about something ▪ to concur with something ➤ Todos estuvimos de acuerdo en pedir una jarra de cerveza, excepto Silvia que quiso un vino blanco. We all agreed on a pitcher of beer, except Silvia, who wanted white wine.

estar **de acuerdo en (hacer) algo** to agree to do something ➤ Estamos de acuerdo en cenar fuera esta noche. We've agreed to go out for supper tonight.

estar **de acuerdo en que...** to be in agreement that...

de acuerdo mutuo by mutual agreement

de adelanto: con un año ~ a year early ▪ a year ahead of schedule

de adelanto: con un poco ~ a little early

de adulto ▪ de mayor ▪ cuando se es adulto ▪ como adulto as an adult ➤ Cuando estaba creciendo prefería los perros, pero de adulto, me han llegado a gustar los gatos por igual. ▪ Cuando estaba creciendo prefería los perros, pero de mayor, me han llegado a gustar los gatos por igual.

de ahí a la realidad *(coloquial)* let's get real

de ahí el nombre (and) hence the name ➤ El nombre del gato es Nat porque le falta parte de su cola, de ahí el nombre. The cat's name is Nat because his tail is not all there, (and) hence the name.

de ahí en adelante **1.** desde allí en adelante from there on **2.** desde entonces en adelante from that point on ▪ from then on

de ahí no salir to get no further than that ➤ De ahí no salí. I got no further than that.

de ahí que hence

de ahora en adelante ▪ desde este momento en adelante ▪ en lo sucesivo from now on

de al lado next door ▪ next door to it ▪ next to it ➤ La casa de al lado es de ladrillo. The house next door to it is brick. ▪ The house next to it is brick.

de alcance global of global proportions ■ global in reach
de algo te conozco ■ te conozco de algo I know you from somewhere
ser **de alguien** ■ pertenecer a alguien ■ *(derecho)* ■ corresponderle a uno to belong to someone
de alguna forma somehow ■ in some way
de alguna importancia ■ de bastante importancia of considerable importance
de alguna manera somehow ■ (in) some way
de alguna manera u otra (in) some way or other ■ somehow or other
de allí para allá ■ de detrás a delante back and forth
de alquiler for rent
ser **de alterne** to be of easy virtue
de alto: tener *x* metros ~ to be *x* meters high ➤ Las piedras de Stonehenge en Inglaterra tienen más de cinco metros de alto y dos y medio de ancho. The stones at Stonehenge in England are more than five meters high and two-and-a-half wide.
de alto caché highly paid ➤ Actriz de alto caché Highly paid actress ➤ Torero de alto caché Highly paid bullfighter
de alto nivel: conversaciones ~ high-level talks
de alto rango: funcionario ~ high-ranking official
¡de amigo nada! friends nothing!
de ancho: tener *x* metros ~ to be *x* meters wide ➤ Las piedras de Stonehenge en Inglaterra tienen más de cinco metros de alto y dos y medio de ancho. The stones at Stonehenge in England are more than five meters high and two-and-a-half wide.
de andar por casa ■ para andar por casa to wear around the house ■ for wearing around the house
de antemano ■ con tiempo beforehand
de antiguo ■ desde antiguo ■ desde que el mundo es mundo from time immemorial
de añadidura ■ por añadidura in addition
de año en año from year to year
de aquí al domingo ■ entre hoy y el domingo between now and Sunday
de aquilatada lealtad of proven loyalty
ser **de armas tomar** ■ ser de llevar armas to be determined ■ to be someone to be reckoned with
de arriba a abajo ■ de arriba abajo from top to bottom ➤ Limpiamos esta cocina de arriba abajo. We cleaned this kitchen from top to bottom.
de arriba abajo ■ de arriba a abajo from top to bottom
de arriba abajo: mirar a alguien ■ mirar a alguien de hito en hito to look someone up and down
de arriba abajo: registrar a alguien to search someone
de arriba abajo: registrar algo to search something from top to bottom
de arribada: entrar to put into port
de aspecto mediterraneo with a Mediterranean look
de aspecto normal average looking
de aspecto sencillo plain-looking
de aúpa: ser un problema ~ *(Esp., coloquial)* ■ ser un problema muy grande ■ ser un problemón to be a big problem
de aúpa: ser una persona ~ *(Esp., coloquial)* ■ ser una persona macanuda ■ ser una persona estupenda to be a great person ■ to be awesome
de ayer a hoy overnight
ser **de ayuda** to be of help
estar **de baja** to be on sick leave
de baja inversión low-budget
de bajo costo low-cost
de bajo presupuesto: película ~ low-budget film ■ low-budget movie
de balde ■ gratis free of charge
¿de barril o de botella? *(Esp.)* ■ ¿de sifón o de botella? draft or bottle?
de bastante importancia ■ de alguna importancia of considerable importance
de batalla: zapatos ~ everyday shoes
de bien lejos from a good distance ■ from a safe distance
de bigote(s) *(Esp.)* ■ estupendo fantastic ■ wonderful ■ great
de bolsillo pocket-size ■ pocket
de boquilla: hablar ~ to talk out of both sides of one's mouth
estar **de botar** to be ready to throw out ■ to be ready throw away
estar **de bote en bote** to be packed ■ to be jam packed ■ to be crowded ■ to be full of people
de bote y voleo instantly
estar **de brazos cruzados** ■ cruzarse de brazos 1. to have one's arms crossed 2. to sit around and do nothing ■ to just sit there
de broma ■ en broma as a joke ■ jokingly
de bruces face down ■ headlong
de bruces: caerse ~ ■ caer de bruces to fall face down
estar **de buen año** to be chubby ■ to have a spare tire
estar **de buen café** to be in a good mood ■ to be in a good humor
ser **de buen conformar** to be easy (to please) ■ to be easy to be around
ser **de buen contento** ■ ser complaciente to be easy to please
de buen grado willingly
estar **de buen humor** to be in a good mood ■ to be in a good humor
ser **de buen nacer** ■ ser de buen nacimiento ■ ser bien nacido to be well born
ser **de buen saque** to have a good appetite ■ to eat a lot
de buen talante willingly ■ good humoredly
estar **de buen talante** to be in a good mood ■ to be in a good humor
ser **de buen tono** to be well bred ■ to be elegant ■ to be (socially) refined
de buen ver good-looking
ser **de buena factura** to be well made
de buena fe: actuar ~ ■ obrar de buena fe to act in good faith
de buena hechura: un traje well-made suit
de buenas a primeras ■ de repente ■ a simple vista ■ a las primeras de cambio ■ sin previo aviso ■ bruscamente right off the bat ■ all at once ■ all of a sudden ■ at first sight ■ point blank
de buenas intenciones está el infierno lleno the road to hell is paved with good intentions
de buenas maneras politely
estar **de buten** to be fantastic ■ to be terrific
de cabo a rabo from one end to the other ■ from head to tail
estar **de cachondeo** to be joking around
de cada out of ➤ Nueve de cada diez Nine out of ten
estar **de caerse para atrás** 1. to be in awe ■ to stand in awe 2. to be drunk
ser **de cajón** to be a matter of course ■ to go without saying
ser **de cal y canto** to be tough ■ to be strong ■ to be firm
estar **de camino** ■ estar en camino to be on the way ■ to be on one's way
estar **de capa caída** ■ andar de capa caída 1. to be crestfallen 2. to be in decline ■ to have seen better days
ser **de capa y espada** to be cloak and dagger
de caparazón dura thick-skinned
de cara a facing
de cara al viento with the wind in one's face
de carga: mozo ~ errand boy
de carnes prietas ■ de carnes duras having a tight, firm body ■ firm-bodied ■ beefy
de casa en casa: ir ~ to go from house to house
de categoría: tener un genio ~ *(Esp.)* to have a terrible temper
de categoría: hotel ~ fashionable hotel
de categoría: político ~ ■ político de no te menees ■ político de agárrate y no te menees ■ pólitico de caerse de culo big-time politician
de categoría: restaurante ~ fashionable restaurant
estar **de caza** to be hunting
de cena for supper ➤ ¿Qué tenemos de cena? What are we having for supper? ■ What's for supper?
de cerca closely
de cero: partir ~ to start from scratch

estar **de cháchara** to be talking away

de chacota: decir algo ~ ■ decir algo en broma to say something in jest ■ to say something as a joke

estar **de chuparse los dedos** to be finger-licking good ■ to be scrumptuous

estar **de cojones** *(subido de tono)* to be fucking great

de color ■ negro **1.** of color ■ black **2.** in color ➤ Thurgood Marshall fue el primer juez de color en el Tribunal Supremo estadounidense. Thurgood Marshall was the first justice of color appointed to the U.S. Supreme Court. ■ Thurgood Marshall was the first black justice appointed to the U.S. Supreme Court. ➤ El pico del ave es (de color) rojo. The beak of the bird is red (in color). ■ The bird's beak in red (in color).

de color cretino with a sallow complexion ■ with a sickly complexion

estar **de compras** to be out shopping ➤ Ella está de compras. She's out shopping.

de compras: ir ~ to go shopping ➤ Ha ido de compras. *(él)* He's gone shopping. ■ *(ella)* She's gone shopping.

de confianza: amigo ~ close friend

de confianza: puesto ~ responsible position ■ responsible post

de confianza: reunión ~ 1. gathering of friends **2.** gathering of family

ser **de confianza** to be in one's confidence ■ to be someone in whom one can trust

de conjunto overall

estar **de coña** to be joking ➤ ¡Estás de coña! You're joking!

de corazón 1. at heart **2.** with all one's heart ➤ Ella es joven de corazón. She's young at heart. ➤ Es un músico de corazón. He's a musician at heart.

de corrido: hacerlo ~ to do it from memory ■ to do it off the top of one's head ➤ Deja, deja, que yo lo hago de corrido. Here let me do it. I can do it off the top of my head.

de corrido: sabérselo ~ to know it by heart

de corte autoritario y patriarcal of an authoritarian and patriarchal stripe ➤ *(noticia)* La reforma política de Vladimir Putin, de corte autoritario y patriarcal... The political reform of Vladimir Putin, of an authoritarian and patriarchal stripe...

ser **de cosecha propia** to be one's own brain child ■ to be original ■ to come from one's own imagination ■ to be from one's own imagination

ser **de costumbres fijas** to have regular habits ■ to be a person of regular habits ➤ El filósofo Immanuel Kant era de costumbres fijas. The philosopher Immanuel Kant was a man of regular habits.

de cuenta y riesgo: hacer algo ~ ■ por cuenta y riesgo ■ a riesgo suyo to do something at one's own risk

estar **de cuerpo presente** to lie in state

de cuerpo y alma wholeheartedly ■ completely

ser **de cuidado** to be someone to be wary of

estar **de culo** *(Esp., ligeramente subido de tono)* to be the pits ■ to be lousy

de culo: ir ~ *(Esp., ligeramente subido de tono)* ■ ir mal to go badly ■ not to go right ■ not to go well

de culo: aparcar ~ *(coloquial)* ■ estacionar en batería marcha atrás to back into a parking place ■ to park backwards ■ to park facing outwards

de dentro ■ desde dentro from inside

ser **de derechas** right of center (politically) ➤ Es un poco de derechas. He's a little right of center.

de derecha a izquierda 1. from right to left **2.** *(al girar un destornillador)* en el sentido contrario de las agujas del reloj counterclockwise

de detrás a delante back and forth

de día ■ durante el día by day ■ during the day

de día en día ■ día a día day by day ■ from day to day

de diario: ropa ~ casual clothes ■ everyday clothes

de diario: vajilla ~ everyday china ■ everyday dishes

ser **de difícil acceso 1.** *(físicamente)* to be difficult to get to ■ to be difficult to reach **2.** *(emocionalmente)* to be difficult to reach ➤ Es un lugar de difícil acceso. It's a place that's very difficult to reach. ■ It's a place that's very difficult to get to. ➤ El joven alienado fue de difícil acceso. The alientated youth was difficult to reach.

de distinta manera: hacer algo ~ ■ hacer algo de otra forma ■ hacer algo de otro modo to do something differently

de diversa consideración of varying degree(s) ■ varying in seriousness ➤ Perdió la vida un hombre de cuarenta años y otras once personas recibieron heridas de diversa consideración. A forty-year-old man lost his life and eleven others suffered injuries of varying degrees.

¿de dónde lo sacaste? ■ ¿dónde lo conseguiste? ■ ¿de dónde lo tienes? where did you get it? ■ where'd you get it?

¿de dónde lo tienes? ■ ¿dónde lo conseguiste? ■ ¿de dónde lo sacaste? where did you get it? ■ where'd you get it?

de donde no hay no se puede sacar you can't squeeze blood out of a turnip

¿de dónde sacaste esa idea? where did you get that idea?

¿de dónde salió? where did it come from?

¿de dónde vienes? ■ ¿dónde has estado? where have you been?

de dos en dos two by two ■ by twos

de dos en dos: subir corriendo los escalones ~ to run up the steps two at a time

ser **de dos haces** to be two-faced

estar **de echar a correr** ■ estar para echar a correr to make one just want to get the hell out of there

estar **de encargo** ■ estar embarazada to be pregnant

estar **de enhorabuena** to be congratulated ➤ Estás de enhorabuena. You're to be congratulated.

de entonces at that age ➤ Lo más interesante del Einstein de entonces... The most interesting thing about Einstein at that age...

de entonces acá since then

de entonces acá ya ha llovido algo a lot of water has passed under the bridge since then

de entonces en adelante 1. from then on **2.** *(formal)* thenceforward

de entrada 1. for openers ■ to start with **2.** *(en un restaurante)* as an entree ■ for an entrée **3.** *(puesto de trabajo)* entry level

de esa envergadura of that magnitude

de esa índole of that kind ■ of that nature ■ like those

de esa manera 1. in that way ■ so that ■ so **2.** by doing so ➤ Incluso si de esa manera... Even if by doing so...

de eso nada ■ nanai de nanai ■ que no nothin' doin' ■ no way ■ forget that

estar **de espalda** to be facing away from someone ■ to have one's back to someone

de espaldas from behind ■ with one's back to something ■ with one's back to someone

de espaldas a with one's back to

estar **de esquina** to sit an angle to the corner ■ to be at an angle to the corner

de esta agua no beberé I don't want anything to do with it ■ I want nothing to do with it ■ I won't have anything to do with it ■ I'll have nothing to do with it

de esta forma in this way

de esta índole of this kind ■ of this nature ■ like these

de esta manera in this way ■ in this manner

de esta no salimos ■ no salimos de esta we're not going to get out of this alive

de estarlo if one is

de este modo in this way

estar **de etiqueta** to be dressed in formal attire

estar **de exámenes** to be in the middle of exams ■ to be taking exams

de extranjis *(Esp., literario)* ■ de hurtadillas secretly ■ on the sly

ser **de fiar** to be trustworthy ■ to be reliable

estar **de fiesta** to be partying

estar **de florero** ■ no hacer nada to be sitting there like a bump on a log ■ to be doing nothing

de fogueo: bala ~ blank (bullet)

de fondo in the background ➤ De fondo se escuchaba... You could hear in the background...

de forma que so that

de forma puntual ■ a tiempo punctually ■ on time ➤ Siempre llega de forma puntual. ■ Siempre llega a tiempo. He always arrives punctually. ■ He always arrives on time.

de forma tajante: negar ~ to deny categorically
de forma tan capciosa in such a deceiving way
de frente ▪ de cara head-on
de gabinete closet ➤ Debajo de la fachada del clasisista latía el corazón de un romántico de gabinete. Beneath the classicist facade beat the heart of a closet romantic.
estar **de gira** to be on tour
de gira: ir ~ to go on tour
de gira por on a tour of
de golpe ▪ de repente ▪ de golpe y porrazo all of a sudden ▪ in one whack ▪ suddenly ➤ Parece que se llenó de golpe. It looks like you got busy all of a sudden.
de golpe y porrazo without warning ▪ just like that
de gorra ▪ de balde ▪ gratis free (of charge)
de gran estatura: hombre ~ very tall man
de gran talla of great stature
de guante blanco *(delito)* nonviolent
estar **de guardia** 1. to be on duty 2. *(médico)* to be on call ➤ ¿Quién está de guardia? Who's on duty? ▪ Who's on call?
de haberlo hecho ▪ si lo hubiera hecho ▪ si lo hubiese hecho 1. *(yo)* if I had done it ▪ had I done it 2. *(él)* if he had done it ▪ had he done it 3. *(ella)* if she had done it ▪ had she done it
de haberlo leído ▪ si lo hubiera leído ▪ si lo hubiese leído *(yo)* if I had read it ▪ had I read it *(él)* if he had read it ▪ had he read it *(ella)* if she had read it ▪ had she read it ➤ De haber leído Kant el *Tratado de la naturaleza humana de Hume...* If Kant had read Hume's *Treatise on Human Nature...* ▪ Had Kant read Hume's *Treatise on Human Nature...*
de haberlo sabido ▪ si lo hubiera sabido ▪ si lo hubiese sabido *(yo)* if I had known (it) ▪ had I known (it) ▪ *(él)* if he had known (it) ▪ had he known (it) ▪ *(ella)* if she had known (it) ▪ had she known (it) ➤ De haberlo sabido, habríamos seguido de movido. If we had known it, we would have kept moving. ▪ Had we known it, we would have kept moving.
de haberme dado tiempo ▪ de haber tenido tiempo ▪ si me hubiera dado tiempo ▪ si hubiera tenido tiempo ▪ si me hubiese dado tiempo ▪ si hubiese tenido tiempo had I had time ▪ if I had had time
de habla española ▪ hispanoparlante ▪ hispanohablante Spanish-speaking
de habla inglesa ▪ angloparlante ▪ anglohablante English-speaking
de hecho ▪ en efecto in fact ▪ as a matter of fact ▪ *(derecho)* de facto
de hecho: inquilino ~ de facto tenant ▪ tenant who is not on the lease
de hecho: matrimonio ~ common-law marriage
de hecho: pareja ~ de facto couple
de hecho y de derecho full-fledged
de hierro made of iron
de hierro: tener una salud ~ to be in robust health
de higos a brevas ▪ de pascuas a ramos ▪ una vez cada muerte de obispo once in a blue moon
de hito en hito: mirar a alguien ~ ▪ mirar a alguien de arriba abajo to look someone up and down
estar **de hombros caídos** ▪ tener los hombros caídos ▪ estar de brazos cruzados to be stooped (over) ▪ to stand stoop shouldered
de hoy today ➤ En los Estados Unidos de hoy... In the United States today...
de hoy a mañana any time now ▪ any day now
de hoy en adelante from today on
de hoy en día ▪ de la actualidad today's
de hoy en una semana ▪ a una semana de hoy a week from today ➤ Los exámenes son de hoy en una semana. Exams are a week from today.
de hoy para mañana: tener algo ~ to have something for tomorrow ▪ to have something here tomorrow ▪ to have something ready tomorrow ➤ Lo tendremos de hoy para mañana. We'll have it for you tomorrow. ▪ It'll be here tomorrow. ▪ It'll be ready tomorrow.
estar **de humor (para hacer algo)** ▪ estar en vena (para hacer algo) to be in the mood to do something ➤ No estoy de humor. I'm not in the mood.
de hurtadillas secretly ▪ on the sly ▪ stealthily
de ida y vuelta round-trip
de ida y vuelta: billete ~ round-trip ticket
de igual a igual: hablar a alguien ~ ▪ hablar con alguien de igual a igual to talk as equals
de igual a igual: tratar a alguien ~ to treat someone as an equal
de igual a igual: ver a alguien ~ to see someone as an equal ▪ to regard someone as an equal
de igual manera ▪ asimismo in the same way ▪ likewise ▪ similarly
de importancia of importance
estar **de impresión** to be really good looking ▪ to be dy-no-mite
ser **de impresión** to be impressive
de improviso ▪ sin previo aviso ▪ de repente ▪ sin mediar palabra unexpectedly ▪ off hand ▪ out of the blue
de improviso: llegar ~ to arrive unexpectedly ▪ to call on someone unexpectedly
de incógnito: ir ~ to go under cover ▪ to go incognito
estar **de infarto** to be heart stopping ➤ *(titular)* Nascar de infarto en Darlington. Heart-stopping Nascar race in Darlington. ➤ La carrera Nascar estuvo de infarto cuando un coche dio vueltas de campana. The Nascar race was heart stopping when a car rolled repeatedly.
ser **de infarto** to be heart stopping
de inicio juvenil: leucemia ~ early onset leukemia
de inmediato ▪ al momento immediately ▪ instantly
de inmediato para...: actuar ~ to act immediately to...
de íntima vinculación a with close ties to
ser **de izquierda(s)** left of center politically ▪ left of center ▪ on the left ▪ of the left ▪ to have leftist tendencies ➤ María es un poco de izquierdas. Maria is a little left of center. ▪ Maria has leftist tendencies.
estar **de juerga** to be out on the town
ser **de juzgado de guardia** to be an outrage
ser **de la acera de enfrente** ▪ ser de la otra acera ▪ estar perdiendo aceite ▪ ser marcha atrás ▪ ser mozo sin bandeja to be gay
de la actualidad ▪ de hoy en día today's
de la Ceca a la Meca ▪ de Herodes a Pilatos from pillar to post ➤ Me tienen de la Ceca a la Meca. ▪ Me tienen de Herodes a Pilatos. They have me running from pillar to post.
ser **de la competencia de uno** to have authority (in a matter) ▪ to be one's responsibility ▪ to be within one's jurisdiction ▪ to be within one's province ➤ No es de mi competencia. I have no authority in the matter. ▪ It's not my responsibility ▪ It's not within my jurisdiction ▪ It's not within my province.
de la derecha on the right ▪ to the right ➤ La ilustración a la derecha. The illustration on the right. ▪ The illustration to the right.
de la época de from the time of ➤ Esta mesa es de la época de Felipe III (tercero). This table is from the time of Felipe III (the third).
de la izquierda on the left ▪ to the left ➤ La ilustración de la izquierda. The illustration on the left. ▪ The illustration to the left.
de la izquierda a la derecha ▪ en el sentido de las agujas del reloj from left to right ▪ clockwise
de la mano con alguien: ir ~ ▪ andar de la mano con alguien to go hand in hand with someone
de la mañana: a la(s) *x* ~ at *x* (o'clock) in the morning ➤ A la una de la mañana At one (o'clock) in the morning ➤ A las seis de la mañana At six (o'clock) in the morning ➤ El vuelo llega a Madrid a las ocho de la mañana. The flight arrives in Madrid at eight in the morning.
ser **de la misma calaña** *(peyorativo)* to be of the same stripe ▪ to be of the same ilk
ser **de la misma escuela** ▪ ser cortado con el mismo patrón que alguien ▪ ser lobos de la misma camada to be cut from the same cloth ▪ to be birds of a feather
ser **de la misma laya** to be of the same stripe ▪ to be of the same ilk
ser **de la misma quinta** to be about the same age

de la nada ■ caído del cielo ■ llovido del cielo from nowhere ■ out of nowhere ■ out of the blue ➤ Salío de la nada y ganó la elección. He came from nowhere to win the election.

de la noche at night ➤ (Él) llegó a las diez de la noche. He arrived at ten at night.

de la noche a la mañana: bailar ~ ■ bailar toda la noche to dance all night

de la noche a la mañana: cambiar to change overnight ➤ Ella cambió de la noche a la mañana. She changed overnight.

de la noche a la mañana: hacer algo ~ to do something overnight ■ to do something by tomorrow ■ to get something done by tomorrow

ser **de la otra acera** ■ ser de la acera de enfrente ■ estar perdiendo aceite ■ ser marcha atrás ■ ser mozo sin bandeja to be gay

de la peor especie of the worst stripe ➤ Es un político de la peor especie. He's a politican of the worst stripe.

de la tarde in the afternoon ■ p.m. ➤ A las tres de la tarde At three (o'clock) in the afternoon ■ At 3 p.m.

ser **de la virgen del puño** ■ ser amarrete ■ ser agarrado al mango to be a tightwad ■ to be tighter than a tick

de lado ■ de soslayo ■ al soslayo ■ de refilón ■ de canto sideways ■ edgewise ➤ Cada décimo ladrillo fue colocado de lado. Every tenth brick was laid sideways.

de lado a lado: andar ~ ■ ir de lado a lado to go (running) all over the place

de lado a lado: bailar to dance side by side

de lance: librería ~ secondhand bookstore

de larga duración: relación ~ long-term relationship

de largo long ■ in length

de las personas consultadas of those surveyed

de las suyas: rabieta ~ 1. *(de él)* one of his tantrums **2.** *(de ella)* one of her tantrums ➤ Nuestra amiga hizo una paella famosa de las suyas. Our friend made one of her famous paellas. ➤ *(noticia)* John McEnroe fingió una rabieta de las suyas. John McEnroe feigned one of his tantrums.

de lava y pon ■ de quita y pon wash and wear ➤ Una camisa de lava y pon A wash and wear shirt

de lejos ■ desde lejos from a distance

de lleno: dar to hit someone directly ■ to hit square ■ to hit right smack ➤ El sol me daba de lleno en los ojos. The sun was hitting me right in the eyes. ■ The sun was hitting me directly in my eyes. ➤ El pastel le dio de lleno en la cara. The pie hit him square in the face ■ The pie hit him right smack in the face.

de lleno a algo: dedicarse ~ to dedicate oneself completely to something ■ to commit oneself to something

de lleno: negar algo ~ to deny something flatly

de lo contrario otherwise ■ or else

ser **de lo más impreciso** ■ no tener nada que ver to be way off ■ to be very incorrect ➤ La medición de Cassini de la distancia entre el Sol y la Tierra en 1677 fue de lo más impreciso, aunque su método era correcto. Cassini's measurement of the Sun's distance from the Earth in 1677 was way off, although his method was correct.

ser **de lo más ocurrente (donde los haya)** ■ ser de lo más gracioso (donde los haya) ■ ser ocurrente donde los haya ■ ser gracioso donde los haya to be as witty as they come ■ to be as witty as can be

ser **de lo más gracioso (donde los haya)** ■ ser de lo más ocurrente (donde los haya) ■ ser ocurrente donde los haya ■ ser gracioso donde los haya to be as witty as they come ■ to be as witty as can be

de lo que than ➤ El senador era más ético de lo que la prensa le daba crédito. The senator was more ethical than the press gave him credit for being. ➤ Más lentamente de lo que me gustaría... Slower than I would like... ■ More slowly than I would like...

de lo que estoy seguro es de que what I'm sure of is that

de lo que fue en realidad than it really was

de lo que fui a la misma edad than I was at that age ■ than I was at the same age

de lo que me doy cuenta es... what I realize is...

de lo que no estoy seguro es de que... what I'm not sure of is... ➤ De lo que no estoy seguro es de que me llegue la pintura. What I'm not sure of is whether I have enough paint.

ser **de lo que no hay** to be the limit ■ to be too much ■ to take the cake

de lo que piensas than you think

de lo que se pensaba than previously thought ■ than previously believed

de lo que se pensaría than one would think ■ than you would think

de lo que va a llegar of what is coming ➤ Parece haberse resignado a la idea de lo que va a llegar. He seems to have resigned himself to the idea of what is coming.

ser **de locos** to be mind-boggling

de los consultados ■ de las personas consultadas of those consulted

de los cuarenta para arriba no te mojes la barriga you're too old for that sort of thing

de los encuestados of those surveyed ■ de las personas encuestadas ➤ El sesenta por ciento de los encuestados... Sixty percent of those surveyed...

ser **de los grandes** to be a big one ➤ Esa paellera es de las grandes. That paella pan is a big one.

de los haya as they come

ser **de los nuestros** to be on our side ➤ Es de los nuestros. He's on our side.

ser **de los pagos de** *(Arg.)* ■ de la misma región que to be from the same area as ■ to be from the same region as ➤ Ariel es de los pagos de Iván. Ariel is from the same area as (is) Iván. ■ Ariel is from the same region as Iván.

ser **de los pocos que 1.** *(refiriéndose a una persona)* to be one of the few who **2.** *(refiriéndose a una cosa)* to be one of the few that

ser **de los que...** to be one of these people who... ■ to be one of those who... ➤ Soy de los que... I'm one of these people who...

de los suyos 1. *(de él)* one of his **2.** *(de ella)* one of hers

de lugar en lugar: ir ~ to go from place to place

de lujo: salir ~ ■ salir muy bien **1.** to turn out great ■ to turn out really well ■ to turn out super deluxe **2.** uncalled-for ➤ La paella salió de lujo. The paella came out super. ■ The paella turned out super.

estar **de luna de miel 1.** *(singular)* to be on one's honeymoon **2.** *(plural)* to be on ones' honeymoon

de lunes a viernes ■ los días laborales Monday through Friday ■ on weekdays

estar **de luto** to be in mourning

de madera made of wood ■ wooden

de madre on one's mother's side (of the family)

de madrugada very early in the morning ■ in the early morning hours ■ in the early hours of the morning ■ in the wee hours

ser **de mal contento** to be hard to please ■ to be difficult to please

de mal efecto in bad taste ■ in poor taste

de mal en peor: ir ~ ■ ir de Guatemala en Guatepeor to go from bad to worse

estar **de mal humor** ■ tener humor de perros to be in a bad mood ■ to be in a foul mood ■ to be in a bad humor

de mal talante: hacer algo to do something unwillingly

estar **de mal talante** to be in a bad humor ■ to be in a bad mood

ser **de mal tono** to be ill bred

de mal vivir: ser una persona ~ ■ ser una persona de mala vida to be a low-life

ser **de mala calaña** to be a shady character

de mala fe out of malice ■ on purpose ■ deliberately ■ in bad faith

estar **de mala gana** not to want to help

de mala gana: hacer algo ~ to do something unwillingly

estar **de mala leche** to be mad ■ to be angry

de mala manera badly

estar **de mala uva** ■ estar de mal humor to be in a bad mood ■ to be in a foul mood

de mala vida: ser una persona ~ ■ ser una persona de mal vivir to be a low-life

estar **de malas** to be in a bad mood

de malas maneras impolitely

de mandato ▪ en el cargo in office ➤ Su último día de mandato His last day in office

de manera expedita in an expeditious manner ▪ expeditiously

de manera extraoficial unofficially

de manera ineluctable: deteriorarse ~ ▪ deteriorarse de manera irreversible to deteriorate irreversibly ➤ Su salud continúa deteriorándose de manera ineluctable. His health continues to deteriorate irreversibly.

de manera inesperada unexpectedly

de manera que... ▪ para que... so that...

de maravilla: irle ~ to be going great (for one) ▪ (for) things to be going great for one ➤ Nos va de maravilla. Things are going great for us.

de materia prima a hecho from raw materials to finished

estar **de maruja** *(Esp., coloquial)* ▪ hacer de maruja to be cleaning the house

de matute: proceder ~ ▪ proceder de incógnito to keep a low profile ▪ to proceed incognito

de mayor 1. cuando crezca uno when one grows up 2. cuando creció uno when one grew up 3. de adulto as an adult ➤ Ella soñaba que de mayor escribiría un libro sobre su infancia. She used to dream that when she grew up, she would write a book about her childhood. ➤ ¿Qué quieres ser de mayor? What do you want to be when you grow up? ➤ Cuando estaba creciendo prefería los perros, pero de mayor, me han llegado a gustar los gatos por igual. ▪ Cuando estaba creciendo prefería los perros, pero de adulto, me han llegado a gustar los gatos por igual.

de media on (the) average

de media almendra parabola-shaped

de mediana edad middle-aged

de medio pelo of no social standing

de memoria by heart ▪ from memory

de memoria: aprender ~ to learn by heart ▪ to memorize

de menos: darle a alguien *x* ~ to short someone *x* ▪ to be *x* short (of a quantity) ▪ to be short *x* ▪ to be missing *x* ➤ Me dieron uno de menos. They shorted me one. ▪ I'm one short. ▪ I'm short one. ▪ I'm missing one. ▪ One is missing. ▪ They gave me one too few. ➤ Un poco de menos A little short (of what I should have been given) ▪ A little less (than what I should have been given)

de mentira: (el) billete ▪ billete de pega play money

de mentira: decir algo ~ to say something in jest

ser **de mentira** to be only joking

de mentirijillas: hacer algo ▪ hacer algo en plan de broma ▪ hacer algo en broma to do something as a joke

de mesa: vino ~ table wine

de mi parte from me ▪ for my part ▪ on my part ▪ for me ▪ on my behalf

estar **de mi parte** to be on my side

estar **de miedo** to be great

de mil amores: llevarse ~ to get along famously ▪ to get along great

de milagro by some miracle ▪ miraculously

estar **de moda** 1. *(ropa)*to be in style ▪ to be in fashion 2. *(manía, furor)* to be a fad ▪ to be the rage ➤ Lo que es moda no incomoda. If it's in style, people will wear it whether it looks good on them or not.

de modo llamativo so as to draw attention ▪ in such a way as to draw attention ▪ *(pasado)* in a way that drew attention

de modo que ▪ de tal manera que so that ▪ so

de momento ▪ en el momento ▪ de pronto at the moment ▪ for the moment ▪ at this juncture *(Nota: en un proceso largo)* ➤ De momento no puedo pensarlo. ▪ No puedo pensarlo de momento. I can't think of it at the moment.

estar **de mona** ▪ estar guapa to be beautiful ▪ to be good-looking ➤ La novia estaba de mona. The bride was beautiful.

estar **de morros con alguien** to be on the outs with someone ▪ to have had a falling out with someone

de mostrador ▪ sin receta over the counter ▪ without a prescription

de mote ▪ para abreviar for short

de motu propio ▪ por su propia cuenta on one's own initiative ▪ of one's own accord ▪ voluntarily

de muchas millas a la redonda for miles around ▪ for miles in every direction

ser **de mucho decir y luego nada** ▪ ser de mucho hablar y poco actuar ▪ ser un(a) cantamañanas ▪ tanto hablar, seca la boca ▪ mucho lirili y poco lerele to be all talk and no action

ser **de mucho hablar y poco actuar** ▪ ser de mucho decir y luego nada ▪ ser un(a) cantamañanas ▪ tanto hablar, seca la boca ▪ mucho lirili y poco lerele to be all talk and no action

de mucho nervio spirited

de mucho pote *(Valle-Inclán)* very special ▪ very important

de muchos bemoles full of difficulties ▪ tricky

de muchos kilómetros a la redonda for kilometers around ▪ for kilometers in every direction

estar **de mudanza** to be in the process of moving

de muerte deadly ▪ deathly

de nacimiento from birth

de natural by nature

de ninguna manera ▪ de ningún modo by no means

de niño(-a) as a child ▪ when I was little ▪ when I was a child

de no haber sido por ▪ si no hubiera sido por ▪ si no llega a ser por if it had not been for ▪ had it not been for ▪ if it hadn't been for ➤ La víctima del derrumbe habría muerto de no haber sido por los servicios de emergencia. ▪ La víctima del derrumbe habría muerto si no hubiera sido por el personal de primeros auxilios. ▪ La víctima del derrumbe podría haber muerto si no llega a ser por los servicios de emergencia. The victim of the collapse would have died had it not been for the paramedics. ▪ The victim of the collapse would have died if it had not been for the paramedics.

de no ser así... 1. if it isn't... ▪ if it's not... 2. *(yo)* if I'm not 3. *(yo)* if I don't

de no ser lo que soy if I weren't what I am

de no ser por ti ▪ si no fuera por ti if it weren't for you ▪ had it not been for you ▪ if it had not been for you ▪ if it hadn't been for you

de no ser porque... if it were not for the fact that... ▪ if it weren't for the fact that... ▪ were it not for the fact that...

de no te menees ▪ de agárrate y no te menees ▪ de caerse de culo ▪ de categoría big-time ➤ Político de no te menees ▪ Político de agárrate y no te menees ▪ Político de caerse de culo ▪ Político de categoría Big-time politician

de noche 1. por la noche at night ▪ by night 2. durante la noche during the night ➤ De noche siempre leemos. ▪ Por la noche siempre leemos. At night we always read. ➤ De noche apagamos la calefacción. At night we turn off the heat. ▪ During the night we turn off the heat.

de nombre by name

de nota well known ▪ noted

estar **de nuestra parte** to be on our side

de nuevo ▪ otra vez again

de nuevo cuño: empleo newly created job ▪ newly created occupation

de nuevo cuño: expresión newly coined expression ▪ new coinage

de nuevo cuño: moda latest style ▪ latest fashion

de ocultis *(culto, literario)* ▪ a solapo on the sly

estar **de oferta** to be on sale ▪ to be on special

de órdago terrific ▪ fantastic

de órdago: baza ~ *(Valle-Inclán)* dirty trick

de órdago: armar un escándolo ~ to cause a huge scandal ▪ to cause a major scandal

de órdago: tener un piso ~ to have a fantastic apartment ▪ to have a beautiful apartment

de otra manera ▪ de otra forma ▪ de otro modo otherwise

de otro modo ▪ de otra manera ▪ de otra forma otherwise

ser **de pacotilla** *(jerga)* ▪ ser de morondanga to be worthless ▪ to be no damned good ▪ to be a piece of junk

de padre on one's father's side of the family

estar **de palique** to talk and talk ➤ Estaban de palique. They talked and talked. ➤ Estuvimos de palique hasta las cinco de la mañana. We talked til 5 in the morning.

estar **de pánico** to be in a panic

de paquete 1. *(pastel, etc.)* made from a mix 2. *(para calentar y servir)* ready made 3. *(ser algo de lujo, o de categoría)* with all the bells and whistles

de par en par wide ▪ wide open ▪ all the way ➤ Abríamos las puertas de par en par We would open the doors wide

de parte de ▪ en nombre de on behalf of

estar **de parte de alguien** to be on someone's side

¿de parte de quién? who shall I say is calling? ▪ who's calling?

¿de parte de quién estás? ▪ ¿a quién apoyas? who are you for?

de parte en parte: ir ~ to go all over the place ▪ to go around

de pasada: decir algo ~ to say something in passing

de pasada: hacer algo ~ to do something in passing

estar **de pasada** to be passing through

de Pascuas a Ramos ▪ de pascuas en flores ▪ de uvas a peras ▪ de uvas a brevas in a month of Sundays ▪ once in a blue moon

de paso ▪ además to boot ▪ on one's way ▪ just passing through ▪ just visiting ➤ Arreglé el frigo y limpié la cocina de paso. I fixed the refrigerator and cleaned the kitchen to boot. ➤ Te pilla de paso. It's on your way. ➤ No somos de aquí, estamos de paso. We're not from here, we're just passing through.

estar **de paso** to stop over ➤ Estuvimos de paso en Atlanta. We stopped over in Atlanta.

de paso: mencionar ~ to mention in passing

de paso: pillarle ~ ▪ quedarle de pasada to be on one's way ➤ ¿Podrías pasar por el correo y mandarme la carta? Te pilla de paso. Would you stop by the post office and mail this for me? It's on your way.

ser **de paso vacilante** to be unsteady on one's feet ➤ El viejo fue de paso muy vacilante. The old man was very unsteady on his feet.

de película: pasarlo ~ ▪ pasarlo de cine ▪ pasarlo grande to have a great time ➤ Los niños lo pasaron de película en el parque de atracciones. ▪ Los niños lo pasaron de cine en el parque de atracciones. The children had a great time at the amusement park.

de penalty: casarse ~ to have to get married ▪ to have a shotgun wedding

de perdidos, al río 1. *(yo)* I might as well ▪ why not? there's nothing to lose ▪ what the heck! 2. *(tú)* you might as well ▪ why not? there's nothing to lose ▪ what the heck!

estar **de perfil a alguien** to stand with one's face turned away from someone

de perlas: venirle ~ ▪ venirle al pelo ▪ venirle como anillo al dedo ▪ quedarle como anillo al dedo to suit one to a T ▪ to be just what the doctor ordered ▪ to come just at the right moment

estar **de permiso** to be on leave

de perros: humor ~ bad mood

de peso: amistades ~ influential friends

de peso: persona ~ influential person

de picos pardos: salir *(Esp.)* ▪ ir de picos pardos to go looking for some action ▪ to cat around

estar **de pie** to be standing (up) ▪ to be on one's feet

de piedra: quedarse ~ to be stunned

de pies a cabeza from head to foot

de pingoneo: ir ~ ▪ ir de cachondeo ▪ ir de juerga to go out on the town

de pingoneo: salir ~ ▪ salir de cachondeo ▪ salir de juerga to go out on the town

ser **de piñón fijo** to be intransigent ▪ to be stubborn ▪ to be unyielding ▪ to be fixed in one's opinions

de plano: cantar ~ to spill the beans ▪ to tell all ▪ to name names ▪ to blow people's cover ▪ *(jerga)* to sing

de plano: negar ~ to deny flatly ▪ to flatly deny

estar **de plantilla** to be on the payroll

estar **de plantón** ▪ estar dejado plantado(-a) to have been stood up ➤ Estoy de plantón. I've been stood up. ▪ *(él)* He stood me up. ▪ *(ella)* She stood me up.

de poca monta *(coloquial)* ▪ de poca importancia of little value ▪ of no account ▪ piddling ▪ petty ➤ Los barones feudales se metían en guerras de poca monta. The feudal barons engaged in little piddling wars.

de por medio 1. along the way ▪ in the process 2. involved ➤ Va a haber bajas de por medio. There are going to be casualties along the way. ▪ There are going to be casualties in the process. ➤ Quieren un divorcio, pero los hijos están de por medio. They want a divorce, but there are children involved.

de por sí in itself ▪ as it is ▪ in and of itself

de por vida for life ▪ for the rest of one's life

de porte digno with a dignified bearing

de posguerra post-war ➤ la Inglaterra de la posguerra Post-war England ➤ la España de la posguerra civil Post-civil war Spain

de postre for dessert ➤ ¿Qué hay de postre? What's for dessert?

de precepto ▪ obligatorio obligatory

de precepto: día ~ *(catolicismo)* holy day of obligation

de prevención as a precaution

de primera fuerza ▪ de primera línea top notch ▪ first rate ➤ Rafa es mecánico de primera fuerza. Rafa is a top notch mechanic.

de primera mano 1. de primeras first hand 2. nuevecito (brand) new ➤ Lo oí de primera mano. I heard it first hand. ➤ Compré el auto de primera mano. I bought the car new.

de primera mano: saber algo ~ ▪ saber algo de primeras to know something first hand ➤ Lo sé de primera mano. ▪ Lo sé de primeras. I know (it) first hand.

de primeras from the outset ▪ from the first ▪ at the outset

de primeras: saber algo ~ ▪ saber algo de primera mano to know something first hand ➤ Lo sé de primeras. ▪ Lo sé de primera mano. I know (it) first hand.

de prisa ▪ con prisa quickly

estar **de prisa** ▪ tener prisa to be in a hurry

de prisa y corriendo: comer ~ to eat on the run ➤ Comimos de prisa y corriendo. We ate on the run.

de profesión by profession ➤ Es contador de profesión. He's an accountant by profession.

de pronto ▪ de repente ▪ de súbito suddenly

de propina for good measure

de prueba: piloto ~ test pilot

de puertas adentro in private

de puertas afuera in public ➤ De puertas afuera, el dictador exhibe una frialdad inmutable, como si nada ocurriera. In public the dictator exhibits an invariable coldness, as if nothing had happened. ➤ De puertas afuera se comporta diferente que con la familia. His public face is different from his private face. ▪ He's different in public than he is in private.

estar **de punta** ▪ de vanguardia state of the art ▪ on the cutting edge

estar **de punta en blanco** ▪ estar todo elegante ▪ estar todo hecho un pincel to be all dressed up ▪ to be dressed to the nines

de puntillas: andar ~ ▪ andar en puntitas to walk on tiptoe

de puntitos ▪ de lunares polka-dotted ▪ with polka dots

de pura cepa ▪ auténtico y genuino authentic and genuine ➤ Arturo es un jarocho de pura cepa. ▪ Arturo es un jarocho auténtico y genuino. Arturo is a native of Vera Cruz, authentic and genuine.

de pura desfachatez ▪ de puro morro ▪ de pura caradura ▪ de puro morro ▪ de pura jeta 1. by (means of) sheer gall ▪ through sheer gall 2. out of sheer gall ▪ motivated by sheer gall ▪ driven by sheer gall

de pura potra *(Esp., argot)* ▪ de pura chorra ▪ de pura leche ▪ de pura suerte by sheer luck

de pura suerte ▪ de pura leche by sheer luck

ser **de puro fácil** ▪ ser tan fácil to be so easy

de puro morro *(pintoresco)* ▪ de pura desfachatez ▪ de pura caradura ▪ de puro morro ▪ de pura jeta 1. by (means of) sheer gall ▪ through sheer gall 2. out of sheer gall

de puta madre *(subido de tono)* ▪ genial ▪ estupendo great ➤ Perdiste un concierto de puta madre. You missed a great concert.

ser **de provecho** to be advantageous

¿de qué altura eres? ▪ ¿cuánto mides? how tall are you? ▪ what is your height?

de que asirse to hold onto ➤ There is no railing to hold onto. No hay pasamano de que asirse.
¿de qué color? what color? ➤ ¿De qué color es? What color is it? ➤ ¿Qué color es este? What color is this? ➤ ¿De qué color los habrías pintado? ■ ¿De qué color los hubieras pintado? What color would you have painted them?
¿de qué das clases? what do you teach?
¿de qué edad? how old?
¿de qué estaba hablando? what was I talking about?
¿de qué estás hablando? ■ ¿de qué hablas? what are you talking about?
¿de qué hablas? ■ ¿de qué estás hablando? what are you talking about?
¿de qué lado está usted? whose side are you on?
¿de qué lado estás? whose side are you on?
¿de qué manera? how so? ■ in what way?
¿de qué me sirve eso? where will that get me? ■ what good will that do me?
¿de qué puede ser? *(al camarero del bar)* ■ ¿qué hay (para tomar)? ■ ¿qué tenéis (para beber)? ■ ¿qué hay para beber? what do you have? ■ what do you have to choose from? ■ what are the choices?
¿de qué se trata esto? what's this all about?
¿de qué te ríes? ■ ¿qué te ha hecho (tanta) gracia? what are you laughing at? ■ what are you laughing about? ■ why are you laughing? ■ what's so funny?
¿de qué va? 1. ¿de qué se trata? what's it about? 2. ¿quién se cree que es? who does he think he is? ➤ ¿De qué va la película? What's the movie about?
¿de qué va todo esto? what's this all about?
¿de qué va (todo) esto que me dicen de...? ■ what's (all) this I hear about...?
¿de qué vas? what's the big idea? ■ what the hell are you doing?
¿de qué vive? 1. *(él)* what does he do for a living? 2. *(ella)* what does she do for a living? 3. *(usted)* what do you do for a living?
¿de qué vives? what do you do for a living?
de quien of anyone who ■ of whoever ■ of the person who ■ of one who ■ of someone who ➤ Habló con la autoridad de quien sabe. He spoke with the authority of one who knows. ■ He spoke with the authority of someone who knows.
¿de quién? whose?
¿de quién es? ■ ¿a quién pertenece esto? whose is this? ■ who does this belong to? ➤ ¿De quién es este libro? Whose book is this? ■ Who does this book belong to?
de quienes of those who ■ of people who ■ of whoever ■ of everyone who ■ of all those who
de quita y pon: una camisa ~ ■ una camisa de lava y pon wash and wear shirt
de raíz: arrancar ~ to pull up by the roots
ser **de rancio abolengo** to be of ancient ancestry ■ of distinguished ancestry ■ from an old and distinguished family
de rato en rato every now and then
de raza *(perros y caballos)* purebred ■ thoroughbred
de rebote by chance ■ on a fly ■ on the rebound
de rebozo secretly ■ in disguise ■ disguised
estar **de rechupete** ■ estar riquísimo to be scrumptuous ■ to be delicious
ser **de recibo** to be acceptable ➤ No es de recibo. It is not acceptable. ➤ No es de recibo que... It is not acceptable that... ■ It is not acceptable for (one to)...
de refilón in passing ■ obliquely
de regalo ■ gratis free
estar **de regreso** ■ estar de vuelta ■ haber vuelto to be back ■ to have returned ➤ Está de regreso. ■ Está de vuelta. ■ Ha vuelto. *(él)* He's back. ■ *(ella)* She's back.
de regulación precisa: instrumento ~ precision instrument
de remate totally ■ hopeless ■ utterly
de remate: comprar algo ~ to buy something at (an) auction ■ to buy something by bidding
de reojo out of the corner of one's eye
de repente ■ de pronto ■ de súbito suddenly
estar **de reposo** to be at rest ■ to be in repose ■ *(té)* to be steeping
estar **de retén** to be on call
de retraso slow ➤ Mi reloj lleva cinco minutos de retraso. My watch is five minutes slow.
de revés *(tenis)* back-handed
de rigor: el traje ~ the required dress (for an occasion) ■ ➤ ¿Cuál es el traje de rigor para la boda? What is the required dress for the wedding?
ser **de rigor** 1. *(esencial)* to be absolutely necessary ■ to be de rigueur 2. *(de costumbre)* to be customary ■ to be traditional ■ to be usual
de rigor: textos ~ required texts ■ required textbooks
de risa me escacho *(Valle-Inclán)* I'm going to bust my gut laughing
estar **de rodillas** 1. to be kneeling ■ to be on one's knees 2. *(suplicando, rogando, o humillándose a alguien)* to be on bended knee
estar **de rodillas** to be kneeling ■ to be on one's knees
de rompe y rasga: decidir ~ to decide on the spur of the moment
de rompe y rasga: decirle a alguien ~ to tell someone flat out
de rompe y rasga: una persona ~ strong-minded person ■ strong-willed person
ser **de sangre azul** to be blue-blooded
de sangre caliente: animal ~ warm-blooded animal
ser **de sangre caliente** to be hot-blooded
de sangre fría: animal ~ cold-blooded animal
de seguir así... ■ si uno sigue así... if one keeps on... ■ if one keeps it up... ➤ De seguir así va a acabar teniendo graves problemas: le da a la botella. ■ Si sigue así va a acabar teniendo graves problemas: le da a la botella. If he keeps on, he's going to have serious problems. (He's hitting the bottle.) ■ If he keeps it up, he's going to have serious problems. (He's hitting the bottle.)
de segunda second-rate
de segunda mano second-hand ■ previously owned
de semana en semana semana a semana (from) week to week ■ week by week
de ser así 1. si es así if so ■ if that's the case ■ if that turns out to be the case ■ if that turns out to be true ■ if that turns out to be so 2. si fuera así if that were so ■ if that were the case 2. *(yo)* if I do ■ if I am ■ if I have ■ if I can *(Nota: Esta frase puede llevar cualquier pronombre o verbo auxiliar. ■ This phrase can take any pronoun or auxiliary verb.)* ➤ Algunos científicos han pronosticado un rápido ascenso de las temperaturas. De ser así, el problema de los incendios forestales veraniegos en la Península Ibérica se recrudecerá. Some scientists have predicted a rapid rise in global temperatures. If that turns out to be the case, the summer brushfire problem on the Iberian Peninsula is going to get a lot worse. ➤ Nada más lejos de mi intención que ofender al jefe al referirme a él como a un "seta". Pero de ser así debería tomárselo como un cumplido. I didn't mean to cause any offense when I called the boss a "turnip," but if I did, he should have taken it as a compliment. ➤ El fontanero cree que las tuberías están completamente echadas a perder; de ser así la reparación será mucho más cara de lo previsto. The plumber thinks the pipes are completely shot. If so, the repair is going to be far more expensive than expected. ➤ La catedrática Rosa Navarro Durán de la Universidad de Barcelona cree haber descubierto que el autor de *El Lazarillo de Tormes* es Alfonso de Valdés. De ser así, habría que replantearse algunos aspectos de la obra. Professor Rosa Navarro Durán of the University of Barcelona believes she has discovered that the author of *Lazarillo de Tormes* is Alfonso de Valdés. If so, some aspects of the novel should be reconsidered. ■ Professor Rosa Navarro Durán of the University of Barcelona believes she has discovered that the author of *Lazarillo de Tormes* is Alfonso de Valdés. If that's the case, some aspects of the novel should be reconsidered.
de ser cierto ■ si es cierto if it's true
de ser posible ■ si fuera posible if possible
de serie as standard equipment ■ built-in ➤ Tiene aire acondicionado de serie. It has built-in air conditioning. ■ It has air conditioning as standard equipment.
de serlo if one is
de siempre usual ■ permanent ■ regular ■ for ever ➤ Te manda muchos saludos tu amigo de siempre, Juan He sends you many

greetings your friend forever, Juan ➤ Cliente de siempre Regular client ■ Long-time client ■ Permanent client

¿de sifón o de botella? *(L.am.)* ■ ¿de barril o de botella? draft or bottle?

estar **de sobra** to be left over

de sobra: haber algo ~ ■ haber más que suficiente more than enough ➤ Había agua de sobra para las plantas. There was water left over after watering the plants. ■ There was more than enough water to water the plants.

ser **de sobra conocido que...** to be common knowledge that...

de sobre mesa ■ de sobremesa right after dinner

de sol a sol from dawn to dusk

ser **de su agrado** to be to one's liking

de su parte 1. *(de él)* on his part ■ on one's behalf 2. *(de ella)* on her part ■ on her behalf

de su pelaje 1. *(de él)* of his ilk ■ of his stripe 2. *(de ella)* of her ilk ■ of her stripe

ser **de su propia cosecha** 1. de su propia huerta to be home grown 2. de su propia imaginación to be out of one's own imagination ■ to be from one's own imagination

de su propia imaginación out of one's own imagination

de súbito ■ de repente ■ de pronto suddenly

de suceder algo así if anything like that should happen

estar **de suerte** to be in luck ➤ Hoy estás de suerte. Today you're in luck.

ser **de suponer que** ■ ser de esperar que... to be expected that ➤ Es de suponer que... ■ Es de esperar que... It's to be expected that... ➤ Era de suponer que... ■ Es de esperar que... It was to be expected that...

de susto en susto one thing after another ■ one nightmare after another

de tacón (alto): zapatos ~ high-heel shoes

de tal manera que ■ de tal modo ■ así in a way that

de tal palo, tal astilla like father, like son

de talión: pena ~ reciprocal punishment ■ punishment identical to the harm inflicted

de tarde en tarde once in a great while

de temporada: verduras ~ green vegetables in season

de tenazón from the hip ■ without taking aim ■ blindly

de tercera third-rate

de ti depende it's up to you

de tiempo en tiempo ■ de cuando en cuando ■ de vez en cuando from time to time

estar **de tiros largos** dressed to kill ■ dressed to the nines

de tiros largos: ponerse ~ to get all dressed up

de toda clase of every kind

de toda laya of all kinds

de todas formas ■ de todos modos in any case ■ anyway

de todas maneras in any case ■ at any rate ■ anyway

de todas partes from everywhere ■ from all over

de todas todas without a shadow of a doubt

de todo como en botica everything under the sun ➤ Hay de todo como en botica. They have everything under the sun.

de todo el mundo from around the world ■ from all over the world ➤ Ante más de ciento cincuenta dirigentes de todo el mundo, el presidente... (Speaking) to more than a hundred and fifty world leaders, the president...

de todo hay en la viña del Señor ■ tiene que haber de todo it takes all kinds (to make a world)

de todo pelaje of every stripe ■ of every kind

de todo punto ■ por completo ■ completamente completely ■ absolutely

de todo un poco ■ un poco de todo a little of everything ➤ ¿Qué has estado haciendo esta mañana?-De todo un poco. ■ ¿Qué has hecho esta mañana?-Un poco de todo. What have you been doing this morning?-A little of everything.

de todos los demonios: hacer un calor ~ to be hot as hell (outside)

de todos los demonios: hacer un frío ~ to be cold as hell (outside)

de todos los tiempos of all time

de todos modos in any case

ser **de toma pan y moja** 1. *(mujer)* to be a dish ■ to be a knockout ■ to be extremely attractive 2. *(hombre)* to be a hunk ■ to be a stud ■ to be extremely attractive

de tomo y lomo: ser mentiroso(-a) ~ to be an out-and-out liar

de turno at the moment ➤ El qué dirán de turno Public opinion at the moment

de última generación ■ de punta ■ de vanguardia state of the art ➤ Radar de última generación State-of-the-art radar

de último minuto last-minute

de un ancho ■ de ancho wide ➤ El puente es de un ancho de tres metros. The bridge is three meters wide.

de un brinco: levantarse ~ to jump to one's feet

de un día day-old ➤ Venden el pan de un día con un descuento. ■ Venden el pan de un día a precio reducido. They sell day-old bread at a discount.

de un extremo a otro from one end to the other ➤ Los fenicios cruzaron el Mediterráneo de un extremo a otro. The Phoenicians sailed the Mediterranean from one end to the other.

de un lado para otro: correr ~ to run all over the place

de un matrimonio anterior: tener hijos ~ to have children from a previous marriage ➤ Tiene otros dos hijos de un matrimonio anterior. He has two other children from a previous marriage.

de un momento a otro 1. en cualquier momento any minute now ■ any time now 2. de repente suddenly

de un plumazo at a stroke ■ in one fell swoop

de un plumazo: tachar algo ~ to reject a written proposal out of hand

de un plumazo: zanjar algo ~ to settle something quickly and decisively

de un tajo: cortar algo ~ to cut something right off ➤ El espadachín cortó la cabeza del dragón de un tajo. The swordsman cut the dragon's head right off.

ser **de un tamaño igual a una vez y media** to be one and a half times as large (as) ■ to be one and a half times the size (of) ➤ *(noticia)* Jamás hasta ahora habían visto los astrónomos algo así en el universo: una burbuja de agua, de un tamaño igual a una vez y media el Sistema Solar. Never before had astronomers seen anything like it in the universe: a bubble of water one and a half times as large as the solar system. ■ Never before had astronomers seen anything like it in the universe: a bubble of water one and a half times the size of the solar system.

de un tiempo a esta parte for some time (now) ■ for a while now

de un tirón 1. de una tacada at a stretch ■ in one fell swoop ■ in one whack ■ in one go ■ all at once 2. leer un libro in one sitting

de un trayecto one way ➤ El pasaje de un trayecto es noventa y cuatro euros y ciento veinte y dos de ida y vuelta. The fare is ninety-four euros one way and one hundred twenty-two round trip.

de una forma o de otra ■ de una forma u otra one way or another

de una forma u otra ■ de una forma o de otra one way or another

de una manera postiva positively

de una manera tajante: decirle algo a alguien ~ to tell someone something in no uncertain terms

de una sentada: leer un libro ~ to read a book in one sitting

ser **de una sola voz** to be of one mind ■ to be of one accord

de una tacada 1. *(en el juego de billar)* in one shot 2. *(leyendo un libro)* in one sitting 3. *(figurativo)* in one go ■ in one whack ➤ Metí tres bolas de una tacada. I sank three balls in one shot. ➤ Hice todas la compras de Navidad de una tacada. I did all my Christmas shopping in one whack. ➤ Ella leyó el libro de una tacada. She read the book in one sitting.

de una tirada ■ en una tirada ■ de un tirón in one go ■ at one go ■ in one fell swoop

de una vez at once ■ in a single action

de una vez para siempre ■ de una vez por todas ■ de una vez once and for all

de una vez por todas ■ de una vez para siempre ■ de una vez once and for all

de uno en uno one by one
de uno para arriba anywhere from one on ▪ at least one
de unos días a esta parte just the other day
estar **de uñas** to be at each other's throats
de uso diario for everyday use
estar **de vacaciones** to be on vacation ▪ to be on holiday
estar **de vacile** *(Esp.)* ▪ estar de vacilón to be pulling the wool over someone's eyes ▪ to be teasing
de vacío empty-handed
de vacío: marcharse ~ to go away empty-handed ▪ to come away empty-handed
de vanguardia ▪ de punta state of the art ▪ on the cutting edge
de venta aquí on sale here
estar **de ver** ▪ quedar por ver to remain to be seen
de veras really ▪ truly ▪ in earnest
¿de veras? ▪ ¿de verdad? ▪ ¿sí? **1.** really? ▪ seriously? **2.** *(en la primera persona singular)* I do?
de verdad truly
¿de verdad? ▪ ¿de veras? really? ▪ do you really? ▪ did you really? ▪ is it?
¿de verdad tanto ciegas por mí? *(Valle-Inclán)* are you really so blinded by love for me?
de vez en cuando ▪ de cuando en cuando ▪ de vez en vez from time to time
de vista by sight
de viva voz: transmitirse ~ to be transmitted by word of mouth
estar **de vuelta** ▪ haber vuelto ▪ volver ▪ estar de regreso to be back ▪ to have returned ▪ to have come back ➤ (Él) está de vuelta. He's back. ▪ He's come back. ▪ He's returned. ➤ It's good to be back. Es bueno estar de vuelta. ▪ Es bueno volver. ➤ (Ella) estará de vuelta en quince minutos. ▪ (Ella) volverá en quince minutos. ▪ (Ella) regresará en quince minutos. ▪ (Ella) estará de regreso en quince minutos. She'll be back in fifteen minutes.
de vuelta a ▪ de regreso a ▪ al volver a ▪ al regresar a back at ▪ on returning to ▪ when I went back to ▪ when I returned to ➤ De vuelta a la tienda de pintura, expliqué por qué tenía que comprar otro paquete de filtros. Back at the paint store, I was explaining why I was buying another set of filters. ▪ On returning to the paint store, I explained why I was buying another set of filters. ▪ When I went back to the paint store I explained why I was buying another set of filters.
de vuelta a casa (on the way) back home ▪ on returning home ▪ *(yo)* when I got home ➤ Mientras conducía de vuelta a casa, pasé a una mofeta. When I was driving back home, I passed a skunk.
estar **de vuelta a la normalidad** ▪ haber vuelto a la normalidad to be back to normal ▪ to have returned to normal ➤ Hoy mi correo electrónico está de vuelta a la normalidad. ▪ Hoy mi correo electrónico ha vuelto a la normalidad. My E-mail is back to normal today.
¡de vuelta al tajo! ▪ ¡de vuelta al trabajo! back to the salt mines! ▪ back to the grind!
¡de vuelta al trabajo! back to work!
de vuelta en ▪ de regreso a ▪ al volver a ▪ al regresar a back at ▪ on returning to ➤ De vuelta en la tienda de pintura, les expliqué por qué tenía que comprar otro paquete de filtros. Back at the paint store, I explained why I was buying another pack of filters.
estar **de vuelta en la ciudad** ▪ haber vuelto a la ciudad to be back in town
estar **de vuelta en la ciudad** ▪ haber vuelto (a la ciudad) to be back in town ➤ Estoy de vuelta en la ciudad. ▪ He vuelto (a la ciudad). I'm back in town.
estar **de vuelta en un lugar** to be back in a place ➤ Ahora estoy de vuelta en España. I'm back in Spain now.
de vuelta y vuelta around and around
de *x* a *y* ▪ (cualquier punto) entre *x* e *y* (anywhere) from *x* to *y* ▪ (anywhere) between *x* and *y* ➤ De diez a veinte ▪ (Cualquier punto) entre diez y veinte (Anywhere) from ten to twenty ▪ Between ten and twenty
de *x* (grados Celsius) bajo cero: la temperatura es ~ the temperature is *x* (degrees Celsius) below zero ➤ La temperatura es de diez (grados Celsius) bajo cero. The temperature is minus ten, Celsius. ▪ The temperature is ten below zero, Celsius.
debajo de ▪ al pie de under ▪ underneath ▪ beneath ▪ below ➤ Viven en el apartamento debajo de este. They live in the apartment under this this one. ▪ They live in the apartment underneath this one. ▪ They leave in the apartment beneath this one. ▪ They live in the apartment below this one.
debajo de este ▪ bajo este under(neath) this one ▪ (just) below this one ▪ beneath this one ➤ Viven en el apartamento debajo de este. ▪ Viven en el apartamento (que hay) bajo este. They live in the apartment under(neath) this one. ▪ They live in the apartment (just) beneath this one. ▪ They live in the apartment (just) below this one.
debajo de la fachada de beneath the façade of
debajo la fachada de ▪ bajo la fachada de ▪ bajo la apariencia de beneath the façade of ➤ Debajo de la fachada clasicista latía el corazón de un romántico encerrado. Beneath the classicist façade, the heart of a closet romantic was beating.
debajo de la mesa under the table ▪ underneath the table ▪ beneath the table
debajo de la superficie: yacer ~ ▪ yacer bajo la superficie to lie beneath the surface
debajo de la superficie: mirar ~ ▪ mirar bajo la superficie to look beneath the surface
debates intensos ▪ densos debates intense debate
debatir a fondo to debate thoroughly ▪ to argue meticulously
debatir si to debate whether
debatirse entre... to be torn between...
debatirse entre la vida y la muerte to fight for one's life ▪ for one's life to hang in the balance ➤ El agredido se debatía entre la vida y la muerte. The attack victim was fighting for his life ▪ the attack victim's life was hanging in the balance.
debe de haber there must be ▪ there has (got) to be ▪ *(coloquial)* there's gotta be ➤ Debe de haber un manual que explica cómo funciona la computadora. There must be a manual that explains how the computer works. ➤ Debe de haber un cajero cerca. There must be an ATM around here (somewhere). ▪ There has to be an ATM around here (somewhere). ▪ *(coloquial)* There's gotta be an ATM around here (somewhere).
debe de ser que no... **1.** *(él)* he must not... **2.** *(ella)* she must not... ➤ Debe de ser que no se lava el pelo. He must not wash his hair.
debe estar para... it's due on...
debe existir (allí) todavía ▪ todavía debe estar allí *(L.am., literario)* ▪ debe haberlo(-a) todavía it must still be there
debe haber there must be ▪ there have to be
debe haber algún error there must be some mistake
debe haber sido it must have been ▪ it had to have been
debe haberlo(-a) todavía *(Arg., literario)* ▪ debe existir (allí) todavía ▪ todavía debe estar allí it must still be there
debe ser de conocimiento público que... it needs to be public knowledge that... ▪ it needs to be publicly known that ▪ the public needs to be aware that...
debe ser un error ▪ debe ser una equivocación **1.** it must be a mistake **2.** there must be some mistake
deber de to have to ▪ must ➤ Debes de comer toda la espinaca antes de poder salir a jugar. You have to eat all your spinach before you can go out and play. ▪ You must eat all your spinach before you can go out and play.
deber haber venido ▪ tener que haber venido to be supposed to be here ➤ ¡Debiste haber venido hace cuatro horas! ▪ ¡Tenías que haber venido hace cuatro horas! You were supposed to be here four hours ago!
deber la vida a to owe one's life to
debería haber there should be ➤ Debería haber un semáforo en esa intersección. There should be a traffic light at that intersection.
debería haber habido there should have been ➤ Debería haber habido más números musicales en el concierto. There should have been more musical numbers at the concert.
debería haberle hecho should have had him ➤ (Yo) debería haberle hecho enviar un mensaje de prueba. I should have had him send a test message.
debería haberme vacunado contra la gripe I should have gotten a flu shot

debería habérmelo imaginado ▪ debería habérmelo supuesto I should have known

debería habérmelo supuesto ▪ debería habérmelo imaginado I should have known

deberías avergonzarte ▪ debería tener vergüenza ▪ tendrías que tener vergüenza you should be ashamed of yourself ▪ you ought to be ashamed of yourself

deberías conocerme mejor you should know me better than that

deberías haberte venido you should have come ▪ you should have come over

deberle dinero a alguien to owe someone money ➤ ¿Cuánto le debo? How much do I owe you? ➤ I owe her fifty euros. Le debo (a ella) cincuenta euros.

deberle disculpas a alguien to owe someone an apology

debía de ser (it) had to be ➤ Aristóteles estaba bastante seguro de que la Tierra debía de ser el centro del sistema planetario y del universo. Aristotle was convinced that the Earth had to be the center of the planetary system and of the universe.

debía participar en: uno ~ one was supposed to participate in ▪ one was set to participate in

debido a because of ▪ owing to ▪ due to ➤ El partido de béisbol fue cancelado debido al mal tiempo. The baseball game was cancelled because of bad weather.

debido a que owing to the fact that ▪ because

debilidad por weakness for ▪ soft spot for

debió de ser una ilusión it must have been an illusion

debo admitir ▪ he de admitir ▪ tengo que admitir I must admit ▪ I have to admit

debo averiguarlo I must find out ▪ I have to find out ▪ I must find that out ▪ I have to find that out

debo confesar que... I must confess that... ▪ I have to confess that...

debo de estar oyendo cosas I must be hearing things

debo de estar viendo cosas I must be seeing things

debo de haber estado ▪ debí haber estado ▪ tengo que haber estado ▪ tuve que haber estado I must have been ➤ Debo de haber estado distraído porque no lo recuerdo. I must have been distracted because I don't remember it.

debo decir que... ▪ tengo que decir que... I must say (that)... ▪ I have to say (that)...

debutar ante las cámaras to debut before the cameras ▪ to make one's first appearance before the cameras ➤ El actor debutó ante las cámaras a los cuatro años. The actor debuted before the cameras at age four. ▪ The actor made his first appearance before the cameras at age four. *(Nota: "Debut" se pronuncia "debiú" y "debuted" se pronuncia "debiúd")*

decaer de poderío to decline in power

decaer en belleza (for) one's beauty to fade

decantarse a favor de algo to go in favor of something ▪ to run in favor of something ▪ to favor something ➤ Public opinion is running in favor of the moderates. La opinión pública se decanta a favor de los moderados.

decantarse como algo to be developing into something ▪ to be becoming something ➤ Se decanta a un pianista hábil. He is developing into an accomplished pianist. ▪ He's becoming an accomplished pianist. ➤ Se decanta a un atleta hábil. He's developing into a skilled athlete. ▪ He's becoming a skilled athlete. ➤ Se decanta a una atleta hábil. She's developing into a skilled athlete. ▪ She's becoming a skilled athlete.

decantarse hacia algo ▪ inclinarse hacia algo to lean toward something ▪ to incline toward something ▪ to tend toward something ▪ to move toward something ➤ Me decanto hacia el candidato de la oposición en estas elecciones. ▪ Me inclino más hacia el candidato de la oposición en estas elecciones. I'm inclining towards the opposition candidate in this election. ▪ I'm leaning towards the opposition candidate in this election. ➤ Me decanto hacia los amarillos. ▪ Me inclino hacia los amarillos. I'm inclining towards the yellow ones. ▪ I'm leaning towards the yellow ones.

decantarse por algo to gravitate toward something ▪ to choose something ▪ to opt for something

decantarse por alguien to gravitate toward someone

decantarse por hacer algo to favor doing something ▪ to be inclined to do something ➤ Me decanto por no exigir la asignatura y dejarla graduarse. I'm inclined to waive the course requirement and let her graduate.

decenas de miles de personas tens of thousands of people

estar **decepcionado con algo** to be disappointed with something ▪ to be disappointed in something

estar **decepcionado(-a) con alguien** to be disappointed in someone ▪ to be disappointed with someone

decíamos ayer *(Fray Luis de León, al volver a su cátedra después de años en prisión)* we were saying yesterday

decididamente es... it's definitely...

estar **decidido a** to be determined to ➤ El piloto estaba decidido a salvar a los alpinistas, pasara lo que pasara. The pilot was determined to save the mountain climbers, no matter what (happened).

estar **decidido a que...** to be determined to...

decidir hacer algo ▪ darse por hacer algo to decide to do something ➤ Decidí regresar. ▪ Decidí volver. I decided to go back.

decidir que to decide to ➤ Decidí que volvería. I decided to go back.

decidirse por algo to decide on something ➤ Me he decidido por jamón serrano. I've decided on country ham.

decidirse por hacer algo to make up one's mind to do something ▪ to decide definitively to do something ▪ to decide definitely to do something ➤ Me decidí por asistir a la universidad. I made up my mind to go to the university. ▪ I decided (definitively) to go to the university. ▪ I decided definitely to go to the university.

decir a alguien que haga algo to tell someone to do something

decir a punto fijo ▪ decir con seguridad ▪ decir por seguro **1.** *(sin el objeto indirecto)* to say for sure ▪ to say for certain ▪ to say exactly **2.** *(con el objeto indirecto)* to tell for sure ▪ to tell for certain ▪ to tell exactly ▪ ➤ No sabría decir a punto fijo cuándo... I couldn't say exactly when... ➤ No te sabría decir a punto fijo cuándo... I couldn't tell you exactly when...

decir a todo amén to be a yes man ▪ to say yes to everything

decir al pan, pan, y al vino, vino ▪ al pan, pan, y al vino, vino to call a spade a spade

decir algo con la boca pequeña ▪ decir algo con la boca chica to say something without really meaning it

decir algo de pasada to say something in passing

decir algo entre burlas y veras ▪ decir algo mitad en serio mitad en broma to say something half seriously, half in jest

decir algo medio en serio, medio en broma ▪ decir algo mitad en serio, mitad en broma to say something half serious, half in jest

decir algo para salir del paso to say something to get out of a jam ▪ to say something to get out of a predicament ▪ to do damage control

decir algo por lo bajinis ▪ decir algo por lo bajini to say something in a whisper ▪ to say something sofly ▪ to say something in a soft voice ▪ to say something in an undertone

decir algo por lo bajo 1. en voz baja to say something in a whisper ▪ to say something softly ▪ to say something in a soft voice ▪ to say something in an undertone **2.** decir algo a sí mismo to say something to oneself

decir algo relacionado con ▪ decir algo sobre to say something about

decir chorradas to talk nonsense ▪ to be full of nonsence

decir con suficiencia to say coolly

decir con toda seguridad 1. to say for sure **2.** to tell one for sure ➤ No puedo decir con toda seguridad. I can't say for sure. ➤ No puedo decirte con toda seguridad. I can't tell you for sure.

decir cosas que levantan ampollas to ruffle someone's feathers ▪ to get someone's hackles up

decir de chacota *(Esp.)* ▪ decir en broma to say (something) in jest

decir de corrido to recite perfectly ▪ to repeat from memory without mistakes

decir en tono suplicante ▪ suplicar ▪ implorar to implore

decir haber hecho algo to say one has done something ▪ to claim to have done something ➤ *(titular)* EE UU dice haber identificado al cerebro del 11-S. US says it has identified the mastermind of 9-11. ▪ US claims to have identified the mastermind of 9-11. ➤ Él dijo haber conseguido el rango de coronel a mediados de los años veinte. He claimed to have achieved the rank of colonel in his midtwenties.

decir la hora to tell time

decir la última palabra to have the last word

decir lo primero que a alguien le viene a la mente to say the first thing that comes to mind

decir lo que se le viene a la boca to say whatever comes to mind

decir mal de alguien to speak badly of someone ▪ to speak ill of someone

decir misa ▪ oficiar misa to say mass ▪ to celebrate mass

decir nombres ▪ dar nombres to name names ➤ No voy a dar nombres. I'm not going to name names.

decir pestes de alguien to heap abuse on someone

decir por lo llano que... ▪ decir a las claras que... ▪ decir sin tapujos que... to say flatly that... ▪ to come right out and say that... ▪ to say flat out that...

decir por todo el morro *(Esp.)* to say flat out ▪ to tell someone flat out ➤ Ella me dijo por todo el morro que los otros estudiantes hablan mejor que yo. She told me flat out that the other students speak better than I do.

decir que no ▪ rehusar ▪ negarse to say no

decir que sí to say yes

decir que uno haga algo to say to do something ➤ Dicen que les esperemos. They said for us to wait (for them).

decir ser *(espurio o poco digno de confianza)* ▪ asegurar ser ▪ afirmar ser to *say* that one is ▪ to *claim* to be

decir sus quejas to air one's grievances

decir tener *(espurio o poco digno de confianza)* **1.** to claim to have **2.** to claim to be ➤ La ciudad dice tener el restaurante más antiguo del mundo. The city claims to have the oldest restaurant in the world. ➤ Decía tener veintiun años. He claimed to be twenty-one.

decir una mentira ▪ mentir to tell a lie ▪ to lie

decir una queja to air a grievance

decirle a alguien cuatro frescas to tell someone where to get off

decirle a alguien lo que tiene que hacer ▪ decirle a alguien qué tiene que hacer ▪ mandar ▪ ordenar ▪ mangonear to tell someone what he has to do ▪ to tell someone what to do

decirle a alguien que haga algo to tell someone to do something ➤ Mi profesor me dijo que lo leyera. My professor told me to read it. ➤ Dile (a ella) que lo haga. ▪ Dígale (a ella) que lo haga. Tell her to (do it). ➤ Le dije (a ella) que lo hiciera. I told her to (do it).

decirle a alguien que no to tell someone no ▪ to turn someone down

decirle a alguien que te ayude to get someone to help you *(Nota: La traducción libre de "decir" como "get" está más próxima al significado verdadero que la traducción literal. ▪ The free translation of "decir" as "get" is closer to the true meaning than a literal translation)* ➤ Dile a Carlos que te ayude con las ecuaciones, a él le salen a primera de cambio. Get Carlos to help you with the equations. He gets them right off the bat. ▪ Get Carlos to help you with the equations. He gets them on the first try. ▪ Get Carlos to help you with the equations. He gets them right off.

decirle a alguien qué tenía que hacer ▪ decirle a alguien lo que tenía que hacer ▪ mandar ▪ ordenar ▪ mangonear to tell someone what he had to do ▪ to tell someone what to do ➤ *(canción popular de los cincuenta)* Y luego el curandero, me dijo qué tenía que hacer. And then the witch doctor, he told me what to do.

decirle adiós a algo to kiss something good-bye ▪ to forget *that*

decirle al oído ▪ contarle al oído to whisper it in someone's ear ➤ Dime al oído. ▪ Cuéntame al oído. Whisper it in my ear.

decirle con toda seguridad 1. *(a usted)* to tell you for sure **2.** *(a él)* to tell him for sure **3.** *(a ella)* to tell her for sure

decirle cuatro cosas a alguien ▪ decirle cuatro frescas a alguien ▪ cantarle las cuarenta to tell someone off

decirle un ejemplo to give an example ➤ ¿Podrías decirme un ejemplo? Could you give me an example?

decírselo a bocajarro a alguien to tell someone something point blank ▪ to tell someone something straight out

decírselo en la cara a alguien to say it (right) to someone's face

decisión acertada right decision ▪ correct decision

decisión de hacer algo decision to do something ➤ *(noticia)* El vicepresidente Al Gore se desmarcó de la decisión de sacar a Elián de la casa de sus primos. Vice president Al Gore distanced himself from the decision to take Elian from his cousins' house.

decisión equivocada wrong decision ▪ incorrect decision

decisión salomónica ▪ decisión sabia wise decision

decisión tomada al instante spur-of-the-moment decision

decisión trascendental ▪ decisión transcendental important decision

declaracion a la prensa ▪ declaración de prensa statement to the press

la **declaración de impuestos** ▪ declaración del impuesto sobre la renta (income) tax return ▪ income tax statement

la **declaración del impuesto sobre la renta** ▪ declaración de impuestos (income) tax return

la **Declaración de los Derechos** *(constitución estadounidense)* Bill of Rights

declaración falsa false statement

declaración jurada sworn statement

ser **declarado culpable de un crimen** ▪ ser condenado por un crimen to be found guilty of a crime ▪ to be convicted of a crime

declarado lo cual... ▪ declarado eso... having stated that...

declarar a alguien inocente to declare someone innocent ➤ El juez lo declaró inocente. ▪ *(Esp. leísmo)* El juez le declaró inocente. The judge declared him innocent. ➤ El juez la declaró inocente. The judge declared her innocent.

declarar ante un gran jurado to testify before a grand jury

declarar contra to testify against ➤ Las subsaharianas que se prostituían en la Casa de Campo se han negado a declarar contra las mafias. The Africans working as prostitutes in the Casa de Campo have refused to testify against the mafiosos.

declarar la guerra a un país to declare war on a country

declarar la quiebra to declare bankruptcy

declararle a alguien culpable to find someone guilty

declararse culpable to plead guilty

declararse en quiebra to declare bankruptcy

declararse un incendio for a fire to break out ➤ *(noticia)* Dos jóvenes reclusos murieron ayer al declararse un incendio en el pabellón de menores de una prisión marroquí. Two young inmates died yesterday when fire broke out in the youth pavillion of a Moroccan prison.

declararse una epidemia for an epidemic to break out

declive medio ▪ descenso medio average decrease

decorado a todo lujo richly decorated ▪ luxuriously decorated ▪ elaborately decorated ▪ finely decorated

decretar que... to decree that...

decretar un edicto to issue a decree

decretar un toque de queda to declare a curfew

decreto de divorcio divorce decree

decúbito prono: estar en ~ *(culto)* ▪ estar boca abajo to lie prone ▪ to lie face down

decúbito supino: estar en ~ *(culto)* ▪ estar boca arriba to lie supine ▪ to lie face up

dedicar el tiempo para hacer algo to take the time to do something

dedicar la vida a algo to dedicate one's life to something ▪ to devote one's life to something

dedicar su tiempo to devote one's time

dedicar tiempo a hacer algo to set aside time to do something ▪ to make time to do something

dedicarse a to be (by profession)... ▪ to do for a living ▪ to dedicate oneself to ▪ to take up

dedicarse en cuerpo y alma a algo to dedicate oneself completely to something

dedo anular ring finger ▪ fourth finger

dedo corazón middle finger

dedo gordo ▪ dedo pulgar ▪ pulgar thumb

dedo gordo del pie big toe

dedo meñique little finger

dedo pulgar ■ dedo gordo ■ pulgar thumb
deducir gran cosa to tell much
deduje eso ■ supuse eso I gathered that
deduzco que... I gather that... ➤ Deduzco que hacer construir una casa lleva menos tiempo que antes. I gather that having a house built takes less time than it used to. ■ I gather that building a house takes less time than it used to.
defender a alguien a ultranza to defend someone tooth and nail
defender a capa y espada to defend with all one's might
defender a muerte to defend to the death
defender algo contra viento y marea to defend something with all one's might
defender con uñas y dientes to defend tooth and nail ■ to fight tooth and nail
defenderse a capa y espada to defend oneself with all one's might ■ to defend oneself with everything one has got
defenderse en un idoma to hold one's own in a language
defenderse muy bien to make a good salary ➤ Se defiende muy bien. *(él)* He makes a good salary. ■ *(ella)* She makes a good salary.
defensa numantina a fight to the death
defensor(a) de la fe defender of the faith
defensores de las libertades civiles civil rights advocates ■ human rights advocates
definitivamente: dejar de fumar ~ ■ dejar de fumar para siempre to quit smoking for good ➤ Espero que hayas dejado de fumar definitivamente. ■ Espero que hayas dejado de fumar para siempre. I hope you've quit smoking for good.
defraudar a alguien to disappointment someone ■ to let someone down ■ to dash one's hopes
defraudar la confianza de alguien to breach someone's confidence
dehesa alpina alpine meadow
¡deja de...! ■ ¡basta de...! ■ ¡para de...! enough of...! ■ that's enough...!
deja de existir ■ ya no existe it no longer exits
¡deja eso! stop that! ■ cut it out!
¡deja la televisión! leave the TV alone! ■ don´t mess with the TV!
¡deja lo que estás haciendo! stop what you're doing!
deja mucho que desear it leaves a lot to be desired
deja que lo diga de otra manera let me rephrase that
deja que empiece diciendo let me say at the outset ■ let me begin by saying
deja que lo haga yo let me do it
deja que me haga una idea let me get an idea
deja que siga adelante 1. *(él)* let him keep doing what he's doing 2. *(ella)* let her keep doing what she's doing
deja que te ayude con el abrigo ■ permíteme el abrigo let me help you with your coat ■ let me take your coat
deja que te lo muestre let me show you
la **dejación de responsabilidad** shirking of responsibility ■ evasion of responsibility
estar **dejado de la mano de Dios** to be abandoned to one's fate
déja(le) que siga adelante 1. *(él)* let him keep doing what he's doing 2. *(ella)* let her keep doing what she's doing
déjalo de mi cuenta ■ déjamelo a mí leave it to me
déjalo estar leave it be! ■ let it be!
déjalo, lo encontré never mind, I found it
déjalo, que se rompe con mirarlo don't touch, it's so fragile you can break it just by looking at it
¡déjame al suelo! let me down!
déjame en paz leave me alone
¡déjame entrar! let me in!
¡déjame fuera de eso! leave me out of it!
déjame que te cuente let me tell you
déjamelo a mí ■ déjalo de mi cuenta leave it to me
¡déjamelo saber! ■ házmelo saber ■ avísame let me know! ➤ Si puedo ayudarte en algo déjamelo saber y haré lo posible por ayudarte. If I can help you with anything, let me know and I'll do what I can to help you.
dejar a alguien a dos velas to leave someone broke
dejar a alguien a la luna de Valencia to leave someone out in the cold
dejar a alguien a su aire to let someone do what he wants ■ to leave someone to one's own devices
dejar a alguien al descubierto to blow someone's cover ■ to leave someone exposed
dejar a alguien algo ■ prestar algo a alguien to lend someone something ➤ Déjame tu boli un momento. Lend me your (ballpoint) pen for a second.
dejar a alguien atrás 1. irse sin alguien to leave someone behind 2. dejar atrás a alguien ■ sacarle distancia a alguien to outdistance someone
dejar a alguien boquiabierto to make someone's jaw drop ■ to leave someone aghast
dejar a alguien como novia de pueblo *(L.am.)* ■ dejar a alguien en el arroyo to ditch someone ➤ Cuando se hizo un actor famoso, dejó a su ex como novia de pueblo, comenzó a salir con una famosa modelo. When he became a famous actor, he ditched his girlfriend and took up up with famous model.
dejar a alguien con la palabra en la boca to cut someone off in mid-sentence ■ to cut off someone in mid-sentence ➤ Me dejó con la palabra en la boca. He cut me off in mid-sentence.
dejar a alguien de la mano de Dios ■ abandonar a alguien a su suerte to abandon someone to his fate
dejar a alguien en bragas *(Esp.)* 1. *(sin dinero)* to fleece someone 2. en apuros to leave someone in a predicament ■ to leave someone in a fix
dejar a alguien en el arroyo to ditch someone ■ to leave someone high and dry
dejar a alguien en la estacada to leave someone high and dry
dejar a alguien en ridículo ■ dejar a alguien por ridículo ■ poner a alguien en ridículo ■ hacer quedar a alguien en ridículo to mock someone ■ to ridicule someone ■ to make a fool of someone
dejar a alguien en su sitio to kill someone dead in his tracks
dejar a alguien esperando ■ tener a alguien esperando to keep someone waiting ➤ Perdone por dejarlo (a usted) esperando. I'm sorry to keep you waiting. ■ Sorry to keep you waiting.
dejar a alguien fuera de algo to leave someone out of something
dejar a alguien fuera de juego ■ cortar a alguien ■ dar un corte a alguien to blank someone out ➤ Cuando reaccionó diciéndote "pobrecito", él te estaba dejando fuera de juego. ■ Cuando reaccionó diciéndote "pobrecito", él te estaba cortando. ■ Cuando reaccionó diciéndote "pobrecito", él te estaba dando un corte. When he reacted by saying "poor baby," he was blanking you out.
dejar a alguien hacer algo ■ dejar que alguien haga algo ■ permitir que alguien haga algo ■ permitir a alguien que haga algo to let someone do something ➤ No sé si mis padres me dejarán ir. I don't know if my parents will let me go. ➤ Ella no me deja que ayude con nada en la cocina. She won't let me help her do anything in the kitchen.
dejar a alguien lleno de estupor to leave someone speechless
dejar a alguien plantado ■ dar a alguien plantón ■ *(L.am.)* dejar a alguien varado to stand someone up ➤ ¡Me dejó plantado(-a)! ■ ¡Me dio plantón! ■ *(L.am.)* Me dejó varado. He stood me up! ➤ *(L.am.)* Ella lo dejó varado. ■ *(Esp., leísmo)* Ella le dejó plantado. She stood him up. ➤ Él la dejó plantada. ■ *(L.am.)* Él la dejó varada. He stood her up.
dejar a alguien por los suelos 1. poner a alguien verde to read someone the riot act 2. hacer a alguien morder el polvo to leave someone in the dust
dejar a alguien quedarse con algo to let someone have something ■ to let someone keep something ➤ Le dejé quedarse con el periódico. 1. *(a él)* I let him have the newspaper. ■ I let him keep the newspaper. 2. *(a ella)* I let her have the newspaper. ■ I let her keep the newspaper.
dejar a alguien sin llave to lock someone out ➤ ¿Por qué nos deja sin llave? Why are you locking us out?
dejar a salvo to set aside ■ to make an exception of
dejar a salvo su derecho de to reserve the right to

dejar a uno cansado ▪ hacer que uno se canse ▪ hacer a uno que se canse to make one tired ➤ The cough has made him tired. La tos le ha dejado cansado. ▪ La tos ha hecho que se canse.

dejar a uno hecho polvo ▪ sacar de onda **1.** to wear someone out **2.** to turn someone off ▪ to be a turnoff ➤ Su mojigatería me deja hecho polvo. His pious sneer is a turnoff.

dejar al perro fuera ▪ sacar al perro to let the dog out ▪ to put out the dog ▪ to put the dog out

dejar algo a alguien ▪ prestar algo a alguien to lend someone something ▪ to lend something to someone ➤ ¿Me dejas este video sólo hasta mañana? Would you lend me this video just until tomorrow? ➤ Déjame tu boli un momento. Lend me your (ballpoint) pen for a second.

dejar algo a la suerte to leave something to chance

dejar algo claro to clarify something ➤ Y para dejarlo más claro todavía... And to clarify it even further...

dejar algo cocinar ▪ proseguir la cocción to let something cook ➤ Dejar cocinar hasta que el pollo esté tierno. ▪ Proseguir la cocción hasta que el pollo esté tierno. Let it cook until the chicken is tender.

dejar algo con alguien to leave something with someone

dejar algo de lado to put something aside ▪ to put aside something ➤ Para concentrarme en mis estudios, necesitor eliminar distracciones, dejando de lado todo lo que no tenga que ver con mi carrera. To concentrate on school, I need to just clear the deck by putting aside all the extraneous activities of daily life. ➤ Necesito dejarlo de lado. I need to put it aside

dejar algo en el aire to leave something up in the air ▪ to leave something unresolved

dejar algo en manos de alguien to leave something in someone's hands ▪ to leave something in the hands of someone

dejar algo intacto to leave something intact

dejar algo para después to leave something for later

dejar algo para mañana to leave something for tomorrow ▪ to put off something until tomorrow

dejar algo para último to leave something until last ▪ to leave something till last ➤ Vamos a entregar los televisores portátiles ahora, el grande lo dejamos para último. Let's deliver the portable TV's first. The big one we'll leave till last.

dejar algo que desear ▪ dejar un poco que desear to leave something to be desired

dejar algo tal como lo había encontrado to leave something exactly as one found it ▪ to return something to its original condition

dejar alguien su marca en algo to leave one's mark on something ➤ En el siglo XIX los respectivos gobiernos de Jefferson, Polk, Lincoln y Hayes dejaron una marca indeleble en los Estados Unidos. In the 19th Century, the administrations of Jefferson, Polk, Lincoln and Hayes left a indelible mark on the United States.

dejar aparte to put aside

dejar atrás to leave behind ▪ to outdistance

dejar bastante que desear ▪ dejar mucho que desear to leave a lot to be desired

dejar bien patente (que...) ▪ dejar bien en claro to make very clear (that...)

dejar buena ventaja ▪ dejar buena ganancia to net a good profit ▪ to bring in a good profit

dejar caer algo to drop something (on purpose) ➤ Galileo dejó caer pesas desde la torre inclinada de Pisa. Galileo dropped weights from the Leaning Tower of Pisa.

dejar caer algo en una conversación to let something drop in a conversation

dejar caer una bomba to drop a bomb

dejar chafado a alguien to take the wind out of someone's sails ▪ to rain on someone's parade

dejar chiquito a alguien to belittle someone

dejar claro que... to make clear that...

dejar cocer a fuego lento to (let) cook on low heat ▪ to (let) cook over low heat

dejar colar ▪ dejar que alguien se cuele to let someone up in line ▪ to let someone up ▪ to let someone break the line ▪ to let someone cut in line

dejar como un colador ▪ acribillar a balazos to riddle with bullets

dejar con la boca abierta ▪ quedarse helado to be flabbergasted

dejar con la carga en las costillas to leave someone holding the bag

dejar con la palabra en la boca to cut someone off (from speaking) ▪ to leave someone hanging

dejar consignado to commit to writing ▪ to put in writing

dejar correr el aire ▪ dejar que corra el aire ▪ airear algo ▪ ventilar algo to air out something ▪ to air something out ▪ to let in some fresh air ▪ to ventilate something ▪ to let (some) fresh air into something

dejar de comer to stop eating (dinner) ▪ to pause from one's dinner ➤ Sin dejar de comer *(él)* Without pausing from his dinner ▪ *(ella)* Without pausing from her dinner

dejar de existir to cease to exist ▪ to cease to be

dejar de fastidiar a alguien to get off someone's back

dejar de fumar de golpe to quit smoking cold turkey

dejar de fumar definitivamente to quit smoking for good

dejar de hacer algo 1. to stop doing something ▪ to no longer do something **2.** *(referido especialmente a costumbres)* to get away from doing something ➤ *(noticia)* Los extranjeros dejan de encabezar la lista de detenidos por tráfico de drogas en Barajas. Foreigners no longer head the list of people arrested for drug trafficking at Barajas. ➤ En los Estado Unidos, la gente ha dejado de decir "señor". In the United States, people have gotten away from saying "sir."

dejar de llover ▪ escampar to stop raining

dejar de ser no longer to be ▪ to no longer exist

dejar de tener no longer to have ➤ Había dejado de tener... *(él)* He no longer had... ▪ *(ella)* She no longer had...

dejar dicho con alguien to leave word with someone

dejar dicho que... to leave word for someone to... ➤ Would you leave word for her to call me? ¿Le puede dejar dicho que me llame?

dejar el abrigo (en la percha) ▪ colgar el abrigo to hang up one's coat

dejar el bigote to grow a mustache

dejar el cargo to leave office ➤ Tras dejar el cargo... After leaving office... ➤ Al dejar el cargo... On leaving office...

dejar el llanto *(literario o médico)* ▪ parar de llorar ▪ dejar de llorar to stop crying

dejar el motor funcionando ▪ dejar el motor andando ▪ dejar el coche en marcha to leave the motor running ▪ to leave the engine running

dejar el poder to leave power ▪ to give up power ▪ to leave office

dejar el teléfono descolgado to leave the telephone off the hook

dejar el tema ▪ abandonar el tema to drop the subject

dejar en alguien una impronta indelible ▪ dejar en alguien una huella indelible to have a lasting impact on someone

dejar en libertad to set free ▪ to free ▪ to release

dejar en porreta ▪ estar en porreta ▪ estar en cueros to be stark naked ▪ to be nude ▪ to be in the nude

dejar en remojo las habas durante la noche to soak the beans overnight

dejar en reposo el té ▪ dejar reposar el té to steep the tea ➤ Déjalo en reposo un momento. ▪ Déjalo reposar un momento. Let it steep for a minute.

dejar la cosa así to let it go ➤ Dejaré la cosa así esta vez. I'll let it go this time.

dejar mancha to stain ▪ to leave a stain

dejar mucho que desear ▪ dejar bastante que desear to leave a lot to be desired

dejar olvidado algo to forget something ▪ to leave something behind ▪ to forget to take something ➤ *(fresas en la frutería)* Las dejó olvidadas. She forgot (to take) them. ▪ She left them behind.

dejar patente que to make clear that ▪ to make obvious that ➤ El líder del partido socialista exigió que el gobierno del País Vasco garantice la seguridad de todos los socialistas que ocupan cargos públicos ya que ETA ha dejado patente que les tiene en el punto de mira. The Socialist party leader demanded that the government of País Vasco guarantee the security of all socialists in government positions since ETA has made clear that it has targeted them.

dejar pisado el embrague to ride the clutch

dejar plantado a alguien ■ dar un plantón a alguien to stand someone up ➤ ¡Me dejó plantada! He stood me up!

dejar por los suelos a alguien to demoralize someone ■ to leave somebody in the dust ➤ Nos dejó por los suelos. He left us in the dust.

dejar puerto ■ zarpar to leave port ■ to set sail

dejar que algo se enfríe *(cocina)* to let something cool down ■ to let something cool off

dejar que alguien se cuele ■ dejar colar to let someone up in line ■ to let someone up ■ to let someone break the line

dejar que alguien se vaya ■ soltarlo a alguien to let go of someone ■ to release someone ■ to let someone go

dejar que corra el aire (para ventilar algo) ■ dejar correr el aire ■ airear algo ■ ventilar algo to air out something ■ to air something out ■ to ventilate something ■ to let in some fresh air ■ to let some fresh air into something ➤ Abre las ventanas para (dejar) que corra el aire en el apartamento. Open the windows and air out the apartment. ➤ Abre las ventanas para (dejar) que corra el aire. Open the windows to air it out.

dejar que el motor funcione ■ dejar que el motor ande to let the motor run ■ to let the engine run ➤ En las mañanas frías, se debe dejar que el motor funcione por cinco minutos antes de manejar. On a cold morning, you should let the motor run for five minutes before driving.

dejar que el pasado permanezca enterrado not to dredge up the past ■ to let the past remain (the) past

dejar que se seque to let it dry ➤ Hay que dejar que se seque antes de saber si necesita otra mano. You have to let it dry before you can tell if it needs a second coat.

dejar quieto to put down something (that one is holding) in one's hand ➤ Deja quieta la escoba y mira quién ha llamado. Put the broom down and see who's at the door.

dejar reposar el té ■ dejar en reposo el té to steep the tea ➤ Déjalo reposar un minuto. ■ Déjalo en reposo un minuto. Let it steep for a minute.

dejar salir al perro to let the dog out ➤ Deja salir al perro. Let the dog out.

dejar su escritorio ■ no estar en su escritorio to be away from one's desk ■ to have stepped away from one's desk ➤ Ha dejado su escritorio un momento. ■ No está en su escritorio en este momento. He's away from his desk at the moment. ■ He's stepped away from his desk for a moment.

dejar su trabajo to quit one's job ➤ Me siento bien por su decisión de dejar su trabajo y montar un negocio por su cuenta. I feel good about his decision to quit his job and go into business for himself.

dejar todo de lado to put everything aside ■ to drop everything

dejar todo de un lado ■ poner todo de un lado to put everything on one side

dejar tras de sí to leave behind

dejar un apartamento *(L.am.)* ■ mudarse de apartamento to move out of an apartment

dejar un cerco en un mueble to leave a ring on a piece of furniture ➤ Please don't put your glass on the piano. It leaves a ring. Por favor, no pongas tu vaso en el piano. Deja un cerco.

dejar un departamento *(Méx.)* to move out of an apartment

dejar un hueco para el postre to leave room for dessert

dejar un mensaje to leave a message ➤ No me acuerdo si dejé mensaje. I can't remember if I left a message.

dejar un piso *(Esp.)* to move out of an apartment ■ to move out of a flat

dejar un puesto to vacate a post

dejar un recado ■ dejar un mensaje to leave a message

dejar un sitio hecho una leonera to make a colossal mess ■ to turn (the place) into a pig pen ➤ Los niños de la guardería dejaron la clase hecha una leonera pero echaron la culpa a la otra clase. The kindergarden children made a colossal mess in the classroom but blamed the other class. ■ The kindergarden children turned the place into a pig pen but blamed the other class.

dejar un tema to drop a subject ■ to get off a subject

dejar una huella duradera a alguien to make a lasting impression on someone ■ to have a lasting influence on someone

dejar una impresión en alguien to make an impression on someone

dejaré la cosa así esta vez ■ por esta vez lo perdono ■ déjalo, así no más I'll let it go this time

dejarle a alguien con la mosca detrás de la oreja to put a bug in someone's ear

dejarle a alguien una nota diciéndole... to leave someone a note saying...

dejarle a uno sin habla ■ quitar el habla a uno to leave one speechless

dejarle a uno sin respiración to make one lose one's breath ➤ El viento ártico le dejó sin respiración. The arctic wind made him lose his breath.

dejarle atónito a alguien to astonish someone

dejarle bien parado en su libro ■ dejarle bien en su libro ■ tenerle en alta estima en su libro to rate high in someone's book ➤ Ella no le deja bien (parado) en su libro. He doesn't rate very high in her book.

dejarle fuera de combate a alguien to put someone out of commission ■ to put someone out of action

dejarle un mal sabor en la boca to leave a bad taste in one's mouth

dejarle un mensaje a alguien ■ dejarle un recado a alguien to leave someone a message

dejarle ver cómo to give you an idea of how ■ to give you some idea of how ➤ Esto te deja ver cómo... This gives you an idea of how... ■ This gives you some idea of how...

dejarlo aquí to call it a day ■ to knock it off ➤ Son las cinco. Dejémoslo aquí. It's five o'clock. Let's call it a day. ■ It's five o'clock. Let's knock it off.

dejarlo descansar to give it a break ■ to give it a rest

dejarlo listo para to get it ready for

dejarlo lo más sencillo posible ■ dejarlo lo más simple posible ■ simplificarlo lo más que se pueda ■ simplificarlo al máximo to keep it simple ■ to keep it as simple as possible

dejarlo lo más simple posible ■ dejarlo lo más sencillo posible ■ simplificarlo lo más que se pueda ■ simplificarlo al máximo to keep it simple ■ to keep it as simple as possible

dejarlo tal cual to leave it the way it is ■ to leave it as it is ■ to leave it like it is

dejarse a la luna de Valencia to be left out in the cold

dejarse avasallar por alguien to let someone push one around ■ to let oneself be pushed around by someone ■ to allow oneself to be pushed around by someone ➤ No te dejes avasallar por él. Don't let him push you around. ■ Don't let yourself be pushed around by him. ■ Don't allow yourself to be pushed around by him.

dejarse caer en ■ visitar to drop by ■ to drop in ➤ Yo pasaba por aquí y decidí dejarme caer en tu casa. I was just passing by and thought I'd drop in.

dejarse caer en el sofá to flop down on the couch

dejarse caer por alguien to descend on someone ■ to impose on someone

dejarse crecer el bigote ■ dejarse el bigote to grow a mustache

dejarse crecer el pelo ■ dejarse el pelo (más) largo to let one's hair grow (longer) ➤ (Ella) debería dejarse crecer el pelo. She should let her hair grow (longer).

dejarse crecer la barba ■ dejar la barba to grow a beard

dejarse decir que... to let it slip that...

dejarse el bigote to grow a mustache ➤ Se dejó el bigote. He grew a mustache.

dejarse el pelo (más) largo ■ dejarse crecer el pelo to let one's hair grow (longer) ➤ (Ella) debería dejarse crecer el pelo. She should let her hair grow (longer).

dejarse llevar (por la corriente) to get carried away ➤ Me dejé llevar. I got carried away.

dejarse oír to make oneself heard

dejarse tiempo suficiente para to allow oneself enough time to ■ to leave oneself enough time to

dejarse una pareja to break up ▪ to split up ➤ María y Anselmo se han dejado. Maria and Anselmo have broken up. ▪ Maria and Anselmo have split up.
dejarse ver to show one's face ▪ to show up
dejarse ver por alguien to get in to see someone ➤ Lincoln despidió a un general cierta vez porque éste no se dejaba ver por nadie. Lincoln fired a general one time because nobody could get in to see him.
dejárselo a cuenta de alguien ▪ quedar a cuenta de alguien to be someone's problem ▪ to be on someone's shoulders ▪ to be up to someone
dejárselo puesto *(refiriéndose al abrigo, por ejemplo)* to leave it on
¡déjate de cumplidos! cut the compliments!
¡déjate de bromas! cut the jokes!
¡déjate de eso! cut it out!
¡déjate de manías! ▪ ¡no seas tonto! ▪ ¡no te pongas tonto! don't be silly!
deje que se lo muestre let me show you
déjelo (usted) a mi cuenta ▪ déjelo de mi cuenta leave it to me
déjelo (usted) de mi cuenta ▪ déjelo a mi cuenta leave it to me
déjeme en paz leave me alone
dejo de comprenderte I don't follow you
del actual ▪ del corriente of this month ➤ El quince del actual The fifteenth of this month
ser **del agrado de uno** to be to one's liking
del agrado de uno: no ser ~ not to be to one's liking
del comienzo from the beginning ➤ El profesor de música dijo, "Practiquemos del comienzo." The music teacher said, "Now, take it from the beginning."
de cero: hacer algo ~ 1. to make something from scratch 2. to make one of a kind ➤ Hice este bizcocho de cero. I made this cake from scratch. ➤ Hice esta maqueta de cero. I scratch-built this model. ➤ Hicieron la casa de cero. They built a one-of-a-kind house.
del corriente ▪ del actual of this month ➤ El quince del corriente ▪ El quince del actual The fifteenth of this month
del cual of which
del demonio: hacer un calor ~ to be hot as hell (outside)
del demonio: hacer un frío ~ to be cold as hell (outside)
del derecho: ponerse una prenda ~ to turn a garment right side out
del día: fruta ~ fresh fruit
del día: pescado ~ today's catch
del día: plato ~ today's special
del dicho al hecho hay mucho trecho ▪ del dicho al hecho hay un largo trecho ▪ es más fácil decirlo que hacerlo it's easier said than done ▪ that's easier said than done
ser **del dominio público** to be in the public domain
estar **del lado de alguien** to be on someone's side
del mismo modo ▪ de la misma forma ▪ de la misma manera in the same way
del pasado of last month
del revés: poner una prenda ~ to turn a garment wrong side out
del talión: la ley ~ an eye for an eye
del tamaño de as big as
del tiempo *(Esp.)* 1. *(fruta)* de temporada in season 2. *(vino)* sin enfriar unchilled ▪ at room temperature 3. *(comida)* sin calentar unheated ▪ at room temperature ➤ ¿Caliente o del tiempo? (Would you like it served) heated or at room temperature?
estar **del todo** to be completely ▪ to be...all over ➤ El cielo está del todo gris. ▪ El cielo está gris por todas partes. ▪ El cielo está gris por todos (los) lados. The sky is gray all over. ▪ The sky is completely gray.
del todo: explicarlo ~ to explain it completely ➤ No lo explica del todo. It doesn't completely explain it.
del todo: tomárselo ~ to drink it all (up) ➤ *(Horacio Quiroga)* La abeja haragana se lo tomaba del todo. The lazy bee would drink it all herself.
del todo cierto: no ser ~ not to be completely true ▪ not to be entirely true ▪ not to be entirely accurate
ser **del todo confuso** to be all a blur ➤ Para mí sus conferencias son del todo confusas. To me his lectures are all a blur.
estar **del todo convencido** to be completely convinced
del uno al diez from one to ten
del *x* in apartment number *x* ▪ in number *x* ➤ El chaval del ocho The guy in apartment number eight ▪ The guy in number eight
delante de in front of
delante de Dios y de todo el mundo in front of God and everybody
estar **delante de las narices** to be right in front of one's nose ▪ to be right at the end of one's nose
estar **delante de los ojos** to be right before one's eyes
estar **delante del altar** ▪ estar ante el altar ▪ estar frente al altar to stand before the altar
delatar a alguien 1. to give someone away 2. to blow someone's cover ➤ Su acento lo delata. *(de él)* His accent gives him away. ▪ *(de usted)* Your accent gives you away. ➤ Su acento la delata. Her accent gives her away. ➤ *(Esp. leísmo)* Su acento le delata. *(de él)* His accent gives him away. ▪ *(de usted)* Your accent gives you away.
déle el pie y se tomará la mano give him an inch and he'll take a mile
déle mis mejores recuerdos 1. *(a él)* give him my best 2. *(a ella)* give her my best
déle un hervor ▪ llévelo a ebullición ▪ póngalo a hervir bring it to a boil
déles un hervor ▪ llévelos a ebullición ▪ póngalos a hervir bring them to a boil
delgada chaqueta ▪ cazadora ▪ campera liviana ▪ chaqueta liviana light jacket ▪ windbreaker
delicado equilibrio entre delicate balance between
delincuente de guante blanco white-collar criminal ▪ non-violent criminal
delineando: irse ~ to be taking shape ➤ El proyecto se va delineando. The project is taking shape.
delirios de grandeza delusions of grandeur
delirios paranoicos paranoid delusions
delirium tremens delirium tremens ▪ the d.t.'s
¡delo por hecho! consider it done!
demanda de demand for ➤ *(noticia)* Demanda de videoconferencias se dispara. Demand for videoconferencing skyrockets. ➤ Hay una mayor demanda de petróleo que (lo que hay) de suministro. There is a greater demand for oil than there is supply.
demanda para demand to ➤ Es mayor la demanda para estudiar español que para estudiar francés. There is a greater demand to study Spanish than French.
demanda se disparó demand skyrocketed ➤ La demanda y los precios se dispararon. The demand and the prices skyrocketed.
estar **demasiado enfermo para viajar** to be too sick to travel ▪ to be too ill to travel ➤ Estuve demasiado enfermo para viajar. ▪ He estado demasiado enfermo para viajar. I was too sick to travel.
estar **demasiado lejos de** to be too far away from ➤ Estuve demasiado lejos del podio para oír bien. I was too far away from the podium to hear well.
ser **demasiado poderoso para suprimir** to be too powerful to suppress
demasiado sé que... ▪ lo sé de sobra que... I know all too well that... ▪ I know only too well that... ▪ I know very well that...
ser **demasiado tarde para hacer algo** to be too late to do something
¡démosle la bienvenida a...! let's welcome...!
demostración de afecto show of affection ▪ expression of affection
demostrar la relevancia de algo to prove the relevance of something
demudársele a uno la cara to turn white in the face
denegar un recurso *(de una solicitud, etc.)* ▪ rechazar un recurso to deny an appeal
denegar una apelación *(en un juicio)* ▪ rechazar una apelación to deny an appeal
denegar una petición *(formal u oficial)* ▪ rechazar una petición to deny a request
denodados esfuerzos tireless efforts

dense prisa, que llegamos tarde (you all) hurry or we'll be late
densos debates ▪ debates intensos intense debate
dentaduras postizas false teeth ▪ dentures
dentro de within ▪ in
ser **dentro de lo posible** within the realm of possibility
dentro de lo que cabe under the circumstances
estar **dentro de mis atribuciones** to be within one's powers ▪ to be within one's province
dentro de nada in no time
dentro de poco ▪ en breve shortly ▪ before long ▪ in a little while
dentro de poco ▪ al poco tiempo ▪ poco tiempo después ▪ en breve a short time later ▪ a little later (on) ▪ shortly afterwards ▪ soon afterwards ▪ in a little while ▪ a short time after that ▪ shortly after that ▪ soon after that ▪ a short time after that ▪ before long
dentro de un plazo de *x* días ▪ en un plazo de *x* ▪ days within (a period of) *x* days ➤ La multa deberá ser pagada en un plazo de treinta días. The fine must be paid within (a period of) thirty days.
dentro de un ratito in a little while ▪ within a short while
dentro de un ratito: te veo ~ I'll see you in a little while
dentro de un año within a year
dentro de unos años ▪ en (unos) pocos años within a few years ➤ Dentro de unos años, las enfermedades retrovirales podrán ser tratadas. ▪ En (unos) pocos años, las enfermedades retrovirales podrán ser tratadas. Within a few years, viral illnesses will become treatable.
dentro de unos pocos minutos within a few minutes ▪ within the next few minutes
dentro de *x* años within *x* years ➤ Algunos expertos dicen que el problema del calentamiento global deberá resolverse dentro de diez años. Some experts say the global warming problem must be solved within ten years.
dentro de *x* horas within *x* hours ➤ Llegarán dentro de dos horas. They'll be here within two hours.
dentro de *x* semanas within *x* weeks
estar **dentro del alcance** to be within reach
dentro del ámbito de uno under one's purview ▪ within one's purview
dentro y fuera de in and around
denunciar a alguien a la policía to report someone to the police
deparar(le) el futuro ▪ aguardar en el futuro (for) one's future to have in store ➤ Who knows what the future has in store? ¿Quién sabe lo que depara el futuro? ➤ I don't know what the future has in store for me. No sé qué me depara el futuro a mí.
depararle la suerte (for one's) luck to have in store ▪ (for one's) destiny to have in store
departamento de facturas billing department
Departamento de Seguridad de la Patria *(EE UU)* Department Of Homeland Security
departir con aguien to converse at length with someone ▪ to have a protracted conversation with someone
depende de cómo se mire it depends on how you look at it
depende de cuánto pueda hacer ▪ depende de hasta dónde llegue 1. *(yo)* it depends on how much I can get done 2. *(él)* it depends on how much he can get done 3. *(ella)* it depends on how much she can get done
depende de hasta dónde llegue ▪ depende de cuánto pueda hacer 1. *(yo)* it depends on how much I can get done 2. *(él)* it depends on how much he can get done 3. *(ella)* it depends on how much she can get done
depende de lo que pase it depends on what happens
depende de los gustos de cada cual it's a matter of individual tastes
depende mucho de it depends a lot on ▪ a lot depends on
depender de 1. to depend on ▪ to be contingent on ▪ to be contingent upon 2. to work out of one's house 3. to come under 4. to depend on the individual ▪ to be a matter of individual preference ➤ Dependerá de que... It will depend on what... ➤ Mi hermano depende de su casa. My brother works out of his house. ➤ La agencia depende del Departamento de Defensa. The agency comes under the Department of Defense. ➤ *(cocinero en la tele)* Depende de cada uno. It's a matter of individual preference. ▪ It's according to taste.
depender de los gustos de cada cual to be a matter of taste ▪ to be a matter of individual tastes ➤ Depende de los gustos de cada cual. It's a matter of (individual) taste.
estar **dependiente de** ▪ depender de to be dependent on ▪ to depend on
depositar la confianza en to place one's confidence in
depositar las ilusiones en to place one's hopes in
depósito lleno ▪ tanque lleno full tank
depreciar el valor ▪ depreciarse to decrease in value ▪ to depreciate ➤ Los carros deprecian su valor con el tiempo. ▪ Los carros se deprecian con el tiempo. Cars decrease in value over time. ▪ Cars depreciate (in value) over time.
depresión suicida suicidal depression
¡deprisa! quick!
depurar el software to debug the software
depurar las partes malas *(ensayo, por ejemplo)* to polish up the bad parts ▪ to polish up the rough parts
derecha más dura *(políticamente)* extreme right ▪ far right ➤ *(titular)* Derecha más dura tiene la llave de la gobernabilidad de Portugal. Extreme right holds the key to the governability of Portugal. ▪ Far right holds the key to the governability of Portugal.
derecho a cocina kitchen privileges
derecho a la cara right to one's face
derecho consuetudinario common law ➤ El derecho consuetudinario inglés English common law
derecho de asilo law of sanctuary
derecho de paso ▪ derecho de tránsito right of way
derecho de tránsito ▪ derecho de paso right of way
derechos de autor royalties
derogar por inconstitucional una ley to declare a law unconstitutional ▪ to rule that a law is unconstitutional
derogar una ley 1. to repeal a law 2. to strike down a law
derramar lágrimas ▪ llorar to shed tears ▪ to cry ▪ to weep
derramar lágrimas de cocodrilo to shed crocodile tears
derrame cerebral ▪ congestión cerebral ▪ infarto cerebral ▪ trombosis cerebral stroke ▪ cerebral hemorrhage
derrapar en una curva to skid on a curve ➤ En los rallies los conductores derrapan en casi todas las curvas. At the auto rallies, the drivers skid on practically all the curves.
derrapar sobre el hielo ▪ patinar sobre el hielo ▪ deslizarse sobre el hielo to skid on the ice
derribar a un oponente *(con un golpe)* ▪ doblegar a un oponente to fell an opponent ▪ to down an opponent ▪ to defeat an opponent
derribar algo el viento to blow something down ▪ to blow down something
derribar un avión ▪ tirar un avión to shoot down an airplane ▪ to down an airplane
derrocar el gobierno to overthrow the government
derrochar energía ▪ desperdiciar energía ▪ malgastar energía ▪ dilapidar energía to waste energy
derrota humillante humiliating defeat
derrotar a la competencia to beat the competition ▪ to defeat the competition
derrotar a un adversario a algo *(política, deporte, ajedrez)* ▪ derrotar a un adversario en algo ▪ ganar a un adversario a algo ▪ ganar a un adversario en algo to defeat an opponent at something ▪ to beat an opponent at something ➤ Me derrota al ajedrez con los ojos cerrados, así que nunca juego con él. ▪ Me derrota en el ajedrez con los ojos cerrados, así que nunca juego con él. ▪ Me gana al ajedrez con los ojos cerrados, así que nunca juego con él. ▪ Me gana en el ajedrez con los ojos cerrados, así que nunca juego con él. He defeats me at chess hands down, so I never play him. ▪ He beats me at chess hands down, so I never play him.
derrumbamiento de tierras ▪ corrimiento de tierras ▪ derrumbe de tierras ▪ desprendimiento de tierras landslide
derrumbar un edificio ▪ tirar un edificio to tear down a building ▪ to tear a building down ▪ to raze a building ➤ Derrumbaron el edificio. ▪ Tiraron el edificio. They tore down the building. ▪ They tore the building down. ▪ They razed the building. ➤ Lo derrumbaron. ▪ Lo tiraron. They tore it down. ▪ They razed it.

derrumbarse bajo el peso de to give way under the weight of ▪ to collapse under the weight of ➤ El puente colgante se derrumbó bajo el peso de los peatones. The suspension bridge gave way under the weight of the pedestrians. ▪ The suspension bridge collapsed under the weight of the pedestrians.

el **derrumbe de la economía** ▪ colapso de la economía ▪ hundimiento de la economía collapse of the economy ▪ sinking of the economy

el **derrumbe de tierras** ▪ derrumbamiento de tierras ▪ corrimiento de terras ▪ desprendimiento de tierras landslide

desabrochar un botón to unbutton a buttton

desafiar la explicación ▪ no tener explicación ▪ no tener arreglo ▪ *(Esp.)* ▪ no tener apaño to defy explanation ➤ El padre le dijo al hijo, "Tu comportamiento desafía la explicación." ▪ El padre le dijo al hijo, "Tu comportamiento no tiene explicación." ▪ El padre le dijo al hijo, "Tu comportamiento no tiene arreglo." ▪ El padre le dijo al hijo, "Tu comportamiento no tiene apaño." The father said to his son, "Your behavior defies explanation."

desahuciar a alguien to take away all hope from someone ➤ Estuvo desahuciada. She was destitute.

desajustarse las coyunturas ▪ sacarle las yugas ▪ hacer sonar los dedos to crack one's knuckles

desalojar un edificio to evacuate a building

desalojo de un edificio evacuation of a building

desandar el camino ▪ desandar sus pasos ▪ deshacer el camino ▪ desandar lo andado to retrace one's steps ▪ to go back over one's steps

desandar lo andado **1.** volver por donde uno fue to retrace one's steps **2.** volver a empezar to start over

desandar sus pasos ▪ desandar el camino ▪ deshacer el camino to retrace one's steps ▪ to go back over one's steps ➤ Mirando este mapa, podemos desandar nuestros pasos de hoy. By looking at this map we can retrace our steps today.

desangrar hasta morir ▪ morir desangrado(-a) to bleed to death

desanimar a alguien para que no haga algo to discourage someone from doing something

desanimarse ▪ abatirse to lose heart

desaparecer de escena to disappear from the scene ▪ to disappear off the scene ▪ to drop out of sight

desaparecer del mapa to disappear off the face of the earth ▪ to vanish from the face of the earth

desaparecer sin dejar rastro to disappear without a trace

desaprovechar el tiempo ▪ malgastar el tiempo ▪ perder el tiempo ▪ desperdiciar el tiempo ▪ despilfarrar el tiempo to waste time

desaprovechar el tiempo de alguien ▪ malgastar el tiempo de alguien ▪ perder el tiempo de alguien ▪ desperdiciar el tiempo de alguien ▪ despilfarrar el tiempo de alguien to waste someone's time

desarmar algo pieza por pieza to take something apart piece by piece ▪ to disassemble something piece by piece

desarticular una red criminal to smash a criminal ring ▪ to dismantle a criminal ring

desarticularse un hueso ▪ dislocarse un hueso to dislocate a bone ▪ *(coloquial)* to pop out of joint ➤ Se le desarticuló el codo. ▪ Se le dislocó el codo. He dislocated his elbow. ▪ *(coloquial)* His elbow popped out of joint.

desatar las iras de alguien ▪ provocar las iras de alguien to unleash someone's anger ▪ to arouse someone's anger ▪ to provoke someone's anger ▪ to unleash someone's ire ▪ to arouse someone's ire ▪ to provoke someone's ire

desatar una ola de ataques to unleash a wave of attacks

desatar una tormenta to stir up a hornet's nest

desatarse un temporal ▪ desatarse una tormenta (for a) storm to break

desatarse una tormenta ▪ desatarse un temporal (for a) storm to break ➤ Se desató una tormenta. A storm broke.

desayunar con algo to have something for breakfast ➤ Vamos a desayunar con huevos. We're having eggs for breakfast.

desayunar fuerte to have a big breakfast

desayuno flojo ▪ desayuno liviano light breakfast

desayuno liviano ▪ desayuno flojo light breakfast

desbancar a alguien ▪ derrocar a alguien to oust someone

desbaratar una manifestación to break up a demonstration

desbastar algo to buff up something ▪ to buff something up ➤ La funda del diente necesita ser desbastada un poco. The cap of the tooth needs to be buffed up a little. ➤ El dentista lo desbastó. The dentist buffed it up.

desbordamiento del Nilo flooding of the Nile

desbordarse (la cañería) to back up (and overflow) ➤ Cuando se atasca la cañería, se desborda el agua. When the pipe is clogged, the water backs up and overflows.

desbordarse (un río) to overflow ▪ to overflow its banks ▪ to back up ➤ El río se desbordó. The river overflowed its banks.

descafeinado a máquina brewed decaf ➤ ¿Tienes descafeinado a máquina? Do you have brewed decaf?

descalzarse los guantes ▪ sacarse los guantes to take off one's gloves ▪ to take one's gloves off

¿descansaste bien? ▪ ¿dormiste bien? did you sleep well?

descanse en paz may he rest in peace ▪ may she rest in peace

descanso eterno eternal rest

descanso refrescante refreshing break

descarga de adrenalina ▪ (el) subidón de adrenalina burst of adrenalin ▪ rush of adrenalin

descargar la conciencia to unburden one's conscience

descargar los remos ▪ remar to swing the oars ▪ to row

descargar sus tensiones sobre uno to take one's frustrations out on someone

descargar un archivo to download a file ➤ Descargué el archivo de Internet. I downloaded the file from the Internet.

descartar algo to rule out something ▪ to rule something out ➤ Lo descarté. I ruled it out.

descartar la idea de to rule out the idea of ▪ to abandon the idea of

descartar la posibilidad de que... to rule out the possibility that...

descartar una hipótesis to rule out a hypothesis

descartar una idea to abandon an idea ▪ to rule out an idea ▪ to rule an idea out ▪ to reject an idea

descender haciendo rapel to rapel down... ▪ to rapel off... ➤ The mountain climbers rapelled down the side of the cliff. ▪ The mountain climbers rapelled off the cliff. Los andinistas descendieron haciendo rapel del precipicio. ▪ Los alpinistas descendieron haciendo rapel del precipicio.

descenso de la temperatura drop in temperature ➤ Un ligero descenso de las temperaturas. A slight drop in temperatures.

descenso del precio de petróleo drop in oil prices

descenso medio ▪ declive medio average decrease

estar **descentrado** to be off center ➤ Ese cuadro está descentrado. That picture is off center.

descolgar el teléfono to take the (tele)phone off the hook ▪ to take the receiver off the hook

descolgar un cartel to take down a sign

descolgarse de algo to break away from something

descolgarse de una huelga to break a strike

la **descomposición del ozono** ozone decay ▪ ozone depletion

estar **desconcertado(-a) ante** ▪ quedarse desconcertado(-a) ante to be baffled by ▪ to be baffled at ➤ Las operadoras extranjeras a veces están desconcertadas ante los listados telefónicos estadounidenses. (The) foreign operators are sometimes baffled by the U.S. directory listings.

desconectarse de algo to tune out something ▪ to tune something out

desconectarse un poco to chill out

descongelar la nevera ▪ descongelar la heladera to defrost the refrigerator

desconocer que... to be unaware that... ▪ not to be aware that... ▪ not to know that... ➤ Muchos aquejados de cáncer desconocen que lo padecen. Many cancer sufferers are unaware that that they have it. ▪ Many cancer sufferers are not aware that they have it. ▪ Many cancer sufferers do not know that they have it.

descorrer la cortina ▪ correr la cortina to open the curtain ▪ to draw back the curtain

descorrer las persianas ▪ abrir las persianas ▪ levantar las persianas to open the blinds ▪ to raise the blinds

descoserse de risa ▪ partirse de risa ▪ desternillarse to be in stitches ▪ to split one's sides laughing
descuartizar a alguien ▪ criticar to tear someone apart ▪ to cut someone to ribbons ▪ to criticize
descubrir cómo hacer algo to figure out how to do something
descubrir el pastel ▪ levantar la liebre to spill the beans ▪ to give away a secret ▪ to let the cat out of the bag
descubrir las cartas to show one's hand ▪ to reveal one's hand
descubrir que... to discover that... ➤ Einstein descubrió que la gravedad hace encorvar la luz. Einstein discovered that gravity bends light.
descubrir sus emociones ▪ desenmascarar sus emociones ▪ traicionar sus emociones to betray one's feelings ▪ to give away one's feelings
descubrir una estatua to unveil a statue
descubrirse sus verdaderos sentimientos ▪ desvelarse sus verdaderos sentimientos to betray one's true feelings ▪ to give away one's true feelings ▪ to give one's true feelings away
¡descuida! ▪ ¡no te preocupes! don't worry! ▪ don't worry about it! ▪ it's okay!
desde afuera 1. from the outside 2. from the outside looking in
desde ahí ▪ a partir de ahí ▪ desde aquí ▪ a partir de aquí from here ➤ Desde ahí, se va a (la) Plaza de Castilla y tira a la derecha. From here, you go to Plaza de Castilla and turn right.
desde ahí en adelante 1. desde aquí en adelante from here on 2. desde ahora en adelante ▪ desde este momento en adelante from now on ▪ from here on out
desde ahora at this point ➤ No sé decirte desde ahora si estaré ese fin de semana. I don't know at this point if I'll be here that weekend.
desde allí ▪ a partir de allí from there on ➤ Desde allí, se va al kilómetro trece y tira en la carretera México-Toluca. From there, you go to kilometer thirteen and turn onto the Mexico-Toluca highway.
desde antes... previously... ▪ already... ▪ prior to
desde aquel día en adelante from that day on
¿desde cuándo recibes clases de inglés? how long have you been taking English?
¿desde cuándo te ocurre? *(dolor de cabeza, por ejemplo)* when did it start? ▪ how long have you had it?
¿desde cuándo vives aquí? how long have you lived here?
desde dentro ▪ de dentro from inside
desde determinada posición from a certain angle ➤ *(Unamuno)* Hay un peñasco que, visto desde determinada posición, guarda una cierta semejanza con la figura de un pájaro. There is a boulder that, seen from a certain angle, gives the appearance of being a (song) bird.
desde distintos puntos de vista from different points of view ▪ from differing points of view
desde el día en que nací since the day I was born
desde el domingo 1. since Sunday 2. ▪ a partir del domingo starting Sunday ▪ as of Sunday
desde el instante en que from the moment (that) ➤ Desde el instante en que te vi... From the moment (that) I saw you...
desde el momento en que te vi from the moment I saw you ▪ (from) the minute I saw you ➤ Desde el momento en que te vi, estuve enamorado. From the moment I saw you, I was in love.
desde el primer momento from the outset ▪ since the outset
desde el principio from the start ▪ from the first ▪ from the beginning ▪ from the outset ▪ *(coloquial)* from the get-go
desde el principio hasta el final from beginning to end
desde el punto de vista de ▪ bajo el punto de vista de from the point of view of
desde entonces since ▪ since then ▪ since that time ➤ No he vuelto desde entonces. I haven't been back since. ▪ I haven't gone back since. ➤ No lo he visto desde entonces. I haven't seen him since (that time). ➤ No la he visto desde entonces. I haven't seen her since (that time).
desde entonces acá from that day to this
desde este momento en adelante ▪ de ahora en adelante ▪ en lo sucesivo from now on
desde finales de... since the late... ➤ Desde finales de los años sesenta... Since the late sixties...
desde fuera from the outside
estar **desde fuera mirando adentro** ▪ estar desde fuera mirando hacia dentro ▪ estar viendo los toros desde la barrera to be on the outside looking in
desde hace años ▪ lleva años for years ➤ Desde hace años va a misa todos los días. For years he has gone to mass every day. ➤ Soy un lector de su revista desde hace años. I have been a reader of your magazine for years.
desde hace más de *x* años for more than *x* years
desde hace meses for months
desde hace mucho tiempo (for) a long time
desde hace muchos años for many years
desde hace tiempo for some time (now)
desde hace *x* años for *x* years ➤ Lo conozco desde hace siete años. I have known him for seven years. ➤ Tengo barba desde hace dos años. I've had a beard for two years.
desde hace *x* días for *x* days
desde hace *x* horas for *x* hours ➤ Marta toca el piano desde hace dos horas. Marta has been playing the piano for two hours.
desde hace *x* meses for *x* months
desde hacía *x* años for *x* years ➤ Él jugaba fútbol desde hacía veinte años. He'd been playing soccer for twenty years.
desde la atalaya de from the vantage point of ➤ Desde la atalaya de la estrella polar, teóricamente, podríamos correlacionar la posición orbital de la Tierra con las estaciones, hasta los meses e incluso los días del año. From the vantage point of the Pole Star, theoretically, we could correlate the Earth's orbital position with the seasons, down to the months and even days of the year.
desde la óptica norteamericana from the American point of view
desde lejos ▪ de lejos from a distance
desde los albores de la civilización since the dawn of civilization
desde los años *x* hasta *y* from the age of *x* to *y* ➤ Viví en esa casa desde los cinco hasta los dieciocho años. I lived in that house from the age of five to eighteen.
desde los tiempos de since the days of ➤ Desde los tiempos del telégrafo. Since the days of the telegraph.
desde luego había there was indeed
desde mi punto de vista ▪ bajo mi punto de vista from my point of view
desde muy cerca: disparar ~ ▪ disparar a escasa distancia to fire at close range ▪ to fire from a short distance ➤ La mayoría de los huesos pertenecen a personas jóvenes que murieron por la destrucción de masa encefálica a causa de disparos de armas de fuego hechos desde muy cerca. Most of the bones are those of youths who died of massive head injuries caused by shots fired at close range.
desde niña since I was a little girl ▪ since I was a child
desde niño since I was a little boy ▪ since I was a child
desde pequeño(-a) from infancy ▪ *(yo)* (ever) since I was a child ➤ Es bilingüe desde pequeña. She is bilingual from infancy.
desde que since ➤ Desde que volví de viaje. Since getting back from my trip. ▪ Since returning from my trip. ➤ Ha vivido en México desde que tenía catorce años. He has lived in Mexico since he was fourteen (years old).
desde que el hombre existe como tal en la tierra since man as such has existed on earth
desde que el mundo es mundo ▪ desde antiguo ▪ de antiguo from time immemorial
desde que me levanté since I got up ➤ Tengo un dolor de garganta desde que me levanté esta mañana. I've had a sore throat since I got up this morning.
desde que tengo memoria for as long as I can remember ▪ for as long as I can recall
desde que tenía uno... since one was... ➤ Él juega al fútbol desde que tenía cinco años. He's been playing soccer since he was five (years old).
desde que tenía memoria for as long a I could remember ▪ for as long as I could recall ➤ I had been a bird watcher for as long as I could remember. Observaba aves desde que tenía memoria.

desde siempre 1. always 2. desde un principio ▪ desde el principio all along ▪ from the start ▪ from the beginning 3. en toda su vida ▪ en toda la vida all one's life ➤ Lo he sabido desde siempre I've always known that. ▪ I've always known it. ➤ Su esposa ha sabido lo de sus escapadas desde siempre. His wife has known about his escapades all along.

desde temprana edad from an early age

desde todo punto de vista ▪ a todas luces any way you look at it

desde un mes atrás for a month ▪ for the past month ▪ for a full month ➤ No he recibido ningún cheque de mi empleador desde un mes atrás. I haven't gotten a check from my employer for a month. ▪ I haven't gotten a check from my employer for the past month. ▪ I haven't gotten a check from my employer for a full month.

desde un principio from the very start

desde ya from this very moment on ▪ from that very moment on

¿desea que lo capturemos? do you want him captured? ▪ do you want us to capture him?

deseaba haberlo hecho 1. *(yo)* I wished I had 2. *(él)* he wished he had 3. *(ella)* she wished she had ➤ Yo mismo había querido pintar mi apartamento, y cuando vi el trabajo que hicieron los pintores, deseaba haberlo hecho. I had wanted to paint the apartment myself, and when I saw the job the painters did, I wished I had.

estar **deseando algo** to be looking forward to something ➤ Estoy deseando mis vacaciones. I am looking forward to my vacation.

desear que... to wish that ▪ to hope that... ➤ Desean que el tiempo cambie para mañana. They hope that the weather will change by tomorrow.

desearle a alguien un feliz cumpleaños to wish someone a happy birthday

desearle a alguien un feliz cumpleaños con retraso to wish someone a belated happy birthday ▪ to wish someone belatedly (a) happy birthday

desechar un mito to dispel a myth

desechos orgánicos organic waste

desembalar una caja to unpack a box ➤ Ahora me toca desembalar mis cajas de libros. Next, I have to unpack my boxes of books.

desembocar con to lead to

desembocar en to lead to ▪ to end at ▪ to "T" into ➤ La calle desemboca en López de Hoyos. The street ends at López de Hoyos. ▪ The street T's into López de Hoyos.

desembocar una amistad to lead to a friendship ➤ La entrevista desembocó en una amistad. The interview led to a friendship.

desempeñar un cargo en la compañía to hold a position in the company

desempeñar un elemento central to play a central role in ▪ to play a pivotal role in

desempeñar un papel to play a role ➤ Desempeñar un papel más activo en To play a more active role in

desencadenar una reacción química to trigger a chemical reaction

desenfundar una pistola to draw a pistol (from a holster) ▪ to pull (out) a pistol ▪ to draw a gun

¡desengáñate! (let's) face it! ▪ just face it!

desenlace (de un chiste) ▪ gracia punch line (of a joke)

desenmascarar a alguien to call someone's bluff

desenmascarar sus emociones ▪ descubrir sus emociones ▪ traicionar sus emociones to betray one's feelings ▪ to give away one's feelings

desentenderse de algo 1. to pretend not to know about something 2. to want nothing to do with something 3. to wash one's hands of something

desentrañar el mensaje to decipher the message

desentrañar el misterio to unravel the mystery

desentrañar la estructura del ADN to unravel the structure of DNA ▪ to piece together the structure of DNA

desenvainar una espada ▪ sacar una espada to draw a sword

desenvolverse bien en algo to take to something ▪ to be a natural at something ▪ to be a quick study in something

desenvolverse bien en to perform very well in ▪ to do very well in

desenvolverse con normalidad ▪ desenvolverse sin incidente to proceed normally

desenvolverse con soltura en un idioma to speak a language fluently

desenvolverse sin incidente ▪ desenvolverse con normalidad to go smoothly

estar **desenvuelto** to be easy-going ▪ to be mellow

el **deseo de que...** the wish that...

deseo frustrado *(sexual)* frustrated urge

estar **deseoso(-a) de** to be anxious to ▪ to be looking forward to ➤ Estoy deseoso de salir. I'm anxious to leave.

estar **deseoso(-a) de que** to be anxious for ▪ to be anxious that ➤ Estoy deseoso de que termine este curso I'm anxious for this course to end. ▪ I'm anxious that this course end.

desequilibrado(-a) mental a mentally unbalanced person

desertar a un país to defect to a country ➤ Lee Harvey Oswald, un inestable ex marine, desertó a la Unión Soviética. Lee Harvey Oswald, an unstable ex-Marine, defected to the Soviet Union.

desertar de un país to defect from a country ➤ Desertó de la Unión Soviéta. He defected from the Soviet Union.

estar **desesperado(-a) por hacer algo** ▪ desesperarse por 1. to be desperate to do something 2. estar que se sale de sus casillas por algo to be climbing the walls to do something ➤ Estaba desesperado por conseguir a alguien que le supliera. He was desperate to get someone to fill in for him. ➤ Están desesperados por lograr que su matrimonio funcione. They are desperate to make their marriage work. ➤ Mucha gente está desesperada por salir de la pobreza. ▪ Mucha gente está que se sale de sus casillas por salir de la pobreza. A lot of people are desperate to get out of poverty. ▪ A lot of people are climbing the walls to get out of poverty.

desestimar una prueba ▪ rechazar una prueba to disallow a piece of evidence ▪ to reject a piece of evidence

desestimar una petición ▪ rechazar una petición to reject a petition ➤ Un juez de Miami desestima la petición de asilo para Elián y dice que debe volver a Cuba. A Miami judge rejects the asylum petition for Elian and says he must return to Cuba.

desfalcar dinero ▪ desfalcar fondos to embezzle money ▪ to embezzle funds

desfallecer de ánimo ▪ desanimarse ▪ abatirse to lose heart

estar **desfasado(-a) con** to be out of phase with ▪ to be out of step with

desfilar en una pasarela to walk up and down a runway

desfondarse bajo el peso de to give way under the weight of ▪ to fall out under the weight of ➤ La caja se desfondó bajo el peso de los libros. The bottom of the box gave way under the weight of the books. ▪ The bottom of the box fell out under the weight of the books.

desgajar a uno de algo to tear someone away from something

desgajar un periódico to tear up a newspaper

el **desgaste de las montañas** wearing away of the mountains ▪ wearing down of the mountains ➤ El desgaste de las montañas es el resultado de millones de años de lluvia y viento. The mountains wore away as the result millions of years of rain and wind.

deshacer el camino ▪ desandar el camino to retrace one's steps ▪ to go back over one's steps

deshacer la maleta to unpack one's suitcase ▪ *(especialmente en el plural)* to unpack ones bags

deshacer una injusticia ▪ enmendar una injusticia to right a wrong

deshacerse de cosas to get rid of things ▪ to get rid of stuff ▪ *(coloquial)* to unload stuff

deshacerse de las formalidades ▪ olvidarse de las formalidades to dispense with the formalities ➤ Vamos a deshacernos de las formalidades e ir al grano. ▪ Vamos a olvidarnos de las formalidades e ir al grano. Let's dispense with the formalities and get down to brass tacks.

deshacerse de sus miedos to shake off one's fears

deshacerse en mil fragmentos to break into a thousand pieces

desinflar un neumático to let air out of a tire ■ to deflate a tire ➤ Desinfla un poco el neumático. Let some air out of the tire.

desistir (el juicio) to drop a case ➤ Una vez admitida a trámite, el juicio debe ser celebrado a menos que el demandante (lo) desista. Once filed, the lawsuit must be heard unless the plaintiff drops it.

desistirse de una búsqueda to suspend a search ■ to call off a search ➤ Al cabo de cuatro días, se desistió de la búsqueda. After four days the search was suspended.

desligarse de algo ■ desmarcarse de algo ■ disociarse de algo to distance oneself from something ■ to dissociate oneself from something ➤ El vicepresidente Al Gore se desligó de la decisión de sacar a Elián de la casa de sus primos. ■ El vicepresidente Al Gore se desmarcó de la decisión de sacar a Elián de la casa de sus primos. ■ El vicepresidente Al Gore se disoció de la decisión de sacar a Elián de la casa de sus primos. Vice president Al Gore distanced himself from the decision to take Elian from his cousins' house. ■ Vice president Al Gore dissociated himself from the decision to take Elian from his cousins' house.

deslizarse hacia el interior de la casa to slip into the house

deslizarse por la barandilla to slide down the bannister

ser **deslucido por** to be marred by ➤ El acto en la universidad fue deslucido por una manifestación estudiantil. The meeting at the university was marred by a student demonstration.

deslucir la imagen de uno to detract from one's appearance ➤ Su corte de pelo desluce su imagen. His haircut detracts from his appearance.

ser **deslumbrado(-a) por la luz** ■ ser cegado por la luz to be blinded by the light

desmarcarse de algo ■ desligarse de algo ■ disociarse de algo to distance oneself from something ■ to dissociate oneself from something ➤ *(noticia)* El vicepresidente Al Gore se desmarcó de la decisión de sacar a Elián de la casa de sus primos. ■ El vicepresidente Al Gore se desligó de la decisión de sacar a Elián de la casa de sus primos. ■ El vicepresidente Al Gore se disoció de la decisión de sacar a Elián de la casa de sus primos. Vice president Al Gore distanced himself from the decision to take Elian from his cousins' house. ■ Vice president Al Gore dissociated himself from the decision to take Elian from his cousins' house.

desmayarse del dolor to pass out from the pain

desmayarse del hambre *(exageración o en serio)* ■ morirse de hambre to be starving ■ to be famished ➤ No como desde ayer en la mañana, estoy que me desmayo del hambre. I haven't eaten since breakfast yesterday, and I'm starving. ■ I haven't eaten since breakfast yesterday, and I'm famished.

desmayarse del susto to pass out from fright

desmentir la información to set the record straight

desmentir una declaración ■ refutar una declaración to correct a statement ■ to refute a statement (with the truth)

desmontar el árbol de Navidad ■ quitar el árbol de Navidad to take down the Christmas tree ■ to take the Christmas tree down ➤ Desmontamos el árbol de Navidad después del seis de enero. ■ Quitamos el árbol de Navidad después del seis de enero. We take down the Christmas tree after January sixth. ■ We take the Christmas tree down after January sixth. ➤ Lo desmontamos después del seis de enero. ■ Lo quitamos después del seis de enero. We take it down after January sixth.

desnudar a un santo para vestir a otro to rob Peter to pay Paul

desnudar su alma to bare one's soul ➤ Ella desnudó su alma a su amiga. She bared her soul to her friend.

desnudarse de cintura para abajo to strip from the waist down

desnudarse de cintura para arriba to strip from the waist up

desobedecer una promesa hecha to break a promise

desolado(-a) por algo: quedarse ~ ■ ser destrozado(-a) por algo to be devastated by something ➤ Se quedó desolado por la repentina muerte de su mujer. ■ Se quedó destrozado por la repentina muerte de su mujer. He was devastated by his wife's sudden death.

desollar vivo a alguien to skin someone alive

estar **despabilado(-a)** 1. to lie awake ■ not to be able to get to sleep 2. not to be the least bit sleepy

ser **despabilado** to be on the ball

despabílate que estamos aquí ■ despiértate que estamos aquí wake up, we're here

despachar a alguien 1. echar a alguien to send someone packing 2. matar a alguien to bump someone off ■ to knock someone off ■ to murder someone

despachar a un cliente to wait on a customer

despachar la correspondencia ~ ■ hacerse cargo de la correspondencia ■ hacerse cargo del correo 1. to handle the mail 2. to send out the mail ■ to send off the mail

despachar a alguien (para el otro barrio) ■ mandar a alguien al otro barrio to knock someone off ■ to bump someone off ■ to murder someone

despachar un asunto to get something done

despachar un mensaje (por mensajero) to send a message via a runner

despachar un paquete to send a package

despachar una botella de vino to polish off a bottle of wine

despacharse a gusto to speak one's mind

despacho oval (del presidente de los Estados Unidos en la Casa Blanca) the Oval Office

desparramar algo por to spill something on

despatarrar a alguien to spread someone's legs

despatarrarse to spread one's legs

despatarrarse de la risa ■ reírse a carcajadas to laugh hard ■ to have a hearty laugh

desperdigar información ■ diseminar información to disseminate information

despedir a alguien con cajas destempladas ■ echar a alguien con cajas destempladas to send someone packing ■ to give someone the boot

despedir a un(-a) empleado(-a) ■ echar a un(-a) empleado(-a) to fire an employee

despedir a un(-a) empleado(-a) con dos semanas de preaviso to give an employee two weeks' notice

despedir el olor a to smell of ■ to give off the smell of

despedir la flema arrancándola ■ arrancar la flema ■ hacer salir la flema arrancándola to loosen the phlegm ■ to cough up the phlegm ■ to bring up the phlegm ➤ El médico le prescribió un expectorante para despedir la flema arrancándola. The doctor prescribed him an expectorant to loosen the phlegm.

despedir partículas *(física)* to give off particles ■ to emit particles ■ to throw particles

despedir un fuerte olor a to smell strongly of

despedir un tufo de alcohol to reek of alcohol

despedir luz to give off light

despedir un fuerte olor a to smell strongly of

despedir un olor hediondo to give off a foul odor

despedirse a la francesa to fly the coop ➤ Hoy la criada se despidió a la francesa. The maid flew the coop today.

despegado: haber ~ to be off the ground ■ to be airborne ■ to have taken off ➤ El avión ha despegado. The airplane is off the ground. ■ The airplane has taken off.

despegarse una etiqueta ■ estirar una etiqueta to peel off a label ➤ Despéguese con cuidado. Peel carefully.

despejar dudas sobre... to clear up doubts about... ■ to dispel doubts about...

despejar el camino hacia to clear the way to ➤ Los jueces despejaron a George W. Bush el camino hacia la presidencia de EE UU. Judges cleared George W. Bush's way to the U.S. presidency.

despejar el camino para (que) to clear the way for ➤ Un tribunal federal de Estados Unidos despejó ayer el camino para que el niño balsero Elián Gonzalez regrese a Cuba con su padre. A U.S. federal court cleared the way yesterday for little rafter Elian Gonzalez to return to Cuba with his father.

despejar el terreno to pave the way for

despejar la incógnita *(matemática)* to find the (value of the) unknown factor

despejar las dudas que to dispel one's doubts that

despejar las dudas sobre to dispel one's doubts about ■ to clear up one's doubts about

despejar un misterio to clear up a mystery
despejarse (el día) *(tiempo)* ■ escampar to clear up
despellejarse el codo ■ rasparse el codo to skin one's elbow ■ to scrape one's elbow
despellejarse la rodilla ■ rasparse la rodilla to skin one's knee ■ to scrape one's knee
despeñarse de la carrete to run off the road
despeñarse por *(un precipicio, etc.)* to throw oneself off of ■ to go over
desperdiciar el tiempo ■ malgastar el tiempo ■ perder el tiempo ■ desaprovechar el tiempo ■ despilfarrar el tiempo to waste time
desperdiciar el tiempo de alguien ■ malgastar el tiempo de alguien ■ perder el tiempo de alguien ■ desaprovechar el tiempo de alguien ■ despilfarrar el tiempo de alguien to waste someone's time
desperdiciar energía ■ derrochar energía ■ malgastar energía ■ dilapidar energía to waste energy
despertar el interés de alguien ■ despertar la curiosidad de alguien to pique one's interest
despertar a la realidad ■ bajar de las nubes ■ bajar a la realidad to wake up to reality ■ to come down out of the clouds
el **despertar de gran sobresalto** ■ el despertar duro rude awakening
el **despertar de las consciencias** awakening of consciousness ➤ *(Arthur Koestler)* Aquel gran siglo del despertar, el sexto a.C. That great century of awakening, the sixth B.C.
despertar duro ■ despertar de gran sobresalto rude awakening ➤ It was a rude awakening. Fue un despertar duro. ■ Fue un despertar de gran sobresalto.
despertar el apetito ■ abrir el apetito to whet one's apetite
despertar sospechas de que... ■ levantar sospechas de que... to awaken suspicion(s) that... ■ to raise suspicion(s) that... ■ to arouse suspicion(s) that... ■ to raise the suspicion that... ■ to arouse the suspicion that... ■ to awaken the suspicion that...
despertarle a alguien 1. to wake someone up ■ to wake up someone ■ to awaken someone **2.** to be awakened by... ➤ Al chico lo despertaron sus padres. ■ *(Esp. leísmo)* Al chico le despertaron sus padres. The boy's parents awakened him. ■ The boy's parents woke him up. ■ The boy was awakened by his parents. ➤ A la chica la despertaron sus padres. The girl's parents woke her up. ■ The girl's parents awakened her. ■ The girl was awakened by her parents. ➤ Nos despertó la tele del vecino. The neighbor's TV woke us up. ■ The neighbor's TV awakened us. ■ We were awakened by the neighbor's TV.
despertarse a la política to become politically conscious
despiadada crítica brutal criticism
despiadado ataque merciless attack ■ savage attack ■ brutal attack
despilfarrar una fortuna to squander a fortune
despilfarrar dinero ■ desperdiciar dinero ■ derrochar dinero to waste money ■ to throw money around
despilfarrar el tiempo malgastar el tiempo ■ perder el tiempo ■ desaprovechar el tiempo ■ desperdiciar el tiempo to waste time
despilfarrar el tiempo de alguien ■ malgastar el tiempo de alguien ■ perder el tiempo de alguien ■ desaprovechar el tiempo de alguien ■ desperdiciar el tiempo de alguien
ser un **despilfarro de dinero** ■ ser un gasto (de dinero) inútil to be a waste of money
estar **despistado(-a)** ■ estar en la luna to be off the track ■ to be a space cadet ■ to be out of it
ser **despistado** to be a little off ■ to be slightly bonkers
estar **desplazado** to be out of place
ser **desplazado de su hogar** to be forced out of one's home
desplazamiento al extranjero ■ viaje al extranjero trip abroad
desplazamiento hacia el azul *(física)* blue shift
desplazamiento hacia el rojo *(física)* red shift
desplazar el agua to displace water
desplazarse la atención hacia to shift one's attention to
desplazarse por la nieve ■ moverse en la nieve to get around in the snow ■ to get about in the snow ➤ Es difícil desplazarse por la nieve. It's hard to get around in the snow. ■ It's hard to get about in the snow.
desplazarse sin coche ■ moverse sin coche to get around without a car ➤ En todas menos las más grandes ciudades estadounidenses, es difícil desplazarse sin coche. ■ En todas menos las más grandes ciudades estadounidenses, es difícil moverse sin coche. In all but the biggest U.S. cities, it's diffcult to get around without a car.
desplegar sus alas ■ extenderse sus alas ■ expandirse sus alas **1.** *(singular)* to spread its wings **2.** *(plural)* to spread their wings
desplegar todas sus armas ■ desplegar todas sus naves ■ desplegar toda su artillería to bring out all one's big guns ➤ Para la misa Navideña, despliegan todas sus armas. ■ Despliegan todas sus naves. For the Christmas mass, they bring out all their big guns.
desplegar tropas to deploy troops
desplegar un ataque a to launch an attack on
despliegue de show of ■ deployment of
despliegue de tropas troop deployment ■ deployment of troops
desplomarse por to be felled by ➤ El deportista es atendido tras desplomarse por un corte de digestión. The athlete is attended after being felled by a stomach cramp.
desplomarse sobre to collapse onto ■ to fall onto ➤ El avión se desploma sobre una pista lateral. The airplane falls onto a parallel runway.
desplumar un pollo to pluck a chicken
despojar a alguien de algo to strip someone of something ➤ Lo despojaron de su título. ■ *(Esp. y L.am., leísmo)* Le despojaron de su título. They stripped him of his title.
despotismo ilustrado ■ dictadura ilustrada benevolent dictatorship
despotricar contra algo to rail at something ■ to rant and rave about something
despotricar contra alguien por algo to rant and rave at someone about something ■ to rant and rave at someone for something ■ to rail at someone for something
desprenderse (de) to come loose (from) ➤ Se desprendió. It came loose.
desprenderse de la ropa to strip off one's clothes ■ to strip one's clothes off
desprenderse de las emociones negativas ■ soltar lastre to get rid of negative emotions
desprenderse de un estudio to emerge from a study ■ to be determined from a study ■ to come out of a study
desprenderse de una encuesta to emerge from a survey ■ to be determined from a survey ■ to be determined by a survey ■ to come out of a survey ➤ Ya es un hecho: los hispanos igualan en número a los negros en EE UU-incluso puede que los superen ya; así se desprende de los primeros datos del censo efectuado el pasado año. It's now a fact: hispanics equal blacks in number in the United States-and might even already outnumber them, according to early data (emerging) from last year's census.
desprendérsele el empaste ■ caérsele el empaste (for) one's filling to come loose ■ (for) one's filling to fall out
desprendimiento de la retina: tener un ~ to have a detached retina
desprendimiento de tierras ■ derrumbe de tierras ■ derrumbamiento de tierras ■ corrimiento de tierras landslide
estar **desprovisto de emoción** ■ carecer de emoción to be devoid of emotion
estar **desprovisto de encanto** ■ carecer de encanto to be devoid of charm ➤ H.L. Mencken, el columnista sindical de los años 20, remarcó que los pueblos acereros del oeste de Pensilvania estaban desprovistos de encanto. H.L. Mencken, the syndicated columnist of the 1920s, noted that the steel towns of western Pennsylvania were devoid of charm.
después de Cristo ■ d.C. Anno Domini ■ A.D.
después de enterarme de lo que había pasado ■ después de saber lo que había pasado after I found out what had happened ■ after I learned what had happened
después de esa hora after that hour ■ after that time ➤ Para contactar conmigo después de esa hora, llámame a este número. To contact me after that hour, call me at this number. ■ To contact me after that time, call me at this number.

después de estar aquejado(-a) de ■ tras estar aquejado(-a) de after being stricken by

después de hacer algo ■ tras hacer algo after doing something ➤ Diez meses después de anunciarlo... ■ Diez meses después de haberlo anunciado... Ten months after announcing it... ➤ Después de anunciar durante meses que se cerraría la escuela, la junta escolar cambió su parecer y decidió renovarla.

después de la cual after which ➤ There will be a lecture at ten a.m., after which refreshments will be served. Habrá una conferencia a las diez de la mañana, después de la cual se servirá un ágape.

después de la medianoche ■ pasada la medianoche after midnight

después de la señal after the tone ➤ Por favor deja tu mensaje después de la señal. Please leave your message after the tone.

después de lo cual after which ➤ Hay que cursar cinco años de estudios en la facultad, después de lo cual se obtiene la diplomatura. You have to take five years of courses, after which the bachelor's degree is conferred.

después de lo ocurrido ■ tras lo ocurrido **1.** after the fact **2.** after what happened **3.** after all that had happened

después de muchos meses de anunciarlo after announcing it for months ■ after months of announcing it ➤ Después de muchos meses anunciándolo, mañana se cierra ya el antiguo instituto. After announcing it for months, tomorrow the old high school will finally close.

después de muerto after death

después de que oscurezca ■ después de que se haga de noche after dark

después de que se haga noche ■ después de que oscurezca after dark

después de rebasar el semáforo after (you go through) the light ■ after (you pass through) the light ➤ Es el primer giro a la derecha después de rebasar el semáforo. It's the first right turn after (you go through) the light.

después de saber lo que había pasado ■ después de enterarme de lo que había pasado after I found out what had happened ■ after I learned what had happened

después de todo 1. after all **2.** in sum ■ to sum up ➤ Después de todo puedo decir... In sum, I can say... ■ To sum up, I can say...

después de un momento al cabo de un momento ■ tras un momento a moment later ■ after a moment

después de unos días ■ pocos días después ■ unos días después ■ a los pocos días a few days later ■ a few days afterwards

después de unos segundos ■ al cabo de unos segundos ■ tras unos segundos after a few seconds ■ a few seconds later

después del cual after which ➤ Habrá un partido a las ocho de la tarde, después del cual, habrá fuegos artificiales. There will be a game at eight p.m., after which there will be fireworks.

despuntar el día (for) the dawn to break

estar **desquiciado por algo** to be in disarray because of something ■ to be chaotic because of something ■ to be all out of whack because of something ■ to be all out of sync ➤ El tráfico vehicular en Madrid está desquiciado este verano por todas las obras. The vehicular traffic in Madrid is chaotic this summer because of the construction everywhere.

destacado empresario ■ destacado hombre de negocios prominent businessman

destacado hombre de negocios ■ destacado empresario prominent businessman

destapar algo to get the top off of something ➤ No puedo destaparlo. I can't get the top off. ➤ Mira a ver si puedes destapar el bote de ketchup. See if you can get the top off (of) this bottle of ketchup.

destapar la olla to open a (big) can of worms

destapar un plan to unveil a plan

destaparse la olla (for) all hell to break loose ➤ Cuando se den a conocer los hallazgos del comité, se destapará la olla. When the findings of the committee become known, all hell's going to break loose.

desternillarse de risa to laugh til it hurts ■ to split one's sides laughing

destilar veneno to be full of poison

estar **destinado(-a) en** to be stationed in

destinatario(-a) desconocido(-a) addressee unknown

destino decretó que...: el azar quiso que... fate decreed that...

destino triste sad fate

destripar el chiste to give away the punch line of the joke ■ to spoil the punch line of the joke

destripar el cuento to give away the ending of the story ■ to spoil the ending of the story

destripar un zancudo to squash a mosquito

estar **destrozado(-a) por algo** ■ quedarse destrozado(-a) por algo ■ estar destruido(-a) por algo ■ estar al borde del abismo to be devasted by something ■ to be crushed by something ➤ Estuvo destrozado por la repentina muerte de su mujer. ■ Se quedó destrozado por la repentina muerte de su mujer. ■ Se quedó desolado por la repentina muerte de su mujer. He was devastated by his wife's sudden death.

ser **destrozado(-a) por algo** ■ ser desolado(-a) por algo ■ estar al borde del abismo to be devastated by something ■ to be crushed by something ➤ Fue destrozado por la repentina muerte de su mujer. He was devastated by his wife's sudden death.

destrozar la lengua ■ cargarse la lengua to butcher the language

ser **destruido por algo** ■ ser desolado por algo ■ ser arrollado por algo to be destroyed by something ■ to be devastated by something ➤ Zonas de Caracas fueron destruidas por las lluvias torrenciales y las riadas. Parts of Caracas were devastated by the torrential rains and flash flooding.

desviación coronaria: cirugía de ~ coronary bypass surgery

desviar atención de to divert attention from

desviar la luz to deflect light

desviar una bala to deflect a bullet

desviar su mirada de alguien to look away from someone

desviarse de la ruta *(vehículos, caminantes, excursionistas)* ■ salirse de ruta ■ desviarse de trayecto ■ salirse de trayecto to go the wrong way ■ to take the wrong route

desviarse del trayecto *(trenes)* **1.** salirse de trayecto ■ desviarse de ruta ■ salirse de ruta to get on the wrong track **2.** descarrilarse to derail

desviarse del rumbo *(aviones, barcos)* to get off course ➤ Lindbergh se desvió sólo sesenta millas de su rumbo durante su vuelo. Lindbergh got only sixty miles off course on his flight.

desvincularse de disassociate oneself from

detallar una cuenta to itemize a bill

¡**detalles ya!** *(en las noticias)* details coming up!

detectar un olor a quemado ■ oler algo que se quema to notice the smell of something burning ■ to detect the smell of something burning ■ to smell something burning

el **detector de metales** metal detector

el **detector de presencias** motion detector

detener a un sospechoso ■ poner a un sospechoso bajo custodia judicial to apprehend a suspect ■ to take a suspect into custody ➤ Algunos potenciales sospechosos fueron detenidos para ser interrogados. ■ Algunos potenciales sospechosos fueron puestos bajo custodia judicial para ser interrogados. Some potential suspects were apprehended for questioning. ■ Some potential suspects were taken into custody for questioning.

detener el avance de una enfermedad to stop the advance of an illness ■ to halt the advance of an illness

detenerse en el camino to stop along the way ■ to stop on the way

deterioro paulatino gradual deterioration ➤ Lo que provoca un deterioro paulatino de... Which causes a gradual deterioration of...

determinado tipo de a certain type of

determinar a alguien a hacer algo to lead someone to do something

detener a un(-a) sospechoso(-a) ■ poner a un(-a) sospechoso(-a) bajo custodia judicial ■ aprehender a un(-a) sospechoso(-a) to detain a suspect ■ to take a suspect into custody ■ apprehend a suspect ➤ Some potential suspects were detained for questioning. ■ Some potential suspects were taken into custoday for questioning. ■ Some potential suspects were apprehended for questioning. Algunos potenciales sospechosos fueron detenidos para ser interrogados. ■ Algunos potenciales sospechosos fueron puestos bajo custodia judicial para ser interrogados. ▪ Algunos potenciales sospechosos fueron aprehendidos para ser interrogados.

detenerse a reflexionar en to stop to think about ➤ Pocas veces se detiene a reflexionar en... We rarely stop to think about...

detenerse a reflexionar en que... to stop to consider that...

el **detergente para la vajilla** dishwashing soap ▪ dishwashing liquid ▪ dish soap

estar **detrás de alguien** 1. ser el siguiente de la fila to be behind someone (in line) ▪ to be after someone (in the line) ▪ to be the next (one) in line 2. ir en persecución de alguien ▪ ir atrás de alguien ▪ estar atrás de alguien to be after someone ▪ to be in pursuit of someone

estar **detrás de una conjura** ▪ estar detrás de una conjuración to be behind a plot

detrito radioactivo ▪ basura radioactiva radioactive waste

deuda saldada retired debt ▪ debt that's been paid (off) ▪ debt that's been settled

devaluar la moneda to devalue the currency

devanarse los sesos to rack one's brains

desvelarse sus verdaderos sentimientos ▪ descubrirse sus verdaderos sentimientos to betray one's true feelings ▪ to give away one's true feelings ▪ to give one's true feelings away

desviarse de su rumbo to get off course ➤ Lindbergh se desvió sólo sesenta millas de su rumbo durante su vuelo transatlántico. Lindbergh got only sixty miles off course on his trans-Atlantic flight.

desviarse del tema 1. apartarse del tema to get off the subject 2. salirse por la tangente to go off on a tangent ➤ Me estoy desviando del tema. ▪ Me estoy apartando del tema. I'm getting off the subject. ➤ No es por desviarme del tema, pero... ▪ No es por apartarme del tema, pero... Not to get off the subject, but... ➤ No quiero desviarme mucho del tema. ▪ No quiero apartarme mucho del tema. I don't want to get too far off the subject.

desvirtuar la objetividad ▪ restar el valor objetivo to detract from the objectivity ➤ La expresión de rabia desvirtúa la objetividad del artículo. ▪ La expresión de rabia resta el valor objetivo del artículo. ▪ La expresión de rabia resta el mérito objetivo del artículo. The expression of anger detracts from the objectivity of the article.

la **devolución de préstamos** check-in desk (at a library)

devolver algo a alguien to give something back to someone ▪ to return something to someone

devolver cambio to give change ➤ Esta máquina devuelve cambio. This machine gives change.

devolver dinero to return money

devolver el servicio *(deportes)* to return the serve

devolver la pelota *(deportes)* to return the ball

devolver la pelota a alguien to give someone a taste of his own medicine

devolver un cumplido to return a compliment ➤ Si alguien te hace un cumplido devuélveselo. If someone pays you a compliment, return it.

devolver una imagen ▪ reflejar una imagen to reflect an image

devolver una invitación to return an invitation ▪ to reciprocate an invitation ➤ La invitación fue aceptada pero no devuelta. The invitation was accepted but not returned. ▪ The invitation was accepted but not reciprocated.

devolverle a uno al principio to take one back to the beginning

devolverle el favor a alguien to return the favor

devolvérselo alguien to pay someone back ▪ to pay it back to someone ➤ Te lo devuelvo mañana ▪ Te lo devolveré mañana. I'll pay you back tomorrow. ▪ I'll pay it back to you tomorrow. ▪ I'll return it to you tomorrow.

devorar a alguien con la mirada to devour someone with a look

devorar un libro to devour a book

di con una tecla por casualidad to hit a key by accident ▪ to hit a key by mistake ➤ Di con la tecla de "enviar" por casualidad. I hit the "send" key by accident. ▪ I hit the "send" key by mistake.

di por supuesto que... I thought for sure (that)... ▪ I just assumed (that)...

el **día abrileño** ▪ día de abril April day

el **día aciago** ▪ aciago día ▪ día fatídico fateful day

el **día ajetreado** hectic day

el **día antes** the day before

el **día anterior** the previous day ▪ the preceding day ▪ the day before

ser un **día asoleado** ▪ ser un día de sol to be a sunny day ➤ Era un día asoleado. ▪ Era un día de sol. It was a sunny day.

un **día caluroso** a hot day

un **día cualquiera** an ordinary day ▪ a day like any other

el **Día de Acción de Gracias** *(EE UU, cuarto jueves de noviembre)* Thanksgiving Day

el **día de autos** day on which a crime was committed ▪ day of the crime

día cálido warm day

día catatónico *(coloquial)* uneventful day ▪ ordinary day

un **día como hoy hace un año (atrás)** ▪ un día tal como hoy hace un año a year ago today ▪ one year ago today ➤ Un día como hoy hace un año atrás, fui a Usuluteca. A year ago today, I went to Usuluteca. ▪ One year ago today, I went to Usuluteca.

el **día de campo** 1. *(de la escuela)* ▪ día de excursión field day 2. *(de relajación)* ▪ día en el campo day in the country

el **día de duelo nacional** day of mourning ➤ *(noticia)* El presidente ruso declara para hoy un día de duelo nacional. Russian president declares today a national day of mourning.

el **día de entresemana** ▪ día entresemana ▪ día de semana weekday

un **día de estos** one of these days

el **día de fiesta** holiday

el **día de hoy** today

el **día de las elecciones** ▪ día de los comicios electorales ▪ jornada de voto election day

el **día de lluvia** ▪ día lluvioso rainy day

el **día de los comicios** ▪ día de las elecciones ▪ jornada de voto election day

el **día de mañana** tomorrow

el **día de mucho calor** ▪ día muy caluroso hot day

el **día de permiso** *(Esp.)* ▪ día libre day off

el **día de Reyes** *(catolicismo)* ▪ epifanía ▪ el seis de enero Epiphany ▪ Feast of the Lights

el **día de temporal** ▪ día tormentoso ▪ día de tormenta stormy day

el **día de trabajo** ▪ día laboral work day

el **día de la raza** *(el doce de octubre)* ▪ día de la hispanidad Columbus Day

el **día de lluvia** rainy day

el **día de los inocentes** *(el veintiocho de diciembre)* April Fool's Day

el **día de los reyes magos** ▪ epifanía ▪ el seis de enero Epiphany ▪ the Feast of Lights

el **día de mañana** ▪ algún día some day

el **día de precepto** *(catolicismo)* ▪ fiesta de precepto holy day of obligation

ser un **día de sol** ▪ ser un día asoleado to be a sunny day ➤ Era un día de sol. ▪ Era un día asoleado. It was a sunny day.

día de tormenta día tormentoso ▪ día de temporal stormy day

el **día de verano** summer day ➤ En un día de verano On a summer day

el **día del Juicio Final** Judgment Day

el **día del Señor** *(catolicismo)* ▪ día de precepto ▪ fiesta de precepto Holy Day of Obligation

día despejado clear day ▪ beautiful day ▪ wall-to-wall sunshine

el **día fatal** a terrible day ▪ an awful day

el **día impar** odd-numbered day

el **día laborable** work day

el **día libre** ▪ día de asueto day off

el **día límite** deadline

día lluvioso ▪ día de lluvia rainy day

el **día menos pensado** when you least expect it ▪ when you least expect

día nefasto: tener un ~ to have a bad day

el **día par** even-numbered day

el **día primaveral** springlike day
día señalado red-letter day
día tormentoso ▪ día de tormenta ▪ día de temporal stormy day
día tras día day after day
día ventoso windy day
día y noche night and day ▪ around the clock
ser el **día y la noche** to be like night and day ▪ to be as different as day and night ▪ to be completely different (from each other) ➤ María y Pablo son el día y la noche. María and Pablo are as different as day and night.
diablo encarnado devil incarnate ▪ devil in the flesh
estar **diáfano que...** to be clear that...
diáfano: ser de carácter ~ to have an excellent character ▪ to be transparent ▪ to be beyond reproach
diagnosticar una enfermedad a alguien to diagnose someone's illness
diagnóstico precoz early diagnosis ▪ early detection
diálogo consigo ▪ diálogo interno internal dialogue ▪ inner dialogue ▪ inner conversation ▪ conversation with oneself
ser un **diamante en bruto** to be a diamond in the rough ▪ to be a rough-cut diamond
ser **diametralmente opuesto en un asunto** ▪ estar a años luz en un asunto to be diametrically opposed on an issue ▪ to be light-years apart on an issue
diaria a day ▪ per day ➤ Este fichero crece al ritmo de una página diaria. This file grows a page a day.
días alternos every other day
los **días cuando** the days when
días laborables weekdays
los **días laborables** ▪ de lunes a viernes on weekdays ▪ Monday through Friday
dibujar el silbido ▪ perder la chaveta ▪ volverse loco to lose one's marbles
dibujo a pulso freehand drawing
dibujo mental ▪ cuadro mental mental picture
dibujos animados: ver ~ to watch cartoons ➤ Veíamos dibujos animados. We were watching cartoons.
dicen las malas lenguas que the gossip is that
dícese de ▪ dicho said of ▪ said in reference to ▪ said with reference to
dicho así when you put it that way
dicho esto 1. having said this ▪ having said that 2. after saying this ▪ after saying that
dicho lo cual 1. dicho eso this being said ▪ having said that ▪ having said it ▪ having said so 2. dicho esto having said this ▪ having said it ▪ having said so
dicho sea en confianza just between you and me
dicho y hecho no sooner said than done
dichoso(-a) tú que... you're lucky that...
dichosos los ojos it's (so) good to see you ▪ it's great to see you ▪ it's wonderful to see you
dictablanda *(de Primo de Rivera en España, 1923-30)* benevolent dictatorship (of Primo de Rivera)
dictadura benévola benevolent dictatorship
dictaminar que... to rule that... ➤ El tribunal supremo de Canadá dictaminó ayer que ni el derecho nacional ni internacional permiten la secesión de Quebec. The Canadian supreme court ruled yesterday that neither national nor international law permits the secession of Quebec.
dictar la ley to lay down the law
dictar una orden to issue an order
dictar una sentencia to impose a sentence
dictarle la ley a alguien to lay down the law to someone
el **diente de león** dandelion
los **dientes de leche** baby teeth
diestro right handed
dieta equilibrada balanced diet
diezmar una población to wipe out a population ▪ to decimate a population ➤ El sarampión diezmó la mitad de la población de Hawai. Measles wiped out half the population of Hawaii.
diferencia horaria time difference ➤ La diferencia horaria juega a favor de España. The time difference works in favor of Spain.
diferencia radical: suponer una ~ to make a critical difference ➤ El reducir la inclinación de la Torre Inclinada de Pisa de 6 a 5,5 grados supone una diferencia radical en su estabilidad. Reducing the tilt of the Leaning Tower of Pisa from 6 to 5.5 degrees has made a critical difference in its stability.
diferenciar entre letra mayúscula y letra minúscula to be case sensitive
diferencias irreconciliables ▪ diferencias insalvables irreconcilable differences
diferencias regionales ▪ diferencias geográficas regional differences ➤ Diferencias regionales en la disponibilidad de atención médica... ▪ Diferencias geográficas en la disponibilidad de atención médica... Regional differences in health care availability...
ser **diferente esta vez** ▪ ser distinta esta vez to be different this time ➤ Por qué será diferente esta vez? ▪ ¿Por qué será distinta esta vez? Why will it be different this time?
diferir una reunión ante to postpone a meeting because of
ser **difícil de acceso** to be hard to get to
ser **difícil de complacer** ▪ ser difícil de contentar to be difficult to please ▪ to be hard to please
ser **difícil de conseguir** to be hard to come by ▪ to be hard to get
ser **difícil de contentar** ▪ ser difícil de complacer to be difficult to please ▪ to be hard to please
ser **difícil de controlar** to be difficult to control ➤ Una clase llena de chicos del séptimo curso pueden ser difíciles con controlar. A classroom full of seven graders can be difficult to control. ➤ El avión se hizo difícil de controlar cuando se acercó al ojo del huracán. The airplane became difficult to control as it approached the eye of the hurricane.
ser **difícil de enfadar** to be slow to anger
ser **difícil que** to be unlikely that
difícilmente transitado nearly impassable ▪ barely passable ➤ Zona difícilmente trasitada Nearly impassable area ▪ Almost impassable area ▪ Barely passable area
difuminarse en la oscuridad ▪ esfumarse en la oscuridad to fade into the darkness
difundir los hechos to report the facts ▪ to get the facts out
diga usted lo que diga whatever you say ▪ say what you will
dígale (usted) de mi parte que... tell him for me that...
digamos ▪ vamos a decir shall we say ▪ let's say
digámoslo así shall we say ▪ let's put it that way
digas lo que digas say what you will ▪ regardless of what you say ▪ no matter what you say ▪ whatever you say
ser **digno de escrutinio** ▪ merecer escrutinio ▪ ser susceptible de escrutinio to deserve scrutiny ▪ to merit scrutiny ▪ to be worthy of scrutiny
ser **digno de ser investigado** ▪ ser digno de investigarlo ▪ ser susceptible de ser investigado ▪ ser susceptible de investigarlo ▪ ser susceptible de investigación ▪ merecer la pena de ser investigado ▪ merecer la pena investigarlo to bear looking into ▪ to be worthy of investigation ▪ to be worthy of being investigated ▪ to bear checking into ▪ to bear checking out
dijo tener (it) reportedly has ▪ (it) is said to have ➤ La policía busca al pirata aéreo que dijo tener problemas familiares. Police are searching for the hijacker, who is said to have family problems. ▪ Police are searching for the hijacker, who reportedly has family problems.
dijo textualmente 1. *(él)* his exact words were 2. *(ella)* her exact words were
dilapidar energía ▪ derrochar energía ▪ desperdiciar energía ▪ malgastar energía to waste energy
dilapidar su herencia (de uno) to squander one's inheritance
dile de mi parte que... tell him for me that...
¡**dime!** tell me! ▪ I'm listening!
dime con quién andas y te diré quién eres ▪ dime con quién vas y te diré quién eres a man is known by the company he keeps
dime de qué presumes y te diré de qué careces tell me what you boast about, and I'll tell you what you lack
¡**dímelo a mí!** you're telling me!
dimensionar en función de to gauge by ▪ to judge from

ser el **diminutivo de** to be short for ➤ Mayte es el diminutivo de María Teresa. Mayte is short for María Teresa.

dimitir de un puesto de trabajo ▪ to resign from a position ▪ to resign from a post ▪ to resign from one's job

dinero a espuertas megabucks ▪ money coming out one's ears

dinero blando ▪ contribuiciones anónimas que no están reguladas por la ley soft money

dinero de bolsillo ▪ calderilla ▪ moneda suelta pocket change ▪ small change ▪ loose change

dinero justo exact change

dinero limpio ▪ dinero en limpio clear money ➤ Después de restar el costo de los materiales, me quedaron limpios doscientos setenta y cinco dólares. ▪ Después de restar el costo de los materiales, me quedaron en limpio doscientos setenta y cinco dólares. After subtracting the cost of materials, I made two hundred seventy-five dollars clear.

dinero negro under-the-table money ▪ hidden money

dinero no crece en las plantas money doesn't grow on trees

dinero no es lo todo money is not everything ▪ money's not everything ▪ money isn't everything

dinero no hace la felicidad money cannot buy happiness ▪ money can't buy happiness

dinero sucio filthy lucre ▪ dirty money

dio la casualidad de que... it happened that... ▪ it just so happened that...

Dios los cría y ellos se juntan ▪ cada oveja con su pareja ▪ cada cual con su cada cual birds of feather flock together

Dios mediante under God ➤ Una nación Dios mediante One nation under God

¡Dios mío! good heavens! ▪ heavens! ▪ Good Lord!

Dios perdone may God forgive

Dios relojero clockmaker God ▪ deistic conception of God

la **dirección asistida** power steering

Dirección de Alimentos y Medicinas *(EE UU)* Food and Drug Administration

dirección de la casa ▪ la seña de la casa the address of the house

dirección temporal temporary address

directamente a la cara right to one's face

directamente al norte ▪ recto al norte due north

directamente por encima directly overhead

director(-a) de la orquesta orchestra conductor ▪ symphony conductor

dirigentes del partido party leaders

dirigentes mundiales world leaders

estar **dirigido a alguien** ▪ ir por alguien to be intended for someone ▪ to be directed at someone ▪ to be aimed at someone ➤ ETA asesina a dos obreros con un coche bomba dirigido a un edil socialista. ETA kills two workers with a car bomb intended for a socialist councilman. ➤ Ese comentario estaba dirigido a mí, ¿verdad? ▪ Ese comentario iba por mí, ¿verdad? That remark was aimed at me, wasn't it?

ser **dirigido por** *(película)* to be directed by ➤ La película *Con faldas y a lo loco* fue escrita y dirigida por Billy Wilder. The film *Some Like It Hot* was written and directed by Billy Wilder.

dirigir el cotarro ▪ llevar la voz cantante ▪ manejar el tinglado to rule the roost

dirigir la palabra to address

dirigirse a alguien 1. to turn to someone ▪ to turn towards someone 2. to go toward someone ▪ to go towards someone ▪ to head for someone 3. to address someone ➤ Se dirigió a su madre y le dijo... She turned to her mother and said...

dirigirse a alguien como ▪ tratar a alguien de to address someone as ➤ En el pasado los niños se dirigían al padre como "usted". ▪ En el pasado los niños trataban al padre de "usted". In the old days, children addressed their fathers as "sir."

dirigirse a casa to head home

dirigirse a la nación ▪ dirigirse al país ▪ dirigirse al pueblo to address the nation ▪ to address the country ➤ El presidente se dirigirá a la nación a las nueve p.m., Franja Horaria de la Costa Este. The president will address the nation at 9 p.m., Eastern Standard Time.

dirigirse a la suya ▪ ir para casa to head home ▪ to head for home

dirigirse a un lugar ▪ llevar a un lugar ▪ conducir a un lugar ▪ salir a un lugar to lead to a place ▪ to go to a place ▪ to take one to a place ➤ Esta carretera se dirige a Valparaíso. ▪ Esta carretera lleva a Valparaíso. ▪ Esta carretera conduce a Valparaíso. This road leads to Valparaiso. ▪ This road goes to Valparaiso. ▪ This road takes you to Valparaiso.

dirigirse a un público ▪ dirigirse a una audiencia to address an audience

dirigirse a una audiencia ▪ dirigirse a un público 1. to address an audience 2. to be aimed at a certain audience ▪ to be geared to a certain audience

dirigirse directamente hacia to go straight towards ▪ to come straight towards ➤ Nos dirigimos directamente hacia ellos. We went straight towards them. ➤ Se dirigieron directamente hacia nosotros. They came straight towards us.

dirigirse para casa to head (for) home ➤ Me dirijo para casa. I'm heading (for) home.

dirigirse una amplia sonrisa to grin at each other ➤ Se dirigieron una amplia sonrisa. They grinned at each other.

disciplina férrea iron discipline

disco de larga duración long playing record ▪ LP

disco duro *(Sp.)* ▪ disco rígido hard drive

disco rayado broken record ▪ person who harps on the same themes repeatedly

disco rígido ▪ disco duro hard drive

el **disco salta** the record skips

disconectársele to get disconnected ➤ Se me disconectó. I got disconnected.

discrepar el compás *(literario)* ▪ perder el compás ▪ perder el ritmo to miss the beat

discrepar sobre algo 1. to have differing accounts of something ▪ to have diverging accounts of something ▪ to have divergent accounts of something 2. to disagree about something

disculpa no me vale: esa ~ that apology doesn't cut it ▪ that apology isn't good enough

disculparse ante alguien to apologize to someone

disculparse tardíamente por ▪ presentar una disculpa tardía por ▪ ofrecer una disculpa tardía por to apologize belatedly for ▪ to make a belated apology for ▪ to offer a belated apology for

discurres como un insensato *(Valle-Inclán)* you're not making any sense

discursante speaker ➤ El presidente es un discursante excelente. The president is an excellent speaker.

discurso de despedida ▪ discurso del adiós farewell address

discurso de investidura: pronunciar el ~ to give the inaugural address ▪ to deliver the inaugural address

discurso flor: pronunciar un ~ to give an outstanding speech

discusión profunda in-depth discussion ➤ *(noticia)* La cumbre fue una discusión profunda sobre desafíos comunes... The summit was an in-depth discussion of common challenges...

discutir por un asunto to argue about a matter ▪ to quarrel about a matter ▪ to argue over a matter ▪ to quarrel over a matter

discutir sobre un asunto to argue over a matter ▪ to quarrel over a matter ▪ to argue about a matter ▪ to quarrel about a matter ➤ Los niños están discutiendo sobre a quién le toca dar a la pelota. The children are arguing over whose turn it is to kick.

diseminar información ▪ desperdigar información to disseminate information

diseñador de moda fashion designer

diseñar un edificio ▪ proyectar un edificio to design a building

diseñar una casa ▪ proyectar una casa to design a house ➤ Thomas Jefferson diseñó Monticello cuando tenía veinticuatro años. ▪ Thomas Jefferson proyectó Monticello cuando tenía veinticuatro años. Thomas Jefferson designed Monticello when he was twenty-four years old.

disfrazarse de ▪ vestirse de to dress up as ➤ ¿De qué te vas a disfrazar en Halloween? ▪ ¿De qué vas a disfrazarte en Halloween? ▪ ¿De qué te vas a vestir en Halloween? ▪ ¿De qué vas a vestirte en Halloween? What are you going to dress up as on Halloween? ➤ Me voy a disfrazar de payaso. ▪ Voy a disfrazarme de payaso.

▪ Me voy a vestir de payaso. ▪ Voy a vestirme de payaso. I'm going to dress up as a clown.

disfrutar haciendo algo to enjoy doing something ➤ Disfruto esquiando. I enjoy skiing. *(Nota: No se puede decir "disfruto esquiar" y el inglés es paralelo: no se puede decir "I enjoy to ski".)*

disfrutar mucho con to get a lot of enjoyment from ▪ to get a lot of enjoyment out of ▪ to get a lot of pleasure from ▪ to get a lot of enjoyment out of

la **disgregación familiar** ▪ atomización familiar breakdown of the family

estar **disgustado(-a) con algo** to be upset about something

estar **disgustado(-a) con alguien** to be upset with someone

disimular la indiferencia to conceal one's indifference ▪ to hide one's indifference ▪ to disguise one's indifference

disimular su acción to cover up one's action ➤ Para disimular su acción, el joven se asomó a la ventana y preguntó qué sucedía. To cover up his action, the youth went to the window and asked what was happening.

disipar las preocupaciones de uno to dispel one's worries

disipar los miedos de uno to dispel one's fears

dislocarse un hueso ▪ desarticularse un hueso to dislocate a bone ▪ *(informal)* to pop out of joint ➤ Se le dislocó el codo. ▪ Se desarticuló el codo. He dislocated his elbow. ▪ His elbow popped out of joint.

la **disminución de la población** ▪ reducción de la población decrease in population

la **disminución de los beneficios comparado con el año pasado** ▪ disminución de los beneficios con respecto al año pasado ▪ disminución de los beneficios en relación al año pasado ▪ disminución de los beneficios del año pasado decrease from last year's profits

la **disminución del paro** ▪ (la) reducción del paro decrease in unemployment ▪ drop in unemployment

disminuirse (de tamaño) to decrease in size ▪ to get smaller ➤ El déficit se ha disminuido. The deficit has decreased in size. ▪ The deficit has gotten smaller.

disminuir(se) de *x* a *y* ▪ bajar de *x* a *y* to decrease from *x* to *y* ➤ Los tipos de interés han disminuido. ▪ Los tipos de interés han bajado. Interest rates have gone down. ➤ Los tipos de interés se han disminuído para el año 2005. ▪ Los tipos de interés han bajado para el año 2005. Interest rates have decreased in 2005. ▪ Interest rates declined in 2005. ▪ Interest rates went down in 2005.

disminuir gradualmente to ease off ➤ Da un aceleración al motor y luego disminuye gradualmente. Gun the engine and then ease off on the accelerator.

disociarse de algo ▪ desmarcarse de algo ▪ desligarse de algo to dissociate oneself from something ▪ to distance oneself from something ➤ *(noticia)* El vicepresidente Al Gore se disoció de la decisión de sacar a Elián de la casa de sus primos. ▪ El vicepresidente Al Gore se desmarcó de la decisión de sacar a Elián de la casa de sus primos. ▪ El vicepresidente Al Gore se desligó de la decisión de sacar a Elián de la casa de sus primos. Vice president Al Gore dissociated himself from the decision to take Elian from his cousins' house. ▪ Vice president Al Gore distanced himself from the decision to take Elian from his cousins' house.

disparar a bocajarro ▪ disparar a mansalva to spray gunfire ▪ to spray bullets

disparar a escasa distancia to fire at close range

disparar a matar to shoot to kill

disparar a tiros ▪ asesinar a tiros to shoot to death

disparar a quemarropa ▪ pegar un tiro a quemarropa ▪ disparar a bocajarro to shoot at point-blank range ▪ to fire (a shot) at point-blank range

disparar a mansalva ▪ disparar a diestro y siniestro ▪ disparar a ciegas to spray gunfire ▪ to spray (with) bullets

disparar desde muy cerca ▪ disparar a escasa distancia to fire at close range ➤ Los jovenes murieron por la destrucción de masa encefálica a causa de disparos de armas de fuego hechos desde muy cerca. The youths died as a result of massive head injuries caused by shots fired at close range.

disparar la bolsa to send stocks soaring ▪ to spark a stock market rally ▪ to spark a rally in the stock market

disparar la tensión con to heighten tensions with

disparar una flecha to shoot an arrow ▪ *(literario)* to loose an arrow

dispararle a alguien to shoot at someone

dispense usted excuse me

disponer de dinero en abundancia to have plenty of money

disponer de poco tiempo not to have much time ▪ to have little time

disponer que... to rule that... ▪ to decree that...

disponerse a abordar la tarea de to set about the task of

disponerse a acostarse to get ready for bed ▪ to get ready to go to bed

disponerse a hacer algo to be about to do something ▪ to get ready to do something ➤ Se disponía a coger la rosa. She was about to pick up the rose. ➤ Se disponía a comprar el periódico cuando... He was about to buy the newspaper when...

dispóngase usted a ▪ dispóngase para ▪ prepárese a ▪ prepárese para ▪ estése listo para ▪ *(literario)* ▪ estése presto a be ready to

disponte a ▪ disponte para ▪ prepárate a ▪ prepárate para ▪ estáte listo para ▪ *(literario)* ▪ estáte presto a be ready to

la **disposición de los billetes** ▪ (la) disponibilidad de los billetes availability of tickets

la **disposición natural a** natural disposition to

la **disposición para hacer algo** willingness to do something

dispositivo de la capa de red network layer device

dispositivos periféricos *(informática)* computer peripherals ▪ peripherals

estar **dispuesto a favor de algo** ▪ estar dispuesto en favor de algo to be biased in favor of something ▪ to have a bias in favor of something

estar **dispuesto a hacer algo** to be willing to do something

estar **dispuesto a todo con tal de...** ▪ estar dispuesto a todo para to do anything to... ▪ to go to any lengths to... ➤ *(La bella y la bestia)* Está dispuesta a todo con tal de salvar a su padre. ▪ Está dispuesta a todo para salvar a su padre. She'll do anything to save her father. ▪ She'll go to any lengths to save her father.

disputa fronteriza ▪ disputa de fronteras border dispute ➤ El Presidente Hayes se puso de parte de Paraguay en la disputa fronteriza sobre el Chaco. President Hayes sided with Paraguay in the border dispute over the Chaco.

distancia a la que distance to which ▪ how far

distancia entre la Tierra y el sol distance from the Earth to the sun ▪ distance between the Earth and the sun ➤ En números redondos la distancia media entre la Tierra y el sol es de 150 millones de kilómetros. In round figures, the mean distance from the Earth to the sun is 150 million kilometers.

la **distancia es el olvido** ▪ ojos que no ven, corazón que no siente out of sight, out of mind

distancia media mean distance ➤ En números redondos la distancia media entre la Tierra y el sol es de 150 millones de kilómetros. In round figures, the mean distance from the Earth to the sun is 150 million kilometers.

estar **distante de** *(emocionalmente)* ▪ estar apartado de to be aloof from ▪ to be distant from

distar bastante de ser perfecto ▪ no ser ni mucho menos perfecto to be far from perfect

distar *x* kilómetros de to be *x* kilometers from ➤ Segovia dista sesenta kilómetros de aquí. Segovia is sixty kilometers from here.

distinguir a los gemelos to tell the twins apart ➤ Mi hermana tiene hijas gemelas, a las que cuesta mucho distinguir. My sister has twin daughters who are difficult to tell apart.

distinguir a los hombres de los chicos to separate the men from the boys

distinguir entre el culo y las cuatro témporas *(Camilo José Cela)* to tell one's ass from a hole in the ground ▪ *(literalmente)* to tell one's ass from the four ember days

estar **distinto de** to be different from ➤ La cocina está distinta de como la dejé. The kitchen is different from the way I left it. ▪ The kitchen is different from how I left it.

ser **distinto de** to be different from ▪ to differ from ➤ El español es distinto del francés en la manera de formar el subjuntivo imperfecto. Spanish is different from French in the way the imperfect subjunctive is formed. ▪ Spanish is different from French in how the imperfect subjunctive is formed. ▪ Spanish differs from French in the way the imperfect subjunctive is formed.

distorsionar los resultados ▪ mediatizar los resultados to distort the results ▪ to bias the results ▪ to skew the results ▪ to doctor the results

distribuir el peso equitativamente to distribute the weight evenly

disuadir a alguien de que haga algo ▪ persuadir a alguien para que no haga algo to dissuade someone from doing something ▪ to talk someone out of doing something

estar **dividido a partes iguales** to be evenly divided ➤ La opinión pública está dividida más o menos a partes iguales. Public opinion is about evenly divided on the issue.

estar **dividido justo a la mitad** ▪ estar partido al medio to be divided down the middle ▪ to be split down the middle

ser **dividido por** ▪ ser dividido entre ▪ entre to be divided by ▪ to be divided into ➤ Treinta (dividido) por seis da cinco. ▪ Treinta (dividido) entre seis toca a cinco. ▪ Treinta entre seis es cinco. ▪ Treinta entre seis cabe a cinco. Thirty divided by six equals five. ▪ Six goes into thirty five times. ▪ Six into thirty goes five times.

estar **dividido por la mitad** to be divided in half ▪ to be evenly divided ➤ El Senado estadounidense estuvo dividido por la mitad, por lo que el vice presidente dio el voto decisivo. The U.S. Senate vote was evenly divided, and the vice president cast the deciding vote.

dividirse en facciones ▪ escindirse en facciones to split (up) into factions ▪ to splinter into factions ▪ to divide (up) into factions

dividirse en grupos to divide up into groups ▪ to split into groups ➤ No me gusta cuando la profesora nos hace dividirnos en grupos. I don't like it when the teacher makes us split into groups. ▪ I don't like it when the teacher makes us divide up into groups. ➤ El pelotón se dividió, un grupo buscando por el río, y el otro tomando el camino de la montaña. The posse split up, one group searching down by the river, the other taking the mountain road.

dividirse en sectores ▪ haber ámbitos ▪ estar dividido en sectores ▪ estar dividido en líneas de pensamiento to be divided into camps ▪ to be divided into schools of thought ➤ El socialismo se divide en dos sectores, uno comunista y otro democrático. ▪ En el ámbito socialista hay dos sectores, uno comunista y el otro democrático. Socialism is divided into two camps, one communist and one democratic. ▪ Socialism is divided into two schools of thought, one communist and one democratic.

divisar a alguien to catch sight of someone ▪ to spot someone (in the distance)

divisar algo de un vistazo to spot something at a glance ➤ Se podía divisar de un vistazo. ▪ Se divisaba de un vistazo. You could spot it at a glance.

divisar algo en la distancia to spot something in the distance ➤ Rodrigo de Triana, desde su puesto de vigía en la Pinta, divisó las fogatas de los nativos americanos en la costa a una distancia de nueve millas y media. Rodrigo de Triana, from the crow's nest of the Pinta, spotted the bonfires of the native Americans along the coast at a distance of about nine miles.

divisar un objeto en la lejanía to make out an object in the distance

divorciarse después de *x* años de casados to get a divorce after *x* years of marriage ➤ Se divorciaron después de cuarenta años de casados. They got a divorce after forty years of marriage.

do re mi fa sol la si do do re mi fa sol (*o* so) la ti do ▪ C D E F G A B C ➤ Concierto en si bemol Concerto in B flat ➤ Concierto en sol menor Concerto in G minor.

do de pecho high C

doblar algo hacia atrás to bend back something ▪ to bend something back

doblar el espinazo to kowtow to someone ▪ to knuckle under to someone

doblar la esquina ▪ dar la vuelta a la esquina to turn the corner

doblar la rodilla a alguien to kowtow to someone

doblar las campanas for the bells to peal ▪ for the bells to ring

doblar las mangas ▪ remangar las mangas ▪ arremangar las mangas to roll up one's sleeves

doblar por la línea de puntos to fold along the dotted line

doblar ropas to fold clothes ➤ ¿Te las doblo? Shall I fold these for you? ▪ Would you like me to fold these for you?

doblar las solapas *(montando una caja)* to fold in the flaps

doblarle la edad a alguien to be twice someone's age ➤ Él le dobla la edad a ella. He's twice her age.

doblarse a la derecha ▪ virar a la derecha to turn (to the) right ▪ to take a right ▪ *(coloquial)* to hang a right

doblarse a la izquierda ▪ virar a la izquierda to turn (to the) left ▪ to take a left ▪ *(coloquial)* to hang a left

doblarse (de dolor) to double over (with pain ➤ Se doblaba (de dolor) cuando le dio el cólico nefrítico. He doubled over with pain during his attack of kidney stones. ➤ Tuve un caso grave de calambres estomacales que me doblaba de dolor. No podía ni ponerme derecho. I had a severe case of stomach cramps that doubled me over. I couldn't even stand up straight.

doble atención: tener ~ to be able to do two things at once

doble de rápido twice as fast

doble fallo dual failure

doble mando: tener ~ to have dual controls

el **doble mentón** double chin

doble que yo twice as much as I do ➤ El gasta por comida el doble que yo. He spends on food twice as much as I do. ▪ He spends twice as much as I do on food.

doce de la medianoche: a las ~ at twelve midnight

doce del mediodía: a las ~ at twelve noon

docena de fraile baker's dozen ▪ thirteen

ser **docto(-a) en** to be knowledgeable about

documentación incautada documents seized

estar **documentado(-a) sobre un tema** to be (well) informed on a subject

documentos fehacientes *(escrituras, contratos, acta de nacimiento, pasaporte, etc.)* irrefutable documents

dolce vita the good life

dolencias cardiacas heart problems

doler el alma to be weary

dolor acerbo sharp pain

el **dolor de cabeza palpitante** throbbing headache

el **dolor no remitía** the pain wouldn't go away

dominar el espacio aéreo de un país to control a country's airspace ▪ to control the airspace of a country

dominar un segmento (de la economía) to lead a sector of the economy ▪ to lead an economic sector ▪ to lead an industry

domingo de ramos Palm Sunday

domingo de resurrección Easter Sunday

dominio público: ser del ~ to be in the public domain

don de gentes: tener ~ to have a way with people

el **don de la comprensión** the gift of understanding

don nadie Mr. Nobody

ser un **don nadie** ▪ *(Arg.)* ser un Juan de los palotes to be a nobody

don sabihondo Mr. Know-it-all

el, la **donante de órganos** organ donor

el, la **donante de sangre** blood donor

donar sangre to donate blood ▪ to give blood

¿dónde andábamos? where were we? ▪ where did we leave off?

donde caben dos, caben tres there's always room for one more

¿dónde coño...? *(subido de tono)* where (in) the hell...? ▪ where'n (the) hell...? ➤ ¿Dónde coño están las tijeras? Where (in) the hell are the scissors? ▪ Where'n (the) hell are the scissors?

estar **donde debe estar** to be where one belongs ➤ Vuelto a mi casa en Vera Cruz me sentí feliz. Estaba donde debía estar. Back in my house in Vera Cruz, I felt happy. I was where I belonged.

disgustarse con alguien to fall out with someone ▪ to have a falling out with someone

¿dónde cuernos has estado? where in the heck have you been?

donde dije digo, digo Diego all bets are off

donde disfrutar where one can enjoy ▪ where you can enjoy

¿dónde estabas? where were you? ➤ Dónde estabas esta mañana? Where were you this morning?

donde estuvieres, haz lo que vieres ■ cuando fueres a Roma vive como romano ■ donde fueres, haz lo que vieres when in Rome, do as the Romans do

¿dónde has estado? ■ ¿de dónde vienes? where have you been?

donde hay la voluntad, hay un camino ■ querer es poder where there's a will there's a way

¿dónde iba ese tren? ■ ¿qué tren se marcha? ■ ¿qué tren acaba de marchar? ■ ¿qué tren acaba de salir? where was that train headed? ■ what train was that? ■ what train just left? ■ which train just left?

donde las dan, las toman two can play that game ■ turnabout is fair play

¿dónde nos avistamos? *(Valle-Inclán)* where shall we meet?

¿dónde nos vemos? ■ ¿dónde nos vemos? ■ ¿dónde quieres quedar? where shall we meet? ■ where do you want to meet?

donde poder descubrir where one can discover ■ where you can discover

donde pone(n) where it says ➤ Sigue por el pasillo a donde ponen "harina". Continue down the aisle to where it says "flour."

¿dónde quedamos? ■ ¿dónde nos vemos? ■ ¿dónde quieres quedar? where shall we meet? ■ where do you want to meet?

¿dónde quieres quedar? ■ ¿dónde quedamos? ■ ¿dónde nos vemos? where do you want to meet? ■ where shall we meet?

donde sale la curva where it curves

¿dónde se fija el límite? ■ ¿dónde se fijan los límites? where do you draw the line?

¿dónde se sacó esta foto? where was this picture taken?

donde sea posible wherever possible

donde una puerta se cierra, se abre una ventana ■ cuando una puerta se cierra, se abre una ventana when one door closes, another opens

¡dónde va a parar! there's no comparison!

¡dónde vas...! you must be joking ■ you must be kidding ■ *(coloquial)* you gotta be joking ■ you gotta be kidding

donde yo quisiera wherever I wanted (to)

dondequiera que estés wherever you are ➤ ¡Buenas noches, Sra. Calabash, dondequiera que estés! Good night, Mrs. Calabash, wherever you are!

dondequiera que voy wherever I go ■ everywhere I go

dorar la píldora to sweeten the pill ■ to sugar-coat the pill

dormí de más ■ me quedé dormido(-a) ■ se me pegaron las sábanas I overslept

dormida de la hija *(Valle-Inclán)* the daughter's sleeping with ■ the daughter's liaison with

dormir a pierna suelta ■ dormir a pierna tendida to sleep comfortably ■ to sleep well

dormir a pierna tendida ■ dormir a pierna suelta to sleep comfortably ■ to sleep well

dormir como un lirón ■ dormir como una leña ■ quedarse como un tronco to sleep like a log

dormir como una leña ■ quedarse como un tronco ■ dormir como un lirón to sleep like a log

dormir de más to oversleep ➤ Dormí de más. I overslept. ➤ Durmió de más. He overslept.

dormir la mona to sleep off a hangover

dormir la siesta ■ tomar una siesta ■ echarse una siesta to have one's nap

dormir menos de lo necesario ■ no dormir lo suficiente not to get enough sleep ➤ *(noticia)* Los jóvenes duermen menos de lo necesario. ■ Los jóvenes no duermen lo suficiente. Young people don't get enough sleep.

dormirse en los laureles ■ dormirse sobre los laureles to rest on one's laurels

dormirse otra vez ■ volver a dormirse ■ conciliar el sueño (de nuevo) to get back to sleep ■ to go back to sleep ■ to fall back to sleep ➤ Después de que la sirena la despertara, no pudo dormirse otra vez. ■ Después de que la sirena la despertara, no pudo volver a dormirse. ■ Después de que la sirena la despertara, no pudo conciliar el sueño (de nuevo). After the siren woke her up, she couldn't get back to sleep.

dormirse sobre los laureles ■ dormirse en los laureles to rest on one's laurels

Dorsal Media del Atlántico *(geología)* Mid-Atlantic Ridge

dorso de la caja ■ la parte posterior de la caja ■ la parte de atrás de la caja ■ el reverso de la caja back of a box ➤ Para receta, ver dorso. For recipe, see back.

dorso de la lata ■ la parte posterior de la lata ■ la parte de atrás de la lata ■ el reverso de la lata back of the can ➤ La receta está en el dorso de la lata. The recipe is on the back of the can.

dorso de la mano ■ (el) envés de la mano back of the hand

dorso de un billete ■ reverso de un billete back of a bill ■ reverse side of a bill *(Nota: En los billetes americanos, el dorso es el lado opuesto al retrato.)*

dorso de un cheque back of a check

dorso del tarro *(L.am.)* ■ (la) parte de atrás del tarro back of the can

dos no riñen si uno no quiere it takes two to tango

dos pantalones two pairs of pants ➤ Hoy me compré dos pantalones. I bought two pairs of pants today.

¡dos por uno! buy one, get one free!

dos terceras partes ■ dos tercios two thirds

dos terceras partes del total two thirds of the total

dos tercios ■ dos terceras partes two thirds

dos veces twice ■ two times

dos veces al día twice a day ■ two times a day ➤ Se les da de comer a los perros dos veces al día. The dogs are fed twice a day. ■ The dogs are fed two times a day.

dos veces más 1. *(singular)* twice as much 2. *(plural)* twice as many

dos veces más que... 1. twice as much as 2. twice as many as 3. twice as often as

ser **dos veces más que ellos** to outnumber them two to one

dos y dos suman cuatro two and two are four ■ two and two makes four ■ two and two equals four

dosificar el tiempo 1. to plan one's time 2. *(deportes)* to allot specific amounts of time

la **dosis de caballo** massive dose

estar **dotado(-a) de** to be endowed with

las **dotes de mando** leadership qualities

drogas blandas soft drugs ■ non-addicting drugs

drogas de diseño designer drugs

drogas duras hard drugs

ducha de agua fría... 1. cold shower 2. *(figurativo)* a good cold douche

estar **ducho(-a) en una materia** to be knowledgeable on a subject ■ to be knowledgeable about a subject

dudar de algo to question something ■ to doubt something

dudar entre not to know whether to

dudar si hacer algo o no not to know whether to do something or not

dudas sobre doubts about ➤ Dudas sobre la suerte de la tripulación Doubts about the fate of the crew

dudoso honor de ser: caberle el ~ to have the dubious honor of being

duelo a muerte fight to the death

dueña y señora lord and mistress

ser **dueño(-a) de sí mismo(-a)** to be in control of oneself ■ to be self-possessed

ser el, la **dueño(-a) de su destino** to be the master of one's fate

ser **dueño(-a) de un secreto** to be the possessor of a secret

dueño y señor lord and master

duplicarse en altura to double in height ➤ Los árboles en Sor Ángela se han duplicado en altura en seis años. The trees on Sor Angela have doubled in height in six years.

duplicarse los gastos(for) one's costs to double ■ (for) one's expenses to double ➤ Se han duplicado mis gastos de comida desde que se instaló el nuevo compañero de piso. My food costs have doubled since the new flatmate moved in.

¿dura mucho? is it long? ■ does it last long? ■ does it go on long?

dura ofensiva major offensive

dura realidad ■ cruda realidad harsh reality

dura resolución tough resolution

durante años for years

durante días enteros for days on end
durante el fin de semana over the weekend ■ during the weekend
durante el primer año de vida ■ en el primer año de vida ■ during the first year of life ■ in the first year of life
durante la mayor parte de during the greater part of ■ for most of ➤ Durante la mayor parte del otoño... For most of the fall... ■ For most of the autumn...
durante la mayor parte del trayecto for most of the way
durante la vida de uno ■ en el curso de la vida de uno during one's lifetime ■ in one's lifetime
durante lapsos de hasta at intervals of up to ➤ Prescribieron un reductor del colesterol a unos ochocientos adultos durante lapsos de hasta un año. They prescribed a cholesterol reducer to some eight hundred adults at intervals of up to a year.
durante las Navidades over Christmas ■ during Christmas
durante las próximas semanas *(futuro)* during the next few weeks ➤ Durante las próximas semanas, tendrás buena suerte. During the next few weeks, you will have good luck.
durante las siguientes semanas *(pasado)* during the next few weeks ➤ Durante las siguientes semanas, su relación cambió por completo. During the next few weeks, their relationship completely changed. ■ During the next few weeks, their relationship changed completely.
durante las últimas semanas during the past few weeks
durante los años que uno lleva viviendo ■ durante los años de vida de uno during one's lifetime ■ in one's lifetime ➤ Durante los años que llevo yo viviendo ■ Durante mis años de vida During my lifetime ■ In my lifetime ➤ Durante los años que llevamos viviendo ■ Durante nuestros años de vida During our lifetimes
durante los *x* años siguientes for the next *x* years
durante los *x* años próximos for the next *x* years
durante mi etapa de estudiante, pagué mis gastos trabajando de pintor I worked my way through college by painting
durante mucho tiempo for a long time
durante períodos de hasta at intervals of up to ➤ Recetaron un reductor del colesterol a unos ochocientos adultos durante períodos de hasta un año. They prescribed a cholesterol reducer to some eight hundred adults at intervals of up to a year.
durante sólo un instante for only an instant
(durante) toda la mañana ■ (en) toda la mañana all morning long ■ the whole morning ■ the entire morning
durante todo el año all year round ■ all year ■ throughout the year ■ all through the year ➤ Ella escucha música navideña durante todo el año. She listens to Christmas music all year round.
durante todo el día ■ todo el día all day long
durante un instante for an instant
durante un momento for a moment
durante un rato *(minutos o horas)* for a while ■ for a time ➤ Leí durante un rato y luego me fui a la cama. I read for a while and then went to bed. ■ I read for a time and then went to bed.
durante un tiempo *(semanas o meses)* ■ por un tiempo for a time ■ for a while ➤ Vivieron en Madrid durante un tiempo. They lived in Madrid for a time. ■ They lived in Madrid for a while.
durante *x* años ■ desde hace *x* años for *x* years ■ over a period of *x* years ➤ Los normandos gobernaron Inglaterra durante setecientos años. The Normans ruled England for seven hundred years.
durar (así) permanecer así to stay that way ➤ Hace fresco fuera. Espero que dure (así.) ■ Hace fresco fuera. Espero que permanezca así. It's nice and cool outside. I hope it stays that way.
durar eternamente to last forever
durar hasta... to last up to... ➤ El efecto puede durar hasta media hora. The effect can last up to half an hour.
durar mucho to last long
durar poco 1. to last a short time ■ not to last long **2.** *(historia)* not to go back very far ■ to be short
duras medidas tough measures
duras represalias stiff reprisals
dureza de su tono harshness of his tone
duro como una piedra: quedarse ~ to be hard as a rock
ser **duro con alguien** ■ tratar duramente a alguien to be hard on someone ■ to be overbearing with someone
ser **duro de corazón** to be hard-hearted
estar **duro de frío** *(coloquial)* ■ estar yerto de frío to be frozen stiff
estar **duro de mollera** ■ estar cerrado de mollera to be thick-headed ■ to be pig-headed
ser **duro de mollera** to be hard-headed
ser **duro de oído 1.** ser tardo de oído ■ ser sordo to be hard of hearing ■ to be deaf **2.** ser insensible ■ ser tozudo to be stubborn ■ to refuse to listen to reason
ser **duro de pelar** to be a hard one to pull off
ser **duro hueso de roer** to be a tough nut to crack ■ to be a tough row to hoe
ser **duro para uno** to be hard on one ➤ La muerte de su madre cuando tenía diez años fue muy duro para él. His mother's death when he was ten was very hard on him.
¡duro y a la cabeza! don't give up!
¡duro y firme! hold it steady!

e incluso and even ▪ or even ➤ Desde la atalaya de la estrella polar, teóricamente, podríamos correlacionar la posición orbital de la Tierra con las estaciones, hasta los meses e incluso los días del año. From vantage point of the Pole Star, theoretically, we could correlate the Earth's orbital position with the seasons, down to the months and even days of the year.

e incluso más and even more

¡**echa el freno, Magdaleno!** cool your jets! ▪ cool it!

echa una firmita aquí (just) sign right here ▪ just sign here

ser **echado(-a) a patadas** ▪ echarle a patadas to get kicked out of ▪ to be bodily removed from ➤ El borracho fue echado a patadas del bar. ▪ Al borracho le echaron a patadas del bar. The drunk got kicked out of the bar. ▪ The drunk was bodily removed from the bar.

estar **echado a perder** ~ 1. *(comida)* estar pasado to be spoiled 2. *(leche, crema)* estar cortada to be sour ▪ to have gone sour 3. estar gastado to be worn out ▪ *(pinturesco)* to be shot ➤ El fontanero cree que las tuberías están completamente echadas a perder. The plumber thinks the pipes are completely shot.

¡**échale el lazo!** ▪ ¡cázale! ▪ ¡a por ello! go for it!

échale un galgo not a chance ▪ no way

échalo(-a) a la ropa sucia throw it in the dirty clothes ▪ put it in the dirty clothes

¡**échame una mano!** help me out! ▪ give me a hand!

estar **echando bombas** to be hopping mad ▪ to be mad as a hornet

estar **echando chispas** ▪ estar que arde to be hopping mad ▪ to be mad as a hornet ▪ to be fuming

echando hostias: ir ~ *(coloquial)* ▪ ir echando leches to haul ass ▪ to go like a bat outta hell

echando leches: ir ~ *(coloquial)* ▪ ir echando hostias to haul ass ▪ to go like a bat outta hell

echar a algo un jarro de agua throw water on something ▪ to douse something (with water)

echar a alguien ▪ despedir a alguien to give someone the boot ▪ to fire someone

echar a alguien a los perros to throw someone to the wolves

echar a alguien con cajas destempladas ▪ despedir a alguien con cajas destempladas to send someone packing ▪ to give someone the boot

echar a alguien contra alguien ▪ poner a alguien en contra de alguien to turn someone against someone

echar a alguien un jarro de agua 1. to throw water on someone ▪ to douse someone with water 2. to squelch someone ▪ to rain on someone's parade

echar a andar ▪ ponerse a andar to start walking

echar a cara o cruz to flip a coin

echar a correr to start running ▪ to break into a run

echar a hacer algo ▪ ponerse a hacer algo to start doing something ➤ Ella echó a correr. She started running.

echar a la calle a alguien 1. despedir a alguien to can someone ▪ to fire someone ▪ to sack someone 2. desalojar a un inquilino to evict someone ▪ to throw someone out ▪ to kick somebody out

echar a patadas a alguien 1. despedir a alguien to give someone the boot ▪ to fire someone 2. echar a alguien del local to kick someone out ▪ to remove someone from the premises ➤ *(Méx.)* Lo echaron a patadas del trabajo. ▪ *(Esp.)* Le echaron a patadas del trabajo. They gave him the boot (at work).

echar a perder algo to destroy something ▪ to ruin something

echar a pique algo to throw something away ▪ to get rid of something

echar a rodar to set in motion

echar a tierra a alguien to bring down someone ▪ to bring someone down

echar a tierra algo to bring something down ▪ to bring down something

echar a un diplomático to expel a diplomat

echar a un lado algo to set something aside

echar a un niño a perder to spoil a child

echar a volar to start flying

echar abajo a alguien to bring down someone ▪ to bring someone down

echar abajo algo to bring down something ▪ to bring something down

echar abajo una propuesta to quash a proposal ▪ to throw out a proposal ▪ to reject a proposal

echar aceite al fuego to add fuel to the flames

echar agua al vino to water down a statement ▪ to qualify a statement

echar agua en el mar ▪ llevar leña al monte to carry coals to Newcastle

echar al correo una carta to mail a letter ➤ Tengo que echar al correo el pago hoy. I have to mail the payment today.

echar al perro (a)fuera to put the dog out

echar algo a la basura to throw something away ▪ to throw something out ➤ Lo eché a la basura. I threw it away. ▪ I threw it out.

echar algo a las espaldas to put something behind one

echar algo al aire to throw something into the air

echar algo al azar to leave something to chance

echar algo al hombro to sling something over one's shoulder ▪ to throw something on one's shoulder

echar algo de baranda ▪ exagerar to exaggerate

echar algo de sí to get rid of something

echar algo en saco roto to let something go to waste

echar algo por alto (just) to let something ▪ (just) to forget something ▪ not to harbor something ➤ Échalo por alto. Just let it go. ▪ Just forget it. ▪ Don't harbor it.

echar algo por la borda ▪ tirar algo por la borda to throw something overboard

echar algo sobre las espaldas de alguien 1. to put something on someone's back 2. echarle una carga a alguien ▪ cargarlo a alguien con algo to saddle someone with something

echar anclas ▪ echar el ancla ▪ echar las anclas to drop anchor

echar balones fuera ▪ achicar balones to dodge the issue ▪ to evade the issue

echar bravatas to talk big

echar camino adelante to strike out

echar candado a la boca ▪ echar candado a los labios to keep one's lips zipped

echar cara a algo ▪ afrontar algo to face something

echar cara a alguien ▪ afrontar a alguien ▪ hacer frente a alguien to face someone

echar carnes to get fat ▪ to gain weight

echar chiribitas to whine

echar cojones to be brave

echar cuentas to figure

echar de comer a los animales ▪ dar de comer a los animales to feed the animals

echar de comer a los niños ■ dar de comer a los niños to feed the children

echar de menos a alguien ■ echar en falta a alguien ■ extrañar a alguien to miss someone ■ to be lonesome for someone ■ to feel lonesome for someone

echar del mundo a algo to get rid of something

echar del mundo a alguien to get rid of someone

echar dinero a algo to throw money at something

echar dinero en algo to put the money in something

echar el agua a su molino ■ llevar el agua a su molino to be on the make ■ to steer the conversation toward one's interests

echar el alma atrás ■ echar el alma a las espaldas to leave one's feelings out of it

echar el ancla ■ echar anclas ■ echar las anclas to drop anchor ■ to cast the anchor(s)

echar el anzuelo to cast the bait ■ to plant the bait

echar el bofe to slog away ■ to slave away

echar el cerrojo to bolt the door

echar el cierre a la investigación sobre to close the investigation of

echar el freno to put on the breaks ■ to slow down

echar el guante to drop the glove

echar el ojo to have a look

echar el ojo a algo ■ tener el ojo echado a algo to have one's eye on something

echar el ojo a alguien ■ tener el ojo echado a alguien to have one's eye on someone

echar el pie adelante ■ dar un paso adelante to take a step forward

echar el resto 1. to do one's utmost ■ to go for broke **2.** to stake all one's money

echar el sello a un pasaporte *(Arg.)* ■ poner el sello a un pasaporte ■ sellar el pasaporte to stamp a passport

echar en cara a alguien to let someone have it ➤ El jefe me echó en cara no haber entregado el informe a tiempo. The boss let me have it for not turning in the report on time.

echar en corro las cosas to round up things

echar encima a alguien to alienate someone ■ to turn someone against you

echar espuma por la boca to foam at the mouth

echar espumarajos por la boca ■ echar espumarajos to foam at the mouth ■ to fume with rage

echar flores a alguien 1. *(literal)* to throw flowers at someone **2.** *(figurativo)* elogiar a alguien to sing someone's praises ■ to lavish praise(s) on someone **3.** *(figurativo)* halagar a alguien to flatter someone ➤ No te lo digo para echarte flores. I'm not saying that just to flatter you. ■ I'm not telling you that just to flatter you.

echar fuego por la boca to spit fire ■ to seethe with anger

echar fuego por los ojos to see red

echar gasolina (al coche) ■ poner gasolina (al coche) to put gas in the tank ■ to get gas ➤ Tenemos que parar y echar gasolina. ■ Tenemos que parar y poner gasolina. We have to stop and get gas.

echar hasta la primera papilla ■ echar la primera papilla to vomit up everything ■ to vomit everything up

echar humo to fume (with anger) ■ to fume (with rage)

echar la bendición a algo to bless something

echar la bendición a alguien to bless someone

echar la buenaventura a alguien to tell someone's fortune

echar la cabeza hacia atrás to throw one's head back

echar la cabeza para adelante to put one's head forward

echar la cabeza para atrás to put one's head back

echar la carga a ■ pasar la cuenta a to pass the buck to

echar la casa por la ventana ■ tirar la casa por la ventana to put the big pot in the little one ■ to spare no expense ■ to go all out ■ to shoot the moon

echar la charla to talk on and on

echar la cremallera to zip one's lips ■ to button one's lips

echar la cuenta 1. sumar la cuenta to total the bill **2.** resumir la situación to sum up the situation

echar la cuenta de la vieja to add up figures one by one

echar la culpa a to put the blame on ■ to lay the blame on

echar la culpa a alguien de algo ■ echar la culpa a alguien por algo ■ culpar a alguien de algo ■ culpar a alguien por algo to blame someone for something ■ to blame something on someone

echar la culpa a alguien por algo ■ echar la culpa a alguien de algo ■ culpar a alguien por algo ■ culpar a alguien de algo to blame someone for something ■ to blame something on someone ■ to deflect the blame onto someone else

echar la culpa de *x* a *y* ■ colgar a alguien un sambenito to shift the blame from *x* to *y*

echar la firma a un documento to sign a document

echar la hiel 1. vomitar to puke **2.** echar el bofe to be winded ■ to be gasping for breath

echar la hueva *(coloquial)* ■ holgazanear en (la) casa ■ flojear por (la) casa ■ andar haciendo el vago por (la) casa to putter around the house

echar la ley a alguien ■ echar a toda ley a alguien to throw the book at someone

echar la mano a la pistola to go for one's gun

echar la primera papilla ■ echar hasta la primera papilla to vomit (up) everything

echar la pota to puke one's guts out

echar la puerta abajo to break down the door

echar la red to cast the net

echar la vista a algo to glance at something

echar la vista a alguien to glance at someone

echar la vista encima to cast a glance ■ to glance ➤ She cast a glance at him. ■ She glanced at him. (Ella) le echó la vista encima (a él). ➤ He cast a glance at her. ■ He glanced at her. (Él) le echó la vista encima (a ella). ➤ He cast a glance around the room. ■ He glanced around the room. Echó la vista encima a la habitación.

echar las anclas ■ echar el ancla ■ echar anclas to drop anchor

echar las campanas al vuelo to ring the bells (in victory)

echar las cartas a alguien to tell someone's fortune (by reading cards)

echar las penas a un lado to forget your troubles

echar las piernas encima de la mesa to put one's feet (up) on the table ■ to prop one's legs on the table

echar las tripas ■ echar la pota to throw up ■ to puke

echar leña al fuego ■ añadir leña al fuego **1.** *(literal)* to put wood on the fire **2.** *(figurativo)* exacerbar la situación ■ empeorar la situación to add fuel to the flames ■ to add fuel to the fire

echar los bofes to huff and puff

echar los bofes por algo to go all out for something

echar los cimientos to lay the foundation

echar los hígados *(argot)* to toss one's cookies ■ to throw up

echar los perros to be furious

echar los pies por alto to be indifferent to what's going on around you

echar los pulmones para to do one's utmost to ■ to give all you've got to

echar lumbre to be furious

echar mano to lend a hand ■ to help out

echar mano a algo to get one's hands on something

echar mano de to make use of

echar marcha atrás su propuesta ■ dar marcha atrás su propuesta ■ replantearse su propuesta ■ retroceder en su propuesta to back away from a proposal

echar más humo que una chimenea to smoke like a chimney ■ to smoke like a train

echar más leña al fuego to put (some) more wood on the fire ■ to add fuel to the flames ■ to add fuel to the fire

echar parches a un prenda 1. poner parches a una prenda to patch an article of clothing **2.** *(cosiendo)* to sew patches on an article of clothing **3.** *(planchando; parches adhesivos)* to iron on patches ■ to iron patches on(to) an article of clothing

echar pelillos a la mar to bury the hatchet

echar pestes to swear ■ to curse ■ *(coloquial)* to cuss

echar por arrobas ■ exagerar to exaggerate

echar por el atajo to take the easy way out

echar por la boca su comida to throw up one's dinner

echar por la borda ■ tirar por la borda to throw overboard

echar por los suelos sus planes ■ echar por tierra sus planes to spoil one's plans ➤ Si continúas con este camino, echarás por los suelos todos tus planes. If you keep going down this road, you're going to spoil all your plans.

echar por tierra ■ echar por los suelos to ruin ■ to wreck ■ to destroy

echar pullas a alguien to needle someone

echar raíces to put down roots

echar rayos y centellas to be hopping mad ■ to be mad as a hornet

echar sangre por los ojos to be torn to pieces ■ to be distraught

echar sapos y culebras por la boca to rant and rave ■ to curse a blue streak ■ to turn the air blue

echar suertes ■ echar a suertes to draw lots

echar tierra a sus planes to scrap one's plans

echar tierra encima de to hush up ■ to cover up

echar todo el chorro ■ irse de la lengua ■ descubrir el pastel to spill the beans

echar tras alguien to go after someone

echar tripa to develop a paunch

echar un barco al agua to launch a boat

echar un barco al fondo ■ dar barreno a un barco to scuttle a ship

echar un discurso to give a speech ■ to make a speech

echar un cable a alguien ■ echar un gancho a alguien to throw someone a lifeline

echar un caliqueño *(subido de tono)* to fuck

echar un candado a la boca ■ poner un candado a la boca to zip one's lips ■ to keep one's trap shut

echar un capote a alguien to give someone a (helping) hand ■ to lend someone a (helping) hand ■ to lend a hand

echar un casquete *(subido de tono)* to fuck

echar un discurso to give a speech ■ to make a speech ■ to deliver a speech

echar un gancho to throw someone a lifeline

echar un guante ■ arrojar el guante to throw down the gauntlet

echar un jarro de agua fría a alguien to rain on someone's parade ■ to throw cold water on someone's hopes

echar un ojo a algo ■ echar un vistazo a algo to glance at something

echar un ojo a alguien ■ echar un vistazo a alguien to glance at someone

echar un parche a una prenda ■ poner un parche a una prenda **1.** to patch an article of clothing **2.** *(cosiendo el parche)* to sew a patch on an article of clothing ■ to sew on a patch ■ to sew a patch on an article of clothing **3.** *(planchando; parches adhesivos)* to iron on a patch ■ to iron a patch on(to) an article of clothing

echar un pasillo ■ mover el esqueleto ■ bailar ■ danzar to dance

echar un polvo *(subido de tono)* ■ echar quiqui to fuck

echar un pulso a alguien ■ echar un pulso con alguien to arm-wrestle someone

echar un quiqui *(subido de tono)* ■ echar un polvo to fuck

echar un rapapolvo ■ dar un rapapolvo ■ reprender ■ regañar to read someone the riot act ■ to give someone hell ■ to tell someone off ■ to reprimand ■ to scold

echar un sermón a alguien to give someone a lecture

echar un último vistazo ■ echar una última ojeada to take one last look around ■ to have a last look around

echar un vistazo (a) ■ dar un vistazo (a) ■ echar una ojeada (a) **1.** to have a look (at) **2.** lanzar una mirada a to cast a glance at ■ to glance at ➤ *(médico al paciente)* Echemos un vistazo. ■ Echemos una ojeada. ■ Veamos. Let's have a look. ➤ Él le echó un vistazo de aprobación a ella. He cast an approving glance at her. ➤ Ella le echó un vistazo igualmente aprobatorio a él. She cast an equally approving glance at him.

echar una bebida de un trago ■ meterse una bebida de un trago to belt down a drink ■ to gulp down a drink

echar una cabezada ■ echar una cabezada ■ dar una cabezadita ■ echar una cabezadita ■ quedarse dormido to doze off ■ to nod off ➤ Intenta no dar una cabezada después de comer. ■ Intenta no echar una cabezada después de comer. ■ Intenta no dar una cabezadita después de comer. ■ Intenta no echar una cabezadita después de comer. ■ Intenta no quedarte dormido después de comer. Try not to doze off after dinner. ■ Try to keep from dozing off after dinner. ■ Try not to nod off after dinner. ■ Try to keep from nodding off after dinner.

echar una charla a alguien ■ echar una charlada a alguien to give someone a lecture

echar una cana al aire ■ echar una canita al aire to have an affair in one's mature years

echar una cortina de humo ■ echar una pantalla de humo to put up a smoke screen ■ to throw up a smoke screen

echar una cuenta to balance an account

echar una filípica to denounce bitterly ■ to harangue

echar una firma ■ firmar to sign

echar una indirecta ■ lanzar una indirecta ■ soltar una indirecta to drop a hint

echar una mano to lend a hand

echar una meada to take a piss ■ to take a leak ■ to take a pee

echar una mirada a to glance at ■ to glance around

echar una moneda al aire to flip a coin ■ to toss a coin

echar una ojeada (a) ■ echar un vistazo (a) to have a look (at) ■ to take a look (at) ➤ *(médico al paciente)* Echemos una ojeada. ■ Echemos un vistazo. Let's have a look.

echar una pantalla de humo ■ echar una cortina de humo to put up a smoke screen ■ to throw up a smoke screen

echar una última ojeada ■ echar un último vistazo to take one last look around

echar vapor 1. *(literal)* to give off steam **2.** *(figurativo)* desahogarse to blow off steam

echarle de la casa a alguien to kick someone out of the house

echarle (del trabajo) a alguien to fire someone

echarle el ojo a alguien to have one's eye on someone ➤ Ella le echa el ojo a él. She has her eye on him.

echarle el perro a alguien to set the dog on someone ■ to sick the dog on someone ■ to sic the dog on someone

echarle la bronca to bawl someone out ■ to tell someone off ■ to let someone have it

echarle la llave to lock (up) ➤ *(tú)* Échale la llave. ■ *(usted)* Échele la llave. Lock it (up).

echarle las cartas a alguien to read someone's cards

echarle los brazos a alguien to throw one's arms around someone

echarle porras a alguien to cheer someone on

echarle un cable a alguien to give someone a hand

echarle un ojo a to keep an eye on ➤ ¿Le echas un ojo a mis cosas mientras hago una llamada? Will you keep an eye on my things while I make a phone call?

echarle un vistazo 1. to have a look at it **2.** *(algo con varias páginas)* to glance through it

echarle una mano a alguien to give someone a hand ■ to help someone out ➤ Claro que te echo una mano, si puedo. Sure I'll give you a hand if I can. ■ Sure I'll help you out if I can.

echarle una zancadilla to trip someone

echarle valor (para) ■ armarse de valor (para) ■ hacer acopio de valor (para) to get up the nerve (to) ■ to get up the courage (to) ■ to pluck up one's courage ■ to get up one's nerve ➤ Cuando tenía trece años tuve que echarle valor para llamarla. When I was thirteen, I had to get up the courage to call her. ■ When I was thirteen, I had to get up the nerve to call her.

echarlo a suertes 1. echar suertes ■ jugárselo a suertes to draw straws ■ to draw lots ■ to cast lots

echarlo todo a perder ■ estropearlo todo to spoil everything ➤ Yo iba a besarla, pero mis padres entraron y lo echaron todo a perder. I was going to kiss her, but my parents came in and spoiled everything.

echarse a... to begin to...

echarse a correr to take off running ■ to break into a run

echarse a hacer algo to start doing something ■ to take off doing something ➤ Se echó a correr. She started running. ■ She took off running. ■ She broke into a run.

echarse a la calle to take to the streets ➤ Los madrileños se echan a la calle. Residents of Madrid take to the streets.
echarse a la derecha 1. *(sentado)* to move over to the right 2. *(conduciendo)* to bear right
echarse a la espalda ▪ echarse a las espaldas to shoulder a responsibility ▪ to shoulder responsibilities
echarse a la izquierda 1. *(sentado)* to move over to the left 2. *(conduciendo)* to bear left
echarse a llorar to start crying
echarse a perder 1. *(alimento)* to spoil 2. *(persona)* to get spoiled 3. to go to the dogs
echarse a reír to start laughing
echarse al agua to take the plunge ▪ to jump into the water
echarse al aire to start flying ▪ to take off
echarse atrás ▪ echarse para atrás 1. retirarse para atrás to back away ▪ to retreat 2. retractarse algo que uno ha dicho o pedido to take back (something one has said or requested) 3. inclinarse hacia atrás to lean back ➤ La ex-presidenta del país suscribió el estatuto, pero el actual se echó atrás y retiró la firma. The former president of the country supported the statute, but the current president has backed away and refused to sign it.
echarse atrás en un contrato *(antes de firmarlo)* to back out of a contract
echarse atrás en un trato to back out of a deal
echarse de cabeza a la piscina to dive into the pool
echarse de cabeza al asunto to throw oneself headlong into the matter
echarse la culpa uno al otro to blame each other
echarse obligaciones ▪ asumir obligaciones to take on responsibilities (for) ▪ to take on the responsibility (to)
echarse para atrás to stay behind
echarse un candado a la boca ▪ echarse un candado a los labios to keep one's lips zipped ▪ to keep one's counsel
echarse una siesta ▪ dormir la siesta ▪ tomar una siesta to take one's afternoon nap ▪ to have one's afternoon nap
echárselas de to brag about ▪ to boast about ▪ to boast of
echárselo a la espalda to sling it on one's back
échate valor y... (just) get up your nerve and...
eche (usted) una firmita aquí sign right here ▪ just sign here
echo de menos saber de ti I've missed hearing from you
el **eclipse total** ▪ eclipse anular total eclipse ▪ annular eclipse
economía de mercado market economy ▪ market-driven economy
ecuación cuadrática ▪ ecuación de segundo grado quadratic equation
ecuación de segundo grado ▪ ecuación cuadrática quadratic equation
la **edad de los metales** bronze age
la **edad de oro** ▪ época dorada golden age ➤ La Primera Guerra Mundial fue la edad de oro de la aviación militar. ▪ La Primera Guerra Mundial fue la época dorada de la aviación militar. World War I was the golden age of military aviation.
la **edad de piedra** stone age
la **edad del pavo** *(adolescencia)* the awkward age
edad media ▪ edad promedio ▪ media de edad average age
la **Edad Media** the Middle Ages
la **edad promedio** ▪ edad media ▪ media de edad average age ➤ La edad promedio de los artífices de la constitución de los Estados Unidos era de aproximadamente cuarenta años. The average age of the framers of the United States' Constitution was about forty years.
edición anterior 1. *(libro)* previous edition ▪ earlier edition 2. *(revista)* previous issue ▪ earlier issue ➤ Una edición anterior An earlier edition ▪ A previous edition ▪ An earlier issue ▪ A previous issue ➤ La edición anterior The previous edition ▪ The previous issue
edición bloqueada *(informática)* ▪ edición protegida contra escritura read-only version
edición de coleccionista collector's edition
edición de un una revista issue of a magazine ▪ edition of a magazine ➤ ¿Cuándo sale la edición de abril? When will be April issue be out? ▪ When does the April issue come out?
edición (en cuadernación) rústica paperback edition
edición rústica paperback edition
edificios colindantes adjacent buildings
la **educación en persona** politeness itself
la **educación sexual** sex education
la **educación superior** higher education
educar a los hijos ▪ educar a los niños to raise children
¡efectivamente! ▪ ¡claro que sí! ▪ ¡eso es! sure enough ▪ that's right
efectivamente, fue así sure enough, it was
ser **efectivo a partir del primero de abril** ▪ entrar en vigor a partir del primero de abril ▪ ser efectivo el primero de abril ▪ entrar en vigor el primero de abril to be effective April first ▪ to go into effect April first ▪ to take effect April first
efecto bola de nieve snowball effect
efecto dominó domino effect
efecto invernadero greenhouse effect
efecto de nube de bala the bullet cloud effect
efecto fugaz efecto pasajero ▪ efecto momentáneo transitory effect ▪ fleeting effect ▪ momentary effect ➤ El medicamento tiene sólo un efecto fugaz. ▪ El medicamento tiene sólo un efecto transitorio. ▪ El medicamento tiene sólo un efecto pasajero. ▪ El medicamento tiene sólo un efecto momentáneo. The medication has only a transitory effect. ▪ The medication has only a momentary effect.
efecto fulgurante en: tener un ~ to have a dramatic effect on ➤ Esa bebida energética tuvo un efecto fulgurante en mi sentido de la atención. That energy drink had a dramatic effect on my alertness.
efecto momentáneo ▪ efecto fugaz ▪ efecto pasajero momentary effect ▪ fleeting effect ▪ transitory effect
efecto secundario side effect
efecto sobre la gente effect on people
efecto transitorio *(que dura horas o días)* transitory effect
efectos de sonido sound effects
efectuar la entrada en to make its entrance into ▪ to enter ➤ El tren va a efectuar su entrada en la estación. The train is going to make its entrance into the station. ▪ The train is going to enter the station.
efectuar parada en to make stops in ➤ Este tren efectua parada en Valdelasfuentes y Alcobendas. This train makes stops in Valdelasfuentes and Alcobendas.
efeméride centenario (one) hundredth anniversary
ser **eficaz contra** to be effective against
ejecutar el anti-virus to run the anti-virus ▪ to run a virus scan
ejecutar un brusco viraje a to make a sharp turn to
el **ejemplar de** 1. example of 2. espécimén de specimen of
ejemplo hipotético ▪ ejemplo anecdótico hypthetical example ▪ anecdotal example
anecdotal example ▪ hypothetical example ejemplo anecdótico ▪ ejemplo hipotético ➤ El ejemplo es hipotético porque la base de datos aún no ha sido creado. ▪ El ejemplo es anecdótico porque la base de datos aún no ha sido creado. The example is hypothetical because the database hasn't been created yet. ▪ The example is anecdotal because the database hasn't been created yet.
ejercer de abogado ▪ ejercer como abogado ▪ ejercer la abogacia to practice law
ejercer la medicina to practice medicine
ejercer (la) presión to exert pressure
ejercer presión sobre alguien para hacer algo ▪ ejercer presión sobre alguien para que haga algo ▪ presionar a alguien para hacer algo ▪ presionar a alguien para que haga algo ▪ hacer presión sobre alguien para hacer algo ▪ hacer presión sobre alguien para que haga algo to pressure someone to do something ▪ to put pressure on someone to do something
ejercer uno el magisterio de algo ▪ alcanzar uno el dominio de algo ▪ alcanzar la madurez to come into one's own
el **ejercicio hace maestro** practice makes perfect
ejercicios de calentamiento: hacer ~ to do warm-up exercises ▪ to do warm-up exercises ▪ to do warm-ups
ejercicios de estiramiento: hacer ~ to do stretching exercises
ejercito del aire air force

el abajo firmante the undersigned

el anterior the previous one ▪ the last one

El amor brujo *(obra de Manuel de Falla)* Love, the magician

El coronel no tiene quien le escriba *(obra de Gabriel García Márquez) No One Writes to the Colonel*

el del medio the one in the middle ▪ the middle one

el día antes the day before

el entonces the then ➤ El entonces consejero de seguridad nacional Colin Powell. The then national security adviser Colin Powell.

él era el que... ▪ él era quien... he was the one who... ▪ *(literario, culto)* it was he who... ➤ Él era el que tocaba el piano. ▪ Él era quien tocaba el piano. He was the one who was playing the piano. ▪ It was he who was playing the piano. ➤ (Él) era el técnico que estuvo ayer aquí. He was the technician who was here yesterday.

él era quien... ▪ él era el que... he was the one who... ▪ *(literario, culto)* it was he who... ➤ Él era quien tocaba el piano. ▪ Él era el que tocaba el piano. He was the one who was playing the piano. ▪ It was he who was playing the piano.

él es el que... ▪ él es quien... he is the one who... ▪ he's the one who... ▪ *(literario, culto)* it is he who... ➤ Él es el que envió la carta. ▪ Él es quien envió la carta. He is the one who sent the letter. ▪ He's the one who sent the letter. ▪ It is he who sent the letter.

él es quien... ▪ él es el que... he is the one who... ▪ *(literario, culto)* it is he who... ➤ Él es quien está tocando el piano. ▪ Él es el que está tocando el piano. He's the one who is playing the piano. ▪ It is he who is playing the piano.

él fue el que... ▪ él fue quien... he was the one who... ▪ *(literario, culto)* it was he who... ➤ Él fue el que escribió el artículo. ▪ Él fue quien escribió el artículo. He was the one who wrote the article. ▪ It was he who wrote the article.

él fue quien... él fue el que... he was the one who... ▪ *(literario, culto)* it was he who... ➤ Él fue quien escribió el artículo. ▪ Él fue el que escribió el artículo. He was the one who wrote the article. ▪ It was he who wrote the article.

el más the most ▪ the best ➤ Éste me gusta más. ▪ El que más me gusta es éste. I like this one the most. ▪ I like this one the best.

el más allá life after death ▪ the hereafter

el más conocido the best known

ser **el más equilibrado** 1. *(informe, debate)* to be the most balanced 2. *(persona)* to be the best all-around ➤ Fue considerado la alumna más equilibrada en el anuario del instituto. She was listed as best all-around in the high school yearbook.

ser **el más parecido a** to be the closest thing to

ser **el más votado** to receive the highest number of votes

el mayor número posible ▪ la mayor cantidad posible ▪ tantos como sea posible ▪ los más posibles ▪ todos los que puedan ▪ todos los que se pueda as many as possible ▪ the greatest possible number

el mejor con diferencia ▪ el mejor con mucho the best by far

el mejor de los dos the better of the two ➤ Ella es el mejor político de los dos. She is the better politician of the two.

el mejor de los tres the best of the three

ser **el mejor que hay** to be the best (one) there is

El mundo como voluntad y representación *(obra de Schopenhauer) The World As Will and Representation*

ser **el no va más** *(Esp.)* ▪ ser el non plus ultra ▪ ser lo máximo ▪ ser a toda madre ▪ ser la repera to be the ultimate

ser **el non plus ultra** *(Esp.)* ▪ ser el no va más ▪ ser lo máximo ▪ ser a toda madre ▪ ser la repera to be the ultimate

ser **el penúltimo** to be the next-to-the-last one

el peor con diferencia the worst by far

ser **el polo opuesto a** to be completely different ▪ to be completely different from ➤ Marco es el polo opuesto a Paco. Marco and Paco are completely different. ▪ Marco is completely different from. Paco.

ser **el que...** 1. to be the one (that)... ▪ to be the one which... 2. ser quien to be the one who... ➤ Su padre era el que lo llevaba peor. ▪ Su padre era quien lo llevaba peor. His father was the one who took it the worst. ➤ Él es el que escribió el artículo. ▪ Él es quien escribió el artículo. He's the one who wrote the article.

¿el qué? oh, and what would that be?

el que... ▪ quien... he who...

el que a hierro mata, a hierro muere he who lives by the sword dies by the sword

el que avisa no es traidor your critic is not your enemy

el que con leche se quema, ve una vaca y llora once bitten, twice shy ▪ an injury makes a person wary of its source

el que debería obedecer, dirige the tail is wagging the dog

el qué dirán what other people say ▪ what anyone says ▪ public opinion ▪ public reaction

el que le pega a su familia se arruina he who bites the hand that feeds him does himself in

ser **el que manda** ▪ ser el jefe to be the boss

el que más y el que menos everybody under the sun

ser **el que mejor lo hace** ▪ ser el que lo hace mejor to be the one who does it best ▪ to be the best there is

el que mucho abarca, poco aprieta don't overdo it ▪ don't spread yourself too thin ▪ don't try to take on too much

el que no hayas your not having ➤ De veras no entendemos el que no hayas escrito. We really don't understand your not having written.

el que no llora no mama the squeaky wheel gets the grease ▪ the wheel that squeaks the loudest is the one that gets the grease ▪ the wheel that squeaks (is the one that) gets the grease ▪

el que ríe último, ríe mejor ▪ quien ríe último, ríe mejor he who laughs last, laughs best

El ruido y la furia *(novela de William Faulkner) The Sound and the Fury*

él se lo guisa y él se lo come he made his bed and now he can sleep in it

ser **el siguiente de la fila** ▪ ir detrás de alguien ▪ estar detrás de alguien to be the next (one) in line ▪ to go after someone (in the line) ▪ to be after someone (in line)

el solo hecho de just ▪ merely ▪ simply ▪ simply by ➤ El solo hecho de conocerte me hace feliz. Just knowing you makes me happy.

el solo hecho de que the mere fact that

El sombrero de tres picos *(obra de Manuel de Falla) The Three-Cornered Hat*

elaborar cerveza to make beer

elección justa ▪ elección reñida close election

elección reñida ▪ elección justa close election

elecciones al congreso congressional races

elecciones al senado Senate races

ser **elegido(-a) por aclamación** to be chosen by acclamation

ser **elegido(-a) sobre otra persona** ▪ eligirle frente a otra persona to be chosen over someone else ➤ Fue elegido sobre otro solicitante. ▪ Le eligieron frente a otro solicitante. He was chosen over another applicant. ▪ They chose him over another applicant.

elegir a alguien a dedo ▪ escoger a alguien a dedo to choose from among an inner circle ▪ to choose someone one already knows

elegir a alguien presidente to elect someone president

elegir con voto secreto to elect by secret ballot

elegir el adecuado to choose the right one ▪ to choose the one that suits one

elegir ropa a dedo ▪ escoger ropa a dedo to choose clothes without trying them on

elegirle frente a otra persona ▪ ser elegido sobre otra persona to choose someone over someone else ➤ Le elegieron frente a otro solicitante. ▪ Fue elegido sobre otro solicitante. They chose him over another applicant. ▪ He was chosen over another applicant.

elevada abstención (de votantes) ▪ baja concurrencia de votantes ▪ escasa participación de electores low voter turnout ▪ light voter turnout ▪ high voter abstention

elevado al cuadrado *(matemáticas)* squared

elevalunas eléctricas power windows

elevar a una potencia *(matemáticas)* to raise to a power ➤ Elevar a la enésima potencia To raise to the *(nth)* power

elevarse por los aires ▪ elevarse en los aires to rise up into the air

elevada concurrencia de votantes ▪ gran número de votantes ▪ alto porcentaje de electores high voter turnout ▪ large voter turnout ▪ heavy voter turnout

ella era la que... ▪ ella era quien... she was the one who... ▪ *(literario, culto)* it was she who... ➤ Ella era la que tocaba el piano. ▪ Ella era quien tocaba el piano. She was the one who was playing the piano. ▪ It was she who was playing the piano.

ella era la técnico que estuvo ayer aquí she was the technician who was here yesterday

ella era quien... ▪ ella era la que... she was the one who... ▪ *(literario, culto)* it was she who... ➤ Ella era quien tocaba el piano. ▪ Ella era la que tocaba el piano. She was the one who was playing the piano. ▪ It was she who was playing the piano.

ella es la que... ▪ ella es quien... she is the one who... ▪ *(literario, culto)* it is she who... ➤ Ella es quien está tocando el piano. ▪ Ella es la que está tocando el piano. She is the one who is playing the piano. ▪ It is she who is playing the piano. ➤ Ella es quien toca el piano. ▪ Ella es la que toca el piano. She is the one who plays the piano. ▪ She's the one who's playing the piano. ▪ It is she who plays the piano.

ella es quien... ▪ ella es la que... she is the one who... ▪ she's the one who... ▪ *(literario, culto)* it is she who... ➤ Ella es quien está tocando el piano. ▪ Ella es la que está tocando el piano. She is the one who is playing the piano. ▪ It is she who is playing the piano. ➤ Ella es quien toca el piano. ▪ Ella es la que toca el piano. She is the one who plays the piano. ▪ It is she who plays the piano.

ella fue la que... ▪ ella fue quien... she was the one who... ▪ *(literario, culto)* it was she who... ➤ Ella fue la que escribió el artículo. ▪ Ella fue quien escribió el artículo. She was the one who wrote the article. ▪ It was she who wrote the article.

ella fue quien... ▪ ella fue la que... she was the one who... ▪ *(literario, culto)* it was she who... ➤ Ella fue quien escribió el artículo. ▪ Ella fue la que escribió el artículo. She was the one who wrote the article. ▪ It was she who wrote the article.

ello se debe a que this is because

eludir la cuestión ▪ lanzar una evasiva to evade the question ▪ to beg the question ➤ Cuando un traductor dice: "Nosotros no decimos eso," está eludiendo la cuestión. ¿Cómo lo explicas entonces? For a translator to say, "We don't say that," begs the question. Then how do you explain it?

eludir la responsabilidad ▪ esquivar la responsabilidad to evade responsibility

eludir un obstáculo to clear a hurdle ➤ El presupuesto eludió su primer obstáculo al ser aprobado por la comisión presupuestaria. The budget cleared its first hurdle when it was passed by the appropriations committee.

embadurnar el maquillaje to smear (the) makeup

embadurnar el pincel de labios ▪ embadurnar el lápiz de labios to smear (the) lipstick

embajador(-a) de ▪ embajador(-a) en ambassador to ➤ Embajador estadounidense de Argentina ▪ Embajador estadounidense en Argentina U.S. ambassador to Argentina

embalar algo con algo ▪ embalar algo en algo to pack something with something ▪ to pack something in something ➤ I'm going to pack the computer and printer with bubble pack. Voy a embalar la computadora con papel de burbujas. ▪ Voy a embalar la computadora en papel de burbujas.

embarazada de *x* meses *x* months pregnant

embarazo indeseado ▪ embarazo no deseado unwanted pregnancy

embarazo no deseado ▪ embarazo indeseado unwanted pregnancy

embarazo tardío pregnancy shortly before menopause

el **embate de las olas** pounding of the waves ▪ breaking of the waves ▪ crashing of the waves

embaucar a alguien to string someone along

ser **embestido por** to be struck by ➤ *(noticia de un accidente)* Tres hombres murieron ayer después de que el turismo en el que viajaban fuera embestido por un camión hormigonera. Three men died yesterday after the sedan in which they were riding was struck by a cement mixer.

embestir a algo to smash into something ▪ to crash into something ▪ to strike something ➤ El coche embistió a la muralla. *(enfoque en el coche)* The car smashed into a wall. ▪ *(enfoque en la muralla)* The car crashed into a wall.

embestir de repente *(toro)* ▪ partir de repente to charge suddenly

el **embrague está sujeto** the clutch is engaged

embromar a alguien 1. burlarse de alguien to make fun of someone ▪ to tease someone 2. timarle a alguien ▪ vender un buzón a alguien to rip someone off ▪ to con someone

emisora de radio radio station

emitir bonos to issue bonds

emitir una advertencia to issue a warning

emitir una noticia en primicia to break the story ▪ to get the scoop ▪ to scoop (the other media)

emitir una tarjeta de crédito to issue a credit card

emitirse por circuito cerrado to be broadcast over closed circuit ▪ to be broadcast via closed circuit

emocionar a alguien vivamente to touch someone deeply ▪ to move someone deeply

emocionarse por to be touched by ▪ to be moved by

estar **empachado(-a) con algo** to be sick and tired of something ➤ Estoy empachada con ser la esposa de un teleadicto al fútbol. I'm sick and tired of being a football widow!

estar **empachado(-a) de algo** ▪ estar harto(-a) de algo to be sick of something ▪ to be fed up with something

estar **empachado(-a) de alguien** ▪ estar harto(-a) de alguien to be sick of someone ▪ to be fed up with someone

empacharse con algo to be worn out with something ▪ to be sick (and tired) of something

empacharse de algo to stuff oneself (to the gills) ➤ En la fiesta de cumpleaños los niños se empacharon de pasteles y helado. At the birthday party, the children stuffed themselves (to the gills) with cake and ice cream.

empalidecerse en comparación a ▪ palidecer ante to pale in comparison to

empantanarse en el tráfico to get bogged down in (the) traffic

empañar las distinciones ▪ hacer las distinciones menos claras ▪ opacar las distinciones to blur the distinctions ➤ Algunas investigaciones médicas empañan las distinciones entre lo ético y lo no ético. Some medical research blurs the distinction between what is ethical and what is unethical.

empañarse con lágrimas to become blurred with tears ▪ to become misty with tears

empaparse de to soak up

empaparse en la lluvia ▪ calarse en la lluvia ▪ ponerse como una sopa ▪ ponerse hecho(-a) una sopa to get drenched in the rain ▪ to get drenched by the rain ▪ to get soaked in the rain ▪ to get soaked by the rain

empaquetar algo en algo to pack something in something ➤ Voy a empaquetar la computadora y la impresora en cajas para el envío. I'm going to pack the computer and printer in boxes for shipping.

emparentar con una familia to marry into a family

empatar a cero *(deportes)* to tie nothing to nothing ➤ Madrid y Manchester empatan a cero. Madrid and Manchester tie nothing to nothing.

el **empate a tres** ▪ triple empate three-way tie

estar **empecinado(-a) en** to be determined to ▪ to have gotten it into one's head to

estar **empeñado(-a) en conseguir algo** to be determined to get something ▪ to be bent on getting something

estar **empeñado(-a) en hacer algo** to be determined to do something ▪ to be bent on doing something

empeñarse en hacer algo 1. insistir en hacer algo to insist on doing something 2. estar aferrado en hacer algo to be bent on doing something ➤ Se empeñaba en acompañarnos. He insisted on going with us. ➤ La Sra. Barrows se empeñaba en reorganizar el deparmento del Sr. Martin. Mrs. Barrows was bent on reorganizing Mr. Martin's department.

empeñarse en saberlo to be determined to find out ▪ to be totally focused on finding out something

empeorar las cosas to make matters worse ▪ to make things worse

emperrarse en hacer algo to persist doggedly in doing something ▪ to be dogged in one's pursuit of something

empezando en la página *x* ▪ empezando por la página *x* ▪ comenzando en la página *x* ▪ ▪ comenzando por la página *x* beginning on page *x* ▪ starting on page *x*

empezando por la página *x* ▪ empezando en la página *x* ▪ comenzando por la página *x* ▪ comenzando en la página *x* beginning on page *x* ▪ starting on page *x*

empezar a afectarle a uno to start to affect one ▪ to begin to affect one ▪ to (start to) catch up with one ➤ Empieza a afectarme la falta de sueño. My lack of sleep is starting to catch up with me. ▪ My lack of sleep is catching up with me. ▪ My lack of sleep is starting to affect me.

empezar a disparar ▪ abrir fuego ▪ romper el fuego to start shooting ▪ to start firing ▪ to open fire

empezar a gustarle a uno algo to start to like something ➤ Le empieza a gustar al perro. *(a él)* The dog is starting to like him. ▪ *(a ella)* The dog is starting to like her. ➤ Le empiezo a gustar al perro. The dog is starting to like me. ➤ Me empieza a gustar el perro. I'm starting to like the dog. ➤ Cuando rondaba los cuarenta me empezó a gustar Mozart. When I was about forty, I started to like Mozart. ▪ When I was about forty, I started liking Mozart.

empezar a hacer algo ▪ comenzar a hacer algo to start to do something ▪ to begin to do something

empezar a moverse to start to pick up ➤ Los negocios empiezan a moverse. Business is starting to pick up.

empezar a pasarse de moda ▪ quedarse viejo to become obsolete

empezar a sospechar de alguien ▪ comenzar a desconfiar de alguien to begin to suspect someone ▪ to become suspicious of someone ▪ to begin to suspect someone

empezar a trabajar ▪ entrar a trabajar to start work ➤ Entro a trabajar a las nueve de la mañana. I start work at nine a.m. ▪ I start work at nine each morning.

empezar a valorar to begin to appreciate

empezar apresuradamente ▪ empezar precipitadamente to begin abruptly ▪ to begin suddenly

empezar con el pie derecho to start off on the right foot ▪ to get off to a good start

empezar con el pie izquierdo to start off on the wrong foot ▪ to get off to a bad start

empezar de cero ▪ empezar desde cero to start at square one ▪ to start from scratch ▪ to start from nothing ▪ to make a clean sweep of ➤ Los nuevos propietarios del edificio empezaron de cero, modernizando la instalación eléctrica, la plomería y remodelando las cocinas y cuartos de baño. The new owners made a clean sweep of the building, upgrading the wiring, plumbing, and remodeling the kitchens and bathrooms.

empezar desde abajo to start at the bottom ▪ to begin at the bottom ➤ Empezó desde abajo y se labró un camino a la cumbre. He started at the bottom and worked his way (up) to the top. ▪ He began at the bottom and worked his way (up) to the top.

empezar desde cero ▪ empezar de cero to start at square one ▪ to start from scratch ▪ to start from nothing

empezar el reloj *(deportes)* ▪ empezar el tiempo to start the clock

empezar en una profesión to get into a profession ▪ to get started in a profession ➤ ¿Cómo empezaste en el periodismo? How did you get into journalism? ▪ How did you get started in journalism?

empezar la carrera (profesional) to begin one's career

empezar la casa por el tejado to put the cart before the horse

empezar la negociación ▪ arrancar la negociación ▪ abrir la negociación to begin negotiations

empezar por abajo to start at the bottom

empezar por el principio to begin at the beginning ▪ to start at the beginning

empezar por to start with ▪ to begin with ➤ El número telefónico empieza por nueve. The phone number starts with nine. ▪ The phone number begin with nine.

empezar precipitadamente ▪ empezar apresuradamente to begin abruptly ▪ to begin suddenly

empezar pronto to get an early start ➤ Aquí nos gusta empezar pronto la Navidad. We like to get an early start on Christmas around here.

empezaron los dobles the bells began to ring ▪ the bells began to peal ▪ the pealing of the bells began ➤ Al mediodía empezaron los dobles. The bells began pealing at noon.

empiezo a ser persona I'm starting to feel like a (new) person ➤ Ahora que me he tomado mi primer café, empiezo a ser persona. Now that I've had my morning coffee, I'm starting to feel like a (new) person.

empinarse una carretera (for) a highway to get steep ▪ (for) a highway to rise ➤ Cuando la carretera se empina... When the highway gets steep... ▪ When the highway begins to rise... ▪ Where the highway is steep...

emplazar a alguien a que haga algo ▪ emplazar a alguien a hacer algo to call on someone to do something ➤ *(titular)* Zapatero emplaza a Batasuna a que condene el terrorismo si quiere participar en la política. Zapatero calls on Batasuna to condemn terrorism if it wants to participate in politics.

empleado de cubierta deck hand

emplearse al fondo to have one's hands full

empleo suplimentario sideline

empollar para un examen to cram for a test

estar **empotrado en la pared** ▪ estar incorporado en la pared to be built into the wall

empotrar el estoque *(tauromaquia)* to embed the sword (in the bull's back)

empotrarse contra ▪ empotrarse en to crash into

emprender el camino de su casa to set out for home ▪ to set out for one's house ▪ to set off on one's way home ▪ to head home

emprender el camino de vuelta a su casa to set out on one's way back home ▪ to set off on one's way back home ▪ to head back home

emprender el regreso to head back

emprender (el) vuelo to take flight

emprender (la) marcha a to set out for

emprender la retirada ▪ batirse la retirada to beat a retreat ▪ to begin to retreat ▪ to start to retreat

emprender marcha a ▪ emprender la marcha a to set out for

emprender un ataque to launch an attack

emprender un hobby to take up a hobby

emprender un proyecto to undertake a project ▪ to take on a project ➤ Cuando emprendí el proyecto no me di cuenta en lo que me estaba metiendo. When I undertook the project, I didn't realize what I was getting (myself) into. ▪ When I took on the project, I didn't realize what I was getting (myself) into.

emprender vuelo ▪ emprender el vuelo to take flight

emprenderla con alguien to take it out on someone ➤ Well, don't take it out on *me*. Bueno, no me la emprendas.

empresa envasadora canning factory

empresa puntera leading company

empresa tapadera front business

empujar con todas sus fuerzas ▪ empujar tan fuerte como uno puede to push with all one's might ▪ to push as hard as one can

en abril pasado ▪ el pasado mes de abril last April

en absoluto 1. para nada not at all ▪ absolutely not 2. ni mucho menos far from it ➤ Por el fallo de la computadora, no pudo trabajar en absoluto. Because of the computer malfunction, he couldn't work at all.

en actividad ▪ andando de acá para allá on the go

en actividades relacionadas con in and around ➤ Estoy pasando dos horas en actividades relacionadas con la cocina para la comida y otra vez para la cena. I'm spending two hours in and around the kitchen at dinner and again at supper.

en achaque de on the pretext of

en adelante henceforth ▪ in the future

en ademán de ▪ como para as if to

en ademán de buena voluntad ▪ en señal de buena voluntad ▪ como gesto de buena voluntad as a gesture of goodwill ▪ as a goodwill gesture

en ademán de protesta as an act of protest ▪ as a form of protest ▪ as a way of protesting ▪ as a protest

estar **en alfa** ▪ estar desenchufado to be off in the ozone ▪ to be in la la land

en algún lugar somewhere
en algún momento at some point ➤ Nos veremos en algún momento. We'll see each other at some point.
en algún momento del día sometime today ▪ sometime during the day
en algún momento en su vida 1. *(singular)* at some point in one's life 2. *(plural)* at some point in their lives
en algún momento u otro at some time or other
estar **en algún sitio** to be somewhere ➤ Tengo que estar en algún sitio para las nueve. I have to be somewhere by nine o'clock.
estar **en alguna cosa** to be at something ▪ to be doing something
en algunos aspectos in some respects
en alta mar at sea ▪ on the high seas ▪ *(literario)* before the mast ➤ La flota entera está en alta mar. The entire fleet is at sea. ➤ *(novela de Richard Henry Dana)* ***Dos años en altamar*** *Two Years Before the Mast*
en alto: colocar los pies ~ to put one's feet up
estar **en alza** to be on the rise ▪ to be rising ▪ to be up and coming
estar **en antecedentes** to know what is really happening ▪ to know what is really going on ▪ to know all about it ➤ Pero yo, que estaba en antecedentes... But I, who knew what was really happening... ▪ But I, who knew what was really going on... ▪ But I, who knew all about it...
estar **en antena** *(radio, televisión)* ▪ estar en el aire to be on the air
en antena: entrar ~ to go on the air
en aplauso de *(Esp.)* in favor of
en aproximadamente un mes ▪ en más o menos un mes ▪ en torno a un mes in about a month ▪ in approximately one month
en aquel entonces at that time ▪ in those days
en aquel mismo momento ▪ en aquel preciso instante at that very moment ▪ at that very instant ▪ at that exact moment ▪ at that exact instant ▪ exactly at that time ▪ at that (exact) moment
en aquel momento at that moment ▪ at that point
en aquel preciso instante *(narración histórica o novelada)* at that instant ▪ exactly at that time ▪ at that (exact) moment ➤ En aquel preciso instante Scrooge oyó un ruido en su habitación. At that instant, Scrooge heard a noise in his room.
en aquella época at that time ▪ in those days ➤ En aquella época las universidades estadounidenses todavía utilizaban impresos perforados para la matrícula. At that time, American universities were still using perforated cards for registration. ▪ In those days, American universities were still using perforated cards for registration
en aquellos días ▪ por aquellos días in those days
en aras de for the sake of ▪ in the interest of ▪ in the service of ▪ in honor of ➤ *(noticia)* El presidente defendió la guerra en aras de la convivencia. The president defended the war for the sake of peaceful coexistence. ▪ The president defended the war for peaceful coexistence's sake.
estar **en arresto domiciliario** ▪ estar en situación de arresto domiciliario to be under house arrest
estar **en ascuas** ▪ estar con el alma en vilo to be on pins and needles ▪ to be in suspense ▪ to be on tenterhooks
en atención a in view of ▪ taking into account ▪ considering
en atención a alguien in honor of someone ▪ for someone ➤ Mañana hay una recepción en atención al rector de la universidad. Tomorrow there's a reception in honor of the rector of the university. ▪ Tomorrow there's a reception for the rector of the university.
estar **en autos de que...** to be aware that... ▪ to be on to the fact that...
estar **en ayunas** ▪ quedarse en ayunas 1. ir sin comer to be fasting 2. no haber desayundo not to have had breakfast
estar **en Babia** ▪ quedarse en Babia to have one's head in the clouds ▪ to be overly idealistic
en balde ▪ en vano ▪ para nada ▪ a lo tonto in vain
en bandolera: llevar algo ~ to wear something across one's chest
en barco by boat
en base a based on
en base a ▪ con base a ▪ basándose en based on ▪ on the basis of ➤ Que los medios de comunicación apunten a un candidato como vencedor en un estado en base a las encuestas a pie de urna es absurdo. ▪ Que los medios de comunicación apunten a un candidato como vencedor con base a las encuestas a pie de urna es absurdo. ▪ Que los medios de comunicación apunten a un candidato como vencedor en un estado basándose en las encuestas a pie de urna es absurdo. For the media to call a state for a candidate based on exit polls is asinine. ▪ For the media to call a state for a candidate on the basis of exit polls is asinine.
en batería: aparcamiento ~ diagonal parking
estar **en blanca** ▪ quedarse sin blanca to be broke
estar **en blanco** ▪ quedarse en blanco to draw a blank ▪ not to be able to think of anything ▪ (for) nothing to come to mind ➤ Estoy en blanco. I'm drawing a blank. ▪ I can't think of anything. ▪ Nothing comes to mind.
en blanco: cheque ~ blank check
en blanco: espacio ~ blank space
en blanco: página ~ blank page
en blanco: quedarse ~ to draw a blank ➤ Me quedé en blanco. I drew a blank. ▪ My mind went blank.
en blanco: (el) papel ~ blank sheet of paper
en bloque en masse
en boca cerrada no entran moscas silence is golden ▪ mum's the word
estar **en boca de la gente** to be the talk of the town
estar **en boga** to be in vogue
estar **en bolas** ▪ estar desnudo to be naked
en bozo just beginning
en bragas: coger a alguien ~ *(Esp.)* ▪ pillar a alguien en bragas to catch someone off guard ▪ to catch someone unprepared ▪ to catch someone off guard ➤ Me cogiste en bragas. ▪ Me pillaste en bragas. You caught me off guard. ▪ You caught me unprepared.
estar **en bragas** to be (completely) destitute ▪ to have absolutely nothing ▪ to be broke
en breve ▪ dentro de poco ▪ en poco tiempo ▪ al poco tiempo 1. *(dentro de días o horas)* soon ▪ before long 2. *(dentro de horas o minutos)* shortly ▪ in a little while ➤ El preso podría ser excarcelado en breve. The prisoner could be released soon. ▪ The prisoner could be released before long. ▪ The prisoner could be released shortly. ▪ The prisoner could be released in a little while.
en breves momentos shortly
en buen lío me he metido it's a fine mess I've gotten myself in
en buen uso being put to good use ➤ Está en buen uso. It is being put to good use. ▪ It's being put to good use.
estar **en buena forma física** to be in good physical condition ▪ to be in good shape physically
en buena lid: ganar ~ *(arcaico)* ▪ ganar con todas las de la ley to win fair and square
en buena medida to a considerable extent
estar **en buenas manos** to be in good hands
estar **en buenos términos** to be on good terms
en busca de in search of
en cabeza: ir ~ ▪ ir por delante ▪ ir en primer lugar to be in the lead ▪ to be first ▪ to be ahead ➤ El caballo con el dorsal número siete va en cabeza. Horse number seven is in the lead.
en cadena: (la) reacción ~ chain reaction
en calidad de amigo: decir a alguien to tell someone as a friend
en calidad de vida in quality of life ➤ *(titular)* Navarra está a la cabeza en calidad de vida. Navarra leads in quality of life.
estar **en cama** to be in bed
en cámara lenta ▪ a cámara lenta in slow motion
en cambio on the other hand
estar **en camino** ▪ estar de camino to be on the way
estar **en camino de desaparecer** to be on the way out ▪ to be on its way out
en canal: abrir ~ dividir en dos to split in two ▪ to split wide open ▪ to split into halves ➤ El carnicero abrió el pollo en canal. The butcher split the chicken in two.

en candelero: poner algo ~ to put something in the spotlight ▪ to make something popular

en candelero: tema ~ hot topic

estar **en capilla 1.** *(en el corredor de la muerte)* to be awaiting execution **2.** *(en gran peligro)* to be in grave danger **3.** *(en vilo)* to be in unbearable suspense ▪ to be on pins and needles ▪ to be on tenterhooks

en carne viva: tener algo ~ to skin something raw ➤ Tenía la rodilla en carne viva cuando me caí de la bicicleta. I skinned my knee raw when I fell off my bicycle.

estar **en carne y hueso** ▪ estar en los huesos ▪ estar en el hueso pelado to be nothing but skin and bone

estar **en carnes** *(poco común)* ▪ estar en cueros ▪ estar en pelotas ▪ estar en bolas to be naked ▪ to be in the buff

estar **en casa** to be at home

en casa de alguien at someone's house ▪ at the home of someone ➤ Cenamos en casa de Carlos. We had supper at Carlos' house. ➤ La recepción se dará en casa de los abuelos de la novia. The reception will be held at the home of the bride's grandparents. ▪ The reception will be held at the bride's grandparents' house.

en casa y en el extranjero at home and abroad

en caso de que in case ▪ in the event that

estar **en choque con alguien** ▪ estar en conflicto con alguien to be in conflict with someone ➤ El gobierno ha estado a veces en choque con la iglesia. The government has sometimes been in conflict with the church.

estar **en ciernes 1.** estar naciente to be budding ▪ to be in the making ▪ to be in its infancy **2.** estar en flor to be in bloom

en ciernes ▪ naciente to be a budding musician ➤ Es una música en ciernes. ▪ Es una música naciente She's a budding musician. ➤ Es músico en ciernes. ▪ Es músico naciente. He's a budding musician.

en cierta forma in a way

en cierta manera in a way ▪ to a certain extent ▪ up to a point

en cierta medida to a certain extent

en cierta ocasión ▪ una vez at one time ▪ once ➤ En cierta ocasión pensamos en colaborar. At one time, we considered collaborating. ▪ We once considered collaborating.

en cierto modo in a way

en cierto momento at one point

en cierto sentido in a sense

en ciertos aspectos in certain respects

en clave de humor on a humorous note

en colaboración con in collaboration with ▪ together with ▪ jointly with

ser **en color** to be in color ➤ ¿La película es en color o en blanco y negro? Is the movie in color or (in) black and white?

estar **en coma** to be in a coma

estar **en coma profunda** to be in a deep coma

en comandita: sociedad ~ limited partnership

en comandita a hacer algo: ir ~ to go as a group to do something ▪ to all go together to do something

en comitiva as a group

en compañía de together with

en comparación a compared to ▪ in comparison to ▪ in comparison with

estar **en compás de espera** ▪ mantenerse en compás de espera to be waiting to hear ▪ to be awaiting word ▪ to be waiting for word ➤ Estoy en compás de espera. I'm waiting to hear.

en compensa de in return for ▪ as a reward for

en conciencia in good conscience

en conclusión in conclusion

estar **en condiciones** to be in good physical condition ▪ to be in good (physical) shape ▪ to be in top form

estar **en condiciones de** to be fit to

en confidencia in confidence

estar **en conflicto con alguien** ▪ estar en choque con alguien to be in conflict with someone ➤ El gobierno ha estado a veces en conflicto con la iglesia. The government has sometimes been in conflict with the church.

en conjunto ▪ en definitiva all in all ▪ all things considered ▪ everything considered

en consecuencia in consequence ▪ as a result of ▪ so

en consecuencia de as a result of

en consideración a algo ▪ en reconocimiento de algo in honor of something ▪ in recognition of something ➤ Mañana hay una recepción en consideración al décimo aniversario del rector al frente de la universidad. Tomorrow there's a reception honoring the rector's tenth anniversary at the helm of the university.

en consignación: mercancías ~ merchandise on consignment ▪ goods on consignment

en consignación: vender algo ~ to sell something on consignment

estar **en construcción** to be under construction

estar **en contacto por radio con alguien** to be in radio contact with someone ➤ ¿Está usted en contacto por radio con sus camiones de reparto? Are you in radio contact with your delivery trucks?

en contadas ocasiones on a few occasions ▪ on a limited number of occasions ▪ a few times ▪ a limited number of times

estar **en contra de algo** ▪ oponerse a algo to be against something ➤ Estoy en contra (de ello). ▪ Me opongo (a ello). I'm against it. ▪ I'm opposed to it.

en contra de algo: no estar ~ not to be against something ▪ *(especialmente al expresar preferencias)* not to be averse to something ➤ No estoy en contra de ir al cine, pero preferiría salir a cenar y charlar un poco. ▪ No es que me moleste ir al cine, pero preferiría salir a cenar y charlar un poco. I'm not averse to going to the movies, but I'd rather go out for dinner and just talk.

en contra de la creencia popular contrary to popular belief

en contra de las reglas: ir ~ to be against the rules ➤ Va en contra de las reglas. It's against the rules.

en contra de lo habitual in contrast to the usual ▪ in contrast to what normally happens

en contra de lo que piensan muchos contrary to popular belief ▪ contrary to what many people think

en contraposición a ▪ a diferencia de ▪ frente a unlike ▪ as opposed to ▪ in contrast to ➤ Los teóricos del dinamismo, en contraposición a los conductistas, creen que es posible analizar los procesos mentales. ▪ Los teóricos del dinamismo, a diferencia de los conductistas, creen que es posible analizar los procesos mentales. The dynamic theorists, as opposed to the behaviorists, believe it is possible to analyze mental processes.

en contraste con in contrast to

en cotas altas in the higher elevations

en cotas bajas in the lower elevations

en cuál línea del metro which metro line ➤ ¿En cuál línea del metro queda la biblioteca pública? -La uno, la parada es Iglesia. Which metro line is the library on? -One; the stop is Iglesia.

en cualquier caso in any case

en cualquier momento any minute ▪ any minute now ▪ at any time

en cuanto 1. tan pronto como ▪ luego que as soon as ▪ the minute ▪ the sooner **2.** siempre que ▪ con tal de que so long as ▪ as long as ➤ En cuanto me levanté, prendí la computadora. As soon as I got up, I turned on the computer. ▪ The minute I got up, I turned on the computer. ➤ En cuanto se compren los billetes aéreos, más baratos son. The sooner you buy the air tickets, the cheaper they are. ➤ El rodaje de la película no empezará en cuanto no se seleccionen todas las localizaciones. The shooting of the movie will not begin until all the locations are selected. ▪ The shooting of the movie will not begin so long as (some) locations remain unselected. ➤ La bolsa seguirá a su ritmo de crecimiento en cuanto la situación económica se mantenga estable. The stock market will continue its rate of growth so long as the economic situation remains stable.

en cuanto a ▪ tocante a ▪ a propósito de regarding ▪ when it comes to ▪ insofar as ▪ pertaining to

en cuanto a lo de regarding (the question of) ▪ with respect to ▪ on the question of ▪ on the matter of

en cuanto a mí 1. as for me ▪ for my part **2.** en lo que a mí concierne as far as I'm concerned

en cuanto a si as to whether

en cuanto cabe alcanzar to the extent that it is possible ▪ to the extent possible ▪ as far as is achievable ▪ as far as is attainable

en cuanto es posible (que) insofar as it's possible (to)

en cuanto estudiante en esta universidad... as a student at this university...

en cuanto hierva ▪ cuando vaya a hervir when it comes to a boil ▪ when it starts to boil ▪ when it begins to boil

en cuanto le sea posible ▪ a la mayor brevedad posible ▪ con la mayor brevedad posible at one's earliest convenience

en cuanto puedas ▪ cuando puedas as soon as you can ▪ when you have a second

en cuanto pueda as soon as I can

en cuanto surja algo te aviso as soon as something comes up I'll let you know

en cuanto te vea ▪ en el momento que te vea the moment I see you ▪ the minute I see you

en cuanto te vi ▪ en el momento que te vi the moment I saw you ▪ the minute I saw you ➤ The minute I saw you, I was in love. En cuanto te vi, estuve enamorado. ▪ En el momento que te vi, estuve enamorado. ▪ En cuanto te vi, me enamoré. ▪ En el momento que te vi, me enamoré

en cuarto curso ▪ en cuarto grado in the fourth grade

en cuarto grado ▪ en cuarto curso in the fourth grade

en cuatro patas ▪ a gatas ▪ a rastras on all fours

estar **en cuerda floja** to be on a tightrope

estar **en cueros (vivos)** ▪ estar en pelotas ▪ estar en bolas to be in the buff ▪ to be (stark) naked ▪ to be in the nude

en cuesta steep

en cuestión in question ▪ at issue ➤ El punto en cuestión es... ▪ El asunto en cuestión es... The point in question is... ▪ The point at issue is...

en cuestión de horas in a matter of hours

en cuestión de minutos in (a matter of) minutes ➤ The aspirin will take away your headache within minutes. La aspirina te quitará el dolor de cabeza en cuestión de minutos. The aspirin will take away your headache within minutes. ▪ The aspirin will take away your headache in minutes.

en cursiva in italics ▪ italicized

en custodia policial ▪ en dependencias policiales in (police) custody

en cuyo caso in which case

estar **en decadencia** to be going out of style ▪ to go out of style ▪ to be on the way out

estar **en declive** 1. to be in decline ▪ to be on the decline 2. estar en cuesta to be sloping

en definitiva 1. definitivamente at last ▪ finally ▪ for good 2. a fin de cuentas in short ▪ finally

estar **en demanda** ▪ estar muy solicitado ▪ estar muy demandado to be in demand ➤ Está en demanda. ▪ Está muy solicitado. It's in demand.

en demasía in excess ▪ too much ▪ to excess

en dependencias policiales ▪ en custodia policial in (police) custody

estar **en desacuerdo con alguien sobre algo** ▪ estar en desacuerdo con alguien por algo ▪ no estar de acuerdo con alguien sobre algo ▪ no estar de acuerdo con alguien por to disagree with someone on something ▪ to disagree with someone about something ▪ not to be in agreement on something ▪ not to be in agreement about something

estar **en desbandada** to be in disarray

estar **en desventaja** to be at a disadvantage

en determinado momento at a certain time

en detrimento de to the detriment of

en diagonal: cortar algo ~ to cross something at an angle ▪ to cross something diagonally ▪ to intersect something at an angle ▪ to intersect something diagonally ➤ El Paseo de la Reforma corta la Avenida Hidalgo en diagonal. The Paseo de la Reforma crosses Hidalgo Avenue at an angle. ▪ The Paseo de la Reforma crosses Hidalgo Avenue diagonally. ▪ The Paseo de la Reforma intersects Hidalgo Avenue at an angle. ▪ The Paseo de la Reforma intersects Hidalgo Avenue diagonally.

estar **en diagonal con la esquina** ▪ quedar en diagonal con la esquina to sit at an angle to the corner ▪ to be situated at an angle to the corner ➤ El edificio está (ubicado) en diagonal con la esquina. The building sits at an angle to the corner. ▪ The building is situated at an angle to the corner.

en días alternos ▪ un día sí y otro no on alternating days ▪ every other day ➤ Durante la crisis petrolera, pudimos comprar gasolina en días alternos. ▪ Durante la crisis petrolera, pudimos comprar gasolina sólo un día sí y otro no. During the oil crisis, we could buy gasoline only on alternating days. ▪ During the oil crisis, we could only buy gasoline every other day.

en diferido *(programa de televisión)* pre-recorded

en dinero B: pagar a alguien ~ ▪ pagar a alguien en negro ▪ pagar a alguien bajo la mesa to pay someone under the table

estar **en dique seco** 1. *(literal)* to be in dry dock 2. *(figurativo)* to be sidelined ▪ to be out of action

en dirección contraria al cuerpo away from one ➤ Al usar el cuchillo, corte en dirección contraria al cuerpo. When you use a knife, cut away from you.

en directo live ➤ Un concierto en directo A live concert

estar **en discusión** to be under discussion

estar **en disposición para hacer algo** to be prepared to do something ▪ to be willing to do something

en distinta medida to varying degrees ➤ Casi cien coches resultaron dañados en distinta medida. Almost a hundred cars were damaged to varying degrees.

en distintos lugares in various places

en distintos lugares del mundo in other parts of the world

en diversas ocasiones on a number of occasions ▪ on various occasions

en donde where ▪ in which ▪ on which

¿en dónde trabajas? where do you work?

en dos zancadas ▪ en menos que canta un gallo in a jiffy ▪ in no time

estar **en edad escolar** to be of school age

en efectivo: pagar ~ ▪ pagar en metálico to pay (in) cash

¿en efectivo o con la tarjeta? cash or charge?

en efecto ▪ de hecho as a matter of fact ▪ in fact

en el acto 1. on the spot ▪ then and there ▪ at once 2. mientros uno espera while you wait ➤ Firmé el documento en el acto, y se lo volví a entregar al mensajero para que se lo devolviera al remitente. I signed the document on the spot and gave it back to the courier (for him) to return to the sender. ▪ I signed the document then and there and gave it back to the courier (for him) to return to the sender. ➤ Llaves hechas en el acto ▪ Copiamos sus llaves en el acto Keys made while you wait

estar **en el aire** to be in the air

estar **en el ajo** *(Esp.)* ▪ andar en el ajo to be in the know

estar **en el albor de la vida** ▪ estar en la flor de la vida to be in one's prime

en el ámbito nacional nationwide

en el amor y la guerra, todo (se) vale all is fair in love and war

en el año de Nuestro Señor... in the year of our Lord

en el ardor de la batalla in the heat of battle

en el aspecto (de) que in that ➤ El diseño es defectuoso en el aspecto (de) que no permite cambiar las piezas deterioradas. The design is defective in that it does not permit the replacement of worn parts.

estar **en el buen camino** to be on the right track

en el buen sentido de la palabra in the true sense of the word

en el calor del momento in the heat of the moment

estar **en el candelero** 1. to be in the limelight 2. estar de moda to be "in"

en el cargo ▪ de mandato in office ➤ Cuando el presidente Obama está a punto de cumplir cinco meses en el cargo... As President Obama nears completion of his fifth month in office...

estar **en el centro** to be downtown

estar **en el derecho de juzgar** ▪ tener el derechar de juzgar to have the right to judge

en el desayuno at breakfast ▪ as part of the breakfast

en el día during the day ▪ during the daytime hours ➤ Vamos a Zaragoza en el día. We're going to Zaragoza during the day.

en el dorso del sobre ▪ por detrás del sobre ▪ en el reverso del sobre ▪ en la parte de detrás del sobre ▪ en la parte trasera del sobre on the back of the envelope ▪ on the reverse side of the envelope

en el entorno familiar within the family ▪ in the home environment

en el examen: salir ~ ▪ poner en el examen to be on the exam(ination) ➤ Va a salir en el examen. ▪ Lo van a poner en el examen. It's going to be on the exam.

estar **en el extremo del corredor** ▪ estar en el fondo del corredor ▪ estar al final del corredor to be at the end of the hall ▪ to be at the end of the hallway ▪ to be at the end of the corridor

estar **en el extremo del pasillo** ▪ estar en el fondo del pasillo ▪ estar al final del pasillo to be at the end of the aisle

en el fondo ▪ en lo hondo fundamentally ▪ basically ▪ at bottom ▪ deep down ▪ at heart ➤ *(editorial)* Las dictaduras son, en el fondo, sistemas muy débiles. Dictatorships are fundamentally very weak systems.

estar **en el fondo del corredor** ▪ estar en el extremo del corredor ▪ estar al final del corredor to be at the end of the hall ▪ to be at the end of the hallway ▪ to be at the end of the corridor

estar **en el fondo del pasillo** ▪ estar en el extremo de pasillo ▪ estar al final del pasillo to be at the end of the aisle

en el fuero interno ▪ en el fondo del corazón ▪ para sus adentros deep down (in one's heart) ▪ deep (down) inside

estar **en el guindo** ▪ estar en la luna to be (off) in the ozone ▪ to be spaced out

en el haber in one's (bank) account ➤ Usted tiene cinco mil pesos en el haber. You have five thousand pesos in your account.

en el habla popular in popular speech

estar **en el hueso pelado** ▪ estar en los huesos to be nothing but skin and bone

en el lapso de varios minutos within a few minutes ▪ within the next few minutes

estar **en el limbo** to be in limbo

estar **en el límite** to be at the limit ➤ Con diez artículos estás en el límite de la caja rápida. With ten items, you're at the limit for the express checkout. ➤ Estoy en el límite o por debajo. I'm at the limit or under it.

estar **en el lugar adecuado en el momento oportuno** to be in the right place at the right time

en el medio de la noche ▪ en la mitad de la noche in the middle of the night

en el medio del invierno ▪ en la mitad del invierno in the middle of winter ▪ in midwinter ▪ half way through the winter

en el mejor de los casos at best

estar **en el mercado** to be priced within the market

estar **en el mismo centro de la ciudad** to be right downtown ▪ to right in the middle of town ▪ to be in the very center of the city

en el mismo momento en que... the minute ▪ at the very moment that... ➤ *(Mark Twain)* Un banquero es un tipo que te presta su paraguas cuando el sol brilla, y lo quiere de vuelta en el mismo minuto en que empieza a llover. A banker is a fellow who lends you his umbrella when the sun is shining and wants it back again the minute it starts to rain.

en el momento ▪ en el instante at the time ➤ Lo haremos en el momento. ▪ Lo haremos en el instante. We'll do it at the time.

en el momento adecuado at the right moment ▪ at the right time

en el momento de at the time of ➤ En el momento de la muerte de Kennedy, la población estadounidense era de ciento ochenta millones de personas. At the time of Kennedy's death, the population of the United States was one hundred (and) eighty million.

en el momento en que te vea ▪ en cuanto te vea the moment I see you ▪ the minute I see you

en el momento en que te vi ▪ en cuanto te vi the moment I saw you ▪ the minute I saw you ➤ El momento en que te vi, estuve enamorado. The moment I saw you, I was in love.

en el mundo in the world ▪ around the world ➤ *(titular)* Más de cinco millones de niños mueren al año en el mundo a causa del hambre. More than five million children around the world die of hunger every year.

en el núcleo de la filosofía de Kant ▪ en el núcleo de la filosofía kantiana at the core of Kant's philosophy ▪ at the heart of Kant's philosophy

estar **en el octavo sueño** ▪ estar dormido profundamente to be in the land of Nod ▪ to be in a sound sleep

en el otro extremo de la calle at the far end of the street

en el país de los ciegos, el tuerto es (el) rey in the land of the blind, the one-eyed man is king

en el paso in the way ➤ Las cajas están en el paso. The boxes are in the way.

estar **en el pellejo del otro** ▪ estar en el pellejo de alguien to be in someone else's shoes

en el peor de los casos ▪ poniéndonos en lo peor if worst comes to worst ▪ at worst ▪ at the very worst

en el peor de los momentos ▪ en el peor momento at the worst possible time

en el peor momento ▪ en el peor de los momentos at the worst possible time

en el plazo de un año within a year

estar **en el poder** to be in power

en el primer año de vida ▪ durante el primer año de vida in the first year of life ▪ during the first year of life

en el próximo futuro ▪ en el futuro cercano in the near future

estar **en el punto de ebullición** to be at the boiling point

estar **en el punto de mira de alguien** to be in someone's sights

en el punto de mira: tener a alguien ~ to target someone ▪ to have someone in one's sights ➤ El líder del partido socialista exigió que el gobierno del País Vasco garantice la seguridad de todos los socialistas que ocupan cargos públicos ya que ETA ha dejado patente que les tiene en el punto de mira. The Socialist party leader demanded that the government of País Vasco guarantee the security of all socialists in government positions since ETA has made clear that it has targeted them. ▪ The Socialist party leader demanded that the government of País Vasco guarantee the security of all socialists in government positions since ETA has made clear that it has them in its sights.

estar **en el punto de mira del público** to be in the public eye

en el que in which

en el que no voy a entrar which I won't go into

estar **en el quinto carajo** *(subido de tono)* ▪ estar en el quinto pino to be in the middle of nowhere

estar **en el quinto coño** *(subido de tono)* ▪ estar en el quinto pino to be in the middle of nowhere

estar **en el quinto infierno** ▪ estar en el quinto pino to be in the middle of nowhere

estar **en el quinto pino** *(Esp.)* **1.** estar en medio de la nada to be in the middle of nowhere **2.** estar donde el aire da vuelta to be way out of the way

en el quinto pino: ir a parar ~ to end up in the middle of nowhere

en el reverso del sobre ▪ por detrás del sobre ▪ en la parte de detrás del sobre ▪ en el dorso del sobre ▪ en la parte trasera del sobre on the back of the envelope ▪ on the reverse side of the envelope

en el sentido de que... in the sense that...

en el sentido más amplio de la palabra in every sense of the word ▪ in the broadest sense of the word

estar **en el séptimo cielo** to be in seventh heaven

estar **en el sitio adecuado en el momento justo** ▪ estar en el sitio oportuno en el momento oportuno to be in the right place at the right time

en el supuesto de que... in the event that... ▪ if... ➤ En el supuesto de que llueva, dormiremos en el refugio. In the event that it rains, we'll sleep in the shelter ▪ In the event that it should rain, we'll sleep in the shelter. ▪ If it rains, we'll sleep in the shelter. ▪ If it should rain, we'll sleep in the shelter.

estar **en el terreno de alguien** to be on someone's turf

estar **en el trabajo** ▪ estar trabajando to be at work ➤ Ella está en el trabajo. ▪ Ella está trabajando. She's at work. ➤ Estoy en mi trabajo. ▪ Estoy trabajando. I'm at work.

en el último minuto ▪ en el último momento ▪ *(coloquial)* ▪ con el tiempo pegado al culo at the very last minute ▪ right at the last minute

en el último término as a last resort

estar **en el umbral de** to be on the threshold of ➤ Estamos en el umbral de un nuevo cambio. We're on the threshold of a new change.

en el vacío in a vacuum ➤ En el vacío la pluma cae igual de rápido que la piedra. ■ La pluma cae al vacío igual de rápido que la pieda. In a vacuum, the feather falls just as fast as the rock.

estar **en entredicho** to be in question ■ to be in doubt

en épocas muy remotas a long, long time ago

en esa época in those days

en esa situación in that situation

en esas circunstancias in those circumstances ■ in that situation

estar **en escena** to be on stage

en ese aspecto in that respect

en ese entonces at that time

en ese instante ■ at that instant ■ just then ■ at that moment

en ese mismo momento at that very moment

en ese momento ■ en ese instante at that moment ■ just then ■ at that instant ➤ En ese momento, la hormigonera circulaba por el sentido contrario. ■ En ese instante, la hormigonera circulaba por el sentido contrario. At that moment, the concrete mixer was going the other way.

en ese preciso instante at that instant ■ at that (exact) moment

en ese tiempo at that time

en esencia in essence ■ essentially ■ basically ➤ Es en esencia un tipo solitario. He's basically a loner.

en eso coincidimos on that we agree ■ we agree on that

en eso coincido I agree on that

en eso coincido contigo I agree with you on that ■ I'm of the same opinion as you

en especie: pagar ~ 1. to pay in kind 2. *(finanza)* pagar una deuda con ovo o plata to pay in specie

estar **en espera** to be on hold

en esta época del año ■ por estas fechas at this time of year

en esta ocasión 1. on this occasion 2. esta vez this time ➤ Vamos a hacer otro viaje, en esta ocasión a Argentina. We're going to take another trip, this time to Argentina.

en estado crítico: encontrarse ~ to be in critical condition

estar **en estado de buena esperanza** ■ estar en estado interesante ■ estar embarazada to be pregnant ■ to be expecting (a baby)

estar **en estado de muerte cerebral** to be brain-dead

estar **en estado de sitio** ■ estar sitiado to be under siege ➤ Me siento como si estuviera en estado de sitio la mitad del tiempo. I feel like I'm under siege half the time.

en este aspecto in this respect

en este momento at this time ■ right now ■ at the moment ➤ Es el único ejemplo que se me ocurre en este momento. That's the only example I can think of at the moment. ➤ En este momento no tenemos gato. At this time we don't have a cat (but we used to).

en este número at this number ➤ Lo puedes localizar en este número. ■ *(Esp. leísmo)* Le puedes localizar en este número. You can reach him at this number. ■ He can be reached at this number. ➤ La puedes localizar en este número. You can reach her at this number. ■ She can be reached at this number.

en este tiempo 1. a esta hora at this time ■ at this hour 2. en esta época at this time ■ at the present time ■ in our time ➤ Normalmente tengo una clase en este tiempo. ■ Normalmente tengo una clase a esta hora. Normally I have a class at this time. ■ Normally I have a class at this hour. ➤ En este tiempo, el país pasa por una mala racha. At this time, the county is having a difficult time.

en estos precisos momentos ■ justo ahora at this very moment ■ right this minute ➤ Estoy trabajando en ello en estos precisos momentos. ■ Estoy trabajando en ello justo ahora. I'm working on it at this very moment. ■ I'm working on it right this minute.

en estos momentos 1. en la actualidad ■ actualmente at the present time ■ at present ■ at this point 2. ahora mismo right now ➤ *(noticia)* En estos momentos, los ciudadanos estadounidenses que viajen a Cuba sin permiso se exponen a tener que pagar entre $7.500 y $8.000 de multa. At the present time, U.S. citizens who travel to Cuba without permission risk having to pay a fine (of) between $7500 and $8000. ■ At present, U.S. citizens who travel to Cuba without permission risk having to pay a fine (of) between $7500 and $8000.

en estos precisos momentos at this very moment

en estrecha asociación in close proximity

en evidencia: dejar ~ to place in evidence

en evitación de accidentes to prevent accidents ➤ *(cartel en una piscina)* En evitación de accidentes los bañistas deben saber nadar. To prevent accidents bathers must know how to swim.

en existencia ■ en depósito in stock

en fase de despegue in take-off mode ■ the moment when the drugs are starting to take effect

estar **en fase terminal** to be in the acute phase (of a terminal illness)

estar **en favor de** ■ estar a favor de to be in favor of

en fe de in witness of

en fecha próxima in the next few days

estar **en filas** to be in ranks ■ to be in the military ■ to be in military service

en fin 1. por fin ■ al fin after all ■ in short ■ finally ■ at the end 2. bueno well ■ well, then

en flagrante delito ■ in fraganti ■ con las manos en la masa in flagrante delicto ■ in the act of commiting a crime ■ in the act ■ red-handed ➤ Agarrar a alguien en flagrante delito ■ Pillar a alguien en flagrante delito. ■ *(Esp.)* Coger a alguien en flagrante delito To catch someone in flagrante delicto ■ To catch someone in the act ■ To catch someone red-handed

estar **en flor** to be in bloom ■ to be in blossom ■ to be in flower ➤ Los manzanos están en flor The apple trees are in bloom.

estar **en forma** to be in shape ■ to be in good physical condition ■ to be physically fit ■ *(coloquial)* to be fit as a fiddle

en forma legal legally

estar **en franca retirada** to be in full retreat

en frío: agarrar a alguien ~ *(L.am.)* to take someone aback ■ to take someone by surprise

en frío: coger a alguien ~ *(Esp.)* to take someone aback ■ to take someone by surprise

en función de depending on ➤ En función de lo que me digan... Depending on what they tell me... ➤ En función de la hora Depending on the time

en función de: actuar ~ ■ actuar según to act according to ■ to act in accordance with

estar **en función de algo** ■ estar relacionado con algo to be related to something ■ to be akin to something ➤ El uno está en función del otro. ■ El uno está relacionado con el otro. One is akin to the other. ■ One is related to the other.

en función de: votar ~ to vote according to ■ to vote based on ■ to vote in view of ➤ *(noticia)* Uno tiene que votar en función no sólo de la resolución del texto en sí mismo sino también en función de lo que está sucediendo en él . One has to vote not only based on the resolution of the text itself, but also in view of what's happening.

en función de algo in accordance with ■ according to ■

estar **en funcionamiento** to be in use

estar **en garantía** to be under warranty ➤ ¿Está en garantía? Is it under warranty? ■ Is it covered by a warranty?

en gran medida in large measure ■ largely

en gran parte in large part

en grupo as a group ■ in a group ■ all together ➤ La clase fue al director en grupo. The class went to the principal as a group.

estar **en guardia** to be on guard ■ to be guarded ■ to be uptight

estar **en guardia (en) contra algo** to be on (one's) guard against something

estar **en guerra con** ■ estar en guerra contra to be at war with

en intervalos regulares ■ a intervalos regulares at regular intervals

estar **en jarras** to stand with one's hands on one's hips ■ to have one's hands on one's hips

estar **en juego** 1. en peligro to be at stake ■ to be at risk 2. *(el balón)* to be in play 3. *(escaño, puesto)* to be up for grabs ➤ El prestigio de la compañía está en juego. The company's reputation is at stake. ➤ El escaño del senador está en juego. The senator's seat is up for grabs.

en la actualidad ■ actualmente at the present time ■ currently ■ at present

estar **en la berza** *(Esp., coloquial)* to be out of it ■ to be in a daze ➤ Está en la berza hoy. He's out of it today.

estar **en la biblioteca** to be at the library

en la boca de la calle ■ en la bocacalle ■ a la boca de la calle ■ al principio de la calle ■ al comienzo de la calle at the beginning of the street

en la bocacalle en la boca de la calle ■ a la boca de la calle ■ al principio de la calle ■ al comienzo de la calle at the beginning of the street

estar **en la brecha** to be in the thick of it ■ to be in the thick of things ■ the be in the middle of it

en la brecha: seguir ~ to stand one's ground ■ to hold one's own

estar **en la brecha de** to be in the thick of ■ to be in the middle of

estar **en la cárcel** ■ estar entre rejas ■ estar tras las rejas ■ *(pintoresco)* ■ estar a la sombra to be in jail ■ to be behind bars ■ *(pintoresco)* to be in the tank ■ to be in the klinker

estar **en la cincuentena** to be in one's fifties

estar **en la Cochinchina** ■ estar en el quinto pinto ■ estar en las quimbambas to be in the middle of nowhere

estar **en la cresta de la ola** 1. to be on the crest of the wave 2. estar en su nivel más alto to be at its peak

estar **en la cuarentena** ■ en sus cuarenta to be in one's forties

estar **en la cuerda floja** to walk a tightrope

estar **en la cumbre de su carrera** ■ estar en la cúspide de su carrera ■ estar en lo más alto de su carrera to be at the height of one's career ■ to be at the peak of one's career

estar **en la cúspide de su carrera** ■ estar en la cumbre de su carrera ■ estar en lo más alto de su carrera to be at the height of one's career ■ to be at the peak of one's career

en la decada de 1890 in the 1890s ■ in the decade of the 1890s

estar **en la duda** to be in doubt ➤ Si estás en la duda... If you're in doubt...

estar **en la edad del pavo** *(adolescencia)* to be at the awkward age

en la emoción del momento ■ en la excitación del momento in the excitement of the moment

en la excitación del momento ■ en la emoción del momento in the excitement of the moment

estar **en la escuela** to be at school

en la espesura del bosque in the depths of the forest ■ in the forest depths

estar **en la esquina de** ■ estar haciendo esquina con ■ hacer esquina con ■ estar en la esquina entre to be at the corner of

estar **en la esquina entre** ■ estar haciendo esquina con ■ estar en la esquina de ■ hacer esquina con to be at the corner of ■ to be on the corner of ➤ La cafetería está en la esquina entre Infanta Mercedes y Gen. Margallo. The restaurant is at the corner of Infanta Mercedes and Gen. Margallo. ■ The restaurant is on the corner of Infanta Mercedes and Gen. Margallo.

estar **en la facultad** to be at school ■ to be at the university ➤ Susana está en la facultad. Susana's at school. ■ Susana's at the university.

estar **en la flor de la vida** ■ estar en el albor de la vida to be in one's prime

estar **en la gloria** 1. to be in heaven 2. estar contentísimo to be overjoyed

estar **en la higuera** ■ estar en alfa ■ to be off in the ozone ■ to be spaced out ■ to have one's head in the clouds

en la hora de la cena at suppertime

estar **en la inopia** 1. no saber to have no clue ■ to have no idea 2. estar distraído ■ estar despistado to be daydreaming ■ to be off in the ozone ■ to be out of it ■ to be in la la land

en la línea enemiga ■ tras las líneas enemigas inside enemy lines ■ behind enemy lines ■ within enemy lines

estar **en la lista** 1. to be on the list 2. *(de estudiantes en una clase)* to be on the roll

estar **en la lista negra de alguien** to be on someone's blacklist ■ to be blacklisted by someone

en la lontananza ■ en el horizante in the far distance ■ a long way off ■ a long way away *(coloquial)* way away ■ way far away

estar **en la luna** 1. estar distraído(-a) ■ estar disorientado(-a) to be lost in one's own thoughts ■ to be distracted ■ to be on the moon ■ to be somewhere else (mentally) 2. no saber lo que está pasando not to know what's going on

en la mano: tener algo ~ to have something in one's hand

en la mañana de on the morning of ➤ Los hechos ocurrieron en la mañana del doce de octubre del año pasado. The incidents occurred on the morning of October twelfth last year.

en la mayoría de los casos in most cases

en la medida de lo posible as far as possible ■ so far as possible ■ to the extent possible ■ so far as is possible ■ to the greatest extent possible ■ to the maximum extent possible

en la medida en que... to the extent that...

en la medida en que sea posible so far as is possible ■ to the extent possible

estar **en la mera esquina** to be right on the corner ➤ Está en la mera esquina. It's right on the corner.

en la mesa de San Francisco, donde comen cuatro comen cinco there's always room for one more

estar **en la misma esquina** ■ estar en la mera esquina to be right on the corner ➤ Está en la misma esquina. ■ Está en la mera esquina. It's right on the corner.

estar **en la misma situación** to be in the same situation ■ to be in the same boat

en la mitad de tiempo 1. in half the time 2. el doble de rápido twice as fast ➤ La nueva computadora nos permite realizar el mismo trabajo de antes en la mitad de tiempo. ■ La nueva computadora nos permite realizar el mismo trabajo de antes el doble de rápido. The new computer enables us to do the same work in half the time. ■ The new computer enables us to do the same work twice as fast.

en la mitad del libro in the middle of the book

en la noche de sábado al domingo Saturday night and early Sunday ■ overnight Saturday

estar **en la onda** to be with it

estar **en la onda de algo** to be (really) into something ➤ Estaba en la onda de música tecno. *(él)* He was really into techno music. ■ *(ella)* She was really into techno music.

en la otra punta de la mesa at the other end of the table

en la otra punta de la ciudad across town ■ on the other side of town ■ on the other end of town ■ across the city ■ on the other side of the city ■ on the other end of the city

en la parte de arriba de la página ■ en la parte superior de la página ■ en lo alto de la página at the top of the page

en la parte de atrás (de) in the back (of) ■ at the back (of) ➤ Estábamos sentados en la parte de atrás del auditorio. We were sitting in the back of the auditorium. ■ We were sitting at the back of the auditorium. ➤ Estuvimos sentados en la parte de atrás del auditorio. We sat in the back of the auditorium. ■ We sat at the back of the auditorium.

en la parte superior at the top

en la parte superior de la página ■ en la parte de arriba de la página at the top of the page

en la parte superior de la pantalla ■ en la parte de arriba de la pantalla at the top of the screen ➤ No hay iconos para alinear el texto a izquierda y derecha en la parte superior de la pantalla. There are no icons for flush left and (flush) right at the top of the screen.

en la parte trasera del sobre ■ en la parte de detrás del sobre ■ en el dorso del sobre ■ por detrás del sobre ■ en el reverso del sobre on the back of the envelope ■ on the reverse side of the envelope

estar **en la pega** *(Uruguay)* ■ estar en el ajo to be in the know

en la práctica in practice ■ in actual practice

estar **en la puerta** ■ estar a la puerta to be at the door ➤ Hay alguien en la puerta. ■ Hay alguien a la puerta. Someone's at the door. ■ There's someone at the door. ➤ Ve a ver quién está en la puerta. ■ Mira a ver quién está en la puerta. Ve a ver quién está a la puerta. ■ Mira a ver quién está a la puerta. Go see who's at the door.

en la puerta de la calle: quedarse ~ to be left out on the street ➤ Se quedó en la puerta de la calle. He was left out on the street.

en la punta de la lengua: tenerlo ~ to be one the tip of one's tongue

en la que in which

en la que no voy a entrar which I won't go into

estar **en la quinta puñeta** ▪ estar en el quinto pino to be in the middle of nowhere

estar **en la retaguardia** *(en una carrera)* to be behind ▪ to be lagging behind ▪ to be in the back

estar **en la senectud de la vida** ▪ estar en la cochera ▪ estar en la chochez to be in one's dotage

estar **en la sombra** to be in the shade

estar **en la sombra de** to be in the shadow of

estar **en la suba** to be on the rise ▪ to be rising ▪ to be on the increase

estar **en la treintena** ▪ estar en los años treinta to be in one's thirties ▪ to be thirty something

estar **en la última semana** to be in the last week ▪ to be down to the last week ➤ Estoy en la última semana de trabajo en mi proyecto. I'm in the last week of work on my project. ▪ I'm down to the last week of work on my project.

estar **en la vanguardía** to be among those on the cutting edge

en la variedad está el gusto ▪ entre col y col, lechuga variety is the spice of life

estar **en la veintena** ▪ estar en los años veinte to be in one's twenties ▪ to be twenty something

en la vejez in old age ▪ in one's old age

en la vida real in real life

estar **en las Chimbambas** ▪ estar en el quinto pino to be in the middle of nowhere

estar **en las faldas de su madre** ▪ estar bajo de las faldas de su madre to be tied to one's mother's apron strings

en las horas intempestivas in the wee hours ▪ in the early morning hours ➤ En las horas intempestivas de la víspera de Navidad, se podían oír las patas de los renos en el tejado. In the wee hours of Christmas Eve, reindeer hooves could be heard on the roof.

estar **en las manos de Dios** to be in God's hands

estar **en las nubes** to be in the clouds

en las postrimerías de at the close of ▪ in the final days of ▪ at the end of

en las propias barbas de alguien: hacer algo ~ to do something right under someone's nose

en las próximas horas in the next few hours ▪ in the next several hours

en las que in which ▪ on which ▪ from which ▪ where ▪ when ➤ Las zonas en las que se puede apreciar el eclipse anular... The areas in which you can see the total eclipse... ▪ The areas where you can see the total eclipse... ▪ The areas from which you can see the total eclipse ▪ The areas in which the total eclipse can be seen...

en las postrimerías del siglo at the end of the century

en las primeras horas de la noche in the early evening ▪ early in the evening

estar **en las últimas** to be about to collapse (from exhaustion)

en lenguaje llano in plain language

en línea recta ▪ recto in a straight line ▪ as the crow flies ➤ Antigua está a como setenta kilómetros de la Ciudad de Guatemala en línea recta. ▪ Antigua está a como sententa kilómetros recto de la Ciudad de Guatemala. Antigua is forty-five miles from Guatemala City as the crow flies.

estar **en litigio** to be in litigation

estar **en llamas** to be in flames

en lo a mi respecta ▪ por lo que a mí respecta as far as I'm concerned

en lo alto 1. muy alto up high **2.** arriba overhead **3.** en la punta ▪ en la cima at the top ➤ En lo alto de la estantería Up high on the shelf ➤ En lo alto se veían las estrellas. The stars were visible overhead.

en lo alto de la escalera at the top of the stairs ▪ at the top of the steps

en lo alto de un despeñadero at the top of a cliff

estar **en lo alto del cielo** to be high in the sky

en lo concerniente a with regard to ▪ concerning

estar **en lo correcto** to be in the right ▪ (for) the argument to be in one's favor

estar **en lo más alto de su carrera** ▪ estar en la cumbre de su carrera ▪ estar en la cúspide de su carrera to be at the height of one's career ▪ to be at the peak of one's career

en lo más minimo in the least

en lo más reñido de la batalla in the heat of battle

en lo posible as far as possible ▪ to the extent possible

en lo que concierne a algo as far as something is concerned ➤ En lo que concierne al sistema solar... As far as the solar system is concerned...

en lo que llevamos de año ▪ en lo que va de año so far this year

en lo que parece in what appears to be ▪ in an apparent ➤ En lo que parece un intento de golpe de estado In what appears to be an attempted coup d'état ▪ In an apparent coup attempt

en lo que pueda to the extent that one can ▪ so far as (is) possible ▪ as far as (is) possible

en lo que se da por seguro es... in what is surely... ▪ in what surely is...

en la que se lee which reads ➤ El manifestante lleva una pancarta en la que se lee... The demonstrator is carrying a placard which reads...

en la que se leía which read ➤ El manifestante llevaba una pancarta en la que se leía... The demonstrator was carrying a placard which read...

en lo que se refiere a in reference to ▪ with reference to ➤ En lo que se refiere a tu otra pregunta In reference to your other question ▪ With reference to your other question

en lo que uno pueda to the extent that one can

en lo que va del año ▪ en lo que llevamos del año so far this year

en lo relacionado a pertaining to ▪ as regards ▪ when it comes to

en lo sucesivo 1. de ahora en adelante in the future ▪ from now on ▪ henceforth ▪ thenceforth **2.** de entonces en adelante thereafter ▪ from that time on

en lo tocante a with respect to

estar **en lo último de algo** to be nearly at the end of something ▪ to nearly have finished something

en lonchas in slices ▪ sliced

en lontananza ▪ a lo lejos in the distance

en los años cincuenta ▪ en los años mil novecientos cincuenta in the 50's ▪ in the 1950's

en los años cuarenta ▪ en los años mil novecientos cuarenta in the 40's ▪ in the 1940's

en los años de la Maricastaña back in the dark ages ▪ eons ago

en los años venideros in the years to come ▪ in the coming years

estar **en los brazos de Morfeo** *(coloquial)* to be asleep

en los buenos tiempos in the good old days

en los celajes: ▪ estar en alfa to be off in the ozone

estar **en los cincuenta** ▪ tener unos cincuenta años to be in one's fifties ▪ to be fifty something

estar **en los cuarenta** ▪ tener unos cuarenta años to be in one's forties ▪ to be forty-something

en los días posteriores in the days following ▪ in the days after

en los dominios del rey de España nunca se pone el sol on the dominions of the Spanish king, the sun never sets ▪ the sun never sets on the Spanish empire *(Nota: Durante el reino de Felipe II)*

estar **en los huesos** ▪ estar en el hueso pelado to be skinny as a rail ▪ to be a bean pole ▪ *(implica enfermedad)* to be nothing but skin and bone ▪ to be emaciated

en los primeros días que lo tuve when I first got this

en los que in which ▪ on which ▪ from which ▪ when ▪ where ➤ *(noticia)* En España, los viernes y los domingos son los días en los que se producen más ataques informáticos. In Spain, Fridays and Sundays are the days on which most computer attacks occur.

en los ratos de ocio ▪ en el tiempo libre ▪ a su aire ▪ a su ritmo at one's leisure ▪ in one's leisure time ▪ in one's free time

en los últimos años in the last few years ▪ in recent years

en los últimos días in the last few days

en los últimos minutos in the last few minutes

estar **en los umbrales de** to border on ▪ to verge on ➤ Eso está en los umbrales de lo ridículo. That borders on the ridiculous ▪ That verges on the ridiculous.

en los viejos tiempos in the old days

en lugar de ▪ en vez de instead of ▪ en lugar de

en mano: entregar algo ~ to hand deliver something

estar **en mano de alguien** to be in someone's possession

en manos de alguien: dejar algo ~ to leave something in someone's hands ▪ to leave something in the hands of someone

en marcha ▪ ¡nos vamos! off ▪ on one's way ➤ ¡En marcha! We're off!

en más de for more than

en más de un sentido in more ways than one

en más o menos un mes ▪ en aproximadamente un mes ▪ en torno a un mes in about a month ▪ in approximately one month

en materia de when it comes to ➤ En materia de los amoríos... When it comes to love affairs...

estar **en medio** to be in the way

estar **en medio de** to be in the middle of

en medio de todo in the middle of everything

en medio de una copiosa lluvia in the pouring rain

en medio del tormento in the midst of one's agony

estar **mejor donde uno está** to be better off as one is ▪ to be better off the way one is ➤ A veces me siento excluido de una conversación, pero cuando la escucho, me doy cuenta de que estoy mejor donde estaba. Sometimes I feel left out of a conversation, but when I listen to it, I realize I'm better off.

estar **en mejor situación** ▪ estar en mejores condiciones ▪ estar mejor to be better off ➤ *(Ronald Reagan)* ¿Están ustedes en mejor situación ahora de la que estaban hace cuatro años? ▪ ¿Están en mejores condiciones ahora de las que estaban hace cuatro años? Are you better off today than you were four years ago?

en mejor situación que in a better position than

en memoria ▪ en recuerdo ▪ in memoriam in memoriam

en memoria de in memory of

en menor medida to a lesser extent

en menos de within ▪ in less than ➤ En menos de veinte minutos Within twenty minutes ▪ In less than twenty minutes

en menos de una hora within an hour ▪ in less than an hour

en menos que canta un gallo ▪ en un abrir y cerrar de ojos in a flash

en metálico: pagar ~ ▪ pagar en efectivo to pay in cash ▪ to pay cash

en mi casa mando yo I'm the master of my own house

en mi descargo by way of explanation (for my failure to acknowledge)

en mi opinión ▪ a mi ver ▪ para mí in my opinion

en mis años mozos in my younger days ▪ in my youth

en mis días in my day

en mis experiencias personales ▪ en mis vivencias ▪ en mi experiencia ▪ en experiencia propia in my experience ▪ in my personal experience ▪ in my own experience

en mis tiempos in my time ▪ in my day

en mis tiempos de... in my time as a... ▪ in my days as a... ▪ in my years as...

en mis viviencias ▪ en mi experiencia ▪ en mis experiencias personales ▪ en experiencia propia in my experience ▪ in my personal experience ▪ in my own experience

en mitad de in the middle of

en mitad de la noche ▪ en el medio de la noche in the middle of the night

en mitad del invierno ▪ en el medio del invierno in the middle of winter ▪ in mid winter ▪ halfway through the winter

en momentos determinados at certain times

estar **en movimiento** to be in motion

en movimiento: poner ~ to set in motion

en muchas millas en torno ▪ en muchas millas a la redonda for (many) miles around ▪ for (many) miles in all directions

en muchos días in a long time ▪ in weeks

en muchos kilómetros en torno ▪ en muchos kilómetros a la redonda for (many) kilometers around ▪ for (many) kilometers in all directions

en nada in anything

en negrita *(informática)* in bold (type)

en negro: pagar a alguien ~ ▪ pagar a alguien en dinero B ▪ pagar a alguien bajo la mesa to pay someone under the table

en ningún caso ▪ bajo ninguna circunstancia ▪ bajo ningún concepto under no circumstances

en ningún momento at no time

en nombrando al ruin de Roma, por la puerta asoma ▪ en nombrando al ruin de Roma, luego asoma we were just talking about you ▪ speaking of the devil

en nombre de ▪ de parte de on behalf of ▪ in the name of

en nuestro próximo encuentro ▪ la próxima vez que nos veamos the next time I see you ➤ Te lo doy en nuestro próximo encuentro. I'll give it to you the next time I see you.

en nuestros días in our day ▪ in our time

en números redondos in round figures ▪ in round numbers ➤ En números redondos la distancia media entre la Tierra y el Sol es de 150 millones de kilómetros. In round figures, the mean distance from the Earth to the sun is 150 million kilometers.

en números rojos in the red ▪ with a deficit

estar **en obras** to be undergoing repairs ▪ to be being renovated ➤ Está en obras. It's undergoing repairs. ▪ It's being renovated.

estar **en oferta** to be on sale ▪ to be on special

estar **en otra parte** to be somewhere else

en otras ocasiónes on other occasions ▪ at other times

en otras tantas ocasiones on so many other occasions

en otro momento ▪ en otra ocasión ▪ otro día some other time ▪ another time ➤ Hablaremos en otro momento. ▪ Hablaremos en otra ocasión. ▪ Hablaremos otro día. We'll talk some other time.

en otro tiempo at one time ▪ in earlier times ▪ formerly ➤ En otro tiempo no habría habido... At one time there would have been no... ▪ In earlier times there would have been no... ▪ Formerly there would have been no...

en otros términos in other words

estar **en pañales** to be a babe in the woods ▪ to be wet behind the ears

en paños menores to be in one's underclothes ▪ to be in one's skivvies ▪ to be in one's undies

estar **en paro** **1.** estar de huelga to be on strike **2.** *(Esp.)* estar sin trabajo to be unemployed ▪ to be out of work

en parte in part ▪ partly

estar **en paz** ▪ estar a mano to be even (Steven) ▪ to be square ➤ Estamos en paz. ▪ Estamos a mano. ▪ No me debes nada. Estamos en paz. ▪ No me debes nada. Estamos a mano. We're even (Steven). ▪ We're square. ▪ You don't owe me anything. We're even (Steven). ▪ You don't owe me anything. We're square.

estar **en pecado** to be in sin

estar **en pedazos** to be in big pieces ▪ to be in chunks

estar **en pedo** **1.** estar borracho to be drunk as a skunk **2.** tener un pedo atravesado en la cabeza to be (flat) out of one's mind ▪ to be out of one's gourd

en pelo ▪ en cueros naked

en pelota ▪ en cueros naked

en pelota picada ▪ en cueros naked

en pelota viva ▪ en cueros naked

estar **en pelotas** ▪ estar en cueros ▪ estar en pelota viva to be in the buff ▪ to be (stark) naked

estar **en penosas condiciones** to be in delapidated condition ▪ falling apart

en pepitoria: pollo ~ chicken in egg and almond sauce

estar **en perfecto estado** to be in perfect condition ▪ to be in excellent condition

estar **en perfecto estado de salud** to be in perfect health

en perpetuo devenir forever in progress (but never in fruition) ▪ ever-evolving ▪ constantly evolving

en persecución de in pursuit of

en persona in person

en pésima forma física in poor (physical) shape ▪ in poor shape physically
en petit comité *(Esp.)* ▪ sólo entre nosotros just 'tween us girls
¡en pie! all rise!
estar **en pie** to be up ▪ to be standing ▪ to be in process
estar **en pie de guerra** to be on a war footing
en piñón fijo stubbornly insistent ▪ unyielding
en plan de broma as a joke
en plan de cachondeo ▪ en plan de broma as a joke
estar **en plantilla** ▪ ser miembro de la plantilla to be on the staff
en plazo de *x* años over an *x*-year period ➤ En plazo de cinco años Over a five-year period ▪ Over a period of five years ➤ En plazo de ocho años Over an eight-year period ▪ Over a period of eight years
en plena actuación *(musical)* right in the middle of the performance
en plena calle right in the middle of the street
en plena depresión económica in the depths of the depression
en plena Edad Media at the height of the Middle Ages
estar **en plena faena** to be hard at work
estar **en plena forma** to be in top form
en plena función *(teatral)* right in the middle of the performance
en plena hora punta at the height of the rush hour
en plena juventud in the flower of youth ▪ in the prime of life
en plena noche ▪ en el medio de la noche in the middle of the night
estar **en pleno apogeo** to be at its height ▪ to be at one's height
en pleno corazón de Madrid in the heart of Madrid
en pleno día ▪ a plena luz del sol ▪ a pleno sol ▪ a las claras in broad daylight
en pocas semanas in a few weeks ▪ over the next few weeks ▪ during the next few weeks
en poco tiempo ▪ a corto plazo on short notice
en pocos años within a few years ➤ En pocos años, las enfermedades retrovirales podrán ser tratadas. Within a few years, retroviral illnesses will become treatable.
en pocos instantes in no time at all
en poco menos de in just under ➤ Lincoln pronunció el discurso de Gettysburg en poco menos de tres minutos. Lincoln delivered the Gettysburg Address in just under three minutes.
en pocos minutos in a few minutes
estar **en poder de** to be under the control of ▪ to be held by ▪ to be in the hands of
en poquísimos casos in very few cases ▪ in very few instances
estar **en porretas** estar en cueros ▪ estar en cueros vivos ▪ estar en pelotas ▪ estar en bolas to be stark naked
en pos de *(Esp., literario, culto)* ▪ para lograr in pursuit of ▪ for the good of
estar **en posesión de** to be in possession of
en potencia in the making ➤ Aristóteles distingue entre *en potencia* y *en acto.* Aristotle distinguishes between *in the making* and *fully existing.*
en primer grado: quemaduras ~ first-degree burns
en primer lugar ▪ en cabeza ▪ a la cabeza ▪ por delante in the first place
estar **en primera fila** 1. *(en un auditorio)* to be on the first row 2. *(en una jerarquía)* to be of the first rank
en primera línea ▪ más acá in the foreground
en primera línea de playa on the beach ➤ El apartamento está en primera línea de playa. The apartment is on the beach. ▪ The apartment faces the beach directly (with nothing in between).
estar **en primera plana** to be on page one (of the newspaper)
en primicia ▪ en secreto off the record
en primicia: emitir una noticia ~ to break the story ▪ to get the scoop ▪ to scoop (the other media)
en primicia: escuchar algo ~ to be the first to hear something
en primicia: recibir algo ~ to be the first to receive something
en principio in principle
en privado ▪ a solas in private ➤ Quiero hablarte en privado. I want to talk to you in private. ▪ I want to speak to you in private. ➤ Quiero hablarle en privado. *(a él)* I want to talk to him in private. ▪ *(a ella)* I want to talk to her in private. ▪ *(a usted)* I want to talk to you in private.
estar **en problemas** to be in trouble
estar **en proceso de recuperación de** to be recovering from
en profundidad thoroughly ▪ in depth
en promedio on the average
en proporción a in proportion to ▪ in proportion as ▪ proportionally as ➤ La ley de Hubble establece que las galaxias se están separando unas de otras y que su velocidad aumenta en proporción a sus distancias. Hubble's law establishes that the galaxies are moving away from each other and that their velocity increases in proportion to the distance between them. ▪ Hubble's law establishes that the galaxies are moving away from each other and that their velocity increases in proportion as the distance between them increases. ▪ Hubble's law establishes that the galaxies are moving away from each other and that their velocity increases proportionally as the distance between them increases.
estar **en prueba** to be in the experimental stage ▪ to be at the experimental stage
en prueba de as proof of
en punto on the dot ➤ A las seis en punto. At six (o'clock) on the dot.
estar **en punto muerto** *(velocidad)* to be in neutral
en puntos dispersos ▪ en varias ubicaciones in various locations
¿en qué consiste el curso? what does the course consist of?
¿en qué me habré metido? what have I gotten myself into?
en qué momento at which time
¡en qué mundo vivimos! ▪ ¡qué mundo este! what a world (we live in)! ➤ ¡Hay que ver, en qué mundo vivimos! Look (at) what a world we live in!
¿en qué se diferencian *x* de *y*? what's the difference between *x* and *y*? ▪ how do you distinguish *x* from *y*?
¿en qué se diferencian *x* y *y*? what's the difference between *x* and *y*? ▪ how do *x* and *y* differ?
¿en qué se parece *x* a *y*? what do *x* and *y* have in common?
¿en qué se ocupa (él)? ▪ ¿a qué se dedica él? what does he do?
¿en qué se ocupa usted? ▪ ¿a qué se dedica usted? what do you do?
en quinto curso ▪ en quinto grado in the fifth grade
estar **en racha** ▪ tener una racha de (buena) suerte to be having a streak of (good) luck ▪ to have a streak of (good) luck
en realidad ▪ realmente really ▪ in reality ▪ in truth ▪ actually ➤ En realidad lo prefiero. ▪ Realmente lo prefiero. I actually prefer it.
en realidad es muy fácil it is really easy ▪ it's really easy
en realidad, no actually, no ▪ not really ▪ not actually
en reata ▪ de reata (in) single file
estar **en receso** to be in recess ▪ to be recessed ➤ El tribunal está en receso. The court is in recess. ▪ The court is recessed.
en recuerdo de in memory of
en redondo flatly
estar **en regla** to be in order
en relación a si ▪ acerca de si about whether ▪ over whether
en relación con ▪ con relación a in relation to ➤ La voz de la cantante necesíta ser más fuerte en relación con el acompañamiento musical. The voice of the singer needs to be louder in relation to the musical accompaniment.
en remojo: poner ~ to soak
estar **en reparación** ▪ estar reparándolo ▪ estar en revisión to be undergoing repairs ▪ to be being repaired ➤ Está en reparación. ▪ Lo están reparando. ▪ Está en revisión. It's being repaired. ▪ It's undergoing repairs.
en repetidas ocasiones on numerous occasions ▪ repeatedly
estar **en reposo** *(física)* to be at rest
en respuesta a in reply to ▪ in response to
en resumen ▪ en corto ▪ en resumidas cuentas ▪ al breve in short ▪ to sum up

en resumidas cuentas *(literario, periodismo)* ■ en corto ■ al breve ■ en resumen to sum up ■ in short

en resumidas cuentas se trata de... ■ en resumidas cuentas es... ■ últimamente es... ■ lo que cuenta es... ■ la última palabra es... ■ lo que vale es... the bottom line is... ➤ The bottom line is money. En resumidas cuentas se trata de dinero. ■ En resumidas cuentas es cuestión de dinero. ■ Lo que cuenta es dinero. ■ Lo que vale es dinero. The bottom line is money.

en retrospectiva in retrospect ■ in hindsight

estar **en revisión** ■ estar en reparación to be undergoing repairs ■ to be being repaired

estar **en riesgo** to be at risk

en rigor 1. en sentido estricto strictly speaking 2. con toda honestidad ■ honestamente in all honesty ■ honestly 3. realmente ■ en realidad really ■ in fact ➤ En rigor, un tomate es una fruta, no un vegetal. Strictly speaking, a tomato is a fruit, not a vegetable. ➤ En rigor, haces demasiadas preguntas personales. In all honesty, you ask too many personal questions. ➤ En rigor, Raquel no debiera dejar que su gata se siente en el alféizar de un piso tan alto. Really, Raquel should not let her cat sit on the window sill so far above the ground.

estar **en ristre** to be at the ready

estar **en rodaje** to be being filmed

en seguida 1. inmediatamente at once ■ immediately ■ right off 2. al principio at first ➤ ¡Ven en seguida! Come at once! ➤ No contestó en seguida. He didn't answer at first.

en seguida echarse de ver que... ■ en seguida poder ver que... ■ inmediatamente poder ver que to (be able to) see right off that... ■ to see straightaway that... ➤ En seguida me echaba de ver que... ■ En seguida pude ver que... ■ Inmediatamente pude ver que... I could see at once that... ■ I could see right off that... ■ I could see straightaway that...

en segundo plano: quedar ~ to remain in the background ■ to stay in the background

en sendos 1. en mismo número de in as many ■ in the same number of 2. en separate in separate ■ on a different 3. uno para cada uno one for each ➤ El tercer ataque en sendos días The third attack in as many days ➤ Los dos montañeros rescatados fueron transportados al hospital en sendos helicópteros. The two rescued mountain climbers were transported to the hospital in separate helicopters. ➤ El coleccionista ha adquirido sendas obras de Picasso para sus tres mansiones en el sur de Francia. The art collector has acquired a work of Picasso for each of his three mansions in southern France.

en sentido humorístico in a humorous vein

en señal de as a sign of

en señal de buena voluntad ■ en ademán de buena voluntad ■ como gesto de buena voluntad as a gesture of goodwill ■ as a goodwill gesture

en sepia sepia

en sepia: retrato ~ sepia portrait

en serio seriously

¿en serio? oh, really? ■ do you?

en sexto curso in the sixth grade

en sí in itself ➤ Esta ensalada es una comida en sí. This salad is a meal in itself. ➤ La tecnología, en sí, no es buena ni mala: todo depende de cómo la apliquemos. Technology in itself is neither good nor bad. It all depends on how we use it.

en sí mismo in itself

estar **en sintonía** to be on the same wavelength

estar **en (situación de) arresto domiciliario** to be under house arrest

en son de broma as a joke

en son de excusa as an excuse

en son de guerra spoiling for a fight

en son de riña spoiling for an argument ■ spoiling for a fight

en su afán por in one's eagerness to

estar **en su ambiente** ■ pegar en su sitio ■ pegar con la gente to fit right in ➤ Estarías en tu ambiente. ■ Pegarías allí. ■ Pegarías con la gente. You'd fit right in.

estar **en su cabal juicio** to have all one's faculties ■ to be in one's right mind

en su contra 1. *(a él)* against him 2. *(a ella)* against her 3. *(a usted)* against you ➤ Al surgir las acusaciones en su contra... When the accusations against him came out...

en su defecto ■ faltando en eso failing that ■ short of that ■ failing this ■ short of this

estar **en su destino** to be in one's destiny ■ *(informal)* to be in the cards for one

en su día in its day ■ in one's day

en su fuero interno in one's heart ■ deep down

en su haber 1. *(positivo)* to one's credit 2. *(positivo o negativo)* behind one ■ under one's belt ➤ Isaac Asimov tine casí cuatro cientos libros en su haber. Isaac Asimov has almost four hundred books to his credit. ➤ Tiene cinco años de cárcel en su haber. He has five years in jail behind him.

estar **en su juicio** to be in one's right mind

en su lugar instead

en su máxima expresión at its best ■ at one's best

en su nombre on one's behalf

en su propia casa *(figurativo)* in one's own back yard

estar **en su (propia) salsa** ■ estar a sus anchas to be in one's element ■ to feel at home ■ to feel at ease

estar **en su propio terreno** to be on one's home turf

estar **en su punto** ■ ni falta más ni falta menos to be just right ■ *(de un filete)* to be cooked medium ➤ ¿Le falta sal? No, está en su punto. Does it need salt? No, it's just right.

estar **en su salsa** ■ estar en su propia salsa ■ estar a sus anchas to be in one's element ■ to feel at home ■ to feel at ease

en su totalidad in its entirety

en sueños in one's dreams ➤ De noche en sueños pronuncio tu nombre. At night, in my dreams, I call your name.

en suma in short

estar **en sus cabales** to be in one's right mind ■ to be in possession of one's faculties

estar **en sus trece** ■ mantenerse en sus trece ■ permanecer en sus trece ■ seguir en sus trece to stick to one's guns ■ to stand firm ■ to stand one's ground

estar **en sus últimas** to be on its last legs

estar **en tablas** to be broke ■ to be destitute

en tal fecha on such and such a date

en tandas de *x* ■ *(menos común)* por tandas de *x* in batches of *x* ■ in units of *x* ■ in quantities of *x* ➤ Las medidas de la receta son para hacer las galletas en tandas de cincuenta. The recipe calls for making the cookies in batches of fifty.

en tanto ■ mientras tanto in the meantime

en tanto que ■ con tal que ■ con tanto que so long as ■ provided that ■ while

en tela de juicio: poner algo ~ to call something into question

estar **en términos amistosos** to be on good terms ■ to be on friendly terms

en términos cotidianos 1. *(en español)* in plain Spanish 2. *(en inglés)* in plain English

en términos generales generally speaking

en terreno de alguien on someone's turf

en territorio estadounidense on American soil ➤ Tras una breve escala en Guam, los tripulantes aterrizaron en territorio estadounidense. After a brief stop in Guam, the crew (members) landed on American soil.

en tiempo de Mari-Castaña ■ en tiempos de Maricastaña back in the dark ages ■ eons ago ■ way before one's time

en tiempo récord in record time

en tiempos antiguos in ancient times

en tiempos de alguien in someone's time ■ during someone's time ➤ En tiempos de mis abuelos... In my grandparents' time...

en tierra firme: estarse ~ to be on solid ground

en toda la extensión de la palabra ■ en todo sentido de la palabra in every sense of the word

(en) toda la mañana ■ (durante) toda la mañana all morning long ■ the whole morning ■ the entire morning

en toda la vida ■ en toda su vida ■ desde siempre all one's life

en toda mi vida in my whole life ■ in all my life ■ *(pintoresco)* in all my born days

en todas partes everywhere

estar **en todo** to think of everything

en todo el contorno ▪ todo alrededor ▪ *(literario)* en derredor throughout the vicinity ▪ throughout the area ▪ all around (the) town ▪ locally

en todo el territorio nacional all over the country ▪ throughout the country

en todo momento at all times ➤ Llévalo contigo en todo momento. Keep it with you at all times.

en todo punto absolutely ▪ completely

en todo sentido de la palabra ▪ en toda la extensión de la palabra in every sense of the word

en todos los sentidos in every way

en tono de enojo in an angry tone (of voice)

en tono suplicante: decir ~ to implore

en torno around ▪ about

en torno a around ▪ approximately

en torno a él ▪ alrededor de él ▪ en torno suyo ▪ alrededor suyo around him

en torno a ella ▪ alrededor de ella ▪ en torno suyo ▪ alrededor suyo around her

en torno a un mes en más o menos un mes ▪ en aproximadamente un mes in about a month ▪ in approximately one month

en torno al fuego: sentarse ~ ▪ sentarse alrededor del fuego to sit around the fire

en torno suyo ▪ alrededor suyo **1.** en torno a él around him **2.** en torno a ella around her

en total ▪ todo dicho ▪ por junto ▪ por mayor in all ▪ all told ➤ ¿Hay tres en total, sí? There are three in all, right?

estar **en trámite** ▪ estar en proceso to be in the pipeline ▪ to be in the mill ▪ to be in process

estar **en trámite parlamentario** to be in the legislative process ▪ *(coloquial)* to be in the legislative mill

estar **en trance de muerte** ▪ estar a punto de morir to be at the point of death

en tren: ir ~ to go by train

en tren: viajar ~ to travel by train

en última instancia ▪ como último recurso as a last resort

en último término in the final analysis ▪ in the last analysis

en un abrir y cerrar de los ojos before you can say Jack Robinson ▪ in a flash

en un ángulo cerrado at a close angle ➤ El cometa rozó la órbita de la Tierra en un ángulo cerrado. The comet grazed the Earth's orbit at a close angle.

en un año in a year

estar **en un apuro** to be in a bind

en un apuro: meterse ~ to get into a bind ▪ to get in a bind

estar **en un brete** to be in a jam ▪ to be in a tight spot ▪ to be in a predicament

en un café rifaron un gato, al que le toque el número cuatro: uno, dos, tres, cuatro *(Esp.)* eenie, meenie, miney, mo, catch a tiger by his toe, if he hollers let him go, eenie, meenie, miney, mo

en un compromiso in a difficult position ➤ Me has puesto en en compromiso. You've put me in a difficult position.

en un día cualquiera on a typical day ▪ on an ordinary day

en un esfuerzo por in an effort to ➤ Alexander Pope escribió *El rapto del rizo* en un esfuerzo por reconciliar a dos familias enemistadas. Alexander Pope wrote *The Rape of the Lock* in an effort to bring two alienated families back together.

estar **en un estado de sitio** to be under siege

en un futuro at some future time ▪ in some future time ➤ Uno espera que la pobreza y el terrorismo desaparezcan de la Tierra en un futuro. Hopefully poverty and terrorism will disappear from the Earth at some future time.

en un futuro inmediato in the immediate future ▪ for the immediate future

en un futuro no muy distante ▪ en un futuro no muy lejano in the not-too-distant future ▪ in the not-very-distant future

en un futuro no muy lejano ▪ en un futuro no muy distante in the not-too-distant future ▪ in the not-very-distant future

en un gesto de mano tendida in a gesture of goodwill ▪ in a goodwill gesture ➤ *(noticia)* En un gesto de mano tendida, el rey de Marruecos anunció ayer que... In a goodwill gesture, the king of Morocco announced yesterday that...

en un intento por in an attempt to ➤ En un intento desesperado por escapar... In a desperate attempt to escape...

en un intervalo de *x* minutos: ocurrir ~ to happen within *x* minutes (of each other) ➤ *(noticia)* Dos espectaculares accidentes de tráfico ocurridos en un intervalo de apenas veinte minutos acabaron con la vida de cuatro jóvenes con edades comprendidas entre diecinueve y veintidós años. Two serious automobile accidents within twenty minutes of each other took the lives of four youths ranging in age from nineteen to twenty two.

estar **en un lugar** to be at a place ▪ to be somewhere ➤ Tengo que estar en el médico a las siete y media. I have to be at the doctor's office at 7:30 p.m.

en un lugar bastante apartado off the beaten path

en un lugar de somewhere in ➤ En un lugar del Pacífico Somewhere in the Pacific

en un marco de within a framework of

en un momento ▪ tan rápido (so) quickly ➤ Me alegro que hayas pillado el error en un momento. ▪ Me alegro que hayas pillado el error tan rápido. I'm glad you caught the error so quickly.

en un momento dado at a given moment ▪ at any given moment

en un momento dado de sus vidas at some time in their lives

en un momento de during

en un momento determinado ▪ en un momento dado ▪ a un momento dado at a given moment ▪ at a given time ▪ at any given moment ▪ at any given time

en un periquete: terminar algo ~ to finish something in no time ▪ *(coloquial)* to finish something in no time flat

en un periquete: volver ~ to be right back ▪ to be back in a second ▪ to be back in a minute ▪ to be back in a jiffy

en un plazo de *x* días within (a period of) *x* days *(Nota: en acuerdos contractuales)*

en un principio at first ➤ En un principio creí correcto hacer la pregunta. At first, I thought it would be okay to ask.

estar **en un punto muerto** *(negociaciones)* to be deadlocked ▪ to be stalemated ▪ to be in a stalemate ▪ to be stalled

en un puño: tener a alguien metido ~ to have someone under one's control

en un quítame allá esas pajas *(Esp.)* ▪ en un santiamén ▪ en un abrir y cerrar de ojos ▪ en un parpadeo ▪ en un pestañazo in a jiffy

en un santiamén ▪ en un abrir y cerrar de ojos in the twinkling of an eye

en un sentido más amplio in a broader sense ▪ in a larger sense

en un solo día in a single day

en un tiempo notablemente corto in a remarkably short time

en un tiempo récord in record time

¡en un tris! ▪ ¡rapidito! ▪ ¡al toque! ▪ ¡al chanfle! ▪ ¡al silbido! quick!

estar **en un tris de** ▪ estar a un tris de ▪ estar a punto de to be within a hair's breadth of ▪ to come very close to

estar **en una categoria aparte** ▪ estar a otro nivel **1.** *(cosa)* to be in a class all by itself **2.** *(persona)* to be in a class all by oneself

en una ocasión one time ▪ on one occasion ▪ once ➤ Trabajo de taxista, y en una ocasión recogí a tres personas que... I drive a taxi, and one time I picked up three people who... ▪ I'm a taxi driver, and on one occasion I picked up three people who... ▪ I work as a taxi driver, and once I picked up three people who...

en una ocasión en que... one time when... ▪ once when... ▪ on one occasion when...

estar **en una posición para hacer algo** to be in a position (to be able) to do something ➤ No estoy en una posición para comentar. I'm not in a position to comment.

en una semana in a week

estar **en una situación apurada** to be difficult situation ▪ to be in a problematic situation

en una situación determinada in a given situation

en una situación en la que in a situation where ▪ in a situation in which

en una sola voz ■ al unísono all together ■ in unison ■ in one voice

estar **en uno de sus mejores momentos** to be at one's best

en unos minutos in a few minutes

en (unos) pocos años ■ dentro de unos años within a few years ➤ En (unos) pocos años, las enfermedades retrovirales podrán ser tratadas. ■ Dentro de unos años, las enfermedades retrovirales podrán ser tratadas. Within a few years, retroviral illnesses will become treatable.

en varias ocasiones on several occasions

en varias ubicaciones ■ en puntos dispersos in various locations

en la vecina Francia in neighboring France

estar **en vena (para hacer algo)** ■ estar de vena (para hacer algo) ■ estar de humor (para hacer algo) to be in the mood (to do something)

estar **en venta** to be for sale

en verano in the summertime

en verdad truly ■ in truth ■ indeed

en verdad os digo *(en la Biblia)* verily I say unto you

en vertical: bajar ~ ■ descender en vertical to go straight down ■ to descend vertically

en vertical: subir ~ ■ elevarse en vertical to go straight up ■ to rise straight up ■ to rise vertically

en vez de eso instead of that ■ instead

estar **en vía muerta** 1. *(negociaciones)* to be deadlocked 2. *(investigación)* to be stymied 3. *(ferrocarril)* to be on the side track

estar **en vías** ■ estar en trámite to be in process

estar **en vilo** ■ estar en ascuas ■ estar en suspenso to be in suspense ■ to be on pins and needles ■ to be holding one's breath

en vilo: mantener a alguien ~ to keep someone in suspense ■ to leave someone up in the air ➤ El libro tiene un final sorprendente que mantiene al lector en vilo hasta el último instante. The book has a surprise ending that keeps the reader in suspense until the very end.

en vísperas de on the eve of

en vista de in view of ■ in light of

estar **en vivo** ■ estar en directo live *(Nota: pronunciado "laiv")* ➤ ¿Está la música en vivo, o es una grabación? Is the music live, or is that a recording?

en voz alta out loud ■ aloud ■ in a loud voice

en voz alta: leerlo ~ to read it out loud ■ to read it aloud

en *x* minutos estoy en tu casa I'll be at your house in *x* minutes

en *x* puntos by *x* points ➤ EE UU recorta en medio punto el tipo de interés. U.S. cuts interest rates by half a point.

estar **enajenado(-a) de furia** ■ estar fuera de sí por enojo ■ estar fuera de sus cabales to be beside oneself with anger

estar **enamorado(-a) de alguien** to be in love with someone

enamorarse de alguien ■ prendarse de alguien to fall in love with someone

enana blanca *(astronomía)* white dwarf

enana marrón *(astronomía)* brown dwarf

enarbolar la bandera to plant the flag (on a staff in the ground)

enarbolar la bandera a media asta to fly the flag at half mast ■ to fly the flag at half staff ➤ The flags were flying at half mast. ■ The flags were flying at half staff. Las banderas se enarbolaban a media asta.

enarbolar una espada ■ blandir una espada to brandish a sword

encabezar la lista ■ ser el primero de la lista to head the list ■ to be at the top of the list ■ to top the list

encajar a la perfección to fit perfectly

encajar críticas ■ aguantar críticas to take criticism

encajar en el grupo to fit into a group ■ to fit the mold

encajar en todo esto to fit into the picture ➤ Hablando de la historia de México, ¿dónde encajan los niños héroes en todo esto? Speaking of Mexican history, where do the heroic children fit into the picture?

encajar la noticia to take the news calmly ■ to take the news in stride

encajar la verdad *(Esp.)* ■ soportar la verdad to bear the truth

encajar con to correspond (exactly) to ■ to fit (perfectly) with ■ to dovetail with ➤ El recorrido anual del sol con respecto al fondo de estrellas llamó la atención de los babilonios porque se fue haciendo evidente que encajaba muy bien con el ciclo completo de las estaciones. The annual movement of the sun against the background of the stars was noticed by the Babylonians because it was becoming evident that this movement corresponded exactly to the cycle of the seasons.

encajar con un perfil to fit a profile ■ to fit a description

encajarle algo a alguien ■ clavarle con algo a alguien ■ *(Arg.)* chantarle algo a alguien to stick someone with (doing) something ■ to get stuck with doing something ➤ Después de la comida me encajaron lavar los platos. ■ Después de la comida me clavaron con lavar los platos. After dinner I got stuck with doing the dishes.

encajarle un gol a un equipo ■ meterle un gol a un equipo ■ hacerle un gol a un equipo to score against a team ➤ El Madrid le encajó dos goles al Barcelona. Madrid scored two goals against Barcelona.

encajarse con alguien *(Méx.)* ■ aprovecharse de alguien ■ ensañarse con alguien to take advantage of someone ➤ Creo que tu jefe se está enseñando contigo. I think your boss is taking advantage of you.

encallarse en 1. *(barco)*to founder on ■ to run aground on ■ to get stranded on ■ to get stranded en 2. *(en trabajo cotidiano, etc.)* to get bogged down 3. *(negociaciones)* to break down

encaminarse para ■ encaminarse a ■ encaminarse hacia to be on one's way to ■ to set off on one's way to ■ to set out for

ser **encandilado(-a) (por las luces)** ■ estar enceguecido por las luces to be blinded (temporarily) by lights ➤ Los faros del auto en sentido opuesto me encandilaron. The headlights of the oncoming car blinded me (temporarily).

encanecerse con el tiempo to go gray gradually ■ to go gray over time ■ to go gray with time

estar **encantado(-a) de concocer a alguien** to be delighted to meet someone ➤ *(a ti, hombre o mujer)* (Estoy) encantado(-a) de conocerte. I'm delighted to meet you. ■ It's good to meet you. ■ It's great to meet you. ■ It's nice to meet you. ➤ *(a usted, hombre)* (Estoy) encantado(-a) de conocerlo (a usted) ■ *(Esp. leísmo)* (Estoy) encantado(-a) de conocerle. I'm delighted to meet you. ■ It's good to meet you. ■ It's great to meet you. ■ It's nice to meet you. ■ ➤ *(a usted, mujer)* (Estoy) encantado(-a) de conocerla (a usted). I'm delighted to meet you. ■ It's good to meet you. ■ It's great to meet you. ■ It's nice to meet you.

estar **encantado(-a) de haber conocido a alguien** to be delighted to meet someone ■ to be delighted to have met someone ➤ *(a ti, hombre o mujer)* (Estoy) encantado(-a) de haberte conocido. It was wonderful to meet you. ■ It was good to meet you. ■ It was great to meet you. ■ It was nice to meet you. ■ I really enjoyed meeting you. ➤ *(a usted, hombre)* (Estoy) encantado(-a) de haberlo conocido (a usted). ■ *(Esp., leísmo)* (Estoy) encantado(-a) de haberle conocido. It was wonderful to meet you. ■ It was good to meet you. ■ It was great to meet you. ■ It was nice to meet you. ■ I thoroughly enjoyed meeting you. ■ I really enjoyed meeting you. ➤ *(a usted, mujer)* (Estoy) encantado(-a) de haberla conocido (a usted). It was wonderful to meet you. ■ It was good to meet you. ■ It was great to meet you. ■ It was nice to meet you. ■ I thoroughly enjoyed meeting you. ■ I really enjoyed meeting you.

encantarle su trabajo to love one's work ➤ A mi marido le encanta su trabajo. My husband loves his work.

encantarle un alimento to love a food ➤ A los caballos les encantan las manzanas. Horses love apples.

estar **encaramado en** to be perched on

estar **encaramado sobre** to be perched above

encarar dos cosas to place two things facing each other ■ to put two things face to face ■ to put two things facing each other ■ to put two things face to face ➤ La costurera encaró las dos piezas simétricas del vestido. The seamstress placed the two symmetrical pieces of the dress facing each other.

encarar una crisis to face up to a crisis ■ to confront a crisis

encararse a alguien ~ 1. to face (up to) someone 2. *(Arg.)* to ask someone out on a date

encargado del patrimonio ■ testamentario executor of an estate

encargar a alguien hacer algo to assign someone the task of doing something ▪ to charge someone with the task of doing something
encargar algo a un suministrador to order something from a supplier
encargar mercancías to order merchandise
encargar una pieza to order a part
encargarse de hacer algo ▪ hacerse cargo de hacer algo to take charge of (doing) something ▪ to take it upon oneself to do something ▪ to take something upon oneself
encargarse de recordarle a alguien to take it upon oneself to remind someone
encariñarse con alguien to grow fond of someone ▪ to become attached to someone ▪ to get attached to someone
encarnar a alguien to play someone ➤ En la película, DiCaprio encarna a un estafador famoso. In the film, DiCaprio plays an infamous con man.
encarnar a la perfección to embody perfectly
encarnar un ideal to embody an ideal
encasillarle a alguien como to pigeonhole someone as ▪ to typecast someone as
ser **encausado(-a) por** ▪ ser acusado(-a) de to be charged with
estar **enceguecido(-a) de rabia** estar enceguecido(-a) de ira to be blinded by rage ▪ to be blind with rage ▪ to fly into a blind rage
estar **enceguecido(-a) por la avaricia** to blinded by greed ▪ to be blind with greed
estar **enceguecido(-a) por las luces** ▪ ser encandilado por las luces to blinded by the lights
encender a alguien ▪ prender a alguien ▪ hacer tilín a alguien ▪ poner a alguien a cien to turn someone on
encender el motor ▪ arrancar el motor to start the engine ▪ to start the motor ➤ Se subió al coche y encendió el motor. He got in the car and started the engine. ▪ He got in the car and started the motor.
encender el ordenador *(Esp.)* ▪ prender la computadora to turn on the computer
encender el piloto to light the pilot
encender la lumbre to light the fire
encender la luz de arriba *(Esp.)* ▪ encender la luz del techo ▪ dar la luz de arriba ▪ dar la luz del techo ▪ prender la luz de arriba ▪ prender la luz del techo to turn on the ceiling light(s) ▪ to turn on the overhead light(s)
encender un cigarro con otro to chain-smoke
encender(se) el entusiasmo sobre algo to get fired up about something ▪ to become enthusiastic about something
encendérsele la bombilla (for) a little light to go on in one's head
estar **encerrado(-a) en un ascensor** to be trapped in an elevator
encerrar a alguien bajo siete llaves to keep someone under lock and key
encerrar la promesa de to hold the promise of
encerrarse en uno mismo to withdraw (into oneself) ▪ to draw into oneself ▪ to become withdrawn
enchinársele el cuero *(Méx.)* ▪ enchinársele la piel ▪ ponérsele la piel de gallina to get goose bumps ▪ to get goose flesh ▪ to give one goose bumps
enchufe con toma de tierra extension cord with a ground ➤ *(instrucciones para prolongador)* Conecte su prolongador a un enchufe con toma de tierra. Plug your extension cord into a grounded outlet.
enchufe eléctrico toma eléctrica electrical outlet ➤ Necesito un alargador con seis tomas y una toma de tierra. ▪ Necesito un alargador con seis enchufes y una toma de tierra. I need an extension cord with three outlets and a ground.
encías desnudas toothless gums
enciclopedia viviente walking encyclopedia
estar **encima de algo** to be on (top of) something ➤ Está encima de la cómoda. It's on (top of) the chest of drawers.
estar **encima de su trabajo** to be on top of one's work
encoger los hombros ▪ encogerse de hombros to shrug one's shoulders
encomendar el alma to commend one's soul to God
enconado enemigo *(literario)* ▪ enemigo enconado bitter enemy
encontrar a un ser que... to meet someone who...
encontrar algo muy divertido to find something very enjoyable ▪ to find something a lot of fun ▪ *(coloquial)* to get one's kicks by doing something ➤ Son un montón de niñatos que encuentran muy divertido ir pintando grafitis por todas partes. They're a bunch of little whippersnappers who get their kicks by writing graffiti all over everything.
encontrar el tema interesante to find the subject interesting
encontrar la horma de su zapato to meet one's match
encontrar la muerte en ▪ encontrar su muerte en to meet one's death in
encontrar por casualidad to chance upon ▪ to hit upon
encontrar trabajo to find work
encontrar un trabajo to find a job
encontrar una manera de hacer algo to find a way to do something
encontrar una manera de poder hacer algo to find a way to (be able to) do something
encontrar una ocasión perseguida to see one's chance ➤ Él encontró entonces una ocasión perseguida. He saw his chance.
encontrar una triquiñuela para no hacer algo ▪ encontrarle la vuelta para no hacer algo to find a way out of doing something ▪ to find a way to get out of doing something ▪ to weasel out of doing something
encontrar su muerte en ▪ encontrar la muerte en to meet one's death in
encontrar tiempo para to find the time to
encontrar un hueco to find a parking place
encontrar un hueco para... to find time to... ▪ to find a moment to
encontrar una ocasión perseguida ▪ encontrar una ocasión buscada ▪ encontrar una ocasión esperada to see one's chance ➤ Él encontró entonces una ocasión perseguida. Then he saw his chance.
encontrarle la manera para no hacer algo ▪ encontrar el truco para no hacer algo ▪ encontrar la maña para no hacer algo ▪ encontar la vuelta para no hacer algo ▪ encontrar una triquiñuela para no hacer algo to find a way out of doing something ▪ to find a way to get out of doing something ▪ to weasel out of doing something
encontrarse bien ▪ sentirse bien to feel well
encontrarse con alguien to meet someone ▪ to run into someone ➤ Juan Bobo iba al mercado cuando se encontró con mucha gente que venía de una boda. Juan Bobo was on his way to the market when he met a lot of people coming from a wedding.
encontrarse con que... to discover that... ➤ El marido se encontró con que su mujer estaba con otro hombre. The husband discovered that his wife was having an affair with another man.
encontrarse con una dificultad ▪ tropezar con una dificultad ▪ dar con una dificultad ▪ dar con un escollo to run into a problem ▪ to hit a snag
encontrarse de vacaciones ▪ estar de vacaciones **1.** *(EE UU)* to be on vacation **2.** *(RU)* to be on holiday
encontrarse en su propia salsa to be in one's element
encontrarse en silla de ruedas to be confined to a wheelchair ▪ to be wheelchair-bound
encontrarse entre la espada y la pared to be between a rock and a hard place ▪ to have one's back to the wall ➤ Me encuentro entre la espada y la pared. I'm caught between a rock and a hard place.
encontrarse fatal to feel terrible ▪ to feel really sick ➤ Me encuentro fatal. I feel terrible. ▪ I feel really sick.
encontrarse mal to feel sick ➤ Me encuentro mal. I feel sick.
encontrárselo casualmente to happen to run into someone ➤ Casualmente me la encontré en la calle. I happened to run into her on the street.
estar **encoñado con alguien** *(subido de tono)* to have the hots for someone
estar **encorvado(-a) sobre su bastón** to be stooped over one's cane
encorvar metal ▪ combar metal ▪ doblar metal to bend metal
encuadrarse en to join ▪ to become part of

encuentro casual ▪ encuentro por azar ▪ encuentro inesperado chance encounter ▪ chance meeting
encuesta de intención de voto voter preference survey ▪ survey of voter preference ▪ survey to determine voter preference ▪ voter preference poll ▪ poll of voter preference ▪ poll to determine voter preference
enderezar una equivocación ▪ rectificar un error to correct a mistake
endulzar el café to sweeten the coffee
endulzar un trato to sweeten a deal
endulzar una oferta to sweeten an offer
endurecer una política to toughen a policy
energía cinética kinetic energy
enésima vez: por ~ for the umpteenth time
enésimo grado nth degree
enfardar el heno to bale hay
enfermarse de muerte to become terminally ill ▪ to fall terminally ill ▪ to develop a terminal illness
enfermarse de una gripe muy fuerte ▪ agarrar una gripe muy fuerte ▪ *(Esp.)* coger una gripe muy fuerte to come down with a bad case of the flu ▪ to develop a bad case of the flu
enfermedad de caballo: padecer de una ~ *(coloquial)* to suffer from a serious illness ▪ to have a serious illness
la **enfermedad de transmisión sexual** sexually transmitted disease ▪ STD
enfermedad mortal: tener una ~ to have a terminal illness
la **enfermedad que pone en riesgo la vida** life-threatening illness
enfermo(-a) cardíaco(-a) ▪ enfermo del corazón heart patient
estar **enfermo(-a) del corazón** to have heart trouble
enfilar algo hacia algo to aim something at something
enfilar hacia to go straight towards ▪ to head straight for ▪ to head straight towards
enfilar la pista to line up with the runway
enfilar la recta final to head down the home stretch
enfilar una calle to go down a street ▪ to go along a street ➤ La procesión está enfilando la Calle Toledo. The procession is going down Toledo Street. ▪ The procession is going along Toledo Street.
enfocar la luz sobre algo to focus the light on something
enfocar un asunto to address a matter
enfocar una lente to focus a lens
enfocarse en un objetivo to focus on a goal
estar **enfrascado en una actividad** to be absorbed in an activity
enfrascarse en una conversación to be engrossed in a conversation ▪ to become engrossed in a conversation
enfrascarse en una riña to be embroiled in an argument ▪ to become embroiled in an argument
estar **enfrentados el uno con el otro** to be at odds with each other
enfrentamiento con la policía clash with the police ▪ confrontation with the police
enfrentarse a un problema ▪ enfrentarse con un problema ▪ sortear un problema to face a problem ▪ to address a problem ▪ to deal with a problem
enfrentarse a ▪ hacer frente a to be faced with ▪ to be facing ➤ El país se enfrenta a un creciente déficit presupuestario. ▪ El país hace frente a un creciente déficit presupuestario. The country is faced with a growing budget deficit. ▪ The country is facing a growing budget deficit.
enfrentarse a la realidad to face (up to) reality
enfrentarse a las consecuencias ▪ dar la cara to face the consequences
enfrentarse a que... to face (up) to the fact that...
enfrentarse con alguien ▪ enfrentarse a alguien ▪ tener un conflicto con alguien **1.** to clash with someone **2.** hacer frente a alguien to confront someone
enfrente de ▪ frente a ▪ delante de across from ➤ Durante la cena, me senté enfrente de Rudolph Serkin. ▪ Durante la cena, me senté frente a Rudolph Serkin. ▪ Durante la cena, me senté delante de Rudolph Serkin. At the dinner, I sat across from Rudolph Serkin.
estar **enfrente uno del otro** to be face to face ▪ to stand face to face ➤ En el baile mexicano la raspa, el hombre y la mujer están enfrente uno del otro y se agarran (de) las manos. In the Mexican dance the shuffle, the man and woman face each other and hold hands.
enfriamiento de la economía cooling off of the economy ▪ cooling down of the economy ▪ slowing of the economy
engalanar con flores to deck with flowers
estar **enganchado(-a) a** ▪ estar colgado(-a) de to be hooked on ▪ to be addicted to ➤ Enganchado al tabaco Addicted to tobacco
ser **engañado(-a) por** to be deceived by ▪ to be fooled by ▪ to be taken in by
engañar el hambre ▪ matar el gusanillo to eat something to tide oneself over til dinner
engarzar el cinturón ▪ abrochar el cinturón to fasten one's seat belt
engatusar a alguien ▪ acaramelar a alguien ▪ hacerle juego a alguien to sweet-talk someone ▪ to coax someone
engatusar a alguien para que haga algo to coax someone into doing something ➤ Le invitamos a la fiesta, pero se hizo de rogar hasta que aceptó. We invited him to the party, but he had to be coaxed into accepting. ➤ Le invitamos a la fiesta, pero se hizo de rogar hasta que accedió a venir. We invited him to the party, but he had to be coaxed into coming.
¡enhorabuena! ¡bien hecho! good for *you*!
enjugar una deuda ▪ liquidar una deuda ▪ saldar una deuda ▪ *(especialmente deudas a plazos)* cancelar una deuda to pay off a debt ▪ to liquidate a debt ▪ to clear (off) a debt
enjugarse la frente ▪ limpiarse la frente to wipe one's brow
el **enlace de los trenes** ▪ (el) intercambiador de los trenes train hub ▪ connecting point of the trains
enmascarar la voz to disguise one's voice
enmendar una injusticia ▪ deshacer una injusticia to right a wrong
enmendarse la plana to turn over a new leaf
enorgullecerse de anunciar que... to be proud to announce that...
enorgullecerse de nombrar a alguien... to be proud to name someone...
enorgullecerse de sus logros to take pride in one's accomplishments
enquistarse en to become entrenched in
enrarecer el aire ▪ contaminar el aire to pollute the air
estar **enredado en** ▪ estar liado en to be caught up in ▪ to be tangled up in
enredar la madeja to complicate matters
enredar la situación to complicate the situation ▪ to complicate matters ➤ Y para enredar la situación... And to complicate the situation... ▪ And to complicate matters...
enredar las cosas ▪ complicar las cosas ▪ liar el tema ▪ rizar el rizo to complicate matters ▪ to complicate things
enredarse al leer las instrucciones ▪ hacerse bolas al leer las instrucciones to get mixed up trying to read the instructions ▪ to get balled up trying to read the instructions ➤ Se enredó al leer las instrucciones del teléfono inalámbrico. He got mixed up trying to read the instructions for the cordless phone.
enredarse en algo to get mixed up in something ▪ to get embroiled in something ▪ to get tangled up in something ➤ El pez espada se enredó en la red de pesca. The swordfish got tangled up in the fishing net.
enredarse la madeja (for) the plot to thicken
enredo de cartas whole mess of letters ➤ Había un enredo de cartas en la mesa. There was a whole mess of letters on the table.
enrolarse en el ejército ▪ alistarse en el ejército ▪ unirse al ejército to enlist in the army ▪ to join the army
enrolarse en un partido político ▪ afiliarse a un partido político to join a political party
estar **enrollado sobre sí mismo** to be wound around itself
enrollarse con alguien *(para romance)* to get it on with someone
enrollarse hablando de algo to get deep into a conversation about something
estar **enroscado para atacar** ▪ estar arrollado sobre sí para atacar to be coiled to strike

ensalzar a alguien to sing someone's praises ▪ to extol someone's virtues ▪ to extol the virtues of someone
ensamblar las partes ▪ montar las partes ▪ armar las partes to assemble the parts ▪ to put together the parts ▪ to put the parts together
ensamblar las piezas ▪ montar las piezas ▪ armar las partes to assemble the pieces ▪ to put together the pieces ▪ to put the pieces together
ensamblar un inglete to cut a mitre joint ▪ to saw a corner piece at a 45º angle
ensamblar una maqueta ▪ armar una maqueta ▪ montar una maqueta ▪ hacer una maqueta to assemble a (scale model) kit ▪ to put together a kit ▪ to put a kit together
ensanchar los horizontes de uno ▪ ampliar los horizontes de uno to broaden one's horizons ▪ to expand one's horizons
ensañarse con alguien 1. to vent one's anger at someone 2. to take something out on someone ➤ ¡No te ensañes conmigo! Don't take it out on me!
ensayar el piano ▪ practicar el piano to practice the piano
ensayo general dress rehearsal ➤ El ensayo general resultó flojo, pero la noche del estreno salió sin ningún contratiempo. The dress rehearsal was rocky, but the opening night came off without a hitch.
enseñar el cobre *(coloquial)* ▪ pelar el cobre ▪ mostrar el verdadero yo to show one's true self ▪ to show one's true colors
enseñarle a alguien a hacer algo to show someone how to do something
enseñarle la ciudad to show someone (around) the city ➤ Le enseñé la ciudad. *(a él)* I showed him around the city. ▪ *(a ella)* I showed her around the city. ➤ Se la enseñé *(a él)* I showed him around (the city). ▪ I showed it to him. ▪ *(a ella)* I showed her around (the city). ▪ I showed it to her.
enseres domésticos housewares
ensillar un caballo to saddle a horse
ensombrecer el futuro to cloud the future ▪ to cast a pall over the future ➤ *(noticia)* Las cuentas suizas del candidato ensombrecen su futuro político. Candidate's Swiss bank accounts cloud his political future. ▪ Candidate's Swiss bank accounts cast a pall over his political future.
ensuciarse las manos to get one's hands dirty ▪ to dirty one's hands
entablar acción ▪ entablar demanda to take legal action
entablar una amistad con alguien to make friends with someone ▪ to become friends with someone
entablar una conversación to engage (in a conversation) ➤ No quiere entablar una conversación. *(él)* He doesn't want to engage. ▪ *(ella)* She doesn't want to engage.
entablar una relación to develop a relationship ▪ to establish a relationship
entablarle pleito a alguien por algo to file suit against someone for something
entender un chiste to catch on to a joke
entenderse bien ▪ llevarse bien to get along well (together) ▪ to get along great ➤ Se entienden muy bien. ▪ Se llevan muy bien. They get along great (together.) ▪ They get along well (together).
entendiendo por tal 1. *(yo)* by which I mean 2. *(él)* by which he means 3. *(ella)* by which she means
estar **enterado(-a) de algo** ▪ ser consciente de algo ▪ constarle algo a alguien ▪ tener conocimiento de algo ▪ tener constancia de algo to be aware of something ▪ to be informed about something ▪ to know about something ➤ Quería decirte algo de lo que probablemente no estés enterado. ▪ Quería decirte algo de lo que puede que no seas consciente. ▪ Quería decirte algo que a ti probablemente no te conste. ▪ Quería decirte algo de lo que probablemente no tengas conocimiento. I wanted to tell you something you may not be aware of. ▪ I wanted to tell you something you might not be aware of. ▪ I wanted to tell you something you're probably not aware of.
enterarse de algo ▪ saber de algo to find out about something ▪ to learn of something ▪ to learn about something ➤ Nos enteramos del accidente al volver de nuestro viaje. We learned of the accident when we got home from our trip. ➤ ¿Cómo te enteraste de ello? ▪ ¿Cómo supiste de ello? How did you find out about it? ➤ ¿Cómo puedo enterarme de ello? ▪ ¿Cómo puedo saber de ello? How can I find out about it? ➤ Esto es de lo que me enteré. ▪ Esto es de lo que me he enterado. ▪ Esto es lo que descubrí. Here's what I found out. ➤ ¿Pudiste enterarte de algo ayer? Were you able to find out anything yesterday?
enterarse de lo que to find out what
enterarse de lo que pasa ▪ enterarse de qué pasa to find out what's going on ▪ to get clued in on what's going on
enterarse de qué pasa ▪ enterarse de lo que pasa to find out what's going on ▪ to get clued in on what's going on
enterarse por alguien de que... to learn from someone that... ▪ to find out from someone that...
enterarse por radio macuto de que... ▪ oír por ahí que... ▪ oír por radio macuto que... ▪ oír por terceras personas que... to hear through the grapevine that...
entidad bancaria banking institution
entidad financiera financial institution
¿entiendes lo que quiero decir? ▪ ¿comprendes? (do you) know what I mean? ▪ see what I mean?
entiendo lo que quieres decir sobre... ▪ sé lo que quieres decir sobre... ▪ sé qué quieres decir sobre... ▪ me hago cargo de lo que dices sobre... I understand what you mean about... ▪ I know what you mean about...
entonar con to go with ▪ to complement each other ▪ to match
entonces no voy a preocuparme I'm not going to worry about it, then
¿entonces qué? 1. then what? ▪ what then? ▪ *what* then? 2. ¿y qué? what about it?
¿entonces vas? so are you going?
entornar los ojos to half close the eyes
entorno doméstico ▪ entorno familiar home environment ▪ home front
entorno familiar ▪ entorno doméstico home environment
entorno social social milieu
entorpecer el paso to get in the way ▪ to be in the way
entorpecer el tráfico ▪ bloquear el tráfico ▪ obstaculizar el tráfico to block traffic
entrada (de coches) driveway
estar **entrada en vigor** to have taken effect ▪ to be in effect ▪ to be in force
entrada gratis ▪ entrada libre free admission
entrada libre ▪ entrada gratis free admission
estar **entrado(-a) en años** to be (getting) on in years ▪ to be up in years ▪ to be getting up there
estar **entrado(-a) en carnes** to have put on a little weight
entramado social social fabric
estar **entrando(-a) en años** ▪ ya ir para viejo ▪ ir envejeciendo to be getting up in years ▪ to be getting old ▪ to be aging
entrañar algo de peligro to involve some danger ▪ to be somewhat dangerous
entrañar riesgo ▪ involucrar riesgo ▪ implicar riesgo to involve risk ▪ to entail risk
entrar a degüello a una ciudad to enter a city by (military) siege ▪ to storm a city
entrar a empujones to push one's way in
entrar a formar parte de un trato ▪ entrar a formar parte de un negocio to get in on the deal
entrar a la fuerza to force one's way in
entrar a saco to enter forcefully
entrar a vivir en un apartamento to move into an apartment
entrar a vivir en un chalet to move into a house
entrar a vivir en un piso ▪ trasladarse a un piso ▪ mudarse a un piso ▪ entrar a vivir en un apartamento ▪ trasladarse a un piso ▪ mudarse a un piso to move into an apartment
entrar a vivir en una casa 1. *(chalet)* to move into a house 2. *(piso; apartamento)* to move into an apartment
entrar a trabajar to start work ➤ Entro a trabajar a las nueve de la mañana. I start work at nine a.m. ▪ I start work at nine each morning.
entrar colándose to get in without paying ▪ to sneak in
entrar con el pie derecho to get off on the right foot
entrar con el pie izquierdo to get off on the wrong foot
entrar de arribada to put into port

entrar de romplón a un edificio ▪ entrar de golpe a un edificio to storm a building

entrar de romplón en el edificio ▪ entrar de golpe en el edificio to storm the building

entrar el coche de culo *(coloquial)* ▪ meter el coche de culo ▪ entrar el coche marcha atrás to back the car in

entrar el coche de morro *(coloquial)* ▪ meter el coche de morro ▪ entrar el coche de punta ▪ entrar el coche de trompa to pull (the car) in

entrar (en) 1. *(ropa)* no caberle to get into ▪ to fit into **2.** *(informática)* to log on ▪ to enter **3.** *(página web, por ejemplo)* to open ▪ to access **4.** acceder a un sitio to enter a place ▪ to go into a place ▪ to go inside a place ➤ No entro en estas botas. ▪ Estas botas no me caben. ▪ No quepo en estas botas. I can't get into these boots. ▪ These boots don't fit (me). ➤ No puedo entrar en la computadora. I can't log onto the computer. ➤ No puedo entrar en esta página web. I can't open this web page. ▪ I can't access this web page. ➤ Vamos a entrar. Let's go in. ▪ Let's go inside.

entrar en acción to get going ▪ to get to work ▪ to get busy

entrar en antena ▪ entrar en el aire ▪ entrar en frecuencia to go on the air

entrar en barrena *(avión)* ▪ caer en barrena to go into a spin ▪ to get into a spin

entrar en calor 1. to get warm ▪ to warm up **2.** *(sexual)* to get hot ▪ to get turned on ➤ Vamos a hacer una fogata para entrar en calor. Let's build a fire to get warm. ▪ Let's build a fire and get warm. ▪ Let's build a fire to warm up. ▪ Let's build a fire and warm up. ➤ A pesar del agua fría, mi cuerpo entró en calor mientras nadaba. In spite of the cold water, my body warmed up quickly as I swam.

entrar en contacto con alguien ▪ contactar con alguien to get in touch with someone ➤ Siento que no haya podido entrar en contacto contigo. I'm sorry I haven't been able to get in touch with you.

entrar en detalles to go into detail

entrar en el agua andando *(Esp.)* ▪ entrar en el agua caminando to wade into the water

entrar en el agua caminando *(L.am.)* ▪ entrar en el agua andando to wade into the water

entrar en el coche ▪ subir al coche ▪ meterse en el coche to get in the car ➤ Ella entró en su coche. She got in her car.

entrar en el mundo de ▪ entrar en el mundillo de ▪ meterse en el mundillo de to get into the world of ▪ to get into the business of

entrar en escena to arrive on the scene

entrar en funcionamiento to begin operations ▪ to begin operating

entrar en juego ▪ ponerse en juego to come into play ▪ to enter into play

entrar en la cuestión to come into question

entrar en (los) detalles to go into detail ▪ to go into the details ▪ to get into details ▪ to go into the particulars

entrar en política ▪ meterse en política ▪ adentrarse en la política to go into politics

entrar en pormenores ▪ pormenorizar to go into minute details

entrar en razón to see the light ➤ Mi hijo adolescente por fin entró en razón. My teenage son finally saw the light.

entrar en situación de suspensión de pagos to default

entrar en una disputa to get into an argument

entrar en una rutina ▪ meterse en una rutina to get into a rut

entrar en vigor *(ley)* to take effect ▪ to go into effect

entrar en volandas to rush in ▪ to come flying in

entrar por el aro ▪ pasar por el aro to fall into line ▪ to knuckle under ▪ to toe the line

entrar por la fuerza to force one's way in

entrar por un oído y salir por el otro to go in one ear and out the other

entrar presuroso to rush in

entrar primero to come in first ▪ to enter first ➤ La novia entra primero, seguida por las damas de honor. ▪ La novia entra primero, seguida de las damas de honor. The bride comes in first, followed by the bridesmaids. ▪ The bride enters first, followed by the bridesmaids.

entrar segundo ▪ llegar segundo to come in second

entrar tercero ▪ llegar tercero to come in third

entrarle a uno cagalera *(subido de tono)* **1.** *(de diarrea)* to have the runs ▪ to have the shits ▪ to have an attack of diarrhea **2.** *(de susto)* to scare the shit out of one ▪ to scare the crap out of one ➤ Me entró cagalera al oír la explosión. The explosion scared the crap out of me.

entrarle a uno hambre ▪ abrirle a uno el apetito to get hungry

entrarle a uno sueño to get sleepy ▪ to become sleepy

entrarle a uno ganas de hacer algo to have the urge to do something

entrarle canguelo ▪ entrarle canguis to get the jitters ▪ to get scared ➤ Me entra canguelo. ▪ Me está entrando canguelo. I'm getting the jitters.

entrarse completamente en ▪ apuntar hacia to zero in on

entre hoy y el domingo ▪ de aquí al domingo between now and Sunday

entre ambos gobiernos ▪ entre los dos gobiernos between the two governments ➤ El presidente abogó por el inicio de un diálogo entre ambos gobiernos. ▪ El presidente abogó por el inicio de un diálogo entre los dos gobiernos. ▪ The president called for a dialogue between the two governments.

entre bastidores ▪ detrás de la cortinas behind the scenes

entre comillas 1. set off by quotation marks ▪ in quotation marks **2.** *(citando a una persona y a menudo señalando con los dedos)* quote unquote

entre cuatro paredes lonely ▪ shut in

estar **entre dos aguas** ▪ nadar entre dos aguas ▪ estar entre Pinto y Valdemoro to straddle the fence

estar **entre el público** to be in the audience ➤ La esposa del especialista estuvo entre el público cuando a su marido le concedieron el premio. The stuntman's wife was in the audience when her husband was awarded the prize.

entre ellos *x* argentinos ▪ incluyendo *x* argentinos among them *x* Argentines ▪ including *x* Argentines

entre fuertes medidas de seguridad ▪ bajo altas medidas de seguridad under tight security

entre horas: comer ~ ▪ comer a destiempo to snack between meals

estar **entre la espada y la pared** ▪ encontrarse entre la espada y la pared to be between a rock and a hard place ▪ to be between the devil and the deep blue sea ▪ *(literario)* to be between Scylla and Charybdis

estar **entre la vida y la muerte** ▪ debatirse entre la vida y la muerte to be fighting for one's life

entre los dos gobiernos ▪ entre ambos gobiernos between the two governments ➤ El presidente abogó por el inicio de un diálogo entre los dos gobiernos. ▪ El presidente abogó por el inicio de un diálogo entre ambos gobiernos. The president called for a dialogue between the two governments.

entre nosotros between you and me

entre nosotros y en confianza between you, me and the gate post ▪ just between us

entre otros among others

entre paréntesis 1. in parentheses **2.** *(corchetes)* in brackets

estar **entre Pinto y Valdemoro** *(Esp.)* **1.** no saber qué hacer to be undecided ▪ not to know what to do **2.** estar achispado(-a) to be high as a kite *(Nota: Pinto y Valdemoro son comarcas vinícolas de España.)*

entre pitos y flautas what with one thing and another

estar **entre rejas** ▪ estar tras las rejas ▪ estar encarcelado ▪ estar encerrado ▪ estar metido ▪ estar dentro ▪ estar en la trena to be behind bars ▪ to be in jail ▪ *(literario)* to be incarcerated ▪ *(coloquial)* to be in the clinker ▪ to be in the tank

entre renglones: leer ~ to read between the lines

estar **entre San Juan y Mendoza** *(Arg.)* **1.** no saber qué hacer not to know what to do **2.** estar achispado(-a) to be high as a kite *(Nota: San Juan y Mendoza son comarcas vinícolas de Argentina.)*

entre semana during the week

estar **entre sueños** ▪ estar medio dormido to be half asleep

entre tanto ▪ mientras tanto in the meantime

entre tú y yo ▪ entre nosotros ▪ esto que quede entre nosotros ▪ entre nos (just) between you and me ▪ this is just between you and me

entre una cosa y otra because of one thing or another

entre uno y dos kilómetros between one and two kilometers

entre *x* e *y* ■ de *x* a *y* (anywhere) between *x* and *y* ■ (anywhere) from *x* to *y* ➤ Entre diez y veinte ■ De diez a veinte (Anywhere) from ten to twenty

entrecerrar los ojos to squint

estar **entregado en mano** to be hand delivered

entregar a alguien a la policía ■ denunciar a alguien to turn someone over to the police ■ to turn someone in to the police ➤ El propio hermano del atracador le entregó. The robber's own brother turned him in.

entregar a alguien el aviso con antelación ■ avisar a alguien con antelación ■ dar a alguien el aviso con antelación to give someone (advance) notice ➤ Le entregó el aviso de (su) renuncia a su jefe con dos semanas de antelación. ■ Le dio el aviso de (su) renuncia a su jefe con dos semanas de antelación. He gave his employer two weeks' (advance) notice that he was going to quit. ■ He gave his employer two weeks' (advance) notice of his resignation.

entregar en el mismo día to deliver on the same day ■ to have same-day delivery

entregar en mano to hand deliver

entregar los deberes to hand in homework ■ to turn in homework ➤ ¿Deberíamos haber entregado nuestros trabajos ayer? Were we supposed to hand in our papers yesterday?

entregar el alma (a Dios) ■ entregar su alma a Dios ■ expirar to give up the ghost

entregar su renuncia ■ renunciar to turn in one's resignation ■ to resign (from a position) ■ to quit (one's job)

entregar su vida a to devote one's life to

entregarse a to indulge in

entrenar al baloncesto to practice basketball

entrenar al fútbol 1. *(EE UU)* to practice football 2. *(Europa)* to practice soccer

entrenar un animal ■ amaestrar un animal ■ enseñar un animal to train an animal ■ to teach an animal ➤ Estoy entrenando a mi caballo para que salte. I'm training my horse to jump. ■ I'm teaching my horse to jump.

entrenador de baloncesto basketball coach

entrenador de fútbol 1. *(EE UU)* football coach 2. *(Europa)* soccer coach

entrevistarse con alguien to meet with someone ➤ El ministro de exteriores se entrevistó con el secretario general. The foreign minister met with the secretary general.

entrometerse en una conversación ■ entremeterse en una conversación to butt into a conversation

enturbiar el futuro to cloud the future

enturbiar la situación to muddy the water

estar **envasado al vacío** to be vacuum-packed

envenenamiento por monóxido de carbono carbon monoxide poisoning

envenenarse con algo to be poisoned by something ■ to get poisoned by something

el **envés de la mano** ■ el dorso de la mano back of the hand

enviar algo como un adjunto ■ enviar algo como datos adjuntos ■ enviar algo como archivos adjuntos to send something as an attachment

enviar de regreso ■ enviar de vuelta to send back ➤ El tío abuelo dice que deben enviarlo (Elián) de regreso a Cuba. The great uncle says that must send him (Elian) back to Cuba.

envío masivo (de cartas) mass mailing

envolverse en la cultura to immerse oneself in the culture

estar **envuelto en llamas** to be enveloped in flames

enzarzarse con alguien ■ enzarzarse en una conversación con alguien ■ enzarzarse en una disputa con alguien to lock horns (with someone)

enzarzarse en una lucha contracorriente ■ enzarzarse en una lucha contra la corriente ■ meterse en una lucha contracorriente ■ meterse en una lucha contra la corriente ■ liarse en una lucha contracorriente ■ liarse en una lucha contra la corriente to engage in an uphill battle ■ to get into an uphill battle ■ to take on an uphill battle

enzarzarse en una pelea ■ verse envuelto en una pelea ■ involucrarse en una pelea to get embroiled in a fight

episodio siguiente next episode ■ upcoming episode ➤ El episodio siguiente del programa fue filmado en nuestra vecindad. The next episode of the program was filmed in our neighborhood. ■ The upcoming episode of the program was filmed in our neighborhood.

época de estudiante student days

época de la cosecha harvest time ■ time of the harvest

época dorada ■ (la) edad de oro golden age ➤ La Primera Guerra Mundial fue la época dorada de la aviación militar. ■ La Primera Guerra Mundial fue la edad de oro de la aviación militar. World War I was the golden age of military aviation.

equilibrar el presupuesto ■ balancear el presupuesto to balance the budget

equilibrar las ruedas ■ balancear la ruedas to balance the wheels

equilibrio ecológico ecological balance

equilibrio electrolítico electrolyte balance

equilibrio entre balance between

equilibrio presupuestario ■ presupuesto equilibrado balanced budget ■ budget in balance

equinoccio vernal ■ equinoccio de primavera vernal equinox ■ spring equinox

el **equipaje de mano** carry-on luggage ■ carry-on(s)

equipamiento estándar standard equipment

equiparar con to liken to ■ to weight academic credit

equipo contrario the other team

equipo de baloncesto basketball team

equipo de fútbol 1. *(EE UU)* football team 2. *(Europa)* soccer team

equipo de salvamento rescue team

equipo de sonido ■ (el) sistema de sonido sound system

equipo de primeros auxilios ■ (el) botiquín de primeros auxilios first-aid kit

equipo de televisión television crew ■ TV crew

equipo de trabajo 1. plantilla work crew ■ staff 2. equipamiento work clothes ■ tools

equipo negociador negotiating team

equivocarse en algo ■ cometer un error en algo to be wrong about something ■ to make a mistake in something

estar **equivocado con alguien** ■ equivocarse con alguien to be wrong about someone ➤ Veo que me he equivocado contigo. ■ Veo que he estado equivocado contigo. I see (that) I was wrong about you.

equivocarse con alguien ■ estar equivocado con alguien to be wrong about someone

equivocarse en algo ■ estar equivocado con algo to be wrong about something ➤ Me equivoqué en la hora. I was wrong about the time.

equivocarse de camino to go the wrong way

era aún muy niña she was still very young ■ I was still very young

era aún muy niño he was still very young ■ I was still very young

era broma ■ sólo estaba bromeando ■ (yo) iba de broma it was just a joke ■ I was just kidding ■ I didn't mean it ■ I was just joking ■ I was only joking

era cristiana *(notación científica)* ■ E.C. Christian Era ■ C.E.

era culpa mía ■ fue culpa mía ■ (yo) tenía la culpa it was all my fault ➤ Todo era culpa mía. ■ Todo fue culpa mía. ■ (Yo) tenía toda la culpa. It was all my fault.

era de esperar que... it was (to be) expected that... ■ that was to be expected that...

era de esperarse ■ era de suponerse it was to be expected ■ that was to be expected

era de lo más frustrante it was really frustrating

era de suponer que... ■ era de esperar que... it was to be expected that...

era de suponerse ■ era de esperarse it was to be expected ■ that was to be expected

¿era ese el autobús que va a...? ■ ¿era ese el autobús para...? was that the bus for...? ➤ Was that the bus for Toluca? ¿Era ese el autobús que va a Toluca? ■ ¿Era ese el autobús para Toluca?

era imposible para... it was impossible for...

era imposible para que... it was impossible to...

era la primera vez en su vida que... 1. *(él)* it was the first time in his life that... **2.** *(ella)* it was the first time in her life that...

era la primera vez que Juan veía a Carmen it was the first time Juan had seen Carmen

era más ético de lo que la prensa le daba crédito he was more ethical than the press gave him credit for being

era mi última oportunidad it was my last chance

era oficial 1. it was official **2.** *(él)* he was an officer **3.** *(ella)* she was an officer

era posterior a la guerra post-war era ➤ Era posterior a la Segunda Guerra Mundial Post-World War Two era ▪ Post-World War II era

¿era tan malo? was it that bad?

era una cosa digna de verse ▪ fue digno de verlo that was something to see ▪ it was a sight to see ▪ that was quite a sight ▪ that was a great sight to see

éramos mi hermano y yo there were (just) myself and my brother ▪ there were just my brother and I

éramos pocos y parió la abuela as if we didn't have enough problems already

éramos *x* there were *x* of us ➤ Éramos seis. There were six of us.

eran más de *x* de la tarde it was after *x* in the afternoon ➤ Eran más de las cinco de la tarde. It was after five in the afternoon.

eran sólo las figuraciones mías ▪ eran sólo las imaginaciones mías it was just my imagination

eran sólo las imaginaciones mías ▪ eran sólo las figuraciones mías it was just my imagination

eran *x* there were *x* of them ➤ Eran seis. There were six of them.

éranse una vez there once were ▪ once upon a time there were

érase que se era ▪ érase una vez ▪ había una vez there once was ▪ once upon a time there was ➤ Érase que se era, vivía... Once upon a time there lived...

érase una vez ▪ érase que se era ▪ había una vez there once was ▪ once upon a time ➤ Érase una vez, vivía... Once upon a time there lived...

eres idealista you're an idealist

¡eres insoportable! ▪ ¡eres intolerable! you're unbearable! ▪ you're intolerable!

¡eres intratable! ▪ ¡eres imposible! you're impossible!

eres tan hermosa you are so beautiful

eres tú ▪ ése eres tú you're the one

¿eres tú el de la foto? is that you in the picture? ▪ are you the one in the picture?

¿eres tú la de la foto? is that you in the picture? ▪ are you the one in the picture?

¡eres un fenómeno! you're a winner!

eres un iluso ▪ eres un soñador ▪ ¡eres un iluso! ▪ ¡pobre iluso! ▪ ¡pedazo de iluso! you're a dreamer ▪ you dreamer!

eres un romántico you're a romantic ▪ you're an incurable romantic

eres un soñador ▪ eres un iluso you're a dreamer

erigirse como to rise to the status of ▪ to hold oneself up as ➤ En el siglo diez y nueve, los Estados Unidos se erigió como una potencia mundial. In the nineteenth century, the United States rose to the status of a world power.

errada ortografía spelling mistakes ▪ spelling errors

errar es de humanos to err is human

errar el punto ▪ errar la diana **1.** to miss the target **2.** *(figurativo)* to miss the mark

errar la diana ▪ errar el punto **1.** to miss the target **2.** *(figurativo)* to miss the mark

errar la vocación to make a wrong career choice ▪ to make an incorrect career choice

errar sin rumbo fijo to wander aimlessly

erre que erre: seguir ~ to continue doggedly ▪ to continue stubbornly ▪ to continue pigheadedly

ser un **error garrafal** to be a glaring mistake ▪ to be a glaring error

¿es a lo mejor...? is it perhaps...?

es absurdo ▪ no tiene ni pies ni cabeza ▪ eso no tiene sentido that's absurd

¡es acojonante! ▪ ¡es asombroso! ▪ ¡qué acojonante! ▪ ¡qué asombroso! it's amazing! ▪ that's amazing!

es agua pasada it's water under the bridge

es algo oficial it's official

¿es allí donde...? is that where...? ➤ ¿Es allí donde vive? Is that where he lives?

es así that's how it is ▪ that's the way it is

es así de fácil it's that simple

es así desde el principio ▪ estaba así cuando lo compré ▪ ya era así cuando lo compré it was like that in the beginning ▪ it was like that when I bought it

es así desde siempre it's always been that way

¡es asombroso! that's amazing!

es asunto mío that's my business ▪ it's my business

es aún pronto para saber ▪ es pronto para saber it's still too early to tell ▪ it's too early to tell

¿es blanco, la gallina lo pone, en la sartén se fríe y por la boca se come? do bears live in the woods? ▪ is the pope Catholic? ▪ is a four-pound robin fat?

es bueno volver it's good to be back

es casi seguro que... it's safe to say that... ▪ it's almost certainly true that...

es como si it is as if ▪ it's as if ➤ Cuando la luz pasa a través de la ranura, es como si los electrones fueran ondas, no partículas. When the light passes through a slit, it is as if the electrons were waves, not particles.

es como si no nos conociéramos ▪ es como si fuéramos dos extraños ▪ cualquiera diría que no somos más que extraños it's as if we didn't even know each other ▪ it's as though we didn't even know each other ▪ we might as well be strangers

es correctísimo it's exactly right ▪ that's exactly right

es cosa fácil there's nothing to it ▪ it's easy

es cosa tuya that's your problem

es coser y cantar ▪ es pan comido it's a cinch ▪ it's a piece of cake

es cuenta mía that's my business

es cuestión de gustos ▪ depende de los gustos de cada cual ▪ sobre gustos no hay nada escrito it's a matter of individual tastes

es culpa mía it's my fault

es de dejar en claro que... it should be made clear that...

es de esperarse that's to be expected

es de lo más frustrante it's really frustrating

es de lo que se trata ▪ es de todo lo que se trata that's what it's all about

es de puta madre *(subido de tono)* it's great!

es de suponer que... it's to be expected that...

es de todo lo que se trata ▪ es de lo que se trata that's what it's all about

es decir 1. esto es ▪ o sea that is **2.** quiero decir I mean **3.** en otras palabras in other words

es (demasiado) pronto para saber ▪ es aún pronto para saber ▪ aún no se puede saber it's too early to tell ▪ it's too soon to tell

es demasiado tarde para eso it's too late for that

es difícil ▪ cuesta it's difficult ▪ it's hard ➤ Es difícil distinguir a los gemelos. It's difficult to tell the twins apart.

es difícil creer que pudiera haber sido it's hard to believe that it could have been

es difícil saberlo it's hard to know ▪ it's hard to say

es dudoso que it's doubtful that ➤ Es dudoso que el presidente haya leído alguna vez el documento. It's doubtful that the president has ever read the document.

¿es eficaz? ▪ ¿sirve? ▪ ¿funciona bien? does it work?

es el caso que ▪ el caso es que ▪ el hecho es que the fact is that

¿es el Corte Inglés? is this Corte Ingles?

es el famoso... so this is... ➤ ¡Es el famoso Javier! ¡Hemos oído hablar mucho de ti! So this is Javier! I've heard so much about you! *(Nota: En español siempre se dice "hemos" aun cuando queremos decir "I". ▪ In Spanish, the expression is always "we" even when the person means "I've heard so much about you!")*

¿es grave? is it serious?

es hora de it's time to ➤ Este mantel está hecho trizas. Pienso que es hora de comprar uno nuevo. This tablecloth has been through the mill. I think it's time to get a new one.
es hora de ir it's time to go
es hora de ir a trabajar it's time to go to work
es importante recordar que... it is important to remember that... ▪ it's important to remember that...
es importante recordarles (a ustedes) que... it is important to remind you that...
es inaudito it's unheard of
es indudable que... unquestionably... ➤ Pero es indudable que... But unquestionably...
es interesante hablar con él he's interesting to talk to
es interesante hablar con ella she's interesting to talk to
es inútil 1. it's useless 2. it's hopeless
es justo decir que... it's fair to say that...
¡es la famosa...! so this is...! ➤ ¡Es la famosa Susana! ¡Hemos oído hablar mucho de ti! So this is Susana! I've heard a lot about you! *(Nota: En español siempre se dice "hemos" aun cuando queremos decir "I". ▪ In Spanish, the expression is alway "we" even when the person means "I've heard so much about you!")*
es la primera vez que veo esto ▪ es la primera vez que lo veo it's the first time I've ever seen that ➤ Es la primera vez en mi vida que veo esto. ▪ Es la primera vez en mi vida que lo veo. It's the first time in my life I've every seen that.
¿es la residencia García Pérez? is this the García Pérez residence?
es largo de contar it's a long story
es lo menos que podía hacer (yo) that's the least I could do ▪ it's the least I could do
es lo menos que puedo hacer that's the least I can do ▪ it's the least I can do
es lo mismo ▪ da lo mismo it doesn't make any difference
es lo primero ▪ es lo principal that's the main thing
es lo principal ▪ es lo primero that's the main thing
es mal momento it's the wrong time ▪ this is the wrong time ➤ No puedo plantearlo ahora; es mal momento. I can't bring it up now; this is the wrong time.
es más 1. besides ▪ furthermore 2. y también and also
es más fácil decirlo que hacerlo ▪ del dicho al hecho hay largo trecho it's easier said than done
es más sano(-a) it's better for you ▪ it's healthier
es más sensato (hacer algo) it makes more sense (to do something) ▪ it's better to
es matemático it's guaranteed ➤ Es matemático... It's guaranteed, the wind blows the minute you leave the hairdresser's.
es mejor que nada ▪ *(Esp.)* menos da una piedra it's better than nothing
es mi deber ▪ es mi obligación it is my duty ▪ it's my duty
es mi hora it's my time ▪ my time has come
es mi obligación ▪ es mi deber it is my duty ▪ it's my duty ➤ Es mi obligación informarles de... It is my duty to inform you of... ➤ Es mi obligación informarles de que... It is my duty to inform you that...
es mucho camino it's a long way
es muy amable por su parte that's very kind of you ▪ it's very kind of you
¡es muy chuli! *(Esp., jerga)* ▪ es guay ▪ es chachi it's cool! ▪ that's cool!
es muy largo de contar it's a very long story
es muy propio de él it's just like him
es oficial 1. it's official 2. *(él)* he's an officer 3. *(ella)* she's an officer
es otra historia ▪ es otro cantar that's another story
es otro cantar that's another story ▪ that's a different story
es para gritar it's enough to make you scream
es para llorar it's enough to make you cry
es para salir corriendo it just makes you want to run away
es para salir llorando it's enough to make you leave in tears
es para salir más que a prisa it just makes you want to get the hell out of there
es para salir pitando it makes you want to get the hell out of there ▪ to make one antsy to leave ➤ Esta reunión es para salir pitando. This meeting makes me want to get the hell out of here. ▪ This meeting makes me antsy to leave.
es para ver 1. *(yo)* I'll have to wait and see 2. *(nosotros)* we'll have to wait and see
es para verlo you have to see it (to understand) ▪ you have to experience it (firsthand)
es peor el remedio que la enfermedad the cure is worse than the disease
es por demás que haga algo It's useless to do anything
es por eso que that is why ▪ that's why
es por lo que that's why ▪ that's the reason why ➤ Es por lo que quería venir a España. That's why I wanted to come to Spain.
es por su propio bien it's for your own good
es posible que no vaya it's possible that I won't go
es probable que it is probable that ▪ it is likely that
es pronto para saber ▪ es aún pronto para saber it's too early to tell ▪ it's still too early to tell
es propicio para... it's a good time to... ➤ Este mes es propicio para prepararse para el invierno. This month is a good time to start preparing for winter.
es pura sugestión it's all in your mind
es que... 1. it's that... 2. *(en situaciones de justificación)* si but ➤ Es que no me da tiempo. It's that I don't have time. ➤ Es que (yo) no quería hacerlo. ▪ Si no quería. But I didn't want to.
es que no doy abasto I just can't cope
es quien es he is what he is ▪ she is what she is
es recomendable (it) is recommended ➤ Es recomendable un enchufe con toma de tierra. A grounded outlet is recommended.
es sólo la punta del iceberg that's just the tip of the iceberg
es tan sencillo como eso it's as simple as that
es temprano it is early (in the morning) ▪ it's early (in the morning)
es todo acostumbrarse it's just a matter of getting used to it
es todo lo contrario it's just the opposite
es todo lo que llevo encima it's all I've got on me
es tres cuartos de los mismos it amounts to the same thing ▪ it's six of one and half a dozen of the other
es un camino que hemos recorrido antes *(literal y figurativo)* ▪ es un camino que ya hemos recorrido it's a road we've been down before ▪ we've been down this road before
es un capítulo aparte that's another thing altogether ▪ that's something else again
es un conocido I recognize him
es un coñazo *(Esp., subido de tono)* 1. *(él)* he's a pain in the ass 2. *(ella)* she's a pain in the ass
es un coñazo de concierto *(Esp., subido de tono)* it's a lousy concert
es un coñazo de conferencia *(Esp., subido de tono)* it's a lousy lecture
es un coñazo de programa *(Esp., subido de tono)* it's a lousy program
es un coñazo de tío *(Esp., subido de tono)* he's a pain in the ass
es un deber que tiene consigo mismo he owes it to himself
es un deber que tienes contigo mismo you owe it to yourself
es un halago it's a compliment
es un hecho conocido que it's a known fact that
es un hecho real it's a true story
es un martirio ▪ es un tormento it's torture
es un patrón que tiene 1. *(él)* it's a pattern of his ▪ it's a pattern that he has 2. *(ella)* it's a pattern of hers ▪ it's a pattern that she has
es un poco tramposo it's a little tricky
es un privilegio it is a privilege ▪ I feel privileged
es un prodigio 1. *(él)* he's a prodigy 2. *(ella)* she's a prodigy
es un soplo it's a breeze ▪ it's a piece of cake ▪ it's easy as pie
es un tanto prematuro it's a little premature ▪ it's a little early
¡es un tormento! ▪ ¡es un martirio! it's torture!
es un tostón it's a hassle ▪ it's a pain ▪ it's a drag

es una bobada it's silly

es una buena señal it's a good sign ▪ that's a good sign

es una conocida I recognize her

es una delicia ▪ es una gozada 1. *(persona)* he's delightful 2. *(comida)* it's delicious

es una faena 1. es una lástima it's too bad ▪ that's too bad ▪ it's the pits 2. es un rollo it's a hassle ▪ it's the pits ➤ Es una faena que no te dejen salir de vacaciones en agosto. It's the pits that they won't let you take your vacation in August.

es una gozada to be (very) enjoyable ▪ to be a (real) treat ➤ Es una gozada conversar con personas inteligentes. It's enjoyable to talk with intelligent people. ➤ El concierto fue una gozada. The concert was a real treat.

es una lástima it's a pity ▪ it's too bad ▪ it's a shame

es una mujer diez she's a ten

es una pena that's too bad

es una pena que... it's too bad that... ▪ it's a pity that...

¡es una raya más para el tigre! what the heck! ▪ I might as well!

es una risa it's a joke ▪ it's laughable ➤ Ir a urgencias en cierto hospital de cuyo nombre no quiero acordarme, es una risa: te tienen esperando hasta la medianoche. The emergency room of a certain hospital whose name I'd rather not recall is a joke: they keep you waiting until midnight.

es una sorpresa permanente it never ceases to amaze me

es una suerte para él que it's lucky for him that

es una temeridad, usted no está para estas cosas it's folly, you are not cut out for these things

es uno por demás that's going too far

es ya de días it's an old one

es *x* horas más tarde it's *x* hours later ➤ Es seis horas más tarde en Madrid que en Nueva York. It's six hours later in Madrid than in New York.

es *x* horas más temprano it's *x* hours earlier ➤ Es seis horas más temprano en Nueva York que en Madrid. It's six hours earlier in New York than in Madrid.

esa noche that night

esbozar iniciativas legislativas to map out legislative initiatives ➤ El presidente electo recibió los líderes del Congreso para esbozar sus primeras iniciativas legislativas. The president elect received Congressional leaders to map out his first legislative initiatives.

esbozar una sonrisa to smile faintly

escabullirse de alguien to slip out of the grasp of someone ▪ to slip out of someone's grasp

escabullirse de hacer algo ▪ escaparse de hacer algo ▪ *(Esp.)* escaquearse de hacer algo to get out of doing something ➤ Se escabulló de sus deudas. She skipped out on her debts.

escabullirse en la multitud to slip through the crowd ➤ Me escabullí en la multitud para volver pronto. I slipped through the crowd (in order) to return quickly.

escabullirse entre la multitud to disappear into the crowd ➤ Me escabullí entre la multitud para que no me vieran. I disappeared into the crowd to that they wouldn't see me.

escala salarial pay scale

escala técnica: hacer una ~ to make a refueling stop ▪ to stop for refueling

escalada al estrellato rise to stardom

escalada (en rocas) rock climbing

estar **escalando las murallas para escapar de allí** ▪ estar saltando las murallas para escapar de allí to be climbing the walls to get out of there

escalar al jefe to go to the boss ▪ to take one's case to the boss ▪ to appeal to the boss

escalar una montaña ▪ subir una montaña to climb a mountain

escalera de caracol spiral staircase

escalera de color color chart ▪ fan deck

un **escalofrío recorrió mi cuerpo** a cold shiver ran through my body ▪ a chill ran through my body

el **escalón de una operación** phase of an operation

escapar ileso ▪ escapar indemne ▪ escapar incólume to escape without injury ▪ to escape uninjured ▪ to escape unhurt ▪ to escape unharmed

escapar incólumne *(culto)* ▪ escapar indemne to escape unscathed

escapar indemne ▪ escapar incólumne to escape unscathed

escapar por los pelos to escape by the skin of one's teeth

escaparse a su control to be beyond one's control ▪ to be out of one's control ➤ Se escapa a mi control. It's out of my control.

escaparse al control de uno to be beyond one's control ➤ Detener el proceso se escapa a su control. Stopping the process is beyond his control.

escaparse con alguien ▪ fugarse con alguien to run off with someone ➤ El jefe se escapó con su secretaria. The boss ran off with his secretary.

escapársele to escape one's notice

escapársele algo to exclaim something without thinking

escapársele de las manos ▪ írsele de las manos to slip away from one ▪ to slip through one's fingers ▪ to get away from one ➤ It slipped away from us. Se nos ha escapado de las manos. ▪ Se nos ha ido de las manos.

escapársele la lengua to elude one ▪ to escape one ▪ to be right on the tip of one's tongue

escaquearse de algo to get out of (doing) something ➤ Estoy intentando escaquearme. I'm trying to get out of it. ▪ I'm trying to get out of doing it.

escaquearse de hacer algo *(Esp., coloquial)* ▪ zafarse de hacer algo ▪ evitar hacer algo ▪ intentar no hacer algo to (try to) get out of doing something ▪ to avoid doing something ➤ Mi compañero de trabajo está siempre escaqueándose. My co-worker always tries to get out of doing things. ▪ My co-worker always tries to avoid doing things. ➤ Se escaquea de pagar siempre que puede. He avoids paying whenever he can.

escaramuza fronteriza border skirmish

escarbar en la herida to rub salt into a wound

escarbar en una vieja herida to re-open an old wound

escarbar la conciencia to sting one's conscience ▪ to make one feel guilty ▪ to prick one's conscience

escarceo amoroso ▪ escarceos amorosos flirtation

escarmentar en cabeza ajena to learn from the mistakes of others ▪ to learn from other people's mistakes

escasa mayoría scant majority ▪ bare majority ▪ narrow majority ▪ slim majority

escasa participación de electores ▪ baja concurrencia de votantes ▪ elevada abstención (de votantes) low voter turnout ▪ light voter turnout ▪ high voter abstention

escasa visibilidad poor visibility

escasas pistas few clues

escasear algo a consecuencia de to become scarce because of ➤ Empieza a escasear el agua a consecuencia de la sequía. Water is becoming scarce because of the drought.

la **escasez de** ▪ carestía de shortage of ▪ scarcity of

la **escasez de agua** ▪ falta de agua water shortage

la **escasez de glóbulos blancos** low white (blood) cell count

la **escasez de puestos de trabajo** job shortage

escena callejera *(pintura)* street scene

escena de un crimen ▪ escenario de un crimen scene of a crime

escena de una batalla ▪ escenario de una batalla scene of a battle ➤ El valle Shenandoah fue la escena de muchas batallas de la guerra civil norteamericana. The Shenandoah Valley was the scene of many American Civil War battles.

escena retrospectiva ▪ (el) analepsis flashback

escenario de un crimen ▪ escena de un crimen scene of a crime

escenario de una batalla ▪ escena de una batalla scene of a battle

escindirse en facciones ▪ dividirse en facciones to split (up) into factions ▪ to splinter into factions ▪ to divide (up) into factions

escisión nuclear nuclear fission

escisión política political splintering

esclarecer la autoría to solve the crime ■ to determine who did it ■ to identify the culprit ➤ Mandaron al FBI para esclarecer la autoría del bombardeo. They sent in the FBI to determine who planted the bomb.

esclarecer un asunto to clear up a matter

escocerle los ojos ■ picarle los ojos to sting one's eyes ■ (for) one's eyes to sting ■ (for) one's eyes to burn ■ (for) one's eyes to smart ➤ Este champú no escuece los ojos. This shampoo doesn't sting your eyes. ➤ Me escuecen los ojos. My eyes are stinging. ■ My eyes are burning. ■ My eyes are smarting.

escolarización obligatoria ■ escolarización mandatoria compulsory schooling ■ compulsory education

escoger a alguien a dedo ■ eligir a alguien a dedo to choose from among an inner circle ■ to choose someone one already knows

escoger al azar to select at random ■ to choose at random ■ *(informal)* to pick (out) at random

escoger ropa a dedo ■ elegir ropa a dedo to choose clothes without trying them on

escoger entre to choose between ■ to pick out

escollo de las negociaciones the stumbling block in the negotiations

esconder la cabeza y las patas to draw in one's head and feet ➤ La tortuga escondió la cabeza y las patas. The turtle drew in its head and feet.

esconderse detrás de algo ■ ocultarse detrás de algo to hide behind something

escorar un avión to bank an airplane ➤ El piloto escoró (el avión) a la izquierda. The pilot banked (the airplane) to the left.

escorarse a la derecha to bank (over) to the right ➤ La avioneta se escoró a la derecha. The (light) airplane banked (over) to the right. ■ The (light) plane banked over to the right.

escorarse a la izquierda to bank (over) to the left ➤ El avión se escoró a la izquierda. The airplane banked (over) to the left. ■ The plane banked (over) to the left.

escoria de la sociedad dregs of society

escribir a máquina con dos dedos to hunt and peck

escribir al correr de la pluma ■ componer al correr de la pluma ■ escribir a vuela pluma ■ componer a vuela pluma to dash off *(Nota: Carta, poema, ensayo, etc.)*

escribir con humo en el cielo to skywrite

escribir en la arena 1. to write in the sand 2. estar perdiendo el tiempo to be wasting one's time ➤ *(tú)* Estás escribiendo en la arena ■ *(usted)* (Usted) está escribiendo en la arena. ■ You're (just) wasting your time.

escribir uno mismo sus canciones to write one's own songs ➤ La cantante escribe ella misma sus canciones. The singer writes her own songs.

escribirse con ■ deletrearse con to be spelled with ➤ Se escribe con una *y*. ■ Se deletrea con una *y*. It's spelled with a *y*.

escribirse el uno al otro to write to each other

escribirse por sí mismo ■ escribirse por sí solo to write itself ➤ *(Richard Rodgers)* Cuando se pone alguna letra de Hammerstein al piano, la canción se escribe por sí misma. ■ Cuando se pone alguna letra de Hammerstein al piano, la canción se escribe por sí sola. When you put a Hammerstein lyric on the piano, the song writes itself.

escrito de discrepancia *(Tribunal Supremo de EE UU)* dissenting opinion ■ minority opinion ➤ En el escrito de discrepancia firmado por los tres magistrados... In the dissenting opinion signed by the three justices... ■ In the minority opinion signed by the three justices...

escrito lo trae en la frente *(de él)* it's written all over his face ■ *(de ella)* it's written all over her face

estar **escrito que...** 1. to be written that... ■ to be in writing that... 2. estar decidido que... to be decided that...

escrutar votos to count votes ■ to tally votes ■ to tally the vote

escuadrilla de aviones squadron of airplanes ■ squadron of planes

escucha telefónica telephone tap

escuchar sin resollar ■ escuchar sin decir palabra to listen without saying a word ■ to listen with bated breath

escuela de enseñanza media middle school ■ junior high school

escuela de oficios trade school

escuela superior ■ preparatoria ■ secundaria ■ *(Esp.)* instituto high school

escupir ceniza *(volcán)* to belch ash ■ to spew ash

escupir humo ■ expulsar humo to belch smoke ➤ Los camiones y autobuses escupían humo de gasoil. The trucks and buses were belching diesel smoke. ➤ Las chimeneas industriales de las acerías solían escupir humo, dejando una patina por todo el polígono industrial. The smoke stacks of the steel mills used to belch smoke, leaving a patina all over the industrial zone.

Escurridizo Willy *(Bill Clinton, para sus enemigos)* Slick Willy

escurrir el bulto ■ esquivar el bulto 1. to weasel out of doing something ■ to duck out 2. evitar el tema to avoid the issue ■ to avoid the subject ➤ No escurras el bulto. ■ No esquives el bulto. Don't avoid the issue.

escurrir el líquido to drain off the liquid ■ to drain the liquid off ➤ Después de triturar el pimiento y la cebolla escurra el exceso de líquido. After pureeing the pepper and onion, drain off the excess liquid.

escurrírsele entre los dedos to slip through one's fingers ➤ El tiempo se me escurrió entre los dedos. The time slipped through my fingers.

ese algo that something

ése eres tú ■ eres tú you're the one ➤ *(melodía de Sesame Street)* Rubber Ducky ése eres tú. Rubber Ducky, you're the one.

ese lunar que tienes, Cielito Lindo, junto a la boca, no se lo des a nadie, que a mí me toca *Cielito Lindo* that beauty spot that you have, Cielito Lindo, beside your mouth, don't give it to anyone, because it belongs to me

ese mismo día that very day ■ that same day

ése no era el trato that wasn't the deal ■ that's not what we agreed on ■ that's not what we agreed to ■ that wasn't what we agreed on ■ that wasn't what we agreed to

ese número se multiplica por *x* the number is *x* times that ➤ El ejército insiste en que ese número se multiplica por diez. The army insists that the number is ten times that.

la **esencia viene en frascos pequeños** good things come in small packages

ser **esencial** to be essential ■ to be critical ➤ En el acueducto de Segovia toda piedra es esencial. In the Segovia aqueduct, every single stone is essential. ■ In the Segovia aqueduct, every single stone is critical.

esfera celeste celestial sphere

esforzarse para ■ hacer un esfuerzo para to make an effort to

esfuerzo diplomático: desplegar un ~ ■ desplegar una labor diplomática to launch a diplomatic effort

esfumarse en la oscuridad to fade into the darkness

esgrimir la espada to draw the sword

eslabón perdido missing link

esmalte sintético latex enamel

esmerarse en hacer algo to take great pains to do something ■ to go to great pains to do something ➤ El chico se esmeró en hacer que la maqueta de la avioneta pareciera auténtica. The boy went to great pains to make the airplane model look completely authentic.

esmerarse para hacer algo to take great pains to do something ■ to go all out to do something

esmerarse para que... to take great pains so that... ■ to go all out so that... ➤ La gente se esmera de verdad para que sus decoraciones sean las mejores. The people really go all out so that their decorations will be the best ones.

eso creía, por lo menos that's what I thought, anyway ■ that's what I thought, at any rate

eso de the matter of ■ the business of ■ this business of ■ that business about

eso de tener que having to

eso depende that depends ■ that all depends ■ it depends

¡eso digo yo! that's what *I* say!

eso equivale a 1. that is equivalent to ■ that amounts to ■ that is tantamount to 2. igual valdría que might as well ➤ Eso equivale a que se queden con todo nuestro dinero. They might as well take all our money.

eso es ■ efectivamente that's right ■ right! ■ correct! ■ that's it

eso es harina de otra costal that's a different kettle of fish

eso es justo lo que pensaba that's just what I was thinking
eso es lo mismo que... that's like... ➤ Eso es lo mismo que decir que... That's like saying...
eso es lo mismo que pretender alcanzar el cielo con las manos that's like trying to reach the sky with your hands ▪ that's impossible
eso es lo que pensaba yo that's what I was thinking
eso es lo que me temía that's what I was afraid of
eso es lo que me temo that's what I'm afraid of
¡eso es lo único que me faltaba! ▪ ¡eso faltaba! that's the last thing I needed! ▪ that was the last thing I needed!
eso es lo último que me esperaba that's the last thing I expected
(eso) es mejor que nada ▪ más vale algo que nada ▪ poco es algo, menos es nada ▪ *(Esp.)* menos da una piedra it's better than nothing
¡eso es mentira! that's a lie!
eso es muy opinable that's debatable
eso es otra cosa that's different
eso es otro canto ▪ otro gallo está cantando that's a different story ▪ that's another story
eso espero ▪ espero que sí I hope so
eso está hecho consider it done
¡eso faltaba! ▪ ¡eso es lo único que me faltaba! that's the last thing I needed! ▪ that was the last thing I needed!
eso fue lo que quise decirte that's what I wanted to tell you ▪ that was what I wanted to tell you
eso hizo el truco that did the trick
eso le pasa hasta al más pintado it happens to the best of us
eso lo dice todo ▪ con eso queda todo dicho that says it all
eso lo resume todo that sums it up
eso me recuerda... that reminds me...
eso no dice mucho a favor de... that doesn't say much for...
(eso) no es decir gran cosa that's not saying a whole lot ▪ that's not saying much
¿eso no más? that's all?
eso no me atañe that's not my concern
eso no tiene ni pies ni cabeza ▪ es absurdo that makes absolutely no sense ▪ that makes no sense whatever ▪ that's absurd
eso no tiene sentido that doesn't make (any) sense ▪ that makes no sense
eso no viene al caso ▪ no viene al cuento ▪ eso no viene al tema ▪ no es relevante that's beside the point ▪ that has nothing to do with it ▪ that's irrelevant
eso no viene al cuento ▪ eso no viene al caso ▪ eso no viene al tema ▪ no es relevante that's beside the point ▪ that has nothing to do with it ▪ that's irrelevant
eso no viene al tema ▪ eso no viene al caso ▪ eso no viene al cuento ▪ no es relevante that's beside the point ▪ that has nothing to do with it ▪ that's irrelevant
eso parece so it seems
eso que ▪ lo que what
eso queda por ver ▪ está por ver that remains to be seen
(eso) se dice pronto ▪ es más fácil decirlo que hacerlo ▪ del dicho al hecho hay un largo trecho to be easier said than done ➤ Es más fácil decirlo que hacerlo. It's easier said than done. ▪ That's easier said than done.
eso si 1. that being the case 2. *(seguido de una cláusula subjuntiva)* if one did something at all ➤ Sólo pediría días libres por una buena razón, eso si los pido. I would request time off only for a very good reason, if at all. ➤ *(Selecciones de Reader's Digest)* Si mi marido saltara en paracaídas, eso si llegara a saltar, sería porque el avión estaría a punto de estrellarse. If my husband took a parachute jump at all, it would be because the airplane was going to crash.
¡eso sí que fue rápido! that was quick!
eso sí que no that's not the point (at all) ▪ you're missing the point ▪ that completely misses the point
¡eso sí que no! ▪ ¡seguro que no! definitely not! ▪ that's out of the question! ▪ *(coloquial)* come on, get real!
¡eso sí que se llama... now that's what I call... ▪ now that's what you call...
¡eso sí que se llama hablar! *now* you're talking!
eso también va por ti ▪ eso va por ti también that goes for you, too ▪ that means you, too
eso te lo tienes que pagar tú that's the price you have to pay
eso te pasa por... ▪ te está bien empleado por that's what happens when... ▪ that's what you get for...
eso va a misa ▪ eso es lo que vamos a hacer that's what we're going to do
eso va por ti también ▪ eso también va por ti that goes for you, too ▪ that means you, too
eso ya es algo that's really something ▪ that's something
¡espabílate! get with it!
espacio de almacenamiento storage space
espacio en blanco blank space
espacio exterior outer space ▪ deep space
espacio sideral outer space
espacio-tiempo *(física)* space-time
espacio vital living space
espada de Damocles sword of Damocles ▪ constant threat
espalda con espalda ▪ espalda contra espalda ▪ trasero contra trasero ▪ *(coloquial)* ▪ culo con culo back to back
espalda contra espalda ▪ espalda con espalda ▪ trasero contra trasero ▪ *(coloquial)* ▪ culo con culo back to back
espalda tensa ▪ espalda en tensión ▪ espalda rígida stiff back ➤ Mi espalda está tensa. ▪ Mi espalda está en tensión. ▪ Mi espalda está rígida. My back is stiff.
espaldas mojadas wetbacks
espantar las moscas to shoo the flies
español chapurreado broken Spanish
español normativo standard Spanish
esparcir la vista *(literario)* ▪ mirar al rededor to look around
esparcir las cenizas de alguien to scatter someone's ashes ➤ Las cenizas del dramaturgo serán esparcidas en el Mediterráneo. The playwright's ashes will be scattered in the Mediterranean.
esparcir pintura encima de todo ▪ esparcir pintura por todas partes ▪ manchar todo de pintura to get paint all over everything
una **especie de** a kind of ▪ like a
espectáculo de magia magic show
espectáculo estrambótico freak show
espectro electromagnético electromagnetic spectrum
especular sobre to speculate about
espejismo de que... wishful thought that... ▪ wishful thinking that...
espejo de cuerpo entero full-length mirror
espejo retrovisor rear-view mirror
¡espera! wait!
espera a ver que... ▪ espérate a ver que... wait till you see what... ▪ wait'll you see what...
espera hasta que te diga lo que... *(yo)* wait till I tell you what...
¡(espera, que) ahora vengo! *(Esp.)* ▪ ¡en seguida vuelvo! ▪ ¡vuelvo en un momento! ▪ *(especialmente L.am.)* ¡en seguida regreso! ▪ ¡regreso en un momento! I'll be right back!
(espera) un momento wait a moment ▪ wait a second ▪ hold on a second
¡espera y verás! wait and see!
esperaba haber sabido de ti a estas alturas I had expected to hear from you by now
esperamos que tu viaje sea agradable we hope you have a pleasant trip
estar **esperando a que alguien haga algo** to be waiting for someone to do something ➤ Estoy esperando a que él me llame. I'm waiting for him to call me.
estar **esperando entre bastidores** to be waiting in the wings
esperando recibir noticias suyas *(despedida de carta comercial)* ▪ quedo a la espera de noticias suyas I look forward to hearing from you
estar **esperando un niño** ▪ estar esperando un bebé ▪ estar esperando un hijo ▪ tener un bebé en camino ▪ tener un hijo en camino to be expecting a baby ▪ to be expecting a child ▪ to have a baby on the way ▪ to have a child on the way

las **esperanzas se desvanecen de (que)...** ▪ las esperanzas se esfuman de (que)... hopes are fading that... ➤ Las esperanzas se desvanecen de que se pueda acordar la paz para la Navidad. Hopes are fading that a peace agreement can be reached by Christmas. ▪ Hopes that a peace agreement can be reached by Christmas are fading.

las **esperanzas se esfuman de (que)...** ▪ las esperanzas se desvanecen de (que)... hopes are fading that... ➤ Se esfuman las esperanzas de encontrar a los mineros atrapados con vida. Hopes of finding the trapped miners alive are fading

esperar a to wait until ▪ to wait till ➤ Tendrás que esperar al lunes próximo para... You'll have to wait till Monday to...

esperar a alguien to wait for someone

esperar a alguien que le lleve a uno ▪ esperar a alguien que le transporte a uno to be waiting for a ride ➤ Espero a alguien que me lleve. ▪ Espero a alguien que me transporte. I'm waiting for a ride.

esperar a que... 1. to anticipate that... ▪ to expect that... 2. to wait until ▪ to wait till ▪ to wait for (it) to... ➤ Los pilotos esperan a que cambie el tiempo. The pilots are waiting for the weather to change. ➤ Espera a que te dé el visto bueno. ▪ Espera hasta que te dé el visto bueno. Wait until I give you the go-ahead. ▪ Wait till I give you the go-ahead. ➤ ¡Espera a que te cuente lo que hizo el jefe en la reunión! Wait till I tell you what the boss did in the meeting! ➤ Tendrás que esperar al lunes próximo para... You'll have to wait until next Monday to...

esperar a que alguien haga algo ▪ esperar hasta que alguien haga algo to wait for someone to do something

esperar afuera to wait outside

esperar con ansia ▪ tener mucha ilusión para to look forward to ▪ to be anxious to ➤ Espero con ansia tu respuesta. I'm looking forward to your reply.

esperar desesperando to hope against hope

esperar el momento oportuno ▪ aguantar la laucha to bide one's time

esperar el pistoletazo de salida para to wait for the green light to ▪ to wait for the go-ahead to

esperar en alguien 1. to put one's hopes in someone 2. *(confianza, fe)* to put one's trust in someone ▪ to put one's faith in someone

esperar hasta que alguien haga algo ▪ esperar a que alguien haga algo to wait for someone to do something

esperar hasta el último momento to wait until the last minute

esperar hasta que... ▪ esperar a que... to wait until... ▪ to wait till... ➤ Espera hasta que te dé el visto bueno. ▪ Espera a que te dé el visto bueno. Wait until I give the go-ahead. ▪ Wait till I give you the go-ahead.

esperar hasta última hora to wait until the last minute

esperar horas to wait for hours

esperar los resultados de las pruebas médicas to wait for the results of the medical tests ▪ to await the results of the medical tests

esperar que... to expect that... ➤ Esperan que el tiempo cambie para mañana. They expect the weather to change by tomorrow.

esperar su turno to wait one's turn

esperar terminar algo to expect to finish something ▪ to expect to have something finished ▪ to expect to have something done ▪ to anticipate having something finished ➤ Espero terminar esto para el dieciocho. I expect to finish this by the eighteenth. ▪ I expect to have this finished by the eighteenth. ▪ I expect to have this done by the eighteenth. ▪ I anticipate having this finished by the eighteenth.

esperar *x* minutos por to wait *x* minutes for

espérate a ver qué... ▪ espera a ver qué... wait till you see what... ▪ wait'll you see what...

espere hasta que le diga lo que... wait till I tell you what...

espero fuera I'll wait outside

espero haber... I hope to have... ➤ Espero haber terminado para finales de abril. I hope to have finished by the end of April.

espero haber sido de alguna ayuda ▪ espero haber sido útil I hope I've helped you ▪ I hope I've been a help

espero haber sido útil ▪ espero haber sido de alguna ayuda I hope I've helped you ▪ I hope I've been a help

espero lo estés pasando bien I hope everything's going okay

espero no... ▪ ojalá no... I hope I don't... ➤ Espero no tener que levantarme temprano mañana. ▪ Ojalá no tenga que levantarme temprano mañana. I hope I don't have to get up early tomorrow.

espero que cumpla *(él)* I hope he does (what he said he would) ▪ I hope he comes through ▪ *(ella)* I hope she does (what she said she would) ▪ I hope she comes through

espero que la respuesta sea fenomenal *(en una carta, por ejemplo)* great, I hope ➤ ¿Qué tal te va todo? Espero que la respuesta sea fenomenal. How's everything going? Great, I hope.

espero que sí ▪ eso espero I hope so

espero que siga así I hope it stays that way

espero que te vayan bien las cosas ▪ espero lo estés pasando bien I hope things are going well for you

espero que venga 1. *(él)* I hope he comes 2. *(ella)* I hope she comes

espero una llamada I'm expecting a call

espesos bosques ▪ tupido bosque dense woods

espesura del bosque: en la ~ in the depths of the forest ▪ in the forest depths

espetarle a alguien algo 1. contrar de buenas a primeras to blurt out something at someone 2. sacar una tema inesperadamente to spring something on someone

espíritu de ayuda spirit of helpfulness

espíritu maligno evil spirit

esplanada del bosque ▪ claro del bosque clearing in the woods ▪ clearing in the forest

ser **espoleado por alguien** to be spurred on by someone ➤ *(noticia)* Turbas espoleadas por Mugabe matan a otro granjero blanco en Zimbabue. Mobs spurred on by Mugabe kill another white farmer in Zimbabwe.

espolear a alguien to spur someone on ▪ to get someone going

espolear al caballo ▪ clavarle espuelas al caballo ▪ meterle espuelas al caballo ▪ picar al caballo to spur the horse

esporas de ántrax anthrax spores

esqueleto de un edificio framework of a building

el **esquema de las cosas** scheme of things ➤ Tiene poca importancia en el esquema eterno de las cosas. It has little importance in the eternal scheme of things.

esquema métrico rhyme scheme ➤ El esquema métrico es ABBA. The rhyme scheme is ABBA.

esquilar ovejas ▪ trasquilar ovejas to shear sheep

esquilmar recursos naturales ▪ agotar recursos naturales to use up natural resources ▪ to exhaust natural resources

esquivar el asunto ▪ evitar el tema to dodge the issue ▪ to avoid the issue ➤ No esquives el asunto. ▪ No evites el tema. Don't dodge the issue. ▪ Don't avoid the issue.

esquivar el bulto ▪ escurrir el bulto 1. to dodge the issue ▪ to avoid the issue 2. escabullirse de hacer algo to weasel out of doing something ➤ No esquives el bulto. ▪ No escurras el bulto. Don't avoid the issue.

esquivar las llamadas telefónicas to dodge telephone calls

esquivar los coches to dodge (the) traffic

esquivar para no chocar con un vehículo que viene en el sentido opuesto to swerve to miss an oncoming vehicle

esquivar una pregunta to dodge a question ▪ to evade a question

¿está abierto(-a)? *(en inglés se usa la segunda persona)* are you open?

está atascado *(videocasete, etc.)* ▪ se ha atascado it's stuck ▪ it's jammed

está bien ▪ no pasa nada ▪ no importa ▪ no hay problema that's okay

está bien que uno... it is right for one to... ▪ it's right for one to...

está bien que uno no... it is right for one not to ▪ it's right for one not to...

está buena *(algo subido de tono)* she's somebody I'd like to go to bed with ▪ she's worth one

está bueno *(algo subido de tono)* he's somebody I'd like to go to bed with ▪ he's worth one

está circulando el rumor que... the rumor is going around that...

está comunicando *(Esp.)* ■ la línea está ocupada the line is busy

esta cuestión presenta dos aspectos there are two sides to this issue

está en la mera esquina it's right on the corner

¡está en su casa! ■ ¡está usted en su casa! make yourself at home!

está entorpeciendo el camino ■ está estorbando it's in the way

esta es la primera vez que... this is the first time that... ➤ Esta es la primera vez que he comido criadillas. This is the first time I've (ever) eaten mountain oysters.

está estorbando ■ está entorpeciendo el camino it's in the way ■ it's blocking the way

esta idea salió de (Paco) it was (Frank's) idea

está justo aquí it's right here

está lloviendo it's raining

está lloviendo desde hace una semana it has been raining for a week ■ it's been raining for a week

está más allá de mí ■ no tengo idea ■ me supera it's beyond me ■ I haven't the slightest (idea)

está medio complicado ■ está un poco complicado ■ está un cachito complicado ■ está un tantito complicado it's a little bit complicated

esta misma mañana just this morning ■ this very morning

está muy espeso(-a) 1. *(salsa)* it's very thick 2. *(neblina)* it's very dense ■ it's like pea soup (out there)

esta noche tonight

está nublado it is cloudy ■ it's cloudy

está por todo el pueblo it's all over town

está por verse ■ eso queda por verse that remains to be seen

está que apesta it stinks ■ it reeks ■ it smells to high heaven

está que arde 1. *(él)* he's furious 2. *(ella)* she's furious 3. *(comida)* ■ está que quema it's burning my mouth ■ my mouth is on fire

está que brinca ■ estar que trina to be hopping mad

está que bufa 1. estar que hiede ■ estar que huele ■ estar que apesta to stink ■ to reek ■ to smell to high heaven 2. *(Arg.)* estar enojado to be in a huff

está que da pena to be in bad shape ■ to be in a sad state

está que echa chispas to be fuming mad

está que echa las muelas to be mad as a hornet ■ to be hopping mad

está que muerde to be mad as hell

está que se le cae la baba to dote on ➤ Están que se les cae la baba con el niño. They dote on the baby.

está que se sale 1. dar lo mejor de sí mismo ■ dar lo mejor de uno mismo ■ estar al cien por cien to be at one's best 2. *(subido de tono)* ■ tener buenas domingas ■ tiene buenas chiches to be stacked ■ to have big boobs ■ to have a nice pair ➤ Los candidatos estaban que se salían durante el debate. ■ Los candidatos dieron lo mejor de sí mismos durante el debate. ■ Los candidatos estuvieron al cien por cien durante el debate. The candidates were at their best during the debate.

está que se sube por las paredes to go through the roof ■ to lose one's temper

está que trina ■ estar que brinca to be hopping mad

está tardando *(él)* he's late ■ he's running late *(ella)* she's late ■ she's running late

está todo bajo control ■ está todo controlado everything is under control ■ everything's under control

está todo controlado ■ está todo bajo control everything is under control ■ everything's under control

esta vez this time

esta vez, no not this time

estaba a lo mío cuando I was minding my own business when

estaba así cuando lo compré ■ ya estaba así cuando lo compré it was like that when I bought it

estaba llegando a casa cuando... 1. *(yo)* I was just getting home when... 2. *(él)* he was just getting home when... 3. *(ella)* she was just getting home when...

estaba pensado que ■ se pensaba que ■ se creía que it was thought that

¡estaba riquísimo! that was delicious!

estaba siendo was being ➤ El barco estaba siendo remolcado hacia un puerto francés. The boat was being towed to a French port.

establecer el récord to set the record

establecer un lazo con to bond with ■ to establish a link with

establecer un precedente ■ sentar un precedente ■ crear un precedente to set a precedent

establacer una relación con alguien ■ llegar a conocer a alguien to get to know someone ➤ Es imposible establecer una relación con ella. ■ Es imposible llegar a conocerla. She's impossible to get to know.

la **estación de ferrocarril** train station ■ railroad station

la **estación de metro más cercana** ■ la estación de metro que está más cerca the closest metro station ■ the nearest metro station ➤ ¿Cuál es la estación de metro más cercana? ■ ¿Qué estación de metro está más cerca? What metro station is the closest? ■ Which metro station is the closest?

la **estación de metro que está más cerca** ■ la estación de metro más cercana the closest metro station ➤ La estación de metro que esta más cerca es División del Norte. ■ La estación de metro más cercana es División del Norte. The closest metro station is División del Norte. ■ The nearest metro station is División del Norte.

estación estival summer season

estacionar en batería ■ estacionar en diagonal to park diagonally ■ to park at an angle (to the curb)

estacionar en diagonal ■ estacionar en batería to park diagonally ■ to park at an angle (to the curb)

¡estad callados! *(Esp., vosotros)* ■ ¡estaos callados! ■ ¡callad! ■ ¡callaos! ■ ¡esténse callados! (you all) be quiet!

¡estad quietos! *(Esp.)* ■ ¡estaos quietos! ■ ¡quédense quietos! (you all) be still!

estadísticas de funcionamiento performance statistics

estado de ánimo: experimentar un ~ ■ sentir un estado de ánimo to be in a mood

estado de ánimo: pasar por un ~ to go through a mood ■ to pass though a mood

estado de buena esperanza: quedarse en ~ to be pregnant ■ to be expecting

estado de deprivación serio dire state of deprivation

estado de excepción ■ (el) toque de queda curfew

estado de sitio: estar en ~ to be under martial law

estado temporal temporary status

ser **estafado por alguien** ■ ser timado por alguien to be cheated by someone ■ to be ripped off by someone ■ to be taken in by someone

estallarle en la cara a alguien to blow up in someone's face ■ to explode in someone's face ■ to go off in someone's face ➤ El petardo le estalló en la cara al niño. The firecracker went off in the boy's face. ■ The firecracker exploded in the boy's face. ■ The firecracker blew up in the boy's face.

estallido de aplausos burst of applause

estallido de carcajadas burst of laughter

estallido de color burst of color

estallido de violencia outbreak of violence

estamos en prueba this is a test

estamos listos para pedir ■ estamos preparados para tomar nota ■ estamos listos para ordenar ■ estamos listos para que nos tome la orden we're ready to order ■ we're ready for you to take our order

estamos preparados para tomar nota ■ estamos listos para pedir we're ready to order

ser la **estampa de algo** to be the epitome of something

ser la **estampa de la miseria** to be the epitome of poverty

estampa de una pintura ■ lámina de una pintura print of a painting

estampa ocurre en the scene takes place in ➤ La estampa ocurre en Buenos Aires. The scene takes place in Buenos Aires.

estamparse contra una pared to crash into a wall
están algo tirantes relations between them are strained
están dándose la gran vida ■ están saliendo con la suya they're sitting pretty ■ they're livin' it up
estando de servicio *(yo)* when I'm on duty ■ when I was on duty
estanque congelado frozen pond
¡estaos callados! *(Esp., vosotros)* ■ ¡estad callados! ■ ¡callad! ■ ¡callaos! (you all) be quiet!
¡estaos quietos! *(Esp., vosotros)* ■ ¡estad quietos! ■ ¡quédense quietos! (you all) be still!
estar meses con pasar meses con to go for months on ➤ Mark Twain dijo, "Puedo estar meses con un buen cumplido." ■ Mark Twain dijo, "Puedo pasar meses con un buen cumplido." Mark Twain said, "I can go for months on a good compliment." ➤ Mark Twain dijo que podía estar meses con un buen cumplido. ■ Mark Twain dijo que podía pasar meses con un buen cumplido. Mark Twain said he could go for months on a good compliment.
estar pendiente de ■ estar atento de ■ estar presto de ■ estar pilas de to watch ■ to monitor ➤ Estoy pendiente de la situación. I'm watching the situation. ■ I'm monitoring the situation.
estar pendiente para ■ estar pendiente para ■ estar atento para ■ estar presto para ■ estar pilas para to be on the lookout for ➤ Estoy pendiente de la confirmación de la reservación. I'm waiting for the confirmation of the reservation.
estar siendo to be being ➤ Hay un niño en este edificio que tal vez esté siendo maltratado. There is a child in this building who may be being abused.
estará cansada she must be tired
estará cansado he must be tired
¡estarás arrepentido(-a)! ■ ¡ya te arrepentirás! you'll be sorry!
estaré de vuelta ■ regresaré ■ volveré I'll be back ■ I'll return ➤ Estaré de vuelta a la una. I'll be back at one (o'clock). ■ I'll return at one (o'clock).
estaré en casa a la(s) *x* I'll be home at *x* o'clock ➤ Estaré en casa a la una. I'll be home at one (o'clock).
estarle bien empleado a alguien ■ merecérselo to serve someone right
estarse batiendo récords to be breaking records
estarse cagando vivo(-a) *(subido de tono)* to have to go to the bathroom so bad one cannot stand it ■ to have to go to the bathroom so bad that one is about to shit in one's pants
estarse calentito to be nice and warm ➤ Se está calentito aquí dentro. It's nice and warm in here.
estarse con *x* horas de antelación ■ estarse con *x* horas de anticipación ■ estarse *x* horas antes to be there *x* hours early ■ to be there *x* hours ahead of time ➤ Estáte en el aeropuerto con dos horas de antelación. Be at the airport two hours early. ■ Be at the airport two hours ahead of time.
estarse días con ■ tirarse días con ■ pasarse días con to go for days on
estarse meses con ■ tirarse meses con ■ pasarse meses con to go for months on ➤ Mark Twain dijo, "Puedo estarme meses con un buen cumplido." ■ Puedo tirarme meses con un buen cumplido. ■ Puedo pasarme meses con un buen cumplido. Mark Twain said, "I can go for months on a good compliment." ➤ Mark Twain dijo que podía estarse meses con un buen cumplido. ■ Mark Twain dijo que podía tirarse meses con un buen cumplido. ■ Mark Twain dijo que podía pasarse meses con un buen cumplido. Mark Twain said he could go for months on a good compliment.
estarse semanas con ■ tirarse semanas con ■ pasarse semanas con to go for weeks on
estársela buscando ■ buscársela to be asking for it
estársele acabando la paciencia ■ estársele agotando la paciencia ■ estar al borde de la paciencia to be at the end of one's patience ■ to be running out of patience ■ *(coloquial)* to be at the end of one's rope ■ to be at the end of one's tether
estársele agotando la paciencia ■ estársele acabando la paciencia ■ estar al borde de la paciencia to be at the end of one's patience ■ to be running out of patience ■ *(coloquial)* to be at the end of one's rope ■ to be at the end of one's tether
¿estás bien? are you (doing) okay? ➤ ¿Estás bien?-¡Como nunca! Are you doing okay?-Better than ever!
estás diciendo lo mismo desde hace veinte años you've been saying that for twenty years ■ that's what you've been saying for twenty years
¡estás en lo cierto! ■ ¡estás en lo correcto! ■ ¡tienes razón! you're right!
¡estás en tu casa! make yourself at home!
estás escribiendo en la arena you're just wasting your time
estás estupendo(-a) you look terrific
estás invitado(-a) you're invited
¿estás listo(-a) para marchar? are you ready to go?
estás malinformado(-a) ■ te han informado mal you're misinformed ■ you've been misinformed
¡estáte aquí! ■ no te muevas de aquí stay right here! ■ stay where you are! ■ you stay put!
¡estáte atento (a él)! watch for him! ■ keep an eye out for him!
¡estáte atento (a ella)! watch for her! ■ keep an eye out for her!
¡estáte atento (a ello) watch for it! ■ keep an eye out for it!
estáte callado(-a) ■ cállate be quiet
estáte listo(-a) para... ■ prepárate para... ■ prepárate a... ■ disponte para... ■ disponte a... ■ *(literario)* estáte presto(-a) a... be ready to...
estáte presto(-a) a... *(literario)* ■ prepárate para... ■ prepárate a... ■ disponte para... ■ disponte a... ■ estáte listo(-a) para... be ready to
¡estáte quieto(-a)! be still! ■ stand still! ■ hold still!
este fin de semana, nunca this weekend is out
este mundo es un pañuelo it's a small world ■ the world is a village
este otro año this coming year
este trocito me encanta *(de la canción)* ■ me encanta este trocito ■ esta parte me encanta I love this part
estela (de un barco) wake (of a boat)
estela (de un jet) vapor trail (of a jet)
estela (de una hélice) prop wash ■ wind blast (of a propeller)
¡esténse callados! *(L.am.)* ■ ¡cállense! (you all) be quiet!
¡esténse quietos! *(L.am.)* ■ ¡quédense quietos! (you all) be still!
¡estése atento (a él)! watch for him! ■ keep an eye out for him!
¡estése atento (a ella)! watch for her! ■ keep an eye out for her!
¡estése atento (a ello) watch for it! ■ keep an eye out for it!
estigma de azafrán stigma of saffron
estilo de vida lifestyle ➤ *(título de un libro) Estilos de vida de los ricos y famosos Lifestyles of the Rich and Famous*
estilo depurado polished style
estilo retorcido convoluted style
estimar en mucho ■ estimar grandemente to esteem highly
estirar la pata ■ estirar la pierna ■ palmarla to kick the bucket ■ to croak
estirar la pierna ■ estirar la pata ■ palmarla to kick the bucket ■ to croak
estirar las piernas to stretch one's legs
esto de this business of
esto es... that is...
esto es así y no hay más cáscaras ■ esto es así y no hay vuelta que darle that's the way it is, and there's nothing more to say about it
esto es así y no hay vuelta que darle ■ esto es así y no hay más cáscaras that's the way it is, and there's nothing more to say about it
esto es el acabóse this is the last straw ■ that's the last straw
esto es jauja this is the life of Riley ■ this is heaven on Earth
esto es lo que hay what you see is what you get
esto es otra cosa that's different
esto me pasa por... that's what I get for...
esto no dice mucho a favor de... it doesn't say much for... ■ that doesn't say much for...
esto no lo cambio por nada I wouldn't trade it for anything

esto no tiene ni pies ni cabeza (para mí) I can't make heads or tails out of this
esto o lo otro this or that
¡esto parece un cine! it's like Grand Central Station in here!
esto que me mandas this thing you sent me ■ the thing you sent me
esto que quede entre nosotros ■ entre tú y yo ■ entre nosotros ■ entre nos this is just between you and me
esto se debe a que... this is because... ■ this is owed to the fact that... ■ this is owing to the fact that...
estorbarle algo (for) something to be in one's way ■ (for) something to be in the way ➤ ¿Le estorban las cajas? Are the boxes in your way? ■ Are the boxes in the way?
¡estos me van a oír! they're going to hear from me! ■ *(coloquial)* they're gonna hear from me!
estos son lentejas (si las quieres las comes, y si no, las dejas) that's how it is, and if you don't like it, tough!
estos zapatos son como barcos ■ me nadan los pies en estos zapatos these shoes are way too big
estoy ansioso(-a) por verte ■ tengo ansias de verte I'm anxious to see you
¡estoy apañado(-a)! I've had it!
estoy a favor I'm for it ■ I'm in favor of it
estoy a punto de acabar ■ estoy a tiro de acabar I'm almost done ■ I'm almost through ■ I'm almost finished
estoy a tiro de acabar ■ estoy a punto de acabar I'm almost done ■ I'm almost through ■ I'm almost finished
estoy aquí desde hace... I've been here for... ➤ Estoy aquí desde hace cinco años y medio. I've been here for five-and-a-half years.
estoy casado(-a) desde hace seis meses I have been married (for) six months
estoy casado(-a) desde junio I have been married since June
estoy completamente de acuerdo contigo ■ estoy totalmente de acuerdo contigo ■ estoy absolutamente de acuerdo contigo ■ coincido completamente contigo I completely agree with you ■ I totally agree with you ■ I agree with you completely ■ I agree with you wholeheartedly
estoy completamente a favor I'm all for it
estoy completamente saturado(-a) I'm completely swamped (with work)
estoy con el agua al cuello I'm down to the wire
estoy con usted (en eso) I'm with you (on that)
estoy confundido I'm confused
estoy contigo 1. *(expresando acuerdo)* I'm with *you*! ■ amen to that! 2. *(dependiente en una tienda)* I'll be right with you ➤ Durante el resto del siglo veintiuno espero que no haya más guerra.-¡Estoy contigo! For the rest of the twenty-first century, I hope there is no more war.-Amen to that! ■ For the rest of the twenty-first century, I hope there is no more war.-I'm with *you*!
estoy convencido(-a) de que ~ 1. I'm convinced that 2. tengo confianza que I'm confident that
estoy curado(-a) de espanto ■ estoy curado contra el espanto nothing shocks me anymore ■ nothing surprises me anymore
estoy de acuerdo I agree
estoy de acuerdo contigo ■ coincido contigo ■ ya somos dos I agree with you ■ that makes two of us
estoy de tu parte I'm on your side
estoy deseando verte (de nuevo) I'm looking forward to seeing you (again)
estoy en desacuerdo ■ no estoy de acuerdo I disagree ■ I do not agree ■ *(coloquial)* I don't agree
estoy en ello I'm working on it ■ I'm in the process
¿estoy en lo cierto? ■ ¿estoy en lo correcto? ■ ¿tengo razón? am I right? ■ am I correct?
¿estoy en lo correcto? ■ ¿estoy en lo cierto? ■ ¿tengo razón? am I right? ■ am I correct?
(estoy) encantado de haberte conocido I enjoyed meeting you
estoy harto(-a) I'm fed up (with it) ■ I'm sick and tired of it
estoy hecho un lío 1. I'm at wit's end 2. I'm torn to pieces ➤ No puedo ni imaginarme qué significan las instrucciones del mando a distancia. Estoy hecho un lío. I can't figure out the instructions for this remote. I'm at wit's end. ➤ ¿Dejo a mi novio? Estoy hecha un lío. Should I break up with my boyfriend? I'm torn to pieces.
estoy hinchado(-a) I'm full *(Nota: Una alternativa más cortés es "no thank you" o "I've had plenty, thanks".)*
estoy liado(-a) ■ estoy ocupado I'm tied up ■ I'm (really) busy ➤ Estoy liado ahora. ¿Te llamo yo luego? I'm tied up at the moment. Can I call you back?
estoy pensando que... I'm thinking that... ■ it sounds like...
estoy pletórico(-a) I'm rarin' to go
estoy positivo(-a) ■ tengo la certeza absoluta ■ tengo la seguridad absoluta I'm positive ■ I'm absolutely certain ■ I'm absolutely sure
estoy preparado(-a) en un soplo I'll be ready in a sec
estoy que me subo por las paredes I'm climbing the walls
estoy todo lo bien que puedo estar (teniendo en cuenta las circunstancias) I'm as well as I can be (under the circumstances)
estoy tirando I'm hanging in there ■ I'm getting by
estoy totalmente de acuerdo contigo ■ estoy completamente de acuerdo contigo I totally agree with you ■ I completely agree with you ■ I agree with you completely ■ I agree with you wholeheartedly
estoy un poco preocupado(-a) al respecto I'm a little concerned about it
estoy un poco preocupado(-a) de que... ■ me preocupa un poco que... I'm a little concerned that...
estar **estagado(-a) después de nueve horas en el avión** to be stiff after nine hours on the airplane
estrato fino thin layer ■ fine layer ➤ Aislaron la proteína por cromatografía de estrato fino. They isolated the protein by means of fine-layer chomatography.
estréchame fuerte ■ agárrame fuerte hold me tight
estrechar el cerco a alguien ■ estrechar el cerco sobre alguien to close in on someone
estrechar el cerco sobre alguien ■ estrechar el cerco a alguien to close in on someone ■ to tighten the noose around someone
estrechar la búsqueda to narrow down the search
estrechar la mano del presidente ■ estrecharle la mano al presidente to shake hands with the president
estrechar las relaciones bilaterales to strengthen bilateral relations
estrechar (las) relaciones entre to strengthen ties between
estrechas relaciones con: mantener ~ to have close ties with ■ to maintain close ties with
estrecheces económicas financial difficulties
estrecho aliado político de close political ally of
estrecho colaborador close collaborator
estrella binaria binary star
estrella cercana neighboring star ■ nearby star
estrella fugaz ■ *(plural)* ■ estrellas fugaces shooting star
estrella de neutrones neutron star
estrella invitada guest star
estrella polar the pole star ■ the North Star ■ Polaris ➤ La Estrella Polar está a 430 años luz, más o menos a cien años luz. ■ La Estrella Polar queda a 430 años luz, más o menos a cien años luz. The Pole Star is 430 light years away, plus or minus a hundred light years. ■ The Pole Star is 430 light years distant, plus or minus a hundred light years.
estrellar contra algo ■ darse contra algo to crash into something ■ to hit something ■ to run into something
estrellarse un avión for an airplane to crash ➤ Se estrelló el avión. The airplane crashed.
estrellas centelleantes twinkling stars
ser **estrenado en el mercado** ■ ser lanzado al mercado ■ salir al mercado to come out ■ to come on(to) the market ■ to be introduced onto the market ➤ Los móviles con tele incorporada fueron estrenados en el mercado en el 2003. ■ Los móviles con tele incorporada fueron lanzados al mercado en el 2003. ■ Los móviles con tele incorporada salieron al mercado en el 2003. Mobile phones with TV's came out in 2003. ■ Mobile phones with TV's came onto the market in 2003. ■ Mobile phones with TV's were introduced onto the market in 2003.

estrenar algo nuevo to try out something new ➤ Estoy estrenando mi nuevo monitor I'm trying out my new TV monitor

estreno más largo en la historia de Broadway the longest-running play in the history of Broadway

estribaciones de una cordillera foothills of a mountain range ▪ spurs of a mountain range

estropear la rosca to strip the thread(s) ➤ La rosca está estropeada. The threads are stripped. ▪ The threading is stripped. ▪ The thread is stripped.

estropear la sorpresa to spoil the surprise

estropear las velocidades to strip the gears

estropearle el final a alguien to spoil the ending for someone ▪ to give away the ending ➤ No quiero estropearte el final. ▪ No quiero estropearle el final. I don't want to spoil the ending for you. ▪ I don't want to give away the ending.

estructurar la pregunta to phrase the question

estrujarle a alguien 1. to squeeze someone 2. *(Chile)* hacer reír a alguien to crack someone up ▪ to double someone over (with laughter) ▪ to have someone in stitches ➤ En los metros de la Ciudad de México, suben, estrujan y bajan. In the Mexico City subways, they get on, they squeeze, and they get off. ➤ Siempre me estruja con los chistes que me cuenta. He cracks me up with the jokes he tells.

estudiar español to take Spanish ▪ to study Spanish

estudiar hacer algo to consider doing something

estudiar inglés 1. to study English 2. recibir una clase de inglés ▪ recibir clases de inglés to take English

estudiar la posibilidad de que ▪ indagar la posibilidad de que to look into the possibility that ▪ to investigate the possibility that

estudio encontró que... study found that... ➤ El estudio encontró que... The study found that...

estudio de gran repercusión important study ▪ major study

estudio en el que participaron study of a certain number of people ▪ study involving a certain number of people ➤ En un reciente estudio en el que participaron trescientos pacientes cardíacos. In a recent study of three hundred heart patients.

estudios posgraduados graduate studies

estar **estupefacto(-a) ante algo** ▪ quedarse estupefacto(-a) ante algo ▪ estar pasmado ante algo ▪ quedarse pasmado ante algo ▪ quedarse anonadado ante algo to be dumbfounded at something ▪ to be astonished at something ➤ *(Esp.)* Te habrás quedado estupefacto ante lo que hice. ▪ *(Méx.)* Has de estar estupefacto ante lo que hice. You must be dumbfounded at what I did.

estupefacto(-a) de que...: quedarse ~ ▪ quedarse pasmado de que... to be dumbfounded that... ▪ to be astounded that...

estupefacto(-a) por algo: quedarse ~ ▪ quedarse pasmado por algo to be dumbfounded by something ▪ to be astounded by something

¡estupendo! ▪ ¡genial! great!

estuve a punto de perder el autobús ▪ casi pierdo el autobús ▪ *pintoresco* ▪ agarré el autobús barriéndome ▪ *España* cogí el (auto)bús por los pelos ▪ casi se me va el (auto)bús I almost missed the bus ▪ I nearly missed the bus ▪ I just barely made it to the bus

estuve cenando con... I had supper with...

estuve comiendo con... I had dinner with...

estuve descansando durante las vacaciones I took it easy during the holidays ▪ I took it easy over the holidays

estuve viviendo allí hasta que cumplí *x* años I lived there until I was *x* years old

etiquetas de correo ▪ etiquetas para sobres mailing labels ▪ address labels

etiquetas para sobres ▪ etiquetas de correo address labels ▪ mailing labels

Europa septentrional northern Europe

evacuar combustible ▪ arrojar combustible to jettison fuel ▪ to dump fuel

evacuar el vientre ▪ exonerar el vientre to have a bowel movement

evaporarse al hervirse to boil away ➤ Toda el agua para el té se ha evaporado al hervirse, y el recipiente está casi al rojo vivo. All the tea water has boiled away, and the pan is practically red hot.

ser **evento para reflexionar** to be food for thought

eventual ataque future attack ➤ El gobierno ha dado el visto bueno a que la aviación militar lanzara un eventual ataque. The government has given the okay for military aircraft to launch a future attack.

evitar a alguien ▪ huir de alguien to avoid someone

evitar a alguien como si fuera la peste ▪ huirle a alguien como la peste to avoid someone like the plague ➤ Le evita como si fuera la peste. ▪ Le huye como la peste. She avoids him like the plague.

evitar aun la apariencia del pecado to avoid even the appearance of evil

evitar el encuentro de alguien ▪ evitar encontrarse a alguien to avoid meeting someone

evitar el tema to avoid the subject ▪ to avoid the topic ▪ to avoid the issue

evitar encontrarse a alguien ▪ evitar el encuentro de alguien to avoid meeting someone

evitar hacer algo ▪ intentar no hacer algo ▪ *(coloquial y el más común)* escaquearse (de hacer algo) to avoid doing something ▪ to get out of doing something ▪ to keep from doing something

evitar la realidad to escape reality ▪ to escape from reality

evitar los baches to avoid the pitfalls ➤ Sus hijos evitaron los baches en los que han caído... Their children have avoided the pitfalls into which other children of celebrities have fallen.

evitar responsabilidades to avoid responsibility ▪ to duck responsibility

evitar sospechas ▪ evitar suspicacias to avoid suspicion(s)

evitar suspicacias ▪ evitar sospechas to avoid suspicion(s)

evitar todo asomo de pecado ▪ evitar todo atisbo de pecado to avoid even the appearance of evil

evitar todo atisbo de pecado ▪ evitar todo asomo de pecado to avoid even the appearance of evil

evitar un desastre *(de origen natural)* ▪ prevenir un desastre to avert a disaster ▪ to prevent a disaster (from happening)

evitar una situación to avoid a situation

evitar ser detectado(-a) por alguien to avoid being detected by someone ▪ to avoid detection by someone

la **evolución del caso** the unfolding of the case

evolucionar con su tiempo to keep up with the times ▪ to keep abreast of the times ▪ to stay abreast of the times ➤ *(noticia)* El presidente de China hace hincapié en la necesaria "transformación del marxismo" a fin de que China evolucione con su tiempo. The president of China emphasizes the necessary "transformation of Marxism" (in order) to keep up with the times. ▪ The president of China emphasizes the necessary "transformation of Marxism" (in order) to keep abreast of the times. ▪ The president of China emphasizes the necessary "transformation of Marxism" (in order) to stay abreast of the times.

evolucionar bien to recover (well) ▪ to progress well ▪ to make (good) progress ▪ to get along well ➤ *(noticia)* El Papa seguirá hospitalizado varios días, aunque evoluciona bien. The Pope will remain hospitalized for several days, even though he is recovering well. ▪ The Pope will remain hospitalized for several days, even though he is progressing well. ▪ The Pope will remain hospitalized for several days, even though he is making (good) progress.

ex-presidente ex-president ▪ former president

exaltar la imaginación to fire up the imagination ▪ to fire up one's imagination

exaltarse por algo ▪ darse manija por algo to get (all) worked up about something ▪ to get (all) worked up over something ▪ to get exercised about something ➤ Se exaltó cuando le dije lo que ella dijo. He got all worked up when I told him what she said. ➤ No te exaltes. Don't get so worked up. ▪ Now, don't get exercised.

examen predeterminado *(TOEFL, GRE, SAT, etc.)* standardized test ▪ standardized exam(ination) ➤ ¿Te has inscrito al examen TOEFL? Have you signed up for the TOEFL test?

excavar su propia tumba to dig one's own grave

excepto para except to

exceder el límite de velocidad to exceed the speed limit

exederse con los preparativos ■ pasarse con los preparativos to outdo oneself ■ to go all out in the preparation

excederse en los elogios a alguien to be lavish in one's praise of someone

excepto con ■ si no es con except with ➤ *(Méx.)* Nunca va a jugar al boliche excepto con sus estudiantes. ■ Nunca va a jugar al boliche si no es con sus estudiantes. ■ *(Esp.)* Nunca va a jugar a los bolos excepto con sus estudiantes. ■ Nunca va a jugar a los bolos si no es con sus estudiantes. He never goes bowling except with his students.

exceso de confianza overconfidence

exceso de confidencia excessive confidence ■ misplaced confidence ➤ Contarle toda tu vida ha sido un exceso de confidencia. Telling him your whole life story was misplaced confidence.

excitación del momento: en la ~ ■ en la emoción del momento in the excitement of the moment

excitar a la chusma to incite the mob ■ to inflame the masses

excluyendo todo lo demás to the exclusion of all else ■ to the exclusion of everything else

exculpar a alguien de algo to exonerate someone of something

excusa no corre: esa ~ that excuse won't fly ■ that excuse doesn't cut it

la **exención de impuestos** tax exemption

la **excrecencia del hueso calcáneo** *(del tálon)* bone spur

exhalar el alma ■ expirar to breathe one's last ■ to expire

exhalar el último suspiro to breathe one's last breath

exhalar un hálito de ■ exhalar una aroma de to give off a scent of ■ to give off an aroma of

la **exhibición de moda** fashion show

la **exhibición de pinturas** exhibit of paintings ■ exhibition of paintings

exigir acatamiento (con) to demand compliance (with)

exigir disculpas a alguien to demand an apology from someone

existen muchas maneras de there are lots of ways to

existir cierta duda sobre (for there) to be some doubt about ➤ Existía cierta duda sobre... There was some doubt about...

éxito de ventas ■ (el) super ventas bestseller

éxito en ventas: convertirse en un ~ to become a bestseller

éxito más vendido bestselling hit

éxito parcial mixed success ■ partial success ■ success mixed with failure ➤ Como mejor se puede describir el éxito de las misiones de exploración de Marte es como parcial. The success of the Mars exploration missions to date can (at) best be described as mixed.

éxodo masivo mass exodus

exonerar el vientre ■ evacuar el vientre to have a bowel movement

expandir sus alas ■ extender sus alas ■ desplegar sus alas to spread its wings

la **expansión del lecho marino** seafloor spreading

expectativa de vida life expectancy

expectativas crecientes rising expectations

expediente de crisis downsizing ■ corporate downsizing

expediente disciplinario 1. historial disciplinario disciplinary history 2. acción disciplinaria disciplinary proceedings

expediente judicial judicial proceedings ■ court proceedings ■ court record

expediente personal personnel file

el **expediente sin tacha** spotless record ■ unblemished record

expedir a alguien un carnet to issue someone an ID card ➤ Deberían expedirle un carnet al matricularse. They should issue you an ID card when you register.

expedir a alguien un pasaporte to issue someone a passport

ser una **experiencia agridulce** to be a bittersweet experience

experiencia desoladora devastating experience

experiencia inolvidable unforgettable experience

experiencia laboral work experience ■ work history

la **experiencia muestra que** experience shows that

experimentar una remontada to experience a rebound ■ to have a rebound ■ to rebound

expiar un delito to expiate a crime ■ to atone for a crime ■ to make reparation for a crime ■ to make restitution for a crime

explayar el mantel ■ tender el mantel ■ poner el mantel to spread the tablecloth ■ to put the tablecloth on the table ■ to lay the tablecloth

explicación: la mejor ~ the best explanation

la **explicación más factible** ■ la explicación más plausible the most plausible explanation

la **explicación más plausible** ■ la explicación más factible the most plausible explanation

la **explicación más posible** ■ la explicación más probable the most likely explanation ■ the most probable explanation

la **explicación más probable** ■ la explicación más posible the most probable explanation ■ the most likely explanation

explicación sencilla simple explanation

explicar del todo to explain completely ➤ No lo explica del todo. It doesn't completely explain it.

explicarlo punto por punto to explain it point by point ■ to spell it out

explicarse cómo funciona alguien to figure someone out ➤ No me explico cómo funciona ese tipo. I can't figure that guy out.

explícate tell me about it ■ tell me more about it ■ elaborate (on that)

explíquese tell me about it ■ tell me more about it ■ elaborate (on that)

la **explotación infantil** child labor

explotar minas de... to mine...

explotar un globo to pop a balloon

exponer su postura to explain one's position ■ to explain one's point of view

exponerse a ser... to risk being... ➤ Los videntes de Elvis se exponen a ser tildados de dementes. Elvis sighters risk being labeled insane.

la **exposición de pinturas** exhibition of paintings

la **exposición temprana** early exposure

expresar sobre papel ■ plasmar sobre papel to express on paper

expresar su agradecimiento to express one's appreciation ■ to express one's gratitude

expresar su descontento ante to express one's displeasure at

expresar su malestar por to express one's displeasure at

expresar un deseo to make a wish

expresarse con gracejo ■ expresarse con gracia ■ expresarse con elegancia ■ expresarse elocuentemente to express oneself eloquently ■ to express oneself clearly

la **expresión de su cara** ■ expresión que uno pone ■ gesto expression on one's face ➤ Deberías haber visto la expresión de su cara. ■ Deberías haber visto la cara que puso. You should have seen the expression on his face.

expresión pintoresca colorful expression

expresión rebuscada stilted expression ■ unnatural expression

exprimirle el cerebro a alguien ■ exprimirle el coco a alguien ■ exprimirle el seso a alguien to pick someone's brain

ser **expulsado de** to be expelled from ■ to get expelled from ■ *(coloquial)* to be kicked out of ■ to get kicked out of ➤ Edgar Allen Poe fue expulsado de la Universidad de Virginia. Edgar Allen Poe was expelled from the University of Virginia. ■ Edgar Allen Poe got expelled from the University of Virginia. ■ Edgar Allen Poe was kicked out of the University of Virginia. ■ Edgar Allen Poe got kicked out of the University of Virginia.

expulsar humo ■ escupir humo to belch smoke ➤ Los camiones y autobuses expulsaban humo de gasoil. The trucks and buses were belching diesel smoke. ➤ Las chimeneas industriales de las acerías solían expulsar humo, dejando una patina por todo el polígono industrial. The smoke stacks of the steel mills used to belch smoke, leaving a patina all over the industrial zone.

extender la alfombra roja to roll out the red carpet

extender la guerra to escalate the war ■ to widen the war ■ to expand the war

extender la loción to spread (on) the lotion

extender la mano to hold out one's hand

extender la manta to spread (out) the blanket ■ to spread a blanket out

extender la mantequilla to spread the butter

extender los documentos to draw up the documents ■ to draw up the papers

extender un cheque to write a check

extender su influencia to extend one's influence ■ to expand one's influence ■ to broaden one's influence

extenderse sus alas ■ desplegar sus alas ■ expandirse sus alas to spread its wings

la **extensión de los daños** extent of the damage

la **extensión de octavas** octave range ➤ El órgano tiene la extensión de octavas más amplia de cualquier instrumento. The organ has the widest octave range of any instrument.

extenderse en una carta ■ expresarse en una carta to write a good, long letter

el **extintor de incendios** fire extinguisher

extirpar un tumor to remove a tumor ■ to extract a tumor ■ to cut out a tumor

¡extra! ¡extra! ¡descúbralo todo! ■ ¡extra! ¡extra! ¡entérense de todo! extra! extra! read all about it!

extracto de cuenta: último ~ ■ último resumen de cuenta ■ resumen de cuenta más reciente most recent bank statement ■ last bank statement

extracto detallado ■ factura detallada ■ factura discriminada itemized statement

extracto mensual ■ resumen mensual monthly statement

extraer un diente ■ extraer una muela ■ sacar un diente ■ sacar una muela to extract a tooth ■ to pull a tooth

extraer una muela ■ extraer un diente ■ sacar una muela ■ sacar un diente to extract a tooth ■ to pull a tooth

extraña habilidad de...: tener la ~ to have an uncanny ability to...

extraña habilidad para...: tener la ~ to have an uncanny ability to...

la **extraña pareja** the odd couple

estar **extrañado ante** to be surprised at

extrarradio de una ciudad outlying areas of a city ■ area surrounding a city

extrema derecha the far right ■ the extreme right

extrema izquierda the far left ■ the extreme left

extremo de la calle ■ fondo de la calle ■ (el) final de la calle end of the street

extremo del pueblo: en el ~ at the edge of town

extremo inferior de la escala ■ (el) límite inferior de la escala lower end of the scale

extremos de un cable ends of a cord ■ ends of a cable

los **extremos se tocan** extremes meet each other

F.A.B. ▪ franco a bordo F.O.B. ▪ free on board

fábrica de guitarras guitar factory

fabricado en México ▪ hecho in México made in Mexico

ser **fácil de armar** to be easy to assemble ▪ to be easy to put together

ser **fácil de complacer** ▪ ser fácil de contentar to be easy to please

ser **fácil de conocer** ▪ ser asequible to be easy to get to know ▪ to be approachable

ser **fácil de contentar** ▪ ser fácil de complacer to be easy to please

ser **fácil de conversación** ▪ ser asequible to be easy to talk to

ser **fácil de entender** ▪ ser asequible to be easy to understand ▪ to be (very) clear ➤ Este manual de informática es fácil de entender. ▪ Este manual de informática es asequible. This computer manual is easy to understand. ▪ This computer manual is very clear.

la **facilidad con la que** *(Esp.)* ▪ facilidad con (la) que ease with which

la **facilidad de idiomas: tener ~** ▪ tener aptitud(es) para los idiomas to have an ear for languages ▪ to have an aptitude for languages

la **facilidad de que** facilidad con que ease with which ➤ La facilidad con que te expresas en español The ease with which you express yourself in Spanish

la **facilidad de que** ease with which ➤ La facilidad de que dispones en la cocina The ease with which you work in the kitchen ▪ Your skill in the kitchen

las **facilidades de pago** easy (payment) terms

facilitar las cosas to make things easier ▪ to facilitate things

facilitar los nombres to divulge the names

factura detallada itemized bill

facturación detallada itemized billing

faja de frequencia ▪ banda de frecuencia waveband ▪ frequency band

fajo de billetes ▪ taco de billetes wad of bills ▪ roll of bills

falda de la colina ▪ (el) pie de la colina foot of the hill ▪ bottom of hill ▪ base of the hill

falda de la montaña ▪ (el) pie de la montaña foot of the mountain ▪ bottom of the mountain ▪ base of the mountain

falda levantada al aire *(como la de Marilyn Monroe en "Con faldas y a lo loco")* billowing skirt

fallar a alguien to let someone down ▪ to disappoint someone

fallar en alcanzar las expectativas de alguien ▪ no satisfacer (las) expectativas (puestas en uno) to fail to meet someone's expectations

fallecer congelado(-a) to freeze to death

fallecer de causas naturales ▪ fallecer de muerte natural to die of natural causes

fallecer víctima de to die a victim of

fallido intento de failed attempt to

fallo del árbitro *(deportes)* incorrect ruling ▪ incorrect call

fallo del motor ▪ paro del motor engine failure

fallo en un programa de computadora ▪ defecto en un programa de computadora bug in a computer program

fallo humano human error

fallo renal kidney failure ➤ Expertos relacionaron las muertes por fallo renal con un nuevo fármaco contra el colesterol. Experts linked the deaths caused by kidney failure to a new anti-cholesterol drug.

falso aviso false alarm ➤ *(noticia)* Detenidos otros dos menores por falso aviso de bomba. Two more minors arrested for a false bomb alarm.

falso testimonio false testimony ▪ perjury

falta de agua ▪ (la) escasez de agua water shortage

falta de equidad miscarriage of justice

falta de juicio lacking in judgment

falta de previsión ▪ imprevisión lack of foresight

falta de respeto lack of respect

falta de sueño lack of sleep ➤ Empieza a afectarme la falta de sueño. My lack of sleep is starting to catch up with me. ▪ My lack of sleep is starting to affect me.

falta de tacto lack of tact ▪ tactlessness

falta mucho por hacer ▪ hay mucho que hacer there's a lot to do

faltaban asientos there weren't enough seats

faltan asientos there are not enough seats ▪ there aren't enough seats

faltar a clase ▪ dejar de asistir a clase to miss class

faltar a la palabra ▪ faltar a su promesa ▪ incumplir un compromiso to break one's promise ➤ Faltó a la palabra. He broke his promise.

faltar a su palabra not to keep one's word

faltar a su promesa not to keep one's promise

faltar a una cita to miss an appointment ▪ to break a date

faltar al colegio to skip school

faltar mucho camino ▪ quedarle a uno mucho camino to have a long way to go

faltar palabras ▪ quedarse sin palabras to be at a loss for words

faltar poco para to be almost ▪ to be nearly

faltar poco para cumplir *x* años ▪ estar a punto de cumplir *x* años ▪ tener casi *x* años to be not quite... ▪ to be almost... *x* years old ➤ Cuando a Marcelino le faltaba muy poco para cumplir cinco años... When Marcelino was not quite five years old... ▪ When Marcelino was almost five years old...

faltar poco para llegar a to be a short distance to

faltar poco para que to be nearly ➤ Faltó poco para que me cayera un rayo cuando estábamos en la playa. I was nearly struck by lightning when we were at the beach.

faltaría más don't mention it

faltarle algún tornillo ▪ faltarle un tornillo to have a screw loose ▪ to have a few loose screws ▪ to have a few screws loose ▪ to be cracked ▪ to be a little nutty

faltarle algunos jugadores (y los que tiene patean en contra) ▪ faltarle un hervor not to be playing with a full deck ▪ to be a couple bricks shy of a load ▪ to be a couple of quarts low ▪ to be half a bubble off plumb

faltarle lo peor for the worst to be yet to come ➤ Me falta lo peor. The worst is yet to come. ➤ Me faltaba lo peor. The worst was yet to come.

faltarle poco para to be about to

faltarle práctica to be out of practice ▪ to need to practice ➤ Me falta práctica. I'm out of practice. ▪ I need to practice.

faltarle un hervor ▪ faltarle algunos jugadores (y los que tiene patean en contra) to be a couple bricks shy of a load ▪ to be a couple quarts low ▪ to be half a bubble off plumb

faltarle un tornillo a alguien to have a screw loose ▪ to have a few loose screws ▪ to have a few screws loose ▪ to be cracked ▪ to be a little nutty

faltarle *x* semanas de gestación to be *x* weeks premature ➤ Al bebé le faltaba seis semanas de gestación. *(él)* The baby boy was six weeks premature. ▪ *(ella)* The baby girl was six weeks premature. ➤ El bebé al que le faltaban seis semanas de gestación... The baby boy, who was six weeks premature... ➤ La bebé, a la que le faltaban seis semanas de gestación... The baby girl, who was six weeks premature...
fama de reputation as
familia acomodada ▪ familia adinerada ▪ familia pudiente ▪ familia rica well-to-do family ▪ wealthy family ▪ rich family ▪ family with money
familia de abolengo distinguished family
familia de bajos recursos ▪ familia de bajos ingresos low-income family
familia de *x* miembros family of *x* ➤ Una familia de cinco miembros A family of five
la **familia es lo primero** the family comes first
familia numerosa large family
familia pequeña ▪ familia corta small family
familia unida close-knit family
familiarizarse con algo to become familiar with something
las **familias de ambas partes** both sides of the family
ser **famoso(-a) por** to be famous for ➤ Bariloche es famoso por el chocolate, y Mendoza por sus vinos. Bariloche is famous for chocolate, and Mendoza for its wines.
ser **fan del baloncesto** ▪ ser aficionado(-a) al baloncesto to be a basketball fan
ser **fan del béisbol** ▪ ser aficionado(-a) al béisbol to be a baseball fan
ser **fan del fútbol** ▪ ser aficionado(-a) al fútbol **1.** *(fútbol americano)* to be a football fan **2.** *(fútbol europeo)* to be a soccer fan
ser una **fantasía de deseo** to be wishful thinking
ser un **fantoche** to be a yes man
farmacia de guardia ▪ farmacia de turno after-hours pharmacy
farmacia de turno ▪ farmacia de guardia after-hours pharmacy
farmacia de turno: tienes la *(Arg., coloquial)* your fly is open
ser el **farolillo rojo** to be the last one in a race
la **fase final 1.** final playoffs ▪ finals **2.** tail end ➤ Sólo vi la fase final del programa. I just caught the tail end of the program
fase final de: estar en la ~ ▪ estar en la última fase de to be in the final stages of
la **fase final de la liga nacional** national league finals
fastidiarse el brazo *(etc.)* ▪ dañarse el brazo to hurt one's arm ➤ Me fastidié el brazo. I hurt my arm.
estar **fatigado(-a) en extremo** *(culto)* ▪ estar muy fatigado to be extremely tired
ser **favorito(-a) a ganar** to be favored to win ➤ Los dos caballos favoritos a ganar van pelo a pelo. The two favored horses are neck and neck.
la **fe de erratas** *(en una publicación)* ▪ fe de errores corrections
la **fe inquebrantable** unshakeable faith
la **fe mueve montañas** faith moves mountains
febrero loco, marzo otro poco *(Méx.)* February's weather is unpredictable, and March's even more so
fecha de corte cutoff date
la **fecha de la muerte de uno** the time of one's death ➤ Hasta la fecha de su muerte **1.** *(de él)* (Up) until the time of his death ▪ Up to the time of his death **2.** *(de ella)* (Up) until the time of her death ▪ Up to the time of her death
fecha de límite ▪ plazo ▪ fecha tope due date
fecha de nacimiento ▪ natalicio date of birth ▪ birth date
fecha de vencimiento expiration date
fecha para: anterior a la ~ before the date on which
fecha tope deadline date ▪ closing date
la **fecundación artificial** ▪ inseminación artificial artificial insemination
la **fecundación in vitro** in vitro fertilization ▪ fertilization outside the womb
¡Felices Pascuas! 1. *(pascua navideña)* Merry Christmas! **2.** *(pascua florida)* Happy Easter!
¡Felices Pascuas y próspero año nuevo! ▪ Feliz Navidad y próspero año nuevo Merry Christmas and Happy New Year
¡felices sueños! sweet dreams!
felicitarle a alguien ampliamente to heartily congratulate someone
ser **feliz como una lombriz** *(Méx.)* to be happy as a clam
el **feliz desenlace** ▪ (el) final feliz happy ending
estar **felizmente casado(-a)** to be happily married
fenómeno fugaz fleeting phenomenon ▪ passing phenomenon *(pintoresco)* (just a) blip on the radar screen
férrea determinación iron determination ▪ fierce determination
férula intermaxilar *(odontología)* bite splint ▪ bitesplint ▪ intermaxillar stress breaker
fiamos en Dios in God we trust
fiar en Dios to trust in God
fiarse de alguien ▪ confiar en alguien ▪ creer en alguien to trust someone ➤ Me fío de él. I trust him. ➤ No me fío de él. I don't trust him.
fiarse de la palabra de uno to take someone's word for it
fiarse de las apariencias to judge by appearances ▪ to go by appearances ➤ No te fíes de las aparencias. Don't judge by appearances.
fiebre porcina swine fever
¿ficción o realidad? fiction or non-fiction?
ficha de setenta y cinco por ciento veinticinco (75 x 125) milímetros three-by-five card ➤ Necesito un paquete de fichas de setenta y cinco por ciento veinte y cinco milímetros. I need a pack of three-by-five cards.
ficha policial police record
fichar (la entrada) to punch in ▪ to clock in
fichar (la salida) to punch out ▪ to clock out
fiebre aftosa foot and mouth disease
fiebre de caballo high fever
fiebre Navideña 1. Christmas fever **2.** pre-Christmas rush
ser **fiel a alguien** to be faithful to someone
ser **fiel a su palabra** ▪ cumplir con su palabra to be true to one's word ▪ to keep one's word
ser **fiel a su promesa** ▪ cumplir con su promesa to be true to one's promise ▪ to keep one's promise
ser una **fiera en la cama** to be a tiger in bed
fiesta de guardar *(catolicismo)* ▪ fiesta de precepto Holy Feast of Obligation ▪ Holy Day of Obligation
fiesta de inauguración housewarming
fiesta de precepto *(catolicismo)* ▪ fiesta de guardar Holy Day of Obligation ▪ Holy Feast of Obligation
fiesta se ha acabado para alguien ▪ es el fin de fiesta para alguien the party's over for someone ➤ La fiesta se ha acabado para los conservadores. The party's over for the conservatives.
figura de autoridad authority figure ➤ La directora le dijo al substituto que Santiago tenía un problema con las figuras de autoridad. The principal told the substitute teacher that Santiago had a problem with authority figures.
figura retórica figure of speech
figurar en el censo to appear in the census ▪ to be listed in the census ▪ to be found in the census
figurar en el directorio to appear in the directory ▪ to be listed in the directory
figurar en la guía telefónica to appear in the telephone directory ▪ to be listed in the telephone directory
figurar entre ▪ figurarse entre to rank among
figurarse que... to imagine that... ➤ *(tú)* Figúrate que caminas por... ▪ *(usted)* Figúrese que camina por... ▪ *(vosotros)* Figuráos que camináis por... ▪ *(ustedes)* Figúrense que caminan por... Imagine that you're walking along...
¡figúrate! just think! ▪ just imagine!
figúrate que... just imagine that...
fijar carteles pegar carteles to put up signs ➤ Prohibido fijar carteles en el túnel. It is prohibited to put up signs. ▪ Putting up signs in the tunnel is prohibited. ▪ Putting up signs is prohibited in the tunnel. ▪ Putting signs up in the tunnel is prohibited.
fijar el precio to set the price
fijar el temporizador to set the timer

fijar la fecha de algo ▪ programar la fecha de algo to set the date of something ▪ to set the date for something

fijar la hora para ▪ establecer la hora para ▪ concretar la hora para ▪ cuadrar la hora para to set a time for ▪ to schedule a time for ▪ to set a time to ▪ to schedule a time to ➤ Necesitamos fijar una hora para la reunión. We need to set a time for the meeting. ➤ Necesitamos fijar una hora para que nos traigan los suministros. We need to set a time to have the supplies delivered. ▪ We need to schedule a time to have the supplies delivered.

fijar límites a to set limits on ➤ *(titular)* Alemania fija fuertes límites a la entrada de ciudadanos de veintidós países. Germany sets strict entry limits on citizens from twenty-two countries.

fijar los límites to set (the) limits ▪ to draw the line ➤ ¿Dónde se fijan los límites? Where do you draw the line?

fijar los márgenes to set the margins

fijar una hora ▪ hacer una cita to make an appointment ▪ to set an appointment

fijar una reunión ▪ programar una reunión to schedule a meeting

fijarse cuando... to notice (it) when...

¡**fíjate en esto!** get this!

fíjate no más (que...) can you imagine... ▪ can you even conceive...

¡**fíjate por donde vas!** ▪ ¡mira por donde vas! ▪ *(Esp.)* ▪ ¡mira por donde andas! watch where you're going!

¡**fíjense en esto!** get this!

¡**fíjese por donde va (usted)!** ▪ ¡mire por donde va (usted)! ▪ *(Esp.)* ▪ ¡mire por donde anda (usted)! watch where you're going!

filo de la navaja razor's edge ▪ edge of the razor (blade)

filo del cuchillo edge of the knife ▪ knife edge ▪ knife's edge

fijo que for sure ▪ surely

fila de coches (long) line of cars ➤ Había un fila de coches retenidos en los puestos de peaje. There was a long line of cars backed up at the toll booths.

fila india: en ~ single file

filete bien hecho ▪ filete muy hecho ▪ bistec bien hecho ▪ bistec muy hecho well done steak

filete de pescado fish fillet

filo mellado ragged edge ▪ jagged edge ▪ nicked edge ▪ chipped edge

el **filón inagotable** ▪ mina inagotable inexhaustible mine ▪ gold mine ➤ Un filón inagotable de expresiones ▪ Una mina inagotable de expresiones An inexhaustible mine of expressions ▪ A gold mine of expressions

filtrarse en la mente de uno to go through one's mind

filtrarse por 1. to filter through ▪ to seep through 2. to leak through

filtro de amor ▪ poción de amor ▪ tónico de amor love potion

filtro mágico ▪ poción mágico ▪ tónico mágico magic potion

el **fin de semana** weekend

ser **fin del camino para alguien** to be the end of the road for someone

fin del final: hasta el ~ until the very end ▪ up to the (very) end ▪ right up to the end ➤ Se murió con noventa y cinco años y fue lúcido y no sordo hasta el fin del final. He died at (age) ninety-five and was lucid and not deaf right up to the end.

el **fin justifica los medios** the ends justify the means

el **fin no justifica los medios** the ends don't justify the means

final de la calle: ir al ~ ▪ ir al fondo de la calle to go to the end of the street ➤ *(tú)* Ve al final de la calle y lo verás justo a la derecha. ▪ Ve al fondo de la calle y lo verás justo a la derecha. *(usted)* Vaya (usted) al final de la calle y lo verá justo a la derecha. ▪ Vaya (usted) al fondo de la calle y lo verá justo a la derecha. Go to the end of the street and you'll see it just off to the right.

el **final de la cama** foot of the bed ▪ end of the bed ➤ Al final de la cama At the foot of the bed

el **final de partido** final score

el **final de su vida** end of one's life ➤ Al final de su vida no ha sufrido. He didn't suffer at the end of his life.

el **final de un libro** end of a book

el **final de una obra (teatral)** end of a play

el **final de una película** end of a movie

el **final de una pesadilla** end of a nightmare

el **final de(l) trayecto** end of the line ➤ San Pablo y Escuela Militar son los finales del trayecto uno. San Pablo and Escuela Militar are the ends of line one.

el **final está próximo** ▪ el final está cerca the end is near

el **final estaba próximo** the end was near

el **final feliz** ▪ feliz desenlace happy ending

el **final sorprendente** surprise ending

la **finalidad de** ▪ (la) intención de ▪ propósito de aim of

finalización del título de uno ▪ terminación del título de uno completion of one's (academic) degree

finalizar algo al cien por cien terminar algo al cien por cien to finish completely

finalmente juntos together at last

finca lechera ▪ granja lechera dairy farm

fingir ignorancia ▪ pretender ignorancia to feign ignorance

firma en blanco carte blanche ▪ full discretionary authority

firma notorial notary's signature

¡**firmes!** *(militar)* attention!

fiscal general ▪ titular de justicia ▪ secretario(-a) de justicia attorney general ➤ La fiscal general Janet Reno... Attorney general Janet Reno...

ser **flaco(-a) como un palillo** to be skinny as a rail

flamante coche deportivo brand-new sports car ➤ Ella acababa de comprarse un flamante coche deportivo. She had just bought a brand-new sports car.

flamante senador(a) newly-elected Senator ▪ freshman Senator

flaqueza moral moral laxity

flautista de Hamelin the Pied Piper

ser un **flechazo** to be love at first sight

flojear por (la) casa ▪ holgazanear en (la) casa ▪ andar haciendo el vago por (la) casa ▪ echar la hueva to putter around the house ▪ to hang around the house ➤ Hemos estado flojeando por (la) casa todo el día. Vamos a jugar un poco de baloncesto. We've been puttering around the house all day. Let's go play a little basketball.

la **flor de la canela** the cream of the crop

la **flor de la juventud** one's prime

ser (una) **flor de un día** to be a flash in the pan

la **flor logra lo que no un diamante** a flower achieves more than a diamond

la **flor y nata de** la crème de la crème of

flores ajadas ▪ flores marchitas withered flowers

flores marchitas ▪ flores ajadas withered flowers

flota de barcos fleet of ships

flotar en el aire 1. *(globo)* ▪ flotar por el aire to float in the air 2. *(humor, olor, etc.)* to hang in the air

fluir a ▪ ser un afluente de to flow into ▪ to be a tributary of ➤ El Río Cifuentes fluye al Tajo. ▪ El Río Cifuentes es un afluente del Tajo. The Cifuentes River flows into the Tagus. ▪ The Cifuentes River is a tributary of the Tagus.

fluir de ideas *(James Joyce)* ▪ fluir de pensamientos ▪ monólogo interior stream of consciousness

flujo continuo de carros ▪ flujo continuo de coches steady stream of cars

flujo continuo de visitantes steady stream of visitors

flujo de caja cash flow

flujo de insultos ▪ rosario de insultos ▪ avalancha de insultos ▪ plétora de insultos ▪ cantidad de improperios stream of insults ▪ barrage of insults

flujo de sangre blood flow ▪ flow of blood ▪ hemorrhage

flujo laminar laminar flow

flujo migratorio flow of immigrants

fogonazo de luz blaze of light

folio en blanco ▪ (el) papel en blanco blank sheet of paper ➤ Por favor, saquen un folio en blanco. ▪ *(Esp., vosotros)* Por favor, sacad un folio en blanco. Please take out a blank sheet of paper. ▪ Please get out a blank sheet of paper.

fondear una mina to plant a mine

fondo de inversión mutual fund

fondo de la calle: ir al ~ ▪ ir al final de la calle to go to the end of the street ➤ *(tú)* Ve al fondo de la calle y lo verás justo a la derecha. ▪ Ve al final de la calle y lo verás justo a la derecha. *(usted)* Vaya (usted) al fondo de la calle y lo verá justo a la derecha. ▪ Vaya (usted) al final de la calle y lo verá justo a la derecha. Go to the end of the street and you'll see it just off to the right.

fondo de la cuestión ▪ fondo del asunto bottom line ▪ heart of the question

fondo de mar ▪ fondo del mar seabed ▪ seafloor

fondo del asunto heart of the matter

fondo del mar ▪ fondo de mar seabed ▪ seafloor

fondo intelectual brain trust

fontanería interna indoor plumbing

forjar el carácter de uno to forge one's character

forjar una excusa ▪ inventar una excusa to make up an excuse ▪ to invent an excuse

forma de enfocar un problema ▪ forma de abordar un problema ▪ forma de enfrentarse a un problema ▪ método de enfocar un problema ▪ método de abordar un problema ▪ método de enfrentarse a un problema ▪ método de enfocar un problema ▪ método de abordar un problema ▪ método de enfrentarse a un problema approach to a problem ▪ way of solving a problem

forma de hacer algo way to do something ▪ way of doing something ▪ way one does something ➤ Me gusta la forma de hablar que tiene el primer ministro británico. I like the way the British prime minister speaks.

forma en (la) que way in which ▪ way (that...) ▪ way ➤ La forma en (la) que me habló me dio buena espina. The way he spoke to me gave me a good feeling.

formación: tener una buena ~ ▪ tener una buena silueta to have a good figure ➤ Tiene una buena formación. She has a good figure.

ser **formado por** to be made up of ➤ El equipo quirúrgico, formado por cincuenta personas... The surgical team, made up of fifty people...

formar agujeros to form holes ➤ Freír la tortita hasta que forme agujeritos en la masa, y darle la vuelta. Fry the pancake until it forms little holes in the batter, and then flip it. ➤ Freír la tortita hasta que se formen agujeritos en la masa, y darle la vuelta. Fry the pancake until little holes form in the batter, and then flip it.

formar un sacerdote to train a priest

formarse: hay que ~ *(Méx.)* ▪ hay que hacer cola to have to get in line ▪ to have to form a line ▪ to have to line up ▪ to have to queue up ➤ Hay que formarse. ▪ Hay que hacer cola. You have to get in line.

formársele un chichón 1. *(en la cabeza)* to get a knot on one's head 2. *(cámara, hernia, etc.)* salírsele algo to balloon out ➤ Después de golpearme la cabeza, se me formó un chichón. I got a knot on my head after I bumped it. ➤ Se me formó un chichón en la hernia. ▪ Se me salió la hernia. My hernia ballooned out.

formarse una opinión to form an opinion ➤ Se formó una opinión equivocada. He formed a mistaken opinion.

formas campestres ▪ hábitos provincianos country ways

formas diferentes de hacer una cosa ▪ formas distintas de hacer una cosa different ways of doing something

formular un deseo ▪ pedir un deseo ▪ pensar en un deseo to make a wish ▪ to think of a wish ➤ *(genio de la lámpara de Aladino)* ¡Formula tres deseos! Make three wishes!

formular una pregunta ▪ hacer una pregunta to ask a question ▪ to pose a question ➤ *(tú)* Déjame formularte esta pregunta. ▪ Permíteme formularte esta pregunta. ▪ *(usted)* Permítame hacerle esta pregunta. ▪ Déjeme que le haga (a usted) esta pregunta. ▪ Let me ask you this question.

formulario de solicitud application form

forofo(-a) del fútbol ▪ fanático(-a) del fútbol ▪ hincha de fútbol soccer fan

estar **forrado(-a) (de dinero)** to be loaded (with money)

forro de madera wood paneling

fortalecer la familia to strengthen the family

fortalecer la seguridad ▪ reforzar la seguridad to beef up security ▪ to increase security ▪ to heighten security

fortaleza inexpugnable invincible fortress ▪ impregnable fortress ▪ unassailable fortress ➤ Ninguna fortaleza es inexpugnable. No fortress is invincible.

fortalezamiento de la familia strengthening of the family

forzar a alguien a hacer algo to make someone do something ▪ to force someone to do something

forzar las normas ▪ forzar las reglas to bend the rules

forzar las reglas ▪ forzar las normas to bend the rules

fosas nasales nasal passages

fosa Marianas *(en el Océano Pacífico)* Marianas Trench

foso de la orquesta orchestra pit

foto de familia family photo

foto suya 1. *(de él)* photo of him ▪ picture of him 2. *(de ella)* photo of her ▪ picture of her

foto trucada doctored photo ▪ doctored photograph

fotocopiadora de color color copier

fracturársele un hueso ▪ rompérsele un hueso to break a bone ▪ to suffer a broken bone ▪ to suffer a bone fracture ➤ En 2004, Fidel Castro se cayó y se le fracturó la rodilla. ▪ En 2004, Fidel Castro se cayó y se le rompió la rodilla. In 2004, Fidel Castro fell and broke his knee.

el **fragor de batalla** din of battle

el **fragor de trueno** clap of thunder ▪ thunderclap

fraguar una alianza to forge an alliance

franco de aduana duty-free

franja de Gaza *(geografía)* Gaza Strip

franja de máxima audiencia prime time

franja del espectro band of the spectrum ▪ spectral bands

franja del espectro político ▪ banda del espectro político band of the political spectrum ➤ El presidente y el primer ministro ocupan la misma franja del espectro político. ▪ El presidente y el primer ministro ocupan la misma franja del espectro político. The president and the prime minister occupy the same band of the political spectrum.

franja lunática lunatic fringe

franquear un pantano to make one's way through a swamp ▪ to make one's way across a swamp

franquear un sobre to put the postage on an envelope ▪ to pay the postage on an envelope

franquear un río to negotiate a river ▪ to ford a river ▪ to make one's way across a river

franquear una carta a to post a letter to ▪ to pay the postage on a letter to ➤ ¿Cuánto cuesta franquear una carta a los Estados Unidos? How much is the postage on a letter to the United States? ▪ What's the postage on a letter to the United States?

frasco de perfume bottle of perfume

frase capicúa ▪ palíndromo palindrome ▪ palindromatic phrase

frase hecha set phrase

frase típica typical phrase

frases cómicas funny lines

el **fraude fiscal** tax evasion

fregar la loza ▪ fregar los cacharros ▪ fregar los platos ▪ fregar la vajilla ▪ lavar la loza to wash the dishes ▪ to do the dishes

fregar la vajilla ▪ lavar los platos ▪ fregar los cacharros ▪ fregar los platos ▪ fregar la loza to wash the dishes ▪ to do the dishes

fregar los cacharros ▪ fregar los platos ▪ fregar la loza ▪ fregar la vajilla to wash the dishes ▪ to do the dishes

fregar los platos ▪ fregar los cacharros ▪ fregar la loza ▪ fregar la vajilla to wash the dishes ▪ to do the dishes

freír a preguntas a alguien ▪ presionar a alguien con preguntas to grill someone ▪ to give someone a grilling

freírse de calor ▪ morirse de calor ▪ asarse de calor to be burning up ➤ *(juego de palabras)* Me frío de calor. I'm burning up.

¡**frena, frena!** hit the brakes! ▪ slow down! ▪ put on the brakes! ▪ apply the brakes!

frenar el crecimiento de to slow (down) the growth of ▪ to retard the growth of

frenar en seco to slam on the brakes ▪ to brake hard

frenar hasta parar to come to a stop

frenar la desbandada to stem the tide

frenar la desbandada de gente to stop the flood of people

frenazo slamming (on) of the brakes

frente a 1. in the face of 2. ante in front of ▪ before 3. enfrente opposite ▪ across from 4. en contraste con in contrast with ▪ as opposed to ▪ as contrasted with ➤ Frente a ellos apareció un tigre. A tiger appeared in front of them. ▪ A tiger appeared before them. ▪ *(literary)* A tiger loomed before them.

frente a ▪ a diferencia de ▪ en contraposición a ▪ en contraste con as opposed to ▪ in contrast to ▪ unlike ➤ El agua dulce frente al agua salada. ▪ Agua dulce a diferencia de agua salada. Fresh water as opposed to salt water. ➤ Un inquilino *de facto* no figura en el contrato, frente al inquilino *de jure*, que sí. ▪ Un inquilino *de facto* no figura en el contrato, a diferencia del inquilino *de jure*, que sí. ▪ Un inquilino *de facto* no figura en el contrato, en contraste con el inquilino *de jure*, que sí. A *de facto* tenant is one who is not on the lease, as opposed to a *de jure* tenant, who is.

estar **frente a** to be facing ▪ to be opposite ▪ to be in front of ▪ to be ahead of ➤ Estamos frente a una crisis ecológica. We are facing an ecological crisis. ➤ ¿Estamos frente a una crisis ecológica? Are we facing an ecological crisis?

frente a frente ▪ cara a cara face to face

frente a frente: hablar ~ to talk face to face

frente a frente: sentarse ~ to sit facing each other

frente a la costa de off the coast of

frente a mí in front of me ▪ before me

estar **frente al altar** ▪ estar ante el altar ▪ estar delante del altar to stand before the altar

frente interno: en el ~ on the domestic front ▪ on the home front

frío: hacer ~ to be cold ➤ Hace frío hoy. It's cold today.

frío: tener ~ to be cold ➤ Tengo frío. I'm cold.

la **frivolización de** trivialization of

frontera entre: servir de ~ to form the border between

frotarse las manos to rub one's hands

frotarse los ojos to rub one's eyes

frustrar la trama ▪ desbaratar la trama to foil the plot

fruta del día fresh fruit

fruto prohibido forbidden fruit

ser **fruto de** to be the fruit of ▪ to be the product of

fue de mentira it was meant only as a joke ▪ it was only a joke ▪ it was just a joke

fue digno de verlo ▪ era una cosa digna de verse ▪ fue algo espectacular it was spectacular ▪ it was a sight to see ▪ it was something to see ▪ it was quite a sight ▪ it was a great sight to see ▪ that was something to see ▪ that was quite a sight ▪ that was a great sight to see

fue él que... it was he who... ▪ *(coloquial)* he was the one who...

fue ella que... it was she who... ▪ *(coloquial)* she was the one who...

fue en ese momento cuando... ▪ fue en ese momento que... ▪ fue ahí que... it was at that moment that...

fue entonces cuando... ▪ fue entonces que... that was when... ▪ it was then that...

fue hecho del comienzo ▪ se comenzó con nada it was made from scratch

fue lo mejor (it) was for the best ▪ (it) was best ➤ Compré esta cámara porque fue lo mejor que encontré. I bought this camera because it was the best one I found. ➤ Se sentía triste al romper con su novia, pero ahora cree que fue lo mejor. He felt sad when he broke up with his girlfriend, but now he believes it was for the best.

fue lo que le consagró 1. *(a él)* it was the making of him 2. *(a ella)* it was the making of her

fue un día caluroso para la época it was a very hot day for this time of year

fue una suerte para él que it was lucky for him that

fue y dijo que 1. *(él)* he went on to say that 2. *(ella)* she went on to say that

fue y sigue siendo ▪ fue y todavía es it was and continues to be ▪ it was and still is

fue y todavía es ▪ fue y sigue siendo it was and still is ▪ it was and continues to be

¡fuego! fire!

fuego cruzado cross fire

fuego amigo friendly fire

fuego cruzado: estar atrapado en el ~ ▪ quedar atrapado en el fuego cruzado to get caught in the cross fire

fuego fatuo will o' the wisp ▪ false expectation

fuego fuerte: cocinar a ~ ▪ cocinar a fuego alto to cook on high heat ▪ to cook over high heat

fuego lento: cocinar a ~ ▪ cocinar a llama baja to cook on low heat ▪ to cook over low heat

fuegos artificiales ▪ fuegos de artificio fireworks

la **fuente de agua** ▪ chorro de agua water fountain ▪ drinking fountain

la **fuente de alimentación** power supply ▪ power source ▪ source of electricity ▪ feed

la **fuente de beber** water fountain ▪ drinking fountain

la **fuente de financiación** source of financing

la **fuente de gelatina** batch of gelatin ▪ batch of Jello ▪ *(hecha de frutas o vegetales)* batch of aspic

la **fuente de horno** oven dish ▪ casserole dish

fuente de ingresos: **la principal ~** the main source of income ▪ the principal source of income

la **fuente de letra** type style

la **fuente de río** headwaters (of a river) ▪ source of a river

la **fuente del señor** *(poético)* ▪ (el) manantial spring

la **fuente de suministro** source of supply

fuente desconocida unknown source

fuente fidedigna ▪ fuente fiable ▪ fuente veraz ▪ fuente reputable reliable source

la **fuente termal** hot spring

fuentes diplomáticas diplomatic sources

fuera como fuera ▪ fuese como fuese however it was

fuera coñas *(Esp., argot juvenil)* ▪ fuera de bromas ▪ bromas aparte all kidding aside

fuera de ▪ además de outside of ▪ out of

estar **fuera de ajuste** ▪ estar mal arreglado to be out of adjustment

fuera de alguna carta *(literario)* ▪ con excepción de una carta ocasional ▪ de no ser por alguna que otra carta ▪ con excepción de una que otra carta except for an occasional letter ➤ Fuera de alguna carta, apenas si tenía noticias suyas. Except for an occasional letter, he rarely heard from her.

fuera de broma ▪ bromas aparte (all) kidding aside ▪ seriously, though

fuera de chiste *(L.am.)* ▪ fuera de broma all kidding aside ▪ all joking aside

estar **fuera de cobertura** *(teléfono móvil)* to be out of range

fuera de combate: dejarle a alguien ~ to put someone out of action ▪ to put someone out of commission

estar **fuera de combate** to be out of action ▪ to be out of commission

fuera de contexto: sacar ~ to take out of context

fuera de eso other than that

estar **fuera de foco** to be out of focus

fuera de horario off-hours ➤ ¿Hay una tienda abierta fuera de horario cerca de aquí? Is there an off-hours store nearby?

estar **fuera de juego** 1. *(deportes)* to be out of play 2. *(referido a la vida social)* to be out of circulation

estar **fuera de la cuestión** 1. to be out of the question 2. no venir al caso to be beside the point ➤ Está fuera de la cuestión. That's beside the point. ▪ It's beside the point

estar **fuera de (la) escena** to be out of the picture ➤ ¿Qué fue de su viejo novio?–Ah, está fuera de escena. Ella tiene un nuevo amor. What happened to her old boyfriend?-Oh, he's out of the picture. She's got a new flame.

estar **fuera de la ley** to be illegal ▪ to be breaking the law

ser un(a) **fuera de la ley** to be an outlaw

ser **fuera de lo común** ▪ ser fuera de lo normal ▪ ser inusual to be out of the ordinary

ser **fuera de lo normal** ▪ ser fuera de lo común ▪ ser inusual to be unusual ➤ Es un poco fuera de lo normal ver una mujer joven pasando un cochecito de bebé con una gata y su camada. It's a little unusual to see a young woman pushing a mother cat and her litter of kittens in a stroller.

estar **fuera de lugar** to be out of place

¡fuera de mi propiedad! get off my property!

fuera de plató off the (movie) set
fuera de que ■ aparte de que ■ además de que besides which
ser un **fuera de serie** ■ ser una persona fuera de serie to be one of a kind ■ to be unique ■ to be exceptional
estar **fuera de servicio 1.** estar cerrado to be out of service **2.** estar estropeado to be out of order
estar **fuera de sí** ■ estar loco de atar to be beside oneself ■ to be fit to be tied
estar **fuera de sí por la preocupación** to be beside oneself with worry
fuera de toda duda without a doubt ■ beyond any shadow of a doubt ■ beyond a shadow of a doubt
fuera de tono off color ■ inappropriate
estar **(fuera) de vacaciones** to be (away) on vacation
fuera lo que fuera whatever it was ➤ Fuera lo que fuera, sirvió. Whatever it was, it worked.
fuera lo que fuera a hacer 1. *(él)* whatever he was going to do **2.** *(ella)* whatever she was going to do
fuero interno inner self ■ voice of conscience
el **fuerte oleaje** high waves ➤ *(noticia)* Los radares no detectaron la patera por el fuerte oleaje. Radars did not detect the dinghy because of the high waves.
fueron felices y comieron perdices ■ y fueron felices por siempre jamás ■ y colorín colorado, este cuento se ha acabado and they lived happily ever after ■ and that's the end of the story
fueron y siguen siendo they were and still are ■ they were and continue to be
fuerte abrazo: darle a alguien un ~ to give someone a big hug
el **fuerte control de seguridad** tight security
estar **fuerte en una asignatura** ■ estar fuerte en una materia ■ estar fuerte en un tema to be strong in a subject ■ to be good in a subject ■ to be good at a subject
fuerte nevada heavy snow
fuerte subida de costos sharp increase in costs
fuerte subida de precios ■ fuerte subida de costes sharp increase in prices
el **fuerte temporal** powerful storm
fuertes lluvias heavy rains
fuertes vientos high winds ■ strong winds
fuerza centrífuga centrifugal force
fuerza centrípeta centripetal force
fuerza de arrastre *(aerodinámica)* (force of) drag
fuerza de gravedad (force of) gravity
fuerza de sus convicciones strength of one's convictions
fuerza de sustentación *(aerodinámica)* (force of) lift
fuerza de voluntad ■ (el) tesón will power
fuerza mayor act of God
fuerza viva life force
fuerza votada voting block ➤ El partido democrático es la fuerza más votada de Hong Kong. The democratic party is the largest voting block in Hong Kong
fuese como fuese ■ fuera como fuera no matter how
fuese por lo que fuera in spite of it all
fugarse con alguien ■ escaparse con alguien to run off with someone ➤ El jefe se fugó con su secretaria. The boss ran off with his secretary.
fugarse de la cárcel to break out of jail ■ to escape from jail ■ to escape from prison
ser **fugitivo de la justicia** to be a fugitive from justice ■ to be on the lam ■ to be on the run
fui a parar al quinto pino I ended up in the middle of nowhere
(Fulano) habla hasta debajo del agua (so-and-so) never stops talking
fulano de tal so-and-so
Fulano, Mengano y Zutano every Tom, Dick and Harry
fulgurante carrera brilliant career
fulminar de un tiro a alguien to shoot someone dead ■ to shoot someone to death
fumador empedernido chain smoker ■ heavy smoker
fumar una pipa to smoke a pipe
fumarse la clase to cut (the) class ■ to skip the class ■ not to attend the class ■ not to go to the class
fumarse las clases ■ hacer novillos ■ volarse las clases to cut class ■ to play hooky ■ to skip school
la **fuente de juventud** fountain of youth
funcionar a pilas ■ funcionar con pilas to run on batteries
funcionar como una pantalla para actividades ilegales ■ funcionar como una pantalla para actividades ilícitas ■ servir como pantalla para actividades ilegales ■ servir como pantalla para actividades ilícitas ■ hacer de pantalla para actividades ilegales ■ hacer de pantalla para actividades ilícitas to serve as a front for illegal activities ■ to serve as a front for illicit activities
funcionar con gas to run on (natural) gas
funcionar con pilas ■ funcionar a pilas to run on batteries
funcionar correctamente 1. to work correctly ■ to work right **2.** to be in working order
funcionar de forma irregular ■ funcionar irregularmente to malfunction ■ to have developed a problem *(coloquial)* to act up ➤ El ascensor ha estado funcionando de forma irregular últimamente. The elevator has been acting up lately. ■ The elevator has developed a problem. ■ The elevator has been malfunctioning.
funcionario: alto ~ ■ funcionario de alto nivel high official ■ high-level official
funcionario de alto rango high-ranking official
funcionario público public official
ser **fundado por** to be founded by ➤ El Colegio Inglés de Valladolid fue fundado por Felipe II. The English College in Valladolid was founded by Felipe II.
estar **fundamentado en** ■ estar basado en ■ tener su base en ■ tener su fundamento en to be based on
fundamentar una teoría en to base a theory on
fundamentarse en to be based on
fundamento lógico logical basis
fundar una opinión en algo 1. to base an opinion on something **2.** *(normalmente tercera persona y voz pasiva)* to found an opinion on something ➤ Se fundó en una opinión equivocada. He based his opinions on misinformation ■ His opinions were based on misinformation ➤ Fundó su opinión con datos falsos. He based his opinion on false information. ■ He formed his opinion with false information. ■ He formed his opinion using false information. ➤ La opinión del comité se fundó en los hallazgos de investigadores especiales. The committee's opinion was founded on the findings of special investigators.
fundarse en to be based on ■ to be founded on
fundarse una opinion en ■ basarse una opinión en algo to base an opinion on
el **furgón de cola** caboose
furia animal ■ rabia animal rage
furor uterino *(arcaico)* ■ ninfomanía nymphomania
fútbol sala indoor football
futuro incierto ■ incierto futuro uncertain future

gafas de leer reading glasses

gafas de sol graduadas ▪ anteojos de sol graduados ▪ anteojos de sol con aumento prescription sun glasses

gafas graduadas ▪ lentes graduados prescription glasses

ser **gajes del oficio** ▪ ser percances del oficio **1.** to be an occupational hazard **2.** to be all in a day's work ▪ to go with the territory ➤ Son gajes del oficio. It's all in a day's work. ▪ It goes with the territory. ▪ Those are the hazards of the occupation.

galardonar a alguien (con el premio) ▪ conceder el premio a alguien ▪ otorgar el premio a alguien ▪ premiar a alguien to award the prize to someone

galimatías legales legal mumbo jumbo

gallina de los huevos de oro the goose that laid the golden egg

gallina en corral ajeno ▪ (el) pez fuera del agua fish out of water

gallina muy ponedora *(Méx., subido de tono)* woman of easy virtue ▪ promiscuous woman

gama completa de opciones complete range of options

gama de octavas ▪ alcance de octavas octave range ➤ El órgano tiene la gama de octavas más amplia de cualquier instrumento. The organ has the widest octave range of any instrument.

gana el sí the ayes have it ▪ the motion is carried

ganado suelto roaming cattle ▪ stray cattle

ganancia política political capital

ganar a alguien *(deportivo)* to beat someone ▪ to win over someone ▪ to defeat someone

ganar a un adversario en algo *(política, deporte, ajedrez)* ▪ derrotar a un adversario a algo ▪ derrotar a un adversario en algo to beat an opponent at something ▪ to defeat an opponent at something ➤ Me gana al ajedrez con los ojos cerrados, así que nunca juego con él. ▪ Me gana en el ajedrez con los ojos cerrados, así que nunca juego con él. ▪ Me derrota al ajedrez con los ojos cerrados, así que nunca juego con él. ▪ Me derrota en el ajedrez con los ojos cerrados, así que nunca juego con él. He beats me at chess hands down, so I never play him. ▪ He defeats me at chess hands down, so I never play him.

ganar a un equipo por goleada *(fútbol, hockey)* to beat a team by a lot of points ▪ *(coloquial)* to smear a team ▪ to whip a team

ganar al año to earn per year ▪ to earn in a year

ganar algo de dinero to earn some money

ganar con el tiempo to get better with age

ganar con todas las de la ley ▪ ganar hecho y derecho to win fair and square

ganar control de ▪ apoderarse de to gain control of

ganar de media *x* por hora to earn an average of *x* per hour ▪ to average *x* per hour ▪ to average *x* hourly ➤ ¿Cuánto ganaste de media por hora en ese trabajo? How much did you average per hour on that job? ➤ Gané de media quince euros por hora. I averaged fifteen euros per hour. ▪ I earned an average of fifteen euros per hour.

ganar dinero to make money ▪ to earn money ➤ Ella gana 2.000 euros mensuales. She makes 2,000 euros a month. ▪ She earns 2,000 euros a month.

ganar dinero a alguien to win money from someone ➤ Le gané diez euros. I won ten euros from him.

ganar el premio ▪ recibir el premio ▪ obtener el premio ▪ concederle el premio to win the prize ▪ to be awarded the prize ▪ to get the prize ▪ to garner the prize ▪ to take the prize

ganar el respeto de alguien to win someone's respect

ganar empuje ▪ cobrar velocidad to gain momentum

ganar hecho y derecho ▪ ganar con todas las de la ley to win fair and square

ganar la elección to win the election

ganar la guerra to win the war

ganar mucho en salud for one's health to improve ➤ He ganado mucho en salud. My health has improved.

ganar peso to gain weight ▪ to put on weight

ganar por el escaso margen de to win by the narrow margin of ▪ to carry by the narrow margin of ➤ Tras la votación, ganada por el escaso margen de tres votos... After the vote, carried by the narrow margin of three votes...

ganar puesto primero to win first place

ganar tiempo to gain time ➤ Ganarás tiempo si coges el metro al aeropuerto. You'll save time by taking the metro to the airport.

ganar tiempo al tiempo to gain time ▪ to try to do too much in too little time

ganar un buen salario to make a good salary

ganar un concurso to win a competition ➤ El diseño de James Hoban ganó el concurso. James Hoban's design won the competition.

ganar un pleito to win a case ▪ to win a lawsuit

ganar un sueldo ▪ ganar un salario ▪ defenderse to make a salary ▪ to get a salary ▪ to earn a salary ➤ Ella gana un buen sueldo. ▪ Ella gana un buen salario. ▪ Ella se defiende muy bien. She makes a good salary. ▪ She gets a good salary. ▪ She earns a good salary. ➤ Gana un sueldo más una comisión. He makes a salary plus commission. ▪ He gets (a) salary plus commission.

ganar una iglesia to take refuge in a church

ganar *x* euros a alguien to win *x* euros from someone ➤ Le gané diez euros. I won ten euros from him.

ganar *x* partidos al hilo to win *x* games in a row

ganarle a alguien to win over someone ▪ to beat someone ▪ to defeat someone

ganarle a alguien por mucho to beat someone hands down ▪ to beat someone handily ▪ to beat someone by a mile

ganarle la partida al tiempo to beat the clock ▪ to win the race against time ➤ James Bond siempre le gana la partida al tiempo, aunque sea por un segundo. James Bond always beats the clock, if only by a second. ▪ James Bond always wins the race against time, if only by a second.

ganarse algo a pulso to earn something with one's own labor ▪ to earn something by one's own labor ▪ to earn it with one's own sweat ➤ *(tú)* Te lo has ganado (a pulso). ▪ *(usted)* Se lo ha ganado (a pulso). You've earned it.

ganarse el aplauso to win applause ➤ Se ganó el aplauso de los reformistas. He won the applause of the reformers.

ganarse el apodo de to earn the nickname of

ganarse el aprecio de ▪ ganarse el respeto de to win esteem of ➤ Se ganó el aprecio de todos. He won the esteem of all.

ganarse el derecho a hacer algo to earn the right to (do) something ➤ Te has ganado el derecho. You've earned the right.

ganarse el respeto de ▪ ganarse el aprecio de to win the respect of

ganarse hasta la casa to get to the house ▪ to make it home

ganarse la confianza de alguien to win someone's confidence ▪ to win someone's trust ▪ to gain someone's confidence ▪ to gain someone's trust

ganarse la gloria to go to heaven

ganarse la vida to earn one's living ▪ *(en preguntas)* to do for a living ➤ El compositor ruso Mussorgsky se ganaba la vida como funcionario. The Russian composer Mussorgsky earned his living as a government official. ➤ ¿Cómo te ganas la vida? What do you do for a living?

ganarse los garbanzos *(coloquial)* ▪ ganarse el pan to bring home the bacon ▪ to earn one's living

ganarse un enemigo to make an enemy

ganarse una bofetada to get a spanking ➤ Jovencito, si le vuelves a dar tu brócoli al perro una vez más, tú vas a ganarte una bofetada. Young man, if you give your broccoli to the dog one more time, you're going to get a spanking.

ganarse una cachetada *(L.am.)* ▪ ganarse un cachetón ▪ ganarse una bofetada to get a spanking

ganarse una reputación honesta to earn a reputation for honesty

gancho de derecha *(boxeo)* right hook

gancho de izquierda *(boxeo)* left hook

garantizar a alguien un asiento ▪ asegurar a alguien un asiento to guarantee someone a seat

ser el **garbanzo negro de la familia** ▪ ser la oveja negra de la familia to be the black sheep in the family ▪ to be the black sheep of the family

garganta irritada: tener la ~ ▪ tener la garganta adolorida to have a sore throat

gargantilla de perlas pearl necklace

el **gas de la risa** ▪ óxido nítrico laughing gas ▪ nitric oxide

gas tenue: con ~ ▪ *(más común)* a fuego lento low flame ▪ low heat ➤ Se cocina con gas tenue. ▪ Se cocina a fuego lento. Cook over low heat. ▪ You cook it over low heat

gastar a manos llenas to spend money hand over fist

gastar bromas to play jokes (on someone)

gastar dinero en algo to spend money on something ➤ Si te tocara la lotería, ¿en qué gastarías el dinero? If you won the lottery, what would you spend the money on? ➤ ¿En qué (te) lo gastarías? What would you spend it on?

gastar frases to waste words

gastar la pólvora a salvas ▪ gastar la pólvora en salvas to waste time and energy

gastar menos que Tarzán en corbatas to be a tightwad

gastar menos que un ciego en novelas to be a tightwad

gastar palabras en balde con alguien ▪ gastar saliva to waste one's words on someone ▪ to talk in vain to someone

gastar por encima de sus posibilidades to spend beyond one's means

gastar saliva ▪ gastar palabras en balde to waste one's words on someone ▪ to talk in vain to someone

gastar tiempo to waste time

gastar una broma a alguien ▪ hacer una burla a alguien to play a joke on someone

gastarle la paciencia a alguien to try someone's patience

gastarle una broma a alguien to play a prank on someone

gastarse de tanto mirar to look a hole (right) through ➤ Los gallos se gastan de tanto mirarlos. You're going to look a hole (right) through that rooster.

ser un **gasto (de dinero) inútil** ▪ ser un despilfarro de dinero to be a waste of money ▪ *(culto)* to be a useless expenditure of money

gasto social social spending ▪ spending on social programs ▪ spending for social programs

gastos de producción: elevarse los ~ (for) production costs to rise

gastos irremediables necessary expenses ▪ unavoidable expenses

gastos superfluos unnecessary expenses ▪ superfluous expenses

gato hidráulico hydraulic jack

gemelos (idénticos) ▪ gemelos hermanos identical twins

gen recesivo ▪ gene recesivo recessive gene

una **generación atrás** a generation ago

género humano human race ▪ humankind ▪ mankind

ser **generosamente recompensado(-a)** to be richly rewarded

¡genial! ▪ ¡estupendo! ▪ ¡maravilloso! (that's) great!

el **genio desdeña el camino trillado** genius disdains a beaten path

la **gente de abajo** poor people

la **gente de barrio** poor people

la **gente de bien** ▪ gente pudiente rich people

la **gente de buen corazón** good-hearted people ▪ good people

la **gente de dinero** ▪ gente pudiente ▪ gente rica people with money ▪ rich people

la **gente de la edad de uno** people one's age

la **gente del segmento de edad de uno** people in one's age group

la **gente de la garra** ▪ gente de mala calaña scary people ▪ people to be wary of

la **gente de mal vivir** low lifes ▪ riff-raff

la **gente de mala calaña** wrong crowd ➤ De joven se juntaba con gente de mala calaña. As a teen-ager he ran (around) with the wrong crowd.

la **gente de medio pelo** people not to be trusted ▪ people you can't trust

la **gente de paz** people of peace ▪ people of good intentions

la **gente de uno** one's kind

la **gente encuestada** the people (who were) surveyed

gente guapa beautiful people

gente marginada people on the fringes

la **gente pudiente** ▪ gente rica ▪ gente de dinero wealthy people ▪ well-to-do people ▪ rich people ▪ people with money

gente que ni siquiera conocía people I didn't even know

la **gente que rodea a uno** the people around one ➤ Mi sueño es ser felíz y hacer felices a quienes me rodean. My dream is to be happy and to make the people around me happy.

la **gente que vive** the people who live

gente rica rich people

gente talluda grown-ups

las **gentes de habla española** ▪ gentes hispanohablantes ▪ gentes hispanoparlantes ▪ pueblos de habla española ▪ pueblos hispanohablantes ▪ pueblos hispanoparlantes Spanish-speaking peoples

las **gentes de habla inglesa** ▪ gentes de habla inglesa ▪ pueblos de habla inglesa ▪ pueblos anglohablantes English-speaking peoples

la **gestión de crisis** crisis management

la **gestión de tiempo** time management ▪ management of one's time

estar **gestionado a fin de lucro** to be operated for profit ▪ to be run for profit

ser **gestionado con fin de lucro por** to be operated for profit by ▪ to be run for profit by

ser **gestionado por el estado** to be state run

gestionar con ánimo de lucro to operate for proft ▪ to run for profit

gesto de amistad expression of friendship

(gesto de) desaire: hacerle a alguien un ~ to snub someone

gesto desdeñoso: hacer un ~ to make a disdainful face ▪ to put on a contemptuous expression

gigante roja: (estrella) ~ *(astronomía)* red giant

gira campestre picnic

gira de Europa tour of Europe ▪ European tour

gira fugaz ▪ gira intensiva ▪ gira a matacaballo whirlwind tour ▪ lightning tour ➤ *(titular)* El cantante norteamericano pone fin a su fugaz gira de España. The American singer winds down his whirlwind tour of Spain.

gira intensiva whirlwind tour

girar alrededor de ▪ girar en torno a to revolve around ➤ La Tierra gira sobre su eje y gira alrededor del sol. ▪ La Tierra gira sobre su eje y gira en torno al sol. The Earth rotates on its axis and revolves around the sun. ➤ Los planetas giran alrededor del sol. The planets revolve around the sun.

girar en torno a ▪ girar alrededor de to revolve around ➤ La Tierra gira sobre su eje y gira en torno al sol. ▪ La Tierra gira sobre su eje y gira alrededor del sol. The Earth rotates on its axis and revolves around the sun.

girar hacia to turn toward ▪ to go toward

girar la vista to look around

girar sobre su eje ▪ rotar sobre su eje to rotate on its axis

girar un bastón ▪ hacer girar un bastón con los dedos ▪ revolear un bastón to twirl a baton

girar un remo to feather an oar
girar y girar to turn round and round ▪ to turn around and around
giro bancario bank money order
giro de posición change of position ▪ about face ▪ change of course ➤ Giro radical de su posición Radical change of position ▪ Complete change of position
giro postal postal money order
glándulas sudoríparas sweat glands
globo aerostático hot-air balloon
globo lunar globe of the moon ▪ lunar globe
globo sonda: lanzarse un ~ ▪ *(plural)* **lanzarse globos sonda** 1. *(meteorología)* to send up a weather balloon 2. *(política)* to send up a trial balloon
globo terráqueo globe of the world ▪ terrestrial globe
gobierno de poder compartido ▪ gobierno de coalición coalition government
el **goce sexual** *(culto)* ▪ gozo sexual sexual pleasure
el **golpe arrollador** crushing blow
el **golpe bajo** low blow
el **golpe de aire frío** blast of cold air ▪ cold air blast ▪ cold blast of air
el **golpe de compás** ▪ tiempo de compás ▪ ritmo de la música beat of the music
el **golpe de estado** coup d'etat
el **golpe de gracia** coup de grace
el **golpe inesperado** ▪ desgracia repentina ▪ suceso inopinado bolt out of the blue
el **golpe de suerte** stroke of luck
el **golpe de tecla** keystroke
golpear contra ▪ dar contra to beat against ➤ La lluvia golpeaba contra el parabrisas. ▪ La lluvia daba contra el parabrisas. The rain was beating against the windshield.
golpear la mesa con el puño to bang one's fist on the table ▪ to bang the table with one's fist
golpear la pared divisoria to pound on the separating wall
golpearse con algo to bump into something ➤ Me golpeé con la mesa y se me hizo un moratón en la cadera. I bumped into the table and bruised my hip.
golpearse en la cabeza ▪ darse (un golpe) en la cabeza to hit one's head
golpearse y quedarse sin aliento ▪ golpearse y quedarse sin poder respirar to get one's breath knocked out ▪ (for) something to knock one's breath out ▪ (for) something to knock the breath out of one
goma de mascar ▪ chicle chewing gum ▪ gum
gorgoteo del agua gurgling of the water
gorguera de encaje lace ruff *(Nota: La gorguera es el adorno de lienzo alrededor del cuello que llevaban los caballeros renacentistas cuyo estilo puede servir para fechar algunos retratos al óleo. ▪ The ruff is the round linen collar worn by Renaissance gentlemen, whose style can be used to date some oil portraits.)*
gota fría cold front
ser la **gota que colma el vaso** ▪ ser la última gota to be the straw that broke the camel's back ▪ to be the last straw ➤ Fue la gota que colmó el vaso. It was the straw that broke the camel's back. ➤ La gota que colmó el vaso fue... The straw that broke the camel's back was... ▪ The last straw was...
gotearle la nariz to have a runny nose ▪ (for) one's nose to run ➤ Me gotea la nariz. I have a runny nose. ▪ My nose is running.
goteras: estar lleno de ~ ▪ tener goteras to have a lot of aches and pains
grabar sonido to record sound
grabar una película ▪ rodar una película to shoot a movie
gracia del chiste point of the joke ▪ meaning of the joke
¡gracias a Dios! ▪ a Dios gracias thank goodness ▪ *(más fuerte)* thank God
gracias a Dios por ser así thank God for that
gracias de nuevo thanks again ▪ thank you again
gracias de todas formas ▪ gracias de todos modos thanks, anyway ▪ thank you, anyway ▪ thanks, just the same ▪ *(frecuentemente irónico)* thank you just the same
gracias de todos modos ▪ gracias de todas formas thanks, anway ▪ thank you, anyway ▪ thanks, just the same ▪ *(frecuentemente irónico)* thank you just the same
gracias por el cumplido thank you for the compliment
gracias por el viaje thanks for the lift ▪ thanks for the ride
gracias por ofrecerte thank you for offering ▪ thanks for offering
gracias por su colaboración thank you for your cooperation
ser **gracioso donde los haya** ▪ ser ocurrente donde los haya ▪ ser de lo más gracioso (donde los haya) ▪ ser de lo más ocurrente (donde los haya) to be as witty as they come ▪ to be as witty as can be
grado de estrés stress level ▪ level of stress ▪ degree of stress
graduar el aire acondicionado to adjust the air conditioning
graduar la calefacción to adjust the heat
graduarse los ojos ▪ graduarse la vista to have one's eyes examined ▪ to have one's eyes checked ▪ to get one's eyes examined ▪ to get one's eyes checked ➤ Tengo que graduarme los ojos. I have to have my eyes examined. ➤ Vengo a graduarme. I've come to have my eyes checked. ▪ I've come to have my eyes examined.
grageas de liberación repetida ▪ píldoras de liberación repetida time-release pills
gran altitud high altitude(s) ➤ A gran altitud quizá sea necesario prolongar el tiempo de cocimiento. At high altitudes, longer cooking times may be necessary.
gran apuesta big gamble ➤ *(titular)* La gran apuesta de Putin. Putin's big gamble.
gran cosa big deal ➤ Lo consideran gran cosa. They think it's a big deal. ▪ It's supposed to be a big deal. ➤ No es (una) gran cosa. It's no big deal. ▪ It's no big thing. ▪ It's not a big deal.
el **gran día** the big day ➤ ¿Cuándo es el gran día? When's the big day?
ser una **gran figura** to be an important figure
ser un **gran fracaso** 1. to be a huge failure ▪ to be a great failure 2. estar chueco to be a big flop ➤ La película fue un gran fracaso. The movie was a big flop.
la **gran manzana** ▪ Nueva York the big apple ▪ New York City
gran mundo ▪ buena sociedad high society
gran número de votantes ▪ elevada concurrencia de votantes ▪ alto porcentaje de electores high voter turnout ▪ large voter turnout ▪ heavy voter turnout
gran oportunidad big break ▪ big opportunity ➤ Su gran oportunidad llegó... His big break came...
gran paso adelante big step forward
gran polémica heated debate
ser una **gran proeza** to be no mean feat
gran público general public
ser una **gran tarea** to be a big job ➤ Es una gran tarea. It's a big job.
granada de mano hand grenade
grandes artistas major artists
las **grandes compañías** ▪ las grandes empresas big business
las **grandes empresas** ▪ las grandes compañías big business
granja lechera dairy farm
grasa corporal body fat
gravedad específica *(física)* specific gravity
gravísima herida severe wound
gravísima lesión serious injury
la **gripe del pollo** avian influenza ▪ bird flu
gripe porcina swine flu
gritar a pleno pulmón to shout at the top of one's lungs
gritar de alegría ▪ gritar de júbilo to shout for joy
gritar hasta roncarse ▪ desgañitarse to shout oneself hoarse
gritar lo más fuerte que uno puede to shout as loud as one can
griterío de los aficionados cheering of the fans
grueso de the bulk of ▪ the majority of ▪ the greater part of
grueso de las tropas most of the troops ▪ the majority of the troops ▪ the major portion of the troops ➤ El gobierno británico retira el grueso de sus tropas de élite. The British government withdraws most of its elite troops.
gruñirle a alguien to growl at someone ➤ Ese perro me gruñe. That dogs growls at me.

grupo de profesores ■ profesorado faculty
grupo que está a favor de la vida pro-life group
grupo sanguíneo ■ tipo de sangre blood type ➤ ¿Cuál es tu grupo sanguíneo?-"A" positivo. What is your blood type?-"A" positive.
grupos ultras extremist groups
guapa de cojones *(subido de tono)* ■ guapa de narices drop dead gorgeous ■ knockout ■ fox
guarda tu recibo save your receipt
guardar ■ conservar ■ abastecer to store
guardar a buen recaudo to keep in a safe place ■ to store in a safe place
guardar a cal y canto ■ guardar bajo llave to keep under lock and key
guardar algo en el buche ■ tener algo en el buche to keep something under one's hat
guardar algo para alguien to save someone something ■ to save something for someone ➤ Nunca compro el periódico, así que mi amigo me guarda el suplemento cultural. I never buy the paper, so my friend saves me the arts section. ■ I never buy the paper, so my friend saves the arts section for me. ➤ Me lo guarda. He saves it for me.
guardar bajo llave ■ guardar a cal y canto to keep under lock and key
guardar cama ■ quedarse en cama ■ permanecer en la cama to stay in bed ■ to remain in bed
guardar distancia to keep one's distance
guardar el secreto to keep it a secret ■ to keep the secret
guardar la compra to put the groceries away ■ to put away the groceries
guardar la lengua to hold one's tongue
guardar las distancias ante to keep one's distance from
guardar las formas to keep up appearances ■ to maintain appearances
guardar todo para uno mismo ■ guardárselo todo ■ guardarse todo para sí to keep something all to oneself
guardar un cierto parecido con to bear a certain resemblance to ■ to bear a superficial resemblance to ➤ Esta ave guarda un cierto parecido con la cigüeña, excepto por su color naranja. This bird bears a superficial resemblance to a stork, except for its orange color.
guardarle el turno a alguien to save someone's place in line ■ to keep someone's place in line
guardarle rencor a alguien por algo ■ tenerle inquina a alguien por algo ■ tenerle tirria a alguien por algo ■ tenerle manía a alguien por algo to bear a grudge against someone for something ■ to harbor a grudge against someone for something ■ to nurse a grudge against someone for something ■ to have a grudge against someone for something
guardarse algo para sí to keep something to oneself ➤ Me lo guardo para mí. I'm going to keep it to myself. ■ I'm going to keep that to myself.
guarde (usted) su recibo save your receipt
guarecerse de ■ resguardarse de ■ buscar refugio de to take shelter from
¡guay de Paraguay! fine as frog's hair! ■ just super!
guerra acérrima ■ guerra sin cuartel all-out war
guerra contra el terrorismo war on terrorism
guerra editorial ■ guerra de editoriales editorial war ➤ *El periodismo en Tennessee* de Mark Twain trata de una guerra editoral entre dos periódicos rurales-es decir, al principio dos. Mark Twain's *Journalism in Tennessee* is about an editorial war between two rural newspapers-two at first, that is.
guerra fronteriza border war
guerra sin cuartel ■ guerra acérrima all-out war
la **guía de conteo de calorías** calorie counter
guía didáctica study guide
guía turística tour guide
el **guía turístico** tour guide
guiar paso a paso por to walk one through ➤ Necesito que alguien me guíe paso a paso por la instalación. I need someone to walk me through the installation.
guiarse por su instinto to follow one's instincts ■ to be guided by one's instincts ➤ Me guié por mi instinto. I followed my instincts. ■ I was guided by my instincts.
guiñar un ojo a alguien ■ guiñar el ojo a alguien to wink at someone
guión bajo *(informática)* underscore ➤ En la dirección de correo electrónico, pones un guión bajo en medio del nombre y el apellido. In the E-mail address, you put an underscore between the first and last names.
el **guión (de cine)** screenplay
guirnalda de margaritas daisy chain
guisar muy bien to be a good cook
gustar de algo to like something
gustar de alguien *(coloquial)* ■ gustarle alguien to like someone (romantically) ➤ Parece que las relaciones sentimentales siempre son complicadas. O bien él gusta de ella y ella no gusta de él, o viceversa. ■ Parece que las relaciones sentimentales siempre son complicadas. O bien a él le gusta ella y él no le gusta a ella, o viceversa. It seems like relationships are always complicated. Either he likes her and she doesn't like him, or viceversa. ➤ Parece que las relaciones sentimentales siempre son complicadas. O bien ella gusta de él, y él no gusta de ella, o viceversa. ■ Parece que las relaciones sentimentales siempre están complicadas. O bien a ella le gusta él y ella no le gusta a él, o viceversa. It seems like relationships are always complicated. Either she likes him and he doesn't like her, or viceversa.
gustarle cada vez más to like something better and better ■ to grow on one ➤ Al principio no me gustaba vivir aquí, pero ahora me gusta cada vez más. I didn't like living here at first, but it's growing on me.
gustarle hacer algo to like to do something ■ to like doing something ■ to enjoy doing something
gustarle las óperas to like opera ➤ Le gustan las óperas. *(a él)* He likes opera. ■ *(a ella)* She likes opera.
gustarle más cada vez to grow on you
gustarle mucho los libros to love books ➤ Le gustaban mucho los libros y dedicaba el tiempo libre a leer. She loved books and spent her free time reading.
el **gusto es mío** ■ es un placer (it's) my pleasure
gusto por interest in
gustos de cada cual individual tastes
gustos depurados refined tastes
gustos refinados refined tastes

ha cambiado el corte *(Valle-Inclán)* he's tampered with the cutting (of the cards)

ha de haber (it) must have been...

ha de llegar el momento en que... the time will come when...

ha de ser... it must be... ➤ Ha de ser el vino It must be the wine

ha de tenerse en cuenta que... ▪ hay que tener en cuenta que... it must be kept in mind that...

ha debido de costar una fortuna it must have cost a fortune

ha debido ser it must have been ➤ Ha debido ser un caso puntual. It must have been an isolated case.

ha estado en la nevera... ▪ lleva en la nevera... it's been in the refrigerator (for)... ➤ Debería estar frío. Ha estado en la nevera cuatro horas. ▪ Debería estar frío. Lleva cuatro horas en la nevera. It should be cold. It's been in the refrigerator for four hours.

¡ha funcionado! *(el truco)* it worked!

ha habido 1. *(singular)* there has been 2. *(plural)* there have been ➤ Ha habido un malentendido. There has been a misunderstanding.

ha habido muchas ocasiones en las que there have been a lot of times when

ha habido un cambio de planes there has been a change of plans ▪ there's been a change of plans

ha hecho que se siente cuando estaba a punto de desmayarse he (the dog) has made her sit down when she was about to faint

ha llegado la ocasión de the time has come to

ha llegado el momento de it's time to ➤ Ha llegado el momento de terminar esta investigación. It's time to end this investigation.

¿ha llegado el avión? has the plane arrived? ▪ has the plane come in?

¿ha llegado mi pedido? has my order come in?

ha pasado lo peor the worst is over

ha pasado un ángel you can hear a pin drop

ha variado el viento ▪ ha cambiado el viento the wind has changed

ha visto tiempos mejores it has seen better days ▪ he has seen better days ▪ she has seen better days

haber andado perdido(-a) to have been at loose ends

haber buen rollo entre dos personas *(coloquial)* ▪ entenderse muy bien con alguien to have a good rapport with someone ➤ Hay buen rollo entre nosotros. ▪ Nos entendemos muy bien. We have a good rapport. ▪ I have a good rapport with...

haber cubierto una buena parte de to be well into ▪ to have covered a good part of ▪ to have covered a lot of ➤ La clase ha cubierto buena parte del libro. The class is well into the book. ▪ The class has covered a good part of the book.

haber de to have to ▪ must ➤ Espero que por eso no haya de enturbiarse nuestra amistrad. ▪ Espero que por eso no se enturbie nuestra amistad. I hope that our friendship will not be troubled by it. ▪ I hope it won't mess up our friendship. ➤ *(canción)* A Pamplona hemos de ir. We must go Pamplona. ▪ We have to go to Pamplona.

haber de hacer algo to have to do something ▪ to need to do something ▪ must do something ➤ Has de estar estupefacto ante lo que hice. You must be dumbfounded at what I did. ➤ Si ha de pasar, pasará. If it's supposed to happen, it will.

haber de todo como en botica *(Esp.)* ▪ haber de todo ▪ haber de lo que te imagines to have everything under the sun ▪ (for) there to be everything under the sun ➤ Hay de todo como en botica. They have everything under the sun.

haber demanda to be in demand

haber demasiado en juego (for) there to be too much at stake ➤ Hay demasiado en juego como para permitirme una demora en la lectura. There's too much at stake to let myself fall behind in the reading. ▪ There's too much at stake to get behind in the reading.

haber desaparecido (de) ▪ haberse extraviado (de) to be missing (from) ▪ to have disappeared (from)

haber estado en el hospital desde... ▪ llevar en el hospital desde... to have been in the hospital since... ➤ Ha estado en el hospital desde el viernes después de tu partida. ▪ Lleva en el hospital desde el viernes después de tu partida. He's been in the hospital since the Friday after you left.

haber estado oyéndolo durante meses ▪ haber venido oyéndolo durante meses to have been hearing that for months ➤ He estado oyéndolo durante meses. ▪ He venido oyéndolo durante meses. I've been hearing that for months.

haber gato encerrado to smell a rat ➤ Aquí hay gato encerrado. I smell a rat.

haber ido a ▪ haber estado en to have been to ➤ Esta mañana he ido a mi proveedor de Internet, a la biblioteca y al laboratorio de informática de la universidad. This morning I've been to my Internet service provider, the library and the university computer lab. ▪ This morning I went to my Internet service provider, the library and the university computer lab.

haber ido conociendo a alguien (gradualmente) ▪ haber ido conociendo a alguien poco a poco to have gradually gotten to know someone

haber llegado al colmo to have had all one can take ➤ He llegado al colmo. I've had all I can take.

haber llovido mucho desde entonces for there to have been a lot of water under the bridge since then ➤ Ha llovido mucho desde entonces. There's been a lot of water under the bridge since then.

haber pasado ya to be over ➤ La temporada de fresas ha pasado ya. ▪ La temporada de las fresas ya ha pasado. The strawberry season is over. ▪ The strawberry season has passed. ▪ The strawberry season has ended.

haber perdido algún tornillo to have a screw loose

haber que to have to ▪ (for one) to need ➤ *(Libro de Snoopy) Hay que ayudarte, Charlie Brown. You Need Help, Charlie Brown.*

haber quedado a ▪ tener hora ▪ tener una cita to have an appointment at

haber recorrido un largo camino to have come a long way ➤ Ha recorrido un largo camino desde que... He's come a long way since...

haber sido cocinero antes que fraile to have been there ▪ to have been in another's situation ▪ to have been in another's shoes ➤ El profesor nos dijo que no intentásemos copiar nuestros trabajos directamente de la enciclopedia, porque él había sido cocinero antes que fraile, y se sabía todos nuestros trucos. The teacher told us not to try to copy our essays directly from the encyclopedia because he's been there before, and he knows our tricks.

haber sido de to become of ▪ to have become of ➤ ¿Qué ha sido de tu amiga mexicana? Whatever became of your Mexican friend? ▪ What has become of your Mexican friend?

haber suficiente profundidad to be too deep to touch bottom ➤ Traté de tocar fondo, pero aún había suficiente profundidad. I tried to touch bottom, but it was still too deep.

haber sus más y sus menos (for) there to be ups and downs

haber tela marinera ■ tener tela marinera (for) something to be very complex ➤ Hay tela marinera. It's complicated ■ There's a lot to it.

haber tomado una copa de más to have had one too many

haber un abismo entre... ■ haber una diferencia abismal entre... (for there) to be a huge difference between...

haber un buen trecho to be a long way

haber un tomate (for) there to be a ruckus ■ (for) there to be a flap ■ (for) there to be a big problem ➤ Ayer en la primera comunión de mi hermano pequeño hubo un tomate cuando uno de los niños le tiró de la coleta a una niña. Yesterday at my little brother's first communion there was a ruckus when one of the boys pulled the ponytail of one of the girls. ■ Yesterday at my little brother's first communion there was a flap when one of the boys pulled the ponytail of one of the girls. ■ Yesterday at my little brother's first communion there was a big problem when one of the boys pulled the ponytail of one of the girls.

haber una incidencia 1. *(neutral)* (for there) to be something to report 2. *(negativo)* (for there) to be a technical problem ■ (for there) to be a snafu ➤ Cuando mi jefe me preguntó si había alguna incidencia le dije que no. When the boss asked me if there was anything to report, I said no. ➤ Cuando llamé a Telefónica para informarles del problema con mi correo electrónico, me dijeron que había una incidencia. When I called Telefónica to report the problem with my E-mail, they told me that there was a technical problem.

haber una marimorena (for) there to be a fuss

haber venido oyéndolo durante meses ■ haber estado oyéndolo durante meses to have been hearing that for months ➤ He venido oyéndolo durante meses. ■ He estado oyéndolo durante meses. I've been hearing that for months.

haber visto mejores días ■ haber visto tiempos mejores to have seen better days

haber visto suceder algo to have seen something happen

haber visto tiempos mejores ■ haber visto mejores días to have seen better days

haber vuelto ■ estar de vuelta ■ estar de regreso to be back ➤ Ha vuelto. ■ Está de vuelta. ■ Está de regreso. *(él)* He's back. ■ *(ella)* She's back.

haber vuelto a la ciudad ■ estar de vuelta en la ciudad to be back in town

haber vuelto la calefacción ■ ya hay calefacción (for) the heat to be back on ➤ Por fin, ha vuelto la calefacción. ■ Ya hay calefacción otra vez. ■ Ya hay calefacción de nuevo. The heat's back on, finally.

haber vuelto a la normalidad ■ estar de vuelta a la normalidad to be back to normal ■ to have returned to normal ➤ Hoy mi correo electrónico ha vuelto a la normalidad. ■ Hoy mi correo electrónico está de vuelta a la normalidad. My E-mail is back to normal today.

haberle quitado los mocos a alguien *(coloquial)* ■ haber criado a alguien (desde la infancia) to have raised someone from infancy

¡**haberlo dicho (antes)!** ■ debería haberlo dicho ■ debería de habérmelo dicho antes you should have told me (about it)!

¡**haberlo sabido!** ■ ¡si lo hubiera sabido! ■ ¡si lo hubiese sabido! if only I had known! ■ if only I'd known! ■ if I had only known! ■ if I'd only known!

haberse agotado algo ■ quedarse sin algo to have run out of something (permanently) ■ to be all gone ■ to be all taken ➤ Se han agotado las entradas. They've run out of tickets. ■ They're out of tickets. ■ The tickets are all gone. ■ The tickets are all taken. ➤ Se ha agotado la gasolina. ■ Nos hemos quedado sin gasolina. We're out of gas. ■ We've run out of gas.

haberse ausentado to have been gone ➤ Tras haberme ausentado un mes... After I had been gone a month...

haberse comprometido to be engaged (to be married) ➤ Se han comprometido. They're engaged.

haberse comprometido (con alguien) a hacer algo to have committed oneself (to someone) to doing something ■ to have made the commitment (to someone) to do something ■ to have promised something to someone

haberse conocido *x* años atrás to have met *x* years earlier ➤ La pareja se había conocido cuatro años atrás. The couple had met four years earlier.

haberse esfumado para entonces ■ haberse volado para entonces to be gone by then ➤ Se habrán esfumado para entonces. ■ Se habrán volado para entonces. They'll be gone by then.

haberse extraviado (de) ■ haber desaparecido (de) to be missing (from) ■ to have disappeared (from)

haberse ganado el derecho (de) to have earned the right (to) ➤ Te has ganado el derecho. You've earned the right.

haberse hecho ■ haber sido de to become of ➤ ¿Qué se ha hecho tu amiga mejicana? Whatever became of your Mexican friend?

haberse ido ya ■ irse ya already to be gone ■ to have already gone ■ to have already left ➤ Ella ya se ha ido. ■ Ella se fue ya. She is already gone. ■ She has already gone. ■ She's already gone. ■ She's already left. ➤ El portero no vuelve hasta el día veinte, y para entonces ya me habré ido. The concierge doesn't get back until the twentieth, and I'll already be gone by then. ■ The concierge doesn't get back until the twentieth, and I'll already have left by then. ■ The concierge doesn't get back until the twentieth, and I'll have already left by then.

haberse puesto un anillo ■ llevar puesto un anillo ■ usar un anillo to be wearing a ring ■ to have put on a ring ➤ (Ella) se ha puesto un anillo. She's wearing a ring.

habérselas con alguien to have it out with someone

habérsele acabado algo ■ quedarse sin algo to be (temporarily) out of something ■ to have run out of something (temporarily) ➤ Se les habían acabado los pedacitos de tocino en la tienda. ■ Se habían quedado sin pedacitos de tocino en la tienda. They were out of bacon bits at the store. ■ They'd run out of bacon bits at the store (when I was there).

había de volver la cabeza it would turn its head *(Nota: Referido a un animal "haber de" expresa comportamiento determinado. ■ Referring to an animal "haber de" expresses determined behavior.)*

había dispuesto para *(Valle-Inclán)* he had arranged for ■ he had given instructions for

había dispuesto que 1. *(él)* he had arranged for 2. *(ella)* she had arranged for

había habido there had been

había ido conociendo had gradually gotten to know ➤ Él había ido conociéndolo. ■ *(Esp., leísmo)* Él había ido conociéndole. He had gradually gotten to know him. ➤ Él había ido conociéndola a ella. ■ Él había ido conociéndola. He had gradually gotten to know her.

había niebla it was foggy

había que... 1. *(yo)* I would have to... 2. *(él)* he would have to... 3. *(ella)* she would have to...

¡**había que verlo!** you should have seen it!

había una vez ■ érase una vez once upon a time ■ there was once ■ there once were

había veces que... there were times when...

¿**habíamos quedado (en) que yo te llamaba?** ■ ¿quedé en llamarte? was I supposed to call you?

habido fuera del matrimonio ■ nacido fuera del matrimonio born out of wedlock

habido y por haber past, present, and future

habiendo declarado que... having stated that...

habiendo dicho eso having said that

habiendo dicho que... having said that...

habiéndome criado en... having been raised in...

las **habilidades de escribir a máquina** typing skills

ser **habildoso con algo** ■ ser hábil con algo to be adept at something ■ to be skillful with something ■ to be skillful at (doing) something ➤ Es muy habilidoso con las computadoras. ■ Es muy hábil con las computadoras. He is very adept at computers. ■ He is very skillful with computers.

habitación abarrotada ■ habitación muy concurrida ■ habitación atestada ■ habitación apiñada ■ habitación llena ■ salón abarrotado ■ salón muy concurrido ■ salón atestado ■ salón apiñado ■ salón lleno crowded room ■ room (jam) packed with people ■ room jammed with people ■ room overflowing with people

la **habitación de al lado** the next room

la **habitación retrete** outhouse

habitar en to inhabit ■ to live in

hábito arraigado ingrained habit

hábitos provincianos ▪ hábitos del pueblo ▪ costumbres rancheras ▪ formas campestres country ways

habitual del local ▪ cliente habitual ▪ parroquiano regular customer

habla coloquial ▪ (el) lenguaje coloquial coloquial speech

habla cotidiana ▪ (el) hablar cotidiano everyday speech

el **lenguaje coloquial** ▪ habla coloquial ▪ habla cotidiana colloquial speech ▪ everyday speech

háblame de... ▪ cuéntame de...tell me about...

¿**hablamos?** shall we talk?

hablando del rey de Roma (que por la puerta asoma) ▪ hablando de Juan y él que se asoma ▪ hablando del rey de Roma y el burro que se asoma ▪ hablando del diablo speaking of the devil

hablando en plata if you'll pardon the expression

hablando mal y pronto ▪ hablando (directamente) al grano ▪ hablando sin tapujos (just) coming right out with it

hablando se entiende la gente let's just calm down and talk this over

háblanos de... ▪ cuéntanos de... tell us about...

hablante desenvuelto(-a) fluent speaker

hablar a borbotones ▪ hablar por los codos to talk a blue streak

hablar a destajo ▪ hablar por los codos to talk a blue streak

hablar a espaldas de alguien to talk behind someone's back

hablar a tontas y locas to talk on and on (without getting to the point)

hablar a voz en grito to talk really loud

hablar al aire to talk to the wind

hablar al caso to speak to the issue

hablar alto ▪ hablar en voz alta to talk out loud

hablar bajo ▪ hablar en voz baja ▪ hablar quedito to whisper

hablar bien to speak well

hablar bien no cuesta dinero *(consejo parental)* speaking without cursing costs nothing

hablar claro 1. hablar claramente to speak clearly 2. hablar sin tapujos to speak candidly ▪ to come out with it

hablar como un descosido to talk a lot

hablar como un libro abierto ▪ expresarse como un libro to speak knowledgeably and clearly

hablar como un nativo ▪ hablar igual que un nativo to speak like a native

hablar como una cotorra ▪ cotorrear ▪ hablar como una lora to talk and talk

hablar como una lora ▪ hablar como una cotorra to talk and talk

hablar con el corazón en la mano to talk sincerely

hablar con gracejo to speak colorfully

hablar con halago a alguien ▪ halagar a alguien to flatter someone

hablar con el Jefe ▪ orar ▪ rezar to talk to the man upstairs ▪ to pray

hablar con los ojos to speak with one's eyes

hablar con muchos giros to speak using a lot of expressions

hablar con propiedad to speak correctly

hablar con propiedad sobre un tema to speak knowledgeably about a subject

hablar con quien le parezca to talk with whoever one wants to ▪ to talk to whoever one wants to ▪ to talk with whoever one feels like (talking to) ▪ *(culto)* to talk with whomever one wants to ▪ to talk to whomever one wants to ▪ to talk with whomever one feels like (talking to)

hablar con voz pausada ▪ hablar despacio to speak slowly

hablar consigo (mismo) to talk to oneself ➤ Habla consigo misma cuando está sola. She talks to herself when she's alone.

el **hablar cotidiano** ▪ (el) habla cotidiano everyday speech

hablar de boquilla 1. fanfarronear to boast 2. fingir que se sabe algo to feign knowledge of something ▪ to pretend to know something

hablar de cosas anodinas to talk about boring things

hablar de igual a igual to talk as equals ▪ to talk without social barriers

hablar de lo mucho y de lo poco to talk about everything

hablar de lo que no te incumbe ▪ hablar de lo que no te corresponde ▪ meterse en lo que no se debe to talk out of school

hablar de lo que no te corresponde ▪ hablar de lo que no te incumbe ▪ meterse en lo que no se debe to talk out of school

hablar de miedo *(coloquial)* to speak very well ▪ to speak very fluently

hablar de perlas *(Esp.)* ▪ hablar de maravilla ▪ hablar que da gusto to speak beautifully

hablar de trivialidades to engage in small talk ▪ to engage in light conversation ▪ to chat ▪ to chitchat

hablar de tú a tú to talk as equals

hablar de vicio to speak very well ▪ to speak beautifully

hablar dormido(-a) ▪ hablar en sueños to talk in one's sleep

hablar (en) cristiano ▪ hablar claro to speak in plain language ▪ to speak in non-technical language

hablar en derechura to be direct ▪ to speak directly (to an issue) ▪ to speak plainly

hablar en nombre de todos to speak for everyone ➤ Creo que hablo en nombre de todos cuando digo que eres el mejor profesor de inglés que jamás hemos tenido. I think I speak for everyone when I say you are the best English teacher we have ever had.

hablar en plata 1. hablar claro to speak clearly 2. hablar sin tapujos to speak candidly ▪ to come out with it

hablar en sueños ▪ hablar dormido to talk in one's sleep

hablar en un idioma to speak in a language ▪ to be speaking (in) a language ➤ El primero, que avisó de que uno de los trenes marchaba en dirección errónea, hablaba en francés, pero el otro le respondía en flamenco. The first (man), who warned that one of the trains was going in the wrong direction, was speaking (in) French, but the other responded in Flemish.

hablar entre dientes ▪ mascullar ▪ murmurar ▪ rezongar to grumble

hablar entre sí to talk among oneselves ➤ Hablábamos entre nosotros. We were talking among ourselves.

hablar ex cátedra to speak with authority ▪ to speak as one having authority

hablar fuerte ▪ hablar recio to talk loud

hablar griego 1. to speak Greek 2. *(figurativo)* to know a lot ▪ to have a tremendous knowledge

hablar igual que un nativo ▪ hablar como un nativo to speak like a native

hablar largo y tendido con alguien to have a leisurely conversation with someone

hablar latín ▪ saber latín 1. to speak Latin 2. to know a lot ▪ to have a tremendous knowledge

hablar mal 1. *(con grámatica incorrecta)* to speak badly 2. *(con desprecio)* to speak ill (of someone)

hablar mal de alguien to speak ill of someone

hablar mal y pronto to come right out with it ▪ to just say it

hablar maravillas de algo to praise something to the skies

hablar maravillas de alguien to praise someone to the skies ▪ to sing someone's praises

hablar más que una cotorra to talk a blue streak

hablar muy alto to talk very loud(ly) ▪ to talk really loud

hablar muy finamente *(saracástico)* to speak very primly and properly

hablar para el cuello de la camisa to talk softly

hablar para sí ▪ hablarse a sí mismo to talk to oneself

hablar por alguien 1. hablar en nombre de alguien to speak for someone ▪ to speak in someone's behalf 2. interceder por alguien ▪ mediar por alguien to put in a good word for someone

hablar por boca de otro to be someone's mouthpiece ➤ Cuando dice que está en contra de la huelga habla por boca de sus jefes. When you say you're against the strike, you're just the boss' mouthpiece.

hablar por los demás ▪ hablar en nombre de todos to speak for the others

hablar por detrás de alguien ▪ hablar por las espaldas de alguien to talk behind someone's back

hablar por hablar ▪ hablar por no estar callado to talk just to talk ▪ to talk just to hear oneself talk

hablar por los codos to talk a blue streak ➤ Habla por los codos. He talks a blue streak.

hablar por no estar callado ▪ hablar por hablar to talk just to talk ▪ to talk just to hear oneself talk

hablar por señas 1. to talk with one's hands 2. *(en el ámbito militar)* to communicate with hand signals

hablar por separado a dos (o más) personas to speak separately to two (or more) people

hablar quedo to speak softly

hablar recio ▪ hablar fuerte to talk loud ▪ to talk loudly

hablar sin ambigüedades ▪ hablar sin vaguedades to speak unambiguously ▪ to speak without equivocation

hablar sin concierto ▪ hablar sin orden ni concierto to talk out of order

hablar sin orden ni concierto ▪ hablar sin concierto to talk out of order

hablar sin sentido not to make any sense

hablar sin vaguedades ▪ hablar sin ambigüedades to speak without equivocation ▪ to speak unambiguously

hablar un idioma to speak a language

hablar un idioma con fluidez ▪ hablar un idioma con soltura to speak a language fluently

hablar un idioma medianamente bien ▪ defenderse en otro idioma to get by in a foreign language

hablar una carraca to talk non-stop

hablar uno to do the talking ➤ Déjame hablar a mí. Let me do the talking.

hablarlo todo to tell everything

hablarse a sí mismo ▪ hablar para sí to talk to oneself

hablarse uno al otro to talk to each other

hablárselo todo a alguien to tell everything to someone

hablé antes de tiempo I spoke too soon

hablo por teléfono I'm on the phone ▪ I'm on the telephone

habló el buey y dijo mu ▪ ¡um dijo el burro! he was full of his usual nonsense

habrá habido there will have been

habrá que dar parte ▪ habrá que reportarlo we'll have to report it

habrá que esperar 1. *(yo)* I'll have to wait 2. *(nosotros)* we have to wait ▪ we'll have to wait 3. *(tú, usted)* you'll have to wait 4. *(ellos)* they'll have to wait

habrá que ver 1. *(yo)* I'll have to wait and see 2. *(nosotros)* we'll have to wait and see 3. *(tú, usted)* you'll have to wait and see 4. *(ellos)* they'll have to wait and see

¿habrá tiempo (para)...? will there be time (to)...?

¿habrá todavía? are there any left? ▪ do you think they still have some?

habrá unos... there must be about... ▪ there must be some...

¡habráse visto semejante insolencia! ▪ ¡habráse visto tal descaro! ▪ ¡qué desfachatez! that's pretty brazen

habré llamado... ▪ habría llamado... I must have called... ➤ Habré llamado a Guatemala treinta veces en agosto. ▪ Yo habría llamado a Guatemala treinta veces en agosto. I must have called Guatemala thirty times in August.

habré visto I must have seen ➤ Habré visto cincuenta películas durante el pasado año. I must have seen fifty movies this year.

habría de estar... ▪ tendría que estar... (it) would have to be... ➤ La farmacia de turno habría de estar abierta esta noche. The on-duty pharmacy would have to be open tonight.

habría de haber... there would have to be...

habría de haberlo there would have to be

habría de ser... ▪ tendría que ser... (it) would have to be... ➤ La fiesta habría de ser después de misa el domingo. The party would have to be after mass on Sunday.

habría de serlo it would have to be

habría habido there would have been

habría ocurrido en it must have occurred in ▪ it must have happened in ▪ it must have taken place in

habría podido esperar *(yo)* I could have waited ➤ Si hubiese sabido que finalmente vendrías, habría podido esperarte a que llegases para cenar. If had known that you would eventually come, I could have waited for you get here to have supper.

habría podido esperar a que alguien hiciese algo ▪ hubiese podido esperar a que alguien hiciese algo *(yo)* I could have waited for someone to do something

habría podido prevenirse it could have been prevented

habría que one ought to ▪ you ought to

habría que preguntárselo 1. *(a él)* you'd have to ask him 2. *(a ella)* you'd have to ask her

habría que señalar que... ▪ conviene señalar que... it should be pointed out that...

habría sido muy útil it would have been very useful ▪ it could have been very useful ➤ Me habría sido muy útil. That could have been very useful to me.

habría tenido que haber *(poco común)* ▪ tendría que haber habido there should have been

habría tenido un accidente should have had an accident

habría visto *(poco común)* ▪ habrá visto 1. *(yo)* I must have seen 2. *(él)* he must have seen 3. *(ella)* she must have seen ➤ Ella habría visto cincuenta películas durante el pasado año. She must have seen 50 movies this year.

hace ahora *x* años it has been *x* years now ▪ it's been *x* years now ▪ *x* years ago now

hace algún tiempo for some time now ▪ for some time

hace años que no la veo I haven't seen her in years ▪ I haven't seen it in years

hace años que no le veo *(Esp., leísmo)* I haven't seen him in years ▪ I haven't seen him for years

hace años que no lo veo I haven't seen him in years ▪ I haven't seen it in years

hace bueno it's nice outside

¿hace cuánto tiempo? how long ago? ➤ ¿Hace cuánto tiempo se fue? How long ago did she leave?

hace falta dinero ▪ hace falta plata 1. se necesita dinero you have to have money ▪ it takes money ▪ *(coloquial)* you gotta have bucks 2. no hay dinero there's no money

hace falta harina 1. se necesita harina you need flour ▪ it takes flour ▪ it requires flour 2. no hay harina there's no flour (in the house) ▪ we don't have any flour (in the house) ➤ Para hacer el pastel, hace falta harina. To make the cake, you need flour.

hace falta mucho arrojo para ▪ hace falta huevos para... it takes a lot of guts to... ▪ you have to have guts to... ▪ you've got to have guts to...

hace falta para (it) is needed to ➤ El poder de convicción hace falta para ganar las elecciones. The strength of one's convictions is needed to win the election.

hace falta que one needs to ▪ it is necessary to ➤ Hace falta que se descubra la verdad. We need to discover the truth. ▪ It is necessary to discover the truth. ➤ Hace falta que vayas a comprar una barra de pan para la comida. You need to go buy the bread for dinner.

hace falta tiempo 1. it takes time ▪ it requires time 2. there's no time

hace falta una hora para 1. se necesita una hora para... an hour is needed to... ▪ we need an hour to... 2. no tenemos una hora para... we don't have the hour we need to...

¡hace la tira que no te veo! I haven't seen you in ages!

hace menos de un año ▪ en el último año within the past year ▪ within the last year ▪ less than a year ago ➤ Se murió hace menos de un año ▪ Se murió en el último año. He died within the past year. ▪ He died within the last year.

hace mucha rasca *(Esp., coloquial)* it's freezing cold (outside) ▪ it's bitterly cold (outside)

hace mucho biruji *(coloquial)* it's cold and windy (outside) ▪ there's an icy wind (outside)

hace mucho tiempo ▪ hace mucho a long time ago

hace mucho tiempo que lo tengo olvidado it's been so long that I've forgotten

hace mucho tiempo que tenía (yo) ganas de... I've wanted for a long time to...

hace muchos, muchos años many, many years ago

hace poco a short time ago ▪ a little while ago ▪ recently

hace poco tiempo a short time ago
hace rato a while ago
hace tiempo ■ hace (un) rato a while ago
hace tiempo que uno está haciendo algo ■ llevar tiempo haciendo algo to have been doing something for a certain time ➤ Hace media hora que estoy preparando la cena. I've been fixing supper for the past half hour.
hace un año a year ago
hace un día de perros the weather is lousy today
hace un frío de mil demonios it's cold as hell (outside)
hace un frío intenso it is extremely cold ■ it's extremely cold
hace un frío que pela it's very cold ■ it's extremely cold
hace un frío que te puedes quedar pajarito *(coloquial)* it's very cold ■ it's extremely cold ■ it's cold as hell (outside)
hace un mes que no it's been a month since ➤ Hace un mes que no voy a Madrid. It's been a month since I visited Madrid.
hace un tiempo atrás some time ago ■ *(coloquial)* some time back
hace un tiempo de perros ■ hace mal tiempo ■ el tiempo está malo the weather is miserable ■ the weather is terrible
hace una esquina (con) to face the corner diagonally ■ to sit an angle to the corner ➤ La entrada a la tienda hace una esquina. The store entrance faces the corner diagonally.
hace una hora que habla por teléfono 1. *(él)* he's been on the phone for an hour 2. *(ella)* she's been on the phone for an hour
hace unas cuantas semanas a few weeks ago ■ a few weeks back
hace unos cuantos meses a few months ago ■ a few months back
hace *x* años *x* years ago ➤ Hace tres años hemos decidido que... We decided three years ago that...
hace *x* años que... it's been *x* years since... ➤ Hace un año que... It's been a year since...
hace *x* domingos ■ *x* domingos atrás *x* Sundays ago ➤ Hace tres domingos ■ tres domingos atrás three Sundays ago
hace *x* grados it's *x* **degrees** ➤ Hace veinte grados centígrados afuera. It's twenty degrees Centigrade outside. *(Nota: 68 grados Fahrenheit)*
hacen falta manos para hacer algo to need help doing something
hacen falta *x* horas para... you need *x* hours to... ■ it takes *x* hours to... ■ *x* hours are needed to ➤ Hacen falta tres horas para dominar un capítulo del libro de cálculo. It takes three hours to master a chapter of the calculus book.
hacer a alguien barruntar que... ■ hacer a alguien sospechar que... ■ hacer a alguien pensar que... to make someone suspicious that... ■ to make someone suspect that...
hacer a alguien pensar que... 1. to make someone think that... 2. hacer a alguien sospechar que... to lead one to think that... ■ to make someone suspect that...
hacer a alguien responable de algo to hold someone responsible for something
hacer a alguien sospechar que... ■ hacer a alguien barruntar que... ■ hacer a alguien pensar que... to make someone suspicious that... ■ to make someone suspect that...
hacer a alguien recordar lo que... to remind someone of what...
hacer a uno que se canse ■ hacer que uno se canse ■ dejarlo a uno cansado to make one tired ➤ La tos (le) ha hecho que se canse. ■ La tos le ha dejado cansado. The cough has made him tired.
hacer acopio de algo ■ abastecer algo ■ abastecerse de algo to store up something ■ to store something up
hacer acopio de valor para... ■ juntar valor para... ■ llenarse de valor para... to get up the nerve to...
hacer acto de presencia to put in an appearance ■ to show up ➤ El alcalde nunca hizo acto de presencia. The mayor never showed up.
hacer ademán de ■ parece que va a to make as if one is about to ■ to look as if one is about to ■ to look like one is about to do something ➤ Hace ademán de estornudar. ■ Parece que va a estornudar He looks like he's going to sneeze.
hacer agua ■ hacer aguas menores ■ orinar to make water ■ to urinate
hacer aguas 1. *(barco)* to take on water 2. *(empresa)* to lose money ➤ Los marineros del Prestige abandonaron el petrolero cuando empezó a hacer aguas. The sailors aboard the Prestige abandoned the tanker when it began taking on water. ➤ Vete buscando otro trabajo porque esta empresa hace aguas. Be looking for a job because this company is losing money.
hacer aguas mayores to have a bowel movement
hacer aguas menores to make water ■ to urinate
hacer alarde de ■ fardar de to boast of ■ to flaunt
hacer algo a alguien to do something to someone ➤ ¿Qué te hizo? What did he do to you?
hacer algo a derechas to do something right ➤ Esta vez sí que lo has hecho a derechas. This time you did it right.
hacer algo a duras penas to do something with difficulty
hacer algo a escondidas to do something secretly ■ to do something in secret
hacer algo a la birlonga to do something sloppily ■ to do something half-assed
hacer algo a la chita callando to do something on the quiet
hacer algo a la chiticallando to do something on the quiet
hacer algo a la fuerza to do something no matter what ■ to do something come rain or (come) shine
hacer algo a la ligera 1. hacer algo rápido to do something quickly 2. ■ hacer algo sin pensar to do something without thinking
hacer algo a la primera (de cambio) to do something right off the bat ■ to do something on the first try ■ to do something right off ➤ Dile a Carlos que te ayude con las ecuaciones, a él le salen a primera de cambio. Get Carlos to help you with the equations. He gets them right off the bat.
hacer algo a las bravas ■ hacer algo con gran esfuerzo to do something with great effort
hacer algo a las mil maravillas to do something perfectly
hacer algo a medias to do something halfway
hacer algo a remolque de alguien 1. to do something because of pressure from someone 2. *(referido especialmente a jóvenes)* to do something because of peer pressure ➤ Ha cambiado su estrategia de marketing a remolque de sus socios. He changed his marketing strategy because of pressure from his associates. ➤ El joven cometió el delito a remolque de las malas compañías. The youth committed the crime because of peer pressure. ■ The youth committed the crime out of peer pressure.
hacer algo a toda vela to do something full sail ■ to do something fast
hacer algo al final ■ hacer algo al último to do something last ➤ Pintaremos la puertas al final. We'll paint the doors last.
hacer algo al respecto ■ hacer algo manos a la obra to do something about it
hacer algo al último ■ hacer algo al final to do something last
hacer algo bueno (por) to do something good (for) ■ to do a good thing (for)
hacer algo bien to do something right ■ to get something right ■ to do something correctly ➤ Lo haré bien esta vez. I'll get it right this time. ■ I'll do it right this time. ■ I'll do it correctly this time.
hacer algo como si nada ■ hacer algo como si tal cosa to do something as if it were nothing
hacer algo como si tal cosa ■ hacer algo como si nada to do something as if it were nothing
hacer algo con cualquier pretexto to do something at the drop of a hat
hacer algo con destreza to do something with finesse ■ to do something with skill
hacer algo con la gorra ■ hacer algo con los ojos cerrados to be able to do something blindfolded ■ to do something with one's eyes closed ■ to do something with no trouble at all ➤ Puedo arreglar esta mesa con la gorra. I can fix this table blindfolded. ■ I can fix this table with my eyes closed. ■ I can fix this table with no trouble at all.
hacer algo contra el reloj to work against the clock
hacer algo contra viento y marea to do something come hell or high water

hacer algo corriendo *(coloquial)* to do something real quick ➤ Quiero revisar corriendo mi correo electrónico antes de irnos. I want to check my E-mail real quick before we go.

hacer algo de la forma más rebuscada ■ hacer algo rebuscadamente to do something the hard way

hacer algo en derechura to do something right away ■ to do something immediately

hacer algo en forma correcta to do something right ■ to do something correctly ■ to do something the right way

hacer algo en las narices de alguien ■ hacer algo en las propias barbas de alguien to do something right under someone's nose

hacer algo en las propias barbas de alguien ■ hacer algo en las narices de alguien to do something right under someone's nose

hacer algo inédito to do something unprecedented ■ to do something as yet untried

hacer algo para la galería to play to the grandstands ■ to play to the gallery

hacer algo para salir de eso ■ concluir algo de una vez (por todas) to get something over with ➤ El dentista me dijo que tenía que sacarme las muelas del juicio en algún momento, así que más me valdría hacerlo para salir de eso. ■ El dentista me dijo que tenía que sacarme las muelas del juicio en algún momento, así que más me valdría concluirlo de una vez. The dentist said I had to have my wisdom teeth out at some point, so I might as well get it over with.

hacer algo para salir del tema ■ hacer algo para cambiar el tema to do something halfheartedly (just to get it done) ■ to do something (just) to get it out of the way

hacer algo por adelantado to do something ahead of time ■ to do something in advance ➤ La profesora prepara sus lecciones por adelantado y desea que los alumnos lo hiciesen también. The teacher prepares her lessons in advance and wishes the students did, too.

hacer algo por alguien to do something for someone ➤ Gracias por todo lo que has hecho por mí. Thank you for all you have done for me.

hacer algo por ce o por be ■ hacer algo por narices ■ hacer algo por fuerzas to do something no matter what ■ to do something come hell or high water

hacer algo por cojones *(subido de tono)* ■ hacer algo por pelotas ■ hacer algo por huevos to do something come hell or high water

hacer algo por despecho to do something out of spite

hacer algo por fuerza ■ hacer algo por narices ■ hacer algo por ce o por be to do something no matter what ■ to do something come hell or high water

hacer algo por gusto hacer algo por placer ■ hacer algo por ganas to do something for pleasure

hacer algo por huevos *(subido de tono)* ■ hacer algo por cojones ■ hacer algo por pelotas to do something come hell or high water ■ to do something no matter what

hacer algo por narices ■ hacer algo por fuerza ■ hacer algo por ce o por be to do something no matter what ■ to do something come hell or high water ➤ Se empeñó en arreglar la tele él sólo por narices. He was determined to fix the TV himself, no matter what.

hacer algo por partes ■ hacer algo paso por paso ■ ir por partes en (hacer) algo ■ ir paso por paso en algo to do something step by step ■ to do something systematically ■ to do first things first ➤ Lo hacemos por partes. Let's do it step by step.

hacer algo por pelotas *(ligeramente subido de tono)* ■ hacer algo por cojones ■ hacer algo por huevos to do something come hell or high water ■ to do something no matter what

hacer algo por placer ■ hacer algo por gusto to do something for pleasure ■ to do something for enjoyment ➤ Escuchamos música clásica por placer. ■ Escucho música clásica por gusto. We listen to classical music for pleasure. ■ I listen to classical music for enjoyment.

hacer algo por puro... to do something out of sheer... ➤ Ella lo hizo por pura vanidad. She did it out of sheer vanity.

hacer algo por sistema ■ hacer algo sistemáticamente to do something systematically

hacer algo por sus cabales to do something in one's right mind ■ to do something in full cognizance

hacer algo por turnos ■ turnarse ■ haciendo algo ■ tomarse turnos haciendo algo ■ alternarse en to take turns doing something ■ to alternate doing something

hacer algo sin que alguien lo sepa to do something without anyone's knowing it

hacer algo sistemáticamente ■ hacer algo por sistema to do something systematically

hacer algo solo ■ hacer algo solito to do something by oneself ■ to do something alone ➤ Fui al cine solo. ■ Fui yo solo al cine. I went to the movies by myself. ■ I went to the movies alone.

hacer algo uno mismo to do something oneself ➤ Yo mismo lo hice. ■ Lo hice yo mismo. I did it myself.

hacer algo volando ■ hacer algo a la rápida to do something in no time

hacer algún avance con to make (some) headway with

hacer añicos de algo to tear something to bits ■ to smash something to bits ■ to smash something to smithereens

hacer ascos de algo to turn one's nose up at something

hacer asiento *(edificio)* to settle

hacer asignaturas to take subjects ■ to take courses

hacer aspavientos to make a fuss

hacer autostop ■ hacer dedo ■ ir a dedo to hitch-hike ➤ Fue a San Sebastián a dedo. He hitch-hiked to San Sebastian.

hacer barquitos *(Esp.)* to sop bread

hacer barullo ■ armar barullo to make a racket

hacer bien en to do well to ■ to be right to ➤ Harías bien en buscar su consejo. You would do well to seek his advice.

hacer bien haciendo algo to be right to do something ➤ Harías bien... You would do well to...

hacer bien to do good deeds

hacer blanco ■ dar en la diana to hit the target ■ to hit the bull's-eye

hacer boca ■ abrir boca ■ abrirse el apetito to work up an appetite ■ to get hungry

hacer bocina con las manos ■ hacer de altavoz con las manos to cup one's hands around one's mouth ➤ Hizo bocina con las manos. ■ Hizo de altavoz con las manos. He cupped his hands around his mouth.

hacer bolillos ■ hacer puñetas to twiddle one's thumbs

hacer borrón y cuenta nueva to wipe the slate clean and start afresh ■ to begin a new page

hacer brecha en alguien ■ abrir brecha en alguien to make an impression on someone

hacer bromas sobre algo to make jokes about something

hacer buen papel to perform well ➤ El jugador hizo buen papel en el torneo. The player performed well in the tournament.

hacer buen tiempo to be nice weather (outside) ➤ Hace buen tiempo hoy. The weather (outside) is nice today.

hacer buen tiempo para to be good weather for

hacer buen uso de algo to make good use of something ■ to put something to good use

hacer buena cosa to do a good thing

hacer buena pareja to work well together

hacer buenas migas con alguien to hit it off with someone ■ to really hit it off with someone

hacer burbujas to make bubbles ■ to form bubbles ■ to bubble

hacer cábalas sobre to conjecture about ■ to speculate on

hacer caer al gobierno to bring down the government ➤ *(noticia)* Dimisión de los laboristas hace caer al gobierno de Israel. Resignation of the laborites brings down the government of Israel.

hacer caer en una trampa a alguien to entrap someone ■ to ensnare someone

hacer caja ■ hacer la caja to count the money

hacer calceta ■ hacer punto to knit

hacer calendarios to build castles in the air

hacer calor to be hot (outside)

hacer caña a alguien ■ machacar a alguien to be hard on someone ■ to come down hard on someone ■ to pressure someone

hacer caso de to heed

hacer caso omiso de algo to ignore something

hacer caso omiso del consejo de alguien to ignore someone's advice
hacer castillos en el aire to build castles in the air
hacer causa para hacer algo to find a pretext for doing something
hacer cautivo a alguien to take someone captive
hacer chaflán to sit at an angle to the corner ➤ La iglesia hace chaflán. The church sits at an angle to the corner.
hacer chapuzas to fix things around the house ▪ to do home repairs
hacer clic en el botón derecho en ▪ pulsar con el botón derecho en ▪ presionar con el botón derecho en ▪ oprimir con el botón derecho en ▪ picar en el botón derecho en to right click on
hacer clic el botón izquierdo en ▪ pulsar con el botón izquierdo en ▪ presionar con el botón izquierdo en ▪ oprimir con el botón derecho en ▪ picar en el botón izquierdo en to left click on
hacer agua la coartada to have cracks in an alibi ▪ (for) an alibi to have cracks in it ➤ Su coartada hace agua. His alibi has cracks in it. ▪ There are cracks in his alibi.
hacer cola ▪ hacer fila ▪ *(Méx.)* formarse to stand in line ▪ to get in line ▪ to line up ▪ to form a line ➤ Estábamos haciendo cola en un cine cuando... We were standing in line at the movies when... ➤ Hay que hacer cola. ▪ Hay que hacer fila. ▪ Hay que formarse. You have to get in line. ▪ You have to line up. ▪ You have to form a line.
hacer como no entiende ▪ hacerse el sueco ▪ no darse por enterado to play dumb ▪ to feign ignorance
hacer como que... to pretend that... ▪ *(coloquial)* to play like...
hacer como que hace algo to look busy ▪ to pretend to be busy
hacer como si to act as if ▪ to pretend (that)
hacer compañía a alguien to keep someone company
hacer composición de (un) lugar to consider the pros and cons ▪ to weigh the pros and cons
hacer con regla y compás to do (something) systematically ▪ to do (something) methodically
hacer conjunto con to go with ▪ to form part of a set with
hacer constar to make known ▪ to express
hacer constar en acta to record in the minutes (of a meeting)
hacer constar que... to state that...
hacer construir una casa ▪ mandar construir una casa ▪ hacer edificar una casa to have a house built ▪ to build a house ➤ Hicimos construir una casa. We had a house built.
hacer correrías en ▪ hacer incursiones en to make incursions into
hacer corro aparte to form a new political faction
hacer corro para ▪ hacer espacio para ▪ hacer sitio para ▪ hacer lugar para ▪ dar cabida a to clear a space for ▪ to make room for
hacer cosquillas a alguien ▪ hacerle el quiliquili a alguien to tickle someone
hacer cualquier cosa con tal de llamar la atención to do anything to get attention
hacer cuenta y borrón to wipe the slate clean ▪ to start afresh
hacer cuentas alegres to count the imaginary proceeds ▪ to dream of big bucks
hacer cumplir la normativa en contra de fumar ▪ aplicar la normativa en contra de fumar to enforce the no smoking rule
hacer de algo to fake being something ▪ to fake doing something ▪ to pretend to be something ▪ to pretend to do something ▪ to act as something ➤ La reportera tuvo que hacer de camarera en la boda de un mafioso a fin de conseguir datos para un artículo. The reporter had to fake being a waitress at the wedding of a mafioso in order to get material for an article. ➤ Hacía de medianero. He acted as a go-between. ▪ He was acting as the go-between.
hacer de altavoz con las manos ▪ hacer bocina con las manos to cup one's hands around one's mouth ➤ Hizo de altavoz con las manos. ▪ Hizo bocina con las manos. He cupped his hands around his mouth.
hacer de amortiguador to act as a buffer ▪ to serve as a buffer
hacer de canguro ▪ estar de niñero(-a) to babysit
hacer de cuenta to suppose ➤ Haz de cuenta que... Suppose...
hacer de cuerpo ▪ hacer de vientre to have a bowel movement
hacer de encargo to make for take out ▪ to make to take home ▪ to make for customer pickup ➤ Se hacen paellas de encargo. Paellas made for take-out. ▪ Paellas special ordered.
hacer de intérprete to act as an interpreter
hacer de las suyas to be up to one's tricks
hacer de pantalla para actividades ilegales ▪ hacer de pantalla para actividades ilícitas ▪ servir como pantalla para actividades ilegales ▪ servir como pantalla para actividades ilícitas ▪ funcionar como pantalla para actividades ilegales ▪ funcionar como pantalla para actividades ilícitas to serve as a front for illegal activities ▪ to serve as a front for illicit activities
hacer de tripas corazón to screw up one's courage ▪ to get up one's nerve ▪ to take a deep breath (and...)
hacer de una pulga un elefante to make a mountain out of a mole hill
hacer de vientre ▪ descargar el vientre ▪ exonerar el vientre to have a bowel movement
hacer dedo ▪ hacer autostop ▪ ir a dedo to thumb a ride ▪ to thumb one's way (to a place)
hacer del comienzo to make from scratch
hacer dengues to be fussy
hacer dinero ▪ hacer plata to make money
hacer doble clic en el ratón to double click on the mouse
hacer doble juego to be two-faced
hacer doblete to moonlight ▪ to work a second job ➤ Hace doblete de camarero. He moonlights as a waiter.
hacer efecto ▪ surtir efecto to take effect
hacer ejercicio to exercise
hacer ejercicios to do exercises
hacer ejercicios de calentamiento to do warm-up exercises ▪ to do warmup exercises ▪ to do warmups
hacer ejercicios de estiramiento ▪ hacer estiramientos to do stretching exercises
hacer el agosto ▪ hacerse la américa to get rich quick ▪ to make a killing overnight ▪ to create a windfall ▪ to feather one's nest
hacer el amor to make love
hacer el artículo a alguien para que haga algo to try to talk someone into doing something
hacer el barbo to lipsync ▪ to move the mouth as if singing
hacer el blanco en los civiles ▪ hacer que los civiles sean el blanco to target civilians
hacer el caldo gordo a alguien to make things easier for someone ▪ to smooth the way for someone ▪ to pave the way for someone
hacer el censo to take the census
hacer el esfuerzo por to make the effort to
hacer el ganso ▪ hacer el tonto to play the fool
hacer el idiota completamente to make a complete fool of oneself
hacer el jaimito *(L.am.)* to horse around
hacer el muerto to float on one's back
hacer el nudo de la corbata ▪ hacerse la corbata to tie a necktie ▪ *(coloquial)* to tie a tie
hacer el oro y el moro to achieve fame and fortune ▪ to win fame and fortune
hacer el paripé to show off
hacer el payaso ▪ hacer payasadas to clown around
hacer el pelo a alguien to do someone's hair
hacer el pino to stand on one's hands ➤ Hizo el pino antes de saltar del trampolín. He stood on his hands before diving off the board.
hacer el primo to be the good guy
hacer el puente a un coche to hotwire a car ▪ to start a car without the ignition key
hacer el quite to lend a helping hand ▪ to lend a hand
hacer el rancho *(coloquial)* to chow down
hacer el reparto de algo to divide up something ▪ to divide something up
hacer el ridículo ▪ ponerse pelmazo to make a fool of oneself ➤ Hice el ridículo ante todo el mundo. I made a fool of myself in front of everybody.

hacer el servicio to serve in the military
hacer el testamento to make one's will
hacer el tonto to fool around ▪ to mess around ▪ to horse around
hacer el vaciado para una estructura to dig the foundation for a structure
hacer el vacío a alguien ▪ darle calabazas a alguien to give someone the cold shoulder ▪ to give someone the brushoff
hacer el vago to goof off
hacer el vago por (la) casa ▪ holgazanear por (la) casa ▪ flojear por (la) casa to hang around the house ▪ to putter around the house
hacer el viacrucis 1. *(catolicismo)* to do the stations of the cross **2.** *(pintoresco)* to go bar hopping
hacer empaquetear y enviar algo 1. to have something packaged and shipped **2.** *(en contenidores de madera)* to have something crated and shipped
hacer en balde alguna cosa to do something in vain
hacer encaje de bolillos 1. to make handmade lace **2.** hacer malabares para lograr algo ▪ hacer malabares para conseguir algo to bend over backwards to ▪ to make every effort to ▪ to go to great lengths to ➤ España ha hecho encaje de bolillos para tener buenas relaciones con el Reino Unido. ▪ España ha hecho malabares para tener buenas relaciones con el Reino Unido. Spain has bent over backwards to have good relations with Britain. ▪ Spain has made every effort to have good relations with Britain. ▪ Spain has gone to great lengths to have good relations with Britain.
hacer encorvar la luz to bend light ➤ Einstein descubrió que la gravedad hace encorvar la luz. Einstein discovered that gravity bends light. ▪ Einstein discovered that gravity causes light to bend.
hacer entender ▪ lograr comunicar ▪ transmitir to get across ▪ to convey
hacer entrar en vereda a alguien ▪ hacer meter en vereda a alguien to bring someone into line
hacer escarceos en la política ▪ hacer escarceos con la política to dabble in politics
hacer eses ▪ hacer zigzag **1.** saltar los coches a la torera to weave (all over the road) ▪ to zigzag (all over the road) **2.** hacer filigranas to stagger (around)
hacer espacio para ▪ hacer sitio para ▪ hacer corro para ▪ dar cabida a to make room for
hacer esquí acuático to water ski
hacer esquina con ▪ estar haciendo esquina con ▪ estar en la esquina de ▪ estar en la esquina entre to be at the corner of ▪ to be on the corner of ➤ El restaurante hace esquina con Gen. Margallo e Infanta Mercedes. The restaurant is at the corner of Gen. Margallo and Infanta Mercedes. ▪ The restaurant is on the corner of Gen. Margallo and Infanta Mercedes.
hacer estallar un artefacto explosivo to set off an explosive device
hacer estallar un petardo to set off a firecracker
hacer estallar una bomba to set off a bomb ▪ to detonate a bomb ▪ to explode a bomb
hacer estiramientos ▪ hacer ejercicios de estiramiento to do stretching exercises
hacer estragos to wreak havoc
hacer estragos con ▪ causar estragos con ▪ crear un caos con to wreak havoc with
hacer estragos entre to wreak havoc among
hacer estremecerse ▪ hacer que uno se estremezca to make one shudder
hacer fachada a ▪ hacer fachada con to face ▪ to be directly across from ➤ La tienda universitaria hace fachada al rectorado. The university store faces the rectory.
hacer falta to be necessary ▪ to be needed ▪ to need ➤ No hace falta que te arregles. You don't need to dress up. ▪ It's not necessary to dress up. ➤ Hace falta una silla. We need a chair. ➤ Hacen falta dos sillas más. We need two more chairs. ➤ Hace falta que te tranquilices. You need to calm down. ➤ Hace falta que nos reunamos. We need to get together. ▪ We need to meet. ➤ Haría falta que... It would be good if...
hacer falta *x* horas para hacer algo to take *x* hours to do something
hacer falta *x* tiempo para hacer algo to take *x* time to do something ➤ Hicieron falta veinte años y veinte mil esclavos para construir la pirámide de Giza. It took twenty years and twenty thousand slaves to build the pyramid at Giza.
hacer feliz a alguien to make someone happy ➤ Mi sueño es ser felíz y hacer felices a quienes me rodean. My dream is to be happy and to make the people around me happy.
hacer flexiones to do pushups
hacer fuego 1. prender fuego to build a fire **1.** disparar to open fire
hacer gala de to display
hacer gamberradas to make trouble
hacer gestiones discretamente to put out feelers
hacer girar un bastón con los dedos ▪ girar un bastón ▪ revolear un bastón to twirl a baton
hacer globos (de chicle) ▪ hacer pompas to blow (gum) bubbles ➤ Hice un globo de goma de mascar y cuando explotó, toda la clase dejó de escribir a máquina, porque creyeron que era la maestra quien les daba la señal para parar. I blew a bubble, and when it popped the whole class stopped typing. They thought the teacher was calling time.
hacer guardia ▪ montar guardia to stand guard
hacer guerra to wage war
hacer hablar a (un instrumento musical) to be able to make (a musical instrument) sing ➤ Hace hablar al piano. She can make a piano sing.
hacer hincapié en ▪ insistir en to make a point of
hacer historia to make history
hacer horas extras to put in overtime ▪ to work overtime
hacer huecos (con un taladro) to drill holes
hacer incursiones en ▪ hacer correrías en to make incursions into
hacer juego to match ▪ to go well together ▪ to complement each other
hacer juego con to match
hacer justicia a algo to do justice to something ▪ to do something justice ➤ La película no hace justicia al libro. The movie doesn't do the book justice. ▪ The movie doesn't do justice to the book. ➤ La película no le hace justicia. The movie doesn't do it justice. ➤ Steven Spielberg y Liam Neeson sin duda alguna harán justicia al tema fascinante de Abraham Lincoln. Steven Spielberg and Liam Neeson will certainly do justice to the fascinating subject of Abraham Lincoln.
hacer la barba a alguien to give someone a shave ▪ to shave someone's beard
hacer (la) caja to count the money
hacer la cama ▪ arreglar la cama to make the bed
hacer la cama a alguien ▪ hacerle la cama a alguien to set someone up
hacer la campana de Gauss to curve the grade
hacer la carrera *(prostitutas)* to ply one's trade
hacer la colada *(Esp.)* ▪ lavar la ropa to do (the) laundry
hacer la compra *(Esp.)* to go grocery shopping ▪ to go to the grocery store ▪ to buy groceries ▪ to do the grocery shopping ▪ to shop for groceries ➤ Voy a hacer la compra. I'm going to the grocery store. ▪ I'm going grocery shopping.
hacer la impresión de que to seem like ▪ to look like ▪ to give the impression that...
hacer la maleta to pack (one's suitcase)
hacer la media (aritmética) to average ▪ to compute the average
hacer la mili to be in military ▪ to be in the service ▪ to do one's tour in the service
hacer la parte de uno to do one's part
hacer la parte más difícil de 1. to do the hardest part of **2.** *(metáfora literaria)* cambiar las tornas en to break the back of ➤ Mark Twain señala que Juana de Arco logró la memorable victoria de Patay sobre los ingleses, cambiando las tornas en la Guerra de los Cien Años. ▪ Mark Twain señala que Juana de Arco logró la memorable victoria de Patay sobre los ingleses y cambió las tornas en la Guerra de los Cien Años. Mark Twain notes that Joan of Arc won the memorable victory of Patay over the English and broke the back of the Hundred Years' War.

hacer la pelota a alguien to butter up someone ▪ to butter someone up

hacer la pirula a alguien *(subido de tono)* ▪ hacerle una faena a alguien to screw somebody over ▪ to fuck somebody over

hacer la prueba con alguien to give someone a try at doing something ▪ to give someone a shot at doing something ➤ Haz la prueba con Mauricio. Give Mauricio a try. ▪ Give Mauricio a shot at it.

hacer la ronda to make rounds ▪ to make one's rounds ➤ El médico está haciendo la ronda. The doctor is making his rounds.

hacer la segunda milla to go the extra mile

hacer la señal de la cruz to make the sign of the cross

hacer la tarea ▪ hacer los deberes to do one's homework ▪ to get one's homework done ➤ Tengo que hacer la(s) tarea(s). ▪ Tengo que hacer los deberes. I have to do my homework. ▪ I have to get my homework done.

hacer la vista gorda ▪ mirar hacia el otro lado to look the other way ▪ to turn a blind eye (to) ▪ to pretend not to notice

hacer la vista gorda a algo to turn a blind eye to something

hacer las compras navideñas con anticipación to do one's Christmas shopping early

hacer las cosas a medias to do things halfway

hacer las cosas a su modo ▪ ser maestrillo que tiene su librillo to do things one's own way

hacer las labores de la casa ▪ hacer las labores domésticas to do housework

hacer las paces to bury the hatchet ▪ to patch up ones' differences

hacer limpieza (en) to clean up ➤ Iván necesita hacer limpieza en su apartamento. Parece que debería solicitar los fondos federales de desastres. Ivan needs to clean up his apartment. It looks like he should apply for federal disaster funds.

hacer lo correcto *(Esp.)* ▪ hacer bien (en) to do the right thing (in)

hacer lo debido ▪ hacer lo que se deba ▪ hacer la parte de uno to do one's duty

hacer lo mejor que uno puede to do the best one can ▪ to do one's best ➤ Estoy haciendo lo mejor que puedo. I'm doing the best I can. ➤ Haré lo mejor que pueda. I'll do the best I can. ▪ I'll do my best. ➤ Hice lo mejor que pude. I did the best I could.

hacer lo mismo que alguien ▪ imitar a alguien ▪ seguir el ejemplo de alguien to follow suit ▪ to follow someone's example ▪ to do the same (thing) ➤ Se unió al baile y llamó a María para que hiciera lo mismo. He joined in the dancing and called to María to follow suit.

hacer lo posible ▪ hacer todo lo posible to do to everything possible

hacer lo que alguien te diga to do what someone tells you ▪ to do whatever someone tells you ➤ Haz lo que te diga la profesora. Do what the teacher tells you.

hacer lo que le dé la gana to do as one pleases ▪ to be a law unto oneself

hacer lo que le dé la real gana to do as one damn well pleases

hacer lo que quiera que... ▪ hacer lo que sea que... to do whatever... ➤ Haz lo que sea que el capitán te ordene. ▪ Haz lo que quiera que el capitán te ordene. You do whatever the captain orders you to do.

hacer lo que sea que... ▪ hacer lo que quiera que... to do whatever... ➤ Haz lo que quiera que el capitán te ordene. ▪ Haz lo que sea que el capitán te ordene. (You) do whatever the captain orders you to do.

hacer lo que uno debe to do what one has to (do) ▪ to do one's duty ▪ to do the right thing

hacer lo que uno predica ▪ predicar con el ejemplo to practice what one preaches ▪ to preach by (one's) example

hacer lo que uno quiera ▪ acamparse como uno quiera ▪ seguir uno mismo to do as one pleases ▪ to do as one likes ➤ *(tú)* Haz lo que quieras. ▪ Acámpate como quieras. ▪ Sigue tú mismo(-a). *(usted)* Haga usted lo que quiera. ▪ Acampe usted como quiera. ▪ Acámpese como quiera. ▪ Siga usted mismo(-a). Do as you please. ▪ Do as you like.

hacer los deberes *(Esp.)* ▪ hacer la tarea to do one's homework ▪ to get one's homework done ➤ Mamá me ha dicho que tengo que hacer los deberes antes de poder ir a esquiar. Mom said I have to do my homework before I can go skiing. ▪ Mom said I have to get my homework done before I can go skiing.

hacer los honores to do the honors

hacer (los) preparativos to make the arrangements ➤ Hicimos (los) preparativos por adelantado. We made (the) arrangements ahead of time.

hacer lugar para ▪ hacer sitio para ▪ hacer espacio para ▪ hacer corro para ▪ dar cabida a to make room for ▪ to clear a space for

hacer mal en hacer una cosa to be a mistake to do something ➤ Harías mal en quejarte. It would be a mistake to complain.

hacer malabares por ▪ hacer todo lo posible por ▪ hacer encaje de bolillos para to bend over backwards to ▪ to make every effort to ➤ España ha hecho malabares para tener buenas relaciones con el Reino Unido. Spain has bent over backwards to have good relations with Britain.

hacer malabarismos 1. to juggle **2.** to jump through a few hoops ➤ Para conseguir un visado estudiantil, hay que hacer malabarismos. To get a student visa you have to jump through a few hoops.

hacer mandados *(esp. para ir al mercado)* to run errands ▪ to go to the store

hacer manualidades to make things with one's hands ➤ A mi hijo le gusta hacer manualidades. My son likes to make things with his hands.

hacer medialunas *(Arg.)* ▪ dar volteretas laterales to do cartwheels

hacer mejoras a la computadora to work on the computer

hacer mella en alguien to make an impression on someone

hacer memoria de to try to remember

hacer meter en vereda a alguien ▪ hacer entrar en vereda a alguien to bring someone into line

hacer mimos a alguien to make a fuss over someone

hacer minucias to do odds and ends

hacer mofa de algo ▪ mofarse de ▪ burlarse de algo to make fun of something

hacer morisquetas a alguien to make faces at someone

hacer muecas a alguien to make faces at someone

hacer nada en absoluto: no~ to do nothing at all ▪ not to do anything at all ➤ No pude hacer nada en absoluto. I couldn't do anything at all.

hacer notar que... ▪ señalar que... to point out that... ▪ to note that... ➤ Hizo notar que el castillo es el símbolo de Castilla y el león de León. ▪ Senaló que el castillo es el símbolo de Castilla y el león de León. He pointed out that the castle is the symbol of Castilla and the lion the symbol of Leon.

hacer obras buenas to do good works ▪ to do good deeds

hacer oídos sordos a alguien to turn a deaf ear to someone

hacer olas to rock the boat ▪ to make waves

hacer palmas to clap rhythmically

hacer papilla a to make mincemeat of ➤ Los Green Bay Packers hicieron papilla al otro equipo. The Green Bay Packers made mincemeat of the other team.

hacer para arreglarse to manage ▪ to get along ➤ Ya sabrá Dios cómo hago para arreglarme. God knows how I'm going to manage.

hacer partícipe en to take part in

hacer pasar a alguien un mal rato to give someone a bad time ➤ Le gusta hacerme pasar un mal rato. He likes to give me a bad time.

hacer pedazos algo to break something all to pieces

hacer peligrar ▪ poner en peligro to put in peril ▪ to imperil ▪ to put at risk ▪ to put in danger ▪ to endanger ▪ *(literario)* to place at risk ➤ *(noticia)* El rechazo de la oposición hace peligrar la reforma fiscal. ▪ El rechazo de la oposición pone en peligro la reforma fiscal. The opposition party's rejection puts economic reform in peril. ▪ The opposition party's rejection imperils economic reform.

hacer pellas *(Esp., coloquial)* ▪ irse de pellas ▪ hacer novillos ▪ irse de pinta to skip school ▪ *(parte occidental de EE UU)* to sluff (school)

hacer pelotas to get brownie points ➤ Haces pelotas trayendo la camiseta de la Universidad de Valladolid. You're getting brownie points wearing the University of Valladolid shirt.

hacer pensar que... ▪ dar que pensar que... to give the impression that...
hacer picadillo de un argumento to make mincemeat of an argument
hacer pie touch bottom
hacer pipí *(lenguaje infantil)* to go pee pee
hacer pis ▪ orinar to urinate
hacer placajes *(deportes)* to block ▪ throw blocks ▪ to make blocking movements
hacer planes to make plans
hacer pleito to pick a fight ▪ to make trouble
hacer por hacer algo to try to do something ▪ to make an effort to do something
hacer posible que alguien haga algo to make it possible for someone to do something ➤ Hizo posible que empezara en los deportes profesionales. He made it possible for me to start in professional sports.
hacer prender a alguien *(literario)* ▪ hacer detener a alguien to have someone arrested ➤ *(Ricardo Palma)* Hizo prender y dar muerte a Don Alonso Yáñez. He had Don Alonso Yáñez arrested and executed.
hacer preparativos con antelación to make arrangements in advance
hacer preparativos de antemano to make arrangements beforehand
hacer preparativos por adelantado to make arrangements ahead of time
hacer presa en alguien *(miedo, pánico, etc.)* to take hold of someone ▪ to seize someone
hacer prisionero(-a) a alguien to take someone prisoner
hacer propósito de to resolve ➤ Hago propósito de enmienda. I resolve to turn over a new leaf
hacer pucheros to pout ▪ to put on a long face
hacer puñetas ▪ hacer bolillos to twiddle one's thumbs
hacer punto ▪ tricotar to knit
hacer que... ▪ hacer ver que... ▪ simular que... ▪ fingir que... to pretend... ➤ Mi hermano hizo que iba al cine. My brother pretended he was going to the movies.
hacer que algo funcione ▪ conseguir que algo funcione to get something to work ▪ to get something to function
hacer que algo haga algo to make something do something
hacer que alguien crea que... to trick someone into believing that... ▪ to fool someone into believing that...
hacer que alguien cumpla una promesa to hold someone to a promise
hacer que alguien haga algo to make someone do something ➤ *(noticia)* El perro ha hecho que se siente cuando estaba a punto de desmayarse. The dog has made her sit down when she was about to faint.
hacer que alguien llegue tarde por su culpa to make someone late ➤ Espero que no hayas llegado tarde por mi culpa. I hope I didn't make you late.
hacer que arranque el motor to get the motor started ▪ to get the engine started
hacer que caiga algo to knock something down ▪ to knock down something ▪ to knock something off (of) something
hacer que den los zapatos de sí ▪ hacer que metan los zapatos en la horma to have a pair of shoes stretched ▪ to get a pair of shoes stretched ➤ Tengo que llevar los zapatos para que me los hagan dar de sí. ▪ Tengo que llevar los zapatos para que los metan en la horma. I've got to take the shoes to get them stretched. ▪ I've got to take the shoes to have them stretched.
hacer que le llame a uno ▪ hacer que lo llame a uno ▪ decirle que le llamo a uno to have someone call someone ➤ *(tú)* Haz que me llame. ▪ *(usted)* Haga que me llame. Have him call me. ▪ Have him give me a call. ▪ Tell him to call me. ▪ Tell him to give me a call.
hacer que le zumben los oídos ▪ hacerle zumbar los oídos to make one's ears ring ➤ Las discotecas hacen que me zumben los oídos. Discotheques make my ears ring.
hacer que los civiles sean el blanco ▪ hacer blanco en los civiles to target civilians
hacer que metan los zapatos en la horma ▪ hacer que den los zapatos de sí to have a pair of shoes stretched ▪ to get a pair of shoes stretched ➤ Tengo que llevar los zapatos para que los metan en la horma. ▪ Tengo que llevar los zapatos para que me los hagan dar de sí.
hacer que no to keep from ▪ to prevent from ➤ ¿Cómo hacéis que no se apaguen la velas afuera? How do you keep the candles from blowing out outside?
hacer que se le queme la sangre a uno ▪ hacer que le hierva la sangre a uno to make one's blood boil
hacer que se vaya el dolor to make the pain go away ➤ Solía estirarme y hacía que se fuera el dolor. I used to stretch, and it would make the pain go away.
hacer que sea necesario make it necessary ➤ Los problemas con el proveedor de Internet han hecho que fuera necesario cambiar. (The) problems with the Internet provider have made it necessary to change.
hacer que suene como si to make it sound like ▪ to make it sound as if ➤ Haces que suene como si fuera algo que se hace todos los días. You make it sound like something you do every day. ▪ You make it sound as if it's something you do every day. ▪ You make it sound like something one does every day. ▪ You make it sound as if it's something one does every day.
hacer que uno se canse ▪ hacer a uno que se canse ▪ dejar a uno cansado to make one tired ➤ La tos (le) ha hecho que se canse. ▪ La tos le ha dejado cansado. The cough has made him tired.
hacer que uno se estremezca ▪ hacer estremecerse to make one shudder ➤ Hace que me estremezca. ▪ Me hace estremecer. It makes me shudder.
hacer quedar a alguien en ridículo ▪ poner a alguien en ridículo ▪ dejar a alguien en ridículo to mock someone ▪ to ridicule someone ▪ to make a fool of someone
hacer rancho aparte **1.** to go one's own way **2.** to keep to oneself
hacer regata to go sailing
hacer ruedas ▪ salir haciendo ruedas to lay rubber ▪ to spin one's wheels ➤ El coche hizo ruedas al salir del semáforo. ▪ El coche salió haciendo ruedas del semáforo. The car laid rubber as it started off from the traffic light. ▪ The car spun its wheels as it started off from the traffic light.
hacer saber to make known
hacer saber algo a alguien ▪ dejar saber algo a alguien ▪ avisarle a alguien algo to let someone know ➤ ¡Hazme saber! ▪ ¡Déjame saber! ▪ ¡Avísame! Let me know! ➤ ¡Hazme saber si puedes venir! ▪ ¡Déjame saber si puedes venir! ▪ ¡Avísame si puedes venir! Let me know if you can come!
hacer salir volando una nidada to flush a covey of birds
hacer saltar el cortacircuitos ▪ hacer saltar el cuadro eléctrico ▪ hacer caer los interruptores ▪ hacer saltar el central to trip the circuit breaker
hacer segunda pregunta a un(a) testigo ▪ repreguntar a un(a) testigo to cross-examine a witness
hacer senderismo to go hiking
hacer sentadillas to do sit-ups
hacer señas a alguien to wave at someone (to get his attention)
hacer sitio para ▪ hacer espacio para ▪ hacer lugar para ▪ dar cabida a to make room for ▪ to clear a space for
hacer sombra a alguien to overshadow someone
hacer su agosto ▪ darse un festín del bueno to have a field day ➤ Los alumnos hacían su agosto con el substituto. ▪ Los alumnos se daban un festín del bueno con el substituto. The students were having a field day with the substitute.
hacer su deber to do one's duty
hacer su santa voluntad to do as one jolly well pleases
hacer sumas ▪ sumar to add (up) ➤ Para hacer sumas de listas de números, es mucho más rápido usar una calculadora. To add (up) columns of figures, it's much faster to use a calculator.
hacer sus necesidades *(mascotas)* to go to the bathroom ▪ to do one's necessities ➤ Hay que sacar a pasear al perro para que haga sus necesidades. You need to take the dog out so he can go to the bathroom.
hacer sus pinitos ▪ dar sus primeros pasitos to take one's first steps
hacer tabla rasa de algo to sweep something aside ▪ to disregard something completely ▪ to clear the deck

hacer tabla rasa de alguien to run roughshod over someone

hacer tablas ▪ acabar en tablas ▪ quedar en tablas **1.** *(ajedrez, negociaciones)* to end in a stalemate ▪ to stalemate **2.** *(deportes)* to (end in a) tie ▪ to end in a draw

hacer tajadas de algo to cut something into pieces

hacer teatro to play-act

hacer temer que... to raise fears that...

hacer tertulia to have a get-together

hacer testamento de to bear witness to ▪ to corroborate

hacer tiempo ▪ rellenar el tiempo ▪ matar el tiempo to kill time ▪ to while away time ▪ to fill the time ▪ to take up the time

hacer todo el trayecto hasta to go all the way to ➤ El metro ahora hace todo el trayecto hasta el aeropuerto. The metro now goes all the way to the airport.

hacer todo lo posible (por) ▪ dar el do de pecho (para que) to do everything possible to ▪ to do one's level best (to) ▪ to do one's very best (to) ▪ to do one's utmost (to)

hacer trabajar el cerebro to exercise the mind ▪ to be good mental exercise

hacer trampas en un acuerdo ▪ traicionar un acuerdo to cheat on an agreement ➤ Los países no deberían hacer trampas en los acuerdos de no proliferación nuclear. ▪ Los países no deberían traicionar los acuerdos de no proliferación nuclear. Countries should not cheat on nuclear non-proliferation treaties.

hacer transbordo de trenes, aviones, subtes, autobuses, *etc.* to change trains, planes, subways, buses *etc.*

hacer transformaciones y arreglos (en la ropa) to do alterations and repairs (on clothes)

hacer trizas de algo to tear something to shreds

hacer trompos *(automóvil)* to spin around

hacer turismo to go sightseeing

hacer un adelantamiento to overtake someone in a race

hacer un ademán de despedida to wave good-bye

hacer un agujero ▪ agujerear **1.** agujerear to dig a hole ▪ to make a hole ▪ to punch a hole **2.** perforar un agujero (a través de) to bore a hole (through) ➤ Los mineros hicieron un agujero a través de la roca. ▪ Los mineros perforaron un agujero a través de la roca. The miners bored a hole through the rock. ➤ Las termitas hicieron un agujero en el suelo de la sala de la prima Mae. ▪ Las termitas perforaron un agujero en el suelo de la sala de la prima Mae. The termites bored a hole through cousin Mae's parlor floor.

hacer un ángulo (diagonal) a la esquina to sit at an angle to the corner ▪ to be situated at an angle to the corner ➤ La iglesia hace un ángulo diagonal a la esquina. The church sits at an angle to the corner. ▪ The church sits at a forty-five degree angle to the corner.

hacer un anuncio to make an announcement

hacer un aprendizaje to serve an apprenticeship

hacer un bis to do an encore ▪ to perform an encore ➤ Hicieron un bis. They did an encore. ▪ They performed an encore.

hacer un buen trabajo to do a good job ➤ Estás haciendo un buen trabajo. You're doing a good job.

hacer un calor bochornoso to be sweltering ▪ to be swelteringly hot ▪ to be oppressively hot

hacer un calor de todos los demonios ▪ hacer un calor de mil demonios to be hot as the hinges of hell ▪ to be blazing hot

hacer un caño *(fútbol)* to pass the ball between the legs of the opposition player

hacer un clavado (al agua) to dive (into the water)

hacer un curso to take a course ▪ to go through a program

hacer un daño tremendo to do tremendous damage

hacer un derrape ▪ derrapar to skid

hacer un dibujo to draw a picture ▪ to make a picture ➤ Me hizo un dibujo de su gato. She drew me a picture of her cat. ▪ She made me a picture of her cat.

hacer un disparo ▪ pegar un tiro ▪ disparar un tiro to fire a shot ➤ ¿Cuántos disparos se hicieron? How many shots were fired?

hacer un examen ▪ presentar un examen ▪ realizar un examen **1.** to take a test **2.** *(esp. parcial o final)* to take an examination ▪ to take an exam

hacer un esfuerzo para ▪ esforzarse para to make an effort to ➤ Hicimos un verdadero esfuerzo por... We made a real effort to...

hacer un flaco favor ▪ hacer un flaco servicio to be of no help

hacer un flaco servicio ▪ hacer un flaco favor to be of no help

hacer un frío de cojones to be cold as a well digger's butt ▪ to be cold as the shady side of a witch's tit

hacer un intento to make an attempt

hacer un mal trabajo ▪ hacer un trabajo de poca calidad to do a poor job ▪ to do an inferior job ▪ to do an unsatisfactory job

hacer un nudo to tie a knot

hacer un paréntesis to take a break ➤ Hagamos un paréntesis. Let's take a break.

hacer un pasaporte to apply for a passport ➤ Cuando estaba haciendo mi pasaporte... When I was applying for my passport...

hacer un pedido a to place an order with

hacer un placaje *(deportes)* to block ▪ to throw a block

hacer un poder (para) to make an effort (to)

hacer un presupuesto para un proyecto de construcción *(pujar privado)* to bid on a construction project

hacer un presupuesto para un trabajo de pintura to bid on a paint job

hacer un propósito para el Año Nuevo to make a New Year's Resolution

hacer un punto *(jugando al baloncesto, balón volea, pero no al fútbol)* to score a point ▪ to make a point

hacer un puré de los aguacates to mash the avocados ▪ to pureé the avocados

hacer un puré de las patatas to mash the potatoes ▪ to pureé the potatoes

hacer un puré de papas ▪ *(Esp.)* hacer un puré de patatas ▪ *(Arg.)* pisar la papas to mash the potatoes ▪ to whip the potatoes

hacer un recado to run an errand

hacer un recorrido de to take a tour of ▪ to go on a tour of

hacer un recuento ▪ llevar a cabo un recuento to do a recount

hacer un refrito de un libro to give a rehash of a book

hacer un refrito de una película to give a rehash of a movie

hacer un registro de to conduct a search of ▪ to search ➤ La policía hizo un registro del edificio. (The) police conducted a search of the building. ▪ (The) police searched the building.

hacer un repaso de **1.** to do a review of **2.** to think back over

hacer un robo de un banco to rob a bank

hacer un seguimiento de un envío to track a shipment

hacer un seguimiento de un paquete to track a package

hacer un signo aprobatorio to give a thumbs up ▪ to nod in approval

hacer un testamento to make a will

hacer un tiempo desapacible ▪ hacer un tiempo de perros ▪ hacer un tiempo desagradable ▪ hacer un tiempo malísimo ▪ hacer un tiempo asqueroso to be bad weather ▪ to be awful weather ▪ to be inclement weather ▪ *(pintoresco)* to be lousy weather

hacer un trabajo de poca calidad ▪ hacer un mal trabajo to do a poor job ▪ to do an unsatisfactory job ▪ to do an inferior job

hacer un trabajo magnífico ▪ hacer un trabajo excelente to do a magnificent job ▪ to do an excellent job ▪ *(coloquial)* to do a bang-up job

hacer un trato to make a deal

hacer un viaje to take a trip ▪ to make a trip

hacer un voto to take a vow

hacer una aparición to make an appearance

hacer una apelación a la calma to appeal for calm

hacer una aseveración to assert ▪ to contend

hacer una auditoria (de los libros de cuentas) to audit the books

hacer una batería de pruebas a algo ▪ hacer un conjunto de pruebas a algo to run a battery of tests on something ▪ to run a series of tests on something

hacer una buena acción ▪ hacer una buena obra to do a good deed

hacer una buena obra ▪ hacer una buena acción to do a good deed

hacer una buena relación con alguien to develop a good friendship with someone ▪ to develop a strong friendship with someone

hacer una burla a alguien ■ gastar una broma a alguien to play a joke on someone ■ to play a trick on someone
hacer una burrada to do something stupid ■ to do a stupid thing
hacer una cama redonda to have group sex
hacer una carajada a alguien *(subido de tono)* to fuck somebody over ■ to screw somebody over
hacer una carrera 1. to race ■ to have a race **2.** hacer una corrida to make a run for it
hacer una chapuza hacer una ñapa to do a makeshift repair
hacer una cita con alguien ■ quedar con alguien ■ concretar una cita con alguien **1.** to make a date with someone **2.** to make an appointment with someone
hacer una corrida ■ hacer una carrera to make a run for it ➤ Quedan sólo unos metros, hagamos una corrida hasta la frontera. ■ Quedan sólo unos metros, hagamos una carrera hasta la frontera. There are only a few yards left. Let's make a run for the border.
hacer una cosa mejor que otra to do one thing better than another ■ to be better at (doing) one thing than at another ➤ Juego al poquer mejor que al bridge. I play poker better than bridge. ■ I'm better at (playing) poker than (I am) at bridge.
hacer una criba to sort through papers
hacer una declaración to make a statement
hacer una declaración jurada 1. to make a sworn statement ■ to make a statement under oath ■ to state under oath **2.** to notarize a document
hacer una derivación en un alambre to tap a wire
hacer una descripción to give a description
hacer una elección ■ elegir to make a choice ➤ Hiciste una buena elección. ■ Elegiste bien. You made a good choice. ➤ Hice una elección incorrecta de carrera cuando era joven, y me costó salir de ello. I made an incorrect career choice early in life and had a hard time getting out of it.
hacer una escapada durante el fin de semana ■ escaparse durante el fin de semana to get away for the weekend ➤ Necesitamos (hacer) una escapada este fin de semana. We need to get away this weekend. ■ We need to get away for the weekend.
hacer una excursión guiada to take a guided tour
hacer una faena a alguien ■ hacer una carajada a alguien to play a dirty trick on someone
hacer una fiesta to have a party
hacer una hipoteca sobre una casa to take out a mortgage on a house ■ to mortgage a house
hacer una imitación divertida de alguien ■ hacer una parodia de alguien to do a humorous imitation of someone ■ to do a takeoff on someone ■ to parody someone ■ to do a spoof of someone ■ to spoof someone
hacer una llamada to make a call ➤ Habré hecho unas treinta llamadas de larga distancia a Chile en agosto. ■ *(Esp.)* Yo haría unas treinta llamadas de larga distancia a Chile en agosto. I must have made thirty long distance calls to Chile in August.
hacer una llamada perdida to (let it) ring once and hang up
hacer una montaña de un granito ■ hacer una montañá de un grano de arena ■ hacer de una pulga un elefante to make a mountain out of a molehill
hacer una mudanza ■ dejar (el piso) to move out (of the apartment)
hacer una mueca ■ poner una mueca to make a face
hacer una ñapa hacer una chapuza to do a makeshift repair
hacer una orgía to have an orgy
hacer una parodia de alguien ■ hacer una imitación divertida de alguien to do a humorous imitation of someone ■ to do a takeoff on someone ■ to parody someone ■ to do a spoof of someone ■ to spoof someone
hacer una pasada to pass a car at high speed
hacer una pausa 1. to pause **2.** to take a break
hacer una picada 1. *(aviación)* to dive **2.** *(comida)* to have a bite to eat (with others) ■ to have a little something to eat (with others) ■ to have a light meal ➤ Vamos a hacer una picada. Let's have a bite to eat.
hacer una pregunta ■ formular una pregunta to ask a question ➤ Déjame hacerte esta pregunta. ■ Permíteme formularte esta pregunta. ■ Déjeme que le haga (a usted) esta pregunta. ■ Permítame formularle esta pregunta. Let me ask you this question.
hacer una prueba *(científica, médica)* to do a test
hacer una reserva con antelación ■ hacer una reserva por adelantado to make a reservation in advance ■ to make reservations in advance ■ to make advance reservations
hacer una seña a alguien con la cabeza to nod at someone
hacer una solicitud to file an application
hacer una sombra to cast a shadow ■ to project a shadow
hacer una suplencia por to substitute for
hacer una teatrada to make a scene ■ to put on an act ■ to make a production out of something
hacer una visita to pay someone a visit
hacer una vivada to pull a fast one ➤ Cuando nadie le miraba hizo una vivada y dio la vuelta donde estaba prohibido. When nobody was looking, he pulled a fast one and did an illegal U-turn.
hacer unos negocios ■ hacer unos trámites to conduct some business ■ to do some business
hacer uso de la palabra ■ tomar la palabra to address the meeting ■ to take the floor
hacer valer su autoridad to assert one's authority
hacer valer sus derechos to assert one's rights
hacer vela to go sailing
hacer ver to point out ■ to expose
hacer ver a alguien quien es to expose someone for what one is ➤ *(homenaje al columnista fallecido Mike Royko.)* Ya no habrá quien haga ver a los idiotas que son idiotas. Now there won't be anybody to expose the idiots for what they are.
hacer ver que... ■ hacer entender que... ■ hacer comprender que... make the point that... ➤ Kant's treatise makes the point that any dispute can be resolved if both parties have the will to resolve it. El tratado de Kant hace ver que cualquier desacuerdo puede resolverse si ambas partes tienen la voluntad de resolverlo.
hacer ver un error ■ señalar un error to expose an error ■ to point out an error
hacer *x* grados to be *x* degrees ➤ Hace veinte grados centígrados afuera. It's twenty degrees Centigrade outside. *(Nota: 68 grados Fahrenheit)*
hacer zapping to flip channels ■ to channel surf
hacer zigzag ■ hacer eses **1.** saltar los coches a la torera to weave (all over the road) ■ to weave (in and out of traffic) ■ to zigzag (all over the road) **2.** hacer filigranas to stagger (around)
hacerla madre to get a woman pregnant ■ *(coloquial, jerga)* to knock a woman up
hacerla una desgraciada to disgrace a woman
hacerle a alguien barruntar cosas to lead someone to imagine things ■ to lead someone to start imagining things
hacerle a alguien barruntar que... to lead someone to suspect that... ■ to make someone suspect that...
hacerle a alguien hacer algo to make someone do something ■ to prompt someone to do something ➤ La guerra le hizo marcharse de casa. The war made him leave home.
hacerle a alguien la cama ■ hacerle pisar el palito to set someone up
hacerle a alguien un cumplido to pay someone a compliment ■ to give someone a compliment
hacerle a alguien un descuento to give someone a discount
hacerle a pelo y a pluma ■ hacer a todo ■ ser bisexual ■ entrarle a todo to go both ways ■ to be AC-DC ■ to be bisexual
hacerle a todo ■ hacer a pelo y a pluma ■ ser bisexual ■ entrarle a todo to go both ways ■ to be AC-DC ■ to be bisexual
hacerle algo a alguien cuesta arriba to make something very heavy going on someone ■ to make something very difficult for someone ➤ "Voy a hacerles esta asignatura muy cuesta arriba," dijo el profesor sádico. "I'm going to make this subject very heavy going," said the sadistic teacher.
hacerle bien a alguien 1. to do someone good **2.** to treat someone well ■ to treat someone right ➤ Te hará mucho bien. It will do you a lot of good. ■ It'll do you a lot of good.
hacerle caso a alguien to pay attention to someone
hacerle conjunto con ■ hacerle juego con ■ combinar con to go with ■ to go together ➤ La corbata le hace conjunto con la camisa. The tie goes with his shirt. ■ His shirt and tie go together.

hacerle desenterrar recuerdos ■ traer recuerdos a la memoria to bring back memories ■ to unearth memories

hacerle el artículo a alguien to pitch merchandise ■ to give someone a pitch ■ to pitch a customer

hacerle el favor a alguien de... to do someone the favor of...

hacerle entrar en razón a alguien to talk some sense into someone

hacerle falta a alguien to miss someone ➤ A Marcelino le hacía falta su mamá. Marcelino missed having a mother.

hacerle falta a alguien que alguien haga algo to need someone to do something ➤ ¿Te hace falta que te ayude? Do you need me to help you? ■ Do you need for me to help you?

hacerle falta algo a alguien to need something ■ to lack something ➤ Al estudiante le hace falta un diccionario. The student needs a dictionary. ■ The student lacks a dictionary.

hacerle falta el dinero ■ necesitar el dinero to need the money ➤ El dinero nos hacía falta. ■ Necesitabamos el dinero. We needed the money.

hacerle gracia a uno to strike someone as funny ■ to hit someone as being funny ■ to hit someone funny ■ to amuse one ■ to be amusing to one ■ to be pleasing to one ➤ A mi mujer la idea no le hace gracia. My wife doesn't like the idea.

hacerle ilusión algo to look forward to something ➤ Me hace mucha ilusión. I'm really looking forward to it. ■ I'm looking forward to it a lot.

hacerle juego a alguien ■ engatusar a alguien ■ acaramelar a alguien to sweet-talk someone

hacerle la cama a alguien ■ hacer la cama a alguien to set someone up

hacerle la pascua a alguien ■ hacerle la puñeta a alguien ■ jugarle una mala pasada a alguien ■ hacerle una jugarreta a alguien to make trouble for someone

hacerle la petaca a alguien to short-sheet someone's bed ■ to make someone an apple-pie bed

hacerle la puñeta a alguien ■ jugarle una mala pasada a alguien ■ hacerle una jugarreta a alguien ■ hacerle la pascua a alguien to make trouble for someone

hacerle parecer to make someone out to be ■ to make someone sound like ➤ Me hizo parecer un mentiroso. He made me out to be a liar. ■ He made me sound like a liar.

hacerle pensar to lead one to believe ➤ Me hace pensar que... It leads me to believe that...

hacerle rabiar a alguien to bait someone

hacerle reproches a alguien to reproach someone

hacerle retroceder a alguien to force someone back ➤ Las olas le hacían retroceder. The waves forced him back.

hacerle sangrar por la nariz a alguien to give someone a bloody nose

hacerle señas para que se detenga *(tiempo presente)* to signal (to) someone to pull over ➤ Te hace señas para que te detengas. He's signalling (to) you to pull over.

hacerle señas para que se detuviera *(tiempo pasado)* to signal (to) someone to pull over ➤ El policía de tráfico me hizo señas para que me detuviera. The traffic policeman signalled (to) me to pull over.

hacerle sombra en algo to have problems in something ➤ Desde el principio le hizo sombra en su negocio. From the start he had problems in his business.

hacerle tilín to turn one on sexually ➤ Ella me hace tilín. She turns me on.

hacerle un arañazo a alguien to scratch someone

hacerle un cheque to write someone a check ■ to make someone out a check ➤ Me hizo un cheque. He wrote me a check. ■ He made out a check to me. ■ He made me out a check.

hacerle un chequeo a alguien to give someone a battery of medical tests ■ to run a battery of tests on someone ■ to run a series of medical tests on someone ■ to give someone a series of medical tests

hacerle un cumplido a alguien to pay someone a compliment ■ to compliment someone ■ to give someone a compliment

hacerle un hijo *(coloquial)* to get her pregnant ➤ Le hizo un hijo. He got her pregnant.

hacerle un lío to throw one for a loop ➤ Esas glorietas me hicieron un lío. Those traffic circles threw me for a loop. *(Nota: El inglés es un retruécano.)*

hacerle un regalo a alguien to give someone a present ■ to give someone a gift

hacerle un reproche a alguien to reproach someone

hacerle una caricia al perro to pet the dog

hacerle una huchita to make a nest egg

hacerle una mala faena a alguien to play a dirty trick on someone

hacerle una reverencia a alguien to bow to someone ➤ Cuando el Sr. Bean le hizo a la reina una reverencia, le pegó con la cabeza y la tumbó. When Mr. Bean bowed to the queen, he bumped her in the head and knocked her down.

hacerle una visita a alguien to pay someone a visit ➤ Iba a hacerte una visita. I was going to pay you a visit.

hacerle la zalá a alguien *(poco común)* ■ hacerle la pelota a alguien ■ adular a alguien to butter someone up ■ *(subido de tono)* to brownnose someone

hacerle una jugarreta a alguien to play a dirty trick on someone

hacerle zumbar los oídos ■ hacer que le zumben los oídos to make one's ears ring ➤ Las discotecas me hacen zumbar los oídos. Discotheques make my ears ring.

hacerlo de buena gana **1.** to do it willingly **2.** to do so willingly

hacerlo de mala gana **1.** to do it unwillingly **2.** to do so unwillingly ➤ Pero lo hizo de mala gana. But he did so unwillingly.

hacerlo a pelo *(jerga)* to have sex in the raw ■ to do it in the raw ■ to have unprotected sex ■ to have sex without a condom

hacerlo por deporte ■ hacerlo porque sí to do it just for fun

hacerlo porque sí ■ hacerlo por deporte to do it just for fun ■ to do it just for the heck of it

hacerlo así to do it this way ■ to do it like this ➤ *(tú)* Hazlo así. ■ *(usted)* Hágalo así. Do it this way. ■ Do it like this.

hacerlos uno por uno to do them one at a time

hacerse carpintero to become a carpenter ➤ Cuando tenía dieciséis años, se hizo carpintero. When he was sixteen (years old), he became a carpenter.

hacerse a base de golpes to become successful through a long, hard struggle

hacerse a la derecha ■ quedarse a la derecha **1.** to bear right ■ to move over to the right ■ to get over to the right **2.** tomar la bifurcación a la derecha to bear right (at the fork) ■ to take the right fork ➤ *(tú)* Hazte a la derecha. ■ Quédate a la derecha. ■ *(usted)* Hágase (usted) a la derecha. ■ Quédese (usted) a la derecha. Bear right. ■ Move over to the right. ■ Get over to the right. ➤ Hazte a la derecha en la bifurcación. ■ Quédate a la derecha en la bifurcación. ■ Toma la bifurcación a la derecha. Bear right at the fork. ■ Take the right fork.

hacerse a la idea de algo ■ acostumbrarse a la idea de algo to get used to the idea of something

hacerse a la izquierda ■ quedarse a la izquierda **1.** to bear left ■ to move over to the left ■ to get over to the left **2.** tomar la bifurcación a la izquierda to bear left (at the fork) ■ to take the left fork ➤ *(tú)* Hazte a la izquierda. ■ Quédate a la izquierda. ■ *(usted)* Hágase (usted) a la izquierda. ■ Quédese (usted) a la izquierda. Bear left. ■ Move over to the left. ■ Get over to the left. ➤ Hazte a la izquierda en la bifurcación. ■ Quédate a la izquierda en la bifurcación. ■ Toma la bifurcación a la izquierda. Bear left at the fork. ■ Take the left fork.

hacerse a la mar ■ zarpar to set sail ■ to go to sea

hacerse a la mar con rumbo a ■ zarpar con rumbo a to set sail for

hacerse a las armas to enlist in the military ■ to join the military ■ to join the service

hacerse a todo to adapt to any situation

hacerse a un lado ■ echarse a un lado **1.** to step aside **2.** to move over

hacerse abogado(-a) to become a lawyer ■ to become an attorney

hacerse agua la boca to make one's mouth water

hacerse al campo ■ salir al campo to set out for the countryside

hacerse amigos to become friends

hacerse amigos de los demás ▪ hacerse amigos de todos ▪ hacerse amigos de todo el mundo to get to know everyone ▪ to get to know everybody

hacerse añicos 1. *(persona)* to be worn to a frazzle **2.** *(cosa)* to be in tatters ▪ to be in rags

hacerse bolas *(Méx.)* ▪ armarse un lío ▪ hacerse un lío to get mixed up ▪ to get confused ▪ to be thrown for a loop ▪ to get thrown for a loop ➤ Me hago bolas. I'm mixed up. ▪ I got mixed up.

hacerse cábalas to wonder ▪ to speculate ▪ to guess

hacerse camino to make way

hacerse cargo to understand a situation ➤ Me hago cargo. I understand. ▪ Don't worry about it.

hacerse cargo de algo ▪ encargarse de algo to take charge of something ➤ El Federal Bureau of Investigation (FBI) se ha hecho cargo del caso. The FBI has taken charge of the case.

hacerse cargo de todo lo que uno hace to assume responsibility for one's actions ▪ to take responsibility for one's actions

hacerse cargo de todo lo que uno le dice to assume responsibility for what one says ▪ to take responsibility for what one says

hacerse carne to become incarnate

hacerse catedrático(-a) to become a university professor ▪ to become a college professor

hacerse cisco *(coloquial)* to break down ▪ to bust

hacerse composición de lugar to take stock of the situation

hacerse con algo 1. conseguir algo to get hold of something **2.** tomar posesión de algo to get possession of something ▪ to take possession of something **3.** dominar un campo de estudio ▪ dominar un campo de conocimiento to get a grasp of an academic subject ▪ to get a grasp of a field of inquiry ➤ Estoy tratando de hacerme con una copia. I'm trying to get hold of a copy. ➤ Ojalá pudiera hacerme con una copia. I wish I could get hold of a copy. ▪ I wish I could get my hands on a copy. ▪ I wish I could obtain a copy. ➤ Los Reyes Católicos se hicieron con buena parte de América del Sur a través de sucesivas conquistas. Ferdinand and Isabella took possession of a good part of South America through a series of conquests. ➤ Por fin me he hecho con la asignatura. I'm finally getting a grasp of the subject.

hacerse con alguien to get hold of somebody ➤ Las cosas estuvieron paradas hasta que nos hicimos con el técnico. Things were at a standstill until we got hold of the technician.

hacerse con el control de algo to get control of something

hacerse con el control de sus sentidos to take control of one's senses ▪ to come to one's senses

hacerse con los servicios de alguien ▪ contratar a alguien to hire someone

hacerse cuenta que 1. to pretend ▪ to act as if ▪ *(coloquial)* to act like **2.** *(forma coloquial e incorrecta de "darse cuenta de que")* to realize ▪ to notice

hacerse cuesta arriba 1. to start to wear one down **2.** to start to get difficult ▪ to start to get hard ▪ *(coloquial)* to turn into a (real) bear ➤ La mudanza se me está haciendo cuesta arriba. This moving is starting to wear me down. ➤ Este asignatura se me está haciendo cuesta arriba. This course is starting to get difficult. ▪ This course is starting to get hard. ▪ This course is turning into a real bear.

hacerse daño to hurt oneself ➤ ¡No te hagas daño! Don't hurt yourself!

hacerse daño en el (brazo) to hurt one's (arm) ➤ Se hizo daño en el brazo jugando al fútbol. He hurt his arm playing football.

hacerse de cruces to be astonished ▪ to be beside oneself ➤ Cuando se enteraron de que su hija adolescente estaba embarazada, los padres se hicieron de cruces. When they learned that their teenage daughter was pregnant, the parents were beside themselves.

hacerse nombre to make a name for oneself

hacerse de oro to get rich ▪ to make a fortune

hacerse de rogar *(Esp.)* ▪ hacerse rogar to have to be coaxed ▪ to have to be pleaded with ▪ to play hard to get ➤ Le invitamos a la fiesta, pero se hizo de rogar hasta que accedió a venir. We invited him to the party, but he had to be coaxed into accepting. ▪ We invited him to the party, but he had to be pleaded with before he would accept.

hacerse dueño de to take possession of

hacerse eco de la notica to spread the news

hacerse eco de la opinión de alguien to echo someone's opinions ▪ to echo someone's sentiments

hacerse eco de las palabras de alguien to echo someone's words

hacerse el cazurro to feign being a hick

hacerse el chulo ▪ hacerse el gallito to act cocky ▪ to be cocky ▪ to act sassy ▪ to get sassy ▪ to be sassy ▪ to sass **2.** juntar valentía to become emboldened ➤ *(madre al hijo)* No te hagas el chulo conmigo. ▪ No te hagas el gallito conmigo. Don't sass me! ▪ Don't get sassy with me!

hacerse el control de su tiempo ▪ controlar su tiempo to get control of one's time

hacerse el desentendido de algo 1. desentenderse de algo to pretend not to hear something ▪ to pretend not to know something **2.** lavarse las manos de algo ▪ lavarse las manos como Poncio Pilato to wash one's hands of something

hacerse el disimulado to pretend not to notice ▪ to pretend not to know

hacerse el encontradizo to "accidentally" meet someone ▪ to "accidentally" cross paths with someone

hacerse el escurridizo to make oneself very hard to catch ▪ to elude a pursuer very skillfully

hacerse el gallito ▪ hacerse el chulo **1.** ser agrandado to act cocky ▪ to be cocky ▪ to act sassy ▪ to be sassy **2.** juntar valentía to become emboldened ➤ *(madre al hijo)* No te hagas el gallito conmigo. ▪ No te hagas el chulo conmigo. Don't sass me! ▪ Don't get sassy with me!

hacerse el ganso to clown around

hacerse el idiota to play the fool

hacerse el interesado to feign interest ▪ to pretend to be interested

hacerse el interesante to try to get attention ▪ to be "on stage"

hacerse el loco ▪ hacerse el tonto to play dumb

hacerse el longui ▪ hacerse el longuis to play dumb

hacerse el muerto 1. to play dead **2.** ignorar a alguien to ignore someone

hacerse el necesario to make oneself useful

hacerse el olvidadizo to pretend to forget ▪ to pretend you forgot

hacerse el pelo to do one's hair ➤ Tengo que hacerme el pelo. I have to do my hair.

hacerse el primo to get taken for a ride ▪ to be taken for a ride ▪ to get suckered into something

hacerse el propósito de to resolve to ▪ to determine to

hacerse el simpático a to ingratiate oneself to someone

hacerse el sueco ▪ hacer como que no comprende ▪ simular no comprender ▪ no darse por enterado to play dumb ▪ to feign ignorance

hacerse el tarado to play dumb

hacerse el tonto ▪ hacerse el bobo ▪ hacerse el distraído ▪ hacerse el sueco ▪ hacerse el loco to play dumb

hacerse entender algo por alguien to get something across to someone ▪ to make oneself understood to someone

hacerse estallar to blow oneself up ➤ *(noticia)* Un terrorista suicida se hizo estallar en Jerusalén. A suicide bomber blew himself up in Jerusalem.

hacerse extensiva una invitación a to tell someone to invite others

hacerse famoso(-a) instantáneamente ▪ alcanzar una pronta fama to become instantly famous ▪ to achieve instant fame

hacerse famoso(-a) (por) to become famous (by)

hacerse fluido en un idioma ▪ volverse fluido en un idioma ▪ soltarse en un idioma ▪ llegar a hacerse fluido en un idioma to become fluent in a language

hacerse fuerte en 1. to become strong in **2.** to entrench oneself in ▪ to barricade oneself in

hacerse ilusiones 1. to get one's hopes up **2.** construir castillos en el aire to engage in wishful thinking ▪ to build castles in the air ➤ No te hagas ilusiones. Don't get your hopes up. ➤

Sólo te hagas ilusiones. ■ Sólo quieres hacerte ilusiones. That's just wishful thinking.

hacerse famoso(-a) ■ llegar a ser famoso(-a) to become famous

hacerse la corbata ■ hacer el nudo de la corbata to tie a necktie ■ *(coloquial)* to tie a tie

hacerse la difícil ■ hacerse la dura ■ hacerse la estrecha to play hard to get

hacerse la estrecha to act like a prude ■ to pretend to be a prude

hacerse las uñas to do one's nails

hacerse lenguas de algo to rave about something

hacerse lenguas de alguien to praise someone to the skies

hacerse más amplio ■ volverse más amplio ■ ampliarse to become wider ■ to get wider ■ to grow wider ➤ Debemos evitar que la disparidad entre los ricos y los pobres se haga más amplio. ■ Debemos evitar que la disparidad entre los ricos y los pobres se amplíe. ■ Debemos evitar que la disparidad entre los ricos y los pobres se vuelva más amplía. We must prevent the disparity between rich and poor from growing wider.

hacerse más intenso ■ ponerse más intenso ■ intensificarse to become more intense

hacerse más mayor to get older ➤ Queremos ir a España cuando nuestra hija se hace un poco más mayor. We want to go to Spain when our daughter gets a little older.

hacerse médico to become a doctor

hacerse migas to be broken all to pieces ■ to be badly broken ➤ Cuando abrí la bolsa, los nachos se habían hecho migas. When I opened the bag, the chips were broken all to pieces. ■ When I opened the bag, the chips were badly broken.

hacerse parte del secreto to get in on the secret

hacerse partícipe de un secreto to stumble across the secret ■ to happen onto the secret

hacerse pasar por to pretend to be ■ to pass oneself off as ■ to pass itself off as ■ to parade as ➤ El periodista se metió a ver a la víctima haciéndose pasar por un médico. The reporter got in to see the victim by passing himself off as a doctor. ■ The reporter got in to see the victim by pretending to be a doctor. ➤ Es un trabajo diario haciéndose pasar por un periódico. It's a daily work of fiction parading as a newspaper. ■ It's a daily work of fiction passing itself off as a newspaper.

hacerse pedazos to break into pieces ➤ *(noticia)* NASA admite que la sonda espacial "Contour" puede haberse hecho pedazos. NASA admits that the space probe "Contour" may have broken into pieces.

hacerse presente to make one's presence felt ➤ Ha querido hacerse presente. He wanted to make his presence felt.

hacerse presidente ■ llegar a ser presidente ■ volverse presidente to become president

hacerse profesor(a) to become a teacher

hacerse público ■ ser hecho público to be made public ➤ Antes de hacerse público Before it was made public ■ Before being made public

hacerse respetar to command respect

hacerse rico(-a) ■ enriquecerse ■ hacerse platudo(-a) to become rich ■ to get rich

hacerse tarde ■ estarse haciendo tarde to be getting late

hacerse tardísimo ■ estarse haciendo tardísimo to be getting very late ■ *(coloquial)* to be getting awful late

hacerse un bufete to build up one's practice

hacerse un chequeo to undergo a battery of medical tests ■ to undergo a series of medical tests

hacerse un esguince en el tobillo to sprain one's ankle

hacerse un esguince en la muñeca to sprain one's wrist

hacérsele un huevo a la cámara *(de una llanta)* to balloon out

hacerse un lío *(Esp.)* ■ liarse ■ trastocarse ■ armarse un lío ■ hacerse un taco ■ hacerse bolas to get mixed up ■ to get confused ■ to be thrown for a loop ■ to get thrown for a loop ➤ Me hago un lío. I'm mixed up. ■ I got mixed up.

hacerse un nombre to make a name for oneself

hacerse un poco más mayor to get a little older ➤ Queremos ir a España cuando nuestra hija se haga un poco más mayor. We want to go to Spain when our daughter gets a little older.

hacerse un procedimiento médico to have a medical procedure ➤ Me hice un TAC por mis dolores de cabeza. ■ Me hice un scanner. I had a CAT scan for my headaches. ➤ ¿Te has hecho un electrocardiograma? Have you had an electrocardiogram (EKG)? ➤ Daniel se hizo un agujero en la lengua. Daniel had his tongue pierced.

hacerse un reproche to berate oneself

hacerse un taco ■ armarse un taco ■ trastocarse to get all mixed up ■ to get muddled ■ to get in a muddle

hacerse una composición de lugar 1. to take stock of the situation 2. to get an idea of ➤ Necesito hacerme una composición de lugar. I need to take stock of the situation. ■ I need to take stock of my situation. ➤ Para que te hagas una composición de lugar de... Just so you can get an idea of...

hacerse una idea de... ■ darse una idea de to get an idea of ■ to imagine what it's like...

hacerse una paja *(subido de tono)* ■ pelársela ■ meneársela ■ cascársela ■ darle al manubrio ■ hacerse una gallola to jack off ■ to jerk off ■ to beat one's meat ■ to beat off

hacerse una prueba de colesterol to have one's cholesterol checked ➤ Hay que hacerse una prueba de colesterol. You should have your cholesterol checked.

hacerse valer to be assertive

hacerse ver del médico to have the doctor examine you ■ to have the doctor check you over ➤ Hazte ver del médico. Have the doctor examine you. ■ Have the doctor check you over.

hacerse visera con los dedos to make a viser with one's hands ■ to cup one's fingers over one's eyes

hacerse visible ■ poder verse to come into view ■ to become visible ➤ Desde la cofa de la Santa María, la tierra llana se hizo visible a una distancia de nueve millas y media. From the crow's nest of the Santa Maria, flat land came into view at a distance of about nine and a half miles.

hacérsele a alguien (muy) cuesta arriba to be heavy going ➤ Se me hace muy cuesta arriba. This is very heavy going.

hacérsele cuesta arriba 1. to start to get difficult ■ to start to get hard ■ to start to get labor intensive ■ to begin to get difficult ■ to begin to get hard ■ to begin to get labor intensive 2. to start to wear one down ■ to begin to wear one down ➤ Esta asignatura se me está haciendo cuesta arriba. This course is starting to get difficult. ■ This course is starting to get hard. ■ This course is starting to get labor intensive. ➤ La mudanza se me haciendo cuesta arriba. The moving is starting to wear me down. ■ The moving is beginning to wear me down.

hacérsele la boca agua a uno ■ hacérsele agua la boca to make one's mouth water ➤ La paella me hizo la boca agua. ■ Se me hizo la boca agua cuando vi la paella. ■ Con la paella se me hizo la boca agua. ■ La paella hizo que la boca se me hiciera agua. The paella made my mouth water.

hacérsele realidad to come true (for one) ■ to become a reality (for one)

hacérsele tarde para hacer algo to get too late to do something ➤ El informático vino esta mañana, pero no terminamos a tiempo y se me hizo tarde para ir a misa a las once. My computer technician came this morning, and we didn't finish in time for me to attend mass at eleven.

hacérsele un nudo en la garganta ■ anudarse la voz to get a lump in one's throat

hacérselo notar a alguien ■ apuntárselo a alguien to point it out to someone

hacia arriba upwards ■ up ■ towards the top

hacia atrás backwards ➤ Si no progresamos, vamos hacia atrás. If we're not gaining ground, we're losing ground.

hacia atrás en el tiempo: llevar a alguien ~ ■ transportar a alguien hacia atrás en el tiempo to take one back in time ➤ Esta película te lleva hacia atrás en el tiempo. ■ Esta película te transporta hacia atrás en el tiempo. This film takes you back in time. ➤ Mirar a través del telescopio te lleva hacia atrás en el tiempo. ■ El telescopio te transporta hacia atrás en el tiempo. Looking through a telescope takes you back in time.

¿hacia dónde? where to?

¿hacia dónde está...? which way is...?

hacia el este ■ rumbo este eastbound

hacia el fin de semana ■ al final de la semana ■ a fines de semana toward the end of the week

hacia el norte ▪ rumbo norte northbound
hacia el oeste ▪ rumbo oeste westbound
hacia el sur ▪ rumbo sur southbound
hacia eso de la(s) *x* ▪ a eso de la(s) *x* around *x* o'clock
hacia la época de ▪ por la época de ▪ sobre la época de ▪ alrededor de la época de around the time of ▪ about the time of ➤ Hacia la época de la Revolución Industrial, comenzaron los problemas de contaminación del aire y del agua. (At) about the time of the Industrial Revolution, the problems of air and water pollution began.
hacia la hora de ▪ sobre la hora de ▪ alrededor de la hora de (at) about the time of ▪ around the time of
hacía mucho tiempo que (no)... ▪ hacía mucho que (no)... it had been a long time since... ➤ Hacía mucho tiempo que no hablaba inglés. It had been a long time since I had spoken English. ➤ Hacía mucho que no lo veía. It had been a long time since I had seen him. ▪ It had been a long time since I'd seen him. ➤ *(Esp. leísmo)* Hacía mucho que no le veía. It had been a long time since I had seen him. ▪ It had been a long time since I'd seen him.
hacía tiempo que for some time
estar **hacinado en** to be crowded together in ▪ to be crammed into
hacinarse en to be crowded together in ▪ to be crammed into
hada madrina fairy godmother
haga buen o mal tiempo come rain or shine
haga el tiempo que haga no matter what the weather is
hágala circular *(usted)* pass it on
hagamos un trato 1. let's make a deal 2. let's make a bet
hagas lo que hagas, no... whatever you do, don't...
¡hágase la luz! let there be light!
hágase tu voluntad thy will be done
hágase tu voluntad y no la mía thy will, not mine, be done
hago lo demás ▪ hago lo que falta ▪ hago lo que queda ▪ hago el resto I'll do the rest ▪ I'll do what's left
hago lo que me da la gana I do as I please
hago lo que me da la real gana I do as I damn well please
¡hala! wow!
halcones y palomas *(los que son pro-guerra y pro-paz)* hawks and doves
hallar difícil creer to find it difficult to believe
hallar indicios de to find evidence of
hallar que... to find that...
hallarse en paradero desconocido to have disappeared ➤ Se halla en para dero desconocido. His whereabouts are unknown. ▪ He has disappeared.
hallarse enfermo(-a) to be ill
hallárselo todo hecho to have smooth sailing ▪ to be smooth sailing ▪ to find smooth sailing
hallazgo de ruinas arqueológicas the discovery of the archeological ruins ▪ the uncovering of archeological ruins
hallazgo que... finding that...
el **hambre atroz** ravenous hunger
hambriento de justicia longing for justice
hamburguesa tal cual hamburger with nothing on it ▪ regular hamburger
hará un año... it'll be a year...
haraganear con mala gente ▪ rondar con mala gente ▪ merodear con mala gente ▪ holgazanear con mala gente ▪ andar con mala gente ▪ reunirse con mala gente to run around with a bad crowd ▪ to hang around with a bad crowd ▪ to hang out with a bad crowd
haré lo demás ▪ hago lo demás I'll do the rest
haré lo posible por ayudarte I'll do what I can to help you ▪ I'll do whatever I can to help you ➤ Si puedo ayudarte en algo déjamelo saber y haré lo posible por ayudarte. If I can help you with anything, let me know and I'll do what I can to help you.
haré lo que pueda I'll do what I can ▪ I'll do whatever I can
haría algo si...: uno ~ one would do something if... ➤ (Yo) iría si me diera tiempo. ▪ (Yo) iría si tuviera tiempo. ▪ (Yo) iría si tuviese tiempo. I would go if I had (the) time. ▪ I'd go if I had (the) time.
haría falta algo para 1. something would be needed to 2. something is lacking ▪ something is missing ➤ Para hacer el pastel, haría falta harina. To make a cake, you would need flour. ▪ I don't have the flour to make the cake. ▪ I don't have the flour in the house to make the cake. ➤ Una alianza entre todos las democracias occidentales haría falta para derrotar el terrorismo. An alliance of all the western democracies would be needed to defeat terrorism. ➤ Haría falta buena voluntad para respetar el cese del fuego. The will to observe the cese fire is lacking. ▪ The will to observe the cease fire is missing.
haría falta que... it would be good if... ➤ Haría falta que nos acompañaras. It would be good if you came with us.
haría falta tiempo para... 1. it would take time to... 2. there's no time to... ▪ we don't have time to...
haría falta una hora para... 1. it would take an hour to... ▪ we would need an hour to... 2. we don't have an hour to...
harina de maíz corn meal
ser **harina de otro costal** ▪ ser sapo de otro pozo ▪ ser un capítulo aparte to be a different kettle of fish ▪ to be a horse of another color ▪ to be a whole different ballgame ▪ to be another thing altogether ▪ to be a different thing altogether ▪ to be altogether different ▪ to be completely different ➤ Eso es harina de otro costal. That's a different kettle of fish.
¡harre! ▪ ¡arre! giddyap!
estar **harto de que...** ▪ estar hasta el gorro de... ▪ estar hasta las narices con... to be fed up with... ▪ to be sick of... ▪ to be sick and tired of
has de saber que... you must know that...
has descubierto la pólvora con eso that's the understatement of the year
¿has disfrutado? did you enjoy it?
¿has estado allí alguna vez? have you ever been there (before)?
¿has oído hablar de...? have you heard about...? ▪ did you hear about...?
¿has pensado alguna vez lo que...? ▪ ¿has pensado alguna vez qué...? have you ever thought about what...?
¿has perdido el juicio? ▪ ¿has perdido la razón? have you lost your senses? ▪ have you lost your mind?
has sido científicamente comprobado que... it has been scientifically proved that... ▪ it has been scientifically proven that...
¿has sido tú quien lo ha hecho? are you the one who did it?
¿has traído tu diccionario? did you bring your dictionary?
¿has visto eso? ▪ ¿has visto? did you see that? ▪ see that?
¿has visto nunca cosa igual? have you ever seen anything like it?
hasta a mí 1. even me 2. *(con gustarle, etc.)* even I ➤ Hasta a mí me gusta algo de la música clásica. Even I like some classical music.
hasta agotar los adjetivos beyond description
hasta ahora until (just) now ➤ No hemos tenido noticias de su estado hasta ahora. We had no word on his condition until (just) now.
¡hasta ahora! see you later! ▪ see you in a bit!
hasta ahora (todo) bien so far so good
hasta ahí voy that's as far as I'm going
hasta aquí up to this point ▪ thus far
estar **hasta aquí (con)** *(haciendo gestos con la mano)* to have had it up to here (with)
hasta bien entrado(-a) en el próximo año ▪ hasta bien entrado en el año que viene until well into next year
hasta cierto grado ▪ hasta cierto punto as far as it goes
hasta cierto punto up to a (certain) point ▪ to a certain extent ▪ as far as it goes
hasta dentro de un rato see you in a while
hasta dentro de una semana see you in a week
hasta donde era posible recordar as far as anyone could recall
hasta donde es posible recordar as far as anyone can recall
¿hasta dónde llega el problema? how serious is the problem?
hasta donde me acuerdo ▪ hasta donde recuerdo ▪ hasta donde puedo acordarme ▪ hasta donde me puedo acordar ▪ que yo recuerde ▪ que (yo) me acuerde as far as I can recall ▪ as best I (can) recall ▪ as far as I can remember ▪ as best I (can) remember ▪ to the best of my recollection

hasta donde recuerdo ▪ hasta donde me acuerdo ▪ hasta donde puedo acordarme ▪ hasta donde me puedo acordar ▪ que yo recuerde ▪ que (yo) me acuerde as far as I can recall ▪ as best I (can) recall ▪ as far as I can remember ▪ as best I (can) remember ▪ to the best of my recollection

hasta donde se pueda as far as possible

¿hasta dónde vas? how far are you going?

hasta donde yo sé ▪ que yo sepa as far as I know ▪ so far as I know

estar **hasta el coco** ▪ estar hasta la cocorota to be up (to here) with

hasta el día de hoy ▪ hasta hoy en día to this day

hasta el domingo until Sunday

hasta el domingo inclusive through Sunday

hasta el fin del final until the very end ▪ up to the (very) end ▪ right up to the end ➤ Se murió con noventa y cinco años y fue lúcido y no sordo hasta el fin del final. He died at (age) ninety-five and was lucid and not deaf right up to the end

estar **hasta el gorro de algo** ▪ estar harto de algo to be fed up (to here) with something ▪ to be sick of something ➤ Estoy hasta el gorro de que la vecina ponga la música a todo volumen. I've had it with the neighbor's turning up her music full blast. ▪ I'm fed up (to here) with the neighbor's turning up her music full blast. ▪ I'm sick of the neighbor's turning up her music full blast.

hasta el infinito ad infinitum

estar **hasta el mismísimo carajo de** *(subido de tono)* ▪ estar hasta el mismísimo coño to be damned sick and tired of

hasta el momento until now ▪ up to now ▪ so far ➤ Hasta el momento los sospechosos se han negado a colaborar con la policía. The suspects have so far refused to cooperate with the police.

estar **hasta el moño de** to be fed up (to here) with

¡hasta el próximo día! see you next time!

hasta el punto de que... to the extent that... ➤ El diseño es defectuoso hasta el punto de que no permite reemplazar piezas deterioradas. The design is defective to the extent that it does not permit the replacement of worn (out) parts.

estar **hasta el tope** ▪ *(con gestos de la mano)* estar así de gente to be packed ▪ to be jam packed

hasta el último detalle (right) down to the last detail

hasta el *x* por ciento de... up to *x* percent of... ▪ up to *x* per cent of...

hasta en las cejas: tener algo ~ to get something all over oneself ➤ Tengo pintura hasta en las cejas. I got paint all over myself.

hasta entonces desconocido previously unknown

hasta fin de existencias while supplies last ▪ as long as supplies last

hasta hace bien poco until very recently

hasta hace poco (tiempo) until recently

hasta hoy en día until the present day ▪ up to the present time

hasta hoy mismo ▪ hasta el día de hoy to this day ➤ Lo recuerdo hasta hoy mismo. ▪ Lo recuerdo hasta el día de hoy. I remember it to this day.

estar **hasta la bandera** to be packed (with people)

estar **hasta la coronilla** to have had it up to here ➤ Estoy hasta la coronilla. I've had it up to here.

hasta la fecha to date ▪ so far ▪ up to now ▪ up to the present

hasta la fecha de su muerte **1.** *(de él)* (up) until the time of his death ▪ up to the time of his death **2.** *(de ella)* (up) until the time of her death ▪ up to the time of her death

hasta la pared de enfrente resolutely

estar **hasta la punta de los pelos con** to be thoroughly fed up with

hasta las altas horas ▪ hasta las horas intempestivas until all hours (of the night) ▪ until the wee hours

estar **hasta las bolas** to be up to one's kiester

estar **hasta las cachas** to be up to here ▪ to be up to one's neck

estar **hasta las cejas de trabajo** to be up to one's eyebrows in work

estar **hasta las narices de** to be fed up with

estar **hasta los moños de** to be sick to death of

hasta las tantas until all hours

hasta le diría (a usted) que I'd even go so far as to say that

hasta los confines de la Tierra ▪ hasta los confines del mundo to the ends of the Earth ▪ to the far corners of the Earth ▪ to the far corners of the world

hasta los confines del mundo hasta los confines de la Tierra to the ends of the Earth ▪ to the far corners of the Earth ▪ to the far corners of the world

estar **hasta los moños de** to be sick to death of

hasta los tuétanos through and through ▪ to the core

hasta luego see you later

hasta mañana see you tomorrow

hasta más no poder to the limit ▪ to the utmost

hasta más ver ▪ hasta la vista so long! ▪ see you later!

hasta muy corrida la noche until the wee hours of the night ▪ (until) far into the night

hasta nueva orden until instructed to do so ▪ until told to do so

hasta nuevo aviso until further notice

¡hasta pronto! see you soon!

hasta que until ▪ before ➤ Hasta que Estados Unidos lo difundió el martes, los servicios secretos rusos no sabían el nombre de su topo en el FBI. Until the United States released it on Tuesday, the Russian secret services did not know the name of their mole in the FBI. ➤ Pasaron cuatro décadas hasta que... Four decades went by before...

hasta que al final until finally

hasta que alguien no haga algo until someone does something *(Nota: Fíjese que en inglés la oración es afirmativa.)* ➤ Hasta que no arreglen el calentador tendremos que apañarnos sin agua caliente. Until they fix the (water) heater, we'll have to do without hot water. ➤ Hasta que no decidáis de qué color queréis el baño, no podemos empezar a pintar. Until you (all) decide what color you want the bathroom, we can't start painting.

hasta que las ranas críen pelo *(Esp.)* ▪ hasta que los pericos mamen until hell freezes over

hasta que los pericos mamen *(L.am.)* ▪ hasta que las ranas críen pelo until hell freezes over

hasta que no se haga algo until something is done *(Nota: Nótese que en inglés la oración es afirmativa. ▪ Note that in Spanish the sentence is negative.)* ➤ Hasta que no se arregle el calentador tendremos que apañarnos sin agua caliente. Until the (water) heater is fixed, we'll have to do without hot water. ➤ Hasta que no se decida el color del baño, no podemos empezar a pintar. Until the color of the bathroom is decided, we can't start painting. ▪ Until the color of the bathroom is decided, we can't start to paint.

hasta que no sea detenido *(él)* until he's arrested ▪ *(ella)* until she's arrested *(Nota: Nótese que en inglés la oración es afirmativa. ▪ Note that in Spanish the sentence is negative.)*

hasta que no veas esto... until you have seen this... ▪ until you've seen this...

hasta que pasara otro año for another year

hasta que pase otro año for another year

hasta qué punto extent to which ▪ to what extent

hasta que se agote algo until something runs out ▪ until something is used up ▪ until something is exhausted

hasta que se corte **1.** *(cualquier utilidad)* before it's cut off **2.** *(suerte, racha)* until it runs out

hasta que todo el líquido se haya absorbido until all the liquid has been absorbed ▪ until all the liquid is absorbed

hasta tal grado que ▪ hasta tal punto que so much so that ▪ to such an extent that

hasta tal punto que ▪ hasta tal grado que so much so that ▪ to such an extent that

hasta te diría que... I'd even go so far as to say that...

hasta yo ▪ incluso yo even I ➤ Hasta yo entiendo las ideas generales de la relatividad, sin las matemáticas. Even I understand the general ideas of relativity, without the math.

estar **hastiado(-a) de algo** to be weary of something

hastiarle algo a alguien to be weary of something

hastiarse de algo to grow tired of something ▪ to grow weary of something ▪ to get tired of something

¿hay alguien aquí? **1.** *(desde afuera)* is anybody there? **2.** *(desde adentro)* is anybody here?

hay algunos que dicen que... ▪ los hay que dicen que... there are some who say that... ▪ there are those who say that...

hay cabida para ▪ hay cupo para there is room for ▪ there is capacity for

hay casos en los que there are cases when ▪ there are cases where

hay cupo para ▪ hay cabida para there is room for ▪ there is capacity for

¿hay de eso en España? does that go on in Spain? ▪ does that happen in Spain?

hay de todo en la viña del Señor ▪ hay de todo como en botica it takes all kinds (to make a world)

hay esfuerzos encaminados para... efforts are underway to... ▪ there are efforts underway to...

¿hay forma de...? is there a way to...? ▪ is there any way to...? ➤ ¿Hay forma de ponerse en contacto con él? Is there any way to get in touch with him?

¿hay huevos? do you have eggs? ▪ do you carry eggs?

hay intentos para... efforts are underway to...

¿hay leche? 1. *(en una tienda)* do you have milk? ▪ do you carry milk? 2. *(en casa)* do we have milk? ▪ is there any milk?

hay más de lo que parece ▪ hay mucho más de lo que parece there's more to it than meets the eye

hay moros en la costa the coast is not clear

hay motivos para creer there is reason to believe

hay motivos para hacer algo to have reasons to do something

hay muchas maneras de matar pulgas there are lots of ways to skin a cat

hay muchas personas que coinciden there are many who (would) agree

hay mucho barullo ▪ hay mucho lío there's a lot of commotion

hay mucho jaleo aquí *(a cliente por teléfono)* it's really busy right now

hay mucho movimiento there's a lot of commotion

hay niebla it is foggy ▪ it's foggy

hay para todos there's enough to go around ▪ there's enough for everybody

¿hay permiso, mi general? *(Valle-Inclán)* may I come in, sir?

hay que you have to ▪ one must ▪ you need ➤ *(Méx.)* Hay que formarse. ▪ *(Esp.)* Hay que hacer cola. You have to get in line.

hay que adaptarse a las circunstancias you have to adapt to the circumstances

hay que averiguarlo you need to find out ▪ it needs to be investigated ▪ it needs to be looked into

Hay que ayudarte, Charlie Brown *(título de un libro) You Need Help, Charlie Brown*

hay que darle su curso ▪ (darle) tiempo al tiempo ▪ hay que esperar to let it take its course ▪ to let it run its course ➤ No hay cura para el resfriado común. Hay que darle su curso. There's no cure for the common cold. You just have to let it take its course. ▪...You just have to let it run its course.

hay que decidirse y montar a caballo *(Valle-Inclán)* we've got to make up out minds and get going

hay que estar loco para... you'd have to be crazy to...

hay que hacerlo inmediatamente it must be done right away ▪ it must be done immediately

¡hay que joderse! we're screwed!

¿hay que llevar algo a la fiesta? *(Esp.)* ▪ ¿hay que traer algo a la fiesta? are we supposed to bring something to the party? ▪ are we supposed to take something to the party?

¿hay que traer algo a la fiesta? are we supposed to bring something to the party? ▪ are we supposed to take something to the party?

¡hay que ver! honestly!

hay que verlo seeing is believing ▪ I'll believe it when I see it

hay quien there are people who ▪ there are those who ▪ some people

hay quien apunta que there are those who suggest that ▪ some people suggest that ▪ some are suggesting that

hay quien dice que... there are people who say that... ▪ there are those who say that... ▪ some are saying that...

hay quien piensa que... there are those who think that... ▪ there are people who think that... ▪ some people think that...

hay quien se pasa la vida entera... there are people who spend their whole lives... ▪ some people spend their whole lives...

hay química entre ellos ▪ hay chispas entre ellos there's chemistry between them

hay rumores de (que haya...) there is talk of... ➤ Hay rumores de (que haya) una guerra civil. There is talk of civil war. ▪ There's talk that there might be a civil war.

hay semanas que... there are weeks when... ➤ Hay semanas que no uso el metro nada. There are weeks when I don't use the metro at all.

hay sol the sun is out ▪ it's sunny out(side)

hay sus prisas y sus carreras there is a lot of hustle and bustle ▪ there's a lot of hustle and bustle

hay tela para rato there's a lot to talk about ▪ we have a lot to talk about

hay trabajo por hacer there's work to be done

hay un modo de... there's a way to...

hay un poco de viento ▪ hay una brisa it's a little windy

hay una inundación en el sótano ▪ el sótano está inundado the basement is flooded

hay una sensación de it feels like

hay veces que... there are times when...

haz a los otros lo que quieras que te hagan a ti do unto others as you would have them do unto you

haz como que no oyes nada a lo que no te agrada turn a deaf ear to unpleasant comments

el **haz de luz** diffusion of light from a central source ▪ *(coloquial)* beam of light ▪ ray of light

haz de cuenta que... *(Méx.)* ▪ supón que... suppose (that)...

el **haz de partículas** *(física)* stream of particles

haz el amor y no la guerra make love, not war

haz lo que yo ▪ haz como yo do like me

¡házmela buena! ▪ ¡ojalá! if only! ▪ I wish!

ser el **hazmereír** to be the laughingstock

hazme un hueco córrete un poco (move over and) make room

¡hazla circular! ▪ ¡hazla pasar! pass it on!

¡hazla pasar! ▪ ¡hazla circular! pass it on!

¡hazla que se pare! make her stop!

¡hazle que se pare! make him stop!

¡hazlo y punto! just do it!

¡hazlo ya! do it now!

hazte una composición del lugar visualize this ▪ form a mental picture of this ▪ imagine this

he aquí 1. *(singular)* aquí hay here is ▪ here's 2. *(plural)* ▪ aquí hay here are 3. *(bíblico)* behold ➤ Y he aquí los cielos se abrieron. And behold the heavens were opened.

he aquí por qué *(esp. científico y derecho)* ▪ (eso) es por qué that is why ▪ that's why ▪ so therefore

he cambiado de idea ▪ he cambiado de parecer ▪ he cambiado de opinión I've changed my mind

he cambiado de opinión 1. I've changed my mind 2. *(opiniones políticas, etc.)* I changed my opinion

he cambiado de parecer I've changed my mind

he de admitir ▪ tengo que admitir I must admit ▪ I have to admit

he cambiado de opinión I've changed my mind ▪ I changed my mind ➤ He cambiado de opinión. Prefiero agua con gas. I've changed my mind. I'll have sparkling water instead.

he de suponer que... I gather that... ▪ I assume that...

¡he dicho! I've told you!

he esperado mucho tiempo el día en el que... I have long awaited the day when... ▪ I have long awaited the day that..

he estado pensando en lo que dijiste I have been thinking about what you said ▪ I've been thinking about what you said

he estado pensando en lo que me dijiste I have been thinking about what you told me ▪ I've been thinking about what you told me

he ido a la playa I've been to the beach ▪ I've been at the beach

he llegado antes ▪ (yo) estoy antes ▪ me toca a mí I was here first ▪ I'm next ▪ I got here first

he llegado pronto I'm early
he quedado I have an appointment ▪ I have a date
¿he tardado mucho? was I long?
he tenido barba durante cinco años I had a beard for five years
hecha la ley, hecha la trampa every law has a loophole
Hechizo de luna *(título de película) Moonstruck*
estar **hecho** *(cocina)* to be done ▪ to completely cooked ▪ to be cooked through
estar **hecho a la medida de uno** to be tailor-made for one ▪ to be perfectly suited to one ➤ Esta trabajo está hecha a mi medida. This job is tailor made for me. ▪ This job is perfectly suited to me.
estar **hecho con buen gusto** to be tastefully done ▪ to be done in good taste
ser un **hecho conocido que** to be a known fact that
estar **hecho el uno para el otro** to be made for each other
hecho en España ▪ fabricado en España made in Spain
el **hecho es que...** ▪ el caso es que... the fact is that...
hecho a mano made by hand ▪ handmade
estar **hecho a medias** to be half done
hecho(-a) a sí mismo(-a) self-made
estar **hecho ascuas** to be glowing
ser un **hecho cierto** ▪ ser un hecho probado to be an established fact ▪ to be an accomplished fact ▪ to be a proven fact
el **hecho (de) que...** the fact that...
hecho delictivo ▪ delito crime
estar **hecho el uno para el otro** to be made for each other
el **hecho es que...** ▪ el caso es que... ▪ es el caso que... the fact is that...
hecho innegable undeniable fact
estar **hecho jirones** to be in rags ➤ Mi partitura de Bach está hecho jirones. My Bach score is just in rags.
estar **hecho(-a) migas** to be beat ▪ to be dog tired ▪ to be whipped
hecho ocurrió ▪ incidente ocurrió ▪ incidente se produjo incident occurred ➤ El hecho ocurrió cuando el primer ministro abandonaba su morada. The incident occurred as the prime minister was leaving his residence.
estar **hecho papilla** ▪ estar hecho puré to be beat ▪ to be dog tired ▪ to be whipped
estar **hecho pedazos** 1. estar hecho trizas to be broken into pieces 2. estar cansado to be beat ▪ to be whipped ▪ to be dog tired ▪ to be knackered 3. *(corazón)* to be broken
estar **hecho(-a) polvo** 1. estar muy cansado ▪ estar molido to be beat ▪ to be whipped ▪ to be dog tired ▪ to be pooped out ▪ to be knackered 2. estar deshecho ▪ estar destrozado to be all torn up ▪ to be distraught ▪ to be crushed ▪ to be torn to pieces ➤ Está deshecho porque su novia le dio calabazas. He's all torn up because his girlfriend jilted him.
estar **hecho por el hombre** to be man-made
ser un **hecho probado** ▪ ser un hecho cierto to be an established fact ▪ to be an accomplished fact ▪ to be a proven fact
ser **hecho público** ▪ hacerse público to be made public ➤ Before it was made public ▪ Before being made public Antes de hacerse público
hecho terrorista ▪ acto terrorista ▪ acción terrorista ▪ atentado terrorista terrorist act ▪ act of terrorism
estar **hecho trizas** 1. to broken to pieces ▪ to be shattered 2. estar desgastado to have been through the mill ▪ to be worn out ➤ Este mantel está hecho trizas. Pienso que es hora de comprar uno nuevo. This tablecloth has been through the mill. I think it's time to get a new one. ▪ This tablecloth is worn out. I think it's time to get a new one.
estar **hecho(-a) un abril** ▪ parecer un abril ▪ estar hermoso to have a beautiful young face ▪ to look vibrant
estar **hecho(-a) un adefesio** to look a sight ▪ to look a fright ▪ to look frightful
estar **hecho(-a) un alfeñique** ▪ ir hecho un riel to be skinny as a rail
estar **hecho(-a) un almíbar** to be sweet as pie ▪ to be a peach ▪ to be a sweetheart
estar **hecho(-a) un andrajo** to be a wreck ▪ to be a sight ▪ to look a sight
estar **hecho(-a) un asco** to be disgusting ▪ to be revolting
estar **hecho(-a) un basilisco** to be hopping mad ▪ to be furious
estar **hecho(-a) un brazo de mar** ▪ ir hecho un brazo de mar ▪ ir muy arreglado(-a) to be dressed to the nines ▪ to be dressed to kill ▪ to look great
estar **hecho un cachas** to be a hunk
estar **hecho un cascajo** to be an old codger
estar **hecho un chaval** to look young for one's age ▪ to be young for one's age
estar **hecho(-a) un cielo** *(dícese de los niños)* to be an angel ▪ to be a love
estar **hecho(-a) un cristo** ▪ estar hecho un trapo ▪ estar hecho un guiñapo to be all banged up ▪ to be badly banged up ▪ to be hurt
estar **hecho(-a) un cromo** to be all banged up
estar **hecho un dandi** to be very elegant
estar **hecho(-a) un demonio** to be a little hellion ▪ to be a little brat
estar **hecho(-a) un espectro** to be a ghost (of oneself) ▪ to be a ghost (of one's old self)
estar **hecho(-a) un esqueleto** to be skin and bone
estar **hecho(-a) un facha** to be an ultra right-wing militant
estar **hecho(-a) un figurín** ▪ estar más bonito que un San Luis de palo to be shined up like a new penny ▪ to look very handsome
estar **hecho(-a) un flan** to be shaking like a leaf
estar **hecho(-a) un guiñapo** to look a wreck
estar **hecho un harapo** to be dressed in rags ▪ to be wearing tattered clothes ▪ to be in tatters ▪ to be in rags
estar **hecho(-a) un harnero** *(dícese de personas, no cosas)* to be all banged up
estar **hecho un hielo** ▪ estar hecho un témpano to be freezing (cold) ➤ Estoy hecho un hielo. I'm freezing.
estar **hecho(-a) un higo** ▪ estar muy arrugado ▪ estar como una pasa 1. to be wrinkled (from old age) 2. to be shriveled (from swimming in cold water)
estar **hecho un hombre** to have grown up ➤ ¡Vaya! ¡Estás hecho un hombre! Wow! You've grown up!
estar **hecho(-a) un humo** to be fuming ▪ to be mad ▪ to be angry
estar **hecho(-a) un lázaro** to be covered with sores
estar **hecho(-a) un manojo de nervios** to be a bundle of nerves ▪ to be a nervous wreck
estar **hecho(-a) un mar de lágrimas** to be flooded with tears ▪ *(poético)* to cry a river ▪ to cry a sea of tears
estar **hecho(-a) un memo** to be a blithering idiot
estar **hecho un mozo** to be well-preserved ▪ to be young for one's age
estar **hecho(-a) un palo** to be a bean pole ▪ to be skinny as a rail
estar **hecho(-a) un sol** to be a peach ➤ Estás hecho un sol. You're a peach.
estar **hecho un toro** 1. estar fuerte to be strong as an ox ▪ to be robust 2. estar enfadado to be mad as a bull ▪ to be mad as a wet hen ▪ to be mad as a hornet
estar **hecho(-a) un trapo** ▪ estar hecho(-a) polvo ▪ estar hecho(-a) un guiñapo to look like a wreck
estar **hecho un trasto** to be a little bundle of mischief
estar **hecho(-a) un truhán** to be corrupted ▪ to have become corrupt
hecho un(-a) truhán: salir ~ to turn out corrupt ▪ to go bad (morally)
estar **hecho(-a) un zorro** to be sly ▪ to be astute
estar **hecho(-a) una bestia** ▪ perder los estribos to have a purple fit ▪ to be out of control (with anger)
hecho(-a) una bestia: ponerse ~to become angry
estar **hecho(-a) una birria** to be a mess
estar **hecho una braga** *(personas y objetos)* to be all banged up
estar **hecho(-a) una braga** to be beat ▪ to be pooped ▪ *(RU)* to be knackered

estar **hecho(-a) una caca** *(subido de tono)* to look like shit ▪ *(alternativo inofensivo)* to look like the dickens

estar **hecho una facha** to look scruffy

estar **hecho(-a) una fiera** to be mad as a bull ▪ to be mad as a hornet ▪ to be mad as a wet hen

estar **hecho(-a) una flauta** to be skinny as a reed

estar **hecho(-a) una furia** to hopping mad ▪ to be mad as a hornet ▪ to be mad as a wet hen

estar **hecho(-a) una lástima** *(dícese de personas y cosas)* to be a total wreck ▪ to look a sight

estar **hecho(-a) una lía** to be soused ▪ to be plastered

estar **hecho(-a) una mierda** *(grosero)* **1.** *(en primera persona)* to feel like shit ▪ *(alternativo inofensivo)* to feel awful ▪ to feel terrible **2.** *(en el resto de los casos)* to look like shit ▪ to be a piece of shit ➤ Estoy hecho una mierda. I feel like shit. ➤ Está hecho una mierda. He looks like shit.

estar **hecho(-a) una pasa 1.** to be wrinkled (from old age) **2.** to be shriveled up like a raisin (after swimming)

estar **hecho(-a) una pena** to be a total wreck

estar **hecho(-a) una piltrafa** ▪ ser muy flaco(-a) to be nothing but skin and bone

estar **hecho(-a) una ruina** to be a wreck ▪ to look (like) a wreck

estar **hecho(-a) una sopa** ▪ estar calado hasta los huesos to be drenched ▪ to be soaked (to the bone) ▪ to get drenched ▪ to get soaked (to the bone) ➤ Me pilló la lluvia y estoy hecho una sopa. I got caught in the rain, and I'm drenched. ▪ I got caught in the rain, and I'm soaked.

estar **hecho(-a) unos zorros** to be a total wreck

hecho y derecho como para hacer algo: ser un hombre ~ not to be a child anymore ▪ to be old enough to know better than to do something ▪ to be too old to act a certain way ➤ Ya eres un hombre hecho y derecho como para ir haciendo esas tonterías. You're not a child anymore. ▪ You're old enough to know better than to act like that.

los **hechos ocurrieron** the incidents occurred

hechos sucedidos de ayer: en los ~ in the events of yesterday

la **hélice de ángulo variable** ▪ hélice de palas orientables variable-pitch propeller ➤ El avioneta tiene una hélice de ángulo variable. The (light) airplane has a variable-pitch propeller.

la **hélice de *x* palas** *x*-bladed propeller ▪ propeller with *x* blades ➤ Una hélice de tres palas A three-bladed propeller

hemisferio del cuerpo ▪ (la) parte del cuerpo side of the body

hemisferio norte northern hemisphere

hemos de suponer que... we are led to conclude that... ▪ let's suppose that... ▪ let's assume that... ▪ we must conclude that... ▪ we are forced to conclude that...

estar **henchido de aire** *(arcaico)* ▪ estar hinchado de aire to be filled with air ➤ El globo está henchido de aire. ▪ El globo está hinchado de aire. The balloon is filled with air.

estar **henchido(-a) de orgullo** ▪ estar colmado(-a) de orgullo ▪ estar lleno de orgullo to be filled with pride

ser **henchido(-a) por el espíritu** *(bíblico)* ▪ estar lleno(-a) del espíritu to be filled with the spirit ➤ Fueron henchidos por el espíritu. They were filled with the spirit.

estar **henchido por las lluvias** ▪ aumentar el caudal a causa de las lluvias to be swollen from the rain(s)

henchir de aire los pulmones to fill with the lungs with air

henchir por to fill with

henchirse de orgullo to swell with pride ▪ to be filled with pride

hendir el agua to part water

hendir el aire con una espada to rend the air with a sword

hendir el mar to part the sea

heredar algo a alguien to inherit something from someone

heredar dinero to inherit money ▪ to come into money

heredar una fortuna to inherit a fortune ▪ to come into a fortune

herencia hispana Hispanic heritage

ser **herido de gravedad** ▪ ser herido gravemente ▪ ser gravemente herido to be seriously injuried

ser **herido gravemente** ▪ ser gravemente herido ▪ ser herido de gravedad to be seriously injured ▪ to be badly injured

herir los sentimientos de alguien to hurt someone's feelings

herir su delicadeza to wound one's pride

hermano mayor mandón bossy big brother

hermosa vivienda beautiful home

hermosa voz beautiful voice ➤ Ella tiene una hermosa voz para el canto. She has a beautiful (singing) voice.

ser un **hermoso día** to be a beautiful day

hernia discal herniated disk

El héroe solitario *(título de película de Billy Wilder)* *The Spirit of Saint Louis*

heroicas proezas heroic deeds

hervir de gente to swarm with people

hervir de odio to seethe with hatred

hervir de rabia to seethe with rage

hervir en deseos de venganza to seethe with desire for revenge

hervirle la sangre a alguien ▪ bullir la sangre a alguien to make someone's blood boil

(hermanos/gemelos) ▪ gemelos (idénticos) identical twins

(hermanos) mellizos fraternal twins

(hermanos) siameses Siamese twins ➤ Las hermanas siamesas estaban unidas por la cabeza. The Siamese twins were joined at the head.

hermosa vivienda beautiful home

ser un **hermoso día** to be a beautiful day

héroe de la patria national hero

héroe olvidado unsung hero ▪ forgotten hero

hervidero de rumores hotbed of rumores

hice lo mejor que pude ▪ (lo) hice lo mejor que pude I did (it) the best I could

hice lo que pude para... I did what I could to...

hiciera lo que hiciera whatever he did

hierba de San Juan St. John's wort

hierro de marcar branding iron

hija de sobrino(-a) ▪ sobrina en segundo grado ▪ resobrina great niece

hija mía ▪ mi cielo my darling

hijo bastardo ▪ hijo ilegítimo illegitimate child

hijo de perra *(subido de tono)* son of a bitch

hijo de puta *(subido de tono)* ▪ hijo de la gran puta son of a bitch ▪ motherfucker

hijo de sobrino(-a) ▪ sobrino en segundo grado ▪ resobrino great nephew

hijo de vecino: cada ~ ▪ cualquier hijo de vecino ▪ todo hijo de vecino every Tom, Dick and Harry

hijo fuera del matrimonio child born out of wedlock

hijo pródigo prodigal son

ser **hijo único** to be an only child ➤ Ella es hija única. She's an only child.

¡**híjole!** *(Méx.)* wow!

hilera de coches *(moving, for instance, funeral procession or motorcade)* (long) line of cars ➤ Había una larga hilera de coches en el funeral. There was a long line of cars in the funeral procession.

hilo conductor 1. conductor wire **2.** common thread ➤ Un hilo conductor une todas estas composiciones. A common thread runs through all these compositions.

¡**híncale el diente!** ▪ ¡hincarles el diente! dig in!

hincar el diente (a la comida) to sink a tooth (into the food) ➤ ¿Quieres hincar el diente? Would you like some?

hincar los codos ▪ romperse los codos ▪ empollar ▪ estudiar to hit the books

hincharse en forma de globo ▪ inflarse en forma de globo to balloon out

la **hinchazón (se) ha bajado** the swelling has gone down

¡**hinquémosle el diente!** let's dig in!

hipoteca: primera ~ first mortgage

hipoteca subsidiaria second mortgage

hipoteca variable adjustable-rate mortgage

ser una **historia de la vida real sobre...** to be a real life story of... ▪ to be a real life story about...

La historia más grande jamás contada *(obra de Oursler y la película basada en ella) The Greatest Story Ever Told*

historia no está del lado de uno history is not on one's side

historia real ■ historia verdadera ■ historia verídica true story ➤ La película está basada en una historia real. The movie is based on a true story.

historia se repite history repeats itself

historia universal 1. world history 2. *(desde el "big bang" hasta ahora)* history of the universe

historia universal de la filosofía *(desde los griegos antiguos hasta el Siglo XXI)* history of philosophy

historia verdadera ■ historia real true story ■ fact ➤ La película está basada en una historia verdadera. The movie is based on a true story.

historietas cómicas funnies ■ funny papers

hito arquitectónico architectural landmark

hito más notable major landmark ■ principal landmark ■ most famous landmark

hizo con ella lo que quiso he had his way with her

hizo que dejara de gustarme ■ hizo que me dejara de gustar it made me stop liking it

hizo que no me gustara it made me not like it

hogar deshecho broken home

hoja de balance ■ (el) balance ■ balance de situación balance sheet

Hoja de Ruta ■ nacia la paz Roadmap to Peace

hoja de un cuchillo blade of a knife

hoja de una hélice *(poco común)* ■ pala de una hélice blade of a propeller ■ propeller blade

hoja plegadiza dropleaf (of a table)

hojear una revista to leaf through a magazine

holgazanear con mala gente ■ rondar con mala gente ■ merodear con mala gente ■ haraganear con mala gente ■ andar con mala gente ■ reunirse con mala gente to run around with a bad crowd ■ to hang around with a bad crowd ■ to hang out with a bad crowd

holgazanear por (la) casa ■ flojear por (la) casa ■ hacer el vago por (la) casa to hang around the house ■ to putter around the house ➤ Hemos estado holgazaneando por (la) casa todo el día. Vamos a jugar un poco de baloncesto.

¡hombre! well!

¡hombre al agua! man overboard!

hombre de armas tomar ■ hombre de Dios es Cristo someone to be reckoned with ■ a force to be reckoned with

hombre de bien a man of principle ■ an honest man ■ an upstanding man ■ a man you can trust

hombre de bigote(s) man with a mustache

hombre de buena pasta *(coloquial)* well-brought-up man

hombre de Dios es Cristo ■ hombre de armas tomar someone to be reckoned with ■ a force to be reckoned with

hombre de doble vida man with a double life ■ man living a double life ■ man who has a double life

hombre de estado statesman

hombre de fondos a man with money

hombre de Iglesia churchman

hombre de la calle street person

hombre de letras man of letters

hombre de mundo man of the world

hombre de negocios businessman

hombre de pelo en pecho he-man ■ real man ■ stud ■ man with hair on his chest

ser **hombre de pocas palabras** to be a man of few words

el **hombre es un animal de costumbres** man is a creature of habit

hombre hecho a sí mismo self-made man

hombre imprescindible ■ hombre indispensable indispensable man

hombre indispensable ■ hombre imprescindible indispensable man

hombre precavido vale por dos forewarned is forearmed

hombre público public figure

hombre que se ha hecho a sí mismo ■ hombre hecho a sí mismo self-made man

hombre, ya te digo man, I tell you

estar **hombro con hombro** 1. estar atestado to be packed (shoulder to shoulder) 2. *(en el trabajo)* to work cooperatively

hombre muy apuesto dashing figure ■ very handsome man

homologar un título to approve a degree ➤ El ministerio de educación homologó mi título y equiparó mis créditos. The education ministry approved my degree and weighted my credits.

hora antes hour early ➤ Llegamos una hora antes. We arrived an hour early.

¡hora de acostarse! ■ ¡a dormir! bedtime! ■ time for bed!

hora de dejar checkout time

hora de llegada arrival time

hora de marchar time to go ■ time to leave

hora de salida departure time

hora de siempre the usual time

hora de verdad the moment of truth ■ *(in bullfighting)* the moment the bull is killed

la **hora es más avanzada de lo que piensas** it's later than you think

ser la **hora justa que el tren debe partir** to be the exact moment the train is supposed to leave

hora mía my time ➤ Llámame a las tres de la tarde hora mía. Call me at three p.m. my time.

hora peninsular española Spain peninsular time ➤ La hora peninsular española es una hora más tarde que la hora de Greenwich. Spain peninsular time is one hour later than Greenwich Mean Time.

hora punta 1. *(electricidad)* peak hour 2. *(tráfico)* rush hour ➤ *(titular)* Un apagón en hora punta provoca el caos en Londres. Power outage at rush hour causes chaos in London. ■ Rush hour power outage causes chaos in London.

hora punta: en plena ~ at the height of the rush hour

ser la **hora que me sienta mejor** ■ ser la hora que me viene mejor ■ ser cuando me sienta mejor ■ ser cuando me viene mejor to be the time that suits me the best ■ to be when it suits me the best ■ to be the time that is most convenient for me ■ to be when it is most convenient for me

ser la **hora que me viene mejor** ■ ser la hora que me sienta mejor ■ ser cuando me viene mejor ■ ser cuando me sienta mejor to be the time that suits me the best ■ to be when it suits me the best ■ to be the time that is most convenient for me ■ to be when it is most convenient for me

horario de actividades schedule of events

horario de clases schedule of classes ■ class schedule

horario de verano Daylight Savings Time ■ DST

horas extras 1. overtime 2. tiempo contado borrowed time ➤ Está viviendo horas extras. He's living on borrowed time.

horas extras sin pagar unpaid overtime

horas intempestivas: estar levantado hasta ~ ■ estar levantado hasta las tantas ■ estar levantado hastas altas horas to be up until all hours (of the night) ■ to be up until the wee hours (of the night) ■ to be up until the middle of the night ➤ Estuvimos levantados hasta horas intempestivas. We were up until the wee hours (of the night). ■ We were up until all hours (of the night). ■ We were up until the middle of the night.

horas muertas hours of inactivity

horas puntas peak hours

horizontales y verticales *(crucigrama)* across and down

hormigueo humano crush of people

ser una **hormiguita para su casa** to be hard-working and thrifty ■ to be a hard-working, thrifty person

hornada de galletas *(Esp.)* ■ bandeja de galletas batch of cookies

horneada de galletas *(Méx.)* ■ bandeja de galletas batch of cookies

el **horno no está para bollos** ■ no está el horno para bollos it's not the right time ■ it's not the right moment

horno para cocer ladrillos kiln

horrores: gustarle ~ ■ gustarle muchisimo to love something ■ to be a freak for something ➤ El café me gusta horrores. I'm a coffee freak. ■ I love coffee.

ser un **hortera** to be tacky ▪ to be uncool ▪ to be lousy

hospedarse en la casa de alguien quedarse en la casa de alguien ▪ alojarse en la casa de alguien to stay at someone's house

hospedarse en un hotel to stay at a hotel ▪ to stay in a hotel ➤ En Madrid, nos hospedamos en un hotel. In Madrid we stayed at a hotel. ➤ En nuestro viaje, yo preferiría hospedarme en un hotel. On our trip, I'd prefer to stay in a hotel.

hospital materno-infantil maternity hospital

hotel de tres al cuarto flop house ▪ fleabag hotel

hoy día ▪ hoy en día today ▪ nowadays ▪ these days

hoy (en) día 1. *(adverbio)* today ▪ nowadays ▪ these days 2. *(adjetivo)* present-day

hoy estreno starts today

hoy mismo ▪ sólo hoy this very day ▪ just today

hoy más que nunca today more than ever

hoy no not today

hoy por hoy at this time ▪ at this point ▪ at present

hoy por ti y mañana por mí you can do the same for me some time

hoy tienes un aspecto fenomenal you look great today

hoyo en uno hole in one

hubiera jurado ▪ hubiese jurado ▪ habría jurado ▪ juraría haber... I could have sworn I... ▪ I'd swear I could have...

hubo que... they had to... ▪ it was necessary to...

hubo un tiempo en (el) que... there was a time when...

hueco del ascensor elevator shaft

hueco libre para aparcar place to park

huele bien it smells good

huele mal it smells bad

huelga de celo *(Esp.)* work slowdown

huelga decir needless to say

huelga decir que... ▪ se sobrentiende que... it goes without saying that...

huelga salvaje wildcat strike

huella genética genetic fingerprint

huellas dactilares fingerprints

ser un **hueso duro de roer** *(Esp.)* ▪ ser un clavo duro de morder to be a tough nut to crack

huevo cocido ▪ huevo duro hard-boiled egg

huevo de cosas por hacer, tener un ~ *(argot)* to have a lot to do ▪ to have a bunch of things to do

huevo duro ▪ huevo cocido hard-boiled egg

huevo estrellado ▪ huevo frito fried egg

huevo frito ▪ huevo estrellado fried egg

huevo pasado por agua soft-boiled egg

huevos revueltos scrambled eggs

huir a la francesa to fly the coop ▪ to quit without notice

huir al amparo de la noche ▪ huir al amparo de la oscuridad to flee under cover of darkness

huir bajo el manto de la oscuridad *(literario)* ▪ huir al amparo de la noche ▪ huir al amparo de la oscuridad to flee under cover of darkness

huir de alguien ▪ evitar a alguien to avoid someone

huir de las garras de alguien ▪ escapar de las garras de alguien to escape from someone's clutches

huir del país to flee the country ▪ to escape from the country

huirle a alguien como la peste ▪ evitar a alguien como si fuera la peste to avoid someone like the plague ➤ Le huye como la peste. ▪ Le evita como si fuera la peste. She avoids him like the plague.

la **humedad en el aire** humidity in the air ▪ water vapor in the air

la **humedad en una esponja, bala de heno, etc.** moisture in a sponge, bale of hay, etc. ▪ amount of water in a sponge, bale of hay etc.

la **humedad relativa** relative humity

humedecerse los labios ▪ mojar el gaznate ▪ refrescar(se) el gaznate to wet one's whistle ▪ to have something to drink

humo denso dense smoke

humo espeso thick smoke

humor burdo coarse humor

humor cáustico ▪ humor mordaz ▪ humor corrosivo biting humor ▪ caustic humor ▪ corrosive humor

humor corrosivo ▪ humor cáustico ▪ humor mordaz corrosive humor ▪ caustic humor ▪ biting humor

humor mordaz ▪ humor cáustico ▪ humor corrosivo biting humor ▪ caustic humor ▪ corrosive humor

hundimiento de la economía ▪ (el) derrumbe de la economía ▪ colapso de la economía sinking of the economy ▪ collapse of the economy

hundir el rostro entre las manos to bury one's face in one's hands

hundirse el tejado ▪ ceder el tejado ▪ caerse el tejado ▪ derrumbarse el tejado (for) the roof to cave in ▪ (for) the roof to collapse ▪ (for) the roof to give way ▪ (for) the roof to fall in ➤ El peso de la nieve hizo que el techo se hundiera. ▪ El peso de la nieve hizo que el techo se cayera. ▪ El peso de la nieve hizo que el techo se derrumbara. ▪ El peso de la nieve hizo que el techo cediera. The weight of the snow caused the roof to cave in.

hundirse en una sima de un lustro to sink to a five-year low

hurgar en el cajón ▪ registrar el cajón to rummage through the drawer

hurgarse las narices to pick one's nose ➤ Se hurgaba las narices. He was picking his nose.

husmear en los asuntos de alguien to pry into someone's business ▪ to pry into someone's affairs ▪ to stick one's nose into someone else's business

huso horario time zone

estar **huyendo** to be on the run ▪ to be fleeing ➤ Los fugitivos están huyendo. The fugitives are on the run. ▪ the fugitives are fleeing.

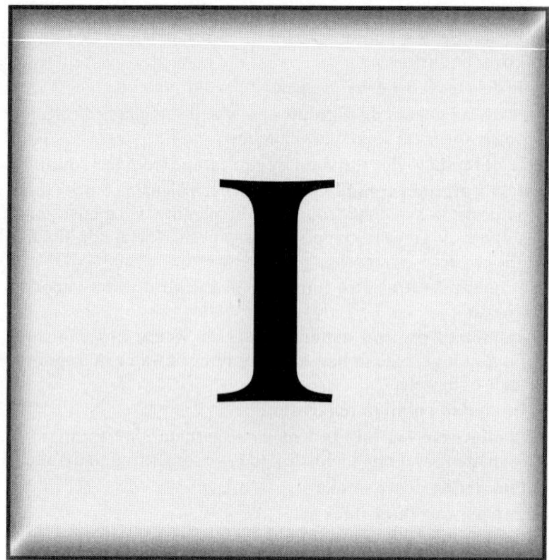

iba a haber 1. there was going to be 2. there were going to be

iba a llegar ▪ llegaría was going to arrive ▪ would arrive ➤ Yo no sabía a qué hora iba a llegar el avión. I didn't know what time the plane was going to arrive. ▪ I didn't know what time the plane would arrive.

iba a ser el mediodía it was going on noon

iba a ser la medianoche it was going on midnight

iba a ser la una it was going on one o'clock

iba a transformar su vida para siempre it would change his life forever

iba sintiéndome aliviar I was beginning to feel better ▪ I was starting to feel better

iba ya a irme cuando... I was about to leave when...

iban a ser las ocho it was going on eight o'clock

IBM (en una oficina) *(Esp.)* ▪ y ve me (office) gofer *(Nota: De "go for".)*

idas y venidas comings and goings

idea muy acertada: no ser una ~ not to be a very good idea ➤ No fue una idea muy acertada. It was not a very good idea. ▪ That was not a very good idea.

idea de bombero ▪ idea peregrina hare-brained idea

idea de que... idea that... ➤ Schopenhauer comparte con Freud la vista que el comportamiento humano se puede explicar en términos de unos pocos instintos básicas. Schopenhauer shares with Freud the view that human behavior can be explained in terms of a few basic drives.

idea descabellada crazy idea ▪ ridiculous idea

idea nebulosa vague idea

idea peregrina ▪ idea más peregrina ▪ idea ridícula ▪ idea absurda ridiculous idea ▪ hare-brained idea ➤ ¡Qué idea peregrina! ▪ ¡Qué idea más peregrina! What a ridiculous idea! ▪ What a hare-brained idea!

identificación de llamadas caller ID

estar **ido(-a)** to be out of it

ser **idóneo(-a) para** to be suitable for ▪ to be suited for

los **idus de marzo** the ides of March ➤ *(El adivino en Julio César de Shakespeare)* Han llegado los idus de marzo. The Ides of March are come.

ser **ignorado por alguien** to be ignored by someone ▪ to get avoidance signals from someone

ignorar que to be unaware that ▪ not to know that ➤ Yo ignoraba que fuera posible perder la visión de color en una sola franja del espectro. I was unaware that it is possible to lose color vision in a single band of the spectrum.

ser **igual de benévolo** to be just as benevolent ▪ to be equally benevolent ▪ to be just as lenient ▪ to be equally lenient

estar **igual de bueno** to be just as good

estar **igual de lleno de** equally full of

igual de rápido just as fast ➤ En el vacío la pluma cae igual de rápido que la piedra. ▪ La pluma cae al vacío igual de rápido que la pieda. In a vacuum, the feather falls just as fast as the rock.

ser **igual de sangriento como** ▪ ser igual de sangriento que 1. to be as bloody as 2. to be as contentious as ➤ Las elecciones (por Nueva York) serán igual de sangrientas o más que las presidenciales. The (New York) elections will be as contentious, or more so, than the presidential elections.

igual le falta sal ▪ aún le falta sal ▪ todavía le falta sal ▪ igual necesita sal it still needs salt

igual me quiere ▪ aún me quiere ▪ todavía me quiere 1. *(él)* he still loves me 2. *(ella)* she still loves me

igual me pasó ▪ me pasó lo mismo the same thing happened to me

igual que like ▪ just like ▪ the same as ➤ Las plantas respiran igual que nosotros. Plants breathe just like we do.

igual que en ▪ como en ▪ de as in ➤ ¿"A" igual que en Alberto? "A" como en Alberto? ▪ ¿"A" de Alberto? "A" as in Albert?

igual que por as one would have for ➤ Cuando atropellaron a nuestra perra, lloré igual que por un miembro de la familia. When our dog got run over, I cried as I would have for a member of the family.

igual que yo like me

igual valer para un roto que para un descosido ▪ valer lo mismo para un fregado que para un barrido ▪ valer igual para un fregado que para un barrido ▪ servir lo mismo para un fregado que para un barrido to be a jack of all trades

igualar la equación a cero to set the equation equal to zero

igualar una oferta para to match an offer to ➤ *(titular)* Putin iguala la oferta de Bush para reducir su arsenal nuclear Putin matches Bush's offer to reduce his nuclear arsenal

igualdad de ánimo equanimity

ilimitadas posibilidades unlimited possibilities

iluminar el camino para to light the way for

iluminar el camino que... ▪ abrir el camino que... ▪ despejar el camino que... to blaze the trail that... ➤ Einstein iluminó el camino que la física ha seguido desde entonces. ▪ Einstein abrió el camino que la física ha seguido desde entonces. ▪ Einstein despejó el camino que la física ha seguido desde entonces. Einstein blazed the trail that physics has followed ever since.

ilusión de óptica ▪ trampantojo optical illusion

la **ilusión de que...** the hope that...

ilustrar a alguien sobre un tema to enlighten someone on a subject

imagen poco atractiva unappealing image ➤ Ver a gente sentada charlando es una imagen poco atractiva para la tele. El espectador opta por hacer zapping. To see people sitting around talking is an unappealing image on a TV screen. The viewer keeps flipping channels.

una **imagen vale más que mil palabras** a picture's worth a thousand words

imágenes de espejo como dos gotas de agua mirror images of each other ➤ Las famosas gemelas de San Francisco son como imágenes de espejo. The famous San Francisco twins are mirror images of each other.

imbuirse en to immerse oneself (in a pursuit)

impaciente por to be impatient to ▪ to be impatient for

impartir un seminario to give a seminar

impedimento para impediment to

impedir a alguien acudir to prevent someone from going ▪ to keep someone from going ▪ to bar someone from going ➤ *(titular)* Las elecciones en Egipto impiden a Mubarak acudir a la ONU. Elections in Egypt prevent Mubarak from going to the UN.

impedir a alguien hacer algo ▪ impedir a alguien que haga algo to prevent someone from doing something ▪ to keep someone from doing something ▪ to bar someone from doing something

impedir a alguien que haga algo ▪ impedir a alguien hacer algo to prevent someone from doing something ▪ to keep someone from doing something ▪ to bar someone from doing something

impedir que ▪ prevenir ▪ evitar to prevent someone from

impedir que alguien se caiga to prevent someone from falling ▪ to break someone's fall

impedir que alguien se cayera to prevent someone from falling ■ to break someone's fall

impedirle prosperar ■ hacerle sombra to be unsuccessful in business ■ to have problems in one's business

imperativo categórico *(en la filosofía de Kant)* categorical imperative ➤ Obra de modo que tu acción pueda servir de norma a todos los hombres. ■ *(más técnico)* Obra de tal manera que tus máximas pueden constituirse por ellas mismas en leyes universales naturales. So act that you could will the maxim of your action to be a universal law.

imperio mediático media empire

Imperio sacroromano Holy Roman Empire

implantación de un plan introduction of a plan ■ establishment of a plan ➤ *(noticia)* La sangría no cesa pese a la implantación de sucesivos planes contra la violencia doméstica. The bloodshed continues despite the introduction of a plan against domestic violence.

los **implantes de silicona** silicon implants

estar **implicado(-a) en el caso** to be involved in the case ➤ Los tres jueces implicados en el caso The three judges involved in the case

implicar un gasto ■ suponer un gasto to involve an expense

implicar amenaza para la vida ■ significar amenaza para la vida to be life threatening

implicar una inversión to involve an investment

imponer un estado de excepción to impose a curfew

imponer las manos *(catolicismo)* to lay one's hands on

imponerle una medalla a alguien to award someone a medal ■ to award a medal to someone

imponerse a un equipo to beat a team ■ to win over a team ■ to be victorious over a team ➤ *(titular)* Real Madrid se impone al Celta. Real Madrid wins over the Celts. ■ Real Madrid beats the Celts.

imponérsele el nombre de to give someone the name ■ to dub someone

importar trabajo to involve work ➤ Importa mucho trabajo. It involves a lot of work.

importarle un bledo not to care less ➤ Me importa un bledo. I couldn't care less. ■ I could care less. ■ I could give a damn.

importarle un carajo not to care less

importarle un pepino ■ importarle un rábano not to care less

imposición de manos *(catolicismo)* the laying on of hands

el **impresionante alquiler** exorbitant rent

imprimir a su voz ■ imprimir a su tono de voz to give one's voice ➤ *(García Marquez)* Imprimió a su voz una severidad convincente. He gave his voice a convincing severity.

imprimir carácter to build character

impronta indeleble: dejar en alguien una ~ to have a lasting impact on someone

impuesto al valor agregado (IVA) *(Méx.)* sales tax ■ value-added tax (VAT)

impuesto de sociedades corporate (income) tax

impuesto sobre el valor añadido (IVA) *(Esp.)* sales tax ■ value-added tax (VAT)

impugnar la elección to contest the election

impulsar a alguien a hacer algo to drive someone to do something ➤ La única hipótesis que se baraja sobre las razones que pudieron impulsarlos a cometer el crimen... The only hypothesis being considered regarding the reasons that could drive them to commit the crime...

estar **imputado(-a) en un delito** to be implicated in a crime

estar **imputado(-a) en conexión con** to be implicated in connection with

in fraganti: agarrar a alguien ~ ■ pillar a alguien in fraganti ■ agarrar a alguien con las manos en la masa ■ pillar a alguien con las manos en la masa ■ agarrar a alguien en flagrante delito ■ pillar a alguien en frangante delito to catch someone red-handed ■ to catch someone in the act *(Nota: En España se puede usar así "coger" como "agarrar" y "pillar".)*

in memoriam ■ en recuerdo in memory of ■ as a memorial to

inauguración de una tienda grand opening of a store

ser **inaugurado como presidente** to be inaugurated as president ➤ James K. Polk fue inaugurado como presidente de los Estados Unidos el día 4 de marzo de 1845. James K. Polk was inaugurated as president of the United States on March 4, 1845.

incautarse de contrabando ■ confiscar contrabando to seize contraband ■ to confiscate contraband ➤ Los policias se incautaron de una cantidad de DVDs apócrifos al allanar un videoclub. Police seized a quantity of unauthorized DVDs when they raided a video rental store.

incendio forestal forest fire

incidencia (con los ordenadores): hay una ~ *(Esp.)* ■ las computadoras están bloqueadas the computers are down

incierto futuro ■ futuro incierto uncertain future

incipiente ciencia de nascent science of

incipiente noviazgo de ambos their recent engagement

incitar a alguien to incite someone ■ to spur someone on

inclinación para hacer una cosa tendency to do a certain thing

estar **inclinado hacia** to be inclined toward(s) ■ to incline toward(s) ➤ El tejado está inclinado hacia el sur para que las células solares reciban la máxima exposición al sol. The roof is inclined toward the south in order for the solar cells to receive maximum exposure to the sun. ■ The roof inclines towards the south in order for the solar cells to receive maximum exposure to the sun.

inclinar la balanza a favor de to tip the scales in favor of

inclinarse hacia abajo to lean down

inclinarse hacia algo ■ decantarse hacia algo to incline toward something ■ to lean toward something ➤ Me inclino hacia el candidato de la oposición en estas elecciones. ■ Me decanto hacia el candidato de la oposición en estas elecciones. I'm inclining towards the opposition candidate in this election. ■ I'm leaning towards the opposition candidate in this election. ➤ Me inclino hacia los amarillos. ■ Me decanto hacia los amarillos. I'm inclining towards the yellows ones. ■ I'm leaning towards the yellow ones.

inclinarse sobre 1. to lean over **2.** to bend over ➤ Galileo se inclinó sobre la barandilla de la torre inclinada de Pisa y dejó caer balas de cañon de distintos pesos y tamaños. Galileo leaned over the railing of the Leaning Tower of Pisa and dropped cannonballs of different weights and sizes. ➤ El padre se inclinó sobre su niño... The father leaned over his little boy... ■ The father bent over his little boy...

incluido el mío ■ incluyendo el mío mine included ■ including mine

incluir algo por el mismo precio to include something additional for the same price ■ *(coloquial)* to throw something into the bargain ➤ No sólo nos vendió el equipo de música, nos incluyó un colección de discos de Beethoven por el mismo precio. He not only sold us the stereo system, he threw a set of Beethoven disks into the bargain.

incluir en la lista ■ sumar a la lista to add to the list

incluso cuando even when

incluso en la actualidad even now

incluso entre even among

incluso que even than ➤ Es más poderoso incluso que... It is more powerful even than...

incluso si even if

incluso sin even without ➤ *(titular)* Aznar apoyará a Bush incluso sin el amparo de la ONU. Aznar will support Bush against Iraq even without UN backing.

incluso yo ■ incluyéndome ■ hasta yo including me ■ myself included

incluyendo el mío ■ incluido el mío including mine ■ mine included

incluyendo el tuyo including yours

incluyendo *x* argentinos ~ ■ entre ellos *x* ■ argentinos including *x* Argentines ■ among them *x* Argentines

incoado debate sobre initial debate on

incómoda explicación embarrassing explanation

estar **incomunicado 1.** *(por el tiempo, etc.)* to be stranded **2.** *(en una prisión)* to be in solitary confinement ➤ Estamos incomunicados en la nieve. We're stranded in the snow. ➤ El prisionero está incomunicado para evitar filtraciones. The prisoner is in solitary confinement to prevent leaks.

el **inconsciente** the unconscious (mind)

incontables veces countless times

estar **incorporado** to be built in

incorporar los ingredientes *(receta)* to add the ingredients ➤ Incorporar los huevos enteros, removiendo enérgicamente hasta integrarlos en la pasta. Add the eggs whole, stirring vigorously until blended into the dough.

incorporarse a to become part of ▪ to join ➤ Me incorporé a trabajar en enero. ▪ Me incorporé a trabajar desde enero. I started working for a company in January. ➤ Se incorporó al ejército en septiembre y le ha ido de maravilla. He joined the army in September, and he's been very successful. ➤ Se incorporó a la causa de los derechos de los animales. He's joined the animal rights cause. ➤ He's joined the ranks of the unemployed. Se ha incorporado a las filas de los desempleados. ▪ *(Esp.)* Se ha incorporado a las filas de los parados.

incorporarse a filas ▪ incorporarse al ejército, marina, fuerza aérea to join the military

incorporarse en la cama to sit up in bed

incremento sobre los beneficios del año pasado ▪ mejora sobre los beneficios del año pasado increase over last year's profits ▪ improvement over last year's profits

estar **incrustado en** to be lodged in ▪ to be embedded in ▪ to be stuck in

incrustársele en la mente la idea de que... to have the idea firmly fixed in one's head that ▪ to get the idea firmly stuck in one's head that...

inculcarle algo to instill something in someone ➤ La profesora le inculcó el amor por la lectura. The teacher instilled in him a love of reading.

incumplir una promesa ▪ faltar a una promesa ▪ no cumplir (con) una promesa ▪ desobedecer una promesa hecha ▪ romper una promesa to fail to keep a promise ▪ not to keep a promise ▪ to break a promise

incurrir en imprecisiones en una encuesta to bias a poll (unintentionally) ▪ to bias a survey (unintentionally)

indagar la posibilidad de que ▪ estudiar la posibilidad de que to look into the possibility that

indesmayable deseo unfaltering desire ▪ unflagging desire

indicador de hasta qué punto... ▪ medida de hasta qué punto... indication of how much... ▪ indication of the extent to which... ▪ indicator of how much... ▪ indicator of the extent to which... ▪ barometer of how much... ▪ barometer of the extent to which... ➤ *(noticia)* La amplitud de la victoria de Blair será un indicador de hasta qué punto ha fracasado la apuesta conservadora de espantar a los británicos con el fantasma de Europa y su moneda. The margin of Blair's victory will be a barometer of the extent to which the conservative ploy of scaring the British with the specter of Europe and its currency has failed.

indicar claramente que... to show clearly that...

el **índice de desempleo** ▪ tasa de desempleo ▪ tasa de paro unemployment rate

el **índice de precios al consumo** consumer price index

el **índice de refracción** *(el cociente entre la velocidad de la luz en vacío y la velocidad de la luz a través de materia)* refractive index ➤ El índice de refracción del agua es 1.333. The refractive index of water is 1.333.

índice escuálido emaciated index finger ➤ *(García Márquez)* Ella dirigió hacia la calle un índice escuálido. She pointed at the street with an emaciated index finger.

indicios de: hallar ~ to find evidence of

indicios vitales ▪ constantes vitales vital signs

ser **indiferente acerca de** to be indifferent to

estar **indignado por** to be indignant at

indignarse de algo to become indignant at something ▪ to be angered by something

ser **indigno(-a) de uno** to be beneath one ▪ to be unworthy of one ➤ El artículo fue indigno de un periodista de su calibre. The article was beneath a journalist of his caliber.

indulto a alguien pardon of someone

indulto a alguien: conceder un ~ ▪ otorgar un indulto a alguien to grant someone a pardon ▪ to grant a pardon to someone ➤ Durante la Guerra Civil Norteamericana, el Presidente Lincoln concedió cientos de indultos a los soldados. During the American Civil War, President Lincoln granted hundreds of pardons to the soldiers.

industria de la ballena whaling industry

infancia feliz happy childhood

infancia infeliz unhappy childhood

infarto cerebral ▪ derrame cerebral ▪ congestión cerebral ▪ trombosis cerebral stroke ▪ cerebral hemorrhage

infarto de miocardio myocardial infarction

infarto leve mild heart attack

infectársele (una herida) ▪ enconarse (una herida) to become infected ▪ to get infected ➤ The injury became infected. La herida se infectó. ▪ La herida se enconó. ➤ La herída se le infectó. ▪ La herida se le enconó. *(a él)* His injury became infected. ▪ His injury got infected. ▪ *(a ella)* Her injury became infected. ▪ Her injury got infected. ➤ La herida se me infectó. ▪ La herida se me enconó. My injury became infected. ▪ His injury became infected.

ser **inferior a alguien en rango** ▪ estar por debajo de alguien en rango to be beneath someone in rank

inferior a lo normal lower than average

una **infinidad de** ▪ un sinfín de an infinite number of ▪ an endless number of

la **inflación de o superior al diez por ciento** double-digit inflation ▪ inflation of ten percent or higher

la **inflamación de la fascia plantar** plantar fascitis

inflar el kilometraje ▪ abultar el kilometraje to inflate the mileage

inflar las urnas to stuff ballot boxes

inflarse como un sapo to balloon out (like a toad)

inflarse de orgullo ▪ hincharse de orgullo to swell with pride

información desde dentro inside information

información sesgada ▪ información parcializada biased information

la **información verosímil** credible information

informar sobre to report on

informarse cómo hacer algo to find out how to do something

informarse de ▪ informarse sobre ▪ aprender sobre to become informed about ▪ to learn about

informe manipulado ▪ informe sesgado biased report ▪ biased report

el **informe mejor de lo que se esperaba** ▪ informe mejor de lo esperado ▪ informe más que favorable better-than-expected report

informe sesgado *(Esp.)* ▪ informe manipulado biased report ▪ biased report

infravalorar a alguien ▪ subestimar a alguien to underestimate someone

infravalorar el efecto de ▪ subestimar el efecto de to underestimate the effect of

infringir la ley ▪ violar la ley to break the law

infringir las reglas to break the rules

infundir confianza a alguien ▪ dar confianza a alguien to instill confidence in someone ▪ to give someone confidence

infundir esperanza a alguien ▪ dar esperanza a alguien to instill hope in someone

la **infusión de manzanilla** ▪ té de manzanilla chamomile tea *("Infusión" se refiere a un té de hierbas ▪ "Infusión" refers to herbal tea)*

ingeniárselas para hacer algo ▪ encontrarle la vuelta para hacer algo ▪ encontrar una manera de hacer algo to figure out a way to do something ➤ Debo ingeniármelas para... ▪ Tengo que ingeniármelas para... I must figure out a way to... ▪ I have to figure out a way to...

ingeniería informática computer science

ingeniero informático computer scientist

ingenio agudo sharp wit ▪ keen wit

inglés chapurreado broken Spanish

inglés normativo standard English

ingrediente activo ▪ principio activo active ingredient

el **ingrediente esencial** essential ingredient

estar **ingresado en el hospital** to be admitted to the hospital ▪ to be in the hospital ▪ to be hospitalized

ingresar a alguien en el hospital to admit someone to the hospital

ingresar dinero a una cuenta bancaria to deposit money in a bank account

ingresar dinero en el banco to deposit money in the bank

ingresos conjuntos combined income ▪ joint income

ingresos per cápita per capita income

inicial del segundo nombre middle initial
iniciar la temporada to open the season
iniciar una conversación aparte de la del grupo to splinter a conversation ➤ No quiero invitarlo porque siempre inicia una conversación aparte de la del grupo en la mesa de comedor. I don't want to invite him because he always splinters the conversation at the dinner table.
iniciar una investigación ▪ abrir una investigación to begin an investigation
Inmaculada Concepción *(catolicismo)* Immaculate Conception
inmediatos a immediately following ➤ *(noticia)* Los días inmediatos a la detención también están cargados de sorpresas. The days immediately following the arrest were also filled with surprises *(Note the difference in tense usage.)*
inmiscuirse en los asuntos de alguien ▪ meterse en los asuntos de alguien to meddle in someone's affairs
inmolarse por to sacrifice oneself for
inquietar a alguien to unsettle someone ▪ to shake someone up ▪ to get to someone
inquilino precario de facto tenant ▪ tenant who is not on the lease
inscribirse a las clases ▪ apuntarse a las clases to register for class(es)
inscribirse en las clases ▪ apuntarse a las clases to register for class(es) ➤ ¿Te has inscrito en las clases ya? ▪ ¿Te has apuntado a las clases ya? Have you registered for classes yet?
la **inseminación artificial** ▪ fecundación artificial artificial insemination
insistir en to insist on
insistir mucho 1. to be very insistent 2. to be very persistent
¡**insisto!** I insist!
inspirarse en to be inspired by ▪ to get inspiration from ▪ to take inspiration from ▪ to receive inspiration from ▪ to find inspiration in
instalarse en un lugar to settle in a place ➤ Después de la guerra los sobrinos del dictador se instalaron en Estados Unidos. After the war the dictator's nephews settled in the United States.
las **instalaciones de fontanería** plumbing
instalarse en to be settled into ▪ to be moved in ▪ to take hold of ➤ ¿Estás bien instalado en tu nuevo piso? Are you (all) moved into your new apartment? ▪ Are you (all) settled into your new apartment? ➤ El presidente intentó hacer frente al clima de desconfianza que se ha instalado en los mercados financieros. The president tried to confront the climate of mistrust that has taken hold of the financial markets.
instar a alguien a hacer algo ▪ instar a alguien a que haga algo to urge someone to do something
instar a alguien a que haga algo ▪ instar a alguien a hacer algo to insist to someone that he do something ➤ *(titular)* Bush insta a la ONU a que desempeñe un mayor papel en Irak. Bush urges the UN to take on a greater role in Iraq. ➤ *(titular)* Bush insta a Zapatero que no retire todavía las tropas de Irak. Bush urges Zapatero not to withdraw troops from Iraq yet.
instar a alguien que haga algo ▪ instar a alguien a hacer algo to urge someone to do something
instinto de instinct for
instituir heredero(-a) a alguien ▪ instituir por heredero(-a) a alguien to designate someone as heir
el, la **instructor(-a) de vuelo** flight instructor
instruida sociedad educated society
instruir un sumario contra alguien ▪ abrir un sumario contra alguien to indict someone ▪ to issue an indictment against someone ▪ to issue an indictment of someone
instrumento de cuerda stringed instrument
instrumento de regulación precisa precision instrument
instrumento de teclado keyboard instrument
insuficiencia personal manpower shortage ▪ personnel shortage
el, la **integrante de su generación** member of one's generation
integrante de un equipo member of a team
integrante de un partido político member of a political party
el, la **integrante de una banda** member of a band
integrarse en la cultura to integrate oneself into the culture
integrismo religioso ▪ fundamentalismo religioso religious fundamentalism
integrista religioso(-a) ▪ fundamentalista religioso(-a) religious fundamentalist
ser **inteligente para saber que...** to be smart enough to know that... ▪ to be intelligent enough to know that...
ser **inteligente un huevo** *(coloquial)* ▪ ser muy inteligente to be really smart
intemperie: estar a la ~ ▪ estar a la merced de los elementos to be at the mercy of the weather ▪ to be at the mercy of the elements
la **intención de** ▪ (la) finalidad de ▪ propósito de intention of ▪ aim of ▪ purpose of
intencion subrepticia *(culto)* ▪ intención trasvestida ▪ intención amarrada ▪ intención escondida hidden intention ▪ hidden agenda
intentar hacer algo ▪ tratar de hacer algo to attempt to do something ▪ to try to do something
intentar hacer algo sin conseguirlo to try unsuccessfully to do something
intentar no hacer algo ▪ evitar hacer algo ▪ escaquearse (de hacer algo) ▪ zafarse de hacer algo to avoid doing something ▪ to weasel out of doing something ▪ to get out of doing something
intentar no pensar en algo ▪ tratar de no pensar en algo to try not to think about something ➤ Intenta no pensar en ello. ▪ Trata de no pensar en ello. Try not to think about it.
intentar otra vez to try again ▪ to give it another try ▪ to have another try
intentar que no haga algo to try not to let it do something ▪ to try to keep it from doing something ➤ Intenta que no se te cale. ▪ Intenta que no se te apague. Try not to let it stall (on you). ▪ Try to keep it from stalling (on you).
intento anterior previous attempt
intento de ▪ intento para attempt to ➤ Los intentos de establecer la Inquisición en Nápoles y Milán fracasaron. ▪ Los intentos de establecer la Inquisición en Nápoles y Milán fracasaron. Attempts to establish the Inquisition in Naples and Milan failed.
intento de agresión attempted assault ▪ assault attempt
intento de suicidio attempted suicide ▪ suicide attempt
intento fallido de... ▪ fallido intento de... failed attempt to... ▪ unsuccessful attempt to...
intento frustrado frustrated attempt
intento golpista ▪ asonada (de estado) attempted coup ▪ coup attempt
intento por: en un ~ in an attempt to
intentona golpista *(Esp.)* ▪ intentona de golpe de estado ▪ intento golpista ▪ asonada (de estado) attempted coup ▪ coup attempt
intentona militar military coup
el **intercambiador de los trenes** ▪ (el) enlace de los trenes train hub ▪ connecting point of the trains
intercambio de ideas exchange of ideas ▪ interchange of ideas ▪ back-and-forth ➤ El intercambio de ideas entre los estudiantes y el profesor debería ser fluido. The back-and-forth between the students and the teacher should be fluid.
intercambiar una mirada to exchange glances ▪ to glance at each other
interceder por alguien to intercede on behalf of someone ▪ to intercede on someone's behalf ▪ to intercede for someone ▪ *(colorful)* ▪ dar la cara por alguien to go to bat for someone
el **interés acumulado en pagos trimestrales** interest compounded quarterly ➤ El fondo devenga un interés de cinco por ciento acumulado en pagos trimestrales. The trust pays five percent interest compounded quarterly.
el **interés por** interest in
interesarse mucho en algo to take a keen interest in something
interesarse por ▪ interesarse en to take an interest in
intereses creados special interests
intereses privados special interests
internarse en el bosque to go into the forest ▪ to go into the woods ▪ to enter the forest ▪ to enter the woods

internarse en el parque to go into the park
estar **intermitente** ■ estar intermitentemente to be off and on
interpolar la puntuación insert punctuation
interpretar a alguien en un cine to play someone in a movie
interpretar el papel de to play the role of
interpretar música to perform music ■ to interpret ➤ Vamos a interpretar unas piezas de Bach. We're going to perform some pieces by Bach.
interrogar a la parte contraria to cross-examine a witness
interrogatorio cruzado cross examination
interrupción voluntaria del embarazo ■ aborto abortion
intervención fiscal tax audit
ser **intervenido(-a) por** to be operated on for...
intervenir en una actividad ■ tomar parte en una actividad to take part in an activity
intervenir en una situación to intervene in a situation
intervenir un alijo de armas to seize a cache of weapons ■ to confiscate a cache of weapons
intervenir un alijo de drogas to seize a cache of drugs ■ to confiscate a cache of drugs ➤ *(titular Intervenido en Ibiza el mayor alijo de éxtasis de este año.* Year's largest cache of extasy seized in Ibiza.
intestino delgado small intestine
intestino grueso large intestine
intimar con alguien to become close friends with someone ■ to establish a close friendship with someone
ser **íntimo(-a) con alguien** to be very close to someone
Intimo y personal *(título de película) Up Close and Personal*
intoxicación alimenticia food poisoning
intoxicarse con algo to be made ill by something ■ to be made sick by something ■ to get sick from something
introducir una moneda to insert a coin
inundaciones asolan la región floods ravage the region ■ floods devastate the region
inundado (de agua) flooding
invadir el carril contrario to enter the lane of (the) oncoming traffic
invadir la intimidad de alguien ■ invadir la privacidad de alguien to invade someone's privacy
¡inventa algo! make up something! ■ make something up! ■ think up something! ■ think something up!
ser **inversamente proporcional a** to be inversely proportional to
investigación y desarrollo ■ I plus D ■ I+D research and development ■ R and D ■ R&D
invicto marte *(Valle-Inclán)* ■ guerrero invicto ■ guerrero sin derrota unbeaten warrior
invierno crudo ■ invierno duro bitter winter ■ harsh winter ■ hard winter
invierno duro ■ invierno crudo hard winter ■ bitter winter ■ harsh winter
invierno sombrío bleak winter
invitación fija standing invitation
¡invítale a pasar! ■ ¡que entre! tell him to come (on) in! ■ have him come in! ■ show him in!
invitar a alguien a entrar to ask someone (to come) in ■ to invite someone (to come) in
invitarle a alguien a beber un café ■ invitarle a alguien a tomar un café to invite someone for a cup of coffee ■ to treat someone to a cup of coffee ➤ Te invito a beber un café. ■ Te invito a tomar un café. I'll buy you a cup of coffee. ■ I'll treat you to a cup of coffee.
estar **involucrado(-a) en una conversación** to be engaged in a conversation ■ to be involved in a conversation
involucrar un riesgo ■ conllevar riesgo to involve risk ■ to involve taking (a) risk
involucrarse en la acción ■ ser parte de la acción to get in on the action
ipso facto ipso facto ■ by its very nature
ir a beber agua ■ ir a tomar agua to get a drink of water ➤ Voy a beber agua. ■ Voy a tomar agua. I'm going to get a drink of water.

ir a buscar to go get ➤ ¿Tienes tiempo para que los vaya a buscar? Do you have time for me to go get them? ■ *(con prisa)* Do you have time for me to run get them?
ir a caballo to go on horseback
ir a capa caída ■ andar a capa caída ■ estar aplanchado to be crestfallen
ir a casa to go home ➤ I'm going home. Voy a casa.
ir a confesarse to go to confession
ir a conocer to go for the first time ■ to visit for the first time ➤ Cuando fuimos a conocer el Museo Smithsonian... When we went for the first time to the Smithsonian Aerospace Museum...
ir a contracorriente ■ ir contra la corriente ■ ir contra corriente to go against the grain ■ to go against the tide ■ to be out of step ■ to resist peer pressure ➤ No tengas miedo de ir a contracorriente. Don't be afraid to go against the grain. ■ Don't be afraid to resist peer pressure.
ir a contrapelo 1. to go against the grain **2.** *(en asuntos públicos)* to go against the current ■ to go against the flow ■ to go against public opinion
ir a cuerpo gentil to go without a coat
ir a dar un vuelco to be headed for disaster ■ to be headed for a catastrophe
ir a dedo a un lugar ■ echar dedo to thumb one's way to a place ■ to hitchhike to a place ➤ Fuimos a Sevilla a dedo. We thumbed our way to Sevilla.
ir a escote to go Dutch
ir a esperar a alguien ■ ir al encuentro de alguien to go meet someone
ir a favor de un grupo político to go with a political faction ■ to side with a political faction ➤ Voy a favor de los políticos moderados. I'm going (to go) with the political moderates. ■ I'm going to side with the political moderates.
ir a hacer algo to be going to do something ➤ Voy a hacer mis deberes esta tarde. I'm going to do my homework this afternoon.
ir a hacer la compra *(Esp.)* ■ ir a hacer los mandados to go grocery shopping ■ to do the grocery shopping
ir a hervir to come to a boil ■ to start to boil ■ to begin to boil ➤ Cuando vaya a hervir, añadir la harina batiendo fuertemente la mezcla. When it comes to a boil, add the flour while beating the mixture vigorously.
ir a intervalos ■ ir y venir ■ estar a veces sí, a veces no to be off again, on again ■ to be on again, off again ■ to be on and off ➤ Their relationship is on again, off again at this point. ■ Their relationship is on and off at this point. En estos momentos su relación va a intervalos. ■ En estos momentos su relación va y viene. ■ En estos momentos, en su relación a veces sí están, y a veces no. Their relationship is on again, off again at this point. ■ Their relationship is on and off at this point.
ir a juego con ■ combinar con to match ■ to go (well) with ➤ Esa corbata va a juego con el saco. That tie goes with the coat.
ir a juicio to go to court
ir a la americana ■ ir a escote to go Dutch ■ to each pay one's own tab
ir a la casa de alguien 1. *(chalet)* to go (over) to someone's house **2.** *(piso)* to go (over) to someone's apartment **3.** *(cualquiera de los dos)* to go (over) to someone's ➤ Voy a la casa de los Vidal. I'm going (over) to the Valdals'.
ir a la estela de un barco ■ ir a rebufo de un barco to travel in the wake of a boat
ir a la imprenta to go to press
ir a la pata coja ■ andar a la pata coja to hop
ir a la última to wear the latest fashions
ir a la vanguardia de ■ estar en primera línea de to be at the forefront of ■ to be on the cutting edge of
ir a la ventura to go without a fixed plan ■ to decide to go along
ir a la zaga to follow the crowd
ir a las chapas por to go barreling down ➤ Los carros van a las chapas por esta calle. The cars really go barreling down this street.
ir a lo concreto ■ ir al grano to get to the point ■ to get down to brass tacks

ir a lo grande con... to (really) go to town on... ➤ Los peques van a lo grande con el helado. The kids are really going to town on the ice cream.

ir a lo largo de to run the length of ➤ En la Autónoma hay una acera que va a lo largo de campus. At the Autonoma there's a sidewalk that runs the length of the campus.

ir a medio gas ▪ ir pisando huevos to poke along ▪ to go poking along ▪ to go way below the speed limit ▪ to drive way below the speed limit

ir a mejor ▪ ponerse cada vez mejor ▪ ser cada vez mejor ▪ estar cada vez mejor to get better and better ➤ Va a mejor. ▪ Se pone cada vez mejor. It gets better and better.

ir a mesa puesta y cama hecha to live in a house with maid service

ir a mirar escaparates to go window shopping

ir a navegar to go boating

ir a pachas (en) *(coloquial)* ▪ ir a escote ▪ ir a medias to go halves (on) ▪ to split the bill (evenly)

ir a parar a **1.** *(sin querer)* to end up in **2.** acabar en ▪ llegar a to end at ▪ to come to an end at **3.** *(dícese de calles)* hacer un T con to tee into **4.** *(dícese de ríos)* desembocar en ▪ ir a dar en to flow into ➤ Nos equivocamos de dirección y fuimos a parar al quinto pino. We took a wrong turn and ended up in the middle of nowhere. ➤ La Avenida Cuba va a parar a la Avenida Arequipa. Cuba Avenue tees into Arequipa Avenue. ➤ El Río Duratón va a parar al Duero. ▪ El Río Duratón va a dar al Duero. The Duraton River flows into the Duero.

ir a parar al medio de la nada ▪ ir a parar en el medio de la nada ▪ ir a parar en el quinto pino ▪ ir a parar por las quimbambas ▪ ir a parar a la conchinchina to end up in the middle of nowhere

ir a parar al quinto pino ▪ ir a parar en el medio de la nada ▪ ir a parar por las quimbambas ▪ ir a parar a la conchinchina to end up in the middle of nowhere

ir a parar en **1.** to come to an end at ▪ to end at **2.** ir a parar sobre to end up on

ir a parar en malas manos to fall into the wrong hands ▪ to end up in the wrong hands

ir a pata *(muy coloquial)* ▪ ir a pie **1.** to go on foot ▪ to walk **2.** to walk all over the place (trying to find something) ▪ to walk all over hell and half of Georgia (trying to find something) ➤ Fuimos a pata tratando de encontrar un regalo de boda. We went all over hell and half of Georgia trying to find a wedding present.

ir a pelo **1.** ir desnudo to go naked **2.** montar a pelo to ride bareback **2.** ir sin suficiente ropa to be insuffcently clad ▪ not to have enough clothes on **3.** ir sin suficiente equipo to be poorly equipped ▪ to be ill-equipped

ir a pie to go on foot ▪ to walk ➤ ¿Es bastante cerca para ir a pie? Is it close enough to walk to? ▪ Is it close enough to go on foot?

ir a por algo *(Esp.)* ▪ ir por algo to go get something ▪ to go for something ➤ Voy a la lavandería a por mis camisas. I'm going to the laundry to get my shirts. ▪ I'm going (to the laundry) for my shirts.

ir a por alguien *(Esp.)* ▪ ir por alguien **1.** to go after someone ▪ to be out to get someone **2.** to go in someone's place ➤ *(noticia)* El policía disparó al asaltante cuando éste les advirtió a sus víctimas "voy a por vosotros." The policeman shot the assailant when he threatened his victims by saying, "I'm gonna get you." ➤ Mi jefe no pudo asistir a la reunión, así que fui por él. My boss couldn't go to the meeting, so I went in his place.

ir a por lana y volver trasquilado *(Esp.)* ▪ ir por lana y salir trasquilado ▪ volver con el rabo entre las piernas ▪ salir con el rabo entre las piernas to come away with one's tail between one's legs ▪ to get a comeuppance ▪ to have the tables turned on one ▪ to get a result opposite of what one wanted

ir a por todas por algo *(Esp.)* ▪ ir a todas por algo ▪ batirse el cobre por algo ▪ batirse en duelo por algo to go all out for something

ir a que le corten el pelo a uno to go get a haircut ➤ Tengo que ir a que me corten el pelo. I have to go get a haircut.

ir a que le den la baja a uno to get medical permission for time off ▪ to get a medical authorization for time off

ir a que le devuelvan el dinero a uno ▪ ir a que le den un reembolso a uno to go (and) get a refund ▪ to go for a refund

ir a que le hagan un análisis de sangre a uno to go get a blood test

ir a que le informen sobre los plazos a uno to get information about the deadlines

ir a que le saquen una muela a uno to have a tooth extracted ▪ *(más coloquial)* to get a tooth pulled

ir a que le tomen las medidas a uno para un traje to (go) get measured for a suit

ir a rebufo *(de una carrera de autos)* to slipstream

ir a rebufo de un avión ▪ ir a la estela de un avión to travel in the wake of an airplane

ir a rebufo de un barco ▪ ir a la estela de un barco to travel in the wake of a boat

ir a remolque de alguien to go in someone's shadow ▪ to be overshadowed by someone

ir a ser la(s) *x* to be going on *x* o'clock ➤ Van a ser las cinco. It's going on five o'clock. ➤ Iban a ser las cinco. It was going on five o'clock. ➤ Iba a ser la una. It was going on one o'clock.

ir a su aire to go off on one's own

ir a su bola *(coloquial)* ▪ ir por libre ▪ ir a su aire **1.** to do one's own thing **2.** to go off on one's own **3.** to ignore everyone ▪ to be very independent ▪ to be very self-centered ▪ to be very self-absorbed ➤ Ese estudiante no le cae bien al profesorado porque quiere ir a su bola. ▪ Ese estudiante no le cae bien al profesorado porque quiere ir por libre. ▪ Ese estudiante no le cae bien al profesorado porque quiere ir a su aire. The faculty doesn't like that student because he wants to do his own thing. ➤ En Segovia el estudiante se separó del viaje organizado por la universidad y fue a su bola. ▪ En Segovia el estudiante se separó del viaje organizado por la universidad y fue por libre. ▪ En Segovia el estudiante se separó del viaje organizado por la universidad y fue a su aire. In Segovia, the student left the university tour group and went off on his own. ➤ Va a su bola. ▪ Va por libre. ▪ Va a su aire. He ignores everyone else.

ir a tirarse en trineo to go sleigh riding ▪ to go sledding

ir a tiro hecho **1.** to go to it (in a determined way) **2.** *(sexual)* to go for it

ir a toda hostia ▪ ir cagando leches ▪ ir en un pispas ▪ ir en un flis to haul ass

ir a toda pastilla ▪ ir a tope ▪ ir a toda prisa ▪ ir al máximo ▪ ir muy de prisa to go full blast ▪ to go full speed

ir a toda vela to go full sail

ir a tomar aire fresco ▪ salir a tomar aire fresco to go out for some fresh air

ir a trompicones *(automóvil)* to chug along ▪ to chug-a-lug ▪ to go in fits and starts

ir a una corrida de toros ▪ *(coloquial)* ir a los toros to go to a bullfight

ir a *x* kilómetros por hora ▪ circular a *x* ▪ kilómetros por hora to go *x* kilometers per hour ▪ to travel at *x* kilometers per hour

ir (a) *x* puntos por delante del otro equipo ▪ llevar *x* ▪ puntos de ventaja sobre el otro equipo ▪ estar (a) *x* ▪ puntos por delante del otro equipo to be *x* points ahead of the other team ▪ to be ahead of the other team by *x* points

ir acompañado de to go hand in hand with

ir adelante to go ahead ▪ to proceed

ir adelante por to proceed across ▪ to proceed along ➤ *(Bernal Díaz)* Ibamos adelante por una ancha calzada. We were proceeding across a wide causeway.

ir al baño to go the bathroom

ir al caso to get to the point

ir al centro to go downtown

ir al cine to go to the movies

ir al encuentro de alguien to go meet someone ➤ Tengo que ir al encuentro de ella en el aeropuerto. ▪ Tengo que ir a su encuentro en el aeropuerto. I have to meet her at the airport.

ir al fin del mundo con alguien to do anything for someone

ir al galope to go at a gallop ▪ to gallop

ir al garete ▪ irse al garete to go to pot

ir al grano ▪ ir lo concreto to get to the point ▪ to get down to brass tacks

ir al quite de alguien to rescue someone from an embarrassing situation ▪ to rescue someone from an unwanted approach (by someone else)

ir al teatro ■ ir a ver una obra de teatro ■ ir a ver una obra teatral to go to a play

ir al trote to go at a trot

ir al trullo *(coloquial y vulgar)* ■ ir al maco to get thrown in the tank ■ to go to jail

ir alto to be high ■ to be up ➤ El arroyo va muy alto. The stream is high. ■ The steam is up.

ir anocheciendo to be getting dark ➤ Va anocheciendo. It's getting dark.

ir armado(-a) to be armed ■ to go armed ➤ Iban armados y ofrecieron resistencia. They were armed and offered resistance.

ir atrás ■ retroceder to back up

ir atrasado(-a) con el trabajo ■ llevar retraso con el trabajo to be running behind in one's work ■ to get behind in one's work

ir averiguando to become informed about ■ to find out about (through investigation) ➤ Tras abundantes lecturas he ido averiguando las verdaderas causas de la revolución francesa. Through extensive reading, I've been becoming informed about the true causes of the French Revolution.

ir besando el culo de un carro *(subido de tono)* ■ ir pegado a un carro ■ ir besando el paragolpes de un carro to tailgate a car

ir bien to go well ■ to be going well ➤ Nos va muy bien. It's going very well for us.

ir bien de tiempo to make good time

ir bien derecho to walk erect

ir bien vestido to be well dressed

ir borrándose to die out

ir cabeza abajo 1. ir mal to go badly 2. ir al revés to be (turned) upside down 3. ir haciendo el pino to walk on one's hands

ir cada cual por su camino ■ ir cada uno por su lado 1. tomar rutas distintas to go off on one's own 2. terminar una relación con alguien to go ones' separate ways

ir cada uno por su lado ■ ir cada cual por su camino 1. tomar rutas distintas to go off on one's own ■ to go around on one's own 2. terminar una relación con alguien to go ones' separate ways ➤ Después del tour guiado, a los estudiantes se les dieron dos horas para ir cada uno por su lado. After the guided tour, the students were given two hours to go (around) on their own.

ir cada vez a más velocidad to get faster and faster ➤ Los nuevos trenes van cada vez a más velocidad. The new trains are getting faster and faster.

ir cagando leches *(subido de tono)* ■ ir a toda hostia ■ *(alternativo inofensivo)* ■ ir en un pispas ■ ir en un flis to haul ass ■ to go like a bat out of hell

ir cobrando pagos con tiempo to collect payments over time

ir como la seda to go smoothly ■ to hum along

ir como oveja al matadero to go like a lamb to the slaughter

ir como perro sin amo to be at loose ends

ir como sardinas en lata to be packed (in) like sardines

ir como un reloj ■ marchar como un reloj 1. ir a la perfección to go like clockwork 2. ir como la seda to run smoothly 3. ser puntual to be punctual 4. ir al baño con regularidad to be regular ■ not to suffer from constipation

ir con algo 1. corresponder a algo to go with 2. combinar con ■ entonar con to go with 2. vestirse de algo ■ ir en algo to be wearing ➤ Las fundas van con las sabanas. The pillowcases go with the sheets. ➤ ¿Qué colores van con el pelo rojo? ■ ¿Qué colores combinan con el pelo rojo? ■ ¿Qué colores entonan con el pelo rojo? What colors go with red hair? ➤ Iba con una bikini. ■ Iba en una bikini. She was wearing a bikini.

ir con alguien 1. acompañar a alguien to go with someone ■ to accompany someone 2. volver con alguien to go to (be with) someone 3. estar con alguien to be with someone ➤ Si no tienes prisa, espérame y voy contigo. If you're not in a hurry, hold on a minute and I'll go with you. ➤ Debes ir con él. You must go to him. ■ You must be with him. ➤ Iba con su mujer en el momento del atentado. He was with his wife at the time of the assassination.

ir con chismes to be armed with gossip

ir con destino a ■ ir destinado a ■ ir con rumbo a to be headed for ■ to be heading for ■ to be bound for

ir con el hatillo a cuestas ■ andar con el hatillo a cuestas ■ llevar el hatillo a cuestas to go with a pack slung over one's back

ir con el pecho al aire to go bare-chested

ir con el rabo entre las piernas *(Esp.)* ■ ir con la cola entre las piernas to go away with one's tail between one's legs

ir con exceso de velocidad to speed ■ to exceed the speed limit ➤ El policía lo paró por ir con exceso de velocidad. The policeman pulled him over for speeding. ■ The policeman pulled him over for exceeding the speed limit.

ir con la cabeza levantada to hold one's head high

ir con la cara descubierta 1. to go with one's face uncovered 2. to have no hidden agendas ■ to have all one's cards on the table

ir con la cola entre las piernas ■ ir con el rabo entre las piernas to go away with one's tail between one's legs

ir con la corriente to go with the flow

ir con la frente muy alta to hold one's head high

ir con la hora pegada al culo *(subido de tono)* ■ ir fatal de tiempo to be pressed for time ■ to be running out of time

ir con la verdad por delante to make no bones about it ■ to be up-front about it

ir con muletas to be on crutches ■ to walk with crutches

ir con pie derecho to be off to a good start ■ to get off on the right foot

ir con pies de plomo to tread lightly ➤ *(tú)* ¡Ve con pies de plomo! ■ *(usted)* Vaya con pies de plomo! Tread carefully!

ir con rumbo a ■ ir con destino a to be headed for ■ to be heading for ■ to be bound for

ir con un equipo to be for a team ➤ Vamos con Alianza Lima. We're for Alianza Lima.

ir conociendo a alguien ■ llegar a conocer a alguien to get to know someone ➤ (Yo) había ido conociéndolo... ■ (Yo) lo había ido conociendo... I had gradually gotten to know him... ➤ (Yo) había ido conociéndola... ■ (Yo) la había ido conociendo... I had gradually gotten to know her... ➤ *(Esp. leísmo)* (Yo) había ido conociéndole... ■ (Yo) le había ido conociéndo... He had gradually gotten to known him...

ir contra corriente ■ ir a contracorriente ■ ir contra la corriente to go against the grain ■ to go against the tide ■ to be out of step

ir contra la corriente ■ ir contra corriente ■ ir a contracorriente to go against the grain ■ to go against the tide ■ to be out of step

ir contra su palabra to go against his word

ir contra una ley to be against the law

ir cuesta abajo to go downhill

ir dando tumbos to encounter lots of obstacles ■ to encounter all sorts of setbacks

ir de 1. ir en to be wearing 2. tratarse de to be about 3. considerarse to consider oneself ➤ Iba de traje de baño. She was wearing a bathing suit. ➤ Fuentes dijo que su próximo libro va de vampiros. Fuentes said his next book is about vampires. ➤ Va de experto. He considers himself an expert.

ir de acampada to go camping

ir de bareo to go bar hopping

ir de bracete to go arm-in-arm ■ to walk arm-in-arm

ir de bruces a to run headlong into

ir de cabeza a to head straight for

ir de camino a to be on one's way to ➤ Ibamos de camino a... We were on our way to...

ir de capa caída *(referido sobre todo a negocios)* to be declining ■ to be going down ■ to be failing

ir de caza ■ salir a cazar to go hunting

ir de compras to go shopping

ir de copas to go (out) for a drink ■ to go have a drink

ir de cráneo to be headed for trouble ■ to be headed for problems ■ to be in a tough spot ■ to be in a predicament

ir de cubaneo en Miami ■ cubanear en Miami to have a night on the town in Miami's Cuban barrio

ir de culo *(ligeramente subido de tono)* ■ ir de cabeza to be headed for trouble ■ to be headed for problems

ir de divo(-a) to be full of oneself

ir de espaldas ■ sentarse de espaldas to ride backwards ■ to sit backwards ➤ No me gusta ir de espaldas en el tren. En los largos viajes me marea. ■ No me gusta sentarme de espaldas en el tren. En los largos viajes me marea. I don't like to ride backwards on the train. On long trips it makes me nauseated. ■ I don't like to sit backwards on the train. On long trips it makes me nauseated.

ir de flor en flor to go from flower to flower

ir de gorra to panhandle ■ to beg

ir de juerga to go out on the town

ir de lado a lado to stagger (from drunkenness)

ir de mal en peor to go from bad to worse

ir de oyente a un curso ■ ir de oyente a una clase ■ ir de oyente a una asignatura to audit a course ■ to audit a class ■ to audit a subject

ir de pachanga to go partying

ir de paseo to go for a walk

ir de picos pardos ■ salir de picos pardos to go looking for some action ■ to cat around

ir de pingo *(de día o de noche)* to go (out) on a lark

ir de polizón to stow away

ir de puta madre *(Esp., subido de tono)* ■ ir que arde to be going great ■ to be going great guns ➤ La venta de entradas va de puta madre. ■ La venta de entradas va que arde. The ticket sales are going great guns.

ir de tascas to go bar hopping

ir de un extremo a otro to go from one end to the other

ir de un lado para (el) otro ■ ir de un lado a otro ■ ir por todas partes ■ ir por todos lados to go all over the place

ir de una carrera *(poco común)* ■ ir rápido ■ ir volando to hurry ■ to be quick ➤ Voy de una carrera. I'll hurry. ■ I'll be quick.

ir de vuelta a ■ volver a to go back to ■ to return to ➤ Mientras iba de vuelta a casa... As I was going back home... ■ As I was returning home...

ir de *x* a *y* to range from *x* to *y* ➤ La cifra va del 25 al 40 por ciento. The figure ranges from 25 to 40 percent.

ir demasiado lejos ■ propasarse to go too far

ir derecho a... to go straight to... ■ to go directly to

ir desaliñado(-a) ■ estar desaliñado to be disheveled

ir descaminado(-a) ■ ir desencaminado to bark up the wrong tree ■ to be off the track ■ to be on the wrong track

ir descamisado 1. to wear one's shirt unbuttoned **2.** to be in rags (from poverty) **3.** to go shirtless

ir desde to range from

ir desencaminado ■ ir descaminado to bark up the wrong tree ■ to be off the track ■ to be on the wrong track

ir destinado(-a) a ■ ir con destino a ■ ir con rumbo a to be headed for ■ to be heading for ■ to be bound for

ir detrás de algo ■ andar detrás de algo **1.** to be after something **2.** to (try to) track down something ➤ Ese novio tuyo anda detrás de tu dinero. Your boyfriend is after your money. ➤ Ando detrás de una primera edición de los ensayos de Emerson. I'm trying to track down a first edition of Emerson's essays.

ir detrás de alguien 1. andar detrás de alguien ■ ir en persecución de alguien ■ ir tras alguien to go after someone **2.** to (try to) track down someone ■ to (try to) track someone down **3.** ser el siguiente de la fila to be after someone in line ■ to be the next person in line ➤ La mujer esa va detrás del futbolista. ■ La mujer esa anda detrás del futbolista. That woman is going after the football player. ➤ La policía va detrás de los atracadores. ■ La policía anda detrás de los atracadores. The police are after the robbers. ➤ La policía va detrás de ellos. The police are trying to track them down.

ir directo al grano to get right to the point ■ to go right to the point

ir dirigido a alguien ■ estar a nombre de alguien to be addressed to someone

ir disminuyendo to be on the decrease ■ to be on the decline

ir embalado por la calle to go barreling down the street ➤ Los coches van embalados por esa calle a noventa kilómetros por hora. The cars go barreling down that street at ninety kilometers per hour.

ir empezando a... ■ estar empezando a... to be starting to... ➤ Voy empezando a entenderlo. I'm starting to get the idea.

ir en ■ ir con ■ ir de ■ vestirse de to be wearing ■ to have on ➤ Iba en una bikini. ■ Iba de una bikini. She was wearing a bikini. ■ She had on a bikini.

ir en autobús to go by bus

ir en avión a ■ coger un avión a to fly to ■ to take a plane to ➤ Fuimos a Madrid en avión. We flew to Madrid.

ir en aumento to be on the increase ■ to be increasing ■ to be rising ➤ La cantidad de quejas va en aumento constante. The number of complaints is constantly on the increase. ■ The number of complaints is steadily increasing. ■ The number of complaints is rising steadily.

ir en ■ ir de to be wearing ➤ Iba en traje de baño. She was wearing a bathing suit.

ir en ascenso 1. to be on the increase ■ to increase **2.** *(especialmente en el futuro)* to begin to increase ■ to start to increase

ir en aumento to be on the increase

ir en cabeza ■ ir por delante ■ ir en primer lugar to go first *(Nota: Especialmente en carreras deportivas como ciclismo ■ Especially in races such as bicycling)*

ir en carro ■ ir en coche ■ ir en auto to go by car

ir en coche *(Esp., Arg.)* ■ ir en carro ■ ir en auto to go by car

ir en contra de las reglas to be against the rules

ir en contra de los principios de uno to go against the grain ➤ Va en contra de mis principios prestar libros y CDs, porque la misma gente que los pide prestados es la misma que no los devuelve. It goes against my grain to lend books and CDs, because the very people who borrow them, are the very ones who don't return them.

ir en el asiento de copiloto to ride shotgun

ir en el coche de San Fernando, un rato a pie y otro andando ■ ir en el coche de San Fernando, un rato a pie y otro caminando ■ ir a pie to go on Shank's mare ■ to go on Shank's pony ■ to go on foot ■ to walk

ir en pareja to go in pairs

ir en perjuicio de to go against ■ to work against

ir en persecución de alguien ■ ir detrás de alguien ■ ir tras alguien to be after someone ■ to be in pursuit of someone

ir en romería to go on a pilgrimage

ir en taxi ■ tomar un taxi to go by taxi ■ to take a taxi ➤ Fuimos en taxi. We went by taxi. ■ We took a taxi.

ir en un flis *(Esp., coloquial)* ■ ir a toda hostia ■ ir cagando leches ■ ir en un pispas to fly ■ to zoom

ir en un pispas *(Esp., coloquial)* ■ ir a toda hostia ■ ir cagando leches ■ ir en un pispas to fly ■ to zoom

ir en una carrera ■ ir de una carrera to hurry ■ to be quick ➤ Voy en una carrera. ■ Voy de una carrera. I'll hurry. ■ I'll be quick.

ir escopetado(-a) to dash off ■ to be off like a shot

ir envejeciendo ■ ya ir para viejo ■ estar entrando en años to be getting old ■ to be getting up in years ➤ Va envejeciendo. *(él)* He's getting old. ■ He's getting up in years. *(ella)* She's getting old. ■ She's getting up in years.

ir fatal de tiempo ■ ir justo de tiempo ■ estar apurado de tiempo ■ andar escaso de tiempo ■ ir con la hora pegada al culo to be (really) pressed for time ➤ Voy fatal de tiempo. I'm (really) pressed for time.

ir follado *(subido de tono)* ■ ir a toda leche ■ ir a toda hostia ■ circular muy de prisa to go like a bat outta hell

ir fuera del camino ■ ir fuera de camino to get off the track ■ to be off the track

ir hacia to go toward ■ to be headed for ■ to go in the direction of

ir haciendo algo to gradually do something ■ gradually to do something

ir haciendo el cabra *(especialmente los motociclistas)* to drive (extremely) dangerously

ir hasta to go as far as

ir hecho un cromo ■ ir hecho un adefesio to look a sight ➤ ¡Vas hecho un cromo! ■ ¡Vas hecho un adefesio! You look a sight!

ir iguales *(deportes)* ■ estar empatados to be tied ➤ Van iguales. ■ Están empatados. They're tied.

ir incluido to be included ■ to come included ➤ Las pilas no van incluidas. Batteries are not included. ➤ El cinturón va incluido en el conjunto. The belt comes included with the set.

ir justo de tiempo ■ ir fatal de tiempo ■ estar apurado de tiempo ■ andar escaso de tiempo ■ ir con la hora pegada al culo to be (really) pressed for time ➤ Voy justo de tiempo I'm (really) pressed for time.

ir la música por dentro ▪ llevar la música por dentro to be lighthearted ▪ to carry one's music inside

ir mal 1. to go badly 2. *(ruedas)* to be out of alignment ▪ to wobble

ir mal vestido(-a) ▪ andar hecho(-a) un pingo to dress shabbily ▪ to be dressed shabbily ➤ Va muy mal vestido. He dresses shabbily. ▪ He is dressed shabbily.

ir más allá to go farther ▪ to go further

ir más allá de... to go beyond...

ir mejor to be getting better ➤ El paciente va mejor. The patient is getting better.

ir mejorando algo to be improving somewhat

ir montado(-a) en burro, caballo, camello, elefante etc. to ride (on) a donkey, horse, camel, elefant etc.

ir muy (bien) escotadas to wear a low-cut dress ▪ to wear a low-cut blouse ▪ to show the cleavage nicely

ir muy por debajo del límite de velocidad to go way below the speed limit ▪ to go far below the speed limit ▪ *(coloquial)* to poke along

ir muy tomado(-a) to be very drunk

ir normalito y bien to be like everybody else ▪ to go with the flow ➤ ¿Por qué no puedes ir normalito y bien? Why can't you be like everybody else?

ir para casa ▪ dirigirse a la suya to head home ▪ to head for home

ir para largo 1. to go on for a long time ▪ to go on and on 2. to be a while ➤ Sus tratamientos para el reumo van para largo. Her treatments for rheumatoid arthritis will go on for a long time. ➤ Estábamos esperando a que saliera nuestro tren, y como iba para largo, decidimos almorzar en la estación. We were waiting for our train to leave, and since it was going to be a while, we decided to get something to eat at the station. ➤ Este discurso podría ir para largo. This speech could go on and on.

ir para los *x* (años) to be going on *x* (years old). ➤ (Ella) va para los treinta. She's going on thirty.

ir para viejo(-a) to be getting old ➤ (Ella) va para vieja. She's getting old.

ir parte por parte to go step by step

ir pasando 1. to come through 2. to go through ➤ Vamos pasando. We're coming through.

ir pegado a la costa 1. *(en coche)* to drive along the coast 2. *(en barco)* to sail along the coast ▪ to hug the coast

ir pegado a un carro *(L.am.)* ▪ ir besando el culo de otro carro to tailgate (a car)

ir pegado a un coche *(Esp.)* ▪ ir besando el culo de otro coche to tailgate (a car)

ir peor ▪ ser peor to go worse ▪ to do (a lot) worse ➤ Puede que no sea el trabajo de tus sueños, pero te podría ir peor. ▪ Puede que no sea el trabajo de tus sueños, pero te podía ser peor. Maybe it's not your dream job, but still, you could do a lot worse. ➤ No es el inquilino perfecto, pero nos podría ir peor. ▪ No es el inquilino perfecto, pero nos podía ser peor. He's not a perfect tenant, but we could do a lot worse.

ir pisando huevos ▪ ir a medio gas to poke along ▪ to go poking along ▪ to go way below the speed limit ▪ to drive way below the speed limit

ir por 1. ir por vía de to go by way of 2. estar dirigido a to be aimed at ▪ to be intended for 3. estar repitiendo to be on... ➤ Ese comentario iba por mí, ¿verdad? That remark was aimed at me, wasn't it? ➤ Va por el tercer plato de paella. ▪ Va por la segunda repetición de paella. He's on his third helping of paella.

ir por algo to (go) get something ▪ *(pintoresco)* to fetch something

ir por alguien 1. ir a buscar a alguien to go (to) get someone ▪ to go for someone ▪ to go pick someone up 2. referirse a alguien to be referring to someone ▪ to mean someone ▪ to be aimed at someone ➤ Fue a la escuela por su hijo. He went to the school to get his son. ➤ Fue por su hijo. He went to get his son. ▪ He went for his son. ➤ Eso no va por él. That's not aimed at him. ▪ That's not a reference to him.

ir por buen camino to be on the right track ▪ to be on the right road

ir por cierto camino to take a certain route

ir por defecto a *(informática)* to default to ➤ El software va por defecto al español, reemplazando "realize" por "realice". The software defaults to the Spanish, changing "realize" to "realice."

ir por delante de alguien 1. to go in front of someone 2. *(a pie)* to walk ahead of someone

ir por el atajo ▪ cortar por el atajo ▪ atajar ▪ ahorrar camino to take a shortcut

ir por (el) buen camino to be on the right track

ir por (el) mal camino to be on the wrong track

ir por el mismo camino to go the same route ▪ to follow suit

ir por ese lado to go that way ➤ No vayas por ese lado. Don't go that way.

ir por este lado to go this way ➤ Vamos por este lado. Let's go this way.

ir por los cerros de Úbeda ▪ dar un rodeo ▪ dar un montón de vueltas ▪ *(L.am.)* dar un gran vueltón to go around Robin Hood's barn ▪ to go way out of the way ▪ *(ligeramente subido de tono)* to go way the hell out of the way

ir por mar to go by sea

ir por partes to go one step at a time ▪ to go step by step ➤ Vamos por partes. Let's go one step at a time. ▪ Let's go step by step. ▪ Let's proceed one step at a time ▪ Let's proceed step by step.

ir por su camino to go one's own way

ir por todas partes ir por todos lados ▪ ir de un lado para otro ▪ ir de un lado a otro to go all over the place

ir por una Coca-Cola to go for a Coca-Cola ▪ to go for a Coke ➤ ¿Tenemos tiempo de ir por una Coca-Cola? ▪ ¿Tenemos tiempo para ir por una Coca-Cola? Do we have time to go for a Coke?

ir puesto(-a) de drogas to be high on drugs ▪ to be under the influence of a drug ➤ Iban puestos de algo. They were on something.

ir que arde to go great guns ➤ Va que arde. It's going great guns.

ir que vuela para to hurry to ▪ *(coloquial)* to hightail it to

ir raleando to thin out

ir seguro de sí to be sure of oneself ➤ Iba muy seguro de sí. He was very sure of himself.

ir según lo previsto to go according to plan ▪ *(coloquial)* to go according to Hoyle

ir todavía más allá to go even further ➤ *(noticia)* El embajador fue todavía más allá y confirmó que la existencia de armas de destrucción masiva fue la razón principal que indujo a España a apoyar la guerra. The ambassador went even further and confirmed that the existence of weapons of mass destruction was the principal reason why Spain supported the war.

ir tras alguien ▪ ir en persecución de alguien ▪ ir detrás de alguien to be after someone ▪ to be in pursuit of someone

ir uno por su camino to go one's own way

ir viento en popa to go smoothly ▪ to be sailing along

ir *x* cursos por delante de alguien en la escuela to be *x* years ahead of someone in school ➤ Iba dos cursos por delante de mí en el colegio. He was two years ahead of me in school.

ir y hacer algo *(Méx.)* to up and do something

ir y venir ▪ pasarse yendo y viniendo to go back and forth ➤ Henry va y viene durante una hora de su habitación al baño. ▪ Se pasa una hora yendo y viniendo de su habitación al baño. Henry goes back and forth from his room to the bathroom for an hour.

el **ir y venir de la gente** ▪ las idas y venidas de la gente the comings and goings of people

ir y venir de un lado para otro to go running around

irle bien a alguien 1. to go well for one ▪ to do someone good 2. quedarle bien ▪ sentarle bien ▪ resultarle muy bien to be (very) becoming to someone ▪ to look good on someone ➤ Ese sombrero no le va bien. That hat does not look good on her. ➤ Ese vestido le va muy bien. ▪ Ese vestido le queda muy bien. ▪ Ese vestido le sienta muy bien. ▪ Ese vestido le resulta muy bien. *(a usted)* That dress is very becoming to you. ▪ The dress looks very good on you. ▪ *(a ella)* That dress is very becoming to her. ▪ That dress looks very good on her.

irle gustando a uno to grow on one ▪ to gradually come to like

ironizar sobre algo to satirize something

irresistible deseo de irresistible urge to

irrumpir en to barge in ■ to burst into

irrumpir en llamas to burst into flames ➤ El avión se desplomó e irrumpió en llamas. The airplane plummeted to ground and burst into flames.

irrumpir en películas to break into films ■ to break into the movies

irrumpir en prensa to break into print

irse a acabar to end ■ to come to an end ➤ No pensé que se fuera a acabar. I thought it was never going to end.

irse a freír espárragos to go jump in a lake

ir(se) a hacer gárgaras ■ ir(se) a hacer puñetas to go jump in a lake

ir(se) a hacer puñetas ■ ir(se) a hacer gárgaras to go jump in a lake

irse a la aventura to go (somewhere) without a fixed plan ■ to go (somewhere) without a set plan

irse a la cama 1. to go to bed **2.** to go to bed (together)

irse a la cama to go to bed ■ to turn in ➤ Es medianoche, me voy a la cama. It's midnight; I'm going to bed. ■ It's midnight; I'm going to turn in.

irse a la cama juntos to go to bed together

irse a la francesa to fly the coop ➤ La chacha se fue a la francesa hoy. The maid flew the coop today.

irse a la guerra ■ marchar a la guerra to go off to war ➤ En la Guerra Civil Americana cientos de miles de jóvenes dejaron sus granjas y se fueron a la guerra. In the American Civil War, hundreds of thousands of young men left their farms and went off to war.

irse a la mierda *(subido de tono)* ■ irse a la porra ■ irse a la eme to go to hell ■ *(alternativa benigna)* to go to blazes ➤ Vete a la mierda. ■ Vete a la porra. ■ Vete a la eme. Go to hell! ➤ Váyase usted a la mierda. ■ Váyase usted a la porra. ■ Váyase usted a la eme. Go to hell! ➤ Dile a tu amigo que se vaya a la mierda. ■ Dile a tu amigo que se vaya a la porra. ■ Dile a tu amigo que se vaya a la eme. Tell your friend to go to hell.

irse a las manos to come to blows

irse a paseo to go take walk ■ to go jump in a lake ➤ ¡Vete a paseo! Go take a walk! ■ Go jump in a lake!

irse a pique 1. *(barco)* hundirse to sink **2.** *(esperanzas)* to be dashed

irse a la porra ■ irse a la eme ■ irse a la mierda to go to hell ■ to go to blazes

irse a tomar por culo *(Esp., subido de tono)* ■ irse a tomar por saco to get screwed ■ to go jump in a lake

irse a tomar por saco *(Esp.)* to go jump in a lake ➤ ¡Vete a tomar por saco! Go jump in a lake!

irse a tomar vientos to go jump in a lake

irse abajo 1. desmoronarse to crumble ■ to go to pieces ■ to fall apart **2.** derrumbarse to collapse **3.** *(planes)* to fall through ■ to fall apart **4.** *(esperanzas)* to be dashed

irse acercando 1. to move (up) closer **2.** *(en contextos militares)* to move in closer ➤ No veo nada. Vamos a irnos acercando. ■ No veo nada. Vamos acercándonos. I can't see. Let's move up closer.

irse al cielo ■ ganarse la gloria to go to heaven

irse al extranjero to go abroad

irse al fondo to go to the bottom ■ to sink

ir(se) al garete to go to pot

irse al sobre ■ ir a la cama to hit the sack ■ to hit the hay ■ to go to bed ➤ Me voy al sobre. ■ Me voy a la cama. I'm going to hit the sack. ■ I'm going to hit the hay. ■ I'm going to bed.

irse al traste to fall through

irse alejando de to get further and further away

irse bien calzado to wear good shoes

irse cada uno por su lado ■ irse cada quien por su lado ■ tomar caminos distintos ■ tomar distintos caminos to go ones' separate ways ➤ Nos fuimos cada uno por su lado. ■ Tomamos (cada uno) caminos distintos. We went our separate ways. ➤ Se fueron cada uno por su lado. ■ Se fueron cada quien por su lado. ■ Tomaron (cada uno) caminos distintos. ■ Tomaron (cada uno) distintos caminos. They went their separate ways.

irse con las manos vacías to come away empty-handed

irse con un escalofrío to get a chill

irse de cabeza to fall down (head first) ■ to fall forward (all the way down) ■ to fall flat ■ to fall headlong ➤ Me fui de cabeza en las escaleras. I fell headlong down the steps. ■ I fell forward down the steps.

irse de juerga to go out on the town

irse de la boca to let the cat out of the bag ➤ Ella se fue de la boca. She let the cat out of the bag.

irse de la lengua to let it slip ■ to let the cat out of the bag

ir(se) de lado a lado *(reflexivo sólo en el infinitivo y primera persona singular y plural)* to stagger (from drunkenness, dizziness)

irse de manos to come to blows ➤ Nos fuimos de manos. We came to blows.

irse de picos pardos *(Esp., coloquial)* to go looking for a good time ■ *(coloquial, chicas)* to go guy hunting ■ to cat around

irse de pinta *(Méx.)* ■ fumarse las clases ■ hacer pellas ■ irse de pellas to skip school

irse de rositas to get off scott free

irse de vacaciones to go on vacation ■ to go away on vacation ➤ Se han ido de vacaciones. They've gone on vacation.

irse la boca a alguien ■ írsele la boca a alguien to shoot off one's big mouth ■ to shoot off at the mouth ■ to run off at the mouth

irse la cabeza 1. to feel dizzy **2.** irse la olla to forget things ■ to be forgetful ➤ Se me va la cabeza. I feel dizzy. ■ I forget things. ■ I'm forgetful.

irse mucho en (for) a lot to depend on ■ (for) a lot to be riding on ➤ Tenemos que esforzarnos porque nos va mucho en este proyecto. We have to apply ourselves because a lot depends on this project. ■ We have to apply ourselves because a lot is riding on this project.

irse para arriba como pedo de buzo *(pintoresco)* to skyrocket ➤ ¡Cuando salga el libro, nuestra fama se va a ir para arriba como pedo de buzo! When the book comes out, our fame is going to skyrocket!

irse por la tangente ■ salirse por la tangente ■ irse por las ramas ■ salir por peteneras to go off on a tangent

irse por las ramas 1. andarse por las ramas ■ andarse con rodeos ■ irse por los cerros de Úbeda ■ marear la perdiz to beat around the bush **2.** irse por la tangente ■ salirse por la tangente ■ salirse por peteneras to go off on a tangent

irse por los cerros de Úbeda *(Esp.)* ■ irse por la tangente ■ salirse por la tangente to digress ■ to get off on a tangent ■ to go off on a tangent

irse por los imbornales *(L.am.)* ■ salirse por la tangente ■ irse por la tangente ■ salirse por peteneras ■ irse por las ramas to go off on a tangent ■ to get off on a tangent

irse pronto ■ salir pronto ■ marcharse pronto to leave early

irse sin ■ partir sin ■ dejar olvidado ■ quedársele to leave behind

irse volando ■ emprender vuelo to fly away

irse ya ■ haberse ido ya to have already gone ■ to have already left ➤ Ella se fue ya. ■ Ella ya se ha ido. She's already gone. ■ She's already left. ➤ El portero no vuelve hasta el día veinte, y para entonces ya me habré ido. The concierge doesn't get back until the twentieth, and I'll already be gone by then. ■ The concierge doesn't get back until the twentieth, and I'll already have left by then. ■ The concierge doesn't get back until the twentieth, and I'll have already left by then.

írsele to lose its punch ■ morirse to pass away ➤ Ella se nos fue el año pasado. She passed away last year.

írsele a uno de la cabeza to slip one's mind ➤ Se me fue de la cabeza. It slipped my mind.

írsele a uno ■ pasarse la mano **1.** to go too far ■ to overdo it **2.** *(con el castigo de un niño)* to be too overbearing

írsele a uno la cabeza ■ marearse to get dizzy

írsele al otro barrio *(coloquial)* to pass on ■ to pass away ■ to die

írsele de la cabeza ■ írsele ■ perder el hilo de las ideas ■ perder el hilo ■ írsele el santo al cielo to lose one's train of thought ■ to forget what one was saying

írsele de las manos 1. escurrírsele de los dedos ■ escurrírsele entre los dedos to slip through one's fingers ■ to slip away from one ■ to get away from one ■ to elude one **2.** escapársele de las manos ■ caérsele de las manos to drop (accidentally) ➤ Se nos ha ido de las manos. ■ Se nos ha escurrido de los dedos. It slipped through our fingers. ■ It slipped away from us. ■

It got way from us. ■ It eluded us. ➤ Se me fue de las manos. I dropped it.

írsele el trabajo a uno por motivo de algo to lose one's job because of something

írsele la boca a alguien ■ irse la boca a alguien to shoot off at the mouth ■ to run off at the mouth

írsele la olla to lose the thread

írsele los ojos tras algo (for) the eyes to be drawn to ➤ Se fueron los ojos tras Isabel. All eyes were drawn to Isabel.

Isla de la Pascua Easter Island

Islas Británicas British Isles

izar la bandera ■ levantar la bandera to raise the flag ■ *(literary)* to hoist the flag ➤ Izaron la bandera a media asta. They raised the flag to half mast. ■ They raised the flag to half staff.

¡ja, ja, ja! ha, ha, ha!

el **jabón de silla de montar** saddle soap

Jack el destripador Jack the Ripper

jalarle el pelo a alguien to pull someone's hair

estar **jalonado de** to be marked by

jalonar una área ■ jalonar un terreno to mark off an area ➤ Están jalonando la parcela donde se va a construir la casa. They're marking off the lot where the house will be built.

jalonear la manga de alguien to tug at someone's sleeve

jamás conocido never before seen ■ previously unknown ■ unlike anything seen before

¡jamás de los jamases! ■ ¡nunca jamás! never ever! ■ not in a million years!

jamás deja de asombrarme it never ceases to amaze me

jamás había visto one had ever seen ➤ Fue la mejor película que jamás había visto. It was the best movie that I had ever seen. ➤ (Ella) estaba más guapa de lo que la había visto jamás. She looked more beautiful than I had ever seen her.

jamás hasta ahora ■ nunca hasta ahora never before

jamás lograr que se olvide never to live something down ➤ Jamás lograré que se olvide. I'll never live it down.

jamás se me ha pasado por cabeza it has never crossed my mind ■ it's never crossed my mind

jamás se me olvidará aquel día ■ jamás olvidaré aquel día I'll never forget that day

jamás se me pasó por cabeza it never crossed my mind

jamás te olvidaré ■ no te olvidaré jamás I will never forget you

jamba de (la) puerta door jamb

jamón con chorreras: y un ~ get serious! ■ *(coloquial)* you gotta be kidding! ■ you gotta get serious!

el **jamón de mono** *(cómico)* ■ cacahuete ■ *(Méx.)* cacahuate ■ *(Arg.)* maní peanut

jamón serrano ■ jamón curado cured ham

jamoncito de pollo (chicken) drumstick

jaque mate a alguien: dar ~ *(juego de ajedrez y figurativo)* to checkmate someone

el **jarabe de arce** ■ (la) miel de arce ■ sirope de arce maple syrup

el **jarabe de pico** bull ■ nonsense ■ blarney ■ poppycock

jarabe tapatío *(baile de la forma de "la raspa")* Jaliscan shuffle

el **jardín de (la parte de) atrás** ■ jardín trasero back yard

jardín delantero front yard

jardín trasero ■ jardín de (la parte de) atrás back yard

jaula abierta, pájaro muerto your fly is open

jaula de oro gilded cage

jefa (mujer) female boss

el **jefe de pista** ringmaster

el **jefe del estado mayor** chief of staff

jefe (hombre) male boss

jeringuilla desechable ■ jeringas desechable disposable needle ■ disposable syringe

jersey de cuello alto ■ jersey de cuello vuelto turtleneck sweater

jeta de cerdo *(popular en bares de tapas españoles y en el sur de los Estados Unidos)* hog jowl

jornada completa eight-hour shift

jornada de reflexión the day before an election

jornada de verano summer schedule

jornada partida split shift

ser **joven de corazón** to be young at heart ➤ Ella es joven de corazón. She's young at heart.

jubilación anticipada early retirement

juego de computadora *(L.am.)* ■ juego de ordenador ■ videojuego computer game

juego de equipo team sport

juego de ingenio guessing game

juego de mesa board game

ser un **juego de niños** ■ ser comida de niños to be child's play

juego de ordenador *(Esp.)* ■ juego de computadora ■ videojuego computer game ■ video game

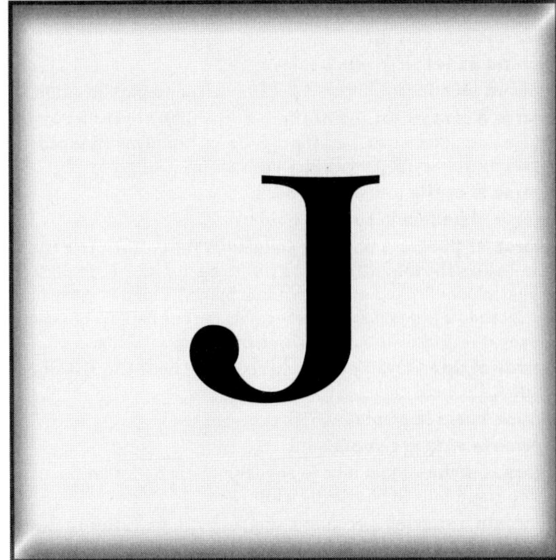

juego de palabras 1. juego de voces ■ retruécano play on words 2. como Scrabble *(crucigramas, etc.)* word game

juego de voces ■ juego de palabras play on words

juego del pasabola passing the buck

juego individual de vajilla place setting

juego limpio fair play

juegos en red games on line

jueves santo *(jueves de Semana Santa)* Maundy Thursday

el **juez de paz** justice of the peace

ser **juez y parte** to be an interested party ■ to be prejudiced ■ to be judge and jury

juez(-a) de paz justice of the peace

jugada a jugada play by play

jugar a cartas vistas to lay one's cards on the table ■ to lay all one's cards on the table

jugar a escondite to play hide and seek

jugar a hacer el cuco to play peek-a-boo

jugar a la baja to speculate on a downturn in prices

jugar a la bolsa to play the stock market

jugar a los bolos *(Esp.)* ■ jugar al boliche to go bowling ■ to bowl

jugar a los sonidos de los animales to make animal sounds

jugar a pillar to play tag

jugar a policías y ladrones to play cops and robbers

jugar al billar ■ billar to play pool ■ to shoot (some) pool

jugar al boliche *(L.am.)* ■ jugar a los bolos to go bowling ■ to bowl

jugar al desencuentro to play telephone tag

jugar al gato y el ratón ■ jugar al juego del gato y el ratón to play (a game of) cat and mouse

jugar al rin-raje to ring the doorbell and run

jugar bien la baza *(Esp.)* ■ jugar bien las cartas to play one's cards right ■ to play one's hand well

jugar bien las cartas to play one's cards right

jugar con fuego to play with fire

jugar con los nervios de uno to rattle one's nerves ■ to jangle one's nerves

jugar contra un equipo to play a team ■ to take on a team ➤ Real Madrid juega contra Barcelona este fin de semana. Real Madrid plays Barcelona this weekend. ■ Real Madrid takes on Barcelona this weekend.

jugar en casa *(deportes)* to play on the home court ■ to play in the home stadium ■ to play at home

jugar fuerte to play for high stakes

jugar la última carta to play one's last card

jugar limpio to play fair

jugar por parejas to play doubles

jugar sucio to play dirty

jugar un papel en to play a role in

jugar un picado *(esp. fútbol y baloncesto)* to play a pickup game

jugarse a cara o cruz to flip a coin over ■ to flip over ➤ Nos lo jugamos a cara o cruz. Let's flip over it. ➤ Nos jugamos la cena a cara o cruz. Let's flip over who'll buy supper.

jugarse el cuello to risk one's neck

jugarse el pellejo to risk one's hide

jugarse el puesto ■ poner su trabajo en riesgo (for) one's job to the on the line ■ (for) one's job to be at risk ➤ Se jugó el puesto por el correo electrónico que mandó a toda la compañía criticando a la gerencia. His job was on the line because of a company-wide E-mail he sent criticizing the top management.

jugarse el tipo ■ jugarse la vida to risk one's neck ■ to risk one's life

jugarse hasta la camisa to risk everything

jugarse la vida to risk one's life

jugarse mucho ■ tener mucho en juego to have a lot on the line ■ to risk a lot ■ to be risking a lot

jugárselo a suertes ■ echarlo a suertes ■ echar suertes to draw straws ■ to draw lots ■ to cast lots ■ *(con una moneda)* to flip a coin

jugárselo todo a una carta ■ jugar al todo o nada ■ jugárselo todo a una baza ■ ir todo en una carta to go all or nothing

jugo de naranja recién exprimido ■ *(Esp.)* zumo de naranja recién exprimido freshly squeezed orange juice

el **juguete hinchable** inflatable toy

junta de dilatación (de un edificio) expansion joint (of a building)

junta de jefes ■ cúpula militar estadounidense the joint chiefs ■ the Joint Chiefs of Staff

junta directiva ■ consejo de administración ■ consejo administrativo board of directors

junta rectora *(Esp.)* ■ consejo rector doctoral committee

juntar las partes ■ ensamblar las partes to assemble the parts ■ to put together the parts ■ to put the parts together

juntar polvo ■ acumular polvo ■ amontonar polvo to collect dust ■ to gather dust

juntarse en Internet ■ verse en Internet to link up on the Internet ➤ Los jóvenes se juntan y charlan en el Internet. Young people link up and chat on the Internet.

junto a algo ■ al lado de algo beside something ■ next to something

junto a la boca ■ al lado de la boca ■ en la boca beside one's mouth ➤ Ese lunar que tienes, Cielito Lindo, junto a la boca, no se lo des a nadie, que a mí me toca. That beauty spot that you have, Cielito Lindo, beside your mouth, don't give it to anyone because it belongs to me.

junto a mi ahora es... joining me now is...

junto al camino beside the road ■ at the side of the road

junto con together with ■ along with ➤ Virginia, junto con Maryland y Delaware, son estados del centro de la costa atlántica. Virginia, along with Maryland and Delaware, are central Atlantic states.

¿juntos o separados? *(la cuenta)* together or separate?

jura presidencial swearing in (of the president)

¿jura usted decir la verdad, sólo la verdad y nada más que la verdad?-sí, lo juro. do you swear to tell the truth, the whole truth and nothing but the truth, so help you God?-I do.

juramento presidencial presidential oath

jurar como un carretero ■ tener una boca de camionero ■ putear to curse like a drunk sailor ■ to swear like a drunk sailor *(informal)* to cuss like a drunk sailor

jurar el cargo to take the oath of office

jurar en falso ■ mentir bajo juramento ■ cometer perjurio ■ perjurarse to lie under oath ■ to commit perjury ■ to perjure oneself

juraría haber... ■ hubiera jurado... I'd swear I could have... ■ I could have sworn I...

juraría que... I could swear (that)... ➤ Juraría que vi que al cerdo le cambiaba la expresión de la cara cuando lo trinchaban. I could swear (that) I saw the expression on that pig's face change when they carved it.

juro a Dios I swear to God

justamente antes de *(implica una secuencia de eventos)* ■ justo antes de just before ➤ Justamente antes del anochecer en Nochebuena, Scrooge volvió a su casa. Just before dark on Christmas Eve, Scrooge returned to his house.

justamente después de *(implica una secuencia de eventos)* ■ justo después de just after

justamente no puedo entenderlo ■ simplemente no puedo entenderlo ■ me cuesta poder entenderlo I just can't understand it ■ I simply can't understand it

justificar algo amparándose en que... to justify something by saying that... ■ to justify something by maintaining that...

estar **justo a la altura de** ■ quedar justo a la altura de to be right near ■ to be right around ■ to be right in the vicinity of ➤ La pastelería está justo a la altura de la boca del metro Alvarado. The store is right near the Alvarado metro entrance . ■ The pastry shop is right around the entrance to the Alvarado metro.

estar **justo a la vuelta de la esquina** to be just around the corner ➤ Hay una tienda que está abierta fuera de hora justo a la vuelta de la esquina. There's an off-hours store just around the corner.

¡justo a tiempo! ■ ¡vaya cálculo! (that was) good timing! ■ (you're) just in time!

justo a tiempo de just in time to

justo ahora ■ en este preciso momento ■ en estos precisos momentos at this very moment ■ right this minute ➤ Estoy trabajando en ello justo ahora. ■ Estoy trabajando en ello en estos precisos momentos. I'm working on it at this very moment. ■ I'm working on it right this minute.

justo al comienzo ■ justo al principio at the very beginning ■ right at the beginning

justo al contrario just the opposite

justo al final at the very end ■ right at the end ➤ Añade el pimiento verde picado justo al final. Es deseable que estén calientes pero a la vez crujientes. Add the chopped green pepper at the very end. You want them to be hot, but still crunchy. ■ Add the chopped green pepper right at the end. You want them to be hot, but still crunchy.

estar **justo al fondo** to be at the very bottom ■ to be right at the bottom

estar **justo al lado de** ■ estar contiguo a ■ estar pegado a ■ estar a continuación de to be right next to ■ to be right beside ■ to be right by ➤ El parque está justo al lado de la biblioteca. ■ El parque está contiguo a la biblioteca. ■ El parque esta pegado a la biblioteca. ■ El parque está a continuación de la biblioteca. The park is right next to the library. ■ The park is right beside the library. ■ The park is right by the library.

estar **justo al otro lado de la calle** ■ estar del otro lado de la calle ■ estar en la acera de enfrente ■ estar en la vereda de enfrente to be right across the street

justo al otro lado de la calle: vivir ~ to live right across the street ■ to live directly across the street

justo al principio ■ justo al comienzo at the very beginning ■ right at the beginning

justo antes de eso right before that ■ just before that ➤ Justo antes de eso, oí el chirrido de los frenos. Right before that, I heard the screeching of the brakes. ■ Just before that, I heard the screeching of the brakes.

justo antes de (que...) ■ un momento antes de que... just before... ■ right before...

justo antes del anochecer ■ justamente antes del anochecer just before dark ■ right before dark

estar **justo aquí** ■ estar aquí mismo to be right here ➤ En este plano estamos justo aquí. ■ En este plano estamos aquí mismo. On this map, we're right here. ➤ En el diagrama estamos aquí mismo. ■ En el diagrama, estamos aquí mismo. In the diagram we're right here.

justo arriba del todo at the very top ■ right at the top

estar **justo con** ■ quedar justo con to be right by ■ to be right beside ➤ Está justo en la esquina con la Plaza San Miguel. ■ Queda justo en la esquina con la Plaza San Miguel. It's on the corner by the Plaza San Miguel.

justo cuando just as ➤ Justo cuando iba a salir, sonó el teléfono. Just as I was about about to leave, the phone rang. ▪ Just as I was leaving, the phone rang.

justo debajo de right under ▪ right underneath ➤ Si pones los refrescos justo debajo del congelador, se enfriarán más rápido pero se no congelarán. If you put the soft drinks right under the freezing compartment, they'll get cold quicker but won't freeze. ▪ If you put the soft drinks right underneath the freezing compartment, they'll get cold quicker but won't freeze.

justo desde el principio right from the start

justo después de right after

justo en la cara right in the face

justo en medio right in the middle

estar **justo encima de la cabeza** ▪ estar directamente encima de la cabeza ▪ tener algo justo encima de la cabeza ▪ estar por encima de la cabeza de alguien to be directly overhead ▪ to be straight overhead ▪ to be straight up ➤ En México, el sol y la luna están casi justo encima de la cabeza. ▪ En México el sol y la luna, los tienes casi justo encima de la cabeza. In Mexico, the sun and moon are almost directly overhead.

estar **justo enfrente de...** ▪ estar directamente enfrente de... to be right across the street from... ➤ Estoy justo enfrente de tu casa. I'm right across the street from your house.

justo enfrente de...: vivir ~ to live right across the street from... ➤ En Valladolid, vivíamos justo enfrente del Hospital Universitario. In Valladolid, we lived right across the street from the University Hospital.

justo entonces just then

justo frente a donde just opposite where ▪ right across from where

justo lo que ▪ exactamente lo que the very one (that) ▪ just what ▪ exactly what ➤ Es justo lo que estaba buscando. That's the very one I was looking for. ▪ That's just what I was looking for.

justo lo que recetó el médico ▪ justo lo que prescribió el médico ▪ justo lo que ha recetado el médico just what the doctor ordered

justo lo que necesito just what I need

justo lo que te faltaba ▪ justo lo que siempre has querido just what you've always wanted

justo para 1. just in time for **2.** just in time to ➤ Vuelvo para el 12 de Abril, justo para Semana Santa. I'll be back by April 12, just in time for Holy Week. ➤ Llego a Madrid justo para coger el tren para Salamanca. I arrive in Madrid just in time to catch the train for Salamanca.

justo por encima de just over the top of ➤ Desde más o menos cien metros de distancia se alcanzan a ver las cabezas de las cigüeñitas justo por encima del nido. From about a hundred meters down the street, you can see the heads of the baby storks just over the top of the nest.

ser **(justo) todo lo contrario** to be just the opposite ▪ to be just the other way around ▪ to be quite the opposite ➤ Es (justo) todo lo contrario. It's just the opposite. ▪ It's just the other way around.

juzga tú mismo judge for yourself

ser **juzgado sobre la base de** to be judged on the basis of

juzgar a la ligera to pass judgment on ▪ to judge superficially

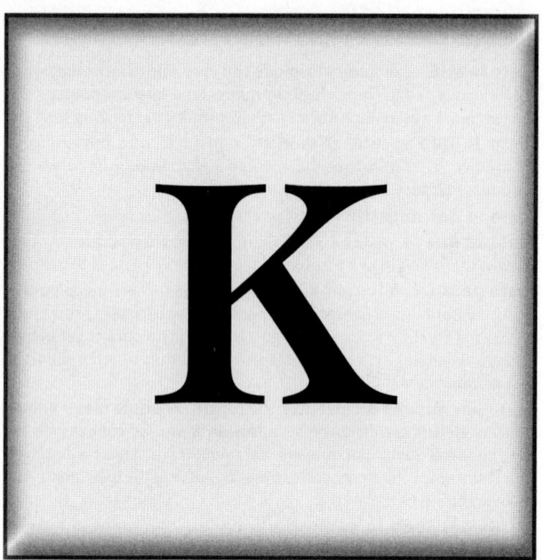

kilómetros al cuadrado kilometers square ➤ El área de este pueblo es de cuatro kilómetros al cuadrado, es decir, cuatro kilómetros por cuatro kilómetros, o dieciséis kilómetros cuadrados. This town is four kilometers square, that is, four kilometers by four kilometers, or sixteen square kilometers in area.

kilómetros cuadrados square kilometers ➤ El pueblo cubre cuatro kilómetros cuadrados, es decir, dos kilómetros por dos kilómetros. The town covers four square kilometers, that is, it is two kilometers by two kilometers.

la anterior the last one ▪ the previous one ▪ the one before this one ▪ ➤ En la clase anterior tuvimos una charla muy interesante. In the last class, we had a very interesting discussion.

La cabalgata de las Walkyrias *(composición de Wagner)* Ride of the Valkyries

la cual which

la cuenta, por favor ▪ la nota, por favor ▪ me cobra(s), por favor the bill, please

la de that of

la de Álvarez ▪ la Sra. Álvarez Mrs. Alvarez

la del alba sería *(de* Don Quixote, *y sólo en tiempo pasado)* ▪ al alba at dawn ▪ at the crack of dawn

la del medio the one in the middle ▪ the middle one ➤ La hija del medio The middle daughter

¡**la he hecho buena!** *(Esp.)* ▪ ¡metí la pata! ▪ ¡metí las cuatro! ▪ ¡buena la hice! ▪ ¡ahora sí que la hice! I've done it now! ▪ look what I've done!

ser **la más mínima de todas la preocupaciones de uno** to be the least of one's worries

la mayor cantidad posible ▪ tantos como sea posible ▪ las más posibles ▪ todas las que puedan ▪ todas las que se pueda as many as possible ▪ the greatest possible number

la mayoría de las cuales 1. *(cosas)* most of which **2.** *(personas)* most of whom

la mayoría de los cuales 1. *(cosas)* most of which **2.** *(personas)* most of whom

la nota, por favor ▪ la cuenta, por favor ▪ me cobra(s), por favor the bill, please

ser **la que... 1.** *(cosa)* to be the one that... ▪ to be the one which... **2.** *(persona)* ser quien to be the one who... ➤ Su madre era la que lo tomó peor. ▪ Su madre era quien lo tomó peor. His mother was the one who took it the worst. ➤ Ella es quien compuso la canción. She is the one who composed the song.

¡**la que está cayendo!** *(Méx.)* **1.** *(del sol)* the sun is really beating down! ▪ the sun is really oppressive! **2.** *(de la lluvia, nieve)* it's really coming down out there!

la que se ha armado ▪ lo que ha pasado what has happened

la que se ha creado ▪ lo que ha pasado what has happened

la que se ha montado ▪ lo que ha pasado that has happened ▪ what has happened

ser **la reoca** ▪ ser lo más ▪ ser lo mero mero to be tops ▪ to be top of the line

la única vía para hacer algo the only way to do something

la vi antes 1. *(persona)* I saw her earlier **2.** *(antecedente femenino como "película")* I saw it earlier

labio inferior lower lip

labio leporino cleft palate ➤ Nació con labio leporino. He was born with a cleft palate.

labio superior upper lip

labor diplomática: desplegar una ~ ▪ desplegar una labor de diplomacia to launch a diplomatic effort

las **labores de** the work of ➤ *(noticia)* Las labores de limpiar el sitio del Centro Mundial de Comercio ya están terminadas. The work of cleaning up the World Trade Center site is now complete.

labrarse un futuro como *(Esp.)* ▪ forjarse un futuro como to carve a niche for oneself as ▪ to establish oneself as

labrarse un porvenir to build a future for oneself ➤ Trato de labrarme un porvenir. I'm trying to build a future for myself.

lacra social social blight ▪ scourge

ladearse a babor *(avión, barco)* to pitch to the left ▪ to list to the left

ladearse a estribor *(avión, barco)* to pitch to the right ▪ to list to the right

ladera de una colina side of a hill ▪ hillside ▪ slope of a hill

ladera de una montaña side of a mountain ▪ mountainside ▪ slope of a mountain ▪ mountain slope

ladera opuesta de una colina far side of a hill

lado del teléfono end of the telephone line ▪ end of the line

lado opuesto de la luna far side of the moon ▪ dark side of the moon ▪ distant side of the moon

lado opuesto de una colina ▪ lado más lejano de una colina far side of a hill ▪ other side of a hill ▪ opposite side of a hill ➤ Los barcos al alcanzar el horizonte desaparecen como si estuviesen descendiendo por el lado opuesto de una colina, mucho antes de alcanzar el punto de fuga de los objetos distantes. Ships as they reach the horizon disappear as if they were descending the far side of a hill, long before they reach the vanishing point of distant objects.

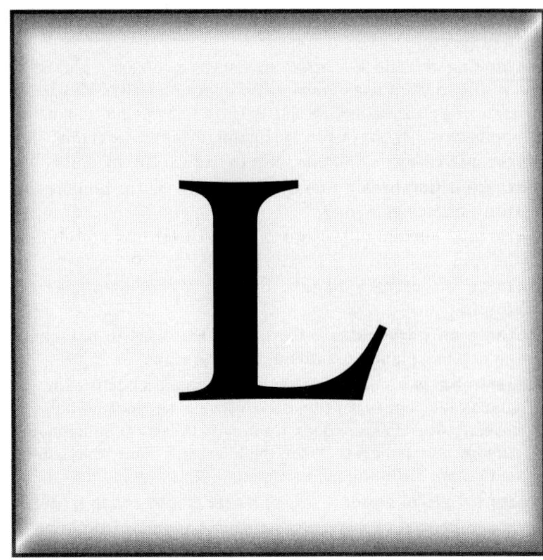

ladrarle a algo (o alguien) to bark at something (or someone) ➤ El perro le ladró al cartero. The dog barked at the postman.

ladrido de un perro barking of a dog

lágrimas de cocodrilo crocodile tears

lagunas (en los conocimientos) gaps in one's knowledge ➤ Todavía tengo lagunas en mis conocimientos de español, pero ando llenándolas. I still have gaps in my knowledge of Spanish, but I'm closing them.

lamentar decirte esto to hate to tell you this ➤ Lamento decirte esto... I hate to tell you this...

lamentar tener que hacer algo ▪ sentir tener que hacer algo to regret (having) to do something ▪ to regret having to do something ➤ Lamentamos tener que informarle a usted que... We regret to inform you that...

lamerle el culo a alguien *(subido de tono)* ▪ hacerle la pelota a alguien ▪ ser chupamedias ▪ ser adulón ▪ ser lisonjero to brown-nose someone ▪ *(alternativa benigna)* to butter up someone ▪ to butter someone up

lana de vidrio fiber glass

lancha neumática a motor motorized rubber raft

ser **lanzado al mercado** ▪ ser estrenado en el mercado ▪ salir al mercado to come out ▪ to come on(to) the market ▪ to be introduced onto the market ➤ Los móviles con tele incorporada fueron lanzados al mercado en el 2003. ▪ Los móviles con tele incorporada fueron estrenados en el mercado en el 2003. ▪ Los móviles con tele incorporada salieron al mercado en el 2003. Mobile phones with TV's came out in 2003. ▪ Mobile phones with TV's came onto the market in 2003. ▪ Mobile phones with TV's were introduced onto the market in 2003.

lanzador de béisbol baseball pitcher

lanzamiento literario literary debut

lanzar al público una revista to put out a magazine

lanzar la pelota ▪ arrojar la pelota ▪ tirar la pelota to pitch the ball

lanzar tropas to deploy troops ▪ to send in troops

lanzar un ataque contra un objetivo to launch an attack on a target ▪ to attack a target

lanzar un aullido to let out a howl

lanzar un grito ▪ dar un grito ▪ gritar to give a shout ▪ to shout

lanzar un rugido ▪ dar un rugido ▪ proferir un rugido to let out a roar

lanzar una bomba ▪ arrojar una bomba to drop a bomb

lanzar una indirecta ■ echar una indirecta ■ soltar una indirecta to drop a hint

lanzar una mirada a ■ echar un vistazo a to cast a glance at ➤ (Él) le lanzó una mirada de aprobación (a ella). He cast an approving glance at her. ➤ Ella le lanzó una mirada igualmente aprobatoria a él. She cast an equally approving glance at him.

lanzar una ráfaga ■ tirar una salva to fire a volley of shots

lanzarse a hombres ■ tirarse a los brazos de los hombres to throw oneself at men

lanzarse al vacío to jump into the void ■ to throw oneself into the void

lanzarse en carrera to take off like a shot ■ to take off running

lanzarse en paracaídas ■ tirarse en paracaídas to parachute out of an airplane ■ to bail out of an airplane

lanzarse hacia ■ salir disparado para to make a beeline for ➤ Cuando los peques llegaron de la escuela, se lanzaron hacia la nevera. ■ Cuando los peques llegaron de la escuela, salieron disparados para la nevera. When the kids came home from school, they made a beeline for the refrigerator.

lanzar un globo sonda ■ *(plural)* lanzar globos sonda **1.** *(meteorología)* to send up a weather balloon **2.** *(política)* to send up a trial balloon **3.** *(general)* to send up a balloon probe

¡**lánzate a por ello(-a)!** go for it!

lapicera descartable *(Arg.)* ■ bolígrafo descartable disposable ballpoint pen

el **portaminas descartable** disposable mechanical pencil

lapidar a alguien por ■ matar a alguien a pedradas por to stone someone to death for

el **lápiz (de cera)** grease pencil

el **lápiz labial** lipstick

el **lapsus entre** gap between ➤ El lapsus entre intención y conducta... The gap between intention and behavior...

larga distancia long distance

larga singladura hacia la recuperación long road to recovery

largarse de casa to storm out of the house

largas horas long hours

¡**largo de aquí!** ■ ¡pírate! ■ ¡sal de aquí! beat it! ■ get out of here!

ser **largo de contar** to be a long story ➤ Es largo de contar. It's a long story.

largo y tendido ■ detalladamente ■ pormenorizadamente at great length

¡**larguémonos!** let's get out of here!

¡**las cosas tuyas!** the things you come up with!

las cuales which

las dos ■ ambas both (of them)

¡**las manos quietas!** keep your hands to yourself!

las más ■ las más veces most of the time

las más veces ■ lás más most of the time

lasca de silicio ■ chip de silicio silicon chip

lastimar la herida to aggravate the wound

lata abollada dented can ➤ La lata está abollada. The can is dented.

lata de cerveza 1. *(llena)* can of beer **2.** *(vacía)* beer can ➤ Alguien ha sugerido poner fotos de los maridos desaparecidos en las latas de cerveza. Someone has suggested putting photos of missing husbands on beer cans.

lata vacía de cerveza beer can

lateral derecho stage right

lateral izquierdo stage left

lavado de dinero ■ blanqueo de dinero money laundering

lavado en seco dry cleaning ➤ ¿Cómo funciona el lavado en seco? How does dry cleaning work?

lavar dinero ■ blanquear dinero to launder money

lavar el cerebro a alguien to brainwash someone

lavar los cacharros to wash the dishes

lavar su imagen to clean up one's image

lavarse las manos to wash one's hands

(le) agradezco su ayuda (a usted) I appreciate your help

(le) agradezco su llamada (a usted) I appreciate your call

¿**le atienden?** *(leísmo)* ■ ¿lo(-a) atienden? are you being helped? ■ is someone helping you?

le cambiará la vida 1. *(a usted)* it will change your life ■ it'll change your life **2.** *(a él)* it will change his life **3.** *(a ella)* it will change her life

le conozco (desde hace) mucho tiempo I have known him (for) a long time

¿**le da (a usted) tiempo a...?** ■ ¿tiene (usted) tiempo para...? do you have time to...?

le da golpes el corazón 1. *(a él)* his heart is pounding **2.** *(a ella)* her heart is pounding

le daba golpes el corazón 1. *(a él)* his heart was pounding ■ his heart pounded **2.** *(a ella)* her heart was pounding ■ her heart pounded

le daré (a usted) la última oportunidad I'll give you one last chance ■ I'll give you one more chance

¿**le despachan?** are you being helped? ■ have you been helped? ■ are you being served?

le dicen 1. *(a él)* they call him ■ he goes by **2.** *(a ella)* they call her ■ she goes by

le dice de mi parte que... ■ dígale de parte mía que... **1.** *(a él)* tell him for me (that) **2.** *(a ella)* tell her for me (that)

le dicen así por 1. *(a él)* he's named for **2.** *(a ella)* she's named for

le dio golpes el corazón 1. *(a él)* his heart pounded **2.** *(a ella)* her heart pounded

le diré que has llamado ■ le diré que llamaste **1.** *(a él)* I'll tell him you called **2.** *(a ella)* I'll tell her you called

le echo unos *x* años ■ le supongo unos *x* años ■ le doy unos *x* años **1.** *(a él)* I'd guess he's about *x* (years old) **2.** *(a ella)* I'd guess she's about *x* (years old)

le guste o no 1. *(a usted)* whether you like it or not **2.** *(a él)* whether he likes it or not **3.** *(a ella)* whether she likes it or not **4.** *(todos los contextos)* like it or not

¿**le han dicho a usted alguna vez que...?** has anyone ever told you that...? ➤ ¿Le han dicho a usted alguna vez que se parece a un famoso? Has anyone ever told you that you look like someone famous?

¿**le importa (a usted)?** would you mind? ➤ *(camarera al cliente)* ¿Le importa quitar las gafas de la mesa? Would you mind moving your glasses off the table?

¿**le importaría (a usted) si...?** *(expresa un poco de impaciencia)* do you *mind* if...

le convendría más (a usted)... ■ le quedaría mejor hacer algo you would be better off... ■ it would be better to... ➤ Le conviene más esperar. ■ Le quedaría mejor esperar. You would be better off waiting. ■ It would be better to wait.

le llaman por teléfono you're wanted on the (tele)phone

¿**le molesta (a usted) que le haga una pregunta?** do you mind if I ask you a question?

¿**le ocurre algo?** ■ ¿le pasa algo? is anything wrong?

le paso I'll connect you ■ I'll put you through

le quedan dos telediarios *(Esp., coloquial)* **1.** *(él)*he's on his last legs **2.** *(ella)* she's on her last legs

le supongo unos *x* años ■ le echo unos *x* años ■ le echaría unos *x* años **1.** *(a él)* I'd guess he's about *x* (years old) ■ I'd say he's about *x* (years old) **2.** *(a ella)* I'd guess she's about *x* (years old) ■ I'd say she's about *x* (years old) **3.** *(a usted)* I'd guess you're about *x* (years old) ■ I'd say you're about *x* (years old) ■ I'd guess you at about *x* (years old)

le tengo manía ■ le tengo tirria ■ me queda gordo ■ me cae gordo **1.** *(él)* I can't stand him **2.** *(ella)* I can't stand her

le va el trabajo en esto ■ se juega el trabajo en esto one's job is on the line because of this

le valió el premio ■ le ganó el premio **1.** *(a él)* it won him the prize ■ it garnered him the prize ■ it got him the prize **2.** *(a ella)* it won her the prize ■ it garnered her the prize ■ it got her the prize

le vendrá muy bien ■ le vendrá como anillo al dedo ■ le vendrá al pelo **1.** *(a él)* that will suit him fine ■ that will suit him to a T **2.** *(a ella)* that will suit her fine ■ that will suit her to a T

lealtades divididas ■ lealtades repartidas divided loyalties ➤ Fue un caso de lealtades divididas. ■ Fue un caso de lealtades repartidas. It was a case of divided loyalties.

leche desnatada skim milk
leche entera whole milk
leche semi-desnatada two-percent milk ▪ milk containing two percent milk fat
lecho de muerte deathbed
lecho de rosas bed of roses ▪ bowl of cherries ➤ La vida no es un lecho de rosas. Life is not a bed of roses. ▪ Life is no bed of roses ▪ Life is not a bowl of cherries. ▪ Life is no bowl of cherries.
lecho del Atlántico sea floor of the Atlantic ▪ Atlantic sea floor
lector asiduo ▪ asiduo lector regular reader ➤ Soy lector asiduo de su periódico. ▪ Soy asiduo lector de su periódico. I am a regular reader of your newspaper.
lector de CD ▪ reproductor de CD CD player
leer algo detenidamente to read something carefully ▪ to take one's time reading something ▪ to take one's time to read something
leer entre líneas to read between the lines
leer un libro de tapa a tapa ▪ leer un libro de cubierta a cubierta ▪ tragarse el libro entero ▪ leer hasta la dedicatoria de un libro ▪ leer un libro de principio a fin ▪ leer un libro de cabo a rabo to read a book from cover to cover ▪ to read a book all the way through ▪ to read a book from beginning to end ➤ Ella leyó el libro de tapa a tapa. ▪ Se tragó el libro. She read the book from cover to cover.
leer todo sobre ello to read all about it
leerle el pensamiento a alguien to read someone's mind ➤ Me estaba leyendo el pensamiento cuando bajó el estéreo. He was reading my mind when he turned down the stereo.
leerle la cartilla ▪ cantarle la cartilla ▪ cantarle las cuarenta to read someone the riot act
legitimar una firma ▪ dar fe de una firma ▪ legitimizar una firma to notarize a signature
leí en alguna parte que... I read somewhere that...
lejos de far from ▪ a long way from ➤ Vivo lejos de aquí. I live a long way from here.
estar **lejos de terminar** to be far from over
lengua bífida forked tongue
lengua desenfrenada: tener una ~ ▪ tener una lengua suelta to have an unbridled tongue ▪ to have a loose tongue
lengua derivada idioma derivado ▪ lengua hermana derivative language
lengua materna ▪ lengua nativa ▪ lengua propia ▪ idioma nativo mother tongue ▪ native language ▪ first language
lengua muerta dead language
lengua nativa ▪ lengua propia ▪ lengua materna native language ▪ first language ▪ mother tongue
lengua oficial ▪ idioma oficial official language
lengua suelta: tener una ~ ▪ tener una lengua desenfrenada to have a loose tongue ▪ to have an unbridled tongue
lengua vituperina acid tongue ▪ sharp tongue
el **lenguaje burdo** coarse language
el **lenguaje coloquial** ▪ (el) habla coloquial ▪ habla cotidiana colloquial speech ▪ everyday speech
el **lenguaje corporal** body language
lenguaje onírico ▪ lenguaje de los sueños language of dreams ▪ dream language ▪ oneiric language
lentes graduados ▪ lentes de prescripción prescription lenses ▪ prescription glasses
la **lentitud del proceso** slowness of the process
ser **lento al reaccionar** to be slow to react ▪ to have a slow reaction time
ser **lento al responder** to be slow to respond ➤ La alianza ha sido lenta al responder militarmente a los ataques. The alliance has been slow to respond militarily to the attacks.
estar **lento de reflejos** to be slow to react
ser **lento en reaccionar** ▪ tardar en reaccionar ▪ ser lento al reaccionar to be slow to react
león marino sea lion
¿les importa que me siente con ustedes? ▪ ¿les importa si me siento con ustedes? ▪ ¿les molesta que me siente con ustedes? ▪ ¿les molesta si me siento con ustedes? do you (all) mind if I sit with you?
les ruego paciencia (please) bear with me ➤ Lleva un minuto explicarlo, por eso les ruego paciencia. It takes a minute to explain this, so please bear with me.
la **lesión cerebral** brain injury
letra de cambio bill of exchange
letra mayúscula capital letter ▪ upper-case letter
letra minúscula lower-case letter ▪ *(coloquial)* little letter
letra muda silent letter ➤ En español, la "h" es muda. In Spanish, the "h" is silent.
letra pequeña fine print
el **letrero dice** ▪ la señal dice ▪ el cartel dice ▪ el letrero pone ▪ la señal pone ▪ el cartel pone the sign says
letrero luminoso 1. lighted sign 2. *(en billetes de dinero)* inscription
el **letrero pone** *(Esp.)* ▪ el letrero dice ▪ la señal pone ▪ la señal dice ▪ el cartel pone ▪ el cartel dice the sign says ➤ Mira, el letrero pone: subida al castillo. Look, the sign says: this way up to the castle.
estar **levantado desde...** to have been up since... ➤ ¿Estás levantado?-Sí, estoy levantado desde las siete menos cuarto. Are you up?-Yes, I've been up since a quarter to seven. ➤ Estoy levantado desde hace una hora. I've been up for an hour.
estar **levantado hasta las tantas** *(con ganas)* to stay up until the middle of the night ▪ to stay up until all hours (of the night) ▪ to stay up until the wee hours (of the night) ▪ to be up until all hours (of the night) ▪ to be up until the wee hours (of the night) ▪ to be up until the middle of the night ➤ En Madrid, solía estar levantado hasta las tres de la mañana para ver un programa de Nueva York. In Madrid, I used to stay up until 3 a.m. to watch a program from New York.
levantado hasta las tantas: quedarse ~ *(con o sin ganas)* to be up until all hours ➤ Anoche me quedé hasta las tantas intentando terminar un trabajo a tiempo para entregarlo hoy. I was up until all hours last night trying to get my paper finished in time to turn it in today. ➤ Me quedé levantado hasta la medianoche para ver el partido. I stayed up until midnight to watch the game.
levantar al público de sus asientos to bring the audience to its feet
levantar atestado de *(derecho)* to write up a report on
levantar campamento 1. levantar el campamento to break camp 2. juntar las cosas y partir (en la playa, por ejemplo) to gather one's things and leave 3. empacar y dejar un apartamento to close shop ➤ Necesito una semana después de que se acaben las clases para levantar campamento. ▪ I need a week after school is out to close shop here.
levantar el ánimo ▪ levantar el espíritu ▪ animar el espíritu to lift one's spirits ▪ to cheer up ➤ Tu carta me levantó el ánimo. Your letter lifted my spirits.
levantar (el) campamento to break camp
levantar en vilo a alguien to lift someone up (in the air)
levantar falso testimonio contra alguien ▪ calumniar a alguien to bear false witness against someone ▪ to slander someone ▪ *(literario)* to calumniate someone
levantar la liebre ▪ descubrir el pastel ▪ delatar to let the cat out of the bag ▪ to spill the beans
levantar la mesa ▪ recoger la mesa to clear the table ▪ to clear off the table ▪ to clean off the table
levantar la mirada ▪ levantar la vista ▪ levantar los ojos to look up
levantar la prohibición de viajar to lift the travel ban ▪ to raise the travel ban ▪ to lift the ban on travel ▪ to raise the ban on travel
levantar la sesión to adjourn the meeting ▪ to recess ➤ Se levanta la sesión. The meeting is adjourned.
levantar la vista ▪ levantar los ojos ▪ levantar la mirada to look up ▪ to raise one's eyes
levantar las sanciones impuestas a un país por to lift the sanctions on a country for ▪ to lift the sanctions against a country for ▪ to raise the sanctions on a country for ▪ to raise the sanctions against a country for
levantar los ojos ▪ levantar la vista ▪ levantar la mirada to look up ▪ to raise one's eyes
levantar polvareda ▪ levantar una polvareda to raise a rumpus ▪ to cause a stir ▪ to create a stir

levantar sospechas de que... ■ despertar sospechas de que... to raise suspicion(s) that... ■ to arouse suspicion(s) that... ■ to awaken suspicion(s) that... ■ to raise the suspicion that... ■ to arouse the suspicion that... ■ to awaken the suspicion that...

levantarle a uno los cascos to make one's head spin

levantarle el castigo a alguien to let someone off ■ to lift someone's punishment

levantarse a duras penas de la cama ■ apenas poder levantarse de la cama ■ casi no poder levantarse de la cama ■ prácticamente no poder levantarse de la cama to barely be able to get out of bed ■ to hardly be able to get out of bed ➤ Se levanta a duras penas de la cama por la mañana. ■ Apenas puede levantarse de la cama por la mañana. ■ Se levanta a duras penas de la cama por la mañana. ■ Casi no puede levantarse de la cama por la mañana. ■ Prácticamente no puede levantarse de la cama por la mañana. He can barely get out of bed in the morning. ■ He can hardly get out of bed in the morning.

levantarse de entre los muertos to rise from the dead

levantarse de la cama to get out of bed ➤ Se levanta a duras penas de la cama por la mañana. He can barely get out of bed in the morning.

levantarse de las cenizas to rise from the ashes

levantarse de un brinco ■ levantarse de un salto to jump to one's feet

levantarse de un salto ■ levantarse de un brinco to jump to one's feet

levantarse de una silla ■ alzarse de una silla to get up out of a chair

levantarse la tapa de los sesos to blow one's brains out

levar anclas to weigh anchor

la **ley de física** law of physics

la **ley de probabilidades** law of averages

ley del gallinero: ser la ~ to be the low man on the totem pole ■ (for) there to be a pecking order ➤ Acá es la ley del gallinero. As a new hire, you're the low man on the totem pole.

la **ley del silencio** silent treatment

la **ley del talón: ojo por ojo y diente por diente** an eye for an eye and a tooth for a tooth

la **ley física** law of physics ■ physical law

la **ley marcial** martial law

la **ley natural** natural law

la **ley seca** *(EE UU, 1920-33)* Prohibition

leyenda de celuloide legendary film ➤ La leyenda de celuloide del *Expreso de Medianoche* palidece ante la realidad de las cárceles turcas. The legendary film *Midnight Express* pales in comparison to the reality of the Turkish jails.

leyenda negra black legend: the tradition of religious and political persecution in Spain

las **leyes del movimiento de los planetas** *(Johannes Kepler)* laws of planetary motion

estar **liado con el trabajo** to be tied up with work ■ to be really busy with work

liar el tema ■ rizar el rizo to complicate matters

liar los bártulos ■ preparar los bártulos to pack up one's belongings ■ to pack up one's things

liarse la manta a la cabeza y... to take the plunge and... ■ to get up one's nerve and...

liberar los fondos to release the funds

la **libertad condicional** parole

la **libertad de moverse** freedom to move about

libra esterlina pound sterling ■ British pound

librarse en to be unleashed in ■ to be let loose in ■ to be fought in ■ to take place in ➤ La batalla por la Casa Blanca se libra mañana en el Tribunal Supremo de Florida. The battle for the White House will be fought tomorrow in the Florida Supreme Court.

librería de ocasión used bookstore ■ secondhand bookstore

ser un **libro abierto** ■ ser como un libro abierto to be an open book

libro de actas the minutes ■ the minutes book ■ the book containing the minutes

libro de apuntes ■ cuaderno de apuntes notebook

ser un **libro de la (misma) hostia** *(subida de tono)* ■ ser un libro jodidamente bueno ■ ser un libro de pinga ■ ser un libro de puta madre *(alternativa benigna)* ■ ser un libro estupendo to be a damned good book ■ to be one hell of a book ■ to be a great book ■ to be a wonderful book

libro de la vida *(secuenciación de ADN)* the blueprint of life ■ DNA map

libro de memorias scrap book

Libro de los muertos de Egipto Egyptian Book of the Dead

libro de oración común book of common prayer

ser un **libro de pinga** *(ligeramente subida de tono)* ■ ser un libro de la (misma) hostia ■ ser un libro jodidamente bueno ■ *(alternativo inofensivo)* ■ ser un libro estupendo to be damned good book ■ to be one hell of a book ■ to be a great book

libro de registro (del avión) log book

libro para colorear coloring book

libro sobre book about

libros sobre el bricolaje ■ libros sobre hágalo usted mismo do-it-yourself books

libros y amigos, pocos y buenos *(proverbio español)* books and friends, few and good

licencia poética poetic license

ser **licenciado(-a) en** to have a bachelor's degree in ➤ Es licenciada en filología hispánica por la Complutense. She has a bachelor's degree in Spanish from the Complutense.

licitar por algo en una subasta ■ pujar por algo en una subasta to bid on something at an auction ➤ Licitó muy alto por el piano alguna vez tocada por Alicia de la Rocha. He bid very high on the piano once played by Alicia de la Rocha.

lid política ■ competición política political contest

líder cívico(-a) ■ líder de la comunidad ■ líder en la comunidad civic leader ■ community leader ➤ Rigoberta Menchú es una líder cívica en su comunidad en Guatemala. ■ Rigoberta Menchú es una líder de su comunidad en Guatemala. Rigoberta Menchu is a leader in her community in Guatemala.

líder nato(-a) born leader ■ natural leader

las **lides del amor** affairs of the heart ■ matters of the heart

ligar bronce *(coloquial)* ■ tostarse ■ broncearse ■ dorarse to get a tan

ligarle las trompas (de Falopio) *(método de control de natalidad para mujeres)* to have one's (Fallopian) tubes tied ➤ Le ligaron las trompas. She had her tubes tied.

ligera pendiente slight slope

ligera ventaja slight advantage

ligeramente distinto slightly different

ser **ligero de cascos** 1. ser alegre de cascos ■ ser un casquivano to be scatterbrained 2. ser promiscuo to sleep around ■ to be promiscuous

lijar hacia la veta de la madera to sand with the grain of the wood ➤ Se lija hacia la veta de la madera. No se lija en contra de la veta. Sand with the grain of the wood. Don't sand across the grain of the wood.

limar diferencias 1. *(singular)*to smooth over one's differences 2. *(plural)* to smooth over ones' differences

limar las asperezas entre ■ limar asperezas entre to ease tensions between ➤ Clinton y Asad intentan limar asperezas entre Israel y Siria. Clinton and Asad try to ease tensions between Israel and Syria.

limitarse a cumplir órdenes simply to be following orders ■ just to be following orders

limitarse a decir que... simply to say that... ■ simply to tell someone that... ➤ Me limité a decirle que *(a él)* I simply told him that... ■ *(a ella)* I simply told her that...

el **límite de** 1. (el) borde de limit of 2. frontera de the border of ■ the border between ➤ En el límite de Virginia y Carolina del Norte On the border of Virginia and North Carolina ■ On the border between Virginia and North Carolina ■ On the Virginia-North Carolina border

el **límite de edad** age limit

el **límite de la propiedad** property line

el **límite de tiempo** time limit

el **límite de velocidad** speed limit

el **límite inferior de la escala** ■ extremo inferior de la escala lower end of the scale

los **límites de la propiedad** property boundaries ■ boundaries of the property

limítrofe con bordering on ➤ Países limítrofes con Colombia, incluyendo Ecuador y el Perú countries bordering on Colombia, including Ecuador and Peru
limpiado de minas mine clearance
limpiar algo a conciencia to clean something thoroughly ▪ to give something a thorough cleaning
limpiar lo que ha dejado alguien to clean up after someone
limpiar lo suyo to clean up after oneself ➤ Siempre limpio lo mío cuando uso la cocina. I always clean up after myself when I use the kitchen
limpiar los zapatos to shine one's shoes
limpieza étnica ethnic cleansing
ser **limpio como el oro** to be clean as a whistle ▪ to be spic and span
limpio como los chorros de oro clean as a whistle
estar **limpio(-a) de culpa** to be free of blame
los **limpios de corazón** the pure in heart
lindar con *(países, propiedades, parcelas, etc.)* ▪ colindar con to have a common border with ▪ to be adjacent to ▪ to have a common property line with
la **linde del bosque** edge of the forest ▪ edge of the woods
línea base baseline ➤ Para medir la distancia entre Marte y la Tierra, Cassini en 1677 utilizó la distancia entre Paris y Cayena, Guyana Francesa, como la línea base. In measuring the distance of Mars from the Earth, Cassini in 1677 used the distance from Paris to Cayenne, French Guiana, as the baseline.
línea de atrás *(tablero de ajedrez, damas)* back row
línea de mira ▪ línea de visión line of sight
línea de puntos: cortar por la ~ to cut along the dotted line
línea de puntos: doblar por la ~ to fold along the dotted line
línea de trabajo ▪ medio de trabajo line of work
línea de tratamiento stage of treatment ➤ En las primeras líneas de tratamiento. In the early stages of treatment.
línea de visión ▪ línea de mira line of sight
línea divisoría dividing line
línea fronteriza: cruzar la ~ to cross the border
línea recta straight line ➤ La línea recta es la distancia más corta entre dos puntos. A straight line is the shortest distance between two points.
linterna de mano flashlight
lío amoroso affair
lipoproteínas de alta densidad ▪ LAD ▪ colesterol bueno good cholesterol ▪ high-density lipoproteins ▪ HDL
lipoproteínas de baja densidad ▪ LBD ▪ colesterol malo bad cholesterol ▪ low-density lipoproteins ▪ LDL
lisiado(-a) de guerra disabled veteran
estar **liso como la mar serena** to be smooth as glass
lista de bodas ▪ listas de boda bridal registry
lista de causas alzadas calendar of appeals
lista negra blacklist
lista negra: poner a alguien en la ~ to blacklist someone ▪ to put someone on the blacklist ▪ to put somone's name on the blacklist
estar **listo(-a)** 1. estar preparado to be ready 2. estar apañado ▪ estar arreglado to be done for ▪ to have had it 3. estar hecho ▪ estar cocinado ▪ estar cocido to be done ➤ Estoy listo. ▪ Estoy preparado. I'm ready. ➤ *(L.am.)* No abras la puerta del horno, el pastel no está listo. ▪ *(Esp.)* No abras la puerta del horno, la tarta no está lista. ▪ Don't open the oven door. The cake's not done. ➤ *(Méx.)* El pay no está listo. ▪ *(Esp.)* El pastel no está listo. The pie's not done. ➤ ¡Estoy listo! ▪ ¡Estoy apañado! ▪ ¡Estoy arreglado! I'm done for! ▪ I've had it!
ser **listo(-a) como el diablo** to be smart as hell ▪ to be smart as the dickens
¡**listo el pollo!** mission accomplished!
estar **listo(-a) para hacer algo** to be ready to do something
estar **listo(-a) para ir** to be ready to go
estar **listo(-a) para pedir** to be ready to order ➤ Estamos listos para pedir. We're ready to order.
llamada del deber call of duty
llamada entrante incoming call
llamada interior inner calling
la **llamada no comunicó** the call didn't go through
llamadas que entraban incoming calls ▪ calls that were coming in ▪ calls which are coming in
llamadas que entran incoming calls ▪ calls that are coming in ▪ calls which are coming in
estar **llamado a fracasar** to be doomed to fail ▪ to be doomed to failure
estar **llamado(-a) a ser...** to be destined to be...
llamado(-a) así por... so named for...
llamado(-a) así porque so called because
llámalo equis ▪ llámalo hache call it what you will ▪ call it whatever you want ▪ call it whatever you will
llámalo hache ▪ llámalo equis call it what you will ▪ call it whatever you want ▪ call it whatever you will
llámame simplemente Paco just call me Frank
llámame y podemos quedar call me and we'll arrange a time to meet ▪ call me and we'll set up a time to meet
llaman a la puerta ▪ tocan a la puerta someone's knocking at the door
llamar a alguien aparte to call someone aside
llamar a alguien a hacer algo to call on someone to do something
llamar a alguien a mala hora ▪ llamar a alguien en mal momento to call someone at a bad time ▪ to catch someone at a bad time
llamar a alguien en el hombro to tap someone on the shoulder
llamar a alguien en mal momento ▪ llamar a alguien a mala hora to call someone at a bad time ▪ to catch someone at a bad time
llamar a alguien la atención por algo to tell someone off (for something he has done)
llamar a alguien por señas para que venga ▪ llamar a alguien por señas para que se acerque to motion to someone to come over ▪ to wave at someone to come over
llamar a cobro revertido ▪ llamar por cobrar to call collect
llamar a declarar to call to testify
llamar a filas to call to arms ▪ to call up reserves
llamar a la puerta to knock on the door
llamar a la unidad to call for unity
llamar a las cosas por su nombre to call a spade a spade
llamar a orden la reunión to call the meeting to order
llamar a voces to call out
llamar a un(-a) médico(-a) ▪ conseguir a un(-a) médico(-a) to call a doctor ▪ to get a doctor
llamar a la palestra a alguien ▪ llevarle a la palestra ▪ amonestar a alguien to call someone into action
llamar al pan, pan, y al vino, vino to call a spade a spade
llamar la atención a ▪ atraer la atención a to call attention to ▪ to draw attention to ▪ to attract attention to
llamar la atención a sí mismo(-a) to call attention to oneself ▪ to draw attention to oneself
llamar Dios a alguien for God to call someone home ▪ to die
llamar Dios a alguien por un camino for God to call someone for some purpose
llamar la atención to stand out ▪ to attract attention ➤ Lo que llevas puesto llama mucho la atención (de la gente). Your outfit is attracting a lot of attention. ▪ Your outfit is attracting people's attention.
llamar la atención de alguien to get someone's attention ▪ to attract one's attention
llamar la atención de alguien sobre algo to call someone's attention to something ▪ to call something to someone's attention ➤ Quiero llamar su atención sobre los cambios en la ley de impuestos. I want to call your attention to the changes in the tax law.
llamar para anular ▪llamar para cancelar to call to cancel ➤ Llamo para anular la reservación. ▪ Llamo para cancelar la reservación. I'm calling to cancel the reservation.
llamar por ayuda to call for help
llamar por lo del anuncio to call about the ad ▪ to call in response to the ad ➤ Llamo por lo del anuncio del piso. I'm calling about the ad in the paper for an apartment ▪ I'm calling in response to the ad in the paper for an apartment

llamar por señas a alguien to motion to someone to come over ■ to wave at someone to come over

llamar y anular llamar y cancelar to call and cancel ➤ Llamé y anulé la cita. ■ Llamé y cancelé la cita. I called and cancelled the appointment.

llamarada solar solar flare

llamarle a alguien por alguien to name someone for someone ■ to name someone after someone ➤ Le llamaron Tomás por su abuelo. They named him Thomas for his grandfather. ■ They named him Thomas after his grandfather.

llamarle la atención a alguien to tell someone off ■ to rebuke someone

llamar la atención de alguien to get someone's attention

llamarse decirle a uno to go by ■ to call ➤ Me llamo Maxwell pero me llaman Max. ■ Me llamo Maxwell pero me dicen Max. My name is Maxwell but I go by Max. ■ My name is Maxwell but they call me Max.

llamarse a sí mismo como to refer to oneself as ➤ Como se llaman a sí mismos As they refer to themselves ■ As they call themselves

llamársele por alguien ■ ponérsele por alguien *(all countries)* to be named after someone ■ *(Estados Unidos)* to be named for someone ➤ Se le llamó Tomás por su abuelo. ■ Se le puso Tomás por su abuelo. He was named Thomas for his grandfather. ■ He was named Thomas after his grandfather. ➤ Se la llama Virginia (el estado norteamericano) por la Reina Isabel Primera de Inglaterra. Virginia (the U.S. state) was named for Queen Elizabeth the First of England. ■ It was named Virginia after Queen Elizabeth the First of England.

llamativa falta de logros conspicuous lack of success

llámelo hache call it what you will ■ call it what you want

llaneza en el trato straightforwardness of manner ■ straightforward manner

llantas de aleación mag wheels

llanto de tambores *(poetic)* weeping of drums

llanura de inundación flood plain

llave completa *(lucha libre)* full nelson ➤ Mi oponente me sujetó con una llave completa. My opponent pinned me with a full nelson.

la **llave de la casa** house key ■ key to the house

la **llave de repuesto** spare key ■ extra key

la **llave del éxito** key to success

la **llave está puesta en la cerradura** the key is in the lock

llegado a este punto ■ llegado este punto ■ llegado tan lejos at this point ■ at this stage (of the game) ■ having come this far ➤ No podemos echarnos atrás llegados a este punto. ■ No podemos echarnos atrás llegado este punto. We can't retreat at this stage (of the game.) ■ We can't retreat at this point. ■ We can't retreat, having come this far. ➤ No puedo dejar mis estudios habiendo llegado tan lejos. ■ No puedo dejar mis estudios habiendo llegado hasta aquí. I can't quit school at this stage (of the game.) ■ I can't quit school at this point. ■ I can't quit school, having come this far.

llegado al caso for that matter ➤ Llegado al caso, no confiaría en el dueño del taller, ni en sus mecánicos. I wouldn't trust the owner of the shop or any of his mechanics, for that matter.

llegado al caso de que if (it happens that) ■ in the event that ➤ Las tarjetas rojas no deberían ser definitivas llegado al caso de que el jugador obtuvo la roja por la acumulación de dos amarillas. Red cards should not be binding if the player got them by accumulating two yellows. ■ A red card should not be binding in the event that the player got it by accumulating two yellows.

llegado este punto ■ llegado a este punto having come this far ■ at this point ■ at this stage (of the game) ➤ No puedo dejar mis estudios llegado este punto. I can't quit school, having come this far. ■ I can't quit school at this point. ■ I can't quit school at this stage (of the game.)

llegar a 1. to arrive in ■ to arrive at 2. llegar hasta ■ durar hasta to last until 3. alcanzar a to reach

(llegar a) acostumbrarse to become accustomed ■ to get accustomed ■ to get used to

llegar a casa to get home ■ to arrive home

llegar a conocer a alguien to get to know someone ■ to get acquainted with someone ■ to become acquainted with someone

llegar a convencerse de algo to become convinced of something

llegar a convencerse de que... ■ convencerse de que... to become convinced that...

llegar a convertirse en una cara familiar para el público to become a familiar face to the public

llegar a dársele muy bien algo to get good at doing something ■ to become proficient in something ■ to become proficient at something ➤ Al joven ha llegado a dársele muy bien las matemáticas. The youth has become very proficient in mathematics. ■ The youth has become very proficient in mathematics.

llegar a dársele muy bien hacer algo to become proficient at doing something ➤ Ha llegado a dársele muy bien lanzar el disco, y a su perro se le ha llegado a dar muy bien cogerlo. He's become very proficient at throwing the frisbee, and his dog has become proficient at catching it.

llegar a decir que... to go so far as to say that... ➤ Llegaría a decir que... I would go so far as to say that...

llegar a decirle a alguien que... to go so far as to tell someone... ➤ Ella llegó a decirme que... She went so far as to tell me that...

llegar a entender algo 1. to come to understand something 2. to figure out something ■ to figure something out ➤ *(el entrevistador al autor famoso)* No he llegado a entender si usted cree en Dios o es Dios quien cree en usted. I haven't figured out whether you believe in God or God believes in you.

llegar a fin de mes to make ends meet ➤ Por ser que son pobres, logran llegar a fin de mes. For being poor, they manage to make ends meet.

llegar a hacerse fluido en un idioma ■ soltarse en un idioma ■ volverse fluido en un idioma ■ hacerse fluido en un idioma ■ to become fluent in a language

llegar a la conclusión de que to come to the conclusion that ■ to arrive at the conclusion that ■ to conclude that

llegar a la escena de un accidente ■ llegar al lugar de un accidente to arrive at the scene of an accident

llegar a la lista de los más vendidos ■ llegar a la lista best-seller to make the best-seller list

llegar a la mayoría de edad to come of age

llegar a la superficie to reach the surface

llegar a las armas to turn into an armed conflict

llegar a las manos ■ llegar a las armas ■ liarse a mamporros to come to blows

llegar a los oídos de alguien que... (for word) to reach someone that... ■ (for someone) to receive word that... ➤ A todo esto, había llegado a oídos del reporteo... While all this was going on, word reached the reporter that... ■ While all this was going on, the reporter received word that...

llegar a manos to come to blows

llegar a mayores to come to blows

llegar a mencionar to go so far as to mention

llegar a mesa puesta ■ venir a mesa puesta to come home to a set table

llegar a obtener un buen manejo de algo to become proficient with something ➤ Mi hermano ha llegado a conseguir un buen manejo del torno. My brother has become very proficient with a lathe.

llegar a saber to come to know

llegar a ser to become ■ to go on to become

llegar a ser famoso(-a) ■ hacerse famoso(-a) to become famous

llegar a ser presidente ■ volverse presidente ■ hacerse presidente to become president

llegar a tanto para to go to such lengths to

llegar a tener to come to have ➤ Un agnóstico de joven, San Agustín llegó a tener una profunda espiritualidad. An agnostic as a young man, St. Augustine came to have a deep spirituality.

llegar a tener fluidez en inglés ■ llegar a tener un buen dominio en inglés ■ llegar a tener un buen dominio del inglés to become fluent in English ■ to become proficient in English ■ to develop a good command of English

llegar a tiempo ■ llegar en punto to arrive on time

llegar a tiempo para algo to arrive in time for something ➤ Llegamos a tiempo para la cena. ■ Llegamos a tiempo para cenar.

We arrived in time for supper. ▪ We arrived in time to have supper. ▪ We arrived in time to eat supper.

llegar a tiempo para hacer algo to arrive in time to do something

llegar a un acuerdo to reach an agreement ▪ to come to an agreement

llegar a un concierto 1. *(literal)* to arrive at a concert **2.** *(arcaico)* llegar a un acuerdo to reach an accord ▪ to reach an agreement

llegar a un lugar 1. *(dentro de una comarca)* to arrive in a place **2.** *(un punto)* to arrive at a place ▪ to get to a place ➤ Llegamos a Atlanta a las 3 p.m. We arrived in Atlanta at 3 p.m. ▪ We arrived at Atlanta at 3 p.m. ▪ We got to Atlanta at 3 p.m. ➤ Llegamos al aeropuerto a las 3 p.m. We arrived at the airport at 8 a.m. ▪ We got to the airport at 8 a.m.

llegar a un punto decisivo to come to a head

llegar a un sitio con alguien 1. avanzar un tema con alguien to get somewhere with someone **2.** arribar con alguien a un lugar to arrive somewhere with someone ➤ ¿Has llegado a algún sitio con el jefe hoy? Did you get anywhere with the boss today?

llegar a una conclusión ▪ sacar una conclusión to come to a conclusion ▪ to arrive at a conclusion ▪ to draw a conclusion ➤ ¿A qué conclusiones has llegado con tu estudio? What conclusions have you drawn from your study? ➤ De nuestro estudio hemos llegado a varias conclusiones. From our study we have arrived at several conclusions.

llegar al colmo to have all one can take ➤ He llegado al colmo. I've had all I can take.

llegar al conocimiento de alguien to come to someone's attention

llegar al fondo del asunto ▪ llegar al punto del asunto to get to the bottom of the matter ▪ to get to the heart of the matter

llegar al fondo del océano to reach the bottom of the ocean ▪ to get to the bottom of the ocean ➤ Una bola de acero de una libra, que se deja caer al océano sobre la Fosa Marianas, tarda sesenta y tres minutos en llegar al fondo. A one-pound steel ball, dropped into the ocean above the Marianas Trench, takes sixty-three minutes to get to the bottom. ▪ A one-pound steel ball, dropped into the ocean above the Marianas Trench, takes sixty-three minutes to reach the bottom.

llegar al lugar del accidente to arrive on the scene of the accident

llegar al mundo ▪ venir al mundo ▪ nacer to come into the world ▪ to be born

llegar al poder ▪ acceder al poder to come to power

llegar al punto de cocción 1. to start to cook ▪ to reach the temperature at which cooking begins **2.** to come to a boil

llegar al punto de ebullición to come to a boil ▪ to reach the boiling point

llegar antes ▪ llegar primero **1.** *(aquí)* to get here first ▪ to arrive (here) first ▪ *(especialmente en una cola o fila)* to be here first **2.** *(allí)* to get there first ▪ to arrive first ➤ Ella llegó antes. She got here first. ▪ She was here first.

llegar antes de lo programado ▪ llegar antes de lo previsto **1.** *(aquí)* to get here ahead of schedule ▪ to get here early ▪ to arrive (here) ahead of schedule ▪ to arrive (there) early **2.** *(allí)* to get there ahead of schedule ▪ to get there early ▪ to arrive (there) ahead of schedule ▪ to arrive (there) early

llegar como bajado del cielo ▪ aparecer como bajado del cielo ▪ venirle como agua de mayo ▪ venirle como caído del cielo ▪ ser agua de mayo to be a Godsend

llegar con dificultad a fin de mes ▪ apenas salir a flote to have a hard time making it to the end of the month ▪ to have a hard time making it through the month

llegar corriendo ▪ llegar a la carrera ▪ llegar deprisa y corriendo to come running in

llegar de improviso to arrive unexpectedly ▪ to call on someone unexpectedly

llegar de regreso de ▪ volver de ▪ regresar de to come back from ▪ to return from

llegar deprisa y corriendo ▪ llegar corriendo to come running in

llegar primero *(en una carrera)* to come in first ▪ to come in in first place ➤ Lance Armstrong llegó primero. Lance Armstrong came in first.

llegar en mal momento to arrive at a bad time ▪ to get here at a bad time ▪ to come at a bad time

llegar hasta ▪ llegar a **1.** to go as far as **2.** to last until ➤ Esta calle sólo llega a Plaza de Castilla. This street only goes as far as the Plaza de Castilla. ▪ This street only goes to the Plaza de Castilla.

llegar para to be enough for

llegar para quedarse to catch on ➤ La canción de Javier llegó para quedarse. Javier's song caught on.

llegar profundamente a alguien ▪ realmente llegar a alguien to (really) get to someone ➤ El libro *(Noche)* de Elle Wiesel llegó profundamente a la clase. Elie Wiesel's *Night* really got to the class. ➤ Esa música realmente me llegó. ▪ Esa música me llegó profundamente. That music really got to me. ➤ *(a él)* Le llegó profundamente. That really got to him. ➤ *(a ella)* Le llegó profundamente. That really got to her.

llegar pronto *(Esp.)* ▪ llegar temprano **1.** *(allí)* to get there early ▪ to be early ▪ to arrive early **2.** *(aquí)* to get here early ▪ to be early ▪ to arrive early

llegar segundo *(en una carrera)* ▪ llegar en segundo puesto to come in second ▪ to come in in second place ➤ Llegó en el puesto dos. He came in second.

llegar tarde a cenar to be late for supper

llegar tarde a comer to be late for dinner

llegar tarde a la escuela to be late for school

llegar tarde a una cita to be late for an appointment ▪ to arrive at one's appointment late

llegar temprano *(L.am.)* ▪ llegar pronto **1.** *(allí)* to get there early ▪ to be early ▪ to arrive early **2.** *(aquí)* to get here early ▪ to be early ▪ to arrive early

llegar y besar al santo 1. to get it right on the first try **2.** to score (sexually) right off the bat

llegaría el avión: (yo)no sabía a qué hora ~ ▪ (yo) no sabía a qué hora iba a llegar el avión I didn't know what time the airplane would arrive ▪ I didn't know what time the airplane was going to arrive

llegarle al alma algo ▪ sentir algo vivamente to really get to someone ▪ to get to someone ▪ to affect someone deeply

llegarle la hora a uno ▪ llegarle su hora (for) one's time to come ➤ Le ha llegado la hora (a él). ▪ Le llegó su hora (a él). His time has come.

llegarse a creer algo to come to believe something

llegarse hasta ▪ llegarse a to run down to ▪ to run over to

llegó la hora this is it

llegué, vi y vencí *(Julio Cesar)* ▪ vine, vi y vencí ▪ vini, vidi, vici I came, I saw, I conquered

llenar de esperanza to fill with hope ➤ Mi amigo me llenó de esperanza. My friend filled me with hope.

llenar el depósito 1. *(Esp.)* to fill the gas tank **2.** *(L.am., se refiere a cualquier líquido)* to fill the tank **3.** llenar la bodega to fill the warehouse

llenar el tanque *(se refiere a cualquier líquido)* to fill the tank

llenar el tanque de combustible to fill the tank (with fuel) ▪ to fill up

llenarse de júbilo al enterarse de que... ▪ llenarse de alegría al enterarse de que... to be overjoyed to learn that... ▪ to be overjoyed to find out that...

llenarse de júbilo al oír que... *(culto, literario)* ▪ alegrarse al oír que... ▪ llenarse de alegría al oír que... to be overjoyed to hear that... ▪ to be overjoyed when one hears that...

llenarse de júbilo al pensar que... *(culto, literario)* ▪ alegrarse al pensar que... ▪ llenarse de alegría al pensar que... to be overjoyed at the thought that... ▪ to be overjoyed to think that...

llenarse de valor para ▪ juntar valor para ▪ hacer acopio de valor para to get up the nerve to...

estar **lleno de desafíos** ▪ estar cargado de desafíos ▪ estar lleno de pruebas y desafíos to be full of challenges ▪ to be filled with challenges

lleva el subjuntivo it takes the subjunctive

lleva en la nevera ▪ ha estado en la nevera it's been in the refrigerator (for)... ➤ Debería estar frío. Lleva cuatro horas en la nevera. ▪ Debería estar frío. Ha estado en la nevera cuatro horas. It should be cold. It's been in the refrigerator for four hours.

lleva por título the title is ▪ it is entitled

llevar a alguien a hacer algo to prompt someone to do something ➤ La Batalla de Antietam fue el punto determinante en la Guerra Civil Americana, llevando a Lincoln a anunciar la Proclamación de Emancipación. The Battle of Antietam was the turning point in the American Civil War, prompting Lincoln to announce the Emancipation Proclamation.

llevar a alguien a juicio ■ llevar a alguien a la barra to take someone to court

llevar a alguien a la barra ■ llevar a juicio a alguien to take someone to court

llevar a alguien a la puerta ■ acompañar a alguien a la puerta to show someone to the door ■ to see someone to the door ■ to go with someone to the door ■ to accompany someone to the door ➤ Los llevó a la puerta. ■ Los acompañó a la puerta ■ *(Esp., leísmo)* Les llevó a la puerta. ■ Les acompañó a la puerta. He showed them to the door. ■ He saw them to the door. ■ He went with them to the door. ■ He accompanied them to the door. ➤ Cuando María me lo pidió, la acompañé a la puerta, y allí me dio un beso. When she asked me (to), I showed Mary to the door, and there she gave me a kiss. ■ When she asked me (to), I saw Mary to the door, and there she gave me a kiss. ■ When she asked me (to), I went with Mary to the door, and there she gave me a kiss. ■ When she asked me (to), I accompanied Mary to the door, and there she gave me a kiss.

llevar a alguien a la vicaria ■ llevar a alguien al altar ■ casarse con alguien to take someone to the altar ■ to marry someone

llevar a alguien a rastras ■ arrastrar a alguien (cogido) por los pelos ■ arrastrar a alguien (cogido) de los pelos to drag someone by the heels ➤ Prácticamente tuvimos que llevar a mi tía a rastras para hacer que vaya al médico. ■ Prácticamente tuvimos que arrastrar a mi tía por los pelos para hacer que vaya al médico. ■ Prácticamente tuvimos que arrastrar a mi tía de los pelos para hacer que vaya al médico. We practically had to drag my aunt by the heels to get her to go to the doctor.

llevar a alguien al huerto to seduce someone ■ to have sex with someone ■ to lead someone down the garden path

llevar a alguien en andas to be very attentive to someone

llevar a alguien en palmitas ■ tener a alguien en palmitas ■ traer a alguien en palmitas ■ tener a alguien entre algodones to wait on someone hand and foot ➤ Ella le lleva en palmitas. ■ Ella le tiene en palmitas. ■ Ella le tiene entre algodones. ■ Ella le trae en palmitas. ■ Ella le tiene entre algodones. ■ Ella le trae entre algodones. ■ Ella le lleva entre algodones. She waits on him hand and foot.

llevar a alguien hacia atrás en el tiempo ■ transportar a alguien hacia atrás en el tiempo to take one back in time ➤ Esta película te lleva hacia atrás en el tiempo. ■ Esta película te transporta hacia atrás en el tiempo. This film takes you back in time. ➤ Mirar a través del telescopio te lleva hacia atrás en el tiempo. ■ El telescopio te transporta hacia atrás en el tiempo. Looking through a telescope takes you back in time.

llevar a alguien al altar ■ llevar a alguien a la vicaría ■ casarse con alguien to take someone to the altar ■ to take someone down the aisle ■ to marry someone

llevar a bordo to carry on board

llevar a cabo ■ llevar al cabo to carry out

llevar a cabo la ley ■ aplicar la ley to enforce the law

llevar a cabo un recuento ■ hacer un recuento to do a recount

llevar a cabo una excelente labor *(florido)* ■ hacer un trabajo excelente to do an excellent job

llevar a cabo una serie de pruebas médicas a alguien to run a battery of (medical) tests on someone

llevar a cabo venturosamente to carry out successfully ■ successfully to carry out

llevar a cuestas la carga ■ aguantar la carga ■ soportar la carga to bear the burden

llevar a juicio a alguien to take someone to court

llevar a la espalda algo to carry something on one's back

llevar a la iglesia a una mujer to march a woman down the aisle ■ to take a woman down the aisle

llevar a un lugar ■ dirigirse a un lugar ■ conducir a un lugar ■ salir a un lugar to go to ■ to take you to ■ to lead to ➤ Esta carretera lleva hasta Toluca. ■ Esta carretera se dirige a Toluca. ■ Esta carretera conduce a Toluca. ■ Esta carretera sale a Toluca. This road goes to Toluca. ■ This road takes you to Toluca. ■ This road leads to Toluca.

llevar a una guerra civil to lead to a civil war

llevar adelante to go on with ■ to proceed with

llevar al cabo ■ llevar a cabo to carry out

llevar al paredón to send before a firing squad

llevar algo a buen puerto to carry something to a successful conclusion

llevar algo a cuestas ■ llevar algo a espaldas to carry something on one's back

llevar algo a efecto ■ llevar algo a cabo to put something into effect ■ to carry out something

llevar algo a la espalda to carry something on one's back

llevar algo a la práctica ■ poner algo en práctica to put something into practice

llevar algo bien to take something well

llevar algo en andas *(implica dos o más personas)* to carry something with a platform on one's shoulders

llevar algo en bandolera to wear something across one's chest

llevar algo entre manos to be working on something ➤ Lo llevamos entre manos. We're working on it.

llevar allí... ■ estar allí desde hace... to have been there for... ➤ Llevan un año allí. ■ Están allí desde hace un año. They've been there for a year.

llevar antifaz ■ llevar disfraz ■ llevar una careta to wear a mask ➤ Llevaban antifaz. ■ Llevaban disfraces They were wearing masks.

llevar aparte a alguien to take someone aside

llevar aquí... ■ estar aquí desde hace... to have been here for... ➤ Llevo cuatro meses aquí. ■ Estoy aquí desde hace cuatro meses. I've been here for four months.

llevar bordado en la manga to be sewn onto the sleeve

llevar cambio consigo ■ llevar cambio ■ tener cambio to have any change on one ■ to have any change ➤ ¿Llevas cambio contigo? ■ ¿Lleva (usted) cambio consigo? Do you have any change on you?

llevar comisión to get a commission

llevar cuentas to keep a record of one's expenses ➤ ¿Llevas cuentas? Do you keep a record of your expenses?

llevar disfraz ■ llevar antifaz to wear a mask ➤ Llevaban disfraces. ■ Llevaban antifacec. They were wearing masks.

llevar el agua a su molino ■ echar el agua a su molino to steer the conversation toward one's interests ■ to be on the make

llevar el ejército a la batalla to lead the army into battle

llevar el gato al agua to pull it off ➤ Oscar llevó el gato al agua. Oscar pulled it off.

llevar el marcador ■ llevar la cuenta (del marcador) ■ llevar el tanteo to keep score

llevar el paso *(se refiere a marchar o bailar)* to keep in step ■ to stay in step

llevar el pelo corto to have short hair ■ to wear one's hair short

llevar el pelo cortado al cepillo to have a crew cut ■ to wear one's hair in a crew cut

llevar el pelo largo to have long hair ■ to wear one's hair long

llevar el pero de una conversación ■ ser el único en hablar to do all the talking

llevar el peso de algo to bear the brunt of something ➤ El presidente lleva el peso de las críticas. The president bears the brunt of the criticism.

llevar el tanteo ■ llevar el marcador ■ llevar la cuenta (del marcador) to keep score

llevar el timón ■ tomar el timón to take the helm

llevar la bandera to fly the flag

llevar la camisa por fuera (del pantalón) to wear one's shirttail out ➤ De todas las camisas que puedo llevar por fuera, ésta es la única que tiene cuello. Of all my shirts that can be worn with the tails out, this (one) is the only one that has a collar.

llevar la batuta to run the show ■ to be the head honcho

llevar la cuenta (de algo) to keep track (of something)

llevar la cuenta (del marcador) ■ llevar el marcador ■ llevar el tanteo to keep score

llevar la guardia alta to keep one's guard up ■ to keep up one's guard

llevar la peor parte ■ llevarse lo peor to get the worst of it

llevar la puntuación ■ llevar el tanteo ■ llevar el marcador to keep score

llevar la voz cantante to call the shots ■ to have the say ■ to be the boss

llevar las de ganar to be favored to win

llevar las de perder to be the underdog ■ to be expected to lose ■ to be predicted to lose

llevar las riendas ■ ejercer el control to take the reins ■ to take command of the situation

llevar lentillas to wear contact lenses

llevar leña al monte ■ echar agua en el mar to carry coals to Newcastle

llevar lo peor to get the worst of it

llevar los pantalones ■ llevar los calzones to wear the pants ➤ Si yo me casara, dejaría que mi mujer llevara los pantalones, siempre que ella me dejase hacer lo que me diera la gana. If I got married, I'd let my wife wear the pants so long as she let me do anything I wanted.

llevar mal una cosa to take something badly ■ to be offended by something

llevar mucho tiempo en algo to have been doing something for a long time ■ to have been at something for a long time ➤ Llevo mucho tiempo en esto. I've been doing this for a long time. ■ I've been at this for a long time.

llevar muletas ■ andar en muletas to walk with crutches ■ to walk on crutches

llevar muy bien sus estudios to do very well in one's studies ■ to do very well in school

llevar por mal camino to lead astray

llevar por título 1. *(libro)* to be entitled **2.** *(persona)* to bear the title (of) ➤ Lleva por título Caballero del Imperio Británico. He bears the title of Knight of the British Empire (KBE).

llevar (puesto) *(ropa, joyería)* ■ tener puesto algo ■ ir en algo ■ ir de algo ■ ponerse algo to have on something ■ to be wearing something ➤ El torero lleva puesta una montera. The bullfighter is wearing a (bullfighter's) cap. ➤ (Ella) llevaba un traje de baño. ■ (Ella) iba de traje de baño. ■ (Ella) iba en traje de baño. She was wearing a bathing suit. ➤ (Ella) llevaba cuero. ■ (Ella) iba de cuero. She was wearing leather. ➤ (Él) llevaba un anillo. ■ (Él) se había puesto un anillo. He was wearing a ring.

llevar retraso en el trabajo ■ estar atrasado con el trabajo to be behind in one's work ➤ Llevo retraso en el trabajo. ■ Estoy atrasado con el trabajo. ■ Estoy atrasado con mi trabajo. I'm behind in my work.

llevar rumbo a un lugar ■ seguir rumbo a un lugar ■ estar de camino a un lugar to be on one's way to a place ➤ Llevamos rumbo al cine. ■ Seguimos rumbo al cine. We're on our way to the movies.

llevar su curso to take its course

llevar tiempo en el hospital desde... ■ haber estado en el hospital desde... to have been in the hospital since... ➤ Lleva en el hospital desde el viernes después de tu partida. ■ Ha estado en el hospital desde el viernes después de tu partida. He's been in the hospital since the Friday after you left.

llevar tiempo haciendo algo ■ hace tiempo que uno está haciendo algo to have been doing something for a certain time ➤ Llevo media hora preparando la cena. I've been fixing supper for the past half hour. ➤ (Él) lleva tres semanas fuera. He's been gone (for) three weeks. ➤ Llevo cinco años usando estos zapatos. I've worn these shoes for five years. ■ I've been wearing these shoes for five years.

llevar tiempo usando ropa to have worn clothes ■ to have been wearing clothes ➤ Llevo cinco años usando estos zapatos. ■ Llevo cinco años usando estos zapatos. I've worn these shoes for five years. ■ I've been wearing these shoes for five years.

llevar tiempo usando un medicamento to have been taking a medication ■ to have been on a medication ➤ Lleva un año usando antiinflamatorios. He's been taking anti-inflammatories. ■ He's been on anti-inflammatories.

llevar un anillo ■ usar un anillo to wear a ring ➤ (Ella) lleva un anillo. She wears a ring.

llevar un día de perros ■ tener un día de perros to have a lousy day

llevar un negocio to run a business

llevar un registro de to keep a record of

llevar un...tren de vida to live a...life

llevar una carga 1. to carry a load **2.** to bear a heavy load

llevar una empresa to run a business ■ to operate a business ➤ La compañía que lleva el aeropuerto The company that runs the airport ■ The company that operates the airport

llevar una mala mano (de cartas) 1. tener una mala mano (de cartas) to have a bad hand (of cards) ■ to be dealt a bad hand of cards **2.** tener cartas que no pueden ganar ni por asomo to have a losing hand (of cards) ■ to be dealt a losing hand of cards

llevar una vida activa to lead an active life

llevar una vida ascética to live an ascetic life

llevar una vida de clase media to live a middle class life ➤ El agente doble llevaba una vida de clase media en uno de los barrios residenciales de las afueras de Washington. The double agent lived a middle class life in a Washington suburb.

llevar una vida de perros ■ llevar una vida perruna to lead a dog's life

llevar una vida normal to lead a normal life

llevar una vida muy corta 1. to live a short life ■ to die young **2.** not to have been living very long ■ to be young

llevar ventaja ■ to be ahead ➤ Boca Juniors llevaba la ventaja en el medio tiempo. Boca Juniors was ahead at halftime.

llevar horas de adelanto sobre to be hours ahead of ■ to be hours later than ➤ Madrid lleva seis horas de adelanto sobre Nueva York. Madrid is six hours ahead of New York. ■ It is six hours later in Madrid than (it is) in New York.

llevar puntos de ventaja sobre el otro equipo ■ estar (a) tantos puntos por delante del otro equipo ■ ir (a) tantos puntos por delante del otro equipo to be so many points ahead of the other team ■ to be ahead of the other team by so many points ➤ Boca Juniors lleva cuatro puntos de ventaja sobre el otro equipo. Boca Juniors is four points ahead of the other team.

llevar tanto tiempo hacer algo ■ tardar tanto tiempo en hacer algo to take a certain time to do something ➤ Después de ser disparado por Bonnie y Clyde, le llevó a una de sus víctimas tres días morir. After being shot by Bonnie and Clyde, it took one of their victims three days to die.

llevar una hora ■ tardarse una hora to take an hour (for) ➤ Lleva una hora en secar la pintura. ■ Lleva una hora para que (se) seque la pintura. ■ Se tarda una hora para que (se) seque la pintura. It takes an hour for the paint to dry.

llevarla con alfileres ■ llevarla cogido con pinzas to just barely get by (in a course)

llevarle a alguien a rastras to drag someone

llevarle a alguien una ventaja to have an advantage over someone

llevarle a la palestra ■ llamarle a la palestra ■ amonestar a alguien to call someone on the carpet

llevarle a uno a creer ■ conducirle a uno a creer to lead one to believe

llevarle a uno a la cima to take one to the top

llevarle años a alguien to many years older than someone ■ to be a lot older than someone

llevarle de paseo 1. *(a él)* to take him for a walk **2.** *(a ella)* to take her for a walk

llevarle la contra a alguien to contradict someone

llevarle la contraria a alguien to keep contradicting someone

llevarle para siempre hacer algo to take forever to do something ➤ Me está llevando para siempre resolver estos problemas de matemáticas. It's taking me forever to do these math problems.

llevarle por el mal camino a alguien to lead someone astray

llevarle una hora ■ tomarle una hora to take an hour (to) ■ to take one hour (to) ➤ Me llevó una hora bajar este puñetero correo electrónico. ■ Me tomó una hora bajar este puñetero correo electrónico. It took me an hour to download this blasted E-mail.

llevarle *x* años a alguien to be *x* years older than someone ➤ Mi hermano me lleva dos años y medio. My brother is two-and-a-half years older than I (am).

llevarle *x* puntos a alguien to be *x* points ahead of someone

llevarlo a uno a preguntarse to prompt one to wonder ➤ Me lleva a preguntarme si... It raises the question (for me) whether... ▪ It prompts me to wonder whether...

llevarlo a uno a un lugar to take one to a place ➤ *(al taxista)* Nos lleva al Hotel Olid Melia, por favor. Take us to the Olid Melia Hotel, please.

llevarlo peor to take it the worst ➤ Su madre era la que lo llevaba peor. His mother was the one who took it the worst.

llevarse a matar con alguien *(Esp.)* ▪ llevarse a las malas con alguien ▪ estar a matar con alguien to be at loggerheads with someone

llevarse algo por delante to run into something ▪ to collide with something ▪ to hit something ➤ Era de noche y me llevé por delante un bache y quedé con la rueda desinflada. ▪ Era de noche y me llevé un bache por delante y quedé con la rueda desinflada. When it was dark I hit a pothole and I got a flat tire.

llevarse bien ▪ entenderse bien to get along well (together) ▪ to get along great (together) ➤ Se entienden muy bien. ▪ Se llevan muy bien. They get along well (together). ▪ They get along great (together.)

llevarse como el perro y el gato to get along like dogs and cats

llevarse de maravilla ▪ llevarse magníficamente bien to get along famously (together) ➤ Nos llevamos de maravilla. ▪ Nos llevamos magníficamente bien. We get along famously.

llevarse el día en algo ▪ llevarse todo el día en algo to spend the (whole) day on something ▪ to spend the (whole) day doing something

llevarse el gato al agua to pull it off

llevarse el primer premio to take first prize ▪ to carry off first prize

llevarse la mayor sorpresa de su vida to get the surprise of one's life ➤ Va a llevarse la mayor sorpresa de su vida. He's going to get the surprise of his life.

llevarse la mejor tajada to get the lion's share

llevarse las miradas de todos to command all eyes

llevarse magníficamente bien ▪ llevarse de maravilla to get along famously (together) ➤ Nos llevamos magníficamente bien ▪ Nos llevamos de maravilla. We get along famously.

llevarse mal not to get along ➤ Se llevan mal. They don't get along.

llevarse su almuerzo a la escuela ▪ llevarse su comida a la escuela to take one's lunch to school

llevarse su merecido to get what ones deserves ▪ to get one's just desserts

llevarse tajada ▪ sacar tajada to get one's share

llevarse todo el día en algo ▪ llevarse el día en algo to spend the (whole) day on something ▪ to spend the (whole) day doing something

llevarse un berrinche ▪ hacer un berrinche ▪ coger un berrinche to have a fit

llevarse un botín de to make off with ▪ to escape with ▪ to get away with ➤ Los atracadores, que consiguieron huir, se llevaron un botín de once millones de pesetas. The assailants, who managed to flee, made off with eleven million pesetas.

llevarse un chasco ▪ llevarse un buen chasco ▪ pegarse un (buen) chasco to be disappointed ▪ to feel let down

llevarse una buena impresión (for) someone to make a good impression on one ▪ to come away with a good expression of someone ▪ to get a good impression of someone ➤ Me llevé una buena impresión del nuevo maestro. The new teacher made a good impression on me. ▪ I came away with a good impression of the new teacher.

llevarse una impresión to get an impression ➤ ¿Cómo te llevaste esa impresión? How did you get that impression?

llevárselo consigo to take it with one ➤ (Ella) se lo llevó consigo. She took it with her. ➤ Me lo llevé conmigo. I took it with me.

llevárselo consigo a casa to take it home with one ➤ Se lo llevó consigo a casa. *(él)* He took it home with him. ▪ *(ella)* She took it home with her.

llevárselo de vuelta a to take it back to

¿llevas cambio (encima)? ▪ ¿tienes suelto (encima)? do you have any change (on you)?

¡llévatelo! take it! ▪ it's yours!

¡llévatelo por sólo diez dolares! it's yours for just ten dollars!

llevo usando ▪ llevo gastando I've worn ▪ I've been wearing ➤ Llevo cinco años usando estos zapatos. ▪ Llevo cinco años gastando estos zapatos. I've worn these shoes for five years. ▪ I've been wearing these shoes for five years.

llorar a lágrima viva to cry like a baby

llorar a moco tendido ▪ darse un hartón de llorar to cry one's eyes out

llorar como una Magdalena to cry and cry

llorar con pena ▪ llorar amargamente ▪ llorar agustiadamente to cry bitterly ▪ to cry hard

llorar de alegría to cry tears of joy ▪ to cry for joy

llorar la muerte de alguien to mourn someone's death ▪ to mourn the death of someone

llorar la pérdida de alguien to mourn the loss of someone ▪ to mourn someone's loss

llorar sin consuelo to cry unconsolably

llorar sus muertos to mourn one's dead ▪ to mourn their dead

llover a cántaros ▪ llover a jarros to rain cats and dogs

llover a raudales to rain in buckets

llover con fuerza ▪ llover a cántaros to rain hard

llover implacablemente to rain relentlessly

llover preguntas a ▪ acribillar a alguien a preguntas to bombard with questions

llover sobre to rain (down) on

llover sobre mojado to be the same old story

lloverle encima to get rained on ▪ to get caught in the rain ➤ No quiero que me llueva encima. I don't want to get rained on. ▪ I don't want to get caught in the rain.

lloverle un aluvión de to be inundated with ▪ to be deluged with

llovido del cielo: venir (como) ~ ▪ venir como caído del cielo to be like manna from heaven ▪ to come as if sent from heaven

llueva o haga sol ▪ pase lo que pase rain or shine ▪ come rain or (come) shine ▪ come what may ▪ no matter what (happens) ➤ Salimos para Ciudad Bolivar mañana, llueva o haga sol. ▪ Salimos para Ciudad Bolivar mañana, pase lo que pase. We're leaving for Ciudad Bolivar tomorrow rain or shine. ▪ We're leaving for Ciudad Bolivar tomorrow come rain or shine. ▪ We're leaving for Ciudad Bolivar tomorrow no matter what.

llueve sobre mojado when it rains, it pours

lluvia a torrentes ▪ lluvia torrencial torrential rain(s)

lluvia de balas hail of bullets

lluvia de estrellas ▪ lluvia de meteoritos meteor shower

lluvia ha remitido ▪ lluvia ha amainado rain has subsided ▪ rain has died down

lluvia torrencial ▪ lluvia a torrentes torrential rain(s)

la **lluvia y el viento golpeando contra la ventana** ▪ hostigo de la lluvia y del viento rain and wind beating against the window

lo acordado what has been agreed to

ser **lo adecuado** ▪ ser lo correcto ▪ ser lo previsto to be the right way ▪ to be the correct way ▪ *(pintoresco)* to be according to Hoyle

lo ajeno what belongs to others ▪ other people's property ➤ Para vivir en comunidad, hay que respetar lo ajeno. To live in a group, one must respect other people's property. ▪ To live in a group, one must respect what belongs to others.

lo alto the upper part ▪ the top

lo anterior 1. the foregoing ▪ this ▪ that 2. what has been said ➤ Lo anterior explica por qué... The foregoing explains why... ▪ This explains why... ▪ That explains why...

lo antes posible ▪ lo más pronto que sea posible ▪ cuanto antes ▪ tan pronto como sea posible ▪ con la mayor brevedad posible as soon as possible

lo antes que pueda uno as soon as one can ➤ Lo haré lo antes que pueda. I'll do it as soon as I can.

lo aprecio ▪ lo agradezco I appreciate it

lo aprendido what is learned ▪ what was learned ▪ what has been learned

lo barato es caro you get what you pay for ▪ "cheap" is expensive in the long run
ser **lo bastante como para...** to be more than enough to...
ser **lo bastante grande como para hacer algo** ▪ ser lo suficientemente grande para to be big enough enough to do something ➤ El niño es lo bastante grande como para ir andando al colegio él solo. The boy is big enough to walk to school by himself.
lo bien que uno hace algo 1. how well one does something 2. as well as one can do something ➤ Depende de lo bien que lo hagas. It depends on how well you do it. ➤ ¿Lo haces lo bien que yo? Can you do it as well as I can?
lo bueno acerca de... *(culto)* ▪ lo bueno de... the good thing about...
lo bueno de... *(coloquial)* ▪ lo bueno acerca de... the good thing about... ▪ what is good ➤ Lo bueno es que... The good thing (about it) is that...
lo bueno pesa más que lo malo the good outweighs the bad
lo bueno que tiene the good thing about ➤ Lo bueno que tiene esto es que... The good thing about this one is that...
lo cansado que how tired
lo chungo es que... ▪ lo malo es que... the bad part is that... ▪ the bad thing about it is that...
lo cierto es que ▪ la verdad es que the truth is ▪ what is certain is that
¡**lo cojo yo!** *(Esp., teléfono o puerta)* ▪ ¡voy! I'll get it!
sale lo comido por lo servido *(Esp.)* ▪ ha sido lo comido por lo servido it's not profitable ▪ it's break even (only) ▪ there's no money in it
lo comprendo *(comprensión de sentimientos, etc.)* I understand
lo consabido 1. lo que es de dominio popular what is well known 2. lo que ambos sabemos what we both know 3. lo que es comúnmente citado what is often cited
lo contrario
ser **lo contrario (de)** 1. to be the opposite (of) ➤ Es simplemente lo contrario. It's just the opposite. ➤ La derecha es lo contrario de la izquierda. Right is the opposite of left.
lo convenido the plan
ser **lo correcto** ▪ ser lo adecuado ▪ ser lo previsto to be the correct one ▪ to be the right one ▪ to be the (correct) way ▪ to be the right way ▪ *(pintoresco)* to be according to Hoyle
lo cortés no quita lo valiente you don't lose anything by being polite
¡**lo creeré cuando lo vea!** I'll believe it when I see it!
lo cual which ▪ the fact of which ▪ which fact
lo cual era which ➤ En el Siglo XIX (Diecinueve) los niños trabajaban en fábricas, lo cual era característico de la época. In the Nineteenth Century, children worked in factories, which was characteristic of the times.
lo cual es which is ➤ Gracias a Carlos, hemos acabado a tiempo, lo cual es muy alentador. Thanks to Carlos, we have finished on time, which is very encouraging.
lo cual es natural which is (only) natural
lo cual fue which was ➤ Me prestó algo de dinero, lo cual fue muy amable (por su parte). ▪ *(coloquial)* Me prestó algún dinero, lo cual fue muy amable (por su parte). She lent me some money, which was very kind (of her).
lo de about ▪ the one about ➤ Siento mucho lo de tu padre. Sorry (to hear) about your father.
lo de abajo what's below the belt ▪ the genitals
ser **lo de menos** 1. to be the least of it ▪ to be the least of one's problems 2. to be the least one can do
lo de siempre *(al pedir en un bar, por ejemplo)* ▪ lo mismo de siempre the usual ▪ my usual ▪ the same as always ➤ Lo de siempre, por favor. The usual, please. ▪ My usual, please. ▪ The same as always, please.
ser **lo de siempre** to be the (same as) usual ▪ to be the same as always
lo dejaremos así ▪ estaremos en paz we'll call it even ▪ we'll be even Steven ➤ Dame mil pesos, y lo dejaremos así. Give me a thousand pesos, and we'll call it even. ▪ Give me a thousand pesos, and we'll be even Steven.
lo dejo a tu criterio ▪ te dejo decidir I'll leave it (up) to you to decide ▪ I'll let you decide
lo desconocido the unknown
lo dicho 1. as I say ▪ as I said ▪ once again 2. what was said 3. that settles it
¡**lo dicho!** let's leave it at that! ▪ that settles it!
lo dicho antes just what we said
lo difícil the hard part ▪ the difficult part ➤ Ahora viene lo difícil. Now comes the hard part.
lo difícil que puede ser how hard it can be ▪ how difficult it can be
lo digo en serio I mean it
lo dije en serio I meant it
lo disfruto ▪ me entretiene I enjoy it
lo dudo ▪ lo estoy dudando I doubt it
lo eché a la basura I threw it away
lo elegí por una razón ▪ lo elegí por un motivo ▪ lo escogí por una razón ▪ lo escogí por un motivo I chose it for a reason
lo encuentro difícil de creer que... ▪ lo veo difícil de creer que... ▪ me parece difícil de creer que... I find it difficult to believe that...
lo encuentro muy entretenido ▪ lo veo muy entretenido ▪ me parece muy entretenido I find it entertaining
lo entiendo *(comprensión intelectual)* I understand
lo eres ▪ tú lo eres that's you
¡**lo es!** it sure is!
lo es todo it's everything ➤ *(anuncio)* La educación lo es todo. Education is everything.
lo escogí por una razón ▪ lo elegí por un motivo ▪ lo elegí por una razón ▪ lo elegí por un motivo I chose it for a reason
lo escrito, escrito está what's in writing is binding
lo esencial the basics
lo estoy dudando ▪ lo dudo I doubt it
lo exterioriza it makes it show (up)
lo gracioso es que... the thing that's so funny is (that)... ▪ the thing that's so comical is (that)...
lo grave es que the serious part is ▪ what's serious about it is
¡**lo guapa que estás!** how beautiful you look!
¡**lo guapo que estás!** how handsome you look!
lo hace difícil... it makes it difficult...
lo haces mal you're doing it wrong
lo haces todo mal you're doing it all wrong
lo hago yo mismo 1. *(por lo general)* I do it myself 2. *(referido a una cosa específica)* I'll do it myself
lo harán siempre they'll do it every time
lo harás bien you'll do fine
lo haré con gusto I'll be glad to ▪ I'd be glad to
lo haré encantado I'd be delighted to (do it) ▪ I'd love to (do it)
lo haré yo mismo I'll do it myself
lo he notado I've noticed ▪ I've noticed that ▪ I've noticed it
lo he pensado mejor I've reconsidered
lo he sabido desde siempre I've always known that ▪ I've always known it
lo hecho the past ▪ what's done ▪ what's been done
lo hecho, hecho está ▪ a lo hecho, pecho what's done is done ▪ there's no use crying over spilled milk
lo hice sin querer ▪ no quería ▪ no lo pretendía I didn't mean to
lo hice yo *I* did (it)
lo ideal y lo real the ideal and the actual
lo importante the important thing
lo imposible: alcanzar ~ to achieve the impossible
lo imposible: emprender ~ to undertake the impossible ▪ to attempt (to do) the impossible
lo juro I swear (it)
lo justo 1. the minimum ▪ as little as possible 2. lo estrictamente necesario the bare essentials 3. justo a tiempo just in time ➤ Yo con fulano me trato lo justo. I have as little to do with John Doe as possible. ➤ Esta cocina está equipada con lo justo, una estufa, un fregadero y un frigorífico, pero sin lavaplatos ni microondas. This kitchen is equipped with the bare essentials, a stove, a sink, and a frigerator, but no dishwasher or microwave.
lo lamento ▪ lo siento I'm awfully sorry
lo malo de... the bad thing about...

lo malo era que... the bad thing about it was that... ▪ the problem was that... ▪ the trouble was that...

lo malo es que... the bad thing about it is that... ▪ the problem is that... ▪ the trouble is that...

lo malo que tiene es que... the bad thing about it is that...

lo malo que uno tiene: aceptar ~ to accept one's weaknesses ▪ to accept one's shortcomings

lo mamé desde pequeño(-a) *(soez)* it was impressed on me from early childhood on

lo más alto que uno puede: saltar ~ to jump as high as one can

lo más de prisa que uno puede: correr ~ to run as fast as one can

lo más emocionante the most exciting thing ➤ Es lo más emocionante que he hecho. It's the most exciting thing that I have (ever) done.

lo más fuerte que uno puede: gritar ~ to shout as loud as one can

lo más parecido a the closest thing (there is) to ➤ El ejercicio es lo más parecido a una panacea médica. Exercise is the closest thing there is to a medical panacea.

lo más probable ▪ lo más fácil the most likely thing ▪ the most likely

lo más pronto ▪ como muy pronto ▪ como muy temprano at the earliest

lo más pronto posible ▪ cuanto antes ▪ lo antes posible ▪ tan pronto como sea posible ▪ a la mayor brevedad posible as soon as possible ▪ as quickly as possible

lo más pronto que sea posible ▪ tan pronto que sea posible ▪ tan pronto como sea posible ▪ lo antes posible ▪ cuanto antes ▪ con la mayor brevedad posible as soon as possible

lo más próximo que llega a lo que se entiende por ▪ lo más parecido a lo que se entiende por the closest thing to what one would call ▪ the closest thing to what would be understood by

lo más próximo que llegó a lo que se entiende por the closest thing to what one would call... ▪ the closest thing to what would be understood by

lo más que puede pasar ▪ lo más que puede ocurrir the most that can happen

lo más que uno puede as hard as one can ➤ Trabajo lo más que puedo. I'm working as hard as I can.

lo más vital para vivir the bare necessities

lo máximo posible as much as possible

lo mejor para: querer ~ to want the best for ➤ Yo siempre quiero lo mejor para mis hijos. I always want the best for my children.

ser **lo mejor** to be for the best ▪ to be the best thing ▪ to be the best thing (to do) ➤ Se sentía infeliz al romper con su novia, pero ahora cree que fue lo mejor. He felt bad when he broke up with his girlfriend, but now he believes it was for the best. ▪ He felt bad when he broke up with his girlfriend, but now he believes it was the best thing.

ser **lo mejor a lo que uno puede aspirar** ▪ ser lo mejor que uno puede esperar to be the most that one can aspire to ▪ to be the most to which one can aspire ▪ *(coloquial)* to be as good as it gets ➤ Para nuestro gato capado, rascarle la espalda es lo mejor a lo que puede aspirar. ▪ Para nuestro gato capado, rascarle la espalda es lo mejor que puede esperar. For our neutered cat, a back scratch is as good as it gets.

lo mejor es it is best to ▪ it's best (to) ➤ Para planear un viaje, lo mejor es consultar el sitio de turismo en el Internet. To plan a trip it's best to consult the tourism site on the Internet.

ser **lo mejor que hay** to be the best (thing) there is

lo mejor que pude as best I could

ser **lo mejor que le pudo pasar a alguien** to be best thing that ever happened to someone ➤ Ella es lo mejor que le pudo pasar. She's the best thing that ever happened to him.

lo mejor que pueda to the best of one's ability ▪ as best one can

ser **lo mejor que puede** to be the best one can do

ser **lo mejor que tiene** to be the best thing about it ➤ Eso es lo mejor que tiene. That's the best thing about it. ➤ Lo mejor que tiene son los efectos especiales, no la historia. The best thing about it are the special effects, not the plot.

ser **lo mejor que uno puede hacer** to be the best one can do ➤ Es lo mejor que puedo hacerlo. That's the best I can do. ➤ ¿No lo puedes hacer mejor? Is that the best you can do? ▪ Can't you do it (any) better than that?

lo mejor que uno podía as best one could ▪ as well as one could

lo mejor sería... it would be best to... ▪ the best would be to...

lo mejor sería no... it would be best not to... ▪ the best would be to not... ▪ it would be best to not...

lo menos... the least...

lo menos posible as little as possible ▪ the least possible

lo menos que sea posible (para) as little as possible (to) ▪ the least possible (to)

ser **lo menos que uno puede hacer** to be the least one can do

lo menos que uno podía as little as one could ▪ the least one could

ser **lo menos que uno podía hacer** to be the least one could do

ser **lo mero mero** to be tops ▪ to be the ultimate ▪ to be top of the line

ser **la reoca** ▪ ser lo más ▪ ser lo mero mero to be tops ▪ to be top of the line ▪ to be the ultimate

lo mínimo que podrías haber hecho es the least you could have done is

ser **lo mismo** ▪ dar lo mismo not to make any difference ▪ to make no difference ➤ Es lo mismo. ▪ Da lo mismo. It doesn't make any difference. ▪ It makes no difference ➤ Para mí es lo mismo. ▪ Me da lo mismo. It doesn't make any difference to me. ▪ It makes no difference to me.

lo mismo algo como algo ▪ tanto algo como algo both something and something ▪ something as well as something ➤ Lo mismo vino rosado como vino tinto está bueno con un filete. ▪ Tanto vino tinto como vino rosado está bueno con un filete. Both red wine and rosé are good with a steak. ▪ Rosé as well as red wine is good with a steak.

lo mismo de siempre ▪ lo de siempre the usual

lo mismo digo ▪ igualmente same here ▪ likewise ▪ I feel the same way

lo mismo hombres que mujeres ▪ tanto hombres como mujeres ▪ ambos hombres y mujeres men and women alike ▪ men as well as women ▪ both men and women

¡lo mismo le digo! ▪ ¡igualmente! same to you!

lo mismo (me) da ▪ me da lo mismo it doesn't matter ▪ it's all the same to me

lo mismo que just as ▪ the same as ➤ Hoy he hecho lo mismo que ayer, fui a clase y luego volví a casa. Today I did the same thing I did yesterday, I went to class and then back home.

¡lo mismo te digo! ▪ ¡igualmente! same to you!

lo mismo uno que otro both one and another ➤ Lo mismo la madre que la hija son buenas cocineras. Both mother and daughter are good cooks.

lo mucho que te guste as much as you like ▪ however much you like

lo notaba (uno) ▪ se notaba ▪ se podía ver one could tell ➤ (Yo) lo notaba. ▪ (Yo) lo podía ver. I could tell.

lo noto I can tell (it) ▪ I can see it ▪ I can sense it

lo otro the other thing ➤ Lo otro que quería decirte es que no voy a poder ir hoy. The other thing I wanted to tell you is that I'm not going to be able to go today.

lo particular de ▪ lo que distingue the unique thing about ▪ what distinguishes ➤ Lo particular de un pound cake es su densidad. ▪ Lo que distingue un pound cake es su densidad. The unique thing about a pound cake is its density. ▪ What distinguishes a pound cake (from other cakes) is its density.

lo pasado what is past ▪ the past

lo pasado, pasado (está) 1. a lo hecho, pecho what's done is done ▪ there's no use crying over spilled milk 2. no guardes rencores let bygones be bygones ▪ don't bear a grudge ▪ don't hold a grudge

lo pensaré I'll think it over

lo peor que puede pasar ■ lo peor que puede ocurrir the worst (thing) that can happen ➤ Lo peor que le puede pasar (a él) es que... The worst thing that can happen to him is that...

lo peor se ha producido the worst has happened ■ the worst has come about ■ the worst has taken place

lo poco que faltó para que... how close one came to... ➤ Lo poco que faltó para que perdiéramos el partido How close we came to losing the game

lo poco que queda de... what little remains of...

lo poco que uno ha cambiado how little one has changed

¿lo pongo en número o en letra? shall I spell out the number or write it (as numerals)?

lo primero es ■ lo principal es the main thing is

lo primero es lo primero first things first

lo primero que hice fue the first thing I did was

lo primero que me impresionó fue... the first thing that struck me was... ➤ Lo primero que me impresionó de... fue The first thing that stuck me about... was

lo primero que noté fue the first thing I noticed was ➤ Lo primero que noté fue el olor de la humedad. The first thing I noticed was the smell of dampness.

lo primero que se le vino a la lengua fue 1. *(él)* the first thing he said was 2. *(ella)* the first thing she said was

lo primero que se me ocurrió fue the first thing I thought of was

lo prometido es deuda a promise is a promise

lo puedo comprender I can understand it ■ I can understand that

¿lo puedo dejar encargado? ■ ¿me lo puede pedir? can you (special) order it for me?

lo puedo entender I can understand it ■ I can understand that

lo que what ■ that which

lo que a ti te vaya mejor whatever works best for you

lo que a uno le parece what one thinks of ➤ Tendrás que contarnos qué te pareció tu viaje a Escandinavia. You'll have to tell us what you thought of your trip to Scandinavia.

lo que conlleva what it involves

lo que depara el futuro what the future holds

lo que dice va a misa 1. *(él)* what he says, goes 2. *(ella)* what she says, goes

lo que digas, vale whatever you say, goes

lo que distingue algo ■ lo particular de algo what distinguishes something (from something else) ■ the unique thing about something ➤ Lo que distingue un pound cake (de otros pasteles) es su densidad. ■ Lo particular de un pound cake es su densidad. What distinguishes a pound cake (from other cakes) is its density. ■ The unique thing about a pound cake is its density.

Lo que el viento se llevó *(novela de Margaret Mitchell) Gone with the Wind*

lo que en realidad... what really...

lo que era 1. en lo que consistía what it was 2. como era what it was like ■ how it was ➤ Recordaba lo que era estar sin un céntimo. He remembered what it was like to be penniless. ■ He remembered how it was to be penniless. ■ He remembered what it was to be penniless.

lo que es what it is (like) ➤ Recuerda lo que es estar sin un céntimo. He remembers what it is (like) to be penniless.

lo que es más ■ más todavía ■ además what's more

lo que está ocurriendo realmente what's really going on

lo que está pasando es que... ■ lo que está ocurriendo es que... what's happening is that...

lo que fuere ■ lo que fuese whatever may be ■ whatever it might be

lo que ha crecido algo *(con un verbo antecedente)* ■ lo mucho que ha crecido algo how much something has grown ➤ ¡Mira lo que ha crecido el Manolito! Look at how Manolito has grown!

lo que ha podido pensar uno what one may have been able to come up with ■ what one may have thought up

lo que hace falta es... ■ lo que se necesita es... what is needed is... ➤ El capitalismo genera riqueza, el socialismo la distribuye, y lo que hace falta es un equilibrio entre ellos. Capitalism creates wealth, socialism distributes it, and what is needed is a balance between them.

¡lo que hace un nombre! ¡that's the power of a name! ■ ¡that's the power in a name!

lo que hace único a algo ■ lo que distingue algo the unique thing about something ■ what is unique about something ■ what distinguishes something (from something else) ➤ Lo que hace única a la música clásica española es su expresividad, su capacidad para evocar lo místico. The unique thing about Spanish classical music is its expressiveness, its ability to evoke mystique.

¡lo que hacen algunos para llamar la atención! what some people won't do to get attention! ■ what some people will do to get attention!

lo que haces a ti te pasará ■ lo que haces se te revierte ■ lo que siembras, cosecharás what goes around comes around ■ you reap what you sow

lo que haces se te revierte ■ lo que haces a ti te pasará ■ lo que siembras, cosecharás what goes around comes around ■ you reap what you sow

lo que haga fulano o mengano me da igual I don't care what other people do

lo que hay que hacer es.... what you have to do is... ■ what has to be done is...

lo que hay que saber sobre... what you need to know about...

lo que le corresponde one's share

lo que le ha tocado a uno en la vida one's lot in life ➤ El destino de los humanos es tener que trabajar. Es lo que nos ha tocado en la vida. The fate of humans is to have to work. It's our lot in life. ➤ Parecen satisfechos con lo que les ha tocado en la vida. They seem satisfied with their lot in life.

lo que les dé la gana 1. *(a ellos)* whatever they feel like doing ■ whatever they want to do 2. *(a ustedes)* whatever you (all) feel like doing ■ whatever you (all) want to do ➤ Les dices que se lo lleven y hagan con él lo que les dé la gana. You tell them to take it away and do whatever they want to with it.

lo que más me gusta de todo es que... what I like most (of all) is that... ■ the thing I like most (of all) is that... ■ what I like best (of all) is that... ■ the thing I like best (of all) is that...

lo que más se aproxima a the closest thing there is to

¡lo que me faltaba! that's all I needed!

¡lo que me faltaba por oír! now I've heard everything!

lo que me gusta y lo que no what I like (about it) and what I don't ■ the thing I like (about it) and the thing I don't

lo que me gustaba y lo que no what I liked (about it) and what I didn't ■ the thing I liked (about it) and the thing I didn't

lo que me ha gustado the thing I liked about it ■ what I liked about it

lo que me ha gustado the thing I liked about it ■ what I liked about it ➤ Lo que me ha gustado fue el final. What I liked about it was the ending. ■ The thing I liked about it was the ending.

lo que me ha llevado a llamarte es que... what prompted me to call you is that...

ser **lo que mejor le viene a uno** ■ ser lo mejor que sienta a uno to be the most convenient for one ■ to be the best for one ■ to suit one the best ➤ Las mañanas son lo que mejor me viene. ■ Las mañanas son lo que mejor me sienta. Mornings are the best for me. ■ Mornings are the most convenient for me. ■ Mornings suit me the best.

ser **lo que mejor le sienta a uno** ■ ser lo que mejor le viene a uno to be the most convenient for one ■ to be the best for one ■ to suit one the best ➤ Las mañanas son lo que mejor me sienta. ■ Las mañanas son lo que mejor me viene. Mornings are the best for me. ■ Mornings are the most convenient for me. ■ Mornings suit me the best.

lo que no debo the wrong things

lo que ocurra primero whichever comes first ➤ La garantía cubre dos años o cincuenta mil millas, lo que ocurra primero. The warranty covers two years or fifty thousand miles, whichever comes first.

lo que parece: en ~ in what appears to be ■ in an apparent ➤ En lo que parece un intento de golpe de estado... In what appears to be an attempted coup d'état...

lo que parece ser what looks like ■ what appears to be ■ what seems to be

lo que pasa es que... it's just that... ➤ Lo que pasa es que no lo conoces. ■ *(Esp., leísmo)* Lo que pasa es que no le conoces. It's just that you don't know him. ■ You just don't know him.

lo que piensen fulano o mengano me importa un bledo I don't give a damn what other people think
lo que queda de... what's left of... ■ what remains of
lo que queda de ello(-a) ■ lo que queda de eso(-a) what's left of it ➤ *(noticia)* La sonda espacial "Contour", o lo que queda de ella, se encuentra en su órbita prevista alrededor del Sol, pero partido en al menos tres trozos. The space probe "Contour," or what's left of it, is in its planned orbit around the sun, but has broken into at least three pieces.
lo que queda del día 1. what remains of the day ■ what is left of the day 2. *(novela de Kazuo Ishugo) The Remains of the Day*
hacer lo que alguien te pida to do whatever someone asks you (to)
lo que quiere decir que which means that ➤ Las llaves del nuevo apartamento finalmente me las entregan el lunes 30 de julio, lo que quiere decir que mis vacaciones las emplearé para hacer la mudanza y montar la casa. I get the keys to the new apartment on Monday, July 30, which means that I will use my vacation to move and set up housekeeping.
lo que se debería hacer what they should do ■ what ought to be done ■ what should be done ■ the thing to do ➤ Es lo que se debería hacer. That's what they should do. ■ That's what they ought to do. ■ That's the thing to do. ■ That's what ought to be done. ■ That's what should be done.
lo que se dice ■ quero decir what you call ■ what you'd call ■ I mean ➤ *(C.J.Cela: La familia de Pascual Duarte)* Muy limpio, lo que se dice muy limpio, no lo fuera nunca. Very clean, I mean very clean, he never was.
lo que se espera de ti what's expected of you
lo que se me ha ocurrido es que what occurred to me is that
lo que se ve es lo que hay ■ esto es lo que hay ■ *(pintoresco)* ■ no hay más cera que la que arde ■ (y) no hay más cáscaras what you see is what you get ■ *(informática)* wysiwyg
lo que sea 1. whatever it is 2. ¡lo que toque! whatever! ➤ Lo que sea, dime en seguida. Whatever it is, tell me quick.
lo que sea que...: hacer ~ ■ hacer lo que quiera que... to do whatever... ➤ Haz lo que sea que el capitán te ordene. ■ Haz lo que quiera que el capitán te ordene. You do whatever the captain orders you to do.
lo que suceda what(ever) happens ➤ Mucho de lo que suceda depende de la elección. Much of what happens depends on the election.
lo que te parezca mejor whatever you think is best ■ whatever seems best to you
¡lo que toque! ■ ¡lo que sea! ■ ¡da igual! whatever!
lo que uno está pasando ■ por lo que uno está pasando what one is going through ➤ Nadie se imagina (por) lo que estamos pasando. No one has any idea what we're going through.
lo que uno haya o no hecho ■ lo que uno haya hecho o no haya hecho what one may or may not have done
lo que uno no debe the wrong thing
lo que uno piensa de what one thinks of ➤ Dinos lo que pensaste del discurso del presidente. Tell us what you thought of the president's speech.
¡lo que va de...! what a difference between...!
lo que ven, lo copian monkey see, monkey do
lo quiero por escrito I want it in writing ■ I want it in black and white
lo quiera o no like it or not
lo recuerdo I remember (it)
lo retiro I take it back
lo rico que soy how rich I am ➤ Verifiqué mi saldo para ver lo rico que soy. I checked my balance to see how rich I am.
¿lo sabías? 1. did you know it? ■ did you know that? 2. ¿sabías algo (sobre esto)? did you know about it?
lo saqué fiado I put it on the bill ■ the store let me take it on credit
lo sé I know (it) ■ I know that
lo sé de sobra ■ lo sé muy bien I know it all too well
lo sentí I was sorry ■ I felt sorry
lo siento ■ lo siento mucho I'm sorry
lo siento de todo corazón 1. *(para pedir disculpas o lamentar un suceso)* I'm very sorry ■ I'm really sorry ■ I'm so sorry 2. *(lamentar un suceso)* I feel it very deeply
lo siento enormemente I'm terribly sorry
lo siento mucho I'm very sorry
lo siento por ti I feel for you
lo siguiente the following
lo siguiente que supe (the) next thing I knew
ser **lo suficiente para** to be enough to
estar **lo suficientemente bien para** to be well enough to
ser **lo suficientemente bueno para** to be good enough to
ser **lo suficientemente grande como para contener algo** ■ ser lo suficientemente grande como para que algo quepa dentro to be large enough to hold something
ser **lo suficientemente grande (como) para hacer algo** to be big enough (potentially) to do something
ser **lo suficientemente grande para hacer algo** to be big enough to do something ➤ Esta puerta no es lo suficientemente grande para que pase el piano. This door is not big enough for the piano to go through. ➤ Jovenzuelo, eres suficientemente grande para saber que no se juega al balón en la casa. Young man, you're big enough to know better than to play ball in the house.
ser **lo suficientemente ligero para llevar a mano** to be light enough to carry
ser **lo suficientemente mayor para votar** ■ tener la edad suficiente para votar ■ tener la edad para votar to be old enough ■ to be of voting age
ser **lo suficientemente pequeño para** to be small enough to ■ to little enough to
ser **lo suficientemente pesado para** to be heavy enough to
lo supe desde un principio I had known it all along
lo suponía (yo) ■ lo supuse I figured as much ■ that's what I figured ■ I assumed as much ■ I guessed as much ■ I guessed that ■ that figures
lo tendré presente I'll keep it in mind ■ I'll keep that in mind
lo tengo en la punta de la lengua it's on the tip of my tongue ■ it's right on the tip of my tongue
lo tenías bien merecido ■ te lo estabas buscando ■ te lo merecías ■ te lo tenías bien merecido you had it coming ■ you got what you deserved ■ you deserved it
¡lo típico! it's just typical! ■ that's just typical! ■ typical!
lo último que hubiese deseado ■ lo último que hubiera deseado the last thing I wanted
ser **lo último que uno necesita** to be the last thing one needs ➤ Es lo último que necesito. That's the last thing I need. ■ It's the last thing I need. ➤ Era lo último que (yo) necesitaba. That was the last thing I needed. ■ It was the last thing I needed.
lo ultísimo ■ lo último de lo último the very latest ■ the newest of the new
lo único the only thing
lo único en que (yo) pensaba era en... only thing I thought about was...
lo único más the only other thing
lo único que decia (yo) era... the only thing I was saying was... ■ all I was saying was...
lo único que dijo (él) fue the only thing he said was... ■ all he said was...
lo único que diría (él) es que... ■ sólo se limitó a decir (que)... ■ sólo se limitó a comentar (que)... the only thing he would say is (that)... ■ all he would say is (that)... ■ the only thing he would say was (that)... ■ all he would say was (that)... *(Inglés puede tomar el presente o el pasado.)*
lo único que diría (él) era que... the only thing he would say was that...
lo único que falta es the only thing missing is
lo único que faltaba era the only thing missing was
lo único que me interesa es... 1. the only thing that interests me is... ■ the only thing I'm interested in is... ■ the only thing I care about is... ■ all I care about is...
lo único que me resta es... my only alternative is to...
lo único que me restaba era... my only alternative was to...
lo único que siquiera está a la altura de algo the only thing that even comes close to something
lo único que tengo es the only thing I've got is ■ the only thing I have is ■ all I've got is ■ all I have is ➤ Lo único que tengo es uno de cincuenta. ¿Puedes cambiármelo? All I've got is a fifty. Can

you change it (for me)? ▪ The only thing I've got is a fifty. Can you change it (for me)? ▪ All I have is a fifty. Can you change it (for me)? ▪ The only thing I have is a fifty. Can you change it (for me)?

lo uno por lo otro y la casa sin barrer we're not resolving the issue ▪ we're just going around in circles ➤ Tú quieres ir en coche, y yo en tren, y lo uno por lo otro y la casa sin barrer. You want to go by car, and I want to go by train, but we're not resolving the issue. ▪ You want to go by car, and I want to go by train, but we're not getting the issue resolved.

lo vas a conseguir 1. you're going to make it ▪ you're going to manage it ▪ you're going to succeed at it. 2. *(amenaza)* you're going to get it!

lo veía venir ▪ ya lo veía venir I could see it coming

lo veo difícil de creer que... ▪ lo encuentro difícil de creer que... ▪ me parece difícil de creer que... ▪ I find it difficult to believe that...

lo veo muy entretenido ▪ lo encuentro muy entretenido ▪ me parece muy entretenido I find it entertaining

lo veo venir I can see it coming

lo vi venir I saw it coming

lo voy a pensar I'll give it some thought

lo voy a pensar I'll give it some thought ▪ I'm going to think about it ▪ I'm going to give it some thought ▪ I'll think it over ▪ I'll think about it

ser un **lobo con piel de cordero** to be a wolf in sheep's clothes ▪ to be a wolf in sheep's clothing

ser **lobos de la misma camada** to be birds of a feather

el **local de alterne** whorehouse ▪ red-light house ▪ house of prostitution

localizarlo con el busca to page someone ➤ ¿Puede localizarla con el busca? Can you page her?

estar **locamente enamorado de** ▪ estar enamorado hasta los tuétanos to be head over heals in love with

estar **loco(-a) de atar** to be fit to be tied

ser un **loco(-a) de atar** to be a nut

estar **loco(-a) de capirote** ▪ estar tonto de capirote to be crazy as a bedbug

estar **loco(-a) de contento** to be happy as a lark ▪ to be very happy

estar **loco(-a) de remate** to be stark raving mad ▪ to be stark raving nuts ▪ to be crazy as a loon

estar **loco(-a) perdido(-a)** to be crazy out of one's mind ▪ to be completely crazy

estar **loco(-a) perdido(-a) por algo** to be crazy about something

estar **loco(-a) perdido(-a) por alguien** to be crazy about someone

estar **loco(-a) de remate** to be stark raving nuts

locomotora de maniobras switch engine

lograr acceso a ▪ conseguir acceso a to gain access to ▪ to get access to ➤ ¿Hay una pista sobre cómo lograron acceso a toda esa munición? ▪ ¿Hay una pista sobre cómo consiguieron acceso a toda esa munición? Is there any indication (as to) how they gained access to all that ammunition? ▪ Is there any indication (as to) how they got access to all that ammunition?

lograr captar ▪ entender ▪ hacerse a una idea to understand exactly ▪ to get a bead on ➤ Las corporaciones multinacionales europeas tratan de lograr captar el mercado de autos eléctricos en los Estados Unidos. The European multinational corporations are trying to get a bead on the U.S. electric car market.

lograr el apoyo de to win the support of ▪ to gain the support of ▪ to get the support of

lograr ponerse al día ▪ lograr ponerse al corriente ▪ poder seguir el ritmo to keep up

lograr que alguien haga algo to get someone to do something ➤ No pude lograr que me dejara de molestar. I couldn't get him to stop bothering me.

lograr que se aprueben to win approval of ➤ *(titular)* Canciller alemán logra que se aprueben las primeras reformas económicas. German chancellor wins approval of his first economic reforms.

lograr salir en la portada de una revista to make the cover of a magazine

lograr su meta ▪ lograr su objetivo to achieve one's goal ▪ to achieve one's objective

lomo de un libro ▪ canto de un libro spine of a book

lomos de visón: abrigo de ~ mink coat

la **longevidad (de la vida de uno)** ▪ longevidad del individuo length of one's life ▪ (personal) longevity ➤ La longevidad de la vida de uno depende así de la genética como de los hábitos personales. ▪ La longevidad del individuo depende tanto de la genética como de sus hábitos personales. The length of one's life depends both on genetics and (personal) habits. ▪ Personal longevity depends both on genetics and habits.

la **longitud de onda** wavelength

loro viejo no aprende a hablar you can't teach an old dog new tricks

los abajo firmantes the undersigned

los de edades (comprendidas) entre ▪ segmento de edad age group ➤ Los de edades (comprendidas) entre cuatro y seis años comen en el primer turno. ▪ El segmento de edad entre cuatro y seis años come en el primer turno. The age group between four and six eats during the first lunch period.

los demás ▪ los otros the others

los días laborables ▪ de lunes a viernes on weekdays ▪ Monday through Friday

los dos both (of them)

los enfermos the sick

los españoles Spaniards ▪ the Spanish (people) ▪ the people of Spain ➤ Los españoles tienen una tasa de natalidad especialmente baja. The Spanish have a unusually low birth rate. ➤ En el restaurante entraron dos españoles hoy. Two Spaniards came into the restaurant today.

los grandes grown-ups

los hay que dicen que... ▪ hay algunos que dicen que... there are those who say that... ▪ there are some who say that...

los más posibles ▪ el mayor número posible ▪ la mayor cantidad posible ▪ tantos como sea posible ▪ todos los que puedan ▪ todos los que se pueda as many as possible ▪ the greatest possible number

los míos ▪ mi gente my people

los que se oponen those opposed ▪ all opposed ➤ Los que se oponen, por favor manifiéstenlo levantando la mano. Those opposed please manifest by a show of hands. ▪ All opposed please manifest by a show of hands.

los suyos 1. los parientes de uno one's people ▪ one's family ▪ one's relatives 2. sus one's own

el **lote de libros** set of books

el **lote de sobres** pack of envelopes ➤ Lote de veinte sobres Pack of twenty envelopes

las **luces de emergencia** panel lights ▪ emergency lights ▪ warning lights

lucha de clases class struggle

luchas internas de un partido political in-fighting

lucir bien *(personas y cosas)* to look good

lucir ocupado(-a) ▪ verse ocupado 1. *(trabajando)* to look busy 2. *(habitado)* to look occupied ➤ Cuando la maestra entró al aula los estudiantes trataron de lucir ocupados. When the teacher entered the classroom, the students tried to look busy. ➤ Los ladrones evitan viviendas que lucen ocupadas. Thieves avoid dwellings that look occupied.

lucirse con un coche nuevo to show off a new car

ser una **lucha contra la corriente** ▪ ser una lucha contracorriente to be an uphill battle

lucha de apareamiento mating battle ➤ Los elefantes están enzarzados en una lucha de apareamiento. The elephants are engaged in a mating battle.

ser una **lucha hasta el final** ▪ ser una lucha hasta sus consecuencias ▪ ser una pelea hasta el final ▪ ser una pelea hasta sus consecuencias to be a fight to the finish

luchar con uñas y dientes ▪ pelear con uñas y dientes to fight tooth and nail

luchar en una guerra to fight in a war ➤ Su abuelo luchó en la Segunda Guerra Mundial. His grandfather fought in the Second World War.

luchar hasta el final ▪ pelear hasta el final to fight to the finish

lucrarse (de) 1. to come out well (from) 2. *(pey.)* to feather one's nest (by)

luego de ▪ a raíz de ▪ a partir de right after ➤ Luego de aquello, cambió mucho. After that, he changed a lot.

luego de esto whereupon ▪ after which

luego me enteré de que... then I found out that...

luego que ▪ en cuanto ▪ tan pronto como as soon as

luego todo all through ▪ the whole time

lugar adecuado right place ▪ suitable place

lugar común commonplace ▪ platitude

lugar correcto right place ▪ correct address ▪ correct location

lugar de encuentro ▪ punto de encuentro meeting place ▪ place to meet ▪ meeting point

el **lugar para pasar la noche** place to spend the night ➤ Necesito un lugar para pasar la noche. I need a place to spend the night.

lugar remoto 1. lugar lejano faraway place ▪ distant place **1.** fuera de casa, oficina, etc. remote location ➤ Deberías poder mirar tu cuenta de correo de la universidad desde lugares remotos. You should be able to check you university e-mail account from remote locations.

lugar seguro safe place

ser una **lumbrera para** to be a whiz at

luna creciente waxing moon

luna delantera *(Esp.)* ▪ (el, los) parabrisas... front windshield

luna llena full moon

luna menguante waning moon

luna nueva new moon

luna trasera *(Esp.)* ▪ (el, los) parabrisas de atrás ▪ luneta rear windshield

luna de miel honeymoon

la **luz a raudales** flooded with light ▪ bathed with light ▪ bathed in light

la **luz al final del túnel** light at the end of the tunnel ➤ Puedo ver la luz al final del túnel. I can see the light at the end of the tunnel.

la **luz de arriba** overhead light ➤ Prendí la luz de arriba. ▪ Encendí la luz de arriba. I turned on the overhead light. ▪ I turned the overhead light on.

la **luz de arriba** overhead light ➤ Prendí la luz de arriba. ▪ Encendí la luz de arriba. I turned on the overhead light.

la **luz de esperanza** beacon of hope

la **luz del techo** ceiling light ➤ Apaga la luz del techo. Turn off the ceiling light. ▪ Turn the ceiling light off.

la **luz deslumbrante** blazing light

la **luz solar** ▪ luz del sol sunlight ▪ the sun's light ▪ the light of the sun

luz velazqueña *(propia de las pinturas de Velázquez)* light of Velázquez

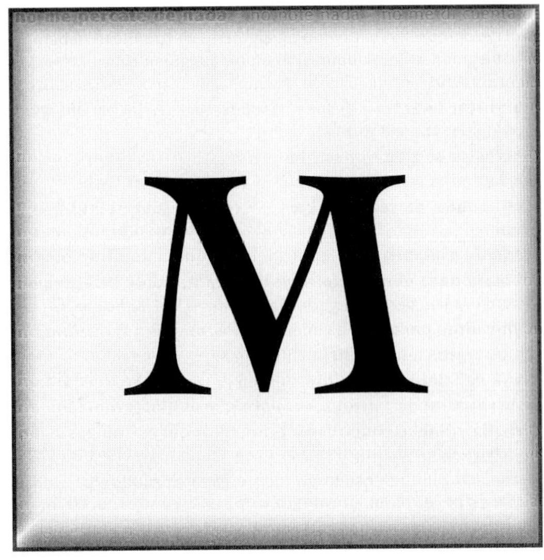

macedonia de frutas *(Esp.)* ■ ensalada de frutas fruit cocktail

machacado por la guerra war torn

madeja de lana ■ ovillo de lana ■ copo de lana ball of yarn

madeja de nervios bundle of nerves

madera densa *(p.ej., ébano, teca)* dense wood

madera labrada ■ madera tallada carved wood

madera tallada ■ madera labrada carved wood

madrastra de la madre (maternal) stepgrandmother ■ mother's stepmother

madrastra del padre (paternal) stepgrandmother ■ father's stepmother

la **madre debería salir de cuentas** ■ *(lenguaje pintoresco)* se espera el bebé the baby is due ➤ Ayer la madre debería haber salido de cuentas. ■ El bebé se esperaba ayer. The baby was due yesterday.

¡**madre mía!** boy oh boy!

madre soltera 1. *(sin casarse)* unwed mother **2.** *(divorciada o viuda)* single mother ■ single mom

magia se deshizo: la ~ the magic spell was broken

magrear a alguien to feel up someone ■ to feel someone up

maíz molido corn meal ■ ground corn

maíz pisingallo popping corn ■ corn for popping

mal aliento: tener ~ to have bad breath

mal barrio ■ barrio peligroso bad neighborhood ■ dangerous neighborhood

mal carácter: tener ~ ■ tener mal genio ■ *(coloquial)* tener mala uva ■ tener malas pulgas to have a bad disposition

el **mal de altura** ■ mal de montaña altitude sickness ■ mountain sickness

estar **mal de la azotea** *(Méx., coloquial)* ■ estar mal de la chaveta to be touched in the head ■ to have bats in one's belfry

el **mal de montaña** ■ mal de altura mountain sickness ■ altitude sickness

el **mal de las vacas locas** ■ encefalopatía esponjiforme bovina mad cow disease

estar **mal del coco** ■ estar mal de la cabeza to be touched in the head ■ *(coloquial)* to be tetched in the head

estar **mal del tarro** to be touched in the head

mal de muchos, consuelo de tontos ■ mal de todos, consuelo de tontos misery loves company

mal de todos, consuelo de tontos ■ mal de muchos, consuelo de tontos misery loves company

ser **mal educado(-a) 1.** faltarle educación to have a poor upbringing ■ to be poorly brought up **2.** ser malcriado to be disrespectful to one's elders ■ to be disrespectful of one's elders ■ to be disrespectful of adults ■ to be disrespectful to adults

estar **mal emparentado** to be ill bred

mal genio: tener ~ ■ tener mal carácter ■ *(coloquial)* ■ tener mala uva ■ tener malas pulgas to have a bad disposition ➤ Algunos perros tienen mal genio. Some dogs have bad dispositions.

estar **mal guisado** to be badly cooked ■ to be poorly cooked

mal hábito ■ mala costumbre ■ manía bad habit

estar **mal hablado** to be poorly spoken ■ to be ill spoken

estar **mal llamado** to be mistakenly called ■ to be incorrectly called ■ to be wrongly called

el **mal menor** the lesser evil ■ the lesser of two evils

estar **mal ordenados** ■ estar descolocados to be out of order ■ to be out of proper sequence ➤ Los papeles de esta carpeta están descolocados. ■ Los papeles en esta carpeta están mal ordenados. ■ Los papeles en esta carpeta están mal ordenados. ■ Los papeles de esta carpeta están descolocados. ■ Los folios de esta carpeta están descolocados. The papers in this folder are out of order. ■ The papers in this folder are out of (their proper) sequence.

estar **mal regulado** ■ estar mal ajustado to be out of adjustment ■ *(coloquial)* out of kilter ■ out of whack ➤ El muelle está mal regulado. The spring mechanism (that keeps the door from slamming) is out of adjustment.

el **mal síntoma** bad sign ➤ Es un mal síntoma, quiere decir que ya empiezas a resignarte. That's a bad sign. It means you're starting to give up.

estar **mal templada la guitarra** ■ estar desafinado (for) the guitar to be out of tune

mal tiempo: hacer ~ ■ tiempo de perros to be bad weather ■ *(culto, literario)* to be inclement weather ➤ Estamos atravesando una ola de mal tiempo. ■ Estamos atravesando una racha de mal tiempo. A period of bad weather has set in. ■ A spell of bad weather has set in. ■ A period of inclement weather has set in.

estar **mal visto** to be out of favor ■ to be frowned on ➤ El gerente del edificio está mal visto por los inquilinos. The building manager is out of favor with the tenants. ➤ No asear el desecho de su perro está mal visto por el ayuntamiento (de la ciudad). Not cleaning up after your dog is frowned on by the city government.

ser una **mala cosa perder** ■ ser una cosa mala perder to be a bad thing to lose ➤ Es una mala cosa perder el pasaporte. ■ Es mala cosa perder el pasaporte. A passport is a bad thing to lose.

mala costumbre ■ mal hábito ■ manía bad habit

mala distribución: tener una ~ to have a bad floor plan ■ to have a bad layout ■ to have a poor layout

mala gestión bad management ■ poor management

mala jugada 1. *(deportes)* bad play **2.** jugarreta dirty trick

mala pasada: hacerle a alguien una ~ *(especialmente en el trabajo)* to cross someone ■ to slight someone

mala sangre: tener ~ ■ tener mala sombra to be crafty ■ to be devious

mala sombra: tener ~ ■ tener mala sangre to be crafty ■ to be devious

mala uva: tener ~ *(Esp., coloquial)* ■ tener malas pulgas ■ tener mal genio to have a bad disposition ■ to be mean tempered ➤ Tiene mala uva. He has a bad disposition. ■ He's mean tempered.

mala vida: llevar una ~ not to live a good life ■ not to live prudently

mala voluntad para con alguien: tener ~ ■ tener mala voluntad hacia alguien to feel ill will toward someone ■ to have ill will for someone

mala yerba nunca muere ■ mala hierba nunca muere mean people never die

malas artes: conseguir algo con ~ to get something through devious means

malas lenguas gossips ➤ Las malas lenguas dicen que tu marido tiene una amante. The gossips say your husband has a lover

malas pulgas: tener ~ ■ tener pocas pulgas to have a bad temper ■ to be bad tempered

maldecir su suerte to curse one's luck

¡**maldita sea!** damn it!

¡**maldita sea tu estampa!** damn you!

¡**maldito seas!** damn you!

malgastar el tiempo ■ perder el tiempo ■ desaprovechar el tiempo ■ desperdiciar el tiempo ■ despilfarrar el tiempo to waste time

malgastar el tiempo de alguien ▪ perder el tiempo de alguien ▪ desaprovechar el tiempo de alguien ▪ desperdiciar el tiempo de alguien ▪ despilfarrar el tiempo de alguien to waste someone's time

malgastar energía ▪ desperdiciar energía ▪ derrochar energía ▪ dilapidar energía to waste energy

malgastar la vida to waste one's life

malhadadas relaciones con... ill-fated relations with...

¡**malhadado de mí!** *(poco común)* ▪ ¡desgraciado de mí! woe is me!

malla de alambre wire mesh

ser **malo para el negocio** to be bad for business ➤ Ese camarero es malo para el negocio. That waiter is bad for business.

malos aires para tough times for

malos tratos a la infancia child abuse

maná del cielo manna from heaven

un **manantial de** a great source of ▪ a source of great

mancha solar sunspot

manchar todo de pintura ▪ salpicar pintura por todas partes ▪ esparcir pintura encima de todo ▪ esparcir pintura por todas partes to get paint all over everything

mancharse algo con algo to get something on something ➤ El pintor manchó el piano con pintura. The painter got paint on the piano. ➤ Cuando comía papas fritas, me manché la camisa con ketchup. While I was eating French fries, I got ketchup on my shirt.

mandar a alguien a hacer algo 1. to send someone to do something 2. to commission someone to do something ➤ Su mamá le mandó a Juan Bobo al mercado a comprar un saco de arroz. Juan Bobo's mother sent him to the market to buy a sack of rice. ➤ Le mandaron a que compusiera la música para la banda sonora de la película. They commissioned him to compose the soundtrack for the film.

mandar a baqueta ▪ mandar a la baqueta to rule tyrannically

mandar a hacer deberes ▪ asignar deberes to assign homework ➤ El catedrático nos mandó hacer tres temas. ▪ El profesor nos asignó tres temas. The professor assigned us three themes.

mandar a mano dura ▪ mandar a mano fuerte to rule with an iron fist ▪ to rule with an iron hand

mandar a zapatazos to rule with an iron fist ▪ to rule with an iron hand

mandar el ejército to lead the army ▪ to command the army

mandar hacer algo to have something done ➤ Mandé hacer esta mesa. I had this table made.

mandar un telegrama ▪ poner un telegrama to send a telegram

mandarle a buscar a alguien ▪ mandarle venir a alguien to send for someone ➤ Le mandé a buscar. I sent for you.

mandarlo a la escuela to send someone to school ➤ Sus padres trabajaron mucho para mandarla a la escuela. Her parents worked hard to send her to school.

mandarlo instalar to have one installed ➤ Mándalo instalar. Have one installed.

mandato (del oficio público) term of office ➤ Clinton es el primer demócrata que gana un segundo mandato desde Franklin Roosevelt. Clinton is the first Democrat since Franklin Roosevelt to win a second term.

mando de la tele ▪ control remoto del televisor TV remote

mando medio middle management

mandonear a alguien ▪ mangonear a alguien to boss someone around

mandos de un avión controls of an airplane

manejar con cuidado to handle with care ▪ *(mandato)* handle with care!

manejar el tinglado ▪ llevar la voz cantante to rule the roost

manejar una máquina to operate a machine ▪ to run a machine

manéjese con cuidado handle with care

manejo del lenguaje de un periodista journalist's ear for the language

manera de enfocar un problema ▪ manera de abordar un problema ▪ manera de enfrentarse a un problema ▪ método de enfocar un problema ▪ método de abordar un problema ▪ método de enfrentarse a un problema ▪ forma de enfocar un problema ▪ forma de abordar un problema ▪ forma de enfrentarse a un problema approach to a problem ▪ way of solving a problem

manera de hacer algo way of doing something

manera de obrar way of doing things ▪ way of going about things ▪ modus operandi

manga ancha: tener ~ ▪ tener la manga ancha to be overly indulgent ▪ to be over-indulgent

manga por hombro: andar ~ ▪ estar manga por hombro to be in (a state of) chaos ▪ to be topsy-turvy

mangonear a alguien ▪ mandonear a alguien ▪ decir a alguien lo que tiene que hacer to boss someone around

manguear a alguien *(Arg., coloquial)* to ask someone for money

manía persecutoria persecution complex

maniático de los árboles de Navidad Christmas tree freak ➤ Soy un maniático de los árboles de Navidad. I'm a Christmas tree freak.

manifestar afecto a alguien to show someone affection ▪ to show affection for someone

manifestar su satisfacción a to express one's satisfaction at

manifestar su sorpresa to express one's surprise

manifestarse contra to demonstrate against ▪ to demonstrate in protest against

maniobra de evasión ▪ maniobra de diversión diversionary tactic

estar **manipulado** to be tampered with ➤ *(noticia)* Aviación Civil aseguraba que el helicóptero no había estado manipulado, pero ahora se abre esta posibilidad. The Civil Aviation Agency had given its assurance that the helicopter had not been tampered with, but now has left open that possibility.

manipular el ordenador *(Esp.)* ▪ trabajar en el ordenador ▪ *(L.am.)* manipular la computadora ▪ trabajar en la computadora to do things to the computer ▪ to work on the computer ➤ El técnico está manípulando el ordenador. ▪ El técnico está trabajando en el ordenador. The technician is doing things to the computer. ▪ The technician is working on the computer.

manipular la computadora *(L.am.)* ▪ hacer mejoras a la computadora ▪ trabajar en la computadora ▪ *(Esp.)* manipular el ordenador ▪ trabajar en el ordenador to do things to the computer ▪ to work on the computer ➤ El técnico está manipulando la computadora. ▪ El tècnico está trabajando en la computadora. The technician is doing things to the computer. ▪ The technician is working on the computer.

manipular los resultados ▪ distorsionar los resultados ▪ tergiversar los resultados ▪ *(Esp.)* ▪ sesgar los resultados to bias the results ▪ to skew the results ▪ to distort the results

manipular para neutralizar to jockey for position

manipular una encuesta ▪ sesgar un encuesta to bias a poll (intentionally) ▪ to bias a survey (intentionally)

manjar espiritual spiritual food ▪ spiritual sustenance

mano a mano 1. *(ellos)* between the two of them 2. *(nosotros)* between the two of us ▪ together ➤ Los dos despacharon mano a mano dos litros de cerveza. ▪ Se despacharon entre los dos dos litros de cerveza. Between (the two of) them, they polished off a pitcher of beer. ▪ Together, they polished off a pitcher of beer. ➤ Nos despachamos mano a mano dos litros de cerveza. ▪ Nos despachamos entre los dos dos litros de cerveza. Between (the two of) us we polished off a pitcher of beer. ▪ Together, we polished off a pitcher of beer.

mano blanda con alguien: tener ~ ▪ tratar a alguien con mano blanda to be (too) lenient with someone ▪ to be (too) easy on someone ▪ to be (too) soft on someone ▪ not to be strict enough with someone

la **mano de hierro** iron hand

ser **mano de santo** to be a sure-fire remedy ▪ to do the trick ➤ La abuela cubana de Susana me dijo que para el resfriado disolviera dos aspirinas en una limonada caliente, y fue mano de santo. Susana's Cuban grandmother told me that for my cold to dissolve two aspirins in a hot lemonade, and it did the trick.

ser la **mano derecha de alguien** to be someone's right-hand man

la **mano dura** iron fist

mano, no te rajes *(Méx.)* don't be shy, brother ▪ let yourself go, brother

manojo de nervios: estar hecho un ~ ▪ ser un manojo de nervios to be a bundle of nerves ▪ to be a nervous wreck

¡manos a la obra! **1.** *(tú)* get to work! **2.** *(vosotros)* (you all) get to work! **3.** *(nosotros)* let's get to work!

¡manos arriba! hands up!

manos en alto hands up ▪ with one's hands up ➤ Salieron manos en alto. They came out with their hands up.

manos golosas *(especialmente de los niños)* ▪ manos pringadas sticky hands

manos pringosas *(Esp., especialmente de los niños)* ▪ manos pegajosas ▪ manos golosas sticky hands

¡manos quietas! hands off! ▪ keep your hands to yourself!

mansa brisa gentle breeze

ser **manso(-a) como un cordero** to be gentle as a lamb

ser **manso(-a) como una oveja** to be gentle as a lamb

manteca blanda *(Arg.)* ▪ mantequilla blanda soft butter ▪ softened butter

manteca clarificada *(Arg.)* ▪ mantequilla clarificada clarified butter

manteca de cerdo bacon grease ▪ bacon fat ▪ lard

mantener a alguien alejado **1.** to keep someone away ▪ to keep away someone **2.** to keep someone back ▪ to keep back someone ▪ to hold someone back ▪ to hold back someone ➤ Al principio, Scrooge quería mantener a las fantasmas alejadas. At first Scrooge wanted to keep the ghosts away. ▪ At first Scrooge wanted to keep away the ghosts. ➤ Al principio, Scrooge quería mantenerlas alejadas. At first Scrooge wanted to keep them away. ➤ La policia mantuvo a los manifestantes alejados de la caravana. Police kept the protesters back from the motorcade. ▪ Police held the protesters back from the motorcade.

mantener a alguien apartado(-a) to keep back someone ▪ to keep someone back ➤ La policía mantuvo a la multitud apartada mientras pasaba la caravana. The police kept the crowd back as the motorcade passed. ➤ La policía la mantuvo apartado. The police kept them back.

mantener a alguien en vilo ▪ tener a alguien en vilo ▪ dar carrete a alguien to keep someone in suspense ➤ El libro tiene un final sorprendente que mantiene al lector en vilo hasta el último instante. The book has a surprise ending that keeps the reader in suspense until the very end.

mantener a distancia a alguien to keep someone at bay ▪ to hold someone at bay ➤ El perro mantuvo a distancia al ladrón. The dog kept the burglar at bay. ▪ The dog held the burglar at bay.

mantener a raya a alguien to keep someone in line ➤ Es bueno que ella sea pesada porque me mantiene a raya. It's good she's overbearing because she keeps me in line. ➤ Ella los mantiene a raya. She keeps them in line

mantener a su familia to support one's family

mantener algo a raya to keep something in line ▪ to keep something at bay

mantener algo en secreto to keep something a secret

mantener atado(-a) a alguien con una correa corta to keep someone on a short leash ▪ to keep a tight rein on someone ▪ not to give someone much wiggle room

mantener bajo los costes to hold down costs ➤ Tenemos que mantener los costes bajos. We've got to keep our costs down.

mantener el motor en marcha to get the motor running ▪ to keep the motor running

mantener el paso ▪ llevar el paso ▪ mantener el ritmo to maintain the pace ▪ to maintain the speed

mantener el ritmo **1.** *(al correr)* to maintain the pace ▪ to maintain the speed **2.** *(al bailar)* to maintain the rhythm

mantener el tipo ▪ aguantar el tipo to keep one's cool ▪ to put on a brave face

mantener entretenido(-a) a alguien to keep someone entertained ➤ Los niños nos mantuvieron entretenidos. The children kept us entertained.

mantener estrechas relaciones con to maintain close ties with ▪ to maintain close relations with

mantener la cabeza fría to keep a cool head

mantener los ojos abiertos ▪ estar pendiente ▪ estar alerta to keep one's eyes open ▪ to keep an eye out ▪ to be on the lookout ▪ to be on the alert

mantener la línea (telefónica) desocupada to keep the line clear

mantener los tiempos que uno gasta to keep track of one's time ➤ Mantén los tiempos que gastas. Keep track of your time.

mantener su palabra ▪ cumplir su palabra to keep one's word

mantener su pulso con alguien ▪ mantener una rencilla con alguien to remain at odds with someone ▪ to be locked in struggle with someone

mantener un trabajo to hold a job ➤ No puede mantener un trabajo. He can't hold a job.

mantener una cita to keep an appointment

mantener una conversación ▪ tener una conversación to have a conversation ➤ Mantuvimos una conversación muy interesante en el camino. We had a very interesting conversation along the way.

mantener una relación de amistad con alguien to be friends with someone

mantener una relación profesional con alguien to have a business relationship with someone

mantener una relación sentimental con alguien to be dating someone ▪ to be involved with someone

mantener una ventaja de *x* puntos sobre to lead someone by *x* points ➤ McCain mantenía una ventaja de 20 puntos sobre Bush. McCain was leading Bush by 20 points.

mantener vivas las tradiciones to keep the traditions alive

mantenerla sencilla to keep it simple

mantenerle informado(-a) ▪ tenerle informado(-a) to keep someone informed

mantenerse aflote to stay afloat

mantenerse a sí mismo(-a) to pay one's own way ▪ to be self-sufficient financially

mantenerse abrigado(-a) ▪ mantenerse caliente to keep warm

mantenerse al día en sus estudios to keep abreast of one's studies ▪ to stay abreast of one's studies ▪ to keep up to date in one's studies ▪ to keep on top of one's studies ▪ to stay on top of one's studies

mantenerse al ritmo de to keep up with ➤ No puedo mantenerme al ritmo de la clase. I can't keep up with the class.

mantenerse al tanto de to keep abreast of ▪ to stay abreast of ▪ to keep up to date on ▪ to stay up to date on ▪ to keep up with ➤ Quiero mantenerme al tanto de los desarrollos en Irak. I want to keep abreast of the developments in Iraq. ▪ I want to stay abreast of the developments in Iraq. ▪ I want to keep up to date on the developments in Iraq. ▪ I want to keep up with the developments in Iraq.

mantenerse alejado(-a) to stay away

mantenerse alejado(-a) de los problemas to keep out of trouble ▪ to stay out of trouble

mantener algo controlado to keep something at bay ▪ to hold something at bay ➤ Beber agua puede mantener controlados los ataques de hambre. Drinking water can keep hunger pangs at bay.

mantenerse apartado(-a) de to remain aloof from ▪ to stand aloof from ▪ to keep aloof from

mantenerse caliente ▪ mantenerse abrigado to keep warm

mantenerse en alerta to stay alert ▪ to keep on one's toes ▪ to stay on one's toes

mantenerse en compás de espera ▪ estar in compás de espera to be waiting to hear ▪ to be waiting for word ▪ to be awaiting word

mantenerse en forma to keep in shape ▪ to stay in shape ➤ Me gusta mantenerme en forma. I like to keep in shape.

mantenerse en pie ▪ permanecer en pie to remain standing

mantenerse en segundo plano to keep a low profile ▪ to stay in the background

mantenerse en sus trece ▪ permanecer en su trece ▪ seguir en sus trece ▪ estar en sus trece to stick to one's guns ▪ to stand one's ground

mantenerse fiel a alguien to remain faithful to someone

mantenerse firme to stand firm

mantenerse sujeto al pasamanos to hold on to the railing ▪ to hold on to the handrail ➤ Manténgase sujeto al pasamanos. Hold on to the railing. ▪ Hold on to the handrail.

¡mantente a raya! ▪ ¡saca las manos (de aquí)! ▪ ¡saca tus pezuñas! ▪ ¡quita tus pezuñas! ▪ ¡quita de ahí tus zarpas! back off!
¡mantente al margen! ▪ ¡tú no te metas! you stay out of this! ▪ you keep out of this!
mantequilla blanda soft butter ▪ softened butter
mantequilla clarificada clarified butter
manto de nieve ▪ capa de nieve blanket of snow
manuscritos del Mar Muerto Dead Sea Scrolls
manutención de los hijos child support
manzana ácida tart apple ➤ La receta exige mazanas ácidas, sin corazón. The recipe calls for cored tart apples. ▪ The recipe calls for tart apples with the core removed.
mañana con neblina foggy morning
mañana mismo no later than tomorrow
mañana posterior a morning after
mañas del oficio tricks of the trade
el **mapa de carreteras** road map
mapa físico topographical map
el **mapa mural** wall map
maqueta de un edificio (scale) model of a building
máquina de escribir typewriter
mar borrascoso ▪ mar tomentoso stormy sea
mar encabritado ▪ mar picado choppy sea
mar picado ▪ mar encabritado choppy sea
mar tormentoso stormy sea ▪ rough sea
maraña de cables tangle of wires
marca de fábrica brand name
marcar algo (con un visto) to put a check mark (by something) ▪ to check off something ▪ to check something off ➤ Ya la he llamado, así que puedes marcar (con un visto) al lado de su nombre. I've already called her, so you can put a check mark by her name. ▪ I've already called her, so you can check her (name) off the list.
marcar algo con una señal *(visto, equis, punto, raya, flecha, etc.)* to put a mark by something
marcar (bien) ▪ remarcar (bien) to press (down) hard ▪ to bear down (hard) ➤ Márcalo bien para que las copias sean legibles. ▪ Remárcalo bien para que las copias sean legibles. Bear down hard so that the copies will be legible. ▪ Press hard so the copies will be legible.
marcar distancias con alguien ▪ marcar distancias hacia alguien to distance oneself from someone
marcar el camino to lead the way
marcar el compás ▪ marcar el ritmo to beat time (to the music) ▪ to mark time (to the music)
marcar el mensaje *(informática)* ▪ resaltar el mensaje ▪ pintar el mensaje ▪ iluminar el mensaje to highlight the message
marcar el paso *(militar)* to mark the beat (of the marching step)
marcar el ritmo ▪ marcar el compás to beat time (to the music) ▪ to mark time (to the music)
marcar las distancias con alguien to distance oneself from someone
marcar las distancias hacia un grupo to distance oneself from a group
marcar las pautas ▪ dar ejemplo to set the example
marcar la(s) *x* *(manecillas de un reloj)* to point to *x*
marcar quinientos en el examen TOEFL ▪ sacar quinientos en el examen TOEFL ▪ obtener quinientos en el examen TOEFL ▪ tener una puntuación de quinientos en el examen TOEFL to score five hundred on the TOEFL test ▪ to get five hundred on the TOEFL test
marcar un gol ▪ anotar un punto **1.** to score a goal ▪ to score a point **2.** *(baloncesto)* to score (a basket)
marcar un hito to reach a milestone ▪ to be a milestone
marcar un jalón en to be a milestone in
marcar un punto de partida to reach a turning point
marcar un tiempo de to clock (a time of)
marcarlo (bien) remarcarlo (bien) to bear down (hard) ▪ to press hard ➤ Márcalo (bien) para que las copias sean legibles. ▪ Remárcalo (bien) para que las copias sean legibles. Bear down (hard) so that the copies will be legible. ▪ Press hard so the copies will be legible.
marcarse como objetivo to set one's sights on
marcarse un farol *(póquer, etc.)* ▪ tirarse un farol ▪ farolear to bluff
¡marcha al trabajo! get back to work!
¡marcha atrás! back up!
marcha de acontecimientos ▪ curso de acontecimientos course of events
marcha sobre Washington march on Washington
¡marchad al trabajo! *(Esp.)* (you all) get back to work!
marchamo de identidad ▪ etiqueta de identidad identification tag ▪ identification label
¡marchemos al trabajo! let's get back to work!
marcharse al exilio to go into exile
marcharse con las manos vacías to go away empty-handed
marcharse pronto ▪ salir pronto ▪ irse pronto to leave early
marcharse sin alguien to leave without someone ➤ Se han marchado sin mí. They left without me.
marco de la puerta door frame
marco de referencia frame of reference
Mare Nostrum ▪ mar Mediterráneo Mediterranean Sea
marea alta high tide
marea baja low tide
marea muerta neap tide
marea negra oil slick
marea viva spring tide
marear la perdiz ▪ andar con vueltas to hem and haw ▪ to beat around the bush
marejada electromagnética electromagnetic storm
el **margen de ganancia** ▪ margen de beneficio profit margin
marquetería de oro gold inlay ▪ gold marquetry
marrar el blanco to miss the target
marrar el golpe to miss (the hit)
marrar el tiro to miss the shot
más the most ▪ the best ➤ Esta camisa me gusta más. ▪ La camisa que más me gusta es ésta. I like this shirt the most. ▪ I like this shirt the best.
más a menudo more often ➤ Deberías escribirles a tus padres más a menudo. You should write your parents more often.
más abajo farther down
ser **más abrigado que...** ▪ ser más cálido que... ▪ abrigar más que... ▪ calentar más que... to be warmer than... ▪ to provide more warmth than... ➤ Las nuevas botas espaciales son más abrigadas que las antiguas (botas) de cuero. ▪ Las nuevas botas espaciales abrigan más que las antiguas (botas) de cuero. ▪ Las nuevas botas espaciales calientan más que las antiguas (botas) de cuero. ▪ Las nuevas botas espaciales son más cálidas que las antiguas (botas) de cuero. The new "moon" boots are warmer than the old leather ones.
ser **más aburrido(-a) que chupar un clavo oxidado** *(Arg.)* ▪ más aburrido(-a) que un hongo to be a crashing bore ▪ to be an insufferable bore
estar **más aburrido(-a) que un hongo** to be bored to death ▪ to be bored silly ▪ to be bored stiff
más acá ▪ en primera línea in the foreground
más adelante **1.** farther on **2.** más tarde ▪ después later on ▪ sometime after that
más admirar de alguien to most admire about someone ➤ Es lo que más admiro de ella. That's what I most admire about her.
más allá beyond ▪ farther on
el **más allá** the hereafter ▪ life after death
más alla de ▪ allende (de) beyond ▪ over and above
estar **más allá de la edad en la cual...** to be beyond the age at which... ➤ El animal está más allá de la edad en la cual (él) pueda defenderse fácilmente de los predadores. The animal is beyond the age at which it can defend itself easily from predators.
estar **más allá de la edad en (la) que...** ▪ estar más allá de la edad donde... to be beyond the age at which... ▪ to be beyond the age where... ➤ El hermanito de Andrés está más allá de la edad en la que sólo se quiere comer perritos calientes y hamburguesas. Andres' little brother is beyond the age where all he wants to eat is hotdogs and hamburgers. ➤ He pasado la edad en que me gustaban las discotecas a noventa decibelios. I'm beyond the age where I like ninety-decibel discotheques.

más allá de la tumba ▪ ultratumba beyond the grave
estar **más allá del alcance de** 1. to be beyond the scope of 2. to be beyond the reach of
ser el **más alto de la gama** to be the top of the line
más anhelado sueño fondest dream
estar **más apretados que sardinas en lata** to packed like sardines
ser **más apto que alguien en algo** to be more qualified than someone at something ▪ to be better qualified than someone at something ▪ to be better than someone at something
más arriba higher up
más atrás farther back
más aún even more ▪ all the more so ➤ Esos pequeños actos son manifestaciones de lo divino, más aún porque son espontáneos. Those little acts are manifestations of the divine, all the more so because they are spontaneous.
más bien 1. sino instead ▪ rather ▪ but rather 2. o sea or to be exact ▪ or more precisely ➤ Me concentré más bien en... I concentrated instead on... ➤ *(juego de palabras)* Llegamos a tierras de indios, más bien, hicimos hincapié. We arrived in Indian territory, or to be exact, stepped on an Inca's foot.
ser **más bien** ▪ parecerse más a to be more like ➤ Una avioneta ultraligera es más bien una cometa grande. ▪ Una avioneta ultraligera se parece más a una cometa grande. An ultralight airplane is more like a big kite.
más bien de: tratarse ~ to be instead ▪ to be rather ➤ El corazón artificial Jarvik 2000 se trata más bien de una pequeña bomba... The Jarvik 2000 artificial heart is rather a small pump...
ser **más bien tarde para** to be pretty late in the day to ▪ to be pretty late to ➤ Es más bien tarde para empezar a cortar el césped. It's pretty late in the day to start cutting the grass.
ser **más bruto(-a) que un arado** to be dumb as an ox ▪ to be dumb as a post
estar **más bueno(-a) que el pan** to be good looking
estar **más cagado que un palo de gallinero** *(L.am., subido de tono)* to be scared shitless
ser **más cálido que...** ▪ ser más abrigado que... ▪ abrigar más que... ▪ calentar más que... to be warmer than... ▪ to provide more warmth than... ➤ Las nuevas botas espaciales son más cálidas que las antiguas (botas) de cuero. ▪ Las nuevas botas espaciales son más abrigadas que las antiguas (botas) de cuero. ▪ Las nuevas botas espaciales abrigan más que las antiguas (botas) de cuero. ▪ Las nuevas botas espaciales calientan más que las antiguas (botas) de cuero. The new "moon" boots are warmer than the old leather ones.
ser **más caro de lo normal** to be more expensive than usual ▪ to be higher than usual
más castigado(-a) hardest hit
el **más cerca de** ▪ el más cercano nearest (to) ▪ closest to
la **más cerca de** ▪ la más cercana nearest (to) ▪ closest to ➤ Queda en la esquina más cerca de la Plaza San Miguel. It's on the corner nearest the Plaza San Miguel. ▪ It's on the corner closest to the Plaza San Miguel.
más cerca de casa closer to home
¡**más claro no canta un gallo!** 1. *(yo)* I hear you loud and clear! 2. *(nosotros)* we hear you loud and clear!
estar **más claro que el agua** to be crystal clear ▪ to be plain as day ▪ to be obvious
estar **más colorado que un pimiento** *(por quemaduras del sol)* to be red as a beet ▪ to be red as a lobster
estar **más colorado que un tomate** *(de quemadura de sol o de vergüenza)* to be red as a beet ▪ to be beet red
ser **más conocido(-a) como** to be better known as ▪ to be best known as ➤ Aunque Jakob Grimm fue un gran lingüista, es más conocido como escritor de fábulas. Although Jakob Grimm was a great linguist, he is best known as a writer of fables.
ser **más conocido(-a) por** to be best known for ➤ Aunque Jakob Grimm fue un gran lingüista, es más conocido por sus fábulas y cuentos de hadas. Although Jakob Grimm was a great linguist, he is best known for his fairy tales and fables.
¿**más cosas?** anything else?
estar **más contento que un chiquillo con zapatos nuevos** to be happier than a kid with new shoes
estar **más contento que unas pascuas** to be happy as a lark
más de la mitad more than half ➤ ¿Te puedes creer que ha pasado ya más de la mitad del año? Can you believe that the year is already more than half over?
más de lo mismo more of the same (thing)
más de lo normal more than usual
más de lo que more than
más de lo que (tú) piensas more than you think
más de lo que uno debiera more than one should have
más de lo que (yo) pueda comer: es ~ it's more than I can eat
más de una vez more than once
más de uno more than one ▪ some
estar **más derecho que una vela** to be ramrod straight
ser **más difícil de encontrar que una aguja en un pajar** to be like trying to find a needle in a haystack
ser **más duro(-a) que un roble** to be strong as an ox
ser **más el ruido que las nueces** ▪ ser menos de lo que parece not to be as bad as it appears to be
más encendido que el carmín: ponerse ~ to turn beet red
estar **más feliz que unas pascuas** *(Esp.)* ▪ estar más feliz como unas pascuas ▪ estar más contento que unas castañuelas to be happy as a lark ▪ to be happy as a clam
el **más grave** ▪ el peor worst ➤ El atentado más grave desde el inicio de la Intifada causa diecisiete muertos en Tel Aviv. The worst terrorist attack since the beginning of the Intifada causes seventeen deaths in Tel Aviv.
ser **más la bulla que la cabuya** to be more hype than substance
más le gustaría a uno ▪ uno prefería one would rather ➤ Más me gustaría salir a cenar y ver una película que ir al partido. ▪ Preferiría salir a cenar y ver una película que ir al partido. I would much rather go out to dinner and a movie than go to the game.
más le habría valido... 1. *(a él)* it would have been better (for him) to... 2. *(a ella)* it would have been better (for her) to 3. *(a usted)* it would have been better (for you) to...
más (le) vale it better
más le vale (a uno) one had better ▪ *(pintoresco)* one damn well better ➤ Más le vale llegar a horario mañana, o le pondré de patitas en la calle. He damn well better get here on time tomorrow, or I'm going to give him his walking papers.
más (le) vale a uno irse a trabajar one had better get to work ▪ one had better leave for work ▪ one had better be on one's way to work. ➤ Más vale que vaya a trabajar. I'd better get to work. ▪ I'd better leave for work. ▪ I'd better be on my way to work.
más le vale a uno que se dé prisa one had better hurry ➤ Más nos vale que no demos prisa. We had better hurry. ▪ We'd better hurry. ➤ Más me vale que me dé prisa. I had better hurry. ▪ I'd better hurry.
más (le) vale a uno que se ponga a trabajar one had better get to work ➤ Más vale que me ponga a trabajar. I'd better get to work.
más (le) vale que... it had better... ▪ *(coloquial)* it better...
más (le) vale que no it had better not ▪ *(coloquial)* it better not
más (le) vale que no... it had better not... ▪ *(coloquial)* it better not... ➤ Después de esperar diez días a que este puñetero aguacate madure, más (le) vale que no se eche a perder para mañana. After waiting ten days for this blasted avocado to ripen, it (had) better not spoil by tomorrow.
más lejos de farther than
más lejos de lo que imaginas farther than you think
ser **más libre que el aire** to be free as a bird
ser **más limpio que los chorros del oro** *(Esp.)* to be clean as a whistle
ser **más malo(-a) que pegarle un palo a un viejo** *(Arg.)* to be worse than stealing candy from a baby
ser **más malo(-a) que un dolor** to be a royal pain
ser **más malo(-a) que un nublado** to be bad news
ser **más manso que un cordero** ▪ ser un pan de Dios to be gentle as a lamb
mas me valdría que me ponga a trabajar I had better get to work ▪ I'd better get to work
más me valdría que me pusiera a trabajar ▪ más me valía que me pusiera a trabajar 1. I had better get to work ▪ I'd better get

to work 2. más me vale que me busque un empleo I had better get a job ■ I had better find work

más (me) vale que ■ haría bien en ■ debería I had better

más (me) vale que ■ haría bien en ■ debería I had better ■ I'd better ➤ Más vale que me dé prisa. ■ Haría bien en darme prisa. ■ Debería darme prisa. I had better hurry ■ I'd better hurry.

más me vale que me ponga a trabajar I had better get to work ■ I'd better get to work

más me valía que me pusiera a trabajar it was better that I got to work

ser la **más mínima de todas mis preocupaciones** to be the least of my worries

estar **más muerto(-a) que una tumba** to be dead as a doornail

estar **más muerto(-a) que vivo** to be more dead than alive

los **más necesitados de nuestra sociedad** the neediest in our society

estar **más negro que el azabache** ■ estar negro como el azabache to be jet-black

más o menos more or less ■ about ■ approximately ■ or so ➤ En una hora más o menos In an hour or so ■ In about an hour

estar **más ocupado(-a) que una colmena** to be busy as a bee ■ to be busier than all get-out

estar **más para abajo** to be farther down ➤ La parada de autobuses está más para abajo. The bus stop is farther down.

estar **más pelado(-a) que el culo de un mandril** not to have a pot to piss in ■ to be destitute

estar **más perdido(-a) que el barco del arroz** ■ estar más perdido(-a) que un turco en la neblina to be completely lost ■ to be totally lost

ser **más pesado que el aire** ■ ser más denso que el aire to be heavier than air ■ *(como un adjetivo antes de un sustantivo)* heavier-than-air ➤ Vuelo con una aeronave más pesada que el aire Flight by means of heavier-than-air aircraft

ser **más pesado(-a) que milanesa de chancho** *(Arg.)* ■ ser más pesado(-a) que una vaca en brazos to be a terrible nag

ser **más pesado(-a) que una vaca en brazos** to be a terrible nag ➤ Eres más pesado que una vaca en brazos. You're a terrible nag.

ser **más pobre que una rata** ■ estar más pobre que una rata to be poor as a church mouse

más pronto sooner (than that) ➤ Aunque no estaré en la facultad hasta el miércoles, podemos quedar más pronto de todas formas si necesitas ayuda con tu trabajo. Even though I won't be on campus until Wednesday, we can still meet if you need help on your paper sooner (than that).

más pronto o más tarde eventually ■ sooner or later

más propenso a more likely to ■ more apt to ■ more prone to

el **más propenso a** the most likely to ■ the most apt to ■ the most prone to

más propenso a que: resultar ~ to be more likely to

más que a uno ■ more than one does ➤ A mí me gusta la comida picante más que a él. I likes spicy food more than he does.

más que nada most of all ■ mostly ➤ Pero más que nada, me gusta la forma en que te mueves. ■ Pero más que nada, me gusta tu forma de moverte. But most of all, I like the way you move.

más que nada por primarily for ■ mostly for ■ more than anything else for ■ most of all for ➤ Lo hice más que nada por el dinero. I did it primarily for the money. ■ I did it mostly for the money. ■ I did it more than anything else for the money. ■ I did it for the money more than anything else.

más que nunca more than ever ➤ Estoy más convencido que nunca de que... I'm more convinced than ever that...

estar **más que satisfecho** to be quite satisfied

más que todo above all

más que yo more than I do ➤ Ella va al cine más que yo. She goes to the movies more than I do.

la **más remota memoria** ■ la memoria más remota one's earliest memory ➤ La más remota memoria de Alberto es de un coche rojo de fórmula uno de juguete con el que jugaba en la cuna. Alberto's earliest memory is of a toy red Formula One race car that he would play with in his crib.

estar **más seco que una pasa** *(anciano)* to be wrinkled

más sencillo que el mecanismo de un chupete as simple as pie ■ simple as pie ■ a piece of cake

mas si... if, however...

el **más significante** ■ el principal the main one ➤ Tengo muchos pasatiempos pero los más significantes son los deportes. I have a lot of hobbies but my main ones are sports.

estar **más solo que la una** to be (completely) alone

estar **más sordo(-a) que una tapia** to be deaf as a post

estar **más sucio(-a) que un palo de gallinero** to be filthy dirty ■ to be a filthy mess

más tarde later ➤ Cuatro años más tarde Four years later

más tarde de lo previsto later than expected ➤ Los científicos dicen que la capa de ozono será restaurada veinte años más tarde de lo previsto. Scientists say the ozone layer will be restored twenty years later than expected.

más tarde supe que... I later found out that... ■ I found out later that...

más te habría valido... it would have been better (for you) to...

más temprano de lo previsto earlier than expected ➤ Llegamos más temprano de lo previsto. We arrived earlier than expected.

más tiempo longer ■ any longer

estar **más tieso que un ajo** ■ sentirse más tieso que un ajo ■ quedarse más tieso que un ajo to be stiff as a board ➤ Ayer fui a una caminata, y hoy me siento más tieso que un ajo. I went hiking yesterday, and today I'm stiff as a board.

estar **más tieso que un palo** ■ estar más tieso que una estaca to be stiff as a board

más todavía ■ lo que es más ■ además what's more ■ furthermore

ser **más tonto que Abundio** to be dumb as a post ■ to be dumber than all get-out

más valdría 1. sería mejor it would be better 2. ser de beneficio a uno ■ ser una raya más para el tigre ■ de perdidos al río (one) might as well ➤ Más valdría venir a Madrid cuando no haga tanto calor. ■ Sería mejor venir a Madrid cuando no haga tanto calor. It would be better to come to Madrid when it's not so hot. ➤ Todo el mundo sabe que lo hiciste, así que más te valdría confesarlo. Everyone knows you did it, so you might as well confess. ➤ Ya que tenemos seis horas entre conexiones, más nos valdría salir a ver un poco de la ciudad. Since we have a six-hour layover, we might as well go see a little of the city. ➤ El dentista me dijo que tenía que sacarme las muelas del juicio en algún momento, así que más me valdría hacerlo ahora para terminarlo de una vez. The dentist said I had to have my wisdom teeth out at some point, so I might as well get it over with. ➤ A las cero horas y un minuto del día del Año Nuevo, me quedaba un cigarrillo en la cajetilla, así que me dije a mí mismo, más me valdría fumármelo. ■ A las cero horas y un minuto del día del Año Nuevo, me quedaba un cigarrillo en la cajetilla, así que me dije a mí mismo, ¿qué es una raya más para el tigre? ■ *(Esp.)* A las doce y uno del día del Año Nuevo, me quedaba un cigarrillo en la cajetilla, así que me dije a mí mismo, "de perdidos al río". At twelve-o-one New Year's Day, I had one cigarette left in the pack, so I said to myself, "What the heck, I might as well smoke it."

más vale it is better ➤ Más vale dar que recibir. It is better to give than to receive.

más vale algo que nada ■ es mejor que nada ■ *(Esp.)* menos da una piedra it's better than nothing ■ something's better than nothing

más vale caer en gracia que ser gracioso better to laugh than be laughed at

más vale dar que recibir it is better to give than receive ■ it is more blessed to give than to receive

más vale estar solo que mal acompañado it is better to be alone than in bad company

más vale maña que fuerza brain is better than brawn ■ brain over brawn

más vale pájaro en mano que ciento volando a bird in the hand is worth two in the bush

más vale predicar con el ejemplo actions speak louder than words

más vale prevenir que curar better safe than sorry ■ an ounce of prevention is worth a pound of cure

más vale que... ■ sería mejor que... ■ sería mejor si... it had better... ■ one had better... ■ you had better... ➤ Más vale que nos pongamos en marcha. We'd better be on our way. ➤ Más vale que tenga una buena excusa. *(él)* His excuse had better be good. ■ *(ella)* Her excuse had better be good. ■ *(usted)* Your excuse had better be good. ➤ Más vale que lo haga. I'd better (do it). ➤ Más vale que preguntes. You'd better ask.

más vale que me marche I'd better get going ■ I'd better be going

más vale que me ponga a trabajar I'd better get to work

más vale que sobre y no que falte 1. better a little extra than not enough ■ better too much than not enough 2. más vale muchos que pocos better too many than too few

más vale tarde que nunca better late than never

más vale que (tú)... ■ harías mejor en... you had better... ■ you'd better...

más vale que (tú) no... ■ harías mejor en no... you had better not... ■ you'd better not...

ser **más viejo que el diluvio universal** to be old as the hills

ser **más viejo(-a) que Matusalén** to be as old as Methuselah

ser **más viejo(-a) que la pana** to be old as the hills ■ to be as old as Methuselah

ser **más viejo(-a) que la sarna** to be old as the hills ■ to be as old as Methuselah

ser **más viejo(-a) que la tos** to be old as the hills ■ to be as old as Methuselah

estar **más visto que un tebeo** to be old hat

ser **más vivo que el hambre** to be very astute

ser el **más votado** to receive the highest number of votes

más y más ■ cada vez más more and more

masa líquida batter

mascador de chicle empedernido inveterate gum chewer

máscara mortuoria death mask

mascullar palabras to mutter words ■ to mutter something

masilla (de calafatear) ■ masilla para rellenar ■ pasta para rellenar caulking compound ■ caulk

el **máster en administración de empresas** masters in business administration ■ MBA

mata de pelo head of hair

matar a alguien a golpes to beat someone to death

matar a alguien a pedradas por... ■ lapidar a alguien por... to stone someone to death for...

matar a alguien a puñaladas to stab someone to death

matar a alguien de hambre to starve someone to death

matar a alguien con arma blanca to kill someone with a bladed weapon

matar dos pájaros de un tiro ■ matar dos pájaros en un tiro to kill two birds with one stone

matar el gusanillo to eat something to tide one over (until the next meal)

matar el hambre to satisfy one's hunger

matar el tiempo to kill time

matar la gallina de los huevos de oro to kill the goose that lays the golden egg

matarlas callando ■ ser un lobo con piel de cordero ■ ser un lobo vestido con piel de oveja to be a wolf in sheep's clothes ■ to be a wolf in sheep's clothing

matarse a hacer algo ■ matarse haciendo algo ■ darse una paliza haciendo algo to knock oneself out doing something

materia gris *(cerebro)* gray matter

la **materia ni se crea ni se destruye, simplemente se transforma** matter can neither be created nor destroyed, only changed in form

materia oscura *(astrofísica)* dark matter

el **material de oficina** office supplies ➤ Tienda de material de oficina Office supplies store

los **materiales de construcción** building materials

materias primas raw materials

matice (usted) eso ■ aclare (usted) eso tell me exactly what you mean ■ clarify that ■ explain that in more detail

matiza eso ■ aclara eso tell me exactly what you mean ■ clarify that ■ explain that in more detail

matizar lo que uno dijo antes to qualify what one said earlier ■ to put a different spin on what one said earlier

matizarle a alguien lo que uno quiere decir ■ aclararle a alguien lo que uno quiere decir to explain to someone (in more detail) what one means

matizarle a alguien lo que uno quiso decir ■ aclararle a alguien lo que uno quiso decir to explain to someone (in more detail) what one meant

matrícula universitaria university tuition fees ➤ ¿Cuánto fue tu matrícula? How much was your tuition?

matrícula de honor honor roll

matrícula de inscripción registration fee(s)

matrícula del coche license number ➤ ¿Cogiste la matrícula? ■ ¿Viste la matrícula? Did you get the license number?

estar **matriculado(-a) en el programa** to be matriculated in the program ➤ ¿Estás matriculado o sin matricular? Are you matriculated or non-matriculated?

matricularse en ■ inscribirse to enroll

matrimonio anterior previous marriage ➤ Tiene otros dos hijos de un matrimonio anterior. He has two other children from a previous marriage.

máximo caché top fee

máximo(-a) experto(-a) en foremost expert on

máximo(-a) sospechoso(-a) del caso ■ sospecho principal del caso prime suspect in the case

el **mayor colectivo de** ■ la mayor concentración de the largest concentration of ■ the greatest concentration of ➤ El mayor colectivo de magrebíes de Madrid vive en Lavapiés. ■ La mayor concentración de magrebíes de Madrid vive en Lavapiés. The largest concentration of northwest Africans in Madrid lives in Lavapiés. ■ The greatest concentration of northwest Africans lives in Lavapiés.

mayor de edad of legal age ■ of age

ser **mayor de x** to be over *x* years old ■ to be over *x* years of age ➤ Es mayor de cuarenta. *(él)* He's over forty. ■ *(ella)* She's over forty.

la **mayor parte de** most of ■ the better part of ■ the greater part of ➤ He pasado la mayor parte de los seis últimos años aquí en España. I have spent most of the last six years here in Spain. ■ I have spent the better the part of the last six years here in Spain. ■ I have spent the greater part of the last six years here in Spain. ➤ Pasamos la mayor parte del fin de semana en casa. We spent the better part of the weekend at home. ■ We spent most of the weekend at home. ■ We spent the greater part of the weekend at home.

la **mayor parte de la gente** ■ la mayoría de la gente most people

la **mayor parte de su vida** (for) most of one's life

la **mayor parte del tiempo** ■ la mayoría del tiempo most of the time

el **mayor problema** the biggest problem

los **mayores de x** people over *x* (years old) ➤ Los mayores de sesenta y cinco deben vacunarse. People over sixty-five should be vaccinated.

mayoría abrumadora overwhelming majority

mayoría absoluta *(con número superior a la mitad)* absolute majority ■ more than half

mayoría de la gente ■ la mayor parte de la gente most people

mayoría de quienes 1. most of those who ■ most of the ones who 1. La mayoría de quienes fueron encuestados prefirieron el chocolate argentino sobre el suizo. Most of those (who were) polled preferred Argentine chocolate to Swiss. 2. most of whom ➤ España tiene ochenta millones de habitantes, la mayoría de quienes son católicos. Spain has a population of eighty million, most of whom are Catholic.

mayoría del tiempo ■ la mayor parte del tiempo most of the time

mayoría relativa *(pero menos de 50%)* plurality ■ relative majority ■ the highest number of votes

me acaba de venir a la mente it just came to me

me acabo de enterar (de que...) ■ acabo de enterarme (de que...) I just found out (that...)

me achicharré *(coloquial)* I got burned to a crisp ■ I got badly sunburned

me acordé de ti cuando... I thought of you when...

me alegra estar aquí I'm glad to be here

me alegraría si... I'd be glad if...

me alegré de recibir noticias tuyas ▪ me alegró recibir noticias tuyas I was glad to hear from you

me alegro I'm glad

me alegro de volverte a ver it's good to see you again ▪ it's nice to see you again

me alegro mucho de que I'm glad that ▪ I'm very happy that

me alegro por ello I'm glad of that

me alegro por ti ▪ estoy contento(-a) por ti I'm happy for you

me alegro que nos hayamos visto ▪ me encantó verte hoy I enjoyed seeing you today

me alegró recibir noticias tuyas ▪ me alegré de recibir noticias tuyas I was glad to hear from you

¡me apunto! count me in!

me aso (vivo) ▪ me estoy asando (vivo) I'm burning up

me atienden, gracias I'm being helped, thank you

me bajo en la próxima I get off at the next stop ▪ I'd like to get off at the next stop

me bastó un vistazo para... all it took was one look (for me) to...

me bastó una mirada para comprobar que... I could see at a glance that...

¡me basto (y me sobro)! I can do it on my own (and I don't need anyone's help)! ➤ Me basto yo solo(-a) para complicarme la vida. No necesito que vengas a complicármela tú. I can complicate my own life. I don't you to do it for me.

me cachis en los moros *(Esp., arcaico)* what a pain! ▪ good grief! ▪ that's terrible!

me cae bien 1. *(él)* I like him 2. *(ella)* I like her

me carga... 1. me cae pesado it bothers me 2. *(él)* he teases me 3. *(ella)* she teases me

me cargan... 1. they bother me 2. they tease me

me chifla ▪ me encanta I love ➤ Me chifla el ceviche. I love ceviche.

me clavaron ▪ me vieron la cara de tonto they gouged me ▪ I paid through the nose

me complace anunciar it gives me great pleasure to announce

¿me comprendes? see what I mean?

¿me concedes este baile, por favor? ▪ ¿por favor me concedes este baile? may I have this dance?

me conoces bien you know me better than that ➤ Me conoces bien. Por supuesto que no. You know me better than that. Of course not!

me consta que... I know for a fact that...

me costó un buen dinero it cost me a pretty penny

me cuesta bastante dar con ello it's hard to put my finger on it

me da corte (hacer algo) ▪ me da vergüenza (hacer algo) I'm not comfortable (doing something) ▪ I'm embarrassed (to do something) ▪ it embarrasses me (to do something)

me da igual 1. me da lo mismo ▪ me es igual it doesn't matter ▪ it doesn't make any difference ▪ I don't care ▪ I have no preference 2. cualquiera de los dos either one

me da la corazonada de que... ▪ me late que... I have a hunch that...

me da la impresión de que... ▪ me da la sensación de que... ▪ me da la corazonada de que... I get the feeling that... ▪ I get the impression that...

me da la sensación de que... ▪ me da la impresión de que... ▪ me da la corazonada de que... I get the feeling that... ▪ I get the impression that...

me da lástima *(él)* I feel sorry for him ▪ *(ella)* I feel sorry for her ▪ *(usted)* I feel sorry for you

me da lo mismo ▪ para mí es lo mismo ▪ me da igual ▪ lo mismo me da it doesn't make any difference to me ▪ it makes no difference to me ▪ it doesn't matter to me ▪ it's all the same to me

me da pena que 1. I feel bad that 2. it grieves me that ➤ Me da pena que no hayas conectado con mis amigos en México. I feel bad that you haven't linked up with my friends in Mexico. ▪ I feel bad that you haven't connected with my friends in Mexico.

me da una rabia (cuando...) ▪ me da una bronca (cuando...) it makes me mad (that...) ▪ it makes me angry (that...) ▪ it makes me mad (when...) ▪ it makes me angry (when...)

¿me da (usted) la hora? ▪ ¿tiene (usted) la hora? could you tell me the time? ▪ could you tell me what time it is? ▪ have you got the time? ▪ do you have the time?

me da vergüenza it embarrasses me

me da vergüenza admitirlo ▪ me da vergüenza decirlo it embarrasses me to admit it

¿me das agua? ▪ ¿me podrías dar agua? could I have a drink of water? ▪ may I have a drink of water? ▪ could I get a drink of water? ▪ may I get a drink of water?

¿me das fuego? ▪ ¿tienes fuego? do you have a light? ▪ have you got a light?

¿me das las señas? ▪ ¿me das tu dirección? would you give me your address?

¿me das una mano? ▪ ¿me echas una mano? would you give me a hand? ▪ can you give me a hand?

me debo estar volviendo loco(-a) I must be losing my marbles

me debo por entero a la patria *(Valle-Inclán)* ▪ la patria es primero my whole duty is to my country

me deja alucinado(-a) it blows me away ▪ it blows my mind

¿me deja pasar? may I get by? ▪ may I get past? ▪ could I get by? ▪ could I get past? ➤ Perdone. ¿Me deja pasar? Excuse me. May I get by? ▪ Excuse me. May I get past?

¿me dejas...? ▪ ¿me prestas...? may I borrow...? ▪ could I borrow...? ▪ can I borrow...? ▪ would you lend me...? ➤ ¿Me dejas tu boli? ▪ ¿Me prestas tu boli? May I borrow your (ballpoint) pen? ▪ Could I borrow your pen? ▪ Can I borrow your pen? ▪ Would you lend me your pen?

¿me dejas mirar tu libro? may I look at your book? ▪ can I look at your book?

me dejé llevar I got carried away

me dejo llevar I get carried away ▪ I let myself get carried away

me dejó alucinado(-a) it blew me away ▪ it blew my mind

me dejó fascinado(-a) I found it (totally) fascinating ▪ I was (totally) fascinated by it

me dejo llevar por la corriente I get carried away

me desborda ▪ me sobrepasa it's beyond me

me despierto en este momento ▪ acabo de despertarme I just woke up

me di cuenta de que... I realized that... ▪ I found myself... ➤ Mientras hacía cola para comprar la entrada, me di cuenta de que no quería ver la película. As I stood in line to buy the ticket, I realized (that) I didn't want to see the movie. ▪ As I stood in line to buy the ticket, I found myself not wanting to see the movie.

me dibujas a mi novia draw me a picture of my girlfriend

me dieron las uvas *(Esp., coloquial)* ▪ se me hizo muy tarde it got very late (on me) ▪ I ran way overtime

me dije I said to myself ▪ I thought to myself

me dijeron que... they told me that... ▪ I was told that...

me dio a entender que... *(él)* I got the impression from him that... ▪ he gave me the impression that... ▪ *(ella)* I got the impression from her that... ▪ she gave me the impression that...

me dio por pensar que... it got me (to) thinking that...

me dio vergüenza it embarrassed me

me dio un vuelco el corazón my heart leaped

me doy por vencido(-a) I give up

me duele la cabeza ▪ tengo un dolor de cabeza I have a headache

¿me echas una mano? ▪ ¿me das una mano? would you give me a hand? ▪ can you give me a hand?

me echo una pensada I'll give it some thought

me encandilaron (las luces) ▪ me enceguecieron (las luces) I was blinded by the lights

me encanta este trocito *(de la canción)* ▪ este trocito me encanta ▪ me encanta esta parte I love this part

me encantaría, gracias I'd love to, thank you

me encantaría saber... I'd love to know...

me encantaría saberlo I'd love to know

me encantó conocerte hoy ▪ encantado de haberte conocido hoy I enjoyed meeting you today
me encantó verte hoy ▪ me alegro que nos hayamos visto hoy I enjoyed seeing you today
me encargo de... I'm in charge of...
me enceguecieron (las luces) ▪ me encandilaron (las luces) I was blinded by the lights
me encuentro fatal I feel terrible ▪ I feel really sick
me enteré por un amigo I heard it from a friend ▪ I found about about it through a friend
me entero I'll know ➤ Me entero en cinco minutos si este programa va a funcionar I'll know in five minutes if this software is going to work.
me entretiene ▪ lo disfruto I enjoy it
me entró algo en el ojo ▪ tengo algo en el ojo ▪ se me cayó algo en el ojo I got something in my eye
me equivoqué I was wrong
me equivoqué contigo I was wrong about you
me es completamente igual it's all the same to me
me es igual 1. me da igual ▪ me da lo mismo ▪ it doesn't matter ▪ it doesn't make any difference ▪ I don't care ▪ I have no preference 2. cualquiera de los dos either one
me es indiferente que... ▪ no me importa que... I don't care whether... ➤ Que les guste o no me es indiferente. ▪ Que les guste o no no me importa. I don't care whether they like it or not.
me es inverosímil (que...) ▪ se me hace inverosímil (que...) I don't think it's true (that...) ▪ I think it's highly unlikely (that...)
¿me escuchan por atrás? can you (all) hear me back there? ▪ can those of you in the back hear me?
me especializo en ▪ me estoy especializando en I'm majoring in
me está chinchando 1. *(él)* he's bothering me 2. *(ella)* she's bothering me
me está rondando un resfriado I'm coming down with a cold ▪ I'm getting a cold ▪ I'm catching a cold ▪ I'm starting to get a cold
me estás gustando I'm really getting to like you
me estás tomando la delantera ▪ te estás adelantando a mí you're getting ahead of me
me estoy adelantando ▪ me estoy adelantando mucho ▪ me estoy adelantando demasiado I'm getting ahead of myself
me estoy adelantando a los acontecimientos I'm getting ahead of myself
me estoy adelantando a ti I'm getting ahead of you
me estoy encontrando mal I feel funny
me estoy especializando en ▪ me especializo en I'm majoring in
¿me explico? ▪ ¿me sigues? do you follow me?
me falta lo peor the worst is yet to come
me faltaba lo peor the worst was yet to come
me fue imposible hacerlo I wasn't able to do it ▪ I didn't get to it ➤ Hoy me fue imposible hacerlo, pero mañana seguro que lo haré. I didn't get to it today, but I will tomorrow for sure.
me fue imposible ir I didn't get to go ▪ I couldn't go ▪ I wasn't able to go
me gané *x* euros hoy I made *x* euros today ➤ Me gané cien euros hoy. I made a hundred euros today.
me gotea la nariz ▪ me moquea la nariz I have a runny nose
me gusta I like it
me gusta cantidad ▪ me gusta mucho ▪ me encanta ▪ me gusta horrores I love it
me gusta cómo lo manejaste I like the way you handled it ▪ I like the way you handled that
me gusta esquiar I like to ski ▪ I enjoy skiing ▪ I like skiing
me gusta que me rasquen la espalda I like to get my back scratched
me gusta tu corte de pelo I like your haircut
me gusta tu peinado I like your hair ▪ I like the way you've fixed your hair ▪ I like the way you've combed your hair
me gustan I like them
me gustaría enmarcar esto ▪ me gustaría encuadrar esto I'd like to get this framed ▪ I'd like to have this framed
me gustaría haber ido ▪ me habría gustado ir ▪ me hubiera gustado ir ▪ me hubiese gustado ir I would like to have gone ▪ I would have liked to go ▪ I'd like to have gone ▪ I'd have liked to go
me gustaría hablar contigo a solas I would like to speak with you alone ▪ I would like to speak to you alone ▪ I would like to talk to you alone ▪ I would like to talk with you alone ▪ I'd like to talk with you alone
me gustaría ir I would like to go ▪ I'd like to go
me gustaría presentarte... I'd like you to meet... ▪ I'd like to introduce you to... ➤ Me gustaría presentarte a mis primas, Emily y Alice. I'd like you to meet my cousins, Emily and Alice. ▪ I'd like to introduce you to my cousins, Emily and Alice.
me gustaría saber qué tienes que decir sobre esto ▪ me gustaría saber qué tienes que decir respecto a esto I'd like to hear what you have to say about that ▪ I'd like to hear what you have to say about it
me gustaría repetir *(comida)* I'd like (to have) some more ▪ I'd like (to have) another helping
me ha pillado el toro *(Esp.)* ▪ se me agotó el tiempo I ran out of time
me habría gustado haber ido I would like to have gone ▪ I'd like to have gone
me habría gustado ir ▪ me hubiese gustado ir I would have liked to go ▪ I'd have liked to go
me hace mucha ilusión I'm really looking forward to it ▪ I'm really excited about it
me hace recordar ▪ me recuerda a it reminds me of
¿me haces un favor? will you do me a favor?
me hago cargo de lo que dices sobre... *(Esp.)* ▪ sé lo que quieres decir sobre... ▪ entiendo lo que quieres decir sobre... ▪ sé qué quieres decir sobre... I know what you mean about... ▪ I understand what you mean about...
¡me han dado! ▪ ¡me dieron! they got me! ▪ they got me good!
¡me han pegado una paliza! ▪ ¡me han dado (una paliza)! they got me! ▪ they got me good!
me han sableado they screwed me (over) ▪ I got screwed (over)
me haría falta dinero ▪ no puedo permitírmelo I can't afford it ➤ Me gustaría ir a recorrer Europa con vosotros, pero me haría falta dinero. Me gustaría ir a recorrer Europa con vosotros, pero no puedo permitírmelo. I'd like to tour Europe with you (all), but I can't afford it.
me has dado mucho en qué pensar you've given me a lot to think about
me has leído el pensamiento cuando you were reading my mind when
¡me has oído! you heard me!
me has picado la curiosidad ▪ ya me has picado el gusanillo you've piqued my curiosity you've got me curious ▪ you've got my curiosity up ▪ you've got my curiosity going
¡me has pillado! ▪ ¡me has cazado! you got me!
me has pillado en un mal momento ▪ me enganchaste en un mal momento you've caught me at a bad time
me he criado en... I grew up in...
me he dejado las llaves dentro de la casa *(Esp.)* ▪ me quedé afuera ▪ me encerré fuera de (mi) casa ▪ me encerré afuera I locked myself out of the house
me he dejado las llaves dentro del auto ▪ me quedé afuera del auto ▪ me encerré fuera del auto I locked myself out of the car ▪ I locked the keys in the car
me he enterado de que... I have learned that... ▪ it has come to my attention that... ▪ it has been brought to my attention that...
me he quedado dudando I'm still not sure
me he quedado pasmado(-a) (de que...) I was astounded (that...)
me hubiera gustado ir ▪ me hubiese gustado ir ▪ me habría gustado ir I would have liked to go ▪ I'd have liked to go
me hubiese gustado ir ▪ me hubiera gustado ir ▪ me habría gustado ir ▪ me gustaría haber ido I would liked to go ▪ I'd have liked to go
me hubiera gustado tanto que... ▪ me hubiese gustado tanto que... I would have liked it so much if... ➤ Me hubiera

gustado tanto que te hubieras quedado. I would have liked it so much if you had stayed.

me huele a chamusquina ■ me huele a gato encerrado there's something fishy about this ■ there's something fishy going on here

me huele a gato encerrado ■ me huele a chamusquina there's something fishy about this ■ there's something fishy going on here

me ilusiona... I am looking forward to...

me imaginé que... I figured (that)... ➤ Me imaginé que no podías quedar. I figured (that) you couldn't meet.

me impactó it made an impression on me

me importa un bledo ■ no me importa un bledo ■ no me importa un comino ■ no me importa un cuerno ■ no me importa un pito ■ no me importa un pepino ■ no me importa un rábano I could give a damn ■ I don't give a damn ■ I could care less

me importa una mierda *(subido de tono)* ■ me la trae floja ■ me la suda ■ me importa un pito I could give a shit ■ I don't give a shit

me coges fuera de juego *(Esp.)* ■ me pillas fuera de juego ■ me agarras deprevenido(-a) you've caught me off guard ■ you've got me on that one

me la encuentro hasta en la sopa 1. I see it all over the place 2. *(ella)* it's almost like she follows me around ■ she's always in my face

me la pela *(subido de tono)* I don't give a damn ■ I could care less ■ I couldn't care less

me la refanfinflas I couldn't care less

¡me la suda! I don't give a damn! ■ I could care less! ■ I couldn't care less!

me la trae floja *(subido de tono)* I could give a shit ■ I don't give a shit

me las arreglaré yo solo(-a) I'll manage somehow ■ I'll get along somehow ■ I'll survive somehow

me llama la atención lo siguiente: the following has come to my attention: ■ it has come to my attention that...

me llama la atención que... I notice that... ■ I've noticed that...

me le encuentro hasta en la sopa *(Esp., leísmo)* it's almost like he follows me around ■ he's always in my face

¡me lo decía el corazón! I knew it deep down!

me lo dijo un pajarito ■ me lo ha contado un pajarito a little bird told me

me lo encuentro hasta en la sopa 1. I see it all over the place 2. *(él)* it's almost like he follows me around ■ he's always in my face

me lo estaba preguntando I was just wondering

¡me lo figuro! ■ ¡ya me imagino! ■ ¡me lo imagino! ■ ¡ya me lo figuro! that's what I figured! ■ that's what I thought!

me lo ha contado un pajarito ■ me lo dijo un pajarito a little bird told me

me lo has puesto en bandeja you made it easy for me

me lo has quitado de la boca you took the words right out of my mouth

¡me lo imagino! 1. I can imagine! 2. ¡me lo figuro! ■ ¡ya me lo imagino! ■ ¡ya me imagino! that's what I figured! ■ that's what I thought!

me lo llevé por la cara *(Esp.)* ■ me lo llevé regalado I got it for free ■ I got it for nothing

me lo llevé regalado ■ me lo llevé gratis ■ lo conseguí gratis I got it for free ■ I got it for nothing

¿me lo puede pedir? ■ ¿lo puedo dejar encargado? can you (special) order it for me?

me lo quedo I'll take it

me mola cantidad ■ me gusta cantidad I love it

me moquea la nariz ■ me gotea la nariz I have a runny nose

me nadan los pies en estos zapatos ■ estos zapatos son como barcos ■ me quedan muy grandes los zapatos these shoes are much too big ■ these shoes are far too big ■ *(coloquial)* these shoes are way too big

me negué I refused ➤ Me negué porque... I refused because...

me niego I refuse

me ocuparé de ello ■ yo me ocuparé de ello I'll take care of it

me parece difícil de creer que... ■ lo encuentro difícil de creer que... ■ lo veo difícil de creer que... I find it difficult to believe that...

me parece muy entretenido ■ lo veo muy entretenido ■ lo encuentro muy entretenido I find it entertaining

me parece que ■ se me figura que ■ se me antoja que it seems to me that

me parece bien it's okay with me ■ it's fine with me ■ fair enough! ■ *(incorrecto pero común)* it's okay by me ■ it's fine by me

me parece muy bien 1. I think it's a good idea 2. it's fine with me ■ it's okay with me ■ that's fine with me ■ *(incorrecto pero común)* it's okay by me ■ it's fine by me

me parece que... ■ se me hace que... ■ se me figura que... it seems to me that...

me parece que más bien es... I think it really *is*...

¿me pasas la sal y pimienta, por favor? would you pass me the salt and pepper, (please)? ■ pass the salt and pepper, (please)

me pasó lo mismo ■ igual me pasó the same thing happened to me

me patea el hígado *(L.am.)* ■ me pone de mala leche it makes me sick ■ it gives me the fantods ➤ La colección de sapos, gusanos y escarabajos de mi hermanito me patea el hígado. My little brother's collection of toads, worms, and beetles makes me sick. ■ My little brother's collection of toads, worms, and beetles gives me the fantods.

me patea el hígado que... it makes me sick that...

¿me permites? 1. *(cortés)* may I? ■ *(informal)* can I? 2. could I see it? ■ could I look at it?

¿me permites la pregunta? ■ ¿te puedo preguntar? might I ask?

¿me permites el bolígrafo? may I use your pen? ■ can I use your pen?

¿me permites ir al baño? may I use the bathroom? ■ may I use your bathroom?

¿me permites pasar? may I get by?

¡me pido prime! *(niños)* I want go to first! ■ I get to go first!

me pilló de sorpresa ■ me agarró de sorpresa it caught me by surprise

me podía haber imaginado ■ me podría haber imaginado ■ tendría que haberlo sabido I might have known

me podría haber imaginado ■ me podía haber imaginado ■ tendría que haberlo sabido I might have known

me podrían persuadir I could be talked into it ■ I could be persuaded

me podrías persuadir you could talk me into it ■ you could persuade me ■ I could be persuaded ➤ Con un poco de labia, me podrías persuadir. With a little cajoling, you could talk me into it. ■ With a little cajoling, you could persuade me.

me pone *(él)* he turns me on ■ *(ella)* she turns me on

me pone a cien 1. it makes me mad ■ it makes me see red ■ *(él)* he makes me mad ■ *(ella)* she makes me mad 2. *(él)* he turns me on ■ *(ella)* she turns me on

me pone enfermo(-a) ■ me enferma it makes me sick

me pone enfermo(-a) que... ■ me enferma que... it makes me sick that... ■ it makes me sick when...

me pone triste it makes me sad

¿me pone una ración de...? ■ ¿me sirve una porción de...? could I have a plate of...?

me produjo tristeza it made me sad

me pude ver a toda mi familia I got to see all my family ■ I got to see my whole family

me pueden esperar sentados (porque parados se van a cansar) I won't be back ■ I'm never going back

me puedo imaginar que a alguien le guste... ■ puedo llegar a imaginarme que a alguien le guste... ■ puedo llegar a entender que a alguien le guste... ■ puedo llegar a comprender que a alguien le guste... ■ puedo entender que a alguien le guste... ■ puedo comprender que a alguien le guste... I can see (somone's) liking it ■ I can imagine (someone's) liking it

me queda bien it fits (me)

me queda mal it doesn't fit (me)

me queda poco tiempo I don't have much time (left) ▪ I'm running out of time
me queda uno I have one left
me quedan *x* I have *x* left ➤ Me quedan diez. I have ten left.
me quedan grandes los zapatos these shoes are too big
me quedé corto 1. no me alcanzó el dinero I came up short (of money) ▪ I didn't have enough money 2. subestimé el impacto I underestimated it
me quedé de piedra I was flabbergasted ▪ I was stunned
me quedé dormido ▪ dormí de más ▪ se me pegaron las sábanas I overslept
me quedé en blanco I drew a bank
me quedé en la de Valencia I was dumbstruck
me quedé fascinado(-a) I was fascinated
me quedo I'm staying
me recuerda a ▪ me hace recordar it reminds me of
¿me regalas agua? ▪¿me das agua? could I have a drink of water? ▪ may I have a drink of water? ▪ could I get a drink of water? ▪ may I get a drink of water?
me repatea que... ▪ me molesta que... it bothers me that... ▪ what bothers me is that... ▪ what gets me is that...
me revienta que... it makes me furious when... ▪ it makes me furious that...
me revuelve la bilis it makes my blood boil
me rindo ▪ me doy por vencido I surrender ▪ I give up
me sale bien I do it well
me salió el contestador I got the answering machine
me sé la canción de memoria I know the song by heart
me sé tu telefóno (de memoria) I know your telephone number (by heart) ▪ I've memorized your phone number
me sé la lección ▪ me he aprendido la lección I know the lesson thoroughly ▪ I know the lesson backwards and forwards
me sentí como un florero I felt completely out of it ▪ I felt excluded
me siento de aquí I feel like I'm from here ▪ I feel like I belong here
me siento muy decaído(-a) sobre eso ▪ me siento muy desconcertado(-a) por eso I feel sick about it ▪ I feel bad about it
me siento muy desconcertado(-a) por eso ▪ me siento muy decaído(-a) sobre eso I feel sick about it ▪ I feel bad about it
me siento (muy) indispuesto(-a) I don't feel up to it ▪ I feel that I can't do it
me siento muy mal con eso ▪ me siento muy mal por eso ▪ me siento muy mal de eso ▪ me siento muy mal sobre eso ▪ me siento muy mal en esto I feel really bad about it
me siento raro(-a) I feel funny
me siento tonto(-a) I feel like a fool
¿me sirve una porción de...? ▪ ¿me pone una ración de...? could I have a plate of...?
me sobrepasa ▪ me desborda it's beyond me
me sonrojé I blushed
¡me suda la polla! *(muy subido de tono)* ▪ I could give a shit!
me suena it rings a bell ▪ it sounds familiar
me suena un montón it sounds really familiar ▪ it definitely rings a bell
me supera ▪ es superior a mis fuerzas it's beyond me
me temo I'm afraid ➤ Es sólo el técnico de la tele, me temo. It's just the TV repairman, I'm afraid.
me temo que no I'm afraid not
me temo que sí I'm afraid so
me tienen de la Ceca a la Meca ▪ me tienen de acá para allá they have me running from pillar to post
me toca a mí ▪ a mí me toca 1. voy yo it's my turn ▪ it's my go 2. he llegado antes ▪ (yo) estoy antes I'm next ▪ I was here first ▪ I got here first
me tocaron *x* dólares I won *x* dollars
me tomaría una bebida ahora mismo I could (really) go for a drink right now
me tuvieron que dar puntos (de sutura) ▪ *(Esp., coloquial)* ▪ me tuvieron que coser I had to have stitches
me va entrando el sueño I'm getting sleepy
me va entrando la curiosidad it's piquing my curiosity
¡me van a oír! I'm going to give them a piece of my mind!
me vendría bien tu ayuda ▪ me vendría bien trabajar contigo I could use your help
me veo... I see myself ▪ I look... ▪ I think I'm... ➤ Me veo un poco gordo. I think I'm getting a little bit fat.
¡me voy! I'm off! ▪ I'm on my way!
me voy a dormir ▪ me voy a la cama I'm going to bed
me voy al sobre I'm going to hit the sack ▪ *(coloquial)* I'm gonna hit the sack
me voy con esto this is my last one
me vuelve loco(-a) it drives me crazy
me zumban los oídos my ears are ringing
mecánica ondulatoria *(física)* wave mechanics
mechero de Bunsen Bunsen burner
el **mechón de pelo** lock of hair
media aritmética arithmetic mean
media de average number of
media de: crecer una ~ to grow an average of
media de: hacer una ~ to do an average of
media de edad de: tener una ~ to have an average age of ➤ Mis compañeros de clase tienen una edad media de veinte años. My classmates have an average age of twenty (years).
media etiqueta *(Esp.)* ▪ corbata y saco coat and tie ➤ Se requiere para la cena media etiqueta. ▪ Se requiere para la cena corbata y saco. The dress for the dinner is coat and tie. ➤ (Yo) llevaba media etiqueta. I was wearing a coat and tie.
media hermana half sister
media jornada: trabajar ~ ▪ trabajar tiempo medio ▪ trabajar medio día to work part time
media llave *(lucha libre)* half nelson ➤ Mi oponente me sujetó con una media llave. My opponent pinned me with a half nelson.
media mañana twelve noon ▪ midday ▪ high noon
media, mediana y moda *(estadística)* mean, median and mode
media naranja: mi ~ ▪ mi cara mitad my other half
mediante un procedimiento sencillo by means of a simple procedure ▪ (by) using a simple procedure ▪ with a simple procedure ▪ through a simple procedure
mediar en la pelea to mediate in the fight ▪ to break up the fight
mediar un abismo entre ▪ estar mundos aparte ▪ estar diametralmente opuestos to be poles apart ➤ Media un abismo entre las facciones políticas. The political factions are poles apart.
mediar un buen trecho to have a long way to go ▪ to have a ways to go
medias: hablar a ~ ▪ not to tell the whole truth ▪ to tell only part of the story ▪ to hem and haw ▪ to beat around the bush ▪ to avoid giving a direct answer
medias tintas: andarse con ~ to hem and haw ▪ to beat around the bush ▪ to avoid giving a direct answer
medias tintas: hablar con ~ to speak ambiguously ▪ to speak in ambiguities
mediatizar los resultados ▪ distorcionar los resultados to bias the results ▪ to skew the results ▪ to doctor the results ▪ to distort the results
médico de cabecera family doctor
médico de confianza personal physician
médico de medicina general general practitioner
médico espiritual ▪ confesor confessor
el **médico me ha recetado antibióticos** the doctor prescribed me antibiotics
medida de choque drastic measure
medida de cintura ▪ talla de cintura waist size
medida de hasta qué punto... ▪ indicador de hasta qué punto... indication of how much... ▪ indication of the extent to which... ▪ indicator of how much... ▪ indicator of the extent to which... ▪ barometer of how much... ▪ barometer of the extent to which... ➤ *(noticia)* La amplitud de la victoria de Blair será una medida de hasta qué punto ha fracasado la apuesta conservadora de espantar a los británicos con el fantasma de Europa y su moneda. ▪ La amplitud de la victoria de Blair será un indicador de hasta qué punto ha fracasado la apuesta conservadora de espantar a los británicos con el fantasma de Europa y su

moneda. The margin of Blair's victory will be a barometer of the extent to which the conservative ploy of scaring the British with the specter of Europe and its currency has failed.

medidas cautelares precautionary measures ▪ preventive measures

medidas correctoras corrective measures

medidas de excepción heightened measures ▪ extraordinary measures

medidas de seguridad security measures

medidas drásticas drastic steps ▪ drastic measures

medio crudo medium rare

medio de trabajo line of work

medio de vida estilo de vida way of life

estar **medio dormido(-a)** ▪ estar entre sueños ▪ estar adormecido to be half asleep

medio en serio, medio en broma: decir algo ~ to say something half seriously, half in jest

medio hermano half brother

medio mundo half the world ▪ half the population ➤ Medio mundo asistió al concierto de Franco de Vita. Half the population was at the Franco de Vita concert.

medio país habla de... half the country is talking about...

medio para conseguir un fin ▪ medio para lograr un fin means to an end

medio para lograr un fin ▪ medio para conseguir un fin means to an end

medio propicio good way ➤ El estudiar es un medio propicio para aprobar el examen. Studying is a good way to pass the exam.

medios de comunicación news media

medios de hacer algo means of doing something

medios de transporte means of transport

medir el tiempo de algo ▪ cronometrar algo ▪ contar el tiempo de algo to time something ➤ Necesitamos que alguien mida el tiempo de los discursos. We need (for) someone to time the talks.

medir la temperatura a alguien ▪ tomar la temperatura a alguien to take someone's temperature ➤ Su madre le midió la temperatura. ▪ Su madre le tomó la temperatura. *(a él)* His mother took his temperature. ▪ *(a ella)* Her mother took her temperature.

medir las cosas por el mismo rasero ▪ medir las cosas por la misma vara to measure things by the same standards ▪ to hold others to the same standard you hold yourself to

medir las cosas por la misma vara ▪ medir las cosas por el mismo rasero to measure things by the same standard

medir las palabras to measure one's words ▪ to be measured in one's words

medir mal sus propias fuerzas to bite off more than one can chew ➤ Ha medidio mal sus propias fuerzas. He's bitten off more than he can chew.

medir sus fuerzas to take each other on ▪ to test each other's mettle ▪ to pit oneself against someone

medirle la tensión a alguien ▪ tomarle la presión a alguien to check someone's blood pressure ▪ to take someone's blood pressure ➤ El médico le midió la tensión (a ella). ▪ El médico le tomó la presión (a ella). The doctor checked her blood pressure.

medirlo a pasos to pace it off ➤ Lo medí a pasos. I paced it off. ➤ Medí la sala a pasos. I measured the living room by pacing it off.

medirse con alguien to take on someone ▪ to take someone on

médula ósea: un transplante de la ~ bone marrow transplant

mejor actriz de reparto best supporting actress

mejor actor de reparto best supporting actor

mejor aún ▪ o mejor aún ▪ (o) mejor todavía better still ▪ better yet

estar **mejor bajo** to be better off under

estar **mejor con** to be better off with

ser **mejor de lo esperado** ▪ ser mejor de lo que se esperaba to be better than expected ➤ La ganancia de este año es mejor de lo esperado. ▪ La ganancia de este año es mejor de lo que se esperaba. This year's earnings were better than expected.

ser **mejor de lo que se esperaba** ▪ ser mejor de lo esperado to be better than expected ➤ La ganancia de este año es mejor de lo que se esperaba. ▪ La ganancia de este año es mejor de lo esperado. This year's earnings were better than expected.

el **mejor de los dos** the better of the two ➤ Ella es el mejor político de los dos. She is the better politician of the two.

ser el **mejor de su clase** ▪ ser el mejor del grupo ▪ ser el mejor del conjunto to be the best of the group ▪ to be the best of the lot ➤ Sara es la mejor de la clase. Sara is the best pupil in her class. ➤ Ese coche de carreras es el mejor de su clase. That race car is the best in its class.

ser el, la **mejor de toda la ciudad** to be the best one in town

el **mejor de todos los mundos posibles** the best of all possible worlds

la **mejor defensa es un buen ataque** the best defense is a good offense

estar **mejor del resfriado** (for) one's cold to be better ➤ Hoy estoy mejor del resfriado. My cold is better today.

mejor del grupo ▪ mejor del conjunto ▪ mejor de su clase best of the group ▪ best of the lot

mejor del conjunto ▪ mejor del grupo ▪ mejor de su clase best of the group ▪ best of the lot

mejor dicho ▪ o mejor dicho or rather

ser el, la **mejor en lo que hace** to be the best there is (at something) ▪ to be the one who does something the best

ser el, la **mejor en todos los aspectos (para las necesidades de uno)** to be the best all around ➤ Es el mejor carro en todos los aspectos para mis necesidades. This is the best all around car for me.

la **mejor explicación** the best explanation

mejor harías... you'd do better (to...)

mejor malo conocido que bueno por conocer better the devil you know than the devil you don't

ser la **mejor manera de hacer algo** to be the best way to do something ➤ ¿Cuál es la mejor manera de mandar este paquete? What's the best way to send this package?

mejor me voy ▪ será mejor que me vaya I'd better leave ▪ I'd better go

ser el **mejor medio para hacer algo** ▪ ser la mejor manera de hacer algo ▪ ser la mejor forma de hacer algo ▪ ser lo más adecuado para hacer algo to be the best way to do something ➤ ¿Cuál es el mejor medio de enviar este paquete? ▪ ¿Cuál es la mejor manera de enviar este paquete? What's the best way to send this package?

mejor no ▪ será mejor que no *(yo)* I'd better not ▪ *(tú)* you'd better not

mejor no menearlo ▪ no tientes al diablo let sleeping dogs lie

la **mejor palabra es la que siempre queda por decir** the best words remain to be said

ser **mejor para alguien que...** to be better for someone than... ➤ Las verduras y hortalizas frescas son mejores para ti que las enlatadas. Fresh vegetables are better for you than canned ones.

mejor prevenir que curar better safe than sorry

mejor que uno... one had better... ➤ Mejor que llegues (aquí) a tiempo. You'd better get here on time. ▪ You'd better be here on time.

ser **mejor que alguien con respecto a algo** ▪ ser mejor que alguien en lo que respecta a algo ▪ ser mejor que alguien cuando se trata de algo ▪ ser mejor que alguien al hacer algo ▪ ser mejor que alguien haciendo algo to be better about something than someone else ➤ Algunos conductores de autobús son mejores que otros con repecto a esperar a los rezagados. Some bus drivers are better than others about waiting for stragglers.

ser el **mejor que hay** to be the best one there is

mejor que mejor so much the better

ser **mejor que mejor** ▪ ser cada vez mejor ▪ estar cada vez mejor ▪ poner cada vez mejor ▪ ir a mejor to get better and better

mejor que no I had better not ▪ I'd better not ▪ *(coloquial)* I better not

ser **mejor que nunca** to be better than ever

ser el **mejor que uno haya probado** to be the best (that) one has ever tasted ➤ Es la mejor paella que haya probado. That's the best paella I've ever tasted.

mejor será si ■ será mejor si it will be better if

mejor sería hacer algo ■ sería mejor hacer algo it would be better to do something ➤ Mejor sería venir a Madrid cuando no haga tanto calor. ■ Más valdría venir a Madrid cuando no haga tanto calor.

mejor sería que uno hiciera algo ■ mejor sería que uno hiciese algo it would be better for one to do something ■ it would be better if one did something ➤ Mejor sería que nos acompañaras. It would be better for you to go with us. ■ It would be better if you went with us.

mejor sería que uno hiciese algo ■ mejor sería que uno hiciera algo it would be better if one did something ■ it would be better for one to do something ➤ Mejor sería que usted la acompañase. It would be better if you went with her. ■ It would be better for you to go with her.

mejor sería si uno hiciera algo ■ mejor sería si uno hiciese algo ■ sería mejor si uno hiciera algo ■ sería mejor si uno hiciese algo it would be if one did something ■ it would be better for one to do something ➤ Mejor sería que esperaras. ■ Mejor sería que esperases. ■ Sería mejor que esperaras. ■ Sería mejor que esperases. It would be better if you waited. ■ It would be better for you to wait.

mejor todavía ■ o mejor todavía ■ (o) mejor aún (or) better still ■ (or) better yet

mejor voy ■ será mejor que vaya I'd better attend ■ I'd better go

mejora sobre los beneficios del año pasado ■ incremento sobre los beneficios del año pasado improvement over last year's profits ■ increase over last year's profits

estar **mejorando** ■ ir mejorando to be getting better ■ to be on the road to recovery ➤ El paciente está mejorando. ■ El paciente va mejorando. The patient is getting better. ■ The patient is on the road to recovery. ➤ Tu inglés está mejorando constantemente. Your English is getting better all the time.

mejorando lo presente.... ■ excluyendo los presentes ■ no agravando a los presentes present company excepted ■ as indeed you are ■ but he hasn't got anything on you

mejorar en una actividad to get better at doing something ➤ Estás mejorando (en esto). You're getting better at this. ➤ Cada semana que pasa mejoras en el piano. You're getting better at the piano by the week.

mejorar la posición económica ■ mejorar la situación económica to better one's fortunes

mejorar la salud ■ ganar mucho en salud (for) one's health to improve ➤ Mi salud ha mejorado. ■ He ganado mucho en salud. My health has improved.

mejorar la situación económica ■ mejorar la posición económica to better one's fortunes

mejorarse uno mismo to better oneself

ser una **memoria agridulce** to be a bittersweet memory

memoria ampliable *(informática)* expandable memory ➤ ¿Es ampliable la memoria? Is the memory expandable? ■ Can the memory be expanded?

memoria de chorlito: tener la ~ ■ tener la memoria de grillo not to be able to remember a thing

memoria de grillo ■ memoria de chorlito not to be able to remember a thing

una **memoria más remota** an earlier memory

la **memoria más remota** ■ la más remota memoria one's earliest memory ➤ La memoria más remota de Alberto es de un coche rojo de fórmula uno de juguete con el que jugaba en la cuna. ■ La más remota memoria de Alberto es de un coche rojo de fórmula uno de juguete con el que jugaba en la cuna. Alberto's earliest memory is of a toy red Formula One race car that he would play with in his crib.

memoria remota early memory

mencionar de paso ■ mencionar de pasada ■ decir de paso ■ decir de pasada to mention in passing

menda lerenda *(masculino o femenino)* ■ menda lironda ■ mendi lerendi ■ *(sólo masculino)* el menda ■ *(sólo femenino)* la menda yours truly

menear el esqueleto ■ mover el esqueleto ■ bailar to dance ■ to kick up a little dust

menear la cabeza to shake one's head

menguada asistencia ■ baja participación ■ alta abstención low turnout

ser **menor de edad** to be under age ■ to be a minor

menos de lo normal *(singular)* less than usual ■ *(plural)* fewer than usual ➤ *(noticia)* Por la huelga esta mañana hay menos taxis de lo normal. Because of the strike this morning there are fewer taxis than usual.

menos mal 1. it's a good thing 2. thank goodness!

menos aún even less

menos cosas que hacer fewer things to do

menos cuarto quarter till ➤ *(conductor de autobús)* Llegamos a la Plaza de Castilla a menos cuarto. We arrive at Plaza de Castilla at a quarter till.

menos da una piedra *(Esp.)* ■ más vale algo que nada ■ es mejor que nada it's better than nothing ■ it could be worse ■ one could do a lot worse ■ you could do a lot worse

menos es nada it's a pittance ■ nothing wouldn't be any less

¡**menos mal!** it's a good thing! ■ thank God (for that)!

menos mal que it's a good thing that ➤ Menos mal que trajiste tu chubasquero. ■ Menos mal que trajiste tu piloto. It's a good thing you brought your raincoat.

ser **menos propenso a (que)** ■ resultar menos propenso a (que) to be less likely to

menos recomendable less desirable

menos tiempo less time

menos veces fewer times

menos violento 1. less violent 2. less awkward ■ less embarrassing

menoscabar la confianza en uno mismo ■ minar la confianza en uno mismo to undermine self-confidence

mensajes sin leer unread messages

mentalizarse de algo ■ hacerse a la idea de algo to make up one's mind about something ■ to make up one's mind to do something ➤ Debes mentalizarte de no verlo más. ■ *(leísmo, España y países andinos)* Debes mentalizarte de no verle más. You have to make up your mind not to see him again.

mentar la soga en casa del ahorcado ■ meter la pata to say the wrong thing

mente de piñón fijo: tener una ~ ■ tener una mente de una línea to have a one-track mind

mente de una línea: tener una ~ ■ tener una mente de piñón fijo to have a one-track mind

mente despejada clear mind

mentir ante un gran jurado to lie to a grand jury

mentir bajo juramento ■ jurar en falso ■ cometer perjurio ■ perjurarse to lie under oath ■ to commit perjury ■ to perjure oneself ➤ Mentir bajo juramento puede costarle caro. Lying under oath can get you in a lot of trouble.

mentir descaradamente to tell a bold-faced lie ■ to tell an out-and-out lie

mentir más que hablar to be an inveterate liar

mentira piadosa white lie

mentira(s) tiene(n) las patas muy cortas the truth will come out

menuda casa this is quite a house ■ that's quite a house

menuda cena an awesome supper

¡**menuda ganga!** ■ ¡vaya ganga! ■ ¡qué ganga! ■ ¡menudo chollo! ■ ¡vaya chollo! ■ ¡qué chollo! what a bargain!

¡**menuda tía!** *(Esp.)* ■ ¡qúe chica! 1. what a girl! ■ what a gal! 2. *(refiriéndose al aspecto físico)* what a fox!

¡**menuda tostada!** *(día caluroso)* ■ ¡qué calorete! what a scorcher!

menudear la lluvia ■ llover torrencialmente to get a lot of rain ■ to have torrential rains

menudear los insultos (for) there to be a barrage of insults ■ (for) there to be a free-for-all of insults ➤ En los programas televisivos de poca categoría siempre menudean los insultos. On trashy TV talk shows, there is always a barrage of insults. ■ On trashy TV talk shows, it's always a free-for-all of insults

¡**menudo alboroto!** ■ ¡qué jaleo! what a racket!

menudo cambio quite a change ➤ Quayaquil está precioso, (hay un) menudo cambio desde la última vez que la visité. Quayaquil is beautiful, quite a change from the last time I was there.

¡menudo cerdo! *(Wilbur de E.B. White)* some pig!
¡menudo chollo! ■ ¡vaya chollo! ■ ¡qué chollo! ■ ¡vaya ganga! ■ ¡menuda ganga! what a deal! ■ what a bargain!
¡menudo elemento! what a character! ➤ ¡Menudo elemento estás tú hecho! What a character you are!
¡menudo lío! ■ ¡qué desbarajuste! ■ ¡qué lío! what a mess!
¡menudo negocio! ■ ¡menudo trato! ■ ¡vaya negocio! ■ ¡vaya trato! ■ ¡qué negocio! ■ ¡qué trato! what a deal!
¡menudo pájaro está hecho! that guy's a little questionable ■ that guy's a little slippery ■ he's a shady character
¡menudo personaje! what a character!
menudo sitio tienes aquí this is quite a place you have here
¡menudo tío! ■ ¡qué tío! what a guy!
ser una **mera casualidad** to be a sheer coincidence ■ to be purely coincidental
mercado a la baja buyer's market
mercado al alza seller's market
mercado de cambio ■ mercado de divisas currency markets
mercado de divisas ■ mercado de cambio currency markets
mercado de trabajo job market
mercado de valores ■ bolsa (de valores) stock market
merced a ■ gracias a ■ debido a thanks to ■ owing to
merecer escrutinio ■ ser digno de escrutinio ■ ser susceptible de escrutinio to deserve scrutiny ■ to merit scrutiny ■ to be worthy of scrutiny
merecer la pena ■ valer la pena to be worth it ■ to be worth the trouble ➤ No merece la pena. It's not worth it. ■ It's not worth the trouble.
merecer la pena investigarlo ■ ser digno de ser investigado ■ ser digno de investigarlo ■ ser digno de ser investigado ■ ser susceptible de investigarlo ■ ser susceptible de ser investigado ■ ser susceptible de investigación to be worthy of investigation ■ to be worthy of being investigated ■ to bear looking into ■ to bear checking out ■ to bear checking into
el **mero hecho de que...** the simple fact that... ■ the mere fact that...
merodear con mala gente ■ rondar con mala gente ■ haraganear con mala gente ■ holgazanear con mala gente ■ andar con mala gente ■ reunirse con mala gente to run around with a bad crowd ■ to hang around with a bad crowd ■ to hang out with a bad crowd
el **mes entrante** next month ■ the coming month
el **mes pasado** last month
la **mesa cojea** ■ la mesa se bambolea the table wobbles ■ the table rocks
mesa de billar pool table ■ billiard table
mesa de diálogo negotiating table
mesa de trabajo ■ escritorio ■ pupitre desk ■ work table
mesa empotrada booth ➤ Preferiríamos una mesa empotrada si hubiera alguna disponible. We'd prefer a booth if one's available.
la **mesa se bambolea** ■ la mesa cojea the table rocks ■ the table wobbles
meses cálidos ■ meses calurosos warm months
meses más calurosos the hottest months
mesilla de noche ■ *(L.am.)* ■ velero ■ mesita de luz bedside table ■ night table ■ *(muy pequeña)* nightstand
meta alcanzable ■ objetivo alcanzable obtainable goal ■ achievable goal
meta en la vida: tener una ~ to have a goal in life
¡mete caña! ■ métele pata step on it! ■ go faster!
¡métele pata! ■ ¡mete caña! step on it! ■ go faster!
meter a alguien bajo el ala ■ poner a alguien bajo el ala to take someone under one's wing
meter a alguien en vereda ■ poner a alguien en vereda to bring someone into line
meter algo de culo en ■ meter marcha atrás en ■ dar marcha atrás en to back onto ➤ Meter el barco de culo en la rampa puede ser complicado. Backing the boat onto the ramp can be tricky.
meter algo de morro *(coloquial)* ■ entrar de morro ■ entrar de frente to pull in ➤ Mete el coche de morro en este hueco. Pull into this parking place.
meter algo para dentro to push something in
meter caña to step on it ■ to go faster ■ to come down hard on someone ■ to mistreat someone ➤ ¡Mete caña! Step on it! ■ Go faster!
meter cisco entre *(coloquial)* ■ meter cizaña entre ■ sembrar cizaña entre to cause trouble between ■ to stir up trouble between ■ to sow discord between
meter cizaña (entre personas) ■ sembrar cizaña entre personas ■ meter cisco to create discord ■ to sow discord ■ to sow disharmony ■ to cause trouble between people ■ to create a rift between people *(Nota: Entre tres personas o más, se usa "among" en vez de "between".)*
meter datos en la computadora *(L.am.)* ■ *(Esp.)* ■ meter datos en el ordenador to enter data into the computer ➤ Mete tu nombre en el campo. Enter your name in the window. ➤ Enter your name in the dialogue box. Mete tu nombre en el cuadro de diálogo. Enter your name in the dialogue box.
meter el dedo a alguien ■ incordiar a alguien ■ molestar a alguien to bother someone
meter el hocico to stick one's nose into other people's business
meter la camisa por dentro ■ meterse la camisa to tuck in one's shirt ■ to tuck in one's shirttail ➤ ¡Mete la camisa por dentro! ■ ¡Métete la camisa! Tuck in your shirt! ■ Tuck in your shirttail!
meter la pata ■ meter la gamba to put one's foot in it ■ to make a faux pas ■ to make a boo-boo
meter la pata al fondo to make a fatal gaffe ➤ Si no hubiera metido la pata hasta el fondo (en aquella ocasión), podría haber ganado las elecciones. If he hadn't made that fatal gaffe, he might have won the election.
meter la primera to shift into low (gear) ■ to shift into first (gear) ■ to put it in low (gear) ■ put it in first (gear)
meter las manos en las bolsillos to put one's hands in one's pockets
meter las narices en todo to be a busybody ■ to stick one's nose into other people's business
meter los zapatos en la horma ■ dar de sí los zapatos to stretch (a pair of) shoes
meter mano a algo ■ toquetear algo to touch something up ■ to touch up something
meter mano a alguien to investigate someone
meter marcha atrás al coche ■ dar marcha atrás al coche por la entrada ■ dar marcha atrás al coche en la entrada to back the car out of the driveway ➤ Metí marcha atrás al coche en la entrada. ■ Di marcha atrás al coche por la entrada. ■ Di marcha atrás al coche en la entrada. I backed the car out of the driveway.
meter marcha atrás ■ poner marcha atrás to shift into reverse ■ to put it in reverse
meter prisa a alguien to rush somebody ■ to hurry someone up
meter un casete en su sitio to put in a cassette
meter un gol *(deportes)* to make goal ■ to score
meter una puya a alguien ■ poner una banderilla a alguien **1.** *(jocosa)* to give someone a bad time ■ to throw barbs at someone **2.** *(con ánimo de herir)* to taunt someone ■ to hit someone where it hurts
meterle espuelas al caballo ■ clavarle espuelas al caballo ■ espolear al caballo ■ picar al caballo to spur the horse
meterle paja a un trabajo to pad a theme
meterlo en la lista to put it on the list
meterse a alguien en el bolsillo to have someone in one's pocket
meterse con alguien **1.** atacar a alguien to pick on someone **2.** gastar bromas a alguien to tease someone ➤ Métete con alguien de tu tamaño. ■ Métete con alguien del mismo tamaño. ■ Métete con alguien de tu edad. Pick on somebody your own size.
meterse el espectáculo en el bolsillo ■ quedarse con el espectáculo to steal the show
meterse en aguas calientes ■ meterse en aguas turbias to get in hot water ■ to get in(to) trouble
meterse en algo **1.** to get involved in something **2.** to get into something ■ to enter something ➤ *Cielito Lindo* es una canción en la que verdaderamente te metes. *Cielito Lindo* is a song you can really get into. ➤ Nunca pensé meterme en política, pero mira por dónde, terminé ministro. I never thought I'd get into

politics, but look where I ended up, being a (government) minister. ➤ Cuando emprendí el proyecto no me di cuenta en lo que me estaba metiendo. When I undertook the project, I didn't realize what I was getting into.

meterse en berenjenales to get oneself into a (real) fix ▪ to get oneself into a (real) pickle ▪ to get oneself in a (real) mess ▪ to get oneself into a jam

meterse en camisa de once varas to be out of one's depth ▪ to get in beyond one's depth

meterse en cinta para hacer algo ▪ prepararse para hacer algo to get ready to do something ➤ Tengo que meterme en cinta para dar una presentación en la reunión. I have to get ready to give a presentation at the meeting.

meterse en cosas que no le incumben ▪ meterse donde no lo llaman to meddle in things that are none of one's business ▪ to meddle in other people's business ▪ to meddle in other people's affairs

meterse en el asiento de atrás to get in the back seat ➤ ¡Métete en el asiento de atrás! Get in the back seat!

meterse en el coche ▪ meterse en el carro ▪ meterse en el auto ▪ entrar en el coche ▪ subir al coche to get in the car ▪ to get into the car ➤ Ella entró en su coche. She got in her car. ▪ She got into her car.

meterse en la cocina to go into the kitchen ▪ *(coloquial)* to go in the kitchen

meterse en las drogas ▪ verse involucrado en drogas to get into drugs ▪ to get involved in drugs ➤ ¿Cómo se metió en las drogas? ▪ ¿Cómo se vio involucrado en las drogas? How did he get into drugs? ▪ How did he get involved in drugs?

meterse en política ▪ entrar en política ▪ adentararse en la política to go into politics

meterse en problemas ▪ tener problemas to get in(to) trouble ➤ Se metió en problemas por hacerlo. ▪ Se metió en problemas por hacer eso. He got in(to) trouble for doing it.

meterse en un apuro to get in a bind

meterse en un embolado ▪ meterse en un jaleo ▪ meterse en un lío ▪ meterse en un mogollón to get into a (big) mess ▪ to get into a tight spot ▪ to get into a jam

meterse en un jaleo ▪ meterse en un embolado ▪ meterse en un lío ▪ meterse en un mogollón to get into a (big) mess ▪ to get into a jam ▪ to get into a tight spot

meterse en un lío ▪ meterse en un jaleo ▪ meterse en un mogollón ▪ meterse en un embolado to get into a (big) mess ▪ to get into a jam ▪ to get into a tight spot

meterse en un mogollón *(Esp.)* ▪ meterse en un jaleo ▪ meterse en un lío ▪ meterse en un embolado to get into a (big) mess ▪ to get into a jam ▪ to get into a tight spot

meterse en una camisa de once varas to be out of one's depths

meterse en una conversación to butt into a conversation

meterse en una discusión to get into an argument

meterse en una lucha contra la corriente meterse contra la corriente to engage in an uphill battle (ahead of one) ▪ to have an uphill battle (ahead of one) ▪ to have got an uphill battle (ahead of one)

meterse en una pelea to get into a fight ▪ *(coloquial)* to get in a fight

meterse en un rutina ▪ entrar en una rutina to get into a rut

meterse en una tormenta *(avión)* to fly into a storm ➤ El avión se metió en una tormenta y cayó. The airplane flew into a storm and crashed.

meterse entre medias *(subido de tono)* ▪ meterse entre las piernas to get in a woman's pants

meter la cabeza to draw in one's head ➤ *(Clement Clark Moore)* Al meter la cabeza y darme la vuelta, Santa Claus bajó por la chimenea dando un golpe. ▪ Cuando meti la cabeza y me daba vuelta, Santa Claus bajó por la chimenea dando un golpe. ▪ Conforme metí la cabeza y me daba vuelta, Santa Claus bajó por la chiminea dando un golpe. As I drew in my head and was turning around, down the chimney St. Nicholas came with a bound.

meterse la camisa ▪ meter la camisa por dentro to tuck in one's shirt ▪ to tuck in one's shirttail ➤ ¡Métete la camisa! ▪ ¡Mete la camisa por dentro! Tuck in your shirt! ▪ Tuck in your shirttail!

meterse las manos en los bolsillos to put one's hands in one's pockets

meterse por la autopista ▪ meterse en la autopista to get on the freeway

meterse por una calle **1.** meterse en una calle to turn onto a street ▪ to turn down a street **2.** doblar y subir por una calle to turn up a street

meterse un pico *(jerga)* to shoot up ▪ to inject drugs

meterse un tiro *(jerga)* to take a hit (of a drug) ▪ to give oneself another hit ➤ (Historias del Kronen *de José Angel Mañas)* Hay que ir al baño para meterse otro tiro. You have to go to the bathroom to take another hit.

meterse una bebida de un trago ▪ echar una bebida de un trago to belt down a drink ▪ to gulp down a drink

meterse una raya *(jerga)* to snort a line (of cocaine) ➤ (Historias del Kronen *de José Angel Mañas)* Manolo me pasa un talego con el que me hago un canutillo bien tensado y me meto la primera raya (de coca). Manolo hands me a big bill and with that I make myself a nice, taut little tube and snort the first line (of cocaine).

metérsele entre ceja y ceja ▪ ponérsele entre ceja y ceja to get a notion in one's head ➤ Cuando algo se te mete entre ceja y ceja, ¡no hay manera! When you get a notion your head, you're impossible! ➤ Al jefe de Carlos se le metió entre ceja y ceja que tenían que parar para reorganizar la oficina...¡otra vez! Carlos' boss got it into his head that they had to stop to reorganize the office... again!

métete con alguien de tu tamaño ▪ métete con alguien del mismo tamaño ▪ prueba con alguien de tu tamaño ▪ prueba con alguien del mismo tamaño pick on somebody your own size

estar **metido(-a) en aguas calientes** estar metido(-a) en aguas turbias to be in hot water ▪ to be in troubled waters ▪ to be in trouble

estar **metido(-a) en aguas turbias** to be in hot water ▪ to be in trouble

estar **metido(-a) en carnes** to be heavyset

estar **metido(-a) en el ajo** ▪ estar metido(-a) en el asunto to be mixed up in something (questionable)

estar **metido(-a) en el asunto** ▪ estar metido(-a) en el ajo to be mixed up in something (questionable)

estar **metido(-a) en harina** to be hard at work ▪ to be down to the nitty-gritty

estar **metido(-a) en problemas** to be in trouble

estar **metido(-a) en un avispero** to have gotten oneself into a mess ▪ to have gotten into a hornet's nest ▪ to have loosed a hornet's nest

estar **metido(-a) en un berenjenal** to be in a (real) pickle ▪ to be in a real mess ▪ to be in a big mess

estar **metido(-a) en un buen lío** to be embroiled in problems

estar **metido(-a) en una conversación** ▪ estar involucrado(-a) en una conversación to be engaged in a conversation

método (de enseñanza) approach ▪ method ➤ El método audiolingüístico frente al método natural en la enseñanza de la lengua The audiolingual approach versus the natural approach to language teaching

método de enfocar un problema ▪ método de abordar un problema ▪ método de enfrentarse a un problema ▪ manera de enfocar un problema ▪ manera de abordar un problema ▪ manera de enfrentarse a un problema ▪ forma de enfocar un problema ▪ forma de abordar un problema ▪ forma de enfrentarse a un problema approach to a problem ▪ way of dealing with a problem

mezclar churras con merinas *(Esp.)* ▪ mezclar peras con manzanas to mix apples and oranges ▪ to compare apples and oranges

mezclar peras con manzanas to mix apples and oranges ▪ to compare apples and oranges

mezclarse con algo to mix with something ▪ to get into something ➤ El separador de agua y combustible extrae agua procedente de la condensación que se haya mezclado con el combustible del depósito. The fuel-water separator extracts any condensed moisture in the fuel tank that has gotten (mixed) into the fuel.

estar **MFT** *(Arg.)* ▪ estar meando fuera del tarro to be off base ▪ to be full of nonsense ▪ not to know what one is talking about

mi boca está que arde *(de comer pimientos picantes)* my mouth is on fire

mi cielo *(puede referirse a hombre o mujer)* ▪ cariño ▪ cielito ▪ amorcito honey

mi corazón se hundió ▪ se me cayó el alma a los pies my heart sank

mi madre y ella she and my mother ➤ Mi madre y ella son amigas. She and my mother are friends.

ser **mi mayor reto de la vida** to be the greatest challenge of my life

mi media naranja ▪ mi cara mitad my other half

mi memoria me dice que ▪ mi recuerdo me dice que ▪ mi recuerdo es que my recollection is that

mi mente divagó my mind wandered

mi padre y él he and my father ➤ Mi padre y él son amigos. He and my father are friends.

mi pregunta de hoy my question today ➤ Mi pregunta de hoy concierne a... My question today concerns...

mi recuerdo es que ▪ mi recuerdo me dice que ▪ mi memoria me dice que my recollection is that

mi recuerdo me dice que ▪ mi memoria me dice que ▪ mi recuerdo es que my recollection is that

mi reina ▪ cariño ▪ cielito ▪ amorcito ▪ mi cielo honey

mi rey ▪ cariño ▪ cielito ▪ amorcito ▪ mi cielo honey

mi único problema my only problem ▪ my only concern

microscopio de *x* de aumento *x*-power microscope ➤ El laboratorio está equipado con un microscopio de 300x de aumento. The lab is equipped with a 300-power microscope.

miedo escénico: entrarle a uno ~ darle a uno miedo escénico ▪ agarrarle a uno miedo escénico ▪ entrarle a uno pánico escénico ▪ darle a uno pánico escénico ▪ agarrarle a uno pánico escénico to get stage fright ➤ I'm getting stage fright. Me está entrando miedo escénico. ▪ Me está entrando pánico escénico.

miedo escénico: tener ~ ▪ tener pánico escénico ▪ darle a uno miedo escénico ▪ agarrarle a uno miedo escénico to have stage fright ➤ Tengo miedo escénico. ▪ Me entra miedo escénico. ▪ Me da miedo escénico. ▪ Me agarra miedo escénico. I have stage fright.

miedo mutuo mutual fear ▪ balance of terror ➤ Los arsenales nucleares de los Estados Unidos y de la Unión Soviética se procuraron un miedo mutuo entre ambos países. The nuclear arsenals of the United States and the Soviet Union maintained a balance of terror between the two countries.

ser **miembro de un club** ▪ ser socio de un club ▪ pertenecer a un club to be a member of a club ▪ to belong to a club

ser **miembro de un partido político** ▪ ser afiliado de un partido político to be a member of a political party ▪ to belong to a political party

mientras lo estoy pensando while I'm thinking about it ▪ while it's on my mind

mientras lo quiera uno as long as one wants it ➤ Me han dicho que el trabajo es mío mientras lo quiera. The told me the job is mine as long as I want it.

mientras más años the more years ▪ the longer ➤ Mientras más años vivimos, más probabilidades tenemos de envejecernos. The longer we live the more likely we are to grow old.

mientras más mejor the more, the better

mientras más uno se acerca a... the closer one gets to... ➤ The closer you get to sixty, the younger it seems. ▪ The closer to sixty you get, the younger it seems. Mientras más te acercas a los sesenta, más joven parece.

mientras más uno se acerca... the closer one... ➤ Mientras más te acercas a los sesenta, más joven parece. The closer to sixty you get, the younger it seems.

mientras me lo estoy pensando ▪ mientras me lo pienso while I'm thinking of it ▪ while I'm thinking about it ▪ while it's occurring to me

mientras ponen los anuncios ▪ durante los comerciales while the commercials are on ▪ during the commercials ▪ during the commercial break

mientras ponían los anuncios while the commercials were on ▪ during the commercials ▪ during the commercial break

mientras (que) ▪ en tanto que whereas

mientras tanto ▪ en tanto in the meantime

miércoles de ceniza *(catolicismo)* Ash Wednesday

las **mil** ▪ las tantas ▪ hasta las mil quinientas the wee hours ▪ all hours of the night ➤ Los niños se quedaron despiertos hasta las mil esperando ver el cometa. ▪ Los niños se quedaron despiertos hasta las tantas esperando ver el cometa. The children stayed up until the wee hours hoping to see the comet.

mil gracias many thanks ▪ thanks a million

mil millones 1. *(inglés americano)* billion 2. *(inglés británico)* thousand million

minar la confianza en alguien ▪ socavar la confianza en alguien to undermine confidence in someone ➤ *(titular)* Las acusaciones de corrupción minan la confianza en el primer ministro. Accusations of corruption undermine confidence in the prime minister.

minar la confianza en uno mismo ▪ menoscabar la confianza en uno mismo to undermine self-confidence ➤ Las sectas fundamentalistas toman control psicológico sobre la gente minando su confianza en sí misma. Fundamentalist sects take psychological control of people by undermining their self-confidence.

el **mínimo del mercado ha caído por el suelo** ▪ el mínimo del mercado está por el suelo the bottom has fallen out of the market

minucias: hacer ~ to do odds and ends

minusvalía física physical disability

mira (a ver) si see if ▪ go and see if ▪ look and see if ➤ Mira (a ver) si puedes adelantar ese coche. See if you can pass that car. ▪ See if you can get around that car. ▪ See if you can get ahead of that car.

¡**mira de lo que sirve!** a lot of good *that* does!

mira de lo que ha servido look at all the good it did ▪ a lot of good it did ➤ Le dije a mi hijo adolescente, "Cuando yo tenía tu edad, mi padre solía decirme que me pusiera derecho." Mi hijo me dijo, "Y mira de lo que ha servido." I told my teenage son, "When I was a teenager, my father used to tell me to sit up straight." My son said, "A lot of good it did." ▪ I told my teenage son, "When I was a teenager, my father used to tell me to sit up straight." My son said, "And look at all the good it did."

mira en el dorso see back

mira en que... look where... ▪ see where...

¡**mira lo que has hecho!** look what you've done!

¡**mira lo que he hecho!** look what I did!

¡**mira por dónde!** *(Esp.)* ▪ ¡fíjate! ▪ ¡no te lo vas a creer! get this! ▪ you won't believe this! ▪ you'll never believe it! ➤ Nunca pensé meterme en política, pero mira por dónde, terminé ministro. I never thought I'd get into politics, but look where I ended up, being a (government) minister.

¡**mira por dónde andas!** ▪ ¡mira por dónde vas! watch where you're going!

¡**mira por dónde vas!** ▪ ¡mira por dónde andas! watch where you're going!

mira que le tomo la palabra okay, I'm going to take your word for it

¡**mira qué suerte!** what luck!

mira qué suerte que as luck would have it ➤ Mira qué suerte que tengo uno para ti. As luck would have it, I have one for you.

mira que te tomo la palabra okay, I'm going to hold you to it

mira quién ha llamado (go) see who's at the door

¡**mira quién habla!** ▪ ¡mira quién fue a hablar! look who's talking!

mirada de asombro look of amazement

mirada de desprecio disdainful look ▪ look of contempt

mirada de odio hateful look ▪ baleful look

mirada de reproche reproachful look ▪ look of reproach

mirada despreciativa disdainful look

mirada fugaz fleeting glance

mirada interrogante questioning look

mirada significativa meaningful look ➤ Nos intercambiamos miradas significativas. We exchanged meaningful looks. ▪ We looked at each other meaningfully. ▪ We gave each other meaningful looks.

mirándolo bien now that I think about it

mirar algo to look at something ➤ *(libro)* Lo miré. I looked at it. ➤ *(revista)* La miré. I looked at it.

mirar a alguien to look at someone ➤ Lo miré. ▪ *(Esp., leísmo)* Le miré. I looked at him. ▪ I looked at it. ➤ La miré. I looked at her. ▪ I looked at it.

mirar a alguien a los ojos (de frente) to look someone (straight) in the eye ➤ Lo miré a los ojos (de frente). I looked him (straight) in the eye. ➤ La miré a los ojos (de frente). I looked her (straight) in the eye. ➤ *(Esp., leísmo)* Le miré a los ojos (de frente). I looked him (straight) in the eye.

mirar a alguien con recelo to look at someone warily ▪ to look at someone with mistrust ▪ to look at someone with suspicion ▪ to regard someone with mistrust ▪ to regard someone with suspicion

mirar a las musarañas to stare into space ▪ to stare vacantly

mirar a las telarañas ▪ mirar las telarañas to have one's head in the clouds ▪ to be off in the ozone

mirar a su alrededor ▪ mirar en sus entornos to look around (one) ➤ Mira a tu alrededor. Look around (you).

mirar a ver ▪ echarle un vistazo a to check on ▪ to have a look at ➤ Pedí que el gerente mirara a ver cómo está el inquilino. I asked the manager to check on the tenant. ➤ El médico le echó un vistazo a las amígdalas del muchacho. the doctor checked the boy's tonsils.

mirar a ver cómo va un pedido *(en un restaurante, tienda, etc.)* ▪ mirar a ver cómo va una orden to check on an order ➤ ¿Podrías (mirar a) ver cómo va nuestro pedido? Ya llevamos veinte minutos (esperando). ▪ ¿Podrías ver cómo va nuestro pedido? Van a hacer veinte minutos. Would you check on our order? It's been over twenty minutes. ➤ ¿Puedes mirar cómo va mi orden del libro? Es ya más de un mes. Would you check on my book order? It's been more than a month.

mirar algo a contraluz to hold something up to the light

mirar algo con detenimiento ▪ mirar algo bien mirado to take a good look at something ▪ to have a good look at something

mirar algo de frente to look straight at something

mirar atentamente to watch carefully ➤ ¡Miren atentamente! ▪ *(Esp., vosotros)* ¡Mirad atentamente! Watch carefully!

mirar bajo el capó ▪ mirar bajo el cofre to look under the hood ▪ to check under the hood

mirar bajo el cofre *(Méx.)* ▪ mirar bajo el capó to check under the hood ▪ to look under the hood

mirar bien a alguien 1. mirar a alguien minuciosamente to look at someone intently 2. estimar a alguien to esteem someone ▪ to have a good opinion of someone ➤ La miró bien de frente. He looked at her intently in the face.

mirar con detenimiento to take a good look

mirar con fijeza a alguien ▪ mirar fijamente a alguien ▪ clavársele la mirada en alguien to stare at someone

mirar con lupa to go over with a fine-tooth comb

mirar con recelo a alguien to look at someone suspiciously ▪ to look at someone with suspicion

mirar de arriba a abajo a alguien 1. to look someone up and down 2. fijarse en la apariencia de la persona to look someone over 3. estudiar detenidamente a una persona to size someone up ▪ to take the measure of a person

mirar de cara al problema ▪ afrontar el problema ▪ mirar al problema cara a cara to look the problem in the face

mirar de cerca to look closely

mirar de frente a alguien to look someone in the eye ➤ Juan lo miró de frente. ▪ *(Esp., leísmo)* Juan le miró de frente. Juan looked him in the eye.

mirar desde to look out from

mirar desde lo alto overlook from a height

mirar detrás de algo to look behind something

mirar el campo palmo a palmo ▪ batir el campo ▪ peinar el campo to comb the area

mirar en sus entornos ▪ mirar a su alrededor to look around (one) ➤ Mira en tus entornos. ▪ Mira a tu alrededor. Look around (you).

mirar fijamente a alguien ▪ mirar con fijeza a alguien ▪ clavarse la mirada en alguien to stare at someone

mirar hacia el otro lado ▪ hacer la vista gorda to look the other way ▪ to turn a blind eye (to) ▪ to pretend not to notice

mirar por encima del hombro to look over one's shoulder

mirar por la ventana ▪ *(L.am.)* aguaitar por la ventana to look out the window ▪ to look out of the window

mirar sombríamente a alguien to glower at someone

mirara a donde mirara ▪ mirase a donde mirase wherever one looked ▪ everywhere one looked ▪ wherever you looked ▪ everywhere you looked

mirarle las piernas a alguien to look at someone's legs ➤ Le mirábamos las piernas y comentábamos... *(nosotros a ella)* We were looking at her legs and commenting... ▪ *(nosotras a él)* We were looking at his legs and commenting...

mirarle a alguien a la cara to look directly at someone

to **look someone in the eye** mirarle a los ojos a alguien to look someone in the eye

mirarle a alguien directamente a los ojos to look someone straight in the eye

mirarle a alguien por el rabillo del ojo ▪ mirar a alguien por la esquina del ojo ▪ mirar a alguien de reojo to look at someone out of the corner of one's eye ▪ to cast a sidelong glance at someone

mirarle feo a alguien to give someone a dirty look

mirarlo en frío to look at it cold

mirarse al espejo ▪ mirarse en el espejo to look at oneself in the mirror

mirarse en el espejo ▪ mirarse al espejo to look at oneself in the mirror

mirarse uno al otro en el espejo ▪ mirarse uno al otro al espejo to look at each other in the mirror

mirase a donde mirase ▪ mirara a donde mirara everywhere you looked ▪ wherever you looked ▪ everywhere one looked ▪ wherever one looked

mire a donde mire everywhere you look ▪ wherever you look ▪ everywhere one looks ▪ wherever one looks

mis abuelos my grandparents

mis tíos my uncle and aunt ▪ my aunt and uncle

misa de gallo ▪ misa del gallo midnight mass

misa cantada ▪ misa mayor ▪ misa solemne high mass

misa mayor ▪ misa cantada ▪ misa solemne high mass

misa solemne ▪ misa cantada ▪ misa mayor high mass

el **misil de largo alcance** long-range missile

el **misil de medio alcance** medium-range missile

el **misil de tierra-aire** surface-to-air missile

el **misil teledirigido con laser** laser-guided missile

ser la **misma cantinela** ▪ ser la misma cantilena ▪ ser la misma canción de siempre to be the same old story ▪ to be the same song, fiftieth verse

ser la **misma historia de siempre** to be the same old story ▪ to be the same song, fiftieth verse

mismamente ayer ▪ ayer mísmo just yesterday ▪ only yesterday

el **mismo día de** the very day of

misterio sin resolver unsolved mystery

Misterios Dolorosos *(catolicismo)* Sorrowful Mysteries

Misterios Gloriosos *(catolicismo)* Glorious Mysteries

Misterios Gozosos *(catolicismo)* Joyful Mysteries

Misterios Luminosos *(catolicismo)* Mysteries of Light

mistificar a alguien to hoodwink someone

mitad en broma half kidding ▪ half in jest

mitad en serio half seriously

mitigar el riesgo ▪ reducir el riesgo to reduce the risk ▪ to lower the risk ▪ to mitigate the risk

la **moción de censura** motion of censure

modales buenos ▪ buenos modales good manners

modales burdos coarse manners ▪ boorish manners

modelo de comportamiento ▪ (el) patrón de comportamiento behavior pattern ▪ pattern of behavior

ser **moderadamente optimista** ▪ ser comedidamente optimista ▪ ser optimista de forma moderada ▪ sentirse moderadamente optimista ▪ ser comedidamente optimista to be guardedly optimistic ▪ to be cautiously optimistic ▪ to feel guardedly optimistic ▪ to feel cautiously optimistic

modestia aparte if I do say so myself ▪ if I may say so (myself)

modestia falsa false modesty

modestia fingida false modesty
módica suma modest sum
módico precio modest price
modo de empleo how to use
modo de salir de esto way out of this
modo de vida way of life
la **modulación de amplitud** ■ AM ■ *(coloquial)* onda media amplitude modulation ■ AM
la **modulación de frecuencia** ■ FM frequency modulation
modus operandi modus operandi ■ way of doing things
mojar el churro *(Esp., subido de tono)* to dip one's wick
mojar el gaznate *(Esp.)* ■ refrescar(se) el gaznate ■ humedecerse los labios to wet one's whistle ■ to have a drink
mojarse de pies a cabeza to be drenched from head to toe
mojarse del todo ■ mojarse entero ■ mojarse completamente ■ mojarse por completo to get all wet ➤ Se me cayeron los deberes en un charco y se mojaron enteros. I dropped the homework assignment in a puddle and it got all wet.
mojarse el culo *(Esp., coloquial)* ■ mojarse los pies to get one's feet wet ■ to try something out ➤ *(hombre conduciendo un coche nuevo, a un amigo)* Me estoy mojando el culo. I'm getting my feet wet. ■ I'm trying it out.
mojarse los pies ■ mojarse el culo to get one's feet wet
molarle mazo *(Esp., coloquial)* ■ ser guay ■ ser la bomba to be awesome
molduras de rodapié ■ molduras del rodapié ■ (los) rodapiés ■ molduras de zócalo ■ zócalo baseboard moldings ■ baseboards
molestar la sensibilidad de alguien to offend someone's sensibilities
molestarse en hacer algo to bother to do something
ser **molido a golpes** to be beaten to a pulp
molinete (chino) *(juguete)* whirligig
ser un **momento agridulce** to be a bittersweet moment
momento álgido ■ punto álgido ■ punto cumbre peak moment ■ climax
momento crucial crucial moment ■ turning point
momento embarazoso ■ momento bochornoso embarrassing moment ■ awkward moment
momento idóneo para ideal moment to ■ perfect time to
momento propicio opportune moment ■ right moment ■ *(culto)* propitious moment
momentos de nervios tense moments
monda y lironda: la verdad ~ the plain truth ■ the unvarnished truth
mondar patatas *(Esp.)* ■ pelar patatas ■ pelar papas to peel potatoes
mondo y lirondo to the bone ■ clean ➤ Comimos el pavo mondo y lirondo. We ate the turkey to the bone. ➤ El perro lamió el plato mondo y lirondo. The dog licked the plate clean.
moneda suelta ■ calderilla ■ dinero del bolsillo small change ■ loose change ■ small change ■ pocket change
monólogo interior *(James Joyce)* ■ fluir de ideas ■ fluir de pensamientos stream of consciousness
montaña rusa roller coaster
montañas rocosas rocky mountains
montar a alguien to have sex with someone
montar a caballo ■ cabalgar to ride a horse ■ to ride horseback
montar a caballo a mujeriegas ■ montar a caballo a la mujeriega to ride sidesaddle
montar a una yegua 1. *(jinete)* to ride a mare 2. *(caballo semental)* to cover a mare
montar en avioneta to ride in an airplane ■ to fly in an airplane ➤ Esa no es la avioneta en la que yo monté. That's not the airplane I flew in. ■ That airplane is not the one I flew in. ■ That airplane is not the one I rode in.
montar en coche ■ andar en coche to ride in a car ➤ ¿Has montado una vez en un Rolls-Royce? Have you ever ridden in a Rolls-Royce?
montar el numerito ■ montar un escándalo to make a scene ■ to carry on ■ to pitch a fit ■ to have a conniption
montar en bicicleta ■ andar en bicicleta to ride a bicycle ■ to ride a bike ➤ Nuestra niña está aprendiendo a montar en bicicleta. Our little girl is learning to ride a bicycle.
montar en cólera to become extremely angry ■ to have a purple fit ■ *(coloquial)* to go ballistic
montar en trineo ■ andar en trineo 1. *(trineo sin tracción animal)* to go sleigh riding ■ to go sledding ■ to sleigh ride ■ to ride on a sled 2. *(trineo tirado por perros)* to ride (on) a dogsled 3. *(trineo tirado por caballos)* to ride in a (horse-drawn) sleigh ➤ Jack London montaba trineos tirados por perros, como muchos de los personajes de sus novelas. Jack London rode a dogsled, like many of the characters in his novels. ➤ Qué divertido es montar en un trineo tirado por un caballo. What fun it is to ride in a one-horse open sleigh. ➤ Me gusta montar en trineo. I like to go sleigh riding. ■ I like to go sledding. ■ I like to sleigh ride. ■ I like to ride on a sled. ➤ A nuestro perro le gusta que le montemos en el trineo. Our dog likes to ride on the sled.
montar en un helicóptero ■ andar en un helicóptero to ride en a helicopter
montar estanterías ■ armar una estantería to put up shelves ■ to put up shelving ■ to put shelves up ■ to put shelving up
montar guardia ■ hacer guardia to stand guard
montar la carrera ■ comenzar la carrera to begin one's career
montar la de San Quintín ■ montar un jaleo to raise holy hell ■ to put up a fight
montar un cisco *(Esp.)* ■ armar un cisco ■ meter un cisco to give someone (a lot of) flack ■ to throw a (temper) tantrum ➤ Sé por experiencia que si le dices que no le puedes dejar dinero, te va a montar un cisco. I know from experience that if you tell him you can't lend him any money, he's going to give you a lot of flack.
montar un fusil ■ armar un fusil to assemble a rifle
montar un negocio por cuenta propia ■ montar un negocio por su cuenta ■ empezar un negocio por cuenta propia ■ empezar un negocio por su cuenta to go into business for oneself
montar un número ■ hacer un número ■ hacer un desplante to make a scene
montar un pollo *(muy coloquial)* ■ montar alguien un cisco a uno ■ ponerse alguien a discutir con uno to get an argument from someone ➤ Sé por experiencia que si le dices que no le puedes dejar dinero, te va a montar un pollo. ■ Sé por experiencia que si le dices que no le puedes dejar dinero, te va a montar un cisco. ■ Sé por experiencia que si le dices que no le puedes dejar dinero, se pondrá a discutir contigo. I know from experience, if you tell him you can't lend him any money, you'll get an argument.
montar una escena to make a scene ■ to throw a fit ➤ El niño montó una escena en el supermercado porque su madre no le quiso comprar chicles. A child made a scene in the supermarket because his mother wouldn't buy him chewing gum.
montar una exposición to set up a display
montar una maqueta ■ armar una maqueta ■ ensamblar una maqueta ■ hacer una maqueta to assemble a kit ■ to put together a kit ■ to put a kit together
montar una tienda (de campaña) ■ armar una tienda (de campaña) ■ armar una carpa to pitch a tent ■ to put up a tent
montarse a un caballo ■ montarse en un caballo ■ subirse a un caballo to get on a horse
montarse en un ascensor ■ subir(se) a un ascensor ■ montarse en un elevador ■ subir(se) a un elevador to get on an elevator
montarse en un caballo ■ montarse a un caballo ■ subirse a un caballo to get on a horse
montarse en un tren ■ subir(se) a un tren to get on a train
montarse la de Dios *(Esp.)* ■ montar una escena ■ *(L.am.)* montar un berrinche ■ montar una pataleta to make a scene ■ *(especialmente los niños)* to have a tantrum ■ to throw a tantrum
montarse una escena (for) there to be a scene ➤ Se montó una escena en el supermercado entre una madre y su hijo porque ella no le quiso comprar chicles. There was a scene in the supermarket today between a mother and her little boy because she wouldn't buy him chewing gum.
montarse una historia ■ contar una historia disparatada to tell a tall tale ■ to tell tales ■ to invent stories ➤ Se monta unas historias para no venir a trabajar que no se las cree nadie. He tells tales in order not to come to work, that no one believes.
montarse una película 1. to make a federal case out of something 2. to make up a cock and bull story ➤ No te montes

películas. Una cosa es que te haya cogido tu puñetero boli sin permiso, otra muy distinta es que como dices tú "haya violado tu derecho a la initimidad." I didn't invade your privacy. You're making a federal case out of it just because I borrowed your blasted ballpoint pen. ➤ Se ha montado una película diciendo al profesor que se perdió el examen por haber presenciado un accidente de coche. He made up a cock and bull story that he missed the exam because he witnessed an automobile accident.

montárselo bien to have it made ▪ to have got it made ➤ Mi amigo se lo monta bien: ha encontrado un trabajo que le deja tiempo libre para ir a la universidad y cubrir sus gastos. My friend has it made. He's found a job that covers his expenses and leaves him enough time to attend the university. ▪ My friend's got it made. He's found a job that covers his expenses and leaves him enough time to attend the university.

montárselo con alguien to get it on (sexually) with someone

montárselo de tal manera que... to work it out so that... ➤ Se lo ha montado de tal manera que sólo trabaja cuatro días a la semana. He's worked it out so that he only works four days a week.

montárselo por su cuenta ▪ hacerlo por su cuenta to go it alone

los **(Montes) Apalaches** Appalachian Mountains

un **montón (de)** a (whole) lot (of) ▪ an awful lot (of)

monturas y cristales *(Esp.)* ▪ monturas y lentes frames and lenses

monturas y lentes ▪ monturas y cristales frames and lenses

moraleja (de la historia) moral of the story

morar en algo to dwell on something

morar en el corazón de uno to dwell in one's heart ▪ to dwell within one's heart

morar en un vivienda to reside in an apartment building ▪ to live in an apartment building

morder algo to bite (on) something ➤ Según ella estaba comiendo su paella, mordió algo duro. As she was eating her paella, she bit on something hard.

morder el anzuelo ▪ dejarse engañar to take the bait

morder el polvo to bite the dust

morder la mano que te da de comer ▪ arrojar piedras contra tu (propio) tejado ▪ tirar piedras contra tu (propio) tejado to bite the hand that feeds you

morderse la lengua 1. to bite one's tongue **2.** *(figurativo)* tragar saliva to swallow hard ▪ to suppress one's reaction ▪ to hold back words ▪ to suppress one's feelings

morderse las manos to wring one's hands (from anxiety)

morderse los labios 1. to bite one's lip(s) **2.** *(figurativo)* tragar saliva to swallow hard ▪ to resist the temptation to say something ▪ to resist the temptation to speak up

ser **mordido(-a) por un perro** to get bitten by a dog ▪ to be bitten by a dog

ser **mordido(-a) por una serpiente** to get bitten by a snake ▪ to be bitten by a snake

morir a causa de to die of ➤ *(titular)* Más de cinco millones de niños mueren al año en el mundo a causa del hambre. More than five million children around the world die of hunger every year.

morir acuchillado(-a) ▪ morir por arma blanca ▪ morir apuñalado(-a) to die of stab wounds ▪ to be stabbed to death

morir ahogado(-a) to drown

morir al pie del cañón ▪ morir con las botas puestas to die with one's boots on ▪ to die in the saddle ▪ to die in harness

morir apedreado(-a) ▪ morir lapidado(-a) to be stoned to death ▪ to die by stoning

morir atropellado(-a) ▪ ser atropellado(-a) to be run over ▪ to get run over ➤ El perro murió atropellado por un coche. The dog was run over by a car and killed. ▪ The dog died from being run over by a car. ▪ The dog got run over by a car.

morir calcinado(-a) ▪ morir carbonizado(-a) to burn to death

morir carbonizado(-a) ▪ morir calcinado(-a) to burn to death

morir como chinches ▪ caer como moscas to drop like flies

morir como moscas ▪ caer como chinches to drop like flies

morir como un perro to die destitute (without family, friends, or money)

morir con el corazón destrozado to die of a broken heart

morir con las botas puestas to die with one's boots on

morir de causas naturales to die of natural causes

morir de éxito to be the victim of one's own success

morir de muerte natural ▪ morir de causas naturales to die of natural causes

morir de sobreparto to die in childbirth

morir desangrado(-a) ▪ desangrar hasta morir to bleed to death

morir en el acto to die instantly

morir en la hoguera to be burned at the stake ▪ to die at the stake

morir en una calle ▪ terminar en una calle to tee into a street ▪ to end at a street ➤ La Avenida de los Shiris muere en la Avenida Seis de Diciembre. ▪ La Avenida de los Shiris termina en la Avenida Seis de Diciembre. ▪ La Avenida de los Shiris ends at Avenida Seis de Diciembre. ▪ La Avenida de los Shiris tees into Avenida Seis de Diciembre.

morir fulminado(-a) to be struck and killed by lightning ▪ to be struck by lightning and killed ▪ to be killed by a lightning strike

morir lapidado(-a) ▪ morir apedreado(-a) to be stoned to death ▪ to die by stoning

morir por to die as a result of ➤ Los jovenes murieron por la destrucción de masa encefálica a causa de disparos de armas de fuego hechos desde muy cerca. The youths died as a result of massive head injuries caused by shots fired at close range.

morir por alguien ▪ morirse por alguien to be crazy about someone

morir por dentro to die inside

morir porque se le rompe el corazón to die of a broken heart

morir toreando to be killed fighting a bull ▪ to die fighting a bull ➤ Manolete murió toreando. Manolete was killed fighting a bull. ▪ Manolete died fighting a bull.

morirse antes de tiempo to die before one's time

morirse de ganas de to be dying to

morirse de risa to die laughing

morirse de viejo to die of old age

morirse por algo to be dying for something

morirse por alguien ▪ morir por alguien to be crazy about someone ▪ to be dying for

morirse por hacer algo to be dying to do something

morirse por saber to be dying to find out ➤ Me muero por saber cómo te fue tu cita a ciegas. I'm dying to find out how your blind date was.

morro de un avión ▪ (la) nariz de un avión nose of an airplane

mortales de espaldas *(buceo)* somersault dive

mortificación personal *(práctica religiosa)* self-mortification

moscas volantes floaters (in the eyes)

mosquear a alguien ▪ fastidiar a alguien to hassle someone

mostrar el verdadero yo ▪ enseñar el cobre ▪ pelar el cobre to show one's true self ▪ to show one's true colors

mostrar lo mejor de sí mismo ▪ sacar lo mejor de sí mismo to put one's best foot forward ▪ to turn on the charm

mostrar las herraduras ▪ huir to beat trail out of Dodge ▪ to beat it

mostrar respeto hacia alguien to show respect for someone

mostrar su preocupación por to express one's concern about ▪ to express one's concern over

mostrar sus cartas ▪ descubrir las cartas to show one's hand ▪ to reveal one's hand

mostrar sus sentimientos ▪ revelar sus sentimientos to show one's feelings

mostrar un pago to show a payment ➤ ¿Se muestra un pago en febrero? ▪ ¿Se muestra algún pago en febrero? Do you show a payment in February? ▪ Does it show a payment in February? ▪ Does it show a payment for February? ➤ No se muestra un pago en Febrero. It does not show a payment in February. ▪ It doesn't show a payment in February. ▪ *(informal)* I don't show a payment in February. ▪ I'm not showing a payment in February.

mostrarse a favor de to come out in favor of

mostrarse centrado to show oneself to be focused

mostrarse reacio a to be reluctant to ▪ to be skittish about

mostrarse remiso ante algo to be resistent to something ▪ to be reluctant in the face of something ▪ to be reluctant when faced with something

mota de polvo speck of dust

motivo de conversación conversation piece

motivo de la porcelana china pattern ➤ Este motivo de la porcelana viene en varios colores. This china pattern comes in a variety of colors.

ser **motivo de orgullo para uno** ▪ ser causa de orgullo para uno to be a source of pride to one

ser **motivo para hacer algo** to be reason to do something

motivo por el cual ▪ (la) razón por la que reason why

motivo subyacente underlying motive

motivos de 1. grounds for 2. causa(s) de cause of ➤ Los investigadores trataban de averiguar anoche los motivos del derrumbe. ▪ Los investigadores trataban de averiguar anoche las causas del derrumbe. Investigators last night were trying to determine the cause of the collapse.

motivos para creer: tener ~ ▪ tener razones para creer to have reason to believe

el **motor de arranque** ▪ burro de arranque starter ▪ starter motor

el **motor de búsqueda** *(informática)* search engine

el **motor de combustión interna** internal combustion engine

el **motor de reacción** ▪ motor de propulsión a chorro jet engine

el **motor fuera borda** outboard engine ▪ outboard motor

mover el esqueleto ▪ menear el esqueleto ▪ bailar *(L.am.)* echar un pasillo to dance

mover el vientre to have a bowel movement

mover la barra de desplazamiento hacia abajo ▪ mover la pantalla hacia abajo to scroll down

mover la barra de desplazamiento hacia arriba ▪ mover la pantalla hacia arriba to scroll up

mover la pantalla hacia abajo ▪ mover la barra de desplazamiento hacia abajo to scroll down

mover la pantalla hacia arriba ▪ mover la barra de desplazamiento hacia arriba to scroll up

mover palancas to pull strings

moverle el interés ▪ tener un interés creado to have an ax to grind ➤ Para que no creas que me mueve el interés, te explico a dónde quiero llegar. So you won't think I have an ax to grind, here's what I'm driving at.

moverse 1. frecuentar to hang out 2. arrimarse ▪ ponerse más allá to move over ➤ Es mi piso en España. Es donde me muevo. This is my home in Spain. This is where I hang out. ➤ *(tú)* Muévete un poco. ▪ *(usted)* Muévase un poco. ▪ *(vosotros)* Moveos un poco. ▪ *(ustedes)* Muévanse un poco. Move over a little

moverse con to be powered by ▪ to be propelled by ➤ Este autobús se mueve con gas natural. This bus is powered by natural gas.

moverse con entera libertad to move about with complete freedom

moverse de espaldas ▪ moverse hacia atrás to move backwards

moverse en la nieve ▪ desplazarse en la nieve to get around in the snow ➤ Es difícil moverse en la nieve. It's hard to get around in the snow.

moverse hacia atrás ▪ moverse de espaldas to move backwards

moverse por to move about ➤ Un adolescente canadiense que se movía por Internet bajo el apodo de Mafiaboy... A Canadian who moved about the Internet under the nickname of Mafiaboy...

moverse respecto al fondo de estrellas to move against the background of the stars ▪ to change position against the background of the stars ➤ Los astrónomos de Babilonia habían notado que el sol se mueve respecto al fondo de estrellas. The Babylonian astronomers had noticed that the sun moves against the background of the stars. ▪ The Babylonian astronomers had noticed that the sun changes (its) position against the background of the stars.

moverse sin coche ▪ desplazarse sin coche to get around without a car ➤ En todas menos las más grandes ciudades estadounidenses, es difícil moverse sin coche. ▪ En todas menos las más grandes ciudades estadounidenses, es difícil desplazarse sin coche. In all but the biggest U.S. cities, it's diffcult to get around without a car.

movimiento diurno de objetos astronómicos diurnal motion of astronomical objects

movimiento propio proper motion ➤ El astrónomo británico Edmond Halley descubrió el movimiento propio de las estrellas. The British astronomer Edmond Halley discovered the proper motion of the stars.

movimiento sumergido ▪ movimiento underground underground movement ➤ El movimiento de los jóvenes católicos era sumergido en la Polonia comunista. The Catholic youth movement was underground in Communist Poland.

mozo de carga ▪ botón ▪ chacho errand boy

mozo de equipajes baggage handler

muchas menudencias a lot of little things ➤ Muchas menudencias causaron las desavenencias en su amistad. A lot of little things caused the rift in their friendship.

muchas otras cosas ▪ otras muchas cosas many other things

muchas veces 1. many times ▪ often ▪ frequently 2. any time ➤ Muchas gracias por tu ayuda.-Muchas veces. Thank you for helping me.-Any time.

muchas veces seguidas ▪ uno tras otro in rapid succession

una **muchedumbre se amontona** ▪ una muchedumbre se está amontonando ▪ una muchedumbre se congrega ▪ una muchedumbre se está congregando ▪ un público se congrega ▪ un público se está congregando a crowd is gathering

mucho antes a long time before

mucho ha llovido desde entonces that's water under the bridge

mucho lirili y poco lerele *(Esp., coloquial)* ▪ tanto hablar, seca la boca ▪ ser de mucho hablar y poco actuar ▪ ser de mucho decir y luego nada ▪ ser un(a) cantamañanas to be all talk and no action

mucho más much more ▪ far more

ser **mucho pedir** to be a lot to ask ▪ to be a tall order

mucho que pensar: darle a alguien ~ to give someone a lot to think about ➤ Ese profesor me dio mucho que pensar. That teacher gave me a lot to think about.

mucho ruido, pocas nueces: hacer ~ to make a big fuss over nothing

ser **mucho ruido y pocas nueces** 1. hablar mucho y no hacer nada to be all talk and no action 2. ser una tempestad en una tetera to be much ado about nothing ▪ *(obra teatral de Shakespeare, mucho ruido y pocas nueces) Much Ado About Nothing*

mucho tiempo 1. a long time ▪ long 2. for a long time ➤ 1. Esperé mucho tiempo. I waited a long time. ➤ ¿Tardé mucho (tiempo)? Was I long? ➤ ¿Tendrá que guardar cama mucho tiempo? Will he be bedridden for a long time?

mucho tiempo: hace ~ a long time ago

mucho va en... ▪ va mucho en... a lot depends on... ▪ it depends a lot on ➤ Mucho va en la persona que lo haga. A lot depends on the person doing it. ▪ It depends a lot on the person doing it.

muchos cocineros dañan el puchero ▪ muchas manos en un plato hacen garabato too many cooks spoil the broth

muchos son los llamados y poco los elegidos many are called, but few are chosen

mudar de aires ▪ cambiar de aires ▪ cambiar de lugar to get a change of scenery ▪ to have a change of scenery

mudarse a un apartamento ▪ trasladarse a un apartamento ▪ entrar a vivir en un apartamento ▪ mudarse a un piso ▪ trasladarse a un piso ▪ entrar a vivir en un piso to move into an apartment

mudarse acá to move here ➤ Cuando nos mudamos acá... When we moved here...

mueble archivador *(Esp.)* ▪ archivador file cabinet

muebles ajados ▪ ajado mobiliario ▪ muebles maltratados beat-up furniture

muebles en estado natural ▪ muebles sin tinte o barníz unfinished furniture

¡**muérete!** drop dead!

ser la **muerte** ▪ ser letal ▪ ser mortal to be fatal ➤ *(titular)* El cáncer a menudo ya no es muerte. Cancer is often no longer fatal. ▪ Cancer is often not fatal any more.

la **muerte a pedradas** death by stoning

la **muerte súbita** sudden death
la **muerte por** death from ➤ *(titular)* Investigadas más muertes por drogas sintéticas More deaths from synthetic drugs being investigated
estar **muerto(-a)** 1. to be dead 2. *(figurativo)* estar cansadísimo to be dead to the world
estar **muerto(-a) de miedo** to be scared to death
estar **muerto(-a) de risa** to be consumed with laughter
estar **muerto(-a) de vergüenza** to be embarrassed to death ■ to be thoroughly ashamed of oneself
¡**muerto el burro, la cebada al rabo!** ■ ¡a buenas horas! ■ ¡a buenas horas, mangas verdes! 1. *now* you show up! 2. *now* you tell me!
muerto(-a) en la travesía who died in the crossing ➤ *(noticia)* La madre de Elián, muerta en la travesía Elian's mother, who died in the crossing
muestra de que... indication that... ■ sign that...
muestra de sangre blood sample
muestra distorsionada biased sample ■ distorted sample ■ defective sample ■ contaminated sample
muestra evidente clear example ■ obvious example
muestra gratuita free sample
muestra mediatizada biased sample
muestra representativa representative sample
muestra sesgada biased sample
muévete un poco move over a little
mujer bella ■ mujer guapa beautiful woman
mujer de armas tomar battle-axe ■ battle-ax ➤ Su profesora de geometría era una mujer de armas tomar. Her geometry teacher was an old battle axe.
mujer de la calle ■ mujer de la vida street walker
mujer de la vida ■ mujer de la calle woman of easy virtue
mujer fatal femme fatale
mujer guapa ■ mujer bella beautiful woman
mujer pública ■ mujerzuela prostitute
mullir una almohada to fluff a pillow
multar con cierta cantidad a alguien por to fine someone a certain amount for
multiplicarse como los conejos ■ procrear como conejos to breed like rabbits
¡**multiplícate por cero!** get lost!
mundialmente conocido known the world over ■ world-renowned
mundialmente famoso(-a) world-famous
mundillo de: entrar en el ~ ■ entrar en el mundo de to get into the business of
mundo al revés: estar el ~ to be topsy turvy
mundo de: entrar en el ~ ■ entrar en el mundillo de to get into the business of
mundo de ensueño ■ reino de la fantasía world of make-believe ■ land of make-believe
mundo de habla hispana Spanish-speaking world
mundo de habla inglesa English-speaking world
mundo de los negocios: en el ~ in the business world
mundo del espectáculo show business
el **mundo es un pañuelo** ■ qué pequeño es el mundo it's a small world
un **mundo por descubrir** a world to discover
mundo venidero world to come
muñeco de nieve snowman
muro de carga load-bearing wall
música celestial celestial music ■ music of the spheres
músico callejero street musician
músico nato born musician
muy a la derecha way over to the right
muy a menudo very often
estar **muy allá** to be a long way off ■ to be a long way away
muy amable that's very kind of you ■ thank you
ser **muy amigo(-a) de** to be a close friend of ➤ En ese entonces era muy amigo de la a familia. At that time he was a close friend of the family.
ser **muy aplicado(-a)** to be very hard working ➤ The pupils are very hardworking. Los alumnos son muy aplicados.
estar **muy bien** 1. tener buena salud to be very well 2. venirle bien ■ quedarle bien to be okay ■ to suit very well 3. vivir muy bien to be very well off (financially) 4. estar guapo(-a) to be very good-looking
estar **muy bien hecho** to be very good ■ to be very well done
estar **muy bonito(-a)** to look very pretty ■ to be very pretty in one's eyes
ser **muy bonito** to be very pretty
estar **muy bueno(-a)** *(subido de tono)* to be very attractive physically ■ to be worth one
estar **muy cambiado(-a)** to have changed a lot ➤ Está muy cambiada. She's changed a lot.
muy cierto, pero... true, but...
estar **muy concurrido** ■ estar muy frecuentado to attract a lot of people ■ to be popular ■ to have a big clientele
ser **muy de adentro** to be like a member of the family
muy de la mañana early in the morning ■ first thing in the morning
muy de mañana ■ muy temprano ■ de madrugada very early in the morning ➤ Muy de mañana ese día Very early that morning ■ Very early in the morning that day
estar **muy de moda** to be very much in style ■ to be quite the thing
muy de su gusto much to one's liking ■ very much to one's taste
muy de vez en cuando very rarely
muy delgada mayoría ■ muy estrecha mayoría wafer-thin majority
estar **muy demandado** ■ estar en demanda ■ estar muy solicitado to be in demand
ser **muy esperado** ■ ser tan esperado to be eagerly awaited ➤ La visita del presidente, que era muy esperada ■ La visita del presidente, que era tan esperada The president's visit, which was eagerly awaited
muy estrecha mayoría ■ muy delgada mayoría wafer-thin majority
muy hombre all man ■ a real he-man
ser **muy largo de contar** to be a long story
estar **muy mentado** to be much in the news ■ to be in the spotlight
estar **muy metido(-a) con algo** to be very involved with something
estar **muy metido(-a) con alguien** to be very involved with someone
estar **muy metido(-a) en algo** to be very involved in something
muy mono ■ muy bonito very pretty ■ really pretty *(Nota: "Mono" es una palabra usada más por las mujeres; un hombre probablemente diría "bonito".)* ➤ Es una camisa muy mona. ■ Es una camisa muy bonita. That's a very pretty shirt. ■ That is a really pretty shirt. ■ That shirt is really pretty.
muy mujer all woman
ser **muy respetado por alguien** to be well respected by someone
muy resumido in a nutshell
ser **muy sentido** to be deeply felt
Muy señor mío Dear Sir
estar **muy solicitado(-a)** *(personas y cosas)* ■ estar en demanda ■ estar muy demandado(-a) to be in demand
estar **muy solo(-a)** to be very much alone
ser **muy sonado** to be much talked-about
ser **muy suyo(-a)** 1. ser propio de alguien ■ ser típico de alguien to be very like someone ■ to be very typical of someone 2. ser muy meticuloso to be particular ■ to like things just so
ser **muy torpe conduciendo** to be a lousy driver
muy viejo(-a) para eso: ya estar ~ to be too old for that ➤ Ya yo estoy muy viejo para eso. I'm too old for that.
ser **muy unido(-a) con alguien** to be very close to someone
muy unidos very close (friends) ➤ Son muy unidos. They are very close.

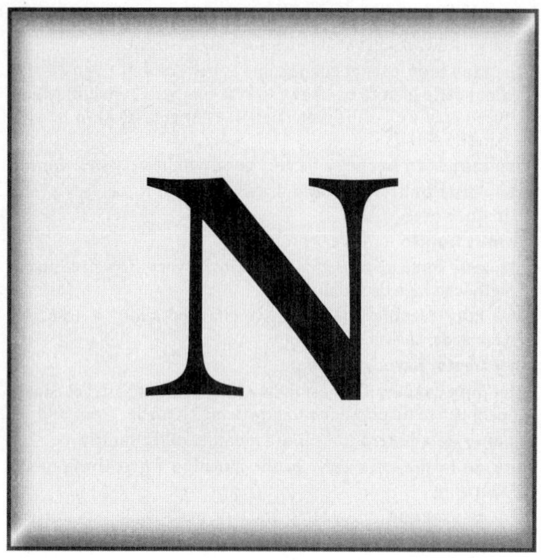

nace un pardillo cada minuto *(P. T. Barnum)* ▪ cada minuto nace un mamón there's a sucker born every minute

nacer con fortuna ▪ nacer con un pan bajo el brazo ▪ nacer en cuna de oro to be born with a silver spoon in one's mouth

nacer de forma prematura to be born prematurely ➤ Los cachorros han nacido de forma prematura. The cubs were born prematurely.

nacer muerto(-a) to be still-born ➤ El infante nació muerto. The infant was still-born.

nacido muerto(-a) still-born

la **nación pujante** booming nation

nada de nada ▪ nada en absoluto nothing at all ▪ anything! ➤ No quiere hablar nada de nada. ▪ No quiere hablar de nada en absoluto. He doesn't want to talk about anything!

nada de particular nothing in particular ▪ nothing special

nada del otro jueves nothing to write home about ▪ nothing special

nada en absoluto nothing at all ▪ absolutely nothing

nada hay nuevo bajo el sol there's nothing new under the sun

nada hay que temer there's nothing to fear ▪ you have nothing to fear ▪ we have nothing to fear

nada más no sooner ▪ as soon as ➤ Nada más bajarme del avión... No sooner had I gotten off the plane... ▪ As soon as I got off the plane...

¿nada más? that's all? ▪ nothing else?

nada más abrir la puerta *(con cualquier sujeto)* no sooner had one opened the door ▪ as soon as one opened the door ▪ the second one opened the door ▪ the instant one opened the door ➤ Nada más abrir la puerta, me topé con Pepe. No sooner had I opened the door than I ran into Pepe.

nada más despegar right after takeoff ▪ immediately after takeoff ▪ on becoming airborne ➤ Nada más despegar, el avión se desplomó tras perder un motor. On becoming airborne, the airplane plummeted to earth after losing an engine. ▪ Immediately after becoming airborne, the airplane plummeted to earth after losing an engine.

nada más entrar *(yo)* as soon as I walked in ▪ the minute I walked in ▪ the second I walked in ▪ the instant I walked in ▪ *(él)* as soon as he walked in ▪ the minute he walked in ▪ the second he walked in ▪ the instant he walked in ▪ (ella) as soon as she walked in ▪ the minute she walked in ▪ the second she walked in ▪ the instant she walked in

nada más lejos de la realidad nothing could be further from the truth ▪ nothing could be farther from the truth

ser **nada más lejos de mi intención** to be the farthest thing from my mind

nada más llegar no sooner had one arrived ▪ as soon as one gets there ➤ Nada más llegar a Madrid, fuimos al Escorial. No sooner had we arrived in Madrid than we went to the Escorial.

nada más que 1. solamente ▪ únicamente only 2. lo que sea menos, sino anything but

nada más que por just because of

nada menos no less

nada menos que no other than ▪ nothing less than

¡nada! (¡nada!) ▪ de nada don't mention it ▪ any time ▪ sure ▪ it was nothing ▪ you're welcome

nada parecido nothing of the kind

nada podría estar más alejado de la verdad ▪ no hay nada más lejos de la verdad nothing could be further from the truth

nada por el estilo nothing of the kind ▪ nothing of the sort ▪ no such thing ➤ No dije nada por el estilo. I said nothing of the kind. ▪ I said no such thing.

nada que me gustara ▪ nada que me gustase nothing that I liked ▪ not any that I liked ▪ none that I liked ➤ Fui a comprar un sofá hoy, pero no vi ninguno que me gustara. ▪ Fui a comprar un sofá hoy, pero no vi ninguno que me gustase. I shopped for a sofa today, but I didn't see any that I liked. ▪ I shopped for a sofa today, but I didn't see one that I liked. ▪ I shopped for a sofa today, but I saw none that I liked.

nada que ponerse nothing to wear ➤ *(artículo deportada)* Jackie Kennedy también sufría de nada que ponerse. Jackie Kennedy also suffered from nothing to wear.

nada que (yo) no pueda solucionar nothing that I can't solve

nada te lo impide nothing's stopping you

nadar contra corriente 1. to swim upstream ▪ to swim against the current 2. to go against the grain ▪ to go against prevailing opinion

nadar en abundancia ▪ nadar en dinero ▪ rebosar en dinero to be rolling in dough

nadar en dinero ▪ nadar en abundancia ▪ rebosar en dinero to be rolling in dough

nadar entre dos aguas ▪ estar entre dos aguas ▪ estar entre Pinto y Valdemoro to straddle the fence

nadar largos to swim laps ➤ Ella ha nadado diez largos. She has swum ten laps.

nadie da nada por nada nobody gives something for nothing ▪ nobody does something for nothing

nadie diga: de esta agua no beberé never say never

nadie en su sano juicio no one in his right mind

nadie es profeta en su tierra no one is a prophet in his own country

nadie escarmienta en cabeza ajena *(dicho español)* no one learns from others' mistakes

nadie está contento(-a) con su suerte no one is happy with his fate

nadie le ha dado vela en este entierro nobody asked him (to stick his nose into it)

nadie lo notará ▪ nadie se va a dar cuenta no one will notice (it) ▪ nobody will notice (it)

nadie más, menos aún no one else, not even ▪ nobody else, not even

nadie pensaba que fuera posible no one thought it was possible

nadie podría decirlo you wouldn't know it

nadie que se le parezca ▪ nadie que ni de lejos sea anyone who even comes close ➤ No sé de nadie que se le parezca como futbolista. ▪ No sé de nadie que sea ni de lejos tan buen futbolista (como él). I don't know of anyone who even comes close to him as a football player. ▪ I don't know of anyone who compares to him as a football player.

nadie que tenga dos dedos de frente nobody with any sense ▪ no one with any sense

nadie sabe ▪ no se sabe no one knows ▪ nobody knows ▪ it is not known ▪ it's not known

nadie salvo no one but ▪ no one except

nadie se atrevía a... no one dared to...

nadie (se) lo nota ▪ no se nota nobody will notice it ▪ you can't see it ▪ you can't tell

nadie se sorprende tanto de algo como... no one is more surprised at something than... ■ no one has been more surprised at something than... ■ no one was more surprised at something than...

nadie se va a dar cuenta ■ nadie lo notará no one will notice (it) ■ nobody will notice (it)

¿nadie te dijo que...? ■ ¿no te dijeron que...? didn't anyone tell you (that)...? ■ they didn't tell you (that)...?

¿nadie te ha dicho que...? ■ ¿no te han dicho que...? hasn't anyone told you (that)...? ■ they haven't told you (that)...? ■ didn't anyone tell you (that)...? ■ they didn't tell you (that)...? ■ no one told you (that)...? ➤ ¿Nadie te ha dicho que dejé de trabajar allí? Didn't anyone tell you that I quit working there?

nadie (te) lo nota ■ nadie te lo notará nobody will notice (it) ■ you can't see it ■ you can't tell (it)

nanai de nanai *(Esp., jerga)* ■ nada de nada ■ que no ■ de eso nada nothin' doin' ■ no way ■ forget that

Naranja mecánica 1. *(título de película)* *A Clockwork Orange* 2. *(deportes)* el nombre por el cual se conoce al equipo de fútbol nacional de Holanda

nata agria ■ crema agria sour cream

nata montada *(Esp.)* ■ crema batida whipped cream

ser **natural de** ■ ser oriundo(-a) de to be a native of

la **naturaleza le tiene horror al vacío** nature abhors a vacuum

naturaleza muerta ■ (el) bodegón still life

navaja de Occam *(filosofía de la ciencia)* ■ principio de economía Ockham's razor ■ law of parsimony ➤ La navaja de Occam reza que la explicación completa más sencilla es la verdadera. Ockham's razor, or the law of parsimony, states that the simplest complete explanation is the true one.

una **nave de andenes** a section of platforms

la **Nave de San Pedro** ■ la Iglesia católica the ship of St. Peter ■ the Roman Catholic Church

la **nave espacial** spaceship ■ spacecraft

la **navegación a estima** dead reckoning

navegar contra el viento to tack

la **necesidad aguza el ingenio** necessity is the mother of invention

la **necesidad de que...** the need for...

necesidades básicas basic necessities

estar **necesitado(-a) de dinero** to be hard-pressed for money ■ to be hard-pressed for cash

necesitar algo to need something ■ to need anything ➤ Si necesitáis algo, estoy fuera. If you need anything, I'm outside.

necesitar un respiro to need a breather ■ to need a breathing spell

necesitarse con urgencia ■ necesitarse desesperadamente ■ necesitarse sin falta to be badly needed ➤ No te haces la más mínima idea de la urgencia con que necesitamos tu presencia entre nosotros. We cannot tell you how badly needed your presence is in our midst.

necesitarse desesperadamente ■ necesitarse con urgencia ■ necesitarse sin falta to be desperately needed ■ to be urgently needed ■ to be badly needed ➤ Por las fotos del satélite, parece que finalmente tenéis la lluvia que tan desesperadamente necesitábais. From the satellite pictures, it looks like you're finally getting some badly needed rain.

necesitarse con urgencia ■ necesitarse desesperadamente ■ necesitarse sin falta to be urgently needed ■ to be desperately needed ■ to be badly needed

necesito toda la ayuda posible I need all the help I can get

el **necio es atrevido y el sabio comedido** fools rush in where angels fear to tread

negar de forma tajante to deny categorically

negar de plano to deny flatly ■ to flatly deny

negar haber hecho algo to deny having done something ■ to deny that one has done something

negarse a colaborar con alguien to refuse to cooperate with someone ➤ Hasta el momento los sospechosos se han negado a colaborar con la policía. The suspects have so far refused to cooperate with the police.

negarse a desaparecer to refuse to go away ➤ Mi resfriado se niega a desaparecer. My cold refuses to go away.

negarse a hacer algo to refuse to do something

negarse a volver a enviarle to refuse to send him back ➤ Al instalar mal el módem el técnico, la tienda se negó a volver a enviarle. After the technician installed the modem wrong, the store refused to send him back.

negarse en rotundo ■ negarse rotundamente to absolutely refuse

negarse rotundamente ■ negarse en rotundo to absolutely refuse

negarse tajantemente a hacer algo to refuse flatly to do something ■ to refuse categorically to do something

negativa de refusal to

las **negociaciones están en un punto muerto** the negotiations are deadlocked ■ the negotiations are stalled

negociar algo 1. *(términos, precios, etc.)* to negotiate something 2. *(sólo precio)* to bargain for something

negociar colectivamente to bargain collectively ➤ El sindicarse permitió a los trabajadores negociar colectivamente sus salarios. Becoming unionized enabled the workers to bargain collectively for their wages.

negociar lo que... to negotiate what... ➤ Los líderes del sindicato negociaron lo que creían que los trabajadores de la planta iban a aceptar. The union leaders negotiated what they thought the plant workers would approve.

negociar los términos de un divorcio to negotiate a divorce settlement

negociar que... to negotiate... ➤ Los líderes del sindicato quieren negociar que los trabajadores de planta tengan dos descansos diarios. The union leaders want to negotiate two breaks a day for the plant workers.

negociar qué... to negotiate what... ■ to work out what... ➤ Después de negociar qué tipo de transporte queríamos, contratamos el viaje. After negotiating what kind of transportation we wanted, we signed the contract for the trip.

negociar un contrato to negotiate a contract

negocio del espectáculo show business

negocio floreciente booming business

negocio redondo sweet deal

estar **negra la situación** (for) the situation not to look good ■ (for) the situation to be very serious

negro como el azabache ■ más negro que el azabache jet-black

estar **negro un asunto** (for) the matter not to look good ■ (for) the matter to be very serious

nervios bien templados nerves of steel

estar **nervioso(-a) por** to be nervous about

neumonía atípica ■ (el) Síndrome Respiratorio Agudo Grave Severe Acute Respiratory Syndrome ■ SARS

neutralizar a alguien to blank someone out ➤ Cuando reaccionó diciéndote "pobrecito", él estaba neutralizándote. When he reacted by saying, "poor baby," he was blanking you out.

neutralizar un plan to foil a plan

ni a la de tres not for the life of me ■ for the life of me

ni a tiros no way ■ under no circumstances

ni afirmar ni negar ■ no afirmar o negar neither to affirm nor deny ■ not to affirm or deny ■ neither to confirm nor deny ■ not to confirm or deny

ni aun not even

ni aunque (lo) quisiera uno not even if one wanted to ➤ Ni aunque yo (lo) quisiera. Not even if I wanted to.

ni bien *(Sudamérica)* ■ nada más ■ apenas no sooner ➤ Ni bien abrí la puerta, me encontré a Gemma. ■ Nada más abrir la puerta, me encontré con Gemma. No sooner had I opened the door than I ran into Gemma. ■ I opened the door, and there was Gemma.

ni bien (yo) llegue allá ■ en cuanto (yo) llegue allá ■ tan pronto (yo) llegue allá as soon as I get there ➤ Le daré de comer al perro ni bien llegue allá. I'll feed the dog as soon as I get there. ■ I'll feed the dog as soon as I arrive (there).

ni con mucho not by a long shot

ni de coña *(Esp., subido de tono)* ■ de ningún modo ■ de ninguna manera ■ ni de broma ■ ni pa' Dios no way! ■ no way, José

ni en sueños not in one's wildest dreams

¡ni hablar! nothing doing! ■ *(coloquial)* nothin' doin'

ni hablarse ■ no hablarse not to be speaking ■ not to be on speaking terms ➤ Ni se hablan. They're not speaking. ■ They're not even speaking to each other. ■ They're not on speaking terms.

ni hostias ■ me importa un bledo I don't give a damn

ni huevos ■ me importa un bledo I don't give a damn

¡ni idea! beats me! ■ it (sure) beats me!

ni inmutarse not to even bat an eye ■ not to so much as bat an eye ■ not to budge (an inch) ■ to be poker-faced ■ to be expressionless ■ to remain expressionless ➤ El presunto culpable ni se inmutó. The accused was poker-faced. ■ The accused was expressionless. ■ The accused remained expressionless

ni la más mínima prueba: no tener ~ ■ no tener ni una sola prueba not to have a shred of evidence ➤ La policía no tiene ni la más mínima prueba. ■ La policía no tiene ni una sola prueba. The police don't have a shred of evidence.

¡ni lo creas! don't you believe it! ➤ Don't you believe it! ¡Ni lo creas, hijo!

ni lo pienses ■ no lo pienses ni tan siquiera ■ no pienses siquiera en una cosa así ■ ni se te ocurra don't even think such a thing

ni lo sé, ni me importa I don't know, and I don't care

¡ni lo sueñes! dream on! ■ fat chance!

ni más faltara *(Esp.)* ■ no hay de que ■ de nada ■ muchas veces you're welcome ■ any time ■ *(común pero menos aconsejable)* don't mention it

ni más ni menos no less ➤ ¡*El diccionario de la música Harvard*, y en español, ni más ni menos! *The Harvard Dictionary of Music*, and in Spanish, no less!

¡ni me preguntes! don't ask!

ni me va ni me viene I don't care one way or the other ■ it makes no difference to me

ni media palabra don't breathe a word of it ■ mum's the word

ni modo 1. no way! **2.** *(Méx.)* no tengo otra alternativa ■ no tengo otra opción I have no other choice ■ I don't have any (other) choice ■ I have no alternative

¡ni mucho menos! far from it!

ser **ni mucho menos perfecto** ■ distar bastante de ser perfecto to be far from perfect

ni muerto ni vivo me verán en... I wouldn't be caught dead at... ■ I wouldn't be caught dead in...

ni...ni neither...nor

ni para remedio for love or money

ni pasarse por la imaginación sugerir que... not to suggest by any stretch of the imagination that... ➤ Ni se me pasa por la imaginación sugerir... I'm not suggesting by any stretch of the imagination that...

¡ni pensarlo siquiera! ■ ¡ni pensarlo! don't even think of it! ■ forget that idea!

ni pincha, ni corta he has no weight

ni pincha, ni corta: ser alguien que ~ to have no weight ■ to be a non-entity

ni pizca ■ ni un ápice not a bit

ni por asomo ■ ni por pienso ■ de ningún modo by no means

ni por el forro not in the slightest ■ not in the least

ni por el torro not in the slightest ■ not in the least

ni por nada del mundo not for anything in the world ■ not for all the tea in China

ni por pienso ■ ni por asomo ■ de ningún modo by no means ■ never!

ni por sombra not a bit

ni por soñación by no means whatsoever

ni puñetera idea I don't have the faintest idea ■ I haven't got the slightest idea ■ I don't have any idea

ni puta idea *(subido de tono)* I don't have any fuckin' idea ■ I got no fuckin' idea

ni que as if

ni que decir tiene (que) ■ huelga decir (que) it goes without saying ■ it goes without saying

ni qué ocho cuartos: qué dieta ~ diet, my foot! ➤ ¡Qué dieta ni qué ocho cuartos! Fue un corto plazo de agonía antes de un rápido aumento de cinco libras. Diet, my foot! It was a short period of starvation preceding a rapid gain of five pounds.

ni quiero hacerlo nor do I want to (do it)

ni quiero oírlo nor do I want to hear it

ni quiero verla nor do I want to see her

ni quiero verle nor do I want to see him

ni quito ni pongo rey I have no say in these matters

ni remotamente not even remotely

ni se alteró ■ ni se inmutó he didn't budge ■ he didn't move a muscle

ni se inmutó ■ ni se alteró he didn't move a muscle ■ he didn't budge

ni se te ocurra ■ no lo pienses ni tan siquiera ■ no pienses siquiera en una cosa así ■ ni lo pienses don't even think such a thing

ni siquiera not even ■ hardly ➤ Ni siquiera estudié para el examen de arte. No había manera de hacerlo. I didn't even study for the art test. There was no way to. ➤ *("Father William", de Lewis Carroll)* Ni siquiera se supondría... One would hardly suppose...

ni siquiera estudié para el examen de arte I didn't even study for the art test

ni siquiera lo había pensado 1. *(yo)* I hadn't even thought of that **2.** *(él)* he hadn't even thought of that

ni siquiera lo noté ■ ni siquiera me di cuenta I didn't even notice

ni siquiera lo pensé I didn't even think of that

ni siquiera me da bola 1. *(él)* he doesn't even know I exist **2.** *(ella)* she doesn't even know I exist

ni siquiera me di cuenta ■ ni siquiera lo noté I didn't even notice

ni siquiera sabía que... I didn't even know that...

ni siquiera se le pasaría a uno por la cabeza one would hardly suppose ■ it would never occur to you that

ni siquiera sé tu nombre I don't even know your name

ni siquiera tengo que... ■ no tengo ni que... I don't even have to... ➤ Los sobres vienen por lotes de veinticinco. Ni siquiera tengo que contarlos. ■ Los sobres vienen por lotes de veinticinco. No tengo ni que contarlos. The envelopes come in lots of twenty-five. I don't even have to count them. ➤ Ni siquiera tengo que ir a la tienda. Con llamar por teléfono basta. ■ No tengo ni que ir a la tienda. Con llamar por telefóno basta. I don't even have to go to the store. I just give them a call.

ni siquiera un poco menos any less so ➤ ¿Dices que tu brazo está todavía dolorido? ¿Ni siquiera un poco menos que la última vez que fuiste al médico? You say your arm is still sore? Any less so than the last time you went to the doctor?

ni sombra de ■ no hay señales de no sign of

ni sombra de duda without a shadow of a doubt

ni soñarlo it's out of the question

ni tanto, ni tan poco it's not that bad ■ neither one extreme nor the other

ni tener tiempo para not even to have time to

ni un ápice ■ ni pizca not a bit

ni una palabra don't say a word

ni una sola prueba: no tener ~ ■ no tener ni la más mínima prueba not to have a shred of evidence ➤ La policía no tiene ni una sola prueba. ■ La policía no tiene ni la más mínima prueba. The police don't have a shred of evidence.

ni uno not a single one

ni uno ni el otro neither one ■ not either one ➤ No podemos permitirnos ni un apartamento ni el otro. We can't afford to buy either condominium. ■ We can afford neither condominium.

ni yo tampoco ■ tampoco I don't either ■ neither do I ■ *(coloquial)* me either

niebla matinal morning fog ➤ La niebla matinal se retira de la Bahía de San Francisco para las once de la mañana. The morning fog burns off the San Francisco Bay by 11 a.m. ■ The morning fog on the San Francisco Bay dissipates by 11 a.m.

ninguna de las dos veces neither time ■ not either time ➤ No votó al titular ninguna de las dos veces. She didn't vote for the incumbent either time. ■ Neither time did she vote for the incumbent.

ninguno de los anteriores none of the above

ninguno de los dos neither of the two

niño(-a) consentido(-a) ■ niño(-a) mimado(-a) ■ niñato(-a) ■ *(Méx., coloquial)* niño(-a) chiple spoiled child ■ *(coloquial)* spoiled brat

niño(-a) de oro golden boy

niño de pecho ▪ niño de teta infant ▪ babe in arms

niño(-a) de sus ojos apple of one's eye

niño(-a) de teta ▪ niño de pecho infant ▪ babe in arms

el **niño Dios** the Christ child

niño en la edad de crecer ▪ niño en la edad de crecimiento growing boy

niño(-a) en la edad del estirón a child at the growing age ▪ a child growing like a weed

niño(-a) mimado(-a) ▪ niño(-a) consentido(-a) ▪ niñato(-a) ▪ *(Méx., coloquial)* niño(-a) chiple spoiled child ▪ *(coloquial)* spoiled brat

niño(-a) prodigio(-a) child prodigy

el **niño que llevamos dentro** the inner child ▪ the child within (each of) us

niños soldados child soldiers

el **nivel cero** ▪ zona cero ground zero

el **nivel de calidad** level of quality

el **nivel de conciencia** level of consciousness ➤ Su nivel de conciencia sigue siendo bajo y sólo despierta a veces. His level of consciousness continues to be low, and he only wakes up now and then.

nivel de crucero *(aeronáutica)* cruising altitude

el **nivel del rocío** dew point

nivelar el presupuesto to balance the budget

no a todo not quite ▪ not completely

no abarcar lo suficiente ▪ no cubrir lo necesario not to go far enough ➤ El nuevo proyecto de ley de salubridad no abarca lo suficiente. ▪ La nueva propuesta de ley de salubridad no abarca lo suficiente. ▪ La nueva propuesta de ley de salubridad no cubre lo necesario. The health care reform bill does not go far enough.

no acabar de to be at a loss to

no aceptar una oferta ▪ rechazar una oferta to decline an offer

no acertaba a explicármelo (yo) ▪ no pude entenderlo completamente ▪ no pude comprenderlo completamente I couldn't quite understand it

no acierto a explicármelo ▪ no puedo entenderlo completamente ▪ no puedo comprenderlo completamente I can't quite understand it ▪ I don't quite get it

no afirmar o negar ▪ ni afirmar ni negar not to affirm or deny ▪ to neither confirm nor deny

no aguantar más la curiosidad not to be able to stand the curiosity any longer ▪ not to be able to bear the curiosity any longer ➤ Ella no aguantó más la curiosidad. She couldn't stand the curiosity any longer. ▪ Her curiosity got the best of her.

no aguantar pulgas not to put up with any nonsense ➤ No aguanta pulgas. She doesn't put up with any nonsense.

no aguanto más ▪ no soporto más I can't stand (it) any more ▪ I can take (it) any more

no ahorrárselas con nadie ▪ no ahorrar con nadie not to be afraid of anybody

no alcancé a hacer todo lo que quería I didn't get done everything that I had wanted to ▪ I didn't get everything done that I had wanted to

no alcanzar a esquivar algo to be unable to get out of the way of something ▪ to be unable to dodge something

no alcanzar a ver *(por obstrucción de la vista)* to be unable to see ▪ to be unable to make out ➤ No alcanza a ver los números de la báscula por su estómago. He can't see the numbers on the scale because of his stomach. ➤ No alcanzo a leer el nombre en el buzón. I can't make out the name on the mail box.

no alterarse ▪ ni inmutarse not to budge ▪ not to move a muscle ➤ Los niños no se alteraron. The children didn't budge.

no anda ▪ no funciona ▪ no va it's not working ▪ it isn't working ▪ it doesn't work

no andar bien de tiempo not to have much time ▪ to be short of time ▪ *(coloquial)* to be short on time

no andar muy bien not to be (doing) very well ➤ Mi abuela no anda muy bien. My grandmother is not (doing) very well.

¡no andes con rodeos! ▪ no te andes por las ramas ▪ no te andes por rodeos ▪ ¡a lo concreto! quit beating around the bush! ▪ get to the point!

no ando muy bien que digamos I'm not doing all that well ▪ I'm not doing all that great

no aparecer ni en los mejores sueños de uno ▪ no poder imaginárselo ni en los mejores sueños de uno ▪ no poder figurárselo ni en los mejores sueños de uno to be beyond one's wildest dreams

no aparentar su edad not to look one's age ➤ No aparenta sus treinta y ocho años. She doesn't look thirty-eight.

no aparentarlo not to look it

no aprobar ▪ desaprobar ▪ no estar de acuerdo con to disapprove of ▪ not to approve of ➤ Los padres no aprobaban la relación de su hija con un hippie. The parents disapproved of their daughter's relationship with a hippie.

no arrepentirse de nada to have no regrets ➤ I have no regrets. No me arrepiento de nada. ➤ You won't regret it. No te vas a arrepentir. ▪ No se va (usted) a arrepentir.

no así 1. but not 2. unlike ➤ Ganaron la guerra, no así la paz. They won the war, but not the peace. ➤ La noche de juerga fue divertida, no así el día siguiente. The night on the town was fun, unlike the next day.

no avanzar lo suficiente not to get far enough ▪ not to make enough progress ▪ not to make enough headway

no avanzar mucho not to get very far

no bastar para que... not to be enough to... ▪ to fail to... ➤ No bastó para que dejaran de creerlo. It wasn't enough to make them stop believing it. ▪ It wasn't enough to convince them. ▪ It failed to convince them.

no bien ▪ luego que ▪ así que ▪ apenas no sooner

no bien hubo... no sooner had...

no bullir ni pie ni mano not to lift a finger

no busques camorra don't go looking for trouble

no cabe duda there's no doubt about it

no cabe duda que... there's no doubt that...

no cabe equivocarse you can't go wrong

no cabe más there's no more room ▪ there's no more space

no cabe olvidar que... ▪ no debería olvidarse que... ▪ no se debería olvidar que... it should not be forgotten that...

no cabe pensar que... there's no question that...

no caber con alguien en un espacio not to (be able to) fit in a space with someone

no caber desear nada más not to be able to wish for anything more ➤ No me cabe desear nada más. I couldn't wish for anything more.

no caber en el pellejo ▪ estar henchido de orgullo to burst with pride ▪ to be bursting with pride

no caber en sí de... to be beside oneself with...

no caber en sí de orgullo ▪ estar rebosante de orgullo ▪ estar derrochando orgullo to be bursting with pride

no caber más for there to be no more room

no caber ni un alfiler to be (jam) packed

no caberle algo ▪ no entrar en algo to outgrow something ➤ Cuando mi hermano mayor no cabe en su ropa, mi padres me la pasan. ▪ Cuando a mi hermano mayor no le cabe su ropa, mis padres me la pasan. ▪ Cuando mi hermano mayor no entra en su ropa, mis padres me la pasan. ▪ Cuando a mi hermano mayor no le entra su ropa, mis padres me la pasan. When my big brother grows out of his clothes, my parents hand them down to me. ▪ When my big brother outgrows his clothes, my parents hand them down to me.

no cabíamos en casa y parió la abuela ▪ éramos pocos y parió la abuela we were already bursting at the seams and in come(s)...

no caerá esa breva fat chance of that (happening)! ▪ one should be so lucky! ▪ *(con sarcasmo)* good luck!

no caerse de un guindo ▪ no nacer ayer not to be born yesterday ➤ No me he caído de un guindo. ▪ No nací ayer. I wasn't born yesterday, (you know).

no caérsele a alguien de la boca algo never to stop talking about something

no caérsele a uno los anillos not to be above doing something ➤ A Jimmy Carter, a pesar de ser un ex-presidente, no se le caían los anillos trabajando de carpintero. Jimmy Carter, though a former president, was not above working as a carpenter.

¿no caes? don't you get it? ▪ don't you catch on?

no caía I didn't get it (at first) ■ I wasn't getting it

no caigo ■ no entiendo I don't get it ■ I don't catch on

no cambiar nada not to change a bit ➤ Al volver a México, todos mis amigos me dijeron que yo no había cambiado nada. When I went back to Mexico, all my friends said I hadn't changed a bit.

no capto (la) onda ■ no lo cojo ■ no chanelo I don't get it ■ I don't catch on

no casar con to clash with ■ not to go with

no ceder un ápice not to budge an inch ■ not to give an inch ■ not to concede an inch

no chanelo I don't get what you mean

no comerse una rosca con ■ no conseguir nada de to get nowhere with

no conocer el patio not to have been around the block yet ➤ El candidato da la impresión de ser como un niño que no conoce el patio. The candidate comes across as a little kid who hasn't been around the block yet.

no conocer límites ■ no tener límites to know no limits ■ to have no limits ■ to know no bounds ■ to have no bounds

no conocer un lugar not to have been to a place (before)

no conoces nuestra nueva casa 1. *(chalet)* you haven't seen our new house **2.** *(piso)* you haven't seen our new apartment

no conocía a nadie cuando llegué I didn't know anybody when I got here

no conocía un alma cuando llegué I didn't know a soul when I got here

no conozco a nadie aquí I don't know anyone here

no conozco a nadie que... I don't know anyone who...

no conozco un alma aquí I don't know a soul here

no conseguí recibir los cursos que quería I didn't get to take the courses I wanted (to)

no conseguir nada de ■ no comerse una rosca con to get nowhere with

no consigo dar con ello ■ no puedo dar con ello I cannot (quite) put my finger on it ■ I can't (quite) put my finger on it ■ it's intangible

no consigo que esto funcione I can't get this thing to work ■ I can't get this to work

no contar not to count ■ not to be important ■ not to matter ➤ Me tratan como si yo no contase. They treat me as if I don't count.

no contestan there's no answer

no convenirle hacerlo one should not do it ➤ No le conviene hacerlo. He shouldn't do it.

no correr not to cut it ➤ Esa excusa no corre. That exuse doesn't cut it.

no correr prisa to be in no hurry

no creas todo lo que se dice don't believe everything you hear

¿no crees que sería mejor...? don't you think it would be better to...? ■ wouldn't it be better to...?

no creí que te fuera a importar ■ no pensé que te fuera a importar ■ no creí que te importara ■ no pensé que te importara I did not think you would mind ■ *(coloquial)* I didn't think you'd mind

no creí que te importara ■ no pensé que te importara ■ no creí que te fuera a importar ■ no pensé que te fuera a importar I did not think you would mind ■ *(coloquial)* I didn't think you'd mind

no creo I don't think so ■ I don't believe so

no creo en ello I don't believe it

no creo que haya la menor duda en que... I don't think there is any doubt that...

no creo que haya ninguna pregunta que... ■ no creo que haya ninguna cuestión que... ■ no creo que haya ninguna aclaración que hacer que I don't think there's any question that...

no creo que lo haga 1. *(él)* I don't think he'll do it **2.** *(ella)* I don't think she'll do it

no creo que sea eso ■ no me parece que sea eso I don't think it's *that*

no creo que sea una buena idea I don't that's a good idea

no creyó sobrevivir he didn't think he'd survive ■ he did not think he would survive

no cuajó it didn't come together ■ it didn't happen ■ it didn't take place ■ it didn't come off

no cuela I don't buy it

no cuelgue (usted) ■ no se retire (usted) don't hang up ■ hold on ■ hold the phone

no cuelgues ■ no te retires don't hang up ■ hold on ■ hold the phone

no cuentes conmigo count me out ■ count me out of the deal

no cuentes, ¿vale? don't tell, okay?

no cumplir not to do what one says he will ■ not to keep one's word ➤ Pero tú no cumples. But you don't do what you say you're going to. ■ But you don't keep your word.

no da abasto there's not enough to go around ■ there's not enough for everybody ■ it won't go around

no daba crédito a mis ojos I couldn't believe my eyes

no dar abasto (con algo) not to be able to cope (with something) ■ not to be able to deal with something ➤ Los hospitales no daban abasto con tantos heridos. The hospitals couldn't cope with so many injured people. ➤ No damos abasto con tantos pedidos. We can't deal with all these orders.

no dar beligerancia a alguien ■ no conceder beligerancia a alguien not to pay any attention to someone ➤ No des beligerancia a él. Don't pay any attention to him.

no dar crédito to believe it

no dar crédito a los ojos ■ no dar crédito a lo que ven los ojos not to be able to believe one's eyes ➤ No doy crédito a mis ojos. I can't believe my eyes. ➤ No daba crédito a mis ojos. *(yo)* I couldn't believe my eyes. ■ *(él)* He couldn't believe his eyes. ■ *(ella)* She couldn't believe her eyes.

no dar crédito a lo ocurrido to believe what happened

no dar crédito a lo que ven sus ojos ■ no dar crédito a sus ojos not to believe one's eyes

no dar cuartel to show no mercy ■ to attack relentlessly

no dar el brazo a torcer not to let one's arm be twisted ■ not to let anyone twist one's arm ■ to stick to one's guns ■ to stand one's ground

no dar la gana hacerlo *(enfático)* not to feel like doing it ■ I don't want to do it

no dar la talla to be up to it

no dar ni clavo not to lift a finger ■ not to do a lick of work

no dar ni chapa not to lift a finger ■ not to do a lick of work

no dar ni golpe not to lift a finger ■ not to do a lick of work

no dar ninguna seña de to show no sign(s) of

no dar para tanto not to stretch far enough ■ not to go far enough ➤ Mis ahorros no darían para tanto, si también venían mis padres. My savings wouldn't stretch far enough if my parents came, too.

no dar paz a algo to go to town with something ■ to go at it with something ■ to give something a workout ➤ Florentina no daba paz a las tijeras. Florentina was going to town with the scissors. ■ Florentina was going at it with the scissors. ■ Florentina was giving the scissors a workout.

no dar pie con bola ■ no acertar en nada ■ no hacer nada a derechas ■ no hacer nada bien not to hit on it ■ not to hit on the right answer ■ not to hit on the solution

no dar resultado not to work ■ not to be successful ■ to be unsuccessful ➤ El tratamiento no dio resultado. The treatment didn't work. ■ The treatment was unsuccessful.

no dar señales de vida to show no signs of life ■ not to show any signs of life

no dar su brazo a torcer to stand firm ■ not to let one's arm be twisted

no dar un paso sin alguien not to go anywhere without someone

no darle bola a alguien to pay no attention to someone ■ not to know that someone exists ➤ Nadie le da bola a ese tarado. Nobody pays any attention to that idiot.

no darle más que penas ■ no darle más que disgustos ■ no reportar nada sino disgustos ■ no hacer nada sino darle problemas to cause nothing but trouble ■ to be nothing but trouble

no darse por aludido to tune out ■ not to internalize ■ not to be engaged by ➤ Los hispanos dicen "¡allá penas!" para no darse por aludidos de lo que la otra persona está diciendo.

Hispanics say "allá penas" (it's not my problem) in order to tune out what the other person is saying.

no darse por enterado(-a) ■ hacer caso omiso de ■ hacerse el sueco to feign ignorance ■ to play dumb

no dársele a uno un pitoche de not to give a damn about

¡no debe de ser! it can't be!

no debe faltar mucho it shouldn't be long (now)

no debe ser... 1. *(conjetura)* (one) can't be... ■ it can't be 2. *(prohibición)* (one) musn't be... ■ it musn't be ■ it can't be ➤ ¿Cómo es Kent de grande?-No sé, pero no debe ser muy grande. How big is Kent?-I don't know, but he can't be very big. ➤ ¿Qué tan grande es Antigua?-No sé, pero no debe ser muy grande. ■ ¿Cómo es de grande Antigua?-No sé, pero no debe ser muy grande. How big is Antigua?-I don't know, but it can't be very big. ➤ No debe ser muy caro. It can't be very expensive. ➤ El trabajo no debe ser entregado más tarde que mañana por la mañana. The paper must not be turned in later than tomorrow morning. ■ The paper musn't be turned in later than tomorrow morning. ■ The paper can't be turned in later than tomorrow morning.

no debe ser muy malo can't be very bad

no debería olvidarse que... ■ no se debería olvidar que... ■ no cabe olvidar que... it should not be forgotten that...

no debes decírselo a ellos cuando te vayas you mustn't tell them when you're leaving

no debes pensar eso you mustn't think that

no decir esta boca es mía not to open one's mouth

no decir más que estupideces ■ no decir más que tonterías ■ no decir más que patochadas to be full of nonsense

no decir más que gillipolleces *(subido de tono)* to be full of shit ■ *(alternativa benigna)* to be full of nonsense

no decir más que patochadas ■ no decir más que tonterías ■ no decir más que estupideces to be full of nonsense

no decir ni esta boca es mía not to say a word

no decir ni jota not to say a word

no decir ni pío for there not to be a peep out of ➤ No dijo ni pío. There wasn't a peep out of him.

no decir palabra not to say a word

no decir tal to say no such thing ■ to say nothing of the sort

no decirle nada a alguien 1. not to say anything to someone ■ to say nothing to someone 2. to be lost on someone ➤ Sus garantías no me dicen nada. No me fío de ellos. Their assurances are lost on me. I don't trust them.

no deja de... it still...

no dejar a alguien ni a sol ni a sombra to attack someone relentlessly ■ not to give someone a moment's rest ■ *(literario, periodísmo)* not to give someone a moment's respite

no dejar a nadie indiferente to leave no one untouched ■ to leave no one unaffected ➤ La película no deja a nadie indiferente. ■ Nadie sale de la película indiferente. The movie leaves no one untouched. ■ The movie leaves no one unaffected. ■ No one is the same after seeing the movie.

¡no dejar caer! do not drop!

no dejar de hacer algo to keep doing something

no dejan de pasar los carros *(L.am.)* ■ no dejan de pasar los coches ■ no dejan de pasar los automóviles there's a solid stream of cars ■ there's a continuous stream of cars ■ there's an unbroken stream of cars

no dejar de preguntarle algo a alguien to keep asking someone something ➤ No dejé de preguntarle... I kept asking him...

no dejar de tener to still have ➤ No deja de tener sus encantos. She still has her charms.

no dejar de venir ■ seguir viniendo ■ seguir acercándose to keep (on) coming

no dejar hueso sano a alguien ■ no dejar un hueso sano a alguien to rake someone over the coals

no dejar meter baza to monopolize the conversation ■ not to let anybody else get a word in edgewise

no dejar nada a la imaginación to leave nothing to the imagination

no dejar nada a la suerte to leave nothing to chance

no dejar nada que desear to leave nothing to be desired

no dejar ni a sol ni a sombra to give one no peace ■ to leave one no peace

no dejar ni un solo cabo suelto not to leave any loose ends

no dejar piedra sin mover to leave no stone unturned

no dejar títere con cabeza ■ no quedar títere con cabeza to turn the place upside down

no dejarle mentir a alguien to bear someone out ■ to back someone up

no dejarse ganar por not to give way to

no dejes de... 1. *(coloquial)* don't fail to... 2. *(por escrito)* do not fail to...

no dejes para mañana lo que puedes hacer hoy don't leave for tomorrow what you can do today ■ don't put off until tomorrow what you can do today

no dejo de pensar... I keep thinking...

no del todo not completely ■ it doesn't quite ■ one doesn't quite ➤ Creía que tenía suficiente dinero, pero no del todo. ■ Creía que tenía suficiente dinero, pero no me llega. I thought I had enough money, but I don't quite

no desaprovechar ocasión para never to miss a chance to

no desearás a la mujer de tu prójimo thou shalt not covet thy neighbor's wife

no despegarle los ojos not to let someone out of your sight ➤ No le despegues los ojos. Don't let him out of your sight.

no destiñe ■ no se destiñe colorfast

no dice la hora it doesn't give the time ■ it doesn't say what time

no dije eso I didn't say that

no dio resultado it didn't work out

no dolerle prendas al reconocer *(C.J. Cela)* ■ no avergonzarse al reconocer not to be ashamed to admit ➤ No me duelen prendas reconocer que... ■ No me avergüenza reconocer que... I'm not ashamed to admit that...

no dormir suficiente ■ dormir menos de lo necesario not to get enough sleep ➤ *(noticia)* Los jóvenes duermen menos de lo necesario. ■ Los jóvenes no duermen lo suficiente. Young people don't get enough sleep.

no dormirse entre los laureles not to rest on one's laurels

no doy crédito a mis ojos I don't believe my eyes

no dudar en... not to hesitate to...

no echarse 1. quedarse levantado to stay up ■ to skip the siesta ■ not to lie down (for a nap) 2. no perder a propósito not to let up ■ not to slack off ■ not to let someone get the best of one

no echarse a perder to keep ■ to prevent from spoiling ➤ ¿No se echa a perder? Will it keep?

¡no empecemos de nuevo! don't start that again!

no, en absoluto absolutely not

no en vano (and) in fact ■ (and) actually ➤ La ciencia ficción se ha convertido en un género muy popular, no en vano muchos escritores utilizan sus reglas tradicionales y técnicas literarias en sus obras. Science fiction has become a very popular genre, and in fact, many non-science fiction writers employ its conventions and techniques in their works.

no encontrar rasgo de to find no trace of

no encontrarse bien ■ no sentirse bien not to feel well ➤ No me encuentro bien. I don't feel well. ■ I'm not feeling well. ➤ ¿Te encuentras bien? Do you feel all right? ■ Do you feel okay? ■ Are you feeling okay?

no encontrarse nada bien not to be at all well ➤ No se encuentra nada bien. *(él)* He's not at all well. ■ *(ella)* She's not at all well.

no encontrarse solo ■ no estar solo ■ no ser el único not to be alone ■ not to be the only one ■ not to be unique ➤ *(noticia)* El agujero negro en la Vía Láctea no se encuentra solo. The black hole in the center of the Milky Way is not alone. ■ The black hole in the center of the Milky Way is not the only one. ■ The black hole in the center of the Milky Way is not unique.

no entender ni jota ■ no entender una jota not to understand a thing ■ not to understand at all

no entender una jota ■ no entender ni jota not to understand a thing ■ not to understand at all

no entendérsele nada a alguien not to be able to understand anything someone says

no entendí ■ no he caído I didn't get it ■ I didn't catch on

no enterarse not to register ■ not to take it in ➤ Al principio no me enteré. At first it didn't register. ■ At first I didn't take it in.

no entiendo por qué... I don't understand why... ■ *(coloquial)* I don't see why...

no entra it doesn't fit ▪ it won't fit ▪ it won't go in

no entrar en algo ▪ no caberle algo to outgrow something ➤ Cuando mi hermano mayor no entra en su ropa, mi padres me la pasan. ▪ Cuando a mi hermano mayor no le entra su ropa, mis padres me la pasan. ▪ Cuando mi hermano mayor no cabe en su ropa, mi padres me la pasan. ▪ Cuando a mi hermano mayor no le cabe su ropa, mis padres me la pasan. When my big brother grows out of his clothes, my parents hand them down to me. ▪ When my big brother outgrows his clothes, my parents hand them down to me.

no entrar ni salir en to play no part in ▪ not to play any part in ▪ to play no role in ▪ not to play any role in

no entrarle ni las balas to be tough as nails ▪ to be thick-skinned

no era eso that wasn't it ▪ it wasn't that

no era más que ▪ no era sino it was nothing more than ▪ it was nothing but

no era para menos it was not without good reason

no era rentable it wasn't profitable

no era sino ▪ no era más que it was nothing but

no era una simple imaginación it was not just my imagination ▪ it was not just our imagination

¡no es así! not so!

¿no es así? isn't that right? ▪ is that not right?

no es así de sencillo it's not that simple

no es así desde siempre it hasn't always been that way

no es asunto tuyo ▪ no es de tu incumbencia ▪ no pintas nada en esto it is none of your business ▪ it's none of your business ▪ it is no concern of yours ▪ it's no concern of yours

no es casualidad que... it is no accident that...

no es cierto it's not true

¿no es cierto? 1. isn't that right? 2. don't you think?

no es como para reírse ▪ no es para reírse ▪ no es nada como para reírse ▪ no es un asunto del que uno se pueda reír it's no laughing matter

no es cosa del otro jueves ▪ no es nada del otro jueves ▪ no es cosa del otro mundo ▪ no es nada del otro mundo it's nothing to write home about

no es de extrañar ▪ es lógico ▪ no me extraña no wonder ➤ Es lógico que conozas este bar. No wonder you know this bar.

no es de extrañar que... it's no wonder that... ▪ it's little wonder that...

no es de tu incumbencia ▪ no es asunto tuyo ▪ no pintas nada en esto it is no concern of yours ▪ it's no concern of yours ▪ it is none of your business ▪ it's none of your business

no es decir gran cosa ▪ eso no es decir gran cosa that's not saying a whole lot ▪ that's not saying much

no es difícil de imaginar it's not difficult to imagine ▪ it's not hard to imagine

no es eso it's not that ▪ that's not it

no es gran cosa it's no big thing

no es justo ▪ no hay derecho ▪ es injusto it's not fair ▪ it's unfair ▪ it's unjust

no es la cosa que tenía en mente that's not what I had in mind

no es lo mío ▪ no es santo de mi devoción it's not my cup of tea

no es lo mismo it's not the same thing ▪ that's different

no es lo que quería decir (yo) ▪ no pretendía decir eso ▪ no iba con esa intención that's not what I meant

no es moco de pavo ▪ esto no es moco de pavo ▪ eso no es moco de pavo it's nothing to sneeze at

no es nada it's nothing ▪ don't worry about it

no es nada como para reírse ▪ no es como para reírse ▪ no es un asunto del que uno se pueda reír it's no laughing matter

no es nada de eso ▪ nada de eso that's not it ▪ it's not like that at all

no es nada del otro jueves ▪ no es cosa del otro jueves ▪ no es nada del otro mundo ▪ no es cosa del otro mundo it's nothing to write home about ▪ it's no big thing

no es nada del otro mundo it's nothing

no es nada personal it's nothing personal

no es ni... it's not even...

no es ninguna vergüenza it's nothing to be ashamed of

no es oro todo lo que reluce all that glitters is not gold

no es para menos not without good reason ▪ not without reason ▪ it's not without good reason

no es para mí it's not for me ▪ it's not intended for me ➤ Este mensaje no es para mí. This message is not for me. ▪ This message is not intended for me.

no es para mí juzgar(lo) it's not for me to judge ▪ that's not for me to judge

no es para tanto ▪ no hay para tanto 1. no es grave it's no big deal ▪ it's no big thing 2. tampoco está tan mal it's not that bad ▪ it's not so bad

no es por falta de ganas it's not because I don't want to ▪ it's not that I don't want to

no es por mí it's not for me ▪ it's not for my benefit ▪ it's not for my sake ▪ it's not as a favor to me

no es por tirarme flores, pero... not to brag, but...

no es preocupante it's nothing to worry about

no es propio de él it's not like him

no es propio de ella it's not like her

no es propio de ti it's not like you

no es rentable it's not profitable

no es que importe ▪ no es que cambie las cosas not that it matters ▪ not that it makes any difference ▪ not that it changes anything

no es que lo crea, es que estoy absolutamente seguro I don't just think so, I know so

no es que sea muy interesante it's not all that interesting

no es tan fiero el león como lo pintan 1. it is not what it is cracked up to be 2. it is not as bad as it is portrayed

no es un asunto del que uno se pueda reír ▪ no es nada como para reírse ▪ no es como para reírse it's no laughing matter

no es una simple imaginación it's not just my imagination ▪ it's not just our imagination

no escatimar esfuerzo(s) para to spare no effort to

no escatimar gastos to spare no expense

no escatimar sus alabanzas de alguien to be unstinting in one's praise of someone

no escribe ▪ no pinta (it) doesn't write ➤ Este bolígrafo no pinta. This ballpoint pen doesn't write.

no escrudiñadero ▪ insondable unfathomable ▪ inscrutable

no escuches lo que diga (él) don't listen to anything he says

no escuches lo que te diga (ella) don't listen to anything she tells you ▪ don't listen to anything she says to you

no escurras el bulto ▪ no esquives el bulto ▪ no evites el tema ▪ no evites el asunto don't evade the issue ▪ don't avoid the issue

no esperar menos de alguien to expect nothing less of someone

no esquives el bulto ▪ no escurras el bulto don't evade the issue ▪ don't avoid the issue

no está bien que uno... it is not right for one to... ▪ it isn't right for one to... ▪ it's not right for one to...

no está bien que uno no... it is not right for one not to ▪ it isn't right for one not to... ▪ it's not right for one not to...

no está el horno para bollos ▪ el horno no está para bollos ▪ no está el patio para bollos this is not the right time ▪ it's not the right time

no está el patio para bollos ▪ no está el patio para bollos this is not the right time ▪ it's not the right time

¡no está mal! not bad!

no está merecido it's not deserved ➤ La crítica no está merecida. The criticism is not deserved.

no está nada mal that's not a bad thing

no estar al día ▪ seguir en la prehistoria to be behind the times ➤ Si no aceptas tarjetas de crédito o débito para compras de 550 euros, es que no estás al día. ▪ Si no aceptas tarjetas de crédito o débito para compras de 550 euros, es que sigues en la prehistoria. If you don't accept credit or debit cards for purchases of 550 euros, you're behind the times.

no estar católico(-a) ▪ no encontrarse bien not to feel well

no estar de acuerdo con alguien sobre algo ▪ estar en desacuerdo con alguien sobre algo to disagree with someone on something ▪ to disagree with someone about something ▪ to disagree with someone over something

no estar de humor para algo ▪ no tener humor para algo not to be in the mood for something

no estar de humor para hacer algo not to be in the mood to do something

no estar en ningún lado to be nowhere to be found ➤ Buscó su collar por todos los rincones, y no estaba en ningún lado. She looked everywhere for her necklace, but it was nowhere to be found. ▪ She looked everywhere for her necklace, but she couldn't find it anywhere.

no estar en su escritorio ▪ dejar el escritorio to be away from one's desk ▪ to have stepped away from one's desk ➤ No está en su escritorio en este momento. ▪ He dejado su escritorio un momento. He's away from his desk at the moment. ▪ He's stepped away from his desk for a moment.

no estar en sus cabales not to be in one's right mind

no estar muy allá ▪ ser cosita de gusto to be nothing to write home about

no estar para bromas to be in no mood for jokes

no estar para fiestas not to be in the mood for fun and games ▪ to be in no mood for fun and games

no estar para una cosa not to be cut out for something ➤ Es una temeridad, usted no está para estas cosas. It's folly, you're not cut out for these things.

no estar por la labor not to have one's mind on the job

no estaría nada mal que it wouldn't be a bad thing if

no este, sino ese not this one, but that one

no estoy allí desde que... ▪ no he estado allí desde que... I have not been there since... ▪ I haven't been there since...

no estoy avergonzado para admitir que... ▪ no me avergüenza admitir que... ▪ no se me rasgan las vestiduras al reconocer que... I'm not ashamed to admit that...

no estoy de acuerdo ▪ estoy en desacuerdo I do not agree ▪ I disagree ▪ *(coloquial)* I don't agree

no estoy diciendo que no (lo) es I'm not saying it's not

no estoy enterado(-a) de eso ▪ no estoy enterado(-a) de ello I don't know about it

no estoy listo(-a) I'm not ready

no estoy muy seguro(-a) que digamos I'm not a hundred percent sure ▪ I'm not completely sure

no estoy ofendido(-a) I'm not offended

no estoy preparado(-a) I'm not prepared

no estoy vestido(-a) I'm not dressed

no evites el tema ▪ no evites el asunto ▪ no esquives el bulto ▪ no escurras el bulto don't evade the issue ▪ don't avoid the issue

¡no exageres! don't overdo it!

no exceder de lo corriente to be just average ▪ to be only average

no existe dicho... there is no such...

no existe posibilidad alguna de... there's no chance of...

no existe posibilidad alguna de que... there's no chance that...

¡no falla! can't miss!

¡no faltaba más! ▪ ¡no faltaría más! **1.** *(asentimiento)* by all means! ▪ of course! ▪ don't mention it! ▪ anything you say! **2.** *(impaciencia)* that's the limit! ▪ that's the last straw!

¡no faltaría más! ▪ ¡no faltaba más! **1.** *(asentimiento)* by all means! ▪ of course! ▪ don't mention it! ▪ anything you say! **2.** *(impaciencia)* that's the limit! ▪ that's the last straw!

¿no fastidies? no kidding? ▪ you're joking!

no figurar en not to appear in ▪ not to be included in

no forzosamente not necessarily

no fue del todo culpa mía it wasn't all my fault

no funciona ▪ no va ▪ no anda it doesn't work ▪ it's not working ▪ it isn't working

no funcionar bien not to work properly ▪ not to work right

no ganar nada con hacer algo not to gain anything by doing something ▪ not to get anywhere by doing something

no ganar ni para pipas to work for peanuts

no ganar un palmo de terreno not to gain an inch of ground

no gustarle ▪ no irle not to like it ▪ not to like something ➤ No me gusta. I don't like it. ➤ No le gustan los quesos (muy) fuertes. He doesn't like strong cheeses.

no gustarle nada alguien not to like someone at all ➤ No me gustó nada (él). I didn't like him at all. ➤ A ella no le gustó nada (él). She didn't like him at all.

no gustarle ni disgustarle una cosa neither to like nor dislike something ➤ No le gustaba ni le disgustaba. He neither liked nor disliked it.

no ha cambiado nada nothing has changed

no ha extrañado a nadie que it has come as no surprise that ▪ it comes as no surprise that

¡no ha sido él! he did not!

¡no ha sido ella! she did not!

no ha terminado it's not over

no haber cambiado un pelo not to have changed a bit

no haber hecho más que empezar to have barely begun ▪ to have barely scratched the surface ➤ Con dieciséis mil lemas, no había hecho más que empezar el diccionario. With sixteen thousand entries, I had barely scratched the surface of the dictionary. ▪ With sixteen thousand entries, I had barely begun the dictionary. ➤ Los genetistas que trabajan en la secuenciación de los genomas de todas las plantas y animales no han hecho más que empezar. The geneticists who are mapping the genomes of all the plants and animals of the world have barely scratched the surface.

no haber inventado la pólvora not to be the brightest person in the world ▪ not to be the sharpest knife in the drawer

no haber más alternativa (que...) ▪ no haber más opción (que...) for there not to be any alternative (but to...) ▪ for there not to be any choice (but to...) ▪ for there not to be much choice (but to...) ▪ for there not to be any alternative (other than to...) ▪ for there not to be any choice (other than to...) ▪ for there not to be much choice (other than to...) ➤ No hay más alternativa que... ▪ No hay más opcion que... There's no choice but to... ▪ There's not much choice but to... ▪ There's no choice other than to... ▪ There's not much choice other than to...

no haber más opción (que...) ▪ no haber más alternativa (que...) for there not to be any choice (but to...) ▪ for there not to be much choice (but to...) ▪ for there not to be any alternative (but to...) ▪ for there not to be any choice (other than to...) ▪ for there not to be much choice (other than to...) ▪ for there not to be any alternative (other than to...) ➤ No hay más alternativa que... ▪ No hay más opcion que... There's no choice but to... ▪ There's not much choice but to... ▪ There's no choice other than to... ▪ There's not much choice other than to...

no haber matado una mosca en su vida never to have hurt a flea

no haber pasado algo **1.** no padecer una enfermedad not to have an illness **2.** no haber ocurrido algo (for) something not to happen ➤ No ha pasado la varicela. She's never had chickenpox. ➤ No ha pasado lo que tenía que pasar. What was supposed to happen, didn't. ➤ No ha pasado el tren. The train hasn't come. ▪ The train hasn't gotten here (yet).

no haber pasado bocado en todo el día ▪ no haber probado bocado en todo el día not to have had a bite to eat all day ▪ no haber por dónde coger a alguien

no haber probado bocado en todo el día ▪ no haber pasado bocado en todo el día not to have had a bite to eat all day

no haber visto nada igual never to have seen anything like it ▪ not to have (ever) seen anything like it ➤ Los médicos no han visto nada igual. The doctors have never seen anything like it.

no había hecho nada más que esperar *(yo)* I had done nothing but wait ▪ the only thing I did was wait ▪ *(él)* he had done nothing but wait ▪ the only thing he did was wait ▪ *(ella)* she had done nothing but wait ▪ the only thing she did was wait

no había nadie nobody was there ▪ there was nobody around

no había podido dejar de ver *(yo)* I couldn't help seeing ▪ *(él)* he couldn't help seeing ▪ *(ella)* she couldn't help seeing

no había tiempo que perder there was no time to lose

no hablar de otra cosa to talk of nothing else ▪ not to talk about anything else ▪ not to talk of anything else ▪ to be all one talks about

no hablar ni una palabra not to say a word

no hablarse ▪ ni hablarse not to be speaking ▪ not to be on speaking terms ➤ No se hablan. They're not speaking. ▪ They're not on speaking terms.

no hablo de nadie en concreto I'm not talking about anyone specifically ▪ I'm not talking about any one person

no habrá tenido tiempo *(él)* he probably hasn't had time ▪ *(ella)* she probably hasn't had time

no hace falta there's no need ▪ you don't need to

no hace falta más que uno ▪ con uno basta all it takes is one ▪ one is all it takes

no hace falta que ▪ no hay que there's no need to ▪ you don't need to ▪ it's not necessary ▪ that's not necessary

no hace falta que me lleves you don't need to give me a ride ▪ I don't need a ride

no hace mucho *(tiempo)* not long ago

no hacer bien con not to go (well) with ▪ not to look good with ➤ La corbata no hace bien con la camisa. The tie doesn't go with the shirt. ▪ The tie doesn't look good with the shirt.

no hacer cosa a derechas ▪ no hacer nada a derechas not to do anything right

no hacer justicia a algo not to do justice to something ▪ not to do something justice ➤ La película no hace justicia al libro. The movie doesn't do the book justice. ▪ The movie doesn't do justice to the book. ➤ La película no le hace justicia. The movie doesn't do it justice.

no hacer justicia a alguien not to do justice to someone ▪ not to do someone justice ➤ La foto del carnet de conducir no le hace justicia a ella. The driver's license photo doesn't do her justice.

no hacer más que ▪ no hacer sino to do nothing but ▪ to only ➤ No hago más que... I do nothing but... ▪ All I do is... ➤ Corregir demasiado no hace más que socavar la confianza en uno mismo. Correcting too much only undermines self-confidence.

no hacer más que despotricar ▪ pasarse el día despotricando to be forever complaining

no hacer nada a derechas ▪ no hacer nada bien ▪ no dar pie con bola not to do anything right

no hacer nada bien ▪ no hacer nada a derechas ▪ no dar pie con bola not to do anything right ➤ Nunca te digas a ti mismo, "Nunca hago nada bien." Never say to yourself, "I don't do anything right."

no hacer nada especial para la ocasión not to be doing anything special for the occasion

no hacer nada en especial ▪ no hacer nada en particular not to be doing anything in particular

no hacer nada más que not to do anything but ▪ to do nothing but ➤ No hago nada más que trabajar. I do nothing but work. ▪ I don't do anything but work. ▪ All I do is work.

no hacer nada para merecerlo not to do anything to deserve it

no hacer nada sino darle problemas ▪ no darle más que penas ▪ no darle más que disgustos ▪ no reportar nada sino disgustos to cause nothing but trouble ▪ to be nothing but trouble

no hacer sino ▪ no hacer más que to do nothing but

no hacerle caso a alguien not to pay any attention to someone

no hacerle mella a alguien not to phase someone

no hacía una cosa desde had not done something since ➤ California no sufría cortes de luz desde la Segunda Guerra Mundial. California had not suffered blackouts since the Second World War.

¡no hagas caso! pay no attention! ▪ don't pay any attention!

no has cambiado un pelo you haven't changed a bit

¿no has visto jamás...? have you ever seen...?

no hay campo there's no room

no hay como... there's nothing like...

no hay cuidado there's nothing to worry about ▪ there's nothing to fear

no hay cuidado alguno there's nothing at all to worry about ▪ there's nothing whatever to fear

no hay de qué ▪ de nada you're welcome

no hay de qué preocuparse there's nothing to worry about

no hay derecho ▪ no es justo ▪ es injusto it's not fair ▪ it's not right ▪ it's unjust

no hay día en que... not a day goes by that... ▪ not a day goes by without...

no hay dos sin tres things always happen in three's ▪ things (always) come in three's

no hay duda de que... there is no doubt that...

no hay duda de que es... there is no doubt that it is... ▪ it is undoubtedly...

no hay escapatoria there's no way out ▪ there's no (way to) escape ▪ there's no escape route

no hay fin a la vista ▪ no se ve el final there's no end in sight

¡no hay localidades! sold out!

no hay mal que por bien no venga every cloud has a silver lining

no hay manera de saber si there is no way to know if

no hay manera de saber si...o no there is no way to know whether...or not

no hay manera de saberlo there's no way of knowing

no hay manera en que... there is no way to ➤ No hay manera en que podamos evitar... There is no way to prevent...

no hay marcha atrás ▪ no hay vuelta atrás there's no turning back ▪ there's no backing out (now)

no hay más cáscaras there's nothing more to say about it ➤ Esto es así y no hay más cáscaras. That's the way it is, and there's nothing more to say about it.

no hay más cera que la que arde what you see is what you get

no hay más que... ▪ no tienes más que... ▪ basta... all you have to do is... ➤ No hay más que enchufarlo. ▪ Basta enchufarlo. All you have to do is plug it in.

no hay más que conformarse we have to get along with it

no hay más que decir that's all there is to it

no hay más que hablar that's all there is to say about it ▪ there's nothing else to say about it

no hay mejor defensa que un buen ataque the best defense is a good offense

no hay moros en la costa the coast is clear

no hay muchas salidas 1. there are not many exits 2. *(figurativo)* there are not many alternatives ▪ there are not many options

no hay nada de qué hablar there's nothing to discuss ▪ there's nothing to talk about

no hay nada estropeado ▪ todo está bien there's nothing wrong with it (mechanically)

no hay nada malo en eso ▪ no hay nada malo en ello there's nothing wrong with that ▪ there's nothing wrong with it ➤ Ah, bueno, menos mal. No hay nada malo en eso. Oh, well, that's good. There's nothing wrong with that.

no hay nada más lejos de la verdad ▪ nada podría estar más alejado de la verdad nothing could be further from the truth

no hay (nada) más que pedir ▪ no podrías pedir nada más you couldn't ask for anything more

¿no hay nada más que te guste? *(dependiente al cliente)* would you like anything else?

no hay nada que me guste más (que...) ▪ a mí no hay nada que me guste más (que...) there's nothing I like better (than...) ▪ I like nothing better (than...)

no hay nada que temer there's nothing to fear

no hay necesidad de explicación there's no need to explain

no hay otra opción there's no other choice

no hay para todos there's not enough for everyone ▪ there's not enough to go around

no hay peor ciego que el que no quiere ver there are none so blind as those who will not see

no hay peor sordo que el que no quiere oír there are none so deaf as those who will not hear

¡no hay pero que valga! no excuses! ▪ no arguments! ▪ I don't want to hear any excuses! ▪ no ifs, ands, or buts!

no hay prisa there's no hurry

no hay puntos intermedios (entre) there is no middle (between)

no hay que it isn't necessary to ▪ one must not ▪ we mustn't ➤ No hay que confundir la simpatía con la debilidad. We mustn't mistake kindness for weakness.

no hay qué comer ■ no hay nada que comer there's nothing to eat ■ there's no food ➤ No hay qué comer en la casa. ■ No hay nada que comer en la casa. There's nothing to eat in the house.

no hay que poner todos los huevos en la misma cesta don't put all your eggs in one basket

no hay quien 1. there is no one who ■ no one 2. no one can ■ it is impossible to

no hay quien le gane *(a él)* there's no one who can beat him ■ no one can beat him ■ *(a ella)* there's no one who can beat her ■ no one can beat her

no hay rasgos de there is no trace of

no hay tal cosa ■ no es cierto there is no such thing ■ there's no such thing

no hay tal cosa como there is no such thing as ■ there's no such thing as

no hay término medio there's no middle ground

no hay tiempo que perder there's no time to lose

no hay vuelta atrás ■ no hay marcha atrás there's no turning back ■ there's no backing out (now)

no he caído ■ no entendí I didn't get it ■ I didn't catch on

no he llegado tan lejos ■ no lo he pensado hasta ese punto I haven't thought that far ahead

no he podido evitar notar que... I couldn't help noticing that...

no he querido ser impertinente, pero... ■ no quiero parecer maleducado, pero... I don't mean to be rude, but...

¡no he sido yo! I did not! ➤ ¡Tú lo has sacado!-¡No he sido yo! You brought it up!-I did not!

no he terminado I haven't finished ■ I'm not finished ■ I'm not through

no he visto nada igual I've never seen anything like it ➤ *(Colin Powell después del tsunami)* No he visto nada igual en mi vida. I've never seen anything like it in my life.

no he vuelto desde entonces I haven't been back since ■ I haven't gone back since ■ I haven't returned since

no hubo caso it was no use

no hubo modo de there was no way to

no hubo ningún detenido there were no arrests

no hubo tiempo there was no time to ■ there wasn't (any) time to

no huelo a nada I don't smell of anything

no iba con esa intención ■ no quería decir eso ■ no pretendía decir eso *(yo)* I didn't mean it that way ■ that's not what I meant ■ *(él)* he didn't mean it that way ■ that's not what he meant ■ *(ella)* she didn't mean it that way ■ that's not what she meant

no importarle un bledo to care less ■ not to care less

no ir a ninguna parte not to go anywhere

no ir a parar en 1. no dejar de not to cease in ■ not to relent in 2. no conformarse con not to settle for

no ir con alguien to be beyond someone ➤ La magnanimidad sencillamente no iba con él. Magnanimity was simply beyond him.

no irla con algo not to go along with something

no írsele a caer la casa encima not to let any grass grow under one's feet ➤ No se le va a caer la casa encima. He doesn't let any grass grow under his feet.

no juzguéis para no ser juzgado judge not that you be not judged

¡no la acoja! *(Valle-Inclán)* don't protect her!

no la aguanto ■ no la soporto ■ no puedo aguantarla ■ no puedo soportarla I can't stand her

no la conozco de vista I don't know her by sight ■ I don't know what she looks like ■ I wouldn't know her if I saw her

no la llegué a ver *(a ella)* I didn't get to see her ■ I never got to see her ■ *(una película)* I didn't get to see it ■ I never got to see it

no la sitúo ■ no la ubico ■ no sé de qué la conozco I can't place her ■ I don't know where I know her from

no la soporto ■ no la aguanto ■ no puedo soportarla ■ no puedo aguantarla I can't stand her

no la ubico ■ no la sitúo ■ no sé de qué la conozco I can't place her ■ I don't know where I know her from

no le conozco de vista *(Esp., leísmo)* ■ no lo conozco de vista *(a él)* I don't know him by sight ■ *(a usted)* I don't know you by sight

no le creo 1. *(a usted)* I don't believe you ■ *(a él)* I don't believe him ■ *(a ella)* I don't believe her 2. no le doy ningún crédito a eso I don't put any stock in it

no le doy ningún crédito a lo que dice I don't put any stock in what he says

no le di ninguna importancia... I didn't think anything of it at the time

no le hace *(L.am.)* ■ no importa it doesn't matter

¡no le hagas caso! 1. *(a él)* pay no attention to him! ■ don't pay any attention to him! 2. *(a ella)* pay no attention to her! ■ don't pay any attention to her!

no le incumbe *(a usted)* it's none of your business ■ *(a él)* it's none of his business ■ *(a ella)* it's none of her business

no le llegué a ver *(Esp., leísmo)* ■ no lo llegué a ver (a él) I didn't get to see him ■ I never got to see him

no le sitúo *(Esp., leísmo)* ■ no le ubico ■ no lo sitúo ■ no lo ubico I can't place him

no le valió que... ■ no ayudó a la situación it didn't help matters that... ■ it didn't help that...

no le veo demasiado *(Esp., leísmo)* ■ no puedo verle mucho ■ no lo veo demasiado ■ no puedo verlo mucho I don't get to see him very often ■ I don't see him very often

no le veo la gracia I fail to see the humor (in that) ■ I don't see what's so funny (about that)

no les veo demasiado *(Esp., leísmo)* ■ no puedo verles mucho ■ no los veo demasiado ■ no puedo verlos mucho I don't get to see them very often

no llegar a hacer algo not to get to something ■ not to get something done ➤ Tuve que preparar tantas clases que no llegué a corregir sus trabajos. I had so many classes to prepare that I didn't get your papers graded.

no llegar para tanto 1. *(dinero)* not to have enough ■ not to go far enough ■ not to be able to afford ■ not to permit 2. *(conocimientos, destreza)* not to be good enough ■ to be insufficient ➤ Mi sueldo no llega para tanto. My salary doesn't permit it. ■ I can't afford it on my salary. ➤ No me atrevo con Lope de Vega. Mi español no llega para tanto. I'm not up to Lope de Vega. My Spanish is not good enough.

no llegarle a los talones a alguien not to (be able) to hold a candle to someone ➤ El talento del discípulo no le llega a los talones al del maestro. The student doesn't hold a candle to his teacher.

no llevar al matrimonio más que su cuerpo 1. *(mujer)* to marry without a dowry 2. *(hombre)* to marry penniless

¡no lleves las cosas demasiado lejos! don't go too far! ■ don't take things too far! ■ don't take liberties!

no llevo la cuenta I'm not keeping track ■ I'm not keeping score ➤ Pero pagaste la última vez. Me toca a mí invitar.-No importa. No llevo la cuenta. But you paid last time. It's my turn to pay.-I don't care. I'm not keeping score.

¿no lo adivinas? can't you guess?

no lo aguanto ■ no lo soporto ■ no puedo aguantarlo ■ no puedo soportarlo I can't stand him

no lo aparentas *(tu edad, por ejemplo)* ■ no lo pareces you don't look it

no lo chanelo ■ no lo cojo ■ no capto (la) onda I don't get it ■ I don't catch on

no lo cojo ■ no lo chanelo ■ no capto (la) onda I don't get it ■ I don't catch on

no lo conozco de vista I don't know him by sight ■ I don't know what he looks like ■ I wouldn't know him if I saw him

no lo consiento I won't stand for it

no lo creo ■ no me lo creo I don't believe it

¡no lo cuentes! *(el secreto)* don't tell! ■ don't give it away!

¡no lo dejes escapar! ■ ¡no te lo pierdas! don't miss it!

no lo digo por decir I'm not just saying that

no lo dudes believe me

¡no lo dudo! ■ ¡sin duda! I'll *bet* you do!

¡no lo eches en saco roto! don't forget! ■ don't forget to!

no lo encuentro por ninguna parte I can't find it anywhere

no lo había notado ▪ no me había dado cuenta ▪ no me había fijado I hadn't noticed

no lo había visto desde esa perspectiva ▪ no lo había visto así I hadn't thought of it that way

no lo he decidido I haven't decided

no lo he pensado hasta ese punto ▪ no he llegado tan lejos I haven't thought that far ahead

no lo llegué a ver *(a él)* I didn't get to see him ▪ I never got to see him ▪ *(un espectáculo)* I didn't get to see it ▪ I never got to see it

no lo notaba I couldn't tell

no lo sé aún ▪ no lo sé todavía ▪ aún no lo sé ▪ todavía no lo sé I don't know yet ▪ I still don't know

no lo tengo I don't have it

no lo tengo muy claro I'm not completely sure ▪ *(EE UU, coloquial)* I'm not real sure

no lo logro entender it baffles me ▪ I'm baffled by it

no lo menciones ▪ ni lo menciones don't mention it ▪ don't bring it up ▪ don't bring the subject up

no lo necesito ▪ no me hace falta I don't need it

no lo noté ▪ no me fijé ▪ no me di cuenta ▪ *(literario, periodismo)* no me percaté I didn't notice

¡no lo olvide! ▪ ¡no lo olvides! don't forget!

no lo pareces *(tu edad, por ejemplo)* ▪ no lo aparentas you don't look it

¡no lo permita Dios! perish the thought!

no lo pienses dos veces don't give it a second thought

no lo pienses ni tan siquiera ▪ ni se te ocurra ▪ no pienses siquiera en una cosa así ▪ ni lo pienses don't even think such a thing

no lo pretendía ▪ no quería *(yo)* I didn't mean to ▪ *(él)* he didn't mean to ▪ *(ella)* she didn't mean to

no lo puedo remediar I can't help it

no lo puedo soportar I can't stand it

no lo quiero ni regalado I wouldn't have it even if they gave it to me

no lo resisto más ▪ no lo aguanto más ▪ no lo soporto más I can't endure it any longer ▪ I can't take it any longer ▪ I can't stand it any longer

no lo resisto ni un minuto más ▪ no lo aguanto ni un minuto más ▪ no lo soporto ni un minuto más I can't endure it another minute ▪ I can't take it another minute ▪ I can't stand it another minute

no lo sabes (tú) bien you're telling me! ▪ yeah, *tell* me about it!

no lo sabía I didn't know

no lo sabría *(con "yo")* I wouldn't know

no lo sé ▪ no sé I don't know ▪ I do not know

no lo sé a ciencia cierta I couldn't swear by it

no lo sé aún ▪ no lo sé todavía I don't know yet ▪ I still don't know ▪ I still haven't heard ▪ I haven't heard yet

no lo sé todavía ▪ no lo sé aún I don't know yet ▪ I still don't know ▪ I still haven't heard ▪ I haven't heard yet

no lo soporto ▪ no lo aguanto ▪ no puedo soportarlo ▪ no puedo aguantarlo *(a él)* I can't stand him ▪ *(ello)* I can't stand it

no lo suficiente 1. not enough 2. *(con "avanzar")* not far enough

no lo suficiente para not enough to

no lo suficiente para... not enough to make any difference

no lo tomes así don't take it that way

no lo veo así I don't look at it that way ▪ I don't see it that way

no lo veo por ninguna parte I don't see it anywhere

no lo vi de esa manera I didn't look at it that way

no lo vuelvas a hacer don't do it again

no lograr hacer algo not to succeed in doing something ▪ not to manage to do something ▪ to fail to do something ➤ El presidente no logró convencer a Rusia. The president failed to convince Russia.

no lograr saber not to manage to find out ▪ not to succeed in finding out

no lograrse saber not to be possible to find out ➤ No se ha logrado saber el contenido exacto y la magnitud del proyecto. So far it has not been possible to find out the exact content and magnitude of the bill. ▪ It has so far not been possible to find out the exact content and magnitude of the bill.

no llegar muy lejos not to get very far

no llegó la sangre al río nothing came of it

no más de no more than

no me acuerdo de tu nombre ▪ no recuerdo tu nombre I can't remember your name ▪ I don't remember your name

no me apetece 1. no gracias I don't care for any 2. no tengo ganas I don't feel like it 3. no quiero I (just) don't want to

no me apetece, gracias I don't care for any, thanks

no me apetece ir I don't feel like going

no me apetecía ir I didn't feel like going

no me atañe it's not my concern

no me avergüenza admitir que... ▪ no estoy avergonzado de admitir que... ▪ *(literario)* no se me rasgan las vestiduras al reconocer que... I'm not ashamed to admit that...

no me cabe decirlo it's not for me to say

no me cabe en la cabeza I can't take it in ▪ I can't believe it ▪ I can't realize it

no me cabe la menor duda que... I have no doubt in my mind that...

no me cabe más alegría I couldn't be happier

no me concentro I can't concentrate

no me cosco ▪ no caigo I don't get it ▪ I don't catch on

no me creo lo que... I can't believe what...

no me da buena espina I don't feel good about it ▪ I don't have a good feeling about it

no me da la gana ▪ no me da la real gana I don't feel like it ▪ I don't want to

no me da miedo ▪ no tengo miedo I'm not afraid

no me da tiempo ▪ no tengo tiempo I can't find the time ▪ I can't find the time ▪ I don't have time

¡no me des por vencido! 1. no dejes de alentarme don't give up on me! 2. no me excluyas don't count me out

no me di cuenta ▪ no me fijé ▪ no lo noté ▪ *(literario, periodismo)* no me percaté I didn't notice

no me di cuenta (de eso) ▪ no lo noté I didn't notice (it)

no me dice nada 1. *(cuando no se refiere a una persona)* it doesn't do anything for me 2. *(él)* he doesn't say anything to me 3. *(ella)* she doesn't say anything to me

¡no me digas! ▪ ¡quién iba a decirlo! well, what do you know?! ▪ you don't say! ▪ you're kidding! ▪ is that right? ▪ is that so? ▪ *(incredulidad)* no!

no me digas que... don't tell me (that)...

no me dio el cambio bien: el camarero ~ the waiter didn't get the change right ▪ the waiter didn't give me the right change

no me duelen prendas al reconocer que... *(Camilo José Cela)* ▪ tengo que admitir que... ▪ tengo que reconocer que... I have to admit that... ➤ No me duelen prendas al reconocer que tienes razón. ▪ Tengo que admitir que tienes razón. I have to admit that you're right.

no me eches la culpa a mí don't blame *me*

no me entiendas mal ▪ no me malinterpretes don't get me wrong ▪ don't misunderstand me

no me estoy metiendo contigo I'm not blaming you ▪ I'm not mad at you ▪ it's not you that I'm blaming ▪ it's not you that I'm mad at

no me extraña (nada) that doesn't surprise me (at all) ▪ that doesn't surprise me (a bit)

no me fastidies ▪ no me molestes ▪ *(Arg., Chi., Uru.)* no (me) jodás don't bother me

no me fijé ▪ no me di cuenta ▪ no lo noté ▪ *(literario, periodismo)* no me percaté I didn't notice

no me fijé mucho en... ▪ no presté mucha atención a... I didn't pay much attention to...

no me fío de él I don't trust him

no me fío de ella I don't trust her

no me gusta ▪ no me va I don't like it ➤ No me gusta. ▪ No me va.

no me gusta algo ▪ no me va algo I don't like something ➤ No me gusta la música rock. ▪ No me va la música rock. I don't like rock music.

no querer que sepa nadie ▪ no querer que se entere nadie not to want anyone to find out ➤ Yo no quería que lo supiera nadie. ▪ Yo no quería que lo supiese nadie. ▪ Yo no quería que se enterara nadie. ▪ No quería que se enterase nadie. I didn't want anyone to find out. ▪ I didn't want anybody to find out.

no querer sino to want only to

no querer ver a alguien ni en pintura ▪ no querer ver a alguien ni pintado not to ever want to see someone again ▪ not to ever want to see the likes of someone ever again ➤ No quiero verlo ni en pintura. ▪ *(Esp., leísmo)* No quiero verle ni en pintura. I don't want to see him ever again. ▪ I don't want to see the likes of him ever again. ➤ No quiero verla ni en pintura. I don't want to see her ever again. ▪ I don't want to see the likes of her ever again.

no quería: (yo) ~ ▪ lo hice sin querer ▪ no lo pretendía I didn't mean to

no quería decirle eso, pero tuve (que...) I didn't want to tell him, but I had to

¿no quieres? don't you want to?

no quiero correr el riesgo I don't want to take the chance ▪ I don't want to risk it ▪ I don't want to take the risk

no quiero correr ningún riesgo I don't want to take any chances

no quiero entrar al trapo I don't want to discuss it

no quiero entrar en ello ▪ no quiero meterme (en ello) I don't want to get into it ▪ I don't want to discuss it

no quiero entretenerte (más) ▪ no quiero retenerte (más) I don't want to keep you (any longer) ▪ I don't want to delay you (any longer) ▪ I don't want to detain you (any longer)

no quiero inmiscuirme, pero... I don't want to pry, but...

no quiero meterme (en ello) ▪ no quiero entrar en ello I don't want to get into it ▪ I don't want to discuss it

no quiero meterme en eso ▪ no quiero entrar en eso I don't want to get into that ▪ I don't want to discuss that

no quiero nada más, gracias I don't care for any more, thank you ▪ I don't care for any more, thanks

no quiero parecer mal educado, pero... ▪ no he querido ser impertinente, pero... I don't mean to be rude, but...

no quiero presionar I don't want to push

no quiero que me llueva encima I don't want to get rained on

no quiero sino que... lo único que quiero es que... ▪ all I want is for... ▪ I only want (for)...

no quiero volver a tenerlo como profesor nunca I don't ever want to have him as a teacher again ▪ I don't ever want to have him for a teacher again ▪ I don't want him for a teacher ever again

no quisiera estar en sus zapatos *(de él)* I wouldn't want to be in his shoes ▪ *(de ella)* I wouldn't want to be in her shoes ▪ *(de usted)* I wouldn't want to be in your shoes

no quitar los ojos de encima a algo ▪ **no quitarle los ojos de encima (a algo)** ▪ **seguir algo con lupa** to watch something like a hawk ▪ not to take one's eyes off of something

no quitar los ojos de encima a alguien not to take one's eyes off of someone

no quitarle más tiempo a alguien not to take any more of someone's time ➤ No te quito más tiempo. I won't take any more of your time.

no rasgársele las vestiduras al reconocerlo to make no bones about it

no recordar haber hecho algo not to remember doing something ▪ not to remember having done something ➤ No recuerdo haber escuchado la pieza de Strauss. I don't remember hearing the Strauss piece. ▪ I don't remember having heard the Strauss piece.

no recuerdo el tiempo cuando ▪ no recuerdo la época cuando I can't remember a time when ➤ No recuerdo el tiempo cuando no teníamos perro. I can't remember a time when we didn't have a dog.

no recuerdo la época cuando ▪ no recuerdo el tiempo cuando I can't remember a time when ➤ No recuerdo la época cuando no teníamos perro. I can't remember a time when we didn't have a dog.

no recuerdo tu nombre ▪ no me acuerdo de tu nombre I don't remember your name ▪ I can't remember your name

no reparar en nada to stop at nothing

no reparar en pelillos ▪ no detenerse en pelillos to let nothing stand in one's way ▪ not to let anything stand in one's way

no reportar nada sino disgustos ▪ no darle más que disgustos ▪ no darle más que penas ▪ no hacer nada sino darle problemas to cause nothing but trouble ▪ to be (a source of) nothing but trouble

no reportarle más que problemas a alguien ▪ no causarle más que problemas a alguien ▪ no darle más que problemas a alguien to cause someone nothing but problems

no reportarle sino disgustos to bring one nothing but trouble ▪ to cause one nothing but trouble

no representar su edad not to look one's age ➤ Ella no representa su edad. She doesn't look her age.

no resistir algo not to withstand something ➤ La explicación ofrecida por el fabricante no resulta especialmente tranquilizadora. The explanation offered by the manufacturer was not particularly reassuring.

no resistir más not to be able to bear it any longer

no respondas y hazlo ▪ te he dicho que lo hagas ▪ haz lo que te he dicho y punto do what you're told and don't answer back ▪ don't argue with me, just do it

no resultar not to work ▪ not to turn out ➤ El experimento no resultó. The experiment didn't work. ➤ La receta no resultó. The recipe didn't turn out.

no resultarle difícil colegir que... ▪ no ser difícil deducir que... not to be hard to figure out that... ➤ No me resultó difícil colegir que... It wasn't hard (for me) to figure out that... ➤ No le resultó difícil colegir que... *(a él)* It wasn't hard (for him) to figure out that... ▪ *(a ella)* It wasn't hard for her to figure out that...

un ***no* rotundo** a resounding *no*

no sabes cuánto me alegro de... you don't know how glad I am to...

no saber a qué atenerse not to know where one stands

no saber a qué carta quedarse **1.** not to know what to think ▪ not to know what to believe **2.** to be of two minds about something

no saber a quién creer not to know who to believe

no saber con certeza ▪ no saber con seguridad ▪ no saber de fijo not to know with (any) certainty ▪ not to know for sure

no saber con seguridad ▪ no saber de fijo ▪ no saber con certeza not to know for sure ➤ Nadie sabe con seguridad. Nobody knows for sure. ➤ No lo sé con seguridad. I don't know for sure. ▪ I don't know with (any) certainty.

no saber de fijo ▪ no saber con seguridad ▪ no saber con certeza not to know for sure ▪ not to know with (any) certainly

no saber de nadie que... not to know of anyone who... ➤ No sabía de nadie que pudiera ayudarme. I didn't know of anyone who could help me.

no saber de qué va la vaina ▪ no saber qué se cuece ▪ no saber por dónde van los tiros ▪ no saber cómo viene la mano not to see the big picture ▪ not to "get it"

no saber dónde meterse not to know what to do with oneself

no saber dónde se mete not to know what one is in for ▪ to have no idea of what one is in for ➤ No sabe dónde se mete. He has no idea of what he's in for.

no saber en qué punto está la relación con alguien not to know where one stands with someone ➤ No sé en qué punto está mi relación con el jefe. I don't know where I stand with the boss.

no saber gran cosa sobre algo not to know a lot about something

no saber hacer la "o" con un canuto to be dumb as a post

no saber lo que es **1.** not to know what it is **2.** no saber cómo es not to know what it's like

no saber lo que es el hombre ▪ no saber cómo son los hombres not to know what men are like

no saber lo que es la mujer ▪ no saber cómo son las mujeres not to know what women are like

no saber lo que se pierde not to know what one is missing ➤ No sabe lo que se pierde. *(él)* He doesn't know what he's missing. ▪ *(ella)* She doesn't know what she's missing. ▪ *(usted)* You don't know what you're missing.

no saber lo que se tiene not to realize what one is on to

no saber lo que se trae entre manos ■ no saber lo que se lleva entre manos ■ no saber lo que uno está tramando not to know what one is up to ➤ No sé lo que se trae entre manos. I don't know what he's up to.

no saber muy bien lo que pasa not to be sure what is happening ■ not to be sure what is going on

no saber muy bien lo que pasaba not to be sure what was happening ■ not to be sure what was going on

no saber de fijo not to know definitely ■ not to know definitively ➤ No sé de fijo si vienen o no. I don't know definitively whether they are coming (or not).

no saber ni la "a" sobre algo ■ no saber ni papa not to know the first thing about something

no saber ni papa ■ no saber ni la "a" sobre algo not to know the first thing about something

no saber ni que hacer ■ ya no hallar la salida ■ no saber qué decir to be at one's wit's end

no saber por dónde van los tiros ■ no saber de qué va la vaina ■ no saber qué se cuece ■ no saber por dónde viene la mano not to see the big picture ■ not to "get it"

no saber por dónde viene la mano ■ no saber de qué va la vaina ■ no saber por dónde van los tiros ■ no saber qué se cuece not to see the big picture ■ not to "get it"

no saber por qué ni cómo not to know why or how

no saber qué decidir not to be able to make up one's mind

no saber qué decir 1. to be at a loss not to know what to say 2. to be drained of ideas to be at one's wit's end

no saber qué se cuece ■ no saber por dónde van los tiros ■ no saber de qué va la vaina not to see the big picture ■ not to "get it"

no saber valorar a alguien ■ no saber apreciar a alguien to take someone for granted

no saberlo con seguridad not to know for sure

no sabes cuánto... you don't know how much...

no sabes cuánto me alegro de... you don't know how pleased I am to... ■ you don't know how glad I am to...

no sabes ni la media you don't know the half of it

no sabía qué esperar: (yo) ~ I didn't know what to expect

no sabía que estuvieras...: (yo) ~ I didn't know (that) you were... ➤ (Yo) no sabía que estuvieras trabajando en Madrid. I didn't know you were working in Madrid.

no sacar nada en claro de ■ no sacar nada en limpio de not to be able to make anything out of ■ not to be able to make heads or tails out of ➤ No saco nada en claro de esta carta. I can't make heads or tails out of this letter.

no sacarle ni la hora a alguien not to give someone the time of day ➤ A ese no le sacas ni la hora. That guy won't give you the time of day.

no saco nada en claro de esta explicación I can't make any sense out of this explanation

no salimos de esta ■ de esta no salimos we'll never get out of this alive

no satisfacer (las) expectativas (puestas en uno) to fail to meet someone's expectations

no se aprecia la diferencia you can't tell the difference

no sé ■ no lo sé I don't know ■ I do not know

no sé cómo explicármelo I don't know what to make of it ■ I can't explain it

no sé cuantito I don't know exactly which one ■ something or other ➤ Alfonso no sé cuantito... Alfonso something or other

no sé cuántos what's his name ■ what's her name ➤ ¿Viste a no sé cuántos en la fiesta? *(a él)* Did you see what's his name at the party? ■ *(a ella)* Did you see what's her name at the party?

no sé de nadie I don't know of anyone

no sé de nadie que... ■ no sé de nadie quien... ■ no conozco a nadie que... I don't know of anyone who... ➤ No sé de nadie que sepa traducir como Cecilia y Iván. I don't know of anyone who can translate like Cecilia and Ivan.

no sé de ninguno I don't know of any ■ I don't know of one

no se debería olvidar que... ■ no debería olvidarse que... ■ no cabe olvidar que... it should not be forgotten that...

no se debiera... one must not ■ one mustn't

no sé decirte ■ no puedo decirte (porque no sé) I can't tell you ■ I couldn't tell you

no se deja notar ■ no se nota you can't tell ■ it isn't apparent

no (se) destiñe colorfast

no se dice por nada que... ■ bien se dice que... it's for good reason that they say (that)... ■ not for nothing do they say (that)...

no se distingue ■ no se nota you can't tell

¿no se echa a perder? will it keep?

no se gana siempre you can't win them all ■ *(coloquial)* you can't win 'em all

no se ganó Zamora en una hora ■ Zamora no se ganó en una hora Rome wasn't built in a day

no se ha hecho esperar it didn't take long ➤ La respuesta al ataque terrorista no se ha hecho esperar. The response to the terrorist attack didn't take long.

¡no se habla! no talking!

no se hable más de ello let's drop the subject

no se hace you mustn't do that ■ don't do that

no se hace así that's not how it's done ■ that's not how you do it

no se hace de rogar ■ no se hace rogar *(a él)* you don't have to ask him twice ■ *(a ella)* you don't have to ask her twice

no se haga de rogar ■ no se haga rogar don't be shy

no se haga ilusiones don't get your hopes up

no se le da mal *(a él)* he's not bad at it ■ *(a ella)* she's not bad at it ■ *(a usted)* you're not bad at it

no se les da mal *(a ellos)* they're not bad at it ■ *(a ustedes)* you (all) are not bad at it

no se lo des a nadie don't give it to anybody

¡no se lo pierda! ■ ¡no te lo pierdas! don't miss it!

no sé lo que hacer con eso ■ no sé lo que hacer al respecto ■ no sé qué hacer con eso ■ no sé qué hacer al respecto I don't know what to do about it

no sé lo que me ha dado ■ no sé qué me ha dado I don't know what's gotten into me ■ I don't know what got into me

no se me da mal I'm not bad at it

no se me ocurre ■ no me sale it's not coming to me ■ I can't think of it

no se me ocurría que it didn't occur to me that

no se me ocurrió preguntar it didn't occur to me to ask

no se me partiría el corazón al... it wouldn't break my heart to...

no se me partiría el corazón si... it wouldn't break my heart if...

no se me rasgan las vestiduras al reconocer que... *(literario)* ■ no estoy avergonzado de admitir que... ■ no me avergüenza admitir que... I'm not ashamed to admit that...

no se moleste don't bother

no se muestra ■ no se ve it doesn't show

no sé nada de eso I don't know about that ■ I'm not informed about that ■ I'm uninformed about that

no sé ni quién eres I don't even know who you are ■ I hardly know who you are ■ I hardly know you

no se nota 1. you can't tell ■ you don't notice it 2. no se ve ■ no se muestra it doesn't show ■ you can't see it

no se nota you can't tell

no se oía nada you couldn't hear a thing ■ there was no sound

no se olvide (usted) de... ■ no olvide (usted)... don't forget to ➤ No se olvide (usted) de llamarme. ■ No olvide (usted) llamarme. Don't forget to call me. ➤ No se olvide (usted) de apagar las luces antes de irse. ■ No olvide (usted) apagar las luces antes de irse. Don't forget to turn off the lights before you leave. ■ Don't forget to turn the lights off before you leave.

no se puede aguantar *(anuncio para donuts)* you can't resist

no se puede decir no one can say

no se puede llevar a cabo it can't be done ■ it cannot be done

no se puede saber it's impossible to know ■ there's no way to know

no se puede tolerar it's intolerable

no sé qué: tener un ~ to have a certain something

no sé qué aspecto tenía *(él)* I don't know what he looked like ■ *(ella)* I don't know what she looked like

no sé qué aspecto tiene *(él)* I don't know what he looks like ■ *(ella)* I don't know what she looks like

no sé qué es lo que debo hacer I don't know what I should do

no sé qué hacer con eso ▪ no sé qué hacer al respecto ▪ no sé lo que hacer con eso ▪ no sé lo que hacer al respecto I don't know what to do about it

no sé qué me ha dado ▪ no sé lo que me ha dado I don't know what's gotten into me ▪ I don't know what got into me

no sé qué me ha pasado ▪ no sé qué me ha podido pasar I don't know what's come over me

no sé qué pensar I don't know what to think

no sé qué pensar de eso ▪ no sé qué pensar sobre eso I don't know what to think about it

no sé qué pensar de esto I don't know what to think of this

no se retire ▪ no cuelgue don't hang up ▪ hold on ▪ hold the phone

no se sabe ▪ nadie sabe it is not known ▪ it's not known ▪ no one knows ▪ nobody knows

no se sabía casi nada sobre... hardly anything was known about...

no sé si creérmelo I don't know if I believe that ▪ I don't *know* about that

no se te da mal you're not bad at it

no se trata de... cualquiera it's not just any...

no sé tú, pero... I don't know about you, but...

no sé usted, pero... I don't know about you, but...

no se va a arrepentir you won't regret it

no se ve el final (de) ▪ no hay fin a la vista there's no end in sight (to) ➤ No se ve el final de la violencia en el Medio Oriente. There's no end in sight to the violence in the Middle East.

no se ven igual los toros desde la barrera que desde la arena ▪ no se ven igual los toros desde la barrera que desde el tendido it's one thing to criticize ▪ it's easy to criticize

no sea (usted) así don't be like that

no sea (usted) bestia don't be crass

no sea (usted) ingenuo(-a) don't be naïve

no sea (usted) irrazonable don't be unreasonable ▪ don't be difficult

no seas así don't be like that

no seas bestia don't be crass

no seas ingenuo don't be naïve

no seas irrazonable don't be unreasonable ▪ don't be difficult

¡no seas tonto(-a)! ▪ ¡déjate de manías! don't be silly!

no sentí ningún ruido I didn't hear anything ▪ I didn't hear a thing

no ser algo del otro jueves ▪ no ser cosa del otro jueves not to be anything to write home about

no ser apto para not to be suitable for ➤ *(en un juguete)* No aptos para menores de treinta y seis meses. Not suitable for children under thirty-six months.

no ser apto para (el) consumo to be unfit for human consumption

no ser capaz de matar una mosca not to be able to hurt a flea ➤ No es capaz de matar una mosca. He couldn't hurt a flea. ▪ He wouldn't hurt a flea.

no ser consecuente con su fe to belie one's faith ▪ to be untrue to one's faith

no ser cosa del otro jueves ▪ no ser nada del otro jueves not to be anything to write home about

no ser de fiar ▪ no ser trigo limpio not to be trustworthy

no ser de piedra not to be made of stone

no ser de su agrado not to be to one's liking

no ser de tono not to be socially acceptable ▪ not to be done

no ser del agrado de uno not to be to one's liking

no ser el caso to be beside the point

no ser más que una coraza to be just a front ▪ to be just a mask (that hides the real person)

no ser otro que... to be none other than...

no ser para menos not to be without good reason ➤ No era para menos. It was not without good reason.

no ser para nada consciente de que... to be completely unaware that...

no ser santo de su devoción not to be one's cup of tea ➤ La música de guitarra eléctrica no es santo de mi devoción. Electric guitar music is not my cup of tea.

no ser todo lo que se dice que es not to be all that it's cracked up to be ▪ not to be all that it is claimed to be

no ser trigo limpio ▪ no ser de fiar not to be trustworthy ➤ Ese tipo no es trigo limpio. ▪ Ese tipo no es de fiar. That guy is not trustworthy.

no serle ajeno a alguien to be no stranger to someone

no servir de nada ▪ no servir para nada not to do any good ▪ to be useless ➤ El presidente se aceró a Miami para echar una mano al candidato, pero al final no le sirvió de nada porque perdió estrepitosamente. The president went to Miami to lend the candidate a hand, but in the end it didn't do any good because he lost overwhelmingly.

no servir para nada to be useless ▪ to be of no use (at all)

no siempre es fácil it's not always easy

no significa nada it's not important

no sin cierta pena not without regrets

no sirve de mucho it doesn't do much good

no sirve de nada it doesn't do any good

no sirve más que para... it just... ▪ it only...

no soler hacer pruebas para not to test routinely for

no sólo a ti te pasa you're not the only one

no sólo no he... not only have I not... ➤ No sólo no he oído la expresión, sino que no viene en ninguno de mis diccionarios. Not only have I not heard the expression, but it is not found in any of my dictionaries. ▪ Not only have I not heard the expression, but neither is it found in any of my dictionaries.

no soltar una perra ▪ no soltar ni un céntimo ▪ no soltar ni una peseta ▪ no soltar un duro to be tight at a tick

no soltar un duro ▪ no soltar ni un céntimo ▪ no soltar ni una peseta to be tight as a tick

no sonar bien not to sound right ▪ to sound funny

no soportar que... to hate it when... ➤ No soporto que cierren el agua mientras me estoy duchando. I hate it when they turn off the water while I'm taking a shower.

no soy de la casa I don't live here

no soy de los que... I'm one of those (people) who...

no soy caído(-a) del catre I wasn't born yesterday

no soy quien para juzgar(lo) I'm not the one to judge

no suponer hacer algo en absoluto not to involve doing something at all

no suponer mucho not to count for much

no surtir efecto to have no effect on ▪ to fail to sway ➤ Las amenazas de Pekín de recurrir a las armas para evitar la secesión formal de Taiwan no surtieron efecto en las elecciones presidenciales celebradas ayer. Beijing's threats to resort to force to prevent the secession of Taiwan had no effect on yesterday's presidential election.

¡no tan deprisa! ▪ ¡no tan rápido! not so fast!

¡no tan rápido! ▪ ¡no tan deprisa! not so fast!

¡no tantas cosas a la vez! ▪ ¡sólo una cosa por vez! ▪ ¡no todo a la vez! one thing at a time!

no tanto not so much ▪ not that much

¡no tardes! don't be long!

no tardó en... it didn't take long to...

no te alarmes don't be alarmed

no te cabrees ▪ no te enojes ▪ no te enfades don't get mad

no te capto ▪ no te entiendo I don't get what you mean

no te consiento juicios sobre mí ▪ no (te) voy a tolerar que me juzgues I won't tolerate your judging me

no te consiento que me hables así ▪ no tolero que me hables así I won't tolerate your speaking to me that way ▪ I won't put up with your speaking to me that way

no te cortes don't be shy ➤ No te cortes. Toma otro donut. Don't be shy. Take another doughnut.

no te creo I don't believe you

no te cueles don't butt in line

no te culpo (por ello) I don't blame you (for it)

no te dejes avasallar por él don't let him push you around

no te eches atrás ▪ no te rajes don't chicken out ▪ don't get cold feet ▪ don't be shy

no te enfades ▪ no te cabrees ▪ no te enojes don't get mad
¡no te ensañes conmigo! don't take it out on me!
¿no te entra en la testa que...? ¿can't you get it into your thick skull that...?
no te escaquees (de hacerlo) don't try to get out of (doing) it ➤ No te escaquees de ir. Don't try to get out of going. ➤ No te escaquees. Don't try to get out of it.
¡no te hagas de rogar! ▪ ¡no te hagas rogar! don't play hard to get!
¡no te hagas el remilgoso! don't be so finicky!
no te hagas ilusiones don't get your hopes up
no te hubiese reconocido I wouldn't have recognized you
¿no te importa si fumo? do you mind if I smoke?
no te incumbe ▪ ¡qué te importa! it's none of your business
¿no te la figuras? 1. ¿no adivinas? can't you guess? 2. *(refiriéndose a sustantivo femenino)* can't you imagine it? 3. *(refiriéndose a una persona femenina)* can't you imagine her? ▪ can't you picture her?
¿no te llama la atención que...? have you ever noticed that... ▪ have you ever noticed how...?
¡¿no te lo crees?! would you believe?!
¿no te lo figuras? 1. ¿no adivinas? can't you guess? 2. *(refiriéndose a sustantivo masculino)* can't you imagine it? 3. *(refiriéndose a una persona masculina)* can't you imagine him? ▪ can't you picture him?
no te lo puedo decir ▪ no puedo contarte I can't tell you ▪ I'm not at liberty to tell you
no te lo tomes como algo personal don't take it personally
no te lo tomes personalmente don't take it personally
no te lo tomes seriamente don't take it seriously
no te lo vas a creer you're not going to believe this ▪ you're not going to believe it ▪ you won't believe this
¡no te marches! ▪ ¡no te vayas! don't go! ▪ don't leave!
no te mates don't go to a lot of trouble ▪ don't knock yourself out ▪ don't go to too much trouble
no te metas en los asuntos ajenos don't meddle in other people's affairs ▪ don't meddle in other people's business
no te molestes don't bother
¡no te ocupes de mí! *(peatón al conductor saltándose el semáforo de peatones)* ▪ ¡no te preocupes por mí! ▪ ¡tú dale! ▪ ¡tú sigue! don't mind *me*! ▪ don't let me cramp your style!
no te olvides de ▪ no olvides don't forget to ➤ No te olvides de llamarme. ▪ No olvides llamarme. Don't forget to call me. ➤ No olvides apagar las luces antes de irte. ▪ No te olvides de apagar las luces antes de irte. Don't forget to turn off the lights before you leave. ▪ Don't forget to turn the lights off before you leave.
¡no te pases! ▪ ¡tampoco te pases! don't overdo it! ▪ don't overstep your bounds!
¡no te pases con la salsa! easy on the salsa! ▪ easy on the sauce!
no te pongas así don't be that way ▪ don't take it personally ➤ Come on, don't be that way! ¡Vamos, no te pongas así!
no te pongas borde ▪ no seas difícil don't get difficult ▪ don't get angry ▪ don't get ticked off ▪ don't give me a bad time ▪ don't hassle me
¡no te pongas chulo conmigo! ▪ no te pases de vivo conmigo don't get smart with me! ▪ don't sass me! ▪ don't get sassy with me!
¡no te pongas tonto(-a)! ▪ ¡no seas tonto(-a)! ▪ ¡déjate de manías! don't be silly!
¡no te preocupes! ▪ ¡tranquilo! ▪ no te comas el coco ▪ pierde cuidado don't worry ▪ don't worry about it
no te puedes perder you can't miss it ➤ Está en la misma esquina. No te puedes perder. ▪ Está en la mera esquina. No te puedes perder. It's right on the corner. You can't miss it.
¡no te quedes como una estatua! don't just stand there!
no te quito más tiempo I won't take any more of your time
¡no te rajes! *(L.am.)* ▪ ¡no te eches atrás! don't be shy! ▪ don't hold back! ▪ let yourself go! ▪ don't get cold feet! ➤ Mano, no te rajes. Brother, don't be shy! ▪ Brother, don't hold back! ▪ Brother, let yourself go!
no te sigo ▪ no te entiendo I don't follow you ▪ I don't understand (you)
¡no te sueltes! don't let go! ▪ hang on!
no te vas a arrepentir you won't regret it
¡no te vayas! ▪ ¡no te marches! don't go! ▪ don't leave!
no te vayas a creer you're not going to believe this
no te vayas muy lejos don't go too far! ▪ stay nearby!
no tendrás ninguna dificultad en localizarlo you won't have any trouble finding it
no tener adónde acudir not to have anywhere to turn ▪ to have nowhere to turn
no tener adónde ir not to have anywhere to go ➤ Lo echaron de su apartamento y ahora no tiene adónde ir. He got evicted from his apartment, and now he doesn't have anywhere to go.
no tener adónde más acudir not to have anywhere else to turn ▪ to have nowhere else to turn ➤ No tenemos adónde más acudir. We don't have anywhere else to turn.
no tener (a) nadie en mente ▪ no tener (a) una persona en especial en mente ▪ no tener (a) una persona específica en mente not to have any one person in mind ▪ to have no one person in mind ▪ not to have anyone specific in mind ➤ No tengo a nadie en concreto en mente. ▪ No tengo a una persona específica en mente. I don't have any one person in mind. ▪ I don't have a specific person in mind.
no tener a quién acudir not to have anyone to turn to
no tener (a) una persona en especial en mente ▪ no tener (a) nadie en mente ▪ no tener (a) una persona específica en mente not to have any one person in mind ▪ to have no one person in mind ▪ not to have anyone specific in mind ➤ No tengo a nadie en concreto en mente. ▪ No tengo a una persona específica en mente. I don't have any one person in mind. ▪ I don't have a specific person in mind.
no tener abuela ▪ no necesitar abuela to blow one's own horn ▪ to brag
no tener agallas para hacer algo ▪ no tener arrestos para hacer algo ▪ no tenerlas bien puestas para hacer algo not to have the guts to do something ▪ not to have the courage to do something
no tener alma to have a heart of stone
no tener apaño *(Esp.)* ▪ no tener arreglo ▪ no tener explicación to defy explanation ➤ El padre le dijo al hijo, "Tu comportamiento no tiene apaño." ▪ El padre le dijo al hijo, "Tu comportamiento no tiene arreglo." ▪ El padre le dijo al hijo, "Tu comportamiento no tiene explicación." The father told his son, "Your behavior defies explanation."
no tener apuro por to be in no hurry to ▪ not to be in any hurry to
no tener arreglo *(dícese ligeramente de personas y situaciones)* ▪ no tener remedio to be hopeless ▪ to be beyond hope ▪ to be a lost cause ➤ Hija mía, es que no tienes arreglo. Young lady, you're hopeless. ▪ Young lady, you're beyond hope. ▪ Young lady, you're a lost cause.
no tener arrestos para hacer algo ▪ no tener agallas para hacer algo ▪ no tenerlas bien puestas para hacer algo not to have the guts to do something ▪ not to have the courage to do something
no tener barba ni bigote to be clean shaven
no tener cabeza to have no brains
no tener cabida to have no place
no tener de qué preocuparse not to have anything to worry about ▪ to have nothing to worry about
no tener dónde caerse muerto(-a) ▪ no tener ni para pipas ▪ no tener ni para petardos ▪ no tener un peso partido por la mitad ▪ ser paupérrimo to be dirt-poor ▪ *(ligeramente subido de tono)* not to have a pot to piss in
no tener dónde estar ▪ no tener que estar en ninguna parte not to have to be anywhere ➤ No tengo dónde estar ahora. Vamos a comer algo. ▪ No tengo que estar en ninguna parte ahora. Vamos a comer algo. I don't have to be anywhere right now. Let's go get something to eat.
no tener dos dedos de frente not to be very bright ▪ not to be very smart ▪ not to be very sharp
no tener el menor reparo en que not to hesitate at all to ▪ not to hesitate in the least to
no tener elección (además de) ▪ no tener elección (que no sea) ▪ no tener opción (además de) to have no choice (but to)

▪ not to have any choice (but to) ▪ to have no choice other than to ▪ not to have any choice other than to

no tener en cuenta los hechos to ignore the facts

no tener ética to have no ethics ▪ not to have any ethics

no tener hiel to be guileless ▪ to have no guile

no tener huesos rotos not to have any broken bones ▪ to have no broken bones

no tener humor para algo ▪ no estar de humor para algo not to be in the mood for something

no tener humor para hacer algo ▪ no estar de humor para hacer algo not to be in the mood to do something

no tener intención de ofender (a nadie) to mean no offense (to anyone) ➤ (Yo) no tenía intención de ofenderte. I meant no offense. ▪ I didn't mean to offend you.

no tener la cabeza de... not to be in the mood to...

no tener la idea más remota ▪ no tener la más remota idea ▪ no tener la más mínima idea ▪ no tener la menor idea not to have the slighest idea ▪ not to have the faintest idea ▪ not to have a clue

no tener la más mínima idea ▪ no tener la menor idea ▪ no tener la más remota idea ▪ no tener la idea más remota not to have the slightest idea ▪ not to have the faintest idea ▪ not to have a clue

no tener la oportunidad de hacer algo not to have the opportunity to do something ▪ not to have the chance to do something ▪ not to get to do something ➤ No tuve la oportunidad de ir a la excursión. I didn't get to go on the tour.

no tener límites ▪ no conocer límites to have no limits ▪ to know no bounds

no tener manera de saberlo to have no way of knowing ➤ No tenemos manera de saberlo. We have no way of knowing.

no tener más que el día y la noche ▪ no tener más que la noche y el día to be dirt-poor ▪ to have nothing

no tener más remedio que ▪ no haber más remedio que not to be able to help but...

no tener mucha sal en la mollera *(Don Quixote, de Sancho Panza)* not to be very smart

no tener nada bueno que decir de... to have nothing good to say about...

no tener nada de particular not to have anything special about it ▪ not to stand out in any way ➤ No tiene nada de particular. There's nothing special about it. ▪ It doesn't stand out in any way.

no tener nada mejor que hacer to have nothing better to do ▪ not to have anything better to do

no tener nada que decir en el asunto ▪ no tener nada que opinar en el asunto to have nothing to say about a matter ▪ not to have anything to say about a matter

no tener nada que opinar en el asunto ▪ no tener nada que decir en el asunto to have nothing to say about a matter ▪ not to have anything to say about a matter

no tener nada que perder not to have anything to lose ▪ to have nothing to lose

no tener nada que ver to be way off ➤ No tiene nada que ver. That's way off.

no tener nada que ver con not to have anything to do with

no tener ni barrunto de lo que se le viene encima ▪ no tener ni idea de lo que se viene encima not to have any idea of what is coming ▪ not to have any idea of what one is in for ▪ to have no idea of what is coming ▪ to have no idea of what one is in for

no tener ni idea to have no idea ▪ not to have any idea ➤ No tengo idea. I have no idea. ▪ I don't have any idea.

no tener ni idea de lo que se le viene encima ▪ no tener ni barrunto de lo que se le viene encima not to have any idea of what is coming ▪ not to have any idea of what one is in for ▪ to have no idea of what is coming ▪ to have no idea of what one is in for

no tener ni la más remota idea not to have the slightest idea ▪ not to have the slightest

no tener ni para petardos ▪ no tener ni para pipas ▪ no tener dónde caerse muerto(-a) ▪ ser paupérrimo to be dirt-poor ▪ *(ligeramente subido de tono)* not to have a pot to piss in

no tener ni para pipas ▪ no tener ni para petardos ▪ no tener dónde caerse muerto(-a) ▪ ser paupérrimo to be dirt-poor ▪ *(ligeramente subido de tono)* not to have a pot to piss in

no tener ni pies ni cabeza to be absurd

no tener ni un minuto de respiro not to have a moment's rest

no tener ni voz ni voto en el asunto ▪ ser como una cuchara, ni pincha, ni corta to have no say in the matter ▪ not to have any say in the matter ➤ No tengo ni voz ni voto. ▪ Soy como una cuchara, ni pincho, ni corto. I have no say in the matter. ▪ I don't have any say in the matter.

no tener ningún lugar en to have no place in

no tener ninguna duda para hacer algo to have no qualms about doing something

no tener ninguna prueba de eso to have no proof of that ▪ not to have any proof of that

no tener ninguna prueba de que... to have no proof that... ▪ not to have any proof that...

no tener opción (además de) ▪ no tener opción (que no sea) ▪ no tener elección (además de) ▪ no tener elección (que no sea) to have no choice but to ▪ not to have any choice but to ▪ to have no choice other than to ▪ not to have any choice other than to

no tener (otra) alternativa ▪ no tener otra opción ▪ no tener otra salida ▪ no quedarle otra to have no alternative ▪ not to have any alternative ▪ to have no choice ▪ not to have any choice ➤ No tengo otra alternativa. ▪ No tengo otra opción. ▪ No tengo otra salida. ▪ No me queda otra. I have no alternative. ▪ I don't have any alternative. ▪ I've got no alternative. ▪ I haven't got any alternative. ▪ I have no choice. ▪ I don't have any choice. ▪ I've got no choice. ▪ I haven't got any choice.

no tener (otra) alternativa que... ▪ no tener otra opción que... ▪ no tener otra salida que... ▪ no quedarle otra que...to have no alternative but to... ▪ not to have any alternative but to... ▪ to have no choice but to... ▪ not to have any choice but to... ▪ to have no alternative other than to... ▪ not to have any alternative other than to... ▪ to have no choice other than to... ▪ not to have any choice other than to... ➤ No tengo otra alternativa que... ▪ No tengo otra opción que... ▪ No tengo otra salida que... ▪ No me queda otra que... I have no alternative but to... ▪ I don't have any alternative but to... ▪ I've got no alternative but to... ▪ I haven't got any alternative but to... ▪ I have no choice but to... ▪ I don't have any choice but to... ▪ I've got no choice but to... ▪ I haven't got any choice but to... ▪ I have no alternative other than to... ▪ I don't have any alternative other than to... ▪ I've got no alternative other than to... ▪ I haven't got any alternative other than to... ▪ I have no choice other than to... ▪ I don't have any choice other than to... ▪ I've got no choice other than to... ▪ I haven't got any choice other than to...

no tener otra salida que... to have no alternative other than to... ▪ to have no alternative but to... ▪ to have no option but to... ▪ to have no option other than to...

no tener palabras para expresar not to have words to express ➤ No tengo palabras para expresarle mi agradecimiento. I don't have words to express to him my appreciation.

no tener para remedios to be in a hopeless situation

no tener pelos en la lengua not to mince words ▪ not to be self-conscious ▪ to shoot from the hip ▪ to talk turkey

no tener por haberse agotado ▪ no tener to be out of

no tener prisa to be in no hurry ▪ not to be in any hurry

no tener que dar cuentas a nadie ▪ no tener que responder a nadie ▪ no tener que rendirle cuentas a nadie not to be answerable to anyone ▪ not to be accountable to anyone

no tener remedio to be a lost cause ▪ to be beyond hope

no tener remedio *(dícese ligeramente de personas y situaciones)* ▪ no tener arreglo to be hopeless ▪ to be beyond hope ▪ to be a lost cause

no tener reparo en hacer algo to have no qualms about doing something

no tener seso *(arcaico)* ▪ no tener cabeza to have no brains

no tener término medio (for) there to be no middle ground ▪ to have no middle ground

no tener tiempo ni para morirse to not have a minute to spare ▪ to be so busy that one can't see straight

no tener todas las luces ▪ faltarle unos jugadores not to be playing with a full deck ▪ to be a couple bricks shy of a load

▪ to be a couple (of) quarts low ▪ to be a half a bubble off plumb

no tener trazas de (for) there to be no signs of ▪ to show no signs of ▪ not to look like ➤ No tiene trazas de llover. There are no signs of rain. ▪ It doesn't look like it's going to rain. ▪ There's no rain in sight. ▪ It shows no sign of raining. ▪ There is no sign that it's going to rain. ➤ No tiene trazas de venir. It doesn't look like he's going to show up. ▪ There's no sign of him.

no tener un céntimo not to have a cent to one's name

no tener zorra idea not to have (got) a clue ▪ to have no idea ➤ No tengo zorra idea cómo desmontarlo. I have no clue how to take it apart. ▪ I haven't got a clue how to take it apart. ▪ I have no idea how to take it apart.

no tenerlas bien puestas para hacer algo ▪ no tener agallas para hacer algo ▪ no tener arrestos para hacer algo not to have the guts to do something ▪ not to have the courage to do something

no tenerse to be worn out ▪ to be beat

no tenerse en pie ▪ estar hecho polvo ▪ estar cansadísimo ▪ estar exhausto ▪ estar agotado to be worn out ▪ to be exhausted ▪ *(coloquial)* to be beat ▪ to be whipped ▪ to be pooped (out) ▪ to be shot

no tengo ▪ no tengo ninguno ▪ no lo tengo ▪ no tengo uno I don't have one

no tengo alternativa ▪ ¡qué remedio! I have no alternative ▪ I don't have any alternative

no tengo cambio ▪ no tengo suelto ▪ no tengo chatarra I don't have any change ▪ I haven't got any change

no tengo chatarra *(poco culto)* ▪ no tengo feria ▪ no tengo cambio ▪ no tengo suelto ▪ no tengo calderilla I don't have any change ▪ I haven't got any change

no tengo feria *(jerga mexicana)* I don't have any change

no tengo ganas I don't feel like it ▪ I don't want to

no tengo intención de inmiscuirme, pero... ▪ no pretendo inmiscuirme, pero... I don't mean to pry, but...

no tengo la más mínima idea ▪ no tengo ni la más remota idea ▪ no tengo ni la más ligera idea ▪ ni idea I don't have the slightest idea ▪ I don't have the vaguest idea ▪ I don't have the foggiest idea ▪ I don't have the foggiest notion

no tengo la menor idea ▪ ni idea I don't have any idea ▪ I have no idea

no tengo nada que pensar I don't feel sorry ▪ I have no regrets ▪ I don't feel bad about it

no tengo ni la más ligera idea ▪ no tengo la más mínima idea ▪ ni idea I don't have the slightest idea ▪ I don't have the vaguest idea ▪ I don't have the foggiest idea ▪ I don't have the foggiest notion

no tengo ni puñetera idea I don't have the foggiest idea ▪ I haven't got the foggiest (idea) ▪ I don't have the slightest idea ▪ I don't have any idea

no tengo ni puta idea *(subido de tono)* I don't have the slightest friggin' idea ▪ I don't have the foggiest idea

no tengo ni que... ▪ ni siquiera tengo que... I don't even have to... ➤ Los sobres vienen por lotes de veinticinco. No tengo ni que contarlos. ▪ Los sobres vienen por lotes de veinticinco. Ni siquiera tengo que contarlos. The envelopes come in lots of twenty-five. I don't even have to count them. ➤ No tengo ni que ir a la tienda. Con llamar por telefóno basta. ▪ Ni siquiera tengo que ir a la tienda. Con llamar por teléfono basta. I don't even have to go to the store. I just give them a call.

no tengo ninguno I don't have any

no tengo sitio donde ponerlo I don't have anywhere to put it ▪ I don't have any place to put it

no tengo suelto ▪ no tengo cambio ▪ no tengo chatarra I don't have any change ▪ I haven't got any change

no tengo zorra idea ▪ no tengo ni idea ▪ no tengo la más mínima idea ▪ no tengo ni pajolera idea I don't have the slightest idea ▪ I haven't got the slightest idea ▪ I haven't got a clue

no tenía ni idea de cómo... I had no idea how... ➤ No tenía ni idea de como... y no tenía ganas de descubrirlo. I had no idea how... and I didn't want to find out.

no tiene aspecto de serlo *(él)* he doesn't look like one ▪ *(ella)* she doesn't look like one

no tiene gracia it's not funny ▪ it isn't funny ▪ that's not funny ▪ that isn't funny

no tiene nada que ver that's way off ▪ that's nowhere close (to being right)

no tiene nada que ver con... it doesn't have anything to do with ▪ *(él)* he doesn't have anything to do with... ▪ *(ella)* she doesn't have anything to do with...

no tiene ni pies ni cabeza ▪ es absurdo ▪ eso no tiene sentido that's absurd

no tiene ninguna gracia that's not one bit funny ▪ that's not funny at all

¿no tiene otra solución? there's no other solution? ▪ there's no other way to do it? ▪ that's the only way?

no tiene pérdida you can't miss it

no tiene por qué... there is no reason to... ▪ there's no reason to...

no tiene por qué (ser así) ▪ no necesariamente not necessarily

no tiene sentido hacer una cosa it makes no sense to do something ▪ it doesn't make any sense to do something ▪ there's no sense in doing something ➤ No tiene sentido salir durante la hora punta. It makes no sense to leave during the rush hour.

no tienes más que... ▪ no hay más que... all you have to do is...

no tienes más remedio que aguantar mecha you'll just have to grin and bear it ▪ there's nothing to do but grin and bear it

no tienes por qué tener miedo you need not be afraid ▪ you needn't be afraid

no tienes remedio you're hopeless

¡no todo a la vez! ▪ ¡sólo una cosa por vez! ▪ ¡no tantas cosas a la vez! one thing at a time!

no tolerar 1. no aguantar not to tolerate 2. no permitir not to allow

no tolero que me hables así ▪ no te consiento que me hables así I won't tolerate your speaking to me that way ▪ I won't put up with your speaking to me that way

no tomarse a la ligera not to be taken lightly ▪ not to be sneezed at

no tomarse molestías con algo ▪ no preocuparse por algo ▪ no molestarse con algo not to worry about something ▪ not to bother ➤ No te tomes la molestia con eso. Ya cuidaré yo de ello. ▪ No te preocupes por eso. Ya cuidaré yo de ello. ▪ No te molestes con eso. Ya cuidaré yo de ello. Don't worry about it. I'll take care of it. ▪ Don't bother. I'll take care of it.

no tomárselo bien not to take kindly to something ➤ La madre...no se lo tomó muy bien que me acercara al ternero cuando ella no estaba allí mismo para protegerlo. The mother cow didn't take too kindly to my approaching the calf when she was not right there to protect him.

no va ▪ no funciona ▪ no anda it's not working ▪ it isn't working ▪ it doesn't work

no va a pasar mucho tiempo antes de que... it won't be long before... ➤ No va a pasar mucho tiempo antes de que haya... It won't be long before there is...

ser el **no va más** ▪ ser el non plus ultra to be the ultimate ➤ El nuevo coche de mi hermano es el no va más de los descapotables. ▪ El nuevo coche de mi hermano es el non plus ultra de los descapotables. My brother's new car is the ultimate convertible. ▪ My brother's new convertible is the ultimate.

no va más para atrás *(asiento de coche)* it won't go back any further or farther ▪ that's as far back as it'll go

no vacilar en not to hesitate to

no vale la pena ▪ no merece la pena it's not worth the trouble ▪ it´s not worth it ▪ it´s not worthwhile

no vale la pena llorar sobre leche derramada ▪ a lo hecho, pecho ▪ agua pasada no mueve molinos there's no use crying over spilled milk ▪ what's done is done

no vale nada it doesn't count ➤ *(Bill Clinton, después de la elección del 2000)* Ningún americano podrá decir jamás: mi voto no vale nada. No American can ever again say: my vote doesn't count. ▪ No American can ever say again: my vote doesn't count.

no valer nada not to count

no valer ni dos reales not to be worth two cents

no valer ni lo que costó bautizarlo to be a no-good

no valorar lo... not to appreciate how... ➤ Ella no valora lo duro que trabaja. She doesn't appreciate how hard he works.

no vaya a ser que... in case one should be... ▪ in case one might be... ▪ in case one is... ▪ *(culto, literario)* lest one be... ➤ Siga al sospechoso una semana entera, no vaya a ser que ande en algo malo o sucio. Tail the suspect for a full week in case he's involved in something bad or dirty.

no vayas tan lejos don't go too far ▪ don't make unwarranted assumptions

no veía one couldn't see ➤ Después de su accidente de bicicleta, José Manuel no veía. After his bicycle accident, José Manuel couldn't see.

no vender una escoba *(Esp., coloquial)* ▪ salir con las manos vacías to get nowhere ▪ not to get anywhere

no venir a cuento *(Esp.)* ▪ no venir al caso ▪ no venir al cuento to be beside the point ▪ to be pointless

no venir al caso ▪ no venir al cuento ▪ no venir a cuento to be beside the point ▪ to be pointless

no venir al cuento ▪ no venir al caso ▪ no venir a cuento to be beside the point ▪ to be pointless ➤ Hablar de nuestros errores del pasado no viene al cuento ahora. Talking about our past mistakes is pointless.

no veo la hora de I can hardly wait

no ver la relación not to see the connection ➤ No veo ninguna relación. I see no connection. ▪ I don't see any connection.

no ver las debilidades de alguien to be blind to someone's faults

no ver más allá de sus narices *(literal y figurado)* not to be able to see beyond the end of one's nose

no ver tres en un burro to be (as) blind as a bat

no volver a oírse nada más never to be heard from again ➤ No volvieron a oírse nada más. They were never heard from again.

no volver a verse en *x* años not to see each other again for *x* years ➤ No volvieron a verse en siete años. They didn't see each other again for seven years.

no voy a ningún lado I'm not going anywhere

la **noche anterior** the night before ▪ the previous night

la **noche de estreno** opening night ➤ El ensayo general resultó flojo, pero la noche del estreno salió sin ningún contratiempo. The dress rehearsal was rocky, but the opening night came off without a hitch.

la **noche de juerga** night on the town

noche en vela: pasar la ~ to have a sleepless night

la **noche está declinando** night is falling

el **nombre de la asignatura** name of the course ▪ title of the course ➤ ¿Cuál es el nombre del la materia? What's the name of the course? ▪ What's the title of the course?

el **nombre en clave** code name

el **nombre le queda** ▪ el nombre le pega the name fits ➤ El nombre Boudreaux le queda al perro perfectamente. ▪ El nombre Boudreaux le pega al perro perfectamente. The name Boudreaux fits the dog perfectly.

el **nombre me suena** the name rings a bell ▪ the name sounds familiar

el **nombre no me suena** the name doesn't ring a bell ▪ the name doesn't sound familiar

nombre supuesto: inscribirse bajo un ~ to register under a fictitious name

ser el **non plus ultra** ▪ ser el no va más to be the ultimate ➤ El nuevo coche de mi hermano es el non plus ultra de los descapotables. ▪ El nuevo coche de mi hermano es el no va más de los descapotables. My brother's new car is the ultimate convertible.

normas contables accounting rules ▪ accounting standards

norte en la vida: tener un ~ ▪ tener un rumbo en la vida to have a direction in life

nos conocemos desde... we've known each other since... ➤ Nos conocemos desde 1990. We've known each other since 1990.

nos conocemos desde hace... we've known each other for... ➤ Nos conocemos desde hace veinte años. We've known each other for twenty years.

nos conocemos desde que teníamos *x* años we've known each other since we were *x* years old ➤ Nos conocemos desde que teníamos diez años. We've known each other since we were ten years old.

nos encantaría, gracias we would love to, thank you ▪ we'd love to, thank you ▪ *(arcaico)* we should love to, thank you

nos es grato... we are pleased to...

nos ha nacido un niño *("Mesías" de Haendel)* (for) unto us a child is born

nos han abierto ya expediente they've begun to investigate us

nos han dejado sin pestañas they cleaned us out ▪ they robbed us blind

¡nos las piramos! we're off!

nos lo jugamos a cara o cruz let's flip over it ▪ let's flip a coin

¿nos toma nota? ▪ ¿nos toma la orden? would you take our order?

¿nos toma la orden? ▪ ¿nos toma nota? would you take our order?

¿nos vamos? shall we be on our way? ▪ are you ready to go?

nota aclaratoria ▪ aclaración explanatory note

notar cómo... to feel something...

notar que... to notice that...

notas altas ▪ agudos high notes

noticia bomba bombshell

noticias al instante ▪ noticias al momento breaking news

noticias al momento ▪ noticias al instante breaking news

noto que I see (that) ➤ Noto que has ordenado la casa. I see (that) you've straightened up the house. ▪ I notice (that) you've straightened up the house. ➤ Noto que alguien me está mirando. I have the feeling that someone is looking at me.

ser **novato(-a) en estas lides** to be new at this game ➤ Soy novata en estas lides. I'm new at this game.

la **novedad es que...** what's new is that... ▪ the news is that...

la **novedad se ha desvanecido** the novelty has worn off

el, la **novelista con éxito de ventas** bestselling novelist

novia desde la infancia childhood sweetheart

novia formal ▪ prometida fiancée

novio formal ▪ prometido fiancé

nube algodonosa billowy cloud

nubes algodonosas ▪ cúmulo billowy clouds ▪ billowing clouds

las **nubes de humo** clouds of smoke ▪ billows of smoke ▪ billowing smoke

nubes dispersas scattered clouds

nubes pasajeras passing clouds ➤ ¿Va a llover? No, son nubes pasajeras. Is it going to rain? No, they're just passing clouds.

nubes y claros: haber ~ ▪ estar parcialmente nublado to be partly cloudy

nudo en la garganta lump in one's throat

nuestros antepasados ▪ nuestros predecesores our ancestors

nuestros predecesores ▪ nuestros antepasados our ancestors

nuevas formas de pensar new ways of thinking

nuevas revelaciones en el caso new revelations in the case ▪ new developments in the case

nueve de cada diez veces ▪ nueve veces de cada diez ▪ nueve veces sobre diez nine times out of ten

nueve veces de cada diez ▪ nueve veces sobre diez ▪ nueve de cada diez veces nine times out of ten

nueve veces sobre diez ▪ nueve veces de cada diez ▪ nueve de cada diez veces nine times out of ten

nuevo aviso: hasta ~ until further notice

nuevo envoltorio 1. new wrapping 2. *(figurativo)* new twist ➤ Hay un nuevo envoltorio en el caso de Anna Nicole Smith. There is a new twist in the Anna Nicole Smith case.

nuevo programa new development

nuevo rico nouveau riche ▪ new rich

nuevos desarrollos en el caso new developments in the case

número aproximado ▪ más o menos ▪ (a) grosso modo ballpark figure ▪ rough estimate

número atrasado back issue

número creciente de growing number of

número de la suerte lucky number

número de seguimiento tracking number

número de un periódico ▪ (la) edición de un periódico issue of a newspaper ▪ edition of a newspaper

número entero whole number

número impar odd number

número no listado ■ número secreto unlisted number

número par even number

número quebrado ■ (la) fracción fraction

número real real number

número secreto ■ número no listado unlisted number

número significativo de personas significant number of people ■ enough people ➤ Si un número significativo de personas... If a significant number of people... ■ If enough people...

número telefónico durante el día daytime telephone number

ser el, la **número uno** to be number one

número uno en ventas number one bestseller

números redondos round numbers

números rojos: estar en ~ 1. *(cuenta corriente)* to be overdrawn ■ (for) one's checking account to be overdrawn **2.** *(empresa)* to be operating in the red

nunca creí que me pudiera pasar a mí I never thought it could happen to me

nunca debió venir aquí he never should have come here ■ he should never have come here

nunca desde not since

nunca digas de este agua no beberé don't be too sure ■ never say never

nunca doy explicaciones *(Mary Poppins)* I never explain anything

nunca es tarde para (que) it's never too late to

nunca estuve enterado ■ nunca supe de eso I was never informed ■ I was never told (about it) ■ I never knew about it ■ nobody told me ■ no one told me ■ they never told me

nunca falta un roto para un descosido ■ siempre hay un roto para un descosido ■ nunca falta un tiesto para una maceta there's someone for everyone ■ there's somebody for everybody

nunca haber visto algo así never to have seen anything like it

nunca haberle ido mejor a alguien to have never had it so good ■ never to have had it so good ➤ Nunca nos ha ido mejor. We've never had it so good. ■ Never have we had it so good. ■ It's never gone better for us.

nunca hacer nada bien never to do anything right ➤ Nunca te digas a ti mismo, "Nunca hago nada bien." Never say to yourself, "I never do anything right."

nunca hasta ahora ■ jamás hasta ahora never before ➤ Nunca hasta ahora habían visto los astrónomos algo así en el universo: una burbuja de agua, de un tamaño igual a una vez y media el Sistema Solar, envolviendo una estrella en formación. Never before had astronomers seen anything like it: a bubble of water one and a half times the size of the solar system surrounding a star in formation.

nunca he llegado a enterarme de cómo... I have never understood how... ■ *(más categoría)* I never have understood how... ➤ Nunca he llegado a enterarme de cómo funciona la Bolsa. I never have understood how the stock market works.

nunca he visto algo semejante I've never seen anything like it

nunca la he visto *(a ella)* I have never seen her ■ I've never seen her ■ *(una película)* I have never seen it ■ I've never seen it

nunca le he visto *(Esp., leísmo)* ■ nunca lo he visto I have never seen him ■ I've never seen him

nunca lo he visto *(a él)* I have never seen him ■ I've never seen him ■ *(un espectáculo)* I have never seen it ■ I've never seen it

nunca lo vi de esa manera I never looked at it that way

nunca más never again ■ not ever again ➤ No quiero volver a tenerla como profesora nunca más. I never want to have her for a teacher again. ■ I don't ever want to have her for a teacher again. ■ Never again do I want to have her for a teacher.

nunca me he enterado I never found out ■ I've never found out ➤ Nunca me he enterado de lo que pasó. I never found out what happened. ■ I've never found out what happened.

nunca me he llegado a enterar de qué... I have never understood what... ➤ Nunca me he llegado a enterar de qué implica la manipulación genética. I have never understood what gene modification involves.

nunca (me) imaginé que... I never dreamed (that)...

nunca me lo hubiese imaginado ■ nunca me lo hubiera imaginado ■ nunca lo habría pensado ■ nunca habría pensado en eso ■ nunca se me hubiera ocurrido I would never have thought of that

¡**nunca mejor dicho!** well put! ■ I couldn't have said it better myself!

nunca olvidaré ■ no me olvidaré jamás de I will never forget ➤ Nunca olvidaré el día... I will never forget the day...

nunca olvidaré aquella vez que... I will never forget the time that... ■ I'll never forget the time that...

nunca pensaba que iba a llegar a eso I never thought it would come to that

nunca pensaba que iba a llegar a esto I never thought it would come to this

nunca quiso hacer algo: uno ~ one never would do something ➤ Nunca quise dárselo. *(a él)* I never would give it to him. ■ *(a ella)* I never would give it to her. ■ *(a ellos)* I never would give it to them.

nunca sabe uno ■ nunca se sabe you never know

nunca se lo ha hecho a *él* *(olvidado el cumpleaños de su marido)* I've never done that to *him*

nunca se me olvidará el día en que... ■ nunca olvidaré el día en que... I'll never forget the day (that)...

nunca se puede predecir you never can tell ■ it's unpredictable

nunca se sabe (lo que...) ■ nunca sabe uno (lo que...) you never know (what...) ■ one never knows (what...)

nunca se sabe qué traerá el nuevo día no one knows what tomorrow will bring ■ you never know what tomorrow will bring ■ one never knows what tomorrow will bring

nunca te rindas ■ nunca hay que darse por vencido never give up

nunca te saldrás con la tuya you'll never get away with it

nunca te vas a creer lo que... you're never going to believe what...

nunca te vas a creer que you're never going to believe (that)...

o al menos a mí me parece ▪ o al menos así yo lo veo or so it seems to me ▪ or at least that's how I see it

o al revés ▪ o viceversa or vice versa

o algo por el estilo or words to that effect ▪ or something like that

o ambas cosas or both

o así or so ▪ or thereabouts

o bien ▪ o either ▪ or ➤ Parece que las relaciones sentimentales siempre son complicadas. O bien a él le gusta ella y él no le gusta a ella, o viceversa. ▪ *(coloquial)* Parece que las relaciones sentimentales siempre son complicadas. O bien él gusta de ella y ella no gusta de él, o viceversa. It seems like relationships are always complicated. Either he likes her and she doesn't like him, or viceversa. ➤ Parece que las relaciones sentimentales siempre son complicadas. O bien a ella le gusta él y ella no le gusta a él, o viceversa. ▪ *(coloquial)* Parece que las relaciones sentimentales siempre son complicadas. O bien ella gusta de él, y él no gusta de ella, o viceversa. It seems like relationships are always complicated. Either she likes him and he doesn't like her, or viceversa.

o eso parece or so it seems ▪ or so it appears

o eso parecía or so it seemed ▪ or so it appeared

¡o jugamos todos, o se rompe la baraja! either we'll all play, or no one is going to play!

o lo uno o lo otro *(obra de Kierkegaard)* either... or...

o mejor aún ▪ (o) mejor todavía better still ▪ better yet

o mejor dicho ▪ mejor dicho or rather

o peor aún or worse yet ▪ or even worse

o por lo menos eso dice él or so he says

os ruego paciencia *(Esp., vosotros)* ▪ sed pacientes conmigo bear with me ▪ please be patient ➤ Me llevará un minuto explicarlo, por eso os ruego paciencia conmigo. ▪ Me llevará un minuto explicarlo, por eso por favor sed pacientes conmigo. It will take a minute to explain this, so please bear with me. ▪ It will take a minute to explain this, so please be patient (with me.) ▪ It takes a minute to explain this, so please bear with me. ▪ It takes a minute to explain this, so please be patient (with me).

¡o se pasa por el aro o ya sabéis! ▪ o sí o sí **1.** either do it or else! ▪ either meet the demand or pay the price! **2.** if you don't like it, tough ▪ if you don't like it, lump it

o sea that is ▪ in other words ▪ or rather

¡o sea que ahora yo tengo la culpa! ▪ ¡a que ahora resulta que la culpa la tengo yo! ▪ ¡ahora resulta que yo tengo la culpa! so now it's my fault!

¿o sí? **1.** *(yo, con el verbo "to be")* am I? **2.** *(yo, con verbos de acción)* do I? ▪ shall I? ▪ can I?

o te pasas o no llegas you go from one extreme to the other ➤ Uno nunca sabe cómo tratar a un adolescente. O te pasas o no llegas. You never know how to deal with teenagers. You're either too strict or too lenient.

ser **o todo o nada** to be all or nothing ▪ to be (either) boom or bust

obcecado con una idea: estar ~ to be obsessed with an idea

obcecado con una idea: volverse ~ to become obsessed with an idea

obcecarse con una idea to become obsessed with an idea

obcecarse en una creencia to be fanatically obsessed with a belief ▪ to be irrationally obsessed with a belief

obedecer a ▪ surgir de ▪ proceder de to arise from ➤ Obedece a una falta de respeto. It arises from a lack of respect.

obedecer la ley ▪ acatar la ley to obey the law ▪ to abide by the law

obedecer una orden to obey an order

objetivo alcanzable ▪ meta alcanzable obtainable goal ▪ achievable goal

objetivo concreto specific target ➤ Los investigadores trabajan con la certeza de que los autores tenían objetivos concretos. The investigators are working with the certain knowledge that the perpetrators had specific objectives.

objetivo convexo *(cámara, telescopio, microscopio)* convex lens

objetos ordinarios ordinary objects

objetos perdidos lost and found ➤ ¿Dónde está objetos perdidos? Where is lost and found? ➤ ¿Hay un objetos perdidos aquí? Is there a lost and found here?

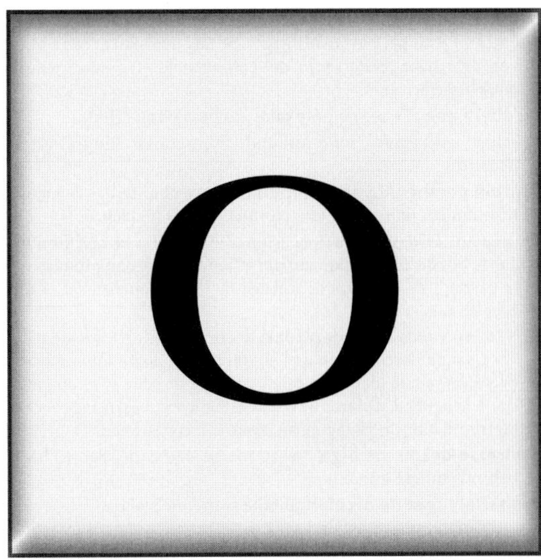

obligación cuyas fluctuaciones dan la tónica del mercado ▪ bono cuyas fluctuaciones dan la tónica del mercado bellwether bond

estar **obligado por un tratado** to be bound by a treaty

estar **obligado por una promesa** ▪ estar atado por una promesa to be bound by a promise

obligar a alguien a hacer algo to force someone to do something ▪ to be forced by something to do something ➤ Las circunstancias lo obligaron a volver de su viaje antes de lo previsto. Circumstances forced him to curtail his trip. ▪ He was forced by circumstance to curtail his trip.

obligar al desalojo to force (the) evacuation ➤ *(noticia)* Una plaga de chinches obligó al desalojo del tren. A bedbug infestation forced the evacuation of the train.

obligarse a hacer algo to force oneself to do something ➤ Me obligaba a levantarme temprano. I would force myself to get up early.

obra de divulgación work for the average reader

obra maestra magnum opus

obra rompedora ▪ obra revolucionaria ground-breaking work ▪ revolutionary work ▪ seminal work

ser **obra suya** to be one's own doing

obra tardía later work

obrar bajo el manto de la noche ▪ obrar con nocturnidad to operate under cover of darkness

obrar con nocturnidad ▪ obrar bajo el manto de la noche to operate under cover of darkness

obrar un cambio to bring about a change ▪ to effect a change ▪ to produce a change ➤ Lo que obró el cambio fue la dieta. What brought about the change was diet.

obras de encargo commissioned works

obras elegidas ▪ obras seleccionadas selected works

obras seleccionadas ▪ obras elegidas selected works

obré como obré porque ▪ actué así porque I acted as I did because

observar las instrucciones ▪ seguir las instrucciones to follow the instructions ▪ to follow the directions

obstinarse en hacer algo ▪ empeñarse en hacer algo ▪ insistir en hacer algo to insist on doing something

obtener el calendario to derive the calendar ➤ Obtenemos el calendario del ciclo anual del sol. We derive the calendar from the sun's yearly cycle.

obtener la luz verde to get the green light ▪ to get authorization ▪ to get approval ▪ to get permission

obtener sus frutos de to reap the benefits of

obtener un buen nivel con to become proficient with

obtener un buen nivel en to become proficient in ▪ to become proficient at

obtener un mayor rendimiento del combustible to be fuel efficient ▪ to get better mileage ➤ Los nuevos coches obtienen un mayor rendimiento del combustible. The new cars are more fuel efficient.

ser **obvio que...** ▪ ser patente que... to be obvious that...

ocasión anhelada long-awaited moment ▪ long-awaited occasion

ocasión perseguida opportune moment ▪ chance ➤ Él encontró entonces una ocasión perseguida. He saw his chance.

ser **ocasionado por** to be occasioned by ▪ to be brought on by ➤ El brindis fue ocasionado por el anuncio del compromiso de la pareja. The toast was occasioned by the announcement of the couple's engagement.

ocultar su verdadera identidad to conceal one's true identity ➤ Cuando descubrieron que era un agente doble intentó ocultar su verdadera identidad cambiando de nombre y de apariencia. When they discovered he was a double agent, he tried to conceal his true identity by changing his name and appearance.

ocultarse detrás de algo ▪ esconderse detrás de algo to hide behind something

ocupar el lugar de alguien to take someone's place

ocupar espacio to take up space

ocupar la cola ▪ estar en último lugar to be in last place

ser **ocurrente donde los haya** ▪ ser gracioso(-a) donde los haya ▪ ser de lo más gracioso(-a) (donde los haya) ▪ ser de lo más ocurrente (donde los haya) to be as witty as they come ▪ to be as witty as can be

¿ocurrió algo? ▪ ¿algo va mal? is something wrong? ▪ is anything wrong?

ocurrió de repente it happened just like that

ocurrir inesperadamente ▪ sobrevenir to happen unexpectedly

ocurrirle un accidente to have an accident ➤ Encárgate del Sr. Bond. Podría ocurrirle un accidente. Look after Mr. Bond. He might have an accident.

odio acerbo bitter hatred

odio admitirlo, pero... ▪ odio reconocerlo, pero... I hate to admit it, but...

ofenderse por algo to be offended by something ▪ to take offense at something ▪ to take exception to something

oferta de estreno ▪ oferta de lanzamiento ▪ oferta por inauguración introductory offer

oferta de lanzamiento ▪ oferta de estreno ▪ oferta por inauguración introductory offer

oferta en firme: hacer una ~ ▪ hacer una oferta firme to make a firm offer

oferta por inauguración ▪ oferta de estreno ▪ oferta de lanzamiento introductory offer

¡oficial! officer!

oficial de mucho, maestro de nada jack of all trades and master of none

oficiar misa ▪ decir misa ▪ celebrar misa to say mass ▪ to celebrate mass

oficina de correos ▪ casa de correos post office

Oficina de Protección Ambiental Environmental Protection Agency (EPA)

Oficina de Protección del Consumidor Better Business Bureau

oficio más antiguo del mundo ▪ prostitución world's oldest profession ▪ prostitution

oficios de la casa housework ▪ household chores ▪ housekeeping (chores)

oficios de la casa: hacer ~ to do housework ▪ to do the household chores

ofrecer una disculpa tardía por ▪ presentar una disculpa tardía por ▪ disculparse tardíamente por to apologize belatedly for ▪ to make a belated apology for ▪ to offer a belated apology for

ofrecer una rueda de prensa ▪ ofrecer una rueda de periodistas to hold a press conference

ofrecer una vista de ▪ tener unas vistas a ▪ tener unas vistas hacia ▪ tener unas vistas de to afford a view of ▪ to have a view of

ofrecerle a alguien un puesto de trabajo to offer someone a job

oía cosas I was hearing things

oído externo outer ear

oído interno inner ear

oído medio middle ear

oír (a) alguien acercarse ▪ oír (a) alguien que se acerca to hear someone coming ▪ to hear someone approaching ➤ La oí acercarse. ▪ La oí que se acercaba. I heard her coming.

oír (a) alguien decir to hear someone say ➤ Oí a Gemma decir que es de Madrid. I heard Gemma say she is from Madrid. ▪ I heard Gemma say she was from Madrid. *(Nota: en inglés, el segundo verbo en pasado también es natural.)*

oír (a) alguien diciendo que... to hear someone saying (that)...

oír (a) alguien haciendo algo ▪ oír (a) alguien que hace algo to hear someone doing something ➤ Los vecinos oían que levantaban la voz. The neighbors heard them raising their voices.

oír (a) alguien llegando ▪ oír a alguien que llega to hear someone coming ▪ to hear someone arriving

oír (a) alguien llorando ▪ oír (a) alguien que llora to hear someone crying

oír (a) alguien que llega ▪ oír (a) alguien llegando to hear someone coming ▪ to hear someone arriving

oír (a) alguien que llora ▪ oír (a) alguien llorando to hear someone crying

oír (a) alguien que se acerca ▪ oír (a) alguien acercándose to hear someone coming ▪ to hear someone approaching

oír (a) alguien que viene ▪ oír (a) alguien viniendo to hear someone coming

oír (a) alguien viniendo ▪ oír (a) alguien que viene to hear someone coming

oír (a) un gato maullando ▪ oír (a) un gato haciendo miau ▪ oír (a) un gato que maúlla ▪ oír a un gato que hace miau to hear a cat meowing ➤ ¿Oyes (a) ese gato maullando? ▪ ¿Oyes (a) ese gato haciendo miau? Do you hear that cat meowing?

oír (a) un perro ladrando ▪ oír (a) un perro que ladra to hear a dog barking

oír algo por radio macuto ▪ oír algo por terceras personas to hear something through the grapevine

oír (decir) que... to hear that... ➤ Oigo (decir) que el jazz cubano es buenísimo. I hear that Cuban jazz is really good. ➤ He oído (decir) que el jazz cubano es buenísimo. I have heard that Cuban jazz is really good.

oír el ruido de un alfiler cayéndose ▪ oír un alfiler cayendo(se) to hear a pin drop ➤ Cuando Mel Blanc les dijo a los niños con la voz de Bugs Bunny "Estad muy, muy callados," se podría haber oído el ruido de un alfiler cayéndose. When Mel Blanc told the kids, in Bugs Bunny's voice, "Be ve-wee, ve-wee qui-et," you could have heard a pin drop.

oír hablar de to hear about

oír (hablar de) lo que pasó to hear about what happened ▪ to hear what happened ➤ ¿Oíste (hablar de) lo que pasó? ▪ ¿Oíste algo de lo que pasó? Did you hear about what happened? ▪ Did you hear what happened?

oír lo último ▪ saber lo último to hear the latest ➤ ¿Has oído lo último? ▪ ¿Sabes lo último? Have you heard the latest?

oír los pasos de alguien to hear someone's footsteps

oír por ahí que... ▪ enterarse por radio macuto de que... ▪ oír por radio macuto que... ▪ oír por terceras personas que... to hear through the grapevine that...

oír por radio macuto que... ▪ enterarse por radio macuto de que... ▪ oír por ahí que... ▪ oír por terceras personas que... to hear through the grapevine that...

oír por terceras personas que... ▪ enterarse por radio macuto de que... ▪ oír por radio macuto que... ▪ oír por ahí que... to hear through the grapevine that...

oír que alguien llama to hear someone calling ➤ Cuando oí que me llamaba... When I heard him calling me...

oír ruido de pisadas to hear footsteps

oír sobre algo to hear about something

oír sobre algo ▪ saber sobre algo ▪ saber de algo to hear about something

oír un alfiler cayendo(se) ■ oír el ruido de un alfiler cayéndose to hear a pin drop ➤ Cuando Mel Blanc les dijo a los niños con la voz de Bugs Bunny "Estad muy, muy callados," se podría haber oído un alfiler cayendo. When Mel Blanc told the kids, in Bugs Bunny's voice, "Be ve-wee, ve-wee qui-et," you could have heard a pin drop.

oír un sonido ■ oír un ruido ■ oír algo to hear a sound ■ to hear a noise ■ to hear something ➤ Oí el sonido de un chotacabras. I heard the sound of a whippoorwill.

ojalá lo tenga *(con "yo" como el sujeto)* I sure hope I have ■ I sure hope I do ■ I sure hope so ➤ ¿Vas a tener vacaciones en Navidad?-No lo sé, pero ojalá las tenga. Do you have a vacation at Christmas time?-I don't know, but I sure hope I do.

ojalá lo tuviera *(con "yo" como el sujeto)* ■ ojalá lo tuviese I sure wish I did ■ I sure wish I had ➤ ¿Vas a tener vacaciones en Navidad?-No, pero ojalá las tuviera. Do you have a vacation at Christmas time?-No, but I sure wish I did.

ojalá no lo hubiera dicho ■ ojalá no lo hubiese dicho I wish I hadn't said it ■ I wish I hadn't said that

ojalá no lo hubiera sabido ■ ojalá no lo hubiese sabido I wish I hadn't known it ■ I wish I hadn't known that

ojalá (que) hubiera alguna manera de... ■ ojalá (que) hubiese alguna manera de... I wish there were some way to... ➤ Ojalá (que) hubiera alguna manera de contactar contigo. ■ Ojalá (que) hubiera alguna manera de conectar contigo. ■ Ojalá (que) hubiera alguna manera de ponerme en contacto contigo. I wish there were some way to get in touch with you.

ojalá (que) hubiera alguna manera de que... ■ ojalá (que) hubiese alguna manera de que... I wish there were some way that... ➤ Ojalá (que) hubiera alguna manera de que contacte contigo. ■ Ojalá (que) hubiera alguna manera de que conecte contigo. ■ Ojalá (que) hubiera alguna manera de que me ponga en contacto contigo. I wish there were some way that I could get in touch with you.

ojiva nuclear nuclear warhead

ojiva química chemical warhead

¡ojo! ■ ¡cuidado! watch it!

ojo a la funerala ■ ojo amoratado e hinchado swollen black eye

ojo amoratado: tener un ~ to have a black eye

ojo amoratado e hinchado ■ ojo a la funerala swollen black eye

ojo por ojo, y diente por diente an eye for an eye, and a tooth for a tooth

ojo, que la vista engaña appearances are deceiving

ojos café ■ ojos morenos ■ ojos negros ■ ojos marrones ■ ojos pardos brown eyes

ojos de carnero degollado doe eyes ■ soulful eyes

ojos de sapo ■ ojos reventones ■ ojos saltones bulging eyes ■ protruding eyes ■ bug eyes

ojos encarnados de llorar eyes red from crying ➤ Tenía los ojos encarnados de tanto llorar. Her eyes were red from so much crying.

ojos entornados half-closed eyes ■ eyes half closed

ojos hundidos deep-set eyes ■ sunken eyes

ojos marrones ■ ojos café ■ ojos morenos ■ ojos negros ■ ojos pardos brown eyes

ojos pardos ■ ojos café ■ ojos morenos ■ ojos negros ■ ojos marrones brown eyes

ojos que no ven, corazón que no siente ■ la distancia es el olvido **1.** out of sight, out of mind **2.** what you don't know won't hurt you

ojos rasgados slanted eyes

ojos relampaguearon de ira le relampagueron los ojos de ira ■ los ojos de alguien relampaguearon con ira eyes flashed with anger ➤ Sus ojos (de ella) le relampaguearon de ira. Her eyes flashed with anger.

ojos reventones ■ ojos saltones ■ ojos de sapo protruding eyes ■ bug eyes

ojos saltones ■ ojos reventones ■ ojos de sapo protruding eyes ■ bug eyes

ojos tapados: tener los ~ **1.** cubrirse los ojos con las manos to cover one's eyes with one's hands **2.** cubrirle los ojos con un paño to blindfold someone **3.** desconectarse de la realidad to have one's head in the sand

ola de calor heat wave ■ hot spell

ola de frío ■ oleada de frío cold wave ■ cold spell ■ cold snap ➤ Tuvimos una ola de frío en noviembre, pero luego volvió a hacer bueno. We had a cold snap in November, but it then it warmed up again.

ola de resaca undertow

¡olé! bravo!

¡olé tus huevos! *(subido de tono)* **1.** *(negativo)* you gotta have it your way, don't ya! **2.** *(positivo)* way to go!

oleada de calor ■ ola de calor heat wave ■ hot spell

oleada de frío ■ ola de frío cold wave ■ cold spell ■ cold snap

oleada de refugiados flood of refugees ■ wave of refugees

oler a algo *(cosa o persona)* to smell like something ■ *(persona)* to smell of something ➤ Huele a tabaco. *(hoja)* It smells like tobacco. *(hombre)* He smells of tobacco. ■ He smells like tobacco. ➤ Huele a regaliz. It smells like licorice. ➤ Hueles a regaliz. You smell like licorice. ➤ He estado cerca de fumadores, y ahora mi ropa huele a tabaco. I've been around smokers, and now my clothes smell of tobacco. ■ I've been around smokers, and now my clothes smell like tobacco. ➤ En este apartamento, huele muchísimo a tabaco. This apartment smells strongly of tobacco.

oler (a) algo que se quema ■ oler (a) algo que se está quemando ■ detectar un olor a quemado ■ sentir el olor de algo quemándose to smell something burning ■ to notice the smell of something burning ■ to detect the smell of something burning ➤ Huelo algo que se quema. ■ Me huele a algo que se quema. I smell something burning. ➤ (Me) huele a madera quemada. I smell wood burning. ➤ Sentí el olor de algo quemándose, y fui a investigar. I noticed the smell of something burning and went to investigate. ■ I detected the smell of something burning and went to investigate.

oler a chamusquina ■ oler a cuerno quemado ■ oler a gato encerrado to smell a rat ■ (for) there to be something fishy going on ➤ (Me) huele a chamusquina. I smell a rat. ■ There's something fishy going on. ■ There's something fishy about it.

oler a cuerno quemado ■ oler a chamusquina to smell fishy ■ (for) there to be something fishy going on

oler a pólvora (for something) fishy to be going on ■ (for) something to smell fishy around here ➤ Aquí huele a pólvora. There's something fishy going on here. ■ Something smells fishy around here.

oler a queso (for one's) feet to stink ➤ Le huelen los pies a queso. His feet stink.

oler a rayos ■ oler a tigre to stink to high heaven ■ to stink like hell ■ *(especialmente de personas)* to be ripe ■ to smell ripe

oler a rosas to smell like roses ■ to smell good ➤ Ella siempre huele a rosas. She always smells good.

oler a tigre ■ oler a rayos to stink to high heaven ■ to stink like hell ■ *(especialmente de personas)* to be ripe ■ to smell ripe

oler bien to smell good

oler(le) a algo to smell something ➤ (Me) huele a pollo frito. I smell fried chicken. ■ It smells like fried chicken (in here). ➤ Me huele a humo. I smell smoke. ➤ (A ella) le huele a humo. She smells smoke. ➤ Olemos a la mofeta, eso es seguro. Esperemos que la mofeta no nos huela a nosotros. We smell the skunk, all right. Let's just hope the skunk doesn't smell us.

olerle a camelo to think somebody's pulling a fast one ➤ Me huele a camelo. (I think) somebody's pulling a fast one.

olla a presión pressure cooker

olor a quemado: haber ~ ■ detectar un olor a quemado to smell something burning ■ to notice the smell of something burning ➤ Hay olor a quemado. I smell something burning. ■ It smells like something is burning.

olor agresivo ■ (el) hedor strong odor

el **olor de santo** odor of sanctity

olvidar las llaves dentro to lock oneself out ■ to forget one's keys

olvidarse de hacer algo to forget to do something

olvidarse de las formalidades ■ deshacerse de las formalidades to dispense with the formalities ➤ Vamos a olvidarnos de las formalidades e ir al grano. ■ Vamos a deshacernos de las formalidades e ir al grano. Let's dispense with the formalities and get down to brass tacks.

la **omisión de hacer algo** failure to do something
onda corta short wave
onda de sonido sound wave
onda expansiva shock wave
onda sónica sound wave
ondas cerebrales brain waves
ondas de radio radio waves
ondear la bandera blanca to raise the white flag (of surrender)
ópera bufa comic opera
ópera prima *(de un artista)* first work
la **operación a corazón abierto** ■ cirugía a corazón abierto open-heart surgery
la **operación de acoso y derribo** search and destroy mission ■ search and destroy operation
operación delicada delicate operation
opinión resentida jaundiced view
la **opinión vertida** opinion expressed
opino lo mismo I think the same (thing) ■ I'm of the same opinion
oponerse a algo ■ estar en contra de algo to be opposed to something ■ to be against something ➤ Me opongo (a ello). ■ Estoy en contra (de ello). I'm against it. ■ I'm opposed (to it).
a la **oportunidad la pintan calva** strike while the iron is hot
oportunidad excepcional ■ oportunidad única rare opportunity
optar por to opt for ■ to choose ■ to select
opuesto a opposite ■ directly across from ➤ En la pared opuesta a la del reloj On the wall opposite the clock
ora pro nobis *(catolicismo)* ■ ruega por nosotros pray for us
orden alfabético: estar en ~ ■ estar por orden alfabético to be (arranged) in alphabetical order
orden alfabético según: poner en ~ to alphabetize by ➤ Las frases están puestas en orden alfabético según la primera palabra y la palabra clave. The phrases are listed in alphabetical order by first word and by key word.
la **orden de registro** search warrant
ordenar a alguien que hagan algo to order someone to do something
ordenar la casa 1. *(chalet)* to tidy up the house 2. *(piso, apartamento)* to tidy up the apartment
ordenar las ideas to collect one's thoughts
orejas agujereadas pierced ears
orejas de burro dunce cap
organismos armados law enforcement
Organización Mundial de Salud ■ OMS World Health Organization ■ WHO
organizarse el tiempo ■ organizar su tiempo to budget one's time ➤ Necesito organizarme el tiempo mejor. ■ Necesito organizar mi tiempo mejor. I need to budget my time better.
orientar sus esfuerzos a to direct one's efforts to ■ to direct one's efforts toward
orientarse en un lugar to get one's bearings in a place ➤ ¿Me podrías ayudar hasta que me oriente? Could you help me until I get my bearings?
Oriente Próximo ■ Medio Oriente Near East ■ Middle East
orilla de la plaza perimeter of the plaza
orilla del camino side of the road ■ roadside
orilla del río river bank
orinarse en la cama to wet the bed
oro fino pure gold
oro negro ■ petróleo black gold ■ oil
os guste o no *(Esp.)* ■ les guste o no whether you (all) like it or not
os invito yo *(Esp.)* ■ les invito yo ■ yo invito it's my treat ■ I'm treating (you)
os lo hacéis fuera, ¿vale? *(Esp.)* ■ háganlo afuera, ¿está bien? do it outside, okay?
os parecéis *(Esp.)* ■ se parecen 1. *(dos personas)* you (two) look alike 2. *(dos o más personas)* you (all) look alike
os ruego paciencia *(Esp., vosotros)* ■ sed pacientes conmigo (please) bear with me ■ please be patient
Osa Mayor Ursa Major ■ Great Bear ■ *(coloquial)* Big Dipper
Osa Menor Ursa Minor ■ Little Bear ■ *(coloquial)* Little Dipper
oscilar entre *x* y *y* años to range in age from *x* to *y* ➤ Trescientos jóvenes cuyas edades oscilaban entre trece y diecinueve años Three hundred teenagers ranging in age from thirteen to nineteen
estar **oscuro como boca de lobo** to be pitch-dark ■ to be pitch-black dark
ostentar cargo público to hold public office
ostentar el título to hold the title
ostentar la presidencia to hold the presidency
ostentar una cicatriz *(como muestra de orgullo)* to sport a scar ■ to display a scar
¡**ostras!** darn it! ■ jeez! ➤ ¡Ostras! Espero que no. Jeez! I hope not.
otorgar de cabeza to nod in agreement
otorgar el perdón to grant forgiveness ➤ Si él te pide perdón, ¿qué ganas con no otorgárselo? If he asks you to forgive him, what's to be gained by not granting it?
otorgar testamento to make a will ■ to make out a will ■ to write a will
¡**otra, otra!** ■ ¡más! ■ ¡bis! encore!
otra cosa además de ■ otra cosa que no sea anything besides ➤ ¿Tienes otra cosa que no sea miel, por ejemplo jarabe de arce? Do you have anything besides honey, like maple syrup?
ser **otra persona** to be a new person ➤ Seré otra persona. I'll be a new person.
otra persona aparte de mí someone (else) besides me ■ someone other than me
la **otra punta** ■ el otro extremo the other end
otra vez ■ de nuevo again ■ some other time
otra vez será 1. quizás la próxima vez maybe next time 2. tal vez en otro momento maybe some other time
la **otra vida** ■ el otro mundo ■ el más allá the next life ■ the next world
otras muchas cosas ■ muchas otras cosas many other things
otras tantas ocasiones so many other occasions
el **otro barrio** ■ el otro mundo ■ el más allá the hereafter ■ life after death ■ the other world
otro cualquiera hubiera... ■ otro cualquiera hubiese... ■ cualquier otro hubiera... ■ cualquier otro hubiese... anybody else would have... ■ anyone else would have... ➤ Otro cualquiera hubiera pedido disculpas. ■ Otro cualquiera se hubiera disculpado. Andybody else would have apologized.
otro cualquiera lo huberia hecho ■ otro cualquiera lo hubiese hecho ■ cualquier otro lo hubiera hecho ■ cualquier otro lo hubiese hecho anybody else would have done it ■ anyone else would have done it
el **otro día** the other day
otro día cualquiera any other day
otro igual another one like it
el **otro mundo** ■ el más allá ■ la otra vida the next world ■ the next life
otro tanto as much again
otros dos two more
otros *x*: tener ~ to have *x* other ■ to have another *x* ➤ Tengo otros dos pantolones en la tintorería. I have two other pairs of pants at the cleaners. ■ I have another two pairs of pants at the cleaners.
ovillo de lana ■ madeja de lana ■ copo de lana ball of yarn
oveja negra 1. *(literal)* black sheep 2. *(figurativo)* oveja negra ■ oveja descarriada ■ garbanzo negro ■ bala perdida black sheep
oveja negra de la familia ■ garbanzo negro de la familia black sheep of the family ■ black sheep in the family
¡**oye, tú!** hey, you!

ser **pa' cagarse** *(subido de tono)* 1. ser terrible to be the shits 2. morirse de miedo to be scared shitless 3. ser espectacular ▪ ser estupendo to be fuckin' great

ser una **pachanga del siglo** *(L.am.)* ▪ ser una juerga monumental to be one hell of a party ▪ to be one hell of a bash ▪ *(alternativo más suave)* to be quite a party ▪ to be quite a bash

ser una **pachanga sideral** *(L.am.)* ▪ ser una juerga monumental to be one hell of a party ▪ to be be one hell of a bash ▪ *(alternativo más suave)* to be quite a party ▪ to be quite a bash ➤ Fue una pachanga sideral. ▪ Fue una juerga monumental. That was one hell of a party.

estar **pachucho(-a)** 1. *(vegetal)* to be overripe ▪ to be a little bit spoiled 2. *(persona)* estar malito ▪ estar un poco pocho to be (a little) under the weather

la **paciencia tiene un límite** there is a limit to one's patience

pactar un gobierno de coalición to form a coalition government

padecer hambre to go hungry ▪ to starve

padrastro de la madre de uno (maternal) stepgrandfather ▪ mother's stepfather

padrastro del padre de uno (paternal) stepgrandfather ▪ father's stepfather

padres al que se les muere un hijo parents who have lost a child

padres autoritarios ▪ padres impositores authoritarian parents

padres impositores ▪ padres autoritarios authoritarian parents

padres primerizos first-time parents

padrino de boda best man

padrón de habitantes register of townspeople

ser una **paella de la (misma) hostia** *(ligeramente subida de tono)* ▪ ser una paella jodidamente buena ▪ *(alternativo inofensivo)* ser una magnífica paella to be damned good paella ▪ to be one hell of a paella ▪ to be great paella ▪ to be delicious paella

paga extraordinaria pay bonus ▪ bonus paycheck

estar **pagado de uno mismo** ▪ estar orgulloso de sí mismo to be proud of oneself ▪ to be pleased with oneself ➤ Estaba muy pagado de sí mismo. He was very proud of himself. ▪ He was very pleased with himself.

pagar a alguien con creces 1. *(venganza)* to pay someone back good (and hard) 2. *(gratitud, poco común)* to repay someone's favor generously ▪ to repay someone's kindness many times over ➤ Le haré pagar con creces lo que ha hecho. I'm going to pay him back good (and hard) for what he has done. ➤ Le pagó con creces a su amigo el favor de financiar su educación. He repaid his friend's favor of financing his education many times over.

pagar a escote to split the bill evenly among everybody ▪ to divide the bill (up) evenly among everybody

pagar a plazos ▪ pagar en abonos ▪ pagar en cuotas to pay in installments

pagar a tocateja to pay hard cash ▪ to pay cold cash ▪ to pay cash on the line

pagar cada uno lo suyo to go Dutch ➤ Que cada uno se pague lo suyo. Let's go Dutch.

pagar con la misma moneda ▪ pagar en la misma moneda 1. *(negativo)* to give someone a dose of his own medicine 2. *(positivo)* to repay a kindness

pagar de adelantado ▪ pagar por adelantado to pay in advance

pagar el pato ▪ pagar los platos rotos ▪ ser el chivo expiatorio ▪ ser cabeza de turco to be the fall guy ▪ to be the scapegoat ▪ to take the rap ▪ to be the fall guy ➤ Le hicieron pagar el pato. ▪ Le hicieron que pagara el pato. They made him the scapegoat.

pagar en abonos ▪ pagar a plazos ▪ pagar en cuotas to pay in installments

pagar en cuotas ▪ pagar a plazos ▪ pagar en abonos to pay in installments

pagar en efectivo to pay cash ▪ to pay in cash

pagar en la misma moneda ▪ pagar con la misma moneda 1. *(negativo)* to give someone a dose of his own medicine 2. *(positivo)* to repay a kindness

pagar en abonos ▪ pagar a plazos to pay in installments

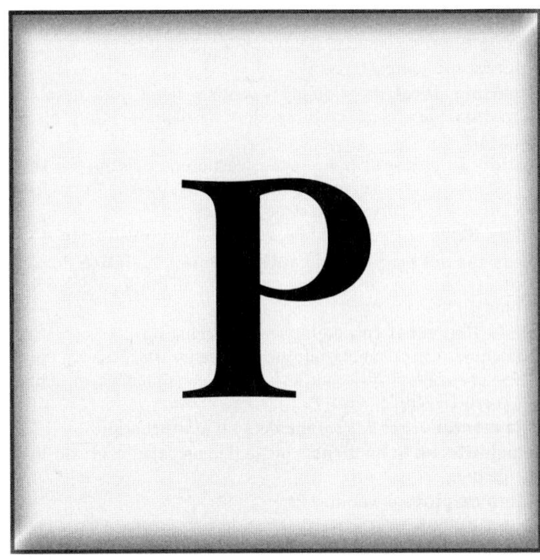

pagar hasta la camisa por to pay through the nose for ▪ to pay way too much for ▪ to pay far too much for

pagar justos por pecadores to pay for the misdeeds of others ▪ to be held accountable for the misdeeds of others ▪ to suffer for the misdeeds of others

pagar la fianza para que alguien salga de la cárcel to bail someone out of jail ▪ to bail out someone from jail

pagar la novatada ▪ aprender de la manera difícil to learn the hard way ▪ to make beginner's mistakes

pagar lo consumido ▪ pagar la consumición to pay the tab

pagar lo que hace falta ▪ abonar la diferencia to pay the difference

pagar los atrasos to pay back pay

pagar los platos rotos ▪ pagar el pato ▪ ser el chivo expiatorio to be the fall guy ▪ to be the scapegoat

pagar por adelantado ▪ pagar de adelantado to pay in advance ▪ to pay ahead

pagar su pecado to pay the piper

pagar un beneficio to pay a benefit

pagar un rescate to pay ransom ▪ to pay ransom money

pagarse los estudios to pay for one's studies

página en blanco blank page

páginas amarillas yellow pages

pago de atrasos back pay

pago domiciliado draft of a bank account ▪ bank account draft

pago final más *(cuantioso que el resto)* ▪ último pago ▪ último plazo balloon payment

páguese a... pay to the order of...

páguese al portador pay to the order of cash

país costero coastal country

el **país de habla española** ▪ país hispanohablante Spanish-speaking country

el **país de habla inglesa** ▪ país anglohablante English-speaking country

el **país de origen** ▪ país de nacimiento ▪ país natal native land ▪ native country ▪ *(literario)* country of one's birth

el **país del tercer mundo** third-world country

el **país en desarrollo** ▪ país en vías de desarrollo developing country

el **país en vías de desarrollo** ▪ país en desarrollo developing country

el **país extranjero** foreign country

el **país sin desarrollo** undeveloped country ➤ El país queda sin desarrollo. The country remains undeveloped.

paisaje adusto ▪ paisaje desolado ▪ tierra dura bleak countryside ▪ desolate countryside ▪ desolate terrain ▪ bleak terrain el **paisaje agreste** wilderness

paisaje boscoso wooded landscape ▪ wooded terrain ▪ forest landscape ▪ forest terrain

el **paisaje desolado** ▪ paisaje adusto ▪ tierra dura desolate countryside ▪ bleak countryside ▪ desolate terrain ▪ bleak terrain

vestido de paisano: ir ~ ▪ andar vestido de paisano ▪ ir vestido de civil ▪ andar vestido de civil to be dressed in civilian clothes ▪ to be dressed in street clothes

Países Bajos *(Bélgica, Luxemburgo y Holanda)* Low Countries

los **países del bloque de la antigua Unión Soviética** former Soviet bloc countries ▪ the countries of the former Soviet bloc

países limítrofes con countries bordering on ➤ Los países limítrofes con Colombia, que incluyen Venezuela, Ecuador, Peru, Panamá, y Brasil The countries bordering on Colombia, including Venezuela, Ecuador, Peru, Panama, and Brazil

paja mental *(subido de tono)* intellectual masturbation

un **pajarito me lo ha dicho** ▪ me lo dijo un pajarito a little bird told me

pájaro carpintero woodpecker

pájaro de cuenta ▪ persona de abrigo ▪ persona de (mucha) cuenta person to be wary of ▪ someone to be wary of ▪ person you can't trust ▪ someone you can't trust

ser un **pájaro de mal agüero** ▪ ser ave de mal agüero to be a prophet of doom

pájaro gordo bigwig ▪ big shot

pájaro marinero the sailor in the crow's nest ▪ the sailor on lookout

pala de un remo blade of an oar

pala de una hélice ▪ paletas de una hélice blade of a propeller ▪ propeller blade

¡**palabra!** honest! ➤ ¡Palabra! no la conozco. Honest, I don't know her!

palabra final: tener la ~ ▪ tener la última palabra to have the last word

palabra por palabra word for word

ser **palabras al aire** it's just a lot of hot air

palabras altisonantes high-sounding words

palabras cruzadas ▪ crucigrama crossword puzzle

palabras hirientes hurtful words

ser **palabras mayores** to be strong words ▪ to be an important matter ▪ to be something serious ➤ Ya son palabras mayores. Those are strong words.

las **palabras me fallaron** words failed me

las **palabras se las lleva el viento** that's a bunch of hot air

palabras sueltas words without context ▪ words removed from their context

palabras textuales exact words

ser **palabras vanas** to be (just) empty words ➤ No son más que palabras vanas. ▪ Son nada más que palabras vanas. They are just empty words.

¡**palabrita del Niño Jesús!** *(dicho por niños)* cross my heart and hope to die!

la **palabrita mágica** *(instando al niño a que diga "gracias")* ▪ ¿qué se dice? what do you say?

palanca de atracción *(poco común)* ▪ incentivo ▪ aliciente enticement ▪ come-on

palanca de cambio *(both straight and automatic shift)* gear shift lever

palanca de cambio(s) manual gear shift lever

palas de una hélice blades of a propeller ▪ propeller blades *(Nota: Véase "aspas" de una hélice.)*

palco de primera fila first-tier box ▪ box in the first tier

paleolítico inferior lower paleolithic (era)

paleolítico superior upper paleolithic (era)

palestra política: entrar a la ~ ▪ salir al ruedo político to enter the political arena ▪ to enter the (political) fray

paleta de albañil ▪ cuchara de albañil mason's trowel

palidecer ante to pale in comparison to ➤ La legendaría película *El expreso de medianoche* palidece ante la realidad de las cárceles turcas. The legendary film *Midnight Express* pales in comparison to the reality of Turkish jails.

palidez acusada pronounced paleness ▪ marked paleness ▪ noticeable paleness ➤ Su palidez era muy acusada. His paleness was very pronounced. ▪ His paleness was very marked.

palillo de dientes ▪ (el) escarbadientes ▪ (el) mondadientes toothpick

palito para tender ▪ pinza clothes pin

ser una **paliza** to be just awful

palmo a palmo: inspeccionar un lugar ~ ▪ inspeccionar un lugar centímetro a centímetro ▪ registrar un lugar palmo a palmo to inspect a place inch by inch ▪ to go over a place inch by inch ▪ to comb an area ➤ Registraron el terreno palmo a palmo. They searched the terrain inch by inch. ▪ They combed the terrain inch by inch.

palo atravesado *(de arco de fútbol, taburete, etc.)* ▪ travesaño crossbar ▪ crosspiece

palo de ciego ▪ bastón de ciego ▪ bastón blanco blind person's cane

un **palo por bogar y por no bogar** to be damned if one does and damned if one doesn't

el **pan ázimo** ▪ pan sin levadura **1.** unleavened bread **2.** *(referido al pan de la eucaristía)* host

pan bendito *(catolicismo)* ▪ hostia ▪ pan ázimo blessed bread ▪ host

ser **pan comido 1.** ser una tarea fácil de hacer to be a piece of cake **2.** ser una tarea divertida ▪ ser una tarea agradable to be duck soup

pan con pan, comida de tontos ▪ pan con pan, comida de bobos ▪ entre col y col, lechuga variety is the spice of life

ser el **pan de cada día** to be an everyday occurrence ▪ to be par for the course

el **pan de hamburguesa** hamburger bun

el **pan de hogaza** large round loaf of bread with a hard crust

el **pan de molde** sandwich bread (pre-sliced at the bakery) *(Nota: En español, la palabra "barra" de pan se refiere solamente al pan que no haya sido cortado en rebanadas. Al pan cortado en rebanadas se le denomina "pan de molde" o "una bolsa de pan de molde". ▪ In Spanish, the word for "loaf" refers only to bread which has not been sliced. A "loaf" of sliced bread is referred to simply as a bag of (sandwich) bread.)*

pan eucarístico ▪ hostia eucharistic bread ▪ communion bread ▪ host

el **pan integral** whole wheat bread

ser el **pan (nuestro) de cada día** to be par for the course

ser **pan para hoy y hambre para manaña** to pay the piper ➤ Es pan para hoy y hambre para mañana. You'll have to pay the piper. ▪ We'll have to pay the piper.

el **pan recién hecho** freshly baked bread

pan y agua bread and water

pan y agua: tener a alguien a ~ to treat someone like dirt ▪ to be mean to someone ▪ to treat someone abusively

panacea para todos nuestros problemas panacea for all our problems

panacea universal cure all ▪ universal panacea

el **panel de stop** ▪ (la) señal de alto stop sign

los **paneles de madera** ▪ planchas de madera wood paneling

pánico bancario ▪ pánico bursátil run on a bank

pánico bursátil ▪ pánico bancario run on a bank

pánico escénico ▪ miedo escénico stage fright

pantalla de humo: echar una ~ ▪ echar una cortina de humo to put up a smoke screen

pantalla grande big screen ▪ silver screen ▪ the movies

pantalla para actividades ilegales: funcionar como ~ ▪ funcionar como pantalla para actividades ilícitas ▪ servir como pantalla para actividades ilegales ▪ servir como pantalla para actividades ilícitas ▪ hacer de pantalla para actividades ilegales ▪ hacer de pantalla para actividades ilícitas to serve as a front for illegal activities ▪ to serve as a front for illicit activities

paño de cocina kitchen towel

ser el **paño de lágrimas de alguien** to be someone's shoulder to cry on

paño de tierra parcel of land

paño listado striped cloth

paños calientes 1. medidas insuficientes ▪ medidas a corto plazo half measures ▪ short-term solutions ▪ a solution that treats the symptoms rather than the cause 2. gran ayuda boon ➤ Pretender arreglar los altos alquileres controlando los precios de alquiler son paños calientes. La solución es construir más viviendas públicas. Trying to solve the problem of unaffordable rent by imposing rent controls is a half-measure. The solution is to build more public housing. ➤ Los descansos entre clase y clase son paños calientes. The breaks between classes are a boon.

paños menores ▪ ropa interior underclothes

pañuelo en los ojos blindfold

papas fritas 1. *(L.am.)* fried potatoes ▪ *(Esp.)* potato chips

papel cuadriculado quadrille paper ▪ grid paper

el **papel de cebolla** onionskin paper

el **papel de diario** ▪ papel de periódico newsprint

el **papel de estaño** tin foil

el **papel de periódico** ▪ papel de diario newsprint

el **papel en blanco** blank sheet of paper

el **papel en sucio** ▪ hoja en sucio ▪ folio en sucio ▪ trozo de papel en sucio (piece of) scratch paper ➤ ¿Tienes (un) papel en sucio? Do you have a piece of scratch paper?

papel milimetrado graph paper

ser **papel mojado** to be worthless ➤ El cese de fuego ya era papel mojado después de que... The ceasefire was worthless after...

papel rugoso coarse paper

papelera de reciclaje *(informática)* recycle bin

papeles de matrícula ▪ hojas de inscripción ▪ ficha de inscripción ▪ solicitud de inscripción application forms for university admission

papeles que corregir: tener ~ to have papers to grade ➤ La profesora tiene muchos papeles que corregir. The teacher has a lot of papers to grade.

papeleta estropeada spoiled ballot

papeleta mariposa butterfly ballot

el **paquete de acciones** stock portfolio

el **paquete de seis (cervezas)** ▪ (el) pack (de cervezas) six-pack (of beer)

el **paquete postal** parcel post

un **par de** a couple of ▪ a pair of ▪ two

par de huevos: tener un ~ *(subido de tono)* ▪ tenerlos bien puestos ▪ tenerlos en su sitio to have balls

par o impar even or odd ▪ odd or even *(Nota: Normalmente esta segunda forma es preferida en el habla inglesa.)*

¿para abajo? *(ascensor)* going down?

para acabar de arreglarlo ▪ para acabarlo de arreglar ▪ ir para acabar de arreglarlo ▪ *(subido de tono)* para acabar de joderlo 1. to make matters worse ▪ to top it all off 2. (in order) to finish fixing it ➤ Ya íbamos tarde y para acabar de arreglarlo, perdimos el último metro. We were already late, and to make matters worse, we missed the last metro. ➤ Faltan aún dos programas por instalar en tu computadora para acabar de arreglarla. There are still two programs to be installed on the computer (in order) to finish fixing it.

para acabar de joderlo *(subido de tono)* and to fuck it up totally

para abrir boca as an appetizer ▪ as appetizers ➤ Tengo estos canapés preparados para abrir boca. I've fixed these hors dóuvres as an appetizer.

para afuera: abrir ~ to open outwards

para ahorrar tiempo (in order) to save time

para andar por casa ▪ de andar por casa to wear around the house ▪ for wearing around the house

para aclararnos for clarity

para acuñar una frase to coin a phrase

ser **para algo** ▪ estar indicado para algo to be intended for algo

para añadir leña al fuego to add fuel to the fire ▪ to add fuel to the flames

¿para arriba? *(ascensor)* going up?

estar **para arriba *x* metros** to be *x* meters up ▪ to be *x* meters high ▪ to be *x* meters off the ground

para averiguarlo (in order) to find out

para ayuda de to help toward ▪ to help with

para bien o para mal for better or worse ▪ for good or ill

para bien y para mal come hell or high water

ser **para caerse de espaldas** to be awe inspiring ➤ El interior de la catedral es para caerse de espaldas. The interior of the cathedral is awe inspiring.

para cerciorarse (in order) to make sure ▪ (in order) to be sure ▪ (in order) to make certain ▪ (in order) to be certain ➤ Para cerciorarme consulté mi plan de clases. To make sure, I checked my class schedule.

para chuparse los dedos finger-licking good

para colmo ▪ para postre ▪ para colmo de males ▪ para no va más to top it all off

para colmo de males ▪ para postre ▪ para no va más to top it all off

estar **para comérselo** 1. *(food)* to look scrumptuous 2. *(person)* drop-dead gorgeous

ser **para como...** to be enough to make you...

para comprobar si to (check to) see if... ▪ to (check to) see whether (or not)...

para complicar las cosas to complicate matters ▪ to complicate things

para con ▪ ante ▪ hacia toward ▪ with respect to

para cuando 1. about the time of ▪ around the time of 2. how late 3. when ▪ by what date

¿para cuándo es? *(bebé, libro de la biblioteca)* 1. *(bebé)* when is it due? ▪ when's it due? 2. *(encargo en la pastelería, etc.)* when do you need it (to be ready)? ▪ when is it for? ▪ when would you like it?

¿para cuándo es el trabajo? ▪ ¿cuándo hay que entregar el trabajo? when is the paper due?

(para) cuando me di cuenta de lo que me había pasado ▪ (para) cuando quise darme cuenta de lo que me había pasado before I knew what (had) hit me

(para) cuando quise darme cuenta de lo que me había pasado ▪ (para) cuando me di cuenta de lo que me había pasado before I knew what (had) hit me

para cuando tú vas, yo ya he venido I pick up where you leave off ▪ you're a babe in the woods compared to me

para dar y tomar: tener ~ to have plenty to spare

para dar y vender: tener ~ to have plenty of them ▪ to have tons of them

para decepción de to the disappointment of

para desgracia mía to my great discomfort

¿para dónde vas? where are you headed?

para el año *x* by the year *x*

estar **para el arrastre** *(metáfora taurina)* 1. *(persona)* to be done for ▪ to have had it ▪ to be all washed up 2. *(cosa)* to have had it

ser **para el caso lo mismo** to be basically the same ▪ to make no difference ➤ En Amsterdam hablan flamenco y holandés, que para el caso es lo mismo. In Amsterdam, they speak Flemish and Dutch, which are basically the same (language). ➤ En la receta puedes usar miel o sirope de arce, para el caso es lo mismo. In the recipe you can use either honey or maple syrup. It makes no difference.

para (el) fin de mes ▪ para el final del mes by the end of the month

para el fin de la semana ▪ para el final de la semana by the end of the week

para (el) fin del año ▪ para los últimos días del año by end of the year ▪ in the final days of the year

para el final de la semana ▪ para el fin de la semana by the end of the week

para el final de mes ▪ para (el) fin de mes by the end of the month

para el final del año ▪ para el fin de año by the end of the year ▪ towards the end of the year ▪ in the final weeks of the year

para el final del día by the end of the day

para el tiempo que venga uno by the time one arrives ➤ Para el tiempo que venga ella, estará fría la cena. By the time she arrives, the supper will be cold.

para el único próposito de for the sole purpose of

para ello to that end ▪ for that purpose

para empezar (in order) to begin ▪ for starters ▪ to begin with ➤ *(Cuento de Navidad de Dickens)* Para empezar, Marley ya estaba muerto. Marley was dead, to begin with.

para entonces by then ■ by that time

para enturbiar las cosas to complicate matters ➤ Para enturbiar aún más las cosas... To complicate matters even more...

para escoger to choose from ➤ Hay alojamientos para escoger. There are (a variety of) lodgings to choose from.

para eso that's why ■ (in order) to do it ■ (in order) to do that ➤ Amontona la arena, para eso necesitas una pala. Pile the sand. You'll need a shovel to do it.

para eso estoy that's what I'm here for

para eso son los amigos that's what friends are for

para estas alturas del año by this time of year

para este viaje no se necesitan alforjas you didn't need to go to so much trouble ■ you shouldn't have gone to so much trouble

para fin de año ■ para Noche Vieja for New Year's Eve ■ on New Year's Eve ➤ Este es el vestido que me pienso poner para fin de año. This is the dress I'm planning to wear on New Year's Eve.

para finales de(l) año toward the end of the year ■ late in the year ➤ Para finales de(l) año, el sol se encuentra próximo al solsticio. Toward the end of the year, the sun is near the solstice. ■ Late in the year, the sun is near the solstice.

para fuera: empujar algo ~ to push something outwards ■ to push something away from you

para gustos están los colores ■ para gustos se hicieron los colores ■ sobre gustos no hay nada escrito **1.** it's a matter of taste ■ beauty is in the eye of the beholder **2.** different strokes for different folks ■ that's what makes horse racing

para gustos se hicieron los colores ■ para gustos están los colores beauty is in the eye of the beholder ■ different strokes for different folks ■ that's what makes horse racing

para hacer tiempo (in order) to fill the time

para hacer una cosa es preciso saber hacerla to do something, you have to know how (to do it)

estar **para hacerla madre** to be so good-looking I'd like to make her a mother

estar **para hacerle un favor** *(subido de tono)* to be so good-looking I'd like to go to bed with her

para ir más alla de lo dicho beyond that ➤ Para ir más alla de lo dicho, le dejo que hable de sí mismo. Beyond that, I'll let him tell you about himself.

para la desdicha de uno to one's sorrow

para las postrimerías del año in the last few days of the year ■ in the final days of the year ■ toward the end of the year ■ by the end of the year

para liar el tema ■ para rizar el rizo to complicate matters

para llevar: comida ~ food to take out ■ food to go ➤ ¿Para tomar o para llevar? To eat here or to go? ■ To stay or to go? ■ For here or to go? ■ For here or to take out?

para lo que es for what it is ■ considering its purpose

para lo que se figura usted: no ser ~ not to be for what one thinks (it is for)

para lo que te figuras: no ser ~ not to be for what you think (it is for)

para los desgraciados todos los días son martes for the unfortunate, every day is a bad day

ser **para los efectos lo mismo** for the effect(s) to be the same ■ for the result(s) to be the same

para los niveles estadounidenses by U.S. standards ➤ *(noticia)* Su casa era modesta para los niveles estadounidenses. His house was modest by U.S. standards.

para los que queremos... for those of us who want...

para los que somos... for those of us who are...

para los que son... for those who are... ■ for the ones who are...

para los restantes for the rest ■ for the others

para luego ■ y luego and then ➤ El todoterreno dio una vuelta en el aire, para luego caer con las ruedas hacia arriba. The all-terrain flipped over forward in the air, and (then) came to rest with its wheels up.

para mayor exasperación de even more exasperating to ■ still more exasperating to

para más inri ■ para colmo to add insult to injury

para más señas ■ por más señas to be exact

ser **para mear y no echar gota** *(subido de tono)* ■ ser el colmo (de la estupidez) to be a joke ■ to be ridiculous ■ to be the height of stupidity

ser **para mearse de miedo** to be scary as hell ■ to be terrifying

ser **para mearse de risa** to laugh so hard one practically pisses in his pants

para mencionar sólo unos cuantos ■ por mencionar sólo unos cuantos to name (just) a few

para menos: no ser ~ not (to be) for nothing ➤ El cliente estaba mosqueado, y no era para menos, pues tenía una mosca en su sopa. The customer was mad as shooed fly, and (it was) not for nothing, because there was a fly in his soup.

para meter esto to fit this ■ that this will fit into ➤ ¿Tiene un sobre para meter esto? Do you have an envelope to fit this? ■ Do you have an envelope that this will fit into?

para mí 1. for me **2.** en mi opinión to me ■ in my opinion

para mi desdicha to my sorrow

para mí es lo mismo ■ me da lo mismo ■ me da igual ■ lo mismo me da it doesn't make any difference to me ■ it doesn't matter to me ■ it's all the same to me

para mí significa mucho it means a lot to me

para mi sorpresa to my surprise

para muestra basta un botón 1. you can see the whole picture at a glance ■ you can get the whole picture at a glance ■ a little example illustrates the point **2.** you don't have to play in the mud to know that it's dirty

para nada ■ en absoluto at all ■ not at all ➤ *(Sánchez Silva)* El alcalde, un hombre piadoso, accedió a ello por su propia cuenta, sin consultar para nada con los concejales. The mayor, a devout man, agreed to it on his own, without consulting with the councilmen at all.

para nada, para nada no, no, that's not necessary

para no ir más lejos ■ sin ir más lejos to cite an obvious example ■ to give you an obvious example

para no sé qué for I don't know what all ➤ Ayer pasó una revisión para no se qué. Yesterday he had a checkup for I don't know what all.

para no sé qué de for whatever ➤ Ayer pasó una revisión para no se qué de la garganta. Yesterday he had a checkup for whatever he had wrong with his throat.

para no ser menos not to be outdone ➤ Nuestros vecinos fueron a Buenos Aires de vacaciones, así que, para no ser menos, fuimos a Santiago de Chile. Our neighbors went to Buenos Aires on vacation, so not to be outdone, we went to Santiago de Chile.

para no variar, siempre lo mismo it's the same song, fiftieth verse

ser **para parar el tráfico** to (really) stop traffic ➤ Está tan buena que para el tráfico. She's so good-looking that she stops traffic.

estar **para parar un tren** ■ para parar tráfico **1.** ser muy guapo(-a) to be drop-dead gorgeous **2.** verse muy guapo(-a) to look stunning ➤ El chico aquel está para parar un carro. ■ El chico aquel está para parar un tren. That guy is gorgeous. ■ That guy really stops the traffic.

para picar: haber algo ~ ■ tener algo para picar to have something to snack on ■ (for) there to be something to eat ■ to have something to nibble on ➤ ¿Hay algo para picar? Is there anything to eat? ■ Is there anything to snack on? ■ Do you have anything to snack on? ■ Do you have anything to nibble on?

para postre 1. para colmo to top it all off **2.** de postre for dessert

para otros 1. for other(s) **2.** to other(s) ➤ Creo que trabajas más cuando trabajas a cuenta propia que cuando trabajas para otros. I think you worker harder when you work for yourself than when you work for others. ➤ Es invisible para otros usuarios. It's invisible to other users.

para que ■ a fin de que so that ■ in order that ■ (in order) to ➤ ¿Qué podemos hacer para que (yo) la conozca? What can we do so that I can meet her?

¿para qué? ■ ¿a qué? what for? ➤ ¿Para qué has hecho eso? What did you do that for?

para que entre un poco de aire fresco in order to let in some fresh air ■ to let in some fresh air ➤ Abre la ventana para que entre un poco de aire fresco. Open the window to let some fresh air into the room.

¡para que escarmientes! ■ ¡para que tengas! let that be a lesson to you! ■ that'll teach you!

para que haya in order for there to be ■ for there to be

para que lo sepas ■ para que sepas just so you know

para que luego digan only to have them say ■ only to have them tell me ➤ Lavé los platos, para que luego (me) dijeran que no ayudo con las tareas de la casa. I washed the dishes, only to have them tell me that I don't help with the housework.

para que no me pille el toro so that I won't have problems (later)

para que resulte for it to work

para que sepas ■ para que lo sepas just so you know

¿para qué sirve? what's it for? ■ what does it do? ■ what's its purpose?

¡para que te empapes! ■ ¡chínchate! take that! ■ so there! ■ up yours!

para que te enteres ■ para que sepas just so you know ➤ Just to give you an idea of the size of the solar system, if the sun were the size of a grapefruit... Para que te hagas una idea del tamaño del sistema solar, si el sol fuera un pomelo... ■ Para que te hagas una idea del tamaño del sistema solar, si el sol fuera una toronja...

para que te jodas *(subido de tono)* ■ para que te chinches ■ para que rabies ■ para que te fastidies so get screwed! ■ so there!

¡para que tengas! ■ ¡para que escarmientes! let that be a lesson to you! ■ that'll teach you!

para que tuviera que... so that I would have to... ➤ El consulado otorgó el visado estudiantil con menos fecha que el de la duración del curso para que tuviera que pagar otra matrícula para extenderlo. The consulate granted the student visa for less than the duration of the course so that I would have to pay tuition again to extend it.

¡para que veas! 1. just to show you! 2. I told you!

para que (yo) pudiera so that I could

para que (yo) pueda so that I can

para quedar bien con alguien to get on someone's good side ■ to humor someone ➤ Para quedar bien con mi suegra, le llevé flores el día de la madre. To get on my mother-in-law's good side, I took her some flowers on mother's day.

para quien for anyone who ■ for whoever ➤ Para quien ha tenido la suerte de... For anyone who has been lucky enough to...

para rato: ir ~ ■ ir para largo to go on and on ➤ Este discurso podría ir para rato. This speech could go on and on.

para remate ■ para colmo to top it all off ➤ Perdí mi trabajo, me suspendieron en la universidad, y para remate, anoche rompí con mi novia. I lost my job and flunked out of the university, and to top it all off, I broke up with my girlfriend.

para retraerse al comienzo to go back to the beginning ■ to return to the beginning ➤ Para retraernos al comienzo... To go back to the beginning...

para ser más exactos: (bueno) ~ (or) to be more precise

para ser sincero ■ en honor a la verdad to tell you the truth

para serlo to be one ■ as such ➤ Quiere ser bombero y para serlo ha de prepararse a conciencia. He wants to be a fire fighter, and to be one you have to train rigorously.

para serte sincero to be honest ■ to be frank

para servir a Dios y a usted *(pasado de moda)* at your service, sir

para servirle ■ servidor de usted at your service

para servirte at your service

para sí to oneself

para siempre 1. forever ■ forever and ever ■ for life 2. definitivamente for good ➤ El matrimonio es para siempre. Marriage is forever. ➤ Dejé de fumar para siempre. ■ Dejé de fumar definitivamente. I quit smoking for good.

para siempre jamás forever and ever

para siempre un(-a) amigo(-a) ■ amigos(-as) para siempre ■ tu amigo(-a) eternamente your friend forever

para sus adentros to oneself

para sus adentros: comprender algo ~ ■ comprender algo en su interior ■ comprender en lo más profundo de sí ■ comprender en lo más profundo de su ser to understand deep down ➤ Colón comprendió para sus adentros que Ptolomeo había creído menor la circunferencia de la Tierra. ■ Colón comprendió en su interior que Ptolomeo había creído menor la circunferencia de la Tierra. ■ Colón comprendió en lo más profundo de sí que Ptolomeo había creído menor la circunferencia de la Tierra. ■ Colón comprendió en lo más profundo de su ser que Ptolomeo había creído menor la circunferencia de la Tierra. Columbus understood deep down that Ptolemy underestimated the Earth's circumference.

para sus adentros: decirse algo ~ ■ decirse algo para sí (mismo) ■ decirse algo para uno (mismo) ■ decirse algo en su interior ■ decirse algo en lo más profundo de sí ■ decirse algo en lo más profundo de su ser to say to oneself ➤ Y me dije para mis adentros... ■ Y me dije para mí (mismo)... ■ Y me dije en mi interior... ■ Y me dije en lo más profundo de mí... ■ Y me dije en lo más profundo de mi ser... And I said to myself...

para sus adentros: guardar(se) algo ~ ■ guardar algo para sí (mismo) ■ guardar algo para uno (mismo) ■ guardar algo en su interior ■ guardar algo en lo más profundo de sí ■ guardar algo en lo más profundo de su ser to keep something to oneself ➤ Guárdatelo para tus adentros. ■ Guárdatelo para ti (mismo). ■ Guárdatelo en tu interior. ■ Guárdatelo en lo más profundo de ti. ■ Guárdatelo en lo más profundo de tu ser. (Just) keep it to yourself.

para sus adentros: pensar ~ ■ pensar algo para sí (mismo) ■ pensar algo para uno (mismo) to think to oneself ➤ Y pensé para mis adentros... ■ Y pensé para mí (mismo)... And I thought to myself...

para sus adentros: saber ~ ■ saber en su interior ■ saber en lo más profundo de sí ■ saber en lo más profundo de su ser to know in one's heart ■ to know deep down ■ to know in one's gut

para sus adentros: sentir ~ ■ sentir en su interior ■ sentir en lo más profundo de sí ■ sentir en lo más profundo de su ser to feel in one's heart ■ to feel in one's gut ➤ Sentí para mis adentros que iba a recibir la beca. ■ Sentí en mi interior que iba a recibir la beca. ■ Sentí en lo más profundo de mí que iba a recibir la beca. ■ Sentí en lo más profundo de mi ser que iba a recibir la beca. I felt in my heart that I would get the scholarship. ■ I felt in my gut that I would get the scholarship.

para tal o para cual... for this or that... ➤ Tenemos que pararnos a pensar qué es mejor para tal o cual invitado si queremos tener una cena perfecta. We have to stop and think, if we want a perfect dinner, what is best for this or that guest.

para ti 1. for you 2. to you ➤ Soy Señora McDougall, Margie para ti. I'm Mrs. McDougall, Margie to you.

para tirar a la chuña *(Esp.)* more than one knows what to do with ➤ Tiene dinero para tirar a la chuña. ■ Tiene dinero para parar un tren. He has more money than he knows what to do with.

estar **para tirársela** *(subido de tono)* to be so good looking I'd like to put it to her

para todos sale el sol ■ el sol sale para todos we're all equals

para un futuro próximo ■ próximamente in the near future ■ soon ➤ No tenemos previsto ningún viaje a Madrid para un futuro próximo. ■ No tenemos previsto ningún viaje a Madrid próximamente. We don't anticipate a trip to Madrid in the near future. ■ We don't anticipate a trip to Madrid soon.

estar **para un polvo** *(subido de tono)* to be someone one would like to get it on with

para una eventual consulta posterior: guardar las instrucciones ~ to save the instructions for future reference ■ to keep the instructions for future reference

para una vez que maté un perro, me llamaron mataperros do something once, and you're labeled forever

para uno solo of one's own ➤ Mi hermana quería tener un perro para ella sola. My sister wanted a dog of her own.

para unos to some people

para (uso) diario for everyday use ■ for day-to-day use ■ for daily use

para variar for a change

ser **para ver** to have to wait and see

para ver lo que hubiera que ver to see what one could see ■ to see what(ever) there was to see

para visitar a amigos to visit friends ➤ El sábado voy a Coslada para visitar a unos amigos de mi pueblo. Saturday I'm going to Coslada to visit some friends from home.

parachoques abollado dented bumper ➤ El parachoques está abollado. The bumper is dented. ➤ El parachoques estaba abollado. The bumper was dented. ➤ Tenía el parachoques abollado. It had a dented bumper. ➤ El parachoques fue abollado. The bumper got dented.

parada cardiaca ▪ paro cardiaco ▪ cardiac arrest

parada cardiorespiratoria ▪ paro cardiorespiratorio cardiopulmonary arrest ▪ cardiorespiratory arrest

la **parada de metro más cercana** ▪ la parada de metro que está más cerca the closest metro stop ▪ the nearest metro stop ➤ ¿Cuál es la parada de metro más cercana? ▪ ¿Qué parada de metro está más cerca? What metro stop is the closest? ▪ Which metro stop is the closest?

la **parada de metro que está más cerca** ▪ la parada de metro más cercana the closest metro stop ▪ the nearest metro stop ➤ La parada de metro que esta más cerca es División del Norte. ▪ La parada de metro más cercana es División del Norte. The closest metro stop is División del Norte. ▪ The nearest metro stop is División del Norte.

parada de taxi taxi stand ▪ taxi stop

parada respiratoria ▪ paro respiratorio respiratory arrest ▪ cessation of breathing

ser un **paradigma de** to be a model of

estar **parado(-a) junto a** ▪ estar de pie junto a to stand beside ▪ to be standing beside

paraíso fiscal tax haven

paraje desolado desolate spot (in the wild)

paraje soleado sunny spot

paraje sombrío gloomy spot

paraje umbrío ▪ paraje sombreado shady spot

estar **paralizado en el día de fiesta** *(poco común)* ▪ cerrado por festivo ▪ cerrado por vacaciones to be closed down for the holiday ▪ to be shut down for the holiday

estar **paralizado** 1. *(persona, animal)* to be paralyzed 2. *(tráfico)* to be at a standstill

estar **paralizado por una huelga** to be paralyzed by a strike

paralizar el recuento (de votos) ▪ parar el recuento (de votos) to stop the recount (of votes) ▪ to halt the recount (of votes)

paralizar el tráfico to stop traffic ▪ to halt traffic ▪ to snarl traffic

parar de hablar to stop talking

parar de hacer ruido to stop making noise

parar de una (buena) vez to knock it off ▪ to cease and desist ➤ Diles a los niños que paren de una (buena) vez. Es hora de irse a la cama. Tell the kids to knock it off. It's time to go to bed.

parar el golpe to ward off the blow ▪ to deflect the blow

parar el recuento ▪ paralizar el recuento to stop the recount ▪ to halt the recount

parar el tiro *(deportes)* to deflect the shot

parar en firme to come to a complete stop ▪ to come to a halt

parar en mal ▪ acabar mal to come to a bad end ▪ to meet an ill fate

parar en seco to stop abruptly ▪ to stop suddenly ▪ to come to a sudden stop

parar en seco a alguien ▪ pararle los carriles a alguien to stop someone dead in one's tracks

parar en seco algo to stop something abruptly ▪ to break something off abruptly

parar la amenaza to ward off the threat

parar la oreja 1. *(refiriéndose a un perro)* to cock its ear 2. poner la oreja to listen to someone else's conversation ▪ *(especialmente refiriéndose al teléfono)* to listen in on someone's conversation

parar los pies a alguien ▪ bajarle los humos a alguien to put someone in his place ▪ to clip someone's wings ▪ to take someone down a notch

parar por alguien to stop for someone ➤ El coche paró por el peatón. The car stopped for the pedestrian. ➤ El coche paró por el funeral. The car stopped for the funeral procession.

parar un taxi to flag a taxi

pararle el carro a alguien to put a stop to something once and for all

pararlo a alguien por ir con exceso de velocidad to stop someone for speeding ➤ El policía me paró por ir con exceso de velocidad. The policeman stopped me for speeding.

pararse a considerar to stop to consider

pararse a fumar ▪ pararse para fumar to stop to smoke ▪ to stop to have a smoke ➤ Me he parado a fumar. I stopped to smoke. ▪ I stopped to have a smoke.

pararse para fumar ▪ pararse a fumar to stop to smoke ▪ to stop to have a smoke

pararse y escuchar to stop and listen ➤ Me paré y escuché la música viniendo de la sala de concierto. I stopped and listened to the music coming from the concert hall.

parársele el coche ▪ calársele el coche (for) the car to stall ➤ Se le paró el coche. ▪ Se le caló el coche. The car stalled (on him).

ser **parcialmente correcto** to be partially correct ▪ to be partly correct ▪ to be correct in part

ser **parcialmente culpable de** ▪ ser en parte culpable de to be partly to blame for ▪ to be partially to blame for

ser **parcialmente responsable de** ▪ tener responsabilidad en parte de to be partially responsible for ▪ to be partly responsible for

parece ayer ▪ parece que fue ayer it seems like just the other day ▪ it seems like yesterday

parece bien ▪ parece que anda bien it seems (to be doing) okay ▪ *(él)* he seems (to be doing) okay ▪ *(ella)* she seems (to be doing) okay

parece como si it seems as if

parece como si hubiese sido ayer (que...) it seems like yesterday (that...) ▪ it seems like (just) the other day (that...)

parece dormida she seems to be asleep

parece dormido he seems to be asleep

parece mentira it seems impossible ▪ it's incredible ▪ I can't believe it

parece mentira que... ▪ no puedo creer que... I can't believe (that)...

parece que... it seems that... ▪ it looks as if... ▪ *(coloquial)* it looks like... ➤ Parece que acaba del venir del pueblo. ▪ *(coloquial)* Parece que se acaba de caer de un guindo. It seems he just came out of the boondocks. ▪ It looks like he just came out of the sticks.

parece que anda bien ▪ parece bien it seems (to be doing) okay ▪ *(él)* he seems (to be doing) okay ▪ *(ella)* she seems (to be doing) okay

parece que está empollando huevos *(él)* I don't think he's up to much ▪ *(ella)* I don't think she's up to much

parece (que fue) ayer it seems like yesterday ▪ it seems like just the other day

parece que ha comido lengua he can't stop running his mouth ▪ he can't stop talking

parece que le han comido la lengua los ratones *(L.am.)* *(él)* he hasn't said a word ▪ *(ella)* she hasn't said a word

parece que le ha comido la lengua un gato *(Esp.)* *(él)* he hasn't said a word ▪ *(ella)* she hasn't said a word

parece que le ha hecho la boca un fraile *(Cervantes)* he's always asking for something ▪ he's always wanting something

parece que te ha dado la noche it looks like you've had quite a night of it

parece que va a llover it looks like it's going to rain ▪ it looks like it might rain ▪ it looks like rain ▪ it's showing signs of rain

parece que va a nevar it looks like it might snow ▪ it shows signs of snowing ➤ Parece que va a nevar esta noche. It looks like it might snow tonight. ▪ It shows signs of snowing tonight.

parece que viene de arar he's a pigpen ▪ he's a sight ▪ he's got dirt all over him

parece ser que it seems that ▪ it appears that ▪ it seems to be that

parecer abanico de tonta to be jumpy as a goat ➤ ¡Estáte quieto! Pareces abanico de tonta. Be still! You're as jumpy as a goat.

parecer de perlas to be great

parecer la casa de tócame Roque to be a madhouse

parecer la radiografía de un silbido ▪ parecer el espíritu de la golosina to be skinny as a rail

parecer mentira to be unbelievable ▪ to seem impossible ➤ Parece mentira. It seems impossible.
parecer mucho mayor to look a lot older ▪ to look much older ▪ to look years older
parecer mucho menor to look a lot younger ▪ to look much younger ▪ to look years younger
parecer no fijarse en to seem not to notice
parecer poca cosa *(personas)* not to be good enough (for someone) ▪ *(cosas)* not to be good enough (for something)
parecer que en su vida ha roto un plato ▪ parecer una mosquita muerta to look innocent ▪ to look naive ▪ to look like a model of perfection
parecer que está empollando huevos not to be up to much (apparently)
parecer que uno está bien to seem okay ➤ Parece que está bien. He seems okay. ➤ Parecía que estaba bien esta mañana. He seemed okay this morning.
parecer un abril ▪ estar hecho un abril to be a sweet young thing ▪ to be a spring chicken
parecer un alfeñique to be a skinny little runt
parecer un alma en pena to look downtrodden
parecer un cine to be like Grand Central Station ➤ ¡Esto parece un cine! It's like Grand Central Station in here! ▪ It's like Grand Central Station around here!
parecer un disco rayado to be like a broken record ▪ to sound like a broken record
parecer un esqueleto ▪ estar hecho un saco de huesos to be skinny as a rail ▪ to be nothing but a skeleton
parecer un gallinero ▪ parecer una pocilga to be a total mess ▪ to be a wreck ▪ to be a pigsty ▪ to be a pigpen
parecer un liliputiense ▪ parecer un Tarzán de bonsai to be a little squirt
parecer un pato mareado to be a total spazz ▪ to be a clutz
parecer un príncipe to be handsome
parecer una casa de locos to be a madhouse
parecer una furia to be furious
parecer una jaula de grillos to be like a madhouse ➤ Ese bar parece una jaula de grillos. Mejor no entramos. That bar is (like) a madhouse. Let's not go in.
parecer una leonera ▪ estar (todo) manga por hombro ▪ estar hecho un desbarajuste to be a mess ▪ to be a wreck to be a pigpen
parecer una Magdalena to be always crying
parecer una mosquita muerta ▪ parecer que en su vida ha roto un plato to look innocent ▪ to look naive ▪ to look like a model of perfection
parecer una pasa to be old and wrinkled ▪ to be shriveled like a raisin
parecer una pocilga ▪ parecer un gallinero to be a total mess ▪ to be a wreck ▪ to be a pigsty ▪ to be a pigpen
parecer una suela de zapato to be tough as shoe leather
parecerá extraño que... it must seem strange that...
parecerse a alguien to look like someone ▪ to resemble someone ➤ Me parezco a mi padre. ▪ Me doy un aire a mi padre. I look like my father. ▪ I resemble my father. ➤ (Él) se parece a ti. ▪ (Él) se te parece. ▪ (Él) se te da un aire. He looks like you. ➤ (Ella) se parece a ti. ▪ (Ella) se te parece. ▪ (Ella) se te da un aire. She looks like you. ➤ Se parece a su padre. He looks like his father.
parecerse a su padre to be like one's father ▪ *(pintoresco)* to be a chip off the old block
parecerse al juego del tira y afloja to be a tug of war
parecerse al perro del hortelano, que ni come ni deja comer to be a dog in the manger
parecerse como dos gotas de agua ▪ parecerse como una gota de agua a otra to be like two peas in a pod
parecerse como un huevo a otro to be like two peas in a pod
parecerse como un huevo a una castaña not to look anything alike
parecerse como una gota de agua a otra ▪ parecerse como dos gotas de agua to be like two peas in a pod
parecerse en algo ▪ tener algo en común to be alike in something ▪ to have something in common
parecerse en el blanco de los ojos y en el blanco de los dientes 1. *(físico)* not to look anything alike **2.** *(personalidad)* not to be anything alike ▪ to be completely different ▪ to have nothing in common
parecerse más a ▪ ser más bien to be more like ➤ Una avioneta ultraligera se parece más a una cometa grande. ▪ Una avioneta ultraligera es más bien una cometa grande. An ultralight airplane is more like a big kite.
parecerse uno al otro to look alike ➤ Ella y su hermana se parecen mucho. ▪ Ella y su hermana se parecen un montón. She and her sister look a lot alike.
parecérsele a alguien to look like someone ▪ to resemble someone
parecía que... it was as if... ▪ it was like...
parecido asombroso amazing resemblance ▪ uncanny resemblance
parecido de los niños a sus padres children's resemblance to their parents
la **pared de carga** ▪ pared maestra load-bearing wall
pared desnuda bare wall
la **pared por medio** *(entre dos apartamentos o edificios)* separating wall
las **paredes oyen** walls have ears ▪ walls can hear
pareja casada married couple
pareja de hecho de facto couple
pareja distanciada ▪ pareja enajenada estranged couple
pareja enajenada *(culto)* ▪ pareja distanciada estranged couple
ser una **pareja eterna** to be an eternal couple
pareja nidificante *(aves)* nesting pair
pareja perfecta perfect match ➤ Ella es una pareja perfecta para mí. She's a perfect match for me.
el **paréntesis en** interruption in
pares o nones: juego de ~ ▪ juego de pares y nones a game of chance to determine which one of two people wins, like flipping a coin. Each player puts a hand behind his back, mentally selects the number of fingers he will show, and extends that number of fingers. The lead player then says either "pares" o "nones" ("even" or "odd"), and both players show their hands simultaneously. If the number of fingers extended by both players corresponds to the lead player's call, he wins.
pares sueltos 1. last remaining pairs (in a certain size) **2.** matching set in which a piece is missing (often sold at close-out prices)
parida mental hare-brained idea
ser **pariente de alguien** ▪ ser familia de alguien to be related to someone ➤ ¿Eres pariente de Alberto? Are you related to Alberto?
parientes políticos in-laws
el **parte de guerra** battle statistics
París bien vale una misa it's worth the effort
paro cardiaco ▪ parada cardiaca cardiac arrest
paro cardiorespiratorio ▪ parada cardiorespiratoria cardiopulmonary arrest ▪ cardiorespiratory arrest
paro de motor(es) engine failure
paro registrado ▪ desempleo registrado unemployment rate ➤ El paro registrado subió en agosto. The unemployment rate increased in August.
paro respiratorio ▪ parada respiratoria respiratory arrest ▪ cessation of breathing
parpadeo en la pantalla del radar ▪ destello en la pantalla del radar blip on the radar screen
párpados se volvieron cárdenos (por falta de sueño) eyes became blue from (lack of sleep)
parque empresarial business park
parque eólico wind farm
la **parte culpable** guilty party
la **parte de atrás** back part ➤ La parte de atrás del monitor es más estrecha que la de delante. The back part of the monitor is narrower than the front part.
la **parte de atrás de un carro** *(L.am.)* ▪ parte trasera de un carro back of a car

la **parte de atrás de un coche** *(Esp.)* ■ parte trasera de un coche back of a car

la **parte de atrás de una casa** ■ parte trasera de una casa ■ parte posterior de una casa back of a house

parte de atrás del sobre: en la ~ ■ en el reverso del sobre ■ por detrás del sobre ■ en el dorso del sobre on the back of the envelope

la **parte de en medio** ■ parte del medio the part in the middle ■ the middle part the one in the middle ■ the piece in the middle

la **parte de la ciudad** part of the city

ser (una) **parte de un acuerdo** to be party to an agreement

ser (una) **parte de un juicio** to be a party in a lawsuit

parte defendida defendant

la **parte del cuerpo** ■ hemisferio del cuerpo side of the body ➤ Tenía la parte derecha de su cuerpo paralizada. ■ Tenía el hemisferio derecho del cuerpo paralizado. The right side of his body was paralyzed.

la **parte del medio** ■ parte de en medio the part in the middle ■ the middle part the one in the middle ■ the piece in the middle

la **parte del problema** part of the problem

la **parte del tiempo** part of the time

la **parte demandante** plantiff

ser **parte en una cosa** ■ tener parte en una cosa ■ tomar parte en una cosa to take part in something

el **parte facultativo** ■ parte médico medical report ■ medical bulletin

parte hablada speaking part

la **parte inferior de la página** ■ el pie de la página foot of the page ■ bottom of the page

parte médico ■ parte facultativo medical report ■ medical bulletin

parte por parte: ir ~ to go step by step

la **parte posterior de la caja** ■ dorso de la caja back of the box

la **parte posterior de la casa** ■ parte de detrás de la casa ■ parte trasera de la casa back part of the house

la **parte posterior de la lata** ■ dorso de la lata back of the can

la **parte trasera de un camión** ■ carga de un camión back of a truck

partes artículadas moving parts

partes constitutivas constituent parts

partes involucradas ■ partidos en juego parties involved

partes privadas ■ partes pudendas private parts

partes pudendas ■ partes privadas private parts

participar en to participate in

participar en concurso público por un proyecto de construcción *(puja pública)* to bid on a construction project

ser **partícipe de un secreto** to be in on a secret

ser **partidario de** to be a proponent of ■ to be in favor of

partidario de que...: mostrarse ~ to come out in favor of...

estar **partido al medio** ■ estar dividido justo a la mitad to be divided down the middle ■ to be split down the middle

partido bisagra *(política)* swing party ■ swing faction ➤ Londres ha pactado con un partido bisagra y salvado la autonomía de Ulster. London formed a pact with a swing faction and saved the autonomy of Ulster.

ser **partido de** *(fracciones)* ■ ser dividio por to be divided by ➤ Cinco partido por diez da un medio. Five divided by ten equals one half.

partido fuera (de casa) *(deportes)* away game

partidos en juego ■ partes involucradas parties involved

partir de algún lugar ■ salir de un lugar to depart from a place ■ to leave a place ➤ El vuelo parte de Caracas a las ocho y media de la mañana. The flight departs from Caracas at eight-thirty in the morning. ■ The flight leaves Caracas at eight-thirty in the morning.

partir a la batalla to go into battle

partir algo to split open something ■ to split something open

partir algo al medio ■ dividir algo al medio ■ partir algo a la mitad to split something down the middle ■ to divide something down the middle ■ to split something in half ■ to divide something in half ➤ Partimos el melón al medio y cada uno se comió una mitad. We split the melon down the middle and each ate half.

partir algo por el medio to split something in half ■ to split something down the middle ■ to split something through the middle ➤ Para preparar un *banana split*, se parte el plátano por el medio. To make a banana split, you split the banana down the middle.

partir algo por entero to break something off of something ➤ Partió el plátano por entero del racimo. She broke the banana off of the cluster.

partir algo por la mitad to cut something in two widthwise ■ *(más técnico)* to cut something in two radially

partir camino con alguien to part company with someone ■ to go ones' separate ways

partir como una bala to be off like a shot ■ to take off like a shot

partir como una exhalación to be off like a shot ■ to take off like a shot

partir como una flecha to be off like a shot ■ to take off like a shot

partir con dirección a ■ partir con destino a ■ salir para ■ salir con destino a to leave for ■ *(especialmente aerolíneas, trenes, etc.)* to depart for

partir de cero ■ empezar de cero to start from scratch ■ to start from nothing ■ to start with nothing

partir de esta vida to depart this life

partir de lo básico to begin with the basics

partir de repente *(toro)* ■ embestir de repente to charge suddenly

partir de un plantamiento erróneo ■ partir de una falsa premisa to begin with a false premise

partir de una premisa falsa ■ partir de un plantamiento erróneo to begin with a false premise

partir el alma ■ causar gran pena to rend one's soul ■ to tear one to pieces

partir el ángulo *(geometría)* to dissect the angle

partir el camino con alguien ■ encontrarse a mitad de camino to meet someone half way

partir la boca ■ partir los morros to hit someone in the mouth ■ to bust someone in the mouth

partir los morros ■ partir la boca to hit someone in the mouth ■ to bust someone in the mouth

partir rieles to split rails

partir un tronco con una hacha to split a log with an ax(e) ■ to split a trunk with an ax(e)

partirle el corazón *(a él)* to break his heart ■ *(a ella)* to break her heart

partirle la boca a alguien *(coloquial)* ■ darle un puñetazo a alguien to hit someone in the mouth ■ *(coloquial)* to bust someone in the mouth

partirle la cara a alguien to smash someone's face ■ to bash someone's face (in)

partirle un pedazo de algo a alguien to break off a piece of something for someone ➤ Párteme un pedazo de chocolate. Break me off a piece of chocolate.

partirle un rayo a alguien to damn someone ➤ ¡Que te parta un rayo! Damn you! ■ May lightning strike you!

partirse con un chasquido to break with a snap ■ to snap when it breaks ■ to snap as it breaks ➤ Pisé una ramita que se partió con un chasquido. I stepped on a twig that broke with a snap. ■ I stepped on a twig that snapped when it broke. ■ I stepped on a twig that snapped as it broke. *(Nota: Se puede usar "which" en vez de "that".)*

partirse de risa ■ descoserse de risa to split one's sides laughing ■ to be in stitches

partirse el corazón to break one's heart ■ to have a broken heart

partirse el culo (de risa) *(subido de tono)* ■ cagarse de risa to laugh one's ass off ■ to shit in one's pants laughing ■ *(alternativo inofensivo)* to laugh one's (fool) head off

partirse el culo (de trabajo) *(coloquial, ligeramente subido de tono)* ■ partirse el culo trabajando to work one's ass off ■ to bust one's ass ■ to bust one's tail

partirse el espinazo (trabajando) ■ romperse la espalda (trabajando) to break one's back working ■ to break one's back with work

partirse el pecho (de risa) to split one's sides laughing ■ to laugh one's head off

partirse por el eje (longitudinal) to be split down the middle (lengthwise)

partírsele el diente to break one's tooth ■ to break a tooth ➤ Se le partió el diente. He broke his tooth.

partitura musical musical score

parto muerto still birth

parto prematuro premature birth

pasa con confianza come in and make yourself at home

pasa de eso ■ apaga y vámonos ■ ignóralo let's just drop it

pasa lo que pasa porque... this happens because... ■ it happens because... ■ it occurs because...

pasa por aquí, por favor step over here, please

pasa un ángel it's so quiet you can hear a pin drop

ser una **pasada** *(Esp., coloquial)* **1.** *(positivo)* to be great **2.** *(negativo)* to be terrible ■ to be too much

pasada de pintura: echar una ~ ■ dar una mano de pintura to apply a coat of paint

pasada la medianoche ■ después de la medianoche after midnight

pasado la flor de la vida: haber ~ ■ haber pasado los años mozos to be past one's prime

el **pasado mes de abril** ■ en abril pasado last April

pasado cercano ■ pasado reciente recent past

estar **pasado de fecha** ■ estar caducado ■ estar vencido out of date ■ expired

estar **pasado de moda** to be out of style ■ to be out of fashion

ser **pasado de padres a hijos** ■ pasarse de padres a hijos to be passed down from father to son ➤ Viticultores de padres a hijos desde 1889 Grape growers from father to son since 1889 ➤ La bodega ha sido pasada de padres a hijos por cuatro generaciones. The winery has been passed down from father to son for four generations.

estar **pasado de rosca 1.** *(tuerca, tornillo)* to be stripped **2.** *(consumidor de drogas)* estar pasado de vueltas to have fried one's brain

pasado mañana day after tomorrow

ser **pasado por alto por alguien** to be overlooked by someone

pasado reciente ■ pasado cercano recent past

pasado remoto remote past ■ distant past

pasado turbio questionable past

pasado un poco más tiempo pretty soon ■ very soon ■ quite soon

pasado un tiempo after a time ■ after a while

pasados unos minutos ■ a los pocos minutos minutes later

pasados unos momentos ■ a los pocos momentos moments later

¡pásala! ■ ¡hazla pasar! ■ ¡hazla circular! pass it on!

¡pásale! *(Méx.)* ■ ¡adelante! ■ ¡pase! come on in! ■ come in!

¡pásalo bien! ■ ¡que te diviertas! have a good time!

pásame eso ■ cógeme eso pass me that ■ pass that to me ➤ Pass me that, would you? Cógeme eso, ¿podrías? ■ Pásame eso, ¿podrías?

pasando por by way of ➤ Fuimos pasando por Atlanta. We went by way of Atlanta.

¡pasando por encima de mi cadáver! over my dead body!

pasapalabra: jugar a ~ to play word guessing

pasar a alguien a un sitio to get someone into a place ➤ Mi amigo nos pasó a la discoteca. My friend got us into the discotheque.

pasar a bordo (del avión) ■ subir a bordo (del avión) ■ embarcar (en el avión) to board the airplane ■ to get on the airplane ■ *(No implica que la persona en cuestión vaya a hacer un viaje)* to go aboard the airplane ➤ Vamos a pasar a bordo. ■ Embarquemos. Let's board the airplane. ■ Let's get on the airplane.

pasar a bordo (del barco) ■ subir a bordo (del barco) ■ embarcar to board the ship ■ to get on the ship ■ *(no implica que la persona en cuestión vaya a hacer un viaje)* to go aboard the ship

pasar a cuchillo a alguien *(coloquial)* ■ acuchillar a alguien to stab someone to death ■ to knife someone to death

pasar a disposición judicial a alguien to start a police record on someone

pasar a entrar en funcionamiento to begin operation ➤ El tren de alta velocidad pasará a entrar en funcionamiento el año que viene. The high-speed train will begin operation next year.

pasar a hablar de... to go on to talk about...

pasar a hacer algo to go on to do something ■ to continue on to do something ➤ Muchos empleados pasan a ocupar cargos más altos en la compañía. Many employees go on to occupy higher positions in the company.

pasar a la clandestinidad to go underground

pasar a la historia como ■ pasar a la posteridad como to go down in history as

pasar a la posteridad to hand down to posterity

pasar a limpio sus apuntes ■ pasar sus apuntes a limpio to make a clean copy of one's notes ■ to organize one's notes ■ to put one's notes in order

pasar a lo siguiente to go on to the next thing

pasar a mayores to become serious ➤ El problema de la piratería está pasando a mayores. The problem of piracy is becoming serious.

pasar a mejor vida to pass away ■ to pass on ■ to die

pasar a otra cosa to go on to something else

pasar a por alguien *(Esp.)* ■ pasar por alguien to come by for someone ■ to go by for someone ➤ Paso a por ti a la una. ■ Paso por ti. I'll come by for you at one (o'clock). ■ I'll go by for you at one (o'clock).

pasar a ser to become ➤ El vicepresidente de la compañía pasó a ser el presidente tras la dimisión de éste. The company vice president became president when the latter resigned.

pasar a su hora *(trenes, etc.)* ■ ser puntual to be right on time ■ *(pintoresco)* to run like clockwork ➤ Los trenes españoles siempre pasan a su hora. ■ Los trenes españoles son puntuales. The Spanish trains are right on time. ■ The Spanish trains run like clockwork.

pasar a uno por las armas to kill someone

pasar agachado(-a) to sneak by (by crouching down)

pasar al abordaje de un barco *(piratas y bucaneros)* to go aboard a ship

pasar al frente de to pass in front of

pasar al torrente sanguíneo to enter the bloodstream ■ to get into the bloodstream

pasar algo de mano en mano to pass something around ■ to pass something among each other ■ to takes turns sharing something ➤ Nos pasábamos los libros de mano en mano. We passed the books around among each other.

pasar algo en silencio ■ soportar algo en silencio ■ sufrir algo en silencio to suffer something in silence

pasar algo por alto to skip over something ■ to omit something

pasar alguien a retiro ■ jubilarse to retire

pasar apuros to go through a difficult time

pasar arrasando ■ venir arrasando to come barreling down ➤ Los carros pasan arrasando por esta calle, ¿verdad? ■ Los carros vienen arrasando por esta calle, ¿verdad? The cars really come barreling down this street, don't they?

pasar carros y carretas ■ aguantar mucho to put up with a lot ■ to endure a lot

pasar como pedo ■ pasar embalado ■ pasar como chiquetazo to go flying by ■ to fly by ■ to go by like a bat outta hell

pasar como un sueño to happen as if it were a dream ■ to pass as if it were a dream

pasar como una sombra to go almost unseen

pasar con el carro *(L.am.)* ■ pasar en el coche to drive by ■ to go by in the car

pasar con el coche *(Esp.)* ■ pasar con el carro to drive by ■ to go by in the car

pasar de to get beyond ➤ Cuando intento ver mi correo electrónico no pasa de "autorizando". When I try to see my E-mail, it doesn't get beyond "authorizing."

pasar de algo *(coloquial)* **1.** to ignore something **2.** no gustar de algo not to like something ➤ Paso de esas cosas. Those things don't interest me. ■ That doesn't interest me. ➤ **Sus padres pasaban de gatos.** His parents didn't like cats. ➤ **Los padres pasaban del gato, pero a los niños les encantaba.** The parents didn't like the (family) cat, but the children loved him.

pasar de alguien ■ ignorar a alguien to ignore someone ➤ Pasa de todo el mundo. He ignores everyone. ■ He ignores everybody.

pasar de castaño oscuro ■ ser la gota que colma el vaso ■ ser el colmo ■ hasta aquí hemos llegado to be the last straw ➤ Esto pasa de castaño oscuro. ■ Esto es la gota que colma el vaso. ■ Esto es el colmo. ■ Hasta aquí hemos llegado. This is the last straw. ■ That's the last straw.

pasar de largo to walk by without speaking ■ to go by without speaking ■ to go by without acknowledging someone ■ to walk by someone without acknowledging him or her

pasar de largo hacia un lugar to go by on one's way to a place ■ to pass by on one's way to a place ➤ Estábamos en la cafetería y Santiago pasó de largo hacia el mercado. We were in the café and Santiago went by on his way to the supermarket. ■ We were in the café and Santiago passed by on his way to the supermarket.

pasar de largo por un lugar to go by a place ■ to pass (by) a place ➤ Pasó de largo por la casa de correos en camino. He went by the post office on the way. ■ He passed (by) the post office on the way.

pasar de página ■ pasar la página ■ pasar la hoja to turn the page

pasar de ser... ■ ya no ser... to no longer be... ■ not to be any more... ■ to cease to be... ➤ Ha pasado de ser el último equipo a ser la revelación de este año. It is no longer the worst team in the league, but this year's sensation. ■ It's not the league's worst team any more. It's this year's sensation. ■ It has ceased to be the league's worst team. It's this year's sensation.

pasar de un estado a otro to go from (being) something to something else ■ to become something else ■ to turn into something else ■ to be converted into something else ➤ Cuando pasó de pinche a cocinero le aumentaron el sueldo. When he went from kitchen helper to cook... ■ When the kitchen helper became a cook... ➤ Al estar sometido a altas presiones durante miles de millones de años, el carbón pasa a (ser) piedras preciosas. ■ Al estar sometido a altas presiones durante miles de millones de años, el carbón se convierte en piedras preciosas. When subjected to great pressure over eons of time, coal turns into precious stones. ■ When subjected to great pressure over eons of time, coal is converted into precious stones.

pasar de un lugar a otro ■ pasar de un sitio a otro to go from one place to another

pasar de una cosa a otra cosa to go from something to something else ■ to become something ➤ Cuando el vehículo anfibio pasa del asfalto al agua... When the amphibious vehicle goes from pavement to water... ■ When the vehicle becomes a boat...

pasar de *x* a *y* to go from *x* to *y* ➤ Gracias a una reforma, el desnivel de la torre inclinada de Pisa ha pasado de 6 a 5,5 grados. Thanks to a repair, the tilt of the Leaning Tower of Pisa has gone from 6 to 5.5 degrees.

pasar desapercibido to go unnoticed

pasar desapercibido para alguien to go unnoticed by someone

pasar el cargo a alguien to pass the position on to one's successor ■ to appoint a successor to one's own position ➤ Cuando el dueño de la compañía se retiró de su puesto de director general, le pasó el cargo a su hijo. When the owner of the company retired from his post as general manager, he passed it on to his son. ■ When the owner of the company retired from his post as general manager, he appointed his son as his successor. ■ When the owner of the company retired from his post as general manager, he appointed his son to succeed him.

pasar el cesto ■ pasar el cestillo to pass the collection basket *(Nota: A menudo es en realidad un plato o una bandeja.)*

pasar el coleto *(Caribe)* ■ pasar el trapeador ■ pasar la fregona to mop (the floor)

pasar el ecuador 1. to cross the equator **2.** *(Esp.)* to compete the third year of one's bachelor's degree studies and to take a trip to celebrate *(Nota: En España, la licenciatura dura cinco años.)*

pasar el fin de semana to spend the weekend ➤ Estuve pasando el fin de semana con mis padres. I spent the weekend with my parents.

pasar el rato (haciendo algo) ■ pasar tiempo (haciendo algo) to spend time (doing something)

pasar el tiempo to spend time

pasar embalado ■ pasar como chiquetazo to go flying by ■ to go barreling down

pasar en ámbar to run the yellow light

pasar en frente de alguien en la autopista to pass someone on the highway ■ to go around someone on the highway

pasar estrecheces ■ estar pasando estrecheces ■ pasar problemas económicos to be in financial straits ■ to be experiencing financial difficulties

pasar frente a ■ pasar delante de to walk past ■ to walk by ➤ Pasé frente a la biblioteca camino de mi clase. I walked past the library on the way to (my) class. ■ I walked by the library on the way to class.

pasar grandes penas to experience great hardship(s) ■ to undergo great hardship(s) ■ to suffer great hardship(s)

pasar hambre to go hungry

pasar harina por un tamiz to sift flour

pasar hoja ■ pasar la página to turn the page

pasar inadvertido ■ pasar desapercibido ■ pasar sin ser notado ■ pasar sin ser visto to go unnoticed

pasar inadvertido en la tanda to get lost in the shuffle

pasar inspección to pass inspection

pasar la aduana pasar por aduanas ■ cruzar la aduana to go through customs

pasar la aspiradora to vacuum

pasar la bola to pass the buck

pasar la cuenta ■ echar la carga to pass the buck

pasar la fregona *(Esp.)* ■ pasar el coleto ■ pasar el trapeador to mop (the floor)

pasar la gorra to pass the hat *(Nota: Se refiere fundamentalmente a espectáculos callejeros.)*

pasar la lista to pass around the roll sheet ■ to pass the roll sheet around

pasar la noche to spend the night

pasar la noche en blanco ■ pasar la noche en vela not to be able to get to sleep (all night) ➤ Pasé la noche en blanco. I couldn't get to sleep last night. ■ I couldn't get to sleep all night (last night).

pasar la página ■ pasar de página ■ pasar la hoja to turn the page

pasar la palabra a alguien ■ dar la palabra a alguien to turn the meeting over to someone

pasar la pena negra to suffer miserably

pasar la vida to spend one's life

pasar la vida a tragos to live one day at a time ■ to take life one day at a time ■ to take one day at a time ■ to live a day at a time ■ to take life a day at a time ■ to take a day at a time

pasar las de Caín ■ pasar por las de Caín to have a rough time ■ to go through hell

pasar las horas muertas to sit around (doing nothing) ■ to waste a lot of time ■ to waste inordinate amounts of time ■ to waste an inordinate amount of time ■ to while away time (doing nothing constructive) ➤ Se pasa las horas muertas mirando la tele. He sits around watching TV all day. ■ He wastes a lot of time watching TV. ■ He wastes inordinate amounts of time watching TV.

pasar las migas to wash down food ➤ ¿Quieres una copa de vino para pasar las migas? Do want a glass of wine to wash it down?

pasar lista to call the roll ■ to take (the) attendance

pasar lo suyo to have a very hard time ➤ Tras la muerte de su esposa y su hijo, ha tenido que pasar lo suyo. Since the deaths of his wife and son, he has had a very hard time. ➤ Pasó lo suyo después de la operación. He had a very hard time after his operation.

pasar los límites de... to cross the line ■ to go overboard ➤ Después de escapar del colegio, ella ha pasado todos los límites. Skipping school was the last straw. She's gone overboard!

pasar más hambre que un maestro de escuela to hardly have a crumb to eat

pasar miedo ■ tener miedo to be fearful ■ to be afraid ➤ Sólo de pensar que tienen que ir al médico, los niños pasan miedo. At the thought of having to go to the doctor, children are fearful. ▪ At the thought of having to go to the doctor, children are afraid.

pasar página to forget it ▪ to turn the page ▪ to put it behind one

pasar por 1. pasar a través de to go through ▪ to walk through ▪ to pass through **2.** pasado al lado de ▪ pasar de largo to go by ▪ to walk by ▪ to pass by **3.** pasar a lo largo de to walk down to **4.** involucar to involve (as an essential step) ➤ Desde el principio la solución pasaba por la devolución de Elián a su padre. Since the beginning, the solution has involved the return of Elian to his father.

pasar por alguien *(L.am.)* ▪ pasar a por alguien *(Esp.)* to come by for someone ▪ to go by for someone ➤ En una hora, paso por ti. I'll come by for you in an hour.

pasar por alto 1. *(con intención de dejar algo de lado)* to put something aside (temporarily) ▪ to set something aside (temporarily) **2.** *(sin intención)* to overlook something ➤ Vamos a pasar por alto los deberes para acabarlos luego y echamos unos tiros. ▪ Vamos a dejar los deberes de lado para acabarlos luego y echamos unos tiros. Let's put aside our homework til later and (go) shoot some hoops. ➤ Pero cuando se pasa por alto todas sus excentricidades, resulta ser un gran artista. But when you overlook all her eccentricities, she is a great artist.

pasar por alto sus defectos to overlook someone's defects

pasar (por aquí) to come (by) ▪ to come along ▪ to be along ▪ to be here ➤ Otro autobús pasará en seguida. Another bus will be along shortly. ▪ Another bus will come along shortly. ▪ Another bus will come by shortly. ▪ Another bus will be here shortly. ▪ Another bus will be by shortly.

pasar por el aro ▪ entrar por el aro **1.** to go through the hoop **2.** ▪ hacer trámites to go through a few hoops ▪ to get through the red tape

pasar por el costado to pass alongside

pasar por el lado de uno to go by someone without speaking ▪ to pass by someone coming the other way ➤ Pasó por mi lado sin saludarme. She went by me without speaking.

pasar por encima de algo 1. *(en la calle)* to go over something ▪ to run over something ▪ to pass over something **2.** *(en un avión)* to fly over something ➤ Pasamos por encima de un bache. We went over a pothole. ▪ We ran over a pothole. ➤ Pasamos por encima del Gran Cañón en un helicóptero. We flew over the Grand Canyon in a helicopter.

pasar por encima de alguien to go over someone's head ▪ to go around one's boss

pasar por grandes penas ▪ pasar por momentos muy duros to suffer great hardship(s) ▪ to experience great hardship(s) ▪ to go through great hardship(s) ▪ to undergo great hardship(s)

pasar la aduana ▪ cruzar la aduana to go through customs

pasar meses con ▪ estar meses con to go for months on ➤ Mark Twain dijo, "Puedo pasar meses con un buen cumplido." ▪ Mark Twain dijo, "Puedo estar meses con un buen cumplido." Mark Twain said, "I can go for months on a good compliment." ➤ Mark Twain dijo que podía pasar meses con un buen cumplido. ▪ Mark Twain dijo que podía estar meses con un buen cumplido. Mark Twain said he could go for months on a good compliment.

pasar por la vicaría ▪ casarse to get hitched ▪ to tie the knot ▪ to get married

pasar por las armas ▪ fusilar to shoot someone

pasar (por) las de Caín to have a rough time ▪ to go through hell

pasar por lo mismo to go through the same thing ➤ Estamos pasando por lo mismo. We're going through the same thing.

pasar por los pelos 1. to make it by the skin of one's teeth **2.** *(semáforo en amarillo)* to run the yellow ▪ to barely make it through the light (before it turns red)

pasar por momentos muy duros ▪ pasar por grandes penas to suffer great hardship(s) ▪ to experience great hardship(s) ▪ to go through great hardship(s) ▪ to undergo great hardship(s)

pasar por su mente to go through one's mind ➤ ¿Qué pasó por tu mente cuando...? What went through your mind when...?

pasar por un trago (amargo) to go through a bad experience

pasar por una etapa en la que to pass through a stage in which ▪ to go through a phase in which

pasar revista a algo to review something ▪ to go over something ➤ *(noticia)* Aznar y Bush pasarán revista hoy en Washington a la situación en Afganistán. Aznar and Bush will review today the situation in Afghanistan. ▪ Aznar and Bush will go over the situation in Afghanistan today.

pasar revista a las tropas to review the troops ➤ La plana mayor del Pentágono pasó revista a las tropas. The top Pentagon brass reviewed the troops.

pasar sin pena ni gloria to barely make a stir ▪ to hardly make a stir ▪ to go virtually unnoticed

pasar tiempo a solas con alguien to spend time alone with someone

pasar tiempo juntos to spend time together

pasar un buen rato ▪ divertirse ▪ pasarlo bien ▪ parsarlo grande to have a good time

pasar un mal rato ▪ pasar las de Caín to have some difficult moments ▪ to have a bad time ➤ Pasó un mal rato cuando le preguntaron por su nivel de inglés en la entrevista. He had some difficult moments in the interview when asked about his English proficiency.

pasar un mal rato haciendo algo ▪ costarle hacer algo to have a hard time doing something ▪ to be hard for one (to) do something ➤ Pasó un mal rato después de su accidente. He had a bad time after his accident. ▪ He went through a difficult time after his accident. ➤ Pasó un mal rato viendo el documental sobre el terremoto en su ciudad natal. It was hard for him to watch the documentary about the earthquake in his hometown. ▪ He had a hard time watching the documentary about the earthquake in his hometown.

pasar un mal trago to go through a bad experience

pasar un periodo de tiempo en blanco ▪ pasar un periodo de tiempo in albis to go through a period of time without any money ▪ to go through a period of time with no money ➤ Está sin trabajo. Ha tenido que pasar el mes en blanco. He's out of work. He's gone through the month without any money.

pasar un rato divertido to have a good time

pasar un tiempo en blanco to go through a period of being broke

pasar un trago amargo to have a rough time

pasar una noche de perros to have a bad night

pasar una noche en blanco to stay up all night

pasar una noche toledana to spend a very cold night

pasar una película ▪ poner una película to show a movie

pasar volando por encima de algo to fly over something

pasará el dolor the pain will go away

pasarlas canutas por hacer algo ▪ vérselas negras para hacer algo to have a terrible time doing something ▪ to have a dickens of a time doing something ▪ to have an awful time doing something ➤ La pasé canutas por intentar comprender cómo funciona el mando (a distancia). I had a terrible time trying to figure out this remote. ▪ I had a dickens of a time trying to figure out this remote. ▪ I had an awful time trying to figure out this remote.

pasarlas más putas que Caín *(subido de tono)* ▪ pasarlas putas ▪ pasar las de Caín to go through hell

pasarlas moradas to have a bad time ▪ to go through a tough time

pasarlas negras to be going through hell

pasarlas putas *(subido de tono)* to have a bad time

pasarle a alguien a su habitación to show someone to one's room

pasarle a alguien el teléfono to hand someone the telephone

pasarle a uno to come over one ▪ to happen to one ➤ No sé qué me está pasando. I don't know what's come over me. ▪ I don't know what's happening to me.

pasarle con su habitación ▪ ponerle con su habitación to put someone through (to someone) ➤ *(operadora del hotel)* Le paso con su habitación. ▪ Le pongo con su habitación. I'll put you through to their room.

pasarle factura a alguien ▪ pasarle recibo a alguien to come back to haunt one ➤ Sus excesos con el alcohol le pasan factura ahora que es mayor en forma de cirrosis. His excessive drinking has come back to haunt him now that he's older. He has developed cirrhosis (of the liver).

pasarle por la cabeza to cross one's mind ➤ Jamás me ha pasado por la cabeza. It never crossed my mind.

pasarle recibo a alguien ■ pasarle factura a alguien to come back to haunt one ➤ Sus excesos con el alcohol le pasan recibo ahora que es mayor en forma de cirrosis. His excessive drinking has come back to haunt him now that he's older. He has developed cirrhosis (of the liver).

pasarlo a lo grande ■ pasarlo (en) grande to have a great time

pasarlo bien to get along well

pasarlo bomba to have a blast ➤ Lo pasamos bomba en la fiesta en la playa. We had a blast at the beach party.

pasarlo de muerte ■ pasarlo grande to have a great time

pasarlo (en) grande ■ pasárselo pipa to have a great time ➤ Lo pasamos en grande en Tío Molonio escuchando a Hakan tocar la guitarra y cantar. We had a great time at Tío Molonio listening to Hakan play the guitar and sing.

pasarlo mal not to have a good time ■ not to enjoy ■ to have a bad time ➤ Lo pasé mal en la fiesta. I didn't have a good time at the party. ■ I didn't enjoy the party. ➤ Lo pasó mal después de la operación. He had a bad time after his operation.

pasarlo muy bien to have a good time

pasarlo pipa ■ pasarlo en grande to have a great time ➤ Los niños lo pasaron pipa en el circo. The children had a great time at the circus.

pasarlo teta *(subido de tono)* ■ pasarlo de puta madre to have a great time

pasaron *x* años *x* years went by ■ *x* years passed ➤ Pasaron dos años. Two years went by. ■ Two years passed.

pasarse to outdo oneself ■ to surpass oneself ■ to run over ➤ ¡Te pasaste! You outdid yourself! ➤ ¡Ay, me pasé! Oops, I ran over!

pasarse a la izquierda *(politicamente)* to move to the left (politically) ■ to become a leftist

pasarse al campo contrario to change loyalties ■ to switch loyalties

pasarse al enemigo to go over to the enemy

pasarse de inteligente to try (unsuccessfully) to look intelligent

pasarse de la raya **1.** cruzar la raya to go too far ■ to cross the line **2.** *(sexualmente)* propasarse to go too far

pasarse de listo ■ pasarse de vivo to go too far ■ to trespass the limits

pasarse de rosca to strip the thread(s)

pasarse de vivo ■ pasarse de listo to go too far ■ to trespass the limits

pasarse días con ■ tirarse días con ■ estarse días con to go for days on

pasarse el desvío to miss the turn ■ to go too far ➤ Nos hemos pasado el desvío. We've gone too far. We've missed the turn.

pasarse el día despotricando ■ no hacer más que despotricar to be forever complaining

pasarse el día en la calle, como los perros ■ pasarse todo el día fuera ■ estar (todo el día) de parranda to stay out all day ■ not to go home at all

pasarse el día tocándose la barriga ■ *(subido de tono)* pasarse el día tocándose los huevos (a dos manos) to sit around doing nothing ■ to vegetate ■ *(subido de tono)* to sit on one's ass

pasarse el semáforo (en rojo) ■ saltarse el semáforo (en rojo) to crash the (red) light ■ to run the (red) light

pasarse la pelota to pass the buck

pasarse la pelota entre ellos to pass responsibility back and forth between them ■ to pass the ball back and forth between them ➤ Los gobiernos que tienen problemas con la inmigración ilegal se pasan la pelota entre ellos. The governments which have problems with illegal immigration pass responsibility back and forth between them.

pasarse la vida entera haciendo una cosa to spend one's whole life doing something ➤ Hay quien se pasa la vida entera... There are people who spend their whole lives...

pasarse las horas muertas to sit around (doing nothing) ■ to waste a lot of time ■ to waste inordinate amounts of time ■ to waste an inordinate amount of time ■ to while away time (doing nothing constructive) ➤ Se pasa las horas muertas mirando la tele. He sits around watching TV all day. ■ He wastes a lot of time watching TV. ■ He wastes inordinate amounts of time watching TV.

pasarse meses con ■ tirarse meses con ■ estarse meses con to go for months on ➤ Mark Twain dijo, "Puedo pasarme meses con un buen cumplido." ■ Puedo tirarme meses con un buen cumplido. ■ Puedo estarme meses con un buen cumplido. Mark Twain said, "I can go for months on a good compliment." ➤ Mark Twain dijo que podía pasarse meses con un buen cumplido. ■ Mark Twain dijo que podía tirarse meses con un buen cumplido. ■ Mark Twain dijo que podía estarse meses con un buen cumplido. Mark Twain said he could go for months on a good compliment.

pasarse o no llegar ■ pasar de un extremo a otro ■ ir de un extremo a otro to go from one extreme to the other

pasarse por el culo *(subido de tono)* not to give a shit ➤ Su opinión me la paso por el culo. I don't give a shit what he thinks. ■ I could give a shit what he thinks. ■ I couldn't give a shit what he thinks.

pasarse por el forro *(subido de tono)* ■ pasarse por el arco del triunfo ■ pasarse por el coño (de la tía Bernarda) *(alternativa benigna)* pasarse algo por debajo del sobaco not to give a (flying) fuck ■ *(alternativa benigna)* not to give a (flying) damn ➤ Su opinión me la paso por el forro. I don't give a (flying) fuck what he thinks. ➤ Su opinión me la paso por el arco del triunfo. I don't give a (flying) fuck what he thinks. ➤ Me paso lo que él dice por el arco del triunfo. ■ Me paso lo que él dice por el forro. I don't give a (flying) fuck what he says. ■ I don't give a (flying) damn what he says.

pasarse por la entrepierna *(subido de tono)* to get in someone's shorts

pasarse por la piedra a alguien *(subido de tono)* to lay someone ■ to shack up with someone ■ to have sex with someone ➤ Se la ha pasado por la piedra. He had sex with her. ■ He shacked up with her. ■ He laid her.

pasarse semanas con ■ tirarse semanas con ■ estarse semanas con to go for weeks on

pasarse sin algo to get along without something ➤ Me he pasado casi dos años sin fumar. I've gotten along for two years without smoking.

pasarse un pelín to go a little too far ■ to go a bit too far

pasarse una temporada **1.** to spend some time **2.** (for) a period of time to pass

pasarse yendo y viniendo ■ ir y venir to go back and forth ➤ Se pasa una hora yendo y viniendo de su habitación al baño. ■ Henry va y viene durante una hora de su habitación al baño. Henry goes back and forth from his room to the bathroom for an hour.

pasársela en blanco to be broke

pasársele la hora to run behind schedule ■ to be late

pasársele por la cabeza ■ pasársele por la imaginación to cross one's mind ➤ Jamás se me pasó por cabeza. It never crossed my mind.

pasársele por la imaginación ■ ocurrírsele to come up with an idea

pasárselo bomba ■ pasárselo pipa ■ pasárselo grande ■ divertirse mucho to have a blast ■ to have a great time ■ to have a lot of fun

pasárselo grande ■ pasárselo pipa ■ pasárselo bomba ■ divertirse mucho to have a blast ■ to have a great time ■ to have a lot of fun

pasárselo pipa ■ pasárselo bomba ■ pasárselo grande ■ divertirse mucho to have a lot of fun ■ to have a great time ➤ Los retoños se lo pasaron pipa en el circo. The kids had a lot of fun at the circus.

Pascua de la Resurrección ■ Pascua Florida Easter (Sunday) ➤ La Pascua de la Resurrección es el domingo siguiente a la primera luna llena después del equinoccio de primavera, fecha establecida como el veinte o veintiuno de marzo. Easter (Sunday) is the first Sunday after the first full moon after the vernal equinox, which always falls on the twentieth or twenty-first of March.

pase de pernocta: tener ~ *(militar)* to have an overnight pass ■ to have overnight leave ■ to have permission to spend the night off base

pase de (una) película ■ pase showing of a movie ➤ El próximo pase de película 7:15 p.m. Next showing 7:15 p.m.

pase lo que pase no matter what happens ■ come what may ■ whatever happens

pase usted con confianza come in and make yourself at home
Paseando a Miss Daisy *(título de película) Driving Miss Daisy*
pasear de arriba a abajo to pace up and down
pasearse en trineo to go sleigh riding ▪ to go sledding
pasearse por el parque to stroll through the park
paseo marítimo boardwalk
pasión por los deportes passion for sports
pasmado(-a) ante algo: quedarse ~ ▪ quedarse estupefacto(-a) ante algo to be astounded at something ▪ to be dumbfounded at something
pasmado(-a) de que...: quedarse ~ ▪ quedarse estupefacto(-a) de que... to be astounded that... ▪ to be dumbfounded that...
pasmado(-a) por algo: quedarse ~ ▪ quedarse estupefacto(-a) por algo to be astounded by something ▪ to be dumbfounded by something
¡**paso a la juventud!** ▪ ¡abran paso a la juventud! make way for the younger generation!
paso a paso ▪ paso por paso step by step
Paso de Calais Strait of Dover
paso de cebra *(Esp.)* ▪ paso de peatones pedestrian crossing ▪ crosswalk
paso de esas historias ▪ no me interesa todo eso I don't care about all that
paso de peatones ▪ *(Esp.)* paso de cebra pedestrian crossing ▪ crosswalk
paso de ti I don't want anything to do with you
paso de un tornado path of a tornado ➤ El tornado aniquiló cuanto encontraba a su paso. The tornado annihilated everything in its path. ▪ The tornado destroyed everything in its path.
paso del ecuador 1. crossing of the equator 2. *(Esp.)* completion of the third year of one's bachelor's degree studies and taking a trip to celebrate *(Nota: En España, la licenciatura dura cinco años, y la culminación del tercer curso es celebrado por los estudiantes por haber pasado el ecuador del curso. ▪ In Spain, the bachelor's degree takes five years, and completion of the third year is celebrated for students having passed the halfway mark.)*
paso del tiempo passage of time
paso en falso false step
paso hacia el camino correcto: dar un ~ to take a step in the right direction
ser un **paso hacia el camino correcto** to be a step in the right direction
paso inferior underpass
paso libre unobstructed passage
estar un **paso por delante** to be a step ahead
paso por delante: dar un ~ to go a step further ▪ to go one step further ▪ to take a step further
estar un **paso por detrás** to be a step behind
paso por detrás: dar un ~ ▪ dar un paso para atrás to take a step backwards ▪ to take a step back
paso por el camino correcto: dar un ~ ▪ ser un paso por el camino correcto to take a step in the right direction ▪ to be a step in the right direction
paso por paso ▪ paso a paso step by step
pasó un año a year went by ▪ a year passed
pasodoble *(baile)* double step ▪ two-step
pasos contados a alguien: tenerle los ~ ▪ contar los pasos a alguien ▪ estar contándole los pasos a alguien to follow someone's movements ▪ to monitor someone's movements
pasta gansa: costarle ~ *(Esp., coloquial)* ▪ costarle un ojo de la cara to cost one a fortune ▪ to cost one a pretty penny
pasta gansa: tener ~ *(Esp., coloquial)* ▪ tener dinero to have plenty of money ▪ to be well-heeled
pastilla de freno brake pad
el **pastizal de vacas** cow pasture
ser **pasto de la actualidad** grist for the media mill ▪ to be constantly in the news ▪ to be the subject of great public interest
ser **pasto de las llamas** to be enveloped in flames
ser **pasto de la(s) murmuración(es)** to be fodder for the tabloids ▪ to be grist for the tabloids ▪ to be the object of gossip ▪ to be the focus of gossip
pata coja: tener la ~ ▪ cojear ▪ *(coloquial)* tener la pata chula to limp ▪ to favor a leg
pata de la mesa table leg
pata de una araña leg of a spider ▪ spider leg ➤ Las arañas tienen ocho patas. Spiders have eight legs. ▪ A spider has eight legs.
pata chula: tener la ~ *(coloquial)* ▪ tener la pata coja ▪ cojear to limp ▪ to favor a leg
patas arriba: dejar algo ~ 1. dejar algo al revés to leave something upside down 2. dejar un sitio hecho una leonera ▪ estar un sitio hecho un desbarajuste to leave something (in) a mess ▪ to leave something a wreck
estar **patas arriba** 1. estar al revés ▪ estar dado la vuelta to be upside down 2. estar hecho una leonera ▪ estar hecho un desbarajuste to be a mess ▪ to be a wreck ➤ La casa está patas arriba. The house is a mess. ▪ The house is a wreck.
patas arriba: poner algo ~ 1. poner algo al revés ▪ darle la vuelta a algo to place something upside down ▪ to put something upside down ▪ to turn something over ▪ to turn something upside down 2. poner un sitio hecho una leonera ▪ poner un sitio hecho un desbarajuste to make a mess ▪ to make a wreck of the place ▪ to turn the place into a wreck
patas de gallo crow's-feet ▪ wrinkles around the eyes
ser una **patata** to be a lemon
patata caliente política ▪ asunto delicado political hot potato
patata caliente a alguien: pasarle la ~ to let someone else handle the hot potato ▪ to give someone else the hot potato
patatas bravas fried potatoes served with spicy brava sauce
patatas fritas *(Esp.)* potato chips
patatín-patatán and so on and so forth ▪ et cetera, et cetera
patatín-patatán: no me vengas con el ~ don't give me all that nonsense
patear el asfalto ▪ patear la calle to pound the pavement ▪ to beat the pavement *(Nota: En inglés se refiere más a buscar empleo pero puede también referirse a buscar alojamiento o caminar mucho por la ciudad [turistas, carteros]).*
patear la calle 1. patear el asfalto to pound the pavement ▪ to beat the pavement 2. patearse la calle to walk up and down the street (hunting for something) *(Nota: En inglés se refiere más a buscar empleo pero puede también referirse a buscar alojamiento o caminar mucho por la ciudad [turistas, carteros]).*
patearse el dinero to blow all one's money
patearse la ciudad ▪ recorrer la ciudad a pie to explore the city on foot ▪ to go around the city on foot ▪ *(coloquial)* to do the city on foot
la **patente en trámite** patent pending
ser **patente que...** ▪ ser obvio que... to be obvious that... ▪ *(literario)* to be patently obvious that...
pátina del tiempo ▪ pátina que deja el tiempo greening of copper because of gradual oxidation
el **patinaje artístico** figure skating
el **patinaje sobre el hielo** ice skating
patinar en seco to just spin one's wheels ➤ Estoy patinando en seco. I'm just spinning my wheels.
patinar sobre hielo to ice skate
patinarle el coco ▪ estar chiflado(-a) to be cracked ➤ Le patina el coco. He's cracked.
patinarle las meninges ▪ estar chiflado(-a) to be cracked
patio de las malvas *(literario)* ▪ cementerio cemetery
ser el **patito feo** to be the ugly duckling
patria celestial heavenly home
patria chica ▪ ciudad natal hometown
patria potestad ▪ custodia legal (legal) custody ▪ (legal) guardianship
patrocinar un proyecto de ley to sponsor a bill
el **patrón de comportamiento** ▪ modelo de comportamiento behavior pattern ▪ pattern of behavior ➤ *(noticia)* Varios expertos creen que el patrón de comportamiento en los cinco crímenes permite anticipar que el asesino volverá a actuar. Several experts believe that the behavior pattern (exhibited) in the five crimes indicates that the killer will act again. ▪ Several experts believe that the pattern of behavior (exhibited) in the five crimes indicates that the killer will act again.
patrón matemático ▪ modelo matemático mathematical model

pauta: detectar una ~ ▪ detectar un patrón ▪ detectar un esquema to discern a pattern ▪ to detect a pattern ➤ ¿Detectas alguna pauta que indique en qué direccion cambiará España en los próximos diez años? Do you detect any patterns that would enable you to predict how Spain will change in the next ten years?

pauta ascendente growing trend

pauta para ▪ modelo para model for ➤ *(titular)* Una pauta europea para la inmigración A European model for immigration

la **pauta empieza a verse** ▪ un patrón empieza a verse ▪ la pauta se empieza a ver ▪ la pauta se nota the pattern is beginning to emerge ▪ the pattern is emerging

pautas del estudio research model ▪ research guidelines ➤ Tenemos que ser más específicos en la clasificación de aves si queremos seguir las pautas del estudio. We have to be more specific in the classification of the birds in order to follow the guidelines of the research. ▪ We have to be more specific in the classification of the birds in order to follow the research model.

pava del cigarro ▪ pava del cigarrillo ▪ pava del pitillo ▪ colilla cigarette butt

pavimentar una calle to pave a street

¡**paz!** peace!

paz duradera lasting peace

la **paz en la tierra a los hombres de buena voluntad** peace on earth, good will toward men

la **paz interior** inner peace

peana de una copa base of a wine glass

el **pecado lleva a la penitencia** sin brings you to penitence ▪ sin brings its own penitence

¡**pecador(a) de mí!** woe is me!

pecar de ignorancia ▪ pecar por ignorancia to sin from ignorance ▪ to sin out of ignorance

pecar por ignorancia ▪ pecar de ignorancia to sin from ignorance ▪ to sin out of ignorance

ser **peccata minuta** to be a lesser sin

pechar con las consecuencias to face (up to) the consequences

pecho caído drooping bosoms

a pecho descubierto *(hombre o mujer)* boldly

pecho desnudo *(hombre o mujer)* bare chest ▪ *(mujer)* bare breast

ser un **pecho lobo** to have a hairy chest

extraño sentido de humor: tener un ~ to have a weird sense of humor

ser un **pedazo de alcornoque** ▪ ser un pedazo de animal to be dumb as a post

pedazo de fiesta *(Esp., coloquial)* great party

ser un **pedazo de pan** 1. piece of bread 2. ser macanudo to be a really great person ▪ to be a peach

pedazo por pedazo piece by piece ➤ El templo de Debot se mandó de Egipto a Madrid pedazo por pedazo. The Temple of Debot was sent from Egypt to Madrid piece by piece.

estar **pendiente de un cabello** ▪ estar pendiente de un hilo ▪ *(Esp.)* estar cogido con pinzas to be hanging by a thread

estar **pendiente de un hilo** ▪ estar pendiente de un cabello ▪ *(Esp.)* estar cogido con pinzas to be hanging by a thread

pedido fijo standing order

pedir a voces to plead ▪ to beg

pedir algo a gritos 1. pedirlo a gritos to be asking for trouble ▪ to be asking for it 2. necesitar algo de forma urgente to cry out for something 3. estar buscándolo to beg for something

pedir comunicación con alguien ▪ pedir hablar con alguien to ask to speak to someone ▪ to ask to speak with someone

pedir consentimiento para hacer algo ▪ pedir permiso para hacer algo to ask (for) permission to do something

pedir consulta to request an appointment ▪ to call for an appointment

pedir cosas prestadas y no devolverlas to borrow things and not return them ▪ to borrow things without returning them ➤ Siempre pedía cosas prestadas y nunca las devolvía. He was always borrowing things and never returning them. ▪ He was always borrowing things and not returning them. ▪ He was always borrowing things without returning them.

pedir cuentas to ask for an explanation

pedir hablar con alguien ▪ pedir comunicación con alguien to ask to speak to someone ▪ to ask to speak with someone

pedir dinero prestado a alguien to ask to borrow money from someone ▪ to ask someone to lend you money

pedir disculpas a alguien por to apologize to someone for

pedir en justicia to ask by rights ▪ to ask in all fairness

pedir encarecidamente to request earnestly

pedir guerra to ask for trouble

pedir hora ▪ preguntar por la hora to ask the time

pedir justicia to call for justice

pedir la luna ▪ pedir el cielo y las estrellas to ask for the moon

pedir la mano de una mujer to ask for a woman's hand in marriage

pedir la medicina con la receta to have a prescription filled ▪ to get a prescription filled

pedir la palabra to ask for the floor

pedir la vez ▪ pedir el turno to ask who's last in line ▪ to ask whose turn it is

pedir leche a las cabrillas ▪ pedir peras al olmo to ask the impossible

pedir limosna to beg ▪ to panhandle

pedir peras al olmo ▪ pedir leche a las cabrillas to ask the impossible

pedir permiso para hacer algo ▪ pedir consentimiento para hacer algo to ask (for) permission to do something

pedir prestado dinero a alguien to borrow money from someone

pedir tregua to call for a truce

pedir un deseo ▪ formular un deseo ▪ pensar en un deseo to make a wish ▪ to think of a wish ➤ *(a un niño frente a su pastel de cumpleaños)* ¡Pide un deseo! Make a wish!

pedir un millón por to ask a fortune for ▪ to ask a ridiculous price for

pedir un préstamo 1. *(banco)* to apply for a loan 2. *(amigo)* to ask to borrow money from someone ▪ to ask for a loan

pedirle a alguien que haga algo 1. to ask someone to do something 2. to be asked to do something *(Nota: El inglés frecuentemente utiliza una construcción pasiva.)* ➤ Le pedí (a ella) que me ayudara con la fiesta. I asked her to help me with the party. ➤ Le pidieron que hablara ante los estudiantes de periodismo. They asked him to speak to the journalism students. ▪ He was asked to speak to the journalism students.

pedirle perdón a alguien por algo to ask someone's forgiveness for something ▪ to ask someone to forgive you for something

pedirlo a gritos *(como una amenaza)* to be asking for it ➤ Lo estás pidiendo a gritos. ▪ Estás pidiéndolo a gritos. You're asking for it!

pegarse a la silla ▪ pegarse al asiento to overstay ▪ to stay too long

estar **pegado(-a) a la tele** to be glued to the TV

estar **pegado(-a) a las faldas de la madre** ▪ estar enmadrado(-a) to be tied to one's mother's apron strings

estar **pegado(-a) a las sábanas** to be too tired to get up ▪ to oversleep ▪ to be glued to the sheets

pegamento en barra glue stick

pegar algo a algo ▪ adosar algo a algo ▪ adjuntar algo a algo to stick something to something ▪ to stick something onto something

pegar brincos de alegría ▪ dar brincos de alegría to jump for joy ▪ to leap for joy

pegar en su sitio ▪ estar en su ambiente ▪ estar en su elemento to fit right in ▪ to be in one's element ➤ Pegarías allí. ▪ Estarías en tu ambiente. ▪ Estarías en tu elemento. You'd fit right in. ➤ Pegarás allí. ▪ Pegarás con la gente. ▪ Estarás en tu ambiente. You'll fit right in.

pegar fuego a algo ▪ prender fuego a algo ▪ incendiar algo to set fire to something ▪ to set something on fire

pegar fuerte a alguien to hit someone hard

pegar la frente a la ventana to press one's face against the window

pegar la hebra to have a conversation

pegar la oreja 1. *(puerta)* to listen through the door 2. *(pared)* to listen through the wall

pegar ojo to doze off ➤ Para no pegar ojo... To keep from dozing off...
pegar saltos to jump up and down
pegar un bajón ■ dar un bajón ■ sufrir on bajón ■ tener un bajón to fall into a depression ■ *(coloquial)* to go down into the dumps ■ to be down in the dumps
pegar un botón *(coloquial)* ■ coser un botón to sew on a button ➤ ¿Me pegarías el bóton del cuello (de la camisa)? Would you sew on this collar button for me?
pegar un brinco ■ dar un brinco to give a start
pegar un estirón to shoot up like a weed ■ to grow like a weed ■ to have a growth spurt
pegar un patinazo ■ derrapar 1. *(vehículo)* to skid ■ to go into a skid 2. *(figurativo)* meter la pata to slip up ■ to put one's foot in it
pegar un salto to jump (from being startled) ➤ El trueno asustó al gato y pegó un salto que casi se muere. The thunder clap spooked the cat, and he practically jumped out of his skin.
pegar un tiro a quemarropa ■ disparar a quemarropa to shoot at point-blank range ■ to fire (a shot) at point-blank range
pegarle a alguien un puñetazo en la nariz to punch someone in the nose ■ to give someone a punch in the nose
pegarle cuatro tiros to shoot someone repeatedly
pegarle un tiro a alguien to shoot someone
pegarle una cornada al torero ■ meterle una cornada al torero to gore the bullfighter ➤ El quinto toro le pegó al torero una cornada en la cara posterior del muslo derecho. The fifth bull gored the bullfighter in the back (side) of the right thigh.
pegarle una torta a alguien to slap someone in the face
pegarse (a alguien) to tag along (with someone) ➤ ¿Os importa si me pego a vosotros? Can I tag along (with you)?
pegarse a la butaca to be glued to one's seat ■ to be captivated by a movie
pegarse al asiento ■ pegarse a la silla to overstay ■ to stay too long
pegarse al claxon ■ pegarse a la bocina ■ quedarse pegado al claxon ■ pitar como (un) loco to ride the horn ■ to lean on the horn ■ to honk (the horn) like crazy
pegarse como una lapa a alguien to latch onto someone
pegarse el lote (con alguien) ■ darse el lote (con alguien) to make out with someone ■ to neck
pegarse fuego ■ prenderse fuego to catch on fire ■ to catch fire
pegarse la gran vida to live the good life ■ to live it up
pegarse la vida padre to live the good life ■ to live it up
pegarse un buen chasco ■ llevarse un buen chasco to be really disappointed ■ to be extremely disappointed ■ to be terribly disappointed ■ to feel really let down ■ to be really let down
pegarse un golpe contra algo ■ pegarse un golpe con algo to bump into something
pegarse un revolcón to have a roll in the hay
pegarse un tiro to shoot oneself
pegarse un tute ■ darse un tute to work hard ■ to bust one's tail
pegarse una enjuagada (en la cara) to splash water (in one's face) ➤ Me enchilé un ojo y me tuve que pegar una enjuagada hasta que se me pasó. I got jalapeño juice in my eye and I had to splash water in my face until it went away.
pegarse una leche ■ pegarse una torta ■ pegarse un tortazo to bump into something really hard
pegársela a alguien 1. to be unfaithful to someone ■ to cheat on someone 2. to deceive someone ■ to double-cross someone ➤ Se la pega a su esposa con la secretaria. He's cheating on his wife with his secretary.
pegársela con queso ■ dársela con queso to cheat someone
pegársele a alguien algo to rub off on someone ■ to pick up (a trait) ➤ La habitación de tu hermano está limpia y ordenada, y la tuya da asco. Se te podría pegar algo de él. Your brother's room is clean and neat, and yours is a disaster. It wouldn't hurt if a little of that could rub off on you. ➤ Se me ha pegado un acento peninsular. I've picked up a peninsular accent.
pegársele a uno las sábanas ■ quedarse dormido to oversleep
pegársele como una lapa a alguien to cling to someone like a leech ■ to latch on to someone
pegársele el sol ■ quemarse del sol ■ quemarse ■ *(coloquial)* achicharrarse to get sunburned
pegársele las sábanas a alguien not to be able to get out of bed ■ not to be able to get up ➤ Llego tarde porque se me han pegado las sábanas. I'm late because I couldn't get out of bed. ■ I'm late because I couldn't get up.
peina ese naipe *(Valle-Inclán)* ■ mezcla bien las cartas ■ baraja bien shuffle those cards good!
peinar canas to get old ■ to be old
peinar el campo ■ batir el campo ■ mirar el campo palmo a palmo to comb the area
pelar el cobre *(coloquial)* ■ enseñar el cobre ■ mostrar el verdadero yo to show one's true self ■ to show one's true colors
pelar la cáscara de un huevo to peel an egg
pelar la pava to whisper sweet nothings (to each other) ■ to say sweet nothings (to each other)
pelar las gambas to peel the shrimp ■ to shell the shrimp ■ to peel the shells off the shrimp
pelarse de frío to be freezing cold
pelarse los cojones de frío *(subido de tono)* to freeze one's balls off
pelear a muerte to fight like cats and dogs
pelear con uñas y dientes ■ luchar con uñas y dientes to fight tooth and nail
pelear hasta el final ■ luchar hasta el final to fight to the finish
película cargada de acción action-packed film ■ action-packed movie
(película de) cortometraje short film
película de indios y vaqueros ■ película de vaqueros Western (movie)
película de intriga ■ película de suspenso thriller
película de largometraje ■ (un) largometraje feature-length film
película de vaqueros ■ película de indios y vaqueros Western (movie) ➤ ¿Te gustan las películas de vaqueros? Do you like Westerns?
película más taquillera de la historia biggest box-office hit in history
película melodramática ■ melodrama melodramatic film
película muy fuerte very violent movie ■ very shocking movie ■ very sexually explicit movie
película que ponen movie that's on ■ movie that's showing
película subida (de tono) 1. *(con cierta calidad artística)* risqué movie 2. *(sin calidad artística)* blue movie ■ dirty movie
película taquillera box office hit ■ hit at the box office
película terminó... movie was over... ■ movie got out... ■ movie ended... ➤ La película terminó a las diez. The movie was over at ten o'clock. ■ The movie got out at ten o'clock. ■ The movie ended at ten o'clock.
película verde blue movie ■ dirty movie
¡pelillos a la mar! let's just let it go ■ let's bury the hatchet
pelillos a la mar: echar ~ to put it to rest ■ to bury the hatchet
un **pelín de nieve** *(Esp.)* ■ un poquito de nieve ■ algo de nieve a trace of snow
pelo a pelo: intercambiar ~ ■ intercambiar pelo por pelo ■ trocar pelo a pelo ■ trocar pelo por pelo to barter for something of equal value ■ to trade something for something of equal value
pelo a pelo: comparar ~ to compare item by item ■ to compare item for item
pelo a pelo: ir ~ 1. to be neck and neck ➤ Los dos caballos favoritos a ganar van pelo a pelo. The two favored horses are neck and neck.
pelo en la sopa fly in the ointment
pelo entrecano graying hair ■ salt and pepper hair
pelo pincho ■ pelo a cepillo stiff hair ■ brushlike hair
pelo por pelo: intercambiar ~ ■ intercambiar pelo a pelo to barter (in minute calculation) ■ to pay in kind (very exactly)
pelo recogido: llevar el ~ to wear one's hair (pulled back) in a bun
pelos en la lengua: no tener ~ not to mince words

pelos y señales: explicar algo con ~ to explain something in minute detail ■ to explain something in great detail ■ to give a blow-by-blow account of something

la **pelota está en tu tejado** the ball is in your court ■ the ball's in your court

el **pelotón de fósiles** fossil squad ■ old folks coterie

peluquería para hombres ■ barbería barber shop

peluquería para mujeres beauty parlor ■ hair dresser's (shop)

pena capital ■ pena de muerte capital punishment ■ death penalty

pena de cárcel: recibir una to receive a jail sentence

pena de cárcel: sentenciar a alguien a to sentence someone to jail

pena de muerte ■ pena capital death penalty ■ capital punishment

pena de prisión prison sentence

ser **pena de talón** ■ ser ojo por ojo y diente por diente to be eye for an eye (and a tooth for a tooth)

pena máxima maximum sentence

pena que me da tener que... how much it hurts (me) to have to... ■ how hard it is (for me) to have to... ➤ No sabes tú la pena que me da tener que castigarte. You don't know how much it hurts me to have to punish you.

pender de un hilo ■ colgar de un hilo ■ estar sujeto con pinzas ■ *(Esp.)* estar cogido con pinzas to hang by a thread ➤ En ese país la dictadura pende de un hilo. In that country the dictatorship is hanging by a thread.

pender sobre ■ colgarse sobre to hang over ■ to hang above ➤ En Navidad el muérdago pende sobre la puerta. At Christmas the mistletoe hangs over the doorway.

estar **pendiente de algo** to keep an eye on something ■ to watch something ➤ Estáte pendiente de la sopa para que no se salga. Watch the soup so (that) it won't boil over. ■ Keep an eye on the soup so (that) it won't boil over. ➤ Estoy pendiente de la radio para ver quiénes son los diez superventas. I'm keeping an ear to the radio to find out who made the top ten.

estar **pendiente de alguien** ■ estar a la espera de saber de alguien **1.** estar a la espera de alguien to be waiting to hear from someone ■ to await word from someone ■ to wait for word from someone **2.** estar mirando para ver cuándo llega alguien to watch out for someone ■ to keep an eye out for someone **3.** parar la oreja to listen (out) for someone **4.** vigilar a alguien to keep an eye on someone ■ to watch someone **5.** prestar muchísima atención a alguien to pay a lot of attention to someone ■ to cater to someone's every whim ■ to be ga-ga over someone ➤ Estoy pendiente de otra persona. I'm awaiting word from someone. ■ I'm waiting to hear from someone. ■ I'm waiting for word from someone. ➤ No puedo salir porque estoy pendiente del repartidor. I can't leave because I'm waiting on the delivery man. ➤ Estáte pendiente del bebé mientras bajo a hacer la compra. Watch the baby while I go to the grocery store. ■ Keep an eye on the baby while I go to the grocery store.

estar **pendiente de una situación** to monitor a situation (closely) ■ to keep a close watch on a situation ➤ Los especuladores de divisas están muy pendientes de las fluctuaciones del dólar. Currency traders closely monitor the fluctuations in the dollar. ■ Currency traders keep a close watch on the fluctuations in the dollar.

estar **pendiente de los labios de alguien** ■ estar colgado de los labios de alguien to hang on every word someone says

estar **pendiente de que...** to be monitoring to be sure that... ■ to be watching to be sure that... ■ to be watching to make sure that... ➤ Hay muchos técnicos pendientes de que todo vaya bien. There are a lot of technicians watching to make sure that everything goes well.

estar **pendiente de que alguien haga algo** to be waiting for someone to do something ➤ Estoy pendiente de que él me llame. I'm waiting for him to call me.

estar **pendiente de un hilo** ■ estar colgado de un hilo to be hanging by a thread

la **pendiente de un tejado** ■ inclinación de un tejado pitch of a roof

pendiente pronunciada steep slope

pendón verbenero *(peyorativo, subido de tono)* ■ pendón desorejado ■ chiruza slut ■ street walker

penetrar en to manage to enter (by getting past a checkpoint) ■ to manage to get into ➤ *(noticia)* Un individuo armado con un cuchillo penetró ayer en una guardería en Seul y acuchilló a diez niños cuando comían. An individual armed with a knife managed to enter a kindergarten in Seoul and stabbed ten children as they were eating lunch.

penetrar en las líneas enemigas to penetrate enemy lines

Península Ibérica Iberian Peninsula

penosa situación económica serious economic situation ■ dire economic straits

estar **pensado para...** to be intended for...

estar **pensando en algo** to be thinking about something ➤ ¿Estás pensando en comprar una casa? Are you thinking about buying a house?

pensando en eso ■ con esto en mente with that in mind

estar **pensando en las musarañas** ■ estar distraído ■ estar despistado to be off in the ozone ■ to be daydreaming

pensándolo bien on second thought

pensar algo detenidamente to think something through ■ to think about something carefully

pensar con el culo *(subido de tono)* not to have shit for sense ■ *(alternativa benigna)* not to be quite with it ➤ Ese tío piensa con el culo. That guy doesn't have shit for sense. ■ That's guy's not quite with it.

pensar con los pies not to have a grain of sense ➤ Ese tío piensa con los pies. That guy doesn't have a grain of sense.

pensar efectivamente en to be actually thinking about ➤ El joven pensaba efectivamente en su novia. The youth was actually thinking about his girlfriend.

pensar en cómo... to think about how...

pensar en las musarañas ■ estar en Babia to be spaced out ■ to be off in the ozone

pensar en lo mucho que... to think about how much...

pensar en un deseo ■ pedir un deseo ■ formular un deseo to think of a wish ■ to make a wish

pensar en voz alta to think out loud

pensar lo mejor de algo to look on the bright side ➤ Hay que pensar lo mejor. You have to look on the bright side.

pensar lo mejor de alguien 1. ver lo bueno de alguien to see someone's good qualities **2.** no juzgar precipitadamente to give someone the benefit of the doubt

pensar que... 1. to think that... **2.** tener en cuenta que... to bear in mind that... ■ to remember that... ■ to keep in mind that... ➤ *(Selecciones de* Reader's Digest*)* Piensa que para un niño es muy difícil aceptar un "no" tajante, así que si le niegas algo, razona tu negativa. Bear in mind that for a child it is very difficult to accept a flat "no," so if you refuse him something, explain your reasons. ■ Remember that for a child it is very difficult to accept a flat "no," so if you refuse him something, explain your reasons.

pensar que algo es gracioso ■ pensar que algo tiene gracia to think something is funny

pensar un deseo ■ pedir un deseo pero no decirlo to make a wish to oneself ■ to make a wish but not say it out loud ■ to make a silent wish ➤ ¡Piensa un deseo! ■ ¡Pide un deseo pero no lo digas! Make a wish to yourself! ■ Make a wish, but don't say it out loud. ■ Make a silent wish.

pensarlo bien 1. pensarlo detalladamente to think it over **2.** tener remordimiento to have second thoughts

pensarlo dos veces (antes de...) to think twice (before...)

pensarlo mejor ■ pensarlo bien ■ pensarlo detalladamente to think it over ➤ Al principio quería matricularme en matemáticas, pero luego lo pensé mejor y me matriculé en español. At first I wanted to major in mathematics, but then I thought better of it and majored in Spanish.

pensarlo un poco to think about it for a moment

pensárselo (bien) ■ pensarlo bien to think of everything ■ to think something out well ➤ Y, se las pensó bien. He thought of everything.

pensé para mí mismo I thought to myself

pensé que seguramente... I thought for sure... ➤ Pensé que seguramente no me iba a gustar. I 7thought for sure I wasn't going to like it.
pensión completa ▪ cuarto y comida room and board
penúltimo puesto: ocupar el ~ to occupy (the) next-to-last place ▪ to hold (the) next-to-last place ➤ *(editorial)* Irak ocupa el penúltimo puesto del índice de desarrollo que elabora Naciones Unidas. Iraq occupies next-to-last place in the United Nations development index.
peña taurina *(Esp.)* bullfighting club
estar **peor del catarro** (for) one's cold to be worse ➤ Hoy estoy peor del catarro. My cold is worse today.
ser **peor el remedio que la enfermedad** (for) the cure to be worse than the disease ➤ Es peor el remedio que la enfermedad. The cure is worse than the disease.
ser **peor lo roto que lo descosido** ▪ el remedio es peor que la enfermedad the cure is worse than the disease
ser **peor que peor** to be even worse ➤ Tu excusa para no haber hecho los deberes es que te has ido a jugar. ¡(Es) peor que peor! Your excuse for not having done your homework is that you went out to play?! That's even worse!
ser la **pequeña cenicienta** to be little Cinderella ▪ *(coloquial)* to take a lot of crap
pequeña economía doméstica household budget
pequeña minoría tiny minority
ser una **pequeña negociación** to be a minor deal ▪ to be an incidental agreement ➤ Fue una pequeña negociación. It was a minor deal. ▪ It was an incidental agreement.
per cápita ▪ por cabeza per capita
per se ▪ por sí mismo per se
los **percances del oficio** *(literario)* ▪ (los) gajes del oficio occupational hazard ▪ all in a day's work
percatarse de (que...) ▪ darse cuenta de (que...) ▪ culto apercibirse de (que...) to realize ▪ to notice ➤ *(noticia)* Al llegar al hotel se percataron de que se habían olvidado de recoger su equipaje en el aeropuerto. When they arrived at the hotel, they realized they had left their luggage at the airport. ➤ Me percaté de que un cliente había dejado su teléfono celular sobre el mostrador. I noticed that a customer had left his cell phone on the counter.
perchas (de ropa) coat hangers
percibir peligro to sense danger
percibir un atisbo de impaciencia en su voz to detect a note of impatience in someone's voice
percibir un atisbo de sarcasmo en su voz to detect a note of sarcasm in someone's voice
perdedor de lujo person valiant in defeat ▪ good loser
perder aceite ▪ perder el aceite to be obviously gay ▪ to betray one's homosexuality ➤ Está perdiendo aceite. He's (obviously) gay.
perder altitud ▪ perder altura to lose altitude ➤ El avión iba perdiendo altitud. The airplane was losing altitude.
perder altura ▪ perder altitud to lose altitude ➤ El avión iba perdiendo altura. The airplane was losing altitude.
perder contacto con la realidad to lose touch with reality
perder el control de algo to lose control of something ➤ *(L.am.)* El conductor perdió el control del carro en el hielo. ▪ *(Esp.)* El conductor perdió el control del coche en el hielo. The driver lost control of the car on the ice. ➤ Perdió el control del brazo derecho después del derrame cerebral. He lost control of his right arm after his stroke.
perder de vista a alguien to lose sight of someone ➤ Lo he perdido de vista. ▪ *(Esp., leísmo)* Le he perdido de vista. I've lost sight of him. ➤ La he perdido de vista. I've lost sight of her.
perder de vista algo to lose sight of something ➤ Desde el nivel del agua, perdí la visión de la costa. ▪ Desde el nivel del agua, perdí de vista la costa. At the water level, I lost sight of the coast. ➤ No pierdas de vista tus objetivos. Don't lose sight of your goal. ➤ Desde el nivel del mar, el náufrago perdió la visión de la costa. From sea level, the shipwrecked sailor lost sight of the coast.
perder (el) aceite to be obviously gay ▪ to be betray one's homosexuality ➤ Está perdiendo el aceite. He's obviously gay.
perder el apetito to lose one's appetite ➤ Perdí el apetito. I lost my appetite.
perder el aplomo ▪ perder la calma to lose one's calm ▪ to lose one's serenity
perder el apoyo popular to lose popular support
perder el calor popular to lose popular esteem ▪ to lose popularity ➤ *(titular)* El primer ministro pierde el calor popular. The prime minister loses popular esteem. ▪ The prime minister loses popularity.
perder el compás 1. *(una vez)* to miss the beat 2. *(de forma continuada)* to lose the beat
perder el conocimiento ▪ perder el sentido ▪ desmayarse to lose consciousness
perder el contacto por radio con to lose radio contact with
perder el control 1. *(conductor)* to lose control 2. *(vehículo)* to go out of control 3. perder los papeles ▪ perder los estribos ▪ perder la compostura to lose control to lose one's temper ➤ El conductor perdió el control del coche y se empotró contra una farola. The driver lost control of the car and crashed into a light post. ➤ *(noticia)* El coche perdió el control y se empotró contra una farola a la altura del número doce. The car went out of control and crashed into a light post by number twelve. ➤ Mi profesora de matemáticas tenía poca paciencia con sus alumnos; perdía el control por menos de un pimiento. My mathematics teacher was impatient with her students. She would lose control at the drop of a hat.
perder el control del poder to lose one's grip on power ▪ to lose one's hold on power
perder el control que uno tiene sobre alguien to lose control over someone ➤ Mi madre perdió el control que tenía sobre mí cuando terminé la secundaria. My mother lost control of me when I finished high school.
perder el equilibrio to lose one's balance
perder el favor de alguien to fall out of favor with someone ▪ to lose favor with someone
perder el hilo (de las ideas) ▪ perder el hilo (de los pensamientos) ▪ írsele de la cabeza ▪ írsele ▪ írsele el santo al cielo to lose one's train of thought ▪ to forget what one was saying
perder el hilo (de los pensamientos) ▪ perder el hilo (de las ideas) ▪ írsele de la cabeza ▪ írsele ▪ írsele el santo al cielo to lose one's train of thought ➤ Perdí el hilo de mis pensamientos. I lost my train of thought.
perder el juicio to lose one's senses ▪ to lose one's common sense ▪ to lose one's reason ▪ to lose one's sanity
perder el norte 1. perder la orientación to lose one's bearings ▪ to lose one's sense of direction 2. no saber qué hacer con la vida de uno mismo to lose one's direction (in life) ▪ to lose one's way 3. perder el sentido común to lose one's marbles
perder el paso to get out of step
perder el rastro de alguien to lose someone's trail
perder el rumbo de uno mismo ▪ perder el norte ▪ no saber qué hacer con la vida de uno mismo to lose one's way ▪ to lose one's direction (in life)
perder el sentido ▪ perder el conocimiento ▪ desmayarse to lose consciousness ▪ to pass out ▪ to faint
perder el sentido común ▪ perder el norte to lose one's marbles ▪ to have lost one's senses
perder el seso ▪ perder la cabeza to lose one's head
perder el sitio en la cola to lose one's place in line
perder el sueño por algo ▪ quitarle el sueño to lose sleep over something ➤ Yo no perdería el sueño por eso si fuera tú. ▪ Yo no dejaría que eso me quitara el sueño. I wouldn't lose any sleep over it if I were you.
perder el tiempo ▪ malgastar el tiempo ▪ desaprovechar el tiempo ▪ desperdiciar el tiempo ▪ despilfarrar el tiempo to waste time
perder el tiempo de alguien ▪ malgastar el tiempo de alguien ▪ desaprovechar el tiempo de alguien ▪ desperdiciar el tiempo de alguien ▪ despilfarrar el tiempo de alguien to waste someone's time
perder el trabajo to lose one's job
perder el tren to miss the train
perder el valor 1. depreciarse to lose its value ▪ to lose its worth 2. perder el arrojo to lose one's nerve
perder estrepitosamente to lose overwhelmingly ▪ to be defeated overwhelmingly ▪ to be beaten overwhelmingly ➤ El presidente se aceró a Miami para echar una mano al candidato,

pero al final no le sirvió de nada porque perdió estrepitosamente. The president went to Miami to lend the candidate a hand, but in the end it didn't do any good because he lost overwhelmingly. ▪ The president went to Miami to lend the candidate a hand, but in the end it didn't do any good because he was defeated overwhelmingly. ▪ The president went to Miami to lend the candidate a hand, but in the end it didn't do any good because he was beaten overwhelmingly.

perder frente a to lose to

perder hasta el culo *(subido de tono, se refiere al dinero)* to lose one's ass ▪ *(alternativa benigna)* to lose one's shirt

perder hasta la camisa to lose one's shirt ▪ to lose everything

perder hasta lo que no tiene to lose everything

perder la autoridad sobre los movimientos de cuerpo to lose control over one's bodily movements

perder la bola ▪ perder la chaveta ▪ perder la olla to lose one's head

perder la brújula to lose one's bearings ▪ to lose one's touch

perder la cabeza ▪ perder la chola to lose one's head ▪ to lose one's cool

perder la calma to lose one's cool

perder la chaveta ▪ perder la olla ▪ perder la bola ▪ volverse loco to lose one's marbles

perder la compostura to lose one's composure

perder la cordura ▪ enloquecerse to lose one's sanity ▪ to go mad ▪ *(coloquial)* to go crazy

perder la cuenta (de) to lose count (of)

perder la dirección de alguien to lose someone's address

perder la honra to lose one's honor

perder la línea to lose one's figure

perder la noción del tiempo to lose track of the time

perder la oportunidad de hacer algo to miss the chance to do something ▪ to miss the opportunity to do something ▪ to lose the chance to do something ▪ to lose the opportunity to do something

perder la paciencia to lose (one's) patience

perder la pista de alguien ▪ perder el rastro de alguien to lose the trail of someone ▪ to lose track of someone ➤ *(titular)* Pentágono pierde la pista de Bin Laden. The Pentagon loses Bin Laden's trail. ▪ The Pentagon loses the trail of Bin Laden. ▪ The Pentagon loses track of Bin Laden.

perder la razón to lose one's sanity ▪ to lose one's reason

perder la tierra to be swept off one's feet

perder la vergüenza to lose one's shyness

perder la vida to lose one's life

perder la virginidad to lose one's virginity

perder la visión ▪ perder la vista ▪ quedarse ciego to go blind ▪ to be blinded ➤ Al caerse de la bici y golpearse la cabeza, el niño perdió la visión temporalmente. The child was blinded temporarily when he fell from his bicycle and hit his head.

perder la visión de un ojo to lose sight in an eye ▪ to lose sight in one eye

perder la vista ▪ quedarse ciego ▪ perder la visión to lose one's sight ▪ to go blind ▪ to lose one's eyesight

perder las ataduras morales to lose one's moral grounding ▪ to lose one's moorings

perder las esperanzas de ▪ renunciar a la esperanza de to give up hope of ▪ to lose hope of

perder los estribos ▪ perder la compostura ▪ perder los nervios ▪ perder los papeles ▪ ponerse como una fiera to blow one's top ▪ to go ballistic ▪ to come unglued ▪ to have a purple fit ▪ to lose one's cool ▪ to lose one's temper ➤ Perdí los estribos y dije un montón de cosas de las que me arrepiento. I went ballistic and said a bunch of things I regret. ▪ I blew my top and said a bunch of things I regret. ▪ I lost my temper and said a bunch of things I regret. ▪ I lost my cool and said a bunch of things I regret.

perder los nervios ▪ perder los estribos ▪ perder la compostura ▪ perder los papeles ▪ enfadarse ▪ enojarse ▪ cabrearse to get angry ▪ to go ballistic ▪ to blow one's top ▪ to lose one's temper ▪ to lose one's cool

perder los papeles ▪ perder los nervios ▪ perder los estribos ▪ perder la compostura to go ballistic ▪ to blow one's top ▪ to lose one's temper ▪ to lose one's cool ▪ to get all bent out of shape

perder pie to lose one's footing

perder por goleada to lose by a huge margin ▪ to suffer an overwhelming defeat ▪ to get thrashed

perder por *x* puntos ▪ perder por *x* puntos to lose by *x* points

perder puntos to lose points

perder puntos ante alguien to lose someone's esteem ▪ to lose someone's regard ▪ to suffer damage to one's reputation ➤ El director de cine perdió puntos ante su público cuando hizo comentarios anti-semíticos. The movie director suffered damage to his reputation when he made anti-semitic remarks.

perder su turno to lose one's turn

perder sueño to lose sleep ➤ Se pierde una noche de sueño volando de Estados Unidos a España. You lose a night's sleep flying from the United States to Spain.

perder terreno to lose ground

perder toda pista de alguien to completely lose track of someone ▪ to lose track of someone completely

perder un tornillo to be a little (bit) wacky ➤ Ha perdido un tornillo. He's a little (bit) wacky.

perder uno su identidad cultural to lose one's cultural identity

perder velocidad de vuelo *(aeronáutica)* to stall ➤ La alarma de velocidad insuficiente suena justo antes de que el avión pierda velocidad de vuelo. The stall warning sounds just before the airplane stalls.

perderle el tiento a algo ▪ perderle el truco a algo to lose the knack of something ▪ to lose one's knack for doing something ▪ to lose one touch for doing something ▪ to lose one's touch at something ▪ not to be as good as something as one used to be ➤ Le he perdido el tiento a la paella. Ya no me sale como antes. I've lost the knack of making paella. ▪ I'm not as good at making paella as I used to be.

perderle la pista a alguien to lose track of someone ▪ to lose the trail of someone ▪ to lose someone's trail ➤ No les pierdas la pista. Don't lose track of them. ▪ Don't lose their trail.

perderse en el horizonte to ride off into the sunset ➤ Al final de la película de vaqueros, el héroe se pierde en el horizonte. At the end of the Western, the hero rides off into the sunset.

perderse la oportunidad de algo to miss out on something ➤ Ella se pierde la oportunidad de una vida. She's missing out on the chance of a lifetime.

perdí el hilo (de las ideas) ▪ se me ha ido (de la cabeza) ▪ se me ha ido la olla ▪ se me ha ido el santo al cielo I lost my train of thought

pérdidas cuantiosas heavy losses ➤ En la Batalla de Chancellorsville durante la Guerra Civil norteamericana, el Norte sufrió pérdidas cuantiosas. In the American Civil War Battle of Chancellorsville, the North suffered heavy losses.

perdí la comunicación *(teléfono)* ▪ se cortó (la comunicación) I got cut off ▪ we got cut off

pérdida de conciencia loss of consciousness

pérdida de memoria de corto plazo short-term memory loss ▪ loss of short-term memory

pérdida de orientación loss of bearings ➤ El arte europeo posterior a la Primera Guerra Mundial refleja la pérdida de orientación de la cultura. European art of the post World War I period reflects the culture's loss of bearings.

ser una **pérdida de tiempo** ▪ ser tiempo perdido to be a waste of time

pérdida temporal de la conciencia temporary loss of consciousness ▪ momentary loss of consciousness

estar **perdidamente enamorado(-a) de alguien** to be hopelessly in love with someone

estar **perdido(-a) al explicar algo** ▪ estar perdido a la hora de explicar algo ▪ estar perdido tratando de explicar algo ▪ no explicarse cómo to be at a loss to explain something ➤ *(noticia)* Los médicos están perdidos a la hora de explicar la alta incidencia de cáncer en el colegio. ▪ Los médicos no se explican la alta incidencia de cáncer en el colegio. The doctors are at a loss to explain the high incidence of cancer at the elementary school.

perdido(-a) de pintura: ponerse ~ to get paint all over oneself ➤ Te has puesto perdido de pintura. You got paint all over yourself. ▪ You're covered with paint.

estar **perdido(-a) de locura** to be absolutely crazy ▪ to be completely crazy

¡perdón! *(general)* ■ *(usted)* perdone ■ *(ustedes)* perdonen ■ *(tú)* perdona ■ *(Esp., vosotros)* perdonad pardon! ■ pardon me! ■ I beg your pardon

el **perdón de los pecados** forgiveness of sins

perdona que te diga esto, pero pardon me for saying so, but ■ pardon me for saying this, but

perdonar el bollo por el coscorrón to realize that something is more trouble than it's worth ■ to realize that something's not worth the trouble

perdonar y olvidar to forgive and forget

pereza va tan lenta que la miseria la alcanza poverty catches up with laziness

perfeccionar su español to perfect one's Spanish

perfil humano humano profile ■ human characteristics

el **perfil inversor** investment needs ■ needs as an investor ■ investor profile ■ investor's characteristics ➤ *(publicidad bancaria)* La mejor selección de fondos para su perfil inversor The best selection of funds for your investment needs

perforar la piel to perforate the skin ■ to break the skin

perforar un agujero a través de algo ■ hacer un agujero a través de algo to bore a hole through something ➤ Los mineros perforaron un agujero a través de la roca. The miners bored a hole through the rock. ➤ Las termitas perforaron un agujero en el suelo de la sala de la prima Mae. The termites bored a hole through cousin Mae's parlor floor.

la **perífrasis nominal** noun periphrasis

la **perífrasis verbal** verb periphrasis

periódico parcial ■ periódico prejuiciado biased newspaper ■ slanted newspaper

periodismo amarillo yellow journalism

periodismo sensacionalista sensationalist journalism ■ sensationalistic journalism

perita en dulce *(frase de Eduardo Mendoza)* ■ guinda confitada very pretty young girl ■ very pretty young damsel ■ very pretty young thing

perito tasador (insurance) claims adjustor

perjudicar la moral del equipo to hurt the morale of the team ■ to damage the morale of the team

ser **perjudicial para las aspiraciones de uno** to be damaging to one's aspirations

permanecer atento a algo ■ seguir atento a algo **1.** to monitor something ■ to watch something continually ■ to watch something without interruption ■ *(coloquial)* to watch something non-stop **2.** *(televisión, radio)* to stay tuned ■ not to go away ■ to stay with one **3.** to still be waiting to... ■ to still be waiting for... ■ to still await word from **4.** to continue to monitor ➤ No te despistes. Permanece atento al guiso hasta que esté hecho o se te quemará. Don't get sidetracked. Keep (on) watching the stew continually until it's done, or it will burn. ■ Don't get sidetracked. Watch the stew continually until it's done, or it will burn. ■ Don't get sidetracked. Watch the stew without interruption until it's done, or it will burn. ■ Don't get sidetracked. Keep watching the stew non-stop, or it will burn. ➤ Permanezca atento a nuestro programa. Stay tuned to our program. ■ Don't go away. ➤ Permanecemos atentos a la respuesta favorable del viñedo español que nos vende el amontillado. ■ Permanecemos atentos a que nos respondan favorablemente del viñedo español que nos vende el amontillado. We are still waiting to hear from the Spanish winery that sells Montilla sherry. ■ We are still awaiting word from the Spanish winery that sells the Montilla sherry. ➤ El gobierno permanece atento a la situación en Oriente Medio. The government continues to monitor the situation in the Middle East.

permanecer en la cama ■ quedarse en la cama ■ *(por enfermedad)* guardar cama to stay in bed ■ to remain in bed

permanecer en pie ■ mantenerse en pie to remain standing

permanecer en silencio ■ permanecer callado to remain silent ➤ (Usted) tiene el derecho de permanecer en silencio. You have the right to remain silent.

permanecer en sus trece ■ seguir en sus trece ■ mantenerse en sus trece ■ estar en sus trece **1.** *(positivo)* to stick to one's guns ■ to stand one's ground **2.** *(positivo o negativo)* to resist stubbornly ■ to refuse to yield ■ to be unyielding **3.** *(negativo)* to be obstinate

permanecer sentado to remain seated

permanezca a la escucha ■ por favor, siga la espera (please) continue to hold

permanezca en espera: por favor ~ please continue to hold ■ please continue to wait

permiso de residencia de menores residence permit for minors ■ residence permit for dependents

permiso de residencia fiscal residence permit based on employment (within the country)

permiso de residencia permanente permanent-residency permit

permiso paterno parental permission

permiso temporal temporary permit

permita Dios God willing

permítame comenzar diciendo... let me begin by saying...

permítame el abrigo ■ deje que le ayude con el abrigo let me take your coat ■ let me help you with your coat

permíteme el abrigo ■ deja que te ayude con el abrigo let me take your coat ■ let me help you with your coat

permitir anticipar ■ llevarle a uno a pensar ■ llevarle a uno a creer to lead one to believe ■ to indicate ➤ *(noticia)* Varios expertos creen que el patrón de comportamiento en los cinco crimenes permite anticipar que el asesino volverá a actuar. The behavior pattern (exhibited) in the five crimes leads experts to believe that the killer will act again. ■ Several experts believe that the behavior pattern (exhibited) in the five crimes indicates that the killer will act again.

permitir realizar to enable one to do ➤ La nueva computadora nos permite realizar el mismo trabajo de antes en la mitad de tiempo. The new computer enables us to do the same work in half the time.

permitirle algo a alguien to let someone have something ➤ Permítemelo un momento. Let me have that for a second. ■ May I have that for a second? ■ Can I have that for a second? ■ Hand me that for a second. ■ Give me that for a second. ■ Lend me that for a second.

permitirse el lujo de to permit oneself the luxury of ■ to indulge (oneself) in

pernocta: tener pase de ~ *(militar)* to have permission to spend the night off base

pero al final but in the end

pero apenas había... *(singular)* but there was hardly any... ■ *(plural)* but there were hardly any...

¡pero bueno! **1.** but what the heck! ■ but shoot! **2.** but I don't know for sure **3.** *(con indignación)* what (the heck) are you *doing*? ■ what in the world are you doing? ■ why... ➤ Me han suspendo. Pero bueno, me esforzaré más en septiembre. I flunked, but what the heck, I'll make a greater effort this fall. ➤ Creo que sí, pero bueno... I think so, but I don't know for sure... ➤ ¡Pero bueno, ¿qué estás haciendo?! What the heck are you doing? ■ What in the world are you doing?

¡pero bueno, no queda nada! why, it's all gone!

pero bueno, veamos... anyway, let's see

¡pero cómo has crecido! my, how you've grown!

pero cuál no sería mi sorpresa cuando... but what was my astonishment when...

pero es así but it is ■ but it does ■ but it has ■ but it will *(Nota: El verbo en inglés depende del antecedente.)*

pero ¿es que...? ...or something? ➤ Pero, ¿es que te has vuelto loco? What! Have you gone crazy or something?

pero nada más but nothing else ■ but that's all ■ but that's about it ➤ Cuando hay niños pequeños los llevamos un rato al desfile, pero nada más. When there are young children, we take them to the parade for a while, but that's about it.

pero no era así **1.** but it wasn't **2.** pero no era verdad ■ pero no era cierto but it wasn't so ■ but it wasn't true ➤ Cuando oyó el coche pensó que era su mujer volviendo a casa del trabajo, pero no era así. When he heard the car, he thought it was his wife coming home from work, but it wasn't. ➤ Dijo que había ido a la biblioteca después de clase, pero no era verdad. He said he went to the library after school, but it wasn't true.

pero no fue así **1.** but it wasn't **2.** pero no fue verdad ■ pero no fue cierto but it wasn't so ■ but it wasn't true ➤ Cuando oyó el coche pensó que era su mujer volviendo a casa del trabajo, pero no fue así. When he heard the car, he thought it was his wife coming home from work, but it wasn't. ➤ Dijo que había ido a la biblioteca después de clase, pero no fue así. He said he went to the library after school, but it wasn't true.

pero pasado eso but more than that

¡**pero por Dios!** please do!

pero por lo demás but otherwise

estar **pero que muy bien** to be really great ➤ La película está pero que muy bien. The movie is really great.

pero que muy bien: hacer algo ~ *(tanto sincero como sarcástico)* to do a great job

pero que muy bien: quedarle algo a alguien ~ 1. to turn out really well 2. to look (really) great ➤ *(Méx.)* El pay les quedó pero que muy bien. ▪ *(Esp.)* La tarta os ha quedado pero que muy bien. Your pie turned out really well. ➤ Este vestido te queda pero muy bien. That dress looks (really) great on you

¡**(pero) qué cambiazo has dado!** my, (how) you've changed!

¡**(pero) qué estirón has pegado!** my, (how) you've grown! ▪ look how you've grown!

pero, ¿qué se ha creído? who does he think he is?

pero se acabó but that was it ▪ but that was the end of it ▪ but that was the end of that

pero, ¿será así? oh, really? ▪ is that possible? ▪ could it be?

pero si lo hice... but if I did... ➤ No quise herir tus sentimientos, pero si lo hice, por favor acepta mis disculpas. I didn't mean to hurt your feelings, but if I did, please accept my apology.

pero si yo... but if I...

pero tampoco but neither

pero tampoco es como para... but then again... ▪ but neither is it as if... ▪ but nor is it as if... ➤ No es gran cosa pero tampoco es como para que pase inadvertido. It's not a big deal, but then again, it shouldn't go unnoticed.

pero todavía sin saberlo but yet unaware ▪ as yet unaware(s)

¡**pero vamos!** 1. but, I'm not sure ▪ but, I don't know for sure 2. *(con indignación)* what are you *doing*? 3. *(como mandato)* let's go! ▪ let's leave! ➤ ¿En qué dirección está la Plaza de Castilla? Creo que por ahí, ¡pero vamos...! Which way is the Plaza de Castilla? I think it's that way, but I'm not sure...

¡**(pero) vaya!** 1. *(sorpresa)* hey! 2. *(resignación)* what the heck! 3. *(indignación)* what?! 4. what a...! ➤ ¡(Pero) vaya, mira quién viene! Hey! Look who's coming! ▪ Hey! Look who's here! ➤ No me ha salido bien el examen, ¡pero vaya! Lo haré mejor la próxima vez. I didn't do well on the exam, but what the heck! I'll do better next time. ➤ ¡Pero vaya! ¡No pretenderá que yo pague lo que él ha roto! What?! He's not wanting me to pay for something he himself broke!

¡**pero ya!** right now! ▪ right this minute!

perra chica *(Esp., arcáico)* ▪ cinco céntimos de peseta five-cent copper coin

perra gorda *(Esp., arcáico)* ▪ perra grande ▪ diez céntimos de peseta ten-cent copper coin

¡**perra mala!** bad dog!

perrito caliente hot dog ➤ Un perrito con chili, mayonesa y cebolla, por favor. A hot dog with chili, mayonnaise, and onions, please.

perro de presa 1. hunting dog 2. *(para aves específicamente)* bird dog

perro de raza purebred dog

perro del hortelano: ser como el ~ to be the dog in the manger

perro educado housebroken dog ➤ Es un perro educado. The dog is housebroken. ▪ It's a housebroken dog.

perro extraviado ▪ perro perdido stray dog

perro faldero lap dog

ser un **perro faldero** to be someone's shadow ▪ to follow someone around all the time

perro guía ▪ perro lázaro seeing-eye dog ▪ guide dog

perro hace "guau-guau" y el gato hace "miau" a dog goes "bow-wow" and a cat goes "meow"

perro ladrador, poco mordedor to be all bark and no bite

perro lázaro ▪ perro guía seeing-eye dog ▪ guide dog

¡**perro malo!** bad dog!

perro viejo 1. old dog 2. *(figurativo)* wise old man

el **perro y el niño donde ven cariño** children and dogs go where they are welcome ▪ we go where we are loved

persecución de alta velocidad high-speed chase

perseguir a alguien to go after someone

perseguir al gato hasta el árbol to chase the cat up the tree

perseguir el cargo de alguien to be after someone's job

perseguir carros, gatos y ardillas *(pasatiempo de los perros)* to chase cars, cats, and squirrels

la **perseverencia da sus frutos** ▪ la constancia da sus frutos persistence pays off

persona acabada has-been

la **persona adecuada para** the right person for

persona anodina dull person

persona asequible approachable person ▪ person who is easy to get to know

persona corriente average person

persona de abrigo ▪ pájaro de cuenta ▪ persona de cuenta person to be wary of

persona de aspecto normal ▪ persona corriente average-looking person

persona de entonces person at that age ➤ Lo más interesante del Einstein de entonces... The most interesting thing about Einstein at that age...

persona de habla española ▪ persona de habla hispana Spanish speaker

persona de la tercera edad ▪ ciudadano de la tercera edad senior citizen ▪ elderly person

persona de (mucha) cuenta 1. pájaro de cuenta ▪ persona de abrigo person to be wary of 2. pez gordo big shot

ser una **persona de pelo en pecho** ▪ ser todo un hombre ▪ ser un hombre hecho y derecho to be a real man

persona de pocas palabras person of few words

persona de poco fiar untrustworthy person

persona de recursos especiales resourceful person

persona del montón average person

persona desaliñada slovenly person ▪ scruffy person ▪ unkempt person

persona encomiable praiseworthy person

ser la **persona idónea para el cargo** ▪ ser la persona idónea para el trabajo ▪ ser la persona idónea para el puesto to be exactly the right person for the job ▪ to be the ideal person for the job

persona inculta ▪ persona zafia uncultured person ▪ uncouth person ▪ coarse person ▪ bumpkin

persona informal ▪ persona poco fiable unreliable person

persona más indicada para... ▪ persona adecuada para... right person for...

persona matutina ▪ persona mañanera morning person

persona non grata persona non grata ▪ unwanted person

la **persona que habla español** the Spanish speaker ▪ the person who speaks Spanish ▪ the Spanish-speaking person ➤ Busco al cajero que habla español. I'm looking for the teller who speaks Spanish. ▪ I'm looking for the Spanish-speaking teller.

una **persona que hable español** a Spanish speaker ▪ a person who speaks Spanish ▪ a Spanish-speaking person ➤ Busco un cajero que hable español. I'm looking for a teller who speaks Spanish. ▪ I'm looking for a Spanish-speaking teller.

persona que te encanta pero no encaja ▪ persona que te encanta pero que no acaba de encajar person you like but who does not fit

persona sin doblez person of impeccable character

persona sin ninguna instrucción uneducated person ▪ person without education

persona torpe awkward person ▪ clumsy person

persona trabajadora industrious person ▪ hard-working person ▪ energetic person

persona vespertina ▪ persona nocturna ▪ persona trasnochadora night person

persona zafia ▪ persona inculta bumpkin ▪ uncouth person ▪ coarse person ▪ uncultured person

personaje sin redondear type character ▪ typecast character

personalidad adecuada right personality ▪ suitable personality

personalidad desabrida ▪ personalidad brusca abrasive personality

perspectiva de tener que... prospect of having to...

perspectiva poco alentadora discouraging outlook

perspectiva poco favorable unfavorable outlook

perspectiva poco halagüeña unfavorable outlook

perspectiva sombría bleak outlook ➤ La perspectiva económica fue sombría durante un tiempo pero ahora ha mejorado. The economic outlook was bleak for a time but has brightened up.

persuadir a alguien para que haga algo to persuade someone to do something ■ to talk someone into something

persuadir a alguien para que no haga algo ■ disuadir a alguien de que haga algo to talk someone out of doing something ■ to dissuade someone from doing something

pertenecer a ■ ser de ■ corresponderle a uno to belong to ■ to be owned by ■ to be those of ➤ La mayoría de los huesos pertenecen a personas jóvenes que murieron por la destrucción de masa encefálica a causa de disparos de armas de fuego hechos desde muy cerca. Most of the bones are those of youths who died of massive head injuries caused by shots fired at close range.

pertinaz lluvia *(literario, poético)* ■ lluvia pertinaz persistent rain

pertrecharse de algo ■ pertrecharse con algo ■ aprovisionarse de algo to equip oneself with something

pesa mucho it's heavy ■ it weighs a lot

pesa un huevo *(subido de tono)* ■ pesa un montón ■ pesa mucho it's heavy ■ it weighs a lot

pesado(-a) con alguien: ser muy ~ ■ ser muy cansino con alguien ■ ser muy plasta con alguien to be wearing on someone ➤ Los ataques incesantes de la prensa han sido muy pesados con el primer ministro. The relentless attacks of the press have been very wearing on the prime minister.

pesar hasta las palabras 1. to weigh everything one says ■ to consider the implications in everything one says **2.** to be very tight (with money)

pesar lo suyo to weigh a ton

pesar menos que una pluma to be (as) light as a feather

pesarle a alguien el alma 1. to weigh (heavily) on someone **2.** *(poético)* to be heavy laden

pesarle a uno ■ preocuparle a uno to weigh on one's mind ■ to weigh on one ➤ La decisión de ir de pesca o construir una casa en el árbol le pesaba al chico. The decision whether to go fishing or build a tree house weighed heavily on the boy's mind.

pesarle a uno haber hecho algo ■ arrepentirse de haber hecho algo to regret doing something ■ to regret having done something ■ to be sorry one did something ➤ Me pesa haberlo hecho. ■ Me arrepiento de haberlo hecho. I regret doing it. ■ I regret having done it. ■ I'm sorry I did it.

ser la **pescadilla que se muerde la cola** to be a Catch-22 ■ to be a catch twenty-two ■ to be a no-win situation ■ to be a vicious circle

pescado del día today's catch

pescar algo al vuelo ■ coger al vuelo ■ pescar a la primera ■ coger a la primera **1.** to catch something on a fly **2.** entender algo con facilidad ■ memorizar algo al instante to catch something on a fly

pescar más que to catch more fish than ➤ Bert estaba pescando más que Ernie. Bert was catching more fish than Ernie.

pescar una gripe to get the flu ■ to catch the flu ■ to come down with the flu

pescar la indirecta ■ captar la indirecta to catch the hint ■ to get the hint

pescar(se) un resfriado to catch a cold

pese a ■ a pesar de despite ■ in spite of ➤ *(titular)* El gobierno británico rechaza trasladar el submarino *Tireless* pese a la petición de Aznar. The British government refuses to move the submarine *Tireless* despite Aznar's request. ■ The British government refuses to move the submarine *Tireless* in spite of Aznar's request.

pese a ello ■ a pesar de eso in spite of that

pese a lo anterior in spite of the foregoing

pese a quien pese no matter who doesn't like it ■ no matter what anybody thinks ■ no matter who opposes it ■ no matter who is against it ■ regardless of who opposes it ■ regardless of who is against it

pese a todo in spite of everything

peso escurrido net weight

peso gallo *(boxeo)* bantam weight

peso medio *(boxeo)* middle weight

peso mosca *(boxeo)* flyweight

peso neto net weight

peso pluma *(boxeo)* featherweight

pestaña de un libro ■ solapa de un libro overleaf of a book jacket

pestaña de zanahoria carrot shaving

la **petición por** request for

pez gordo ■ pez gordísimo ■ mero mero big shot ■ bigwig ➤ ¿Cuándo se va a presentar el pez gordo de St. Louis? When's the bigwig from St. Louis going to show up?

petición cursada application in process

estar **pez en algo** ■ estar pez de algo to be completely uninformed about something

el **pez gordo se come al chico** the strong devour the weak

pica, pica ■ doble click double click ■ click twice

picada maestra *(L.am.)* ■ vía principal main road

picado de viruela scarred from smallpox ■ pockmarked from smallpox

picadura de abeja beesting

picadura de avispa wasp sting

picadura de tarántula tarantula sting

estar **pícame Pedro que picarte quiero** ■ chincharse to poke (at) each other ➤ Los hermanos han estado todo el día pícame Pedro que picarte quiero. ■ Los hermanos están todo el día chinchándose uno al otro. The brothers have been poking at each other all day.

picar al caballo ■ espolear al caballo to spur the horse

picar alto *(Esp.)* to aim high

picar billetes to punch tickets ➤ El revisor vino por todo el tren picando los billetes de los pasajeros. The conductor came through the train car punching the passengers' tickets.

picar el anzuelo ■ tragar el anzuelo to swallow the bait ■ to take the bait

picar el sol en la piel (for) the sun to sting the skin

picar en *(informática)* ■ hacer clic en ■ pinchar en to click on ➤ *(tú)* Pica en E-mail. ■ *(usted)* Pique en E-mail. Click on E-mail.

picar (la) comida en bocaditos *(lechuga, cebolla, etc.)* ■ picar (la) comida en trocitos to cut the food into bite-size pieces ■ to chop the food into bite-size pieces ■ *(coloquial)* to cut the food in bite-size pieces ■ to chop the food in bite-size pieces

picar la curiosidad to pique one's curiosity ■ to arouse one's curiosity

picar la piedra to break up stone with a pickax

picar la retaguardia de un enemigo to be in close pursuit of a retreating enemy

picar más que la pimienta to be hotter than pepper

picar muy menudito to chop very finely

pico de oro: tener un ~ ■ tener un piquito de oro ■ tener (mucha) labia to have the gift of gab

pico y pala: trabao de ~ menial work

pide por esa boca ■ pide por esa boquita just ask me (and I'll do whatever you like)

estar **pidiéndolo a gritos** ■ estar pidiéndolo a voces to be asking for it ■ to be begging for it

estar **pidiéndolo a voces** ■ estar pidiéndolo a gritos to be asking for it ■ to be begging for it

pie a tierra: echar el ~ ■ apearse ■ descabalgar to get (down) off the back of an animal ■ to jump down off the back of an animal *(caballo, burro, mula, elefante, camello, etc.)*

el **pie de ducha** shower stall

el **pie de foto** picture caption ■ caption under the picture

pie de guerra: estar en ~ to be on a war footing

el **pie de la colina** ■ falda de la colina foot of the hill ■ bottom of the hill ■ base of the hill

el **pie de la montaña** ■ falda de la montaña foot of the mountain ■ bottom of the mountain ■ base of the mountain

el **pie de la página** ■ la parte inferior de la página foot of the page ■ bottom of the page

pie derecho: empezar con el ~ ■ empezar con buen pie to get off on the right foot ■ to get off to a good start

pie izquierdo: levantarse con el ~ ▪ tener un mal día to get out of the wrong side of the bed ▪ to get up on the wrong side of the bed ▪ to have a bad day

piedra angular cornerstone

piedra de toque touchstone ▪ criterion

piedra de tripi ▪ tripi tab of LSD ▪ LSD

piedra filosofal philosopher's stone

piedra movediza nunca moho cobija a rolling stone gathers no moss

la **piel curtida** tanned hide

piel de Barrabás: ser de la ~ *(dícese de los niños)* ▪ ser el bicho que picó al tren ▪ ser de la piel del diablo to be very naughty ▪ to be very bad ▪ to be a terror

la **piel de melocotón** smooth skin ▪ *(tipo de tela)* peach skin

la **piel de naranja** *(coloquial)* ▪ celulitis cellulitis

la **piel del toro** *(Esp., nombre metafórico del país)* Spain

¡**piensa algo!** *(tú)* think of something!

piensa el ladrón que todos son de su condición the thief believes everyone is like him ▪ he who thinks everyone is a knave is one himself

piensa mal y acertarás think ill, and you'll be right ▪ suspicions are often correct

piensa por ti think for yourself

¡**piénsalo!** ▪ ¡imagínate! just think!

¡**piense algo!** *(usted)* think of something!

pienso luego existo ▪ cogito ergo sum *(Descartes)* I think therefore I am ▪ cogito ergo sum

¡**piérdete!** ▪ ¡lárgate! get lost! ▪ beat it!

pierna de cordero leg of lamb

piernas bien torneadas shapely legs ▪ well-shaped legs ▪ well-turned legs

piernas de ensueño beautiful legs

pies descalzos *(cartel de piscina)* no shoes

pies ¿para qué os quiero? ▪ ¡huyamos! let's get out of here! ▪ let's beat it! ▪ *(pintoresco)* let's beat a trail outta Dodge!

pies planos flat feet

pieza de repuesto spare part ▪ replacement part

pieza de al lado ▪ (la) habitación de al lado next room

pieza inmediata *(L.am., en museos, etc.)* ▪ sala contigua ▪ habitación contigua adjoining room

pieza por pieza ▪ paso a paso step by step

piezas que se mueven moving parts

pila alkalina *(redonda, con 1,5 voltios)* alkaline battery

pila para linterna de mano flashlight battery

píldora del día siguiente morning-after pill ➤ La Conferencia Episcopal arremetió contra el gobierno por haber autorizado la píldora del día siguiente. The Conference of Bishops attacked the government for authorizing the morning-after pill.

piloto de (autos de) carreras race car driver

piloto de aviones airplane pilot

piloto de avionetas airplane pilot ▪ pilot of light airplanes ▪ private pilot

piloto de pruebas test pilot

ser **pillado con el culo al aire** ▪ ser pillado con los pantalones bajados ▪ ser pillado en bragas to get caught with one's pants down

ser **pillado(-a) con las manos en la masa** to be caught red-handed ➤ *(titular)* Los cacos fueron pillados con las manos en la masa. The burglars were caught red-handed.

ser **pillado con los pantalones bajados** ▪ ser pillado en bragas to get caught with one's pants down

ser **pillado en bragas** ▪ ser pillado con los pantalones bajados ▪ ser pillado con el culo al aire to be caught with one's pants down

ser **pillado(-a) en fragante** *(derecho)* to be caught in the act

ser **pillado(-a) in fraganti** to be caught in the act

ser **pillado(-a) por la policía** ▪ ser trincado por la policía ▪ ser cogido por la policía to get busted by the police

pillar a alguien a base de bien *(Esp.)* ▪ pegarle a alguien bien to get someone good ➤ Esa maldita ave nos pilló a base de bien. That damned bird got us good.

pillar a alguien con las manos en la masa *(Esp.)* ▪ coger a alguien con las manos en la masa ▪ agarrar a alguien con las manos en la masa to catch someone red-handed

pillar a alguien de sorpresa to catch someone by surprise

pillar a alguien en bragas ▪ pillar a alguien en pelotas ▪ *(Esp.)* coger a alguien en bragas to catch someone with his pants down

pillar a alguien en mal momento ▪ *(Esp.)* coger a alguien en mal momento to catch someone at a bad time

pillar a alguien in fraganti ▪ pillar a alguien en flagrante delito ▪ pillar a alguien con las manos en la masa ▪ coger a alguien en el acto to catch someone red-handed ▪ to catch someone in the act

pillar a alguien por sorpresa ▪ agarrar a alguien por sorpresa ▪ tomar a alguien por sorpresa to catch someone by surprise ▪ to take someone by surprise

pillar algo de paso ▪ *(Esp.)* coger algo de paso to catch something in passing

pillar el toro a alguien ▪ coger el toro a alguien (for) the bull to gore someone

pillar un resfriado to catch a cold ▪ to catch cold

pillar una mona ▪ pillar una turca ▪ embriagarse to get drunk

pillar una turca ▪ pillar una mona ▪ embriagarse to get drunk

pillar una tajada to get smashed ▪ to get drunk

pillarle a alguien en una mentira to catch someone in a lie

pillarle cagando *(subido de tono)* ▪ pillarle in fraganti ▪ cogerle cagando ▪ verle cagando to catch someone red-handed

pillarle por banda a alguien to corner someone

pillarse los cojones con las tapas de un baúl: como ~ *(subido de tono)* ▪ como pillarse los cojones con la tapa de un piano (de cola) like I want a hole in the head ➤ Me apetece ir a cenar con ellos como pillarme los cojones con las tapas de un baúl. I want to have supper with them like I want a hole in the head.

pillarse los dedos to get (one's fingers) burned ▪ to get in trouble

pillarse un globo *(coloquial)* **1.** *(alcohol)* to get drunk **2.** *(drogas)* to get stoned **3.** *(Esp.)* to go ballistic ▪ to get mad as a hornet

pillemos un mini y unas bravas *(Historias del Kronen de José Ángel Mañas)* let's have a beer and some fried potatoes

¡**pim, pam, pum!** ▪ ¡pun, pun, pun! **1.** bang, bang, bang! **2.** bam, bam, bam!

pinchar algo con un tenedor ▪ perforar algo con un tenedor to pierce something with a fork ▪ to perforate something with a fork ➤ Pincha la papa con un tenedor para asegurarte que esté hecha. Pierce the potato with a fork to make sure it's done.

pinchar con un tenedor 1. *(al comer)* to take (food) on a fork ▪ to pick up (food) with a fork **2.** *(antes de cocinar)* to perforate with a fork **3.** *(para comprobar que está hecho)* to test with a fork

pinchar un teléfono to bug a telephone

pincharse el dedo to prick one's finger

pinchársele una rueda to have a blowout ▪ for a tire to blow out ➤ En el viaje a Valencia se me pinchó una rueda. On the trip to Valencia, I had a blowout. ▪ On the trip to Valencia, a tire blew out.

pinta lluvia ▪ parece que va a llover it looks like it's going to rain ▪ it looks like rain

ser **pintado(-a) a alguien** ▪ ser el mismísimo(-a) doble de alguien ▪ ser idéntico a alguien to be the spitting image of someone

pintan bastos *(pintoresco)* ▪ la cosas se están saliendo de control things are getting out of hand ▪ things are getting out of control

pintar (de) negro to paint a bleak picture ➤ El informe pinta de negro el futuro del planeta de aquí a medio siglo como no detengamos el calentamiento global. The report paints a bleak picture of the environment in half a century if we don't reverse the trend of global warming.

pintarse los labios to put on one's lipstick ▪ to put one's lipstick on ➤ Tengo que pintarme los labios. ▪ Me tengo que pintar los labios. I have to put on my lipstick. ▪ I have to put my lipstick on.

pinto, pinto, gorgorito, vende las vacas a veinticinco, ¿en qué lugar?, en Portugal, ¿en qué calleja?, Moraleja; esconde la mano que viene la vieja eenie, meenie, miney, mo, catch a tiger by his toe; if he hollers, let him go; eenie, meenie, miney, mo

pintor(a) de acuarelas watercolor artist

pintor(a) de brocha gorda house painter

pintura al óleo oil painting

pintura ha empeorado paint has deteriorated

¡pío, pío! tweet, tweet!

ser un **piojo resucitado** 1. ser un don nadie ▪ ser un Juan de los palotes to be a wannabe ▪ to be a nobody 2. ser rico por medios dubiosos to be someone who has become rich (quickly) by obscure or dishonorable means

Piolín y Silvestre Tweety and Sylvester

piquito de oro: tener un ~ ▪ tener un pico de oro ▪ tener (mucha) labia to have the gift of gab

estar **pirado(-a) por alguien** to be crazy about someone

pirarse de allí en cuanto poder ▪ rajarse de allí en cuanto poder to get the hell out of there ▪ *(pintoresco)* to beat a trail outta Dodge ➤ Nos piramos de allí en cuanto pudimos. We got the hell out of there.

pisando huevos: ir ~ 1. pasar de puntillas to tread lightly 2. ir muy despacio to go too slowly

estar **pisando los talones a alguien** ▪ estar sobre los talones de alguien ▪ estar sobre las pistas de alguien ▪ estar tras (de) las pisadas de alguien ▪ estar tras (de) las huellas de alguien to be hot on someone's heels

pisándose los cojones: ir ~ *(subido de tono)* ▪ ir pisando huevos ▪ ir muy despacio to go too slow ▪ to go too slowly

pisar a fondo el acelerador ▪ pegar a fondo to floor the accelerator

pisar algo 1. *(sobre)* to step on something 2. *(meterse)* to step in something ➤ Pisé una cucaracha. I stepped on a cockroach. ➤ Pisé una catalina. ▪ Pisé estiércol de vaca. I stepped in a cow pie. ▪ I stepped in (some) cow plop.

pisar buena hierba ▪ haber pisado buena hierba 1. to get somewhere (now) 2. to be a good move ➤ La investigación arroja buenos resultados. Estamos pisando buena hierba. The research is yielding good results. (Now) we're getting somewhere. ➤ Con la compra de este coche pisamos buena hierba, nunca nos ha dado un problema. Buying this car was a good move. It's never given us a problem.

pisar el embrague to depress the clutch (pedal) ▪ to step on the clutch pedal ▪ to disengage the clutch

pisar firme to be a force to be reckoned with ➤ El Real Madrid pisa fuerte en la liga europea. Real Madrid is a force to be reckoned with in the European League.

pisar fuerte ▪ pisar firme to be in one's element ➤ En la industria automovilística, los orientales han pisado fuerte. In the automobile industry, the Orientals are in their element.

pisar las pistas de un crimen ▪ pisar sobre las pistas de un crimen ▪ pisar por las pistas de un crimen ▪ destruir las evidencias de un crimen to trample evidence of a crime ▪ to destroy criminal evidence ▪ to destroy the evidence in a crime

pisar las tablas to go onstage

pisar mala hierba 1. no servir de nada not to get anywhere 2. meter la pata to be a bad move ➤ Con este curso en cestería ando pisando mala hierba. This course in basketweaving is not getting me anywhere. ➤ Al contratar al baterista de la banda de rock como percusionista de la sinfonía pisamos mala hierba. Hiring the rock band's drummer as the percussionist for the symphony was a bad move.

pisar terreno firme ▪ saber el terreno que uno pisa to know one's ground on an issue

pisar un clavo to step on a nail

pisar una catalina to step in a cow pie ▪ to step in (a pile of) cow dung ▪ *(pintoresco)* to step in (a pile of) cow plop ➤ Pisé una catalina. I stepped in a cow pie. ▪ I stepped in (a pile of) cow dung. ▪ I stepped in (a pile of) cow plop.

pisarle los talones a alguien to be hot on someone's heels ➤ Estamos pisándoles los talones. We're hot on their heels.

pisarle una idea a alguien to beat someone to (the idea) ➤ Iba a escribir un trabajo comparando a Shakespeare y Calderón para mi clase de teatro, pero otro estudiante me ha pisado la idea. I was going to write a paper comparing Shakespeare and Calderón for my theatre course but another student beat me to it.

piso bajo *(Esp.)* ▪ planta baja ground floor ▪ first floor

piso bajo continuo *(en los autobuses)* wheelchair access

piso de abajo 1. next floor down ▪ floor below this one ▪ one floor down 2. *(Esp., apartamento directamente debajo de éste)* apartment below this one ▪ apartment under(neath) this one 3. *(Esp., cualquier apartamento)* apartment downstairs

piso de arriba 1. *(planta)* next floor up ▪ one floor up ▪ floor above this one 2. *(Esp., apartamento directamente arriba de éste)* apartment above this one ▪ apartment over this one 3. *(Esp., cualquier apartamento)* apartment upstairs

piso de dos ambientes one-bedroom apartment ▪ two-room apartment

piso de tierra ▪ suelo de tierra dirt floor ▪ earthen floor

piso de tres ambientes three-room apartment

piso de un solo ambiente ▪ estudio studio apartment ▪ one-room apartment

pisos de madera sin revestir bare wood flooring

pisos que se alquilan apartments for rent

pista al dinero ▪ pista sobre el dinero money trail ➤ *(titular)* Barricadas para seguir la pista al dinero. Obstacles to following the money trail.

pista de patinaje skating rink

pista desapercibida hidden clue

pista falsa false lead

pista *x* *(en un disco compacto)* track *x* ▪ band *x* ➤ La canción está en la pista seis. The song is on track six. ▪ The song is on band six.

pistola cargada loaded pistol ▪ loaded gun

pistola de fulminantes ▪ pistola de pistones cap pistol ▪ cap gun

pistola para masilla ▪ pistola para calafateo caulking gun ▪ calking gun

pistoletazo de salida: dar el ~ to give the starting signal ▪ to fire the opening shot ▪ to fire the beginning shot ▪ to begin the race ▪ to kick off ➤ La ciencia ha dado el pistoletazo de salida en la carrera por encontrar las claves del comportamiento. Science has begun the race to find the keys to behavior. ➤ Se ha dado el pistoletazo de salida para las rebajas de este año. They've kicked off the January sales.

pitar falta *(deportes)* ▪ indicar falta to call a foul

pito, pito, colorito, ¿dónde vas tan bonito? *(Esp.)* ▪ pito, pito, gongorito, ¿dónde vas tan bonito? eenie, meenie, miney, mo, catch a tiger by his toe; if he hollers, let him go; eenie, meenie, miney, mo

con todos los pitos y flautas with all the bells and whistles ▪ with all the extras

pitos y flautas: tener todos los ~ to have all the bells and whistles ▪ to have all the extras

pizca de sal pinch of salt ➤ Échale una pizca de sal. Put in a pinch of salt. ➤ Añade una pizca de sal. Add a pinch of salt.

placas invisibles de hielo (en la carretera) black ice ▪ invisible (sheet of) ice

plan pionero groundbreaking plan ▪ pioneer plan ➤ Ha comenzado un plan pionero contra el cáncer en Madrid. A groundbreaking plan has been introduced in Madrid to fight cancer.

placa (de grasa) en las paredes arteriales plaque (made of fat) on the arterial walls ➤ Hay nuevos medicamentos que impiden la formación de placas de grasa en las arterias del cerebro. There are new drugs which prevent the formation of plaque in the arterial walls of the brain.

placa de hielo patch of ice ➤ El coche pasó por una placa de hielo y se derrapó saliéndose de la carretera. ▪ El coche cogió una placa de hielo y se derrapó saliéndose de la carretera. The car hit a patch of ice and slid off the road.

placa de mármol ▪ plancha de mármol slab of marble ▪ marble slab

placas de madera plank paneling

placas de matrícula *(de un coche)* license plates

el **placer es mío** *(culto)* ▪ el gusto es mío ▪ es un placer (it's) my pleasure ▪ it's a pleasure

plácido vuelo smooth flight

el **plan a largo plazo** long-range plan

el **plan de ajuste** economic recovery plan ➤ Decenas de miles de personas protestaron en Buenos Aires contra el duro plan de ajuste. Tens of thousands of people protested in Buenos Aires against the harsh economic recovery plan.

plan de arreglo recovery plan ➤ Ante la crisis económica, el gobierno fomentó un plan de arreglo único. In the face of economic crisis, The government promoted a unique recovery plan.

el **plan de choque** ▪ plan de ataque plan of attack ➤ Bruselas lanza un plan de choque contra el mal de las "vacas locas." Brussels launches a plan of attack against "mad cow" disease.

el **plan de financiación de** plan to finance ▪ plan for the financing of

el **plan de negocios** business plan

plancha caliente 1. *(para la comida)*hot plate 2. *(para la ropa)* hot iron

plancha de mármol ▪ placa de mármol slab of marble ▪ marble slab

planear algo to plan something

planear por el aire to glide through the air

planear sobre 1. *(positivo)* to soar over ▪ to soar above 2. *(negativo)* to hang over ➤ Las cigüeñas planeaban tranquilamente sobre las torres de las iglesias de Salamanca. The storks were soaring peacefully above the church steeples of Salamanca. ➤ *(noticia)* Un ajuste de cuentas planea sobre las bombas de Galicia. A settling of accounts hangs over the bombings in Galicia.

el **planeta exterior** outer planet

el **planeta interior** inner planet

el **planeta menor** ▪ (el) asteroide minor planet ▪ asteroid

planisferio Mercator ▪ mapamundi Mercator Mercator projection map of the world ▪ Mercator projection world map

plano callejero street map

plano de casa house plan ▪ floor plan of a house

plano de sustentación *(aerodinámica)* airfoil

plano de sustentación alabeado ▪ ala de avión cambered airfoil ▪ airplane wing ➤ El plano de sustentación alabeado fue inventado por Horatio Phillips en 1884. The cambered airfoil was invented by Horatio Phillips in 1884. ▪ The airplane wing was invented by Horatio Phillips in 1884.

planos sociales social circles

planta baja ground floor

planta de oportunidades bargain basement *(Nota: En Estados Unidos la planta de oportunidades suele estar en el sótano.)*

planta de un edificio floor plan of a building

planta envasadora bottling works ▪ bottling plant

planta superior next floor up ▪ floor above

plantar a alguien ▪ dejar plantado a alguien 1. to stand someone up 2. *(figurativo)* to abandon someone ➤ Me di cuenta de que me había dejado plantado después de estar dos horas esperándolo. I realized he had stood me up after waiting for him for two hours. ➤ *(noticia)* Zapatero planta a Aznar en su apoyo a la guerra. Zapatero abandons Aznar in his support of the war.

plantar a alguien en el arroyo ▪ poner a alguien en el arroyo to ditch someone ➤ Cuando su carrera como actor despegó, plantó a su novia en el arroyo y se casó con una modelo. When his acting career took off, he ditched his girlfriend and married a model.

plantar cara a alguien ▪ hacer frente a alguien 1. to take someone on ▪ to take on someone 2. to face the situation ➤ *(titular)* La actriz mexicana Salma Hayek planta cara a Schwartzenegger. The Mexican actress Salma Hayek takes on Schwartzenegger. ➤ No tenemos más remedio que plantar cara. We have no choice but to face the situation.

plantar sus estudios to abandon one's studies ➤ Marcos plantó los estudios antes de terminar la carrera. Marcos abandoned his studies before he finished his degree.

plantar un pino 1. to plant a pine tree 2. *(vulgar)* defecar to take a crap

plantas y alzados *(de un edificio)* plans and elevations

plantarse ante to take positions (just) outside ➤ *(titular)* Tropas de EE UU se plantan ante Bagdad. U.S. troops take positions (just) outside Baghdad.

plantarse con alguien ▪ presentarse con alguien 1. to show up with someone 2. *(sin invitación)* to crash (a party) ➤ Aunque no lo habían invitado a la cena, se plantó allí con su novia. ▪ Aunque no lo habían invitado a la cena, se presentó allí con su novia. Even though he wasn't invited to the dinner party, he showed up with his girlfriend. ▪ Even though he wasn't invited to the dinner party, he and his girlfriend crashed it.

plantarse delante de to take (up) a position in front of ▪ to stake out a position in front of ➤ Se plantó delante de la entrada del edificio de pisos para martillarme dinero. He took up a position in front of the apartment building to hit me up for some money. ▪ He staked out a position in front of the apartment building to hit me up for some money.

plantarse en un lugar ▪ llegar a un lugar to get to a place ▪ to arrive in a place ➤ En el tren de alta velocidad te plantas en Sevilla en menos de tres horas. On the bullet train you arrive in Seville in less than three hours.

plantarse justamente al lado de alguien to come up and stand right next to someone ➤ En la cena de gala el presidente de la fundación se plantó justo a mi lado. At the formal dinner the president of the foundation came up and stood right next to me.

plantarse justamente delante de alguien to stand right in front of someone

plantarse justamente detrás de alguien to stand right behind someone

plantarse por encima de to stand over ➤ Me planté por encima del hombro de Carlos para ver lo que estaba escribiendo en su cuadernillo. I stood over Carlos' shoulder to see what he was writing in his little notebook.

plantarse sobre to stand (right) on something ➤ La gata se plantó sobre el periódico mientras lo leía para llamar mi atención. The cat stood (right) on the newspaper I was reading in order to get my attention.

planteamiento erróneo false premise ➤ Partiste de un planteamiento erróneo. You started with a false premise.

plantear a alguien un ultimátum to give someone an ultimatum ▪ to deliver (someone) an ultimatum

plantear algo 1. proponer algo to propose something 2. poner sobre el tapete to bring up something (for discussion) ▪ to bring something up (for discussion) ➤ No puedo plantearlo ahora. No es el momento adecuado. It can't bring it up now. It's the wrong time.

plantear dudas sobre algo to raise doubts about something ▪ to raise questions about something

plantear la cuestión 1. to raise the question 2. *(ley parlamentaria)* to call for a vote

plantear objecciones to raise objections

plantear una pregunta ▪ plantear una cuestión to pose a question ▪ to give rise to a question ▪ to raise a question ➤ Nos confundieron las especificaciones, las cuales plantearon más preguntas de las que respondieron. We were baffled by the specifications, which raised more questions than they answered.

plantear problemas 1. hablar sobre problemas to discuss (some) problems 2. causar problemas to cause (a lot of) problems ▪ to cause (a lot of) trouble ➤ Ahora que estamos todos los socios reunidos me gustaría plantear algunos problemas. Now that all of the partners are together, I'd like to discuss some problems. ➤ Los continuos robos en la zona nos están causando problemas. The continual robberies in the area are causing (a lot of) problems. ▪ The continual robberies in the area are causing a lot of trouble.

plantear que... 1. to propose that... ▪ to advance the idea that... 2. *(ante un tribunal)* to argue that...

plantear un debate to trigger a debate

plantear una dificultad to raise difficulties ▪ to cause difficulties

plantear un problema to pose a problem

plantear una queja to lodge a complaint ▪ to make a complaint ▪ to file a complaint

plantearse algo to consider something

planteárselo a alguien to explain it to someone ▪ to show it to someone

plantilla de un equipo *(deportes)* ▪ (los) integrantes de un equipo members of team ▪ team members

plantilla de una fábrica work force of a factory ▪ a factory's work force ▪ crew of a factory ▪ factory crew

plantilla de una oficina office staff

plantilla para rotular template

estar **plasmado por todos lados** ▪ estar plasmado por todas partes to be broadcast all over the place ▪ to be bandied about ▪ to be blasted all over the place ▪ to be spouted all over the place

plasmar algo con las manos ■ forjar algo con las manos to shape something with one's hands
plasmar en historietas to caricature (in cartoons)
plasmar sobre papel ■ expresar sobre papel to express on paper
plasmar la visión de to express the vision of ■ to give expression to ➤ Las obras de Miguel Delibes plasman la visión de un católico liberal. The works of Miguel Delibes express the vision of a liberal Catholic.
plasta con alguien: ser muy ~ ■ ser muy cansino(-a) con alguien ■ ser muy pesado(-a) con alguien to be wearing on someone
plástico biodegradable biodegradable plastic
plata, de la que cagó la gata *(subido de tono)* **1.** *(literal)* silver, my ass! **2.** *(figurativo)* I lost my ass on that job ■ I didn't make squat on that job.
plataforma de radar radar installation
plato combinado *(Esp.)* **1.** *(cena)* single-course supper **2.** *(comida)* single-course dinner
plato de degustación ■ plato degustación sampler plate
plato de gusto de uno: no ser ~ ■ no ser santo de la devoción de uno not to be one's cup of tea
plató de rodaje movie set
ser **plato de segunda mesa** to be second best ■ to feel second best
plato del día today's special
plato fuerte 1. plato principal ■ segundo (plato) main course **2.** atracción principal ■ el no va más main attraction **3.** el punto más importante del orden del día main order of business ■ main item on the agenda ➤ Nacho pidió gazpacho para empezar y de plato fuerte paella. Nacho ordered gazpacho as an appetizer, and paella as his main course. ➤ El plato fuerte del espectáculo era la increíble mujer contorsionista. The show's main attraction was the incredible female contortionist. ➤ El plato fuerte de la reunión fue la remodelación del sistema de pagos. The main order of business at the meeting was the revamping of the system of making payments.
plato (hondo) de sopa bowl of soup
playa de estacionamiento parking lot
Playa Girón *(Cuba, nombre verdadero de "Bahía Cochinos")* Bay of Pigs
playa nudista nude beach
plaza de armas parade ground
plaza de la villa village square ■ town square
plaza mayor main square
plegarse a la presión ■ ceder ante la presión to buckle under pressure ■ to bow to pressure ■ to give in to pressure
ser **plena noche** ■ ser noche cerrada to be (in) the middle of the night ➤ Ya era plena noche cuando oímos el ruido. ■ Ya era noche cerrada cuando oímos el ruido. It was the middle of the night when we heard the noise.
la **plenitud sexual** sexual prime ■ sexual peak
pleno de la cámara legislative session
estar **pleno de suspense** ■ estar lleno de suspense suspense-filled ■ filled with suspense ➤ Es una novela plena de suspense. It is a suspense-filled novel. ■ It is a novel filled with suspense.
pleno del tribunal session of the court
pleno extraordinario special session
pleno invierno depths of winter
pleno Manhattan midtown Manhattan
pleno verano ■ (el) rigor del verano hottest part of the summer ■ height of the summer ■ depths of summer
plétora de insultos ■ cantidad de improperios ■ rosario de insultos ■ avalancha de insultos ■ retahila de insultos barrage of insults ■ stream of insults
la **pléyade de** illustrious group of ■ illustrious collection of ■ star-studded group of ■ star-studded collection of
plica: mandar un manuscrito bajo (sistema de) ~ ■ mandar un manuscrito anónimamente to submit a manuscript anonymously ➤ Nicanor Parra, el autodenominado "antipoeta" chileno, al mandar tres manuscritos bajo plica, ganó el primero, segundo y tercer puesto de un concurso literario. Nicanor Parra, the self-styled Chilean "antipoet," on submitting three manuscripts anonymously to a literary competition, won first, second and third prize.
plus fiscal: obligación con ~ security containing tax incentives ■ security which contains tax incentives ➤ La compañía emite obligaciones con un plus fiscal. The company issues securities which contain tax incentives.
Plus Ultra *(lema de España establecida por Carlos V, también escrito Plvs Vltra)* to new heights ■ *(arcaico, literalmente)* farther beyond
pobre de... poor...
ser **pobre de espíritu** to be poor in spirit
pobre de mí poor me!
pobre de ti poor you!
ser un **pobre hombre** ■ ser un don nadie to be a nobody
pobre que una rata: ser más ~ ■ ser más pobre que las ratas ■ no tener dónde caerse muerto(-a) to be (as) poor as a church mouse ■ *(coloquial, ligeramente subido de tono)* not to have a pot to piss in
pobreza abyecta ■ pobreza extrema ■ vil pobreza abject poverty ■ extreme poverty
pobreza extrema ■ pobreza abyecta ■ vil pobreza extreme poverty ■ abject poverty
poca cosa not much ➤ ¿Qué pasa?-Poca cosa What's going on? -Not much.
ser **poca cosa** (for) there not to be ➤ Es poca cosa lo que pueda hacer el gobierno a estas alturas. There's not much the government can do at this point.
poca idea tiene que... little does he know (that)...
pocas veces (only) rarely
poco a poco little by little
¡**poco a poco!** take it easy! ■ go easy!
poco a poco llegaremos antes ■ lento pero seguro slowly but surely
ser **poco amigo(-a) de** not to be at all fond of ■ not to be very keen on ■ not to be too keen on ➤ Es poco amigo(-a) de cocinar. He's not at all fond of cooking. ■ He's not too keen on cooking. ➤ Es poco amiga de cocinar. She's not at all fond of cooking. ■ She's not too keen on cooking.
poco antes de que...: (muy) ~ shortly before...
ser **poco brillante** ■ ser poco inteligente not to be too bright ■ not to be very bright ■ not to be very intelligent
ser **poco cortés** ■ ser descortés to be impolite ➤ Ella es poco cortés. ■ Ella es descortés. She's impolite.
poco después ■ al poco tiempo soon afterwards ■ shortly afterwards
poco después de shortly after ■ soon after ➤ El avión se estrelló poco después de despegar. The airplane crashed shortly after takeoff. ■ The airplane crashed shortly after taking off. ■ The airplane crashed soon after takeoff ■ The airplane crashed soon after taking off.
estar **poco dispuesto(-a) a hacer algo** ■ estar reacio(-a) a hacer algo ■ estar renuente a hacer algo to be reluctant to do something
(poco es algo,) menos es nada ■ *(Esp.)* menos da una piedra it's better than nothing ■ at least it's something
ser **poco ético** to be unethical
ser **poco exigente** to be lenient ■ to be easygoing ■ not to be (very) demanding ➤ Es un jefe poco exigente (con sus empleados). He's not a very demanding boss.
ser **poco fanático de** not to be fond of ■ not to like to ➤ Es poco fanático de cocinar. He is not fond of cooking. ■ He doesn't like to cook. ➤ Es poco fanático del orden. He's doesn't like to clean up.
ser **poco favorecido por la madre naturaleza** to be short on looks ■ to be very homely
ser **poco hombre** ■ ser un calzonazos to be a wimp
poco importa si it matters little whether ■ it makes little difference whether ■ it doesn't make much difference whether ■ it doesn't matter much whether ➤ Poco importa si vamos en tren o en autobús. It matters little whether we go by train or bus.
(poco) más o menos more or less
poco menos de gente: hay un ~ there are not quite as many people ➤ Hay un poco menos de gente en el pase de esta noche que en el de anoche. There are not quite as many people at tonight's performance as last night's.

poco público low turnout ■ small audience ■ minimal attendance

un **poco raro** a bit odd ■ a little odd ➤ A sus vecinos les parecía un poco rara. Her neighbors thought she was a bit odd. ■ Her neighbors thought her a bit odd. ■ To her neighbors, she seemed a bit odd.

poco sabía ■ no tenía idea de lo que ■ cuán lejos estaba de saber que little did he know

poco sueldo low pay

poco tiempo después ■ dentro de poco ■ al poco tiempo ■ en breve a short time later ■ a little later (on) ■ shortly afterwards ■ soon afterwards ■ in a little while ■ a short time after that ■ shortly after that ■ soon after that ■ a short time after that

poco y malo *(especialmente comida)* measly (helping), poorly prepared ➤ Lo que nos pusieron en aquel restaurante era poco y malo. What we were served in that restaurant was measly and poorly prepared.

pocos días después a few days later

pocos y bien avenidos few and well-matched

pocos y buenos few and good ➤ *(proverbio español)* Libros y amigos, pocos y buenos. Books and friends, few and good.

poder aquisitivo buying power ■ purchasing power

poder alzar la frente ■ poder llevar la frente bien alta ■ poder llevar la cabeza bien alta to be able to hold one's head high

poder comerse un estribo de cobre *(L.am.)* ■ tener el estómago a prueba de bomba to have a cast-iron stomach

poder con algo 1. poder llevar algo que pesa mucho ■ poder levantar algo que pesa mucho to be able to manage something heavy **2.** poder aguantar un prueba o desafío ■ lidiar con algo to weather a test ■ to prevail in the face of adversity ➤ ¿Puedes tú solo con el baúl o te ayudo a llevarlo? ■ ¿Puedes llevar tú solo el baúl o te ayudo? Can you carry the trunk by yourself, or would you like me to help you with it? ■ Can you manage the trunk by yourself, or would you like me to help you with it?

poder con algo pesado to be able to manage something heavy ➤ I need to move the piano, but I can't manage it by myself. Necesito mover el piano, pero no puedo con él yo solo.

poder con alguien 1. ganar a alguien to get the best of someone ■ to beat someone **2.** superarle a alguien to be beyond someone ■ to be more than one can deal with **3.** lidiar con alguien ■ defenderse de alguien to hold one's own with someone ■ to deal with someone ➤ Yo puedo contigo. ■ Yo te puedo. I can whip you! ■ I can beat you! ➤ Mi hermano mayor y yo nos peleábamos mucho de pequeños pero él siempre podía conmigo. ■ Mi hermano mayor y yo nos peleábamos mucho de pequeños pero él siempre me podía. My big brother and I used to fight all the time when we were kids, but he always got the best of me. ➤ No sé cómo tratar a los niños pequeños en clase. Pueden conmigo. ■ No sé cómo tratar a los niños pequeños en clase. Me pueden. ■ I don't know how to deal with small children in a classroom situation. They are beyond me. ■ I don't know how to deal with small children in a classroom situation. They are more than I can deal with. ➤ No creo que sea un adversario tan difícil, seguro que podré con él. I don't think he is a difficult opponent, I'm sure I can hold my own (with him) ■ I don't think he is a difficult opponent, I'm sure I can deal with him.

poder contarse con los dedos de la mano to be able to count something on one's fingers ■ to be few in number

el **poder de veto** veto power ■ power to veto

el **poder ejecutivo** executive branch

poder es querer ■ donde hay voluntad, hay un camino where there's a will, there's a way

poder esperar sentado not to hold one's breath ➤ ¿Quieres salir con ella? ¡Ja! Puedes esperar sentado. You want to go out with her? Well, don't hold your breath.

poder hacer algo 1. to be able to do something **2.** to get to do something ➤ ¿Puedes montar en bicicleta? Can you ride a bicycle? ➤ *(queja de niños)* ¿Por qué ella puede ir y yo no? Why does she get to go and not me? *("Not me" es coloquial. La forma correcta es "not I".)*

el **poder judicial** judicial branch

poder leerse como si de un libro se tratara ■ ser un libro abierto to read someone like a book ■ to be an open book

el **poder legislativo** legislative branch

el **poder mental** brain power

poder negro ■ black power black power

poder oír el vuelo de una mosca to be able to hear a pin drop

poder permitirse algo ■ poderse permitir algo ■ poder afrontar algo ■ poder costear algo to be able to afford something ➤ ¿Podemos permitírnoslo? Can we afford it? ➤ No puedo permitírmelo. ■ No me lo puedo permitir. ■ No puedo afrontarlo. ■ No me lo puedo costear. I can't afford it.

poder ser tratado to become treatable ➤ En pocos años, las enfermedades retrovirales podrán ser tratadas. Within a few years, retroviral illnesses will become treatable.

poder verse to be able to be seen ➤ Por medio del diagrama, puede verse cómo montar la maqueta. From the diagram, you can see how to assemble the kit. ■ From the diagram, one can see how to assemble the kit.

poderse ver desde to be visible from ■ to be able to be seen from ➤ Desde la habitación de nuestro hotel, se podía ver el bosque del Retiro. From our hotel room, you could see the woods of the Retiro Park.

los **poderes fácticos** the powers that be

poderes públicos (public) authorities

poderío de un país power of a country ➤ El poderío de España en la Comunidad Europea se irá consolidando con el tiempo. Spain's power in the European Community is strengthening over time.

poderío económico de un país economic power of a country

poderío militar de un país military power of a country

poderosa razón compelling reason

poderoso caballero es don dinero *(Quevedo)* money talks

poderse permitir algo ■ poder permitirse algo ■ poder afrontar algo ■ poder costear algo to be able to afford something ➤ No me lo puedo permitír. ■ No puedo afrontarlo. ■ No me lo puedo costear. I can't afford it.

podía haber asegurado que...: (yo) ~ I could have sworn (that)...

podía haber bailado toda la noche: (yo) ~ I could have danced all night

podía haber tenido en cuenta: (yo) ~ I might have considered

¡**podía haberlo dicho (yo)!** ■ ¡dime algo que no sepa! I could have said that myself! ■ so, what else is new?! ■ tell me something I don't know!

podía hacerlo: uno ~ one could do it ➤ Todo el mundo le dijo a Phileas Fogg que era imposible dar la vuelta al mundo en ochenta días, pero él sabía que podia hacerlo. Everyone told Phileas Fogg that it was impossible to go around the world in eighty days, but he knew (that) he could do it.

uno **podía tener** one could have ■ one might have ➤ Fue preocupante enterarnos de que había una posibilidad de que nuestra hija podía tener la misma enfermedad. It was worrisome to find out that our daughter might have the same condition. ■ It was worrisome to find out that our daughter could have the same condition. ➤ Mi abuela me contó que en aquella época nadie podía tener un coche sin levantar envidias. My grandmother told me that in those days, you couldn't have a car without making people envious.

uno **podría añadir** ■ (yo) podría agregar I might add ➤ Ella siempre pedía lo más caro que había en la carta, y podría añadir, nunca devolvió el favor. She always ordered the most expensive thing on the menu, and, I might add, she never returned the favor.

podría argüirse que... ■ se podría argüir que... it could be argued that...

podría debatirse (si...) ■ se podría debatir (si...) it is debatable (whether...) ■ that's debatable

podría decirse que... ■ se podría decir que... it could be said that... ■ it is safe to say that...

podría entenderse it could be understood

podría entenderse como... it could be understood as... ■ it could be interpreted as...

podría haber there could be ➤ Basándose en el tipo de la reducción del deficit, la Junta de la Reserva Federal predice que podría haber una subida del dólar en los próximos meses. Based on the rate of deficit reduction, the Federal Reserve Board predicts there could be a rise in the dollar in the coming months.

uno **podría haber...** one could have... ➤ Yo podría haber jurado que la expresión de la cara del cerdo se alteró cuando el chef lo cortó. I could have sworn that the expression on that pig's face changed when he carved it. ➤ Enrique dijo que su padre podría haber sido un gran futbolista, pero se lesionó siendo muy joven. ■ Enrique dijo que su padre pudo haber sido un gran futbolista, pero se lesionó siendo muy joven. Enrique said his father could have been a great football player, but he was injured at a very young age. ➤ Si no hubiera metido la pata hasta el fondo, podría haber ganado las elecciones. If he hadn't made the fatal gaffe, he could have won the election.

uno **podría haber hecho mucho más** ■ uno pudo haber hecho mucho más one could have done much more

uno **podría haber muerto** ■ uno pudo haber muerto **1.** one could have died **2.** one could have been killed ➤ La víctima del derrumbe podría haber muerto si no llega a ser por los servicios de emergencia. The victim of the collapse might have died if it had not been for the paramedics. ➤ Si el equipo de rescate lo hubiera encontrado apenas unos minutos más tarde, la víctima podría haber muerto. The victim could have died if the rescuers had found him even a few minutes later. ➤ Ese escritor que mencionas podría haber muerto el año pasado, pero no estoy seguro. The writer you're referring to may have died last year, but I'm not sure (of that). ➤ La víctima podría haber muerto o por los golpes sufridos o por parada cardiorespiratoria. The victim could have died either from the blows suffered or from heart failure.

podría haber sido... 1. it could have been... **2.** *(uno)* one could have been...

podría haberlo there could be

uno **podría ir** one could go ■ one would be able to go ➤ Podría ir si fuéramos el viernes por la noche. I could go if we went on Friday night. ■ I would be able to go if we went on Friday night. ■ I'd be able to go if we went on Friday night. ➤ Volví a llamarla para decir que finalmente sí podría ir. I called her back and said (that) I could go after all.

podría no haber 1. there might not be **2.** *(uno)* one might not have... ➤ Vamos a darnos prisa. Podría no haber más asientos. Let's hurry. There might not be any more seats. ➤ Yo podría no haberla conocido si no hubiera ido a la fiesta. I might not have met her if I hadn't gone to the party.

podría no haberlo hecho 1. *(yo)* I might not have (done it) **2.** *(él)* he might not have (done it) **3.** *(ella)* she might not have done it

podría no parecer mucho, pero... ■ puede no parecer mucho, pero... it might not seem like much, but...

podría ser 1. it could be **2.** tal vez sea ■ puede que sea ■ quizás sea it might be ➤ Podría ser difícil reunir tantos voluntarios. ■ Tal vez sea difícil reunir tantos voluntarios. ■ Puede que sea difícil reunir tantos voluntarios. ■ Quizás sea difícil reunir tantos voluntarios. It could be difficult to get that many volunteers. ■ It might be difficult to get that many volunteers.

podríamos decir ■ como si dijéramos ■ por así decir ■ por decirlo así so to speak ■ as it were

podríamos llamar shall we say ■ let's say ➤ Nos encontramos en el triste colectivo de las, podríamos llamar, víctimas de las cuentas mal hechas. We find ourselves among the sad collection of those who, shall we say, are victims of improper accounting.

podrían pasar meses that could take months ■ it could take months ■ it could be months

podrían pasar meses para it could takes months to... ■ it could be months before...

¡**podrías!** you *could* (if you wanted to)

estar **podrido(-a) de dinero** to be filthy rich

estar **podrido(-a) hasta la médula** to be rotten to the core

el **poema de amor** love poem ➤ Quevedo escribió el poema de amor más hermoso de la lengua española. Quevedo wrote the most beautiful love poem in the Spanish language.

el **poema infantil** nursery rhyme

polarizar la atención de los medios de comunicación to receive media attention ➤ La ejecución polarizó la atención de los medios de comunicación. The execution received widespread media attention.

polémico entrevistador de televisión controversial television interviewer

polémico viaje controversial trip

policía antidisturbios riot police

policía encubierto ■ agente encubierto undercover agent

policía vestido de civil plainclothes policeman ■ plainclothes police officer

policías y ladrones: jugar a ~ to play cops and robbers

política de acoso politics of intimidation

política de apaciguamiento ■ política de confraternización policy of appeasement ■ appeasement policy

política de confraternización ■ política de apaciguamiento policy of appeasement ■ appeasement policy

política de devolución return policy ➤ Compro ahí porque tienen una política de devolución muy flexible. I shop there because they have a liberal return policy.

política de echar parches patchwork policy

política exterior foreign policy

política para la galería playing to the crowd

política partidista partisan politics

ser la **polla** *(subido de tono)* to be a kick *(Nota: La expresión inglesa no resulta tan subida de tono como la española.)* ➤ La última peli que vimos era la polla. Acción, humor-no le faltaba de nada. The last flick we saw was a kick. Action, humor-it had it all.

ser el **polo opuesto** to be completely different from ■ to be exact opposites ➤ Nacho es el polo opuesto a Paco. Nacho and Paco are completely different. ■ Nacho is completely different from Paco. ■ Nacho and Paco are exact opposites.

ser **polos opuestos 1.** *(referido a la personalidad)* to be exact opposites ■ to be completely different **2.** *(referido a los puntos de vista)* to be poles apart

polos opuestos se atraen opposites attract

polvareda política political rumpus

polvo eres y en polvo te convertirás ashes to ashes, dust to dust

polvo salvaje: echar un ~ *(subido de tono)* to have wild sex

polvos de picapica *(para bromas pesadas)* itching powder

polvos de talco talcum powder

pomo de la puerta ■ picaporte de la puerta doorknob

¡**pon dos!** ■ ¡que sean dos! make it two! ■ make that two!

¡**pon cuatro!** ■ ¡que sean cuatro! make it four! ■ make that four!

el **ponche de huevo** eggnog

ponderar la nota to weight the grade

ponderación de la nota weighting of the grade ■ adjustment of the grade ➤ Con la pequeña ponderación de la nota With the little weighting of the grade ■ With the little adjustment of the grade

ponderar la cantidad ■ ponderar la suma to ponder the sum

ponencia económica economic report

ponencia universitaria convocation ■ (special) university lecture ■ special (academic) presentation ■ (academic) assembly

poner a alguien a buen recaudo 1. to put someone where he can do no harm **2.** to put someone where he cannot escape

poner a alguien a caer de un burro ■ poner a alguien a caldo ■ poner a alguien verde to rake someone over the coals

poner a alguien a caldo ■ poner a alguien a caer de un burro ■ poner a alguien verde to rake someone over the coals

poner a alguien a cien 1. enfadar a alguien to make someone mad ■ to drive someone up the wall **2.** encender a alguien ■ prender a alguien to really turn someone on (sexually) ■ to give someone the hots ➤ Los hijos de mi hermana me ponen a cien. Están muy mimados. My sister's children make me mad. They are so spoiled. ■ My sister's children drive me up the wall. They are so spoiled. ➤ Tú me pones a cien cuando me acaricias. Your caresses really turn me on. ➤ Lo puso a cien. She turned him on.

poner a alguien a prueba to put someone to the test

poner a alguien a raya to bring someone into line

poner a alguien a tono 1. poner a alguien cachondo to make someone horny **2.** dejar a alguien colocado to make someone high (on drugs) **3.** poner las pilas a alguien to build a fire under someone **4.** poner a alguien en forma to put someone in good (physical) shape

poner a alguien a trabajar to put someone to work

poner a alguien a un paso de... to put someone on the verge of... ■ to bring someone to the verge of...

poner a alguien a un paso de la muerte to bring someone to the verge of death ➤ Su enfermedad lo puso a un paso de la muerte. ■ *(Esp., leísmo)* Su enfermedad le puso a un paso de la muerte. His illness brought him to the verge of death. ■ His illness brought him to the point of death. ➤ Su enfermedad la puso a un paso de la muerte. Her illness brought her to the verge of death. ■ Her illness brought her to the point of death.

poner a alguien a un paso del suicidio to bring someone to the verge of suicide ➤ Una terrible depresión lo puso a un paso del suicidio. A terrible depression brought him to the verge of suicide.

poner a alguien al corriente de algo ■ poner a alguien al día de algo ■ poner a alguien al tanto to catch someone up on something ➤ Hace la tira que no te veo. Ponme al corriente de tu vida. I haven't seen you in ages. Catch me up on yourself.

poner a alguien al día de algo ■ poner a alguien al corriente de algo to catch someone up on something ➤ Hace la tira que no te veo. Ponme al día de tu vida. I haven't seen you in ages. Catch me up on yourself.

poner a alguien al tanto con algo ■ poner a alguien al tanto de algo to bring someone up to date on something

poner a alguien al teléfono to get someone on the phone ➤ Póngame a su jefe al teléfono. Get me his boss on the telephone. ■ Get his boss for me on the telephone.

poner a alguien bajo el ala ■ meter a alguien bajo el ala to take someone under one's wing

poner a alguien cara de culo *(soez)* ■ poner cara de desagrado ■ poner cara de descontento to give someone a dirty look

poner a alguien como ejemplo a alguien to hold up someone as an example to someone ■ to hold someone up as an example to someone

poner a alguien como un Cristo to mistreat someone badly (physically or verbally) ■ to call someone every name in the book

poner a alguien como un trapo ■ criticar a alguien con mucha dureza to give someone a dressing down ■ to chew someone out ■ to give someone a withering blast (of criticism)

poner a alguien contra la pared *(literal y figurativo)* to back someone up against a wall

poner a alguien de mala leche *(subido de tono)* ■ enojar a alguien ■ enfadar a alguien ■ cabrear a alguien to make someone mad

poner a alguien de mil colores 1. *(con bochorno)* to embarrass someone ■ to turn someone crimson 2. *(con ira o rabia)* to make someone flush with anger

poner a alguien de parte de uno to get someone on one's side

poner a alguien de patitas en la calle ■ poner a alguien en la calle 1. despedir a alguien to fire someone ■ to sack someone ■ to give someone his walking papers ■ to put somebody out on the street 2. desahuciar a alguien to put someone out on the street ■ to evict someone

poner a alguien de testigo to be one's witness ■ to call on someone as a witness ■ to call on someone to corroborate one's story ■ to call on someone to back one up ➤ ¿Cómo que no soy capaz de encestar tres triples seguidos? Ven conmigo a la cancha que te voy a poner de testigo. What do mean I can't make three baskets in a row? Come to the court with me and be my witness.

poner a alguien de todos los colores to make someone blush ■ to embarrass someone

poner a alguien de vuelta y media to chew someone out ■ to give someone a dressing down

poner a alguien derecho to set someone straight ■ to correct someone

poner a alguien en antecedentes to brief someone

poner a alguien en contra de algo to turn someone against something

poner a alguien en contra de alguien ■ echar a alguien contra alguien to turn someone against someone

ponerse a alguien en contra de uno mismo to turn someone against oneself ■ to alienate someone ➤ Al no invitar a mi suegra a ir a la playa con nosotros, me la he puesto en contra. By not inviting my mother-in-law to go to the beach with us, I've turned her against me. ➤ Al no invitar a su suegra a ir a la playa con ellos, se la ha puesto en contra. By not inviting his mother-in-law to go to the beach with them, he's turned her against him.

poner a alguien en cuarentena to place someone in quarantine ■ to quarantine someone

poner a alguien en el arroyo ■ plantar a alguien en el arroyo to ditch someone ■ to leave someone high and dry ➤ Cuando su carrera como actor despegó, plantó a su novia en el arroyo y se casó con una modelo. When his acting career took off, he ditched his girlfriend and married a model.

poner a alguien en guardia contra algo 1. alertar a alguien to put someone on alert against something ■ to warn someone about something 2. hacer desconfiar a alguien to put someone on (one's) guard ■ to make someone (feel) guarded ➤ En la tercera parte de Saga de los Forsyte, Irene trata, muy sutilmente, de poner en guardia a su hijo Jolyon contra su compromiso con Fleur. ■ En la tercera parte de Saga de los Forsyte, Irene, muy sutilmente, trata de alertar a su hijo Jolyon contra su compromiso con Fleur. In the third volume of the Forsyte Saga, Irene tries to warn her son in subtle ways about his engagement to Fleur. ➤ Las miradas que me echaba aquel chico en el metro me pusieron en guardia. ■ Las miradas que me echaba aquel chico en el metro me hizo desconfiar de él. The sidelong glances of that guy in the subway put me on my guard. ■ The sidelong glances of that guy in the subway made me feel guarded.

poner a alguien en jaque ■ poner en jaque a alguien ■ poner a alguien en una situación difícil 1. dejar a alguien sin saber qué hacer to put someone in a quandary 2. poner a alguien en apuros to put someone in jeopardy ■ to get the best of someone ■ to outfox someone ➤ La fiebre del pollo ha puesto en jaque a las autoridades sanitarias. The bird flu has the authorities in a quandary. ➤ El fútbol es un deporte impredecible: un equipo de segunda puede poner en jaque a los grandes en el momento más inesperado. Football is an unpredictable sport. A second rate team can put a major team in jeopardy at the most unexpected moment. ➤ El detective le dijo a su compañero: El asesino nos ha puesto en jaque; no tenemos ni una sola pista sobre su paradero. The detective said to his partner, "The killer has outfoxed us. We have no clue as to his whereabouts."

poner a alguien en la calle ■ poner a alguien de patitas en la calle 1. despedir a alguien to fire someone ■ to sack someone ■ to give someone his walking papers ■ to put somebody out on the street 2. desahuciar a alguien to put someone out on the street ■ to evict someone

poner a alguien en la lista negra to blacklist someone ■ to put someone on the blacklist ■ to put someone's name on the blacklist

poner a alguien en la mitad del arroyo to ditch someone ■ to leave someone high and dry

poner a alguien en la picota ■ someter a alguien al escarnio público to hold someone up to public scorn ■ to make an example of someone ➤ Algunos periódicos pusieron en la picota a la directiva de la entidad bancaria que quebró por fraude. Some newspapers held the managers of the failed bank up to public scorn for (having committed) fraud.

poner a alguien en la sombra *(coloquial)* ■ encarcelar a alguien to throw someone in the klinker ■ to put someone in jail

poner a alguien en libertad to release someone (from detention) ■ to free someone ■ to set someone free

poner a alguien en relación con alguien ■ poner a alguien en contacto con alguien to put someone in touch with someone ➤ Un vecino mío me puso en relación con un club de amantes de los pájaros. My neighbor put me in touch with a birdwatchers club.

poner algo en ridículo ■ dejar algo en ridículo ■ dejar algo por ridículo ■ hacer el ridículo sobre algo to make a mockery of something ■ to make something look ridiculous

poner a alguien en ridículo ■ dejar a alguien en ridículo ■ dejar a alguien por ridículo ■ hacer quedar a alguien en ridículo to mock someone ■ to ridicule someone ■ to make a fool of someone ■ to make someone look ridiculous

poner a alguien en su lugar ■ poner a alguien en su sitio ■ bajarle los humos a alguien ■ bajarle el copete a alguien to put someone in his place

poner a alguien en su sitio ■ poner a alguien en su lugar ■ bajar los humos a alguien ■ bajar el copete a alguien to put someone in his place ■ to take someone down a peg

poner a alguien en un brete ■ poner a alguien en un compromiso to put someone on the spot

poner a alguien en un compromiso ■ poner a alguien en un brete to put someone on the spot

poner a alguien en un pedestal ■ poner a alguien en un altar to put someone on a pedestal

poner a alguien en vereda ■ meter a alguien en vereda ■ meter a alguien en vara to bring someone into line

poner a alguien (enfermo) de los nervios to get on someone's nerves ➤ La grosería de los camareros de este restaurante me está poniendo (enfermo) de los nervios. The rude waiters in this restaurant get on my nerves.

poner a alguien fuera de combate to put someone out of action ■ to put someone out of commission

poner a alguien negro ■ tener a alguien harto ■ hartar a alguien to make someone mad ■ to upset someone ■ to get on someone's nerves ➤ La vecina de al lado con la "música" a toda pastilla, me pone negro. ■ La vecina de al lado con la "música" a toda pastilla, me tiene harto. My nextdoor neighbor, with her "music" turned up full blast, gets on my nerves.

poner a alguien por las nubes to praise someone to the skies

poner a alguien por testigo to be one's witness ➤ *(Scarlet O'Hara)* A Dios pongo por testigo que nunca volveré a pasar hambre. As God is my witness, I'll never go hungry again.

poner a alguien un par de banderillas ■ poner a alguien una banderilla ■ tirar una puya a alguien ■ meter una puya a alguien 1. *(jocoso)* to give someone a bad time ■ to throw barbs (at someone) 2. *(con ánimo de herir)* to taunt someone ■ to provoke someone ■ to pick on someone 3. ponerle los cuernos a alguien to cheat on one's (sexual) partner

poner a alguien una banderilla ■ poner a alguien un par de banderillas ■ tirar una puya a alguien ■ meter una puya a alguien 1. *(jocoso)* to give someone a bad time ■ to throw barbs (at someone) 2. *(con ánimo de herir)* to taunt someone 3. ponerle los cuernos a alguien to cheat on one's (sexual) partner

poner a alguien verde ■ echar una bronca a alguien ■ poner a alguien a caldo ■ poner a alguien a caer de un burro 1. to bawl someone out (to his face) 2. to bad-mouth someone (in his absence)

poner a alguien verde de envidia *(coloquial)* ■ ponerle los dientes largos a alguien to make someone envious ■ to turn someone green with envy

poner a mal tiempo buena cara to put on a brave face ■ to grin and bear it ■ to make the best of a bad situation

poner a parir a alguien *(Esp.)* ■ criticar a alguien to cut someone to ribbons ■ to criticize someone

poner a precalentar el horno to preheat the oven ➤ Pon a precalentar el horno a 350°F. Pre-heat the oven to 350°F.

poner a prueba a alguien to put someone to the test ➤ Los alumnos pusieron a prueba a la sustituta. The students put the substitute teacher to the test.

poner a prueba la paciencia de alguien to try someone's patience ➤ Los de sexto pusieron a prueba la paciencia del sustituto. The sixth graders tried the substitute's patience.

poner a punto un motor to tune (up) an engine

poner a raya to bring into line

poner a remojo los frijoles ■ poner en remojo los frijoles to soak the beans ➤ Tienes que poner los frijoles en remojo toda la noche antes de cocinarlos. You have to soak those beans overnight before you cook them.

poner a toda pastilla ■ poner a todo volumen to turn up full blast ➤ Su madre, que no oye bien, pone la tele a toda pastilla. His mother, who does not hear well, turns the TV up full blast.

poner a trabajar a alguien to put someone to work

poner a un sospechoso bajo custodia judicial ■ detener a un sospechoso ■ aprehender a un sospechoso to take a suspect into custoday ■ to detain a suspect ■ to apprehend a suspect ➤ Algunos potenciales sospechosos fueron puestos bajo custodia judicial para ser interrogados. ■ Algunos potenciales sospechosos fueron detenidos para ser interrogados. ■ Algunos potenciales sospechosos fueron aprehendidos para ser interrogados. Some potential suspects were taken into custody for questioning. ■ Some potential suspects were detained for questioning. ■ Some potential suspects were apprehended for questioning.

poner algo a alguien en una bandeja de plata ■ poner algo a alguien en una bandeja ■ servir algo a alguien en bandeja de plata to hand someone something on a silver platter ■ to serve something (up) to someone on a silver platter

poner algo a buen recaudo to put something in a safe place ■ to put something under lock and key

poner algo a derecho to stand something upright

poner algo a disposición de alguien to put something at someone's disposal ■ to put something at the disposal of someone

poner algo a escurrir to let something drain

poner algo a la sombra to put something in the shade ■ to put something out of the (direct) sunlight

poner algo a la venta to put something on sale

poner algo a la vista de alguien to put something where someone can see it

poner algo a nivel 1. to place something level ■ to level 2. nivelar algo to level something ■ to make something level ➤ Cuanto más alto el edificio, más importante es que las vigas estén puestas a nivel con exactitud milimétrica. The taller the building (is), the more important it is that the beams be placed perfectly level to within thousandths of an inch. ■ The taller the building (is), the more important it is that the beams be leveled to within thousandths of an inch (on either end of the building). ➤ El albañil puso el suelo a nivel llenando con agua una manguera transparente. The carpenter leveled the floor by filling a transparent hose with water. ■ The carpenter made the floor level by filling a transparent hose with water.

poner algo a prueba to put something to the test

poner algo a prueba to put something to the test ■ to try something out ■ to try out something ■ to test something ➤ En una estancia de 117 días, los astronautas pondrán a prueba el mayor ingenio orbital de la historia. For 117 days, the astronauts will put to the test the largest orbiting device in history.

poner algo a subasta ■ *(más común)* subastar algo ■ sacar algo a subasta to place something at auction ■ to auction off something ■ to auction something off ■ to sell something at auction ➤ La familia puso a subasta parte del mobiliario para no pagar el impuesto de sucesión. ■ La familia subastó parte del mobiliario para no pagar el impuesto de sucesión. ■ La familia sacó a subasta parte del mobiliario para no pagar el impuesto de sucesión. The family auctioned off some off their furniture to avoid paying inheritance taxes. ■ The family auctioned some of their furniture off to avoid paying inheritance taxes. ➤ La familia lo puso a subasta. ■ La familia lo subastó. ■ La familia lo sacó a subasta. The family auctioned it off.

poner algo a tono con to make something in keeping with

poner algo al alcance de alguien to put something within someone's reach ■ to put something within reach of someone

poner algo al descubierto to lay something bare

poner algo al remojo to soak something ➤ Se ponen los frijoles al remojo. (You) soak the beans.

poner algo bajo siete llaves to put something under lock and key

poner algo boca abajo ■ colocar algo boca abajo to put something face down ■ to place something face down

poner algo boca arriba to put something face up ■ to place something face up

poner algo claro to make something clear

poner algo como estaba to put something back the way it was ■ to put back something the way it was ➤ Por favor pon los CDs como estaban. Please put the CDs back the way they were. ■ Please put back the CDs the way they were. ➤ Por favor ponlos como estaban. Please put them back the way they were.

poner algo como nuevo ■ dejar algo como nuevo to make something like new

poner algo de relieve ■ destacar algo to highlight something ■ to emphasize something ■ *(culto)* to put something into relief

poner algo delante de los ojos de alguien to dangle something before someone's eyes ➤ Le pusieron un Cadillac reluciente delante de los ojos del cantante y lo cambió por los derechos de autor de su canción más famosa. They dangled a shiny Cadillac before the singer's eyes, and he sold the rights to his most famous song for it.

poner algo derecho to place something level ▪ to place something (vertically) straight ▪ to place something upright ➤ Asegúrate de que las copas no toquen las servilletas sino que estén puestas derechas. Make sure the wine glasses don't touch the napkins, but are placed level on the table.

poner algo en bandeja a alguien 1. to hand something to someone 2. to walk into that one ➤ Me puso el gol en bandeja. He (practically) handed me the goal. ➤ *(tirando pullas)* ¡Me lo has puesto en bandeja! I walked into that one!

poner algo en claro to make something clear

poner algo en conocimiento de alguien ▪ llamar a alguien la atención por algo ▪ llamar a alguien la atención sobre algo to make someone aware of something ▪ to call something to someone's attention ▪ to call someone's attention to something ▪ to bring something to someone's attention ➤ Carlos me puso en conocimiento (de eso). Carlos made me aware of it. ▪ Carlos brought it to my attention.

poner algo en cuestión to call something into question

poner algo en duda ▪ poner algo en tela de juicio to cast doubt on something ▪ to call something into question

poner algo en evidencia to place something in evidence

poner algo en la calle to put something in the street

poner algo en marcha to put something into effect ▪ to initiate ▪ to start ▪ to introduce ➤ La Unión Europea ha puesto en marcha un plan contra el terrorismo biológico. The EU has put into effect a plan against biological terrorism. ▪ The EU has initiated a plan against biological terrorism.

poner algo en peligro to put something in jeopardy ▪ to put something at risk

poner algo en práctica ▪ llevar algo a la práctica to put something into practice ▪ to put something into effect ▪ to make ▪ to effect ➤ Hay que poner en práctica los cambios necesarios para mejorar la distribución de nuestros productos. We need to make the necessary changes to improve the distribution of our products.

poner algo en relieve *(mapas, máscaras, descripción, etc.)* ▪ poner algo en tres dimensiones to put something in relief ▪ to make something three-dimensional ▪ to make something graphic

poner algo en remojo ▪ poner algo a remojo to soak something ▪ to leave something to soak ➤ Pon las alubias en remojo toda la noche. Soak the beans overnight.

poner algo en riesgo to put at risk ▪ to place at risk

poner algo en su sitio to put something (back) where it belongs ▪ to put something (back) where it goes

poner algo en sucio ▪ poner algo en borrador to put something in draft form ▪ to put something in rough form ▪ to make a draft of something

poner algo en tela de juicio ▪ poner algo en entredicho ▪ poner algo en duda to call something into question ▪ to cast doubt on something ➤ Todos los rumores sobre sus amoríos en el pasado ponen en tela de juicio la credibilidad de su matrimonio. Todos los rumores sobre sus amoríos en el pasado ponen en entredicho la credibilidad de su matrimonio. All the gossip about his past love affairs call into question the legitimacy of his marriage. ▪ All the gossip about his past love affairs casts doubt on the legitimacy of his marriage.

poner algo por encima de algo to put something before something else

poner algo por las nubes to praise something to the skies

poner bajo la jurisdicción de jurado de acusación ▪ remitir al jurado de acusación to bind over to the grand jury

poner banderillas a alguien ▪ poner a alguien un par de banderillas ▪ tirar una puya a alguien ▪ meter una puya a alguien 1. *(jocoso)* to give someone a bad time ▪ to throw barbs (at someone) 2. *(con ánimo)* de herir to taunt someone ▪ to provoke someone ▪ to pick on someone 3. ponerle los cuernos a alguien to cheat on one's (sexual) partner

poner buena cara to put on a happy face

poner cara de asco to grimace

poner cara de circunstancias to have the proper bearing (for the occasion)

poner cara de cordero degollado to put on an innocent face ▪ to feign innocence ▪ to put on a long face ▪ to put on a sad face

poner cara de culo *(subido de tono)* ▪ poner mala cara ▪ poner cara de desagrado ▪ poner cara de descontento to give someone a dirty look

poner cara de mala leche to look pissed off

poner cara de pocos amigos to look angry ▪ *(coloquial)* to look mad

poner cara larga to put on a long face

poner caras con nombres ▪ poner las caras con los nombres to put names with faces ▪ to match names with faces ➤ Te mando una foto para que pongas caras con nombres. ▪ Te mando una foto para que pongas las caras con los nombres. I'm sending you a photo so (that) you can put names with faces.

poner casa a alguien ▪ darle casa a alguien to give someone a place to live

poner celoso a alguien ▪ dar celos a alguien ▪ dar achares a alguien to make someone jealous

poner cocodrilos ▪ colocar cocodrilos to attach jumper cables

poner colorado(-a) a alguien ▪ poner rojo(-a) a alguien ▪ avergonzar a alguien to make someone blush ▪ to embarrass someone

poner como ejemplo ▪ poner de ejemplo to give as an example ▪ to cite as an example

poner coto a algo ▪ poner alto a algo ▪ poner fin a algo ▪ dar fin a algo to put a stop to something

poner cubiertos en una mesa de comedor to set places at a dinner table. ➤ Pon seis cubiertos. Set six places.

poner de ejemplo ▪ poner como ejemplo to cite as an example ▪ to give as an example ➤ *(titular)* Francia ha bloqueado la liberalización energética y ha puesto de ejemplo los cortes de luz en California. France has blocked energy reform and has cited as an example the power outages in California.

poner de ejemplo a alguien to make an example of someone ▪ to hold someone up as an example

poner de malas a alguien ▪ hacer enojar a alguien ▪ desesperar a alguien ▪ sacar de quicio a alguien to infuriate someone

poner de manifiesto 1. to make clear 2. to bring out into the open

poner el cascabel al gato ▪ arrojarse a alguna acción atrevida to bell the cat ▪ to do something daring

poner el corazón en algo to set one's heart on something ▪ to have one's heart set on something

poner el crédito en la cuenta to credit the account

poner el culo como un tomate a alguien *(coloquial)* ▪ calentar el culo a alguien ▪ dar unos azotes (en el culo) a alguien ▪ dar a alguien en el culo ▪ azotar a alguien (en el trasero) ▪ zurrar a alguien ▪ dar una zurra a alguien ▪ dar una azotaina a alguien to tan someone's hide ▪ to give someone a spanking ▪ to spank someone

poner el dedo en la llaga ▪ abordar un tema delicado to touch a sore spot ▪ to hit a sore spot ▪ to touch on something unpleasant

poner el despertador a... to set the alarm (of an alarm clock) for... ➤ Siempre pongo el despertador a las seis y cuarenta y cinco. I always set the alarm for 6:45 a.m. ▪ Six forty-five a.m. is the time I always set the alarm for.

poner el dinero to put up the money ▪ to provide the funds

poner el examen to make the exam ➤ Por fáciles que ponga los examenes, tendré que suspender a algún alumno. No matter how easy I make the exams, I'll have to flunk somebody.

poner el grito en el cielo por to scream bloodly murder because of ▪ to scream bloody murder over ▪ to scream bloody murder for

poner el listón muy alto to set the bar high ▪ to aim high

poner el mantel ▪ tender el mantel ▪ explayar el mantel to put the tablecloth on the table ▪ to spread the tablecloth ▪ to lay the tablecloth

poner el número en letra to spell out the number (in letters) ➤ ¿Lo pongo en número o en letra? Shall I write the number in numerals or spell it out?

poner el ojo en alguien ▪ poner los ojos en alguien ▪ tener el ojo puesto en alguien ▪ tener los ojos puestos en alguien to have one's eye on someone

poner el puñal en el pecho a alguien to hold a gun to someone's head

poner el sambenito a alguien *(Esp.)* to point the finger at someone ▪ to accuse someone

poner el sello a un sobre ▪ poner la estampilla a un sobre to put the stamp on an envelope ▪ to stamp an envelope

poner empeño en to put a lot of effort into

poner en alerta to place on alert ▪ to put on alert ➤ *(noticia)* Siria pone en alerta a 35.000 soldados tras el ataque israelí. Syria places 35,000 troops on alert following the Israeli attack.

poner en aprietos a alguien to put someone in a difficult situation

poner en boca de alguien palabras que no ha dicho to put words into someone's mouth

poner en circulación to put in circulation ▪ to put into circulation

poner en el disparadero a alguien to wear someone out ▪ to drive someone to distraction ➤ Me pone en el disparadero que tengamos tantas reuniones de personal. It drives me to distraction that we have so many staff meetings. ▪ It wears me out that we have so many staff meetings. ▪ All the staff meetings wear me out.

poner en entredicho ▪ poner en tela de juicio to call into question ▪ to cast doubt on ➤ Todos los rumores sobre sus amoríos en el pasado ponen en entredicho la credibilidad de su matrimonio. ▪ Todos los rumores sobre sus amoríos en el pasado ponen en tela de juicio la credibilidad de su matrimonio. All the gossip about his past love affairs calls into question the legitimacy of his marriage. ▪ All the gossip about his past love affairs casts doubt on the legitimacy of his marriage.

poner en entredicho (que...) ▪ poner en tela de juicio (que...) to call into question (whether) ▪ to cast doubt on (whether) ➤ Recientes estudios ponen en entredicho que el cannabis tenga tantas propiedades curativas como hasta ahora se había pensado. ▪ Recientes estudios ponen en tela de juicio que el cannabis tenga tantas propiedades curativas como hasta ahora se había pensado. Recent research calls into question whether cannabis has the curative properties it was previously thought to have. ▪ Recent research casts doubt on whether cannabis has the curative properties it was previously thought to have.

poner en escena un ballet to put on a ballet ▪ to stage a ballet ▪ to present a ballet

poner en escena un espectáculo to put on a show ▪ to stage a show

poner en escena una obra de teatro to put on a play ▪ to stage a play ▪ to stage a theatrical production ▪ to present a play

poner en juego 1. to put into play 2. to put at risk ▪ to place at risk

poner en las nubes to extol ▪ to praise

poner en libertad a alguien to release someone (from detention) ▪ to free someone

poner en marcha un motor ▪ arrancar un motor to start the engine ▪ to start the motor ➤ Puse el motor en marcha. ▪ Arranqué el motor. I started the engine. ▪ I started the motor.

poner en marcha una empresa to start a business ▪ to start up a business

poner en movimiento to set in motion

poner en negrita el texto ▪ poner el texto en negrita to put text in bold type

poner en órbita to put into orbit ▪ to send into orbit

poner en orden alfabético según to alphabetize by ➤ Las frases están puestas en orden alfabético según la primera palabra o una palabra clave. The phrases are alphabetized by the first word, or a key word.

poner en tela de juicio (que...) ▪ poner en entredicho (que...) to call into question (whether) ▪ to cast doubt on (whether) ➤ Recientes estudios ponen en tela de juicio que el cannabis tenga tantas propiedades curativas como hasta ahora se había pensado. ▪ Recientes estudios ponen en entredicho que el cannabis tenga tantas propiedades curativas como hasta ahora se había pensado. Recent research calls into question whether cannabis has the curative properties it was previously thought to have.

poner escolta a alguien to provide an escort for someone

poner fecha a to set a date for

poner fin a algo to put an end to something ▪ to put a stop to something

poner fin a su vida ▪ suicidarse to take one's own life ➤ Aquejada de cáncer, ella puso fin a su vida. Suffering from cancer, she took her own life.

poner firme a alguien 1. *(militar)* to call someone to attention 2. *(coloquial)* to crack the whip on ➤ El capitán puso firme a la compañía. The captain called the company to attention. ➤ El entrenador puso firmes a los jugadores menos disciplinados. The trainer cracked the whip on the less disciplined players.

poner freno a algo 1. poner fin a algo to put a stop to something 2. reducir algo to cut down on something ▪ to curb something ➤ Hay que poner freno a las llamadas a larga distancia. We need to put a stop to the long-distance calls. ▪ We need to cut down on the long-distance calls.

poner freno a la boca to control one's tongue

poner freno a lo que... 1. poner fin a lo que... to put a stop to what... 2. reducir lo que... to cut down on what... ▪ to curb what...

poner gasolina (al coche) ▪ echar gasolina (al coche) to put gas in the car ▪ to get gas ➤ Tenemos que parar y poner gasolina. ▪ Tenemos que parar y echar gasolina. We have to stop and get gas.

poner gesto a alguien to smirk at someone

poner haldas en cinta para hacer algo *(arcaico)* ▪ meterse en cinta para hacer algo to get ready to do something

poner la calefacción to turn on the heat

poner la cara larga to put on a long face

poner la casa to offer one's house ➤ Si queréis yo pongo mi casa para la fiesta de Navidad. If you'd like me to, I'll offer my house for the Christmas party.

poner la casa patas arriba ▪ voltear la casa al revés to turn the house upside down ➤ Pusimos la casa patas arriba hasta que dimos con el comprobante. We turned the house upside down until we found the receipt.

poner la estampilla a un sobre ▪ poner el sello a un sobre to put the stamp on an envelope

poner la mano en el fuego por algo to be able to vouch for something ➤ Pongo la mano en el fuego por la veracidad de sus afirmaciones. I can vouch for the truth of what he is saying.

poner la mano en el fuego por alguien to be able to vouch for someone ▪ to be able to recommend someone ➤ Pongo la mano en el fuego por ella. I can vouch for her.

poner la mesa to set the table

poner la mira en algo ▪ tener las miras puestas en algo to set one's sights on something ▪ to have one sights set on something

poner la mira en hacer algo ▪ tener las miras puestas en hacer algo to set one's sights on doing something ▪ to have one's sights set on doing something

poner la oreja to listen to someone else's conversation

poner la otra mejilla to turn the other cheek

poner la primera piedra to lay the first stone

poner la ropa a hacer ▪ dar a lavar y planchar las ropas ▪ dar a hacer la colada to send out the laundry ▪ to send the laundry out ▪ to have the laundry done

poner la rúbrica a algo ▪ firmar algo 1. to sign (one's name to) something 2. poner el sello personal de uno en algo to put one's personal stamp on something ➤ El presidente puso su rúbica al proyecto de ley. The president signed the bill (into law). ➤ Katherine Hepburn pone su rúbica a todas sus interpretaciones. Katherine Hepburn puts her personal stamp on all her performances.

poner la vista en algo ▪ echarle el ojo a algo to have one's eye on something ➤ Mi mujer ha puesto la vista en una casa que quiere que su marido le compre. Pero te aseguro que su marido piensa bien distinto. My wife has her eye on a house she wants her husband to buy (for) her. But her husband, take it from me, has other ideas.

poner las cartas boca arriba ▪ poner las cartas cara arriba ▪ parar las cartas sobre la mesa to lay one's cards (on the table) face up ▪ to put one's cards (on the table) face up

poner las cartas sobre las mesa ▪ poner las cartas boca arriba to lay one's cards on the table ▪ to put one's cards on the table

poner las cosas en orden to put things in order

poner las cosas en su sitio 1. to put things where they belong ▪ to put things up ▪ to put things away **2.** poner las cosas en claro to get something straight ➤ La madre le dijo a su hijo adolescente, "Pon tus cosas en su sitio". The mother told her teenage son, "Put your things away." ➤ Más vale que pongamos las cosas en su sitio, ¿cuánto estás dispuesto a pagar? We'd better get this straight. How much are you willing to pay?

poner las orejas tiesas 1. *(refiriéndose a los animales)* to prick up one's ears **2.** ponerse en alerta to become alert

poner leña al fuego ▪ echar leña al fuego **1.** to put kindling on the fire **2.** empeorar un problema o conflicto to add fuel to the flames

poner los cimientos de 1. *(de un edificio)* to lay the foundation for **2.** *(de un pacto, tratado)* to lay the groundwork for ▪ to lay the foundation for ➤ Acaban de poner los cimientos para un nuevo centro comercial. They just laid the foundation for a new shopping center. ➤ Los negociadores ponen los cimientos de un alto el fuego entre palestinos e israelíes. The negotiators are laying the groundwork for a ceasfire between the Palestinians and the Israelis.

poner los cinco sentidos en algo ▪ tener puestos los cinco sentidos en algo to focus all one's attention on something ▪ to have all one's attention focused on something ▪ to concentrate all one's attention on something

poner los codos en la mesa ▪ clavar codos ▪ poner los codos ▪ estudiar to hit the books ▪ to study

poner los cojones encima de las mesa ▪ poner los cojones en la mesa **1.** imponer la voluntad to impose one's will on someone **2.** imponer la opinión to impose one's opinion on someone

poner los cordones a las zapatillas to lace (up) a pair of athletic shoes

poner los cordones a los zapatos to lace (up) a pair of shoes

poner los huevos en la mesa ▪ poner los cojones encima de la mesa **1.** imponer la voluntad to impose one's will on someone **2.** imponer la opinión to impose one's opinion on someone

poner los ojos bizcos to cross one's eyes ▪ to look cross-eyed

poner los ojos en blanco to turn up the whites of one's eyes ▪ to roll one's eyes

poner los peros to find fault

poner los pies en alto ▪ colocar los pies en alto to put one's feet up

poner los pies en el suelo to come down to Earth ▪ to come down to reality

poner los puntos sobre las íes to dot all the i's and cross all the t's

poner los sellos a un sobre ▪ franquear un sobre to put the stamps on an envelope ▪ to stamp an envelope

poner mala cara (for) one's look to turn sour ▪ (for) one's look to turn angry

poner manos a la obra to get to work

poner morro to smirk

poner nervioso(-a) a alguien to make someone nervous

poner nota a un ejercicio to grade an exercise

poner nota a un examen 1. *(examen final)* to grade an exam **2.** *(control semanal)* prueba semanal to grade a test ▪ to grade a quiz ➤ El profesor aún no ha puesto las notas. The teacher hasn't graded the tests yet. ▪ The teacher still hasn't graded the tests.

poner nota a un trabajo to grade a paper

poner orden en algo to give (logical) order to something

poner paños calientes a algo to apply half measures (to the solution to a problem)

poner parches a una prenda ▪ echar parches a una prenda **1.** to patch an article of clothing **2.** *(cosiendo)* to sew patches on an article of clothing **3.** *(planchando parches adhesivos)* to iron on patches ▪ to iron patches on an article of clothing

poner patas arriba 1. to turn upside down **2.** *(una silla)* to turn the legs upright ▪ to turn the chair upright ➤ He puesto la casa patas arriba buscando el recibo y no consigo encontrarlo. I've turned the house upside down looking for the receipt, and I can't find it. ➤ Pon la silla patas arriba para barnizarla. Turn the chair upright to varnish it. ➤ El bar ha cerrado. Los taburetes están patas arriba encima de las mesas. That bar is closed. The stools are turned upright on the tables.

poner paz to make peace ▪ to call a truce ➤ Había en el parque dos niños peleándose y me fui hacia ellos a poner paz. There were two children in the park fighting, and I went over to them to make peace. ▪ There were two children in the park fighting, and I went over to them to call a truce.

poner pegas a algo 1. entorpecer o dificultar una acción to make something difficult ▪ to make something as difficult as possible ▪ to put obstacles in someone's way ▪ to hinder something **2.** encontrar defectos a algo to find fault with something

poner pegas a alguien 1. poner trabas a alguien ▪ entorpecer la acción de alguien ▪ complicarle la existencia a alguien to make trouble for someone ▪ to put obstacles in someone's way **2.** encontrar defectos a alguien to find fault with someone

poner películas ▪ pasar películas ▪ dar películas to show movies

poner peros a algo to find fault with something ▪ to nitpick

poner peros a alguien to find fault with someone

poner pies en polvorosa *(coloquial)* ▪ tomar las de Villadiego ▪ salir pitando ▪ salir echando chispas ▪ *(L.am.)* mostrar las herraduras ▪ *(Venezuela)* marcar la milla to get the hell out of a place ▪ to beat a trail out of Dodge

poner pleito a alguien to file suit against someone ▪ to take someone to court ▪ to bring an action against someone

poner por los suelos to criticize stridently

poner por obra algo to get something done ▪ to put something into effect ➤ Pongámoslo por obra. Let's get it gone. ▪ Let's do it.

poner por tierra un argumento ▪ echar por tierra un argumento ▪ rebatir un argumento to throw cold water on an argument ▪ to shoot down an argument ▪ to discredit an argument ▪ to demolish an argument ▪ *(coloquial)* to make mincemeat of an argument

poner precio ▪ fijar precio to set the price

poner presión a alguien ▪ presionar a alguien to put pressure on someone ▪ to bear down on someone ➤ Los jefes están poniendo mucha presión a la plantilla. ▪ Los jefes están presionando a la plantilla. The bosses are putting a lot of pressure on the staff. ▪ The bosses are bearing down on the staff.

poner puertas al campo to be impossible ▪ to stop the unstoppable ▪ to (try to) prevent the inevitable ▪ to be impossible to stem the tide ➤ Pretender que ese chico no se vea con su novia es como poner puertas al campo. To try to keep that boy from seeing his girlfriend is impossible. ➤ No se pueden poner puertas al campo. The tide cannot be stemmed. ▪ The tide cannot be turned.

poner punto a ▪ poner punto final a to put an end to

poner punto en boca ▪ echar cremallera to zip one's lips ▪ to button one's lips

poner punto final a ▪ poner punto a to put an end to

poner reparos a algo to raise doubts about something ▪ to raise questions about something

poner rúbrica a algo to sign something ▪ to sign off on something

poner rumbo para 1. to set out for **2.** *(barcos)* to set sail for

poner sobre aviso to warn ▪ to alert

poner sobre aviso a los competidores to alert the competition

poner sobre el tapete to lay one's cards on the table

poner su granito de arena to do one's part ▪ to put in one's five cents' worth

poner término a algo ▪ poner fin a algo to put a stop to something ▪ to put an end to something ▪ to stop something

poner tibio a alguien to singe someone's ears ▪ to give someone a verbal lashing

poner tierra de por medio *(coloquial)* to get out of there ➤ Cuando vimos que el otro conductor se ponía agresivo pusimos tierra de por medio. When we saw that the other driver was becoming aggressive, we got out of there.

poner toda la carne en el asador ▪ echar toda la carne al asador to go all out

poner todos los medios para hacer algo to provide all the means possible to do something

poner trabas to make something difficult ■ to make something as difficult as possible ■ to put obstacles in someone's way

poner un alto precio para to put a high price on ➤ *(titular)* Hezbolá ha puesto un alto precio para entregar a sus tres rehenes israelíes. Hezbollah has put a high price on handing over its three Israeli hostages. ■ Hezbollah has put a high price on returning its three Israeli hostages.

poner un dicho en la boca de alguien ■ atribuir un dicho a alguien to credit someone with a saying ■ to attribute a saying to someone

poner un ejemplo ■ decirle un ejemplo ■ dar un ejemplo **1.** to give an example ■ to cite an example **2.** *(la persona está conscientemente contando)* to give one example ➤ (Te) pongo un ejemplo. I'll give you an example. ➤ Este libro de matemáticas sólo pone un ejemplo, pero se necesitan dos o tres. This math text gives (only) one example, but two or three are needed. ➤ ¿Podrías decirme un ejemplo? Could you give (me) an example? ➤ Déjame ponerte un ejemplo. ■ Déjame darte un ejemplo. Let me give you an example. ➤ Déjame ponerte esto como ejemplo. Let me give you this example. ■ Let me cite this as an example.

poner un huevo 1. *(literal)* to lay an egg **2.** meter la pata to make a faux pas ■ to commit a gaffe

poner un negocio en manos de alguien to turn a business over to someone ➤ Javi, pongo el negocio en tus manos. Javi, I'm turning the business over to you.

poner un par de banderillas a alguien ■ poner una banderilla a alguien ■ poner banderillas a alguien ■ tirar una puya a alguien ■ meter una puya a alguien **1.** *(jocoso)* to give someone a bad time ■ to throw barbs (at someone) **2.** *(con ánimo de herir)* to taunt someone ■ to provoke someone ■ to pick on someone **3.** ponerle los cuernos a alguien to cheat on one's (sexual) partner

poner un parche a una prenda ■ echar un parche a una prenda **1.** to patch an article of clothing **2.** *(cosiendo el parche)* to sew a patch on an article of clothing ■ to sew on a patch ■ to sew a patch on an article of clothing **3.** *(parches adhesivos)* to iron on a patch ■ to iron a patch on an article of clothing

poner un pie en 1. *(dentro)* to set foot in **2.** *(sobre)* to set foot on

poner un puñal en el pecho a alguien to hold a knife to someone's chest

poner un reloj en hora 1. to set a clock **2.** *(de pulsera)* to set a watch

poner un telegrama ■ mandar un telegrama to send a telegram

poner un video to put on a video ■ to play a video

poner una banderilla a alguien ■ poner un par de banderillas a alguien ■ poner banderillas a alguien ■ tirar una puya a alguien ■ meter una puya a alguien **1.** *(jocoso)* to give someone a bad time ■ to throw barbs (at someone) **2.** *(con ánimo de herir)* to taunt someone ■ to provoke someone ■ to pick on someone **3.** ponerle los cuernos a alguien to cheat on one's (sexual) partner

poner una cosa en manos de alguien to put it in someone else's hands ■ to leave it to someone else (to do)

poner una cosa en tela de juicio to call something into question

poner una cosa por delante de otra ■ dar prioridad a algo to put something before something else ■ to give priority to something ■ to give something priority over something else ■ to give something a higher priority than something else ➤ *(consejo paterno a menudo obviado)* A tu edad deberías poner tus estudios por delante de las chicas. ■ A tu edad deberías dar prioridad a tus estudios sobre las chicas. At your age, you should put your studies before girls. ■ At your age, you should give your studies a higher priority than girls.

poner una cosa por las nubes 1. alabar a alguien to praise something to the skies **2.** subir el precio de algo to raise the price of something sky high

poner una hora ■ fijar una hora **1.** *(toque de queda; hora de los adolescentes para volver a casa)* to set a curfew (for adolescents imposed by the parents) **2.** to set a time

poner una mueca ■ hacer una mueca to make a face

poner una multa a alguien 1. multar a alguien to fine someone ■ to give someone a fine ■ to impose a fine on someone **2.** dar una citación to give (someone) a ticket **3.** to get a ticket ➤ Me pusieron una multa por exceso de velocidad. I got a speeding ticket.

poner una película ■ pasar una película to show a movie

poner una prenda bien ■ poner una prenda del derecho to turn a garment right side out ➤ *(calcetín)* Ponlo bien. ■ *(camiseta)* Ponla bien. Turn it right side out.

poner una vela a un santo to light a candle to a saint ■ to invoke good luck (for some enterprise)

poner una venda en los ojos a alguien 1. taparle los ojos a alguien to blindfold someone **2.** engatusar a alguien to pull the wool

poner unas líneas to write a few lines

poner uno de su parte to do one's part ■ to do one's share ➤ No basta con que ayudemos a nuestros hijos con los deberes. Ellos tienen que poner de su parte para sacar buenas notas. It's not enough for us to help our children do their homework. They have to do their part in order to make good grades. ■ It's not enough for us to help our children do their homework. They have to do their share in order to make good grades.

poner verde a alguien *(Esp.)* to bawl someone out

ponerle a alguien al corriente ■ ponerle a alguien al día to bring someone up to date ■ to give someone an update ➤ Sólo quería ponerte al corriente. I just wanted to bring you up to date. ■ I just wanted to give you an update.

ponerle a alguien al día ■ ponerle a alguien al corriente to bring someone up to date ■ to give someone an update ➤ Sólo quería ponerte al día. I just wanted to bring you up to date. ■ I just wanted to give you an update.

ponerle a alguien cara de asco to turn one's nose up at someone

ponerle a alguien el culo como un tomate ■ darle una azotaina a alguien ■ darle una nalgada a alguien to tan someone's hide ■ to give someone a spanking ➤ Como te sigas portando mal, te voy a poner el culo como un tomate. If you keep acting that way, I'm going to tan your hide.

ponerle a alguien la ceniza en la frente (en miércoles de ceniza) to put the ashes on someone's forehead (on Ash Wednesday)

ponerle a alguien la cornamenta ■ ponerle a alguien los cuernos to cheat on someone ■ to be unfaithful to someone

ponerle a alguien los nervios de punta 1. to put someone on edge **2.** to be hysterical ➤ A mí, que soy de un pueblo pequeño, la gran ciudad, con sus ruidos, la gente y la contaminación me pone los nervios de punta. Because I come from a small town, the big city, with all its noises, people and pollution puts me on edge. ➤ *(periodístico)* Después de presenciar aquel accidente tan cerca, a los testigos se les pusieron los nervios de punta. After witnessing the accident close up, several witnesses were hysterical.

ponerle a alguien los pelos de punta to make someone's hair stand on end

ponerle a alguien mala cara to give someone a dirty look ■ *(literario)* to give someone a baleful look

ponerle a alguien un cero grande como una casa ■ ponerle a alguien un cero como una catedral ■ ponerle a alguien un cero patatero to give someone a flat F ■ to flunk someone flat

ponerle a alguien un compañero ■ asignarle a alguien un compañero to assign someone a companion

ponerle a alguien un ojo a la funerala ■ ponerle a alguien un ojo morado to give someone a black eye

ponerle a alguien un ojo morado ■ ponerle a alguien un ojo a la funerala to give someone a black eye

ponerle a alguien un sobresaliente to give someone an A ➤ Me han puesto un sobresaliente en el examen, no te creas. ■ Saqué un sobresaliente en el examen, no te creas. They gave me an A on the test, would you believe. ■ I got an A on the test, would you believe.

ponerle a mal con alguien to cause a rift between two people

ponerle a parir a alguien *(Esp., leísmo)* ■ ponerle verde ■ *(L.am.)* ponerlo a parir a alguien ■ ponerlo verde to bawl someone out

ponerle a un animal una inyección letal ■ sacrificar un animal to give an animal a lethal injection ■ to put an animal to sleep ▪ to euthanize an animal ➤ Después de que el animal fuera herido, el veterinario le puso una inyección con un barbitúrico de acción rápida. ▪ Después de que el animal fuera herido, el veterinario lo sacrificó con un barbitúrico de acción rápida. After the animal was injured, the veterinarian put it to sleep with a fast-acting barbiturate.

ponerle algo a huevo a alguien ▪ ponerle algo a tiro a alguien to make oneself an easy mark ▪ to be (just) asking for it ➤ Llevando esa camiseta de "Yo he visto a Elvis," te has puesto las bromas a huevo. By wearing the "I-Saw-Elvis" T-shirt, you've made yourself an easy mark for people's jokes. ▪ By wearing the "I-Saw-Elvis" T-shirt, you're asking for it.

ponerle asco ▪ darle asco to be revolting ▪ to revolt someone ➤ Él me pone asco. ▪ Él me da asco. He's revolting. ▪ He revolts me. ▪ He's revolting to me.

ponerle banderillas a alguien ▪ poner una banderilla a alguien ▪ poner un par de banderillas a alguien ▪ tirar una puya a alguien ▪ meter una puya a alguien **1.** *(jocoso)* to give someone a bad time ▪ to throw barbs (at someone) **2.** *(con ánimo de herir)* meterse con alguien to taunt someone ▪ to provoke someone ▪ to pick on someone **3.** ponerle los cuernos a alguien to cheat on one's (sexual) partner

ponerle en (la) situación to draw one into the situation ➤ La música de *La bella y la bestia* te pone en la situación. The music of the *Beauty and the Beast* really draws you into the situation.

ponerle falta a alguien to mark someone absent

ponerle fin to put an end to it

ponerle freno a alguien to rein someone in ▪ to check someone

ponerle gusto a algo ▪ hacer que alguien disfrute (de) algo to make something enjoyable ➤ Al tocar el piano así, le pones gusto a la música clásica. When you play the piano like that, you make classical music enjoyable.

ponerle la cara a alguien como un mapa to smash someone's face

ponerle la mano encima a alguien to lay a hand on someone ➤ Ni se te ocurra ponerme la mano encima, o grito. Don't even think of laying a hand on me or I'll scream.

ponerle la zancadilla a alguien 1. to trip someone (by sticking one's foot out) **2.** entorpecer la tarea a alguien to screw somebody over

ponerle las pilas a alguien to build a fire under someone ▪ to get someone moving

ponerle los cuernos a alguien to cheat on someone ▪ to be unfaithful to someone ▪ *(literary)* to make a cuckhold of someone

ponerle los dientes largos a alguien *(coloquial)* ▪ poner a alguien verde de envidia to make someone envious ▪ to turn someone green with envy

ponerle los trastos en la calle ▪ poner a alguien de patitas en la calle to throw someone out ▪ to put someone out on the street ▪ to turn someone out

ponerle música a algo to set something to music ➤ Se le ha puesto música al poema. The poem was set to music.

ponerle triste a uno ▪ entristecerle a uno to make one sad ▪ to sadden one ➤ Me pone triste ver tanta pobreza. It makes me sad to see so much poverty. ▪ It saddens me to see so much poverty. ➤ La noticia me entristeció. The news made me sad. ▪ I was saddened by the news.

ponerle un compañero a alguien ▪ asignarle a alguien un compañero to assign someone a companion ➤ Le pusieron un compañero al policía. ▪ Le asignaron un compañero al policía. They assigned the police officer a companion. They assigned the police officer a companion.

ponerle un pañuelo en los ojos to blindfold someone ➤ Darle vueltas con un pañuelo puesto en los ojos. Spin her around blindfolded.

ponerle un pleito a alguien ▪ demandar a alguien **1.** *(contencioso civil o penal)* to take someone to court **2.** *(contencioso económico)* to sue someone

ponerle un sobresaliente to give someone an A ➤ El catedrático le puso un sobresaliente al estudiante. The professor gave the student an A. ▪ The student got an A. ➤ Me han puesto un sobresaliente en el examen, no te creas. I got an A on the test, would you believe. ▪ Would you believe I got an A on the test?

ponerle una multa a alguien to give someone a ticket

ponerle una pistola en el pecho a alguien to stick a gun in someone's ribs

ponerles los cordones a unas zapatillas (de deporte) to lace up a pair of athletic shoes

ponerle los cordones a unos zapatos to lace up a pair of shoes

ponerlo a parir a alguien to cut someone to ribbons ▪ to criticize someone ▪ to be critical of someone

ponerlo a prueba to put it to the test

ponerlo donde estaba ▪ reponerlo to put it back (where it was)

ponerlo en marcha ▪ prenderlo to turn it on

ponerlos en orden to put them in order ▪ to place them in order

ponerse a hacer algo to begin to do something ▪ to start doing something ▪ to set about doing something

ponerse a actuar (para hacer algo) ▪ ponerse en acción (para hacer algo) ▪ ponerse en camino (para hacer algo) to get going (on something) ▪ to get busy (on something) ▪ to get to work (on something) ➤ Tenemos que ponernos a actuar para acabar el informe a tiempo. We'd better get going if we're going to finish the report on time. ▪ We'd better get going on this report if we're going to finish it on time. ▪ We'd better get busy if we're going to finish the report in time. ▪ We'd better get busy on the report if we're going to finish it on time. ▪ We'd better get to work if we're going to finish the report in time. ▪ We'd better get to work on the report if we're going to finish it on time.

ponerse a bien con alguien to get on good terms with someone ▪ to establish a rapport with someone

ponerse a bien con Dios to start toeing the line ▪ to get right with God

ponerse a cien 1. *(sexual)* to get (sexually) excited ▪ to get turned on ▪ to get horny **2.** *(enfado)* to get really mad

ponerse a cubierto to take cover ▪ to get under cover

ponerse a dieta ▪ ponerse a régimen to go on a diet

ponerse a hacer algo ▪ echarse a hacer algo to start doing something ▪ to set about doing something ▪ to get to the doing of something ▪ to get to doing something ➤ Se puso a llorar. ▪ Se echó a llorar. She started crying. ➤ Él se puso a pitar. He started honking. ➤ Empezaré a consultar bibliografía para mi tesis este verano, pero no me pondré a redactar hasta principios del año que viene. ▪ Empezaré la lectura para mi tesis este verano, pero no me pondré a redactar hasta principios del año que viene. I'll start reading on my thesis this summer, but I won't get to the writing of it until early next year. ▪ I'll start reading on my thesis this summer, but I won't get to writing it until early next year.

ponerse a la altura de ▪ situarse a la altura de ▪ ponerse al lado de ▪ situarse al lado de to pull up alongside of ▪ to come up alongside of ➤ La patrulla policial se puso a la altura del vehículo sospechoso. ▪ La patrulla policial se situó al lado del vehículo sospechoso. The police car pulled up alongside the suspicious vehicle.

ponerse a la cola ▪ ponerse en la cola ▪ ponerse en fila ▪ *(Méx.)* formarse to get in line ➤ Hay que ponerse a la cola. ▪ Hay que formarse. You have to get in line.

ponerse a la de Dios es Cristo *(coloquial)* ▪ ponerse muy alterado to get all bent out of shape

ponerse a la defensiva to go on the defensive

ponerse a la faena *(coloquial)* ▪ ponerse las pilas to get cracking ▪ to get to work ➤ Si planeas acabar eso para mañana, más vale que te pongas a la faena. If you plan to finish that by tomorrow, you'd better get cracking.

ponerse a mal con alguien ▪ ponerse a malas to get on bad terms with someone

ponerse a pitar como (un) loco to start honking like crazy

ponerse a régimen ▪ ponerse a dieta to go on a diet

ponerse a salvo to take refuge ▪ to find shelter ➤ Cuando empezó a llover durante la excursión nos pusimos a salvo en un viejo refugio de montaña. When it started raining during our hike, we took refuge in an old mountain retreat. ▪ When it began to rain during our hike, we found shelter in an old mountain retreat.

ponerse a trabajar en ▪ poner por obra to get to work on

ponerse a tiro ■ ponerse en el punto de mira ■ ponerse en la mira to come into view ■ to enter into one's sights ➤ El faisán se puso a tiro y el cazador abrió fuego. The pheasant came into view, and the hunter opened fire. ■ The pheasant entered the hunter's sights, and he opened fire.

ponerse a tono 1. ponerse cachondo to get horny 2. *(drogas, alcohol)* ■ colocarse to get stoned 3. *(alcohol)* to get drunk 4. ponerse las pilas to get fired up ■ to get motivated 5. ponerse en forma to get in shape 6. ponerse al día con el trabajo to get caught up on work

ponerse a tope 1. ponerse atestado de gente to get crowded ■ to get (jam) packed ■ to get packed like sardines 2. agotarse las entradas to get completely booked (up) 3. ponerse hasta el culo (de drogas) to get stoned (on one's ass) ■ to get coked to the gills

ponerse a trabajar para una empresa to start working for a company ■ to go to work for a company ■ to start working at a company

ponerse agresivo to become aggressive

ponerse (al aparato) ■ ponerse (al teléfono) to come to the phone ■ to get the phone ➤ Dile que se ponga al aparato. ■ Dile que se ponga. Tell him to come to the phone. ■ Tell him to get the phone.

ponerse al cabo de la calle ■ ponerse al día to get up to date ■ to get current

ponerse al corriente to bring oneself up to date

ponerse al día to get caught up ■ to bring oneself up to date ■ to get current

ponerse al frente to take charge

ponerse al frente de algo to take charge of something ➤ Se puso al frente del negocio. He took charge of the business.

ponerse al lado de alguien 1. to side with someone ■ to take someone's side (in a difference of opinions) 2. *(de pie)* to go up (and stand) next to someone ■ to go over (and stand) next to someone 3. *(sentado)* to go over and sit next to someone 4. *(en un vehículo)* to pull up alongside someone ■ to come up alongside someone ➤ Me he puesto al lado de los moderados políticos. I've sided with the political moderates. ➤ La patrulla policial se puso al lado del vehículo sospechoso. ■ La patrulla policial se situó al lado del vehículo sospechoso. The police car pulled up alongside the suspicious vehicle.

ponerse al sol to go out in the sun ■ to sunbathe ➤ Cómo se me ocurre ponerme al sol sin protector solar. ■ Vaya idea la mía de ponerme al sol sin protector solar. I should know better than to go out in the sun without sunscreen.

ponerse (al teléfono) ■ ponerse al aparato to come to the phone ■ to get the phone ➤ Dile a Juan que se ponga (al teléfono). Tell Juan to come to the phone. ■ Tell Juan to get the phone.

ponerse al volante to get behind the wheel

ponerse algo *(ropa)* to put on something ■ to get into something ➤ I want to get into something more comfortable. ■ I want to put on something more comfortable. ■ I want to change into something more comfortable. Quiero ponerme algo más cómodo.

ponerse algo de un color to turn something a color ➤ La boca se nos puso verde de comer caramelos. The candy turned our mouths green.

ponerse a discutir con alguien ■ montarle un cisco a alguien ■ montarle un pollo a alguien to start arguing with someone ■ to get into an argument with someone

ponerse alguien hombro con hombro con otro to collaborate closely with someone ■ to work in close cooperation with someone

ponerse ante el espejo to stand in front of the mirror

ponerse bien to get well ■ to recover

ponerse berraco(-a) 1. ponerse cachondo(-a) to get horny 2. ponerse agresivo to get aggressive

ponerse blanco(-a) como la cera ■ ponerse más blanco(-a) que la cera to turn white as a sheet ➤ Al oír la noticia mi marido se puso blanco como la cera. When my husband heard the news, he turned white as a sheet.

ponerse borde con alguien *(coloquial)* ■ ser cortante to be curt ■ to get ugly ➤ No te pongas borde. Don't be curt. ■ Don't get ugly.

ponerse bruto(-a) ■ ponerse burro(-a) 1. ponerse berraco(-a) to get horny ■ to get hot as firecracker 2. ponerse agresivo to get aggressive ■ to become aggressive

ponerse burro(-a) ■ ponerse bruto(-a) 1. ponerse berraco(-a) ■ ponerse cachondo(-a) to get horny ■ to get hot as a firecracker 2. ponerse agresivo to get aggressive ■ to become bullheaded

ponerse cachondo(-a) to get horny

ponerse cada vez más interesante to get more and more interesting

ponerse cada vez mejor to get better and better ➤ Se pone cada vez mejor. It gets better and better.

ponerse chulo(-a) ■ pasarse de vivo to be a smart aleck ➤ No te pongas chulo. ■ No te pases de vivo. Don't be a smart aleck.

ponerse ciego(-a) 1. ponerse como el Quico ■ ponerse las botas ■ ponerse morado(-a) to eat like a horse ■ to eat one out of house and home 2. to get blind drunk (on alcohol) ■ to get stoned (on drugs)

ponerse ciego(-a) de rabia ■ ponerse ciego de furia ■ ponerse ciego de ira to fly into a blind rage

ponerse colorado(-a) ■ ponerse como la grana ■ ponerse como un tomate to blush ■ to turn beet red ■ to turn red as a beet ■ to turn red in the face

ponerse como el Quico ■ comer como un descosido ■ comer como lima nueva ■ ponerse las botas ■ ponerse ciego(-a) ■ ponerse morado(-a) to eat like a horse

ponerse como la grana ■ ponerse colorado(-a) ■ ponerse como un tomate to blush ■ to turn red as a beet

ponerse como objetivo ■ ponerse la meta de to set the goal of ➤ *(noticia)* El jefe de la policía se pone como objetivo acabar con las mafias. The police chief sets the goal of finishing off the mafia.

ponerse como si le fuera la vida en ello to act as if one's life depended on it ➤ Se pusieron como si les fuera la vida en ello. They acted as if their lives depended on it.

ponerse como un basilisco ■ ponerse hecho(-a) un basilisco to go ballistic ■ to blow a fuse ■ to hit the ceiling ■ to get all bent out of shape

ponerse como un camarón to turn red as a lobster

ponerse como un Cristo ■ ponerse en un estado lamentable to get all banged up ■ to get badly banged up ■ to get hurt

ponerse como un globo to get (all) huffed up ➤ El actor se puso como un globo cuando un paparazzi le sacó una foto. The actor got all huffed up when a paparazzi took a photograph of him.

ponerse como un tomate ■ ponerse como la grana ■ ponerse colorado(-a) to blush ■ to turn red as a beet ■ to get red as a beet

ponerse como un toro ■ ponerse hecho(-a) un toro to get (as) strong as an ox

ponerse como una fiera ■ ponerse como una furia to go ballistic ■ to come unglued ■ to come unhinged ■ to blow a fuse ■ to hit the ceiling ■ to get all bent out of shape

ponerse como una moto *(Esp.)* 1. *(sexualmente, etc.)* to get excited ■ to get hot 2. *(emocionalmente)* to get excited ■ to get all fired up

ponerse como una sopa ■ ponerse hecho(-a) una sopa ■ calarse hasta los huesos to get soaked (to the bone) ■ to get drenched

ponerse cómodo(-a) to make oneself comfortable ➤ ¡Ponte cómodo(-a)! Make yourself comfortable!

ponerse con los brazos en jarras ■ ponerse en jarras to put one's hands on one's hips

ponerse crespo(-a) *(L.am.)* ■ ponerse bravo(-a) ■ *(Esp.)* ponerse de uñas ■ ponerse farruco(-a) ■ ponerse flamenco ■ ponerse chulo(-a) to get exercised ■ to get one's nose out of joint ■ to get one's shirt in a knot ➤ No te pongas crespo. Don't get exercised. ■ Don't get your nose out of joint. ■ Don't get your shirt in a knot.

ponerse de acuerdo ■ llegar a un acuerdo ■ llegar a un concierto to reach an agreement ■ to come to an agreement

ponerse de baja to take time off from work

ponerse de domingo ■ vestirse de domingo ■ endomingarse to dress (up) in one's Sunday best ■ to get dressed up in one's Sunday best

ponerse de lado de algo to side with something ■ to be on the side of something ■ to take sides with something ➤ Hay que ponerse de lado de la democracia en cualquier circunstancia. We have to side with democracy no matter what. ■ We have to be on the side of democracy no matter what. ■ We have to take sides with democracy no matter what.

ponerse de lado de alguien ■ ponerse del lado de alguien to side with someone ■ to take sides with someone

ponerse de largo ■ vestirse de gala to put on a long (evening) dress ■ to put on a long (formal) dress

ponerse de listo con alguien ■ ser atrevido con alguien to get fresh with someone

ponerse de mala leche *(coloquial)* ■ ponerse de mal humor to get hostile ■ to become hostile

ponerse de manifiesto que... to become clear that...

ponerse de mil colores ■ ponerse de veinticinco colores ■ ponerse como un tomate ■ ruborizarse to turn every color in the rainbow ■ to turn (beet) red ■ to turn red in the face ■ to flush with embarrassment ■ to blush

ponerse de moños to sulk

ponerse de morro to stick one's lips out ■ to pout

ponerse de parte de alguien to be on someone's side ■ to side with someone

ponerse de parto to start giving birth ■ to begin giving birth ➤ Al sentir que se ponía de parto... After feeling the beginning of the birth...

ponerse de pie ■ ponerse en pie to stand up ■ to stand

ponerse de punta en blanco ■ ponerse todo elegante ■ ponerse todo hecho(-a) un pincel to get (all) dressed up ■ to get dressed to the nines ➤ Nos pusimos de punta en blanco para ir a la boda de mi hermano. ■ Nos pusimos de largo para ir a la boda de mi hermano. We got all dressed up to go my brother's wedding.

ponerse de rodillas ■ arrodillarse to kneel ■ to kneel down ■ to get (down) on one's knees

ponerse de rodillas ante el altar ■ ponerse de rodillas frente al altar ■ ponerse de rodillas delante del altar ■ arrodillarse ante el altar ■ arrodillarse frente al altar ■ arrodillarse delante del altar to kneel before the altar

ponerse de rodillas ante el obispo ■ arrodillarse ante el obispo to kneel before the bishop

ponerse de veinticinco colores ■ ponerse de mil colores ■ ponerse como un tomate to turn every color in the rainbow ■ to turn (beet) red ■ to turn red in the face ■ to flush with embarrassment ■ to blush

ponerse de(l) lado de algo to side with something ■ to be on the side of something ■ to take sides with something ➤ Hay que ponerse de(l) lado de la democracia en cualquier circunstancia. We have to side with democracy no matter what. ■ We have to be on the side of democracy no matter what. ■ We have to take sides with democracy no matter what.

ponerse de(l) lado de alguien to side with someone ■ to take sides with someone

ponerse derecho to stand up straight ➤ La madre le dijo a su hijo, "Ponte derecho". The mother said to her son, "Stand up straight."

ponerse dura una cosa ■ endurecerse to get hard ■ to harden ■ to set (up) ➤ He puesto los jarrones de arcilla en el horno pero aún no se han puesto duros. I've put the clay vases in the kiln, but they haven't hardened yet. ■ I've put the clay vases in the kiln, but they haven't gotten hard yet. ■ I've put the clay vases in the kiln, but they haven't set (up) yet.

ponerse el mundo por montera ■ llevarse el mundo por delante to throw caution to the wind

ponerse el pene erecto ■ empinársele ■ ponerse dura ■ *(Esp.)* empalmarse to get an erection ■ *(jerga)* to get a hard-on

ponerse en armas *(arcaico)* ■ tomar armas to take up arms

ponerse en cabeza ■ progresar ■ prosperar to get ahead

ponerse en camino (para hacer algo) ■ ponerse en acción (para hacer algo) ■ ponerse a actuar (para hacer algo) to get going (on something) ■ to get busy (on something) ■ to get to work (on something)

ponerse en camino (para una destinación) ■ emprender viaje para to start out (for a destination) ■ to set off down the road (for a destination) ■ to set out (for a destination)

ponerse en común para... to coordinate ones' efforts (in order) to... ➤ Tenemos que ponernos en común para rematar el proyecto. We have to coordinate our efforts (in order) to finish off the project.

ponerse en contacto con alguien to get in touch with someone ➤ ¿Hay forma de ponerse en contacto con él? Is there any way to get in touch with him?

ponerse en cuclillas to squat (down)

ponerse en el medio to get in the way ➤ No te pongas en el medio. Don't get in the way.

ponerse en fila to line up ■ to get in line

ponerse en forma to get in shape ■ to get fit ➤ Necesita perder peso y ponerse en forma. He needs to lose weight and get in shape.

ponerse en formación *(militar)* to get into formation ■ to fall in

ponerse en guardia 1. *(psicológicamente)* to put up one's guard ■ to become guarded **2.** *(militar)* to put up one's guard ➤ Cada vez que su cuñado se le acerca se pone en guardia. Normalmente sólo se dirige a él para darle sablazos. Every time his brother-in-law comes around, he puts up his guard. Usually he only goes to him to hit him up for some bucks. ■ Every time his brother-in-law comes around, he becomes guarded. Usually he only goes to him to hit him up for some bucks.

ponerse en jarras ■ ponerse con los brazos en jarras to put one's hands on one's hips

ponerse en juego ■ entrar en juego to come into play ➤ En la regulación de las emociones se pone en juego, sobre todo, el cortex prefrontal. In the regulation of the emotions the prefrontal cortex, above all, comes into play.

ponerse en la mira ■ ponerse en el punto de mira to come into view ■ to enter into one's sights ➤ El faisán se puso en la mira y el cazador abrió fuego. The pheasant came into view, and the hunter opened fire. ■ The pheasant entered the hunter's sights, and he opened fire.

ponerse en lo peor to imagine the worst ■ to imagine a worst-case scenario

ponerse en lugar de otro to put oneself in another's place ■ *(coloquial)* to put oneself in another's shoes

poner algo en manos de alguien ■ delegar algo a alguien to delegate something to someone ■ to put something in another's hands

ponerse en manos de alguien to put oneself in another's hands ➤ Al aceptar la cirugía, se puso en manos del curandero. On agreeing to the surgery, he put his life in the witch doctor's hands.

ponerse en marcha 1. arrancar (for) something to start (up) ■ (for) something to start running **2.** salir (for) something to start off ■ to leave **3.** *(por una acción externa)* ser activado por to be activated by ■ to be set in motion **4.** *(por sí mismo)* prenderse automáticamente to go on ■ to turn on ■ to activate itself **5.** ponerse en movimiento to begin moving ■ to start moving ➤ A pesar de que hacía frío por la mañana, el motor se puso en marcha de primera. In spite of the cold morning, the engine started right up. ➤ La lavadora se puso en marcha cuando apreté el botón de encendido. The washing machine started running when I pressed the "on" button. ➤ Después de las once, los radiadores se ponen en marcha solos. After eleven, the radiators turn themselves on. ➤ A la hora convenida el autobús se puso en marcha. At the specified time, the bus started off (on its route). ➤ El tren no se pone en marcha hasta la una. ■ El tren no sale hasta la una. The train doesn't leave until one. ➤ Hay que ponerse en marcha antes de que salga el sol. *(tú)* You need to leave before sunup. ■ *(nosotros)* We need to leave before sunup. ■ *(general)* It's essential to leave before sunup. ➤ El sistema de iluminación se pone en marcha mediante un sencillo mecanismo. The lighting system is activated by a simple mechanism. ■ The lighting system is turned on by a simple mechanism. ■ The lighting system activates itself. ■ The lighting system turns itself on. ➤ La noria se pone en marcha a través de un complejo sistema de cables y poleas. The Ferris Wheel is operated by (means of) a complex system of cables and pulleys. ■ The Ferris Wheel is set in motion by a complex system of cables and pulleys. ■ The Ferris Wheel runs on a complex system of cables and pulleys. ➤ Las atracciones del parque se ponen en marcha después del toque del silbato, así se previenen los accidentes. The amusement park rides begin moving after the sound of a whistle, which prevents accidents. ■ The amusement park rides start moving after the sound of a whistle, which prevents accidents.

ponerse en medio de alguien to get in someone's way

ponerse en movimiento to start moving

ponerse en pie ■ ponerse de pie to stand up ■ to stand

ponerse en pie de guerra to prepare for war ■ to get on a war footing

ponerse en rojo *(semáforo)* ■ ponerse la (luz) roja to turn red ➤ ¿Qué puñetas haces? ¡Se ha puesto la luz roja! ■ ¿Qué puñetas haces? ¡Se ha puesto en rojo! What the heck are you doing? The light's turned red!

ponerse en verde *(semáforo)* ■ ponerse la (luz) verde to turn green ➤ Cuando se ponga en verde... When it turns green... ➤ Se ha puesto en verde. It's (turned) green.

ponerse enfermo ■ enfermarse to get sick

ponerse enfrente de alguien to get in front of someone

ponerse flamenco *(Esp.)* ■ ponerse gallito ■ ponerse chulo to get sassy

ponerse frenético to get frantic ■ to become frantic

ponerse fuera de quicio por algo to get all worked up over something ■ to get all bent out of shape over something ■ to get all worked up about something ■ to get all bent out of shape about something

ponerse fuera de sí por algo to get all worked up over something ■ to get exercised about something ■ *(coloquial)* to get all bent out of shape about something ■ to get all bent out of shape over something ■ to get one's nose out of joint ■ to get one's shirt in a knot ➤ No te pongas fuera de ti. Don't get all worked up. ■ Don't get all bent out of shape. ■ Don't get your nose out of joint. ■ Don't get your shirt in a knot.

ponerse gallito ■ ponerse flamenco ■ ponerse chulo(-a) to get sassy

ponerse hasta el culo ■ ponerse ciego(-a) **1.** *(comida)* ponerse morado(-a) ■ ponerse como el Quico to eat like a horse ■ to eat someone out of house and home **2.** *(drogas)* to get stoned

ponerse hecho(-a) un basilisco ■ ponerse como un basilisco ■ ponerse hecho(-a) un energúmeno ■ ponerse hecho una fiera ■ ponerse hecho(-a) una furia to blow a fuse ■ to hit the ceiling ■ to go ballistic ➤ Yo que tú, no me pondría hecho un basilisco. ■ No merece la pena que te pongas como un basilisco. I wouldn't get all bent out of shape (over it) if I were you.

ponerse hecho(-a) un Cristo ■ ponerse como un Cristo ■ ponerse hecho(-a) un guiñapo ■ ponerse hecho(-a) un trapo to get all banged up ■ to get badly banged up ■ to get hurt

ponerse hecho(-a) un energúmeno ■ ponerse hecho(-a) un basilisco ■ ponerse como un basilisco ■ ponerse hecho(-a) una furia to blow a fuse ■ to hit the ceiling ■ to go ballistic

ponerse hecho(-a) un guiñapo ■ ponerse hecho(-a) un trapo ■ ponerse hecho(-a) un Cristo ■ ponerse como un Cristo **1.** to get all banged up ■ to get badly banged up **2.** *(por enfermedad)* to look terrible

ponerse hecho(-a) un toro ■ ponerse como un toro to get (as) strong as an ox

ponerse hecho(-a) una furia ■ ponerse hecho(-a) un energúmeno ■ ponerse hecho(-a) un basilisco ■ ponerse como un basilisco to fly into a rage ■ to have a purple fit ■ to blow a fuse ■ to hit the ceiling ■ to go ballistic

ponerse hecho(-a) una sopa ■ ponerse como una sopa ■ calarse hasta los huesos to get soaked (to the bone) ■ to get drenched

ponerse histérico(-a) to get hysterical ■ to become hysterical

ponerse imposible to become impossible ■ to be impossible ■ to get impossible ➤ Te pones imposible cuando te enfadas. You become impossible when you get mad.

ponerse interesante to get interesting

ponerse junto a alguien to stand next to someone

ponerse juntos de portero *(dicho por niños)* to both be the goalkeeper ➤ ¿Nos ponemos juntos de portero? Shall we both be the goalkeeper (on this end)? ■ Can we both be the goalkeeper (on this end)?

ponerse (la luz) roja *(semáforo)* ■ ponerse en rojo to turn red ➤ ¿Qué puñetas haces? ¡Se ha puesto la luz roja! ■ ¿Qué puñetas haces? ¡Se ha puesto en rojo! What the hell are you doing? The light's turned red!

ponerse la meta de ■ ponerse como objetivo to set the goal of

ponerse la ropa ■ vestirse to put on one's clothes ■ to put one's clothes on ■ to get dressed

ponerse las botas **1.** to put on one's boots **2.** ponerse como el Quico ■ ponerse ciego ■ ponerse morado to eat like a horse **3.** salir con muchas ganancias to (really) clean up

ponerse (los huevos) de corbata *(subido de tono)* ■ ponerse los cojones de corbata to be scared shitless ➤ La montaña rusa nos los puso de corbata. The rollercoaster made us scared shitless.

ponerse los ojos como platos (for) one's eyes to get as big as saucers ➤ Se le pusieron los ojos como platos. *(a él)* His eyes got as big as saucers. ■ *(a ella)* Her eyes got as big as saucers.

ponerse los pelos de punta to make one's hair stand up straight ■ to make one's hair stand on end ➤ Me puso los pelos de punta. It made my hair stand up straight. ■ My hair stood on end.

ponerse mal to take a turn for the worse ➤ Las cosas se han puesto mal. Things have taken a turn for the worse.

ponerse mala ■ tener la regla ■ tener la menstruación to have one's menstrual period ■ to have one's period

ponerse malo **1.** enfermarse to get sick **2.** echar a perder to go bad ■ to turn bad ➤ El pavo aguantará dos o tres días hasta que se ponga malo. The turkey will keep two or three days before it goes bad.

ponerse más blanco(-a) que la cera ■ ponerse blanco(-a) como la cera to turn white as a sheet

ponerse más colorado(-a) que un tomate to turn red as a beet

ponerse más cómodo(-a) to get more comfortable

ponerse más intenso(-a) ■ hacerse más intenso(-a) ■ intensificarse to become more intense

ponerse mejor to get better ➤ Según pasan las semanas, el libro se poner mejor. As the weeks go by, the book gets better and better.

ponerse morado(-a) ■ ponerse como el Quico ■ ponerse las botas ■ ponerse ciego to eat like a horse ■ to eat one out of house and home

ponerse muy a la derecha to get way over to the right ➤ Ponte muy a la derecha. Get way over to the right.

ponerse muy a la izquierda to get way over to the left

ponerse muy ancho(-a) ■ engreírse to feel very self-important

ponerse nervioso to get nervous

ponerse pálido(-a) to turn pale ■ to become pale ■ to get pale

ponerse pelma to be a drag

ponerse por (en) medio to get in the way

ponerse por las nubes to become very expensive ■ *(coloquial)* to go through the roof ➤ En Navidad el marisco se pone por las nubes. At Christmastime, seafood becomes very expensive. ■ At Christmastime, the price of seafood goes through the roof.

ponerse ralo(-a) ■ enralecer **1.** *(cabello, pelo)* to lose hair ■ (for) one's hair to thin ■ (for) one's hair to get thin **2.** *(cerdas de un cepillo)* to lose bristles ➤ Se le pone el cabello ralo. His hair is thinning. ➤ Esta brocha de pintura se está poniendo rala. This paintbrush is losing its bristles.

ponerse rojo(-a) **1.** *(semáforo)* ponerse la luz roja to turn red **2.** ponerse colorado(-a) to blush ■ to turn red (in the face) ■ to turn beet red

ponerse rojo(-a) de ira to have a purple fit

ponerse rojo(-a) de la pena to turn red with embarrassment ■ to blush

ponerse ropa ■ usar ropa to put on clothes ■ to wear clothes ➤ Hace dos días que no me pongo un abrigo. ■ Hace dos días que no uso un abrigo. ■ No me he puesto un abrigo en dos días. ■ No he usado un abrigo en dos días. For two days (now), I have not put on a coat. ■ For two days (now), I haven't put on a coat. ■ For two days (now) I have worn no coat. ■ For two days (now) I haven't worn a coat. ■ I haven't worn a coat for two days (now).

ponerse tenso(-a) **1.** ponerse nervioso(-a) to tense up ■ to get uptight **2.** tensarse to become taut ■ to get taut ➤ No te pongas tenso. Don't get uptight. ➤ Se puso tenso antes de su examen oral. He tensed up before his oral examination. ➤ Enrolla la línea hasta que se ponga tensa. Reel in the line until it becomes taut. ■ Reel in the line until it gets taut.

ponerse tibio to become lukewarm

ponerse tiesa *(subido de tono)* ▪ ponerse dura ▪ ponerse como un canto ▪ tener una erección to get a hard-on ▪ to get a boner ▪ to get hard as rock ▪ to get an erection ▪ to have an erection

ponerse todo elegante ▪ ponerse todo hecho(-a) un pincel ▪ ponerse de punta en blanco to get (all) dressed up ▪ to get dressed to the nines ➤ Nos pusimos todo elegantes para ir a la boda de mi hermano. ▪ Nos pusimos de punta en blanco para ir a la boda de mi hermano. We got all dressed up to go my brother's wedding.

ponerse todo hecho(-a) un pincel ▪ ponerse de punta en blanco ▪ ponerse todo elegante to get all dressed up ▪ to get dressed to the nines

ponerse tonto(-a) to get silly ▪ to start acting silly

ponerse triste to become sad ▪ to be saddened

ponerse un anillo ▪ llevar un anillo to be wearing a ring ➤ (Él) se había puesto un anillo. ▪ (Él) llevaba un anillo. He was wearing a ring.

ponerse un candado en la boca to shut your trap ▪ to shut up ➤ ¡Ponte un candado en la boca y no cuentes más mentiras! Shut your trap, and don't tell me any more lies!

ponerse un lacito en el dedo to tie a little bow around one's finger (as a reminder)

ponerse uno a huevo 1. to make oneself an easy mark 2. to make oneself an easy target ➤ El ladrón se puso a huevo al atracar a un tío justo enfrente de la comisaría. The robber made himself an easy mark when he held up a guy right in front of the police station. ➤ El turista, que llevaba una cartera inmensa en el bolsillo de atrás, se puso a huevo para los carteristas. The tourist wearing a large wallet in his back pocket made himself an easy target for pickpockets.

ponerse uno en el lugar de otro to put oneself in someone else's place ▪ to put oneself in someone else's shoes

ponerse verde de envidia to turn green with envy

ponerse vertical to stand up straight ➤ Después de su operación por una hernia, no pudo ponerse vertical por un par de días. After his hernia operation, he couldn't stand up straight for a couple days.

ponerse violento to become violent

ponérsele a alguien el cabello de punta (for) one's hair to stand on end ▪ (for) one's hair to stand up straight ➤ Se me puso el cabello de punta al ver al perro salir corriendo delante del coche. My hair stood on end when I saw the dog run out in front of the car. ▪ My hair stood up straight when I saw the dog run out in front of the car.

ponérsele algo a huevo a alguien to be a shoo-in for one ➤ Aquel trabajo se me puso a huevo y no me lo pensé dos veces. That job was a shoo-in for me, and I didn't have to think twice (about applying for it).

ponérsele como un canto *(subido de tono)* to get a hard-on ▪ to get hard as a rock

ponérsele delante de las narices a alguien to get in someone's face ▪ to shove it in someone's face ▪ to flaunt one's contempt

ponérsele dura a uno *(subido de tono)* ▪ ponérsele tiesa a uno ▪ empinársele ▪ ponérsele como el cuello de un cantaor ▪ ponérsele como una viga ▪ *(Esp.)* empalmarse to get a hard on

ponérsele en el moño ▪ ponérsele entre ceja y ceja to get it into one's head ▪ to get an idea into one's head ➤ A mi mujer se le puso en el moño que quería ir de vacaciones a la playa, y a la playa tuvimos que ir. My wife got it into her head that she wanted to go to the beach on vacation, and to the beach we went. ▪ My wife got the idea into her head that she wanted to go to the beach on vacation, and to the beach we went.

ponérsele entre ceja y ceja que... ▪ metérsele entre ceja y ceja que... to get a notion in one's head that... ▪ to get it into one's head that... ➤ Al jefe de Carlos se le puso entre ceja y ceja que tenían que parar para reorganizar la oficina...¡otra vez! Carlos' boss got it into his head that they had to stop to reorganize the office... again!

ponérsele infectado ▪ infectarse to get infected ▪ to become infected

ponérsele la carne de gallina ▪ ponerse la piel de gallina to get goose bumps ▪ to get goose flesh ▪ to be given goose bumps ▪ to be given goose flesh ➤ Se me pone la carne de gallina cada vez que oigo el cuarto concierto para piano de Beethoven. I get goose bumps when I hear Beethoven's fourth piano concerto. ▪ It gives me goose bumps to hear Beethoven's fourth piano concerto.

ponérsele la piel de gallina ▪ ponérsele la carne de gallina to get goose bumps ▪ to get goose flesh ▪ to give one goose bumps ➤ Se me pone la piel de gallina cuando escucho el Réquiem de Mozart. I get goose bumps when I listen to Mozart's Requiem.

ponérsele los cojones de corbata *(subido de tono)* to scare the shit out of somebody

ponérsele los dientes largos ▪ ponerse verde de envidia to be green with envy ➤ Se le pusieron los dientes largos cuando me vio con mi flamante deportivo rojo pasión. He was green with envy when he saw my brand-new bright red sports car.

ponérsele los nervios de punta to get extremely tense

ponérsele los pelos de punta for one's hair to stand on end ▪ for one's hair to stand up straight ➤ Al oír la noticia, se le pusieron los pelos de punta. His hair stood on end when he heard the news.

ponérsele mala cara to grimace ➤ Se le puso mala cara cuando olió el queso de Cabrales. He grimaced when he smelled the Cabrales cheese.

ponérsele nada por delante not to let anything stop one ▪ not to let anything get in his way ▪ to press on regardless ➤ No se le pone nada por delante. He doesn't let anything stop him. ▪ He doesn't let anything get in his way. ▪ He presses on regardless.

ponérsele por alguien ▪ ponerle nombre por alguien ▪ llamársele por alguien to name someone after someone ▪ to name someone for someone ➤ Se le puso Tomás por su abuelo. ▪ Le pusieron Tomás por su abuelo. ▪ Se le llamó Tomás por su abuelo. He was named Thomas for his grandfather. ➤ *(chiste)* Al niño le hemos puesto gafas.-¡Vaya nombre más feo! We named our little boy "Glasses."-What an ugly name!

ponérsele un nudo en la garganta to get a knot in one's throat ▪ to give one a knot in one's throat

ponérselo fácil a alguien to make it easy for someone ▪ to make it easy on someone ➤ *(publicidad navideña)* Nadie se lo pone tan fácil a los Reyes Magos. No one else makes it so easy for the Three Wise Men.

ponérselo a huevo a alguien *(subido de tono)* ▪ ponérselo a tiro a alguien to make something easy for someone ▪ to make it a cinch for someone ▪ to make it a pushover for someone ➤ Al cometer el robo delante de la cámara de seguridad, el ladrón se lo puso a huevo a la policía. By committing the robbery in front of the security camera, the thief made it easy for the police. ▪ By committing the robbery in front of the security camera, the thief made it a cinch for the police. ▪ By committing the robbery in front of the security camera, the thief made it a pushover for the police.

ponérselo difícil para que alguien haga algo ▪ dificultar el que alguien haga algo to make it difficult for someone to do something ➤ Mis ingresos me están poniendo muy difícil pedir un crédito. My salary makes it difficult for me to get a loan. ➤ The preference to hire within the European Union makes it more difficult for Americans to get work permits to teach English in Europe. La predilección de contratar gente de la Unión Europea pone muy difícil el que los americanos consigan los permisos de trabajo para dar clases de inglés en Europa. ▪ La predilección de contratar gente de la Unión Europea dificulta mucho el que los americanos consigan los permisos de trabajo para dar clases de inglés en Europa.

ponérselo fácil a alguien to make it easy for someone ➤ Te lo ponemos fácil. We make it easy for you.

¡póngame al corriente! catch me up! ▪ what's the latest?

pongamos por caso ▪ pongamos por ejemplo let's take for example ▪ let's take as an example

pongamos que let's say (that) ▪ let's assume (that)

¡póngase más allá! ▪ ¡córrase más allá! move over!

pongo por caso ▪ pongo por ejemplo I'll give you an example

pongo por ejemplo ▪ pongo por caso I'll give you an example

poniendo a uno en lo peor ▪ en el peor de los casos if worst comes to worst ▪ at (the very) worst ➤ Poniéndonos en lo peor ▪ En el peor de los casos If worst comes to worst ▪ At the very worst

ponle pausa *(video, etc.)* put it on pause

estar **poniéndole los cuernos a alguien** to be cheating on someone

ponlo bien 1. ponlo del derecho turn it right side up **2.** *(ropa)* dale la vuelta turn it right side out

¡ponme al corriente! catch me up! ▪ tell me the latest! ▪ bring me up to date! ▪ what's the latest?

¡ponme al corriente sobre ti! catch me up on yourself!

ponme x ▪ dame x give me x ➤ Ponme cinco tomates. Give me five tomatoes.

ponte cómodo(-a) make yourself comfortable

ponte en mi lugar put yourself in my place

¡ponte más allá! move over!

¡ponte serio! get serious!

¡póntelo! put it on!

popularidad afianzada abiding popularity ▪ secure popularity ▪ unwavering popularity

ser **poquita cosa** to be a pipsqueak ▪ to be a no count ➤ Eres muy poquita cosa como para darme miedo, forastero. I'm not afraid of a little squirt like you, pardner. ▪ I'm not afraid of a no count like you, pardner.

por abril del año que viene around April of next year

por accesión by acquiecence

por accidente ▪ por casualidad by accident ▪ by chance ▪ by happenstance

por aclamación by acclamation

por activa o por pasiva 1. con intención o sin ella whether one meant to or not ▪ by intent or by default **2.** por las buenas o por las malas willingly or unwillingly

por adarmes in a trickle ▪ in bits and pieces ▪ in dribs and drabs

por adelantado ▪ anticipadamente in advance ➤ Hicimos (los) preparativos por adelantado. We made (the) arrangements ahead of time.

por afición ▪ de afición as a hobby ▪ just for fun ▪ just for the fun of it

por ahí 1. en alguna parte por aquí somewhere around here ▪ nowhere in particular ▪ wherever **2.** *(señalando)* over there ▪ around there ▪ that way **3.** más o menos about ➤ ¿Adónde te vas a ir a pasear?-No sé. Por ahí. Where are you going on your walk?-I don't know. Wherever. ➤ ¿Dónde están las llaves?-No sé. Mira por ahí. Where are the keys?-I don't know. Have a look around there. ➤ ¿Por dónde se fue el ladrón?-Por ahí. Which way did the thief go?-That way. ➤ ¿Cuánto te costó?-Veinte euros, por ahí. How much did it cost?-About twenty euros.

por ahí adelante *(con insolencia)* somewhere ➤ ¿De dónde lo sacaste?-No sé. Por ahí adelante. Where'd you get that?-Oh, somewhere.

estar **por ahí atrás** ▪ estar por ahí detrás ▪ estar por allí atrás ▪ estar por allí detrás to be back there somewhere ➤ Está por ahí atrás. ▪ Está por ahí detrás. ▪ Está por allí atrás. ▪ Está por allí detrás. He's back there somewhere.

estar **por ahí detrás** ▪ estar por ahí atrás ▪ estar por allí detrás ▪ estar por allí atrás to be back there somewhere ➤ Está por ahí detrás. ▪ Está por ahí atrás. ▪ Está por allí detrás. ▪ Está por allí atrás. He's back there somewhere.

estar **por ahí en algún lado** to be around here somewhere ▪ to be around here someplace ➤ Sé que está por aquí en algún lado. I know it's around here somewhere. ➤ Sabía que estaba por ahí en algún lado. I knew it was around here someplace.

por ahí va la cosa ▪ por ahí van los tiros that's about right ▪ you're not too far off ▪ I think you are right

por ahí van los tiros ▪ por ahí va la cosa that's about right ▪ you're not too far off ▪ I think you are right

por ahora for the time being ▪ for the present ▪ for the moment ➤ Por ahora no tenemos gato. For the time being, we don't have a cat. ▪ For the time being, we have no cat. ▪ For the present, we don't have a cat. ▪ For the present, we have no cat. ▪ For the moment, we don't have a cat. ▪ For the moment, we have no cat.

ser **por algo que...** to be for a reason (that)... ▪ to be for good reason (that)... ▪ not to be for nothing (that)... ➤ Es por algo que dicen que... It's for a reason that they say (that)... ▪ It's for good reason that they say (that)... ▪ It's not for nothing that they say (that)...

por algo se empieza (well) it's a start ▪ (well) it's a beginning

por algo y para algo as the result of something and for the sake of some end ➤ Todo existe por algo y para algo. Everything exists as the result of something and for the sake of some end. ▪ Everything exists because of something and for a purpose. ➤ Todo lo que hago lo hago por ti y para ti. Everything I do, I do it because of you and for you.

estar **por alguien** to have a crush on someone ▪ to like someone ➤ Sally Brown está por Linus. Sally Brown has a crush on Linus.

por algún motivo ▪ por alguna razón for some reason

por alguna parte somewhere

por alguna que otra razón for some reason or other

por alguna razón ▪ por algún motivo for some reason

por allá around there

por allí over there

estar **por allí atrás** ▪ estar por allí detrás ▪ estar por ahí atrás ▪ estar por ahí detrás to be back there somewhere ➤ Está por allí atrás. ▪ Está por allí detrás. ▪ Está por ahí atrás. ▪ Está por ahí detrás. He's back there somewhere.

estar **por allí detrás** ▪ estar por allí atrás ▪ estar por ahí detrás ▪ estar por ahí atrás to be back there somewhere ➤ Está por allí detrás. ▪ Está por allí atrás. ▪ Está por ahí detrás. ▪ Está por ahí atrás. He's back there somewhere.

por alto: pasar ~ ▪ pasar por encima to overlook ➤ Disculpe, pero creo que ha pasado usted por alto la importancia de Ibsen en el teatro moderno. Excuse me, but I think you overlooked the importance of Ibsen in modern drama.

por amor a for love of ▪ out of love for

por amor al arte: hacer algo ~ to do something for free ▪ to do something just for the fun of it

por amor de ▪ por causa de for the love of ▪ because of the love of ▪ out of love for ▪ for the sake of love ➤ Eduardo VIII de Inglaterra abdicó por el amor de Wallis Simpson. Edward VIII of England abdicated the throne for the love of Wallis Simpson.

por amor de Dios ▪ por el amor de Dios for God's sake

por amplia mayoría by a wide majority ▪ by a large majority

por anticipado ▪ con atelación in advance

por antonomasia ▪ por excelencia par excellence ➤ El artista colombiano Fernando Botero es el pintor por antonomasia de los cuerpos rellenitos. The Colombian artist Fernando Botero is the artist par excellence of the plump human body.

por añadidura ▪ de añadidura in addition

por (aquel) entonces *(narración histórica)* ▪ por aquella época ▪ sobre estos días around that time ▪ around this time ▪ at about that time ▪ at about this time ▪ back then ➤ Por (aquel) entonces, vivíamos en Colonia Vertiz Narvarte. At that time we lived in Colonia Vertiz Narvarte. ▪ At that time we were living in Colonia Vertiz Narvarte.

por aquella época *(narración histórica)* ▪ por (aquel) entonces ▪ sobre estos días around that time ▪ around this time ▪ at about that time ▪ at about this time

por aquellos días ▪ en aquellos días in those days

por aquí around here ▪ this way

estar **por aquí** ▪ quedar por aquí to be around here ▪ to be this way

por aquí en algún sitio: quedar ~ ▪ estar por aquí en algún sitio to be around here somewhere

por aquí se va a... this is the way to...

por arrobas: darle algo ~ *(coloquial)* ▪ darle algo a lo pavote to give someone something by the ton ▪ to give someone loads of something ➤ La profesora nos da tareas por arrobas. The teacher gives us homework by the ton. ▪ The teacher gives us loads of homework.

por arte de birlibirloque ▪ por arte de magia by magic

por así decir ▪ por decirlo así ▪ por así decirlo ▪ podríamos decir ▪ como si dijéramos ▪ como si dijesemos so to speak ▪ as it were

por así decirlo ▪ por decirlo así so to speak ▪ as it were

por aventura perchance ▪ perhaps ▪ maybe ▪ possibly

por azar ▪ por suerte by chance ▪ by accident ▪ accidentally

por barba ▪ por persona a head ▪ per person ▪ per head ➤ La comida nos ha salido a treinta y cinco euros por barba. The dinner has come out to thirty-five euros a head. ▪ The dinner has come out to thirty-five euros per person. ▪ The dinner has come out to thirty-five euros per head.

por buena fe: actuar ~ ▪ actuar de buena fe to act on good faith ▪ to act out of good faith ➤ El médico que ayudó a la víctima no debería haber sido castigado por su buena fe. The doctor who helped the victim should not have been punished for his good faith.

por buena razón for good reason

por cabeza ■ por barba per person ■ per head ➤ El convite nos ha salido a cuarenta euros por cabeza. The get-together has come out to forty euros per head. ■ The get-together has come out to forty euros per person.

por cada acción hay una reacción de igual magnitud y (en) sentido opuesto *(Tercera Ley de Newton)* for every action there is an equal and opposite reaction

por casualidad ■ por carambola by chance

por causa de because of

por causas mayores because of extreme circumstances

por causas que se desconocen because of unknown causes

por ce o por be *(coloquial)* ■ en cualquier circunstancia come hell or high water ■ no matter what ■ no matter what the circumstances ■ in spite of all obstacles ➤ Se empeñó en llegar al refugio de noche por ce o por be. He was determined to reach shelter by dark, come hell or high water. ■ He was determined to reach shelter by dark, no matter what. ■ He was determined to reach shelter by dark, in spite of all obstacles.

por chiripa ■ de chiripa ■ de potra ■ de casualidad by a fluke ■ by chance ■ by pure luck ■ through pure luck

por cierto 1. to be sure ■ for sure ■ indeed **2.** a propósito by the way ➤ Por cierto, ya aprovecho, ¿cómo traducirías...? By the way, while I'm at it, how would you translate...?

por cojones *(soez)* ■ te guste o no like it or not

por compasión: hacer algo ~ to do something out of compassion

por completo ■ completamente completely

por conducto de by way of ■ through

por conducto de uno: rogarle a alguien ~ to ask someone to convey to someone else ➤ Le ha rogado por mi conducto que... He asked me to convey to you...

por conductos oficiales through channels

por consecuencia ■ *(más común)* como consecuencia as a consequence ■ as a result

por consejo de alguien on the advice of someone ■ on someone's advice

por consiguiente as a result ■ therefore

por control remoto ■ dirigido by remote control

por correo aéreo by air mail

por cualquier lado que se mire however you look at it ■ whichever way you look at it

por cualquier medio by whatever means

por cualquier quítame allá esas pajas ■ por lo más mínimo over the least little thing ■ over nothing ■ over any little thing ■ over any little picayune thing ■ for nothing ➤ Se enfada por cualquier quítame allá esas pajas. He gets angry over the least little thing.

por cuanto in view of the fact that ■ considering the fact that ■ given that ➤ Conceden gran valor a la opinión del agente por cuanto le consideran el máximo experto en antiterrorismo del FBI. They give great weight to the agent's opinion, in view of the fact that he is the FBI's top antiterrorism expert. ■ They give great weight to the agent's opinion, considering the fact that he is the FBI's top antiterrorism expert. ■ They give great weight to the agent's opinion, given that he is the FBI's top antiterrorism expert.

por cuenta ajena at the expense of someone else ■ at someone else's expense

por cuenta de at the expense of

por cuenta y riesgo de uno ■ de cuenta y riesgo ■ a riesgo suyo at one's own risk

ser **por culpa suya** to be one's fault ■ because of one ■ to be on one's account ➤ Por culpa suya, he perdido el autobús. Because of you I missed the bus. ■ It's your fault that I missed the bus. ■ It's because of you that I missed the bus. ■ I missed the bus on your account.

por cumplir just to be polite

por de pronto ■ por lo pronto **1.** for now ■ right now **2.** for one thing ➤ Por de pronto, nos vamos a poner a trabajar y luego ya veremos si nos da tiempo a tomar un café. For now, let's get to work, and later we'll see if we have time (to go) for a cup of coffee. ■ Right now, let's get to work, and later we'll see if we have time (to go) for a cup of coffee.

estar **por debajo de algo** to be under something ■ to be underneath something ■ to be beneath something

estar **por debajo de alguien en rango** ■ ser inferior a alguien en rango to be beneath someone in rank

estar **por debajo de la media 1.** estar por debajo del promedio to be below average **2.** estar por dentro del calcetín to be in one's sock ➤ Tengo una uña por debajo de la media. I've got a fingernail in my sock.

estar **por debajo del nivel de la tierra** to be below ground level ➤ Los primeros cinco pies de la pared están por debajo del nivel de la tierra. The first five feet of the wall is below ground level.

estar **por debajo del promedio** ■ estar por debajo de la media to be below average

por decirlo así ■ por así decirlo ■ por así decir ■ podríamos decir ■ como si dijéramos so to speak ■ as it were

por decirlo de alguna manera in a manner of speaking

por decreto ■ por real decreto by (royal) decree

por defecto by default ➤ Esta aplicación gestiona el programa de correo electrónico por defecto. This application is the manager of the e-mail program by default.

por delante: tener un mes ~ to have a month to go ➤ Tenemos un mes por delante hasta las vacaciones navideñas. We have a month to go until Christmas vacation.

estar **por delante de alguien (en la fila)** ■ preceder a alguien (en la fila) to be ahead of someone (in line) ■ to be in front of someone (in line) ■ to be before someone (in line) ➤ Hay dos personas delante de mí en la fila. ■ Hay dos personas delante de ti en la cola. There are two people ahead of me in (the) line. ■ There are two people in front of you in (the) line. ■ There are two people before you in (the) line.

por delante: ir ~ ■ estar por delante **1.** *(deporte)* to be ahead ■ to be leading **2.** *(en una cola o lista)* to be ahead of someone ■ to be in front of someone

por demanda popular ■ por petición popular by popular demand

ser **por demás que** to be useless to

por dentro on the inside ■ inside ■ in the interior ■ inwardly

por deporte: hacer algo ~ to do something (just) for the fun of it ■ to do something just for enjoyment *(Nota: En español implica un deporte o actividad física. ■ In Spanish this expression refers only to a sport or physical activity.)* ➤ Hago baloncesto por deporte. No soy miembro de un equipo. I play basketball (just) for fun. I'm not a member of a team.

por derecho propio in its own right

por descontado ■ ni que decir tiene of course ■ granted

estar **por descubrir** ■ quedar por descubrir to be yet to be discovered

por descuido when one wasn't looking ■ when one didn't keep an eye on it ■ because of carelessness ➤ La leche se puso a hervir y se salió del cazo por descuido. The milk boiled over when I wasn't looking. ■ The milk boiled over when I didn't keep an eye on it. ■ I carelessly let the milk boil over.

por desgracia unfortunately

por despecho: hacer algo ~ to do something out of spite

por determinar to be determined ■ to be arranged

estar **por detrás del resto del mundo** to be behind the rest of the world ■ to lag behind the rest of the world

por detrás del sobre ■ en el reverso del sobre ■ en la parte de atrás del sobre ■ en el dorso del sobre ■ en la parte trasera del sobre on the back of the envelope ■ on the reverse side of the envelope

¡**por Dios!** for heaven's sake

por Dios, por la Patria y por el Rey *(himno de Riego)* for God and country

por diversión ■ para divertirse ■ por deporte just for fun

por doble for double that amount ■ for twice that amount

por donde because of which

¿**por dónde?** which way? ■ where to?

¿**por dónde iba?** ■ ¿qué estaba diciendo? where was I? ■ what was I saying?

¿**(por) dónde queda...?** ■ ¿dónde está...? where is...?

por donde se mire everywhere you look ■ wherever you look

¿por dónde se va a...? ■ ¿cómo se llega a...? how do you get to...? ➤ Perdone, ¿por dónde se va a la Plaza Mayor? Excuse me, how do you get to the Plaza Mayor?

por donde van los tiros whichever way the wind blows ■ the way the wind blows

por duplicado in duplicate

por ejemplo ■ p.ej. ■ verbigracia for example ■ for instance ■ exempli gratia ■ e.g.

por excelencia ■ por antonomasia par excellence

por el amor de Dios ■ por amor de Dios for the love of God ■ for God's sake

por el aro: pasar ~ ■ pasar por el tubo to toe the line

por el camino along the way

por el campo de ■ por los pagos de around ■ in the vicinity of ➤ Oí decir por el campo de Salamanca que... They say around Salamanca that...

por el canto de un duro ■ por los pelos by the skin of one's teeth

por el contrario on the contrary

por el cual because of which

por el estilo of the sort ■ of the kind

por el interés de in the interest of

por el interés, te quiero Andrés to be a fair-weather friend ■ to be an opportunistic friend

por el mismo caso by the same token

por el mismo rasero: medir a alguien ~ to measure someone by the same standard(s)

por el mismo rasero: medir algo ~ to measure something by the same standard(s)

por el momento so far ■ up to now ➤ No han establecido por el momento lazo alguno. So far no link has been established.

por el momento no ■ por ahora no ■ todavía no not so far ■ not yet ■ not at this time ■ not as yet ■ not as of now ➤ No sabemos nada de su estado por el momento. ■ No sabemos nada de su estado por ahora. We have no word on his condition as yet. ■ We have no word on his condition as of now.

por el morro: hacer algo ~ to do something out of pure gall ■ to do something out of sheer gall

por el placer de hacerlo ■ por gusto for the fun of it

por el tubo: pasar ~ ■ pasar por el aro to toe the line ■ to fall into line ■ to knuckle under

por ello because of it ■ because of that ■ for that reason

estar **por en medio** to be underfoot ➤ Es difícil hacer las tareas (del hogar) con niños y perros por en medio. It's hard to do housework with children and dogs underfoot.

por en medio de la acera: ir ~ to walk in the middle of the sidewalk *(Nota: Especialmente de una manera que bloquea el paso ■ Especially in a way that blocks people)*

por en medio de la calle: cruzar ~ to jaywalk ➤ Se puso a cruzar por en medio de la calle sin mirar si venían coches. She jaywalked (across the street) without looking to see if there were any cars.

por encima: cruzar to cross (over) ➤ Cruzamos por encima del Potomac por el puente de la Calle Catorce. We crossed (over) the Potomac River on the Fourteenth Street Bridge.

por encima: ir ~ to go over

por encima: pasar algo ~ 1. *(en la calle)* to go over something ■ to run over something ■ to pass over something 2. *(en un avión)* to fly over something ➤ Pasamos por encima de un bache. We went over a pothole. ■ We ran over a pothole. ➤ Pasamos por encima del Gran Cañón en un helicóptero. We flew over the Grand Canyon in a helicopter.

estar **por encima de la ley** to be above the law ➤ Nadie está por encima de la ley. No one is above the law.

estar **por encima de la media** to be above average

por encima de la tempestad above the weather ➤ Fuimos en avión por encima de la tempestad. We flew above the weather.

por encima de las nubes above the clouds ➤ El avión voló por encima de las nubes. The airplane flew above the clouds.

estar **por encima de las posibilidades de uno** to be beyond one's means ■ to be more than one can afford ➤ El Rolls-Royce está por encima de nuestras posibilidades. The Rolls-Royce is beyond our means. ■ The Rolls-Royce is more than we can afford.

por encima de las posibilidades de uno: vivir ~ to live beyond one's means

¡por encima de mi cadáver! ■ ¡sobre mi cadáver! over my dead body!

por encima de todo more than anything else ■ above all

por encima de un puente: pasar ~ ■ cruzar un puente to go over a bridge ■ to cross a bridge

por encima del nivel del mar above sea level ➤ La ciudad está a quinientos metros por encima del nivel del mar. The city is at five hundred meters above sea level.

por enésima vez for the umpteenth time

por entero ■ enteramente entirely ■ wholly ■ completely

por entero a algo: dedicarse ~ to dedicate oneself exclusively to something

por entonces *(narración histórica)* ■ por aquel entonces around that time ■ at about that time ■ at about this time

por esa época around that time ➤ Por esa época (durante la Segunda Guerra Mundial) las mujeres empezaron a llevar pantalones. Around that time (World War II) women began to wear pants.

por equivocación ■ por error by mistake

por error ■ por equivocación by mistake

por esa regla de tres... using that line of reasoning... ■ using the same argument... ■ well, if *that* were the case...

por escrito in writing ■ in black and white

por ese lado in that way

por eso 1. therefore 2. that's why ■ for that reason 3. so ➤ *(Valle-Inclán)* Por eso el número es sagrado. That's why the number is sacred.

por eso es que... that's why... ➤ *(Ogden Nash)* Una primordial termita madera tocó, la probó y le gustó, y es por eso que tu prima Mae, por el suelo de la sala hoy se coló. Some primeval termite knocked on wood, and tasted it and found it good. And that is why your cousin Mae fell through the parlor floor today.

por eso mismo ■ precisamente por eso for that very reason ■ that's the very reason why

por esos mundos de Dios: ir ~ to wander all over the place

por estas fechas ■ en esta época del año at this time of year

por excelencia ■ por antonomasia par excellence

por exceso de confianza because of overconfidence ■ from overconfidence ➤ Perdieron el partido por exceso de confianza. They lost the game because of overconfidence.

por exceso de peso because of overloading ■ from overloading ➤ El ascensor se paró entre dos plantas por exceso de peso. The elevator stopped between floors because of overloading. ■ The elevator stopped between floors because it was overloaded.

por experiencia from experience ➤ Sé por experiencia que... I know from experience that...

por experiencia propia: saber ~ to know from personal experience ■ to know from one's own experience ➤ Sé por experiencia propia que... I know from personal experience that... ■ I know from my own experience that...

por extensión by extension

por extraño que parezca strange as it may seem

por falta de because of lack of ➤ El servicio está interrumpido por falta de suministro eléctrico. Service has been interrupted because of a lack of electricity.

por falta de un término mejor for want of a better term ■ for lack of a better term

por favor please

por favor, espere a recibir asiento please wait to be seated

¿por favor, me concedes este baile? may I have this dance?

por favor llamar al timbre ■ por favor tocar el timbre please ring the bell

por favor, permanezca a la escucha ■ por favor, siga en la línea please continue to hold

por favor tocar el timbre ■ por favor llamar al timbre please ring the bell

por fin ■ al fin ■ en fin ■ en resumen at last ■ finally ■ in the end ■ after all

¡por fin! at last! ■ it's about time! ■ it's high time!

por fortuna ▪ afortunadamente fortunately ▪ luckily

por fuera on the outside

por fuerza of necessity ▪ necessarily ➤ Por fuerza las consecuencias siguen a las acciones. The consequences necessarily follow from the action.

por gusto 1. por el placer de hacerlo for the fun of it 2. por propia elección by choice

estar **por hacer algo** to be about to do something

por hache o por be ▪ por las buenas o por las malas 1. te guste o no ▪ quieras o no quieras whether you like it or not 2. como sea by any means whatever ▪ by whatever means ▪ by hook or by crook

por iniciativa propia on one's own initiative

por instantes ▪ por momentos and the next minute ▪ next thing I knew ▪ all of a sudden ▪ in an instant ▪ in the next instant ▪ suddenly

por instinto ▪ instintivamente by instinct ▪ instinctively

por la boca muere el pez put up or shut up

por (la) casa *(interior de la casa)* ▪ alrededor de la casa around the house

por la cual because of which ▪ as a result of which

por la cuenta que le tiene 1. *(él)* if he knows what's good him 2. *(ella)* if she knows what's good for her

por la derecha from the right ➤ Einstein es el tercero por la derecha. Einstein is third from the right.

por la dormida del expediente *(Valle-Inclán)* because of the inactive state of the case

por la época de alrededor de la época de ▪ hacia la época de ▪ sobre la época de around the time of ▪ at about the time of

por la fuerza ▪ por las bravas 1. by force 2. adamantly 3. of necessity ▪ necessarily ➤ El cliente reclamó por la fuerza la devolución del importe. The customer adamantly demanded a refund.

por la fuerza: tomar ~ to take by force ➤ La banda de Robin Hood tomó el castillo por la fuerza. Robin Hood's band took the castle by force.

por la fuerza de la costumbre from force of habit ▪ out of force of habit ▪ through force of habit

por la izquierda from the left ➤ Quiroga es el tercero por la izquierda en la foto. Quiroga is the third from the left in the photo.

por la jeta *(coloquial)* ▪ por la cara ▪ por la patilla for free

por la labor de: no estar ~ ▪ no estar dispuesto a 1. not to be up to doing something 2. not to be up for something ➤ No estoy por la labor de asistir a tres horas más de clase. I'm not up for three more hours of class today. ➤ No estoy por la labor de ir al cine esta noche. I'm not up to going to the movies tonight.

por la noche ▪ de noche at night ▪ during the night ▪ in the night

por la noche: el *x* ~ on the night of *x* ➤ El dieciocho de diciembre por la noche On the night of December eighteenth

por la mañana in the morning ▪ during the morning ➤ Salimos mañana por la mañana. We're leaving tomorrow morning.

por la mañana temprano early in the morning

por la noche at night ▪ during the night

por la otra punta 1. by the other end 2. on the other end ➤ Coge la rama por la otra punta, que por esta tiene espinas. Pick the branch up by the other end. This end has thorns. ➤ La entrada a la biblioteca es por la otra punta del edificio. The entrance to the library is on the other end of the building. ▪ The library entrance is on the other end of the building.

por la presente hereby ➤ Por la presente se les comunica que... You are hereby notified that...

por la presente te invito I hereby invite you

por la puerta grande: salir ~ ▪ salir en loor de multitudes to finish to great acclaim

por la tarde 1. *(hasta que anochezca)* in the afternoon 2. *(hasta la cena)* in the evening

por largo tiempo for a long time

por las bravas ▪ a las bravas ▪ por la fuerza 1. brazenly ▪ adamantly ▪ without regard for the consequences 2. unprotected ➤ Se presentó en mi fiesta por las bravas. He brazenly crashed my party. ➤ El cliente vino reclamando la devolución del importe por las bravas. The customer adamantly demanded a refund. ➤ Los albañiles que trabajan en los rascacielos cruzan la vigas suspendidas en el aire por las bravas: sin arnés ni ningún tipo de seguridad. The construction workers who build skyscrapers walk across the beams in the open air unprotected: no harness, ropes or rescue lines.

por las buenas: hacer algo ~ to do something in a nice way

por las buenas: hacer política ~ to play politics fairly

por las buenas o por las malas ▪ por hache o por be 1. te guste o no ▪ quieras o no quieras whether you like it or not 2. como sea by hook or by crook ▪ by any means whatever ▪ by whatever means

por las claras: hablarle a alguien ~ ▪ hablarle a alguien sin tapujos ▪ hablarle a alguien sin pelos en la lengua to tell someone without holding back anything ▪ to tell someone without hiding anything ▪ to tell someone up front ▪ not to mince words ▪ *(coloquial)* to tell someone flat out ➤ Háblame por las claras... Tell me without holding anything back... ▪ Tell me up front...

por las malas ▪ por la fuerza by force

por las noches at night ▪ in the evenings

estar **por las nubes** *(precio)* to be sky-high

por las nubes: poner a alguien ~ to praise someone to the skies

por lejano que sea su origen no matter how far back its origin

por ley by law

por libre: hacer algo ~ ▪ hacer algo por decisión propia to do something on one's own ▪ to do something independently ▪ to do something at one's own behest

por libre: ir ~ ▪ ir a su aire ▪ ir solo(-a) to go on one's own ▪ to go by oneself

por libre: presentar un examen ~ to take an examination after studying on one's own ▪ to take an examination after studying independently

por libre: trabajar ~ ▪ ser trabajador(-a) autónomo(-a) to freelance

por lo común ▪ por lo general ▪ generalmente generally ▪ as a rule

por lo cual ▪ por lo que because of which ▪ as a result of which

por lo del anuncio about the ad ▪ in response to the ad ➤ Llamo por lo del anuncio en el periódico. I'm calling about the ad in the paper. ➤ Escribo por lo del anuncio en el periódico. I am writing in response to the ad in the paper.

por lo demás ▪ sin incluir eso ▪ además de eso apart from that ▪ other than that ▪ otherwise ▪ in all other respects ➤ Por lo demás, tu español es muy correcto. Apart from that, your Spanish is completely correct. ▪ Other than that, your Spanish is completely correct. ▪ Otherwise, your Spanish is completely correct. ▪ In all other respects, your Spanish is completely correct.

por lo general 1. en general ▪ por lo común ▪ comúnmente in general 2. por regla general as a general rule ▪ generally ▪ in general 3. usualmente ▪ normalmente usually

por lo menos ▪ al menos ▪ siquiera at least ➤ ¡Por lo menos estudia un poco! At least he studies a little! ➤ El ataque ha causado por lo menos trece muertes. ▪ El ataque ha causado al menos trece muertos. The attack caused at least thirteen deaths.

por lo menos por ahora at least for now

por lo menos todavía at least not yet

por lo mismo for that very reason

por lo pronto ▪ por ahora ▪ por de pronto for now ▪ right now ➤ Por lo pronto, nos vamos a poner a trabajar y luego ya veremos si nos da tiempo a tomar un café. For now, let's get to work, and later we'll see if we have time (to go) for a cup of coffee. ▪ Right now, let's get to work, and later we'll see if we have time (to go) for a cup of coffee.

por lo que ▪ por lo cual so (that) ▪ because of which ▪ for which ▪ as a result of which ➤ *(noticia)* El Supremo de Florida sentenció que las célebres papeletas mariposas de Palm Beach son legales, por lo que no hay razones para celebrar allí nuevas elecciones. The Florida Supreme Court ruled that the famous Palm Beach butterfly ballots are legal, so that there is no reason to hold new elections. ➤ La sartén tiene una capa antiadherente por lo que los alimentos no quedan pegados a ella. The frying pan has a non-stick surface so (that) food won't stick to it. ➤ Se trata de una calle muy corta por lo que espero que no tengas ninguna dificultad en localizarlo. It's a very short street so I hope you won't have any trouble finding it. ➤ Llegué a Madrid con tres horas de retraso por lo que en casa estuve a las catorce horas. I arrived in Madrid three hours late, so I got home at two p.m. ■ I arrived in Madrid three hours late, as a result of which I reached the house at two p.m.

por lo que a mí atañe ■ en lo que a mí concierne as far as I'm concerned

por lo que a mí respecta ■ en lo a mí respecta as far as I'm concerned

por lo que a mí se refiere as far as I'm concerned

por lo que más quieras ■ por favor, por favor, por favor please, please, please ■ I beg you ■ *(arcaico)* I beg of you

por lo que pudiera valer for what it's worth

por lo que recuerdo ■ por lo que puedo recordar ■ de lo que me puedo acordar as far as I can remember ■ my recollection is

por lo que respecta a algo ■ en lo que respecta a algo as far as something is concerned

por lo que respecta a alguien ■ en lo que respecta a alguien as far as someone is concerned

por lo que se dice the scuttlebutt is that ■ the rumor is that ■ rumor has it that ■ it's been going around that

por lo que se refiere a ■ en cuanto a ■ referente a ■ concerniente a as regards ■ in regard to ➤ Por lo que se refiere al pago, será efectuado. In regard to your payment, it will expedited.

por lo que se ve ■ a lo que se ve ■ aparentemente apparently

por lo que veo as far as I can see ■ as far as I can tell ➤ Por lo que veo, no hay forma de acabar esto. There's no way to finish this, as far as I can see. ➤ Por lo que veo no habéis hecho ni el huevo. As far as I can see, you haven't done a lick of work.

por lo que yo sé as far as I know ■ so far as I know

por lo que yo veo ■ por lo que veo I see that ■ I see ➤ Por lo que veo, te gusta el azul. I see (that) you like blue. ➤ Por lo que yo veo, no te has ido. I see you haven't left.

por lo regular as a (general) rule ■ usually

por lo tanto consequently ■ so

por lo visto ■ al parecer apparently ■ from the looks of it

por los cerros de Úbeda: irse ~ ■ irse por las ramas to go off on a tangent ■ to get (way) off the subject

¡por los clavos de Cristo! *(arcaico)* ■ ¡caracoles! good grief!

por los cojones: pasarse algo ~ *(subido de tono)* not to give a (flying) damn about something ➤ Cariño, mi madre me ha dicho que viene mañana.-Me lo paso por los cojones. Yo mañana voy de pesca. Honey, mother said she's coming over tomorrow.-I don't give a damn. I'm going fishing tomorrow.

por los cuatro costados through and through ■ to the core

por los pelos by the skin of one's teeth ■ in the nick of time ■ just in time ■ just barely

por los que luchar ■ por los que merece la pena luchar worth fighting for ➤ Creo que aún quedan ideales por los que luchar. I believe there are still ideals worth fighting for.

por los siglos de los siglos ■ en los siglos de los siglos ■ in secula seculorum forever and forever

estar **por los suelos** **1.** *(precios)* to hit bottom ■ to be at their lowest **2.** *(estado de ánimo)* tener la moral por los suelos to be down in the dumps ■ to be really down ■ to be depressed ➤ En enero y febrero los pasajes de avión están por los suelos. In January and February (the) air fares hit bottom. ■ In January and February air fares are at their lowest. ➤ El perro está por los suelos desde que su "frisbee" aterrizó en el tejado. The dog is down in the dumps since his frisbee landed on the roof. *(Nota: "Frisbee" es el disco de plástico que se lanza al perro.)*

por malas artes ■ por artimañas by trickery

por más amenazador(a) que parezcan ■ por más amenazador(a) que se vean no matter how threatening... ➤ Mi instructor de vuelo me enseñó que las nubes altas no dan lluvia, por más amenazadoras que parezcan. ■ Mi instructor de vuelo me enseñó que las nubes altas no dan lluvia, por más amenazadoras que se vean. My flight instructor taught me that high clouds won't rain, no matter how threatening they look.

por más que... the more... ■ no matter how much...

por más que intento... the more I try... ■ no matter how much I try... ■ no matter how hard I try...

por más que miré... the harder I looked... ■ no matter how hard I looked... ■ I looked and looked...

por más señas **1.** para ser más exacto ■ para ser más preciso ■ para ser más concreto to be exact ■ to be precise ■ to be specific **2.** sin ir más lejos... (and) just to prove it...

por mayoría de votos by a majority vote

por medio de ■ mediante ■ a través de through ■ by means of

estar **por venir** ■ deparar el futuro to lie ahead ■ to have in store ➤ No sabemos lo que está por venir, pero somos optimistas. ■ No sabemos lo que nos depara el futuro, pero somos optimistas. We don't know what lies ahead, but we're optimistic. ■ We don't know what the future has in store, but we're optimistic.

por mejor decir ■ mejor dicho better said ■ rather

por mencionar algunos to mention a few

por menos de for less than ➤ Se consiguen por menos de diez dólares. You can get them for less than ten dollars.

por mes ■ al mes ■ mensual per month ■ a month ■ monthly ➤ El parking es veinte euros por mes. ■ El parking es veinte euros al mes. The parking space is twenty euros a month. ■ The parking space is twenty euros per month.

por mí on my account ■ because of me

por mi cara bonita for free *(Nota: Se puede usar cualquier pronombre. ■ Any pronoun can be used.)*

¡por mí, como si se la machaca! *(subido de tono)* I don't give a damn! ■ color me impressed! ■ yeah, well so what?!

¡por mí, como si se la pilla con la tapa del water! *(subido de tono)* I don't give a damn! ■ color me impressed! ■ yeah, well so what?!

por mí, como si te operas I don't care ■ I don't give a damn

por mi cuenta on my own

por mi cuenta: trabajar ~ to be self-employed ■ to work for oneself

por mi parecer ■ a mi parecer to my of thinking

por mi parte as far as I'm concerned ■ so far as I'm concerned ■ for my part

¡por mi vida! for the life of me!

por miedo a ■ por temor a for fear of ■ out of fear of ■ because of the fear of ➤ Judíos y palestinos acaparan comida por miedo a la guerra. Jews and Palestinians hoard food for fear of war.

por mis cojones *(subido de tono)* ■ por mis huevos ■ por mis narices come hell or high water ■ *(alternativa benigna)* no matter what ■ come what may ➤ Voy a acabar esto esta noche por mis cojones. I'm going to finish this tonight come hell or high water. ■ I'm going to finish this tonight no matter what.

por momentos ■ por instantes at times

por mor de *(arcaico de "por amor de")* ■ por causa de ■ con motivo de because of ■ on the occasion of ■ occasioned by ■ by virtue of ➤ Me acuerdo del viaje que hice a la capital por mor de las quintas. I remember the trip I took to the capital occasioned by my military service.

por mor de la amistad *(arcaico de "por amor de")* ■ en nombre de la amistad (que nos une) ■ por el valor de la amistad (que nos une) out of friendship ■ for the sake of friendship

por mor de la verdad *(arcaico de "por amor de")* ■ en honor a la verdad ■ con toda honestidad in all honesty ■ for the sake of the truth

por mor del que dirán *(arcaico de "por amor de")* ■ por el qué dirán because of what people will say ■ because of the gossip mill ■ because of all the gossip it will generate ➤ La recién divorciada no quiere que la vean con su nuevo novio por mor del qué dirán. The newly divorced woman doesn't want to be seen with her new boyfriend because of what people will say. ■ The newly divorced woman doesn't want to be seen with her new boyfriend because of the gossip mill. ■ The newly divorced woman doesn't want to be seen with her new boyfriend because of all the gossip it will generate.

por mucho que ■ por más que no matter how much ■ however much

por mucho que intento... no matter how hard I try...

por muchos años for many years

por muy fácil no matter how easy ➤ Por muy fáciles que ponga los exámenes, hay algún alumno que reprobará. No matter how easy I make the exam, some student will flunk.

por muy sucia que esté, no digas nunca de esta agua no beberé never say never

por nada 1. casi gratis for peanuts **2.** por ningún motivo for no reason in particular **3.** *(Sudamérica, coloquial)* de nada you're welcome ➤ Nos lo vendieron por nada. ■ Nos lo dieron casi gratis. They sold it to us for peanuts. ■ They let us have it for peanuts. ➤ ¿Por qué me lo preguntas?-Por nada, por curiosidad. Why do you ask?-For no reason in particular. I was just curious.

por naturaleza by nature ➤ El carácter de su padre alegre por naturaleza resulta contagioso. His father's temperament, easy-going by nature, is infectious.

por necesidad of necessity ■ out of necessity

por ninguna parte nowhere ■ not anywhere

por no hablar de not to mention

por no tener que... ■ al no tener que... by not having to...

¡por nosotros! *(un brindis)* here's to us!

por obra y gracia de thanks to the efforts of ➤ El museo de Felipe II en Valladolid se inauguró por obra y gracia de Su Majestad. The museum of Phillip the Second in Valladolid was established thanks to the efforts of His Majesty.

por obra y gracia del Espíritu Santo *(catolicismo)* by the power of the Holy Spirit

por orden first one and then the other

por orden de alguien at someone's order ■ on someone's command ■ on someone's order ■ at someone's command ■ *(culto)* at someone's behest

por otra parte 1. en cambio on the other hand **2.** además what's more ■ besides **3.** aparte ■ entonces well, anyway ■ so anyway

por otro for another thing ■ for another ➤ ¿Por qué no quieres ir?-Bueno, por un lado, tengo demasiadas tareas, y por otro, no tengo (el) dinero. ■ ¿Por qué no quieres ir?-Bueno, por una parte, tengo demasiadas tareas, y por otra, no tengo (el) dinero. Why don't you want to go?-Well, for one thing, I've got too much homework, and for another (thing), I don't have the money.

por otro lado ■ en cambio on the other hand

por parte de uno ■ por parte suya ■ de parte de uno ■ de parte suya on someone's part ➤ Fue una reacción muy rápida por parte tuya. That was quick thinking on your part. ■ That was a quick reaction on your part.

por parte de su madre on one's mother's side (of the family) ➤ Mi tío por parte de mi madre My uncle on my mother's side (of the family)

por parte de su padre on one's father's side (of the family) ➤ Mi prima por parte de mi padre My cousin on my father's side (of the family)

por parte suya ■ de parte tuya ■ por parte de uno ■ de parte de uno on one's part ➤ Fue muy inteligente por parte tuya. That was clever thinking on your part.

por partida doble: cobrar ~ to get paid double (what one anticipated) ■ to get paid twice as much as one anticipated

por partida doble: disfrutar algo ~ to enjoy something twice as much ■ to enjoy something two-fold ➤ Me encanta Buenos Aires, y me encanta un asado con chimichurri, así que disfruté mi viaje a Argentina por partida doble. I love Buenos Aires, and I love steak with chimichurri sauce, so I enjoyed my trip to Argentina two-fold.

por partida doble: tener que hacer algo ~ to have to do something all over again ■ to have to re-do something ■ to have to do something over (again) ■ to have to do something a second time

por pedido popular by popular demand

por perdonado: dar algo ~ to be forgiven ➤ Dalo por perdonado. You're forgiven.

por petición popular ■ por demanda popular by popular demand

por piernas: salir ~ ■ salir por pies ■ salir corriendo **1.** *(de aquí)* to get out of here ■ to make a beeline out of here **2.** *(de allí)* to get out of there ■ to make a beeline out of there

por piezas ■ pieza por pieza piece by piece ■ disassembled ➤ La maqueta del avión vino por piezas. The airplane model came disassembled. ➤ La mesa vino pieza por pieza. The table came disassembled.

por pitos o por flautas for some reason or other

por poco almost ■ nearly ■ practically ■ *(muy coloquial)* darn near ■ *(muy coloquial y ligeramente subido de tono)* damn near

por poco darle un síncope ■ por poco darle un ataque ■ *(más antiguo)* por poco darle un telele to almost give one a heart attack ■ to practically give one a heart attack ➤ Cada vez que veo a los peatones cruzar la calle por en medio sin mirar, por poco me da un síncope. When I see the pedestrians jaywalking without looking, it almost gives me a heart attack. ■ When I see pedestrians jaywalking without looking, it practically gives me a heart attack.

por poco me caígo ■ casi me caigo ■ por poco me caí I almost fell

por poco perder la vida 1. *(literal)* to almost die **2.** *(figurativo)* casi dar a alguien un soponcio to nearly die ■ to almost die ➤ Por poco perdió la vida en el accidente. He almost died in the accident. ➤ Cuando la vi por poco perdí la vida. ■ Cuando la vi por poco me dio un soponcio. When I saw her I nearly died.

por poco pierdo el avión ■ casi pierdo el avión ■ estuve a punto de perder el avión ■ *(el mismo día, o recientemente)* he estado a punto de perder el avión I almost missed the plane

por poderes: autorizar ~ to authorize by proxy

por poderes: casarse ~ to get married by proxy

por poderes: votar ~ to vote by proxy

por poquito almost ■ nearly ■ practically ■ *(coloquial)* darn near ■ *(coloquial y un poco subido de tono)* damn near ➤ Por poquito me caigo. I almost fell. ■ I nearly fell. ■ I darn near fell. ■ I damn near fell.

por porfiar y por fiar te puedes arruinar two things can lead you to bankruptcy, stubbornness and lending (people) money

por preguntar nada se pierde ■ preguntando se llega a Roma there's no harm in asking ■ it doesn't hurt to ask ■ it never hurts to ask

por presiones de because of pressure from

por principios on principle ➤ Por principios creo que la pena capital debería ser abolida. On principle, I think that capital punishment should be abolished.

por propia elección ■ por elección propia ■ por propia voluntad ■ por voluntad propia by (one's own) choice ■ of one's own free will ➤ Estoy aquí por mi propia elección. ■ Estoy aquí por mi elección propia. I'm here by choice. ■ I'm here by my own choice. ■ I'm here of my own free will.

por prueba y error ■ a prueba y error by trial and error ➤ Iván encontró la respuesta del problema de física por prueba y error. ■ Iván encontró la respuesta del problema de física a prueba y error. Iván found the answer to the physics problem by trial and error.

por pudor out of modesty

¿por qué? why?

¿por qué a mí? why me?

¿por qué debería? why should I?

¿por qué estás tan triste? why are you so sad? ■ *(puede ser acusatorio)* what are you so sad about?

¿por qué has hecho eso? why did you do that? ■ what did you do that for?

¿por qué me (lo) preguntas? why do you ask?

¿por qué no? why not?

¿por qué no...? why don't you...?

¿por qué yo? why me?

por más que digas no matter what you say

por más que digas no podrás convencerme no matter what you say, you can't convince me ■ nothing you say can possibly convince me ■ no matter how hard you try, you can't convince me ■ no matter what you say, you'll never convince me

¿por qué regla de tres...? why on earth...?

¿por qué tarda tanto? ■ ¿por qué toma tanto tiempo? ■ ¿por qué se tarda tiempo? why is it taking so long?

¿por qué te pones así? why are you making such a fuss? ■ what's the big deal?

¿por quién me has tomado? ■ ¿quién te piensas que soy? who do you think I am?

por quítame allá esas pajas: reñir ~ to quibble over nothing ■ to argue over nothing ■ to argue about nothing

por razones más que obvias for obvious reasons ➤ Por razones más que obvias no puedo entrar en detalles. ■ For obvious reasons, I can't go into details.

por razones personales for personal reasons

por real decreto by royal decree

por referencia: oír algo ~ to hear something secondhand ■ to be hearsay ■ to get something as hearsay ➤ Lo oí por referencia. I heard it secondhand. ■ It was hearsay. ■ I got it as hearsay.

por regla general as a general rule ■ as a rule

¡por San Jorge! by George!

por seguro le digo (a usted) que... I can tell you for sure that... ■ I can tell you for certain that... ■ I can tell you for a fact that...

por seguro te digo que... I can tell you for sure that... ■ I can tell you for certain that... ■ I can tell you for a fact that...

por señas pedir a alguien que venga to wave at someone to come over ➤ Por señas le pedí al camarero que viniera... I waved at the waiter to come over...

por separado separately ■ each one individually ■ each individually

por ser feriado *(L.am.)* ■ por ser fiesta because of the holiday ■ because it's a holiday ■ because of its being a holiday

por ser fiesta ■ por ser feriado because of the holiday ■ because it's a holiday ■ because of its being a holiday

por ser vos quien sois... *(arcaico, usado con ironía)* but since it's *you*...

por si in case ➤ He traído el paraguas por si llueve. I brought my umbrella in case it rains.

por si acaso *(coloquial)* ■ por si las moscas just in case ■ if by any chance

por si cuela ■ si cuela, cuela ■ a ver si cuela ■ por si suena la flauta (just) to see if someone will do it ■ (just) to see if someone will go for it ■ (just) to see if it'll fly ■ (just) to see if it flies ➤ Pídele a Alfredo que nos ponga unas raciones gratis, por si cuela. Ask Alfredo to give us a free serving, just to see if he'll go for it. ■ Ask Alfredo to give us a free serving, just to see if he'll do it. ■ Ask Alfredo to give us a free serving, just to see if it'll fly.

por si eso no fuera poco ■ por si eso no fuera suficiente as if that weren't enough

por si eso no fuera suficiente ■ por si eso no fuera poco as if that weren't enough

por si faltara poco ■ por si fuera poco **1.** as if that weren't enough **2.** at that ➤ La cañería del agua caliente empezó a fugar y por si faltara poco, el ascensor se ha atorado. The hot water pipe has sprung a leak, and as if that weren't enough, the elevator has gone out. ➤ Es escritora y con mucho talento por si faltara poco. She's a writer, and a very talented one at that.

por si fuera poco ■ por si faltara poco **1.** as if that weren't enough **2.** at that ➤ La cañería del agua caliente tiene una pérdida y por si fuera poco han cortado la luz por una avería. The hot water pipe has sprung a leak, and as if that weren't enough, the lights have gone out. ➤ Es escritora y con mucho talento por si fuera poco. She's a writer, and a very talented one at that.

por si hay ■ por si acaso hay **1.** *(singular)* in case there is **2.** *(plural)* in case there are

por si hubiera alguna duda as if there were any doubt

por si las moscas *(coloquial)* ■ por si acaso just in case ➤ Vamos a llevar pan de más por si las moscas. Let's take some extra bread with us just in case.

por si le interesa 1. *(a usted)* in case you're interested **2.** *(a él)* in case he's interested **3.** *(a ella)* in case she's interested

por si no lo sabías in case you didn't know

por si no te diste cuenta in case you haven't noticed

por si no te enteraste in case you haven't heard ■ in case you hadn't heard

por si no te vuelvo a ver in case I don't see you again

por si pasa algo ■ por si las moscas in case something happens ➤ Lleva otra tarjeta de crédito por si no aceptan ésta. ■ Lleva otra tarjeta de crédito por si las moscas. Take another credit card in case they don't accept this one.

por sí solo by oneself

por si te interesa in case you're interested

(por) si te sirve de consuelo if it's any consolation to you

por siempre *(poético)* ■ para siempre forever

por siempre jamás for ever and ever

por sistema: hacer algo ~ ■ hacer algo sistemáticamente to do something systematically

por su causa because of it ■ on account of it ➤ Es mejor consultar las cosas con la almohada a tiempo que perder el sueño por su causa después. It's better to sleep on it than (to) lose sleep because of it. ■ It's better to sleep on it than (to) lose sleep on account of it.

por su cuenta ■ por su propia cuenta on one's own ■ by oneself ➤ Accedió a ello por su propia cuenta. He agreed to it on his own.

por su gusto (just) to please one ■ in order to please one

por su lado de la acera on one's side of the sidewalk

por su parte (de usted) ■ de su parte (de usted) of you ■ on your part ➤ Fue muy generoso por su parte traer el vino para la fiesta. It was generous of you to bring the wine for the party. ➤ Fue bueno por su parte que usted ayudara. It was good of you to help. ➤ Fue desconsiderado por su parte sonarse la nariz en medio del aria. It was inconsiderate of you to blow your nose in the middle of the aria. ➤ Fue irresponsable por su parte dejarse la llave en la cerradura. It was irresponsible of you to leave the key in the lock.

ser **por su propio bien** to be for one's own good

por su propio pie unaided ■ on his own ■ under his own power ■ *(coloquial)* under his own steam ➤ *(noticia)* El Papa bajó por su propio pie de la escalerilla del avión. The Pope came down the steps of the airplane unaided. ➤ El piloto salió del auto siniestrado por su propio pie. The (race car) driver got out of wreckage unaided. ■ The (race car) driver got out of wreckage on his own. ■ The (race car) driver got out of the wreckage by himself. ■ The (race car) driver got out of the wreckage under his own steam.

por suerte 1. afortunadamente fortunately **2.** por azar by chance ■ by accident ■ accidentally

por suerte para ■ afortunadamente para fortunately for ■ luckily for

por supuesto ■ ¡seguro (que sí)! ■ ¡claro que sí! ■ ¡cómo no! of course!

por supuesto que lo haré ■ claro que lo haré of course I will (do it) ■ of course I'll do it

por supuesto que puedo ■ claro que puedo of course I can

por sus obras los conoceréis *(Mateo 7:15)* by their works you shall know them

por tal arte (de) ■ de tal manera in such a way (as) ➤ *(Abraham Lincoln al Gen. Hooker)* He oído por tal arte de ser creíble de sus comentarios recientes de que el ejército y el gobierno ambos necesitan un dictador. I have heard in such a way as to believe it of your recently saying that both the army and the government needed a dictator.

por tal lo tengo *(culto)* ■ o por tal lo tengo ■ o así me parece a mí or so I take it ■ or so it seems to me ■ that's what I take it to mean

por tal motivo for that reason ■ so ■ therefore ➤ Por tal motivo le rogamos que durante las obras dejen los grifos bien cerrados. For that reason, we ask that during the repairs you keep your taps turned completely off. ■ So we ask that during the repairs you keep your taps turned completely off.

por tal razón... that is why... ■ that's why...

por tandas de *x* ■ en tandas de *x* in batches of *x* ■ in units of *x* ■ in quantities of *x* ➤ Las medidas de la receta son para hacer las galletas por tandas de cincuenta. The recipe calls for making the cookies in batches of fifty.

por tanteos by trial and error

por tanto so ■ therefore ■ because of that ■ consequently ■ on that account ➤ Quiero, por tanto, enviar una nota por correo electrónico a todo el mundo comunicando mi nueva dirección. So I want(ed) to send everyone a note via E-mail with my new address. ➤ El desarrollo de muchos paises dependerá por tanto de su política interna y no sólo de la intervención de la ONU. The development of many countries will depend therefore on their own domestic policy and not just on UN intervention. So the development of many countries will depend on their own domestic policy and not just on UN intervention. ➤ Por tanto, ¿qué ha ido mal y qué se puede hacer todavía? So what went wrong, and what do we do now?

por temor a for fear of ■ out of fear for ➤ España ha cerrado sus fronteras a reses de Francia e Irlanda por temor a las "vacas locas". Spain has closed its borders to French and Irish beef for fear of "mad cows."

por temor a que... for fear that... ▪ fearing that... ▪ afraid that... ▪ out of fear that...

por temporadas on and off ▪ occasional

por terceras personas ▪ por terceros from a third party ▪ from someone else ➤ No me lo dijiste tú. Me enteré por terceras personas. You didn't tell me. I heard it from a third party. ▪ You're not the one who told me. I heard it from someone else.

por término medio on average

por tiempo indefinido for an indefinite time ▪ for an undefined time

por tierra overland ▪ by land

por toda la mañana all morning ▪ (for) the whole morning ▪ (for) the entire morning

por todas las cosas equivocadas for all the wrong things

por todas las razones equivocadas for all the wrong reasons

estar **por todas partes** ▪ estar por todos lados to be everywhere ▪ to be all over the place

por todo el morro: decir algo ~ *(Esp.)* ▪ pregonar algo por todas partes ▪ pregonar algo a todo el mundo to broadcast something all over the place ▪ to bandy something about ▪ to tell something to everybody ▪ to tell something indiscriminately

por todo el oro del mundo for all the money in the world ▪ for all the tea in China

estar **por todo el pueblo** to be all over town ➤ El rumor está por todo el pueblo. The rumor is all over town. ➤ He estado por todo el pueblo tratando de encontrar un regalo de boda. I've been all over town trying to find a wedding present. ➤ El virus de la gripe está por todo el pueblo. This flu bug is all over town.

por todo el territorio nacional ▪ por toda la nación around the country ▪ around the nation ▪ nationwide ▪ countrywide

por todo lo alto ▪ a lo grande whole hog ➤ Para dar la bienvenida al año nuevo por todo lo alto hemos contratado a una banda de mariachis. To celebrate the New Year whole hog we've hired a mariachi band.

por todo lo alto: una fiesta ~ a big bash ▪ *(ligeramente subido de tono)* one hell of a bash ▪ one hell of a party

estar **por todos lados** ▪ estar por todas partes to be everywhere ▪ to be all over the place

por todos los medios by every means possible ▪ by every means available

por todos los rincones on all sides ▪ everywhere you look

¡**por todos los santos!** ▪ ¡santo cielo! good heavens!

por tu culpa because of you

por tu parte ▪ de tu parte of you ➤ Fue muy generoso por tu parte traer el vino para la fiesta. It was generous of you to bring the wine for the party. ➤ Fue bueno por tu parte que ayudaras. It was good of you to help. ➤ Fue desconsiderado por tu parte sonarte la nariz en medio del aria. It was inconsiderate of you to blow your nose in the middle of the aria. ➤ Fue irresponsable por tu parte dejarte la llave en la cerradura. It was irresponsible of you to leave the key in the lock.

por última vez last ▪ for the last time ➤ ¿Cuándo la viste por última vez? When did you last see her?

por último finally ▪ last ▪ at last ▪ lastly

por un caso de in a case involving ▪ because of a case involving ▪ because of a case of ➤ Relevados dos guardias civiles en Bosnia por un caso de prostitución. Two civil guardsmen relieved of their posts in Bosnia in a case involving prostitution.

ser **por un casual** *(Esp.)* ▪ ser por una casualidad to be by any chance ▪ to happen to be ➤ ¿No será esta calle por un casual Avenida Sor Ángela pero con un nombre distinto? Is this street by any chance the same street as Sor Ángela Avenue, only with a different name? ▪ Does this street happen to be the same as Sor Ángela Avenue, only with a different name?

por un casual: tener ~ *(Esp.)* ▪ tener por una casualidad to have by any chance ▪ to happen to have ➤ ¿No tendrás por un casual un cigarrillo? You don't happen to have a cigarette, do you? ➤ ¿Tienes celos, por un casual? ▪ ¿Estás celoso, por un casual? Are you jealous, by any chance?

por un garbanzo no se echa a perder el cocido 1. un voto en contra no cambia la voluntad de la mayoría one dissenting vote won't override the will of the majority 2. no vamos a dejar que un amargado nos arruine la fiesta we're not going to let one party pooper ruin our party

por un lado ▪ por una parte for one thing ➤ ¿Por qué no quieres ir?-Bueno, por un lado, tengo demasiadas tareas, y por otro, no tengo (el) dinero. ▪ ¿Por qué no quieres ir?-Bueno, por una parte, tengo demasiadas tareas, y por otra, no tengo (el) dinero. Why don't you want to go?-Well, for one thing, I've got too much homework, and for another, I don't have the money.

por un lado... y por otro ▪ por una parte... y por otra on the one hand... and on the other

por un ligero margen by a small margin

por un oído le entra y por otro le sale it went in one ear and out the other

por un oído me entra y por otro me sale it went in one ear and out the other

por un perro que maté, mataperros me pusieron for having done it once, now I'm labeled

por un quítame allá esas pajas ▪ por una pavada over nothing ▪ over any little (picayune) thing

por un tubo: saber algo ~ to know something upside down and backwards

por un tubo: tener dinero ~ ▪ estar podrido en plata to be filthy rich ▪ to have megabucks ▪ to have money up the wazoo

por un tubo: vender algo ~ to sell as fast as the supply can keep up with the demand ▪ to sell briskly

por una buena razón for a good reason

por una razón u otra for some reason or other

por una simpleza ▪ por una pavada over nothing ➤ ¿Por qué te pones así por una simpleza? Why do you get so worked up over nothing?

por una vez for once ➤ Por una vez me alegré de verlo. For once I was glad to see him. ➤ Por una vez me alegré de verla. For once I was glad to see her. ➤ Por una vez me alegré de verle. *(leísmo, España y países andinos)* For once I was glad to see him. ➤ Por una vez, haz los deberes por ti mismo. For once, do your homework by yourself.

por una vez que... for the one time that... ▪ for having once...

por unanimidad unanimously

por uno de esos azares del destino by one of those vicissitudes of fate

por valor de at the price of ➤ Se compró un cuadro por valor de un millón de euros. He bought a painting at the price of one million euros.

por valor de: tener una deuda ~ to owe ➤ Tiene una deuda con hacienda por valor de diez mil euros. He owes ten thousand euros in taxes.

por ventura *(arcaico)* ▪ por suerte ▪ por casualidad ▪ por fortuna ▪ por azar by chance

estar **por ver algo** ▪ quedar por ver algo to still have to see something ▪ not to have seen something yet ➤ Los museos quedan por ver. We still have to see the museums. ▪ We haven't seen the museums yet.

estar **por verse** ▪ quedar por verse to remain to be seen ➤ Eso queda por verse. ▪ Eso está por verse. That remains to be seen.

por vía legal: llegar a un país ~ to enter a country legally

por vía marítima by ship ▪ by surface mail

por vía oral: comunicar algo ~ to communicate something by word of mouth ▪ to spread something by word of mouth

por vía oral: tomar ~ *(medicamento)* to take by mouth ▪ to take orally ➤ Tómese este jarabe para la tos por vía oral. Take this cough syrup by mouth. ▪ Take this cough syrup orally.

por vía rectal: administrar ~ to take rectally

por vivienda per household

por *x* veces *x* times over ➤ Ganamos esa cantidad de dinero por tres veces más. We made that much money three times over.

por *x* votos contra *y* ▪ por *x* votos frente a *y* by a vote of *x* to *y* ➤ *(Esp., titular)* El (Tribunal) Constitucional rechaza la recusación de su presidente por seis votos contra cinco. The Constitutional Court rejects the recusal of its chief justice by a vote of six to five.

porcelana cascada ▪ porcelana picada ▪ porcelana mellada ▪ porcelana saltada chipped china

el **porcentaje de acierto** hit ratio

la **porción de culpa** share of the blame

pormenorizar: no hay que ~ ▪ no hace falta que pormenorices there's no need to go into detail ▪ you don't need to go into detail

porque lo digo yo because I say so ▪ because I'm telling you to

porque no 1. just because 2. *(yo)* I just don't ▪ just because I don't 3. *(él)* he just doesn't ▪ just because he doesn't 4. *(él)* she just doesn't ▪ just because she doesn't

porque sí 1. just because 2. *(yo)* I just do ▪ just because I do

porque si no ▪ que, si no 1. (because) otherwise 2. *(tú, usted)* because if you don't 3. *(él)* because if he doesn't ▪ *(ella)* because if she doesn't ➤ Dile que me llame antes de las nueve, porque si no, no me pasan el mensaje. Tell him to call me before nine, (because) otherwise I won't get the message. ▪ Tell him to call me before nine, because if he doesn't, I won't get the message.

porrada de gente ▪ (un) montón de gente ▪ gentío whole bunch of people ▪ mob

un **porrón de cosas** *(Esp.)* ▪ un montón de cosas a whole bunch of things

un **porrón de gente** *(Esp.)* ▪ un gentío ▪ un montón de gente a whole bunch of people ▪ a lot of people ▪ a crowd (of people) ▪ quite a crowd

portada de una revista cover of a magazine ▪ magazine cover ➤ Su imagen fue portada de *TIME*. His picture was on the cover of *TIME*.

el **portal educativo** *(informática)* educational web site

el **portal de Belén** ▪ (el) Belén ▪ (el) pesebre Nativity scene ▪ crèche

el **portaminas desechable** ▪ lapicero desechable disposable mechanical pencil

portarse bien to behave oneself ➤ ¡Pórtate bien! Behave yourself!

portarse bien con alguien to be nice to someone ▪ to be good to someone ➤ *(Bill Gates a un público de estudiantes de secundaria)* Portáos bien con los tragas. Probablemente acabaréis trabajando para uno. Be nice to nerds. You'll probably end up working for one.

portarse mal con alguien ▪ comportarse mal to misbehave toward someone ▪ to act up ➤ Los niños se portaron muy mal en el colegio con el sustituto. The children at school misbehaved toward the substitute.

¡**pórtate bien!** behave yourself! ▪ *(a un perro que gruñe)* be nice!

posar para un retrato to sit for a portrait

posarse en to perch on

poseer lo que se requiere (para triunfar) ▪ poseer lo que se necesita (para triunfar) ▪ tener lo que se requiere (para triunfar) ▪ tener lo que se necesita (para triunfar) to have what it takes (to succeed) ➤ Posees lo que se requiere para triunfar. ▪ Posees lo que se necesita para triunfar. ▪ Tienes lo que se requiere para triunfar. ▪ Tienes lo que se necesita para triunfar. You have what it takes to succeed.

poseer propiedad ▪ tener propiedad ▪ ser el dueño de propiedad to own property ▪ to have property ▪ to be the owner of property ➤ Ella posee muchas propiedades. She owns a lot of property. ➤ Ella tiene muchos bienes inmuebles. She has a lot of real estate. ▪ She owns a lot of real estate. ➤ El hotel es propiedad de la compañía ferroviaria. The hotel is owned by the railroad. ➤ ¿Quién es el dueño del edificio? ▪ ¿A quién pertenece este edificio? ▪ ¿De quién es el edificio? Who owns this building? ➤ Esta no es la residencia del Sr. Ortiz. Es sencillamente un piso del edificio de su propiedad. This is not Mr. Ortiz's residence. This is just a flat in the building he owns.

la **posibilidad de que...** the possibility that...

la **posibilidad de que eso suceda** ▪ la probabilidad de que eso suceda ▪ las probabilidades de que eso suceda the chance(s) of that happening ➤ La probabilidad de que eso suceda no es muy alta. ▪ Las probabilidades de que eso suceda no son muy altas. The chances of that happening are not very good.

la **posibilidad es escasa (de que...)** the chances are remote (that...)

posibilidad lejana ▪ posibildad remota remote possibility

posibilidad remota ▪ posibilidad lejana remote possibility

posición económica economic status

la **posición inicial** entry-level position

la **posición social** social status

la **posición vertical** upright position

el **poste telefónico** ▪ poste de teléfono telephone pole

estar **postrado(-a) en la cama** to be bedridden

postura de vida ▪ modo de vida way of life

postura del misionero missionary position

potencia mundial world power ➤ En el siglo quince, España se erigió como una potencia mundial. In the fifteenth century, Spain became a world power.

potenciar el crecimiento ▪ promover el crecimiento to promote growth

potenciar los efectos de to heighten the efects of

potente explosión powerful explosion

potente explosivo powerful explosive ➤ *(noticia)* Un potente explosivo causa destrozos en la Embajada de España en Caracas. A powerful explosive damages Spain's embassy in Caracas.

potro arisco unruly colt ▪ hostile colt

el **poyete de la ventana** ▪ (el) alféizar window sill

pozo de ciencia pillar of knowledge

pozo de sabiduría pillar of wisdom

ser una **práctica común** ▪ ser una costumbre muy común to be (a) common practice

prácticamente en cada... in almost every...

prácticamente no haber suficiente ▪ casi no haber suficiente ▪ apenas haber suficiente ▪ a duras penas haber suficiente (for) there barely to be enough ➤ Prácticamente no había suficiente agua caliente para afeitarme esta mañana. ▪ Casi no había suficiente agua caliente para afeitarme esta mañana. ▪ Apenas había suficiente agua caliente para afeitarme esta mañana. ▪ A duras penas había suficiente agua caliente para afeitarme esta mañana. There was barely enough hot water to shave this morning. ▪ There was hardly enough hot water to shave this morning.

prácticamente no hablar un idioma ▪ **apenas hablar un idioma** ▪ **a duras penas hablar un idioma** ▪ **casi no hablar un idioma** to barely speak a language ▪ to hardly speak a language ➤ Prácticamente no hablaba español cuando llegó a Buenos Aires. She barely spoke Spanish when she arrived in Buenos Aires. ▪ She hardly spoke Spanish when she arrived in Buenos Aires.

prácticamente no poder levantarse de la cama ▪ casi no poder levantarse de la cama ▪ apenas poder levantarse de la cama ▪ levantarse a duras penas de la cama to be barely able to get out of bed ▪ to be hardly able to get out of bed ➤ Prácticamente no puede levantarse de la cama por la mañana. ▪ Casi no puede levantarse de la cama por la mañana. ▪ Apenas puede levantarse de la cama por la mañana. ▪ Se levanta a duras penas de la cama por la mañana. He can barely get out of bed in the morning. ▪ He can hardly get out of bed in the morning.

prácticamente no tener suficiente ▪ casi no tener suficiente ▪ apenas tener suficiente ▪ a duras penas tener suficiente to have barely enough ▪ to have hardly enough ➤ Prácticamente no tenía suficiente agua caliente para afeitarme esta mañana. ▪ Casi no tenía suficiente agua caliente para afeitarme esta mañana. ▪ Apenas tenía suficiente agua caliente para afeitarme esta mañana. ▪ A duras penas tenía suficiente agua caliente para afeitarme esta mañana. I barely had enough hot water to shave this morning. ▪ I hardly had enough hot water to shave this morning.

prácticamente sin tocar ▪ casi sin tocar practically untouched ▪ barely touched ▪ hardly touched ➤ Hay partes de este libro prácticamente sin tocar. There are places in this book we've barely touched. ▪ There are places in this book we've hardly touched.

practicar deportes ▪ hacer deportes to play sports

practicar lo que uno predica to practice what one preaches

practicar una autopsia ▪ realizar una autopsia to perform an autopsy ▪ to do an autopsy

practicar una detención ▪ arrestar a alguien to make an arrest ▪ to arrest someone ➤ La policía practicó más de cien detenciones. The police made more than a hundred arrests.

practicarle a alguien un examen to give someone a physical (examination)

prado alpino alpine meadow

precaver de ▪ precaver contra ▪ guardarse de to guard against

estar **precedido de** to be preceded by

preceptiva bíblica biblical precepts ▪ biblical injunction

precepto bíblico biblical precept

preciarse de to pride oneself on

precintar una bolsa de plástico ■ sellar una bolsa de plástico to seal a plastic bag ➤ Por favor, no precintes la bolsa; voy a comerlos ahora mismo. Please don't seal the bag; I'm going to eat them right now.
precio al por mayor wholesale price
precio al por menor ■ precio de venta al público ■ PVP retail price ■ store price ■ *(especialmente de carros)* sticker price
precio arreglado set price ■ fixed price
precio asequible affordable price
precio de lista ■ precio de venta al público ■ PVP list price ■ retail price
precio de venta al público ■ PVP ■ precio de lista retail price ■ list price
precio dispara price skyrockets ➤ *(titular)* El precio de viviendas dispara en Madrid. Price of housing skyrockets in Madrid.
precio habitual regular price ➤ El precio será habitual. This will be the regular price.
precio por la cabeza de alguien price on someone's head ➤ Hay un precio por su cabeza. There's a price on his head.
precio que normalmente tiene regular price
precio razonable reasonable price
precio sideral astronomical price
precio venta al público ■ PVP retail price
precios de saldo closeout prices
preciosa casa beautiful house
precipitarse a una conclusión to jump to conclusions
precipitarse al vacío 1. caerse al vacío to fall into the void 2. saltar desde ■ tirarse al vacío to jump into the void ■ to throw oneself into the void
precipitarse desde 1. caerse desde to fall from 2. saltar desde ■ tirarse desde to jump from ■ to throw oneself from
precipitarse hacia la recesión to plunge into a recession ■ to plunge into recession ➤ *(titular)* El mundo se precipita hacia la recesión. The world plunges into (a) recession.
precipitarse por un barranco to tumble down a slope
precisamente por eso ■ por eso mismo for that very reason ■ that's the very reason why
precisamente tú 1. *(presente)* in fact, it is you who 2. *(pasado)* in fact, it was you who
precisamente usted 1. *(presente)* in fact, it is you who 2. *(pasado)* in fact, it was you who
precisar algo ■ especificar algo ■ detallar algo to specify something ■ to give the specifics of something ■ to go into specifics ■ to give the details of something ■ to go into the details of something ➤ Todavía no se han precisado los pormenores de la sentencia. They still haven't specified the details of the sentence. ■ They still haven't given the specifics of the sentence. ■ They still haven't given the details of the sentence.
precisar que... to indicate that... ➤ El emisor árabe Al Yazira precisó que la grabación fue realizada antes de que los pilotos suicidas se trasladaran a EE UU. The Arab broadcaster Al Jazira indicated that the recording was made before the suicide pilots moved to the U.S.
preconizar una reforma ■ abogar por una reforma ■ encomiar una reforma to advocate a reform
el **predicador fundamentalista** fundamentalist preacher
predicar con el ejemplo ■ hacer lo que uno predica to preach by (one's) example ■ to practice what one preaches
predilección por predilection for
predio rústico soil ■ field for cultivation
predisponerse en contra de algo to be biased against something ■ to be predisposed against something
predisponerse en contra de alguien to be biased against someone ■ to be predisposed against someone
predominar sobre algo ■ prevalecer sobre algo to prevail over something
predominar sobre alguien ■ prevalecer sobre alguien to prevail over someone
ser la **preferencia de paso de alguien** ■ tener el derecho de paso for the right of way to favor someone ■ to have the right of way ➤ *(noticia de un accidente)* Los semáforos de ambos sentidos estaban en verde, pero la preferencia de paso era de la hormigonera. The traffic light was green in both directions, but the right of way favored the cement mixer.

preferiría decir I should say ➤ El programa es un documental-un documento, preferiría decir. The program is a documentary, a document, I should say.
preferiría que... *(cuando "yo" es el sujeto)* I would prefer that... ■ I would rather... ■ I'd prefer that... ■ I'd rather ➤ Prefería que no llamaras antes de las ocho de la mañana. I would prefer that you not call before 8 a.m. ■ I would rather you didn't call before 8 a.m. ■ I would rather you not call before 8 a.m. ■ I'd prefer that you not call before 8 a.m. ■ I'd rather you didn't call before 8 a.m. ■ I'd rather you not call before 8 a.m.
pregonar a los cuatro vientos ■ pregonar a los gritos pelados to blab something all over the place ➤ Le conté un secreto a mi vecina y lo pregonó a los cuatro vientos. I told my neighbor a secret, and she blabbed it all over the place.
pregunta capciosa trick question
pregunta de reflexión matter for reflection
pregunta doble intencionada loaded question
pregunta elemental elementary question ■ basic question ➤ Al principio me pareció una pregunta muy elemental; luego lo pensé mejor. At first I thought it was an elementary question, but then I thought better of it.
la **pregunta está muy bien hecha** ■ es una buena pregunta that's a good question
pregunta incómoda embarrassing question
pregunta obligada obligatory question ■ mandatory question ➤ Una pregunta obligada en toda entrevista de trabajo es "¿Cuál es su disponibilidad de tiempo?" An obligatory question in every job interview is, "What is your availability?"
pregunta ociosa idle question
pregunta ofensiva ■ pregunta que ofende offensive question
pregunta que ofende offensive question
pregunta sin responder ■ respuesta en blanco unanswered question ■ question left blank
pregunta sin respuesta ■ pregunta que no tiene respuesta unanswerable question
pregunta tramposa trick question ■ question with a catch ■ catch question ➤ Los abogados soltaron muchas preguntas tramposas al testigo principal en el caso. The lawyers threw a lot of trick questions at the principal witness in the case.
pregunta y respuesta ■ P&R question and answer ■ Q&A
preguntando se va a Roma ■ preguntando se llega a Roma anyone can tell us how to get there ■ anyone can tell you how to get there ■ just ask anybody on the street
preguntar a alguien algo personal to ask someone a personal question
preguntar algo a alguien a bocajarro to ask someone something point-blank ➤ Le pregunté a bocajarro lo que haría si... ■ Le pregunté a bocajarro qué haría si... I asked him point-blank what he would do if...
preguntar por alguien to ask for someone ➤ Vaya al servicio al cliente y pregunte por el gerente. Go to customer service and ask for the manager.
preguntar por la hora ■ pedir hora to ask the time
preguntar por la salud de alguien to inquire after someone's health ■ to ask about someone's health
preguntar sobre algo to ask about something
preguntar sobre alguien to ask about someone ➤ Preguntaron sobre ti. They asked about you.
preguntarle a alguien por algo to ask someone about something
preguntarle a alguien por alguien to ask someone about someone
preguntarle a alguien qué... to ask someone what... ➤ Les pregunté a mis alumnos qué verduras se ponen en la paella. I asked my students what vegetables you put in paella.
preguntarse a sí mismo to ask oneself
preguntarte unas cuantas cosas to ask you a few things
premiado: guión ~ award-winning script
premio codiciado coveted award ■ coveted prize
premio gordo jackpot
¡**premio para...!** ■ ¡un tanto para...! score one for...!
premisa insoslayable unquestionable premise ■ absolute requirement ■ unavoidable premise ■ inescapable premise ➤ El presidente del gobierno está exigiendo un cambio de

rumbo en la política vasca que se base en tres premisas insoslayables. The president of the government is demanding a change of direction in Basque politics which he bases on three absolute requirements.

prenda corta light clothing ■ summer clothes *(referido a mangas cortas, pantalones cortos, minifaldas, etc. ■ referring to short sleeves, short pants, miniskirts, etc.)*

prenda raída frayed garment ■ frayed article of clothing

prendarse de algo to be captivated by something

prendarse de alguien ■ enamorarse de alguien to fall in love with someone ■ to be captivated by someone

prendas de vestir articles of clothing

prender a alguien *(L.am.)* ■ encender a alguien ■ hacer tilín a alguien ■ poner a alguien a cien to turn someone on

prender algo con alfileres to do a lousy job on something ■ *(ligeramente soez)* to do a half-assed job on something

prender la computadora *(L.am.)* ■ encender el ordenador to turn on the computer

prender la luz *(L.am.)* ■ encender la luz to turn on the light

prender la luz de arriba ■ prender la luz del techo ■ encender la luz de arriba ■ encender la luz del techo to turn on the ceiling light(s) ■ to turn on the overhead light(s)

prenderle fuego a algo ■ pegar fuego a algo to set something on fire ■ to set fire to something ■ to ignite something ➤ Cuando se prepara un café irlandés se le prende fuego al whiskey. When you make Irish coffee, you ignite the whiskey.

prenderse fuego ■ incendiarse to catch (on) fire ➤ Durante la Batalla de la Tierra Virgen en la Guerra Civil Americana, los bosques se prendieron fuego y muchos soldados murieron calcinados. During the American Civil War Battle of the Wilderness, the woods caught (on) fire, and many of the soldiers burned to death.

prenderse fuego a lo bonzo ■ quemarse a lo bonzo to set oneself on fire ■ to incinerate oneself

estar **prendido con alfileres** 1. to be shoddily made ■ to be shoddily built ■ to be poorly made 2. *(dicho de deberes escolares)* to be shoddily prepared 3. estar pendiente de un hilo to be hanging by a thread

prensa amarilla yellow journalism

prensa del corazón human interest press ■ *(despectivo)* gossip rags

prensa rosa human interest press ■ *(despectivo)* gossip rags

prensado en frío: aceite de oliva ~ cold-pressed olive oil

preocuparle a uno ■ pesarle a uno to worry one ■ to weigh on one's mind ■ to weigh on one

preocuparse de ■ intranquilizarse to worry about

preparado de pastel ■ preparado para bizcocho cake mix

estar **preparado para el despegue** to be ready for takeoff ➤ Seis, cuatro, cinco Delta, preparado para el despegue.-Cuatro, cinco Delta, adelante. Six four five Delta, ready for takeoff.-Four five Delta, go ahead.

preparado(-a) para lo que venga ready for whatever comes one's way

¡preparados, listos, ya! on your mark, get set, go! ■ ready, aim, fire!

preparar el terreno para algo to lay the groundwork for something ➤ Los diplomáticos están preparando el terreno para el encuentro de la cumbre. The diplomats are laying the groundwork for the summit meeting.

preparar la cena to fix supper ■ to prepare supper ■ to make supper ■ to get supper (ready) ■ to fix dinner ■ to prepare dinner ■ to make dinner ■ to get dinner (ready) *(Nota: "Supper" y "dinner" suelen coincidir en los Estados Unidos, ya que "dinner" es la comida principal del día, normalmente servida entre las seis y siete de la tarde, así que "preparar la cena" se puede traducir bien como "to fix dinner".)*

preparar la comida to fix dinner ■ to prepare dinner ■ to make dinner ■ to get dinner (ready)

preparar la nómina to do the payroll

preparar los bártulos ■ liar los bártulos to pack up (one's things) ■ to pack up (one's belongings)

preparar un asalto ■ preparar un atraco to plan a robbery ■ to plan a holdup

preparar una encerrona a alguien ■ preparar una trampa a alguien to set a trap for someone ■ to lay a trap for someone ■ to put someone in a tight spot ■ to put someone in a difficult predicament ■ to put someone in a difficult situation

preparar una trampa para un animal to set a trap for an animal

prepararse a hacer algo to prepare to do something

prepararse para to train to be

prepárate a ■ prepárate para ■ disponte a ■ disponte para ■ estáte listo para ■ *(culto)* estáte presto a be ready to

preparativos bélicos preparations for war

prescindir de alguien 1. no necesitar de alguien to do without someone 2. despedir a alguien to fire someone ➤ Puedo prescindir de ese tipo. I can do without that guy. ➤ *(noticia)* El obispo de Vigo ha prescindido de una profesora de religión tras separarse de su marido. The Bishop of Vigo (has) fired a teacher after she separated from her husband.

por prescripción médica on doctor's orders ■ on the doctor's orders

presenciar un accidente to witness an accident

presenciar un acontecimiento histórico to witness a historical event

presenciar un suceso to witness a (tragic) event

presenciar un evento to witness an event

presentación en sociedad ■ puesta de largo ■ quinceañera young woman's debut ■ young woman's presentation to society ■ young woman's coming out in society

presentar a una joven en sociedad to present a young woman to society

presentar armas *(militar)* to present arms ➤ ¡Presenten armas! Present arms!

presentar batalla ■ hacer frente to put up a fight

presentar cargos contra alguien por to press charges against someone for

presentar los papeles para matricularme en el master en filogía hispánica to apply for the master's program in Spanish

presentar pruebas determinantes to present conclusive proof

presentar signos de to show signs of ➤ El cuerpo no presentaba signos de violencia. The body showed no signs of violence.

presentar su renuncia ■ presentar su dimisión to offer one's resignation ■ to tender one's resignation ■ to submit one's resignation

presentar sus condolencias a alguien ■ dar sus condolencias a alguien to express one's condolences to someone ■ to give one's condolences to someone ➤ Voy a presentar mis condolencias a la familia. I am going to express my condolences to the family.

presentar sus respetos to pay one's respects

presentar un examen ■ tomar un examen 1. to take a test 2. *(esp. parcial o final)* to take an examination ■ to take an exam

presentar un plan de vuelo *(aviación)* to file a flight plan

presentar un proyecto de ley to introduce a bill

presentar una demanda judicial (contra alguien) ■ presentar un juicio (contra alguien) ■ admitir un juicio a trámite (contra alguien) to file a lawsuit (against someone) ■ to file suit (against someone)

presentar una denuncia sobre to lodge a complaint about ■ to file a complaint about ■ to make a complaint about

presentar una película to premiere a movie ➤ *(noticia)* Tom Cruise y Penélope Cruz presentaron ayer en Madrid *Vanilla Sky*. Tom Cruise and Penelope Cruz yesterday premiered *Vanilla Sky* in Madrid.

presentar una reclamación sobre ■ presentar una denuncia to lodge a complaint about

presentar y admitir un juicio (contra alguien) ■ presentar y admitir una demanda contra alguien to file a lawsuit (against someone) ■ to file suit against someone ➤ Una vez presentado y admitido a trámite, el juicio debe ser celebrado a menos que el demandante desista. Once filed, the lawsuit must be heard unless the plaintiff drops it.

presentarse a la reelección *(Esp.)* ■ presentarse para reelección to run for reelection ■ to stand for reelection

presentarse a presidente *(Esp.)* ■ presentarse para presidente to run for president

presentarse a su hora to show up on time

presentarse a trabajar to show up for work ➤ No se presentó a trabajar ayer. He didn't show up for work yesterday.

presentarse a un tercer mandato to run for a third term

presentarse a una audición para el papel de... to audition for the part of...

presentarse a una audición para un papel de... to audition for a part as...

presentarse ante el juez to go before the judge

presentarse como *(Esp.)* to run for ➤ Cuando se presentó como senador... When he ran for Senator... ▪ When he ran for the Senate...

presentarse como candidato a *(Esp.)* to run as a candidate for

presentarse en público to appear en public ▪ to make public appearances ➤ El músico joven empezó a presentarse en público cuando tenía ocho años. The young musician began to appear in public at the age of eight.

presentarse para reelección *(Esp.)* to run for reelection ▪ to stand for reelection

presentarse para presidente *(Esp.)* ▪ presentarse a presidente to run for president

presentarse para un cargo público *(Esp.)* to run for public office

presentarse para un tercer mandato *(Esp.)* to run for a third term

presentársele ▪ tener por delante to have ahead of one ➤ Se nos presenta un verano maravilloso. ▪ Tenemos un verano maravilloso por delante. We have a wonderful summer ahead of us.

presentársele la oportunidad to have the opportunity ▪ to have the chance ➤ Cuando se me presentó la oportunidad... When I had the opportunity... ▪ When the opportunity presented itself... ▪ When the opportunity arose... ▪ When the opportunity came along... ▪ When I had the chance...

presente histórico historic present (tense)

el **presidente de la Reserva Federal** chairman of the Federal Reserve Board

el **presidente de turno** current president ➤ José María Aznar es el presidente de turno de la Unión Europea. José María Aznar is the current president of the European Union.

presidente del comité chairman of the committee ▪ committee chairman

presidente saliente outgoing president

presión arterial ▪ presión de la sangre ▪ presión sanguínea ▪ (la) tensión blood pressure ➤ El médico tomó su presión arterial. *(de él)* The doctor took his blood pressure. ▪ *(de ella)* The doctor took her blood pressure.

la **presión de la sangre** ▪ presión sanguínea ▪ presión arterial ▪ (la) tensión blood pressure ➤ ¿Qué tensión tienes? What's your blood pressure? ➤ ¿Qué tal la tensión? How's your blood pressure?

presión sanguínea ▪ presión de la sangre ▪ presión arterial ▪ tensión blood pressure ➤ El médico dijo que su presión sanguínea estaba en el rango normal. The doctor said his blood pressure is in the normal range.

presión sanguínea límite borderline blood pressure ➤ El médico dijo que su presión sanguínea estaba al límite. ▪ El médico dijo que su presión sanguínea estaba en el límite. The doctor said his blood pressure was borderline.

presionar a alguien ▪ poner presión a alguien to put pressure on someone ▪ to bear down on someone ➤ Los jefes están presionando a la plantilla. ▪ Los jefes están poniendo mucha presión a la plantilla. The bosses are putting a lot of pressure on the staff. ▪ The bosses are bearing down on the staff.

presionar a alguien para hacer algo ▪ presionar a alguien para que haga algo ▪ ejercer presión sobre alguien para hacer algo ▪ ejercer presión sobre alguien para que haga algo ▪ hacer presión sobre alguien para hacer algo ▪ hacer presión sobre alguien para que haga algo to pressure someone to do something ▪ to put pressure on someone to do something

presionar el botón derecho en ▪ pulsar el botón derecho en ▪ *(coloquial)* cliquear el botón derecho en to right click on

presionar el botón izquierdo en ▪ pulsar el botón izquierdo en ▪ *(coloquial)* cliquear el botón izquierdo en to left click on

presionar en exceso a algo to put excessive pressure on something ▪ to put excessive pressure against something

presionar en exceso a alguien to put excessive pressure on someone

presione cualquier tecla para continuar press any key to continue

estar **preso(-a)** to be in jail

preso(-a) huido(-a) escaped convict ▪ prison escapee ▪ escaped prisoner

prestar algo a alguien ▪ dejar algo a alguien to lend someone something ▪ to lend something to someone

prestar atención ▪ hacer caso ▪ prestar oídos to pay attention

prestar declaración ▪ to testify to give evidence

prestar el juramento to take the oath ➤ El presidente de los Estados Unidos presta el juramento de servicio el veinte de enero al mediodía. The president of the United States takes the oath of office at noon on January the twentieth.

prestar juramento to take an oath ▪ to take the oath ➤ El presidente de los Estados Unidos presta juramento (de servicio) el veinte de enero al mediodía. The president of the United States takes the oath of office at noon on January the twentieth.

prestar oídos ▪ prestar atención ▪ hacer caso to pay attention

prestar un flaco favor a alguien ▪ hacer un flaco favor a alguien 1. to do someone no favors 2. to be of little help ▪ to be of no help ▪ to be no help at all ➤ Los padres que sobreprotegen a sus hijos les prestan un flaco favor. Overprotective parents do their children no favors. ➤ Acordamos repartir el dinero, pero el tipo me prestó un flaco favor. We agreed to spit the money, but the guy was no help at all.

prestarse a to be party to

prestarse a hablar to agree to speak ➤ *(noticia)* La pareja se prestó a hablar por separado y en calidad de testigos con la policía. The couple agreed to speak separately to the police as witnesses.

prestarse a ser usado(-a) por... to let oneself be used by... ▪ to allow oneself to be used by...

prestarse bien a algo 1. ser apto para algo to lend itself well to something ▪ to be suitable for something ▪ to be appropriate for something 2. satisfacer bien las necesidades de uno to meet one's needs well ➤ Este proyecto se presta muy bien al trabajo en equipo. This project lends itself very well to teamwork. ➤ Este traje se presta (bien) para la boda. This suit is (very) appropriate for the wedding. ➤ Esta casa se presta muy bien a nuestras necesidades. This house meets our needs very well.

presteza mental ▪ presencia de ánimo presence of mind

estar **presto(-a) a** to be poised for ➤ Los soldados están prestos al combate. The soldiers are poised for combat.

prestigio en la comunidad ▪ reconocimiento en la comunidad standing in the community ➤ Goza de un gran prestigio en la comunidad. ▪ Goza un gran reconocimiento en la comunidad. He enjoys a high standing in the community. ▪ He has a high standing in the community.

presumir de ser to claim to be ▪ to boast of being

presunto(-a) terrorista alleged terrorist

presuntos implicados en un delito suspects implicated in a crime

presupuesto ajustado: tener un ~ to be on a tight budget ➤ Este año tengo un presupuesto muy ajustado. I'm on a really tight budget this year.

presupuesto de tiempos de guerra wartime budget

presupuesto equilibrado ▪ equilibrio presupuestario balanced budget

presupuesto gratis free estimates

pretender hacer algo 1. to aim to do something 2. to pretend to do something

pretender ignorancia ▪ fingir ignorancia to feign ignorance

pretender que algo no ocurra 1. intentar de que algo no ocurra to try to keep something from happening ▪ to try to prevent something from happening 2. asumir que algo no ocurra to assume that something is not going to happen ▪ to assume that something is not going to be the case ➤ El presidente pretende que su salida del gobierno no merme su liderazgo político. The president is trying to keep his leaving office from weakening his political leadership.

prevenir un desastre *(de origen natural)* ▪ evitar un desastre to avert a disaster ▪ to prevent a disaster (from occurring)

previa petición *(Esp.)* ▪ previa cita necesaria ▪ por cita previa by appointment (only) ▪ appointment required

previo a prior to ➤ Los técnicos del ayuntamiento descartan que el bloque tuviese grietas previas al derrumbamiento. The city's inspectors rule out the possibility that the building had cracks prior to its collapse.

primar sobre *(Esp.)* ▪ tener precedencia sobre ▪ tener prioridad sobre a to take precedence over

la **primavera la sangre altera** to get spring fever

la **primavera se siente en el aire** spring is in the air

el **primer atisbo de** the first indication of ▪ the first sign of ▪ the first hint of ▪ the first sight of

primer borrador first draft

primer esbozo first strokes of a sketch

primer espada ▪ torero bullfighter

¡**primer fallo!** *(béisbol)* strike one!

primer impulso ▪ impulso espontáneo first impulse ▪ spontaneous impulse ➤ Al hablar en un idioma extranjero, tu primer impulso es casi siempre el que vale. When speaking a foreign language, your first impulse is almost always the right one. ▪ When speaking a foreign language, your spontaneous impulse is almost always the right one.

primer plano closeup ➤ La tercera escena de la película empieza con un primer plano de la protagonista. The third scene of the movie begins with a closeup of the main character.

primer plano de...: estar en el ~ to be in the forefront of... ➤ *(noticia)* El embajador ha estado en el primer plano de la actualidad defendiendo las posiciones del gobierno en relación con la guerra. The ambassador has been in the forefront of events defending the government's position on the war.

primer sol de la mañana early morning sun

primer(-a) sospechoso(-a) ▪ sospechoso(-a) principal prime suspect

primer tiempo *(deportes)* **1.** *(fútbol)* first half **2.** *(baloncesto)* first quarter

primera dama first lady

primera elección de la camada pick of the litter

primera hipoteca first mortgage

primera impresión: causar una ~ to make a first impression ➤ Causó una primera impresión excelente. She made a very good first impression. ➤ La primera impresión que me causó Madrid fue la de una ciudad que conserva su atractivo histórico. My first impression of Madrid was (that) of a city that has preserved its historical beauty.

la **primera impresión que se experimenta** the first sensation that you experience ➤ La primera impresión que se experimenta durante un despegue es de vértigo. The first sensation that you experience when taking off is vertigo.

primera infancia early childhood

primera manga *(deportes)* first classification round

primera minoría largest minority ➤ *(noticia)* Los hispanos, la primera minoría de EE UU, será clave en las elecciones de noviembre. Hispanics, the largest minority in the U.S., will be key in the November elections.

primera oración opening prayer ▪ first sentence

primera señal de que... ▪ primera indicación de que... first sign that... ▪ first indication that... ➤ La primera señal de que había... *(singular)* The first sign that there was... ▪ The first indication that there was... ▪ *(plural)* The first sign that there were... ▪ The first indication that there were...

primera vez que uno hacía una cosa the first time one had done something ➤ Era la primera vez que Jim veía a Hanna. It was the first time Jim had seen Hanna. ➤ Eramos los primeros occidentales que iban a esa tierra indómita en años. We were the first Westerners who had gone to that untamable land in years.

primeras personas en hacer algo: ser de las ~ to be one of the first (people) to do something ▪ to be among the first (people) to do something ➤ Fui una de las primeras personas en inscribirme. I was one of the first (people) to sign up. ▪ I was among the first to sign up.

primeras relaciones first sexual experience

primero de ▪ en un principio ▪ al principio ▪ para empezar at first

ser el **primero de la fila** ▪ estar a la cabeza de la cola to be first in line ▪ to be at the head of the line ▪ to be at the front of the line ▪ to be at the beginning of the line

primero de todo first of all ▪ *(coloquial)* first off

primero dije que sí at first I said yes

ser el **primero en hacer una cosa** to be the first one to do something

ser el **primero empezando por la cola** to be the last one in line ▪ to be at the end of the line

primero es la obligación que la devoción ▪ primero la obligación y después la devoción work before play ▪ first things first

primero la obligación y después la devoción ▪ primero es la obligación que la devoción work before play ▪ first things first

primero les dije que sí at first I said yes

primeros ancestros: nuestros ~ ▪ nuestros primeros ascendientes ▪ nuestros primeros antepasados our earliest ancestors

primeros antepasados: nuestros ~ ▪ nuestros primeros ascendientes ▪ nuestros primeros ancestros our earliest ancestors

primeros años early years ▪ early life

primeros ascendientes: nuestros ~ ▪ nuestros primeros antepasados ▪ nuestros primeros ancestros our earliest ancestors

los **primeros cristianos** the early Christians

primeros puestos de la escala: estar en los ~ to be in the top percentile

primeros puestos de la escala: estar muy cerca de los ~ to be near the top of the scale

ser **primo hermano una cosa de otra** to be the first cousin of something ➤ El español y el portugués por sus orígenes latinos son primos hermanos. Spanish and Portuguese are, by virtue of their Latin roots, first cousins.

primo lejano distant cousin

ser **primordial** to be top priority

la **principal fuente de ingresos** main source of income ▪ principal source of income

la **principal hipótesis con la que se trabaja es...** the main hypothesis they're working on is...

príncipe azul prince charming

príncipe de las tinieblas prince of darkness

Príncipe destronado *(novela de Miguel Delibes)* *Dethroned Prince* *(Nota: Puede refeirirse a un niño que, por el nacimiento de un hermano, pierde su estatus de "benjamín". ▪ This term can refer to a child who, through the birth of a sibling, loses his status as the youngest.)*

príncipe heredero crown prince

principio activo ▪ ingrediente activo active ingredient

principio de economía *(filosofía de la ciencia)* ▪ navaja de Occam law of parsimony ▪ Ockham's razor ➤ El principio de economía, o la navaja de Occam, dice que la explicación completa más sencilla es la verdadera. The law of parsimony, or Ockham's razor, states that the simplest complete explanation is the true one.

principio de los tiempos beginning of time

ser el **principio del fin (de)** to be the beginning of the end (of)

prisas son malas consejeras haste makes waste

prisas y carreras hustle and bustle ➤ Había prisas y carreras. There was a lot of hustle and bustle.

prisión incondicional para alguien: imponer ~ to impose a mandatory jail sentence

prisión preventiva preventive detention

prisionero(-a) en el corredor de la muerte death-row inmate

privar a alguien de hacer algo ▪ reprimir a alguien de hacer algo to prohibit someone from doing something ▪ to forbid someone to do something ▪ to stop someone from doing something

privarle a alguien de algo *(Esp., leísmo)* ▪ privarlo a alguien de algo to deprive someone of something

privarle a alguien de su libertad *(Esp., leísmo)* ▪ privarlo a alguien de libertad to take away someone's freedom ▪ to take someone's freedom away

privarlo a alguien de hacer algo ■ reprimir a alguien de hacer algo to stop someone from doing something

privarlo a alguien de su libertad *(L.am.)* ■ *(Esp., leísmo)* privarle a alguien de libertad to take away someone's freedom ■ to take someone's freedom away

pro indiviso *(herencias)* joint property ■ jointly owned property

la **probabilidad de que eso suceda** ■ las probabilidades de que eso suceda ■ la posibilidad de que eso suceda the chance(s) of that happening ➤ La probabilidad de que eso suceda no es muy alta. ■ Las probabilidades de que eso suceda no son muy altas. ■ La posibilidad de que eso suceda no es muy alta. The chances of that happening are not very good. ■ The probability of that happening are not very high.

las **probabilidades de que** the probability that

ser **probado en** to be tested on ➤ *(noticia)* Europa prohíbe los cosméticos probados en los animales. Europe prohibits cosmetics from being tested on animals.

probar a hacer algo to try doing something ➤ Probé a escribirle a ella, y resultó que... I tried writing to her, and what happened was...

probar cómo está to do a taste test

probar con algo to try something ■ to try one's hand at something ■ to give something a try ➤ Tras un período en el teatro, se trasladó a Hollywood para probar con el cine. After a stint in theater, she moved to Hollywood to try (her hand at) films. ■ After a stint in theater, she moved to Hollywood to give films a try.

probar con alguien de tu tamaño to pick on somebody your own size ➤ ¡Prueba con alguien de tu tamaño! Pick on somebody your own size!

probar de manera determinante ■ probar determinantemente to prove conclusively

probar determinantemente ■ probar de manera determinante to prove conclusively

probar fortuna ■ probar suerte to try one's luck

probar la suerte con to try one's luck with

probar suerte en ■ probar fortuna en to try one's luck

probarse nuevas ropas to try on new clothes ➤ Me he probado unos zapatos nuevos, pero me quedaban chicos. I tried on a pair of new shoes, but they were too small.

problema de fondo ■ problema subyacente underlying problem

problema gordo big problem

un **problema ha surgido** a problem has come up ■ a problem has arisen

el **problema subyacente** ■ problema de fondo underlying problem

el **problema trascendental** major problem

los **problemas ambientales** environmental problems

problemas cardiacos heart problems ■ cardiac problems ■ *(coloquial)* heart trouble

los **problemas con el coche** car trouble

los **problemas de comunicación** breakdown in communications ■ communications breakdown

problemas evolutivos ■ problemas de desarrollo developmental problems

procedente de a native of ■ originating in ■ which originated in ■ from ➤ procedente de Tejas a native of Texas ■ a Texas native ■ a Texan ➤ El presunto terrorista llegó a Madrid en un vuelo procedente de Düsseldorf, Alemania. The suspected terrorist arrived in Madrid on a flight from Düsseldorf, Germany.

proceder con algo to proceed with something ■ to go about something

proceder de to grow out of ■ to arise from

proceder de algo ■ venir de algo ■ provenir de algo to grow out of something ■ to arise from something ➤ La crisis política procede de la frustración del régimen dictatorial. The political crisis has grown out of frustration with the dictatorial regime. ■ The political crisis has arisen from frustration with the dictatorial regime.

proceder de matute ■ proceder de incógnito to keep a low profile ■ to proceed incognito ■ to maintain a low profile

proceder en marcha to go on ■ to continue

procedimiento de destitución de impeachment procedure against

procedimiento debido due process

procedimiento sencillo simple procedure ➤ Mediante un procedimiento sencillo... Using a simple procedure... ■ Through a simple procedure...

procedimientos del juzgado court procedures

procesar a alguien por un delito to try someone for a crime ➤ La justicia chilena ordena que se procese a Pinochet por secuestro y homicidio. The Chilean judiciary orders that Pinochet be tried for kidnapping and homicide.

la **procesión va por dentro** **1.** *(él)* he carries his burdens silently ■ he doesn't talk about his problems **2.** *(ella)* she carries her burdens silently ■ she doesn't talk about her problems **3.** *(yo)* I carry my burdens silently ■ I don't talk about my problems

procrear como conejos to breed like rabbits

procura lo mejor, espera lo peor y toma lo que viniere try for the best, expect the worst, and take what comes

procurar que algo no... to try not to let something...

procurar que no se le interponga en su camino to keep it from getting in your way

procurar tener to try to have ➤ El librero siempre procuraba tener libros nuevos para ella. The bookseller always tried to have new books for her.

prodigarle consejos a alguien to deluge someone with advice

prodigarle halagos a alguien to shower someone with compliments

prodigarse en alabanzas hacia algo to shower something with praise ■ to heap praise on something

prodigarse en alabanzas hacia alguien to shower someone with praise ■ to heap praise on someone

ser un **prodigio de** to be a prodigy in ■ to be a genius at ➤ Carlos es un prodigio de las matemáticas. Carlos is a prodigy in math. ➤ Mi hijo pequeño es un prodigio de la informática. My little boy is a genius at computers.

prodigio de la naturaleza natural wonder

prodigio de la tecnología technological marvel

ser **pródigo en algo** **1.** to have a lot of something **2.** *(connotaciones negativas)* to be characterized by a lot of something ■ to witness a lot of something ➤ Don Juan fue pródigo en amores. Don Juan had a lot of affairs. ➤ Jorge Luis Borges fue pródigo en virtudes, excelente profesor, conferenciante, escritor por antonomasia y humilde. Jorge Luis Borge had many virtues. He was an excellent professor, lecturer, a great writer, and very unassuming. ➤ *(noticia)* Este fin de semana ha sido pródigo en accidentes por toda Europa. This weekend has witnessed accidents all over Europe. ➤ Esta semana en Oriente Medio ha sido pródiga en acciones violentas. This week in the Middle East has been characterized by numerous acts of violence.

producir daños ■ causar heridas ■ causar lesiones to cause injury ■ to cause injuries

producir dolor (emocional) ■ ser hiriente ■ causar dolor (emocional) to cause (emotional) pain ■ to be hurtful

producir una guerra ■ causar una guerra to cause a war

producirle una impresión a uno ■ causarle una impresión to make an impression (on one)

producirle náuseas ■ darle náuseas to make one feel sick (to one's stomach) ■ to make one (feel) nauseated ➤ El olor de algunos quesos le produce náuseas. The smell of some cheeses makes him feel sick (to his stomach). ■ The smell of some cheeses makes him (feel) nauseated.

producirse (algo no previsto) to happen ■ to occur ➤ El accidente se produjo cerca de Jaén. The accident occurred near Jaén. ■ The accident happened near Jaén. ➤ El incidente se produjo mientras abandonaba su oficina. The incident occurred as he was leaving his office.

producirse un crimen (for) a crime to be committed ➤ Poco después de que se produjera el crimen Shortly after the crime was committed

producirse una aglomeración en torno a... (for) a crowd to gather around...

producto de la venta proceeds from the sale ➤ El producto de la venta no me llegaba para liquidar mis deudas. Proceeds from the sale were not sufficient to pay off my debts.

producto derivado de ■ sub-producto de by-product of ■ derivative of ■ derived from ➤ La cuajada y el suero son productos derivados de la leche. Curds and whey are by-products of milk. ■ Curds and whey are derivatives of milk.■ Curds and whey are derived from milk.

producto interior bruto ■ (PIB) gross domestic product ■ (GDP)

ser **profano en la materia** to know little about the subject ■ not to know very much about the subject

profecía según la cual prophecy that ■ prophecy according to which

proferir un gruñido to growl ■ to let out a growl ■ to utter a growl ➤ El olor del hombre hizo que el tigre profiriera un gruñido de advertencia. The man's scent made the tiger let out a warning growl.

proferir un rugido ■ lanzar un rugido ■ dar un rugido to let out a roar

ser **profesional muy completo(-a)** to be a total professional

ser **profesor(-a) de primaria** to be an elementary school teacher

ser **profesor(-a) de primero** ■ ser maestro(-a) de primer grado to be a first grade teacher ■ to teach first grade ➤ Soy profesora de primero. I'm a first grade teacher. ■ I teach first grade.

la **profundidad de la crisis** ■ (el) alcance de la crisis depth of the crisis ■ extent of the crisis

profundo cambio profound change ■ great change ➤ Fue una época de profundo(s) cambio(s). It was a time of profound change(s). ■ It was a time of great change(s).

el **programa de reconocimiento de voz** voice recognition software

el **programa de reformas** a series of reforms

programa de televisión ■ programa televisivo television program ■ television show ■ TV show ➤ Pasan mi programa de televisión favorito a las ocho. My favorite TV show comes on at eight.

programa informático computer program

programar el contador ■ programar el temporizador to set the timer

programar el temporizador ■ programar el contador to set the timer

programar la fecha de algo ■ fijar la fecha de algo to set the date of something

programar una reunión ■ fijar una reunión to schedule a meeting

progresar a buen ritmo to progress steadily

prohibido el paso no trespassing ■ keep out

prohibido el paso a toda persona ajena (a la obra) authorized personnel only (on the construction site)

prohibido fumar ■ se prohíbe fumar no smoking

prohibido hacer aguas mayores y menores no urinating or defecating

prohibido verter basuras ■ prohibido arrojar basura no dumping

prohibido verter escombros no dumping

prolongada espera long wait

prolongada estancia lengthy stay ■ prolonged stay

el **promedio de** ■ la media de the average number of ➤ El promedio de alumnos en las clases de español es de veinticinco. The average number of pupils in the Spanish classes is twenty-five.

promedio de edad average age ➤ El promedio de edad de los artífices de la constitución de los Estados Unidos era de aproximadamente cuarenta años. The average age of the framers of the United States' Constitution was about forty years.

promesa rota broken promise

promesa vana empty promise

prometer el oro y el moro to promise the moon

prometer (ser) to have promise ■ to have potential ➤ Esa niña promete (ser). That child has promise. ➤ La niña promete mucho. The child has a lot of promise. ■ The child has great promise.

prometerse (en matrimonio) ■ comprometerse para casarse to get engaged ■ to become engaged

prometérselas felices con ■ tener grandes expectativas por to have high hopes for

promover la tolerancia to promote tolerance ■ to increase tolerance

promover los derechos de la mujer to promote women's rights

promover una causa to advance a cause ■ to promote a cause

promulgar una ley ■ aprobar una ley to pass a law ■ to enact a law

pronóstico a largo plazo extended forecast

pronóstico del tiempo ■ pronóstico meteorológico weather forecast ➤ ¿Cuál es el pronóstico (del tiempo) para este fin de semana? ■ ¿Cuál es el pronóstico meteorológico para este fin de semana? What's the weather forecast for this weekend? ➤ El pronóstico para mañana es de tiempo parcialmente nuboso. ■ Para mañana se espera tiempo parcialmente nuboso. The weather forecast for tomorrow is partly cloudy.

pronóstico reservado: quedarse ingresado de ~ to be admitted for observation ➤ Se quedó ingresado de pronóstico reservado. *(él)* He was admitted for observation. ■ *(ella)* She was admitted for observation.

pronto habrá there will soon be ■ there will be soon

pronunciar un discurso ■ dar un discurso to deliver a speech ■ to give a speech ■ to deliver an address ➤ Lincoln pronunció el discurso de Gettysburg en poco menos de tres minutos. Lincoln delivered the Gettysburg Address in just under three minutes.

pronunciar un nombre to call a name ➤ Cuando el profesor pronunció el nombre de la alumna, ella se sonrojó. When the teacher called the pupil's name, she blushed. ➤ De noche en sueños pronuncio tu nombre. At night, in my dreams, I call your name.

pronunciar una conferencia ■ dar una conferencia to give a lecture

pronunciarse en la misma línea que to take the same position as ➤ Aznar y Blair se pronunciaron en la misma línea que Bush respecto a la guerra de Irak. Aznar and Blair have taken the same position as Bush on the war in Iraq.

propagarse como la pólvora ■ correr como la pólvora to spread like wildfire ➤ La noticia se propagó como la pólvora. The news spread like wildfire.

propasarse con alguien to go too far (sexually) with someone ➤ Él intentó propasarse, y ahora ella no le dirige la palabra. He tried to go to far, and now she won't speak to him.

ser **propenso(-a) a accidentes** to be accident-prone

propiamente dicho strictly speaking ➤ El conflicto en Irlanda del Norte no tiene nada que ver con la religión, propiamente dicha. The conflict in Northern Ireland has nothing to do with religion, strictly speaking.

propias caracteristicas *(de un automóvil)* ■ características de maniobrabilidad ■ caracteristicas de conducción handling characteristics

propiciar la formación de ■ facilitar la formación de to facilitate the formation of

propiciar un debate ■ provocar un debate to touch off a debate ■ to spark a debate ■ to cause a debate

propiciar una crisis to touch off a crisis

propiciar una infección to promote infection

ser **propiedad de** to be owned by ➤ El Hotel Roanoke fue originariamente la propiedad del ferrocarril. The Hotel Roanoke was owned by the railroad originally.

propiedad de la comunidad ■ propiedad comunal community property

propietario del local owner of the premises ■ owner of the place

propietario en derecho legal owner

propinarle un codazo a alguien ■ darle un codazo a alguien to jab someone with one's elbow ■ to give someone a jab with one's elbow

propinarle una derrota a alguien to hand someone a defeat ➤ *(noticia)* La última derrota se la propinó el viernes el Supremo de Florida. The Florida Supreme Court handed him his latest defeat Friday.

propinarle una paliza a alguien ■ darle una paliza a alguien to give someone a beating

propio de su edad normal for one's age

ser **propio de la edad de uno** to be normal for one's age ➤ El médico dijo que su costumbre de chupar el dedo era propio de su edad. The doctor said his thumbsucking was normal for his age.

el **propio hermano de uno** one's own brother ➤ El propio hermano del ladrón lo entregó. The robber's own brother turned him in.

el **propio rey** the king himself ➤ En la Edad Media algunos nobles tuvieron más poder que el propio rey. In the Middle Ages some nobles had more power than the king himself.

ser **propio de alguien 1.** to be characteristic of one **2.** to be like one ➤ La simpatía es propia de los españoles. Friendliness is characteristic of the Spanish. ➤ No es propio de ti. It's not like you.

proponer un brindis to propose a toast

proponer una invitación ■ extender una invitación to issue an invitation ■ to extend an invitation

proporcionar casa a to provide housing for

proporcionar los materiales ■ suministrar los materiales to furnish the materials

proporcionar potencia para ■ suministrar potencia para to provide power to ■ to furnish power to ■ to give power to ➤ Igor Sikorsky desarrolló el primer helicóptero que, con un único rotor, proporcionaba suficiente potencia para elevarse. Igor Sikorsky developed the first helicopter with a single rotor that furnished enough power to lift off.

proporcionar un ambiente to lend an atmosphere

propósito de ■ (la) finalidad de ■ (la) intención de purpose of ■ aim of ■ intention of

propuesta de compra: presentar una ~ ■ hacer una propuesta de compra to present an offer ■ to make an offer

propuesta de resolución proposed resolution ➤ *(titular)* Annan critica la propuesta de resolución de Bush sobre Irak por no recoger sus recomendaciones. Annan criticizes Bush's proposed resolution on Iraq for not taking his recommendations into account.

la **propulsión a gas natural** natural gas propulsion

prórroga de estancia visa extension ■ extension of the period during which foreign visitors can stay in a country

pros y contras pros and cons

proseguir con to go on with ■ to continue with

proseguir la cocción ■ dejar algo cocinar to let something cook ➤ Proseguir la cocción hasta que la carne esté tierna. ■ Dejar cocinar hasta que la carne esté tierna. Let it cook until the meat is tender.

protagonista femenina female lead ■ female star ■ leading lady

protagonista masculino male lead ■ male star ■ leading man

protagonizar un regreso to make a comeback

protagonizar una película to star in a film ■ to star in a movie

ser **protegido con** to be protected by ➤ Fueron protegidos con trajes ignífugos. They were protected by fireproof suits.

protegido contra escritura *(informática)* ■ (edición) bloqueada read-only

protegido de toda perturbación *(frase de la misa católica)* protected from all anxiety

¡**protesta aceptada!** objection sustained!

ser una **protesta en contra** to be a protest against (it) ➤ Votar por la reforma es un voto de protesta contra el gobierno actual. To vote for the reform is a vote of protest against the present government.

¡**protesta rechazada!** objection overruled!

protestar contra algo to protest against something ➤ Tenemos que protestar contra la morralla que inunda nuestro salón cada vez que encendemos la tele. We need to protest against the sewage that pours into our living room every time we turn the TV on.

protestar por algo to protest because of something ➤ Tenemos que protestar por la morralla que inunda nuestro salón cada vez que encendemos la tele. We need to protest because of the sewage that pours into our living room every time we turn the TV on. ➤ Los sindicatos se echaron a la calle para protestar por la nueva ley. The unions took to the streets to protest because of the new law. ■ The unions took to the streets to protest against the new law.

protesto, (su) señoría I object, your honor ➤ Protesto, (su) señoría.-Se acepta (la protesta). I object, your honor.-(Objection) sustained. ➤ Protesto, (su) señoría.-Protesta denegada. ■ Queda denegada. I object, your honor.-(Objection) overruled.

proveedores extranjeros foreign suppliers

proveer una fortaleza to provision a fort

proveniente de coming from ➤ Apenas me encontré solo comencé a oír ruidos extraños provenientes del piso de al lado. No sooner was I alone than I began to hear strange noises coming from the apartment next door.

proveniente de los sentidos proceeding from the senses ■ coming from the senses ■ empirical

provenir de ■ ser de to come from ➤ Proviene de una familia muy unida. He comes from a very close family. ➤ Proviene de una familia numerosa. She comes from a large family.

estar **provisto de** ■ estar equipado con to be equipped with

estar **provisto de sus cabales** to be in possession of one's faculties ■ to be mentally competent ➤ El tribunal rechazó el alegato de insania mental después de que psiquiatras forénsicos testificaran que el acusado estaba provisto de sus cabales. The court rejected the insanity plea after forensic psychiatrists testified that the defendant was mentally competent.

ser **provocado por** to be caused by ➤ Los inmigrantes murieron asfixiados como consecuencia del humo provocado por un cortocircuito en el interior del remolque. The immigrants were asfixiated by the smoke caused by a short circuit inside the tugboat. ■ The immigrants suffocated on smoke from a short circuit inside the tugboat.

provocar agresión to provoke aggression

provocar alergias a alguien to cause allergies in someone ➤ *(noticia)* La droga provoca alergias sobre todo a las mujeres. The drug causes allergies especially in women.

provocar dolor (físico) ■ causar dolor (físico) to cause (physical) pain

provocar las iras de alguien ■ desatar las iras de alguien to provoke someone's anger ■ to unleash someone's anger ■ to arouse someone's anger ■ to provoke someone's ire ■ to unleash someone's ire ■ to arouse someone's ire

provocar un auténtico delirio to bring down the house

provocar un debate ■ propiciar un debate to touch off a debate ■ to spark a debate ■ to cause a debate

provocar un efecto ■ producir un efecto ■ causar un efecto to produce an effect ■ to cause an effect

provocar un incendio ■ causar un incendio to cause a fire

provocar un tumulto to cause an uproar

ser la **próxima cosa mejor** to be the next-best thing

próximamente en... coming soon to... ➤ ¡Próximamente en Madrid! Coming soon to Madrid!

próximo a ■ cerca de near ■ close to ■ not far from ■ *(culto)* in close proximity to ➤ La bomba cayó próximo a su casa. The bomb landed near his house. ■ The bomb landed close to his house. ■ The bomb landed not far from his house.

estar **próximo a quedar terminado** ■ estar a punto de estar listo to be almost finished ■ to be about finished ■ to be almost ready ■ to be about ready

el **próximo día** the next time ➤ El próximo día de clase habrá un examen. The next time we have class there will be a test. ■ The next time we meet there will be a test.

el **próximo fin de semana** next weekend ■ *(a partir del miércoles)* this weekend

el **próximo tren** the next train ➤ ¿Cuándo sale el próximo tren? When does the next train leave?

proyectar un edificio ■ diseñar un edificio to design a building ➤ El arquitecto italiano Francisco Sabatini proyectó la madrileña Puerta de Alcalá y el Palacio Real. The Italian architect Francisco Sabatini designed the Alcalá Gate and the Royal Palace in Madrid.

proyectar una casa ■ diseñar una casa to design a house ➤ Thomas Jefferson proyectó Monticello cuando tenía veinticuatro años. ■ Thomas Jefferson diseñó Monticello cuando tenía veinticuatro años. Thomas Jefferson designed Monticello when he was twenty-four years old.

proyectar una sombra to cast a shadow

proyecto bursátil stock transaction

proyecto de alto(s) vuelo(s) ■ proyecto de alcance ■ proyecto de importancia very important project

proyecto de investigación: realizar un ~ to carry out a research project ■ to conduct a research project

proyecto de ley bill ■ legislation

proyecto de resolución draft resolution

proyecto político domestic program and foreign policy (taken as a whole) ➤ Blair se moviliza para frenar el creciente descrédito de su proyecto político. Blair moves to check the growing unpopularity of his domestic and foreign policies.

el **proyector de diapositivas** slide projector

prudencia es la madre de la ciencia prudence is the mother of science

prueba contundente strong evidence

prueba de embarazo pregnancy test

prueba de fuego baptism by fire ▪ acid test ➤ Superó con éxito la prueba de fuego. He came through his baptism by fire. ▪ He passed the acid test.

prueba de maratón marathon test

prueba de selectividad university placement test

prueba de su gestión ▪ prueba de su liderazgo test of one's leadership

prueba de su liderazgo ▪ prueba de su gestión test of one's leadership

prueba definitiva definitive proof

prueba inadmisible inadmissible evidence

prueba inculpatoria conclusive evidence

prueba insostenible evidence that cannot be corroborated ➤ La prueba es insostenible. The evidence cannot be corroborated.

pruebas abrumadoras overwhelming evidence

pruebas clínicas 1. *(de una persona)* medical tests 2. *(previas al lanzamiento de un medicamento)* clinical tests ▪ clinical trials

pruebas de galera galley proofs

pruebas determinantes: presentar ~ to present conclusive proof

psicología conductista behavioral psychology

psicología evolutiva developmental psychology

psicología inversa: usar ~ ▪ usar psicología revertida to use reverse psychology ➤ Mary Poppins usaba psicología inversa para conseguir que los niños se durmieran. Mary Poppins used reverse psychology to get the children to go to sleep.

publicar la historia to carry the story ➤ El *New York Times* publicó la historia en primera plana. The *New York Times* carried the story on the front page.

publicar un artículo to publish an article ▪ to run an article

publicidad subliminal subliminal advertising

público se congrega ▪ un público se está congregando ▪ un público está congregándose ▪ gente se congrega ▪ gente se está congregando ▪ gente está congregándose crowd is gathering

pude ir I was able to go ▪ I could, and did, go ➤ Finalmente sí pude ir. I was able to go after all. ▪ I could-and did-go after all.

pude ver a toda mi familia I was able to see all my family ▪ I got to see all my family ▪ I got to see my whole family ▪ I was able to see my whole family ▪ *(implica sobrepasar obstáculos)* I managed to see all my family

pude ver cómo... I could see how... ➤ Pude ver cómo llegaron a esa conclusión. I could see how they came to that conclusion. ▪ I could see how they arrived at that conclusion.

pudiera haber habido there might have been ▪ there could (possibly) have been ➤ Pudiera haber habido un antiguo asentamiento aquí aunque los restos arqueológicos no son especialmente concluyentes. There could have been an ancient settlement here, but the archeological evidence is inconclusive. ➤ En Marte, en un momento dado, pudiera haber habido vida. There might at one time have been life on Mars. ▪ There could (possibly) have been life on Mars at one time.

pudiera haber sido it could have been ▪ it might have been ➤ Plutón pudiera haber sido en un momento dado un satélite de Neptuno, pero puede que nunca lo sepamos. Pluto could at one time have been a satellite of Neptune, but we may never know. ▪ Pluto might at one time have been a satellite of Neptune, but we may never know.

pudiera ser que sí it could be possible ▪ it could be so ▪ maybe so

pudieras si no fuera... ▪ pudieras de no ser por... you could, if it were not for... ▪ you could, if it weren't for... ▪ you could, were it not for...

pudo causar ▪ pudo haber causado 1. it could have caused 2. *(él)* he could have caused 3. *(ella)* she could have caused

pudo haber habido there could have been ▪ there might have been ▪ there may have been

pudo haber hecho mucho más ▪ podría haber hecho mucho más 1. *(él)* he could have done much more 2. *(ella)* she could have done much more

pudo haber muerto: uno ~ ▪ uno podría haber muerto 1. *(implica que sigue vivo)* one could have died ▪ one could have been killed ▪ one might have died ▪ one might have been killed 2. *(no sabemos si sigue vivo o no)* one could have died ▪ one may have died 3. *(implica que está muerto)* one could have died ➤ *(sigue vivo)* ¡Dios mío, pudo haber muerto en esa curva! ▪ ¡Dios mío, podría haber muerto en esa curva! Good grief, he could have been killed on that curve! ➤ La víctima del derrumbe pudo haber muerto si no llega a ser por los servicios de emergencia. ▪ La víctima del derrumbe podría haber muerto si no llega a ser por los servicios de emergencia. The victim of the collapse might have died if it had not been for the paramedics. ▪ The victim of the collapse could have died had it not been for the paramedics. ➤ Si el equipo de rescate lo hubiera encontrado apenas unos minutos más tarde, la víctima pudo haber muerto. ▪ Si el equipo de rescate lo hubiera encontrado apenas unos minutos más tarde, la víctima podría haber muerto. The victim could have died if the rescuers had found him even a few minutes later. ➤ *(no sabemos si sigue vivo)* Ese escritor que mencionas pudo haber muerto el año pasado, pero no estoy seguro. Quizás sigue vivo. ▪ Ese escritor que mencionas podría haber muerto el año pasado, pero no estoy seguro. Quizás sigue vivo. The writer you're referring to may have died last year, but I'm not sure (of that). He might still be living. ➤ *(está muerto)* La víctima pudo haber muerto bien por los golpes sufridos o bien por paro cardiorespiratoria. ▪ La víctima podría haber muerto bien por los golpes sufridos o bien por paro cardiorespiratoria. The victim could have died either from the blows suffered or from heart failure.

pudo haber sido ▪ podría haber sido it could have been ▪ it might have been ▪ *(él)* he could have been ▪ he might have been ▪ *(ella)* she could have been ▪ she might have been ▪ *(usted)* you could have been ▪ you might have been

pudo haberse formado: la vida ~ life could have (been) formed

pudo morir ▪ pudo haber muerto ▪ podría haber muerto (one) could have died ▪ (one) might have died ▪ (one) may have died ➤ *(noticia)* La víctima pudo morir el mismo día de la desaparición, hace once meses. The victim may have died the day of his disappearance eleven months ago.

pudo ser ▪ podría haber sido (it) could have been ➤ La intensa lluvia pudo ser la causa del accidente. The heavy rain could have been the cause of the accident.

pudo ser peor it could have been worse

pueblo más próximo nearest town

pueblos de habla española ▪ pueblos hispanohablantes ▪ (las) gentes de habla española ▪ gentes hispanohablantes Spanish-speaking people

pueblos de habla inglesa ▪ pueblos anglohablantes ▪ (las) gentes de habla inglesa ▪ gentes anglohablantes English-speaking people

pueblo minero mining town

pueblo vecino neighboring town

puede it might ➤ ¿Va a llover?-Puede. Is it going to rain?-It might.

puede decirse it can be said

puede contarse ▪ puede ser contado ▪ puede ser dicho ▪ puede decirse it can be told

puede haber there can be

puede haber sido 1. it might have been 2. *(él)* he might have been 3. *(ella)* she might have been 4. *(usted)* you might have been ➤ El fuego puede haber sido provocado por un cortocircuito. The fire might have been caused by a short circuit.

puede no parecer mucho, pero... ▪ podría no parecer mucho, pero... it might not seem like much, but...

puede ocurrir ▪ puede suceder it might happen ▪ it could happen ▪ it is possible ➤ Puede ocurrir que no se presenten. ▪ Puede suceder que no se presenten. It's possible that they won't show up. ▪ They might not show up. ➤ Con la lluvia que está cayendo, puede ocurrir que no se presenten. ▪ Con la lluvia que está cayendo, puede suceder que no se presenten. With the rain, they might not show up. ➤ (Aún) puede ocurrir otro ataque terrorista a gran escala. ▪ (Aún) puede suceder otro ataque terrorista a gran escala. Another large-scale terrorist attack could happen. ➤ El fin de la pobreza puede ocurrir en el siglo veintiuno. The elimination of poverty could happen in the twenty-first century.

puede que... maybe... ▪ perhaps...

puede que así sea that could be ▪ that's possible

puede que haya... there might be... ▪ there may be... ➤ Puede que haya más refrescos en la heladera. There might be (some) more soft drinks in the refrigerator.

puede que llegue aquí ▪ quizás llegue aquí ▪ quizás esté ▪ tal vez llegue aquí ▪ tal vez esté one might arrive ▪ one might get here ▪ one might be here ➤ Quizás llegue mañana. ▪ Quizás esté aquí mañana. ▪ Tal vez esté aquí mañana. ▪ Puede que esté aquí mañana. *(él)* He might arrive tomorrow. ▪ He might get here tomorrow. ▪ He might be here tomorrow. ▪ *(ella)* She might arrive tomorrow. ▪ She might get here tomorrow. ▪ She might be here tomorrow.

puede que lo sepa 1. *(él)* he might know (it) 2. *(ella)* she might know (it) 3. *(usted)* you might know (it)

puede que me guste ▪ tal vez me guste ▪ a lo mejor me gusta I might like it ▪ maybe I'll like it

puede que me hubiera gustado si... I might have liked it if... ➤ Puede que me hubiera gustado la tarta de calabaza si le hubieran puesto un poco de crema batida. I might have liked the pumpkin pie if they had put a little whipped cream on it.

puede que no fuera tan buena idea maybe it wasn't such a good idea ▪ maybe that wasn't such a good idea

puede que no llegue 1. *(carta, paquete, etc.)* it might not make it 2. *(yo)* I might not make it 3. *(él)* he might not make it 4. *(ella)* she might not make it

puede que no lo sepas, pero... you might not know it, but... ▪ you might not know this, but...

puede que no pueda asistir *(yo)* I might not be able to attend

puede que no pueda ir *(yo)* I might not be able to go

puede que no pueda pasar *(yo)* I might not be able to come

puede (que) no sea ▪ tal vez no sea ▪ quizás no sea... it might not be...

puede que no sea tan buena idea maybe it isn't such a good idea ▪ maybe that isn't such a good idea

puede que no sepas que... you might not know that...

puede que no venga 1. it might not come 2. *(yo)* I might not come 3. *(él)* he might not come 4. *(ella)* she might not come

puede que nunca... 1. it may never... 2. *(yo)* I may never... 3. *(él)* he may never... 4. *(ella)* she may never...

puede que nunca lo sepamos we may never know

puede que nunca sepamos qué... ▪ puede que nunca sepamos lo que... we may never know what...

puede que sea... ▪ tal vez sea... ▪ quizás sea... it might be...

puede que sea ese ▪ quizás sea ese that might be the one ▪ it might be (that one) ▪ that could be the one ▪ it could be (that one) ▪ maybe it's that one

puede que sean... they may be... ▪ they might be... ▪ maybe they're... ➤ Puede que sean gemelas idénticas, pero son diferentes como de la noche al día. They may be identical twins, but they're as different as night and day.

puede que sepa... 1. *(él)* he might know... 2. *(ella)* she might know...

puede que sepan 1. *(ellos, ellas)* they might know 2. *(ustedes)* you (all) might know

puede que sí, puede que no ▪ igual sí, igual no ▪ tal vez sí, tal vez no maybe, maybe not

puede que tenga que... one may have to ▪ one might have to ➤ Puedo ir a la reunión, pero puede que tenga que salir si me llaman. I can go to the meeting, but I may have to leave if they page me. ▪ I can go to the meeting, but I might have to leave if they page me.

puede que ya lo tenga ▪ quizá(s) ya lo tenga ▪ tal vez ya lo tenga I might already have it

puede retirarse you may go

¿puede ser? could you? ▪ would you? ➤ Otro potecito de chimichurri, ¿puede ser? Bring us another ramekin of chimichurri, would you? ▪ Could you bring us another ramekin of chimichurri? ▪ Would you bring us another ramekin of chimichurri?

puede ser mortal it can be fatal

¿puede ser o no? 1. ¿se puede hacer o no? is it possible or not? 2. ¿puedes hacerlo o no? can you do it or not?

puede ser que ▪ quizá ▪ tal vez perhaps ▪ maybe

puede servirse con you can serve it with ▪ it can be served with ➤ Puede servirse con arroz o papas. You can serve it with rice or potatoes. ▪ It can be served with rice or potatoes.

puede usted cambiar(me) un billete de cincuenta euros? can you change a fifty-euro bill (for me)? ▪ do you have change for a fifty-euro bill? ➤ ¿Puedes cambiar(me) un billete de cincuenta? Can you change a fifty (for me)?

¿puedes cambiar(me)...? can you change...? ➤ ¿Puedes cambiar(me) un billete de cincuenta? Can you change a fifty (dollar bill/euro bill)?

¡puedes conseguirlo! you can do it! ▪ you're up to it!

¿puedes devolvérmelo? can I have it back? ▪ may I have it back? ▪ can you return it to me?

¡puedes esperar sentado! don't hold your breath! ➤ ¿Quieres salir con ella? ¡Ja! Puedes esperar sentado. You want to go out with her? Well, don't hold your breath.

puedes estar seguro you can be sure ▪ you can depend on it

¿puedes ir a buscarme...? ▪ ¿puedes ir a traerme...? can you get me...? ▪ can you bring me...?

puedes suponer lo que pasó you can guess what happened ▪ you can just about guess what happened ▪ you can pretty well guess what happened

puedo asegurar(te) que ▪ te aseguro que I can assure you

puedo comprender que a alguien le guste... ▪ puedo entender que a alguien le guste... ▪ puedo llegar a comprender que a alguien le guste... ▪ puedo llegar a entender que a alguien le guste... ▪ puedo llegar a imaginarme que a alguien le guste... ▪ me puedo imaginar que a alguien le guste... I can see liking... ▪ I can imagine liking...

puedo con ello ▪ yo puedo con ello ▪ (yo) puedo solo ▪ (yo) me encargo solo ▪ (yo) me apaño solo ▪ (yo) solo me apaño I can handle it ▪ I can deal with it

¿puedo devolverte la llamada? ▪ ¿puedo llamarte luego? can I call you back later? ▪ may I call you back (later)?

puedo comprender cómo... I can understand how... ▪ I can see how... ▪ I can appreciate how...

puedo entender eso I can understand that

¿puedo hacerle (a usted) una sugerencia? may I make a suggestion?

¿puedo hacerte una sugerencia? ▪ ¿puedo darte una sugerencia? may I make a suggestion?

¿puedo llamarte luego? can I call you later?

puedo llegar a entender que a alguien le guste... ▪ puedo llegar a comprender que a alguien le guste... ▪ puedo llegar a imaginarme que a alguien le guste... ▪ puedo entender que a alguien le guste... ▪ puedo comprender que a alguien le guste... ▪ me puedo imaginar que a alguien le guste... I can see liking... ▪ I can imagine liking...

¿puedo pasar? ▪ ¿se puede? may I come in?

¿puedo pasar al baño? may I use your bathroom? ▪ may I use the bathroom?

puedo prometer y prometo... *(Adolfo Suárez, primer presidente democrático de España tras la muerte de Franco)* I can promise, and I promise... ▪ I can and do promise...

puedo tener que... I may have to... ▪ I might have to... ➤ Puedo tener que salir temprano. I may have to leave early. ▪ I might have to leave early.

¿puedo traerte algo? can I get you anything?

¿puedo unirme a ti? may I join you?

¿puedo unirme a ustedes? may I join you (all)?

puedo ver cómo... I can see how...

puedo ver eso I can see that

puedo ver la luz al final del túnel I can see the light at the end of the tunnel

puedo ver lo que... I can see what... ➤ Puedo verlo que habéis montado aquí. I can see what a fuss you've made here.

puedo ver que... I can see that...

¡puedo visualizarlo! I can just picture it! ▪ I can picture it now! ▪ I can see it now!

¿puedo volverte a llamar? ▪ ¿puedo volver a llamarte? may I call you again?
puente aéreo air shuttle service ▪ shuttle ▪ (continual) commuter flights
el **puente colgante** suspension bridge ➤ El puente colgante cedió un poco bajo el peso de la muchedumbre. ▪ El puente colgante cedió ligeramente bajo el peso de la muchedumbre. The suspension bridge gave a little under the weight of the crowd. ▪ The suspension bridge gave slightly under the weight of the crowd.
puente levadizo drawbridge
el **puente sobre el río** bridge across the river ▪ bridge over the river
puentear a alguien to bypass someone ▪ to pass over someone
¡puerta! out! ▪ get out!
puerta a puerta door to door
puerta conduce a door leads to
puerta de atrás ▪ puerta trasera back door
puerta de la calle ▪ puerta principal front door
puerta principal ▪ puerta de la calle front door
puerta que abre hacia door opening onto ➤ La puerta que abre hacia el balcón. The opening onto the balcony. ▪ The door that opens onto the balcony.
puerta que comunica con door between ▪ door from ▪ door opening into ▪ door that opens into ➤ La puerta que comunica la cocina con el comedor The door between the kitchen and the dining room ▪ The door from the kitchen to the dining room
puerta trasera ▪ puerta de atrás back door
puerto de mar seaport
puerto de montaña ▪ puerto montañoso mountain pass
puerto fluvial river port
Puerto Príncipe, Haití Port-au-Prince, Haiti
pues aquí no venga(n) con... well, don't come in here with...
pues bien well, then
pues bueno well, then
¡pues claro! well, of course!
pues de lo contrario because if it weren't
pues el caso es que... for the fact is that...
pues eso ▪ lo dicho well, that's what we'll do ▪ and that's it ➤ Bueno, pues eso. ▪ Bueno, lo dicho. Okay, well, that's what we'll do.
pues menuda te perdiste, tronco *(Esp., jerga juvenil)* well, you missed a good one, dude
pues muchas gracias por la invitación well, thanks for the invitation
pues, nada well, that's okay
pues, no well, no ▪ why, no
pues no me digas que... well, don't tell me that...
pues no pretenderá que *yo* he's not expecting *me* to... ➤ ¡Pero vaya! ¿Pues no pretenderá que le pague lo que él mismo ha roto? What?! He's not expecting me to pay for something he himself broke!
pues, realmente ▪ bueno, en realidad well, actually
pues que since
¿pues qué (entonces)? what, then?
pues será que... ▪ pues quizás... then one must have... ➤ *(Valle-Inclán)* Pues será que le mataron por (una) venganza. Then they must have killed him in reprisal.
¡pues sí! yeah!
pues sí que... it's really... ➤ Pues sí que llueve. It's really coming down out there.
puesta a punto *(de un motor)* tune-up
puesta al día de los archivos updating of the files ▪ update of the files
puesta de largo ▪ quinceañera ▪ presentación en sociedad young woman's debut ▪ young woman's presentation to society ▪ young woman's coming out in society
puesta en común: quedar para la ~ to meet to coordinate ones' efforts ➤ Quedamos mañana en mi casa para la puesta en común. Let's meet at my house tomorrow to coordinate our efforts.
puesta en escena (de una obra teatral) production of a play ▪ the staging of a play
puesta en libertad release from detention ▪ release
estar **puesta en marcha** 1. *(motor)* to be idling 2. *(aparato eléctrico en general)* to be (turned) on
puesta en venta introduction on the market ▪ appearance in the stores
puesta más larga en la historia del cine longest-running movie in the history of cinema
ser **puesto a prueba** to be put to the test
puesto conlleva ▪ puesto involucra job involves
puesto de trabajo job ▪ position ▪ post
(puesto de) trabajo estresante stressful job
ser **puesto en arresto domiciliario** ▪ quedar en (situación de) arresto domiciliario to be placed under house arrest ▪ to be put under house arrest ➤ *(noticia)* El ex-presidente de Yugoslavia, Slobodan Milosevic, fue puesto a la 1.30 de hoy en arresto domiciliario. Ex-president Slobodan Milosevic of Yugoslavia was placed under house arrest at 1:30 p.m. today.
estar **puesto en el mercado** to be on the market ➤ Su casa está puesta en el mercado. Their house is on the market.
estar **puesto en escena** to be staged ▪ to be presented as a stage play ▪ to be presented on (the) stage ➤ *El violinista sobre el tejado* está ahora (puesta) en escena en Nueva York. *Fiddler on the Roof* is currently being staged in New York. ▪ *Fiddler on the Roof* is currently being presented as a stage play in New York. ▪ *Fiddler on the Roof* is currently being presented on (the) stage in New York.
ser **puesto(-a) en libertad** to be set free
estar **puesto(-a) en un tema** ▪ estar al tanto en un tema to be up on a subject ▪ to be informed on a subject
puesto número *x* *x*th place ➤ Entre las naciones con la renta per cápita más alta, España ocupa el puesto número trece. Among nations with the highest per capita income, Spain is in thirteenth place.
puesto que ▪ ya que since ▪ as
puja benéfica ▪ (el) remate a beneficio ▪ subasta a beneficio benefit auction ➤ *(noticia)* Los calzoncillos de la estrella británica del pop Robbie Williams fueron adjudicados ayer en una puja benéfica celebrada en Londres por 6.300 dólares (1,2 millones de pesetas). British pop star Robbie Williams' briefs were sold yesterday at a benefit auction in London for $6,300 (1.2 millon pesetas).
la **pujante ciudad** booming city ▪ thriving city
pujar a la alta por algo ▪ pujar fuerte por algo ▪ pasar un presupuesto alto por algo to bid high on something
pujar a la baja por algo ▪ pujar flojo por algo ▪ pasar un presupuesto bajo por algo to bid low on something
pujar en una subasta por algo to bid at an auction on something ▪ to bid on something at an auction ▪ to bid at an auction for something ➤ Pujé hasta dos mil dólares por un hermoso carillón, pero alguien pujó más fuerte. I bid two thousand dollars on a beautiful grandfather clock, but somebody outbid me.
pujar flojo por algo ▪ pujar a la baja por algo to bid low on something
pujar fuerte por algo ▪ pujar a la alta por algo to bid high on something
pulsador de alarma ▪ (el) botón de alarma alarm button
pulsar el botón derecho en ▪ presionar el botón derecho en ▪ *(coloquial)* cliquear el botón derecho en to right-click on
pulsar el botón izquierdo en ▪ presionar el botón izquierdo en ▪ *(coloquial)* cliquear el botón izquierdo en to left-click on
pulsar una tecla ▪ presionar una tecla ▪ apretar una tecla ▪ empujar una tecla ▪ marcar to press a key ➤ Para conservar el mensaje, pulse dos. To save the message, press two.
la **pulsión de muerte** *(psicoanálisis)* death instinct
pulso bajo: tener el ~ to have a weak pulse
pulso de la América profunda: tomar el ~ to take the pulse of middle America ▪ to take the pulse of the American heartland ➤ La película toma el pulso de la América profunda. The films takes the pulse of middle America. ▪ The film takes the pulse of the American heartland.
pulso firme steady hand ▪ firm hand
pulso militar show of force ▪ sabre rattling
¡pun, pun, pun! ▪ ¡pim, pam, pum! bang, bang, bang!

punta afilada sharp point ➤ Me gusta dibujar con este portaminas porque tiene la punta más afilada que el otro. I like to draw with this (mechanical) pencil because it has a sharper point than the other one.

punta de la lengua: tenerlo en la ~ to be (right) on the tip of one's tongue ▪ to have it (right) on the tip of one's tongue

ser la **punta del iceberg** to be (just) the tip of the iceberg ➤ Es la punta del iceberg. That's just the tip of the iceberg. ▪ That's the tip of the iceberg.

puntas del pelo ends of the hair

punto álgido ▪ momento álgido ▪ punto culminante ▪ momento culminante high point ▪ culminating moment

punto bueno good point ➤ Uno de los puntos buenos de Carlos como traductor es su increíble conocimiento de las literaturas escritas en español e inglés. One of Carlos' good points as a translator is his incredible knowledge of both Spanish- and English-language literature.

punto caliente 1. hot spot 2. *(en un debate)* disputed point ▪ point in dispute

punto cardinal cardinal point ▪ important point

punto céntrico central point ➤ El Zócalo es el punto céntrico de la Ciudad de México. The Zócalo is the central point of Mexico City. ➤ La simplicidad del motivo es el punto céntrico de la filosofía de Schopenhauer, que el repertorio de conducta humana puede reducirse a unos pocos impulsos básicos. The simplicity of motive is the central point of Schopenhauer's philosophy, that the repertory of human behavior can be reduced to a few basic drives.

punto ciego: tener un ~ to have a blind spot ➤ Tengo un punto ciego en el ojo izquierdo, a la derecha de mi perspectiva, o a la izquierda desde la del doctor. I have a blind spot in my left eye, at about three o'clock from my perspective, or about nine o'clock from the doctor's.

el **punto conflictivo es...** the point at issue is...

punto culminante ▪ momento culminante ▪ punto álgido ▪ momento álgido culminating moment ▪ high point

punto de apoyo fulcrum

punto de condensación ▪ el nivel del rocío dew point

punto de ebullición boiling point

punto de encuentro ▪ lugar de encuentro ▪ sitio de encuentro meeting point ▪ meeting place ▪ place to meet

punto de equilibrio point of equilibrium ▪ center of equilibrium

punto de fuga vanishing point ➤ Los barcos al alcanzar el horizonte desaparecen como si estuviesen descendiendo el lado opuesto de una colina, mucho antes de alcanzar el punto de fuga de los objetos distantes. Ships as they reach the horizon disappear as if they were descending the far side of a hill, long before they reach the vanishing point of distant objects.

punto de mira: tener a alguien en el ~ to have someone in one's sights ▪ to target someone ➤ El líder del partido socialista exigió que el gobierno del País Vasco garantice la seguridad de todos los socialistas que ocupan cargos públicos ya que ETA ha dejado patente que los tiene en el punto de mira. The Socialist party leader demanded that the government of País Vasco guarantee the security of all socialists in government positions since ETA has made clear that it has them in its sights. ▪ The Socialist party leader demanded that the government of País Vasco guarantee the security of all socialists in government positions since ETA has made clear that it has targeted them.

punto de partida point of departure ➤ Sirve del punto de partida para la discusión. It serves as a point of departure for the discussion.

punto (de) penal *(fútbol)* ▪ punto de penalty penalty point

punto de penalty *(fútbol)* ▪ punto (de) penal penalty point

punto de referencia point of reference

punto de venta point of sale

punto de vista point of view ▪ frame of reference ➤ Desde mi punto de vista... From my point of view...

punto de vista ciego blind spot ➤ Tengo un punto de vista ciego cuando se refiere al separatismo político. ¿Por qué es más importante eso que tener una buena vida? I have a blind spot when it comes to political separatism. Why is it more important than having a good life?

ser el **punto débil** ▪ ser el punto flaco de uno ▪ ser el talón de Aquiles to be one's weak point ▪ to be one's Achilles' heel

punto del entorno feature in the landscape ▪ point of reference ➤ Al alcanzar la cresta de la montaña, escudriñé el horizonte buscando puntos del entorno, pero no reconocí ninguno. ▪ Al alcanzar la cresta de la montaña, escudriñé el horizonte buscando puntos del entorno, pero no reconocí ningún punto del entorno. As I reached the ridge I scanned the horizon for recognizable features of the landscape but saw none. ▪ As I reached the ridge I scanned the horizon for points of reference but recognized none.

punto en boca mum's the word

punto final *(dictado)* period, end of dictation

ser el **punto flaco de uno** ▪ ser el punto débil to be one's weak point

ser el **punto fuerte de uno** ▪ ser el fuerte to be one's strong point ▪ to be one's strong suit ▪ to be one's forte

punto menos que ▪ poco menos que almost ▪ practically ➤ Era punto menos que ilegible. It was almost illegible. ▪ It was practically illegible.

punto muerto 1. *(literal)* dead center 2. *(en una caja de cambios)* neutral

punto negro 1. marca negra ▪ mancha negra black spot 2. lado malo ▪ aspecto malo bad part

punto neurálgico defining moment ➤ El punto neurálgico de la Revolución Francesa fue la toma de la Bastilla. The defining moment of the French Revolution was the storming of the Bastille.

punto neurálgico de la economía ▪ sistema central de la economía backbone of the economy

punto neurálgico de tránsito transportation hub

punto neurálgico de una ciudad heart of a city

punto neurálgico de una negociación topic of a negotiation

punto neurálgico de una organización core of an organization

punto neurálgico del movimiento heart of the movement ▪ core of the movement ➤ El punto neurálgico del movimiento hippy fue la sensación de alienación por parte de la gente joven. The heart of the hippie movement was a sense of alienation on the part of young people.

punto por punto: ir ~ to go (over something) point by point ➤ Vamos punto por punto. Let's go over this point by point.

punto y aparte 1. *(dictado, redacción)* period, paragraph 2. end of discussion!

punto y coma *(dictado, redacción)* semicolon

punto y seguido *(dictado, redacción)* period, next sentence

puntos a tratar ▪ asuntos a discutir things to discuss

puntos de nieve *(clara de huevo batida)* stiff peaks

puntos en común points in common ▪ things in common

puntos en contra: tener ~ to have strikes against it

puntos suspensivos dot, dot, dot

estar **puntuable para algo** to count toward something ▪ to be countable toward something ➤ ¿Están estos créditos puntuables para el título? Do these credits count toward the degree? ▪ Are these credits countable toward the degree?

puntualidad inglesa: llegar con ~ to arrive exactly on time

puñado de algo handful of something ➤ Un puñado de camarones, por favor. A handful of shrimp, please. ➤ La teoría de cuerdas fue desarollada por un puñado de hombres. String theory was developed by a handful of men.

puñalada trapera: darle a alguien ~ ▪ darle a alguien una puñalada por la espalda ▪ darle a alguien una puñalada por atrás to be a stab in the back ▪ to stab someone in the back ➤ Decirle al jefe que tu compañero de trabajo llegó atrasado fue una puñalada en la espalda. Telling the boss that your co-worker was late was a stab in the back.

puñalada por la espalda stab in the back

¡puñetas! ▪ ¡pucha! darn! ▪ aw, heck! ▪ shoot!

puñetero caballo lousy horse ▪ blasted horse

pupilo(-a) del rey one favored by the king

pura sensatez del niño pure sensibility of the child

ser la **pura verdad** to be the absolute truth ▪ to be the honest-to-God truth

pura voluntad sheer determination

pura y lisa falsedad out-and-out lie

pureza de sangre: tener ~ 1. *(Esp.)* Edad Media to be of pure Christian stock (without Jewish or Arabic blood) **2.** *(referido a animales)* to be thoroughbred ▪ to be purebred

purgar el radiador to bleed a radiator

purgar los frenos to bleed the brakes

puritanos de conducta *(Valle-Inclán)* self-rightous types

ser **puro chiste** to be a joke ➤ Ese curso en la teoría literaria es puro chiste. That literary theory course is a joke.

ser **puro hueso** to be (nothing but) skin and bone

puro nervio *(persona enérgica)* live wire

¡**puro pedo!** *(subido de tono)* bullshit!

puro teatro (pure) theatrics ▪ an act ➤ *(noticia)* El gobierno de Bush calificó de "puro teatro" el rechazo por parte del parlamento de Irak de la última resolución. The Bush Administration labeled as "(pure) theatrics" the Iraqui parliament's rejection of the latest resolution.

que a mí me toca *(el lunar de Cielito Lindo)* because it belongs to me

¡qué agarrado al mango! *(Arg.)* ▪ ¡qué tacaño! what a tightwad!

¡qué agradecimiento!*(sarcástico)* that's gratitude for you! ▪ what an ingrate!

¿qué almorzaste? *(L.am.)* what did you have for lunch?

qué amable de tu parte that's very kind of you

¡qué ambientazo! what a great atmosphere! ▪ what a perfect atmosphere! ➤ ¡Jolín, qué ambientazo! Wow, what a great atmosphere!

¡qué andar ni qué andar! what's all this about walking? ➤ ¡Qué andar ni qué andar si yo tengo coche! What's all this (talk) about walking? I have a car.

¡qué animal eres! ▪ ¡eres una bestia ▪ ¡qué bruto eres! you're a tiger! ▪ what a tiger (you are)!

¡que aproveche! ▪ ¡buen provecho! bon appetite ▪ enjoy your dinner ▪ enjoy your meal

¡qué asco! ▪ ¡huácala! ▪ ¡fuchi! ugh! ▪ yuck! ▪ that's gross! ▪ *(refiriéndose al hedor)* peee-yuuu!

¿qué aspecto tenía él? ▪ ¿cómo se veía él? ▪ ¿cómo lucía él? what did he look like?

¿qué aspecto tenía ella? ▪ ¿cómo se veía ella? ▪ ¿cómo lucía ella? what did she look like?

¿qué aspecto tiene él? ▪ ¿cómo se ve él? ▪ ¿cómo luce él? what does he look like?

¿qué aspecto tiene ella? ▪ ¿cómo se ve ella? ▪ ¿cómo luce ella? what does she look like?

que aún vive that still exists

qué bajo how low ➤ ¿Has visto qué bajos son nuestros precios? Have you seen how low our prices are?

¡qué bajón! ▪ ¡vaya chasco! ▪ ¡qué rollo! **1.** what a bummer! **2.** what a comedown! **3.** damn it!

¡qué barbaridad! how awful!

¡qué bárbaro! how incredible!

¡Qué bello es vivir! *(título de película) It's a Wonderful Life*

¿qué bicho te ha picado? what's bugging you?

¡qué bien! *(Esp.)* ▪ ¡qué bueno! (very) good! ▪ great!

¡qué bien huele aquí! it smells good (in) here

qué bien que... *(Esp.)* ▪ qué bueno que... it's a good thing (that)... ➤ Qué bien que llegaran en ese momento. It's a good thing they got there when they did. ▪ It's a good thing they got there at that moment.

qué bien que me llamaste ▪ me alegra que hayas llamado I'm glad you called

qué bien se siente that feels so good ▪ it feels so good

¡qué bocas el menda! *(1990s slang)* ▪ ¡qué boca de jarro! what a big mouth!

¡qué bochorno! ▪ ¡qué corte! ▪ ¡qué quemo! how embarrassing! ▪ what an embarrassment!

¡qué bonito! that's pretty! ▪ isn't that lovely! ▪ how pretty!

¡qué botón eres! *(Arg.)* ▪ ¡qué chivato eres! ▪ ¡qué soplón! tattletale! ▪ you're a tattletale!

¡qué bruto eres! ▪ ¡qué animal eres! ▪ ¡eres una bestia! you're a tiger! ▪ what a tiger (you are)!

¡qué buen pájaro! ▪ ¡menudo pájaro está hecho! what a strange bird! ▪ what a weirdo!

¡qúe buena pinta! ▪ ¡qué pinta tiene! ▪ tiene una pinta... **1.** *(comida)* that looks delicious! **2.** *(persona)* what a knockout!

¡qué buenas noticias lo de la beca! that's good news about your scholarship

¡qué bueno! *(L.am.)* ▪ ¡qué bien! good! ▪ great!

¡qué bueno haberte visto! *(L.am.)* it was good to see you ▪ it's been good to see you

¡qué bueno que... ▪ menos mal que... it's a good thing that... ➤ Qué bueno que llegaran en ese momento. It's a good thing they got there when they did.

qué bueno es estar en casa, ¿verdad? ▪ ¿qué rico es estar en casa, ¿verdad? it's great to be home, isn't it?

¡qué bueno verte! *(L.am.)* (it's) good to see you!

¡qué burrada! ▪ ¡qué estupidez! what a stupid thing to do! ▪ what a dumb thing to do!

que cada palo aguante su vela we have to take what comes our way ▪ we must bear our own burdens

que cada uno se pague lo suyo let's go Dutch

¡qué calor hace! ▪ ¡qué día de calor! what a hot day! ▪ what a scorcher!

¿qué carajo quieres? *(muy subido de tono)* what the fuck do you want? ▪ *(alternativa benigna)* what the heck do you want? ▪ what in the world do you want?

¡qué caramba! *(L.am.)* ▪ ¡qué caray! ▪ ¡caramba! ▪ ¡caray! **1.** *(positivo)* wow! ▪ amazing! **2.** *(negativo)* for crying out loud!

¿qué carrera estudias? ▪ ¿qué es lo que estudias? what are you majoring in? ▪ what's your major?

¡qué casualidad! what a coincidence!

¿qué causa...? ▪ ¿cuál es la causa de...? what causes...? ▪ what accounts for...? ▪ what explains...? ➤ ¿Qué causa el color azulado? ▪ ¿Cuál es la causa del color azulado? What accounts for the bluish color? ▪ What explains the bluish color? ▪ What causes the bluish color?

¡qué cenar ni qué cenar si... why have supper now? ▪ why eat supper now?... ➤ ¡Qué cenar ni qué cenar si son las cinco! Why have supper now? It's only five o'clock! ▪ Why eat supper now? It's only five o'clock!

¡qué chachi! ▪ ¡qué bien! ▪ ¡excelente! that's great!

¡qué chasco se va a llevar! **1.** *(él)* what a bummer that's going to be for him ▪ that's going to be a (real) bummer for him **2.** *(ella)* what a bummer that's going to be for her ▪ that's going to be a (real) bummer for her

¡qué chivato eres! what a tattletale (you are)! ▪ tattletale!

¡qué chorra! ▪ ¡qué coña! ▪ ¡qué suerte! what luck!

¡qué chorradas (me) dices! ▪ ¡qué pavadas me dices! what a bunch a nonsense (you're telling me)! ▪ you're feeding me a bunch of nonsense ▪ what a line! ▪ you're feeding me a line

¡qué coche ni qué coche si estamos aquí al lado! why take the car if we're (so) close by ▪ why take the car if we're practically next door?

¡qué cojones! *(subido de tono)* what the hell!

¿qué cojones es eso? *(subido de tono)* ▪ ¿qué coño es eso? what (in) the hell is that?

¿qué cojones haces? *(subido de tono)* what (in) the hell are you doing?

que, como yo who, like me

qué comprar what to buy ➤ Trato de decidir qué computora comprar. I'm trying to decide what computer to buy.

que comprende ▪ que incluye which includes ▪ including ➤ Hay mucha vida cultural, que comprende teatro y ballet. There is a lot of cultural life, including theatre and ballet.

¡qué compromiso! ▪ ¡qué vergüenza! how embarrassing!

que con su pan se lo coma ▪ que le aproveche **1.** *(de él)* it's his funeral **2.** *(de ella)* it's her funeral

que con tu pan te lo comas it's your funeral

¡qué confianzas son esas! 1. what a lot of nerve! 2. *(tú)* you've got a lot of nerve! 3. *(él)* he's got a lot of nerve! 4. *(ella)* she's got a lot of nerve! 5. *(usted)* you've got a lot of nerve!

que conste en acta 1. *(tribunal)* let it be stated in the record ▪ let it be noted in the record 2. *(reunión)* let it be entered in the minutes ▪ let it be stated in the minutes ▪ include it in the minutes 3. *(coloquial)* mark my word

que conste que to set the record straight ▪ make note of the fact that ➤ Que conste que yo no se lo he dicho. To set the record straight, I did not say that.

que conste que ya te dije I told you so

¡qué coña! *(jerga juvenil de los años 90)* ▪ ¡qué chorra! ▪ ¡qué suerte! what luck! ▪ we're in luck! ▪ you're in luck!

¡qué coñazo de tío! *(Esp.)* ▪ ¡qué tipo aburridísimo! what a crashing bore! ▪ what a dreary character!

¡qué coño! *(subido de tono)* what the fuck!

¿qué coño es eso? ▪ ¿qué cojones es eso? what (in) the hell is that?

¡qué corte! ▪ ¡qué quemo! ▪ ¡qué bochorno! how embarrassing! ▪ what an embarrassment!

¿qué cosa será? what could it be? ▪ what is it? ➤ P: ¿Qué cosa será, y es de entender, que cuanto más le quitan, más grande será?-R: Un agujero. Q: What could it be, that the more you take away, the bigger it gets?-A: A hole.

¡qué cosa tan rara! that's weird! ▪ (how) weird! ▪ how odd!

¿qué cosecha es el vino? ▪ ¿qué reserva es el vino? what year is the wine? ▪ what year was the wine made? ▪ how many years has the wine been aged?

¡¿qué crees que estás haciendo?! what do you think you're doing!?

¡qué cuento! what a crock! ▪ that's a crock! ▪ that's a lie!

¿qué cuernos es eso? ▪ ¿qué rayos es eso? what (in) the hell is that?

¿qué cuernos quieres? ▪ ¿qué diablos quieres? what the hell do you want? ▪ *(alternativa benigna)* what the heck do you want?

¡que cumplas muchos más! and (may you have) many happy returns!

¡qué curioso! that's funny ▪ that's strange ➤ ¡Qué curioso! Podría jurar que dejé las llaves aquí. That's funny; I could swear I left my keys here.

¡qué de coches! *(coloquial, pero incorrecto)* ▪ ¡cuántos coches! what a lot of cars!

¡qué de comida! *(coloquial, pero incorrecto)* ▪ ¡cuánta comida! what a lot of food!

¡qué de cosas! *(coloquial, pero incorrecto)* ▪ ¡qué montón de cosas! ▪ ¡qué cantidad de cosas! what a bunch of stuff! ▪ what a lot of stuff!

¡qué de gente! *(coloquial, pero incorrecto)* ▪ ¡qué gentío! ▪ ¡que montón de gente! ▪ ¡qué cantidad de gente! what a mob scene!

¡que dé la cara! show yourself! ▪ own up! ▪ (whoever did it) come forward!

¡qué de prisa pasa el tiempo! how quickly time passes! ▪ how quickly time goes (by)! ▪ time goes so quickly!

¿qué debo hacer? what must I do? ▪ what do I have to do? ▪ what do I do?

¡qué descaro! what gall! ▪ what nerve! ▪ what a lot of nerve!

¿qué desea usted? 1. *(restaurante)* ¿qué se le ofrece? what would you like? ▪ what'll you have? 2. *(tienda, oficina)* how may I help you?

¡qué desfachatez! ▪ ¡qué confianzas son esas! what nerve! ▪ he's got a lot of nerve!

¡qué desgracia! 1. that's too bad ▪ that's unfortunate ▪ how unfortunate 2. ¡qué mala pata! what rotten luck!

¡qué desvarío! that's madness!

¡qué detallazo! awesome! ▪ how nice! ▪ what a nice gesture

¡qué detallazo de...! what a great...!

¡qué detalle! that's nice of you! ▪ how nice!

¡qué día de calor! ▪ ¡qué calor hace! what a hot day! ▪ what a scorcher!

¿qué día es hoy, (me refiero al número de día)? ▪ ¿a cuánto estamos? ▪ ¿a qué día estamos hoy? what's today's date? ▪ what day is it today? ▪ what's the date (of) today?

¡qué día tengo! I'm having quite a day (of it)! ▪ what a day!

¡qué día tienes! you're having quite a day (of it)! ▪ what a day!

¡qué diablos! what the hell!

que dice ser 1. *(cosa)* which is said to be ▪ that is said to be 2. *(persona)* who is said to be

que dicen ser 1. *(cosa)* which are said to be ▪ that are said to be 2. *(persona)* who are said to be

¿qué dices? what?

que dijo alguien as someone once said ▪ as somebody once said

que dijo ser 1. *(cosa)* which was said to be ▪ that was said to be 2. *(persona)* who was said to be

que Dios la tenga en Su gloria ▪ que Dios la acoja en Su seno may she rest in peace

que Dios le acoja en Su seno 1. *(él)* may he rest in peace 2. *(ella)* may she rest in peace

que Dios le ampare ▪ que Dios le socorra 1. *(él)* may God protect him 2. *(ella)* may God protect her

que Dios le bendiga (a usted) 1. may God bless you 2. gracias! bless you!

que Dios lo tenga en Su gloria ▪ que Dios lo acoja en Su seno may he rest in peace

¡que Dios nos ayude! God help us!

¡que Dios nos coja confesados! *(Esp.)* ▪ ¡que Dios nos encuentre confesados! ▪ ¡Dios nos pille confesados! God help us!

que Dios te bendiga 1. may God bless you 2. *(gracias!)* bless you!

¡que Dios te lo pague! thank you very much ▪ may God bless you for your help ▪ may God repay you

el **qué dirán** 1. public reaction 2. public opinion

el **qué dirán de turno** public opinion at the moment

que dirige 1. leading 2. *(cosa)* that is leading ▪ which is leading 3. *(persona)* who is leading

que dirigía 1. leading 2. *(cosa)* that was leading ▪ which was leading 3. *(persona)* who was leading

¡qué dolor! what pain!

¡qué emocionante! how exciting! ▪ that's exciting! ➤ ¡Vaya! ¡Qué emocionante! Wow! How exciting!

que en gloria esté ▪ que en paz descanse 1. *(él)* may he rest in peace 2. *(ella)* may she rest in peace

que en paz descanse ▪ que en gloria esté 1. *(él)* may he rest in peace 2. *(ella)* may she rest in peace

que en seguida cae bien instantly likeable ▪ who you like right away

que entre 1. *(él)* have him come in ▪ tell him to come in 2. *(ella)* have her come in ▪ tell her to come in

¡qué entretenido ni qué entretenido si casi me duermo! what do you mean fun, I almost fell asleep!

que envuelve el asunto surrounding the matter

¡qué equivocado estaba (yo)! how wrong I was!

¿qué es de tu vida? ▪ ¿qué hay de nuevo? what's new with you?

¿qué es esa locura de...? ▪ ¿qué se te ha dado por...? ▪ ¿qué se te ha dado con...? whatever possessed you to...?

¿qué es esto? what is this? ▪ what's this?

que es gerundio: andando ~ get going! ▪ get moving! ▪ hurry it up!

¿qué es lo que estudias? ▪ ¿qué carrera estudias? what are you majoring in? ▪ what's your major?

¿qué es lo que haces? what in the world are you doing? ▪ what *are* you doing?

¿qué es lo que quiere? 1. *(él)* what does he want? 2. *(ella)* what does she want?

¿qué es lo que se le ofrece? ▪ ¿qué se le ofrece? what can I do for you? ▪ how can I help you?

¿qué es lo que te preocupa? what's on your mind?

¿qué es lo que tienes en la mano? what do you have in your hand?

que es por lo que which is why ➤ En la distancia, las montañas tienen un tono azulado que es por lo que se llaman La Cresta Azul. From a distance, the mountains have a bluish cast, which is why they're called the Blue Ridge.

¿qué es todo esto? what is all this? ▪ what's all this?

¿qué esperabas? what were you expecting?

¿qué esperas obtener (de esto)? ▪ ¿qué esperas sacar (de esto)? what do you hope to get out of it?

¿qué esperas sacar (de esto)? ▪ ¿qué esperas obtener (de esto)? what do you hope to get out of it?

que espere sentado(-a) it will be a long wait ▪ it will take a long time ▪ don't hold your breath

¡qué estafa! what a racket! ▪ what a scam!

¿qué están dando en la tele? ▪ ¿qué están poniendo en la tele? ▪ ¿qué dan en la tele? ▪ ¿qué ponen en la tele? what's on TV?

¿qué estás cursando? **1.** ¿qué carrera (de universidad) estás haciendo? what's your major? **2.** ¿en qué curso estás? ▪ what year are you? **3.** ¿qué asignaturas estás dando? ▪ ¿qué asignaturas tienes? what courses are you taking?

que esté(n) pendiente de uno to be the center of attention ➤ A los bebés les gusta que todos estén pendientes de ellos. Babies like to be the center of attention. ▪ Babies like (for) people to make a fuss over them.

¡qué estupidez! ▪ ¡qué burrada! what a stupid thing to do! ▪ what a dumb thing to do!

¡qué experiencia! what an experience!

¡qué facha! **1.** what a fascist! **2.** ¡vaya fachas! what a sight!

¡qué faena! **1.** ¡qué lata! ▪ ¡qué marrón! what a pain! **2.** what a lot of work!

¿qué fecha es hoy? ▪ ¿a cuánto estamos? what's today's date? ▪ what's the date today? ▪ what is the date of today? ➤ Hoy es el seis. Today is the sixth.

¡qué follón! **1.** what a mess! **2.** what (a lot of) excitement!

¡qué forma de...! what a way to...!

¿qué fue de? whatever happened to? ▪ whatever became of? ➤ *(título de película) ¿Qué fue de Baby Jane? Whatever Happened to Baby Jane?*

¡qué fuerte! **1.** that's harsh **2.** what (brute) strength!

¿qué función tiene? ▪ ¿qué hace? ▪ ¿para qué sirve? what is its function? ▪ what's its function? ▪ what does it do?

¡qué gallo le ha salido! what a sour note! ▪ what a flat note!

¡qué gracia! ▪ ¡qué gracioso! **1.** how funny! **2.** *(con sarcasmo)* very funny!

¡qué gran noticia! ▪ ¡qué notición! what great news!

¿qué grosor tiene? how thick is it?

¿qué ha de ser? what could it be?

¿qué ha ido mal? what went wrong?

que ha parido madre known to man(kind) ➤ Es la persona más antipática que ha parido madre. He's the meanest person known to man(kind).

¿qué ha sido de...? what has become of...?

¿qué ha sido eso? what was that?

¿qué hace? ▪ ¿qué función tiene? ▪ ¿para qué sirve? what does it do? ▪ what is its function? ▪ what's its function?

¿qué hacemos? what shall we do?

¿qué hacemos con eso? what shall we do with that?

¿qué hago? what shall I do?

¿qué has almorzado? *(Esp., se refiere al tentempié durante la mañana)* what did you have to eat?

¿qué has cenado? what did you have for supper?

¿qué has comido? **1.** *(en todos los países)* what did you have to eat? **2.** *(Esp.)* what did you have for dinner?

¿qué has desayunado? what did you have for breakfast?

¿qué has dicho? what did you say?

¿qué hay? **1.** ¿qué pasa? what's up? **2.** ¿qué tienes? ▪ ¿qué te pasa? what's the matter? **3.** *(al pedir en un restaurante)* ¿qué tienes? ▪ ¿de qué puede ser? what do you have? ▪ what are the choices?

¿qué hay de contradictorio en eso? what's contradictory about that?

¿qué hay de nuevo? ▪ ¿qué novedades me traes? what's new?

¿qué hay de nuevo, viejo? *(Bugs Bunny)* what's up, doc?

¿qué hay de postre? what's for dessert?

¿qué hay de ti? what's going on (with you)?

¿qué hay de tu sonrisa? what are you smiling about?

¿qué hay detrás de...? what's behind...? ➤ ¿Qué hay detrás del sofa? What's behind the sofa? ➤ ¿Qué hay detrás de los comentarios del presidente? What's behind the president's remarks?

¿qué hay en la cartelera? ▪ ¿qué echan? what's on at the movies? ▪ what's playing at the movies?

¿qué he roto? what did I break?

¡qué hermoso! that's beautiful! ▪ how beautiful! ▪ that's lovely! ▪ how lovely!

¿qué hora es? what time is it?

¿qué horas son esas (de venir)? what do you mean showing up so late?

¡qué horror! how awful! ▪ how horrible! ▪ that's terrible

¿qué hubiese querido sino que...? what would he have wanted more than...?

¿qué hubo? what happened here? ▪ what took place here? ▪ what transpired here?

¿qúe hubo de lo de Fulano? ▪ ¿qué hubo de tal y cuál? what was that about so-and-so? ▪ what was that about what's his name?

¿qué húbole? *(Méx.)* ▪ ¿qué hubo? what's up?

¡qué huevos! *(subido de tono)* what balls!

¿qué importancia tiene? what's its importance? ▪ why is it important (to...)? ▪ what importance does it have?

¡qué inoportuno! what bad timing! ▪ *(coloquial)* what lousy timing ▪ *(culto)* how inopportune! ➤ El teléfono sonó justo cuando me metía en la ducha. "¡Qué inoportuno!" pensé. The phone rang just as I was getting into the shower. "What lousy timing!" I thought.

¡qué jaleo! what a racket! ▪ what a lot of noise! ▪ what a lot of hubbub! ▪ what a din!

que jamás había visto **1.** that one had ever seen **2.** than one had ever seen ➤ Fue la mejor película que jamás había visto. It was the best movie that I had ever seen. ➤ (Ella) estaba más guapa de lo que la había visto jamás. She looked more beautiful than I had ever seen her.

¡que la fuerza te acompañe! *(La guerra de las galaxias)* may the force be with you!

¡qué largo me lo fiáis! *(Don Juan, dicho con sarcasmo a Dios)* ▪ ¡tan largo me lo fiáis! ▪ ¡cuán largo me lo fiáis! what a long time you give me! *(Nota: Esta frase también se encuentra en Tirso de Molina y otros autores.)*

¡qué lástima! what a pity! ▪ that's too bad!

que le atraviesa a uno el tímpano ▪ que taladra los oídos earsplitting

¡que le cunda! make the most of it!

¡que le cunda el tiempo ▪ aproveche el tiempo ▪ *(Bol.)* saque el jugo make the most of your time

que le den dos duros *(Esp.)* ▪ que no le den ni la hora I wouldn't give him the time of day

que le es ajeno ▪ que no tiene nada que ver con alguien **1.** *(a él)* which has nothing to do with him **2.** *(a ella)* which has nothing to do with her **3.** *(a él)* he knows nothing about that ▪ he doesn't know anything about that **4.** *(a ella)* she knows nothing about that ▪ she doesn't know anything about that

¿qué le ha parecido...? **1.** *(usted)* how did you like...? ▪ what did you think of...? **2.** *(él)* how did he like...? ▪ what did he think of... **3.** *(ella)* how did she like...? ▪ what did she think of...?

¡qué le hagamos! *(L.am.)* ▪ ¡qué le vamos hacer! there's nothing we can do about it

¿qué le has puesto? *(receta, etc.)* what did you put in it?

¿qué le impulsó a...? what prompted you to...?

que le llueva encima to get rained on ▪ to get caught in the rain ➤ No quiero que me llueva encima. I don't want to get rained on. ▪ I don't want to get caught in the rain.

¿qué le parece? how about it? ▪ what do you think? ▪ what do you think of it? ➤ ¿Qué te parece este traje? ▪ ¿Qué le parece (a usted) este traje? How about this suit? ▪ What do you think of this suit?

¿qué le parece a usted? what do you think of it?

¿qué le pongo? *(Esp., especialmente en un bar de tapas)* ▪ ¿qué se le ofrece? ▪ ¿qué desea? what'll you have? ▪ what would you like?

¡qué le vamos a hacer! ▪ ya no tiene remedio ▪ hay que aceptar las cosas como vienen there's nothing we can do about it

¡qué le vas a hacer! there's nothing you can do about it

¡qué le voy a hacer! there's nothing I can do about it

¡que leche tienes! ▪ ¡qué suertudo! you lucky dog!

¡qué leches...! ■ ¡qué diablos...! what the hell...!

que llegamos tarde or we'll be late ➤ Venga, venga, que llegamos tarde. Come on, or we'll be late.

¿qué lleva alguien a hacer algo? what brings someone to do something? ■ what causes someone to do something?

que lo diga otro that's for somebody else to say

que lo digan los demás that's for others to say

¡que lo intente! just let him try!

que lo pases bien have a good time

que lo castiguen si lo hizo he should be punished if he did it

¡que lo haga Rita! ■ ¡que lo haga Montoto! let somebody else do it!

¡que lo hagas otra vez! do it again!

¿qué locura te ha entrado de...? ■ ¿qué se te ha dado por...? ■ ¿qué se te dio por...? ■ ¿qué ralle se te ha dado por...? whatever possessed you to...?

¡que los chinguen! *(Méx., subido de tono)* ■ ¡que se jodan! they can get screwed! ➤ Si no les gusta, ¡que los chinguen! ■ Si no les gusta, ¡que se jodan! If they don't like it they can get screwed!

¡que los follen! *(Esp., subido de tono)* ■ ¡que se jodan! they can get screwed! ➤ Si no les gusta, ¡que los follen! ■ Si no les gusta, ¡que se jodan! If they don't like it they can get screwed!

¡qué madrugador! ¿verdad? up awfully early, aren't you?!

¡qué mala suerte! that's too bad!

¡qué mala suerte nos ha tocado! what rotten luck (we're having)!

¡qué malo! that's mean!

¿qué manda usted? ■ ¿qué desea usted? what would you like?

¡qué manera de perder el tiempo! ■ ¡qué pérdida de tiempo! what a waste of time!

¡qué mañoso!(-a) **1.** ¡qué astuto! how clever! ■ that's very clever **2.** ¡qué molesto! what a pain to deal with! **3.** ¡qué porquería! what a finicky... ■ it sucks! ➤ ¡Qué mañoso eres! How clever you are! ■ You're very clever! ➤ ¡Qué mañoso es ese profesor (universitario)! That professor is a pain (to deal with). ➤ ¡Qué mañoso es este coche! What a finicky car! ■ This car's really finicky. ■ This car sucks!

¡qué mañoso(-a) eres! how clever you are! ■ you're very clever!

¡qué marchoso(-a)! ■ ¡qué fiera! what a party animal! ■ what a partier!

¡qué marrón! ■ ¡qué bajón! what a bummer!

¿qué más da? **1.** ¿qué más vale? what difference does it make? **2.** ¿a quién le importa? who cares? **3.** ¿y qué? so what?

¿qué más daría? what difference would it make?

¿qué más daría eso? what difference would that make?

¡qué más podrías pedir! what more could you ask!

¿qué más quieres? what else do you want?

¡qué más quisiera yo que fuera posible! how I wish it were possible ■ *(coloquial)* I sure wish I could

¡que me ahorquen si...! ■ ¡que me aspen si...! damned if I can...! ➤ ¡Que me ahorquen si entiendo estas instrucciones! Damned if I can understand these instructions!

¡que me aspen! **1.** well, I'll be damned ■ I'll be damned **2.** just let 'em try!

¡que me aspen si...! ■ ¡que me ahorquen si...! (I'll be) damned if... ➤ ¡Que me aspen si entiendo estas instrucciones! Damned if I can understand these instructions!

¡que me aspen si lo sé! (I'll be) damned if I know!

¿qué me cuentas? you don't say!

¿qué me dices de...? what do you think of...? ■ what do you think about...? ■ what's your opinion of...? ➤ ¿Qué me dices de lo que pasó ayer? What do you think about what happened yesterday?

que me embrome por... that's what I get for...

¿qué me ha cundido? ■ ¿cómo me ha servido? what good has it done me? ■ what good has it been?

¿qué me ha cundido?-a fin de cuentas, nada what do I have to show for it?-nothing! ■ I don't have anything to show for it ➤ He pasado seis años en esta puñetera universidad, y ¿qué (poco) me ha cundido? ■ He pasado seis años en esta puñetera universidad, y ¿cómo me ha servido? I've spent six years at this blasted university, and what do I have to show for it?

que me maten si... damned if I...

que me muera de repente si... ■ que me parta un rayo si... may God strike me dead if...

que me muera si... cross my heart and hope to die if...

que me parta un rayo si... damned if I can...

que me plazca: haré lo ~ ■ haré lo que me dé la gana I'll do as I please

¿qué me pongo? what shall I wear?

que me quiten lo bailado no one can take that away from me ➤ Simón no tiene ni coche ni casa, pero como dice él, que le quiten lo bailado. Simon doesn't have a house or (a) car, but as he says, he's lived it up, and no one can take that away from him.

¡que me salga a la suerte! I hope I get lucky

¿qué mérito tiene eso? what merit is there in that?

¡qué miedo tendrán...! they must be terrified

¡qué modales! what (bad) manners! ■ that's bad manners

¡qué molestarle ni qué molestarle! **1.** *(a él)* why bother him (with it) ■ why bother him (about it) **2.** *(a ella)* why bother her (with it)? ■ why bother her (about it)?

¡qué molestarlo ni qué molestarlo! why bother

¡qué montón de mierda! *(subido de tono)* what a crock of shit!

¡qué morro! what cheek! ■ what gall!

¡qué morro tienes! *(Esp.)* ■ ¡qué descaro tienes! ■ ¡qué descarado(-a)! you've got a lot nerve! ■ what cheek (you have)!

¿qué mosca le habrá picado? ■ ¿qué mosca le ha picado? **1.** *(a él)* what's bugging him? **2.** *(a ella)* what's bugging her? **3.** *(a usted)* what's bugging you?

¿qué mosca te ha picado? what's bugging you? ■ what's with you?

¡qué mundo este! ■ ¡en qué mundo vivimos! what a world (we live in)!

¡qué mundo este! ■ ¡en qué mundo vivimos! what a world (we live in)! ➤ ¡Qué mundo este! ■ ¡Hay que ver, en qué mundo vivimos! What a world we live in! ■ Look (at) what a world we live in!

que nada se pierde con ignorar what you don't know won't hurt you

¿que nada te niega? you mean he never refuses you anything?

¿qué narices...? what (in) the heck...? ■ what in the world...? ➤ ¿Qué narices es eso? ■ ¿Qué porras es eso? What (in) the heck is that? ■ What in the world is that?

¡qué...ni qué ocho cuartos! ■ ¡qué... ni qué niño muerto! my foot! ■ nothing! ➤ Qué deberes ni que ocho cuartos, vas a ordenar tu habitación. Homework, my foot! Clean your room! ■ Homework, nothing! Clean your room! ➤ Qué dieta ni que ocho cuartos, te comes el broculí. Diet, my foot! Eat your broccoli! ■ Diet, nothing! Eat your broccoli. ➤ Qué ladrones ni que ocho cuartos, no me vengas con esas, te lo has gastado en el bingo. Thieves, my foot! Don't give me that. You spent it playing bingo! ■ Thieves, nothing! Don't give me that. You spent it playing bingo.

que ni por mano de santo not to have a prayer ➤ Que ni por mano de santo te salvas. You don't have a prayer. ➤ Que ni por mano de santo van a ganar. They don't have a prayer of winning.

que ni te imaginas that you wouldn't believe ➤ Ha habido un accidente que ni te imaginas. There was an accident that you wouldn't (even) believe.

que no abandones tus cánones don't abandon your standards

¡que no cunda el pánico! please remain calm! ■ don't panic!

¡que no decaiga la fe! ■ ¡no pierda la fe! don't lose faith!

¡que no dejes caer los ánimos! ■ ¡no pierdas ánimo! don't lose heart!

que no es ■ equivocado the wrong one ■ that isn't the (right) one

que no era ■ equivocado the wrong one ■ that wasn't the (right) one ➤ Tomé el paraguas que no era. ■ Tomé el paraguas equivocado. I took the wrong umbrella. ➤ Tomé el autobús que no era. ■ Tomé el autobús equivocado. I took the wrong bus.

¡que no eres capaz! ■ ¡apuesto a que no! bet you can't!

que no es de fiar: una fuente ~ unreliable source

que no es de fiar: un(a) testigo ~ unreliable witness

que no es por nada no offense ■ it's nothing against you ➤ No es por nada pero ella tiene razón. No offense, but she's right.

¡que no falte! 1. *(él)* make sure he's here 2. *(ella)* make sure she's here 3. make sure there's enough
que no las hubo no, there weren't
que no me dieron ni la hora they wouldn't give me the time of day ■ they didn't give me the time of day
que no se casa con nadie uncompromising
que no se puede aguantar unbearable
que no se puede olvidar ■ inolvidable unforgettable
que no se vuelva a repetir don't let it happen again
que no sea other than ➤ ¡La burocracia de esta ciudad es para los habitantes de algún planeta que no sea la Tierra! The bureaucracy of this city is for the inhabitants of some planet other than Earth!
que no son pocos numerous ■ which are not hard to come by ■ which are not lacking (by any means) ■ which are plentiful ➤ Es un político que ha sabido capear los temporales del tiempo, que no son pocos, y llegar a la cima. He's a politician who has managed to weather the numerous controversies of the day and make it to the top.
que no tardaría en volverse... which would not take long to become... ■ that would not take long to become...
¡que no te cuenten la película! don't let them feed you a line
¡que no te decaigas! ■ ¡que no te des por vencido! don't lose faith! ■ keep your chin up! ■ don't give up!
¡que no te enteras, Contreras! you don't get it
¡que no te entre el pánico! don't panic!
¡que no te tomen el pelo! don't let them fool you! ■ don't let them kid you! ■ don't let them pull your leg!
que no te vaya mal: espero ~ I hope there are no problems ■ I hope you don't have any problems
¡qué noche tienes! you're having quite a night of it!
¿qué noticias tienes de Lalo? what do you hear from Ed?
¿qué onda? what's up?
¿qué ondón, Ramón? *(Méx.)* ■ ¿qué patín, hijín? what's up, dude?
qué oscuro está aquí dentro it's dark in here
¿qué otra cosa? what else?
¿qué otras personas? who else?
¡qué paliza de...! what an exhausting...!
¿qué parte ha dado? what does it say?
¿qué parte han dado los guardias? *(Valle-Inclán)* ■ ¿qué informe han dado los guardias? what does the police report say?
¿qué pasa? what's happening? ■ what's going on? ➤ ¿Qué pasa?-Poca cosa. What's going on?-Not much.
¿qué pasa aquí? what's going on here?
¿qué pasa de nuevo contigo? what's new with you?
que pase un momento a conferenciar conmigo el coronel *(Valle-Inclán)* have the colonel come talk to me for a minute
que pase una feliz noche have a good evening
que pase (usted) una feliz noche ■ que tenga (usted) una buena noche have a good evening
que pases una feliz noche ■ que tengas una buena noche have a good evening
¿qué patín, hijín? *(Méx.)* what's up, dude?
¡qué pedazo de animal! ■ ¡so bestia! what an animal!
que pela: un frío ~ bitter cold
¡qué pena! that's too bad ■ what a pity! ■ what a shame!
qué pequeño how small
qué pequeño es el mundo ■ el mundo es un pañuelo it's a small world
¡qué pérdida de tiempo! ■ ¡qué manera de perder el tiempo! what a waste of time!
¿qué perimetro tiene? what's the perimeter? ■ how big around is it?
¡qué pero ni qué ocho cuartos! there's no excuse
¡qué pícaro! ■ ¡menudo canalla! ■ ¡menudo pájaro está hecho! what a rogue!
¿qué pides? ■ ¿cuánto pides? what do you want for it? ■ what are you asking for it? ■ how much do you want for it? ■ how much are you asking for it?
¿qué pides por...? ■ cuánto pides por...? what do you want for...? ■ what are you asking for...? ■ how much do you want for...? ■ how much are you asking for...?
¿qué piensas al respecto? what do you think about it? ■ what do you think of it? ■ what do you think?
¿qué piensas hacer? what do you plan to do? ■ what are you planning to do?
¿qué piensas hacer al respecto? ■ ¿qué piensas hacer sobre ello? what do you plan to do about it? ■ what are you planning to do about it?
¡qué pinta tiene! 1. *(food)* ¡qúe buena pinta! ■ tiene una pinta... that looks delicious! 2. *(people)* he's good-looking ■ she's good-looking
¡qué piquito tienes! you've got a lot of lip! ■ you're in a foul mood!
¡qué poco! *(ración de comida, cantidad de pago, etc.)* that's pretty skimpy ■ that's measley ■ that's pretty paltry
qué poco hay de... there's hardly any... ➤ Qué poco pan hay. There's hardly any bread.
¡qué poco interés hay en este tema! no one's interested in this subject
¡qué poco trabajas! you're barely working!
¡qué poco dura...! (how) short-lived is...! ➤ ¡Qué poco dura la alegría en casa de los pobres! (How) short-lived is the joy of the poor!
¡qué polvo tiene! *(subido de tono)* ■ ¡está para un buen polvo! 1. *(él)* he's worth one ■ I'd like to get it on with him 2. *(ella)* she's worth one ■ I'd like to get it on with her
¿qué ponen en la tele? ■ ¿qué están dando en la tele? what's on TV?
¡qué porras! what the heck!
¿qué porras es eso? ■ ¿qué narices es eso? what in the world is that?
¿qué posibilidades hay? what are the odds? ■ what are the prospects?
¿qué posibilidades tenemos de...? what are the chances of our...?
¿qué posibilidades tenemos de que...? what are the chances that we...?
¿qué precio tiene? ■ ¿cuánto cuesta? what's the price? ■ how much does it cost? ■ how much is it?
¡qué pregunta difícil! it's hard to say ■ that's a difficult question (to answer)
¿qué pretendías? what were you expecting?
¿qué pretendes? what do you expect?
que pudiera hallarse that could be found
que pueda conseguir ■ asequible available
¿qué puede ser? ■ ¿qué será? what could it be?
¿qué puedo hacer por ti? what can I do for you?
¡qué puñetas! what the heck!
que quede claro let me make this (perfectly) clear
que quema: el sol está ~ it's blistering hot ■ it's a scorcher
¡qué quemo! ■ ¡qué bochorno! ■ ¡qué vergüenza! ■ ¡qué compromiso! how embarrassing! ■ what an embarrassment!
que quepa that will fit this ■ that this will fit into ■ to fit this ➤ ¿Tiene usted un sobre en (el) que quepa esto exactamente? ■ ¿Tiene usted un sobre del tamaño de esto? Do you have an envelope to fit this (exactly)? ■ Do you have an envelope that will fit this (exactly)?
que quiera, que no quiera, el asno ha de ir a la feria *(pintoresco)* you have to, like it or not
¿qué quieres decir? what do you mean?
¿qué quieres decir con eso? what do you mean by that?
¿qué quiere decir eso? what does that mean?
¡qué quieres! *(pesadez)* what do you want?!
¿qué quieres? what do you want?
¿qué quieres que haga (al respecto)? what do you want me to do (about it)?
¿qué quieres que le haga? what do you want *me* to do?
¿qué quieres ser cuando seas grande? ■ ¿qué quieres ser de mayor? what do you want to be when you grow up?
¿qué quieres ser de mayor? ■ ¿qué quieres ser cuando seas grande? what do you want to be when you grow up?
¿qué rayos es eso? ■ ¿qué cuernos es eso? what (in) the world is that?

¿qué recompensa tiene eso? ▪ ¿de qué sirve? what good is that?

¡qué remedio! **1.** there's nothing I can do about it **2.** there's nothing anyone can do about it

¿qué remedio me queda? what else can I do?

¿qué reserva es el vino? ▪ ¿qué cosecha es el vino? what year is the wine? ▪ what year was the wine made? ▪ how many years has the wine been aged?

qué rico es estar en casa, ¿verdad? ▪ ¿qué bueno es estar en casa, ¿verdad? it's great to be home, isn't it?

¡qué rollo! **1.** what a hassle **2.** ¡qué cuento! what a crock! ▪ that's a crock! ▪ that's a lie!

¿qué rollo? *(Méx., jerga)* what's up?

¿qué sacaste por ello? how much did you get for it?

que se deja intimidar: no ser una persona ~ not to be a person who is easily intimidated

que se dejaba intimidar: no ser una persona ~ not to be a person who was easily intimidated

¿qué se dice? *(instando al niño a que diga "gracias")* ▪ la palabrita mágica what do you say?

que se dice pronto ▪ que se dice rápido it's easy to criticize ▪ it's easy to judge

que se dice rápido ▪ que se dice pronto it's easy to criticize ▪ it's easy to judge

¿qué se espera obtener? **1.** what do you hope to get out of it? **2.** what do expect to get out of it?

¡que se fastidie! ▪ ¡que se jorobe! **1.** *(él)* too bad for him! **2.** *(ella)* too bad for her!

¿qué se ha de hacer? ▪ ¿qué se le ha de hacer? what's to be done? ▪ what can be done about it?

¿qué se ha roto? ▪ ¿qué se rompió? what broke? ▪ what got broken?

¡que se jodan! *(L.am., subido de tono)* ▪ ¡que los chinguen! ▪ ¡que los follen! they can get screwed! ➤ Si no les gusta, ¡que los jodan! If they don't like it, they can get screwed!

¡que se la pega! **1.** he's going to crash **2.** he's going to hit it ▪ he's going to run into it

(que) se la pone *(Arg.)* ▪ (que) se va a ir a la porra **1.** he's going to crash ▪ he's going to have a wreck **2.** he's going to hit it ▪ he's going to run into it ➤ Si sigue manejando así, se la va a poner. If he keeps driving like that, he's going to crash.

que se las trae that's a tough one ➤ Es un encargo que se las trae. That's a difficult assignment.

¿qué se le ha de hacer? ▪ ¿qué se ha de hacer? what's to be done? ▪ what can be done about it? ▪ what can we do about it?

¿qué se le ofrece? ▪ ¿qué desea? what'll you have? ▪ what would you like?

¿qué se le va a hacer? *(frustración)* what can you do?

¿qué se les ocurrirá después? ▪ ¿qué vendrá después? ▪ ¿qué será lo siguiente? what'll they think of next?! ➤ ¿Metrosexuales y tecnosexuales? ¡Dios mío! ¿Qué se les ocurrirá después? Metrosexuals and technosexuals? Eee-gad! What'll they think of next?!

¡que se lo creyó! ▪ ¡que se lo ha creído! **1.** *(él)* he fell for it! **2.** *(ella)* she fell for it **3.** *(usted)* you fell for it!

¡que se lo cuente a su abuela! ▪ ¡a otro perro con ese hueso! go tell it to the Marines!

¡que se lo ha creído! ▪ ¡que se lo creyó! **1.** *(él)* he fell for it! **2.** *(ella)* she fell for it **3.** *(usted)* you fell for it!

¿qué se necesita para...? what does it take to...? ▪ what is needed to...? ▪ what do you need to...?

que se parece mucho a... **1.** *(cosa)* which looks a lot like **2.** *(persona)* who looks a lot like

¿qué se parece mucho a...? what looks a lot like...

que se pudo encontrar that could be found

¿qué se quiere obtener? ▪ ¿qué se quiere sacar de eso? what do you want to get out of it?

¿qué se rompió? ▪ ¿qué se ha roto? what broke? ▪ what got broken?

¿qué se supone que deba hacer? ▪ ¿qué se supone que tenga que hacer? what do you think I should do?

¿qué se supone que debiera haber hecho? ▪ ¿qué se supone que debiese haber hecho? what was I supposed to do?

¿qué se supone que debo hacer? what am I supposed to do?

¿qué se supone que haga (yo) ahora? what am I supposed to do now?

¿qué se supone que tenga que hacer? ▪ ¿qué se supone que deba hacer? what do you think I should to do?

¿qué se suponía que íbamos a hacer? **1.** what were we supposed to do? ▪ what were we going to do? **2.** what could we have done? ➤ ¿Qué se suponía que íbamos a hacer hoy? What were we supposed to do today? ▪ What were we going to do today? ▪ What did we have planned for today? ➤ ¿Qué se suponía que íbamos a hacer para impedirlo? What were we supposed to do to prevent it? ▪ What could we have done to prevent it?

¿qué se suponía que debía hacer? **1.** *(yo)* what was I supposed to do? **2.** *(él)* what was he supposed to do? **3.** *(ella)* what was she supposed to do?

¿qué se te da bien? what are you good at? ▪ what do you do well?

¿qué se te ha dado por...? ▪ ¿qué se te ha dado con...? ▪ ¿qué es esa locura de...? whatever possessed you to...? ▪ whatever made you...? ▪ whatever prompted you to...? ➤ ¿Qué se te ha dado por renunciar a un trabajo de cien mil dólares al año y tomar un trabajo de veinticinco mil dólares al año? Whatever possessed you quit your one-hundred-thousand-dollar-a-year job and take a twenty-five-thousand-dollar-a-year job?

¿qué se te ha perdido? what have you lost? ➤ ¿Qué has perdido?-He perdido mi boli. What did you lose?-I lost my (ballpoint) pen. ➤ ¿Qué has perdido por preguntar?-Nada. What have you lost by asking?-Nothing.

¿qué se te ofrece? ▪ ¿qué te pongo? what'll you have? ▪ what would you like?

¡qué sé yo! ¡yo qué sé! how would I know? ▪ how should I know? ▪ search me!

que sea leve I hope it goes well

¡que sean dos! make that two!

¿qué será? what could it be?

¿qué será eso? what would that be? ▪ what could that be?

¿qué sería de...? what would have become of...?

¡que *sí*! *(al contradecir)* yes, it *is*!

que si esto, que si lo otro either way, I don't care ▪ either way, it doesn't make any difference

que si patatín, que si patatán say whatever, but this is the way it has to be done

que si quieres arroz I said, would you like rice? ▪ I said, do you want rice?

¡que siga el espectáculo! get on with the show!

¡qué sitio más cutre! ▪ ¡qué sitio más tirado! what a dive!

que son de suponer that one might expect ▪ that you might expect ▪ which one might expect ▪ which you might expect

¿qué son estas cosas? what are these things?

¡qué susto me has dado! you scared me!

¡qué tacaño! what a tightwad! ▪ *(más despectivo)* what a cheapskate!

¡qué tajante! how strict! ▪ what a strict...!

¿qué tal? how's it going? ▪ how are things going?

¿qué tal ahí? how about in there?

¿qué tal andas? how's everything going?

¿qué tal de...? how are you fixed for...? ▪ do you have enough...? ➤ ¿Qué tal de dinero? How are you fixed for money? ▪ Do you have enough money?

¿qué tal es? **1.** what's it like? **2.** *(él)* what's he like? **3.** *(ella)* what's she like?

¿qué tal estás? ▪ ¿cómo estás? how are you?

¿qué tal estoy? ▪ ¿cómo estoy? ▪ ¿cómo me veo? how do I look?

¿qué tal has pasado la semana? how was your week?

¿qué tal la escuela? ▪ ¿qué tal va la escuela? how is school?

¿qué tal le fue a Juan? how did Juan do?

¿qué tal lo has pasado? **1.** *(L.am.)* ¿te divertiste? ▪ ¿cómo te lo has pasado? did you have a good time? **2.** *(Esp.)* ¿cómo has estado? how have you been?

¿qué tal lo llevas? how are you getting along?

¿qué tal me fue? ▪ ¿qué tal me ha ido? how did I do? ▪ how'd I do?

¿qué tal me ha ido? ■ ¿qué tal me fue? how did I do? ■ how'd I do?

¿qué tal me queda? how does it look on me?

¿qué tal saliendo a cenar? how was your dinner out? ■ how was your supper out?

¿qué tal si? ■ ¿qué te parece si? ■ ¿y si...? what if...? ■ how about if...? ■ what do you say we...?

¡qué suerte! what luck!

¿qué tal te ha ido? how did it go?

¿qué tal te han quedado? *(ropas)* how did they fit (you)?

¿qué tal va? ■ ¿cómo te va? how's it going?

¿qué tal vamos de tiempo? ■ ¿cómo vamos de tiempo? how are we doing on the time?

¿qué tal voy? how am I doing?

¿qué tal voy de tiempo? ■ ¿cómo voy de tiempo? how am I doing on the time?

que taladra los oídos ■ que le atraviesa a uno el tímpano ear-splitting

qué tan bueno how good ➤ Depende de qué tan buenos amigos seáis. It depends on how good friends you are.

¿qué tan lejos está? ■ ¿a qué distancia está? ■ ¿a cuánto está? how far away is it? ■ how far is it?

¿qué tan pronto...? ■ ¿cuándo...? how soon...?

que te aproveche ■ que con tu pan te lo comas you made your bed, now you can sleep in it

¿qué te apuestas a que...? ■ ¿qué te va a que...? what do you bet...?

¡que te aspen! *(Esp.)* ■ ¡vete al cuerno! to hell with you!

¡que te chinguen! *(Méx., subido de tono)* ■ ¡que te jodan! (you can) get screwed! ■ *(alternativa benigna)* go take a walk! ■ go jump in a lake! ➤ Si no te gusta, ¡que te chinguen! ■ Si no te gusta, ¡que te jodan! If you don't like it you can get screwed!

¡que te crees tú eso! you're not going to fall for that, are you?

¡que te cunda! ■ ¡que te rinda! I hope you make a killing ■ I hope you clean up ■ I hope you make a bundle

que te den dos duros they better not give you very much

¡que te den morcilla! go jump in a lake! ■ go take a walk!

¡que te den por el culo! *(muy subido de tono)* up yours! ■ get screwed! ■ *(alternativa benigna)* go jump in a lake!

que te des cuenta de que... ■ date cuenta de que... (just) be aware that...

¡que te diviertas! ■ ¡pásalo bien! have a good time!

¡que te follen! *(Esp., subido de tono)* ■ ¡que te jodan! (you can) get screwed! *(alternativa benigna)* go take a walk! ■ go jump in a lake! ➤ Si no te gusta, ¡que te follen! ■ Si no te gusta, ¡que te jodan! If you don't like it (you can) get screwed!

¿qué te ha entrado a hacer eso? whatever possessed you to do that?

¿qué te ha hecho (tanta) gracia? ■ ¿de qué te ríes? what are you laughing at? ■ what are you laughing about? ■ why are you laughing? ■ what's so funny?

¿qué te ha parecido...? how did you like...? ■ how'd you like...? ➤ ¿Qué te ha parecido ese tiro? How'd you like that shot?

¿qué te habrá pasado? what has come over you? ■ what's come over you?

¡qué te habrás creído! what you must have thought!

¿qué te incumbe a ti? what business is it of yours? ■ what's it to you?

¡que te jodan! *(L.am., subido de tono)* ■ ¡que te chinguen! ■ ¡que te follen! (you can) get screwed! ➤ Si no les gusta, ¡que los jodan! If they don't like it, they can get screwed!

que te lo paso ■ ya te lo doy here, I'm handing it to you

¡que te mejores pronto! get well soon!

¿qué te parece? how about it? ■ what do you think? ■ what do you think of it? ■ how does that sound? ➤ ¿Qué te parece este traje? How about this suit? ■ What do you think of this suit?

¡qué te parta un rayo! damn you!

¿qué te pasa? what's the matter? ■ what's wrong? ■ what's the matter with you?

¿qué te pongo? ■ ¿qué se te ofrece? what'll you have? ■ what would you like?

que te puedes morir that can be fatal ■ which can be fatal ■ that can kill you

que te quiten lo bailado no one can take that away from you

¿qué te respondí? what did I tell you? ■ what'd I tell you?

que te sea leve don't work too hard

¿qué te va a que...? ■ ¿qué te apuestas a que...? what do you bet...?

¿qué te va en ello? ■ ¿qué te importa? what's in it for you? ■ what does it matter to you? ■ what difference does it make to you?

se la pela *(subido de tono)* **1.** *(él)* he doesn't give a damn **2.** *(ella)* she doesn't give a damn

¿qué te va en eso? what does that matter to you? ■ what difference does that make to you?

que te vaya bien I hope everything goes well for you ■ good luck

que te vaya bonito *(sarcasmo)* have a nice life

que te vaya de lujo *(sarcasmo)* have a nice life

que te zurzan go jump in a lake ■ go take a walk

¿qué tendrá que ver el culo con las témporas? what's *that* got to do with it?

¿qué tenemos aquí? what have we here?

que tengas una buena noche ■ que pases una feliz noche have a good evening

que tenga (usted) una buena noche ■ que pase (usted) una feliz noche have a good evening

¿qué tiene de duro? ■ ¿qué tiene de chungo? what's hard about it? ■ what's difficult about it?

¿qué tiene de extraño? whats so strange about that?

¿qué tiene de malo? what's wrong with ➤ ¿Qué tiene de malo decir... What's wrong with saying...?

que tiene premio it'll get the prize

¿qué tienes? what's the matter? ■ what's wrong?

¡qué timo! what a ripoff!

¡qué tío! *(Esp.)* ■ ¡qué tipo! what a guy!

¡qué tío más rancio! what a stuffed shirt! ■ what a party pooper!

¡qué tipo aburridísimo! what a crashing bore! ■ what a dreary character!

¿qué tipo de coche es? what kind of car is it?

que tira para atrás *(hedor)* (bad) enough to make you reel back ■ (bad) enough to floor you ■ (bad) enough to make you flinch

que todavía no ha cumplido *x* años who is not yet *x* years old ➤ Nuestro sobrino que todavía no ha cumplido tres años. Our nephew who is not yet three years old.

¡que trabaje Rita! let somebody else do it!

¡qué trabajo ímprobo! what an enormous task!

¿qué tren acaba de marchar? ■ ¿qué tren se marcha? ■ ¿a dónde iba ese tren? where was that train headed? ■ what train was that? ■ which train was that? ■ what train just left? ■ which train just left?

¿qué tripa se te ha roto? *(de padre a hijo)* ■ ¿qué tripa se te ha pasado? ■ ¿qué te ha pasado? ■ ¿qué necesitas? what's *happened* to you?

¡qué trucho! *(Arg.)* ■ ¡qué timo! what a ripoff!

que uno haya hecho algo 1. one's doing something **2.** one's having done something ➤ Realmente apreciamos que te hayas mantenido en contacto con nosotros. ■ Realmente agradecemos que te hayas mantenido en contacto con nosotros. We really appreciate your staying in touch with us. ➤ El que hayas abandonado la clase me sorprendió. ■ El que te hayas retirado de la clase me sorprendió. Your dropping out of the class surprised me.

¡qué va! *(coloquial)* heck no ■ no, no ■ nah

¡qué va a ser cierto! *(irónico)* yeah, sure!

¡qué valor! 1. what nerve! ■ what gall! ■ *(él)* he's got a lot of nerve ■ that guy's got a lot of nerve! ■ *(ella)* she's got a lot of nerve **2.** that took (a lot of) guts! ■ what guts! ■ what courage!

¿qué vamos a hacerle? what are we going to do about it?

¿qué vas a hacer al respecto? what are you going to do about it?

¡que vaya Rita! ■ ¡que vaya Rita la cantaora! let somebody else go!

que venga 1. *(él)* have him come in **2.** *(ella)* have her come in

¡que vengan! let them come! ■ bring them on!

¿qué ventolera te ha entrado de ponerte a organillero? *(Valle-Inclán)* whatever possessed you to become an organ grinder?

¡qué vergüenza! **1.** qué avergonzante how embarrassing! **2.** debería darte vergüenza shame on you! **3.** ¡qué deshonroso! what a disgrace! ■ that's disgraceful! ■ that's a disgrace!

¿qué ves de malo? what's wrong with that? ■ what objection do you have to that?

¡qué vidita tienes! ■ ¡qué vida llevas! ■ ¡qué nivel! what a life you lead!

¡que viene el lobo! *(Fábulas de Esopo)* ■ ¡que le vas a ver las orejas al lobo! be extremely careful!

¿qué voy a hacer contigo? what am I going to do with you?

que ya es decir and that's saying something

que ya es mucho decir ■ ya es decir mucho and that's saying a lot

que ya es tuyo ■ que ya estás a punto de conseguirlo **1.** you've already got it **2.** *(a él)* you've already got him **3.** *(a ella)* you've already got her

que yo **1.** than I do **2.** than I am **3.** as I am **4.** than I am ➤ Es más alto que yo. He's taller than I (am). *(Nota: "Than me" es coloquial pero incorrecto. "Than" es una conjunción, por lo tanto no puede llevar un objeto.)*

que jamás había visto **1.** that one had ever seen **2.** than one had ever seen ➤ Fue la mejor película que jamás había visto. It was the best movie that I had ever seen. ➤ (Ella) estaba más guapa de lo que la había visto jamás. She looked more beautiful than I had ever seen her.

que (yo) me acuerde ■ que yo recuerde ■ hasta donde me acuerdo ■ que (yo) me acuerde as far as I can recall ■ as far as I can remember ■ as best I (can) recall ■ as best I (can) remember ■ to the best of my recollection

que yo recuerde ■ que (yo) me acuerde ■ hasta donde recuerdo ■ hasta donde me acuerdo ■ hasta donde puedo recordar ■ hasta donde me puedo acordar ■ as far as I can recall ■ as far as I can remember ■ as best I (can) recall ■ as best I (can) remember ■ to the best of my recollection

que yo sepa that I know of ■ as far as I know ■ so far as I know ➤ No hay ninguno que yo sepa. There isn't one that I know of. ■ There aren't any that I know of.

que yo sepa, no ■ no que yo sepa not that I know of ■ not so far as I know ■ so far as I know, no

que yo supiera ■ que yo supiese **1.** that I knew of **2.** as far as I knew

que yo supiese ■ que yo supiera **1.** that I knew of **2.** as far as I knew

quebrantamiento de las normas de etiqueta ■ quebrantamiento de las reglas de etiqueta breach of etiquette

quebradero de cabeza ■ (el) rompecabezas brainteaser ■ puzzle

quebrantar la ley ■ romper la ley to break the law

quebrar un negocio to bankrupt a business

quebrarle la cabeza a alguien to baffle someone

quebrarle las alas a alguien ■ acortarle las alas a alguien to clip someone's wings

quebrarse la voz (for) the voice to break

quebrársele la voz (for) one's voice to break

¿queda claro? is that clear?

¡queda cumplido! *(las últimas palabras de Jesús)* it is finished!

quedar el rabo por desollar the worst is yet to come ■ the worst is still to come ■ the hardest part is yet to come ■ the hardest part is still to come

queda entre nosotros it's our own little secret

queda mucho por hacer a lot remains to be done ■ there's still a lot to do

queda poco it's almost all gone

¿quedamos en eso? shall we leave it at that? ■ does that work for you? ■ does that sound like a plan?

quedan *x* semanas para there are *x* weeks until

estar **quedándose sordo** to be going deaf ■ to be losing one's hearing ➤ Se está quedando sordo. He's going deaf. ■ He's losing his hearing.

quedarle cierto tiempo to have a certain amount of time left ■ (for) a certain amount of time to remain ➤ Le quedan quince años antes de que se jubile. He has fifteen years left until he retires.

quedar a la altura del betún ■ quedar mal to be really embarrassing

quedar a la cuarta pregunta to be broke

quedar a mano ■ quedar en paz to be even (Steven) ■ to call it even ➤ Dame diez pesos y quedamos a mano. ■ Dame diez pesos y quedamos en paz. Give me ten pesos and we'll be even (Steven). ■ Give me ten pesos and we'll call it even.

quedar a una calle ■ estar a una calle to be a block away ■ to be a block over ■ to be a block from here

quedar a *x* años luz ■ estar a *x* años luz to be *x* light-years away ■ to be *x* light-years distant

quedar aislado(-a) por la nieve to be snowed in

quedar anonadado(-a) ■ quedar atontado to be stunned

quedar asentado(-a) en to give in to ■ just to give in to ■ simply to give in to

quedar asentado(-a) en el expediente permanente to be put into the permanent record

quedar aterrado(-a) to be terrified

quedar atontolinado to be dazed ■ to be in a daze

quedar atrapado en una tormenta de nieve to get stranded in a snowstorm ■ to get stranded in a blizzard ■ to be stranded in a snowstorm ■ to be stranded in a blizzard

quedar atrapado en una inundación to get stranded in a flood ■ to be stranded in a flood ➤ Muchas personas quedaron atrapadas cuando la inundación sumergió Nueva Orleans. Many people got stranded when the flood engulfed New Orleans. ■ Many people were stranded when the flood engulfed New Orleans.

quedar atrás ■ rezagarse to remain behind ■ to lag behind other students

quedar bien **1.** salir bien to turn out well ■ to come out well **2.** tener buen corte to fit well ■ to fit (just) right ➤ Lo importante es que quede bien. The important thing is to get it right. ➤ Que quede bien. Do it just right. ■ Make it perfect. ■ I hope it comes out just right. ➤ Este pantalón me queda bien. These pants fit (me) just right.

quedar bien con alguien **1.** causar una buena impresión to make a good impression **2.** ser visto favorablemente por alguien to get on someone's good side ➤ Para quedar bien con el jefe, le fui a comprar su café. To get on the boss' good side, I went and bought his coffee.

quedar con alguien ■ citarse con alguien to have an appointment with someone ■ to have a date with someone ■ to make an appointment with someone ➤ Ha quedado con María a las cinco. He has a date with María at five. ➤ He quedado con el médico mañana. I have a doctor's appointment tomorrow. ■ I have an appointment with the doctor tomorrow.

quedar calentorro(-a) *(sexual)* to get hot (as a firecracker)

quedar cegado(-a) to be blinded momentarily (by bright light)

quedar claro que... to be clear that...

quedar compensado(-a) (por) to be compensated for (by) ➤ Los episodios incompletos quedan compensados por la literatura apócrifa. The incomplete biblical accounts are compensated for by apocryphal literature.

quedar con alguien ■ concretar una cita con alguien ■ hacer una cita con alguien **1.** *(social)* to meet someone ■ to make a date with someone **2.** *(negocio, médico, etc.)* to make an appointment with someone ➤ Quedamos debajo del reloj en el Biltmore. Let's meet under the clock in the Biltmore. ■ Meet me under the clock in the Biltmore.

quedar de perlas to be total perfection ■ to be absolutely perfect ➤ Quedó de perlas. It was total perfection. ■ It was absolutely perfect.

quedar demasiado lejos para ir caminando ■ quedar demasiado lejos para ir andando to be too far (away) to walk to ■ to be too far away to go on foot

quedar desmembrado to be dismembered

quedar detenido to be under arrest ■ to be arrested

quedar (el) primero *(en la puntuación)* to come in first ➤ Boca Juniors quedó (el) primero. Boca Juniors came in first.

quedar embarazada to get pregnant ■ to become pregnant

quedar en agua de borrajas ■ terminar en agua de borrajas to fizzle out ■ for nothing to come of it ■ to come to nothing ➤ Quedó en agua de borrajas. It fizzled out. ■ Nothing came of it.

quedar en agua de cerraja *(rare)* ■ quedar algo en agua de borrajas to fizzle out ■ to come to nothing ➤ Quedó en agua de cerraja. ■ *(más común)* Quedó en agua de borrajas It fizzled out. ■ Nothing came of it.

quedar en algo ■ estar de acuerdo en algo to agree on something

quedar en descubierto to be exposed ■ to be found out

quedar en el objetivo to be on target

quedar en estado to get pregnant ■ to become pregnant

quedar en las mismas **1.** to keep doing what one is doing **2.** to stay where one is

quedar en libertad to be set free ■ to be released

quedar en libertad bajo fianza to be free on bail ■ to be free on bond

quedar en limpio to clear one's name ➤ Quedó en limpio después del juicio. His name was cleared after the trial.

quedar en nada to come to nothing ➤ Las conversaciones bilaterales quedaron en nada. The bilateral talks came to nothing.

quedar en paz **1.** quedarse tranquilo to be at peace **2.** *(Esp.)* quedar a mano to be even (Steven) ■ to call it even

quedar en ridículo haciendo algo to make a fool of oneself doing something ➤ Quedé en ridículo bailando la Macarena. I made a fool of myself doing the Macarena.

quedar en (situación de) arresto domiciliario ■ ser puesto en arresto domiciliario to be placed under house arrest ■ to be put under house arrest ➤ *(noticia)* El ex presidente de Yugoslavia Slobodan Milosevic quedó a la 1.30 de hoy en situación de arresto domiciliario. Former Yugoslav president Slobodan Milosevic was placed under house arrest at 1:30 a.m. today. ➤ Galileo fue puesto en arresto domiciliario. Galileo was placed under house arrest. ■ Galileo was put under house arrest.

quedar en suspenso to remain in suspense ■ to be in suspense

quedar en tablas to be deadlocked

quedar encallado **1.** *(barco)* to be stranded ■ to be run aground **2.** *(negociaciones)* to be bogged down ■ to be stymied **3.** *(artilugio, dispositivo)* to be jammed ■ to be stuck ■ to get stuck

quedar encantado(-a) por alguien to be enchanted by someone

quedar envuelto en llamas to be engulfed in flames ■ to be enveloped in flames ➤ El avión se desploma sobre una pista lateral, queda partido en tres trozos y envuelto en llamas. The airplane falls onto a parallel runway, breaks into three pieces and is engulfed in flames.

quedar esparcido por to be scattered all over ■ to be scattered over ➤ La carga de la camión quedó esparcida por la carretera. The truck's freight was scattered (all) over the highway.

quedar fascinado(-a) to be fascinated

quedar hechizado(-a) por alguien **1.** quedar bajo el sortilegio de alguien to be under someone's spell **2.** quedar encantado por alguien to be enchanted by someone ■ to be charmed by someone

quedar huérfano to be orphaned

quedar intacto to remain intact ■ to be left intact

quedar lavado to go through the wash ➤ Por descuido dejé un billete de cincuenta dólares en mi bolsillo y quedó lavado. I accidentally left a fifty-dollar bill in my pocket, and it went through the wash.

quedar lejos to be far away

quedar libre ■ salir en libertad to go free

quedar mal si to look bad if

quedar mejor to look better ➤ Le queda mejor el rojo que el azul. She looks better in red than in blue.

quedar mirando a alguien de hito a hito ■ mirar a alguien de arriba a abajo ■ recortar a alguien to look someone up and down

quedar momentos duros ■ quedar momentos difíciles to have hard times ahead ■ to have tough times ahead

quedar motivo(s) para creer que... to still have reason to believe that...

quedar para el arrastre **1.** estar acabado to be all washed up ■ to have had it ■ to be finished **2.** estar cansadísimo to be pooped ■ to be beat ■ to be whipped ■ to be knackered **3.** quedar por muerto to be left for dead ➤ El pueblo quedó para el arrastre después del terremoto. The town was left ravaged after the earthquake.

quedar partido ■ quedar partido en trozos to break apart ■ to break into pieces ➤ El avión se desploma sobre una pista lateral, queda partido en tres trozos y envuelto en llamas. The airplane falls onto a parallel runway, breaks into three pieces and bursts into flames.

quedar perfecto ■ salir perfecto to come out perfect ■ to look great ➤ El pastel quedó perfecto. The cake came out perfect. ➤ Quedó perfectamente explicado en el trabajo. It was perfectly explained in his paper.

quedar por demostrar to remain to demonstrated ■ to remain to be proved

quedar por explicar to remain unexplained ■ to have yet to be explained ■ to be yet to be explained ➤ El apagón queda por explicar. The power outage remains unexplained. ■ The power outage has yet to be explained. ■ The power outage is yet to be explained.

quedar por ver ■ (aún) estar por ver to still have to see something ■ not to have seen something yet ➤ Los museos quedan por ver. We still have to see the museums. ■ We haven't seen the museums yet.

quedar por verse ■ quedarse por ver ■ estar por verse to remain to be seen ➤ Eso queda por verse. ■ Eso está por verse. That remains to be seen.

quedar primero *(en la puntuación)* ■ quedar el primero to come in first ➤ Boca Juniors quedó primero. ■ Boca Juniors quedó el primero. Boca Juniors came in first.

quedar privado de juicio ■ quedar privado de razón to lose one's reason

quedar privado de razón ■ quedar privado de juicio to lose one's reason

quedar prohibido terminantemente ■ estar prohibido terminantemente to be strictly prohibited ➤ Queda prohibido terminantemente permanecer junto al borde del andén. It is strictly prohibited to stand at the edge of the platform.

quedar que ni pintado a alguien to not want to see someone ever again

quedar sacudido a los cimientos to be shaken to one's foundations ■ to be shaken to its foundations

quedar sin aliento ■ dejar a alguien sin aliento **1.** to be out of breath **2.** to to be breathless ➤ Me quedé sin aliento después de subir corriendo seis plantas de escaleras. I was out of breath after running up six flights of stairs. ➤ Quedamos sin aliento al ver la vista desde Pikes Peak. ■ Nos dejó sin aliento la vista de Pikes Peak. The view from Pikes Peak left us breathless.

quedar sin castigo to go unpunished ➤ Un informe de la ONU revela que el 98% de los delitos quedan sin castigo en ese país. A UN report reveals 98% of crimes go unpunished in that country.

quedar sin hacer to be left undone ■ to remain undone

quedar sin realizar **1.** quedar sin llevarse a cabo never to be carried out **2.** *(sueño)* not to come true ■ not to be realized

quedar sólo un mes para (for there) to be only a month left until ■ to be only a month until

quedar sólo una semana hasta que to be only a week until

quedar suelto ■ aflojarse to come loose ➤ Quedó suelto. ■ Se aflojó. It came loose.

quedar sumido en el caos to be plunged into chaos

quedar tendido to be stretched out ➤ El gato quedó tendido en la alfombra. The cat was stretched out on the rug.

quedar varado **1.** quedar encallado to run aground **2.** estar en dique seco to be in drydock **3.** *(en todos los contextos)* quedar tirado to be stranded

quedar zanjado **1.** quedar cerrado (el tema, caso) to be settled **2.** quedar sin empleo to be terminated ➤ Quedó zanjado el tema. The matter was settled. ➤ Los obreros quedaron zanjados sin pago alguno. The workers were terminated without being paid.

quedaré como un idiota I'll look like an idiot ■ you'll make me look like an idiot

quedarle bien **1.** irle bien ■ sentarle bien ■ resultarle bien to look good on someone ■ to be (very) becoming to someone ➤ Ese vestido le queda muy bien. *(a usted)* That dress is very becoming to you. ▪ That dress looks good on you. ▪ *(a ella)* That dress is very becoming to her. ▪ That dress looks good on her.

quedarle caña to have energy left ▪ to have some steam left ▪ not to have run out of steam yet

quedarle corto a alguien to be too short (on someone) ➤ Me quedaron cortos los pantolones. The pants are too short (on me).

quedarle de pasada ▪ pillarle de paso to be on your way ▪ to be along your route ▪ to be along your path ➤ ¿Podrías pasar por el correo y mandarme esto? Te queda de pasada. Would you stop by the post office and mail this for me? It's on your way.

quedarle de pena to look awful on someone ▪ to look terrible on someone ▪ to look dreadful on someone ➤ Ese sombrero le queda de pena. That hat looks awful on her. ▪ That hat looks terrible on her. ▪ That hat looks dreadful on her.

quedarle dos telediarios *(Esp., coloquial)* to be on one's last legs ▪ not to have much time left ➤ Le quedan dos telediarios. **1.** *(él)* He's on his last legs. **2.** *(ella)* She's on her last legs.

quedarle grande ▪ no estar a la altura de la situación to be out of one's depth ➤ En el trabajo todo le queda grande. ▪ Le queda todo grande en el trabajo. *(a él)* He's out of his depth in the job. ▪ *(a ella)* She's out of her depth in the job.

quedarle grande la ropa (for) clothes to be too big ➤ Me queda todo un poco grande. All the clothes I've tried on are a (little) bit too big (for me). ▪ Everything I've tried on is a (little) bit too big (for me).

quedarle mucho camino ▪ faltar mucho camino to have a long way to go ➤ Nos queda mucho camino. We have a long way to go. ▪ We still have a long way to go.

quedarle muchos años to have many years left ➤ *(médico a paciente)* Le quedan muchos años. You have many (good) years left.

quedarle muy agradecido por sus atenciones to appreciate all one's attention ▪ to appreciate all the things one has done (for one) ▪ to appreciate everything one has done (for one) ➤ Le quedo muy agradecido por sus atenciones. **1.** *(a él)* I really appreciate all the things he has done for me. **2.** *(a ella)* I really appreciate all the things she has done for me. **3.** *(a usted)* I really appreciate all the things you have done for me.

quedarle muy reconocido(-a) por su ayuda to appreciate one's help ➤ Te quedo muy reconocido por su ayuda. I really appreciate your help.

quedarle pequeño 1. quedarle chico to be too small for one **2.** *(comida, etc.)* no ser suficiente para uno not to be enough for one **3.** *(niños)* to outgrow one's clothes ▪ *(adultos)* to get too fat for one's clothes

quedarle pequeña la ropa to outgrow clothes ➤ Este abrigo me ha quedado pequeño. I've outgrown this coat.

quedarle poco tiempo not to have much time left ▪ to have little time left ➤ Nos queda poco tiempo. We don't have much time left. ▪ We have little time left.

quedarle por to still have to ➤ Nos queda por comprar el vino para la fiesta. We still have to buy the wine for the party.

quedarle por ver to have yet to see ▪ to still have to see ➤ Nos quedan por ver los museos. We have yet to see the museums. ▪ We still have to see the museums.

quedarle *x* años hasta que... to have *x* years left until...

quedarse a dos velas to be broke

quedarse a la derecha ▪ hacerse a la derecha **1.** to bear right ▪ to move over to the right ▪ to get over to the right **2.** tomar la bifurcación a la derecha to bear right (at the fork) ▪ to take the right fork ➤ *(tú)* Quédate a la derecha. ▪ Hazte a la derecha. ▪ *(usted)* Quédese (usted) a la derecha. ▪ Hágase (usted) a la derecha. Bear right. ▪ Move over to the right. ▪ Get over to the right. ➤ Quédate a la derecha en la bifurcación. ▪ Hazte a la derecha en la bifurcación. ▪ Toma la bifurcación a la derecha. Bear right at the fork. ▪ Take the right fork.

quedarse a la izquierda ▪ hacerse a la izquierda **1.** to bear left ▪ to move over to the left ▪ to get over to the left **2.** tomar la bifurcación a la izquierda to bear left (at the fork) ▪ to take the left fork ➤ *(tú)* Quédate a la izquierda. ▪ Hazte a la izquierda. ▪ *(usted)* Quédese (usted) a la izquierda. ▪ Hágase (usted) a la izquierda. Bear left. ▪ Move over to the left. ▪ Get over to the left. ➤ Quédate a la izquierda en la bifurcación. ▪ Hazte a la izquierda en la bifurcación. ▪ Toma la bifurcación a la izquierda. Bear left at the fork. ▪ Take the left fork.

quedarse a (la) mitad del camino 1. to be halfway finished ▪ to be halfway done **2.** to be halfway to a place ➤ Me quedo a (la) mitad del camino. I'm halfway done. ➤ Nos quedamos a (la) mitad de camino. We're halfway there.

quedarse a la providencia de Dios to be up to the will of Providence ▪ to be left to the will of Providence

quedarse a medias to get (only) halfway ▪ to make it only halfway ▪ to run out of steam halfway (through)

quedarse a medio camino to be halfway

quedarse a oscuras to remain in the dark

quedarse a piñón fijo 1. ser intransigente to remain intransigent **2.** ser cabeza dura to be impervious to reason **3.** tener una laguna mental to have a mental block

quedarse a verlos venir to wait for them to get here ▪ to wait for them to arrive

quedarse absorto(-a) con algo ▪ quedarse absorto(-a) en algo ▪ estar absorto(-a) en algo ▪ quedarse embobado en algo ▪ quedarse embobado con algo to be absorbed in something ▪ to be engrossed in something ▪ to be fascinated by something ➤ Me quedé absorto con la conferencia de ayer. I was absorbed in yesterday's lecture. ▪ I was engrossed in yesterday's lecture. ▪ I was fascinated by yesterday's lecture.

quedarse afónico ▪ quedarse sin voz ▪ tener la voz tomada to lose one's voice ▪ to get hoarse ▪ to become hoarse ▪ to be hoarse

quedarse al descubierto ▪ quedarse sin protección to be left exposed ▪ to be left unprotected

quedarse algo para sus adentros ▪ quedarse algo para sí (mismo) ▪ guardarse algo para sí (mismo) to keep something to oneself ▪ not to tell anyone something

quedarse alguien sin habla to be left speechless ▪ to remain speechless

quedarse apaciblemente dormido(-a) to fall peacefully asleep

quedarse atónito al descubrir que... ▪ estar atónito al descubrir que... to be astonished to discover that...

quedarse atónito(-a) ante ▪ quedarse estupefacto(-a) ante ▪ quedarse patitieso ante ▪ estar atónito ante ▪ estar estupefacto ante ▪ estar patitieso(-a) ante to be astonished at

quedarse atónito(-a) de que... ▪ quedarse patitieso(-a) de que... to be astonished that... ➤ Me quedé atónito de que tomara el carro familiar para salir a pasear. ▪ *(Esp.)* Me quedé atónito de que cogiera el coche familiar para ir a dar una vuelta. I was astonished that he would take the family car and go joy riding. ➤ Se quedó atónito de que le subieran el sueldo después de un mes trabajando. He was astonished that they gave him a raise after one month on the job.

quedarse atrás ▪ quedarse rezagado to get behind ▪ to fall behind ▪ to lag behind ➤ *(reportero tomando notas de lo que dice un entrevistado)* Lo siento, me he quedado algo atrás. ▪ Lo siento, me he quedado algo rezagado. I'm sorry, I got behind you a little bit.

quedarse bien parado to be well-off

quedarse bizco(-a) 1. to be cross-eyed **2.** quedarse pasmado to be at a loss for words

quedarse blanco(-a) como la cal ▪ quedarse blanco(-a) como la cera ▪ quedarse pálido(-a) ▪ (em)palidecer (for) one's face to go white ▪ to turn white as a sheet ➤ Cuando supo la noticia, se quedó pálida. ▪ Cuando supo la noticia, se quedó blanca como la cal. ▪ Cuando supo la noticia, empalideció. When she heard the news, her face went white. ▪ When she heard the news, she turned white as a sheet.

quedarse boquiabierto(-a) ante algo ▪ quedarse boquiabierto(-a) con algo ▪ estar boquiabierto ante algo (for) one's jaw to drop ▪ to be flabbergasted at something ▪ *(culto)* to be agape ➤ Me quedé boquiabierto ante la noticia. My jaw dropped when I heard the news. ▪ I was flabbergasted at the news. ▪ I was agape when I heard the news.

quedarse boquiabierto(-a) por algo to be flabbergasted by something ▪ (for) one's jaw to drop because of something ➤ Me quedé boquiabierto por la noticia. I was flabbergasted by the news. ▪ My jaw dropped when I heard the news.

quedarse calvo(-a) ▪ quedarse pelado(-a) ▪ quedarse pelón to go bald

quedarse chafado(-a) 1. *(emocionalmente)* to be thrown for a loop ▪ to be crushed 2. *(enfermedad)* to have a lot taken out of one ➤ Me quedé chafado. It threw me for a loop. ➤ Mis accesos de bronquitis me han chafado. My bouts with bronchitis have taken a lot out of me.

quedarse ciego(-a) to go blind

quedarse colgado to get hung up ▪ to hang up something ▪ to hang something up ➤ La computadora se quedó colgada. Tal vez tengamos que reiniciarla. The computer has gotten hung up. We might have to restart it. ▪ Something has hung the computer up. We might have to restart it. ▪ Something has hung up the computer. We might have to restart it.

quedarse como quien ve visiones to be left seeing stars

quedarse como un pasmarote ▪ quedarse como un tarado to stand there like an idiot

quedarse como un témpano to be frozen stiff ▪ to be chilled to the bone ▪ to be chilled to the quick

quedarse como un tronco ▪ dormir como un tronco to sleep like a log

quedarse como una pasa to be wrinkled

quedarse compuesta y sin novio ▪ estar compuesta y sin novio to be a happily single woman

quedarse con to have ▪ to keep ▪ to end up with ➤ Puedes quedarte con el periódico. You can have the newspaper. ▪ You can keep the newspaper. ➤ *(tú)* Quédate con el cambio. ▪ *(usted)* Quédese con el cambio. Keep the change.

quedarse con alguien to stay with someone ➤ Me quedé con amigos en San Martín de los Andes. I stayed with friends in San Martín de los Andes.

quedarse con el culo en el aire *(soez)* to be left with one's ass uncovered ▪ to be exposed

quedarse con el día y la noche ▪ quedarse en la calle ▪ quedarse sin un mango ▪ quedarse sin un peso ▪ quedarse partido por la mitad to be left penniless

quedarse con el espectáculo ▪ meterse el espectáculo en el bolsillo to steal the show ➤ Gracias al sorteo, el concursante menos conocido consiguió la primera pregunta, y básicamente se quedó con el espectáculo. By the luck of the draw, the little-known candidate got the first question, and she basically stole the show.

quedarse con la boca abierta to be left speechless

quedarse con la copla to get the idea

quedarse con la mente en blanco ▪ quedarse en blanco to draw a blank

quedarse con la sangre en el ojo *(Arg.)* ▪ tener sed de venganza ▪ tener ganas de vengarse to thirst for revenge ▪ to lust for revenge ▪ to burn with the desire for revenge ▪ to burn for revenge

quedarse con las ganas to not have it out of one's system ➤ Me quedé con las ganas de ir a Disneyland. I haven't gotten going to Disneyland out of my system.

quedarse con las manos cruzadas ▪ quedarse con los brazos cruzados just to stand there (and do nothing)

quedarse (con la mente) en blanco ▪ quedarse en albis to draw a blank ▪ (for) one's mind to go blank

quedarse con la vena ▪ guardar rencor to harbor resentment ▪ to hold a grudge ▪ to bear a grudge ▪ to nurse a grudge

quedarse con los brazos cruzados ▪ quedarse con las manos cruzadas just to stand there (doing nothing)

quedarse con todos los demás to keep the rest

quedarse con una buena impresión de alguien to come away with a good impression of someone

quedarse cortado con to be stunned by

quedarse corto 1. no ser suficiente to fall short of something ▪ not to be enough 2. subestimar algo to underestimate something ➤ A pesar de mis esfuerzos, me quedé corto. In spite of my efforts I fell short. ▪ My efforts were not enough. ➤ Me quedé corto al comprar vino para la cena. I underestimated when I bought wine for supper.

quedarse en la casa de alguien ▪ alojarse en la casa de alguien ▪ hospedarse en la casa de alguien to stay at someone's house

quedarse de brazos cruzados to stand there and do nothing ▪ to stand by and do nothing ▪ to fiddle while Rome burns

quedarse de hielo por... ▪ quedarse helado(-a) por... to be stunned by...

quedarse de juerga to stay out with friends ➤ Nos quedamos de juerga hasta las cinco de la mañana. We stayed out with our friends until five in the morning.

quedarse de pie to remain standing

quedarse de piedra to be flabbergasted ▪ to be stunned ▪ to be really surprised

quedarse de Rodríguez to be left at home alone while one's parents are away

quedarse de una pieza 1. quedarse helado to be dumbstruck ▪ to be dumbfounded 2. salir ileso to escape injury 3. permanecer intacto to remain intact

quedarse dentro (de la casa) to stay indoors ▪ to stay in

quedarse desconcertado ante ▪ estar desconcertado ante to be baffled by ▪ to be baffled at ➤ Las operadoras extranjeras a veces se quedan desconcertadas ante los listados telefónicos estadounidenses. (The) foreign operators are sometimes baffled by U.S. directory listings.

quedarse doblado(-a) to be pooped out ▪ to be pooped

quedarse dormido(-a) ▪ dormirse ▪ dar una cabezada ▪ dar una cabezadita ▪ echar una cabezada ▪ echar una cabezadita to fall asleep ▪ to doze off ▪ to nod off ➤ Intenta no quedarte dormido después de comer. ▪ Intenta no dar una cabezada después de comer. ▪ Intenta no echar una cabezada después de comer. ▪ Intenta no dar una cabezadita después de comer. ▪ Intenta no echar una cabezadita después de comer. Try not to fall asleep after dinner. ▪ Try not to doze off after dinner. ▪ Try to keep from dozing off after dinner. ▪ Try not to nod off after dinner. ▪ Try to keep from nodding off after dinner.

quedarse dormido(-a) durante to sleep through

quedarse dueño y señor del campo to remain in charge

quedarse embarazada *(Esp.)* ▪ quedar embarazada to get pregnant ▪ to become pregnant

quedarse en albis ▪ quedarse (con la mente) en blanco to draw a blank

quedarse en Babia ▪ estar en Babia to have one's head in the clouds ▪ to be unrealistically idealistic

quedarse en blanco ▪ quedarse con la mente en blanco to draw a blank ➤ Me quedé en blanco. I drew a blank. ▪ My mind went blank.

quedarse en bolas ▪ quedarse sin nada to end up with nothing

quedarse en el acto ▪ morir en el acto to drop dead ▪ to collapse and die ▪ to die instantly

quedarse en el camino not to make it ▪ to be left along the way ▪ not to finish ➤ Me quedé en camino. I didn't make it. ➤ Cuarenta por ciento de los estudiantes de quinto se quedaron en el camino. Forty percent of the senior class didn't graduate.

quedarse en el pellejo to finish on the bell ▪ to make it by a hair

quedarse en el sitio to die on the spot ▪ to die instantly ▪ to die in the place where one is injured

quedarse en la calle to be left out on the street ▪ to be out on the street

quedarse en la luna de Valencia to have one's head in the clouds

quedarse en la puerta de la calle to be left out on the street ➤ Se quedó en la puerta de la calle. He was left out on the street.

quedarse en los huesos to be nothing but skin and bone

quedarse en pelotas to be in the buff ▪ to be nude

quedarse en tierra *(dícese de barcos y aviones)* to stay behind

quedarse en un término medio to be about average ▪ to be statistically average ➤ Los españoles se quedan en un término medio de altura entre todas las poblaciones mundiales, no son los más altos pero tampoco los más bajos. The Spanish are of average height among the peoples of the world, not the tallest but also not the shortest.

quedarse enganchado(-a) a algo to get caught up in something ➤ Carlos se quedó enganchado al libro *Pedro Páramo* de Juan Rulfo. Carlos really got caught up in the book *Pedro Páramo* by Juan Rulfo.

quedarse estancado(-a) en los detalles to get bogged down in details

quedarse estupefacto(-a) ante ■ estar estupefacto(-a) ante ■ quedarse atónito(-a) ante ■ estar atónito(-a) ante to be dumbfounded at ➤ Te habrás quedado estupefacto ante lo que hice. ■ *(L.am.)* Has de estar estupefacto ante lo que hice. You must be dumbfounded at what I did.

quedarse flipado(-a) *(Esp., jerga)* **1.** estar falopeado(-a) to be high on drugs **2.** estar pasmado(-a) to be amazed ■ to be astounded

quedarse frío(-a) to be stunned ■ to be numb

quedarse frito(-a) *(coloquial)* ■ quedar agotado(-a) ■ estar agotado(-a) to be whipped ■ to be beat ■ to be dog tired ■ to be knackered ■ to be exhausted

quedarse fuera de to get left out of ■ to be left out of ➤ La última vez, me quedé fuera de la porra de la oficina. Last time, I got left out of the office (football) pool.

quedarse fuera del sol to stay out of the sun

quedarse hablando con las paredes ■ hablar solo como loco malo to be left hanging ➤ Escuché un clic en el teléfono y me quedé hablando con las paredes. There was a click in the telephone, and I was just left hanging.

quedarse hasta tarde ■ salir hasta tarde to stay out late ➤ Tengo que trabajar mañana así que no puedo quedarme hasta tarde. ■ Tengo que trabajar mañana así que no puedo salir hasta tarde. I have to work tomorrow, so I can't stay out late.

quedarse hecho(-a) una sopa to get drenched ■ to get soaked (to the bone) ■ to be drenched ■ to be soaked (to the bone)

quedarse helado(-a) 1. tener mucho frío to be freezing cold **2.** estar asombrado to be stunned **3.** estar muerto de miedo to be scared stiff

quedarse hierático(-a) to remain impassive

quedarse impresionado con... to be impressed with... ➤ Quedé impresionado con el nuevo auto eléctrico. I was impressed with the new electric car. ➤ Quedamos impresionados con el nuevo recluta. *(presente)* We are impressed with the new recruit. ■ *(pretérito)* We were impressed with the new recruit.

quedarse incomunicado(-a) to be stranded ➤ Nos hemos quedado incomunicados por el tiempo. We've been stranded by the weather. ➤ Nos hemos quedado incomunicados en la nieve. ■ Estamos incomunicados en la nieve. We're stranded in the snow.

quedarse ingresado(-a) de pronóstico reservado ■ quedarse internado(-a) para observación to be admitted for observation ➤ Se quedó ingresado de pronóstico reservado. He was admitted for observation.

quedarse internado(-a) para observación ■ quedarse internado(-a) de prognóstico reservado to be admitted (to the hospital) for observation ➤ Quería saber si se quedó para observaciones. I wanted to know if he was admitted for observation.

quedarse levantado(-a) to stay up

quedarse levantado(-a) hasta las mil quinientas (estudiando) *(especialmente estudiantes)* to stay up until all hours studying

quedarse limpio(-a) de una acusación to be cleared of an allegation

quedarse más blanco(-a) que el papel ■ quedarse más blanco que la pared to have no idea

quedarse más fresco(-a) que una lechuga to be pleased as punch

quedarse medio muerto(-a) to be dead tired ■ to be beat ■ to be whipped ■ to be exhausted

quedarse mirándole a alguien to stare at someone ➤ Luego se me queda mirando. Then he stares at me.

quedarse muy pancho(-a) *(Arg.)* ■ quedarse tan ancho to act as if nothing (has) happened ■ to be oblivious to the situation

quedarse obsoleto to become obsolete

quedarse para vestir santos ■ quedarse soltera to become a spinster ■ to become an old maid

quedarse pasmado(-a) 1. to be awed ■ to be amazed **2.** to be at a loss for words

quedarse parado(-a) sobre sus huellas ■ quedarse parado(-a) en sus huellas to stop dead in one's tracks

quedarse patitieso(-a) ■ quedarse mudo(-a) ■ quedarse atónito(-a) to be speechless ■ to be astonished

quedarse pegado(-a) a la butaca to be glued to one's seat

quedarse pegado(-a) a la superficie to stick to the surface

quedarse pegado(-a) al claxon ■ pegarse al claxon ■ pitar como (un) loco to ride the horn ■ to lean on the horn ■ to honk (the horn) like crazy

quedarse pelado(-a) ■ quedarse calvo(-a) ■ quedarse pelón to go bald

quedarse pelón ■ quedarse pelado(-a) ■ quedarse calvo(-a) to go bald

quedarse pensativo un momento to think about it for a moment ■ to think about it for a second ➤ Se quedó pensativo un momento y luego dijo... He thought about it for a moment and then said...

quedarse pequeño en to not be big enough for ➤ *(titular)* La catedral de la Almudena se quedó pequeña en el funeral. The Almudena Cathedral was not big enough for the funeral.

quedarse perplejo(-a) al... to be perplexed to... ➤ Me quedé perplejo al saber que... I was perplexed to learn that... ■ I was perplexed on learning that... ■ I was perplexed when I found out that...

quedarse planchado(-a) ■ quedarse apesadumbrado(-a) **1.** *(sentido metafórico, positivo o negativo)* to be bowled over ■ to be floored **2.** *(sentido literal)* to be flattened

quedarse plasmado en 1. to be expressed in ■ to be manifested in **2.** to be set forth in **3.** to become a reality in ➤ El realismo mágico de Gabriel García Márquez se queda plasmado en su máxima expresión en *Cien años de soledad*. The magical realism of Gabriel Garcia Marquez reached its height in *One Hundred Years of Solitude*.

quedarse por ver ■ quedar por verse to remain to be seen

quedarse rezagado(-a) ■ quedarse atrás to get behind ■ to fall behind ■ to lag behind ➤ Lo siento, me he quedado algo rezagado. ■ Lo siento, me he quedado algo atrás. I'm sorry, I got behind you a little bit.

quedarse roque to be in deep slumber ■ *(coloquial)* to be zonked (out)

quedarse seco(-a) to be broke

quedarse sin aire to be out of air ➤ Me quedo sin aire. I'm out of air.

quedarse sin algo not to get any of something ■ to go without something ➤ Me quedó sin nieve. I didn't get any ice cream.

quedarse sin aliento to be out of breath ■ to get out of breath ➤ Me quedé sin aliento cuando corrí para agarrar el autobús. I got out of breath when I ran to catch the bus.

quedarse sin blanca 1. estar sin blanca ■ quedarse sin medio ■ quedarse sin un centavo to be broke **2.** irse a la quiebra to go broke

quedarse sin entradas 1. quedarse sin boletos to be sold out (of tickets for an event) **2.** no conseguir entradas to end up without tickets

quedarse sin empleo ■ quedarse sin trabajo to lose one's job

quedarse sin gas 1. *(gasolina, nafta)* to run out of gas ■ to be out of gas **2.** *(tanque de propano utilizado para cocinar)* to be out of (propane) gas

quedarse sin habla to be speechless ■ to be left speechless ■ to be dumbstruck

quedarse sin mercancías ■ quedarse sin mercadería ■ agotar la mercancía to run out of merchandise ■ to run out of stock

quedarse sin moverse to be motionless

quedarse sin nada to lose everything ➤ En el incendio la familia se ha quedado sin nada. The family lost everything in the fire.

quedarse sin palabras ■ faltar palabras to be at a loss for words

quedarse sin saber qué hacer not to know what to do ➤ Me quedé sin saber qué hacer. I didn't know what to do.

quedarse sin trabajo to be out of work ■ to be left jobless

quedarse sin voz to lose one's voice

quedarse solo ■ estar solo del todo to be left all alone ■ to be left alone ➤ Me quedé solo. I was left (all) alone.

quedarse solo haciendo algo to be left alone doing something

quedarse sopa to go out like a light ■ to crash and burn ■ to fall asleep instantly

quedarse sordo(-a) to go deaf ▪ to lose one's hearing ▪ to suffer hearing loss

quedarse sumido en el caos to degenerate into chaos

quedarse tan ancho ▪ estar tan ancho ▪ quedarse tan campante ▪ estar tan campante ▪ quedarse tan tranquilo ▪ estar tan tranquilo ▪ quedarse tan pancho ▪ quedarse muy pancho ▪ estar tan pancho ▪ quedarse tan pimpante ▪ estar tan pimpante ▪ no mover (ni) un músculo de la cara ▪ no movérsele ni un músculo de la cara ▪ *(Esp.)* quedarse tan pichi ▪ estar tan pichi to act as if nothing had happened ▪ to be oblivious to the situation ▪ to go on as if nothing had happened ▪ not to bat an eye ➤ Se quedó tan ancho. ▪ Estaba tan ancho. ▪ No movió (ni) un músculo de la cara. ▪ No se le movió (ni) un músculo de la cara. He acted as if nothing had happened. ▪ He went on as if nothing had happened. ▪ He didn't bat an eye.

quedarse tan campante 1. not to bat an eye 2. not to give a damn

quedarse tan fresco(-a) to be pleased as punch ▪ to be delighted with oneself

quedarse tan pancho(-a) ▪ quedarse muy pancho(-a) ▪ quedarse tan fresco(-a) ▪ quedarse tan tranquilo(-a) 1. to act as if nothing had happened ▪ to go on as if nothing had happened ▪ not to bat an eye 2. to be cool as a cucumber ▪ to be unflappable ➤ James Bond se queda tan pancho bajo presión. ▪ James Bond está tan pancho bajo presión. James Bond is cool as a cucumber under pressure. ▪ James Bond is unflappable under pressure.

quedarse tieso(-a) to not know what to do ▪ to not know where to turn ▪ to be at a loss ➤ Se quedó tieso y no dio una respuesta. He was at a loss to (know how to) respond.

quedarse tieso(-a) para saber lo que hacer ▪ quedarse tieso(-a) para saber qué hacer to be at a loss to know what to do

quedarse tirado(-a) to be stranded ▪ to get stranded ➤ Nos hemos quedado tirados en Carretera Nacional Uno (la de Burgos). We were stranded on the Burgos Highway.

quedarse trabado(-a) to be tongue-tied ▪ to stumble on the words ▪ to stumble over the words

quedarse un poco triste to be a little (bit) down ▪ to be a little (bit) sad ➤ Me he quedado un poco triste. I've been a little bit down.

quedarse viendo las estrellas to see stars

quedársele mirando a alguien to keep staring at someone ➤ Luego se me queda mirando y dice algo. Then he keeps staring at me and says something.

quedársele pequeñas las ropas to outgrow one's clothes

quedárselo para sí to keep it to oneself

quédate a mi lado stay at my side ▪ stay beside me

quédate con el vuelto *(L.am.)* ▪ ¡quédate con la vuelta! ▪ ¡quédate con el cambio! keep the change!

¡**quédate con la vuelta!** *(Esp.)* ▪ ¡quédate con el vuelto! ▪ ¡quédate con el cambio! keep the change!

¿**quedé en llamarte?** ▪ ¿habíamos quedado que yo te llamaba? was I supposed to call you?

quedo a la espera de noticias suyas *(despedida de carta comercial)* ▪ esperando recibir noticias suyas I look forward to hearing from you

quejarse airadamente to complain angrily

¡**quejica!** ▪ ¡llorica! ▪ ¡llorón! crybaby!

quemaduras en primer grado first-degree burns

quemar a alguien en la hoguera to burn someone at the stake

quemar etapas to try to be older than one's age

quemarle a uno sólo de pensarlo *(Esp., leísmo)* ▪ quemarlo a uno sólo de pensarlo to burn one up just thinking about it ▪ to burn one up just to think about it

quemarlo a uno sólo de pensarlo to burn one up just thinking about it ▪ to burn one up just to think about it ➤ Me quema sólo de pensar lo que ha pasado. It burns me up just thinking about it. ▪ It burns me up just to think about it. ➤ Me quema sólo de pensar que haya podido hacerlo. It burns me up just to think that he could have done it.

quemarse a lo bonzo ▪ prenderse fuego a lo bonzo to set oneself on fire

quemarse las cejas to burn the midnight oil

querellarse contra alguien por algo to file suit (in court) against someone for something ▪ to file a court suit against someone ▪ to bring an action (in court) against someone for something

queremos que vengáis a cenar *(Esp.)* ▪ queremos que (ustedes) vengan a cenar we want you (all) to come over for supper

queremos que vengas a cenar we want you to come over for supper

querer algo de vuelta to want something back (again) ➤ *(Mark Twain)* Un banquero es un tipo que te presta su paraguas cuando el sol brilla, y lo quiere de vuelta en el mismo minuto en que empieza a llover. A banker is a fellow who lends you his umbrella when the sun is shining and wants it back again the minute it starts to rain.

querer comerse el mundo to be mad at the whole world

querer decir to mean ➤ ¿Qué quieres decir? What do you mean? ➤ Quiero decir que... I mean that...

querer decir con eso (que...) to mean by that (that...) ➤ ¿Qué quieres decir con eso? What do you mean by that? ➤ Quiero decir con eso que... By that I mean that...

querer el oro y el moro to want everything

querer es poder ▪ donde hay voluntad hay un camino where there's a will there's a way

querer fiesta to want to party

querer llegar y besar el santo to want to everything all at once

querer llevárselos to want custody (of the children) ➤ En el trámite de divorcio la esposa quiere llevárselos (a los hijos). In the divorce proceeding, the wife wants custody (of the children).

querer salir corriendo to want to run the other way ➤ Cuando vi la cocina después de la fiesta, quise salir corriendo. When I saw the kitchen after the party, I just wanted to run the other way.

querer ser la novia en una boda y el muerto en un entierro to want to be the center of attention

querer ser más católico(-a) que el Papa to try to be more Catholic than the Pope ▪ to be holier than thou

quererle a alguien to love someone

quererse como dos tortolitos to be like two peas in a pod ▪ to be like two lovebirds

queso para untar cheese spread ▪ spreadable cheese

el **quid de la cuestión** the heart of the matter ▪ (at) the heart of the issue

quien a hierro mata, a hierro muere he who lives by the sword dies by the sword ▪ he who lives by the sword dies by it

quien busca halla ▪ quien busca encuentra seek and ye shall find ▪ seek and you will find

quien calla ortorga ▪ callar es otorgar silence implies consent

quien canta, sus males espanta he who sings scares his woes away

¿**quién cree que es?** 1. *(él)* who does he think he is? 2. *(ella)* who does she think she is?

¿**quién da más?** ▪ ¿quién puja más alto? ▪ ¿alguien ofrece más? do I hear *x*? ➤ ¿Quien da más? ¿Nadie? Do I hear... ➤ ¿Quién da cincuenta? ¿Nadie? Do I hear fifty? Anyone?

¿**quién engaña a quien?** ▪ de pillo a pillo entre dos timadores who do you think you're fooling?

¿**quién es el hombre ese?** who is that man?

quien está a las duras, está a las maduras adversity makes the person

quien esté libre de pecado, que tire la primera piedra the one who is free of sin can cast the first stone ▪ people who live in glass houses shouldn't throw stones

quien evita la ocasión, evita el peligro discretion is the better part of valor

¿**quién excepto...?** ▪ ¿quién sino...? ▪ ¿quién salvo...? who but...? ➤ ¿Quién excepto Shakespeare pudo haberlo escrito? Who but Shakespeare could have written it?

¿**quién ha sido?** who was it?

quien hace mal espere otro tal what goes around comes around ▪ you reap what you sew

¿**quién hubiera pensado que...?** ▪ ¿quién hubiese pensado que...? who would have thought that...?

¿**quién iba a comprenderte?** who could possibly understand you?

quien la sigue, la consigue persistence pays off

¿quién llegó primero? who got here first?

¡quién lo dijera! who would have said...?

¡quien lo diría! who would have said...?

¿quién lo habrá escrito? who could have written it?

¿quién manda aquí? who's in charge here?

¿quién marcó? who scored?

¿quién me llamará? who could be calling me? ▪ who could that be?

quien menos te lo esperas the person you least expect ▪ the person of whom you least expect it

quien mucho abarca, poco aprieta 1. he who takes on too much, spreads himself too thin 2. aprendiz de mucho, maestro de nada jack of all trades and master of none ▪ he who tries to become expert in all fields, masters none

¿quién no? 1. who doesn't? 2. who wouldn't?

quien no se arriesga, no pasa la mar ▪ quien nada arriesga, nada gana nothing ventured, nothing gained

¡quién pudiera patinar sobre hielo así! what I wouldn't give to ice skate like that!

¡quién pudiera tocar el piano así! what I wouldn't give to play the piano like that!

¿quién puede culparle? 1. *(a él)* who can blame him? 2. *(a ella) who can blame her?* 3. *(a usted)* who can blame you?

¿quien puede culparte? who can blame you?

¿quién puja más alto? ▪ ¿quién da más? ▪ ¿alguien ofrece más? do I hear *x*? ➤ ¿Quien puja más? ¿Nadie? Do I hear...? Anyone? ➤ ¿Quién puja cincuenta? ¿Nadie? Do I hear fifty? Anyone?

quien quiera... ▪ si alguien quiere... whoever might want to... ▪ if anyone wants to... ➤ Quien quiera hacer una pregunta, que la haga ahora, porque no se permiten preguntas durante el examen. ▪ Si alguien quiere hacer una pregunta, que la haga ahora, porque no se permiten preguntas durante el examen. Whoever might want to ask a question, do so now, because no questions are permitted during the examination. ▪ If anyone wants to ask a question, this is the time to ask it because no questions are permitted during the examination.

quien ríe el último, ríe mejor ▪ él que ríe último ríe mejor ▪ reirá mejor el que ría último he who laughs last laughs best

quien rompe, paga you break it, you've bought it

¿quién sale en la película? ▪ ¿quién trabaja en la película? who's in the movie?

¿quién salvo...? ▪ ¿quién sino...? ▪ ¿quién excepto...? who but...? ➤ ¿Quién salvo Shakespeare pudo haberlo escrito? Who but Shakespeare could have written it?

¿quién se lo dice? who's going to tell him? ▪ who wants to tell him?

¡quién se lo iba a imaginar! who would have thought it? ▪ who would have believed it?

quien se quiere morir se muere it's a self-fulfilling prophecy

¿quién se va por ahí? *(arcaico)* ▪ ¿quién vive? who's there?

¿quién seguirá recordando todavía? who can forget? ▪ who still remembers?

¿quién será? who could it be? ▪ who could that be? ▪ who *is* it? ➤ ¿Quién será? ¿Who could be? ▪ Who *is* it? ➤ Pues, si no es él, ¿quién será? Well, if he's not the one, who *is* it then? ▪ Well, if he's not the one, who could it be?

¿quién será ese? who could that be? ▪ who is that?

quien siembra, cosecha you reap what you sew ▪ what goes around comes around

¿quién sigue? ▪ ¿a quién le toca? ▪ ¿quién va? who's next?

¿quién sino...? ▪ ¿quién salvo...? ▪ ¿quién excepto...? who but...? ➤ ¿Quién sino Shakespeare pudo haberlo escrito? Who but Shakespeare could have written it?

¿quién te da la clase de álgebra? who do you have for algebra?

¿quién te ha dado permiso para...? who gave you permission to...?

¿quién te ha dado vela en este entierro? who asked *you*? ▪ what business is it of *yours*?

¡quién te ha visto y quién te ve! you've come a long way, baby

¿quién te lo ha contado? who told you?

¿quién te lo prohíbe? who's going to stop you?

quien tiene boca, se equivoca we all make mistakes ▪ nobody's perfect

quien tiene el tejado de vidrio no tire piedras al de su vecino people who live in glass houses shouldn't throw stones

¿quién trabaja en la película? ▪ ¿quién sale en la película? who's in the movie?

¿quién va? 1. ¿a quién le toca? whose turn is it? 2. ¿quién es? ▪ ¿quién vive? who is it? ▪ who's there? ▪ who goes there? ▪ who is that? ▪ who's that?

¡quién va a ser! who do you *think*!?

¿quién viene? who is that? ▪ who's that? ▪ who is coming? ▪ who's coming?

quienes me rodean the people around me ➤ Mi sueño es ser feliz y hacer felices a quienes me rodean. My dream is to be happy and to make the people around me happy.

quienquiera que haya estado whoever has been ➤ Quienquiera que haya estado en Nueva York o México, D.F., queda impresionado por la vastedad de ambas ciudades. Whoever has been to New York or Mexico City has been impressed by the vastness of the two cities.

quienquiera que haya hecho esto whoever did this ▪ whoever has done this

quienquiera que haya sido whoever it was ➤ No sabemos quién ha compuesto esta pieza, pero quienquiera que haya sido tiene un talento desbordante. We don't who composed this piece, but whoever it was was a prodigious talent.

quienquiera que haya sido el que whoever it was who ➤ Quienquiera que haya sido la que empezó el movimiento sufragista en Europa... Whoever it was who started the (women's) suffrage movement in Europe...

quienquiera que se acerque anyone who even comes close ➤ Quienquiera que se acerque a este castillo recibirá una flecha que atraviese su corazón. Anyone who even comes close to this castle is going to get an arrow through the heart. ▪ Anyone who gets anywhere near this castle is going to get an arrow through the heart.

quiera Dios ▪ Dios mediante ▪ primero Dios God willing

quiera o no 1. *(yo)* whether I want to or not 2. *(él)* whether he wants to or not 3. *(ella)* whether she wants to or not

quieras o no whether you want to or not

quieras que no even though you wish it weren't ▪ even though you want the opposite ➤ Quieras que no, debes reconocer que es posible. Even though you wish it weren't, you have to realize that it's possible.

quiere que 1. (it) has it that 2. *(él)* he wants (for) it to 3. *(ella)* she wants for it to ➤ Su versión quiere que... His versión has it that...

¿quiere tener la bondad de...? would you please...? ▪ *(más culto)* would you kindly...?

¿quieres algo especial para tener? do you want me to get you something special?

¡¿quieres dejar?! would you stop that?!

¿quieres probarlo? ▪ ¿quieres un poco? ▪ ¿te apetece un trozo? ▪ ¿te gustaría un pedazo? want a bite? ▪ want a (little) piece?

¿quieres provocarme? are you trying to provoke me?

¿quieres que...? would you like (for) me to...? ➤ ¿Quieres que (yo) te llame? Would you like (for) me to call you?

¿quieres que me quite? do you need to me to move?

¿quieres que te lleve? do you want a ride? ▪ would you like a ride ▪ want a ride?

¿quieres un poco? ▪ ¿quieres probarlo? ▪ ¿te apetece un trozo? want a bite? ▪ want a (little) piece? ▪ would you like some?

quiero atreverme ▪ me animo I want to give it a shot ▪ I want to give it a go ▪ I want to give it a try ▪ I want to give it a whirl

quiero decir I mean ▪ what I mean is ▪ what I'm trying to say is

quiero decir con estas palabras que... ▪ con eso quiero decir que... by that I mean (that)...

quiero decir que... I mean that... ▪ what I'm trying to say is that...

quiero hablar contigo a solas I want to talk to you alone ▪ I want to talk with you ▪ I want to speak with you alone ▪ I want to speak to you alone

quiero pensar que... I'd like to think that...

quiero por tanto so I want ➤ Quiero, por tanto, enviar una nota por mail a todo el mundo comunicando mi nueva dirección. So I want to send everyone an E-mail with my new address.

quiero que vengáis a cenar *(Esp.)* ▪ quiero que vengan a cenar I want you (all) to come over for supper

quiero recordar 1. I'm trying to remember **2.** I want to remember

ser un **quiero y no puedo** to be pie in the sky

quinta columna fifth column

quinta esencia quintessence

quinto pino: ir a parar al ~ ▪ ir a parar al medio de la nada to end up in the middle of nowhere

quise haber hecho algo I wished I had done something

quise hacerlo I wanted to do it

quisiera haber podido I wish I could have

quisiera haber podido ir I wish I could have gone

quisiera poder I wish I could

quisiera poder ir I wish I could go

quisquilloso(-a): estar (un poco) ~ to be picky ▪ to be finicky ▪ to be fussy ▪ to be overly fastidious

¡quita de allá! get out of the way!

¡quita tus pezuñas! ▪ ¡quita tus zarpas de...! ▪ ¡saca las manos (de aquí)! ▪ ¡saca tus pezuñas! back off!

¡quita tus zarpas de...! keep your hands off... ▪ keep your mitts off...

quita y pon: de ~ ▪ de lava y pon wash and wear

quitar a alguien de la boca una cosa to take the words right out of someone's mouth ➤ Me lo quitaste de la boca. You took the words right out of my mouth.

quitar a alguien de la cabeza alguna cosa to get a notion out of someone's head

quitar a alguien la capa to expose someone

quitar algo de encima ▪ acabar algo ▪ concluir algo de una vez (por todas) ▪ hacer algo para salir de eso to get something over with ➤ Quitémonos esto de encima de una vez por todas. ▪ Concluyamos esto de una vez (por todas). Let's get it over with once and for all.

quitar algo soplando ▪ volarle algo to blow something off of something ➤ El viento le quitó el sombrero al muñeco de nieve. ▪ El viento le voló el sombrero al muñeco de nieve. The wind blew the snowman's hat off.

quitar el árbol de Navidad ▪ desmontar el árbol de Navidad to take down the Christmas tree ▪ to take the Christmas tree down ➤ Quitamos el árbol de Navidad después del seis de enero. We took down the Christmas tree after January sixth. ▪ We took the Christmas tree down after January sixth. ➤ Lo quitamos después del seis de enero. We took it down after January sixth.

quitar el habla a alguien ▪ dejarle sin habla a alguien **1.** to leave someone speechless **2.** to blank someone out

quitar el hipo a alguien to take someone's hiccups away ▪ *(figurativo)* to take someone's breath away

quitar el polvo ▪ sacar el polvo to dust ➤ Necesito quitar todo de estos estantes y quitarles el polvo. I need to take everything off these shelves and dust them.

quitar el récord a alguien to break the record set by someone

quitar el sueño to keep one awake (at night)

quitar hierro al asunto 1. to downplay a matter ▪ to play down a matter **2.** to avoid the central point of the matter ➤ *(titular)* El gobierno español quita hierro a la amenaza del terrorista Bin Laden. The Spanish government downplays threats by the terrorist Bin Laden. ▪ The Spanish government plays down threats by the terrorist Bin Laden.

quitar la cabezuela al vino ▪ quitar el corcho al vino to remove the cork ▪ *(cava, champaña)* to pop the cork

quitar la mesa ▪ levantar la mesa to clear off the table ▪ to clear the table

quitar la palabra a alguien to interrupt someone

quitar la palabra de la boca to cut someone off

quitar lo superficial 1. remover la superficie ▪ remover lo superficial to strip the surface **2.** deshacerse de lo superfluo to dispense with the superficial

quitar los mocos ▪ hurgarse la nariz to pick one's nose

quitar sospechas sobre algo to quell one's suspicions about something

quitar un embargo ▪ levantar un embargo to lift an embargo ▪ to end an embargo

quitar valor de algo 1. restar(le) valor a algo to downplay the importance of something ▪ to play down the importance of something **2.** devaluar algo to reduce the value of something

quitarle a uno el apetito to spoil one's appetite

quitarle a uno las amígdalas ▪ quitarle a uno las anginas to have one's tonsils out ➤ Me quitaron las amígdalas. ▪ Me quitaron las anginas. I had my tonsils out.

quitarle años (de encima) to take years off (of) one ▪ to make one look years younger

quitarle de la boca a alguien to take the words (right) out of someone's mouth

quitarle de la cabeza a alguien to get the idea out of someone's head

quitarle el pan de la boca a alguien to deprive someone of his or her livelihood to hit someone right in the teeth

quitarle las palabras de la boca to take the words (right) out of someone's mouth

quitarlo de la lengua to take the words right out of one's mouth ➤ Me lo acabas de quitar de la lengua. You took the words right out of my mouth.

quitarse algo de en medio ▪ quitarse algo de encima to get something out of the way ➤ Voy a hacer la compra esta mañana y quitármelo de en medio. ▪ Voy a hacer la compra esta mañana y quitármelo de encima. I'm going to do my grocery shopping this morning and get it out of the way. ➤ De ese modo, me lo quito de en medio. ▪ De ese modo, me lo quito de encima. That way, I'll get it out of the way.

quitarse años to drop year's off one's age ▪ to lie about one's age

quitarse de cuentos to quit rambling on

quitarse de en medio ▪ quitarse del camino ▪ apartarse del camino to get out of the way

quitarse de encima a alguien to get rid of someone

quitarse de encima algo to get rid of something

quitarse de la boca una cosa to take something out of one's mouth

quitarse de la cabeza la idea de que... to get the idea out of one's head that... ▪ to get it out of one's head that...

quitarse de las manos algo to wash one's hands of something

quitarse de una costumbre ▪ alejarse de un hábito ▪ librarse de un hábito to break a habit

quitarse el amargor a la boca to take away the bitter taste

quitarse el sombrero to take off one's hat ▪ to take one's hat off ➤ Se quitó el sombrero. He took off his hat. ▪ He took his hat off. ➤ Se lo quitó. He took it off.

quitarse la borrachera ▪ sacarse la borrachera to sober up

quitarse la careta ▪ quitarse la máscara to take off the mask ▪ to take the mask off ➤ Se quitó la careta. He took off the mask. ▪ He took the mask off. ➤ Se la quitó. He took it off.

quitarse la máscara ▪ quitarse la careta to take off the mask ▪ to take the mask off

quitarse la ropa to take one's clothes off

quitarse un peso de encima to get a weight off one's shoulders

quitársele de la cabeza to get it out of one's head

quitárselo de la boca to take the words right out of someone's mouth ➤ Me lo has quitado de la boca. You took the words right out of my mouth.

quitárselo del pecho to get it off one's chest

quizá(s) fuese provechoso perhaps it would be advantageous ▪ it might be advantageous

quizá(s) ya lo tenga ▪ tal vez ya lo tenga ▪ puede que ya lo tenga I might already have it

racha de empates spate of ties

racha de mala suerte: tener una 1. to have a streak of bad luck **2.** *(deportes, apuestas, etc.)* to have a losing streak

racha de suerte: tener una ~ 1. to have a streak of good luck ▪ to be having a lucky streak **2.** *(deportes, apuestas, etc.)* to be having a winning streak ▪ to be on a winning streak ➤ Tengo una racha de suerte. I'm having a streak of good luck. ▪ I'm having a lucky streak. ▪ I'm having a winning streak.

rachas moderadas ▪ vientos suaves ▪ vientos leves light winds

racimo de uvas bunch of grapes

la **ración de** ▪ porción de serving of ▪ plate of ➤ Me pones una ración de anchoas, por favor. I'll have a serving of anchovies, please. ▪ I'll have a plate of anchovies, please.

estar **radicalmente en desacuerdo con alguien sobre algo** ▪ estar radicalmente en desacuerdo con alguien por algo to be in sharp disagreement with someone over something ▪ to disagree sharply with someone over something ▪ to be in sharp disagreement with someone about something ▪ to disagree sharply with someone about something ▪ to be at odds with someone over something ▪ to be odds with someone because of something

radiación (cósmica) de fondo *(astrofísica)* background (cosmic) radiation

radio macuto: oír algo por ~ ▪ oír algo extraoficialmente to hear something through the grapevine ➤ Lo oí por radio macuto. I heard it through the grapevine.

ráfaga de actividad flurry of activity ▪ burst of activity

ráfaga de disparos ▪ ráfaga de tiros burst of gunfire ▪ volley of shots

ráfaga de inspiración burst of inspiration ▪ flash of inspiration

ráfaga de rayos gamma burst of gamma rays

ráfaga de tiros ▪ ráfaga de disparos burst of gunfire

ráfaga de viento ▪ racha gust of wind

raíz cuadrada square root

raíz cúbica cube root

la **ralentización de la economía** slowdown in the economy ▪ slowing down of the economy

ralladura de limón grated lemon peel ▪ grated lemon rind ▪ lemon zest

rallar en un tema to be a broken record ▪ to go and on about a subject

rama de apio stalk of celery ▪ celery stalk

el **ramiquín de salsa** little dish of salsa ▪ ramekin of salsa *(también escrito "ramequin")*

ramita de perejil sprig of parsley ▪ parsley sprig

ramo de flores bouquet of flowers

rampa de lanzamiento launch pad ▪ launching pad

rancio abolengo: una familia de ~ family of ancient lineage ▪ family of aristocratic lineage

rango normal: estar en el ~ to be in the normal range ➤ El médico dijo que su presión sanguínea estaba en el rango normal. The doctor said his blood pressure is in the normal range.

raparle algo a alguien to swipe something from someone

la **rapidez de lectura** reading speed ➤ Tu rapidez de lectura en inglés ha mejorado mucho. Your reading speed in English has improved a lot.

ser **rápido como el viento 1.** trabajar eficazmente to be a fast worker ▪ to work very efficiently ▪ to be efficient **2.** ser listo to be (mentally) quick ▪ to have a quick, clear mind

rápido como un rayo quick as a flash ▪ like a flash

rápido como una flecha like an arrow

rara especie 1. *(literal)* rare species **2.** *(figurativo)* rare breed of ➤ Gabriel García Márquez es una rara especie de cuentista y periodista. Gabriel García Márquez is a rare breed of story teller and journalist.

rara vez ▪ casi nunca hardly ever ▪ rarely ➤ Rara vez voy al cine. I hardly ever go to the movies. ▪ I rarely go to the movies.

rara vez o nunca rarely if ever

ser **raro de cojones** *(subido de tono)* ▪ ser raro de narices to be weird

ser **raro de narices** to be weird

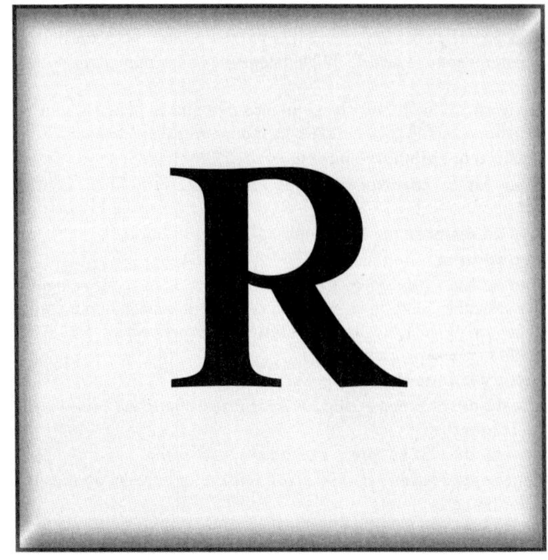

estar **rascándose la barriga** ▪ estar tocándose la barriga to be sitting on one's ass ▪ to be sitting on one's duff

rascarle la espalda a alguien to scratch someone's back ▪ to give someone a back scratch ➤ Le gusta que le rasquen la espalda. He likes to get his back scratched. ▪ He likes to have his back scratched. ➤ ¿Me rascas la espalda? Would you scratch my back?

rascarse la barriga ▪ tocarse la barriga to sit on one's butt ▪ *(subido de tono)* to sit on one's ass

rascarse la cabeza 1. *(literal y figurativo)* to scratch one's head **2.** *(figurativo)* to be baffled

rasgarse las vestiduras 1. to tear one's clothing ▪ to rend one's garments **2.** *(figurativo)* to get indignant ▪ to get all bent out of shape ➤ Ella vino aquí gritando y rasgándose las vestiduras. She came shouting and all bent out of shape. ➤ Reconoció que había sido él y no se le rasgaron las vestiduras. He acknowledged that it was he himself, and he made no bones about it.

rasgo del comportamiento behavioral trait

rasgos afilados fine features ▪ chiseled features

raso como la palma de la mano *(Sancho Panza)* completely flat ▪ completely level ▪ completely smooth

rasparse el codo ▪ despellejarse el codo to scrape one's elbow ▪ to skin one's elbow

rasparse la rodilla ▪ despellejarse la rodilla to scrape one's knee ▪ to skin one's knee

rastrear las aguas to dredge a waterway

rastrear los pasos de alguien ▪ controlar los pasos de alguien to trace someone's steps ▪ to track someone's movements

rastrear una llamada to trace a (telephone) call

rastreo de llamadas search of telephone records

rastro de: no encontrar ~ to find no trace of

rastro de pruebas shread of evidence

rastro perdido lost trail

rata de biblioteca bookworm

ratificar que... to confirm that...

ratificar un contrato to ratify a contract

ratificar un tratado to ratify a treaty

ratificarse en la idea to uphold the idea ▪ to reaffirm the idea ▪ *(coloquial)* to second the motion

un **rato largo** a good while ▪ quite a while

ser un **ratón de biblioteca** to be a bookworm ▪ to be a book lover

ratón de un solo agujero, pronto lo pilla el gato don't put all your eggs in one basket

ratos de ocio leisure time

ratos libres ▪ tiempo libre free time

ratos perdidos idle moments

raya de cocaína ■ tiro de cocaína ■ rayote hit of cocaine

raya en un pantalón crease in a pair of pants ➤ La lluvia está estropeando la raya de mi pantalón. The rain is ruining the crease in my pants.

rayar en to border on ➤ El médico dijo que su gripe raya en la neumonía. The doctor said his flu is bordering on pneumonia.

rayar en lo ridículo to border on the ridiculous

rayas en la carretera ■ rayas en la autopista lines on the highway

rayo de esperanza ray of hope ■ glimmer of hope

rayo de luna moonbeam

rayo de luz ■ (el) haz de luz beam of light ➤ Cuando tenía dieciséis años, Einstein se preguntó cómo sería cabalgar en un rayo de luz. When he was sixteen, Einstein wondered what it would be like to ride on a beam of light.

¡**rayos y truenos!** oh, my gosh!

raza de perro breed of dog ➤ ¿Qué raza de perro es? What breed of dog is that?

la **razón de ello es que...** the reason for it is that...

la **razón de estado** raison d'être ■ reason for existence ■ reason for being

la **razón de peso** compelling reason

la **razón de sobra para** reason enough to ■ good reason to ■ sufficient reason to

estar la **razón de su parte** to be in the right ■ to have the best case

la **razón de verdad** ■ la razón verdadera ■ la razón real the real reason

la **razón no quiere fuerza** reason needs no force

razón oculta ■ motivo oculto ■ segunda intención ulterior motive

la **razón para** the reason for

la **razón real** ■ la razón de verdad ■ la verdadera razón the real reason

la **razón social** 1. trade name 2. company name

la **razón verdadera** ■ la verdadera razón ■ la razón de verdad ■ la razón real the real reason

razonamiento convincente ■ argumento convincente convincing argument

razonamiento erróneo faulty reasoning ■ faulty argument

razones para creer: tener ~ ■ tener motivos para creer to have reason to believe

reabastecer de combustible ■ repostar combustible ■ rellenar de combustible to refuel

reacción airada: provocar una ~ to provoke an angry reaction

reacción en cadena chain reaction

reacción retardada delayed reaction

reaccionar ante el estrés to react under stress ■ to deal with stress

reactivación de los incendios resurgence of the fires ■ revival of the fires

reactor atómico atomic reactor

el **reactor de fisión** fission reactor ■ atom smasher

real decreto royal decree

real rollo royal hassle ■ royal pain

un **real tostón** *(titular deportivo)* a royal pain ■ a real drag

realizar los preparativos para to lay the groundwork for

realizar un ataque to carry out an attack ➤ Los bombardeos de represalia fueron realizados el día previo. The reprisal bombings were carried out the day before.

realizar un examen ■ hacer un examen ■ presentar un examen 1. to take a test 2. *(esp. parcial o final)* to take an examination ■ to take an exam

realizar un experimento to conduct an experiment ■ to perform an experiment ■ to do an experiment ■ to carry out an experiment

realizar un llamamiento to make an appeal ■ to issue an appeal

realizar un proyecto de investigación to do a research project

realizar un trabajo impecable to do an excellent job ■ to do an impeccable job

realizar una autopsia ■ practicar una autopsia to perform an autopsy ■ to do an autopsy

realizar una buena acción to do a good deed ■ to do a good turn ➤ Satisfecho por su buena acción realizada... Pleased with himself for having done a good turn...

realizar una comida to hold a meal ■ to hold meals ➤ La comida se realizaba en el refectorio. Meals were held in the refectory (of the monastery).

realizar una entrevista to conduct an interview

realizar una gran tarea to carry out a big project

realizar una intervención 1. to perform surgery 2. to conduct a police raid

realizar una investigación to conduct an investigation ■ to carry out an investigation ➤ Las investigaciones realizadas por Otto Hahn y Lise Meitner condujeron al descubrimiento de la fisión nuclear. The research conducted by Otto Hahn and Lise Meitner led to the discovery of nuclear fission.

realizarle una operación a alguien to perform surgery on someone ■ to perform an operation on someone ➤ Van a realizarle una operación seria en el hombro. They're going to perform major surgery on his shoulder.

realizar una prueba to do a test ■ to perform a test

ser **realmente antipático** ■ ser realmente desagradable to be downright mean

ser **realmente extraño** ■ ser categóricamente extraño to be downright strange ➤ El médico me puso una prueba de fibra óptica muy profunda en las fosas nasales que me hizo sentir categóricamente extraño. The doctor put a fiberoptic probe way up into my nasal passage that felt downright strange.

realmente llegar a alguien to really get to someone ➤ Esa obra teatral realmente me llegó. That play really got to me.

realmente me impresiona I'm really impressed by ■ I'm really impressed at ➤ Realmente me impresiona lo bueno que es tu español. I'm really impressed by how good your Spanish is. ■ I'm really impressed at how good your Spanish is.

realzar el sabor de algo ■ potenciar el sabor de algo ■ aumentar el sabor de algo ■ darle más sabor a algo to enhance the flavor of something ➤ Hacer las verduras a la plancha realza su sabor. ■ Hacer las verduras a la plancha potencia su sabor. ■ Hacer las verduras a la plancha aumenta su sabor. ■ Hacerlos a la plancha da más sabor a los vegetales. Grilling brings out the flavor of the vegetables.

realzar la base enterrada *(p.ej. de la torre de Pisa)* to strengthen the foundation

realzar la figura to enhance the figure

realzar la imagen ■ dar realce a la imagen to enhance the image ■ to enhance one's image

reanimar a alguien to revive someone

reanudar el trabajo después de las vacaciones to go back to work after one's vacation

reanudar la conversación to resume the conversation

reanudarse pruebas nucleares to resume nuclear tests

rebaja fiscal tax cut ➤ *(noticia)* El gobierno alemán aplaza la rebaja fiscal para reconstruir las zonas arrasadas por las riadas. German government delays tax cut (in order) to rebuild flood-torn areas.

rebasados los niveles de ozono high ozone levels ■ high levels of ozone ■ excessive ozone levels ■ excessive levels of ozone ➤ *(titular)* Rebasados los niveles de ozono en Aranjuez, Alcobendas y Fuenlabrada. High levels of ozone in Aranjuez, Alcobendas and Fuenlabrada.

rebajar el precio to lower the price

rebajar las exigencias to relax the requirements

rebajar un plan to scale back a plan

rebajar un requisito to relax a requirement

rebajarse un poco to relax a little

rebasar las expectativas to exceed one's expectations ■ to surpass one's expectations

rebasar un carro en la carretera *(L.am.)* ■ adelantar un coche en la carretera ■ pasar un coche en la carretera to pass a car on the highway ■ to overtake a car on the highway

rebasarlo a alguien en la carretera *(L.am.)* ■ adelantarle a alguien en la carretera ■ pasarle a alguien en la carreterra to pass someone on the highway

rebelarse contra ▪ alzarse en rebelión contra ▪ levantarse en rebelion contra to rebel against ▪ to rise up in rebellion against
rebobinar (una cinta) to rewind (a tape) ➤ Te ovidaste de rebobinar el vídeo. You forgot to rewind the video.
el **reborde alrededor de un cojín** piping around the edge of a cushion
estar **rebotado con alguien** to be put out with someone ▪ to be upset with someone
estar **rebotado por algo** to be upset about something
estar **rebosante de orgullo** ▪ no caber dentro de sí de orgullo ▪ estar derrochando orgullo to be bursting with pride
rebosar dinero ▪ nadar en dinero ▪ nadar en abundancia to be rolling in dough
el **rebote de la bolsa** stock market rebound ▪ rebound of the stock market ▪ rebound in the stock market
rebosar seguridad en sí mismo to exude self-confidence
rebozar el pollo ▪ apanar el pollo ▪ empanar el pollo ▪ empanizar el pollo to coat the chicken with batter ➤ Reboza el pollo y colócalo en una bandeja de Pyrex. Coat the chicken with the batter and place it in a Pyrex dish.
recabar apoyo para to win support for ▪ to garner support for ▪ to gather support for
recabar apoyo contra to win support against ▪ to garner support against ▪ to gather support against
recabar datos sobre algo ▪ recabar información sobre algo to gather information about something
recabar firmas to collect signatures ▪ to get signatures
recabar fondos para to raise funds for
recaer en alguien 1. *(sospechoso)* to fall upon someone **2.** *(premio)* ▪ concedérsele a alguien to be awarded to someone ▪ to go to someone
recaer en una enfermedad ▪ sufrir una recaída to relapse (into an illness) ▪ to suffer a relapse (into an illness)
recalcado de facciones with prominent features
recalcar algo ▪ enfatizar algo ▪ hacer resaltar algo ▪ hacer hincapié en algo to emphasize something ▪ to stress something
recalcar que... ▪ enfatizar que... ▪ hacer resaltar que... to emphasize that...
recapacitar sobre algo to think over something ▪ to think something over ▪ to reflect on something
recapacitar sobre una propuesta to think over a proposal ▪ to reflect on a proposal
recargar las tintas ▪ cargar las tintas ▪ exagerar to stretch the truth ▪ to lay it on (pretty) thick ▪ to exaggerate
recatarse de hacer algo to shy away from doing something
recaudación de fondos collection of funds ▪ collecting of funds ▪ raising of funds ▪ fundraising
recaudar dinero to collect money
recaudar impuestos to collect taxes
recaudar una deuda to recover a debt ▪ to collect on a debt
recelar de algo to be suspicious of something ▪ to distrust something ▪ to mistrust something ➤ *(titular)* El presidente venelozano recela del gobierno español. The Venezuelan president distrusts the Spanish government. ▪ The Venezuelan president mistrusts the Spanish government.
recelar de alguien to be suspicious of someone ▪ to distrust someone ▪ to mistrust someone
recelar que ▪ sospechar que to suspect that
recelos sobre suspicions about ▪ suspicions regarding
receta de antes policies of the past
recetar medicamento to prescribe medication ➤ El médico me ha recetado antibióticos. The doctor prescribed me antibiotics.
rechazar a golpes to beat back
rechazar algo de plano to reject something flatly
rechazar algo tajantemente to reject something categorically ▪ to reject something emphatically ▪ to reject something flatly
rechazar el emplazamiento de diálogo to reject the call for dialogue
rechazar el emplazamiento para dialogar to reject the call to (have a) dialogue
rechazar hacer algo to refuse to do something
rechazar la idea de sí ▪ rechazar la idea sin más ▪ apartar la idea de sí to reject the idea (out of hand) ▪ to dismiss the idea (out of hand) ➤ Rechacé la idea de mí. ▪ Aparté la idea de mí. ▪ I dismissed the idea out of hand.
rechazar la pelota to pass ▪ to decline ▪ to say no
rechazar por to reject on grounds of being ▪ to reject as being ▪ to reject because of
rechazar una invitación to decline an invitation ▪ to turn down an invitation ▪ to turn an invitation down
rechazar una petición to decline a request ▪ to turn down a request ▪ to turn a request down ▪ to deny a request
rechazo mayoritario rejection by the majority
rechazo paterno paternal rejection
rechinar los dientes to grind the teeth
reciba mi más sincero pésame I want to express my deepest sympathy ▪ I want to express my deepest condolences
reciba un cordial saludo *(cierre de una carta)* sincerely yours
recibir a alguien con los brazos abiertos to receive someone with open arms
recibir a alguien en el aeropuerto to meet someone at the airport
recibir algo con escepticismo ▪ acoger algo con escepticismo to greet something with skepticism
recibir algo consternado to greet something with dismay ▪ to greet something with consternation ▪ to react to something with dismay ▪ to react to something with consternation
recibir bien la medida to welcome the measure ➤ *(noticia)* Algunos pasajeros recibieron bien la medida, otros no tanto. Some passengers welcomed the measure, but others did not.
recibir clases ▪ tomar clases to take classes ➤ Recibo tres clases de español. I'm taking three Spanish classes.
recibir el alta hospitalaria to be released from the hospital ➤ El atleta recibió el alta hospitalaria al mes de su grave accidente. The athlete was released from the hospital a month after his serious accident.
recibir el alta médica to get medical authorization to return to work ▪ to receive medical authorization to go back to work
recibir el impacto de algo to get hit with something ➤ Clinton recibió el impacto de un huevo en Polonia. Clinton got hit with an egg in Poland.
recibir el pago de atrasos ▪ recibir los pagos atrasados to receive back pay ▪ to get back pay
recibir el pistoletazo de salida para to get the green light to ▪ to get the go-ahead to
recibir el valor de su dinero get one's money's worth
recibir la baja médica to be granted medical leave
recibir la señal de un transmisor to receive the signal from a transmitter
recibir lo que merece uno to get what one deserves
recibir lo que uno nunca imaginó to get more than one bargained for
recibir más (de lo) que uno quiere to get more than one bargained for ➤ Cuando compraron el apartamento, recibieron más que quisieron. Había un gravamen desconocido en la propiedad. When they bought the condo(minium), they got more than they bargained for. There was a lien on the property. ▪ When they bought the condo(minium), they got more than they bargained for. There was an encumbrance on the property.
recibir respuesta ▪ contestarle to get an answer ➤ No he recibido respuesta. ▪ No me han contestado. I haven't gotten an answer. ▪ They haven't answered me. ➤ No he podido recibir respuesta. I haven't been able to get an answer.
recibir un encargo del suministador to receive an order from the supplier
recibir una cornada to be gored ▪ to get gored ➤ El torero recibió una cornada en la pierna. The bullfighter was gored in the leg. ▪ The bullfighter got gored in the leg.
recibir una ducha de agua fría to get a wake-up call
recibir una liquidación ▪ recibir un finiquito to receive a severance package ▪ to get a severance package ▪ to be given a severance package
recibir una mano de bofetadas to get slapped around
recibir una paliza to be beaten (up) ▪ to get beaten (up) ▪ to get a beating ▪ to be beat up ▪ to get beat up ➤ Recibió una

paliza. He was beaten (up). ■ He got beaten (up) ■ He was beat up. ■ He got beat up

recibir una tunda *(muebles)* **1.** to be beat(en) up ■ to take a beating **2.** to get a lot of wear (and tear) ■ to take a beating ➤ Cuando estábamos creciendo, el sofá recibía buenas tundas. When we were growing up, the sofa got pretty beat(en) up. ■ When we were growing up, the sofa took quite a beating. ■ When we were growing up, the sofa got quite a beating ■ When we were growing up, the sofa got a lot of wear and tear. ■ When we were growing up, the sofa took a beating.

recién casados newlyweds

¡**recién casados!** just married!

recién llegado newcomer

recién salida: planta ~ ■ retoño plant that has just come up ■ plant that has just sprouted ■ volunteer

recién salido de la imprenta recently released

estar **recién salido del cascarón** to be green behind the ears ■ to be wet behind the ears

recientemente estrenado recently released ■ newly released ■ just released

recinto universitario university campus

recintos feriales fairgrounds

la **reclamación de equipajes** baggage claim

reclamar algo a alguien to demand something from someone

reclamar la inocencia de alguien to claim the innocence of someone ■ to maintain the innocence of someone ■ to declare the innocence of someone

reclamarle para trabajar en algo 1. *(a él)* to get him back to work on something **2.** *(a ella)* to get her back to work on something

reclamo al seguro insurance claim

reclamo de equipaje baggage claim

reclamo (para pájaros) bird call ■ birdcall

reclinar la frente sobre las manos to bury one's head in one's hands

recluir a alguien en un manicomio to commit someone to an asylum

recobrar el aliento ■ recobrar la respiración to catch one's breath

recobrar el ánimo to recover one's spirits

recobrar el conocimiento ■ recobrar el sentido to regain consciousness

recobrar el habla 1. to recover one's voice ■ to recover one's speech **2.** to re-enter the conversation

recobrar el sentido ■ recobrar el conocimiento ■ volver en sí to regain consciousness

recobrar fuerzas: hacerle ~ ■ hacerle cargar las pilas ■ hacerle cobrar fuerzas to recharge one's batteries ➤ Las dos semanas en Acapulco me hicieron recobrar fuerzas. The two weeks in Acapulco recharged my batteries.

recobrar la compostura ■ recuperar el aplomo ■ reponerse to regain one's composure ■ to recover one's composure ■ to pull oneself back together

recobrar la respiración ■ recobrar el aliento to catch one's breath

recobrar la sensación de to recover the sensation in ■ to recover the feeling in ➤ Después del accidente, recobró gradualmente la sensación de su brazo. After the accident, he gradually recovered the feeling in his arm. ■ After the accident he gradually recovered the sensation in his arm.

recobrar el sentido común ■ recuperar la cordura to recover one's sanity ■ to regain one's sanity

recobrarse de una enfermedad ■ restablecerse de una enfermedad ■ reponerse de una enfermedad to recover from an illness

recodo del camino ■ recodo en el camino sharp curve in the road ■ hairpin turn in the road

recodo del río bend in the river

recoger a los peques to get the kids ■ to pick up the kids

recoger a un niño huérfano ■ acoger a un niño huérfano ■ albergar a un niño huérfano to take in an orphan ■ to shelter an orphan

recoger agua to absorb water

recoger bayas to pick berries

recoger el guante to take up the gauntlet

recoger el relevo to take the baton (and run with it) ■ to take over

recoger filtraciones to receive leaked information

recoger firmas ■ recolectar firmas to gather signatures ■ to circulate a petition

recoger la aceituna *(coloquial)* ■ recoger el fruto de su trabajo ■ recoger los frutos de su trabajo to reap the benefits of one's efforts ■ to reap the benefits of one's labors

recoger la casa to straighten up the house

recoger la mesa ■ levantar la mesa to clear the table ■ to clear off the table ■ to clean off the table

recoger la recomendación to incorporate the recommendation ➤ *(titular)* Annan critica la propuesta de resolución de Bush sobre Irak por no recoger sus recomendaciones. Annan criticizes Bush's proposed resolution on Iraq for not incorporating his recommendations.

recoger lo que uno siembra ■ recogerse lo que se siembra to reap what one sows ➤ Recogemos lo que sembramos. We reap what we sow.

recoger los bártulos to gather up one's things

recoger los platos to put away the dishes ➤ Por favor, recoge los platos que están en el escurridor. Please put away the dishes in the drainer.

recoger muestras de un crimen to gather evidence of a crime

recoger sus pertenencias to gather up one's belongings ■ to gather up one's things ■ to pack up one's belongings

recoger velas to back down

recogerlos uno a uno to pick them up one at a time

recogerse lo que se siembra ■ recoger lo que uno siembra to reap what one sows ➤ Se recoge lo que se siembra. You reap what you sow.

recogida: acordar una ~ to schedule a pickup ■ to arrange a pickup ➤ Vamos a acordar una recogida. Let's arrange a pickup.

ser **recolectado a mano** to be hand picked ■ to be picked by hand ■ to be gathered by hand

recolectar a mano to pick by hand ■ to hand pick ■ to gather by hand

recolectar firmas ■ recoger firmas to gather signatures ■ to circulate a petition

recomendar a alguien para un trabajo ■ recomendar a alguien para un puesto de trabajo to recommend someone for a job

recomendar hacer to recommend doing... ■ to recommend that one do... ■ to advise doing ■ to advise that one do... ➤ ¿Qué recomiendan hacer los expertos? What do the experts recommend that we do? ■ What do the experts advise that we do?

reconciliar puntos de vista en conflicto to reconcile conflicting points of view ■ to reconcile differing points of view

reconciliarse con la iglesia to reconcile oneself with the church

reconfortar a alguien to comfort someone ■ to make someone feel better ➤ Una taza de té te reconfortará. A cup of tea will make you feel better.

reconocer a alguien a simple vista to recognize someone right off ■ to recognize someone immediately

reconocérsele como to be recognized as

¿**reconoces haber...?** do you realize that you have...?

reconocimiento de la voz: (el) programa para el ~ voice recognition software

reconocimiento médico medical checkup ■ physical examination ■ medical examination

la **reconstrucción policial** ■ retrato robot police artist's sketch

recordar a alguien ■ acordarse de alguien to remember someone ■ to call someone to mind

recordar a alguien con cariño ■ acordarse de alguien con cariño **1.** to remember someone fondly ■ to remember someone with affection

recordar el pasado to reminisce

recordar que... ■ tener en mente que... ■ tener en cuenta que... to bear in mind that... ■ to keep in mind that... ➤ Recuerda que mañana tienes que madrugar. ■ Ten en mente que tienes que madrugar mañana. ■ Ten en cuenta que tienes que madrugar mañana. Remember, you have to get up early tomorrow. ■ Bear in mind that you have to get up early tomorrow. ■ Keep in mind that you have to get up early tomorrow.

recordarlo es importante it's important to remember it ■ to remember it is important

recordárselo 1. *(a él)* to remind him of it 2. *(a ella)* to remind her of it 3. *(a usted)* to remind you of it

recorrer a pie ■ patearse to go around on foot

recorrer antes de lo programado to run ahead of schedule

recorrer de parte a parte to go from one place to another ■ to walk around

recorrer en una y otra dirección to wander around

recorrer todo el país to travel all over the country

recorrer un largo camino to come a long way ➤ El peregrino recorrió un largo camino, desde Bayona en Francia hasta Santiago de Compostela en España. The pilgrim came a long way, from Bayonne in France to Santiago de Compostela in Spain. ➤ Has recorrido un largo camino, guapita. You've come a long way, baby.

recorrer un sendero to walk a path ■ to walk along a path ■ to walk down a path ■ to walk up a path

recorrerse la ciudad de punta en punta ■ recorrerse la ciudad de cabo a rabo ■ recorrerse la ciudad de un lado a otro to run all over town ■ to go all over town

recorrido aéreo ■ en línea recta air miles ■ as the crow flies ■ in a straight line ➤ Washington está a un recorrido aéreo de doscientos siete millas de Nueva York. ■ Washington está a doscientos siete millas en línea recta de Nueva York. Washington is two hundred and seven air miles from New York. ■ Washington is 207 miles from New York as the crow flies. ■ Washington is 207 miles from New York in a straight line.

recorrido de despegue take-off roll

recorrido del Palacio Real en Madrid tour of the Royal Palace in Madrid

recortar con tijeras to cut out with scissors ■ to clip ➤ Recorte y envíe el cupón a... Cut out the coupon and send it to... ■ Cut out and send the coupon to...

recortar el tipo de interés to cut the interest rate ➤ *(noticia)* EE UU recorta en medio punto el tipo de interés. U.S. cuts interest rate(s) by half a point.

recortar empleos ■ recortar trabajos to cut jobs

recortar los tipos de interés to cut interest rates

el **recorte de empleos** ■ supresión de empleos ■ recorte de puestos de trabajo ■ supresión de puestos de trabajo elmination of jobs ■ *(coloquial)* axing of jobs

el **recorte de empleados** ■ (la) supresión de empleados laying off of employees ■ *(coloquial)* axing of employees

el **recorte de la noticia** newspaper clipping

el **recorte de los tipos de interés** cut in interest rates ■ interest rate cut

el **recorte de plantilla** reduction in the workforce ■ personnel reduction

el **recorte de puestos de trabajo** ■ supresión de puestos de trabajo ■ recorte de empleos ■ supresión de empleos elimination of jobs ■ *(coloquial)* axing of jobs

recorte presupuestario ■ recorte de presupuesto budget cut

estar **recostado en** to be sitting against ➤ Estaba recostado en el tronco. I was sitting against the tree trunk.

recostarse en ■ recostarse sobre to lean on

recovecos del alma depths of the soul

recrear la vista to watch girls ■ to enjoy the "scenery"

recta final final stretch ■ home stretch

recto al norte ■ directamente al north due north

rectifícame si me equivoco ■ corrígeme si me equivoco correct me if I'm wrong

rectificar el punto de sal to get the amount of salt right

rectificar un error ■ corregir un error ■ enderezar una equivocación to correct a mistake

recta final home stretch ■ final stretch ■ last leg

¡recuerde! ■ ¡recordatorio! reminder!

recuerdo de memory of ■ recollection of

recuerdo haber pensado... I remember thinking...

recuerdo imborrable indelible memory

recuerdo nítido vivid recollection ■ vivid memory

recuerdo que te dije I remember telling you

un **recuerdo único** a singular memory

recuéstate y disfruta el espectáculo sit back and enjoy the show

recula un poco ■ retrocede un poco ■ da marcha atrás un poco ■ ve marcha atrás un poco back up a little (bit)

recular con un vehículo to rear-end a vehicle ■ to collide with a vehicle from behind ■ to hit a vehicle from behind

la **recuperación de interés en** revival of interest in

recuperación de la economía ■ recuperación económica economic recovery

recuperación paulatina gradual recovery

recuperar (el) contacto con alguien to get back in touch with someone ■ to reestablish contact with someone ➤ Espero que hayas recuperado contacto con tus amigos. I hope you've gotten back in touch with your friends. ■ I hope you've reestablished contact with your friends.

recuperar cuerpos ■ rescatar cadáveres to recover bodies

recuperar el aliento to catch one's breath ■ to get one's breath (back) ■ to recover one's breath

recuperar el aplomo ■ recobrar la compostura ■ reponerse to recover one's composure ■ to regain one's composure ■ to pull oneself back together

recuperar el control de to regain control of ➤ Los moderados recuperaron el control de la asamblea legislativa. The moderates regained control of the legislature.

recuperar el cuerpo ■ recuperar la postura to sit up

recuperar el dinero to get one's money back

recuperar el documento *(informática)* to retrieve the document ■ to recover the document ➤ ¿Crees que puedes recuperar el documento? Do you think you can retrieve the document?

recuperar el sueño perdido to get caught up on one's sleep ■ to catch up on one's sleep ➤ Este fin de semana recuperé el sueño perdido. I got caught up on my sleep this weekend. ■ I caught up on my sleep this weekend. ➤ He recuperado el sueño (perdido). I've caught up on my sleep. ■ I've gotten caught up on my sleep.

recuperar el terreno perdido to recover lost ground

recuperar el tiempo perdido to make up for lost time ➤ Reemprendió su camino, como queriendo recuperar el tiempo perdido. He got back on the road, as if trying to make up for lost time.

recuperar la conexión to re-establish the connection

recuperar la consciencia ■ volver en sí to regain consciousness

recuperar la cordura ■ recobrar el sentido común to regain one's sanity

recuperar la postura ■ recuperar el cuerpo ■ incorporarse to sit up

recuperar los gastos to recover expenses

recuperar su aspecto habitual to recover one's usual appearance ■ to regain one's usual appearance

recuperar su dinero to get one's money back

recuperar su cuerpo ■ incorporarse ■ aderezarse to sit up

recuperar terreno to regain ground

recuperar un examen to make up an exam(ination) ■ to make up a test

recuperarse de un shock ■ superar un trauma to get over a trauma ■ to recover from a trauma ■ to get over a shock to the system ■ to recover from a shock to the system ■

recuperarse hasta el punto de que to recover to the point of

recurrir a alguien para algo ■ acudir a alguien para algo to turn to someone for something ■ to go to someone for something ➤ No sé a quién recurrir. ■ No sé a quién puedo recurrir. I don't know who to turn to. ➤ I went to my friend to ask him to fill in for me. Recurrí a mi amigo para pedirle que me supliera.

recurrir a expedientes radicales to resort to radical measures ■ to take radical measures

recurrir a la estratagema de ■ recurrir a la táctica de to resort to the stratagem of ■ to resort to the tactic of

recurrir a la fuerza ▪ recurrir a las armas to resort to force ➤ Cuando faltó la diplomacia, el gobierno recurrió a la fuerza. When diplomacy failed, the government resorted to force.

recurrir a la táctica de to resort to the tactic of

recurrir al expediente de to resort to the expedient of

recurrir la condena to appeal the conviction

recurrir la denegación to appeal the denial

recurrir contra... to appeal...

recurrir notarialmente a alguien to file suit against someone

recurrir primero a before doing anything else ▪ to go first to

rechazar preguntas ▪ reprimir preguntas to squelch questions

recta larga straight stretch

la **red de prostitución** prostitution ring

la **red de venta** ▪ (el) personal de venta **1.** sales force **2.** *(en un sentido negativo)* trafficking ring ▪ ring of traffickers

las **redes neuronales** neural networks

redactar los papeles to draw up the papers ➤ Haré que nuestro abogado redacte los papeles. I'll have our lawyer draw up the papers. ➤ (Ella) ha contratado a un abogado para redactar los papeles de divorcio. She's hired a lawyer to draw up the divorce papers.

redactar un acuerdo to draw up an agreement

redactar una carta to draft a letter

redactor jefe editor-in-chief

redada de llamadas ▪ batida de llamadas search of telephone records

redada policial police raid ▪ police round-up

redimir una hipoteca ▪ cumplir una hipoteca to pay off a mortgage

el **redoble de (los) tambores** beating of drums

la **reducción de la población** ▪ disminución de la población decrease in population

la **reducción de sueldo** decrease in pay ▪ reduction in pay ▪ cut in pay ▪ pay cut ➤ A los empleados les aplicaron una reducción de sueldo. The employees were given a decrease in pay.

la **reducción del paro** ▪ (la) disminución del paro decrease in unemployment ▪ drop in unemployment

reducir a alguien a cama to lay someone low ▪ to be laid low by ➤ La gripe lo redujo a la cama. He was laid low by the flu. ➤ *(Esp. leísmo)* La gripe le redujo a la cama He was laid low by the flu. ➤ La gripe la redujo a cama. She was laid low by the flu.

reducir a cenizas to reduce to ashes

reducir el flujo sanguíneo ▪ bajar el flujo sanguíneo to decrease the flow of blood ▪ to reduce the flow of blood ▪ to decrease (the) blood flow ▪ to reduce (the) blood flow

reducir el riesgo ▪ mitigar el riesgo to reduce the risk ▪ to lower the risk ▪ *(culto)* to mitigate the risk

reducir una ecuación a la mínima expresión to reduce an equation to its simplest form

reducir una fracción al mínimo denominador to reduce a fraction to its lowest common denominator

reducirse a to reduce to ▪ to boil down to ▪ to add up to ➤ Se reduce a un gran lío. It adds up to a big mess. ▪ It boils down to a big mess.

reducirse al hecho de que... to boil down to the fact that...

ser un **reducto de** ▪ ser un bastión de to be a bastion of ▪ to be a stronghold of ➤ Durante la Guerra Civil norteamericana, la parte este de Tennessee fue un reducto de sentimiento unionista dentro de la Confederación. ▪ Durante la Guerra Civil norteamericana, la parte este de Tennessee fue un bastión de sentimiento unionista dentro de la Confederación. During the American Civil War, East Tennessee was a bastion of Unionist sentiment within the Confederacy. ▪ During the American Civil War, East Tennessee was a stronghold of Unionist sentiment within the Confederacy.

redundar en el beneficio de alguien ▪ convenirle a alguien to be to someone's advantage ▪ to play into someone's hands ▪ to play into the hands of someone

redundar en beneficio suyo ▪ convenirle a uno to be to one's advantage ➤ Redunda en beneficio tuyo... It's to your advantage to...

redundar en lo que... to have a bearing on what...

ser **reelegido para otro mandato (como)** to be re-elected to another term (as)

reemprender el camino to get back on the road ▪ to get back on one's way ➤ Reemprendió su camino, como queriendo recuperar el tiempo perdido. He got back on the road, as if trying to make up for lost time. ▪ He got back on his way, as if trying to make up for lost time.

reemprender el trabajo to get back to work

reemprender la carrera 1. retomar los estudios to resume one's studies **2.** retomar la carrera profesional to resume one's career **3.** *(competición deportiva)* ▪ volver a la carrera to get back into the race

referente a ▪ que tiene que ver con having to do with

referirse a alguien to mean someone ▪ to refer to someone ➤ Pensé que te referías a mí. I thought you meant me. ▪ I thought you were referring to me.

referirse a que ▪ señalar que to point out that

reflejar una imagen ▪ devolver una imagen to reflect an image

reflexionar un momento to think for a moment ▪ to reflect for a moment ➤ Ella reflexionó un momento y luego dijo... She thought for a moment and then said... ▪ She reflected for a moment and then said...

reforma del barrio urban renewal

reformar conciencia *(Lazarillo de Tormes)* to salve one's conscience

reformar la constitución to amend the constitution

reformar un edificio to remodel a building ▪ to renovate a building

reforzar la presencia militar to beef up the military presence ➤ Las dos naciones están reforzando su presencia militar a lo largo de la frontera. The two nations are beefing up their military presence along the border.

reforzar la seguridad ▪ fortalecer la seguridad to beef up security ▪ to increase security ▪ to heighten security

reforzar las fuerzas armadas to beef up the armed services ▪ to beef up the military

refregar algo a alguien por las narices to rub someone's nose in something ▪ to hold something up to someone

refrendar el testimonio de alguien ▪ corroborar el testimonio de alguien ▪ apoyar el testimonio de alguien to corroborate someone's testimony ▪ to support someone's testimony ▪ to affirm someone's testimony ▪ to back up someone's testimony

refrendar una ley to sign a bill into law

refrendar un pasaporte to stamp a passport

refrendo de un testimonio ▪ corroboración de un testimonio corroboration of testimony ▪ affirmation of testimony

refrescar los conocimientos de una materia ▪ recuperar los conocimientos de una materia to brush up on a subject ▪ to bone up on a subject

refrescarle la memoria a uno ▪ reivindicar la memoria to refresh one's memory

refrescar(se) el gaznate ▪ mojar el gaznate ▪ humedecerse los labios to wet one's whistle

refuerzo de firme substantial reinforcement

refugiarse en to take refuge in

refugio seguro: buscar ~ to seek safe haven

regalar el oído to serenade someone with beautiful music ▪ to delight someone with beautiful music

regalar entradas gratis to give away free tickets

regalarle a alguien el oído ▪ regalarle a alguien los oídos ▪ lisonjearle a alguien ▪ halagar a alguien to flatter someone

regalarle a alguien los oídos lisonjearle a alguien ▪ halagar a alguien to flatter someone

regalarse algo to treat oneself to something ➤ ¡Regálate un helado! Treat yourself to an ice cream!

regalárselo a alguien ▪ dárselo a alguien to give it to someone

el **regaliz de palo** licorice stick ▪ stick of licorice

regalo de cumpleaños birthday present ▪ birthday gift

regalo de despedida going-away present

ser un **regalo de Dios** ▪ ser una bendición (de Dios) to be a blessing ▪ to be a Godsend

regalo intemporal ▪ regalo para toda la vida timeless gift

regalo para toda la vida ▪ regalo intemporal timeless gift

regar comida ■ pasar las migas to wash down food ➤ ¿Quieres una copa de vino para regar la comida? Do you want a glass of wine to wash it down?

regatear a alguien *(fútbol)* to get past someone ■ to get around someone ■ to outmaneuver someone

el **régimen de ascenso** *(aviación)* climb rate ■ rate of climb

el **régimen del verbo** preposition that necessarily follows the verb *(Por ejemplo, "a" después de "ir", y "de" después de "estar harto" ■ For example "a" after "ir", and "de" after "estar harto")*

régimen retrógrado backward regime

la **región colindante** neighboring region

la **región en su conjunto** surrounding region

La ***región más transparente*** *(novela de Carlos Fuentes) Where the Air Is Clear*

región vecina ■ región colindante neighboring region ■ adjoining region

estar **registrado en 1.** to be felt **2.** to be detected

registrar de arriba abajo to search from top to bottom

registrar llamadas ■ rastrear llamadas to search telephone records

registrar palmo a palmo to search inch by inch

registrar un edificio to search a building

registrarse los bolsillos to search one's pockets ■ to look through one's pockets

registrarse *x* casos de la enfermedad (for) *x* cases of the illness to be reported

registro de llamadas realizadas 1. record of calls made ■ roster of calls **2.** search of telephone records

registro de los pagos record of the payments

registro de morosos list of people in arrears ■ list of payment delinquencies

registro electoral voter list ■ list of registered voters

registro preliminar preliminary search

registro visual de: tener un ~ to have a panoramic view of

registros muestran que... the records show that...

regla cardinal cardinal rule

regla de cálculo slide rule

regla de oro golden rule

regla no escrita unwritten rule

el **reglaje de altímetro** *(aeronáutica)* altimeter setting

reglamento determina que... rule states that...

reglas de compromiso rules of engagement

reglas del juego rules of the game

regodearse en algo ■ regodearse con algo **1.** *(en sentido negativo)* to gloat over something **2.** *(en sentido positivo)* to delight in something ➤ ¡No te regodees! Don't gloat! ➤ Se regodea mucho con su hijita, especialmente cuando ella dice nuevas palabras. He delights in his little daughter, especially when she says new words.

regresar al trabajo ■ regresar al tajo ■ regresar a la faena to get back to work ➤ *(tú)* ¡Regresa al trabajo! ■ *(usted)* ¡Regrese al trabajo! ■ *(vosotros)* ¡Que regreséis al trabajo! ■ ¡Regresad al trabajo! Get back to work!

regresarse caminando ■ volverse andando to walk back ■ to return on foot ➤ Me regresé a casa caminando. I walked back home. ■ I returned home on foot.

Regreso al futuro *(título de película) Back to the Future*

reguero de trickle of ■ trail of

reguero de gasóleo: verter un ~ ■ dejar un reguero de gasóleo **1.** *(para calefacción)* to spill a trail of heating oil ■ to leave a trail of heating oil **2.** *(para motores)* to spill a trail of diesel fuel ■ to leave a trail of diesel fuel ➤ *(noticia)* El carguero portugués que se hundió el pasado día diecisiete frente a la costa vizcaína ha empezado a verter algunos regueros de gasóleo. The Portuguese tanker which sank on the seventeenth of this month off the Biscayan coast has begun to spill a trail of diesel fuel.

reguero de sangre: dejar un ~ to leave a trail of blood

regulador de tiempo timer

regular el botón en la posición deseada to set the dial in the desired position

regularizar a los ciudadanos de otro país to regularize the situation of citizens of another country

rehacerse de la pérdida de un ser querido to get over the loss of a loved one ■ to recover from the loss of a loved one ➤ Le costó rehacerse de la pérdida de su esposa. He had a hard time getting over the death of his wife. ➤ Le costó rehacerse. It took him a long time to get over it.

rehuir algo to avoid something

rehuir el carril lento to avoid the slow lane

rehuir hablar de to avoid talking about

rehusar un ofrecimiento to decline an offer

reinado de un(a) monarca rule of a monarch ■ reign of a monarch

el **Reino de España** *(nombre oficial de España)* Kingdom of Spain

reino de la fantasía ■ mundo de ensueño ■ mundo de las maravillas world of make-believe ■ land of make-believe

reino insular island kingdom

reinstalar el programa to reinstall the software

reír a alguien las gracias to encourage someone by laughing

reír a mandíbula batiente ■ partirse de risa to laugh one's head off

reír por no llorar to laugh to keep from crying

reirá mejor el que ría el último ■ quien ríe el último, ríe mejor he who laughs last laughs best

reírle a alguien la gracia to encourage someone by laughing

reírse a carcajada limpia to have a good laugh

reirse con, no reirse de to laugh with, not at ➤ Me río contigo, no me río de ti. I'm laughing with you, not at you.

reírse con toda la boca to laugh one's head off

reírse de algo to laugh at something

reírse de alguien 1. *(literal)* to laugh at someone **2.** burlarse de alguien to make fun of someone

reírse de alguien en su cara to laugh at someone to his face ■ to laugh in someone's face

reírse de los peces de colores not to care less

reírse de sí mismo to laugh at oneself

reírse del mundo entero to laugh at the world

reírse del vecino de enfrente ■ reírse de alguien en su cara to laugh at someone to his face ■ to laugh in someone's face

reírse por dentro to laugh to oneself

reiterados fallos repeated failures

reivindicar (la autoría de) un ataque ■ atribuirse un ataque to claim responsibility for an attack

reivindicar la memoria ■ refrescar la memoria to refresh one's memory

rejilla de ventilación air vent

relación a distancia long-distance relationship

relación con alguien: tener ~ to be acquainted with someone ■ to be on pleasant terms with someone

la **relación de nombres** list of names

la **relación (entre ideas)** connection (between ideas) ■ relation ■ relationship ➤ Sigo sin ver la relación. I still don't see the connection. ■ I still don't get the connection.

la **relación hombre mujer** male-female relationships

relación *x* a *y* ratio of *x* to *y*

estar **relacionado con algo** ■ estar en función de algo to be related to something ■ to be akin to something ➤ El uno está relacionado con el otro. ■ El uno está en función del otro. One is akin to the other. ■ One is related to the other.

relacionar algo con algo to link something to something ■ to link something with something ➤ Expertos relacionaron las muertes por fallo renal con un nuevo fármaco contra el colesterol. Experts linked the deaths caused by kidney failure to a new anti-cholesteral drug.

relaciones en el entorno de trabajo relationships at work ■ relationships in the work environment

relaciones estrechas close relations

relaciones extranjeras ■ relaciones internacionales foreign relations

relaciones internacionales ■ relaciones extranjeras foreign relations

relaciones públicas public relations

relajarse el estómago ■ estragarse ■ atracarse a comer to stuff oneself ■ to stuff oneself to the gills

relamerse de gusto to smack one's lips (from enjoyment of the food)

relampagueos de dolor ▪ punzadas de dolor shooting pains ▪ jolts of pain

relatividad general *(Einstein)* general relativity

relatividad restringida *(Einstein)* special relativity

relato compacto concise account

relato de la policía police account

relato de primera mano firsthand account

Relato de un náufrago *(obra de Gabriel García Márquez) Account of a Shipwrecked Sailor* ▪ *(True) Story of a Shipwrecked Sailor*

relato objetivo de los hechos balanced account of events ▪ unbiased account of the events

ser **relevado de** to be dismissed from ▪ to be relieved from ▪ to be fired from ➤ Relevados dos guardias civiles en Bosnia por un caso de prostitución. Two civil guardsmen relieved of their posts in Bosnia in a case involving prostitution.

relevo de alguien someone's replacement ▪ replacement of someone

relevo de la guardia changing of the guard

el **relieve del país** geography of the country

reliquia del pasado relic of the past

el **reloj a pilas** ▪ reloj de pilas battery-powered clock ▪ clock that runs on batteries ➤ Necesito un reloj a pilas para los viajes y para los cortes de luz. I need a battery-powered clock for traveling and power outages.

el **reloj de arena** hourglass

el **reloj de pilas** ▪ reloj a pilas battery-powered clock ▪ clock that runs on batteries ▪ battery-powered watch

el **reloj está detenido** ▪ el reloj está parado the clock has stopped ▪ the clock is stopped

el **reloj marca *x* p.m.** ▪ el reloj tiene *x* p.m. the clock says *x* p.m. ▪ the clock reads *x* p.m.

rellenar de combustible ▪ repostar combustible ▪ reabastecer de combustible to refuel

rellenar los espacios en blanco ▪ llenar los espacios en blanco to fill in the blanks

rellenar los huecos to fill in the blanks

rellenar un agujero to fill a hole

rellenar un impreso ▪ llenar un impreso to fill out a form

relucir como una espada to gleam like a sword

relucir el pelo (for one's) hair to shine

remachar el clavo to drive home the main point

remangarse la camisa y ponerse a currar ▪ remangarse las mangas y a trabajar to roll up one's sleeves and get to work ➤ Remanguémonos las mangas y a trabajar. Let's roll up our sleeves and get to work.

remanso de paz quiet place ▪ peaceful haven ▪ escape ▪ refuge

remanso de serenidad haven of peace and tranquility ➤ El pueblo hoy es un remanso de serenidad. The village today is a haven of peace and tranquility.

remanso para fauna haven for wildlife

remarcar (bien) ▪ marcar (bien) to bear down (hard) ▪ to press (down) hard ➤ Remárcalo bien para que las copias sean legibles. ▪ Márcalo bien para que las copias sean legibles. Bear down hard so that the copies will be legible. ▪ Press (down) hard so that the copies will be legible.

rematar con ▪ acabarse con to culminate in ▪ to finish off with ▪ to be capped by ▪ to be crowned by ▪ to end in ▪ to end with ➤ La marcha de los zapatistas en México remató con una manifestación gigantesca en la Plaza de la Constitución. The march of the Zapatistas culminated with a gigantic demonstration in the Plaza of the Constitution.

rematar de cabeza por encima de... to head the ball over...

rematar el libro to finish up the book ➤ *(profesora a la clase)* Remataremos el libro el jueves. We'll finish up the book on Thursday.

rematar la cuesta de una loma to reach the crest of a hill

rematar la juerga to cap the night ▪ to finish off the night

remedar a alguien ▪ imitar a alguien ▪ copiar a alguien to mimic someone ▪ to imitate someone

remedio casero home remedy ➤ He aquí un artículo interesante sobre remedios caseros. Here's an interesting article about home remedies.

remedio contra ▪ cura contra cure for

el **remedio es peor que la enfermedad** ▪ cuesta más el remedio que la enfermedad the cure is worse than the disease

remedio para el resfriado cold remedy

rememorar sobre to reminisce about

la **remisión de los pecados** remission of sins

ser **remilgado con algo** ▪ ser muy especial para algo to be fussy about something ➤ Es remilgada con la comida. She's fussy about food.

remitente: devolver al ~ to return to (the) sender

remite el temporal storm lets up ▪ storm subsides ▪ storm loses its punch

remitir al jurado de acusación ▪ poner bajo la jurisdicción de jurado de acusación to bind over to the grand jury

remolacha azucarera sugar beet

remolcar un vehículo to tow a vehicle

el **remolque de un camión** trailer of a truck

remontar a los tiempos en que... to go back to the time when...

remontar el oleaje to ride the waves

remontar el vuelo to take flight ▪ to start flying ▪ to take off

remontar un gol ▪ igualar el tanteo to even the score

remontar una crisis to recover from a crisis

remontarse a 1. ▪ datar de to date from ▪ to date back to ▪ to date back **2.** to go back (to) ➤ El conflicto actual se remonta a enero del año pasado. The present conflict goes back to January of last year. ➤ Nuevas dataciones en Francia indican que el inicio del arte se remonta a más de 35,000 años. New dating estimates in France indicate that the beginning of art dates back more than 35,000 years. ➤ Mis recuerdos se remontan a los años cuarenta. My memories go back to the forties.

remontarse al cielo to soar up into the sky

remontarse al futuro to go back to the future

remonte (mecánico) ski lift

remorder la conciencia to weigh on one's conscience ▪ to gnaw at one's conscience

remorderse la conciencia to weigh on one's conscience ➤ Me remuerde la conciencia. It weighs on my conscience.

remover enérgicamente to stir vigorously ➤ Incorporar los huevos enteros, removiendo enérgicamente hasta integrarlos en la pasta. Add the eggs whole, stirring vigorously until blended into the dough.

remover la ensalada to toss the salad

remover de vez en cuando to stir occasionally ➤ Llevarlo a ebullición removiendo de vez en cuando. Bring it to a boil, stirring occasionally.

remover Roma con Santiago ▪ revolver Roma con Santiago to explore every avenue

renace como el ave Fénix to rise like a Phoenix from the ashes

la **rendición sin condiciones** unconditional surrender

rendido(-a) (de cansancio): caer ~ to collapse from exhaustion

estar **rendido(-a) de trabajo** to be exhausted from work

rendimiento físico physical performance

rendir bajo presión to perform well under pressure ➤ No rindo muy bien si estoy bajo presión. I don't perform well under pressure.

rendir cuentas de algo to give an accounting of something

rendir fruto(s) ▪ dar fruto(s) to bear fruit

rendir gracias por ▪ dar gracias por to give thanks for ▪ to express one's gratitude for

rendir homenaje a alguien ▪ rendir pleitesía a alguien to pay homage to someone

rendir las armas to surrender one's weapons

rendir tributo a alguien to pay tribute to someone ▪ to pay one's last respects to someone

rendirle mucho el tiempo ▪ cundirle mucho el tiempo to get a lot done ➤ Nos rindió mucho el tiempo. We got a lot done.

rendirse sin condiciones to surrender unconditionally

renegar de alguien ■ desheredar a alguien to renounce someone ■ to disown someone ■ to disinherit someone

renegar de la hora en que nació alguien to curse the day someone was born

renegar de sus circunstancias to curse one's circumstances

renegar de una promesa ■ no cumplir una promesa ■ no guardar una promesa to renege on a promise ■ to break a promise ■ not to keep a promise ■ to go back on one's promise ■ to fail to keep a promise

renovar la herida ■ reabrir la herida to reopen the wound

renovar una póliza de seguro to renew an insurance policy

renovarse o morir to change or die ■ to adjust to the times or perish

renta de un fondo interest from a trust ■ interest on a trust ➤ Vive de la renta de un fondo. He lives on the interest from a trust.

renta per cápita per-capita income

renta vitalicia pension ■ annuity

rentabilidad del dinero return on one's money ■ return on one's investment

renuncia de alguien a someone's withdrawal from

renunciar a casarse to renounce marriage

renunciar a la esperanza de to give up hope of

renunciar a su cargo de to resign from one's post as ➤ *(titular)* Pinochet renuncia a su cargo de senador. Pinochet resigns from his senate post. ■ Pinochet resigns from his post as senator.

renunciar a un puesto de trabajo ■ dimitir de un puesto de trabajo ■ dejar un (puesto de) trabajo to quit one's job ■ to resign from a job ■ to resign from a position ■ to quit one's post

renunciar a una opción ■ dejar una opción ■ abandonar una opción to waive an option

renunciar al derecho de to waive the right to

renunciar al pacto to renounce the agreement

renunciar la mano a alguien to reject a (marriage) proposal ■ to refuse a (marriage) proposal

renunciarse a sí mismo to deny oneself

ser la **repanocha 1.** ser el colmo to be the limit ■ to be too much **2.** ser gracioso to be a scream ➤ Eres la repanocha. You're the limit. ■ You're too much. ■ You're a scream.

repantigarse en el suelo ■ echarse en el suelo to sprawl out on the floor ➤ De niño, me repantiguaba en el suelo y leía los comics en el periódico. As a kid, I used to sprawl out on the floor and read the funnies.

reparaciones provisionales makeshift repairs

reparar en la mirada de alguien to care what someone thinks ■ to care about someone's opinion of one

reparo sobre ■ duda persistente sobre lingering doubt about ■ qualms about

la **repartición de la riqueza** distribution of wealth

repartir algo to share something ■ to divide something ■ to distribute something ➤ ¿Quieres repartir el resto del helado? Do you want to share the rest of the ice cream (with me)? ➤ ¿Quieres repartir lo que queda del helado? Do you want to share what's left of the ice cream?

repartir el tiempo entre... to divide the time between...

repartir la riqueza to distribute (the) wealth

reparto a domicilio home delivery

reparto de mercado market share

repetid después de mí *(Esp., vosotros)* repeat after me

repetir como un papagayo to parrot *(Dar la respuesta sin entenderla ■ To give the answer without actually understanding it)*

repetir mandato to win again

repiqueteo de la lluvia sobre el tejado ■ repiqueteo de la lluvia en el tejado pattering of (the) rain on the roof ■ patter of (the) rain on the roof

repitan (ustedes) después de mí repeat after me

replantear su ofensiva to rethink one's offensive

replantearse una propuesta ■ recapacitar sobre una propuesta ■ retroceder en una propuesta ■ dar marcha atrás una propuesta ■ echar marcha atrás una propuesta to back away from a proposal ■ to withdraw a proposal ■ to rethink a proposal

estar **repleto de** to be packed with

replicarle a alguien to talk back to someone ➤ ¡No me repliques! Don't talk back to me!

reponer algo que se rompe to replace something (that's been) broken ■ to replace something which has been broken

reponer que... ■ replicar que... to reply that...

reponerse de un susto to recover one's composure after a scare

reponerse de una enfermedad ■ restablecerse de una enfermedad to recover from an illness

reponerse de una herida to recover from a wound

reponerse de una trauma to recover from a trauma

reportaje gráfico graphic reporting

reportarle beneficio a uno to be beneficial

reportarle dinero a uno to bring in money ■ to land money

reportero a pie de calle reporter on his beat ■ reporter out on his beat

reportero asignado a una determinada sección beat reporter ➤ El periódico tiene una serie de reporteros que no tienen asignada una sección en concreto a la par que tiene reporteros ya asignados que cubren el ayuntamiento, los juzgados, la policía, los negocios, la religión, la medicina y la ciencia. The newspaper has a number of general assignment reporters as well as beat reporters who cover city hall, courts, police, business, religion, medicine and science.

reportero gráfico news photographer ■ photojournalist

reposar en paz ■ descansar en paz to rest in peace

la **reposición de un programa anterior** rerun of an earlier program

reposo absoluto complete rest

repostar combustible ■ rellenar de combustible ■ reabastecer de combustible to refuel

repreguntar a un(a) testigo ■ hacer segunda pregunta a un(a) testigo to cross-examine a witness

representante diplomático(-a) diplomatic representative

representar a alguien en una obra teatral to play (the role of) somone in a play

representar de... to stand for in... ➤ ¿Qué representa la C de tu segundo nombre? What does the C in your middle name stand for?

representar mucho para uno ■ significar mucho para alguien to mean a lot to one ➤ Representa mucho para mí. ■ Significa mucho para mí. It means a lot to me.

representar a todas las clases sociales to come from all walks of life

¡**reprímete!** *(de "reprimirse")* control yourself!

¡**reprimíos!** *(Esp., de "reprimirse")* ■ ¡reprímanse! control yourselves!

reprimir a alguien de hacer algo ■ privar a alguien de hacer algo to stop someone from doing something

reprimir una revuelta ■ sofocar una revuelta to put down a rebellion ■ to put down a revolt ■ to suppress a rebellion ■ to suppress a revolt

repuesto(-a) de su enfermedad having recovered from one's illness

requerimiento a la copa *(Valle-Inclán)* sipping his drink

requiéscat in pace ■ R.I.P. rest in peace

requisito previo prerequisite

resaca feroz bad hangover

resaltar la importancia de to stress the importance of

resaltar una información to highlight...

resarcir a alguien de algo to compensate someone for something

resarcirse de ■ compensar to make up for ■ to compensate for

resbalar sobre el hielo to slide on the ice *(Nota: "Resbalar" siempre se refiere a una acción no voluntaria. ■ "Resbalar" always refers to an involuntary action.)*

resbalarle algo a alguien to go right by one ➤ A mí me resbaló todo lo que dijo el profesor ayer. Everything the teacher said yesterday went right by me.

resbalarse en el hielo to slip on the ice

resbalarse en una superficie resbaladiza to slide on a slick surface

ser **rescatado con vida** to be rescued alive

rescatar cadáveres ■ recuperar cuerpos to recover bodies

rescindir un contrato to cancel a contract ▪ to rescind a contract

estar **resentido(-a) con alguien** to be upset with someone

resentimiento soterrado hidden resentment

reseña entusiasta rave review ➤ La película está recibiendo reseñas entusiastas. The movie is getting rave reviews.

reserva para dos a reservation for two ▪ reservations for two

reservado el derecho de admisión the right to admit selectively is reserved

reservados todos los derechos ▪ todos los derechos reservados all rights reserved

reservar algo para una ocasión especial to save something for a special occasion ➤ Estaba reservando este disco para mis nuevos altavoces. I was saving this disc for my new speakers.

reservar con *x* días de antelación ▪ hacer una reserva con *x* días de antelación ▪ hacer una reserva *x* días por adelantado to make reservations *x* days in advance ▪ to make reservations *x* days ahead

reservar tiempo para to set aside time for ▪ to allow time for ➤ Yo reservaría tres días para el viaje. I would allow three days for the trip. ▪ I would set aside three days for the trip.

reservar tiempo para que to set aside time to ▪ to allow time to ➤ Yo reservaría suficiente tiempo para que seque. I would allow plenty of time for it to dry.

reservas comprobadas petroleras known oil reserves ▪ known reserves of oil

resguardo de ingreso deposit slip

residir por temporadas to live part of the year

residuos nucleares nuclear waste

estar **resignado(-a) a su destino** to be resigned to one's fate ▪ to be resigned to one's plight

resignarse a su suerte to be resigned to one's fate

resistir el impacto to withstand the impact

resistir hasta la muerte to fight to the death

resistir la tentación to resist temptation ▪ to withstand temptation

resistirse a apoyar to refuse to support

resistirse a cooperar to refuse to cooperate

resistirse a creerlo to refuse to believe it ➤ Nos resistimos a creerlo. We refuse to believe it.

resistírsele algo ▪ no cogerle el truquillo a algo not (to be able) to get the hang of something ▪ to struggle with something ➤ Se me resiste. I can't get the hang of it. ▪ I'm not getting the hang of it. ➤ Se me resiste el cálculo. I'm struggling with calculus.

la **resolución de la corte** the findings of the court

resolver el caso to solve the case ▪ to crack the case

resolver el problema ▪ solucionar el problema to solve a problem ▪ to take care of a problem

resolver un problema de matemáticas ▪ solucionar un problema de matemáticas to solve a mathematics problem ▪ to solve a math problem ▪ to work a mathematics problem ▪ to work a math problem

resolver los papeleos to clear up the paperwork

resolver un problema solucionar un problema to solve a problem

resolver un problema de matemáticas ▪ solucionar un problema de matemáticas to solve a mathematics problem ▪ to solve a math problem ▪ to work a mathematics problem ▪ to work a math problem

resolver unos asuntos to take care of some business

resolverse a hacer algo to resolve to do something ▪ to make up one's mind to do something

resolverse en to come (down) to ▪ to boil down to

resolverse solo to take care of itself

resonancia magnética magnetic resonance imaging ▪ MRI

respaldar un proyecto to back a proposal

respaldo de arriba: tener el ~ to have the backing of one's superiors ▪ to have the support of one's superiors ▪ to be backed by one's superiors

respecto a 1. with respect to ▪ regarding ▪ in reference to **2.** compared to

respeta a tus mayores y te respetarán tus menores respect your elders and young people will respect you

respetar a los mayores de uno to respect one's elders

respetar el ceda el paso ▪ ceder el derecho de paso to yield the right of way ▪ to respect the right of way ➤ *(noticia de un accidente)* El conductor del turismo no respetó el ceda el paso y comenzó a girar. The driver of the sedan failed to yield the right of way and began to turn.

respetar el resultado ▪ atenerse al resultado ▪ atenerse a los resultados ▪ aceptar los resultados to abide by the result ➤ Ortega dijo que si el proceso electoral fuera observado por Jimmy Carter, que él (Ortega) respetaría los resultados. ▪ Otega dijo que si el proceso electoral fuera observado por Jimmy Carter, que él (Ortega) se atendría a los resultados. Otega said if the election were monitored by Jimmy Carter, he (Ortega) would abide by the result.

respetar la norma to obey the law

estar **respetuoso(-a) con** to be respectful to

la **respiración boca a boca** mouth-to-mouth resuscitation

la **respiración de fuelle** wheezing sound ▪ metallic sound in the breathing

respirar hondo ▪ respirar profundo to take a deep breath ▪ to breathe deep(ly)

respirar profundamente 1. to breathe deeply **2.** to take a deep breath ➤ Respiré profundamente. I took a deep breath.

respirar por la herida to betray one's bitterness ▪ to reveal the pain beneath the surface

respirar profundo ▪ respirar hondo to take a deep breath

respirarse ambiente de tragedia to have an air of tragedy

resplandor de la luna moonlight

responder a la acusación de ▪ responder bajo la acusación de to answer to the charge of

responder a la defensiva to answer defensively

responder a la demanda ▪ cubrir la demanda to answer the demand ▪ to meet the demand ▪ to cover the demand ➤ No hay suficiente petróleo en el mundo para responder a la demanda. ▪ No hay suficiente petróleo en el mundo para cubrir la demanda. There is not enough petroleum in the world to answer the demand. ▪ There is not enough petroleum in the world to meet the demand.

responder a un anuncio 1. to answer an ad ▪ to respond to an ad **2.** to respond to an announcement ▪ to react to an announcement ➤ El rey respondió con orgullo al anuncio del compromiso del príncipe. The king responded with pride to the announcement of the prince's engagement. ▪ The king reacted with pride to the announcement of the prince's engagement.

responder a una descripción to answer a description ▪ to fit a description ▪ to match a description ▪ to correspond to a description ➤ Un sospechoso que respondía a esa descripción fue detenido hoy. A suspect answering that description was arrested today.

responder al mismo nivel ▪ responder de la misma manera to respond in kind

responder algo to say something in response ➤ El indio, maravillado, quiso responder algo, pero no pudo. The Indian, in awe, tried to say something in response, but he couldn't.

responder bajo la acusación de ▪ responder a la acusación de to answer to the charge of

responder con cautela to answer guardedly

responder con retraso ▪ responder tardíamente to answer belatedly ▪ to respond belatedly

responder de forma afirmativa ▪ responder afirmativamente to answer in the affirmative ▪ to answer affirmatively

responder de forma negativa ▪ responder negativamente to answer in the negative

responder por alguien ▪ responder en nombre de alguien ▪ contestar por alguien ▪ contestar en nombre de alguien **1.** to answer for someone ▪ to speak for someone ▪ to answer in someone's behalf ▪ to answer on someone's behalf **2.** to be accountable for someone ▪ to answer for someone ➤ No puedo responder por ella, pero... I can't answer for *her*, but... ➤ Los oficiales de bajo rango no deberían responder por los errores del comandante. The low-level officers should not have to answer for the commander's mistakes.

responder sin vacilar to answer without hesitation

responder tardíamente ▪ responder con retraso to answer belatedly ▪ to respond belatedly

responsabilidad abrumadora awesome responsibility ▪ overwhelming responsibility ▪ crushing responsibility

responsabilizar a alguien de algo to hold someone responsible for something

responsabilizarse de algo to accept responsibility for something ▪ to take responsibility for something

responsabilizarse de sí mismo to be responsible for oneself ▪ to be responsible for one's actions

respuesta adecuada ▪ respuesta correcta right answer ▪ correct answer

respuesta concreta definite answer ▪ specific answer ▪ concrete answer

respuesta correcta ▪ respuesta adecuada correct answer ▪ right answer

respuesta definitiva: dar la ~ to give the definitive answer ➤ Kant dio la respuesta definitiva a la pregunta de si se puede probar la existencia de Dios. Kant gave the definitive answer to the question whether the existence of God can be proved.

respuesta evasiva evasive answer

respuesta equivocada ▪ respuesta incorrecta wrong answer ▪ incorrect answer

respuesta incorrecta ▪ respuesta equivocada incorrect answer ▪ wrong answer

respuesta segura safe answer

respuesta solapada evasive answer

respuesta tajante 1. respuesta contundente categorical answer ▪ categorical reply **2.** respuesta áspera harsh answer

resquebrajarle el frío (for the) cold to incapcitate someone

resquicio de esperanza glimmer of hope ▪ ray of hope

restablecerse de una enfermedad ▪ recuperarse de una enfermedad ▪ reponerse de una enfermedad to recover from an illness

hacer **restallar un látigo** to crack a whip

restañar la sangre ▪ parar el flujo sanguíneo to stem the flow of blood ▪ to stop the flow of blood ▪ to halt the flow of blood

restar el valor objetivo ▪ restar el mérito objetivo ▪ desvirtuar la objetividad to detract from the objectivity ➤ La expresión de rabia resta el valor objetivo del artículo. ▪ La expresión de rabia desvirtúa la objetividad del artículo. ▪ La expresión de rabia resta el mérito objetivo del artículo. The expression of anger detracts from the objectivity of the article.

restar expectativas to reduce one's expectations

restar importancia a to play down

restar méritos a alguien to belittle somebody ▪ to run somebody down

restar valor de 1. quitarle valor a to minimize the importance of ▪ to downplay the importance of **2.** devaluar algo to reduce the value of something

restarle importancia to minimize the importance of ▪ to downplay the importance of

restarle importancia a un asunto ▪ *(coloquial)* quitarle paja a un asunto to downplay the importance of a matter ▪ to play down the importance of a matter

restaurar el fluido eléctrico ▪ restaurar el servicio eléctrico to restore power ▪ to restore the flow of electricity ▪ (for) the power to come back on ▪ (for) the electricity to come back on ➤ Restauraron el fluido eléctrico. The power came back on. ▪ The electricity came back on. ▪ They restored (the) power. ▪ They restored the electricity. ▪ They restored the flow of electricity.

resto del tiempo rest of the time

resto somos rest of us are

restos de supernova *(astronomía)* remnant(s) of a supernova ▪ aftermath of a supernova explosion

restos mortales mortal remains

restregar algo a alguien por las narices ▪ refregar algo a alguien por las narices to hold something up to someone ▪ to rub someone's nose in something

restringir la libertad de imprenta to limit (the) freedom of the press

resucitar a los muertos to raise the dead ▪ to resurrect the dead

resucitar de entre los muertos 1. to be raised from the dead **2.** to rise from the dead ➤ Al tercer día resucitó On the third day He rose again

resulta que... it turns out that...

resulta ser que... it turns out that... ▪ as it turns out ➤ Resulta ser que tengo que trabajar este domingo. It turns out that I have to work this Sunday. ▪ As it turns out, I have to work this Sunday.

resultado infructuoso unfruitful result ▪ unprofitable outcome ▪ unproductive result

resultados del escrutinio election results ▪ election returns

resultados electorales al Congreso (detallados) por comunidades autónomas *(Esp.)* breakdown of the Congressional races by autonomous region

resultados electorales al Congreso (detallados) por estados *(Estados Unidos, México)* breakdown of the Congressional races by state ▪ breakdown of the Congressional races state by state

resultar ameno ▪ ser ameno to be enjoyable ▪ to have an enjoyable time ➤ Nuestra conversación resultó amena. We had a very enjoyable conversation.

resultar bien to come together right ▪ to come together ▪ to turn out ➤ No resultó (bien). It didn't turn out. ▪ It didn't come together (right).

resultar contraproducente to be counterproductive

resultar difícil to turn out to be difficult ▪ to be difficult ➤ Va a resultar difícil, por no decir imposible. That is going to be difficult if not impossible.

resultar herido(-a) to be injured ▪ to be hurt ➤ Veinte personas resultaron heridas. Twenty people were injured.

resultar ileso(-a) to be unhurt ▪ to be unharmed ▪ to escape injury

resultar inútil to turn out to be useless ▪ to (turn out to) be in vain

resultar mortal to be fatal

resultar muerto(-a) to be killed

resultar muy raro que... to be strange that...

resultar peor el remedio que la enfermedad for the cure to be worse than the disease ➤ Resultó peor el remedio que la enfermedad. The cure was worse than the disease.

resultar que to turn out that

resultar ser to turn out to be

resultar ser cierto to turn out to be true

resultar un incordio to be a pain ▪ to be a nuisance

resultar un tanto impactante to come as something of a shock ➤ La noticia le resultó un tanto impactante. The news came as something of a shock.

resultar una birria ▪ resultar un desastre to come out a mess ▪ to come out terrible

resultarle curioso a alguien que... ▪ parecerle curioso a alguien que... to seem odd to someone that

resultarle difícil hacer algo to find it difficult to do something ▪ to be difficult for one to do something

resultarle duro a uno to be hard on one ➤ Dejar a tanta familia me resultó especialmente duro. Leaving so many family (members) behind was really hard on me. ▪ To leave so many family (members) behind was really hard on me.

resultarle fácil decir eso to be easy for someone to say that ➤ Te resulta fácil a ti decir eso. ▪ A ti te resulta fácil decir eso. It's easy for *you* to say that.

resultarle interesante (for someone) to find something interesting ➤ Me ha resultado muy interesante. I found it very interesting.

resultarle más a cuenta... to be better to...

resultó que... it turned out that...

resurgir como to come back as ▪ to come back in the form of

retar a alguien a un debate ▪ desafiar a alguien a un debate to challenge someone to a debate

retazos del pasado de uno isolated incidents from one's past

el **retén militar** military checkpoint

el **retén policial** police roadblock

las **retenciones al salario** deductions from one's salary

retenciones de tráfico: haber ~ ▪ estar atascado el tráfico (for) traffic to be backed up

retener a alguien ▪ detener a alguien ▪ parar a alguien to hold up someone ▪ to hold someone up ▪ to keep someone ➤ No quiero retenerte más. I don't want to hold you up any longer. ■ I don't want to keep you any longer.

retener a alguien como rehén to hold someone hostage

retener (la) comida ■ retener los alimentos to hold down food ■ to hold food down ■ to keep down food ■ to keep food down ➤ No puede retener la comida. La vomita. He can't hold down food. It just comes back up. ■ He can't keep food down. It just comes back up.

retener la onda expansiva to block the shock wave ■ to deflect the shock wave

retirada a tiempo es una victoria ■ retirarse a tiempo es una victoria ■ salida a tiempo es una victoria timely withdrawal is (a) victory

retirada de escombros removal of debris ■ clearing of debris

retirada de poder withdrawal from power

retirada militar military withdrawal

retirar de (la) circulación to take out of circulation ■ to withdraw from circulation

retirar dinero ■ sacar dinero to withdraw money ■ to take out money

retirar el coche 1. correr el coche to move the car (out of the way) 2. ir a buscar el coche (al mecánico) to pick up the car (from the shop)

retirar el saludo ■ retirar la palabra to stop speaking to someone ➤ Le retiró el saludo. She's no longer speaking to him. ■ She doesn't speak to him any more. ■ She no longer speaks to him.

retirar la palabra ■ retirar el saludo to stop speaking to someone

retirar lo dicho to take back what one said ■ to take back a remark

retirar los impuestos to take out (for) taxes ■ to withhold taxes ■ to withhold the tax

retirar una proposición to withdraw a proposal

retirarle una invitación to withdraw an invitation ➤ Cuando el invitado preguntó quién venía, el anfitrión le retiró la invitación. When the prospective guest asked who was coming, the host withdrew the invitation.

retirarse a un segundo plano 1. to withdraw into the background ■ to move into the background 2. to recede into the background

retirarse con las manos vacías to go away empty-handed

retirarse de algo to back away from something ■ to get back from something ■ to get away from something ➤ Retírate de la hoguera, que te vas a quemar. Back away from the fire, or you'll burn yourself. ■ Get back from the fire, or you'll burn yourself. ■ Get away from the fire, or you'll burn yourself.

retirarse de una competencia ■ abandonar una competencia to withdraw from a competition

retirarse de una situación ■ romper un compromiso ■ echarse atrás ■ volverse atrás to back out of a situation

retirarse del bordillo ■ separarse del bordillo ■ to back away from the curb ■ to pull back from the curb ➤ Retírate un poco del bordillo. Estás muy cerca. ■ Sepárate un poco del bordillo. Estás muy cerca. Back away from the curb a little (bit). You're too close. ■ Pull back from the curb a little bit. You're too close.

retirarse del cordón *(Arg., Chi.)* ■ separarse del cordón ■ retirarse del bordillo ■ separarse del bordillo to back away from the curb ■ to pull back from the curb

retiro forzoso forced withdrawal

retiro lo que dije I take it back

reto pendiente en the challenge facing ➤ El reto pendiente en la cumbre es el lanzamiento de un nuevo tratado que aborde la reforma de las instituciones comunitarias de la Unión Europea en previsión de futuras ampliaciones. The challenge facing the summit is the creation of a new treaty that deals with reforming the European Union's institutions in anticipation of future expansion.

retomar el caso to reopen the case

retomar los estudios ■ reanudar los estudios to resume one's studies

retomar una clase ■ volver a tomar una clase to retake a course ➤ Me hicieron retomar la clase de teoría literaria cuando ya la había tomado y sacado un muy bien. They made me retake literary theory even though I had already taken it and gotten a B in it.

retomar una conversación to resume a conversation ■ to pick up where (the conversation) left off

retorcer a alguien el pescuezo to wring someone's neck

retorcerse de risa ■ desternillarse de risa to split one's sides laughing

retorcerse en la tumba to turn over in one's grave ➤ *(comentario)* Bismarck se retorcerá en la tumba si un bávaro llega a canciller. Bismarck will turn over in his grave if a Bavarian becomes chancellor.

retorcidas ramas del árbol twisted branches of the tree

retornar a alguien *(secuestrado, tomado como rehén)* to return someone (who has been kidnapped or held hostage)

retornar algo *(tomado prestado o alquilado)* ■ devolver algo to turn something back in ■ to return something (borrowed or rented) ■ to take back something (borrowed or rented)

retorno del hijo pródigo return of the prodigal son

el **retortijón de tripas** stomach cramp

retractarse de una acusación to retract an allegation

retractarse de una afirmación to retract a statement

retractarse de una concesión to retract a concession

retractarse de una confesión to retract a confession

retrasar a alguien ■ detener a alguien to delay someone ■ to hold someone up ■ to hold up someone

retrasar el reloj to set one's watch back

retrasar una enfermedad to slow down the progress of an illness

retrasarse en el pago to fall behind in one's payments ■ to get behind in one's payments

retrasarse en el trabajo ■ atrasarse en el trabajo ■ atrasarse con el trabajo to get behind in one's work ■ to fall behind in one's work

retraso mental limítrofe ■ leve retraso mental mild mental retardation ■ borderline mental retardation

retratarse así to describe in that way

retrato de grupo group portrait

retrato en sepia sepia portrait

ser un **retrato ajustado** ■ ser un retrato preciso ■ ser un retrato exacto to be an accurate portrayal

ser un **retrato exacto** ■ ser un retrato ajustado ■ ser un retrato preciso to be an accurate portrayal

ser un **retrato preciso** ■ ser un retrato ajustado ■ ser un retrato exacto to be an accurate portrayal

retrato reconstruido ■ retrato robot ■ reconstrucción policial police artist's sketch

retrato robot ■ retrato reconstruido police artist's sketch

el **retrete se desbordó** ■ el water se desbordó the toilet overflowed ■ the commode overflowed

retrocede un poco ■ recula un poco ■ da marcha atrás un poco ■ ve marcha atrás un poco back up a little (bit)

retroceder ante algo ■ dar marcha atrás ante algo ■ retirarse de algo ■ separarse de algo to back away from something ➤ Retrocedimos ante la serpiente. We backed away from the snake.

retroceder ante alguien ■ dar marcha atrás ante alguien to back away from someone

retroceder en una propuesta ■ recapacitar sobre una propuesta ■ replantearse una propuesta ■ dar marcha atrás una propuesta ■ echar marcha atrás una propuesta to back away from a proposal ■ to withdraw a proposal

retunda importancia overriding importance

estar **reunido(-a)** to be in a meeting ➤ Está reunida. She's in a meeting.

la **reunión de emergencia** ■ reunión de urgencia emergency meeting

la **reunión de urgencia** ■ reunión de emergencia emergency meeting

la **reunión familiar** ■ tertulia familiar family get-together

reunir unos voluntarios ■ juntar algunos voluntarios to round up some volunteers ■ to get together some volunteers

reunirse (como un grupo) 1. *(una clase, negocio, etc.)* to meet 2. *(tribunal o legislativo)* to convene ➤ La clase se reúne tres veces por semana. The class meets three times a week. ➤ El comité se reúne todos los lunes. The committee meets every Monday.

reunirse en torno suyo to gather around someone

reunirse por separado(-a) con personas to meet separately with people

reunirse *x* veces a la semana to meet *x* times a week ➤ La clase se reúne tres veces a la semana. The class meets three times a week.

revalorizarse frente a (una moneda) to rise against (a currency) ➤ El euro se revaloriza frente al dólar. The euro is rising against the dollar.

revelar fotos to develop photos ▪ to develop pictures ➤ Fotos reveladas en 45 minutos Photos developed in 45 minutes

revelar la verdadera naturaleza de uno to reveal one's true nature

revelarse como 1. *(persona)* to show oneself to be 2. *(cosa)* to show itself to be

reventar de risa to burst out laughing

reventar en colores brilliantes to burst (out) into brilliant colors ▪ to burst with brilliant colors

reventar por hacer algo ▪ morirse por hacer algo to be bursting to do something ▪ to be dying to do something

ser el **reverso de la medalla** to be the other side of the coin ▪ to be the exact opposite

reverso de la moneda other side of the coin ▪ reverse side of a coin

reverso de un billete ▪ dorso de un billete back of a bill ▪ reverse side of a bill *(En billetes estadounidenses, el dorso es el lado opuesto al retrato.)*

revertir a to revert to

revertir al punto de partida to end up (back) where one started ▪ to go back to square one

revertir el daño resultante de... to reverse the damage resulting from... ▪ to reverse the damage caused by...

revertir en beneficio de uno to be to one's advantage ▪ to be to the advantage of one

revertir en perjuicio de uno to be to one's detriment ▪ to be to the detriment of one

revestimiento antiadherente non-stick coating

revestimiento de planchas de madera plank paneling ▪ paneling of wood planks

revestimiento de madera wood paneling

revestimiento de un edificio ▪ fachada de un edificio facade of a building

revestimiento de una superficie surface coating

revestir con to back with ➤ Reviste con cartulina. Back with posterboard.

revestir una pared to panel a wall

revisar a alguien con un detector de metales to check someone over with a metal detector ▪ to check over someone with a metal detector ➤ Los agentes los revisaron con un detector de metales. ▪ *(Esp., leísmo)* Los agentes les revisaron con un detector de metales. The officers checked them over with a metal detector.

revisar a ver si... to check to see if... ▪ to check to see whether (or not)... ▪ to check to see that... ➤ Antes de conectar el tostador, revisa a ver si el voltaje es el mismo que indica la placa de características. Before connecting the toaster, check to see that the voltage is the same as that indicated on the characteristics plaque.

revisar el correo electrónico ▪ mirar el correo electrónico ▪ ver el correo electrónico ▪ mirar si uno tiene correo electrónico to check one's E-mail

revisar el producto acabado to look over the finished product ▪ to check (over) the finished product

revisar la ortografía to check the spelling

revisar los mensajes telefónicos ▪ comprobar el buzón de voz ▪ comprobar los mensajes de voz ▪ comprobar si se tienen mensajes de voz to check one's voice mail ▪ to check one's (tele)phone messages

revisar un manuscrito (por si hay errores) to proofread a manuscript

la **revisión anual** annual checkup ▪ yearly checkup

revisión rutinaria routine inspection ▪ routine checkup

la **revisión del automóvil** ▪ inspección del automóvil automobile inspection

revistar las tropas to review the troops

revocar una orden to countermand an order

revolcarse con alguien to have a roll in the hay with someone

revolcarse en el fango *(cerdos)* ▪ revolcarse en el lodo ▪ revolcarse en el barro to wallow in the mud

revolear un bastón ▪ girar un bastón ▪ hacer girar un bastón con los dedos to twirl a baton

revolotear por el aire de la tarde *(el murciélago de Ogden Nash)* ▪ hacer eses en el aire de la tarde ▪ serpentear por el aire de la tarde ▪ zigzaguear en el aire de la tarde to zigzag through the evening air

revolotear por encima de sus cabezas to flutter around over their heads ▪ to zigzag around over their heads

Revolución Industrial Industrial Revolution ➤ El historiador Bruce Catton dijo que la Guerra Civil norteamericana se produjo porque la Revolución Industrial llegó al norte antes que al sur, creando al gobierno federal demandas en conflicto. Historian Bruce Catton said the American Civil War came about because the Industrial Revolution reached the North before the South, creating conflicting demands on the federal government.

las **revoluciones por minuto** ▪ RPM ▪ vueltas por minuto revolutions per minute ▪ RPM

revolver el estómago de uno to upset one's stomach ▪ to make one nauseated ➤ Ciertas cosas revuelven el estómago del bebé. Certain things will upset the baby's stomach.

revolver la casa ▪ poner la casa patas arriba ▪ voltear la casa al revés to turn the house upside down

revolver un avispero ▪ alborotar un avispero to stir up a hornets' nest

revolverle el estómago a uno to turn one's stomach

revolverle la bilis to make someone's blood boil ➤ Le revuelve la bilis (a él). It makes his blood boil. ➤ Le revuelve la bilis (a ella). It makes her blood boil.

revolverle las tripas to turn one's stomach

revolverse en su tumba to turn over in one's grave

revuelta estudiantil student riot

¡**rey de mambo!** twinkle toes!

reza como reads like ➤ Tu carta reza como una novela de Julio Verne. Your letter reads like a Jules Verne novel.

reza la antigua frase (que...) ▪ (tal) como dice el refrán as the old saying goes

rezar por alguien to pray for someone

rezar que... to state that... ➤ El principio de economía, o la navaja de Occam, reza que la explicación completa más sencilla es la verdadera. The law of parsimony, or Ockham's razor, says that the simplest complete explanation is the true one.

rezar la misa to say mass ➤ El obispo rezó la misa hoy. The bishop said mass today.

riada de humanidad flood of humanity

ricacho donostiarra *(Valle-Inclán)* a rich man from San Sebastian

ser **rico en contenido** to be rich in meaning ▪ to be rich in content ➤ Las obras de Shakespeare son ricas en contenido. The works of Shakespeare are rich in meaning.

riego sanguíneo ▪ corriente sanguínea ▪ flujo sanguíneo bloodstream

riesgos derivados de risks associated with

el **rifi-rafe** ▪ intercambio de ideas ▪ *(formal)* ▪ intercambio dialéctico back and forth (between student and teacher)

el **rifle de asalto** assault rifle

la **rigidez del clima** the harshness of the climate

ser el **rigor de las desdichas** to be very unfortunate

el **rigor del verano** ▪ pleno verano the hottest part of the summer ▪ in the depths of summer

rigor mortis rigor mortis

rima asonante vowel rhyme

rima consonante repetition of consonants ▪ consonance ▪ consonant rhyme

¡**ríndete!** give up!

río abajo downriver

río arriba upriver

río henchido ▪ río subido swollen river

río se desbordó river overflowed its banks

río y mar fresh water and salt

risa desternillante side-splitting laughter

risa sardónica sardonic laughter ■ derisive laughter

ritmo ajetreado hectic pace

ritmo de ascenso climb rate ➤ El avión lleva un ritmo de ascenso de ciento cincuenta metros por minuto. The airplane is climbing at a rate of a hundred and fifty meters (four hundred ninety-one point eight feet) per minute.

ritmo de crecimiento de rate of growth in ■ growth rate in

ritmo de descenso rate of descent ➤ El avión lleva un ritmo de descenso de quinientos pies (ciento cincuenta y dos metros) por minuto. The airplane is descending at a rate of five hundred feet per minute.

ritmo de la música ■ (el) golpe de compás ■ tiempo de compás beat of the music

ritmo de la vida pace of life ➤ Dicen que el ritmo de la vida es más lento en Madrid que en Barcelona. They say the pace of life is slower in Madrid than in Barcelona.

ritmo mareante ■ ritmo vertiginoso dizzying rate

ritmo vertiginoso ■ ritmo mareante dizzying rate

rito de la elección *(catolicismo)* rite of election

el **rival de cuidado** ■ rival formidable formidable rival ■ formidable opponent ➤ Tiene que enfrentar a un(a) rival de cuidado. He has to face a formidable rival.

el **rival formidable** ■ rival de cuidado formidable rival ■ formidable opponent

rizar el rizo 1. to gild the lily 2. liar el tema to complicate matters 3. *(aviación)* to loop the loop

robaparcelas land grabber

robar en tiendas to shoplift

robar una carta de una baraja ■ tomar una carta de la baraja ■ robar un naipe de una baraja to draw a card from a deck ➤ Robé un as a tu sota, así que gano yo. I drew an ace to your jack, so I win.

robarle la cartera a alguien to steal someone's wallet ■ to pick someone's pocket

robarle el pensamiento a alguien to steal someone's thought

robarle tiempo a alguien to take someone's time ➤ No quiero robarle más tiempo. I don't want to take any more of your time.

robársele por la fuerza a alguien *(Esp., leísmo, se refiere al robo de niños para el comercio de esclavos)* ■ robárselo(-a) a alguien ■ secuestrar a alguien to kidnap someone ■ to abduct someone

robo a mano armada ■ timo highway robbery ■ rip-off

rocambolesca sucesión de hechos ■ inverosímil sucesión de hechos unlikely series of events ■ far fetched... ■ bizarre...

roce con alguien: tener un ~ to have a brush with someone

roce con el fracaso: tener un ~ to have a brush with failure

roce con la muerte: tener un ~ to have a brush with death

roce con la policía: tener un ~ to have a brush with the law

el **roce de la tela** ■ roce del tejido the feel of the fabric ■ the feel of the cloth

el **roce de su mano** touch of one's hand

el **roce del tejido** ■ roce de la tela the feel of the fabric ■ the feel of the cloth

rocoso desfiladero rocky ravine

rodada suave: tener una ~ to have a smooth ride

rodamientos sellados sealed ball bearings

rodar cabezas to roll heads

rodar por el mundo to wander the world ■ to trot the globe

rodar íntegramente to film entirely

rodar sobre algo to roll over something

rodar una película ■ grabar una película to shoot a movie

estar **rodeado(-a) de** to be surrounded by

rodearle el cuello con los brazos to put one's arms around someone's neck

roer la conciencia to gnaw on one's conscience ■ to weigh on one's conscience

rogar por to pray for ➤ Ruega por nosotros. Pray for us.

rogar que to ask that... ■ to please... ■ to request that...

rogarle a alguien por conducto de uno to ask someone to convey to someone

rogarse que please ➤ Se ruega que... Please...

rojo brilliante vermillion

rojo chillón bright, bright red ■ screaming red

estar **rojo como la grana** to be beet red

rojo fuego fiery red

ser un **rollo** to be a hassle ➤ Es un rollo. It's a hassle.

rollo de película ■ (el) carrete roll of film

rollo macabeo real drag ■ killer

ser un **rollo patatero** *(Esp.)* ■ ser aburridísimo to be extremely boring

Romano Pontífice ■ el Papa the Pope

romper a cantar to break into (a) song

romper a hervir *(Esp.)* ■ romper el hervor ■ empezar a hervir to come to a boil ■ to start to boil ■ to start boiling

romper a llorar ■ romper en llanto ■ irrumpir en llanto to burst into tears

romper aguas (for) one's water to break ➤ Rompió aguas. Her water broke.

romper con alguien ■ cortar con alguien ■ terminar con alguien to break up with someone ■ to break off one's relationship ➤ Jill rompió con su novio. Jill broke up with her boyfriend. ➤ Han roto. ■ Han cortado. ■ Han terminado. They broke up. ■ They've broken up.

romper con el pasado to break with the past

romper con la idea de que... to break with the idea that...

romper con la rutina to break the routine

romper con la tradición ■ apartarse de la tradición to break with tradition ■ to depart from tradition

romper con el pasado to break with the past ■ to make a break with the past

romper el día ■ romper la aurora ■ rayar el alba (for) dawn to break ➤ Rompía el día. Dawn was breaking.

romper el fuego ■ abrir fuego ■ empezar a disparar 1. to open fire 2. *(figurado)* to start the questions ■ to fire away (with questions)

romper el hervor ■ romper a hervir ■ empezar a hervir to come to a boil ■ to start to boil ■ to start boiling ➤ Cuando rompa el hervor, bajar el fuego. When it comes to a boil, reduce the heat.

romper el hielo *(literalmente y en una conversación)* to break the ice

romper el precinto to break the seal

romper el secreto de la confesión *(por un confesor)* to violate the secrecy of the confessional ■ to breach a confidence

romper el silencio to break the silence

romper en llanto ■ romper a llorar ■ irrumpir en llanto to burst into tears

romper filas ■ romper formación to break ranks ■ to fall out

romper formación ■ romper filas to break ranks ■ to fall out

romper la aurora ■ desapuntar la aurora ■ romper el día ■ rayar el alba for dawn to break ➤ Rompía la aurora. The dawn was breaking.

romper la baraja to end hostilities

romper las olas contra ■ estrellarse las olas contra (for) the waves to break against or on ■ (for) the waves to crash against

romper los esquemas de alguien to shatter someones illusions ■ to ruin someone's plans ■ to foul up someone's plans

romper moldes 1. to break out of the mold 2. to rewrite the history books 3. to rewrite the record books 4. to break with tradition

romper por todo to press on regardless

romper previsiones to exceed expectations

romper sus lazos con alguien to break one's ties with someone

romper una promesa ■ desobedecer una promesa hecha ■ faltar a una promesa ■ no cumplir (con) una promesa ■ incumplir una promesa to break a promise ■ not to keep a promise ■ to fail to keep a promise

romper vínculos con alguien to part company with someone ■ to terminate a friendship

romperle la cara a alguien ■ partirle la cara a alguien to smash someone's face

romperle la crisma a alguien ■ romperle la cabeza to knock someone's block off

romperle la piel to break the skin ➤ Me mordió el perro, pero no me rompió la piel. The dog bit me, it didn't break the skin.

romperle las narices a alguien to punch someone in the nose

romperle los dientes a alguien to bash someone's teeth in ▪ *(coloquial)* to bust someone's teeth in

romperse con una fractura seria (for a) bone to be badly broken ➤ Se rompió el hueso con una fractura seria. The bone was badly broken.

romperse el culo to bust one's butt ▪ to bust one's ass ▪ to work one's ass off

romperse en pedazos to fall apart

romperse la espalda (trabajando) ▪ partirse el espinazo (trabajando) to break one's back working ▪ to break one's back with work

romperse los codos ▪ hincar los codos ▪ empollar ▪ estudiar to hit the books

romperse los cojones *(subido de tono, coloquial)* to bust one's tail ▪ to bust one's ass ▪ to bust one's balls

romperse un bolsillo (for) a pocket to wear through ➤ Se me rompió el bolsillo del pantalón. My pants pocket wore through.

romperse un hueso to break a bone ➤ Se rompió la muñeca. He broke his wrist.

rompérsele la espalda to suffer a broken back ➤ Se le rompió la espalda en un accidente. His back was broken in an accident.

ronda de aplausos: darle a alguien una ~ to give someone a round of applause ➤ Démosles a la plantilla de la cocina una ronda de aplausos. Let's give the kitchen crew a round of applause.

rondar con mala gente ▪ merodear con mala gente ▪ holgazanear con mala gente ▪ haraganear con mala gente ▪ andar con mala gente ▪ reunirse con mala gente to run around with the wrong crowd ▪ to hang around with the wrong crowd ▪ to hang out with the wrong crowd ▪ to run around with a bad crowd ▪ to hang around with a bad crowd ▪ to hang out with a bad crowd

rondar (ya) los *x* (años) to be around *x* (years old) ➤ Ronda los treinta. ▪ *(él)* He's around thirty (years old). ▪ *(ella)* She's around thirty.

ropa blanca 1. lienzo linen(s) **2.** vestimenta blanca white clothes ▪ white clothing

ropa de abrigo warm clothes ▪ warm clothing

ropa de cama bedclothes ▪ covers

ropa de la tintorería clothes from the dry cleaner ▪ dry cleaning ➤ Tengo que ir a reocoger mi ropa de la tintorería. I have to go pick up my clothes from the dry cleaner. ▪ I have to go pick up my dry cleaning.

ropa de mesa table linen

ropa de negocios business attire

ropa desgreñada disheveled clothes

ropa harapienta ▪ ropa andrajosa ▪ ropa deshilachada ragged clothes ▪ tattered clothes

ropa inservible clothes that don't fit any more ▪ outgrown clothes ▪ old clothes

ropa interior underclothes

ropa protectora protective clothing

ropa que lleva uno clothes one is wearing

la **ropa sucia se lava en casa** don't wash your dirty linen in public

estar **roque** to be out like a light ▪ to be zonked out ➤ Se acaba de acostar y ya está roque. He just went to bed and he's already out like a light.

rosario de abundance of ▪ string of ▪ barrage of ▪ flood of ▪ *(culto)* plethora of

rosario de insultos ▪ cantidad de improperios ▪ flujo de insultos ▪ avalancha de insultos ▪ plétora de insultos barrage of insults ▪ stream of insults

rosario de libros (whole) lot of books ▪ bunch of books ▪ abundance of books

rosca al revés ▪ rosca a izquierdas reverse thread ▪ left-handed thread ➤ La rosca al revés se aprieta hacia la izquierda. You tighten a reverse thread counterclockwise. ▪ You tighten a left-handed thread counterclockwise.

rosca de reyes *(Arg.)* ▪ (el) roscón de reyes large ring-shaped cake baked for Epiphany (January 6 Christian celebration)

rosca desgastada *(tornillo)* stripped threads

rosca gastada *(tornillo)* worn threads

el **roscón de reyes** *(Esp.)* large ring-shaped cake baked for Epiphany (January 6 Christian celebration)

rostro a rostro ▪ cara a cara face to face

rostro curtido ▪ cara curtida leathery face

rostro de miedo ▪ cara de miedo fearful face

rostro hermético poker face ➤ Estaba rodeado de rostros herméticos. He was surrounded by poker faces.

la **rotación de cosechas** crop rotation

rotar cosechas to rotate crops

rotar sobre su eje ▪ girar sobre su eje to rotate on its axis

rotundidad de la explicación completeness of the explanation

rotundidad del informe completeness of the report

rozamiento del aire resistance of the air ▪ friction of the air

rozar de ramas rustling of the branches ▪ rustling of the leaves ➤ Al oír el rozar de ramas On hearing the rustling of the branches ▪ *(yo)* When I heard the rustling of the branches ▪ *(él)* When he heard the rustling of the branches

rozar el fracaso to have a brush with failure

rozar *x* euros to inch toward *x* euros

rubricar un acuerdo ▪ firmar un acuerdo to sign an agreement

rueda de auxilio ▪ rueda de repuesto spare tire

rueda de la fortuna wheel of fortune

rueda de prensa ▪ rueda de periodistas news conference ▪ press conference

rueda de reconocimiento police lineup

rueda de repuesto ▪ rueda de auxilio spare tire

ruedas delanteras front wheels

ruedas traseras rear wheels

ruedo político ▪ palestra política political arena

rugir el tigre *(Esp.)* ▪ oler mal el inodoro (for) the toilet to reek ▪ (for) the toilet to stink

la **rugosidad del papel** coarseness of the paper

ruido de fondo ▪ ruido en el fondo background noise

ruido de los sables ▪ ruido de sables ▪ ruido de los cuarteles ▪ pulso militar saber rattling

ruido en el fondo ▪ ruido de fondo background noise

ruinas cataclísmicas catastrophic destruction ▪ catastrophic damage

ruleta rusa Russian roulette

rumbo de la vida direction of one's life

rumbo en la vida: tener un ~ ▪ tener un norte en la vida to have a direction in (one's) life

rumbo este ▪ hacia el este eastbound

rumbo norte ▪ hacia el norte northbound

rumbo oeste ▪ hacia el oeste westbound

rumbo sur ▪ hacia el sur southbound

el **rumor de la lluvia** ▪ tamborileo de la lluvia patter of the rain ➤ Los durmió el rumor de la lluvia. The patter of the rain lulled them to sleep.

el **rumor del viento** rustling of the wind

ruptura material material breach

ser la **ruta más corta** ▪ ser la ruta más directa to be the shortest way ▪ to be the most direct route

S.A. ■ sociedad anónima Inc. ■ incorporated

sábana de contour fitted sheet

sabe Dios God knows ■ God only knows

¿sabe (usted) cómo ir? ■ ¿sabe (usted) el camino? do you know how to get there? ■ do you know the way?

¿sabe (used) el camino? ■ ¿sabe (usted) cómo ir? do you know the way? ■ do you know how to get there?

saber a to taste like ➤ Esto sabe a ron cubano. This tastes like Cuban rum.

saber a ciencia cierta que... to know with absolute certainty that...

saber a cuerno quemado 1. to be a slap in the face 2. to sound fishy

saber a gloria to taste divine ■ to taste great

saber a poco to be a disappointment ➤ La película me supo a poco. The movie was a disappointment. ➤ La asignatura me supo a poco. The course was a disappointment.

saber a qué atenerse to know what to expect

saber a rayos (y centellas) ■ saber penoso ■ saber terriblemente mal ■ saber terroríficamente mal to taste terrible ■ to taste awful

saber algo a papagayo ■ saber de memoria to be able to reel off from memory

saber algo a priori ■ saber algo con antelación ■ saber algo de antemano to know something a priori ■ to know something before the fact ■ to know something beforehand

saber algo al dedillo 1. to know something by heart 2. to know something thoroughly

saber algo como el Ave María ■ saber algo como el Padrenuestro (for) something to be second nature

saber algo con antelación ■ saber algo de antemano ■ saber algo a priori to know something beforehand

saber algo de antemano ■ saber algo con antelación ■ saber algo a priori to know beforehand

saber algo de boca de otro to know something from word of mouth ■ to have found out something from someone else ■ to learn of something from someone else ■ to hear (of) something from someone else

saber algo de buena tinta to have it straight from the horse's mouth ■ to have (it) on good authority ■ to know from reliable sources

saber algo de carrerilla to be able to reel off something ■ to be able to reel something off

saber algo de memoria to know something by heart ■ to know something by rote

saber algo de primera mano ■ saber algo de primeras to know something firsthand ➤ Lo sé de primera mano. ■ Lo sé de primeras. I know (it) firsthand.

saber amargo to taste bitter

saber andar por un sitio to know one's way around a place

saber bastante para sus años ■ saber bastante para su edad to know a lot for one's age

saber bien 1. *(conocimientos)* to know well 2. *(sabor)* to taste good

saber callarse to know when to keep quiet ■ knowing when to keep quiet ■ knowing how to keep quiet

saber capear los temporales to know how to weather the storms

saber (cómo) moverse to know one's way around ➤ Ese chico realmente sabe (cómo) moverse. That guy really knows his way around.

saber cómo conseguir que se hagan las cosas to know how to get things done ➤ El Presidente Polk, dijo el historiador Bernard DeVoto, supo cómo conseguir que se hicieran las cosas. President Polk, said historian Bernard DeVoto, knew how to get things done.

saber cómo salirse con la suya con alguien ■ saber cómo lograr que alguien haga lo que uno quiere ■ saber cómo manejar a alguien ■ tener mano con alguien to know how to get one's way with someone

saber con qué buey ara ■ saber con qúe bueyes ara ■ saber con los bueyes que ara to know who one's friends are ■ to know who your friends are

saber cuál es el sentido de su vida to know one's purpose in life ■ to have direction ■ to know where one is going

saber cuál es la diferencia entre ■ conocer la diferencia entre to know the difference between ➤ ¿Sabes cuál es la diferencia entre "en decúbito prono" y "en decúbito supino"? Estar en decúbito prono es estar boca abajo. Estar en decúbito supino es estar boca arriba. ■ ¿Conoces la diferencia entre "en decúbito prono" y "en decúbito supino"? Estar en decúbito prono significa estar boca abajo. Estar en decúbito supino significa estar boca arriba. Do you know the difference between "prone" and "supine"? To lie prone means to lie face down. To lie supine means face up.

saber de algo 1. tener conocimiento de algo to know of something 2. enterarse de algo to know about something 3. recibir noticias de algo to hear about something ➤ ¿Sabes de alguna juguetería en esta zona? Do you know of a toy store in this area? ➤ No sé nada de eso. I don't know anything about that. ➤ Quiero que me cuentes qué tal fue tu viaje. ■ Quiero oír cómo te fue el viaje. I want to hear about your trip.

saber de alguien ■ oír de alguien to hear from someone ➤ Es bueno saber de ti. ■ ¡Qué bien que te oigo! ■ ¡Qué bien saber de ti! ■ ¡Qué bueno es saber de ti! ■ ¡Qué bueno es oírte! It's good to hear from you. ➤ Era bueno saber de ti. ■ ¡Qué bueno fue oírte! ■ ¡Qué bien que te oí! ■ ¡Qué bueno fue saber de ti! It was good to hear from you! ➤ ¿Qué sabes de Miguel? ■ ¿Qué has oído de Miguel? What do you hear from Miguel? ➤ Sabrás de mí la semana que viene. You'll hear from me next week.

saber de antemano (uno) ■ tener conocimiento previo to know beforehand ■ to know in advance ■ to have previously known ■ to have prior knowledge of

saber de boca de otro que... to learn from someone that...

saber de fijo to know for sure ■ to know definitely ➤ No lo sé de fijo. I don't know for sure.

saber de la experiencia que... ■ saber por la experiencia que... to know from personal experience that... ■ to know from personal experience (that...) ■ to know from one's own experience (that...) ➤ Sé de la experiencia que la comida mexicana está buenísima. I know from personal experience that Mexican food is delicious.

saber de lo que se trata *(libro, película)* ■ saber de qué se trata ■ saber de qué va to know what it's about

saber de lo que uno es capaz to know what one is capable of

saber de qué pie cojea ■ saber cuál es el punto débil de alguien ■ saber cuál es el talón de Aquiles de alguien to know someone's weaknesses ■ to know someone's defects ■ to know someone's weak points ■ to know someone's vulnerabilities

saber de qué va *(libro, película)* ■ saber de lo que se trata ■ saber de qué se trata to know what it's about

saber desde dentro qué... to find out for oneself what... ■ to see for oneself what... ■ to see firsthand what...

saber desde un principio to know all along ➤ (Yo) lo sabía desde un principio. I knew it all along. ➤ Lo supe desde un principio. I had known it all along.
saber dónde aprieta el zapato 1. *(literal)* to know where the shoe pinches 2. *(figurativo)* to know (better than others) what one's own problems are ■ to know one's own mind
saber dónde le aprieta el zapato a uno 1. *(literal)* to know where the shoe pinches ■ to know where the shoe is too tight 2. *(figurativo)* saber cuál es el punto débil de alguien ■ saber cuál es el talón de Aquiles de alguien to know someone's weakness ■ to know someone's Achilles' heel
saber dónde se mete ■ saber en que se mete uno to know what one is getting into ➤ Yo sabía donde me metía. I knew what I was getting into.
saber el guión ■ saberse el guión to know the script
saber el método de algo to know how to go about doing something
saber el terreno que pisa to know one's ground on an issue
saber entrar to know how to get in
saber es poder knowledge is power
saber hacer algo to know how to do something
saber hacerla bien ■ saber montárselo bien to know how to put on a good show
saber hacerlo con los ojos cerrados to be able to do it with one's eyes closed ■ to be able to do it blindfolded ➤ Sé hacerlo con los ojos cerrados. I can do it with my eyes closed. ■ I can do it blindfolded.
saber hasta de even to know (about) ➤ Valdano sabe hasta de baloncesto. Valdano even knows basketball.
saber ir a un sitio ■ saber por dónde se va a un sitio to know how to get to a place ■ to know the way to a place ➤ ¿Sabes ir? Do you know how to get there? ■ Do you know the way?
saber la tierra que pisa to know one's ground on an issue
saber la vida y milagros de alguien to know someone's life history
saber latín ■ saber mucho latín 1. conocer el latín to know Latin 2. ser despierto to be sharp ■ to be astute ➤ Emmanuel sabe Latín. Emmanuel knows Latin. ■ Emmanuel is sharp.
saber llevar bien a alguien ■ saber aguantar a alguien ■ saber lidiar con alguein to know how to cope with someone ■ to know how to deal with someone
saber llevar algo to know how to cope with something
saber lo que conlleva ■ saber lo que implica ■ saber lo que involucra to know what it involves
saber lo que es bueno para uno to know what's good for one ➤ Harás la tarea si sabes lo que bueno para ti. You'll do your homework if you know what's good for you.
saber lo que es propio *(protocolo)* ■ saber lo es correcto to know what's proper ■ to know the correct protocol ■ to know what's correct
saber lo que se lleva entre manos ■ saber lo que se trae entre manos to know what someone is up to
saber lo que se trae entre manos ■ saber lo que se lleva entre manos to know what someone is up to
saber lo último ■ oír lo último to hear the latest ➤ ¿Sabes lo último? ■ ¿Has oído lo último? Have you heard the latest?
saber los resultados de algo ■ oír los resultados de algo to know the results of something ■ to know the decision on something ■ to hear (the decision) on something ➤ Todavía no sé nada de mi solicitud de residencia. ■ Todavía no he oído nada sobre mi solicitud de residencia. I still don't know the decision on my residency application. ■ I still haven't heard anything on my residency application.
saber más que Lepe *(Esp.)* ■ ser muy astuto y perspicaz to be astute ■ to be cunning
saber mejor que nadie que... to know as well as anyone that... ■ to know perfectly well that... ■ to know very well that...
saber mucho latín ■ saber latín to be very astute ■ to be very sharp ■ to be super sharp
saber muy bien lo que hace to know exactly what one is doing ➤ Los saboteadores sabían muy bien lo que hacían. The saboteurs knew exactly what they were doing.
saber no ocupa lugar: el ~ get an education! ■ improve yourself! ■ knowledge takes up no space
saber pasarlo bien to know how to have fun ■ to know how to have a good time
saber penoso ■ saber a rayos (y centellas) ■ saber terroríficamente mal ■ saber terriblemente mal to taste terrible ■ to taste awful
saber perfectamente que... to know perfectly well (that)... ■ to know full well (that)... ■ to know very well (that)... ➤ *(editorial)* Sabe perfectamente que perdería una elección abierta, con voto secreto. He knows perfectly well that he would lose an open election by secret ballot.
saber por boca de otro que... ■ saber de boca de otro que... to learn from someone else that...
saber que algo anda mal to know something is wrong ➤ Su padre supo que algo andaba mal al encontrar a su hijo recostado en la cama llorando. His father knew something was wrong when he found his son lying on the bed crying.
saber si to figure out whether
saber su recorrido por un lugar to know one's way around a place ➤ Sé mi recorrido por Jalapa. I know my way around Jalapa.
saber terriblemente mal ■ saber terroríficamente mal ■ saber penoso ■ saber a rayos (y centellas) to taste terrible ■ to taste awful
saber terroríficamente mal ■ saber terriblemente mal ■ saber penoso ■ saber a rayos (y centellas) to taste terrible ■ to taste awful
saber tocar el piano to know how to play the piano ■ to be able to play the piano ➤ Mary sabe tocar el piano. Mary knows how to play the piano. ■ Mary can play the piano.
saber un huevo *(argot)* to know a lot
saber usar to know how to use
saber vivir to know how to live
saberlo por to find it out from ■ to find out from
saberlo por boca de alguien to hear it from someone
saberse al dedillo to know by heart
saberse algo ■ salir algo a la luz ■ trascenderse algo to become known ■ to come to light ■ to get out ➤ No podemos dejar que esto se sepa. ■ No podemos dejar que esto salga a la luz. ■ No podemos dejar que esto se trascienda. We can't let this become known. ■ We can't let this come to light. ■ We can't let this get out.
saberse algo de corrido to know something by heart
saberse la cartilla ■ tener aprendida la cartilla to able to reel off
saberse las frases ■ saberse las líneas to know one's lines
saberse las líneas ■ saberse las frases to know one's lines
saberse los entresijos to know the ins and outs
sabérselas todas to know every trick in the book
sabérselo hacer to know how to do it
sabérselo todo to know everything ➤ Parece que se lo sabe todo. *(él)* He seems to know everything. ■ *(ella)* She seems to know everything.
sabes a qué me refiero you know what I'm taking about ■ you know what I'm referring to ■ you know what I mean
¿sabes a quién me haces recordar? ■ ¿sabes a quién me recuerdas? ■ ¿sabes en quién me haces pensar? (do) you know who you remind me of?
¿sabes a quién me recuerdas? ■ ¿sabes a quién me haces recordar? ■ ¿sabes en quién me haces pensar? do you know who you remind me of? ■ do you know who you made me think of?
¿sabes algo? 1. (do) you know something? 2. do you know anything about it?
¿sabes algo de...? have you heard anything from...? ➤ ¿Sabes algo de tus primos? Have you heard anything from your cousins?
¿sabes alguna cosa de...? do you know anything about...?
¿sabes cómo llegar? ■ ¿sabes ir? do you know how to get there? ■ do you know the way?
sabes de sobra que no he sido yo you know it wasn't I ■ *(coloquial pero incorrecto)* you know it wasn't me
sabes efectivamente que... you know damned well that...
¿sabes en quién me haces pensar? (do) you know who you made me think of? ■ do you know who you remind me of?
¿sabes ir? ■ ¿sabes cómo llegar? do you know how to get there? ■ do you know the way?

¿sabes lo que te digo? you know what I'm saying?
sabes que sí 1. you know it is 2. you know I do *(puede ir con cualquier pronombre)*
¿sabes ya el día? do you know the day yet?
sabía que vendrías *(con "yo")* I knew you would come ▪ I knew you'd come
¿sabías algo (sobre esto)? ▪ ¿lo sabías? did you know about it?
¿sabías eso? did you know that?
¿sabes por casualidad...? ▪ ¿sabes por algún casual...? do you happen to know...? ▪ do you by any chance know...?
¿sabes por casualidad si...? ▪ ¿sabes por algún casual si...? do you happen to know if...?
¿sabes por casualidad si (o no)...? ▪ ¿sabes por algún casual si (o no)...? do you happen to know whether (or not)...?
sabes tanto como yo you know as much as I do ▪ your guess is as good as mine
¿sabías que...? did you know that...?
sabor acerbo sharp taste
sabor amargo bitter flavor
sabor intenso strong flavor
saborear las mieles del triunfo to savor the triumph
¿sabrías por casualidad...? ▪ ¿sabrías por algún casual...? would you happen to know...?
¿sabrías por casualidad si...? ▪ ¿sabrías por algún casual si...? would you happen to know if...?
¿sabrías por casualidad si (o no)...? ▪ ¿sabrías por algún casual si (o no)...? would you happen to know whether (or not)...
¡saca la cabeza afuera! ▪ ¡saca las manos (de aquí)! ▪ ¡saca tus pezuñas! ▪ ¡quita tus pezuñas! ▪ ¡quita de ahí tus zarpas! ▪ ¡mantente a raya! back off!
saca las manos (de aquí) ▪ saca la cabeza afuera ▪ saca tus pezuñas ▪ quita tus pezuñas ▪ ¡quita de ahí tus zarpas! ▪ ¡mantente a raya! back off!
¡sácalo de aquí! 1. *(a él)* get him out of here! 2. *(a ella)* get her out of here!
sacar a alguien de la cama con grúa to drag someone out of bed ➤ Los lunes por la mañana, hay que sacar a los niños de la cama con grúa. We have to drag the kids out of bed on Monday morning.
sacar a alguien de un apuro to get someone out of a jam ▪ to save someone from a predicament ▪ to bail someone out of a predicament
sacar a alguien del error to set someone straight
sacar a bailar a alguien to ask someone to dance ▪ to take someone out onto the dance floor
sacar a colación to bring up ▪ to mention first ➤ ¡Tú lo has sacado a colación!-¡No he sido yo! You brought it up!-I did not!
sacar a golpes a alguien to remove someone by force ▪ to eject someone by force
sacar a hombros a alguien to carry someone out on one's shoulders
sacar a la palestra un asunto to bring a matter up for discussion ➤ Sacaron a la palestra el asunto. They brought the matter up for discussion.
sacar a lucir algo to show off something ▪ to show something off
sacar a luz to bring to light ▪ to reveal
sacar a pasear al perro ▪ sacar al perro a dar una vuelta to take the dog (out) for a walk ▪ to walk the dog
sacar a plomo ▪ quitar valor a ▪ restar valor a to make light of ▪ to play down the importance of
sacar algo a pública subasta to put something up for public auction
sacar a subasta to put up for auction ▪ to auction
sacar agua de ▪ recoger agua de to draw water from ▪ to get water from
sacar agua de las piedras to squeeze blood out of a turnip
sacar al perro a dar una vuelta ▪ sacar a pasear al perro to take the dog out for a walk ▪ to take the dog for a walk ▪ to walk the dog
sacar algo a alguien a correazos to beat it out of someone
sacar algo a flote 1. to bring something to light 2. to restore profitability
sacar algo a la luz to bring something to light
sacar algo a la venta ▪ poner algo a la venta to introduce something on the market ▪ to put something on the market
sacar algo a relucir to bring something up ▪ to mention something
sacar apuntes to take notes
sacar beneficio de algo to get benefit from something ▪ to benefit from something
sacar buenas notas to make good grades ▪ to get good grades
sacar de madre a alguien *(coloquial)* to madden someone
sacar de quicio a alguien ▪ poner de los nervios a alguien to exasperate someone ▪ to get on one's nerves ▪ to get under one's skin ▪ to get under someone's skin ➤ Tener a mi abuela en casa todo el día me saca de quicio. Having my grandmother at home all day gets on my nerves. ▪ Having my grandmother at home all day gets under my skin.
sacar del buche to come out with it ➤ ¡Sácatelo del buche! Out with it! ▪ Just say it!
sacar dinero de una cuenta ▪ retirar dinero de una cuenta to withdraw money from an account ▪ to take money out of an account ▪ to take out money from an account ▪ to take money from an account
sacar el canario a pasear *(pintoresco)* to shake the dew off the rose ▪ to take a leak
sacar el coche de culo hasta la calzada *(Esp.)* ▪ dar marcha atrás hasta la calzada to back (out) onto the street
sacar el jugo a la naranja to juice (an orange)
sacar el látigo (a alguien) to crack the whip on someone ➤ Parece que el catedrático ha sacado el látigo y tenemos que ponernos las pilas. That professor (really) cracks the whip, and we have to bust our butts.
sacar el mejor partido posible de la situación to make the best of a situation
sacar el tema a colación ▪ mencionar la cuestión to bring up the subject ➤ Fue el General Lee quien sacó el tema de la rendición. It was General Lee who brought up the subject of the surrender.
sacar en claro ▪ sacar en limpio to learn from something that... ▪ to get out of it that... ▪ to be clear to one... ▪ to be able to get something out of something ➤ Saqué en claro que... I got out of it that... ▪ I understood from it that... ➤ Lo único que saqué en claro fue... The only thing that was clear (from it) was... ▪ The only thing I could get out of it was...
sacar en limpio ▪ sacar en claro to learn from something that... ▪ to get out of it that... ▪ to be clear to one... ▪ to be able to get something out of something ➤ Saqué en limpio que... I got out of it that... ▪ I understood from it that... ➤ Lo único que saqué en limpio fue... The only thing that was clear was... ▪ The only thing I could get out of it was...
sacar fuera de contexto to take out of context
sacar información de alguien to get information out of someone
sacar la basura 1. to take out the trash 2. *(especialmente materia orgánica que puede pudrirse)* to take out the garbage
sacar la cabeza to stick one's head out ➤ No saques la cabeza por la ventana. Don't stick your head out (of) the window.
sacar la cabeza de aquí to back off
sacar la cara por alguien ▪ salir a defender a alguien ▪ apoyar a alguien to stick one's neck out for someone ▪ to come to someone's defense ▪ to back someone up ➤ Si el jefe te reta, sacaré la cara por ti. ▪ Si el jefe te reta, yo te apoyaré. If the boss challenges you, I'll back you up.
sacar la conclusión to arrive at the conclusion ▪ to come to the conclusion
sacar la consecuencia de que... to gather that...
sacar la flema tosiendo ▪ arrancar la flema ▪ despedir la flema tosiendo to loosen the phlegm ▪ to cough up phlegm ▪ to bring up phlegm ➤ El médico le recetó un expectorante para hacerle sacar la flema. The doctor prescribed him an expectorant to loosen the phlegm.
sacar la idea de hacer algo de... to get the idea to do something from...

sacar la lengua a alguien to stick one's tongue out at someone

sacar la puerta de las bisagras to take the door off the hinges ➤ Voy a sacar la puerta de sus bisagras para poderla pintar. I'm going to take the door from the jamb so I can paint it. ▪ I'm going to take the door off the hinges so I can paint it.

sacar la tarjeta amarilla a un jugador to flash the yellow card at a player ▪ to yellow-card a player

sacar la vergüenza a alguien ▪ avergonzar a alguien ▪ ruborizar a alguien to make someone blush

sacar lápiz y papel to take out pencil and paper

sacar las cosas de quicio 1. dejar que todo se vaya a la miércoles to let things get out of hand ▪ to let things go to the dogs ▪ to let things go to hell 2. hacer una montaña de un grano de arena to blow things out of proportion ▪ to make a mountain out of a molehill

sacar las vergüenzas a alguien to embarrass someone (by revealing secrets)

sacar lo mejor de alguien to get the best out of someone

sacar lo mejor de sí mismo ▪ mostrar lo mejor de sí mismo to put one's best foot forward ▪ to turn on the charm

sacar lo que uno sabe *(por coacción)* to force the information out of someone ▪ to coerce the information out of someone

sacar los pies de las alforjas to go off on a different track ▪ to go off on a different tack

sacar malas notas to make bad grades ▪ to make poor grades ▪ to get bad grades ▪ to get poor grades

sacar más provecho de algo to get more out of something ➤ Sacarás más provecho (de eso) que los otros. You'll get more out of it than the others.

sacar partido a algo ▪ sacar partido de algo to make the most of something ➤ *(anuncio)* Saca partido al ocio en Internet. Make the most of your leisure time on the Internet.

sacar partido de algo ▪ sacar partido a algo to make the most of something ➤ *(anuncio)* Saca partido del ocio en Internet. Make the most of your leisure time on the Internet.

sacar provecho de ▪ beneficiarse de ▪ beneficiarse con ▪ coloquial sacar tajada de to benefit from ▪ to profit from

sacar tajada de *(coloquial)* ▪ sacar provecho de ▪ beneficiarse de ▪ beneficiarse con to benefit from ▪ to profit from

sacar trabajo adelante to get accomplished ➤ No saqué adelante todo el trabajo que esperaba. I didn't get accomplished all I had hoped to accomplish.

sacar un corner *(fútbol)* to do a corner kick

sacar un curso ▪ crear un curso to introduce a course

sacar un diente ▪ extraer un diente to pull a tooth ▪ to extract a tooth

sacar un puñal ▪ blandir un puñal to draw a daggar ➤ Sacó su puñal. He drew his daggar.

sacar un sobresaliente ▪ ponerle un sobresaliente to get an A ➤ Saqué un sobresaliente en el examen, no te creas. ▪ Me han puesto un sobresaliente en el examen, no te creas. I got an A on the test, would you believe.

sacar una conclusión ▪ llegar a una conclusión to come to a conclusion ▪ to arrive at a conclusion ▪ to draw a conclusion ➤ ¿Qué conclusiones has podido sacar de tu estudio? What conclusions have you been able to draw from your study?

sacar una copia to make a copy

sacar una espada ▪ desenvainar una espada to draw a sword

sacar una hoja en blanco to get out a piece of paper ▪ to take out a piece of paper

sacarle una impresión a algo to make an impression of something ▪ to make a mold of something ➤ El dentista me sacó una impresión a mis dientes. The dentist made an impression of my teeth. ▪ The dentist made a mold of my teeth.

sacar una nota to get a grade ➤ Saqué un sobresaliente en el examen. ▪ Saqué una A en el examen. I got an A on the test.

sacar una publicación to get out a publication ▪ to get a publication out ➤ Tenemos que sacar este número. We've got to get this issue out. ▪ We've got to get out this issue. ➤ Tenemos que sacarlo. We've got to get it out.

sacar *x* en el examen to get *x* on the exam

sacarle de quicio to get on someone's nerves ▪ to make someone see red ➤ Era algo que me sacaba de quicio. It was getting on my nerves. ▪ It was making me see red. ➤ Nos sacamos de quicio el uno al otro. ▪ Nos sacamos de quicio (mutuamente). We get on each other's nerves.

sacarle de sus casillas a alguien to drive someone up the wall ➤ Le saca de sus casillas, llamándolo, enviándole correos electrónicos y interrumpiendo su trabajo. She drives him up the wall, calling, sending E-mails, and interrupting his work.

sacarle de tino a alguien ▪ exasperar a alguien to exasperate someone

sacarle dinero a alguien to get money out of someone ➤ No vas a sacarle dinero a ella. You won't get any money out of her.

sacarle una fotografía a alguien ▪ tomarle una fotografía a alguien to take someone's picture

sacar(le) en claro ▪ dar(le) a entender ▪ decir claro to make clear

sacarle información a alguien con un tirabuzón ▪ sacarle información a alguien con un sacacorchos to drag information out of someone

sacarle partido a algo to make the most of something ➤ Sácales partido a tus estudios. Make the most of your studies. ➤ ¡Sácate partido! Make the most of it!

sacarle punta a lo que dice alguien to twist someone's words

sacarle todo con tirabuzón to drag it out of someone

sacarlo a alguien de su error to set someone straight

sacarse algo del buche to come out with something ➤ ¡Sácatelo del buche! Out with it! ▪ Just say it! ▪ Come on, tell me! ▪ Come on, tell us!

sacarse de quicio el uno al otro ▪ sacarse de quicio mutuamente to get on each other's nerves

sacarse la borrachera ▪ quitarse la borrachera to sober up

sacarse la camisa to pull out one's shirttail(s) ▪ to pull one's shirttail(s) out

sacarse la tensión to get something out of one's system

sacarse las yugas ▪ desajustarse las coyunturas to crack one's knuckles

sacarse los guantes ▪ descalzarse los guantes to take off one's gloves

sacarse un diente ▪ sacarse una muela ▪ tener una extracción dental to have a tooth pulled ▪ to have a tooth extracted

sacarse una foto(grafía) ▪ tomarse una foto(grafía) to have one's picture taken ➤ Me saqué una foto. I had my picture taken.

sacarse una muela ▪ sacarse un diente ▪ tener una extracción dental to have a tooth pulled ▪ to have a tooth extracted

¡sácate partido! make the most of it!

¡sácatelo del buche! out with it! ▪ tell me! ▪ tell us!

saco de dormir sleeping bag

saco roto 1. comilón ▪ cubo de basura ▪ tragaldabas ▪ tragón(a) bottomless pit ▪ vacuum cleaner 2. pozo sin fondo drain on one's resources 3. comprador compulsivo spendthrift ▪ compulsive spender

saco de arena sandbag

sacrificar a un animal (para el consumo humano) to slaughter an animal (for human consumption)

sacrificar a un animal (para que no sufra) ▪ darle a un animal una inyección letal to put an animal to sleep ▪ to euthanize an animal ➤ Después de que el animal fuera herido, el veterinario lo sacrificó con un barbitúrico de acción rápida. After the animal was injured, the veterinarian put it to sleep with a fast-acting barbiturate.

sacrificar muchas cosas to make a lot of sacrifices

¡sacúdete la pereza de los huesos! get the lead out of your butt! ▪ get off your duff!

sacudirse la pereza to get the lead out of one's butt ➤ ¡Sacúdete la pereza! Get the lead out of your butt!

sacudirse la tiranía de to shake off the tyranny of

sacudirse los efectos de la droga to shake off the effects of the drug

Sagrada Biblia ▪ Santa Biblia Holy Bible

sagrada familia holy family

sagrada forma *(catolicismo)* ▪ hostia host ▪ communion wafer

¡sal de aquí! ▪ ¡largo de aquí! get out of here!

la **sal de la tierra** salt of the earth

sala de montaje film-editing room

salario neto take-home pay ▪ net pay ▪ net salary

saldar cuentas to get even ▪ to get revenge ▪ to settle accounts

saldar la cuenta to pay off the account

saldar la deuda to pay off the debt

saldar una cuenta 1. vengarse to get revenge ▪ to get even ▪ to settle accounts **2.** liquidar una deuda to pay off an account ▪ to settle an account ▪ to liquidate a debt

saldar una deuda to pay off a debt ▪ to settle a debt

saldar uno todas sus deudas to get out of debt

saldo a favor positive balance ▪ balance in favor

saldo actual present balance ▪ current balance ➤ Su cuenta arroja un saldo actual de 30.000 pesetas. Your account shows a current balance of 30,000 pesetas.

saldo de la cuenta bancaria bank (account) balance

saldo de una cuenta ▪ saldo a favor positive balance ▪ balance in favor ▪ balance of an account

saldo deudor ▪ saldo en contra balance owed ▪ negative balance ▪ balance on an account

saldo en contra ▪ saldo deudor balance owed ▪ negative balance ▪ balance on an account

sale más barato it's cheaper in the long run ▪ it comes out cheaper in the end

salga lo que salga ▪ cueste lo que cueste no matter how much it costs ▪ (the) money is not an issue ▪ money's not an issue ▪ price is no object

sálgase (usted) con la suya ▪ puede (usted) salirse con la suya have it your way ▪ you can have it your way

salida de emergencia emergency exit

salida de la situación ▪ forma de salir de la situación way out of the situation

salida de socorro *(Esp.)* ▪ salida de emergencia emergency exit

salida de tono impertinence ▪ outburst ➤ ¡Menuda salida de tono! What an outburst! ▪ That was quite an outburst!

salida en el control de seguridad security loophole

salida fácil: hay una ~ there's an easy way out

salida fácil: tomar la ~ to take the easy way out

salida más próxima nearest exit

salida para setting for

salida transitoria temporary development ▪ temporary situation

salido(-a): estar muy ~ *(Esp.)* ▪ estar muy salido **1.** to be horny **2.** to be a sex maniac ▪ to be a sex fiend

salido(-a) en ▪ que se estrenó en which came out in ▪ which was released in ▪ which was introduced onto the market in ➤ El filme, salido en 1967... The film, which came out in 1967... ▪ The film, released in 1967...

salir a ▪ llevar a to lead to

salir a caminar *(L.am.)* ▪ salir a dar un paseo ▪ salir de paseo ▪ salir a dar una vuelta to go out for a walk

salir a cazar ▪ ir de caza to go hunting

salir a cenar ▪ cenar fuera to go out for supper ▪ to go out for (evening) dinner ▪ to dine out

salir a comer ▪ comer fuera to go out for lunch ▪ to go out for (afternoon) dinner ▪ to dine out

salir a cuerpo gentil to go out without a coat ▪ to go outside without a coat

salir a dar un paseo ▪ salir de paseo ▪ salir a caminar to go out for a walk

salir a escena por primera vez to make one's first appearance in the play ➤ Falstaff sale a escena en el segundo acto. Falstaff makes his first appearance in the second act.

salir a flote 1. seguir adelante to land on one's feet **2.** darse a conocer to come out ➤ Tras la ruina de su negocio, él salió a flote y terminó por convertirse en millonario. After his business failure, he landed on his feet and ended up a millionaire. ➤ La verdad finalmente sale a flote. The truth eventually comes out.

salir a hacer algo to go do something ➤ ¡Sal a llamarlo! Go call him!

salir a la calle 1. to go out (into the street) **2.** to go out on the town

salir a la calle para algo to go out for something ▪ to go out to get something ➤ Cesar salió a la calle para comprar el pan. Cesar went out for some bread. ▪ Cesar went out to get some bread.

salir a la luz ▪ saberse algo ▪ trascenderse algo to come to light ▪ to become known ▪ to get out ➤ No podemos dejar que esto salga a la luz. ▪ No podemos dejar que esto se sepa. ▪ No podemos dejar que esto se trascienda. We can't let this come to light. ▪ We can't let this get out. ▪ We can't let this become known.

salir a la palestra to enter the fray ▪ to enter the (political) arena

salir a la superficie to come to the surface

salir a las *x* esta noche to leave at *x* o'clock tonight

salir a pedir de boca to turn out perfectly

salir a todo correr to leave in a rush

salir a tomar aire 1. salir para tomar aire to go out for some fresh air **2.** escaparse de algo aburrido to come up for air

salir a un lugar ▪ llevar a un lugar ▪ conducir a un lugar ▪ dirigirse a un lugar to lead to a place ▪ to go to a place ▪ to take you to a place ➤ Esta carretera sale a Cárdenas. ▪ Esta carretera lleva a Cárdenas. ▪ Esta carretera conduce a Cárdenas. ▪ Esta carretera se dirige a Cárdenas. This road leads to Cardenas. ▪ This road goes to Cardenas. ▪ This road takes you to Cardenas.

salir adelante to move forward

salir airoso de algo to come out of something with flying colors

salir airoso de un examen detallado to bear up under scrutiny ▪ to stand up under scrutiny

salir al encuentro de alguien to go meet someone

salir al exterior to go outside

salir al mercado ▪ ser lanzado al mercado ▪ ser estrenado en el mercado to come out ▪ to come on(to) the market ▪ to be introduced onto the market ➤ Los móviles con tele incorporada salieron al mercado en el 2003. ▪ Los móviles con tele incorporada fueron lanzados al mercado en el 2003. ▪ Los móviles con tele incorporada fueron estrenados en el mercado en el 2003. Mobile phones with TVs came out in 2003. ▪ Mobile phones with TVs came onto the market in 2003. ▪ Mobile phones with TVs were introduced onto the market in 2003.

salir al paso de algo to move to block something ➤ *(noticia)* Los empresarios vascos salen al paso del Plan Ibarretxe y advierten de sus peligros Basque businessmen move to block the Ibarretxe Plan (for Basque independence) and warn of its dangers

salir algo de algo to come of it ➤ No salió nada de aquello. Nothing came of it. ➤ Espero que no salga nada de eso. I hope nothing comes of it.

salir beneficiado ▪ salir ganando to come out ahead ➤ Saldrás beneficiado. ▪ Saldrás ganando. You'll come out ahead.

salir bien parado(-a) to come off well

salir cagando leches *(Esp., subido de tono)* ▪ *(alternativa benigna)* salir echando leches to go like a bat out of hell ▪ *(coloquial)* to go like a bat outta hell

salir caro to cost a lot

salir con destino a ▪ salir para to leave for ➤ Salieron con destino a Buenos Aires el veinte y tres. They left for Buenos Aires on the twenty-third.

salir con los pies por delante ▪ estirar la pata ▪ morirse to kick the bucket ▪ to croak ▪ to die

salir con un domingo siete *(en una conversación o charla)* to come up with something completely unrelated

salir con ventaja en una carrera to get a head start in a race

salir de ▪ quitarse de encima to get rid of ➤ Sales inmediatamente de esos zapatos. You get rid of those shoes immediately.

salir de casa to leave home

salir de compras to go out shopping ➤ Ella ha salido de compras. She's gone out shopping.

salir de copas 1. salir a tomar to go out for a drink **2.** hacer la gira de bares to go bar hopping

salir de cuentas *(dícese de madres en estado)* to be due ➤ Mi hermana salió de cuentas ayer. My sister's baby was due yesterday.

salir de debajo de la cama to come out from under the bed ➤ No puedo conseguir que la gata salga de debajo de la cama. I can't get the cat to come out from under the bed.

salir de debajo de las piedras to come out of the woodwork

salir de este mundo ▪ morirse to depart this life

salir de Guatemala y entrar en Guatepeor to go from bad to worse

salir de la cantera *(deportes)* ▪ salir de los suplentes to come from the reserve team

salir de la cárcel to get out of jail

salir de la escena 1. *(en teatro)* to exit (from) the scene ▪ to leave the stage ▪ to go out **2.** no ser parte de algo to bow out ▪ to count oneself out

salir de los suplentes *(deportes)* ▪ salir de la cantera to come from the reserve team

salir de lujo to turn out better than expected ▪ to outdo oneself ▪ *(figurativo)* to hit a home run

salir de moda to go out of style

salir de nada to come out of the blue ▪ to come out of left field ▪ to come out of nowhere ➤ Su insulto salió de nada. His insult came out of the blue. ▪ His insult came out of left field.

salir de paseo ▪ salir a dar un paseo ▪ salir a dar una vuelta to go out for a walk

salir de pena ▪ salir mal to turn out badly ▪ to come out badly

salir de pena en un examen ▪ andar mal en un examen to do badly on a test ▪ to do poorly on a test ▪ not to do well on a test

salir de pena en una foto ▪ salir mal en una foto to look bad in a photo

salir de peña to go with a group of people

salir de picos pardos *(Esp.)* ▪ ir de picos pardos to go looking for some action ▪ to cat around

salir de trabajar to get off (work) ➤ ¿A qué hora sales de trabajar? What time do you get off?

salir de un apuro ▪ salir de un predicamento ▪ salir de un atolladero ▪ salir del paso to get out of a jam ▪ to get out of a fix ▪ to get out of a tight spot ▪ to get out of a predicament

salir de un atolladero ▪ salir del paso ▪ salir de un apuro to get out of a jam ▪ to get out of a fix ▪ to get out of a tight spot ▪ to get out of a predicament

salir del armario (para alguien) to come out (of the closet) to someone ▪ to disclose one's homosexuality to someone ➤ El homosexual salió del amario para su familia y amigos. The gay came out (of the closet) to his family and friends.

salir del arroyo to rise above humble circumstances

salir del ascensor to get off the elevator ➤ Gira a la izquierda cuando salgas del ascensor. Turn left when you get off the elevator. ▪ Turn left as you get off the elevator.

salir del carro ▪ bajar(se) del carro ▪ salir del coche ▪ bajar(se) del coche to get out of the car

salir del corazón to come from the heart

salir del paso to get out of a tight spot ▪ to get oneself out of a jam ▪ to get out of a fix ▪ to get out of predicament

salir del salario de uno to come out of one's salary ➤ Incluso cuando tu empleador paga la mitad de tu asistencia médica, aún sigue saliendo de tu salario. Even when your employer pays for half your medical care, it still comes out of your salary.

salir despedido por los aires to go flying through the air

salir disparado ▪ salir volando **1.** to be off and running **2.** to be off like a shot ➤ El presidente de la Bolsa de Nueva York le pagó al joven Thomas Edison cuarenta mil dólares por el teletipo, y desde ese momento Edison salió disparado. ▪ El presidente de la Bolsa de Nueva York le pagó al joven Thomas Edison cuarenta mil dólares por el teletipo, y desde ese momento Edison salió volando. The president of the New York Stock Exchange paid the young Thomas Edison forty thousand dollars for the stock ticker, and from that moment Edison was off and running. ➤ Sonó la corneta, y los caballos salieron disparados. The bugle sounded, and the horses were off like a shot. ▪ The bugle sounded, and the horses were off and running.

salir disparado hacia ▪ lanzarse hacia to make a beeline for ➤ Cuando los peques llegaron de la escuela, salieron disparados para la nevera. ▪ Cuando los peques llegaron de la escuela, se lanzaron hacia la nevera. When the kids came home from school, they made a beeline for the refrigerator.

salir echando leches to go like a bat out of hell ▪ *(coloquial)* to go like a bat outta hell

salir el sol (for) the sun to come up ▪ (for) the sun to rise

salir el tiro por la culata to backfire

salir en el periódico to be carried in the newspaper ▪ to come out in the newspaper

salir en la escena (de una obra teatral o película) to appear in the scene (of a play or movie)

salir en la primera plana to make the front page ▪ to make page one ▪ to make front page news ▪ to come out on the front page ▪ to come out on page one

salir en libertad ▪ quedar libre to go free

salir en persecución de alguien to go after someone ▪ to run after someone

salir en tromba contra algo to come out swinging against something ➤ *(titular)* El gobierno sale en tromba contra la fusión de la policía y la Guardia Civil. The government comes out swinging against the merging of the police and Civil Guard.

salir en una escena ▪ aparecer en una escena to appear in a scene ➤ Las brujas salen en la primera escena del primer acto. ▪ Las brujas aparecen en la primera escena del primer acto de Macbeth. The witches appear in the first scene of the first act of Macbeth.

salir ganando ▪ salir beneficiado to come out ahead ➤ Saldrás ganando. ▪ Saldrás beneficiado. You'll come out ahead.

salir haciendo ruedas ▪ hacer ruedas ▪ salir pelando ▪ salir arando to lay rubber ➤ El carro salió haciendo ruedas del semáforo. The car laid rubber as it started off from the traffic light.

salir hasta las altas horas de la mañana to stay out until all hours ▪ to stay out until the wee hours

salir hasta tarde ▪ quedarse hasta tarde to stay out late ➤ Tengo que trabajar mañana así que no puedo salir hasta tarde. ▪ Tengo que trabajar mañana así que no puedo quedarme hasta tarde. I have to work tomorrow, so I can't stay out late.

salir herido(-a) to be injured ▪ to suffer injuries

salir ileso(-a) to come away uninjured ▪ to come away unharmed ▪ to come away unscathed ▪ to come away without a scratch ▪ to walk away without a scratch

salir incólume ▪ salir ileso to come away unscathed ▪ to come out unscathed

salir impune de ▪ salirse con la suya to get away with

salir indemne to escape unhurt ▪ to escape unharmed ▪ to escape uninjured ▪ to escape without injury

salir mal to turn out badly

salir mal parado to come off badly

salir marcha atrás de un lugar ▪ salir marcha atrás de un hueco ▪ salir reculando de un lugar ▪ salir reculando de un hueco ▪ salir de culo de un lugar ▪ salir de culo de un hueco to back out of a parking place

salir más barato to be cheaper in the long run ▪ to come out cheaper (in the long run) ➤ Sale más barato comprar un bónobus. It's cheaper in the long run to buy a bus pass. ▪ It comes out cheaper to buy a bus pass.

salir para ▪ salir con destino a to leave for ▪ to leave bound for ➤ Salieron para Buenos Aires el veinte y tres. They left for Buenos Aires on the twenty-third.

salir para coger aire *(Esp.)* **1.** salir a tomar aire to go out for some (fresh) air **2.** escaparse de algo aburrido to come up for air

salir para tomar aire 1. salir a tomar aire to go out for some fresh air **2.** escaparse de algo aburrido to come up for air

salir para un lugar to leave for a place

salir pitando ▪ salir zumbando ▪ salir disparado ▪ marcharse a toda prisa ▪ salir como pedo de indio to be off like a shot

salir por la tele to be on TV ▪ to appear on TV

salir por piernas (de allí) to get out of there ▪ *(pintoresco)* to beat a trail out of Dodge ▪ to get the hell out of there

salir por piernas (de aquí) to get out of here ▪ *(pintoresco)* to beat a trail out of Dodge ▪ to get the hell out of here

salir pronto ▪ irse pronto ▪ marcharse pronto to leave early ▪ *(especialmente para un viaje)* to get an early start ➤ Necesitamos salir pronto por la mañana. We need to leave early tomorrow. ▪ We need to get an early start in the morning.

salir publicado to be published ▪ to appear in print ▪ to come out

salir reculando de un aparcamiento ▪ salir marcha atrás de un aparcamiento ▪ salir de culo de un aparcamiento to back out of a parking place

salir rentable ▪ ser rentable to be profitable

salir según lo previsto to go according to plan ▪ to go as planned

salir sin algo to walk off without something ▪ to leave without something ▪ to forget to bring something ➤ Salí sin mis gafas. I walked off without my glasses. ▪ I left without my glasses. ▪ I forgot to bring my glasses.

salir sin ningún contratiempo ▪ llevarse a cabo sin ningún contratiempo ▪ suceder sin ningún contratiempo to come off without a hitch ➤ El ensayo general resultó flojo, pero la noche del estreno salió sin ningún contratiempo. The dress rehearsal was rocky, but the opening night came off without a hitch.

salir sin que nadie se dé cuenta to slip away unnoticed ▪ to leave without being noticed

ponerse de moda to come into style

salir volando 1. to fly off 2. to blow away 3. to be off and running 4. to be off like a shot ➤ ¡Ay, el yo-yo salió volando! Oops, the yo-yo flew off (the string)! ➤ El montón entero de hojas salió volando. The whole pile of leaves blew away. ➤ El presidente de la Bolsa de Nueva York le pagó al joven Thomas Edison cuarenta mil dólares por el teletipo, y desde ese momento Edison salió volando. ▪ El presidente de la Bolsa de Nueva York le pagó al joven Thomas Edison cuarenta mil dólares por el teletipo, y desde ese momento Edison salió disparado. The president of the New York Stock Exchange paid the young Thomas Edison forty thousand dollars for the stock ticker, and from that moment Edison was off and running. ➤ Sonó la corneta, y los caballos salieron volando. ▪ Sonó la corneta, y los caballos salieron disparados. The bugle sounded, and the horses were off like a shot. ▪ The bugle sounded, and the horses were off and running.

salir y ponerse to rise and set ➤ Hoy (el siete de agosto) el sol sale a las 6,30 y se pone a las 20,37. The sun rises today (August seventh) at 6:30 a.m. and sets at 8:37 p.m.

salir ya to leave right now ➤ ¿Ya sale? Are you leaving right now? ▪ Are you about to leave?

salir zafo de algo ▪ salir zafo en algo to come away from something unscathed ▪ to come out of something unscathed ▪ to come away from something intact ▪ to come away unhurt from

salir zumbando ▪ salir pitando ▪ salir disparado ▪ marcharse a toda prisa ▪ salir como pedo de indio to be off like a shot

salirle al paso to intercept someone ▪ to catch up with someone and stop him or her

salirle bien to turn out well (for someone) ▪ to get it right ➤ Esta salsa de chimichurri me salió bien. This chimichurri sauce turned out well. ➤ ¿Te salió bien (en el examen)? Did you get it right (on the test)? ➤ Lo importante es que salga bien. ▪ Lo importante es que quede bien. The important thing is to get it right. ➤ ¿Te salieron bien las cosas? Did things turn out okay? ▪ Did everything turn out okay?

salirle de pura chapupa *(Esp.)* ▪ salirle de pura chiripa to be sheer luck ▪ to be pure luck ➤ Le salió de pura chapupa. ▪ Nos salió de pura chapupa. It was sheer luck. ▪ We were just lucky.

salirle el tiro por la culata a alguien 1. petardear ▪ hacer explosiones to recoil ▪ to kick ▪ to backfire 2. tener el efecto contrario al deseado to backfire (on someone) ➤ El candidato abandonó sus principios por sacar ventaja política, y le salió el tiro por la culata. The candidate abandoned principle for political expediency, and it backfired on him. ➤ Se le salió el tiro por la culata. It backfired on him. ➤ Se me salió el tiro por la culata. It backfired on me. ➤ Al intrigante le salió el tiro por la culata. ▪ Al intrigante le saltaron sus planes en sus mismas narices. ▪ Los planes saltaron ante los mismos ojos del intrigante. The schemer's plans blew up in his face.

salirle erupciones en la piel ▪ salirle un salpullido en la piel ▪ tener picores to have a rash ▪ to break out

salirle los dientes to cut teeth ▪ to teethe

salirle una letra ilegible to write illegibly

salirse con la suya 1. hacerse la voluntad de uno ▪ prevalecer to get one's way 2. salirse con la suya en un artimaña to get away with something *("La suya" refers to "la intención".)* ➤ El niño salió con la suya, fuimos a tomar un helado. The child got his way. We went for ice cream. ➤ Nunca te saldrás con la tuya. You'll never get away with it!

salirse de to depart from ▪ to be a departure from ➤ Se saldría de la lógica del libro. It would depart from the book's logic. ▪ It would be a departure from the logic of the book.

salirse de la carretera to run off the road ➤ El conductor volanteó para no atropellar al perro y se salió de la carretera. The driver swerved to miss the dog and ran off the road.

salirse de la pista to run off the runway ➤ El avión se salió del extremo de la pista, chocó contra una valla y dio una vuelta de campana. The airplane ran off the end of the runway, hit a fence and flipped over.

salirse de un acuerdo to back out of an agreement

salirse de un compromiso to get out of a commitment

salirse del libreto to depart from the script

salirse del molde ▪ salirse de lo normal to break out of the mold

salirse por una tangente to go off on a tangent

salírsele el tiro por la culata to backfire on someone ➤ El candidato abandonó sus principios por sacar ventaja política, y el tiro le salió por la culata. The candidate abandoned principle for political expediency, and it backfired on him. ➤ Se le salió el tiro por la culata. It backfired on him. ➤ Se me salió el tiro por la culata. It backfired on me.

salírsele una hernia ▪ saltársele una hernia ▪ abrírsele una hernia (for) a hernia to balloon out ➤ Se le salió la hernia. ▪ Se le saltó la hernia. ▪ Se le abrió la hernia. The hernia ballooned out. ▪ *(a él)* His hernia ballooned out. ▪ *(a ella)* Her hernia ballooned out.

salón abarrotado ▪ salón muy concurrido ▪ salón atestado ▪ salón apiñada ▪ salón lleno ▪ habitación abarrotada ▪ habitación muy concurrida ▪ habitación atestada ▪ habitación apiñada ▪ habitación llena crowded room ▪ room (jam) packed with people ▪ room jammed with people

el **salón comedor independiente** *(anuncio inmobiliario)* separate dining room

el **salón de belleza** beauty parlor

estar **salpicado de** to be cluttered with ▪ to be dotted with

salpicar pintura por todas partes ▪ manchar todo de pintura ▪ esparcir pintura encima de todo ▪ esparcir pintura por todas partes to get paint all over everything ▪ to get paint everywhere

salsa de la sopa ▪ condimento de la sopa the liquid part of the soup

salsa Perrins Worcestershire sauce

estar **saltando las murallas para escapar de allí** ▪ estar escalando las murallas para escapar de allí to be climbing the walls to get out of there

saltar a cordel ▪ saltar la soga to jump rope ▪ to skip rope

saltar a la palestra ▪ salir a la palestra to enter the fray ▪ to jump into the fray

saltar al claro to jump out (into the open)

saltar arriba y abajo to jump up and down

saltar de la sartén y dar en las brasas ▪ saltar del sartén y dar en las brasas to go from the frying pan to the fire ▪ to go from the frying pan into the fire

saltar en pedazos to blow to pieces ▪ to blow to smithereens ▪ to blow all to smithereens

saltar la liebre ▪ descubrir el pastel ▪ levantar la liebre ▪ delatar algo to let the cat out of the bag ▪ to spill the beans ▪ to give something away

saltar la soga ▪ saltar a cordel to jump rope ▪ to skip rope

saltar lo más alto que uno puede to jump as high as one can

saltar por la ventana to jump out the window ➤ Pedrito Conejo se escapó saltando por la ventana. Peter Rabbit escaped by jumping out the window.

saltar por los aires 1. volar en pedazos ▪ volar por los aires to blow up into a thousand pieces 2. hacerse humo to go up in smoke ➤ *(titular)* La tregua de EE UU y el líder chíe Al Sader salta por los aires. The truce between the U.S. and Shiite leader Al Sadr goes up in smoke.

saltar una valla limpiamente ▪ saltar una valla sin tocarla ▪ hacer un salto limpio to clear a hurdle ➤ Los atletas españoles saltaron limpiamente todas las vallas en veinte segundos. The Spanish runners cleared all the hurdles in twenty seconds.

saltarle a la vista ▪ llamarle la atención to jump out at one ▪ to catch one's eye ➤ Me saltó a la vista la palabra. The word jumped out at me. ▪ The word caught my eye.

saltarle un ojo a alguien to put someone's eye out

saltarse al jefe ▪ saltearse al jefe to do an end run ▪ to go to your boss' boss ▪ to go around your boss
saltarse algo a la torera *(pintoresco)* ▪ hacer caso omiso de algo to neglect something
saltarse el guión ▪ improvisar to abandon one's script
saltarse el límite de velocidad ▪ sobrepasar el límite de velocidad to break the speed limit ▪ to exceed the speed limit ▪ *(especialmente el gerundio)* to speed
saltarse el procedimiento to bypass the procedure
saltarse el turno ▪ arrancar antes de tiempo to go out of turn
saltarse la cola ▪ colarse ▪ romper la cola to cut in line ▪ to jump the queue ▪ to jump the line ▪ to butt in line
saltarse la patente to infringe on a patent
saltarse la tapa de los sesos ▪ volarse la tapa de los sesos ▪ volarse los sesos to blow one's brains out
saltarse las normas ▪ no seguir las reglas to break the rules ➤ Las carreteras están llenas de conductores que se saltan las normas. The highways are filled with drivers who break the rules. ▪ The highways are populated by drivers who break the rules. ▪ The highways are full of drivers who break the rules.
saltarse las reglas to get around the rules ➤ Tendremos que imaginar algún modo de saltarnos las reglas. We'll have to figure out some way to get around the rules. ▪ We'll have to figure out some way of getting around the rules.
saltarse las vallas ▪ romper las vallas to disregard social conventions ▪ to flaunt social conventions
saltarse un semáforo to crash a (traffic) light ▪ to run a (traffic) light ➤ El otro coche se saltó el semáforo. The other car crashed the light. ▪ The other car ran the red light.
salte con la tuya ▪ puedes salirte con la tuya have it your way ▪ you can have it your way
salto a la fama se debe a que... rise to fame is owed to... ▪ rise to fame can be attributed to... ▪ rise to fame is attributable to...
salto cuántico quantum leap
salto de mata: andar a ~ ▪ vivir a salto de mata to live from hand to mouth
salto de página: insertar un ~ to insert a page break ▪ to put in a page break
salto de tiempo time warp
salto de viento ▪ cambio de viento shifting of the wind ▪ shift in the wind ▪ change in the (direction of the) wind
salto mortal ▪ cabriola somersault
salúdale de mi parte **1.** *(a él)* say hello to him for me ▪ tell him hello for me ▪ give him my best **2.** *(a ella)* say hello to her for me ▪ tell her hello for me ▪ give her my best
saludar a alguien **1.** dar saludos a alguien to greet someone **2.** agitar la mano a alguien ▪ señalar a alguien to wave to someone ➤ Los candidatos saludan a sus seguidores en Austin. The candidates are waving to their fans in Austin.
saludar a alguien con los brazos abiertos to greet someone with open arms
saludarle a alguien de mi parte to say hello to someone for me ▪ to give someone my regards to remember me to someone
saludos entrañables: mis ~ my heartfelt greetings
salvar el pellejo ▪ salvar su propio pellejo to save one's (own) skin
salvarle la campana a uno to be saved by the bell
salvarle la vida a alguien to save someone's life ➤ Le salvaron la vida. They saved his life.
salvarle la vista a uno to save one's eyesight
salvarse por los pelos to escape by the skin of one's teeth
sálvate tú mismo ▪ sálvese quien pueda ▪ sálvese el que pueda it's every man for himself
sálvese el que pueda ▪ sálvese quien pueda ▪ sálvate tú mismo it's every man for himself
sálvese quien pueda ▪ sálvese el que pueda ▪ sálvate tu mismo it's every man for himself
San Martín de la Vega St. Martin of the Fields
¡san seacabó! **1.** done! **2.** never again!
sancionar a alguien con trabajos sociales to require someone to perform community service
saneamiento de las cloacas clearing of the (blocked) sewers
saneamiento de un edificio upgrading of a building ▪ restoration of a building
sanear las cuentas to organize the books ▪ to do the financials
sangrar a borbotones to bleed profusedly
sangrar a chorros to spurt blood
sangrar a raudales to bleed profusely
sangrar los frenos ▪ purgar los frenos to bleed the brakes
sangrar por la nariz to have a bloody nose ▪ to have a nosebleed ▪ (for) one's nose to be bleeding
sangrar por la nariz: hacerle a alguien ~ to give someone a bloody nose ▪ to bloody someone's nose
sangrar un párrafo to indent a paragraph ➤ Este puñetero software está sangrando los párrafos e insertando numeraciones por defecto. This blasted software is indenting the paragraphs and inserting numbering by default.
sangrar una línea de texto to indent a line of text
sangre azul: tener ~ ▪ ser de sangre azul to be blue-blooded
sangre de horchata: tener (la) ~ ▪ tener horchata en las venas to be cold-hearted ▪ to be cold-blooded
sangre fría: matar a alguien a ~ to kill someone in cold blood
sangre tira: la ~ blood is thicker than water
ser una **sangría de recursos** to be a drain on one's resources
ser una **sangría (económica) para algo** to bleed the lifeblood out of something ▪ to bleed something dry ➤ El gasto militar ha sido una sangría para la economía del país. Military spending has bled the lifeblood out of the economy. ▪ Military spending has bled the economy dry.
estar **sano y salvo** to be safe and sound
sanseacabó: y ~ and that's that!
¡santa palabra! (that's) music to my ears! ▪ I second the motion! ▪ I'll drink to that!
Santa Rita, Santa Rita, lo que se da no se quita it's mine now!
Santas Pascuas let it go at that ▪ and that's it ▪ and be done with it ➤ Deja que el niño se vaya al cine, y Santas Pascuas. Let the boy go to the movies, and be done with it.
santificado sea tu Nombre hallowed be Thy name
santificar las fiestas to keep the holy feasts
¡santo cielo! ▪ ¡por todos los santos! good heavens!
santo de la devoción de uno: no ser (el) ~ ▪ no ser plato del gusto de uno not to be one's cup of tea ➤ La "música" heavy no es santo de mi devoción. Heavy metal "music" is not my cup of tea.
¡santo Dios! good God!
el **Santo Padre** ▪ el Papa the Holy Father ▪ the Pope
Santo Tomás, una y no más just one more! ➤ ¿Quieres otra copa?-Santo Tomás, una y no más. Do you want another drink?-Just one more!
santo varón ▪ tío estupendo great guy
santo y bueno well and good
santo y seña *(militar, reunión secreta)* password
saña de los ataques aéreos brutality of the air attacks ▪ brutality of the aerial attacks
sapos y culebras: echar ~ to curse a blue streak ▪ to turn the air blue
el **saque de banda** *(fútbol)* throw-in
el **saque de centro** *(fútbol)* kickoff
el **(saque de) corner** *(fútbol)* ▪ saque de esquina corner kick
el **saque de esquina** *(fútbol)* ▪ (saque de) corner corner kick
el **saque inicial** *(fútbol)* kickoff
el **saque de mano** *(fútbol)* throw-in
el **saque de puerta** *(fútbol)* ▪ saque de portería ▪ saque de meta goal kick
¡saque la cabeza de fuera! back off!
¡sáquese partido! make the most of it!
sargento instructor drill sergeant
sarta de mentiras pack of lies
la **sartén anti-adherente** non-stick frying pan ▪ no-stick frying pan ▪ non-sticking frying pan
la **sartén de hierro fundido** cast-iron skillet

satisfacer las expectativas de alguien to meet someone's expectations
satisfacer un deseo to grant a wish
se abrieron las puertas del infierno ▪ se armó una gran barahunda all hell broke loose
se acaba el tiempo ▪ el tiempo se acaba time is running out
se acabó ▪ acabóse it's over ▪ that's all there is to it
se almacenan los recuerdos 1. memories are stored 2. *(hablando colectivamente del cerebro)* memory is stored
se alza there stands ▪ stands ➤ A poca distancia del bosque se alza una gran roca. A short distance from the forest there stands a large rock.
se alzaba there stood ▪ stood ➤ A poca distancia del bosque se alzaba una gran roca. A short distance from the forest there stood a large rock.
se armó un gran cacao all hell broke loose
se armó una gran barahúnda ▪ se abrieron las puertas del infierno all hell broke loose
se arrienda habitación ▪ alquilo habitación room for rent
se aventó un churro it was a fluke
se bifurca la calle ▪ se bifurca el camino ▪ calle se bifurca ▪ camino se bifurca the road forks ➤ Donde se bifurca la calle, una ramificación lleva a Salamanca, y la otra a Valladolid. Where the road forks, one fork leads to Salamanca, and the other (fork leads) to Valladolid.
sé buen chico y... ▪ sé un buen chico y... be a good boy and...
se busca vivo o muerto wanted dead or alive
¡se cae! you could fall! ➤ *(padre a su niño)* ¡Se cae!-*(y el niño responde)* ¡No se cae! You could fall!-I won't fall!
se calcula que... it is estimated that...
se calculó en was computed at ➤ El consumo de combustibles se calculó en 50 millas por galón. Fuel consumption was computed at the rate of 50 miles per gallon.
se comenzó a... (it) was first... ➤ *(noticia)* La contaminación del agua se comenzó a detectar en el verano de 2000. The water contamination was first detected in the summer of 2000.
se conoce por... you can tell by...
se cortó el teléfono ▪ se cortó la línea the (tele)phone went dead ▪ the phone was cut off
sé cortó (la comunicación) *(teléfono)* ▪ perdí la comunicación we got cut off ▪ I got cut off
se cortó la línea ▪ se cortó el teléfono the telephone went dead ▪ the phone went dead
se cree que es... it is believed to be...
se creyó que era... it was believed to be...
se cruzaron las miradas they exchanged glances
se cruzaron los ojos their eyes met
se da la clase hoy (the) class meets today ▪ we have class today ▪ there is (a) class today
se dan las condiciones para conditions are right for ➤ *(noticia)* Se dan las condiciones para llegar a un "acuerdo histórico" entre los palestinos y los israelíes. (The) conditions are right for coming to a historic agreement between the Palestinians and Israelis.
sé de sobra que... ▪ demasiado sé que... I know all too well ▪ I know only too well
se decidió que... it was decided that...
se desplomó el avión the airplane plummeted to the ground
se desplomó el techo the ceiling fell in ▪ the ceiling collapsed
se desprendió it came loose
se dice que... they say that... ▪ people say that... ▪ *(en escritura formal)* it is said that...
se diría que you could say that... ▪ it could be said that... ▪ one can say that...
¿se dirige (usted) a mí? are you speaking to me?
se echa de ver que... you can see that... ▪ one can see that...
se enciende esta lucecita this little light went on in my head
se engaña quien piense así anyone who thinks that is kidding himself ▪ whoever thinks that is kidding himself
se entiende it's understandable
se entiende que... it's understandable that...
se espera al bebé (para) la semana que viene the baby is due next week
se espera que... it is hoped that...
se está haciendo tarde ▪ se hace tarde it's getting late
se está mejor en casa que en ningún otro sitio *(Dorothy en "El mago de Oz")* ▪ no hay ningún sitio como la propia casa there's no place like home
se estima que... it is estimated that...
se exterioriza it shows
¡sé formal! ▪ ¡ten formalidad! ▪ ¡compórtate! behave yourself!
se gasta de tanto mirarlo you're going to wear it out looking at it ➤ La foto se gasta de tanto mirarla. You're going to wear that photograph out looking at it.
se ha atascado *(videocasete, etc.)* ▪ está atascado it's stuck
se ha consolado de la pérdida antes de la pérdida *(Valle-Inclán)* he's accepted his loss before the fact
se ha demostrado que it has been shown that
se ha ido la luz the power's gone off
se ha levantado el viento the wind is picking up ▪ the wind is getting up ▪ it's starting to get windy ▪ it's getting windy ▪ the wind is starting to blow
se ha perdido el encanto it has lost its charm ▪ it's lost its charm
se ha quedado sin batería ▪ batería está descargada the battery is dead ▪ the battery has lost its charge
se había cansado de vivir solo he had grown tired of living alone
se habló de ello it was discussed
¿se habrá olvidado? 1. *(él)* do you think he's forgotten? ▪ could he have forgotten? 2. *(ella)* do you think she's forgotten? ▪ could she have forgotten?
¿se habrá perdido? 1. *(él)* do you think he's gotten lost? 2. *(ella)* do you think she's gotten lost?
se hace así you do it like this ▪ this is how you do it
se hace tarde it's getting late
se hace un largo silencio there is a long silence ▪ there was a long silence
se han vuelto las tornas the shoe's on the other foot ▪ it's now a whole new ball game ▪ it's another story now
se hizo it was done
sé honesto(-a) be honest
se impone decir que... it must be said that...
se la pela *(subido de tono)* 1. *(él)* he doesn't give a damn ▪ he could care less 2. *(ella)* she doesn't give a damn ▪ she could care less
se las trae that's a tough one ➤ Es una situación que se las trae. It's a nightmare secenario. ➤ Ella tiene un jefe que se las trae. Her boss is a nightmare.
se le acaba el tiempo a alguien time is running out (for someone) ▪ someone's time is running out
se le considera is considered ➤ A Barcelona se le considera una de las ciudades más bella de Europa. Barcelona is considered one of the most beautiful cities in Europe.
se le demudó la cara his face went white
se le pasaron los síntomas a alguien one's symptoms disappeared ▪ one's symptoms went away ➤ Después de tomarme el medicamento, se me pasaron los síntomas. When I took the medicine, my symptoms disappeared. ▪ When I took the medicine, my symptoms went away.
se le pasó el arroz 1. one overcooked the rice 2. *(figurativo)* she has passed the marrying age
se le supone... it is thought to be... ▪ it is believed to be...
se le va la fuerza por la boca ▪ perro ladrador, poco mordedor 1. *(él)* he's all bark and no bite ▪ his bark is worse than his bite 2. *(ella)* she's all bark and no bite ▪ her bark is worse than her bite
se le ve el plumero he's not fooling anybody
se les dice... they call them...
se levanta la sesión 1. *(reunión)* the meeting is adjourned 2. *(tribunal)* court is adjourned
se llegó a creer que... ▪ llegó a creerse que... it came to be believed that... ▪ people came to believe that...
se lo agradezco I appreciate it
se lo cobro *(a usted)* I'll have to charge you for it

se lo dejo a cuenta ■ anótelo en la cuenta ■ apúntelo en la cuenta ■ póngalo en la cuenta put it on the bill

se lo dejo a mi cuenta ■ anótelo en mi cuenta ■ apúntelo en mi cuenta ■ póngalo en mi cuenta put it on my bill

se lo dejo a usted I'll leave it to you

¿se lo doblo? shall I fold it for you? ■ would you like me to fold it for you? ➤ *(referido a camisas)* ¿Se las doblo? Shall I fold them for you? ■ Would you like me to fold them? ■ Do you want me to fold them?

se lo doy a usted ■ puede quedarse con ello you can have it ■ you can keep it

se lo prometo (a usted) I promise

sé lo que estás pensando I know what you're thinking

sé lo que hago I know what I'm doing

sé lo que quieres decir sobre... ■ entiendo lo que quieres decir sobre... ■ me hago cargo de lo que dices sobre... ■ sé qué quieres decir sobre I know what you mean about... ■ I understand what you mean about...

¿se lo rebano? ■ ¿se lo troceo? shall I slice it for you? ■ would you like me to slice it for you? ■ do you want me to slice it for you?

se lo sugeriré 1. *(a él)* I'll suggest it to him 2. *(a ella)* I'll suggest it to her

se lo tomaba del todo *(la abeja haragana de Quiroga)* she would drink it all herself

¿se lo troceo? ■ ¿se lo rebano? shall I slice it for you? ■ would you like me to slice it for you? ■ do you want me to slice it for you?

se me acaba el tiempo ■ se me agota el tiempo I'm out of time

se me agota el tiempo ■ se me acaba el tiempo I'm out of time

se me cayó algo en el ojo *(Méx.)* ■ me entró algo en el ojo ■ tengo algo en el ojo I got something in my eye

se me cayó el alma a los pies my heart sank

se me cayó el empaste my filling came out ■ I lost a filling ■ my filling fell out

se me encogió el corazón cuando... my heart shrank when...

se me cumplió el sueño my dream came true

se me fue el santo al cielo ■ se me fue ■ se me pasó it slipped my mind ■ I forgot ■ *(argot)* I spaced it

se me fue la olla *(coloquial)* ■ entró por una oreja y salió por la otra ■ se me fue la pinza ■ se me olvidó ■ se me pasó it went in one ear and out the other ■ I forgot

¡se me ha adelantado (usted)! you beat me to it!

se me ha atravesado en la garganta it got caught in my throat

se me ha hecho tarde I'm running late ■ it's gotten late on me

se me ha ido de la cabeza ■ se me ha ido ■ perdí el hilo de las ideas ■ perdí el hilo ■ se me ha ido el santo al cielo I lost my train of thought ■ I forgot what I was saying

se me ha preguntado si I've been asked if ■ I've been asked whether

se me había olvidado que... I had forgotten that...

se me hace indispensable I can't do without it

se me hace la boca agua it makes my mouth water

se me hace que... *(Méx.)* ■ me parece que... it seems to me that...

se me hace tarde I'm running late ■ it's getting late on me

se me ocurre una idea ■ tengo una idea I have an idea ■ I've got an idea

se me ocurrió... it occurred to me...

se me olvidaría la cabeza si no la tuviese pegada a los hombros I'd forget my head if it weren't attached

se me olvidó conseguir algo ■ se me pasó conseguir algo I forgot to get something

se me olvidó de plano ■ se me olvidó por completo I completely forgot (about it)

se me olvidó por completo ■ se me olvidó de plano I completely forgot (about it)

se me olvidó preguntar I forgot to ask

se me olvidó su nombre 1. *(de usted)* I forgot your name 2. *(de él)* I forgot his name 3. *(de ella)* I forgot her name

se me olvidó tu nombre I forgot your name

se me pasa I forget

se me pasó conseguir algo ■ se me olvidó conseguir algo I forgot to get something

se me pasó por completo I forgot all about it

se me pegaron las sábanas me quedé dormido ■ dormí de más I overslept

se me pidió que... I was asked to...

se me pierde (it) is lost to me

se me pinchó una rueda I had a blowout ■ a tire blew out (on me) ➤ En el viaje a Valencia se me pinchó una rueda. On the trip to Valencia, I had a blowout. ■ On the trip to Valencia, a tire blew out (on me).

se me ponen los pelos de punta 1. *(de miedo)* it makes my hair stand up straight 2. *(de emoción)* it makes chills run up and down my spine

se me sigue olvidando I keep forgetting

se merece un aplauso 1. *(él)* let's give him a round of applause 2. *(ella)* let's give her a round of applause

sé mirada *(Valle-Inclán)* be considerate!

se mire por donde se mire however you look at it

se muestra it shows

se necesita (que) 1. *(singular)* there needs to be 2. *(plural)* there need to be ➤ Se necesita un semáforo en ese cruce. There needs to be a traffic light at that intersection.

se nos hacen indispensables *(Valle-Inclán)* we can't do without them

se nos pidió we were asked for

se nos presenta un gran verano we have a wonderful summer ahead (of us)

se oía you could hear

se oye demasiado it's too noisy ■ there's too much noise

se pasa todo el día 1. *(él)* he spends the whole day 2. *(ella)* she spends the whole day ➤ Se pasa todo el día trabajando ante el ordenador. He spends the whole day working at the computer.

se pensó que... it was thought that...

se podía haber oído caer un alfiler al suelo you could have heard a pin drop

¡se podrán comer, pero buenas! *(Valle-Inclán)* they might be edible, but *good*?

se podría dar con un canto en los dientes ■ se podría dar con una piedra 1. *(usted)* you should count yourself lucky ■ you should consider yourself lucky 2. *(él)* he should count himself lucky ■ he should consider himself lucky 3. *(ella)* she should count herself lucky ■ she should consider herself lucky

se podría decir que... ■ podría decirse que... it is safe to say that...

se podría pedir (que)... you might as well ask (that)... ■ you might as well request (that)...

se podría pensar que... ■ uno podría pensar que... ■ cabe pensar que... ■ cabría pensar que... one would think that... ■ you would think that...

se podría preguntar you might ask ■ one might ask

se pondrá furiosa she'll be furious

se pondrá furioso he'll be furious

sé por lo que estás pasando I know what you're going through

se produjo el accidente the accident occurred

¿se puede? ■ ¿puedo pasar? may I come in?

se puede arreglar con it's a question of

se puede conseguir ■ puedes conseguirlo it can be done ■ you can do it

se puede llevar a todas partes you can take it anywhere ■ you can take it everywhere

¿se puede saber a qué has venido? may I ask what you're doing here?

¿se puede saber por qué? may I ask why?

se puso los ojos como platos 1. *(él)* his eyes got as big as saucers 2. *(ella)* her eyes got as big as saucers

sé que lo hará 1. I know you'll do it 2. I know you will

se quedaron sin... they were out of... ➤ Se quedaron sin agua mineral en la tienda. They were out of mineral water at the store.

se recoge lo que se siembra you reap what you sow

se reduce a que it adds up to the fact that ■ the bottom line is that

se remonta al tiempo en que it goes back to the time when

se ruega contestación ■ SRC R.S.V.P. ■ the favor of a reply is requested

se ruega paciencia ■ les ruego paciencia ■ sean pacientes conmigo (please) bear with me ■ please be patient ➤ Me llevará un minuto explicarlo, por eso se ruega paciencia. It takes (me) a minute to explain this, so please bear with me. ■ It takes (me) a minute to explain this, so please be patient (with me).

se ruega que... please... ■ kindly...

se ruega que no... ■ se pide que no... ■ favor de no... please do not ■ please refrain from ■ kindly refrain from

se siente como si pasara un ángel it's so quiet you can hear a pin drop

se sirve a domicilio we deliver ■ home delivery available

se solicita que... ■ se ruega que... we ask that... ■ we request that...

se supo que... it was learned that... ■ it became known that... ■ it was found out that...

se supone que debería estar it is supposed to be ■ it's supposed to be ➤ Se supone que el auto debería estar listo para esta tarde. The car is supposed to be ready this afternoon.

se supone que debería ser it is supposed to be ■ it's supposed to be ➤ Se supone que el auto alquilado debería ser un sedán de cuatro puertas y no dos. The rental car is supposed to be a four-door and not two. *(In Latin America and Europe, the trunk or hatchback is counted as a door, so it is important to specify a "four-door sedan.")*

¿se supone que debiéramos llevar algo a la fiesta? are we supposed to bring something to the party?

¡(se suponía que) tendrías que haber estado aquí hace cuatro horas! ■ ¡tendrías que haber venido hace cuatro horas! you were supposed to be here four hours ago! ■ you were supposed to have been here four hours ago!

¿(se suponía que) tendríamos que haber entregado nuestros trabajos ayer? ■ ¿deberíamos haber entregado nuestros trabajos ayer? we were supposed to turn in our papers yesterday?

se tarda mucho it takes a long time

¡se te ocurren! the things you come up with! ■ the things you think of!

se te ocurrirá algo you'll think of something

se te suben los ceros a la cabeza you've got rocks in your head

se te va a escapar el pájaro ■ tu bragueta está desabrochada your fly is open ■ *(Literalmente, "Your songbird is going to escape.")* ➤ Se te va a escapar el pájaro.-Ya volverá porque los huevos están aquí. Your songbird is going to escape.-It'll come back because the eggs are here.

se teje una crisis a crisis is brewing

se terminó de construir ■ se acabó de construir construction was completed ➤ En 1819 se terminó de construir el edificio que albergaría la colección de arte real español (el Prado). ■ En 1819 se acabó de construir el edificio que albergaría la colección de arte real español (el Prado). In 1819 construction was completed on a building that would house the Spanish royal art collection.

se tiene la sensación de que... you get the feeling that... ■ one gets the feeling that...

se trata de una calle muy corta it's a very short street ➤ Se trata de una calle muy corta por lo que aunque no recuerde yo ahora el número espero que que preguntando no tengas ninguna dificultad en localizarlo. It's a very short street, so even though I don't remember the number, I expect that by asking (someone), you won't have any trouble finding it.

se trata de una profesión muy interesante it's a very interesting profession

sé tú mismo be yourself

sé (un) buen chico y... be a good boy and...

se va a armar la grande all hell's going to break loose ■ *(subido de tono)* the shit's going to hit the fan ■ *(más benigno)* the Moregrow's going to hit the Mixmaster

se va a cagar la perra *(subido de tono)* **1.** vamos a tirar la casa por la ventana we're going to shoot the moon ■ we're going to go all out **2.** *(referido a fiestas)* there's going to be one hell of a party ■ we're going to throw one hell of a party

se va a celebrar (it) will be held

se va enredando la madeja ■ se está enredando la madeja the plot thickens

¡se va, se va, se va, a la de una, a la de dos, a la de tres, adjudicado! going, going, going, gone! ➤ ¡Se va, se va, se va, a la una, a la de una, a la de dos, a la de tres, adjudicado al señor de la corbata verde. Going, going, going, gone! Sold to the gentleman in the green necktie!

se ve el final the end is in sight

se ve que... **1.** you can see that... ■ one can see that... **2.** it shows that...

se veía you could see ■ one could see ➤ Desde Marbella se veía Gibraltar. From Marbella you could see Gibraltar.

¡se viene el agua! **1.** it's going to rain any minute now ■ it's going to start pouring any second now **2.** *(deportes)* the tide's going to turn in our favor! ■ we're going to get you now! ➤ ¡Ahora que llegó Iván, se viene el agua! Now that Ivan's here, we're going to get you!

se vino el cielo abajo it was pouring down rain ■ it was pouring rain ■ the rain was pouring down

sea como sea no matter how ■ at any cost ■ one way or another ■ somehow or other ➤ Sea como sea, terminaré mi carrera. One way or another, I'm going to finish my schooling.

sea cual sea ■ sin importar cuál sea **1.** no matter what ■ regardless of who is ■ regardless of which one is ➤ Sea cual sea su aspecto *(de él)* No matter what he looks like ■ *(de ella)* No matter what she looks like ■ *(de ello)* No matter what it looks like ➤ El nuevo gobierno, sea cual sea el ganador final... The new government, regardless of which one is the winner...

sea cual sea el caso ■ sea lo que sea ■ aun así whatever the case may be ■ be that as it may ■ even so

sea cual sea el resultado whatever the result ■ whatever the outcome ■ however it turns out

sea cual sea el rumbo que decidas tomar en la vida whatever (the) direction you decide to take in life ■ whatever path you choose in life

sea de donde sea no matter where you're from ➤ *(publicidad de Telefónica)* Sea de donde sea, hablamos su idioma. No matter where you're from, we speak your language.

sea de donde seas no matter where you're from

sea honesto(-a) be honest

sea lo que fuere be that as it may

sea lo que sea ■ fuera lo que fuera ■ sea cual sea el caso ■ aun así be that as it may ■ even so ■ whatever the case may be ■ whether that is the case or not

sea necesario que... se requiera que... (it) may be necessary (for one) to...

sea que uno haga algo depende de whether one does something depends on whether ➤ Sea que yo vaya a Puerto Vallarta depende de si termine mi trabajo. Whether I go to Puerto Vallarta depends on whether I get my paper done.

sea usted mismo be yourself

sean pacientes conmigo ■ les ruego paciencia ■ se ruega paciencia (please) bear with me ■ please be patient ➤ Me llevará un minuto explicarlo, por eso por favor sean pacientes conmigo. It takes (me) a minute to explain this, so please bear with me. ■ It takes (me) a minute to explain this, so please be patient (with me).

la **sección de amenidades** ■ cartelera entertainment section

las **secciones móviles del ala** control surfaces of the wing

estar **seco** to be broke ■ to have dry pockets

secreto de la confesión *(catolicismo)* secrecy of the confessional ■ sacramental silence

secreto del oficio trade secret

sector automovilístico automobile industry

ser **secuela de...** to be the result of...

ser la **secuela de una enfermedad** to be the result of an illness

secuencia principal *(astrofísica)* main sequence

secuenciar el genoma humano to map the human genome

la **secuenciación del genoma humano** the mapping of the human genome

secuestrar a alguien to kidnap someone

secuestrar un avión to hijack an airplane ■ to hijack a plane

la **sed de aprender** thirst for learning

la **sed de vivir** lust for life

sed pacientes conmigo *(Esp.)* ■ os ruego paciencia bear with me ■ please be patient ➤ Me llevará un minuto explicarlo, por eso por favor sed pacientes conmigo. ■ Me llevará un minuto explicarlo, por eso os ruego paciencia. It takes a minute to explain this, so please bear with me. ■ It takes a minute to explain this, so please be patient (with me).

la **sede de una diócesis** seat of a diocese

la **sede de una empresa** headquarters of a business

la **sede de una monarquía** seat of a monarchy

la **sede del juzgado** courthouse

segar el césped ■ cortar el césped to mow the lawn ■ to cut the grass

segmento de edad ■ los de edades (comprendidas) entre age group ➤ El segmento de edad entre cuatro y seis años come en el primer turno. ■ Los de edades (comprendidas) entre cuatro y seis años comen en el primer turno. The age group between four and six eats during the first lunch period.

segmento lúdico recess ■ play period

seguía esperándola: él ~ he was still waiting for her

seguían esperándola: ellos ~ they were still waiting for her

estar **seguido de** to be followed by ➤ La reunión estuvo seguida de una comida. The meeting was followed by a luncheon.

ser **seguido por** ■ ser perseguido por to be followed by ■ to be pursued by ➤ El fugitivo fue seguido por la policía. ■ El fugitivo fue perseguido por la policía. The fugitive was followed by the police.

seguir a alguien hasta el interior de to follow someone into ➤ No siguió a sus compañeros hasta el interior de la iglesia. He didn't follow his companions into the church.

seguir adelante 1. progresar to keep on ■ to go forward ■ to progress **2.** prosperar ■ comunicar to go through ➤ La propuesta no siguió adelante. The proposal didn't go through.

seguir adelante con to go ahead with

seguir andando *(Esp.)* ■ seguir caminando to keep walking ■ to walk on

seguir atento to follow with interest

seguir atento a algo ■ permanecer atento a algo **1.** to keep an eye on something ■ to watch something (continually) **2.** *(televisión, radio)* to stay tuned ■ not to go away ■ to stay with us **3.** to still be waiting to... ■ to still be waiting for... ■ to still await word from **4.** to continue to monitor ➤ No te despistes. Sigue atento al guiso hasta que esté hecho o se te quemará. Don't get sidetracked. Keep (on) watching the stew continually until it's done, or it will burn. ■ Don't get sidetracked. Watch the stew continually until it's done, or it will burn. ■ Don't get sidetracked. Watch the stew without interruption until it's done, or it will burn. ■ Don't get sidetracked. Keep watching the stew non-stop, or it will burn. ➤ Siga atento a nuestro programa. Stay tuned. ■ Don't go away. ➤ Seguimos atentos a la respuesta favorable del viñedo español que nos vende el amontillado. ■ Permanecemos atentos a que nos respondan favorablemente del viñedo español que nos vende el amontillado. We are still waiting to hear from the Spanish winery that sells Montilla sherry. ■ We are still awaiting word from the Spanish winery that sells Montilla sherry. ➤ El gobierno sigue atento a la situación en Oriente Medio. The government continues to monitor the situation in the Middle East.

seguir caminando ■ seguir andando to keep walking ■ to walk on

seguir cerrado to remain closed ■ to stay closed ➤ *(noticia)* Los bancos argentinos seguirán cerrados hasta el viernes. Argentine banks will remain closed until Friday.

seguir con algo to continue with something ■ to continue doing something ■ *(coloquial)* to get on with something ➤ Necesito seguir con mis deberes. Te llamo más tarde. I need to get on with my homework. I'll call you later.

seguir con el cuento ■ continuar con el cuento to go on with the story

seguir con lupa to scrutizine ■ to watch like a hawk

seguir con vida still to be alive ■ *(literario, poético)* to be yet alive ➤ Sigue con vida. He's still alive.

seguir dale que dale sobre algo to go on and on about something

seguir de cerca to keep track of ■ to follow closely

seguir de largo to go one's own way

seguir de movida to keep partying ■ to keep on partying (after the party is over or the bar is closed)

seguir de una pieza still to be in one piece

seguir derecho to keep (going) straight ahead ■ to continue (going) straight ahead

seguir el consejo de alguien ■ llevarse del consejo de alguien to take someone's advice

seguir en still to be in ➤ Cuando Eduardo Mendoza escribió *La verdad sobre el caso Savolta* y *La cripta*, seguía en Nueva York. When Eduardo Mendoza wrote *The Truth About the Savolta Case* and *The Crypt*, he was still in New York.

seguir en contacto to keep in touch ➤ Seguimos en contacto. Let's keep in touch. ■ Keep in touch.

seguir en la brecha to keep at it ■ to go on about one's business ■ to stand one's ground

seguir en la prehistoria ■ no estar al día to be behind the times ➤ Si no aceptas tarjetas de crédito o débito para compras de 550 euros, es que sigues en la prehistoria. ■ Si no aceptas tarjetas de crédito o débito para compras de 550 euros, es que no estás al día. If you don't accept credit or debit cards for purchases of 550 euros, you're behind the times.

seguir las huellas de alguien to follow in someone's footsteps ■ to follow in the footsteps of someone

seguir en libertad ■ *(Esp.)* andar suelto to remain at large

seguir en sus trece ■ permanecer en sus trece ■ mantenerse en sus trece ■ estar en sus trece to stick to one's guns

seguir haciendo algo to keep on doing something ■ to go on doing something ■ to continue doing something

seguir la pisada de alguien to follow in someone's footsteps

seguir la ruta del dinero *(en investigaciones criminales)* to follow the money

seguir las instrucciones ■ observar las instrucciones to follow the instructions ■ to follow the directions ➤ Cuando todo lo demás falla, sigue las instrucciones. When all else fails, follow the instructions.

seguir los cauces reglamentarios to go through proper channels

seguir mirando to keep looking (at) ➤ Sigue mirándolo. She keeps looking at him.

seguir olvidándosele a uno to keep forgetting ➤ Se me sigue olvidando. I keep forgetting.

seguir oyendo to keep hearing

seguir pegado a to hang onto

seguir siendo still to be ■ to continue to be

seguir sin descartar not to have been ruled out

seguir su sugerencia de to follow someone's suggestion to

seguir teniendo to continue to have ■ to continue to be having ■ still to be having ➤ Seguía teniendo problemas con la computadora incluso después de que la repararan. He was still having problems with the computer even after they repaired it. ■ He continued to have problems with the computer even after he got it back from the shop. ■ He continued having problems with the computer even after they repaired it.

seguir uno mismo ■ hacer lo que uno quiera ■ acamparse como uno quiera to do as one pleases ■ to do as one likes ➤ *(tú)* Sigue tú mismo(-a). ■ Haz lo que quieras. ■ Acámpate como quieras. ■ *(usted)* Siga usted mismo(-a). ■ Haga usted lo que quiera. ■ Acampe usted como quiera. ■ Acámpese como quiera. Do as you please. ■ Do as you like.

seguir viviendo to go on living ■ to live on ➤ Su legado sigue viviendo. His legacy lives on.

seguiré adelante y... I'll go ahead and...

seguirle el humor a alguien to humor someone

seguirle haciendo algo to go along with someone's doing

seguirle la corriente a alguien to go along with whatever someone says ■ to follow someone's lead ■ to humor someone

seguirle la pista a alguien ■ no perder la pista de alguien ■ vigilar a alguien ■ controlar a alguien to keep tabs on someone ■ to keep track of someone

según contó 1. *(él)* as he told it 2. *(ella)* as she told it
según cuenta 1. *(él)* as he tells it 2. *(ella)* as she tells it
según el criterio de uno at one's discretion
según el cual by which
según el programa ■ según lo previsto on schedule
según el punto de vista according to one's point of view ■ depending on how you look at it
según estamos hablando (en estos precisos momentos) ■ conforme hablamos ■ conforme estamos hablando (en estos precisos momentos) as we speak ➤ Estoy trabajando en ello según estamos hablando (en estos precisos momentos). I'm working on it as we speak.
según están as they are ■ the way the are ■ in the order they are (now) in
según están las cosas the way things are
según fueron pasando los años as the years went passing by
según iban pasando los años as the years passed (by) ■ as the years went passing by
según la cual by which
según las cuales by which
según lo acordado as agreed
según lo entendido as understood
según lo pactado as stipulated ■ as contracted for
según lo planeado: ir ~ ■ andar según lo planeado to go according to plan
según lo previsto: salir ~ ■ salir según el programa to go according to plan ■ to go as planned ■ to proceed on schedule ■ to go according to schedule ■ to proceed according to (the) schedule
según lo veo ■ desde mi punto de vista ■ a mi parecer ■ en mi opinión as I look at it ■ the way I look at it ■ from my point of view ■ in my opinion
según los conocimientos actuales according to present-day knowledge
según los cuales by which
según mi leal saber y entender to the best of my knowledge
según parece ■ al aparecer apparently
según pasan los años ■ a medida que pasan los años ■ conforme pasan los años ■ as the years go by ■ as the years pass by
según sales as you leave ■ as you're leaving ➤ El complejo queda en la salida a Valencia a mano izquierda según sales de Madrid. The complex is at the Valencia exit, on the left-hand side as you leave Madrid. ■ The complex is at the Valencia exit, on the left-hand side as you're leaving Madrid.
según se mire depending on how you look at it
según sopla el viento depending on the way the wind blows
según supe después as I found out later
según un estudio reciente according to a recent study
según uno in one's opinion
según van pasando los años ■ conforme van pasando los años ■ a medida que van pasando los años as the years go passing by
según van pasando los días ■ a medida que van pasando los días ■ conforme van pasando los días as the days pass ■ as the days go by ■ as the days go passing by
Segunda Guerra Mundial ■ II Guerra Mundial Second World War ■ World War II ➤ California no sufría cortes de luz desde la Segunda Guerra Mundial. California had not suffered blackouts since the Second World War.
segunda intención ulterior motive ■ hidden agenda
segunda repisa desde abajo ■ segundo estante desde abajo second shelf (up) from the bottom ■ next-to-the-bottom shelf ■ second-from-the-bottom shelf ➤ Está en la segunda repisa desde abajo. ■ Está en el segundo estante desde abajo. It's on the second shelf (up) from the bottom. ■ It's on the next-to-the-bottom shelf. ■ It's on the second-from-the-bottom shelf.
segunda repisa desde arriba ■ segundo estante desde arriba next-to-the-top shelf ■ second shelf (down) from the top ■ next-to-the-top shelf ■ second-from-the-top shelf ➤ Está en la segunda repisa desde arriba. ■ Está en el segundo estante desde arriba. It's on the second shelf (down) from the top. ■ It's on the next-to-the-top shelf. ■ It's on the second-from-the-top shelf.
segunda vuelta electoral ■ segunda vuelta runoff election
segundo de arco *(geometría)* second of an arc ■ arc second
segundo estante desde arriba ■ segunda repisa desde arriba next-to-the-top shelf ■ second shelf (down) from the top ■ next-to-the-top shelf ■ second-from-the-top shelf ➤ Está en el segundo estante desde arriba. ■ Está en la segunda repisa desde arriba. It's on the second shelf (down) from the top. ■ It's on the next-to-the-top shelf. ■ It's on the second-from-the-top shelf.
segundo favorito second favorite ➤ Woody Allen dijo que el cerebro era su segundo órgano favorito. Woody Allen said the brain was his second favorite organ.
segundo hombre más poderoso second most powerful man
ser el **segundo por abajo** ■ ser el segundo desde abajo ■ ser lo que está inmediatamente encima de lo más bajo to be (the) second from the bottom ■ to be the second one (up) from the bottom ■ to be just above the bottom one
seguramente será... for sure it's...
la **seguridad en sí mismo(-a)** self-confidence
la **seguridad vial** highway safety ■ road safety
estar **seguro(-a) de que...** to be sure that...
ser **seguro(-a) de sí mismo** to be sure of oneself
seguro de vida life insurance
ser **seguro hacer una cosa** to be safe to do something ➤ ¿Es seguro andar por la noche en este barrio? Is it safe to walk in this neighborhood at night?
seguro médico health insurance ■ medical insurance
seguro que... for sure ■ surely ➤ Seguro que hay otras civilizaciones como la nuestra, y aún más avanzadas en nuestra propia Vía Láctea. For sure there are other civilizations like our own, and even more advanced, in our own Milky Way. ■ Surely there are other civilizations like our own, and even more advanced, in our own Milky Way.
seguro que estás contento(-a) (que...) I bet you're glad (that...)
¡**seguro que no!** ■ ¡eso sí que no! definitely not!
seguro que se lo pueden arreglar I'm sure it can be arranged
la **selección (nacional)** national team ➤ *(titular)* La selección cae otra vez en cuartos tras perder en los penaltis ante Corea. The (Spanish) national team loses again in the quarterfinals after losing the penalty round against Korea.
seleccionado aleatoriamente ■ seleccionado al azar selected at random ■ randomly selected
sellar el labio ■ sellar los labios to seal one's lips
sello de correos postage stamp
semáforo está en verde, rojo etc. traffic light is green, red, etc. ➤ *(noticia de un accidente)* Los semáforos de ambos sentidos estaban en verde, pero la preferencia de paso era de la hormigonera. The traffic light was green in both directions, but the cement mixer had the right of way.
semáforo peatonal walk light
semana a semana ■ de semana en semana (from) week to week ■ week by week
la **semana anterior** the week before
Semana Blanca dead week
Semana de Pasión ■ Semana Santa Holy Week
semana entre medias intervening week ➤ Durante la semana entre medias tendré que volver a formatear el documento. In the intervening week, I have to reformat the document.
semana intermedia intervening week
semana laboral workweek
Semana Santa ■ Semana de Pasión Holy Week
semana trascendental critical week ■ very important week
el **semblante alegre** 1. *(habitual)* cheerful countenance 2. *(en el momento)* cheerful look
el **semblante radiante** 1. *(habitual)* radiant countenance 2. *(en el momento)* radiant look
estar **sembrado** to be at one's best ■ to be witty ■ *(jerga)* to be on a roll
sembrar cizaña (entre personas) ■ meter cizaña entre personas ■ meter cisco to create discord ■ to sow discord ■ to sow disharmony ■ to cause trouble between people ■ to create a rift between people ■ to cause trouble between people ■ to create rifts between people *(Nota: Entre tres personas o más, se usa "among" en vez de "between".)*

sembrar semillas to sow seeds ▪ to plant seeds
sembrar un árbol to plant a tree
semejante cosa: hacer ~ to do a thing like that
estar **semi-cerrado** to be half-closed
semillas germinan ▪ semillas están germinando seeds sprout ▪ seeds germinate ▪ seeds are sprouting ▪ seeds are germinating
sémola de maíz hominy grits
senda de planeo *(aeronáutica)* glide path
sendero de menos resistencia ▪ camino de menos resistencia path of least resistance
sendero se bifurcaba path forked
sendos: en ~ in as many ▪ in separate ▪ on a different ▪ something for each ➤ Los dos montañeros rescatados fueron transportados al hospital en sendos helicópteros. The two rescued mountain climbers were transported to the hospital in separate helicopters. ➤ El coleccionista ha adquirido sendas obras de Picasso para sus tres mansiones en el sur de Francia. The art collector has acquired a work of Picasso for each of his three mansions in southern France. ➤ Los cazas fueron transportados por sendos portaaviones. Each fighter jet was transported on a different aircraft carrier. ➤ La actriz y su acompañante llegaron en sendas limusinas al estreno. The actress and her companion arrived in separate limousines.
la **sensación de soledad** lonely feeling
sensación térmica windchill factor
sentada la base de que... ▪ suponiendo que (es cierto que)... granted that...
estar **sentados frente a frente** to be sitting face to face
sentar la cabeza ▪ volverse sensato ▪ centrarse ▪ hacerse sensato to get one's act together ▪ to come to one's senses ▪ to get oneself together
sentar las bases de to lay the groundwork for
sentar un precedente ▪ establecer un precedente ▪ crear un precedente to set a precedent
sentarle bien a alguien ▪ irle bien ▪ quedarle bien ▪ resultarle bien to be (very) becoming to someone ▪ to look good on someone ➤ Ese vestido le sienta muy bien. ▪ Ese vestido le va muy bien. ▪ Ese vestido le queda muy bien. ▪ Ese vestido le resulta muy bien. *(a usted)* That dress is very becoming to you. ▪ That dress looks good on you. ▪ *(a ella)* That dress is very becoming to her. ▪ That dress looks good on her.
sentarle bien algo a alguien *(ropa)* to look good on you ▪ to go well on you
sentarle como a un Cristo dos pistolasa uno ▪ caerle a uno tan bien como a un Santo Cristo dos pistolas to be ridiculous ▪ to be absurd
sentarle como jarro de agua fría a uno to hit one like a bucket of cold water ▪ to come as a shock to one ▪ to come as a nasty surprise to one
sentarle como un guante a uno ▪ quedarle como un guante a uno to fit one like a glove
sentarle como un tiro to make one feel sick ▪ to disagree with one ➤ La salsa picante me sentó como un tiro. The hot sause didn't agree with me.
sentarle como un tiro a uno *(Esp.)* to need it like (one needs) a hole in the head ▪ to need that like (one needs) a hole in the head
sentarle como una patada en el estómago a uno to be like a kick in the stomach ▪ to be like a kick in the teeth
sentarse a la mesa to sit down at the table
sentarse a negociar to sit down and negotiate ▪ to sit down to negotiate
sentarse adelante to sit in front ▪ to sit up front ▪ to sit in the front seat
sentarse al amor de la lumbre ▪ sentarse junto al fuego to sit by the fire
sentarse atrás to sit in back ▪ to sit in the back seat
sentarse bien to sit tight
sentarse de espaldas ▪ ir de espaldas to sit backwards ▪ to ride backwards ➤ No me gusta sentarme de espaldas en el tren. En los viajes largos me marea. ▪ No me gusta ir de espaldas en el tren. En los viajes largos me marea. I don't like to sit backwards on the train. On long trips it makes me nauseated. ▪ I don't like to ride backwards on the train. On long trips it makes me nauseated.
sentarse en torno al fuego to sit around the fire
sentarse enfrente de alguien ▪ sentarse frente a alguien ▪ sentarse delante de alguien to sit across from someone
sentarse erguido(-a) to sit up straight
sentarse frente a frente to sit face to face
sentarse junto al fuego ▪ sentarse al amor de la lumbre to sit by the fire
sentencia de muerte death sentence
sentido común common sense ➤ El sentido común es el menos común de los sentidos. Common sense is not so common.
sentido contrario opposite direction ▪ opposite way
sentido de atención alertness ➤ La bebida energética tuvo un efecto fulgurante en mi sentido de la atención. The energy drink had a dramatic effect on my alertness.
sentido de la vida meaning of life
sentido de orientación sense of direction ➤ Tiene un mal sentido de orientación. He has a poor sense of direction. ➤ He perdido mi sentido de orientación. I've lost my sense of direction. ▪ I've lost my bearings.
sentido de pertenencia sense of belonging ▪ feeling of belonging
sentido del gusto y olfato más desarrollados ▪ sentido del gusto y olfato realzados heightened sense of taste and smell ▪ enhanced sense of taste and smell ➤ Al dejar de fumar, el sentido del gusto y olfato están más desarrollados. When you quit smoking, the senses of taste and smell are heightened. ▪ When you quit smoking, the senses of taste and smell are enhanced.
sentimiento cálido warm feeling
sentimientos contrapuestos: tener ~ ▪ tener sentimientos enfrentados to have mixed feelings ▪ to have conflicting feelings ▪ to have contradictory feelings ▪ to have ambivalent feelings ▪ (for) one's feelings to be mixed ➤ Tengo sentimientos contrapuestos al respecto. ▪ Tengo sentimientos enfrentados al respecto. I have mixed feelings about it. ▪ My feelings about it are mixed.
sentimientos enfrentados ▪ sentimientos contrapuestos mixed feelings ➤ Mis sentimientos están enfrentados. My feelings are mixed. ▪ I have mixed feelings.
sentir afecto hacia alguien ▪ sentir cariño hacia alguien to feel affection for someone
sentir antipatía por alguien to feel animosity toward someone ▪ to feel antipathy for someone
sentir atracción por alguien to be attracted to someone ▪ to feel attraction to someone
el **sentir general** the general feeling ▪ the common feeling ▪ the general view ▪ the common view
sentir indiferencia hacia alguien ▪ tener indiferencia por alguien to have no use for someone ▪ not to have any use for someone
sentir morriña ▪ tener morriña **1.** to feel homesick **2.** to have the blues
sentir mucha pena cuando se entera de to be sorry to hear about ➤ Sentí mucha pena cuando me enteré de tu abuelo. I was sorry to hear about your grandfather.
sentir nostalgia to feel nostalgia
sentir nostalgia de algo to feel nostalgia for something ▪ to feel nostalgic about something
sentir que uno está desmayándose to feel faint
sentir un trasfondo de to feel an undercurrent of ▪ to sense an undercurrent of
sentir una corriente de aire to feel a draft
sentir ver to be sorry to see ➤ Sentía ver... He was sorry to see...
sentirse a disgusto to feel uncomfortable
sentirse a gusto con ▪ sentirse a gusto en to be comfortable with ➤ El filósofo Kant se sentía tan a gusto con la abstracción que rara vez utilizaba ejemplos. ▪ El filósofo Kant se sentía tan a gusto en la abstracción que rara vez utilizaba ejemplos. The philosopher Kant was so comfortable with abstraction that he hardly used any examples.
sentirse atraído(-a) por alguien to be attracted to someone ▪ to feel attracted to someone

sentirse bien ▪ encontrarse bien **1.** to feel well **2.** to feel good ➤ No me siento bien. I don't feel well. ➤ El agua caliente de la ducha se siente bien contra mi espalda. The warm water of the shower feels good on my back.

sentirse bien por to feel good about ➤ Me siento bien por su decisión de dejar su trabajo y montar un negocio por su cuenta. I feel good about his decision to quit his job and go into business for himself.

sentirse como nuevo(-a) to feel like a new person

sentirse comprimido to feel crowded ▪ to feel squeezed

sentirse con confianza al respecto to feel confident about it ➤ ¿Te sientes con confianza al respecto? ¿Do you feel confident about it?

sentirse con libertad de to feel free to

sentirse de maravilla to feel great ▪ to feel wonderful

sentirse desasosegado to feel uneasy ▪ to feel restless ▪ to feel on edge

sentirse desganado ▪ estar desganado not to have much of an appetite ▪ to feel listless

sentirse desgraciado to feel miserable

sentirse en tensión ▪ estar en vilo to be in suspense ➤ Es una película estupenda. Te sientes en tensión todo el rato. It's a great movie. You're in suspense the whole time.

sentirse entonado to feel perked up ▪ to feel inspirited

sentirse exhausto to feel exhausted

sentirse fatal ▪ estar fatal to feel awful

sentirse feliz to feel happy

sentirse frustrado to get frustrated ▪ to feel frustrated ➤ Me sentía muy frustrado intentando explicarlo en inglés. I used to get really frustrated trying to explain it in English.

sentirse fuera de lugar ▪ sentirse fuera del tiesto to feel out of place

sentirse fuera del tiesto ▪ sentirse fuera de lugar to feel out of place

sentirse gran orgullo en to take great pride in

sentirse igual to feel the same way ➤ Yo en tu lugar me habría sentido igual. ▪ Yo en tu lugar me hubiera sentido igual. In your place, I would have felt the same way.

sentirse incómodo con la situación to feel uncomfortable with the situation ▪ to be uncomfortable with the situation

sentirse mal ▪ encontrarse mal to feel ill ▪ not to feel well

sentirse mal por algo ▪ tener cargo de conciencia por algo ▪ darle cargo de conciencia por algo to feel bad about something ➤ No quiero que te sientas mal por ello. I don't want you to feel bad about it.

sentirse orgullo en to take pride in

sentirse ser to feel like to be ▪ to be like to be ➤ ¿Qué se sentirá ser perro o gato? What would it feel like to be a dog or a cat? ▪ What would it be like to be a dog or cat?

seña de la casa ▪ (la) dirección de la casa address of the house

señal acústica: al oírse la ~ ▪ al oírse el tono at the sound of the tone ▪ at the sound of the beep ▪ when you hear the tone ➤ Al oírse la señal acústica ▪ Al oírse el tono When you hear the tone ▪ At the sound of the tone ▪ When you hear the beep ▪ At the sound of the beep

la **señal de humo** smoke signal

señal entrecortada broken up signal ▪ interference in the signal

estar **señalado por** to be indicated by ➤ Los archivos señalados por las banderas blancas que aparecen momentariamente en el escritorio, desaparecen solos cuando cierras adecuadamente el programa cada vez. The files indicated by the white flags which appear momentarily on the desktop disappear by themselves, each time you exit the program correctly.

señalar al norte ▪ apuntar al norte to point north ➤ Las brújulas utilizadas en los barcos de Colón aún señalan al norte. ▪ Las brújulas utilizadas en los barcos de Colón aún apuntan al norte. The compasses used on Columbus' ships still point north.

señalar algo to point out something ▪ to point something out ➤ Señaló un error en mi trabajo. He pointed out an error in my paper.

señalar con el dedo a to point at ➤ Que no señales a las personas con el dedo. Es descortés. Don't point at people. It's impolite.

señalar con precisión un lugar to pinpoint a place

señalar el texto *(procesamiento de textos)* to block text

señalar en el mapa to pinpoint on the map ▪ to indicate on the map ▪ to point out on the map

señalar los errores to point out the mistakes ▪ to point the mistakes out ➤ ¿Me los señalarías? Would you point them out for me?

señalar que... to point out that... ➤ Señaló que el castillo es el símbolo de Castilla y el león de León. He pointed out that the castle is the symbol of Castile and the lion the symbol of Leon.

señalarle un error a alguien to point out someone's mistake

señas particulares ▪ los detalles the particulars ▪ the details

señas personales distinguishing features ▪ identifying marks

Señor Cascarrabias *(protagonista de* Cuento de Navidad *de Dickens)* Mr. Scrooge

ser un **señor coche** to be quite a car ➤ Es un señor coche. That's quite a car.

señor juez ▪ señoría your honor

señor mayor older gentleman

separar el arroz con un tenedor to fluff the rice with a fork

separar el grano de la paja ▪ separar la paja del grano ▪ apartar el grano de la paja to separate the wheat from the chaff ▪ to separate the sheep from the goats

separar la paja del grano ▪ separar el grano de la paja ▪ apartar el grano de la paja to separate the wheat from the chaff ▪ to separate the sheep from the goats

separar los residuos para reciclar to separate the trash in order to recycle

separarse de to separate from ▪ to split off from

separarse de alguien to separate from one's spouse ▪ to leave someone ➤ Se separó de su marido. She left her husband.

separarse del bordillo ▪ retirarse del bordillo to back away from the curb ▪ to pull back from the curb ➤ Sepárate del bordillo un poco. Estás muy cerca. ▪ Retírate un poco del bordillo. Estás muy cerca. Back away from the curb a little (bit). You're too close. ▪ Pull back from the curb a little bit. You're too close.

¡separe! *(técnica dental al paciente al atar el babero)* lift up! ▪ lift your head up! ▪ make a space!

septo desviado *(médico)* deviated septum

ser de 1. provenir de to be from ▪ to come from **2.** sumar a to be ➤ Catalina es de Antigua, Guatemala. Catalina is from Antigua, Guatemala. ➤ El agente doble, cuyo sueldo en el FBI era de 100.000 dólares anuales. The double agent whose salary at the FBI was $100,000 a year.

el **ser humano** human being

ser querido loved one

ser quien habla to do all the talking ➤ Él es quien habla. He does all the talking.

ser normal: ser su ~ to be oneself ▪ to be one's normal self ▪ to be one's usual self

ser *x* (for) there to be *x* (in number) ➤ Somos cinco. There are five of us.

¿será así? is it? ▪ is that really the case? ➤ Pero, ¿será así? But is it?

será eso that could be ▪ maybe so

será mejor que... it would be better if... ➤ Será mejor que vayas conmigo. It would be better if you went with me.

será mejor que me vaya ▪ será mejor que me marche I'd better go ▪ I'd better leave

será mejor que (yo) vaya ▪ será mejor que (yo) asista I'd better go ▪ I'd better attend ▪ I'd better be there

¿seré yo el que...? could I have been the one who...?

¿seré yo la que...? could I have been the one who...?

seres queridos ▪ seres más queridos loved ones

sería como la una it must have been about one o'clock

sería conveniente it would be a good idea ▪ it would be good ➤ Sería conveniente llegar pronto. It would be a good idea to arrive early. ▪ It would be good to arrive early.

sería genial that would be great ▪ that would be perfect

sería inútil that would be useless ▪ it would be useless ▪ it wouldn't do any good

sería lo más atinente *(Valle-Inclán)* the best thing to do would be

sería mejor hacer algo ■ mejor sería hacer algo ■ más valdría hacer algo it would be better to do something ➤ Sería mejor venir a Madrid cuando no haga tanto calor. ■ Más valdría venir a Madrid cuando no haga tanto calor. It would be better to come to Madrid when it's not so hot.

sería mejor que uno haga algo it would be better for one to do something

sería mejor que uno hiciera algo ■ sería mejor que uno hiciese algo ■ sería mejor si uno hiciera algo ■ sería mejor si uno hiciese algo it would be better if one did something ■ it would be better for one to do something ➤ Sería mejor que la acompañaras. ■ Sería mejor que la acompañases. ■ Sería mejor si la acompañaras. ■ Sería mejor si la acompañases. It would be better if you went with her. ■ It would be better for you to go with her.

sería mejor si uno hiciera algo ■ sería mejor si uno hiciese algo ■ sería mejor que uno hiciera algo ■ sería mejor que uno hiciese algo it would be better if one did something ■ it would be better for one to do something ➤ Sería mejor si esperaras. ■ Sería mejor si esperases. ■ Sería mejor que esperaras. ■ Sería mejor que esperases. It would be better if you waited. ■ It would be better for you to wait.

serían como las *x* it must have been about *x* o'clock ➤ Serían como las dos cuando... It must have been about two o'clock when...

la **serie de instrucciones** set of instructions ➤ Necesito una serie de instrucciones infalibles. I need a perfect set of instructions.

la **serie (de televisión)** television series ■ TV series

serle de ayuda a alguien to be helpful to someone ■ to help someone ➤ Celebro que te sea de ayuda. I'm delighted that it's helpful to you. ■ I'm delighted that it helps you.

el **Sermón de la Montaña** Sermon on the Mount

serpentear por to wind through ➤ Los caminos comarcales serpentean incesantemente por las montañas de esa región. ■ Las carreteras comarcales serpentean incesantemente por las montañas de esa región. The country roads wind endlessly through the mountains of that region.

la **serpiente multicolor** *(carreras de bicicleta)* multicolor string of bicycles

la **serpiente venenosa** poisonous snake

servicio a clientes ■ servicio al cliente ■ (la) atención al cliente customer service

servicio al cliente ■ servicio a clientes ■ (la) atención al cliente customer service

servicio de cobro de facturas (bill) collection agency

servicio de espionaje intelligence agency

Servicio de Impuestos Interior Internal Revenue Service

servicio de tiempo time service ➤ ¿Tiene España un servicio de tiempo?-Sí, desde todos los sitios se marca 093. Does Spain have a time service?-Yes, from all locations dial 093.

servicio doméstico domestic help

servidor de usted ■ para servirle at your service

servir a la patria *(Esp.)* ■ servir al rey to serve in the military ■ to serve one's country

servir a manera de to serve as

servir al rey *(Esp.)* ■ servir a la patria to serve in the military

servir algo a alguien en bandeja de plata servir algo a alguien en bandeja ■ poner algo a alguien en una bandeja de plata to hand someone something on a silver platter

servir como algo to serve as something ➤ La licuadora sirve como picadora tambien. The blender serves as a chopper, too.

servir como pantalla para actividades ilegales ■ servir como pantalla para actividades ilícitas ■ funcionar como pantalla para actividades ilegales ■ funcionar como pantalla para actividades ilícitas ■ hacer de pantalla para actividades ilegales ■ hacer de pantalla para actividades ilícitas to serve as a front for illegal activities ■ to serve as a front for illicit activities

servir de to serve as ■ to act as

servir de colchón para ■ hacer de amortiguador to act as a buffer against ■ to serve as a buffer against

servir de pauta para to serve as a guideline for

servir de prueba de to serve as proof of

servir de prueba de que to serve as proof that

servir de sangre a to be the lifeblood of

servir de válvula de escape to be an escape valve ■ to serve as an escape valve

servir lo mismo para un fregado que para un barrido ■ valer lo mismo para un fregado que para un barrido to be a jack-of-all-trades

servir para hacer algo ■ servir como algo to be usable to do something ■ to serve as something ➤ La licuadora también sirve para picar. The blender can be used as a chopper. ■ The blender serves as a chopper, too. ■ The blender chops, too.

servirle a alguien para hacer algo to help someone do something

servirle a uno to work for one ■ to meet one's needs ➤ Creo que el programa de la UNAM te servirá. I believe the program at UNAM will work for you.

servirle mucho a alguien to work well for someone ■ to serve someone well

servirse de algo para hacer algo to use something to do something ■ to make use of something to do something ■ to utilize something to do something

servirse de alguien to patronize someone

sesgar un encuesta *(Esp.)* ■ manipular una encuesta to bias a poll (intentionally) ■ to bias a survey (intentionally)

sesgo de una muestra estadística bias in a statistical sample

la **sesión de tarde** matinée ■ matinee

la **sesión doble** double feature

sesión fotográfica picture-taking session

sesión movida tumultuous meeting ➤ Tuvimos una sesión movida en el último consejo de administración. The last board meeting was tumultuous.

sexo débil weaker sex

sexo seguro: practicar el ~ to practice safe sex

sexto sentido sixth sense

si... why... ➤ ¡Si nos conocemos de antiguo! Why, we've known each other for ages!

si algo así sucediera ■ si sucediera algo así ■ si sucediera semejante cosa ■ si semejante cosa sucediera if anything like that happened ■ if anything like that were to happen

si algo así sucede ■ si sucede algo así ■ si sucede semejante cosa ■ si semejante cosa sucede if anything like that happens ➤ Si algo así sucede, recibirás de regreso el doble de tu dinero. If anything like that happens, you get double your money back.

si algo así sucediera ■ si algo así llegara a pasar if anything like that happened

si alguien quiere... ■ quien quiera... if anyone wants to... ■ whoever might want to... ➤ Si alguien quiere hacer una pregunta, que la haga ahora, porque no se permiten preguntas durante el examen. ■ Quien quiera hacer una pregunta, que la haga ahora, porque no se permiten preguntas durante el examen. If anyone wants to ask a question, this is the time to ask it because no questions are permitted during the examination. ■ Whoever might want to ask a question, do so now, because no questions are permitted during the examination.

si alguna vez descubro ■ si alguna vez me entero if I ever find out

si alguna vez me entero ■ si alguna vez descubro if I ever find out

un **sí apabullante** a resounding yes

si apenas but hardly

si así lo deseas if you want to

si bemol b-flat

si bien 1. but rather **2.** *(aunque)* although

si bien es cierto ■ si bien es verdad if that's really true ■ if it's really true

si bien es verdad ■ si bien es cierto if that's really true ■ if it's really true

si cabe que if there is a question that

si conoce la extensión, márquela (ahora) ■ si sabe la extensión, márquela (ahora) if you know the extension, dial it now

si crees que puedes con ello... if you think you can handle it...

sí da you *can* catch it ■ it *is* contagious *(Pun found on an AIDS-prevention poster, SIDA being the Spanish acronym)*

si de hecho era cierto if it was really true

si de hecho es cierto if it's really true
si de mí dependiera if it were up to me
si de verdad estás interesado ■ si de verdad te interesa if you're really interested
si de verdad (usted) está interesado ■ si usted de verdad está interesado ■ si de verdad le interesa (a usted) if you're really interested
si Dios quiere God willing
sí efectivamente 1. *(yo, presente)* I do indeed 2. *(yo, pasado)* I did indeed 3. *(él, presente)* he does indeed ■ *(él, pasado)* he did indeed 4. *(ella, presente)* she does indeed 5. *(ella, pasado)* she did indeed ➤ Sí efectivamente recibí el CD. I did indeed receive the CD.
si el río suena, piedras lleva where there's smoke, there's fire
si, en cambio ■ si, por otra parte if, on the other hand ■ if, however
si es así if so ■ if that's the case
si es cierto ■ de ser cierto if it's true
si es de tu interés ■ si estás interesado if it interests you ■ if you're interested
si es mucho pedir if that's asking too much ■ if that's too much to ask ■ if it's too much to ask
si es que if one should ➤ Si es que consigo este trabajo, pagaré todas mis deudas. If I should get the job, I'll pay all my debts.
si es que a más no se propasa if he doesn't take any more liberties
si es que era eso if you could call it that
si es que eran eso if you could call them that
si es que es eso if you can call it that
si es que si no but if not
si es que tiene alguno if (it has) any ➤ Es de poca importancia, si es que tiene alguna. It is of little, if any, importance. ■ It is of minor, if any, importance.
si es tan amable if you would be so kind as to
si esto cuela if one can get away with it
si esto no da resultado if this doesn't work ■ if that doesn't work
si existe alguna posibilidad (por remota que sea) ■ si existe alguna (remota) posibilidad if at all possible
si existe alguna (remota) posibilidad ■ si existe alguna posibilidad (por remota que sea) if at all possible
si fracaso, ni caso if it doesn't work out, don't worry about it
si fue así if it was
si fuera así if it were
si fuera posible ■ de ser posible if possible
si fuiste tú if it was you ➤ No sé si fuiste tú pero alguien dejó los platos sucios en el fregadero. I don't know if it was you, but somebody left dirty dishes in the sink.
si hay una conclusión de if any conclusion can be drawn from ➤ Si hay una conclusión de lo ocurrido, ésta es que... If any conclusion can be drawn from what happened, it is that...
si hubiera estado en mis cabales ■ si hubiese estado en mis cabales if I had had my wits about me
si hubiera habido if there had been
si hubera sabido... ■ de haber sabido... if I had known... ■ had I known... ➤ Si hubiera sabido lo malo que iba a ser, no habría pagado por verlo. ■ De haber sabido lo malo que iba a ser, no habría pagado por verlo. ■ De haber sabido lo malo que iba a ser, no habría pagado por verlo. If I had known how bad it was going to be, I wouldn't have paid to see it. ■ Had I known how bad it was going to be, I wouldn't have paid to see it. ■ If I had known how bad it would be, I wouldn't have paid to see it. ■ Had I known how bad it would be, I wouldn't have paid to see it.
si la envidia fuera tiña, cuántos tiñosos habría if envy were dirt, the whole world would be dirty
si la hay if there is one ➤ La sucursal del banco estaría en esta calle, si la hay. The branch of the bank would be on this street if there is one.
si la memoria no me engaña if my memory serves me (correctly)
si las hay if there are any
si las miradas matasen... if looks could kill...
si las paredes hablaran... if walls could talk...
si le dan la ocasión given the chance
si le quita *x* a *y*, te quedan *z* *y* minus *x* equals *z* ➤ Si le quitas sesenta a cien, te quedan cuarenta. One hundred minus sixty equals forty. ■ One hundred take away sixty leaves forty.
si le surge algo if anything comes up
si llega a eso if it comes to that
si llegara a eso ■ si llegase a eso if it came to that
si lo consigo ■ si lo logro if I can make it happen ■ if I can manage it ■ *(coloquial)* if I can swing it ■ if I can pull it off
sí lo es *(agreeing)* ■ sí que lo es yes, it is
si lo fuera a acabar if I thought I would finish it
si lo hay if there is one
sí lo hice I *did*
si lo hubiera hecho ■ de haberlo hecho 1. *(yo)* if I had done it 2. *(él)* if he had done it 3. *(ella)* if she had done it 4. *(usted)* if you had done it ➤ Yo me habría sorprendido si él lo hubiera hecho. I would have been surprised if he had (done it).
si lo hubiera sabido ■ de haberlo sabido 1. *(yo)* if I had known it 2. *(él)* if he had known it 3. *(ella)* if she had known it 4. *(usted)* if you had known it
si los hay if there are any
si lo hay if there is one
sí lo hice 1. I *did*! 2. I *did* do it.
si lo logro ■ si lo consigo if I can make it happen ■ if I can manage it ■ *(coloquial)* if I can swing it ■ if I can pull it off
si lo sé if I had known
si lo tengo 1. if I have it 2. if I have one ■ if I have any
si los gillipollas volaran, estaría todo el día nublado ■ si los gillipollas volaran, estaría todo el cielo nublado if assholes flew, it would be cloudy all day ■ if assholes could fly, it would be cloudy all day
si los hay ■ if there are any ■ if there ever was one
si los perros ladran, señal que cabalgamos *(Don Quixote)* if there are lots of obstacles, it's a sign we're making progress ■ there is no advancement without resistance
si mal no recuerdo ■ *(Esp.)* ■ si mal no me acuerdo if I remember right ■ if I remember correctly ■ if my memory serves me (correctly)
sí me alegra de eso I *am* glad of that
si me apuras para... if you try to bulldoze me into... ➤ Si me apuras para comprar el auto, me voy a otro concesionario. If you try to bulldoze me into buying the car, I'm going to another dealership.
si me da tiempo if I have time ➤ Si me da tiempo, iré. If I have time, I'll go. ■ If I have time, I will go.
si me diera tiempo if I had time ➤ Si me diera tiempo, iría. If I had time, I'd go. ■ If I had time, I would go.
si me disculpa (usted) if you'll excuse me
si me disculpan if you'll excuse me ■ if you all will excuse me
si me disculpas if you'll excuse me
si me disculpáis *(Esp., vosotros)* if you'll excuse me ■ if you all will excuse me
si me haces el favor would you? ■ if you would, (please) ■ ➤ Entrégame eso, si me haces el favor. Hand me that, would you?
si me hubiera dado tiempo ■ si hubiera tenido tiempo if I had had time ■ had I had time *("If I would have had time" es de uso común en los Estados Unidos pero incorrecto y además confunde la diferencia importante entre el condicional ("habría tenido, would have had") y el subjuntivo ("hubiera tenido, had had").* ■ *"If I would have had time" is common in the United States but incorrect and loses the important distinction between the conditional (would have had, habría tenido) and subjunctive ("had had, hubiera tenido").)* ➤ Si me hubiera dado tiempo habría ido. If I had had time, I'd have gone ■ If I had had time, I would have gone.
si me permites *(expresando impaciencia)* (I would appreciate it) if you'll allow me ■ (I would appreciate it) if you would let me ➤ Si me permites explicar... If you'll let me explain... ■ I would appreciate it if you'd let me explain...
si me permites decirlo ■ si puedo decir así if I may say so
si me lo propongo, lo logro if I put my mind to it, I could do it ➤ Si me lo propongo, lo logro. If I put my mind to it, I could do it.
si muerde la lengua se muere she has a vicious tongue ■ she is extremely mean ■ she says extremely hurtful things

si no otherwise ➤ Dile que me llame antes de las nueve, que si no, no me pasan el mensaje. Tell him to call me by nine, (because) otherwise I won't get the message.
si no cambias con el cambio, el cambio te cambia if you don't change with the times, the times will change you
si no es con ■ excepto con except with ➤ Nunca juega al boliche si no es con sus estudiantes. ■ *(Méx.)* Nunca va a jugar al boliche si no es con sus estudiantes. ■ Nunca va a jugar al boliche excepto con sus estudiantes. ■ *(Esp.)* Nunca va a jugar a los bolos si no es con sus estudiantes. ■ Nunca va a jugar a los bolos excepto con sus estudiantes. He never goes bowling except with his students.
si no es mía la culpa but it's not my fault
si no es mucho pedir if it's not too much trouble ■ if it isn't too much trouble
si no estuviera, déjale un mensaje en su contestadora if he's not there, leave a message on his answering machine
si no fuera porque if it were not for the fact that ■ if it weren't for the fact that
si no hay tropiezos barring the unforeseen ■ if there are no trip ups
si no hubiera sido por ■ de no haber sido por if it had not been for ■ if it hadn't been for ■ had it not been for ➤ La víctima del derrumbe habría muerto si no hubiera sido por los servicios de emergencia. ■ La víctima del derrumbe habría muerto de no haber sido por los servicios de emergencia. The victim of the collapse would have died if it had not been for the paramedics. ■ The victim of the collapse would have died had it not been for the paramedics.
si no interviene ningún factor adverso ■ si no hay contratiempos ■ si no aparecen contratiempos ■ si todo sale como estaba planeado ■ si todo sale como estaba previsto all things being equal ➤ Si no interviene ningún factor adverso, preferiría vivir aquí en Jalapa. All things being equal, I'd prefer to live here in Jalapa.
si no le importa if you don't mind
si no llega a ser por ■ de no ser por ■ a no ser por if it were not for ■ if it weren't for ■ were it not for ➤ La víctima del derrumbe podría haber muerto si no llega a ser por los servicios de emergencia. The victim of the collapse could have died if it had not been for the paramedics. ■ The victim of the collapse might have died if it had not been for the paramedics.
si no lo haces if you don't do it ■ if you don't
si no más if not more so ➤ Es tan importante, si no más, como... It is as important, if not more so, than...
si no me engaño if I'm not mistaken
si no me equivoco if I'm not mistaken
si no me falla la memoria if my memory serves me ■ if I remember correctly ■ if I remember right
si no puedes con ellos, úneteles if you can't beat 'em, join 'em
si no quería but I didn't mean to
si no te gusta, te chinchas if you don't like it, you can lump it
si no te importa if you don't mind
¡si nos conocemos de antiguo! why, we've known each other forever!
si paso de hoy if I (can) get through today
si persisten las dudas if you still have questions ➤ Si persisten las dudas, házmelas llegar. If you still have questions, send them to me.
si podemos extraer una conclusión de lo ocurrido, es que... ■ si podemos extraer una conclusión de lo que ocurrió, es que... ■ si podemos sacar una conclusión de lo ocurrido, es que... ■ si podemos sacar una conclusión de lo que ocurrió, es que... if any conclusion can be drawn from what happened, it is that... ■ if we can draw any conclusion from what happened, it is that...
si podemos sacar una conclusión de lo ocurrido, es que... ■ si podemos sacar una conclusión de lo que ocurrió, es que... ■ si podemos extraer una conclusión de lo ocurrido, es que... ■ si podemos extraer una conclusión de lo que ocurrió, es que... if any conclusion can be drawn from what happened, it is that... ■ if we can draw any conclusion from what happened, it is that...
si por algún motivo ■ si por alguna razón if for some reason
si por alguna razón ■ si por algún motivo if for some reason
si por casualidad alguna if by (any) chance
si por cualquier motivo ■ si por cualquier razón if for any reason
si por cualquier razón ■ si por cualquier motivo if for any reason
si, por otra parte ■ si, en cambio if, on the other hand ■ if, however
si pudiera pensar en algo (para) ■ si se me ocurriera algo (para) if I could just think of something (to)
si pudiera volver a hacerlo ■ si tuviera la oportunidad de volver a hacerlo if I could do it all over again ■ if I had it to do all over again ■ if I had the chance to do it all over again ■ if I had the opportunity to do it all over again
si puedo ayudarte en algo if I can help you with anything ➤ Si puedo ayudarte en algo déjamelo saber y haré lo posible por ayudarte. If I can help you with anything, let me know and I'll do what I can to help you.
si puedo decir así ■ si me permites decirlo if I may say so
sí que... of course... ■ I *do*... ■ certainly ■ indeed
¡sí que cocina! ■ ¡cómo cocina! **1.** *(él)* can he ever cook! **2.** *(ella)* can she ever cook!
sí que las hubo ■ sí que había yes, there were
sí que lo era 1. *(yo)* yes, I was **2.** *(él)* yes, he was **3.** *(ella)* yes, she was **4.** *(usted)* yes, you were
sí que me acuerdo ■ por supuesto que me acuerdo I *do* remember ■ of course I remember
sí que me alegro de eso I *am* glad of that
sí que me gustaría saber... I'd sure like to know...
sí que tengo I do have
si quiere (usted) if you want to ■ if you like ■ if you prefer
si quiere, que lo haga let him do it if he wants to ■ let her do it if she wants to
si quieres if you want to ■ if you like ■ if you prefer
si quieres que te diga la verdad... if you want me to tell you the truth... ■ if you want to know the truth...
si quisiera Dios ■ si Dios quiera God willing
si sale algún tema if anything comes up
si sale cierto ■ si llega a ser verdad if it turns out to be true ■ if it proves to be true
si se considera que... if you consider that... ■ if you take into consideration that...
si se consiguiese algo if you achieved something ■ if you managed something ➤ El helicóptero de Leonardo da Vinci funcionaría si se consiguiese el giro rápido de la hélice. Leonardo da Vinci's helicopter would work if you achieved a rapid rotation of the rotor.
si se consiguiese que hiciera algo if you got it to do something ■ if you made it do something ■ if it were made to ➤ El helicóptero de Leonardo da Vinci funcionaría si se consiguiese que la hélice girara rápidamente. Leonardo's da Vinci's helicopter would work if you got the the rotor to spin fast. ■ Leonardo's helicopter would work if you made the rotor spin fast. ■ Leonardo's helicopter would work if the rotor were made to spin fast.
si se corta la línea ■ si se corta la comunicación if you get disconnected
sí se da la clase hoy class does meet today ■ we do have class today ■ there *is* a class today
si se detiene a pensarlo bien if you stop to think about it
si se encarta ■ si se tercia if the occasion should arise ■ should the occasion arise ■ if the occasion arises
si se hiciera a mi manera ■ si se hiciese a mi manera ■ si se hiciera como yo digo ■ si se hiciese como yo digo if I had (it) my way
si se me ocurriera algo (para) ■ si pudiera pensar en algo (para) if I could just think of something (to)
si se me permite hacer una sugerencia if I might make a suggestion
si se me permite la pregunta if you don't mind my asking ■ if I might ask ■ might I ask
si se me presenta la oportunidad if the opportunity arises ■ if I get the chance ■ if I have the chance
si se pudiera conseguir que if you could get it to ➤ El helicóptero de Leonardo da Vinci funcionaría si se pudiera conseguir que

la hélice girara rápidamente. Leonardo da Vinci's helicopter would work if you could get the rotor to spin fast.

sí, se puede 1. *(lema de United Farm Workers)* yes, we can ▪ yes, it can be done 2. sí, se puede entrar yes, you can come in ▪ yes, you may come in

si se tercia ▪ si se encarta should the occasion arise ▪ if the occasion should arise ▪ if the occasion arises

si semejante cosa sucede ▪ si sucede semejante cosa ▪ si algo así sucede ▪ si sucede algo así if anything like that happens

si semejante cosa sucediera ▪ si sucediera semejante cosa ▪ si algo así sucediera ▪ si sucediera algo así if anything like that happened

si sólo supieran ▪ tan sólo supieran if only they knew

si sucede algo así ▪ si algo así sucede ▪ si semejante cosa sucede ▪ si sucede semejante cosa if anything like that happens

si sucede semejante cosa ▪ si semejante cosa sucede ▪ si sucede algo así ▪ si algo así sucede if anything like that happens

si sucediera algo así ▪ si algo así sucediera ▪ si sucediera semejante cosa ▪ si semejante cosa sucediera if anything like that happened

si sucediera semejante cosa ▪ si semejante cosa sucediera ▪ si sucediera algo así ▪ si algo así sucediera if anything like that happened

si te he visto no me acuerdo *(como promesa de no chivar)* if I saw it, I don't remember ▪ I'll look the other way ▪ I'll pretend it never happened

si te parece if it's convenient ▪ if you like ➤ Si te parece, empiezo a trabajar este lunes. If it's convenient, I'll start work this Monday. ➤ Si te parece, iremos a cenar a la mexicana esta noche. If you like, we'll have Mexican food tonight.

si te parece bien if you like

si te sirve de consuelo ▪ por si te sirve de consuelo if it's any consolation to you

si te surge algo if anything comes up ➤ Si te surge algo, llámame. If anything comes up, call me.

si te vuelvo a coger haciendo eso *(Esp.)* ▪ si te vuelvo a pillar haciendo eso if I catch you doing that again

si te vuelvo a pillar haciendo eso ▪ *(Esp.)* ▪ si te vuelvo a coger haciendo eso if I catch you doing that again

si todo lo demás falla if all else fails

si todo marcha según lo planeado if everything goes according to plan ▪ if everything goes as planned

si tú lo dices if you say so

si tuviera la oportunidad de volver a hacerlo si pudiera volver a hacerlo if I had it to do all over again ▪ if I had the chance to do it all over again ▪ if I had the opportunity to do it all over again ▪ if I could do it all over again

si tuviera su año 1. *(de él)* if his year were up 2. *(de ella)* if her year were up

si uno podría hacer algo if one could do something ➤ Si pudieras ir, yo podría llevarte. If you could go, I could take you. ▪ If you could go, I could give you a ride.

si uno pudiera hacer algo if one could do something ▪ if one were able to do something ➤ Si pudieras ir, yo podría llevarte. If you could go, I could take you. ▪ If you could go, I could give you a ride.

si uno sigue así... ▪ de seguir así... if one keeps on... ▪ if one keeps it up... ▪ if one keeps (on) doing what one is doing ➤ Si sigue así va a acabar teniendo graves problemas: le da a la botella. ▪ De seguir así va a acabar teniendo graves problemas: le da a la botella. If he keeps on, he's going to have serious problems. He's hitting the bottle. ▪ If he keeps it up, he's going to have serious problems. He's hitting the bottle.

si usted lo dice if you say so

si vamos a eso for that matter

si viene alguna carta para mí if I get any mail

si y sólo si *(lógica simbólica)* if and only if

¡si ya lo sé! I know, I know! (you don't need to belabor the point)

si yo decía if I would say

si yo estuviera en su pellejo ▪ si yo fuera él if I were in his shoes ▪ if I were he

si (yo) hubiera podido hacerlo, lo hubiera hecho if I could have done it, I would have

si (yo) hubiera sabido cómo if I had known how

si (yo) hubiera sabido lo... if I had known how...

si (yo) hubiera sabido lo que... if I had known what...

si (yo) hubiera sabido qué... if I had known what...

si (yo) lo hubiera hecho ▪ de haberlo hecho if I had done it ▪ had I done it

si (yo) lo hubiera sabido ▪ de haberlo sabido if I had known

si yo no estuviera cuando vayas if I'm not there when you go

si yo no estuviera cuando vengas if I'm not here when you come

si yo pudiera decir lo mismo... if I could say the same thing... ▪ if I were able to say the same thing...

si (yo) pudiera volver a hacerlo ▪ si (yo) tuviera la oportunidad de volver a hacerlo if I could do it over again ▪ if I had it to do all over again ▪ if I had the chance to do it over again ▪ if I had the opportunity to do it over again

si (yo) tuviera la oportunidad de volver a hacerlo ▪ si (yo) pudiera volver a hacerlo if I had the chance to do it over again ▪ if I had the opportunity to do it over again ▪ if I had it to do all over again ▪ if I could do it over again

estar **siempre a la entera disposición de alguien** ▪ estar todo el tiempo detrás de alguien to be at someone's beck and call

siempre está allí cuando se le necesita he's always there when you need him ▪ he's always there when he's needed

siempre está allí donde se le necesita he's always there where you need him ▪ he's always there where he's needed

siempre desde que ever since

siempre es puntual *(él)* he is always on time ▪ he is (very) punctual ▪ *(ella)* she is always on time ▪ she is (very) punctual

siempre hay un roto para un descosido ▪ nunca falta un roto para un descosido there's someone for everyone

siempre me toca... I always...

siempre que ▪ cada vez que ▪ cuandoquiera whenever ▪ every time ▪ as often as

siempre que iba... *(yo)* 1. whenever I would go... ▪ whenever I was going 2. whenever I went

siempre que puedo whenever I can ▪ as often as I can

siempre que quieras whenever you want (to)

siempre que sea posible whenever possible

siempre que (yo) venía aquí... whenever I used to come here...

siempre se encuentra argumentos... one always find reasons...

siempre se puede mejorar there's always room for improvement

siempre tener una ocurrencia ▪ tener cada salida to come out with the funniest things ➤ Ella siempre tiene una ocurrencia. ▪ Ella tiene cada salida. She comes out with the funniest things.

siempre y cuando so long as ▪ whenever ▪ if and when ▪ if and only if

estar **siendo analizado minuciosamente** to be under scrutiny

estar **siendo atacado** to be under attack ▪ to be being attacked

estar **siendo discutido** to be under discussion ➤ El asunto está siendo discutido. ▪ Se está discutiendo. The matter is under discussion.

siendo él aún un bebé when he was still a baby

siendo ella aún un bebé when she was still a baby

siendo lo que es being what it is ➤ Mi comprensión de la química siendo lo que es... My understanding of chemistry being what it is...

siendo que... ▪ dado que... given (the fact) that... ▪ *(muy coloquial)* seeing as how... ➤ Siendo que este tema es muy complejo ▪ Dado que este tema es muy complejo... Given (the fact) that this matter is very complex... ▪ Given the complexity of this matter... ▪ Seeing as how this matter is very complex...

siendo quien era *(él)* considering who he was ▪ *(ella)* considering who she was ▪ *(refiriéndose a la posición u ocupación de la persona)* considering who it was ▪ considering who he was ▪ considering who she was

siendo quien es *(él)* considering who he is ▪ *(ella)* considering who she is ▪ *(refiriéndose a la posición u ocupación de la persona)* considering who it is ▪ considering who he is ▪ considering who she is

las **sienes chorreantes** temples dripping with perspiration
siento como si fuera a... I feel like I'm...
siento haber llegado tarde I'm sorry I'm late ■ *(informal)* sorry I'm late
siento haberte hecho esperar I'm sorry to keep you waiting
siento llegar tarde (I'm) sorry I'm late
siento no haberte escrito antes sorry I haven't written sooner
siento no poder ayudarte I'm sorry I can't help you
siete pecados capitales seven deadly sins
siga mi consejo take my advice
sigilo sacramental ■ secreto de la confesión secrecy of the confessional
significar algo para uno to mean a lot to one ➤ Significa algo para mí. It means a lot to me.
significar amenaza para la vida ■ implicar amenaza para la vida to be life threatening
signo de igual equals sign
signo de mayor que ■ (>) symbol for greater than
signo de menor que ■ (<) symbol for less than
signo de admiración exclamation mark
signo de riqueza symbol of wealth ➤ Un Rolls-Royce es el signo de la riqueza. A Rolls-Royce is the symbol of wealth.
sigo sin hacerlo ■ todavía no lo he hecho ■ aún no lo he hecho I still haven't done it ■ I haven't done it yet
sigo sin saber... I still don't know... ➤ Sigo sin saber por qué hice eso. I still don't know why I did that.
sigo sin ver la relación I still don't see the connection
¡**sigue así!** ■ ¡consérvalo así! keep it up!
sigue comunicando it's still busy
¡**sigue con el buen trabajo!** keep up the good work!
sigue entero (it) is still in one piece ➤ *(L.am.)* Quiero prender la tele un momento para ver si el mundo sigue entero. ■ *(Esp.)* Quiero encender la tele un momento para ver si el mundo sigue entero. I want to turn on the TV for a second to see if the world is still in one piece.
¿**sigue habiendo...?** is there still...? ➤ ¿Sigue habiendo un mercado al aire libre cerca del metro Tetuán? Is there still an open air market on Sundays near the Tetuán metro?
sigue habiendo mucho ■ aún hay mucho there's still a lot of
sigue la vida life goes on
sigue mi consejo take my advice
sigue sentado ■ no se levante ■ no te levantes keep your seat
sigue siendo 1. it is still ■ it continues to be 2. *(él)* he is still ■ he continues to be 3. *(ella)* she is still ■ she continues to be
sigue sin... it still hasn't...
sigue sin venir it still hasn't come in ■ it hasn't come in yet ■ it's not here yet
estar **siguiendo un régimen** to be on a diet
el **siguiente día que me llames** the next time you call me
siguiente fase: iniciar la ~ to begin the next phase
siguiente paso next step
siguiente pregunta next question
silenciar algo to hush up something ■ to hush something up ➤ El alcalde intenta silenciar el escándalo de corrupción. The mayor is trying to hush up the corruption scandal. ■ They mayor is trying to hush the corruption scandal up. ➤ El alcalde intenta silenciarlo. They mayor is trying to hush it up.
silencio de muerte dead silence
el **silencio vale oro** silence is golden
silueta delgada slim figure ■ trim figure ■ good figure
silla de ruedas: encontrarse en ~ to be wheelchair-bound ■ to be confined to a wheelchair
silla plegable folding chair
simbología onírica dream symbolism ■ symbolism in dreams ■ symbolism of the dream
estar **simpático(-a) con alguien** to be nice to someone
simpático hipermercado del barrio your friendly neighborhood supermarket
ser **simpatizante de** to be sympathetic to ➤ Es simpatizante de los palestinos. He is sympathetic to the Palestinians.
el **simple hecho de que...** the simple fact that...
simple idea simplistic idea
simplemente dejar ser a alguien to just let someone be
simplemente no puedo I just can't
simplemente no puedo entenderlo ■ justamente no puedo entenderlo ■ me cuesta poder entenderlo I just can't understand it ■ I simply can't understand it
simplificarlo al máximo ■ simplificarlo lo más que se pueda dejarlo lo más sencillo posible ■ dejarlo lo más simple posible to keep it simple ■ to keep it as simple as possible ■ to simplify it as much as possible
simplificarlo lo más que se pueda ■ simplificarlo al máximo ■ dejarlo lo más sencillo posible ■ dejarlo lo más simple posible to keep it simple ■ to keep it as simple as possible
simulacro de examen mock exam
simulacro de fuego fire drill
simular estar to fake being ■ to feign being
simular que... to fake that... ■ to feign that... ■ to pretend that...
estar **sin algo** to be out of something ➤ La tienda está sin agua embotellada. The store is out of bottled water.
estar **sin aliento** ■ estar sin resuello to be out of breath ■ to be breathless
sin aliento: quedarse ~ to get out of breath
sin ambages: hablar ~ to get to the point ➤ ¡Habla sin ambages! Get to the point!
sin antes decirte: no hacer algo ~ not to do something until I tell you ■ not to do something unless I tell you (first)
sin apenas resistencia: caer ~ to fall with hardly any resistance
estar **sin apetito** ■ estar desganado to have no appetite ■ not to have any appetite ■ not to have an appetite
sin ataduras no strings attached
estar **sin blanca** ■ estar sincero to be penniless ■ to be (completely) broke
sin causa for no good reason ■ without cause
sin comentarios no comment
sin complejos without hangups
sin compromiso with no obligation
sin compromisos ■ sin ataduras no strings attached
sin conseguirlo unsuccessfully
sin conseguirlo: intentar hacer algo ~ to try unsuccessfully to do something
sin consuelo: llorar ~ to cry inconsolably
sin contar ■ excluyendo not counting ■ excluding
sin contratiempos without a hitch ■ without snags
sin cortapisas with no strings attached ■ without (any) strings attached ■ without restrictions ■ without conditions
sin darse cuenta ■ sin enterarse without realizing it ■ without being aware of it
sin decir agua va without (any) warning ■ without any advance warning ■ with no advance warning ■ suddenly
sin decir esta boca es mía without saying a word
sin decir una palabra without saying a word
sin dejar de comer without pausing from one's dinner
sin dejar rastro without a trace
sin descuidar los movimientos (de) without taking one's eyes off (of)
sin duda no doubt ■ undoubtedly
sin duda alguna without any doubt ■ without the slightest doubt ■ with no doubt(s) whatever
sin el más mínimo atisbo de without the slightest hint of ➤ Sin el más mínimo atisbo de una sonrisa Without the slightest hint of a smile
sin embargo however ■ nevertheless
sin embargo, tenía la intención *(yo)* I meant to, though
sin encontrar rastro de without finding a trace of
sin enterarse ■ sin darse cuenta without realizing it ■ without being aware of it
sin esperanza de with no hope of ■ without any hope of ➤ Estaban atrapados en el submarino sin esperanza de poder salir nunca. They were trapped in the submarine with no hope of ever getting out.

sin esperar más without waiting any longer
estar **sin fuerzas** to be completely exhausted
sin gastos adicionales ▪ gratis at no extra charge ▪ free
sin haber apenas barely having ▪ hardly having ➤ *(noticia)* Sin haber dormido apenas, la prima de Elián González se desmayó ayer. Barely having slept, the cousin of Elián González fainted yesterday. ▪ Hardly having slept, the cousin of Elián González fainted yesterday.
sin haber hecho nada 1. without having done anything **2.** through no fault of one's own
sin hablar palabra ▪ sin decir nada ▪ sin decir ni una palabra without saying a word
sin hacer nada para without doing anything for ▪ without doing anything to ➤ Siempre tiene suerte sin hacer nada para merecerla. He's always lucky without doing anything to deserve it.
sin hacerse el menos daño ▪ sin dañarse para nada without hurting oneself at all
sin hielo, por favor no ice, please
sin huesos without hidden strings
sin imaginar siquiera qué... without even imagining what...
sin importar los gastos ▪ sin reparar en gastos ▪ cueste lo cueste ▪ el costo no obstante regardless of the cost ▪ no matter how much it costs ▪ sparing no expense
sin incluir eso ▪ además de eso ▪ por lo demás other than that ▪ apart from that ▪ otherwise ▪ in (all) other respects ➤ Sin incluir eso, tu español es muy correcto. Apart from that, your Spanish is completely correct. ▪ Other than that, your Spanish is completely correct. ▪ Otherwise, your Spanish is completely correct. ▪ In all other respects, your Spanish is completely correct.
sin igual without equal ▪ without peer
sin inmutarse without batting an eye
sin intromisiones without interference
sin ir más lejos ▪ para no ir más lejos **1.** as it happens ▪ in fact **2.** to cite an obvious example ▪ to give you an obvious example
sin ir tan lejos more to the point
sin lugar a dudas ▪ sin ninguna duda no doubt about it ▪ without a doubt ▪ undoubtedly
sin más ▪ sin más ni más just like that ▪ immediately
sin más demora ▪ sin tardar más without further delay
sin más (ni más) ▪ sin más ni menos just like that ▪ without further ado
sin más ni menos ▪ sin más ni más without further ado
sin mencionar not to mention
sin mirar en barras without giving special consideration to social class ▪ without deferring to social class
sin necesidad de without the necessity of ▪ with no need for
sin ningún compromiso with no obligation
sin ningún disimulo blatantly ▪ openly
sin ningún pudor without (any) embarrassment ▪ with no embarrassment
sin ninguna duda ▪ sin lugar a dudas no doubt about it
estar **sin oficio ni beneficio** ▪ no tener ni oficio ni beneficio to be out of work
sin orden ni concierto any old way
sin par unequalled
sin parar without delay
sin pararse en barras *(Esp.)* ▪ sin mirar en barras ▪ sin reparar en barras ▪ sin tropezar en barras stopping at nothing ▪ not letting anything stop one ▪ not letting anything get in one's way
sin pasar por la iglesia out of wedlock
sin pena ni gloria without distinction
sin pena ni gloria: pasar ~ to go unnoticed ▪ to go almost unnoticed ▪ to go virtually unnoticed ▪ hardly to make a stir
sin pensarlo on the spur of the moment
sin pensárselo dos veces ▪ sin pensárselo más without giving it a second thought ▪ without giving it another thought
sin pensárselo más ▪ sin pensárselo dos veces without giving it another thought ▪ without giving it a second thought
sin pestañear ▪ sin inmutarse without batting an eye
sin piedad 1. *(adjetivo)* without pity ▪ unmerciful **2.** *(adverbio)* without pity ▪ unmercifully
sin poder disimular unable to get over
sin poner objecciones without protest
sin precedentes all-time high ▪ without precedents
sin precisar ninguna fecha without setting a date
sin previo aviso without notice ▪ unexpectedly ▪ out of the blue
sin prisa, pero sin pausa slow but steady ▪ slowly but steadily
sin probar untasted ▪ unsampled ➤ *(Ricardo Palma)* Tiene el hábito de no dejar ninguna botella sin probar. It is his custom to leave no bottle untasted.
sin pronunciar una palabra ▪ como el convidado de piedra without saying a word
sin que parezca que vaya a terminar with no end in sight ➤ La insurgencia continúa sin que parezca que vaya a terminar. The insurgency continues with no end in sight.
sin que se le acuse a alguien por without accusing someone of
sin que se sepa si without its being known whether ▪ and it remains unknown whether
sin que uno se dé cuenta without one's realizing it ▪ without one's being aware of it ▪ unbeknownst to one ➤ Sin que (yo) me dé cuenta Unbeknownst to me ▪ Without my being aware of it ▪ Without my realizing it
sin querer without meaning to ▪ unintentionally
sin quererla ni beberla: involucrarse en algo ~ to get roped into something
sin quererla ni beberla: quedarse ~ to be left high and dry
sin rastro (de) without a trace (of)
sin rayas ▪ lisas unlined ➤ Fichas sin rayas ▪ Fichas lisas Unlined index cards ▪ Blank index cards
sin rebozo openly ▪ frankly
sin receta ▪ de mostrador without a prescription ▪ over the counter ➤ Las píldoras del día siguiente ahora están disponibles sin receta en algunos países. Morning-after pills are now available without a prescription in some countries. ▪ Morning-after pills are now (available) over-the-counter in some countries.
sin recurrir a without resorting to ▪ without recourse to ▪ without having recourse to
sin referirse a without reference to
sin reflexión: hacer algo ~ to do something without thinking
sin reparar en barras *(Esp.)* ▪ sin reparar en nada ▪ sin mirar en barras ▪ sin pararse en barras ▪ sin tropezar en barras stopping at nothing ▪ without stopping at anything
sin reparar en gastos ▪ cueste lo cueste ▪ sin importar los gastos regardless of the cost ▪ no matter how much it costs
sin reparo without difficulty
sin reserva without qualification ▪ without holding back
sin respaldo legal without (a) legal basis
estar **sin resuello** ▪ estar sin aliento to be out of breath ▪ to be breathless
sin saber qué hacer not knowing what to do ▪ without knowing what to do
sin saber qué hacer ni decir not knowing what to do or say
sin saberlo yo without my knowledge ▪ without my knowing it
sin salir siquiera without ever leaving
sin siquiera without even ▪ without so much as ▪ without even so much as
sin solución por continuidad uninterrupted
sin son ▪ sin razón without reason ▪ without basis
sin son ni ton: actuar ~ ▪ sin ton ni son without rhyme or reason
sin tacha flawless ▪ unblemished
sin tapujos: decirle a alguien ~ ▪ decirle a alguien llanamente to tell someone flat out ▪ to tell someone without hiding anything
sin tocar untouched
estar **sin trabajo** to be out of work ▪ to be without work
sin trabas: acceso ~ unfettered access ▪ free access
sin tropezar en barras ▪ sin mirar en barras ▪ sin reparar en barras ▪ sin pararse en barras ▪ no pararse en barras to stop at nothing

estar **sin un arma encima** ■ estar desarmado(-a) to be unarmed
sin un arma encima: ir ~ ■ ir desarmado to go unarmed
estar **sin un cuarto** ■ estar sin un real not to have a penny (to one's name) ■ not to have a dime (to one's name)
estar **sin un real** ■ estar sin un cuarto not to have a penny (to one's name) ■ not to have a dime (to one's name)
sin verificar unverified
sincerarse con alguien to open up to someone ■ to confess the truth ■ to divulge the truth ■ to come clean ➤ ¿Por qué no te sinceras y lo admites? Why don't you just come clean and admit it?
estar **sincronizado para explotar en...** to be timed to go off in...
sincronizar algo ■ *(coloquial)* ajustar algo to time something ■ to adjust the timing of something ➤ Hay que sincronizar el encendido del distribuidor. ■ Hay que ajustar el encendido del distribuidor. The timing (of the firing) of the distributor needs to be adjusted.
el **síndrome de abstinencia** withdrawal symptoms ■ withdrawal
el **síndrome de inmunodeficiencia adquerida SIDA** acquired immune deficiency syndrome ■ AIDS
el **Síndrome Respiratorio Agudo Grave** ■ neumonía atípica Severe Acute Respiratory Syndrome ■ SARS
sine die sine die ■ without setting the date for the next meeting
sine qua non sine qua non ■ essential condition ■ necessary condition
un **sinfín de** ■ una infinidad de an endless number of ■ an infinite number of
Sinfonía inconclusa ■ Sinfonía inacabada *(Schubert)* Unfinished Symphony
ser un **siniestro total** to be totalled ➤ El coche es un siniestro total. The car was totalled.
sino más bien but rather
sino más bien que but rather that
sino: no... ~ anything but... ➤ *(Horacio Quiroga)* El cachorro no quiere comer sino huevos de pájaro. The cub doesn't like to eat anything but bird eggs.
sino que but also ■ but even ■ but rather
sino tampoco nor even ■ *(cuando la negación precede el propio verbo)* or even
sintonizar una emisora de radio to tune in to a radio station ➤ Si acaban de sintonizar... If you just tuned in...
sinuoso camino winding road
el **sinvergüenza** scoundrel ■ skunk ■ person without shame
¿sírvase decirme...? would you tell me...?
¡sirve! *(mi idea, invención, etc.)* it's working!
sirve para... it's for...
el **sistema anticongelante** de-icing system
el **sistema de aspersión** sprinkler system
el **sistema de coordinadas** *(física y matemáticas)* system of coordinates
el **sistema de partido único** one-party system
el **sistema de sonido** ■ equipo de sonido sound system
el **sistema dental** set of teeth
el **sistema solar** solar system
sitiar a alguien to corner someone
sitiar una ciudad to lay siege to a city
estar **sitiado** to be under siege ■ to be cornered ■ to be hemmed in
ser un **sitio concurrido** to be a busy place ➤ Es un sitio concurrido. It's a busy place.
sitio de encuentro ■ lugar de encuentro ■ punto de encuentro place to meet ■ meeting place ■ meeting point
sitio suficiente para nosotros dos room enough for both of us
sitios donde encuentras... places to find... ■ places where you can find...
sito en situated in ■ located in ■ situated on ■ located on
situación absurda ■ situación muy caricaturesca ■ situación ridícula ridiculous situation
situación avergonzante ■ situación embarazosa ■ situación bochornosa ■ situación violenta embarrassing situation
situación bochornosa ■ situación embarazosa ■ situación violenta embarrassing situation ■ awkward situation
la **situación de prueba** probationary status ■ probation
situación determinada given situation
situación embarazosa ■ situación bochornosa ■ situación avergonzante ■ situación violenta embarrassing situation ■ awkward situation
la **situación en la que** situation in which ■ *(coloquial)* situation where
la **situación en que quedo** situation in which I find myself ■ situation I find myself in
la **situación estresante** stressful situation
la **situación ganar-ganar** win-win situation
la **situación límite** 1. extreme situation 2. life-threatening situation
la **situación muy caricaturesca** ■ situación absurda ■ situación ridícula ridiculous situation
la **situación reinante** prevailing situation ■ overall situation
situación ridícula ■ situación caricaturesca ■ situación absurda ridiculous situation
situación violenta ■ situación embarazosa ■ situación bochornosa ■ situación avergonzante embarrassing situation
situarse a la altura de ■ situarse al lado de ■ ponerse a la altura de ■ ponerse al lado de
situarse a la derecha to stand to the right
situarse a la izquierda to stand to the left
situarse al lado de ■ situarse a la altura de ■ ponerse al lado de ■ ponerse a la altura de 1. *(de pie)* to come up and stand next to someone 2. *(sentado)* to sit next to someone 3. *(vehículo)* to pull up alongside of someone ■ to come up alongside of someone ➤ La patrulla policial se situó al lado del vehículo sospechoso. ■ La patrulla policial se situó a la altura del vehículo sospechoso. The police car pulled up alongside the suspicious vehicle.
situarse atrás to stand back ■ to get back ➤ ¡Sitúense atrás! ■ ¡Atrás! Stand back! ■ Get back!
situarse con las piernas abiertas to stand with one's legs apart
situarse debajo de to drop below ➤ El paro masculino se sitúa debajo del diez por ciento en España por primera vez en veinte años. Male unemployment drops below ten percent for the first time in twenty years.
situarse en los pulmones ■ asentarse en los pulmones ■ colocarse en los pulmones to settle in one's lungs ➤ La infección se ha situado en los pulmones. ■ La infección se ha asentado en los pulmones. ■ La infección se ha colocado en los pulmones. The infection has settled in his lungs.
¡so animal! ■ ¡pedazo de animal! what an animal!
so capa de ■ con pretexto de under the guise of ■ under the pretense of
so pena de under penalty of
so penas de at the risk of
so pretexto de *(derecho)* ■ con pretexto de ■ en achaque de on the pretext of ■ under the pretext of
sobar la badana a alguien ■ zurrar la badana a alguien ■ calentar la badana a alguien to tan someone's hide ■ to rake someone over the coals
sobrarle motivos para to have more than enough reason to ■ to have more than sufficient to
sobre acolchado ■ sobre guateado ■ sobre acolchonado padded envelope
sobre acolchonado *(Méx.)* ■ sobre acolchado ■ sobre guateado padded envelope
sobre apaisado ■ sobre rectangular oblong envelope
estar **sobre ascuas** to be on pins and needles
estar **sobre aviso (contra algo)** ■ andar sobre aviso to be on the alert (against something) ■ to be on the lookout (against something) ■ to be on guard (against something)
sobre aviso: ponerle a alguien ~ to forewarn someone
el **sobre con polvos blancos** envelope of white powder
sobre el fuego: poner algo ~ to put something on the stove ■ to put something on the burner

sobre el nivel del mar: situarse ~ ▪ estar situado sobre el nivel del mar to be above sea level ➤ Sepúlveda está situada a 1.014 metros sobre el nivel del mar. Sepulveda is 1,014 meters above sea level.

sobre el papel ▪ en teoría on paper ▪ in theory

sobre estos días ▪ sobre estas fechas around this time

sobre guateado ▪ sobre acolchado ▪ sobre acolchonado padded envelope

sobre gustos no hay nada escrito it's a matter of taste ▪ beauty is in the eye of the beholder ▪ different strokes for different folks ▪ that's what makes horse racing

sobre haz on the face of it

sobre la base de que... on the assumption that...

sobre la época de ▪ hacia la época de ▪ alrededor de la época de ▪ por la época de around the time of ▪ at about the time of

sobre la hora de ▪ hacia la hora de ▪ alrededor de la hora de (at) about the time ▪ around the time ➤ Sobre la hora del comienzo de la convención, una gran multitud empezó a congregarse fuera del auditorio. At about the time the convention started, a large crowd began gathering outside the auditorium.

sobre la marcha along the way ▪ as one goes along ➤ Lo haremos sobre la marcha. We'll do it along the way. ➤ Hans Christian Andersen inventó muchos de sus cuentos sobre la marcha. Hans Christian Andersen invented many of his stories as he went along.

sobre la que about which

sobre la tierra above ground ➤ El metro en Batán está sobre la tierra. The metro at Batán is above ground.

estar **sobre las huellas de alguien** ▪ estar pisando las huellas a alguien ▪ estar pisando las huellas de alguien ▪ estar sobre las huellas de alguien ▪ estar tras (de) las huellas de alguien ▪ estar (por) detrás de las huellas de alguien to be on somone's trail ▪ to be on someone's tracks

estar **sobre las pisadas de alguien** ▪ estar tras (de) las pisadas de alguien ▪ estar (por) detrás de las pisadas de alguien to be on someone's tracks

estar **sobre las pistas de alguien** ▪ estar sobre la pista de alguien ▪ estar tras (de) las pistas de alguien ▪ estar (por) detrás de las pistas de alguien to be on someone's trail

sobre lo que about which

estar **sobre los talones de alguien** ▪ estar pisando los talones a alguien ▪ estar pisando los talones de alguien ▪ estar sobre los talones de alguien ▪ estar tras (de) los talones de alguien ▪ estar (por) detrás de los talones de alguien to be hot on somone's heels

sobre mediados de mes around mid-month

¡**sobre mi cadáver!** ▪ ¡por encima de mi cadáver! over my dead body!

sobre prefranqueado pre-stamped envelope

sobre rotulado... envelope marked... ▪ envelope labeled...

sobre todas las demás cosas above everything else

sobre todo 1. above all ▪ above everything else 2. *(especialmente)* especially ➤ Sobre todo si son otros que las imponen Especially if they are imposed by others

sobre todo lo demás above all else

sobre *x* about *x* o'clock

sobre una base de against a background of

sobrecarga sensorial: sufrir ~ to suffer from sensory overload

sobremanera exceedingly

sobrepasar el límite de velocidad ▪ saltarse el límite de velocidad to exceed the speed limit ▪ to break the speed limit

sobreponerse a las circunstancias to surmount the (adverse) circumstances ▪ to overcome the (adverse) circumstances

sobreponerse a un estado de ánimo to overcome an attitude

sobresalir en to excel at ▪ to excel in

sobresaltarse ante el comentario ▪ recular ante el comentario ▪ dar una reculada ante el comentario to flinch at the remark

sobrevenir y ceder *(enfermedad)* to strike and abate ➤ La enfermedad puede sobrevenir y ceder inesperadamente. The illness can strike, and abate, unexpectedly.

sobrevive el más fuerte the strongest survives

sobrevivir a algo to survive something ▪ to live through something

sobrevivir a muchos altibajos to survive a lot of ups and downs

sobrino(-a) segundo(-a) *(hijo[-a] del primo hermano[-a])* ▪ sobrino(-a) en segundo(-a) (grado) first cousin once removed

socavar la confianza en alguien ▪ minar la confianza en alguien to undermine confidence in someone

socavar la confianza en sí mismo ▪ socavar la confianza en uno mismo to undermine self-confidence

socavar la moral to hurt morale ▪ to undermine morale

socavar un túnel ▪ excavar un túnel to dig a tunnel ▪ to excavate a tunnel

sociedad anónima ▪ S.A. incorporated ▪ Inc.

sociedad bien educada ▪ sociedad bien instruida educated society

sociedad bien instruida ▪ sociedad bien educada educated society

la **sociedad en comandita** limited partnership

ser **socio de un club** ▪ ser miembro de un club to be a member of a club

socio del gremio de organistas estadounidenses member of the American Guild of Organists

socios de plenos derechos equal partners

¡**socorro!** help!

sofocar un incendio to extinguish a fire

sofocar una revuelta ▪ reprimir una revuelta to suppress a revolt ▪ to put down a revolt ▪ to suppress a rebellion ▪ to put down a rebellion ▪ to suppress an uprising ▪ to put down an uprising

la **soga quiebra por lo más delgado** a chain is no stronger than its weakest link

el **sol abrasador** burning sun

sol de punta a punta wall-to-wall sunshine

el **sol está luciendo** the sun is shining

el **sol matinal** morning sun

el **sol naciente** rising sun

el **sol poniente** setting sun

el **sol sale para todos** ▪ para todos sale el sol we're all equals

solamente tendría una explicación there could only be one explanation

solapa de un libro ▪ pestaña de un libro overleaf of a book jacket

soldadito de plomo tin soldier

soldadura blanda soldering

soldadura dura welding

soler hacer pruebas para to test routinely for

soler hacer una cosa to usually do something ▪ to generally do something ▪ to typically do something ▪ to habitually do something

soler ser to tend to be ▪ usually to be ➤ Suele ser lento. It tends to be slow.

solía decir... 1. *(yo)* I used to say... 2. *(él)* he used to say... 3. *(ella)* she used to say... ➤ Mi padre solía decir... My father used to say...

solía ser que... it used to be that...

solicitar la admisión en una universidad ▪ solicitar el ingreso en una universidad to apply (for admission) to a university ➤ Él solicitó la admisión en la Universidad Nacional Autónoma de México. ▪ Él solicitó el ingreso en la Universidad Nacional Autónoma de México. He applied (for admission) to the National Autonomous University of Mexico.

solicitar un nuevo juicio to seek a new trial ➤ Tenía toda razón al solicitar un nuevo juicio. He had good reason to seek a new trial.

solicitar una beca to apply for a scholarship

solicitar unirse con alguien to request a meeting with someone

la **solicitud de información** request for information

sólo a causa de eso that alone

sólo a unos minutos in just a few minutes

sólo así... that's the only way... ▪ only in that way ▪ only thus

sólo bromearle ▪ sólo vacilarle ▪ sólo tomarle el pelo ▪ sólo ser de mentira to be just joking ▪ to be just kidding ▪ to be only joking ▪ to be only kidding ➤ Sólo te bromeaba. ▪ Sólo te

estaba vacilando. ■ Sólo te estaba tomando el pelo. I was just joking. ■ I was just kidding. ■ I was only joking. ■ I was only kidding.
sólo comprobando ■ probando just checking
sólo cuatro líneas just a short note ■ a few lines
ser **sólo cuestión de tiempo el que...** to be only a matter of time before...
sólo (de) pensar just the thought of ■ just thinking about ■ merely the thought of ■ merely thinking about ■ at just the thought of ➤ Sólo de pensar que tienen que ir al médico, los niños pasan miedo. Just the thought of having to go to the doctor makes children fearful. ■ At just the thought of having to go to the doctor, children are fearful.
sólo de pensarlo... just thinking about it... ■ just the thought of it... ■ the very thought of it... ■ merely thinking of it...
estar **solo del todo** ■ quedarse solo to be all alone ■ to be left all alone
ser **sólo el principio** to be just the beginning
sólo en abril 1. only in April **2.** in April alone ■ just in April ➤ Diez por ciento de descuento sólo en abril Ten percent discount only in April ➤ *(noticia)* Sólo en abril en España se ha registrado un consumo de paella de entre setenta y ochenta toneladas. ■ Sólo en abril en España se ha registrado un consumo de paella de entre setenta y ochenta toneladas. In April alone, the Spanish consumed between seventy and eighty tons of paella. ■ Just in April, the Spanish consumed between seventy and eighty tons of paella.
sólo en *x* in *x* alone ■ just in *x* ➤ Sólo en Nepal han aparecido veinte lagos nuevos. In Nepal alone twenty new lakes have appeared. ■ Just in Nepal, twenty new lakes have appeared ➤ Sólo en 2004... In 2004 alone... ➤ Sólo en Chile... In Chile alone... ■ Just in Chile...
sólo entonces... only then...
sólo entonces caí en la cuenta only then did I realize it ■ only then did I realize that
sólo entonces caí en la cuenta de que... only then did I realize that...
sólo entonces se inmutó only then did he budge ■ only then did he react
sólo estaba bromeando ■ (yo) iba de broma ■ era broma I was just kidding ■ I didn't mean it ■ I was just joking ■ I was only joking
sólo estar de paso ■ sólo estar de visita to be just passing through ■ to be just visiting ➤ Sólo estoy de paso. ■ Sólo estoy de visita. I'm just passing through. ■ I'm just visiting.
sólo estar de visita ■ sólo estar de paso to be just visiting ■ to be just visiting ➤ Sólo estoy de visita. ■ Sólo estoy de paso. I'm just visiting. ■ I'm just passing through.
sólo hace unos días just the other day ➤ La vi sólo hace unos días. I saw her just the other day. ➤ Sólo hace unos días ella decía que... Just the other day she was saying that...
el **solo hecho de** just ■ merely ➤ El solo hecho de estar con ella... Just being with her...
el **solo hecho de que...** ■ solo el hecho de que... the mere fact that...
sólo hoy ■ hoy mismo just today ■ this very day
ser **sólo la punta del iceberg** to be just the tip of the iceberg
sólo llegar a ■ sólo llegar hasta to only go as far as ■ to only go to ➤ Esta calle sólo llega a la Plaza de Castilla. ■ Esta calle sólo llega hasta la Plaza de Castilla. This street only goes as far as the Plaza de Castilla. ■ This street only goes to the Plaza de Castilla.
sólo llevaba una semana trabajando allí cuando... I had only been working there a week when...
sólo me gusta a mí I'm the only one who likes it ➤ Yo no hago casi nunca gazpacho porque en casa sólo me gusta a mí. I almost never make gazpacho because at my house I'm the only one who likes it.
sólo para que te hagas una idea (de...) just so you can get an idea (of...) ➤ Sólo para que te hagas una idea del tamaño del sistema solar, si el sol fuera del tamaño de una toronja... Just so you can get an idea of the size of the solar system, if the sun were the size of a grapefruit...
sólo para recordarte just to remind you...
sólo personal autorizado ■ prohibido la entrada a personal no autorizado authorized personnel only
sólo por esta vez just this once
sólo porque just because ➤ Sólo porque tienes el poder no significa que tengas derecho. Just because you have the power doesn't mean you have the right.
sólo pretendía ayudar I was just trying to help
sólo que just because ➤ Sólo que algo sea imposible no quiere decir que nadie intente hacerlo. Just because something is impossible doesn't mean that somebody won't try to do it.
sólo que ahora... only now... ■ but now... ➤ Sólo que ahora hay medicamentos que controlan... Only now there are medications that control...
sólo quería ponerte al corriente ■ sólo quería ponerte al día I just wanted to bring you up to date ■ I just wanted to give you an update
sólo quería que estuvieras enterado de...: (yo) ~ I just wanted you to be aware of...
sólo quería que estuvieras enterado de que...: (yo) ~ I just wanted you to be aware that...
sólo quería recordarte que... I just wanted to remind you that...
solo salario block grant
sólo se limitó a comentar all he would say was ■ all he said was
sólo se necesita all you need is
sólo se veía all you could see was
sólo se vive una vez you only live once ■ you only go around once
sólo soy un(-a) mandado(-a) I'm just doing what I was told ■ I'm just doing what I was told to do
¡sólo tienes que enchufarlo! ■ ¡basta enchufarlo! just plug it in! ■ all you have to do is plug it in!
¡sólo una cosa por vez! ■ ¡no todo a la vez! ■ ¡no tantas cosas a la vez! one thing at a time!
sólo una pizca just a touch
sólo yo I was the only one who ■ only I ➤ Sólo yo asistí a la clase. ■ Fui el único que asistí a la clase. I was the only one who went to class. ■ Only I went to class.
soltar el embrague 1. to release the clutch pedal ■ to take one's foot off the clutch pedal ■ to engage the clutch **2.** *(de golpe)* to pop the clutch ➤ Para arrancar el coche de tirón, gira la llave, mete segunda, déjalo caer unos metros por la pendiente y suelta el embrague de golpe. To jump-start the car, turn on the ignition, put it in second, let it coast downhill for a few yards and pop the clutch.
soltar el freno to release the brake
soltar un trompetazo to give a blast on the trumpet ■ to give a blast on one's trumpet ■ to sound the trumpet ■ to sound one's trumpet
soltar una indirecta ■ lanzar una indirecta ■ echar una indirecta to drop a hint
soltar la sin hueso to shoot one's mouth off ■ to run off at the mouth
soltar la tela to fork over the dough ■ to fork it over
soltar lastre ■ largar lastre **1.** to drop ballast **2.** to get rid of the dead weight ■ to clear the deck **3.** dejar de guardar rencores to stop harboring grievances
soltar un gallo *(pintoresco)* ■ cantar una nota desafinada to loose a flat note ■ to sing a flat note ➤ Soltó un gallo. He loosed a flat note. ■ He sang a flat note.
soltar un suspiro ■ dar un suspiro to heave a sigh ■ to sigh ➤ Ella soltó un profundo suspiro. She heaved a deep sigh. ■ She sighed deeply. ■ She sighed heavily.
soltar una indirecta to drop a hint
soltar una parrafada to go on and on
soltar una pluma to make an effeminate gesture
soltar una retahíla de to reel off a bunch of ■ to let fly ➤ Soltó una retahila de estadísticas. He reeled off a bunch of statistics.
soltar vapores to give off fumes
soltarse a andar to start walking
soltarse a hablar to start talking
soltarse del todo ■ desprenderse ■ deshacerse to come off (completely) ■ to come undone
soltarse el moño 1. *(literal)* to let one's hair fall naturally **2.** *(figurativo)* desinhibirse to let one's hair down
soltarse el pelo *(literal)* to let one's hair fall naturally

soltarse en un idioma ■ volverse fluido en un idioma ■ hacerse fluido en un idioma ■ llegar a hacerse fluido en un idioma to become fluent in a language

soltarse la melena to let one's hair down

soltero empedernido ■ solterón confirmed bachelor

la **solución por continuidad** interruption

solucionar un problema de matemática(s) ■ resolver un problema de matemática(s) to solve a mathematics problem ■ to solve a math problem ■ to work a mathematics problem ■ to work a math problem

solvencia de un informe reliability of a report

ser la **sombra de alguien** to be someone's shadow

sombra de ojos *(maquillaje)* eye shadow

sombrero de la N tilde on the N ➤ La N con sombrero es la Ñ. The N with the tilde is Ñ.

someter el nombramiento a votación to put the nomination to a vote ■ to vote on the nomination

someterse a tratamientos por una enfermedad ■ ser sometido a tratamientos por una enfermedad ■ estar sometido a tratamientos por una enfermedad to undergo treatments for an illness

ser **sometido a exámenes médicos** to undergo (medical) tests ■ to undergo a medical examination ■ to receive a medical examination ➤ *(noticia)* Pinochet será sometido a exámenes médicos Pinochet will undergo medical tests ■ Pinochet will be given medical tests

ser **sometido a tratamientos por una enfermedad** ■ estar sometido a tratamientos por una enfermedad ■ someterse a tratamientos por una enfermedad to undergo treatments for an illness

ser **sometido a una operation** to undergo surgery ■ to have an operation

somos de la misma opinión we are of the same opinion ■ we are in agreement (on that)

somos los dos optimistas we're both optimists

somos *x* there are *x* of us ➤ Somos seis. There are six of us.

son más de las *x* it's after *x* ➤ Son más de las cinco. It's after five.

son muchas las personas que there are so many people who

son *x* there are *x* of them ➤ Son cinco. There are five of them.

sonado caso well-known case ■ notable case ■ famous case

sonar a chino to be all Greek to one

sonar a música celestial to be music to one's ears

sonar bien ■ parecerle bien to sound good ➤ Suena bien. ■ Me parece bien. That sounds good.

sonar chistoso *(L.am.)* ■ sonar gracioso to sound comical ■ to sound funny

sonar cierto a uno ■ sonar verdadero a uno to ring true to one

sonar cómico ■ sonar gracioso ■ *(L.am.)* sonar chistoso to sound comical ■ to sound funny

sonar raro to sound strange ■ to sound funny

sonar el estéreo to play the stereo

sonar la radio to play the radio

sonar mal not to sound like a good idea

sonar la flauta por casualidad to make a lucky guess

sonar verdadero a uno ■ sonar cierto a uno to ring true to one

sonarle a uno to sound familiar ➤ El apellido me suena. The name sounds familiar.

sonarse la nariz to blow one's nose

sonda espacial space probe

sondeo a pie de urna exit poll

sondeo de opinión opinion poll

sonido de gorgoteo ■ sonido de gárgaras gurgling sound

sonido envolvente wrap-around sound ■ wraparound sound

el **sonido se transmite** sound carries ➤ El sonido se transmite especialmente bien sobre el agua. Sound carries especially well across water.

sonreír de felicidad to smile happily

sonreír sin la mayor gana ■ sonreír sin la menor gana to feign a smile ■ to smile dryly ■ to smile an empty smile

sonrisa de oreja a oreja ear-to-ear grin ■ big grin ■ wide grin

la **sonrisa en la cara** ■ la sonrisa que se dibuja en el rostro the smile on one's face

sonrisa forzada ■ sonrisa sujeta forced smile

sonrisa sujeta ■ sonrisa forzada forced smile

soñar con alguien to dream about someone ■ to have a dream about someone

soñar despierto sobre to daydream about

soñé estar... I dreamed I was...

soñé ser... I dreamed I was...

¡soooo! whoa! ■ slow down! ■ hold on a second!

sopesar algo to see how heavy something is

sopesar las opciones to weigh the options

sopesar los pros y contras to weigh the pros and cons

soplar y resoplar to huff and puff

el **soplete soldador** welding torch

soplo en el corazón: tener un ~ to have a heart murmur

soportar críticas to endure criticism

soportar dificultades to endure hardship

soportar el peso to support the weight ■ to bear the weight

soportar la carga ■ aguantar la carga ■ llevar a cuestas la carga to bear the burden

soportar la verdad ■ encajar la verdad to bear the truth

soportar su propio peso to carry one's own weight

sorber el café to sip one's coffee

sorber las palabras de alguien to drink in someone's words

el **sorbete de limón al cava** lemon sherbert and champagne

sorprender a alguien que to surprise someone that ➤ Me sorprendió que tan poca gente acudiese. ■ Me sorprendió que tan poca gente acudiera. It surprised me that so few people showed up.

sorpresa desagradable unpleasant surprise

sortear el día to get through the day

sortear el tráfico to make one's way through (the) traffic ■ to get through the traffic

sortija de diamantes diamond ring

sospecho bien fundado well-founded suspicion

sospechoso máximo del caso ■ sospechoso principal del caso prime suspect in the case ■ number one suspect in the case

sospechoso principal del caso ■ máximo sospechoso del caso prime suspect in the case ■ number one suspect in the case

sostener que... to maintain that... ➤ El autor sostiene que... The author maintains that...

sostenerse a duras penas barely to survive ■ *(coloquial)* to eke out a living ➤ Se sostiene a duras penas con lo que gana... He barely survives by doing odd jobs. ■ He ekes out a living doing odd jobs.

sota, caballo y rey ■ siempre lo mismo the same old thing ■ same old, same old

sótano está inundado ■ hay una inundación en el sótano the basement is flooded

soy como todo el mundo I'm like everyone else

soy de los que... I'm one of those (people) who...

soy incapaz I can't do it

soy incapaz de decirlo I can't say

SRC ■ se ruega contestación R.S.V.P. ■ the favor of a reply is requested

su caso of one ■ in one's case ■ for one

su época (de uno) one's time

su gasto one's cost ➤ No debería hacer yo el gasto. El casero debería pagarlo. It shouldn't be my cost. The landlord should pay for it.

su opinión vale tanto como el mío your guess is as good as mine

su señoría your honor

su verdadero yo one's true self

¡suave! ¡suave! easy! easy!

el **suavizante para ropa** fabric softener

suavizar una declaración to water down a statement ■ to water a statement down ■ to qualify a statement ■ to soften a statement

¡suba! *(taxista)* hop in! ■ get in! ■ come on up!

¡sube al carro! ▪ ¡métete en el carro! ▪ *(Esp.)* ¡sube al coche! ▪ ¡métete en el coche! get in the car!

subestimar el efecto de ▪ menospreciar el efecto de to underestimate the effect of

subestimar a alguien ▪ infravalorar a alguien to underestimate someone

subestimar el efecto de ▪ infravalorar el efecto de to underestimate the effect of

subestimar el tiempo que lleva ▪ subestimar el tiempo que requiere to underestimate the time it takes ▪ to underestimate how long it takes ▪ to underestimate the time required ➤ Subestimé el tiempo que me llevaría llegar aquí. I underestimated how long it would take (me) to get here.

subida al castillo this way up to the castle

subida de la inflación ▪ el alza de la inflación rise in inflation ▪ increase in inflation ▪ uptick in inflation

subida de la temperatura rise in temperature

subida de presión rise in blood pressure ▪ increase in blood pressure

subida de tensión power surge

subida del alquiler ▪ aumento del alquiler rent increase ▪ increase in the rent

subida del desempleo ▪ subida del paro rise in unemployment ▪ increase in unemployment

subida del paro ▪ subida del desempleo rise in unemployment ▪ increase in unemployment

el **subidón de adrenalina** ▪ descarga de adrenalina rush of adrenalin ▪ burst of adrenalin

subiendo *x* planta(s) (to be) *x* floors up ➤ ¡Subiendo una planta! (It's) one floor up. ➤ ¡Subiendo dos plantas! (It's) two floors up.

subir a bordo de un avión ▪ embarcarse en un avión to board an airplane

subir a bordo de un barco ▪ embarcarse en un barco to board a ship

subir a lo alto to climb to the top

subir al coche ▪ meterse en el coche ▪ entrar en el coche to get in the car ➤ Ella entró en su coche. She got in her car.

subir al escenario to go on stage ➤ Dígale al Sr. Sinatra que sube al escenario en cinco minutos. Tell Mr. Sinatra he goes on in five minutes.

subir al tren ▪ subirse al tren ▪ montarse en el tren to board the train ▪ to get on the train

subir cada vez más algo to rise higher and higher

subir corriendo to run upstairs

subir corriendo los escalones de dos en dos to run up the steps two at a time

subir de un salto al coche to hop into the car ▪ to jump into the car

subir por el centro *(fútbol, soccer)* to run up center field toward the goal ▪ to run down the center of the field toward the goal

subir por la banda *(fútbol, soccer)* to run up the side of the field toward the goal ▪ to run down the side of the field toward the goal

subir el dobladillo to take up the hem

subir en avión to go up in an airplane ▪ to go up in a plane

subir los escalones to climb the steps

subir los escalones de dos en dos to climb the steps two at a time ▪ to go up the steps two at a time ▪ to run up the steps two at a time

subir otra (planta) más to go up one more (floor) ➤ Hay que subir otra más. You have to go up one more.

subir por alguien to go up and get someone ➤ Sube por él. Go up and get him. ➤ *(Valle-Inclán)* ¡Suba usted por el Batuco! Go up and get Batuco.

subir una montaña ▪ escalar una montaña to climb a mountain

subiré y lo buscaré I'll go up and get it

subirle el dobladillo *x* centimetros to take up the hem on it *x* centimeters

subirle el sueldo a alguien to raise someone's salary

subirlo a punto de cocción ▪ darle un hervor ▪ hervirlo to bring it to a boil

subirlo a toda flama to turn it up to high heat

subirlo a toda pastilla to turn it up full blast

subirlo a toda potencia *(electricidad)* to turn it up to full power

subirlo a todo vatio to turn it up as high as it will go ▪ to turn it to full wattage ▪ to turn it up to full power

subirlo a todo volumen ▪ to turn up the volume as high as it will go ▪ to turn the volume up as high as it will go

subirlo a tope *(todos los contextos)* ▪ subirlo al máximo ▪ subirlo hasta donde se pueda ▪ subirlo a la máxima potencia to turn it up as high as it will go ▪ to turn it up as high as it'll go

subirlo al máximo *(todos los contextos)* ▪ subirlo a tope ▪ subirlo a la máxima potencia ▪ subirlo hasta donde se pueda to turn it up as high as it will go ▪ to turn it up as high as it'll go

subirlo hasta donde se pueda to turn it up as far as it will go ▪ to turn it up as far as it'll go

subirse a la parra to blow one's top

subirse a un caballo ▪ montarse a un caballo ▪ montarse en un caballo to get on a horse ▪ to mount a horse

subir(se) al tren ▪ montarse en el tren to get on the train

subirse al tren de to get in on ▪ to be included in ▪ to be part of

subirse el cuello to put up the collar

subirse el sueldo to give oneself a raise ➤ *(anuncio)* Si pudieras subirte el sueldo con tan sólo una llamada de teléfono, ¿lo harías? If you could give yourself a raise with just a telephone call, would you do it?

subirse en el coche to get in the car

subirse la mangas to roll up one's sleeves ➤ *(médico al prepararse para ponerle una inyección al paciente)* Súbete la manga. Roll up your sleeve.

subirse por las paredes to be climbing the walls

subirse por las paredes: hacer a uno ~ to drive one up the wall

subírsele to flip up ➤ Cuando intento clavar esta ele en la pared, se me sube. When I try to nail this L into the wall, it flips up (on me).

subírsele a la cabeza to go to one's head ➤ El vino se me sube a la cabeza. The wine goes to my head.

subírsele al pantalón to climb up one's pants leg ➤ Unas hormigas se me subieron al pantolón. Some ants climbed up my pants leg.

subírsele los ceros a la cabeza to have got rocks in one's head ➤ Se te subieron los ceros a la cabeza. You've got rocks in your head.

subírsele un tufo a las narices to get one's nose out of joint ▪ to get mad

sublevarse en armas *(dícese especialmente de las fuerzas armadas)* to stage a coup ▪ to mutiny

sublimar a alguien ▪ ensalzar a alguien ▪ enaltecer a alguien to exalt someone ▪ to extol someone ▪ to revere someone

sublimar los deseos to sublimate one's wishes

subsanar el problema ▪ rectificar el problema to rectify the problem

sucede a veces que... it sometimes happens that...

sucede que... ▪ da la casualidad de que... it (so) happens that...

suceder algo sin ningún contratiempo ▪ salir algo sin ningún contratiempo to come off without a hitch

suceder por poco (for something) to almost happen ➤ Encontré algunas expresiones interesantes no relatadas que por poco hizo que se me olvidara lo que estaba haciendo. I found some unrelated interesting expressions, which almost made me forget what I was doing.

sucesos de altura ▪ sucesos más relevantes ▪ sucesos más importantes major events ➤ Sucesos de altura del Siglo XX Major events of the 20th Century

sudar a mares to sweat profusely

sudar como un descosido to sweat profusely

sudar como un pollo to sweat profusely

sudar el calcetín to sweat profusely

sudar hiel to sweat blood *(literalmente "to sweat bile")*

sudar la camiseta 1. sudar a mares to sweat profusely 2. esforzarse en algo to bust one's butt

sudar la gota gorda ▪ sudar tinta to sweat blood

sudar sangre para hacer algo to sweat blood to do something

sudar tinta ▪ sudar la gota gorda to sweat blood *(literalmente "to sweat ink")*

sueldo neto take-home pay ▪ net pay ▪ salary after deductions

sueldos de hambre y miseria: pagar ~ to pay starvation wages

suele ser mortal *(enfermedad)* it is usually fatal ▪ it's usually fatal

suelo de tierra ▪ piso de tierra dirt floor ▪ earthen floor

suelo de un planeta surface of a planet ➤ *(titular)* La sonda europea "Beagle 2" inicia la recta final hacia el suelo de Marte. The European (space) probe "Beagle 2" begins the home stretch toward the surface of Mars. ▪ The European (space) probe "Beagle 2" begins its final descent toward the surface of Mars.

suelo estadounidense ▪ suelo norteamericano American soil

¡suelta la lana! hand over the dough!

¡suena bien! sounds good!

sueño de la liebre feigned sleep

sueño dorado greatest dream

sueño hecho realidad: ser (para alguien) un ~ to be a dream come true (for someone)

sueño premonitorio prophetic dream

sueño realizado a dream come true

la **suerte está echada** *(de Julius Caesar de Shakespeare)* the die is cast

suerte inesperada ▪ algo caído del cielo ▪ fruta caída windfall

suerte para otra vez better luck next time

suficientemente bien well enough

ser (lo) **suficientemente grande para que quepa** to be big enough to fit

ser **suficiente para vivir** ▪ alcanzar para vivir to be enough to live on ➤ No es un gran salario, pero es suficiente para vivir. ▪ No es un gran salario, pero alcanza para vivir. It's not a big salary, but it's enough to live on.

suficiente(s) para todos: haber ~ (for) there to be enough to go around ▪ (for) there to be enough for

ser **suficiente(s) para todos** to be enough to go around ▪ to be enough for everyone

sufragar los costos de ▪ sufragar los gastos de to defray the cost of ▪ to offset the cost of ➤ La beca ayudó a sufragar los costos de su educación. The scholarship helped defray the cost of his education. ▪ The scholarship helped offset the cost of his education.

sufragar por alguien ▪ votar por alguien to vote for someone

sufragios emitidos a favor de algo votes cast in favor of something ▪ votes cast for something

sufragios emitidos en contra de algo votes cast against something

sufrir dificultad respiratoria to have breathing problems ▪ to have trouble breathing

sufrir el bochorno to suffer the embarrassment ➤ Tras sufrir el bochorno After suffering the embarrassment

sufrir un accidente to have an accident

sufrir un ataque de apoplejía to have a seizure

sufrir un rasguño to suffer a scratch ➤ Él sufrió un rasguño en el pómulo. He suffered a scratch on the cheek.

sufrir una cogida ▪ sufrir una cornada to be gored by a bull ▪ to get gored by a bull

sufrir una cornada ▪ sufrir una cogida to be gored by a bull ▪ to get gored by a bull

sufrir una contrariedad to suffer a disappointment

sufrir una desilusión to suffer a disappointment ▪ to be disappointed ▪ to be chagrined

sufrir una recaída to suffer a relapse ▪ to have a relapse

sufrir una transformación to undergo a transformation

¡sugiéraselo (usted)! 1. *(a él)* suggest it to him! 2. *(a ella)* suggest it to her!

¡sugiéreselo! 1. *(a él)* suggest it to him! 2. *(a ella)* suggest it to her!

sujételo bien hold it tight ▪ hold onto it tight ▪ get a firm grip on it ▪ grip it firmly

sujétame esto hold this for me

sujetar el embrague to engage the clutch

sujetársele sin cinturón to stay up without a belt ➤ Quiero un pantalón que se me sujete sin cinturón. I want a pair of pants that will stay up without a belt. ▪ I want a pair of pants that'll stay up without a belt.

sujéteme (usted) esto hold this for me

estar **sujeto por** ▪ estar vinculado por to be bound by ➤ En algunos tribunales españoles, el juez no está sujeto por la decisión del jurado. In some Spanish courts, the judge is not bound by the jury's decision.

suma y sigue *(arimética)* carried forward

sumar a la lista ▪ incluir en la lista to add to the list

sumar de cabeza una columna de números ▪ sumar de cabeza una serie de números to add a column of figures in one's head ▪ to add a series of numbers in one's head

sumar la cuenta to add up the bill ▪ to figure up the bill

sumar una columna de números to add up a column of figures ▪ to add up a column of numbers ➤ Esta columna de números da seiscientos cuarenta y cinco. This column of figures adds up to six hundred forty-five. ➤ Tengo un amigo ciego que puede sumar una columna de números en su cabeza. I have a blind friend who can add (up) a column of figures in his head.

sumar *x* ▪ dar *x* to add up to *x* ▪ to total *x* ➤ Estos dígitos suman nueve. ▪ La suma de estos dígitos da nueve. These digits add up to nine. ▪ The sum of these digits totals nine.

sumarse a alguien to join someone

sumido(-a) en: quedar ~ to be plunged into

estar **sumido(-a) en dudas sobre algo** ▪ quedar sumido(-a) en dudas sobre algo to be wracked by doubts about something ▪ to be filled with doubts about something ▪ to be consumed with doubt about something ▪ to be plagued by doubts about something ▪ to be plunged into doubt about something

suministrar a alguien la resucitación cardiopulmonar ▪ suministrar a alguien RCP to give someone cardiopulmonary resuscitation ▪ to give someone CPR ▪ to administer cardiopulmonary resuscitation ▪ to administer CPR

suministro eléctrico ▪ suministro de la electricidad electric power suppy ▪ electrical power supply ➤ *(titular)* Estado de emergencia en California por el colapso del suministro eléctrico. State of emergency in California over the disruption of the electrical power suppy.

suministros eléctricos electrical supplies

suministros médicos medical supplies

sumirse en el caos más absoluto to be plunged into total chaos

sumo pontífice the Pope

estar **supeditado a** ▪ depender de to be subject to ▪ to be contingent on ▪ to be subordinate to ▪ to be dependent on ▪ to depend on ▪ to be subordinate to ➤ Está supeditado a lo que decidan. ▪ Depende de lo que decidan. It's subject to what they decide. ▪ It's contingent on what they decide. ▪ It's dependent on what they decide. ▪ It depends on what they decide. ▪ It's subordinate to their decision.

superar a alguien ▪ ganar a alguien ▪ hacer algo mejor que alguien to outdo someone ▪ to surpass someone ➤ No sé de nadie que la pueda superar como cocinera. ▪ No sé de nadie que la pueda ganar como cocinera. ▪ No sé de nadie que cocine mejor que ella. I don't know of anyone who can outdo her as a cook. ▪ I don't know of anyone who surpasses her as a cook. ➤ No sé de nadie que lo pueda superar en los juegos de computadora. ▪ No sé de nadie que lo pueda ganar en los juegos de computadora. ▪ No sé de nadie que juegue los juegos de computadora mejor que él. ▪ *(Esp. leísmo)* No sé de nadie que le pueda superar en los juegos de ordenador. ▪ No sé de nadie que le pueda ganar en los juegos de ordenador. ▪ No sé de nadie que juegue los juegos de ordenador mejor que él. I don't know of anyone who can outdo him at computer games. ▪ I don't know of anyone who surpasses him at computer games.

superar el límite to exceed the limit ▪ to be over the limit

superar el límite de velocidad to exceed the speed limit ▪ to speed

superar en número al enemigo to outnumber the enemy

superar la prueba to pass the test
superar un trauma ■ recuperarse de un shock to get over a trauma ■ to recover from a trauma ■ to get over a shock to the system ■ to recover from a shock to the system
superar una revisión to pass inspection ■ to clear inspection
superávit en la cuenta surplus in the account ■ account surplus ■ positive balance
superficie rugosa rough surface
superior a lo normal higher than average
suplantar a alguien para falsificar un cheque to impersonate someone ■ to forge a check
suplemento dominical *(de un periódico)* Sunday supplement
suplicar el perdón de alguien to ask someone's forgiveness ■ to ask someone to forgive one
suplicar piedad to ask for mercy ■ to beg for mercy
ser un **suplicio de tántalo** to be just beyond one's reach
suplico que... ■ ruego que... ■ imploro que... ■ pido que... I ask that...
suplir algo por algo to substitute something for something
suponer la práctica de to involve (the practice of)
suponer un gasto ■ implicar un gasto to involve (an) expense
suponer un gran ahorro de tiempo ■ ahorrar mucho tiempo to save a lot of time
suponer una diferencia radical to make a critical difference ➤ El reducir la inclinación de la Torre Inclinada de Pisa de 6 a 5,5 grados supone una diferencia radical en su estabilidad. Reducing the tilt of the Leaning Tower of Pisa from 6 to 5.5 degrees has made a critical difference in its stability.
suponer una dificultad para to be a challenge for
suponer una senda hacia to provide an avenue for ■ to provide a way to ■ to provide a means of ➤ La democracia supone una senda hacia la denuncia y enmienda de los perjuicios. Democracy provides an avenue for the open expression and redress of grievances.
supongamos que... let's assume that... ■ let's suppose that...
supongamos que haya... let's suppose (that) there is... ■ let's assume (that) there is...
supongamos que hubiera... ■ supongamos que hubiese... let's suppose (that) there were... ■ let's assume (that) there were...
supongamos que hubiese... ■ supongamos que hubiera... let's suppose (that) there were... ■ let's assume (that) there were...
supongo que bien okay, I guess
supongo que deberíamos... ■ creo que deberíamos... I guess we better... ■ I guess we should...
supongo que lo que... I guess the thing that...
supongo que no I guess not ■ apparently not ■ I suppose not
supongo que sí I guess so ■ I suppose so
suponiendo que... 1. supposing that... 2. on the chance that... 3. granted that...
suponiendo que (es cierto que)... ■ sentada la base de que... granted that...
supresión de empleos ■ supresión de puestos de trabajo axing of employees ■ laying off of employees
supresión de puestos de trabajo ■ supresión de empleos axing of jobs ■ elimination of jobs
suprimir la página to skip over the page
suprimir las configuraciones por defecto *(informática)* ■ anular las configuraciones por defecto to turn off the defaults ■ to remove the defaults ■ to eliminate the defaults ■ to delete the defaults
supuestamente debiera (uno) estar aquí ■ (uno) tenía que haber estado ■ uno tenía que haber venido ■ (uno) tenía que haber llegado ■ *(más lejos en el tiempo)* tendrías que haber venido (one) was supposed to be here ➤ ¡Supuestamente debieras estar aquí hace cuatro horas! You were supposed to be here four hours ago!
supuesto terrorista alleged terrorist
supuse eso ■ deduje eso I gathered that
surcar las olas to ride the waves
surcar los mares to ply the seas
surgir un contratiempo a alguien 1. (for) something to come up ■ to have something come up 2. to have an emergency ■ to have a problem ➤ Me ha surgido un contratiempo al ir a tu casa. I've run into a problem on my way to your house. ■ I've encountered a problem on my way to your house.
surtidor de gasolina gas pump
surtir a alguien de algo to supply someone with something
surtir efecto *(medicina)* to take effect
surtir el mercado to supply the market
surtir un pedido ■ dar abasto a un pedido to fill an order
surtir una receta to fill a prescription
susceptible: ser muy ~ to be easily offended
ser **susceptible de escrutinio** ■ merecer escrutinio ■ ser digno de escrutinio to deserve scrutiny ■ to merit scrutiny ■ to be worthy of scrutiny
ser **susceptible de ser investigado** ■ ser digno de ser investigado ■ merecer la pena de ser investigado ■ ser susceptible de investigarlo ■ ser digno de investigarlo ■ merecer la pena investigarlo to bear looking into ■ to be worthy of investigation ■ to bear checking out ■ to bear checking into ➤ Esto es susceptible de ser investigado. ■ Esto es susceptible de investigación. This bears looking into. ■ This is worthy of investigation. ■ This is worthy of being investigated. ■ This bears checking out. ■ This bears checking into.
suscitar una violenta reacción ■ provocar una violenta reacción to stir up a violent reaction
suspender una asignatura to fail a course ➤ Me han suspendido. They failed me. ➤ Me he suspendido. I failed.
suspender el juicio to drop the case
suspender la boda to call off the wedding
suspirar por ■ anhelar to long for
suspirar por alguien ■ beber los vientos por alguien to pine for someone ■ to long for someone ■ to feel lonesome for someone
suspiro de alivio sigh of relief
suponer que to be supposed to ➤ No se supone que capitulemos ante el mundo como está, se supone que lo hagamos de la forma que debería ser. We're not supposed to capitulate to the world as it is. We're supposed to make it the way it ought to be.
sustituir a to take the place of ■ to replace ➤ Las cadenas de televisión han sustituido a los diarios escritos en el protagonismo de pifias monumentales. The television networks have taken the place of the written dailies as the authors of monumental blunders. ■ The television networks have replaced the written dailies as the authors of monumental blunders.
sustituir algo por algo to substitute something for something ■ to substitute something with something ➤ En una receta se puede sustituir dos cucharadas de harina por una de fécula de maíz. In a recipe you can substitute a tablespoon of cornstarch for two tablespoons of flour.
susurro de las hojas rustling of the leaves
susurro del arroyo murmur(ing) of the stream ■ murmur(ing) of the creek ■ murmur(ing) of the brook
susurro del viento whistling of the wind ■ whisper of the wind
sustraer algo to heist something ■ to steal something (with cunning) ■ *(galleta)* to snitch a cookie ➤ Un cargamento de Viagra fue sustraído en el puerto. A shipment of Viagra was heisted at the harbor.
suyo afectísimo sincerely yours ■ affectionately
tabaco rubio light tobacco
tabla de contar ■ tablero contador abacus
tabla de cortar cutting board
tabla de dibujo drawing board
tabla de ejercicios workout board
tabla de materias table of contents
tabla de picar cutting board
tabla de salvación last hope ■ last resort
tablero contador ■ tabla de contar abacus
tablero de instrumentos instrument panel
el **tablón de anuncios** bulletin board
tachar a alguien de algo ■ tildar a alguien de algo ■ caracterizar a alguien de algo to label someone as something
tachar una palabra to draw a line through a word ■ to cross out a word ➤ El editor tachó la palabra. The editor drew a line through the word. ■ The editor crossed out the word.

¡**tachín, tachán!** hooray, hooray!

táctica dilatoria ■ táctica retardatoria delaying tactic ■ delay tactic

táctica retardatoria ■ táctica dilatoria delaying tactic ■ delay tactic

taco de billetes wad of bills

taco de jamón small cube of ham

taco de papel pad of paper

tacones altos high heels

tácticas para amedrentar scare tactics

tacto político political correctness

tachar algo to cross out something ■ to cross something out ■ to cross off something ■ to cross something off ■ to *x* out something ■ to *x* something out

Tacita de Plata *(nombre coloquial)* Cádiz, Spain

tajada de pescado piece of fish ■ slab of fish

ser **tajante contra algo** to be vehemently opposed to something

tajo profundo deep cut

tajo profundo: darse un ~ to suffer a deep cut

tal como ■ como just as

tal como había dicho 1. *(yo)* just as I had said 2. *(él)* just as he had said 3. *(ella)* just as she had said

Tal como éramos *(título de película)* *The Way We Were*

tal como le dije (a usted) 1. as I told you 2. as I told you I would

tal como me lo imaginaba ■ así como me lo imaginaba just as I thought

tal como te dije 1. as I told you 2. as I told you I would

tal cosa such a thing

tal cual: beber algo ~ ■ beber algo a palo seco to drink something straight

tal cual: citar algo ~ to quote something exactly ■ to quote something word for word

tal cual: comer algo ~ 1. comer algo como te lo sirven to eat something as it is ■ to eat something as served 2. comerlo crudo to eat something raw

tal cual: dejar algo ~ to leave something the way it is ■ to leave something as it is ■ to leave something like it is

tal cual: una hamburguesa ~ a hamburger with nothing on it ■ a plain hamburger

tal día on such and such a day

tal era su odio hacia... 1. *(de él)* such was his hatred toward... ■ so fierce was his hatred toward... 2. *(de ella)* such was her hatred toward... ■ so fierce was her hatred toward...

tal era su valor que 1. *(de él)*such was his courage that... ■ so great was his courage that... ■ his courage was so great that... 2. *(de ella)* such was her courage that... ■ so great was her courage that... ■ her courage was so great that...

ser **tal para cual** 1. to be two of a kind ■ to be birds of a feather 2. to be tit for tat ■ to be retaliation in kind ➤ Son tal para cual. They're two of a kind.

tal vez perhaps ■ maybe

tal vez haya there might be ■ there may be

tal vez haya habido there might have been ■ there may have been

tal vez me guste ■ puede que me guste I might like it

tal vez no me creyeras si te dijera... you might not believe me if I told you...

tal vez ya lo tenga ■ puede que ya lo tenga ■ quizá(s) ya lo tenga I might already have it

tal y como ■ tal como exactly as ■ exactly the way ■ just as

tal y como debe ser the way it has to be ■ as it has to be

tal y como debería ser (just) as it should be

tal y como están las cosas under the circumstances ■ (given) the way things are

tal y como están yendo las cosas... ■ tal y como están marchando las cosas... ■ tal y como van las cosas... the way things are going...

tal y como (lo) dijiste just as you said

tal y como (lo) planteaste just as you proposed

tal y como (lo) sugeriste just as you suggested

tal y como se planeó originalmente as originally planned ■ as it was originally planned

talante agradable good mood

talentos desconocidos hidden talents

tales cosas such things ■ things like that

talla de cintura ■ medida de cintura waist size

talla de cristal glass sculpture

talla moral moral stature

talle de avispa: tener un ~ to have an hourglass figure

el **talle de una copa** stem of a wine glass ➤ Me gustaría comprar unas copas de vino bonitas que tengan el talle corto. I'd like some pretty wine glasses with short stems. ■ I'd like some pretty short-stemmed wine glasses.

el **talón de Aquiles** Achilles' heel

tamaño de letra type size

también actor fellow actor

también hijo de Dios fellow creature

también me acuerdo I remember that, too

los **tambores de guerra** ■ ruido de los sables ■ ruido de los cuarteles ■ pulso militar saber rattling

tamborileo de la lluvia sobre el tejado ■ tamborileo de la lluvia en el tejado drumming of the rain on the roof ■ beating of the rain on the roof ■ pounding of (the) rain on the roof

tampoco lo creo ■ yo tampoco lo creo I don't think so, either

tampoco lo sé I don't know, either

tampoco me gusta ■ no me gusta tampoco ■ a mí tampoco me gusta I don't like it, either

¡**tampoco te pases!** ■ ¡no te pases! don't overdo it!

estar **tan allá** *(al señalar en una dirección)* ■ estar tan lejos to be so far away ➤ Los bafles están tan allá que no puedo oírlos. The speakers are so far away (that) I can't hear them.

estar **tan atrasado(-a)** to be so far behind

ser **tan cierto como me he de morir** to cross my heart and hope to die

estar **tan claro como el agua** *(texto, instrucciones, direcciones)* to be crystal clear

ser **tan diferentes como el día y la noche** to be as different as night and day ➤ Puede que sean gemelas idénticas, pero son tan diferentes como el día y la noche. They may be identical twins, but they're as different as night and day.

ser **tan esperado** ■ ser muy esperado to be eagerly awaited ➤ La visita del presidente, que era tan esperada ■ La visita del presidente, que era muy esperada The president's visit, which was eagerly awaited

ser **tan fácil** ■ ser de puro fácil to be so easy

¡**tan fácil decirlo!** that's easy for *you* to say!

tan largo como uno quiera as long as one likes ➤ Deje un mensaje tan largo como quiera. Leave a message as long as you like.

¡tan largo me lo fiáis! *(Tirso de Molina, Zorrilla y otros autores)* ■ ¡cuán largo me lo fiáis! ■ ¡qué largo me lo fiáis! what a long time you give me!

estar **tan limpio como una patena** ■ estar tan limpio como los chorros del oro to be clean as a whistle ■ to be spick-and-span ■ to be spotless

estar **tan oscuro como la boca de un lobo** to be pitch-dark ■ to be pitch-black dark

tan pequeño como un ratón, y cuida la casa como un león *(acertijo cuya respuesta es "la llave")* as small as a mouse, and it guards the house like a lion

ser **tan pobre como un ratón de sacristía** ■ ser tan pelado como una rata to be poor as a church mouse

tan pronto como ■ en cuanto ■ luego que as soon as

tan pronto como pueda *(yo)* ■ en cuanto pueda as soon as I can

tan pronto como sea posible ■ lo más pronto posible ■ cuanto antes ■ lo antes posible ■ a la mayor brevedad posible as soon as possible ■ as quickly as possible

tan rápido como sus patas se lo permitían: el animal corrió ~ the animal ran as fast as its legs would carry it

tan rápido como sus piernas se lo permitían: (él) corrió ~ he ran as fast as his legs would carry him

tan siquiera at least ■ only

tan sólo *(enfatiza lo positivo)* **1.** only ■ just **2.** if only ➤ ¡Tan sólo cien pesos por mes te consigue un auto cero kilómetro!-Sí, ¿pero por cuántos meses? Just one hundred pesos per month gets you a brand-new car!-Yes, but for how many months? ➤ La Navidad está a tan sólo dos semanas. Christmas is just two weeks away. ■ Christmas is only two weeks away. ➤ ¡Tan sólo supieran! If only they knew! ➤ Tan sólo basta con un simple mirada para que... Just a glance is enough to...

tan sólo con with nothing but ■ with only

tan sólo has de... you only have to... ■ you just have to... ➤ Tan sólo has de prometerme que... You only have to promise me that... ■ You just have to promise me that...

tan sólo horas después ■ tan sólo horas más tarde only hours later

tan sólo me permito... if I may... ■ just let me... ■ if you would allow me to... ■ if you would permit me to... ➤ Tan sólo me permito subrayar un rasgo... Just let me draw attention to one feature... ■ If I may draw attention to one feature... ■ Allow me to draw attention to one feature... ■ Permit me to draw attention...

tan sólo pudiera... if only I could...

tan sólo supieran if only they knew

tan sólo *x* de *y* only *x* (out) of *y* ➤ *(noticia)* Tan sólo veintinueve de trescientos cincuenta diputados pertenecen a formaciones que han manifestado su apoyo a la toma en consideración del proyecto. Only twenty-nine (out) of three hundred and fifty legislators belong to groups that have expressed their support for considering the bill.

tan, tan, tan grande soooooo big

tanda de billar game of billiards ■ game of pool

tanda de golpes series of blows

tanda de ladrillos layer of bricks ■ course of bricks

tanda de noche night shift

tanta categoría such class

las **tantas** ■ las mil the wee hours ■ all hours of the night ➤ Los niños se quedaron despiertos hasta las tantas esperando ver el cometa. ■ Los niños se quedaron despiertos hasta las mil esperando ver el cometa. The children stayed up until the wee hours hoping to see the comet. ■ The children stayed up until all hours of the night hoping to see the comet.

tantear a alguien to sound someone out

tantear el suelo con un bastón to feel one's way along with a cane ➤ El ciego tanteaba el suelo con el bastón. The blind man felt his way along with his cane.

tantear el terreno 1. to see how the land lies **2.** to check out the terrain

tanteo final final score ➤ ¿Cuál ha sido el tanteo final? ■ *(más común)* ¿Cómo han quedado (al final)? What was the final score?

tanto dinero so much money

¡tanto bueno por aquí! so good to see you! ■ it's great to see you!

tanto hablar, seca la boca ■ ser de mucho hablar y poco actuar ■ ser de mucho decir y luego nada ■ ser un(a) cantamañanas ■ mucho lirili y poco lerele to be all talk and no action

tanto hombres como mujeres ■ lo mismo hombres que mujeres ■ ambos hombres y mujeres men as well as women ■ men and women alike ■ both men and women

tanto lo bueno como lo malo the good as well as the bad ■ both the good and the bad

tanto lo dulce como lo salado sweet as well as well salty ■ both sweet and salty

tanto más cuanto (más) however many (more) ■ regardless of how many (more) ■ no matter how many (more) ➤ Linus van Pelt ha sacado un sobresaliente en el examen de geografía solamente por saber dónde está Ipanema, y tanto más cuanto más puntos obtuvo por el resto del examen, no cambia su nota. Linus van Pelt got an A on the geography test by knowing where Ipanema was, and however many more points he got on the rest of the exam didn't change his grade.

tanto mejor all the better ■ so much the better

tanto monta ■ da igual it makes no difference ■ it doesn't make any difference ■ it's all the same ■ it comes out to the same thing

tanto monta, monta tanto (Isabel como Fernando) 1. both parties are equal **2.** all parties are equal

tanto peor so much the worse ■ all the worse

tanto por saber: hay ~ there's so much still to know ■ there's so much yet to know ■ there's so much still to learn

tanto que so much that ■ so long that ■ so far that ■ so often that ■ to such an extent that

tanto si lo necesita como si no whether one needs it or not ➤ Le damos un baño a nuestro perro una vez al año tanto si lo necesita como si no. We give our dog a bath once a year whether he needs it or not.

tanto tiempo 1. such a long time **2.** so much time

tanto (tiempo) como haga falta for as long as it takes

tanto va el cántaro a la fuente (que se rompe) the chickens finally come home to roost ■ your misdeeds finally catch up with you

tanto *x* como *y* ■ lo mismo *x* que *y* both *x* and *y* ■ *x* as well as *y* ■ *x* and *y* alike

tantos como sea posible ■ el mayor número posible ■ la mayor cantidad posible ■ todos los que puedan ■ todos los que se pueda as many as possible ■ the greatest possible number

tañidos de campana 1. *(todas ocasiones)* pealing of bells ■ ringing of bells **2.** *(especialmente ocasiones tristes)* tolling of bells

tapadera antiproyección *(para una sartén)* splatter guard

tapar la boca a alguien to silence someone ■ to shut someone up

tapar un agujero to fill a hole

tapar una grieta to seal a crack

taparse los oídos ■ taparse las orejas to hold one's ears ■ to cover one's ears

tapas cojonudas *(subido de tono, pintoresco)* damned fine tapas ➤ Hay tapas cojonudas en los bares en la calle Paraíso en Valladolid. There are damned fine tapas in the bars on Paraiso Street in Valladolid.

tardar demasiado to take too long ➤ Tardaba demasiado. It was taking too long.

tardar el doble de lo normal to take twice as long as it usually does

tardar el doble de lo previsto to take twice as long as expected ■ to take twice as long as anticipated

tardar el doble en hacer algo de lo que to take twice as long to do something as ➤ Tardo el doble en preparar la cena de lo que tardo en comerla. It takes me twice as long to fix supper as it does to eat it.

tardar el triple to take three times as long

tardar en acostumbrarse to take a while to get used to

tardar en reaccionar 1. ser lento de reacción to be slow to react **2.** tardar en reconocer o asociar algo o alguien to do a double take

tardar más de lo debido to take longer than it should

tardar mucho en to take a long time to

tardar tiempo en to take time to ➤ Tardamos una semana en quitar el olor a humo de las cortinas. It took us a week to get the smell of smoke out of the curtains.

tardar un poco ▪ tardar un poquito to be a little (bit) late ▪ to be going to be a little (bit) late ➤ Ella tarda un poquito. She's going to be a little bit late.

tardarse más en hacer una cosa que en hacer otra to take longer to do something than to do something else ➤ Se tarda más en preparar la comida que en limpiar la cocina. It takes longer to fix dinner than (it does) to clean the kitchen.

tardarse una hora ▪ llevar un hora to take an hour (for) ➤ Se tarda una hora para que (se) seque la pintura. ▪ Lleva una hora para que seque la pintura. It takes an hour for the paint to dry. ▪ It takes the paint an hour to dry.

tarde desierta desolate afternoon ➤ Era una tarde desierta. It was a desolate afternoon.

¿tardé mucho? was I long? ▪ did I take a long time?

tarde o temprano ▪ a la corta o a la larga ▪ a la larga o a la corta ▪ antes o después sooner or later

ser **tardo(-a) de oído** ▪ ser duro(-a) de oído ▪ ser sordo to be hard of hearing ▪ to be deaf

tarea doméstica household chore

tarea imposible impossible task

tareas de rescate y recuperación search and rescue operations

tarima flotante ▪ entarimado hardwood floor(s)

tarjeta de visita business card

tarjetas surtidas assorted cards ➤ Tarjetas de Navidad surtidas Assorted Christmas cards

tarro de pintura ▪ (el) bote de pintura can of paint

tarta de chocolate al estilo alemán German chocolate cake

tasa bruta overall rate

(tasa de) aceleración rate of acceleration ▪ acceleration rate ➤ La aceleración de un objeto cayendo es de dieciséis pies por segundo al cuadrado, en vacío. The accelertion rate of an object falling in a vacuum is 16 feet per second squared. ▪ The rate of acceleration of an object falling in a vacuum is sixteen feet per second squared.

(tasa de) cambio exchange rate

tasa de desempleo ▪ (el) índice de desempleo ▪ tasa de paro ▪ índice de paro unemployment rate

tasa de divorcio ▪ (el) índice de divorcio divorce rate ➤ *(titular)* El RU registra una tasa de divorcios del 40 por ciento de los enlaces. The UK has a divorce rate of 40 percent.

tasa de embarque ▪ tarifa de embarque departure tax (paid on leaving a country) *(Las tasas de embarque son comunes en los países sudamericanos, Japón y en algunos países europeos.)*

tasa de natalidad birth rate ➤ España tiene una tasa baja de natalidad. Spain has a low birth rate.

tasa de paro ▪ tasa de desempleo ▪ (el) índice de desempleo unemployment rate

tasa más alta de highest rate of ▪ highest incidence of ➤ *(titular)* Madrid tiene la tasa de sida más alta de Europa. Madrid has the highest rate of AIDS in Europe. ▪ Madrid has the highest incidence of AIDS in Europe.

tasa anual annual rate

tasa media mensual average monthly rate

tasa mensual monthly rate

tasa postal *(L.am.)* ▪ tarifa postal postal rate

tasador(-a) de hacienda ▪ asesor(-a) de impuestos tax assessor

tasador(-a) de inmobiliaria real estate appraiser

tasas universitarias university fees ➤ *(noticia)* Blair subirá las tasas universitarias pese a la oposición de su partido. Blair will raise university fees despite opposition from his (own) party.

taza de café cup of coffee

taza de té cup of tea

te abro I'll let you in

te acompaño a casa I'll take you home ▪ *(anticuado)* I'll see you home

te acompaño en el sentimiento you have my deepest sympathy ▪ my condolences

(te) agradezco tu ayuda I appreciate your help

(te) agradezco tu llamada I appreciate your call

te alcanzo después ▪ te alcanzo más tarde I'll catch up with you later

¡te apuesto que no adivinas quién soy! *(niño trayendo disfraz)* ▪ ¡a que no sabes quien soy! bet you can't guess who I am! ▪ you'll never guess who I am!

té al limón lemon-flavored tea ▪ tea with lemon

te alcanzo después ▪ te alcanzo más tarde I'll catch up with you later

te amo I love you ➤ Te amo.-Y yo a ti. I love you.-I love you, too.

¿te apetece que...? do you want to...? ▪ would you like to...? ▪ do you feel like...? ➤ Te apetece que vayamos a la corrida de toros? Do you want to go to the bullfight? ▪ Would you like to go to the bullfight? ▪ Do you feel like going to the bullfight?

¿te apetece un trozo? ▪ ¿quieres un poco? ▪ ¿quieres probarlo? want a bite? ▪ want a (little) piece?

te apuesto que, si me pongo, lo logro I bet you (that), if I put my mind to it, I could

te apuesto *x* dólares a que... ▪ van *x* dólares a que... I bet you *x* dollars that...

¡te arrepentirás! ▪ ¡te vas a arrepentir! you'll be sorry!

te aseguro que me apetece of course I want to! ▪ of course I do!

¿te atienden? are you being helped? ▪ have you been helped? ▪ are you being waited on? ▪ have you been waited on? ▪ is someone helping you? ▪ has someone taken your order?

te avisaré if... I'll let you know if...

¿te ayudo en algo? can I help you with anything?

¡te busques la vida! ▪ ¡búscate la vida! get a life!

te cambiará la vida it will change your life ▪ it'll change your life

¡te cogí! gotcha!

te comento que... I wanted to tell you that...

te confiaré un secreto I'll tell you a secret

te conozco de algo ▪ de algo te conozco I know you from somewhere

te corresponde ▪ te toca a ti ▪ es tu turno it's your turn ▪ it's your go

¿te cuento un chiste? (do you) want to hear a joke?

te da miedo it's scary

¿te da tiempo a...? ▪ ¿tienes tiempo para...? do you have time to...?

te daré otra oportunidad I'll give you another chance ▪ I'll give you another try

te daré tres oportunidades de adivinar I'll give you three guesses

te dejo con lo que estabas I'll leave you to it

te dejo decidir ▪ lo dejo a tu criterio I'll let you decide ▪ I'll leave it (up) to you to decide

te dejo que pruebes tres veces I'll give you three tries

¿te despachan? are you being assisted? ▪ are you being helped? ▪ have you been helped?

te digo en serio ▪ te lo digo en serio I'm serious ▪ I mean it ▪ *(pintoresco)* I kid you not

te dije así ▪ te dije que sí ▪ ya te lo dije I told you so ▪ I told you

te diré lo que haremos I'll tell you what let's do ▪ I'll tell you what we'll do

¿te diriges a mí? are you speaking to me?

te doy una explicación let me explain

te empiezo a creer I'm beginning to believe you ▪ I'm starting to believe you

(te) engancha it gets in your blood ➤ La caída libre (te) engancha. Skydiving gets in your blood.

¡te enterarás! you'll find out!

(te) entiendo I understand

te entiendo perfectamente I know exactly what you mean ▪ I understand you perfectly

te equivocas you are wrong ▪ you're wrong *(más cortés)* you are mistaken ▪ you're mistaken

te está poniendo los cuernos 1. *(a él)* she's cheating on you ▪ she's stepping out on you 2. *(a ella)* he's cheating on you ▪ he's stepping out on you
te están contando un cuento ▪ te están contando una película they're feeding you a line
te están contando una película ▪ te están contando un cuento they're feeding you a line
te estás adelantando a mí ▪ me estás adelantando ▪ me estás tomando la delantera you're getting ahead of me
¡te estás pasando! 1. you're going to far! 2. *(al pintar)* you're running over a little bit
te ficharán it'll go on your record ➤ Una vez que cumplas dieciséis años, te ficharán. Once you turn sixteen it'll go on on your record.
¿te gustaría? ▪ ¿te apetece? would you like to? ▪ do you want to? ➤ ¿Te gustaría ir al cine? ▪ ¿Te apetece ir al cine? Would you like to go to the movies? ▪ Do you want to go to the movies?
te guste o no whether you like it or not
¿te ha gustado? did you like it?
te ha hecho la boca un fraile *(coloquial)* to ask for things constantly ▪ constantly to be asking for something
¿te han dicho alguna vez que...? has anyone ever told you that...? ➤ ¿Te han dicho alguna vez que te pareces a un famoso? Has anyone ever told you that you look like someone famous?
te han informado mal ▪ estás malinformado you've been misinformed ▪ you're misinformed ▪ they've misinformed you
(te) has cargado con demasiado you've taken on too much
¿te has dado cuenta alguna vez...? ▪ te has fijado alguna vez...? have you ever noticed...?
¿te has dañado? did you hurt yourself?
¿te has fijado alguna vez (en que...)? ▪ ¿te has dado cuenta alguna vez (de que...)? have you ever noticed (that...)?
te has vuelto loco you've lost your marbles
te he dicho que no lo sé I told you, I don't know
¿te importa? do you mind?
¿te importa si...? do you mind if...?
te interesa más... 1. it interests you more... 2. it would be better for you to... ▪ you would be better off to... ▪ it is more in your interest to... ➤ Te interesa más esperar. You would do better to wait. ▪ You'd do better to wait. ▪ You would be better off waiting. ▪ You'd be better off waiting. ▪ It is more in your interest to wait. ▪ It's more in your interest to wait.
te invitamos it's our treat ▪ we're treating you
te invito it's my treat ▪ I'm treating (you)
te invito a tomar un café I'll treat you to a cup of coffee ▪ I'll buy you a cup of coffee
¿te invito a tomar un café? can I buy you a cup of coffee?
te iré mandando más I'll be sending you (some) more ➤ Te iré mandando más fotos con los días. I'll be sending you (some) more photos in the coming days.
te juro por Dios I swear to God
¡te la estás buscando! you're asking for it!
¡te la vas a cargar! ¡you're in for it (now)! ▪ you're going to get it! ➤ Te la vas a cargar si no te corriges You're going to get it if you don't straighten up.
te llaman por teléfono you're wanted on the (tele)phone ▪ you have a phone call
¡te lo advertí! I warned you!
te lo agradezco I appreciate it
te lo agradezco un montón ▪ te lo agradezco mucho I appreciate it a bunch ▪ I appreciate it a lot
te lo cobro I'll have to charge you for it
te lo comenté I told you about it
te lo dejo a cuenta ▪ anótalo en la cuenta ▪ apúntalo en la cuenta ▪ ponlo en la cuenta ▪ put it on the bill
te lo dejo a mi cuenta ▪ anótalo en mi cuenta ▪ apúntalo en mi cuenta ▪ ponlo en mi cuenta put it on my bill
te lo dejo a ti I'll leave it to you
te lo dejo en... I'll leave it for you in...
te lo dejo con... I'll leave it for you with...
te lo digo aparte this is just between you and me
¡te lo digo yo! I'm telling you!
te (lo) dije así I told you so ▪ I told you
¿te lo doblo? shall I fold it for you? ▪ would you like me to fold it for you?
te lo doy ▪ puedes quedarte con ello I'll give it to you ▪ you can have it ▪ you can keep it
¡te lo estás buscando! you're asking for it!
¡te lo has buscado! you asked for it!
¡te lo has creído! you fell for it!
te lo has ganado a pulso you've earned it
te lo juro I swear (it)
te lo mereces you deserve it
te lo paso I'll pass it to you
te lo prometo I promise
¿te lo rebano? ▪ ¿te lo troceo? shall I slice it for you? ▪ would you like me to slice it for you?
¿te lo troceo? ▪ te lo rebano? shall I slice it for you? ▪ would you like me to slice it for you?
¡te me anticipaste! you beat me to it!
¡te me has adelantado! ▪ ¡me ganaste de mano! you beat me to it!
¿te ocurre algo? ▪ ¿algo va mal? ▪ ¿ocurrió algo? is anything wrong?
te oigo a duras penas ▪ casi no te oigo ▪ apenas te oigo I can barely hear you ▪ I can hardly hear you
te oigo alto y claro ▪ más claro no canta un gallo I hear you loud and clear
¿te parece bien que (yo)...? do you think I should...?
¡te parece bonito! how do you like *that*?!
¡te pasaste! 1. ¡te superaste! you outdid yourself! 2. cruzaste la raya ▪ te pasaste de castaño a oscuro you went too far
te paso I'll connect you ▪ I'll put you through
te pedí que no lo hicieras ▪ te pedí que no lo hicieses I asked you not to (do that)
te pedí que no hicieras tanto ruido I asked you not to make so much noise
te pega tanto it looks really good on you
¡te pido que no lo hagas! please don't!
te pilla de camino *(Esp.)* ▪ te pilla de paso ▪ te queda de paso it's on your way ➤ ¿Me echas esto al buzón? Te pilla de camino. Would you put this in the mailbox for me? It's on your way.
te pilla de paso *(Esp.)* ▪ te queda de paso ▪ te pilla de camino it's on your way ➤ ¿Echas esta carta al buzón? Te pilla de paso. Would you put this letter in the mailbox? It's on your way.
te podrías dar con un canto en los dientes ▪ te podrías dar con una piedra you should count yourself lucky ▪ you should consider yourself lucky
te propongo un trato I'll make you a deal
¿te provoca? *(Méx.)* ▪ ¿te gustaría? do you want to? ▪ would you like to? ➤ Te provoca ir al cine? Do you want to go to the movies? ▪ Would you like to go to the movies? ➤ ¿Te provoca un tinto? Would you like a glass of red wine?
te queda de paso ▪ te pilla de paso ▪ te pilla de camino it's on your way
te recuerdo que... I wanted to remind you that... ▪ I just wanted to remind you that... ▪ just to remind you...
te resulta fácil a ti decir eso ▪ a ti te resulta fácil decir eso it's easy for *you* to say that.
te reto a que... I dare you to...
¿te rindes? 1. ¿te das por vencido? do you give up? 2. *(en contexto militar)* do you surrender?
¡te superaste! ▪ ¡te pasaste! you outdid yourself!
te suponía... I thought you were... ▪ I took you to be...
te tengo calado(-a) ▪ veo por dónde vienes I've got you pegged ▪ I've got your number ▪ I know what you're up to
te toca (a ti) ▪ a ti te toca it's your turn ▪ it's your go
te toca jugar it's your turn to play
te tomo la palabra I take your word for it ▪ I'll take your word for it
te va a dar que hablar it will give you something to talk about
¡te vas a acordar de mí! you're going to hear from me about this!
te vendrá muy bien it will do you good ▪ it will do you a lot of good

te veo cansado(-a) you look tired
te veo dentro de un ratito I'll see you in a little while
te veo venir I (can) see you coming
¿te veré otra vez? ▪ ¿te voy a volver a ver? ▪ ¿volveré a verte? will I see you again? ▪ am I going to see you again?
¿te vienes a (mi) casa? can you come over?
te vienes conmigo you're coming with me
¿te voy a volver a ver? ▪ ¿volveré a verte? ▪ ¿te veré otra vez? am I going to see you again? ▪ will I see you again?
teatrada publicitaria publicity stunt
teatro español del siglo veinte twentieth century Spanish drama ▪ twentieth century Spanish theater
techo falso drop ceiling
la **techumbre a dos aguas** ▪ tejado a dos aguas gable roof
tecla errónea *(informática)* wrong key
teclear de nuevo to re-key ▪ to re-enter
tecnología aplicada applied technology
tecnología punta ▪ tecnología vanguardista ▪ último grito de la tecnología state-of-the-art technology ▪ cutting-edge technology ▪ latest technology
tejado a dos aguas ▪ (la) techumbre a dos aguas gable roof
tejado plano flat roof
el **tejemaneje** behind-the-scenes maneuvering
tejido adiposo fatty tissue ▪ fat tissue
tejido cicatrizado scar tissue
tejido inflamado inflamed tissue
tela marinera: tener ~ ▪ tener tela que cortar ▪ tener tela to be a long story
tela metálica wire mesh ▪ screen ▪ screening material
teléfono de disco dial telephone
teléfono de teclas push-button phone ➤ Aunque es un teléfono de teclas, en su electrónica interna es un teléfono de disco. Even though it's a push-button phone, in its internal electronics it is a dial telephone.
teléfono inalámbrico cordless telephone ▪ cordless phone
teléfono rojo hot line
televisión basura trash TV
el **telón de acero** *(frontera entre países comunistas y no comunistas)* iron curtain
tema árido dry subject
el **tema de un libro** ▪ argumento de un libro subject of a book
tema deprimente ▪ tema depresivo depressing subject
el **tema en candelero** hot topic
el **tema es que...** ▪ el asunto (en cuestión) es que... the issue is that...
ser un **tema escabroso** to be a delicate subject ▪ to be a sensitive subject
el **tema espinoso** thorny issue
ser un **tema familiar** to be a family matter
el **tema musical** theme song
tema polémico controversial subject
el **tema recurrente** ▪ tema reiterativo recurrent theme
tema reiterativo ▪ tema recurrente recurrent theme
los **temas de actualidad** current events
temblar de miedo to tremble with fear ▪ to tremble with fright ▪ to tremble from fright
temblar las carnes to shake ▪ to tremble ▪ to shudder
temblarle las piernas (for) one's knees to tremble ➤ Me temblaban las piernas. My knees were trembling.
temblor me recorrió todo el cuerpo: un ▪ un temblor recorrió todo mi cuerpo a shudder ran (up and) down my spine ▪ a shiver ran up my spine ▪ a shudder convulsed me
temer por su vida to fear for one's life
temer que... to be afraid that... ➤ Temía que la empresa lo incluyera en el recorte del personal. ▪ Temía que la empresa lo incluyese en el recorte del personal. He was afraid (that) the company would include him in the personnel cutbacks.
temerse lo peor to fear the worst
temeroso de Dios god-fearing
estar **temeroso de que** to be fearful that
el **temor a la oscuridad** fear of the dark
el **temor al fracaso** fear of failure
temor y asco fear and loathing
temperatura ambiente ▪ temperatura ambiental ambient temperature ▪ room temperature
temperatura corporal body temperature
temperatura exterior outside air temperature ▪ temperature outside
temperaturas por debajo del punto de congelación below-freezing temperatures
temperaturas por encima de lo normal above-average temperatures
una **tempestad en un vaso de agua** a tempest in a teapot
templar el carácter de alguien ▪ forjar el carácter de alguien ▪ desarrollar el carácter de alguien to develop someone's character ▪ to refine someone's character
temporada de esquila sheep-shearing season ▪ shearing season
temporada de mala suerte ▪ racha de mala suerte streak of bad luck
temporada navideña Christmas season
el **temporal de lluvia** rain storm
el **temporal de nieve** ▪ tormenta de nieve snow storm
tempranas memorias early memories
ten cabeza *(Valle-Inclán)* ▪ ¡ten (mucho) ojo! keep your wits about you!
ten con ten: tener ~ ▪ ser diplomático ▪ tener tacto to have tact ▪ to be tactful ▪ to be diplomatic ▪ to have savoir faire
ten en cuenta que... ▪ toma en cuenta que... ▪ considera que... ▪ te advierto que... bear in mind that... ▪ keep in mind that... ▪ mind you... ➤ Ten en cuenta que tenemos que estar en el aeropuerto en dos horas. Mind you! We have to be at the airport in two hours. ▪ Bear in mind that we have to be at the airport in two hours. ▪ Keep in mind that we have to be at the airport in two hours.
ten esto hold this ▪ hold onto this ▪ take this
¡ten formalidad! ▪ ¡sé formal! ▪ ¡compórtate! behave yourself!
tender a ▪ tirar a to tend to ▪ to incline towards ▪ to verge on ▪ to border on
tender el mantel ▪ explayar el mantel ▪ poner el mantel to spread the tablecloth ▪ to lay the tablecloth ▪ to put the tablecloth on the table
tender el vuelo to take flight
tender la mano to hold out one's hand
tender la mano a alguien ▪ echar la mano a alguien to reach out to someone ▪ to extend one's hand to someone ▪ to outstretch one's hand to someone ▪ to offer one's hand to someone ➤ *(titular)* Los chiíes tienden la mano a la minoría suní tras las elecciones en Irak. The Shiites reach out to the Sunni minority after the elections in Iraq.
tender la ropa a secar ▪ tender la ropa para que se seque to hang out clothes to dry ▪ to hang up clothes to dry
tender las redes to cast (the) nets
tender puentes to build bridges ▪ to establish ties
tender puentes a alguien to reach out to someone (in friendship)
tender puentes entre to build bridges between ➤ *(titular)* Blair tiende puentes entre Estados Unidos y Europa. Blair builds bridges between the United States and Europe.
tender un cable a alguien ▪ echar un cable a alguien to give someone a hand
tender un lazo a alguien to set a trap for someone
tender una mano a alguien ▪ echar una mano a alguien to lend someone a hand ▪ to give someone a hand
tenderle una trampa a alguien to lay a trap for someone
tenderle las redes a alguien 1. tratar de atrapar a alguien to lay a trap (for someone) ▪ to try to trap someone ▪ to try to snare someone **2.** tratar de seducir a alguien to try to seduce someone
estar **tendido a lo largo** to be stretched out
tendrá que haber there will have to be
tendría que haber there would have to be
tendría que haber habido there should have been ➤ Tendría que haber habido alguien encargado de traer los refrescos. There should have been someone in charge of bringing the soft drinks.

■ Someone should have been (put) in charge of bringing the soft drinks.

tendría que haberlo sabido ■ me podría haber imaginado ■ me podía haber imaginado I might have known

¿tendría que hacerlo? am I supposed to? ➤ *Mordred:* ¿Me reconoces?- *El rey Arturo:* Tendría que hacerlo? *Mordred:* Do you recognize me?-*King Arthur:* Am I supposed to?

¡tendría que ser tú! it would be you!

tendría *x* años cuando... **1.** *(yo)* I must have been (about) *x* years old when... **2.** *(él)* he must have been (about) *x* years old when... **3.** *(ella)* she must have been (about) *x* years old when... ➤ (Yo) tendría diez años cuando... I must have been (about) ten years old when...

¡tendrías que haber venido hace cuatro horas! ■ ¡tendrías que haber estado hace cuatro horas! you were supposed to be here four hours ago!

¡tendrías que haberlo visto! you should have seen *that*!

tenemos que conformarnos con lo que tenemos ■ a falta de pan buenas son tortas we'll have to make do with what we have

tenencia de armas bearing of arms

la **posesión (ilegal) de armas** (illegal) weapons possession ■ (illegal) possession of weapons

tener a alguien a pan y agua to treat someone like dirt

tener a alguien cagando aceite *(subido de tono)* ■ tener a alguien de hijo to have someone at one's beck and call ■ to be at someone's beck and call ➤ El jefe quiere tenerme cagando aceite. The boss wants me at his beck and call. ■ The boss wants to have me at his beck and call.

tener a alguien con quien hablar to have someone to talk to

tener a alguien de su parte to have someone on your side

tener a alguien en palmitas ■ tener a alguien entre algodones ■ traer a alguien en palmitas ■ llevar a alguien en palmitas to wait on someone hand and foot ➤ Ella lo tiene en palmitas. ■ Ella lo tiene entre algodones. ■ Ella lo trae en palmitas. ■ Ella lo lleva en palmitas. ■ Ella lo tiene entre algodones. ■ Ella lo trae entre algodones. ■ Ella lo lleva entre algodones. She waits on him hand and foot. ➤ La tiene en palmitas. ■ La trae en palmitas. He waits on her hand and foot.

tener a alguien en un puño ■ tener a alguien metido en un puño ■ tener mano con alguien to have someone wrapped around one's little finger ➤ La clase tiene al profesor en un puño. The class has that teacher wrapped around its little finger. ➤ Los estudiantes tienen al profesor en un puño. The students have the teacher wrapped around their little finger.

tener a alguien entre algodones ■ traer a alguien entre algodones ■ tener a alguien en palmitas ■ traer a alguien en palmitas ■ llevar a alguien en palmitas to pamper someone ■ to wait on someone hand and foot ➤ Ella lo tiene entre algodones. She pampers him. ■ She waits on him hand and foot.

tener a alguien entre ceja y ceja not to like someone ■ to dislike someone ➤ El jefe lo tiene entre ceja y ceja. ■ *(Esp. leísmo)* El jefe le tiene entre ceja y ceja. The boss doesn't like him. ■ The boss dislikes him.

tener a alguien esperando **1.** to have someone waiting **2.** to keep someone waiting ➤ Usted tiene a alguien esperando (para) verlo. You have someone waiting to see you. ➤ Perdone por tenerlo a usted esperando. (I'm) sorry to keep you waiting.

tener a alguien fichado **1.** to have someone's number ■ to have someone pegged **2.** to have a (police) record on someone

tener a alguien metido en un puño ■ tener a alguien en un puño ■ tener mano con alguien to have someone wrapped around one's little finger

tener a bien hacer algo to see fit to do something

tener a dieta a alguien to have someone on a diet

tener adonde ir ■ tener algún sitio donde ir to have somewhere to go ➤ Tengo adonde ir esta tarde. I have to go somewhere this afternoon. I have somewhere to go this afternoon. ➤ ¿Tienes adonde ir esta tarde? *(pregunta neutral o dudosa)* Do you have anywhere to go this afternoon? ■ *(él que pregunta cree que sí)* Do you have somewhere to go this afternoon?

tener a la vista to have within sight

tener a mano to have on hand

tener a mucha honra to feel very proud of...

tener a quien salir to resemble someone

tener a su favor a otro to be in someone's favor

tener acierto to be right on

tener agallas ■ tener muchas agallas to have guts ■ to have a lot of guts ■ to have got a lot of guts ➤ Ese tipo tiene muchas agallas. That guy's got a lot of guts. ■ That guy has a lot of guts. ■ That guy's got guts.

tener agarrado a alguien por los huevos *(subido de tono)* ■ tener agarrado a alguien por los cojones to have someone by the balls ■ *(alternativa benigna)* to have someone over a barrel

tener aguante **1.** tener resistencia to have (good) endurance **2.** tener paciencia to have patience ■ to be able to put up with a lot ➤ Los corredores de larga distancia tienen mucho aguante. Long-distance runners have good endurance.

tener agujetas to have stiffness in the muscles ■ to have stiff muscles ■ to be stiff (from exercise)

tener al alcance de su mano ■ tener a mano to have at one's fingertips ■ to have at hand ■ to have within easy reach ■ to have readily available ➤ Es información que cualquier gerente de banco tendría que tener al alcance de su mano. ■ Es información que cualquier gerente de banco tendría que tener a mano. That's information that any bank manager would have to have at his fingertips.

tener al niño enfermo to have a sick child

tener algo a gala to pride oneself on something ■ to be proud of something

tener algo a huevo *(subido de tono)* to have something in the bag ■ to have something sewn up ➤ Cuando vi el puntaje de mi examen, supe que tenía la beca a huevo. When I saw my score on the exam, I knew I had the scholarship in the bag. ■ When I saw my test score, I knew I had the scholarship sewn up.

tener algo a la mano to something have at hand ■ to have something in readiness

tener algo a mal a alguien ■ tomar algo a mal a alguien ■ tomarse algo mal to take something the wrong way ■ to take offense ➤ No me tengas a mal lo que voy a decirte, pero... ■ No me tomes a mal lo que voy a decirte, pero... ■ No te tomes mal lo que voy a decirte, pero... Don't take it the wrong way, but... ■ No offense, but... ■ Don't take offense, but...

tener algo atorado en la garganta to have something caught in one's throat

tener algo consigo to have something with one ■ to have something on one ■ *(culto)* to have something on one's person ➤ No tiene el pasaporte consigo. He doesn't have his passport with him. ■ He doesn't have his passport on him. ■ He doesn't have his passport on his person. ➤ No tengo el pasaporte conmigo. I don't have my passport with me. ■ I don't have my passport on me. ■ I don't have my passport on my person. *("On one's person" se usa con más frecuencia en contextos legales y policiales.)*

tener algo de dinero ■ tener algún dinero to have some money

tener algo de dramático to be pretty exciting ➤ Su vida siempre ha tenido algo de dramático. Her life has always been pretty exciting.

tener algo en común ■ parecerse en algo to have something in common ■ to be alike in something

tener algo en el buche ■ guardar algo en el buche to keep something under one's hat

tener algo en la mente to have something on one's mind

tener algo en la punta de la lengua to have something on the tip of one's tongue

tener algo en marcha to have something underway

tener algo hecho un lío to have something in a mess

tener algo muy presente to have something at heart ➤ Tiene muy presente lo que es mejor para ti. He has your best interests at heart.

tener algo todo para uno mismo to have something all to oneself

tener algo por (ser) to consider something (to be)

tener algo preparado para alguien to have something ready for someone ➤ Lo tendremos preparado para usted para el viernes. We'll have it ready for you by Friday.

tener algo que anunciar to have an announcement to make

tener algo que decir **1.** tener algo que expresar to have something to say **2.** tener mucho que decir to have a lot to say

tener algo que perder to have something to lose

tener algo que ver con... to have something to do with...

tener alguien delante to have someone ahead of someone ➤ Lo atenderé tan pronto como pueda, pero tienes dos personas delante. I'll help you as soon as I can, but I have two people ahead of you. ■ I'll help you as soon as I can, but there are two people ahead of you.

tener alguien que cuidar to have someone to take care of ➤ Tenía tres hijos que cuidar. ■ Tenía tres niños que cuidar. She had three children to take care of.

tener algún dinero ■ tener algo de dinero to have some money

tener algunos kilos de más to be a few pounds overweight

tener ambas partes el mismo voto ■ tener ambas partes los mismos derechos to be equals in a situation ■ to be a two-way street ➤ En el matrimonio los dos tienen el mismo voto. ■ En el matrimonio los dos tienen los mismos derechos. In marriage, both partners are equals. ■ Marriage is a two-way street.

tener anginas *(Méx.)* to have tonsilitis

tener ansias de verlo a alguien ■ estar ansioso por verlo a alguien to be anxious to see someone

tener ante sí to have before one

tener antecedentes de to have a history of ➤ Su familia tiene antecedentes de problemas cardiacos. His family has a history of heart problems.

tener apego a to have an attachment to ➤ No tiene ningún apego a las cosas materiales. He has no attachment to material things.

tener apenas *x* años to be barely *x* years old ➤ Su madre murió cuando tenía apenas once años. His mother died when he was barely eleven.

tener aprecio a alguien to hold someone in high esteem ■ to esteem someone highly

tener apuro por to be in a hurry to

tener arreglos con alguien to have dealings with someone

tener arrestos para hacer algo ■ tener agallas para hacer algo to have the guts to do something ■ to have the courage to do something

tener asco a to be sickened by ■ to be repelled by

tener asuntos importantes que atender to have important matters to attend to

tener atadas las manos to have one's hands tied

tener bajo consumo ■ tener buen consumo ■ *(coloquial)* consumir como un mechero to get good mileage ■ to have good fuel efficiency ■ to be (very) fuel efficient

tener bajo control to have under control

tener bemoles ■ tener tres pares de bemoles to be fraught with difficulties ■ to be a tricky business

tener bien cubiertos los riñones to be well-heeled ■ to be well off financially

tener bien de algo *(L.am.)* to have a lot of something ■ to have something in abundance

tener buen aspecto *(especialmente refiriéndose a la salud)* to look good ■ to look healthy

tener buen conformar *(más común)* ■ ser de buen conformar to be easygoing ■ to be easy to be around ■ to be easy to please

tener buen consumo ■ tener bajo consumo ■ *(coloquial)* consumir como un mechero to get good mileage ■ to have good fuel efficiency ■ to be (very) fuel efficient

tener buen corazón to have a good heart ■ to be kind

tener buen gusto con to have good taste in

tener buen humor to be in a good mood

tener buen oído to have good hearing

tener buen oído para la música ■ tener un buen oído para la música to have a good ear for music

tener buen oído para los idiomas ■ tener un buen oído para los idiomas to have a good ear for languages

tener buen perder to be a good sport ■ to be a good loser

tener buen pulso to have a steady hand

tener buen saque 1. ser comilón to (be able to) eat like a horse **2.** *(tenis)* to have a good serve ➤ Tiene buen saque. ■ Es comilón. He can eat like a horse. ■ He eats like a horse.

tener (buen) tino para hacer algo to have knack for doing something

tener buen tipo to have a good figure

tener buena acogida to be well received

tener buena boca *(vino)* ■ tener buen sabor to have a good flavor

tener buena facha to have a good visage ■ to have a handsome face ■ to have a beautiful face

tener buena fama to be highly regarded

tener buena figura to have a good figure

tener buena mano con algo to have a knack for something

tener buena mano con la cocina to be a good cook

tener buena mano con los niños to have a way with children

tener buena mollera to have brains ■ to be brainy ■ to be smart

tener buena percha ■ tener una buena percha to look (really) sharp ■ *(culto)* to cut a fine figure

tener buena pinta to have a good (overall) appearance ■ to cut a fine figure

tener buena planta ■ tener una buena planta to cut a fine figure

tener buena presencia to look really nice ■ to look good ■ to look smart

tener buena racha to have a streak of (good) luck

tener buena traza para algo to be good at something

tener buenas domingas *(subido de tono)* ■ tener unas buenas glándulas mamarias ■ estar que se sale to have big boobs ■ to be stacked

tener buenas espaldas to be broad shouldered ■ to have broad shoulders

tener buenas posibilidades de to stand a good chance of ■ to have a good chance of

tener buenos cimientos to have a solid foundation

tener buenos cuartos to have a lot of bucks ■ to have a lot of dough ■ to be well-heeled

tener cabeza to have brains ■ to be sensible

tener cabeza de chorlito to be a birdbrain

tener cabeza para los estudios to be a good student ■ to be a fast learner ■ to be a quick study

tener cabeza para los negocios to have a head for business

tener cabida to be able to accommodate

tener cabida para to have room for

tener cabida en alguna parte to fit somewhere

tener cada salida ■ siempre tener una ocurrencia to come out with the funniest things ➤ Ella tiene cada salida. ■ Ella siempre tiene una ocurrencia. She comes out with the funniest things.

tener calentura ■ tener fiebre to have a fever

tener callos to have calluses

tener calma to be calm

tener cambio de un billete to have change for a bill

tener cambio de una moneda to have change for a coin

tener canguelo ■ tener canguis to have the jitters ■ to have got the jitters ➤ Tengo canguelo. I have the jitters. ■ I've got the jitters.

tener canguis ■ tener canguelo to have the jitters ■ to have got the jitters ➤ (Él) tiene canguis. He has the jitters. ■ He's got the jitters.

tener cara de cemento armado to have a lot of gall

tener cara de cordero degollado to look sad ■ to have a sad face

tener cara de loco to look like a madman

tener cara de palo to have a (very) straight face ■ to put on a straight face

tener cara de perro to look unfriendly

tener cara de pocos amigos to have an angry look (on one's face) ■ to look angry ■ *(coloquial)* to look mad

tener cara de póquer to be poker-faced ■ to have a poker face

tener cara de vinagre to look bitter

tener cara para hacer algo to have the nerve to do something

tener cartas en la manga ■ tener un as en la manga ■ tener un as bajo la manga to have an ace up one's sleeve ■ to have an ace in the hole ■ to have something up one's sleeve

tener casi olvidado ■ casi haberse olvidado ■ ya casi no acordarse to have almost forgotten ■ barely to remember ➤ Tengo casi olvidado cómo suena el inglés por haber estado fuera tanto tiempo. ▪ Casi me he olvidado de cómo suena el inglés por haber estado fuera tanto tiempo. ▪ Ya casi no me acuerdo de cómo suena el inglés por haber estado fuera tanto tiempo. I've almost forgotten what English sounds like, I've been away so long. ▪ I barely remember what English sounds like, I've been away so long.

tener cauces para la expresión de algo ▪ poder encauzar la expresión de algo to have an avenue for the expression of something ➤ Sin tener cauces para su expresión ▪ Sin poder encauzar su expresión Without having any avenue for its expression

tener celos de alguien to be jealous of someone

tener chispa to be witty ▪ to have a lot of spark

tener cita con alguien ▪ quedar con alguien **1.** *(negocio, médico, social)* to have an appointment with someone **2.** *(con posibilidades románticas)* to have a date with someone ➤ Tuve cita con el médico ayer. I had a doctor's appointment yesterday. ▪ I had an appointment with the doctor yesterday.

tener cogido por los cojones a alguien *(Esp., subido de tono)* ▪ tener a alguien cogido por los huevos ▪ tener agarrado a alguien por los huevos ▪ tener a alguien agarrado por los cojones to have someone by the balls ▪ *(alternativa benigna)* to have someone over a barrel ➤ El capataz de la construcción tenía al prestamista cogido por los cojones. The general contractor had the construction lender by the balls. ▪ The general contractor had the construction lender over a barrel.

tener cola ▪ traer cola to have serious consequences ▪ to have grave consequences

tener coleta ▪ traer coleta ▪ tener cola ▪ traer cola to have serious consequences

tener comida de sobra to have more than enough food ▪ to have plenty of food

tener como marco ▪ estar ambientado en to be set in ▪ to take place in ➤ La historia tenía como marco una pequeña aldea. The story took place in a small village.

tener como norma to make a practice of

tener con qué comprarlo ▪ poder permitírselo to be able to afford it

tener conciencia cabal de to be fully aware of

tener conciencia de to be aware of

tener conciencia de que to be aware that ➤ Tenía conciencia de que... He was aware that...

tener conciencia laxa ▪ tener conciencia ancha to have a weak conscience ▪ to have a lax conscience

tener confianza de que... ▪ tener la confianza de que... to be confident that... ➤ Tengo (la) confianza de que... I am confident that...

tener confianza en to have confidence in

tener conocimiento de algo ▪ estar enterado de algo ▪ ser consciente de algo ▪ constarle algo a alguien ▪ tener constancia de algo to be aware of something ▪ to know about something ➤ Quería decirte algo de lo que posiblemente no tengas conocimiento. ▪ Quería decirte algo de lo que probablemente no estés enterado. ▪ Quería decirte algo de lo que puede que no seas consciente. I wanted to tell you something you may not be aware of. ➤ No tengo conocimiento de que se esté impartiendo ninguna clase de inglés en este edificio. ▪ No sé de ninguna clase de inglés que se esté impartiendo en este edificio. I'm not aware of any English classes being taught in this building.

tener constancia de algo to aware of something ▪ (for) something to have come to one's attention ➤ No tengo constancia de que el archivo haya sido entregado. ▪ No me consta que el archivo haya sido entregado. I'm not aware that the file has been delivered. ▪ It has not come to my attention that the file has been delivered.

tener corazón to have a heart

tener correa para rato to have (physical) endurance

tener cosas más importantes que hacer to have more important things to do

tener cosquillas to be ticklish

tener costumbres muy arraigadas to be set in one's ways

tener costumbres persistentes to have regular habits

tener cuartos to have money ▪ to have wealth

tener cubierto el riñón ▪ tener bien cubierto el riñón to be well-heeled ▪ to be well off financially

tener cuenta con to be careful of

tener cuerda para rato to go on for a while

tener cuidado to be careful

tener cuidado con el hielo to be careful on the ice

tener cupo para *x* personas to have room for *x* people ▪ to hold *x* people ➤ Cada tren tiene cupo para mil personas. Each train holds a thousand people.

tener de diferente to be different about one ➤ No sé qué ella tiene de diferente. I don't know what's different about her.

tener de largo ▪ ser de largo to be a certain length

tener de particular to be unusual

tener de sobra to have more than enough

tener de todo to have everything ➤ Esa tienda tiene de todo. That store has everything.

tener deberes para casa *(Esp.)* ▪ tener tarea to have homework (to do)

tener declarada la guerra con alguien to be in conflict with someone ▪ to be at loggerheads with someone

tener derecho a to have a right to ▪ to have the right to ▪ to be entitled to

tener derecho de pernada droit de seigneur ▪ the presumed right of a feudal lord to have sex with the bride of a vassal on her wedding night

tener dificultad en hacer algo to have trouble doing something ▪ to have difficulty doing something ➤ Se trata de una calle muy corta por lo que aunque no recuerde yo ahora el número espero que preguntando no tengas ninguna dificultad en localizarlo. It's a very short street, so even though I don't remember the number, I expect that by asking (someone), you won't have any trouble finding it.

tener dificultad para entender to have a hard time understanding ▪ to have difficulty understanding

tener dolores por todas partes to ache all over

tener don de gentes to have a way with people

tener dos dedos de frente ▪ no tener ni dos dedos de frente to be a lowbrow ▪ to be slow

tener dudas con lo de... to have doubts about...

tener duende to have a certain enchanting quality

tener dura la mollera to be pigheaded

tener eco ▪ tener éxito ▪ cuajar ▪ volverse popular to catch on ▪ to become popular

tener edad para ser el padre de alguien to be old enough to be someone's father

tener edad para ser la madre de alguien to be old enough to be someone's mother

tener edad suficiente para to be old enough to

tener el cenizo to be jinxed

tener el coche en doble fila to be double parked

tener el corazón puesto en algo to have one's heart set on something

tener el corazón en un puño to be anxious

tener el cuartel general en *(militar)* to be based in ▪ to have its headquarters in

tener el deber de to be one's duty to ▪ to have the obligation to

tener el derecho a esperar to be entitled to ▪ to have the right to expect ➤ Tenía el derecho a esperar una respuesta. You were entitled to an answer. ▪ You had the right to expect an answer.

tener el disco rayado ▪ ser como un disco rayado to be a broken record ▪ to keep repeating oneself

tener el mejor aspecto posible to look one's best ➤ Quiero tener el mejor aspecto posible. I want to look my best.

tener el número correcto ▪ tener el número que es to have the right number

tener el oído duro to be hard of hearing ▪ to be deaf

tener el ojo echado a algo ▪ echar el ojo a algo to have one's eye on something

tener el ojo echado a alguien ▪ echar el ojo a alguien to have one's eye on someone

tener el pago domiciliado cobrarle el pago domiciliado to draft one's bank account ▪ to do a draft of one's bank account

tener el pie en el suelo to have one's feet on the ground

tener el presentimiento de que... to have the presentiment that... ▪ to have the feeling that... ➤ *(Dorothy en Mago de Oz)* Toto, tengo el presentimiento de que ya no estemos en Kansas. Toto, I've a feeling we're not in Kansas anymore.

tener el récord to hold the record

tener el riñón (bien) cubierto ▪ tener cubierto el riñón to be well-heeled

tener el tejado de vidrio for the pot to call the kettle black ➤ Tiene el tejado de vidrio. The pot is calling the kettle black.

tener el tiempo justo para algo to have just enough time for something

tener el tiempo justo para hacer algo to have just enough time to do something

tener el valor de hacer algo to have the nerve to do something ▪ to have the gall to do something

tener empeño en to be determined to

tener en alta estima to rate very high in someone's book ➤ Ella no me tiene en alta estima. I don't rate very high in her book.

tener en consideración to take into consideration ▪ to take into account

tener en contra de uno to have against one

tener en cuenta que... ▪ tener en mente que... ▪ recordar que... to bear in mind that... ▪ to keep in mind that... ➤ Ten en cuenta que mañana tienes que madrugar. ▪ Ten en mente que tienes que madrugar mañana. ▪ Recuerda que tienes que madrugar mañana. Bear in mind that you have to get up early tomorrow. ▪ Keep in mind that you have to get up early tomorrow.

tener en donde agarrarse ▪ tener donde agarrarse to have an anchor

tener en el bolsillo a alguien to have someone in one's pocket

tener en jaque a alguien 1. *(ajedrez)* to put someone in check **2.** to checkmate someone ▪ to put someone in an untenable position ▪ to have somone over a barrel

tener en la punta de la lengua una cosa to have something on the tip of one's tongue ▪ for something to be on the tip of one's tongue

tener en marcha to have underway

tener en mente que... ▪ tener en cuenta que... ▪ recordar que... to bear in mind that... ▪ to keep in mind that... ▪ to remember that... ➤ Ten en mente que mañana tienes que madrugar. ▪ Ten en cuenta que tienes que madrugar mañana. ▪ Recuerda que tienes que madrugar mañana. Bear in mind that you have to get up early tomorrow. ▪ Keep in mind that you have to get up early tomorrow. ▪ Remember that you have to get up early tomorrow.

tener en poco a alguien to be contemptuous of someone ▪ to regard someone with contempt

tener en que apoyarse to have something to lean on

tener enchufe to have connections

tener energía contenida to have energy bottled up inside (one) ▪ to have bottled up energy

tener entendido que... to understand that... ➤ Tengo entendido que... I understand that...

tener entidad propia to have one's own life

tener entradas (para) to have tickets (to)

tener espaldas anchas ▪ ser ancho de espaldas to have broad shoulders ▪ to be broad shouldered

tener estrella to be lucky

tener estudios to have an education

tener facilidad de palabra to have a way with words

tener fama de ser to be famous for being ▪ to be famous as

tener fiebre ▪ tener calentura to have a fever

tener figura de algo to have the shape of something ▪ to be shaped like something ▪ to be something-shaped ➤ Tiene figura de L. It's L-shaped. ▪ It's shaped like an L. ▪ It has the shape of an L.

tener flojos los tornillos to have a few screws loose ▪ to have a few loose screws

tener frío to be cold ➤ Tengo frío. I'm cold.

tener fuerzas to be up to it ▪ to be ready for it ➤ ¿Tienes fuerzas? Are you up to it?

tener fuerzas para algo to be up to something ▪ to be up for something ➤ ¿Tienes fuerzas? Are you up to it? ▪ Are you up for it?

tener ganas de 1. to feel like **2.** estar deseando to look forward to ➤ No tengo ganas. I don't feel like it. ➤ Tengo ganas de verte. I'm looking forward to seeing you. ▪ I look forward to seeing you.

tener gracia to be funny ➤ No tiene gracia. It's not funny.

tener gran capacidad to have a lot on the ball

tener graves problemas 1. tener problemas serios to have serious problems **2.** estar en aprietos to be in big trouble

tener gripa *(Méx., Col.)* ▪ tener la gripe to have the flu

tener gusto to have (good) taste

tener hambre to be hungry

tener hecho algo to have something accomplished ▪ to have something made ➤ *(editorial)* Entre la marea negra y la guerra contra Irak, los socialistas van a tener hecha la campaña electoral. Between the oil slick and the war against Iraq, the socialists will have the election campaign made.

tener hipo to have the hiccups ▪ to have the hiccoughs

tener honra en to be honored to

tener huevo para ▪ tener agallas para to have the balls to ▪ *(alternativa benigna)* to have the guts to

tener huevos ▪ tener cojones ▪ tenerlas bien puestas to have balls ▪ *(alternativa benigna)* to have guts

tener humor de perros ▪ estar de mal humor to be in a bad mood ▪ to be in a foul mood ▪ to be in a bad humor

tener inconveniente en que to object to

tener indiferencia por alguien ▪ sentir indiferencia hacia alguien to have no use for someone ▪ not to have any use for someone

tener influencias to have connections

tener ínfulas to put on airs

tener intriga por saber to be dying to find out

tener jeta to have cheek ▪ to be cheeky

tener la antena puesta to eavesdrop

tener la base en ▪ tener la sede en to be based in ▪ to have its headquarters in

tener la cabeza a pájaros to be an airhead

tener la cabeza cargada to have a lot on one's mind

tener la cabeza como una jaula de grillos ▪ estar chiflado ▪ estar tocado (de la cabeza) to be cracked ▪ to be touched in the head

tener la cabeza cuadrada to be narrow-minded

tener la cabeza en su sitio to have one's head on straight

tener la cabeza llena de pájaros to be a dreamer

tener la cabeza sobre los hombros to have a head on one's shoulders

tener la capacidad de hacer algo to have the ability to do something

tener la competencia para to be within one's jurisdiction to ▪ to come within one's jurisdiction to ▪ to fall within one's jurisdiction to

tener la conciencia limpia ▪ tener la conciencia tranquila to have a clear conscience

tener la conciencia tranquila ▪ tener la conciencia limpia to have a clear conscience

tener (la) confianza de que... to be confident that...

tener la culpa to be at fault

tener la culpa de algo to be to blame for something ▪ to bear the blame for something ▪ to be at fault for something

tener la culpa del accidente to cause the accident ▪ to be the cause of the accident ▪ to be at fault in the accident

tener la depre ▪ estar depre to be down in the dumps

tener la despensa repleta to have a full pantry ▪ to have plenty to eat in the house

tener la despensa vacía to have an empty pantry ▪ to have nothing to eat in the house ▪ not to have anything to eat in the house

tener la edad para votar ▪ tener la edad suficiente para votar ▪ ser lo suficientemente mayor para votar to be old enough to vote ▪ to be of voting age ➤ En 1960, mi abuelo estaba a favor de Kennedy, pero no tenía la edad para votar. ▪ En 1960, mi abuelo estaba a favor de Kennedy, pero no era lo suficientemente mayor para votar. In 1960 my grandfather was for Kennedy, but he wasn't old enough to vote.

tener la espalda mal to have a bad back ➤ Él tiene la espalda mal. He has a bad back.

tener la esperanza puesta en to have one's hopes set on

tener la fea costumbre de to have a bad habit of

tener la fuerza de sus convicciones to have the strength of one's convictions

tener la gripe to have the flu

tener la habilidad de hacer algo to have the ability to do something

tener la impresión de que... 1. to have a feeling (that)... ▪ to have the feeling (that)... 2. to have the impression that...

tener la llave de to hold the key to ➤ *(titular)* Derecha más dura tiene la llave de la gobernabilidad de Portugal. Extreme right holds the key to the governability of Portugal. ▪ Far right holds the key to the governability of Portugal.

tener la manga ancha to be overly indulgent ▪ to be over-indulgent

tener la marca ▪ trabajar una marca to carry the brand ➤ Tenemos la marca pero no el artículo. We carry the brand but not the item.

tener la mente ocupada en muchas cosas to have a lot on one's mind

tener la mente puesta en otras cosas to have one's mind on other things

tener la misma tesis to have the same point of view

tener la negra ▪ tener una racha de mala suerte to have a streak of bad luck

tener la osadía de... to have the audacity to...

tener la paciencia de hacer algo *(as a character trait)* to have the patience to do something

tener la paciencia para hacer algo *(en situaciones)* to have the patience to do something

tener la plena confianza de que... to be very confident that...

tener la sartén por el mango ▪ tomar la sartén por el mango ▪ *(Esp.)* coger la sartén por el mango to call the shots

tener la sede en ▪ tener la base en to be based in ▪ to have its headquarters in

tener la sensación de que... ▪ tener la impresión de que... to have the feeling that...

tener la situación bajo control to have the situation under control

tener la suerte de to have the good fortune to

tener la última palabra to have the last word

tener la vida en un hilo (for) one's life to be hanging by a thread

tener la virtud de to have the power to ➤ Superman tiene la virtud de ver a través de las paredes. Superman has the power to see through walls.

tener la voz ronca *(como Louis Armstrong)* ▪ tener la voz grave to have a gravelly voice ▪ to have a rasping voice

tener la voz tomada ▪ tener mala voz ▪ estar ronco to be hoarse (temporarily)

tener lana to have money

tener las manos libres para to have one's hands free to ▪ to be free to ▪ to have the option of

tener las mismas comodidades que to have the same conveniences as

tener las miras puestas en algo ▪ poner la mira en algo to have one sights set on something ▪ to set one's sights on something

tener las miras puestas en hacer algo ▪ poner la mira en hacer algo to have one's sights set on doing something ▪ to set one's sights on doing something

tener las pilas puestas ▪ venir con las pilas puestas to be ready for action ▪ to be ready to go ▪ to be champing at the bit

tener lengua de trapo to be tongue-tied

tener lo que se requiere (para triunfar) ▪ tener lo que se necesita (para triunfar) ▪ poseer lo que se requiere (para triunfar) to have what it takes (to succeed) ➤ Tienes lo que se requiere para triunfar. ▪ Tienes lo que se necesita para triunfar. ▪ Posees lo que se requiere para triunfar. ▪ Posees lo que se necesita para triunfar. You have what it takes to succeed.

tener los días contados (for) one's days to be numbered ➤ Mi carro tiene los días contados. My car's days are numbered.

tener los hombros caídos ▪ estar de hombros caídos ▪ estar cruzado de brazos to be standing around doing nothing

tener los huesos húmedos ▪ estar hecho una sopa to be soaked to the bone ➤ La lluvia me pilló desprevenido(-a), y tengo los huesos húmedos. I got caught in the rain, and I'm soaked to the bone.

tener los huesos molidos to be bone tired

tener los nervios crispados to be on edge ▪ to be edgy

tener los nervios de punta to be on edge

tener los ojos cerrados a algo to be in denial about something

tener los ojos clavados en algo ▪ mirar fijamente a algo to stare at something ▪ to have one's eyes fixed on something

tener los ojos clavados en alguien ▪ mirar fijamente a alguien to stare at someone ▪ to have one's eyes fixed on someone

tener los ojos como platos (for) one's eyes to be as big as saucers

tener los ojos en alguna cosa to be looking at something ▪ to have one's heart set on something

tener los ojos puestos en algo to have one's eyes fixed on something

tener los ojos vendados to be blindfolded

tener los pies sobre el suelo to have one's feet on the ground

tener lugar ▪ tener cabida to be acceptable ▪ to be suitable ▪ to fit in

tener lugar en ▪ celebrarse en 1. to take place in ▪ to be held in 2. to take place at ▪ to be held at ➤ La reunión tendrá lugar en Madrid. The meeting will take place in Madrid. ➤ La reunión tendrá lugar en el Hotel Meliá Castilla. The meeting will take place at the Melia Castilla Hotel.

tener madera to have talent ▪ to be a natural

tener madera de actor to have the makings of an actor

tener madera de algo to have the makings of something

tener madera para to have a talent for

tener mal apecto 1. not to look well ▪ to look sick 2. to look sloppy ▪ to look ill-kempt ▪ to look ill-kept

tener mal de lejos 1. sólo ver de cerca to be near-sighted 2. verse mal de lejos not to look good from a distance

tener mal fario 1. to have bad luck ▪ to be unlucky 2. to be mean ▪ to be nasty

tener mal perder to be a poor loser ▪ to be a sore loser

tener mal vino not to be able to hold one's liquor ▪ to become aggressive when drunk ▪ to become quarrelsome when drunk

tener mala boca to be foul-mouthed ▪ to bad-mouth people

tener mala cara to look sick ▪ not to look well ▪ to look unwell

tener mala idea ▪ tener mala intención to have bad intentions ▪ to be malicious

tener mala leche to be mean ▪ to be hateful ▪ to be twisted

tener mala memoria to have a poor memory

tener mala opinión de to think badly of

tener mala pata ▪ tener mala suerte to have bad luck ▪ to be unlucky

tener mala racha to be down on one's luck ▪ to be going through a difficult time

tener mala sangre to be mean-spirited

tener mala sombra to be unlucky

tener mala traza para algo to be bad at doing something ▪ not to be good at doing something

tener mala voz ▪ tener la voz tomada ▪ estar ronco to be hoarse (temporarily)

tener mala(s) noticia(s) ▪ traer mala(s) noticia(s) to have (some) bad news

tener malas pulgas to have a bad temper ▪ to be bad tempered

tener manga ancha to be overly indulgent ▪ to be over-indulgent ▪ to be very flexible

tener manía de hacer algo to have a passion for something ▪ to be bent on something ▪ to be a fool for something ➤ *(Forrest Gump)* Qué manía de correr tiene ese niño. That kid's a running fool.

tener mano con alguien ▪ tener a alguien (metido) en un puño to have influence on someone ▪ to have pull with someone ▪

to have an in with someone ■ to know how to get one's way with someone

tener mano dura to be strict ■ to be firm

tener mano en una cosa to have a hand in something

tener mano izquierda to be clever ■ to be sly ■ to be astute

tener mano para una cosa to be good at something ■ to have a knack for something

tener manos de trapo to be clumsy ■ to be all thumbs

tener maña para hacerlo to have the knack of it

tener marcha to be lively ■ to have lots of energy ■ to be a partier ■ to be in the mood for a party

tener mariposas en el estómago to have butterflies in one's stomach

tener más años que Matusalén to be as old as Methuselah

tener más cara que espalda to be brazen ■ to be cheeky ■ to be shameless

tener más cojones que el caballo de Espartero to have balls ■ to have guts

tener más cojones que el caballo de Santiago to have balls ■ to have guts

tener más cojones que un toro to be as brave as a bull

tener más cuento que Calleja 1. to be a cumpulsory liar ■ to be an inveterate liar 2. to be baloney ■ to be crap

tener más espolones que un gallo to be as old as the hills ■ to be old as the hills

tener más hambre que maestro de escuela to be as hungry as a bear ■ to be starving ■ to be famished

tener más moral que el Alcoyano *(Esp.)* to have strong morale ■ to maintain high spirits

tener más paciencia que el santo Job to have the patience of Job

tener más razón que un santo to be as right as rain

tener más visitas que un ministro to be very popular

tener memoria de elefante to have the memory of an elephant

tener menos seso que un mosquito to be pea-brained

tener menos suerte not to be so lucky ➤ Tuvo menos suerte. He wasn't so lucky.

tener mente propia to have a mind of one's own

tener miedo a alguien to be afraid of someone

tener miedo de algo to be afraid of something

tener miedo de que... to be afraid that...

tener miedo hasta de su sombra ■ estar asustado hasta de su propia sombra to be afraid of one's (own) shadow ➤ Tiene miedo hasta de su sombra. He's afraid of his (own) shadow.

tener mierda en la cabeza *(subido de tono)* not to have shit for brains

tener molidos los huesos to be worn to a frazzle

tener morbo 1. to arouse sexual curiosity 2. (for) there to be more to something than meets the eye ➤ La cosa tiene morbo. There's more to it than meets the eye.

tener morriña ■ sentir morriña 1. to be homesick 2. to have the blues

tener morro ■ tener mucho morro to have (a lot of) cheek ■ to have (a lot of) gall

tener motivos de sobra por hacer algo to have more than sufficient reason for doing something ■ to be more than justified in doing something

tener motivos para creer ■ tener razones para creer to have reason to believe

tener mucha correa to be witty ■ to be imaginative ■ to be creative

tener mucha cuerda to have a lot of energy ■ to be hyperactive ■ to be witty

tener mucha escuela ■ tener mucha experiencia to be well-educated ■ to be worldly ■ to be streetwise ■ to be crafty

tener mucha ilusión... 1. to be excited... 2. to be very hopeful... ➤ Javier tiene mucha ilusión al asistir a la universidad. Javier is very excited about going to the university. ➤ Javier tiene mucha ilusión de llegar a ser catedrático universitario. Javier is very hopeful that he will become a university professor.

tener mucha labia to have the gift of gab

tener mucha mollera ■ tener mucho coco ■ tener un gran coco to be a brain ■ to be a genius ■ *(coloquial)* to be a smart cookie ■ to be smart as hell

tener mucha raigambre to be deeply rooted

tener mucha trastienda to be crafty ■ to play one's cards close to one's chest

tener muchas escamas to be a chameleon

tener muchas tablas to be resourceful ■ to have a lot of experience ■ to be crafty

tener mucho coco ■ tener mucho tarro to be a brain

tener mucho cuento to be all talk ■ to be unreliable

tener mucho de alguien to be a lot like someone ➤ Tiene mucho de su madre. She's a lot like her mother.

tener mucho en juego ■ jugarse mucho to have a lot on the line ■ to risk a lot ■ to be risking a lot ➤ Tengo mucho en juego. ■ Me juego mucho. I have a lot on the line. ■ I'm risking a lot.

tener mucho morro ■ tener morro to have a lot of nerve ■ to have a lot of gall

tener mucho mundo to have been around ➤ Tiene mucho mundo. *(él)* He's been around. ■ *(ella)* She's been around.

tener mucho que comentar ■ tener tema para rato to have a lot to talk about ➤ Tenemos mucho que comentar sobre mi viaje reciente a Guatemala y El Salvador. We have a lot to talk regarding my recent trip to Guatemala and El Salvador.

tener mucho que perder to have a lot to lose

tener mucho rostro to have a lot of gall ■ to have a lot of nerve ■ to have a lot of cheek

tener mucho talento to have a lot of talent ■ to be very talented

tener mucho tarro ■ tener mucho coco to be a brain

tener mucho teatro to be given to histrionics ■ to always be on stage

tener mucho tiempo por delante to have plenty of time

tener muchos entresijos to have a lot of ins and outs ■ to have a lot of twists and turns ■ to have a lot of intricacy

tener muchos humos to put on airs ■ to have an exaggerated opinion of oneself

tener muchos marrones *(coloquial)* tener muchos problemas to have a lot of problems

tener muchos motivos para dar gracias to have a lot to be thankful for

tener muchos problemas ■ *(coloquial)* tener muchos marrones to have a lot of problems

tener muchos recovecos 1. *(casa)* to have a lot of nooks and crannies 2. *(camino)* to have a lot of twists and turns 3. *(ley)* to be convoluted ■ to have a lot of ins and outs

tener narices to have a lot of nerve

tener nervios de acero to have nerves of steel

tener nieves perpetuas to be covered with snow (all) year round

tener ocasión de to have occasion to

tener oído para la música to have an ear for music

tener ojeriza a alguien to have it in for someone ■ to be nursing a grudge against someone

tener ojo clínico to have a sharp eye

tener ojos de carnero degollado 1. to have a lovesick look 2. to have an innocent look

tener olfato para una ganga to have a nose for a bargain

tener otitis to have an ear infection ■ to have an inflammation of the inner ear ■ *(término médico)* to have otitis

tener otro compromiso to have another commitment ➤ No puedo ir porque tengo otro compromiso. I can't go because I have another commitment.

tener paciencia to be patient ➤ *(tú)* Ten paciencia. ■ *(usted)* Tenga paciencia. ■ *(vosotros)* Tened paciencia. ■ *(ustedes)* Tengan paciencia. Be patient.

tener padrinos to have connections ■ to have well-connected friends

tener pájaros en la cabeza to have bats in one's belfry

tener palanca to have pull ■ to have connections

tener para dar y tomar to have plenty to spare

tener para rato to have enough to last a while

tener pelotas to have balls ■ to have guts

tener pena to be sad
tener perspectiva (sobre...) ▪ tener perspectiva (de...) ▪ tener una visión global (de...) to get the big picture (of...) ▪ to get the big picture (when it comes to...)
tener picores to have a rash ▪ to itch
tener plan to have a date ▪ to have plans
tener pluma to be nellie ▪ to be camp ▪ to be effeminate
tener poca aceptación to be unpopular
tener poca cabeza not to be very smart ▪ not to be very bright ▪ *(coloquial)* not to be real bright
tener poca correa to have a short fuse
tener poca hambre ▪ no tener mucha hambre not to be hungry ➤ Tenía poca hambre. ▪ No tenía mucha hambre. I wasn't very hungry.
tener poca vergüenza to have no shame ➤ ¿No te da vergüenza? ▪ ¿No tienes vergüenza? Have you no shame?
tener pocas barbas to be green behind the ears ▪ to be inexperienced
tener pocas luces not to be very bright ▪ *(coloquial)* not to be very bright ▪ not to be real bright
tener poco que perder to have little to lose ▪ not to have much to lose
tener por cierto ▪ tener por seguro to know for sure ▪ to be sure ▪ to be certain
tener por delante ▪ presentársele to have ahead of one ➤ Tenemos un gran verano por delante. ▪ Se nos presenta un gran verano. We have a great summer ahead of us.
tener por objetivo to have as one's objective ▪ to have as one's goal
tener posiciones opuestas con alguien ▪ estar en conflicto con alguien ▪ estar en desacuerdo con alguien to be at cross purposes with someone ▪ to be at loggerheads with someone ▪ to have a disagreement with someone ▪ to be having a disagreement with someone
tener presente to keep in mind ▪ to bear in mind ▪ to remember ➤ Tenía presente sus palabras. I kept his words in mind. ▪ I bore his words in mind. ▪ I bore in mind his words. ▪ I remembered his words.
tener previsto to plan to ▪ to anticipate ▪ to expect ➤ Clinton tiene previsto reunirse con líderes del partido hoy. Clinton plans to meet with party leaders today. ➤ Lo tiene previsto. He plans to. ➤ No tengo previsto ningún viaje a Madrid próximamente. I don't anticipate a trip to Madrid in the near future.
tener prevista la llegada a la una to be scheduled to arrive at one
tener prevista la salida a la una to be scheduled to depart at one ➤ El vuelo tiene prevista la salida a las cinco en punto. The flight is scheduled to depart at five o'clock on the dot.
tener prioridad sobre alguien to have priority over someone ▪ to be ahead of someone ➤ Tiene prioridad sobre mí. He has priority over me. ▪ He's ahead of me.
tener prisa to be in a hurry
tener problemas con la justicia to be in trouble with the law
tener propensión a hacer algo to tend to do something ➤ Gore, según Bush, tiene propensíon a exagerar. Gore, according to Bush, tends to exaggerate.
tener pudor to feel modest ▪ to feel modesty
tener pudor de confesarlo to be embarrassed to admit it
tener puesto ▪ vestirse de ▪ llevar to wear ▪ to have on ➤ Tiene puesto un abrigo. She's wearing a coat. ▪ She has on a coat.
tener pulgas to have fleas ▪ to have a quick temper
tener que comentar muchas cosas de to have a lot to talk about regarding ▪ to have a lot to talk about concerning
tener que estar en un sitio to have to be somewhere ➤ Tengo que estar en un sitio para las nueve. I have to be somewhere by nine o'clock.
tener que haber venido ▪ deber haber venido to be supposed to be here ➤ ¡Tenías que haber venido hace cuatro horas! You were supposed to be here four hours ago!
tener que habérselas con alguien to have to deal with someone ▪ to have someone to deal with
tener que hacer algo to have to do something
tener que ir a algún sitio to have to go somewhere ➤ Tengo que ir a algún sitio para las nueve. I have to be somewhere by nine o'clock.
tener que operarse to have to have an operation ▪ to have to have surgery ▪ to have to undergo surgery ▪ to have to be operated on
tengo que reconocer... I'd have to say... ▪ I have to say ▪ I have to acknowledge
tener que ser así to have to be just so ➤ Su café tiene que ser así. Her coffee has to be just so.
tener que tragar saliva to have to swallow hard ▪ to have to swallow one's feelings
tener que ver con ▪ atañer to have to do with ➤ No tiene nada que ver contigo. It has nothing to do with you.
tener que volver to have to go back ➤ Tengo que volver allí. I have to go back there.
tener quebraderos de cabeza to have worries ▪ to have problems
tener química con alguien (for there) to be chemistry between two people
tener rabia a alguien to be angry with someone
tener razón to be right ▪ to be correct ➤ Tienes razón. You're right. ▪ You're correct. ➤ Tienes razón en tu apreciación. You're correct in your analysis.
tener razón al to be right when ▪ to have good reason when ➤ Tenía razón al solicitar un nuevo juicio. He had good reason when he sought a new trial.
tener razón de to be right to ▪ to have good reason to
tener razones para creer ▪ tener motivos para creer to have reason to believe
tener reflejos lentos to have slow reflexes ▪ to have poor reflexes
tener remedios a manta to have a cure for everything ▪ to have a solution to everything
tener resonancia to strike a nerve with ▪ to cause a sensation
tener respeto por alguien to have respect for someone ➤ The young people in the town have no respect for the colonel. Los jóvenes el pueblo no tienen ningún respeto por el coronel.
tener retraso to be late
tener rostro to have nerve ▪ to have gall
tener salida para todo to be able to talk one's way out of anything ▪ to know how to talk one's way out of anything
tener sangre azul to be blue-blooded
tener sangre caliente to be hot-blooded ▪ to have a quick temper ▪ to be impetuous
tener sangre de horchata ▪ no tener sangre en las venas to be unfeeling ▪ to be unemotional
tener sangre fría **1.** to be cold-blooded ▪ to be (emotionally) cold **2.** to have sangfroid ▪ to be calm, cool and collected
tener santos en la corte to have friends in high places
tener sed de venganza ▪ tener ganas de vengarse ▪ *(Arg.)* quedarse con la sangre en el ojo to thirst for revenge ▪ to lust for revenge ▪ to burn with the desire for revenge ▪ to burn for revenge
tener segundas intenciones to have an ulterior motive ▪ to have a hidden agenda
tener sentimientos encontrados to have mixed feelings ▪ to have conflicting feelings
tener siete vidas como los gatos to have nine lives like a cat
tener sorbido el seso a alguien to have someone under one's spell
tener su aquél to have that certain something ▪ to have a certain something
tener su base en ▪ tener su fundamento en ▪ estar fundamentado en ▪ estar basado en to be based on
tener su cara y su cruz to have its good and bad points ▪ to have its pros and cons
tener su fundamento en ▪ tener su base en ▪ estar fundamentado en ▪ estar basado en to be based on
tener su pro y su contra to have its pros and cons
tener sueño to be sleepy
tener suerte to be lucky
tener sus bemoles **1.** to be tricky **2.** to have its drawbacks

tener sus entresijos to be a complex person ■ to be a deep person ■ to be hard to fathom ➤ Tiene sus entresijos. He's a very complex person. ■ He's a very deep person. ■ He's hard to fathom

tener sus manías to be odd ■ to be peculiar

tener sus más y sus menos to have (its) pros and cons ■ to have its good points and bad points

tener sus orígenes to have its origins ➤ El órgano de cañones tiene sus orígines en la Roma del Siglo V (cinco) y lo utilizaban para atraer a la gente al circo. The pipe organ has its origins in fifth-century Rome, where it was used to attract people to the circus.

tener sus prontos de enojo ■ tener sus prontos to have a quick temper ■ to be quick-tempered ■ to have a short fuse

tener sus propias ideas ■ tener sus propias opiniones to have a mind of one's own ➤ Ella tiene sus propias ideas. ■ Ella tiene su propias opiniones. She has a mind of her own.

tener sus propias opiniones ■ tener sus propias ideas to have a mind of one's own

tener sus motivos para hacer algo ■ tener sus razones para hacer algo to have one's reasons for doing something ➤ Tuve mis motivos para escogerlo. ■ Tuve mis razones para elegirlo. I had my reasons for choosing it.

tener sus razones para hacer algo ■ tener sus motivos para hacer algo to have one's reasons for doing something ➤ Tuve mis razones para escogerlo. ■ Tuve mis motivos para elegirlo. I had my reasons for choosing it.

tener sus sospechas to have one's suspicions ➤ No sé quién atasca el fregadero todo el tiempo, pero tengo mis sospechas. I don't know who's stopping up the sink all the time, but I have my suspicions.

tener suerte de no... to be lucky not to...

tener suficientes cojones para... ■ tener suficientes narices para... to have enough guts to... ■ to have the guts to...

tener suficientes narices para... ■ tener suficientes cojones para... to have enough guts to... ■ to have the guts to...

tener tablas *(sobre todo en el espectáculo)* to have stage presence ■ to be an experienced performer

tener talante para to have a talent for ■ to have a gift for

tener tela ■ tener tela que cortar ■ tener tela marinera to be a long drawn-out affair ➤ Tiene tela. It's a long drawn-out affair.

tener tela para rato ■ tener mucho que hacer to have a lot (of work) to do ■ to have plenty (of work) to do ■ to have a lot of work on one's hands ■ to have plenty or work on one's hands

tener temor to feel apprehensive that ■ to be afraid that ■ to worry that

tener temperamento to have a strong character

tener ten con ten to have savoir faire ■ to have tact ■ to be tactful ■ to find the middle ground

tener tendencia a ■ tener propensión a to have a tendency to

tener tiempo de hacer algo ■ tener tiempo para hacer algo to have time to do something

tener tino para hacer algo ■ tener buen tino para algo to have a knack for doing something

tener toda la intención de to have every intention of ➤ Ceci dijo que durante las vacaciones tiene toda la intención de estar lo más alejada de la computadora que pueda. Ceci said that during her vacation she has every intention of staying as far from a computer as possible.

tener toda la pinta de to have all the earmarks of ➤ Esto tiene toda la pinta de un ataque terrorista. This has all the earmarks of a terrorist attack.

tener toda razón al to have good reason to ➤ Tiene toda razón al solicitar un nuevo juicio. He has good reason to seek a new trial.

tener todo lo que uno puede manejar ■ tener todo lo que uno puede acaparar ■ tener todo lo que uno puede controlar to have (got) all one can handle ■ to have all one can manage ■ to have all one can deal with ➤ Tengo todo lo que puedo manejar en este momento. I've got all I can handle right now.

tener todos los papeles hechos un lío ■ tener un lío de papeles to have all one's papers in a mess ■ for one's papers to be in a mess

tener tomate (for) there to be a ruckus ■ (for) there to be a flap ■ (for) there to be a big problem ➤ Ayer en la primera comunión de mi hermano pequeño hubo un tomate cuando uno de los niños le tiró de la coleta a una niña. Yesterday at my little brother's first communion there was a ruckus when one of the boys pulled the ponytail of one of the girls. ■ Yesterday at my little brother's first communion there was a flap when one of the boys pulled the ponytail of one of the girls. ■ Yesterday at my little brother's first communion there was a big problem when one of the boys pulled the ponytail of one of the girls.

tener tos to have a cough

tener trabajo que hacer to have work to do

tener tres pares de bemoles ■ tener bemoles to be fraught with difficulties ■ to be tricky

tener un aire de desconcierto to have a disconcerted look ■ to look disconcerted

tener un aforo de *x* personas to have a seating capacity of *x* people ■ to seat *x* people

tener un as en la manga ■ tener un as bajo la manga ■ tener cartas en la manga **1.** have an ace up one's sleeve ■ to have an ace in the hole **2.** to have something up one's sleeve

tener un aspecto fenomenal to look great ■ to look wonderful ➤ Hoy tienes un aspecto fenomenal. You look great today. ■ You look wonderful today.

tener un bebé en camino ■ tener un hijo en camino ■ estar esperando un bebé ■ estar esperando un hijo to have a baby on the way ■ to have a child on the way ■ to be expecting a baby ■ to be expecting a child

tener (un) bombo *(mujer embarazada)* ■ ponerse como un globo to balloon out ➤ Está (embarazada) de ocho meses y tiene un buen bombo. ■ Está (embarazada) de ocho meses y se está poniendo como un globo. She's eight months pregnant and really ballooning out.

tener (un) buen oído para... to have a good ear for... ➤ (Ella) tiene (un) buen oído para la música. She has a good ear for music. ➤ (Él) tiene (un) buen oído para los idiomas. He has a good ear for languages.

tener un buen palmito *(subido de tono)* to have a nice little butt ■ to have a nice ass

tener un cacao mental ■ tener un quilombo en la cabeza to be in a fog ■ not to know whether one is coming or going ➤ Tiene un cacao mental. He's in a fog. ■ He doesn't know whether he's coming or going.

tener un comienzo avanzado ■ comenzar avanzado ■ salir con ventaja (en una carrera) to get a head start ■ to have a head start

tener un corazón blando ■ ser blando de corazón to be tender hearted

tener un corazón de oro to have a heart of gold ■ to be golden hearted

tener un detalle contigo to give you a present ■ to give you a gift ➤ Mi familia quiere tener un detalle contigo. My family wants to give you a present. ■ My family wants to give you a gift.

tener un dolor de garganta to have a sore throat ➤ Tengo un dolor de garganta desde que me levanté esta mañana. I've had a sore throat since I got up this morning.

tener un empacho de algo to have one's fill of something

tener un error de *(cálculo)* to be off by ■ to be in error by ➤ El cálculo de Cassini de la distancia desde la Tierra hasta el Sol tuvo un error de aproximadamente seis millones de millas. Cassini's 1677 estimate of the distance from the Earth to the sun was off by about six million miles. ■ Cassini's 1677 estimate of the distance from the Earth to the sun was in error by about six million miles.

tener un golpe de suerte to have a stroke of luck ■ to get lucky

tener un gran impacto sobre alguien to have a great influence on someone

tener un hambre canina to be hungry as a bear

tener un hijo en camino ■ tener un bebé en camino ■ estar esperando un hijo ■ estar esperando un bebé to have a child on the way ■ to have a baby on the way ■ to be expecting a child ■ to be expecting a baby

tener un hueco para ver a alguien to get by to see someone ■ to go by to see someone ■ to go by and see someone

tener un humor de perros to be in a bad mood

tener un hijo enfermo to have a sick child ■ (for) one's child to be sick ➤ Tengo la hija enferma. My daughter is sick.

tener un interés creado to have an ax to grind

tener un interés personal ■ actuar de manera interesada to have an ax to grind

tener un lío con alguien to have an affair with someone

tener un montón de cosas que decirle a alguien to have a lot of things to tell someone ▪ to have a whole bunch of things to tell someone

tener un muy mal concepto de to have a poor opinion of ▪ to have a low opinion of

tener un niño de camino to have a child on the way ▪ to have a baby on the way

tener un par de cojones *(ligeramente subido de tono)* ▪ tener un par de huevos ▪ tenerlos bien puestos ▪ tenerlos en su sitio to have balls

tener un par de huevos *(subido de tono)* ▪ tener un par de cojones ▪ tenerlos bien puestos ▪ tenerlos en su sitio to have balls

tener un pedo atravesado en la cabeza *(subido de tono)* ▪ tener tremendo pedo atravesado en la cabeza ▪ tener un pedón atravesado en la cabeza ▪ tener mierda en la cabeza to have shit for brains ▪ *(alternativa benigna)* not to have the sense God gave an animal cracker

tener un pico de oro ▪ tener un piquito de oro ▪ tener (mucha) labia to have the gift of gab

tener un pinchazo 1. to have a flat (tire) 2. *(figurativo)* to fail

tener un piquito de oro ▪ tener un pico de oro ▪ tener (mucha) labia to have the gift of gab

tener un plan 1. to have a plan 2. *(tener perspectivas de sexo)* to have a hot date

tener un pluriempleo to work two jobs ▪ to moonlight ▪ to have a second job

tener un polvo to be a hot number ▪ to be (sexually) hot ➤ Esa tía rubia tiene un polvo. That blond chick is a hot number. ▪ That blond chick is really hot.

tener un porrazo to have an accident ▪ to have a crash

tener un pronto to have a quick temper

tener un quilombo en la cabeza ▪ tener un cacao mental not to know whether one is coming or going ➤ Tiene un quilombo en la cabeza. He doesn't know whether he's coming or going.

tener un ramalazo to be effeminate

tener un saber de to have a knowledge of

tener un sentimiento inquietante acerca de algo to have an uneasy feeling about something

tener un sueño muy ligero to be a very light sleeper

tener un tema *(Esp., coloquial)* ▪ tener un plan to have a hot date

tener un tipo bonito to have a good figure

tener un tomate to have a ruckus ▪ to have a flap ▪ to have a problem

tener una altitud baja to be at a low elevation ▪ to be close to sea level

tener una altitud elevada to be at a high elevation ▪ to be high above sea level

tener una boca como un buzón (de correos) 1. tener la boca grande ▪ darle un bocado a un cartón y sacar una visera to have a big mouth 2. ser un bocazas to be a big mouth

tener una bronca formada to pitch a fit ▪ to have a fit ▪ to throw a fit

tener una buena comunicación con alguien to have a good rapport with someone

tener una buena educación ▪ ser muy culto to have a good education ▪ to be well educated

tener una buena relación to have a good relationship

tener una cabeza bien amueblada to have one's head on straight ▪ to have it together ▪ to have (really) got it together

tener una cabeza privilegiada ▪ tener un cráneo privilegiado 1. to have a lot on the ball 2. *(con sarcasmo)* ▪ tener un cabezón to be pigheaded ▪ to be unreasonably obstinate

tener una calva to have a bald spot

tener una carrera to have a race ➤ Vamos a tener una carrera de cien metros lisos mañana a las nueve. We are having a hundred-yard dash tomorrow at nine. ▪ There's going to be a hundred-yard dash tomorrow at nine.

tener una cita con alguien 1. *(social o negocio)* quedar con alguien to have an appointment with someone 2. *(con potencial romántico)* to have a date with someone

tener una conexión fuerte con una audiencia to have audience appeal ➤ El organista Virgil Fox tenía una conexión fuerte con audiencias de jóvenes. The organist Virgil Fox had a tremendous audience appeal with young people.

tener una corazonada que ▪ latirle a uno que to have a hunch that

tener una cosa en la punta de la lengua to have something on the tip of one's tongue

tener una cosa entre manos ▪ llevar una cosa entre manos to have a deal going ▪ to be working on something ▪ to have a deal in progress ➤ Tenemos una venta de diez mil unidades entre manos. ▪ Tenemos entre manos una venta de diez mil unidades. We've got a deal going for ten thousand units.

tener una discusión to have an argument

tener una espina clavada en el corazón to have a heartache ▪ to have an aching heart

tener una extracción dental ▪ sacarse un diente ▪ sacarse una muela to have a tooth extracted ▪ to have a tooth pulled

tener una gran salida to be off to a good start ▪ to get off to a good start ➤ Ha tenido una gran salida. He's off to a good start.

tener una mala racha 1. to be down on one's luck 2. to be going through a difficult time

tener una mentalidad abierta to be open-minded ▪ to have an open mind

tener una mentalidad cerrada to be close-minded ▪ to have a closed mind

tener una noción del vocabulario to have a smattering of vocabulary ➤ Tengo sólo una noción de vocabulario japonés. ▪ Tengo sólo una noción del vocabulario de japonés. I have just a smattering of Japanese vocabulary. ▪ I have just a smattering of the vocabulary of Japanese.

tener una panorámica a vista de pájaro to have a bird's-eye view ▪ to get a bird's-eye view

tener una puntuación de quinientos en el examen TOEFL ▪ sacar quinientos en el examen TOEFL to score five hundred on the TOEFL test

tener una racha de (buena) suerte 1. to be having a streak of (good) luck ▪ to get lucky 2. to be having a winning streak ▪ to be on a winning streak

tener una reputación local to have a local reputation ▪ to be well known around town ▪ *(coloquial)* to be the big fish in a little pond

tener (una) respuesta ▪ contestarle to hear (back) from someone ▪ to receive an answer from somone ▪ to get back to someone ➤ No he tenido (una) respuesta todavía. ▪ No me han contestado todavía. I haven't heard (back) from them yet. ▪ I haven't received an answer from them yet. ▪ They haven't gotten back to me yet.

tener una reunión to have a meeting

tener una rodada suave to have a smooth ride

tener una sola oportunidad para to have only one chance to ▪ to have only one opportunity to

tener una sonrisa de oreja en oreja to grin from ear to ear

tener una visión global ▪ tener perspectiva sobre un asunto ▪ tener perspectiva de un asunto to get the big picture ▪ to see things in perspective ▪ to grasp the implications of a matter

tener unas buenas glándulas mamarias *(subido de tono)* ▪ tener unas buenas domingas ▪ estar que se sale to have big boobs ▪ to be stacked ▪ *(muy subido de tono)* to be built like a brick shithouse

tener unas vistas a algo ▪ tener unas vistas hacia algo ▪ tener unas vistas de algo ▪ ofrecer una vista de algo to have a view of something ▪ to afford a view of something ▪ to command a view of something ➤ The house commands a fine view of the river and woodlands. La casa tiene unas vistas preciosas del río y de los bosques.

tener vacaciones to have a vacation ➤ ¿Vas a tener vacaciones en Navidad?-Ojalá las tuviera. Do you have a vacation at Christmas time?-I sure wish I did. ▪ Do you have a vacation at Christmas time?-I sure hope so.

tener vergüenza ▪ darle vergüenza to be ashamed

tener vida propia to have a life of its own

tener vista para ▪ ser avispado(-a) to be shrewd in ▪ to be shrewd when it comes to

tener *x* años ▪ contar *x* años ▪ *(coloquial)* tener *x* tacos to be *x* years old ➤ Tiene treinta años. He's 30 years old.

tener *x* años de antigüedad to be *x* years old ➤ La catedral tiene quinientos años de antigüedad. The cathedral is five hundred years old.

tener *x* años luz de un extremo a otro 1. to be *x* light-years across 2. ser del diámetro de *x* años luz to be *x* light-years in diameter ➤ La Vía Láctea tiene trescientos mil años luz de un extremo al otro. ▪ El diametro de la Vía Láctea es de trescientos mil años luz. The Milky Way is three hundred thousand light-years across. ▪ The Milky Way is three hundred thousand light-years in diameter.

tener *x* faltas 1. to have *x* errors ▪ to have *x* mistakes 2. *(deportes)* ▪ tener *x* fallos to have *x* fouls

tener *x* faltas de asistencia to be absent *x* times ▪ to have *x* absences

tener *x* metro(s) de longitud to be *x* meter(s) long ▪ to be *x* meter(s) in length

tenerla tomada con alguien ▪ tenerle declarada la guerra ▪ tenerle ganas to have it in for somebody

tenerlas bien puestas *(eufemismo)* ▪ tener huevos ▪ tener cojones to have balls ▪ to have guts

tenerle a alguien de hijo to be at someone's beck and call ▪ to have someone at one's beck and call ➤ El jefe me tiene de hijo. The boss has me at his beck and call. ➤ El jefe lo tiene de hijo. ▪ *(Esp., leísmo)* El jefe le tiene de hijo. He's at the boss' beck and call. ➤ El jefe la tiene de hija. The boss has her at his beck and call.

tenerle a alguien en alta estima en su libro ▪ dejarle bien (parado) en su libro to rate high in someone's book ➤ Ella no le tiene en alta estima en su libro. He doesn't rate very high in her book.

tenerle agarrado por los cojones *(Esp., leísmo)* ▪ tenerlo agarrado por las pelotas to have someone by the balls ▪ to have got someone by the balls

tenerle bien enseñado(-a) a alguien *(el camarero, p.ej.)* ▪ tenerle bien amaestrado to have (got) someone trained ➤ Le tengo al camarero bien enseñado. I've got the waiter trained. ▪ I have the waiter trained.

tenerle bronca a alguien to have it in for someone

tenerle cariño a alguien to feel affection for someone ▪ to be attached to someone

tenerle informado(-a) ▪ mantenerle informado(-a) to keep someone informed

tenerle inquina a alguien *(literario)* ▪ tomarle manía a alguien to have a grudge against someone ▪ to feel ill-will toward someone

tenerle inquina a alguien por algo ▪ tenerle tirria a alguien por algo ▪ tenerle manía a alguien por algo ▪ guardarle rencor a alguien por algo to bear a grudge against someone for something ▪ to harbor a grudge against someone for something ▪ to nurse a grudge against someone for something ▪ to have a grudge against someone for something

tenerle manía a alguien to dislike someone intensely ▪ not to be able to stand someone ➤ Le tengo manía a él. I can't stand him. ▪ I intensely dislike him. ➤ Le tengo manía a ella. I can't stand her. ▪ I intensely dislike her.

tenerle por turista to think someone is a ▪ to take someone for ➤ Te tienen por turista. They think you're a tourist. ▪ They take you for a tourist.

tenerle preocupado(-a) to have someone worried ➤ Su silencio me tiene preocupado. *(de él)* His silence has me worried. ▪ *(de ella)* Her silence has me worried.

tenerle tirria a alguien por algo ▪ tenerle inquina a alguien por algo ▪ tenerle manía a alguien por algo ▪ guardarle rencor a alguien por algo to bear a grudge against someone for something ▪ to harbor a grudge against someone for something ▪ to nurse a grudge against someone for something ▪ to have a grudge against someone for something

tenerlo decidido to have one's mind made up ➤ Todavía no lo tengo decidido. I still haven't made up my mind.

tenerlo en el bote to have it in the bag ▪ to have it all sewn up ▪ to have it sewn up

tenerlo en la punta de la lengua to be (right) on the tip of one's tongue ➤ Lo tengo en la punta de la lengua. It's on the tip of my tongue. ▪ It's right on the tip of my tongue.

tenerlo merecido to have it coming

tenerlos bien puestos ▪ tenerlos en su sitio ▪ tener un par de huevos ▪ tener un par de cojones to have balls

tenerlos en su sitio ▪ tenerlos bien puestos ▪ tener un par de huevos ▪ tener un par de cojones to have balls

tenerse por descendiente de alguien to claim to be a descendent of someone

tenerse que fastidiar to have to put up with it

tenérselo creído ▪ ser vanidoso to be conceited ▪ *(coloquial)* to be stuck up ➤ (Ella) se lo tiene creído. ▪ Es vanidosa. She's conceited. ▪ She's stuck up.

tengamos la fiesta en paz cut it out! ▪ none of that! ▪ cool it! ▪ enough of that!

tengo algo en el ojo ▪ me entró algo en el ojo ▪ *(Méx.)* se me cayó algo en el ojo I got something in my eye ▪ I have something in my eye

tengo algunas ideas sobre... 1. I have some ideas about... 2. I have some thoughts about...

tengo algunas ideas sobre eso 1. I have some ideas about that 2. I have some thoughts about that

tengo algunas opiniones sobre eso I have some opinions about that ▪ I have some thoughts about that

tengo ansias de verte ▪ estoy ansioso por verte I'm anxious to see you

tengo carro *(Esp.)* ▪ tengo carro I have a car ▪ I own a car ▪ I've got a car

tengo dinero I have some money ▪ I've got some money

tengo dos noticias, una buena y una mala I have some good news and some bad news

tengo el deber de it is my duty to ▪ I have the obligation to

tengo entendido que... I understand that...

tengo ideas encontradas al respecto I'm of two minds about that

tengo la impresión contraria I have the opposite impression

tengo la impresión de que se me olvida algo ▪ tengo la impresión de que se me pasa algo I have the feeling I'm forgetting something

tengo la impresión en mis adentros I (can) feel it in my bones

tengo la sensación de que... ▪ tengo la impresión de que... ▪ me da la impresión de que... I have the feeling that...

tengo más hambre que el perro de un ciego I'm hungry as a bear

tengo mis razones I have my reasons

tengo mis sospechas I have my suspicions ➤ No sé quién atasca el fregadero continuamente, pero tengo mis sospechas. I don't know who's stopping up the sink all the time, but I have my suspicions.

tengo mucho gusto en ello I'll be glad to

tengo por objetivo my objective is

tengo que admitir ▪ debo admitir ▪ he de admitir I must admit ▪ I have to admit

tengo que apurarme *(L.am.)* ▪ tengo que darme prisa I've got to hurry ▪ I have to hurry

tengo que darme prisa *(Esp.)* ▪ tengo que apurarme I've got to hurry ▪ I have to hurry

tengo que irme I have to go ▪ I have to leave

tengo que volver allí I have to go back there ▪ I have to return there

¿tengo razón? ▪ ¿estoy en lo cierto? ▪ ¿estoy en lo correcto? am I right? ▪ am I correct?

tengo sentimientos encontrados sobre... I have mixed feelings about...

tengo un amigo que... I have a friend who...

tengo un dolor de cabeza ▪ me duele la cabeza I have a headache

tengo un juicio I have to go to court

tengo un lío de papeles ▪ tengo los papeles hechos un lío my papers are in a mess

tengo una barba desde hace cinco años I have had a beard for five years ▪ I've had a beard for five years

tengo una cita esta noche ▪ voy a salir con alguien esta noche I have a date tonight

tengo una idea ▪ se me ocurre una idea I have an idea ▪ I've got an idea

tengo una inquietud ▪ tengo una preocupación I have a concern

tengo (yo) la culpa si... can I help it if...? ▪ is it my fault if...?

tenía el deber de 1. *(yo)* it was my duty to 2. *(él)* it was his duty to 3. *(ella)* it was her duty to 4. *(usted)* it was your duty to

tenía la culpa 1. *(yo)* it was my fault 2. *(él)* it was his fault 3. *(ella)* it was her fault 4. *(usted)* it was your fault

tenía la esperanza de saber de ti a estas alturas I had hoped to hear from you by now ▪ I was hoping to hear from you by now

tenía la intención de decir que... I meant to say (that)...

tenía la intención de decirte que... I meant to tell you (that)...

tenía la intención de preguntarte... I meant to ask you...

tenías que haber oído... you should have heard...

tenía que haber traído mi abrigo ▪ debería haber traído mi abrigo I should have worn my coat

tenías que haberme llamado ▪ deberías haberme llamado you were supposed to call me ➤ Tenías que haberme llamado esta mañana, pero si lo hiciste, no me enteré. ▪ Tenías que haberme llamado esta mañana, pero si lo hiciste, no me di cuenta. You were supposed to call me this morning, but if you did, I'm not aware of it.

teniente de alcalde vice mayor

tensar un arco to draw a bow ▪ to draw back a bowstring ▪ to draw a bowstring back ➤ Robin Hood colocó una flecha en la cuerda y tensó el arco. ▪ Robin Hood puso una flecha en la cuerda y tensó el arco. Robin Hood placed an arrow on the string and drew the bow.

tensión alta: tener la ~ to have high blood pressure

tensión baja: tener la ~ to have low blood pressure

la **tensión se ha reducido** tensions have been reduced ▪ tensions have lessened

tentar a la suerte to tempt fate ▪ to press one's luck ➤ ¡No tientes a la suerte! Don't press your luck! ▪ Don't tempt fate. ➤ Vamos a esperar el semáforo. No quiero tentar a la suerte con mi rodilla. Let's wait for the light. I don't want to tempt fate with my knee.

tentativa de asesinato attempted murder ▪ attempted homicide

tentativa de suicidio suicide attempt ▪ attempted suicide

un **tente en pie** ▪ tentempié snack ▪ something to hold you over ▪ a little something to give you a lift

estar **teñido de sangre** to be bloodstained

teñirse el pelo ▪ teñirse el cabello to dye one's hair ➤ Sr. Stewart le dio la vena y se tiñó el pelo de verde. Sr. Stewart upped and dyed his hair green.

teoría de conjuntos *(matemática y lógica)* set theory

teoría de Copérnico Copernican theory ▪ theory of Copernicus ➤ La teoría de Copérnico afirma que el Sol, y no la Tierra, es el centro del sistema planetario. Copernican theory asserts that the Sun, and not the Earth, is the center of the planetary system.

teoría de cuerdas *(física)* string theory

teoría y la práctica theory and practice ▪ theory and fact ➤ No sólo en la teoría sino en la práctica. Not just in theory but in practice. ▪ Not just in theory but in fact.

terapia genética gene therapy

tercer curso: estar en el ~ to be in the third grade

tercer mundo third world

tercera edad: ser de la ~ to be over sixty-five

la **tercera parte** one third ▪ a third

tercera persona third party ▪ third person

tercero en discordia three's a crowd

ser el **tercero en discordia** to be the odd man out

terciar con alguien to have a word with someone

terciarse el rifle a la espalda to sling the rifle on one's back

ser **terco como una mula** to be stubborn as a mule

tergiversar la historia to distort history

tergiversar la verdad to distort the truth ▪ to twist the truth

la **terminación del título de uno** ▪ (la) finalización del título de uno completion of one's (academic) degree

terminar algo al cien por cien finalizar algo al cien por cien to finish completely

terminar con to put an end to

terminar con alguien ▪ cortar con alguien ▪ romper con alguien to break up with someone ▪ to break off one's relationship ▪ to split up ➤ Jill terminó con su novio. Jill broke up with her boyfriend. ➤ Han terminado. ▪ Han cortado. ▪ Han roto. They broke up. ▪ They've broken up.

terminar (con) la discriminación to end discrimination

terminar de to stop short of

terminar de hacer algo ▪ acabar de hacer algo to finish doing something ➤ Hemos terminado de cenar hace un momento. ▪ Acabamos de cenar hace un momento. We just finished eating supper (a short time ago). ▪ We just finished supper (a few minutes ago).

terminar diciendo to conclude by saying ▪ to finish by saying

terminar el diploma de estudios avanzados (DEA) ▪ acabar el diploma de estudios avanzados ▪ terminar el master ▪ acabar el master 1. to complete a master's ▪ to finish a master's 2. diplomarse en estudios avanzados to get a master's

terminar el doctorado 1. acabar el doctorado to finish one's doctorate ▪ to finish one's doctoral degree ▪ to complete one's doctorate

terminar en una calle ▪ morir en una calle to end at a street ▪ to tee into a street ➤ La Avenida de los Shiris termina en la Avenida Seis de Diciembre. ▪ La Avenida de los Shiris muere en la Avenida Seis de Diciembre. La Avenida de los Shiris ends at Avenida Seis de Diciembre. ▪ La Avenida de los Shiris tees into Avenida Seis de Diciembre.

terminar el master 1. acabar el master ▪ terminar el diploma de estudios avanzados (DEA) ▪ acabar el diploma de estudios avanzados (DEA) to complete one's master's (degree) ▪ to finish one's master's (degree) 2. diplomarse en estudios avanzados to get a master's (degree)

terminar en agua de borrajas ▪ quedar en agua de borrajas to come to nothing ▪ to fizzle ▪ (for) nothing to come of it ➤ Terminó en agua de borrajas. Nothing came of it.

terminar en una calle ▪ morir en una calle ▪ hacer una T en una calle to end at a street ▪ to tee into a street ➤ La Avenida de los Shyris termina en la Avenida Seis de Diciembre. Shyris Avenue ends at Sixth of December Avenue. ▪ Shyris Avenue tees into Sixth of December Avenue.

terminar la licenciatura ▪ acabar la licenciatura 1. to complete one's bachelor's (degree) ▪ to finish one's bachelor's (degree) 2. licenciarse to get a bachelor's (degree)

terminar leyendo to conclude by reading... ▪ to finish by reading...

terminar los estudios ▪ acabar los estudios to complete one's degree ▪ to finish one's degree

terminar un libro ▪ acabar un libro to finish reading a book ▪ to finish a book

terminarse de imprimir to be out of print

terminé I'm through ▪ I'm done

término medio: alcanzar un ~ ▪ llegar a un término medio to hit a happy medium

término medio: encontrar un ~ to find a happy medium

termómetro de hasta qué punto barometer of how much ▪ barometer of the extent to which ➤ *(noticia)* La amplitud de la victoria de Blair será un termómetro de hasta qué punto ha fracasado la apuesta conservadora de espantar a los británicos con el fantasma de Europa y su moneda. The margin of Blair's victory will be a barometer of the extent to which the conservative ploy of scaring the British with the specter of Europe and its currency has failed.

terreno abonado para hotbed of

terreno abrupto ▪ terreno quebrado ▪ terreno escabroso ▪ terreno desigual ▪ vericuetos rugged terrain ▪ uneven terrain

terreno de béisbol baseball diamond

terreno de juego playing field

terreno de hombre man's territory

terreno escabroso ▪ terreno abrupto ▪ terreno quebrado rugged terrain ▪ rough terrain ▪ uneven terrain

terreno quebrado ▪ terreno abrupto ▪ terreno desigual ▪ vericuetos uneven terrain ▪ rugged terrain

terreno resbaladizo: pisar ~ to tread on slippery ground ➤ Hablar de la política es pisar terreno resbaladizo. To talk about politics is to tread on slippery ground.

territorio inexplorado unexplored territory ■ uncharted territory

el **terrón (de azúcar)** sugar lump ■ lump of sugar

el, la **terrorista suicida** suicide bomber

test de (los) antecedentes de alguien: hacer un ~ ■ realizar un test de (los) antecedentes de alguien ■ llevar a cabo un test de (los) antecedentes de alguien to run a background check on someone ■ to do a background check on someone

testamento vital living will

testificar ante el tribunal *(Esp.)* ■ testificar ante la corte to testify in court ■ to testify before the court

testificar ante la corte *(L.am.)* ■ testificar ante el tribunal to testify in court ■ to testify before the court

ser **testigo de algo** ■ atestiguar algo to bear witness to something

testigo de cargo witness for the prosecution ■ prosecution witness

testigo de descargo ■ testigo de defensa witness for the defense ■ defense witness

ser **testigo de que...** to bear witness that... ➤ Los estudiantes eran testigos de que el profesor había cubierto la materia adecuadamente. The students bore witness that the teacher had covered the material adequately.

testigo impertinente uncooperative witness

testigo material material witness

testigo ocular ■ testigo presencial ■ testigo visual eyewitness

testigo presencial ■ testigo visual ■ testigo ocular witness on the scene ■ eyewitness

testigo principal principal witness ■ star witness

testigo visual ■ testigo ocular ■ testigo presencial eyewitness ■ witness on the scene

testimonio arrollador ■ testimonio devastador devastating testimony ➤ El testimonio fue arrollador. The testimony was devastating.

texto asequible clear textbook ■ easy-to-understand textbook ■ textbook that is easy to understand

tía abuela great aunt

tiazos del ruedo manchego *(Valle-Inclán)* dudes from around la Mancha

ser **tibio en materia de la religión** to be lukewarm toward religion

el **tic nervioso** nervous tic

el **ticket (de compra)** ■ (el) comprobante (cash register) receipt ■ ticket

¡tiempo! time out!

tiempo agradable ■ tiempo benigno balmy weather

¡tiempo al tiempo! give it some time!

tiempo al tiempo: ganar ~ to beat time ■ to race against time

tiempo aplicado the time involved

tiempo aproximado de llegada estimated time of arrival (E.T.A.)

tiempo benigno ■ tiempo agradable balmy weather ■ mild weather

tiempo cálido ■ buen tiempo ■ tiempo caluroso warm weather

tiempo caluroso ■ tiempo cálido ■ buen tiempo warm weather

tiempo completo full time

ser el **tiempo de actuar** ■ ser el momento de actuar to be time to act ➤ Es el tiempo de actuar. It is time to act. ■ It's time to act. ➤ El tiempo de actuar es ahora. The time to act is now.

tiempo de cocción cooking time

tiempo de compás ■ (el) golpe de compás ■ ritmo de la música beat of the music

tiempo de hacer algo time to do something ➤ ¿Tenemos tiempo de ir por una cerveza? Do we have time to go for a beer?

tiempo de ocio leisure time

tiempo de perros ■ mal tiempo ■ intemperie bad weather ■ miserable weather ■ *(coloquial)* lousy weather

tiempo de respuesta response time ➤ ¿Por qué es el tiempo de respuesta tan lento? Why is the response time so slow?

tiempo de secado drying time

tiempo desapacible awful weather

tiempo es oro time is money

tiempo establecido time allotted ➤ El tiempo establecido para el examen es dos horas. The time allotted for the test is two hours.

tiempo frío cold weather

tiempo libre ■ ratos libres free time ■ spare time

tiempo lluvioso rainy spell

el **tiempo lo dirá** ■ dale tiempo al tiempo time will tell

tiempo muerto *(deportes)* time out

tiempo para el destino time to destination ■ time remaining until arrival

tiempo para hacer algo: tener ~ to have time to do something ➤ ¿Tenemos tiempo para ir a tomar una cerveza? Do we have time to go for a beer?

ser **tiempo perdido** to be time lost ■ to be time wasted ■ *(especialmente en el pasado)* to be a waste of time

tiempo perfecto 1. tiempo compuesto perfect tense ■ compound tense **2.** momento perfecto perfect time ■ perfect moment

tiempo perro miserable weather ➤ Hace un tiempo perro. The weather is miserable.

tiempo que emplea time it takes ➤ Un año es el tiempo que emplea la Tierra en dar una vuelta alrededor del Sol. A year is the time it takes the Earth to go around the sun. ■ A year is the time it takes the Earth to circle the sun.

tiempo radiante ■ clima maravilloso beautiful weather ■ magnificent weather ■ wall-to-wall sunshine ➤ El tiempo está radiante hoy. ■ El clima está maravilloso hoy. The weather is beautiful today. ■ The weather is magnificent today. ■ It's wall-to-wall sunshine today.

tiempo restante ■ tiempo que queda time remaining ■ time left ➤ Por el tiempo restante, responderé preguntas de la audiencia. For the time remaining, I'll take some questions from the audience. ➤ *(profesor a los estudiantes que hacen un examen)* Les quedan diez minutos. You have ten minutes (left). ■ There are ten minutes left. ■ There are ten minutes remaining.

el **tiempo se acaba** ■ se acaba el tiempo time is running out

el **tiempo que haga falta para...** ■ el tiempo que sea necesario para however long it takes to...

el **tiempo que sea necesario para...** ■ el tiempo que haga falta para however long it takes to...

tiempo restante time remaining

el **tiempo se le acaba a alguien** time is running out for someone ■ someone's time is running out

tiempo sombrío bleak weather

tiempo todo lo cura time heals all wounds

tiempo tormentoso stormy weather

tiempo transcurrido elapsed time

el **tiempo vuela** time flies

tiempos de Maricastaña: en los ~ eons ago ■ back in the dark ages

tienda de ultramarinos ■ tienda de comestibles grocery store

tienda libre de impuestos duty-free shop ■ duty-free store

tiene cara de (ponerse a) llover ■ tiene pinta de llover it looks like it's going to rain

tiene cierta musicalidad it has a ring to it ■ there's a ring to it

tiene muchas maneras de entenderla *(referido a una canción)* there are a lot of ways to interpret it

tiene que haber... 1. *(singular)* there has to be... **2.** *(plural)* there have to be...

tiene que haber de todo ■ de todo hay en la viña del Señor it takes all kinds (to make a world)

tiene que haber habido there has to have been ■ there have to have been

tiene que haberlo there has to be (one)

tiene que haberlos there have to be

tiene que ocurrir it's bound to happen ■ it has to happen ■ it's going to happen

tiene sentido para mí ■ para mí, tiene sentido it makes sense to me

tiene tan mal vestir, que hasta la ropa se le quiere ir he dresses so badly that even his clothes try to get away from him

tiene (una) pinta... 1. *(él)* he's handsome ▪ he's good-looking ▪ he's dynamite 2. *(ella)* she's beautiful ▪ she's good-looking ▪ she's a fox
¿tiene (usted) carro? do you have a car? ▪ do you own a car?
¿tiene (usted) hora? ▪ ¿me da usted la hora? do you have the time? ▪ have you got the time?
¿tiene (usted) tiempo para...? ▪ ¿le da (a usted) tiempo a...? do you have time to...?
tiene ya it now has ➤ El diccionario tiene ya más de ochenta mil voces. The dictionary now has more than eighty thousand entries.
¿tienes coche? do you have a car? ▪ do you own a car?
¿tienes cosquillas? are you ticklish?
¿tienes fuego? ▪ ¿me das fuego? do you have a light? ▪ have you got a light?
¿tienes fuerzas? are you up to it? ▪ are you up for it?
¿tienes hora? ▪ ¿me das la hora? do you have the time? ▪ have you got the time?
¡tienes que matizar! clean up your act!
¡tienes razón! ▪ ¡estás en lo cierto! ▪ ¡estás en lo correcto! you're right!
¿tienes tiempo para...? ▪ ¿te da tiempo a...? do you have time to...?
¡tienes toda la razón! ▪ ¡estás en lo cierto! ▪ ¡tienes razón! right you are! ▪ you're exactly right! ▪ you're right!
tienes un aspecto fenomenal you look great ▪ you look wonderful
tierra de nadie no man's land
tierra dura ▪ paisaje adusto ▪ paisaje desolado desolate terrain ▪ bleak terrain ▪ desolate countryside ▪ bleak countryside
tierra firme terra firma ▪ dry land
tierra sagrada hallowed ground
tierra sin cultivar ▪ (el) erial ▪ eriazo uncultivated land ▪ untilled land
¡tierra, trágame! ▪ ¡trágame tierra! I just want to go run and hide, I feel so embarrassed! ▪ I just want to disappear, I feel so embarrassed!
Tierras de penumbra *(título de película) Shadow Lands*
tierras de ultramar lands across the sea ▪ lands over the sea
tierras lejanas distant lands ▪ far-off lands ▪ faraway lands
estar **tieso como un palo** to be stiff as a board
tieso y parejo flat out
tildar de ▪ tachar de to label someone as ➤ Los videntes de Elvis se exponen a ser tildados de dementes. Elvis sighters risk being labeled insane.
ser **timado(-a) por alguien** ▪ ser estafado(-a) por alguien to be cheated by someone ▪ to be ripped off by someone ▪ to be taken in by someone
timar a alguien to rip off someone ▪ to rip someone off
el **timón de profundidad** *(aeronáutica)* horizontal stabilizer ▪ elevator
el **tinte para madera** ▪ (el) colorante wood stain ▪ stain
tinta apenas se había secado y... ink had barely dried when... ▪ ink was barely dry when... ▪ ink had barely dried before... ➤ La tinta apenas se había secado en el acuerdo entre los países y los firmantes ya empezaban a atacar el acuerdo. The ink had barely dried on the agreement between the two counties when the signatories started attacking it.
tinte racista: tener un ~ to have a racist tinge ▪ to be tinged with racism
tinto de verano *(Esp.)* ▪ vino tinto con gaseosa red wine spritzer
tío abuelo ▪ tío segundo great uncle
tío cachas beefcake ▪ hunk
tío formidable great guy ▪ awesome dude
tío genial ▪ tío estupendo ▪ tío cojonudo ▪ tío brillante great guy ▪ awesome dude
¡tío lila! you old fool!
tío(-a) segundo(-a) *(primo(-a) hermano(-a) del padre o de la madre de uno)* first cousin once removed
tipo de cambio exchange rate ▪ rate of exchange ➤ ¿Cuál es el tipo de cambio de la euro al dólar hoy? What is the euro-to-dollar exchange rate today?
tipo de letra type style
tipo duro tough guy
tipo medio average person
tipo solitario loner ▪ lone wolf ➤ Es en esencia un tipo solitario. He's basically a loner.
¡tira! *(al conductor de un carro)* go!
¡tira a la derecha! turn right! ▪ *(jerga)* hang a right!
¡tira a la izquierda! turn left! ▪ *(jerga)* hang a left!
tira adelante *(Esp.)* ▪ sigue adelante ▪ dale para adelante go straight ahead ▪ keep going straight (ahead)
tira cómica ▪ historieta comic strip
tira de amigos: tener la ~ ▪ tener un montón de amigos to have thousands of friends ➤ Tiene la tira de amigos. He has thousands of friends.
tira de beicon *(Esp.)* slice of bacon ▪ rasher of bacon
tira de película roll of film ▪ strip of film ▪ *(de rayos X)* radiographic film
tira de sellos roll of stamps *(literalmente un "rollo de sellos")*
tira de tocineta *(Sudamérica)* slice of bacon ▪ rasher of bacon
tira de tocino *(Méx.)* slice of bacon ▪ rasher of bacon
tira magnética magnetic strip
¡tira, tira! harder, harder!
tirada de un libro printing of a book ➤ La primera tirada fue de diez mil ejemplares. The first printing was ten thousand copies.
tirada de un periódico circulation of a newspaper
ser un(-a) **tirador(-a) certero(-a)** to be a good shot ▪ to be a crack shot
tirador de béisbol baseball pitcher
tirador(-a) de poca calidad poor shot ➤ Es tirador de poca calidad. He's a poor shot.
tirador(-a) experto(-a) expert marksman ▪ crack shot
tirando getting by ▪ so-so ▪ pretty good ➤ ¿Qué tal?-¡Tirando! How are you doing?-(I'm) getting by.
estar **tirante con alguien** to have a strained relationship with someone ▪ (for) a relationship to be strained ▪ (for) relations to be strained ➤ Estamos algo tirantes. Relations between us are strained.
tirar a ▪ tender a to verge on ▪ to border on ▪ to incline towards
tirar a amarillo to be yellowish
tirar a azul to be bluish
tirar a la borda ▪ echar a la borda to throw overboard
tirar a la chuña to squander
tirar a rojo to be reddish
tirar abajo la puerta ▪ tirar la puerta abajo to break down the door ▪ to break the door down ➤ Los agentes tiraron abajo la puerta. ▪ Los agentes tiraron la puerta abajo. The police officers broke down the door. ▪ The police officers broke the door down. ➤ Los agentes tiraron abajo la puerta del apartamento sospechoso. The police officers broke down the door of the suspects' apartment. ➤ Los agentes la tiraron. The police officers broke it down.
tirar adelante to go straight (ahead) ▪ to keep going straight ahead
tirar al amarillo to be yellowish
tirar al azul to be bluish
tirar al balón 1. chutar al balón ▪ darle al balón to kick the ball 2. arrojar el balón to throw the ball
tirar al gol to shoot for a goal
tirar al rojo to be reddish
tirar algo por la borda ▪ echar algo por borda to throw something overboard
tirar chinas a algo to throw rocks at something
tirar de to tear off
tirar de algo *(coloquial)* ▪ darle a algo to hit something (pretty hard) ▪ to use something ▪ to resort to something ➤ Cuando quiero mantenerme despierto para estudiar, tiro de café. ▪ Cuando quiero mantenerme despierto para estudiar, le doy al café. When I have to stay up late to study, I hit the coffee (pretty hard). ➤ Cuando me quedo sin efectivo, tiro de tarjeta de crédito. ▪ Cuando me quedo sin efectivo, le doy a la tarjeta. When I'm out of cash, I hit the credit cards. ▪ When I'm out of cash, I resort to plastic.
tirar de bebida to hit the bottle (to forget one's troubles) ▪ to drink (as an escape) ▪ to resort to drink

tirar de la manta ■ levantar la liebre ■ descubrir el pastel ■ tirar el diablo de la manta to let the cat out of the bag
tirar de la palanca ■ jalar la palanca to pull the lever
tirar el arado to pull the plow
tirar la casa por la ventana ■ echar la casa por la ventana to put the big pot in the little one ■ to shoot the moon ■ to go all out ■ to spare no expense
tirar la descargada *(Valle-Inclán)* to cheat
tirar la pelota 1. arrojar la pelota ■ lanzar la pelota to pitch the ball 2. dar a la pelota ■ chutar a la pelota to kick the ball
tirar la piedra y esconder la mano to be a snake in the grass ➤ Él tira la piedra y esconde la mano. He's a snake in the grass.
tirar la primera piedra ■ arrojar la primera piedra to cast the first stone
tirar la puerta abajo ■ tirar abajo la puerta to break the door down ■ to break down the door
tirar la toalla ■ arrojar la toalla ■ arrojar la esponja to throw in the towel
tirar los tejos a alguien ■ tirar los trastos a alguien to make a pass at someone ■ to come on to someone ■ to hit on someone
tirar piedras contra to throw stones at ■ to throw rocks at
tirar piedras contra el propio tejado ■ arrojar piedras contra el propio tejado to bite the hand that feeds you
tirar piedras contra su (propio) tejado ■ arrojar piedras contra su (propio) tejado to bite the hand that feeds you
tirar un arado to pull a plow
tirar un avión ■ derribar un avión to shoot down an airplane ■ to down an airplane ➤ Tiraron una avioneta civil. ■ Derribaron una avioneta civil. They shot down a civilian light airplane.
tirar un edificio ■ derrumbar un edificio to tear down a building ■ to tear a building down ■ to raze a building ➤ Tiraron el edificio. ■ Derrumbaron el edificio. They tore down the building. ■ They tore the building down. ■ They razed the building. ➤ Lo tiraron. ■ Lo derrumbaron. They tore it down. ■ They razed it.
tirar una calle to take a street ■ to go up a street ■ to go down a street ➤ *(tú)* ¡Tira esa calle! ■ *(usted)* ¡Tire esa calle! Take that street! ■ Go up that street! ■ Go down that street!
tirar una copa de vino to knock over a glass of wine ■ to turn over a glass of wine ■ to overturn a glass of wine
tirar una oportunidad to blow a chance ■ to lose another opportunity ➤ *(titular)* Madrid tira otra oportunidad en Atenas. Madrid blows another chance in Athens.
tirar una salva ■ lanzar una ráfaga to fire a volley of shots
tirarle de la lengua a alguien to try to get someone to talk ■ to try to get information from someone ■ to try to elicit information from someone ■ to try to draw someone out
tirarle flores a alguien to praise someone ■ to sing someone's praises ■ to say complimentary things about someone
tirarle un mordisco a alguien *(perro)* to snap at someone
tirarlo contra to throw it at ➤ Ella lo tiró conta él. She threw it at him.
tirarse a alguien *(subida de tono)* to lay someone ■ to screw someone ■ to get laid
tirarse a la piscina to take the plunge
tirarse de cabeza to dive in head first
tirarse días con ■ pasarse días con ■ estarse días con to go for days on
tirarse el pisto ■ tirarse el moco ■ tirarse el folio ■ tirarse el pegote ■ tirarse el rollo ■ enrollarse 1. to lighten up ■ to loosen up 2. to brag ■ to lay it on too thick ■ to blab ■ to harp ■ to shoot one's mouth off ➤ Venga, hombre, tírate el pisto y déjame la moto. C'mon, man, lighten up, and lend me your motorcycle. ■ C'mon, man, loosen up, and lend me your motorcycle.
tirarse en trineo: ir a ~ to go sleigh riding
tirarse meses con ■ pasarse meses con ■ estarse meses con to go for months on ➤ Mark Twain dijo que podía tirarse meses con un buen cumplido. ■ Mark Twain dijo que podía pasarse meses con un buen cumplido. ■ Mark Twain dijo que podía estarse meses con un buen cumplido. Mark Twain said he could go for months on a good compliment.
tirarse por cabeza to dive in head first
tirarse semanas con ■ pasarse semanas con ■ estarse semanas con to go for weeks on
tirarse un cuesco ■ tirarse un pedazo to cut a loud fart
tirarse un examen to flunk a test
tirarse un farol *(póquer)* ■ marcarse un farol ■ farolear ■ engañar to bluff
tirarse un pedo to cut a fart
tirarse una plancha to make a big mistake ■ to put one's foot in it
tiritas adhesivas Band-Aids ■ adhesive bandage strips
ser un **tiro al aire** not to have it together
tiro al plato ■ tiro al pichón skeetshooting
tiro con arco archery
tiro de cocaína ■ raya de cocaína ■ rayote hit of cocaine
tiro de gracia coup de grace ■ coups de grace ■ death blow
tirón de orejas: darle a alguien un ~ to tweak someone's ears
titular de justicia ■ fiscal general ■ secretario(-a) de justicia attorney general ➤ La titular de justicia Janet Reno Attorney General Janet Reno ➤ El titular de justicia Robert Kennedy Attorney General Robert Kennedy
titular de la Casa Blanca the occupant of the White House
título de degree in ➤ Un título de geólogo A degree in geology
título de licenciado ■ licenciatura bachelor's degree
(título de) licenciatura bachelor's degree
título de propiedad title deed
tiznar la reputación de alguien to stain someone's reputation ■ to damage someone's reputation
to' quisqui everybody ➤ ¡Aquí a trabajar to' quisqui! Everybody get to work!
toca irse a la cama it's bedtime
toca jugar it's time to play
¡**toca madera!** knock on wood!
estar **tocado de la cabeza** to be touched in the head
estar **tocado de (una enfermedad)** to feel (an illness) coming on
estar **tocado del ala** to be wacky ■ to have bats in one's belfry
tocar a alguien en la herida to touch someone's sensitive spot
tocar a alguien un pelo to lay a finger on someone ➤ No le toques ni un pelo. Don't (you) lay a finger on him! ➤ No se te ocurra tocarle un pelo. Don't you dare lay a finger on him.
tocar a su fin ■ llegar al final to come to an end
tocar alguna tecla ■ mover alguna cuerda to pull a few strings
tocar bailar con la más fea to be stuck holding the bag ■ to get the short end of the stick ➤ Siempre nos toca bailar con la más fea. We always get the short end of the stick.
tocar bien *(instrumento musical)* to play well
tocar de cerca a uno to hit (close to) home
tocar de oído to play by ear
tocar el ala de su sombrero to tip one's hat
tocar el cielo con las manos to experience ecstasy
tocar el claxon to honk the horn ■ to sound the horn
tocar el frente to feel one's forehead
tocar el fondo de algo to touch the bottom of something ➤ Toqué el fondo de la piscina. I touched the bottom of the swimming pool.
tocar el piano que da gusto to play the piano beautifully
tocar el timbre y echar a correr ■ jugar al rinraje ■ hacer un rinraje to ring the doorbell and run
tocar a alguien en la herida ■ meter el dedo en la llaga to touch someone's senstive spot ■ to touch someone's sore spot
tocar en lo vivo to touch a sore spot ■ to strike a nerve
tocar fondo 1. *(bolsa de valores, por ejemplo)* to hit rock bottom 2. *(depresión)* to be very depressed
tocar la batería to play (the) drums
tocar mal *(instrumento musical)* to play badly
tocar muchas teclas to try to do too many things at once
tocar tierra 1. *(avión)* to touch down ■ to land 2. *(barco)* to pull into port
tocarle a cualquier otro to be somone else's turn ➤ Respondió que fregó los platos ayer y hoy le toca a cualquier otro de sus hermanos. He answered that he washed the dishes yesterday, and today it's one of his brothers' or sisters' turn.

tocarle el mochuelo a uno ▪ tocarle la china a uno ▪ cargar con el mochuelo to get stuck doing something ▪ to get stuck with having to do something ▪ to get the short end of the stick ➤ Siempre nos toca el mochuelo de hacer las tareas de la casa. We always get stuck doing the household chores. ▪ We always get stuck with having to do the household chores.

tocarle hacer to be called upon to do ▪ to have to do ▪ to be one's turn to do

tocarle hacer algo to fall to one's lot to do something ▪ to be one's responsibility to do something ▪ to be one's turn to do something ▪ to have to do something ▪ to be called upon to do something ➤ Me tocó hacerlo. It fell to me to do it. ▪ It devolved upon me to do it. ▪ It devolved on me to do it. ▪ It fell to my lot to do it. ➤ Me tocó ser él que tenía que decírselo a ella. Me tocó tener que decírselo a ella. ▪ It fell to my lot to be the one to tell her.

tocarle de cerca to hit close to home

tocarle el mochuelo ▪ echarle el mochuelo ▪ cargar con el mochuelo to have the finger pointed at you ▪ to get the finger pointed at you

tocarle la lotería to win the lottery

tocarse la barriga ▪ rascarse la barriga to sit on one's butt ▪ to sit on one's ass

toda clase de all kinds of

toda clase de formas de lots of ways to ▪ all kinds of ways to ▪ all sorts of ways to

toda la extensión entire expanse ➤ Si fuera posible mirar hacia abajo a nuestro sistema solar desde la estrella polar, toda la extensión a través de la órbita de Plutón parecería un mero punto. If it were possible to look down on our solar system from the Pole Star, the entire expanse across Pluto's orbit would appear to be a mere speck.

toda la mañana all morning ▪ the entire morning ▪ the whole morning

toda la noche ▪ a lo largo de toda la noche all night long ▪ (all) through the night ➤ El bebé nos tuvo despiertos toda la noche. The baby kept us up all night long. ▪ The baby kept us up through the night.

toda la verdad the whole truth

toda una aventura quite an adventure ▪ a real adventure

toda una empresa ▪ toda una aventura quite an undertaking ▪ a real project

toda una hora a whole hour

toda una generación a whole generation ▪ an entire generation ➤ Para toda una generación For a whole generation ▪ For an entire generation ▪ To a whole generation ▪ To an entire generation

todas las tardes every afternoon

todas las variedades de ▪ todos los tipos de all kinds of

todavía debe estar allí ▪ debe existir allí todavía ▪ *(Sudamérica)* debe haberlo(-a) todavía it must still be there

todavía estoy en... I'm still in... ➤ Todavía estoy en Texas por una semana más. I'm still in Texas for another week. ▪ I'm still in Texas for one more week.

todavía fresco(-a) en mi memoria still fresh in my memory

todavía me queda trayecto por recorrer I still have a ways to go

todavía no lo sé ▪ aún no lo sé ▪ no lo sé todavía ▪ no lo sé aún I don't know yet ▪ I still don't know

todavía no lo tengo decidido I still haven't decided

todavía nos queda trayecto por recorrer we still have a ways to go

¿todavía sigues allí? are you still there?

todavía te queda trayecto por recorrer you still have a ways to go

todo a una carta: jugárselo ~ to go all or nothing

todo abril y mayo all of April and May

todo bicho viviente every living soul ▪ everybody under the sun

estar **todo bien con** ▪ venirle bien to be all right with ▪ to be okay with ▪ to suit well ▪ to suit fine ➤ Todo está bien conmigo, pero necesito consultar con el portero. It's all right with me, but I need to check with the concierge.

ser **todo corazón** to be all heart

todo cuanto quería all one wanted ➤ El elefante bebió del estanque todo cuanto quería y luego barritó su satisfacción con su trompa. The elephant drank all he wanted from the pond, and then trumpeted his satisfaction with his trunk.

todo de él everything about him

todo de ella everything about her

todo dicho ▪ en total all told ▪ in all

ser **todo dulzura y encanto** to be all sweetness and light

todo el día all day ▪ all day long

todo el maldito día the whole damned day

todo el mundo everybody

todo el puto día the whole fucking day ▪ *(alternativa benigna)* (all) the livelong day

todo el que all (those) who ▪ everyone who

todo el rato the whole time ➤ *(película)* Te sientes en tensión todo el rato. You're in suspense the whole time.

todo el rato mientras uno hacía una cosa the whole time one was doing something

todo el santo día all the livelong day ▪ the whole damned day ▪ all day long

todo el tiempo ▪ todo el rato the whole time ▪ the entire time ▪ *(menos claro)* all the time ➤ Con todo el tiempo que ha pasado en España, todavía no ha visto una corrida de toros. For all the time she's spent in Spain, she has yet to see a bull fight. ➤ Pensé que iba a tener que llamar a un cerrajero, y estuviste en casa todo el tiempo. I thought I was going to have to get a locksmith, and you were in the house all the time. ▪ I thought I was going to have to get a locksmith, and you were in the house the whole time. ▪ I thought I was going to have to get a locksmith, and you were in the house the entire time. ▪ I thought I was going to have to get a locksmith, and you were in the house all the time.

todo el tiempo que necesites all the time you need ▪ as much time as you need ➤ Tómate todo el tiempo que necesites. Take all the time you need. ▪ Take as much time as you need.

todo el viaje the whole trip

estar **todo elegante** ▪ estar de punta en blanco ▪ estar todo hecho un pincel ▪ estar ataviado ▪ ataviarse to be all dressed up ▪ to be dressed to the nines

todo empezó con it all began with ▪ it all started with

todo en él everything about him

todo en ella everything about her

todo en una carta: ir ~ to go all or nothing

todo en uno all in one ➤ Es una galleta (dulce) y un comprimido de vitaminas todo en uno. It's a cookie and a vitamin pill all in one.

todo encaja it all fits together

todo está bien ▪ no hay nada estropeado there's nothing wrong with it (mechanically)

todo está en su sitio everything is in order ▪ everything's in order

todo está vendido ▪ no quedan existencias sold out

todo este rollo de *(coloquial)* this whole business of ▪ the whole business of

estar **todo hecho(-a) un pincel** ▪ estar de punta en blanco ▪ estar todo elegante to be all dressed up ▪ to be dressed to the nines

ser **todo igual** to be all the same ➤ Quiero una caja de Crismas que sean todos iguales. I want a box of Christmas cards that are all the same.

ser **todo interés** to be all business

todo listo (everything is) all set ▪ (we're) all set

todo lo anterior having said (all) this ▪ having said as much ▪ the foregoing

todo lo concerniente a all matters concerning ▪ all matters relating to

todo lo contrario quite the opposite ▪ quite (to) the contrary

todo lo cual all of which

todo lo demás everything else

todo lo habido y por haber (en el universo) everything under the sun

todo lo hecho con everything made with

todo lo más 1. como máximo at most ▪ at the most 2. all the more ser **todo lo más resaltable** ▪ ser todo lo más remarcable ▪ ser todo lo más remarcado ▪ ser todo lo más resaltado to be all the more remarkable ➤ Una confianza duradera acompañó a Lincoln. Esto es lo más resaltable en tiempos de desorden civil. An abiding public trust attended Lincoln. This is all the more remarkable in times of civil unrest.

ser **todo lo mismo** to be all the same thing

todo lo pasado all that has happened

todo lo que concierne algo ▪ todo lo que implica algo what something is all about ➤ Los países se replantean todo lo que concierne la alianza. ▪ Los países se replantean todo lo que implica la alianza. The countries are re-thinking what the alliance is all about.

todo lo que haga algo anything that does something ▪ whatever does something ➤ Todo lo que active la circulación en los músculos ayuda a mantenerlos en forma. Anything that stimulates the circulation in the muscles helps keep them in shape.

todo lo que hago ▪ cada cosa que hago every move I make ▪ everything I do ➤ Critica cada cosa que hago. He criticizes every move I make.

todo lo que hay en la tienda everything in the store

todo lo que implica algo ▪ todo lo que concierne algo what something is all about ➤ Los países se replantean todo lo que implica la alianza. ▪ Los países se replantean todo lo que concierne la alianza. The countries are rethinking what the alliance is all about.

todo lo que percibía uno *(literario)* ▪ todo lo que uno podía ver ▪ todo lo que veía uno ▪ todo lo que se veía all (that) one could see... ▪ all (that) one could observe

ser **todo lo que queda** to be all that's left ➤ Es todo lo que queda. It's all that's left. ▪ That's all that's left.

todo lo que representa uno everything one stands for ➤ La ex primera ministra sigue sin dejar a nadie indiferente: los conservadores aún la adoran y los liberales siguen odiando todo lo que representa. The former prime minister still leaves no one indifferent: conservatives still adore her, and liberals continue to hate everything she stands for.

todo lo que uno quería all one wanted

todo lo que uno quiera all one wants (to) ➤ Puedes comer todo lo que quieras. You can eat all you want. ➤ Puedes racionalizar todo lo que quieras, pero el hecho es que... You can rationalize all you want to, but the fact of the matter is...

todo lo que uno quiso all one wanted ➤ El niño comió todas las galletas que quiso. ▪ El niño comió cuantas galletas quiso. The boy ate all the cookies he wanted.

todo lo vimos muy bien *(Bernal Díaz)* ▪ veíamos todo muy bien we could see everything really well

todo o nada all or nothing

ser **todo oídos** ▪ ser todo orejas to be all ears

ser **todo orejas** ▪ ser todo oídos to be all ears

ser **todo oscuridad** to be completely dark ➤ La ciudad era todo oscuridad. The city was completely dark.

todo parece indicar que... all indications are that...

todo por el pueblo pero sin el pueblo *(lema de los ilustrados, Siglo XVIII)* for the people without the people

todo se andará all in good time ▪ it will come out all right in the end

todo se pega menos la hermosura all the bad rubs off

todo se reduce a... it all boils down to...

todo se remonta a it all goes back to

ser **todo un éxito** to be a complete success ▪ to be a total success

todo un hombre ▪ muy hombre ▪ muy macho all man ▪ a real man ▪ a he-man ▪ very macho

todo un milagro quite a trick ➤ Fue todo un milagro conseguir que la tumbona pasara por la puerta principal. It was quite a trick getting the chaise lounge through the front door.

ser **todo un personaje** to be quite a character ➤ Ella es todo un personaje. She is quite a character. ▪ She's quite a character.

ser **todo un reto** to be quite a challenge

todo va a salir bien everything's going to be okay ▪ everything's going to be all right

todos los años every year

todos los caminos conducen a Roma ▪ todos los caminos llevan a Roma ▪ todos los caminos van a Roma all roads lead to Rome

todos los demás 1. *(cosas)* everything else ▪ all the other ones ▪ all the others ▪ all the rest 2. *(personas)* everyone else ▪ all the others ▪ all the other people

todos los demás juntos all the others combined ▪ all the rest combined

todos los derechos reservados ▪ reservados todos los derechos all rights reserved

todos los días every day

todos los días lo mismo it's the same every day ▪ just like I do every day ▪ just like I always do

todos los días se aprende una cosa nueva you learn something new every day

todos los domingos every Sunday

todos los públicos for all audiences

todos (los) que pude as many as I could

todos los que puedan ▪ la mayor cantidad posible ▪ el mayor número posible ▪ tantos como sea posible ▪ los más posibles as many as possible

todos los que se pueda todos los que puedan j el mayor número posible ▪ la mayor cantidad posible ▪ tantos como sea posible ▪ los más posibles as many as possible ▪ the greatest possible number

todos los sistemas funcionan all systems are working ▪ *(jerga de NASA)* all systems are go

todos los tipos de ▪ todas las variedades de all kinds of

todos mis conocidos everybody I know ▪ everyone I know

todos presentes y contados all present and accounted for

todos quedan invitados everyone is invited

todos sin excepción everyone without exception ▪ *(coloquial)* all and sundry

todos tenéis all of you have ▪ you all have ▪ you have

todos tienen they all have ▪ all of them have

todos tenemos all of us have ▪ we all have

estar **todos vendidos** ▪ agotarse las entradas to be sold out ➤ El concierto, en el que todas las localidades están vendidas... ▪ El concierto, en el que se agotaron las entradas... The concert, which was sold out...

toga y birrete cap and gown *(Literalmente "birrete y toga". La borla es "the tassle".)*

tolerar el dolor to stand the pain ▪ to tolerate the pain

¡toma! *(al entregar algo a alguien)* here!

toma de decisiones decision making

toma de posesión (de un mandato) taking of office ▪ assumption of command

toma de tierra ground wire ▪ ground ➤ Necesito una base con seis tomas y un toma de tierra. I need an extension cord with six outlets and a ground.

toma de una ciudad *(militar)* seizure of a city ▪ fall of a city ▪ taking of a city

toma en cuenta que... ▪ ten en cuenta que... ▪ considera que... ▪ te advierto que... bear in mind that... ▪ keep in mind that... ▪ mind you... ➤ Ten en cuenta que tenemos que estar en el aeropuerto en dos horas. Mind you! We have to be at the airport in two hours. ▪ Bear in mind that we have to be at the airport in two hours. ▪ Keep in mind that we have to be at the airport in two hours.

¡toma nota! make a note of it!

toma tu tiempo ▪ coge tu tiempo take your time

ser un **toma y daca** to be a trade-off

toma y daca política political give and take

tomado en su conjunto ▪ tomado en su totalidad taken as a whole ▪ taken in its entirety

tomado en su totalidad ▪ tomado en su conjunto taken as a whole ▪ taken in its entirety

ser **tomado(-a) por sorpresa** ▪ ser cogido(-a) por sorpresa ▪ ser cogido(-a) en frío ▪ cogerle en frío to be taken by surprise ▪ to be caught by surprise

tomar a alguien como rehén ▪ agarrar a alguien como rehén to take someone hostage

tomar a alguien por alguien to take someone for someone else ▪ to confuse someone with someone else

tomar a alguien por tonto to take someone for a fool
tomar algo a chacota ■ tomar algo a la chunga to take something as a joke
tomar algo a la chunga ■ tomar algo a chacota to take something as a joke
tomar algo a mal to take something badly
tomar algo a pachas *(Esp.)* ■ tomar algo a medias to split something ■ to divide something ➤ ¿Quieres tomar un postre a pachas? ■ ¿Quieres tomar un postre a medias? Do you want to split a dessert? ■ Do you want to divide a dessert?
tomar algo a pecho to take something to heart
tomar algo con filosofía to take something philosophically
tomar algo con un poco de sal to take something with a grain of salt
tomar algo de algo to take something from something ■ to derive something from something ➤ Carlos se pregunta si Dylan Thomas tomó el título de su poema "Do Not Go Gentle into That Good Night" de San Juan de la Cruz. Carlos wonders whether Dylan Thomas took the title of his poem, "Do Not Go Gentle into That Good Night" from St. John of the Cross.
tomar algo por la tremenda ■ dar algo por la tremenda to make a big fuss about something ■ to raise a big stink about something
tomar aliento to catch one's breath
tomar altitud ■ tomar altura ■ *(Esp.)* coger altitud to gain altitude
tomar altura ■ tomar altitud ■ *(Esp.)* coger altitud to gain altitude ➤ El avión volvió a tomar altura. The airplane regained altitude.
tomar apuntes ■ *(Esp.)* coger apuntes to take notes
tomar armas to take up arms
tomar asignaturas to take subjects ➤ Tomo cinco asignaturas. I'm taking five subjects.
tomar (cada uno) caminos distintos tomar distintos caminos 1. elegir otra ruta to take a different route 2. separarse ■ irse cada uno por su lado ■ irse cada quien por su lado to go one's separate ways 3. llevar sus propios senderos en la vida to take different paths in life ■ to go in different directions (in life) ➤ Tomaron caminos distintos para llegar a Toluca. ■ Tomaron distintos caminos para llegar a Toluca. They each took a different route to Toluca. ➤ Tomaron caminos distintos. ■ Tomaron distintos caminos. ■ Se fueron cada uno por su lado. ■ Se fueron cada quien por su lado. They went their separate ways. ➤ Tomamos caminos distintos. ■ Tomamos distintos caminos. ■ Nos fuimos cada uno por su lado. We went our separate ways.
tomar cartas en un asunto to take matters into one's own hands ■ to intervene in a matter ➤ *(noticia)* La Guardia Civil ha decidido tomar cartas en el asunto. The Civil Guard has decided to take matters into its own hands. ■ The Civil Guard has decided to intervene in the matter.
tomar color 1. *(frutas)* to ripen 2. *(proyectos)* to take shape ■ to come to fruition
tomar el sol ■ tumbarse al sol ■ ser como un lagarto ■ tumbarse al sol como un lagarto to bask in the sun ■ *(coloquial)* to soak up some rays
tomar conciencia de algo to take stock of something ■ to become cognizant of something ■ to become aware of something ➤ Los hispanos empiezan a tomar conciencia de su potencia electoral (en EE UU) y exigen ser escuchados. Hispanics begin to take stock of their electoral clout and demand to be heard.
tomar conciencia de que... to take stock of the fact that... ■ to be cognizant (of the fact) that... ■ to be aware (of the fact) that... ■ to take cognizance of the fact that...
tomar consistencia *(una hipótesis)* to take shape
tomar el aire to get some (fresh) air
tomar el control de la situación to take control of the situation
tomar el desayuno ■ desayunar to have breakfast ■ to eat breakfast
tomar el fresco to get some fresh air ■ to get a breath of fresh air ■ to take some fresh air
tomar el olivo to beat it ■ to flee for cover ■ *(torero)* to take cover behind the barrier
tomar el mando to take command
tomar el pelo to pull someone's leg
tomar el pedido to take the order
tomar el pulso a alguien to take someone's pulse ■ to sound someone out
tomar el pulso sanguineo ■ tomar el pulso to take one's pulse ■ to take someone's pulse
tomar el rábano por las hojas to get the wrong end of the stick
tomar el relevo to take over
tomar el relevo de alguien to take over from someone ■ to pick up where someone leaves off ■ to take the relay from
tomar el remedio to take one's medicine ➤ Tengo que tomar el remedio. I have to take my medicine.
tomar la sartén por el mango ■ tener la sartén por el mango ■ *(Esp.)* coger la sartén por el mango to call the shots
tomar el sol ■ tumbarse al sol ■ ser como un lagarto ■ tumbarse al sol como un lagarto to sunbathe ■ to get some sun ■ to bask in the sun ■ *(coloquial)* to soak up some rays
tomar el tiempo como viene ■ tomar el tiempo conforme viene to take one day at a time
tomar el timón ■ llevar el timón to take the helm
tomar el trabajo de to take on the task of
tomar empeño en to take pains to
tomar en consideración to take into consideration ■ *(al calificar papeles)* to count
tomar en cuenta to take into account
tomar en serio to take seriously
tomar la calle equivocada to take the wrong street
tomar la bifurcación a la derecha ■ quedarse a la derecha en la bifurcación ■ hacerse a la izquierda en la bifurcación to take the right fork ■ to bear right at the fork
tomar la bifurcación a la izquierda ■ quedarse a la izquierda en la bifurcación ■ hacerse a la izquierda en la bifurcación to take the left fork ■ to bear left at the fork
tomar la disparada to take off like a shot
tomar la iniciativa to take the initiative
tomar la horizontal ■ coger la horizontal to catch some Z's ■ to take a snooze
tomar la medida ■ medir to take the measurement ■ to measure
tomar la ofensiva to take the offensive ■ to go on the offensive
tomar la palabra ■ hacer uso de la palabra to take the floor
tomar la primera bocacalle a la derecha to take the next right to take the next right
tomar la primera bocacalle a la izquierda to take the next left to take the first left
tomar la salida fácil to take the easy way out
tomar la sopa boba ■ andar a la sopa boba to scrounge ■ to eke out an existence
tomarle la tensión a alguien ■ medirle la tensión a alguien to check someone's blood pressure ■ to take someone's blood pressure ➤ El médico me tomó la tensión. ■ El médico me midió la tensión. The doctor checked my blood pressure. ➤ El médico le tomó la tensíón. ■ El médico le midió la tensión. The doctor checked her blood pressure.
tomar las afufas *(coloquial)* ■ huir to flee ■ to beat it
tomar las aguas to bathe in a warm spring ■ to go to a spa
tomar las armas to take up arms
tomar las calles ■ *(Esp.)* coger las calles to control the streets ■ to take possession of the streets ■ to rule the streets
tomar las cenizas to receive the ashes on Ash Wednesday
tomar las de Villadiego ■ marcharse precipitadamente ■ salir pitando ■ marcharse huyendo ■ *(Esp.)* coger las de Villadiego to beat a trail out of Dodge
tomar las duras con las maduras to take the bitter with the sweet
tomar las medidas de algo to take the measurements of something ■ to measure something
tomar las riendas de su vida to take control of one's life ➤ ¡Toma las riendas de tu vida! Take control of your life!
tomar lecciones to take lessons
tomar medidas para ■ adoptar medidas para to take steps to

tomarse muchas molestías para hacer algo to go to a lot of trouble to do something ➤ (Él) se tomó muchas molestias para persuadirlo. ▪ *(Esp., leísmo)* (Él) se tomó muchas molestías para persuadirle. He went to a lot of trouble to persuade him. ➤ (Él) se tomó muchas molestias para persuadirla. ▪ *(Esp., leísmo)* Se tomó muchas molestías para persuadirle. He went to a lot of trouble to persuade her.

tomar parte por alguien (en un asunto) to side with someone (in a matter)

tomar partido en una discusión to take sides in an argument

tomar partido en una disputa to take sides in a dispute

tomar por la fuerza un edificio to storm a building

tomar posesión de la casa ▪ adueñarse de la casa ▪ aposentarse en la casa to take possession of the house ▪ to take over ➤ Mi gata entró cierto día y tomó posesión de la casa. My cat just walked in one day and took over.

tomar posesión del cargo to take office ▪ to be inaugurated

tomar prestado ▪ pedir prestado to borrow

tomar reprisalias contra to retaliate against

tomar su café to have one's coffee ➤ Ya he tomado mi café. I've already had my coffee.

tomar su curso to take its course ➤ No hay cura para el resfriado. Hay que dejarlo tomar su curso. There's no cure for the common cold. You just have to let it take its course.

tomar su tiempo ▪ *(Esp.)* coger su tiempo to take one's time

tomar un año de descanso ▪ tomar un año sabático to take a year off

tomar un taxi ▪ ir en taxi to take a taxi ▪ to go by taxi

tomar un bocado to have a bite to eat

tomar un buche (de agua) to take a mouthful (of water)

tomar un examen *(L.am.)* ▪ presentarse a un examen to take an exam(ination)

tomar un giro favorable to take a turn for the better

tomar un recado ▪ tomar un mensaje to take a message

tomar una calle equivocada to take a wrong street

tomar una materia to take a course ▪ to take a class ▪ to take a subject ➤ Tomo cinco materias. I'm taking five subjects.

tomar una resolución to make a decision

tomar una siesta ▪ echarse una siesta ▪ dormir la siesta to take one's afternoon nap ▪ to have one's afternoon nap

tomar unas copas to have a few drinks

tomar velocidad to gain speed

tomar vida propia to take on a life of its own ➤ El rumor ha tomado vida propia. The rumor has taken on a life of its own.

tomarla contra alguien to pick on someone ▪ to have a grudge against someone

tomarle a alguien de instrumento to use someone as a tool

tomarle aversión a algo to become averse to something ▪ to develop an aversion to something ➤ En su vejez le tomó aversión al peine. In his old age he has become very averse to a comb. ▪ In his old age he has developed an aversion to a comb.

tomarle el pelo ▪ estarle vacilando to pull someone's leg ▪ to be kidding someone ▪ to kid someone ➤ ¡Estás tomándome el pelo! You're pulling my leg! ▪ You're kidding me!

tomarle el pulso a algo to gauge something

tomarle el pulso a alguien to take someone's pulse

tomarle la delantera ▪ *(Esp.)* cogerle la delantera to take the lead

tomarle la mano a algo to take to something (that was difficult at first) ▪ to get into something (that was difficult at first)

tomarle la palabra a alguien to take someone's word for something ➤ Te tomo la palabra. I take your word for it. ▪ I'll take your word for it.

tomarle la presión ▪ tomarle la tensión to take someone's blood pressure

tomarle la temperatura a alguien *(Esp.)* ▪ medir la temperatura a alguien to take someone's temperature ➤ Su madre le tomó la temperatura. ▪ Su madre le midió la temperatura. *(a él)* His mother took his temperature. ▪ *(a ella)* Her mother took her temperature.

tomarle la tensión a alguien ▪ tomarle la presión a alguien ▪ medirle la tensión a alguien ▪ medirle la presión a alguien to take someone's blood pressure ▪ to check someone's blood pressure ➤ El médico me tomó la tensión. ▪ El médico me midió la tensión. The doctor checked my blood pressure. ➤ El médico le tomó la tensión. ▪ El médico le midió la tensión. The doctor checked her blood pressure.

tomarle manía a alguien *(literario)* ▪ tenerle inquina a alguien to be down on someone ▪ to be on someone's case

tomarle nota a alguien to take someone's order ➤ *(tú)* ¿Nos tomas nota? ▪ *(usted)* ¿Nos toma nota? Would you take our order? ➤ ¿Le han tomado nota? Has anyone already taken your order? ▪ Has your order been taken?

tomarlo a alguien en la confianza de uno to take into one's confidence ➤ Quiero tomarte en mi confianza. I'd like to take you into my confidence.

tomarlo a mal ▪ tomárselo a mal to take it the wrong way ➤ Ella lo tomó a mal. ▪ Ella se lo tomó a mal. She took it the wrong way.

tomarlo como un cumplido to take it as a compliment

tomarlo como un insulto to take it as an insult

tomarlo con tiempo to take one's time

tomarlo con un poco de sal to take it with a grain of salt

tomarse a la ligera to take lightly

tomarse algo con filosofía to take something philosophically

tomarse algo con humor to take something good humoredly ▪ to take something in good humor

tomarse algo en serio to take something seriously

tomarse como lo que es to be taken for what it is

tomarse confianzas to take liberties ▪ to be fresh

tomarse confianzas para hacer algo ▪ tomarse confianzas ▪ propasarse to take liberties ➤ Se toma muchas confianzas en mi casa, cogiéndose Cocas, contestando el teléfono y entrando sin llamar. ▪ Se toma muchas licencias en mi casa, cogiéndose Cocas, contestando el teléfono y entrando sin llamar. He takes a lot of liberties in my house, getting Cokes, answering the phone, and coming in without ringing the doorbell. ➤ *(Ricardo Palma)* Si es que a más no se propasa... If he doesn't take any more liberties...

tomarse el trabajo de... to take the trouble to... ▪ to go to the trouble to...

tomarse en serio 1. to take oneself seriously **2.** to be taken seriously

tomarse la libertad de ▪ tomarse la licencia de to take the liberty of ➤ Me tomé la libertad de enseñarle tu carta. ▪ Me tomé la licencia de enseñarle tu carta. I took the liberty of showing her your letter.

tomarse la licencia de ▪ tomarse la libertad de to take the liberty of ➤ Me tomé la licencia de enseñarle su carta. ▪ Me tomé la libertad de enseñarle su carta. I took the liberty of showing her your letter.

tomarse la medicación to take one's medication ▪ to take one's medicine

tomarse licencias para hacer algo ▪ tomarse confianzas ▪ propasarse to take the liberty of doing something ➤ Se toma muchas licencias en mi casa, cogiéndose refrescos, contestando el teléfono y entrando sin llamar. ▪ Se toma muchas confianzas en mi casa, cogiéndose refrescos, contestando el teléfono y entrando sin llamar. He takes a lot of liberties in my house, getting soft drinks, answering the phone, and coming in without ringing the doorbell.

tomarse los dichos to exchange (marriage) vows

tomarse muchas molestías para... to go to a lot of trouble to...

tomarse su responsabilidad en serio to take one's responsibility seriously

tomarse tiempo para ▪ concederse tiempo para to take time off to ➤ Me tomé tiempo para salir a comer con Susana. ▪ Me concedí tiempo para salir a comer con Susana. I took time off to go out to dinner with Susana.

tomarse todo el tiempo para hacer algo to take one's time doing something ▪ to take a good long time to do something ▪ to take plenty of time to do something ▪ to take plenty of time doing something

tomarse un respiro to take a breather

tomarse licencias para hacer algo to take the liberty of doing something

tomarse una pastilla to take a pill
tomarse unos días (libres) to take some time off
tomarse vacaciones to take a vacation ■ to take a day off
tomárselo a mal ■ tomarlo a mal to take it the wrong way ➤ Ella se lo tomó a mal. ■ Ella lo tomó a mal. She took it the wrong way.
tomárselo al dedillo to take it literally
tomárselo como algo personal to take it personally ➤ No te lo tomes como algo personal. Don't take it personally.
tomárselo mal to take it badly
tómate el tiempo que te haga falta take your time ■ take all the time (that) you need
el **tonel de cerveza** keg of beer
tónica actual current trend
tónica general general trend
tono mayor major key
tono menor minor key
tonos tierra earth tones
¡**tonterías!** nonsense!
¡**tonto!** silly!
ser **tonto(-a) de capirote** ■ ser loco(-a) de capirote to be a blithering idiot ■ to be a hopeless case
tonto del pueblo village idiot
el **top secret** top secret
toparse con alguien *(literal y figurativo)* to bump into someone ■ to run into someone
el **tope de salario** maximum salary
el **toque de queda** curfew
torcer el gesto to make an angry face
torcer el morro to make an angry face
torcerle el pescuezo a alguien to wring someone's neck
torcerse el tobillo to twist one's ankle
¡**torero!** way to go!
tormenta de arena sandstorm
tormenta de ideas brainstorm
tormenta de nieve ■ temporal de nieve snowstorm
tormenta en un vaso de agua tempest in a teapot
tormenta irrumpió storm broke
tornar a surgir ■ volver a aparecer to reappear
Toro Sentado *(el indio norteamericano)* Sitting Bull
ser la **torre de Babel** to be a Tower of Babel ■ to be a scene of noise and confusion
la **torre de control** control tower
la **torre inclinada de Pisa** the Leaning Tower of Pisa ➤ Galileo dejó caer pesas desde la torre inclinada de Pisa. Galileo dropped weights from the Leaning Tower of Pisa.
torrente sanguíneo: pasar al ~ to enter the bloodstream ■ to get into the bloodstream
Torres gemelas del Centro de comercio mundial Twin Towers of the World Trade Center
tortilla (española) egg and potato omelet ➤ Un pincho de tortilla, por favor. A slice of potato omelet, please.
tortilla francesa omelet ■ omelette ➤ Una tortilla francesa, por favor. An omelet, please.
tortura de un oso ■ espectáculo en que se tortura a un oso bear baiting ➤ Los Puritanos odiaban los espectáculos en que se torturan a los osos, no por el dolor que se infligía al oso, sino por el placer que les producía a los espectadores. *(Carlysle)* The Puritans hated bear baiting, not because it gave pain to the bear, but because it gave pleasure to the spectators.
tos perruna ■ tos de perros bad cough
la **tos pertinaz** persistent cough
tostado a la francesa: el café ~ French roast coffee
ser un **tostón** 1. ser una patata to be a lemon 2. ser un fastidio to be a hassle
total de la obra ■ totalidad de la obra the body of one's work
estar **totalmente a favor de algo** ■ estar a favor de algo al cien por cien to be completely in favor of something ■ to be all for something ➤ Estoy totalmente a favor. ■ Estoy a favor al cien por cien. ■ Lo apruebo al cien por cien. I am completely in favor of it. ■ I'm all for it.

tour operator travel agent
trabajaba el endoso *(Valle-Inclán)* he was working the deal
trabajador a sueldo wage earner
trabajador de la construcción construction worker
trabajador indocumentado undocumented worker
trabajador por cuenta ajena worker who is not self-employed ■ wage earner
estar **trabajando** 1. to be working 2. estar en el trabajo to be at work ➤ Ella está trabajando. ■ Ella está en el trabajo. She's at work.
trabajar a cuenta ajena to work for someone else
trabajar a cuenta propia ■ trabajar por su propia cuenta to be self-employed
trabajar a destajo 1. to work by the job (as opposed to earning a fixed salary) ■ to do piecework ■ to work by the piece 2. trabajar sin descanso to work without letup ➤ Los pintores normalmente trabajan a destajo. Painters normally work by the job. ➤ Furniture refinishers work by the piece. ■ Los restauradores de muebles trabajan a destajo. Furniture refinishers do piecework. ➤ Las inundaciones provocadas por la lluvia hicieron trabajar a los bomberos a destajo. The flooding caused by the rain caused the firemen to work without letup.
trabajar a la par de alguien to work as hard as someone ■ to work with the same intensity as someone
trabajar a pérdida to operate at a loss ■ to run at a loss
trabajar a tope to operate at full capacity ■ to run at full capacity
trabajar afanosamente to work diligently ■ to work painstakingly ■ to work laboriously ■ to work feverishly
trabajar al lado de to work with ➤ Nunca he trabajado a su lado. I've never worked with him.
trabajar al sol to work in the sun
trabajar bien juntos to work well together ➤ Javier y yo trabajamos bien juntos. Javier and I work well together.
trabajar como un burro ■ trabajar como un buey ■ trabajar como un condenado ■ currar (de sol a sol) to work like a dog ■ to slave away
trabajar como un condenado ■ trabajar como un burro ■ trabajar como un buey ■ currar (de sol a sol) to work like a dog ■ to slave away
trabajar con el ordenador *(Esp.)* to work at the computer
trabajar con la computadora to work at the computer
trabajar con mimo en algo to work lovingly on something
trabajar contra el reloj to work against the clock
trabajar de to work as ➤ Trabajo de taxista. I work as a taxi driver.
trabajar de firme to work hard
trabajar en algo to work on something
trabajar en contra de algo to work against something
trabajar en el ordenador *(Esp.)* 1. trabajar con el ordenador ■ trabajar en la computadora ■ trabajar con la computadora to work at the computer 2. hacerle mejoras al ordenador to work on the computer ■ to do things to the computer
trabajar en la computadora 1. trabajar con la computadora to work at the computer 2. hacerle mejoras a la computadora to work on the computer ■ to do things to the computer
trabajar en una película to be in a movie ■ to be in a film
trabajar hasta echar la gota to work up a sweat
trabajar hasta tarde to work late
trabajar jornada completa ■ trabajar tiempo completo to work full time
trabajar jornada partida to work a split shift
trabajar media jornada ■ trabajar medio turno to work part time
trabajar muchas horas to put in a long day ■ to work long hours
trabajar mucho to work hard
trabajar lo más que uno pueda to work as hard as one can
trabajar por su cuenta ■ trabajar a cuenta propia to be self-employed
trabajar por una causa to work for a cause
trabajar sobre to work on

trabajar tiempo completo ▪ trabajar jornada completa to work full time

trabajarlo más to work on it some more ▪ to do some more work on it

trabajo anodino boring job

trabajo arduo arduous task

trabajo atrasado backlog of work

trabajo chapuza low-paying job without medical or retirement benefits

trabajo de clase class assignment ➤ Se negó rotundamente a hacer el trabajo de clase. He absolutely refused to do his class assignment.

trabajo de impresión print jobs ▪ print work

trabajo de su vida one's life's work

trabajo desafiante challenging job

trabajo en equipo teamwork

trabajo es placer: mi ~ my work is play

trabajo estable: tener un ~ to have a steady job

trabajo estresante ▪ puesto de trabajo estresante stressful job

¡**trabajo hecho!** mission accomplished!

trabajo para toda la vida lifetime job

ser un **trabajo perdido** ▪ ser un indeseable to be an undesirable ➤ Él es un trabajo perdido. He's a lost cause.

trabajo que conlleva ▪ trabajo que se supone work that involves

el **trabajo que se supone** ▪ el trabajo que conlleva the work that it involves

trabajo retrasado work to catch up on ▪ backlog of work ➤ Tengo mucho trabajo retrasado. I have a lot of work to catch up on.

trabar amistad to strike up a friendship

trabar conversación con alguien to strike up a conversation with someone ▪ to get into a conversation with someone ➤ Marta y yo trabamos conversación sobre la cultura musical en Madrid hoy en día. Marta and I got into a conversation about the musical culture of present-day Madrid. ➤ Ella habló, él respondió, y trabaron conversación. She spoke, and he spoke back, and they got into a conversation.

trabársele la lengua to get tongue-tied ▪ to be tongue-tied ➤ Se me trabó la lengua. I got tongue-tied.

la **tracción a cuatro ruedas** four-wheel drive

tracción delantera front-wheel drive

traducirse por to be translated as

traer a alguien cogido de la mano, oreja, pelo ▪ traer a alguien agarrado de la mano, oreja, pelo to bring someone, pulling by the hand, ear, hair

traer a la memoria to bring to mind

traer algo entre manos to have something up one's sleeve ▪ to have an ulterior motive ▪ to have a hidden agenda

traer cola ▪ tener cola to have serious consequences ▪ to have grave consequences

traer consigo to carry with one ▪ to carry on one's person ▪ to have with one ▪ to have on one's person ▪ to carry with it ➤ *(Juan Montalvo)* La fama de Bolívar trae consigo el ruido de las armas. Bolivar's fame carries with it the thunder of arms.

traer escrito en la frente to be written all over...

traer las pilas ▪ venir con las pilas to come with batteries

traer mal fario to bring bad luck

traer mala(s) noticia(s) ▪ tener mala(s) noticia(s) to have (some) bad news

traer un lío con alguien to have an illicit affair with someone

traer una presentación to do a presentation

traerle a alguien en palmitas to wait on someone hand and foot ➤ Ella lo trae en palmitas. She waits on him hand and foot.

traerle a alguien noticias to have some news for someone ➤ Te traigo noticias. I have some news for you. ▪ I've got some news for you.

traérsele flojo not to give a damn

tráfico de influencias influence peddling

tráfico pesado heavy traffic

tráfico vespertino evening traffic

trágame tierra ▪ tierra, trágame I was so embarrassed, I just wanted to run and hide

tragar bilis to swallow one's anger

tragar carros y carretas ▪ aguantar carros y carretas to put up with murder

tragar con algo to put up with something (stoically)

tragar con todo lo que le echen a alguien to deal with anything they throw at him ▪ to deal with whatever they throw at someone ▪ to handle anything they throw at him ▪ to handle whatever they throw at him ▪ to deal with anything that comes his way ▪ to deal with whatever comes his way ➤ Él traga con todo lo que le echen. He can deal with anything they throw at him. ▪ He can deal with whatever they throw at him. ▪ He can handle anything they throw at him. ▪ He can handle whatever they throw at him. ▪ He can deal with anything that comes his way. ▪ He can deal with whatever comes his way.

tragar el anzuelo ▪ caer en el anzuelo ▪ picar en el anzuelo to swallow the bait

tragar el medicamento ▪ bajar la medicina to swallow the medicine ▪ to get the medicine down

tragar quina to grin and bear it

tragar saliva ▪ morderse la lengua to swallow hard ▪ to suppress one's feelings

tragarse el anzuelo to swallow the bait ▪ to take the bait

tragarse la historia to swallow the story ▪ to believe the story

tragarse un billete to take a bill ➤ ¿Se traga la máquina un billete de cinco dólares? Will the machine take a five-dollar bill?

tragarse un libro entero ▪ leer un libro de tapa a tapa ▪ leer un libro de cubierta a cubierta ▪ leer hasta la dedicatoria de un libro to read a book from cover to cover ▪ to read a book all the way through

tragarse una mentira ▪ tragarse una trola to swallow a lie ▪ to fall for a lie

tragarse una moneda to take a coin ➤ Este teléfono no se traga monedas, sólo tarjetas. This phone doesn't take coins, only cards.

tragarse una trola ▪ tragarse una mentira to swallow a lie ▪ to fall for a lie

tragárselo la tierra to disappear off the face of the earth

trago amargo: pasar un ~ to have a rough time

ser un **trago amargo** bitter pill (to swallow)

traicionar a alguien to betray someone ➤ En la Última Cena, Jesús dijo, "Uno de vosotros me traicionará." At the Last Supper, Jesus said, "One of you will betray me."

traicionar la confianza depositada en alguien to betray someone's trust

traicionar sus emociones ▪ desenmascarar sus emociones ▪ descubrir sus emociones to betray one's feelings ▪ to give away one's feelings

traicionar un acuerdo ▪ hacer trampas en un acuerdo to cheat on an agreement ➤ Los países no deberían hacer trampas en los acuerdos de no proliferación nuclear. ▪ Los países no deberían traicionar los acuerdos de no proliferación nuclear. Countries should not cheat on nuclear non-proliferation treaties.

traído por los cabellos far-fetched

estar **traído por los pelos** to be far-fetched

el **traje con raya diplomática** pinstriped suit

el **traje de Adán** birthday suit

el **traje de luces** bullfighter's suit

el **traje de pengüino** *(coloquial)* monkey suit ▪ tails

traje entallado tailored suit ▪ tailor-made suit

traje ignífugo fireproof suit ▪ fire-resistant suit

el **traje intachable** immaculate suit

tramo de base *(aeronáutica)* base leg

tramo de viento en cola *(aeronáutica)* downwind leg

tramo despejado open stretch

trampa mortal death trap

trampa mortífera death trap

¡**tranquilo!** ▪ ¡no te preocupes! don't worry!

transbordador que cubre el recorrido entre Santander y Plymouth the ferry from Santander to Plymouth

transgredir la ley to transgress the law ▪ to infringe the law

transitar hacia un lugar 1. to go toward a place 2. *(a pie)* to walk toward a place
transitar por un lugar 1. to go by a place 2. *(a pie)* to walk by a place
la **transmisión de entendimiento** mental telepathy
transmisión entrecortada broken (up) transmission ▪ interference in the transmission ▪ interference on the line
el **transmisor-receptor** two-way radio
transmitirse de boca a boca to spread by word of mouth
transmitirse de generación en generación en la familia to run in the family ➤ Los trastornos de sangre se transmiten de generación en generación en su familia. Blood disorders run in her family.
transportar a alguien hacia atrás en el tiempo ▪ llevar a alguien hacia atrás en el tiempo to take one back in time ➤ Esta película te transporta hacia atrás en el tiempo. ▪ Esta película te lleva hacia atrás en el tiempo. This film takes you back in time. ➤ El telescopio te transporta hacia atrás en el tiempo. ▪ Mirar a través del telescopio te lleva hacia atrás en el tiempo. Looking through a telescope takes you back in time.
el **transporte terrestre** ground transportation
tras desplomarse por after being felled by ▪ after being stricken by ➤ El deportista es atendido tras desplomarse por un corte de digestión. The athlete is attended after being felled by a stomach cramp.
tras estar aquejado de ▪ después de estar aquejado de after being stricken by
tras hacer algo ▪ después de hacer algo after doing something
tras la ruptura 1. after the breakup 2. *(nosotros)* after we broke up 3. *(ellos)* after they broke up
tras la toma de la ciudad after the fall of the city ▪ after the taking of the city
tras las líneas enemigas ▪ en la línea enemiga behind enemy lines ▪ within enemy lines ▪ inside enemy lines
estar **tras las rejas** ▪ estar entre rejas ▪ estar en la cárcel ▪ estar a la sombra to be behind bars ▪ to be in jail ▪ *(pintoresco)* to be in the clinker ▪ to be in the tank
tras licenciarse en la universidad after graduating from the university
tras lo ocurrido ▪ después de lo ocurrido after the fact
tras siete llaves under lock and key
tras un momento ▪ al cabo de un momento ▪ después de un momento a moment later ▪ after a moment
tras unos segundos ▪ al cabo de unos segundos ▪ después de unos segundos a few seconds later ▪ after a few seconds
tras *x* días de *x* days after ➤ Tras cuarenta días de la llegada del euro... Forty days after the arrival of the euro...
trascenderse algo ▪ saberse algo ▪ salir algo a la luz to become known ▪ to get out ▪ to come to light ➤ No podemos dejar que esto se trascienda. ▪ No podemos dejar que esto salga a la luz. ▪ No podemos dejar que esto se sepa. We can't let this become known. ▪ We can't let this get out. ▪ We can't let this come to light.
tras consultar con ▪ tras asesorarse con in consultation with
trasero contra trasero ▪ espalda contra espalda ▪ espalda con espalda back to back
trasfondo moral moral overtones
trasladar a un empleado to transfer an employee
trasladarse a un apartamento ▪ mudarse a un apartamento ▪ entrar a vivir en un apartamento ▪ trasladarse a un piso ▪ mudarse a un apartamento ▪ entrar a vivir en un piso to move into an apartment
traspapelar algo to lose something in the shuffle ▪ to put something in the wrong place ▪ to mislay something ➤ Me parece que se ha traspapelado el mensaje mío. I think my message got lost in the shuffle. ▪ I think my message must have been put in the wrong place. ▪ My message must have been mislaid. ▪ My message must have gotten put in the wrong place.
traspasarle la pena el corazón to be grief-stricken ▪ to be pierced with sorrow
traspaso de poder transfer of power
trasquilar ovejas ▪ esquilar ovejas to shear sheep
trastornar sus planes to upset one's plans
trastorno emocional emotional disorder
trastorno de aprendizaje learning disorder
trastorno de sangre blood disorder
trastornos de espalda back problems
trasvasar el agua to divert the water
¡trata de pararme! try and stop me!
tratamiento de textos word processing
tratar a alguien a puntapiés to kick somebody around
tratar a alguien con guantes de seda ▪ tratar a alguien con mano blanda to treat someone with kid gloves ▪ to handle someone with kid gloves
tratar a alguien de ▪ dirigirse a alguien como to address someone as ➤ En el pasado los niños trataban al padre de "usted". ▪ En el pasado los niños se dirigían al padre como "usted". In the old days, children addressed their fathers as "sir."
tratar a zapatazos ▪ amedrentar to push around
tratar de ▪ intentar ▪ pretender ▪ procurar to try to ➤ El gobierno pretendió mantener el orden. The government tried to maintain order.
tratar de hacer memoria de algo to try to remember something ▪ to try to recall something
tratar de no pensar en algo ▪ intentar no pensar en algo to try not to think about something ➤ Trata de no pensar en ello. ▪ Intenta no pensar en ello. Try not to think about it.
tratar de no perderse to try not to miss ➤ Trataré de no perderme la actuación del viernes. I'll try not to miss Friday's performance.
tratar de un tema ▪ tratar sobre un tema ▪ tratar de una materia ▪ tratar sobre una materia to deal with a subject ▪ to deal with a topic
tratar de no to try not to ➤ Trata de no moverte. Try not to move. ▪ Try to hold still.
tratar las dudas de alguien to address someone's doubts ▪ to address someone's concerns
tratar las inquietudes de alguien ▪ tratar las preocupaciones de alguien to address someone's concerns
tratar las preocupaciones de alguien ▪ tratar las inquietudes de alguien to address someone's concerns
tratar por activa y por pasiva de to try everything to
tratarlo como tal to treat it as such
tratarlo de to address someone as
tratarlos como tales to treat them as such
tratarse de to be ▪ to be a question of ▪ to deal with ➤ Se trata de una profesión muy divertida. It's a very enjoyable profession.
tratársele como tal to be treated as such
trato carnal sexual relationship ▪ carnal knowledge
¡trato hecho! it's a deal!
¿trato hecho? ¡trato hecho! done? done! ▪ is it a deal? it's a deal!
trato vejatorio humiliating treatment ▪ degrading treatment
traumatizarse de to be devastated by
travesaño del taburete crossbar of the stool
trayecto (de un viaje) leg (of a trip) ➤ En el viaje de Valladolid a Toledo, hay un trayecto corto entre las estaciones de ferrocarril de Chamartín y Atocha en Madrid. On the trip from Valladolid to Toledo, there is a short leg between the Chamartín and Atocha train stations in Madrid.
trayecto recto straight stretch
trayectoría de una bala path of a bullet
trayectoría personal personal journey
trazar paralelos con algo to draw parallels with something
trazar un paralelo entre dos cosas to draw a parallel between two things
trazo de pluma stroke of the pen
trazo grueso 1. broad brush 2. *(chistes)* off color ▪ in bad taste ➤ Sus posiciones editoriales son de trazo grueso. Her editorial positions are pretty broad brush. ➤ Su hermano siempre cuenta chistes de trazo grueso. Her brother is always telling off-color jokes. ▪ Her brother's jokes are in very bad taste.
los **trece caballeros de la fama** Pedro de Candía and the twelve other followers who remained loyal to Pizarro
trecho recto straight stretch

el **tren anterior** the earlier train
un **tren antes** an earlier train
el **tren de aterrizaje** landing gear ➤ El tren de aterrizaje está fuera. The landing gear is down.
el **tren de aterrizaje plegable** ▪ tren de aterrizaje replegable ▪ tren de aterrizaje retráctil retractable landing gear
el **(tren de) mercancías** freight train
el **tren de primera hora** the early train ➤ No pude comprar un billete para el tren de primera hora. Estaban todos vendidos. I couldn't get a ticket for the early train. They were sold out.
tren de vida muy ajetreado: llevar un ~ to live a very hectic life
el **tren con destino a** train for ▪ train to
el **tren ya está puesto (en el anden)** the train is at the platform
trepar por el árbol to climb (up) the tree
tres adivinanzas three guesses
tres cuartas partes del total three-fourths of the total
ser **tres cuartos de lo mismo** ▪ (venir a) ser lo mismo ▪ implicar lo mismo ▪ suponer lo mismo ▪ suponer la misma cosa to amount to the same thing ➤ No lo despidieron, pero le bajaron el sueldo a la mitad y le dieron una oficina en el sótano, lo cual es tres cuartos de lo mismo. ▪ No lo despidieron, pero le bajaron el sueldo a la mitad y le dieron una oficina en el sótano, lo cual viene a ser lo mismo. They didn't fire him, but they cut his salary in half and gave him an office in the basement, so it amounts to the same thing.
tres en raya tic-tac-toe
tres es multitud three's a crowd
los **tres primeros** the first three ➤ Tenemos que leer los tres primeros capítulos. We have to read the first three chapters.
triángulo amoroso love triangle
triángulos homologados regulation triangles
el **tribunal de apelaciones** court of appeals ▪ appeals court
El **Tribunal Supremo de los Estados Unidos** ▪ El Tribunal Supremo de EE UU United States Supreme Court ▪ U.S. Supreme Court
tributar homenaje a to pay tribute to
trigo integral whole wheat
trillar trigo to thresh wheat
ser **trincado(-a) por la policía** to be nabbed by the police ▪ to be picked up by the police
trincar a alguien to nab someone
trinchar un asado ▪ cortar un asado to carve a roast
trinchar un pavo ▪ cortar un pavo to carve a turkey
trinchar una pierna de cordero ▪ cortar una pierna de cordero to carve a leg of lamb
trio amoroso ménage à trois ▪ three-way
tripa cervecera beer gut
el **triple empate** three-way tie
triturar papel to shred paper
trivial: jugar al ~ to play trivial pursuit
trocear en daditos una zanahoria to dice a carrot
trocear un plátano to slice a banana
trocear una cebolla to chop an onion ▪ to cut up an onion
trocito desprendido dimpled chad
trocitos de jamón ham bits
tromba de agua cloudburst (with flash flooding) ▪ deluge of water ▪ torrent of water ▪ downpour ➤ La tromba de agua me caló. I got soaked in the cloudburst. ▪ I got drenched in the cloudburst.
la **trombosis cerebral** ▪ infarto cerebral ▪ derrame cerebral ▪ congestión cerebral stroke ▪ cerebral hemorrhage
tronco familiar family tree
¡tronco va! timber!
tronador rugido thunderous roar ▪ deafening roar
tropas curtidas en la batalla battle-hardened troops
tropas terrestres ground troops
tropezar algo ▪ chocar contra algo ▪ topetear contra algo to bump something ➤ Detesto cuando tropiezo algo, y toda la jodida computadora se vuelve loca. ▪ Detesto cuando tropiezo contra algo, y todo el puñetero ordenador enloquece. I hate it when I bump something, and the whole damn computer goes haywire.
tropezar con una dificultad ▪ dar con una dificultad ▪ dar con un escollo ▪ encontrarse con una dificultad to run into difficulty ▪ to hit a snag
tropezar con una oposición to run into opposition ➤ El proyecto de ley tropezó con una fuerte oposición en el Comité Bancario del Senado. The bill ran into strong opposition in the Senate Banking Committee.
trozo a trozo piece by piece
trozo de madera block of wood
trozo raquítico measly helping
trucar una fotografía to doctor a photograph ➤ Esta foto está trucada. This photo is doctored.
truco sucio dirty trick
trucos del oficio tricks of the trade
¡tú, aquí, ni entras ni sales! you stay out of this! ▪ you keep out of this!
tu bragueta está desabrochada ▪ se te va a escapar el pájaro your fly is open
tú déjame hablar a mí let me do the talking
tu estancia aquí your being here ➤ Agradecemos tu estancia aquí. We appreciate your being here.
¡tú la ligas! *(en un juego de cogidas, por ejemplo)* ▪ *(tú)* la pegas you're it!
(tú) lo eres that's you
¡tú lo has sacado!-¡no he sido yo! you brought it up!-I did not!
¡tú me has hecho a mí! you made me!
¡tú mismo (y tu mecanismo)! ▪ ¡allá tú! the ball's in your court! ▪ I've been here the whole time! ▪ I haven't gone anywhere!
tú no sabes qué alegría me da you don't know how glad I am ▪ you don't know how pleased I am ▪ you don't know how delighted I am ▪ I can't tell you how glad I am
¡tú no te metas! ▪ ¡mantente al margen! you stay out of this! ▪ you keep out of this!
tu opinión vale tanto como el mío your guess is as good as mine
¡tú por aquí! what are you doing here?!
¿tú qué te crees? ▪ ¿tú quién te crees que eres? who do you think you are?
¿tú quién te crees que eres? ▪ ¿tú qué te crees? who do you think you are?
¡tú te arreglas siempre para tirar la descargada! *(Valle-Inclán)* you always manage to get away with cheating!
¿tú te crees? ▪ ¿qué te parece? how do you like *that*?
tuerca floja ▪ tornillo suelto screw loose ➤ Tiene una tuerca floja. He has a screw loose.
tumbado(-a) boca abajo lying facedown
tumbar algo ▪ derrumbar algo ▪ derribar algo ▪ abatir algo to knock down something ▪ to knock something down
tumbarse a la bartola ▪ echarse a la bartola ▪ tenderse a la bartola to take it easy
tumbarse al sol (como un lagarto) ▪ tomar el sol ▪ ser como un lagarto to bask in the sun ▪ to sunbathe ▪ to get some sun ▪ *(coloquial)* to soak up some rays
tumbarse boca abajo to lie down on one's stomach ▪ to lie down facedown
tumbarse boca arriba to lie down on one's back ▪ to lie down faceup
tumbarse en un trineo to lie down on a sled
tupida alfombra de nieve deep blanket of snow
tupido bosque dense forest ▪ dense woods ▪ *(literario)* dense wood
turnarse ▪ alternarse en to take turns
turno de preguntas question-and-answer period ▪ question-and-answer session
tuve mis motivos para ▪ tuve mis razones para I had my reasons for

tuve mis razones para ▪ tuve mis motivos para I had my reasons for ➤ Tuve mis razones para escogerlo. ▪ Tuve mis motivos para elegirlo. I had my reasons for choosing it.

tuve mucho que explicar I had a lot of explaining to do

tuve que madurar mucho I had a lot of growing up to do

tuvo que haber ▪ debe haber 1. there had to be 2. there had to have been ▪ there must have been ➤ Tuvo que haber una tormenta aquí, a juggar por todas las ramas caídas. There had to have been a storm here, judging from the fallen branches. ▪ There must have been a storm here, judging from the fallen branches.

tuvo que ser planeado it had to have been planned ▪ it must have been planned

tuyo afectísimo sincerely yours ▪ affectionately

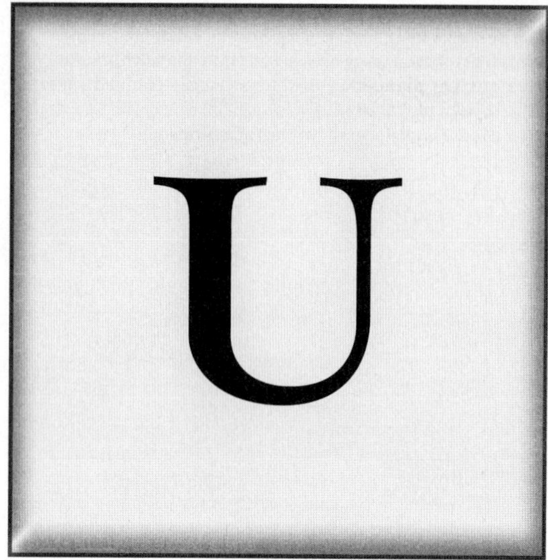

estar **(ubicado) en diagonal con respecto a la esquina** to sit at an angle to the corner ➤ El edificio está (ubicado) en diagonal con respecto a la esquina. The building sits at an angle to the corner.

ubicar algo ▪ colocar algo en orden to place something in (its proper) order

¡Uf, qué calor! Ugh, it's hot!

última fase de: estar en la ~ ▪ estar en la fase final de to be in the final stage(s) of

última fila *(teatro, cine)* back row

ser la **última gota** ▪ ser la gota que rebalsó el vaso ▪ ser el colmo to be the last straw

última palabra: quedarse con la ~ to always have to have the last word ▪ to always have to be one up ➤ Siempre tiene que quedarse con la última palabra. He always has to have the last word.

última palabra: tener la ~ to have the last word

última película latest film

última plaza last place ➤ Va a ser difícil abandonar la última plaza. It's going to be difficult to get out of last place.

última voluntad (antes de morir) last wish (before dying) ▪ final wish

ultimar el asalto final to plan the final assault ▪ to plan the final strike

ultimar un plan to finalize a plan ▪ to put the finishing touches on a plan

ultimar una reunión to conclude a meeting ➤ *(titular)* Aznar y Zapatero ultiman una reunión para salvar el pacto contra el terrorismo Aznar and Zapatero conclude (their) meeting to save the anti-terrorism pact

último aliento: dar el ~ to breathe one's last breath

último asidero last recourse ▪ last possible option ▪ last possible means

último cambio de sentido las 20 (veinte) próximas millas last turnaround next 20 (twenty) miles

último cuarto de hora final hours ➤ Clinton está aprovechando su última cuarto de hora en la Casa Blanca para lanzar iniciativas muy criticadas por los conservadores. Clinton is taking advantage of his final hours in the White House to launch initiatives highly criticized by the conservatives.

último cuarto de hora: al ~ at the eleventh hour ▪ final hours

el **último de lo último** ▪ lo ultísimo the very latest ▪ the newest of the new

último desmentido latest denial

último extracto de cuenta most recent bank statement ▪ latest bank statement ▪ last bank statement

ser el **último grito** to be the very latest

ser el **último grito de la tecnología** ▪ tecnología punta ▪ tecnología vanguardista to be the (very) latest technology

el **último instante** the very end ➤ El libro, *La vuelta al mundo en ochenta días*, tiene un final sorprendente que mantiene al lector en vilo hasta el último instante. The book, *Around the World in Eighty Days*, has a surprise ending that keeps the reader in suspense until the very end.

último intento de golpe de estado latest coup attempt

último intento para last-minute attempt to

último lanzamiento latest release ▪ new release

ser el **último mono** to be the low man on the totem pole

último pago *(más cuantioso que el resto)* ▪ pago final más ▪ último plazo balloon payment

último piso top floor

el **último que haya...** whoever was last... ➤ El último que haya estado en el baño se ha dejado la luz encendida. ▪ El último en estar en el baño se ha dejado la luz encendida. Whoever was in the bathroom last left the light on.

último recurso last resort ▪ last-minute appeal

último reducto last stronghold ▪ last holdout

último suspiro: respirar el ~ to take one's last breath ▪ to breathe one's last breath

último tramo de su salida a final stretch... ▪ home stretch...

últimos flecos de la operación last-minute details of the operation

últimos meses que le quedan de presidente last months as president

últimos retoques ▪ los remates finishing touches ▪ final touches ➤ Michael está poniendo los últimos retoques en el modelo del San Felipe. Michael is just putting the finishing touches on the model of the San Felipe. ➤ Miguel da los últimos retoques a su avión. Miguel is putting the finishing touches on his airplane.

últimos sacramentos last rites

los **últimos serán los primeros en el reino de los cielos** *(Nuevo Testamento)* the last shall be first in the kingdom of heaven

el **ultraje a la bandera** desecration of the flag ▪ defiling of the flag

el **ulular del viento** howling of the wind

un balance de a total of ➤ *(noticia)* Un balance de noventa personas murieron en el choque. A total of ninety people died in the crash.

ser **un bestia en** to be a whiz at ▪ to be a whiz in ➤ Ella es un bestia en las matemáticas. She's a whiz at math. ▪ She's a whiz in math.

¡un bledo! nonsense! ▪ sure, sure!

un buen pellizco ▪ una buena tajada a tidy sum ▪ a pretty penny

un buen día one fine day

un buen rato quite a while

un buen trecho a ways ▪ quite a ways ➤ Ya llevo un buen trecho andado así que quizá termine mis estudios aquí. I'm already down the track a ways, so I'll probably finish my degree here.

un catorceavo a fourteenth ▪ one fourteenth

un centésimo a hundredth ▪ one one hundredth

un cincuentavo a fiftieth ▪ one fiftieth

un cincuentiunavo a fifty-first ▪ one fifty-first

un día sí y otro no ▪ en días alternos every other day ▪ on alternating days ➤ Durante la crisis petrolera, pudimos comprar gasolina sólo un día sí y otro no. ▪ Durante la crisis petrolera, pudimos comprar gasolina en días alternos. During the oil crisis, we could buy gasoline only on alternating days. ▪ During the oil crisis, we could only buy gasoline every other day.

un dieciochavo ▪ un dieciochoavo an eighteenth ▪ one eighteenth

un cuarentavo a fortieth ▪ one fortieth

un cuarto a fourth ▪ one fourth

ser **un deber** to be a must ➤ Es un deber. It's a must.

un décimo a tenth ▪ one tenth

un día de estos one of these days

un día y otro día day in, day out ▪ day after day

un diecinueveavo a nineteenth ▪ one nineteenth

un dieciochoavo an eighteenth ▪ one eighteenth

un dieciseisavo a sixteenth ■ one sixteenth
un diecisieteavo a seventeenth ■ one seventeenth
un doceavo a twelfth ■ one twelfth
un, dos, tres, al escondite inglés ■ uno, dos y tres, al escondíte inglés one, two, three, here I come!
un gol de... ■ un gol para... a goal for... ■ a goal by...
un hombre, un voto ■ un hombre, un sufragio one man, one vote
un lugar para cada cosa y cada cosa en su lugar a place for everything, and everything in its place
un medio a half ■ one half
un medio para hacer algo a way to do something
¡un momento! 1. ¡espera un momento! just a moment! ■ just a minute! ■ wait a moment! ■ just a second ■ wait a second ■ hold on a second 2. ¡no tan de prisa! not so fast! ➤ ¡Un momento! ¿Qué pasa aquí? Just a minute! What's going on here?
un momento antes a moment before
un momento antes de (que)... ■ justo antes de que... a moment before... ■ just before... ➤ Un momento antes de perder contacto con el transbordador, el comandante transmitió a los controladores que había un incremento en la presión de uno de los neumáticos. ■ Un momento antes de que los controladores perdiesen contacto con el transbordador, el comandante transmitió que había un incremento en la presión de uno de los neumáticos. A moment before the controllers lost contact with the shuttle, the commander radioed that there was an increase in the pressure in one of the tires. ■ Just before the controllers lost contact with the shuttle, the commander radioed that there was an increase in the pressure of one of the tires.
un montón a lot ■ a whole lot ■ an awful lot ➤ Ha estado tosiendo un montón. He's been coughing a lot. ■ He's been coughing an awful lot.
un *no* contundente ■ un *no* rotundo ■ un *no* resonante a resounding *no*
un *no* rotundo a resounding *no*
un *no* tajante a flat *no* ■ an unequivocal *no*
un noveno a ninth ■ one ninth
un noventavo a ninetieth ■ one ninetieth
un número de ■ diversos ■ varios a number of ➤ Según un número de estudios... ■ Según diversos estudios... ■ Según varios estudios... According to a number of studies...
un ochentavo an eightieth ■ one eightieth
un octavo an eighth ■ one eighth
un onceavo an eleventh ■ one eleventh
un par de a couple of ➤ *(L.am)* Compré un par de rollos de película para el campamento. ■ *(Esp.)* Compré un par de rollos de película para el camping. I bought a couple of rolls of film for the camping trip.
un poco menos de gente not quite as many people ➤ Hubo un poco menos de gente en asistencia este año que la que hubo el año pasado. There weren't quite as many people in attendance this year as there were last year.
un poco de todo ■ de todo un poco a little of everything ➤ ¿Qué has estado haciendo esta mañana?-Un poco de todo. ■ ¿Qué has hecho esta mañana?-De todo un poco. What have you been doing this morning?-A little of everything.
un poco extrañado: quedarse ~ to be a little surprised
un poco más adelante 1. un poco más lejos a little farther on 2. un poco más tarde a little later on
ser **un poco disticoso(-a)** 1. *(refiriéndose a comida)* to be a little bit picky 2. *(refiriéndose a orden y limpieza)* to be fastidious 3. *(refiriéndose a susceptibilidad e irritabilidad)* to be a little bit finicky
ser **un poco raro(-a)** ■ ser un poco fuera de lo común to be a bit odd ■ to be a little odd ➤ Me parecía un poco raro. It seemed a little (bit) odd. ➤ A sus vecinos les parecía un poco rara. Her neighbors thought she was a bit odd. ■ Her neighbors thought her a bit odd. ■ To her neighbors, she seemed a bit odd.
un poco triste: quedarse ~ to be a little (bit) down ■ to be a little (bit) sad ➤ Me he quedado un poco triste. I've been a little bit down.
¡un punto para...! ■ ¡un tanto para...! 1. a point for...! 2. score one for...!
un puñado de gambas, por favor a handful of shrimp, please
un quinceavo a fifteenth ■ one fifteenth
un quinto a fifth ■ one fifth
un rato después a while later
¡un respeto! show a little respect!
¡un segundín! just a second!
un séptimo a seventh ■ one seventh
un sesentavo a sixtieth ■ one sixtieth
un setentavo a seventieth ■ one seventieth
un sexto a sixth ■ one sixth
¡un sinfín! an endless supply ■ a huge quantity
un solo Dios one God ➤ *(frase religiosa)* Creo en un solo Dios... I believe in one God...
un solo estudiante one student ➤ "Quiero que un solo estudiante maneje el video," dijo el maestro suplente. "I want one student to operate the video machine," said the substitute.
supongamos que... let's say... ■ for instance... ■ let's suppose...
ser **un tal y un cual** ■ ser un charlatán to be a charlatan
un... tan such a... ➤ Un animal tan pequeño Such a small animal
un tanto rather ■ somewhat
un tanto desconcertado a little disconcerted
un tanto difícil rather difficult ■ a little difficult
un tanto dormido a little sleepy
¡un tanto para...! 1. ¡un punto para...! a point for...! 2. anota uno para...score one for...!
ser **un tanto prematuro** to be a little premature ■ to be too early
un tercio a third ■ one third
un treceavo a thirteenth ■ one thirteenth
un treintaidosavo a thirty-second ■ one thirty-second
un treintaiunavo a thirty-first ■ one thirty-first
un treintavo a thirtieth ■ one thirtieth
un veinteavo a twentieth ■ one twentieth
un veintidosavo a twenty-second ■ one twenty-second
un veintiunavo a twenty-first ■ one twenty-first
una bonita mañana one fine morning
una buena cantidad a large quantity ■ a lot
una cosa así ■ algo así a thing like that ■ such a thing
una cosa es decirlo y otra hacerlo ■ del dicho al hecho hay un largo trecho it's one thing to say it and another thing to do it ■ it's one thing to talk and another to act
una cosa es predicar y otra es dar trigo it's one thing to talk and another to produce results
una cosa es que it's one thing for ➤ Una cosa es que nos importe el otro, pero otra es adueñarse de su libertad. It's one thing for someone to be important to us, but it's another to take over their freedom.
una cosa llevó a la otra one thing led to another
una cosa sí te digo I'll tell you one thing ■ I'll say one thing
una cosa sí te diré I'll tell you one thing ■ I'll say one thing ➤ Una cosa sí te diré que no me gusta de este nuevo refrigerador, que ya está empezando a formar hielo. I'll tell you one thing I don't like about this new refrigerator, it's already starting to ice up.
ser **una cualquiera** to be a woman of easy virtue
dar una de cal y otra de arena to apply a policy of carrot and stick
una de dos 1. *(preferencia)* one or the other ■ take your pick 2. *(decisión)* make up your mind ➤ Tengo cerveza y vino. Elige una de dos. I've got beer and wine. Take your pick. ➤ Una de dos: te vas con nosotros o te quedas. Make up your mind: either come with us or stay.
una de las razones por la que one of the reasons that
una de las razones por las que one of the reasons why
una especie de 1. a sort of 2. a type of ■ one type of ■ a kind of
una manera de... 1. *(una como un artículo)* a way to... 2. *(una como un número)* one way to...
una noche de viernes on a Friday night
una pareja de a couple of
una planta más arriba ■ un piso más arriba one floor up
una poca cantidad a small quantity ■ a little thing of it ➤ Una poca cantidad cuesta 245 pesetas. A little thing of it costs 245 pesetas.
¡una polla (como la manga de un abrigo)! *(subido de tono)* no fuckin' way!

¡una polla (como una olla)! *(subido de tono)* no fuckin' way!

¡una polla (de aquí a Lima)! *(subido de tono)* no fuckin' way!

una que otra palabra a (very) few words

una que otra palabra: escribir ~ to jot a few things down

una que otra vez 1. *(adverbio)*(every) once in a while ▪ occasionally **2.** *(adjetivo)* an occasional ➤ Tomo cervezas una que otra vez. I drink a beer every once in a while. ▪ I drink a beer occasionally ▪ I drink an occasional beer.

una semana antes a week before

una sola persona one person ▪ a single person ▪ a single individual ➤ "Quiero una sola persona para manejar el reproductor de DVD," le dijo el sustituto a la clase. "I want *one* person to operate the DVD player," said the substitute teacher to the class.

una sola vez ▪ una única vez a single time ▪ one time ▪ once

una única vez ▪ una sola vez a single time ▪ one time ▪ once

una vez at one time ▪ once

una vez a la semana once a week

una vez a las quinientas very rarely ➤ Yo viajo en avión una vez a las quinientas. I travel by plane very rarely. ▪ I rarely travel by plane.

una vez a salvo once safe ▪ on reaching safety

una vez al año una vez por año once a year

una vez de más once too often ➤ Ella se insubordinó una vez demás, y ello le costó su trabajo. She was insubordinate once too often, and it cost her her job.

una vez más ▪ de nuevo ▪ otra vez ▪ por enésima vez one more time ▪ all over again ➤ La serie de la *Guerra de las Galaxias* es sólo los buenos y los malos una vez más. ▪ La serie de la *Guerra de las Galaxias* es sólo los buenos y los malos de nuevo. ▪ La serie de la *Guerra de las Galaxias* es sólo los buenos y los malos otra vez. ▪ La serie de la *Guerra de las Galaxias* es sólo los buenos y los malos por enésima vez. The *Star Wars* series is just the good guys and and the bad guys all over again.

una vez que la conozcas once you get to know her

una vez que le conozcas *(Esp., leísmo)* ▪ una vez que lo conozcas once you get to know him

una vez que lo conozcas once you get to know him

una vez que lo había leído (yo) once I had read it *(pronunciado "red")*

una vez que lo haya leído (yo) once I have read it *(pronunciado "red")*

una vez que lo lea (yo) once I read it *(pronunciado "rid")*

una vez que lo leí once I read it *(pronunciado "red")*

una vez que uno haya... ▪ cuando uno haya... once one has... ▪ when one has... ➤ Una vez que yo haya leído el artículo, puedo darte mi opinión. Once I have read the article, I can give you my opinion. ▪ When I have read the article, I can give you my opinion.

una vez que uno hubo... ▪ cuando uno hubo... once one had... ▪ when one had... ▪ after one had... ➤ Una vez que Lincoln hubo escrito la carta al Gen. Meade, decidió no mandarla. Once Lincoln had written the letter to Gen. Meade, he decided not to send it.

una vez superado once you get past ▪ when you get past ➤ Una vez superada la política y la religión, es claro que la gente es simplemente la gente. When you get past politics and religion, people are just people.

una vez tenía *(yo)* I once had

una y no más (Santo Tomás) 1. just one more! **2.** but not a second time ▪ but not again ➤ ¿Quieres otra copa?-Una y no más, Santo Tomás. Do you want another drink?-Just one more! ➤ Esta te la dejo pasar, pero una y no más. I'll let it go this time, but not the next time. ▪ I'll overlook it this time, but not again.

una y otra vez again and again ▪ over and over again ▪ time and again ▪ time and time again ▪ repeatedly

unas cuantas a few

unas cuantas cosas a few things

unas cuantas cosas: preguntarte ~ ▪ hacerte unas cuantas preguntas to ask you a few things ▪ to ask you a few questions

unas cuantas veces a few times

unas décimas slight temperature ▪ mild temperature ▪ low fever ➤ (Ella) tiene unas décimas. She has a slight temperature.

unas décimas de segundo a fraction of a second

única alternativa es (que...): la ~ the only alternative is (to)...

única manera de: la ~ the only way to

única vía para: la ~ the only way to

ser el **único en hablar** ▪ llevar el pero de una conversación to do all the talking

único(-a) que queda only surviving ▪ only one left ➤ Mi abuela es la única que queda. My grandmother is my only surviving grandparent. ▪ My grandmother is my only grandparent left.

unidad astronómica ▪ UA astronomical unit ▪ AU ➤ Una unidad astronómica (UA) es la distancia media entre la Tierra y el Sol, 149.587.870,691 millones de kilómetros (92,955,807 millones de millas). One astronomical unit (AU) is the mean distance between the Earth and the sun, 149.587.870,691 million kilometers (92,955,807 miles).

unidad de cuidados intensivos ▪ UCI intensive care unit ▪ ICU

unidad de vigilancia intensiva *(Esp.)* ▪ UVI ambulance ▪ mobile emergency treatment unit ▪ mobile clinic

unido a together with ▪ combined with ▪ along with ➤ La niebla, unida al exceso de velocidad y a la falta de distancias de seguridad causó catorce muertos y setenta heridos como balance provisional. Fog, together with excessive speed and lack of safe distances between cars, caused fourteen deaths and an estimated seventy injuries...

estar **unidos por** *(hermanos siameses)* to be joined at ➤ Las hermanas siameses estaban unidas por la cabeza. The Siamese twins were joined at the head. ▪ The Siamese twin sisters were joined at the head.

la **unión de facto** ▪ unión de hecho ▪ concubinato ▪ pareja de hecho common-law marriage ▪ de facto union ▪ concubinage

la **unión de hecho** ▪ unión de facto ▪ concubinato ▪ pareja de hecho common-law marriage ▪ de facto union ▪ concubinage

la **unión hace la fuerza** there is strength in numbers ▪ there's strength in numbers

unir a las personas to bring people together ▪ to unite people

unir fuerzas contra to join forces against ➤ Conservadores y socialistas unen fuerzas contra el voto de miedo en Euskadi. Conservatives and socialists join forces against the rule of fear in País Vasco.

unir (sus) fuerzas con to join forces with

unirse a los voluntarios to join the volunteers

unirse a un coro to join a choir

unirse a una empresa to join a firm ➤ Cuando se unió a la empresa, era el miembro más joven. When he joined the firm, he was its youngest member.

unirse a una clase to join a class ➤ ¿Quieres unirte a nuestra clase? Do you want to join our class?

unirse al circo to join the circus ➤ Huyó de su casa para unirse al circo. He ran away from home to join the circus.

unirse para hacer algo to join forces to do something

universidad a distancia open university

universidad estatal state university ➤ Universidad Estatal de Pensilvania Pennsylvania State University ▪ Penn State

universo en sí mismo: ser un (auténtico) ~ to be a world in oneself ➤ San Francisco, Juana de Arco, Miguel de Cervantes, el filósofo Immanuel Kant y Abraham Lincoln son auténticos universos en sí mismos. Figuran entre las grandes personalidades del segundo milenio. St. Francis, Joan of Arc, Miguel de Cervantes, the philosopher Immanuel Kant and Abraham Lincoln are worlds in themselves. They rank among the great personalities of the second millenium.

uno a continuación del otro ▪ uno al lado del otro ▪ juntos beside each other ▪ next to each other ▪ together

uno a la vez one at a time

uno al lado del otro ▪ uno a continuación del otro ▪ juntos beside each other ▪ next to each other ▪ together

uno de esos one of those ➤ He debido tragar uno de esos chiles picantes. ▪ He debido haber tragado uno de esos chiles picantes. I must have swallowed one of those hot peppers.

uno de esos tipos aventureros one of those adventurous types

ser **uno de esos tíos que...** to be the kind of guy who... ▪ to be one of those guys who...

ser **uno de los nuestros** to be one of us ➤ Es uno de los nuestros. He's one of us. ➤ Es una de las nuestras. She's one of us.

uno de los pocos one of the few

uno detrás de otro one after another

uno en uno: (de) ~ one at a time ▪ one by one ➤ Subieron los muebles de uno en uno. They took the pieces of furniture up(stairs) one at a time. ▪ They took the pieces of furniture up(stairs) one by one.

ser **uno entre un millón** to be one in a million

uno haría bien en... ▪ se haría bien en... one would do well to... ➤ Te harías bien en... You would do well to...

uno igual one like it

ser **uno mismo** to be oneself ➤ Soy yo mismo a pesar de mi mismo, pero me gustaría ser yo mismo adrede. I'm myself in spite of myself, but I'd like to be myself on purpose.

uno nunca sabe one never knows

uno o el otro either one ➤ Podemos permitirnos comprar un apartamento o el otro. We can afford to buy either condominium.

uno podría pensar que... ▪ se podría pensar que... ▪ cabe pensar que... ▪ cabría pensar que... one would think that... ▪ you would think that...

uno por uno one by one ▪ one at a time

uno sobre uno one on one

uno tras otro 1. one after the other 2. en rápida sucesión in rapid succession

uno y otro ▪ tanto el uno como el otro ▪ ambos both ▪ each ➤ El español y el francés son lenguas romances. Uno y otro proceden del latín. Spanish and French are Romance languages. Both come from Latin. ▪ Spanish and French are Romance languages. Each comes from Latin. ➤ Una y otra (compañía) pertenecen al mismo conglomerado. Both (companies) belong to the same conglomerate. ▪ Each (company) belongs to the same conglomerate.

unos cuantos a few ➤ Trajo unos cuantos libros consigo. He brought a few books with him.

unos pocos más ▪ unos cuantos más a few more

untar el filete con ajos machacados to rub the fillet with crushed garlic ▪ to rub the crushed garlic into the fillet ▪ to massage crushed garlic over the fillet ➤ Untar el filete con los ajos machacados y dejarlo una hora. Rub the crushed garlic into the fillet and let it rest for an hour.

untarle la mano a alguien ▪ sobornar a alguien to grease someone's palm ▪ to bribe someone

uña encarnada ingrown nail ➤ (Él) tiene una uña encarnada en el dedo del pie. He has an ingrown toenail.

uña está arañando *(de la mano)* (finger)nail is snagging ▪ (finger)nail is catching

ser **uña y carne** ▪ ser como uña y carne ▪ ser inseparables to be thick as thieves ▪ to be inseparable

urdir robarle a alguien to plot to rob someone ▪ to scheme to rob someone

urdir un atentado to plot an assassination

urdir un crimen to plot a crime

usando los poderes de que me invisten by virtue of the powers invested in me

usar algo como un elemento de presión en una negociación ▪ utilizar algo como un elemento de presión en una negociación to use something as leverage in a negotiation ▪ to use something as a bargaining chip in a negotiation

usar de su derecho to exercise one's right

usar el látigo con alguien ▪ usar el látigo contra alguien to whip someone

usar tiempo de manera eficiente to make good use of one's time ➤ Connie usa su tiempo de manera eficiente. Connie makes good use of her time.

usar un anillo ▪ llevar un anillo to wear a ring

uso del matrimonio use of marriage as a means

usos intelectuales *(culto)* ▪ tendencias intelectuales intellectual tendencies

usos y costumbres: decidir según (sus) ~ to decide on the basis of one's roots and traditions

usos y costumbres: vivir según (sus) ~ to live according to one's roots and traditions

usted debe tener dieciocho años de edad o más you must be eighteen (years old) ▪ you must be over eighteen ▪ you must be eighteen or over ▪ you must be eighteen or older

usted se está adelantando a mí ▪ usted me está tomando la delantera you're getting ahead of me

usted lo es you are

usted me está tomando la delantera ▪ usted se está adelantando a mí you're getting ahead of me

utilizar a alguien como correo 1. utilizar a alguien como mensajero to use someone as a courier 2. to use someone as a conduit for drugs 3. utilizar a alguien para actividades ilegales to use someone as a conduit for illegal activities

utilizar algo como un elemento de presión en una negociación ▪ usar algo como un elemento de presión en una negociación to use something as leverage in a negotiation ▪ to use something as a bargaining chip in a negotiation

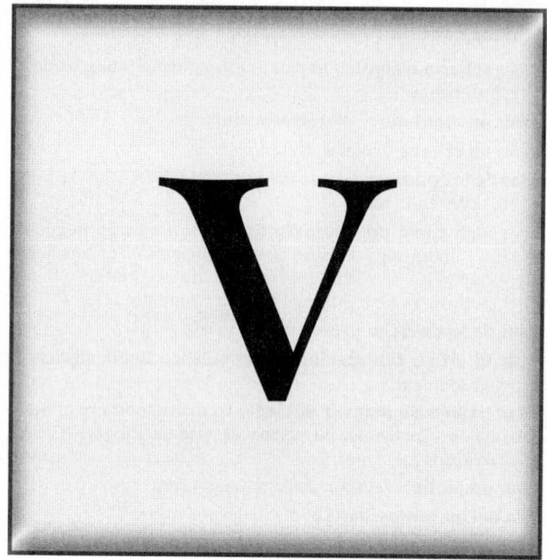

va a dar mucho (de) que hablar there's going to be a lot of talking ▪ it's going to provoke a lot of controversy

va a haber ▪ habrá **1.** *(singular)* there is going to be ▪ there will be **2.** *(plural)* there are going to be ▪ there will be

va a haber hule there is going to be trouble ▪ *(coloquial)* there's gonna be trouble

va a ponerse bien 1. *(él)* he's going to be okay ▪ he's going to recover ▪ he'll recover **2.** *(ella)* she's going to be okay ▪ she's going to recover ▪ she'll recover

va a resultar complicado, por no decir imposible that will be difficult if not impossible

va bien 1. (it) is going well **2.** funciona bien (it) is working well ▪ (it) is doing well

va de cuento que the story goes that ▪ the story is that ▪ the story is told that

va de que: el cuento ~ ▪ el cuento trata de the story is about

va en contra de las reglas it's against the rules

va incluido it is included ▪ it comes with ➤ La pila va incluída. The battery is included. ▪ It comes with the battery.

va mucho en... ▪ mucho va en... it depends a lot on... ▪ a lot depends on... ➤ Va mucho en la persona que lo haga. It depends a lot on the person doing it. ▪ A lot depends on the person doing it.

va para *x* (años) 1. *(él)* he's going on *x* (years of age) **2.** *(ella)* she's going on *x* (years of age) ➤ Ella va para cincuenta. She's going on fifty.

va para *x* años que... it's going on *x* years since... ➤ Va para ocho años que vine a España. It's going on eight years since I came to Spain.

va por ti también ▪ eso va por ti también ▪ eso también va por ti that goes for you, too ▪ that means you, too

va que arde it's as good as it gets

va que chuta ▪ va que se mata that should do it ▪ that should cover it ▪ that should be more than enough ▪ that should be plenty

va que se mata ▪ va que chuta that should do it ▪ that should cover it ▪ that should be more than enough ▪ that should be plenty

va sin explicación it needs no explanation

va y va 1. *(él)* he goes and goes ▪ he's always on the go ▪ he keeps on the go ▪ he stays on the go **2.** *(ella)* she goes and goes ▪ she's always on the go ▪ she keeps on the go ▪ she stays on the go

vacaciones estivales summer vacation ▪ summer holidays

vacas flacas lean years ▪ years of (financial) hardship

vacas gordas years of prosperty ▪ time of prosperity ▪ prosperous years ▪ prosperous times ▪ boom

vaciar el costal a alguien ▪ vaciar el saco a alguien to unburden oneself to someone ▪ to tell someone everything

vaciar los bolsillos to empty one's pockets

vaciarse un recinto to let out ▪ to get out ➤ Según se vaciaba el recinto del concierto nos encontramos con unos amigos. ▪ Conforme se vaciaba el recinto del concierto nos encontramos con unos amigos. As the concert was letting out, we ran into some friends. ▪ As the concert was getting out, we ran into some old friends.

vacilar entre to hesitate between

vacío de poder power vacuum

estar **vacunado contra** to be vaccinated against

vadear un río a pie ▪ cruzar un río vadeando ▪ apear un río ▪ franquear un río to ford a river ▪ to wade across a river

¡**vado permanente!** *(Esp.)* keep clear!

vagar por to wander (around)

ser un **vago de siete suelas** to be a good-for-nothing bum

el **vagón de primera** first-class (railroad) car

el **vagón restaurante** dining car

el **vagón de segunda** second-class (railroad) car

¡**vale!** *(Esp.)* **1.** está bien ▪ conforme ▪ órale okay! **2.** ¡muy bien! good!

vale más el remedio que la cura an ounce of prevention is worth a pound of cure

vale la pena it's worth it ▪ it's worth the trouble

vale la pena intentarlo it's worth a try

vale más (hacer algo) it is better (to do something)

vale más hacer que mandar if you want something done right, it's better to do it yourself

¡**vale, tío!** *(Esp.)* okay, José!

vale todo ▪ todo vale anything goes

valer igual para un fregado que para un barrido ▪ valer lo mismo para un fregado que para un barrido ▪ servir lo mismo para un fregado que para un barrido to be a jack-of-all-trades

valer la pena to be worthwhile ▪ to be worth the trouble

valer lo mismo para un fregado que para un barrido ▪ servir lo mismo para un fregado que para un barrido to be a jack-of-all-trades

valer más hacer algo ▪ ser mejor hacer algo to be better to do something ➤ Más valdría venir a Madrid cuando no haga tanto calor. ▪ Sería mejor venir a Madrid cuando no haga tanto calor. It would be better to come to Madrid when it's not so hot.

valer más que uno haga algo to be better for one to do something ▪ to be better that one do something

valer para to be good for ➤ *(farmacéutico)* La ibuprofena vale para los músculos adoloridos. Ibuprofen is good for sore muscles.

valer su peso en oro to be worth one's weight in gold

valer tanto como pesa to carry one's weight ➤ Vale tanto como pesa. He carries his weight.

valer un brindis ▪ merecer un brindis to deserve a toast ➤ Eso vale un brindis. ▪ Eso merece un brindis. That deserves a toast.

valer un huevo y la yema del otro *(subido de tono)* to cost an arm and a leg

valer un imperio to be worth a fortune

valer un ojo de la cara to cost an arm and a leg

valer un potosí ▪ valer su peso en oro to be worth its weight in gold

valer un riñón to cost an arm and a leg

valer *x* puntos to be worth *x* points

valerle a alguien to get into ▪ to fit someone ➤ Estas botas no me valen. ▪ No entro en estas botas. ▪ No quepo en estas botas. I can't get into these boots. ▪ These boots don't fit (me). ▪ I can't get these boots on.

valerle a alguien el premio to win someone the prize ▪ to get someone the prize ▪ to garner the prize ➤ Las obras de Rigoberta Menchú sobre los mayas le valieron el Premio Nobel. The works of Rigoberta Menchú about the Mayans won her the Nobel Prize. ▪ The works of Rigoberta Menchú about the Mayans got her the Nobel Prize. ▪ The works of Rigoberta Menchú about the Mayans garnered (her) the Nobel Prize.

valerle a alguien un premio to earn someone a prize ▪ to garner someone a prize ▪ to get someone a prize

valerse de algo para algo 1.to make use of something for some purpose ▪ to use something for some purpose ▪ to avail oneself of something to do something **2.** to claim responsibility

➤ Se valió de sus encantos personales para engatusar al guarda. She used her charms to sweet-talk the guard. ➤ Ningún grupo se ha valido del ataque. No group has claimed responsibility for the attack (in order to exert pressure on the government).

valerse de toda su fuerza interior to muster all of one's inner strength

valerse de un pretexto to seize on an excuse ➤ Se valió del pretexto deprisa, como si lo buscara. She seized on the excuse hastily, as if she were looking for one.

valerse de una oportunidad to seize (on) an opportunity

valerse por sí mismo to get along by oneself ▪ to manage by oneself ▪ to fend for oneself

valerse solo to get along by oneself ▪ to manage by oneself ▪ to fend for oneself

¡**válgame el cielo!** good heavens!

¡**válgame Dios!** good heavens!

¡**válgate Dios!** heaven help you!

valía la pena intentarlo it was worth a try

¡**valiente amiga!** 1. *(tú)* some friend you are! 2. *(ella)* some friend she is!

¡**valiente amigo!** 1. *(tú)* some friend you are! 2. *(él)* some friend he is!

valla de protección guard rail

el **valle de lágrimas** (this) vale of tears

valor alimenticio food value ▪ nutritional value

valor fiduciario 1. bank note ▪ treasury bill 2. intrinsic value

el **valor nominal** face value ▪ nominal value

el **valor superior** higher value

el **valor tiene su recompensa** courage is its own reward ▪ virtue is its own reward

valoración objetiva de los hechos objective appraisal of the facts ▪ objective assessment of the facts

valorar que to appreciate the fact that

valorar una propiedad to appraise a piece of property

los **valores en cartera** investment portfolio ▪ holdings

los **valores inmuebles** real estate

los **valores superiores** finer virtues

vamos a aclarar una cosa let's get one thing straight ▪ let's make one thing clear

¡**vamos a casarnos!** we're engaged! ▪ we're going to get married!

vamos a decir ▪ digamos ▪ supongamos let's say

vamos a ir a barullos there will be a lot of us ▪ there will be a big group of us

vamos a medias let's go halves ▪ let's split the bill

vamos a meternos aquí let's go in here

vamos a por el niño *(Esp.)* ▪ vamos por el niño 1. we're going to try for a boy 2. let's try for a boy 3. pasemos por el niño let's go get the little boy ▪ let's go pick up the little boy

vamos a por la niña *(Esp.)* 1. we're going to try for a girl 2. let's try for a girl 3. pasemos por la niña let's go get the girl ▪ let's go pick up the little girl

vamos a por un café *(Esp.)* ▪ vamos a tomar un café let's go have a cup of coffee ▪ let's go get a cup of coffee ▪ let's go for a cup of coffee

vamos a tomar un café let's go have a cup of coffee ▪ let's go get a cup of coffee ▪ let's go for a cup of coffee

vamos al caso ▪ vamos al grano let's get to the point

vamos al grano ▪ vamos al caso let's get to the point

¡**vamos allá!** here we go!

vamos allí ▪ vamos para allí let's go there

¡**vamos, anda!** come on, now! ▪ c'mon now!

vamos haciéndonos menos *(Méx.)* 1. let's have fewer children 2. let's humble ourselves *(Juego de palabras utilizado en vallas publicitarias para contrarrestar el machismo como valor social)*

vamos para allá (en seguida) *(coloquial)* we'll be (right) over

vamos para allí ▪ vamos pa allá let's go there!

vamos por buen camino now we're on the right track ▪ now we're getting somewhere ▪ now we're in business ▪ now we're cooking with gas

vamos por partes let's go one step at a time ▪ let's take one thing at a time

¡**vamos tirando!** we're getting by! ▪ we're hanging in there!

¡**vamos viento en popa!** we're cooking with gas! ▪ we're going great guns!

van a rodar cabezas heads are going to roll ▪ *(coloquial)* heads are going to roll

van iguales *(deportes)* ▪ (van) empatados they're tied ▪ the score is even ▪ it's a draw

van incluidos it comes with ➤ Con la ensaladera van incluidos una cuchara y un tenedor de madera. The salad bowl comes with a wooden spoon and fork.

van *x* dólares a que... ▪ te apuesto *x* dólares a que... I bet (you) *x* dollars that...

vanidad y pobreza, en una pieza: tener ~ to be vain and poor at the same time

vapulear a alguien 1. ganar sobradamente to trounce someone 2. dar una paliza a alguien to give someone a beating

vara mágica ▪ varita mágica magic wand

las **variaciones sobre el mismo tema** *(música)* themes and variations

variar el viento (for) the wind to change ➤ Ha variado el viento. The wind has changed.

varias alternativas para several alternatives to

varias alternativas para que several alternatives for

variedad en la unidad unity in diversity

varilla de aceite dipstick

varios años several years ➤ Los restos llevaban allí varios años. The remains had been there for several years.

varita mágica ▪ vara mágica magic wand

varón esclarecido great man

vas a ponerte bien you're going to be okay ▪ you're going to recover

vas a ver lo que es bueno ▪ te vas a llevar una buena you're going to get it ▪ *(coloquial)* you're gonna get it ▪ you're gonna enjoy it

vaso capilar capillary (vein)

vaso sanguíneo blood vessel

vástago de émbolo piston rod

vaticinar los resultados de las elecciones to predict the election results

¡**vaya alucine!** ▪ ¡vaya flipe! ▪ ¡menudo flipe! what a trip! ▪ what an experience!

¡**vaya bicho!** ▪ ¡vaya trasto! what a brat!

¡**vaya bodrio!** 1. *(habitación)* what a mess! 2. *(bar o disco cutre)* what a dive! 3. *(cachivaches)* what a bunch of junk! 4. *(tonterías)* that's a crock! ▪ what a crock! ▪ that's (a bunch of) nonsense ▪ that's a bunch of bull ▪ that's baloney ▪ that's a bunch of hooey

¡**vaya cálculo!** what timing!

¡**vaya cálculo en el riñón!** *(cómico)* what timing!

¡**vaya chasco!** 1. what a bummer! ▪ what a downer! 2. what a letdown! ▪ what a comedown!

¡**vaya chollo!** what a deal! ▪ what a bargain! ➤ ¡Vaya chollo de coche! What a deal (you got) on that car! ▪ You got a good deal on that car!

vaya con... I can't believe...

vaya con Dios go with God

¡**vaya coñazo!** *(subido de tono)* 1. what a pain in the ass! 2. what a crashing bore!

¡**vaya coñazo de...!** what a lousy...! ▪ what a crappy...! ▪ what a rotten...! ➤ ¡Vaya coñazo de película que nos han hecho tragar! What a crappy movie they made us watch!

¡**vaya cosa!** what a piece of work! ▪ what a disaster!

¡**vaya cuervo!** ▪ ¡vaya pendejo! ▪ ¡vaya fiasco! what a turkey! ▪ what a jerk!

¡**vaya desbarajuste!** ▪ ¡vaya lío! ▪ ¡qué lío ▪ ¡menudo lío! ▪ ¡qué follón! what a mess!

¡**vaya día!** what a day!

vaya donde vaya uno wherever one goes ➤ Ella va a triunfar vaya donde vaya. She'll be successful wherever she goes.

¡**vaya dos!** ▪ ¡vaya par de dos! what a pair! ▪ what a couple!

¡**vaya flipe!** ▪ ¡vaya alucine! ▪ ¡menudo flipe! what a trip! ▪ what an experience! ▪ oh, wow!

¡**vaya fracaso!** what a bomb! ▪ what a flop!

¡**vaya horas!** at last!

¡vaya impresión que me llevé! I was very impressed! ▪ it made quite an impression on me

¡vaya locura! talk about crazy!

¡vaya noche ha sido para...! it's been quite a night for... ▪ what a night it's been for... ➤ ¡Vaya noche ha sido para Real Madrid! It's been quite a night for Real Madrid! ▪ What a night it's been for Real Madrid!

¡vaya nombre! what a name!

¡vaya novedad! ▪ ¡qué novedad! what a novelty!

¡vaya papeleta! ▪ ¡qué problema! what a predicament! ▪ what a situation!

¡vaya par de dos! ▪ ¡vaya dos! what a pair! ▪ what a couple! ▪ what a duo! ▪ what a twosome!

vaya perro con to be hell bent on ▪ to be bound and determined to ➤ Vaya perro con irse a España. He's hell bent on going to Spain.

¡vaya por Dios! ▪ ¡ay, Dios mío! oh, good God! ▪ oh, my God!

¡vaya por dónde! ▪ ¡mira por dónde! ▪ ¡imagínate! fancy that! ▪ imagine that!

¡vaya problema! what a problem! ▪ what a lot of trouble!

¡vaya ritmo! what a pace! ➤ ¡Vaya ritmo llevan tus amigos! What a bunch of partiers your friends are! ➤ ¡Vaya ritmo de trabajo que se lleva en esta oficina! What a beehive (of activity) this office is!

¡vaya si! of course

¡vaya sitio! 1. *(negativo)* what a dump! ▪ what a dive! 2. *(positivo)* what a great place!

¡vaya sitio este! what a dive! ▪ what a dump!

¡vaya susto! that's scary ▪ what a scare! ▪ what a fright!

¡vaya tanque! *(al servirse un café)* ▪ ¡vaya taza! ▪ ¡qué taza! what a big cup! ▪ that's a big cup!

¡vaya tela! ▪ ¡tiene tela! amazing! ▪ incredible! ▪ unbelievable!

¡vaya trasto! 1. ¡qué porquería! what a piece of junk! 2. *(de un coche)* ¡qué cascajo! what a heap! ▪ what a piece of junk! 3. ¡qué mal criado(-a)! what a brat!

¡vaya un folletín! *(Valle-Inclán)* what a soap opera!

¡vaya una cosa! ▪ ¡gran cosa! big deal!

¡vaya una sombra negra! *(Valle-Inclán)* what rotten luck!

vaya usted a saber ▪ cualquiera sabe ▪ ¡ande! ¿quién sabe? who knows? ▪ who's to say? ▪ there's no telling ▪ it's anyone's guess ▪ God knows! ▪ goodness knows!

¡vaya, vaya! well, well!

¡vaya zafarrancho! ¡qué desmadre! what an uproar! ▪ what a circus! ▪ this is total chaos!

váyase lo ganado por lo perdido ▪ váyase lo uno por lo otro *(Esp.)* there's no gain or loss ▪ we're at even stakes ▪ it's even stakes ▪ it's fifty-fifty ▪ it's quits

váyase (usted) a paseo *(Esp.)* ▪ váyase de paseo ▪ váyase a freír churros ▪ váyase a freír espárragos go jump in a lake ▪ go take a flying leap

ve pensando en be thinking of ➤ Ve pensando en un sitio para ir a cenar. Be thinking of a place to go have supper. ▪ Be thinking of a place to go have dinner.

veces más times as ➤ El olfato canino es al menos trescientas veces más agudo que el humano. A dog's sense of smell is at least three hundred times as sharp as a human's.

vecindario cómodo (para vivir) ▪ barrio cómodo (para vivir) convenient neighborhood ➤ Este es un vecindario muy cómodo (para vivir). This is a very convenient neighborhood.

vecino de al lado next-door neighor

vecino del edificio occupant of the building

la **vegetación exuberante** lush vegetation ▪ luxuriant vegetation

vehículo contrario oncoming vehicle

una **veintena de personas** some twenty people

veinticuatro horas tiene el día you've had enough time to do it

vela mayor main sail

velada agradable ▪ velada amena enjoyable evening

velada alusión a veiled reference to

velada amena ▪ velada agradable enjoyable evening

velar algo por turnos to take turns watching something

velar por la salud ▪ cuidar la salud to guard one's health ▪ to look after one's health ▪ to be careful about one's health

velar por la seguridad 1. to look out for one's safety 2. to look after one's security

ser una **veleta** *(políticamente)* to change with the (political) winds ▪ to be a chameleon

velo de niebla thin layer of fog ▪ light layer of fog ▪ thin cover of fog ▪ light cover of fog

velocidad absoluta groundspeed ▪ ground speed

velocidad controlada por radar speed checked by radar

la **velocidad de combate** intensity of the combat ▪ fierceness of the combat

la **velocidad de crucero** cruising speed

la **velocidad de escape** escape velocity

la **velocidad del sonido** speed of sound ▪ velocity of sound ➤ Los trenes alcanzarán velocidades varias veces superiores a la del sonido. The trains will reach speeds several times that of sound.

la **velocidad límite** terminal velocity

velocidad relativa airspeed ▪ air speed

¡ven a conocerlo! come and check it out!

¡ven a tomar parte! come and join in!

¡ven a ver! come and see!

¡ven a vivirlo! come and experience it!

¡ven acá! come here!

¡ven por otra! come get another one! ▪ come have another one!

ven y únete a nosotros come (and) join us

ven y tráete (a) tus amigos ▪ ven y tráete (a) unos amigos come and bring your friends ▪ come and bring some friends

ven y tráete (a) un amigo come and bring a friend

¡ven y verás! come and see (for yourself)

el **vencedor se queda con todo** the winner takes all

vencer a alguien con contundencia to roundly defeat someone ▪ to defeat someone roundly

vencer a alguien por *x* puntos ▪ ganar a alguien por *x* puntos ▪ derrotar a alguien por *x* puntos to beat someone by *x* points ▪ to win over someone by *x* points ▪ to defeat someone by *x* points ➤ Real Madrid vence a Barcelona por seis puntos. Real Madrid beats Barcelona by six points. ▪ Real Madrid wins over Barcelona by six points.

vencer el *x* de abril ▪ caducar el *x* de abril to expire (on) the *x*th of April ➤ Mi prórroga de estancia vence el veinte y seis de julio. My visa extension expires (on) July twenty-sixth.

vencer la timidez to overcome shyness

vencer sus miedos to conquer one's fears

vencido la fecha de entrega: haber ~ ▪ haber vencido el plazo to be overdue ➤ La fecha de entrega ha vencido. ▪ El plazo ha vencido. It's overdue.

vendar una herida to bandage a wound ▪ to bind (up) a wound ➤ El equipo de primeros auxilios vendó la herida de la víctima. The paramedics bandaged the victim's wound. ▪ The paramedics bound up the victim's wound.

vendarle los ojos a alguien to blindfold someone

el **vendedor ambulante** 1. traveling salesman 2. door-to-door salesman

vender algo al por mayor to sell something wholesale

vender algo al por menor to sell something retail

vender algo bien ▪ vender algo a buen precio to sell something for a good price ▪ to get a good price for something

vender algo por chauchas y palitos *(Arg.)* ▪ vender algo por una tontería to sell something for a song ▪ to sell something for peanuts

vender algo por lo que te den to sell something for whatever you can get (for it)

vender algo por una tontería to sell something for a song ▪ to sell something for peanuts

vender caro to sell high ▪ to sell above the market price ▪ to sell above market ➤ Pedro tuvo suerte. Vendió la casa cara, y se salió con la suya. Pedro was lucky. He sold the house for above market, and got away with it.

vender el oro y el moro to sell someone a bill of goods

vender hasta la camisa to (practically have to) sell the shirt off one's back ➤ Está tan mal que ha tenido que vender hasta la camisa. He's is so badly off financially that he (practically) had to sell the shirt off his back.

vender la burra *(arcaico)* ■ vender la moto ■ *(Arg.)* dorarle la píldora to talk someone into something ➤ (Ya) le vendió la burra. ■ (Ya) le vendió la moto. *(a él)* He's (already) talked him into it. ■ *(a ella)* He's (already) talked her into it.

vender la moto ■ vender la burra to talk someone into something ➤ (Ya) le vendió la moto (a él). He's (already) talked him into it.

vender la piel del oso antes de cazarlo to count one's chickens before they hatch

vender una cinta pirata 1. to pirate a video 2. to pirate a tape ➤ Vende vídeos piratas. He sells pirated videos.

venderle un buzón a alguien ■ timar a alguien ■ embromar a alguien to rip someone off ■ to con someone

venderse caro *(a un posible jefe)* to sell oneself ■ to tout one's strengths ■ to tout one's virtues

venderse como churros ■ venderse como pan caliente to sell like hotcakes ➤ El libro se vende como churros. The book is selling like hotcakes.

venderse como pan caliente ■ venderse como churros to sell like hotcakes

veneno potente powerful poison

venero de información ■ (la) gran fuente de información mine of information ■ gold mine of information

venga a nosotros tu reino thy kingdom come

¡venga, coño! come on, damn it!

¡venga, dímelo! ■ ¡dale, dímelo! come on, tell me!

¡venga la música! let's have some music!

venga lo que venga ■ pase lo que pase come what may

venga lo que viniere ■ venga lo que venga come what may

¡venga, vámonos! ■ ¡venga, vamos! ■ ¡venga ya! come on, let's go! ■ c'mon, let's go!

¡venga, vamos! ■ ¡venga, vámonos! ■ ¡venga ya! ■ ¡dale, vámonos! ■ ¡dale ya! come on, let's go! ■ c'mon, let's go!

¡venga! ¡venga! ¡venga! ¡venga! go! go! go! go!

¡venga ya! 1. ¡me estás vacilando! ■ ¡estás de coña! ■ ¡te estás quedando conmigo! come on! ■ you're pulling my leg! ■ noooo! ■ get real! 2. ¡venga, vámonos! ■ ¡venga, vamos! come on, let's go! ■ c'mon, let's go!

¡vengan las preguntas! bring on the questions! ■ let's have the questions!

vengarse de alguien por algo to get even with someone for something ■ to get revenge on someone for something ■ to take revenge on someone for something

vengo a graduarme (la vista) I'm here to get my vision checked ■ I'm here to get (some) glasses ■ I'm here to get a pair of glasses

vengo de afuera I just came in (from outside)

venir a buscar a alguien ■ pasar por alguien ■ *(Esp.)* venir a por alguien to come (by) for someone ■ to come get someone ➤ Me vienen a buscar a las siete. They're coming (by) for me at seven. ■ They're coming to get me at seven.

venir a cenar a casa *(en casa)* come have supper with us ■ come on over for supper

venir a cenar con nosotros *(en casa o fuera de casa)* let's have supper together

venir a contrapelo a alguien 1. to go against the grain 2. to rub someone the wrong way ➤ Como (gran) amante de la música clásica, el *heavy metal* me viene a contrapelo. As a classical music lover, heavy metal goes against my grain.

venir a la cabeza to come to mind

venir a la memoria to come to mind

venir a las manos ■ llegar a mis manos to fall into one's hands

venir a mano ■ venir bien to come in handy

venir a menos 1. *(persona)* to come down in the world 2. *(barrio viejo)* to go to seed

venir a mesa puesta ■ llegar a mesa puesta to come home to a set table

venir a parar a to end up in

venir a parar a las manos de uno to come into one's possession

venir a por alguien *(Esp.)* ■ venir a buscar a alguien ■ pasar por alguien to come by for someone ■ to pick someone up ➤ ¿Puedes venir a por mí? Can you come by for me? ■ Can you pick me up?

venir a que to come to... ■ to come for the purpose of... ➤ Vine a que me gradúes la vista. ■ Vine para un examen de la vista. ■ Vine a recibir una revisión de los ojos. I came to get my vision checked. ■ I came to get my eyes checked. ■ I came to have my eyes examined. ■ I've come for the purpose of having my eyes examined.

venir a que... to come to (do something) ■ to come by (with some objective in mind) ➤ Va a venir a que le des dinero. He's going to come (to) hit you up for some bucks.

venir a ser lo mismo ■ ser lo mismo ■ ser tres cuartos de lo mismo ■ implicar lo mismo ■ suponer la misma cosa ■ suponer lo mismo to amount to the same thing ➤ No lo despidieron, pero le bajaron el sueldo a la mitad y le dieron una oficina en el sótano, lo cual viene a ser lo mismo. They didn't fire him, but they cut his salary in half and gave him an office in the basement, which amounts to the same thing.

venir a toda pastilla to come full blast

venir a todo galope to come full blast ■ to come at a gallop

venir al caso to be relevant

venir al mundo ■ llegar al mundo ■ nacer to come into the world ■ to be born

venir al pelo ■ venir de perlas ■ venir de perilla to suit one to a T ➤ Me viene al pelo. It suits me to a T.

venir arrasando ■ pasar arrasando to come barreling down ➤ Los coche vienen arrasando por esta calle, ¿verdad? ■ Los coches pasan arrasando por esta calle, ¿verdad? The cars really come barreling down this street, don't they?

venir bien ■ venir a mano to come in handy

venir cagando leches *(Esp., subido de tono)* ■ venir corriendo ■ venir a las chapas to come running

venir clavada una cosa a otra to come nailed together

venir como agua de mayo to be a godsend ■ to be just what one needs

venir como caído del cielo to fall like manna from heaven ■ to be a godsend

venir con historias a alguien ■ venir con cuentos a alguien to feed someone a line ■ to be fed a line

venir con las pilas ■ traer las pilas to come with batteries

venir con las pilas puestas ■ tener las pilas puestas to be ready for action ■ to be ready to go ■ to be champing at the bit

venir con suplicaciones to come begging

venir cuatro gatos to stay away in droves ➤ Vinieron cuatro gatos. People stayed away in droves.

venir de familia ■ venir en la familia ■ correr en la sangre to run in the family ➤ Los trastornos de sangre vienen de su familia. Blood disorders run in her family.

venir de familia de bien to come from a wealthy family

venir de nuevas ■ venir de nuevo to come back ■ to come again

venir de un lugar 1. provenir de un lugar ■ ser de un lugar ■ ser oriundo de un lugar to be from a place ■ to come from a place ■ to hail from a place 2. regresar de un lugar ■ volver de un lugar to come (back) from a place ■ to return from a place ■ to get back from a place 3. estar regresando de un lugar ■ estar volviendo de un lugar to be coming back from a place ■ to be returning from a place ■ to be on one's way back from a place ➤ Vine de Barcelona a las 5:30 a.m. I got back from Barcelona at 5:30 a.m. ■ I arrived from Barcelona at 5:30 a.m. ➤ Venía de Barcelona cuando lo vi. I was coming back from Barcelona when I saw it. ■ I was on my way back from Barcelona when I saw it. ■ I was returning from Barcelona when I saw it.

venir de un medio muy pobre to come from a (very) poor background

venir de un origen humilde to come from a humble background ■ to be of humble origins

venir de una familia acomodada ■ venir de una familia acaudalada ■ nacer en cuna de oro to come from wealthy family

venir de una familia numerosa to come from a large family

venir de una familia pudiente to come from a wealthy family

venir de una familia unida to come from a close family

venir del arroyo to come from a poor background

venir derrapando ■ venir lanzado to careen out of control

venir dirigido a nombre de alguien ▪ estar a nombre de alguien to be addressed to someone ➤ El inquilino al que viene dirigida esta carta se mudó hace cinco años. ▪ El inquilino a nombre del cual viene esta carta se mudó hace cinco años. The tenant that this letter is addressed to moved out five years ago. ▪ The tenant to whom this letter is addressed moved out five years ago.

venir embalado por la calle to come barreling down the street ➤ Los coches vienen embalados por esta calle a noventa kilómetros por hora. The cars come barreling down this street at ninety kilometers per hour.

venir en la familia ▪ venir de familia ▪ correr en la sangre to run in the family ➤ Los trastornos de sangre vienen en la familia. Blood disorders run in the family.

venir en seguida to be along shortly ▪ to be here in a minute ▪ to get here in a minute ➤ Otro autobús vendrá en seguida. Another bus will be along shortly. ▪ Another bus will be here in a minute. ▪ Another bus will get here shortly. ▪ Another bus will get here in a minute.

venir en son de paz to come in peace

venir en un amplio surtido de colores to come in a wide variety of colors

venir en varios colores to come in a variety of colors ➤ Este motivo de la porcelana viene en varios colores. This china pattern comes in a variety of colors.

venir incluido to be included

venir lanzado ▪ venir derrapando to careen out of control

venir pegado a algo to come attached to something ➤ Los pequeños radios venían pegados a los tarros de crema de cacahuete. The little radios came attached to the jars of peanut butter.

venir por to come because of ▪ to come in response to ➤ Vengo por el anuncio en el periódico. I've come because of the ad in the newspaper. ▪ I've come in response to the ad in the newspaper.

venir rodado ▪ venirle fácil a uno to come easily to one ▪ come easily for one ▪ to come without effort

venirle a alguien con exigencias to make demands on someone

venirle a la atención que... ▪ recibir información de que... ▪ informarle a alguien (de) que... to come to one's attention that... ▪ to be brought to one's attention that... ➤ Ha venido a mi atención que... ▪ He recibido información de que... ▪ Alguien me ha informado (de) que... It has come to my attention that... ▪ It has been brought to my attention that...

venirle a la boca a alguien to come to one ➤ Acaba de venirme a la boca. It just came to me.

venirle a recoger a alguien to come by for someone

venirle a uno ▪ salirle a uno to come to one ▪ to come to one's mind

venirle a uno con cuentos (chinos) ▪ venirle a uno con historias **1.** to feed one a line ▪ to be fed a line ▪ to feed someone a bunch of bull ➤ No me vengas con cuentos chinos. ▪ No me vengas con historias. Don't give me that. ▪ Don't give me that nonsense. ▪ Don't feed me that nonsense.

venirle a uno con monsergas ▪ venirle a uno con sermones to give one a (moral) lecture ➤ Mi suegra nos viene con monsergas cuando dejamos que los niños se acuesten tarde. My mother-in-law gives us a lecture when we let the children stay up late.

venirle a uno con sermones to give one a (moral) lecture

venirle a uno que ni pintado to be picture perfect ▪ to be made to order ▪ to fit perfectly ➤ Este traje me viene que ni pintado. This suit fits (me) perfectly. ▪ This suit is perfect for me.

venirle al pelo ▪ irle que ni pintado **1.** to suit one to a T **2.** to be just what one needs ➤ Me viene al pelo. ▪ Me va que ni pintado It suits me to a T.

venirle ancho a uno **1.** *(ropa)* to be too big for one **2.** *(figurativo)* to be too much for someone to handle ▪ to be too much for someone

venirle angosto ▪ estar angosto to be cramped ▪ to be too small ➤ Esta oficina me viene angosta. This office is too cramped for me. ➤ Este aparcamiento nos viene muy angosto para el coche familiar. This parking space is too narrow for the station wagon.

venirle besando el culo a otro coche to tailgate a car ➤ Miré por el retrovisor y vi que el coche de detrás venía besándome el culo. I looked in the rearview mirror and saw that the car behind me was tailgating me.

venirle bien ▪ estar todo bien con ▪ parecerle muy bien to be all right with ▪ to be okay with ▪ to suit well ▪ to suit fine ➤ Me viene bien, pero necesito ver con el portero. It's all right with me, but I need to check with the concierge. ➤ La cena a las nueve nos viene muy bien. ▪ La cena a las nueve nos parece muy bien. Supper at nine suits us fine. ▪ Supper at nine is perfect. ▪ Supper at nine is great.

venirle como agua de mayo ▪ venirle como caído del cielo ▪ ser agua de mayo to be a Godsend

venirle como anillo al dedo a uno **1.** to fit hand in glove **2.** venirle al pelo a uno to suit one to a T

venirle de casta a uno to be in one's blood

venirle de familia to come from one's family (influences) ▪ to run in the family

venirle el Andrés to be that time of the month ▪ to have one's (menstrual) period

venirle el primo de América to have one's menstrual period ▪ to have one's period

venirle enorme ▪ quedarle enorme to be much to big for one ▪ to be far too big for one ▪ to be way too big for one ➤ A la edad de cuatro años Yo-Yo Ma tocaba el violonchelo aunque le venía enorme. At the age of four, Yo-Yo Ma was playing the cello even though it was way too big for him.

venirle rodado algo a alguien ▪ venirle algo servido en bandeja a alguien **1.** to fall into one's lap ▪ to come to one without effort **2.** to go smoothly (for one) ➤ La oportunidad le vino rodada. The opportunity fell into his lap. ➤ Las cosas nos vienen rodando en nuestro plan para establecer un restaurante americano que no sirva comida rápida. Our plans to establish a American restaurant that does not serve fast food are shaping up.

venirle una factura to get a bill ▪ to receive a bill ➤ No me ha venido la factura de teléfono. I haven't gotten the phone bill. ▪ I haven't received the phone bill.

venirlo consiguiendo to be getting it ▪ to be catching on ➤ Y lo vengo consiguiendo. ▪ Y vengo consiguiéndolo. I'm getting it. ▪ I'm catching on.

venirse a tierra ▪ venirse abajo ▪ derrumbarse to collapse

venirse abajo **1.** venirse a tierra ▪ hundirse ▪ derrumbarse ▪ desplomarse to collapse ▪ to fall down **2.** *(persona)* to go to pieces ▪ to be devastated ▪ to be crushed ▪ to cave in ➤ El edificio se vino abajo durante el terremoto. ▪ El edificio se derrumbó durante el terremoto. The building collapsed during the earthquake. ➤ Cuando recibió la noticia de su despido, se vino abajo. ▪ Cuando recibió la noticia de su despido, se derrumbó. When she found out she had been fired, she went to pieces. ▪ When she found out she had been fired, she was devastated. ➤ El testigo se vino abajo durante el interrogatorio del abogado de la otra parte. ▪ El testigo cedió ante el interrogatorio del abogado de la otra parte. The witness caved in under cross-examination.

venirse de vacío ▪ volver con las manos vacías to come away empty-handed ▪ to come back empty-handed

venirse el cielo abajo ▪ caer la lluvia a torrentes to pour down rain ➤ Se venía el cielo abajo. The rain was pouring down. ▪ It was pouring down rain.

venírsele a la memoria to come to mind

venírsele el mundo encima (for) the world to cave in on one ➤ Se me vino el mundo encima. The world caved in on me.

venírsele encima to be in for ➤ No tiene ni barrunto de lo que se le viene encima. ▪ No tiene ni idea de lo que se le viene encima. He has no idea what he's in for.

venta a plazos installment sale

venta al contado cash sale

venta al por mayor wholesale

venta al por menor retail sales

venta de billetes *(avión, tren, etc.)* ticket sales

venta de boletos *(todos los contextos)* ticket sales

venta de entradas *(concierto, museo, etc.)* ticket sales

venta de tickets *(Esp., todos los contextos)* ▪ venta de boletos ticket sales

venta por balance sales asset

ventana de doble cristal ▪ ventana de doble vidrio double-glazed window

ventana (en) saliente ▪ mirador bay window

ventana ojival pointed window

ventana vestida de luna *(poetic)* window with moonlight shining through

ventanilla de atención customer service window ▪ drive-through window

ventas al menudeo ▪ venta al por menor retail sales

ventilar sus diferencias to air one's differences

ventolera de sus pulmones *(de Louis Armstrong, el trompetista, por ejemplo)* ▪ capacidad pulmonar lung power ▪ wind power

veo borroso my eyes are blurry

veo con sorpresa... I was surprised to see... ➤ Veo con sorpresa en el periódico... I was surprised to see in the newspaper...

ver a alguien hacer algo ▪ ver a alguien haciendo algo to see someone do something ▪ to see someone doing something ➤ La vi salir. ▪ La vi saliendo. I saw her leave. ▪ I saw her leaving. ➤ Lo vi salir. ▪ Lo vi saliendo. I saw him leave. ▪ I saw him leaving. ➤ *(Esp., leísmo)* Le vi salir. ▪ Le vi saliendo. **1.** *(a él)* I saw him leave. ▪ I saw him leaving. **2.** *(a ella)* I saw her leave. I saw her leaving.

ver algo con buenos ojos to look approvingly on something

ver algo con malos ojos to take a dim view of something

ver algo de cerca to see something close up

ver algo de lejos to see something at a distance ▪ to see something from a distance ▪ to see something from afar

ver algo negro to see no possibility of something ➤ Veo muy negro que terminemos a tiempo. I see no possibility of finishing on time. ➤ Veo tu futuro muy negro si sigues desperdiciando tu tiempo. I see a bleak future for you if you keep on wasting your time.

ver (algo) venir to see something coming ➤ Lo veía venir. I could see it coming. ▪ I saw it coming. ➤ Veía venir los resultados de los exámenes porque no había estudiado. He could see the exam results coming because he hadn't studied.

ver dibujos animados to watch cartoons ➤ Veíamos dibujos animados. We were watching cartoons.

ver el juego ▪ caerse del guindo to see through someone's ploy ▪ to get wise to something ▪ *(Gran Bretaña)* to cotton on

ver el lado bueno de todo to see the bright side of everything ▪ to look on the bright side of everything

ver el lado malo de todo to see the down side of everything ▪ to see the black side of everything

ver el mundo to see the world

ver el mundo de color de rosa to see the world through rose-colored glasses

ver el plumero a alguien **1.** to see someone's real intentions **2.** to sense someone's political stance

ver la luz **1.** to see the light ▪ finally to see the truth **2.** to come to fruition ▪ to begin

ver la luz al final del túnel to see the light at the end of the tunnel

ver la matrícula ▪ anotar la matrícula ▪ coger la matrícula to get the license number ➤ ¿Viste la matrícula? Did you see the license number? ▪ Did you get the license number?

ver la paja en el ojo ajeno, y no la viga en el propio to see the straw in the other person's eye, but not to see the beam in your own

ver la suya *(Méx., deportes)* **1.** to meet one's match **2.** to have a difficult time

ver la tele to watch TV ➤ Están viendo la tele. They're watching TV.

ver las barbas al lobo to see the handwriting on the wall ➤ Puedo ver las barbas al lobo. I can see the handwriting on the wall.

ver las cosas de color de rosa to see the world through rose-colored glasses

ver las cosas de forma global ▪ ver las cosas en perspectiva to get the big picture ▪ to see the big picture

ver las cosas de otro modo to see things differently

ver las cosas en perspectiva ▪ ver las cosas de forma global to get the big picture ▪ to see the big picture

ver las estrellas *(de dolor)* to see stars

ver las orejas al burro ▪ ver las orejas al lobo to smell trouble ▪ to see trouble coming

ver las orejas al lobo ▪ ver las orejas al burro to smell trouble ▪ to see trouble coming

ver los toros desde la barrera *(taurino)* **1.** carecer de la información suficiente como para juzgar u opinar to be on the outside looking in **2.** presumir de más conocimiento del que realmente se tiene to be a grandstand quarterback ▪ to be a backseat driver

ver llegar algo to see something coming ➤ No vio llegar el tren. He didn't see the train coming.

ver más allá de su nariz to see beyond the end of one's nose ➤ Raramente ve más allá de su nariz. He rarely sees beyond the end of his nose.

ver menos que Pepe Leches ▪ no ver un burro a dos pasos ▪ no ver tres en un burro to be blind as a bat

ver mundo to see the world

ver negro to see no possibility of... ▪ to see no possibility that... ▪ not to think (that)... ➤ Mira la hora que es, lo veo negro que lleguemos a tiempo. Look what time it is. I don't think we're going to make it. ▪ Look what time it is. I see no possibility of getting there on time.

ver para creer seeing is believing

ver que... ▪ comprobar que... to see that...

ver quién hay en la puerta ▪ atender la puerta ▪ abrir la puerta to see who's at the door ▪ to answer the door ➤ Vete a ver quién hay en la puerta. ▪ Vete a atender la puerta. ▪ Vete a abrir la puerta. Go see who's at the door. ▪ Go answer to the door.

ver visiones to have visions

veranillo de San Miguel ▪ el veranillo de San Martín Indian summer

veranillo del membrillo ▪ septiembre September

¡verás! ▪ ¡ya verás! you'll see!

verbena de San Isidro *(santo patrón de Madrid)* street festival in honor of San Isidro

la **verdad a medias** half truth

verdad amarga bitter truth

la **verdad como la copa de un pino** unvarnished truth ▪ plain truth ▪ undeniable truth

la **verdad como un templo** inescapable truth

la **verdad como un puño** hard-hitting truth

la **verdad como una casa** inescapable truth

verdad desnuda the naked truth ▪ the unvarnished truth

la **verdad es que...** **1.** lo cierto es que... the truth is (that)... **2.** en realidad actually ➤ La verdad es que el término "friqui" (free kick) no es extraño, lo entiende casi todo el mundo. Actually the term "friqui" (free kick) is not rare. Almost everyone understands it.

la **verdad es hija del tiempo** the truth eventually comes to light

la **verdad lisa y llana** ▪ la verdad monda y lironda the unvarnished truth

verdad monda y lironda ▪ verdad lisa y llana the unvarnished truth

verdad no tiene más que un camino there are no alternatives to the truth

la **verdad ofende** the truth hurts

la **verdad por delante** the truth up front

la **verdad pura y dura** the plain, hard truth

¿verdad, que sí? it is, isn't it ? ▪ it was, wasn't it?

la **verdad, sólo la verdad y nada más que la verdad** the truth, the whole truth, and nothing but the truth

el **verdadero significado de...** the true meaning of...

verdadero yo: su ~ one's true self

las **verdades como puños** hard-hitting truths

estar **verdoso y desmochado** to be greenish and worn (down) ➤ La alfombra, por haber estado durante años en una casa húmeda, está verdosa y desmochada. The rug, for having remained for years in a humid house, is greenish (from mold) and worn.

verduguear a alguien *(Arg.)* to show someone up

verduras al vapor steamed vegetables ▪ *(coloquial)* steamed veggies

vergüenza ajena: sentir ~ to feel embarrassed for someone ▪ to feel ashamed for someone ➤ Los invitados del programa de entrevistas soltaban tantas intimidades que (yo) sentía vergüenza ajena. The talk show guests came out with so many personal revelations that I felt embarrassed for them.

ser una **vergüenza para uno** to be an embarrassment to one ■ to be an embarrassment for one

verlas venir 1. to sit and wait for something to happen 2. to be flat (out) broke ➤ Pasa su tiempo libre viéndolas venir. He just sits around waiting for something to happen. ➤ Estoy en el paro y viéndolas venir. I'm unemployed and flat (out) broke.

verle a alguien como a uno más to see someone as being like everyone else

verle antes a alguien to see someone earlier ➤ Lo vi antes. ■ *(leísmo)* Le vi antes. I saw him earlier. ➤ La vi antes. I saw her earlier.

verle el juego a alguien ■ conocerle el juego a alguien to be onto someone

verle las orejas al lobo ■ verle las orejas al burro to smell trouble ■ to realize that something is wrong

verlo negro to see no future in it ■ to see no possibility in it ■ to see no hope in it

verlo todo (de) color de rosa to see the world through rose-colored glasses

verlo todo negro ■ ser pesimista to have a pessimistic outlook

verlo venir to see it coming ■ to be able to see it coming ➤ Lo veo venir. I can see it coming. ➤ Lo venía venir. I could see it coming. ➤ Lo vi venir. I saw it coming. ■ I could see it coming.

verruga pilosa hairy wart ■ *(medical)* pilose wart

estar **versado en la materia** to be versed in the subject

verse ante un dilema to face a dilemma ■ to be faced with a dilemma ■ to be on the horns of a dilemma

verse afectado(-a) to be affected ➤ *(gazapo de periódico)* El hombre fue disparado en la cabeza, pero ningún órgano vital se vio afectado. The man was shot in the head, but no vital organs were affected.

verse afectado(-a) por algo ■ estar afectado por algo to be affected by something

verse ahogado(-a) ■ estar ahogado 1. no tener aire to be suffocating 2. estar agobiado con deudas to be overwhelmed with debt 3. estar agobiado con responsabilidades to be overwhelmed with responsibilities

verse alejado(-a) de alguien to be separated from someone (against one's will) ■ to find oneself separated from someone ➤ Después del divorcio el padre se vio alejado de los niños. After the divorce the father was separated from his children. ■ After the divorce the father found himself separated from his children.

verse alejado(-a) del caso to be removed from the case (against one's will) ■ to be taken off the case (against one's will) ➤ El inspector se vio alejado del caso y fue restituido. The inspector was taken off the case and reassigned.

verse anegado ■ verse inundado to be flooded ■ to get flooded ➤ El garaje se vio anegado por la lluvia. The garage was flooded by the rain. ■ The garage got flooded by the rain.

verse arrastrado a algo to get dragged into something ■ to be dragged into something ➤ Algunos países vecinos se vieron arrastrados al conflicto. Some of the neighboring countries got dragged into the conflict. ■ Some of the neighboring countries were dragged into the conflict.

verse arrastrado a la discusión to get dragged into the argument

verse atacado por los dos lados to be attacked by both sides (in a dispute) ■ to get caught in the cross fire

verse con fuerzas para to feel up to ■ to be up to

verse constreñido a hacer algo to be compelled to do something ■ to be obligated to do something ■ to feel obligated to do something

verse de Pascuas a Ramos to see each other once in a blue moon ■ to see each in a month of Sundays

verse deslucido 1. to be overshadowed 2. to look run down ➤ El festival se vio deslucido por el mal tiempo. The festival was overshadowed by bad weather. ➤ Después de su enfermedad se le veía muy deslucido. After his illness, he looked run down.

verse empañado to be blemished ➤ Su historial académico se vio empañado por la puntuación del examen final. His academic record was blemished by his score on the final (exam).

verse empañado por vinculación con... to be tainted by association with...

verse en bragas to be caught with one's pants down

verse en dificultades to be in dire straits

verse en Internet ■ juntarse en Internet to link up on the Internet

verse en las garras del lobo to be in the wolf's mouth

verse envuelto(-a) en ■ verse involucrado en to be involved in

verse impotente para hacer algo to be powerless to do something

verse involucrado(-a) en las drogas ■ meterse en las drogas to get involved in (taking) drugs ■ to get into drugs ➤ ¿Cómo se vio involucrado en las drogas? ■ ¿Cómo se metió en las drogas? How did he get into drugs? ■ How did he get involved in (taking) drugs?

verse las caras to face each other

verse las caras con algo ■ dar la cara por algo to face up to something

verse las caras con alguien to face up to someone ➤ Me tendré que ver las caras con mis deudores. I have to face up to my debtors.

verse mermado por to be diminished by ➤ El beneficio se vio mermado por la inflación. The profits were diminished by inflation.

verse negro para hacer algo to find it extremely difficult to do something ➤ Me vi negro para terminar el partido. I found it very difficult to finish the match.

verse obligado(-a) a to be forced to ■ to feel obligated to ■ to find oneself forced to ➤ Al Gore se vio obligado ayer a poner una fecha a su rendición. Al Gore was forced to put a date on his concession.

verse sobrecogido to be overwhelmed by ➤ Londres se vio ayer sobrecogido por el estreno de uno de los filmes más esperados del momento, *Harry Potter y la piedra filosofal*. London was overwhelmed by the premier of one of the most awaited films of the season, *Harry Potter and the Philosopher's Stone*.

verse sorprendido(-a) ■ quedarse sorprendido(-a) to be surprised

vérselas con alguien to face someone ➤ *(titular)* Un Madrid épico se la verá con el Barça en las semifinales. An epic Madrid will face Barcelona in the semifinals. ➤ *(titular)* El actor se las verá con la justicia. The actor will (have to) face justice. ■ The actor will face a court proceeding.

vérselas negras para hacer algo to go through hell to do something ■ to go through hell doing something ■ to have a hell of a time doing something ➤ El taxista se las vio negras para llegar al aeropuerto a tiempo. The taxi driver went through hell to get to the airport on time. ■ The taxi had a hell of a time getting to the airport on time.

vérselas y deseárselas to go through hell to do something ■ to go through hell doing something ■ to have a hell of a time doing something ➤ Me las vi y me las deseé para conseguir una entrada para el concierto de Paul McCartney. I went through hell getting tickets for the Paul McCartney concert. ■ I had a hell of a time getting tickets for the Paul McCartney concert. ➤ El taxista se las vio y se las deseó para llegar al aeropuerto a tiempo. The taxi driver went through hell to get to the airport on time. ■ The taxi had a hell of a time getting to the airport on time.

vérsele muy acelerado ■ estar acelerado to be hyper

vérsele el plumero to give oneself away ■ not to fool anybody ➤ Se le ve el plumero. He's not fooling anybody. ➤ Se te ha visto el plumero. You've given yourself away. ■ You haven't fooled anybody.

vérsele una actitud to show an attitude ■ to display an attitude

vertedero de basura garbage dump

verter a cuentagotas ■ verter con cuentagotas to pour a drop at a time ■ to pour drop by drop

verter el contenido del sobre to pour the contents of the envelope ■ to pour the contents of the packet ➤ Verter el contenido del sobre en un litro de agua templada. ■ Verter el contenido del sobre en un litro de agua tibia. Pour the contents of the envelope into one liter of lukewarm water. ■ Pour the contents of the packet into a liter of tepid water.

verter opiniones ■ expresar opiniones to spout off opinions ■ to bandy about opinions ■ to express opinions ■ to voice opinions ■ to state opinions ➤ Opiniones que se vertían a favor y en contra de... The opinions bandied about for and against...

¿ves lo que (te) quiero decir? see what I mean? ▪ (do you) see what I mean?
¿ves qué fácil? ▪ ¿ves cómo es de fácil? see how easy it is?
estar **vestido(-a) con** to be wearing ➤ Estaba vestido con parjarita. He was wearing a bow tie.
vestido (con un cuello de) palabra de honor *(Esp.)* ▪ vestido de noche sin tirantes stapless evening gown
estar **vestido(-a) de** to be dressed in ▪ to be wearing
estar **vestido(-a) de civil** to be dressed in civilian clothes
estar **vestido(-a) de paisano** ▪ vestirse de paisano to be dressed in civilian clothes ▪ not to be wearing a uniform
vestido(-a) (muy) escotado low-cut dress
vestir con la estación to dress for the weather
vestir de civil to wear civilian clothes
vestir de forma anodina to wear drab clothes ▪ to dress austerely ▪ to wear dowdy clothes
vestir ropa to wear clothes ➤ *(noticia)* El jugador no volverá a vestir la camisa de Madrid. The player will not wear the Madrid jersey again.
vestir una prenda to wear a garment
vestirse de ▪ disfrazarse de to dress up as ➤ ¿De qué te vas a vestir en Halloween? ▪ ¿De qué vas a vestirte en Halloween? ▪ ¿De qué te vas a disfrazar en Halloween? ▪ ¿De qué vas a disfrazarte en Halloween? What are you going to dress up as on Halloween? ➤ Me voy a vestir de payaso. ▪ Voy a vestirme de payaso. ▪ Me voy a disfrazar de payaso. ▪ Voy a disfrazarme de payaso. I'm going to dress up as a clown.
vestirse de domingo ▪ ponerse de domingo ▪ endomingarse to dress (up) in one's Sunday best ▪ to get dressed up in one's Sunday best
vestirse (de forma) elegante ▪ arreglarse to dress up
vestirse de luto to be dressed in mourning ▪ to be dressed in black (from head to toe)
vestirse de punta en blanco to be dressed to the nines ▪ to be decked out in one's finest
vestirse por la cabeza to put the cart before the horse ▪ to build the house roof first
vestirse por los pies ▪ ser hecho y derecho to be honest and wholesome ▪ to be upright and honest ➤ Se viste por los pies. He's very upright and honest.
veta mezquina mean streak ▪ streak of meanness
estar **vetado al público** to be forbidden to the public ▪ to be concealed from the public
vetar la votación to veto the proposal approved in the vote ➤ La votación va a ser vetada por el presidente. The proposal approved in the vote will be vetoed by the president.
vete a abrir 1. *(para él)* go open the door (for him) **2.** *(para ella)* go open the door (for her)
¡vete a freír espárragos! ▪ ¡a freír espárragos! ▪ ¡a freír monas! ▪ ¡vete a freír churros! go jump in a lake! ▪ go take a walk!
¡vete a fumar por ahí! get lost! ▪ beat it! ▪ scram!
¡(vete) a hacer puñetas! ▪ ¡vete a hacer gárgaras! get lost! ▪ beat it! ▪ scram!
¡vete a la cama! go to bed!
¡vete a la porra! get lost! ▪ beat it! ▪ scram!
¡vete a paseo! ▪ ¡vete de paseo! go take a walk!
¡vete a saber! ▪ ¡anda a saber! **1.** ¿quién sabe? who knows? ▪ who's to say? ▪ there's no telling ▪ it's anyone's guess ▪ God knows! ▪ goodness knows! **2.** *(cuando la situación es absurda)* go figure!
¡vete al carajo! *(subido de tono)* get the hell out of here!
¡vete al cuerno! *(subido de tono)* get the hell out of here!
¡vete al guano! *(L.am.)* get lost!
¡vete al pasillo! go stand in the hall!
vete pensando en *(Esp.)* ▪ ve pensando en be thinking of ➤ Vete pensando en un sitio para ir a cenar. ▪ Ve pensando en un sitio para ir a cenar. Be thinking of a place to go have supper. ▪ Be thinking of a place to go have dinner.
¡vete por ahí! get out of here!
vete preparado(-a) be prepared
¡vete (tú) a saber! who knows? ▪ who's to say? ▪ there's no telling ▪ it's anyone's guess ▪ God knows! ▪ goodness knows!
¡vete de paseo! ▪ vete a paseo go take a walk!
vía crucis *(catolicismo)* ▪ viacrucis ▪ estaciones de la cruz **1.** Stations of the Cross **2.** road to Calvary **3.** *(figurativo)* ordeal
vía de comunicación avenue of communication
vía de gran tránsito major traffic artery
vía de servicio ▪ vía del servicio service road
vía de urgencia: hacerse por la ~ to be done quickly ▪ to be done summarily ➤ Moscú expulsará, ya sin recurso a la vía de urgencia, a otros cuarenta y seis estadounidenses. Moscow will summarily expel without appeal forty-six U.S. diplomats.
vía libre a: dar ~ 1. to give free rein to **2.** dar luz verde a to give the go-ahead for ▪ to give the green light to
vía libre para: dar ~ to give free rein to
vía muerta: estar en ~ to be deadlocked ▪ to have come to a dead end
vía satélite by satellite ▪ via satellite ➤ Hay veinte y seis nuevos canales de televisión vía satélite. There are twenty-six new satellite TV channels. ▪ There are twenty-six new TV channels available by satellite. ▪ There are twenty-six new TV channels transmitted by satellite.
viajar a rincones lejanos ▪ viajar a lugares remotos ▪ viajar a lugares lejanos to travel to faraway places ▪ to travel to the far corners of the Earth
viajar al extranjero to go abroad
el **viaje de ida** the trip over ➤ El viaje de ida llevó más tiempo que el de vuelta. The trip over took longer than the trip back.
el **viaje de negocios** business trip
el **viaje de novios** honeymoon (trip) ▪ wedding trip
el **viaje de vuelta** return trip ▪ trip back ➤ El viaje de vuelta fue más rápido que el de ida. The return trip was faster than the trip over. The trip back was faster than the trip over.
viaje organizado package holiday (trip)
¡viajeros al tren! all aboard!
vías de comunicación avenues of communication
vías digestivas digestive tract
víbora mortífera deadly snake
víbora se enrosca snake coils
vibrar con to be alive with
víctima mortal victim ▪ fatality ➤ El brote de legionella se ha cobrado su quinta víctima mortal. The outbreak of Legionnaire's disease has claimed its fifth victim. ▪ The outbreak of Legionnaire's disease has claimed its fifth fatality.
victoria aplastante crushing victory
victoria arrolladora overwhelming victory ▪ crushing victory
victoria demoledora overwhelming victory
victoria pírrica Pyrrhic victory
vida accidentada troubled life
vida amorosa love life
vida anodina humdrum existence
vida anterior previous life
vida canonical ▪ vida de canónigo canonical life
vida comunitaria 1. vida en comunidad community life **2.** vida en común communal life
vida conyugal ▪ vida de casados married life
vida cotidiana ▪ vida diaria everyday life ▪ daily life
vida de canónigo ▪ vida canonical canonic life ▪ canonical life
vida de currante worker's life
vida de perros dog's life
vida de verdad: conseguir una ~ to get a life
vida diaria ▪ vida cotidiana everyday life ▪ daily life
vida en rosa the good life
vida errante: llevar una ~ to be a wanderer ▪ to have wanderlust
la **vida es un soplo** ▪ la vida es breve ▪ la vida es efímera life is short
la **vida es una caja de sorpresas** ▪ la vida siempre da sorpresas ▪ la vida está llena de sorpresas life is full of surprises
la **vida es una tómbola** life is like a fortune wheel ▪ life is a crap shoot
la **vida está llena de sorpresas** ▪ la vida siempre da sorpresas ▪ la vida es una caja de sorpresas life is full of surprises
la **vida hay que tomarla como viene** you have to take life as it comes ▪ you have to take things in stride

vida íntima: preservar su ~ to protect one's privacy
vida laboral work life ➤ Al recuperar la salud, reanudó su vida laboral. When he recovered his health, he went back to work.
vida mía *(apelativo cariñoso)* darling ▪ sweetheart
la **vida nos golpea** life deals us some harsh blows ▪ life just belts it out ▪ life just throws it at us
vida cenobítica monastic life
vida padre: pegarse la ~ to live it up ➤ Se está pegando la vida padre. He's living it up.
vida pasa tan deprisa life goes (by) so quickly
la **vida pasada** one's past life
vida perruna dog's life
la **vida pudo haberse formado...** life could have begun...
vida rutinaria ▪ vida cotidiana everyday life ▪ daily life
vida salvaje wildlife
vida salvaje: gestión de ~ wildlife management
vida sexual sex life
la **vida siempre da sorpresas** ▪ la vida es una caja de sorpresas ▪ la vida está llena de sorpresas life is full of surprises
vida vegetativa: tener una ~ to be a vegetable ▪ to be completely incapacitated
vida y milagros: contarle a alguien su ~ to tell someone one's life story ➤ Me contó su vida y milagros. He told me his life story.
vidrio opaco frosted glass ▪ opaque glass
viejo que se cura, cien años dura those who take care of themselves live longer
viejo verde dirty old man
estar **viendo los toros desde la barrera** ▪ estar desde fuera mirando adentro ▪ estar desde fuera mirando hacia dentro to be on the outside looking in
viene a ser lo mismo it comes to the same thing ▪ it amounts to the same thing
¿vienes mucho por aquí? do you come here often?
¿vienes o te quedas? are you coming or staying (here)?
viento cruzado crosswind ➤ El compensador del timón compensa el efecto del viento cruzado. The rudder trim tab corrects for the crosswind.
viento de cola ▪ viento en popa tailwind
viento de frente ▪ viento frontal headwind
viento de levante east wind ▪ wind from the east ▪ wind out of the east
viento de poniente west wind ▪ wind from the west ▪ wind out of the west
viento en popa ▪ viento de cola tailwind
viento en popa: ir ~ 1. to go very well ▪ to go full sail ▪ to go great **3.** *(pintoresco)* to be cooking with gas ➤ Mis negocios van viento en popa. Business is going very well. ▪ Business is going full sail. ▪ Business is (going) great. ➤ Nuestra relación va viento en popa. Our relationship is going great. ➤ ¡Vamos viento en popa! ▪ ¡Esto va viento en popa! (Now) we're cooking with gas!
viento helado ▪ viento siberiano icy wind
viento lateral cross wind ▪ crosswind
viento siberiano ▪ viento helado icy wind
vientos alisios trade winds
vientos del cambio: los ~ the winds of change
vientos fuertes strong winds ▪ high winds
vientos racheados 1. ráfagos de viento gusty winds **2.** *(en un avión)* turbulencia turbulence
vientos suaves light winds
el **viernes pasado** last Friday
Viernes Santo *(viernes de Semana Santa)* Good Friday
el **vigente campeón** reigning champion
la **vigente campeona** reigning champion
viga atravesada crossbeam
vigilante nocturno night watchman
vigilar mis cosas ▪ echarle un ojo a mis cosas to keep an eye on my things
vigilar estrechamente to keep a close eye on ▪ to monitor closely ▪ to watch closely
vigilar si... to monitor to be sure that... ➤ Bruselas vigilará si las petroleras españolas pactan las subidas. Brussells monitors the Spanish oil companies to be sure that they are not fixing price increases.
vigilar un examen ▪ administrar un examen to proctor an examination
el **vil metal** ▪ dinero money ➤ Lo hago por el vil metal. I'm doing it for the money.
la **vil pobreza** ▪ pobreza abyecta ▪ pobreza extrema abject poverty ▪ extreme poverty
vilipendiar a alguien to vilify someone
vincular a alguien con algo to link someone to something ▪ to link someone with something ➤ Los investigadores han vinculado a los terroristas con el crimen organizado. Investigators have linked the terrorists to organized crime. ➤ *(noticia)* La policía vincula con Al Qaeda a un detenido en Detroit con doce millones de dólares falsos. Police link a detainee with twelve million counterfeit dollars in Detroit to Al Qaeda. ▪ Police link a detainee with twelve million counterfeit dollars in Detroit with Al Qaeda.
vincularse a to become part of
vínculo estrecho con alguien: tener un ~ to have a close relationship with someone
vine en coche *(Esp.)* ▪ vine conduciendo ▪ *(L.am.)* vine en carro ▪ vine en auto ▪ vine manejando I came by car ▪ I drove
vine en carro *(L.am.)* ▪ vine en auto ▪ vine manejando. ▪ *(Esp.)* vine conduciendo ▪ vine en coche I came by car ▪ I drove
(vino) amontillado *(Esp., jerez elaborado de uvas de la región de Montilla, Andalucía)* amontillado ▪ sherry
vino añejo ▪ vino de solera vintage wine
vino blanco ▪ vino claro white wine
vino cabezón wine that gives you a headache
(vino) clarete ▪ (vino) rosado rosé (wine)
vino de mesa table wine
vino de solera ▪ vino añejo vintage wine
vino fuerte full-bodied wine
vino generoso full red wine
vino joven wine of recent vintage
vino para guisar cooking wine
vino peleón ▪ vinazo rotgut wine ▪ Ripple®
(vino) rosado ▪ (vino) clarete rosé (wine)
vino tinto red wine
vino vigoroso strong drink
viña del Señor: de todo hay en la ~ it takes all kinds (to make a world)
violación de la libertad condicional parole violation
violar un bloqueo 1. to run a blockade **2.** to violate the embargo ▪ to break the embargo ▪ to defy the embargo
violencia de género gender violence
violencia permanente permanent violence ▪ continuous violence ▪ unending violence ➤ En muchos países latinoamericanos ha existido una violencia institucionalizada permanente. In many Latin American countries there has existed a permanent form of institutionalized violence.
virar a la derecha ▪ girar a la derecha ▪ doblar a la derecha to turn (to the) right ▪ to take a right ▪ *(jerga)* to hang a right
virar a la izquierda ▪ girar a la izquierda ▪ doblar a la izquierda to turn left ▪ to turn to the left ▪ to take a left ▪ *(jerga)* to hang a left
la **virtud es su propia recompensa** virtue is its own reward
la **virtud no se logra en un cuarto de hora** virtue is not achieved overnight ▪ virtue is not acquired overnight
virus informático computer virus
vis a vis 1. face to face **2.** prison visit where physical contact is permitted
visible a larga distancia visible from a (long) distance ▪ visible from afar ▪ which can be seen from a long way off
ser **visible a simple vista** to be visible to the naked eye ▪ to be visible with the unaided eye ▪ to be visible without a telescope ▪ to be visible without binoculars
visiblemente emocionado(-a) visibly affected
la **visión de la sangre** sight of blood
visión somera ▪ visión de conjunto ▪ vistazo overview
la **visión túnel** tunnel vision
visita de cumplido obligatory visit ▪ visit out of kindness
visita domiciliaria home visit

visitar al señor Roca to go to the bathroom ■ *(en un edificio público)* to go to the restroom

visitar los altares to go to mass

visitar por sorpresa a to pay a surprise visit to

vislumbrar a lo lejos to make out in the distance ■ to discern in the distance

vista de águila sharp vision ■ acute vision

vista de lince sharp vision ■ acute vision

vista de perfil side view

ser una **vista hermosa** to be a beautiful view ➤ La vista desde lo alto de la montaña es hermosa. The view from the mountaintop is beautiful.

vista oral: celebrar la ~ 1. to hear oral arguments **2.** tener una junta preliminar to hold a preliminary hearing

vístame despacio que tengo prisa haste makes waste

vistas hermosas: tener unas ~ ■ tener unas vistas preciosas ■ tener bellas vistas to have a beautiful view ■ to command a beautiful view ■ to offer a beautiful view ■ to have a fine view ■ to command a fine view ■ to offer a fine view ➤ La habitación del hotel tiene unas vistas preciosas. ■ La habitación del hotel ofrece unas vistas preciosas. The hotel room has a beautiful view.

visto bueno 1. aprobación approval **2.** (el) tic check (mark)

visto de ■ visto desde as seen from ➤ Los planetas giran alrededor del sol en sentido contrario de las agujas del reloj, visto de la estrella polar. The planets orbit the sun counterclockwise as seen from the North Star.

visto desde ■ visto de as seen from ➤ La tierra gira sobre su eje en sentido contrario de la aguas del reloj, visto desde la estrella polar. The Earth rotates on its axis counterclockwise as seen from the North Star.

estar **visto para sentencia** to be ready for sentencing

visto que in view of the fact that ■ considering that

visto y no visto ■ ahora lo ves, ahora no now you see it, now you don't

vitola internacional cigar band

¡viva! long live! ■ hurrah!

ser la **viva imagen de algo** to look exactly like something

ser la **viva imagen de alguien** ■ ser el clavadito de alguien ■ ser la estampa de alguien to be the spitting image of someone

¡viva la madre que te parió! *(piropo)* hurrah for the mother who gave birth to you!

¡viva la Pepa! to hell with everybody else!

ser un **viva la virgen** to be a person who does not give a damn

¡viva yo! hurrah for me (and to hell with everybody else)!

¡vivan los novios! long live the bride and groom!

¡vive Dios! ■ ¡Dios mío! good God! ■ good heavens!

víveres para *x* meses provisions for *x* months ■ *x* months' provisions

vivía una huelga it was experiencing a strike ■ it was having a strike ➤ La base (naval de Rota) vivía la huelga más larga de su historia. The (Rota naval) base was experiencing its longest strike in history.

vivienda(s) asequible(s) affordable housing

vivir a cuenta de otro ■ vivir por cuenta de otro to live off someone (else)

vivir a cuerpo de rey ■ vivir como un rajá to live like a king

vivir a expensas de to live at the expense of ■ to live off the back(s) of

vivir a la buena de Dios to live with no worries

vivir a lo de Dios es Cristo to live it up

vivir a lo grande ■ darse la gran vida to live it up

vivir a lo loco to live for the moment

vivir a pecho descubierto to live bravely and with integrity

vivir a salto de mata ■ andar a salto de mata to live each day as it comes ■ to take each day as it comes

vivir a su aire ■ vivir a sus anchas to live as one likes ■ to do what one wants ■ to do what one likes ■ to do as one likes ➤ Vivo a mi aire. I live as I like. ■ I do what I want. ■ I do what I like. ■ I do as I like.

vivir a sus anchas ■ vivir a su aire to live as one likes ■ to do what one wants ■ to do what one likes ■ to do as one likes ➤ Vivo a mis anchas. I live as I like. ■ I do what I want. ■ I do what I like. ■ I do as I like.

vivir al día to live from hand to mouth

vivir al lado de alguien to live next door to someone

vivir al máximo cada día to live each day to the fullest

vivir algo to live through something ■ to experience something ■ to have been in something ➤ Una vez viví una inundación. I lived through a flood once. ■ I experienced a flood once. ■ I've been in a flood.

vivir de una forma austera to live conservatively

vivir como Dios to live like a king

vivir como Dios manda to live according to the dictates of society

vivir como Dios quiere *(más común)* ■ vivir como Dios manda to live according to the dictates of society

vivir como perros y gatos to fight like cats and dogs ➤ Viven como perros y gatos. They fight like cats and dogs.

vivir como un abad ■ vivir como un rey to live luxuriously ■ to live in luxury ■ to live like a king

vivir como un cura ■ vivir sin cuidado to live without financial worries

vivir como un rajá ■ vivir a cuerpo de rey to live like a king

vivir como un rey to live like a king

vivir con desahogo to live comfortably

vivir con muy pocos recursos to live on very little ➤ La familia se las arreglaba para vivir con muy pocos recursos. The family managed to live on very little.

vivir con su pareja ■ vivir en pareja con alguien to live together (out of wedlock) ■ to cohabit

vivir de to make a living by ■ to earn one's living by ■ to do something for a living

vivir de la sopa boba ■ andar a la sopa boba to live off one's parents ■ to scrounge

vivir de las rentas de un fondo to live off the interest from a trust

vivir de milagro to barely make ends meet ■ to just (barely) make ends meet

vivir de prisa ■ vivir a prisa to live life in the fast lane

vivir de puta madre *(subido de tono)* to live it up

vivir de su pluma to make a living as a writer

vivir del aire to live off the fat of the land

vivir del cuento to live without working ■ to live off the fat of the land

vivir en la mentira to live a lie

vivir en las nubes to have one's head in the clouds

vivir en otro mundo to live in another world ■ to have one's head in the clouds

vivir en pareja con alguien ■ vivir con su pareja to live together (out of wedlock) ■ to cohabit

vivir en sí mismo to be alive in the fullest sense ■ to be alive within oneself ➤ *(Unamuno)* El hombre que no se contradice a sí mismo en rigor no vive; por lo menos no vive en sí mismo. The man who doesn't contradict himself is in the fullest sense not living, or at least, not within himself.

vivir en su mundo to be in one's own little world ■ to live in one's own little world

vivir en un estado de shock to be in a state of shock

vivir entre... to live amidst... ➤ *(titular)* Los políticos argentinos viven entre sobresaltos. Argentine politicians experience one jolt after another.

vivir fuera de casa to live away from home ➤ Durante muchos años (ella) ha vivido fuera de casa. For many years she has lived away from home.

vivir justo enfrente to live right across the street ■ to live straight across the street ■ to live directly across the street

vivir la vida al límite to live life to the full ■ to live life to the fullest ➤ La vida hay que vivirla al límite. Life must be lived to the full. ■ One must live life to the full.

vivir muy separado de alguien to live a long way from someone ■ to live far from someone

vivir numerosas especies de peligros to experience many kinds of dangers ■ to live with many kinds of dangers ➤ *(noticia)* Alrededor de Kandahar viven numerosos especies de peligros. Around Kandahar, people experience many kinds of dangers. ▪ Around Kandahar, people live with many kinds of dangers.

vivir otra vida a través de alguien to live through someone else ▪ to live through the experiences of someone else

vivir para contarla to live to tell about it

¡vivir para ver! 1. ¡va a suceder! it's going to happen, mark my words! **2.** ¡quién lo creería! who would believe it! **3.** mejor suerte para la próxima better luck next time! ▪ live and learn!

vivir por encima de sus posibilidades to live beyond one's means

vivir solo to live alone ▪ to live by oneself ➤ Vive sola. She lives alone. ▪ She lives by herself.

vivir sólo de sus ingresos to live within one's income

vivir un amor desgraciado to have a sad experience in love ➤ El vivió un amor desgraciado en la adolescencia. He had a sad experience in love in his youth.

vivir un período de tiempo to experience a certain period of time ▪ to live through a (period of) time ▪ to have... ➤ *(noticia)* Wall Street vive su peor semana en setenta años. Wall Street has its worst week in seventy years. ➤ *(noticia)* El turismo está viviendo un mal verano. The tourist industry is having a bad summer. ▪ The tourist industry is going through a bad summer. ▪ The tourist industry is experiencing a bad summer.

vivir una experiencia to live through an experience

vivir una jornada de luto to have a day of morning ▪ to spend a day in mourning

vivir una situación de crisis to experience a crisis

vivir uno de sus mejores momentos to experience a high point

vivir unos momentos duros ▪ vivir unos momentos difíciles to be going through hard times ▪ to experience a low point

vivir *x* puertas más abajo to live *x* doors down ➤ (Él) vive dos puertas más abajo. He lives two doors down.

vivir *x* puertas más arriba to live *x* doors up ➤ (Ella) vive tres puertas más arriba. She lives three doors up (the street).

estar **vivito y coleando** to be alive and kicking

el **vivo al hoyo, y el muerto, al bollo** there's no use crying over spilled milk

vivo aquí toda la vida ▪ vivo aquí desde siempre I have lived here all my life ▪ I've lived here all my life

vivo en España desde 1998 I have lived in Spain since 1998 ▪ I've lived in Spain since 1998

ser el **vivo ejemplo de algo** to (perfectly) exemplify something ▪ to be the epitome of something ➤ Antonio Banderas es el vivo ejemplo del amante latino. Antonio Banderas perfectly exemplifies the Latin lover. ▪ Antonio Banderas is the epitome of the Latin lover.

ser el **vivo retrato de alguien** to be the spitting image of someone

vocación unilateralista unilateral stance ▪ unilateral position

voladura controlada de un edificio ▪ demolición controlada de un edificio ▪ implosión controlada de un edificio controlled demolition of a building (using explosives)

volar a ciegas *(aeronáutica)* to fly blind

volar a ras del agua to fly just above (the level of) the water ▪ to fly at close to water level ▪ to fly just off the water

volar algo to blow something off ➤ Los fuertes vientos volaron el techo de la casa. The high winds blew the roof off the house. ▪ The strong winds blew the roof off the house.

volar desnudo(-a) ▪ volar en pelotas ▪ volar encuerado(-a) to go naked ▪ to parade around in the buff

volar encuerado(-a) *(L.am.)* ▪ volar desnudo(-a) ▪ volar en pelotas to go naked ▪ to parade around in the buff

volar por los aires ▪ saltar por los aires ▪ saltar en pedazos to blow up (into a thousand pieces) ➤ El almacén de combustible voló por los aires al ser alcanzado por un rayo. The fuel storage depot blew up when it was struck by lightning. ➤ Los técnicos de demolición volaron por los aires el viejo hotel histórico para construir una plaza de estacionamiento. The demolition experts blew up the historic old hotel to build a parking garage.

volar sobre el océano to fly over the ocean

volar un edificio 1. *(demolición)* to raze a building ▪ to tear down a building **2.** hacer saltar por los aires to blow up a building ▪ to blow a building up

volarle un miembro to lose a limb ➤ Le volaron la mano derecha en la segunda Guerra Mundial. He lost his right hand in the Second World War.

volarse la tapa de los sesos ▪ saltarse la tapa de los sesos to blow one's brains out

volarse por la ventana to go out the window ➤ Y todos los planes que hicimos se volaron por la ventana. And all the plans we made went out the window.

volarse una clase *(L.am.)* to cut a class

volcar de campana *(vehículo)* ▪ dar vuelcos de campana to roll over repeatedly ▪ to roll over and over

volcar un mueble to knock over a piece of furniture ▪ to knock a piece of furniture over ➤ El gato volcó el velero. The cat knocked over the nightstand. ▪ The cat knocked the nightstand over. ➤ El gato lo volcó. The cat knocked it over.

volcarse a algo to turn all (of) one's attention to something ▪ to make something one's exclusive focus ➤ Se ha volcado (de lleno) a la literatura argentina. She has turned all (of) her attention to Argentine literature. ▪ She has made Argentine literature her exclusive focus.

volcarse para hacer algo ▪ salir de su paso para hacer algo to go out of one's way to do something ▪ to knock oneself out to ▪ to go way beyond the call of duty to ➤ La doctora se ha volcado para conseguir atender a todos los pacientes. The doctor has gone (way) out of her way to attend all the patients.

el **volcán está en erupción** the volcano is erupting

voltear la cabeza to turn one's head ▪ to spin one's head around

voltear la casa al revés ▪ poner la casa patas arriba to turn the house upside down

voluntad de hablar willingness to talk

voluntad de hierro: tener la ~ to be iron willed

la **voluntad popular** the will of the people

volver a arrancar el motor to restart the engine ▪ to restart the motor ▪ to start the engine back up ▪ to start the motor back up

volver a calentar comida to reheat food ▪ to heat food back up. ➤ Vuelve a calentar la sopa. Los invitados a la cena por fin han llegado. Warm the soup back up. Our supper guests have finally arrived. ▪ Reheat the soup. Our supper guests have finally arrived.

volver a captar to recapture

volver a crecer *(pelo)* to grow back ➤ Volverá a crecer. It'll grow back.

volver a dormirse ▪ dormirse otra vez ▪ conciliar el sueño (de nuevo) to get back to sleep ▪ to go back to sleep ▪ to fall back to sleep ➤ Después de que la sirena la despertara, no pudo volver a dormirse. ▪ Después de que la sirena la despertara, no pudo dormirse otra vez. ▪ Después de que la sirena la despertara, no pudo conciliar el sueño (de nuevo). After the siren woke her up, she couldn't get back to sleep.

volver a empezar to start over (again)

volver a encontrar el norte to get back on track ▪ to get back on the right track ▪ to regain one's bearings ▪ to recover one's sense of direction

volver a estar de moda to be back in style ▪ to come back in style

volver a estar en circulación to get back in(to) circulation

volver a haber (for) there to be... again ▪ (for) there again to be ▪ (for) there to be another ➤ Vuelve a haber un descubrimiento importante en la lucha contra el cáncer. Another important breakthrough in cancer research is taking place. ➤ Va a volver a haber una edad de oro. There's going to be another golden age.

volver a hacer buen tiempo *(clima)* to warm back up ▪ to turn nice again ➤ Tuvimos una ola de frío en noviembre, pero luego, volvió a hacer buen tiempo. We had a cold spell in November, but then it warmed back up. ▪ We had a cold spell in November, but then it turned nice again.

volver a hacer de las suyas ▪ volver a las andadas **1.** *(como fumar, por ejemplo)* to go back to one's old habits ▪ to go back to one's old ways ▪ to backslide **2.** *(como comer la comida de los compañeros* *de piso, por ejemplo)* to be back to one's old tricks ■ to go back to one's old tricks

volver a intentarlo to try it again ■ to give it another try

volver a invitar a alguien to invite someone back ■ to ask someone back

volver a la carga to get back to the task

volver a la misma canción ■ volver al mismo cuento to continue with the same old story ■ to be the same old story

volver a la normalidad ■ normalizarse to get back to normal ■ to return to normal ➤ La vida vuelve a la normalidad tras las devastadoras inundaciones. Life is getting back to normal after the devastating floods. ■ Life is returning to normal after the devastating floods.

volver a la tarea ■ volver a las labores ■ volver al trabajo to get back to work ➤ ¡Vuelve a la tarea! Get back to work!

volver a las andadas ■ volver a hacer de las suyas **1.** *(como fumar, por ejemplo)* to go back to one's old habits ■ to go back to one's old ways ■ to backslide **2.** *(como comer la comida de los compañeros de piso, por ejemplo)* to be back to one's old tricks ■ to go back to one's old tricks

volver a las labores ■ volver a la tarea ■ volver al trabajo to get back to work

volver a meterse en el coche to get back in the car ■ to get back into the car ➤ ¡Vuelvan a meterse en el coche! ■ *(Esp.)* ¡Volved a meteros en el coche! (You all) get back in the car!

volver a nacer 1. to have a narrow escape ■ narrowly to escape **2.** to be born again ➤ Volví a nacer después del accidente. I had a narrow escape in the accident. ■ I had a narrow escape from the accident. ■ I narrowly escaped injury in the accident

volver a poner en marcha algo to start something back up

volver a ponerse en contacto con alguien to get back to someone ■ to get back in touch with someone

volver a por aire *(Esp.)* to come up for air

volver a producirse ■ volver a ocurrir ■ volver a suceder to happen again ■ to occur again ➤ Este fenómeno no volverá a producirse. This phenomenon will not happen again.

volver a repetir *(de comida)* to have three helpings ■ to have a third helping ■ to have (yet) another helping ➤ He vuelto a repetir. I've had three helpings. ➤ Voy a volver a repetir. I'm going to have (yet) another helping.

volver a su ser to put back the way it was ■ to restore to its original condition

volver a tiempo de ■ volver a tiempo para ■ regresar a tiempo para to be back in time for ➤ ¿Vas a volver a tiempo de cenar? ■ ¿Vas a volver a tiempo de la cena? Will you be back in time for supper?

volver a tiempo para ■ volver a tiempo de ■ regresar a tiempo para to be back in time for ■ to return in time for ➤ ¿Vas a volver a tiempo de cenar? ■ ¿Vas a volver a tiempo de la cena? Will you be back in time for supper?

volver a uno loco to drive one crazy

volver al asunto ■ volver al tema to come back to the subject ■ to return to the subject ■ to get back to the subject

volver al comienzo to return to the beginning ■ to go back to the beginning

volver al orden to return to normal

volver al redil to return to the fold

volver al tema ■ volver al asunto to come back to the subject ■ to return to the subject ■ to get back to the subject

volver al trabajo to go back to work

volver algo a su ser to restore something to its original condition ■ to restore something to the way it was

volver como el ave fénix to rise like a phoenix from the ashes

volver de vacío ■ volver con las manos vacías to come away empty-handed

volver en blanco lo negro to turn black into white

volver en pie ■ volver a ponerse en pie to get back on one's feet ■ to get back up ➤ El boxeador volvió en pie antes de que el árbitro contara (hasta) diez. The boxer got back on his feet before the count of ten. ■ The boxer got back up before the count of ten. ■ The boxer got back on his feet before the referee reached the count of ten. ■ The boxer got back up before the referee reached the count of ten.

volver en sí to come to ■ to regain consciousness ➤ El boxeador volvió en sí antes de la cuenta de diez. The boxer came to before the count of ten.

volver (hacia) atrás to turn back ➤ Es demasiado tarde para volver (hacia) atrás. It's too late to turn back now.

volver la cara ■ mirar hacia el otro lado to look away ➤ Volvió la cara para no saludar. He looked away to avoid saying hello.

volver la espalda a algo 1. dar media vuelta to turn one's back (to something) **2.** ignorar algo ■ darle la espalda a algo to turn one's back on something

volver la espalda a alguien ■ darle la espalda a alguien ■ traicionar a alguien to turn one's back on someone

volver la mirada 1. mirar hacia atrás ■ voltear la mirada to look back **2.** mirar hacia el pasado to look into the past **3.** remontarse al pasado to look to the past (for answers)

volver la tortilla *(Esp., coloquial)* ■ darle la vuelta a la tortilla to turn the tables ■ to change the status quo

volver la vista atrás to look back

volver las aguas a su cauce ■ volver las aguas por su cauce ■ volver las aguas por donde solían (for) things to return to normal ■ (for) things to get back to normal ■ (for) things to settle down

volver las aguas por donde solían ir ■ volver las aguas por su cauce (for) things to return to normal ■ (for) things to get back to normal ■ (for) things to settle down

volver las aguas por su cauce ■ volver las aguas por donde solían (for) things to return to normal ■ (for) things to get back to normal ■ (for) things to settle down

volver las tornas (a alguien) to turn the tables (on someone) ■ to reverse an unfavorable situation ■ to gain the upper hand in a situation

volver lo de abajo arriba to turn something upside down ■ *(literalmente)* to turn the bottom side up

volver lo de arriba abajo to turn something upside down ■ *(literalmente)* to turn the top side down

volver pie atrás ■ retroceder **1.** to step back ■ to step backwards **2.** to back off

volver sobre sí ■ volver sobre sus pasos to retrace one's steps

volver sobre sus pasos ■ volver sobre sí to retrace one's steps ■ to go back over one's steps

volver uno a su casa to return home ■ to come home ➤ ¡Vuelve a casa ahora mismo! Come home this minute!

volver uno a sus orígenes ■ volver uno a sus raíces to return to one's origins ■ to return to one's roots ■ *(coloquial)* to come home ■ to go home

volver uno a sus raíces ■ volver uno a sus orígenes to return to one's roots ■ to return to one's origins ■ *(coloquial)* to come home ■ to go home ➤ Al venir a España siento como si volviera a mis raíces. By coming to Spain, I feel as if I've come home. ■ By coming to Spain, I feel as if I'm returning to my roots. ■ By coming to Spain, I feel as if I've returned to my roots.

¿volveré a verte? ■ ¿te voy a volver a ver? ■ ¿te veré otra vez? will I see you again? ■ am I going to see you again?

volverle a uno el juicio to come to one's senses ■ to return to one's senses ■ to come back to one's senses

volverle loco ■ chiflarle to drive one crazy ➤ Me vuelve loco. It drives me crazy. ■ *(él)* He drives me crazy. ■ *(ella)* She drives me crazy.

volverse a medias ■ dar media vuelta ■ voltearse a medias to turn (halfway) around

volverse agresivo *(gradualmente, con el tiempo)* to become aggressive ■ to turn aggressive

volverse atrás ■ dar marcha atrás ■ recoger velas ■ echarse atrás to back down ■ to turn back ■ to change one's mind

volverse aún mejor to get even better

volverse cada vez más grande to get bigger and bigger

volverse contra alguien to turn against someone ■ to turn on someone

volverse fluido(-a) en un idioma ■ soltarse en un idioma ■ hacerse fluido(-a) en un idioma ■ llegar a hacerse fluido(-a) en un idioma to become fluent in a language

volverse gilipollas *(subido de tono)* to turn into a real asshole

volverse instintivo ■ convertirse en instintivo to become second nature ■ to become instinctive ➤ Para un piloto aterrizar se vuelve instintivo. ■ Para un piloto aterrizar se convierte en algo instintivo. To a pilot, landing becomes second nature. ■ To a pilot, landing becomes instinctive.

volverse intensa sexualmente (una relación) to become sexual ■ to become physical ■ to get physical

volverse loco(-a) enloquecerse ■ chiflarse ■ to go crazy

volverse loco de contento to be happy as a lark ■ to be happy as a clam

volverse más amplio ■ ampliarse ■ hacerse más amplio to become wider ■ to get wider ■ to grow wider ➤ Debemos evitar que la disparidad entre los ricos y los pobres se vuelva más amplio. ■ Debemos evitar que la disparidad entre los ricos y los pobres se amplíe. ■ Debemos evitar que la disparidad entre los ricos y los pobres se haga más amplia. We must prevent the disparity between rich and poor from growing wider.

volverse mico para to be champing at the bit to ➤ Cuando se sacó el carnet de conducir Juan se volvió mico para comprarse un coche. When he got his driver's license, Juan was champing at the bit to buy a car.

volverse muy amable to suddenly become very nice ■ to become very nice all of a sudden ■ to turn very nice all of a sudden ■ to suddenly turn very nice

volverse obcecado(-a) con una idea ■ obcecarse con una idea to become obsessed with an idea

volverse presidente ■ llegar a ser presidente ■ hacerse presidente to become president ➤ Rutherford Hayes se volvió presidente de los Estados Unidos en 1877. Rutherford Hayes became president of the United States in 1877.

volverse tarumba to go nuts ■ to go bonkers

volverse un hábito to become a habit

volviendo a lo que le iba diciendo getting back to what I was telling you

volviendo a lo que te iba diciendo getting back to what I was telling you

vomitar hasta la primera papilla to throw up everything in one's stomach ■ *(coloquial)* to puke one's guts out ➤ Ha vomitado hasta la primera papilla. He vomited up everything in his stomach. ■ He threw up everything in this stomach. ■ *(coloquial)* He puked his guts out.

la **votación del nombramiento** vote on the nomination

votar con la billetera ■ votar con el bolsillo to vote one's pocketbook ➤ La gente vota con la billetera, generalmente. ■ La gente vota con el bolsillo, generalmente. People vote their pocketbooks, generally.

votar con el bolsillo ■ votar con la billetera to vote one's pocketbook ➤ La gente vota con el bolsillo, generalmente. ■ La gente vota con la billetera, generalmente. People vote their pocketbooks, generally.

votar contra 1. *(una persona)* to vote against **2.** *(un distrito electoral entero)* to vote down ➤ Dinamarca votó ayer contra el euro. Denmark yesterday voted down the euro.

votar en contra de to vote against

votar en función de to vote based on ■ to vote depending on ■ to vote in view of ➤ *(noticia)* Uno tiene que votar en función no sólo de la resolución del texto en sí mismo sino también en función de qué está sucediendo en Irak. One has to vote not only depending on the resolution of the text itself, but also in view of what's happening in Iraq.

votar por alguien to vote for someone

votar por correo to vote by absentee ballot ➤ Votó por correo. He voted by absentee ballot.

voté a favor de... I cast my vote for... ■ I cast my vote in favor of... ➤ Voté a favor del candidato moderado. ■ Voté a favor de la candidata moderada. I voted for the moderate candidate.

voto bisagra swing vote

voto de calidad ■ voto del desempate ■ voto de gracia tie-breaking vote

voto de castidad vow of chastity

voto de celebato vow of celibacy

voto de censura vote of no confidence ■ no-confidence vote ■ vote of censure

voto de confianza vote of confidence

voto de gracia ■ voto del desempate ■ voto de calidad tie-breaking vote

voto del desempate ■ voto de calidad ■ voto de gracia tie-breaking vote

voto del miedo rule of fear ■ vote out of fear ■ vote of fear ➤ Conservadores y socialistas unen fuerzas contra el voto del miedo en Euskadi (País Vasco). Conservatives and socialists join forces against the rule of fear in the Basque region.

voto por correo ■ *(menos común)* papeleta en ausencia absentee ballot

¡voy! *(puerta o teléfono)* ■ ¡yo lo cojo! ■ ¡yo contesto! I'll get it!

¡voy! ■ ¡va! coming!

voy a abandonar mientras estoy ganando I'm going to quit while I'm ahead

voy a echarte de menos ■ voy a extrañarte I'm going to miss you

voy a explicarme I'll explain ■ let me explain

voy a extrañarte ■ voy a echarte de menos I'm going to miss you

voy a ir para Navidad(es) I'm going for Christmas

voy a salir I'm going out

voy a salir con alguien esta noche ■ tengo una cita esta noche I have a date tonight

voy a ver I'll go see ■ I'll see ■ I'll look and see ■ I'll go look ■ *(coloquial)* I'm going to go see

voy allí de vez en cuando I go there sometimes ■ I go there from time to time

voy cogiendo el truco *(Esp.)* ■ voy cogiendo el truquillo ■ le voy agarrando la mano I'm getting the hang of it

voy para I'm on my way to

voy para allá I'm on my way ■ I'm coming

voy para casa I'm on my way home.

voy por ahí I'll drop by ■ I'll come by ■ I'll drop over ■ I'll come over ■ I'll pop in

voy sintiéndome mejor I'm starting to feel better ■ I'm beginning to feel better

voy tarde ■ se me hace tarde ■ se me ha hecho tarde I'm late ■ I'm running late

voy tirando I'm hanging in there

voz afónica ■ voz ronca hoarse voice

voz áspera rough voice

la **voz cantante** leading voice

la **voz de bajo** bass voice

la **voz de cautela** voice of caution

la **voz de la conciencia** voice of conscience

la **voz de mando** commanding voice

la **voz de pito** shrill voice ■ high-pitched voice

ser la **voz de su amo** to be his master's voice

voz de trueno: tener una ~ to have a booming voice

la **voz del pueblo** voice of the people

la **voz en el desierto** voice in the wilderness

voz estentórea ringing voice

la **voz grave** deep voice

voz ronca ■ voz afónica hoarse voice

voz rugosa gravelly voice

la **voz titubeante** faltering voice

voz tomada: tener la ~ ■ quedarse afónico ■ tener la voz empañada to be hoarse ■ to lose one's voice

voz vaga vague (tone of) voice

vuelco electoral electoral upset

vuelo acrobático aerobatic flying

vuelo con ala delta hang gliding

vuelo de conexión connecting flight

vuelo nivelado level flight

vuelo no tripulado unmanned flight

vuelo procedente de flight from ■ flight originating in ■ flight which originated in ➤ El presunto terrorista llegó a Madrid en un vuelo procedente de Düsseldorf, Alemania. The suspected terrorist arrived in Madrid on a flight from Düsseldorf, Germany.

vuelo rasante low-level flight

vuelos continuos ■ vuelos a cada equis tiempo continual flights ■ flights at regular intervals ➤ El puente aéreo provee vuelos continuos entre Madrid y Barcelona. ■ El puente aéreo provee vuelos a cada equis tiempo entre Madrid y Barcelona. The air shuttle provides continual flights between Madrid and Barcelona. ■ The air shuttle provides flights at regular intervals between Madrid and Barcelona.

vuelos programados scheduled flights

vuelta a España *(carrera de bicicletas)* tour of Spain

vuelta al cole back to school

vuelta al mundo ■ noria Ferris Wheel

vuelta ciclista bicycle tour ■ bicycle race

vuelta de espaldas *(salto de trampolín)* back flip ➤ *(comentarista de las Olimpiadas)* Tres vueltas y media de espaldas Three-and-a-half back flips

vuelta del camino turn in the road

vuelta en avióneta: llevar a alguien a dar una ~ ■ llevar a alguien a dar un paseo en avioneta to take someone for an airplane ride ➤ Me llevó a dar una vuelta en avioneta. ■ Me llevó a dar un paseo en avioneta. She took me for an airplane ride.

vuelta en avioneta: ir a dar una ~ ■ ir a dar un paseo en avioneta to go for an airplane ride

vuelta y vuelta *(filete)* rare ■ lightly browned on each side ➤ ¿Cómo te gustaría tu filete?-Vuelta y vuelta. How would you like your steak?-Rare. Lightly browned on each side.

vueltas por minuto ■ revoluciones por minuto ■ RPM revolutions per minute ■ RPM

estar **vuelto de costado** ■ estar vuelto de lado to be turned sideways ■ to be turned on one's side ■ to be turned on its side

vuelve a haber there is once again ■ there are once again

vuelve a intentarlo try it again

¡**vuelve al trabajo!** ■ ¡vuelve a trabajar! get back to work!

vuelve cuando quieras come back anytime ■ drop in anytime

vuelvo a señalar I repeat

la **vuestra** yours ■ belonging to (all of) you

vulnerar la ley to break the law ■ to violate the law ■ to be in violation of the law

vulnerar un pacto to violate a pact ■ to violate an agreement

el **wáter se desbordó** ▪ el retrete se desbordó the toilet overflowed

***x* a cero** *x* to nothing ➤ Nos ganaron diez a cero. They beat us ten to nothing.

***x* al cuadrado** ▪ *x* elevado al cuadrado *x* squared ▪ *x* to the second power

***x* al cubo** ▪ *x* elevado al cubo *x* cubed ▪ *x* to the third power

***x* años atrás** ▪ *x* años antes *x* years earlier ▪ *x* years before ➤ La pareja se había conocido cuatro años atrás. The couple had met four years earlier.

x* de cada *y *x* out of *y* ➤ Nueve de cada diez Nine out of ten

***x* de más** *x* too many ➤ Ella trató de colarse en la caja rápida con quince artículos de más. She tried to get in the express line with fifteen items too many.

***x* más de los necesarios** *x* more than needed ▪ *x* more than necessary ➤ Dos más de los necesarios Two more than necessary

x* menos *y* iguala *z ▪ *x* menos *y* es igual a *z* *x* minus *y* equals *z* ▪ *x* minus *y* is equal to *z*

***x* metros de longitud: tener ~** to be *x* meters long ▪ to be *x* meters in length

***x* minutos más de camino** *x* minutes farther along

***x* pies de longitud: tener ~** to be *x* feet long ▪ to be *x* feet in length

el ***x* por la noche** on the night of *x* ➤ El dieciocho de diciembre por la noche On the night of December eighteenth

los ***x* primeros** the first *x* ➤ Tenemos que leer los tres primeros capítulos para el lunes. We have to read the first three chapters for Monday.

los ***x* primeros capítulos** the first *x* chapters ➤ Tenemos que leer los tres primeros capítulos para el lunes. We have to read the first three chapters for Monday.

***x* primeras partes** the first *x* parts ➤ Tenemos que leer las tres primeras partes. We have to read the first three parts.

***x* puntos de ventaja** *x* points ahead

***x* veces al día** *x* times a day ▪ *x* times per day

***x* veces más** 1. *(singular)* *x* times as much 2. *(plural)* *x* times as many ➤ Tres veces más Three times as much

***x* veces más rápido que** *x* times as fast as

***x* veces más agudo que** *x* times as sharp as ▪ *x* times as sensitive as ➤ El olfato canino es al menos trescientas veces más agudo que el humano. A dog's sense of smell is at least three hundred times as sharp as a human's. ▪ A dog's sense of smell is at least three hundred times as sensitive as a human's.

***x* veces mayor** *x* times as large ▪ *x* times as big

x* votos frente a *y ▪ por *x* votos contra *y* by a vote of *x* to *y* ➤ *(noticia)* El Tribunal Constitucional rechazó ayer en un pleno muy dividido-seis votos frente a cinco-la recusación que presentó el Gobierno vasco al presidente de dicha institución. The Constitutional Court (of Spain) in a very contentious full session, yesterday rejected-by a vote of six to five-the Basque government's appeal to the court's presiding judge.

***x* y tantos** *x* odd ▪ *x* some odd ➤ Veinte y tantos... Twenty odd... ▪ Twenty some odd...

¡y a buen entendedor! and a word to the wise!
y a continuación and coming up... ■ and then ■ and next
¿¡y a eso lo llamas arte!? and you call that art?!
y a la verdad and indeed
y a los demás que los parta un rayo and to hell with everybody else
y a más... and the more... ➤ Y a más trabajo, más dinero And the more work, the more money
¿y a mí que me cuentas? what are you telling *me* for?
¡y a mucha honra! ■ ¡y orgulloso de serlo! and proud of it! ■ and proud to be one!
y a otra cosa, mariposa 1. (and) moving right along... 2. let's move on
y a propósito de... and speaking of...
y a usted, ¿quién le presenta? what's it got to do with you? ■ who asked you?
y acertaste and you were right
y acerté and I was right
y acertó ■ y le pegó *(él)* and he hit the nail on the head ■ *(ella)* and she hit the nail on the head ■ *(usted)* and you hit the nail on the head
y además and besides
¿y ahora qué hacemos? now what do we do? ■ what do we do now?
y al no serlo ■ y ya que no lo soy ■ y puesto que no lo soy and since I'm not
y aparte... and besides...
y aquí and at this point
¡y aquí estoy yo! ■ ¡y hasta hoy! and here I am today!
y aquí no ha pasado nada 1. everything's just fine (here) 2. nobody's doing anything about it
y aquí paz, y después, gloria and that's the end of the discussion
y así en adelante ■ y así sucesivamente and so on
y así lo hizo *(él)* and he did ■ and so he did ■ *(ella)* and she did ■ and so she did ■ *(usted)* and you did ■ and so you did
y así me va and that's what I get
y así te va and that's what you get
y así sucesivamente ■ y así en adelante ■ etcétera and so on ■ et cetera ■ *(coloquial)* and whatnot ■ and what have you
y así te luce el pelo and it shows ■ and you can tell ➤ Juan lleva tres meses sin trabajar y sin hacer nada y así le luce el pelo. Juan has not worked or done anything for three months, and it shows.
y así te quedó and it shows
y así te va and that's what you get ➤ No terminaste tus estudios, y así te va. You didn't finish school, and that's what you get.

y aún lo es ■ y aún lo sigue siendo ■ y aún sigue siéndolo and it still is
y aún lo hace ■ y aún lo sigue haciendo ■ y aún sigue haciéndolo and it still does
y basta and that's enough
y, bueno, sí (lo hice)... well, and I did... ■ and, well, I did...
¡y bien! now! ➤ Y bien, ¿hay algo de mí que sí te gusta? Now, is there anything about me that you *do* like?
y Cía. and Co. ■ and Company
y, claro,... and, of course,...
y colorín colorado, este cuento se ha acabado ■ fueron felices y comieron perdices ■ y fueron felices por siempre jamás and that's the end of the story ■ and they lived happily ever after
y como and as if ■ and as though ➤ Y como diseñado al más mínimo detalle por una computadora... And as if designed down to the last detail by a computer...
¡y cómo! and how!
y como era de esperar and sure enough ■ and as (was) expected ■ and as was (to be) expected
y como es de esperar and sure enough ■ and as (is) expected
y como fin de fiesta to cap the event ■ as the climax
¿y cómo iba a saberlo? how was I supposed to know?
y como si fuera poco and as if that weren't enough
y con razón and rightly so ■ and for good reason
y conste que and let it be known that ■ and let it be shown that
y cosas de estas and things of this sort ■ and the like
y cuál no sería mi sorpresa cuando and what to my surprise ■ when to my surprise
y da gracias... ■ y gracias... and (just) be glad that... ➤ Te has portado muy mal y hoy no podrás salir a jugar y da gracias que sólo es hoy. You have behaved very badly today, so you can't go out to play, and (just) be glad that it's only for today.
¡y dale! *(él)* there he goes again! ■ *(ella)* there she goes again!
y dale que dale *(él)* he keeps going on and on ■ *(ella)* she keeps going on and on
y de éste and thereby ■ and with reference to the latter
y de hecho ■ y en realidad and, in fact,
y de improviso and suddenly ■ then suddenly
y de repente caí en la cuenta (de que...) ■ y de repente me di cuenta (de que...) and all at once it hit me (that...)
y de ser así ■ y si es así ■ y si fuera así and if so
y demás ■ y así sucesivamente ■ etcétera and everything else ■ and so on ■ et cetera ■ and the like
y después está... and then there's...
y dicho sea de paso and incidentally ■ and let me say in passing
y en cambio and instead
y en cierta forma ■ y en cierto modo and in a way
y en cierto modo ■ y en cierta forma and in a way
y en concreto ■ y especificamente and specifically
y en lugar de ello ■ y en vez de ello and instead of that
y en paz and that's it
y en realidad ■ y realmente ■ y de hecho and actually, ■ and, in fact,
y en vez de ello ■ y en lugar de ello and instead of that
¿y enterrarlo en el jardín? *(Valle-Inclán)* how about burying him in the garden?
y entonces hay... ■ y luego hay... and then there's...
¿y entonces qué se supone que hago (yo) ahora? so what am I supposed to do now?
y es lo que hay ■ y no hay más ■ y punto and that's that ■ and that's all there is to it
y es lo que había ■ y no había más ■ y punto and that was (the end of) that ■ and that's all there was to it
y es más... and what's more...
y es que... and it's because... ■ it's (just) that... ➤ No me apetece ir al cine esta noche y es que he estado trabajando mucho. I don't feel like going to the movies tonight. It's just that I've been working hard (today).
¿y eso? (and) how come?

¿y eso cómo se come? what do you make of it? ▪ how would you explain it?

y eso es decir mucho ▪ y eso ya es decir mucho ▪ y eso ya es mucho decir and that's saying a lot ▪ and that's going some

¿y eso cómo se come? ▪ ¿cómo te explicas esto? ▪ ¿cómo te lo explicas? ▪ ¿qué te parece esto? what do you make of it?

y eso que **1.** even though ▪ even if **2.** in spite of the fact that

¿y eso se consiente? *(Valle-Inclán)* and that's allowed?

y eso ya es mucho ▪ y eso es decir mucho ▪ y eso ya es decir mucho ▪ y eso ya es mucho decir and that's going some ▪ and that's saying a lot

y específicamente ▪ y en concreto and specifically

y fueron felices por siempre jamás ▪ fueron felices y comieron perdices ▪ y colorín colorado, este cuento se ha acabado and they lived happily ever after ▪ and that's the end of the story

¡y gordo! *(Valle-Inclán)* a big one! ▪ major! ➤ He pescado un pez y bien gordo además. I've caught a fish, and a big one at that.

y gracias... ▪ y da gracias... and (just) be glad that...

¡y hasta hoy! ▪ ¡y aquí estoy yo! and here I am today!

y hasta puede que más ▪ y puede que incluso más ▪ y quizás más and maybe (even) more ▪ and perhaps even more

(y) lo consigo that works for me ▪ that does it for me

y lo demás es cuento **1.** y lo demás es historia and the rest is history **2.** y lo demás son tonterías and the rest is nonsense

y lo demás son tonterías and the rest is nonsense

y lo logró and it worked ▪ and it was successful

y lo pasado, pasado let bygones be bygones

y lo que es más and what's more

y lo que es peor and worse ▪ and what's worse

y lo sigo estando ▪ y sigo estándolo and I still am

y lo sigo haciendo ▪ y sigo haciéndolo and I still do

y lo sigo siendo ▪ y sigo siéndolo ▪ y sigo así and I still am ▪ and I continue to be

y lo sigo teniendo ▪ y sigo teniéndolo and I still have one ▪ and I still do (have one) ▪ and I still have it ▪ and I still do (have it)

¿y luego? ▪ ¿y qué paso? and then? ▪ what then?

y luego de esto and then... ▪ and so... ➤ Y luego de esto decidí... And then I decided... ▪ And so I decided...

y luego hay... ▪ y entonces hay... and then there's...

y más cosas that and other things

y mira de lo que ha servido and look at all the good it did ▪ a lot of good it did ➤ Le dije a mi hijo adolescente, "Cuando yo tenía tu edad, mi padre solía decirme que me sentase derecho." Mi hijo me dijo, "Y mira de lo que ha servido." I told my teenage son, "When I was a teenager, my father used to tell me to sit up straight." My son said, "And look at all the good it did." ▪ I told my teenage son, "When I was a teenager, my father used to tell me to sit up straight." My son said, "A lot of good it did."

y mucho menos much less ➤ Es imposible que un cohete alcance la velocidad de la luz, y mucho menos sobrepasarla. It is impossible for a rocket to reach the speed of light, much less exceed it.

y mucho menos con especially with ▪ much less with ➤ Por favor no saquen fotos durante la actuación, y mucho menos con flash. Please do not take photographs during the performance, especially with a flash.

y ni aun así and not even then

y no al revés and not the other way around

y no digamos (and) not to mention ➤ Está prohibido fumar en el colegio, y no digamos en los baños. Smoking is prohibited in the school, not to mention in the bathrooms.

y no había más ▪ y es lo que había ▪ y punto ▪ y es lo que había **1.** and that was that **2.** and that's all there was to it ▪ and that was all there was to it

¡y no hablemos más! and let's leave it at that! ▪ and we both know it! ➤ Estamos de acuerdo en que no podemos permitirnos la reforma y no hablemos más (del tema). We agree that we can't afford the remodeling, and let's leave it at that.

y no hay Dios que le convenza *(Esp., leísmo)* **1.** *(a él)* nothing will convince him ▪ you'll never convince him **2.** *(a ella)* nothing will convince her ▪ you'll never convince her

y no hay Dios que lo convenza *(L.am.)* nothing will convince him ▪ you'll never convince him

y no hay más ▪ y es lo que hay ▪ y punto and that's that ▪ and that's all there is to it

y no otra cosa and not anything else ▪ and nothing else

y no sé qué **1.** and I don't know what else **2.** y así sucesivamente and so forth

y no sé qué (tanto) más and I don't know what all (else) ▪ and I don't know what else ➤ En su bolsa Connie guarda su cartera, gafas, lápiz labial, agenda, llave universal y no sé qué (tanto) más. In her pocketbook Connie keeps her wallet, glasses, lipstick, appointment book, real estate key, and I don't know what all else.

y no tengo la intención and I don't intend to

y no tengo tampoco la intención nor do I intend to

y no tenía ganas de descubrirlo and I didn't want to find out ➤ No tenía ni idea de cómo... y no tenía ganas de descubrirlo. I had no idea how... and I didn't want to find out.

¡y orgulloso de serlo! ▪ ¡y a mucha honra! and proud of it! ▪ and proud to be one!

y otras hierbas and so on and so forth ▪ and so on ▪ and on and on and on

y para abreviar to make a long story short

y para de contar and that's it ▪ and that's all ➤ Somos tú, Matías y yo, y para de contar. There are just you, Mathias, and myself, and that's it.

¡y pensar que eras tú! and to think (that) it was you!

¡y pensar que fuiste tú! and to think (that) it was you!

¡y pensar que podría haber sido usted! and to think (that) it could have been you! ▪ and to think (that) it might have been you!

¡y pensar que podrías haber sido tú! and to think (that) it could have been you! ▪ and to think (that) it might have been you!

y peor de todo and worst of all

y por eso and that's why ▪ so ▪ and so ▪ and therefore

y por lo mismo and for that (very) reason ▪ and therefore ▪ and thus ▪ and hence

y por (lo) tanto and therefore ▪ and so

y por si fuera poco and as if that weren't enough

y por último and last ▪ and finally ➤ Se añade seis cucharadas de harina y por último un chorrito de leche. Add six tablespoons of flour, and last, a splash of milk.

y por una buena razón and for (a) good reason

y posteriormente and subsequently ▪ and later ▪ and then ➤ La secretaria aplazó, y posteriormente suspendió, la reunión. The secretary postponed, and subsequently cancelled, the meeting.

y precisamente en aquel instante and just at that moment

y puede que incluso más ▪ y hasta puede que más ▪ y quizás más and maybe (even) more ▪ and perhaps (even) more

y puesto que no lo soy ▪ y ya que no lo soy ▪ y al no serlo and since I'm not

y punto **1.** y no hay más ▪ y es lo que hay and that's it ▪ and that's that ▪ and that's final **2.** y no había más ▪ y es lo que había and that was that ▪ and that was the end of it

¿y qué? so? ▪ so what? ▪ what of it? ▪ what then?

¿y qué es entonces? and what is it then?

¿y qué fue lo que vi? and what did I see? ▪ and what was it that I saw?

¡y que lo digas! you can say that again!

¡y qué más! **1.** is that all? **2.** *(sarcástico)* yeah, sure! **3.** so, what else is new?

¡y que me quiten lo bailado! and no one can take that away from me!

y que no falte and may it always be so ▪ and may it always be that way ➤ Tengo mucho trabajo.-Y que no falte. I have a lot of work to do.-And may it always be that way.

y que no se diga más ▪ y que no se hable más and that's it ▪ and that's final

y que no se hable más ▪ y que no se diga más and that's it ▪ and that's final

y que no tenga que... **1.** *(yo)* and I don't want to have to... **2.** *(él)* and I don't want him to have to... **3.** *(ella)* and I don't want her to have to... **4.** *(usted)* and I don't want you to have to...

¿y qué se hace? *(Valle-Inclán)* and what are we going to do? ▪ what's to be done?

¡y que sea usted! and to think it was you!

¿y qué tal entonces? ▪ ¿qué tiene? ▪ ¿entonces qué? ▪ ¿qué te parece? what about it?

¡y que te quiten lo bailado! and no one can take that away from you!

¡y que tenga que...! and to think...!

¿y qué va a hacerle? ▪ ¿y qué remedio? and what can you do about it?

¿y qué remedio? ▪ ¿y qué va a hacerle? and what can you do about it?

¿y qué ventolera te ha entrado a ponerte a organillero? *(Valle-Inclán)* whatever possessed you to become an organ grinder?

y quizás más y puede que incluso más ▪ y hasta puede que más and maybe (even) more ▪ and perhaps (even) more

y realmente y en realidad and actually ▪ and in fact

¡y sanseacabó! and that's that!

¡y santas Pascuas! and that's that!

y santo remedio and that did the trick ➤ Me dolía mucho el oído, le eché unas gotas de aceite de oliva y santo remedio. I had a bad earache, I put in a couple drops of olive oil, and that did the trick.

y se acabó lo que se daba ▪ se acabó and that's it

y se nota and it shows

y según eso and accordingly

y según lo hacía (yo) and as I did

y según parece and by all appearances ➤ Se va a presentar un nuevo modelo de ordenador portátil, y según parece, es mucho mejor que todos los anteriores. They're coming out with a new laptop computer, and by all appearances, it is much better than any of the old(er) ones.

¿y si...? ▪ ¿qué tal si...? what if...?

y si no... and if you don't believe me...

y si no, al tiempo you'll see in the end

y si no, tiempo al tiempo you'll see in the end

y si otro se tira por un barranco, ¿te tiras tú también? just because somebody throws himself off a cliff, are you going to do it, too? *(Admonición paterna para no dejarse influir por las actitudes de otros niños ▪ Parental admonition to resist peer pressure)*

y si te gusta whatever floats your boat

y sigo así ▪ y lo sigo siendo ▪ y sigo siéndolo and I still am ▪ and I continue to be

y sigo estándolo ▪ y lo sigo estando and I still am

y sigo haciéndolo ▪ y lo sigo haciendo ▪ y aún lo hago and I still do

y sigo teniéndolo ▪ y lo sigo teniendo and I still have one ▪ and I still do (have one) ▪ and I still have it ▪ and I still do (have it)

y sigue haciéndolo ▪ y lo sigue haciendo ▪ y aún lo hace ▪ y aún sigue haciéndolo and it still does

y sigue siendo... and still is...

y sigue siéndolo ▪ y aún lo es and it still is... ▪ *(él)* and he still is... ▪ *(ella)* and she still is...

y sin embargo and yet

y sobre todo and above all ▪ and most of all

y sonó la flauta por casualidad **1.** it was just a stroke of luck **2.** it was a fluke (that I got it right) ▪ it was just a lucky guess

y tal como había dicho *(él)* and just as he had said ▪ *(ella)* and just as she had said

¡y tan derecho! nice and straight!

¡y tan fácil! nice and easy!

y tan posible very possibly ▪ quite possibly ▪ it's very possible

¡y tanto! and how!

¡y tengamos la fiesta en paz! cut it out!

y tenía razón *(él)* and he was right ▪ *(ella)* and she was right ▪ *(usted)* and you were right

y toda esa historia and all that jazz ▪ and all that stuff

y toda la hostia *(subido de tono)* **1.** and all that crap ▪ and all that shit **2.** and all those assholes ▪ and all the rest of those jerks

y toda la pesca ▪ y todo eso and all that (stuff) ▪ and the whole business ▪ and whatnot

y todo and all ▪ and everything

y todo cuento **1.** *(presente)* and all of it is nonsense **2.** *(pasado)* and all of it was nonsense

y todo ese rollo ▪ y todo eso all that (jazz)

y todos tan amigos ▪ y todos tan contentos and nothing came of it ▪ and it was as if nothing had ever happened ▪ and it was like nothing had happened ➤ Tres meses después de la pelea, se volvieron a ver y todos tan amigos. Three months after the fight, they met again, and it was as if nothing had happened.

y todos tan contentos ▪ y todos tan amigos ▪ y todos tan tranquilos (it's) as if nothing ever happened

¿y tú? ▪ ¿y a ti? what about you? ➤ Fui al Escorial el sábado. ¿Y tú? I went to the Escorial Saturday. What about you? ➤ Me gusta el jazz. ¿Y a ti? I like jazz; what about you?

y tú, más and you, even more (so) ▪ and you're even more so ➤ Es buena cocinera, y tú más. She's a good cook, and you're an even better one. ▪ She's a good cook, and you're even better.

¿y tú qué crees? ▪ ¿a ti qué te parece? do bears live in the woods? ▪ is the pope Catholic? ▪ is a four-pound robin fat? ▪ what do you *think*?

¡y tú que lo digas! ▪ ¡muy bien dicho! ▪ ¡así se habla! right on! ▪ well said!

¡y un cojón! *(subido de tono)* (that's) bullshit!

¡y un huevo! *(subido de tono)* (that's) bullshit!

¡y un jamón! (that's) baloney!

¡y un jamón con chorreras! you gotta be serious! ▪ get serious!

¡y un pimiento! (that's) baloney

¡y una mierda! *(subido de tono)* (that's) bullshit!

¡y una polla! subido de tono (that's) bullshit!

¡y vaya fiesta! **1.** and what a party! **2.** and what a festival!

¡y vaya si...! and boy, can... ➤ ¡Y vaya si canta (ella)! And boy, can she sing!

y viceversa ▪ y al revés and vice versa

y voy yo y me lo creo and I fell for it

¡y ya está! and there you are! ▪ and it's done!

y ya que de esto hablamos and while we're on the subject ▪ and since we're talking about it

y ya que no lo soy ▪ y puesto que no lo soy ▪ y al no serlo and since I'm not

y yo me lo creo, ¿no? ▪ ¡y yo voy y me lo creo! and you expect me to believe that?

¡y yo voy y me lo creo! ▪ y yo me lo creo, ¿no? and you expect me to believe that?!

¿ya? ▪ ¿está bien? okay?

ya a la venta now on sale

ya ahora now ➤ Pero ya ahora hay una mujer nueva en mi corazón. But *now* there's a new woman in my heart.

ya aprovecho while I'm at it ➤ Por cierto, ya aprovecho, ¿Cómo traducirías...? By the way, while I'm at it, how would you translate...?

ya bien sea whether it be ▪ whether it is ▪ whether ➤ Ya bien sea expresado o implícito Whether (it be) expressed or implied ▪ Whether explicit or implicit

¡ya caigo! now I get it! ▪ I get it! ▪ now I know!

ya casi era de noche cuando... it was almost dark when...

ya casi no acordarse ▪ casi haberse olvidado ▪ tener casi olvidado barely to remember ▪ to have almost forgotten ➤ Ya casi no me acuerdo de cómo suena el inglés por haber estado fuera tanto tiempo. ▪ Casi me he olvidado de cómo suena el inglés por haber estado fuera tanto tiempo. ▪ Tengo casi olvidado cómo suena el inglés por haber estado fuera tanto tiempo. ▪ I've almost forgotten what English sounds like, I've been away so long. ▪ I barely remember what English sounds like, I've been away so long.

¡ya comenzamos! here we go again!

ya cuando no sooner than ➤ Ya cuando empezó la película se cortó la electricidad. No sooner had the movie started than the power went out.

ya de antes ▪ que desde antes which had previously ➤ Brotó el cristianismo de la confluencia de dos grandes corrientes espirituales, la una judaica y la otra helénica, ya de antes influidas mutualmente. *(Unamuno)* Christianity grew out of the confluence of two great spiritual currents, the Judaic and Hellenic, which had previously influenced each other.

(ya) de paso 1. and while you're at it 2. on one's way ➤ Ya de paso que vas al mercado, cómprame una botella de vino. While you're at the market, get me a bottle of wine. ➤ ¿(Ya) de paso me echas esto en el buzón? Would you mail this for me on your way?

ya duró bastante it's been through the mill ▪ it's lasted a long time

ya en 1. una vez en once in 2. tan temprano como as early as 3. ahora en now in ➤ Ya en Madrid fue directamente a su hotel. Once in Madrid he went straight to his hotel. ➤ María trabajaba en el departamento ya en 2004, ¿verdad? María was working in the department as early as 2004, wasn't she?

ya en esto 1. by this time 2. now that 3. while one is at it ▪ while one is in the process (of doing something) ▪ while one is in the midst of (doing something) ➤ Ya en esto, estaría bien que llegásemos hoy a Barcelona. Now that we're on our way, it would be good if we could get to Barcelona today.

ya en una ocasión once before

¡ya entiendo! ▪ ¡ahora (lo) entiendo! ▪ *(Esp.)* ¡(ah,) ya lo cojo! now I get it! ▪ (oh,) I get it!

ya entonces ▪ para entonces by then

ya entrado el año 1. once the year has begun 2. once the year had begun

ya era así cuando lo compré ▪ es así desde el principio ▪ *(Méx.)* es así de factura it was like that when I bought it

ya era tarde para it was too late to

ya es decir ▪ que ya es decir (and) that's saying something

ya es decir mucho ▪ ya es mucho decir (and) that's saying a lot

ya es historia it's history ▪ it's over ➤ La crisis ya es historia. The crisis is over.

ya es hora it's about time ▪ it's high time

ya es hora de que... it's high time that... ▪ it's about time that...

ya es hora de volver al trabajo it's time we got back to work

ya es hora de empezar a trabajar it's time we got down to work

ya es hora que llegaras it's about time you got here ▪ it's high time you got here

ya es hora que nos vayamos a casa it's time we went home

ya es mucho decir ▪ ya es decir mucho (and) that's saying a lot

ya es un hecho it's now a fact

¡ya está! 1. ¡no hagas eso! cut it out! 2. ¡(y) ya está! (and) there you are! ▪ that's it! 3. ¡entiendo! (I) got it!

¡ya está bien! ▪ ¡ya vale! knock it off! ▪ enough is enough! ▪ enough of that! ▪ that's enough!

¡ya está bien de...! that's enough of...!

ya está fuera de duda there's no longer any doubt

ya está puesto(-a) 1. *(mesa)* it's already set 2. *(tren)* to be at the platform ▪ to be ready to board ➤ El tren ya está puesto. The train is at the platform.

ya está resuelto it's already been taken care of

ya estaba armada that did it ▪ now it was war ▪ now the war was on

ya estaba levantado(-a) *(yo)* I was already up ▪ *(él)* he was already up ▪ *(ella)* she was already up

ya estar aquí ▪ ya haber llegado already to be here ➤ Ya estabas aquí. ▪ Ya habías llegado. You were already here. ▪ You were here earlier.

ya estar (con algo) ▪ ya estar en ello to go at it ▪ to be going at it ➤ Ya están otra vez el perro y el gato. The dog and the cat are going at it again. ▪ The dog and the cat are fighting again. ➤ Ya están los niños con el nuevo videojuego. The kids with the new video game are really going at it.

ya estar en ello to go at it ▪ to be going at it ➤ Anoche ya estaban mis vecinos en ello. My neighbors were really going at it last night.

ya estar criado(-a) to be grown ➤ Sus hijos ya están criados. Their children are grown.

ya estar disponible to be available now ➤ Ya está disponible. It's now available ▪ It's become available.

ya estar pillado(-a) to be in for it now ➤ ¡Ya estamos pillados! We're in for it now!

ya estar puesto already to be in place ▪ *(tren)* to be (waiting) at the platform ➤ El tren ya está puesto. The train is at the platform.

ya estar todo visto to have seen what there is to see ➤ Ya está todo visto. *(yo)* I've seen what there is to see. ▪ *(nosotros)* We've seen what there is to see.

¡ya estoy aquí! I'm here! ▪ I'm home!

ya falta menos we're getting closer (to the end)

ya fuera este o ese whether it was this one or that one ▪ whether it was one or the other

ya ha pasado lo peor the worst is over now ▪ the worst part is over now

ya haber cumplido con esperar to have waited long enough ➤ Ya he cumplido con esperar. I've waited long enough.

ya haber estado casado(-a) to have been married before ▪ to have been previously married

ya haber hecho algo to have already done something ➤ Si todavía no ha preguntado, no se lo menciones. ▪ Si no ha preguntado aún, no se lo digas. If he hasn't asked already, don't mention it. ▪ If he hasn't already asked, don't mention it.

ya haber llegado ▪ ya estar aquí to already be here ➤ Ya habías llegado. ▪ Ya estabas aquí. You were already here. ▪ You were here earlier.

ya hace años many years ago ▪ years ago

ya hay calefacción ▪ haber vuelto la calefacción (for) the heat to be back on ➤ Ya hay calefacción otra vez. ▪ Ya hay calefacción de nuevo. ▪ Por fin, ha vuelto la calefacción. The heat's back on, finally.

¡ya he tenido bastante! ▪ ¡estoy harto! ▪ ¡se acabó! I've had it! ▪ I'm through!

¡ya iba siendo hora! at last! ▪ finally! ▪ it's high time! ▪ it's about time!

ya ir para allá to be on one's way (over) ➤ Ya voy para allá. I'm on my way. ▪ I'm on my way over.

ya ir para viejo ▪ estar entrando en años ▪ ir envejeciendo to be getting old ▪ to be getting up in years ▪ to be aging ➤ Ya va para viejo. ▪ Está entrando en años. ▪ Va envejeciendo. He's getting old. ▪ He's getting up in years. ➤ Ya va para vieja. ▪ Está entrando en años. ▪ Va envejeciendo. She's getting old. ▪ She's getting up in years.

ya la tengo I already have it ➤ ¿Tienes la última película de Antonio Banderas?-Sí. Ya la tengo. Do you have the latest Antonio Banderas film?-Yes, I already have it.

ya le pondré al día *(a él)* I'll give him an update ▪ I'll bring him up to date ▪ *(a ella)* I'll give her an update ▪ I'll bring her up to date

ya le leeré la cartilla 1. *(a él)* I'm going to read him the riot act ▪ I'm going to give him a piece of my mind 2. *(a ella)* I'm going to read her the riot act ▪ I'm going to give her a piece of my mind

¡ya la veo! 1. *(persona)*I can (just) see her now! 2. *(susantivo femenino)*I can (just) see it now!

ya le ajustaré luego las cuentas 1. *(a él)* I'll deal with him later 2. *(a ella)* I'll deal with her later

¡ya le arreglaré! *(Esp., leísmo)* ▪ ¡ya lo arreglaré! I'll fix him

¡ya te arreglaré! I'll fix you!

ya le pondré las cosas claras *(a él)* I'm going to give him a piece of my mind ▪ *(a ella)* I'm going to give her a piece of my mind

¡ya le veo! *(Esp., leísmo)* I can just see him now!

¡ya lo arreglaré! I'll fix him!

¡ya lo creo! you bet (your life)!

¡ya lo has dicho! you said it! ▪ you can say that again!

¡ya lo veo! I can just see him now!

¡ya llegará la mía! I'll get lucky some day!

¡ya lo cojo! *(Esp.)* ▪ ¡ah, ya lo cojo! ▪ ¡ahora (lo) entiendo! ▪ ¡ya entiendo! (now) I get it! ▪ oh, I get it!

¡ya lo creo! I'll say! ▪ of course! ▪ yes, indeed!

¡ya lo creo que...! I'll say it's... ➤ ¡Ya lo creo que hace calor! I'll *say* it's hot.

ya lo decía yo I *told* you ▪ I told you so

¡ya lo estoy visualizando! ▪ ¡ya puedo visualizarlo! I'm getting the picture!

ya lo haré I'll get (around) to it ▪ I'll get to it later ▪ I'll do it later

¡ya lo has dicho! you said it!

ya lo hice una vez I did that once before ▪ I've already done that once

ya lo pondré al día ▪ ya lo actualizaré I'll update it

ya lo sabía (yo) that's what I thought ▪ I thought as much ▪ I already knew it ▪ I had already realized it

¡ya lo sabrás! *you'll* find out!

ya lo sé I do know

ser **ya lo suficientmente grande para** to be just big enough to

¡ya lo tengo! ▪ ¡ya sé! I've got it! ▪ *I* know! ▪ I've figured it out! ▪ I've solved it!

ya lo veo 1. *(él)* I can just see him now ▪ *(ello)* I can just see it now 2. ya me doy cuenta I can tell

¡ya lo veremos! we'll see about that!

ya lo ves you see

ya me apañaré 1. I'll manage, (don't worry) 2. I'll take care of it ▪ (just) leave it to me ➤ Ya me apañaré para terminar el informe hoy. I'll manage to get the report finished today. ➤ ¿Quieres que lave los cacharros?-Ya me apañaré. Do you want me to wash the dishes?-I'll take care of it. ▪ Just leave to me.

ya me contarás tell me (all) about it ➤ Ya me contarás luego cómo te fue la cita a ciegas. Tell me all about your blind date when you get back.

ya me doy cuenta ▪ ya lo veo ▪ lo noto ▪ se nota I can tell

ya me entero y te lo comento ▪ yo ya me entero y te lo comento I'll find out for you

¡ya me estoy haciendo una idea! ▪ ¡ya me lo estoy imaginando! ▪ ¡ya me puedo hacer una idea! ▪ ¡ya me lo puedo imaginar! I'm getting the idea! ▪ I'm getting an idea! ▪ I can imagine!

ya me lo figuraba ▪ ya me parecía ▪ me lo estaba imaginando ▪ me lo estaba figurando ▪ lo pensaba yo I thought as much ▪ I figured as much ▪ that's what I thought ▪ that's what I figure

ya me gusta now I like it ➤ Ya me gusta la literatura del siglo diez y nueve. Now I like ninteenth-century literature.

ya me gustaría I'd like nothing better

ya me has picado el gusanillo *(coloquial)* ▪ me has picado la curiosidad you've piqued my curiosity ▪ you've got me curious ▪ you've got my curiosity up

ya me he dado cuenta I realize that ▪ I realize it ▪ I can tell that

ya me he dado cuenta de que... now I've realized that...

¡ya me imagino! ▪ ¡me lo imagino! ▪ ¡me lo figuro! ▪ ¡ya me lo imagino! I can imagine!

¡ya me (lo) imagino! ▪ ¡me lo figuro! ▪ ¡me lo imagino! I can imagine!

¡ya me lo puedo imaginar! ▪ ¡ya me puedo hacer una idea! ▪ ¡ya me estoy haciendo una idea! ▪ ¡ya me lo estoy imaginando! ▪ ¡ya puedo visualizarlo! ▪ ¡ya lo estoy visualizando! I can just picture it now! ▪ I can picture it now!

ya me paso I'm overdoing it ▪ I've outdone myself

ya me pasó it's happened to me before

ya me podías haber llamado ▪ bien podías haberme llamado you could have called me

¡ya me puedo hacer una idea! ▪ ¡ya me lo puedo imaginar! ▪ ¡ya me estoy haciendo una idea! ▪ ¡ya me lo estoy imaginando! ▪ ¡ya puedo visualizarlo! ▪ ¡ya lo estoy visualizando! I can just picture it now! ▪ I can picture it now! ▪ I'm getting the picture!

ya me veía... I could see myself...

ya me veo haciendo eso I can see myself doing that

ya me voy I'm leaving

ya me voy a la cama I'm going to bed

¡ya mero! *(Méx.)* 1. in a second 2. *(en el momento álgido)* I'm almost there

ya mero llega 1. *(él)* he'll be here any minute (now) 2. *(ella)* she'll be here any minute (now)

¡ya nada se me da! *(Valle-Inclán)* I don't succeed in anything any more!

ya ni siquiera don't even ➤ Ya ni siquiera me acuerdo. ▪ Ya ni siquiera recuerdo. I don't even remember.

¡ya ni vergüenza tiene! 1. *(él)* he's got a lot of nerve! 2. *(ella)* she's got a lot of nerve!

ya no not any more ▪ no longer

ya no aguantar más ▪ ya no poder más to be at the end of one's rope ▪ to be at the end of one's tether

ya no cabía duda... there was no longer any doubt that...

ya no contaba contigo I'd given you up ➤ Ya no contaba contigo. Creí que no ibas a venir. I'd given you up. I didn't think you were coming. ➤ Ya no contaba contigo. Creí que no ibas a llamar. I'd given you up. I didn't think you were going to call.

ya no es lo que era it's not what it used to be ▪ it's not what it once was

ya no está con nosotros 1. está muerto he's gone 2. está muerta she's gone

ya no existir to no longer exist

ya no hallar la salida ▪ no saber ni qué hacer ▪ no saber qué decir to be at one's wit's end

ya no me apetece más gracias I don't care for any more, thank you ▪ I don't care for any more, thanks

ya no poder más ▪ ya no aguantar más to be at the end of one's rope ▪ to be at the end of one's tether

ya no poder volverse atrás to be beyond the point of no return ➤ Cuando no podamos pagar el interés de la deuda, no podremos volvernos atrás. When we can no longer pay the interest on the debt, we will be beyond the point of no return.

ya no puede caminar he can't walk anymore

ya no queda sino 1. there's no one left but... 2. there's nothing left but...

ya no quedan sino there are only... left

ya no se toma a la mujer como antes *(titular con doble sentido)* 1. women are no longer viewed the way they used to be 2. women are no longer seduced the way they used to be

ya no ser niños to no longer be children ➤ Ya no somos niños. We're no longer children.

(ya) no tengo ni que... ▪ ni siquiera tengo que... I don't even have to... ➤ Los sobres vienen por lotes de veinticinco. Ya no tengo ni que contar. The envelopes come in lots of twenty-five. I don't even have to count them.

ya nos conocemos 1. I know you better than that 2. we already know each other 3. ya nos hemos conocido we've already met

ya nos hemos conocido we've already met

ya pasar to wear off ➤ Por lo menos ya pasó el susto inicial de la noticia. At least the initial shock of the news has worn off.

ya pasó todo everything's okay

ya pensaba que te habías olvidado del tema I thought you'd (you had) forgotten about it

ya podías haber empezado por ahí you could have said that to begin with ▪ why didn't you say that to begin with?

ya puedes suponer lo que... you can imagine how...

¡ya puedo visualizarlo! ▪ ¡ya lo estoy visualizando! I can just see it! ▪ I'm getting the picture!

ya que now that ▪ since ▪ as long as ➤ Ya que estoy aquí... As long as I'm here... ▪ Since I'm here... ➤ Ya que se empeña en saberlo... *(él)* Since he's so determined to find out... ▪ *(ella)* Since she's so determined to find out... ▪ *(usted)* Since you're so determined to find out...

ya que estás en ello while you're at it

ya que estoy en ello ▪ puesto a ello while I'm at it ▪ since I'm already doing it

ya que has venido... since you're here...

ya quedó dicho as was said ▪ as was said earlier

ya regreso *(L.am.)* ▪ espera que ya regreso ▪ espera que ya vengo ▪ espera que ahora vengo ▪ ya vuelvo ▪ espera que ya vuelvo I'll be right back

ya sabe usted this is your house ▪ you are welcome here anytime

ya sabes this house is your house

ya sabes lo que es eso you know what *that's* like

¡ya sé! ▪ ¡ya lo tengo! *I* know! ▪ I've got it!

ya se ha dicho todo lo que se tenía que decir everything that can be said has been said

¡ya se la escacharraron! *(Valle-Inclán)* ▪ ya le partieron la cabeza ▪ ya le rompieron la cabeza they've split his head

ya se le ha hecho todo lo que se ha podido everything that can be done has been (done) ▪ we've done all we can

ya se (le) notaba you could tell (that he...) ▪ you could tell (that she...) ➤ Ya se le notaba que estaba mal de salud. *(a él)* You could tell he was in poor health. ▪ *(a ella)* You could tell she was in poor health.

ya sé lo que quiero *(al mesero)* ▪ ya sé qué es lo que quiero I already know what I want

ya se nota you can tell

ya se notaba you could tell

ya se ve you can see ▪ you can tell

ya se ve que... by now you realize that... ▪ by now you have realized that...

ya se verá you'll see ▪ we'll see

ya sea whether it be

ya ser muy otro(-a) to be a very different person ▪ to be a completely different person ▪ to have changed a lot ▪ to have changed a great deal

ya será para menos it can't be that bad

estar **ya sobre** to be upon

ya somos dos 1. yo también that makes two of us ▪ so am I ▪ I am, too 2. estoy de acuerdo contigo that makes two of us ▪ I'm with you ▪ I agree with you ➤ Tengo mucha hambre.-Ya somos dos. I'm really hungry.-That makes two of us. ➤ Estoy harto de esta reunión.-Yo también. I'm tired of this meeting.-That makes two of us.

¡ya son horas! at last! ▪ it's about time! ▪ it's high time!

ya soy mayorcito(-a) para eso I'm too old for that

ya te acordarás you'll think of it later ▪ you'll remember (it) later ▪ *(advertencia)* it's going to come back to haunt you! ▪ the chickens are going to come home to roost! ▪ you'll be sorry!

¡ya te arreglaré yo! *(amenaza)* you're going to get it! ▪ I'll deal with you later!

¡ya te arrepentirás! ▪ ¡estarás arrepentido(-a)! you'll be sorry!

¡ya te digo! 1. I agree 2. boy, I'll say!

ya te diré I'll let you know

ya te entiendo I get what you mean ▪ I catch your drift ▪ I hear you!

ya te lo dije I told you so

¡ya te pondré al día! I'll tell you all about it ▪ I'll bring you up to date ▪ I'll give you the skinny

¿ya te retiras? ▪ ¿ya te vas? ▪ ¿ya sales? are you leaving (so soon)? ▪ are you leaving (already)?

¡ya te tengo acorralado(-a)! I've got you cornered!

ya te tocará your turn is coming ▪ your turn will come

ya tenemos la fiesta armada everything's under way ▪ everything's rolling

ya tener bastantes preocupaciones ▪ ya tener suficientes preocupaciones to have enough to worry about ➤ Que no se lo digas. Ya tiene bastantes preocupaciones en este momento. Don't tell him. He has enough to worry about right now.

ya tengo uno(-a) I already have one

ya va siendo hora 1. it's getting to be time 2. *(con impaciencia)* ya es hora it's high time ▪ it's about time ➤ Ya va siendo hora de salir. It's getting to be time to leave. ▪ It's high time we got out of here.

¡ya vale! ▪ ¡basta! ▪ ¡se acabó! I'm through! ▪ I've had it!

¡ya vale, ya vale! all right, all right!

ya vendrá ▪ ya vendrá algún día *(él)* someday he'll show up ▪ he'll show up at some point ▪ *(ella)* someday she'll show up ▪ she'll show up at some point

ya veo cómo es 1. *(él)* I know what he's like 2. *(ella)* I know what she's like 3. *(ello)* I know what it's like

ya veo que no it certainly isn't

ya veremos we shall see ▪ we'll see

ya vuelvo *(Esp.)* ▪ espera que ya vuelvo ▪ espera que ya vengo ▪ espera que ahora vengo ▪ ya regreso ▪ espera que ya regreso I'll be right back

¡ya, ya! I get it ▪ got it!

yacer desmayado(-a) to lie unconscious

yacer en el suelo to lie on the floor

yacimiento arqueológico archeological site

yacimiento petrolífero ▪ campo petrolífero oil field

yacimiento de carbón coal field

yacimientos de empleo ▪ mina de empleo labor pool

yaya y yayo grandma and grandpa

yema del dedo ▪ *(plural)* yemas de los dedos fingertip ▪ *(plural)* fingertips

yema mejida ▪ (el) ponche de huevo ▪ ronpopo eggnog

yendo y viniendo back and forth ▪ to and fro ➤ Se pasa una hora yendo y viniendo de su habitación al baño. He goes back and forth from his room to the bathroom for an hour.

los **yentes y vinientes** ▪ (los) transeúntes passersby

estar **yerto de frío** to be frozen stiff

yo con fulano me trato lo justo I have as little to do with John Doe as possible

(yo) daría cualquier cosa por I'd give anything to

(yo) daría un ojo de la cara por I'd give my eyeteeth to

yo en mi caso I personally ➤ Yo en mi caso voy a trabajar ese día. I personally am going to work that day.

yo en tu lugar if I were in your place ▪ if I were in your shoes

(yo) encantado(-a) I'd love to ▪ I'd be delighted to

yo habitualmente... I habitually... ▪ I routinely...

(yo) hubiera jurado que... ▪ (yo) podría haber jurado que... ▪ (yo) podría haber asegurado que... ▪ (yo) hubiera asegurado que... ▪ (yo) podría haber afirmado que... ▪ (yo) hubiera afirmado que... I could have sworn that...

(yo) iba de broma ▪ era broma ▪ sólo estaba bromeando I was just kidding ▪ I didn't mean it ▪ I was just joking ▪ I was only joking

¡yo, ídem de ídem! ditto!

(yo) la cojo *(con antecedente femenino)* I'll get it

(yo) la he fastidiado ▪ (yo) la he organizado ▪ (yo) lo monté I caused this problem

(yo) la he organizado ▪ (yo) la he fastidiado ▪ (yo) lo monté I caused this problem

yo lo cojo *(Esp.)* 1. *(teléfono)* yo contesto ▪ yo respondo I'll get it 2. *(objeto)* yo lo tomo I'll take hold of it

yo lo hago encantado I'd love to do it

(yo) lo monté ▪ (yo) la he organizado ▪ (yo) la he fastidiado I caused this problem

(yo) me apaño solo ▪ (yo) solo me apaño ▪ (yo) puedo con ello ▪ (yo) puedo solo ▪ (yo) me encargo solo I can handle it ▪ I can deal with it

yo me basto (y me sobro) I can do it myself

(yo) me encargo solo ▪ (yo) puedo solo ▪ (yo) puedo con ello ▪ (yo) me apaño solo ▪ (yo) solo me apaño I can handle it ▪ I can deal with it

yo me lavo las manos I'm washing my hands of it ▪ I want nothing to do with it

yo me lo guiso, yo me lo como: ser como Juan Palomo ~ to be a lone wolf ▪ to be a loner ▪ to do one's own thing ▪ to follow one's own instincts

yo me lo sabía de memoria I used to know it by heart

yo me ocuparé de ello ▪ yo me ocupo I'll take care of it

yo me ocupo ▪ yo me ocuparé I'll take care of it

yo me sabía eso de memoria I used to know that by heart

yo mero I myself

(yo) no acertaba a explicármelo ▪ no pude entenderlo completamente ▪ no pude comprenderlo completamente I couldn't quite understand it

(yo) no acierto a explicármelo ▪ no puedo entenderlo completamente ▪ no puedo comprenderlo completamente I can't quite understand it ▪ I don't quite get it

yo no I don't ▪ not I

(yo) no hago casi nunca... I almost never make... ▪ I hardly ever make... ▪ I almost never do... ▪ I hardly ever do... ➤ Yo no hago casi nunca gazpacho porque en casa sólo me gusta a mí. I almost never make gazpacho because at home I'm the only one who likes it.

(yo) no me siento diferente I don't feel any different (from anyone else)

yo no sé tú, pero... I don't know about you, but...

(yo) podría haber jurado que... ▪ (yo) hubiera jurado que... ▪ (yo) podría haber asegurado que... ▪ (yo) hubiera asegurado que... ▪ (yo) podría haber afirmado que... ▪ (yo) hubiera afirmado que... I could have sworn that...

(yo) puedo con ello ■ (yo) puedo solo ■ (yo) me encargo solo ■ (yo) me apaño solo ■ (yo) solo me apaño I can handle it ■ I can deal with it

(yo) puedo con ello, gracias ■ yo puedo solo, gracias I can handle it, thanks

(yo) puedo decirte que... ■ (yo) te puedo decir que... I can tell you that...

(yo) puedo solo, gracias ■ yo puedo con ello, gracias I can handle it, thanks

¡yo qué sé! ■ ¡qué sé yo! how would I know? ■ how should I know? ■ search me!

yo qué tú ■ si yo fuera tú ■ yo en tu lugar if I were you

yo que tú tendría ojo ■ tendría cuidado si fuera tú ■ yo que tú tendría cuidado ■ yo que tú me andaría con ojo ■ yo que tú me andaría con cuidado I'd be careful if I were you

yo sabía que vendrías I knew you would come ■ I knew you'd come

yo sí que ■ yo sí I certainly do

yo siempre... I always...

yo soy así ■ así soy that's (just) the way I am ■ that's just how I am

yo soy el que soy I am what I am ■ with me, what you see is what you get

yo soy yo y mi circunstancia *(Ortega y Gasset)* I am myself and my circumstances

yo solo no puedo hacerlo I can't do it by myself ■ I can't do it alone

yo también I do, too ■ so do I ■ *(coloquial, pero incorrecto)* me, too

yo también puedo I can, too

(yo) tampoco lo creo I don't think so, either

(yo) te puedo decir que... ■ (yo) puedo decirte que... I can tell you that...

(yo) ya me entero y te lo comento I'll find out for you

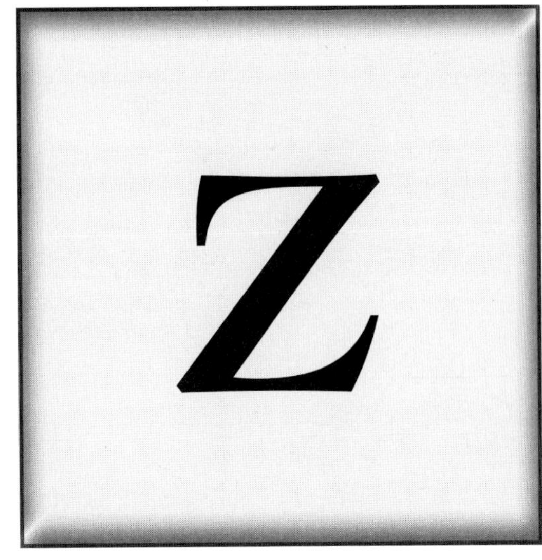

zafarrancho de combate: ordenar ~ to order soldiers to their battle stations

zafarrancho de limpieza 1. general cleaning **2.** blizzard of laundry ▪ barrage of laundry

zafarse de alguien to get rid of someone

zafarse de hacer algo ▪ escaquearse de hacer algo ▪ evitar hacer algo to get out of doing something ▪ *(coloquial)* to weasel out of doing something

zafarse de los escombros to get clear of the debris

Zamora no se ganó en una hora ▪ Roma no se hizo en un día Rome wasn't built in a day

zanjar algo de plano to settle something once and for all ▪ to settle something definitively

zanjar el tema to settle the question

zanjar los rumores sobre to quash the rumors about ▪ to dispel the rumors about

zapatas de freno(s) brake shoes ➤ Las zapatas se utilizan en los frenos de tambor. ▪ Las zapatas se emplean en los frenos de tambor. Brake shoes are used on drum brakes.

¡zapatero a tus zapatos! mind your own business!

zapatillas de deporte athletic shoes

zapatos de batalla everyday shoes

zapatos de caña alta high-top shoes

zapatos de charol patent leather shoes

zapatos de deporte athletic shoes

zapatos del carajo *(subido de tono)* ▪ zapatos cojonudos fucking great new shoes

zapatos estrechos tight shoes

zarpar con rumbo a ▪ hacerse a la vela con rumbo a to set sail for

zarza ardiendo burning bush

zona cero ▪ nivel cero ground zero

zona circundante surrounding area

zona comprendida entre area bound by

zona con solera historic area ▪ historic district ▪ historic zone

zona del edificio part of the building ➤ Estaba en otra zona del edificio. He was in another part of the building.

zona este *(de Nueva York)* East Side

zona infantil playground

zona oeste *(de Nueva York)* West Side

zona mal delimitada ▪ zona de límites confusos gray area

zona no fumadores no smoking area

zonas circundantes surrounding areas

zonas de difícil acceso hard-to-reach areas

zorro viejo (sly) old fox

zuecos de madera wooden clogs

zumbar como la *s* de *desde* to buzz like the *s* in *desde*

zumbarle a alguien los oídos (for) one's ears to ring

zumo de naranja recién exprimido *(Esp.)* ▪ jugo de naranja recién exprimido freshly squeezed orange juice

zurrarle la badana a alguien ▪ calentar la badana a alguien ▪ sobar la badana a alguien to tan someone's hide ▪ to rake someone over the coals

little off. *(at the moment)* No está muy centrada. ▪ Está un poco chiflada. ▪ *(all the time)* Es un poco chiflada. ▪ Está un poco ida de la cabeza. ▪ No está muy centrada. ▪ Está un poco loca. ▪ Está un poco p'allá. ➤ The measurement is a little off. La medida no es muy exacta. ▪ La medida es un poco imprecisa. ▪ La medida no está muy ajustada. ▪ La medida no es muy correcta.

to be **a little out of it** estar medio chiflado(-a) ▪ estar medio loco(-a)

to be **a little out of sorts 1.** to be cranky estar un poco gruñón ▪ estar un poco irritable **2.** to be feeling unwell no encontrarse bien ▪ *(Sp., coll.)* no estar muy católico ➤ The child is a little out of sorts because his mother would not buy him candy at the grocery store. El niño está un poco gruñón porque su madre no le ha comprado caramelos en la tienda. ➤ I'm (feeling) a little out of sorts today so I'm going to skip the gym. Hoy no me encuentro muy bien, así que me voy a saltar el gimnasio.

to be **a little premature 1.** *(judgment)* to be too hasty ▪ to rush to judgment ser un poco prematuro ▪ ser un poco pronto **2.** *(birth)* ser un tanto prematuro ▪ ser un poco pronto ➤ It's a little premature to say that the policy is a failure. Es un poco prematuro afirmar que la política ha sido un fracaso. ➤ The baby was a little premature. El bebé fue un poco prematuro. ➤ The baby was two months premature. El bebé fue sietemesino.

to be **a little steep 1.** *(in price)* ser un poco caro ▪ ser un poco alto ▪ ser un poco elevado ▪ ser un poco excesivo **2.** *(in angle)* ser (muy) inclinado ▪ estar (muy) inclinado ▪ tener (mucha) pendiente ▪ tener (demasiada) pendiente ➤ That agent's fee is a little steep for us right now. Los honorarios de ese agente son un poco altos para nosotros en este momento. ➤ This path is a little steep to climb without mountaineering equipment. Este sendero está un poco inclinado como para escalar sin equipo de alpinismo.

a little strange: to act ~ ▪ to act a little strangely estar un poco raro ▪ estar un poco extraño

a little thing of it una poca cantidad ▪ un poco sólo ➤ A little thing of it costs a hundred dollars. Una poca cantidad cuesta cien dólares. ▪ Un poco sólo cuesta cien dólares.

a little while ago ▪ a short time ago hace poco tiempo ▪ hace poco ▪ hace un poco

a little while later al poco tiempo

a lot bastante ▪ mucho ▪ un montón ➤ She looks a lot older than her sister. Parece mucho mayor que su hermana. ▪ Parece bastante mayor que su hermana. ➤ I like it a lot. Me gusta mucho. ▪ Me gusta un montón. ▪ Me gusta bastante.

to be **a lot alike** parecerse mucho en su forma de pensar ▪ parecerse mucho (en su mentalidad) ▪ ser muy parecidos ▪ tener ideas muy parecidas ➤ Oscar and Diego are a lot alike. Oscar y Diego se parecen mucho.

a lot alike: to look ~ parecerse mucho (físicamente) ▪ ser muy parecidos ▪ ser como dos gotas de agua ➤ She and her sister look a lot alike. Ella y su hermana se parecen mucho (físicamente). ▪ Ella y su hermana son como dos gotas de agua. ▪ Ella y su hermana son muy parecidas.

a lot depends on mucho depende de (si) ➤ For a new artist, a lot depends on the first release. Para un(-a) nuevo(-a) artista, mucho depende de su primer corte.

a lot fewer muchos menos ➤ I have traveled to Mexico a lot fewer times than Marta has. He viajado a México muchas menos veces que Marta. ➤ There were a lot fewer people there than I had expected. Había mucha menos gente allí de la que esperaba.

a lot going for one: to have ~ haber nacido con estrella

a lot is riding on ▪ a lot depends on hay mucho en juego en ▪ nos jugamos mucho en ▪ se va mucho en ➤ A lot is riding on this election. Hay mucho en juego en estas elecciones. ▪ Nos jugamos mucho en estas elecciones. ➤ We have to apply ourselves because a lot is riding on this project. ▪ We have to apply ourselves because a lot depends on this project. Tenemos que esforzarnos porque nos va mucho en este proyecto.

to be **a lot like someone** tener mucho de alguien ➤ She's a lot like her mother. Tiene mucho de su madre.

a lot more 1. much more mucho más **2.** many more muchos más ➤ There were a lot more (many more) people there than I had expected. ▪ There were a lot more people than I was expecting. Había mucha más gente de la que esperaba. ➤ There were a lot more guests than I was expecting. Había muchos más invitados de lo que esperaba.

a lot less mucho menos ➤ It cost a lot less than I had thought it would. Costó mucho menos de lo que pensaba.

a lot of ▪ a great deal of mucho(-a) ▪ cantidad de ▪ *(coll.)* una bestialidad de ➤ A lot of food Mucha comida ▪ Cantidad de comida ▪ Una bestialidad de comida ➤ A lot of money Mucho dinero

a lot of explaining to do: to have ~ tener mucho que explicar

a lot of fun: to have ~ ▪ to have a great time divertirse mucho ▪ pasarlo grande ▪ *(coll., said especially of children)* pasárselo pipa ➤ The kids had a lot of fun at the circus. Los peques se lo pasaron pipa en el circo.

a lot of good it did ▪ and look at all the good it did y mira de lo que ha servido ➤ I told my teenage son, "When I was a teenager, my father used to tell me to sit up straight." My son said, "A lot of good it did." Le dije a mi hijo adolescente, "Cuando yo tenía tu edad, mi padre solía decirme que me sentase derecho". Mi hijo me dijo, "Y mira de lo que ha servido".

a lot of good *that* does! ¡mira de lo que sirve!

a lot on the line: (for) there to be ~ haber mucho en juego ➤ There is a lot on the line. Hay mucho en juego.

a lot on the line: to have ~ ▪ to risk a lot tener mucho en juego ▪ jugarse mucho ➤ I have a lot on the line. ▪ I'm risking a lot. Tengo mucho en juego. ▪ Me juego mucho.

a lot remains to be done ▪ there's still a lot to do queda mucho por hacer

to be **a matter of** ser cosa de ▪ ser cuestión de

to be **a mere** no pasar de ser un mero ▪ ser un mero

to be **a mile away** estar a una milla (de distancia)

a mile away: to see someone coming ~ ▪ to see someone coming a mile off vérsele venir a la legua ▪ vérsele venir a los dos kilómetros ➤ You can see him coming a mile away. ▪ You can see him coming a mile off. Se lo ve venir a la legua. ➤ You could spot his dishonesty a mile away. Se podían ver sus intenciones a la legua.

a mile away: to spot something ~ ▪ to spot something a mile off **1.** *(literal)* to come into view divisar algo a la legua ▪ ver algo a la legua **2.** *(figurative)* to sense dishonesty ver algo a la legua ▪ ver las intenciones de alguien a la legua ▪ divisar algo a la legua ➤ You could spot his phoniness a mile away. ▪ You could spot his phoniness a mile off. Se podía divisar su falsedad a la legua.

a moment before ▪ a moment earlier un momento antes

a moment before... ▪ just before... un momento antes de (que)... ➤ A moment before the controllers lost contact with the shuttle, the commander radioed that there was an increase in the pressure in one of the tires. Un momento antes de perder contacto con el transbordador, el comandante transmitió a los controladores que había un incremento en la presión de uno de los neumáticos. ▪ Un momento antes de que los controladores perdiesen contacto con el transbordador, el comandante transmitió que había un incremento en la presión de uno de los neumáticos.

a moment later ▪ after a moment un momento después ▪ al cabo de un momento ▪ un momento más tarde

a month before ▪ a month earlier un mes antes

a month before... un mes antes de (que)...

a month later un mes después ▪ al mes siguiente ▪ pasado un mes ▪ al mes

a month later to the day ▪ exactly a month later justo en un mes

to be **a must** ser un deber ➤ It's a must. Es un deber.

to be **a must-see** ser para no perderse ▪ ser una visita obligada ▪ deberse ver ▪ no podérselo perder ➤ The movie is a must-see. La película es una visita obligada. ▪ Esa película se debe ver. ▪ Esa película no te la puedes perder. ➤ The Prado is a must-see. El Prado es una visita obligada.

a number of diversos ▪ un número de ▪ varios ➤ According to a number of studies... Según diversos estudios... ▪ Según un número de estudios...

a particular one ▪ a specific one uno(-a) muy concreto(-a) ➤ I was looking for a particular one. Buscaba uno muy concreto. ➤ I was looking for a particular pattern. Estaba buscando un patrón en concreto.

a particular person una persona en particular ▪ una persona concreta

a perfectly good... ...que está perfecto ▪ ...que está en perfectas condiciones ➤ Why throw away a perfectly good sponge just because it's a little ripe? ¿Por qué tirar una esponja que está perfecta sólo porque huele un poquito a rancio?

a short distance away a poca distancia

a short time ago ▪ a little while ago hace poco ▪ *(literary)* poco tiempo ha

a single 1. a lone ▪ the same un(-a) simple ▪ un(-a) mismo(-a) **2.** one un(-a) solo(-a) ➤ A single error could cost me my job. Un simple error podría costarme el trabajo. ➤ A single bullet wounded both people. Una misma bala fue la que hirió a ambas personas. ➤ Monotheism is the belief in one God. Monoteísmo es la creencia en un solo Dios.

a single time una sola vez ▪ una única vez

a sort of una especie de

a sure thing una cosa cierta

a tenth una décima parte

a ways *(coll.)* un buen trecho ➤ I'm already down the track a ways, so I'll probably finish my degree here. Ya llevo un buen trecho recorrido así que quizá termine mis estudios aquí.

a ways to go: to have ~ *(coll.)* **1.** *(literal and figurative)* quedarle un buen trecho ▪ quedarle bastante ▪ un largo camino por recorrer **2.** *(literal)* quedarle un buen trecho por recorrer ➤ The swelling has gone down some, but it still has a ways to go. La hinchazón se ha disminuido algo, pero todavía le queda bastante. ➤ We still have a ways to go. Nos queda un buen trecho.

a week ▪ per week a la semana ▪ por la semana ▪ cada semana ➤ The class meets three times a week. La clase se reúne tres veces a la semana. ▪ La clase se reúne tres veces por semana. ➤ She has to go to the doctor a couple times a week. Cada semana tiene que ir al médico un par de veces.

a week before una semana antes

a week before... una semana antes de (que)...

a week from today de hoy en una semana

a week later una semana después ▪ una semana más tarde ▪ pasada una semana

a while ago hace tiempo ▪ hace (un) rato

a while later un rato después

a while longer un rato más ▪ aún un rato ▪ todavía un rato ➤ Do you want to stay a while longer? ▪ *(informal)* Do you want to stick around a while longer? ¿Quieres quedarte un rato más?

a whole generation ▪ an entire generation toda una generación ➤ For a whole generation Para toda una generación

a whole hour: to take ~ ▪ to take an entire hour llevarle a uno toda una hora ▪ llevarle a uno una hora entera ▪ tardar toda una hora ▪ tardar una hora entera ▪ tardar una hora completa ➤ It took a whole hour. Llevó toda una hora. ▪ Llevó una hora entera. ▪ Llevó una hora completa. ➤ It took a whole hour to download this E-mail. Tardó toda una hora descargar este correo electrónico. ▪ Llevó toda una hora descargar este correo electrónico. ➤ It took me a whole hour. Tardé toda una hora. ▪ Me llevó toda una hora. ▪ Tardé una hora entera. ▪ Me llevó una hora entera. ▪ Tardé una hora completa. ▪ Me llevó una hora completa.

a whole hour: to shoot ~ *(coll.)* ▪ to waste a whole hour tirarse toda una hora ▪ tirarse una hora entera ➤ He shot a whole hour making the salad. Se tiró toda una hora preparando la ensalada. ▪ Se tiró una hora entera preparando una ensalada.

a work in progress una obra en proceso

a year ▪ per year anuales ▪ al año ➤ *(news item)* The double agent, whose salary at the FBI was $100,000 a year... El agente doble, cuyo sueldo en el FBI era de $100.000 dólares anuales...

a year ago hace un año

a year ago today ▪ exactly one year ago hoy hace un año ▪ al año exactamente ▪ al año justo

a year later un año después ▪ al año

to **abandon a search** abandonar una búsqueda

to **abandon an idea** abandonar una idea

to **abandon one's script** saltarse el guión ➤ There were two stellar moments when the rivals abandoned their scripts. Hubo dos momentos estelares en los que los rivales se saltaron el guión.

to **abandon someone to his fate** ▪ to leave someone to his fate abandonar a alguien a su suerte ▪ dejar a alguien de la mano de Dios

abandoned streets ▪ deserted streets calles abandonadas ▪ calles fantasmas ▪ calles olvidadas

to **abdicate the throne** abdicar el reino

to **abide by the agreement** atenerse al convenio ▪ cumplir con el acuerdo ▪ acatar el pacto

to **abide by the decision** acatar la decisión ▪ atenerse a la decisión

to **abide by the law** ▪ to obey the law acatar la ley ▪ obedecer la ley

to **abide by the result** ▪ atenerse al resultado ▪ respetar el resultado ➤ Ortega said if the election were monitored by Jimmy Carter, he (Ortega) would abide by the result. Ortega dijo que si el proceso electoral fuera observado por Jimmy Carter, que él (Ortega) respetaría los resultados. ▪ Ortega dijo que si el proceso electoral fuera observado por Jimmy Carter, que él (Ortega) se atendría a los resultados. *(Both "resultado" and "resultados" are correct.)*

to **abide by the rules** ▪ to go by rules ▪ to obey the rules **1.** atenerse a las normas ▪ cumplir con las normas **2.** *(games)* cumplir las reglas ▪ atenerse a las reglas

abiding trust ▪ unwavering trust confianza inquebrantable ➤ An abiding public trust attended Lincoln, despite the controversy and calumny he endured. A pesar de las calumnias que tuvo que soportar, Lincoln fue asistido por la confianza inquebrantable de la gente.

ability to: to have the ~ tener la capacidad de

abject coward *el, la* vil cobarde

abject poverty vil pobreza ▪ pobreza abyecta ▪ pobreza extrema

abject slavery esclavitud abyecta

to be **able-bodied** estar capacitado ➤ Why do you beg? You're able-bodied. ¿Por qué mendigas? Estás capacitado.

to be **able to** ser capaz de ▪ poder ➤ If the interview subject says, after an interruption, "Where was I?," the reporter should always be able to tell him. Si el entrevistado dice, después de una interrupción, "¿Por dónde iba?" el reportero debe ser siempre capaz de decírselo.

to be **able to count something on one's fingers** ▪ to be few in number poder contarse con los dedos de la mano

to be **able to do something blindfolded** ▪ to know how to do something blindfolded saber hacer algo con los ojos cerrados

to be **able to manage something heavy** poder con algo pesado ➤ I need to move the piano, but I can't manage it by myself. Necesito mover el piano, pero no puedo con él yo solo.

to be **able to talk one's way out of anything** ▪ to know how to talk one's way out of anything tener salida para todo

to be **able to tell that...** (poder) darse cuenta de... ➤ I can tell that you haven't done your homework. Me doy cuenta de que no has hecho tu tarea. ➤ I could tell that he hadn't done his homework. Me di cuenta de que no había hecho su tarea. ▪ Pude darme cuenta de que no había hecho su tarea.

to **abort a fetus** abortar un feto

to **abort a mission** abortar una misión

to **abort a takeoff** abortar una maniobra de despegue

aborted attempt intento abortado

aborted landing aterrizaje frustrado

abortive attempt intento frustrado

to be **about** tratar de ▪ ir de ▪ estar sobre

about face! *(military command)* ¡media vuelta!

about-face: to do an ~ **1.** *(military facing movement)* darse la media vuelta **2.** to do a one-eighty ▪ to adopt the very position that one had earlier opposed dar un giro de ciento ochenta (grados) ▪ adoptar la postura a la que uno previamente se opuso **3.** to turn one's life around dar un giro de ciento ochenta grados

about it al respecto ■ a ese respecto ■ con eso ■ sobre eso ➤ I don't know anything about it. No sé nada al respecto. ➤ I can't do anything about it. No puedo hacer nada al respecto. ➤ I don't know what to do about it. No sé qué hacer con eso. ■ No sé qué hacer a ese respecto.

about it: the thing I liked ~ 1. *(recent)* lo que me ha gustado 2. *(less recent)* lo que me gustó ➤ The thing I liked about it was the ending. Lo que me ha gustado fue el final. ■ Lo que me gustó fue el final.

about it?: what did you like ~ ¿qué es lo que te ha gustado?

to be **about like** ser más o menos como ■ ser parecido a ➤ The weather there is about like it is here. El tiempo allí es más o menos como aquí. ■ El tiempo allí es parecido al de aquí.

to be **about out** 1. to be almost out ■ to be almost used up estar a punto de acabarse ■ casi agotárlele a uno 2. to be about over ■ to be almost over estar a punto de terminar ➤ We're about out of sugar. ■ We're almost out of sugar. El azúcar está a punto de acabarse. ■ Casi se nos agota el azúcar. ➤ School is about out. Las clases están a punto de terminar.

about something: to like a lot of things ~ gustar muchas cosas de algo ➤ I like a lot of things about this condo, but the other one has bigger bedrooms. Me gustan muchas cosas de este apartamento, pero el otro tiene recámaras más grandes.

to be **about the same age** ser más o menos de la misma edad

about the time of ■ around the time of ■ at about the time of para cuando ■ hacia la época de ■ alrededor del tiempo de

to be **about this big** *(motioning with the hands)* ser así de grande

to be **about this size** *(motioning with the hands)* ser así de este tamaño

about time: it's ~ ya es hora ■ ya va siendo hora ■ por fin

to be **about to** estar a punto de ■ estar para ■ disponerse a

to be **about to arrive** estar a punto de llegar ■ estar al caer ■ estar para llegar

to be **about to begin** estar a punto de empezar ■ estar a punto de comenzar

to be **about to change** estar a punto de cambiar ➤ Our lives were about to change forever. Nuestras vidas estaban a punto de cambiar para siempre.

about whether ■ over whether acerca de si ■ en relación a si

about which sobre lo que ■ sobre la que

to be **about *x* (years old)** 1. tendrá *x* años 2. *(said of older people)* to be pushing *x* andar pisando los *x* años ➤ She's about five. Ella tendrá cinco. ➤ He's about eighty. ■ He's pushing eighty. Anda pisando los ochenta.

above a store ■ over a store encima de una tienda ➤ When the writer Isaac Asimov was a child, his family lived above their candy store. De niño el escritor Isaac Asimov y su familia vivían encima de su propia tienda de golosinas.

above all sobre todo

above all else sobre todo lo demás

above and beyond the call of duty más allá de la llamada del deber

to be **above average** 1. *(in terms of a specific number or benchmark)* estar por encima de la media ■ estar por encima del promedio 2. *(as a general observation)* estar superior a la media ■ estar superior al promedio 3. *(especially in medical description)* estar más alto de lo común ➤ His white cell count was above average, indicating an infection. Su cuenta de glóbulos blancos estaba más alto de lo común, indicando una infección.

above-average intelligence 1. *(casual observation) la* inteligencia superior a lo normal ■ inteligencia más alta de lo común 2. *(as measured)* inteligencia por encima de la media ■ inteligencia por encima del promedio

above-average temperatures temperaturas por encima de lo normal

above everything else sobre todas las demás cosas

to be **above ground** estar al ras de la tierra ➤ The metro at Batán is above ground. El metro en Batán hace su recorrido al ras de la tierra.

to be **above normal** estar por encima de lo normal ■ ser por encima de lo normal ■ ser más de lo normal ■ ser superior a lo normal ➤ The rainfall for the year is several (cubic) inches above normal. Las precipitaciones de este año han sido de algunas pulgadas por encima de lo normal. ➤ We have had a period of above-normal temperatures. Hemos tenido un período de temperaturas por encima de lo normal. ■ Hemos tenido un período de temperaturas superiores a lo normal.

to be **above sea level** estar sobre el nivel del mar ➤ The city is at five hundred meters above sea level. La ciudad está a quinientos metros por encima del nivel del mar.

to be **above suspicion** estar fuera de toda sopecha ■ estar fuera de sospecha ■ estar libre de sospechas

above the clouds por encima de las nubes ➤ The airplane flew above the clouds. El avión voló por encima de las nubes.

above the earth por encima de la tierra ■ sobre la tierra ➤ The satellites orbit high above the earth. Los satélites orbitan muy por encima de la tierra.

to be **above the national average** estar por encima de la media nacional ■ estar por encima del promedio nacional

above the weather por encima de las tempestades ➤ We flew above the weather. Fuimos en avión por encima de las tempestades.

abrasive personality personalidad desabrida ■ personalidad brusca

absence makes the heart grow fonder cuanto más lejos el santo, más cerca la devoción

to be **absent-minded** ser distraído ■ ser despistado

to be **absent without leave** ■ to be AWOL estar ausente del (puesto de) servicio (militar) ■ haber abandonado el puesto de servicio

absent without leave: to go ~ ■ to go AWOL abandonar el (puesto de) servicio (militar)

to be **absent without permission** estar ausente sin permiso

absentee ballot voto por correo

absentee ballot: to vote by ~ votar por correo

absenteeism (from work) absentismo laboral ➤ Alcoholism is one of the principal causes of absenteeism (from work). El alcoholismo es una de las principales causas de absentismo laboral.

absolute majority ■ fifty percent plus one, with all possible voters voting mayoría absoluta ➤ An absolute majority in the U.S. Senate, which has one hundred senators, is fifty-one votes. Una mayoría absoluta en el senado estadounidense, el cual tiene cien senadores, es cincuenta y un votos.

absolute zero ■ temperature at which a substance would have no thermal energy, −273°C, −459.67°F, or 0°K cero absoluto ■ temperatura en la cual una substancia no tendría energía termal

to be **absolutely essential** ser primordial ■ *(said of attire)* ser de rigor

to be **absolutely necessary** ser imprescindible ■ ser absolutamente necesario

absolutely not no en absoluto ■ no en lo absoluto

to **absolutely refuse to do something** negarse en rotundo a hacer algo ■ negarse rotundamente a hacer algo ■ negarse en redondo a hacer algo ➤ He absolutely refused to do his class assignment. Se negó rotundamente a hacer el trabajo de clase. ■ Se negó en redondo a hacer el trabajo de clase.

to be **absolutely right** tener toda la razón ■ *(coll.)* dar en el clavo ➤ You are absolutely right, in fact. De hecho, tiene usted toda la razón. ■ De hecho, usted ha dado en el clavo.

to **absorb water** absorber el agua

to be **absorbed in something** ■ *(coll.)* to be wrapped up in something quedarse absorto con algo ■ quedarse absorto en algo ■ estar absorto en algo ■ quedarse embobado con algo ■ quedarse embobado en algo ■ estar embobado con algo ➤ I was absorbed in yesterday's lecture. Me quedé absorto con la conferencia de ayer. ■ Me quedé embobado con la conferencia de ayer.

to be **absorbed in an activity** estar absorto en una actividad ■ estar ensimismado en una actividad ■ estar enfrascado en una actividad

to be **absurd** ser absurdo ■ no tener ni pies ni cabeza ■ no tener ninguna consistencia ➤ That's absurd. Eso es absurdo. ■ Eso no tiene ni pies ni cabeza. ■ Eso no tiene ninguna consistencia.

abuse of authority abuso de superioridad

abuse of power abuso de poder

academic adviser consejero académico

academic credit crédito (académico)

academic deficiency mal expediente ➤ The student was dropped for academic deficiency, but on appeal, given academic probation. Al estudiante lo echaron por su mal expediente, pero recurrió, y le otorgaron un período de prueba.

academic degree título universitario

academic discipline disciplina académica

academic environment medio académico ▪ ámbito académico

academic field campo académico ▪ ámbito académico

academic performance rendimiento académico

academic probation: to be put on ~ ▪ to be placed on academic probation poner a alguien en un período de prueba ▪ poner a alguien en una situación de prueba ➤ The student was put on academic probation. ▪ The student was placed on academic probation. Al estudiante lo pusieron en un período de prueba. ▪ Al estudiante lo pusieron en una situación de prueba. ➤ The student was taken off academic probation when he brought his grades up. El estudiante salió de su período de prueba cuando mejoró sus calificaciones. ▪ El estudiante salió de su situación de prueba cuando mejoró sus calificaciones.

academic question cuestión sin aplicación práctica ▪ cuestión teórica

academic records expediente académico ▪ certificado de notas

acceleration due to gravity la aceleración de la gravedad

acceleration rate ▪ rate of acceleration (tasa de) aceleración ➤ The acceleration rate of an object falling in a vacuum is sixteen feet per second squared. ▪ The rate of acceleration of an object falling in a vacuum is 16 feet per second squared. La aceleración de un objeto cayendo es dieciséis pies por segundo al cuadrado, en vacío.

accent mark: to have an ~ ▪ to be accented tener tilde ▪ llevar tilde ▪ acentuarse ▪ *(coll.)* llevar acento ▪ tener acento ➤ Does the "a" have an accent mark? ¿Tiene la "a" tilde? ▪ ¿Lleva la "a" tilde? ▪ ¿Se acentúa la "a"? ▪ ¿Lleva la "a" acento? ▪ ¿Tiene la "a" acento?

to **accept an apology** aceptar una disculpa ▪ aceptar sus disculpas

to **accept an invitation** aceptar una invitación

to **accept an offer** aceptar una propuesta

to **accept defeat** aceptar la derrota

to **accept one's (own) weaknesses** ▪ to accept one's (own) shortcomings aceptar las debilidades de uno mismo

to **accept someone's weaknesses** ▪ to accept someone's shortcoming aceptar las debilidades de alguien

to **accept people the way they are** ▪ to accept people as they are aceptar a las personas tal (y) como son

to **accept someone the way he is** ▪ to accept someone as he is aceptar a alguien por lo que es

to **accept something philosophically** ▪ to come to terms with something aceptar algo con filosofía ▪ aceptar algo filosóficamente ▪ tomar algo filosóficamente ➤ He has accepted philosophically being confined to a wheelchair. ▪ He has come to terms with his being confined to a wheelchair. Ha aceptado con filosofía (el) estar confinado a una silla de ruedas. ▪ Ha aceptado filosóficamente (el) estar confinado a una silla de ruedas. ▪ Se ha tomado con filosóficamente (el) estar confinado a una silla de ruedas.

to **accept (the) responsibility for something** **1.** to take on an obligation for something asumir la responsabilidad por algo **2.** to accept the blame for something asumir la culpabilidad por algo ➤ *(news item)* Aznar accepts responsibility for the decision to move the damaged oil tanker away from the coast. Aznar asume la culpabilidad por la decisión de alejar el petrolero averiado de la costa.

to **accept the responsibility to do something** ▪ to accept the responsibility for doing something aceptar la responsabilidad de hacer algo ▪ asumir la responsabilidad de hacer algo ➤ If we get a dog, the children have accepted the responsibility to feed it. Si conseguimos un perro, los niños han aceptado la responsabilidad de darle de comer. ▪ Si conseguimos un perro, los niños asumen la responsabilidad de darle de comer.

to **accept willingly** ▪ to willingly accept ▪ willingly to accept aceptar de buen grado ▪ aceptar a buen grado

to **access a database** *(computers)* acceder a una base de datos

accessible (location) (lugar) accesible ➤ The game preserve is not very accessible from the highway. La reserva de animales no es muy accesible de la carretera.

accessible person ▪ person who is easy to talk to ▪ person who is easy to get to know ▪ down-to-earth person persona accesible ▪ persona asequible ➤ He is a very accessible person. Él es una persona muy accesible. ▪ Él es una persona muy asequible.

accident at work ▪ accident on the job ▪ on-the-job accident ▪ accident while at work *el* accidente laboral

to be **accident prone** ser propenso a los accidentes

to **accidentally bump into something** chocar accidentalmente con algo ▪ dar a algo sin querer ▪ darse contra algo sin querer ▪ *(with much force)* golpear algo sin querer ➤ I accidentally bumped the E-mail icon when I was trying to save to the hard drive. Le he dado al icono del E-mail sin querer cuando intentaba guardar al disco rígido.

to be **accompanied by someone** estar acompañado de alguien

to be an **accomplished fact** ▪ to be a proven fact ▪ to be an established fact ser un hecho probado ▪ ser un hecho cierto ➤ Some newspapers treat a politically motivated accusation as if it were an accomplished fact. Algunos periódicos tratan las acusaciones de tipo político como si fueran hechos probados. ▪ Algunos periódicos tratan las acusaciones en el ámbito político como si fueran hechos ciertos.

accomplished pianist experto(-a) pianista ▪ consumado(-a) pianista

according to **1.** in accordance with ▪ commensurate with a medida que **2.** in the way that de acuerdo con ▪ según ▪ a tenor de **3.** as explained by según explicó ▪ según explicaron

according to a recent study según un estudio reciente

according to her según ella

according to him según él

according to Hoyle: to be ~ ▪ to follow the rules ▪ to be in accordance with the rules ser lo correcto ▪ ser lo adecuado ➤ It's not according to Hoyle. No es lo correcto. ▪ No es lo adecuado.

according to Hoyle: to go ~ *(coll.)* ▪ to go according to plan ▪ to go the way one planned ir según lo previsto ▪ ir de acuerdo con el plan ▪ ir de acuerdo con lo planeado ➤ If everything goes according to Hoyle... Si todo va según lo previsto...

according to one's own lights: to judge something ~ juzgar algo hasta donde uno llega a entender ▪ valorar algo hasta donde uno llega a entender ▪ juzgar algo según el propio entender de uno

according to plan: to go ~ ir según lo previsto ▪ ir por sus cabales ▪ ir según lo planeado ➤ If everything goes according to plan... Si todo va según lo previsto...

according to which según el cual ▪ según la cual ▪ según los cuales ▪ según las cuales ➤ I read a book according to which the first humans were extraterrestrials. He leído un libro según el cual los primeros humanos eran extraterrestres.

to **account for the fact that** ▪ to explain the fact that explicarse el hecho que *("el hecho de que" is common but incorrect.)* ➤ How do you account for the fact that...? ¿Cómo te explicas el hecho que...?

to **account for one's actions** ▪ to give an accounting of one's actions dar cuentas de sus actos ▪ rendir cuentas de sus actos

to **account for people** dar cuenta de alguien ▪ responder de las personas ➤ I wish we could make the fanatics account for all the hostages they are holding. Ojalá pudiéramos hacer que los fanáticos den cuenta de los rehenes que retienen.

to **account for something** **1.** to give account for something dar cuenta de algo **2.** to explain something explicar algo

account is current ▪ account is up to date cuenta está al día

Account of a Shipwrecked Sailor *(book by Gabriel García Márquez)* ▪ *Story of a Shipwrecked Sailor* ***Relato de un náufrago***

to be **accounted for** ser encontrados ▪ ser contabilizados ➤ All the passengers are accounted for. Todos los pasajeros han sido contabilizados.

accounting rules ■ accounting standards normas de contabilidad
accurate description descripción precisa
accurate impression una impresión precisa ■ una impresión exacta ■ una impresión acertada
accurate map plano exacto ■ plano muy preciso ■ plano detallado
to be an **accurate portrayal** ser una representación precisa ■ ser una interpretación precisa ■ ser un retrato preciso
accurate scale báscula precisa ■ báscula exacta
to be **accustomed to** ■ to be used to soler ■ estar acostumbrado a ■ estar habituado a ■ tener la costumbre de ➤ That's what I'm accustomed to, too. Eso es a lo que yo también estoy acostumbrado.
accustomed to: to get ~ ■ to get accustomed to acostumbrarse a ■ llegar a acostumbrarse a
ace up one's sleeve: to have an ~ ■ to have an ace in the hole tener un as en la manga ■ tener un as bajo la manga
to **ache all over** tener dolores por todas partes
aches and pains: to have (a lot of) ~ estar lleno de goteras ■ tener goteras ■ tener muchos achaques
to **achieve fame and fortune** ■ to win fame and fortune hacerse rico y famoso ■ ganarse el oro y el moro
to **achieve one's goal** ■ to achieve one's objective lograr su meta ■ lograr su objetivo
to **achieve success** lograr éxito
to be **achieved through** ■ to be achieved by means of conseguirse mediante ■ lograrse mediante ➤ The reader's interest in *Charlotte's Web* is achieved through the believability of the talking farm animals. La tensión narrativa en *La telaraña de Charlotte* se consigue mediante la verosimilitud de los animales de granja que hablan.
acid test prueba de fuego
acid tongue lengua viperina
to **acknowledge one's (own) fault** reconocer la propia culpa ■ reconocer su propia culpa
to **acknowledge someone's fault** reconocer la culpa de uno
to **acknowledge receipt of** acusar recibo de
to **acknowledge that one is wrong** reconocer que uno está equivocado
acknowledgment of receipt ■ letter received acuse de recibo
to **acquire a liking for** ■ to acquire a taste for adquirir el gusto por
to **acquire a taste for** ■ to acquire a liking for adquirir el gusto por ■ tomarle el gusto a
to **acquire property** adquirir propiedades ■ hacendar
acquired immune deficiency syndrome ■ AIDS *el* síndrome de inmunodeficiencia adquerida ■ SIDA
acquired taste gusto adquirido
acrid remark ■ caustic remark comentario con acritud ■ comentario cáustico
acrid smell un olor acre
acrid smoke humo acre
acrimonious debate ■ bitter debate debate reñido
acrimonious discussion discusión reñida
acrimonious dispute disputa acalorada
across and down *(crossword puzzle)* horizontales y verticales
across from enfrente de ■ frente a ■ delante de ➤ At the dinner, I sat across from Rudolph Serkin. Durante la cena, me senté enfrente de Rudolph Serkin. ■ Durante la cena, me senté frente a Rudolph Serkin. ■ Durante la cena, me senté delante de Rudolph Serkin.
across the board general ■ lineal
across the board tax cut *el* recorte de impuestos general
across the country: to travel ~ atravesar el país ■ viajar atravesando el país
to be **across (the street) from something** estar en frente de algo ■ estar al otro lado de la calle ■ estar al cruzar la calle ■ estar cruzando la calle ■ *(L. Am.)* estar a través de la calle de algo ➤ In Valladolid, we lived across (the street) from University Hospital. En Valladolid, vivíamos en frente del Hospital Universitario. ■ En Valladolid, vivíamos a través (de la calle) del Hospital Universitario. ■ En Valladolid, vivíamos al cruzar la called del Hospital Universitario. ■ En Valladolid, vivíamos cruzando la calle del Hospital Universitario.
across town ■ on the other side of town (from here) ■ on the other end of the city en la otra punta de la ciudad
to **act according to someone's instructions** ■ to act in accordance with someone's instructions actuar de acuerdo con las instrucciones de alguien
to **act as a go-between** hacer de intermediario ■ servir de intermediario
to **act as a buffer against** hacer de amortiguador ■ servir de colchón a
to **act as if...** ■ to act as though... ■ to pretend that... ■ to act like... hacer como si... ■ actuar como si... ■ fingir que...
to **act as if nothing had happened** ■ to go on as if nothing had happened actuar como si nada ■ quedarse tan ancho ■ hacer como si nada hubiera ocurrido ■ hacer como si nada hubiese ocurrido
to **act as if nothing has happened** quedarse tan ancho ■ actuar como si nada haya ocurrido ■ hacer como si nada haya ocurrido ■ obrar como si nada haya ocurrido
to **act as if one's life depends on it** actuar como si la vida dependiera en eso ■ actuar como si le vaya la vida en ello ■ actuar como si le fuera la vida en ello ■ actuar como si se jugase la vida con eso
to **act as master of ceremonies** ser maestro de ceremonias
to **act as one does** actuar así ■ actuar como uno (lo) hace ■ obrar como uno obra ➤ I acted as I did because... Actué así porque... ■ Actué como lo hice porque... ■ Obré como obré porque...
to **act as one's attorney** actuar del abogado de uno
to **act childishly** ■ to be childish ser infantil ■ resultar infantil ■ aniñarse
to **act decisively** actuar con decisión
to **act in accordance with** ■ to act according to actuar de acuerdo con ■ actuar en función de ■ actuar según
to **act in accordance with someone's instructions** ■ to act according to someone's instructions actuar de acuerdo con las instrucciones de alguien ■ actuar según las instrucciones de alguien
to **act in behalf of someone** actuar en nombre de alguien ■ actuar de parte de alguien ■ actuar en favor de alguien
to **act in collaboration with someone** actuar en colaboración con alguien
to **act in conjunction** ■ to act together ■ to act in concert actuar en conjunto ➤ In a guitar, the strings and sound chamber act in conjunction to enrich and project the sound. En una guitarra, las cuerdas y la caja de resonancia actúan en conjunto enriqueciendo y proyectando el sonido.
to **act in conjunction with someone** actuar conjuntamente con alguien
to **act in good faith** actuar de buena fe ■ actuar en buena fe
to **act in self-defense** actuar en defensa propia
to **act like** ■ to act as if ■ to act as though actuar como si ■ hacer como si ■ dárselas de ➤ He acts like he's never heard of... Hace como si no lo hubiera oído... ■ Actúa como si no lo hubiera oído... ➤ He always acts like a know-it-all. Siempre se las da de listo.
to **act like one** comportarse como tal
act of courage ■ courageous act ■ valiant act acto de valentía ■ acto de coraje
act of defiance ■ defiant act ■ defiant action acto desafiante
act of faith acto de fe
act of God caso de fuerza mayor
act of God: by an ~ por causas de fuerza mayor
act of kindness acto de bondad
act of terrorism ■ terrorist act acto terrorista
act of vandalism acto vandálico
act of war acto de guerra
act of will: as an ~ como un acto de voluntad
to **act on a force** actuar sobre una fuerza
to **act on behalf of someone** ■ actuar de parte de alguien ■ actuar en nombre de alguien ■ representar a alguien ■ actuar en representación de alguien

to **act on impulse** actuar por impulso propio

to **act one's age** comportarse de acuerdo con su edad

to **act out** imitar ▪ parodiar ➤ The psychiatrist guessed correctly that the child was acting out something she had seen on TV. El psiquiatra supuso correctamente que la niña estaba imitando algo que había visto en la tele.

to **act out of desperation** ▪ to do something in desperation hacer algo por desesperación ➤ He acted out of desperation. Lo hizo a la desesperada.

to **act out of fear for one's life** actuar por miedo a la vida ▪ actuar por miedo de la vida ▪ actuar por miedo de perder la vida ▪ actuar por miedo a perder la vida

to **act out of fear of** actuar por miedo a ▪ actuar por miedo hacia ▪ actuar por miedo de

to **act out of hatred for** actuar por odio a ▪ actuar por odio hacia

to **act out of love for** actuar por amor a ▪ actuar por amor hacia ▪ actuar por amor por

to **act out of the necessity for** actuar por necesidad de

to **act out of the necessity to** actuar por necesidad de

to **act under someone's direction** actuar bajo la dirección de alguien

to **act up 1.** to function incorrectly ▪ to have developed a problem funcionar de forma irregular ▪ funcionar irregularmente **2.** to misbehave portarse (tan) mal ▪ comportarse mal **3.** to flare up molestar ▪ doler ➤ The elevator has been acting up lately. ▪ The elevator has developed a problem. El ascensor ha estado funcionando de forma irregular últimamente. ➤ Quit acting up, or I'm going to suspend your allowance. Deja de comportarte tan mal o te quito la paga. ➤ My arthritis has been acting up again. La artritis me está molestando de nuevo.

to **act with leniency toward someone** actuar con benevolencia hacia alguien ▪ actuar con benevolencia para alguien

to **act without thinking** actuar sin reflexión ▪ actuar irreflexivamente

acting out imitación ▪ parodia ▪ *el* imitar ▪ *el* parodiar

action-packed adventure aventura cargada de la acción

action-packed film ▪ action-packed movie película cargada de la acción

actions speak louder than words las acciones hablan más que las palabras ▪ las acciones dicen más que las palabras ▪ más vale predicar con el ejemplo

active ingredient ingrediente activo ▪ principio activo

active volcano volcán activo

actual connection conexión efectuada ➤ The phone company here charges for the attempts to connect to the server as well as for the actual connect. La compañía telefónica te cobra tanto los intentos de conexión con el servidor como la conexión efectuada.

actual footage *las* imágenes reales ➤ The movie *Pearl Harbor* contains actual footage. La película *Pearl Harbor* contiene imágenes reales.

actual practice: in ~ en la práctica

actually: and ~ ▪ (and) in fact no en vano ➤ Science fiction has become a very popular genre, and actually, many non-science fiction writers employ its conventions and techniques in their works. La ciencia ficción se ha convertido en un género muy popular, no en vano muchos escritores utilizan sus convenciones en sus obras.

to **actually do something** realmente hacer algo ▪ de hecho hacer algo ▪ de veras hacer algo ▪ verdaderamente hacer algo ➤ How does a tachometer actually count the revolutions per minute of an engine? ¿Cómo cuenta realmente un tacómetro las revoluciones de un motor? ➤ My sympathies were with Bello until I actually read his article. Me inclinaba hacia la postura de Bello hasta que realmente leí su artículo.

to **actually feel** alcanzar a sentir ➤ I can actually feel... Alcanzo a sentir...

acute phase of an illness fase aguda de una enfermedad

ad campaign campaña publicitaria

ad for anuncio de ➤ I'm calling in response to the ad in the paper for an apartment. Llamo por lo del anuncio del apartamento.

ad infinitum hasta el infinito

to be **adamantly opposed to** ▪ to adamantly oppose oponerse rotundamente a

to **adapt to any situation** hacerse a todo ▪ adaptarse a cualquier situación

to **add a column of figures** sumar una columna de números

to **add fuel to the flames** ▪ to add fuel to the fire ▪ to inflame the situation echar leña al fuego ▪ añadir leña al fuego

to **add in one's head** sumar en la cabeza ➤ He added (up) the column of figures in his head. Sumó la columna de números en su cabeza.

to **add insult to injury** ▪ to rub salt into the wound echar sal en la herida ▪ echar vinagre a la herida ➤ That just adds insult to injury. Sólo echa sal en la herida.

to **add one's name to the list** incluir su nombre en la lista

to **add onto a building** ampliar un edificio ▪ añadir un ala a un edificio

to **add onto a house** ampliar una casa ▪ añadir un ala a una casa

to **add, subtract, multiply, and divide** sumar, restar, multiplicar y dividir

to **add to the list** sumar a la lista ▪ incluir en la lista

to **add up** *(intransitive verb)* ▪ to make sense cuadrar ▪ tener sentido

to **add up (numbers)** ▪ to perform addition ▪ to add sumar ➤ He can add (up) a column of four-digit figures in his head. Puede sumar una columna de números de cuatro dígitos en la cabeza.

to **add up the bill 1.** *(restaurant, grocery store)* bill with a fixed sum sumar la cuenta **2.** *(involving the computation of labor)* running bill sumar la factura

to **add up to 1.** to total sumar a ▪ dar **2.** to reduce to ▪ to boil down to reducirse a ➤ These digits add up to nine. Estos dígitos suman a nueve. ▪ La suma de estos dígitos da nueve. ➤ It adds up to a big mess. ▪ It boils down to a big mess. Se reduce a un gran lío.

to **add up to the fact that** reducirse a que

to be **added to something** ▪ to come already added to something venir agregado a algo ➤ In this pill (that) I take, the antihistamine is already added (in)to it. En esta pastilla que tomo yo, viene ya agregado el antihistamínico.

to be **addicted to drugs** estar adicto a las drogas ▪ ser adicto a las drogas ▪ estar enganchado a las drogas

to be **addicted to tobacco** estar adicto al tabaco ▪ ser adicto al tabaco ▪ estar enganchado al tabaco

addition to a house añadido a una casa

addition, subtraction, multiplication, and division suma, resta, multiplicación y división

to **address a concern** ▪ to address an issue abordar una preocupación ▪ tratar una preocupación ▪ abordar una preocupación ▪ tratar una duda ➤ We need to address the sales force's concerns. Necesitamos abordar las preocupaciones del equipo de ventas. ▪ Necesitamos tratar las preocupaciones del equipo de ventas. ▪ Necesitamos abordar las dudas del equipo de ventas. ▪ Necesitamos tratar las dudas del equipo de ventas.

to **address an assembly** *(all contexts)* dirigirse a la asamblea ▪ *(student body)* dirigirse al cuerpo estudiantil

to **address an audience** dirigirse a un público ▪ dirigirse a una audiencia ➤ President Kennedy addressed an audience of four million (people) in Berlin. El presidente Kennedy se dirigió a un público de cuatro millones de personas en Berlín.

to **address an envelope** poner la dirección en un sobre

to **address an envelope to someone** dirigir el sobre a alguien

to **address an issue 1.** to address a concern abordar una duda ▪ tratar una duda ▪ abordar una preocupación ▪ tratar una preocupación **2.** to address a topic abordar un tema ▪ abordar un asunto ▪ tratar un tema ▪ tratar un asunto

address labels ▪ mailing labels etiquetas de correo ▪ etiquetas para sobres

to **address one's concerns** tratar las inquietudes de uno ▪ tratar las preocupaciones de uno ▪ tratar las dudas de uno

to **address one's needs** satisfacer sus necesidades ➤ Their program didn't address our needs as students. Su programa no satisfacía nuestras necesidades como estudiantes. ▪ Su programa no satisfacía nuestras necesidades de estudiantes.

to **address someone as** dirigirse a alguien como ▪ tratar a alguien de ➤ In the old days, children addressed their fathers as "sir." En el pasado los niños se dirigían al padre como "usted". ▪ En el pasado los niños trataban al padre de "usted".

to **address someone by name** ▪ to call someone by name llamar a alguien por su nombre

to **address the meeting** *(parliamentary procedure)* hacer uso de la palabra

to **address the nation** ▪ to address the country pronunciar un discurso ante la nación ▪ dirigirse al país ▪ dirigirse a la nación ▪ dirigirse al pueblo ➤ The president will address the nation at 9 p.m., Eastern Standard Time. El presidente se dirigirá a la nación a las nueve p.m., Franja Horaria de la Costa Este.

to **address the needs of someone** ▪ to address someone's needs cubrir las necesidades de ➤ The course didn't address the needs of the students. El curso no cubría las necesidades de los estudiantes.

to **address the problem** enfrentarse a ▪ enfrentarse con

to be **addressed to someone** estar dirigido a alguien ▪ ir dirigido a nombre de alguien ▪ venir dirigido a nombre de alguien ➤ The tenant that this letter is addressed to moved out five years ago. ▪ The tenant to whom this letter is addressed moved out five years ago. El inquilino al que viene dirigida esta carta se mudó hace cinco años. ▪ El inquilino a nombre del cual viene esta carta se mudó hace cinco años.

addressee unknown destinatario desconocido

to be **adept at (doing) something** ▪ to be skillful at (doing) something ser hábil con algo ▪ ser habilidoso con algo ➤ Iván is very adept at computers. Iván es muy hábil con las computadoras. ▪ Iván es muy habilidoso con las computadoras.

to be **adequate time to** ▪ to be sufficient time to ser tiempo suficiente para ▪ ser suficiente tiempo para ▪ bastar ➤ This has taken two months; two weeks should have been adequate. Esto ha tardado dos meses, dos semanas deberían haber sido suficientes. ▪ Esto ha tardado dos meses, dos semanas deberían haber bastado.

to **adhere to** adherirse a ▪ cumplir con ➤ Women in some parts of the world must adhere to a strict dress code. Las mujeres en algunas partes del mundo deben cumplir con un estricto código de vestimenta. ▪ Las mujeres en algunas partes del mundo deben adherirse a un estricto código de vestimenta.

adjacent building edificio colindante ▪ edificio adyacente ▪ edificio contiguo

adjacent property propiedad colindante ▪ propiedad adyacente

adjacent region ▪ neighboring region región colindante ▪ región adyacente

to be **adjacent to** ▪ to be (right) next to ▪ to be (right) beside ▪ to be (right) by estar contiguo a ▪ estar justo al lado de ▪ estar pegado a ▪ estar a continuación de ➤ The park is adjacent to the library. ▪ The park is (right) next to the library. ▪ The park is (right) beside the library. ▪ The park is (right) by the library. El parque está contiguo a la biblioteca. ▪ El parque está justo al lado de la biblioteca. ▪ El parque está pegado a la biblioteca. ▪ El parque está a continuación de la biblioteca.

adjoining room *(in museums, palaces, etc.)* ▪ next room pieza inmediata ▪ pieza de al lado

to **adjourn the meeting** levantar la sesión

to **adjust for inflation** tomar en cuenta la inflación

to **adjust the air conditioning** graduar el aire condicionado

to **adjust the heat** graduar la calefacción

to **adjust the timing of something** sincronizar algo ▪ ajustar algo ➤ The timing of the firing of the distributor needs to be adjusted. Hay que sincronizar el encendido del distribuidor. ▪ Hay que ajustar el encendido del distribuidor.

adjustable lamp *(Sp.)* flexo

adjustable-rate mortgage hipoteca variable

to be **adjusted for inflation** estar ajustado por concepto de inflación ➤ Today's cost of living in the United States, adjusted for inflation, is about the same as in 1960. El coste de la vida en los Estados Unidos, ajustado por concepto de inflación, es más o menos lo mismo que en 1960.

to **administer an oath to someone** ▪ to swear someone in tomarle a alguien el juramento

to **administer last rites** *(Catholicism)* ▪ to administer extreme unction administrar la extrema unción

to **admire someone** admirar a alguien

to **admit a student non-matriculated** ▪ to admit a student on a non-matriculated basis admitir a un estudiante no matriculado

to **admit someone to the hospital** ingresar a alguien en el hospital

to **admit that...** admitir que... ▪ dar la razón... ▪ confesar que... ➤ You have to admit that I'm right. ▪ You've got to admit that I'm right. Tienes que admitir que tengo razón. ▪ Me tienes que dar la razón que tengo razón.

to be **admitted for observation** quedarse ingresado de pronóstico reservado

to be **admitted to the hospital** ▪ to be in the hospital ▪ to be hospitalized estar ingresado en el hospital

to be **adrift** estar a la deriva ➤ The shipwrecked sailor was adrift in a raft for ten days. El náufrago estuvo diez días a la deriva en una balsa.

adult life vida adulta ➤ Erich Fromm lived most of his adult life in Mexico City. Erich Fromm vivió la mayor parte de su vida adulta en la Ciudad de México.

to **advance a cause** ▪ to promote a cause promover una causa

to **advance farther than** avanzar más de lo que ➤ Columbus told his sailors they had advanced farther than they really had. A sus marineros Colón les dijo que habían avanzado más de lo que realmente habían hecho.

to **advance in one's career** avanzar en su carrera

to **advance in rank** ascender de un rango a otro

(advance) notice: to give someone ~ avisar a alguien con antelación ▪ entregar a alguien el aviso con antelación ▪ dar a alguien el aviso con antelación ▪ dar a alguien el aviso con anticipación ➤ He gave his employer two weeks' (advance) notice that he was going to quit. Le entregó el aviso de (su) renuncia a su jefe con dos semanas de antelación. ▪ Le dio el aviso de (su) renuncia a su jefe con dos semanas de antelación. ➤ She gave her landlord a month's (advance) notice. Avisó (de su mudanza) a su casero con un mes de antelación. ➤ I gave the power company a month's (advance) notice of our change of address. Avisé a la compañía eléctrica con un mes de antelación del cambio de dirección. ▪ Avisé del cambio de dirección a la compañía eléctrica con un mes de antelación. ▪ Avisé a la compañía eléctrica del cambio de dirección con un mes de antelación.

advance payment antesala ▪ adelanto ▪ anticipo

advance team equipo por delante ▪ *(military)* avanzadilla

to **advance through the ranks** ascender a través de los rangos ▪ escalar posiciones

advice column consultorio sentimental

to **advise someone to do something** aconsejar a alguien hacer algo

to **advise that someone do something** aconsejar que alguien haga algo

to **advocate a reform** preconizar una reforma ▪ abogar por una reforma ▪ promover una reforma

aerobatic flying vuelo acrobático

affairs of the heart ▪ matters of the heart asuntos del corazón ▪ las lides del amor

to be **affected by** verse afectado por ▪ estar afectado por

affection for: to feel ~ sentir cariño por ▪ sentir cariño hacia ▪ sentir afecto por ▪ sentir afecto hacia

affection for: to have ~ tener cariño por ▪ tener cariño hacia

to be **affiliated with** estar afiliado a ▪ ser colaboradores de

to be **afflicted with** ▪ to be suffering from ▪ to suffer from sufrir de ▪ estar aquejado de ➤ She was afflicted with cancer. ▪ She was suffering from cancer. Estaba aquejada de cáncer.

to **affirm someone's testimony** ▪ to corroborate someone's testimony corroborar el testimonio de alguien ▪ refrendar el testimonio de alguien ▪ apoyar el testimonio de alguien

affirmation of testimony ▪ corroboration of testimony corroboración de un testimonio ▪ refrendo de un testimonio

affirmation of the old reafirmación de lo antiguo ➤ It is at once an affirmation of the old and a celebration of the new. Es al mismo tiempo una reafirmación de lo antiguo y una celebración de lo nuevo.

afford something: to be able to ~ ■ to have the money to pay for something poderse permitir algo ■ poder permitirse algo ■ afrontar algo ■ poder costear algo ➤ I can't afford it. No me lo puedo permitir. ■ No puedo permitírmelo. ■ No puedo afrontarlo. ■ No me lo puedo costear. ➤ We simply can't afford it. Simplemente no podemos permitírnoslo. ■ *(Sp.)* Sencillamente no podemos permitírnoslo.

to **afford a view of** ofrecer una vista de ■ tener unas vistas a ■ tener unas vistas hacia ■ tener unas vistas de

to **afford someone an opportunity to** darle a alguien la oportunidad de ■ ofrecerle a alguien la oportunidad de ■ darle a alguien la posibilidad de ■ ofrecerle a alguien la posibilidad de ■ permitirle a alguien la oportunidad de ■ darle a alguien la ocasión de

affordable price precio asequible ■ precio asumible

to be **afraid of one's shadow** ■ to be afraid of one's own shadow estar asustado hasta de su propia sombra ■ tener miedo hasta de su propia sombra

after a few seconds al cabo de unos segundos ■ después de unos segundos ■ tras unos segundos

after a moment ■ a moment later al cabo de un momento ■ después de un momento ■ tras un momento

after a while ■ a while later al poco rato ■ al cabo de un rato ■ después de un rato ■ pasado un rato

after a fashion ■ in a way en cierto modo ■ de cierta manera

after a time ■ after a while pasado un tiempo ■ *(in literary narrative)* sucedió tiempo después que

after all **1.** a la larga ■ al final **2.** después de todo **3.** al fin y al cabo ■ finalmente ➤ I ended up going out to dinner after all. A la larga acabé saliendo a comer. ■ Al final acabé saliendo a comer. ➤ I'd like to take courses year round. After all, I live here. Me gustaría tomar cursos durante todo el año. Después de todo, vivo aquí. ➤ The actress didn't care that they didn't call her for the audition. After all, she didn't like working for that director. A la actriz no le importó que no la hubieran llamado para la audición, al fin y al cabo no le gustaba trabajar para ese director.

after all is said and done ■ when all is said and done al fin de cuentas ■ al final de cuentas ■ en fin ■ cuando todo está dicho y hecho

after all was said and done ■ when all was said and done cuando todo estaba dicho y hecho ■ al fin de cuentas ■ en fin

after doing something después de hacer algo ■ tras hacer algo ➤ Ten months after announcing it... Diez meses después de anunciarlo... ■ Diez meses después de haberlo anunciado... ➤ After announcing for months that the school would close, the board changed its mind and decided to renovate it. Después de anunciar durante meses que se cerraría la escuela, la junta escolar cambió su parecer y decidió renovarla.

after being felled by tras desplomarse por ■ después de desplomarse por ➤ *(picture caption)* The athlete is attended to after being felled by a stomach cramp. El deportista es atendido tras desplomarse por un corte de digestión.

after being stricken by después de estar aquejado de ■ tras estar aquejado de

after dark después de que oscurezca ■ después de que se haga de noche

after-dinner drink bebida de sobremesa ■ copa de sobremesa ■ chupito ■ *el* pluscafé

after doing something después de hacer una cosa ■ al hacer una cosa ➤ After leaving the office I went for a drink. Después de abandonar la oficina me fui a tomar algo. ➤ After I found out what had happened... Al saber lo que había pasado... ■ Al descubrir lo que había pasado...

after graduating from the university después de acabar la universidad ■ después de graduarse en la universidad ■ al graduarse en la universidad ■ tras graduarse en la universidad ■ después de titularse en la universidad ■ al titularse en la universidad ■ tras titularse en la universidad ■ después de licenciarse en la universidad ■ al licenciarse en la universidad ■ tras licenciarse en la universidad ■ después de diplomarse en la universidad

after hearing the news después de oír la noticia ■ tras oír la noticia

after hours después de la hora de cierre de las tiendas

after I found out what had happened ■ after I learned what had happened después de saber lo que había pasado ■ después de enterarme de lo que había pasado

after I had read the article ■ once I had read the article ■ when I had read the article cuando hube leído el artículo

after I have read the article ■ once I have read the article ■ when I have read the article cuando (yo) haya leído el artículo

after I read the article ■ once I read the article ■ when I read the article **1.** *(past, pronounced "red")* cuando leí el artículo ■ al leer el artículo **2.** *(future, pronounced "reed")* cuando (yo) lea el artículo ■ al leer el artículo

after it was discovered that... tras descubrirse que...

after losing to tras perder frente a ■ tras haber perdido frente a ■ después de perder frente a ■ después de haber perdido frente a

after midnight pasada la medianoche ■ después de la medianoche

after next después del próximo ➤ School starts Monday after next. El colegio comienza el lunes después del próximo.

after school después de clase ■ después del colegio ■ después del cole ➤ Can you meet me after school? ¿Podemos quedar después del colegio? ➤ I have to stay after school. Me tengo que quedar después de clase.

to be **after someone** **1.** to be in pursuit of someone ir en persecución de alguien ■ ir detrás de alguien ■ ir tras alguien **2.** to be the next person in line ir detrás de alguien ■ estar detrás de alguien ■ ser el siguiente de la fila

to be **after someone's job** estar detrás del puesto de alguien ■ estar detrás del cargo de alguien ■ estar tras el puesto de alguien

to be **after someone's money** andar detrás del dinero de alguien ➤ She's just after his money. Ella sólo anda detrás de su dinero.

after taxes después de los impuestos

after that ■ afterwards ■ then después ➤ We went out for supper, and after that (we went) to the movies. ■ We went out for supper, and afterwards (we went) to the movies. ■ We went out to supper, and then (we went) to the movies. Salimos a cenar y después fuimos al cine.

after that date después de esa fecha ■ después ■ más tarde ■ posteriormente ➤ To contact me after that date, my cell phone number will be... Para contactar conmigo después de esa fecha, mi móvil será...

after that hour ■ after that time después de esa hora ➤ To contact me after that hour, call me at this number... ■ To contact me after that time, call me at this number... Para contactar conmigo después de esa hora, llámame a este número...

after the fact después de lo ocurrido ■ tras lo ocurrido

after the fashion of ■ in the style of a la moda de ■ al estilo de ■ en el estilo de

after the tone ■ after the beep después de la señal ➤ Please leave your message after the tone. Por favor deja tu mensaje después de la señal.

after which **1.** después del cual ■ después de la cual ■ después de lo cual **2.** whereupon luego de esto ➤ There will be a game at 8 p.m., after which there will be fireworks. Habrá un partido a las ocho de la tarde, después del cual, habrá fuegos artificiales. ➤ There will be a lecture at 10 a.m., after which refreshments will be served. Habrá una conferencia a las diez de la mañana, después de la cual se servirá un ágape. ➤ You have to take five years of courses, after which the bachelor's degree is conferred. Hay que cursar cinco años de estudio en la facultad, después de lo cual se obtiene la diplomatura.

after *x* years of doing something después de *x* años de hacer algo

after years of después de años de ➤ After years of financial struggle, he made a fortune. Después de años de luchas financieras, él hizo una fortuna.

after you! *(tú)* ¡después de ti! ▪ *(usted)* ¡después de usted!
after (you go through) the light ▪ after (you pass through) the light después de rebasar el semáforo ➤ It's the first right turn after you go through the light. Es el primer giro a la derecha después de rebasar el semáforo.
after which ▪ whereupon después del cual ▪ luego de esto
after *x* years 1. después de *x* años **2.** *x* years later a los *x* años ➤ After ten years in the newspaper business, he made the transition to script writing. Después de diez años en el negocio del periodismo, él se pasó a la escritura de guión.
after *x* years of después de *x* años de ▪ a los *x* años de
aftermath of a supernova explosión *(astronomy)* las repercusiones de una explosión de supernova ▪ secuela de una explosión supernova
aftermath of the attack, bombing, earthquake, flood, revolt, riot situación de caos que sigue al ataque, bombardeo, terremoto, diluvio, rebelión, disturbio
again and again ▪ over and over (again) ▪ repeatedly repetidas veces
against a background of sobre una base de
against all odds contra toda probabilidad
to be **against it** ▪ to be opposed (to it) estar en contra de ello ▪ oponerse a ello ➤ I'm against it. ▪ I'm opposed (to it). Estoy en contra (de ello). ▪ Me opongo (a ello).
against one en contra de uno ▪ en su contra ➤ When the accusations against him came out... Al surgir las acusaciones en su contra...
against one's better judgment contra su buen juicio
against one's will *(with coercion)* contra su voluntad ▪ *(without coercion)* a disgusto
against one's wishes contra los deseos de uno
against the current aguas arriba
against the current: to go ~ ir a contra corriente ▪ ir en contra de la corriente
against the grain: to go ~ ir contra los principios de uno ➤ It goes against the grain for me to lend books and CDs, because the very people who borrow them are the very ones who don't return them. Va contra de mis principios prestar libros y CDs, porque la misma gente los piden prestados son los mismos que no los devuelven.
to be **against the rules** ir en contra de las reglas ▪ estar en contra de las reglas ➤ He said it was against the rules. Dijo que eso va en contra de las reglas.
age group segmento de edad ▪ los de edades (comprendidas) entre ➤ The age group between four and six eats during the first lunch period. El segmento de edad entre cuatro y seis años come en el primer turno. ▪ Los de edades (comprendidas) entre cuatro y seis años comen en el primer turno.
to **age wine** añejar el vino ▪ criar el vino ➤ How many years has the wine been aged? ¿Cuántos años ha estado añejando el vino? ▪ ¿Cuántos años ha añejado el vino? ▪ ¿Cuántos años ha estado criando el vino? ▪ ¿Cuántos años ha criado el vino?
to **aggravate a wound** empeorar una herida
to **aggravate someone** agraviar a alguien ▪ causar perjuicio a alguien
aging of the skin envejecimiento de la piel
aging of the wine envejecimiento del vino
aging process: to slow down the ~ ▪ to retard the aging process frenar el proceso de envejecimiento
ago: *x* Sundays ~ hace *x* domingos ▪ *x* domingos atrás ➤ Three Sundays ago Hace tres domingos ▪ Tres domingos atrás
to **agree in person, number, and gender with...** concertar en persona, número y género con ▪ concertar en persona, número y género entre...
to **agree on something** ▪ to be in agreement on something ▪ to concur with something estar de acuerdo en algo ▪ coincidir en algo ▪ ponerse de acuerdo en algo ▪ avenirse a algo ▪ quedar en algo ➤ We all agreed on a pitcher of beer, except Silvia, who wanted white wine. Todos estuvimos de acuerdo en pedir una jarra de cerveza, excepto Silvia que quiso un vino blanco. ▪ Todos estábamos de acuerdo en pedir una jarra de cerveza, excepto Silvia que quiso un vino blanco. ➤ The board of directors agreed to introduce onto the market a car that runs on organic fuel. La junta directiva coincidió en introducir al mercado un carro que funciona con combustible orgánico. ➤ My wife and I agreed, after a spirited discussion, that I could decorate the house. Mi esposa y yo nos pusimos de acuerdo, después de una discusión fogosa, en que yo podía decorar la casa. ➤ They couldn't agree on the place for the Olympics. No se avinieron a elegir la sede para los Juegos Olímpicos.
to **agree that...** ▪ to be in agreement that... coincidir en que... ▪ estar de acuerdo en que... ➤ (The) scientists are in agreement that... ▪ (The) scientists agree that... Los científicos coinciden en que...
to **agree to anything** ▪ to agree to everything ▪ to say yes to anything ▪ to say yes to everything comprometerse a todo
to **agree to do something** quedar en hacer algo ▪ aceptar hacer algo ▪ acceder a hacer algo ➤ I agreed to take a salad to the picnic. Quedé en llevar una ensalada para el picnic. ➤ The Israelis and Palestinians agreed to negotiate. Los israelis y los palestinos aceptaron negociar. ➤ He agreed to it on his own. Accedió a ello por su propia cuenta. ➤ Did we really agree to buy magazine subscriptions when we bought the computer? ¿En serio quedamos en comprar subscripciones de revistas cuando compramos la computadora?
to **agree to everything** ▪ to agree to anything ▪ to say yes to anything ▪ to say yes to everything comprometerse a todo
to **agree to something** acceder a algo ▪ acordar algo ➤ He agreed to it on his own. Accedió a ello por su propia cuenta. ▪ Lo acordó por su propia cuenta.
to **agree to hear the case** acordar oír el caso
to **agree to hold** acordar celebrar ➤ The candidates agreed to hold three debates. Los candidatos acordaron celebrar tres debates.
to **agree to it on one's own** acceder a ello por su propia cuenta
to **agree to negotiate** aceptar negociar ▪ acordar negociar ➤ The two sides agreed to negotiate. Las dos partes aceptaron negociar. ▪ Las dos partes acordaron negociar.
to **agree with** ▪ to go with ▪ to be in concordance with concordar con ➤ "No hay" doesn't agree with "disculparte." You have two equally valid options: "no hay que disculparse" or "no tienes que disculparte." "No hay" no concuerda con "disculparte". Tienes dos opciones igualmente válidas: "no hay que disculparse" o "no tienes que disculparte".
to **agree with someone** estar de acuerdo con alguien ▪ coincidir con alguien ▪ opinar lo mismo que alguien
agreeable climate *el* clima amable
to be **ahead** llevar ventaja ➤ Boca Juniors was ahead at halftime. Boca Juniors llevaba la ventaja en el intermedio.
ahead of another time zone: hours ~ estar *x* horas adelantado (con) respecto a otro huso horario ▪ llevar *x* horas de adelanto (con) respecto a otro huso horario ▪ ir *x* horas adelantado (con) respecto a otro huso horario ➤ Spain is six hours ahead of the east coast of the United States. ▪ It is six hours later in Spain than (it is) on the east coast of the United States. España está seis horas adelantada con respecto a la costa este de los Estados Unidos. ▪ España lleva seis horas de adelanto (con) respecto a la costa este de los Estados Unidos. ▪ España va seis horas adelantada con respecto a la costa este de los Estados Unidos.
behind another time zone: hours ~ estar *x* horas atrasado (con) respecto a otro huso horario ▪ llevar *x* horas de atraso (con) respecto a otro huso horario ▪ ir *x* horas atrasado con respecto a otro huso horario
to be **ahead of its time** estar avanzado para su tiempo ▪ estar avanzado para su momento ▪ estar adelantado a su tiempo ▪ estar por delante de su tiempo ➤ Thomas Jefferson's house, Monticello, was a hundred years ahead of its time. La casa de Thomas Jefferson, Monticello, estaba cien años adelantada a su tiempo.
to be **ahead of one 1.** to be in front of one estar delante de uno **2.** to be in the future estar por venir ➤ There are a lot of people ahead of us in line. ▪ There are a lot of people in front of us in line. Hay muchas personas delante de nosotros en la fila. ▪ *(coll.)* Hay muchas personas delante nuestro en la fila. ▪ *(L. Am.)* Hay muchas personas delante de nosotros en la cola. ➤ The best days of our lives are ahead of us. Los mejores días de nuestra vida están por venir.

ahead of one: to have something ~ presentársele ■ tener por delante ➤ We have a great summer ahead of us. Se nos presenta un gran verano. ■ Tenemos un gran verano por delante.

to be **ahead of one's time** estar adelantado al tiempo de uno

ahead of oneself: to get ~ estar adelantándose ➤ I'm getting ahead of myself; I was going to say that... Me estoy adelantando, (yo) iba a decir que...

ahead of schedule: to arrive ~ llegar antes de tiempo ■ llegar antes de lo programado ■ llegar adelantado ➤ Because of a tailwind, we arrived in Madrid a half hour ahead of schedule Por viento de cola, llegamos a Madrid media hora antes de lo programado. ■ Por viento de cola, llegamos a Madrid media hora adelantado.

to be **ahead of schedule** estar antes de lo programado ■ estar de lo previsto ■ estar antes de tiempo

to be **ahead of someone 1.** to be in front of someone (in line) estar a delante de alguien (en la fila) ■ preceder a alguien (en la fila) **2.** *(in school)* ir *x* cursos por delante **3.** to have a higher priority than someone ■ to have priority over someone tener prioridad sobre alguien ➤ There are two people ahead of you in line. Hay dos personas delante de ti en la fila. ■ Hay dos personas delante de ti en la cola. ➤ He was two years ahead of me in school. Iba dos cursos por delante de mí en el colegio. ➤ He's ahead of me. ■ He has priority over me. Tiene prioridad sobre mí.

ahead of someone: to get ~ adelantarse a alguien ➤ She keeps trying to get ahead of me in line. Ella sigue tratando de adelantárseme en la fila. ■ Ella sigue tratando de adelantárseme en la cola.

ahead of someone: to have someone ~ tener alguien delante ➤ I'll help you as soon as I can, but I have two people ahead of you. ■ I'll help you as soon as I can, but there are two people ahead of you. Le atenderé tan pronto como pueda, pero tienes dos personas delante.

to be **ahead of someone in line** *(Mex.)* estar delante de alguien en la cola ■ *(Sp.)* estar delante de alguien en la fila

ahead of someone in line: to get ~ *(Mex.)* adelantarse de alguien en la cola *(Sp.)* estar delante de alguien en la fila

ahead of something: to get ~ adelantar a algo ➤ See if you can get ahead of that other car. Mira si puedes adelantar a ese otro coche.

ahead of the deadline ■ before the deadline antes de la fecha límite ■ antes de la fecha tope ■ previamente a la fecha límite ■ previamente a la fecha tope ➤ I'd like to turn this book in ahead of the deadline. ■ I'd like to turn this book in before the deadline. Me gustaría entregar este libro antes de la fecha límite. ■ Me gustaría entregar este libro previamente a la fecha tope.

to be **ahead of the game** estar adelantado

ahead of the game: to get ~ ir adelantando

to be **ahead of the other team** ■ to lead the other team llevar la delantera sobre el otro equipo ■ llevar ventaja sobre el otro equipo ■ estar por delante del otro equipo ■ ir por delante del otro equipo ■ liderar el partido ■ liderar la clasificación *(The last refers to all teams or games taken together.)* ➤ Real Madrid is ahead of the other team. Real Madrid va por delante del otro equipo ■ Real Madrid lleva ventaja sobre el otro equipo.

to be **ahead of the other team *x* points** llevar *x* puntos de ventaja sobre el otro equipo ■ estar (a) *x* puntos por delante del otro equipo ■ ir (a) *x* puntos por delante del otro equipo

ahead of time 1. con tiempo **2.** con antelación ■ de anticipación **3.** con tiempo de sobra **4.** por adelantado **5.** antes ➤ I'll let you know ahead of time. *(tú)* Te aviso con tiempo. ■ Te lo haré saber con tiempo. ■ *(usted)* Le aviso con tiempo. ■ Se lo haré saber con tiempo. ➤ The appointment was made two weeks ahead of time. La cita fue acordada con dos semanas de antelación. ➤ We finished ahead of time. ■ We finished with time left over. ■ We finished with time to spare. Terminamos con tiempo de sobra. ➤ The payment must be made ahead of time. ■ The payment must be made in advance. El pago se debe realizar por adelantado. ➤ We made (the) arrangements ahead of time. Hicimos (los) preparativos por adelantado. ➤ How far ahead of time did they call you? ¿Cuánto tiempo antes te han llamado?

to **aid and abet a crime** promover un crimen

to **aim a weapon at a target** apuntar con un arma a un objetivo ■ apuntar con un arma a un blanco

aim of *la* finalidad de ■ propósito de ■ *la* intención de

to **aim high** picar alto ■ aspirar a mucho

to **aim to do something** ■ to intend to do something pretender hacer algo ■ tener la intención de hacer algo

to be **aimed at someone** ■ to be intended for someone estar dirigido a alguien ■ ir por alguien ➤ That remark was aimed at me, wasn't it? Ese comentario estaba dirigido a mí, ¿verdad? ■ Ese comentario iba por mí, ¿verdad?

to **air a grievance** presentar una queja ■ decir una queja

air conditioning as standard equipment ■ built-in air conditioning aire condicionado de serie

air cover cobertura aérea ➤ The fighter jets provided air cover for the advancing ground troops. Los cazas proveen cobertura aérea para el avance de (las) tropas terrestres.

air force ejército del aire

air intake toma de aire

air miles ■ as the crow flies ■ in a straight line recorrido aéreo ■ en línea recta ➤ Washington is two hundred and seven air miles from New York. ■ Washington is two hundred and seven miles from New York as the crow flies. Washington está a doscientos siete millas en línea recta de Nueva York. ■ Washington está a un recorrido aéreo de doscientos siete millas de Nueva York.

air of sophistication *el* aire de sofisticación

air of superiority *el* aire de superioridad

to **air one's differences** ventilar sus diferencias

to **air one's dirty linen in public** airear los trapos sucios en público

to **air one's grievances** ventilar sus quejas ■ quejarse

to **air out something** ■ to air something out ■ to ventilate something ■ to let some fresh air into something dejar que corra el aire (para ventilar algo) ■ airear algo ■ ventilar algo ■ dejar correr el aire ➤ Open the windows and air out the apartment. Abre las ventanas para dejar que corra el aire en el apartamento. ➤ Open the windows to air it out. Abre las ventanas para dejar que corra el aire.

air pocket bolsa de aire ■ vacío de aire ■ *el* bache

air pollution contaminación del aire ■ contaminación ambiental

air shuttle (service) ■ commuter flights ■ commuter (flight) service puente aéreo

air strikes ataques aéreos

air traffic controller controlador aéreo

air vent rejilla de ventilación

airborne virus virus llevado por el viento ■ virus transportado por el viento

aircraft carrier *el* portaaviones ■ *el* portaaeronaves ■ *(plural) los* portaaviones ■ *los* portaaeronaves

airfare tarifa aérea ■ pasaje aéreo

to be an **airhead** tener una cabeza de chorlito ■ tener una cabeza hueca

airmail: by ~ por correo aéreo

airplane crash ■ plane crash *el* accidente de aviación ■ siniestro ■ *(Mex.)* avionazo

the **airplane crashed** se estrelló el avión

the **airplane pancaked** ■ the airplane belly landed **1.** *(large airplane)* el avión aterrizó de panza **2.** *(light airplane)* la avioneta aterrizó de panza

airplane ride vuelta en avioneta ➤ Martha Anne Woodrum took us for an airplane ride. Martha Anne Woodrum nos llevó a dar una vuelta en una avioneta.

airplane ticket ■ plane ticket *el* billete de avión ■ *el* pasaje de avión

airport beacon baliza

airport shuttle *(ground transportation between hotels and airport)* traslado aeropuerto ➤ Door-to-door airport shuttle Traslado aeropuerto puerta a puerta

airspeed *la* velocidad relativa

to be **akin to something** ■ to be related to something estar relacionado con algo ■ estar en función de algo ➤ *(new* *customers and earnings, for example)* One is akin to the other. ■ One is related to the other. El uno está relacionado con el otro. ■ El uno está en función del otro.

alas ¡ay! ■ ¡ay de mí! ■ desafortunadamente ■ por desgracia

to **alert the competition** poner sobre aviso a los competidores

Alexander the Great Alejandro Magno

to be **alive and kicking** estar vivito y coleando

to be **alive and well** estar bien vivo

to be **alive with activity** ■ to be buzzing with activity ser un hervidero de actividad ■ bullir de actividad ➤ Santa's workshop is alive with activity. ■ Santa's workshop is buzzing with activity. El taller de Papá Noel es un hervidero de actividad. ■ El taller de Papá Noel bulle de actividad.

alkaline battery pila alkalina ■ batería alkalina

to be **all a blur** ser una confusión total ■ ser un borrón ➤ His lectures are all a blur. Sus clases son una confusión total. *(Spanish has no generic word for "lecture" and borrows either "clase," "lección," "conferencia," or "charla.")*

all aboard! ¡(viajeros) al tren!

all about: what something is ~ todo lo que implica algo ■ todo lo que concierne a algo ➤ The countries are re-thinking what the alliance is all about. Los países se replantean todo lo que implica la alianza. ■ Los países se replantean todo lo que concierne a la alianza.

all about it: to find out ~ **1.** *(by investigating)* averiguar todo sobre eso **2.** *(by being told)* enterarse de todo

all about it: to forget ~ ■ to completely forget olvidarse de plano ■ pasarse de largo ➤ I forgot all about it. ■ I completely forgot. Se me olvidó de plano. ■ Se me pasó de largo. ■ *(accepts more responsibility for forgetting)* Me olvidé de plano.

all about it: to know ~ saber todo sobre ello ■ saber todo acerca de ello ■ saber todo referente a ello ➤ He already knew all about it. Ya sabía todo sobre ello.

all about it: to read ~ **1.** leer todo sobre ello **2.** *(newspaper boys)* descubrir toda la verdad ■ enterarse de todo ■ enterarse de toda la verdad ➤ Extra, extra! Read all about it! ¡Extra! ¡Extra! ¡Descubra toda la verdad! ■ ¡Extra! ¡Extra! ¡Entérense de todo!

all agree that... ■ all are in agreement that... **1.** *(they)* todos coinciden en que... ■ todos están de acuerdo en que... **2.** *(we)* todos coincidimos en que... ■ estamos todos de acuerdo en que...

all agreed that... ■ all were in agreement that... **1.** they all agreed that... todos coincidían en que... ■ todos estaban de acuerdo en que... **2.** we all agreed that... ■ all of us agreed that... todos coincidíamos en que... ■ estábamos todos de acuerdo en que...

to be **all alone** estar completamente solo ■ estar solo del todo

all alone: to be left ~ **1.** *(temporarily)* ser dejado(-a) solo(-a) ■ quedarse solo(-a) **2.** *(permanently)* to be orphaned quedar huérfano(-a) ➤ In the movie *Home Alone* Kevin was left all alone at home when his family went on Christmas vacation without him. En la película *Solo en casa* Kevin fue dejado solo en casa cuando su familia salió de vacaciones de Navidad sin él. ➤ The child was left all alone when his parents and siblings died in an automobile accident. El niño quedó huérfano cuando sus padres y hermanos murieron en un accidente automovilístico.

all along ■ from the start desde siempre ■ desde un principio ■ desde el principio ➤ His wife has known about his escapades all along. Su esposa ha sabido lo de sus escapadas desde siempre. ➤ This article confirms what I've been saying all along. Este artículo confirma lo que he venido diciendo desde el principio.

all and sundry *(coll.)* ■ everybody, collectively and individually todos sin excepción

all at once 1. suddenly de buenas a primeras ■ de repente ■ de pronto **2.** at the same time de una vez ➤ All at once it hit me De repente me di cuenta ■ Se me ocurrió de repente ■ De repente me vino a la mente ■ De pronto me vino a la mente ➤ Don't eat it all at once; save half for later. No lo comas de una vez. Deja la mitad para más tarde.

all balled up: to get ~ hacerse un lío ➤ I got all balled up trying to solve this calculus problem. Me hice un lío tratando de resolver este problema de cálculo.

all balled up: to get someone ~ ■ to have someone all balled up tener a alguien hecho un lío ➤ I had the class all balled up trying to explain "could" without using any Spanish. Tuve a la clase hecha un lío tratando de explicarles "could" sin usar el español.

to be **all bark and no bite** ser perro ladrador poco mordedor ■ *(L. Am.)* perro que ladra no muerde

all bent out of shape: to get ~ *(coll.)* ■ to lose one's composure perder la compostura ■ perder los papeles ➤ Well, don't get all bent out of shape over it. Bueno, no pierdas la compostura. ■ Bueno, no pierdas los papeles.

all bets are off ■ what I agreed to previously no longer applies *(Sp.)* donde dije digo, digo Diego

to be **all bundled up in** *(for cold weather)* estar bien abrigado(-a) con

to be **all business** ser todo interés

all but ■ nearly casi ➤ By morning the campfire had all but died out. Para la mañana la hoguera del campamento casi se había aplacado. ➤ He's all but finished in politics. Está casi acabado en la política.

all by oneself 1. without assistance por sí solo(-a) **2.** alone solito(-a)

to be **all cooped up** estar todo arrinconado(-a) ➤ I dislike being all cooped up in a little seat for nine hours on the trans-Atlantic flight. No me gusta estar todo arrinconado en un pequeño asiento por nueve horas en el vuelo transatlántico.

all day 1. the whole day todo el día **2.** in the course of the day en todo el día ➤ He spent the whole day playing video games. (Él) pasó todo el día jugando videojuegos. ➤ I haven't seen her all day. No la he visto en todo el día.

all day long todo el día ■ durante todo el día

to be **all dressed up** estar de punta en blanco ■ estar todo elegante ■ estar todo hecho un pincel ➤ What are you doing all dressed up? ¿Qué hace así todo elegante?

all dressed up: to get ~ ponerse de punta en blanco ■ ponerse (todo) hecho un pincel ■ ponerse (todo) elegante

to be **all ears** ser todo oídos

all-encompassing ■ all-inclusive ■ comprehensive omnicomprensivo

all expenses paid: (with) ~ con todos los gastos pagados

to be **all fixed up** *(coll.)* ■ to be all taken care of estar todo arreglado ■ *(L. Am.)* estar todo resuelto ■ *(Sp.)* estar todo apañado ■ estar todo aviado ➤ He's brought the coffee, put in the hot milk, added the sweetener and brought the croissant. We're all fixed up. ■ We're all taken care of. Nos trajo el café, puso la leche caliente, agregó el edulcorante y nos trajo el croissant. Estamos todos arreglados.

to be **all for something** estar totalmente a favor de algo ■ estar a favor de algo al cien por cien ■ aprobar algo al cien por cien ■ aprobar al cien por cien algo ➤ I'm all for it. Estoy totalmente al favor. ■ Estoy a favor al cien por cien. ■ Lo apruebo al cien por cien.

all (four) of his grandparents ■ all (of) his grandparents ■ each of his (four) grandparents todos sus abuelos ■ cada uno de sus (cuatro) abuelos ■ todos y cada uno de sus abuelos ➤ This baby looks like all four of his grandparents. Este bebé se parece a todos y cada uno de sus abuelos.

to be **all gone** estar terminado ■ acabarse ■ no quedar nada ➤ The paella is all gone, darn it. La paella se acabó, caramba. ■ La paella se ha terminado, narices. ■ La paella se ha terminado, demonios.

to be **(all) Greek to one** sonar a chino

all he wants to do is ... ■ he only wants to... lo único que quiere hacer es... ■ *(literary)* (él) no quiere sino...

all he would say was (that)... sólo se limitó a decir que... ■ sólo se limitó a comentar que... ■ lo único que diría era que... ■ simplemente diría que...

to be **all heart** ser todo corazón

all hell is going to break loose se va a armar la gorda ■ se va a armar la grande ■ *(S.A.)* se va a armar la podrida

all hell broke loose se abrieron las puertas del infierno ▪ se armó una gran barahúnda ▪ se armó un gran cacao

all hot and bothered over something: to get ~ ▪ to get all bent out of shape about something ▪ (for) something to get under one's skin calentarse por algo ▪ perder los papeles ▪ irritarse por algo ▪ sofocarse por algo ▪ *(L. Am.)* molestarse por algo ▪ enojarse por algo ▪ *(Sp.)* enfadarse por algo ▪ cabrearse por algo ➤ Don't get all hot and bothered over it. ▪ Don't let it get under your skin. No te calientes por eso. ▪ No te irrites por eso. ▪ No te sofoques por eso.

all I care about is... ▪ the only thing I care about is... lo único que me importa es...

all I have is... ▪ all I've got is... ▪ the only thing I've got is... sólo tengo... ▪ lo único que tengo es... ➤ All I have is a fifty. Can you change it (for me)? Sólo tengo un billete de cincuenta. ¿Puede cambiármelo?

all I have left is... lo único que me queda es...

all I need is... lo único que necesito... ▪ lo único que me hace falta... ➤ All I need is a good night's sleep. Lo único que necesito es una buena noche de sueño. ▪ Lo único que me hace falta es una buena noche de sueño.

all I wanted was... todo lo que deseaba era... ▪ todo lo que quería era...

to be **all in a day's work** ser (los) gajes del oficio ➤ It's all in a day's work. Son gajes del oficio.

all in all ▪ all things considered ▪ everything considered en definitiva ▪ en conjunto ▪ mirándolo bien ▪ en general

all in good time todo vendrá a su debido tiempo ▪ todo se andará

all in one todo en uno ➤ It's a cookie and a vitamin pill all in one. Es una galleta (dulce) y un comprimido de vitaminas todo en uno.

to be **all in one piece 1.** to be intact estar todo de una pieza ▪ estar en una pieza ▪ estar intacto **2.** to be uninjured estar ileso

all-inclusive ▪ all-encompassing ▪ comprehensive omnicomprensivo

all indications are that... ▪ everything seems to indicate that... todo parece indicar que...

all it takes is one no hace falta más que uno ▪ con uno basta

all it took was one look (for me) to... me bastó un vistazo para...

all it's cracked up to be: not to be ~ *(coll.)* ▪ not to be all that it's claimed to be ▪ not to be all that it's reputed to be no ser todo lo que se dice que es

all it's good for is to... ▪ the only thing it's good for is to... sólo sirve para...

all I've got is... ▪ the only thing I've got is... ▪ all I have is... lo único que tengo es... ➤ All I've got is a fifty. Can you change it? Lo único que tengo es uno de cincuenta. ¿Puedes cambiármelo? ▪ Lo único que tengo son cincuenta. ¿Puedes cambiármelo? ▪ Lo único que tengo es uno de cincuenta. ¿Me lo puedes cambiar? ▪ Lo único que tengo son cincuenta. ¿Me lo puedes cambiar?

all joking aside ▪ all kidding aside *(L. Am., Sp.)* bromas aparte ▪ *(L. Am.)* fuera de chiste ▪ fuera de broma ▪ *(Sp., slang)* fuera coñas

all kidding aside ▪ all joking aside bromas aparte ▪ *(L. Am.)* fuera de chiste ▪ fuera de bromas ▪ *(Sp., slang)* fuera coñas

all kinds of todos los tipos de ▪ todas las variedades de

all kinds of things toda clase de cosas

all kinds of time: to have ~ *(coll.)* ▪ to have all the time in the world tener todo el tiempo del mundo ➤ School is out, so I have all kinds of time. Se acabaron las clases así que tengo todo el tiempo del mundo. ➤ I don't have all kinds of time. No tengo todo el tiempo del mundo.

all man todo un hombre ▪ muy hombre ▪ muy macho

all matters concerning ▪ all matters relating to todo lo concerniente a

to be **all mixed up** estar confundido

all morning ▪ the entire morning ▪ the whole morning toda la mañana ▪ la mañana entera

all morning long ▪ the whole morning ▪ the entire morning (durante) toda la mañana ▪ (en) toda la mañana

all night long ▪ (all) through the night (a lo largo de) toda la noche ➤ The baby kept us up all night long. ▪ The baby kept us up through the night. El bebé nos tuvo despiertos toda la noche.

all of a sudden de repente ▪ repentinamente ▪ de pronto ▪ de sopetón ▪ de golpe ▪ de golpe y porrazo

all of April and May todo abril y mayo

all of his grandparents ▪ all four of his grandparents cada uno de sus abuelos y sus abuelas ▪ cada uno de sus (cuatro) abuelos ▪ *(emphasizing)* todos y cada uno de sus abuelos ➤ This baby looks like all (four) of his grandparents. Este bebé se parece a todos y cada uno de sus abuelos.

all of them todos ➤ It's the source of all of them. Es la fuente de todos.

all of us todos nosotros

all of which todo lo cual ▪ todo la cual ▪ todos los cuales ▪ todas las cuales

all of you ▪ you all *(L. Am., familiar and formal)* todos ustedes ▪ *(Sp., familiar)* todos vosotros ▪ *(formal)* todos ustedes

all one can deal with: to have (got) ~ ▪ to have (got) all one can handle ▪ to have (got) all one can manage tener todo lo que uno puede manejar ▪ tener todo lo que uno puede acaparar ▪ tener todo lo que uno puede controlar

all one can handle: to have (got) ~ ▪ to have (got) all one can manage ▪ to have (got) all one can deal with tener todo lo que uno puede manejar ▪ tener todo lo que uno puede acaparar ▪ tener todo lo que uno puede controlar ➤ I've got all I can handle right now. Tengo todo lo que puedo manejar en este momento. ▪ Tengo todo lo que puedo acaparar en este momento. ▪ Tengo todo lo que puedo controlar en este momento.

all one can manage: to have (got) ~ ▪ to have (got) all one can deal with ▪ to have (got) all one can handle tener todo lo que uno puede manejar ▪ tener todo lo que uno puede acaparar ▪ tener todo lo que uno puede controlar ➤ I've got all I can manage right now. Tengo todo lo que puedo manejar en este momento.

to be **all one talks about** ▪ not to talk of anything else but... ▪ to talk of nothing but... no hablar de otra cosa que... ▪ ser lo único de lo que uno habla

all one wanted todo lo que uno quería ▪ todo lo que uno quiso ➤ The elephant drank all he wanted from the pond, and then trumpeted his satisfaction with his trunk. El elefante bebió del estanque todo cuanto quería y luego barritó su satisfacción con su trompa. ➤ The boy ate all the cookies he wanted. El niño comió todas las galletas que quiso. ▪ El niño comió cuantas galletas quiso.

all one wants todo lo que uno quiera ➤ You can eat all you want. Puedes comer todo lo que quieras. ➤ You can have all you want to eat. Puedes comer cuanto quieras. ➤ I've had all I want, thank you. ▪ I don't care for any more, thank you. No me apetece más, gracias. ▪ Estoy satisfecho, gracias. ▪ He comido lo que he podido, gracias. ➤ You can rationalize all you want to, but the fact of the matter is... Puedes racionalizar todo lo que quieras, pero el hecho es que...

all one's life en toda su vida ▪ en toda la vida ▪ desde siempre

all opposed ▪ those opposed ▪ all who are opposed los que se oponen ➤ All opposed please indicate by a show of hands. ▪ Those opposed please indicate by a show of hands. Los que se oponen, por favor manifiéstenlo levantando la mano.

all or nothing: to go ~ ir a todo o nada ▪ jugarse a todo o nada

all-out effort ▪ total effort esfuerzo total

all-out war ▪ total war guerra acérrima

all over: it's ~ se acabó

to be **all over 1.** to be the end ▪ to be curtains acabarse ▪ estar acabado **2.** to be everywhere estar por todas partes ▪ estar del todo ▪ estar por todos (los) lados ➤ If the violence continues, the peace process is all over. ▪ If the violence continues, it's the end of the peace process. ▪ If the violence continues, it's curtains for the peace process. Si la violencia continúa, el proceso de paz está acabado. ➤ The sky is gray all over. El cielo está del todo gris. ▪ El cielo está gris por todas partes. ▪ El cielo está gris por todos (los) lados.

all over again una vez más ▪ de nuevo ▪ otra vez ▪ por enésima vez ➤ The *Star Wars* series is just the good guys and the bad guys all over again. La serie de la *Guerra de las Galaxias* es sólo los buenos y los malos una vez más. ▪ La serie de la *Guerra de las Galaxias* es sólo los buenos y los malos de nuevo. ▪ La serie de la *Guerra de las Galaxias* es sólo los buenos y los malos otra vez. ▪ La serie de la *Guerra de las Galaxias* es sólo los buenos y los malos por enésima vez.

all over everything: to get paint ~ manchar todo de pintura ▪ esparcir pintura encima de todo ▪ esparcir pintura por todas partes ➤ The painter got paint all over everything. El pintor manchó todo de pintura. ▪ El pintor esparció pintura por todas partes.

all over oneself: to get something ~ cubrirse de algo (hasta las cejas) ▪ llenarse de algo (hasta las cejas) ➤ I got paint all over myself. Me cubrí de pintura (hasta las cejas). ▪ Me llené de pintura (hasta las cejas).

all over the country ▪ throughout the country ▪ nationwide ▪ far and wide en todo el territorio nacional ▪ a lo largo y ancho del país

to be **all over the front page** estar a toda plana ➤ The story was all over the front page. La primicia estaba a toda plana.

to be **all over the place** estar por todas partes ▪ estar por todos lados

all over the place: to run ~ correr de un lado para otro ▪ correr por todos lados ▪ correr por todas partes

all over the world en todo el mundo ▪ por todo el mundo

to be **all over town 1.** estar por todas partes ▪ estar por toda la ciudad **2.** *(little town)* estar por todo el pueblo ➤ The rumor is all over town. El rumor está por todas partes. ▪ El rumor está por toda la cuidad ▪ El rumor está por todo el pueblo. ➤ This flu bug is all over town. ▪ This flu bug is all over the city. Este virus está por toda la ciudad.

all present and accounted for todos presentes y contados

all-purpose word palabra multi-uso

all right 1. okay! ▪ agreed! está bien ▪ *(Mex.)* ¡órale! ▪ *(Sp.)* ¡vale! ▪ ¡claro! **2.** for sure ▪ undoubtedly claro que ▪ por supuesto que **3.** well ▪ okay bien ➤ Come with us!-All right! *(Sp.)* ¡Vente con nosotros!-¡Vale! ▪ *(Mex.)* ¡Vente con nosotros!-¡Órale! ➤ He's dead, all right. Claro que está muerto. ➤ Are you feeling all right? ¿Te encuentras bien?

all right: that's ~ ▪ that's okay no pasa nada ▪ está bien ▪ no hay problema

all right, all right! ▪ stop! stop! ¡bueno! ¡bueno! ▪ ¡ya vale, ya vale! ▪ ¡para! ¡para!

to be **all right with** ▪ to be okay with estar todo bien con ▪ venirle bien ➤ It's all right with me, but you need to check with the concierge. Todo está bien conmigo, pero necesitas consultar con el portero. ▪ Me viene bien, pero necesitas consultar con el portero.

all rights reserved reservados todos los derechos ▪ todos los derechos reservados

all rise! ¡en pie! ▪ ¡todos de pie! ▪ ¡todos se pongan de pie!

all roads lead to Rome todos los caminos llevan a Roma ▪ todos los caminos van a Roma ▪ todos los caminos conducen a Roma

to be **all set (to) 1.** to be ready (to) estar listo (para) ▪ estar preparado (para) ▪ estar dispuesto (para) **2.** to be arranged (for) estar arreglado (para) ➤ Everything's all set. Todo listo.

all she wants to do is... ▪ she only wants to... ▪ the only thing she wants to do is... lo único que quiere hacer es... ▪ *(literary)* (ella) no quiere sino...

all she was wearing ▪ the only thing she was wearing todo lo que llevaba puesto ▪ todo lo que traía puesto ▪ lo único que traía ▪ lo único que llevaba puesto

all sorts of toda clase de ▪ todo tipo de ➤ All sorts of things Toda clase de cosas ▪ Todo tipo de cosas ➤ There are all sorts of factors to take into account. Hay toda clase de factores a tener en cuenta. ▪ Hay todo tipo de factores a tener en cuenta. ➤ There are all sorts of activities planned. Hay todo tipo de actividades planeadas.

all sorts of ways to ▪ lots of ways to toda clase de formas de

all-star cast reparto estelar ▪ elenco de estrellas

to be **all sweetness and light** ser todo dulzura y encanto

all systems are go *(NASA jargon)* ▪ all systems are working todos los sistemas funcionan

to be **all talk** ▪ to be unreliable tener mucho cuento

to be **all talk and no action** ser un(a) cantamañanas ▪ ser de mucho decir y luego nada ▪ ser de mucho hablar y poco actuar ▪ tanto hablar, seca la boca ▪ *(archaic)* mucho lirili y poco lerele

all that... tan... ➤ I'm not all that well-versed in math. No estoy tan puesto en matemáticas. ➤ I'm not all that in demand. No estoy tan solicitado. ➤ The concert was not all that great. El concierto no estuvo tan bien. ➤ That beggar doesn't seem all that ill-fed to *me*. Ese mendigo no me parece muerto de hambre del todo. ▪ Ese mendigo no me parece tan muerto de hambre. ➤ The newspaper doesn't seem all that leftist to *me*. El periódico no me parece izquierdista del todo. ▪ El periódico no me parece tan izquierdista.

all that glitters is not gold no todo lo que brilla es oro ▪ no es oro todo lo que reluce

all that has happened todo lo pasado

all that jazz: and ~ y todo ese rollo ▪ y todo eso

to be **all that's left** ▪ to be all that remains ser todo lo que queda ▪ así haber quedado ➤ That's all that's left of the stew. ▪ That's all that remains of the stew. Es todo lo que queda del cocido. ▪ Es todo lo que queda del guisado. ➤ That's all that's left of the building after the bombing. ▪ That's all that remains of the building after the bombing. Así ha quedado el edificio tras el bombardeo.

all the answers: to have ~ **1.** tener todas las respuestas **2.** *(sarcastic)* to be a know-it-all saberlo todo ▪ ser un(a) sabelotodo ➤ You seem to have all the answers. Parece que tienes todas las respuestas.

all the better ▪ so much the better tanto mejor

all the earmarks of: to have ~ tener toda la pinta de ➤ This has all the earmarks of a terrorist attack. Esto tiene toda la pinta de un ataque terrorista.

all the livelong day todo el santo día

all the more reason! ¡con más motivo! ▪ ¡es razón de más!

to be **all the more reason that one should** ▪ to be all the more reason to ser toda la razón de más para (que)

to be **all the more reason to** ▪ to be all the more reason that one should ser toda la razón de más para (que)

to be **all the more remarkable** ser todo lo más resaltable ▪ ser todo lo más remarcable ▪ ser todo lo más remarcado ▪ ser todo lo más resaltado ➤ An abiding public trust attended Lincoln. This is all the more remarkable in times of civil unrest. Una confianza duradera acompañó a Lincoln. Esto es lo más resaltable en tiempos de desorden civil.

all the more so más aún ➤ Those little acts are manifestations of the divine, all the more so because they are spontaneous. Esos pequeños actos son manifestaciones del divino, más aún porque son espontáneos.

all the others combined ▪ all the rest combined todos los demás juntos

all the rage ▪ the latest fad el último grito de la moda ➤ High heels were all the rage back in the seventies. Los tacones altos fueron el último grito de la moda allá en los setenta.

all the rest combined ▪ all the others combined todos los demás juntos

to be **all the same 1.** ser todo igual ▪ ser todo lo mismo **2.** darle (todo) igual ▪ darle (todo) lo mismo ➤ I want a box of Christmas cards that are all the same. Quiero una caja de tarjetas navideñas que sean todas iguales. ➤ If it's all the same to you, I'd rather stay home and watch TV. Si todo te da igual, prefiero quedarme en casa y ver la tele.

all the time 1. constantly ▪ continuously constantemente ▪ continuamente ▪ siempre **2.** the whole time ▪ the entire time todo el tiempo ➤ They correct me all the time. Me corrigen constantemente. ➤ He eats there all the time. Come y cena allí constantemente. ▪ Come y cena allí continuamente. ➤ I do it all the time. Lo hago siempre. ▪ Lo hago constantemente. ▪ Lo hago continuamente. ➤ For all the time she's spent in Spain, she has yet to see a bullfight. Con todo el tiempo que ha pasado en España, todavía no ha visto una corrida de toros.

➤ I thought I was going to have to get a locksmith, and you were in the house all the time. ▪ I thought I was going to have to get a locksmith, and you were in the house the whole time. Pensé que iba a tener que llamar a un cerrajero, y estuviste en casa todo el tiempo.

all the trouble one had todos los problemas que uno tuvo ▪ todo lo que le costó a uno ➤ After all the trouble we had getting here, you mean to say we're leaving again? ¡Después de todo lo que nos costó llegar hasta aquí, quieres decir que nos vamos otra vez?

all the way 1. todo el camino **2.** del todo ▪ totalmente ▪ de par en par ➤ Even with the stitches out, I still can't open my mouth all the way. Incluso sin los puntos, yo todavía no puedo abrir la boca del todo. ➤ Open your hand all the way. Abre la mano totalmente. ➤ The crowds lined the Gran Vía all the way from the Plaza de España to Alcalá Street. La multitud llenaba las aceras de la Gran Vía totalmente desde la Calle Alcalá hasta la Plaza de España. ➤ I can't open this window all the way. No puedo abrir esta ventana de par en par.

all the way: to go ~ 1. llegar hasta el final **2.** *(sexually)* llegar hasta el final

all the way down hasta el fondo ➤ I couldn't get these blinds to go all the way down. No pude hacer que estas persianas bajaran hasta el fondo.

all the way down (to the end) al fondo ➤ Go all the way down (to the end) and turn right. Vaya al fondo y gire a la derecha.

all the way through: to read a book ~ ▪ to read a book from cover to cover tragarse un libro ▪ leer un libro hasta las tapas

all the way to a place: to go ~ hacer todo el trayecto hasta el final ➤ The metro now goes all the way to the airport. El metro ahora hace todo el trayecto hasta el aeropuerto.

all the way to the top: to climb ~ escalar del todo hasta el final ➤ We climbed all the way to the top of the Washington Monument. Escalamos del todo hasta la cima del Monumento de Washington.

all the way up: to go ~ subir hasta arriba del todo ➤ I can't get the (car) window to go all the way up. No puedo hacer subir la luna hasta arriba del todo.

all the while ▪ the whole time todo el rato

all things being equal si no interviene ningún factor adverso ▪ si no intervienen otros factores ➤ All things being equal, I'd prefer to live here in Jalapa. Si no interviene ningún factor adverso, preferiría vivir aquí en Jalapa.

all things considered ▪ all in all ▪ everything considered en definitiva ▪ en conjunto ▪ mirándolo bien ▪ teniendo todo en cuenta ▪ pensándolo bien

all (those) who ▪ everyone who todos los que ▪ cuantos

all through 1. the whole time durante todo ▪ todo el tiempo **2.** all the way through ▪ all the way along a lo largo ▪ en el transcurso de ➤ All through the movie a couple behind us was yakking. Durante toda la película teníamos una pareja detrás cotorreando. ➤ All through the book A lo largo del libro ▪ En el transcurso del libro

to be **all thumbs** ser un manazas ▪ ser manazas ➤ I'm all thumbs when it comes to trying to put a doorknob back together. Soy un manazas a la hora de volver a armar el pomo en la puerta.

an **all-time high** un máximo sin precedentes ▪ máximo de todos los tiempos ▪ máximo histórico

to be **an all-time low** estar en mínimos históricos

(all-time) record cifras récord

all to oneself: to have something ~ tener todo para uno mismo

all to oneself: to keep something ~ guardar todo para uno mismo ▪ guardárselo todo

all to the good, but: that's ~ todo eso está muy bien, pero

all together 1. in a unified action todos juntos ▪ todos a la vez **2.** in unison al unísono ▪ a una (sola) voz **3.** of one mind de una sola voz

all told ▪ in all en total

all too soon: to end ~ hacerse corto(-a) ▪ saberle a poco ▪ terminar demasiado pronto ➤ Our first date ended all too soon. Nuestra primera cita se nos hizo corta. ▪ Nuestra primera cita nos supo a poco. ▪ Nuestra primera cita terminó demasiado pronto.

all too well: to know ~ ▪ to know only too well saber demasiado ▪ saber de sobra

to be **all torn up 1.** to be distraught ▪ to be upset estar desecho ▪ estar hecho polvo ▪ estar destrozado **2.** to be in the throes of construction estar levantado ▪ estar en obras ➤ He's all torn up because his girlfriend jilted him. Está desecho porque su novia le dio calabazas. ➤ The Alonso Martínez metro station is all torn up right now because of the construction. La estación de Alonso Martínez está toda levantada por las obras.

all walks of life: to come from ~ representar todas clases sociales

to be **all washed up** ▪ to have had it estar acabado

to be **all wet 1.** to be soaked estar todo mojado ▪ estar empapado ▪ estar calado ▪ estar chorreando **2.** to be dead wrong estar completamente equivocado ➤ Don't let the dog in; he's all wet. No dejes entrar al perro; está empapado. ➤ I could be all wet, but that's my gut feeling. Podría estar completamente equivocado, pero es mi sentimiento más profundo.

all who todos los que ▪ todos aquellos que ▪ cuantos

all woman muy mujer ▪ mucha mujer

all work and no play makes Jack a dull boy tanto trabajo acabará haciéndose aburrido

all worked up over: to get ~ ▪ to get all bent out of shape over ponerse como loco ▪ perder los estribos

all year round (durante) todo el año ➤ She listens to Christmas music all year round. Ella escucha música navideña durante todo el año.

all you could see was... ▪ sólo se veía... ▪ todo lo que se podía ver era... ➤ All you could see was smoke. Sólo se veía humo. ▪ Todo lo que se podía ver era humo.

all you ever do is... ▪ all you do is... ▪ you only... no haces más que... ▪ lo único que haces... ➤ You only hurt people. No haces más que hacer daño a la gente. ➤ All you ever do is talk about yourself. Lo único que haces es hablar de ti mismo.

all you can eat todo lo que puedas comer

all you can drink 1. bebe todo lo que puedas **2.** all you are permitted to drink todo lo que te dejemos beber ➤ The lemonade stand sign says, "All you can drink, ten cents." But when the customer tried to drink all the lemonade for ten cents, Dennis the Menace said to the customer, "*I* said it's all you can drink, that's who." El letrero del puesto de limonada dice, "Bebe todo lo que puedas por diez céntimos". Pero cuando el cliente intenta beberse toda la limonada por sólo diez céntimos, Daniel el Travieso le dice, "Soy yo el que dice cuánto es todo lo que puedes beber".

all you ever hear about now is... ▪ now all you ever hear about is... ▪ now all anybody ever talks about is... ahora sólo se habla de...

all you have to do is... ▪ just... todo lo que hay que hacer es... ▪ no tienes más que... ▪ no hay más que... ▪ basta con... ➤ All you have to do is plug it in. ▪ Just plug it in. No hay que hacer más que enchufarlo. ▪ Basta con enchufarlo.

all you need is... 1. all that is needed is... ▪ the only thing you need is... ▪ all one needs is... sólo se necesita ▪ único que se necesita es... **2.** the only thing you (personally) need is... sólo necesitas... ▪ sólo necesita (usted)...

alleged terrorist presunto terrorista ▪ *(formally charged)* acusado de terrorismo

Allen screw tornillo para una llave allen

Allen wrench ▪ hex wrench *la* llave allen

to **allot time for** reservar (el) tiempo para

to **allow enough time for something** ▪ dejarse suficiente tiempo para ▪ calcular tiempo suficiente para ➤ I didn't allow enough time to compensate for the rush-hour traffic. No calculé el tiempo suficiente para compensar el tráfico de las horas punta.

to **allow for** ▪ to make allowance for ▪ to take into account considerar ▪ tener en cuenta ➤ The property tax appraisal must allow for the depreciation of the vehicle. El impuesto de propiedad debe considerar la devaluación del vehículo.

allow me to say (that)... let me say (that)... *(tú)* permíteme decir ▪ *(usted)* permítame decir to **allow someone to do something** ▪ to let someone do something permitir que alguien haga algo ➤ You shouldn't allow your dogs to run loose like that. No deberías permitir que tus perros anden sueltos así.

to **allow time for something** dejar tiempo para algo ▪ reservar tiempo para algo ➤ I would allow three days for the trip. Yo reservaría tres días de viaje. ➤ I would allow plenty of time for it to dry. (Yo) dejaría amplio tiempo para que seque.

to **allow time to do something** dejar tiempo para hacer algo ▪ calcular suficiente tiempo para ➤ I didn't allow enough time to get to the airport on time. No dejé suficiente tiempo para llegar al aeropuerto a tiempo.

to **almost do something** por poco hacer algo ▪ casi hacer algo ➤ I almost fell. Por poco me caigo. ▪ Casi me caigo. ➤ I found some unrelated interesting expressions which almost made me forget what I was doing. Encontré algunas expresiones interesantes no relacionadas que por poco hicieron que se me olvidara lo que estaba haciendo ➤ When the dog ran out in front of the car, it almost gave me a heart attack. Cuando el perro cruzó corriendo delante del carro, por poco me da un síncope. ▪ Cuando el perro cruzó corriendo delante del carro, casi me dio un ataque.

almost wasn't casi no fue ▪ casi no llegó a ser ➤ *(title) The Christmas That Almost Wasn't La Navidad que casi no fue* ▪ *La Navidad que casí no llegó a ser*

almost without realizing it casi sin darme cuenta

to be **almost *x* years old** ▪ to be nearly *x* years old ▪ to be not quite *x* years old tener casi *x* años ▪ faltar poco para cumplir *x* años ▪ estar a punto de cumplir *x* años ➤ When Marcelino was almost five years old... Cuando Marcelino estaba a punto de cumplir cinco años... ▪ Cuando Marcelino tenía casi cinco años... ▪ Cuando a Marcelino le faltaba muy poco para cumplir cinco años...

almost forgotten: to have ~ tener casi olvidado ▪ casi haberse olvidado ▪ ya casi no acordarse ➤ I've almost forgotten what English sounds like, I've been away so long. ▪ I hardly remember what English sounds like, I've been away so long. Tengo casi olvidado cómo suena el inglés por haber estado fuera tanto tiempo. ▪ Casi me he olvidado de cómo suena el inglés por haber estado fuera tanto tiempo. ▪ Ya casi no me acuerdo de cómo suena el inglés por haber estado fuera tanto tiempo.

almost from the moment that... casi desde el momento en que... ▪ prácticamente desde el momento en que...

almost from the time that... casi desde que...

to **almost have a heart attack** ▪ to almost give one a heart attack ▪ to practically have a heart attack por poco darle un síncope ▪ casi darle un síncope ▪ casi darle un ataque al corazón ▪ por poco darle un ataque al corazón

to be **almost here** estar casi aquí ▪ estar prácticamente aquí ➤ The weekend is almost here. El fin de semana está casi aquí. ▪ El fin de semana está prácticamente aquí.

almost never ▪ hardly ever ▪ rarely casi nunca ▪ casi no ▪ rara vez ▪ apenas ➤ He is almost never home. ▪ He is hardly ever home. Casi nunca está en casa. ▪ Casi no está en casa. ▪ Rara vez está en casa. ▪ Apenas está en casa.

almost no one ▪ hardly anyone casi nadie ▪ apenas nadie

almost nothing is known of casi nada se sabe de

along came a spider se acercó una araña

to be **along in a minute** ▪ to be along shortly pasar en un minuto ▪ pasar en un momento ➤ The bus will be along in a minute. ▪ The bus will be along shortly. El bus pasará en un minuto. ▪ El bus pasará en un momento.

to be **along shortly** ▪ to arrive shortly ▪ to be here shortly ▪ to get here shortly ▪ to be along soon ▪ to arrive soon ▪ to be here soon ▪ to get here soon llegar dentro de poco ▪ llegar en breve ➤ Another bus will be along shortly. ▪ Another bus will arrive shortly. ▪ Another bus will be here shortly. ▪ Another bus will get here shortly. Dentro de poco llegará otro autobús.

along the edge (of) 1. a lo largo del borde (de) ▪ a lo largo de los límites (de) ▪ a lo largo de la orilla (de) 2. *(of a blade)* a lo largo del filo (de) ➤ We planted a hedge along the edge of the property. Plantamos un seto a lo largo del borde de la propiedad. ➤ There are nicks along the edge of the knife blade. Hay melladuras a lo largo del filo del cuchillo.

along the length of a lo largo de

along the side of something: to walk ~ caminar al costado de algo ▪ andar al costado de algo ➤ We walked along the side of the Escorial. Caminamos a lo largo del costado del Escorial. ▪ Andamos a lo largo del costado del Escorial.

along the street calle adelante ▪ por la calle

along the way 1. as one goes along en el camino ▪ sobre la marcha 2. en route por el camino ➤ There are many interesting sights along the way. Hay muchas vistas bonitas en el camino. ➤ We'll stop for lunch along the way. Pararemos por el camino para comer.

along with ▪ together with junto con ▪ así como ➤ Virginia is geographically a Central Atlantic state, along with Maryland and Delaware. Geográficamente, Virginia es un estado del centro de la costa atlántica, así como Maryland y Delaware. ➤ Virginia, along with Maryland and Delaware, are Central Atlantic states. Virginia, junto con Maryland y Delaware, son estados del centro de la costa atlántica.

alongside of: to come up ~ ponerse a la altura de ▪ situarse a la altura de ➤ The Spanish runner came up alongside of the French runner, passed him, and went on to win the race. El corredor español se puso a la altura del corredor francés, le adelantó y pasó a ganar la carrera. ▪ El corredor español se situó a la altura del corredor francés, le adelantó y pasó a ganar la carrera.

alongside of: to pull up ~ ▪ to pull up next to ponerse a la altura de ▪ situarse a la altura de ▪ ponerse al lado de ▪ situarse al lado de ➤ The police car pulled up alongside the suspicious vehicle. La patrulla policial se puso a la altura del vehículo sospechoso. ▪ La patrulla policial se situó al lado del vehículo sospechoso.

to be **aloof from** estar distante de ▪ estar apartado de

aloof from: to remain ~ ▪ to keep aloof from ▪ to stand aloof from mantenerse apartado de

alpha and omega ▪ the beginning and the end ▪ the all-encompassing el principio y el fin

alphabetical order: to be in ~ estar en orden alfabético ▪ estar por orden alfabético

to **alphabetize by** poner en orden alfabético según ➤ The phrases are alphabetized by the first word and by key word. Las frases están puestas en orden alfabético según la primera palabra y la palabra clave.

alpine meadow dehesa alpina ▪ prado alpino

to be **already being helped** ya estar atendido ➤ I'm already being helped, thank you. Ya me atiende, gracias. ▪ Ya me están atendiendo, gracias. ▪ Ya fui atendido, gracias.

already done something: to have ~ ya haber hecho algo ➤ If he hasn't asked already, don't mention it. ▪ If he hasn't already asked, don't mention it. Si todavía no ha preguntado, no se lo menciones. ▪ Si no ha preguntado aún, no se lo digas.

to be **already gone** ▪ to have already gone ▪ to have already left haberse ido ya ▪ irse ya ➤ The concierge doesn't get back until the twentieth, and I'll already be gone by then. ▪ The concierge doesn't get back until the twentieth, and I'll already have left by then. El portero no vuelve hasta el día veinte, y para entonces ya me habré ido.

to be **already here** ya estar aquí ▪ ya haber llegado ➤ You were already here. ▪ You were here earlier. Ya estabas aquí. ▪ Ya habías llegado.

already left: to have ~ ▪ to already be gone ▪ to have already gone irse ya ▪ haberse ido ya ➤ She's already left. Ella se fue ya. ▪ Ella ya se ha ido. ▪ Ella se ha ido ya.

already-tense situation situación ya tensa

to be an **also ran** ser un no electo ▪ ser una no electa

altar boy ▪ acolyte monaguillo ▪ acólito

to **alter a photograph** ▪ to doctor a photograph trucar una fotografía

to **alter clothes** arreglar ropa ➤ I need to have these pants altered. Necesito que me arregle este pantalón. ▪ Necesito arreglar este pantalón.

alterations and repairs (on clothes): to do ~ hacer transformaciones y arreglos (en la ropa)

alternate rate tarifa alternativa ➤ Do you have an alternate rate for long-term rentals? ¿Tiene usted una tarifa alternativa para alquileres de largo plazo?

alternating current ■ AC corriente alterna

although it might not look like it ■ although it might not seem like it aunque no lo parezca ■ aunque parezca mentira

although it might not seem like it aunque no lo parezca ■ aunque parezca mentira

altimeter setting *(aeronautics) el* reglaje de altímetro ■ *el* ajuste de altímetro

altitude sickness 1. mountain sickness mal de montaña **2.** *(associated with flying)* mal de alturas

to be **altogether impossible** ■ to be completely impossible ser completamente imposible

to **always be able to** siempre ser capaz de ■ siempre poder

to **always be doing something** estar siempre haciendo algo

to **always be willing to do something** siempre estar dispuesto a hacer algo

to be **always on the go** no parar (un segundo) ■ estar siempre en movimiento ■ ser muy activo

to be **always on time** ■ to be (very) punctual ser muy puntual ■ estar a hora exacta ■ ser muy preciso en la hora ■ *(coll.)* estar como un clavo ➤ He's always on time. ■ He's (very) punctual. Es muy puntual. ■ Está a hora exacta. ■ Es muy preciso en la hora. ■ Está como un clavo.

am I ever glad to see you! ¡vaya si me alegro de verte!

am I glad to see you! ¡cuánto me alegro de verte! ■ ¡qué bueno verte!

am I right? ¿estoy en lo cierto? ■ ¿estoy en lo correcto? ■ ¿tengo razón?

am I supposed to? ■ should I? ¿tendría que hacerlo? ■ ¿debería hacerlo? ■ ¿debiera de hacerlo? ■ ¿debiese de hacerlo? ➤ *Mordred:* Do you recognize me?-*King Arthur:* Am I supposed to? *Mordred:* ¿Me reconoces?-*El rey Arturo:* ¿Tendría que hacerlo?

to **amass a fortune** amasar una fortuna ➤ He had amassed a small fortune by the time he was thirty. El había amasado una pequeña fortuna para la edad de treinta.

to **amaze someone 1.** *(always positive)* dejarle maravillado a alguien **2.** *(usually positive)* dejarle asombrado a alguien **3.** *(positive or negative)* dejarle con la boca abierta a alguien ➤ You amaze me. Me dejas asombrado. ■ Me dejas maravillado.

to be **amazed at** quedar asombrado de ➤ Mark Twain said that when he was fifteen, he thought his father was stupid. But when he was twenty-five he was amazed at how much his father had learned in ten years. Mark Twain dijo que cuando tenía quince años pensaba que su padre era estúpido, pero cuando tenía veinticinco quedó asombrado de todo lo que había aprendido su padre en diez años.

the **amazing thing is** lo asombroso es

Amazon basin cuenca del Amazonas

ambassador to embajador de ■ embajador en ■ embajador ante ➤ U.S. ambassador to Argentina Embajador estadounidense de Argentina ■ Embajador estadounidense en Argentina ➤ Spanish ambassador to the United States Embajador español de los Estados Unidos ■ Embajador español en los Estados Unidos ➤ *(news item)* The Spanish ambassador to the United Nations admits that everything will be called into question if the Iraqi arsenal does not turn up. El embajador español ante las Naciones Unidas admite que si no aparece el arsenal iraquí todo estará en tela de juicio.

ambient temperature temperatura ambiente

ambivalent feelings ■ mixed feelings ■ contradictory feelings sentimientos contradictorios ■ sentimientos contrapuestos

ambivalent relationship conflicto en el apego ■ conflicto de apego ambivalente

ambulance chaser *(opportunistic lawyer) el* picapleitos

amen amen ■ que así sea

amen to that! ■ I'm with *you*! ¡estoy contigo! ■ ¡así sea! ➤ For the rest of the twenty-first century, I hope there is no more war.-Amen to that! Durante el resto del siglo veintiuno espero que no haya más guerra.-¡Estoy contigo!

to **amend the constitution** reformar la constitución

American Bar Association Colegio de abogados de los Estados Unidos

American citizen ■ citizen of the United States ■ U.S. citizen cuidadano norteamericano ■ ciudadano de los Estados Unidos ■ ciudadano estadounidense ➤ Are you an American citizen? ¿Eres un cuidadano de los Estados Unidos?

American soil suelo estadounidense

among other things entre otras cosas

among others entre otros

to be **among the first (people) to do something** ■ to be one of the first people to do something ser de las primeras personas en hacer algo ➤ I was among the first (people) to sign up. ■ I was one of the first to sign up. Fui una de las primeras personas en inscribirme.

among them entre ellos ■ entre ellas ➤ *(news item)* Twenty people kidnapped in the Philippines, including three American tourists Secuestradas veinte personas en las Filipinas, entre ellas tres turistas estadounidenses

amount owed 1. *(by the payer)* (cantidad) a pagar ■ *(to the payee)* (cantidad) a cobrar

to **amount to the same thing** venir a ser lo mismo ■ ser lo mismo ■ ser tres cuartos de lo mismo ■ implicar lo mismo ■ suponer la misma cosa ■ suponer lo mismo ➤ It cost me a thousand pesetas, or six euros. It amounts to the same thing. Me costó mil pesetas o seis euros. Es lo mismo. ➤ They didn't fire him, but they cut his salary in half and gave him an office in the basement, so it amounts to the same thing. No le despidieron, pero le bajaron el sueldo a la mitad y le dieron una oficina en el sótano, lo cual viene a ser lo mismo. ■ No le despidieron, pero le bajaron el sueldo a la mitad y le dieron una oficina en el sótano, lo cual es tres cuartos de lo mismo.

to **amount to (a quantity)** ■ to add up to (a quantity) ascender a (una cantidad) ■ sumar (una cantidad) ■ suponer (una cantidad) ■ terminar siendo una cantidad ■ terminar resultando una cantidad ➤ Fifty dollars a week compounded over forty years amounts to a great deal of money. ■ Interest on fifty dollars a week compounded over forty years amounts to a great deal of money. Los intereses de cincuenta dólares a la semana ascienden en cuarenta años a muchísimo dinero. ■ Los intereses de cincuenta dólares a la semana se incrementan en cuarenta años a muchísimo dinero.

amount to anything: not to ~ no llegar a nada ■ nunca ir a llegar a nada ➤ And you thought he wasn't going to amount to anything. Y tú pensaste que él no iba a llegar a nada.

to **amount to something** llegar a ser algo ■ alcanzar algo en la vida

amplitude modulation ■ AM **1.** *(adjective)* de amplitud modulada **2.** *(noun)* modulación de amplitud ➤ An AM radio Una radio de amplitud modulada

amusement park *el* parque de atracciones ■ parque de diversiones

amusing anecdote anécdota graciosa ■ chascarrillo

an awful lot (of) un montón (de) ■ una barbaridad (de) ➤ He's been coughing an awful lot. Ha estado tosiendo un montón. ➤ You've eaten an awful lot of ice cream. Te has comido una barbaridad de helado.

an hour ago hace una hora

to **analyze in detail** analizar pormenorizadamente ■ analizar detalladamente

ancestor worship culto a los antepasados

anchorman presentador

anchorperson presentador(a)

ancient civilizations civilizaciones antiguas

ancient ruins antiguas ruinas ■ antiguos restos

and accordingly y según eso

and actually ■ (and) in fact y en realidad ■ y realmente ■ no en vano ➤ Science fiction has become a very popular genre, and actually, many non-science fiction writers employ its conventions and techniques in their works. La ciencia ficción se ha convertido en un género muy popular, no en vano muchos escritores utilizan sus convenciones en sus obras.

and all con todos ■ hasta con ■ y todo ➤ Here's your watermelon, seeds and all. Aquí tienes la sandía, hasta con semillas.

and all at once y repentinamente ■ y de súbito

and all at once I realized that... y repentinamente me di cuenta de que... ■ y de súbito me di cuenta de que...

and all at once it came to me (that...) y repentinamente me vino a la mente (que...)

and all at once it hit me (that...) y de repente caí en cuenta (de que...) ▪ y de repente me di cuenta (de que...)
and all that jazz y toda esa historia
and all that stuff y cosas de esas ▪ y todo ese rollo ▪ y toda esa historia
and all this time y todo este tiempo ➤ And all this time I thought you were doing your homework. Y todo este tiempo pensaba que estabas haciendo tu tarea.
and also y también ▪ es más
and another thing! ¡y otra cosa!
and as I did y según lo hacía (yo)
and as if ▪ and as though y como si ➤ And as if designed down to the last detail by a computer Y como si diseñado al más mínimo detalle por una computadora
and as if that weren't enough y por si fuera poco
and at that point y en ese momento ▪ y al llegar a ese punto ➤ The conversation became heated and at that point they came to blows. La conversación se tornó acalorada y al llegar a ese punto se fueron a las manos.
and at this point y aquí ▪ y llegado a este punto
and be done with it y acabar con eso
and besides y además
and besides that y además de eso
(and) don't forget it! 1. don't leave it behind ▪ don't forget to take it! ¡(y) no vayas a olvidártelo! 2. (and) don't you forget it! ¡y no lo vayas a olvidar! ▪ ¡y no lo olvides!
and don't you forget it! ¡y no lo vayas a olvidar! ▪ ¡y no lo olvides!
and even e incluso ➤ From the vantage point of the Pole Star, we could correlate the Earth's orbital position with the seasons, down to the months and even days of the year. Desde la atalaya de la estrella polar, podríamos correlacionar la posición orbital de la Tierra con las estaciones, hasta los meses e incluso los días del año.
and even more e incluso más ▪ y aun más
and everything ▪ and all y todo
and everything else y todo lo demás ▪ y demás
and finally ▪ and last y por último ➤ Add six tablespoons of flour, and finally, a splash of milk. Se añade seis cucharadas de harina y por último un chorrito de leche.
and following that y luego de eso
and following this y luego de esto
and for good reason y por buena razón
and for that very reason ▪ and for that (same) reason y por lo mismo
and he did y así lo hizo
and he was right y acertó ▪ y tenía razón
(and) hence the name a ello(-a) se debe su nombre ▪ de ahí el nombre ➤ Monticello, Thomas Jefferson's house, is situated on the summit of a small mountain, and hence the name. Monticello, la casa de Thomas Jefferson, está situated en la cumbre de una pequeña montaña, y a ella se debe su nombre. ➤ The cat's name is Nat because his tail is not all there, (and) hence the name. El nombre del gato es Nat porque le falta parte de su cola, de ahí el nombre.
and here I am today y hasta hoy ▪ y aquí estoy yo
and hopefully y espero que ▪ y con suerte
and how! ¡y cómo! ▪ ¡y tanto!
and I can tell you right now... y (que) conste que...
and I could go on and on y así puedo seguir indefinidamente ▪ y así podría seguir indefinidamente
and I didn't want to find out y no tenía ganas de descubrirlo ➤ I had no idea how... and I didn't want to find out. No tenía ni idea de como... y no tenía ganas de descubrirlo.
and I don't intend to y no tengo la intención
and I don't know what all (else) y no sé qué (tanto) más ➤ In her pocketbook Connie keeps her wallet, glasses, lipstick, appointment book, real estate key, and I don't know what all else. En su bolsa Connie guarda su cartera, gafas, lápiz labial, agenda, llave universal, y no sé qué (tanto) más.
and I don't want to have to y no quiero tener que ▪ y que no tenga que
and I still am y sigo así ▪ y lo sigo siendo ▪ y sigo siéndolo ▪ y lo sigo estando ▪ y sigo estándolo
and I still do y sigo haciéndolo ▪ y lo sigo haciendo
(and) in fact ▪ (and) actually y de hecho ▪ y en realidad ▪ no en vano ➤ Science fiction has become a very popular genre, and in fact, many non-science fiction writers employ its conventions and techniques in their works. La ciencia ficción se ha convertido en un género muy popular, no en vano muchos escritores utilizan sus reglas tradicionales y técnicas literarias en sus obras.
and incidentally y dicho sea de paso
and indeed y a la verdad
and instead y en cambio
and instead of that y en lugar de ello ▪ y en vez de ello
and if so y de ser así ▪ y si es así ▪ y si fuera así
and if so, what? y si fuera así, ¿qué? ▪ y si es así, ¿qué?
and if so, why? y si fuera así, ¿por qué? ▪ y si es así, ¿por qué? ➤ And if so, why did you? Y si es así, ¿por qué lo hiciste?
and if you don't believe me... y si no me crees...
and in a way y en cierta forma ▪ y en cierto modo
and it goes on to say that... y sigue para decir que... ▪ y continúa para decir que... ▪ y sigue para añadir que... ▪ y continúa para añadir que...
and it shows y se nota ▪ y así te quedó
and it still does y aún lo hace ▪ y aún lo sigue haciendo ▪ y aún sigue haciéndolo
and it still is y sigue siéndolo ▪ y lo sigue siendo ▪ y aún lo es
and it worked ▪ and it was successful y lo logró ▪ y tuvo éxito ▪ y resultó ▪ y funcionó
and it's because... y es que...
and just as I had said y tal y como (yo) había dicho
and just as I had said it would (be) y tal y como (yo) había dicho que sería
and just as I had said it would (turn out) y tal y como (yo) había dicho que resultaría
and just at that moment y precisamente en ese instante ▪ y justo en ese momento
and last ▪ and finally y por último ➤ Add six tablespoons of flour, and last, a splash of milk. Se añade seis cucharadas de harina y por último un chorrito de leche.
and look at all the good it did ▪ a lot of good it did y mira de lo que ha servido ➤ I told my teenage son, "When I was a teenager, my father used to tell me to sit up straight." My son said, "And look at all the good it did." Le dije a mi hijo adolescente, "Cuando yo tenía tu edad, mi padre solía decirme que me sentase derecho". Mi hijo me dijo, "Y mira de lo que ha servido".
and maybe (even) more ▪ and perhaps (even) more y puede que incluso más ▪ y hasta puede que más ▪ y quizás más
and mind you *(tú)* y ten en cuenta ▪ *(usted)* y tenga en cuenta
and most of all y sobre todo
and not even then y ni aun así
and not only that... 1. and in addition... y no sólo eso... 2. and as if that weren't enough... y por si fuera poco...
and not the other way around y no al revés
and now for bueno, vamos con
and, of course,... y, claro,...
and on you go to... *(tú)* y te vas luego a... ▪ *(usted)* y se va luego a...
and perhaps even more ▪ and maybe even more y puede que incluso más ▪ y hasta puede que más ▪ y quizás más
and proud of it ▪ and proud to be one y orgulloso de serlo ▪ ¡y a mucha honra!
and rightly so y con razón
and since I'm not y ya que no lo soy ▪ y puesto que no lo soy ▪ y al no serlo
and so así que ▪ y así
and so forth ▪ and so on ▪ et cetera y así sucesivamente ▪ etcétera
and so I did y así lo hice
and so on ▪ and so forth y así sucesivamente ▪ etcétera
and so on and so forth y demás ▪ *(colorful)* y otras hierbas
and some y pico ▪ y algo ➤ In 1800 and some... En mil ocho cientos y pico...

and specifically y específicamente ▪ y en concreto
and still does y aún lo hace ▪ y aún sigue haciéndolo
and still is y sigue siéndolo ▪ y aún lo es
and subsequently ▪ and later ▪ and then y posteriormente ➤ The secretary postponed, and subsequently cancelled, the meeting. ▪ The secretary postponed, and later cancelled, the meeting. ▪ The secretary postponed, and then cancelled, the meeting. La secretaria aplazó, y posteriormente suspendió, la reunión.
and suddenly ▪ then suddenly y de repente ▪ *(more coll.)* y de golpe ▪ *(coll.)* y de golpe y porrazo ▪ *(more formal)* y de improviso
and sure enough y como era de esperar
and that was that y punto ▪ y no había más ▪ y es lo que había
and that was the end of that y eso fue todo
and that's all there is to it ▪ and it's as simple as that y es lo que hay ▪ y es así de simple
and that's going some y eso ya es mucho ▪ y eso ya es decir mucho
and that's just how it is ▪ and that's just the way it is y no hay vuelta que darle
and that's saying a lot y eso es decir mucho
and that's that y ya está ▪ y punto aparte ▪ y punto ▪ y no hay más ▪ y sanseacabó ▪ y santas Pascuas
and that's the end of that y eso es todo
and the like ▪ and so on ▪ et cetera y así sucesivamente ▪ y demás
and the rest is history y lo demás es historia
and then y entonces ▪ y a continuación ▪ y luego de esto ➤ And then I decided... ▪ And so I decided... Y luego de esto decidí...
and then it goes on y luego sigue
and then it goes on to add that... y luego continúa para decir que... ▪ y luego sigue para añadir que... ▪ y luego continúa para añadir que...
and then it goes on to say that... y luego sigue para decir que...
and then some y algo más ➤ As soon as school is out, I'll write you a long letter and then some. En cuanto acaben las clases, te escribiré una carta extensa y algo más.
and then there's... y luego hay... ▪ y entonces hay...
and then to... 1. and after that to y después 2. and on top of that y encima ▪ y además ▪ *(coll.)* y para colmo ➤ He went first to the Caribbean, and then to Los Angeles. Fue primero al Caribe y luego a Los Ángeles. ➤ They come late to class and never do their homework, and then to complain about the teacher... Llegan tarde a clase, nunca hacen los deberes, y encima se quejan del profesor... ▪ Llegan tarde a clase, nunca hacen los deberes, y encima se quejan del profesor... ▪ Llegan tarde a clase, nunca hacen los deberes, y para colmo se quejan del profesor...
and there you have it! ¡y ahí tienes! ▪ ¡y ahí lo tienes! ▪ ¡y ya está!
and thereby y de esto
and therefore ▪ and thus ▪ and hence ▪ and for that reason y por ello ▪ y por eso ▪ y por lo tanto ▪ y por lo mismo
and they lived happily ever after ▪ and they lived happily forever after y fueron felices y comieron perdices ▪ y fueron felices por siempre jamás ▪ y colorín colorado, este cuento se ha acabado
and to think it was you! ▪ and to think that it was you! *(tú)* ¡y pensar que eras tú! ▪ ¡y pensar que fuiste tú! ▪ *(usted)* ¡y pensar que era usted! ▪ ¡y pensar que fue usted!
and to think it was you the whole time! ¡y pensar que eras tú todo el tiempo!
and to think that...! ¡y pensar que...!
and to think (that) it could have been you! ▪ and to think (that) it might have been you! *(tú)* ¡y pensar que podrías haber sido tú! ▪ *(usted)* ¡y pensar que podría haber sido usted!
and to think (that) it was you! *(tú)* ¡y pensar que eras tú! ▪ *(usted)* ¡y pensar que era usted!
and to top it all off ▪ to top it all off y para rematarla ▪ y para rematar la faena ▪ y para rematar ▪ y para acabar ▪ y para terminar
and up a partir de ▪ o más ➤ For five students and up, the fee is fifty euros per hour. A partir de cinco estudiantes, la tarifa es cincuenta euros por hora. ▪ Para cinco estudiantes o más, la tarifa es cincuenta euros por hora.
and vice versa y viceversa ▪ y al revés ▪ y al contrario ▪ y a la inversa
and we both know it! ¡y no se hable más! ▪ ¡y no hay más que hablar! ▪ ¡y ya ambos lo sabemos! ▪ ¡y no hablemos más!
and, well, I did... ▪ well, and I did... y, bueno, sí...
and what can you do about it? ¿y qué va a hacerle? ▪ ¿y qué remedio?
and what did I see? ¿y qué fue lo que vi?
and what have you ▪ and what not ▪ and so on y así sucesivamente
and what is it then? ¿y qué es entonces?
and what of it? ▪ (and) so what? ¿y qué?
and what's more y lo que es más ▪ y más aún
and when I do 1. cuando lo hago 2. and when that happens (to me) cuando me pasa (eso) ➤ I go surfing once or twice every summer, and when I do, I feel like the happiest guy on Earth. Voy a surfear una o dos veces cada verano, y cuando lo hago, me siento el tío más feliz de la tierra. ➤ I get sunburned on the top of my head sometimes, and when I do, I rub in some aloe vera gel, and it really helps it. Me quemo la calva de vez en cuando, y cuando me pasa, me froto algún gel de aloe vera y realmente ayuda.
and worse ▪ and what's worse y lo que es peor
and worse yet y aún peor
and worst of all y lo peor de todo
and yet y sin embargo
anecdotal example ▪ hypothetical example ejemplo anecdótico ▪ ejemplo hipotético ➤ The example is anecdotal because the database hasn't been created yet. El ejemplo es anecdótico porque la base de datos aún no ha sido creado.
anecdotal material material anecdótico ➤ The series has a lot of anecdotal material, but not a very good exposition of the philosophy. La serie tiene mucho material anecdótico pero no una buena exposición de la filosofía.
to **angle for something** *(coll.)* ▪ to angle at something andar buscando algo ▪ planear algo ➤ What are you angling for? ▪ What are you angling at? ¿Qué andas buscando? ▪ ¿Qué estás planeando?
angle of attack *(angle at which the wing of an airplane or bird is tilted into the ambient air during flight)* ángulo de ataque ➤ In flight, an airplane's angle of attack coincides with the angle of incidence except during landing, when it is greater. En el vuelo, el ángulo de ataque de un aeroplano coincide con el ángulo de incidencia excepto durante el aterrizaje, cuando es mayor.
angle of incidence (of a propeller) ▪ (angle of) pitch of a propeller ángulo de incidencia (de una hélice)
angle of incidence (of a wing) ▪ *(angle at which the wing of an airplane or bird tilts downward into its direction of thrust)* ángulo de incidencia
(angle of) pitch 1. *(of a roof)* ángulo de inclinación 2. *(of a propeller)* angle of incidence ángulo de incidencia
to be **angry at oneself** *(L. Am., Sp.)* estar molestado consigo mismo ▪ *(Mex.)* estar enojado con uno mismo ▪ *(Sp.)* estar enfadado con uno mismo
angry at oneself: to get ~ *(L. Am., Sp.)* molestarse consigo mismo ▪ *(Mex.)* enojarse con uno mismo ▪ *(Sp.)* enfadarse con uno mismo
angry look: with an ~ con una mirada asesina ▪ con (muy) mala cara ▪ *(coll.)* con cara de mala leche
angry reaction: to provoke an ~ provocar una reacción airada
to be **angry with someone** estar molesto con alguien ▪ *(Sp.)* estar enfadado con alguien ▪ *(L. Am.)* estar enojado con alguien
animal rights advocate defensor(a) de los derechos de los animales
anniversary (of a historical event) *la* efeméride ▪ aniversario
anniversary of a wedding ▪ wedding anniversary aniversario de bodas

to **announce one's engagement** anunciar su compromiso matrimonial

to **announce shortly** estar a punto de anunciar ➤ The president will announce shortly. El presidente está a punto de anunciar.

annual checkup *(medical)* ▪ yearly checkup revisión anual

annual rate taza anual

another chance otra oportunidad

another day ▪ at a later date ▪ another time ▪ some other time otro día

another helping: to go for ~ ir a repetir ➤ I'm going for another helping. Voy a repetir.

another helping: to have ~ ▪ to have some more repetir ➤ I'd like (to have) another helping. ▪ I'd like (to have) some more. Me gustaría repetir.

another one like it ▪ another like it otro igual

to be **another question altogether** ▪ to be a different question altogether ▪ to be a whole different kettle of fish ser capítulo aparte ▪ ser harina de otro costal

another thing I did was this otra cosa que hice fue ésta

another thing I do is this otra cosa que hago es ésta

another thought coming: to have (got) ~ ir a averiguarlo ➤ If you think you can do that and get away with it, you've got another thought coming. Si tú piensas que puedes hacer eso y salirte con la tuya, vas a averiguarlo.

another time **1.** again otra vez ▪ de nuevo **2.** (at) some other time en otra ocasión ➤ Play that piece another time. ▪ Play that piece again. Toca esa pieza otra vez. ▪ Toca esa pieza de nuevo. ➤ We can program the phone another time. Podemos programar el teléfono en otra ocasión.

another *x* people ▪ *x* more people otras *x* personas ▪ *x* personas más ➤ We're expecting another six people. ▪ We're expecting six more people. Esperamos otras seis personas. ▪ Esperamos seis personas más.

to **answer a description** ▪ to match a description ▪ to correspond to a description ▪ to answer to a description responder a una descripción ➤ A suspect answering that description was arrested today. Un sospechoso que respondía a esa descripción fue detenido hoy.

to **answer a question** responder (a) una pregunta ▪ contestar (a) una pregunta

to **answer an ad** ▪ to respond to an ad responder a un anuncio

to **answer for one's actions** **1.** responder por un hecho **2.** *(during interrogation)* to give an accounting of one's actions rendir cuentas ➤ He's going to have to answer for the dent in the car. Va a tener que responder por el abollón en el coche. ➤ To answer for one's actions before a grand jury Rendir cuentas ante el gran jurado

to **answer for someone** **1.** to be accountable for someone responder por alguien **2.** to speak for someone responder por alguien ➤ The low-level officers should not have to answer for the commander's mistakes. Los oficiales de bajo rango no deberían responder por los errores del comandante. ➤ I can't answer for *her*, but... No puedo responder por ella, pero...

to **answer defensively** responder a la defensiva

to **answer guardedly** responder con cautela

to **answer in the affirmative** responder de forma afirmativa ▪ responder afirmativamente

to **answer in the negative** responder de forma negativa ▪ responder negativamente

to **answer someone** responder a alguien ▪ *(L. Am.)* contestar a alguien

to **answer the call for** acudir a la llamada para

to **answer the door** ▪ to go to the door ▪ to (go) see who's at the door atender la puerta ▪ abrir la puerta ▪ ver quien hay en la puerta ➤ Go answer the door. ▪ Go see who's at the door. Vete a atender la puerta. ▪ Vete a abrir la puerta. ▪ Vete a ver quien hay en la puerta.

to **answer the objection** responder a la objeción

to **answer the question** responder a la pregunta ▪ contestar a la pregunta

to **answer (to) a description** ▪ to match a description ▪ to correspond to a description responder a una descripción

to **answer to someone** responder a alguien ▪ estar subordinado a alguien ➤ The attorney general answers to the president. El fiscal general responde al presidente. ➤ Can't you report the problem to whomever you answer to? ¿No puedes informar del problema a quien sea que estés subordinado?

to **answer to the charge of** responder a la acusación de ▪ responder bajo la acusación de

answer to the problem ▪ solution to the problem solución al problema ➤ I don't know the answer to the problem. No sé la solución al problema.

answer to the question respuesta a la pregunta ➤ What's the answer to the question? ¿Cuál es la respuesta a la pregunta? ➤ I don't know the answer to the question. No sé la respuesta a la pregunta.

to **answer unwillingly** ▪ to answer reluctantly contestar con reservas ▪ contestar con recelo ▪ contestar con desgana

to **answer without hesitation** contestar sin dudar ▪ contestar sin titubear

to **answer your question** contestarle la pregunta a alguien ▪ responder a su pregunta ➤ Did I answer your question? ¿Contesté tu pregunta? ▪ ¿Te contesté la pregunta? ➤ You didn't answer my question. No respondiste a mi pregunta. *(See also "to answer your question" alphabetized under "to.")*

answering machine contestador automático

antennae of a crayfish ▪ feelers of a crayfish bigotes de un langostino

antennae of an insect ▪ feelers of an insect antena de un insecto

anthrax spores esporas de ántrax

anti-cholesterol drug fármaco contra el colesterol ➤ Experts linked the deaths caused by kidney failure to a new anti-cholesterol drug. Los expertos relacionaron las muertes por fallo renal con un nuevo fármaco contra el colesterol.

anti-trust laws leyes anti-monopolio

to **anticipate that** ▪ to expect that esperar a que

antique(s) dealer comerciante de antigüedades

Anvil Chorus *(from Verdi's "Il trovatore")* El coro de los gitanos ▪ El coro del yunque ▪ El coro de la fragua

to be **anxious for something to happen** estar deseoso de que ocurra algo ➤ I'm anxious for this course to end. Estoy deseoso de que termine este curso.

to be **anxious to do something** estar animado por hacer algo ▪ estar ansioso por hacer algo ▪ estar deseoso de hacer algo ▪ tener ganas de hacer algo ▪ tener apuro por hacer algo ➤ I'm really anxious to get started. Estoy muy animado por empezar. ➤ I'm anxious to get there. Estoy ansioso(-a) por llegar. ➤ I'm anxious to leave. Estoy deseoso de salir.

to be **any damned good** **1.** *(Sp., off-color)* ser de la hostia **2.** *(L. Am., off-color)* ser de pinga ➤ If it were any damned good, I would have heard about it. Si fuera algo de la hostia, ya habría oído algo acerca de ello. ▪ Si fuera algo de pinga, ya habría oído algo acerca de ello.

any day now cualquier día de éstos ▪ de hoy a mañana

"Any Dream Will Do" *(Andrew Lloyd Webber song)* "Cualquier sueño me valdrá"

(any) further word on ▪ (any) further information on algún dato (nuevo) ▪ algún dato (más reciente) ➤ Do you have any further word on when the new drug will be on the market? ¿Tiene usted algún dato más reciente sobre cuando estará en el mercado el nuevo medicamento?

any indication alguna indicación ➤ Did he give you any indication...? ¿Te dio él alguna indicación...? ➤ Have you had any indication...? ¿Has recibido alguna indicación...?

any less so ni siquiera un poco menos ➤ You say your arm is still sore? Any less so than the last time you went to the doctor? ¿Dices que tu brazo está todavía dolorido? ¿Ni siquiera un poco menos que la última vez que fuiste al médico?

any longer más ➤ I don't want to keep you any longer. No quiero retenerte más.

any minute (now): to be along ~ llegar de un momento a otro ▪ llegar en cualquier momento ▪ venir de un momento a otro ▪ venir en cualquier momento ▪ entrar de un momento a otro ▪ entrar en cualquier momento ▪ estar al caer (de un momento a otro) ▪ estar al caer (en cualquier momento) ▪

estar por caer (de un momento a otro) ▪ estar por caer (en cualquier momento) *("Rato" can be substituted for "momento" in all examples.)* ➤ The train will be along any minute now. El tren llegará en cualquier momento. ▪ El autobús llegará de un momento a otro.

any minute (now): to be here ~ ▪ to be about to arrive estar al caer ▪ estar por caer ➤ They'll be here any minute. Están al caer. ▪ Están por caer.

any more than someone else: not to want to do something ~ no tener más ganas de hacer algo que alguien ➤ I don't want to go any more than you do. No tengo más ganas de ir de las que tienes tú.

any number of ▪ quite a few ▪ several varios ▪ unos cuantos ➤ There are any number of ways to solve this algebra problem. Hay varias maneras de solucionar este problema de álgebra. ▪ Hay unas cuantas formas de solucionar este problema de álgebra.

any of them **1.** ninguno de ellos **2.** alguno de ellos ➤ I don't like any of them. No me gusta ninguno de ellos. ➤ Do you like any of them? ¿Te gusta alguno de ellos?

any old algún cualquiera ▪ alguna cualquiera ➤ *(woman to her husband)* Any old father will spend time with his children. Algún padre cualquiera pasaría tiempo con sus niños. ➤ Any old ice cream shop will give you two scoops. Alguna heladería cualquiera te dará dos bolas.

any old time ▪ just any old time ▪ whenever you feel like (it) cuando a uno le dé la gana ▪ cuando a uno le guste ▪ cuando a uno le apetezca ➤ You think you can hand in your homework (just) any old time. Well, you can't. It's due today! Crees que puedes entregar los deberes cuando te dé la gana. Bueno, pues no (puedes). ¡Es para hoy!

any old way ▪ every which way así como así ▪ sin orden ni concierto

any one person in mind: not to have ~ ▪ not to have a specific person in mind no tener (a) nadie en concreto en mente ▪ no tener (a) una persona en especial en mente ▪ no tener (a) una persona específica en mente ➤ I don't have any one person in mind. ▪ I don't have a specific person in mind. No tengo a nadie en concreto en mente. ▪ No tengo a una persona específica en mente.

any other cualquier otro ➤ Does she go by any other name? ¿Responde ella a cualquier otro nombre? ➤ A rose by any other name would smell as sweet. Una rosa con cualquier otro nombre olería igual de dulce.

any other day otro día cualquiera ➤ I'm on call Saturday. (So) in short, I would prefer any other day. Estoy de guardia el sábado. Total que prefiero otro día cualquiera.

any other person ▪ anyone else **1.** *(positive, or question)* cualquier otra persona ▪ alguna otra persona ▪ alguien más **2.** *(negative)* ninguna otra persona ▪ nadie más ➤ Do you know anyone else who plays the piano as well as she does? ¿Conoces a cualquier otra persona que toque el piano tan bien como ella? ▪ ¿Conoces a alguna otra persona que toque el piano tan bien como ella? ▪ ¿Conoces a alguien más que toque el piano tan bien como ella? ➤ I've never heard that last name in any other person. ▪ I've never heard that last name in anyone else. No he oído ese apellido jamás en ninguna otra persona. ▪ No he oído ese apellido en nadie más *(Note that "en cualquier otra persona" would equate to "in some other person.")*

any other way **1.** alguna otra manera ▪ alguna otra forma **2.** *(route)* algún otro camino ▪ alguna otra vía ➤ Is there any other way to solve this algebra problem? ¿Existe alguna otra manera de solucionar este problema de álgebra? ➤ Is there any other way to do this job? ¿Hay alguna otra forma de hacer este trabajo? ➤ How could they feel any other way? ¿Cómo podrían sentirse de alguna otra forma? ➤ Is there any other way to get there? ¿Existe alguna otra vía para llegar ahí?

any possibility alguna posibilidad ▪ *(L. Am.)* algún chance ➤ Is there any possibility of finding them? ¿Existe alguna posibilidad de encontrarlos? ▪ *(Sp., leísmo when referring to people)* ¿Existe algún chance de encontrarles?

any questions?: are there ~ ¿hay preguntas? ▪ ¿(hay) alguna duda?

any questions?: do you have ~ *(tú)* ¿tienes preguntas? ▪ *(usted)* ¿tiene usted preguntas? ▪ *(ustedes)* ¿tienen ustedes preguntas? ▪ *(Sp., vosotros)* ¿tenéis (vosotros) preguntas?

any remaining questions ▪ any additional questions ▪ any remaining doubts algo que no ha quedado claro ▪ alguna duda restante ▪ alguna otra duda ▪ cualquier pregunta restante ▪ cualquier duda restante ➤ If there are any remaining questions, you can come by my office after class. Si hay cualquier pregunta restante, podéis pasar por mi oficina después de la clase. ➤ (Do you have) any remaining doubts? ▪ Anyone still have (any) questions? ▪ Any questions? ¿Hay alguna pregunta restante? ▪ ¿Algo que no ha quedado claro? ▪ ¿Tienes alguna duda restante? ▪ ¿Tienes alguna otra duda? ➤ I'd like to clear up any remaining doubts that the class might have. Me gustaría aclarar alguna duda restante que la clase pueda tener. ➤ The European Union is trying to dispel any remaining doubts about the new currency. La Unión Europea está intentando disipar alguna duda restante acerca de la nueva moneda.

any remaining items of business algunas diligencias restantes ▪ algunos asuntos (de negocios) restantes

any semblance of something cualquier apariencia de algo ▪ cualquier asomo de algo ▪ cualquier semejanza de algo ▪ *(coll.)* cualquier pizca de algo ▪ *(literary)* cualquier vestigio de algo ➤ The terrorists want to sabotage any semblance of progess. Los terroristas quieren sabotear cualquier asomo de progreso.

any such subject tal asignatura ➤ I never took any such subject. Nunca hice tal asignatura. ▪ Nunca cursé tal asignatura.

any such thing ▪ anything of the sort tal cosa ▪ nada por el estilo ➤ I never said any such thing. ▪ I never said anything of the sort. Nunca dije tal cosa. ▪ Nunca dije nada por el estilo.

any suggestions?: (are there) ~ ¿(hay) alguna sugerencia? ▪ ¿(hay) sugerencias?

any that I liked: not ~ ▪ none that I liked nada que me gustara ▪ nada que me gustase ➤ I shopped for a sofa today, but I didn't see any that I liked. ▪ I shopped for a sofa today, but I didn't see one that I liked. Fui a comprar un sofá hoy, pero no vi ninguno que me gustara. ▪ Fui a comprar un sofá hoy, pero no vi ninguno que me gustase.

any three: choose ~ *(tú)* elige cualquier trio ▪ elige cualquier grupo de tres ▪ *(usted)* elija cualquier trio ▪ elija cualquier grupo de tres

any too soon: not ~ ▪ none too soon ▪ in the nick of time por los pelos ▪ a tiempo ➤ I didn't take these beers out of the freezer any too soon. Saqué estas cervezas del congelador por los pelos.

any way you look at it a todas luces ▪ a toda luz ▪ desde todo punto de vista

anybody else would have ▪ anyone else would have otro cualquiera lo habría hecho ▪ otro cualquiera lo hubiera hecho ▪ otro cualquiera lo hubiese hecho

anybody else would have... ▪ anyone else would have... otro cualquiera hubiera...

anyone? ¿alguno de vosotros? ▪ ¿alguno de ustedes?

anyone can see that ▪ anyone can see it cualquiera se da cuenta ▪ cualquiera puede verlo *("Lo" is more natural in Spanish than "eso.")*

anyone can see that... cualquiera se da cuenta de que... ▪ cualquiera puede ver que...

anyone I know? ▪ anybody I know? ¿alguien que conozca? ▪ ¿alguien conocido?

anyone (else) to turn to a quien (más) acudir ➤ I didn't have anyone to turn to. No tenía a quien acudir. ➤ I didn't have anyone else to turn to. No tenía a quien más acudir.

anyone who (even) comes close... **1.** nadie que ni de lejos sea... ▪ nadie que se le parezca... **2.** quienquiera que se acerque... ➤ I don't know of anyone who even comes close to him as a football player. ▪ I don't know of anyone who compares to him as a football player. No sé de nadie que sea ni de lejos tan buen futbolista (como él). ▪ No sé de nadie que se le parezca como futbolista. ➤ Anyone who even comes close to this castle is going to get an arrow through the heart. ▪ Anyone who gets anywhere near this castle is going to get an arrow through the heart. Quienquiera que se acerque a este castillo recibirá una flecha que atraviese su corazón.

anyone who thinks that... ▪ whoever thinks that... quien piense así... ➤ Anyone who thinks that is kidding himself. ▪ Whoever thinks that is kidding himself. Se engaña quien piense así.

anyone with a brain can see that... ▪ anyone who has a brain can see that... cualquiera con dos dedos de frente se da cuenta de que...

anything about: to know ~ **1.** *(usu. things)* saber algo de **2.** *(usu. people)* to hear anything about saber alguna cosa de ▪ haber oído algo de alguien ➤ Do you know anything about Windows? ¿Sabes algo de Windows? ➤ Do you know anything about Stephen? ▪ Have you heard anything about Stephen? ¿Sabes alguna cosa de Esteban?

anything besides otra cosa además de ▪ otra cosa que no sea ➤ Do you have anything besides honey to put on it, like maple syrup? ¿Tienes otra cosa que no sea miel, por ejemplo sirope de arce?

anything but nada más que ▪ *(literary, journalistic)* sino ➤ I don't do anything but work. No hago nada más que trabajar. ➤ *(Horacio Quiroga)* The cub doesn't like to eat anything but bird eggs. El cachorro no quiere comer sino huevos de pájaro.

anything but! ¡cualquier cosa menos eso! ▪ ¡no, en absoluto! ➤ Is that a good movie for children?-It's anything but! ¿Es una buena película para los niños?-No, cualquier cosa menos eso. ▪ ¿Es una buena película para los niños?-No, en absoluto.

anything can happen cualquier cosa puede suceder ➤ Anything can happen between now and then. Cualquier cosa puede pasar desde ahora. ➤ Anything can happen in my life right now. Cualquier cosa puede suceder en mi vida en estos momentos.

anything else? 1. *(asked by a store clerk)* ¿alguna cosa más? **2.** *(physician taking patient's medical history)* ¿más cosas?

anything goes vale todo ▪ todo vale

anything interesting algo interesante ➤ Is there anything interesting in the paper today? ¿Hay algo interesante en el periódico hoy?

anything that does something ▪ whatever does something todo lo que haga algo ➤ Anything that stimulates circulation in the muscles helps keep them in shape. Todo lo que active la circulación en los músculos ayuda a mantenerlos en forma.

anything to drink algo de beber ▪ algo para beber ➤ Do you want anything to drink? ¿Quieres algo de beber? ▪ ¿Quieres algo para beber? ➤ I haven't had anything to drink. *(liquid of any kind)* No he bebido nada. ▪ *(alcohol specifically)* No he probado ni una gota (de alcohol). ▪ No he probado trago.

anything to eat algo de comer ▪ algo para comer ➤ Do you want anything to eat? ¿Quieres algo de comer? ▪ ¿Quieres algo para comer?

anything to wear algo que ponerse ▪ algo para ponerse ➤ Do you have anything to wear to the wedding? ▪ Do you have anything to wear for the wedding? ¿Tienes algo que ponerte para la boda? ➤ I don't have anything to wear to day. No tengo nada que ponerme hoy.

anything will do (for me) cualquier cosa (me) valdrá

anything wrong 1. *(with "do you see")* algo fuera de lugar ▪ algo que no cuadra ▪ algo que no va **2.** *(with "is there")* algo mal ➤ Do you see anything wrong here? ¿Ves algo fuera de lugar? ▪ ¿Ves algo que no cuadra? ▪ ¿Ves algo que no va? ➤ Is there anything wrong? ▪ Is something wrong? ¿Hay algo mal?

anytime! *(informal)* ▪ you're welcome! ▪ don't mention it! ¡cuando quieras! ▪ ¡muchas veces! ▪ ¡de nada! ➤ Thank you for helping me.-Anytime. Muchas gracias por tu ayuda.-Cuando quieras. ▪ Muchas gracias por tu ayuda.-Muchas veces. ▪ Muchas gracias por tu ayuda.-De nada.

anytime now en cualquier momento a partir de ahora ▪ en cualquier momento a partir de ya ▪ de un momento a otro ▪ any day now de hoy a mañana

anytime of day or night a cualquier hora del día ➤ You can call me at anytime of day or night. Me puedes llamar a cualquier hora del día.

anytime one wants (to) ▪ whenever one wants to a la hora que uno quiera ▪ cuando (así lo) quiera ➤ We can leave anytime you want (to). Podemos irnos a la hora que quieras. ▪ Podemos irnos cuando (así lo) quieras.

anytime soon en breve ▪ pronto ▪ a corto plazo ➤ The government is not going to make the information public anytime soon. El gobierno no hará la información pública en breve.

anyway, as I was saying... aparte, como decía... ▪ en fin, como decía...

anyway, getting back to what I was saying... aparte, volviendo a lo que estaba diciendo... ▪ aparte, como iba diciendo

anywhere between cualquier lugar entre ▪ cualquier sitio entre ➤ We can stop anywhere between Madrid and Barcelona. Podemos parar en cualquier lugar entre Madrid y Barcelona. ▪ Podemos parar en cualquier sitio entre Madrid y Barcelona.

anywhere else to turn: not to have ~ no tener a donde acudir ➤ I didn't have anywhere else to turn. No tenía a donde acudir.

anywhere from *x* to *y* (cualquier punto) entre *x* e *y* ▪ de *x* a *y* ➤ Anywhere from ten to twenty. (Cualquier punto) entre diez y veinte. ▪ De diez a veinte.

anywhere: to have to go ~ ▪ to have to be anywhere tener que ir a algún lado ➤ Do you have to be anywhere this afternoon? ¿Tienes que ir a algún lado esta tarde?

anywhere to go: to have ~ tener adonde ir ▪ tener algún sitio donde ir ➤ Do you have anywhere to go this afternoon? ¿Tienes adonde ir esta tarde? ▪ ¿Tienes algún sitio donde ir esta tarde?

apart from ▪ except for a excepción de ▪ a parte de eso

apart from that ▪ other than that ▪ otherwise ▪ except for that aparte de eso ▪ además de eso

apartment building edificio de apartamentos ▪ *el* bloque de pisos ▪ *(especially studios and one-bedroom apartments)* bloque de apartamentos

apartment complex *la* urbanización

apartments for rent apartamentos para alquilar ▪ apartamentos que se alquilan ▪ *(Sp.)* pisos de alquilar ▪ pisos que se alquilan ▪ *(L. Am., less common)* departamentos para alquilar

apex of a triangle *la* cúspide de un triángulo

apocryphal story cuento apócrifo ▪ historia apócrifa

to **apologize for something** pedir disculpas por algo ▪ disculparse por algo ➤ We apologize for any inconvenience caused by the airport security procedures. Nos disculpamos por cualquier molestía causada por los procedimientos de seguridad aeroportuaria. ➤ I apologize for being late. Discúlpame por llegar tarde.

to **apologize to someone for something** pedir disculpas a alguien por algo ▪ disculparse con alguien por algo ▪ disculparse ante alguien por algo

Appalachian chain Sierra de los Apalaches ▪ Cordillera de los Apalaches

Appalachian Mountains *(range extending from Quebec to northern Alabama) los* (Montes) Apalaches

Appalachian Trail Senda de los Apalaches ➤ The Appalachian Trail is an ancient Native American trail extending from Quebec to Alabama. La Senda de los Apalaches es una sende antigua de los norteamericanos nativos que se extiende desde Quebec hasta Alabama.

apparently not parece que no ▪ por lo visto, no ▪ según parece, no

apparently so parece que sí ▪ aparentemente sí ▪ por lo visto, sí ▪ según parece, sí

to **appeal a case** apelar un caso

to **appeal a decision to a higher court** apelar una decisión a un tribunal superior ▪ apelar una decisión a un tribunal de (una) instancia más alta ➤ The lawyers appealed the decision in the case to a higher court. Los abogados apelaron la decisión del caso a un tribunal superior. ▪ Los abogados apelaron la decisión del caso a un tribunal de (una) instancia más alta.

to **appeal a ruling** apelar un decreto

to **appeal for calm** llamar a la calma ▪ hacer un llamamiento a la calma ▪ hacer una invitación a la calma

to **appeal the conviction** recurrir la condena ▪ apelar la condena

to **appeal to a higher authority** apelar a una instancia superior to **appeal to an audience** interesarle a una audiencia ➤ Classical organists don't usually appeal to young people, but Virgil Fox with his laser light show was the notable exception. Los organistas clásicos no suelen interesarle a los jóvenes, pero Virgil Fox con su espectáculo de luces láser era la excepción notable.

to **appeal to the emotions** apelar a las emociones ➤ Advertisers often very successfully appeal to our emotions. Los publicistas apelan a menudo exitosamente a nuestras emociones.

appeals court ▪ court of appeals *el* tribunal de apelaciones

to **appear at a press conference** comparecer ante la prensa

to **appear at the door** ▪ to stand in the doorway ▪ to come to the door asomarse a la puerta ▪ aparecer en la puerta

to **appear at the scene** aparecer en el lugar ▪ aparecer en la escena ➤ Many onlookers appeared at the scene of the accident. Muchos curiosos aparecieron en el lugar del accidente. ➤ The criminal later appeared at the scene of his crime. El delincuente apareció después en la escena del crimen.

to **appear before a (Congressional) committee** comparecer ante un comité (del Congreso)

to **appear before Congress** ▪ to go before Congress comparecer ante el Congreso

to **appear before the judge** comparecer ante el juez ▪ presentarse ante el juez

to **appear in a scene** salir en una escena ▪ aparecer en una escena ➤ Falstaff appears in the first scene of the first act. Falstaff sale en la primera escena del primer acto. ▪ Falstaff aparece en la primera escena del primer acto.

to **appear in court** comparecer ante el tribunal ▪ presentarse ante el tribunal

to **appear in public** ▪ to make public appearances presentarse en público ➤ The young musician began to appear in public at the age of eight. El joven músico empezó a presentarse en público cuando tenía ocho años.

to **appear in the census** ▪ to be listed in the census ▪ to be found in the census figurar en el censo

to **appear in the directory** ▪ to be listed in the directory ▪ to be found in the directory figurar en el directorio

to **appear in the telephone directory** ▪ to be listed in the telephone directory ▪ to be found in the telephone directory figurar en la guía telefónica

to **appear in the window** ▪ to come to the window asomarse a la ventana ➤ The superstar came to the window to wave to her fans. La superestrella se asomó a la ventana para saludar (con la mano) a sus aficionados.

to **appear on a list** figurar en una lista ➤ Her name doesn't appear on the list. Su nombre no figura en esta lista.

to **appear on the balcony** ▪ to come out onto the balcony asomar al balcón ▪ salir al balcón ➤ The Real Madrid players appeared on the balcony to greet their fans. Los jugadores del Real Madrid se asomaron al balcón para saludar a sus seguidores.

to **appear on the scene** tener sus orígenes ▪ aparecer en escena ▪ entrar en escena ➤ The pipe organ appeared on the scene in fifth-century Rome to attract people to the circus. El órgano de cañones tiene sus orígines en la Roma del Siglo V (quinto) y lo utilizaban para atraer a la gente al circo.

to **appear out of nowhere** ▪ to appear out of the blue salir de la nada ▪ aparecer de la nada ▪ aparecer de Dios sabe dónde

to **appear out of the blue** ▪ to appear out of nowhere salir de la nada ▪ aparecer de la nada ▪ aparecer de Dios sabe dónde

to **appear to be** parecer

appearance before Congress intervención ante el Congreso ➤ In his last appearance before Congress, the president... En su última intervención ante el Congreso, el presidente...

appearance before the court ▪ court appearance comparecencia ante el tribunal

appearance before the press comparecencia ante la prensa

appearances are deceiving las apariencias engañan ▪ ojo, que la vista engaña

appeasement policy ▪ policy of appeasement política de apaciguamiento ▪ política de aplacamiento

to **applaud something** ▪ to praise something alabar algo

to **applaud in unison** ▪ to applaud in rhythm aplaudir al compás ▪ aplaudir al unísono ➤ After the show the audience applauded in unison. Después del espectáculo la audiencia aplaudió al compás.

apple of one's eye la niña de los ojos de uno

to be an **apple polisher** *(L. Am.)* jalar bolas ▪ *(Sp.)* ser un(a) pelota

apples and oranges: to mix ~ ▪ to compare apples and oranges mezclar churras con merinas ▪ mezclar peras con manzanas

application fee tasa de solicitud de inscripción

application form: to fill out the ~ rellenar el formulario de solicitud

application forms (for university admission) **1.** *los* papeles de matrícula ▪ hojas de inscripción ▪ ficha de inscripción ▪ solicitud de inscripción **2.** application packet *el* sobre de matrícula

application forms for the graduate program in Spanish hojas de solicitud para el programa de postgrado en Filología Hispánica

application packet *(containing all the forms) el* sobre de matrícula

applied technology tecnología aplicada

to **apply for a job** solicitar un trabajo

to **apply for a loan** solicitar un préstamo

to **apply for a passport** hacer el pasaporte ▪ *(L. Am.)* sacarse el pasaporte ➤ When I was applying for my passport... Cuando estaba haciendo mi pasaporte... ▪ Cuando me estaba sacando el pasaporte...

to **apply for a scholarship** solicitar una beca

to **apply for admission to the graduate program in Spanish** solicitar admisión en el programa de postgrado en Filología Hispánica

to **apply (for admission) to a university** solicitar la admisión a una universidad ▪ solicitar el ingreso a una universidad

to **apply for the master's program** introducir los papeles para matricularse en el máster ➤ I would like to apply for the master's program in Spanish. Me gustaría introducir los papeles para el programa de máster en Filología Hispánica.

to **apply medicine to the skin** aplicar medicamento a la piel

to **apply oneself** aplicarse

to **apply paint, lacquer, etc.** aplicar la pintura, laca, etc. ➤ The best method is to thin the lacquer and apply several light coats. ▪ The best method is to thin the lacquer and apply several thin coats. La mejor manera de aplicar la laca es diluirla y aplicar varias capas finas.

to **apply pressure to a wound** ▪ to apply pressure on a wound hacer un torniquete ➤ The paramedics applied pressure to the wound to stop the bleeding. El equipo de primeros auxilios hizo un torniquete para detener la hemorragia.

to **apply pressure to something** ▪ to put pressure on something aplicar presión a algo ▪ ejercer presión a algo ▪ poner presión a algo ▪ aplicar presión sobre algo ▪ ejercer presión sobre algo ▪ poner presión sobre algo ➤ The pressure applied by the clamps to the glued pieces will make them stronger when the glue is dry. La presión aplicada por las abrazaderas a las piezas encoladas las reforzará una vez secas.

to **apply to a circumstance** aplicarse a una circunstancia ➤ The "s" on third-person singular verbs applies only to the present tense. La letra "s" en los verbos de tercera persona singular se aplica sólo al tiempo presente.

to **apply to a university** ▪ to apply for admission to a university solicitar la admisión en una universidad ▪ solicitar el ingreso en una universidad ➤ He applied (for admission) to the National Autonomous University of Mexico. Él solicitó la admisión en la Universidad Nacional Autónoma de México. ▪ Él solicitó el ingreso en la Universidad Nacional Autónoma de México.

appraisal of performance ▪ performance appraisal evaluación de rendimiento (del empleado)

appraisal of the situation evaluación de la situación ➤ What's your appraisal of the situation? ¿Cuál es tu apreciación de la situación?

to **appraise a piece of property** valorar una propiedad ▪ *(especially for tax purposes)* tasar una propiedad

to **appraise property** valorar propiedades *(especially for tax purposes)* tasar propiedades

to **appraise the situation** evaluar la situación

appraised value valor tasado

to **appreciate someone's help** agradecerle la ayuda a alguien ▪ *(archaic)* quedarle muy reconocido por su ayuda ➤ I appreciate your help. Te agradezco la ayuda. ▪ Te quedo muy reconocido por su ayuda.

appreciate the fact that... valorar que...

to **appreciate the importance of** valorar la importancia de

to be **appreciative of** ▪ to be grateful for quedar agradecido de ▪ valorar (mucho) ➤ He was very appreciative of your efforts. Él quedó muy agradecido de tus esfuerzos. ▪ Él valoró mucho tus esfuerzos.

to **apprehend a suspect** ▪ to detain a suspect ▪ to take a suspect into custody aprehender a un sospechoso ▪ detener a un sospechoso ▪ poner a un sospecho bajo custodia justicial ➤ Some potential suspects were apprehended for questioning. ▪ Some potential suspects were detained for questioning. ▪ Some potential suspects were taken into custody for questioning. Algunos potenciales sospechosos fueron aprehendidos para ser interrogados. ▪ Algunos potenciales sospechosos fueron detenidos para ser interrogados. ▪ Algunos potenciales sospechosos fueron puestos bajo custodia judicial para ser interrogados.

to **approach a deadline 1.** acercarse a la fecha límite ▪ acercarse a la fecha tope **2.** *(imminent)* aproximarse a la fecha límite ➤ We are rapidly approaching the April 15 deadline. ▪ The April 15 deadline is rapidly approaching. Nos acercamos rápidamente a la fecha límite del quince de abril. ▪ Nos aproximamos rápidamente a la fecha límite del quince de abril.

approach-avoidance conflict *(psychology)* conflicto de aproximación-evitación

approach lights *(to a runway) las* luces de posición ▪ luces de acercamiento

to **approach someone about a matter** ▪ to approach someone with a matter abordarle a alguien con un asunto

to **approach someone about something** acercarse a alguien (sobre algo) ▪ mostrarse interesado en ➤ The South American player approached Real Madrid. El jugador sudaméricano se mostró interesado en (jugar para) el Real Madrid.

to **approach someone for money** pedir dinero prestado a alguien

to **approach the problem** ▪ to deal strategically with the problem manejar el problema ▪ abordar el problema ➤ You'll know how to approach the problem. Sabrás cómo manejar el problema.

approach to a problem ▪ way of solving a problem enfoque de un problema ▪ método de abordar un problema ▪ método de enfrentarse a un problema ▪ manera de enfocar un problema ▪ manera de abordar un problema ▪ manera de enfrentarse a un problema ▪ forma de enfocar un problema ▪ forma de abordar un problema ▪ forma de enfrentarse a un problema

approach to teaching ▪ teaching method método de enseñanza ➤ Audiolingual approach versus the natural approach to language teaching El método audiolingüístico en contra del método natural en la enseñanza de la lengua

appropriate authorities ▪ relevant authorities *las* autoridades pertinentes

appropriate behavior conducta apropiada

appropriate dress for the occasion vestido indicado para la ocasión

approval of one's superiors: to have the ~ ▪ to be in the good graces of one's superiors tener la aprobación de los superiores ▪ tener el visto bueno de sus superiores ➤ You need the approval of the boss. Necesitas la aprobación del jefe. ▪ Necesitas el visto bueno del jefe.

to **approve a degree** homologar un título ➤ The education ministry has to approve my degree and weight my credits. El ministerio de educación tiene que homologar mi título y equiparar mis créditos.

to **approve of** aprobar ▪ estar de acuerdo con

to **approve of one's performance** aprobar su gestión ➤ Sixty-three percent of Americans approve of the president's performance. Sesenta y tres por ciento de estadounidenses aprueban la gestión del presidente.

to **approve of wholeheartedly** ▪ to approve wholeheartedly of ▪ to endorse without reservations aprobar sin reservas

approved absence justificativo de ausencia ▪ justificante de ausencia ➤ The student must present an approved absence form. El estudiante debe presentar un justificativo de ausencia. ▪ El estudiante debe presentar un justificante de ausencia.

to be **approved of** ▪ to be well seen estar bien visto ▪ estar bien considerado

April day un día abrileño

April Fool's Day *(its Spanish equivalent falls on December 28) el* Día de los Inocentes

April showers bring May flowers marzo ventoso, y abril lluvioso, sacan a mayo florido y hermoso

apropos of ▪ concerning ▪ with regard to ▪ regarding ▪ with reference to a propósito de ➤ Apropos of your suggestion... ▪ Regarding your suggestion... A propósito de su sugerencia...

apt comment comentario acertado

apt phrase ▪ appropriate phrase ▪ suitable phrase frase acertada

to be **apt to** ser apto para ▪ ser propenso a ▪ ser facilque ▪ ser probable que ➤ The coiled snake is apt to strike at any moment. La víbora enroscada es propensa a arremeter en cualquier momento.

arc second *(geometry)* ▪ second of an arc segundo de arco

architect of the policy *el* artífice de la política

architectural landmark hito arquitectónico

ardent Catholic ▪ devout Catholic católico ferviente ▪ católico devoto ▪ católico apostólico romano

ardent fan fanático efusivo

arduous task trabajo arduo

are both coinciden ➤ *(headline)* Woody Allen and Bruce Springsteen are both in Madrid today. Woody Allen y Bruce Springsteen coinciden en Madrid hoy.

are there any questions? ▪ do you have any questions? ¿hay preguntas? ▪ ¿alguna pregunta?

are they not? ▪ aren't they? ¿no? ▪ ¿no, los son? ▪ ¿no, lasson? ▪ ¿verdad? ▪ ¿es verdad? ▪ ¿no es verdad? ▪ ¿no le parace? ▪ ¿no crees? ➤ The commemorative coins you need are quarters, are they not? Las monedas comemorativas que necesitas son cuartos de dólar, ¿no (las son)?

are we on for tomorrow? ¿quedamos mañana? ▪ ¿está en pie lo de mañana?

are we still on for tomorrow? *(coll.)* ¿sigue en pie lo de mañana? ▪ ¿todavía estamos para mañana? ▪ ¿aún estamos para mañana?

are we supposed to bring something to the party? ¿se supone que hay que llevar algo a la fiesta? ▪ ¿se supone que tenemos que llevar algo a la fiesta?

are you asleep? ¿duermes? ▪ ¿estás dormido?

are you awake? ¿estás despierto?

are you being helped? ▪ have you been helped? *(tú)* ¿te atienden? ▪ *(usted)* ¿le atienden? ▪ *(between tú and usted)* ¿lo atienden? ▪ ¿la atienden? ▪ ¿lo han atendido? ▪ ¿la han atendido?

are you coming or staying? ¿vienes o te quedas?

are you decent? ▪ is it safe to come in? ¿se puede pasar?

are you doing okay?-better than ever! ¿estás bien?-¡como nunca!

are you feeling okay? ¿te encuentras bien?

are you hungry? *(tú)* ¿tienes hambre? ▪ *(usted)* ¿tiene (usted) hambre? ➤ Are you hungry?-Not very. ¿Tienes hambre?-Poca. ➤ Are you hungry?-Very. ¿Tienes hambre?-Mucha.

are you in line? ¿está usted en la cola? ▪ *(Sp.)* ¿está usted en la fila? ▪ *(L. Am.)* ¿está usted haciendo la cola?

are you in this class? ¿estás en esta clase? ▪ ¿estás en este curso?

are you just going to sit there and keep bawling? ¿vas a quedarte ahí llorando?

are you moving? 1. are you going to move? ¿te mudas? ▪ ¿te trasladas? ▪ ¿te cambias? 2. are you in the process of moving? ¿te estás mudando?

are you new? ▪ is this your first time here? ¿eres nuevo(-a) por aquí?

are you on...? 1. *(asking a person over the telephone his or her location)* ¿estás (situado) en...? ▪ ¿está usted (situado) en...? 2. *(asking over the telephone the location of a business)* ¿está la tienda (situada) en... ➤ Are you on Constitution? ▪ Are you located on Constitution Ave.? ¿Está (situado) en la Avenida Constitución?

are you open? ¿está abierta (la tienda)? ▪ ¿está abierto (el taller)? ▪ ¿están abiertos? ➤ Are you open on Sundays? ¿Están abiertos los domingos?

are you presentable? ¿estás presentable?

are you ready? ¿estás listo? ▪ ¿estás preparado?

are you ready to go? 1. *(a él)* ¿estás listo para marchar? ▪ *(a ella)* ¿estás lista para marchar? 2. shall we be on our way? ¿nos vamos (yendo)? ▪ ¿vamos saliendo?

are you related to...? ¿estás familiarizado con...?

are you speaking to me? *(tú)* ¿te diriges a mí? ▪ *(usted)* ¿se dirige (usted) a mí?

are you still serving? ¿está abierta la cocina? ▪ ¿tienes cocina ahora? ▪ ¿están sirviendo aún? ▪ ¿todavía están sirviendo? ➤ Are you still serving breakfast? ¿Están sirviendo el desayuno aún? ▪ ¿Todavía están sirviendo el desayuno?

are you still there? ¿todavía sigues allí?

are you the one who did it? ¿ha sido tú que lo ha hecho? ▪ *(to a man)* ¿has sido tú el que lo ha hecho? ▪ *(to a woman)* ¿has sido tú la que lo ha hecho

are you trying to provoke me? ¿quieres provocarme?

are you up? ¿estás levantado(-a)?

area map ▪ map of the area 1. *(street map)* plano de la zona 2. *(geopolitical and highway map)* mapa de la zona

area of discussion tema específico de la discusión

area of high pressure *(weather)* ▪ high pressure area *el* anticiclón

area of low pressure *(weather)* ▪ low pressure area borrasca

area surrounding a city ▪ outlying areas of a city ▪ outlying areas around a city extrarradio de una ciudad

aren't we all! who isn't? ▪ you're not the only one! ¿quién no lo está? ▪ ¡no eres el único! ▪ ¿no lo estamos todos?

argue a case before a court debatir el caso ante el tribunal ▪ debatir el caso ante la corte

to **argue about** discutir sobre ➤ *(playing kick ball)* The children are arguing about whose turn it is to kick. Los niños están discutiendo sobre a quien le toca dar la pelota.

to **argue back to someone** ▪ to take issue with someone ▪ to take the opposite point of view llevar la contraria a alguien ▪ contestarle a alguien

to **argue heatedly** discutir acaloradamente ▪ andar en dares y tomares

to **argue meticulously** discutir meticulosamente

to **argue that...** *(before a court, etc.)* plantear que...

argument against argumento contra

the **argument has holes in it** el argumento tiene agujeros

the **argument is full of holes** el argumento está lleno de agujeros

the **argument stands up** el argumento se sostiene

the **argument would stand up better...** el argumento se sostendría más...

argyle socks calcetines de rombos

to **arise from** obedecer a ▪ surgir de ▪ proceder de ▪ venir de ➤ It arises from a lack of respect. Obedece a una falta de respeto. ▪ Surge de una falta de respeto. ▪ Procede de una falta de respeto.

arithmetic mean media aritmética

Ark of the Covenant Arca de la Alianza

arm in arm: to go ~ ▪ to walk arm in arm ir del bracete ▪ ir cogidos del brazo

arm of a chair brazo de una silla

to **arm oneself to the teeth** armarse hasta los dientes

arm twisting: to engage in ~ ▪ to twist someone's arm torcerle el brazo a alguien

to **arm wrestle** echar un pulso

to be **armed and dangerous** estar armado y ser peligroso ➤ The police described the assailants as armed and dangerous. La policía describió a los atracadores como armados y peligrosos.

armed camp campamento armado

to be **armed to the teeth** estar armado hasta los dientes

armor plated ▪ armored ▪ plated blindado ▪ acorazado

armored truck camión blindado ▪ camión acorazado

armpit of the world culo del mundo

arms race carrera armamentista ▪ carrera armamentística

army ants hormigas legionarias

army ants: invasion of ~ marabunta ➤ The invasion of army ants levelled the grazing field. La marabunta arrasó el pasto.

army brat *(coll.)* hijo(-a) de un miembro de las fuerzas armadas

army green *el* verde caqui

around and around: to go ~ dar vueltas y vueltas ➤ We went around and around and never resolved anything. Dimos vueltas y vueltas y nunca resolvimos nada. ➤ We went around and around, but never spotted the house. Dimos vueltas y vueltas, pero nunca ubicamos la casa.

around April of next year por abril del año que viene

around her en torno a ella ▪ en torno suyo ▪ alrededor de ella ▪ alrededor suyo

around here (por) aquí ➤ How do you get waited on around here? ¿Cómo hago para ser atendido aquí? ➤ Is there anybody around here? ¿Hay alguien (por) aquí? ➤ What have they got against street numbers around here? ¿Qué tienen en contra de los números de la calle por aquí?

to be **around here somewhere** ▪ to be around here someplace estar por aquí en algún lado ▪ quedar por aquí ▪ estar en alguna parte por aquí cerca ➤ It's around here somewhere. Está por aquí en algún lado. ➤ I knew it was around here someplace. Sabía que estaba por ahí en algún lado. ➤ The ATM machine is around here somewhere. El cajero automático queda en algún sitio por aquí. ▪ El cajero automático está en algún sitio por aquí.

around him en torno a él ▪ en torno suyo ▪ alrededor de él ▪ alrededor suyo

around one: the people ~ la gente que rodea a uno ➤ *(quote cited in a newspaper)* My dream is to be happy and to make the people around me happy. Mi sueño es ser feliz y hacer felices a quienes me rodean.

around Robin Hood's barn: to go ~ ▪ to go way out of the way dar un gran rodeo ➤ To drive from Roanoke, Virginia, to Pittsburgh, Pennsylvania, you have to go around Robin Hood's barn. ▪ To drive from Roanoke, Virginia, to Pittsburgh, Pennsylvania, you have to go way (the hell) out of the way. Para conducir desde Roanoke, Virginia, a Pittsburgh, Pensilvania, hay que dar un gran rodeo.

around that time ▪ at about that time 1. *(all contexts)* por entonces ▪ por aquel entonces 2. *(minutes or hours)* alrededor de esa hora

to be **around the block** *(Sp.)* estar al otro lado de la manzana ▪ quedar al otro lado de la manzana ▪ *(L. Am.)* estar al otro lado de la cuadra ▪ quedar al otro lado de la cuadra ➤ The hardware store is around the block from here. La ferretería está al otro lado de la manzana. ▪ La ferretería queda al otro lado de la manzana. ▪ La ferretería está al otro lado de la cuadra. ▪ La ferretería queda al otro lado de la cuadra.

around the block: not to have been ~ no conocer el patio ➤ The candidate comes across like a little kid who hasn't been around the block yet. El candidato da la impresión de ser como un niño que no conoce el patio.

around the block: to drive ~ *(L. Am.)* conducir (alrededor de) la cuadra ▪ *(Sp.)* conducir alrededor de la manzana ➤ I'll drive around the block while you go in. Conduzco alrededor de la manzana mientras tú entras. ▪ Conduzco (alrededor de) la cuadra mientras entras.

around the block: to go ~ *(L. Am.)* recorrer la cuadra ▪ *(Sp.)* recorrer la manzana

around the block: to live ~ *(L. Am.)* vivir al otro lado de la cuadra ▪ *(Sp.)* vivir al otro lado de la manzana ➤ They live around the block from here. Viven al otro lado de la manzana desde aquí. ▪ Viven al otro lado de la cuadra desde aquí.

around the campfire: to huddle ~ agacharse alrededor de la fogata ▪ *(poetic)* agacharse alrededor de la hoguera

around the clock continuamente ▪ a todas horas ➤ Her father has required around-the-clock care since his stroke. Su padre (de ella) ha requerido atención continua desde su derrame.

to be **around the corner** estar a la vuelta de la esquina ▪ quedar a la vuelta de la esquina ➤ The hardware store is right around the corner from here. La ferretería está justo a la vuelta de la esquina desde aquí. ▪ La ferretería queda justo a la vuelta de la esquina desde aquí.

around the corner: to go ~ ir a la vuelta de la esquina

around the corner: to live ~ vivir a la vuelta de la esquina

around the country ▪ around the nation ▪ nationwide ▪ countrywide por todo el territorio nacional

around the fire: to sit ~ sentarse en torno al fuego

around the house 1. *(inside)* por (la) casa ▪ alrededor de la casa **2.** *(outside)* alrededor de la casa

around the house: to go ~ dar la vuelta a la casa ▪ ir alrededor de la casa

around the house: to hang ~ holgazanear por (la) casa ▪ hacer el vago por (la) casa ▪ flojear por (la) casa ➤ We've been hanging around the house all day. Let's go play some basketball. Hemos estado holgazaneando alrededor de la casa todo el día. Vamos a jugar un poco de baloncesto.

around the house: to putter ~ estar en casa relajándose

around the mountain alrededor de la montaña

around the time of ▪ about the time of hacia la época de

around the world 1. *(refers to travel and takes the verb "dar")* la vuelta al mundo **2.** all over the world ▪ throughout the world en el mundo ▪ en todo el mundo ➤ *(Jules Verne novel) Around the World in Eighty Days La vuelta al mundo en ochenta días* ➤ *(headline)* More than five million children around the world die of hunger every year. Más de cinco millones de niños mueren al año en el mundo a causa del hambre.

around there por allá

around this time 1. about this time ▪ right about now ahora ▪ a eso de la(s) *x* horas **2.** *(historical narrative)* alrededor de este tiempo ▪ por aquel entonces ▪ por aquella época ▪ sobre esos días

around this time last year el año pasado por estas fechas

around this time (of year): to happen ~ ocurrir por estas fechas

around to it: to get ~ ponerse con algo ➤ I still haven't gotten around to it. Todavía no me he puesto con ello. ➤ I hadn't gotten around to it. No me había puesto con ello.

around town ▪ locally en toda la ciudad ▪ en todo el pueblo ▪ en los alrededores ▪ *(literary, journalistic)* en todo el contorno

around *x* dollars a barrel en torno a *x* dólares por barril ▪ alrededor de los *x* dólares por barril

around *x* o'clock ▪ at about *x* o'clock ▪ at around *x* o'clock a eso de la(s) *x* ▪ *hacia eso de la(s) x* ▪ alrededor de la(s) *x* de la tarde ➤ Around two in the afternoon ▪ At about two in the afternoon A eso de dos de la tarde ▪ Alrededor de las dos de la tarde ▪ Aproximadamente a las dos de la tarde ▪ Más o menos a las dos de la tarde

to be **around *x* years old** ▪ to be around *x* years of age rondar (ya) los *x* años ➤ She's around twenty. ▪ She's about twenty. Ronda ya los veinte años.

to **arouse a feeling of** provocar un sentimiento de ▪ surgir un sentimiento de

to **arouse one's curiosity** ▪ to pique one's curiosity ▪ to get one's curiosity up picar la curiosidad

to **arouse someone sexually** excitar a alguien sexualmente

to **arouse someone's anger** ▪ to provoke someone's anger desatar la ira de alguien ▪ provocar la ira de alguien

to **arouse suspicion(s) that...** ▪ to raise suspicion(s) that... ▪ to awaken suspicion(s) that... ▪ to arouse the suspicion that... ▪ to raise the suspicion that... ▪ to awaken the suspicion that... ▪ to provoke the suspicion that... despertar sospechas de que... ▪ levantar sospechas de que... ▪ causar sospechas de que...

to **arrange a pickup** ▪ to schedule a pickup acordar para que vengan a recoger algo ▪ acordar para que vengan a buscar algo

to **arrange a time** acordar una hora

to **arrange (for)** acordar (para que) ➤ I'd like to arrange (for) a pickup. Me gustaría acordar una recogida. ➤ I'd like to arrange for UPS to pick it up. Me gustaría acordar con UPS para que lo recoja. ➤ I'd like to arrange for someone to get me at the airport. Me gustaría acordar con alguien para que pasen por mí al aeropuerto. ▪ Me gustaría acordar con alguien para que me busquen al aeropuerto.

arrange music arreglar música ▪ adaptar música

to **arrange the delivery for a certain day** ▪ to set the delivery for a certain day acordar la entrega para un día específico

to **arrange to meet** cuadrar (con alguien) para quedar ▪ acordar cuando nos encontramos ➤ Call me and we can arrange to meet. Llámame y podemos cuadrar para quedar.

arrested development desarrollo limitado ▪ desarrollo lento

arrival time hora de llegada

to **arrive at a conclusion** llegar a una conclusión ▪ sacar una conclusión

to **arrive at a place** ▪ to get to a place llegar a un lugar ➤ We arrived at the airport at 3 p.m. ▪ We got to the airport at 3 p.m. Llegamos al aeropuerto a las 3 p.m.

to **arrive at the scene of an accident** llegar a la escena de un accidente ▪ llegar al lugar de un accidente

to **arrive early 1.** to arrive ahead of schedule *(L. Am.)* llegar temprano ▪ *(Sp.)* llegar pronto **2.** to arrive before one is supposed to llegar antes de tiempo ▪ llegar con anticipación ▪ llegar adelantado

to **arrive in a place** ▪ to get to a place llegar a un lugar ▪ llegar a un sitio ➤ We arrived in Atlanta at 3 p.m. ▪ We got to Atlanta at 3 p.m. Llegamos a Atlanta a las 3 p.m.

to **arrive in time for something** llegar a tiempo para algo ➤ We arrived in time for supper. Llegamos a tiempo para la cena.

to **arrive in time to do something** llegar a tiempo para hacer algo ➤ We arrived in time to have supper. Llegamos a tiempo para cenar.

to **arrive late 1.** *(planes, trains, buses, etc.)* to arrive behind schedule *(L. Am.)* llegar atrasado ▪ *(Sp.)* llegar con retraso **2.** *(social or business)* to arrive after one is supposed to llegar tarde

to **arrive on the scene** entrar en escena

to **arrive on the scene of the accident** ▪ to arrive at the scene of an accident llegar al lugar del accidente

to **arrive on time** llegar a tiempo ▪ llegar puntualmente ▪ llegar en forma puntual

arriving late ▪ who arrive late que llegue(n) tarde ▪ que llegue(n) retrasados ▪ *(journalistis, litarary)* llegar en forma impuntual ➤ Students arriving late must get permission to enter class. Los estudiantes que lleguen tarde deben obtener un permiso para entrar a clase.

art for art's sake ▪ l'art pour l'art el arte por el arte

art lover *el, la* amante del arte

article of clothing prenda (de vestir)

Articles of Confederation *(U.S. governmental charter from 1776 to 1789)* Artículos de Confederación

artificial sweetener endulzante ▪ edulcorante

the **artists of the world are never puritans, and seldom even ordinarily respectable** *(H. L. Mencken)* los artistas del mundo nunca son (unos) puritanos, y rara vez resultan siquiera medianamente respetables

arts and crafts artes y oficios

as a child de niño ▪ cuando niño ▪ de pequeño

as a consequence of ▪ as a result of como consecuencia de ▪ a consecuencia de ▪ en consecuencia de ▪ como fruto de ▪ por consecuencia de

as a favor (for) como un favor (por) ▪ como una atención (por)

as a friend siendo un(-a) amigo(-a) ▪ en calidad de amigo(-a) ▪ por ser un(-a) amigo(-a) ▪ *(Sp., literary)* a título de amigo(-a)

as a (general) rule ▪ usually por lo general ▪ como regla general ▪ en general ▪ normalmente

as a gesture of goodwill ▪ as a goodwill gesture en señal de buena voluntad ▪ en ademán de buena voluntad

as a group en grupo ➤ The class went to the principal as a group. La clase fue al director en grupo.

as a hobby: to do something ~ hacer algo como hobby ▪ hacer algo como afición

as a joke de mentirijillas ▪ en plan de broma ▪ en plan de cachondeo

as a last resort como último remedio ▪ como último recurso ▪ como última opción ▪ cuando la otra opción es mucho peor ▪ en última instancia

as a matter of course como cosa corriente y normal

as a matter of fact ▪ in fact en efecto ▪ de hecho

as a matter of principle por principios ▪ por pudor

as a matter of routine por rutina ▪ por costumbre

as a Mexican (myself) siendo yo (mismo) Mexicano ▪ siendo yo (misma) Mexicana

as a practical matter como un asunto práctico

as a precaution de prevención ▪ como precaución ▪ como prevención ▪ de precaución

as a result ▪ in consequence ▪ therefore en consecuencia ▪ por consiguiente

as a result of ▪ as a consequence of en consecuencia de ▪ como consecuencia de ▪ por ▪ *(literary)* como fruto de ➤ In 1865 as a result of the assassination of President Abraham Lincoln, conspiracy theories were focused on the Confederate leaders. En 1865, como consecuencia del asesinato del presidente Abraham Lincoln, las teorías de la conspiración se enfocaron en líderes de la Confederación sureña. ➤ An eleven-year-old boy died Friday night as the result of an explosion of a sack of firecrackers. Un niño de once años murió la noche de viernes por la explosión de un saco de cohetes. ➤ As a result of the accident, Pedro received a compensation of fifty thousand pesos. A consecuencia del accidente sufrido, Pedro recibió una indemnización de cincuenta mil pesos.

as a reward for en recompensa de

as a rule ▪ as a general rule por lo general ▪ como regla general ▪ en general ▪ normalmente

as a sequel to como secuela a

as a set: to be sold ~ venderse en conjunto ▪ venderse como un set ▪ venderse como un juego

as a set: to come ~ ▪ to form a set ▪ to make up a set venir en conjunto ➤ The dress, the shoes, and the pocketbook come as a set. El vestido, los zapatos y el bolso vienen en conjunto. ➤ The bow tie and cummerbund come as a set. La corbata de moño y la faja vienen en conjunto. ▪ *(Sp.)* La pajarita y la faja vienen en conjunto.

as a sign of respect en señal de respeto

as a Spaniard (myself) siendo yo (mismo) español ▪ siendo yo (misma) española

as a student at this university como estudiante de esta universidad ▪ como estudiante de esta casa de estudios

as a whole como un todo

as agreed según lo acordado

as an adult de adulto ▪ de mayor ▪ cuando se es adulto ▪ como adulto ➤ When I was growing up I liked dogs (the) best, but as an adult I have come to like cats just as much. Cuando estaba creciendo prefería los perros, pero de adulto, me han llegado a gustar los gatos por igual.

as an act of will como un acto de voluntad

as an American (myself) siendo yo (mismo) un norteamericano ▪ siendo yo (mismo) un estadounidense ▪ siendo yo (misma) una norteamericana ▪ siendo yo (misma) una estadounidense

as an aside como un aparte

as an attachment: to send something ~ enviar algo como un adjunto ▪ enviar algo como datos adjuntos ▪ enviar algo como archivos adjuntos

as an encore: to play something ~ tocar algo como un bis ▪ interpretar algo como un bis

as an entrée ▪ for an entrée de entrada

as an example ▪ by way of example ▪ (just) to give you an example como un ejemplo ▪ por ejemplo ▪ para dar un ejemplo ▪ a guisa de ejemplo

as an expression of en ademán de ▪ como una expresión de ➤ We sent flowers as an expression of sympathy. Mandamos flores en ademán de condolencia.

as befits someone como le corresponde a alguien ➤ I bought a cheap dining table, as befits a student living in a studio apartment. Compré una mesa de comedor barata, como le corresponde a un estudiante viviendo en un apartamento tipo estudio.

as before como la vez anterior

as before: same place ~ el mismo lugar que antes

as before: same time ~ a la misma hora que antes ▪ a la misma hora de antes

as best I can recall ▪ as far as I can recall ▪ to the best of my recollection ▪ as far as I can remember hasta donde puedo recordar ▪ hasta donde puedo acordarme ▪ que yo recuerdo ▪ que (yo) me acuerdo ▪ hasta donde me acuerdo

as best I could lo mejor que pude

as big as tan grande como

as big as saucers: my eyes got ~ mis ojos se pusieron tan grandes como platos

(as) big as saucers: my eyes were ~ mis ojos estaban tan grandes como platos ▪ mis ojos quedaron tan grandes como platos ▪ me quedaron los ojos como platos

as bloody as 1. igual de sangrientos que **2.** *(exaggerated metaphor)* ▪ as contentious as igual de reñido ▪ tan encarnizado como ➤ The (New York) elections will be as bloody or more so than the presidential elections. Las elecciones (por Nueva York) serán igual de sangrientas o más que las presidenciales.

as carefully as possible con todo el cuidado posible

(as) compared to ▪ as distinguished from ▪ compared to comparado con

as contracted for ▪ as stipulated según lo pactado

to be **(as) cool as a cucumber** ▪ to be unflappable quedarse tan pancho ▪ quedarse tan fresco ▪ quedarse tan tranquilo ➤ James Bond is as cool as a cucumber under pressure. James Bond está tan pancho bajo presión. ▪ James Bond se queda tan pancho bajo presión. ▪ James Bond está tan fresco bajo presión. ▪ James Bond se queda tan fresco bajo presión. ▪ James Bond está tan tranquilo bajo presión. ▪ James Bond se queda tan tranquilo bajo presión.

to be **(as) dead as a doornail** estar más muerto que una tumba

to be **as different as night and day** ▪ to be as different as day and night ser (tan) diferentes como el día y la noche ➤ They may be identical twins, but they're as different as night and day. Puede que sean gemelas idénticas, pero son diferentes como de la noche al día.

as distinguished from ▪ (as) compared to comparado con

to be **(as) easy as pie** ▪ to be a piece of cake ser pan comido

as everyone knows como sabe todo el mundo

as something goes ▪ as far as something goes como corresponde a algo ▪ en contraste a algo ▪ comparado con algo ➤ The president's salary is low, as executive salaries go. El salario del presidente es poco comparado con otros salarios de los ejecutivos.

as expected como esperado

as was to be expected como se había de esperar

as something as something can be más algo que algo ➤ The flowers are as fake as fake can be. Las flores son más falsas que falsas. ▪ Las flores son más falsas que la falsedad.

as far as hasta ➤ I'll go with you as far as the corner. Te acompaño hasta la esquina.

as far as anyone can recall ▪ as far as anyone can remember hasta donde es posible recordar

as far as anyone can tell ▪ so far as anyone can tell hasta donde alguien pueda decir

as far as anyone could recall hasta donde era posible recordar

as far as I can recall ▪ as far as I can remember ▪ as best I can recall ▪ to the best of my recollection que yo recuerdo ▪ hasta donde me acuerdo ▪ que (yo) me acuerdo ▪ hasta donde puedo recordar ▪ hasta donde puedo acordarme

as far as I can see hasta donde puedo ver

as far as I can tell ▪ so far as I can tell hasta donde yo pueda decir

as far as I knew que yo supiera ▪ por lo que yo supiera

as far as I know ▪ so far as I know que yo sepa ▪ por lo que yo sé ▪ hasta donde yo sé

as far as I remember ▪ as far as I can remember ▪ as far as I (can) recall que yo recuerde

as far as I'm concerned en lo que a mí concierne ▪ por lo que a mí se refiere ▪ en lo que a mí respecta ▪ por lo que a mí me atañe

as far as it goes dentro de lo que cabe ▪ hasta cierto punto ▪ hasta cierto grado ➤ It's a good text as far as it goes, but it doesn't cover everything. Es un buen texto dentro de lo que cabe, pero no cubre todo.

as far as possible 1. so far as possible ▪ to the extent possible en lo posible ▪ en la medida de lo posible **2.** as far in the distance as possible hasta donde se pueda

as far as something is concerned en lo que concierne a algo ➤ As far as the solar system is concerned... En lo que concierne al sistema solar...

as far as the eye can see ▪ as far as you can see ▪ as far as one can see hasta donde alcanza la vista

to be **as far away from something as** ▪ to be as far from something as estar la distancia que hay entre ➤ Copernicus determined that Venus is not quite three-fourths as far from the sun as the Earth is. Copérnico determinó que Venus no está del todo a tres cuartos de la distancia que hay entre el sol y la tierra.

as far back as 1. *(in time)* ya en **2.** *(in space)* tan atrás como

as fast as I can 1. *(present)* tan rápido como puedo **2.** *(future)* tan rápido como pueda ➤ I'm going as fast as I can. Voy tan rápido como puedo. ➤ I'll get there as fast as I can. Llegaré tan rápido como pueda.

as fast as I could ▪ as quickly as I could ▪ as rapidly as I could tan rápido como pude ➤ I ran as fast as I could. Corrí tan rápido como pude.

as fast as his legs would carry him: he ran ~ corrió tan rápido como sus piernas se lo permitían ▪ corrió tan de prisa como sus piernas se lo permitían

as fast as its legs would carry it: the animal ran ~ el animal corrió tan rápido como sus patas se lo permitían ▪ el animal corrió tan de prisa como sus patas se lo permitían

to be **as fit as a fiddle** estar tan sano como un roble

as follows a continuación ▪ como sigue

as for en cuanto a ➤ As for me, I still wonder. En cuanto a mí, todavía me pregunto.

as for what I know en cuanto yo sé ▪ que yo sepa ➤ As for what I know about the subject... En cuanto yo sé del tema...

to be **(as) free as a bird** ser (tan) libre como un pájaro ▪ ser (tan) libre como un ave

to be **(as) fresh as a daisy** estar tan fresco como una rosa

as God is my witness a Dios pongo por testigo que ➤ As God is my witness, I'll never go hungry again. *(Scarlett O'Hara)* A Dios pongo por testigo que nunca volveré a pasar hambre.

to be **as good a place as any** ser tan buen lugar como cualquier otro

to be **as good a time as any** ser tan buen momento como cualquier otro ▪ ser tan buena hora como cualquier otra

to be **as good as** ser tan bueno como ➤ I want to see if it's as good as he says. Quiero ver si es tan bueno como dice.

to be **as good as done** ser dado por hecho

to be **as good as gold** *(said of children)* ser más bueno que el pan

to be **as good as it gets** ser lo mejor a lo que uno puede aspirar ▪ ser lo mejor que uno puede esperar ▪ ser lo mejor que puede pasar a uno ➤ For our neutered cat, a back scratch is as good as it gets. Para nuestro gato capado, rascarle la espalda es lo mejor a lo que puede aspirar. ▪ Para nuestro gato capado, rascarle la espalda es lo mejor que puede esperar.

as had been thought ▪ as was supposed como se había pensado ▪ como se suponía ➤ There are probably not as many coding genes as had been thought. Probablemente no haya tantos genes de codificación como se había pensado.

to be **as happy as a lark** *(Sp.)* estar tan feliz como unas pascuas ▪ estar más feliz que unas pascuas ▪ estar más contento que unas castañuelas

as hard as one can lo más que uno pueda ➤ "I'm wishing as hard as I can," said Cinderella. "Estoy deseándolo lo más que pueda", dijo la Cenicienta. ➤ I'm working as hard as I can. Trabajo lo más que pueda.

as hard as one has tried lo más que uno ha intentado ▪ lo más que uno ha intentado

as he likes to be called como (a él) le gusta que le llamen

as he refers to himself como se llama a sí mismo

to be **as high as a kite** ▪ to be high as a kite ▪ to be feeling no pain estar achispado

as high as it will go: to turn it up ~ ▪ to turn it up as high as it'll go ▪ to turn it all the way up ▪ to turn it up full blast **1.** *(all contexts)* subirlo a tope ▪ subirlo al máximo **2.** *(sound only)* subir lo a todo volumen ▪ subirlo a toda potencia *(Sp., colorful)* subirlo a toda pastilla **3.** *(Sp., gas)* subirlo a todo gas ▪ *(flame)* subirlo a toda llama **4.** *(electric power)* subirlo a toda potencia ➤ In the summer we have to turn up the refrigerator as high as it will go to keep everything good and cold. En el verano tenemos que subir la temperatura de la heladera al máximo para conservar todo bien frío. ➤ Our neighbor, who is deaf, turns the TV up as high as it'll go. Nuestra vecina, quien es sorda, sube el volumen de la tele a toda pastilla.

as high as it would go: to turn it up ~ subirlo al máximo ▪ *(Sp., colorful)* subirlo a toda pastilla ➤ Our neighbor, who was deaf, would turn the TV up as high as it would go. Nuestra vecina, quien era sorda, subía el volumen de la tele a toda pastilla.

to be **(as) hungry as a bear** tener más hambre que un lobo ▪ tener tanta hambre que me podría comer un caballo ▪ *(Madrid)* estar canino

as I did: to act ~ ▪ to do what I did ▪ to do as I did **1.** *(on a single occasion)* obrar como obré ▪ hacer lo que hice **2.** *(on more than one occasion)* obrar como yo obraba ▪ obrar como yo solía ➤ I acted as I did because I was desperate. ▪ I did what I did because I was desperate. Obré como obré porque estaba desesperado. ▪ Hice lo que hice porque estaba desesperado. ➤ In those days, I acted as I did because I was young. En aquella época obré como obraba, porque era joven. ➤ If I acted that way in those days, it was because I was very young. Si en aquella época obré como solía, fue porque era muy joven.

as I do como yo ▪ *(after "gustar," "encantar," etc.)* como a mí ➤ Do it as I do it. ▪ Do it the way I do it. Hazlo como yo. ➤ Catalina likes the music of Astor Piazzola as much as I do. A Catalina le gusta la música de Astor Piazzola tanto como a mí.

as I found out later según supe después ▪ como supe después ▪ según me enteré después ▪ como me enteré después ▪ según descubrí después ▪ como descubrí después *("Más tarde" can be substituted for "después" in all examples.)*

as I go along conforme avanzo ➤ I'm developing the course as I go along. Estoy desarrollando el curso conforme avanzo.

as I have said many times como he dicho muchas veces

as I have said on numerous occasions como he dicho en reiteradas ocasiones

as I have said repeatedly como he dicho repetidas veces

as I look at it 1. in the process of looking at it conforme lo miro **2.** as I see it ▪ the way I look at it ▪ in my view ▪ from my point of view en mi opinión ▪ desde mi punto de vista ▪ a mi parecer ▪ según lo veo (yo)

as I look through it conforme le echo un vistazo ▪ conforme lo hojeo ▪ conforme le doy una vuelta

as I promised (you) tal y como te (lo) prometí ➤ I'm returning this early, as I promised you I would. Te lo devuelvo temprano, tal y como te lo prometí.

as I recall según recuerdo

as I said ▪ once again como he dicho ▪ lo dicho

as I say ▪ once again como he dicho ▪ lo dicho

as I told you I would *(a ti)* tal como te dije que lo haría ▪ *(a usted)* tal como le dije (a usted) que lo haría

as I was 1. como era yo **2.** como lo estaba ➤ She's as cute as I was when I was her age. Ella es tan bonita como era yo cuando tenía su edad. ➤ He was as confused about the explanation as I was. Él estaba tan confundido con la explicación como lo estaba yo.

as I was saying como decía ▪ como (yo) iba diciendo

as I would have for igual que por ➤ When our dog got run over, I cried as I would have for a member of the family. Cuando atropellaron a nuestro perro, lloré igual que por un miembro de la familia.

as I write this 1. *(at the time of writing this)* mientras escribo esto **2.** *(in the process of writing this)* conforma escribo esto ▪ cuando escribo esto ➤ It is Wednesday morning as I write this. Es la mañana del miércoles mientras escribo esto. ▪ Es la mañana del miércoles cuando escribo esto.

as if ▪ as though como si ➤ He studied as if his whole future depended on it. ▪ He studied as though his whole future depended on it. Estudió como si su futuro dependiera de ello. ➤ As if I cared what he thinks! ¡Como si me importara lo que piensa (él)!

as if by magic como por arte de magia ▪ como por ensalmo

as if from como de ➤ The country awoke from the revolution as if from a nightmare. El país se despertó de la revolución como de una pesadilla.

as if he owned the place como Pedro por su casa

as if I didn't have anything else to do como si no tuviera otra cosa que hacer

as if it were nothing como si fuera nada ▪ como quien no dice nada

as if it were yesterday como si fuera ayer

as if nothing had happened: to act ~ actuar como si tal cosa no hubiese pasado ▪ actuar como si nada hubiese pasado ▪ actuar como si nada hubiera pasado ▪ comportarse como si nada hubiese pasado ▪ comportarse si nada hubiera pasado

as if nothing has happened: to act ~ actuar como si tal cosa no hubiese pasado ▪ actuar como si nada haya pasado ▪ comportarse como si nada haya pasado

as if one were a friend como si fuera un amigo ▪ como si fuera una amiga ➤ He spoke to me as if he were a friend. Me habló como si fuera un amigo.

as if she owned the place como Pedro por su casa

as if that weren't bad enough... como si no fuera (eso) lo suficientemente malo...

as if that weren't enough... como si eso no fuera bastante...

as if there were any doubt por si hubiera alguna duda ▪ por si hubiese alguna duda

as if to illustrate the point that... como para ilustrar la idea que... ▪ como para ulustrar el concepto que... ▪ como para ilustrar el argumento que...

as if to say como para decir ▪ como si fuera decir

as if we didn't have enough problems (already) ▪ as if we didn't have enough problems as it is ▪ that's all we needed (y) por si fuera poco ▪ como si no tuvieramos bastantes problemas

as if we had known each other all our lives como si nos hubiésemos conocido toda la vida ▪ como si nos conociésemos de toda la vida ▪ como si nos conociéramos de toda la vida

as in de ▪ como en ▪ igual que en ➤ "A" as in "Alberto"? ¿"A" de "Alberto"? ▪ ¿"A" como en "Alberto"? ▪ ¿"A" igual que en "Alberto"?

as is 1. the way it is como está ▪ como es ▪ así **2.** in its present condition tal como está ▪ tal y como lo ve ▪ como se encuentra ➤ Just leave it as is. Sólo déjalo así. ▪ Déjalo como está. ▪ Déjalo como es. ➤ Just send it as is; there's no need to wrap it. Sólo envíalo como está. No hay que envolverlo.

as (is) expected ▪ as is to be expected como es de esperar

as it appears ▪ as it appears to be como aparenta

as it can be: to be as easy no poder ser más fácil ▪ ser de lo más fácil ▪ estar chupado

as it has to be ▪ the way it has to be ▪ the way it's got to be como debe ser

as it is 1. the way it is ▪ like it is **1.** *(as a temporary condition)* como está ▪ tal como está ▪ tal y como está ▪ tal (y) como están las cosas ▪ dadas las circunstancias **2.** *(as a permanent state)* como es ▪ tal como es ▪ tal y como es ▪ según es **3.** in itself ▪ in and of itself de por sí I like it as it is. Me gusta tal (y) como esta. Yo no lo cambiaría. Lo dejaría tal (y) como está. ➤ Leave the subject as it is. Deja el tema tal y como está. ➤ I don't have enough time as it is, much less to take on an additional project. No tengo suficiente tiempo tal y como están las cosas, mucho menos para emprender un proyecto nuevo. ▪ No tengo mucho tiempo dadas las circunstancias, mucho menos para emprender nuevos proyectos.

as it should be ▪ the way it should be ▪ the way it ought to be ▪ like it ought to be **1.** *(as a temporary condition)* como debería estar ▪ tal (y) como debería estar **2.** *(as a permanent state, as is customary)* como debería ser ▪ tal (y) como debería ser ➤ I hung the picture over the mantle, as it should be. He colgado el cuadro sobre la repisa, tal y como debería estar. ➤ And that's as it should be. Y es tal (y) como debería ser. ➤ The bride will wear white as is customary. Tal y como debería ser, a novia vestirá de blanco.

as it stands ▪ as things stand tal como está (la cosa) ➤ As it stands right now... Tal como está en este momento...

as it says in... como dice en... ➤ As it says in the Bible... Como dice en la Biblia...

as it states in... *(in a legal document)* ▪ as stated in... ▪ as recorded in... como consta en... ▪ como se manifiesta en... ➤ As it states in the public record... Como consta en el registro civil... ➤ As it states in the Declaration of Independence... Como se manifiesta en la Declaración de la Independencia...

as it usually is 1. como suele ser (normalmente) ▪ como es normalmente **2.** como suele estar (normalmente) ▪ como normalmente está ➤ Madrid is all lighted up, as it usually is at Christmas time. Madrid está muy iluminada como normalmente está en tiempo de Navidad.

as it was 1. tal y como era **2.** tal y como estaba **3.** tal y como fue **4.** tal y como estuvo ➤ As it was, I didn't have enough time, much less to take on an additional project. No tenía suficiente tiempo tal y como estaban las cosas, mucho menos para emprender un proyecto nuevo. ▪ No tenía mucho tiempo dadas las circunstancias, mucho menos para emprender nuevos proyectos. ➤ I had gotten up at 6 a.m., as it was, and by the time of the party, I could hardly keep my eyes open. Tal y como estaban las cosas me levanté a las seis, para cuando empezó la fiesta, casi no pude tener los ojos abiertos.

as it was called que es como se le llamaba

as it were ▪ so to speak digamos ▪ por así decir ▪ por decir así ▪ por así decirlo así ▪ por decirlo así ▪ a lo que se dice ▪ como si dijéramos ▪ podríamos decir

to be **(as) light as a feather** pesar menos que una pluma

as likely as not tan probable como no

to be **as likely to do something** tener la misma probabilidad de hacer algo ▪ haber hecho algo igual que ➤ In the days of sailing ships, passengers on long voyages were as likely to die from disease as from shipwreck. En los tiempos de los barcos de velas, los pasajeros en largas travesías, tenían tantas posibilidades de morir de una enfermedad como por un naufragio.

as little as possible lo menos posible

as long as 1. so long as ▪ provided that con tal de que **2.** since ya que ▪ con que **3.** while mientras (que) **4.** for as long as en tanto ▪ en cuanto ▪ siempre y cuando **5.** the same length as tan largo como ▪ tanto como ➤ You can fold the curtains as long as they don't get wrinkled. ▪ You can fold the curtains so long as they don't get wrinkled. Puedes doblar las cortinas con tal de que no se arruguen. ➤ As long as I'm here, I might as well... Ya que estoy aquí, más me valdría... ➤ As long as they live in that house, I'll never set foot in it. Mientras vivan en esa casa, jamás pondré un pie en ella. ➤ They told me that the job is mine as long as I want it. Me han dicho que el trabajo es mío siempre y cuando (yo) lo quiera. ➤ This route is not as long as the other. ▪ This route is not so long as the other. Esta ruta no es tan larga como la otra. ▪ Esta ruta es no tan larga como la otra. ➤ The Beethoven fourth piano concerto is not quite as long as the fifth. ▪ The Beethoven fourth piano concerto is not quite so long as the fifth. El cuarto concierto de piano de Beethoven no es, por poco, tan largo como el quinto.

as long as I remain here mientras me quede aquí ▪ en tanto me quede aquí

as long as I'm here 1. since I'm here ya que estoy aquí ▪ con que estoy aquí **2.** while I'm here mientras que (yo) esté aquí

as long as one likes ▪ as long as one wants to tan largo como uno quiera ▪ tanto como uno quiera ▪ cuanto uno quiera ➤ Leave a message as long as you like. *(tú)* Deja un mensaje tan largo como quieras. ▪ *(usted)* Deje un mensaje tan largo como quiera.

as long as supplies last ▪ while supplies last hasta (el) fin de existencias ➤ Offer valid until Christmas or as long as supplies last. Oferta válida hasta la Navidad o fin de existencias.

as long as you're here... con que estés... ▪ ya que estás

as luck would have it ▪ luckily por suerte

to be **(as) mad as a hatter** ▪ (as) crazy as a loon ▪ (as) crazy as a bedbug estar (tan) loco(-a) como una cabra ▪ estar más loco(-a) que una cabra

to be **(as) mad as a hornet** ▪ to be (as) mad as a wet hen estar como una fiera ▪ estar hecho una furia

(as) mad as a hornet: to get ~ ▪ to get mad (as) a wet hen ponerse como una fiera ▪ ponerse hecho una furia ▪ ponerse como una exhalación

to be **(as) mad as a wet hen** ▪ to be (as) mad as a hornet estar como una fiera ▪ estar hecho una furia

(as) mad as a wet hen: to get ~ ▪ to get mad as a hornet ponerse como un toro ▪ ponerse como una fiera ▪ ponerse hecho una exhalación

as many as tantos como ▪ tantas (as) como ➤ Take as many as you want. Toma tantos como quieras. ▪ Toma tantas como quieras.

as many as I could 1. todos los que pude 2. todos los que podía 3. todos los que podría

as many as possible el mayor número posible ▪ la mayor cantidad posible ▪ tantos como sea posible ▪ todos los que puedan ▪ los más posibles ▪ todos los que se pueda ➤ Urban apartment building architecture puts as many people as possible in(to) a small space. La arquitectura urbana pone el mayor número de gente posible en el menor espacio posible.

as many (of something) as will 1. tantos (algo) como 2. todos los (algo) que ➤ Take as many oranges as will fit in the basket. Toma tantas naranjas como quepan en la cesta. ▪ Toma todas las naranjas que quepan en la cesta. ▪ *(Sp.)* Coge tantas naranjas como quepan en la cesta. ▪ Coge todas las naranjas que quepan en la cesta.

as marked como en la etiqueta ➤ Are the prices as marked, or 10 percent off that? In other words, does the marked price include the discount? ¿Están los precios como en la etiqueta, o un diez porciento menos? En otras palabras, ¿la etiqueta incluye el descuento?

as much again otro tanto

as much as tanto como ➤ *(wildlife expert)* The bears trusted us as much as they trusted each other. Los osos confían en nosotros tanto como se fían entre ellos.

as much as anyone tanto como cualquier otro(-a) ➤ She deserves a scholarship as much as anyone. Ella merece una beca tanto como cualquier otro.

as much as I would like tanto como me gustaría

as much as I would like to ▪ por mucho que me gustara ▪ por mucho que me gustarse

as much as possible tanto como sea posible ▪ lo máximo posible ▪ cuanto más

as much as you like ▪ however much you like lo mucho que te guste

as much as you would think tanto como se pensaría ➤ It didn't hurt as much as you would think it would because the endorphins kick in right away. No me dolió tanto como se pensaría porque las endorfinas reaccionan inmediatamente.

to be **as much one thing as another** ser tanto lo uno como lo otro ➤ The elimination of poverty is as much a technological problem as a social one. La eliminación de la pobreza es tanto un problema tecnológico como uno social.

as much time as possible el mayor tiempo posible

as much to do with: to have ~ tener que ver con ➤ The Inquisition in Spain had as much to do with the monarchy as with the Catholic Church. La Inquisición española tuvo tanto que ver con la monarquía como con la iglesia católica.

to be **(as) neat as a pin** *(Sp.)* estar tan limpio como los chorros del oro ▪ estar tan limpio como la patena ▪ estar tan limpio como una patena ▪ *(L. Am.)* estar tan limpio como una tazita de plata ➤ She keeps the house as neat as a pin. Ella mantiene la casa tan limpia como los chorros del oro. ▪ Ella tiene la casa tan limpia como la patena. ▪ Ella tiene la casa tan limpia como una patena.

as never before ▪ more than ever before como nunca ➤ We've enjoyed this Christmas as never before. Nos hemos divertido como nunca esta Navidad. ▪ Esta Navidad nos hemos divertido como nunca.

(as) nice as one could be tan agradable a más no poder ➤ The lady at the commissary was (as) nice as she could be. La señora en la comisaría fue tan agradable a más no poder.

as of April first a partir del primero de abril ▪ a partir del uno de abril

as of now hasta el momento ▪ desde ahora ➤ As of now there's no word from the explorers. Hasta el momento no se sabe ni una palabra de los exploradores ➤ As of now we have no plans. Hasta el momento no tenemos planes. ▪ Desde ahora no tenemos planes.

as of today ▪ starting today a partir de hoy

as of yesterday 1. hasta ayer 2. since yesterday desde ayer ➤ As of yesterday the account had not been credited. Hasta ayer, no habían hecho un ingreso. ➤ *(headline)* Sanitation department, on strike as of yesterday La sanidad, desde ayer en huelga

as of yet ▪ so far ▪ yet por ahora ▪ todavía ➤ As of yet, there's no word from the rescue team. No hay noticias del equipo de rescate por ahora.

as often as I can siempre que puedo

as often as not la mitad de las veces ▪ un día sí y un día no ➤ He's late as often as not. Llega tarde un día sí, un día no.

as often as possible tan a menudo como sea posible

to be **as old as Methuselah** ser más viejo(-a) que Matusalén

to be **(as) old as the hills** tener más espolones que un gallo

as one can be: to be as crazy ser de lo más loco ▪ no poder ser más loco ▪ ser loquísimo ▪ ser loco como uno solo ▪ ser requeteloco ▪ estar requeteloco ➤ That cat is as crazy as she can be. Esa gata es de lo más loca. ▪ Esa gata no podría estar más loca. ▪ Esa gata es loquísima. ▪ Esa gata es loca como ella sola.

as one does como uno ➤ I don't have as much free time as he does. No tengo tanto tiempo libre como él.

as one does something ▪ in the process of one's doing something conforme uno hace algo ➤ As my little daughter turns the pages, she mentions the objects missing from the pictures. Conforme pasa las hojas, mi hijita menciona los objetos ausentes de los dibujos.

as one goes along sobre la marcha ▪ mientras uno va avanzando ➤ Hans Christian Andersen invented many of his stories as he went along. Hans Christian Andersen inventó muchos de sus cuentos sobre la marcha. ➤ The teacher is creating the course as he goes along. El profesor está creando el curso mientras él va avanzando.

as one might think ▪ as you might think como se podría pensar ▪ como se podría imaginar ▪ como sería de imaginar ▪ como sería de pensar ➤ Learning to fly airplanes is not so difficult as one might think. ▪ Learning to fly airplanes is not as difficult as one might think. Aprender a volar aviones no es tan difícil como se podría pensar.

as one nears ▪ as one approaches ▪ as one reaches conforme uno se acerca ▪ a medida que uno se acerca

as one pleases como uno quiera ▪ lo que le parezca a uno ▪ a su antojo

as one pleases: to do ~ hacer como uno quiere ▪ hacer como uno quiera ▪ hacer lo que le parezca ▪ hacer su antojo ▪ hacer su santa gana

as one puts it como uno lo dice ▪ como uno lo expresa

as one still is igual que a día de hoy ▪ como aún uno está ▪ como aún uno es ➤ She was, as she still is, always reading. Ella siempre estaba, igual que a día de hoy, leyendo. ▪ Ella estaba, como aún está, siempre leyendo. ➤ He was as a child, as he still is in old age, a very jolly person. Él era de niño, igual que a día de hoy, una persona jovial.

as one usually is como uno suele ser ▪ como uno suele estar ▪ como uno suele tener ▪ como uno acostumbra ➤ I'm not as hungry tonight as I usually am. No tengo tanta hambre esta noche como suelo tener. ➤ Today I am not as rushed as I usually am. Hoy no estoy tan apurado como suelo estar. ▪ Hoy no estoy tan apurado como acostumbro.

as one would expect ▪ as you would expect ▪ as you'd expect como cabría esperar ▪ como cabría suponer ▪ como cabe esperar ▪ como cabe suponer ▪ como sería de esperar ▪ como sería de suponer ▪ como se podría esperar ▪ como se podría suponer

as opposed to ▪ in contrast to ▪ unlike frente a ▪ a diferencia de ▪ en contraposición a ▪ en contraste con ➤ Fresh water as opposed to salt water El agua dulce en contraste al agua salada ▪ Agua dulce a diferencia del agua salada ➤ The dynamic psychological theorists, as opposed to the behaviorists, believe it is possible to analyze mental processes. Los teóricos de la psicología dinámica, en contraposición a los conductistas, creen que es posible analizar los procesos mentales. ➤ A *de facto* tenant is one who is not on the lease, as opposed to a *de jure* tenant, who is. Un inquilino *de hecho* no figura en el contrato, a diferencia del inquilino *de jure,* que sí.

as opposed to what? ¿a diferencia de qué? ▪ ¿en contraposición a qué?

as originally conceived como originalmente concebido

as originally planned ▪ as was originally planned tal como se planeó originalmente ▪ *(Sp.)* tal y como se planeó originalmente

as per your request for ▪ regarding your request for *(familiar)* con respecto tu petición ▪ en respuesta a tu petición ▪ *(formal)* con respecto a su petición ▪ en respuesta a su petición

as president *(man)* de presidente ▪ como presidente *(woman)* de presidenta ▪ como presidenta ➤ *(Lincoln)* Just think of a sucker like me as president! ¡Imagínate a un pardillo como yo de presidente!

as pretty as tan bonito como ➤ Is the house as pretty inside as out? ▪ Is the house as pretty on the inside as it is on the outside? ¿Es la casa tan bonita por dentro como por fuera?

as proof of en prueba de

as regards por lo que se refiere a ▪ en cuanto a

to be **as right as rain** tener más razón que un santo

as seen from visto desde ▪ visto de ➤ The planets orbit the sun counterclockwise as seen from the North Star. Los planetas giran alrededor del sol en sentido contrario a las agujas del reloj, vistos desde la estrella polar.

as seen in the photo como se ve en la foto

as she likes to be called como (a ella) le gusta que le llamen

as she refers to herself como se llama a sí misma

as shown in the photo como muestra la foto

to be **as skinny as a rail** estar en los huesos ▪ estar tan flaco como un palo ▪ parecer un esqueleto andante ▪ estar como un palillo

as some of you already know como algunos de ustedes ya saben ▪ *(Sp., vosotros)* como algunos de vosotros ya saben

as someone else is ▪ the way someone else is al igual que ➤ I'm in the process of learning Spanish as Marta is English. Estoy en el proceso de aprender el español al igual que Marta está aprendiendo inglés.

as someone once said ▪ as somebody has said como alguien dijo una vez ▪ que dijo alguien

as something goes para como están ➤ That's pretty cheap as airfares go. Es muy barato para como están las tarifas aéreas.

as soon as en cuanto ▪ tan pronto como ▪ luego que ➤ As soon as I left, I felt better. En cuanto me marché, me sentí mejor.

as soon as I can en cuanto (yo) pueda ▪ lo antes que pueda

as soon as I get there en cuanto (yo) llegue ▪ así que (yo) llegue

as soon as possible lo más pronto posible ▪ cuanto antes ▪ lo antes posible ▪ tan pronto como sea posible ▪ a la mayor brevedad posible

as soon as something comes up I'll let you know en cuanto surja algo te aviso

as stated in... ▪ as it states in... ▪ as recorded in... como consta en... As stated in the minutes Como consta en acta

as stipulated según lo estipulado

as stipulated in the contract ▪ as specified in the contract como estipulado en el contrato ▪ como especificado en el contrato

to be **as strong as an ox** ser tan fuerte como un toro

as such como tal

as sure as my name is... tan cierto como que me llamo...

as that of tan como el de ▪ tan como la de ➤ The wine of Spain is as good as that of France. El vino de España es tan bueno como el de Francia. ➤ The music of Hummel was, in his time, as famous as that of Chopin. En su época la música de Hummel era tan famosa como la de Chopin.

as the case may be según el caso

as the crow flies en línea recta ➤ Washington is one hundred and fifty miles from Roanoke as the crow flies. Washington está a ciento cincuenta millas de Roanoke en línea recta.

as the day goes by como pasa el día ▪ a medida que pasa el día ▪ como siga el día ▪ según pasa el día ▪ según va pasando el día ▪ a medida que el día pasa ▪ conforme pasa el día ▪ conforme va pasando el día

as the day progresses a medida que el día avanza ▪ a medida que avanza el día

as the days pass ▪ as the days go by según pasan los días ▪ según van pasando los días

as the name implies como el nombre implica

as the old saying goes como reza la antigua frase ▪ como suele decirse

as the weeks go by ▪ as the weeks pass según pasan las semanas ▪ conforme pasan las semanas ▪ a medida que pasan las semanas

as the years pass ▪ as the years go by según pasan los años ▪ según van pasando los años ▪ a medida que pasan los años ▪ a medida que los años pasan ▪ a medida que los años van pasando ▪ conforme pasan los años ▪ conforme van pasando los años

as the years passed ▪ as the years went by conforme pasaban los años ▪ conforme fueron pasando los años ▪ conforme los años pasaban ▪ conforme iban pasando los años ▪ *("Conforme" can be replaced by "a medida que" or "según" in all examples.)*

as they come: to be as witty ~ ser de lo más agudo ▪ ser tan agudo como los que hay

as things stand (tal) como están las cosas ▪ tal como las cosas se perfilan

as those of como los de ▪ como las de ➤ The piano concertos of Saint-Saëns are not so complex as those of Beethoven. Los conciertos de piano de Saint-Saëns no son tan intrincados como los de Beethoven.

as though ▪ like ▪ as if como si ➤ It feels as though it's ninety degrees in here. ▪ It feels like it's ninety degrees in here. Aquí dentro se siente como si hiciera noventa grados.

to be **(as) tight as a tick** ser (un) tacaño ▪ ser (un) agarrado ▪ no soltar un duro ▪ ser (un) roñoso

as time goes by ▪ as time passes **1.** *(present)* conforme pasa el tiempo ▪ a medida que pasa el tiempo ▪ según pasa el tiempo ▪ con el paso del tiempo **2.** *(future)* conforme pase el tiempo ▪ a medida que pase el tiempo ▪ según pase el tiempo ▪ con el paso del tiempo ➤ It's getting warmer as time goes by. Hace más calor conforme pasa el tiempo. ➤ As time goes by, I'm forgetting him. A medida que pasa el tiempo, me voy olvidando de él. ➤ You'll get better as time goes by. Te sentirás mejor conforme pase el tiempo. ➤ The situation will improve as time goes by. La situación mejorará a medida que pase el tiempo.

as to ▪ about ▪ over con respecto a ▪ en lo que respecta a ➤ The employee was confused as to the grounds for his dismissal. El empleado estaba confuso con respecto a la causa de su despido. ▪ El empleado estaba confuso en lo que respecta a la causa de su despido.

as to whether en cuanto a si

as understood según lo entendido

as usual como siempre ▪ como de costumbre ▪ a la rutina

as was expected como era de esperar

as was I ▪ as I was ▪ as I had been como lo fui yo
as (was) originally planned tal y como se planeó originalmente
as was said (earlier) ya quedó dicho
as we all know ▪ as all of us know como todos sabemos
as we always have ▪ as we have always done como lo hemos hecho siempre
as we get older conforme envejecemos ▪ a medida que nos hacemos mayores ▪ a medida que uno envejece ▪ a medida que envejecemos
as we had agreed como habíamos acordado ▪ como habíamos quedado
as we had discussed como habíamos hablado
as we have seen como hemos visto
as we speak ▪ at this exact moment en este mismo momento
as we were saying yesterday como decíamos ayer *(Fray Luis de León uttered these words on returning to his professorship at the University of Salamanca in 1576 after five years' imprisonment by the Inquisition for using the Hebrew Bible instead of the Vulgate.)*
as well ▪ too ▪ also también
as well as 1. as proficiently as tan bien como ▪ igual de bien que **2.** in addition to ▪ both... and así como ▪ tanto como ➤ I can't skateboard as well as Jaime can. No puedo montar en monopatín tan bien como Jaime. ➤ She can sing as well as an opera singer. Ella canta tan bien como una cantante de ópera. ▪ Ella canta igual de bien que una cantante de ópera.
as yet por el momento ▪ por ahora ➤ We have no word on his condition as yet. No sabemos nada de su estado por el momento. ▪ No sabemos nada de su estado por ahora.
as yet undetermined ▪ still to be determined ▪ yet to be determined aún por determinar
as you might expect ▪ as one might expect ▪ as you would expect ▪ as one would expect como cabría esperar ▪ como cabría suponer ▪ como cabe esperar ▪ como cabe suponer ▪ como sería de esperar ▪ como sería de suponer
as you might think ▪ as one might think como se podría pensar ▪ como sería de pensar
as you pointed out *(tú)* (tal y) como apuntaste ▪ *(usted)* (tal y) como apuntó (usted)
as you probably guessed como ya habrás supuesto ▪ como te habrás imaginado
as you probably know as you probably already know *(tú)* como ya sabrás ▪ *(usted)* como usted ya sabrá
as you probably realize como te habrás dado cuenta
as you put it ▪ as you expressed it tal como (lo) dijiste ▪ tal como lo expresaste ▪ *(Sp.)* tal y como (lo) dijiste ▪ tal y como lo expresaste
as you see fit ▪ as you deem appropriate *(tú)* de acuerdo a como lo veas tú ▪ como te parezca bien ▪ *(usted)* de acuerdo a como lo vea usted ▪ como le parezca bien
as you well know *(tú)* como tú bien sabes ▪ *(usted)* como usted bien sabe
as you would expect ▪ as you'd expect ▪ as one would expect como cabría esperar ▪ como cabría suponer ▪ como cabe esperar ▪ como cabe suponer ▪ como sería de esperar ▪ como sería de suponer
as you've probably noticed como habrás notado ▪ como habrás advertido
to be **ashamed of** avergonzarse de
to be **ashamed of oneself** avergonzarse de sí mismo(-a) ▪ estar avergonzado(-a) de sí mismo(-a) ▪ caérsele la cara de vergüenza ➤ You should be ashamed of yourself. Deberías avergonzarte de ti mismo. ▪ Se te debería caer la cara de vergüenza.
ashamed of oneself: to be thoroughly ~ estar muerto de vergüenza
ashamed to admit that...: not to be ~ no avergonzarse de reconocer (que...) ➤ I'm not ashamed to admit that I once put walnuts in (the) paella. No me avergüenza reconocer que una vez puse nueces en la paella. ▪ No me avergüenzo de reconocer que una vez puse nueces en la paella.
to be **ashamed to say that...** avergonzarse de decir que... ➤ I'm not ashamed to say that... No me avergüenzo de decir que...
to be **ashamed to show one's face in public** avergonzarse de mostrarse en público
aside from aparte de ➤ Aside from that, how did you like it? Aparte de eso, ¿cómo te gustaba?
aside from the fact that ▪ apart from the fact that aparte de que
to **ask a favor of someone** ▪ to ask someone a favor pedirle un favor a alguien ➤ I'd like to ask you a favor. ▪ I'd like to ask a favor of you. *(tú)* Me gustaría pedirte un favor. ▪ *(usted)* Me gustaría pedirle un favor.
to **ask a question** hacer una pregunta ▪ *(in an academic setting)* formular una pregunta ➤ Let me ask you this question. Déjame que te haga esta pregunta. ▪ Permítame que le haga esta pregunta. ▪ Déjame hacer te esta pregunta. ▪ Permítame hacer le esta pregunta.
to **ask about someone** preguntar sobre alguien ➤ They asked about you. Preguntaron sobre ti.
to **ask about something** ▪ to inquire about something preguntar sobre algo ▪ preguntar por algo
ask about it infórmate ▪ pregúntale a alguien
to **ask directions (of someone)** ▪ to ask someone directions preguntar (por) una dirección a alguien ➤ When you get near the palace, just stop and ask directions of someone on the street. Cuando llegues cerca del palacio, pregúntale (por) la dirección a alguien. ▪ Cuando llegues cerca del palacio, pregunta a alguien.
to **ask for (a) time out** *(sports)* ▪ to request (a) time out pedir tiempo ▪ pedir que se corte el juego
to **ask for a woman's hand in marriage** pedir al padre la mano de la novia
to **ask for it by name** pedirlo por su nombre
to **ask (for) permission to do something** pedir permiso para hacer algo ▪ pedir consentimiento para hacer algo
to **ask (for) permission to speak** ▪ to request permission to speak pedir permiso para hablar
to **ask for someone** preguntar por alguien ➤ Go to customer service and ask for the manager. Vaya al servicio al cliente y pregunte por el gerente.
to **ask for someone by name** preguntar por alguien específicamente ➤ When you get to the store, ask for Mr. Álvarez by name. Cuando llegues a la tienda, pregunta específicamente por el Señor Álvarez. ▪ Cuando llegues a la tienda, pregunta por el Señor Álvarez específicamente.
to **ask for something** pedir algo
to **ask for the moon** ▪ to make unmeetable demands pedir la luna ▪ pedir el cielo y las estrellas
to **ask for time off (from work)** pedir tiempo libre
to **ask for trouble** buscarse líos ▪ buscar pleitos
ask her to call me pídele (a ella) que me llame ▪ pídale (a ella) que me llame
ask him to call me pídele (a él) que me llame ▪ pídale (a él) que me llame
to **ask permission** ▪ to ask for permission to ▪ to request permission to pedir permiso ➤ The student asked the substitute's permission to go to the library. La alumna le pidió permiso al substituto para ir a la biblioteca.
to **ask somone a favor** pedir a alguien un favor ➤ Could I ask you a favor? ¿Podría pedirte un favor?
to **ask someone a personal question** hacerle a alguien una pregunta personal
to **ask someone a pointed personal question** hacerle a alguien una pregunta personal directa ➤ He asks pointed personal questions. Él hace preguntas personales directas.
to **ask someone a question** hacerle una pregunta a alguien ➤ Do you all want to ask our guest any questions? ¿Queréis hacerle alguna pregunta a nuestro invitado?
to **ask someone about someone** ▪ to inquire about someone preguntarle a alguien por alguien ➤ I saw Marta today, and she asked me about you. Vi a Marta hoy, y ella me preguntó por ti.
to **ask someone about something** preguntarle a alguien por algo
to **ask someone back** ▪ to invite someone back volver a invitar a alguien

to **ask someone for permission to do something** ▪ to ask someone's permission to do something pedir a alguien permiso para hacer algo

to **ask someone for something** pedirle algo a alguien ➤ He asked her for her phone number. Le pidió (a ella) su número telefónico. ➤ The policeman asked her for her driver's license. El policía le pidió (a ella) su carnet de conducir. ➤ She asked me for my book. Ella me pidió mi libro.

to **ask someone if** preguntarle a alguien si ➤ Ask him if an error message accompanies the bounced E-mail. Pregúntale si un mensaje de error acompaña al correo devuelto.

to **ask someone in** ▪ to ask someone to come in ▪ to invite someone (to come) in invitar a alguien a entrar

to **ask someone over** ▪ to invite someone to come over ▪ to ask someone (to come) over invitar a alguien a casa

to **ask someone out on a date** ▪ to ask someone out ▪ to invite someone out on a date invitar a alguien a salir ▪ *(coll.)* pedirle a alguien salir ▪ *(old-fashioned)* pedirle a alguien una cita ➤ He asked her out (on a date). Él le pidió una cita. ▪ Él le pidió (a ella) a salir. ▪ Él le invitó (a ella) a salir.

to **ask someone pointedly** preguntar a alguien directamente ▪ preguntar a alguien sin rodeos

to **ask someone something** preguntarle algo a alguien

to **ask someone something point blank** preguntar algo a alguien a bocajarro

to **ask someone (to come) in** ▪ to invite someone (to come) in invitar a alguien a entrar

to **ask someone to do something** pedirle a alguien que haga algo ➤ I asked her to help me with the party. Le pedí (a ella) que me ayudara con la fiesta. ➤ The technician has done more things to the computer than I asked him to. El técnico le ha hecho más cosas al ordenador de las que le he pedido que haga.

to **ask someone to forgive one** ▪ to ask (for) someone's forgiveness pedir el perdón de alguien

to **ask someone to lend you money** ▪ to ask someone for a loan ▪ to ask to borrow money from someone pedir dinero prestado a alguien

to **ask someone up** ▪ to invite someone up pedir a alguien que suba ➤ She asked him up for a glass of wine. Ella le pidió que subiera a tomar una copa de vino.

to **ask someone what...** preguntarle a alguien qué... ➤ I asked my students what vegetables you put in paella. Le pregunté a mis alumnos qué verduras se ponen en la paella. ➤ I asked him what I wanted to. Le pregunté lo que quise. ➤ I asked him what he wanted. Le pregunté qué quería.

to **ask someone which...** preguntarle a alguien cual...

to **ask someone's forgiveness for something** ▪ to ask someone to forgive one for something suplicar el perdón de alguien por haber hecho algo

to **ask the doctor about it** preguntárselo al médico ▪ preguntárselo al doctor ➤ I'm going to ask the doctor about it tomorrow. Le voy a preguntar al médico (por esto) mañana. ➤ I'm going to ask the doctor tomorrow about changing my medication. Le voy a preguntar al médico mañana si puedo cambiar la medicación.

to **ask the impossible** pedir peras al olmo ▪ *(L. Am.)* pedir leche a las cabrillas

to **ask whose turn it is** ▪ to ask who's next in line pedir la vez ▪ pedir el turno

to be **asked to...** solicitarse que... ▪ rogarse que... ➤ Candidates are asked to bring a recent photo (with them). Se solicita que los candidatos traigan (consigo) una foto reciente. ▪ Se solicita que los candidatos vengan con una foto reciente. ▪ Se solicita que los candidatos lleven (consigo) una foto reciente.

to be **asking for it** ▪ to be asking for trouble ▪ to be begging for it estárselo buscando ▪ buscárselo ▪ pedirlo a gritos ➤ You're asking for it, buddy. ¡Te lo estás buscando, tío! ▪ ¡Estás pidiéndolo a gritos, tío! ➤ He's been asking for it, and now he's going to get it! ¡Se lo estaba buscando, y ahora va a tener lo suyo! ▪ ¡Se lo estaba buscando, y ahora va a recibir (de lo lindo)!

asking price precio que se pide ▪ a cuánto va

aspect of one's character ▪ character traits rasgo de su carácter ➤ Lincoln's sadness and his humor are intriguing aspects of his character. La tristeza de Lincoln por un lado y su sentido de humor por otro son rasgos intrigantes de su carácter.

aspect of one's personality ▪ personality trait rasgo de (la) personalidad

to be **assailed by doubts** ▪ to begin to have doubts acometerle dudas ➤ She was assailed by doubts. A ella le acometieron dudas.

assassination attempt intento de asesinato

assassination plot conjura para asesinar alguien ▪ conjura para matar a alguien ▪ el complot para esesinar a alguien

assault rifle *el* rifle de asalto

to **assemble a kit** ▪ to put together a kit armar una maqueta ▪ ensamblar una maqueta ▪ montar una maqueta ▪ hacer una maqueta

to **assemble a phrase** construir una frase ▪ hacer una frase

to **assemble peacefully** congregarse... ▪ reunirse...

to **assemble the parts** ▪ to put together the parts ▪ to put the parts together ensamblar las piezas ▪ juntar las piezas

to **assemble the pieces** ▪ to put together the pieces ▪ to put the pieces together juntar las piezas ▪ ensamblar las piezas

assembly line cadena de montaje ▪ línea de montaje

to **assess a situation** evaluar una situación ▪ valorar una situación

to **assess real estate** *(for tax purposes)* valorar una propiedad ▪ tasar una propiedad

to **assess the damage** evaluar el daño ▪ evaluar los daños ▪ valorar el daño ▪ valorar los daños

asshole: to turn into a real ~ *(off-color)* volverse gillipollas ▪ volverse un hijo de puta ▪ *(benign alternative)* volverse un desgraciado

to **assign a reporter to a beat** asignar a un periodista una sección específica ➤ The reporter was assigned to the police beat. Al reportero le asignaron la sección de sucesos. ▪ Al reportero le asignaron la sección policiaca.

to **assign a seat** asignar un sitio ▪ asignar un asiento

to **assign for homework** ▪ to give for homework *(Sp.)* poner de deberes ▪ mandar de deberes ▪ *(L. Am., Sp.)* poner de tarea ▪ mandar de tarea ➤ What did he assign us for homework? ▪ What's our homework? ¿Qué nos ha puesto de deberes? ▪ ¿Qué nos ha mandado de deberes? ▪ ¿Qué nos ha puesto de tarea? ▪ ¿Qué nos ha mandado de tarea?

to **assign homework** ▪ to give homework dar tarea(s) ▪ dejar tarea(s) ▪ *(Sp.)* dar deberes ▪ dejar deberes ➤ Did the teacher assign us any homework? ¿Nos dio tarea(s) la profesora?

to **assign someone a companion** asignarle a alguien un compañero ▪ ponerle un compañero a alguien ➤ They assigned the police officer a companion. Le asignaron un compañero al policía. ▪ Le pusieron un compañero al policía.

to **assign someone as a companion (to someone else)** asignarle a alguien de compañero ▪ ponerle a alguien de compañero ➤ I was assigned the newcomer as a companion. Me asignaron de compañero al nuevo. ▪ Me pusieron de compañero al nuevo.

to **assign someone the task of doing something** ▪ to charge someone with the task of doing something asignarle a alguien la tarea de hacer algo ▪ asignarle a alguien el cometido de hacer algo ▪ encargarle a alguien hacer algo ▪ encargarle a alguien que haga algo

to **assign someone to a diplomatic post** asignar un puesto diplomático a alguien ➤ The diplomat was assigned to a new embassy. El diplomático fue asignado a una nueva embajada.

assigned seat asiento designado ➤ Are the seats assigned? ¿Están designados los asientos?

to **assimilate information** asimilar información

assisted-living facility complejo residencial para la tercera edad

to **associate with someone 1.** *(on a personal basis)* relacionarse con alguien **2.** *(in business)* asociarse con alguien ➤ He didn't associate with anybody. No se relacionaba con nadie.

to be **associated with** estar asociado a ➤ Teodora contributed to the greatness of the reign of Justinian, with which she was always associated. Teodora contribuyó a la grandeza del reinado de Justiniano, al que siempre estuvo asociada.

assorted cards tarjetas surtidas

assortment of cards surtido de tarjetas

to **assume responsibility for something (that has happened)** asumir la responsabilidad por algo (que ha sucedido)

to **assume responsibility to do something** ■ to take on responsibility to do something asumir la responsabilidad de hacer algo ■ aceptar la responsabilidad de hacer algo ■ tomar sobre sí la responsabilidad de hacer algo

to **assume that...** asumir que... ■ suponer que... ■ dar por hecho que... ➤ When you brought the side dish of guacamole, I assumed it was part of the meal. Cuando trajiste el acompañamiento de guacamole asumí que era parte de la comida. ■ Cuando trajiste el acompañamiento de guacamole supuse que era parte de la comida. ■ Cuando trajiste el acompañamiento de guacamole di por hecho que era parte de la comida.

asthma attack *el* ataque de asma ■ *la* crisis de asma ➤ She had an asthma attack. ■ She suffered an asthma attack. Sufrió un ataque de asma. ■ Sufrió una crisis de asma.

to **astonish someone** ■ to leave someone astonished dejarle a alguien atónito

to be **astonished at** quedarse atónito ante

astonished look ■ look of astonishment cara de asombro ➤ I saw the astonished look on her face. ■ I saw the look of astonishment on her face. Observé su cara de asombro.

to be **astonished that...** quedarse atónito de que... ■ quedarse sin palabras ■ quedarse boquiabierto ➤ I was astonished that he would take the family car and go joy riding. Me quedé atónito de que tomara el carro familiar para salir a pasear. ■ *(Sp.)* Me quedé atónito de que cogiera el coche familiar para ir a dar una vuelta. ➤ He was astonished that they gave him a raise after one month on the job. Se quedó atónito de que le subieran el sueldo después de un mes trabajando.

to be **astonished to...** quedarse atónito al ■ quedarse turulato ➤ The Supreme Court nominee said he was astonished to receive the nomination. El nominado al Tribunal Supremo dijo que se quedó atónito al recibir la nominación.

to be **astonished when...** ■ to be astonished that... quedarse atónito cuando... ■ estar atónito cuando... ➤ He was astonished when they gave him a raise after one month on the job. ■ He was astonished that they gave him a raise after one month on the job. Quedó atónito cuando le subieron el sueldo después de un mes trabajando.

to be **astounded at something** ■ to be dumbfounded at something quedarse pasmado ante algo ■ quedarse estupefacto ante algo ■ quedarse con la boquiabierto ante algo

to be **astounded by something** ■ to be dumbfounded by something quedarse pasmado por algo ■ quedarse estupefacto por algo

to be **astounded that...** ■ to be dumbfounded that... quedarse pasmado de que... ■ quedarse estupefacto de que...

astronomical cost costo astronómico ■ coste astronómico

astronomical price precio astronómico ■ precio sideral

astronomical sum suma astronómica ■ suma sideral

astronomical unit ■ AU unidad astronómica ■ UA ➤ One astronomical unit is the mean distance between the Earth and the sun, 149,587,870 million kilometers. Una unidad astronómica es la distancia media entre la Tierra y el Sol, 149.587,870 millones de kilómetros.

at a canter: to go ~ *(horseback riding)* ■ to canter ir a medio galope

at a certain time en determinado momento

at a close angle: to cross one's path ~ pasarle a alguien rozándole ■ cruzarle a alguien rozándole ➤ He cut across my path at a close angle. Me pasó rozándome. ■ Me cruzó rozándome.

to be **at a crossroads** estar en una encrucijada ➤ The country is at a crossroads. El país está en una encrucijada.

to be **at a disadvantage** estar en desventaja

at a distance a la distancia ■ a distancia

at a dizzying rate: to increase ~ alcanzar cotas de infarto ➤ Real estate prices in Madrid are increasing at a dizzying rate. El precio de la propiedad inmobiliaria en Madrid está alcanzando cotas de infarto.

at a fast pace: to walk ~ ■ to walk at a rapid pace caminar a buen ritmo ■ caminar a buen paso ■ *(Sp.)* andar a buen ritmo ■ andar a buen paso

to be **at a full stop** ■ to be at a standstill estar completamente parado

at a gallop: to go ~ ir al galope

at a given moment en un momento dado ■ en un momento determinado

at a given time en un momento determinado

at a glance de un vistazo

to be **at a loss to explain something** estar perdido al explicar algo ■ estar perdido a la hora de explicar algo ■ estar perdido tratando de explicar algo ■ no explicarse cómo ➤ *(news item)* The doctors are at a loss to explain the high incidence of cancer at the elementary school. Los médicos están perdidos a la hora de explicar la alta incidencia de cáncer en el colegio. ■ Los médicos no se explican la alta incidencia de cáncer en el colegio.

to be **at a loss to know what to do or say** quedarse en blanco (sin saber que hacer o decir) ■ quedarse pasmado (sin saber que hacer o decir)

at a mere glance a simple vista

at a profit: to sell something ~ ■ to sell something for a profit vender algo con beneficio ■ vender algo con provecho ■ vender algo y sacar (un buen) beneficio de la venta ■ vender algo y sacar provecho de la venta ➤ We bought an old rundown house, remodeled it, and sold it at a profit. Compramos una casa vieja y destartalada, la remodelamos, y al venderla le sacamos un (buen) beneficio. ■ Compramos una casa vieja y destartalada, la remodelamos, y al venderla le sacamos provecho. ➤ The house was remodeled and sold at a profit. La casa fue remodelada y vendida con beneficio.

at a rapid rate a buen ritmo

at a set time ■ at a fixed time ■ at a regular time a una hora fija ■ a una determinada hora ■ a una hora determinada

at a snail's pace a paso de tortuga ■ a paso de cangrejo

at a specific time a una hora concreta

at a specified time a una hora en concreto ➤ Does the bus pass by here at a specified time? ¿El autobús pasa a alguna hora en concreto?

to be **at a standstill** ■ to be at a full stop estar (completamente) parado ➤ Things were at a standstill until we got hold of the technician. Las cosas estuvieron (completamente) paradas hasta que nos hicimos con el técnico.

at a stroke ■ in one fell swoop de un solo golpe ■ de una tocada

at a time 1. at a stretch de un tirón **2.** at a moment (when) en un momento (en que) **3.** singly por vez ➤ We work eight hours at a time. ■ We work eight hours at a stretch. Trabajamos ocho horas de un tirón. ■ Podemos trabajar ocho horas de un tirón.

at a time: for days ~ durante días ■ durante días enteros ■ durante varios días seguidos ➤ The power would go off for days at a time. La electricidad se iba durante días enteros. ■ La electricidad se iba durante varios días seguidos.

at a time: for months ~ durante meses ■ durante meses seguidos ■ durante meses enteros ➤ It rains in northern California for months at a time. En el norte de California llueve durante meses seguidos. ■ En el norte de California llueve durante meses enteros.

at a time when en un tiempo cuando

at a trot: to go ~ ir al trote ➤ The cow was coming at me at a trot, mooing. La vaca venía hacia mí al trote, mugiendo.

at a walk: to go ~ *(horseback riding)* ■ to walk ir al paso

at about that time ■ around the time por entonces ■ por aquella época

(at) about the time of ■ around the time of **1.** *(within days, weeks, months, etc.)* hacia la época de ■ por la época de ■ sobre la época de ■ alrededor de la época de **2.** *(within hours or minutes)* hacia la hora de ■ sobre la hora de ■ alrededor de la hora de ➤ (At) about the time of the Industrial Revolution, the problems of air and water pollution began. Hacia la época de la Revolución industrial, comenzaron los problemas de contaminación del aire y del agua. ➤ At about the time the convention started, a large crowd began gathering outside the auditorium. Hacía la hora del comienzo de la convención una gran multitud se congregó fuera del auditorio. ■ Sobre la hora del comienzo de la convención... ■ Alrededor de la hora del comienzo de la convención...

at about this time *(present)* por ahora ■ *(past)* por entonces

at about *x* o'clock 1. *(singular)* a eso de la *x* ■ sobre la *x* **2.** *(plural)* a eso de las *x* ■ sobre las *x* ➤ At about one o'clock A eso de la una ■ Sobre la una ➤ At about two o'clock A eso de las dos ■ Sobre las dos

at age *x* ■ at the age of *x* a los *x* años ➤ *(headline)* Schoolchildren begin smoking at age thirteen Los escolares empiezan a fumar a los trece años

at all: not ~ en absoluto ■ nada ■ ni un pelo ■ *(L. Am.)* para nada ➤ Because of computer problems, I couldn't work at all. Por problemas con el ordenador, no pude trabajar en absoluto. ■ Por problemas con el ordenador, no pude trabajar para nada. ➤ You haven't changed at all. No has cambiado nada. ■ No has cambiado ni un pelo.

at all costs ■ at any cost a toda costa

at all hours (of the night) a las tantas (horas de la noche) ■ a las horas intempestivas ■ a todas horas (de la noche)

at all times en todo momento ■ a toda hora ■ a todas horas ➤ Keep it with you at all times. Llévalo contigo en todo momento.

at an alarming rate a una tasa alarmante ■ a un índice alarmante ➤ New cases of the virus were being reported at an alarming rate. Se han registrado nuevos casos del virus a una tasa alarmante.

at an angle: to cross something ~ ■ to cross something obliquely cruzar algo en diagonal ■ cortar algo en diagonal ➤ The Paseo de la Reforma crosses the Avenue Hidalgo at an angle. El Paseo de la Reforma corta la Avenida Hidalgo en diagonal.

at an angle: to see something ~ ■ to see something from an angle ver algo desde un ángulo ➤ The philosopher Immanuel Kant said the faint oval patches of light in the night sky were disks seen at an angle. ■ The philosopher Immanuel Kant said the faint oval patches of light in the night sky were disks seen from an angle. El filósofo Immanuel Kant dijo que las tenues superficies luminosas ovales en el cielo nocturno son discos vistos desde un ángulo.

at an angle to the corner: to sit ~ hacer ángulo diagonal con la esquina ➤ The church sits at an angle to the corner of Jefferson and McClanahan streets. La iglesia hace un ángulo diagonal con la esquina de las calles de Jefferson y McClanahan.

at an angle to the curb: to be parked ~ estar aparcado en batería ➤ The car is parked at an angle to the curb. El coche está aparcado en batería.

at an early age ■ from an early age desde temprana edad

at an exorbitant price a peso de oro

at any cost ■ at all costs a toda costa

at any given moment ■ at any given time en un momento dado

at any given time ■ at any given moment en un momento dado

at any moment en cualquier momento ➤ They could arrive at any moment. Podrían llegar en cualquier momento.

at any price a cualquier precio

at any price: peace ~ la paz a cualquier precio

at any rate ■ anyway de todas maneras ■ como sea

to be **at arm's length** estar a mano

at arm's length: to hold someone ~ ■ to keep someone at arm's length mantener las distancias con alguien

at around *x* (o'clock) ■ at about *x* (o'clock) ■ around *x* (o'clock) a eso de la(s) *x* ■ alrededor de la(s) *x* ➤ At around two (o'clock) in the afternoon. A eso de las dos de la tarde.

at bay: to keep someone ~ ■ to hold someone at bay mantener a alguien a raya ■ contener a alguien ■ mantener a alguien a distancia ➤ The dog kept the burglar at bay. ■ The dog held the burglar at bay. El perro mantuvo a distancia al ladrón.

at bay: to keep something ~ ■ to hold something at bay mantener algo controlado ➤ Drinking water keeps hunger pangs at bay. Beber agua puede mantener controlados los ataques de hambre.

at best en el mejor de los casos ■ como mejor ➤ The success of the Mars exploration missions to date can (at) best be described as mixed. Como mejor se puede describir el éxito de las misiones de exploración de Marte como parcial.

at birth 1. al nacer **2.** since birth ■ from birth de nacimiento ➤ *(news item)* Doctors have succeeded in keeping alive a baby weighing only three hundred ninety grams at birth. Los médicos han logrado que un bebé que pesó al nacer tan sólo trescientos noventa gramos sobreviva.

at both ends en cada extremo ■ en los extremos ■ a cada extremo ■ a los extremos ➤ Elephants are useful friends, equipped with handles at both ends. *(Ogden Nash)* Los elefantes son amigos muy útiles, equipados con asas en cada extremo.

at breakneck speed: to go ~ ir a una velocidad de vértigo

at certain times en momentos determinados

to be **at church** estar en la iglesia ■ *(to be at Mass)* estar en misa

at clearance sale price a precio de saldo

at close range: to fire ~ disparar desde muy cerca ■ disparar a escasa distancia ➤ The youths died as a result of massive head injuries caused by shots fired at close range. Los jóvenes murieron por la destrucción de masa encefálica a causa de disparos de armas de fuego hechos desde muy cerca.

at considerable cost con gastos considerables ➤ They rebuilt the bridge at considerable cost. Reconstruyeron el puente con gastos considerables.

at cost a precio de costo

to be **at cross purposes with someone with respect to something** tener posiciones opuestas con alguien sobre algo ■ estar a la grena con alguien sobre algo

at dawn al alba

at daybreak a primera luz del día ■ al rayar el alba

at different times a distintas horas

at dusk ■ at twilight al crepúsculo ■ al caer la noche ■ al ocaso

at each other: to look ~ **1.** *(two people)* mirarse el uno al otro **2.** *(several people)* to look at one another mirarse entre ellos ➤ They looked at each other. Se miraron el uno al otro. ■ *(two females)* Se miraron la una a la otra.

at each other: to shout ~ gritarse el uno al otro ■ gritarse entre sí ➤ They ended up shouting at each other. Acabaron gritándose el uno al otro. ■ Acabaron gritándose entre sí. ■ *(two females)* Acabaron gritándose la una a la otra.

to be **at each other's throats** tenerse de punta

at every step of the way a cada paso

at every turn a cada vuelta de la esquina

at face value al valor nominal

to be **at fault** tener la culpa

at first 1. at first, but no longer primero **2.** early on en un principio **3.** in the first instance al principio **4.** immediately ■ right off the bat a la primera ➤ At first I said yes. Primero dije que sí. ➤ At first he was a philosophy major. En un principio era estudiante de filosofía. ➤ I didn't see her at first. Al principio no la vi. ➤ At first, I couldn't believe it. Al principio me costó creerlo. ➤ At first it was funny. ■ In the beginning it was funny. Al principio resultó gracioso. ➤ He didn't answer at first. No contestó a la primera.

at first glance a primera vista ■ al primer golpe de vista

at fixed times ■ at set times ■ at regular times a horas fijas ➤ Does the bus come by here at fixed times? ¿Pasa el autobús por aquí a horas fijas?

(at) full blast ■ at top volume ■ (turned) all the way up a todo volumen ■ a toda pastilla

(at) full gallop: to go ~ ir a todo galope

at full gallop: to take off ~ partir a galope tendido

(at) full sail: to go ~ ir a toda vela

at full speed: to go ~ ir a toda máquina ■ ir a toda velocidad ■ ir a toda pastilla ■ ir a las chapas ■ ir a fondo ■ *(Sp., slang)* ir a toda hostia

(at) full steam: to go ~ ir a todo vapor

at full throttle: to go ~ ir a todo gas

at great length: to speak ~ ■ to expound at great length hablar largo y tendido ■ expandirse

at gunpoint: to hold someone ~ detener a alguien a punta de pistola

at half mast: to fly the flag ~ ■ *(both transitive and intransitive)* to fly the flag at half staff volar la bandera a media asta ➤ The flags were flying at half mast. Las banderas volaban a media asta.

to be **at hand** ■ to be within easy reach estar a mano ■ estar al alcance de la mano ➤ In my house, I like for everything to be at hand. En mi casa, me gusta que todo esté a mano. ➤ Peace is at hand. La paz está al alcance de la mano.

at hand: to have something ~ ■ to have within (easy) reach tener algo a mano

at heart: to be something ~ ser algo de corazón ➤ She's young at heart. (Ella) es joven de corazón. ➤ He's a musician at heart. Es un músico de corazón.

at heart: to have something ~ tener algo muy presente ➤ He has your best interests at heart. Tiene muy presente lo que es mejor para ti.

at high speed a gran velocidad

at his insistence ■ at his urging a instancias suyas

to be **at home** estar en casa

at home and abroad en casa y en el extranjero

at intervals of up to durante períodos de hasta ➤ They prescribed a cholesterol reducer to some eight hundred adults at intervals of up to a year. Recetaron un reductor del colesterol a unos ochocientos adultos durante períodos de hasta un año.

at issue: to be (the point) ~ ser el asunto en cuestión ■ ser el punto conflictivo ➤ At issue in the general election is whether... El asunto en cuestión en las elecciones generales es si... ➤ The point at issue is... El punto conflictivo es...

to be **at it again** ya estar haciendo algo otra vez ■ estar dale que dale con algo ➤ My neighbor's at it again, playing her blasted stereo at midnight. Ya está otra vez mi vecina, poniendo el puñetero equipo de música a las doce de la noche. ➤ My neighbors are at it again. Mis vecinos están dale que dale. ➤ My grandfather's at it again, reliving the Spanish Civil War. Ya está mi abuelo, dale que dale con la Guerra Civil Española. ■ Ya está otra vez mi abuelo con la Guerra Civil Española.

at its best en su máxima expresión

to be **at its height** estar en pleno apogeo

to be **at large** andar suelto ■ estar prófugo

at large: to remain ~ ■ still to be at large continuar sin ser aprendido ■ continuar prófugo

at last por fin

at last! ■ finally! ■ it's high time! ■ it's about time! ¡por fin! ■ ¡ya es hora! ■ ¡ya son horas! ■ ¡vaya horas! ■ ¡ya iba siendo hora! ■ ¡a buenas horas (mangas verdes)!

at least al menos ■ por lo menos ■ a lo menos ➤ The attack caused at least thirteen deaths. El ataque ha causado al menos trece muertes. ➤ At least that motorcycle has a muffler. Al menos esa moto tiene un silenciador. ➤ At least he studies a little. Por lo menos estudia un poco. ➤ At least the dog obeys you, but not me. El perro a lo menos te obedece a ti, pero no a mí.

at least for now por lo menos por ahora

at least a little al menos un poco

at least not yet por lo menos todavía

at least that's what I thought al menos así lo he creído

at least to some extent al menos en cierto modo ■ al menos en cierta parte

to be **at loggerheads with someone** ■ to be at cross purposes with someone estar a la greña con alguien ■ andar a la greña con alguien ■ andar a palos con alguien ■ tener posiciones opuestas con alguien ■ estar en conflicto con alguien ■ estar en desacuerdo con alguien ➤ *(news item)* President Bush and Federal Reserve chairman Alan Greenspan are at loggerheads over the size of the tax cut. El presidente Bush y el presidente de la Reserva Federal, Alan Greenspan, andan a la greña por la cuantía de la rebaja fiscal.

to be **at loose ends** haber andado perdido

at mid morning a media mañana

at midnight a medianoche

at midweek ■ in the middle of the week a mediados de la semana

at most como máximo ■ a lo sumo ■ a todo tirar ■ como mucho ■ cuando más

at my age a mi edad ■ a estas alturas

to be **at my expense 1.** *(dinner, drink, etc.)* correr por cuenta mía **2.** *(joke)* ser a costa mía ■ ser a mi costa ➤ The dinner was at my expense. La cena corrió por cuenta mía. ➤ The joke was at my expense. El chiste fue a costa mía.

at night de noche ■ de la noche ■ por la noche ■ por las noches ➤ He arrived at night. Llegó por la noche. ➤ The attack began at ten at night. El ataque empezó a las diez de la noche. ➤ We always read at night. Siempre leemos por las noches. ➤ At night we always read. De noche siempre leemos. ■ Por la noche siempre leemos.

at nightfall a la caída de la noche ■ al anochecer

at no extra charge sin gastos adicionales ■ sin cargos adicionales ■ sin cargos extras

at no time en ningún momento

to be **at odds with each other** estar enfrentados el uno con el otro

to be **at odds with someone** estar enfrentado con alguien

to be **at odds with someone over something** ■ to be at odds with someone because of something estar en desacuerdo con alguien por algo ■ haber llegado a conclusiones distintas sobre algo

at off times a deshora ■ a deshoras ➤ Diabetics have to eat at off times. ■ A diabetic has to eat at off times. El diabético tiene que comer a deshora.

at once 1. immediately ■ this minute de una vez (por todas) ■ inmediatamente ■ en seguida ■ al punto **2.** at the same time a la vez ■ al mismo tiempo ➤ Come home at once! ■ Come home this minute! ¡Vuelve a casa de una vez! ➤ Straighten up your room this minute, will you! ¡Quieres recoger tu cuarto de una vez (por todas)! ➤ She would paint two pictures at once, alternating between the two. Solía pintar dos cuadros a la vez, alternando uno y otro. ➤ It is at once an affirmation of the old and a celebration of the new. Es al mismo tiempo una reafirmación de lo antiguo y una celebración de lo nuevo. ■ Es al mismo tiempo una confirmación de lo antiguo y una celebración de lo nuevo.

at one another: to look ~ *(more than two people)* mirarse entre ellos ■ mirarse entre sí

at one another: to shout ~ *(more than two people)* gritarse entre sí

at one point en cierto momento

at one time 1. once en cierta ocasión **2.** formerly en otro(s) tiempo(s) ➤ At one time we considered collaborating. En cierta ocasión pensábamos en colaborar. ➤ At one time, the justice would have been swift and severe. En otros tiempos la justicia habría sido más rápida y contundente.

to be **at one's best** dar lo mejor de sí mismo ■ dar lo mejor de uno mismo ■ estar a la altura de uno mismo ■ dar a la altura de uno mismo ■ estar al cien por cien ■ *(Sp., coll.)* estar uno que se sale ■ *(refers especially to wittiness)* estar sembrado ➤ The candidates were at their best during the debate. Los candidatos dieron lo mejor de sí mismos durante el debate. ■ Los candidatos estuvieron a su (propia) altura durante el debate.

at one's discretion según el criterio de uno

at one's disposal: to be (completely) ~ ■ to be (entirely) at one's disposal estar (cien por cien) a la disposición de uno

at one's earliest convenience en cuanto le sea posible ■ a la mayor brevedad posible

at one's expense a su costa ■ a costa suya ➤ They laughed at my expense. Se rieron a mi costa.

at one's fingertips: to have ~ tener a mano ■ tener al alcance de su mano ➤ That's information that any bank manager would have to have at his fingertips. Es información que cualquier gerente de banco tendría que tener a mano. ■ Es información que cualquier gerente de banco tendría que tener al alcance de su mano.

to be **at one's height** estar en pleno apogeo

at one's leisure ■ in one's leisure time ■ at times of one's own choosing en los ratos de ocio ■ en el tiempo libre ■ a su aire ■ a su ritmo

at one's own pace: to work ~ trabajar a su propio ritmo

at one's own request a petición propia ➤ The president will appear before Congress at his own request. El presidente comparecerá en el Congreso, a petición propia.

at one's own risk a riesgo suyo ■ por cuenta y riesgo ■ de cuenta y riesgo ➤ Enter at your own risk. *(tú)* Entra a riesgo tuyo. ■ *(usted)* Entre a riesgo suyo.

at one's request ■ at the request of one a petición suya ➤ The meeting was called at her request. La reunión fue convocada a petición suya. ➤ She came at my request. Vino a petición mía.

to be **at one's wit's end** ya no hallar la salida ■ no saber ni que hacer ■ no saber qué decir

at other times ■ on other occasions en otras ocasiones

at others' expense ■ at other people's expense a costa ajena ➤ Sponges live at others expense. ■ Leeches live at other's expense. El gorrón vive a costa ajena.

at planeside a pie de avión ➤ Can we get our bags at planeside? ¿Podemos recoger el equipaje a pie de avión?

at pointblank range: to fire (a shot) ~ pegar un tiro a quemarropa ■ disparar a quemarropa

at present ■ at the present time en este momento ■ actualmente ■ en la actualidad ■ en estos momentos

at press time al cierre de la edición ■ al cierre de esta edición

at random al azar ■ aleatoriamente

at regular intervals ■ continual a intervalos regulares ■ a determinados intervalos ■ *(Sp.)* a cada equis tiempo ➤ The air shuttle provides flights at regular intervals between Madrid and Barcelona. ■ The air shuttle provides continual flights between Madrid and Barcelona. El puente aéreo provee vuelos continuos entre Madrid y Barcelona. ■ El puente aéreo provee vuelos a intervalos regulares entre Madrid y Barcelona. ■ El puente aéreo provee vuelos a cada equis tiempo entre Madrid y Barcelona.

at regular times ■ at set times ■ at fixed times a unas horas fijas ■ a unas determinadas horas ■ a unas horas determinadas ➤ Does the bus come by here at regular times? ¿Pasa el autobús a unas horas fijas? ■ ¿Pasa el autobús a unas horas determinadas?

to be **at rest** *(physics)* estar en reposo

to be **at right angles** estar en ángulo recto ■ formar (una) escuadra

to be **at risk** estar en riesgo

at risk: to put ~ ■ to place at risk poner en riesgo

at room temperature 1. a temperatura de ambiente 2. *(food)* unheated del tiempo ➤ ¿Heated?-No thanks, unheated is fine. ¿Se lo caliento?-No gracias, del tiempo está bien.

at rush hour en hora punta ➤ *(headline)* Power outage at rush hour causes chaos in London ■ Rush-hour power outage causes chaos in London Un apagón en hora punta provoca el caos en Londres

to be **at school** 1. *(primary and secondary)* estar en la escuela 2. *(university)* estar en la facultad ■ estar en la universidad ➤ He's at school right now. Está en la escuela en este momento. ■ Está en la facultad en este momento.

to be **at sea** 1. *(literal)* estar en alta mar 2. to flounder estar a la deriva ➤ The entire fleet is at sea. La flota entera está en alta mar. ➤ He's been at sea since he flunked out of school. Ha estado a la deriva desde que lo suspendieron de la universidad.

at set times ■ at fixed times ■ at regular times a unas horas fijas ■ a unas determinadas horas ■ a unas horas determinadas ➤ Does the bus come by here at set times? ¿Pasa el autobús a unas horas fijas? ■ ¿Pasa el autobús a unas horas determinadas?

at (sign) ■ @ *(computers)* arroba

at so many dollars per hour a tantos dólares por hora ➤ Let's say you calculated twenty-four hours of work at so many dollars per hour. Digamos que calculaste veinticuatro horas de trabajo a tantos dólares por hora.

at some future time en un futuro

at some point en algún momento ➤ We'll see each other at some point. Nos veremos en algún momento.

at some point in one's life en algún momento en su vida

at some point in their lives en algún momento en su vida

at some time alguna vez

at some time in their lives en un momento dado de sus vidas

at some time or other en algún momento u otro

at someone else's expense at another's expense a costa ajena

at someone's behest a instancias de alguien ■ por orden de alguien

at someone's request a petición de ➤ Dreadlocks went to the barber at his boss' request. Rastas fue al peluquero a petición de su jefe.

to be **at someone's side** estar al lado de alguien

at something for a long time: to have been ~ ■ to have been doing something for a long time llevar mucho tiempo en algo ➤ I've been at this for a long time. ■ I've been doing this for a long time. Llevo mucho tiempo en esto.

to be **at stake** estar en juego ➤ The company's reputation is at stake. El prestigio de la compañía está en juego.

at stake: (for) there to be too much ~ haber demasiado en juego ➤ There's too much at stake to let myself fall behind in the reading. Hay demasiado en juego como para permitirme una demora en la lectura.

at such and such times en tal o cual momento ■ en tales o cuales momentos

at sunrise ■ at sunup al salir el sol ■ a la salida del sol

at sunset ■ at sundown al ponerse el sol ■ a la puesta del sol ■ en el ocaso

at suppertime a la hora de la cena

to be **at the other end of the street** estar al otro extremo de la calle. ■ *(coll.)* estar a la otra punta de la calle

at the very end ■ right at the end justo al final ➤ Add the chopped green pepper at the very end. ■ Add the chopped green pepper right at the end. Añade el pimiento verde picado justo al final.

at that 1. in addition además 2. in response ■ immediately y al instante ■ acto seguido 3. in place, agreed upon en eso ➤ She's a writer, and a very talented one at that. Es escritora y además de mucho talento. ➤ Aunt Polly turned her back, and at that, Tom fled out the kitchen door. La tía Polly se dio la vuelta, y acto seguido, Tom salió volando por la puerta de la cocina. ➤ We'll leave it at that. Quedamos en eso.

at that age a esa edad

at that instant ■ at that moment en ese preciso instante ■ *(historical or fictional narrative)* en aquel preciso instante ➤ At that instant, Scrooge heard a noise in his room. En aquel preciso instante Scrooge oyó un ruido en su habitación.

at that moment ■ just then 1. en ese instante ■ en ese momento 2. en aquel instante ■ en aquel momento ➤ At that moment, the concrete mixer was going the other way. En ese momento, la hormigonera circulaba por el sentido contrario.

at that point *("at that point in time" is common but redundant)* en aquel momento

at that time en ese entonces ■ en aquel entonces ■ por entonces ■ por aquel entonces ■ por esa época ■ en ese tiempo ■ *(literary)* a la sazón ➤ At that time, we lived in Colonia Vertiz Narvarte. Por aquel entonces vivíamos en Colonia Vertiz Narvarte. ➤ At that time, universities were still using perforated cards for registration. En aquella época las universidades todavía utilizaban impresos perforados para la matrícula.

at that very moment ■ at that very instant ■ at that exact moment ■ at that exact instant en aquel preciso instante ■ en aquel mismo momento ■ en ese mismo momento

at the age of *x* ■ at age *x* a los *x* (años) ■ con los *x* (años) ➤ At (the age of) fourteen... A los catorce (años)... ➤ *(Valladolid headline)* Schoolchildren begin smoking at the age of thirteen Los escolares empiezan a fumar a los trece años

at the appointed hour a la hora prevista ■ a la hora señalada ➤ He makes an appointment, and then at the appointed hour he doesn't show up. Hace la cita y luego no se presenta a la hora prevista.

at the back (of) ■ in the back of en la parte de atrás (de) ➤ We were sitting at the back of the auditorium. ■ We were sitting in the back of the auditorium. Estábamos sentados en la parte de atrás del auditorio.

at the beginning of a principios de ▪ al comienzo de ▪ *(a street)* a la boca de ▪ en la bocacalle ➤ At the beginning of the century... A principios del siglo ➤ At the beginning of the twentieth century... A principios del Siglo XX... ➤ At the beginning of the movie... Al principio de la película... ▪ Al comienzo de la película... ➤ At the beginning of the street... En la bocacalle... ▪ A la boca de la calle... ▪ Al principio de la calle... ▪ Al comienzo de la calle...

to be **at the beginning of the line** ▪ to be at the head of the line ▪ to be at the front of the line ▪ to be first in line estar el primero de la fila ▪ estar a la cabeza de la cola

at the beginning of the page al principio de la página

at the beginning of the year al comienzo del año ▪ al inicio del año

to be **at the boiling point** estar en el punto de ebullición

at the bottom (of) al fondo (de)

at the bottom of the hour ▪ at the end of the hour al final de la hora

at the bottom of the ninth (inning) *(baseball)* ▪ at the end of the ninth (inning) al final del noveno tiempo

at the bottom of the page ▪ at the foot of the page al pie de la página ▪ al final de la página

to be **at the controls** estar al mando

at the core of Kant's philosophy ▪ at the heart of Kant's philosophy en el núcleo de la filosofía de Kant ▪ en el núcleo de filosofía Kantiana ▪ en el centro de la filosofía de Kant

to be **at the corner of** estar haciendo esquina con ▪ hacer esquina con ▪ estar en la esquina de ▪ estar en la esquina entre ➤ The restaurant is at the corner of Sor Ángela and Infanta Mercedes. El restaurante está haciendo esquina con Sor Ángela e Infanta Mercedes. ▪ El restaurante hace esquina con Sor Ángela e Infanta Mercedes. ▪ El restaurante está en la esquina entre Sor Ángela e Infanta Mercedes.

at the crack of dawn al rayar el alba ▪ *(from Don Quijote, and only in past tense)* la del alba sería ➤ He's up every morning at the crack of dawn. Cada día se levanta al rayar el alba. ➤ I got up at the crack of dawn. La del alba sería cuando me levanté.

at the customer's request 1. a petición del cliente **2.** at the customer's disposal a disposición del cliente ➤ The pianist played Happy Birthday at the customer's request. El pianista tocó Feliz Cumpleaños a petición del cliente. ➤ We have a large variety of condiments at the customer's request. Tenemos un amplio surtido de guarniciones a disposición del cliente.

at the dinner table: to be sitting ~ ▪ to be seated at the dinner table estar sentado a la mesa ➤ We were sitting at the dinner table when the doorbell rang. Estábamos comiendo sentados a la mesa cuando sonó el timbre. ▪ Estabamos sentados a la mesa cuando llamaron a la puerta. *("Mesa de comedor" means "dining room table." For "dinner table," Hispanics just say "mesa.")*

to be **at the door** estar en la puerta ▪ estar a la puerta ➤ Someone's at the door. Hay alguien en la puerta. ▪ Hay alguien a la puerta. ➤ Go see who's at the door. Ve a ver quien está en la puerta. ▪ Mira a ver quien está en la puerta. ▪ Ve a ver quien está a la puerta. ▪ Mira a ver quien está a la puerta.

at the drop of a hat: to do something ~ *(coll.)* ▪ as if it were nothing hacer algo sin más ni más ▪ hacer algo al toque ▪ hacer algo al menor pretexto ▪ hacer algo sin pretexto alguno ▪ hacer algo con la mínima excusa ➤ Jet-setters fly all over the world at the drop of a hat. La gente del "jet set" vuela por todo el mundo al menor pretexto.

at the earliest lo antes posible ▪ *(Sp.)* como muy pronto

to be **at the edge of the abyss** estar al borde (del abismo)

to be **at the end of one's patience** ▪ to be running out of patience acabársele la paciencia ▪ agotársele la paciencia ▪ estar al borde de la paciencia ➤ I'm at the end of my patience. Se me acaba la paciencia.

to be **at the end of one's rope** ▪ to be at the end of one's tether ya no poder más ▪ ya no aguantar más

to be **at the end of one's tether** ▪ to be at the end of one's rope ya no poder más ▪ ya no aguantar más

to be **at the end of the aisle** estar en el fondo del pasillo ▪ estar en el extremo del pasillo ▪ estar al final del pasillo

at the end of the century en las postrimerías del siglo ▪ al final del siglo

at the end of the concert al final del concierto ➤ At the end of the concert, the audience demanded an encore. Al final del concierto, el público pidió un bis.

at the end of the day 1. *(literal)* at the conclusion of the day al fin del día ▪ al final del día **2.** *(figurative)* in the final analysis a fin de cuentas

at the end of the hall al fondo del corredor ▪ en el extremo del corredor ▪ al final del corredor ▪ al fondo del pasillo ▪ en el extremo del pasillo ▪ al final del pasillo

at the end of the month al final del mes ▪ a fin de mes

at the end of the street al final de la calle ▪ al fondo de la calle

at the end of the summer al final del verano

at the end of the week al final de la semana

at the end of the year a fin de año ▪ al final del año

at the end of *x* months al cabo de *x* meses

at the expense of someone 1. *(literal)* at someone's expense a expensas de alguien **2.** *(negative)* a costa(s) de alguien ➤ We went out to dinner at my expense. (I paid for the dinner.) Comimos afuera a mis expensas. (Pagué la cuenta.) ➤ The joke was at my expense. El chiste fue a costa mía.

to be **at the far end of the street** estar en el otro extremo de la calle ➤ The butcher shop is at the far end of the street. La carnicería está en el otro extremo de la calle.

at the first opportunity a la primera oportunidad

at the first shot 1. *(literal)* al primer tiro ▪ al primer balazo **2.** *(figurative)* on the first try al primer intento **3.** *(of a cannon)* a la primera descarga

at the first sign of trouble al primer indicio de problemas

at the foot of the page ▪ at the bottom of the page al pie de la página ▪ al final de la página

to be **at the forefront of** ▪ to be on the cutting edge of estar a la vanguardia de ▪ estar en primera línea de ➤ He's at the forefront of his field. Él está a la vanguardia en su campo.

to be **at the front of...** ▪ to be at the head of estar al frente de ➤ The captain was at the front of the squadron. ▪ The captain was at the head of the squadron. El capitán estaba al frente del escuadrón.

to be **at the front of the line** ▪ to be at the head of the line ▪ to be at the beginning of the line ▪ to be first in line estar el primero de la fila ▪ estar a la cabeza de la cola

at the hands of a manos de ➤ The fall of Constantinople at the hands of the Muslims marked the end of the Middle Ages. La caída de Constantinopla a manos de los musulmanes marcó el final de la Edad Media.

to be **at the head of the line** ▪ to be at the front of the line ▪ to be at the beginning of the line ▪ to be first in line estar el primero de la fila ▪ estar a la cabeza de la cola ➤ She's at the head of the line. ▪ She's at the front of the line. ▪ She's the first (one) in line. Está la primera de la fila. ▪ (Ella) está a la cabeza de la cola.

(at) the heart of the issue *el* quid de la cuestión ▪ al centro del asunto ▪ *(Sp., coll.)* meollo de la cuestión

to be **at the height of one's career** estar en la cúspide de su carrera ▪ estar en la cumbre de su carrera ▪ estar en lo más alto de su carrera

at the height of the Middle Ages en plena Edad Media

at the height of the rush hour en plena hora punta

at the highest point on ▪ at the highest point of en lo alto de

at the home of en casa de ➤ The reception will be held at the home of the bride's grandparents. La recepción se dará en casa de los abuelos de la novia.

at the instigation of ▪ at the urging of ▪ at the insistence of ▪ at the suggestion of ante la insistencia de ▪ a instancias de ➤ I went to the art exhibit at the instigation of a couple of my friends. ▪ I went to the art exhibit at the urging of a couple of my friends. ▪ I went to the art exhibit at the insistence of a couple of my friends. Fui a la exposición ante la insistencia de un par de amigos.

at the invitation of someone: to go ~ ▪ to be invited by someone invitar a alguien ➤ I went to the party at the invitation of a couple of my friends. Un par de amigos me invitaron a la fiesta.

at the last minute a última hora ▪ *(coll.)* con el tiempo pegado al culo

at the latest a más tardar ▪ como muy tarde

at the level of the water table ▪ at water-table level a nivel freático

to be **at the library** estar en la biblioteca ➤ She's at the library. Está en la biblioteca. ➤ There's an exhibit on Ogden Nash at the library. Hay una exhibición sobre Ogden Nash en la biblioteca.

to be **at the limit** estar en el límite ➤ With ten items, you're at the limit for the express checkout. Con diez artículos estás en el límite de la caja rápida. ➤ I'm at the limit or under it. Estoy en el límite o por debajo.

to be **at the limit(s) of one's endurance** estar al límite de su resistencia ➤ The mountain climbers were at the limit(s) of their endurance. Los montañeros estaban al límite de su resistencia.

to be **at the mercy of the elements** estar a merced de los elementos ▪ estar a la intemperie

at the moment 1. at this instant de momento ▪ en este momento ▪ en el momento 2. for the time being por ahora ▪ en este momento 3. currently de turno 4. *(in past narrative)* en el momento ➤ I can't think of it at the moment. De momento no puedo pensarlo. ▪ No puedo pensarlo de momento. ▪ No puedo pensarlo en el momento. ➤ That's the only example I can think of at the moment. ▪ Es el único ejemplo que se me ocurre en este momento. ➤ That's all I need at the moment. Es todo lo que necesito por ahora. ▪ Es todo lo que necesito en este momento. ➤ Public opinion at the moment El qué dirán de turno ➤ At the moment of the explosion, I was busy at home and was unaware of it. En el momento de la explosión, yo estaba ocupada en mi casa y no me di cuenta.

at the most todo lo más

at the outset ▪ at the start ante todo ▪ de primeras

at the outside *(coll.)* ▪ at maximum ▪ at most a lo máximo ▪ *(Sp.)* como mucho ➤ There's a metro train every five minutes at the outside, and usually every one to three minutes. Hay un tren de metro cada cinco minutos como mucho, y normalmente pasa entre uno y tres minutos.

to be **at the point of** estar a pique de ▪ estar a dedos de

to be **at the point of death** estar en trance de muerte ▪ estar a punto de morir

to be **at the point of no return** estar a punto de no poder volver atrás

at the present time ▪ at present en estos momentos ▪ en la actualidad

at the price of 1. for por ▪ a razón de ▪ a precio de 2. by sacrificing aunque cueste ➤ I bought the tomatoes at the price of two dollars per pound. ▪ I bought the tomatoes for two dollars per pound. Compré los tomates a razón de dos dólares la libra. ➤ Certainty at the price of honesty Certeza aunque nos cueste la honestidad

at the rate of al ritmo de ▪ a un ritmo de ▪ a razón de

at the rate of *x* 1. a razón de *x* 2. al ritmo de *x* ➤ Labor was computed at the rate of fifteen dollars per hour. El trabajo se calculó a razón de quince dólares la hora. ➤ The tanker truck dispenses fuel at the rate of one hundred liters per minute. El camión cisterna descarga el combustible a razón de cien litros el minuto. ➤ This file grows at the rate of a page every two days. Este fichero crece al ritmo de una página cada dos días.

at the rate of *x* miles per gallon: to consume fuel ~ consumir combustible a razón de *x* galones por milla ▪ consumir *x* galones de combustible por milla

at the rate of *x* percent annually a una tasa anual del *x* por ciento

at the rate one is going al paso que uno va ➤ At the rate we're going, we'll never get there. Al paso que vamos, nunca llegaremos.

at the request of a petición de ▪ a instancia(s) de

at the request of one ▪ at one's request a petición suya

at the right time en el momento adecuado

at the risk of so pena de ▪ al riesgo de

at the same time al mismo tiempo ▪ a la vez ▪ a un tiempo ▪ al tiempo ▪ paralelamente

at the side of the road ▪ beside the road junto al camino

at the sound of the beep al oírse la señal (acústica)

at the stroke of midnight al filo de la medianoche

at the stroke of twelve al filo de las doce

at the suggestion of a la indicación de

at the thought of... al pensar en...

at the thought that... al pensar que...

at the time 1. *(future or past)* en el momento ▪ en el instante 2. *(when)* cuando 3. *(at the same time)* sobre la marcha ▪ al mismo tiempo ➤ We'll do it at the time. Lo haremos en el momento. ▪ Lo haremos en el instante. ➤ The bank mistakingly changed the account number at the time it issued the new card. El banco cambió por error el número de cuenta cuando emitió la nueva tarjeta. ➤ We'll do it at the (same) time. Lo haremos sobre la marcha. ▪ Lo haremos al mismo tiempo.

at the time of en el momento de ▪ al momento de ➤ At the time of Kennedy's death, the population of the United States was one hundred (and) eighty million. Al tiempo de la muerte de Kennedy, la población estadounidense era de ciento ochenta millones de habitantes.

at the time that... 1. *(precise)* en el momento en que... 2. *(general)* al tiempo que...

at the top of a cliff ▪ at the top of a precipice en lo alto de un precipicio ▪ en lo alto de un acantilado ▪ en lo alto de un despeñadero

at the top of a mountain en la cima de una montaña

at the top of one's lungs: to cry ~ llorar a grito limpio ▪ llorar a grito pelado ➤ The child was crying at the top of his lungs. El niño lloraba a grito limpio. ▪ El niño lloraba a grito pelado.

at the top of one's lungs: to shout ~ ▪ to shout at the top of one's voice gritar a pleno pulmón ▪ decir a grito pelado ▪ decir a grito limpio ➤ He was shouting at the top of his lungs. Gritaba a pleno pulmón.

at the top of the hour ▪ at the beginning of the hour al principio de la hora ▪ al comienzo de la hora ▪ al empezar la hora

to be **at the top of the list** ▪ to head the list ▪ to be the first one on the list estar al principio de la lista ▪ encabezar la lista ▪ estar primero en la lista

at the top of the ninth (inning) *(baseball)* ▪ at the beginning of the ninth (inning) al principio del noveno tiempo ▪ al comienzo del noveno tiempo

at the top of the page en la parte superior de la página ▪ en la parte de arriba de la página

at the top of the screen en la parte superior de la pantalla ▪ en la parte de arriba de la pantalla ➤ There are no icons for flush left and right at the top of the screen. No hay iconos para alinear el texto a izquierda y derecha en la parte superior de la pantalla.

at the top of the stairs ▪ at the top of the steps en lo alto de la escalera

at the very beginning justo al comienzo ▪ justo al principio

at the very bottom justo al fondo

at the very end ▪ right at the end justo al final ➤ Add the chopped green pepper at the very end. You want them to be hot, but still crunchy. Añade el pimiento verde picado justo al final. Es deseable que estén calientes pero a la vez crujientes.

at the very last minute ▪ right at the last minute en el último minuto ▪ *(coll.)* con el tiempo pegado al culo

at the very moment that... en el mismo momento en que...

at the very top justo arriba del todo

at the worst possible time en el peor momento ▪ en el peor de los momentos ➤ They dropped in on us at the worst possible time. Se presentaron en el peor momento.

at the wrong time a destiempo ▪ a deshora

at this hour a estas horas ➤ What are you doing up at this hour? ¿Qué haces despierto(-a) a estas horas? ▪ ¿Qué haces levantado(-a) a estas horas?

at this moment ▪ right now en este momento

at this number en este número ➤ He can be reached at this number. Puede ser contactado en este número. ➤ She can be reached at this number. Puede ser contactada en este número.

at this point a estas alturas ▪ en este momento ➤ I think I have sufficient mastery at this point. Creo que ya tengo suficiente dominio a estas alturas. ➤ I don't know at this point if I'll be here that weekend. No sé decirte desde ahora si estaré aquí ese fin de semana.

at this rate a este paso ■ a este ritmo ➤ At this rate we'll never get there. A este paso nunca llegaremos. ■ A este ritmo nunca llegaremos. ➤ At this rate we'll never finish. A este paso no vamos a terminar nunca. ■ A este ritmo no vamos a terminar nunca.

at this stage (of the game) ■ at this point ■ having come this far llegado a este punto ➤ We cannot retreat at this stage (of the game). No podemos echarnos atrás llegados a este punto. ➤ I can't quit school at this stage (of the game). ■ I can't quit school at this point. ■ I can't quit school, having come this far. No puedo dejar mis estudios habiendo llegado tan lejos. ■ No puedo dejar mis estudios habiendo llegado hasta aquí.

at this time 1. at this exact moment en este momento **2.** at this juncture en este momento **3.** at this hour a esta hora **4.** for the time being por el momento ■ por ahora ➤ Normally I have a class at this time. ■ Normally I have a class (at) this hour. Normalmente tengo una clase a esta hora. ➤ We don't have a cat at this time, but we used to. En este momento no tenemos un gato, pero solíamos tenerlo. ➤ We don't have a cat at this time, but we're going to get one. Por ahora no tenemos un gato, pero vamos a conseguir uno.

at this time of year por estas fechas ■ en esta época del año ■ a estas alturas del año

at this very moment ■ as we speak en estos precisos momentos ■ justo ahora ■ conforme hablamos ➤ I'm working on it at this very moment. ■ I'm working on it as we speak. Estoy trabajando en ello justo ahora. ■ Estoy trabajando en ello en estos precisos momentos. ■ Estoy trabajando en ello conforme hablamos.

at times ■ occasionally ■ sometimes a veces

at twilight 1. at dawn (morning) al alba **2.** at dusk (evening) al crepúsculo

to be **at war with** estar en guerra con ■ estar en guerra contra

at water level: to fly ~ ■ to fly slightly above the surface of the water volar a ras del agua

at what cost? *(literal and figurative)* ¿a qué precio? ➤ He has an interesting career.-Yes, but at what cost? He's sacrificed his personal life. Tiene una carrera profesional muy interesante.-Sí, ¿pero a qué precio? Ha sacrificado su vida personal.

at which point ■ whereupon con lo cual

at which time en que momento

at will 1. a voluntad ■ a placer ■ a su voluntad **2.** whenever one wants cuando (uno) quiera ■ cuando le de la gana a uno **3.** whenever one wanted cuando (uno) quería ■ *(formal)* cuando le place a uno ■ cuando le placía a uno ➤ A century ago, people couldn't listen to a Beethoven concerto at will, but might have to wait years to hear it. Cien años atrás, las personas no podían escuchar un concierto de Beethoven a su voluntad, pero hubiesen tenido que esperar años para ello.

to be **at work** estar en el trabajo ■ estar trabajando ➤ She's at work. (Ella) está en el trabajo. ■ (Ella) está trabajando. ➤ I'm at work. Estoy en el trabajo.

at worst ■ at the very worst en el peor de los casos ■ poniéndonos en lo peor

at your earliest convenience a la mayor brevedad posible ■ con la mayor brevedad posible

at your service para servirle ■ servidor de usted

at *x* percent al *x* por ciento

athletic shoes zapatillas de deporte

ATM (machine) ■ automated teller machine cajero automático

atmosphere conducive to talks ambiente propicio para el diálogo

atmosphere of distrust *el* ambiente de recelo ■ ambiente de desconfianza

atmospheric conditions condiciones atmosféricas

atom smasher *(coll.)* ■ particle accelerator *el* acelerador de partículas

atomic reactor reactor atómico

to **attach jumper cables** poner cocodrilos ■ colocar cocodrilos

to **attach something to something 1.** to stick something to something pegar algo a algo ■ adosar algo a algo **2.** to tie, nail, or hook something to something sujetar algo a algo ■ agregar algo a algo **3.** to connect something to something adjuntar algo a algo ➤ A limpet bomb (stick-on bomb) attached to the underside of the car exploded. Una bomba lapa adosada a los bajos del coche hizo explosión. ➤ There was no receipt attached to the box. No había ningún recibo pegado a la caja. ■ No había ningún recibo adosado a la caja. ➤ The disks are separate from, but attach to, the bar of the dumbbells. Los discos son separables, pero vienen sujetos a la barra de las mancuernas. ➤ The hose needs to be attached to the spigot. La manguera necesita estar adjuntada a la boca de riego.

to be **attached to someone** *(emotionally)* tenerle cariño a alguien

attached to someone or something: to get ~ ■ to become attached to someone encariñarse con alguien o algo ➤ Children get attached to pets. Los niños se encariñan con las mascotas.

to be **attached to something** estar adjunto a algo ■ estar agregado a algo

attached to something: to come ~ venir pegado a ■ venir con ➤ The little radios came attached to the jars of peanut butter. Los pequeños radios venían pegado a los tarros de crema de cacahuete. ■ Los pequeños radios venían con los tarros de crema de cacahuete.

attachment to an E-mail ■ E-mail attachment anexo a un correo electrónico ➤ You shouldn't open E-mail attachments from strangers. No deberías abrir anexos a los correos electrónicos que vengan de desconocidos.

to **attack a target** atacar un objetivo ■ atacar un blanco

attack on a target ataque a un objetivo ■ atentado contra un objetivo ➤ Attack on a U.S. destroyer in Yemen Ataque a un destructor de EE UU en Yemen ➤ In the alliance, an attack on one is considered an attack on all. En la alianza atacar a uno sólo se considera como un ataque al resto.

attack on a target: to launch an ~ lanzar un ataque contra un objetivo ■ lanzar un ataque contra un blanco

attack on civilians atentado contra civiles

to **attack someone 1.** to mug someone agredir a alguien ■ atacar a alguien ■ atracar a alguien **2.** to criticize someone agredir verbalmente a alguien ■ criticar

attack victim ■ mugging victim agredido

attainable goal objetivo alcanzable ■ meta alcanzable

attainable growth crecimiento alcanzable ■ crecimiento posible ■ crecimiento realista

attempt to: in an ~ en un intento por ➤ In a desperate attempt to escape En un intento desesperado por escapar

to **attempt to do something** ■ to try to do something intentar hacer algo

attempts to ■ efforts to intentos de ■ intentos para ➤ Attempts to establish the Inquisition in Naples and Milan failed. Los intentos de establecer la Inquisición en Nápoles y Milán fracasaron. ■ Los intentos para establecer la Inquisición en Nápoles y Milán fracasaron.

attempted assault intento de agresión

attempted coup ■ coup attempt intentona golpista ■ intentona de golpe de estado

attempted murder ■ attempted homicide ■ homicide attempt intento de homicidio ■ tentativa de asesinato

attempted suicide ■ suicide attempt intento de suicidio ■ tentativa de suicidio

to **attend a meeting** asistir a una reunión

to **attend a public event 1.** *(formal event)* concurrir a un evento ■ concurrir a un acto público **2.** *(entertainment event)* asistir a un espectáculo ■ presenciar un espectáculo ➤ All the European delegates attended the summit. Todos los delegados europeos concurrieron a la cumbre. ➤ Percival has never been to a bullfight. Percival nunca ha asistido a una corrida de toros. ■ Percival nunca ha presenciado una corrida de toros.

to **attend class** asistir a clase

to **attend Mass** asistir a misa

to **attend regularly** asistir con regularidad

to **attend someone 1.** to attend to someone atender a alguien **2.** *(literary)* ■ to accompany someone amparar a alguien ➤ The nurse attended (to) the patient. La enfermera atendió al paciente. ➤ An abiding public trust attended Lincoln, despite the controversy he endured. Lincoln se vió amparado por la confianza inquebrantable de la gente, a pesar de la controversia que sufrió.

attention! *(military)* ¡firmes!

attention deficit disorder trastorno por déficit de atención

attention span índice de atención ➤ A study has shown that reading to children increases their attention span at school. Un estudio ha demostrado que leerle a los niños aumenta su índice de atención en clase.

attention to this matter: thank you for your ~ agradeciéndole la atención prestada a este asunto

attitude toward ▪ attitude towards *la* actitud hacia

attorney general fiscal general ▪ titular de la justicia ▪ secretario(-a) de justicia

to **attract attention** llamar la atención

to **attract one's attention** llamarle la atención

to **attract flies** atraer a las moscas

to be **attracted to someone** ▪ to feel attracted to someone ▪ to feel attraction for someone sentirse atraído por alguien ▪ sentir atracción por alguien

to **attribute human qualities to animals** asignárseles atributos humanos a los animales

to **auction (off) something** ▪ to auction something off subastar algo ▪ sacar algo a subasta ➤ For tax purposes, the family auctioned off items of furniture, jewelry, and clothes. La familia subastó artículos de mobiliario, de joyería y de ropa por motivos fiscales. ➤ For tax purposes, the family auctioned the items off. La familia subastó los artículos por motivos fiscales. ➤ For tax purposes, the family auctioned them off. La familia los subastó por motivos fiscales.

to **audit a course** ▪ to audit a class ▪ to audit a subject ir de oyente a un curso ▪ ir de oyente a una clase ▪ ir de oyente a una asignatura

to **audit the books** hacer una auditoría (de los libros de cuentas)

to **audition for a part as...** presentarse a una audición para un papel de...

to **audition for the part of...** presentarse a una audición para el papel de...

aunt and uncle: my ~ mis tíos

aurora borealis ▪ northern lights ▪ aurora polaris aurora boreal

authentic and genuine auténtico y genuino ▪ de pura cepa ➤ Arturo is a native of Vera Cruz, authentic and genuine. Arturo es un jarocho de pura cepa. ▪ Arturo es un jarocho auténtico y genuino.

author of such notable works as autor(-a) de obras entre las que se destacan

authoritarian parents padres impositores ▪ padres autoritarios

authority figure figura de autoridad

authorized personnel only prohibido el paso a toda persona ajena

automobile industry sector automovilístico

to **avail oneself of** *(literary)* ▪ to take advantage of valerse de

availability of something: to check on the ~ comprobar la disponibilidad de algo ▪ comprobar si se tiene algo ➤ I need to check on the availability of fresh strawberries at this time of year. Necesito comprobar la disponibilidad de fresas frescas en esta época del año.

availability of tickets: to check on the ~ comprobar la disponibilidad de los billetes

avenue for: to provide an ~ ▪ to provide a way to ▪ to provide a means of suponer una senda hacia ➤ Democracy provides an avenue for the open expression and redress of grievances. La democracia supone una senda hacia la denuncia y enmienda de los perjuicios.

avenue for the expression of something: to have an ~ tener cauce para la expresión de algo ▪ dar cauce a la expresión de algo ▪ dar cauce a la imaginación de uno ➤ Without having any avenue for its expression Sin tener cauce para su expresión ▪ Sin poder dar cauce a su imaginación

avenue for the expression of something: to provide an ~ dar cauce a algo

avenues of communication vías de comunicación

average age edad promedio ▪ edad media ▪ media de edad ➤ The average age of the framers of the United States' Constitution was about forty years. La edad promedio de los artífices de la constitución de los Estados Unidos era de aproximadamente cuarenta años. ➤ My classmates have an average age of twenty (years). Mis compañeros de clase tienen una edad media de veinte años.

average build: to be of ~ ▪ to have an average build ser de complexión media

average decrease descenso medio ▪ declive medio

average family familia media

average increase ascenso medio ▪ aumento medio

average-looking person persona de aspecto normal ▪ persona corriente

average monthly consumption of electricity consumo medio mensual de electricidad

average monthly payment for electricity pago medio mensual de electricidad

average monthly rate tasa media mensual

average number of media de ▪ promedio de ➤ The average number of pupils in the Spanish classes is twenty-five. El promedio de alumnos en las clases de español es de veinticinco. ➤ The average number of children per family in China is one. ▪ In China couples have one child per family on (the) average. En China tienen un hijo por familia como media.

average of: to do an ~ hacer una media de

average of: to grow an ~ crecer una media de

to **average per hour** ganar de media por hora ➤ How much did you average per hour on that job? ¿Cuánto ganaste de media por hora en ese trabajo?

average person tipo medio ▪ persona del montón

averse to doing something: not to be ~ no estar en contra de hacer algo ➤ I'm not averse to going to the movies, but I'd rather go out for dinner and just talk. No estoy en contra de ir al cine, pero preferiría salir a cenar y charlar un poco. ▪ No es que me moleste ir al cine, pero preferiría salir a cenar y charlar un poco.

averse to: to become ~ tomarle aversión a algo ▪ *(Sp.)* cogerle aversión a algo ➤ In his old age he has become very averse to a comb. En su vejez le tomó aversión al peine. ▪ *(Sp.)* En su vejez le cogió aversión al peine.

to **avert a crisis** ▪ to head off a crisis evitar una crisis

to **avert a disaster** ▪ to prevent a disaster (from happening) ▪ to head off a disaster evitar un desastre ▪ prevenir un desastre

to **avert an accident** ▪ to prevent an accident (from happening) evitar un accidente ▪ prevenir un accidente

to **avert one's gaze** ▪ to avert one's eyes ▪ to look away apartar la vista

avian influenza ▪ bird flu *la* gripe del pollo

to **avoid a person** evitar a una persona ▪ huir de una persona

to **avoid a situation** evitar una situación

to **avoid being detected by someone** ▪ to avoid detection by someone evitar ser detectado por alguien

to **avoid doing something** ▪ to get out of doing something intentar no hacer algo ▪ evitar hacer algo ▪ *(coll.)* escaquearse (de hacer algo) ➤ He avoids paying whenever he can. Se escaquea de pagar siempre que puede. ➤ My co-worker always tries to avoid doing things. ▪ My co-worker always tries to get out of doing things. Mi compañero de trabajo está siempre escaqueándose.

to **avoid meeting someone** evitar el encuentro con alguien ▪ evitar encontrarse a alguien

to **avoid responsibility for** evitar responsabilidad por

to **avoid someone like the plague** huirle como la peste ▪ evitar a alguien como si fuera la peste ➤ She avoids him like the plague. Le huye como la peste. ▪ Le evita como si fuera la peste.

to **avoid something** evitar algo ▪ escapar de algo ▪ rehuir de algo ➤ He avoids work like the plague. Le escapa al trabajo como la peste. ▪ Le escapa al trabajo que da miedo.

to **avoid suspicion by someone** ■ to avoid being suspected by someone conseguir que no se sospeche de alguien ➤ For fifteen years the spy managed to avoid suspicion by the FBI. Durante quince años el espía consiguió que el FBI no sospechara de él.

to **avoid talking about something** rehuir hablar de algo ■ rehusar hablar de algo ■ evitar hablar del tema ■ evadir el tema

to **avoid the issue** ■ to dodge the issue evitar el tema ■ esquivar el asunto ■ cambiar de tema ■ *(coll.)* escurrir el bulto ➤ Don't avoid the issue. ■ Don't dodge the issue. No evites el tema. ■ No esquives el asunto. ■ No cambies de tema. ■ No escurras el bulto.

to **avoid the pitfalls** evitar los baches ➤ Their children avoided the pitfalls into which the children of other celebrities have fallen. Sus hijos evitaron los baches en los que han caído los hijos de otros celebridades.

avowed atheist ateo(-a) declarado(-a)

avowed communist comunista declarado(-a)

to **await the results of the medical tests** ■ to wait for the results of the medical tests esperar los resultados de las pruebas médicas

to be **awaiting word** ■ to be waiting to hear estar en compás de espera ■ estar a la espera

to **awaken someone** ■ to wake someone up ■ to wake up someone despertar a alguien ➤ The alarm clock awakens me at 6:45 each morning. ■ The alarm clock wakes me up at 6:45 each morning. El reloj despertador me despierta cada mañana a las siete menos cuarto.

to **awaken suspicion(s) that...** ■ to raise suspicion(s) that... ■ to arouse suspicion(s) that... ■ to arouse the suspicion that... ■ to raise the suspicion that... ■ to awaken the suspicion that... despertar sospechas de que... ■ levantar sospechas de que...

to be **awakened by someone** despertarle a alguien ➤ The boy was awakened by his parents. ■ The boy's parents awakened him. ■ *(coll.)* The boy's parents woke him up. El chico fue despertado por sus padres. ■ Los padres del chico lo despertaron. ■ *(Sp., leísmo)* Los padres del chico le despertaron. ➤ The girl was awakened by her parents. ■ The girl's parents awakened her. ■ The girl's parents woke her up. La chica fue despertada por sus padres. ■ Los padres de la chica la despertaron.

to be **awakened by something** despertarle a alguien ➤ He was awakened by the neighbor's TV. ■ The neighbor's TV awakened him. ■ The neighbor's TV woke him up. Lo despertó la tele del vecino. ■ *(Sp., leísmo)* Le despertó la tele del vecino. ➤ She was awakened by the neighbor's TV. ■ The neighbor's TV awakened her. ■ The neighbor's TV woke her up. La despertó la tele del vecino.

awakening (of consciousness) *el* despertar (de las conciencias) ➤ That great century of awakening, the 6th B.C. *(Arthur Koestler)* Aquel gran siglo del despertar, el sexto a.C.

to **award a contract to someone** ■ to award someone a contract adjudicarle un contrato a alguien

to **award a medal to someone** ■ to award someone a medal imponerle una medalla a alguien

to **award a prize to someone** ■ to award someone a prize conceder un premio a alguien ■ galardonar a alguien (con un premio) ■ otorgar un premio a alguien ■ premiar a alguien ➤ The Spanish poet Vicente Aleixandre was awarded the Nobel prize in 1977. En 1977 se le concedió el premio Nobel al poeta español Vicente Aleixandre. ■ En 1977 se galardonó con el premio Nobel al poeta español Vicente Aleixandre. ■ En 1977 galardonaron con el premio Nobel al poeta español Vicente Aleixandre. ■ En 1977 le fue otorgado el premio Nobel al poeta español Vicente Aleixandre. ■ En 1977 le otorgaron el premio Nobel al poeta español Vicente Aleixandre. ■ En 1977 se le otorgó el premio Nobel al poeta español Vicente Aleixandre.

to **award someone a medal** concederle una medalla a alguien ■ entregarle una medalla a alguien ■ imponerle una medalla a alguien

award-winning journalist periodista premiado(-a)

to be **awarded a prize** concederle un premio ■ serle concedido un premio ■ ser galardonado con un premio ➤ John F. Kennedy was awarded the Pulitzer Prize for literature for his book *Profiles in Courage*. A John F. Kennedy le concedieron el Premio Pulitzer de literatura por su libro *Perfiles en Valor*. ■ A John F. Kennedy le fue concedido el Premio Pulitzer de literatura por su libro *Perfiles en Valor*. ■ John F. Kennedy fue galardonado con el Premio Pulitzer de literatura por su libro *Perfiles en Valor*.

to be **aware of something** estar enterado de algo ■ ser consciente de algo ■ constarle algo a alguien ■ tener conocimiento de algo ■ tener constancia de algo ■ saber algo ➤ I wanted to tell you something you may not be aware of. Quería decirte algo de lo que probablemente no estés enterado ■ Quería decirte algo de lo que puede que no seas consciente. ■ Quería decirte algo que a ti probablemente no te conste. ■ Quería decirte algo de lo que probablemente no tengas conocimiento. ➤ Are you aware of what you did? ¿Eres consciente de lo que has hecho? ➤ I'm not aware that the file has been delivered. ■ It has not come to my attention that the file has been delivered. No tengo constancia de que el archivo haya sido entregado. ■ No me consta que el archivo haya sido entregado.

aware of something: to become ~ enterarse de algo ■ darse cuenta de algo

to be **aware that...** ser consciente de que... ■ tener constancia de que... ■ saber que... ■ constarle a alguien que... ■ tener conocimiento de que... ➤ Were you aware that her brother is ill? ¿Eras consciente de que su hermano está enfermo? ■ ¿Sabías que su hermano estaba enfermo? ➤ I'm not aware of any English classes being taught in this building. No sé de ninguna clase de inglés que se esté impartiendo en este edificio. ■ No tengo conocimiento de que se esté impartiendo ninguna clase de inglés en este edificio. ➤ Aware that he was being followed, the secret agent turned abruptly and headed for the police station. Consciente de que lo seguían, el agente secreto giró bruscamente y se dirigió a la comisaría. ■ *(Sp., leísmo)* Consciente de que le seguían, el agente secreto giró bruscamente y se dirigió a la comisaría.

to be **away from home** ■ to be away from the house ■ not to be at home estar fuera de casa

away from home: to live ~ vivir fuera ➤ For many years she has lived away from home. Durante muchos años (ella) ha vivido fuera.

to be **away from one's desk** ■ to have stepped away from one's desk no estar en su escritorio ■ dejar el escritorio ➤ He's away from his desk at the moment. ■ He's stepped away from his desk for a moment. No está en su escritorio en este momento. ■ Ha dejado su escritorio un momento.

away from you: to cut ~ cortar hacia fuera ➤ When carving with a knife, cut away from you. *(tú)* Al cortar con un cuchillo, corta hacia fuera. ■ *(usted)* Al cortar con un cuchillo, corte hacia fuera.

away game partido fuera

to be **(away) on vacation** estar (fuera) de vacaciones

to be **awe-inspiring** ser sublime

an **awesome computer** *(L. Am.)* computadora padrísima ■ computadora espectacular ■ *(Arg.)* computadora grosa ■ *(Sp.) el* ordenador guay ■ *(off-color)* ordenador de puta madre

awesome dude tipo macanudo ■ tipo genial ■ tipo estupendo ■ *(Mex.)* chavo genial ■ chavo estupendo ■ *(Sp.)* tío genial ■ tío estupendo ■ *(coarse)* tío cojonudo ■ tío brillante ■ *(Arg.)* flaco genial ■ flaco macanudo ■ pibe macanudo ■ chavón macanudo

awesome supper menuda cena

awesome responsibility responsabilidad abrumadora

awful early: to be up ~ *(coll.)* ■ to be up mighty early levantarse pronto ■ levantarse temprano ➤ Up awful early, aren't you? ¡Qué pronto te has levantado hoy! ■ ¡Qué temprano te has levantado hoy! ■ ¡Qué madrugador!

awful early: to get up ~ *(coll.)* **1.** to get up mighty early madrugar mucho ■ ser muy madrugador ■ levantarse muy pronto ■ levantarse muy temprano ■ levantarse muy de mañana **2.** to get up early habitually ■ to be an early riser ser muy tempranero ■ ser muy mañanero

awful late: to be getting ~ *(coll.)* ■ to be getting mighty late ■ to be getting very late hacerse tardísimo ■ estarse haciendo tardísimo ➤ It's getting awful late. ■ It's getting mighty late. ■ It's getting very late. Se está haciendo tardísimo. ■ Se ha hecho tardísimo.

to be **awful weather** ■ to be lousy weather ■ (for) the weather to be terrible hacer un tiempo feo ■ hacer un tiempo asqueroso ■ hacer un tiempo de perros

awful weather: to have ~ tocarle un tiempo asqueroso ■ tocarle un tiempo feo ■ tocarle un tiempo de perros ➤ We had terrible weather for the trip. Nos tocó un tiempo asqueroso para el viaje.

awkward age ■ adolescence *la* edad del pavo

awkward moment ■ embarrassing moment momento embarazoso

awkward situation situación violenta

ax to grind: to have an ~ estar motivado por interés ■ estar movido por interés

axing of employees *(coll.)* ■ laying off of employees *el* recorte de empleados ■ *la* supresión de empleados

axing of jobs *(coll.)* ■ elimination of jobs *el* recorte de puestos de trabajo ■ *la* supresión de puestos de trabajo

the **ayes have it** ■ the motion is carried gana el sí

b-flat si bemol

babe in arms niño(-a) de pecho ■ niño(-a) de teta

babe in the woods pipiolo(-a)

baby boy niño ➤ She just had a baby boy. Acaba de tener un niño.

baby face cara de crío(-a) ■ cara de niño(-a)

baby girl niña

to be the **baby of the family** ■ to be the baby in the family *(boy)* ser el benjamín de la familia ■ *(girl)* ser la benjamina de la familia

the **baby is due 1.** *(now)* el bebé está a punto de nacer ■ ya llega el bebé **2.** *(in the future)* (la madre) sale de cuentas ➤ The baby is due. El bebé está a punto de nacer. ■ El bebé va a nacer. ➤ The baby is due next week. (La madre) sale de cuentas la semana que viene. ➤ The baby is due in November. (La madre) sale de cuentas en noviembre.

baby on the way: to have a ~ ■ to have a child on the way estar esperando un bebé ■ estar esperando un hijo ■ tener un bebé en camino ■ tener un hijo en camino

baby teeth ■ milk teeth *los* dientes de leche

baby was due se esperaba al bebé ■ la madre salió de cuentas ➤ The baby was due yesterday. Se esperaba al bebé ayer. ■ La madre salió de cuentas ayer.

baby's bottom colita del bebé ■ *(Sp.)* culito del bebé

baby's butt: to be as smooth as a ~ estar suave como el culito de un niño

bachelor's degree licenciatura ■ título de licenciado

to be **back** ■ to have come back estar de vuelta ■ haber vuelto ■ estar de regreso ➤ He's back. ■ He's come back. Está de vuelta. ■ Ha vuelto. ■ Está de regreso.

to **back a candidate for** ■ to support a candidate for apoyar a un candidato para

to **back a proposal** respaldar un proyecto

back and forth: to go ~ 1. *(walking, debating, etc.)* ir y venir ■ pasarse yendo y viniendo **2.** *(on a swing)* hamacarse ➤ One of the housemates goes back and forth from his room to the bathroom for an hour. Uno de los compañeros de casa se pasa una hora yendo y viniendo de su habitación al baño. ■ Uno de los compañeros de casa va y viene durante una hora de su habitación al baño. ➤ The children went back and forth on the swing. Los niños se hamacaban en el columpio.

back and forth: to pace ~ andar de adelante a atrás ■ andar de un lado a otro ■ *(coll.)* andar de alante a tras ➤ The groom was pacing back and forth waiting for the bride. El novio andaba de adelante a atrás esperando a la novia. ➤ He paces back and forth like a caged lion. Anda de un lado a otro como un león enjaulado.

back and forth (between student and teacher) intercambio de ideas ■ *(formal)* intercambio dialéctico

back at ■ on returning to de vuelta en ■ de regreso a ■ al volver a ■ al regresar a ➤ Back at the paint store, I explained why I was buying another pack of filters. De vuelta en la tienda de pintura, les expliqué porqué tenía que comprar otro paquete de filtros.

to **back away** dar pasos hacia atrás ■ retroceder

to **back away from a proposal** echarse atrás en una propuesta ➤ After consultation with his advisers, the prime minister backed away from the proposal. Después de consultar con sus consejeros, el primer ministro se echó atrás en su propuesta.

to **back away from someone** ■ to step backwards away from somone retroceder ante alguien ■ dar marcha atrás ante alguien ■ dar un paso atrás ante alguien ➤ What did you do to make him back away? ¿Qué hiciste para hacerle retroceder? ■ ¿Cómo conseguiste que retrocediera?

to **back away from something** retroceder ante algo ■ dar marcha atrás al ver algo ■ retirarse de algo ■ separarse de algo ➤ We backed away from the snake. Retrocedimos ante la serpiente. ➤ Back away from the fire, or you'll burn yourself. ■ Get back from the fire, or you'll burn yourself. Retírate de la hoguera, que te vas a quemar.

to **back away from the curb** alejarse del cordón ■ *(Sp.)* alejarse del bordillo ■ separarse del bordillo ■ retirarse del bordillo ■ ➤ Back away from the curb a little bit. You're too close. Retírate del bordillo un poco. Estás muy cerca. ■ Sepárate del bordillo un poco. Estás muy cerca.

back channels canales internos

back cover contraportada

back door puerta de atrás ■ puerta trasera

to **back down** desdecirse ■ ceder ■ echarse atrás ■ volverse atrás ■ *(on a demand)* echarse atrás

back flip *(diving)* vuelta de espaldas ➤ *(Olympic commentator)* Three and a half back flips Tres vueltas y media de espaldas

back-handed *(tennis)* de revés

back-handed compliment cumplido malintencionado ■ cumplido ambiguo ■ cumplido envenenado

back home de vuelta a casa ➤ When I was driving back home, I passed a skunk. Mientras conducía de vuelta a casa, adelanté a una mofeta.

back home we have a saying allá en mi pueblo tenemos un dicho

to be **back in a place** estar de vuelta en un lugar ➤ I'm back in Spain now. Ahora estoy de vuelta en España.

to be **back in business 1.** to reopen estar abierto de nuevo **2.** to be back to one's routine volver las andadas (de cada día) ➤ They've shut down for the remodeling, but they'll be back in business in a couple months. Han cerrado por remodelaciones, pero estarán abiertos de nuevo en un par de meses. ➤ I've been out with a cold, but I'm back in business. He estado resfriado, pero estoy de vuelta a las andadas de cada día.

to be **back in style** volver a estar de moda

back in the fifties, sixties, seventies, etc. allá en los cincuenta, sesenta, setenta, etc.

back in the old days ■ in the old days ■ in the olden days allá en... ■ antaño

back in those days allá en esos tiempos ■ *(literary, poetic)* allá en aquellos tiempos

back in time: to take one ~ llevar a alguien hacia atrás en el tiempo ■ transportar a alguien hacia atrás en el tiempo ➤ This film takes you back in time. Esta película te lleva hacia atrás en el tiempo. ■ Esta película te transporta hacia atrás en el tiempo. ➤ Looking through a telescope takes you back in time. Mirar a través del telescopio te lleva hacia atrás en el tiempo. ■ El telescopio te transporta hacia atrás en el tiempo.

to be **back in time for** estar de vuelta a tiempo de ■ volver a tiempo de ➤ Will you be back in time for dinner? ¿Vas a estar de vuelta a tiempo de cenar? ■ ¿Vas a volver a tiempo de cenar? ■ ¿Vas a volver a tiempo de la cena?

to be **back in town** estar de vuelta (en la ciudad) ■ haber vuelto (a la ciudad) ➤ I'm back in town. Estoy de vuelta en la ciudad. ■ He vuelto a la ciudad.

back issue ■ back copy número atrasado

back of a bill reverso de un billete ■ dorso de un billete ➤ A portrait of Francisco Pizarro is on the back of the old 1000-peseta bill. Hay un retrato de Francisco Pizarro en el reverso del viejo billete de mil pesetas. ■ Hay un retrato de Francisco Pizarro en el dorso del viejo billete de mil pesetas.

back of a box dorso de la caja ■ *la* parte posterior de la caja ➤ For recipe, see back. Para receta, ver dorso.

back of a can dorso de la lata ■ *la* parte de atrás de la lata ➤ The recipe is on the back of the can. La receta está en el dorso de la lata. ■ La receta está en la parte de atrás de la lata.

back of a car *(L. Am.)* parte de atrás de un carro ■ parte trasera de un carro ■ *(Sp.) la* parte de atrás de un coche ■ parte trasera de un coche

back of a check dorso de un cheque ➤ Endorse the check on the back. Endose el cheque en el dorso.

back of a house *la* parte de atrás de una casa ➤ The mudslide damaged the back of the house. La avalancha de fango dañó la parte de atrás de la casa.

back of a truck carga de un camión ■ *la* parte trasera de un camión

back of an animal lomo de un animal

back of the envelope: on the ~ en el reverso del sobre ■ en la parte de atrás del sobre ■ por detrás del sobre

back of the hand *el* envés de la mano ■ dorso de la mano

back of the thigh ■ back side of the thigh cara posterior del muslo ➤ The fifth bull gored the bullfighter in the back (side) of the right thigh. El quinto toro le pegó al torero una cornada en la cara posterior del muslo derecho.

to **back off 1.** to get back alejarse **2.** to stop pressuring dejar de insistir

back off! ¡córtala! ■ ¡para! ¡mantente a raya! ■ ¡quita tus pezuñas! ■ ¡quita de aquí tus zarpas!

to be **back on** haber vuelto ya haber otra vez ■ ya haber de nuevo ➤ The heat's back on, finally. Ya hay calefacción otra vez. ■ Ya hay calefacción de nuevo. ■ Por fin, ha vuelto la calefacción.

back on track: to get something ~ volver a poner en marcha ■ reencaminar algo ■ reencauzar algo ➤ The president hopes to get the legislation back on track in the next session of Congress. El presidente quiere volver a poner en marcha la legislación en la próxima sesión del Congreso.

to **back onto something 1.** *(driving a vehicle)* meter el vehículo de culo hacia algo ■ dar marcha atrás hacia algo ■ sacar el vehículo de culo hacia algo ■ sacar el vehículo de retroceso hacia algo ■ recular hacia algo **2.** *(for the back of something to face something)* lindar con algo ■ colindar con algo ■ dar a algo (por la parte de atrás) ➤ Backing a boat onto a boat ramp can be tricky. Meter el barco de culo en la rampa puede ser complicado. ➤ Back (the car) onto the street. Da marcha atrás hasta la calzada. ■ Saca el carro de culo hasta la calzada. ➤ Back the boat trailer onto the ramp. Da marcha atrás al remolque con el barco sobre la rampa. ➤ The property backs onto a lake. ■ The back (part) of the property faces a lake. La parte de atrás de la propiedad linda con un lago. ■ La parte de atrás de la propiedad colinda con un lago. ■ La parte de atrás de la propiedad da a un lago.

to **back onto the street** dar marcha atrás hasta la calle ■ sacar el coche de culo hasta la calle

to **back out of a contract** *(before signing it)* echarse atrás (en un contrato)

to **back out of a deal** echarse atrás en un trato

to **back out of a decision** echarse atrás en una decisión

to **back out of a driveway** salir reculando de una entrada ■ dar marcha atrás por una entrada ■ dar marcha atrás en una entrada ■ dar marcha atrás a una entrada ➤ The car backed out of the driveway. El coche dio marcha atrás en la entrada. ➤ I backed the car out of the driveway. Di marcha atrás al coche por la entrada. ■ Metí marcha atrás al coche en la entrada.

to **go in reverse** ir marcha atrás

to **back out of a parking space** salir de un estacionamiento marcha atrás ■ *(Sp.)* salir reculando de un aparcamiento ■ salir marcha atrás de un aparcamiento ■ salir de culo de un aparcamiento *(In Spain, "hueco" can replace "aparcamiento" in all examples.)*

to **back out of a situation** retirarse de una situación ■ salirse de una situación

to **back out of an agreement** salirse de un acuerdo

back part *la* parte de atrás ➤ The back part of the computer monitor is narrower than the front part. La parte de atrás del monitor es más estrecha que la de delante.

back pay: to pay ~ pagar cuotas atrasadas

back pay: to get ~ ■ to receive back pay recibir los pagos atrasados ■ recibir el pago de atrasos

back pocket bolsillo de atrás ■ bolsillo trasero

back problems trastornos de espalda

back row 1. *(of a theater)* última fila **2.** *(of a chess board)* línea de atrás

back scratch: to give someone a ~ rascarle la espalda a alguien ➤ Would you give me a back scratch? ■ Would you scratch my back? ¿Me rascas la espalda? ➤ Would you like a back scratch? ¿Quieres que te rasque la espalda?

back scratched: to get one's ~ ■ to get a back scratch rascarle la espalda ■ que le rasquen la espalda ➤ He likes to get his back scratched. Le gusta que le rasquen la espalda.

back seat asiento trasero ■ asiento de atrás ➤ I was riding in the back seat. (Yo) viajaba en el asiento trasero.

back (side) of the thigh cara posterior del muslo ➤ *(news item)* The bull gored the bullfighter in the back (side) of the right thigh. El toro le dio al torero una cornada en la cara posterior del muslo derecho. ■ El toro le pegó al torero una cornada en la cara posterior del muslo derecho.

to **back someone for a post** ■ to back someone for a position apoyar a un candidato para un puesto de trabajo

to **back someone (up) against a wall** poner a alguien contra la pared

back talker *(he)* respondón ■ *(she)* respondona

back then ■ back in those days por aquel entonces ■ por aquellos días

to be **back there somewhere** estar por ahí atrás ■ estar por ahí detrás ➤ He's back there somewhere. Está por ahí atrás.

back to: to drive ~ conducir de vuelta a ■ conducir de regreso a ■ manejar de regreso a ■ manejar de vuelta a ➤ As I was driving back home... ■ As I was driving back to my house... Mientras conducía de vuelta a mi casa...

back to: to go ~ ir de vuelta ■ volver ➤ As I was going back home... Mientras iba de vuelta a casa...

back to: with one's ~ de espaldas a

back to back espalda contra espalda ■ espalda con espalda ■ trasero con trasero ■ *(coll.)* culo con culo

back to basics: to get ~ ■ to return to the basics volver a lo esencial

back to front ■ from the back ■ from behind de atrás a delante ➤ In this drawing, you're looking at it back to front. En este dibujo, estás mirando de atrás a delante.

to be **back to normal** haber vuelto a la normalidad ■ estar de vuelta a la normalidad ➤ My E-mail is back to normal today. Hoy, mi correo electrónico ha vuelto a la normalidad. ■ Hoy, mi correo electrónico está de vuelta a la normalidad.

back to normal: to get ~ ■ to return to normal volver a la normalidad ■ normalizarse ■ volver a su cauce

back to normal: when things get ~ cuando todo vuelva a la normalidad ■ cuando todo se haya tranquilizado ■ *(Sp.)* cuando las aguas vuelvan a su cauce

to be **back to one's old tricks** ■ to be back to one's (old) shenanigans volver a las andadas ■ volver a hacer de las suyas ■ *(Sp.)* volver a sus jugaretas

back to school vuelta al cole

back to sleep: to get ~ ■ to go back to sleep volver a dormirse ■ dormirse otra vez ■ conciliar el sueño (de nuevo) ➤ After the siren woke her up, she couldn't get back to sleep. Después de que la sirena la despertara, no pudo volver a dormirse. ■ Después de que la sirena la despertara, no pudo dormirse otra vez. ■ Después de que la sirena la despertara, no pudo conciliar el sueño de nuevo.

Back to the Future *(film title) Regreso al futuro*

back to the salt mines! *(coll.)* ■ back to the grind! ■ back to work! ¡de vuelta al tajo!

back to work! ■ get back to work! ¡de vuelta al trabajo!

back to work: to get ~ volver al trabajo ▪ regresar al trabajo ▪ *(coll.)* volver a la faena ▪ regresar a la faena ▪ *(construction work especially)* volver al tajo ▪ regresar al tajo ➤ Get back to work. *(tú)* ¡Regresa al trabajo! ▪ *(usted)* ¡Regrese al trabajo! ▪ *(vosotros)* ▪ ¡Regresad al trabajo! ➤ Get back to work! *(tú)* ¡Marcha al trabajo! ▪ *(vosotros)* ¡Marchad al trabajo!

back to work: to go ~ volver al trabajo ➤ I have to go back to work. Tengo que volver al trabajo.

back up! ¡marcha atrás!

to **back up** *(intransitive verb)* **1.** to move in reverse ir marcha atrás ▪ dar marcha atrás ▪ retroceder ▪ ir hacia atrás ▪ recular **2.** to explain prior facts ir para atrás ▪ retroceder **3.** *(traffic)* retenerse ▪ ponerse en cola **4.** *(drainage pipes)* ▪ to clog up ▪ to get clogged up estancarse ➤ Back up a little bit. Recula un poco. ▪ Retrocede un poco. ▪ Da un poco marcha atrás. ▪ Ve un poco marcha atrás. ➤ Let me back up a little bit. Déjame ir un poco para atrás. ▪ Déjame retrodecer un poco. ▪ Déjame que retroceda un poco. ➤ When it rains, the rush-hour traffic backs up. Cuando llueve, el tráfico en hora punta se pone en cola. ➤ When the pipe is clogged, the water backs up. Cuando se atasca la cañería el agua se estanca.

back up: to start something ~ volver a poner en marcha algo ▪ *(engine)* volver a arrancar

back up: to warm ~ **1.** *(weather)* volver a hacer calor **2.** *(food, etc.)* to reheat recalentar ▪ volver a calentar ➤ We had a cold snap in November, but then it warmed back up. Tuvimos una ola de frío en Noviembre, pero luego volvió a hacer calor. ➤ Warm the soup back up. ▪ Reheat the soup. Recalienta la sopa. ▪ Vuelve a calentar la sopa.

to **back up a car** ▪ to back a car up dar marcha atrás un coche ▪ recular ➤ Back up a little (bit). Recula un poco. ▪ Da marcha atrás un poco.

to **back up someone** *(transitive verb)* ▪ to back someone up ▪ to support someone respaldar a alguien ▪ dar la cara por alguien ▪ apoyar a alguien ➤ If the boss challenges you, I'll back you up. Si el jefe te reta, te respaldaré. ▪ Si el jefe te reta, sacaré la cara por ti. ▪ Si el jefe te reta, yo te apoyaré.

backbone of the organization *el* pilar de la organización

to be **backed up 1.** *(traffic)* haber retenciones de tráfico ▪ estar atascado **2.** *(kitchen sink)* estar atascado ▪ *(when it's bubbling back)* regurgitar ▪ *(includes flooding)* estar inundado por estar atascado ▪ *(L. Am.)* estar atorado ➤ The traffic was backed up for a block on three streets leading into the intersection. Hubo retenciones a lo largo de una manzana en las tres calles que se juntan en el cruce. ➤ The kitchen sink is backed up. ▪ The kitchen sink is stopped up. El fregadero está atascado.

to **backfire on someone** salirle el tiro por la culata ➤ The politician abandoned principle for political expediency, and it backfired on him. El político abandonó sus principios por sacar ventaja política, y le salió el tiro por la culata. ➤ It backfired on him. Se le salió el tiro por la culata. ➤ It backfired on me. Me salió el tiro por la culata.

background check on someone: to run a ~ ▪ to do a background check on someone realizar un test de (los) antecedentes ▪ hacer un test de (los) antecedentes ▪ llevar a cabo un test de (los) antecedentes

background noise ruido en el fondo ▪ ruido de fondo

background radiation *(astrophysics)* ▪ background cosmic radiation radiación cósmica de fondo

backhand *(tennis) el* golpe de revés ➤ She has a good backhand. Tiene un buen golpe de revés.

backlog of calls: to have a ~ tener una acumulación de llamadas ▪ tener muchas llamadas en espera

backlog of orders: to have a ~ tener una acumulación de pedidos

backlog of work: to have a ~ tener trabajo acumulado ▪ tener trabajo amontonado ▪ tener mucho trabajo para poner a uno al día

backslash barra para atrás ▪ barra inclinada para la izquierda

backstreets callejas ▪ callejas pequeñas y poco frecuentadas

backup copy copia de seguridad ▪ copia de respaldo

backwards: to be printed ~ estar impreso al revés ▪ estar impreso a la inversa ➤ This picture is printed backwards. They reversed the negative. La foto está (impresa) al revés. Le han dado la vuelta al negativo. ▪ La foto está (impresa) a la inversa. Le han dado la vuelta al negativo.

backwards: to be written ~ estar escrito al revés ▪ estar escrito a la inversa ➤ The word "ambulance" is written backwards on the front of the ambulance so that it will appear frontwards when seen through a rearview mirror. La palabra "ambulancia" está escrita al revés en el frente de la ambulancia para que parezca al derecho cuando se vea por el espejo retrovisor. ▪ La palabra "ambulancia" está escrita a la inversa en el frontal de la ambulancia para que parezca al derecho cuando se vea por el espejo retrovisor.

backwards: to do something ~ **1.** *(as the mirror of something)* hacer algo a la inversa ▪ hacer algo al revés **2.** to go in reverse direction ir desde atrás hacia adelante ▪ ir de detrás hacia adelante ➤ *(Bob Theves)* Ginger Rogers not only did everything Fred Astaire did, but backwards and in high heels. No sólo hizo Ginger Rogers lo mismo que Fred Astaire, lo hizo además a la inversa y con tacones altos. ➤ You untie the knot the same way you tied it, only backwards. Se desata el nudo igual que como lo ataste, sólo que al revés. ▪ Se desata el nudo igual que como lo ataste, sólo que a la inversa. ➤ Let's repeat the dance steps starting at the end, that is, backwards. Vamos a repetir la coreografía empezando desde el final, esto es, desde atrás hacia adelante.

backwards: to move ~ moverse de espaldas ▪ moverse hacia atrás

backwards: to run ~ correr de espaldas ➤ Baseball players sometimes have to run backwards to catch the ball in the outfield. Los jugadores de béisbol a veces tienen que correr de espaldas para coger la bola en el campo exterior.

backwards: to walk ~ caminar de espaldas ▪ *(Sp.)* andar de espaldas ➤ As he left his boyhood home for the last time, he walked backwards down the road with tears in his eyes. Cuando marchó por última vez del hogar de su niñez, caminaba de espaldas por el camino con lágrimas en los ojos.

backward(s) regime régimen retrógrado

to be **backwoods** ser rústico

backyard *el* jardín de (la parte de) atrás ▪ jardín trasero

bacon grease ▪ bacon fat manteca de cerdo

bacteria causing... ▪ bacteria which causes... bacterias causantes de...

bad breath ▪ halitosis mal aliento

bad case caso grave ➤ He has a bad case of the flu. Tiene un caso grave de gripe. ➤ That editorial writer has a bad case of selective inattention. Ese editorialista sufre un caso grave de falta de atención selectiva.

bad cholesterol ▪ low-density lipoproteins ▪ LDL colesterol malo ▪ lipoproteínas de baja densidad ▪ LBD

bad cold: to get a ~ ▪ to come down with a bad cold ▪ to catch a bad cold *(L. Am.)* agarrar un resfriado fuerte ▪ agarrar un resfriado grave ▪ agarrar un resfriado serio ▪ *(coll., and used always in third person)* pescarse un mal resfrío ▪ *(Sp.)* coger un resfriado fuerte ▪ coger un resfriado grave ▪ coger un resfriado serio ▪ pillar un resfriado

bad cold: to have a ~ ▪ to have got a bad cold tener un catarro fuerte ▪ tener un catarro grave ▪ tener un catarro serio ▪ tener un resfriado fuerte ▪ tener un resfriado grave ▪ tener un resfriado serio ➤ I have a bad cold. ▪ I've got a bad cold. Tengo un catarro fuerte. ▪ Tengo un catarro grave. ▪ Tengo un catarro serio.

bad day día nefasto

bad disposition: to have a ~ tener mal genio ▪ tener mal carácter ▪ *(coll.)* tener mala uva ▪ tener malas pulgas ➤ He has a bad disposition. Tiene mal genio. ▪ Tiene mala uva. ▪ Tiene malas pulgas. ➤ Some dogs have bad dispositions. Algunos perros tienen mal genio.

bad dog! ¡perro malo!

to be **bad for business** ser malo para el negocio ➤ That waiter is bad for business. Ese camarero es malo para el negocio.

bad habit mal hábito ▪ mala costumbre ▪ manía

bad management ▪ poor management mala gestión

bad mood: to be in a ~ estar de mal humor ▪ tener un humor de perros to **bad-mouth someone** *(coll.)* poner a alguien verde ▪ poner a alguien a caldo ▪ poner a alguien a caer de un burro ▪ poner a alguien a parir

to **bad-mouth something** *(coll.)* poner algo verde ▪ poner algo a caldo ▪ poner algo a parir

bad neighborhood mal barrio

bad news: to have (some) ~ traer mala(s) noticia(s) ▪ tener mala(s) noticia(s) ➤ I have some bad news. Traigo una mala noticia. ▪ Traigo malas noticias.

to be **bad news** *(coll.)* no ser de fiar ▪ no ser trigo limpio ➤ That guy is bad news. Ese tipo no es de fiar. ▪ Ese tipo no es trigo limpio.

to be a **bad news bear** ▪ to be bad news ser un ave de mal agüero ➤ He's a bad news bear. Es un ave de mal agüero.

the **bad part (about it) is that...** ▪ the bad thing about it is that... lo malo es que... ▪ el mal asunto es que... *(coll.)* lo chungo es que...

bad sign mal señal ▪ mal indicio ▪ *(Sp.)* mal síntoma ➤ That's a bad sign, it means you're starting to give up. Eso es mal síntoma, quiere decir que ya empiezas a resignarte.

to be **bad tempered** ▪ to have a bad temper ▪ to be ill tempered ser de mal talante ▪ *(colorful)* tener malas pulgas ▪ tener pocas pulgas ▪ ser de pocas pulgas

the **bad thing about it is that...** lo malo del asunto es que... ➤ This telephone is easy to use. The bad thing about it is that it has limited features. Este teléfono es fácil de usar. Lo malo del asunto es que tiene pocas opciones.

to be a **bad thing to lose** ser una cosa que no se puede perder ➤ A passport is a bad thing to lose. El pasaporte es un documento que no se puede perder.

bad time: to call someone at a ~ llamar a alguien en mal momento ➤ Am I calling you at a bad time? ¿Te llamo en mal momento?

bad time: to catch someone at a ~ pillar a alguien en mal momento ▪ *(Sp.)* coger a alguien en mal momento ➤ Am I catching you at a bad time? ¿Te pillo en mal momento? ▪ ¿Te cojo en mal momento?

bad time: to give someone a ~ hacer pasar a alguien un mal rato ➤ He likes to give me a bad time. Le gusta hacerme pasar un mal rato.

bad time: to have a ~ pasar un mal rato ➤ He had a bad time after his operation. Lo pasó mal después de la operación.

bad timing!: that was ~ ¡qué puntería! ▪ ¡qué inoportuno! ▪ ¡qué justo! ➤ The doorbell rang just as I was getting into the shower. "That's bad timing," I thought. El timbre sonó justo cuando me metía en la ducha. "¡Qué puntería!" pensé.

bad weather mal tiempo ▪ *(coll.)* tiempo de perros ➤ A period of bad weather has set in. Estamos atravesando una ola de mal tiempo. ➤ A spell of bad weather has set in. ▪ A period of bad weather has set in. Estamos atravesando una racha de mal tiempo.

to be **badly broken** **1.** *(bones)* sufrir una fractura grave **2.** *(chips, crackers)* estar hecho migas ➤ The bone was badly broken. Sufrió una fractura grave. ➤ When I opened the bag, the chips were badly broken. Cuando abrí la bolsa, los totopos se estaban hechos migas.

to be **badly injured** ▪ to be seriously injured ser herido gravemente

to be **badly needed** necesitarse con urgencia ▪ necesitarse desesperadamente ▪ necesitarse sin falta ➤ From the satellite pictures, it looks like you're finally getting some badly needed rain. Por las fotos del satélite, parece que finalmente tenéis la lluvia que tan desesperadamente necesitábais. ➤ We cannot tell you how badly needed your presence is in our midst. No te haces la más mínima idea de la urgencia con que necesitamos tu presencia entre nosotros.

to be **badly shaken** estar conmocionado ▪ estar trastocado

to be **badly shaken by the news** quedar conmocionado por la noticia *(or "las noticias" depending on the situation)*

to be **badly upset** estar destrozado

to be **baffled by** ▪ to be baffled at quedarse desconcertado ante ▪ estar desconcertado ante ➤ The foreign telephone operators are sometimes baffled by the U.S. directory listings. Las operadoras extranjeras a veces se quedan desconcertadas ante los listados telefónicos estadounidenses.

bag with handles bolsa con asas

baggage carousel cinta de equipajes ➤ Can we get our bags at planeside or do we have to get them off the carousel? ¿Podemos recoger el equipaje a pie de avión o tenemos que recogerlo en la cinta?

baggage claim reclamación de equipajes

baggage handler mozo de equipajes

to **bail out of an airplane** saltar del avión (por una emergencia)

to **bail out water from a boat** ▪ to bail water out of a boat achicar el agua de un barco

to **bail someone out of a predicament** ▪ to save someone from a predicament ▪ to get someone out of a jam sacar a alguien de un apuro

to **bail someone out of jail** ▪ to bail out someone from jail pagar la fianza (para que alguien salga en libertad de la cárcel)

to **bait a bull** ▪ to incite a bull ▪ to wave the cape at a bull incitar a un toro

to **bait a hook (with)** cebar el anzuelo (con)

to **bait an animal** citar a un animal

to **bait someone** hacerle rabiar a alguien

baker's dozen ▪ thirteen una docena de fraile ▪ trece

to **balance a checkbook** cotejar un talonario (con el extracto de cuenta) ▪ actualizar un talonario

to **balance an account** echar una cuenta

balance between equilibrio entre

balance of an account: positive ~ ▪ balance in the account ▪ positive account balance ▪ balance in favor saldo de una cuenta ▪ saldo a favor

balance of payments balanza de pagos

balance of power: to shift the ~ ▪ to change the balance of power ▪ to alter the balance of power alterar el equilibrio de poder

balance of terror ▪ mutual fear miedo mutuo ▪ recelo mutuo ▪ reticencia mutua ▪ desconfianza mutua ➤ The nuclear arsenals of the United States and the Soviet Union maintained a balance of terror, each country being afraid to attack the other. Los arsenales nucleares de los Estados Unidos y de la Unión Soviética procuraron un miedo mutuo, temiendo cada uno de los países atacar al otro.

balance on an account ▪ balance owed saldo en contra ▪ saldo deudor

balance owed ▪ balance (owed) on an account saldo en contra ▪ saldo deudor

balance sheet *el* balance ▪ hoja de balance ▪ balance de situación

to **balance the budget** equilibrar el presupuesto

to **balance the wheels** equilibrar las ruedas

balanced account of the events ▪ account of the events that presents both sides of an issue valoración objetiva de los hechos

balanced budget presupuesto equilibrado

balanced diet dieta equilibrada

balanced meal comida balanceada ▪ comida equilibrada ➤ I want a balanced meal with a green vegetable, a carbohydrate, and meat. Quiero una comida balanceada con verduras, carbohidrato y carne.

to be a **balancing act** ser un acto de equilibrio ▪ acto de balanceo ➤ To work one's way through the university is a balancing act between the pressures of work and school. Pagarse los estudios universitarios trabajando es un acto de equilibrio entre las presiones laborales y las académicas.

bald spot: to have a ~ tener una calva

bale of hay bala de heno

baleful look ▪ hateful look mirada de odio ▪ mirada de desprecio

the **ball is in your court** ▪ the ball's in your court ▪ it's your move la pelota está en tu tejado ▪ la pelota está en tu lado de la cancha ▪ te toca a ti

ball of yarn ovillo de lana ▪ madeja de lana

balled up: to get ~ *(Mex.)* hacerse bolas ■ *(Sp.)* hacerse un lío ➤ I got all balled up. Me hice bolas. ■ Me hice un lío.

balloon: comic strip ~ bocadillo ■ globo

to **balloon out** hincharse en forma de globo ■ inflarse en forma de globo

balloon payment *(final payment, larger than the rest)* pago final ■ último pago ■ último plazo

ballpark figure número aproximado ■ más o menos ■ (a) grosso modo

ballroom dance *el* baile de salón ➤ The tango is a ballroom dance. El tango es un baile de salón.

ballroom dancing baile de salón ➤ I need to take a class in ballroom dancing. Necesito recibir clases de baile de salón.

balmy weather tiempo benigno ■ tiempo agradable

band: wave ~ *(radio wave or frequency)* banda de frequencia

Band-Aids® ■ bandage strips tiritas adhesivas

band of the political spectrum franja del espectro político ■ banda del espectro político ➤ The president and the prime minister occupy exactly the same band of the political spectrum. El presidente y el primer ministro ocupan exactamente la misma franja del espectro político. ■ El presidente y el primer ministro ocupan exactamente la misma banda del espectro político.

band of the spectrum franja del espectro ■ banda del espectro

band of thieves banda de ladrones

bandage strips: adhesive ~ tiritas adhesivas

to be the **bane of one's existence** ser la cruz de uno ■ amargar la existencia de uno ■ ser la pesadilla de uno ■ ser la ruina de uno ➤ The violin lessons were the bane of the boy's existence. Las clases de violín eran la cruz del chico. ■ Las clases de violín amargaban la existencia del chico.

bandwidth ancho de banda ■ *la* amplitud de la franja

bang, bang, bang! ¡pim, pam, pum! ■ ¡pun, pun, pun!

bank account cuenta bancaria

bank (account) balance saldo de la cuenta bancaria

to **bank an airplane** escorar un avión ■ *(light airplane)* escorar una avioneta ➤ The pilot banked to the left. El piloto escoró (el avión) a la izquierda.

to **bank on someone** ■ to count on someone ■ to rely on someone contar con alguien

to **bank on something** contar con algo ➤ I wouldn't bank on his being here on time. (Yo) no contaría con que (él) llegue a tiempo. ➤ I wouldn't bank on it. (Yo) no contaría con ello. ■ (Yo) no contaría con eso.

to **bank to the left or right** ■ to bank over to the left or right escorarse a la izquierda o a la derecha ➤ The airplane banked (over) to the left. El avión se escoró a la izquierda. ➤ The airplane banked (over) to the right. El avión se escoró a la derecha.

to **bang one's fist on the table** dar un puñetazo en la mesa

bank robber atracador de bancos

bank statement: most recent ~ ■ last bank statement (one) received último extracto de cuenta

banking institution entidad bancaria

bar code código de barras

bar none ■ without exception ■ taking all into account de todos ■ contándolos todos ➤ This is the best Argentine restaurant in Madrid, bar none. Contándolos todos, éste es el mejor restaurante argentino de Madrid.

bar scene ambiente de bares ➤ If you like the bar scene, you'll love Spain. The whole country is a bar. Si te gusta el ambiente de bares, te va a encantar España. Todo el país es un bar.

to **bar someone from doing something** prohibir que alguien haga algo ■ no autorizar a alguien que haga algo ■ impedir a alguien hacer algo ■ impedir a alguien que haga algo ➤ The doctor was barred by the court from assisting suicides. El tribunal prohibió al médico que ofreciera asistencia en el suicido. ■ El tribunal impidió al médico que ofreciera asistencia en el suicidio. ➤ The protestors were barred from entering the building. A los manifestantes se les prohibió el acceso al edificio. ■ A los manifestantes se les impidió el acceso al edificio. ➤ The bouncer barred the drunk from entering the bar. El gorila prohibió al borracho que entrara en el bar. ■ El gorila impidió al borracho que entrara en el bar.

to **bar the door** atrancar la puerta

barbershop peluquería para hombres ■ peluquería para caballeros ■ barbería

bare breasted pecho desnudo

bare chested: to go ~ ir a pecho descubierto ■ ir con el pecho al aire

bare essentials: the ~ lo justo ■ lo estrictamente necesario ➤ This kitchen is equipped with the bare essentials, a stove, a sink, and a refrigerator, but no dishwasher or microwave. Esta cocina está equipada con lo justo, una estufa, un fregadero y un frigorífico, pero sin lavaplatos ni microondas.

bare necessities: the ~ lo mínimo imprescindible

to **bare one's chest** despechugarse

to **bare one's soul to someone** abrirle uno el corazón a alguien ➤ She bared her soul to her friend. Ella la abrió su corazón a su amigo.

bare walls paredes desnudas

bare wood flooring pisos de madera sin revestir

to **barely be able to get out of bed** levantarse a duras penas de la cama ■ casi no poder levantarse de la cama ■ prácticamente no poder levantarse de la cama ■ apenas poder levantarse de la cama ➤ He can barely get out of bed in the morning. Se levanta a duras penas de la cama por la mañana.

to **barely have enough to** ■ to hardly have enough to ■ for there barely to be enough to tener apenas lo suficiente para ■ casi no tener lo suficiente para ■ tener a duras penas lo suficiente para

to **barely have time to do something** ■ to hardly have time to do something ■ to scarcely have time to do something apenas tener tiempo para hacer nada ■ casi no tener tiempo para hacer nada ■ prácticamente no tener tiempo para hacer nada ■ a duras penas tener tiempo para hacer nada *("De" can replace "para" in all examples.)*

barely having done something apenas sin haber hecho algo ➤ *(news item)* Barely having slept, the cousin of Elián González fainted yesterday. Sin apenas haber dormido, la prima de Elián González se desmayó ayer. ■ Habiendo apenas dormido, la prima de Elián González se desmayó ayer.

to **barely make a stir** ■ to hardly make a stir ■ to go virtually unnoticed pasar sin pena ni gloria ■ pasar desapercibido

to **barely scratch the surface of something** ■ to have barely scratched the surface of something ■ to have barely begun something haber pasado sólo por encima de un asunto ■ apenas haber empezado algo ➤ The geneticists who are mapping the genomes of all the plants and animals have barely scratched the surface. Los genetistas que trabajan en la secuenciación de los genomas de todas las plantas y animales apenas han pasado por encima del asunto.

to **barely speak Spanish** ■ to hardly speak Spanish apenas hablar español ■ casi no hablar español ■ no hablar casi español ■ prácticamente no hablar español ■ hablar a duras penas español ➤ She barely spoke Spanish when she arrived in Buenos Aires. Apenas hablaba español cuando llegó a Buenos Aires. ■ Casi no hablaba español cuando llegó a Buenos Aires.

to **barely touch** ■ to hardly touch casi no tocar ■ practicamente estar sin tocar ■ apenas tocar ➤ He barely touched his supper. Apenas tocó su cena. ■ Casi no tocó su cena. ➤ There are places in this book we've barely touched. Hay partes de este libro que casi no hemos tocado. ■ Hay partes de este libro que practicamente están sin tocar.

barely *x* meters from a escasos *x* metros de

to be **barely *x* years old** tener apenas *x* años ➤ His mother died when he was barely eleven. Su madre murió cuando él tenía apenas once años.

bargain: to throw something into the ~ *(coll.)* ■ to include something extra for free incluir algo de yapa ■ incluir algo por el mismo precio ➤ He not only sold us the stereo system, he threw a set of Beethoven disks into the bargain. No sólo nos vendió el equipo de música, sino que nos incluyó una colección de discos de Beethoven por el mismo precio.

bargain basement planta de oportunidades *(In Hispanic countries, the bargain section can be on any floor.)*

to **bargain collectively** negociar colectivamente ➤ Becoming unionized enabled the workers to bargain collectively for their wages. Sindicarse permitió a los trabajadores negociar colectivamente sus salarios.

to **bargain for something 1.** to negotiate the price of something negociar el precio de algo **2.** to haggle over the price of something regatear por algo

bargain items artículos de oferta ▪ artículos rebajados ▪ artículos de bajo precio ➤ Let's go check out the bargain CDs. Vamos a echar un vistazo a los CDs de bajo precio.

to **bargain on** prever ▪ contar con ➤ I didn't bargain on having to drive all the way to Alcalá de Henares to deliver the translation. No contaba con tener que conducir hasta Alcalá de Henares para entregar la traducción. ▪ No preveía tener que conducir hasta Alcalá de Henares para entregar la traducción.

bargain prices gangas ▪ precios rebajados

bargain was struck: the ~ ▪ the deal was struck el trato quedó cerrado ▪ el acuerdo quedó cerrado

bargained for: to get more than one ~ recibir más de lo que uno esperaba ➤ When we bought this apartment, we got more than we bargained for. There was an undetected encumbrance on the property. Cuando compramos este apartamento, recibimos más de lo que esperábamos. Había un gravamen que pasó inadvertido en la propiedad.

bargaining chip: to use something as a ~ ▪ to use something as leverage usar algo como elemento de presión en una negociación ▪ utilizar algo como elemento de presión en una negociación

to **bark at something** ladrar a algo ➤ The dog barked at the postman. El perro ladró al cartero.

bark is worse than one's bite: one's ~ perro ladrador, poco mordedor ▪ se le va la fuerza por la boca

to **bark up the wrong tree** ir descaminado

barking of a dog ladrido de un perro

barn dance *(19th-century rural U.S.)* fiesta con baile que acontece en un granero

barometer of how much ▪ barometer of the extent to which ▪ indicator of how much ▪ indicator of the extent to which *un* indicador de hasta que punto ➤ The margin of the prime minister's victory will be a barometer of the extent to which... La amplitud de la victoria del primer ministro será un indicador de hasta que punto...

barrage of books ▪ string of books ▪ flood of books ▪ abundance of books ▪ a bunch of books ▪ *(literary)* ▪ plethora of books avalancha de libros ▪ *un* aluvión de libros ▪ rosario de libros

barrage of criticism ▪ torrent of criticism avalancha de críticas ▪ *el* aluvión de críticas ▪ el torrente de críticas ➤ A barrage of criticism is being leveled at the government for... Una avalancha de críticas está cayendo sobre el gobierno por...

barrage of insults ▪ stream of insults *el* torrente de insultos ▪ avalancha de insultos ▪ rosario de insultos ▪ *la* cantidad de improperios ▪ plétora de insultos ▪ *(Sp.)* retahíla de insultos

barrage of questions batería de preguntas ▪ avalancha de preguntas ▪ *el* torrente de preguntas

to **barrage someone with criticism** ▪ to heap criticism on someone acosar a alguien con críticas

to **barrage someone with questions** abrumar a alguien con preguntas

to be **barred from** serle a alguien impedido el acceso a ➤ The protesters were barred from entering the chamber. A los protestantes se les impidió el acceso a la cámara.

barrel of a gun *el* cañon de una pistola

barrel of monkeys: to be having more fun than a ~ pasárselo pipa ▪ pasárselo bomba ▪ pasárselo grande

barrel of oil ▪ drum of oil *el* barril de petróleo

barrel of rum *el* barril de ron

barrel of wine 1. *(placed horizontally)* ▪ cask of wine barrica de vino **2.** *(placed vertically)* cuba de vino ➤ The wine is aged in oak barrels. El vino se envejece en barricas de roble.

barreling down: to come ~ pasar arrasando ▪ venir arrasando ➤ The cars really come barreling down this street, don't they? Los coches pasan arrasando por esta calle, ¿verdad? ▪ Los coches vienen arrasando por esta calle, ¿verdad?

barring the unforeseen si no hay imprevistos

to **base a theory on** basar una teoría en ▪ fundamentar una teoría en

base camp campamento base

base leg *(aviation)* tramo de base ➤ The landing sequence includes downwind leg, base leg, and final approach. La secuencia de aterrizaje incluye el tramo a favor de viento, el tramo de base y el acercamiento final.

base of a wine glass peana de una copa

base of the mountain ▪ foot of the mountain *el* pie de la montaña

to **base one's opinion on something** ▪ to base an opinion on something fundar la opinión en algo ▪ basar la opinión en algo

base rate cuota básica ➤ We divided the base rate of the telephone among all the apartment mates. Repartimos la cuota básica del teléfono entre los compañeros del apartamento. ➤ What is the base rate if I don't make any long distance calls? ¿Cuál es la cuota básica si no hago llamadas a larga distancia?

baseball diamond campo de béisbol

to be a **baseball fan** ser aficionado al béisbol ▪ ser fan del béisbol

(baseball) pitcher lanzador de béisbol

baseboard (molding) moldura(s) de rodapié ▪ moldura(s) del rodapié

based in ▪ with headquarters in con sede en ▪ con base en ➤ The company, based in Seattle... La empresa, con sede en Seattle...

to be **based in** ▪ to have its headquarters in tener la sede en ▪ tener la base en ▪ *(military)* tener el cuartel general en

based on ▪ on the basis of basándose en ▪ en base a ▪ a base de ➤ For the media to call a state for a candidate based on exit polls is asinine. ▪ For the media to call a state for a candidate on the basis of exit polls is asinine. Que los medios de comunicación apunten a un candidato como vencedor en un estado basándose en las encuestas a pie de urna es absurdo. ▪ Que los medios de comunicación apunten a un candidato como vencedor en un estado en base a las encuestas a pie de urna es absurdo. ▪ Que los medios de comunicación apunten a un candidato como vencedor en un estado a base de las encuestas a pie de urna es absurdo.

to be **based on** estar basado en ▪ tener su base en ▪ estar fundamentado en ▪ tener su fundamento en

to be **based on a true story** estar basado en una historia verdadera ▪ estar basado en una historia real ▪ estar basado en una historia verídica

to be **based on fact** estar basado en hechos reales

based on my experience basado en mi experiencia

based on what I've read basado en lo que he leído

based on what I've seen basado en lo que he visto

baseline línea base ➤ In measuring the distance of Mars from the Earth, Cassini in 1677 used the distance between Paris and Cayenne as the baseline. Para medir la distancia entre Marte y la Tierra, Cassini en 1677 utilizó la distancia entre Paris y Cayena como la línea base.

the **basement is flooded** el sótano está inundado ▪ hay una inundación en el sótano

basic necessities necesidades básicas

basics: the ~ lo esencial

basis for comparison: to have a ~ tener una base de comparación

to **bask in the glow of success** saborear las mieles del éxito ▪ probar las mieles del éxito

to **bask in the sun** ▪ to sunbathe ▪ to get some sun ▪ *(coll.)* to soak up some rays tumbarse al sol (como un lagarto) ▪ ser como un lagarto ▪ tomar el sol

basketball coach entrenador(-a) de baloncesto

basketball court cancha de baloncesto

basketball fan aficionado al baloncesto ▪ fan del baloncesto

basketball team equipo de baloncesto

Basque Region *(of northern Spain)* País Vasco ▪ *(in the Basque language)* Euskadi

to be a **bastion of** ▪ to be a stronghold of ser un reducto de ▪ ser un bastión de ➤ During the American Civil War, East

Tennessee was a bastion of Unionist sentiment within the Confederacy. Durante la Guerra Civil norteamericana, la parte este de Tennessee fue un bastión de sentimiento unionista dentro de la Confederación.

to **bat someone on the head** dar a alguien un golpe suave en la cabeza ▪ dar a alguien un suave capirotazo ➤ My cat bats the other cat on the head just to get him going. Mi gata le da un suave capirotazo en la cabeza al otro gato sólo para provocarlo.

to **bat something around** manotear algo ➤ Cats like to bat things around. A los gatos les gusta manotear cosas.

batch of cookies bandeja de galletas ▪ hornada de galletas ▪ horneada de galletas

batch of Jell-O® ▪ batch of gelatin *la* fuente de gelatina

batter: cake ~ masa líquida (de bizcocho)

batter: pancake ~ masa líquida (de tortitas) ▪ *(S.A., where the pancake is a crepe)* masa de panqueques

batter for coating 1. *(general)* rebozado **2.** *(fish, vegetables)* tempura *(derives its name from the fish often cooked in this manner)*

battery is dead: the ~ la batería está descargada ▪ la batería se ha quedado sin carga

battery of medical tests: to give someone a ~ ▪ to run a series of medical tests on someone hacerle a alguien una serie de estudios médicos

battery of medical tests: to undergo a ~ ▪ to undergo a series of medical tests hacerse una serie de estudios médicos ▪ someterse a una serie de estudios médicos

battery of psychological tests: to give someone a ~ hacerle una batería de estudios psicológicos a alguien

battery of psychological tests: to undergo a ~ hacerse una batería de estudios psicológicos ▪ someterse a una batería de estudios psicológicos

battery of psychometric tests: to give someone a ~ hacerle una batería de estudios psicotécnicos a alguien

battery of psychometric tests: to undergo a ~ hacerse una batería de estudios psicotécnicos

battery of questions: to ask someone a ~ hacerle a alguien una batería de preguntas

battery of tests on someone: to run a ~ *(medical tests)* llevar a cabo una serie de estudios médicos a alguien ▪ llevar a cabo una serie de pruebas médicas a alguien

battery of tests on something: to run a ~ *(on equipment, mechanical devices, commercial products)* hacer una batería de pruebas a algo ▪ hacer un conjunto de pruebas a algo

to be **battery operated** ▪ to be battery powered funcionar con pilas ▪ funcionar a pilas

to be **battery powered** ▪ to be battery operated funcionar con pilas ▪ funcionar a pilas

battery-powered clock ▪ clock that runs on batteries reloj a pilas ▪ reloj de pilas

battle axe 1. *(weapon)* hacha de batalla **2.** *(unmother-like woman)* mujerer de armas tomar ➤ My geometry teacher was an old battle axe. Mi profesora de geometría era una mujer de armas tomar.

battle for batalla por ➤ *(noticia)* The battle for the White House ends tomorrow in the Florida Supreme Court. La batalla por la Casa Blanca se libra mañana en el Tribunal Supremo de Florida.

battle-hardened troops tropas curtidas en la batalla

Battle of Britain: the ~ *(in World War II)* la batalla de Inglaterra

battle is raging: the ~ la batalla está en su punto álgido

battle raged on: the ~ la batalla seguía en su punto álgido

to **bawl someone out** poner a alguien a parir ▪ poner a alguien verde ➤ When the guy ran over me on the sidewalk, I bawled him out. Cuando ese tío me arrolló en la acera, lo puse a parir. ▪ Cuando me arrolló en la acera lo puse verde.

Bay of Pigs *(Cuba)* bahía Cochinos ▪ *(true name)* Playa Girón

bay window ventana (en) saliente ▪ mirador

be a good boy and... sé (un) buen chico y...

be able to *(tú)* sé capaz de ▪ *(usted)* sea capaz de ➤ When you're interviewing someone, and there's an interruption, the subject will often say, "Where was I?" Always be able to tell him or her. Cuando se está entrevistando a alguien, y hay una interrupción, el sujeto a menudo dirá, "¿Dónde estaba?" Siempre sea capaz de decirle.

to **be along 1.** to catch up with someone alcanzar a alguien **2.** to be here pasar (por aquí) ➤ You all go ahead. I'll be along in a few minutes. ▪ You all go ahead. I'll catch up with you in a few minutes. Vayan saliendo. Los alcanzo en unos pocos minutos. ▪ *(Sp., vosotros)* Id saliendo. Os alcanzo en unos pocos minutos. ➤ Another bus will be along shortly. ▪ Another bus will be here shortly. Otro autobús pasará en seguida.

to **be asked to do something** pedirle a alguien que haga algo ➤ He was asked to speak to the journalism students. Le pidieron que hablara ante los estudiantes de periodismo.

to **be at a place** estar en un lugar ➤ I have to be at the doctor's at 7:30 p.m. Tengo que estar en el médico a las siete y media.

be aware that...: (just) ~ *(tú)* date cuenta (de) que ... ▪ que te des cuenta (de) que... ▪ *(usted)* dese cuenta (de) que... ▪ que se de cuenta (de) que...

to **be back** regresar ▪ estar de regreso ▪ *(Sp.)* volver ▪ estar de vuelta ➤ She'll be back in 15 minutes. Volverá en quince minutos. ▪ Estará de vuelta en quince minutos. ▪ Regresará en quince minutos. ▪ Estará de regreso en quince minutos.

to **be being** estar siendo ➤ There is a child in this building who may be being abused. Hay un niño en este edificio que podría estar siendo maltratado.

to **be careful with** tener cuidado con

to **be careful of** tener cuidado con ➤ Be careful of what you say. Ten cuidado con lo que dices.

to **be careful on the ice** tener cuidado en el hielo

to **be given** recibir

to **be here next** ▪ to be coming back volver ▪ estar de nuevo aquí ▪ estar otra vez aquí ➤ When will you be here next? ▪ When are you coming back? ¿Cuándo volverás? ▪ ¿Cuándo estarás de nuevo aquí? ▪ ¿Cuándo estarás otra vez aquí?

be honest *(tú)* sé honesto ▪ *(usted)* sea honesto ▪ *(vosotros)* sed honestos ▪ *(ustedes)* sean honestos

to **be like** sentirse ➤ What would it be like to be a dog or cat? ¿Qué se sentirá ser un perro o un gato?

be nice! *(to a growling mutt)* ¡pórtate bien!

to **be oneself** ser uno mismo ➤ Be yourself. *(tú)* Sé tú mismo. ▪ *(usted)* Sea usted mismo. ➤ I'm myself in spite of myself, but I'd like to be myself on purpose. Soy yo mismo a pesar de mi mismo, pero me gustaría ser yo mismo adrede.

be patient *(tú)* ten paciencia ▪ *(usted)* tenga paciencia ▪ *(vosotros)* tened paciencia ▪ *(ustedes)* tengan paciencia

be quiet ¡silencio!

be ready to... 1. *(tú)* estate listo para... ▪ disponte para... ▪ prepárate para... **2.** *(usted)* dispóngase para... ▪ prepárese para... ▪ estese listo para... **3.** *(ustedes)* dispónganse para... ▪ prepárense para... ▪ estense listos para... **4.** *(Sp., vosotros)* disponeos para... ▪ preparáos para... ▪ estáos listos para... ➤ Be ready to leave at five o'clock. Estate listo para salir a las cinco.

be right back! ▪ I'll be right back! ~ *(L. Am.)* ¡en seguida regreso! ▪ ¡regreso en un momento! ▪ *(Sp.)* ¡en seguida vuelvo! ▪ ¡vuelvo en un momento! ▪ ¡(espera) que ahora vengo! ▪ *(Mex.)* ¡ahorita vengo! ▪ ¡ahorita vuelvo! ▪ ¡ahorita regreso!

be still! ▪ hold still! *(tú)* ¡estate quieto(-a)! ▪ *(usted)* ¡estese quieto(-a)! ▪ *(vosotros)* ¡estáos quietos! ▪ *(vosotras)* ¡estáos quietas! ▪ *(ustedes)* ¡estense quietos!

to **be sure and do something** ▪ to be sure to do something asegurarse de que uno haga algo ▪ asegurarse de hacer algo ➤ Be sure and bring it back. ▪ Be sure to bring it back. Asegúrate de que lo traigas de vuelta. ▪ Asegúrate de devolverlo. ➤ Be sure and call me. ▪ Be sure to call me. Asegúrate de llamarme. ➤ Be sure and tell him what a great hit his present was. ▪ Be sure to tell him what a great hit his present was. Asegúrate de decirle qué gran éxito fue su regalo.

to **be sure to do something** ▪ to be sure and do something asegurarse de hacer algo

be that as it may ▪ even so ▪ whether that's the case or not sea lo que sea ▪ sea cual sea el caso ▪ fuera lo que fuera ▪ aun así

to **be there 1.** to attend allí estar ▪ estar allí **2.** to exist haber ▪ estar ➤ I'll be there! ¡Allí estaré! ➤ I'll be there at five. Estaré allí a las cinco. ➤ The little rural school house she attended as a child in Argentina must still be there. La pequeña escuela rural a la que asistió de niña debe estar allí aún. ▪ La pequeña escuela rural a la que asistió de niña debe existir todavía.

➤ The old schoolhouse must still be there. La vieja escuela debe estar allí todavía. ▪ La vieja escuela debe existir todavía. ▪ Aún debe estar allí la vieja escuela. ▪ Aún debe existir la vieja escuela. ▪ *(S. Am.)* Debe haberla todavía.

to **be there for someone** estar al lado de alguien ➤ She was there for him when his sister died. Ella estuvo a su lado cuando su hermana murió.

to **be there *x* hours early** ▪ to be there *x* hours ahead of time estar *x* horas antes ▪ estar con *x* horas de anticipación ▪ estar con *x* horas de antelación ➤ Be at the airport two hours early. ▪ Be at the airport two hours ahead of time. Estate en el aeropuerto dos horas antes. ▪ Estate en el aeropuerto con dos horas de anticipación. ▪ Estate en el aeropuerto con dos horas de antelación.

be thinking of *(tú)* ve pensando en ▪ *(Sp.)* vete pensando en ▪ *(usted)* vaya pensando en ▪ *(Sp.)* váyase pensando en ➤ Be thinking of a place to go have dinner. Ve pensando en un lugar para ir a comer. ▪ Vete pensando en un lugar para ir a comer. ➤ Be thinking of one. Velo pensando. ▪ *(Sp.)* Vételo pensando.

to **be to be** haber de ser ➤ I'm to be the team director for the next six months. Habré de ser el director del equipo durante los próximos seis meses. ➤ The president was to greet the shuttle crew on its arrival. El presidente habría de saludar a la tripulación del transbordador a su llegada.

be yourself *(tú)* sé tú mismo ▪ *(usted)* sea usted mismo

beacon of hope *la* luz de esperanza

to **beam into a transmitter** ▪ to lock onto a transmitter fijarse en la señal de un transmisor

beam: laser ~ 1. *(coll.)* rayo laser **2.** *(scientific and technical) el* haz de laser

beam of light rayo de luz ▪ *el* haz de luz ➤ When he was sixteen, Einstein wondered what it would be like to ride on a beam of light. Cuando tenía dieciséis años, Einstein se preguntó cómo sería cabalgar en un rayo de luz.

to be a **bean pole** ▪ to be skinny as a rail ▪ to be a toothpick estar en los huesos ▪ estar muy flaco ▪ estar hecho un fideo

to **bear a burden** aguantar una carga ▪ soportar una carga

to **bear a child** ▪ to give birth to a child dar a luz a un(-a) niño(-a)

to **bear a grudge against someone for something** ▪ to nurse a grudge against someone for something ▪ to harbor a grudge against someone for something ▪ to have a grudge against someone for something guardarle rencor a alguien por algo ▪ tenerle inquina a alguien por algo ▪ tenerle tirria a alguien por algo

to **bear a certain resemblance to** guardar un cierto parecido con ▪ tener un cierto parecido con ➤ This bird bears a certain resemblance to a stork, except for its orange color. Este ave guarda un cierto parecido con la cigüeña, excepto por su color naranja.

to **bear a resemblance to** guardar parecido con ▪ tener un parecido con

bear baiting 1. *(the practice)* tortura de un oso **2.** *(the entertainment event)* espectáculo en que se tortura a un oso ➤ *(Carlyle)* The Puritans hated bear baiting, not because it gave pain to the bear, but because it gave pleasure to the spectators. Los Puritanos odiaban los espectáculos en donde se torturaban a los osos, no por el dolor que se inflingía al oso, sino por el placer que le producía a los espectadores.

to **bear down (hard)** *(when writing)* ▪ to press hard marcarlo (bien) ▪ remarcarlo (bien) ➤ Bear down (hard) so that the copies will be legible. ▪ Press hard so the copies will be legible. Márcalo (bien) para que las copias sean legibles. ▪ Remárcalo (bien) para que las copias sean legibles.

to **bear down on someone** ▪ to put a lot of pressure on someone poner presión a alguien ▪ presionar a alguien ➤ The managers are really bearing down on the office staff. ▪ The managers are really putting a lot of pressure on the office staff. Los jefes le están poniendo mucha presión al personal. ▪ Los jefes están presionando al personal.

to **bear false witness against someone** ▪ to slander someone ▪ *(journalistic and literary)* to calumniate someone dar falso testimonio contra alguien ▪ levantar falso testimonio contra alguien ▪ calumniar a alguien

to **bear fruit** dar frutos ▪ rendir frutos

to **bear in mind that...** ▪ to keep in mind that... tener en cuenta que... ▪ tener presente que... ▪ pensar que... ▪ recordar que... ➤ *(selections from* Reader's Digest*)* Bear in mind that for a child it is very difficult to accept a flat "no," so if you refuse him something, extenuate your negative. Piensa que para un niño es muy difícil aceptar un "no" tajante, así que si le niegas algo, razona tu negativa.

to **bear left** mantenerse a la izquierda ▪ hacerse a la izquierda ▪ quedarse a la izquierda ➤ Bear left. *(tú)* Mantente a la izquierda. ▪ Hazte a la izquierda. ▪ Quédate a la izquierda. ▪ *(usted)* Manténgase a la izquierda. ▪ Hágase (usted) a la izquierda. ▪ Quédese (usted) a la izquierda.

to **bear looking into** ▪ to bear checking out valer la pena investigarlo ▪ ser digno de ser investigado ▪ ser digno de investigarse ➤ This bears looking into. ▪ This bears checking out. Esto vale la pena ser investigado. ▪ Esto es digno de ser investigado.

to **bear out something** ▪ to bear something out ▪ to confirm something ▪ to corroborate something confirmar algo ▪ comprobar algo ▪ corroborar algo ➤ The experiment bore out what Einstein knew all along, that gravity bends light. El experimento confirmó lo que Einstein sabía desde un principio, que la gravedad modifica la trayectoria de la luz. ▪ El experimento comprobó lo que Einstein sabía desde un principio, que la gravedad modifica la trayectoria de la luz. ▪ El experimento corroboró lo que Einstein sabía desde un principio, que la gravedad modifica la trayectoria de la luz.

to **bear right** mantenerse a la derecha ▪ hacerse a la derecha ▪ quedarse a la derecha ➤ Bear right. *(tú)* Manténte a la derecha ▪ Hazte a la derecha. ▪ Quédate a la derecha. ▪ *(usted)* Manténgase a la derecha ▪ Hágase (usted) a la derecha. ▪ Quédese (usted) a la derecha.

to **bear scrutiny** merecer escrutinio ▪ ser digno de escrutinio ▪ ser susceptible de escrutinio

to **bear the brunt of something** ser el centro de algo ➤ The president bears the brunt of the criticism. El presidente es el centro de todas las críticas.

to **bear the burden of something** soportar la carga de algo ▪ aguantar la carga de algo

to **bear the cost of something** ▪ to bear the expense of something asumir el costo de algo ▪ asumir el gasto de algo ▪ correr con el costo de algo

to **bear the expense of something** ▪ to bear the cost of something asumir el gasto de algo ▪ asumir el costo de algo

to **bear the responsibility** ▪ to shoulder a responsibility asumir la responsabilidad ▪ cargar con la responsabilidad ▪ *(Sp., coll.)* apencar con la responsabilidad

to **bear the strain** soportar la tensión ▪ aguantar la tensión

to **bear the title (of)** llevar por título ➤ He bears the title of Knight of the British Empire (KBE). Lleva por título Caballero del Imperio Británico.

to **bear the weight** ▪ to support the weight soportar el peso

to **bear up under scrutiny** ▪ to stand up under scrutiny salir airoso de un examen detallado ▪ pasar un escrutinio riguroso

to **bear up under the strain** aguantar la presión ➤ The prime minister has borne up very well under the strain of his office. El primer ministro ha aguantado muy bien la presión del cargo.

bear with me les ruego paciencia ▪ se ruega paciencia ▪ sean pacientes conmigo ▪ *(Sp., vosotros)* os ruego paciencia ▪ sed pacientes conmigo ➤ It takes a minute to explain this, so please bear with me. Me llevará un minuto explicarlo, por eso les ruego paciencia.

to **bear witness that...** ser testigo de que... ▪ *(in legal parlance)* dar fe de que... ➤ Students bore witness that the teacher had covered the material adequately. Los estudiantes eran testigos de que el profesor había cubierto la materia adecuadamente.

to **bear witness to something** ser testigo de algo ➤ The Old Testament's prophets bore witness to the truth of the ancient teachings. Los profetas del Antiguo Testamento eran testigos de la verdad de las antiguas enseñanzas.

to **beat a dead horse** machacar en hierro frío ▪ arar en el mar ➤ My grandfather said when they moved from Pennsylvania to Virginia in 1912, people were still fighting the Civil War.

Talk about beating a dead horse! Mi abuelo dijo que cuando se mudaron de Pensilvania a Virginia en 1912, la gente seguía aún con la Guerra Civil. ¡Para que luego digan de machacar en hierro frío! ➤ There are people who are still mentally rehashing the Spanish Civil War. Talk about beating a dead horse! Hay gente que sigue dándole vueltas a la Guerra Civil Española. Para que luego digan de machacar en hierro frío.

to **beat a (hasty) retreat** batirse en retirada

to **beat a trail out of Dodge** *(coll.)* ■ to get the hell out of a place ■ to vamoose tomar las de Villadiego ■ salir pitando ■ pirarse de allí en cuanto poder ■ salir echando chispas ■ salir echando leches ■ salir como alma que lleva el diablo ■ *(off-color)* salir echando hostias ■ *(L. Am.)* mostrar las herraduras

to **beat against** golpear contra ■ dar contra ➤ The rain beat against the windshield. La lluvia golpeaba contra el parabrisas. ■ La lluvia daba contra el parabrisas.

to **beat an egg** batir un huevo

to **beat an opponent at something** *(politics, sports, chess)* ■ to defeat an opponent at something ganarle a un oponente a algo ■ ganarle a un oponente en algo ■ derrotar a un oponente a algo ■ derrotar a un oponente en algo ➤ He beats me at chess hands down, so I never play him. Me gana al ajedrez con los ojos cerrados, así que nunca juego con él. ■ Me gana en el ajedrez con los ojos cerrados, así que nunca juego con él. ■ Me derrota al ajedrez con los ojos cerrados, así que nunca juego con él. ■ Me derrota en el ajedrez con los ojos cerrados, así que nunca juego con él. *("Oponente" can be replaced by "contrincante" in this context.)*

to **beat around the bush** andarse por las ramas ■ andarse con rodeos ■ *(Sp.)* irse por los cerros de Úbeda ■ marear la perdiz ■ andarse con medias tintas

to **beat back something** ■ to beat something back repeler algo ➤ When the woods caught on fire, the soldiers took off their coats and tried to beat back the flames. ■ When the woods caught on fire, the soldiers took off their coats and tried to beat the flames back. Cuando los bosques se incendiaron, los soldados se quitaron los abrigos y trataron de repeler las llamas. ➤ The soldiers tried to beat them back. Los soldados trataron de repelerlas. ➤ The campers tried in vain to beat back the invasion of ants. Los campistas intentaron en vano repeler la invasión de hormigas. ➤ The victim tried to beat back her attackers with her pocketbook. La víctima intentó repeler a sus asaltantes con su bolsa.

to **beat down on** caer a plomo ➤ The speaker fainted as the noonday sun was beating down on the square. El orador se desmayó al mediodía cuando el sol caía de plomo en la plaza. ■ El orador sufrió el vahído al mediodía cuando el sol caía a plomo en la plaza.

to **beat down the door** ■ to beat the door down derribar la puerta a golpes ➤ The police beat down the door. ■ The police beat the door down. La policía derribó la puerta a golpes.

beat it! ¡largo de aquí! ■ ¡pírate! ■ ¡esfúmate! ■ ¡multiplícate por cero!

beat of the music *el* compás de la música ■ tiempo del compás ■ ritmo de la música

to **beat one's head against a (brick) wall** darse de cabeza contra un muro ■ darse la cabeza contra la pared

beat reporter reportero asignado a una determinada sección ➤ The newspaper has a number of general assignment reporters as well as beat reporters who cover city hall, courts, police, business, religion, medicine, and science. El periódico, tiene una serie de reporteros que no están asignados a una sección en concreto además de los reporteros ya asignados que cubren el ayuntamiento, los juzgados, la policía, los negocios, la religión, la medicina y la ciencia. ➤ A reporter out on her beat Una reportera a pie de calle

to **beat someone 1.** to defeat someone ganarle a alguien **2.** *(in sports that have goals)* to defeat by a wide margin golear a alguien **2.** to beat someone up ■ to give someone a beating golpear a alguien ■ darle una paliza a alguien ➤ They beat us ten to nothing. Nos ganaron diez a cero. ➤ The robbers beat the victim and left him for dead. Los atracadores golpearon a la víctima dejándolo por muerto.

to **beat someone by *x* points** ■ to win over someone by *x* points vencer a alguien por *x* puntos ➤ Real Madrid beats Barcelona by six points. Real Madrid vence a Barcelona por seis puntos.

to **beat someone to it** ganarle de mano a alguien ■ adelantarse a alguien ■ anticiparse a alguien ➤ You beat me to it! ¡Me ganaste de mano! ■ ¡Te me has adelantado! ■ ¡Te me anticipaste! ■ ¡Te me adelantaste!

to **beat something with a mixer** batir algo con un batidor ■ batir algo con una batidora eléctrica ➤ Beat the egg whites until the peaks are stiff. Batir las claras a punto de nieve.

to **beat the clock** ganarle al reloj ➤ James Bond always beats the clock, if only by a second. James Bond siempre le gana al reloj, aunque sea por un segundo.

to **beat the competition** ■ to defeat the competition derrotar a la competencia ■ ganarle a la competencia

to **beat the light** ganarle al semáforo

to **beat the pavement** ■ to pound the pavement ■ to job hunt patearse (toda) la calle

to **beat the rush** adelantarse a la multitud

to **beat their wings** ■ to flap their wings aletear ■ batir las alas ➤ Leonardo da Vinci recognized that, except during take-off, birds beat their wings for propulsion, not lift. Leonardo da Vinci se dio cuenta de que, excepto durante el despegue, las aves aletean para propulsarse, no para mantenerse en el aire.

to **beat time 1.** to race against time ganar tiempo al tiempo ■ correr contra el tiempo **2.** to mark time (to music) marcar el compás

to **beat time to the music** marcar el compás de la música ■ marcar el paso de la música

to **beat to death** matar a golpes ■ apalear hasta la muerte

beat-up car ■ rattletrap ■ clunker ■ bucket of bolts ■ rolling ghetto carro chatarra ■ tartana ■ auto cascajo

beat-up furniture ■ worn (out) furniture muebles ajados ■ ajado mobiliario ■ muebles hechos pelota

to **beat up someone** ■ to beat someone up darle una paliza a alguien ■ *(off-color)* darle de hostias a alguien ➤ The robbers who beat up the couple were recorded by the security camera. Los atracadores que le dieron una paliza a la pareja fueron grabados por la cámara de seguridad. ➤ The robbers beat them up. Los ladrones les dieron una paliza.

beaten path camino trillado ➤ Genius disdains a beaten path. El genio desdeña el camino trillado. ➤ It's off the beaten path. ■ It's out of the way. Está alejado del camino.

beating of drums *el* redoble de tambores

beating of (the) rain on the roof ■ pounding of (the) rain on the roof ■ drumming of (the) rain on the roof tamborileo de la lluvia sobre el tejado

beats me! ■ it (sure) beats me! ni idea ■ no tengo ni idea ■ *(off-color)* no tengo ni puta idea

to be a **beautiful day** ser un día hermoso

beautiful face: to have a ~ tener una cara preciosa ■ tener una cara hermosa ■ tener una cara linda ➤ She has a beautiful face. Ella tiene una cara preciosa. ■ Ella tiene una cara hermosa. ■ Ella tiene una cara linda.

beautiful home lindo hogar ■ bello hogar ■ hermoso hogar

beautiful house casa linda ■ casa preciosa ■ casa hermosa ■ bella casa

beautiful people gente guapa ■ gente hermosa ■ linda gente

beautiful view vista hermosa ➤ The view from the mountaintop is beautiful. La vista desde lo alto de la montaña es hermosa.

beautiful view: to have a ~ *(usually plural in Spanish)* tener unas vistas preciosas ■ tener unas vistas hermosas ■ tener bellas vistas ➤ The hotel room has a beautiful view. La habitación del hotel tiene unas vistas preciosas. ■ La habitación del hotel tiene unas vistas hermosas. ■ La habitación del hotel tiene bellas vistas.

beautiful voice voz hermosa ■ linda voz ➤ She has a beautiful singing voice. Ella tiene una voz hermosa para el canto.

beautiful weather ■ wall-to-wall sunshine tiempo hermoso ■ tiempo radiante ■ clima maravilloso ➤ The weather is beautiful today. El clima es maravilloso hoy. ■ El tiempo está radiante hoy.

beautiful woman mujer bella ■ mujer hermosa ■ mujer linda ■ mujer guapa

beauty is in the eye of the beholder la belleza está en los ojos del que mira

beauty pageant concurso de belleza

beauty parlor *el* salón de belleza

because if it weren't pues de lo contrario ■ (porque) de no ser así ■ porque si no fuese así ■ porque si no fuera así

because if you don't ■ because otherwise porque si no ➤ Please E-mail me at this address because if you don't I can't answer you. Por favor mándame los correos electrónicos a esta dirección porque si no, no te puedo contestar.

because of 1. por ■ a causa de ■ por causa de **2.** owing to debido a ➤ *(Julio Iglesias song)* Because of Her Por ella ➤ The baseball game was cancelled because of bad weather. El partido de béisbol fue cancelado debido al mal tiempo. ➤ The classes were cancelled because of snow. Las clases fueron anulados a causa de la nieve. ➤ He resigned from his job because of a conflict with his boss. Renunció a su trabajo por causa de un conflicto con su jefe.

because of it ■ because of that ■ on account of it por eso ■ por su causa ■ por culpa de eso ➤ It's better to sleep on it than (to) lose sleep because of it. Es mejor consultar las cosas con la almohada a tiempo que perder el sueño por su causa después.

because of pressure from por presiones de

because of that ■ because of it por eso ■ *(literary)* por ende

because of the holiday por ser día festivo ■ por ser fiesta ■ por ser feriado

because of which ■ through which ■ by means of which **1.** por el cual **2.** por la cual

because otherwise ■ because if someone doesn't porque si no ■ que, si no ➤ Tell him to call me by nine, because otherwise I won't get the message. ■ Tell him to call me by nine, because if he doesn't, I won't get the message. Dile que me llame antes de las nueve, porque si no, no me pasan el mensaje. ➤ Please E-mail me at this address because otherwise I can't answer you. Por favor mándame los correos electrónicos a esta dirección porque si no, no te puedo contestar.

beck and call: to be at someone's ~ estar siempre a disposición de alguien ■ estar todo el tiempo detrás de alguien

to **become a bestseller** convertirse en un éxito de ventas

to **become a composer** hacerse compositor ➤ Rimsky-Korsakov became a professional composer after years as a naval officer. Rimsky-Korsakov se hizo compositor tras años de oficial de la marina.

to **become a distinguished professor of** hacerse catedrático de...

to **become a doctor** hacerse médico

to **become a familiar face to the public** llegar a convertirse en una cara familiar para el público

to **become a fatality** convertirse en una víctima mortal ➤ A ten-year-old boy became this summer's first shark fatality in the United States. Un niño de diez años se convirtió en la primera víctima mortal de un tiburón en los Estados Unidos este verano.

to **become a habit** volverse un hábito ■ hacerse un hábito

to **become a lawyer** ■ to become an attorney hacerse abogado

to **become a member of** ■ to join hacerse socio de ■ asociarse a

to **become a professor** hacerse profesor(-a) universitario(-a)

to **become a reality (for one)** ■ to come true (for one) hacérsele realidad

to **become a scarce commodity** convertirse en un bien escaso

to **become a teacher** hacerse profesor(-a)

to **become accustomed to** ■ to get accustomed to ■ to get used to acostumbrarse ■ llegar a acostumbrarse

to **become aggressive** ■ to turn aggressive **1.** *(suddenly)* ponerse agresivo **2.** *(over time)* volverse agresivo

to **become alarmed** ■ to get alarmed alarmarse ➤ Don't become alarmed. No te alarmes.

to **become an attorney** ■ to become a lawyer hacerse abogado

to **become attached to someone** ■ to get attached to someone ■ to grow fond of someone encariñarse con alguien ➤ Children often become very attached to pets. Muy a menudo los niños se encariñan con los mascotas.

to **become available** estar disponible ➤ Affordable solar energy systems for houses will become available some day. Algún día sistemas solares económicos para las casas estarán disponibles.

to **become aware of** enterarse de

to **become aware that...** darse cuenta de que...

to **become clear** ponerse de manifiesto

to **become close friends with someone** ■ to establish a close friendship with someone intimar con alguien ■ llegar a ser buenos amigos con alguien ■ entablar una estrecha relación de amistad on alguien

to **become conscious (of oneself)** concientizarse (de sí mismo) ➤ The computer HAL became conscious of himself. La computadora HAL se concientizó (de sí mismo).

to **become convinced** llegar a convencerse ■ convencerse

to **become incarnate** volverse carne

to **become entrenched in something** atrincherarse en algo ■ enquistarse en algo ➤ The Republicans became entrenched in power after the Civil War. Después de la Guerra Civil los Republicanos se atrincheraron en el poder. ■ Después de la Guerra Civil los Republicanos se enquistaron en el poder.

to **become expert at something** llegar a ser un experto en algo ■ hacerse un experto en algo

to **become familiar with** familiarizarse con

to **become famous** hacerse famoso(-a) ■ llegar a ser famoso(-a)

to **become flooded** inundarse ➤ The streets became flooded during the hurricane. Las calles se inundaron durante el huracán. ➤ The basement became flooded during the hurricane. El sótano se inundó durante el huracán.

to **become fluent in a language** soltarse en un idioma ■ volverse fluido en un idioma ■ hacerse fluido en un idioma ■ llegar a hacerse fluido en un idioma ■ volverse docto en un lenguaje

to **become friends** hacerse amigos

to **become heated** enconarse ■ acalorarse ➤ The discussion became heated. La discusión se enconó.

to **become indignant at** ■ to get indignant at indignarse de

to **become infected** ■ to get infected infectársele ■ enconarse ➤ The wound became infected. La herida se infectó. ■ La herida se enconó. ➤ His wound became infected. ■ His wound got infected. La herida se le infectó. ■ La herida se le enconó. ➤ My wound became infected. ■ His wound became infected. La herida se me infectó. ■ La herida se me enconó.

to **become inflamed** ■ to get inflamed inflamarse

to **become insane** ■ to go mad enloquecerse ■ perder la cordura ■ volverse loco ■ perder la razón

to **become instantly famous** ■ to achieve instant fame alcanzar una pronta fama ■ hacerse famoso instantáneamente

to **become known** saberse ■ conocerse ➤ When it became known that... Al saberse que... ■ Al ser conocido que... ■ Cuando se supo que... ■ Al haberse conocido que... ➤ When it becomes known that... Al saberse que... ■ Al ser conocido que... ■ Cuando se sepa que... ■ Cuando se conozca que...

to **become lethargic** aletargarse ■ achancharse ■ aplatanarse

to **become more intense** ■ to get more intense intensificarse ■ hacerse más intenso ■ ponerse más intenso

to **become obsolete** quedarse anticuado ■ quedarse obsoleto

to **become of** ■ to have become of haber sido de ■ *(archaic)* haberse hecho ■ ser de ➤ Whatever became of your Mexican friend? ¿Qué ha sido de tu amigo mexicano? ■ ¿Qué se ha hecho de tu amigo mejicano? ➤ Without their mother, what will become of them? Sin su madre, ¿qué va a ser de ellos?

to **become overcast** nublarse ■ ponerse el cielo oscuro

to **become pale** ■ to turn pale ■ to get pale ponerse pálido ■ empalidecerse

to **become part of** incorporarse a

to **become physical** ■ to get physical volverse sexualmente intenso

to **become polarized** polarizarse

to **become politically conscious** despertarse a la política to **become pregnant** **1.** *(human beings)* to get pregnant quedar embarazada **2.** *(Biblical)* to be with child quedar en cinta **3.** *(animals)* quedar preñada

to **become president** **1.** hacerse presidente **2.** *(especially in past narrative)* llegar a (ser) presidente **3.** *(by succession)* pasar a ser presidente

to **become proficient at doing something** llegar a dársele muy bien hacer algo ➤ He's become very proficient at throwing the frisbee, and his dog has become proficient at catching it. Ha llegado a dársele muy bien lanzar el disco, y a su perro se le ha llegado a dar muy bien cogerlo.

to **become proficient in something** llegar a dársele muy bien algo ▪ llegar a ser muy bueno en algo ➤ The youth has become very proficient in mathematics. Al joven ha llegado a dársele muy bien las matemáticas. ▪ El joven ha llegado a ser muy bueno en matemática.

to **become proficient in Spanish** ▪ to become fluent in Spanish llegar a ser proficiente en español ▪ llegar a tener fluidez en español ▪ llegar a tener un buen dominio del español

to **become proficient with** llegar a ser competente con ➤ My teenage son has become very proficient with a camera. Mi hijo adolescente ha llegado a ser muy competente con la cámara.

to **become proficient with something** llegar a obtener un buen manejo de algo ➤ My brother has become very proficient with a lathe. Mi hermano ha llegado a conseguir un buen manejo del torno.

to **become saddled with debt** ▪ to go deep into debt meterse en deudas (hasta el cuello) ▪ cargarse de deudas (hasta el cuello) ▪ *(Mex.)* endrogarse

to **become second nature** volverse instintivo ▪ convertirse en instintivo ➤ To a pilot, landing becomes second nature. Para un piloto aterrizar se vuelve algo instintivo. ▪ Para un piloto aterrizar se convierte en algo instintivo.

to **become stronger** ▪ to get stronger ▪ to gain strength **1.** *(from lifting weight, etc.)* fortalecerse **2.** *(after an illness)* recuperarse **3.** *(hurricane, etc.)* arreciar ➤ He's becoming stronger after his recent surgery. ▪ He's getting stronger after his recent surgery. ▪ He's gaining strength after his recent surgery. Se está fortaleciendo después de su reciente cirugía. ➤ The winds are becoming stronger. ▪ The winds are getting stronger. ▪ The winds are gaining strength. Los vientos están arreciando.

to **become suspicious** ▪ to get suspicious comenzar a sospechar ▪ comenzar a desconfiar

to **become suspicious of someone** ▪ to begin to suspect someone comenzar a sospechar de alguien ▪ comenzar a desconfiar de alguien ▪ empezar a sospechar de alguien ▪ empezar a desconfiar de alguien

to **become suspicious that...** ▪ to begin to suspect that... comenzar a sospechar(se) que... ▪ empezar a sospechar(se) que...

to **become the focal point of attention** ▪ to become the center of attention convertirse en el foco de atención ▪ convertirse en el centro de atención

to **become the focal point of the debate** convertirse en el foco del debate ▪ convertirse en el centro del debate

to **become the focal point of the discussion** convertirse en el foco de la charla ▪ convertirse en el centro de la charla

to **become treatable** poder ser tratado(-a) ➤ Within a few years, viral illnesses will become treatable. En pocos años, las enfermedades retrovirales podrán ser tratadas.

to **become violent** ▪ to turn violent ponerse violento

to **become withdrawn** ▪ to withdraw (into oneself) ▪ to draw into oneself encerrarse en uno mismo

to be **becoming to someone** ▪ to look good on someone quedarle bien ▪ irle bien ▪ sentarle bien ▪ resultarle ➤ That dress is very becoming to you. Ese vestido le queda muy bien. ▪ Le va muy bien. ▪ Le sienta muy bien.

bed of roses ▪ bowl of cherries lecho de rosas ➤ Life is no bed of roses. La vida no es un lecho de rosas.

bed to sleep in cama donde dormir ▪ cama para dormir

bedroom community ciudad dormitorio

bedside table ▪ nightstand ▪ night table mesilla de noche ▪ *(S. Am.)* mesita de luz ▪ *(Mex.)* buró ▪ *(archaic)* velero

bedtime! ▪ time for bed! ¡a dormir! ▪ ¡hora de acostarse!

bedtime story cuento antes de dormir ▪ cuento antes de ir a dormir

to **beef up security** reforzar la seguridad ▪ fortalecer la seguridad

beef jerky carne seca ▪ carne deshidratada

to **beef up the military** ▪ to beef up the armed forces reforzar las fuerzas armadas ➤ The two nations are beefing up their military presence along the border. Las dos naciones están reforzando su presencia militar a lo largo de la frontera.

been hearing that for months: to have ~ haber estado oyéndolo durante meses ▪ haber venido oyéndolo durante meses ➤ I've been hearing that for months. He estado oyéndolo durante meses. ▪ He venido oyéndolo durante meses.

been here for: to have ~ llevar aquí ▪ estar aquí desde hace ➤ I've been here for four months. Llevo cuatro meses aquí. ▪ Estoy aquí desde hace cuatro meses.

been in the hospital: to have ~ haber estado en el hospital ▪ llevar (tiempo) en el hospital ➤ He's been in the hospital since the Friday after you left. Ha estado en el hospital desde el viernes después de tu partida. ▪ Lleva en el hospital desde el viernes después de tu partida.

been there, done that: to be a case of ~ necesitar un nuevo reto ▪ afrontar un nuevo reto ▪ enfrentarse a un nuevo reto ▪ hacer algo que uno no haber hecho antes ▪ haber superado una etapa profesional ➤ The screenplay writer became a director. He said it was just a case of been there, done that. El guionista se hizo director. Dijo que sencillamente era una cuestión de afrontar un nuevo reto.

been there for: to have ~ llevar allí ▪ estar allí desde hace ➤ They've been there for a year. Llevan un año allí. ▪ Están allí desde hace un año.

been through the mill: to have ~ estar hecho trizas ▪ estar muy desgastado ▪ estar hecho polvo ➤ This tablecloth has been through the mill. I think it's time to get a new one. Este mantel está hecho trizas. Pienso que es hora de comprar uno nuevo.

been to: to have ~ haber ido a ➤ This morning I've been to my Internet service provider, the library, and the university computer lab. Esta mañana he ido a mi proveedor de Internet, a la biblioteca y al laboratorio de informática de la universidad.

beer can lata (vacía) de cerveza ➤ Someone suggested putting photos of missing husbands on beer cans. Alguien ha sugerido poner fotos de los maridos desaparecidos en las latas de cerveza.

beer gut ▪ beer belly panza de cerveza ▪ *(Sp.)* tripa cervecera ▪ *(Mex., coll.)* panza de pulquero

before anyone else antes que nadie ➤ I heard the news before anyone else. ▪ I was the first to hear the news. Me enteré de las noticias antes que nadie.

before Christ (B.C.) antes de Cristo (a.C.)

before Christmas antes de la Navidad

before dark ▪ before it gets dark antes (de) que se haga de noche ▪ antes (de) que anochezca ▪ antes (de) que se ponga el sol ▪ *(literary)* antes del crepúsculo ▪ antes del ocaso

before dawn ▪ before daybreak ▪ before the sun comes up antes (de) que se haga de día ▪ antes (de) que amanezca ▪ antes (de) que salga el sol ▪ antes del amanecer ▪ antes del día ▪ *(literary)* antes del alba ▪ antes de la aurora

before I could... antes de que (yo) pudiera... ➤ Before I could recover from my astonishment... ▪ Before I could recover my composure... Antes de que pudiera salir de mi asombro... ➤ Before I could answer... Antes de que (yo) pudiera responder...

before I could even antes de que (yo) pudiera siquiera

before I could stop him antes de que (yo) pudiera pararlo ▪ *(Sp., leísmo)* antes de que (yo) pudiera pararle *("Pudiese" can replace "pudiera" in both examples.)*

before I do antes que yo (lo hago) ➤ My mother gets up an hour before I do. Mi madre se levanta una hora antes que yo.

before I did antes que yo (lo hiciera) ➤ They got here before I did. Llegaron antes que yo.

before I knew it antes de darme cuenta ▪ cuando me quise dar cuenta ▪ cuando quise acordarme

before I knew what had happened ▪ before I realized what had happened antes de que pudiera darme cuenta de lo que había pasado

before I knew what had hit me (para) cuando me di cuenta de lo que me había pasado

before I knew what hit me (para) cuando me di cuenta de lo que me pasó

before I was born antes de que (yo) naciese ▪ antes de que (yo) naciera

before (it gets) dark antes de que se haga de noche ▪ antes de que anochezca ▪ antes de que se ponga el sol ▪ antes del ocaso

before last: the one ~ el penúltimo ▪ la penúltima ➤ We arrived here Monday before last. Llegamos aquí el penúltimo lunes. ➤ Christmas before last La penúltima Navidad

before long 1. *(future)* shortly ▪ soon ▪ in a little while en breve ▪ dentro de poco ▪ en poco tiempo ▪ al poco tiempo ▪ antes de poco **2.** *(past)* in a little while ▪ soon afterwards ▪ shortly afterwards poco (tiempo) después ▪ al poco tiempo ▪ dentro de poco

to be **before me in (the) line** ▪ to be in front of me in (the) line ▪ to be ahead of me in (the) line estar antes de mí en la cola ▪ estar antes que yo en la cola ▪ estar primero en la cola ▪ ir primero en la cola ▪ ir antes de mí en la cola ▪ ir antes que yo en la cola ▪ ir delante de mí en la cola ▪ estar delante de mí en la cola ▪ *(coll.)* ir delante mío en la cola ▪ estar delante mío en la cola ➤ She was before me in (the) line. ▪ She was in front of me in (the) line. ▪ She was ahead of me in (the) line. ▪ She was first. Ella estaba antes de mí en la cola. ▪ Ella iba antes de mí en la cola. ▪ Ella estaba antes que yo en la cola. ▪ Ella iba antes que yo en la cola. ▪ Ella estaba primero. ▪ Ella iba primero.

before one was born antes de que naciera uno ▪ antes de que naciese uno ➤ Before you were born *(tú)* Antes de que (tú) nacieras ▪ *(usted)* Antes de que (usted) naciera

before that 1. sooner than that antes (de eso) ▪ más pronto **2.** prior to that antes de eso ▪ anteriormente ➤ We can meet before that if you need to. ▪ We can meet sooner (than that) if you need to. Podemos encontrarnos antes si lo necesitas. ▪ Podemos encontrarnos más pronto si lo necesitas. ➤ Before that, he worked in Washington. ▪ Prior to that, he worked in Washington. Antes de eso, (él) trabajaba en Washington. ▪ Anteriormente, (él) trabajaba en Washington.

before the altar: to stand ~ estar frente al altar ▪ estar delante del altar ▪ estar ante el altar

before the altar: to kneel ~ arrodillarse frente al altar ▪ arrodillarse delante del altar ▪ ponerse de rodillas frente al altar ▪ ponerse de rodillas delante del altar

before the count of ten antes de (llegar a) la cuenta de diez ▪ antes de llegar al conteo de diez ▪ antes del conteo de diez ➤ After being knocked out, the boxer came to before the count of ten. El boxeador volvió en sí antes de llegar a la cuenta de diez

before the court: to testify ~ testificar ante el tribunal ▪ *(L. Am.)* testificar ante la corte

before the end of the year antes de que (se) acabe el año ▪ antes del fin del año

before the mast ▪ as a sailor at sea en alta mar ➤ *(Richard Henry Dana novel) Two Years Before the Mast Dos años en altamar*

before too long ▪ before long sin dejar pasar mucho tiempo ➤ We'll get together before too long. No dejemos pasar mucho tiempo antes de que nos juntemos.

before which *(varies according to the gender and number of the antecedent)* antes del cual ▪ antes de la cual ▪ antes de los cuales ▪ antes de las cuales ➤ The label indicates the date before which the food should be consumed. La etiqueta indica la fecha antes de la cual la comida debe ser consumida.

before you can say Jack Robinson en un abrir y cerrar de ojos

before you know it *(tú)* antes de que te des cuenta ▪ antes de que te enteres ▪ sin que te des cuenta ▪ sin que te enteres ▪ *(usted)* antes de que se dé cuenta ▪ antes de que se entere ▪ sin que se dé cuenta ▪ sin que se entere ➤ Christmas will be here before you know it. La Navidad llegará antes de que te des cuenta. ▪ La Navidad llegará antes de que te enteres. ▪ La Navidad llegará sin que te des cuenta. ▪ La Navidad llegará sin que te enteres.

before you were born *(tú)* antes de que nacieras ▪ antes de que nacieses ▪ *(usted)* antes de que naciera ▪ antes de que naciese

before *x* o'clock antes de la(s) *x* ➤ Tell him to call me before nine, (because) otherwise I won't get the message. Dile que me llame antes de las nueve, porque si no, no me pasan el mensaje. ➤ Tell him to call me before one, (because) otherwise I won't get the message. Dile que me llame antes de la una, porque si no, no me pasan el mensaje.

beforehand: to make arrangments ~ hacer preparativos de antemano ▪ hacer preparativos por adelantado ▪ hacer preparativos con antelación

to **beg off** ▪ to pass ▪ to decline pasar (de algo)

to **beg someone for forgiveness** implorar (por) perdón a alguien ▪ suplicar perdó a alguien

to **beg someone for mercy** suplicar por piedad a alguien

to **beg the question** ▪ to assume the truth of the point in question ▪ to evade the issue eludir la pregunta ▪ rehuir la pregunta ➤ For a translator to say, "We don't say that," begs the question. Then how do you explain it? Cuando un traductor dice: "Nosotros no decimos eso", está eludiendo la pregunta. ¿Cómo lo explicas entonces?

to be **begging for it** estar pidiéndolo a gritos ➤ He's just begging for it. Lo está pidiendo a gritos.

to **begin a new page** ▪ to wipe the slate clean ▪ to start afresh hacer borrón y cuenta nueva ▪ zanjar el asunto definitivamente

to **begin abruptly** ▪ to begin suddenly empezar precipitadamente ▪ empezar apresuradamente

to **begin an investigation** iniciar una investigación ▪ abrir un investigación ▪ *(of a criminal case)* abrir expediente

to **begin at the beginning** ▪ to start at the beginning empezar desde el principio ▪ comenzar desde el principio

to **begin at the bottom** empezar desde abajo ➤ He began at the bottom and worked his way up. Empezó desde abajo y se labró un camino a la cumbre.

to **begin doing something** ponerse a hacer algo ▪ echarse a hacer algo ➤ He began honking the horn. ▪ He started honking the horn. Se puso a pitar. ➤ She began running. ▪ She started running. ▪ She broke into a run. ▪ She took off running. Se echó a correr.

to **begin negotiations** iniciar las negociaciones ▪ arrancar las negociaciones ▪ empezar las negociaciones ▪ abrir las negociaciones

to **begin one's career** empezar la carrera (profesional)

to **begin operations** ▪ to begin operating entrar en funcionamiento

to **begin practicing law** ▪ to open a law practice abrir (un) bufete ▪ abrir una firma

to **begin to appreciate** empezar a valorar *(The Spanish, like the English, refers to gratitude and monetary value.)*

to **begin to do something** empezar a hacer algo ▪ comenzar a hacer algo ➤ He began to read. Empezó a leer. ▪ Comenzó a leer.

to **begin to get difficult** ▪ to begin to get hard ▪ to start to get difficult ▪ to start to get hard hacérsele cuesta arriba ➤ This course is beginning to get difficult. ▪ This course is beginning to get hard. *(Mex.)* Este curso se me está haciendo difícil. ▪ *(Sp.)* Esta asignatura se me está haciendo difícil.

to **begin to like** ▪ to start to like empezarle a gustar a ▪ empezarle a caer bien a ➤ The dog is beginning to like him. ▪ The dog is starting to like him. Le empieza a gustar al perro. ▪ Le empieza a caer bien al perro. ➤ The dog is beginning to like me. ▪ The dog is starting to like me. Le empiezo a gustar al perro. ▪ Le empiezo a caer bien al perro.

to **begin to suspect someone** ▪ to start to suspect someone ▪ to become suspicious of someone comenzar a sospechar de alguien

to **begin with** ▪ to start with empezar por ➤ The phone number begins with nine. ▪ The phone number starts with nine. El número telefónico empieza por nueve.

to **begin with a false premise** partir de un plantamiento erróneo ▪ partir de una falsa premisa

to **begin with the basics** partir de lo básico
beginning of the document comienzo del documento
beginning of the end principio del fin
beginning of time principio de los tiempos
beginning on page *x* empezando en la página *x* ■ empezando por la página *x* ■ comenzando en la página *x* ■ comenzando por la página *x*
beginning today ■ starting today a partir de hoy ■ de hoy en más
behave yourself! ¡pórtate bien! ■ ¡compórtate! ■ ¡sé formal! ■ ¡ten formalidad!
behavior pattern ■ pattern of behavior *el* patrón de comportamiento ■ modelo de comportamiento ➤ *(news item)* Several experts believe that the behavior pattern (exhibited) in the five crimes indicates that the killer will act again. Varios expertos creen que el patrón de comportamiento en los cinco crímenes permite anticipar que el asesino volverá a actuar.
behavioral psychology psicología conductista
behavioral trait rasgo del comportamiento
to be **behind a plot** estar detrás de una conspiración ■ estar detrás de una conjura ➤ I think bin Laden was behind the terrorist plot. Creo que bin Laden estaba detrás de la conjura terrorista. ➤ Who do you think was behind the plot? ¿Quién estaba detrás de la conspiración?
to be **behind bars** ■ to be in jail estar entre rejas ■ estar tras las rejas ■ estar en la cárcel ■ *(coll.)* estar a la sombra
behind closed doors a puerta cerrada ➤ The Supreme Court permitted the trials to be held behind closed doors. La Corte Suprema aceptó que los juicios se celebren a puerta cerrada.
behind enemy lines ■ within enemy lines ■ inside enemy lines tras las líneas enemigas
to be **behind in one's reading** ir atrasado en mi lectura
to be **behind in one's work** ■ to be behind with one's work ■ to be behind on one's work estar atrasado con el trabajo ■ llevar retraso con el trabajo ➤ I'm behind in my work. Estoy atrasado con el trabajo. ■ Llevo retraso con mi trabajo.
behind in one's work: to get ~ atrasarse con el trabajo ■ retrasarse con el trabajo
behind me ■ to my back detrás de mí ■ a mis espaldas ➤ *(TV news reporter)* The Windsor tower, which you can see behind me... La Torre Windsor, que puedes ver a mis espaldas...
to be **behind schedule 1.** *(with work)* estar por detrás de lo previsto ■ ir por detrás de lo previsto **2.** to be late arriving llegar tarde ■ estar retrasado ■ *(L. Am.)* estar demorado ■ venir demorado **3.** to be late leaving ■ to be postponed ■ to be delayed estar pospuesto ■ estar aplazado ➤ *(news item)* Oil production in Iraq is behind schedule because of the constant acts of sabotage. La producción de petróleo en Irak está por detrás de lo previsto debido a los constantes sabotajes. ■ La producción de petróleo en Irak va por detrás de lo previsto debido a los constantes sabotajes. ➤ The flight is behind schedule. ■ The flight is late arriving. El vuelo llega tarde. ■ El vuelo está atrasado. ➤ The flight is behind schedule. ■ The flight is late leaving. ■ The flight has been delayed. ■ The flight has been postponed. El vuelo está pospuesto. ■ El vuelo está aplazado.
behind someone's back: to do something ~ hacer algo a espaldas de alguien ■ hacer algo a escondidas de alguien ➤ He did it behind his wife's back. Lo hizo a espaldas de su esposa.
to be **behind the eight ball** ■ to be in a tough spot ■ to be in a difficult predicament estar con el agua al cuello ■ estar en apuros ■ estar en un apuro
to be **behind the rest of the world** ■ to lag behind the rest of the world estar por detrás del resto del mundo
behind the scenes: to go ~ ir entre bastidores ■ ir atrás de la escena ■ ir atrás (del telón)
to be **behind the times 1.** to be antiquated no estar al día ■ seguir en la prehistoria **2.** to be out of touch with what's going on estar atrasado de noticias ➤ If you can't take debit and credit cards for purchases of 550 euros, you're behind the times. Si no aceptas tarjetas de crédito o débito para compras de 550 euros, es que no estás al día. ■ Si no aceptas tarjetas de crédito o débito para compras de 550 euros, es que sigues en la prehistoria.
being the traditionalist that he is con lo tradicional que es ■ con lo clásico que es
to be **being shown 1.** *(movie)* proyectarse **2.** *(house)* enseñarse ■ mostrarse ➤ The theatre where the film is being shown La sala donde se proyecta la película ➤ The houses are being shown this weekend. Las casas se enseñarán este fin de semana. ■ Las casas se mostrarán este fin de semana.
to be **being watched** mirarle a alguien ■ estar siendo observado ➤ We're being watched. Nos están mirando. ■ Estamos siendo observados. *(Spanish typically uses active voice to express this English passive.)*
being what it is siendo lo que es ■ tal como es ➤ My understanding of chemistry being what it is... Mi comprensión de la química siendo lo que es... ■ Mi comprensión de la química tal como es...
belated apology: to offer a ~ ■ to make a belated apology presentar una disculpa tardía ■ ofrecer una disculpa tardía ■ disculparse tardíamente
belated happy birthday: to wish someone a ~ desearle a alguien un feliz cumpleaños con retraso
belatedly: to answer ~ ■ to respond belatedly responder tardíamente ■ responder con retraso
to **belch ash** *(volcanos)* escupir ceniza
to **belch smoke** *(smokestacks, vehicles, etc.)* escupir humo ■ expulsar humo ➤ The trucks and buses were belching diesel smoke. Los camiones y autobúses escupían humo de gasoil. ➤ The smokestacks of the steel mills used to belch smoke, leaving a patina all over the industrial zone. Las chimeneas industriales de las acerías solían expulsar humo, dejando una patina por todo el polígono industrial.
to **belie one's feelings 1.** to hide one's feelings ocultar los sentimientos ■ no dejar traslucir los sentimientos **2.** to give away one's true feelings desenmascarar sus emociones ➤ His trembling hands belied his steady voice. Sus manos temblorosas desenmascararon el aplomo de su voz.
to **belie one's faith** ■ to be untrue to one's faith no ser consecuente con su fe
believe it or not aunque parece mentira ■ aunque parezca mentira ■ aunque no lo creas
believe me no lo dudes
not to believe one's eyes no creer lo que uno ve ■ no dar crédito a los ojos ➤ I can't believe my eyes. No creo lo que veo. ■ No doy crédito a mis ojos. ➤ I couldn't believe my eyes. No daba crédito a mis ojos.
to **believe one knows** creer saber ➤ We believe we know where... Creemos saber donde...
to **believe the story** ■ to swallow the story creerse la historia ■ tragar(se) la historia
to **bell the cat** ■ to attempt something daring poner el cascabel al gato ■ arrojarse a alguna acción atrevida
bells and whistles: to have all the ~ ■ to have all the extras tener todos los pitos y flautas
bells and whistles: with ~ con todos los pitos y flautas
bellwether bond bono cuyas fluctuaciones dan la tónica del mercado ■ obligación cuyas fluctuaciones dan la tónica del mercado
bellwether stock *la* acción indicadora ■ acción de referencia ■ acción cuyas fluctuaciones dan la tónica del mercado
belly dance danza de vientre
belly flop: to do a ~ echarse un panzazo ■ echarse un barrigazo
belly landing *el* aterrizaje de panza ■ *el* aterrizaje sin tren
to **belong to** pertenecer a ■ ser de ■ *(in a legal sense)* corresponderle a uno ➤ Who does this belong to? ■ Whose is this? ■ To whom does this belong? ¿A quién pertenece esto? ■ ¿De quién es esto? ➤ The painting, the oriental rug, and the grandfather clock belong to the eldest son. La pintura, la alfombra oriental y reloj de péndulo le corresponden al hijo mayor.
to **belong to a club** ser miembro de un club ■ ser socio de un club ■ ser miembro de una sociedad ■ ser socio de una sociedad
to **belong to a political party** ser miembro de un partido político ■ estar afiliado(-a) a un partido político

to be **below average** estar por debajo del promedio ▪ estar por debajo de la media ▪ estar inferior al promedio ▪ estar inferior a la media

below-freezing temperatures temperaturas bajo cero ▪ temperaturas por debajo del punto de congelación

to be **below ground level** estar por debajo del nivel de la tierra ➤ The first five feet of the wall are below ground level. Los primeros cinco pies de la pared están por debajo del nivel de la tierra.

below this one ▪ under this one ▪ beneath this one ▪ underneath this one debajo de éste(-a) ➤ They live in the apartment below this one. ▪ They live in the apartment under this one. ▪ They live in the apartment beneath this one. ▪ They live in the apartment underneath this one. Viven en el apartamento debajo de éste.

to be ***x* below zero** ▪ to be minus *x* ser de *x* bajo cero ➤ It's ten below zero, centigrade. ▪ It's minus ten, centigrade. La temperatura es de diez bajo cero, centígrados. ▪ La temperatura es de diez grados centígrados bajo cero.

below zero: to drop to *x* ~ ▪ to drop to minus *x* ▪ to fall to *x* below zero ▪ to drop to minus *x* bajar hasta *x* bajo cero ▪ *(more abrupt)* caer hasta *x* bajo cero ➤ The temperature last night dropped to ten below zero, Celsius. ▪ The temperature last night dropped to ten below. Anoche la temperatura bajó hasta los diez bajo cero, centígrados. ▪ Anoche la temperatura cayó hasta los diez bajo cero, centígrados.

to **belt down a drink** meterse una bebida de un trago ▪ echar una bebida de un trago ➤ The cowboys in the old westerns can (really) belt 'em down. Los vaqueros de las viejas películas del Oeste (bien que) se meten las bebidas de un trago.

to **belt out a song** cantar una canción a pleno pulmón ▪ cantar una canción a todo pulmón

belt loop trabilla

to **bend back something** ▪ to bend something back doblar algo hacia atrás

to **bend down** agacharse

bend in the river recodo del río

bend in the road curva en la carretera ▪ curva en la ruta

to **bend light** ▪ to cause light to bend hacer encorvar la luz ➤ Einstein discovered that gravity bends light. ▪ Einstein discovered that gravity causes light to bend. Einstein descubrió que la gravidad hace encorvar la luz.

to **bend metal** encorvar el metal ▪ combar metal

to **bend the rules** forzar las reglas ▪ *(Sp.)* forzar las normas

to **bend over** inclinarse

to **bend over backwards to** ▪ to make every effort to hacer malabares para ▪ hacer todo lo posible por ▪ hacer todo lo posible para ▪ *(Sp.)* hacer encaje de bolillos para

to **bend over someone** inclinarse sobre alguien ➤ The paramedics bent over the victim. El equipo de primeros auxilios se inclinó sobre la víctima.

bends: the ~ *la* enfermedad de descompresión ▪ enfermedad del buzo

to be **beneath one** ▪ to be unworthy of one ser indigno de uno ▪ no estar a la altura de uno ➤ The article was beneath a journalist of his caliber. El artículo era indigno de un periodista de su calibre. ▪ El artículo no estaba a la altura de un periodista de su calibre.

beneath one to do something: not to be ~ no caérsele los anillos por hacer algo ▪ no ser indigno de uno hacer algo ➤ Though he is a former president, it is not beneath Jimmy Carter to work as a carpenter. Aunque haya sido presidente de Estados Unidos, a Jimmy Carter no se le caen los anillos por trabajar de carpintero.

beneath the façade of bajo la fachada de ▪ debajo de la fachada de ▪ bajo la apariencia de ➤ Beneath the classicist façade, the heart of a romantic was beating. Debajo de la fachada clasicista latía el corazón de un romántico.

beneath the surface bajo la superficie ▪ debajo de la superficie

beneath the table ▪ underneath the table ▪ under the table (por) debajo de la mesa *("Por" implies movement.)* ➤ They were playing footsie under the table. Se acariciaban el uno al otro con los pies por debajo de la mesa.

to be **beneath someone in rank** ▪ to be under someone in rank ser inferior a alguien en rango ▪ estar por debajo de alguien en rango

beneath the top one: to be (just) ~ ▪ to be second from the top ▪ to be (just) below the top one ser el segundo por arriba ▪ ser el segundo desde arriba ▪ ser lo que está inmediatamente debajo de lo más alto ➤ It's the shelf just beneath the top one. ▪ It's the second shelf from the top. ▪ It's the second from the top shelf. ▪ It's the shelf just below the top one. Es la segunda estantería por arriba. ▪ Es la estantería que está inmediatamente debajo de la más alta.

beneath this one ▪ below this one ▪ under this one ▪ underneath this one debajo (de) este ➤ They live in the apartment beneath this one. ▪ They live in the apartment below this one. ▪ They live in the apartment under this one. ▪ They live in the apartment underneath this one. Viven en el apartamento debajo de este. ▪ Viven en el apartamento (que hay) bajo este. ➤ They live in the apartment beneath mine. ▪ They live in the apartment directly below mine. Viven en el apartamento que está debajo del mío.

beneficiary of an insurance policy, trust, will, etc. beneficiario de una poliza de seguros, fondo, testamento, etc.

to **benefit from** ▪ to profit from **1.** *(in a positive sense)* beneficiarse de ▪ beneficiarse con **2.** *(implies unfair advantage or at someone's expense)* sacar provecho de ▪ sacar tajada de

benefit of the doubt: to give someone the ~ concederle a alguien el beneficio de la duda ▪ darle a alguien el beneficio de la duda

benevolent dictatorship **1.** dictadura benévola **2.** *(Primo de Rivera in Spain, 1923–30)* dicta blanda ▪ *(late 18th-century, early 19th-century Europe)* despotismo ilustrado

to be **bent on** estar empeñado en ▪ empeñarse en ▪ estar resuelto a

to be **bent out of shape over** ▪ to get upset over estar todo ofuscado por ➤ I wouldn't get all bent out of shape over it (if I were you). Yo que tú, no estaría todo ofuscado.

to **berate oneself** hacerse un reproche

Berlin Airlift *(1948–49)* Transporte aéreo de Berlín ▪ Reparto aéreo de Berlín ▪ Abastecimiento aéreo de Berlín

to be **beset by problems** ser asediado por problemas ▪ ser acosado por problemas ▪ *(Sp.)* ser acuciado por problemas

to be **beside each other** ▪ to be next to each other estar uno al lado del otro ▪ estar uno a continuación del otro

beside one's mouth junto a la boca ▪ al lado de la boca ➤ That beauty spot that you have, Cielito Lindo, beside your mouth, don't give it to anyone because it belongs to me. Ese lunar que tienes, Cielito Lindo, junto a la boca, no se lo des a nadie, que a mí me toca.

to be **beside oneself with worry** estar fuera de sí por la preocupación

beside something ▪ next to something junto a algo ▪ al lado de algo

to be **beside the point** no venir al caso ▪ *(coll.)* no venir a cuento ➤ That's beside the point. No viene al caso. ▪ Está fuera de la cuestión. ▪ Eso no tiene nada que ver.

beside the road ▪ at the side of the road junto al camino ▪ *(highway)* en la cuneta

besides: and ~ y además

besides which fuera de que ▪ aparte de que ▪ además de que

to be the **best all around... for** **1.** *(of things)* ser el mejor... para **2.** *(of people)* ser el más equilibrado ➤ This is the best all-around car for me. Es el coche mejor diseñado para mis necesidades. ➤ He was listed as best all-around in the high school yearbook. Fue considerado el alumno más equilibrado en el anuario de la preparatoria.

best defense is a good offense: the ~ la mejor defensa es un buen ataque

best explanation ▪ most likely explanation ▪ most plausible explanation ▪ most probable explanation *la* mejor explicación ▪ explicación más probable ▪ explicación más factible ▪ explicación más plausible

to be the **best for one** ▪ to be the most convenient for one quedarle mejor algo ▪ ser algo que le viene bien a alguien ▪ ser algo que le sienta bien a alguien ➤ Mornings are the best for me. ▪ Mornings are the most convenient for me. Me queda mejor en las mañanas. ▪ Las mañanas son lo que mejor me viene. ▪ Las mañanas son lo que mejor me sienta.

best friend ▪ closest friend mejor amigo(-a)

to be the **best I've ever tasted** ser el mejor que haya probado ▪ ser la mejor que haya probado ➤ It's the best chimichurri sauce I've ever tasted. Es la mejor salsa chimichurri que haya probado.

to be **best known as** ser más conocido como ➤ Although Jakob Grimm was a great linguist, he is best known as a writer of fables. Aunque Jakob Grimm fue un gran lingüista, es más conocido como escritor de fábulas.

to be **best known for** ser más conocido por ➤ Although Jakob Grimm was a great linguist, he is best known for his fairy tales and fables. Aunque Jakob Grimm fue un gran lingüista, es más conocido por sus fábulas y cuentos de hadas.

best man padrino de boda

the **best of all possible worlds** el mejor de todos los mundos posibles

to be the **best one can do** ser lo mejor que uno puede hacer ➤ That's the best I can do. ▪ I can't do it (any) better than this. No puedo hacerlo mejor que esto. ➤ Is that the best you can do? ▪ Can't you do it any better than that? ¿No lo puedes hacer mejor?

the **best one in town** el mejor de toda la ciudad ▪ la mejor de toda la ciudad

to be the **best one there is** *(This phrase does not occur in this form in Spanish. Hispanics prefers to say "to be the best of a particular thing there is.")* ➤ For Peruvian cuisine, this cookbook is the best one there is, in my opinion. Para cocina peruana, éste es el mejor recetario que hay, en mi opinión.

a **best-seller** un éxito de ventas ▪ un super ventas

the **best-seller** el número uno en ventas

best-selling hit éxito más vendido

a **best-selling novel** una novela éxito de ventas

the **best-selling novel** la novela más vendida

a **best-selling novelist** un(a) novelista con éxito de ventas

best supporting actor mejor actor de reparto

best supporting actress mejor actriz de reparto

to be the **best that one can do** ser lo mejor que uno puede hacer

to be the **best thing about something** ser lo mejor que tiene algo ➤ That's the best thing about it. Eso es lo mejor que tiene. ➤ The best thing about the movie is the special effects, not the plot. Lo mejor que tiene la película son los efectos especiales, no la trama.

to be the **best thing that ever happened to someone** ser lo mejor que le pudo pasar a alguien ➤ She's the best thing that ever happened to him. Ella es lo mejor que le pudo pasar.

to be the **best thing there is** ser lo mejor que hay

to be the **best thing to do** ▪ to be the best course of action ser lo mejor que se puede hacer ▪ ser el mejor plan ▪ ser la mejor estrategia ▪ ser la mejor opción ▪ ser la mejor elección ➤ The best course of action would be to hurry up! ¡Lo mejor que se puede hacer es darse prisa!

to be the **best time for me** ▪ to be the most convenient time for me ▪ to be the time that suits (me) best ser la hora que me viene mejor ▪ ser cuando me viene mejor ▪ ser la hora que mejor me conviene ▪ ser la hora que más me conviene

to be the **best way to do something** ser el mejor medio para hacer algo ▪ ser la mejor manera de hacer algo ▪ ser la mejor forma de hacer algo ▪ ser lo más adecuado para hacer algo ➤ What's the best way to send this package? ¿Cuál es el mejor medio de enviar este paquete? ▪ ¿Cuál es la mejor manera de enviar este paquete?

to **bet heavily on** apostar fuerte por ▪ apostar fuerte a ➤ The bettors are betting heavily on one particular horse. Están apostando fuerte por un caballo en concreto. ▪ Están apostando fuerte a un caballo en concreto.

bet I can! ¡a que sí!

to **bet on a horse** apostar a un caballo ▪ apostar por un caballo ➤ Which horse are you betting on? ¿A qué caballo vas a apostar? ▪ ¿Por qué caballo vas a apostar?

bet you ▪ I bet you ▪ I'll bet you a que ▪ apuesto a que

bet you *can*! ¡a que sí puedes!

bet you *can't*! ¡a que no puedes! ▪ ¡a que no eres capaz!

bet you can't catch me! ¡a que no me alcanzas! ▪ ¡a que no me agarras ▪ *(Sp.)* ¡a que no me pillas! ▪ ¡a que no me coges!

bet you can't guess who *I* am! *(child wearing a mask)* ¡a que no puedes adivinar quien soy! ▪ ¡a que no sabes quien soy!

to **betray one's anger** *(L. Am.)* dar señas de enojo ▪ *(Sp.)* dar señas de enfado

to **betray one's true feelings** ▪ to give away one's true feelings ▪ to give one's true feelings away descubrir sus verdaderos sentimientos ▪ revelar sus verdaderos sentimientos

to **betray someone** traicionar a alguien

to **betray someone's trust** traicionar la confianza (depositada) en alguien

better a little extra than not enough ▪ better too many than not enough más vale que sobre y no que falte

to be **better about something than someone (else)** ser mejor que alguien con respecto a algo ▪ ser mejor que alguien en lo que respecta a algo ▪ ser mejor que alguien cuando se trata de algo ▪ ser mejor que alguien al hacer algo ▪ ser mejor que alguien haciendo algo ➤ Some bus drivers are better than others about waiting for stragglers. Algunos conductores de autobús son mejores que otros con respecto a esperar a los rezagados.

better and better: to get ~ ponerse cada vez mejor ▪ ser cada vez mejor ▪ estar cada vez mejor ➤ It just gets better and better. Se pone cada vez mejor. ▪ Va a mejor.

to be **better at one thing than another** hacer una cosa mejor que otra ➤ He's better at poker than he is at bridge. Juega al poquer mejor que al bridge.

better be...: one had ~ más vale que... ➤ We'd better be on our way. Más vale que nos pongamos en marcha. ➤ His excuse had better be good. ▪ *(coll.)* His excuse better be good. Más vale que tenga una buena excusa.

Better Business Bureau oficina de protección del consumidor *(Spanish businesses must maintain a "libro de reclamación," or complaint book. In the event of a complaint, ask for it and write your complaint there, or go to the local consumer protection office.* ▪ *En Estados Unidos las empresas no tienen libros de reclamación, pero toda ciudad tiene un Better Business Bureau que investiga las quejas del consumidor.)*

to be **better for one than** ser mejor para uno que ➤ Fresh vegetables are better for you than canned ones. Las verduras y hortalizas frescas son mejores para ti que las enlatadas.

to be **better for one to do something** ser que alguien haga algo lo mejor ➤ I think it's better for the concierge to have the key. Creo que lo mejor es que tenga la llave el portero.

better get to work: one had ~ **1.** one had better get busy más le vale a uno que se ponga a trabajar **2.** one had better leave for work más le vale uno irse a trabajar ➤ I'd better get to work. ▪ I'd better get busy. Más vale que me ponga a trabajar. ➤ I'd better get to work. ▪ I'd better leave for work. ▪ I'd better be on my way to work. Más vale que vaya a trabajar. ▪ Más me vale irme a trabajar.

better half: one's ~ su media naranja ➤ And this is my better half, Isabel. Y ésta es mi media naranja, Isabel.

better hurry: one had ~ más vale que uno se apure ▪ *(Sp.)* más le vale a uno que se dé prisa ➤ We had better hurry. ▪ We'd better hurry. Más nos vale que nos demos prisa. ➤ I had better hurry. ▪ I'd better hurry. Más me vale que me dé prisa.

to be **better known as** ser más conocido como ➤ The linguist Jakob Grimm was better known as a storyteller. El lingüista Jakob Grimm era más conocido como cuentista.

better late than never más vale tarde que nunca

to be **better left unsaid** valer más no hablar ▪ haber (de) cosas de las que no se puede hablar ➤ Some things are better left unsaid. Hay cosas de las que más vale no hablar.

better luck next time más suerte para la próxima vez ▪ mejor suerte para la próxima

better not: it had ~ *(coll.)* ▪ it better not más (le) vale que no

better not...: it had ~ *(coll.)* ▪ it better not más (le) vale que no... ➤ After waiting ten days for this blasted avocado to ripen, it (had) better not spoil by tomorrow. Después de esperar diez días a que este puñetero aguacate madure, más (le) vale que no se eche a perder para mañana.

better of the two el mejor de los dos ▪ la mejor de las dos ➤ She is the better politician of the two. Ella es el mejor político de los dos.

to be **better off** estar en mejores condiciones ➤ *(presidential campaign rhetoric)* Are you better off now than you were four years ago? ¿Están en mejores condiciones ahora que en las que estaban hace cuatro años? ▪ ¿Están en mejor situación ahora de la que estaban hace cuatro años? ▪ ¿Estáis mejor ahora que donde estaban hace cuatro años? ▪ ¿Están mejor ahora que hace cuatro años? ➤ Sometimes I feel left out of a conversation, but then when I listen to it, I realize I'm better off. A veces me siento excluído de una conversación, pero cuando la escucho, me doy cuenta de que estoy en mejor donde estaba. ➤ My adviser thinks I'd be better off changing majors. Mi consejero universitario opina que (yo) estaría mejor si cambiara de carrera.

to be **better off under** estar mejor bajo

to be **better off with** estar mejor con

to **better one's fortunes** mejorar la situación (económica) ▪ mejorar la posición (económica)

to **better oneself** mejorarse a uno mismo

the **better part of** ▪ the greater part of la mayor parte de ➤ I have spent the better part of a decade here in Spain. He pasado la mayor parte de una década aquí en España. ➤ We spent the better part of the weekend at home. Pasamos la mayor parte del fin de semana en casa.

better safe than sorry ▪ it is better to be safe than sorry mejor prevenir que curar ▪ más vale prevenir que lamentar ▪ *(buying an extra one just in case)* más vale que sobre y no que falte

better still: (or) ~ ▪ (or) better yet (o) mejor aún ▪ (o) mejor todavía

better than another: to do one thing ~ hacer una cosa mejor que otra ➤ She speaks Spanish better than (she speaks) French. Habla español mejor que francés.

better than ever mejor que nunca ▪ como nunca ➤ Are you doing okay?-Better than ever! ¿Estás bien?-¡Como nunca! ▪ ¿Estás bien?-¡Mejor que nunca!

to be **better than ever 1.** ser mejor que nunca **2.** estar mejor que nunca ➤ The new James Bond movie is better than ever. La nueva película de James Bond es mejor que nunca. ➤ Things are better than ever between my girlfriend and me. Las cosas están mejor que nunca entre mi novia y yo.

to be **better than expected 1.** ser mejor de lo que se esperaba ▪ ser mejor de lo esperado **2.** estar mejor de lo que se esperaba ▪ estar mejor de lo esperado ➤ This year's earnings were better than expected. Las ganancias de este año son mejor de lo que se esperaba. ▪ Las ganancias de este año son mejor de lo esperado. ➤ The Christmas bonus this year was better than I expected. El aguinaldo de este año estuvo mejor de lo que esperaba.

better-than-expected report *el* informe mejor de lo que se esperaba ▪ informe mejor de lo esperado ▪ informe más que favorable ➤ It was a better-than-expected report. ▪ The report was better than expected. El informe fue mejor de lo que se esperaba. ▪ El informe fue mejor de lo esperado.

better the devil you know than the devil you don't mejor malo conocido que bueno por conocer ▪ más vale malo conocido que bueno por conocer

to be **better to** valer más ▪ ser mejor ➤ It would be better to come to Madrid when it's not so hot. Más valdría venir a Madrid cuando no haga tanto calor. ▪ Sería mejor venir a Madrid cuando no haga tanto calor.

better too many than not enough ▪ better a little extra than not enough más vale que sobre y no que falte

better yet: (or) ~ (o) mejor aún ▪ (o) mejor todavía ➤ We need a turkey for the turkey biscuits. Better yet, buy two chickens. Necesitamos un pavo para los bollitos de pavo. Mejor aún, compra dos pollos.

between a rock and a hard place: to be (caught) ~ ▪ to have one's back to the wall encontrarse entre la espada y la pared ➤ I'm caught between a rock and a hard place. Me encuentro entre la espada y la pared.

between now and Sunday de aquí al domingo ▪ entre hoy y el domingo

between one and two kilometers entre uno y dos kilómetros

to be **between Scylla and Charybdis** *(literary)* ▪ to be between a rock and a hard place encontrarse entre la espada y la pared ▪ encontrarse entre Escila y Caribdis

to be **between the devil and the deep blue sea** encontrarse entre la espada y la pared

between the two governments entre los dos gobiernos ▪ entre ambos gobiernos ➤ The president called for a dialogue between the two governments. El presidente abogó por el inicio de un diálogo entre los dos gobiernos. ▪ El presidente abogó por el inicio de un diálogo entre ambos gobiernos.

between the two of them mano a mano, (ellos) ▪ entre los dos ➤ Between the two of them they polished off two liters of beer. Los dos se despacharon mano a mano dos litros de cerveza. ▪ Se despacharon entre los dos dos litros de cerveza.

between the two of us mano a mano, (nosotros) ▪ entre nosotros ➤ Between the two of us we polished off two liters of beer. Nos despachamos mano a mano dos litros de cerveza. ▪ Nos despachamos entre los dos dos litros de cerveza.

between us 1. just between you and me entre nosotros **2.** together ▪ among us entre nosotros **3.** in the middle ▪ separating que hay entre nosotros ➤ Just between us, I don't like the new boss. Entre nosotros, no me cae bien el nuevo jefe. ➤ Between us, we can finish it. Entre nosotros podemos terminarlo. ➤ The empty seat between us Asiento vacío que hay entre nosotros ▪ Asiento libre que hay entre nosotros

between you and me: (just) ~ ▪ (just) between the two of us entre tú y yo ▪ entre nosotros ▪ esto que quede entre nosotros ▪ *(coll.)* entre nos ➤ Just between you and me, I don't like the new boss. Entre tú y yo, no me cae bien el nuevo jefe.

to **bevel the edge** biselar el borde ➤ I didn't want you to bevel the edge. I wanted it flat. No quería que biselara el borde, lo quería plano.

beveled edge borde biselado

beware of the dog cuidado con el perro

beyond a shadow of a doubt ▪ beyond any shadow of a doubt sin lugar a duda ▪ fuera de toda duda

to be **beyond description** ser más allá de toda descripción ▪ ser hasta agotar los adjetivos ▪ no alcanzar las palabras para describirlo(-a) ▪ no haber descripción alguna

to be **beyond hope 1.** *(situations and people, said lightly)* no tener remedio ▪ no tener arreglo **2.** *(people only, said seriously)* to be irredeemable ser un(a) bala perdida ▪ ser carne de cañón

to be **beyond one's control** ▪ to be out of one's control escapársele al control de uno ▪ escaparse a su control ▪ estar más allá del control de uno ➤ Stopping the process is beyond his control. Detener el proceso se le escapa al control. ▪ Detener el proceso se escapa a su control.

to be **beyond one's wildest dreams** no aparecer ni en los mejores sueños de uno ▪ no poder imaginárselo ni en los mejores sueños de uno ▪ no poder figurárselo ni en los mejores sueños de uno

to be **beyond reproach** ser irreprochable

beyond that... para ir más allá de lo dicho... ➤ Beyond that, I'll let him tell you about himself. Para ir más allá de lo dicho, lo dejo que hable de sí mismo. ▪ *(Sp., leísmo)* Para ir más allá de lo dicho, le dejo que hable de sí mismo.

beyond that (time) de ahí en más ➤ They'll be here in Madrid until the end of the year. Beyond that (time), I have no idea what's going to happen. Estarán aquí en Madrid hasta finales de año. De ahí en más, no tengo ni idea de lo que va a pasar.

to be **beyond the age at which...** estar más allá de la edad en la cual... ➤ The animal is beyond the age at which it can defend itself easily from predators. El animal está más allá de la edad en la cual (él) pueda defenderse fácilmente de los predadores.

to be **beyond the age where...** estar más allá de la edad en (la) que... ▪ estar más allá de la edad donde... ➤ Andres' little brother is beyond the age where all he wants to eat is hot dogs and hamburgers. El hermanito de Andrés está más allá de la edad en la que sólo se quiere comer perritos calientes y hamburguesas. ➤ I'm beyond the age where I like ninety-decibel discotheques. He pasado la edad en que me gustaban las discotecas a noventa decibelios.

beyond the grave más allá de la tumba ▪ ultratumba

to be **beyond the pale** ser intolerable ▪ ser inaceptable ▪ ser inadmisible ▪ estar más allá del límite de lo aceptable ➤ *(TV pundit's wordplay)* The pale which we are all beyond El aceptable límite más allá del cual todos estamos

to be **beyond the point of no return** ya no poder volverse atrás ➤ When we can no longer pay the interest on the debt, we will be beyond the point of no return. Cuando no podamos pagar el interés de la deuda, no podremos volvernos atrás.

to be **beyond the scope of** estar más allá del alcance de ➤ To get into that is beyond the scope of my paper. Entrar en eso está más allá del alcance de este trabajo.

to **bias a poll** **1.** to tamper with a poll manipular una encuesta ▪ *(Sp.)* sesgar una encuesta **2.** to fail to take into account lurking variables incurrir imprecisiones en una encuesta

bias against something: to have a ~ ▪ to be biased against something tener una prejuicio contra algo

bias in a newspaper *la* parcialidad en un periódico ▪ *la* tergiversación de datos en un periódico

bias in a statistical sample **1.** *(intentional)* manipulación en una muestra estadística ▪ tergiversación de una muestra estadística ▪ *(Sp.)* sesgo de una muestra estadística **2.** *(unintentional) la* imprecisión de una muestra estadística

bias in favor of something *la* parcialidad a favor de algo

to **bias the results** ▪ to skew the results ▪ to distort the results manipular los resultados ▪ distorsionar los resultados ▪ tergiversar los resultados ▪ *(Sp.)* sesgar los resultados

biased account informe distorsionado ▪ relato distorsionado ▪ *(Sp.)* informe sesgado ▪ relato sesgado

to be **biased against something** ▪ to have a bias against **1.** *(general, overall)* tener un prejuicio contra algo **2.** *(specific, particular aspects)* tener un prejuicio en contra de algo

to be **biased in favor of something** estar dispuesto a favor de algo ▪ estar dispuesto en favor de algo

biased information datos prejuiciados ▪ información sesgada

biased newspaper ▪ slanted newspaper periódico muy parcial ▪ periódico prejuiciado

biased sample muestra distorsionada ▪ muestra sesgada

biblical injunction mandato bíblico

biblical precept precepto bíblico

biblical precepts preceptiva bíblica

to **bid high on something** pujar a la alta por algo ▪ pujar fuerte por algo

to **bid low on something** pujar a la baja por algo ▪ pujar flojo por algo

to **bid on a construction project** **1.** *(public bidding)* participar en concurso público por un proyecto de construcción **2.** *(private bidding)* hacer un presupuesto para un proyecto de construcción

to **bid on a paint job** hacer un presupuesto para un trabajo de pintura

to **bid on something at an auction** licitar por algo en una subasta ▪ hacer una oferta en una subasta ▪ *(Sp.)* pujar en una subasta por algo ➤ I bid very high on the piano once played by Artur Rubinstein. Licité muy alto por el piano alguna vez tocado por Artur Rubinstein. ➤ I bid two thousand dollars on a beautiful grandfather clock, but somebody outbid me. Pujé hasta los dos mil dólares por un hermoso carillón, pero alguien pujó más fuerte.

bidding (process) ▪ taking of bids ▪ bid taking la recepción de pujas ➤ The bidding (process) on the construction project has begun. ▪ The taking of bids has begun. ▪ The bid taking has begun. ▪ Bids are now being accepted. La recepción de pujas ha empezado.

to **bide one's time** esperar el momento oportuno

big around is it?: how ~ **1.** *(circle)* ¿cuánto tiene de circunferencia? ▪ ¿qué circunferencia tiene? **2.** *(any figure)* ¿cuánto tiene de perímetro? ▪ ¿qué perímetro tiene?

big around it is: how ~ **1.** *(circle)* la circunferencia que tiene ▪ la circunferencia que tenga **2.** *(any figure)* el perímetro que tiene ▪ el perímetro que tenga ➤ I don't know how big around the tree is, but for sure it's big enough for a tree house. No sé la circunferencia que tiene el árbol, pero seguro que es suficiente para construir una casita. ▪ No sé el perímetro que tiene el árbol, pero seguro que es suficiente para construir una casita. ➤ I don't know if we can get a Christmas tree in the trunk. It depends on how big around it is. No sé si podemos meter un árbol de Navidad en el baúl. Depende de la circunferencia que tenga. ▪ No sé si podemos meter un árbol de Navidad en el baúl. Depende del perímetro que tenga.

big break *la* gran oportunidad ➤ His big break came... Su gran oportunidad llegó

big business grandes empresas ▪ grandes compañías

big day *(one's wedding day, for example) el* gran día ➤ When's the big day? ¿Cuándo es el gran día?

big deal! ¡vaya cosa!

Big Dipper *(coll.)* ▪ Ursa Major Osa Mayor

to be **big enough for** ▪ to have room (enough) for ▪ to fit con cabida para ▪ con espacio suficiente para ▪ lo suficientemente grande para

to be **big enough to fit** **1.** to be just big enough ser (lo) suficientemente grande para que quepa **2.** to be plenty big ser bastante grande para que quepa

to be a **big fan of** ser muy aficionado a ➤ He's not a big fan of computer games. No es muy aficionado a los juegos de ordenador.

to be a **big fish in a little pond** tener una reputación local

to be a **big flop** ser un gran fracaso ➤ The movie was a big flop. La película fue un gran fracaso.

big gamble una gran apuesta ➤ *(headline)* Putin's big gamble La gran apuesta de Putin

big guns: to bring out all one's ~ desplegar todas sus armas ▪ desplegar todas sus naves ▪ desplegar toda su artillería ➤ For the Christmas season, the department stores bring out all their big guns. Para las Navidades, los grandes almacenes despliegan todas sus armas. ▪ Para las Navidades, los grandes almacenes despliegan todas sus naves. ▪ Para las Navidades, los grandes almacenes despliegan toda su artillería.

big hug: to give someone a ~ darle a alguien un fuerte abrazo

to be a **big job** ser una tarea grande ▪ ser una gran tarea

big kiss beso fuerte ➤ Give me a big kiss. Dame un beso fuerte.

big mouth **1.** big mouth ▪ large mouth boca grande **2.** bigmouth ▪ loose talker bocazas ▪ boca de jarro

to be a **big one** ser de los grandes ➤ That paella pan is a big one. Esa paellera es de las grandes.

big picture: to get the ~ tener perspectiva sobre un asunto ▪ tener perspectiva de un asunto ▪ tener una visión global ➤ He doesn't get the big picture. No tiene perspectiva (sobre este asunto).

big picture: to see the ~ ▪ to get the big picture ▪ to look at the big picture ver las cosas en perspectiva ▪ ver las cosas de forma global ➤ You have to see the big picture. ▪ You have to look at the big picture. Hay que ver las cosas en perspectiva. ▪ Hay que ver las cosas de forma global. ➤ He doesn't see the big picture. ▪ He doesn't get the big picture. No ve las cosas en perspectiva. ▪ No ve las cosas de forma global.

big problem problema gordo ▪ gran problema

big screen ▪ the movies pantalla grande

big shot ▪ big wig pez gordo ▪ señorón ▪ pájaro gordo

big smile ▪ ear-to-ear grin ▪ wide smile ▪ broad smile sonrisa de lado a lado ▪ sonrisa de oreja a oreja ▪ amplia sonrisa ➤ Give me a big smile. ▪ Let's have a big smile. Dame una sonrisa de lado a lado. ▪ A ver esa sonrisa de lado a lado.

big step forward gran paso hacia adelante

big-time a lo grande ➤ A big-time politician Un político a lo grande

big toe dedo gordo del pie

big wig ▪ big shot pez gordo ▪ señorón ▪ pájaro gordo ➤ When's the big wig from St. Louis going to show up? ¿Cuándo se va a presentar el pez gordo de St. Louis?

bigger and bigger: to get ~ volverse cada vez más grande

to be **bigger than life** ser lo más grande que hay ▪ ser un (auténtico) universo en sí mismo ➤ St. Francis, Joan of Arc, Cervantes, the philosopher Immanuel Kant, and Lincoln are bigger than life. They are five of the great personalities of the ages. San Francisco, Juana de Arco, Cervantes, el filósofo Immanuel Kant y Lincoln son lo más grande que hay. Son cinco de las grandes personalidades de todos los tiempos.

bigger the better: the ~ cuanto más grande, mejor ▪ *(coll.)* caballo grande, ande o no ande

biggest problem: the ~ el problema mayor ▪ el problema más importante ▪ el mayor problema

bilateral accord ▪ bilateral agreement acuerdo bilateral ▪ convenio bilateral

bilateral agreement ▪ bilateral accord convenio bilateral ▪ acuerdo bilateral

bill me ▪ send me a bill *(tú)* envíame una cuenta ▪ *(usted)* envíeme una cuenta

bill of exchange letra de cambio

bill of lading *(contract between sender and shipper)* manifiesto de embarque ▪ conocimiento de embarque

Bill of Rights *(first ten amendments to the Constitution of the United States)* Declaración de los Derechos

bill, please: the ~ la nota, por favor ▪ la cuenta, por favor ▪ me cobra, por favor ▪ *(if the waiter is young)* me cobras, por favor

billing department departamento de facturas

billion dollars mil millones de dólares *("Un billón" in Spanish means a "million millions" and has twelve zeroes.)*

billowing clouds ▪ billowy clouds nubes algodonosas

billowing skirt *(like Marilyn Monroe's in* The Seven Year Itch*)* falda con mucho vuelo ▪ falda levantada al aire ▪ con faldas al aire

billowing smoke ▪ billows of smoke ▪ thick clouds of smoke *las* nubes de humo

billowy clouds ▪ billowing clouds nubes algodonosas

binary star estrella binaria

to **bind a case over to the grand jury** ▪ to bind over a case to the grand jury remitir el caso al jurado de acusación ▪ poner el caso bajo la jurisdicción del jurado de acusación

to **bind and gag someone** atar y amordazar a alguien

to **bind over a case to the grand jury** ▪ to bind a case over to the grand jury remitir el caso al jurado de acusación ▪ poner el caso bajo la jurisdicción del jurado de acusación

to **bind someone's hands and feet** atar de pies y manos

to **bind (up) someone** ▪ to bind someone up ▪ to tie up someone ▪ to tie someone up atar a alguien ➤ The robbers bound and gagged the victim. Los ladrónes ataron y amordazaron a la víctima. ➤ The robbers bound and gagged him. ▪ The robbers bound him up and gagged him. Los ladrónes lo ataron y lo mordazaron. ▪ *(Sp., leísmo)* Los ladrónes le ataron y le mordazaron.

to **bind (up) a wound** ▪ to bandage a wound **1.** vendar una herida **2.** *(mainly figurative)* sanar una herida ➤ The paramedics bound (up) the victim's wound. ▪ The paramedics bandaged the victim's wound. El equipo de primeros auxilios vendaron la herida de la víctima. ➤ *(Lincoln)* To bind up the nation's wounds Sanar las heridas de la nación

binding agreement acuerdo vinculante

binding contract contrato vinculante

biodegradable plastic plástico biodegradable

to be a **bird brain** tener cabeza de chorlito

bird flu ▪ avian influenza gripe aviar ▪ gripe avícola ▪ gripe del pájaro ▪ gripe del pollo

bird in the hand is worth two in the bush: a más vale pájaro en mano que cien volando

birdcall reclamo (para pájaros)

bird's-eye view: to have a ~ ▪ to get a bird's-eye view tener una panorámica a vista de pájaro

to be **birds of a feather** estar cortado con el mismo patrón que alguien ▪ ser de la misma escuela ▪ ser lobos de la misma camada ➤ Those two are birds of a feather. Los dos esos están cortados con el mismo patrón.

birds of a feather flock together cada oveja con su pareja ▪ cada cual se arrima a su cada cual ▪ Dios los cría y ellos se juntan

of the sort ▪ of the kind por el estilo

birth certificate acta de nacimiento ▪ partida de nacimiento

birth date ▪ date of birth ▪ DOB fecha de nacimiento ▪ natalicio

birth rate tasa de natalidad ➤ Spain has a low birth rate. España tiene una tasa baja de natalidad.

birthday present ▪ birthday gift regalo de cumpleaños

birthday suit: to be wearing one's ~ ▪ to have on one's birthday suit **1.** *(he)* estar como su madre lo trajo al mundo ▪ *(Sp., leísmo)* estar como su madre le trajo al mundo **2.** *(she)* estar como su madre la trajo al mundo

bit odd: a ~ ▪ a little odd un poco raro ➤ It seemed a bit odd. Me parecía un poco raro. ➤ Her neighbors thought she was a bit odd. ▪ Her neighbors thought her a bit odd. A sus vecinos les parecía un poco rara.

to **bite into something** dar un mordisco a algo ▪ morder algo ➤ Snow White bit into the apple. Blancanieves dio un mordisco a la manzana. ▪ Blancanieves mordió la manzana.

to **bite on something** morder algo ➤ I bit on something hard. Mordí algo duro.

to **bite off a piece** ▪ to bite a piece off arrancar un trozo de un mordisco ▪ arrancar un trozo con los dientes ➤ He bit off a piece of the candy bar. ▪ He bit a piece off (of) the candy bar. Arrancó un trozo de la chocolatina de un mordisco. ▪ Arrancó un trozo de la chocolatina con los dientes. ➤ He bit it off. Lo arrancó de un mordisco.

to **bite off more than one can chew** medir mal sus propias fuerzas ▪ abarcar mucho y apretar poco ➤ He has bitten off more than he can chew. Ha medido mal sus propias fuerzas. ▪ Quien mucho abarca poco aprieta.

to **bite one's lip** morderse los labios

to **bite one's tongue 1.** *(literal)* morderse la lengua **2.** to suppress one's reaction ▪ to hold back words morderse la lengua ▪ tragar saliva

bite-size pieces: to cut food into ~ cortar (la) comida en bocaditos ▪ cortar (la) comida en trocitos ▪ *(lettuce, onion, etc.)* picar (la) comida en bocaditos ▪ picar (la) comida en trocitos ▪ cortar la comida en pedacitos ➤ Cut the lettuce into bite-size pieces to make it easier to eat. Pica la lechuga en bocaditos para que sea más fácil de comer.

to **bite someone's head off** echarle a alguien una bronca

bite splint *(dentistry)* ▪ intermaxillar stress breaker férula intermaxilar

to **bite the hand that feeds you** morder la mano que te da de comer

biting humor ▪ caustic humor ▪ corrosive humor humor mordaz ▪ humor cáustico ▪ humor corrosivo

to be **bitten by a snake** ▪ to get bitten by a snake ser mordido(-a) por una serpiente ▪ ser mordido(-a) por una víbora

bitter: to taste ~ saber amargo

bitter cold frío tajante ▪ frío cortante ▪ frío ártico

bitter enemy enemigo rencoroso ▪ enemigo implacable ▪ *(literary)* enconado enemigo ▪ enemigo enconado

bitter feud amarga disputa

bitter flavor ▪ bitter taste sabor amargo

bitter hatred odio acerbo ▪ odio implacable ▪ odio rencoroso

to be a **bitter pill (to swallow)** ser un trago amargo

bitter winter ▪ harsh winter ▪ hard winter invierno crudo ▪ invierno duro

to be a **bittersweet experience** ser una experiencia agridulce

bittersweet feeling emoción agridulce ▪ sentimiento agridulce

bittersweet taste ▪ sweet and sour taste *el* sabor agridulce

bizarre twist: to take a ~ ▪ dar una gira grotesca ▪ dar un giro grotesco ▪ tomar un cariz dantesco ▪ tomar un cariz grotesco ▪ tomar un cariz esperpéntico ▪ tomar un giro dantesco ▪ tomar un giro grotesco ▪ tomar un giro esperpéntico ▪ dar un giro esperpéntico

black coffee café solo

black eye: to get a ~ quedar con un ojo negro ➤ I got a black eye when I was playing baseball. Quedé con un ojo negro cuando jugaba al béisbol.

black eye: to give someone a ~ dejarle a alguien un ojo morado ➤ The Senator has given the whole party a black eye. El senador ha dejado con un ojo morado a todo su partido político.

black eye: to have a ~ tener un ojo morado ▪ llevar un ojo morado ▪ *(comical, and best said when one is poking fun at oneself)* tener un ojo a la funerala ▪ llevar un ojo a la funerala

black ice ▪ invisible ice on pavement placa de hielo invisible (en la carretera) ▪ placa invisible de hielo (en la carretera) ▪ capa fina de hielo ▪ capa invisible de hielo ➤ The car hit a patch of black ice and skidded off the road and struck a telephone pole. El coche dio con unas placas de hielo invisible, derrapó saliéndose de la carretera y chocó con un poste de teléfonos.

to **blacklist someone** ▪ to put someone on the blacklist ▪ to put someone's name on the blacklist poner a alguien en la lista negra

to **black out** ▪ to faint ▪ to lose consciousness temporarily desmayarse ▪ *(L. Am.)* perder el conocimiento temporariamente ▪ *(Sp.)* perder el conocimiento temporalmente

black power poder negro ▪ "black power"

black sheep 1. *(literal)* oveja negra 2. *(figurative)* oveja negra ▪ garbanzo negro ▪ oveja descarriada ▪ bala perdida

to **blacken fish** churruscar pescado

blade of a knife hoja de un cuchillo

blade of an oar pala de un remo

blade of grass hoja de pasto ▪ brizna de hierba ▪ *(on a lawn)* hoja de cesped

blades of a fan ▪ fan blades aspas de un ventilador

blades of a propeller ▪ propeller blades palas de una hélice ▪ hojas de una hélice

to **blame someone for something** ▪ to blame something on someone culpar a alguien de algo ▪ culpar a alguien por algo ▪ echarle la culpa a alguien de algo ▪ echarle la culpa a alguien por algo ➤ *(headline)* Putin blames Chechin terrorism for the carnage in the Moscow subway. Putin culpa al terrorismo checheno de la matanza en el metro de Moscú. ➤ He blames her for everything. (Él) la culpa de todo. ▪ (Él) la culpa por todo. ▪ *(Sp., leísmo)* (Él) le echa la culpa (a ella) por todo. ➤ She blames him for everything. (Ella) lo culpa de todo. ▪ (Ella) lo culpa por todo. ▪ *(Sp., leísmo)* (Ella) le culpa de todo. ▪ (Ella) le culpa por todo. ▪ (Ella) le echa la culpa por todo.

to **blame something on someone** ▪ to blame someone for something culpar a alguien de algo ▪ culpar a alguien por algo ▪ echar la culpa a alguien de algo ▪ echar la culpa a alguien por algo

to be **blamed for** ▪ to get blamed for ser culpado de

bland diet dieta blanda

bland (tasting) food comida insípida ▪ comida sosa

blank (bullet) bala de fogueo

blank check cheque en blanco

blank page página en blanco

blank sheet of paper hoja en blanco ▪ folio en blanco ▪ *el* papel en blanco ➤ Please take out a blank sheet of paper. *(L. Am.)* Por favor, saquen un folio en blanco. ▪ *(Sp., vosotros)* Por favor, sacad un folio en blanco.

to **blank someone out** cortar a alguien ▪ dar un corte a alguien ▪ dejar a alguien fuera de juego ➤ When he reacted by saying, "poor baby," he was blanking you out. Cuando reaccionó diciéndote "pobrecito", él te estaba cortando. ▪ Cuando reaccionó diciéndote "pobrecito", él te estaba dando un corte. ▪ Cuando reaccionó diciéndote "pobrecito", él te estaba dejando fuera de juego.

blank space espacio en blanco

blanket of snow manto de nieve ▪ capa de nieve

blast of cold air ▪ cold air blast ▪ cold blast of air ráfaga de aire frío

blaze of light fogonazo de luz

to **blaze the trail** ▪ to light the way iluminar el camino ▪ abrir el camino ▪ despejar el camino ➤ Einstein blazed the trail that physics has followed ever since. Einstein iluminó el camino que la física ha seguido desde entonces. ▪ Einstein abrió el camino que la física ha seguido desde entonces. ▪ Einstein despejó el camino que la física ha seguido desde entonces.

blazing light *la* luz deslumbrante

bleak outlook perspectiva sombría ▪ perspectiva poco halagüeña ▪ perspectiva poco alentadora ▪ perspectiva poco favorable ➤ The economic outlook was bleak for a time but has brightened up. La perspectiva económica fue sombría durante un tiempo pero ahora es luminosa.

bleak terrain ▪ bleak countryside ▪ desolate terrain ▪ desolate countryside paisaje adusto ▪ paisaje desolado ▪ tierra inhóspita

bleak weather tiempo sombrío

bleak winter invierno sombrío

to **bleed a radiator** purgar el radiador

to **bleed profusely** 1. sangrar a chorros ▪ sangrar a raudales 2. to spurt blood sangrar a borbotones

to **bleed the brakes** sangrar los frenos ▪ purgar los frenos

to **bleed the lifeblood out of** ▪ to bleed dry ser una sangría (ecónomica) ➤ The military spending has bled the lifeblood out of the country's economy. El gasto militar ha sido una sangría para la economía del país.

to **bleed to death** morir desangrado ▪ desangrar hasta morir

bless you! 1. *(to a person who has sneezed)* Gesundheit! ¡salud! ▪ ¡Jesús! 2. *(expression of appreciation)* ¡que Dios te bendiga!

blessed are the losers, for they determine the winners *(T-shirt slogan)* bienaventurados sean los perdedores porque determinan los ganadores

blessed are the meek, for they shall inherit the Earth bienaventurados sean los mansos, porque ellos heredarán la Tierra

to be **blessed with** estar bendecido por ▪ tener la bendición de tener ➤ At ninety, she is still blessed with good health. Con noventa años, tiene la bendición de tener buena salud.

blind alley callejón sin salida ➤ The policy has led the country down a blind alley. La política ha llevado al país por un callejón sin salida.

to be **blind as a bat** ▪ to be as blind as a bat no ver tres en un burro ▪ ser más ciego que un topo

blind date cita a ciegas

blind eye to something: to turn a ~ hacer la vista gorda a algo

blind letter *(letter starting "dear sir," "dear madam," or "to whom it may concern")* carta sin destinatario explícito (que empieza por "a quien pueda interesar" o "a quien pueda resultar de interés", etc.)

blind rage: to fly into a ~ ponerse ciego de rabia ▪ ponerse ciego de ira ▪ ponerse ciego de furia

blind spot 1. *(literal)* punto ciego 2. *(figurative)* punto de vista ciego ➤ I have a blind spot in my left eye, at about three o'clock from my perspective, or about nine o'clock from the doctor's. Tengo un punto ciego en el ojo izquierdo, a la derecha de mi perspectiva, o a la izquierda desde la del doctor. ➤ I have a blind spot when it comes to political separatism. Why is it more important than having a good life? Tengo un punto de vista ciego cuando se refiere al separatismo político. ¿Por qué es más importante eso que tener una buena vida?

to be **blind to reason** estar obcecado ▪ estar cerrado en banda ▪ estar obstinado ▪ no hacer caso a razones

to be **blind to someone's faults** ▪ to be blind to someone's defects estar ciego a los defectos de alguien ▪ no ver las debilidades de alguien

to be **blind to the fact that...** obviar el hecho de que... ▪ ignorar el hecho de que...

blinded: to be (permanently) ~ quedarse ciego ➤ He was (permanently) blinded by looking directly at the sun. Se quedó ciego por mirar directamente al sol. ➤ He was blinded by shrapnel. Se quedó ciego por la metralla.

blinded: to be (temporarily) ~ 1. *(by an accident or stroke)* perder la visión ▪ quedar cegado 2. *(by a flash of bright light)* quedar deslumbrado por la luz ▪ ser deslumbrado por la luz ▪ quedar cegado por la luz ▪ ser cegado por la luz ➤ The child was blinded temporarily when he fell from his bicycle and hit his head. Al caerse de la bici y golpearse la cabeza, el niño perdió la visión temporalmente. ➤ He was momentarily blinded by the flashbulb of the camera. Quedó momentáneamente deslumbrado por el "flash" de la cámara. ▪ Quedó momentáneamente cegado por el "flash" de la cámara. ➤ He was blinded by the headlights of the oncoming car. Quedó deslumbrado por los faros del coche que venía de frente. ▪ Quedó cegado por los faros del coche que venía de frente.

to **blindfold someone** vendar los ojos a alguien ▪ ponerle un pañuelo en los ojos ➤ She spun him around blindfolded. Ella le dio vueltas con los ojos vendados. ▪ Ella le dio vueltas con un pañuelo puesto en los ojos.

blindfolded: to lead someone ~ ▪ to lead someone with one's eyes closed llevar alguien con los ojos cerrados ➤ I could lead you there blindfolded. Te podría llevar allí con los ojos cerrados.

blinding flash *el* resplandor cegador

blinding light luz cegadora

blinding of a person ceguera de una persona ➤ The blinding of Samson La ceguera de Sansón

blinking light una luz intermitente ▪ una luz parpadeante

blip on the radar screen 1. parpadeo en la pantalla del radar ▪ destello en la pantalla del radar 2. *(figurative)* fenómeno fugaz ▪ acontecimiento fugaz

to be **blistering hot** ▪ to be a scorcher estar que quema ▪ ser abrasador ▪ ser atorrante ▪ ser un horno ➤ It's blistering hot. El día está que quema. ▪ El día es abrasador. ▪ El día es atorrante. ▪ El día es un horno.

to **blitz this thing** ▪ to get it done quickly, in a concentrated effort despachar algo ➤ We just need to blitz this thing. Sólo necesitamos despachar esto.

blizzard of mail ▪ avalanche of mail ▪ barrage of mail avalancha de correo ▪ *el* aluvión de correo ▪ aluvión de cartas ➤ That editorial prompted a blizzard of mail. El editorial provocó avalancha de correo. ▪ El editorial provocó un aluvión de correo. ▪ El editorial provocó un aluvión de cartas.

to **block a move** bloquear un movimiento ➤ You blocked my next move. Has bloqueado mi próximo movimiento.

to **block a player** *(sports)* ▪ to make a blocking movement bloquear un jugador ▪ *(rugby)* hacer un placaje ▪ *(often plural)* hacer placajes

to be a **block away** *(L. Am.)* estar a una cuadra de distancia ▪ *(Sp.)* estar a una manzana de distancia ➤ It's a block and a half away. Está a una manzana y media de distancia. ▪ Está a una cuadra y media de distancia.

to be a **block from here** *(L. Am.)* estar a una cuadra de aquí ▪ *(Sp.)* estar a una manzana de aquí ➤ It's just a block from here. Está sólo a una manzana de aquí. ▪ Está sólo a una cuadra de aquí.

block grant un salario en un solo pago

to **block in someone** ▪ to block someone in encerrar a alguien ▪ bloquear a alguien ▪ cerrar a alguien dejar encerrado a alguien ▪ bloquear el paso a alguien ➤ Someone has double parked and blocked me in. Alguien ha aparcado en doble fila y me ha encerrado.

block of ice témpano

block of voters *el* bloque de electores

block of wood trozo de madera

to **block off a street** cortar la calle ➤ They block off the street every Sunday for the open air market. Cortan la calle todos los domingos para el mercadillo.

to **block someone** bloquear a alguien

to **block someone's view** no dejar ver a alguien

to **block text** *(word processing)* señalar el texto

to **block the long-distance calls** bloquear (las) llamadas de larga distancia ➤ I'd like to block the long-distance calls except for calling card calls. Me gustaría bloquear las llamadas de larga distancia excepto cuando se hacen a través de tarjeta.

to **block traffic** bloquear el tráfico ▪ entorpecer el tráfico ▪ colapsar el tráfico

blood boil: to make one's ~ hacer que se le queme la sangre a uno

blood cell count: to do a ~ hacer un recuento de glóbulos en la sangre

blood clot coágulo de sangre

blood donor *el, la* donante de sangre

blood flow *la* circulación de la sangre ▪ *el* torrente sanguíneo

blood is thicker than water la sangre tira

blood pressure presión sanguínea ▪ presión de sangre ▪ presión arterial ▪ tensión ➤ How's your blood pressure? ¿Qué tal la tensión? ➤ What's your blood pressure? ¿Qué tensión tienes? ➤ The doctor said his blood pressure is in the normal range. El médico dijo que su presión sanguínea estaba en el rango normal.

blood pressure: to take someone's ~ tomarle la presión (arterial) a alguien ▪ tomarle la tensión a alguien ➤ The doctor took her blood pressure. El médico tomó su presión arterial. ▪ El médico le tomó su presión arterial.

blood relative consanguíneo

blood run cold: to make one's ~ hacer que se le hiele la sangre a alguien

blood sample muestra de sangre

blood-stained teñido de sangre ➤ A blood-stained coat was found at the crime scene. Un abrigo teñido de sangre fue hallado cerca de la escena del crimen.

to be **blood stained** ▪ to be stained with blood estar teñido de sangre ➤ The coat was blood stained. ▪ The coat was stained with blood. El abrigo estaba teñido de sangre.

blood type ▪ blood group grupo sanguíneo ▪ tipo de sangre ➤ What is your blood type?-A positive. ¿Cuál es tu grupo sanguíneo?-A positivo.

blood vessel vaso sanguíneo

bloodbath baño de sangre

bloodletting ▪ spilling of blood derramamiento de sangre ➤ The political analyst predicted there would be some bloodletting by the Democrats after losing the election. Los analistas políticos predicen un derramamiento de sangre entre los Demócratas tras perder las elecciones.

bloody nose: to give someone a ~ ▪ to bloody someone's nose hacerle sangrar por la nariz a alguien

bloody nose: to have a ~ ▪ to have a nosebleed sangrar por la nariz

to **bloody someone's nose** ▪ to give someone a bloody nose hacerle sangrar por la nariz a alguien

to **blot ink** secar la tinta (con un papel secante)

to **blot out something** ▪ to blot something out 1. *(literal)* eclipsar a algo 2. *(figurative)* reprimir algo ➤ The shadow blotted out the image. La sombra eclipsó a la imagen. ➤ The sunlight blotted out the stars. ▪ The sunlight eclipsed the stars. La luz del sol eclipsó a las estrellas. ➤ I can't think about that. I blot it out. No puedo pensar en eso. Lo reprimo.

to **blow a fuse** 1. to melt a fuse fundirse un fusible ▪ hacer saltar un fusible ▪ fundirse los plomos 2. to blow one's top ▪ to hit the ceiling ponerse como un basilisco ▪ ponerse hecho un basilisco ➤ The microwave and toaster used at the same time will blow the fuse. ▪ Using the microwave and the toaster at the same time will blow the fuse. Utilizar el microondas y el tostador a la vez hará que se salte un fusible.

to **blow a hole in something** abrir un agujero en algo (por explosión) ➤ The mortar shell blew a hole in the side of the building. La explosión del mortero abrió un agujero en un lado del edificio. *(Spanish prefers the indefinite article: "a side" instead of "the side.")*

to **blow a ship out of the water** mandar a pique un barco ▪ hacer saltar un barco por los aires ➤ The squadron of fighters blew the destroyer out of the water. El escuadrón de cazas mandó a pique al destructor. ▪ El escuadrón de cazas hizo saltar el destructor por los aires.

to **blow apart something** ▪ to blow something apart reventar algo

to **blow all one's money** *(coll.)* undirse todo su dinero ▪ pelarse todo su dinero ▪ pulirse todo su dinero

to **blow around like a leaf** revolotear como una hoja ➤ An airplane doesn't blow around like a leaf because the center of gravity coincides with the center of air pressure. Un avión no revolotea como si fuera una hoja porque el centro de gravedad coincide con el centro de la presión del aire.

to **blow away** salir volando ➤ The whole pile of leaves blew away. La pila entera de hojas salió volando. ▪ El montón entero de hojas salió volando.

to **blow bubbles** 1. *(soap)* hacer burbujas 2. *(gum)* hacer pompas ▪ hacer globos (de chicle) ➤ I blew a bubble, and when it popped the whole class stopped typing. They thought the teacher was calling time. Hice un globo de chicle y cuando explotó, toda la clase dejó de escribir a máquina, porque creyeron que era la maestra quien les daba la señal para parar.

blow-by-blow account of something: to give someone a ~ contarle algo a alguien con pelos y señales

to **blow down a sign** ■ to blow a sign down **1.** *(mounted or hanging)* tirar abajo el cartel ■ volcar el cartel ■ llevarse el cartel (por delante) **2.** *(attached to the ground)* to blow over a sign arrancar un cartel (de cuajo) *("Letrero" can be substituted for "cartel." Road signs are "las señales.")* ➤ The wind blew down the sign. ■ The wind blew the sign down. El viento tiró abajo el cartel. ■ El viento volcó el cartel. ■ El viento se llevó el cartel (por delante) ➤ The wind blew it down. El viento lo tiró abajo. ■ El viento lo volcó. ■ El viento se lo llevó (por delante). ➤ The wind blew the sign down. ■ The wind blew down the sign. ■ The wind blew the sign over. ■ The wind blew over the sign. El viento arrancó el cartel. ➤ The wind blew it down. El viento lo arrancó.

to **blow down a tent** ■ to blow a tent down ■ to blow over a tent echar al suelo la carpa ■ echar al suelo la tienda de campaña ■ tirar la carpa ■ tirar la tienda ■ levantar la tienda de campaña ➤ The high winds blew down the tent. Los fuertes vientos echó al suelo la carpa.

to **blow hot and cold** ■ to run hot and cold dar una de cal y otra de arena

to **blow off steam** ■ to let off steam desahogarse

to **blow off the dust from something** ■ to blow the dust off (of) something quitar el polvo de un soplido ➤ He leaned over and blew a thick layer of dust off the tabletop. Se inclinó y quitó de un soplido una gruesa capa de polvo de encima de la mesa. ➤ He blew it off the tabletop. Lo quitó de un soplido de encima de la mesa.

to **blow on** soplar (sobre) algo ➤ He blew on the spoonful of steaming soup to cool it. Sopló la cucharada de sopa humeante para enfriarla.

to **blow one's brains out** saltarse la tapa de los sesos ■ volarse la tapa de los sesos ■ levantarse la tapa de los sesos

to **blow one's mind** alucinarle ■ chiflarle ■ parecerle alucinante ■ *(L. Am.)* barrer la mente ➤ The Smithsonian Air and Space Museum blew my mind. El Museo Aeroespacial del Smithsonian me alucinó. ■ El Museo Aeroespacial del Smithsonian me pareció alucinante. ■ El Museo Aeroespacial del Smithsonian me chifló.

to **blow one's nose** sonarse la nariz

to **blow one's own horn** echarse flores ■ sacar a relucir sus éxitos ■ darse bombo ■ tirarse el folio ■ tirarse el pisto ■ darse ínfulas

to **blow one's paycheck** pulirse el cheque de la paga ■ fundirse el cheque de la paga ■ pelarse el cheque de la paga ➤ He blew his whole paycheck in one night on the town. Se pulió el cheque de la paga entero en una noche de juerga. ➤ He blew his whole paycheck on one night on the town. Se pulió el cheque de la paga entero en una noche de juerga.

to **blow one's top** ■ to blow a fuse ■ to hit the ceiling ■ to go ballistic perder los estribos ■ perder el temperamento ■ perder el control ■ *(archaic)* ponerse hecho un basilisco ■ ponerse como un basilisco

to **blow oneself up** hacerse estallar (a sí mismo) ➤ *(news item)* A suicide bomber blew himself up in Jerusalem. Un terrorista suicida se hizo estallar (a sí mismo) en Jerusalén.

to **blow out** reventarse ➤ The left rear tire blew out (on me). Se me reventó la llanta trasera izquierda.

to **blow out a candle** ■ to blow a candle out apagar una vela soplando ■ apagar una vela de un soplido ➤ The child blew out all the candles on his birthday cake. El niño apagó las velas de su tarta de cumpleaños soplando. ➤ He blew them all out in one breath. Las apagó todas de un soplido.

to **blow over** *(a storm)* ■ to pass disiparse ■ *(hard feelings)* olvidarse ■ pasar(se) ➤ The storm clouds will blow over in a few minutes. Las nubes de tormenta se disiparán en unos pocos minutos. ➤ Just be patient; it'll blow over. ■ Just be patient; it'll pass. Sé paciente. Ya pasará.

to **blow someone away** *(coll.)* **1.** to astonish someone dejar a alguien de una pieza ■ dejar a alguien alucinado ■ dejar a alguien encantado ■ dejar a alguien fuera de sí ■ dejar a alguien anonadado **2.** to shoot someone to death reventar a alguien (con arma de fuego) ■ destrozar a alguien (con arma de fuego) ■ aniquilar a alguien (con arma de fuego) ■ acabar con alguien (con arma de fuego) ➤ The organ accompanied by the orchestra just blew the whole audience away. El órgano acompañado por la orquesta dejó a toda la audiencia de una pieza. ■ El órgano acompañado por la orquesta dejó encantada a toda la audiencia. ■ El órgano acompañado por la orquesta dejó a toda la audiencia fuera de sí misma. ➤ The gangster opened fire and blew his compatriot away. El pistolero abrió fuego y reventó a su compatriota. ■ El pistolero abrió fuego y destrozó a su compatriota. ■ El pistolero abrió fuego y aniquiló a su compatriota. ■ El pistolero abrió fuego y acabó con su compatriota.

to **blow someone out of the water** hundir a alguien ■ mandar a pique a alguien ■ sacar a alguien de la cancha ■ sacar a alguien del terreno de juego ■ dejar a alguien fuera de juego ➤ The debater blew his opponent out of the water by making mincemeat of his argument. El polemista hundió a su oponente haciendo picadillo sus argumentos. ■ El polemista mandó a pique a su oponente haciendo picadillo sus argumentos. ■ El polemista sacó a su oponente de la cancha haciendo picadillo sus argumentos.

to **blow someone's brains out** reventarle los sesos a alguien ■ volarle los sesos a alguien ■ levantarle a alguien la tapa de los sesos

to **blow someone's cover** dejar a alguien al descubierto ■ *(off-color)* dejar a alguien con el culo al aire

to **blow something (all) out of proportion** ■ to make a mountain out of a molehill hacer una montaña de un grano de arena

to **blow something away** ■ to sweep away alejar algo ■ arrastrar algo ■ barrer algo ➤ The wind and rain blew the air pollution away. ■ The wind and rain swept the air pollution away. El viento y la lluvia alejaron la contaminación. ■ El viento y la lluvia arrastraron la contaminación. ■ El viento y la lluvia barrieron la contaminación.

to **blow something down** ■ to blow down something **1.** derribar algo soplando **2.** derribar algo el viento ➤ The big bad wolf blew the little pig's house down. El lobo derribó soplando la casa del cerdito. ➤ The hurricane blew the house down. El huracán derribó la casa.

to **blow something off (of) something** quitar algo soplando ■ volarse ➤ The wind blew the snowman's hat off. El viento le quitó el sombrero al muñeco de nieve. ■ El viento le voló el sombrero al muñeco de nieve. ➤ The high winds blew the roof off the house. Los fuertes vientos volaron el techo de la casa.

to **blow the dust off (of) something** quitar el polvo de un soplido ➤ He leaned over and blew a thick layer of dust off the tabletop. Se inclinó y quitó de un soplido una gruesa capa de polvo de encima de la mesa.

to **blow the horn** ■ to sound the horn tocar el claxon ■ *(Arg., Uru.)* tocar (la) bocina

to **blow the whistle 1.** *(referee, policeman, et al.)* tocar el silbato ■ sonar el silbato ■ tocar el pito **2.** to blow the whistle on someone or something ■ to expose someone or something destaparle la olla a alguien ■ aletar sobre algo ■ denunciar una situación de incompetencia (normalmente en la administración pública) ■ *(Arg., Uru.)* levantar la perdiz

to **blow through** soplar entre ■ soplar a través de ➤ In *Lauriers* by Saint-Saëns, I think the trumpets symbolize the wind blowing through leaves and branches. En *Lauriers* de Saint-Saëns, creo que las trompetas simbolizan el viento soplando entre las hojas y las ramas.

blow to one's career ■ setback to one's career *el* golpe a la carrera (profesional) de alguien

blow to one's ego *el* golpe a su ego ■ *(Sp.)* mazazo a su ego

blow to one's pride *el* golpe a su orgullo ■ *(stronger)* mazazo a su orgullo

to **blow up 1.** to explode explotar (por los aires) ■ saltar por los aires ■ estallar **2.** to hit the ceiling ■ to pitch a fit perder los estribos **3.** to go completely out of control salirse de control ■ irse a la miércoles ➤ The talks blew up. Las conversaciones se fueron a la miércoles.

to **blow up a balloon** ■ to blow a balloon up ■ to inflate a balloon inflar un globo ➤ We blew up fifty balloons for the birthday party. ■ We blew fifty balloons up for the birthday party. Inflamos cincuenta globos para la fiesta de cumpleaños. ■

Hinchamos cincuenta globos para la fiesta de cumpleaños. ➤ We blew up fifty of them. ▪ We blew fifty of them up. Inflamos cincuenta de ellos. ▪ Hinchamos cincuenta de ellos. ➤ We blew them up. Los inflamos. ▪ Los hinchamos.

to **blow up a building** ▪ to blow a building up explotar un edificio ▪ volar un edificio ▪ hacer volar un edificio ▪ hacer saltar un edificio por los aires ➤ The terrorists blew up the building. ▪ The terrorists blew the building up. Los terroristas volaron el edificio. ➤ They blew it up. Lo volaron.

to **blow up a photograph** ▪ to blow a photograph up ▪ to enlarge a photograph ampliar una fotografía ➤ The shop blew up the photograph. ▪ The shop blew the photograph up. La tienda amplió la fotografía. ➤ The shop blew it up. La tienda la amplió.

to **blow up a tire** ▪ to blow a tire up ▪ to inflate a tire inflar una rueda

to **blow up an air mattress** ▪ to blow an air mattress up ▪ to inflate an air mattress inflar un colchón de aire ➤ The camper blew up the air mattress. ▪ The camper blew the air mattress up. El campista infló el colchón de aire. ➤ The camper blew it up. El campista lo infló.

to **blow up in someone's face 1.** *(literal)* estallarle en la cara a alguien **2.** *(figurative)* salirle el tiro por la culata ▪ saltarle en las mismas narices (a alguien) ▪ saltar ante los mismos ojos de alguien ➤ The firecracker blew up in the boy's face. El petardo le estalló en la cara al niño. ➤ The schemer's plans blew up in his face. Al intrigante le salió el tiro por la culata. ▪ Al intrigante le saltaron sus planes en sus mismas narices. ▪ Los planes saltaron ante los mismos ojos del intrigante.

to **blow up into a thousand pieces** saltar por los aires ▪ saltar en pedazos

to be **blown up 1.** ser explotado **2.** *(balloon)* ▪ to be inflated estar inflado ▪ ser inflado **3.** *(photograph)* to be enlarged estar ampliada ▪ ser ampliada ➤ The airplane was blown up by terrorists. El avión fue explotado por terroristas.

blown up: to have a photograph ~ ▪ hacer ampliar una fotografía

to be **blue blooded** tener sangre azul

blue-chip stocks *(stock market)* valores seguros ▪ acciones seguras

blue-collar job trabajo manual

blue-collar worker *el* trabajador manual ▪ *la* trabajadora manual

blue in the face: until one is ~ hasta quedarse azul ▪ hasta ponerse azul ▪ hasta quedarse sin aire ➤ The substitute teacher shouted at the pupils until she was blue in the face. La profesora substituta gritó a los alumnos hasta quedarse azul. ▪ La profesora substituta gritó a los alumnos hasta ponerse azul. ▪ La profesora substituta gritó a los alumnos hasta quedarse sin aire. ➤ I've sanded that wall until I'm blue in the face. He raspado esa pared hasta quedarme sin aire.

blue moon: in a ~ ▪ in a month of Sundays en una eternidad ▪ en la tira de tiempo ➤ I haven't seen you in a blue moon. No te he visto en una eternidad. ▪ No te he visto en la tira de tiempo.

blue moon: once in a ~ una vez cada muerte de obispo ▪ de pascuas a ramos ▪ de tarde en tarde

blue movie ▪ porno flick película verde ▪ película porno ▪ *el* peliporno

Blue Ridge Mountains *(Virginia)* Sierra de la Cresta Azul

blue shift *(physics)* desplazamiento hacia el azul

blueprint of life ▪ DNA map libro de la vida ▪ secuenciación de ADN

to **bluff an opponent in poker** ir de farol ▪ tirarse un farol ▪ echarse un farol ▪ marcarse un farol

bluish cast tono azulado ➤ From a distance, the mountains have a bluish cast, which is why they're called the Blue Ridge. En la distancia, las montañas tienen un tono azulado que es por lo que se llaman La Cresta Azul.

to **blur the distinctions** empañar las distinciones ▪ hacer las distinciones menos claro ▪ opacar las distinciones ➤ Some medical research blurs the distinction between what is ethical and what is unethical. Algunas investigaciones médicas empañan las distinciones entre lo ético y lo no ético.

to **blurt out something** ▪ to blurt something out soltar algo (al hablar) ▪ escapársele algo (al hablar) ▪ *(Mex.)* chispoteársele algo (al hablar) ➤ She blurted out the truth. ▪ She blurted the truth out. Soltó la verdad. ➤ She blurted it out. La soltó. ▪ Se le escapó. ▪ Se le chispoteó.

to **board an airplane, boat, train, etc.** embarcarse a un avión, barco, tren, etc. ▪ subir a bordo de un avión, etc.

board game juego de mesa

board of directors junta directiva ▪ consejo de administración ▪ consejo administrativa

boarding pass tarjeta de embarque

boarding school colegio interno ▪ internado

to **bode ill for** ▪ to spell trouble for ser mal presagio para ➤ The falling dollar bodes ill for her plans to buy a condo in Madrid. La caída del dólar es un mal presagio para sus planes de comprar un apartamento en Madrid.

to be **bodily thrown out of a bar** ▪ to get bodily thrown out of a bar echar a alguien a la fuerza de un bar ➤ The rowdies were bodily thrown out of the bar by the bouncer. Los camorristas fueron echados a la fuerza del bar por el gorila.

body building *la* musculación ▪ físico culturismo

body fat grasa corporal

body language *el* lenguaje corporal

body odor ▪ "B.O." *el* olor corporal ▪ *(colorful)* olor a chivo (que mata) ▪ *(politically correct)* olor a traspiración

body odor: to have ~ tener olor corporal ▪ *(colorful)* oler a chivo (que mata) ▪ *(politically correct)* tener olor a traspiración

body of one's work *el* total de la obra ▪ *la* totalidad de la obra (de un artista)

body temperature temperatura corporal

body-tight ▪ skin-tight ceñido (al cuerpo) ▪ apretado (al cuerpo) ▪ pegado al cuerpo ▪ ajustado ▪ *(spectacularly tight)* ajustadísimo ➤ She wore a body-tight T-shirt. Llevaba una camiseta ceñida.

to be **bogged down 1.** to be swamped ▪ to be bogged down estar empantanado ▪ estar hasta arriba ▪ estar hasta el cuello ▪ estar desbordado **2.** to be deadlocked ▪ to be stalled ▪ to be stymied ▪ to have run aground estar en punto muerto ▪ estar atascado ▪ haber quedado encallado **3.** to be stuck estar atascado ▪ estar atrapado ➤ He's bogged down with work. Está empantanado de trabajo. ▪ Está hasta arriba de trabajo. ▪ Está hasta el cuello de trabajo. ▪ Está desbordado por el trabajo. ➤ The negotiations are bogged down. Las negociaciones están en punto muerto. ▪ Las negociaciones han quedado atascadas. ▪ Las negociaciones han quedado encalladas. ➤ The car is bogged down in the mud. El coche está atascado en el lodo.

bogged down in details: to get ~ quedarse atascado en los detalles ▪ quedarse estancado en los detalles ➤ Doing this research, we get bogged down in details. Haciendo esta investigación, nos quedamos atascados en los detalles.

bogged down in traffic: to get ~ quedar atrapado en un atasco ▪ quedar atrapado en tráfico ➤ Sorry I'm late; I got bogged down in the rush-hour traffic. Perdón por la tardanza. Quedé atrapado en un atasco en la hora punta.

to **boggle the mind** no caber en la cabeza ▪ dejarle alucinado

bogus bill ▪ counterfeit bill *el* billete de pega ▪ billete falso ▪ *(Arg.)* billete trucho

to **boil away** evaporarse al hervir ▪ evaporar al hervirse ➤ All the tea water has boiled away, and the pan is damned near red hot. Toda el agua para el té se ha evaporado al hervir, y el recipiente está casi al rojo vivo.

to **boil down a liquid** ▪ to boil a liquid down ▪ to reduce a liquid reducir un líquido (hirviéndolo) ➤ Boil it down until it has about half as much liquid as you started with. ▪ Boil it down to half the volume. Redúcelo (hirviéndolo) hasta la mitad.

to **boil down something** ▪ to boil something down condensarlo ➤ You're over the thousand-word limit. You need to boil it down. Te has pasado del límite de mil palabras. Necesitas condensarlo. ➤ I'm going to boil this list of questions down to ten. Voy a condensar esta lista de preguntas a diez.

to **boil down to** reducirse a ➤ It all boils down to... Se reduce a... ➤ What it boils down to is... A lo que se reduce es...

to **boil over** salirse por ebullición ▪ rebosar por ebullición ➤ Watch the soup and make sure it doesn't boil over. Vigila la sopa y asegúrate de que no se sale. ➤ Since the invention of the microwave, we Spanish have lost one of our traditions: letting the milk boil over. Desde que se inventó el microondas, los españoles hemos perdido una de nuestras tradiciones: dejar que la leche se salga (del cazo).

boiled water ▪ water that's been boiled ▪ water which has been boiled *el* agua hervida ➤ I only drink boiled water. ▪ I only drink water that's been boiled. Sólo tomo agua hervida. ▪ Sólo bebo agua hervida.

boiling point punto de ebullición

boiling point: to be at the ~ 1. estar en el punto de ebullición **2.** to be at the point of revolt estar a punto de estallar

boiling point: to reach the ~ 1. to come to a boil alcanzar el punto de ebullición ▪ levantar el hervor **2.** to reach the point of revolt llegar al punto donde no da para más

boiling water *el* agua hirviendo

to be **bold enough to do something** ▪ to be daring enough to do something ▪ to have the guts to do something tener agallas para hacer algo ▪ tener narices para hacer algo ▪ *(off-color)* tener los huevos para hacer algo ▪ tener los cojones para hacer algo

to be a **bold-faced liar** ser un mentiroso descarado ▪ ser un embustero ▪ ser un cuentista ▪ ser un trolero

to be a **bold-faced lie** ▪ to be an out-and-out lie ser una mentira descarada ▪ ser un embuste (descarado) ▪ ser un cuento ▪ ser una trola descarada ▪ mentir descaradamente

bold (type): in ~ en negrita ▪ en negrilla

boldness of his actions atrevimiento en sus acciones ▪ *el* coraje en sus acciones

bolt of lightning ▪ lightning bolt **1.** *(cloud to cloud)* relámpago **2.** *(cloud to ground)* rayo ➤ He was struck by lightning while walking the dog. Le cayó un rayo mientras paseaba al perro. ▪ *(coll.)* Lo partió un rayo cuando paseaba al perro.

to be a **bolt out of the blue** ▪ to come like a bolt out of the blue ser un golpe inesperado ▪ caer como una bomba

to **bolt the door** echar el cerrojo

bomb disposal expert ▪ explosives expert artificiero

bomb squad brigada de explosivos ▪ brigada de desactivación de bombas ▪ brigada del desmantelamiento de bombas

to **bombard someone with questions** acribillar a alguien a preguntas ▪ bombardear con preguntas a alguien

bombastic sermon sermón ampuloso

bombastic style estilo ampuloso

bon appetit buen provecho ▪ que aproveche

to **bond with 1.** *(people, animals)* establecer un lazo con **2.** *(glue)* pegar con

bone marrow transplant *el* transplante de la médula ósea

bone of contention with someone: to have a ~ ▪ to have a bone to pick with someone tener un caballo de batalla con alguien ▪ tener una manzana de la discordia con alguien

bone spur *(of the heel bone)* excrecencia del hueso calcáneo

bone to pick with someone: to have a ~ ▪ to have a bone of contention with someone tener un caballo de batalla con alguien ▪ tener una manzana de la discordia con alguien

to **bone up on a subject** *(coll.)* ▪ to brush up on a subject refrescar los conocimientos de una materia ▪ recuperar los conocimientos de una materia

bonus paycheck ▪ pay bonus paga extraordinaria

boob tube ▪ idiot box caja tonta

book about libro sobre ▪ libro acerca de ▪ libro de ➤ It's a book about African art. Es un libro sobre el arte africano.

to **book a flight** sacar un billete ▪ reservar un billete

book on ▪ book about libro acerca de ▪ libro sobre ▪ libro de

to be **booked on the flight** tener un asiento reservado en el vuelo ▪ tener una reservación en el vuelo ➤ We're not showing you as booked on this flight. ▪ We don't show you as (being) booked on this flight. No aparece que usted tenga un asiento reservado en este vuelo.

to be **booked solid** no quedar localidades ▪ no tener un hueco ▪ estar completo ➤ The concert was booked solid. No quedó ninguna localidad para el concierto. ➤ The doctor is booked solid til Tuesday. El doctor no tiene un hueco hasta el martes. ➤ I'm booked solid through May. No tengo un hueco hasta mayo.

to be **booked (up) until** no tener un hueco (en la agenda) hasta ▪ no tener lugar hasta ▪ no poder acaptar más compromisos hasta

to be **boom or bust** ser auge o caída ▪ ser todo o nada ▪ no haber término medio ▪ no tener término medio

booming business negocio floreciente ▪ negocio en auge

booming voice: to have a ~ tener una voz de trueno

boorish manners ▪ coarse manners modales burdos ▪ modales toscos

to **boost a campaign** impulsar a una campaña

booster rocket *el* cohete propulsor

booster shot inyección de refuerzo ▪ vacuna de refuerzo ▪ refuerzo ▪ revacunación ▪ segunda dosis de una vacunación

booth (in a restaurant) mesa empotrada ➤ We'd prefer a booth if one's available. Preferiríamos una mesa empotrada si hubiera alguna disponible.

booth in an exposition ▪ booth at an exposition ▪ exposition booth caseta en una exposición

border between: to form the border between ~ servir de la frontera entre

border dispute disputa fronteriza ▪ disputa de fronteras ➤ U.S. President Hayes sided with Paraguay in its border dispute over the Chaco. El presidente Hayes se puso de parte de Paraguay en su disputa fronteriza sobre el Chaco. ▪ El presidente Hayes se puso de parte de Paraguay en su disputa de fronteras sobre el Chaco.

to **border on 1.** to verge on bordear ▪ tirar a ▪ tender a ▪ rayar en ▪ picar en ▪ estar en los umbrales de **2.** to have a common border with limitar con ▪ hacer frontera con **3.** to have a common property line with lindar con ▪ estar colindante con ➤ The doctor said his flu is bordering on pneumonia. El médico dijo que su gripe raya en la neumonía. ➤ El Salvador borders on Guatemala, Honduras, and the Pacific Ocean. El Salvador limita con Guatemala, Honduras y el Océano Pacífico. ➤ His farm borders on ours. ▪ His farm and our farm have a common border. Su granja linda con la nuestra.

to **border on the ridiculous** rayar en lo ridículo ▪ rozar lo ridículo ▪ *(literary)* estar en los umbrales de lo ridículo ▪ estar a las puertas de lo ridículo ▪ frisar en lo ridículo ➤ That borders on the ridiculous. Eso raya en lo ridículo. ▪ Eso roza lo ridículo. ▪ Eso está en los umbrales de lo ridículo.

border skirmishes escaramuzas fronterizas

Border States *(U.S. Civil War era)* los estados esclavistas que hacían frontera con el Norte antes de la Guerra Civil Estadounidense: Delaware, Maryland, Kentucky, Missouri y Virginia, de los cuales sólo Virginia se separó de la Unión Federal.

border wars guerras fronterizas

to be **bordered by 1.** estar rodeado de **2.** tener una frontera con ➤ The garden is bordered by tall hedges. El jardín está rodeado de setos altos. ➤ Virginia is bordered on the south by North Carolina. Virginia tiene una frontera al sur con Carolina del Norte.

bordering (on) limítrofe con ➤ Countries bordering (on) Colombia, including Ecuador and Peru Países limítrofes con Colombia, incluyendo Ecuador y el Perú

to be a **borderline case** ser un caso límite

borderline blood pressure presión sanguínea límite ➤ The doctor said his blood pressure was borderline. El médico dijo que su presión sanguínea estaba al límite. ▪ El médico dijo que su presión sanguínea estaba en el límite.

to be **borderline pneumonia** estar al borde de la neumonía ▪ ser prácticamente una neumonía

to be a **borderline student** ser un estudiante de aprobado raso ▪ ser un estudiante de aprobar por los pelos ▪ ser un estudiante aprobar justo en el límite ➤ He used to be a borderline student. Era un estudiante de aprobado raso. ▪ Era un estudiante de aprobado por los pelos. ▪ Era un estudiante de aprobar por los pelos. ▪ Era un estudiante de aprobado justo en el límite. ▪ Era un estudiante de aprobar justo en el límite.

to **bore a hole through something** perforar un agujero a través de algo ▪ hacer un agujero a través de algo ➤ The miners bored a hole through the rock. Los mineros perforaron un agujero a través de la roca. ➤ The termites bored a hole through cousin Mae's parlor floor. Las termitas perforaron un agujero en el suelo de la sala de la prima Mae.

to be **bored by** estar aburrido con ▪ sentirse aburrido con ▪ sentirse aburrido por ➤ The poet John Ciardi once said he was bored by his students. El poeta John Ciardi dijo que estuvo aburrido con sus estudiantes. ▪ El poeta John Ciardi dijo una vez que se sintió aburrido con sus estudiantes. ▪ El poeta John Ciardi dijo una vez que se sintió aburrido por sus estudiantes.

to be **bored stiff** ▪ to be bored to death ▪ to be bored silly estar aburrido como una ostra

boring job trabajo anodino

to be **born and raised** nacer y crecer ➤ She was born and raised in Managua, Nicaragua. Ella nació y creció en la Managua, Nicaragua.

born athlete atleta nato ▪ atleta nata

born criminal criminal nato(-a)

born leader ▪ natural leader líder nato(-a)

to be **born lucky** nacer con suerte ▪ nacer con estrella

born musician músico(-a) nato(-a)

to be **born of** ▪ to be caused by ▪ to be the result of ser causado por

to be **born out of wedlock** nacer fuera del matrimonio ▪ ser habido fuera del matrimonio

to be **born prematurely** nacer de forma prematura ➤ The cubs were born prematurely. Los cachorros han nacido de forma prematura.

to be **born with a silver spoon in one's mouth** nacer en cuna de oro ▪ nacer con fortuna ▪ nacer con un pan bajo el brazo

born writer escritor nato ▪ escritora nata

born yesterday: not to be ~ no nacer ayer ▪ no caerse de un guindo ➤ I wasn't born yesterday, you know. No nací ayer. ▪ No me he caído de un guindo, sabes.

to be **borne out by** ▪ to be confirmed by ▪ to be corroborated by ▪ to be supported by ser confirmado por ▪ ser corroborado por ➤ The paternity allegation was borne out by the DNA test. ▪ The paternity allegation was confirmed by the DNA test. La reclamación de paternidad fue confirmada por el examen de ADN. ▪ La reclamación de paternidad fue corroborada por el examen de ADN.

to be **borne out by the facts** ser confirmado por los hechos ▪ ser corroborado por los hechos

to **borrow money** pedir dinero prestado

to **borrow something from someone** tomar prestado algo de alguien ▪ pedir prestado algo de alguien

borrowed time: to be living on ~ tener el tiempo contado ▪ tener los días contados

to be the **boss** ser el jefe ▪ ser el que manda ▪ *(coll.)* llevar la batuta

to **boss someone around** mangonear a alguien ▪ caciquear a alguien

to be **bossed around** ser mangoneado ▪ ser caciqueado ➤ I don't like to be bossed around. No me gusta que me mangoneen. ▪ No me gusta que me caciqueen.

bossy big brother hermano mayor mandón

botched job chapuza

both he and she ▪ he as well as she ▪ tanto él como ella ▪ ambos él y ella ▪ así él como ella

both men and women ▪ men and women alike ▪ men as well as women ambos hombres y mujeres ▪ tanto hombres como mujeres ▪ lo mismo hombres que mujeres

both mother and daughter ▪ the mother as well as the daughter tanto la madre como la hija ▪ lo mismo la madre como la hija ▪ lo mismo la madre que la hija ➤ Both mother and daughter are good cooks. Lo mismo la madre que la hija son buenas cocineras.

both (of) my parents tanto mi padre como mi madre ➤ Both my parents worked when I was a child. Tanto mi padre como mi madre trabajaban cuando yo era pequeño(-a).

both (of them) ▪ they both los dos ▪ las dos ▪ ellos dos ▪ ellas dos

both of us ▪ we both nosotros dos ▪ ambos ▪ los dos ➤ Both of us make the same mistakes. Nosotros dos cometemos los mismos errores. ▪ Ambos cometemos los mismos errores. ▪ Los dos cometemos los mismos errores.

to be **both one thing and another** ser tanto una cosa como la otra ➤ She's both a student and a teacher. Es tanto estudiante como profesora.

both (one's) parents ambos padres ▪ sus dos padres ▪ los dos padres de uno

both sides of the family ambas partes de la familia

both sides of the issue ambas partes del asunto ▪ las dos versiones del asunto

both sides of the question las dos caras de la cuestión ▪ las dos versiones de la cuestión

to **bother someone 1.** to annoy someone dar la lata ▪ fastidiar a alguien ▪ molestar a alguien ▪ irritar a alguien ▪ incordiar a alguien ▪ *(Sp.)* dar la brasa a alguien ▪ dar la vara a alguien **2.** to worry someone preocupar a alguien ➤ Stop bothering me. Deja ya de dar la lata. ▪ Deja ya de dar la vara.

to **bother to do something** molestarse en hacer algo

to **bother with** ▪ to mess with molestarse con ▪ tomarse molestias con ➤ Don't bother with it at all, I'll take care of it. No te molestes con eso. Ya cuidaré yo de ello. ▪ No te tomes la molestia con eso. Ya cuidaré yo de ello. ➤ Don't bother with the settings. You'll get it out of whack. No te molestes con las configuraciones, que las vas a fastidiar.

bottle of perfume frasco de perfume

bottled-up emotions ▪ pent-up emotions emociones contenidas

bottled-up rage ▪ pent-up rage rabia contenida

to be **bottled up inside (one)** estar conteniéndose ▪ estar guardado dentro

bottled up inside (one): to have energy ~ ▪ to have bottled-up energy tener energía contenida

bottling works ▪ bottling plant planta envasadora ▪ planta embotelladora

the **bottom has fallen out of the market** el mínimo del mercado está por los suelos ▪ el mínimo del mercado ha caído por los suelos

the **bottom line is...** a fin de cuentas se trata... ▪ en resumidas cuentas se trata de... ▪ en resumidas cuentas es... ▪ últimamente es... ▪ la última palabra es... ➤ The bottom line is money. En resumidas cuentas se trata de dinero. ▪ En resumidas cuentas es cuestión de dinero. ▪ Lo que cuenta es dinero.

the **bottom line is that...** se reduce a que...

bottom of the barrel: to scrape the ~ estar en las últimas ▪ prescindir de los recursos necesarios ▪ *(off-color)* andar como puta por rastrojo

bottom of the hill: at the ~ al pie de la colina

bottom of the list: at the ~ al final de la lista

bottom of the mountain: at the ~ al pie de la montaña

bottom of the ninth inning: in the ~ *(baseball)* al final de la novena entrada ▪ al final de la novena manga

bottom of the page: at the ~ ▪ at the foot of the page al pie de la página

bottom of the steps: at the ~ ▪ al pie de la escalera ▪ al pie de los escalones

bottom of the tree *la* parte inferior del árbol

to **bottom out** ▪ to hit the lowest point tocar fondo ▪ alcanzar el punto más bajo ➤ I hope the dollar has bottomed out. Espero que el dólar haya tocado fondo.

bottom shelf estantería de abajo ▪ *el* estante de abajo

to be a **bottomless pit** ser un barril sin fondo ▪ ser un pozo sin fondo ➤ Teenagers' stomachs are bottomless pits. Los estómagos de los adolescentes son barriles sin fondo.

bottoms up! ¡arriba, abajo, al centro, al dentro! ▪ ¡hasta la última gota!

bouillon cube cubito de caldo ▪ pastilla de caldo

to **bounce an E-mail** devolver un correo electrónico ➤ The server bounces the E-mails to certain addresses. El servidor me devuelve los correos electrónicos que mando a ciertas direcciones.

to **bounce a check** devolver un cheque ➤ The bank bounced the check. El banco devolvió el cheque.

to **bounce around between** ir dando tumbos entre ➤ I've been bouncing around between academic advising, international students, the dean's office, and the language center trying to find the forms for graduate school. He ido dando tumbos entre negociado (académico), estudiantes internacionales, la oficina del decano y el centro de idiomas intentando encontrar los formularios para estudios de posgrado.

to **bounce back** salir a flote ▪ recuperarse

to **bounce back to you** rebotar hasta donde tú estás ➤ If you drop a German word on the floor, it goes *thud* like a rock; if you drop a French word, it makes a puddle on the floor; but if you drop a Spanish word, it bounces back to you, and you can catch it in midair. Si tiras una palabra alemana al suelo, hace *pum* como una piedra; si tiras una palabra francesa, hace un charco en el suelo, pero si tiras una palabra española, rebota hasta donde estás, y puedes tomarla al vuelo.

to **bounce off (of)** ▪ to rebound off (of) dar un rebote en

bounced check ▪ returned check cheque devuelto ➤ The rent check bounced. ▪ The rent check was returned (unpaid). El cheque por la renta se ha devuelto al dueño.

bounced E-mail correo electrónico devuelto ▪ *(coll.) el* mail devuelto

to be **bound and determined to do something** vaya perro con hacer algo ➤ He's bound and determined to go to Spain. Vaya perro con irse a España.

to be **bound by a condition** estar obligado por una condición ▪ estar atado por una condición

to be **bound by a contract** estar obligado por contrato ➤ You're bound by the contract so long as the other party meets its legal requirements. Estás obligado por el contrato siempre que la otra parte cumpla los requisitos legales.

to be **bound by** estar vinculado por ➤ In some Spanish courts, the judge is not bound by the jury's decision. En algunos tribunales españoles, el juez no está vinculado por la decisión del jurado.

to be **bound by a promise** estar atado por una promesa ▪ estar obligado por una promesa

to be **bound by a treaty** estar obligado por un tratado

bound by rules and regulations estar obligado por normas y reglamentos

to be **bound for** ▪ to be headed for ▪ to be heading for ir con destino a ▪ ir destinado a ▪ ir con rumbo a

to be **bound to** estar condenado a ▪ ser algo inevitable ➤ His insubordination is bound to have serious consequences. Su insubordinación inevitablemente le acarreará serias consecuencias. ▪ Su insubordinación está condenada a acarrearle serias consecuencias. ➤ The capture of Saddam Hussein is bound to have an impact on the average citizen of Iraq. La captura de Saddam Hussein está condenada a tener un impacto en el ciudadano medio iraqui.

to be **bound up with** **1.** to be tied with estar atado con **2.** to be related to estar relacionado con

boundary layer *(physics)* capa límite ➤ One of the great advances in fluid dynamics was Ludwig Prandtl's discovery of the boundary layer. Uno de las grandes avances en la dinámica de fluidos fue el descubrimiento de Ludwig Prandtl de la capa límite.

bounty hunter cazar recompensas ▪ cazador(a) de recompensas

bouquet of flowers ramo de flores

bout with a pneumonia: to have a ~ tener un acceso de neumonía

bouts with fever: to have ~ tener accesos de fiebre ▪ *los* ataques de fiebre

to **bow out** ▪ to withdraw voluntarily retirarse ➤ The marginal candidates bowed out of the race. Los candidatos marginales se retiraron de la carrera (electoral).

to **bow to someone** hacerle una reverencia a alguien ➤ When Mr. Bean bows to the queen, he hits her in the head and knocks her down. Cuando Sr. Bean le hace a la reina una reverencia, le pega con la cabeza y la tumba.

to **bow to pressure** ceder ante la presión ▪ plegarse a la presión

bowels of the earth las entrañas de la tierra

bowl of cherries ▪ bed of roses lecho de rosas ➤ Life is not a bowl of cherries. ▪ Life is not a bed of roses. La vida no es ningún lecho de rosas.

bowl of soup plato (hondo) de sopa ▪ *(L. Am.) el* tazón de sopa

box for mailing ▪ box to send it in ▪ caja para envíos

box in the first tier ▪ first-tier box palco en la primera fila

box office taquilla

box office bomb ▪ box office flop ▪ box office failure ▪ failure at the box office fracaso de taquilla

box office hit película taquillera

box that something comes in caja en la que viene algo ▪ caja que trae algo ➤ I need some boxes like the ones the turrones come in. Necesito unas cajas como las que traen los turrones.

box to send it in ▪ box for mailing ▪ caja para envíos

boxing ring cuadrilátero

boy, I'll say ¡y tú que lo digas!

boy oh boy madre mía

boxer shorts pantalón corto ▪ calzón corto ➤ I would like a bathing suit more like boxer shorts than briefs. Me gustaría un bañador tipo pantalón corto, no tipo calzoncillo.

to **brag about something** ▪ to boast about something ▪ to boast of something jactarse de algo ▪ fanfarronear de algo ▪ echárselas de algo ▪ dárselas de algo

brain damage daño cerebral

to be **brain dead** estar en estado de muerte cerebral

brain injury *la* lesión cerebral

brain power *el* poder mental

brain trust fondo intelectual

brain waves ondas cerebrales

brake pads **1.** pastillas de freno **2.** *(the heat-resistant material on all brakes including bicycle brakes)* pastillas (de freno) ➤ Brake pads are used on disk brakes. Las pastillas de freno se utilizan en los frenos de disco. ▪ Las pastillas de freno se emplean en los frenos de disco.

brake shoes zapatas (de freno) ➤ Brake shoes are used on drum brakes. Las zapatas se utilizan en los frenos de tambor. ▪ Las zapatas se emplean en los frenos de tambor.

brakes failed frenos fallaron

to **branch out** expandir ▪ diversificar ➤ He wants to get his feet on the ground before branching out in his business. Quiere asentarse bien antes de expandir su negocio.

brand name marca de fábrica

brand new nuevecito ▪ flamante ▪ recién comprado ➤ Your shoes look brand new. Tus zapatos parecen nuevecitos. ➤ She had just bought a brand new sports car. Ella acababa de comprarse un flamante carro deportivo. ➤ The kids spilled a soft drink on the brand new sofa. Los niños vertieron un refresco en el sofá recién comprado.

brand new car auto cero kilómetro ▪ coche flamante ▪ carro nuevecito ➤ Just one hundred pesos per month gets you a brand new car!-Yes, but for how many months? ¡Tan sólo cien pesos por mes te consigue un auto cero kilómetro!-Sí, ¿pero por cuántos meses?

branding iron hierro de marcar

to **brandish a dagger** blandir una daga ▪ blandir un puñal

to **brandish a pistol** blandir una pistola

to **brandish a sword** blandir una espada ▪ enarbolar una espada

to be **brass-plated** estar chapado en latón ▪ tener un plaqué de latón ➤ Are these candlesticks plated, or are they solid brass? Estos candelabros, ¿están chapados o son mazizos?

to **breach a confidence** defraudar una confianza ▪ *(by a confessor)* romper el secreto de confesión

breach birth nacimiento de nalgas

breach of confidence **1.** violación de un secreto **2.** *(by a confessor)* violación a un secreto de confesión

breach of contract incumplimiento de contrato

breach of etiquette quebrantamiento de las reglas de etiqueta ▪ quebrantamiento de las normas de etiqueta

breach of trust abuso de confianza

to **break a bone** fracturarse un hueso ▪ romperse un hueso ➤ Castro fell and broke his knee. Castro se cayó y se fracturó la rodilla. ▪ Castro se cayó y se rompió la rodilla.

to **break a case** resolver un caso ➤ The FBI finally broke the case. El FBI finalmente resolvió el caso.

to **break a code** desentrañar una clave ▪ desentrañar un código ➤ William Friedman succeeded in breaking the Japanese purple code. William Friedman logró desentrañar el código púrpura japonés.

to **break a date** cancelar una cita

to **break a habit** quitarse de un hábito ▪ dejar un hábito ▪ quitarse de una costumbre ▪ dejar una costumbre ▪ alejarse de un hábito ▪ librarse de un hábito

to **break a horse** domar un caballo

break a leg! *(in theatre)* ▪ good luck! ¡buena suerte!

to **break a promise** romper una promesa ▪ incumplir un compromiso ▪ desobedecer una promesa hecha

to **break a record 1.** romper un récord ▪ batir un récord ▪ alcanzar un récord ▪ superar un récord **2.** *(phonograph record)* romper un disco de sonido

to **break a story** ▪ to be the first to report a story destapar una noticia ➤ The *Washington Post* broke the Watergate story. The *Washington Post* destapó la noticia del Watergate.

to **break a strike** romper una huelga

to **break all to pieces** hacerse trizas ▪ hacerse añicos ➤ When I dropped it, it broke all to pieces. Cuando lo tiré se hizo trizas. ▪ Cuando se me cayó se hizo añicos. *(See also "break something all to pieces.")*

to **break apart** ▪ to break into pieces quedar partido ▪ quedar partido en trozos ➤ The airplane fell onto a parallel runway, broke into three pieces, and burst into flames. El avión se desplomó sobre una pista lateral, quedó partido en tres trozos y explotó en llamas.

to **break away 1.** escindirse ▪ segmentarse ▪ fragmentarse ▪ separarse **2.** to leave escabullirse ➤ Large chunks of the polar ice caps are breaking away. Grandes segmentos de la capa de hielo polar se están escindiendo. ➤ Several socialists have broken away from the party, splintering the coalition of the left. Unos cuantos socialistas se han escindido del partido, fragmentando la coalición de la izquierda. ➤ We have another party to go to, so let's try to break away a little early. ▪ We have another party to go to, so let's try to get away a little early. Tenemos que ir a otra fiesta, así que intentemos escabullirnos pronto.

break-away republic república escindida

to **break camp** levantar (el) campamento

to **break down** *(intransitive verb)* **1.** to malfunction estropearse ▪ fallar ▪ romperse ▪ averiarse ▪ *(coll.)* hacerse cisco **2.** to break down (and cry) venirse abajo ▪ hundirse **3.** to disintegrate chemically descomponerse ➤ He got frustrated when his E-mail broke down on him. ▪ He got frustrated when his E-mail went out on him. Fue muy frustrante para él que su correo electrónico se estropeara. ➤ The car broke down. El coche se averió. ▪ El coche se estropeó. ▪ El coche se rompió. ▪ El coche falló. ➤ The elevator broke down. El ascensor se rompió. ▪ El ascensor se averió. ▪ El ascensor se estropeó. ▪ El ascensor falló. ➤ She broke down and cried when she heard the news. Ella se vino abajo y lloró cuando oyó las noticias. ▪ Ella se hundió y lloró cuando oyó las noticias. ➤ He broke down and confessed (to) what he had done. Él se vino abajo y confesó lo que había hecho. ▪ Él se hundió y confesó lo que había hecho. ➤ Alcohol breaks down at high temperatures. El alcohol se descompone a altas temperaturas.

to **break down something** *(transitive verb)* **1.** to dismantle something desarticular algo **2.** to itemize something detallar algo ▪ especificar algo ▪ desglosar algo ▪ dar algo en detalle ➤ The government troops have broken down the resistance fighters. Las tropas del gobierno han desarticulado a los guerrilleros de la resistencia. ➤ The American TV news did not break down the Spanish congressional races. La televisión norteamericana no desglosó las carreras al Congreso español. ▪ La televisión norteamericana no dio en detalle las carreras al Congreso español. ➤ The Madrid paper has not broken down the U.S. Senate races. El periódico de Madrid no ha detallado las carreras electorales al Senado Estadounidense.

to **break down the door** ▪ to break the door down tirar la puerta abajo ▪ tirar abajo la puerta ▪ echar la puerta abajo ▪ echar abajo la puerta ▪ tumbar la puerta ➤ The police officers broke down the door. ▪ The police officers broke the door down. Los agentes tiraron la puerta abajo. ▪ Los agentes tiraron abajo la puerta. ▪ Los agentes echaron la puerta abajo. ▪ Los agentes echaron abajo la puerta. ➤ The police officers broke it down. Los agentes la tiraron abajo. ▪ Los agentes la echaron abajo.

to **break even** cubrir (los) gastos ▪ no tener perdidas ni beneficios ▪ llegar a fin de mes ➤ Even a student needs to earn about a thousand dollars or euros a month to break even. Hasta un estudiante necesita ganar más o menos mil dólares o euros al mes para cubrir gastos.

to **break ground 1.** *(on a construction project)* cavar para los cimientos ▪ dar la primera pala **2.** *(in technology, literature, music)* ser un pionero ▪ abrir camino ▪ ser el primero en

to **break in 1.** *(with or without criminal intent)* entrar a la fuerza ▪ forzar **2.** *(with criminal intent)* asaltar ▪ allanar ➤ I've forgotten my key, so I've got to figure out a way to break in. Me he olvidado la llave, así que tendré que buscar la manera de entrar a la fuerza en la casa. ▪ Me he olvidado la llave, así que tendré que buscar la manera de forzar la casa. ➤ The burglars broke in while the owners were on vacation. Los ladrones asaltaron la casa mientras los propietarios estaban de vacaciones. ▪ Los ladrones allanaron la casa mientras los propietarios estaban de vacaciones. ▪ Los ladrones forzaron la casa mientras los propietarios estaban de vacaciones.

break in a case prueba determinante (en un caso)

to **break in a new car** estrenar un coche flamante ▪ hacer el rodaje

to **break in a new employee** hacerle el rodaje a un nuevo empleado

to **break in a pair of blue jeans** domar unos pantalones vaqueros

to **break in a pair of shoes** domar un par de zapatos

break in the case prueba determinante (en el caso)

break in the routine respiro en la rutina

break in the weather mejora en el tiempo

to **break into a conversation** interrumpir para intervenir en una conversación

to **break into a house** ▪ to enter a house by force ▪ to force one's way into a house *(with or without criminal intent)* entrar a la fuerza en una casa ▪ *(with criminal intent)* asaltar una casa ▪ allanar una casa ➤ I've forgotten my key, so I've got to figure out a way to break into the house. Me he olvidado la llave, así que tendré que entrar a la fuerza en la casa. ➤ The burglars broke into the house while the owners were on vacation. Los ladrones asaltaron la casa mientras los propietarios estaban de vacaciones. ▪ Los ladrones allanaron la casa mientras los propietarios estaban de vacaciones.

to **break into a song** irrumpir en una canción

to **break into a telephone call** interrumpir la operadora una llamada telefónica

to **break into a thousand pieces** deshacerse en mil fragmentos

to **break into films** irrumpir en el cine

to **break into pieces** hacerse pedazos ➤ *(news item)* NASA admits that the space probe "Contour" may have broken into pieces. NASA admite que la sonda espacial "Contour" puede haberse hecho pedazos.

to **break into print** irrumpir en la prensa ➤ I see you finally broke into print! ¡Veo que por fin has irrumpido en la prensa!

to **break loose 1.** to come loose soltarse **2.** to free oneself from desencadenarse ➤ During the winds, the parked aircraft broke loose from its moorings. Durante el vendaval, la avioneta aparcada se soltó de sus anclajes. ➤ James Bond broke loose from his handcuffs by altering the path of a laser beam. James Bond se desencadenó de sus esposas alterando el curso de un rayo láser.

to **break off** quebrarse ▪ partirse ➤ The branches broke off during the thunderstorm. Las ramas se quebraron durante la tormenta. ▪ Las ramas se partieron durante la tormenta.

to **break off a piece of something for someone** partirle a alguien un pedazo de algo ➤ Break me off a piece of almond brittle. ▪ Break off a piece of almond brittle for me. Párteme un pedazo de turrón de Alicante.

to **break off a relationship** acabar una relación ▪ terminar una relación

to **break off an engagement** anular un compromiso ➤ They have broken off their engagement. Han anulado su compromiso. ➤ They broke off their engagement last weekend. Anularon su compromiso el fin de semana pasado.

to **break (off) diplomatic relations with** romper relaciones diplomáticas con

to **break off negotiations with** romper las negociaciones con

to **break someone of a habit** quitar a alguien un hábito ▪ quitar a alguien una costumbre ➤ My professor broke me of the habit in one quarter. El profesor me quitó el hábito en un trimestre.

to **break one's back** rompérsele la espalda a alguien ▪ partírsele la espalda a alguien ➤ He broke his back in an accident. ▪ His back was broken in an accident. Se (le) rompió la espalda en un accidente. ▪ Se (le) partió la espalda en un accidente.

to **break one's back with work** deslomarse ▪ matarse a trabajar ▪ partirse el espinazo

to **break one's back working** partirse el espinazo (trabajando)

to **break one's fall** 1. to cushion one's fall amortiguar la caída de uno 2. to stop one's fall parar la caída de uno

to **break one's promise** ▪ to go back on one's word faltar a su promesa ▪ faltar a un compromiso ▪ incumplir un compromiso ▪ faltar a la palabra ➤ He broke his promise. Faltó a su promesa. ▪ Faltó a la palabra.

to **break out** 1. *(war)* estallar 2. *(fire)* desatarse 3. *(rash)* salirle a alguien ▪ ponerse con ➤ War has broken out between the warlords. La guerra ha estallado entre los señores de la guerra. ➤ After the fire broke out, the train kept going for several kilometers. Después de que el fuego se desatara, el tren siguió avanzado durante unos kilómetros. ➤ He's broken out with either chicken pox or measles, I can't tell which. Le ha salido o varicela o sarampión, no sé decir cuál. ▪ Se ha puesto con varicela o sarampión, no sé decir cuál.

to **break out of jail** ▪ to break jail ▪ to escape from jail escaparse de la cárcel

to **break out of prison** ▪ to escape from prison escaparse de la prisión

to **break out of the mold** salirse del molde ▪ salirse de lo normal

to **break out with a rash** ▪ to break out in a rash salirle granitos ▪ *(medical)* salirle un salpullido

to **break over the shoe** ▪ to buckle over the shoe caer sobre el empeine del zapato ➤ I don't want the pants to break over the shoe. It makes them look too long. No quiero que el bajo de los pantolones caiga sobre el empeine del zapato. Los hace parecer muy largos.

to **break ranks** ▪ to fall out romper filas ▪ romper formación

to **break ranks with someone** desmarcarse de alguien

to **break something** romper algo ▪ cargarse algo ▪ *(in one place, like a bone)* quebrar algo

to **break something all to pieces** hacer añicos de algo

to **break the back of** hacer la parte más difícil de ▪ cambiar las tornas en ➤ Mark Twain notes that Joan of Arc won the memorable victory of Patay over the English and broke the back of the Hundred Years' War. Mark Twain señala que Juana de Arco logró la memorable victoria de Patay sobre los ingleses y cambió las tornas en la Guerra de los Cien Años. ▪ Mark Twain señala que Juana de Arco logró la memorable victoria de Patay sobre los ingleses, cambiando las tornas en la Guerra de los Cien Años.

to **break the bank** *(coll.)* dejarle a uno en quiebra ▪ quedar sin un duro en el banco ▪ no quedar con un peso partido en la mitad ➤ Your Christmas shopping spree is going to break the bank. Tu fiebre de compras navideña va a dejarte en quiebra.

to **break the door down** ▪ to break down the door tirar la puerta abajo ▪ echar la puerta abajo ▪ tirar abajo la puerta ▪ echar abajo la puerta ➤ They had to break the door down. ▪ They had to break down the door. Tuvieron que tirar la puerta abajo. ▪ Tuvieron que echar la puerta abajo. ▪ Tuvieron que tirar abajo la puerta. ▪ Tuvieron que echar abajo la puerta. ➤ They had to break it down. Tuvieron que tirarla abajo. ▪ Tuvieron que echarla abajo.

to **break the ice** *(literal and figurative)* romper el hielo

to **break the impasse** romper el bloqueo (de una negociación)

to **break the law** ▪ to violate the law infringir la ley ▪ quebrantar la ley ▪ vulnerar la ley ▪ delinquir ▪ estar fuera de la ley

to **break the line** ▪ to butt in line ▪ to cut into the line colarse ▪ saltarse la cola

to **break the logjam** agilizar el trámite ▪ agilizar el proceso ▪ *(coll.)* deshacer el embrollo

to **break the news** dar la noticia ➤ You need to break the news gently. Necesitas dar la noticia con delicadeza.

to **break the record** ▪ to set the record alcanzar el récord ▪ batir el récord ▪ superar el récord

to **break the record set by someone** quitar el récord a alguien

to **break the routine** romper con la rutina

to **break the rules** infringir las reglas ▪ romper las reglas

to **break the seal** romper el precinto

to **break the skin** penetrarle la piel ▪ traspasarle la piel ➤ When the dog bit you, did it break the skin? Cuando te mordió el perro, ¿te penetró la piel?

to **break the sound barrier** romper la barrera del sonido

to **break the speed limit** ▪ to exceed the speed limit saltarse el límite de velocidad ▪ sobrepasar el límite de velocidad

to **break the spell** deshacer el hechizo ▪ romper el hechizo ▪ romper el encanto ▪ deshacerse el encanto

to **break the story** ▪ to get the scoop ▪ to scoop (the other media) dar la primicia ▪ tener la primicia ▪ emitir una noticia en primicia

to **break through one's skin** vérsele el hueso a alguien ➤ The bone broke through the skin. ▪ The bone broke through his skin. Se le veía el hueso.

to **break up** 1. to break up with each other romper ▪ cortar ▪ dejarse 2. to break into pieces estallar en pedazos 3. to scatter ▪ to disperse desbandarse ▪ dispersarse 4. *(radio transmission)* entrecortarse ➤ The teenagers broke up following an argument. Los adolescentes rompieron después de una discusión. ▪ Los adolescentes cortaron después de una discusión. ▪ Los adolescentes se dejaron después de una discusión. ➤ Maria and Anselmo have broken up. ▪ Maria and Anselmo have split up. María y Anselmo han roto. ▪ María y Anselmo han cortado. ▪ María y Anselmo se han dejado. ➤ The space shuttle broke up on re-entry. ▪ The space shuttle broke into pieces on re-entry. El transbordador espacial estalló en pedazos durante la reentrada. ➤ At the sound of the bugle, the formation broke up. ▪ At the sound of the bugle, the formation scattered. ▪ At the sound of the bugle, the formation dispersed. Después del toque de corneta, la formación se desbandó. ▪ Después del toque de corneta, la formación se dispersó. ➤ You're breaking up. Can you hear me? Se te oye entrecortado. ¿Me oyes tú? ▪ Te oigo entrecortado. ¿Me oyes tú?

to **break up a demonstration** dispersar una manifestación ▪ desbaratar una manifestación ➤ The police broke up the demonstration. La policía dispersó la manifestación. ▪ La policía desbarató la manifestación.

to **break up a fight** ▪ to stop a fight parar una pelea ➤ During the brawl, several people who tried to break up the fight were also hurt. Durante la reyerta también resultaron heridas varias personas que intentaron parar la pelea.

to **break up in confusion** ▪ to break up in disarray acabar en confusión

to **break up with one's boyfriend** cortar con su novio ▪ romper con su novio ▪ dejarlo con su novio ➤ Jill broke up with her boyfriend. Jill cortó con su novio. ▪ Jill rompió con su novio. ▪ Jill lo dejó con su novio.

to **break up with one's girlfriend** cortar con su novia ▪ romper con su novia ▪ dejarlo con su novia

to **break with a snap** ▪ to snap when it breaks ▪ to snap as it breaks partirse con un chasquido ➤ I stepped on a twig that broke with a snap. ▪ I stepped on a twig which snapped when it broke. Pisé una ramita que se partió con un chasquido.

to **break with someone** apartarse de (las tesis de) alguien ➤ President Polk broke with former president Jackson on the issue of the national bank. El presidente Polk se apartó de (las tesis de) el ex-presidente Jackson con respecto al banco nacional.

to **break with the past** ▪ to make a break with the past romper con el pasado

to **break with tradition** romper con la tradición ▪ apartarse de la tradición

breakdown in communications ▪ communications breakdown problemas de comunicación

breakdown of mechanical equipment avería mecánica

breakdown of the congressional races 1. *(U.S., Mex.)* resultados electorales al Congreso (detallados) por estados ▪ *(Sp.)* resultados electorales al Congreso (detallados) por comunidades autónomas

breakdown of the family disgregación familiar ▪ atomización familiar

breakdown of the grades lista detallada de las calificaciones

breaking news información en directo ▪ noticias al instante ▪ últimas noticias

breakneck speed: at ~ a una velocidad de vértigo ➤ The car was going at breakneck speed. El coche iba a una velocidad de vértigo.

breast stroke *(swimming)* brazada

to be a **breath of fresh air** ser una bocanada de aire fresco ➤ Our substitute teacher was (like) a breath of fresh air. El profesor substituto fue (como) una bocanada de aire fresco.

breath of fresh air: to get a ~ tomar una bocanada de aire fresco ▪ tomar aire ▪ respirar hondo

breath of fresh air: to need a ~ necesitar una bocanada de aire fresco ▪ necesitar un poco de aire fresco ▪ necesitar algo de aire fresco ➤ I need a breath of fresh air. Necesito una bocanada de aire fresco. ▪ Necesito un poco de aire fresco. ▪ Necesito algo de aire fresco. ▪ Necesito que me dé el aire.

to **breathe a sigh of relief** suspirar de alivio ▪ suspirar con alivio ▪ respirar aliviado

to **breathe deep** respirar hondo

to **breathe deeply** respirar profundamente

to **breathe down someone's neck** estar encima de alguien

to **breathe easier 1.** to breathe a sigh of relief respirar con calma ▪ suspirar de alivio ▪ suspirar con alivio ▪ suspirar con calma **2.** to breathe more easily respirar más fácilmente ▪ respirar sin dificultad ▪ respirar con menos dificultad

to **breathe easy** respirar tranquilo

to **breathe more easily** ▪ to breathe easier respirar más fácilmente ▪ respirar con menos dificultad ➤ When they put the patient in an oxygen tent, he was able to breathe more easily. ▪ When they put the patient in an oxygen tent, he was able to breathe easier. Cuando pusieron al paciente en una cámara de oxígeno fue capaz de respirar más fácilmente.

to **breathe one's last** expirar (el último aliento)

breathing spell ▪ chance to relax respiro

breathtaking scenery escenografía que quita el aliento ▪ escenografía que deja sin aliento

breathtaking view vista que quita el aliento ▪ vista que deja sin aliento

to **breed animals** criar animales

to **breed crime** fomentar el crime ➤ Squalid ghettos breed crime. Los guetos depauperados fomentan el crimen.

to **breed like rabbits** procrear como conejos ▪ multiplicarse como los conejos

breed of dog raza de perro ➤ What breed of dog is that? ¿Qué raza de perro es?

to be a **breeding ground for** ser un caldo de cultivo para ▪ ser un lugar de cría para ▪ ser un lugar de fomentación para

to **breeze through** ▪ to sail through avanzar sin dificultad ▪ moverse sin dificultad

to **brew a pot of coffee** preparar café de máquina

to **brew an elixir** fabricar un elixir ▪ elaborar un elixir ▪ hacer un elixir

to **brew beer** fabricar cerveza ▪ elaborar cerveza ▪ hacer cerveza

brewed decaf descafeinado de máquina ▪ descafeinado de cafetera ▪ descafeinado natural, no de sobre ➤ Do you have brewed decaf? *(tú)* ¿Tienes descafeinado de máquina? ▪ ¿Tienes descafeinado de cafetera? ▪ *(usted)* ¿Tiene (usted) descafeinado de máquina? ▪ ¿Tiene (usted) descafeinado de cafetera?

briar patch espinar ➤ "Please don't throw me into that briar patch," said Br'er Rabbit to Br'er Fox. "Por favor, no me tires en ese espinar", le dijo 'Mano Conejo a 'Mano Zorro.

brick house casa de ladrillo (visto)

brick works fábrica de ladrillos

bridal registry lista de boda ▪ listas de boda

bride and groom los novios ▪ *(more formally)* los esponsales

bridge across the river ▪ bridge over the river *el* puente sobre el río

bridge of the nose *el* caballete de la nariz

brief history of Mexico historia breve de México

brief sketch ▪ short sketch **1.** *(written)* crónica **2.** *(drawn)* boceto

to **brief the president on** informarle al presidente de ▪ informarle al presidente sobre ➤ The president's advisers briefed him on the situation in Iraq. Los asesores del presidente le informaron de la situación en Irak. ▪ Los asesores del presidente le informaron sobre la situación en Irak.

bright and early radiante y fresca ➤ Bright and early one sunny Saturday morning Una radiante y fresca soleada mañana de sábado

bright, clear day *el* día despejado ▪ día asoleado

bright colors colores vistosos ▪ colores brillantes

bright countenances of the children luminosos semblantes de los niños

bright idea *(sarcastic)* genial idea ▪ idea peregrina ➤ He had the bright idea for a helicopter with an ejection seat. Ha tenido la genial idea de un helicóptero con un asiento de eyección.

bright lights luces brillantes ▪ *(of a car)* high beam luces largas ▪ luces altas

to **brighten one's day** alegrar el día a uno ➤ Your E-mail message really brightened my day. Tu mensaje de correo electrónico me alegró el día de verdad.

brightly colored vistoso ▪ llamativo

to be **brimming with** ▪ to be full of rebosar de ▪ estar lleno de ➤ The pond at the Monasterio de Piedra near Zaragoza was crystal clear and brimming with beautiful trout. El estanque del Monasterio de Piedra cerca de Zaragoza tenía las aguas cristalinas y rebosaba de preciosas truchas.

to **bring a friend** traerse a un amigo ➤ Come and bring a friend. Ven y se trae un amigo.

to **bring a nation to the brink of war** poner a una nación al borde de la guerra

to **bring about** determinar ▪ causar ▪ obrar ▪ lograr que ▪ ocasionar ▪ provocar

to **bring about a change** ▪ to produce a change ▪ to effect a change obrar un cambio ▪ provocar un cambio ▪ efectuar un cambio ➤ What brought about the change was diet. Lo que obró el cambio fue la comida.

to **bring along someone** ▪ to bring someone along ▪ to bring someone with you traerse a alguien consigo

to **bring along something** ▪ to bring something along ▪ to bring something with you traerse algo consigo

to **bring an account current** ▪ to bring the payments on an account up to date poner los pagos (de una cuenta) al día ▪ actualizar los pagos (de una cuenta)

to **bring around someone** ▪ to bring someone around **1.** to persuade someone atraer a alguien a una posición ▪ acercar a alguien a una postura ▪ convencer **2.** to revive someone reanimar a alguien

to **bring back something** ▪ to bring something back **1.** traer algo de vuelta **2.** to return something devolver algo ➤ Be sure and bring it back. Asegúrate y devuélvelo. ▪ Asegúrate de devolverlo.

to **bring back memories** ■ to take one back to traerle recuerdos a uno ■ hacer a alguien volver al pasado ➤ Just seeing her handwriting after all these years brought back so many memories. Sólo ver su letra después de tantos años me trajo tantos recuerdos. ■ Sólo ver su letra después de tantos años me hizo volver al pasado.

to **bring bad luck** dar mala suerte ■ *(coll.)* traer mal fario

to **bring closure to a matter** poner punto final a un asunto

to **bring down something** ■ to bring something down bajar algo ➤ Bring down the clothes you want me to wash. Baja la ropa que quieres que lave. ➤ Bring them down. Bájala.

to **bring down the government** ■ to bring the government down **1.** to force a change of leadership by democratic means hacer caer al gobierno **2.** to overthrow the government (by force) derrocar al gobierno ➤ *(news item)* Resignation of the Laborites brings down the government of Israel. Dimisión de los laboristas hace caer al gobierno de Israel. ➤ The rebels brought down the government. Los rebeldes derrocaron al gobierno.

to **bring down the house** provocar un (auténtico) delirio ■ hacer venirse abajo el sitio (en cuestión) ➤ Kennedy could bring down the house at a press conference. Kennedy podía provocar el delirio en una rueda de prensa.

to **bring (in) a good profit** ■ to net a good profit obtener un buen beneficio

to **bring it to a boil** llevarlo a ebullición ■ darle un hervor ■ subirlo a punto de cocción ■ hervirlo ➤ Bring it to a boil, stirring occasionally. Déle un hervor, removiendo de vez en cuando. ■ Llevarlo a ebullición, removiendo de vez en cuando.

to **bring itself out** ■ to stand out by itself ■ to emphasize itself destacar por sí mismo(-a) ■ resaltar por sí mismo(-a) ■ sobresalir por sí mismo(-a) ➤ You don't need to put the word in italics. It brings itself out. No necesitas poner la palabra en cursiva. Destaca por sí misma.

bring me... acércame... ■ tráeme... ➤ Bring me the medicine, please. Acércame la medicina, por favor.

to **bring off something** ■ to bring something off montar algo ■ organizar algo ➤ The entertainment committee brought off the Christmas bazaar with flying colors. El comité de recreo montó una venta benéfica navideña a lo grande. ■ El comité de recreo organizó una venta benéfica navideña a lo grande.

to **bring on something** ■ to bring something on ■ to cause something causar algo ■ provocar algo ■ originar algo ■ desatar algo

bring on the questions! ■ let's have the questions! ¡vengan las preguntas!

to **bring one nothing but trouble** ■ to cause one nothing but trouble no causar más que problemas ■ *(literary)* no reportarle sino disgustos

to **bring one's order** traerle el pedido a alguien ➤ They still haven't brought us our order. ■ They still haven't brought our order. Todavía no nos han traído el pedido.

bring oneself to do something: not to be able to ~ no tener presencia de ánimo para hacer algo ➤ He couldn't bring himself to tell his friend that his mother had just died. No tuvo la presencia de ánimo para decirle a su amigo que su madre había muerto. ➤ He couldn't bring himself to the realization of what had happened. No tuvo la presencia de ánimo para darse cuenta de lo que había pasado.

to **bring oneself up to date on something** ponerse al corriente con algo ■ ponerse al tanto de algo

to **bring out something** ■ to bring something out **1.** to highlight something resaltar algo ■ destacar algo **2.** to bring in something traer algo ■ sacar algo ➤ The red in the carpet brings out the red flowers in the curtains. El rojo de la alfombra resalta las flores rojas de las cortinas. ➤ The red in the carpet brings it out. El rojo de la alfombra la resalta. ➤ We're ready for you to bring out the birthday cake. ■ We're ready for you to bring the birthday cake out. Estamos listos para que traigas la torta.

to **bring out one's best self** sacar lo mejor de uno mismo

to **bring out the best in someone** destacar lo mejor en alguien ■ sacar (a la luz) lo mejor que hay en alguien ■ sacar lo mejor de los demás ➤ Connie brought out the best in people. Connie destacó lo mejor que hay en la gente.

to **bring out the best in something** sacar (a la luz) lo mejor que hay en algo ■ sacar el mayor partido de algo ■ hacer relucir la mayor parte de algo ➤ This "Lauriers" CD by Saint-Saëns will bring out the best in your new speakers. Este disco compacto de "Lauriers" de Saint-Saëns sacará lo mejor que hay en tus nuevos altavoces.

to **bring out the flavor of something** ■ to bring the flavor of something out ■ to enhance the flavor of something realzar el sabor de algo ■ potenciar el sabor de algo ■ aumentar el sabor de algo ■ darle más sabor a algo ➤ Stir frying brings out the flavor of the vegetables. Hacer las verduras a la plancha realza su sabor.

to **bring out the food** ■ to bring the food out sacar la comida

to **bring out the worst in someone** sacar lo peor de uno ■ sacar lo peor que hay en uno

to **bring out the worst in something** sacar lo peor de algo ■ sacar lo peor que hay en algo

to **bring peace** instaurar la paz ■ traer la paz ■ restaurar la paz ➤ The negotiators are trying to bring peace to the region. Los negociadores están intentando instaurar la paz en la región.

to **bring people back together 1.** to reunite people reunir a la gente **2.** to reconcile people reconciliar a la gente ➤ After the war, the families were brought back together. Después de la guerra las familias se reunieron juntas. ➤ In the movie *Paradise,* the child, played by Elijah Wood, brings the estranged couple back together. En la película *Paraíso*, el niño, interpretado por Elijah Wood, reconcilia a una pareja distanciada.

to **bring people together 1.** to gather people together reunir gente **2.** to unite people unir a las personas ➤ The conference brought together the top medical experts from around the world. El congreso reunió a las eminencias médicas de todo el mundo. ➤ The demonstration brought people together against world famine. La manifestación unió a la gente contra el hambre mundial.

to **bring security** aportar seguridad ➤ Violence will not bring security to the region. La violencia no aportará seguridad a la región.

to **bring someone into line** hacer meter en vereda a alguien ■ hacer entrar en vereda a alguien ■ poner a alguien a raya

to **bring someone to justice** dejar a alguien en manos de la justicia

to **bring someone up to speed** mejorar el rendimiento de alguien ■ poner a alguien al día ■ poner a alguien al corriente

to **bring something downstairs** bajar algo

to **bring something on** ■ to bring on something provocar algo ■ causar algo ■ desatar algo ■ originar algo ➤ What brought this on? ¿Qué ha provocado esto? ➤ I wonder what brought that on. Me pregunto qué provocó aquello. ■ Me pregunto qué desató aquello.

to **bring something on oneself** buscárselo uno mismo ➤ He brought it on himself. Se lo buscó.

to **bring something to a boil** poner algo a hervir ■ llevar algo a punto de ebullición ■ poner algo a cocer ■ llevar algo a punto de cocción ■ darle un hervor ➤ Wash the carrots and zucchinis, and bring them to a boil in the broth together with the garlic cloves. Limpie las zanahorias y los calabacines y déles un hervor en el caldo junto a los dientes de ajo.

to **bring something to a close** ■ to bring to an end ■ to end dar por concluido ➤ Portuguese voters have brought the socialist period to a close with the narrow victory of the Social Democrats. Los votantes portugueses han dado por concluido un ciclo socialista con el ajustado triunfo de los socialdemócratas.

to **bring something to a head** llevar algo a un punto crítico ■ llevar algo a un estado crítico

to **bring something to an end** ■ to bring something to a close ■ to end something dar por concluido

to **bring something to bear on something** movilizar algo para presionar en algo ➤ The full weight of European diplomacy was brought to bear on the trade issue. Todo el peso de la diplomacia europea se movilizó para presionar en el asunto del comercio.

to **bring something to life** dar algo a la vida ▪ animar algo ▪ volver a la vida algo ➤ Grandma Moses' paintings bring to life American Christmases of the nineteenth century. Las pinturas de Grandma Moses dan vida a las Navidades norteamericanas del siglo diecinueve.

to **bring something to light** ▪ to reveal something ▪ to discover something sacar algo a la luz

to **bring something to mind** traer algo a la memoria

to **bring something to one's attention** llamar algo a la atención de alguien

to **bring something upstairs (with one)** subir(te) algo ➤ Hey, honey, bring the newspaper upstairs with you. Cariño, súbete el periódico.

to **bring something with one** traerse algo ➤ I brought these turrones with me from Spain. Me traje estos turrones de España. ➤ He brought it with him. Se lo trajo.

bring that back here! *(tú)* ¡trae eso aquí! ▪ *(usted)* ¡traiga (usted) eso aquí! ➤ Bring that back here! The waiter took the salt shaker. ¡Trae eso aquí! El camarero se llevó el salero.

to **bring the audience to its feet** levantar al público de sus asientos

to **bring the news that** conocerse la noticia de que

bring them on! ¡que vengan!

bring them to a boil déles un hervor ▪ llévelos a ebullición ▪ póngalos a hervir ➤ Bring it to a boil, stirring occasionally. Déle un hervor, removiendo de vez en cuando. ▪ Llevarlo a ebullición, removiendo de vez en cuando.

to **bring things to a head** llevar las cosas a un punto crítico ▪ llevar las cosas a un estado crítico ➤ The expulsion of the early Christians from the temple, and the spreading out of the church from Jerusalem, brought things to a head. La expulsión de los primeros cristianos del templo, y la expansión de la iglesia de Jerusalén, llevaron las cosas a un punto crítico.

to **bring traffic to a halt** ▪ to halt traffic ▪ to snarl traffic colapsar el tráfico ▪ parar el tráfico ▪ detener el tráfico

to **bring up a child** criar un niño

to **bring up a grade** ▪ to bring a grade up subir una nota ▪ subir una calificación ➤ She gave students the opportunity to take a second exam to bring up their grade. Dio a los estudiantes la oportunidad de hacer un segundo examen para subir la nota.

to **bring up a matter for discussion** plantear un asunto de debate ▪ poner un asunto sobre el tapete ➤ I can't bring it up now; it's the wrong time. No puedo plantearlo ahora; es mal momento.

to **bring up a question** suscitar una pregunta ➤ That brings up a question. Eso suscita una pregunta.

to **bring up a subject** ▪ to bring a subject up ▪ to first mention a subject ▪ to be the first to mention a subject sacar un tema ▪ sacar un tema a colación **2.** to propose ▪ to bring up for discussion plantear un tema ➤ You brought it up!-I did not! ¡Tú lo has sacado!-¡No he sido yo! ➤ I can't bring it up now; it's the wrong time. No puedo plantearlo ahora; es el mal momento.

to **bring up a subject for discussion** ▪ to bring a subject up for discussion sacar un tema ▪ plantear un asunto ➤ Why don't you bring it up at the next meeting? ¿Por qué no lo planteas en la próxima reunión?

to **bring up children** ▪ to raise children criar niños

to **bring up one's grades** ▪ to bring one's grades up ▪ to improve one's grades subir sus notas ▪ subir sus calificaciones

to **bring up someone** ▪ to bring someone up ▪ to raise someone criar a alguien ▪ educar a alguien ➤ After his parents died, he was brought up by his godparents. Después de que sus padres murieron, fue criado por sus padrinos. ➤ His godparents brought him up. ▪ His godparents raised him. Sus padrinos le educaron.

to **bring up something from downstairs** ▪ to bring something up from downstairs subir(se) algo de abajo ➤ Would you bring the newspaper upstairs? ¿Puedes subir el periódico? *(Spanish prefers "can" rather than the conditional "would" in this case.)* ➤ Would you bring the newspaper up with you? ¿Puedes subirte el periódico? ➤ Would you bring it up with you? ¿Puedes subírtelo?

to **bring up the subject** sacar el tema ▪ mencionar la cuestión ➤ It was Lee who finally brought up the subject of the surrender to Grant. Fue Lee quien sacó el tema de la rendición a Grant.

brink of war: to be on the ~ estar al borde de la guerra ▪ estar al filo de la guerra

brink of war: to bring a country to the ~ llevar a un país al borde de la guerra ▪ llevar a un país al filo de la guerra

British Isles Islas Británicas

to **broach a subject** abordar un tema (espinoso)

broad brush ▪ lacking in specifics trazo grueso ➤ Her editorial positions are pretty broad brush. Sus posiciones editoriales son de trazo grueso.

broad outlines líneas maestras ➤ The broad outlines of the movie are accurate, but Hollywood has taken some license with the specifics. Las líneas maestras de la película son correctas, pero Hollywood se ha tomado alguna licencia con los detalles.

to be **broad shouldered** ▪ to have broad shoulders ser ancho de espaldas ▪ tener espaldas anchas

broadband satellite dish antena parabólica de banda ancha

to **broadcast a program** retransmitir un programa

to **broadcast a secret** contar un secreto a los cuatro vientos ➤ Did you have to broadcast it all over the school? ¿Tenías que contarlo a los cuatro vientos por todo el instituto?

to **broaden one's horizons** ▪ to expand one's horizons ampliar los horizontes ▪ ensanchar los horizontes

to be **broader in scope** ser de más amplio alcance

to **broadside someone with a criticism** dar un golpe abajo

to **broadside someone with an unfair question** dar un golpe abajo

to **broadside a vehicle** ▪ to hit a vehicle from the side golpear un vehículo de costado ➤ The car was broadsided by a drunken driver. El coche fue golpeado de costado por un conductor ebrio.

broccoli stem tallo de(l) brócoli

broccoli tops hojas de brócoli ▪ *(Sp.)* hojas de brécol

to be **broke** ▪ to be penniless estar a dos velas ▪ estar seco ▪ estar sin blanca ▪ estar sincero ▪ estar planchado ▪ *(Mex., coll.)* estar sin lana

to be **broken all to pieces** estar hecho trizas ▪ estar hecho añicos ▪ *(crackers, cookies)* estar hecho migas ▪ estar hecho migajas ➤ I bought a box of crackers, and when I opened them up they were broken all to pieces. Compré una caja de galletitas saladas, y cuando la abrí, estaban hechas migas.

to be **broken by** ▪ to be interrupted by romperse en ▪ ser roto por ➤ The darkness was broken by flashes of lightning. La oscuridad se rompió en relámpagos. ➤ The dreamy silence was broken by the sound of reindeer pawing on the roof. El silencio soñador fue roto por el ruido de unos renos tocando el tejado con sus patas.

to be **broken down 1.** *(car)* to be dilapidated estar destartalado **2.** to be itemized estar detallado

broken English inglés chapurreado

broken heart corazón roto ▪ corazón partido

broken home hogar desecho

to be **broken off 1.** interrumpirse **2.** romperse un trozo de algo **3.** desprenderse ▪ soltarse ▪ caerse ➤ The negotiations were broken off. Las negociaciones se interrumpieron. ➤ This piece is broken off of this table; can it be glued back on? Esta pieza de la mesa se ha roto. ¿Se puede volver a pegar?

broken promise promesa rota

to be a **broken record** parecer un disco rallado ▪ contar siempre la misma canción ➤ He's like a broken record. Parece un disco rallado. ▪ Cuenta siempre la misma canción.

broken Spanish español chapurreado

to be **broken up 1.** *(eletronic transmission)* haber interferencias **2.** *(sound)* estar entrecortado ▪ oírse entrecortado **3.** to be distraught estar destrozado (emocionalmente) ➤ I can barely hear you. The line is broken up. Casi no te puedo oír. Hay interferencias en la línea. ➤ The connection is bad. Your voice is breaking up. La conexión es mala. Tu voz se oye entrecortada. ➤ The mother was really broken up over her daughter's divorce. La madre estaba destrozada por el divorcio de su hija.

to **broker a peace** mediar en una paz ➤ *(editorial)* Aznar, as president of the European Union, might be exactly the right person to broker a Middle East peace. Aznar, como presidente de la Unión Europea, podría ser justo la persona adecuada para mediar en la paz del Oriente Medio.
to **broker an agreement** mediar en un acuerdo
Bronze Age *la* edad de los metales
brotherly love *el* amor fraternal
to be **brought before a judge** presentarse ante un(-a) juez(-a) ➤ The accused man was brought before the judge. El acusado se presentó ante la jueza.
to be **brought in on a stretcher** traer en una camilla ➤ The victim was brought in on a stretcher. Trajeron a la víctima en camilla.
to be **brought in on a tray** ser traído en una bandeja ➤ The canapés were brought in on silver platters by waiters in livery. Los canapés fueron traídos en bandejas de plata por camareros en librea.
to be **brought into question** ■ to be called into question ponerse en duda ■ traerse a colación
to be **brought on by** estar ocasionado por
brought to you by...: this program has been ~ este programa ha sido patrocinado por... ■ este programa se les ofrece...
brought to you live from Madison Square Garden en directo desde el Madison Square Garden
to be **brought up in luxury** estar criado entre algodones
brown dwarf *(astronomy)* enana marrón
brown eyes ojos castaños ■ ojos marrones ■ ojos negros
brown paper ■ manila paper papel madera ■ papel de estraza
brown rice *el* arroz integral
brownie points: to get ~ recibir favoritismos
to **brownnose someone** *(off-color)* ■ to butter up someone ■ to butter someone up lamerle el culo a alguien ■ *(benign alternative)* hacerle la pelota a alguien
to be a **brownnoser** *(off-color)* ■ to be an apple polisher ■ to be a bootlicker ser un(-a) lameculos ■ *(benign alternatives)* ser un(-a) pelota ■ ser un(-a) adulón(a) ■ ser un(-a) lamesuelas ■ ser un(-a) chupamedias ■ chuparle las medias a alguien ■ *(Mex.)* hacerle la barba a alguien
brunt of his forces grueso de sus fuerzas
to **brush away something** ■ to brush something away quitar algo (con un cepillo) ➤ *(James Whitcomb Riley poem)* Little Orphan Annie brushed the crumbs away. ■ Little Orphan Annie brushed away the crumbs. Annie la huerfanita quitaba las migas (con un cepillo). ➤ She brushed them away. Ella las barría.
brush fire 1. incendio de maleza **2.** *(for the purpose of controlled burning of weeds and brush)* quema de abrojos ➤ Everyone hopes there won't be any brush fires this summer. Se espera que no haya incendios de maleza este verano.
brush off: to give someone the ~ dar calabazas a alguien
to **brush off a suit** cepillar un traje
to **brush off an incident** ■ to brush an incident off dejar pasar un incidente ■ restar importancia a un incidente ➤ He brushed it off. Lo dejó pasar. ■ Lo restó importancia.
to **brush one's hair** cepillarse el pelo
to **brush one's teeth** cepillarse los dientes ■ lavarse los dientes
to **brush up (on) something** poner algo al día ■ ponerse al día con algo ➤ Mayte wants to brush up (on) her English before going to the United States. Mayte quiere poner su inglés al día antes de ir a los Estados Unidos. ■ Mayte quiere ponerse al día con su inglés antes de ir a los Estados Unidos.
brush with death *el* roce con la muerte
brush with failure *el* roce con el fracaso
brush with someone: to have a ~ tener un roce con alguien
brush with the law: to have a ~ *el* tener un roce con la policía ■ tener un roce con la ley ■ tener un encuentro con la policía ■ tener un encuentro con la ley
brushstroke pincelada
bubble gum chicle globo
bubbles: to blow ~ *(with bubble gum)* hacer globos (con el chicle) ■ *(with soap bubbles)* hacer pompitas de jabón
bubbles: to make ~ 1. *(washing machine)* to produce bubbles hacer espuma **2.** *(sparkling wine)* to fizz ■ to give off bubbles hacer burbujas
to **buck a trend** resistirse a la moda
bucket of bolts ■ beat-up car ■ rattletrap ■ rolling ghetto tartana ■ chatarra
bucket of ice cubo de hielo ➤ Would you send a bucket of ice (up) to our room? ¿Nos subiría un cubo de hielo a la habitación?
bucket of paint cubo de pintura ■ *el* tambor de pintura
to **buckle down** centrarse ➤ Now buckle down and get to work! Ahora céntrate y ponte a trabajar. ➤ I need to buckle down and get to work. Necesito centrarme y ponerme a trabajar.
buckle of a belt ■ belt buckle hebilla
to **buckle one's seat belt** ■ to buckle one's safety belt abrochar el cinturón de seguridad
to **buckle under** ceder
buckle up! ¡abróchate el cinturón!
budding musician músico(-a) en ciernes
budget cut recorte presupuestario
to **budget one's time** organizar el tiempo ➤ I need to budget my time better. Necesito organizar mi tiempo mejor.
budget surplus: with a ~ ■ in the black con un excedente (de dinero) ■ con un superávit ➤ The company finished the year with a surplus of five million dollars. La compañía acabó el año con un superávit de cinco millones de dólares. ➤ The company finished the year with a surplus. La compañía acabó el año con superávit.
to **buff off something** ■ to buff something off pulir algo ■ limar algo ■ abrillantar algo ➤ The cap of the tooth needs to be buffed off a little. La funda del diente necesita ser limada un poco. ➤ The dentist buffed it off. El dentista la desbastó.
buffing wheel ■ buffer **1.** *(in a machine shop)* desbastadora ■ rueda pulidora ■ rodillo pulidor **2.** *(used by dentists)* torno pulidor
to **bug a telephone** pinchar un teléfono
to be **bug-eyed** ■ to have protruding eyes ■ to have bulging eyes tener ojos saltones ■ tener ojos de sapo ■ tener ojos reventones
bug eyes ■ protruding eyes ■ *(coll.)* pop eyes ojos saltones ■ ojos de sapo ■ ojos reventones
bug in a computer program fallo en un programa de computadora ■ error en un programa de computadora ■ defecto en programa de computadora
to **bug someone 1.** to pester someone picarlo(-a) a alguien ■ chinchar a alguien ■ tocar las narices a alguien ■ molestar a alguien ■ irritar a alguien ■ *(off-color, but common)* tocar los cojones a alguien ■ tocar los huevos a alguien ■ tocar las pelotas a alguien ■ tocar la polla a alguien ➤ What's bugging him? ¿Qué mosca le habrá picado?
bugging device ■ bug escucha
to **build a bridge 1.** *(literal)* construir un puente **2.** *(figurative)* tender un puente
to **build a fence around someone** levantar un muro para proteger a alguien ■ levantar una barda para proteger a alguien ➤ The secretary builds a fence around her boss. La secretaria ha levantado un muro para proteger a su jefe. ■ Ella levantó una barda para proteger a su jefe.
to **build a fire** ■ to make a fire ■ to get a fire going preparar un fuego ■ hacer fuego ➤ I need to build a fire in the fireplace before the company comes. Necesito preparar un fuego en la chimenea antes de que vengan los invitados.
to **build a fire under someone** ponerle las pilas a alguien ■ apretar las clavijas a alguien
to **build a future for oneself** labrarse un porvenir ➤ I'm trying to build a future for myself. Trato de labrarme un porvenir.
to **build bridges between 1.** *(literal)* construir puentes entre **2.** *(figurative)* tender puentes entre ➤ The diplomats are trying to build bridges between India and Pakistan. Los diplomáticos están intentando tender puentes entre India y Pakistan.
to **build castles in the air** hacer castillos en el aire ■ hacer castillos de arena
to **build character** imprimir carácter
to **build in** empotrar en ■ incorporar

to **build morale** infundir moral ➤ Blair visited the British troops overseas to build morale. Blair visitó a la tropas británicas de ultramar para infundir moral.

build of a person ▪ constitution of a person físico de una persona ▪ *la* complexión de una persona ➤ He has a strong build. ▪ He has a good build. ▪ He has a strong constitution. Tiene una complexión fuerte. ▪ Es de fuerte complexión.

to **build on 1.** construir (algo) sobre **2.** *(figurative)* atenerse a algo ➤ *(political platitude)* A record is not something to stand on, it's something to build on. Un historial de éxitos no es algo en lo que quedarse, es algo sobre lo que construir. ➤ I wouldn't worry about not feeling guilty about the affair, just make your decision and build on it. Yo no me preocuparía por no sentirme culpable por lo de tu amante, sencillamente toma tu decisión y atente a ella.

to **build one's practice** ▪ to build up one's practice establecerse por su cuenta ▪ establecerse por cuenta propia

to **build onto a house** añadir a una casa ➤ They built a garage and a den onto their house. Añadieron un garage y un cuarto de estar a la casa.

to **build something back** ▪ to rebuild something reconstruir ▪ volver a construir ➤ After the earthquake of 1755 knocked down the left tower of the cathedral in Valladolid, they didn't rebuild it. Después de que el terremoto de 1755 derribara la torre izquierda de la catedral de Valladolid, no la volvieron a construir. ▪ Después de que el terremoto de 1755 derribara la torre izquierda de la catedral de Valladolid, no la reconstruyeron.

to **build toward** *(historical or fictional narrative)* estar encaminado hacia ➤ The whole movie builds toward a scene that it omits. Toda la película está encaminado hacia una escena que acaba por omitir.

to **build up 1.** to accumulate acumularse **2.** to increase aumentar ➤ This dental rinse keeps plaque from building up. Este colutorio evita que la placa se acumule. ➤ The pressure on the government is building (up). La presión sobre el gobierno aumenta.

to **build up a fortune** ▪ to amass a fortune amasar una fortuna ➤ He built up a fortune by perseverance and hard work. Amasó una fortuna con perseverancia y duro trabajo.

to **build up fortifications** ▪ to build fortifications up levantar fortificaciones ▪ levantar fortines ▪ levantar fuertes ➤ The army is building up its fortifications around the perimeter of the city. El ejército está levantando sus fortines a lo largo del perímetro de la ciudad.

to **build up one's business** ▪ to build one's business up ▪ to expand one's business ampliar el negocio ➤ We have built up our business. ▪ We have built our business up. Hemos ampliado nuestro negocio. ➤ We have built it up. Lo hemos ampliado.

to **build up one's practice** ▪ to build one's practice up ▪ to expand one's practice *(doctors, lawyers, architects, etc.)* ampliar el negocio ▪ ampliar la actividad profesional ▪ crecer profesionalmente

to **build up security forces** ▪ to build security forces up fortalecer los efectivos de seguridad ➤ The government has built up the security forces. El gobierno ha fortalecido los efectivos de seguridad.

building blocks of life ▪ essential components of life *los* componentes esenciales de la vida

building materials *los* materiales de construcción

to be **built around** estar construído en torno a ➤ The whole movie is built around a scene that it omits. Toda la película está construida en torno a una escena que acaba por omitir.

to be **built in** estar empotrado ▪ estar incorporado ➤ La caja fuerte está empotrada. The safe is built in.

built-in obsolescence (of a product) duración media (de un producto) prevista por el fabricante

to be **built into the wall** estar empotrado en la pared ▪ estar incorporado en la pared

the **bulk of** el grueso de ➤ The bulk of the estate went to the grandchildren. El grueso de la propiedad fue a los nietos.

to be a **bull in a china shop** ser como un elefante en una cacharrería

bullet through the chest bala que le atraviesa el pecho ➤ The Red Baron's plane crashed after he was struck by a single bullet through the chest. El avión del Barón Rojo se estrelló tras recibir el piloto una única bala que le atravesó el pecho.

bulletin board *el* tablón de anuncios

bulletproof vest chaleco antibalas

bullfight: to go to a ~ ir a la corrida de toros

bullfighter's cap *(black, worn as part of the suit of lights)* montera

bullfighter's hat *(gray, brimmed hat worn by the mounted bullfighter who uses a lance)* sombrero andaluz

bullfighter's suit ▪ suit of lights *el* traje de luces

bull's-eye: to hit the ~ dar en el blanco

bullshit! *(off-color)* ▪ nonsense! ¡qué gilipollez! ▪ ¡vaya gilipollez! ▪ ¡gilipolleces! ▪ *(benign alternative)* ¡chorradas!

bullshit excuse *(off-color)* excusa de mierda ▪ *(benign alternative)* porquería de excusa

to **bum a cigarette** ▪ to mooch a cigarette off someone gorronear un cigarrillo

bum steer: to give someone a ~ *(coll.)* dar a alguien malas indicaciones ▪ dar a alguien malas direcciones ▪ indicar mal ▪ dirigir mal ➤ He gave us a bum steer. Nos indicó mal.

bum wrap: to get a ~ *(coll.)* comerse un marrón

bum wrap: to give someone a ~ *(coll.)* meterle un marrón a alguien ▪ echarle un marrón a alguien

to be **bummed out** estar depre ▪ estar chungo

to **bump into someone 1.** to collide with someone chocarse con alguien ▪ darse con alguien **2.** to chance to see someone ▪ to run into someone toparse con alguien ▪ encontrarse con alguien **3.** *(both literal and figurative)* darse de narices con alguien ➤ I bumped into Elisa at the market yesterday. ▪ I collided with Elisa at the market yesterday. (Me) choqué con Elisa en el mercado ayer. ➤ I bumped into Elisa at the market yesterday. ▪ I met Elisa by chance at the market yesterday. Me encontré con Elisa ayer en el mercado. ➤ I bumped into Elisa at the market yesterday. Me di de bruces con Elisa ayer en el mercado.

to **bump into something 1.** to hit something golpearse con algo ▪ chocarse con algo ▪ pegarse (un golpe) con algo **2.** to hit on darse un golpe con algo ▪ toparse con algo **3.** to run into encontarse con algo ➤ I bumped into the table and bruised my hip. Me golpeé con la mesa y se me hizo un moratón en la cadera. ➤ The cyst on his arm was caused by bumping into the door handles. Se le había formado un quiste en el brazo por chocarse con las manijas de las puertas. ➤ When I speak Spanish, I bump into things I can't say. Cuando hablo español me topo con cosas que no sé decir.

to **bump off someone** ▪ to bump someone off ▪ to murder someone dar el pasaporte a alguien ▪ achicharrar a alguien ▪ despachar a alguien

bump on the head testarazo ▪ el chichón

to **bump one's head** ▪ to hit one's head darse un coscorrón ▪ darse una testarazo ➤ I bumped my head on the door frame. ▪ I hit my head on the door frame. Me he dado un coscorrón en el marco de la puerta.

to **bump something** chocar con algo ▪ dar con algo ▪ *(on the computer keyboard)* rozar una tecla ➤ I hate it when I bump something, and the whole damn computer goes haywire. Detesto cuando rozo una tecla y toda la maldita computadora se hace una locura. ▪ Detesto cuando rozo una tecla y toda la maldita computadora se echa a perder. ▪ *(Spain)* Detesto cuando rozo una tecla y toda el maldita ordenador se vuelve una locura. ▪ Detesto cuando rozo una tecla y todo el maldito ordenador se echa a perder.

to be **bumped around** ser llevado a trompicones

bumped around: to get ~ ▪ to get jostled around llevarse trompicones ▪ recibir trompicones

bumper cars coches de choque

bumper sticker pegatina

bumpy ride ▪ rough ride **1.** viaje escabroso ▪ viaje accidentado **2.** difficult time mala racha ➤ It's a bumpy ride from Madrid to Cuenca on the train. De Madrid a Cuenca en tren es un viaje muy escabroso. ➤ When I lost my job, I had a bumpy ride there for a while. Cuando perdí mi trabajo, pasé por una mala racha.

bumpy road *(literal and figurative)* ■ rough road camino fragoso ■ camino de cabras ■ camino pedregoso ■ camino de piedras ■ camino accidentado

bunch of books *(coll.)* ■ barrage of books ■ string of books ■ flood of books ■ abundance of books ■ *(literary)* plethora of books rosario de libros

bunch of grapes racimo de uvas

bunch of hooey ■ bunch of nonsense ■ word salad un sinsentido ■ un despropósito ■ tonterías

to be a **bunch of hot air** ser palabrería

a **bunch of idiots** un montón de idiotas

bunch of spoiled brats atajo de niñatos

bunch of stuff to do: to have a ~ *(coll.)* ■ to have a lot (of things) to do tener que hacer la tira de cosas ➤ I've got a bunch of stuff to do to get ready. Tengo que hacer la tira de cosas para prepararme.

to **bunch them** *(coll.)* ■ to lump them all together meter a todos en el mismo carro ■ meter a todos en el mismo saco ➤ *(H.L. Mencken)* A man remembers his first love with special tenderness, but after that he begins to bunch them. Un hombre recuerda a su primer amor con especial ternura, pero después empieza a meterlos todos en el mismo carro. ■ Un hombre recuerda a su primer amor con especial ternura, pero después empieza a meterlos todos en el mismo saco.

to be a **bundle of nerves** ■ to be a nervous wreck estar hecho un manojo de nervios ■ ser un manojo de nervios

to **bundle up** *(in an overcoat)* arrebujarse

Bunsen burner *(chemistry)* mechero (de) Bunsen ■ mechero de alcohol

burden of proof carga de la prueba ■ peso de la prueba ➤ The burden of proof lies with the accuser. Quien acusa lleva la carga de la prueba.

the **burden of proof is on the accuser** aportar la pruebas es la responsabilidad del acusador

to be a **burden on society** ser una carga para la sociedad ■ ser un peso para la sociedad ■ ser un lastre para la sociedad

to be a **burden on the government** ser una carga para el gobierno ■ ser un peso para el gobierno ■ ser un lastre para el gobierno

bureaucratic mill *(coll.)* trama burocrática ■ entramado burocrático ■ procedimiento burocrático ■ burocracia ➤ The bureaucratic mill could take months. La trama burocrática podría llevar meses. ■ El entramado burocrático podría llevar meses.

to be **buried in (one's) work** estar enfrascado en (su) trabajo

to **burn a hole in one's pocket** quemarle el bolsillo ■ tener un agujero en el bolsillo ➤ Money burns a hole in his pocket. El dinero le quema en el bolsillo. ■ Tiene un agujero en el bolsillo.

to **burn a hole in something** hacer un agujero (quemando) ➤ He burned a hole in his suit with his cigarette. Se hizo un agujero en el traje con un cigarrillo.

to **burn down 1.** *(building)* to burn to the ground arder hasta los cimientos ■ quemarse **2.** *(candle)* consumirse ➤ The barn burned down after it was struck by lightning. El granero ardió (hasta los cimientos) después de que le cayera un rayo. ➤ The candle has burned down. La vela se ha consumido.

to **burn off** *(fog)* ■ to dissipate ■ to lift retirarse ■ disiparse ■ levantarse ➤ The morning fog burns off the San Francisco Bay by 11 a.m. ■ The morning fog on the San Francisco Bay dissipates by 11 a.m. ■ The San Francisco Bay's morning fog lifts by 11 a.m. La niebla matinal se retira de la Bahía de San Francisco hacia las once de la mañana. ■ La niebla matinal de la Bahía de San Francisco se disipa hacia las once de la mañana. ■ La niebla matinal de la Bahía de San Francisco se levanta para las once de la mañana.

to **burn one's bridges (behind one)** quemar las naves ■ desapegarse de alguien ➤ Don't burn your bridges (behind you). No quemes las naves. ■ Que no quemes las naves. ➤ He's burned his bridges with his family. Él se ha desapegado de la familia.

to **burn out 1.** *(lightbulb)* fundirse **2.** *(star)* consumirse ➤ The lightbulb burned out. La bombilla se fundió. ➤ Big stars are too hot and burn out too quickly for advanced life to evolve on the planets around them. La grandes estrellas están demasiado calientes y se consumen demasiado rápido como para que la vida evolucionada prospere en los planetas de alrededor.

to **burn someone at the stake** quemar a alguien en la hoguera

to **burn someone up** ■ to make someone indignant sacar a alguien de sus casillas ■ sacar a alguien de quicio ■ hacer perder los estribos a alguien ■ cabrear a alguien ■ *(off-color)* poner a alguien de mala hostia ➤ It burns me up that the space program has a higher priority than national health insurance. Me saca de mis casillas que el programa espacial tenga mayor prioridad que la sanidad nacional.

to **burn something to a crisp** chamuscar algo ➤ They burned these pork rinds to a crisp. Han chamuscado estas cortezas. ■ Han chamuscado los pellejos del cerdo.

to **burn the candle at both ends** hacer de la noche día ■ andar de cabeza

to **burn the midnight oil** quemarse las cejas

to **burn to death** morir carbonizado ■ morir calcinado ■ morir abrasado

to **burn up** *(intransitive verb)* **1.** to swelter ■ to feel miserably hot asarse vivo ■ estar asándose **2.** to be consumed by fire arder hasta consumirse ➤ I'm burning up. Me aso (vivo). ■ Me estoy asando. ➤ The woods burned up. El bosque ardió hasta consumirse.

to **burn up something** *(transitive verb)* to burn something up *(transitive)* quemar hasta consumirse ➤ He burned the papers up in the fire. ■ He burned up the papers in the fire. Quemó los papeles hasta que se consumieron. ➤ He burned them up. Los quemó hasta que se consumieron. ■ Los quemó hasta que se volvieron cenizas.

to **burn up the pavement** ■ to pound the pavement ■ to beat the pavement ■ to hunt for a job patearse la calle

to be **burned at the stake** morir en la hoguera

to be **burned to a crisp 1.** to be charred from overcooking estar chamuscado **2.** to get badly sunburned darse una tremenda quemadura de sol ■ darse una tremenda asoleada ➤ These pork rinds are burned to a crisp. Estas cortezas están chamuscadas. ➤ I got burned to a crisp at the beach. Me di una tremenda quemadura de sol en la playa. ■ Me di una tremenda asoleada en la playa.

burned to a crisp: to get ~ chamuscarse ➤ At the beach yesterday, I got burned to a crisp. Ayer en la playa me chamusqué.

to be **burned to death** estar calcinado(-a) ■ estar carbonizado(-a)

burner of a stove *el* quemador

burning bush *(from the Book of Exodus)* arbusto ardiente

burning sun *el* sol abrasador

burnout: to suffer from ~ *(coll.)* estar extenuado(-a)

to **burp the baby** hacer eructar al bebé

to **burrow into the ground** escarbar en el suelo

to **burrow into the skin** escarbar en la piel

to **burrow under the ground** escarbar bajo el suelo

to **burrow under the skin** escarbar bajo la piel

burst: the blood vessel ~ el vaso sanguíneo se rompió

burst: the bubble ~ la burbuja explotó ■ la burbuja se reventó

burst: the dam ~ la presa reventó

to **burst at the seams** estar lleno de bote en bote ■ estar que ya no cabe un alfiler ■ *(literal, when a dress is too small)* reventar por las costuras

to **burst a balloon** ■ to pop a balloon explotar un globo

to **burst a bubble** ■ to pop a bubble reventar una burbuja ■ *(bubble gum)* reventar un globo de chicle

to **burst into a room** ■ to rush into a room ■ to enter a room abruptly irrumpir en un cuarto ➤ I burst into the kitchen and said, "Guess who I just saw?" Irrumpí en la cocina y dije, "¡Adivina a quién he visto!"

to **burst into flames** estallar en llamas

to **burst into tears** ■ to start crying saltársele a alguien las lágrimas ■ saltarle las lágrimas ■ romper en llanto ■ prorrumpir en llantos ■ romper a llorar ■ soltar el llanto

burst of adrenalin ■ rush of adrenalin descarga de adrenalina ■ *el* subidón de adrenalina

burst of color estallido de color

burst of energy estallido de energía ■ descarga de energía

burst of gunfire ráfaga de tiros ▪ ráfaga de disparos
burst of inspiration ráfaga de inspiración
to **burst (out) into brilliant colors** ▪ to burst with brilliant colors reventar en colores brillantes
to **burst out laughing** estallar en carcajadas ▪ romper a reír ▪ echarse a reír
to **burst upon the scene** irrumpir en escena
to be **bursting at the seams** estar como piojos en costura
to be **bursting to do something** estar que se muere por hacer algo
to be **bursting with energy** estar desbordante de energía ▪ estar rebosante de energía
to be **bursting with enthusiasm** estar desbordante de entusiasmo ▪ estar rebosante de entusiasmo
to be **bursting with pride** estar rebosante de orgullo ▪ no caber dentro de sí de orgullo ▪ estar derrochando orgullo ▪ estar pavoneándose de orgullo ▪ estar como un pavo real de orgullo
to **bury one's face in one's hands** hundir el rostro entre las manos
to **bury the hatchet** hacer las paces ▪ echar pelillos a la mar
bus fare tarifa del autobús
bus for ▪ bus to autobús para ▪ autobús a
bus from autobús (que viene) de ▪ autobús que viene desde
bus pass *el* bónobus
bus schedule horario de los autobuses
bus to ▪ bus for *el* autobús a ▪ autobús para
business as usual: to be (just) ~ ser el plan nuestro de cada día ▪ ser la historia de siempre
business appointment cita de negocios
business attire ropa de negocios ▪ atuendo de negocios
business dealings tratos de negocio
business hours: during durante el horario de comercio ▪ durante las horas de comercio ▪ durante las horas laborales
business is booming el negocio sube como la espuma
business is down ▪ business is off el negocio va a la baja ▪ el negocio va a peor
business is good el negocio va bien
business is off ▪ business is down el negocio va a la baja ▪ el negocio va a peor
business is picking up el negocio remonta
business is prospering el negocio prospera
business has been good lately el negocio va bien últimamente
business has been lousy lately *(coll.)* ▪ business has been bad lately el negocio va de pena últimamente
business partner socio
business sense sentido comercial ▪ olfato comercial
business tycoon *el* magnate
business world: in the ~ en el mundo de los negocios
to **bust one's ass** *(mildly off-color)* ▪ to bust one's butt ▪ to bust one's tail ▪ to work one's ass off partirse el culo de trabajo ▪ partirse el culo trabajando
to **bust someone in the mouth** *(coll.)* partirle la boca a alguien
to **bustle about a place** ajetrearse en un lugar ➤ The elves were bustling about Santa's workshop. Los elfos se ajetreaban en el taller de Papa Noel.
to **bustle with activity** bullir de actividad
to **bustle with energy** bullir de energía
to **bustle with excitement** bullir de excitación
bustling city bulliciosa ciudad
bustling street bulliciosa calle
to be **busy as a bee** estar ocupado como una abeja ▪ estar hacendoso(-a)
busy person persona ocupada
busy restaurant restaurante concurrido ➤ This restaurant is very busy. Este restaurante está muy concurrido.
busy signal: to get a ~ sonar ocupado ▪ *(Sp.)* recibir la señal de comunicando ▪ estar comunicando ➤ It's busy. ▪ The line's busy. Está comunicando.
busy street calle muy transitada ▪ calle concurrida ➤ One of the busiest streets in the city Una de las calles más concurridas de la ciudad
but also sino también ▪ sino que ▪ pero también
but anyway pero en cualquier caso ▪ pero de todas formas
but are siendo
but even sino que
but hardly si apenas
but here's the thing ▪ but here's my issue pero ésta es la cosa
but I didn't pero no lo hice
but I could say the same thing si yo pudiera decir lo mismo
but I couldn't **1.** pero no pude **2.** pero no podía **3.** pero no podría ➤ I wanted to go, but I couldn't. Quería ir pero no pude. ➤ My drill sergeant told me to run faster, but I couldn't. Mi sargento instructor me decía que corriera más rápido, pero yo no podía. ➤ My little sister swipes cookies from grandma's cookie jar, but I (just) couldn't. Mi hermanita menor se robaba galletas del tarro de la abuela, pero yo (sencillamente) no podía. ➤ She's always flirting with all the men, but I couldn't. Ella siempre está coqueteando con todos los hombres, pero yo no podría hacerlo.
but I couldn't (even) if my life depended on it pero yo no podría (ni) aunque mi vida dependiera de ello ▪ pero yo no podría por más que mi vida dependiera de ello
but I didn't mean to pero no quería ▪ (pero) si no quería
but I do pero yo, sí ▪ pero a mí, sí ▪ yo, sí ▪ a mí, sí ▪ *(Mex.)* cuando a mí, sí ➤ I don't like hamburgers.-But I do. No me gustan las hamburguesas.-Pero a mí, sí. ▪ No me gustan las hamburguesas.-Cuando a mí, sí.
but I don't want to pero no quiero hacerlo ▪ es que no quiero hacerlo
but if I am pero de estarlo ▪ pero de serlo ➤ I don't know at this point if I'll be here that weekend, but if I am, count me in. No sé decirte desde ahora si estaré ese fin de semana, pero de estarlo cuenta conmigo. ➤ I don't think it's true, but if it is, I would break off the relationship with him. No creo que sea verdad eso, pero de serlo, yo cortaría con él.
but in the end pero al final
but instead pero en lugar de eso ▪ pero en vez de eso ▪ pero en cambio ▪ pero en su lugar
but is siendo ▪ pero es
but is it? ▪ but is that really the case? pero, ¿será así? ▪ pero, ¿será ése el caso?
but it does pero es así
but it doesn't pero no es así ▪ pero no... *(The verb can vary.)* ➤ That museum should interest me, I guess, but it doesn't. Supongo que ese museo debería interesarme, pero no es así. ▪ Supongo que ese museo debería interesarme, pero no me interesa.
but it is pero es así
but it's not my fault pero no es culpa mía
but I've never *been* to Paris pero no conozco Paris ▪ (pero) si no conozco Paris
but more than that ▪ but not only that pero además de eso ▪ pero aparte de eso
but neither... pero tampoco... ➤ He hasn't said yes, but neither has he said no. No ha dicho que sí, pero tampoco ha dicho que no.
but no sooner had I... pero apenas (yo) había... ▪ pero en cuanto (yo) había...
but not que no ➤ I addressed him cordially, but not necessarily as a friend. Me dirigía a él cordialmente, que no (necesariamente) como amigo.
but... not pero... no ▪ *(more formal)* no así ➤ Barions and leptons obey Pauli's principle of exclusion, but fotons and mesons do not. Los bariones y los leptones obedecen el principio de exclusión de Pauli, no así los fotones y los mesones.
but once again pero una vez más
but other than that pero además de eso
but rather sino que ▪ más bien ▪ si bien ▪ sino más bien
but rather than... pero en lugar de... ▪ pero en vez de... ➤ I felt sleepy after dinner, but rather than take a nap, I went for

a walk. Me sentí soñoliento después de la comida, pero en lugar de echarme a la cama, fui a dar un paseo.

but rather that... sino más bien que...

but still pero a la vez ▪ pero al mismo tiempo ➤ Add the chopped green pepper at the very end. You want them to be hot, but still crunchy. Añade el pimiento verde picado justo al final. Es deseable que estén calientes pero a la vez crujientes. ▪ Añade el pimiento verde picado justo al final. Es deseable que estén calientes pero al mismo tiempo crujientes.

but that was it pero se acabó

but that's about it pero nada más ➤ The Spanish have coffee and a little piece of pound cake for breakfast, but that's about it. Los españoles desayunan con café y una magdalena, pero nada más.

but then again ▪ but on the other hand pero por otra parte ➤ I like to make paella, but then again, I like to cook in general. A mi me gusta hacer paella, pero por otra parte, me gusta cocinar en general.

but to ▪ other than to más que ➤ I don't have any choice but to pay it. ▪ I don't have any choice other than to pay it. No tengo más alternativa que pagarlo.

but unquestionably... pero es indudable que...

but wait! ¡pero espérate! ▪ ¡pero un momento! ▪ ¡aunque no!

but what if... pero qué pasaría si... ▪ pero, y si...

but what was my astonishment when... *(literary)* ▪ I was astonished when... pero cuál no sería mi sorpresa cuando...

to **butcher the language** cargarse el idioma ▪ destrozar el idioma

to **butt heads** **1.** *(animals in mating and territorial battles)* darse de cabezazos el uno al otro ▪ darse de cornadas el uno al otro ▪ darse de testarazos el uno al otro **2.** *(people arguing)* contraponerse

to **butt in line** ▪ to break the line saltarse la cola ▪ colarse ➤ Please don't butt in line. No te saltes la cola, por favor. ▪ No te cueles, por favor.

to **butt into a conversation** entrometerse en una conversación

butt of the joke blanco de la puya ▪ *la* víctima de bromas

to **butter someone up** ▪ to butter up someone hacerle la pelota a alguien ▪ adular a alguien ▪ *(rare)* hacer la zalá a alguien ➤ The class buttered up the teacher. ▪ The class buttered the teacher up. La clase le hizo la pelota a la profesora. ➤ The class buttered her up. La clase le hizo la pelota.

(butter) spreader ▪ butter knife cuchillo para untar ▪ cuchillo de la mantequilla

to **butter up someone** ▪ to butter someone up hacerle la pelota a alguien ▪ *(Sp., archaic)* darle jabón a alguien

butterfly ballot papeleta mariposa

to **button a button** abrochar un botón

button-down collar cuello (de camisa) con botones

to **button (down) one's collar** abrochar el cuello

to **button one's lips** ▪ to zip one's lips echar la cremallera

to **button the collar** abrocharse el cuello ➤ I didn't wear a tie because I couldn't button the collar of this shirt. No llevé corbata porque no me podía abrochar el cuello de la camisa.

to **button up one's overcoat** abrocharse el abrigo

to **buy a chance to win the lottery** ▪ to buy a lottery ticket comprar un billete de lotería

to **buy a pig in a poke** ▪ to buy something sight unseen comprar algo a ciegas

to **buy a season ticket for...** ▪ to buy a season ticket to... abonarse a... ▪ comprarse un abono para... ➤ We bought season tickets to the symphony. Nos abonamos a la temporada sinfónica. ▪ Nos compramos un abono para la temporada sinfónica. ➤ Adolfo bought a season ticket to the bullfights. Adolfo se abonó a los toros. ▪ Adolfo se compró un abono para los toros.

to **buy groceries** ▪ to do the grocery shopping hacer la compra

buy one and get one free! ▪ get two for the price of one! ¡compre uno y llévese otro de regalo! ▪ ¡compre uno y llévese otro gratis! ▪ ¡dos por uno!

to **buy something (for oneself)** comprarse algo ➤ I bought (myself) a new car. Me he comprado un coche nuevo. ➤ I bought a new car yesterday. ▪ I bought myself a new car yesterday. Ayer me compré un coche nuevo.

to **buy something for someone** ▪ to buy someone something comprar algo para alguien ▪ comprarle algo a alguien ➤ He bought his son a car. ▪ He bought a car for his son. Compró un coche para su hijo. ▪ Le compró un coche a su hijo. ➤ He bought him a car. Le compró un coche.

to **buy something from someone** comprarle algo a alguien ➤ He bought the car from his son. ▪ His son sold him the car. Le compró el carro a su hijo. ▪ Su hijo le vendió el carro. ➤ He bought the car from the dealership. (Le) compró el carro al concesionario. ➤ He bought it from the dealership. Se lo compró al concesionario. ➤ I bought the car from the dealership. (Le) compré el carro al concesionario. ➤ I bought it from the dealership. Se lo compré al concesionario.

to **buy something on credit** comprar algo al fiado ▪ comprar algo a crédito

to **buy something on impulse** comprar a barullo ▪ comprar sin ton ni son ▪ comprar sin reflexionar

to **buy something outright** comprar algo en un solo pago ➤ Catalina financed the piano by teaching lessons, even though her husband could have bought it for her outright. Catalina financió el piano dando clases, aunque su marido se lo podía haber comprado en un solo pago.

to **buy someone a cup of coffee** invitarle a alguien a beber un café ▪ invitarle a alguien a tomar un café ➤ Come on, I'll buy you a cup of coffee. Venga, le invito a tomar un café.

buyer and seller vendedor y comprador *(literally "seller and buyer" in Spanish)*

buyer (for a store) comprador(a) al por mayor ➤ She's a buyer for a department store. Ella es compradora al por mayor para unos grandes almacenes.

buyers' market mercado a la baja

buyer's remorse: to have ~ lamentar haber comprado algo

buying power ▪ purchasing power poder adquisitivo

to **buzz like a bee** zumbar como una abeja

to **buzz like the *s* in *desde*** zumbar como la *s* de *desde*

by a majority of votes por mayoría de votos

by a majority vote por mayoría de votos

by a vote of *x* to *y* por *x* votos contra *y* / *x* votos frente a *y* ➤ *(headline)* The Constitutional Court refuses to recuse its chief justice by a vote of six to five. El Constitucional rechaza la recusación de su presidente por seis votos contra cinco.

by a wide majority ▪ by a large majority por amplia mayoría ▪ por gran mayoría

by accident **1.** by chance por casualidad **2.** absent-mindedly sin darse cuenta **3.** without meaning to sin querer **4.** carelessly a lo tonto

by air **1.** by airplane por aire ▪ vía aérea ▪ en avión **2.** by means of air por el aire ▪ gracias al aire ▪ por efecto del aire ➤ We sent the package by air. Enviamos el paquete por aire. ▪ Enviamos el paquete vía aérea. ▪ Enviamos el paquete en avión. ➤ Honolulu is six hours by air from San Francisco. Honolulu está a seis horas en avión de San Francisco. ➤ Airplanes are supported in flight by air. Los aviones se mantienen en vuelo por el aire. ▪ Los aviones se mantienen en vuelo gracias al aire. ▪ Los aviones se mantienen en vuelo por efecto del aire.

by airmail por correo aéreo ▪ por avión

by airplane ▪ by plane en avión

by all means por supuesto

by allowing doctors to see... al permitir a los médicos ver...

by and by *(southern U.S., coll.)* ▪ presently ▪ soon ▪ shortly a poco tiempo ▪ poco tiempo después

by and large a grandes rasgos ▪ en general

by any chance acaso ▪ por casualidad ▪ *(Sp.)* por un casual ➤ Did you see him, by any chance? ¿Acaso lo viste? ▪ ¿Por casualidad lo viste? ▪ *(Sp., leísmo)* ¿Por casualidad, le viste? ➤ Are you jealous, by any chance? ¿Tienes celos, por un casual? ▪ ¿Estás celoso, por un casual?

by any other name con cualquier otro nombre ➤ A rose by any other name would smell as sweet. Una rosa con cualquier otro nombre olería igual de dulce.

by any other name: to go ~ atender por (algún) otro nombre ▪ atender a (algún) otro nombre ▪ atender por algún alias

▪ atender a algún alias ➤ Does he go by any other name? ¿Atiende por (algún) otro nombre? ▪ ¿Atiende a (algún) otro nombre? ▪ ¿Atiende por algún alias? ▪ ¿Atiende a algún alias?

by any stretch of the imagination that...: not to suggest ~ ni pasarse por la imaginación sugerir que... ➤ I'm not suggesting by any stretch of the imagination that... Ni se me pasa por la imaginación sugerir que...

by appointment previa petición de hora ▪ previa petición de cita

by boat: to go ~ ir en barco

by calling for something ▪ with a call for something con un llamamiento a algo ➤ The French president opened the European Council by calling for dialogue. ▪ The French president opened the European Council with a call for dialogue. El presidente francés abrió el Consejo europeo con un llamamiento al diálogo.

by calling for something to happen con un llamamiento a que suceda algo ▪ con una llamada a que suceda algo ➤ French chief of state Jacques Chirac opened the European Council by calling for France and Germany to maintain their fundamental agreement. El jefe de estado francés, Jacques Chirac, abrió ayer el Consejo Europeo con un llamamiento a que se mantenga el acuerdo fundamental entre Francia y Alemania.

by chance por casualidad ▪ por carámbola

by choice ▪ voluntarily por propia elección ▪ por propia decisión ▪ por propia voluntad ▪ por propio deseo ▪ por gusto ➤ I'm here by choice. Estoy aquí por mi propia elección. ▪ Estoy aquí por mi propia decisión. ▪ Estoy aquí por mi propia voluntad. ▪ Estoy aquí por mi propio deseo.

by coincidence de casualidad ▪ por casualidad

by day ▪ during the day de día ▪ durante el día

by default por defecto ▪ por omisión ➤ This application is the manager of the E-mail program by default. Esta aplicación gestiona el programa de correo electrónico por defecto.

by default rather than intent porque no quedaba más remedio

by doing so ▪ in doing so ▪ in so doing ▪ in that way ▪ thereby haciendo eso ▪ de esa manera ▪ de esa forma ▪ con ese hecho ➤ According to Isaac Asimov, Galileo introduced precision measurement into experimental science, and by doing so, turned the qualitative description of the Greeks into quantitative description. Según Isaac Asimov, Galileo introdujo la medida de precisión en la ciencia experimental, y haciendo eso cambió la descripción cualitativa de los griegos por una descripción cuantitativa.

by doing something al hacer algo ▪ haciendo algo ➤ By leaving at seven forty-five, I have time for a cup of coffee before my nine o'clock class. Al marcharme a las ocho menos cuarto, tengo tiempo de tomarme un café antes de la clase de las nueve. ▪ Marchándome a las ocho menos cuarto, me da tiempo tomarme un café antes de la clase de las nueve.

by extension por extensión

by eye a ojo (de buen cubero)

by far ▪ far and away por mucho ▪ *(Sp.)* con mucho ▪ con diferencia

to be **by far the best** ▪ to be the best by far ▪ to be far and away the best ser con mucho el mejor ▪ ser el mejor con diferencia

by fits and starts ▪ in fits and starts a trompicones ▪ a tontas y locas ▪ a empujones ▪ a saltos y corvos

by force por la fuerza ▪ a la fuerza ▪ por las malas ▪ a las malas

by fortunate coincidence ▪ by a happy coincidence por una afortunada coincidencia ▪ por una feliz coincidencia

by George! ¡por San Jorge!

by golly ¡madre de Dios!

by hand: to deliver something ~ ▪ to hand deliver something entregar algo en propia mano ▪ entregar algo en mano ➤ I delivered it to him by hand. ▪ I hand delivered it. *(envelope)* Se lo entregué en su propia mano. ▪ *(letter)* Se la entregué en su propia mano.

by hand: to do something ~ hacer algo a mano

by hand: to make something ~ hacer algo a mano

by hook or by crook por las buenas o por las malas

by its very nature ▪ ipso facto ipso facto

by itself (por sí) solo

by (medical) prescription bajo prescripción médica ▪ bajo prescripción facultativa ➤ The only way to get this medicine is by prescription. La única forma de conseguir este medicamento es bajo prescripción médica. ▪ La única forma de conseguir este medicamento es bajo prescripción facultativa.

by means of por medio de ▪ mediante

by midnight ▪ before the clock strikes midnight para la medianoche ➤ Cinderella had to leave by midnight. Cenicienta tenía que salir para la medianoche.

by mistake: to do something ~ hacer algo por equivocación ▪ hacer algo por error

by moonlight a la luz de la luna

by mutual agreement de acuerdo mutuo ▪ de mutuo acuerdo

by my side ▪ at my side ▪ beside me a mi lado ▪ *(poetic and in songs)* a la vera mía ▪ a mi vera

by my watch por mi reloj ▪ según mi reloj ➤ We left at 11 a.m. on the dot, by my watch. Salimos a las 11 en punto, por mi reloj. ▪ Salimos a las 11 en punto, según mi reloj.

by name de nombre(s) ▪ por el nombre ▪ por los nombres ➤ He whistled and shouted and called them by name. Silbó, gritó y los llamó por sus nombres.

by name: to call someone ~ llamar a alguien por su nombre

by name: to know someone ~ conocer a alguien por el nombre ▪ conocer a alguien de nombre

by nature de natural

by night ▪ at night ▪ during the night de noche ▪ durante la noche

by no means ni modo ▪ ni por asomo ▪ de ninguna manera

by no means whatsoever ni en sueños ▪ ni loco ▪ *(colorful)* ni harto de vino ▪ ni modo

by noon para las doce del mediodía ▪ a las doce del mediodía

by not doing something al no hacer algo ▪ no haciendo algo ➤ By not inviting my mother-in-law to go to the beach with us, I've turned her against me. Al no invitar a mi suegra a ir a la playa con nosotros, me la he puesto en contra. ▪ No invitando a mi suegra a ir a la playa con nosotros, me la he puesto en contra.

by not having to... al no tener que... ▪ por no tener que...

by now ya ▪ a estas alturas ➤ They should be here by now. Ya deberían estar aquí. ▪ Deberían estar aquí ya. ▪ A estas alturas deberían estar aquí. ▪ Deberían estar aquí a estas alturas. ➤ They should have been here by now. Deberían haber llegado ya. ▪ Deberían haber llegado a estas alturas. ➤ I had expected to hear from you by now. Esperaba haber sabido de ti a estas alturas.

by occupation de oficio

by one's standards para la norma ▪ para la costumbre ▪ para el hábito ➤ People in the United States eat supper early by Spanish and Mexican standards. Los estadounidenses cenan pronto para la norma española y mexicana. ▪ Los estadounidenses cenan pronto para la costumbre española y mexicana. ▪ Los estadounidenses cenan pronto para el hábito español y mexicano.

by oneself: to do something ~ **1.** to do something alone hacer algo solo **2.** to do something without help ▪ to do something unassisted hacer algo solo ▪ hacer algo solito ➤ I went to the movies by myself. ▪ I went to the movies alone. Fui al cine solo. ▪ Fui yo solo al cine. ➤ Our six-year-old rode his bicycle by himself today for the first time. Hoy por primera vez nuestro hijo de seis años montó en bicicleta solo.

by plane ▪ by airplane en avión

by popular demand por demanda popular ▪ por petición popular

by prescription (only) *(medicine)* únicamente bajo receta (médica) ▪ sólo bajo receta (médica) ▪ sólo con la receta médica ➤ Morphine is available by prescription only. La morfina se consigue únicamente bajo receta médica. ▪ La morfina se consigue únicamente con la receta médica.

by-product ▪ derivative product producto derivado ▪ sub-producto ➤ Curds and whey are by-products of milk. La cuajada y el suero son productos derivados de la leche.

by profession de profesión ➤ An accountant by profession Contable de profesión

by request por petición ▪ a súplica

by return mail 1. a vuelta de correo 2. *(payments)* contra reembolso
by rote de memorieta
by secret ballot: to elect ~ elegir con voto secreto
by sheer chance ▪ by sheer happenstance de pura casualidad
by sheer coincidence de pura coincidencia
by sheer gall ▪ out of sheer gall ▪ through sheer gall de pura desfachatez ▪ *(colorful)* de puro morro ▪ de pura caradura ▪ *(slang)* de pura jeta
by sheer happenstance ▪ by sheer chance de pura casualidad
by sheer luck ▪ through sheer luck de pura suerte ▪ de pura leche *(Sp., slang)* de pura potra ▪ de pura chorra
by sheer obstinacy de pura obstinación
by sheer tenacity de pura tenacidad
by some time in en algún momento de ▪ en algún punto de ➤ We should finish by some time in April. Deberíamos acabar en algún momento de abril. ▪ Deberíamos acabar en algún punto de abril.
by someone to do something por alguien para hacer algo ➤ The car was souped up by the teenagers to go faster. El coche fue trucado por el mecánico para que corriera más rápido.
by surface mail ▪ by ship por vía marítima
by surprise: to be taken ~ ▪ to be caught by surprise ser tomado por sorpresa ▪ ser cogido por sorpresa ▪ ser cogido en frío ▪ cogerle en frío
by surprise: to take someone ~ ▪ to catch someone by surprise *(L. Am.)* tomar a alguien por sorpresa ▪ *(Sp.)* coger a alguien por sorpresa
by telephone ▪ by phone por teléfono ➤ I reached him by phone. Lo localizé por teléfono. ▪ *(Sp., leísmo)* Le localizé por teléfono. ➤ I reached her by telephone. La localizé por teléfono.
by that I mean (that)... con eso quiero decir que... ▪ quiero decir con estas palabras que...
by that name con ese nombre ▪ *(with the verb "atender")* por ese nombre ▪ a ese nombre ➤ There's no one here by that name. Aquí no hay nadie con ese nombre. ➤ We don't have anyone by that name. No tenemos a nadie con ese nombre. ▪ No tenemos nadie que atienda por ese nombre. ▪ No tenemos nadie que atienda a ese nombre.
by that time ▪ by then para entonces
by the end of the day para el final del día
by the end of the month para fin de mes ▪ para el final de mes
by the end of the week para el fin de la semana ▪ para el final de la semana
by the end of the year ▪ on or before December 31 para el final del año ▪ para el final de año ➤ By the end of the year, I will have saved five thousand dollars. Para el final del año, habré ahorrado cinco mil dólares.
by the firelight ▪ by the light of the fire a la luz del fuego ▪ al resplandor del fuego
by the hardest: to do something ~ ▪ to play hell doing something hacer algo contra viento y marea ➤ I managed to get here by the hardest. ▪ I played hell getting here. He conseguido llegar aquí contra viento y marea.
by the hour: to be paid ~ ▪ to get paid by the hour ser pagado por horas
by the hundreds a centenares ▪ a cientos ➤ The troops stormed the beach by the hundreds. Las tropas irrumpieron en la playa a centenares.
by the light of the fire ▪ by firelight a la luz del fuego ▪ al resplandor del fuego
by the look(s) of it por la pinta que tiene ➤ By the look(s) of it, I'd say it's a picture of Granada. Por la pinta que tiene, yo diría que es una foto de Granada.
by the luck of the draw ▪ by sheer luck ▪ by sheer happenstance gracias al sorteo ▪ por la suerte del bombo ➤ By the luck of the draw, the little-known candidate got the first question, and she basically stole the show. Gracias al sorteo, el concursante menos conocido consiguió la primera pregunta, y básicamente se quedó con el espectáculo.
by the river ▪ beside the river ▪ next to the river al lado del río ▪ junto al río ▪ *(poetic)* a la vera del río
by the same token por el mismo caso ▪ así como
by the seat of one's pants 1. *(without instruments)* a la buena de Dios ▪ como Dios le dio a entender ▪ al buen tuntun 2. *(by trial and error)* como Dios le dio a entender ▪ tanteando ▪ probando ▪ haciendo pruebas ▪ haciendo ensayos ➤ The pilot flew the course by the seat of his pants. El piloto hizo el trayecto a la buena de Dios. ➤ I built the tree house by the seat of my pants. Construí la casa del árbol como Dios me dio a entender.
by the skin of one's teeth por los pelos ▪ por el canto de un duro ➤ We escaped by the skin of our teeth. Nos salvamos por los pelos. ▪ Nos salvamos por el canto de un duro.
by the sweat of one's brow con el sudor de la frente
by the time 1. para cuando... ▪ para el tiempo que... 2. cuando 3. *(referring to age)* a ➤ She was gone by the time I got there. Se había ido para cuando yo llegué. ➤ By the time I get back... Para el tiempo que venga... ➤ By the time the symptoms appear... Para cuando los síntomas aparezcan... ➤ If he hadn't managed it by the time the last petal fell... Si no lo conseguía cuando cayera el último pétalo... ➤ In Biblical times people married in their early teens. You were dead by (the time you were) forty, so you had to get on with it. En la época de la Biblia, la gente se casaba en su temprana adolescencia. Te morías a los cuarenta, así que había que tirar para adelante. ➤ The doctor recommended against removing the child's tonsils, saying he would outgrow the problem by the time he was seven. El médico recomendó no quitarle las amígdalas al niño puesto que superaría el problema a los siete años.
by the truckload 1. a camiones 2. *(figurative)* por un tubo ▪ a punta (de) pala ▪ a porrillo ▪ a mansalva ▪ a tutiplén ▪ a discreción ➤ They brought in fertilizer by the truckload. Trajeron fertilizante a camiones.
by the way por cierto ▪ a propósito ➤ By the way, while I'm at it, how would you translate...? Por cierto, ya aprovecho, ¿cómo traducirías...?
by the year *x* para el año *x*
by their works you shall know them *(Matthew 7:15)* por sus obras los conoceréis
by themselves (ellos) solos ▪ ellos mismos
by then ▪ by that time para entonces
by this time ya en esto
by this time next week la semana que viene a estas alturas
by this time next year el año que viene a estas alturas ▪ el año que viene por estas fechas
by today's standards para la norma de hoy (en día) ▪ para la costumbre de hoy (en día) ▪ para el hábito de hoy (en día) ▪ para el nivel de hoy (en día) ▪ para las normas de hoy (en día) ▪ para las costumbres de hoy (en día) ▪ para los hábitos de hoy (en día) ▪ para los niveles de hoy (en día)
by train: to go ~ ir en tren
by train: to travel ~ viajar en tren
by trial and error por prueba y error ▪ a prueba y error ▪ tanteando ▪ por tanteos ▪ *(scientific method)* método ensayo-error ➤ We found the solution by trial and error. Encontramos la solución tanteando. ▪ Encontramos la solución por tanteos.
by two's ▪ two by two ▪ two at time ▪ in pairs a pares ▪ de dos en dos
by U.S. standards para el nivel estadounidense ▪ para la norma estadounidense ▪ para la costumbre estadounidense ▪ para el hábito estadounidense ▪ para los niveles estadounidenses ▪ para las normas estadounidenses ▪ para las costumbres estadounidenses ▪ para los hábitos estadounidenses ➤ *(Madrid news item)* His house was modest by U.S. standards. Su casa era modesta para los niveles estadounidenses.
by the window pegado a la ventana ▪ junto a la ventana ▪ en la ventana ➤ Tell the movers to put the sofa by the window. Dile a los mozos que pongan el sofá pegado a la ventana. ➤ We'd like a table by the window. Queremos una mesa pegada a la ventana. ▪ Queremos una mesa junto a la ventana. ▪ Queremos una mesa en la ventana.
by way of pasando por ➤ We went by way of Atlanta. Fuimos pasando por Atlanta.
by way of an answer por (toda) respuesta
by way of example ▪ as an example ▪ (just) to give you an example a guisa de ejemplo ▪ a modo de ejemplo ▪ de muestra valga un botón ▪ valga un botón de muestra

by way of explanation por (toda) explicación
by way of introduction a título de introducción
by way of review como un repaso
by what right? ¿con qué derecho? ■ ¿con qué título?
by whatever means por cualquier medio
by which por el cual ■ por la cual ■ por los cuales ■ por las cuales ■ por el que ■ por la que ■ por los que ■ por las que
by which I mean entendiendo por tal
by word of mouth por vía oral
by virtue of the powers invested in me usando los poderes que me envisten
by *x* o'clock para la(s) *x* ➤ Tell him to call me by nine, (because) otherwise I won't get the message. Dile que me llame para las nueve, porque si no, no me pasan el mensaje. ➤ Tell him to call me by one. Dile que me llame para la una.
by *x* point(s) en *x* punto(s) ➤ U.S. cuts interest rates by half a point. EE UU recorta en medio punto el tipo de interés.
bygone days días pasados ■ días del ayer ■ días que se fueron ➤ *(Ogden Nash)* When I remember bygone days, I think how evening follows morn; so many I loved were not yet dead, so many I love were not yet born. Cuando recuerdo los días pasados, pienso en como la tarde sigue a la mañana; tantos que amé aún no habían muerto, tantos que amo aún no habían nacido.
to **bypass the procedure** saltarse el procedimiento

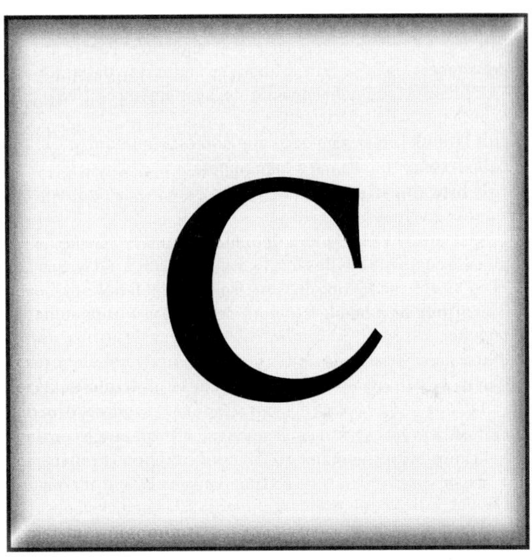

C D E F G A B C ▪ do re mi fa so (sol) la ti do *(musical scale)* do re mi fa sol la si do ➤ Concerto in B-flat Concierto en si bemol ➤ To brighten that chord up, hit an A. Para dar más vida al acorde, ponle un la. ▪ Para dar más vida al acorde, añádele un la.

C-drive unidad C ▪ unidad de disco de tres cuartos

cab of a truck cabina de un camión

cabinet appointments nombramientos del gabinete presidencial ➤ The president's cabinet appointments have been good. Los nombramientos del gabinete presidencial han resultado buenos. ▪ La adjudicación de carteras ministeriales ha resultado buena.

cable car teleférico

cable TV televisión por cable

cache of drugs alijo de drogas ➤ *(headline)* Year's largest cache of ecstasy seized in Ibiza Intervenido en Ibiza el mayor alijo de éxtasis de este año

cache of weapons alijo de armas ▪ alijo de armamentos

cake batter mezcla (del pastel) ▪ masa líquida *(The bread of the baked cake is "el bizcocho del pastel.")*

the **cake fell** se cayó el pastel ▪ el pastel se hundió

cake mix preparado para bizcocho ▪ preparado de pastel

to **cake up** ▪ to get caked up **1.** apelmazarse ▪ apelotonarse **2.** acumularse ▪ apelotonarse ➤ Clean the paintbrush well after each use to keep the paint from caking up (in it). ▪ Clean the paintbrush well after each use to keep the paint from getting caked up (in it). Limpia bien la brocha después de usarla para que la pintura no se apelmace (en ella). ➤ You need to use distilled water in the iron, or mineral deposits will cake up inside it. ▪ You need to use distilled water in the iron, or mineral deposits will get caked up inside it. Necesitas usar agua destilada en la plancha, o el residuo mineral se acumulará dentro.

to **calculate the odds** calcular las probabilidades ▪ calcular las posibilidades

calendar of appeals lista de causas alzadas ▪ calendario de apelaciones

calendar year año civil ▪ año natural ▪ año continuo

caliber of a person *el* calibre de una persona ▪ catadura de una persona

caliber of a rifle *el* calibre de un rifle

calking compound ▪ caulking compound ▪ caulk ▪ calk masilla (de calefatear)

calking gun ▪ caulking gun pistola para masilla ▪ pistola para calafateo

to **call a cab** ▪ to call a taxi llamar a un taxi ▪ avisar a un taxi

to **call a foul** *(sports)* pitar falta ▪ indicar falta

to **call a joint session** convocar un pleno

to **call a meeting** convocar una reunión ▪ convocar una sesión

to **call a spade a spade** llamar a las cosas por su nombre ▪ llamar al pan, pan y al vino, vino

to **call a taxi** ▪ to call a cab avisar a un taxi ▪ llamar a un taxi

to **call a time out** ▪ to call time out pedir un tiempo muerto

to **call a truce** pedir una tregua

to **call about the ad** ▪ to call in response to the ad ▪ to call regarding the ad ▪ to call on the ad llamar por el anuncio ▪ llamar por lo del anuncio ➤ I'm calling about the ad for an apartment. *(under 50 square meters)* Llamo por el anuncio del apartamento. ▪ Llamo por lo del anuncio del apartamento. ▪ *(over 50 square meters)* Llamo por lo del anuncio del piso. ▪ *(studio apartment)* Llamo por el anuncio del estudio. ▪ Llamo por lo del anuncio del estudio.

to **call about the tickets** ▪ to call regarding the tickets llamar por los billetes ▪ llamar por lo de los billetes

to **call ahead** llamar con antelación ➤ When he neared the end of his line, the truck driver would call ahead and order his supper at the diner down the road. Cuando se acercaba al final del trayecto, el camionero llamaba con antelación para pedir su merienda en un restaurante camino adelante.

to **call an election 1.** to order that an election be held convocar una elección **2.** to declare the winner of an election declarar a alguien el ganador de una elección ▪ aventurar el ganador de la elección ▪ aventurar el resultado de la elección ➤ For the media to call a state for a candidate based on exit polls is asinine. El que los medios de comunicación aventuren el ganador de un estado basándose en sondeos a pie de urna es una solemne tontería.

to **call and cancel** llamar y anular ▪ llamar y cancelar ➤ I called and cancelled the appointment. Llamé y anulé la cita. ▪ Llamé y cancelé la cita.

to **call around** llamar a todas partes ➤ It took a lot of calling around the university to locate you. Me ha llevado llamar a todas partes en la universidad para localizarte.

to **call attention to something** llamar la atención sobre algo ➤ The presence of homeless people on the streets calls attention to the need for some kind of reform. La presencia de personas sin hogar en las calles llama la atención sobre la necesidad de algún tipo de reforma.

to **call attention to oneself** llamar la atención sobre sí mismo

to **call attention to the fact that...** llamar la atención sobre el hecho de que...

to **call collect** llamar por cobrar ▪ *(Sp.)* llamar a cobro revertido

the **call didn't go through** la llamada no estableció comunicación

to **call elections** convocar elecciones

to **call for 1.** to urge abogar por **2.** to require exigir ▪ requerir **3.** to telephone for the purpose of llamar para ➤ The president called for the beginning of a dialogue between the two governments. El presidente abogó por el inicio de un diálogo entre los dos gobiernos. ➤ This shrimp chowder recipe calls for cream of chicken soup! ¡Esta sopa de camarón exige sopa de crema de pollo! ➤ This situation calls for immediate action. La situación exige acción inmediata. ▪ La situación requiere acción inmediata. ➤ They called me (to come in) for an interview, so that's a good sign. Me han llamado para una entrevista, así que eso es buena señal.

to **call for a truce** pedir una tregua ▪ solicitar una tregua

to **call for an appointment** ▪ to call to make an appointment llamar para una ata ▪ pedir consulta ▪ pedir cita ▪ pedir hora

call for help: to make a ~ hacer una llamada pidiendo ayuda ➤ She made a call for help. Hizo una llamada pidiendo ayuda.

to **call for help** llamar pidiendo ayuda

to **call for unity** llamar a la unidad ▪ hacer un llamamiento a la unidad

to **call in someone** ▪ to call someone in ▪ to have a meeting with someone reunirse con alguien ➤ You need to call in all the people who deal with international students. ▪ You need to call all the people who deal with international students in. Necesitas reunirte con todo el personal encargado de los estudiantes internacionales. ➤ You need to call them in. Necesitas reunirte con ellos.

to **call in response to the ad** ▪ to call about the ad ▪ to call regarding the ad llamar por el anuncio ▪ llamar por lo del anuncio ➤ I'm calling about the ad in the paper for an apartment. Llamo por el anuncio del apartamento. ▪ Llamo por lo del anuncio del apartamento.

to **call in sick** llamar para decir que uno está enfermo

to **call in time to...** llamar a tiempo para...

to **call into question** ▪ to cast doubt on poner en entredicho ▪ poner en cuestión

to **call it a day** considerar la jornada acabada ▪ considerar la jornada completa ➤ It's five to five. Let's call it a day. Son las cinco menos cinco. Consideremos la jornada acabada.

call number of a book signatura de un libro ▪ asignatura de un libro

call of a bird reclamo de un ave

call of duty llamada del deber ➤ His heroism was beyond the call of duty. Su heroismo iba más allá de la llamada del deber.

to **call off a meeting** ▪ to call a meeting off ▪ to cancel a meeting cancelar una reunión ➤ The boss called off the meeting. ▪ The boss cancelled the meeting. La jefa canceló la reunión. ➤ She called it off. ▪ She cancelled it. Ella la canceló.

to **call off a search** abandonar una búsqueda ▪ desistir de una búsqueda ➤ The search was called off because of bad weather. Abandonaron la búsqueda por el mal tiempo. ▪ Se desistió de la búsqueda por el mal tiempo.

to **call off the dog** ▪ to call the dog off mandar al perro que no ataque ➤ He called off the dog. Mandó al perro que no atacara. ➤ The dog's master called him off. El dueño del perro le mandó que no atacara.

to **call off the wedding** suspender la boda

to **call on someone 1.** to ask someone to give the answer requerir a alguien **2.** to pay a visit to someone visitar a alguien ▪ ir a ver a alguien ➤ Please wait until I call on you. Por favor espera hasta que te requiera. ▪ Por favor espera hasta ser requerido. ➤ The instructor calls mostly on one student that she particularly likes. La instructora requiere fundamentalmente a un estudiante que le cae bien. ➤ An agent from your company called on me several weeks ago. Un agente de su compañía vino a verme hace unas semanas.

to **call on someone to do something** emplazar a alguien que haga algo ▪ emplazar a alguien a hacer algo ▪ apelar a alguien para que haga algo ➤ *(headline)* Zapatero calls on Batasuna to condemn terrorism if it wants to participate in politics. Zapatero emplaza a Batasuna a que condene el terrorismo si quiere participar en la política. ▪ Zapatero emplaza a Batasuna a condenar el terrorismo si quiere participar en la política.

to **call one's attention to something** llamarle la atención sobre algo

to **call out** llamar a voces

to **call outside** ▪ to get outside llamar afuera ➤ To call outside, dial nine. ▪ To get outside, call nine. Para llamar afuera, marca el nueve.

to **call regarding something** ▪ to call about something llamar en referencia a algo ▪ llamar con respecto a algo ▪ llamar por algo ▪ llamar por lo de algo ➤ I'm calling regarding the tickets. ▪ I was calling regarding the tickets. Llamo en referencia a los billetes. ▪ Llamo con respecto a los billetes. ➤ I'm calling regarding the ad in the paper for an apartment. Llamo por el anuncio del apartamento. ▪ Llamo por lo del anuncio del apartamento.

to **call someone a name** llamarle a alguien una cosa ▪ decirle a alguien una cosa ▪ ponerle a alguien un mote despectivo ▪ ponerle a alguien un mote ridículo ➤ *(school squabble)* Ma'am, Carlos called me a name! Seño, ¡Carlos me ha llamado una cosa!

to **call someone as a witness** llamar a alguien de testigo ▪ citar a alguien de testigo

to **call someone aside** ▪ to take someone aside llamar a alguien aparte

to **call someone back 1.** to call someone (again) later llamarle luego **2.** to return someone's call regresarle la llamada a alguien ▪ *(Sp.)* devolver la llamada a alguien ➤ I'm in a meeting. Can I call you back? Estoy reunido. ¿Te llamo luego? ▪ Estoy reunido. ¿Te llamo en un segundo? ▪ Estoy reunido. ¿Te llamo más tarde? ➤ I called him back. ▪ I returned his call. Le devolví la llamada. ➤ I called her back. ▪ I returned her call. Le devolví la llamada.

to **call someone down** ▪ to call down someone ▪ to reprimand someone regañar a alguien ➤ If the teacher calls you down three times in one class, you must leave for ten minutes if the teacher requires you to. Si el profesor te regaña tres veces en la clase, la abandonarás si el profesor te lo exige.

to **call someone names** llamarle a alguien "cosas" ▪ decirle a alguien "cosas" ➤ *(Rudolph)* All of the other reindeer used to laugh and call him names. Todos los otros renos solían reírse y llamarle "cosas".

to **call someone on the carpet** amonestar a un empleado ▪ llamar a alguien a la palestra

to **call someone to testify** llamar a alguien a declarar

to **call someone to the telephone** ▪ to call someone to the phone avisar a alguien que venga al teléfono

to **call someone (up) on the phone** ▪ to call someone (up) on the telephone ▪ to telephone someone ▪ to give someone a call llamar a alguien por teléfono ➤ I'd call him (up) and tell him what you just told me. Yo lo llamaría y le contaría lo que me acabas de decir. ▪ *(Sp., leísmo)* Yo le llamaría y le contaría lo que me acabas de decir.

to **call someone's attention to something** ▪ to call something to someone's attention ▪ to bring something to someone's attention llamar la atención de alguien sobre algo ➤ I want to call your attention to the changes in the tax law. ▪ I want to bring to your attention to the changes in the tax law. Quiero llamar la atención sobre los cambios en la ley de impuestos.

to **call someone's bluff** desenmascararle a alguien

to **call something to someone's attention** ▪ to call someone's attention to something llamar la atención de alguien sobre algo

to **call the roll** ▪ to take (the) attendance ▪ to call roll pasar lista ➤ I'm going to call the roll. Voy a pasar lista.

to **call the shots** ▪ to have the say ▪ to be the boss llevar la voz cantante ▪ tomar la sartén por el mango ▪ tener la sartén por el mango ▪ cortar el bacalao ▪ tener al toro (cogido) por los cuernos ▪ *(Sp.)* coger la sartén por el mango

to **call time** dar la señal para parar ➤ I blew a bubble, and when it popped the whole class stopped typing. They thought the teacher was calling time. Hice un globo de goma de mascar y cuando explotó, toda la clase dejó de escribir a máquina, porque creyeron que era la maestra quien les daba la señal para parar.

to **call time out** pedir tiempo muerto

to **call to ask someone out (on a date)** llamar para pedirle salir a alguien

to **call to invite someone to do something** llamar para invitar a alguien a hacer algo ➤ I'm calling (you) to invite you to come over and have paella with us tonight. Os llamo para invitaros a que vengáis y os toméis una paella con nosotros.

to **call to make an appointment** ▪ to call for an appointment llamar para pedir una cita ▪ llamar para pedir hora ▪ *(medical doctor)* llamar para pedir consulta

to **call to order** llamar al orden ➤ I hereby call the meeting to order. Por la presente llamo la sesión al orden.

to **call up** *(computers)* acceder ➤ After I call up the message, I have to press V to read it. Después de acceder al mensaje, tengo que pulsar V para poder leerlo.

to **call up reserves (to active duty)** *(military)* llamar a los reservistas (a filas)

to **call up someone (on the phone)** ▪ to call someone up (on the phone) llamar a alguien por teléfono ➤ I called her up and talked to her. La llamé y hablé con ella. ➤ Do you want me to call you? ¿Quieres que te llame?

to be **called by one's first name** ser llamado por el nombre de pila ➤ They are usually called by their first names. Se les suele llamar por el nombre de pila.

to be **called off** ▪ to be suspended cancelarse ➤ The meeting was called off because of the snowstorm. La reunión se canceló a causa de la tormenta de nieve. ➤ After four days the search was called off. Al cabo de cuatro días, se canceló la búsqueda.

to be **called up for military duty** llamarle (para ir) a filas ➤ He was called up for military duty. Le llamaron (para ir) a filas.

caller ID identificación de llamadas

calling card tarjeta de visita

callow youth ▪ inexperienced youth **1.** *(time of life)* la inocente juventud **2.** *(person)* el joven inocente **3.** *(youth collectively)* la inocente juventud

calls will be taken in the order received se atenderán las llamadas en orden de recepción

calm before the storm calma antes de la tormenta

to **calm down** ▪ to settle down tranquilizarse ▪ calmarse ➤ Calm down! ▪ Settle down! ¡Tranquilízate! ▪ ¡Cálmate!

calorie counter guía de conteo de calorías

cambered airfoil *(technical name of the airplane wing)* plano de sustentación alabeado ▪ *el* ala del avión ➤ The cambered airfoil was not invented by the Wright Brothers or by Santos-Dumont, but by Horatio Phillips in 1884. El plano de sustentación alabeado no fue inventado por los hermanos Wright ni por Santos-Dumont, sino por Horatio Phillips en 1884.

came and went se fue igual que llegó ➤ The deadline came and went. La fecha tope se fue igual que llegó.

cameo appearance: to make a ~ hacer un cameo ➤ Alfred Hitchcock made cameo appearances in his own films. Alfred Hitchcock hacía cameos en sus propias películas.

to be a **camera hog** ▪ to hog the camera chupar cámara ➤ Don't be a camera hog. No chupes cámara. ➤ Quit hogging the camera. Deja de chupar cámara.

campaign appearance ▪ campaign stop acto de campaña

to be **campaign driven** ser electoralista ▪ ser impulsado por la campaña (electoral) ➤ *(Bill Clinton)* I do not want a campaign-driven cold war with China in 2000. No quiero una guerra fría electoralista con China en el 2000. ▪ No quiero una guerra fría con China impulsada por la campaña electoral en el 2000.

campaign headquarters *(political) la* sede de la campaña

campaign stop ▪ campaign appearance acto de campaña

camping trip *(L. Am.)* campamento ▪ *(Sp.)* camping

campsite parcela de un camping

can and will: we ~ podremos y lo haremos ➤ I'm not prepared to discuss money at this point, but down the road we can and will. No estoy preparado para hablar de dinero ahora, pero más adelante podremos y lo haremos.

can barely get out of bed in the morning: one ~ se levanta a duras penas de la cama por la mañana

can be told: the secret ~ se puede contar el secreto

can be told: the story ~ se puede contar la historia ➤ The story can be told to music. ▪ The story can be told in music. ▪ The story can be put to music. Se puede contar la historia en música.

can be told: the truth ~ se puede contar la verdad

can best be described as... como mejor se puede(n) describir es como... ➤ The success of the Mars exploration missions to date can best be described as mixed. Como mejor se puede describir el éxito de las misiones de exploración de Marte es como parcial.

can breathe easily again: one ~ uno puede volver a respirar bien otra vez

can do it blindfolded: one ~ uno lo puede hacer con los ojos cerrados

can do no wrong (even if he tries): one ~ a uno nada le puede salir mal (ni aunque quisiera) ▪ no poder salirle nada mal (ni aunque quisiera) ▪ no le sale nada mal (ni aunque quisiera) ▪ nada le sale mal (ni aunque quisiera)

can hardly tell the difference between: one ~ apenas se nota la diferencia entre ▪ apenas se ve la diferencia entre ▪ apenas se distingue entre ➤ You can hardly tell the difference between rib steak and sirloin. Apenas se nota la diferencia entre entrecote y solomillo.

can I borrow...? *(informal)* ▪ may I borrow... ? ▪ would you lend me...? ▪ could you lend me...? ¿me dejas...? ▪ ¿me prestas...? ▪ ¿puedes dejarme...? ▪ ¿puedes prestarme...? ▪ ¿te importa si tomo...? ▪ ¿me permites tomar...? ▪ *(Sp.)* ¿te importa si cojo...? ▪ ¿me permites coger...?

can I call you again? ▪ may I call you again? ¿puedo volverte a llamar? ▪ ¿puedo volver a llamarte?

can I call you (back) later? ¿puedo llamarte más tarde?

can I get you anything? *(a ti)* ¿puedo traerte algo? ▪ *(a usted)* ¿puedo traerle algo?

can I have it back? ¿puedes devolvérmelo? ▪ ¿puede usted devolvérmelo?

can I have that for a second? *(informal)* ▪ would you hand me that for a second? ▪ may I have that for a second? ¿me permites eso un momento? ▪ ¿me dejas eso un momento?

can I help it if...? ▪ is it my fault if...? ¿tengo (yo) la culpa si...?

can I help you with anything? ¿te ayudo en algo?

can of beer lata de cerveza

can of paint *el* bote de pintura ▪ lata de pintura

can of worms: to be a (big) ~ ▪ to open a (big) can of worms ser la caja de los truenos ➤ The president's gaffe has opened a big can of worms. El desliz del presidente ha abierto la caja de los truenos.

can only do so much: one ~ uno puede hacer sólo hasta un límite ▪ uno puede hacer sólo hasta cierto punto

can only hold so much puede llevar hasta un límite ▪ puede contener hasta un límite ▪ puede llevar hasta cierto punto ▪ puede contener hasta cierto punto ➤ A cloud can only hold so much water. Una nube puede llevar agua hasta un límite. ▪ Una nube puede contener agua hasta un límite. ▪ Una nube puede llevar agua hasta cierto punto. ▪ Una nube puede contener agua hasta cierto punto.

can only take so much: one ~ ▪ one can take only so much ▪ one can take just so much uno puede aguantar sólo hasta un límite ▪ uno puede soportar sólo hasta un límite ▪ uno puede tolerar sólo hasta un límite ▪ uno puede aguantar sólo hasta cierto punto ▪ uno puede soportar sólo hasta cierto punto ▪ uno puede tolerar sólo hasta cierto punto

can only stand so much...: something ~ ▪ something can stand only so much... ▪ something can take only so much... algo sólo puede resistir cierto... ➤ The body can only stand so much exposure to cold temperatures. El cuerpo sólo puede resistir cierta exposición al frío. ▪ El cuerpo sólo puede resistir una determinada exposición al frío.

can play the piano: one ~ ▪ one knows how to play the piano uno sabe tocar el piano ➤ Mary can play the piano. ▪ Mary knows how to play the piano. María sabe tocar el piano.

can see: one ~ ▪ one can make out ▪ one manages to see uno alcanza a ver ▪ uno llega a ver ➤ He can't see the numbers on the bathroom scale because of his stomach. No alcanza a ver los números de la báscula por su estómago. ▪ No llega a ver los números de la báscula por su estómago. ➤ I can't make out the name on the mailbox. No alcanzo a leer el nombre en el buzón.

can she ever cook! ¡sí que cocina! ▪ ¡cómo cocina!

can take only so much: one ~ ▪ one can take just so much ▪ one can only take so much ▪ one can just take so much uno puede aguantar sólo hasta un límite ▪ uno puede soportar sólo hasta un límite ▪ uno puede tolerar sólo hasta un límite ▪ uno puede aguantar sólo hasta cierto punto ▪ uno puede soportar sólo hasta cierto punto ▪ uno puede tolerar sólo hasta cierto punto

can you beat that? ▪ can you top that? ¿puedes superarlo?

can you believe (that)? ¿te lo puedes creer?

can you bring me...? can you (go) get me...? ¿puedes (ir a) traerme...? ▪ ¿puedes (ir a) buscarme...?

can you change...? ▪ do you have change for...? *(tú)* ¿puedes cambiar...? ▪ ¿puedes dar cambio de...? ▪ ¿tienes cambio de...? ▪ *(usted)* ¿puede (usted) cambiar...? ▪ ¿puede (usted) dar cambio de...? ▪ ¿tiene (usted) cambio de...? ➤ Can you change a fifty (for me)? ▪ Do you have change for a fifty? ¿Puedes cambiarme cincuenta? ▪ ¿Me puedes dar cambio de cincuenta? ▪ ¿Tienes cambio de cincuenta?

can you come over? ¿puedes venir a mi case? ▪ ¿te vienes a (mi) casa?

can you get me...? ▪ can you bring me...? ¿puedes (ir a) buscarme...? ▪ ¿puedes (ir a) traerme...?

can you give me a hand? ▪ can you lend me a hand? ¿me echas una mano?

can you handle it? ▪ can you manage it? ¿puedes con ello?

can you hear me back there? *(tú)* ¿me escuchas por atrás? ▪ *(usted)* ¿me escucha por atrás? ▪ *(ustedes)* ¿me escuchan por atrás? ▪ *(Sp., vosotros)* ¿me escucháis por atrás?

can you lend me a hand? ▪ can you give me a hand? ¿me echas una mano?

can you manage it? ▪ can you handle it? ¿puedes con ello?

can you order them for me? ▪ can you special order them for me? ¿me los puede pedir? ▪ ¿los puedo dejar encargados?

can you pass it to me? ¿puedes pasármelo?

can you reach it for me? ¿puedes alcanzármelo?

can you read this? ¿puedes leer esto? ▪ ¿puedes leerlo?

can you ring this up for me? *(tú)* ¿puedes cobrarme esto? ▪ *(usted)* ¿puede cobrarme esto?

can you shed any light on...? *(tú)* ¿puedes arrojar algo de luz en...? ▪ *(usted)* ¿puede (usted) aclarar...?

can you (special) order it for me? ¿me lo puede pedir de encargo? ▪ ¿lo puedo dejar encargado?

can you tell? ¿se nota? ▪ ¿lo ves? ➤ Did you dye your hair?-Yes, can you tell? ¿Te has teñido el pelo?-Sí, ¿se nota? ▪ ¿Te has teñido el pelo?-Sí, ¿lo ves?

can you think of anybody who...? ¿no se te ocurre nadie que...? ▪ ¿se te ocurre alguien que...?

to **cancel a debt** ▪ to forgive a debt condonar una deuda ▪ perdonar una deuda

to **cancel a reservation** anular una reserva ▪ cancelar una reserva ➤ Don't cancel the reservation. *(tú)* No anules la reserva. ▪ *(usted)* No anule la reserva. ➤ Don't cancel it. *(tú)* No la anules. ▪ *(usted)* No la anule.

to **cancel an appointment** anular una cita ▪ cancelar una cita

cancellation of a debt condonación de una deuda ▪ *el* perdón de una deuda ➤ *(news item)* Spain announces the cancellation of 200 million dollars in debts by sub-Saharan countries. España anuncia la condonación de 200 millones de dólares de deuda a los países subsaharianos.

cancer screen revisión para detección de cáncer ▪ chequeo para detección de cáncer

to **be a candidate for** ser candidato a

candlelight vigil vigilia (con velas)

canned goods conservas alimenticias

canning factory empresa envasadora

cannon fodder *la* carne de cañón ➤ Amnesty International yesterday denounced the growing use of children as cannon fodder. Amnistía Internacional denunció ayer la creciente utilización de niños como carne de cañón.

cannot read: one ~ ▪ one is unable to read **1.** *(because of poor eyesight)* no puede leer **2.** *(because of illiteracy)* not to know how to read no sabe leer **3.** *(because the view is blocked)* no alcanza a leer ➤ He can't read without glasses. No puede leer sin gafas. ➤ Many third-world poor people can't read. Muchos pobres del tercer mundo no saben leer. ➤ He can't read the numbers on the bathroom scale because of his stomach. No alcanza a ver los números de la báscula por su estómago.

can't even: one ~ uno ni siquiera puede

can't even begin to compare: one ~ uno no tiene ni punto de comparación ▪ uno no puede ni comparar

can't get anyone to...: one ~ uno no puede conseguir que nadie... ▪ uno no consigue que nadie... ➤ I can't get anyone to help me. No puedo conseguir que nadie me ayude. ▪ No consigo que nadie me ayude.

can't get anywhere with...: one ~ no puede con... ➤ I can't anywhere with the university's bureaucracy. No puedo con toda la burocracia universitaria.

can't get it out of one's head: one ~ uno no puede quitarse algo de la cabeza ▪ uno no puede sacarse algo de la cabeza

can't handle it: one ~ uno no puede con ello ▪ uno no puede manejarlo ▪ uno no puede lidiarlo ▪ uno no puede lidiar con ello

can't help but...: one ~ ▪ one cannot help but... uno no puede evitar sino... ▪ uno no puede evitar más que... ▪ uno no puede más que...

can't help but wonder: one ~ uno no puede evitar preguntarse ▪ uno no puede evitar más que preguntarse ▪ uno no puede más que preguntarse ▪ uno no puede evitar sino preguntarse

can't keep up with: one ~ uno no puede seguir al ritmo de ▪ uno no puede mantenerse al ritmo de

can't make anything out of: one ~ ▪ one can't make heads or tails out of no sacar nada en claro de ▪ no conseguir comprender ➤ I can't make anything out of this letter. No saco nada en claro de esta carta. ▪ No consigo comprender esta carta.

can't make heads or tails out of: one ~ uno no puede sacar nada en claro ▪ uno no saca nada en claro

can't make it to an event: one ~ ▪ one can't attend an event uno no puede asistir ▪ uno no puede ir ▪ uno no puede venir ➤ I can't make it to the party tonight. ▪ I can't attend the party tonight. No puedo asistir a la fiesta esta noche. ▪ No puedo ir a la fiesta esta noche. ▪ No puedo venir a la fiesta esta noche.

can't make out: one ~ uno no alcanza a leer (con claridad) ▪ uno no alcanza a ver (con claridad) ➤ I can't make out the name on the mailbox. No alcanzo a leer el nombre en el buzón.

can't miss! ¡no falla!

can't not do something: one ~ no puede no hacer algo ▪ no puede negarse a hacer algo

can't place him: one ~ uno no lo sitúa ▪ *(Sp., leísmo)* uno no le sitúa ➤ I recognize the name, but I can't place him. Reconozco el nombre, pero no lo sitúo. ▪ Reconozco el nombre, pero no le sitúo.

can't see the forest for the trees: one ~ los árboles no le dejan ver el bosque a uno

can't stand: one ~ no soporta ▪ no aguanta ▪ no puede ni ver

can't stand the thought of...: one ~ uno no puede soportar (ni) pensar en...

can't stand the thought of it: one ~ uno no soporta ni pensar en ello

can't take a joke: one ~ uno no aguanta una broma ▪ uno no soporta una broma ➤ He can't take a joke. Él no aguanta una broma. ➤ Can't you take a joke? ¿No aguantas una broma?

can't take it any longer: one ~ no puede aguantarlo más ▪ no puede soportarlo más

can't tell: one ~ uno no lo nota ➤ I can't tell whether... No puedo notar si... ➤ You can't tell. No se nota.

can't you get it into your thick skull that...? ▪ can't you get it into your thick head that...? ¿no te entra en la testa que...? ▪ ¿no te entra en la cabezota que...? ▪ ¿no te entra en el melón que...?

can't you guess? ¿no lo adivinas? ▪ ¿no te lo figuras?

can't you think of anybody who? *(tú)* ¿no se te ocurre nadie que...? ▪ *(usted)* ¿no se le ocurre nadie que...?

cap and gown toga y birrete *(literally gown and cap; the tassle is "la borla")*

cap pistol ▪ cap gun pistola de fulminantes ▪ *(Sp.)* pistola de pistones

to be **capable of** ser capaz de ➤ You don't know what people are capable of until they are tested. No sabes de lo que la gente es capaz hasta que los pones a prueba. ➤ There is no technology capable of solving that problem. No hay tecnología capaz de resolver ese problema.

capability to do something: to have the ~ tener (la) capacidad de hacer algo ▪ tener (la) capacidad para hacer algo ▪ tener (los) medios para hacer algo ➤ This computer has the capability to run several programs at the same time. Esta computadora tiene capacidad para ejecutar varios programas a la vez. ➤ Does the Internet café store have the capability to scan pictures? ¿Tiene el ciber-café los medios para escanear fotos?

capability of a computer capacidad de una computadora ▪ capacidad de un ordenador ➤ This tests your computer's memory capabilities. Esto comprueba la capacidad de memoria de tu ordenador.

capillary (vein) vaso capilar

capital flight fuga de capital

capital inflow entrada de capital ▪ afluencia de capital ➤ The net capital inflow into the country is still weak, suppressing the value of its currency. La afluencia de capital neta al país es todavía débil, manteniendo a la baja el valor de su divisa.

capital outflow salida de capital

Captains Courageous *(Kipling novel) Capitanes intrépidos* to be **captivated by someone** ser cautivado por alguien ▪ *(literary)* prendarse de alguien ➤ The prince was captivated by Cinderella. El príncipe fue cautivado por Cenicienta. ▪ El príncipe se prendió de Cenicienta.

to **capture the sense of** captar el sentido de

car bomb coche bomba ▪ *(pl.)* coches bomba

car broke down *(L. Am.)* carro se estropeó ▪ carro se rompió ▪ carro se averió ▪ carro se descompuso ▪ *(Sp.)* coche se estropeó ▪ coche se rompió ▪ coche se averió

car dealer ▪ automobile dealer *(L. Am.)* concesionario de autos ▪ concesionario de automóviles ▪ concesionario de carros ▪ *(Sp.)* concesionario de coches ➤ *(news item)* A new strike in the transportation sector has led auto plants to the verge of bankruptcy, leaving dealers without inventory. Una nueva huelga en el sector del transporte ha colocado a las plantas automovilísticas al borde del colapso, dejando sin existencias a los concesionarios.

car dealership *(L. Am.)* ▪ automobile dealership ▪ auto dealership concesionario de autos ▪ concesionario de automóviles ▪ concesionario de carros ▪ *(Sp.)* concesionario de coches

car parts ▪ automobile parts repuestos de automóvil ▪ *(L. Am.)* repuestos de carros ▪ repuestos de autos ▪ *(Sp.)* repuestos de coche

car rental agency ▪ rental car agency *(L. Am.)* agencia de alquiler de carros ▪ *(Sp.)* agencia de alquiler de coches

car stalled *(L. Am.)* se caló el carro ▪ *(Sp.)* se caló el coche

car that was to take them ▪ the car that would take them *(L. Am.) el* carro que los llevaría ▪ carro que los iba a llevar ▪ *(Sp.)* coche que los llevaría ▪ coche que los iba a llevar

car trouble *(L. Am.)* problemas con el carro ▪ *(Sp.)* problemas con el coche

car was totalled *(L. Am.) el* carro quedó un siniestro total ▪ *(Sp.) el* coche quedó un siniestro total ➤ The car was declared totalled. El carro ha sido declarado un siniestro total. ▪ El coche ha sido declarado un siniestro total.

car with good pickup ▪ car with rapid acceleration *(L. Am.)* carro con reprise ▪ carro con nervio ▪ *(Sp.)* coche con reprise ▪ coche con nervio ➤ This car has good pickup. Este carro tiene mucho reprise. ▪ Este coche tiene mucho reprise.

carbon copy copia al carbón

carbon monoxide poisoning envenenamiento por monóxido de carbono

carbonated water ▪ sparkling water *el* agua con gas ▪ agua mineral con gas

card stock *(for business cards)* cartulina

cardboard box caja de cartón

cardiac arrest paro cardiaco

cardinal rule regla cardinal

cardinal virtue *una* virtud cardinal

cardiopulmonary resuscitation ▪ CPR reanimación cardiorespiratoria

cards are stacked against one uno tiene las cartas en contra ▪ uno tiene las de perder ▪ uno lleva las de perder ➤ He hopes to become an Air Force pilot, but with his excessive height, I think the cards are stacked against him. Espera convertirse en un piloto de la Fuerza Aérea, pero con su excesiva altura, creo que tiene las cartas en contra. ▪ Espera convertirse en un piloto de la Fuerza Aérea, pero con su excesiva altura, creo que tiene las de perder. ▪ Espera convertirse en un piloto de la Fuerza Aérea, pero con su excesiva altura, creo que lleva las de perder.

care anything about...: not to ~ no importarle a uno absolutamente nada algo ▪ no importarle a uno lo más mínimo algo

care less: not to ~ ▪ not to give a (flying) damn importarle a uno un bledo ▪ no importarle a uno un pepino ▪ no importarle a uno un comino ▪ no importarle a uno unas narices ➤ I couldn't care less. ▪ I don't give a (flying) damn. Me importa un bledo.

to **care for 1.** to want ▪ to like querer ▪ apetecer **2.** to take care of cuidar ➤ Would you care for (some) dessert? ▪ Would you care for any dessert? ▪ Would you like (some) dessert? ¿Quieres postre? ▪ ¿Te apetece postre? ➤ We take care of our aging parents. Cuidamos a nuestros padres ancianos.

care of ▪ c/o a la atención de ▪ al cuidado de

to **care to...** ▪ to want to gustarle ➤ Would you care to take off your coat? ▪ Would you like to take off your coat? ¿Le gustaría quitarse el abrigo?

to **care to elaborate** querer dar más detalles ▪ querer entrar en detalles ▪ querer ser más preciso ▪ querer especificar más ➤ Would you care to elaborate? ¿Querrías dar más detalles? ▪ ¿Querrías entrar en detalles? ▪ ¿Querrías ser más preciso? ▪ ¿Querrías especificar más? ➤ I wouldn't care to elaborate. No querría dar más detalles. ▪ No querría entrar en detalles. ▪ No querría ser más preciso. ▪ No querría especificar más.

to **careen around the corner** escorarse al girar en la esquina

to **careen around the curve** ▪ to careen on the curve escorarse al tomar la curva

to **careen out of control** perder (un vehículo) la estabilidad (por la velocidad)

to be **careful about one's health** ▪ to guard one's health ▪ to look after one's health velar por la salud

careful driver conductor(-a) prudente ▪ conductor(-a) cuidadoso(-a)

to be **careful of** tener cuidado con ▪ tener cuidado de ▪ andar con cuidado ▪ *(colorful)* andar(se) con ojo ➤ In Mexico City, Tepito was the place you had to be most careful of. En la Ciudad de México, Tepito era el lugar con el que tener mayor cuidado. ▪ En la Ciudad de México, Tepito era el lugar del que tener mayor cuidado. ▪ En la Ciudad de México, Tepito era el lugar en el que andar con mayor cuidado. ▪ En la Ciudad de México, Tepito era el lugar en el que andar(se) con más ojo.

careful on the ice! *(tú)* ¡(ten) cuidado con el hielo! ▪ *(usted)* ¡(tenga) cuidado con el hielo!

to **caricature (in cartoons)** plasmar en historietas

carpe diem ▪ seize the day aprovecha la flor del día ▪ vive el momento

to **carpet bomb** ▪ to saturate bomb bombardear masivamente ▪ bombardear por saturación

carpet bombing ▪ saturation bombing bombardeo masivo ▪ bombardeo por saturación ▪ bombardeo de saturación

carried forward suma y sigue

to be **carried in a newspaper** salir en el periódico ➤ Mafalda, the Argentine comic strip, is also carried in a Mexico City paper. Mafalda, la historieta argentina, también sale en los periódicos de la Ciudad de México.

carrot and stick: to apply a policy of ~ dar una de cal y otra de arena

carrottop ▪ redhead pelirrojo(-a)

to **carry a gene** portar un gen ➤ If both parents carry the gene, the child may have medical problems. Si ambos progenitores portan el gen, el niño podría tener problemas de salud.

to **carry a story** publicar una historia ➤ The *New York Times* carried the story on the front page. El *New York Times* publicó la historia en primera plana.

to **carry a virus** ser portador de un virus

to **carry an item** ▪ to carry merchandise haber un artículo ▪ tener un artículo ➤ We carry the brand, but not the item. Tenemos la marca pero no el artículo. ➤ Do you carry milk? ¿Hay leche? *("¿Tiene usted leche?" means "Are you lactating?")* ➤ Do you carry eggs? ¿Hay huevos?

to **carry coals to Newcastle** ▪ to provide something already available in abundance llevar leña al monte ▪ echar agua en el mar ▪ llevar hierro a Vizcaya ▪ llover sobre mojado

to **carry merchandise** ▪ to carry an item llevar mercancías ▪ *(coll.)* trabajar mercancías ➤ We don't carry the wide mattresses. No trabajamos los colchones anchos.

to **carry on 1.** to make a scene armar un follón ▪ liarla ▪ liar un cisco ▪ montar un cisco ▪ liar una zapatiesta ▪ montar una zapatiesta ▪ liar un zipizape ▪ montar un zipizape **2.** to continue forward seguir adelante ➤ Quit carrying on (so)! ¡Deja de armar follón! ▪ ¡Deja de liarla! ➤ Carry on! ¡Adelante! ▪ ¡Sigue!

carry-on luggage ▪ carry-on baggage ▪ carry-on(s) *el* equipaje de mano

to **carry on board** llevar a bordo

to **carry on one's suitcase** ▪ to carry one's suitcase on llevar la maleta en el avión ➤ I carried on my suitcase. Llevé mi maleta en el avión. ➤ I had carried on my suitcase, so I didn't have to get it off the baggage carousel. Llevé mi maleta en el avión, así que no tuve que cogerla de la cinta. ➤ I carried it on. La llevé en el avión.

to **carry one's burdens quietly** ▪ to bear one's burdens quietly ir la procesión por dentro ➤ He carries his burdens quietly. ▪ He bears his burdens quietly. La procesión va por dentro.

to **carry one's lunch** *(to work or school)* ▪ to take one's lunch llevarse su almuerzo

to **carry one's (own) weight** responder de uno mismo ➤ He carries his weight in the company. Responde de sí mismo en la compañía.

to **carry out a number to *x* decimal places** sacar *x* decimales ➤ Carry it out to three decimal places. That's accurate enough for our purposes. Saca tres decimales. Es lo suficientemente preciso para nuestros propósitos.

to **carry out an attack** realizar un ataque ➤ The attack was carried out the day before. El ataque fue realizado el día previo.

to **carry out an experiment** ▪ to conduct an experiment llevar a cabo un experimento ➤ Cavendish carried out one of the greatest experiments in physics, in which he determined the gravitational constant. Cavendish llevó a cabo uno de los más grandes experimentos en física, con el que determinó la constante gravitacional.

to **carry out something** ▪ to take out something ▪ to remove something retirar los platos ▪ sacar los platos ➤ Would you help me carry out the dishes? ¿Me ayudarías a retirar los platos? ➤ *(news item)* The heroic mother cat returned to the burning house repeatedly to carry out her kittens. La heroica mamá gato volvió a la casa en llamas repetidas veces para sacar a sus gatitos. ➤ The mother kitten carried them out. La mamá gato los sacó.

to **carry something a step further** ▪ to take something a step further llevar algo un paso más allá ▪ llevar algo un paso más adelante ▪ llevar algo un paso más lejos ➤ Jung carried Freud's dream theory a step further. Jung llevó la teoría de los sueños de Freud un paso más allá. ▪ Jung llevó la teoría de los sueños de Freud un paso más adelante. ▪ Jung llevó la teoría de los sueños de Freud un paso más lejos.

to **carry over into** transferirse a ➤ The problems at home carry over into the classroom. Los problemas en el hogar se transfieren al aula.

to **carry something on one's side** cargar algo a un lado ▪ cargar algo en un lado ▪ cargar algo sobre un lado ➤ I was carrying the knapsack on my right side. Yo cargaba la mochila al lado derecho. ▪ Cargaba la mochila en el lado derecho. ▪ Cargaba la mochila sobre el lado derecho.

to **carry something on one's back** llevar algo a cuestas

to **carry something on one's shoulders** cargar algo sobre los hombros

to **carry something upstairs** ▪ to take something upstairs ▪ to bring something upstairs subir algo

to **carry the ball 1.** *(American football)* llevar el balón ▪ llevar la pelota **2.** *(figurative)* ▪ to bear the responsibility cargar la responsabilidad

to **carry the day** ▪ to make an occasion a success hacer de la ocasión un éxito ➤ Carlos' witty repartee carried the day. He made the whole party a success. Las ingeniosas réplicas de Carlos hicieron de la ocasión un éxito.

to **carry with it** traer consigo ➤ Bolivar's fame carries with it the thunder of arms. *(Juan Montalvo)* La fama de Bolivar trae consigo el ruido de las armas.

carrying case *el* neceser

to **carve a ham** trinchar un jamón ▪ cortar un jamón

to **carve a niche for oneself** ▪ to carve out a niche for oneself hacerse un hueco ▪ labrarse una carrera ▪ labrarse un futuro

to **carve a roast** trinchar un asado ▪ cortar un asado

to **carve a turkey** trinchar un pavo ▪ cortar un pavo

to **carve (out) a niche for oneself** hacerse un hueco ▪ labrarse una carrera ▪ labrarse un futuro

to **carve out a position** labrarse una posición ▪ hacerse un hueco ➤ *(news item)* The Russian president is carving out a position between those of the U.S. and France. El presidente ruso se está labrando una posición entre la postura americana y la francesa.

to **carve wood** trabajar la madera ▪ tallar (la) madera ▪ labrar (la) madera

carved wood madera labrada ▪ madera tallada

carved wooden figurine figurilla de madera labrada ▪ estatuilla tallada en madera

carved wooden statue estatua de madera (labrada)

case of an ailment caso de una enfermedad ➤ She has a mild case of the flu. Tiene un caso leve de gripe.

to be **case sensitive** *(computers)* diferenciar entre letra mayúscula y letra minúscula

to **case the joint** percatarse de cómo está el patio ▪ percatarse de cómo está el percal

to **cash a check** cobrar un cheque ▪ cambiar un cheque ▪ hacer efectivo un cheque

cash account cuenta en la que el cliente mantiene un saldo positivo en efectivo en un establecimiento

cash cow 1. *(lucrative business)* fábrica de dinero ▪ máquina de hacer dinero **2.** *(rich person)* ricachón ▪ ricachona ➤ That restaurant chain is a cash cow. Esa cadena de restaurantes es una fábrica de dinero. ▪ Esa cadena de restaurantes es una máquina de hacer dinero. ➤ He's not the cash cow that everyone thinks he is. Él no es el ricachón que todos piensan.

cash flow flujo de caja ➤ The business had negative cash flow the first year, then broke even for a year, then had positive cash flow. La empresa tuvo un flujo de caja negativo el primer año, luego cubrió gastos durante un año, y luego marchó en positivo.

cash flow problems: to have ~ tener problemas con el flujo de caja

to **cash in on something** ▪ to profit from something **1.** to make money on something rentabilizar algo **2.** to take advantage of something sacar partido de algo ➤ *(headline)* Opposition parties fail to cash in on the oil slick Partidos de la oposición no rentabilizan la marea negra ▪ Partidos de la oposición no sacan partido de la marea negra

cash on one's person: to have ~ tener efectivo (encima) ▪ llevar efectivo (encima) ➤ I don't have any cash on me. No llevo efectivo (encima). ➤ I have some cash. ▪ I've got some cash. Tengo algo de efectivo.

cash or charge? ¿(en) efectivo o con tarjeta? ▪ ¿(en) efectivo o lo cargo a cuenta?

to be **cash poor** tener problemas de liquidez ▪ no tener líquido ▪ no disponer de efectivo ➤ He owns real estate, but he's cash poor. Tiene propiedades, pero tiene problemas de liquidez. ▪ Tiene propiedades pero no tiene líquido. ▪ Tiene propiedades pero no dispone de efectivo.

cash register caja registradora

cash sale venta al contado

"Cask of Amontillado: The ~" *(Edgar Allan Poe story)* "El tonel de amontillado" ▪ "La barrica de amontillado" ➤ Poe wrote "The Cask of Amontillado" in 1846. Poe escribió "El tonel de amontillado" en 1846. *("Amontillado" is a sherry, usually dry, whose grapes are grown near Montilla, Andalucía.)*

Caspar Milquetoast *(character created by H.T. Webster)* ▪ milquetoast persona apocada ▪ persona pusilánime

to **cast a fishing line into the water** lanzar un sedal al agua

to **(cast a) glance at** echar un vistazo a ▪ lanzar una mirada a ▪ mirar ➤ He cast an approving glance at her. (Él) le lanzó una mirada de aprobación (a ella). ➤ She cast an equally approving glance at him. Ella le lanzó una mirada igualmente aprobatoria a él.

to **cast a mold** hacer un molde ▪ *(made out of metal)* fundir un molde

to **cast a pall over something** ensombrecer algo ➤ The car bombing just four blocks away cast a pall over our dinner party. El coche bomba a sólo dos manzanas de distancia nos ensombreció la cena.

to **cast a pall over the future** ensombrecer el futuro ➤ *(noticia)* The candidate's Swiss bank accounts cast a pall over his political future. Las cuentas suizas del candidato ensombrecen su futuro político.

to **cast a shadow on** ■ to project a shadow on proyectar una sombra sobre ➤ During a lunar eclipse, the Earth casts a shadow on the moon. ■ During a lunar eclipse, the Earth projects its shadow onto the lunar surface. Durante un eclipse lunar, la Tierra proyecta una sombra sobre la luna.

to **cast a shadow over** ■ to cast a pall over arrojar una sombra sobre ■ proyectar una sombra sobre ➤ The death of her cat cast a shadow over the girl's birthday. La muerte de su gato arrojó una sombra de tristeza sobre el cumpleaños de la niña.

to **cast a sidelong glance at someone** echarle un vistazo disimulado a alguien ■ mirar disimuladamente a alguien ■ observar disimuladamente a alguien ➤ He cast a sidelong glance at her. Le echó un vistazo disimuladamente (a ella). ■ La miró disimuladamente. ■ La observó disimuladamente.

to **cast a spell on someone** ■ to put someone under a spell hacerle un hechizo a alguien ■ hechizar a alguien

to **cast around for excuses** ■ to cast about for excuses ■ to look for excuses buscar excusas

to **cast aside something** ■ to cast something aside hacer algo a un lado ■ dejar algo a un lado ➤ She cast aside the magazine. ■ She cast the magazine aside. Hizo a un lado la revista. ➤ She cast it aside. La hizo a un lado.

to **cast aspersions on someone** poner a alguien en entredicho ■ difamar a alguien ■ calumniar a alguien

to **cast doubt on** ■ to call into question poner en entredicho ■ poner en cuestión

to be **cast in the same mold** ■ to be cut from the same cloth estar sacado del mismo molde ■ estar cortado por el mismo patrón

cast-iron skillet *la* sartén de hierro fundido *("Sartén" can be masculine, especially in the southern cone of South America.)*

cast-iron stomach: to have a ~ tener un estómago a prueba de bomba ■ *(L. Am.)* poder comerse un estribo de cobre

to **cast lots** echar a suertes

cast of mind mentality *la* mentalidad

to **cast off a spell** ■ to break a spell romper un sortilegio ■ romper un hechizo ■ romper un encantamiento

to **cast off bonds** ■ to cast the bonds off ■ to cast off shackles deshacerse de las ligaduras ■ liberarse de las ataduras ➤ All countries must help Africa cast off the bonds of oppression. ■ All countries must help Africa cast off the shackles of oppression. Todos los países deben ayudar a África a deshacerse de las ligaduras de la opresión. ■ Todos los países deben ayudar a África a liberarse de las ataduras de la opresión.

to **cast off shackles** ■ to cast shackles off ■ to cast off bonds deshacerse de las ligaduras ■ liberarse de las ataduras

to **cast one's vote for someone** ■ to vote for someone darle el voto a alguien ■ votar a alguien

to **cast one's vote for the measure** ■ to cast one's vote in favor of the measure votar a favor de la medida

to **cast out demons** expulsar a los demonios ■ echar fuera a los demonios ■ conjurar a los demonios ■ arrojar a los demonios fuera

to be **cast out into the street** 1. *(from a bar, etc.)* to be cast out onto the street ■ to be thrown out ■ to be kicked out ser echado 2. to be evicted or dispossessed of housing ser desahuciado ■ ser echado de casa ■ ser expulsado ■ ser arrojado

to **cast out someone** ■ to cast someone out ■ to force someone to leave ■ to expel someone expulsar a alguien ■ echar a alguien

to **cast someone as someone** dar a alguien el papel de alguien ➤ Steven Spielberg cast Liam Neeson as Abraham Lincoln. Steven Spielberg dio a Liam Neeson el papel de Abraham Lincoln.

to **cast someone into a dungeon** arrojar a alguien a una mazmorra

to **cast someone into prison** arrojar a alguien a prisión ■ meter a alguien en prisión

to **cast the first stone** tirar la primera piedra ■ arrojar la primera piedra

to **cast the net** echar la red ■ tender la red

to be **casual about...** ser informal para...

casual acquaintance conocido circunstancial

casual attire ■ casual dress ■ casual wear atuendo informal ■ atuendo "de sport" ■ atuendo desenfadado ■ ropa informal ■ ropa "de sport"

casual attitude *la* actitud poco formal ■ actitud poco seria ■ actitud de desinterés ■ actitud de desapego ■ (actitud de) indiferencia

casual clothes ■ street clothes ropa de la calle ■ vestimenta casual ■ ropa desenfadada

casual conversation: to engage in ~ ■ to engage in light conversation ■ to engage in small talk tener una conversación ligera ■ tener una conversación desenfadada ■ tener una conversación informal ■ mantener una conversación ligera ■ mantener una conversación desenfadada ■ mantener una conversación informal

casual dress ■ casual attire ■ casual wear atuendo informal ■ atuendo "de sport" ■ atuendo desenfadado ■ vestido informal ■ vestido "de sport" ■ vestido desenfadado ➤ Dress for the dinner party is casual. A la fiesta trae un atuendo informal. ■ El atuendo de la fiesta es informal.

casual greeting saludo informal ■ saludo desenfadado

casual look aspecto informal ■ aspecto desenfadado

casual wear ■ casual attire ■ casual dress atuendo informal ■ atuendo "de sport" ■ atuendo desenfadado ■ vestido informal ■ vestido "de sport" ■ vestido desenfadado

cat and mouse: to be a game of ~ ser un juego del gato y el ratón

cat and mouse: to play (a game of) ~ jugar al gato y el ratón ■ jugar al juego del gato y el ratón

cat litter ■ kitty litter arena para gatos

cat nap: to take a ~ echar una cabezadita ■ echar una siesta fugaz ■ echar un sueñecito

cat scratch: to get a ~ ■ to get scratched by a cat ■ to be scratched by a cat recibir un arañazo de gato ■ recibir un zarpazo de gato ■ ser arañado por un gato

to be **catapulted to fame** dar el salto a la fama ■ salir catapultado a la fama ■ estar catapultado a la fama

catastrophic damage daños catastróficos

catastrophic destruction ■ catastrophic damage cataclismo ■ destrucción catastrófica

to **catch a ball** agarrar la bola ■ agarrar la pelota ■ tomar la bola ■ tomar la pelota ■ *(soccer, rugby, basketball)* agarrar el balón ■ tomar el balón ■ *(Sp.)* coger la bola ■ coger la pelota ■ coger el balón

to **catch a bus** tomar el autobús ■ *(colorful)* pillar el autobús ■ agarrar el autobús ■ *(Sp.)* coger el autobús

to **catch (a) cold** agarrarse un resfriado ■ resfriarse ■ *(Sp.)* pillar un resfriado ■ coger un resfriado ■ pillar un trancazo ■ coger un trancazo ➤ I got one of those end-of-January colds. Me agarré un resfriado de final de enero.

to **catch a flight** tomar un vuelo ■ *(Sp.)* coger un vuelo ➤ I have to catch a flight at 2:30 p.m. ■ I have to catch a 2:30 p.m. flight. Tengo que tomar un vuelo a las 2:30 p.m. ■ Tengo que coger un vuelo a las 2:30 p.m.

to **catch a glimpse of each other** verse de refilón ■ verse de pasada ➤ We caught a glimpse of each other at the concert. Nos vimos de refilón en el concierto. ■ Nos vimos de pasada en el concierto.

to **catch a glimpse of someone** ver a alguien de lejos ■ ver a alguien de pasada ■ ver a alguien por un momento

to **catch a mistake** ■ to catch an error detectar un error ■ ver un error ■ detectar un fallo ■ ver un fallo

to **catch an error** ■ to catch a mistake detectar un error ■ ver un error ■ detectar un fallo ■ ver un fallo

to **catch fire** ■ to catch on fire prenderse fuego ■ arder ➤ During the American Civil War Battle of the Wilderness, the woods caught (on) fire, and many of the soldiers burned to death. Durante la Batalla de Wilderness en la Guerra Civil Americana, los bosques se prendieron fuego y muchos soldados murieron abrasados. ■ Durante la Batalla de Wilderness en la Guerra Civil Americana, los bosques ardieron y muchos soldados murieron abrasados.

to **catch fish** pescar (peces) ➤ *(Sesame Street episode)* Bert caught all the fish. Bert pescó todos los peces. ➤ Bert was catching more fish than Ernie. Bert estaba pescando más que Ernie. ▪ Bert pescaba más que Ernie.

to **catch flack** recibir críticas ▪ recoger críticas

to **catch hold of something** ▪ to catch onto something agarrarse a algo ▪ sujetarse a algo

Catch Me If You Can *(film title) Atrápame si puedes*

catch me up on yourself! ¡ponme al día con tu vida! ▪ ¡ponme al corriente de tu vida!

to **catch mice** *(referring to cats)* cazar ratones

to **catch my drift** *(colorful)* agarrar la onda ▪ *(Sp.)* pillar la onda ▪ coger la onda ➤ Do you catch my drift? ▪ Do you get what I'm saying? ¿Agarras mi onda? ▪ ¿Entiendes lo que te digo?

to **catch on** *(intransitive verb)* ▪ to take hold despegar ▪ calar en la gente ▪ cuajar ▪ volverse popular ▪ *(style, fad)* tener éxito

to **catch (on) fire** prenderse fuego ➤ During the American Civil War Battle of the Wilderness, the woods caught (on) fire, and many of the soldiers burned to death. Durante la Batalla de la Tierra Virgen en la Guerra Civil Americana, los bosques se prendieron fuego y muchos soldados murieron calcinados.

to **catch on to a joke** entender un chiste ▪ comprender un chiste ▪ pillar un chiste ▪ *(Sp.)* coger un chiste ➤ I didn't catch on. No he entendido el chiste. ▪ No he comprendido el chiste. ▪ No he pillado el chiste. ▪ No he cogido el chiste.

to **catch onto something** ▪ to catch hold of something agarrarse a algo ▪ sujetarse a algo ➤ He broke his fall by catching onto the railing. ▪ He broke his fall by catching hold of the railing. Detuvo su caída agarrándose al pasamanos. ▪ Detuvo su caída sujetándose al pasamanos.

to **catch one by surprise** pillar a uno de sorpresa ▪ pillar a uno por sorpresa ▪ *(Sp.)* coger a uno de sorpresa ▪ coger a uno por sorpresa ➤ The change to Daylight Savings Time caught him by surprise. El cambio al horario de verano lo pilló de sorpresa. ▪ *(Sp., leísmo)* El cambio al horario de verano le cogió de sorpresa.

to **catch one off (one's) guard** agarrar a uno desprevenido ▪ *(Sp.)* cogerle a uno desprevenido ➤ You caught me off guard. Me has agarrado desprevenido. ▪ Me has cogido desprevenido.

to **catch one's attention** llamarle a uno la atención ▪ llamar la atención de uno ▪ atraer la atención de uno ➤ The newspaper article about the late Spanish author Camilo José Cela caught my attention. El artículo de periódico sobre el fallecido escritor español Camilo José Cela llamó mi atención.

to **catch one's breath** ▪ to get one's breath (back) ▪ to recover one's breath recuperar aire ▪ recuperar el aliento ▪ recobrar la respiración ▪ recobrar el aliento

to **catch one's eye 1.** to attract one's attention cruzar la mirada con alguien **2.** to exchange glances cruzar la mirada con alguien **3.** to take a fancy to someone sentirse atraído(-a) a una persona ▪ llamar la atención de uno ▪ hacerle a alguien fijarse en algo ➤ See if you can catch the waiter's eye. Mira a ver si puedes llamar la atención del camarero. ▪ Mira a ver si puedes hacer que el camarero se fije en nosotros. ➤ I caught the waiter's eye. Llamé la atención del camarero. ▪ Hice que el camarero se fijase en mí. ➤ In Ogden Nash's poem, one small fossil caught his eye. En el poema de Ogden Nash, un pequeño fosil le hizo fijarse (en él). ➤ In Ogden Nash's poem, the small fossil caught the museum visitor's eye. En el poema de Ogden Nash, un pequeño fosil cruzó la mirada con el visitante el museo.

to **catch oneself** contenerse ➤ She was about to spill (all) the beans, but she caught herself. ▪ She was about to give away the secret, but she caught herself. Iba a descubrir el pastel, pero se contuvo. ▪ Iba a delatar el secreto, pero se contuvo.

catch phrase ▪ slogan *el* lema ▪ *el* eslogan

to **catch sight of someone** ▪ to spot someone divisar a alguien

to **catch someone at a bad time** pillar a alguien en mal momento ▪ *(Sp.)* coger a alguien en mal momento ➤ Have I caught you at a bad time? ▪ Am I catching you at a bad time? ¿Te pillo en mal momento? ▪ ¿Te cojo en mal momento?

to **catch someone at home** ▪ to find someone at home enganchar a alguien en casa ▪ agarrar a alguien en casa ▪ encontrar a alguien en casa ▪ *(Sp.)* pillar a alguien en casa ▪ coger a alguien en casa ➤ I'm sorry to call you so early, but it's hard to catch you at home. Siento llamarte tan pronto, pero es difícil pillarte en casa. ▪ Siento llamarte tan pronto, pero es difícil cogerte en casa.

to **catch someone by surprise** agarrar a alguien por sorpresa ▪ tomar a alguien por sorpresa ▪ *(Sp.)* pillar a alguien por sorpresa ▪ coger a alguien por sorpresa ➤ It caught him by surprise. Lo pilló por sorpresa. ▪ *(Sp., leísmo)* Le pilló por sorpresa. ▪ Le cogió por sorpresa. ➤ It caught her by surprise. La pillé por sorpresa. ▪ La cogió por sorpresa.

to **catch someone in a good mood** ▪ to find someone in a good mood encontrar a alguien de buen humor ▪ agarrar a alguien de buen humor ▪ agarrar a alguien de buenas ▪ *(Sp.)* pillar a alguien de buenas ▪ pillar a alguien de buen humor ▪ coger a alguien de buenas ▪ coger a alguien de buen humor

to **catch someone in a lie** agarrar a alguien en una mentira ▪ pillar a alguien en una mentira ▪ *(Sp.)* coger a alguien en una mentira ➤ The teacher caught him in a lie. La profesora le agarró (a él) en una mentira. ➤ The teacher caught her in a lie. La profesora le agarró (a ella) en una mentira.

to **catch someone in the act 1.** *(coll.)* agarrar a alguien in fraganti ▪ pillar a alguien in fraganti ▪ atrapar a alguien in fraganti ▪ *(Sp.)* coger a alguien in fraganti **2.** *(law)* agarrar a alguien en flagrante delito ▪ pillar a alguien en flagrante delito ▪ atrapar a alguien en flagrante delito ▪ *(Sp.)* coger a alguien en flagrante delito *("In fraganti" can be written "infraganti.")*

to **catch someone lying** agarrar a alguien mintiendo ▪ pillar a alguien mintiendo ▪ *(Sp.)* coger a alguien mintiendo ➤ The teacher caught him in a lie. La profesora le agarró (a él) mintiendo. ➤ The teacher caught her in a lie. La profesora le agarró (a ella) mintiendo.

to **catch someone off guard** agarrar a alguien desprevenido ▪ agarrar a alguien de sorpresa ▪ agarrar a alguien bajo de guardia ▪ agarrar a alguien con la guardia baja ▪ pillar a alguien desprevenido ▪ pillar a alguien bajo de guardia ▪ pillar a alguien con la guardia baja ▪ *(Sp.)* coger a alguien desprevenido ▪ coger a alguien bajo de guardia ▪ coger a alguien con la guardia baja ➤ The candidate was caught off guard by the question. Agarraron al candidato desprevenido por la pregunta. ▪ Pillaron al candidato desprevenido por la pregunta. ▪ Cogieron al candidato desprevenido por la pregunta.

to **catch someone red-handed** *(coll.)* ▪ to catch someone in the act agarrar a alguien con las manos en la masa ▪ pillar a alguien con las manos en la masa ▪ atrapar a alguien con las manos en la masa ▪ *(Sp.)* coger a alguien con las manos en la masa

to **catch someone unawares** ▪ to take someone unawares ▪ to catch someone by surprise ▪ to take someone by surprise tomar a alguien de imprevisto ▪ tomar a alguien de improviso ▪ *(Sp.)* coger a alguien de imprevisto ▪ coger a alguien de improviso

to **catch someone with his pants down** pillar a alguien en bragas ▪ pillar a alguien con el culo al aire ▪ pillar a alguien con los pantalones bajados ▪ *(Sp.)* coger a alguien en bragas ▪ coger a alguien con el culo al aire ▪ coger a alguien con los pantalones bajados

to **catch someone's attention** ▪ to get someone's attention atraer la atención de alguien ▪ llamar la atención de alguien ➤ An item in the newspaper caught my attention. ▪ An item in the newspaper got my attention. Una noticia en el periódico atrajo mi atención. ▪ Una noticia en el periódico llamó mi atención. ▪ Una noticia en el periódico me llamó la atención. ➤ See if you can catch that waiter's attention. ▪ See if you can get that waiter's attention. Mira si puedes atraer la atención del mesero. ▪ Mira si puedes llamar la atención de ese mesero. ▪ Mira si puedes agarrar la atención de ese mesero. ▪ *(Sp.)* Mira si puedes llamar la atención de ese camarero.

to **catch something in passing** pillar algo de paso ▪ *(Sp.)* coger algo de paso

to **catch something on the fly 1.** *(baseball, softball)* agarrar algo al vuelo ▪ *(Sp.)* coger algo al vuelo **2.** *(idea)* agarrar algo a la primera ▪ entender algo a la primera ▪ pillar algo a la primera ▪ agarrar algo al vuelo ▪ *(Sp.)* coger algo a la primera ▪ coger algo al vuelo ➤ He caught the ball on the fly. Agarró la bola al vuelo. ▪ Cogió la bola al vuelo. ➤ My Spanish teacher told me she likes the way I catch things on the fly. Mi profesora de español me dijo que le gustaba la forma en que agarraba las cosas a la primera. ▪ Mi profesora de español me dijo que le gustaba la forma en que agarraba las cosas al vuelo.

to **catch the bouquet** agarrar el ramo de novia ▪ *(Sp.)* coger el ramo de novia

to **catch the drift** *(colorful)* ▪ to get what someone is saying ▪ to understand what someone is getting at agarrar la idea ▪ *(Sp.)* coger la idea ➤ Do you catch my drift? ▪ Do you get what I'm saying? ¿Agarras mi idea? ▪ ¿Coges la idea?

to **catch the hint** ▪ to get the hint captar la indirecta ▪ pescar la indirecta

to **catch the tail end of something** pillar el final de algo ▪ coger el final de algo ▪ escuchar el final de algo ➤ I caught the tail end of it on the news. Pillé el final de ello en las noticias. ▪ *(Sp.)* Cogí el final de ello en las noticias. ➤ I only caught the tail end of the conversation. Sólo pillé el final de la conversación. ▪ Sólo cogí el final de la conversación.

to be a **catch twenty-two** *(Joseph Heller)* ▪ to be a Catch-22 ▪ to be a no-win situation ▪ to be a vicious circle ser la pescadilla que se muerde la cola ➤ In Mexico they tell you (that) you have to be hired by a firm in the United States and sent to Mexico, and in the United States they tell you the hiring in Mexico is all done locally, so it's a catch twenty-two. En México te dicen que tienes que ser contratado por una empresa en los Estados Unidos y ser trasladado a México, y en los Estados Unidos te dicen que la contración en México es local, así que es la pescadilla que se muerde la cola.

to **catch up on each other** ▪ to catch up on each other's news ponerse al día (el uno al otro) ➤ We have to catch up on each other. Tenemos que ponernos al día (el uno al otro).

to **catch up on one's homework** ▪ to get caught up on one's homework ponerse al día con las tareas ▪ *(Sp.)* ponerse al día con los deberes ➤ I've got to catch up on my homework. Tengo que ponerme al día con las tareas. ▪ *(Sp.)* Tengo que ponerme al día con los deberes.

to **catch up on one's sleep** ▪ to get caught up on one's (lost) sleep recuperar el sueño (perdido) ➤ I've gotten caught up on my sleep. ▪ I've caught up on my sleep. He recuperado el sueño (perdido).

to **catch up on someone** ponerse al tanto con alguien

to **catch up with one** empezar a afectar a uno ➤ My lack of sleep is catching up with me. ▪ My lack of sleep is starting to catch up with me. Empieza a afectarme la falta de sueño.

to **catch up (with someone)** alcanzar a alguien ➤ You all go on ahead, and I'll catch up (with you) later. Vayan ustedes delante, que los alcanzaré más tarde. ▪ Vayan ustedes delante, que los alcanzaré luego. ▪ *(Sp., vosotros)* Idos delante, que os alcanzaré más tarde. ▪ Idos delante, que os alcanzaré luego. ▪ *(Sp., leísmo)* Vayan ustedes delante, que luego les alcanzaré. ▪ Vayan ustedes delante, que luego les cojo. ➤ We're going to catch up with him later. Lo alcanzaremos más tarde. ▪ *(Sp., leísmo)* Le alcanzaremos más tarde. ➤ We caught up with him in the lobby. Lo alcanzamos en el vestíbulo. ▪ *(Sp., leísmo)* Le alcanzamos en el vestíbulo.

to **catch what someone said** oír lo que alguien ha dicho ▪ entender lo que alguien ha dicho ➤ Sorry, I didn't catch what you said. Perdona, no oí lo que dijiste. ▪ Perdona, no entendí lo que dijiste.

to **catch you at home** pillarte en casa ▪ *(Sp.)* cogerte en casa ➤ I didn't think I'd catch you at home on Saturday night. No pensé que te pillaría en casa un sábado por la noche. ▪ No pensé que te cogería en casa un sábado por la noche.

catchall phrase frase polisémica ➤ "Research and development" is a catchall phrase that covers multiple activities, depending on what the company manufactures. "Investigación y desarrollo" es una frase polisémica que cubre actividades multiples, según lo que fabrica la compañía.

Catcher in the Rye *(J.D. Salinger novel)* *El guardián entre el centeno*

catching up with someone acortar distancias con alguien ➤ We're catching up with them. Acortamos distancias con ellos.

catchy tune melodía pegajosa ▪ *(Sp.)* melodía que se pega

categorical answer ▪ categorical reply respuesta tajante ▪ repuesta categórica ▪ respuesta rotunda ▪ respuesta taxativa

categorical denial un "no" categórico ▪ negativa categórica ▪ negación categórica ▪ negativa rotunda ▪ negación rotunda ▪ negativa tajante ▪ negación tajante ➤ The accusation met with a categorical denial by the defendant. ▪ The accusation was met by a categorical denial from the defendant. La acusación se encontró con una negativa rotunda del acusado. ▪ La acusación se encontró con una negación categórica del acusado. ▪ La acusación se encontró con una negativa rotunda del acusado.

categorical imperative *(in Kant's philosophy)* imperativo categórico ➤ Kant's categorical imperative states: So act that you could will the maxim of your action to be a universal law. El imperativo categórico kantiano afirma: Obra de tal manera que tus máximas puedan constituirse por ellas mismas en leyes universales naturales. ▪ *(as paraphrased by Unamuno)* Obra de modo que tu acción pueda servir de norma a todos los hombres.

categorical reply ▪ categorical answer respuesta tajante ▪ repuesta categórica ▪ respuesta rotunda ▪ respuesta taxativa

to **cater to someone's every whim** consentir a alguien todos los caprichos ▪ satisfacer todas las necesidades de alguien ➤ He wants a wife who will cater to his every whim, and she wants a husband who will cater to her pocketbook. Quiere una esposa que consienta todos sus caprichos, y ella quiere un marido que satisfaga las necesidades de su chequera.

to **cater to tourists** satisfacer las necesidades de los turistas

Catholic Church la Iglesia Católica ▪ la Nave de San Pedro

the **cat's out of the bag** el secreto está a los cuatro vientos

cattle rustlers cuatreros

to be **caught in a snowstorm** estar atrapado en una tormenta de nieve

caught in a snowstorm: to get ~ quedar atrapado en una tormenta de nieve

to be **caught in a traffic jam** estar atrapado en el tráfico

caught in a traffic jam: to get ~ quedar atrapado en un embotellamiento ▪ quedar atrapado en un atascado ▪ quedar atascado

to be **caught in traffic** estar atrapado en el tráfico ▪ quedar atrapado en el tráfico

caught in something: to get one's finger ~ pillarse un dedo con algo ▪ atorarse un dedo con algo ➤ Marcus got his finger caught in the basket crank on the outdoor court. A Marcus se le pilló un dedo con la manivela que sube las canastas en concha descubierta.

to be **caught in the act** ▪ to get caught in the act ser agarrado in fraganti ▪ agarrarse in fraganti ▪ ser pillado in fraganti ▪ pillarse in fraganti ▪ ser atrapado in fraganti ▪ atraparse in fraganti ▪ *(Sp.)* ser cogido in fraganti ▪ cogerse in fraganti ▪ *(law)* ser agarrado en flagrante delito ▪ agarrarse en flagrante delito ▪ ser pillado en flagrante delito ▪ pillarse en flagrante delito ▪ ser atrapado en flagrante delito ▪ atraparse en flagrante delito ▪ ser cogido en flagrante delito ▪ cogerse en flagrante delito *("In fraganti" can be written "infraganti.")*

to be **caught in the crossfire** estar atrapado en un fuego cruzado

caught in the crossfire: to get ~ quedar atrapado en un fuego cruzado

to be **caught in the middle** estar atrapado en (el) medio ➤ The new prime minister was caught in the middle of the dispute. El nuevo primer ministro quedó atrapado en (el) medio de la disputa.

caught in the middle: to get ~ quedar atrapado en el medio

to be **caught in the throat** estar atravesado en la garganta ➤ The way people say "luego" around here sounds like they've got a bone caught in their throat. La manera en que la gente dice "luego" aquí suena como si tuvieran un hueso atravesado en la garganta.

to be **caught in the rain** ▪ to get caught in the rain estar atrapado en la lluvia

to be **caught in traffic** estar (atrapado) en un embotellamiento ▪ estar (atrapado) en un atasco ▪ estar atascado ➤ I don't want to get caught in the rush-hour traffic. No quiero quedar atrapado en el atasco de la hora punta.

caught in traffic: to get ~ ▪ to get stuck in traffic quedar atrapado en un embotellamiento ▪ quedar atrapado en un atasco ▪ quedar atascado to be **caught red-handed** ser pillado con las manos en la masa ▪ pillarse con las manos en la masa ▪ ser agarrado con las manos en la masa ▪ agarrarse con las manos en la masa ▪ ser atrapado con las manos en la masa ▪ atraparse con las manos en la masa ▪ *(Sp.)* ser cogido con las manos en la masa ▪ cogerse con las manos en la masa

to be **caught up in a book** estar enganchado en un libro

caught up in a book: to get ~ quedarse enganchado en un libro ➤ Carlos really got caught up in the book *Pedro Páramo* by Juan Rulfo. Carlos se quedó enganchado al libro *Pedro Páramo* de Juan Rulfo.

caught up in a net: to get ~ ▪ to get tangled up in a net estar enredado en una red ➤ The bear was caught up in the net. El oso estuvo enredado en la red.

to be **caught up in the excitement** ser llevado por la emoción

caught up in the excitement: to get ~ dejarse llevar por la emoción ➤ The football fans got caught up in the excitement of Real Madrid's winning the Champion's League. Los aficionados al fútbol se dejaron llevar por la emoción de la victoria del Real Madrid en Liga de Campeones.

caught up on one's sleep: to get ~ recuperar el sueño ➤ I got caught up on my sleep this weekend. Recuperé mi sueño atrasado este fin de semana.

to be **caught up on something** estar al día con algo ➤ I'm caught up on my reading finally. Por fin estoy al día con mis lecturas.

caught up on something: to get ~ 1. ponerse al día con algo **2.** recuperar ➤ I need to get caught up on my reading for school this weekend. Necesito ponerme al día con mis lecturas para clase este fin de semana. ➤ We need to get caught up on all the goings on while we were away. Necesitamos ponernos al día con todo lo que ha pasado mientras estábamos fuera.

caulking compound ▪ caulk ▪ calk masilla (de calafatear)

caulking gun ▪ calking gun pistola para masilla ▪ pistola para calafateo

to **cause a commotion** provocar agitación ➤ The anti-war protestors caused a lot of commotion downtown. Los manifestantes en contra de la guerra provocaron mucha agitación en el centro de la ciudad. ➤ Tom Cruise's visit to downtown Madrid caused a lot of commotion. La visita de Tom Cruise al centro de Madrid provocó una gran agitación.

to **cause a lot of comment** ▪ to generate a lot of comment dar mucho que hablar

to **cause a problem** causar un problema ▪ provocar un problema ▪ dar origen a un problema ▪ originar un problema ▪ dar lugar a un problema ▪ suscitar un problema ▪ producir un problema

to **cause a reaction** causar una reacción ▪ provocar una reacción ▪ dar origen a una reacción ▪ originar una reacción ▪ dar lugar a una reacción ▪ suscitar una reacción ▪ producir una reacción

to **cause a ruckus** ▪ to raise a ruckus armar jaleo ▪ armar bulla ▪ montar jaleo ▪ montar bulla ▪ armar mogollón

to **cause a sensation** tener resonancia ▪ causar revuelo

to **cause a stir** ▪ to create a stir levantar (una) polvareda ▪ causar conmoción

to **cause a war** producir una guerra

to **cause allergies in someone** provocar alergias a alguien ➤ The drug causes allergies, especially in women. La droga provoca alergias, sobre todo a mujeres.

to **cause an uproar** ▪ to provoke an uproar ▪ to create an uproar provocar un tumulto ➤ I caused an uproar by putting walnuts in the paella. Provoqué un tumulto por poner nueces en la paella.

to **cause damage to** ▪ to damage producir daños (físicos) en ▪ producir daños materiales ▪ causar desperfectos en ➤ The explosion caused some damage but not victims. La explosión causó algunos desperfectos pero no víctimas.

to **cause deaths** ▪ to result in deaths provocar muertes ➤ The fire levelled an asylum for the mentally ill, causing at least 25 deaths. ▪ The fire levelled an asylum for the mentally ill, resulting in at least 25 deaths. El fuego arrasó un asilo para enfermos mentales provocando al menos 25 muertes.

to **cause (emotional) pain** ▪ to be hurtful ser hiriente ▪ causar dolor ▪ ser doloroso ▪ producir dolor (emocional)

to be (a) **cause for concern** ser motivo de preocupación ▪ ser causa de preocupación

cause for concern: to give one ~ darle a uno motivo de preocupación ▪ darle a uno causa de preocupación ➤ The thing that gives me cause for concern is (that)... ▪ What gives me cause for concern is (that)... Lo que me da motivo de preocupación es (que)...

to **cause injury** ▪ to cause injuries producir daños ▪ causar heridas ▪ causar lesiones

to **cause nothing but trouble** ▪ to be nothing but trouble no darle más que penas ▪ no darle más que disgustos ▪ no reportar nada sino que disgustos ▪ no hacer nada sino darle problemas

to be the **cause of someone's jealousy** ▪ to be the reason for someone's jealousy ser la causa de los celos de alguien ▪ ser el origen de los celos de alguien ▪ ser el motivo de los celos de alguien ▪ tener la culpa de los celos de alguien ➤ He is the cause of my husband's jealousy. ▪ He is the reason for my husband's jealousy. Él tiene la culpa de los celos de mi marido. ▪ Él es la causa de los celos de mi marido.

cause of the collapse motivo(s) del derrumbe ▪ causa(s) del derrumbe ➤ Investigators last night were trying to determine the cause of the collapse. Los investigadores trataban de averiguar anoche los motivos del derrumbe. ▪ Los investigadores trataban de averiguar anoche las causas del derrumbe.

cause of the problem causa del problema ▪ *el* origen del problema ➤ The cause of the problem with the shuttle was a nick in one of the heat-resistant tiles. La causa del problema de transbordador fue una muesca en una de las láminas resistentes al calor.

to **cause physical pain** causar dolor físico ▪ provocar dolor físico

to **cause problems** causar problemas ▪ provocar problemas

to **cause psychological damage to someone** ▪ to traumatize someone producir daños psicológicos a alguien ▪ causar daños psicológicos a alguien ▪ dejar secuelas (psicológicas) a alguien

to **cause rifts between people** ▪ to sow discord ▪ to create dissension between people ▪ to cause trouble between people meter cizaña (entre personas) ▪ sembrar cizaña (entre personas) ▪ meter cisco (entre personas)

to **cause someone a lot of problems** producirle muchos problemas a alguien

to **cause someone nothing but problems** no reportarle más que problemas a alguien ▪ no causarle más que problemas a alguien ▪ no traerle más que problemas a alguien

to **cause someone to do something** provocar que alguien haga algo ▪ hacer que alguien haga algo ➤ A death in the family caused him to fall behind in school. Una muerte en la familia hizo que se quedara rezagado en el colegio.

to **cause something to happen** ▪ to make something happen hacer que algo pase ▪ hacer que algo suceda ➤ The excessive rotational speed caused the propeller to explode. La excesiva velocidad de rotación hizo que la hélice explotara. ▪ La excesiva velocidad de rotación hizo que la hélice explotase.

to **cause the accident** ▪ to be the cause of the accident causar el accidente ▪ ser la causa del accidente

to **cause trouble (between people)** ▪ to sow discord meter cizaña ▪ sembrar cizaña ▪ sembrar discordia ▪ malmeter ▪ malquistar

caustic humor ▪ biting humor ▪ corrosive humor humor cáustico ▪ humor mordaz ▪ humor corrosivo

caustic remark ▪ acrid remark comentario mordaz

to be **cautiously optimistic** ▪ to be guardedly optimistic ▪ to feel cautiously optimistic ▪ to feel guardedly optimistic ser moderadamente optimista ▪ ser comedidamente optimista ▪ sentirse moderadamente optimista ▪ sentirse comedidamente optimista ▪ ser optimista de forma moderada

to **cave in 1.** to collapse ▪ to give way hundirse ▪ caerse ▪ derrumbarse ▪ ceder **2.** to break down and confess ▪ to give in venirse abajo ▪ ceder ➤ The weight of the snow caused the roof to cave in. El peso de la nieve hizo que el techo se hundiera. ▪ El peso de la nieve hizo que el techo se cayera. ▪ El peso de la nieve hizo que el techo se derrumbara. ▪ El peso de la nieve hizo que el techo cediera. ➤ The witness caved in under cross-examination. El testigo se vino abajo durante el interrogatorio del abogado de la otra parte. ▪ El testigo cedió ante el interrogatorio del abogado de la otra parte.

to **cave in to demands for something** ceder ante las demandas de algo

to **cave in to demands for something to be done** ▪ to cave in to demands that something be done ceder ante las demandas para que se haga algo

caveman hombre de las cavernas ➤ It's so easy even a caveman can do it. Es tan fácil que aún el hombre de las cavernas puede hacerlo.

CD and tape player ▪ combination CD and tape player *el* lector de discos compactos y reproductor de casetes ▪ aparato de música ▪ tocadiscos

CD jacket funda para un CD

CD jewel case caja de un CD

CD player lector de CD ▪ reproductor de CD

cease-fire *el* cese de fuego ▪ alto de fuego

to **cease to exist** dejar de existir

the **ceiling fell in** ▪ the ceiling collapsed se desplomó el techo ▪ el techo vino abajo

ceiling of a room techo de una habitación

to **celebrate Mass** ▪ to say Mass celebrar misa ▪ decir misa ▪ oficiar misa

to **celebrate one's anniversary** celebrar el aniversario de uno

to **celebrate one's birthday** celebrar el cumpleaños de uno

celebrated city ▪ much-discussed city ▪ famous city ciudad famosa

celery stalk ▪ stalk of celery rama de apio

celestial sphere esfera celeste

cell phone ▪ cellular telephone *(Mex.)* un celular ▪ *(Sp.)* un móvil

to **center around** centrarse en torno a

center of gravity centro de gravedad

central command *(military)* ▪ CentCom *el* cuartel general (de la campaña)

central point punto céntrico ➤ The Zócalo is the central point of Mexico City. El Zócalo es el punto céntrico de la Ciudad de México. ➤ The simplicity of motive is the central point of Schopenhauer's philosophy, that the repertory of human behavior can be reduced to a few basic drives. La simplicidad del motivo es el punto céntrico de la filosofía de Schopenhauer, que el repertorio de conducta humana puede reducirse a unos pocos impulsos básicos.

centrifugal force fuerza centrífuga

centripetal force fuerza centrípeta

cerebral hemorrhage ▪ stroke *el* derrame cerebral ▪ hemorragia cerebral ▪ infarto cerebral ▪ trombosis cerebral ▪ hemiplejía ▪ *la* congestión cerebral ▪ embolia

certain constraints ciertas limitaciones ▪ ciertas ataduras *(literary)* ciertas coacciones

certain death muerte segura

certain something: to have a ~ tener un no sé qué

certain things ciertas cosas ➤ Certain things will upset the baby's stomach. Ciertas cosas revuelven el estómago del bebé.

a **chain is no stronger than its weakest link** la soga quiebra por lo más delgado

chain of events *(literary)* ▪ concatenation of events concatenación de sucesos ▪ concatenación de eventos ▪ concatenación de hechos

chain reaction *la* reacción en cadena

chain reaction collision *el* accidente en cadena

to **chain-smoke** encender un cigarro con otro ▪ fumar un cigarro tras otro ➤ He chain-smokes. Enciende un cigarro con otro.

to be a **chain-smoker** ▪ to be a heavy smoker ser fumador empedernido

to **chair a committee** ▪ to preside over a committee presidir un comité

chairman of the committee ▪ committee chairman presidente del comité

chairman of the Federal Reserve Board presidente de la Reserva Federal ▪ presidente de la mesa directiva de la Reserva Federal

chairman of the Joint Chiefs of Staff presidente de la Junta de Jefes de Estado Mayor ▪ jefe del Estado Mayor Conjunto

challenge facing reto que enfrenta ▪ reto pendiente en

to **challenge someone to a debate** retar a alguien a un debate

to **challenge someone to a duel** retar a alguien a duelo ▪ retar a alguien en duelo

to **challenge someone to do something** retar a alguien a hacer algo ▪ retar a alguien a que haga algo

challenging job trabajo desafiante

chamomile tea manzanilla ▪ infusión de manzanilla ▪ té de manzanilla

to be **champing at the bit to...** venir con las pilas puestas para... ▪ tener las pilas puestas para...

chance encounter ▪ chance meeting encuentro casual ▪ encuentro por azar ▪ encuentro inesperado

the **chance is remote** la posibilidad es escasa

chance meeting ▪ chance encounter encuentro casual ▪ encuentro por azar ▪ encuentro inesperado

to be the **chance of a lifetime** ▪ to be the opportunity of a lifetime ser la oportunidad de una vida ▪ ser la ocasión de una vida ➤ It's the chance of a lifetime. Es la oportunidad de mi vida. ▪ Es la ocasión de mi vida.

chance of that happening probabilidad de que eso suceda ▪ posibilidad de que eso suceda

chance to prove oneself oportunidad de probarse a uno mismo ▪ oportunidad de ponerse a prueba uno mismo

chance to prove something to oneself oportunidad de demostrarse algo a uno mismo

to **chance upon** encontrar por casualidad ▪ deparar la suerte

chances are remote ▪ the chance is remote probabilidad es escasa ▪ posibilidad es escasa

chances are slim *(coll.)* ▪ chances are remote ▪ the chance is remote probabilidades son escasas ▪ posibilidades son escasas

the **chance(s) of that (happening)** la probabilidad de que eso suceda ▪ la posibilidad de que eso suceda ▪ las probabilidades de que eso suceda ➤ The chances of that are not very good. La probabilidad de que eso suceda no es muy alta. ▪ Las probabilidades de que eso suceda no son muy altas.

to **change a tire** cambiar una rueda ▪ *(Mex.)* cambiar una llanta ▪ cambiar un neumático

to **change allegiances** cambiar de lealtad ▪ *(colorful)* cambiar de chaqueta

to **change clothes** cambiarse (de ropa) ▪ *(to the skin)* mudarse (de ropa)

to **change course** cambiar de rumbo ▪ cambiar el curso

to **change directions** ▪ to turn around and go the other way cambiar de sentido

to **change dollars into pesos** ▪ to exchange dollars for pesos cambiar dólares por pesos

to **change everything** cambiar (radicalmente) las cosas ➤ That changes everything. Eso cambia (radicalmente) las cosas.

change for a bill: to have ~ tener cambio de un billete

change for a coin: to have ~ tener cambio de una moneda

to be a **change for the better** ser una mejora ▪ ser un cambio a mejor ▪ ser un cambio para bien ▪ *(of a medical condition)* mejoría

to **change for the better** cambiar a mejor ▪ cambiar para bien ▪ *(of a medical condition)* to get better experimentar mejoría

change for the worse cambio a peor ▪ cambio para mal ▪ *(of a medical condition)* empeoramiento

to **change for the worse** cambiar a peor ▪ cambiar para mal ▪ *(of a medical condition)* to get worse sufrir un empeoramiento

to **change hands** ▪ to change ownership cambiar de manos ▪ cambiar de dueños ➤ That restaurant has changed hands half a dozen times. Este restaurante ha cambiado de manos media docena de veces. ▪ Este restaurante ha cambiado de dueños media docena de veces.

to **change hats** ▪ to change occupations cambiar de profesión

change in the wind ■ shift in the wind ■ shifting of the wind cambio en la dirección del viento ■ salto de viento

to **change jobs** cambiar de trabajo ■ pasarse de un trabajo a otro

change of course *(politically)* ■ change of direction *el* viraje ■ giro

change of direction *(politically)* ■ change of course *el* viraje ■ giro

change of heart: to have a ~ tener una mejora de actitud

change of scene ■ change of scenery cambio de aire ■ cambio de ambiente

change of venue cambio de jurisdicción ➤ The case is heard in the jurisdiction where the crime is committed, unless there is a change of venue. La vista del caso se celebra en la jurisdicción donde se ha cometido el crimen a menos que haya un cambio de jurisdicción.

to **change one's clothes to the skin** ■ to change one's clothes completely mudarse ➤ He changed his clothes to the skin after taking a shower. *(Mex.)* Se mudó después de darse un regaderazo. ■ *(Sp.)* Se mudó después de ducharse.

to **change one's expression** ■ to alter one's expression inmutarse ■ cambiar de cara ■ mudar el gesto

to **change one's major** cambiar de carrera

to **change one's mind** cambiar de opinión ■ cambiar de idea ■ cambiar de parecer ➤ I've changed my mind. I'll have carbonated water instead. He cambiado de opinión. Prefiero agua con gas. ➤ I've changed my mind about going home on vacation. He cambiado de idea con respecto a volver a casa en vacaciones.

to **change one's plans** cambiar los planes ■ cambiar de planes

to **change one's position on a matter** dar un giro a su posición sobre un asunto ➤ The government changed its position. El gobierno dio un giro a su posición.

to **change one's tune** cambiar de cantinela ■ cambiar de parecer ➤ He may not be a musician, but he knows how to change his tune. Tal vez no sea músico, pero bien que cambia de cantinela.

to **change one's ways** ■ to turn over a new leaf cambiar uno de hábitos ■ cambiar uno de costumbres ■ pasar página ➤ It's never too late to change your ways. Nunca es tarde para cambiar de hábitos. ■ Nunca es tarde para cambiar de costumbres. ■ Nunca es tarde para pasar página.

to **change places with someone** ocupar el lugar de alguien ■ ocupar el lugar de otra persona ■ cambiar de sitio con alguien ■ cambiar de sitio con otra persona ➤ Would you like to change places with someone you know? ■ Would you like to take the place of someone you know? ¿Te gustaría ocupar el lugar de otra persona a la que conoces? ■ Te gustaría ocupar el lugar de alguien al que conoces?

to **change planes** ■ to make a connecting flight cambiar de avión ■ transbordar ■ hacer transbordo ■ hacer una conexión

to **change sides** *(in a debate)* ■ to switch sides cambiar de parecer ■ cambiar de camisa

change that takes place when cambio que sucede cuando ■ cambio que ocurre cuando

to **change the furniture around** ■ to change around the furniture cambiar los muebles de sitio

to **change the grounds of the discussion** llevar la conversación a otros terrenos

to **change the room around** ■ to change around the furniture in the room cambiar los muebles de sitio

to **change the subject** cambiar de tema ■ cambiar el asunto

to **change the time (for someone)** cambiársele la hora ➤ The students have requested that the time of the class be changed. ■ The students have requested that we change the time of the class. Los estudiantes han pedido que se les cambie la hora de la clase.

to **change trains** cambiar de trenes ■ transbordar a otro tren ■ hacer transbordo a otro tren ■ hacer una conexión con otro tren ■ tomar otro tren ■ *(Sp.)* coger otro tren

to **change with the political winds** ■ to be an opportunist arrimarse al sol que más calienta ■ ser oportunista

changed a lot: to have ~ estar muy cambiado ➤ She's changed a lot. Está muy cambiada.

changing of the guard relevo de la guardia

changing patterns pautas cambiantes

changing times cambio de los tiempos ■ tiempos cambiantes ➤ In a clear example of the changing times, the TV networks have replaced daily newspapers in the commission of glaring mistakes. En una muestra evidente del cambio de los tiempos, las cadenas de televisión han substituido a los diarios escritos en el protagonismo de pifias monumentales.

to **channel surf** ■ to flip channels ■ to flip through (the) channels ■ to change channels in rapid succession cambiar de canales velozmente ■ *(Sp.)* hacer zapping

character flaw ■ flaw of character ■ flaw in one's character defecto del carácter

character from a novel *el* personaje de una novela ■ personaje novelesco ➤ Jane Eyre is a character from a novel by Charlotte Brontë. Jane Eyre es un personaje de una novela de Charlotte Brontë. ➤ He looked like a character from a Dickens novel. Parecía un personaje de una novela de Dickens. ➤ Who is the main character? ¿Quién es el protagonista?

character is formed tiene el carácter formado ■ tiene la personalidad formada ➤ It's not a question of not forgiving him. His character is formed. He is what he is. No se trata de no perdonarle. Él ya tiene el carácter formado. Es lo que es. ■ No se trata de no perdonarle. Él ya tiene la personalidad formada. Es lo que es.

character trait rasgo del carácter

to be **characteristic of** ser propio de ➤ Friendliness is characteristic of the Spanish. La simpatía es propia de los españoles.

to **characterize something as** ■ to describe something as calificar algo de ➤ The president has characterized the elections in Iraq as a success. El presidente ha calificado las elecciones en Irak como un éxito.

to be **characterized by** caracterizarse por

to be a **charge** *(as opposed to cash payment)* ser una compra a crédito ■ ser una compra a cuenta ■ ser una compra con tarjeta ➤ It was a charge, so the store should have a record. Fue una compra a cuenta, así que la tienda debería tener un comprobante.

to **charge a battery** **1.** *(small battery, e.g., cell phone)* cargar una pila **2.** *(large battery, e.g., car)* cargar una batería

charge account cuenta (de crédito)

to **charge for something** cobrar por algo ➤ Did you charge me for the envelope? ¿Me cobró por el sobre? ➤ What would you charge me to print this and bind it? ■ How much would you charge me to print and bind this? ¿Cuánto me cobraría por imprimir esto y encuadernarlo? ■ ¿Cuánto me cobraría por imprimir y encuadernar esto? ➤ How much did you charge me for February? ¿Cuánto me cobró usted por el mes de febrero?

charge it, please *(tú)* cárgalo a la cuenta, por favor ■ cárgalo en mi cuenta, por favor ■ *(usted)* cárguelo en mi cuenta, por favor

to **charge merchandise on an account** ■ to charge merchandise to an account cargar mercancías en una cuenta ■ apuntar mercancías en una cuenta ■ cargar bienes en una cuenta ■ apuntar bienes en una cuenta ➤ Charge it to my account. *(tú)* Cárgalo en mi cuenta. ■ Apúntalo en mi cuenta. ■ *(usted)* Cárguelo en mi cuenta. ■ Apúntelo en mi cuenta.

charge of a bull embestida

charge per kilowatt hour ■ price per kilowatt hour precio (del) kilovatio hora ➤ What is the charge per kilowatt hour for electricity in Madrid? ¿Cuál es el precio (del) kilovatio hora en Madrid?

to **charge someone for something** cobrar a alguien por algo ➤ Did you charge me for the bread? ¿Me cobró por el pan? ➤ Do you charge for the bread, or is that included in the dinner? ¿Cobran por el pan o está incluido en la cena?

to **charge someone with a crime** acusar a alguien de un crimen ■ levantar el cargo de un crimen contra alguien

to **charge someone with a felony** acusar a alguien de un delito mayor ■ levantar el cargo de un delito mayor contra alguien

to **charge someone with a misdemeanor** acusar a alguien de un delito menor ■ levantar el cargo de un delito menor contra alguien to **charge something on someone's account** ■ to put something on someone's account cargar algo en la cuenta de alguien ➤ I'd like to charge this on my account, please. Me gustaría cargar esto en mi cuenta, por favor.

to **charge suddenly** *(bull)* embestir de repente

to **charge the batteries** ■ to charge up the batteries *(small batteries used in radios, cell phones, etc.)* cargar las pilas

to **charge the battery** ■ to charge up the battery *(larger battery used in cars, motorcycles, etc.)* cargar la batería

to **charge the long-distance rate** aplicar la tarifa de larga distancia

to **charge with electricity** cargar de electricidad

to be **charged with a crime** acusarle a alguien con un crimen ➤ He was charged with disorderly conduct. Le acusaron de alteración del orden público.

charge(s) stemming from... acusación derivada de... ■ acusaciones derivadas de...

charity begins at home la caridad bien entendida empieza por uno mismo

charley horse *(coll.)* ■ muscle cramp *el* tirón ■ *el* calambre

charming bum golfo encantador ■ viva la Virgen encantador ➤ She fell for a charming bum. Quedó prendada de un golfo encantador. ■ Quedó prendada de un viva la Virgen encantador.

to **chart a course** ■ to plot a course trazar un curso

to **chase a fugitive** perseguir a un fugitivo

to **chase cars, cats, and squirrels** *(dogs' occupation)* perseguir carros, gatos y ardillas ■ ir tras carros, gatos y ardillas

to **chase someone off** ■ to run someone off ahuyentar a alguien ➤ My big brother chased them off. Mi hermano mayor los ahuyentó.

to **chase the cat up the tree** perseguir al gato hasta el árbol

chastity belt *el* cinturón de castidad

cheap imitation burda imitación ■ *(Mex.)* imitación chafa

cheap shot ■ low blow golpe bajo

to be **cheaper by the dozen** ser más barato por docenas

to be **cheaper in the long run** salir más barato a la larga ➤ It's cheaper in the long run to buy a bus pass. Sale más barato a la larga comprar un bónobus.

to **cheat on a test 1.** *(by copying)* copiar del examen de alguien **2.** *(with hidden notes)* sacar chuletas ■ llevar chuletas **3.** *(with pre-written answers)* dar el cambiazo

to **cheat on an agreement** traicionar un acuerdo ■ hacer trampas en un acuerdo ➤ Countries should not cheat on nuclear non-proliferation treaties. Los países no deberían traicionar los acuerdos de no proliferación nuclear. ■ Los países no deberían hacer trampas en los acuerdos de no proliferación nuclear.

to **cheat on one's husband** ■ to be unfaithful to one's husband ■ to stray engañar a su marido ■ ser infiel a su marido ■ *(colorful)* ponerle los cuernos al marido ■ *(L. Am.)* meterle los cachos al marido

to **cheat on one's spouse** ■ to be unfaithful to one's spouse ■ to stray engañar a su cónyuge ■ ser infiel a su cónyuge ■ *(colorful)* ponerle los cuernos al cónyuge ■ *(L. Am.)* meterle los cachos al cónyuge

to **cheat on one's wife** ■ to be unfaithful to one's wife ■ to stray engañar a su esposa ■ ser infiel a su esposa ■ *(colorful)* ponerle cuernos a la esposa ■ *(L. Am.)* meterle los cachos a la esposa

to **cheat on one's taxes** defraudar a hacienda ■ defraudar a la hacienda pública

to **cheat someone** estafar a alguien ■ timar a alguien ■ *(Mex., coll.)* hacer (una) transa a alguien

to **check and see...** echarle un ojo a... ■ ir a mirar si... ➤ Check and see if the rice is done, would you? Échale un ojo al arroz para ver si está cocido, ¿quieres? ■ Ve a mirar si el arroz está cocido, ¿quieres?

to **check baggage** ■ to check (the) suitcases facturar el equipaje ■ facturar las maletas ➤ Are you going to check your suitcase or carry it on? ¿Vas a facturar tu maleta o llevarla en el avión?

check for a certain amount: to make out a ~ ■ to write a check for a certain amount extender un cheque por cierta cantidad ➤ She made the check for two hundred dollars. ■ She wrote the check for two hundred dollars. Extendió el cheque por valor de doscientos dólares ➤ She made out a check for the balance owed. (Ella) extendió un cheque por el saldo que se debía.

to **check for mistakes** ■ to check it for mistakes revisar para ver si hay errores ➤ Did you check (it) for spelling mistakes? ¿Lo has revisado para ver si hay errores de ortografía?

to **check in at a hotel** ■ to check into a hotel registrarse en un hotel

to **check in at a library** hacerse socio de una biblioteca

to **check in at the (airline) ticket counter** facturar en el mostrador (de facturación) ■ presentarse en el mostrador de facturación ■ registrarse en el mostrador de facturación

to **check in at the gate (just before boarding an airplane)** registrarse en la puerta de embarque (inmediatamente antes de embarcar en el avión) ■ confirmar pasaje en la puerta de embarque (inmediatamente antes de embarcar en el avión) ➤ Do I need to check in with you, or am I all set? ¿Necesito (volver a) registrarme con usted o está todo listo? ■ ¿Necesito (volver a) confirmar pasaje con usted o está todo listo?

to **check instructions** comprobar las instrucciones

to **check into a hotel** registrarse en un hotel

to **check into a report** comprobar algo en un informe ■ averiguar algo en un informe ■ enterarse de algo en un informe ➤ It's the first I've heard of it. I'll check into it. Es la primero vez que oigo eso. Lo comprobaré.

the **check is in the mail** el cheque está en el correo ■ el cheque viene en el correo

to **check it out 1.** *(what's happening)* ver qué pasa **2.** *(library book)* sacarlo ➤ They're shouting "campeones, campeones, olé, olé, olé." I gotta go down and check it out. Están gritando, "campeones, campeones, olé, olé, olé". Tengo que bajar a ver qué pasa. ➤ It was like that when I checked it out. Ya estaba así cuando (yo) lo saqué.

to **check it to make sure** comprobarlo para asegurarse ■ verificarlo para asegurarse ➤ Check it to make sure I counted right. Compruébalo para asegurarte de que conté bien. ■ Compruébalo para asegurarte de que conté bien. ■ Verifícalo para asegurarte de que conté bien.

check (mark) visto bueno ■ una equis ■ una cruz ■ marca de verificación ■ *(Mex.)* paloma ➤ Put a check mark by her name. Pon una marca a (lado de) su nombre. ■ Haz una marca a (lado de) su nombre. ■ Pon una marca de verificación al lado de su nombre.

check me out! ¡ven a conocerme! ■ ¡conóceme! ➤ The little diamond in the earlobe says, "Check me out!" Ese pequeño diamante en el lóbulo de la oreja, va diciéndo: "ven a conocerme".

to **check off something** ■ to check something off **1.** to put a mark by something marcar algo (con un visto) ■ marcar algo (con una señal) ■ hacer una marca en algo ■ verificar algo **2.** to cross off something ■ to cross something off ■ to cross out something ■ to cross something out tachar algo ➤ I've already called her, so you can check her name off the list. Ya la he llamado, así que puedes hacer una marca al lado de su nombre. ➤ She can't come, so you can check her off the list. ■ You can cross her name off the list. No puede venir, así que puedes tacharla de la lista.

to **check on an order 1.** *(from the customer's point of view)* verificar un pedido ■ mirar a ver como va un pedido ■ ver como va la orden (de comida) ■ *(Mex.)* checar un pedido **2.** *(from the waiter's point of view)* mirar a ver como va una comanda ➤ Would you check on our order? It's been over twenty minutes. ¿Podrías comprobar cómo va nuestro pedido? Ya llevamos veinte minutos (esperando). ■ ¿Podrías ver cómo va nuestro pedido? Van a hacer veinte minutos.

to **check on someone** mirar a ver a alguien ■ echarle un vistazo a alguien ■ constatar si alguien está bien ➤ I asked the manager to check on the tenant. Pedí que el gerente mirara a ver como está el inquilino.

to **check on something** comprobar algo ■ echarle un vistazo algo ➤ Would you check on the dog for me? ¿Me mirarías el perro? ■ ¿Le echarías un vistazo al perro (por mí)? ■ ¿Me controlarías al perro? ■ ¿Me vigilarías al perro?

to **check one's E-mail** *(Mex.)* chequear el correo electrónico ■ revisar el correo electrónico ■ *(Sp.)* comprobar el correo electrónico ■ mirar si se tiene correo electrónico

to **check one's (telephone) messages** ■ to check one's voice mail revisar los mensajes telefónicos ■ comprobar el buzón de voz ■ comprobar los mensajes de voz ■ comprobar si se tiene mensajes de voz

to **check out a book (from the library)** ■ to check a book out of the library ■ to take out a book (from the library) sacar un libro de la biblioteca

to **check out a lead** comprobar la veracidad de una pista

to **check out of a hotel** marcharse de un hotel ■ dejar la habitación

to **check over someone** *(coll.)* ■ to check someone over ■ to examine someone hacerle un chequeo a alguien ■ revisar a alguien ➤ The doctor checked the patient over and sent him home. ■ The doctor checked over the patient and sent him home. El médico le hizo un chequeo al paciente y le mandó a casa. ➤ The doctor checked him over and sent him home. El médico le hizo un chequeo y le mandó a casa. ➤ The security guard checks the customers over with a metal detector before entering the café. El guardia de seguridad revisa a los clientes con un detector de metales antes de entrar en el café. ➤ The security guard checks them over. El guardia los revisa. ■ *(Sp., leísmo)* El guardia les revisa.

to **check someone's homework** *(L. Am.)* revisar la tarea ■ *(Sp.)* revisar los deberes ➤ Would you check (over) my homework? ■ Would you check my homework over? ¿Comprobarías mi tarea? ■ ¿Me comprobarías la tarea? ■ ¿Me revisas la tarea? ➤ Would you check it over (for me)? ¿Los comprobarías? ■ ¿Me los comprobarías?

to **check someone's blood pressure** ■ to take someone's blood pressure tomarle la tensión a alguien ■ medirle la tensión a alguien ➤ The doctor checked my blood pressure. El médico me tomó la tensión. ■ El médico me midió la tensión. ➤ The doctor checked her blood pressure. El médico le tomó la tensión. ■ El médico le midió la tensión.

to **check someone's tonsils** echarle un vistazo a las amígdalas ■ revisarle las amígdalas a alguien ➤ The doctor checked the boy's tonsils. El médico le echó un vistazo a las amígdalas del muchacho.

to **check the mail** ver si hay correo ■ comprobar si hay correo ■ comprobar si hay correspondencia ■ fijarse si hay correo ■ fijarse si hay correspondencia ➤ I'm going to go down and check the mail. Voy a bajar y comprobar si tengo correo. ■ Voy a bajar y ver si hay correo.

to **check the number** comprobar el número ➤ Please check the number and try again. Por favor, compruebe su número y vuelva a intentarlo.

to **check the oil** revisar el aceite ■ revisar el nivel de aceite ■ comprobar el (nivel del) aceite

to **check the proper functioning of something** comprobar el buen funcionamiento de algo ➤ It concerned airplanes whose proper functioning had been checked as they came off the assembly line. Se trataba de aviones cuyo buen funcionamiento había sido comprobado al salir de la cadena de montaje.

to **check the spelling** revisar la ortografía

to **check the spread of something** ■ to put the spread of something in check ■ to stop the spread of something atajar la expansión de algo ➤ New vaccines have checked the spread of the contagion. Las nuevas vacunas han atajado la expansión del contagio. ➤ European jurists require one percent of tax revenues to check the spread of domestic violence. Juristas europeas exigen el uno por ciento de los presupuestos para atajar la violencia doméstica.

to **check the time** comprobar la hora ■ ver la hora

to **check to be sure (that)...** ■ to check to make sure (that)... ■ to check to see that... comprobar que... ■ comprobar para estar seguro que... ■ comprobar para asegurarse que... ➤ Before connecting the toaster, check to be sure (that) the voltage is the same as that indicated on the identification plate. Antes de conectar el tostador, compruebe que la tensión corresponde con la indicada en la placa de características.

to **check to make sure (that...)** ■ to check to be sure (that...) ■ to check to see that... ■ to check that... comprobar para estar seguro de que... ■ comprobar que... ➤ Before connecting the toaster, check to make sure (that) the voltage is the same as that indicated on the identification plate. Antes de conectar el tostador, compruebe que la tensión corresponde con la indicada en la placa de características. ➤ Check to make sure I counted right. Comprueba para asegurar que conté bien. ➤ Check it to make sure I counted right. Compruébalo para asegurar que conté bien.

to **(check to) see if...** comprobar (para ver) si... ■ revisar a ver si... ➤ I was just checking to see if my order is on time. Sólo estaba comprobando para ver si mi pedido estará a tiempo. ➤ Check to see if it's done. Comprueba para ver si está hecho. ■ Comprueba que está hecho.

to **check to see that...** ■ to check to make sure (that)... ■ to check to be sure (that)... ■ to check that... comprobar que... ■ revisar a ver si... ➤ Before connecting the toaster, check to see that the voltage is the same as that indicated on the identification plate. Antes de conectar el tostador, revisa a ver si el voltaje es el mismo que indica la placa de características.

to **(check to) see whether or not...** comprobar (para ver) si... o no

to **check under the hood** mirar bajo el capó ■ revisar bajo el capó ■ *(Mex.)* mirar bajo el cofre

to **check with someone** consultar con alguien ➤ I need to check with my friends to make sure we can all go at 8 p.m. Necesito consultar con mis amigos para asegurarme de que todos podemos ir a las ocho. ➤ Check with a video store to see if the movie is available in DVD in several languages. Consulte con el videoclub para ver si tienen la película en DVD con varios idiomas. ➤ Check with the boss before you order any new stock. Consulta con el jefe antes de ordenar cualquier nueva existencia.

to **check with the bank** consultar con el banco ■ comprobar en el banco ■ verificar con el banco ➤ I checked with the bank, and they said my account has not been credited. Consulté con el banco y me dijeron que no se ha producido ningún ingreso en mi cuenta. ➤ I just checked with the bank, and the deposit is showing this morning. Acabo de comprobar en el banco, y el ingreso consta esta mañana.

checked shirt ■ plaid shirt camisa a cuadros

checking account cuenta corriente

checklist lista de comprobación ■ lista para comprobar ■ lista de verificación

to **checkmate someone** dar jaque mate a alguien

checkout period período de préstamo ➤ How long is the checkout period for this book? ■ What is the checkout period for this book? ¿Cuál es el período de préstamo de este libro?

checkout time hora de salir ■ hora de irse ■ hora de dejar el hotel

checkout time at a hotel hora de dejar la habitación ■ hora de desocupar la habitación ➤ What's the checkout time (at this hotel)? ¿A qué hora hay que dejar la habitación (en este hotel)? ■ ¿A qué hora hay que desocupar la habitación?

checkup: medical ~ ■ medical exam ■ physical exam chequeo general ■ revisión médica ■ reconocimiento médico

cheek by jowl: to live ~ ■ to live hand to mouth vivir con una mano detrás y otra delante ➤ The people of the undeveloped countries sort of live cheek by jowl. La gente de los países subdesarrollados medio vive con una mano detrás y otra delante.

to **cheer up** ■ to take heart animarse

to **cheer up someone** ■ to cheer someone up animar a alguien ■ alegrar a alguien

cheer up! *(tú)* ¡anímate! ■ *(usted)* ¡anímese!

cheerful countenance *el* semblante alegre ■ rostro alegre ■ cara alegre

cheerful demeanor figura alegre

cheering of the fans griterío de los aficionados

cheers! ¡salud!

cheese spread queso para untar

chemical property propiedad química ➤ Denatured alcohol has the property of dissolving latex paint. El alcohol desnaturalizado tiene la propiedad química de disolver esmaltes sintéticas.

chemical warhead ojiva química

to **cherish a friendship** tener una amistad en alta estima
cherished memory recuerdo grato ▪ recuerdo placentero ▪ recuerdo profundo
to **chew tobacco** mascar tabaco ▪ *(Cuba, Mex.)* mascar andullo
chicken broth caldo de pollo
to **chicken out** *(coll.)* ▪ to get cold feet ▪ to back out acoquinarse ▪ rajarse ▪ *(standard)* echarse atrás
chief executive officer ▪ CEO director general
chief financial officer ▪ CFO director general de finanzas
chief of protocol *el* jefe de protocolo
chief of staff **1.** *(military)* *el* jefe del estado mayor **2.** *(business)* director del personal
chief operations office ▪ COO director general de operaciones
child abuse malos tratos al niño
to be a **child at heart** ser niño de corazón
child at heart: to remain a ~ seguir teniendo el corazón de un niño ▪ seguir siendo un niño de corazón
child care cuidado infantil
child labor *la* explotación infantil
child molester pederasta ▪ pedófilo
child prodigy niño prodigio
child soldier niño soldado ➤ *(picture caption)* A group of child soldiers marches through the streets of Goma Un grupo de niños soldados desfila por las calles de Goma
child support manutención de los hijos
the **child within (each of) us** ▪ the child in all of us ▪ the inner child el niño que llevamos dentro
children's resemblance to their parents parecido de los niños a sus padres
to be **child's play** ser un juego de niños
childhood hero héroe de la infancia ▪ héroe desde la infancia
childhood heroine heroína de la infancia ▪ heroína desde la infancia
childhood sweetheart novio(-a) desde la infancia ▪ novio(-a) de la infancia
childish behavior comportamiento infantil
to **chill out** desconectarse un poco ▪ tranquilizarse ▪ descansar
a **chill ran through my body** ▪ a cold shiver ran through my body un escalofrío recorrió mi cuerpo
chilly reception: to get a ~ ▪ to be given a chilly reception recibir una fría acogida
china pattern motivo de la porcelana
chink in the armor ▪ Achilles heel punto débil ▪ punto flaco ▪ *el* talón de Aquiles
to be **chintzy with something** *(coll.)* ser tacaño con algo ▪ *(Mex.)* ser codo con algo ➤ The waiter was chintzy with the wine. El camarero fue tacaño con el vino. ▪ El mesero fue codo con el vino.
chip: computer ~ ▪ microchip *el* microchip ▪ *el* chip de computadora ▪ *(Sp.)* chip de ordenador
to **chip in** ▪ to contribute aportar ▪ contribuir ▪ poner ➤ Do you want to chip in on a present for our English teacher? ¿Quieres aportar para un regalo para el profesor de inglés? ▪ ¿Quieres contribuir para un regalo para el profesor de inglés? ▪ ¿Quieres poner para un regalo para el profesor de inglés?
to **chip in on something** ▪ to go in together on something ▪ to go in on something together ▪ to share the cost of something aportar para algo ▪ contribuir con algo para algo ▪ poner algo para algo ➤ We all chipped in (some money) on a present for our English teacher. Todos aportamos (algún dinero) para el regalo del profesor de inglés. ▪ Todos contribuimos (con algún dinero) para el regalo del profesor de inglés. ▪ Todos pusimos (algún dinero) para el regalo del profesor de inglés.
to be a **chip off the old block** **1.** *(looks)* parecerse a su padre **2.** *(personality and looks)* ser clavadito a su padre ▪ ser igualito a su padre
chipped china porcelana cascada ▪ porcelana picada ▪ porcelana mellada ▪ porcelana saltada
chipped glass cristal cascado ▪ cristal picado ▪ cristal mellado ▪ cristal saltado
chips and dip ▪ chips and salsa *(Mex.)* totopos y salsa ▪ *(Sp.)* nachos y salsa
chips are down: when the ~ en la hora de la verdad ▪ en el momento de jugarse el todo por el todo
chiseled features ▪ finely chiseled features rasgos marcados (como a cincel) ▪ rasgos cincelados ▪ rasgos esculpidos
chiseled profile ▪ finely chiseled profile perfil marcado (como a cincel) ▪ perfil cincelado ▪ perfil esculpido
chloroform in print *(Mark Twain's description of a boring book)* cloroformo impreso
to be a **chocaholic** *(coll.)* ▪ to be addicted to chocolate gustarle el chocolate horrores ▪ ser adicto al chocolate ➤ I'm a chocaholic. Me gusta el chocolate horrores. ▪ Soy adicto al chocolate.
chocolate syrup *el* sirope de chocolate ▪ *el* jarabe de chocolate
choice between: (for) there to be a ~ poder elegir entre ➤ Is there a choice between white bread and whole wheat? ¿Se puede elegir entre pan blanco y pan integral?
choice of someone as something: to be one's ~ ser su elección como algo ▪ ser su selección como algo ▪ ser su preferencia como algo ➤ She would be my choice as director of the project. Ella sería mi selección como directora del proyecto. ▪ Ella sería mi preferencia como directora del proyecto.
choice of someone to be something: to be one's ~ ser la selección como algo ➤ We applaud the choice of María to be the new dance instructor. Aplaudimos la selección de María como la nueva instructora de danza.
choice of subjects ▪ choice of courses *la* elección de asignaturas ▪ elección de cursos *(In Spain, "curso" means "academic program.")*
choice of what...: to have a ~ poder elegir ➤ Do we have a choice of what to wear? ▪ Can we choose what to wear? ¿Podemos elegir qué ropa llevar?
choice of words *la* selección de las palabras ▪ uso de palabras ➤ It was a poor choice of words. Fue un uso poco afortunado de las palabras. ➤ It was a beautiful choice of words. Fue un bello uso de las palabras. ▪ Fue un hermoso uso de las palabras.
to **choke on something** ahogarse con algo ▪ atragantarse con algo
choking smoke humo asfixiante
to **choose a candidate** ▪ to select a candidate ▪ to pick a candidate ▪ to decide on a candidate elegir un candidato
to **choose a necktie** ▪ to select a necktie ▪ to pick (out) a necktie escoger una corbata ▪ elegir una corbata
to **choose a restaurant** ▪ to pick a restaurant elegir un restaurante
to **choose between two things** elegir entre dos cosas
to **choose from more than two things** elegir (de) entre más de dos cosas ➤ There is a large selection to choose from. Hay una gran variedad de entre la que elegir. ➤ He chose the shirt from among a large selection. Eligió la camisa (de) entre una gran variedad.
to **choose someone over someone else** eligir a alguien frente a otra persona ▪ ser elegido frente a otra persona ➤ They chose him over another applicant. Le eligieron frente a otro solicitante. ➤ He was chosen over another applicant. Fue elegido frente a otro solicitante.
to **choose the right one** ▪ elegir el adecuado ▪ elegir la adecuada
to **chop a carrot lengthwise** ▪ to cut a carrot into strips ▪ to cut a carrot transversally cortar la zanahoria de largo
to **chop a carrot widthwise** ▪ to cut a carrot crosswise ▪ to cut a carrot radially cortar la zanahoria en rodajas
to **chop an onion** trocear una cebolla ▪ picar una cebolla
to **chop down a tree** ▪ to cut down a tree cortar un árbol ▪ talar un árbol
to **chop very finely** picar muy menudito
chopped onion cebolla troceada ▪ cebolla picada
choppiness of the financial markets *la* inquietud de los mercados financieros ▪ *la* inestabilidad de los mercados financieros
choppy sea mar picado ▪ mar encabritado ▪ mar rizado
choppy water *el* agua picada ▪ agua revuelta ▪ *las* aguas picadas ▪ aguas revueltas
choral work obra coral ▪ trabajo coral
the **chosen** ▪ the elect *(one person)* el elegido ▪ el escogido ▪ *(more than one person)* los elegidos ▪ los escogidos

the **chosen few** los pocos elegidos ■ los pocos escogidos

to be **chosen over someone else** ser elegido frente a otra persona ■ eligirle a alguien frente a otra persona ➤ He was chosen over another applicant. Fue elegido frente a otro solicitante. ■ Le eligieron frente a otro solicitante.

to **chow down** *(coll.)* hacer el rancho

chrism Mass *(Catholicism)* misa del santo crisma

the **Christ child** el niño Dios

to **christen a baby** ■ to christen an infant bautizar a un bebé

to **christen a ship** bautizar un barco ■ dar en llamar a un barco ■ botar un barco

Christian era ■ C.E. era cristiana ■ E. C.

Christmas bonus aguinaldo

Christmas card tarjeta de navidad ■ tarjeta navideña

Christmas carol villancico (navideño)

Christmas Eve *la* noche buena ■ víspera de navidad

the **Christmas holidays** las navidades ■ las fiestas navideñas

the **Christmas season** la temporada navideña ■ temporado de navidad

Christmas tip aguinaldo

Christmastime la navidad

Christmastime: at ~ over Christmas ■ during Christmas ■ *(Sp.)* en navidades ■ en navidad

to **chug along** *(automobile)* ■ to go in fits and starts ir a trompicones

church year ■ ecclesiastical year año santo ■ año litúrgico

cinnamon powder ■ ground cinnamon canela en polvo ➤ Sprinkle cinnamon powder on top. Espolvorear canela en polvo por encima.

cinnamon stick ■ stick of cinnamon rama de canela

to **circle an airfield** ■ to circle a field sobre volar en círculo el aeropuerto

to **circle around** hacer un círculo alrededor de ➤ The hyenas circled around the wounded animal. Las hienas hicieron un círculo alrededor del animal herido.

circle of friends círculo de amigos ■ grupo de amigos ■ *(Sp., coll.)* peña

to **circle overhead** dar vueltas por lo alto ■ dar vueltas en lo alto ■ dar vueltas a lo alto ■ dar vueltas por arriba ➤ The airplane was circling overhead. El avión daba vueltas por lo alto. ■ El avión daba vueltas en lo alto. ■ El avión daba vueltas a lo alto. ■ El avión daba vueltas por arriba.

to **circle the globe** dar la vuelta al globo

circuit breaker automático general ■ enchufe general ■ el cortacircuitos ➤ A short circuit in the hot water heater tripped the circuit breaker. Saltó el automático general por una derivación en el termo de agua caliente.

to **circulate a flyer** ■ to distribute a flyer distribuir un folleto

to **circulate a petition** ■ to gather signatures recoger firmas para una petición ■ recolectar firmas para una petición

circulation department *(of a newspaper or magazine)* departamento de difusión

circulation of a newspaper tirada de un periódico

circulation of the blood circulación de la sangre

to **circumnavigate the globe** ■ to sail around the world circunnavegar el globo

circumstances beyond one's control circunstancias ajenas a la voluntad de uno ➤ Owing to circumstances beyond my control Debido a circunstancias ajenas a mi voluntad

circumstantial evidence prueba circunstancial

to **cite an obvious example** ■ to give you an obvious example para poner un ejemplo obvio ■ para no ir más lejos ■ sin ir más lejos

to **cite as an example** ■ to give as an example poner como ejemplo

to be **cited by the judge for contempt** ■ to be cited for contempt by the judge ser citado por el juez por desacato ➤ He was cited by the judge for contempt. ■ He was cited for contempt by the judge. Fue citado por el juez por desacato. ■ Fue citado por desacato por el juez.

citizen's band radio ■ CB *el* radio civil ■ RC

city center ■ downtown *(road sign)* centro ➤ Mendoza city center ■ Downtown Mendoza Mendoza centro

city councilman ■ town councilman *el, la* concejal ■ *el, la* edil

city desk *(in a newspaper office)* sección de local

city editor *(of a newspaper)* editor(a) de local

city limits *los* límites de la ciudad ■ *(of an ancient city, as it originally existed)* casco histórico ■ casco antiguo

city map ■ map of the city ■ street map plano callejero *el* mapa de la ciudad

city state *(in ancient Greece)* ciudad estado

civic leader ■ community leader *el, la* líder cívico ■ líder de la comunidad ➤ Rigoberta Menchu is a civic leader in her community in Guatemala. ■ Rigoberta Menchu is a leader in her community in Guatemala. Rigoberta Menchú es una líder en su comunidad en Guatemala.

civil ceremony ceremonia civil

civil marriage casamiento por lo civil ■ boda civil

civil rights advocate ■ human rights advocate ■ civil liberties advocate defensor de las libertades civiles ■ defensor de los derechos civiles

civil rights demonstration *la* manifestación por los derechos civiles

civil service servicio civil

civil service reform reforma del servicio civil

civilian clothes: to be dressed in ~ ■ to be wearing civilian clothes estar vestido de civil ■ ir vestido de civil ■ andar vestido de civil ■ estar vestido de paisano ■ ir vestido de paisano ■ andar vestido de paisano

to **claim a prize** reclamar un premio ➤ If you win the lottery, how do you go about claiming the prize? Si ganas la lotería, ¿cómo se reclama el premio?

to **claim a victim** ■ to claim a fatality cobrarse una víctima mortal ■ cobrarse una víctima ➤ *(news item)* The outbreak of legionella claims its fifth victim. ■ The outbreak of legionella claims its fifth fatality. El brote de legionella se cobra su quinta víctima mortal. ➤ The epidemic claimed a new victim. La epidemia se cobró una nueva víctima.

to **claim not to...** ■ to claim one does not... alegar no... ■ alegar que no...

to **claim responsibility for an attack** reinvindicar (la autoría de) un ataque ■ atribuirse (la autoría de) un ataque ➤ No group has claimed responsibility for the attack. Ningún grupo ha reinvindicado la autoría del ataque. ■ Ningún grupo se ha atribuido la autoría del ataque.

to **claim that...** alegar que... ■ afirmar que... ■ asegurar que... ■ aseverar que... ■ decir que... ■ mantener que... ➤ He claims that he is innocent. Él asegura que es inocente. ■ Él afirma que es inocente. ■ Él dice que es inocente.

to **claim to be...** ■ to say that one is... decir ser... ■ tenerse por... ➤ He claims to be innocent. ■ He claims he's innocent. Dice ser inocente. ➤ She claims to be a descendent of Charlemagne. Se tiene por (una) descendiente de Carlomagno.

to **claim to be twenty-one (years old)** ■ to claim to be twenty-one years of age decir tener veintiuno ■ decir tener veintiun años

claim to fame: to be one's (chief) ~ destacarse más que nada por ➤ Columnist Marilyn vos Savant's claim to fame is that she has the highest IQ ever measured. Marilyn vos Savant se destaca más que nada por tener el cociente intelectual más alto que jamás haya sido medido.

to **claim to have...** decir tener... ➤ Madrid claims to have the oldest restaurant in the world. Madrid dice tener el restaurante más antiguo del mundo.

to **claim to have done something** decir haber hecho algo ➤ He claimed to have achieved the rank of colonel in his mid twenties. Él dijo haber conseguido el rango de coronel a mediados de los años veinte.

claim to ownership: to have a ~ tener el derecho legal a reclamar la propiedad de algo ➤ Does a university have any legal claim to the ownership of a student's thesis or dissertation? ¿Tiene la universidad algún derecho legal a reclamar la propiedad total o parcial del trabajo de investigación o de la tesis de un estudiante?

claimed articles artículos reclamados ➤ Have these articles been claimed? ¿Han sido estos artículos reclamados?

claims adjustor: (insurance) ~ perito tasador

clap of thunder ▪ thunderclap ▪ sound of the thunder trueno ➤ The horses were stunned by the clap of thunder. Los caballos se asustaron del trueno.

to **clap rhythmically** hacer palmas

clarified butter mantequilla clarificada

to **clarify something** dejar algo claro ➤ And to clarify it even further... Y para dejarlo más claro todavía...

clarion call *el* toque de atención ▪ *el* clamor ➤ *(British commentator)* Gore heard, and heeded, the Democrats' clarion call to concede to Bush. Gore oyó y cedió al toque de atención de los Demócratas de conceder la victoria a Bush. ▪ Gore oyó y cedió al clamor de los Demócratas de conceder la victoria a Bush. ➤ The general strike was seen as a clarion call by the workers not to be forgotten as Europe becomes prosperous. La huelga general fue vista como un toque de atención de los trabajadores para no ser olvidados conforme Europa se vuelve más próspera. ▪ La huelga general fue vista como un clamor de los trabajadores para no ser olvidados conforme Europa se vuelve más próspera.

to **clash with a color** darse de bofetadas con un color ▪ no casar (bien) con un color ▪ no combinar bien con un color ▪ desentonar ➤ The fuchsia tie clashes with the orange shirt. La corbata fucsia se da bofetadas con la camisa naranja.

to **clash with the police** tener un enfrentamiento con la policía ▪ tener un encontronazo con la policía

clashes with the police ▪ confrontations with the police enfrentamientos con la policía ▪ encontronazos con la policía ➤ *(news item)* Thirteen Algerian Muslims die in clashes with the police Trece islamistas argelinos mueren en enfrentamientos con la policía

class action (law)suit demanda conjunta

class assignment trabajo de clase ➤ He absolutely refused to do his class assignment. Se negó rotundamente a hacer el trabajo de clase.

class is over la clase se ha terminado ▪ la clase se ha acabado ▪ la clase se terminó ▪ la clase se acabó

class meets three times a week hay clase tres veces a la semana ▪ la clase se reúne tres veces a la semana

class meets today se reúne la clase hoy ▪ la clase se reúne hoy ▪ hoy hay clase ▪ se da la clase hoy

classes resume in late August se reanudan las clases a finales de agosto

classes resume on August twenty-fifth se reanudan las clases el veinticinco de agosto

classified ads anuncios breves ▪ anuncios por palabras

claws of a bear, cat, lion, tiger garras de un oso, gato, león, tigre

claws of a lobster ▪ pincers of a lobster pinzas de una langosta ▪ pinzas de una bogavante

clean airplane: aerodynamically ~ avión aerodinámico ▪ *(light airplane)* avioneta aerodinámica ➤ The Ercoupe is a very clean airplane. El Ercoupe es una avioneta muy aerodinámica.

to be **clean as a whistle** ser (más) limpio que los chorros del oro ▪ ser como los chorros del oro ▪ estar tan limpio como la patena

clean bill of health chequeo médico inmejorable ▪ chequeo médico intachable ➤ The doctor gave him a clean bill of health. El doctor le dio unos resultados del chequeo inmejorables.

clean break with someone: to make a ~ romper totalmente con alguien

clean driving record: to have a ~ tener un expediente de circulación intachable

clean copy of one's notes: to make a ~ ▪ to organize one's notes pasar a limpio sus apuntes ▪ pasar sus apuntes a limpio

to **clean fish** *(at home)* limpiar pescado ▪ *(at the grocery store or market)* vaciar pescado

to **clean house** ▪ to clean the house limpiar la casa

to **clean off the table** ▪ to clean the table off ▪ to clear off the table ▪ to clear the table (off) recoger la mesa ▪ levantar la mesa ▪ limpiar la mesa

to **clean out someone** ▪ to clean someone out **1.** to take everything of value limpiarle a alguien ▪ dejar a alguien limpio **2.** to exact an exorbitant price ▪ to take someone to the cleaners ▪ to gouge someone limpiarle a alguien ▪ *(coll.)* pelar a alguien ▪ clavar a alguien ▪ meter un clavo a alguien ▪ meter una clavada a alguien ➤ The burglars cleaned them out. Los ladrones los limpiaron. ▪ Los ladrones los dejaron limpios. ▪ *(Sp., leísmo)* Los ladrones les limpiaron. ▪ Los ladrones les dejaron limpios. ➤ The hotel really cleaned us out. ▪ The hotel really took us to the cleaners. El hotel nos limpió bien. ▪ El hotel nos peló bien. ▪ El hotel nos clavó bien. ▪ El hotel nos metió un buen clavo. ▪ El hotel nos metió una buena clavada.

to **clean out something** ▪ to clean something out organizar algo ▪ ordenar algo ▪ hacer limpieza en algo ➤ I need to clean out these drawers. Necesito organizar estos cajones. ▪ Necesito ordenar estos cajones. ▪ Necesito hacer limpieza en estos cajones. ➤ If I don't clean out the closet, my wife's going to shoot me. Como no organice el armario, mi mujer me mata. ▪ Como no ordene el armario, mi mujer me mata. ▪ Como no haga limpieza en el armario, mi mujer me mata. ➤ If I don't clean out my desk, my boss is going to shoot me. Como no organice el escritorio, mi jefe me mata. ▪ Como no ordene el escritorio, mi jefe me mata. ▪ Como no haga limpieza en el escritorio, mi jefe me mata.

clean record *el* expediente sin tacha ▪ expediente sin mancha

to be **clean shaven** no tener barba ni bigote ▪ ni tener barba ni bigote

to **clean (out) a wound** ▪ to clean a wound out limpiar una herida ➤ The doctor cleaned and bandaged the wound. ▪ The doctor cleaned the wound and bandaged it. ▪ El médico limpió y vendó la herida. ▪ El médico limpió la herida y la vendó.

to **clean something thoroughly** ▪ to give something a thorough cleaning limpiar algo a conciencia

clean sweep (of something): to make a ~ arrasar con algo ▪ empezar de cero ➤ The film made a clean sweep of the Oscars, winning in all categories. La película arrasó con todo los Oscars, ganando en todas las categorías. ➤ The moderate candidates made a clean sweep of the elections, winning in all ten districts. Los candidatos moderados arrasaron con las elecciones, ganando todos los diez distritos. ➤ The new owners made a clean sweep of the building, upgrading the wiring, plumbing, and remodeling the kitchens and bathrooms. Los nuevos propietarios del edificio empezaron de cero, modernizando la instalación eléctrica, la plomería, y remodelando las cocinas y los cuartos de baño.

to **clean the house** limpiar la casa

to **clean up** hacer limpieza (en) ➤ Ivan needs to clean up his apartment. It looks like he should apply for federal disaster funds. Iván necesita hacer limpieza en su apartamento. Parece que debería solicitar los fondos federales de desastres.

to **clean up after oneself** limpiar lo suyo ➤ I always clean up after myself when I use the kitchen. Siempre limpio lo mío cuando uso la cocina.

to **clean up after somone** limpiar lo que ha dejado alguien

to **clean up on** ▪ to receive an abundance of hacer limpieza de ▪ arrasar en

to **clean up one's image** lavar su imagen

to **clean up the house** recoger la casa

clean up your act! ¡compórtate!

to **clear a hurdle** **1.** saltar una valla limpiamente ▪ saltar una valla sin tocarla ▪ hacer un salto limpio **2.** *(figurative)* eludir un obstáculo ➤ The Spanish runners cleared all the hurdles in twenty seconds. Los atletas españoles saltaron limpiamente todas las vallas en veinte segundos. ➤ The budget cleared its first hurdle when it was passed by the appropriations committee. El presupuesto eludió su primer obstáculo al ser aprobado por la comisión presupuestaria.

to **clear a space for** ▪ to make room for hacer sitio para ▪ hacer corro para

clear agreement acuerdo nítido ➤ The prime minister reminded the king that the agreement is clear and needs only to be honored. El primer ministro recordó al rey que el acuerdo es "nítido" y sólo debe cumplirse.

clear and present danger peligro tangible e inminente

clear conscience: to have a ~ tener la conciencia limpia ▪ tener la conciencia tranquila

clear-cut bien delimitado

clear day día despejado ▪ día claro ▪ día diáfano

 clear head 1. *(alert)* cabeza despejada 2. *(organized in thought)* cabeza bien amueblada

to **clear it with someone** ▪ to get someone's authorization ▪ to get someone's approval ▪ to get someone's permission ser autorizado por alguien ▪ conseguir el visto bueno de alguien ▪ solicitar el permiso de alguien ▪ pedir permiso a alguien ▪ consultar un asunto con alguien ➤ I need to clear it with the boss. ▪ I need to get the boss's approval. Necesito que me autorice el jefe. ▪ Necesito (conseguir) el visto bueno del jefe. ▪ Necesito solicitar el permiso del jefe. ▪ Necesito pedir permiso al jefe. ▪ Necesito consultarlo con mi jefe.

clear mind mente despejada

clear money dinero (en) limpio ➤ After subtracting the cost of materials, I made two hundred seventy-five dollars clear. Después de restar el costo de las materiales, me quedaron limpios doscientos setenta y cinco dólares. ▪ Después de restar el costo de las materiales, me quedaron en limpio doscientos setenta y cinco dólares.

to **clear off** *(intransitive verb)* ▪ to clear up despejarse ➤ The weather is clearing off. ▪ The weather is clearing up. El tiempo se está despejando.

to **clear (off) the table** ▪ to clear the table (off) ▪ to clean off the table ▪ to clean the table off quitar la mesa ▪ recoger la mesa ▪ levantar la mesa

to **clear one's head** despejarse ➤ She has a cup of coffee every morning to clear her head. Toma un café todas las mañanas para despejarse.

to **clear one's mind** despejar la mente

to **clear one's nose** ▪ to clear one's nasal passages descongestionar la nariz

to **clear one's throat** carraspear ▪ aclararse la voz

to **clear one's way to** despejarle a alguien el camino hacia ➤ Judges have cleared George W. Bush's way to the U.S. presidency. Los jueces han despejado a George W. Bush el camino hacia la presidencia de EE UU.

clear skies *(literary)* ▪ limpid sky cielos despejados ▪ cielo límpido

clear statement declaración clara ➤ The candidates made very clear statements of their positions on the issues. Los candidatos hicieron declaraciones muy claras sobre sus posturas en los diferentes asuntos. ➤ The terrorists have made a clear statement of their intentions. Los terroristas han hecho una declaración de intenciones bien clara.

to be **clear that...** estar claro que...

to **clear the deck** ▪ to put everything to one side dejar todo de lado

to **clear the deck** 1. despejar la cubierta (de un barco) 2. *(figurative)* eliminar distracciones ➤ To concentrate on school, I need to just clear the deck by putting aside all the extraneous activities of daily life. Para concentrarme en mis estudios, necesito eliminar distracciones, dejando de lado todo lo que no tenga que ver con mi carrera.

to **clear the table** ▪ to clear off the table ▪ to clean off the table quitar la mesa ▪ recoger la mesa ▪ levantar la mesa

to **clear the way for** despejar el camino para (que) ▪ despejar el camino hacia ▪ despejar el camino de ➤ A U.S. federal court has cleared the way for the little rafter Elián González to return to Cuba with his father. Un tribunal federal de los Estados Unidos ha despejado el camino para que el niño balsero Elián González regrese con su padre a Cuba.

to **clear up** ▪ to clear off ▪ for the sun to come out despejarse ▪ abrirse el día ➤ The weather is clearing up. El tiempo se está despejando.

to **clear up a matter** esclarecer un asunto ▪ poner en claro un asunto ▪ zanjar un asunto

to **clear up a misconception** aclarar un concepto equivocado ▪ aclarar una impresión equivocada

to **clear up a misunderstanding** arreglar un malentendido

to **clear up a mystery** despejar un misterio

to **clear up doubts** despejar las dudas ➤ I hope I have cleared up any doubts that are troubling the students. Espero haber podido despejar las dudas que aquejan a los estudiantes.

to **clear up everything** ▪ to clear everything up aclararlo todo ➤ That clears up everything. ▪ That clears everything up. Eso lo aclara todo. ▪ Eso aclara muchas cosas. ➤ That clears it all up. Eso lo aclara todo.

clearance sale ▪ liquidation sale *la* liquidación

clearance for takeoff autorización para el despegue ▪ autorización para despegar

to be **cleared for takeoff** estar autorizado para el despegue ▪ estar autorizado para despegar ➤ Pilot to passengers: we've been cleared for takeoff. Comandante a los pasajeros: estamos autorizados para el despegue. ▪ Estamos autorizados para despegar. ▪ Nos han autorizado para el despegue. ▪ Nos han autorizado para despegar.

to be **cleared to register for classes** tener via libre para matricularse (en la universidad) ▪ tener el camino despejado para matricularse (en la universidad)

clearing in the woods ▪ clearing in the forest claro del bosque ▪ esplanada del bosque

clearing of debris ▪ removal of debris retirada de escombro ▪ retirar escombro

to **clench one's fist** apretar el puño

to **clench one's teeth** apretar los dientes

to clench the railing to hold onto the railing ▪ to grip the railing 1. *(on stairs)* agarrar el pasamanos ▪ agarrar la baranda 2. *(of a ship, bridge, balcony)* agarrar la baranda ▪ aferrarse a la baranda

clever comeback respuesta aguda

clever deception astuto engaño

clever nonsense absurdo genial ➤ Nash and Thurber were the masters of clever nonsense. Nash y Thurber fueron maestros del absurdo genial.

to **click on** *(computers)* hacer clic en ▪ picar en ▪ pulsar en ➤ Click on E-mail. *(tú)* Pica en E-mail. ▪ Haz clic en E-mail. ▪ *(usted)* Pique en E-mail. ▪ Haga clic en E-mail.

click, click *(on a computer mouse)* pica, pica ▪ (hacer) doble click

to **climb a ladder** subirse a una escalera ▪ trepar una escalera

to **climb a mountain** subir una montaña ▪ escalar una montaña

to **climb a tree** trepar un árbol

to **climb down out of the tree** ▪ to climb down from the tree ▪ to come down out of the tree ▪ to come down from the tree bajar del árbol

climb rate *(aviation)* ▪ rate of climb *el* régimen de ascenso

to **climb steps** subir (los) escalones

to **climb to the top** subir a lo (más) alto ➤ We climbed to the top of the mountain. Subimos a lo (más) alto de la montaña. ➤ He climbed to the top of the corporate ladder. Subió a lo (más) alto del escalafón de la compañía.

to **climb up one's pants leg** subírsele por el pantalón ➤ Some ants climbed up my pants leg. Unas hormigas se me subieron por el pantalón.

to be **climbing the walls** 1. to be driven to distraction salirse de las casillas 2. to be desperate to estar desesperado por ▪ desesperarse por ➤ A lot of people are climbing the walls to get out of poverty. Mucha gente está que se sale de sus casillas para salir de sus países. ▪ Mucha gente está desesperada por salir de la pobreza.

climbing vine parra

to **clinch an argument** remachar un argumento ▪ terminar un argumento ➤ Nothing clinches an argument like the facts. Nada remacha un argumento como los hechos.

to **clinch the deal** to close the deal cerrar el trato ▪ cerrar el acuerdo

to **clinch the title** to win the title hacerse con el título ▪ ganar el título

to **cling to someone like a leech** ▪ to latch on to someone pegársele como una lapa a alguien

to **cling to the hope that...** aferrarse a la esperanza de que...

to be **clinging to life** estar aferrado a la vida

clinical trials pruebas clínicas

clinically tested clínicamente probado

to **clip someone's wings** cortar las alas a alguien ▪ quebrar las alas a alguien ▪ atar en corto a alguien ▪ parar los pies a alguien

to **clock (a time of)** marcar un tiempo de

the **clock has stopped** ■ the clock is stopped el reloj está detenido
to **clock in** fichar (a la entrada) ■ fichar (al entrar)
to **clock out** fichar (a la salida) ■ fichar (al salir)
clock says ■ clock reads *el* reloj marca ➤ The clock says 2 p.m. El reloj marca las dos en punto. ➤ The clock says midnight. El reloj marca la medianoche. ➤ The clock says noon. El reloj marca las doce del mediodía.
clock struck midnight ■ clock struck twelve midnight el reloj dio las doce de la noche
clockmaker God *(deistic conception of God)* Dios relojero
clockwise: to turn something ~ girar algo en el sentido de las agujas del reloj ■ *(referring to a screwdriver or wrench)* girar algo a la derecha ■ *(in card and board games)* girar a derechas
Clockwork Orange *(Burgess novel and Kubric film)* *Naranja mecánica*
to **clog (up) a drain** atascar el desagüe ■ tapar el desagüe ■ tapar el caño
to **clog (up) an artery** atascar una arteria ■ obstruir una arteria
to **clog (up) an engine** cegar un motor ➤ They have ruled out that a flock of birds clogged the engine of the airplane. Han descartado que una bandada de pájaros cegara el reactor del avión.
to **close a deal** cerrar un trato
to **close a sale** cerrar una venta
to be **close at hand** estar al alcance de la mano ➤ For the Fisher King the grail was close at hand yet unattainable. Para el Rey Pescador el Santo Grial estaba al alcance de la mano, y sin embargo inalcanzable.
to be **close behind someone** ■ to be right behind someone estar justo detrás de alguien ■ estar pegado a alguien
to be **close by** ■ to be nearby ■ to be very close (to a place) estar a cuatro pasos ■ estar muy cerca ■ estar cercano
to be a **close call** ■ to be a close shave (salvarse) por los pelos ➤ That was a close call! ¡Por los pelos!
close collaborator colaborador estrecho
close contact with contacto estrecho con
close cooperation cooperación intensa ■ cooperación cerrada
to **close down** *(intransitive verb)* ■ to go out of business ■ to shut down cerrar
to **close down a business** ■ to close a business down ■ to shut down a place ■ to shut a place down cerrar un negocio ■ clausurar un negocio ➤ The utility company wants to close down its coal-fired power plants. La compañía de electricidad quiere cerrar su plantas de producción alimentadas por carbón. ➤ The air conditioning went out at the convenience store, and they actually closed the place down for three months. El aire acondicionado de la tienda se estropeó y de hecho tuvieron que cerrar el local durante tres meses. ➤ They closed it down. Lo cerraron.
close election elección justa ■ elección reñida
close enough 1. near enough lo suficientemente cerca (de) **2.** accurate enough lo suficientemente preciso (para) ➤ We didn't sit close enough to the front. ■ We didn't sit near enough to the front. No nos sentamos lo suficientemente cerca de la parte de delante. ➤ We didn't sit close enough. No nos sentamos lo suficientemente cerca. ➤ The figure is carried out to three decimal places, which is close enough for our purposes. ■ The figure is carried out to three decimal places, which is accurate enough for our purposes. La cifra tiene tres decimales, que es lo suficientemente preciso para nuestras necesidades.
to **close for the day** ya haber cerrado ■ haber echado el cierre ➤ We've closed for the day. Could someone return your call tomorrow? Ya hemos cerrado. ¿Podemos llamarle mañana? ■ Ya hemos echado el cierre. ¿Podemos llamarle nosotros mañana?
to be a **close friend of** ser muy amigo de ➤ At that time he was a close friend of the family. En ese entonces era muy amigo de la familia.
to be **close friends** ■ to be good friends ser amigos entrañables ■ estar muy unidos ■ comer en un mismo plato ■ *(Mex., coll.)* ser cuates
to **close in on someone** estrechar el cerco a alguien ■ estrechar el cerco sobre alguien ➤ The police are closing in on the prison escapee. La policía está estrechando el cerco al fugitivo. ■ La policía está estrechando el cerco sobre el fugitivo.
to **close in on the gaps in one's knowledge** andar rellenando las lagunas ➤ I still have a lot of gaps in my Spanish, but I'm closing in on them. Todavía tengo muchas lagunas en español, pero ando rellenándolas.
close-knit family familia unida
close-knit group grupo unido
to be **close minded** tener una mentalidad cerrada
to **close off 1.** to limit access to ■ to restrict access to limitar el acceso a ■ restringir el acceso a ■ acotar a **2.** to enclose acotar ➤ This section of the building is closed off. ■ Access to this section of the building is restricted. El acceso a esta parte del edificio está limitado. ■ El acceso a esta parte del edificio está restringido. ■ Esta parte del edificio está acotada. ➤ They should close off the classical music area and soundproof it. ■ They should enclose the classical music area and soundproof it. Deberían acotar la parte de música clásica e insonorizarla.
to **close one's eyes** ■ to shut one's eyes cerrar los ojos
close political ally of estrecho aliado político de
to **close ranks** cerrar (las) filas
to **close ranks around someone** cerrar filas en torno a alguien
to **close ranks behind someone** cerrar filas a favor de alguien
close relations with: to maintain ~ ■ to maintain close ties with mantener relaciones estrechas con ■ mantener estrechas relaciones con
close relative pariente cercano(-a)
close relatives parientes cercanos ■ primeras relaciones
to be a **close second** no llegar primero por los pelos ■ no ser el primero por los pelos
to be a **close shave** ■ to be a close call (salvarse) por los pelos ➤ That was a close shave! ¡Por los pelos!
to **close shop** ■ to pack up and move levantar campamento ■ empacar y dejar un piso ■ empacar y dejar un apartamento ➤ I need a week after school is out to close shop here. Necesito una semana después de que se acaben las clases para levantar campamento.
to **close slightly higher** *(stock market)* cerrar con ligeras alzas
to **close slightly lower** *(stock market)* cerrar con ligeras caídas
to **close something tight(ly)** ■ to close something securely cerrar algo apretadamente ■ cerrar algo a cal y canto ➤ Make sure the refrigerator door is closed tightly. Asegúrate que la puerta del refrigerador esté cerrada apretadamente. ■ Asegúrate de apretar la puerta del refrigerador al cerrar. ➤ I closed up the apartment tight before leaving for work. Cerré el apartamento a cal y canto antes de salir para trabajar.
to **close the curtains** ■ to draw the curtains cerrar las cortinas ■ echar las cortinas ■ correr las cortinas
to **close the door** ■ to shut the door cerrar la puerta
close ties with: to have ~ ■ to have close relations with tener estrechos lazos con
to be **close to a certain age** ■ to be pushing a certain age andar rondando cierta edad ■ rondar cierta edad ■ *(Cervantes)* frisar cierta edad ➤ She's close to forty. ■ She's pushing forty. Anda rondando los cuarenta. ■ Ronda los cuarenta. ➤ Our knight (Don Quijote) was close to fifty years old. Frisaba la edad de nuestro hidalgo con los cincuenta años.
to be **close to a draw** estar prácticamente empatado ➤ Neither party corners the market on ethical problems. It's closer to a draw. Ningún partido copa el mercado en lo que se refiere a ética. Están prácticamente empatados.
to be **close to someone** ■ to be close friends with someone estar muy unido a alguien ■ *(Mex.)* ser muy cuates de alguien
to be **close together** estar cerca una cosa de otra ■ estar cerca varias cosas entre sí ■ *(usually means touching)* estar varias cosas juntas ➤ The branches of a magnolia tree are close to the ground and close together, which make them great for climbing. Las ramas del magnolio están cerca del suelo y cerca unas de otras, lo que las hace perfectas para escalar. ■ Las ramas del magnolio están cerca del suelo y cerca entre sí, lo que las hace perfectas para escalar. ➤ The ceiling would be prettier if the beams were closer together. El techo estaría más bonito si las

vigas estuvieran más juntas (entre sí). ■ El techo estaría más bonito si las vigas estuvieran más cerca unas de otras.

closed circuit: to be broadcast over ~ ■ to be broadcast via closed circuit emitirse por circuito cerrado

to be **closed for repairs** estar cerrado a causa de reparaciones ■ *(Sp.)* estar cerrado por reformas

to be **closely monitored** ser observado minuciosamente ■ ser inspeccionado minuciosamente ■ ser vigilado minuciosamente ■ ser controlado minuciosamente ➤ The elections should be closely monitored. Las elecciones deberían ser observadas minuciosamente. ■ Las elecciones deberían ser inspeccionadas minuciosamente. ■ Las elecciones deberían ser vigiladas minuciosamente. ■ Las elecciones deberían ser controladas minuciosamente.

closeout prices precios de liquidación ■ *(Sp.)* precios de saldo

closer look: to get a ~ tener una vista más cercana ■ tener una vista más de cerca

closer look (at): to take a ~ mirar con mayor detenimiento

the **closer one gets to...** mientras más uno se acerca a... ➤ The closer to sixty you get, the younger it seems. ■ The closer you get to sixty, the younger it seems. Mientras más te acercas a los sesenta, más joven parece.

closer to home más cerca de casa

closer to the front 1. in the foreground en primera línea ■ más acá **2.** nearer the front más adelante ■ más cerca ➤ You can see it in the foreground. Puedes verlo en primera línea. ■ Puedes verlo más acá. ➤ Let's sit closer to the front. Vamos a sentarnos más adelante. ■ Vamos a sentarnos más cerca.

closest ally aliado(-a) más cercano(-a)

closest friend ■ best friend amigo(-a) más cercano(-a) ■ amigo(-a) más íntimo(-a) ■ mejor amigo(-a)

the **closest metro station is...** ■ the nearest metro station is... estación de metro más cercana es... ■ estación de metro que queda más cerca es... ■ estación de metro que está más cerca es... ➤ The closest metro station to the Museo Teresa Carreño is Bellas Artes. La estación de metro más cercana al Museo Teresa Carreño es la de Bellas Artes.

to be the **closest one there is to 1.** *(resemblance)* ser el más parecido a ■ ser la más parecida a **2.** *(distance)* ser el más cercano ■ ser la más cercana

closest star ■ nearest star estrella más cercana ■ estrella que está más cerca ■ estrella más próxima ■ estrella que está más próxima

to be the **closest thing (there is) to 1.** ser lo que más se aproxima a **2.** ser lo más parecido a ➤ Exercise is the closest thing there is to a medical panacea. El ejercicio es lo más parecido a una panacea médica. ➤ *(ad for cheap flights)* The closest thing to having wings. Lo más parecido a tener alas.

closest thing to what one would call... lo más próximo que llega a lo que se entiende por... ■ lo más próximo que llegó a lo que se entiende por ■ lo más cerca a lo que uno llamaría ■ lo más cerca a lo que uno diría

closest thing you have to lo más parecido a ■ la cosa más parecida a ➤ What's the closest thing you have to patatas bravas? ¿Qué es lo más parecido que tienen a las patatas bravas?

to be a **closet case** ■ to be in the closet ser un gay encubierto ■ ser un gay que no ha salido del armario

closing date ■ deadline fecha tope ■ fecha de vencimiento ■ fecha tope ■ fecha límite

closing of ranks by ■ closing of ranks on the part of *el* cierre de filas de

clothes don't make the man el hábito no hace al monje

clothes one is wearing ropa que lleva uno ■ ropa que tiene presto uno

clothespin pinza (de ropa) ■ palito para tender

cloud ceiling techo de nubes ■ *la* altitud de las nubes ➤ The cloud ceiling this morning is 1,500 meters, high enough to go flying. El techo de nubes esta mañana es de mil quinientos metros, suficientemente alto como para ir a volar.

cloud cover capa nubosa ➤ The cloud cover extends over most of the state. La capa nubosa se extiende sobre la mayor parte del estado. ➤ The cloud cover consists mostly of high diffuse clouds. La capa nubosa está compuesta en la mayor parte de nubes altas y difusas.

cloud has a silver lining: every ~ no hay mal que por bien no venga ➤ Probably the worst single action of a nineteenth-century American president was Franklin Pierce's signing of the Kansas-Nebraska Bill in 1854, but the cloud had a silver lining: it brought Abraham Lincoln back into politics. Probablemente el peor acto de un president norteamericano del siglo XIX fue cuando Franklin Pierce firmó el proyecto de ley Kansas-Nebraska, aunque no hay mal que por bien no venga: provocó la vuelta de Lincoln a la política.

cloud of dust *la* nube de polvo ■ *(Sp.)* polvareda

cloud nine: to be on ~ estar por las nubes ■ estar pletórico

to **cloud the future** ■ to cast a pall over the future ensombrecer el futuro ■ enturbiar el futuro ➤ *(news item)* The candidate's Swiss bank accounts cloud his political future. ■ The candidate's Swiss bank accounts cast a pall over his political future. Las cuentas suizas del candidato ensombrecen su futuro político.

to **cloud one's judgment** empañar el juicio

to **cloud the issue** complicar el asunto ■ embrollar el asunto

cloud with tears: (for) the eyes to ~ empañársele los ojos de lágrimas

clouds above the ocean ■ clouds over the ocean nubes sobre el océano

clouds of smoke ■ billows of smoke ■ billowing smoke nubes de humo

clouds over the ocean ■ clouds above the ocean nubes sobre el océano

to **clown around** hacer el payaso ■ hacer el ganso ■ hacer el indio

to **club someone to death** matar a alguien a palos

to **clue someone in** *(coll.)* poner a alguien al corriente de algo ➤ She clued me in. The real reason for the invitation was that it was a surprise birthday party. Ella me puso al corriente. La verdadera razón de la invitación era una fiesta sorpresa de cumpleaños. ➤ I haven't heard about it. Clue me in. No sé nada. Ponme al corriente.

to **cluster around** amontonarse en torno a ■ amontonarse alrededor de ■ agruparse alrededor de ■ apinarse alrededor de ➤ We clustered around the campfire. Nos amontonamos en torno a la hoguera de campamento. ■ Nos amontonamos alrededor de la hoguera de campamento.

to be **clustered around** apretados alrededor ➤ We were clustered around the campfire. Estábamos apretados alrededor de la hoguera.

the **clutch is engaged** el embrague está sujeto

the **clutch is released** el embrague está suelto

the **clutch is slipping** el embrague está deslizándose ■ el embrague se está deslizando

c'mon now! ■ come on, now! ¡vamos anda!

to **co-opt the opposition** ■ to neutralize opposition by adopting its stand ■ to assimilate the opposition ■ to preempt the opposition anticiparse a la oposición ■ copar (a) la oposición ■ copar las medidas de la oposición ■ adelantarse a la oposición

to **co-star with someone** ■ to star with someone compartir el papel protagonista con alguien ■ compartir el papel estelar con alguien

coal field yacimiento de carbón

coarse humor humor burdo

coarse language lenguaje burdo ■ lenguaje tosco ■ *(Mex.)* lenguaje grosero ■ lenguaje pesado

coarse manners ■ boorish manners modales burdos ■ modales toscos

coarse paper papel rugoso ■ papel basto

coarse sandpaper lija rugosa

coarseness of the language *la* tosquedad del lenguaje

coarseness of the paper *la* rugosidad del papel

coarseness of the sandpaper *la* rugosidad de la lija

to **coast downhill** (dejar) caer cuesta abajo ■ (dejar) caer por una pendiente ➤ To jump-start the car, turn on the ignition, put it in second, let it coast downhill a few feet, and pop the clutch. ■ To jump-start the car, turn on the ignition, put it in second, coast it downhill a few feet, and pop the clutch. Para arrancar el coche, gira la llave, mete segunda, déjalo caer unos metros cuesta abajo y pica embrague. ▪ Para arrancar el coche, gira la llave, mete segunda, déjalo caer unos metros por la pendiente y soltar embrague de golpe.

the **coast is clear** no hay moros en la costa

coastal plain llanura costera

coat and tie *(L. Am., Sp.)* chaqueta y corbata ▪ media etiqueta ▪ *(Mex.)* corbata y saco ➤ The dress for the dinner is coat and tie. Se requiere para la cena corbata y saco. ▪ Se requiere para la cena media etiqueta. ➤ I was wearing a coat and tie. Llevaba media etiqueta.

coat hangers percha

coat of paint capa de pintura ▪ una mano de pintura ▪ pasada de pintura

coat of paint: to give it a ~ darle una pasada de pintura

to **coat something with batter** rebozar algo *(The batter is "el rebozado.")*

to **coat something with breadcrumbs** empanar algo con migas ▪ empanar algo con migajas

to **coat something with egg** rebozar algo (en huevo)

to **coat something with flour** rebozar algo (en harina) ▪ enharinar algo

to **coat something with liquid (for cooking purposes)** bañar algo *(Except for egg, which is "rebozar.")*

to **coat something with paint** ▪ to give something a coat of paint dar a algo una mano de pintura ▪ dar a algo una capa de pintura

to be **coated with batter** estar rebozado en

to be **coated with chocolate** estar bañado en chocolate ▪ estar cubierto de chocolate

to be **coated with glaze** ▪ to be glazed estar bañado en glaseado ➤ Which do you like better, the apples coated with caramel or with red glaze? ¿Qué te gusta más? Las manzanas bañadas en caramelo o glaseado rojo. ➤ The ham is coated with a glaze. ▪ The ham is glazed. El jamón está bañado en glaseado. ➤ For breakfast I had coffee and a glazed doughnut. Desayuné un café y un donut glaseado.

coatrack perchero

to **coax someone into doing something** engatusar alguien para que haga algo ➤ We invited him to the party, but he had to be coaxed into accepting. Le invitamos a la fiesta, pero se hizo de rogar hasta que aceptó. ➤ We invited him to the party, but he had to be coaxed into coming. Le invitamos a la fiesta, pero se hizo de rogar hasta que accedió a venir.

cobblestone street *la* calle empedrada ▪ calle adoquinada

to **cock a pistol** **1.** *(revolver)* amartillar un revólver **2.** *(clip pistol)* amartillar una pistola

to **cock a rifle** amartillar un rifle

to **cock his leg** *(male dog)* levantar la pata ▪ alzar la pata

cockadoodle-do *(rooster call)* kikirikí *(The sound of a hen is "corro-clo-clo.")*

C.O.D. ▪ collect on delivery C.A.E. ▪ cobra al entregar ▪ cobrar a la entrega ▪ a contrarrembolso ▪ *(Sp.)* contra reembolso

code name nombre en clave

code of laws fuero

to **coerce someone into doing something** coaccionar a alguien para que haga algo

coffee cake bizcocho de café ▪ *el* pastel de café

coffee beans granos de café

coffee grounds molienda del café

coffee percolator cafetera de émbolo ▪ cafetera eléctrica

coffee with brandy flambee *(Sp.)* carajillo

coffeepot cafetera

to **coil and strike** *(snake)* enroscarse y atacar

to be **coiled to strike** estar enroscado para atacar ▪ estar arrollado sobre sí para atacar

to **coin a phrase** acuñar una frase

to **coin a word** acuñar una palabra

to **coincide with** coincidir con

to be **coin-operated** funcionar con monedas ➤ I'm looking for a laundromat with coin-operated machines. Busco una lavandería con máquinas que funcionen con monedas.

to be **cold as a well digger's butt** *(off-color)* ▪ to be cold as the shady side of a witch's tit hacer un frío de cojones

to be **cold as ice** *(person)* estar helado ▪ estar congelado ▪ estar hecho un témpano

to be **cold as the shady side of a witch's tit** *(off-color)* ▪ to be cold as a well digger's butt hacer un frío de cojones

cold-blooded animal *el* animal de sangre fría

cold-blooded killer asesino de sangre fría

cold case *(in a grocery store)* ▪ cooler cámara frigorífica

cold cash: to pay ~ ▪ to pay hard cash ▪ to pay cash on the line pagar dinero contante y sonante ▪ *(Sp.)* pagar a tocateja

cold cuts *los* fiambres ▪ *(pork)* embutidos

cold fish témpano ▪ persona sin sentimientos

cold front *(weather)* frente frío

cold is better today: one's ~ estar mejor del catarro hoy ➤ My cold is better today. Estoy mejor del catarro hoy.

cold is worse today: one's ~ estar peor del catarro hoy ➤ My cold is worse today. Estoy peor del catarro hoy.

cold-pressed olive oil *el* aceite de oliva prensado en frío

cold remedy remedio para el resfriado

a **cold shiver ran through my body** ▪ a chill ran through my body un escalofrío recorrió mi cuerpo

cold snap ▪ cold spell ▪ cold wave ola de frío ➤ We had a cold snap in November, but then it warmed up again. Tuvimos una ola de frío en noviembre, pero luego volvió a hacer bueno.

cold sore pupa ▪ *(L. Am.)* fuego

cold spell ▪ cold snap ▪ cold wave ola de frío ▪ oleada de frío ➤ We had a cold spell in November, but then it warmed back up (again). Tuvimos una ola de frío en noviembre, pero luego volvió a hacer bueno.

cold stare: to give someone a ~ ▪ to stare coldly at someone dirigir a alguien mirada fría ▪ echar a alguien una mirada fría

cold turkey: to quit smoking ~ dejar de fumar de golpe ➤ The best way to quit smoking is cold turkey. La mejor manera de dejar de fumar es de golpe.

cold wave ▪ cold snap ▪ cold spell ola de frío

cold weather tiempo frío

to **collaborate with** colaborar con

to **collapse in an earthquake** derrumbarse durante un terremoto ▪ venirse abajo durante un terremoto ➤ The building collapsed during the earthquake. El edificio se derrumbó durante el terremoto. ▪ El edificio se vino abajo durante el terremoto.

collapse of the economy hundimiento de la economía ▪ colapso de la economía ▪ *el* derrumbe de la economía

to **collapse under its own weight** caerse de su propio peso ▪ caerse por su propio peso

collar button *el* botón del cuello (de la camisa) ➤ Would you sew on this collar button for me? ¿Podrías coserme este botón del cuello? ▪ ¿Podrías pegarme este botón del cuello?

collateral damage daños colaterales

to **collect baggage** ▪ to retrieve baggage ▪ to pick up baggage ▪ to get baggage recoger el equipaje

to **collect dust** acumular polvo ▪ juntar polvo

to **collect one's thoughts** ordenar sus ideas ➤ I need to collect my thoughts. Necesito ordenar mis ideas.

to **collect oneself** ▪ to pull oneself together recapacitarse ➤ Collect yourself! ▪ Pull yourself together! *(tú)* ¡Recapacítate! ▪ *(usted)* ¡Recapacítese!

to **collect money for** reunir dinero para ▪ recaudar dinero para ▪ hacer una colecta para ▪ *(L. Am., coll.)* hacer una vaca para

to **collect payments in installments** cobrar pagos a plazos

to **collect people** *(coll.)* **1.** to pick people up ▪ to pick up people recogerle a alguien ▪ buscarle a alguien **2.** to attract people atraer a la gente ➤ She's gone to collect the kids at school. Ha ido a recoger a los niños al colegio. ➤ She makes friends so easily that she just seems to collect people. Hace amigos con tanta facilidad que parece que atrae a la gente. ➤ The newspaper boy collects all the children and dogs on the block, and they follow him down to the end of the street. El chico de los periódicos atrae a los niños y a los perros, y le siguen hasta el final de la calle.

to **collect signatures** ▪ to get signatures recabar firmas

to **collect stamps** coleccionar sellos ▪ coleccionar estampillas

to **collect taxes** recaudar impuestos

to **collect the rent from the tenants** cobrar el alquiler a los inquilinos ▪ cobrar los alquileres a los inquilinos ➤ The landlord comes around once a month to collect the rent from the tenants. El dueño pasa por aquí una vez al mes para cobrar el alquiler a los inquilinos.

collection agency servicio de cobro de facturas

collection of paintings pinacoteca

collective farm *(1930s USSR)* ▪ kolkhoz koljós

collective security agreement acuerdo colectivo de seguridad

collector's edition edición de coleccionista

collector's item artículo de colección

College of Cardinals *(Catholicism)* Colegio cardenalicio

to **collide head-on with** chocar de frente con ▪ chocar de frente contra ▪ colisionar de frente con

to **collide with** chocar con ▪ chocar contra ▪ colisionar con

colloquial speech *el* lenguaje coloquial ▪ *el* habla coloquial ▪ *la* conversación coloquial

color blindness daltonismo ➤ He's color-blind. Es daltónico. ▪ Es daltoniano.

color chart escalera de color

to be **color coded** ser codificado por colores

color copier fotocopiadora de color

color runs *el* color destiñe ▪ pierde color ▪ se le va el color ➤ When I washed these socks, the colors ran. Cuando lavé estos calcetines, los colores destiñeron. ▪ Cuando lavé estos calcetines, perdieron color. ▪ Cuando lavé estos calcetines, se les fue el color.

colorfast yarn hilaza que no (se) destiñe

colorful expression expresión pintoresca

colorful yarns: to spin ~ hilar historias pintorescas ➤ Lincoln spun colorful yarns. Lincoln hilaba historias pintorescas.

coloring book libro para colorear

to be **colossal in size** ser colosal ➤ The castle is colossal in size. El castillo es colosal.

colossal mess: to make a ~ ▪ to make a terrible mess ▪ to turn (the place) into a pigpen ▪ to turn the place into a pigsty montar un estropicio ▪ dejarlo todo revuelto ▪ montar un desbarajuste ▪ poner algo patas arriba ▪ dejar algo hecho una leonera ➤ The kindergarten children made a colossal mess but point the finger at the other class. ▪ The kindergarden children turned the place into a pigpen but pointed the finger at the other class. Los niños de la guardería montaron un estropicio pero cargaron con el mochuelo a la otra clase.

colossal miscalculation *el* error de cálculo colosal ▪ error de cálculo garrafal

colossal mistake *el* error colosal ▪ error garrafal

Columbus Day *(Oct 12 or second Monday in October) (Mex.)* el día de la raza ▪ *(Sp.)* el día de la hispanidad

column of figures columna de números ▪ lista de números ▪ suma ➤ This column of figures adds up to six hundred forty-five. Esta lista de (los) números suma a seiscientos cuarenta y cinco.

to **comb one's hair** peinarse el pelo ▪ peinarse el cabello

to **comb the area** ▪ to comb the vicinity ▪ to scour the area rastrear la zona ▪ batir el campo ▪ peinar el campo ▪ mirar el campo palmo a palmo ▪ hacer una batida por el campo ➤ The police combed the area (looking) for possible clues. La policía rastreó la zona buscando posibles pistas.

to **comb the classifieds for jobs** rastrear los anuncios buscando trabajo

(combination) CD and tape player aparato de música ▪ (combinación de un) lector de discos compactos y reproductor de casetes

combination lock candado de combinación

combination plate ▪ sampler plate plato de degustación ▪ plato de combinación

to **combine the ingredients (of a recipe)** aunar los ingredientes de una receta ▪ combinar los ingredientes de una receta

combined incomes ingresos conjuntos ➤ My wife and I can just barely get by on our combined incomes. Mi mujer y yo a duras penas llegamos al fin de mes con nuestros ingresos conjuntos.

to **come a long way (from...)** *(literal and figurative)* recorrer un largo camino (desde...) ➤ The pilgrims came from all over the Christian world, to Santiago de Compostela in Spain. Los peregrinos recorrieron un largo camino desde todas partes del mundo cristiano hasta Santiago de Compostela en España. ➤ You've come a long way, baby. Has recorrido un largo camino, guapita.

to **come about** ▪ to come to pass ▪ to happen producirse ▪ originarse ▪ ocasionarse ➤ This change has come about because... Este cambio se ha producido porque... ➤ Exactly how did this come about? ¿Cómo se produjo esto exactamente?

to **come added to something** ▪ to be added to something venir agregado a algo ➤ In this pill that I take, the antihistamine is already added into it. En esta pastilla que tomo yo, viene agregado el antihistamínico.

to **come alive 1.** to come to life cobrar vida **2.** to become animated salir del cascarón ▪ florecer ▪ perder la timidez ➤ In "The Nutcracker" ballet, the toys come alive. En el ballet "El cascanueces" los juguetes cobran vida. ➤ She was a very timid child, but when she took ballet, she really came alive. Era una niña muy tímida, pero cuando recibió clases de ballet, salió de su cascarón.

to **come along 1.** to come venir **2.** to appear surgir ▪ aparecer **3.** to progress progresar ▪ avanzar **4.** to accompany ▪ to go with acompañar ➤ Come along (now)! ¡Venga! ➤ Literary figures of the magnitude of Cervantes and Shakespeare come along once in a thousand years. Figuras de la literatura de la talla de Cervantes y Shakespeare surgen una vez cada mil años. ▪ Figuras de la literatura de la talla de Cervantes y Shakespeare aparecen una vez cada mil años. ➤ The house is coming along, isn't it? La casa progresa, ¿verdad? ▪ La casa avanza, ¿verdad? ➤ Would you like to come along? ▪ Would you like to come with us? ▪ Would you like to go with us? ¿Te gustaría acompañarnos? ▪ ¿Nos acompañas?

to **come already added to something** ▪ to be added to something venir agregado a algo ➤ In this pill (that) I take, the antihistamine comes already added (in)to it. ▪ In this pill (that) I take, the antihistamine is added (in)to it. En esta pastilla que tomo yo, viene agregado el antihistamínico.

come and see! ¡ven y verás!

to **come apart** deshacerse ▪ caerse (a pedazos) ▪ desmontarse

to **come across** ▪ to be understood dar la impresión ➤ It doesn't come across right. No da la impresión correcta.

to **come across as...** dar la impresión de... ▪ parecer que... ➤ In the polemic both Sarmiento and Bello come across as being right. En la polémica tanto Sarmiento como Bello dan la impresión de tener la razón. ➤ When you're begging, don't come across as demanding. Cuando pides, que no parezca que lo exiges.

to **come across something** ▪ to find something dar con algo ▪ encontrarse con algo ▪ tropezar con algo ➤ I came across it as I was cleaning out the closet. Di con ello mientras limpiaba el armario.

come and bring a friend! ven(te) y tráete un amigo

come and check it out! ¡ven a conocerlo!

come and experience it! ¡ven a vivirlo!

to **come and go** irse algo como viene ▪ pasar de largo ➤ The appointed day came and went. El día señalado vino tal como se fue. ▪ El día señalado pasó de largo.

to **come and go when I want** ▪ to come and go as I please ir y venir cuando yo quiero

come and get it! ▪ dinnertime! ▪ suppertime! ¡a comer!

to **come (and) get something** venir a buscar algo ▪ venir por algo

come and join in! ¡ven a tomar parte!

come (and) join us ven y únete a nosotros

come and see! ¡ven a ver!

come and see for yourself! ¡ven y verás!

to **come and see you** ir a verte ➤ I'd like to come and see you. Me gustaría ir a verte.

to **come around 1.** dejarse caer por algún sitio ▪ pasarse por algún sitio **2.** volver al buen camino ▪ volver al redil ➤ The mailman will come around eventually. Just be patient. El cartero se dejará caer de un momento a otro. Ten paciencia. ▪ El cartero se pasará por aquí de un momento a otro. Ten paciencia. ➤ He's a good kid. He'll come around eventually. Es un bueno chico. Volverá al buen camino. ■ Es un buen chico. Volverá al redil.

to **come as a blow** ■ to come as a shock sentar como golpe ■ sentar como un tiro

to **come as a shock** ■ to come as a blow sentar como golpe ■ sentar como un tiro

to **come as a surprise to one** llegarle de sorpresa a uno ■ ser un sorpresa ■ pillar de sorpresa ■ llegar de sorpresa ■ *(L. Am.)* caerle de sorpresa ■ pescarle de sorpresa ■ *(Sp.)* coger de sorpresa

to **come as no surprise** no sorprender en absoluto ■ no sorprender lo más mínimo ➤ It comes as no surprise that Mozart was a child prodigy. No me sorprende en absoluto que Mozart fuera un niño prodigio. ■ No me sorprende lo más mínimo que Mozart fuera un niño prodigio.

to **come as something of a shock** resultar un tanto impactante ➤ The news came as something of a shock. La noticia le resultó un tanto impactante.

to **come as something of a surprise** ser medio sorpresa ■ pillar medio de sorpresa ■ llegar medio de sorpresa ■ *(L. Am.)* cachar medio de sorpresa ■ caer medio de sorpresa ■ *(Sp.)* coger medio de sorpresa

to **come ashore** desembarcar

to **come at a bad time** ■ to get here at a bad time ■ to arrive at a bad time llegar en mal momento

to **come at a gallop** venir galopando

to **come at a price** ■ to exact a price costar algo ■ pagar un alto precio por algo ■ pasar factura (en forma de...) ➤ Our advanced standard of living has, so far, come at the price of global warming. Nuestra avanzada forma de vida nos ha costado, a día de hoy, un calentamiento global.

to **come at one** venirle a uno ■ llegarle a uno ➤ It seemed like the bullets were coming at us from all sides. Parecía que las balas nos venían de todos lados. ■ Parecía que las balas nos llegaban de todos lados. ➤ I've heard that the pickpockets there have a technique for coming at you from the front. He oído que los carteristas en ese sitio tienen una técnica para venirte de frente. ■ He oído que los carteristas en ese sitio tienen una técnica para llegarte de frente.

to **come attached to something** venir pegado a algo ➤ The little radios came attached to the jars of peanut butter. Los pequeños radios venían pegados a los tarros de crema de cacahuete.

to **come away empty-handed** volver de vacío ■ volver con las manos vacías

to **come away with** salir con ➤ Heilbroner's *The Worldly Philosophers* reads like a Jules Verne novel, and you come away with an education. *Los filósofos que se dedicaron a asuntos mundiales* de Heilbroner se lee como una novela de Julio Verne, y sales con una formación.

to **come away uninjured** ■ to escape injury ■ to escape unharmed ■ to be unharmed salir ileso

to **come back** ■ to return *(L. Am.)* regresar ■ *(Sp.)* volver ■ regresar ■ volver de nuevo ■ volver de nuevas ➤ Shane, come back! Shane, ¡regresa! ■ Shane, ¡retorna! ■ *(Sp.)* Shane, ¡vuelve! ➤ You all come back and see us! Regresen a visitarnos. ■ Vuelvan a visitarnos. ■ *(Sp.)* Volved a visitarnos.

to **come back from** ■ to return from llegar de regreso de ■ regresar de ■ *(Sp.)* volver de

to **come back on** ■ to come on again ■ to be restored haber vuelto ■ volver ■ restaurar ➤ The electricity came back on three days after the power outage. La electricidad ha vuelto tres días después del apagón. ➤ The electricity just came back on. Acaba de volver la luz. ■ Acaban de restaurar el fluido eléctrico.

to **come back to haunt one** pasarle factura a alguien ➤ His excessive drinking when he was younger has come back to haunt him in old age. He has developed cirrhosis (of the liver). Los excesos de joven con el alcohol han venido ahora a pasarle la factura. Ahora tiene cirrosis.

to **come back to life** regresar a la vida ■ volver a la vida ➤ In the Biblical account, Lazarus comes back to life. El relato Bíblico nos dice que Lázaro vuelve a la vida.

to **come back to someone** volver con alguien ➤ You've come back to me. Has vuelto conmigo.

to **come back to something** ■ to come home to something recurrir a algo ➤ Young people, even though they rebel, need an anchor to come back to. Los jóvenes, aunque se rebelan, necesitan un asidero al que recurrir.

to **come back to the subject** ■ to return to the subject ■ to get back to the subject volver al tema ■ volver al asunto

to **come barreling down the street** venir embalados por la calle ■ venir a bocajarro por la calle ■ venir lanzado por la calle ■ venir arrasando por la calle ■ pasar arrasando por la calle ➤ The teenagers come barreling down this street at ninety kilometers per hour. Los jóvenes vienen embalados por esta calle a noventa kilómetros por hora. ➤ The cars really come barreling down this street, don't they? Los carros pasan arrasando por esta calle, ¿verdad? ■ Los carros vienen arrasando por esta calle, ¿verdad?

to **come begging** venir con ruegos ■ venir con súplicas

to **come between two people** entremeterse entre dos personas ■ entremeterse con dos personas ➤ You shouldn't come between them. No deberías entremeterte entre ellos.

to **come by** **1.** *(for a visit)* to drop by pasar por aquí ■ caerle a alguien **2.** to pass by ■ to come near acercarse a **3.** to come pick up (someone) ■ to be by (for someone) venir a buscar a alguien ■ pasar por alguien ■ venir por alguien ➤ I was in the neighborhood, and thought I'd come by. Estaba por el barrio y pensé pasar por aquí. ➤ The waitress comes by periodically to refill our coffee. La camarera se acerca frecuentemente a ofrecernos más café. ➤ I'll come by for you in an hour. En una hora paso por ti. ■ En una hora vengo por ti.

to **come by and get...** ■ to come by to get... ■ to come over and get... ■ to come over to get... pasar y... ■ pasar para... ■ acercarse a... ■ acercarse para... ■ venir y... ■ venir para... ➤ I'll come by and get it this afternoon. ■ Pasaré esta tarde y lo recogeré.

to **come by for someone** pasar por alguien ■ venir a por alguien ■ venir a buscar a alguien ➤ I'll come by for you at one o'clock. Paso por ti a la una. ➤ Can you come by for me? ¿Puedes venir a por mí?

to **come by for something** ■ to come by to get something pasar para recoger algo ■ acercarse para recoger algo ■ pasar para buscar algo ➤ I'll come by for it this afternoon. ■ I'll come by to get it this afternoon. Pasaré para recogerlo esta tarde. ■ Me acerco a recogerlo esta tarde. ■ Me acerco para recogerlo esta tarde.

to **come clean** ■ to tell the truth ■ to be honest ■ to confess the truth ■ to divulge the truth sincerarse con alguien ➤ Why don't you just come clean and admit it? ¿Por qué no te sinceras y lo admites?

to **come close (to something)** acercarse (a algo) ■ aproximarse (a algo) ➤ In the professor's opinion, there is an excellent American piano concerto, Gershwin's *Rhapsody in Blue*, and a number of others come close. En la opinión del catedrático existe un excelente concierto de piano norteamericano, *Rapsodia en azul* de Gershwin, y otros pocos que se le aproximan en excelencia.

to **come closer** acercarse más ■ aproximarse más ➤ "Come closer, my dear," said the wolf to Little Red Riding Hood. "Acércate más, pequeñita", le dijo el lobo a Caperucita Roja. ■ "Aproxímate más, pequeñita", le dijo el lobo a Caperucita Roja.

to **come down hard on someone** ser severo con alguien ■ ser duro con alguien ■ regañar mucho a alguien ■ *(Sp., coll.)* dar caña a alguien ➤ Manolo is messier than I am, but you don't come down on him as hard. Manolo es más desordenado que yo, pero no eres tan severo con él. ➤ I'm sorry, I came down on you too hard. Siento haber sido demasiado severo contigo. ■ Siento haberte regañado demasiado.

to **come down in the world** venir a menos

to **come down out of the clouds** ■ to wake up to reality bajar de las nubes ■ despertar a la realidad ■ bajar a la realidad

to **come down with a cold** ■ to catch a cold ■ to get a cold pescar un resfriado ■ *(Sp.)* coger un resfriado

to **come down with a fever** ■ to develop a fever ■ to get a fever darle fiebre a uno ■ tener fiebre ■ *(Sp.)* coger una fiebre to **come down with a headache** ▪ to develop a headache darle un dolor de cabeza ▪ dolerle la cabeza

to **come down with the flu** ▪ to get the flu darle una gripe ▪ agarrar una gripe muy fuerte ▪ *(Sp.)* coger la gripe fuerte

to **come easy for one** ▪ to come without effort ▪ (for someone) to be good at hacérsele fácil a uno ▪ dársele bien algo a alguien ➤ English comes easy for Carlos. ▪ English comes without effort for Carlos. ▪ Carlos is good at English. El inglés se le da bien a Carlos.

to **come easy to one** ▪ to come without effort hacérsele fácil a uno ▪ dársele fácil a uno ➤ Languages come easy for Andrés. A Andrés se le dan fácil los idiomas.

to **come face to face with** darse cara a cara con ▪ *(Sp.)* plantarse cara a cara con ➤ In the battle of Lepanto, Cervantes came face to face with death. En la batalla de Lepanto, Cervantes se dio cara a cara con la muerte. ▪ En la batalla de Lepanto, Cervantes se plantó cara a cara con la muerte. ▪ En la batalla de Lepanto, Cervantes le plantó cara con la muerte.

come fall ▪ come autumn ▪ when fall comes ▪ when autumn comes cuando llegue el otoño

to **come first** ▪ to have a higher priority ser lo primero ▪ ser prioritario ▪ ser la prioridad

to **come flying at** venir volando a ▪ venir volando hacia ➤ Here we are, innocent bystanders, and it just comes flying at us. Aquí estamos inocentes transeuntes y de repente viene volando a nosotros. ▪ Aquí estamos inocentes transeuntes y de repente viene volando hacia nosotros.

to **come flying in** entrar volando ➤ A damned fat pigeon came flying in and crapped on my futon. Una gorda maldita paloma entró volando y se hizo en mi futón.

to **come for something** ▪ to come to pick up something venir a recoger algo ▪ *(Sp.)* venir a por algo ▪ *(literary)* acudir a recoger algo ▪ acudir a por algo ➤ I've come for the moldings. ▪ I've come to pick up the moldings. Vengo a recoger las molduras. ▪ Vengo a por las molduras.

to **come forward** dar el primer paso ➤ After the first accuser came forward, others followed. Después de que el primer acusador diera el primer paso otros (le) siguieron.

to **come from 1.** venir de ▪ provenir de **2.** to be from ser de ➤ He comes from a very poor background. Viene de un medio muy pobre. ▪ Viene de un origen humilde. ▪ *(coll.)* Viene del arroyo. ➤ He comes from a very close family. Proviene de una familia muy unida. ➤ She comes from a large family. Proviene de una familia numerosa. ➤ He comes from a wealthy family. Viene de una familia acomodada. ▪ Viene de una familia pudiende. ➤ Marta comes from Lima. ▪ Marta is from Lima. Marta es de Lima.

to **come full blast** venir a toda pastilla

to **come full circle 1.** to return to the starting point volver al lugar de origen **2.** to return to one's original idea retomar una idea (que se había abandonado) ▪ retomar un principio (que se había abandonado) ▪ retomar una ideología (que se había abandonado)

to **come get** venir a buscar ▪ venir (a) por ➤ Come get me! ¡Ven a buscarme! ▪ ¡Ven (a)por mí! ➤ Please come get the printer, take it to your shop and fix it; I'm tired of trying to fix it over the phone. Por favor venga a buscar la impresora, llévesela a la tienda y arréglela; estoy cansado de intentar de solucionar esto por teléfono. ▪ Por favor venga a por la impresora, llévesela a la tienda y arréglela; estoy cansado de intentar de solucionar esto por teléfono.

come get another one! ▪ come have another one! ¡ven por otro!

come have another one! ▪ come get another one! ven por otro!

come hell or high water: to do something ~ ▪ to do something no matter what it takes ▪ to do something whatever it takes ▪ to do something whatever the cost ▪ to do something at all cost ▪ to do something no matter what the cost hacer algo contra viento y marea ▪ hacer algo por narices ▪ *(slightly off-color)* hacer algo por pelotas ▪ hacer algo por huevos ▪ *(off-color)* hacer algo por cojones

come here! ¡ven acá!

to **come home 1.** volver uno a su casa **2.** to return to one's roots volver uno a sus raíces ▪ volver uno a sus orígenes ➤ Come home this minute! ¡Vuelve a casa ahora mismo! ➤ By coming to Spain, I feel as if I've come home. Al venir a España siento como si volviera a mis raíces.

come home to: to be there ~ permanecer para poder recurrir ➤ We want the ideal to be there so they come home to it one day. Queremos que los ideales permanezcan para poder recurrir a ellos algún día.

come in! ¡adelante! ▪ *(tú)* ¡pasa! ▪ ¡entra! ▪ *(usted)* ¡pase! ▪ ¡entre! ▪ *(Mex., coll.)* ¡pásale!

to **come in 1.** to enter entrar en ▪ entrar a ▪ pasar **2.** to arrive llegar ➤ The dog came in(to) the house carrying his bone. El perro entró en la casa llevando consigo su hueso. ➤ Has my order come in? ▪ Has my order arrived? ¿Ha llegado mi pedido? ➤ Has the plane come in? ▪ Has the plane arrived? ¿Ha llegado el avión?

to **come in a variety of colors** ▪ to come in various colors venir en una amplia gama de colores ▪ venir en un amplio surtido de colores ▪ venir en varios colores ➤ This china pattern comes in a variety of colors. Este motivo de la porcelana viene en varios colores.

to **come in all sizes 1.** *(clothes)* venir en todas las tallas **2.** *(people)* ser cada uno de su padre y su madre

to **come in first 1.** *(in scoring)* quedar (el) primero **2.** *(in a race)* llegar (en el puesto) primero ▪ llegar (el) primero **3.** to enter first entrar primero ➤ Boca Juniors came in first. Boca Juniors quedó (el) primero. ➤ The bride comes in first, followed by the bridesmaids. ▪ The bride enters first, followed by the bridesmaids. La novia entra primero, seguida por las damas de honor. ▪ La novia entra primero, seguida de las damas de honor.

to **come in handy** venirle bien ▪ venirle a mano ➤ This little microwave oven sure does come in handy. Este pequeño microondas nos viene muy a mano. ▪ Este pequeño microondas nos viene muy bien.

to **come in peace** venir en son de paz

to **come in second** entrar segundo ▪ llegar (en el puesto) segundo ▪ llegar (el) segundo

to **come in third** entrar tercero ▪ llegar (en el puesto) tercero ▪ llegar (el) tercero

to **come into a fortune** ▪ to inherit a fortune heredar una fortuna

to **come into being** originarse ▪ nacer ➤ How did the modern nation of Israel come into being? ¿Cómo se originó el estado moderno de Israel? ▪ ¿Cómo nació el estado moderno de Israel?

to **come into focus 1.** *(literal)* quedar enfocada (una imagen) **2.** *(figurative)* cobrar perspectiva ➤ By adjusting the microscope, the image comes into focus. Al ajustar el microscopio, la imagen queda enfocada. ➤ It takes about a generation for a president's historical impact to come into focus. Lleva más o menos una generación que el impacto histórico de un presidente cobre perspectiva.

to **come into money** ▪ to inherit money heredar dinero

to **come into one's own** alcanzar uno el dominio de algo ▪ alcanzar uno el magisterio de algo ▪ alcanzar la madurez ➤ Einstein had come into his own as a physicist by the time he was sixteen. Einstein a los dieciséis años ya había alcanzado el dominio de la física.

to **come into one's possession** venir a parar a las manos de uno

to **come into one's stride** ▪ to hit one's stride ▪ to achieve a steady pace ▪ to reach one's optimal performance alcanzar uno su rendimiento óptimo

to **come into play** entrar en juego ▪ ponerse en juego ➤ In the regulation of the emotions the prefrontal cortex, above all, comes into play. En la regulación de las emociones se pone en juego, sobre todo, el cortex prefrontal.

to **come into someone's life** cruzarse en la vida ▪ entrar en la vida

to **come into the world** ▪ to be born llegar al mundo ▪ venir al mundo ▪ nacer

to **come into view** hacerse visible ▪ poder verse ➤ From the crow's nest of the Santa María, flat land came into view at a distance of about nine and a half miles. Desde la cofa de la

Santa María, la tierra llana se hizo visible a una distancia de nueve millas y media.

come join us ▪ come and join us ven y únete a nosotros

to **come loose** 1. quedar suelto ▪ aflojarse 2. to come completely off desprenderse ▪ deshacerse ▪ soltarse del todo ➤ It came loose. Quedó suelto. ▪ Se aflojó. ▪ Se desprendió. ▪ Se deshizo.

to **come of age** llegar a la mayoría de edad

to **come of it** salir algo de algo ➤ Nothing came of it. No salió nada de aquello. ➤ I hope nothing comes of it. Espero que no salga nada de eso.

to **come off** desprenderse ▪ desprenderse de ▪ soltarse ▪ caerse ➤ The engine came off the airplane. El motor se desprendió del avión. ➤ It's just a thin brass plating that comes off if you chip it. Es sólo un baño muy fino de latón que se desprende si lo picas. ➤ That's the plane that the propeller came off of. Ésa es la avioneta de la que se desprendió la hélice. ➤ The collar button came off. El botón del cuello de la camisa se soltó. ▪ El botón del cuello de la camisa se cayó.

come off it! ▪ get real! ¡anda ya!

to **come off well** ▪ to come out well ser bien llevado a la práctica ➤ The plan came off well. El plan fue bien llevado a la práctica.

to **come off without a hitch** suceder sin ningún contratiempo ▪ salir sin ningún contratiempo ➤ The dress rehearsal was rocky, but the opening night came off without a hitch. El ensayo general resultó flojo, pero la noche del estreno salió sin ningún contratiempo.

come on! 1. hurry! ¡venga! ▪ ¡vamos! ▪ *(tú)* ¡anda! ▪ *(usted)* ¡ande! ▪ *(Mex., tú)* ¡ándale, vamos! ▪ *(usted)* ¡ándele, vamos! 2. you're pulling my leg! ▪ noooo! ▪ get real! ¡venga ya! ▪ ¡anda ya!

come-on ▪ enticement palanca de atracción ▪ aliciente ▪ incentivo ▪ reclamo ▪ invitación

to **come on** *(TV show)* pasar ➤ My favorite TV show comes on at eight. Pasan mi programa de televisión favorito a las ocho.

come on, damn it! *(off-color)* ¡venga, coño! ▪ ¡ándale, carajo!

come on, I'll buy you a cup of coffee venga, te invito a un café ▪ vamos, te invito a tomar un café

come on, let's go! ▪ c'mon, let's go! ¡venga, vamos! ▪ ¡venga, vámonos! ▪ ¡venga ya!

come on, now! ▪ c'mon now! ¡vamos anda!

come on over! ¡vente a casa (ahora)!

come on, tell me! ¡venga, dímelo! ▪ *(Mex.)* ¡ándale, dímelo!

to **come on to hard times** ▪ to hit hard times venir a menos

to **come on to someone (sexually)** ▪ to make a pass at someone ▪ to hit on someone arrastrarle el ala ▪ menearle el ala ▪ tirarse el lance con alguien ▪ *(Sp.)* tirarle los tejos a alguien

come on up! *(tú)* ¡sube! ▪ *(usted)* ¡suba! ▪ *(ustedes)* ¡suban! ▪ *(vosotros)* ¡subid!

to **come onto the market** ▪ to come out ▪ to be introduced (onto the market) salir al mercado ▪ ser lanzado al mercado ▪ ser estrenado al mercado

to **come out** 1. *(movie)* to premier estrenar ▪ salir 2. *(merchandise)* to come onto the market salir (al mercado) ▪ ser lanzado (al mercado) ▪ ser estrenado ▪ salir a la luz 3. *(photograph)* to turn out salir ➤ The film, which came out in 1967... El filme, estrenado en 1967... ➤ Mobile phones with TVs came out in 2003. Los móviles con tele incorporada salieron (al mercado) en el 2003. ▪ Los móviles con tele incorporada fueron lanzados (al mercado) en el 2003. ▪ Los móviles con tele incorporada fueron estrenados (en el mercado) en el 2003. ➤ How did the pictures come out? ▪ How did the pictures turn out? ¿Cómo salieron las fotos?

to **come out ahead** salir ganando ▪ salir beneficiado ➤ You'll come out ahead. Saldrás ganando. ▪ Saldrás beneficiado.

to **come out from under the bed** salir de debajo de la cama ➤ I can't get the cat to come out from under the bed. No puedo conseguir que la gata salga de debajo de la cama.

to **come out in favor of** mostrarse a favor de

to **come out (in the newspaper)** salir (en el periódico) ▪ salir (publicado) en el periódico ➤ It came out in the paper last week. Salió publicado en el periódico la semana pasada.

to **come out (into the open)** ▪ to become known darse a conocer ▪ salir a flote ➤ The truth eventually comes out. La verdad finalmente sale a flote. ▪ La verdad finalmente se da a conocer. ➤ It's already come out. Ya se ha dado a conocer.

to **come out monthly, weekly, etc.** *(publication)* ▪ to come out once a month, once a week, etc. salir una vez al mes, a la semana, etc. ➤ The magazine comes out monthly. ▪ The magazine comes out once a month. La revista sale una vez al mes.

to **come out of a study** ▪ to emerge from a study desprenderse de un estudio

to **come out of a survey** ▪ to emerge from a survey desprenderse de una encuesta ➤ It's now a fact: Hispanics equal blacks in number in the United States, and might even already outnumber them, according to early data coming out of last year's census. Ya es un hecho: los hispanos igualan en número a los negros en EE UU. Incluso puede que los superan ya; así se desprende de los primeros datos del censo efectuado el pasado año.

to **come out of one's shell** salir de su cascarón

to **come out of something with flying colors** salir airoso de algo

to **come out (of the closet)** ▪ to declare publicly one's homosexuality salir del armario ▪ hacerse conocer su homosexualidad ▪ declararse homosexual ➤ The gay came out to his family and friends. El homosexual salió del armario para su familia y amigos.

to **come out(side)** salir ➤ Come out and look at the flowers I just planted. Sal y mira las flores que acabo de plantar.

to **come out of one's salary** salir del salario de uno ➤ Even when your employer pays for half your medical care, it still comes out of your salary. Incluso cuando tu empleador paga la mitad de tu asistencia médica, aún sigue saliendo de tu salario.

to **come out of the woodwork** salir de debajo de las piedras

to **come out on top** llevarse la mejor parte

to **come out strongly against** ▪ to be adamantly opposed to salir en tromba contra

to **come out swinging against something** ▪ to be totally against something, with no possibility of discussion salir en tromba contra algo ➤ *(headline)* The government comes out swinging against the merging of the police and Civil Guard. El gobierno sale en tromba contra la fusión de la policía y la Guardia Civil.

to **come out well** ser bien llevado a la práctica ➤ The plan came out well. El plan fue bien llevado a la práctica.

to **come out with it** ▪ to come out and say it hablar claro ▪ hablar sin tapujos ▪ expresar lo que uno siente ➤ I should have just come out with it. Debería haber expresado lo que sentía.

to **come out with the funniest things** tener cada salida ▪ siempre tener una ocurrencia ➤ She comes out with the funniest things. Ella tiene cada salida. ▪ Ella siempre tiene una ocurrencia.

to **come over for dinner** *(afternoon)* venirse a comer ▪ *(evening)* venirse a cenar ➤ We'd like you to come over for dinner. *(afternoon)* Queremos que se vengan a comer. ▪ *(evening)* Queremos que te vengas a cenar.

to **come over for supper** venirse a cenar ➤ We'd like you all to come over for supper. Queremos que se vengan a cenar. ▪ *(Sp., vosotros)* Queremos que os vengáis a cenar.

to **come over one** ▪ to happen to one pasarle a uno ➤ I don't know what's come over me. ▪ I don't know what's happening to me. No sé qué me está pasando.

come rain or (come) shine ▪ rain or shine ▪ no matter what llueva o haga sol ▪ pase lo que pase ➤ We're leaving for Ciudad Bolívar tomorrow come rain or come shine. ▪ We're leaving for Ciudad Bolívar tomorrow no matter what. Salimos para Ciudad Bolívar mañana, llueva o haga sol. ▪ Salimos para Ciudad Bolívar mañana, pase lo que pase.

to **come right back** ▪ come straight back regresar aquí derechito ▪ volver aquí ahora mismo.

to **come right out and say it** ▪ to just say it hablar mal y pronto

to **come running (in)** ▪ to run in llegar corriendo ▪ entrar corriendo to **come storming in** ■ to storm in entrar a degüello a ■ *(Sp.)* entrar a degüello en

to **come straight towards one** dirigirse directamente hacia uno ➤ They came straight towards us. Se dirigieron directamente hacia nosotros.

to **come through 1.** to fulfill one's promise cumplir **2.** to pass through ir pasando ➤ I hope she'll come through. Espero que ella cumpla. ➤ We're coming through. Vamos pasando.

to **come to 1.** to regain consciousness volver en sí **2.** to total ■ to come out to salir a ■ ascender a ➤ After being knocked out, the boxer came to before the count of ten. El boxeador volvió en sí antes de llegar a la cuenta de diez. ➤ What does the bill come to? ¿A cuánto sale la cuenta? ■ ¿A cuánto asciende la cuenta?

to **come to a bad end** ■ to meet an ill fate acabar mal ■ parar en mal ■ acabar en mal

to **come to a boil** ■ to start to boil ■ to begin to boil empezar a hervir ■ romper el hervor ■ ir a hervir ■ llegar al punto de cocción ➤ When it comes to a boil, reduce the heat. Cuando rompa el hervor, bajar el fuego. ➤ When it comes to a boil, add the flour while beating the mixture vigorously. Cuando vaya a hervir, añadir la harina batiendo fuertemente la mezcla.

to **come to a complete stop** ■ to come to a dead stop parar en firme ■ parar en seco

to **come to do something** ■ to come for the purpose of doing something venir a que haga algo ➤ I came to get my eyes checked. ■ I came to have my eyes examined. ■ I came for an eye examination. Vine a que me gradúes la vista.

to **come to a head** llegar a un punto decisivo

to **come to a stop** ■ to come to a full stop ■ to come to a complete stop frenar hasta parar ■ pararse

to **come to an agreement** ■ to reach an agreement llegar a un acuerdo ■ ponerse de acuerdo

to **come to an end** concluir

to **come to be** llegar a ser ➤ I've come to be very skeptical of this plan. He llegado a ser muy escéptico de este plan.

to **come to believe** llegarse a creer

to **come to blows** llegar a (las) manos ■ darse de bofetadas ■ liarse a mamporros ■ llegar a las armas

to **come to grips with** abordar ■ ponerse a tono con ■ luchar con

to **come to have 1.** venir a que... **2.** llegar a tener... ➤ I've come to have my eyes examined. ■ I've come for an eye examination. ■ I've come to get my eyes examined. Vine a que me gradúes la vista. ■ Vine para un examen de la vista. ■ Vine a recibir una revisión de los ojos.

to **come to life** cobrar vida

to **come to light** salir a la luz

to **come to mind 1.** to remember ■ to recall venírsele a la memoria ■ acudirle a la memoria **2.** to occur to one ■ to think of venirle a la cabeza ■ venirle a la mente ■ ocurrírsele ■ venirle a la boca ➤ What came to mind when you mentioned Bariloche was the excellent chocolate. Lo que me vino a la memoria cuando mencionaste Barriloche fue el chocolate excelente. ➤ What comes to mind when you look at this ink blot? ¿Qué se te ocurre cuando miras esta mancha de tinta?

to **come to one** ■ to come to mind venirle a la boca a alguien ➤ It just came to me. Acaba de venirme a la boca.

to **come to power** llegar al poder ■ acceder al poder

to **come to one's attention that...** venirle a la atención que... ■ recibir información de que... ■ informarle a alguien (de) que... ➤ It has come to my attention that... ■ It has been brought to my attention that... Ha venido a mi atención que... ■ He recibido información de que... ■ Alguien me ha informado (de) que...

to **come to one's senses** ■ to recover one's senses hacerse con el control de sus sentidos

to **come to someone's aid** acudir en la ayuda de alguien

to **come to terms with** reconciliarse a algo ■ asimilar algo

to **come to the conclusion that...** ■ to arrive at the conclusion that... ■ to conclude that... llegar a la conclusión de que... ■ sacar la conclusión de que... ■ concluir que...

to **come to the phone** ponerse (al aparato) ➤ Tell Paco to come to the phone. Dile a Paco que se ponga (al aparato).

to **come to the door** asomarse a la puerta

to **come to the surface** salir a la superficie

to **come to the window** asomarse a la ventana

come to think of it ahora que lo pienso

to **come together 1.** to materialize cuajar ■ resultar ■ salir **2.** to unite juntarse ➤ It just didn't come together. ■ It just didn't materialize. No resultó. ■ No salió. ■ No cuajó. ➤ To make progress on social issues, all classes of society need to come together. Para progresar en cuestiones sociales, todas las clases de la sociedad necesitan juntarse.

to **come true (for)** ■ to become a reality (for one) hacérsele realidad (para)

to **come unglued** ■ to come unhinged ■ to go ballistic perder los estribos ■ ponerse como una fiera

to **come unhinged** ■ to come unglued ■ to go ballistic perder los estribos ■ ponerse como una fiera

to **come up for air** salir para tomar aire ■ *(Sp.)* salir para coger más aire ■ volver a por aire

to **come up next to** ■ to draw (up) level with emparejar con ■ ir a continuación a

to **come up to one** acercarse a uno ■ ir al encuentro de uno ➤ They come up to you on the street. Van a tu encuentro en la calle.

to **come up with an idea** ■ to hit on an idea dar con una idea ■ sacar una idea ➤ Where did you come up with that idea? ¿Dónde sacaste esa idea?

to **come upon** *(literary)* ■ to run into ■ to meet ■ to encounter ■ to come across ■ to run across encontrarse con ■ dar con ■ toparse con

to **come very close to...** ■ to come within a hair's breadth of... estar en un tris de... ■ faltarle el canto de un duro para que...

come what may venga lo que venga ■ pase lo que pase ■ venga lo que viniere

to **come with batteries** venir con las pilas ■ traer las pilas

come with me *(restaurant host to diner)* acompaña(me) ■ ven conmigo

to **come with something** llevar algo ➤ It comes with a belt. Lleva cinturón.

to **come within a hair's breadth of...** ■ to come very close to... faltarle el canto de un duro para que...

to **comfort someone 1.** to make someone feel better reconfortar a alguien ■ darle consuelo a alguien ■ consolar a alguien **2.** to console someone darle consuelo a alguien ■ consolar a alguien

to be **comfortable with** sentirse a gusto con ■ sentirse a gusto en ➤ The philosopher Immanuel Kant was so comfortable with abstraction that he hardly used any examples. El filósofo Immanuel Kant se sentía tan a gusto con la abstracción que rara vez utilizaba ejemplos.

comic book (revista de) caricaturas ■ *(Sp.)* tebeo ➤ Have you seen my comic book? ¿Has visto mi revista de caricaturas?

comic opera ópera cómica ■ ópera bufa

comic strip tira cómica

coming! ¡voy! ■ ¡(ya) va!

coming back from ■ on the way back from ■ on returning from *(L. Am.)* al regresar de ■ cuando regresaba de ■ mientras regresaba de ■ *(Sp.)* al volver de ■ cuando volvía de ■ mientras volvía de ■ *(literary)* al retornar de ■ cuando retornaba de ■ mientras retornaba de ➤ Coming back from the airport, we stopped to buy some film. ■ On the way back from the airport, we stopped to buy some film. ■ On returning from the airport, we stopped to buy some film. Al regresar del aeropuerto, paramos para comprar película. ■ Al volver del aeropuerto, paramos para comprar película. ■ Al retornar del aeropuerto, paramos para comprar película.

coming from proveniente de ➤ No sooner was I alone than I began to hear strange noises coming from the apartment next door. Apenas me encontré solo comencé a oír ruidos extraños provenientes del piso de al lado.

coming soon to Montevideo próximamente en Montevideo

coming to vendrá ➤ Coming to Santiago in October Vendrá a Santiago en octubre

coming up! *(on the news)* ya ➤ Details coming up! ¡Detalles ya!

the **coming year** el año venidero ▪ el año que viene ▪ el año que (se) avecina
comings and goings of people el ir y venir de la gente ▪ las idas y venidas de la gente
to **command all eyes** llevarse las miradas de todos
to **command attention** acaparar la atención
command center *(military)* complejo de mando
command of a language dominio de un idioma
command of a language: to have a ~ dominar un idioma ➤ María Luisa has an excellent command of English. María Luisa domina muy bien el inglés.
to **command respect** hacerse respetar
to **commend one's soul to God** comendar el alma
commission or omission acción u omisión
commissioned works obras de encargo
to **commit a bank robbery** ▪ to rob a bank hacer un robo de un banco
to **commit a crime** producir un crimen ➤ Shortly after the crime was committed Poco antes de que se produjera el crimen
to **commit perjury** ▪ to perjure oneself ▪ to lie under oath cometer perjurio ▪ perjurarse ▪ mentir bajo juramento ▪ jurar en falso
to **commit someone to an asylum** internar a alguien en un manicomio
to **commit something to writing** ▪ to put something in writing dejar algo consignado
to **commit suicide** ▪ to kill oneself ▪ to take one's own life suicidarse ▪ matarse
to be **committed to** estar comprometido con
commitment to compromiso con
committee chairman ▪ chairman of the committee presidente de comité
common ailment *la* afección común
common consent asentimiento común
common feeling ▪ common view ▪ general feeling ▪ general view *el* sentir general
common knowledge that... ser bien sabido que... ▪ ser de sobra conocido que...
common law derecho consuetudinario
common-law marriage ▪ de facto union ▪ concubinage unión de hecho ▪ unión de facto ▪ concubinato ▪ pareja de hecho
to be a **common practice** ser una práctica común ▪ ser una costumbre muy común
common sense sentido común ➤ Common sense is not so common. El sentido común es el menos común de los sentidos.
common thread hilo conductor ➤ A common thread runs through all these compositions. Un hilo conductor une todas estas composiciones.
common wall pared divisoria
to be a **commonplace** ser de cajón
communal life vida comunitaria
to **communicate with hand signals** *(military)* ▪ to communicate using hand signals ▪ to signal with one's hands hablar por señas
communion wafer ▪ host sagrada forma ▪ hostia
community property *la* propiedad de la comunidad ▪ propiedad comunal
commuter flights ▪ air shuttle service puente aéreo
commuter train *el* (tren de) cercanías
compact (car) carro pequeño ▪ carro compacto ▪ *el* mini ▪ *(Sp.)* *el* coche pequeño ▪ coche compacto
compact disc ▪ compact disk ▪ CD disco compacto ▪ CD
company he keeps: a man is known by the ~ dime con quien andas y te diré quien eres ▪ dime con quien vas y te diré quien eres
to **compare apples and oranges** mezclar las churras con las merinas
compared to ▪ in comparison to ▪ in comparison with en comparación a
to be **compelled to do something** verse obligado a hacer algo ▪ verse forzado a hacer algo
compelling argument ▪ convincing argument ▪ forceful argument ▪ weighty argument argumento de peso ▪ argumento convincente
compelling reason motivo obligatorio ▪ *la* razón de peso
to **compete for the prize** ▪ to contend for the prize ▪ to vie for the prize competir por el premio
to **compete in the elections** competir en las elecciones
to **compete with each other** competir el uno contra el otro
to **complain about something** ▪ to complain of something quejarse de algo ▪ quejarse sobre algo
to **complain angrily** quejarse airadamente
to **complain of something** ▪ to complain about something quejarse de algo
complaint about queja sobre ➤ I want to make a complaint about... ▪ I want to lodge a complaint about... Quiero hacer una queja sobre... ➤ What's the complaint about? ¿Sobre qué es la queja? ▪ ¿De qué es la queja?
complementary angles ▪ angles whose sum equals ninety degrees ángulos complementarios ▪ ángulos cuya suma es noventa grados
complementary colors colores complementarios
to **complete one's degree** ▪ to finish one's degree acabar los estudios ▪ terminar los estudios
to **complete one's bachelor's (degree)** acabar la licenciatura ▪ licenciarse ▪ terminar la licenciatura
to **complete one's doctoral degree** ▪ to complete one's doctorate acabar el doctorado ▪ doctorarse ▪ terminar el doctorado
to **complete one's master's degree** acabar el master ▪ acabar el diploma de estudios avanzados (DEA) ▪ diplomarse en estudios avanzados ▪ terminar el master ▪ terminar el diploma de estudios avanzados (DEA)
to **complete one's studies** ▪ to finish one's studies terminar los estudios
complete range of options gama completa de opciones
to be **completely convinced** estar del todo convencido
to be **completely crazy** ▪ to be completely nuts estar loco perdido
to be **completely different (from each other)** ser el polo opuesto a ➤ Marco and Paco are completely different. Marco es el polo opuesto a Paco.
to be a **completely different situation** ser una situación completamente diferente ▪ ser una situación completamente distinta
to be **completely exhausted** ▪ to have reached the limits of one's endurance estar al límite de sus fuerzas ▪ estar muerto de cansancio
to **completely explain** explicar del todo ▪ explicar por completo ▪ explicar completamente ➤ It doesn't completely explain it. No lo explica del todo.
to be **completely dark** ser todo oscuridad ➤ The city was completely dark. La ciudad era todo oscuridad.
to **completely lose track of someone** perder toda pista de alguien
to be **completely nuts** ▪ to be completely crazy estar loco perdido ▪ estar loco de remate ▪ estar loco de atar ▪ *(Sp.)* estar más loco que una cabra
to be **completely unaware of** no ser para nada consciente de
to be **completely unaware that...** no ser para nada consciente de que...
completion of a contract cumplimiento de un contrato
completion of one's degree finalización del título de uno ▪ terminación del título de uno
to be a **complex person** ▪ to be a deep person ser una persona compleja ▪ tener sus entresijos ➤ He's a very complex person. ▪ He's a very deep person. Es una person muy compleja. ▪ Tiene sus entresijos.
to **complicate matters** complicar las cosas ▪ liar el tema ▪ rizar el rizo ▪ enredar las cosas *(See also "to complicate matters" under "to.")*
complicated matter asunto complicado ▪ asunto intrincado
to **comply with** cumplir con
to **comply with the building codes** 1. to be in compliance with the building codes cumplir con la normativa referente

a edificios **2.** to obey the building codes seguir la normativa referente a edificios

to **compose music** componer música

to be **composed mostly of** estar compuesto en su mayoría de

to be **composed of the following ingredients** ▪ to contain the following ingredients ▪ to be made up of the following ingredients estar compuesto de los siguientes ingredientes

to **compound the difficulty** agravar la dificultad

compound verb perífrasis verbal

comprehensive guide *la* guía completa

comprehensive list listado extenso ▪ listado amplio ▪ listado exhaustivo ▪ lista completa

compressed air aire comprimido

to be **comprised of** componerse de ▪ estar compuesto

compulsory sterilization ▪ forced sterilization esterilización forzosa ➤ The country's government ordered the compulsory sterilization of 200,000 women. El gobierno del país ordenó la esterilización forzosa de 200.000 mujeres.

compulsory schooling compulsory education escolarización obligatoria

to be **computed at 1.** *(the rate of)* calcularse en **2.** *(at the cost of)* contabilizarse a razón de ➤ Fuel consumption was computed at the rate of 50 miles per gallon. El consumo de combustibles se calculó en 50 millas por galón. ➤ Labor was computed at the rate of $15 per hour. El trabajo se contabilizaba a razón de $15 por hora.

computer chip lasca ▪ *el* chip

computer game *(L. Am.)* juego de computadora ▪ *(Sp.)* juego de ordenador

computer peripherals dispositivos periféricos

computer program programa informático

computer science ingeniería informática

computer scientist ingeniero informático

computer technician informático

computer virus virus informático

the **computers are down** *(L. Am.)* las computadoras están bloqueadas ▪ *(Sp.)* los ordenadores tienen una incidencia ▪ hay una incidencia (con los ordenadores)

con artist ▪ con man estafador(-a)

to **con someone** ▪ to rip someone off vender un buzón a alguien ▪ timar a alguien

concave mirror espejo cóncavo

to **conceal one's indifference** ▪ to hide one's indifference ▪ to disguise one's indifference ▪ to feign interest disimular la indiferencia

to **concede defeat** darse por derrotado

to **concede (the point) that...** ▪ to acknowledge (the point) that... conceder (el punto que) que... ▪ reconocer (el punto) que...

to **concelebrate Mass** *(more than one priest officiating)* concelebrar la misa

to **concentrate on one thing** ▪ to focus on one thing ▪ to limit oneself to one main focus concentrarse en una sola cosa ▪ ceñirse a un tema

concentration of: the largest ~ ▪ the greatest concentration of el mayor colectivo de ➤ The largest concentration of northwest Africans in Madrid lives in Lavapiés. ▪ The greatest concentration of northwest Africans lives in Lavapiés. El mayor colectivo de magrebíes en Madrid vive en Lavapiés.

to **concern one 1.** to worry one concernirle a uno **2.** to have to do with one ▪ to be one's concern atañerle a uno ➤ It concerns him very much. Le concierne muchísimo. ➤ It doesn't concern me. ▪ It's not my concern. (Eso) no me atañe. ➤ As far as I'm concerned Por lo que a mí atañe

concise account relato compacto

to **conclude a meeting** concluir una reunión ▪ ultimar una reunión ➤ *(headline)* Aznar and Zapatero conclude their meeting to save the anti-terrorism pact. Aznar y Zapatero ultiman su reunión para salvar el pacto contra el terrorismo.

to **conclude a peace agreement** ▪ to draw up and sign a peace agreement acordar la paz ➤ The presidents concluded a peace agreement. Los presidentes acordaron la paz.

to **conclude by saying** terminar diciendo

conclusive evidence pruebas concluyentes

conclusive proof pruebas contundentes ▪ pruebas concluyentes

concrete mixer hormigonera ▪ *(truck)* camión hormigonera

condescending attitude ▪ patronizing attitude *la* actitud condescendiente

condition of a patient estado de un paciente

conditions are right for se dan las condiciones para ➤ *(news item)* Sharon says conditions are right for coming to a historic agreement with the Palestinians. Sharon dice que se dan las condiciones para llegar a su "acuerdo histórico" con los palestinos.

to **conduct a search of** ▪ to search hacer un registro de ➤ The police conducted a search of the building. ▪ The police searched the building. La policía hizo un registro del edificio.

to **conduct a test** realizar una prueba

to **conduct a trial** ▪ to hold a trial celebrar un juicio

to **conduct an experiment** ▪ to perform an experiment ▪ to do an experiment ▪ to carry out an experiment realizar un experimento

to **conduct an interview** ▪ to do an interview realizar una entrevista ▪ hacer una entrevista

to **conduct research** realizar investigaciones ➤ The research conducted by Otto Hahn and Lise Meitner led to the discovery of nuclear fission in 1939. Las investigaciones realizadas por Otto Hahn y Lise Meitner condujeron al descubrimiento de la fisión nuclear.

to **conduct some business** ▪ to do some business hacer unas gestiones ➤ I'm going to the bank to conduct some business. ▪ I'm going to the bank to do some business. Voy al banco a hacer unas gestiones.

conductor of an orchestra ▪ orchestra conductor director de una orquesta

conference proceedings ▪ proceedings of the conference las actas de la reunión

to **confess without holding anything back** confesarse a cara descubierta ▪ confesarse sin tapujos

confessed murderer ▪ confessed killer asesino confeso

to **confide in someone** confiarse a alguien ▪ confiarse con alguien ▪ hacer confidencias a alguien

to **confide something to someone** confiar algo a alguien ▪ contar algo en confianza a alguien

confidence in one's abilities: to have ~ confiar en sus habilidades

confidence in oneself ▪ self-confidence confianza en uno(-a) mismo(-a) ▪ confianza en sí mismo(-a) ➤ He has a lot of confidence in himself. ▪ He has a lot of self-confidence. Tiene mucha confianza en sí mismo.

to **confirm that...** confirmar si... ➤ Please confirm that you got this E-mail. Por favor confirma si recibiste este correo electrónico.

confirmed bachelor soltero empedernido

conflicting accounts relatos contradictorios

conflicting advice consejos contradictorios

confrontation with the police ▪ clash with the police enfrentamiento con la policía ➤ *(headline)* Thirteen Algerian Muslims die in confrontations with the police. Trece islamistas argelinos mueren en enfrentamientos con la policía.

to **confuse someone with someone else** ▪ to confuse someone for someone else ▪ to take someone for someone else ▪ to think someone is someone else confundirle a alguien por otra persona ▪ tomar a alguien por otra persona ▪ pensar que alguien es otra persona ▪ creer que alguien es otra persona ➤ Pardon me. I confused you with someone else. ▪ Pardon me. I thought you were someone else. ▪ Pardon me. I took you for someone else. ▪ Pardon me. I thought you were someone else. ▪ *(to a man)* Perdone, lo confundí por otra persona. ▪ Perdone, lo tomé por otra persona. ▪ Perdone, pensé que era otra persona. ▪ Perdone, creí que era otra persona. ▪ *(Sp., leísmo)* Perdone, le confundí por otra persona. ▪ Perdone, le tomé por otra persona. ▪ *(to a woman)* Perdone, la confundí por otra persona. ▪ Perdone, la tomé por otra persona.

to **confuse something with something else** ▪ to take something for something else confundir algo con otra cosa ➤ I confused the copy with the original. ■ I took the copy for the original. Confundí la copia con el original.

to **confuse the issue** confundir la cuestión ■ confundir el asunto

to be **confused** hacerse un lío ■ armarse un lío

congratulations! ¡enhorabuena! ■ ¡felicitaciones!

congressional races las carreras al congreso ■ las carreras hacia el congreso

to **connect cables, cords, wires** conectar cables ➤ Connect the extension cord to an outlet with a ground. Conecte el prolongador a un enchufe con toma de tierra.

to **connect the dots** ■ to see the overall picture concatenar los hechos

to **connect two parts of a building** comunicar dos partes de un edificio ➤ That door connects the office with the rest of the house. Esa puerta comunica la oficina con el resto de la casa.

to **connect two things** ■ to associate two things conectar dos cosas ➤ At first, police didn't connect the star witness to the crime itself. Al principio la policía no conectó el testigo estrella al propio crimen.

connecting flight vuelo de conección

connection (between ideas) relación (entre ideas) ➤ I still don't see the connection. Sigo sin ver la relación.

to **conquer one's fears** ■ to overcome one's fears vencer sus miedos

consecrated communion wafer hostia consagrada ■ *(literary)* forma consagrada

to **consider an option** considerar una opción ■ barajar una opción

to **consider doing something** ■ to think about doing something pensar en hacer algo ➤ We have considered buying a microwave. Hemos pensado en comprar un microondas.

consider it done! *(tú)* ¡dalo por hecho! ■ *(usted)* ¡delo por hecho!

to **consider oneself lucky** darse con un canto en los dientes

to **consider scenarios** ■ to explore scenarios barajar escenarios ➤ Analysts are considering several scenarios. ■ Analysts are considering a number of scenarios. Los analistas barajan diversos escenarios.

to **consider several possibilities** considerar varias posibilidades ■ barajar varias posibilidades ➤ Analysts are considering several possibilities. ■ Analysts are considering a number of possibilities. Los analistas están barajando varias posibilidades.

to **consider someone a friend** ■ to consider someone to be a friend considerar a alguien un amigo

to **consider something (to be)** considerar que algo es ■ tener algo por ser

to **consider the matter settled** dar el asunto por zanjado ■ dar el asunto por concluido ■ dar el asunto por finalizado ■ dar el asunto por resuelto ■ considerar el capítulo como cerrado

to **consider the possibility (that...)** considerar la posibilidad (de que...)

to **consider the pros and cons** hacer composición de lugar

to be **considered** considerársele ➤ Madrid is considered one of the most interesting cities in Europe. A Madrid se le considera una de las ciudades más interesantes de Europa.

to be **considered regarding** barajarse sobre ➤ The only hypothesis being considered regarding the reasons that could drive them to commit the crime... La única hipótesis que se baraja sobre las razones que pudieron impulsarlos a cometer el crimen...

considering one's age tomando en cuenta su edad ➤ Considering her age, she's lucky to be doing as well as she is. Tomando en cuenta su edad, tiene suerte de encontrarse tan bien.

considering the fact that... ■ in view of the fact that... ■ since... tomando en cuenta (el hecho de) que... ■ teniendo en cuenta (el hecho de) que... ■ en vista de que... ■ comoquiera que...

considering who he is siendo quien es ■ tomando en cuenta quien es

considering who he was siendo quien era ■ tomando en cuenta quien era

considering who it is siendo quien es ■ tomando en cuenta quien era

considering who it was siendo quien era ■ tomando en cuenta quien era

considering who she is siendo quien es ■ tomando en cuenta quien es

considering who she was siendo quien era ■ tomando en cuenta quien era

consignment of goods consignación de mercancías ■ partida de bienes

to **consist of** consistir en ■ constar de

to be **consistent throughout** ser coherente en su totalidad

to be **consistent with** *(coll.)* ■ to jibe with concertar con

to be **conspicuous by one's absence** brillar por su ausencia

conspicuous lack falta llamativa de ■ falta conspicua de ■ llamativa falta de ■ carencia conspicua de

constituent parts partes constitutivas ■ piezas constitutivas

construction foreman *el* capataz de obras de construcción

construction was completed on se terminó de construir ■ la construcción fue terminada en ➤ In 1819 construction was completed on a building that would house the Spanish royal art collection—the Prado. En 1819 se terminó de construir el edificio que albergaría la colección de arte real español—el Prado.

construction worker trabajador de la construcción

constructive criticism críticas constructivas

to **consult with one's advisers** consultar con los consejeros de uno ■ consultar a los consejeros de uno

to **consume *x* gallons of fuel per mile** consumir *x* galones de combustible a la milla

to be **consumed with envy** comerse de envidia ■ comérselo la envidia

consumer goods los bienes de consumo

consumer price index *el* índice de precios al consumo

to **consummate a marriage** consumar un matrimonio

consumption of energy ■ energy consumption consumo energético

contact lenses *los* lentes de contacto

to **contact someone** contactar con alguien

to be **contacted by telephone** ■ to be contacted by phone ser contactado por teléfono ■ ser contactado telefónicamente

to **contain a fire** atajar un fuego

to **contain life** ■ to have life albergar la vida ➤ Does Mars contain life? ■ Does Mars have life? ■ Is there life on Mars? ¿Alberga Marte la vida?

to **contain the following ingredients** ■ to be composed of the following ingredients ■ to be made up of the following ingredients componerse de los siguientes ingredientes

contemporary writer escritor(-a) de hoy ➤ Contemporary women writers Escritoras de hoy

to be **contemptuous of someone** ■ to regard someone with contempt tener en poco a alguien

to **contend for the prize** ■ to compete for the prize concurrir al premio

to **contest an election** impugnar una elección

to be **contingent on** ■ to be contingent upon ■ to be subject to ■ to be dependent on ■ to be dependent upon ■ to be subordinate to ■ to be conditioned on estar supeditado a ■ depender de ➤ It's contingent on what they decide. ■ It's contingent upon what they decide. ■ It's subject to what they decide. ■ It's dependent on what they decide. ■ It's dependent upon what they decide. ■ It depends on what they decide. ■ It's subordinate to their decision. Está supeditado a lo que deciden. ■ Depende de lo que deciden.

continual flights ■ flights at regular intervals vuelos continuos ■ vuelos a cada equis tiempo ➤ The air shuttle provides continual flights between Madrid and Barcelona. El puente aéreo provee vuelos continuos entre Madrid y Barcelona.

to **continue for** prolongarse durante ■ continuar durante

to **continue straight ahead** ■ to keep going straight (ahead) seguir derecho ➤ Continue straight ahead. ■ Keep going straight (ahead). *(tú)* Sigue derecho. ■ *(usted)* Siga derecho.

continue to hold: please ~ *(telephone recording)* por favor, permanezca en espera

to **continue walking** ■ to keep walking ■ to walk on seguir caminando ■ *(Sp.)* seguir andando

continuous flow of water ■ continuous stream of water flujo continuo de agua

continuous stream of cars ■ solid stream of cars ■ unbroken stream of cars rodar continuo de carros ■ rodar continuo de automóviles ■ *(Sp.)* rodar continuo de coches

contour sheet ■ fitted sheet sábana elástica ■ sábana funda ■ sábana de contour ➤ A contour sheet is one that fits over the sides of the mattress. Una sábana elástica es la que forra directamente el colchón.

to **contract for a service** ■ to sign up for a service darse de alta en un servicio ■ contratar un servicio ■ apuntarse a un servicio

to **contract with someone for something** ■ to enter into a contract with someone for something ■ to hire someone to do something contratar algo a alguien

to be a **contradiction in terms** ser una contradicción de términos

contradictory feelings ■ mixed feelings ■ ambivalent feelings sentimientos contradictorios ■ sentimientos contrapuestos

contrary to popular belief ■ contrary to what most people think en contra de la creencia popular ■ en contra de lo que piensan muchos ■ contrario a lo que piensan muchos

contrary to what most people think al contrario de lo que piensa la mayoría

to **control one's temper** controlar su genio

to **control oneself** controlarse ■ reprimirse ■ contenerse ■ reportarse ➤ Control yourself! ¡Contrólate! ■ ¡Reprímete!

control surfaces of the wing *(ailerons, flaps, air brakes)* secciones móviles del ala

to **control the airspace of a country** ■ to control a country's airspace controlar el espacio aéreo de un país

control tower *la* torre de control

controlled demolition of a building (with explosives) voladura controlada de un edificio

controls of an airplane mandos de un avión ■ *(light airplane)* mandos de una avioneta

controversial figure figura controversial ■ polémica figura

controversial subject materia controvertida ■ tema controvertido ■ materia polémica ■ tema polémico

controversy surrounding controversia en torno a

to **convene a summit** convocar una cumbre

convenient neighborhood vecindario cómodo (para vivir) ■ vecindad cómoda (para vivir) ➤ This is a very convenient neighborhood. ■ This neighborhood has all the conveniences. Éste es un vecindario muy cómodo (para vivir).

conversation partner compañero(-a) de conversación

conversation piece motivo de conversación

to **converse at length with someone about something** ■ to have a protracted conversation with someone about something hablar detenidamente con alguien sobre algo ■ *(formal, as dialogues between governments)* departir con alguien de algo

convex lens *(camera, telescope)* objetivo convexo

to **convey a message** hacer llegar el mensaje

to **convey the meaning** hacer llegar el significado ■ hacer entender el significado

to be **convicted of a crime** ■ to be found guilty of a crime ser condenado por un crimen ■ ser declarado culpable de un crimen

to be **convinced that...** estar convencido de que...

convincing argument razonamiento convincente ■ argumento convincente

convincing argument: to make a ~ hacer un argumento convincente

convincing case for: to make a ~ hacer un caso convincente para ■ exponer las razones convincentes para

to be a **convoluted law** ser una ley con muchos recovecos

convoluted style estilo retorcido

to **cook something (for a period of time)** ■ to let something cook proseguir la cocción ➤ Cook until the hen is tender. Proseguir la cocción hasta que la gallina esté tierna.

to **cook something on low heat** ■ to cook something over low heat dejar cocer a fuego lento

to be **cooked through** estar cocinado por dentro

cooking time tiempo de cocción ■ tiempo de cocimiento ➤ At high altitudes, longer cooking times may be necessary. A gran altitud quizá sea necesario prolongar el tiempo de cocimiento.

cooking wine vino para guisar

cooking with gas!: (now) we're ~ ■ we're rolling! ¡vamos viento en popa! ■ ¡todo marcha sobre ruedas!

to **cool off** 1. *(food)* to cool down enfriarse 2. *(person)* refrescarse

cooling down of the economy ■ cooling off of the economy ■ slowing down of the economy ■ economic slowdown enfriamiento de la economía

cooling off of the economy ■ cooling down of the economy ■ slowing down of the economy ■ economic slowdown enfriamiento de la economía

coordination between correlación entre

Copernican theory ■ theory of Copernicus teoría de Copérnico ■ teoría copernicana ➤ Copernican theory asserts that the sun, and not the Earth, is at the center of the planetary system. La teoría de Copérnico afirma que el sol, y no la Tierra, está en el centro del sistema planetario.

cops and robbers: to play ~ jugar a policías y ladrones

copy! *(radio communication)* ¡copiado!

to **copy and paste** copiar y pegar

cordless telephone ■ cordless phone teléfono inalámbrico

corduroy pants *el* pantalón de pana

the **core of Kant's philosophy** ■ the heart of Kant's philosophy el nucleo de la filosofía de Kant ■ el nucleo de filosofía Kantiana

Coriolis effect efecto coriolis

corned beef *(beef cured in brine and spices)* carne de vaca curada en salmuera y especias

corned beef brisket pecho delantero curado en salmuera y especias ■ cuarto delantero curado en salmuera y especias

corner kick *(soccer) el* saque de banda ■ saque de esquina ■ (saque de) corner

corner of a field *el* rincón de un campo ➤ *(Rupert Brooke)* If I should die, think only this of me, that there's some corner of a foreign field that is forever England. Si me muero, sólo piensa esto sobre mí, que hay algún rincón de un campo extranjero que será por siempre Inglaterra.

corners of the Earth: to travel to the far ~ viajar a los confines del mundo ■ viajar a lugares remotos ■ viajar a rincones remotos

to **corner someone** acorralar a alguien ➤ I've got you cornered now! ¡Ya te tengo acorralado!

to **corner the market** copar el mercado

corners of the mouth comisuras (de los labios)

coronary bypass surgery cirugía de derivación coronaria

corporate downsizing *el* expediente de crisis

corporate headquarters ■ main office *la* cede

corporate income tax impuesto de sociedades

correct answer *(on a test)* acierto ■ respuesta adecuada

to **correct for (the effect of)** compensar (el efecto de) ■ sopesar (el efecto de) ➤ The rudder trim (tab) corrects for crosswind and torque. El compensador del timón compensa el efecto del viento cruzado y la torsión.

to be **correct in one's analysis** tener razón en su apreciación ➤ You're correct in your analysis. Tienes razón en tu apreciación.

correct me if I'm wrong *(tú)* corrígeme si me equivoco ■ rectifícame si me equivoco ■ corrígeme si estoy equivocado ■ *(usted)* corríjame si me equivoco ■ rectifíqueme si me equivoco ■ corríjame si estoy equivocado

to **correct the spelling** corregir la ortografía

correction in a newspaper *la* fe de errata ■ fe de errores

corrective measures medidas correctivas ■ medidas correctoras

to be **correctly adjusted** ▪ to be properly adjusted ▪ to be in proper adjustment estar bien ajustado ▪ estar bien regulado

to **correspond (regularly) with someone** ▪ to write to each other ▪ to have a correspondence with someone ▪ to correspond with each other ▪ to exchange letters (regularly) cartearse con alguien

correspondence course curso a distancia

correspondent bank banco asociado

to **corroborate someone's testimony** ▪ to support someone's testimony ▪ to affirm someone's testimony ▪ to back up someone's testimony corroborar testimonio ▪ apoyar el testimonio de alguien ▪ refrendar el testimonio de alguien ➤ The pathologist corroborated the defendant's testimony. El patólogo corroboró el testimonio del defendido. ▪ El patólogo corroboró el testimonio del acusado.

corrosive humor ▪ biting humor ▪ caustic humor *el* humor corrosivo ▪ humor mordaz ▪ humor cáustico

to **cost a bundle** costar una burrada ▪ costar un montón ▪ costar una pasta

to **cost a lot** ▪ to be expensive costar mucho ▪ costar caro

to **cost an arm and a leg** costar un ojo de la cara ▪ valer un ojo de la cara ▪ costar un riñón ▪ *(off-color)* costar un huevo ▪ valer un huevo y la yema del otro

to be **cost effective** resultar económico ▪ *(business, economics)* tener una buena relación costo-valor ➤ If it's cost effective, I'd rather use a small space heater than (use) the larger built-in unit. Si resulta económico, preferiría usar el pequeño calentador que la unidad de calefacción incorporada.

to **cost lives** cobrar vidas

cost of living costo de la vida

to **cost one a pretty penny** costarle un buen dinero ➤ It cost me a pretty penny. Me costó un buen dinero.

to **cost someone his life** costarle a alguien la vida

to **cost the life of someone** ▪ to take the life of someone ▪ to take someone's life cobrarse la vida de alguien ▪ costar la vida a alguien ➤ The violence between Palestinians and Israelis has so far cost the lives of seventeen children. La violencia entre palestinos e israelis se ha cobrado ya la vida de diez y siete niños.

cost overrun exceso de costos en relación a lo previsto

costly mistake ▪ costly error **1.** *(financially)* error costoso **2.** *(in terms of consequences)* grave error

costs have more than doubled los costes se han más que duplicado

costume jewelry bisutería

coterie of professional liars atajo de mentirosos profesionales

cotton candy *el* algodón de azúcar

cotton swab *el* algodón de cura ▪ algodón para limpiar la zona de la inyección

to **cotton to the idea** ▪ to like the idea gustarle la idea a uno ➤ I'm starting to cotton to the idea. ▪ I'm starting to like the idea. ▪ I'm taking a liking to the idea. Me va gustando la idea. ▪ La idea me está empezando a gustar. ➤ We don't cotton to smear tactics in politics. No nos gusta el juego sucio en la política.

to be a **couch potato** encantarle a alguien pasar tiempo arrellanado en el sofá

cough syrup *el* jarabe para la tos

to **cough up phlegm** expulsar la flema ▪ *(subido de tono)* echar un gapo

to **cough up the money** acoquinar la pasta ▪ acoquinar el dinero ▪ pagar ➤ C'mon, cough it up! Págame.

could have been killed: one ~ uno pudo haber muerto ➤ Good grief, you could have been killed on that curve. Dios mío, pudiste haber muerto en esa curva. ▪ Dios mío, podrías haber muerto en esa curva.

could have died: one ~ uno pudo haber muerto ▪ uno podría haber muerto ➤ The victim of the collapse could have died if it hadn't been for the paramedics. ▪ The victim of the collapse might have died if it hadn't been for the paramedics. La víctima del derrumbe pudo haber muerto si no llega a ser por los servicios de emergencia. ▪ La víctima del derrumbe podría haber muerto si no llega a ser por los servicios de emergencia. ➤ The victim could have died if the rescuers had found him even a few minutes later. Si el equipo de rescate le hubiera encontrado apenas unos minutos más tarde, la víctima pudo haber muerto. ▪ Si el equipo de rescate le hubiera encontrado apenas unos minutos más tarde, la víctima podría haber muerto. ➤ The writer you're referring to could have died last year, but I'm not sure. ▪ The writer you're referring to may have died last year, but I'm not sure. He may still be living. Ese escritor que mencionas pudo haber muerto el año pasado, pero no estoy seguro. Igual sigue vivo. ▪ Ese escritor que mencionas podría haber muerto el año pasado, pero no estoy seguro. Igual sigue vivo. ➤ The victim could have died either from the blows suffered or from heart failure. La víctima pudo haber muerto o por los golpes sufridos o por parada cardiaca. ▪ La víctima podría haber muerto o por los golpes sufridos o por parada cardiaca.

could have done something: one ~ uno podía haber hecho algo ▪ uno podría haber hecho algo ▪ uno pudo haber hecho algo ➤ The prime minister said his counterpart could have done much more to facilitate a reconciliation. El primer ministro dijo que su homólogo podía haber hecho mucho más para facilitar una reconciliación. ▪ El primer ministro dijo que su homólogo podría haber hecho mucho más para facilitar una reconciliación. ▪ El primer ministro dijo que su hómologo pudo haber hecho mucho más para facilitar una reconciliación. ➤ You could have done your homework if you hadn't spent the whole evening watching TV. Si no te hubieras pasado toda la tarde viendo la tele, podrías haber hecho los deberes. ▪ Si no te hubieras pasado toda la tarde viendo la tele, podías haber hecho los deberes.

could he have forgotten? ▪ do you think he's forgotten? ¿se habrá olvidado?

could I get by? ▪ may I get by? ▪ can I get by? ¿me permite (pasar)? ▪ ¿se puede pasar? ▪ ¿podría pasar? ▪ *(Mex.)* con permiso ▪ *(Sp.)* permiso ▪ disculpe

could I have been the one who...? ¿seré yo el que...? ▪ ¿seré yo la que...?

could I really? ¿realmente podría?

could it be...? ¿será...? ▪ ¿podría ser...?

could not have done something: one ~ uno no podía haber hecho algo ▪ uno no podría haber hecho algo ▪ uno no pudo haber hecho algo ➤ I could not have done that without your help. No podía haber hecho aquello sin tu ayuda. ➤ I could not have done this without your help. No podría haber hecho esto sin tu ayuda. ➤ The DNA evidence proves that the defendant could not have committed the crime. Las pruebas de ADN demuestran que el acusado no pudo cometer el crimen.

could see: one ~ *(as a past continuous)* podía ver ➤ From his deck, Thomas Jefferson could see the construction of the buildings of the University of Virginia through his telescope. Desde su terraza, Thomas Jefferson podía ver la construcción de los edificios de la Universidad de Virginia por su telescopio.

could you come here for a second? ▪ could you come here for a moment? ¿podrías venir aquí un segundo? ▪ ¿podrías venir aquí un momento? ▪ *(L. Am.)* ¿podrías venir acá un segundo? ▪ ¿podrías venir acá un momento?

could you help me for a second? ¿podrías ayudarme un segundo?

Council of Nicea *(325 A.D.)* Concilio de Nicea ➤ The Council of Nicea established the date of Easter as the first Sunday after the first full moon after the vernal equinox (which falls on the twentieth or twenty-first of March), so that Easter falls between March 22 and April 25. El Concilio de Nicea estableció que La Pascua de la Resurrección es el domingo siguiente a la primera luna llena después del equinoccio de primavera (fecha-establecida como el veinte o veintiuno de marzo), así que la Pascua de la Resurrección cae entre el veintidós de marzo y el 25 de abril.

Council of Trent *(1545-1563)* Concilio de Trento ➤ The Council of Trent standardized the Mass worldwide and produced the catechism of the Catholic Church. El Concilio de Trento estandardizó la misa en todo el mundo y produjo el catecismo de la inglesia católica.

counsel in a law case ▪ legal counsel letrado

the **count and countess** los condes

to **count by *x*'s to *y*** contar de *x* en *x* hasta *y* ➤ Count by fives to one hundred. *(ustedes)* Cuenten de cinco en cinco hasta cien. ▪ *(Sp., vosotros)* Contad de cinco en cinco hasta cien.

count me in! inclúyeme ▪ me apunto ▪ *(tú)* cuenta conmigo ▪ *(usted)* inclúyame ▪ cuente conmigo ➤ I don't know at this point if I'll be here that weekend, but if I am, count me in. No sé decirte desde ahora si estaré aquí ese fin de semana, pero de estarlo cuenta conmigo.

count me out! *(tú)* exclúyeme ▪ no cuentes conmigo ▪ *(usted)* exclúyame ▪ no cuente conmigo ➤ Count me out of the deal. No cuentes conmigo.

count of ten: on the ~ al contar hasta diez ➤ On the count of ten, open your eyes. Al contar hasta diez, abre los ojos.

count of ten: before the ~ antes de que uno cuente hasta diez ➤ The boxer came to before the count of ten. ▪ The boxer came to before the referee reached the count of ten. El boxeador volvió en sí antes de que el árbitro contara hasta diez. ➤ The boxer got back on his feet before the count of ten. ▪ The boxer got back on his feet before the referee reached the count of ten. El boxeador volvió en pie antes de que el árbitro contara diez.

to **count on someone for something** contar con alguien para algo ➤ Can I count on you to help me move this Saturday? ¿Cuento contigo para la mudanza el sábado?

to **count one's chickens before they hatch** hacer las cuentas de la lechera ▪ vender la piel del oso antes de cazarlo ➤ Don't count your chickens before they hatch. *(tú)* No hagas las cuentas de la lechera. ▪ *(usted)* No haga las cuentas de la lechera.

to **count the money** hacer (la) caja

to **count toward something** ▪ to be countable toward something estar puntuable para ➤ Do these credits count toward the degree? ▪ Are these credits countable toward the degree? ¿Están estos créditos puntuables para el título?

to **count votes** ▪ to tally votes ▪ to tally the vote escrutar votos

counter: kitchen ~ encimera

counter: store ~ mostrador

counter: ticket ~ mostrador

to **counter the torque** contrarrestar la fuerza de torsión ➤ Wheel bolts have reversed threads to counter the torque. Los tornillos de ruedas tienen las roscas al revés para contrarrestar la fuerza de torsión.

counterclockwise: to turn something ~ girar algo de derecho a izquierda ▪ girar algo en el sentido contrario de las agujas del reloj ▪ *(screwdriver, wrench)* girar a la izquierda

counterfeit bill ▪ bogus bill *el* billete de pega ▪ billete falso

counterfeit money dinero falso ▪ dinero contrahecho ▪ dinero falsificado

to **countermand an order** revocar una orden

countertop encimera

countless times ▪ innumerable times incontables veces ▪ innumerables veces

countries bordering on *los* países limítrofes con ➤ Countries bordering on Colombia... Países limítrofes con Colombia...

country bumpkin paleto tosco

country house casa de campo ▪ casa rural

country road camino comarcal ▪ carretera comarcal ➤ The country roads wind endlessly through the mountains of that region. Los caminos comarcales serpentean incesantemente por las montañas de esa región.

coup attempt ▪ attempted coup intentona golpista ▪ intentona de golpe de estado ▪ asonada

coup de grâce tiro de gracia

coup de grâce: to perform a ~ ▪ to do a coup de grâce dar la puntilla

to be a **couple bricks shy of a load** ▪ to be a couple of quarts low ▪ to be half a bubble off plumb ▪ to be dim-witted faltarle un hervor

a **couple of** un par de ➤ I bought a couple of rolls of film for the camping trip. *(L. Am.)* Compré un par de rollos de película para el campamento. ▪ *(Sp.)* Compré un par de rollos de película para el camping.

to be a **couple quarts low** **1.** *(engine)* to be two quarts low hacer falta un par de litros de aceite **2.** *(person)* to be dim-witted ▪ to be a couple bricks shy of a load ▪ to be half a bubble off plumb faltarle un hervor ▪ faltarle un tornillo

courageous act ▪ act of courage acto de valentía

course in an academic subject asignatura ➤ María is taking a math course. María hace una asignatura de matemática.

course of action curso de acción ▪ línea de acción

course of bricks ▪ layer of bricks camada de ladrillos

course of events marcha de acontecimientos ▪ curso de los acontecimientos

course offerings oferta de asignaturas ▪ catálogo de asignaturas ➤ The academic advisor said they would post a list of the course offerings. El asesor académico dijo que pondría en el tablón de anuncios una lista de la oferta de asignaturas.

court is adjourned se levanta la sesión

court of appeals ▪ appeals court ▪ appelate court *el* tribunal de apelaciones

court procedures procedimientos del tribunal

to **cover a beat** *(journalism)* cubrir una sección

to **cover a mare** montar a una yegua

to **cover a story** cubrir una noticia ▪ cubrir una información ▪ cubrir un acontecimiento

to **cover all the bases** tenerlo todo cubierto ▪ cubrir todos los puntos ▪ tocar todos los puntos ➤ This baby looks like both his parents and all four of his grandparents. She really covers all the bases. Este bebé se parece a ambos su padre y su madre, y a cada uno de sus abuelos. Ella lo tiene todo cubierto. ➤ In the letter I made sure I covered all the bases. En la carta me aseguré de cubrir todos los puntos. ▪ En la carta me aseguré de tocar todos los puntos.

cover letter carta de presentación

cover (of a computer processor) carcasa

cover of a book ▪ book cover ▪ book jacket forro de un libro

cover of a magazine portada de una revista

to **cover one's ass** ▪ to cover one's backside tener seguras las espaldas

to **cover one's backside** ▪ to cover one's ass tener seguras las espaldas

to **cover something with something** cubrir algo con algo ➤ I do think it would be a good idea if you covered the furniture with a plastic tarp before you paint the ceiling. Pienso que sería una buena idea si cubres los muebles con una lona de plástico antes de pintar el cielorraso.

to **cover the cost of something** costear algo ▪ pagar algo

to **cover the waterfront** ▪ to take into account all the possibilities cubrir el espectro ▪ cubrir el terreno ▪ cubrir los frentes ▪ tomar en consideración todas las posibilidades

cover to cover: to read a book (from) ~ leer un libro hasta las tapas ➤ Leyó el libro hasta las tapas. He read the book (from) cover to cover.

to **cover up a lie** cubrir una mentira ▪ *(Sp.)* encubrir una mentira

to **cover up one's action** cubrir su acción ▪ disimular su acción ➤ *(news item)* To cover up his action, the youth went to the window and asked what (had) happened. Para disimular su acción, el joven se asomó a la ventana y preguntó qué sucedía.

coverage of the news ▪ news coverage cobertura informativa ▪ cobertura de una información

to be **covered with blood** estar ensangrentado

to be **covered with paint** ▪ to have (got) paint all over one estar cubierto de pintura ▪ estar perdido de pintura ➤ He's covered with paint. ▪ He has paint all over him. ▪ He's got paint all over him. Está cubierto de pintura. ▪ Está perdido de pintura.

to be **covered with snow** estar cubierto de nieve

to be **covered with snow all year round** tener nieves perpetuas

coveted award ▪ coveted prize premio codiciado

cow pasture *el* pastizal de vacas

cow pie: to step in a ~ ▪ to step in (a pile of) cow dung ▪ to step in (a pile of) cow plop pisar una catalina ▪ pisar bosta ➤ I stepped in a cow pie. ▪ I stepped in (a pile of) cow dung. ▪ I stepped in (a pile of) cow plop. Pisé una catalina.

cowboy boots botas camperas

to **crack a book** *(colorful)* ▪ to open a book abrir un libro (para estudiar) ➤ I haven't cracked a book all weekend. I need to get busy. No he abierto un libro todo el fin de semana. Necesito ponerme a trabajar.

to **crack a joke** ▪ to tell a joke contar un chiste

to **crack a whip** restallar un látigo

to **crack an egg** cascar un huevo

to **crack jokes** ▪ to tell jokes contar chistes

to **crack one's knuckles** sacarle las yugas ▪ desajustarse las coyunturas

to **crack one's rib** ▪ to crack a rib ▪ to suffer a cracked rib hacérsele una fisura de la costilla ➤ I cracked my rib. ▪ I cracked a rib. ▪ My rib was cracked. Se me hizo una fisura de la costilla.

to **crack one's tooth** ▪ to crack a tooth partírsele el diente ➤ He cracked a tooth. Se le partió un diente.

to be a **crack shot** ▪ to be a good shot ser un tirador certero

to **crack the books** ▪ to hit the books estudiar ➤ I've really got to crack the books this weekend. ▪ I've really got to hit the books this weekend. Realmente tengo que estudiar este fin de semana. ➤ He hasn't cracked a book all weekend. No ha estudiado nada en todo el fin de semana.

cracks in an alibi: to have ~ hacer agua la coartada ➤ His alibi has cracks in it. ▪ There are cracks in his alibi. Su coartada hace agua.

cradle song ▪ lullaby canción de cuna

to **cram for a test** empollar para un examen

to **cram it down someone's throat** ponérsele delante de las narices a alguien

to **cramp one's style** estrujar el modo de ser de uno

to be **cramped** venir angosto ▪ estar angosto ➤ This office is too cramped for me. Esta oficina me viene muy angosta. ➤ This parking space is too small for the station wagon. ▪ This parking space is too narrow for the station wagon. Este aparcamiento nos viene muy angosto para el coche familiar.

to **crank the handle** dar al manubrio

to **crash a light** ▪ to run a (red) light ▪ to jump a (red) light saltarse el semáforo ▪ pasar un semáforo en rojo ➤ The car crashed the light. ▪ The car ran the red light. El coche se saltó el semáforo. ▪ El coche pasó el semáforo en rojo. ➤ The car jumped the red light. ▪ The (stopped) car did not wait for the light to change before going through the intersection. El coche (parado) no esperó a que el semáforo se pusiera verde.

to **crash a party** ▪ to attend a party without being invited colarse de rondón en una fiesta ➤ They crashed the party. Se colaron de rondón en la fiesta.

to **crash and burn** ▪ to fall instantly into a sound sleep quedarse frito ➤ When I get home I'm going to crash and burn. Al llegar a casa voy a quedarme frito.

to **crash into a wall** estamparse contra una pared

crashing bore seta ▪ muermazo ▪ pelmazo ▪ rollazo ▪ plomo

to be **crazy about** estar loco por ▪ morirse por

crazy idea ▪ ridiculous idea idea descabellada

to **cream the butter** ▪ to whip the butter batir la mantequilla

crease in a pair of pants raya en un pantalón ➤ The rain is ruining the crease in my pants. La lluvia está estropeando la raya de mi pantalón.

to **create a mortgage** ▪ to take out a mortgage constituir una hipoteca ▪ obtener una hipoteca

to **create a problem** ▪ to cause a problem ▪ to present a problem causar un problema ▪ provocar un problema

to **create a sensation** ▪ to cause a sensation causar una sensación ➤ Mr. Bean created a sensation when he knocked down the queen. Sr. Bean causó una sensación cuando tumbó a la reina.

to **create a stir** ▪ to cause a stir levantar (una) polvareda

creature of habit animal de costumbres ▪ burro de costumbres ➤ Man is a creature of habit. El hombre es un animal de costumbres. ▪ El hombre es un burro de costumbres.

credible information información creíble ▪ información verosímil

credible threat amenaza creíble

credit for something: to give someone ~ darle crédito a alguien por algo ➤ He was more ethical than the press gave him credit for being. Era más ético de lo que la prensa le daba crédito.

to **credit it to the account** abonarlo en la cuenta

credit on the account crédito en la cuenta ▪ abono en la cuenta ➤ I have a credit on the account. Tengo crédito en mi cuenta.

to **credit the account** poner el crédito en la cuenta ▪ abonarle (un pago) en la cuenta ➤ I don't want a refund. Just credit the account. No quiero un reembolso. Sólo ponga el crédito en la cuenta. ➤ They credited my account. Me abonaron en la cuenta.

credit towards: hours of ~ créditos de ➤ She has nine hours of credit towards the master's. Ella tiene nueve créditos (acumulados) del master.

crème de la crème ▪ cream of the crop *la* flor y nata

crest of a hill cima de una colina

crew member *el, la* tripulante

crime of passion *el* crimen pasional

criminal record: to have a ~ tener antecedentes penales

a **crisis is brewing** se teje una crisis ▪ una crisis se está cociendo ▪ una crisis se está tramando

crisis management *la* gestión de crisis

critic is not your enemy: your ~ *(proverb)* el que avisa no es traidor

critical difference: to make a ~ suponer una diferencia radical ➤ Reducing the tilt of the Leaning Tower of Pisa from 6 to 5.5 degrees has made a critical difference in its stability. El reducir la inclinación de la Torre Inclinada de Pisa de 6 a 5,5 grados supone una diferencia radical en su estabilidad.

critical period período trascendental ▪ período crítico

critical phase fase crítica ➤ The peace process has entered a critical phase. El proceso de paz ha entrado en una fase crítica.

critical week ▪ very important week semana trascendental

crop rotation *la* rotación de cosechas

cross between *el* cruce de ➤ A mule is a cross between a horse and a donkey. La mula es un cruce de un caballo y un burro.

cross-cultural validity *la* validez intercultural

to **cross-dress** travestirse

cross examination interrogatorio cruzado

to **cross-examine a witness** interrogar a la parte contraria ▪ repreguntar a un(-a) testigo ▪ hacer segunda pregunta a un(-a) testigo

to be **cross-eyed** ser bizco ▪ *(less common)* ser bisojo

cross my heart and hope to die! ¡palabrita del Niño Jesús!

to **cross off something from a list** ▪ to cross something off (of) a list tachar algo de una lista

to **cross one's arms** ▪ to fold one's arms cruzarse de brazos

to **cross one's eyes** poner los ojos bizcos

to **cross one's mind** pasársele por la cabeza ➤ It never crossed my mind. Jamás se me pasó por la cabeza.

to **cross oneself** ▪ to make the sign of the cross asignarse ▪ santiguarse

cross-reference *la* remisión

to **cross reference the entries** hacer una remisión de una cosa a otra

cross section 1. representative sample muestra representativa **2.** cutaway *el* corte

to **cross swords with someone** cruzar la espada con alguien

to **cross the border** cruzar la línea fronteriza ▪ cruzar la frontera

to **cross the entire width of something** atravesar algo en su mayor anchura

to **cross the finish line** cruzar la meta final

to **cross the line 1.** atravesar la línea ▪ cruzar la línea **2.** to go too far pasar la raya

to **cross the Atlantic Ocean** atravesar el océano Atlántico ▪ *(coll.)* cruzar el charco

crossbar of a stool ▪ crosspiece of a stool travesaño de un taburete ▪ palo atravesado de un taburete

crossfire fuego cruzado

crossfire: to get caught in the ~ **1.** estar atrapado en el fuego cruzado ▪ quedar atrapado en el fuego cruzado **2.** *(figurative)* verse atacado por los dos lados

crossing of the equator paso del ecuador

crosswind ▪ crosswind viento cruzado ▪ viento lateral ➤ The rudder trim tab corrects for the crosswind. El compensador del timón compensa el efecto del viento cruzado.

crow's nest (of a ship) *la* torre de vigía ▪ cofa de vigía ▪ puesto de vigía ➤ From the crow's nest of the Pinta, Rodrigo de Triana, at 2 a.m. on October 12, 1492, spotted the Indian bonfires at a distance of about 9.5 miles, and shouted, "Land, land!" Desde su puesto de vigía en la Pinta, Rodrigo de Triana, a las dos de la mañana el doce de octubre de 1492, divisó las fogatas de los indios a una distancia más o menos de 9.5 millas, y gritó, "¡Tierra!, ¡Tierra!"

to **crowd around** aglomerarse alrededor (de...) ▪ congregarse alrededor (de...)

a **crowd gathered** una muchedumbre se amontonó

a **crowd is gathering** una muchedumbre se congrega ▪ una muchedumbre está congregándose ▪ una muchedumbre se amontona ▪ una muchedumbre se está amontonando ▪ un público se congrega

crowd of people afluencia de gente

crowd of young people ▪ crowd of teenagers mocerío

crowd one hangs out with ▪ crowd one runs with ▪ circle of friends peña

crowded room ▪ room (jam) packed with people ▪ room jammed with people habitación abarrotada ▪ habitación muy concurrida ▪ habitación llena ▪ habitación atestada ▪ habitación apiñada ▪ salón abarrotado ▪ salón muy concurrido ▪ salón lleno ▪ salón atestado ▪ salón apiñado

crown prince príncipe heredero

crowning of a career *la* consagración de una carrera

crush of people hormigueo humano

crushing blow *el* golpe arrollador

cruising altitude *el* nivel de crucero

cruising speed *la* velocidad de crucero

crusty old man un viejo amargado

crux of the issue ▪ the crux of the matter *el* quid del asunto

to **cry and cry** llorar y llorar ➤ *(song lyrics)* To cry and cry because you're going away Llorar y llorar porque te vas

to **cry bitterly** ▪ to cry hard llorar con pena

to **cry inconsolably** llorar sin consuelo

to **cry like a baby** llorar a lágrima viva

to **cry one's eyes out** darse un hartón de llorar ▪ llorar a moco tendido

to **cry quits** clamor por una pausa ▪ implorar una pausa

to **cry tears of joy** ▪ to cry for joy llorar de alegría

crying of an infant vagido

crying over spilled milk: there's no use ~ it's no use crying over spilled milk a lo hecho, pecho

to be **crystal clear** ▪ to be plain as day ▪ to be obvious estar claro como el agua ▪ estar más claro que el agua

cuadrille paper ▪ grid paper papel cuadriculado *(whose lines are all the same intensity, as opposed to "graph paper," which has dark and light lines)*

cube root raíz cúbica

to **culminate with** ▪ to culminate in ▪ to finish off with ▪ to be capped by ▪ to be crowned by ▪ to end with ▪ to end in rematar con ➤ The march (of the Zapatistas in Mexico) which crossed half the country, culminated with a gigantic demonstration in the Plaza of the Constitution, better known as the Zócalo, in Mexico City. La marcha (de los zapatistas en México) que cruzó medio país, remató con una manifestación gigantesca en la Plaza de la Constitución, mejor conocido como el Zócalo, en la Ciudad de México.

cultivated field campo de cultivo

cultural icon ▪ icon of the culture símbolo de la cultura

culture of the bell-shaped vase cultura de el vaso campaniforme

culture shock *el* choque cultural

cultured person ▪ refined person persona cultivada ▪ persona culta ▪ persona refinada

cup of coffee taza de café ▪ un café ▪ un cafecito ➤ Do you want to go have a cup of coffee? ▪ Do you want to go for a cup of coffee? ¿Quieres ir a tomar un café? ▪ ¿Tomamos un café? ▪ ¿Tomamos un cafecito? ➤ Would you like a cup of coffee? ¿Te apetece un café? ▪ ¿Un cafecito? ▪ ¿Tomas café?

cup of tea: not to be one's ~ no ser el santo de uno devoción

to **cup one's ears** ahuecar las manos detrás de los oídos

to **cup one's fingers over one's eyes** ▪ to make a visor with one's hands hacerse visera con los dedos

to **cup one's hand behind one's ear** ahuecar la mano detrás del oído

to **cup one's hands** ahuecar las manos

to **cup one's hands around one's mouth** hacer bocina con las manos ▪ hacer de altavoz con las manos ➤ He cupped his hands around his mouth. Hizo bocina con las manos. ▪ Hizo de altavoz con las manos.

cure for cura contra ▪ remedio contra

the **cure is worse than the disease** cuesta más el remedio que la enfermedad ▪ el remedio está peor que la enfermedad

cured ham jamón curado ▪ jamón serrano

curiosity got the best of one uno no aguantó más la curiosidad ➤ His curiosity got the best of him. No aguantó más la curiosidad.

curiosity seekers: crowd of ~ *la* muchedumbre de curiosos

to be **curious to know** tener curiosidad por saber ▪ tener ganas de saber

currency markets mercado de divisas ▪ mercado de cambios ▪ mercado monetario

current balance (on an account) ▪ present balance saldo actual (en una cuenta)

current events *los* temas de actualidad

current events: to be up on ~ ▪ to be up on what's going on ▪ to be (well) informed about current events estar al corriente con los temas de la actualidad ▪ estar al día con los temas de la actualidad

current trend tónica actual ▪ pauta actual

to **curse one's circumstances** renegar de sus circunstancias

to **curse one's luck** maldecir uno su suerte

cursor is blinking *(computers) el* cursor está parpadeando

to **curtail someone's freedom** ▪ to impose limits on someone's freedom ▪ to curtail civil liberties cercenar la libertad de alguien ▪ cercenar de las libertades de alguien

curtain up! ¡arriba el telón!

to **curve the grades** ▪ to grade on a curve hacer la campana de Gauss

to **cushion the blow** **1.** *(physical impact)* to cushion the impact ▪ to minimize the impact amortiguar el golpe **2.** *(emotional impact)* to soften the blow disminuir la pena

to **cuss like a drunk sailor** *(coll.)* ▪ to curse like a drunk sailor echar sapos y culebras ▪ jurar en arameo

cuss word *(coll.)* ▪ curse word ▪ profanity taco ▪ palabrota

to **custom build something** construir algo a la medida

customer service atención al cliente ▪ servicio al cliente ▪ servicio a clientes

customs agent aduanero

to **cut a fart** *(off-color)* ▪ to cut one ▪ to fart ▪ to cut the cheese echar un pedo ▪ tirarse un pedo ▪ tirarse un cuesco

to **cut a piece of pizza for someone** ▪ to cut someone a piece of pizza cortar un trozo de pizza a alguien ➤ Would you cut me a piece of pizza? ¿Me cortarías un trozo de pizza?

to be a **cut above the others** ▪ to be a cut above the rest ser superior a los demás ▪ ser de mejor categoría que los demás

to **cut and paste** cortar y pegar

to **cut class** faltar a clase ▪ fumarse una clase ▪ pirarse una clase ▪ correrse una clase ▪ hacer novillos

to **cut down on the noise** ▪ to reduce the noise disminuir el ruido

to be **cut from the same cloth** ▪ to be cast from the same mold ▪ to cast in the same mold estar cortado por el mismo patrón ▪ ser harina del mismo costal ▪ ser de la misma escuela ▪ criarse en la misma escuela ➤ We were cut from the same cloth. Nos criamos en misma escuela.

to **cut in line** ▪ to butt in (line) ▪ to break the line colarse

cut in interest rates ▪ interest rate cut *el* recorte de los tipos de interés

to **cut interest rates** recortar los tipos de interés

to **cut into pieces** cortar en pedazos

to **cut into someone's lead** ▪ to cut into someone's advantage acortar la ventaja de alguien

cut it: not to ~ no correr ➤ That exuse doesn't cut it. Esa excusa no corre.

cut it out! ▪ none of that! ▪ enough of that! ▪ cool it! ¡deja eso! ▪ ¡ya está! ▪ ¡no hagas eso! ▪ ¡tengamos la fiesta en paz! ▪ ¡quita!

to **cut it short enough** cortarlo lo suficientemente (corto) ➤ You didn't cut it short enough last time. No me lo cortaste lo suficientemente (corto) la última vez.

to **cut it so close on the time** ser tan justo con el tiempo

to **cut jobs** recortar empleos

cut (of meat) *el* corte (de carne) ➤ Sirloin is a better cut than rib steak. Solomillo es un corte mejor que entrecot.

to **cut off the telephone** ▪ to cut the telephone off cortar la línea ➤ They'll cut off the phone if we can't pay these long distance bills. ▪ They'll cut the phone off if we can't pay these long distance bills. Cortarán la línea si no podemos pagar estas facturas por las llamadas de larga distancia. ➤ They'll cut it off if we don't pay the bill. La cortarán si no podemos pagar la factura.

to be **cut out for something** estar para algo ➤ I'm not cut out for this kind of work. No estoy para este tipo de trabajo.

to **cut out something (with scissors)** ▪ to cut something out (with scissors) recortar algo (con tijeras) ➤ Cut out the coupon and send it to... Recorte y envíe el cupón a... ➤ Cut it out and send it to... Recórtelo y envíelo a...

to **cut someone off in mid-sentence** ▪ to cut off someone in mid-sentence dejar a alguien con la palabra en la boca ➤ He cut me off in mid-sentence. Me dejó con la palabra en la boca.

to **cut something in half** cortar algo por la mitad ▪ cortar algo en dos mitades

to **cut something in two** partir algo

to **cut teeth** ▪ to teethe salirle los dientes

to **cut the bonds** ▪ to cut the cords ▪ to cut the ropes cortar las ligaduras

to **cut the cards** ▪ to cut the deck alzar los naipes

to **cut the grass** ▪ to mow the lawn cortar el césped ▪ segar el césped

to **cut vegetables lengthwise** ▪ to cut vegetables transversally ▪ *(especially carrots, celery, and peppers)* to julienne vegetables cortar las verduras a lo largo ▪ cortar las verduras a la juliana

cutoff date fecha de corte

cutaway drawing *el* corte ▪ *la* sección

cutting board tabla de cortar

cutting edge 1. *(of a blade)* filo **2.** *(of scientific research)* vanguardia ▪ punta de lanza

cutting edge: to be on the ~ estar en la vanguardia ➤ Contemporary Cuban jazz is on the cutting edge. El jazz cubano contemporáneo está en la vanguardia. ▪ El jazz cubano actual está en la vanguardia.

cutting edge technology ▪ state-of-the-art technology ▪ latest technology tecnología vanguardista ▪ tecnología punta ▪ último grito de la tecnología

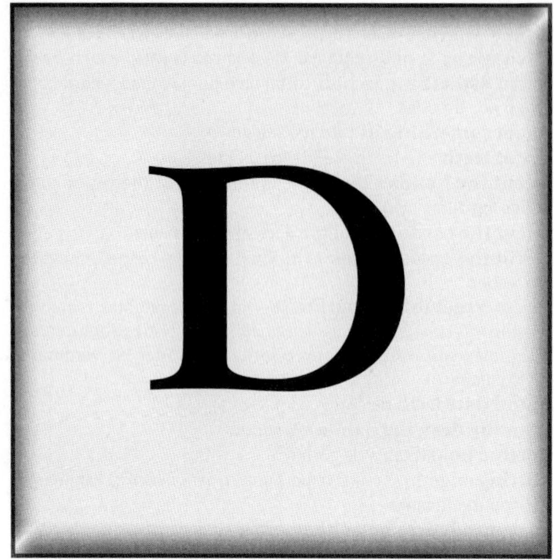

to **dabble in politics** hacer escarceos en la política ▪ hacer escarceos con la política

daily bread pan de cada día

daily life ▪ everyday life vida cotidiana

dairy farm granja lechera

daisy chain guirnalda de margaritas

to **damage someone's reputation** ▪ to hurt someone's reputation ▪ to hurt someone's good name ▪ to stain someone's reputation ▪ to tarnish someone's reputation manchar la reputación de alguien ▪ tiznar la reputación de alguien

damage to something: to cause ~ ▪ to damage something causar daños en algo ➤ The drought has caused damage to the olive trees. ▪ The drought has damaged the olive trees. La sequía ha causado daños en los olivos.

to be **damaging to one's aspirations** ser perjudicial para las aspiraciones de uno

damn it! ¡maldita sea!

to **damn someone with faint praise** cargarse a alguien con un sutil elogio ▪ despachar a alguien con un sutil elogio

damn well better más le vale (a uno) ➤ He damn well better get here on time tomorrow, or I'm going to give him his walking papers. Más le vale llegar puntual mañana, o le pondré de patitas en la calle.

damned fine cojonudo ➤ They have (some) damned fine tapas in Valladolid. Tienen tapas cojonudas en Valladolid.

to be a **damned good book** *(L. Am., mildly off-color)* ser un libro de pinga ▪ *(Sp.)* ser un libro de la (misma) hostia ▪ ser un libro jodidamente bueno ▪ *(benign alternative)* ser un libro estupendo

to be **damned good paella** *(mildly off-color)* ser una paella de la (misma) hostia ▪ *(Sp.)* ser una paella jodidamente buena ▪ *(benign alternative)* ser una magnífica paella

damned if I can understand it ▪ I'll be damned if I can understand it que me aspen si lo entiendo ▪ que me ahorquen si lo entiendo

damned if I can't...: (I'll be) ~ que me aspen si no... ▪ que me ahorquen si no... ▪ que me maten si no...

damned if I know! ▪ I'll be damned if I know! ¡que me aspen si lo sé!

to be **damned if one does and damned if one doesn't** ser condenado por lo que se haga o se deje de hacer ▪ ser condenado de todas maneras

to **dare to do something** osar hacer algo ▪ atreverse a hacer algo

to be **daring enough to do something** ▪ to be bold enough to do something ▪ *(coll.)* to have the guts to do something tener agallas para hacer algo ▪ tener arrestos para hacer algo ▪ *(vulgar)* tener huevos para hacer algo

dark beer cerveza oscura

to be **dark in here** estar oscuro aquí (dentro) ➤ Turn on the light, it's dark in here. Enciende la luz, que está oscuro aquí (dentro). ➤ I don't want it to be dark in here. No quiero que esté oscuro aquí (dentro).

dark matter *(astrophysics)* materia oscura

dark red granate ▪ burdeos ▪ bergandín

dark side of the moon ▪ far side of the moon ▪ other side of the moon ▪ back side of the moon lado opuesto de la luna

darn it! ¡puñales!

dash of olive oil ▪ splash of olive oil chorrito de aceite de oliva

to **dash off** *(a letter, poem, essay, etc.)* escribir al correr de la pluma ▪ componer al correr de la pluma ▪ escribir o componer a vuela pluma

to **dash one's hopes** defraudar a alguien ▪ truncar las esperanzas de alguien ▪ fulminar cualquier esperanza ▪ irse al traste (las esperanzas)

dashing man hombre muy apuesto

data base *(computers) la* base de datos

to **date back to** ▪ to date from remontarse a ➤ New (dating) estimates in France indicate that the beginning of art dates back more than 35,000 years. Nuevas dataciones en Francia indican que el inicio del arte se remonta a más de 35.000 años.

to **date from** ▪ to date back to remontarse a

date of birth ▪ birth date natalicio

date on which: before the ~ anterior a la fecha para

dating of ancient objects and events datación de objetos y acontecimientos antiguos ➤ Precise dating of ancient historical events is often possible when they coincide with eclipses or appearances of comets. La datación precisa de acontecimientos antiguos a menudo es posible cuando coinciden con eclipses y con la aparición de algún cometa. ➤ Carbon dating is a way of dating fossils and rock formations. Datación con carbono es una manera de datar los fósiles y las formaciones de roca.

to be **dating someone** salir con alguien ➤ Chespirito and Doña Florinda are dating. Chespirito y Doña Florinda están saliendo.

daughter-in-law nuera

dawn of civilization los albores de la civilización

dawn was breaking el alba rayaba ▪ amanecía ▪ rompía el día ▪ rompía la aurora

day after day ▪ day in, day out ▪ day in and day out día tras día ▪ a diario ▪ un día y otro día

day after tomorrow pasado mañana

the **day before** ▪ the previous day ▪ the preceding day el día antes ▪ el día anterior

the **day before I left** el día antes de que (yo) saliera

day before yesterday anteayer ▪ hace dos días ▪ antes de ayer

day by day de día en día ▪ día a día

day care center ▪ nursery guardería

a **day early** un día antes ➤ We returned from our trip a day early. Volvimos de nuestro viaje un día antes. ▪ Regresamos de nuestro viaje un día antes.

day in, day out ▪ day in and day out ▪ day after day un día y otro día ▪ día tras día

day of mourning duelo ▪ *el* día de luto (oficial) ➤ *(news item)* Russian president declares today a national day of mourning El presidente ruso declara para hoy un día de luto nacional

day off día libre ▪ día asueto ▪ día de asueto ▪ día de descanso

day off: to take the ~ tomar el día libre

day-old de un día ➤ They sell day-old bread at a discount. Venden el pan de un día con un descuento. ▪ Venden el pan de un día a precio reducido.

day planner ▪ appointment book agenda

day shift turno del día

to **daydream about** soñar despierto sobre

Daylight Savings Time ▪ DST horario de verano ➤ To change to Daylight Savings Time in early spring, you set the clock one hour ahead. Para cambiar al horario de verano a principios de la primavera, se adelanta el reloj una hora.

daylights out of something: to chew the ~ masticar algo a lo bestia ➤ Boy, that kid's chewing the daylights out of that bubble gum. Mira, ese niño está masticando ese chicle a lo bestia.
daylights out of someone: to scare the ~ darle a alguien un susto de muerte ➤ When that dog crossed the street in front of all that traffic, it scared the daylights out of me. Cuando el perro cruzó la calle con todo ese tráfico, me dio un susto de muerte.
days on end: for ~ durante días enteros
the **days when** los diás cuando ▪ los días en que
days to be numbered: (for) one's ~ tener los días contados ➤ His days are numbered. Tiene los días contados.
daytime telephone number número telefónico durante el día
de facto ▪ existing without lawful authority de hecho
de facto couples ▪ (unmarried) couples living together ▪ couples cohabiting parejas de hecho
de facto tenant ▪ tenant who is not on the lease inquilino de hecho
de facto union ▪ common-law marriage la unión de facto ▪ derecho consuetudinario del casamiento ▪ unión libre
de jure ▪ according to law ▪ existing legally de derecho ➤ De jure tenant ▪ Tenant who is on the lease Inquilino de derecho
to be **dead as a doornail** estar más muerto que una tumba
dead calm calma chica
dead comet ▪ spent comet cometa extinguido
dead-end street ▪ dead end vía muerte ▪ *la* calle que no tiene salida
dead heat *el* virtual empate
dead reckoning navegación a estima
Dead Sea Scrolls manuscritos del Mar Muerto ▪ rollos del Mar Muerto
dead silence silencio de muerte
dead spot (in a car's rearview mirror) ángulo muerto
dead weight *el* lastre
to be **dead tired** ▪ to be dog tired ▪ to be pooped (out) estar molido ▪ estar hecho polvo
deadline (date) ▪ final date fecha límite ▪ fecha tope
deadly attack ataque mortífero
deadly snake víbora mortífera
deafening roar rugido tronador
to **deal in** comerciar con ➤ He deals in out-of-print books. Comercia con libros fuera de catálogo.
to **deal someone a mortal blow** ▪ to deal someone a fatal blow ▪ to strike someone a mortal blow ▪ to strike someone a fatal blow asestarle un golpe mortal
to **deal the cards** dar las cartas ▪ repartir los naipes ▪ dar los naipes
the **deal was struck** ▪ the bargain was struck quedó cerrado el acuerdo ▪ quedó hecho el acuerdo ▪ se cerró el trato ▪ quedó hecho el trato
to **deal with someone** abordar a alguien ▪ tratar a alguien ➤ How do you deal with a difficult boss? ¿Cómo se trata a un jefe difícil?
to **deal with a topic** tratar de un tema ▪ tratar sobre un tema
to **deal with stress** ▪ to react under stress reaccionar ante el estrés
to be **dealt a good hand** salirle un buen juego
dear friend amigo entrañable
death by stoning *la* muerte a pedradas
death from *la* muerte por ➤ *(headline)* More deaths from synthetic drugs being investigated Investigadas más muertes por drogas sintéticas
death from natural causes *la* muerte natural ▪ muerte por causas naturales
death mask máscara mortuoria
death row *los* corredores de la muerte
death-row inmate prisionero en el corredor de la muerte
death sentence sentencia de muerte
death toll cifra de los muertos ➤ The death toll in the embassy bombings has passed 140. La cifra de los muertos en el bombardeo de las embajadas ha pasado de 140.
death trap trampa mortal ▪ trampa mortífera
death wish *(psychoanalysis) la* pulsión de muerte
to **debate something thoroughly** debatir a fondo
to **debate whether** debatir si
to **debug the software** depurar el software
to **debunk a myth** desacreditar un mito ▪ desenmascarar un mito
to **decide on something** decidirse por algo ➤ I've decided on country ham. Me he decidido por jamón serrano.
to **decide on the spur of the moment to do something** decidir sin pensar hacer algo ▪ decidir súbitamente hacer algo ▪ decidir abruptamente hacer algo ▪ decidir apresuradamente hacer algo ➤ We decided on the spur of the moment to go Guayaquil. Decidimos sin pensar marcharnos a Quayaquil. ▪ Decidimos súbitamente marcharnos a Quayaquil.
to **decide to do something 1.** decidir hacer algo **2.** to make up one's mind to do something ▪ to decide on something decidirse por hacer algo ➤ I decided to go back. Decidí regresar. ▪ Decidí volver. ➤ I decided (definitively) to go to the university. ▪ I made up my mind to go to the university. Me decidí por asistir a la universidad. ➤ The company decided to dismantle the plant gradually. La compañía decidió desmantelar paulatinamente la planta.
deciduous tree ▪ tree that sheds its leaves annually árbol de hoja caduca
decision making toma de decisiones
decision to do something decisión de hacer algo ➤ *(news item)* Vice president Al Gore distanced himself from the decision to take Elián from his cousins' house. El vicepresidente Al Gore se desmarcó de la decisión de sacar a Elián de la casa de sus primos.
deck of cards baraja de cartas
to **deck with flowers** engalanar con flores
deckhand empleado de cubierta
to **declare a law unconstitutional** ▪ to rule that a law is unconstitutional derogar por inconstitucional una ley
to **declare bankruptcy** declararse en quiebra ▪ declarar la quiebra
to **declare someone innocent** declarar a alguien inocente ➤ The jury declared him innocent. El jurado le declaró (a él) inocente ➤ The jury declared her innocent. El jurado le declaró (a ella) inocente.
to **declare war on a country** declarar la guerra a un país
to **decline an invitation** rechazar una invitación ▪ *(rare)* declinar una invitación
to **decline an offer** no aceptar una oferta ▪ rechazar una oferta ▪ rehusar una oferta ▪ declinar una oferta ▪ rehusar un ofrecimiento
declining interest ▪ dwindling interest ▪ waning interesting *el* interés disminuyente
decrease: to be on the ~ ir disminuyendo
to **decrease blood flow** ▪ to decrease the flow of blood reducir el flujo sanguíneo ▪ bajar el flujo sanguíneo
to **decrease by** ***x*** bajar *x* ▪ disminuir un *x*
decrease from last year's profits disminución de los beneficios comparado con año pasado ▪ disminución de los beneficios con respecto al año pasado ▪ disminución de los beneficios en relación al año pasado ▪ disminución de los beneficios del año pasado
to **decrease from** ***x*** **to** ***y*** diminuir(se) de *x* a *y* ▪ bajar de *x* a *y* ➤ Interest rates have gone down. Los tipos de interés han disminuído. ▪ Los tipos de interés han bajado. ➤ Interest rates have decreased in 2005. ▪ Interest rates declined in 2005. ▪ Interest rates went down in 2005. Los tipos de interés se han disminuido para el año 2005. ▪ Los tipos de interés han bajado para el año 2005.
to **decrease in size** disminuirse (de tamaño) ➤ The deficit has decreased in size. El déficit se ha diminuido.
decrease in pay ▪ reduction in pay ▪ cut in pay ▪ pay cut *la* reducción de sueldo ➤ The employees were given a decrease in pay. A los empleados les aplicaron una reducción de sueldo.
decrease in population *la* disminución de la población ▪ *la* reducción de la población

decrease in speed *la* disminución de la velocidad ■ *la* reducción de la velocidad

decrease in unemployment ■ drop in unemployment *la* disminución del paro ■ *la* reducción del paro ■ disminución del paro ■ reducción del paro

to **decrease in value** ■ to depreciate depreciar el valor ■ depreciarse ➤ Cars decrease in value over time. ■ Cars depreciate (in value) over time. Los carros deprecian su valor con el tiempo. ■ Los carros se deprecian con el tiempo.

to **decree that...** decretar que...

deductions from one's salary *las* retenciones al salario

deep blanket of snow manto espeso de nieve ■ capa espesa de nieve ■ tupida alfombra de nieve

deep coma: to be in a ~ estar en profunda coma

deep down en el fondo

deep down ■ deep inside ■ in one's heart ■ deep down inside ■ deep down in one's heart en el fondo del corazón de uno ■ en el fuero interno ■ para sus adentros

deep fryer freidora

deep-set eyes ■ sunken eyes ojos hundidos

deep space ■ outer space profundo espacio

to **deepen the division between** ahondar la división entre

to be **deeply felt** ser muy sentido

to be **deeply rooted (in)** tener mucha raigambre (en)

to be **deeply touched** estar profundamente compadecido

to **default to** *(computers)* ir por defecto a ➤ The software defaults to Spanish, changing "realize" to "realice." El software va por defecto al español, reemplazando "realize" por "realice".

default setting *(computers)* configuración por defecto ■ configuración predeterminada

to **defeat an opponent at something** ■ to beat an opponent at something derrotar a un(-a) oponente a algo ■ ganarle a un(-a) oponente en algo ➤ He defeats me at chess hands down. Me derrota al ajedrez con los ojos cerrados. ■ Me gana al ajedrez con los ojos cerrados.

to **defeat an opponent in something** ■ to beat an opponent in something derrotar a un(-a) oponente en algo ■ ganar a un(-a) oponente en algo ➤ Our school defeated our number one rival in football. Nuestra escuela derrotó a nuestro rival número uno en fútbol americano.

to **defeat someone roundly** ■ to roundly defeat someone vencer a alguien contundentemente ■ *(especially in Spain)* vencer a alguien con contundencia

to **defect from a country** desertar de un país ➤ He defected from the Soviet Union. Desertó de la Unión Soviéta.

to **defect to a country** desertar a un país ➤ He defected to the Soviet Union. Desertó a la Unión Soviética.

defender of the faith defensor(-a) de la fe

defense witness ■ witness for the defense **1.** *el, la* testigo de la defensa **2.** *(especially to counter testimony)* rebuttal witness testigo de descargo

definitely (yes)! ¡seguro que sí!

definitely not! ■ absolutely not! ¡eso sí que no! ■ ¡seguro que no! ■ ¡en absoluto!

definitive answer: to give the ~ dar la respuesta definitiva ➤ Many philosophers think that Immanuel Kant gave the definitive answer to the question whether the existence of God can be proved. Muchos filósofos opinan que Immanuel Kant dio la respuesta definitiva a la pregunta de si se puede probar la existencia de Dios.

definitive proof prueba definitiva

to **deflect a bullet** desviar una bala

to **deflect light** desviar la luz

to **deflect the blame onto someone (else)** echarle la culpa a alguien

to **deflect the shot** *(sports)* desviar el tiro

to **defray the cost** ■ to offset the cost costear los gastos ■ sufragar los costos ■ sufragar los gastos ➤ The scholarship helped defray the cost of his education. ■ The scholarship helped offset the cost of his education. La beca ayudó a sufragar los costos de su educación.

to **defrost the refrigerator** descongelar la nevera

to **defy explanation** *(L. Am.)* escaparse a toda explicación ■ desafiar la explicación ■ no tener explicación ➤ The father said to his son, "Your behavior defies explanation." El padre le dijo al hijo, "Tu comportamiento desafía la explicación". ■ El padre le dijo al hijo, "Tu comportamiento no tiene explicación".

degrading treatment ■ affront ■ humiliating treatment trato degradante ■ trato vejatorio

deicing system *el* sistema anticongelante

to **delay an execution** aplazar una ejecución

delayed reaction *(noun phrase)* reacción retrasada ■ reacción atrasada ■ acción retardada

delayed-reaction *(adjective phrase)* de acción retardada ■ de reacción retrasada ■ de reacción atrasada ➤ A delayed-reaction detonator Un detonador de acción retardada

delaying tactic táctica dilatoria

to **delete the default settings** *(computers)* ■ to delete the defaults ■ to turn off the defaults ■ to remove the defaults ■ to eliminate the defaults suprimir las configuraciones por defecto ■ anular las configuraciones por defecto

deliberate act ■ willful act acto deliberado ■ acto con intención ■ acción deliberada ■ acción a propósito ■ acción adrede ➤ We cannot rule out (the possibility of) a deliberate act of sabotage. No podemos descartar la posibilidad de una acto deliberado de sabotaje.

deliberate aggression *la* agresión deliberada ■ agresión intencionada

deliberate attempt intento deliberado

delicate balance between equilibrio delicado entre

delicate mission misión delicada ➤ It's a very delicate mission. Es una misión muy delicada.

delicate operation operación delicada

to be a **delicate subject** ■ to be a sensitive subject ser un tema delicado

to **delight in** ■ to take great pleasure in complacerse con ■ complacerse de ■ complacerse en ■ disfrutar de ■ sentir placer por ■ regodearse en ➤ He delights in his little daughter, especially when she says new words. Se regodea mucho con su hijita, especialmente cuando ella dice nuevas palabras.

delinquent account ■ account in arrears cuenta morosa

delirium tremens ■ the D.T.'s delirium tremens

to **deliver a speech** ■ to deliver an address ■ to give a speech pronunciar un discurso ■ dar un discurso

to **deliver an address** ■ to deliver a speech ■ to give a speech dar un discurso ■ pronunciar un discurso ➤ Lincoln delivered the Gettysburg Address in just under three minutes. Lincoln dio el discurso de Gettysburg en poco menos de tres minutos.

to **deliver an ultimatum** *(literary, journalistic)* ■ to give an ultimatum dar un ultimatum ■ plantear un ultimatum

delivery man repartidor

delivery truck camión de reparto ➤ Are you in radio contact with the driver of the delivery truck? ¿Está usted en contacto por radio con el conductor del camión de reparto?

to be **deluged with** ■ to be inundated with caerle un aluvión de ■ prodigarle con avalancha de ➤ Ricky Martin was deluged with requests for his autograph. A Ricky Martin le cayó un aluvión de pedidos por su autógrafo.

delusions of grandeur delirios de grandeza

to **demand an apology from someone** ■ to demand that someone apologize exigir disculpas de alguien ■ exigirle a alguien que se disculpe ■ requerir disculpas de alguien

to **demand compliance (with)** exigir acatamiento (con)

demand for demanda de ➤ *(news item)* Demand for videoconferencing skyrockets La demanda de videoconferencias se dispara

to **demand that someone apologize** ■ to demand an apology from someone exigirle a alguien que se disculpe ■ exigir disculpas de alguien ■ requerir disculpas de alguien

demand to demanda para ➤ There is a greater demand to study Spanish than French. Es mayor la demanda para estudiar español que para estudiar francés.

demand skyrocketed: the ~ la demanda se disparó

to **demand something back** ■ to demand that someone return something ■ to demand that someone give something back exigir el retorno de algo ■ exigir la devolución

de algo ▪ *(jur.)* demandar el retorno de algo ▪ demandar la devolución de algo
to **demand something from someone** exigirle algo a alguien ▪ exigir algo de alguien ▪ reclamarle algo a alguien ▪ reclamar algo de alguien ▪ requerirle algo a alguien ▪ requerir algo de alguien
to **demand something of someone** exigirle algo a alguien ➤ He demands loyalty of his employees. Exige lealtad a sus empleados.
to **demand the safe return of someone** demandar el regreso de alguien sano y salvo
demanding teacher profesor(-a) exigente ▪ maestro(-a) exigente
demands that are placed on you *(tú)* exigencias que se te plantean ▪ *(usted)* exigencias que se le plantean
demolition of a building la demolición de un edificio ▪ derribo de un edificio
den of iniquity antro de perdición
den of thieves cueva de ladrones
dense forest ▪ dense woods bosque espeso ▪ bosque tupido
dense smoke humo denso
dense wood *(ebony, teak, etc.)* madera densa
dense woods ▪ dense forest bosque espeso ▪ bosque tupido
dented can lata abollada ▪ *(Sp., large can such as a paint can)* bote abollado
dented fender parachoques abollado ▪ paragolpes abollado ➤ The fender is dented. El parachoques está abollado. ➤ The fender was dented. El parachoques estaba abollado. ➤ The fender got dented. Se abolló el parachoques. ➤ It had a dented fender. Tenía el parachoques abollado.
to **deny a request** 1. *(personal request)* rechazar una petición 2. *(official request)* negar una petición ▪ *(Sp.)* denegar una petición ➤ They denied my residency application. Me denegaron la solicitud de residencia.
to **deny an appeal** 1. *(of a residency application, etc.)* denegar un recurso 2. *(in a court case)* denegar una apelación ▪ negar una apelación
to **deny having done something** ▪ to deny that one has done something negar haber hecho algo
to **deny something categorically** negar algo categóricamente ▪ negar algo de forma tajante ▪ negar algo rotundamente
to **depart from the script** salirse del libreto
to **depart from tradition** ▪ to break with tradition apartarse de la tradición ▪ romper con la tradición ▪ salirse de la tradición
to **depart on a mission** partir en una misión ➤ *(news item)* The first crew to inhabit the International Space Station departed at 8:53 a.m. yesterday. La primera tripulación que habitará la Estación Espacial Internacional partió a las 8.53 de ayer.
Department of Homeland Security *(USA)* Departamento de Seguridad de la Patria
to be a **departure from** ser un alejamiento de ▪ salirse de ➤ That would be a departure from the logic of the book. Se saldría de la lógica del libro.
to be a **departure from the mainstream** ser un apartarse de la corriente principal ▪ ser un apartarse de la corriente dominante ➤ The new physics represented a departure from the mainstream. La física nueva representaba un apartarse de la corriente principal.
departure time hora de salida
to **depend a lot on** depender mucho de ▪ irse mucho en ➤ The success of our vacation at the beach depends a lot on the weather. El éxito de nuestras vacaciones en la playa depende mucho del buen tiempo.
to **depend on someone (for something)** 1. to trust that someone will come through for you confiar en alguien 2. to be dependent on someone depender de alguien ➤ I need someone I can depend on. Necesito a alguien en quien pueda confiar. ➤ Children depend on their parents for almost everything. Los niños dependen de sus padres para casi todo.
to **depend on something** depender de algo ➤ How much wine shall I buy?-Well, it depends on how many people show up. ¿Cuánto vino compro?-Bueno, depende de cuánta gente venga.
to **depend on what...** depender de que...
to be **dependent on...** estar supeditado(-a) a... ▪ estar subordinado(-a) a...
depending on how you look at it según cómo lo veas ▪ según cómo se mire
depending on one's individual tastes ▪ depending on the person's tastes ▪ depending on the tastes of the individual según sean los gustos de cada cual
depending on the time en función de la hora
depending on what... en función de lo que... ▪ dependiendo de lo que... ➤ Depending on what they tell me... En función de lo que me digan... ▪ Dependiendo de lo que me digan...
to **deplete one's savings** mermar los ahorros de uno ▪ reducir los ahorros de uno
to be **depleted by** verse mermado por
to **deploy ground troops** ▪ to deploy the infantry desplegar la infantería
to **deploy troops** desplegar tropas
to **deposit money in a bank account** depositar dinero en una cuenta bancaria ▪ *(Sp.)* ingresar dinero a una cuenta bancaria
to **deposit money in the bank** depositar dinero en el banco ▪ meter dinero en el banco ▪ ingresar dinero en el banco
deposit slip resguardo de ingreso
depressing subject tema depresivo ▪ tema deprimente
to **deprive someone of something** privar a alguien de algo ▪ privarle de algo a alguien
depth charge *(military)* carga de profundidad
depth of the crisis ▪ extent of the crisis *la* profundidad de la crisis ▪ *el* alcance de la crisis
depths of one's ignorance: the los alcances de la ignorancia de uno ▪ los rincones de la ignorancia de uno
depths of one's soul fondo del alma ▪ recovecos del alma
depths of the forest: in the ~ bosque adentro ▪ en la espesura del bosque
depths of winter: in the ~ ▪ in midwinter en pleno invierno
derailed train tren descarrilado
derisive laughter ▪ mocking laughter ▪ sardonic laughter risa burlona ▪ risa sardónica
to **derive comfort from** ▪ to take comfort in consolarse en ▪ encontrar consuelo en
to **derive pleasure from** deleitarse en ▪ *(literary)* encontrar gozo en
to **derive profit from** sacar ganancia de
to **derive the calendar** derivar el calendario ▪ obtener el calendario ➤ We derive the calendar from the sun's yearly cycle. Obtenemos el calendario del ciclo anual del sol.
to be **derived from** provenir de ▪ derivarse de ▪ obtenerse de ➤ The calendar is derived from the sun's yearly cycle. El calendario proviene del ciclo anual del sol.
to **descend on someone** ▪ to impose on someone caerle de imprevisto a alguien
to **describe someone as something** calificarlo(la) a alguien algo ➤ Whom he described as a good friend Al que calificó de un buen amigo
to **desecrate a flag** ultrajar una bandera
desecration of the flag ▪ defiling of the flag *el* ultraje a la bandera
deserted streets ▪ abandoned streets calles abandonadas
to **deserve a toast** valer un brindis ▪ merecer un brindis ➤ That deserves a toast. Eso vale un brindis. ▪ Eso merece un brindis.
to **design a building** proyectar un edificio ▪ diseñar un edificio ➤ Thomas Jefferson designed Monticello when he was twenty-four years old. Thomas Jefferson proyectó Monticello cuando tenía veinticuatro años.
to **designate someone as heir to** nombrar a alguien heredero a ▪ instituir heredero a ▪ instituir por heredero a
designer drugs drogas de diseño
desire for revenge deseo de venganza ▪ *el* afán de revancha
desolate terrain ▪ desolate countryside ▪ bleak terrain ▪ bleak countryside paisaje adusto ▪ paisaje desolado
desolate day día desierto
desolate spot paraje desolado ▪ lugar desolado

desperate attempt intento desesperado ➤ In a desperate attempt to escape En un intento desesperado por escapar

to be **desperate to do something** estar desesperado por hacer algo ➤ He was desperate to get someone to fill in for him. Estaba desesperado por conseguir a alguien que le supliera.

to be **destined to** estar destinado a ■ estar predestinado a

to **displace water** desplazar el agua

detached retina: to have a ~ tener un desprendimiento de retina

to **detain a suspect** ■ to take a suspect into custody ■ to apprehend a suspect detener a un sospechoso ■ poner a un sospechoso bajo custodia judicial ■ aprehender a un sospechoso ➤ Some potential suspects were detained for questioning. Algunos potenciales sospechosos fueron detenidos para ser interrogados.

to **detect a pattern** detectar una pauta ■ detectar un esquema ■ detectar un modelo

to **detect an odor** detectar un olor

to **detect an undercurrent of** ■ to sense an undercurrent of ■ to feel an undercurrent of sentir un trasfondo de ■ detectar un trasfondo de

to **detect the smell of something burning** ■ to notice the smell of something burning ■ to smell something burning detectar un olor a quemado ■ oler algo que se quema

to **deteriorate irreversibly** deteriorarse de manera ineluctable ■ deteriorarse irreversiblemente ➤ His health continues to deteriorate irreversibly. Su salud continúa deteriorándose de manera ineluctable.

to **determine the cause of** ■ to determine the reason for determinar las causas de ■ averiguar los motivos de ➤ Investigators were trying to determine the cause of the collapse. Los investigadores trataban de averiguar los motivos del derrumbe.

to **determine the reason for** ■ to determine the cause of determinar la razón por ■ averiguar los motivos de

to **determine to** ■ to resolve to hacerse el propósito de

to **determine who did it** ■ to solve the crime ■ to find the perpetrator(s) esclarecer la autoría ➤ They sent in the FBI to determine who planted the bomb. Mandaron al FBI para esclarecer la autoría del bombardeo.

to be **determined to** estar decidido a ■ estar empeñado en ■ tener empeño en ■ estar empecinado en ➤ The pilot was determined to save the mountain climbers, no matter what (happened). El piloto estaba decidido a salvar a los alpinistas, pasara lo que pasara.

to be **determined to find out** empeñarse en saberlo

to **detonate a bomb** ■ to set off a bomb ■ to explode a bomb detonar una bomba ■ hacer estallar una bomba

to **detonate an explosive** ■ to set off an explosive activar un explosivo ■ detonar un explosivo

to **detract from** deslucir ■ desvirtuar ■ restarles valor ➤ His haircut detracts from his appearance. Su corte de pelo desluce su imagen. ➤ The expression of anger detracts from the objectivity of the article. La expresión de rabia desvirtúa la objetividad del artículo. ■ La expresión de rabia resta el valor objetivo del artículo. ■ La expresión de rabia resta el mérito objetivo del artículo.

to **devalue the currency** devaluar la moneda

to be **devastated by something** 1. ser desolado por algo ■ ser arrollado por algo ■ ser destruido por algo 2. *(personal tragedy)* quedarse desolado por algo ■ quedarse destrozado por algo ➤ Parts of Caracas were devastated by the torrential rains and flash flooding. Zonas de Caracas fueron destruidas por las lluvias torrenciales y las riadas. ➤ He was devastated by his wife's sudden death. Se quedó desolado por la repentina muerte de su mujer. ■ Se quedó destrozado por la repentina muerte de su mujer.

devastating experience experiencia desoladora

to **develop a friendship with someone** entablar una amistad con alguien ➤ We have developed a good friendship. ■ We have developed a strong friendship. Hemos entablado una buena amistad. ■ Hemos creado una fuerte amistad.

to **develop a good relationship with someone** entablar una buena relación con alguien ➤ I have developed a good working relationship with my boss. He creado una buena relación de trabajo con mi jefe.

to **develop a medical condition** desarrollar una afección médica ■ desarrollar un cuadro médico

to **develop a paunch** echar tripas

to **develop heart problems** contraer afecciones cardiacas

to **develop normally** evolucionar sin problemas ➤ Thanks to a delicate treatment, the doctors managed to get the premature baby's organs to develop normally. Gracias a un complejo tratamiento, los médicos lograron que los órganos del bebé prematuro evolucionasen sin problemas.

to **develop photographs** revelar fotos ➤ Photos developed en 45 minutes Fotos reveladas en 45 minutos

to **develop someone's character** templar el carácter de alguien

developing countries los países en vía de desarrollo

development bank banco de fomento

developmental problems problemas evolutivos

developmental psychology psicología evolutiva

deviated septum *(medical)* septo desviado

devil's advocate abogado del diablo

devious tactics: to use ~ ■ to employ devious tactics usar técnicas malignas ■ usar malas artes ■ usar mañas ■ usar argucias

devious means: to get something through ~ conseguir algo con malas artes ■ conseguir algo con mañas ■ conseguir algo con argucias

to be **devoid of charm** carecer de encanto ■ estar desprovisto de encanto ➤ H.L. Mencken, the syndicated columnist of the 1920s, noted that the steel towns of western Pennsylvania were devoid of charm. H.L. Mencken, el columnista sindical de los años veinte, remarcó que los pueblos de acero del oeste de Pensilvania carecían de encanto.

to be **devoid of emotion** carecer de emoción ■ estar desprovisto de emoción

to **devote one's life to** dedicar su vida a ■ entregar su vida a ■ *(in third-person only)* dedicarle la vida a

to **devour a book** leer vorazmente un libro

dew point punto de condensación ■ el nivel del rocío

dial telephone teléfono de disco

dialogue box *(computers)* cuadro de diálogo

diamond in the rough ■ rough-cut diamond *el* diamante en bruto

diamond ring anillo de diamantes ■ sortija de diamantes

to **dice a carrot** trocear en daditos una zanahoria ■ cortar en cubos una zanahoria

did indeed claro que

did you bring...? *(tú)* ¿has traído...? ■ ¿trajiste...? ■ *(usted)* ¿ha traído (usted)...? ■ ¿trajo (usted)...? ➤ Did you bring your dictionary with you? ¿Trajiste tu diccionario? ■ ¿Has traído su diccionario? *(The use of the present perfect instead of the preterite is common in Spain.)*

did you catch on? ■ did you get it? *(tú)* ¿lo pillas? ■ ¿lo coges? ■ ¿lo entiendes? ■ ¿lo has entendido? ■ ¿lo has cogido? ■ *(usted)* ¿lo ha cogido (usted)? ■ ¿lo ha entendido? ■ ¿lo entiende?

did you enjoy it? *(tú)* ¿lo has disfrutado? ■ *(usted)* ¿lo ha disfrutado?

did you ever imagine that...? *(tú)* ¿alguna vez te imaginaste que...? ■ *(usted)* ¿alguna vez se imaginó usted que...?

did you get it? 1. *(joke)* did you catch on? *(tú)* ¿lo entendiste? ■ *(usted)* ¿lo entendió (usted) ■ *(Sp., tú)* ¿lo has entendido? ■ *(usted)* ¿lo ha entendido (usted)? 2. *(homework problem, etc.)* did you solve it? *(tú)* ¿lo resolviste? ■ *(usted)* lo resolvió (usted)? ■ *(informal)* ¿lo sacaste? ■ ¿te salió? 3. did you receive it? *(tú)* ¿ lo recibiste? ■ *(usted)* ¿lo recibió (usted)? 4. did you obtain it? *(tú)* ¿lo conseguiste? ■ *(usted)* ¿lo consiguió (usted)?

did you get my E-mail? *(tú)* ¿recibiste mi correo electrónico? ■ ¿recibiste mi mail? ■ *(usted)* ¿recibió (usted) mi correo electrónico? ■ ¿recibió (usted) mi mail?

did you hear about...? *(tú)* ¿has oído hablar de...? ■ ¿te has enterado de lo de...? ■ ¿has oído lo de...? ■ *(usted)* ¿ha oído (usted) hablar de...? ■ ¿se ha enterado (usted) de lo de...? ■ ¿ha oído (usted) lo de...? ➤ Did you hear about the ship from the Philippines loaded with yo-yo's?-It sprang a leak and sank fifteen times. ¿Te has enterado de lo del barco filipino cargado de yoyos?-Se le abrió una vía de agua y se hundió quince veces. ➤ Did you hear about the kid getting nabbed by the cops for stealing candy? ¿Has oído lo del chaval que han pillado los polis por robar caramelos?

did you hear it? ▪ did you hear that? *(tú)* ¿lo has oído? ▪ ¿has sentido? ▪ *(usted)* ¿lo ha oído (usted)? ▪ ¿ha sentido (usted)?

did you hear me?! ¡¿me has oído?!

did you hear the one about...? *(tú)* ¿has oído el de...? ▪ ¿te sabes el de...? ▪ *(usted)* ¿ha oído el de...? ▪ ¿se sabe el de...? ▪ *(ustedes)* ¿han oído el de...? ▪ ¿se saben el de...? ▪ *(Sp., vosotros)* ¿habéis oído el de... ▪ ¿os sabéis el de...

did you hurt yourself? *(tú)* ¿te has dañado? ▪ *(usted)* ¿se ha dañado (usted)?

did you know about it? *(tú)* ¿lo sabías? ▪ ¿sabías algo sobre esto? ▪ ¿sabías algo? ▪ *(usted)* ¿lo sabía (usted)? ▪ ¿sabía (usted) algo sobre esto? ▪ ¿sabía (usted) algo?

did you know it? *(tú)* ¿lo sabías? ▪ *(usted)* ¿lo sabía (usted)?

did you know that? *(tú)* ¿sabías eso? ▪ ¿lo sabías? ▪ *(usted)* ¿sabía (usted) eso? ▪ ¿lo sabía (usted)?

did you know that...? *(tú)* ¿sabías que...? ▪ *(usted)* ¿sabía (usted) que...

did you like it? *(tú)* ¿te gustó? ▪ ¿te ha gustado? ▪ *(usted)* ¿le gustó? ▪ ¿le ha gustado?

did you lose? *(tú)* ¿perdiste? ▪ ¿has perdido? ▪ *(usted)* ¿perdió (usted)? ▪ ¿ha perdido (usted)?

did you lose it? *(tú)* ¿lo has perdido? ▪ *(usted)* ¿lo ha perdido (usted)?

did you really? ¿de verdad?

did you see that? ▪ see that? *(tú)* ¿has visto (eso)? ▪ *(usted)* ¿ha visto (usted) eso?

did you see the way...? ▪ did you see how...? *(tú)* ¿te has fijado en cómo...? ▪ *(usted)* ¿se ha fijado (usted) en cómo...? ➤ Did you see the way he looked at me? ¿Te has fijado en cómo me miró?

didn't anyone tell you (that)...? *(tú)* ¿nadie te ha dicho que...? ▪ ¿no te han dicho que...? ▪ ¿no te habían dicho que...? ▪ ¿no te ha dicho nadie que...? ▪ ¿nadie te dijo que...? ▪ *(usted)* ¿nadie le ha dicho (a usted) que...? ▪ ¿nadie le dijo (a usted) que...? ➤ Didn't anyone tell you that he quit working there? ¿Nadie te ha dicho que (él) dejó de trabajar allí?

didn't anyone tell you to...? *(a ti)* ¿nadie te ha dicho que...? ▪ *(a usted)* ¿nadie le ha dicho que...? ➤ Didn't anyone tell you that the time of the meeting was changed? ¿Nadié le ha dicho que cambiaron la hora de la reunión?

didn't even ni siquiera ➤ I didn't even study for the art test. There was no way to. Ni siquiera estudié para el examen de arte. No había manera de hacerlo.

didn't I? 1. ¿verdad? **2.** ¿no? **3.** ¿no es así?

to **die as a result of** ▪ to die of morir por ▪ fallecer víctima de ➤ *(report)* The youths died as a result of massive head injuries caused by shots fired at close range. Los jovenes murieron por la destrucción de masa encefálica a causa de disparos de armas de fuego hechos desde muy cerca.

to **die before one's time** morirse antes de tiempo

to **die down** *(fire, wind)* amainar ▪ *(wind)* calmarse ➤ Overnight, the campfire died down. Durante la noche amainó la hoguera del campamento. ➤ The breeze died down. Amainó la brisa. ▪ Se calmó la brisa.

to **die in childbirth** morir de sobreparto ▪ morir de parto

to **die inside** morir por dentro

to **die instantly** morir en el acto

the **die is cast** *(alea jacta est-Julius Caesar)* la suerte está echada

to **die laughing** ▪ to die with laughter estar muerto de la risa ▪ *(Sp., off-color)* estar descojonado (de risa)

to **die of** morir a causa de ▪ fallecer de ➤ *(headline)* More than five million children around the world die of hunger every year Más de cinco millones de niños mueren al año en el mundo a causa del hambre

to **die of a broken heart** morir de corazón roto ▪ morir porque se le rompe el corazón

to **die of causes incident to age** *(journalistic)* ▪ to die of old age morir de causas relacionadas a la edad ▪ morir de viejo

to **die of natural causes** fallecer de causas naturales ▪ fallecer de muerte natural

to **die of old age** morirse de viejo

to **die of stab wounds** morir acuchillado(-a) ▪ morir por arma blanca ▪ morir apuñalado(-a)

to **die out 1.** *(fire, wind)* apagarse ▪ extinguirse **2.** *(traditions)* ir borrándose ▪ extinguirse

to **die with one's boots on** morir con las botas puestas

diesel fuel *el* gasoil ▪ *el* diésel

to be **different about one** tener de diferente ➤ I don't know what's different about her. No sé que tiene ella de diferente

to be **different from** ser distinto de ▪ ser diferente de

to be a **different kettle of fish** ▪ to be a whole different kettle of fish ▪ to be a horse of another color ▪ to be another thing altogether ▪ to be a different thing altogether ser harina de otro costal ▪ ser un capítulo aparte

to be a **different question altogether** ▪ to be another question altogether ser capítulo aparte

to be **different than** ser diferente a ➤ Fifty years ago, the country was completely different than it is today. Cuando yo era joven, el país era completamente diferente a hoy.

to be **different this time** ser diferente esta vez ▪ ser distinta esta vez ➤ Why will it be different this time? ¿Por qué será diferente esta vez? ▪ ¿Por qué será distinta esta vez? *("Distinta" is feminine because the implicit referent is "situación.")*

to be a **different way of** ser una manera diferente de ▪ ser una forma diferente de ▪ ser un medio diferente de ➤ It's a different way of doing things. Es una manera diferente de hacer las cosas. ▪ Es una manera distinta de hacer las cosas. ▪ Es una forma distinta de hacer las cosas.

different ways of: there are ~ existen diferentes maneras de ▪ existen distintas maneras de ▪ hay diferentes maneras de ▪ hay distintas maneras de

differential calculus cálculo diferencial

to be **difficult if not impossible** resultar complicado, por no decir imposible ▪ ser complicado, por no decir imposible ➤ That is going to be difficult if not impossible. Va a resultar difícil, por no decir imposible.

to be **difficult to control** ser difícil de controlar ➤ A classroom full of seventh graders can be difficult to control. Una clase llena de chicos del séptimo curso puede ser difícil de controlar. ➤ The airplane was difficult to control as it approached the eye of the hurricane. El avión se hizo difícil de controlar cuando se acercó al ojo del huracán.

to be **difficult to deal with** ▪ to be unyielding ser difícil de abordar ▪ hacerse de rogar

to be **difficult to get to** ▪ to be difficult to reach ser de difícil acceso ▪ ser difícil de alcanzar

to be **difficult to please** ▪ to be hard to please ser difícil de complacer

to be **difficult to reach 1.** to be difficult to get to ser de difícil acceso **2.** to be difficult to establish rapport with ser difícil de alcanzar ➤ It's a place that's very difficult to reach. ▪ It's a place that's very difficult to get to. Es un lugar de difícil acceso. ➤ The alientated youth was difficult to reach. El joven alienado fue difícil de alcanzar.

to be **difficult to understand** ▪ to be hard to understand difícil de entender

to **dig a hole** hacer un agujero

to **dig down into one's pockets** ▪ to rummage through one's pockets hurgar en los bolsillos

dig in! *(tú)* ¡híncale el diente! ▪ *(vosotros)* ¡hincadle el diente! ▪ *(ustedes)* ¡hínquenle el diente! ▪ *(nosotros)* let's dig in ¡vamos a hincarle el diente! ▪ ¡hinquémosle el diente!

to **dig in one's heels** empecinarse ▪ cerrarse a la banda ▪ cerrarse en banda

to **dig one's own grave** cavar(se) su propia fosa ▪ cavar(se) su propia sepultura ▪ cavar(se) su propia tumba ▪ excavar su propia tumba

to **dig the foundation for a structure** excavar para los cimientos de una estructura

digestive track vías digestivas

diminishing returns: the law of ~ la ley de rendimiento decreciente

dimpled chad *(on a ballot)* trocito desprendido
din of battle *el* fragor de batalla
dining car *el* vagón restaurante
dining room *el* salón comedor ➤ *(real estate ad)* Separate dining room Salón comedor independiente
dinner table mesa de comedor
to **dip one's wick** *(off-color)* mojar el churro
diplomatic effort: to launch a ~ desplegar un esfuerzo diplomático ▪ desplegar una labor diplomática
diplomatic efforts esfuerzos diplomáticos
diplomatic representative representante diplomático(-a)
diplomatic sources fuentes diplomáticas
to be **dipped in (white chocolate)** estar bañado en (chocolate blanco)
dire consequences consecuencias sombrías
dire state of deprivation estado de deprivación serio
dire straits: to be in ~ estar en un serio apuro
direct current ▪ DC corriente continua
to **direct one's efforts to** ▪ to direct one's efforts toward(s) dirigir sus esfuerzos a ▪ orientar sus esfuerzos a
direct physical contact contacto de piel a piel
direct quotation cita literal
to be **directed by** *(film)* ser dirigido por ➤ The film *Some Like It Hot* was written and directed by Billy Wilder. La película *Con faldas y a lo loco* fue escrita y dirigida por Billy Wilder.
direction in life: to have a ~ tener un rumbo en la vida ▪ tener un norte en la vida
directions for making something instrucciones para hacer algo
directions to a place las direcciones (para llegar a un sitio)
to be **directly above one's head** ▪ to be right above one's head ▪ to be directly over one's head ▪ to be right over one's head estar justo encima de la cabeza de uno ➤ Was the apple really directly over Newton's head? ¿Estaba la manzana realmente justo encima de la cabeza de Newton?
to be **directly overhead** ▪ to be straight overhead ▪ to be straight up estar justo encima de la cabeza ▪ estar directamente encima de la cabeza ▪ tener algo justo encima de la cabeza ▪ estar por encima de la cabeza de alguien ➤ In Mexico City, the sun and moon are almost directly overhead. En la Ciudad de México, el sol y la luna están casi justo encima de la cabeza. ▪ En la Ciudad de México el sol y la luna los tienes casi justo encima de la cabeza.
dirt floor ▪ earthen floor piso de tierra ▪ suelo de tierra
to be **dirt poor** ▪ to be in abject poverty ser paupérrimo ▪ no tener más que el día y la noche ▪ no tener más que la noche y el día ▪ no tener donde caerse muerto
dirty look: to give someone a ~ mirar a alguien mal ▪ mirar a alguien de mal modo
dirty money ▪ filthy lucre dinero sucio
dirty old man viejo verde ▪ viejo lépero
dirty trick mala pasada ▪ truco sucio
to **disagree with someone about something** ▪ to disagree with someone on something no estar de acuerdo con alguien sobre algo ▪ estar en desacuerdo con alguien sobre algo ▪ discrepar con alguien sobre algo ▪ discrepar con alguien de algo
to **disappear off the face of the earth** ▪ to vanish from the face of the earth ▪ to vanish without a trace tragárselo la tierra ▪ desaparecer del mapa ➤ He has disappeared off the face of the earth. Se lo ha tragado la tierra.
to **disappear without a trace** desaparecer sin dejar rastro alguno
to **disapprove of** no estar de acuerdo con ▪ no aprobar de ▪ desaprobar de ▪ ➤ The parents disapproved of their daughter's relationship with a hippie. Los padres no aprobaban la relación de su hija con un hippie.
to **disassociate oneself from** ▪ to dissociate oneself from desvincularse de ▪ desmarcarse de
to **discern in the distance** ▪ to make out in the distance vislumbrar a lo lejos ▪ atisbar a lo lejos
to **discharge someone from military service** darle de baja a alguien del servicio militar
disciplinary action against someone: to take ~ aplicarle un correctivo a alguien
disconcerted look: to have a ~ ▪ to look disconcerted tener un aire de desconcierto
to **discourage someone from doing something** desanimar a alguien para que no haga algo
discouraging outlook ▪ bleak outlook perspectiva poco alentadora ➤ The outlook for progress in the talks is discouraging. ▪ The outlook for progress in the talks is bleak. La perspectiva de progreso en las negociaciones es poco alentadora.
to **discover that...** descubrir que... ➤ Einstein discovered that gravity bends light. Einstein descubrió que la gravedad curva la luz. ▪ Einstein descubrió que la gravedad hace curvarse la luz.
to **discuss a matter** hablar de un asunto
to **discuss something with someone** hablar de algo con alguien ➤ There's something I need to discuss with you. Hay algo de lo que necesito hablar contigo. ▪ Hay algo de lo que necesito hablar con usted.
to **discuss the details** hablar de los detalles ▪ comentar los detalles ▪ especificar los detalles ➤ We need to discuss the details of the plan. Necesitamos comentar los detalles del plan.
disdainful look mirada despreciativa ▪ mirada desdeñosa ▪ mirada de desdén
to **disengage the clutch** ▪ to depress the clutch pedal pisar el embrague ▪ desembragar
to **disguise one's indifference** disimular la indiferencia
to **disguise one's voice** enmascar la voz
disheveled clothes ropa desgreñada
disheveled hair cabello desgreñado ▪ pelo desgreñado
dishwashing soap ▪ dishwashing liquid ▪ dish soap *el* detergente para la vajilla
to **dislike someone** ▪ not to like someone caerle mal a uno ▪ no caer bien a uno ▪ caerle gordo a uno ▪ tenerle manía a alguien ▪ tenerle entre ceja y ceja ➤ She dislikes him. ▪ She doesn't like him. Él le cae mal (a ella). ▪ Él le cae gordo (a ella). ▪ Ella le tiene manía (a él). ▪ Ella lo tiene entre ceja y ceja. ➤ The boss dislikes him. El jefe lo tiene entre ceja y ceja. ▪ El jefe le tiene manía. ▪ El jefe le tiene ojeriza. ▪ Le cae mal al jefe. ▪ No le cae bien al jefe. ➤ He dislikes me. ▪ He doesn't like me. Le caigo mal. ▪ Le caigo gordo. ▪ No le caigo bien. ▪ Me tiene manía.
to **dislocate one's elbow** desarticularse el codo ▪ dislocarse el codo ➤ He dislocated his elbow. Se desarticuló el codo. ▪ Se dislocó el codo.
to **dismantle a criminal ring** ▪ to smash a criminal ring desarticular una red criminal
to **dismiss a matter** dar por terminado un asunto ▪ dar por concluido un asunto
to **dismiss an appeal** *(of a court decision)* desestimar una apelación ▪ desestimar un recurso ▪ descartar una apelación
to **dismiss the case** absolver la instancia ▪ absolver el caso ▪ anular el caso
to **dismiss the idea (out of hand)** rechazar la idea de sí ▪ apartar la idea de sí ➤ I dismissed the idea out of hand. Rechacé la idea de mí. ▪ Aparté la idea de mí.
to **dismiss the possibility of** rechazar la posibilidad de ▪ descartar la posibilidad de
to **dismiss the possibility that...** rechazar la posibilidad de que... ▪ descartar la posibilidad de que...
disorders: blood ~ trastornos de sangre
disorders: emotional ~ trastornos emocionales
to **dispel a myth** desechar un mito
to **dispel one's doubts** despejar las dudas de uno ▪ disipar las dudas de uno ▪ quitar las dudas de uno
to **dispel one's doubts about** despejar las dudas sobre ▪ disipar las dudas sobre ▪ quitar las dudas sobre
to **dispel one's doubts that...** despejar las dudas que... ▪ disipar las dudas que... ▪ quitar las dudas que...
to **dispel one's fears** disipar los miedos de uno
to **dispel (the) rumors about** ▪ to quash (the) rumors about ▪ to put to rest (the) rumors about zanjar los rumores sobre
to **dispel one's worries** disipar las preocupaciones de uno
to **dispense fuel** descargar combustible ▪ descargar carburante ➤ The injector dispenses fuel at the rate of one hundred

liters per minute. El inyector descarga el combustible a razón de cien litros el minuto.

to **dispense with something 1.** to do without something ▪ to manage without something ▪ to get along without something prescindir de algo **2.** to get rid of something deshacerse de algo

to **dispense with the formalities** deshacerse de las formalidades ▪ olvidarse de las formalidades ➤ Let's dispense with the formalities and get down to brass tacks. Vamos a deshacernos de las formalidades e ir al grano. ▪ Vamos a olvidarnos de las formalidades e ir al grano.

dispenser for tape ▪ tape dispenser portarollo para cinta (adhesiva) ▪ portarollo de cinta ▪ portacinta

to **displace water** desplazar el agua

display of merchandise *la* exposición de mercancías ➤ There was a display of knives in the show window. Había una exposición de cuchillos en el escaparate.

disposable mechanical pencil *el* portaminas desechable ▪ lapicera de un solo uso ▪ lapicera para usar y tirar

disposable needles ▪ disposable syringes jeringuillas desechables

disposable razors maquinillas de afeitar desechables

disrepair: to fall into ~ deteriorarse ➤ The cabin has fallen into disrepair. La cabaña se ha deteriorado.

disruption of the electrical power supply ▪ disruption in the supply of electrical power colapso del sumistro eléctrico ▪ el corte del suministro eléctrico ➤ State of emergency in California over the disruption of the electrical power supply Estado de emergencia en California por el colapso del suministro eléctrico

to **disseminate information** diseminar información ▪ desperdigar información

dissenting opinion *(U.S. Supreme Court and other panels of judges)* ▪ minority opinion escrito de discrepancia ➤ In the dissenting opinion signed by the three justices... ▪ In the minority opinion signed by the three justices... En el escrito de discrepancia firmado por los tres magistrados...

dissenting voice *la* voz discrepante ▪ voz en contra ▪ voz disidente

to **dissociate oneself from** ▪ to disassociate oneself from desvincularse de ▪ desmarcarse de

distance (away) ▪ proximity ▪ closeness ▪ nearness cercanía ➤ At the moment of choosing a restaurant, the distance (away) and the type of cuisine are the most common factors taken into account by customers. A la hora de elegir un restaurante, la cercanía y el tipo de cocina son los criterios más tenidos en cuenta por los clientes.

distance from the Earth to the sun ▪ distance between the Earth and the sun distancia entre la Tierra y el sol ➤ In round figures, the mean distance from the Earth to the sun is 150 million kilometers. En números redondos la distancia media entre la Tierra y el sol es de 150 millones de kilómetros.

to **distance oneself from a group** marcar las distancias hacia un grupo ▪ alejarse de un grupo

to **distance oneself from someone** marcar distancias con alguien

to **distance oneself from something** desmarcarse de algo ▪ desligarse de algo ▪ deslindarse de algo ➤ *(news item)* Vice president Al Gore distanced himself from the decision to remove Elián González (from the home of his cousins). El vicepresidente Al Gore se desmarcó de la decisión de sacar a Elián González (de la casa de sus primos).

distant cousin primo(-a) lejano(-a)

distant lands ▪ far-off lands tierras lejanas

distant memory recuerdo lejano

distant person persona distante ▪ persona fría

distant planet planeta lejano

distant relative pariente lejano(-a)

distinguished family familia de rancio abolengo ▪ familia de renombre

distinguished-looking de aspecto distinguido

distinguishing features señas personales ▪ facciones distinguidas ▪ rasgos distintivos

to **distort the results** ▪ to render the results less accurate ▪ to skew the results ▪ to bias the results distorcionar los resultados ▪ sesgar los resultados ▪ intervenir en los resultados ▪ mediar en los resultados

to **distort the history** tergiversar la historia ▪ cambiar la historia

to **distort the truth** tergiversar la verdad

to **distribute a flyer** ▪ to circulate a flyer distribuir un folleto

to **distribute wealth** repartir la riqueza

distribution of wealth repartición de la riqueza

to **disturb the neighbors** molestar a los vecinos

to **disturb the peace** turbar la paz

to be **disturbed about** estar preocupado por

disturbing development acontecimiento preocupante

ditto! ¡ídem! ▪ yo lo mismo ▪ y yo ▪ yo también ▪ *(replying to "me gusta")* a mí también

diurnal animal ▪ animal active during the day animal diurno

diurnal motion of astronomical objects ▪ daily motion of astronomical objects movimiento diurno de objetos astronómicos

to **dive for cover** tirarse cuerpo a tierra ➤ Dive for cover! ¡Cuerpo a tierra!

to **dive for treasure** ▪ to dive in search of treasure bucear en busca de tesoro ➤ They dive for pearls and treasure. Bucean en busca de perlas y de tesoro.

to **dive into the water** ▪ to dive in zambullirse al agua ▪ hacerse un clavado en el agua

to **dive in head first** zambullirse de cabeza

diversionary tactic maniobra de diversión

to **divert (one's) attention from** desviar la atención de

to **divert (the) funds** desviar los fondos

to **divert (the) traffic** desviar el tráfico

to **divert (the) water** desviar el agua ▪ trasvasar el agua

to **divide one's time between...** repartir el tiempo entre...

to **divide the bill (up) evenly among everybody** ▪ to split the bill evenly among everybody dividir la cuenta entre todos en partes iguales ▪ pagar a escote

to **divide (up) something** ▪ to divide something up hacer el reparto de algo ▪ repartirse algo ➤ The thieves divided up the booty. Los ladrones hicieron el reparto del botín. ▪ Los ladrones se repartieron el botín.

to **divide up into groups** dividirse en grupos

to **divide up the estate** ▪ to divide the estate up hacer el reparto de la herencia ▪ repartirse la herencia

to be **divided by** ▪ to be divided into ser dividido por ▪ ser dividido entre ➤ Thirty divided by six equals five. ▪ Six goes into thirty five times. ▪ Six into thirty goes five times. Treinta (dividido) entre seis da cinco. ▪ Treinta entre seis toca a cinco. ▪ Treinta entre seis es cinco. ▪ Treinta entre seis cabe a cinco. ➤ Five divided by ten equals one half. Cinco partido por diez da un medio.

divided highway carretera separada por una isleta ▪ *(L. Am.)* autopista ▪ *(Sp.)* autovía ➤ It's a four-lane divided highway with limited access. Es una autopista con cuatro carriles separados por una isleta. ▪ Es una autovía con cuatro carriles separados por una isleta.

to be **divided into camps** estar dividido en sectores ▪ haber ámbitos ➤ Socialists are divided into two camps, one communist and one democratic. Los socialistas se dividen en dos sectores, uno comunista y otro democrático. ▪ En el ámbito socialista hay dos sectores, uno comunista y el otro democrático.

divided loyalties: to be a case of ~ ser un caso de lealtades divididas ▪ ser un caso de lealtades repartidas ➤ It was a case of divided loyalties. Fue un caso de lealtades divididas.

dividing line between línea divisoria entre

dividing up of the estate *la* división de la herencia

divorce decree decreto de divorcio

divorce rate tasa de divorcios ➤ *(news item)* The UK (United Kingdom) has a divorce rate of forty percent. El RU (Reino Unido) registra una tasa de divorcios del cuarenta por ciento de los enlaces.

divorce settlement acuerdo de divorcio

to **divorce someone** ▪ to get a divorce from someone divorciarse de alguien ➤ His wife divorced him. Su mujer se divorció de él.

to **divulge information** divulgar información

to **divulge the names** divulgar los nombres ➤ The police would not divulge the names. La policía se negaba a divulgar los nombres.

dizzy spell: to have a ~ ▪ to suffer a dizzy spell sufrir un vahído ▪ sufrir un mareo

dizzying rate: at a ~ ▪ at a very rapid rate a un ritmo vertiginoso ▪ a un ritmo mareante

to **do a bang-up job** *(coll.)* ▪ to do a magnificent job ▪ to do an excellent job hacer un trabajo magnífico ▪ hacer un trabajo excelente

to **do a brisk business** tener mucho movimiento ➤ That restaurant does a brisk business. Ese restaurante tiene mucho movimiento.

to **do a coup de grâce** ▪ to perform a coup de grâce dar un golpe de gracia ▪ asestar un golpe de gracia

to **do a double take** tardar en procesar(lo)

to **do a good business** hacer un buen negocio ▪ ir bien ▪ marcha bien ➤ That restaurant does a good business. Ese restaurante hace un buen negocio. ▪ Ese restaurante va bien. ▪ Ese restaurante marcha bien.

to **do a good deed** hacer una buena obra ▪ hacer una buena acción ▪ hacer una obra de caridad

to **do a good job** hacer un buen trabajo ➤ You're doing a good job. Haces un buen trabajo.

to **do a good thing** hacer algo bueno

to **do a humorous imitation of someone** ▪ to do a takeoff on someone ▪ to parody someone hacer una imitación divertida de alguien

to **do a lot of something** hacer algo mucho ➤ He used to do a lot of painting. Solía pintar mucho. ➤ We have to do a lot of correcting of the draft. Tenemos que hacer muchas correcciones del borrador.

to **do a lot of walking** caminar mucho ▪ *(colorful)* andar una barbaridad

to **do a lot worse** ir peor ▪ ser peor ➤ Maybe it's not your dream job, but still, you could do a lot worse. Puede que no sea el trabajo de tus sueños, pero te podría ir peor. ▪ Puede que no sea el trabajo de tus sueños, pero podría ser (mucho) peor.

to **do a lousy job** hacer una chapuzada

to **do a number on someone** *(coll.)* ▪ to do a number on someone's head perjudicar a alguien ▪ afectar a alguien de manera negativa ▪ dañar a alguien

to **do a poor job** hacer un mal trabajo ▪ hacer un trabajo de poca calidad ▪ hacer un trabajo deplorable

to **do a recount** hacer un recuento ▪ llevar a cabo un recuento

to **do a spoof of someone** ▪ to spoof someone hacer una parodia de alguien ▪ hacer una imitación de alguien ▪ parodiar a alguien

to **do a spoof on something** ▪ to spoof something hacer una parodia de algo ▪ hacer una imitación de algo

to **do a story on something** escribir un artículo sobre algo ▪ escribir un reportaje sobre algo ➤ The reporter did several stories on stem cell research. El reportero escribió varios reportajes sobre la investigación con células madre.

to **do a stupid thing** ▪ to do something stupid hacer una tontería ▪ hacer una estupidez

to **do a takeoff on someone** ▪ to do a humorous imitation of someone ▪ to do a parody of someone ▪ to parody someone hacer una imitación divertida de alguien

to **do a taste test** hacer una prueba de gusto

to **do all the talking** ser el único en hablar ▪ solamente hablar uno ▪ no dejar hablar a nadie

to **do an about face 1.** *(military facing movement)* to turn around 180° dar media vuelta **2.** to reverse one's position on an issue cambiar de opinión (sobre un asunto) **3.** to change one's direction (for the better) cambiar su vida para bien

to **do an encore** hacer un bis ▪ bisar

to **do an end run 1.** *(American football)* to run with the ball toward the goal correr hacia la meta con la pelota en mano **2.** *(figurative)* to go to your boss's boss ▪ to go over your boss's head ▪ to go around your boss saltarse al jefe ▪ ir por encima del jefe

to **do an excellent job** ▪ to do an impeccable job hacer un trabajo excelente ▪ hacer un trabajo impecable ▪ realizar un trabajo excelente ▪ llevar a cabo una excelente labor

to **do an experiment** ▪ to perform an experiment ▪ to conduct an experiment hacer un experimento ▪ realizar un experimento

to **do an impeccable job** ▪ to do an excellent job hacer un trabajo impecable ▪ realizar un trabajo impecable

do any better than: not to be able to ~ 1. no poder mejorar ▪ no poder hacer mejor ▪ ser lo mejor que uno puede hacer **2.** no poder haber hecho algo mejor ➤ I can't do any better than that. No puedo hacerlo mejor. ▪ Es lo mejor que puedo hacer. ➤ *(in a positive sense)* You can't do any better than that. No podías haberlo hecho mejor.

to **do anything to...** ▪ to go any lengths to... estar dispuesto a todo con tal de... ▪ estar dispuesto a todo para... ➤ *(Beauty and the Beast)* She'll do anything to save her father. Está dispuesta a todo con tal de salvar a su padre. ▪ Está dispuesta a todo para salvar a su padre.

to **do anything to get attention** hacer cualquier cosa con tal de llamar la atención ▪ hacer cualquier cosa para llamar la atención

to **do as one pleases** ▪ to do as one likes hacer lo que uno quiera ▪ acamparse como quiera ▪ seguir uno mismo ▪ hacer lo que a uno le da la gana ▪ vivir a su aire ➤ Do as you please. *(tú)* Haz lo que quieras. ▪ Acámpate como quieras. ▪ Sigue tú mismo(-a). ▪ *(usted)* Haga usted lo que quiera. ▪ Acámpese como quiera. ▪ Acámpese como quiera. ▪ Siga usted mismo(-a). ▪ Haga usted lo que le da la santa gana.

to **do away with someone** acabar con alguien

to **do away with something** acabar con algo

do bears live in the woods? ▪ obviously! *(tú)* ¿y tú qué crees? ▪ ¿a ti qué te parece? ▪ *(usted)* ¿y usted qué cree? ▪ ¿a usted qué le parece? ▪ lo que se ve no se pregunta

to **do cartwheels** dar volteretas (laterales) ▪ hacer volteretas ▪ hacer la rueda

to **do everything possible (to)** hacer todo lo posible (para)

to **do exactly what...** ▪ to do the very thing (that)... hacer exactamente lo que... ▪ no hacer sino... ▪ no hacer ni más ni menos lo que... ▪ hacer justo lo que... ➤ You do exactly what you accuse me of doing. ▪ You do the very thing you accuse me of doing. Haces exactamente lo mismo de lo que me acusas. ▪ No estás haciendo sino lo mismo de lo que me acusas. ▪ No haces ni más ni menos que lo mismo de lo que me acusas. ▪ Haces justo lo mismo de lo que me acusas.

to **do for someone** hacer por alguien ➤ Thank you for all you have done for me. Gracias por todo lo que has hecho por mí. ➤ Thank you for all you do for me. Gracias por todo lo que haces por mí.

to **do good deeds** ▪ to do good works hacer obras buenas ▪ hacer obras de caridad

to **do housework** hacer las labores de la casa ▪ hacer las labores domésticas ▪ hacer los quehaceres domésticos

do I hear *x*? *(at an auction)* ¿oigo *x*? ▪ ¿quién da *x*? ▪ ¿alguien ofrece *x*? ➤ Do I hear fifty? Anyone? ¿Oigo cincuenta? ¿Nadie? ▪ ¿Quién da cincuenta? ¿Nadie? ▪ ¿Quién ofrece cincuenta? ¿Nadie?

to **do it just for fun** hacerlo por gusto ▪ hacerlo por divertirse ▪ hacerlo por deporte ▪ hacerlo porque sí

to **do it like this** ▪ to do it this way hacerlo así ➤ Do it like this. ▪ Do it this way. *(tú)* Hazlo así. ▪ *(usted)* Hágalo así.

do it now! ¡hazlo ya!

to **do it one's own way** hacerlo a su manera ▪ hacerlo a su modo

to **do it this way** ▪ to do it like this hacerlo así ➤ Do it this way. ▪ Do it like this. *(tú)* Hazlo así. ▪ *(usted)* Hágalo así.

do-it-yourself books libros sobre hágalo usted mismo ▪ *(Sp.)* libros sobre el bricolaje ▪ ➤ *(book title) Do-It-Yourself for Klutzes Bricolaje para manazas*

to **do its job** valer para hacer

to **do justice to something** ▪ to do something justice hacer justicia a algo ➤ The movie doesn't do the book justice. ▪

The movie doesn't do justice to the book. La película no hace justicia al libro. ➤ The movie doesn't do it justice. La película no le hace justicia.

do like me ■ do as I do *(tú)* haz lo que yo ■ haz como yo ■ haz lo mismo que yo ■ *(usted)* haga (usted) lo que yo ■ haga (usted) como yo ■ haga (usted) lo mismo que yo

do not drop no dejar caer

do not enter no pasar

to **do nothing but** ■ not to do anything but no hacer (nada) más que ➤ I do nothing but work. ■ I don't do anything but work. No hago nada más que trabajar.

to **do one good** irle bien a uno

to **do one thing at a time** ■ to do things one at a time hacer las cosas una a la vez

to **do one's best** hacer lo mejor posible ■ dar el do de pecho

to **do one's best (to)** hacer lo mejor que uno pueda (para) ➤ We'll do our best, sir. Haremos lo mejor que podamos, señor.

to **do one's Christmas shopping early** hacer las compras navideñas temprano

to **do one's duty** cumplir con su deber

to **do one's hair** hacerse el pelo ➤ I have to do my hair. Tengo que hacerme el pelo.

to **do one's homework** *(L. Am.)* hacer la tarea ■ *(Sp.)* hacer los deberes

to **do one's job** cumplir con su trabajo

to **do one's level best** dar el do de pecho

to **do one's nails** hacerse las uñas

to **do one's own thing** hacer lo suyo ■ hacer lo propio ■ andar en su onda

to **do one's part** hacer lo que toca a uno ■ hacer lo que le corresponda a uno ➤ We'll do our part, sir. Haremos lo que nos toca, señor. ■ Haremos lo que nos corresponda, señor.

to **do one's utmost (to)** dar el do de pecho

to **do one's very best (to)** hacer todo lo posible (para)

to **do piecework** ■ to work by the piece trabajar a destajo ■ trabajar por unidad ➤ Furniture refinishers do piecework. ■ Furniture refinishers work by the piece. Los restauradores de muebles trabajan a destajo.

to **do pushups** hacer flexiones

do re mi fa so (or **sol**) **la ti do** ■ C D E F G A B C do re mi fa sol la si do ➤ Concerto in b-flat Concierto en si bemol ➤ To brighten that chord up, hit an A. Para dar más vida al acorde, ponle una la. ■ Para dar más vida al acorde, añádale una la.

to **do research** hacer investigaciones

to **do sit-ups** hacer sentadillas

to **do so** hacerlo ➤ But he did so unwillingly. Pero lo hizo de mala gana.

to **do some cooking** estar cocinando ■ estar de cocinero(-a) ➤ I did some cooking this weekend. Estuve cocinando este fin de semana. ■ Estuve de cocinera este fin de semana.

to **do some more work on it** ■ to work on it some more trabajar más en ello

to **do some work** ■ to get some work done trabajar un poco ■ trabajar algo

to **do someone good** hacerle bien a alguien ➤ It will do you a lot of good. ■ It'll do you good. Te hará mucho bien. ■ Le hará (a usted) mucho bien.

to **do someone in** jorobar a alguien ■ cargárselo a alguien ➤ They did him in. Se lo cargaron.

to **do someone out of something** birarle de algo a alguien ■ quitarle de algo a alguien ➤ He did me out of a twenty. Me birló uno de veinte. ■ Me quitó uno de veinte.

to **do someone's hair** peinarle ■ hacer el pelo a alguien ➤ Who does your hair? ¿Quién te peina?

to **do something about it** hacer algo al respecto

to **do something behind someone's back** hacer algo a espaldas de alguien ➤ He did it behind his wife's back. Lo hizo a espaldas de su esposa.

to **do something correctly** hacer algo correctamente ■ *(Sp.)* hacer algo adecuadamente ➤ When you exit from the program correctly... Cuando cierras correctamente el programa...

to **do something deliberately 1.** *(in a positive or negative sense)* hacer algo con intención ■ hacer algo con premeditación **2.** *(in a negative sense only)* hacer algo adrede

to **do something for a living** ■ to live off the income from something ganarse la vida haciendo algo ■ vivir de algo ➤ The artist said she doesn't plan to paint for a living. ■ The artist said she doesn't plan to live off the income from painting. La artista dijo que no piensa ganarse la vida pintando. ■ La artista dijo que no piensa vivir de pintura.

to **do something for others** hacer algo por los demás

to **do something for pleasure** ■ to do something for enjoyment hacer algo por placer ■ hacer algo para gozar ➤ We listen to classical music for pleasure. ■ We listen to classical music for enjoyment. Escuchamos música clásica por placer.

to **do something for someone** hacer algo por alguien ■ hacerle algo a alguien ➤ I have to cut the neighbor's lawn this week. Tengo que cortarle el césped a la vecina esta semana.

to **do something gradually** hacer algo gradualmente ■ hacer algo paulatinamente ➤ The company decided to dismantle the plant gradually. La compañía decidió desmantelar la planta paulatinamente.

to **do something last** hacer algo al último ■ hacer algo al final ➤ We'll paint the doors last. Pintaremos las puertas al último. ■ Pintaremos las puertas al final.

to **do something new** hacer algo nuevo ■ hacer algo no visto ■ hacer algo inédito

to **do something out of spite** hacer algo por despecho

to **do something real quick** *(Southern U.S., coll.)* ■ to do something (very) quickly hacer algo volando ■ hacer algo corriendo

to **do something really dumb** cometer un solemne disparate ■ cometer un tremendo disparate

to **do something right** ■ to do something correctly ■ to do something the right way hacer algo de forma correcta

to **do something right under someone's nose** hacer algo en las propias narices de alguien ■ hacer algo en las propias barbas de alguien

to **do something stupid** ■ to do a stupid thing hacer una burrada ■ hacer una tontería ■ hacer algo estúpido ■ hacer una estupidez

to **do something systematically** ■ to go about something systematically hacer algo sistemáticamente ■ *(Sp.)* hacer algo por sistema

to **do something the hard way** hacer algo de la forma más complicada

to **do something to one's hair** hacerse algo con el pelo ➤ Look what he's done to his hair! ¡Mira lo que se ha hecho con el pelo!

to **do something to someone** hacer algo a alguien ➤ What did he do to you? ¿Qué te hizo?

to **do something unaided** hacer algo por su propio pie ➤ The (race car) driver left his car unaided. El piloto salió del auto por su propio pie.

to **do something without anyone's knowing it** hacer algo sin que nadie lo sepa ■ hacer algo sin que nadie se entere

to **do something wrong 1.** to do something incorrectly ■ to make a mistake equivocarse ■ cometer un error **2.** to sin pecar ■ hacer algo malo

to **do the best one can** ■ to do one's best hacer lo mejor que uno pueda ➤ I'm doing the best I can. Estoy haciendo lo mejor que puedo. ➤ I'll do the best I can. ■ I'll do my best. Haré lo mejor que pueda. ➤ I did the best I could. Hice lo mejor que pude.

to **do the dishes** lavar la vajilla ■ lavar los trastes ■ *(Sp.)* fregar los cacharros ■ fregar los platos

to **do the grocery shopping** ■ to buy (the) groceries hacer las compras ■ *(Sp.)* hacer la compra

to **do (the) laundry** ■ to do the wash lavar la ropa ■ hacer el lavado (de la ropa) ■ *(Sp.)* hacer la colada

to **do the payroll** preparar la nómina

to **do the right thing** hacer lo justo ■ hacer lo correcto

do the talking: to let one ~ dejar que uno le hable a alguien ➤ Let me do the talking (to him). Déjame que yo le hable.

to **do things halfway** hacer las cosas a medias

to **do things one by one** hacer las cosas uno por uno

to **do things one's own way** hacer las cosas a su modo ■ *(Sp.)* ser maestrillo que tiene su librillo

to **do two things at once** hacer dos cosas al mismo tiempo ■ hacer dos cosas a la vez ■ *(colorful)* estar con un ojo al gato y el otro al garabato

do unto others as you would have them do unto you haz a los otros lo que quieras que te hagan a ti

to **do well to** hacer bien en ➤ You would do well to seek his advice. Harías bien en buscar su consejo.

to **do what one must (do)** ■ to do what one has to do hacer lo que uno tiene que hacer ■ hacer lo que uno debe

do you happen to know...? ¿sabes por casualidad...? ■ *(Sp., coll.)* ¿sabes por algún casual...?

do you happen to know if...? ¿sabes por casualidad si...? ■ *(Sp., coll.)* ¿sabes por algún casual si...?

do you happen to know whether (or not)...? ¿sabes por casualidad si (o no)...? ■ *(Sp., coll.)* ¿sabes por algún casual si (o no)...?

to **do well in school** andar muy bien en la escuela ■ llevar muy bien los estudios

to **do what one can (to)** hacer lo que uno pueda (para)

to **do what one is told** hacer lo que le digan (a uno) ■ cumplir con lo cometido

to **do without something** ir sin algo ■ prescindir de algo ■ pasarse sin algo ➤ I can do without it. Puedo prescindir de eso.

do you? ¿sí? ■ ¿verdad? ■ ¿en serio? ■ ¿de verdad?

do you come here often? ¿frecuentas mucho este lugar? ■ ¿vienes mucho por aquí?

do you feel okay? ■ are you feeling okay? ¿te encuentras bien? ■ ¿te sientes bien?

do you follow me? *(tú)* ¿me sigues? ■ ¿me entiendes? ■ *(usted)* ¿me sigue (usted)? ■ ¿me entiende (usted)? ■ *(polite because it puts the onus on oneself)* ¿me explico?

do you have a car? ■ do you own a car? *(tú)* ¿tienes carro? ■ ¿tienes coche? ■ *(usted)* ¿tiene usted carro? ■ ¿tiene usted coche?

do you have a light? ■ have you got a light? ■ could you give me a light? ¿tienes fuego? ■ ¿me das fuego?

do you have any change on you? ¿llevas cambio (encima)? ■ ¿tienes cambio (encima)?

do you have any money on you? ■ do you have any money with you? ■ have you got any money on you? ■ have you got any money with you? ¿llevas dinero? ■ ¿tienes dinero?

do you have (any) plans this weekend? ■ have you got (any) plans this weekend? *(tú)* ¿tienes planes este fin de semana? ■ ¿tienes planes para el fin de semana? ■ *(usted)* ¿tiene usted planes este fin de semana? ■ ¿tiene usted planes para el fin de semana?

do you have any questions? *(tú)* ¿tienes preguntas? ■ ¿tienes dudas? ■ *(usted)* ¿tiene (usted) preguntas? ■ ¿tiene (usted) dudas? ■ *(ustedes)* ¿tienen (ustedes) preguntas? ■ ¿tienen (ustedes) dudas? ■ *(Sp., vosotros)* ¿tenéis preguntas? ■ ¿tenéis dudas?

do you have change for a fifty-euro bill? ■ can you change a fifty-euro bill? *(tú)* ¿puedes cambiar un billete de cincuenta euros? ■ *(usted)* ¿puede usted cambiar un billete de cincuenta euros?

do you have eggs? *(to a store clerk)* ■ do you carry eggs? ¿hay huevos?

do you have milk? *(to a store clerk)* ■ do you carry milk? ¿hay leche?

do you have the time? ■ have you got the time? ■ could you tell me what time it is? *(tú)* ¿tienes hora? ■ ¿me das la hora? ■ *(Arg.)* ¿me tirás las agujas? ■ *(usted)* ¿tiene usted hora? ■ ¿me da usted la hora?

do you have time (to...)? ■ have you got time (to...)? **1.** *(tú)* ¿tienes tiempo (para...)? ■ ¿te da el tiempo (para...)? **2.** *(usted)* ¿tiene (usted) tiempo (para...)? ■ ¿le da (a usted) el tiempo (para...)?

do you know anything about...? ¿sabes alguna cosa de...? ■ ¿sabes algo de...?

do you know how to get there? ■ do you know the way? *(tú)* ¿sabes cómo ir? ■ ¿sabes el camino? ■ *(usted)* ¿sabe (usted) cómo ir? ■ ¿sabe (usted) el camino?

do you know the way? ■ do you know how to get there? *(tú)* ¿sabes el camino? ■ ¿sabes cómo ir? ■ *(usted)* ¿sabe usted el camino? ■ ¿sabe (usted) cómo ir?

(do) you know who you made me think of? ¿sabes de quién me recordó?

do you know who you remind me of? ¿sabes a quién me recuerdas? ■ ¿sabes a quién me haces recordar?

do you mind if...? ¿te importa si...?

do you mind if I ask you a question? ¿le molesta que le haga una pregunta? ■ ¿le molesta si le hago una pregunta?

do you mind if I sit with you (all)? ¿les importa que me siente con ustedes? ■ *(Sp., vosotros)* ¿os importa que me siente con vosotros?

do you mind if I smoke? ¿te importa si fumo? ■ ¿le importa (a usted) si fumo?

do you need a ride? ¿necesitas que te lleve? ■ ¿necesitas que te alcance? ■ ¿necesitas que te acerque? ■ *(Mex.)* ¿necesitas un aventón?

do you really? ¿de verdad?

(do you) see what I mean? ¿ves lo que (te) quiero decir?

do you swear to tell the truth, the whole truth, and nothing but the truth, so help you God?-I do. ¿jura usted decir la verdad, sólo la verdad y nada más que la verdad?-sí, lo juro.

do you think he's forgotten? ■ could he have forgotten? ¿se habrá olvidado? *(The feminine form is identical.)*

do you think he's gotten lost? ¿se habrá perdido? *(The feminine form is identical.)*

do you think I should...? ¿te parece que (yo) deba...?

do you think there are any left? ¿habrá todavía?

do you think there is any left? ¿habrá todavía?

do you think we should...? ¿te parece que debamos...?

do you understand? ¿me explico? ■ ¿entiendes? ■ ¿entiende usted?

do you want a ride? ¿quieres que te lleve? ■ ¿quieres que te alcance? ■ ¿quieres que te acerque? ■ *(Mex.)* ¿quieres un aventón?

do you want him captured? ¿desea que lo capturemos? ■ *(Sp., leísmo)* ¿desea que le capturemos?

do you want to come with me? ■ want to come? ¿quieres acompañarme? ■ ¿me acompañas? ■ ¿vas conmigo?

do you want to go to the movies? ■ would you like to go to the movies? ¿te gustaría ir al cine? ■ ¿te provoca ir al cine?

to **doctor a photograph** alterar una fotografía ■ trucar una fotografía ➤ This photo is doctored. Esta foto está alterada. ■ Esta foto está trucada.

the **doctor prescribed me antibiotics** el médico me ha recetado antibióticos

to **doctor the results** ■ to skew the results ■ to bias the results ■ to distort the results mediatizar los resultados ■ distorcionar los resultados ■ tergiversar los resultados

doctoral committee mesa de profesores

doctored photograph foto trucada

doctor's orders: on the ~ por prescripción facultativa ■ por prescripción médica

to **dodge a question** ■ to evade a question contestar con una evasiva ■ contestar con evasivas ■ esquivar una pregunta ➤ He dodged the question. Contestó con una evasiva. ■ Esquivó la pregunta.

to **dodge telephone calls** esquivar las llamadas telefónicas

to **dodge the issue** ■ to evade the issue evadir el tema ■ echar balones fuera

to **dodge (the) traffic** esquivar los coches

doe eyes ojos de carnero degollado

does it fit? ■ is it the right size? ¿te queda bien?

does it happen in Spain? ■ does that happen in Spain? ■ does that go on in Spain? ¿hay de eso en España? ■ ¿ocurre eso en España?

does it work? ¿vale para hacerlo? ■ ¿es eficaz? ■ ¿sirve? ■ ¿funciona (bien)?

does that go on in Spain? ■ does that happen in Spain? ¿hay de eso en España? ■ ¿pasa eso en España?

does this belong to you? ■ is this yours? *(tú)* ¿te pertenece esto? ■ ¿es tuyo? ■ *(usted)* ¿le pertenece esto? ■ ¿es suyo?

dog breeder criador(-a) de perros

a **dog goes "bow-wow" and a cat goes "meow"** el perro hace "guau-guau" y el gato hace "miau"

dog in the manger perro del hortelano

dog is housebroken perro(-a) es educado(-a)

to be **dog tired** ■ to be pooped ■ to be beat ■ to be whipped estar con la lengua fuera ■ estar hecho unos zorros

dog's life: to lead a ~ llevar una vida de perros ■ llevar una vida perruna

to be **doing something** estar haciendo algo ➤ His New Year's resolution is to be teaching in September. Su resolución de año nuevo es estar dando clases en septiembre.

domestic front: on the ~ ■ on the home front en el frente interno

domestic help servicio doméstico

to **donate blood** ■ to give blood donar sangre

to be **done 1.** to be finished haber terminado ■ haber acabado **2.** to be completely cooked estar hecho ➤ I'll be done sometime next week. Habré terminado (para) la semana que viene. ■ Habré acabado (para) la semana que viene. ➤ Don't open the oven door. The cake's not done. No abras la puerta del horno, la tarta no está hecha. ➤ The pie's not done. No está hecho el pay. ■ *(Sp.)* No está hecho el pastel.

to be a **done deal** ser un trato hecho ■ ser cosa hecha

done?-done! ■ is it a deal?-it's a deal! ¿trato hecho?-¡trato hecho!

to be **done for** ■ to have had it estar listo ■ estar fusilado ■ estar apañado ■ estar arreglado ➤ I'm done for! ■ I've had it! ¡Estoy listo! ■ ¡Estoy fusilado! ■ ¡Estoy apañado! ■ ¡Estoy arreglado!

don't argue with me no me lleves la contraria ■ no pretendas llevarme la contraria ■ no pretendas hacerme ver lo que no es ■ no me discutas lo evidente ■ no pretendas discutirme lo evidente

don't ask! ¡ni me preguntes!

don't ask *me*! ¡a mí no me preguntes! ■ no tengo ni idea ■ yo que sé

don't avoid the issue! ■ don't evade the issue! ■ don't change the subject! ¡no evites el asunto! ■ ¡no cambies de tema!

don't be afraid to... *(tú)* no temas... ■ no tengas miedo de... *(usted)* no tema... ■ no tenga miedo de...

don't be alarmed *(tú)* no te alarmes ■ *(usted)* no se alarme (usted)

don't be crass no seas bestia ■ no seas burro ■ no seas cafre

don't be like that no seas así ■ no te pongas así

don't be long! *(tú)* ¡no tardes! ■ ¡no demores! ■ ¡no te tardes! ■ *(usted)* ¡no tarde! ■ ¡no demore! ■ ¡no se tarde (usted)

don't be naïve ■ don't be naive *(tú)* no seas ingenuo ■ *(usted)* no sea (usted) ingenuo

don't be shy! ■ let yourself go! ¡no seas tímido(-a)! ■ ¡qué no te dé vergüenza! ■ ¡no te cortes! ■ ¡no te rajes! ■ ¡no seas corto(-a)! ➤ Don't be shy about asking questions. No se den vergüenza hacer preguntas. ■ No os dé vergüenza hacer preguntas.

don't be silly *(tú)* no seas tonto ■ no te pongas tonto ■ déjate de manías ■ déjate de tonterías ■ *(usted)* no sea (usted) tonto ■ no se ponga (usted) tonto ■ déjese (usted) de manías ■ déjese (usted) de tonterías

don't be so finicky! *(tú)* no te hagas el remilgoso ■ no te remilgues ■ *(usted)* no se haga el remilgoso ■ no se remilgue

don't be so obvious! ¡no seas tan obvio(-a)! ■ ¡disimuladamente! ■ ¡no exageres!

don't be surprised if... *(tú)* (que) no te sorprendas si... ■ (que) no te extrañes si... ■ que no te coja de sorpresa si... ■ *(usted)* (que) no se sorprenda si... ■ (que) no se extrañe si... ■ que no se coja de sorpresa si...

don't be too sure ■ don't be so sure no estés tan seguro(-a) ■ ¡no te creas! ■ ¡no te vayas a creer! ■ nunca digas de esta agua no beberé

don't be unreasonable *(tú)* no seas irrazonable ■ no seas tarado ■ *(usted)* no sea irrazonable

don't believe everything you hear no creas todo lo que se dice

don't bet on it ■ don't count on it ■ don't bank on it no te apuestes por eso ■ no cuentes con ello ■ no cuentes con eso

don't bother *(tú)* no te molestes ■ *(usted)* no se moleste (usted)

don't bother me no me fastidies ■ no me molestes

don't bother to... no te molestes en ■ no se moleste (usted) en...

don't breathe a word of it (to anyone) de esto ni una palabra (a nadie) ■ no se lo digas a nadie

don't chicken out! ■ don't be shy! ■ don't get cold feet! ■ don't be intimidated ¡no te rajes! ■ ¡no te eches atrás! ■ ¡no te amilanes! ■ ¡no te desanimes!

don't count your chickens before they hatch no eches las campanas al vuelo ■ no cantes victoria

don't cut me any slack no respondas y hazlo ■ te he dicho que lo hagas ■ haz lo que te digo y punto ■ haz lo que te he dicho y punto

don't do anything except what I tell you no hagas nada más que lo que yo te diga

don't do as I do, do as I say haz lo que yo diga, no lo que yo haga

don't do it yet *(tú)* no lo hagas aún ■ no lo hagas todavía ■ *(usted)* no lo haga (usted) aún ■ no lo haga (usted) todavía

don't do that *(tú)* no hagas eso ■ *(usted)* no haga eso ■ *(to a child)* eso no se hace

don't do that again no lo vuelvas a hacer ■ no vuelvas a hacerlo

don't evade the issue! ■ don't avoid the issue! ¡no esquives el bulto! ■ ¡no escurras el bulto! ■ ¡no te eches atrás!

don't even ni siquiera ■ ya ni siquiera ➤ I don't even remember. Ya ni siquiera me acuerdo. ■ Ya ni siquiera recuerdo.

don't even think about it! ■ don't even think of it! ¡ni lo pienses! ■ ¡ni siquiera lo pienses!

don't even think such a thing ni siquiera pienses tal cosa ■ ¡que ni se te ocurra tal cosa!

don't ever do that again! ■ never do that again! ¡nunca vuelvas a hacer eso!

don't fail to... no dejes de... ➤ Don't fail to visit the Teatro Colón when you're in Buenos Aires. No dejes de ver el Teatro Colón cuando estés en Buenos Aires.

don't feel that way no te sientas así

don't fight! *(especially to children)* ¡no se peleen! ■ *(Sp.)* ¡no os peleéis!

don't forget! *(tú)* ¡no lo olvides! ■ *(usted)* ¡no lo olvide!

don't forget to... *(tú)* no te olvides (de)... ■ *(usted)* no se olvide (de)... ■ no olvides ➤ Don't forget to turn the lights off before you leave. No te olvides de apagar las luces antes de irte. ➤ Don't forget to call me. No te olvides de llamarme.

don't forget your keys! *(tú)* no te olvides tus llaves ■ *(usted)* no se olvide usted sus llaves

don't get fresh with me! ¡no te pongas chulo conmigo! ■ no seas fresco

don't get gored by a bull! *(advice to a tourist)* ¡que no te pille un toro! ■ *(usted)* ¡que no le pille un toro!

don't get mad no te enojes ■ *(coll.)* no te piques ■ no te cabrees ■ no te mosquees ■ *(Sp.)* no te enfades

don't get me going on that ■ don't get me started on that no me hagas acordar ■ no me des manija

don't get me wrong ■ don't misunderstand me *(tú)* no me entiendas mal ■ no me interpretes mal ■ no me mal interpretes ■ *(usted)* no me entienda mal ■ no me interprete mal ■ no me mal interprete

don't get the idea that... ■ don't you go thinking that... no te vayas a figurar que...

don't get the wrong idea! no te hagas ideas equivocadas ■ no saques conclusiones equivocadas ■ no te pienses lo que no es

don't get up! *(tú)* ¡no te levantes! ■ *(usted)* ¡no se levante (usted)!

don't get upset! ¡no te ofendas! ■ ¡no te molestes!

don't get your hopes up *(tú)* no te hagas ilusiones ■ *(usted)* no se haga ilusiones

don't give in to... *(tú)* no te abandones a... ▪ *(usted)* no se abandone (usted) a...

don't give it a second thought ▪ don't give it another thought no (te) lo pienses dos veces

don't give it a thought 1. you're welcome de nada ▪ no hay de que 2. don't worry about it no te preocupes 3. don't even consider it ni lo consideres ▪ ni lo pienses

don't give it away! *(a secret)* ¡no lo cuentes! ▪ ¡no se lo digas a nadie! ▪ *(thing)* no lo regales

don't give it to anybody ▪ don't give it to anyone no se lo des a nadie ➤ That beauty spot that you have, Cielito Lindo, beside your mouth, don't give it to anyone, because it belongs to me. Ese lunar, que tienes, Cielito Lindo, junto a la boca, no se lo des a nadie, que a mí me toca.

don't give me a bunch of nonsense no me vengas con memeces ▪ no me vengas con sandeces ▪ no me vengas con cuentos

don't give me any lip ▪ don't give me any sass no me repliques ▪ no me respondas

don't give me that! ¡no me vengas con eso! ▪ *(Sp.)* ¡a mí no me la cuelas!

don't give up *(tú)* no te rindas ▪ no te des por vencido ▪ no te desesperes ▪ *(usted)* no se rinda ▪ no se dé por vencido ▪ no se desespere

don't go! 1. don't leave! ¡no te vayas! ▪ ¡no te marches! 2. don't make the trip ▪ don't go to that place ¡no vayas!

don't go away! ¡no te vayas! ▪ ¡no se retire!

don't go looking for trouble no busques camorra

don't go to a lot of trouble ▪ don't knock yourself out ▪ don't go to too much trouble no te mates ▪ no te incomodes ▪ no te preocupes

don't go to any trouble on my account no te tomes molestias por mí ▪ no te molestes por mí

don't go to too much trouble ▪ don't knock yourself out no te mates ▪ no te incomodes

don't go too far! 1. stay nearby! ¡no te vayas muy lejos! 2. don't take liberties! ¡no te pases de largo!

don't hang up *(tú)* no cuelgues ▪ no te retires ▪ *(usted)* no cuelgue ▪ no se retire

don't hesitate to... *(tú)* no dudes en... ▪ *(usted)* no dude (usted) en... ➤ Don't hesitate to call me. *(tú)* No dudes en llamarme. ▪ *(usted)* No dude en llamarme. ➤ Don't hesitate to ask me anything you need to. ▪ Don't hesitate to consult (with) me about anything you need to. No dudes en consultarme lo que te haga falta. ➤ Don't hesitate to stop me if you don't understand something I said. No dudéis en interrumpirme si no entendéis algo (que yo diga).

don't hold your breath! puedes esperar sentado ➤ You want to go out with her? Well, don't hold your breath. ¿Quieres salir con ella? ¡Ja! Puedes esperar sentado.

don't just stand there, do something! ¡no te quedes ahí quieto (como una estatua...)! ▪ ¡no te quedes ahí parado (como una estatua...)! ▪ ¡no te quedes como una estatua...!

don't kid yourself! ¡no te engañes!

don't knock yourself out ▪ don't go to too much trouble no te mates

don't laugh! *(tú)* ¡no te rías! ▪ *(usted)* ¡no se ría (usted)!

don't let him out of your sight no le quites los ojos de encima

don't let him push you around no te dejes avasallar por él

don't let it bother you no permitas que te incomode ▪ no permitas que te moleste ▪ no permitas que te inquiete

don't let it get to you no dejes que te afecte

don't let it go to your head que no se te suba a la cabeza ▪ no dejes que (se) te suba a la cabeza

don't let it happen again que no se vuelva a repetir

don't let that happen to you *(tú)* no dejes que eso te pase ▪ no permitas que eso te suceda (a ti) ▪ *(usted)* no deje que eso le pase ▪ no permita que eso le suceda (a usted)

don't let the bedbugs bite! *(children's "good night!")* ¡que no te piquen los chinches!

don't look! *(tú)* ¡no mires! ▪ *(usted)* ¡no mire (usted)!

don't look at me like that ▪ don't look at me that way no me mires así ▪ no me mires de ese modo

don't look now, but... *(tú)* no mires ahora, pero... ▪ no te des vuelta, pero... ▪ *(usted)* no mire ahora, pero... ▪ no se dé vuelta, pero...

don't make a scene no montes un numerito ▪ no hagas un espectáculo ▪ no me hagas una escena ▪ no me hagas una escenita ▪ no me vengas con ese rollo

don't make an issue (out) of it no insistas

don't make it too tough on me no lo hagas muy difícil para mí ▪ no me pongas muy duro

don't meddle in other people's affairs ▪ don't meddle in other people's business no te metas en los asuntos ajenos ▪ no intervengas en los asuntos de otros

don't mention it! 1. don't bring it up! ¡no lo menciones! ▪ ¡ni lo menciones! 2. you're welcome no hay de qué ▪ de nada ▪ no faltaba más ▪ *(Sp.)* ni más faltaba *("You're welcome" is preferable to "don't mention it.")*

don't mind *me*! *(pedestrian to driver crashing the walk light)* ▪ don't let *me* cramp your style! ¡no te preocupes por mí! ▪ ¡tú dale! ▪ ¡tú sigue!

don't miss it! *(tú)* ¡no te lo pierdas! ▪ ¡no te dejes escapar! ▪ *(usted)* ¡no se lo pierda! ▪ ¡no le deje escapar!

don't move! *(tú)* ¡no te muevas! ▪ *(usted)* ¡no se mueva! ▪ ¡todos quietos! ▪ ¡que no se mueva nadie! ➤ "Don't move!" said the bank robber. "No se muevan", dijo el ladrón. ▪ "Todos quietos", dijo el ladrón. ▪ "Que no se mueva nadie", dijo el ladrón.

don't overdo it! ▪ don't go overboard! ¡no te pases! ▪ ¡tampoco te pases!

don't overdo it on... ¡no te pases con...! ➤ Don't overdo it on the garlic. ¡No te pases con el ajo!

don't overstep your bounds! ▪ don't get out of bounds! ¡no te pases (ni un pelo)! ▪ ¡quédate en tu sitio!

don't panic! ¡que no te entre el pánico!

don't patronize me no te pongas paternalista

don't say a word! ¡ni una palabra!

don't say a word about it (to anyone)! ▪ don't say a word about this (to anyone) de esto, ¡ni una palabra (a nadie)!

don't scare me like that 1. *(by an action)* no me des esos sustos 2. *(by telling something)* no me asustes ▪ no me espantes

don't settle for less *(tú)* no te conformes con menos ▪ *(usted)* no se conforme con menos

don't start that again! ¡no empecemos de nuevo!

don't sweat the small stuff no te preocupes por los detalles ▪ no te compliques la existencia con los detalles

don't take it out on me! ¡no te ensañes conmigo! ▪ ¡no la tomes conmigo!

don't take it personally no te lo tomes personalmente ▪ no te lo tomes como algo personal ▪ no te lo tomes a pecho ▪ no te pongas así

don't take it seriously no te lo tomes en serio ▪ no te lo tomes seriamente

don't take it that way *(tú)* no lo tomes así ▪ *(usted)* no lo tome (usted) así

don't take *no* for an answer no admitas un *no* por respuesta

don't take things too far! ▪ don't go too far! ¡no lleves las cosas demasiado lejos!

don't talk back to me no me repliques ▪ *(Mex., coll.)* no me resongues

don't tell *(tú)* no lo cuentes ▪ no te chives ▪ no digas nada ▪ *(usted)* no lo cuente ▪ no se chive ▪ no diga nada ➤ Don't tell, okay? No lo cuentes, ¿vale? ▪ No te chives, ¿vale? ▪ No digas nada, ¿vale? ➤ Don't tell my mom, okay? No se lo cuentes a mi madre, ¿vale? ▪ No te chives a mi madre, ¿vale?

don't tell me (that)... *(tú)* no me digas que... ▪ *(usted)* no me diga (usted) que...

don't think about it *(tú)* no pienses en ello ▪ *(usted)* no piense (usted) en ello

don't wash your dirty linen in public los trapos sucios se lavan en casa

don't work too hard! ¡que te sea leve! ▪ no trabajes mucho ▪ no trabajes arduamente

don't worry no te preocupes ▪ tranquilo ▪ pierde cuidado

don't worry about it ▪ don't worry no te preocupes ▪ no te comas el coco ▪ pierde cuidado

don't you believe it! ¡no te lo creas!

don't you get it? ▪ don't you catch on? ¿no lo entiendes? ▪ *(Sp.)* ¿no caes? ▪ ¿no lo coges? ▪ ¿no lo pillas?
don't you go gettin' any big ideas *(coll.)* no te des tantos humos ▪ no te des tantos aires
don't you think? ¿no es cierto?
don't you think it would be better to...? ▪ wouldn't it be better to...? ¿no crees que sería mejor...?
don't you want to? ¿no quieres?
to be **doomed from the start** estar destinado al fracaso desde un principio
to be **doomed to failure** estar destinado al fracaso
doomsday cult secta del último día ▪ secta del juicio final ▪ secta del fin del mundo ▪ secta apocalíptica
door between ▪ door leading from puerta que comunica con ➤ The door between the kitchen and the dining room ▪ The door leading from the kitchen to the dining room La puerta que comunica la cocina con el comedor
door handle *el* picaporte
door jamb jamba de (la) puerta
door leading from ▪ door between puerta que comunica con ➤ The door leading from the library into the garden La puerta que comunica la biblioteca con el jardín
door leads to puerta conduce a ▪ puerta lleva a
door-to-door salesman vendedor ambulante
door to the patio ▪ patio door puerta del patio ▪ puerta que da al patio
doorknob pomo de la puerta
doors down: to live *x* ~ *(street or hall)* vivir *x* puertas más abajo ➤ He lives two doors down. Vive dos puertas más abajo.
doors up: to live *x* ~ vivir *x* puertas más arriba ➤ She lives three doors up (the street). Vive tres puertas más arriba...
dormer (window) buhardilla ▪ lucerna
to **dot all the i's and cross all the t's** poner los puntos sobre las íes
dot dot dot puntos suspensivos
to **dot the landscape** salpicar el paisaje ➤ Houses dotted the rural landscape. Las casas salpicaban el paisaje.
dotted line: to cut along the ~ cortar por la línea de puntos
dotted line: to fold along the ~ doblar por la línea de puntos
dotted line: to tear along the ~ rasgar por la línea de puntos
double-barrel shotgun escopeta de dos cañones
double bed cama de matrimonio ▪ cama matrimonial ▪ cama doble
double boiler ▪ bain marie baño María
to **double check** revisar
double chin *el* doble mentón ▪ dos papadas ▪ papada doble
to **double click on the mouse** hacer doble clic en el ratón ▪ hacer doble clic en el mouse
double decker bus autobús de dos pisos
double decker hamburger hamburguesa de dos pisos ▪ hamburguesa doble
double-digit inflation ▪ inflation of ten percent or higher *la* inflación de o superior al diez por ciento
double-edged sword arma de doble filo
double feature dos (películas) seguidas ▪ programa doble
to be **double first cousins** *(children of brothers whose wives are sisters)* dos veces primos
double-glazed window ventana de doble cristal
double helix *la* doble hélice ➤ The DNA molecule has a double helix structure. La molécula de AND tiene estructura de doble hélice.
to **double in cost** duplicarse ➤ My food costs have doubled since our new apartment mate moved in. Se han duplicado mis gastos de comida desde que nuestro nuevo compañero de piso se mudó con nosotros.
to **double in height** duplicarse en altura ➤ The trees on Sor Ángela have doubled in height in six years. Los árboles en Sor Ángela se han duplicado en altura en seis años.
double meaning doble significado ▪ doble sentido
double or nothing: to go ~ ir a doble o nada
to **double over (with pain)** doblarse (de dolor) ➤ He doubled over with pain during his attack of kidney stones. Se doblaba (de dolor) cuando le dio el cólico nefrítico. ➤ I had a severe case of stomach cramps that doubled me over. I couldn't even stand up straight. Tuve un caso grave de calambres estomacales que me doblaba de dolor. No podía ni ponerme derecho.
to **double park** estacionar en doble fila ▪ *(Sp.)* aparcar en doble fila
to be **double parked** tener el coche en doble fila
double space doble espacio ▪ el renglón doble
to be **double spaced** ser redactado a doble espacio ➤ The document is double spaced. El documento ha sido redactado a doble espacio.
double spacing espacio doble
double standard *el* doble moral
double take: to do a ~ tardar en reaccionar
to **double the cost of...** doblar el costo de... ▪ duplicar el costo de...
to **double the time it takes to...** doblar el tiempo que lleva hacer... ▪ duplicar el tiempo que lleva hacer...
to **double up** ▪ to squeeze in together ▪ *(coll.)* to scrunch up apretujarse ➤ If we double up, we can all fit. ▪ If we squeeze in together, we can all fit. ▪ If we scrunch up, we can all fit. Si nos apretujamos (un poco), cabremos todos.
to be a **double whammy** llevarse dos palos ➤ Coming to class late and without your book is kind of a double whammy. Llegar tarde a clase y sin libro es como llevarse dos palos.
doubt about whether (or not): to cast ~ ▪ to cause doubt about whether (or not) sembrar duda de si
doubts about dudas sobre ➤ Doubts about the fate of the crew. Dudas sobre la suerte de la tripulación.
doubt(s) about whether duda(s) de si ▪ duda(s) sobre si
to **dovetail with something** encajar con algo ➤ The course in twentieth-century theatre dovetails nicely with my interest in the contemporary spoken language. Su interés por el teatro del siglo XX encaja bien con mi interés por el lenguaje oral contemporario.
dowdy clothes ropa desaliñada ▪ ropa sin gracia
dowdy woman desaliñada
to be **down 1.** to be out of service no estar en servicio ▪ no estar en función ▪ estar bloqueado ▪ *(Sp.)* haber una incidencia **2.** to be sad estar triste ▪ *(Sp.)* estar abatido(-a) ▪ estar bajeras ▪ *(Mex.)* estar agüitado(-a) ➤ The computers are down. Las computadoras están bloqueadas. ▪ Los ordenadores tienen una incidencia. ➤ The dog is always a little bit down until the children get home from school. El perro siempre está un poco triste hasta que los niños vuelven del colegio.
to be **down (in the dumps)** estar depre ▪ tener la depre ▪ estar bajo (de ánimo) ▪ *(Sp., coll.)* estar chungo ▪ estar bajeras
to be **down on one's luck** ▪ to be going through a difficult time tener mala racha
to be **down on someone** ▪ to be on someone's case tomarle manía a alguien ▪ tenerle idea a alguien
down pat: to have (got) something ~ saberse algo al dedillo ▪ saberse algo al pelo ➤ He has quadratic equations down pat. ▪ He's got quadratic equations down pat. Se sabe las ecuaciones cuadráticas al dedillo. ▪ Se sabe las ecuaciones cuadráticas al pelo.
down payment dinero por adelantado ▪ *el* enganche ▪ *(Sp.)* entrada
down river río abajo
down the street calle abajo
down the road 1. farther along the road camino adelante **2.** from now ▪ in the future en el futuro
down there ahí abajo ▪ allí abajo
down to hasta ➤ From the vantage point of the Pole Star, theoretically, we could correlate the Earth's orbital position with the seasons, down to the months and even days of the year. Desde la atalaya de la estrella polar, teóricamente, podríamos correlacionar la posición orbital de la Tierra con las estaciones, hasta los meses e incluso los días del año.
to be **down to earth** ▪ to be approachable ser macanudo(-a) ▪ ser asequible ▪ ser simpático(-a)
down to the last detail con todo lujo de detalle
to be **down to the last week** estar en la última semana ➤ I'm down to the last week. Estoy en la última semana.

to be **down to the nitty-gritty** estar con lo más duro (de la tarea) ➤ We're down to the nitty-gritty. Estamos con lo más duro (de la tarea).

down with...! ¡abajo...!

downed tree trunk ▪ fallen tree trunk tronco caído

to **download a file** descargar un archivo ➤ I downloaded the file from the Internet. Descarqué el archivo de Internet.

to **downplay a threat** ▪ to play down a threat restarle importancia a una amenaza ▪ quitarle hierro a una amenaza ➤ Some people downplay the terrorist threat. Algunas personas le restan importancia a la amenaza terrorista.

to **downplay the importance of a matter** ▪ to play down the importance of a matter restarle importancia a un asunto ▪ *(coll.)* quitarle paja a un asunto

to be **downright abnormal** ser completamente fuera de lo normal ▪ ser completamente anormal

to be **downright absurd** ser completamente absurdo

to be **downright mean** ser realmente desagradable ▪ ser realmente antipático ▪ ser de lo más antipático

to be **downright ridiculous** ser completamente ridículo

to be **downright scary** ser aterrador

to be **downright strange** ser realmente extraño ▪ ser categóricamente extraño ➤ The fiberoptic probe that the doctor put way up into my nose felt downright strange. La prueba de fibra óptica que el médico me puso muy profunda en la nariz que me hizo sentir realmente extraño.

downwind leg *(aviation)* tramo a favor de viento ▪ tramo de viento en cola ➤ The landing sequence consists of the downwind leg, base leg, and final approach. La secuencia de aterrizaje incluye el tramo a favor de viento, el tramo de base y el acercamiento final.

to **doze off** echar una cabezada ▪ dar una cabezada ▪ quedarse traspuesto ➤ Try to keep from dozing off after dinner. Intenta no echar una cabezada después de comer. ▪ Intenta no dar una cabezada después de comer.

a **dozen roses** una docena de rosas

dozens of docenas de

to **draft a customer's bank account** ▪ to withdraw money from a customer's bank account cobrarle un pago directo (de la cuenta corriente) ▪ *(Sp.)* cobrarle el pago domiciliado ➤ The telephone company, utility companies, and my medical insurance provider all draft my bank account each month. La compañía de teléfono, las utilidades y mi proveedor de seguro médico todos me cobran pagos domiciliados.

to **draft a letter** redactar una carta ▪ hacer el borrador de una carta

draft dodger ▪ draft evader evasor(-a) del servicio militar

draft of a letter *el* borrador de una carta

draft of a paper *el* borrador de un ensayo ▪ *(Sp.)* borrador de un trabajo

draft of a bank account *(made by a customer-approved third party)* ▪ bank account draft pago domiciliado

draft or bottled? ¿sifón o de botella? ▪ *(Sp.)* ¿caña o botellín? ▪ ¿de barril o de botella?

draft resolution proyecto de resolución

to **drag and drop** *(computers)* arrastrar y soltar

to **drag (from weariness)** arrastrarse (de cansancio) ➤ She's dragging a little. Se arrastra (de cansancio) un poco.

to **drag information out of someone** sacarle información a alguien con un tirabuzón ▪ sacarle información a alguien con un sacacorchos

to **drag on too long** alargarse ▪ hacerse pesado ➤ The meeting dragged on too long. La reunión se alargó demasiado.

to **drag one's feet 1.** to shuffle one's feet arrastrar los pies ▪ lerdear ▪ lerdearse ▪ andar a rastras **2.** to act slowly and reluctantly hacer algo desganado ▪ hacer algo de mala gana ➤ He drags his feet (when he walks). Anda a rastras.

to **drag someone by the heels** arrastrar a alguien (cogido) por los pelos ▪ arrastrar a alguien (cogido) de los pelos ▪ llevar a alguien a rastras ➤ We practically had to drag my aunt by the heels to get her to go to the doctor. Prácticamente tuvimos que arrastrar a mi tía de los pelos para hacer que vaya al médico. ▪ Prácticamente tuvimos que arrastrar a mi tía por los pelos para hacer que vaya al médico. ▪ Practicamente tuvimos que llevar a mi tía a rastras para hacer que vaya al médico.

to **drag someone to something** arrastrar a alguien a algo ▪ llevar a alguien a rastras a algo ➤ I had to drag my husband to my mother's birthday party. Tuve que arrastrar a mi marido a la fiesta de cumpleaños de mi madre. ▪ Tuve que llevar a mi marido a rastras a la fiesta de cumpleaños de mi madre.

to **drag something across the floor** arrastrar algo por el suelo ➤ Would you help me move this table? I don't want to drag it across the floor. ¿Me ayudarías a mover esta mesa? No quiero arrastrarla por el suelo.

to **drag the icon (over) to where it says...** desplazar el icono a dónde dice... ▪ arrastrar el icono a dónde dice...

dragged into the conflict: to get ~ *(coll.)* ▪ to get drawn into the conflict verse arrastrado al conflicto ➤ Some of the neighboring countries got dragged into the conflict. ▪ Some of the neighboring countries got drawn into the conflict. Algunos países vecinos se vieron arrastrados al conflicto.

to **drain off the liquid** ▪ to drain the liquid off escurrir el líquido ➤ After pureeing the pepper and onion, drain off the excess liquid. Después de hacer puré del pimiento y la cebolla escurra el exceso de líquido.

to be a **drain on one's resources** ser un desgaste de los recursos de uno ▪ ser una sangría de los recursos de uno

dramatic effect on: to have a ~ tener un efecto fulgurante en ➤ Exercise has a dramatic effect on my alertness. Exercise tiene un efecto fulgurante en mi sentido de la atención.

drastic measures: to adopt ~ ▪ to put into effect drastic measures ▪ to put drastic measures into effect tomar medida drástica ▪ tomar acción de consecuencia grave

drastic steps: to take ~ tomar medidas drásticas

to **draw a blank** quedarse en blanco ▪ *(Mex.)* írsele la onda a alguien ➤ I drew a blank. ▪ My mind went blank. Me quedé en blanco. ▪ Se me fue la onda.

to **draw a bow (string)** ▪ to draw back a bow (string) tensar un arco ➤ Robin Hood placed an arrow on the string and drew back the bow. Robin Hood colocó una flecha en la cuerda y tensó el arco.

to **draw a card (from a deck)** robar una carta (de una baraja) ▪ robar un naipe (de una baraja)

to **draw a card from the deck** *(on the table after the cards have been dealt)* tomar una carta (de la baraja) ▪ sacar una carta (de la baraja) ▪ *(Sp.)* coger una carta (de la baraja) ➤ I drew an ace to your jack, so I win. Tomé un as y tú tomaste una sota, así que gano yo.

to **draw a conclusion** sacar una conclusión ▪ llegar a una conclusión

to **draw a crowd** atraer una multitud ➤ The dinosaur movie drew a bigger crowd. La película sobre los dinosaurios atrajo una mayor multitud. ➤ The antique motorcycle display was drawing an appreciative crowd. La muestra de motos antiguas atrajo a una considerada multitud. ▪ La muestra de motos antiguas atrajo a una multitud interesada.

to **draw a dagger** ▪ to pull a dagger sacar una daga ▪ sacar un puñal ➤ He drew his dagger. ▪ He pulled his dagger. Sacó su puñal.

to **draw a line through a word** tachar una palabra ➤ The editor drew a line through the word. El editor tachó la palabra.

to **draw a parallel between two things** trazar un paralelo entre dos cosas

to **draw a parallel with** trazar un paralelo con

to **draw a picture 1.** *(of an object or scene)* hacer un dibujo **2.** *(of a person)* hacer un retrato ▪ dibujarle a alguien ➤ Draw me a picture of my girlfriend. Me dibujas a mi novia. ➤ She drew me a picture of her cat. Me hizo un dibujo de su gato.

to **draw a pistol (from a holster)** desenfundar una pistola ▪ sacar una pistola

to **draw a sword** desenvainar una espada ▪ sacar una espada

to **draw attention to** ▪ to attract attention to llamar la atención a ▪ atraer la atención a

to **draw back the curtains** ▪ to open the curtains abrir las cortinas

to **draw blood** *(to get a blood sample for medical purposes)* sacar sangre to **draw in one's head** **1.** *(turtle)* esconder la cabeza **2.** *(after leaning out the window)* retirar la cabeza ➤ The turtle drew in its head and feet. La tortuga escondió la cabeza y las patas. ➤ *(from Clement Clark Moore's "Night Before Christmas")* As I drew in my head and was turning around, down the chimney St. Nicholas came with a bound. Conforme retiré la cabeza y me daba la vuelta, Papá Noel bajó por la chimenea con un salto.

to **draw (in) people** ▪ to draw people in (close around one) ▪ to draw people close to one atraer a la gente hacia ➤ The charismatic leader drew in the crowd around him. ▪ The charismatic leader drew the crowd in around him. El líder carismático atrajo hacia él a la multitud.

to **draw into oneself** encerrarse en uno mismo

to **draw lots** echarlo a suertes

to **draw parallels between** trazar paralelos entre

to **draw parallels with** trazar paralelos con

to **draw someone out** hacer que alguien se suelte a hablar ▪ *(Sp., leísmo)* tirarle a alguien de la lengua ▪ soltarle la lengua a alguien

to **draw the conclusion that...** ▪ to come to the conclusion that... ▪ to arrive at the conclusion that... sacar la conclusión de que... ▪ llegar a la conclusión de que...

to **draw the curtains** **1.** *(either direction)* correr las cortinas **2.** to close the curtains cerrar las cortinas **3.** to open the curtains ▪ to draw back the curtains abrir las cortinas

to **draw the eye** ▪ to attract the eye ▪ to appeal to the eye atraer la mirada ➤ The painting drew my eye. La pintura atrajo mi mirada.

to **draw to a close** ▪ to come to an end acercarse a su fin ▪ acercarse al final ➤ As the year draws to a close, I have begun to think about my plans and resolutions for the new year. Conforme el año se acerca a su fin ▪ Conforme el año se acerca al final, he empezado a pensar en mis planes y propósitos para el año nuevo.

to **draw together diverse groups** ▪ to bring together diverse groups aglutinar diversos grupos

to **draw the line** **1.** *(literal)* trazar la línea **2.** *(figurative)* set the limits fijar los límites ➤ Where do you draw the line? ▪ Where does one draw the line? ¿Dónde se fijan los límites? ▪ ¿Dónde se fija uno los límites? ➤ Where do you (personally) draw the line? ¿Dónde te fijas los límites?

to **draw up a chair** ▪ to pull up a chair acercar una silla ▪ jalarse una silla ➤ Draw up a chair! ▪ Pull up a chair! ¡Acerca una silla! ▪ ¡Jálate una silla!

to **draw up a list** ▪ to make up a list ▪ to make a list confeccionar una lista

to **draw up an agreement** redactar un acuerdo

to **draw up the papers** ▪ to draw up the documents redactar los papeles ▪ redactar los documentos ➤ I'll have our lawyer draw up the papers. Haré que nuestro abogado redacte los papeles. ➤ She's hired a lawyer to draw up the divorce papers. (Ella) ha contratado a un abogado para redactar los papeles de divorcio.

to **draw water** sacar agua

drawbridge puente levadizo

drawing board tablero de diseño ▪ tabla de dibujo ▪ mesa de dibujo ➤ The Pentagon has two new aircraft on the drawing board. El Pentágono tiene dos nuevas naves sobre el tablero de diseño.

to **dread having to...** darle pavor a uno tener que... ▪ darle miedo a uno tener que...

to **dread (the thought of) having to...** echarse a temblar cada vez que uno piensa que... ▪ darle pavor a uno al pensar que... ➤ When our grandparents were children, they dreaded having to go to the dentist. Cuando nuestros abuelos eran niños, se echaban a temblar de pensar que tenían que ir al dentista.

dreadlocks rastas ▪ trencitas

to **dream about someone** ▪ to have a dream about someone soñar con alguien

to be a **dream come true (for someone)** ser (para alguien) un sueño hecho una realidad ▪ ser (para alguien) un sueño realizado

dream date cita de ensueño ▪ cita de mis sueños

dream house casa de ensueño

dream on! ▪ fat chance! ¡ni lo sueñes!

dream symbolism ▪ symbolism in dreams simbología onírica ▪ simbología de los sueños

to **dream that...** soñar que...

dreary weather ▪ lousy weather tiempo desapacible ▪ tiempo deprimente ▪ *(informal)* tiempo de perros

dregs of society escoria de la sociedad

to be **drenched in sweat** estar empapado en sudor

drenched in the rain: to get ~ empaparse en la lluvia ▪ ponerse hecho(-a) una sopa en la lluvia

to **dress a salad** ▪ to put dressing on a salad ▪ to put oil and vinegar on a salad aliñar una ensalada ▪ arreglar una ensalada ➤ Does the salad already have dressing on it? ¿Está arreglada la ensalada? ▪ ¿Está aliñada la ensalada?

dress code código de vestimenta

to **dress for the occasion** vestirse para la ocasión ➤ I can see you're dressed for the occasion! Ya veo que te has vestido para la ocasión.

to **dress in one's Sunday best** llevar ropa de domingo ▪ irse bien vestido

to **dress poorly** ir mal vestido ▪ andar hecho un pingo ➤ He dresses poorly. Va mal vestido. ▪ Anda hecho un pingo.

dress rehearsal ensayo general ➤ The dress rehearsal was rocky, but the opening night came off without a hitch. El ensayo general resultó flojo, pero la noche del estreno salió sin ningún contratiempo.

to **dress (up)** *(for an occasion)* arreglarse ▪ vestirse (de forma) elegante

to **dress up as** vestirse de ▪ disfrazarse de ➤ What are you going to dress up as on Halloween? ¿De qué te vas a vestir en Halloween? ▪ ¿De qué vas a vestirte en Halloween? ▪ ¿De qué te vas a disfrazar en Halloween? ▪ ¿De qué vas a disfrazarte en Halloween? ➤ I'm going to dress up as a clown. Voy a disfrazarme de payaso.

to be **dressed in (a) uniform** ▪ to be wearing a uniform ir de uniforme ➤ He was dressed in uniform. ▪ He was wearing a uniform. Iba de uniforme.

to be **dressed in black** ▪ to be wearing black estar vestido de negro

to be **dressed in civilian clothes** ▪ to be wearing civilian clothes estar vestido de civil ▪ vestirse de civil ▪ ir (vestido) de civil ▪ andar vestido de civil ➤ He was dressed in civilian clothes. ▪ He was wearing civilian clothes. Estaba vestido de civil.

to be **dressed in formal attire** estar (vestido) de etiqueta

to be **dressed to kill** ▪ to be dressed to the nines estar (vestido) de tiros largos

to be **dressed to the nines** ▪ to be all gussied up estar vestido(-a) de punta en blanco ▪ *(Sp.)* estar hecho(-a) un brazo de mar ▪ ir hecho(-a) un brazo de mar ▪ estar vestido(-a) de lujo

dressing down: to give someone a ~ ▪ to chew someone out echar una bronca a alguien ▪ *(Sp.)* echar un rapapolvo a alguien ➤ The drill sergeant dressed down the new recruit. El sargento instructor echó un rapapolvo al cadete nuevo. ▪ El sargento instructor echó una bronca al cadete nuevo.

dressing room vestuario ▪ *(in a clothing store) el* probador

to **drill holes** hacer huecos ▪ hacer hoyas

drill sergeant sargento instructor

to **drink from the bottle** beber de la botella ▪ beber a morro

to **drink it down in one gulp** tomárselo de un tirón ▪ tomárselo de un trago

to **drink like a fish** beber como una esponja

to **drink to one's health** beber por la salud de alguien

to **drink too much** abusar de la bebida ▪ beber demasiado

drinking fountain ▪ water fountain la fuente de beber ▪ fuentesilla

(drinking) straw *(Mex.) el* popote ▪ *(Sp.) el* sorbete ▪ pajita ▪ caña

drinking water *el* agua potable

to **drive a car** conducir un carro ▪ manejar un carro ▪ *(Sp.)* conducir un coche ▪ dirigir un coche ▪ guiar un coche to **drive a certain make of car** pasearse con un coche ▪ pasearse en un coche ➤ She drives a Lincoln. Se pasea con un Lincoln. ▪ Se pasea en un Lincoln.

to **drive away** alejarse en coche ▪ salir manejando

to **drive away business** ▪ to drive away the clientele alejar el comercio ▪ desalentar el comercio ▪ alejar la clientela ▪ desalentar a la clientela

to **drive by** ▪ to go by in the car pasar con el carro ▪ *(Sp.)* pasar con el coche

to **drive dangerously** ▪ to drive recklessly ▪ to drive unsafely conducir peligrosamente ▪ manejar peligrosamente ▪ ir haciendo el loco ▪ *(motorcyclists)* ir haciendo el cabra

to **drive down to** *(downhill or south)* conducir a ▪ conducir hasta ▪ bajarse a ▪ bajarse hasta ➤ We drove down to Málaga on the south coast of Spain. Condujimos a Málaga en la costa sur de España.

to **drive home the (main) point** remachar el clavo

to **drive in the snow** conducir en la nieve ➤ The snow is beautiful, but I don't like to drive in it. La nieve es hermosa, pero no me gusta conducir en ella.

to **drive on the left** conducir por la izquierda ➤ In Great Britain you drive on the left. En Gran Bretaña se conduce por la izquierda.

to **drive one crazy** volverle loco ▪ chiflarle ➤ It drives me crazy. Me vuelve loco. ▪ Me chifla.

to **drive one up the wall** hacer a uno subirse por las paredes

to **drive out the invaders from a country** ▪ to drive the invaders out of a country echar a los invasores de un país ▪ expulsar los invasores de un país

to **drive over to** *(east, west, or across a mountain)* conducir a través de ▪ conducir hasta ➤ We drove over the mountains from Madrid to Segovia. Condujimos a través de la montaña desde Madrid hasta Segovia.

to **drive recklessly** conducir imprudentemente ▪ conducir de forma temeraria

to **drive someone crazy** volver loco a alguien

to **drive someone to do something** impulsar a alguien a hacer algo ➤ The only hypothesis being considered regarding the reasons that could drive them to commit the crime... La única hipótesis que se baraja sobre las razones que pudieron impulsarlos a cometer el crimen...

to **drive someone up the wall** sacarle a alguien de sus casillas ▪ sacar a alguien de quicio

drive-through window *(virtually unknown in Hispanic countries)* ventanilla de atención al público desde el coche

to **drive to work** conducir al trabajo

to **drive up alongside of** ▪ to drive up next to conducir a continuación a ▪ conducir al lado de

to **drive up next to** ▪ to drive up alongside of conducir a continuación a ▪ conducir al lado de ➤ They drove up next to him. Condujeron a continuación a él.

to **drive up to** conducir a ➤ We drove up to Valladolid. Condujimos a Valladolid. ▪ Condujimos hasta Valladolid. ▪ (Nos) subimos a Valladolid. ➤ We drove up to the Pyrenees. Condujimos a los Pirineos. ▪ Condujimos hasta los Pirineos. ➤ We drove up to the Pyrenees from Madrid. Condujimos de Madrid a los Pirineos. ▪ Condujimos desde Madrid hasta los Pirineos.

driver's license: to get one's ~ obtener su licencia de conducir ▪ *(Sp.)* obtener su permiso de conducción ▪ obtener su permiso de conducir ▪ carné (de conducir)

driver's license manual código de circulación

Driving Miss Daisy *(film title)* *Paseando a Miss Daisy*

to **drizzle lightly** chispear

droit du seigneur *(the alleged right of a feudal lord to have sex with the bride of a vassal on her wedding night)* derecho de pernada

to **drop a bomb** dejar caer una bomba

to **drop a case** desistir (el juicio) ➤ Once filed, the lawsuit must be heard unless the plaintiff drops it. Una vez admitido a trámite, el juicio debe ser celebrado a menos que el demandante (lo) desista.

to **drop a course** dejar una clase ▪ abandonar una clase ▪ *(Sp.)* cargar una clase

to **drop a hint** soltar una indirecta ▪ lanzar una indirecta ▪ echar una indirecta

to **drop anchor** ▪ to cast the anchor(s) echar el ancla ▪ echar (las) anclas

to **drop below** ▪ to fall below situarse debajo de ➤ *(news item)* Male unemployment in Spain drops below ten percent for the first time in twenty years. El paro masculino se sitúa debajo del diez por ciento en España por primera vez en veinte años.

to **drop by** ▪ to drop in ▪ to stop by **1.** *(from the point of view of the visitor)* pasar ▪ visitar **2.** *(from the point of view of the person being visited)* caer(le) ➤ I was in the neighborhood and thought I'd drop by. Yo estaba en la vecindad y decidí pasar por tu casa. ➤ Guess who dropped by today? ¿Adivina quién cayó hoy?

drop ceiling techo falso

to **drop dead** caerse muerto ▪ quedarse en el acto

drop dead! ¡muérete! ▪ ¡muérase!

to **drop everything** soltarlo todo

to **drop everything and** dejar todo y ➤ I dropped everything and went straight to the hospital. Dejé todo y me lancé al hospital.

to **drop from exhaustion** caer rendido ▪ caer exhausto

drop in interest rates bajada de los tipos de interés ▪ baja en la tasa de interés

drop in oil prices descenso del precio de petróleo ▪ caída del precio de petróleo

to **drop in on someone by surprise** caerle a alguien de sorpresa

drop in temperature descenso de la temperatura ➤ A slight drop in temperatures. Un ligero descenso de las temperaturas

drop in unemployment ▪ decrease in unemployment baja en el desempleo ▪ bajada en el desempleo ▪ *la* reducción en el desempleo ▪ *la* disminución del paro ▪ reducción del paro ▪ disminución en el paro

to **drop like flies** caer como chinches ▪ morir como chinches ▪ caer como moscas ▪ morir como moscas

to **drop out of (high) school** *(L. Am.)* abandonar la secundaria ▪ *(Sp.)* abandonar el instituto

to **drop out of the university** ▪ to drop out of school abandonar la universidad

to **drop sharply** ▪ to nose-dive ▪ to plunge caer en picado ➤ The president has dropped sharply in the polls. El presidente ha caído en picado en los índices.

to **drop someone off** ▪ to let someone off dejarle a alguien ➤ She dropped me off at the airport. Me dejó en el aeropuerto. ➤ *(to a taxi driver)* Drop us off at Sanborns. Nos deja en Sanborns.

to **drop something 1.** *(by accident)* to fall out of one's hand(s) caérsele de las manos **2.** *(on purpose)* to let something drop ▪ to let something fall dejar caer ➤ Oops, I dropped it! ▪ Oops, it fell out of my hand! ¡Ay, se me cayó! ▪ ¡Ay, se me cayó de las manos! ➤ Galileo dropped weights from the Leaning Tower of Pisa. Galileo dejó caer pesos desde la torre inclinada de Pisa.

to **drop the case** dejar el juicio ▪ desistir el juicio

to **drop the charges** anular los cargos ▪ dejar los cargos

drop the gun! ▪ drop your gun! ¡baje el arma! ▪ ¡baje la pistola! ▪ ¡suelte el arma! ▪ ¡suelte la pistola!

to **drop the subject** dejar de hablar del asunto ▪ dejar de hablar del tema

to **drown out the sound** ahogar el sonido ➤ The organ on the final verse needs to be loud without drowning out the choir. El órgano en la estrofa final necesita estar fuerte sin ahogar al coro. ➤ The sound of the helicopter drowned out the TV. El ruido del helicóptero ahogó el sonido de la televisión.

drug addiction ▪ addiction to drugs adicción a las drogas

drug dealer *el, la* narcotraficante ▪ *el, la* traficante de drogas ▪ *(Sp., slang) el, la* camello

drumming of (the) rain on the roof ▪ beating of (the) rain on the roof ▪ rain beating on the roof tamborileo de la lluvia sobre el tejado ▪ tamborileo de la lluvia contra el tejado ▪ golpeteo de la lluvia en el tejado

drunk driver ▪ intoxicated driver conductor(-a) ebrio(-a) ▪ borracho(-a) al volante

dry cleaning 1. *(process)* lavado en seco **2.** *(cleaned articles)* ropa de la tintorería ➤ How does dry cleaning work? ¿Cómo funciona el lavado en seco? ➤ I have to go pick up my dry cleaning. Tengo que ir a recoger mi ropa de la tintorería.

dry land ▪ terra firma tierra firme

dry riverbed cauce seco

dry sherry *(wine)* fino ▪ jerez seco ▪ *(whose grapes come from the Montilla area of Andalucía)* amontillado seco

dry subject tema seco ▪ tema aburrido

drying time tiempo de secado

dual controls: to have ~ tener doble mando

dual failure doble falla ▪ *(Sp.)* doble fallo

to **dub someone a knight** ▪ to knight someone armar a alguien caballero

dubious honor of being: to have the ~ tener el dudoso honor de ser ▪ caberle el dudoso honor de ser

duck! ▪ get down! *(tú)* agáchate ▪ *(usted)* agáchese ▪ *(ustedes)* agáchense ▪ *(Sp., vosotros)* agachaos

to be **duck soup** ser pan comido

duct tape cinta aislante ▪ *(Mex.)* cinta adhesiva plateada (de sellado)

to be **due on a certain date 1.** *(payment)* vencerse **2.** *(homework)* ser para ▪ haber que entregar **3.** *(baby)* tener fecha para ▪ salir (la madre) de cuentas ➤ The payment is due on the fifteenth. El pago se vence el día quince. ➤ When is the paper due? ¿Para cuándo es el trabajo? ▪ ¿Cuándo hay que entregar el trabajo? ➤ Our baby is due tomorrow. ▪ My wife is due to deliver tomorrow. Mi esposa sale de cuentas mañana.

due date (fecha de) vencimiento ▪ fecha de límite ▪ fecha tope ▪ plazo

due north directamente al norte ▪ justo hacia el norte ▪ derecho al norte ▪ recto al norte ➤ Pittsburgh, Pennsylvania is due north of Roanoke, Virginia. Pittsburgh, Pensilvania está justo hacia el norte de Roanoke, Virginia.

due process procedimiento debido

due to 1. scheduled to programado para ▪ fijado para ▪ previsto para **2.** because of ▪ owing to debido a ▪ por *("Due to" is hackneyed when it means "because of.")* ➤ The plane is due to arrive at 5 p.m. ▪ The plane is scheduled to arrive at 5 p.m. El avión está programado para llegar a las cinco de la tarde. ➤ We arrived late due to a headwind. ▪ We arrived late because of a headwind. Llegamos tarde debido a un viento de proa.

due to bad weather ▪ because of bad weather debido al mal tiempo

to be **due to have one's baby** ▪ to be due to deliver salir de cuenta ➤ She's due to have her baby on the thirtieth. Ella sale de cuenta el treinta.

due to the fact that... *(hackneyed phrase)* ▪ because of ▪ as a result of por el hecho de que ▪ por lo que ▪ por lo de

dug-up earth tierra removida

dull person persona aburrida ▪ persona anodina

to be **dumb as a post** ser tonto de capirote ▪ ser más burro que el burro ▪ ser más tonto que Abundio ▪ no saber hacer la "o" con un canuto

to be **dumbfounded at** quedarse estupefacto ante ▪ estar estupefacto ante ▪ quedarse atónito ante ▪ estar atónito ante ▪ quedarse con la boca abierta ➤ You must be dumbfounded at what I did. Te habrás quedado estupefacto ante lo que hice. ▪ *(L. Am.)* Has de estar estupefacto ante lo que hice.

to **dump fuel** ▪ to jettison fuel arrojar el combustible ▪ tirar el combustible ▪ botar el combustible ▪ evacuar el combustible ➤ The airplane was dumping kerosene before the crash. El avión arrojaba queroseno antes del siniestro.

dunce cap orejas de burro

dunning letter carta de acosación

durable goods bienes duraderos

during one's lifetime 1. *(one's present lifetime)* durante los años que uno lleva vivo **2.** *(a past lifetime)* durante los años de vida de uno ➤ During my lifetime Durante los años que llevo (yo) vivo ▪ Durante mis años de vida ➤ During Sarmiento's lifetime Durante los años de vida de Sarmiento

during the 1950s ▪ in the 1950s en los años cincuenta ▪ en los años mil novecientos cincuenta

during the day ▪ during the daytime hours ▪ by day en el día ▪ durante el día ➤ We're going to Zaragoza during the day. Vamos a Zaragoza en el día.

during the first year of life ▪ in the first year of life durante el primer año de vida ▪ en el primer año de vida

during the greater part of ▪ for most of durante la mayor parte de

during the next few weeks ▪ in the next few weeks ▪ over the next few weeks ▪ in the ensuing few weeks **1.** *(past)* durante las siguientes semanas **2.** *(future)* durante las próximas semanas ➤ During the next few weeks, their relationship completely changed. Durante las semanas siguientes, su relación cambió por completo. ➤ During the next few weeks, you will have good luck. Durante las semanas próximas, tendrás buena suerte. ▪ Durante las próximas semanas siguientes, tendrás buena suerte.

during the last few weeks durante las últimas semanas

during the night durante la noche ▪ por la noche

during the week entresemana ▪ durante la semana

during the weekend ▪ over the weekend durante el fin de semana

duty-free shop ▪ duty-free store tienda libre de impuestos

duty-free zone zona libre de impuestos ▪ zona franca

to **dwell in one's heart** morar en el corazón de uno

to **dye one's hair** teñirse el pelo ▪ teñirse el cabello ➤ Patrick upped and dyed his hair green. Patrick le dio la vena y se tiñó el pelo de verde.

to be **dying for** morirse por

dying person *el, la* agonizante ▪ moribundo(-a)

to be **dying to do something** morirse de ganas de hacer algo

to be **dying to find out** morirse por saber ▪ morirse por ganas de saber ➤ I'm dying to find out how your blind date went. Me muero por saber cómo te fue tu cita a ciegas.

E-drive *la* unidad E

E-mail ▪ electronic mail **1.** *(the system)* correo electrónico **2.** *(the message itself)* correo (electrónico) ▪ *el* mail ▪ *(colorful)* emilio ➤ Do you have E-mail? ¿Tienes correo electrónico? ➤ I got your E-mail. ▪ I got the E-mail that you sent me. Recibí tu correo. ▪ Recibí tu mail. ▪ Recibí tu emilio. ➤ All my E-mails to you have bounced. Me han devuelto todos los correos (electrónicos) que te he enviado.

each day brings cada día trae ▪ a cada día le corresponde

each day that passed ▪ each passing day cada día que pasaba

each day that passes ▪ each passing day cada día que pasa

each in his own way cada uno a su propia manera

each of them ▪ each one of them ▪ they each cada uno de ellos

each of us ▪ each one of us ▪ we each cada uno de nosotros

each (one) of them ▪ they each cada uno de ellos

each (one) of us ▪ we each cada uno de nosotros

each passing day 1. each day that passes cada día que pasa **2.** each day that passed cada día que pasaba

each to his own taste ▪ each to his own liking cada uno a su gusto ▪ cada quien su gusto

each way cada trayecto ➤ It's half an hour each way. Lleva media hora cada trayecto. ▪ Se tarda media hora por cada trayecto.

to be **eagerly awaited** ser tan esperado ▪ ser muy esperado ➤ The president's visit, which was eagerly awaited... La visita del president, que era muy esperada...

eagerness to please *el* afán de agradar ▪ deseo de agradar

ear for languages: to have an ~ ▪ to have an aptitude for languages tener facilidad de idiomas ▪ tener aptitud(es) para los idiomas

ear for music: to have an ~ tener oído para la música

ear of corn *(Mex.) el* elote ▪ *(Sp.)* mazorca (de maíz)

ear-splitting que taladra los oídos ▪ que le atraviesa a uno el tímpano

ear-to-ear grin ▪ broad smile sonrisa de oreja a oreja

earlier edition *(book, newspaper)* ▪ previous edition edición anterior ➤ An earlier edition ▪ A previous edition Una edición anterior

earlier issue *(magazine)* ▪ previous issue número anterior ▪ edición anterior ➤ An earlier issue Una edición anterior ➤ The earlier issue La edición anterior

an **earlier train** un tren antes ▪ un tren previo

the **earlier train** el tren anterior

earliest memories primeros recuerdos

earliest memory: one's ~ la memoria más remota de uno ▪ *(poetic)* la más remota memoria de uno ➤ Alberto's earliest memory is of a toy red Formula One race car that he would play with in his crib. La memoria más remota de Alberto es de un coche rojo de fórmula uno de juguete con el que jugaba en la cuna.

early bird gets the worm a quien madruga, Dios le ayuda

early childhood primera infancia

the **early Christians** los primeros cristianos

early edition edición anterior

early exposure exposición temprana

early in the evening ▪ in the early evening a prima noche ▪ en las primeras horas de la noche

early in the month a principios del mes

early in the morning por la mañana temprano ▪ muy de mañana ▪ muy temprano ▪ a primeras horas de la mañana

early in the year a principios de año

early last fall ▪ early last autumn a principios del otoño pasado

early last spring a principios de la primavera pasada

early last summer a principios del verano pasado

early last winter a principios del invierno pasado

early last year a principios del año pasado

early life ▪ early years primeros años

early memories tempranas memorias

early morning sun primer sol de la mañana

early next evening ▪ early the next evening a primeras horas de la noche siguiente

early next week a principios de la semana que viene

early on en un principio

early on the evening of en las primeras horas de la noche de

early onset leukemia leucemia de inicio juvenil

early popes primeros papas ➤ Some of the early popes were married. Algunos de los primeros papas estuvieron casados.

early retirement jubilación temprana ▪ jubilación anticipada ▪ jubilación antes de tiempo ➤ They gave him early retirement. Le dieron una jubilación temprana.

to be an **early riser** ser muy tempranero(-a) ▪ ser muy mañanero(-a) ▪ ser madrugador(-a)

early that morning muy de mañana ese día

early the next morning a la mañana siguiente muy temprano

the **early train** el tren de primera hora ➤ I couldn't get a ticket for the early train. They were sold out. No pude comprar un billete para el tren de primera hora. Estaban todos vendidos.

early years: one's ~ ▪ one's early life los primeros años de uno

to **earn a reputation for honesty** ganarse una reputación de honestidad ▪ ganarse una reputación por honestidad

to **earn (a salary of)** ▪ to make (a salary of) ganar (un salario de) ▪ cobrar (un salario de) ➤ He earns four thousand dollars a month. Gana cuatro mil dólares mensuales. ▪ Cobra cuatro mil dólares mensuales.

to **earn interest on** ganar interés en ▪ *(from the bank's point of view)* devengar interés en ➤ We earn interest on our savings. Ganamos interés en nuestros ahorros.

to **earn one's living as** ganarse la vida como ➤ The Russian composer Mussorgsky earned his living as a government official. El compositor ruso Mussorgsky se ganaba la vida como funcionario.

to **earn some money** ganar algo de dinero

to **earn someone the prize** ▪ to get someone the prize ▪ to garner someone the prize valerle a alguien el premio

to **earn the right** ganarse el derecho ➤ You've earned the right. Te has ganado el derecho.

ears are ringing: my ~ me zumban los oídos

ears ring: to make one's ~ hacerle zumbar los oídos ▪ hacer que le zumben los oídos

earth tones tonos tierra ▪ tonos en la gama de marrón y beige

earthen floor ▪ dirt floor piso de tierra

Earth's crust ▪ crust of the Earth corteza terrestre

to **ease off** disminuir gradualmente ➤ Gun the engine and then ease off on the accelerator. Dale una aceleración al motor y luego disminuye gradualmente.

to **ease up on someone** ▪ not to be so hard on someone aflojarle la cuerda a alguien ▪ no ser tan duro con alguien ▪ *(Sp.)* abrir la mano con alguien ➤ You should ease up on your students. You're too hard on them. Deberías abrir la mano con tus alumnos. Eres muy duro con ellos. ➤ You should ease up on them. Deberías abrirles la mano.

to **ease sanctions against** suavizar las sanciones a

to **ease tensions between** limar asperezas entre ➤ *(headline)* Clinton and Asad try to ease tensions between Israel and Syria. Clinton y Asad intentan limar asperezas entre Israel y Siria.

to **ease the embargo on** ▪ to ease the embargo against ▪ to relax the embargo against suavizar el embargo a ▪ disminuir el embargo a ➤ *(news item)* The U.S. House of Representatives early yesterday approved a legislative package to ease the embargo on Cuba. La Cámara de Representantes del Congreso de EE UU aprobó en la madrugada de ayer un paquete de medidas para suavizar el embargo a Cuba.

to **ease up** ▪ to ease off abrir la mano ▪ tomarse las cosas con más calma

ease with which facilidad con la que ▪ facilidad con la cual ➤ The ease with which you express yourself in Spanish La facilidad con que te expresas en español ➤ The ease with which you work in the kitchen La facilidad con la cual haces tu trabajo en la cocina

easier said than done: it's ~ ▪ that's easier said than done es más fácil decirlo que hacerlo ▪ (eso) se dice pronto ▪ del dicho al hecho hay mucho trecho

to be **easily offended** ser ofendido fácilmente ▪ ser muy susceptible

East Side *(New York City)* la zona este

east wind ▪ wind from the east ▪ wind out of the east viento del este ▪ viento de levante

Easter Island Isla de Pascua

Easter (Sunday) Domingo de Resurrección ▪ Pascua Florida ▪ Pascua de Resurrección ➤ Easter (Sunday) falls on the first Sunday after the first full moon after the vernal equinox. El Domingo de Resurrección cae al domingo siguiente de la primera luna llena después del equinoccio de primavera.

easy as it can be: to be (as) ~ ▪ to be as easy as pie no poder ser más fácil ▪ ser pan comido ▪ ser muy fácil ▪ *(Sp., coll.)* estar chupado ➤ It's as easy as it can be. ▪ It's as easy as pie. No puede ser más fácil. ▪ Está chupado (de hacer).

to be **easy as pie** ▪ to be (as) easy as it can be ser pan comido ▪ ser coser y cantar ▪ estar chupado ▪ no poder ser más fácil

easy does it! *(when moving furniture, etc.)* ▪ ¡easy! easy! ¡suave! ¡suave! ▪ ¡tranquilo, tranquilo!

to be **easy-going 1.** to be mellow ser de trato fácil ▪ *(Sp.)* ser asequible **2.** to be lenient ser poco exigente

easy on the salsa! ▪ go easy on the salsa! ¡no te pases con la salsa! ▪ ¡tranquilo con la salsa!

easy (payment) terms las facilidades de pago

to be **easy to assemble** ▪ to be easy to put together ser fácil de armar

to be **easy to get to know** ▪ to be approachable ser fácil de conocer ▪ ser asequible

to be **easy to please** ser fácil de contentar

to be **easy to put together** ▪ to be easy to assemble ser fácil de armar

to be **easy to talk to someone** ser fácil de conversar con alguien ▪ ser asequible ➤ She's easy to talk to. Es muy fácil de conversar con ella.

to be **easy to understand** ▪ to be clear ser fácil de entender ▪ ser asequible ➤ This computer manual is easy to understand. ▪ This computer manual is very clear. Este manual de informática es fácil de entender. ▪ Este manual de informática es asequible.

easy way out: there's an ~ hay salida fácil

easy way out: to take the ~ tomar la salida fácil

to **eat a fire** *(colorful)* ▪ to eat hot-spiced food comer brasas ➤ She used to live in Mexico. She can eat a fire. Ella vivía en México, puede comer brasas.

to **eat alone** ▪ to eat by oneself ▪ to dine alone comer solo ▪ comer en solitario

to **eat between meals** comer entre comidas

to **eat humble pie** ▪ to swallow one's pride comerse una rebanada de humildad ▪ comerse el orgullo

to **eat like a horse** comer como un muerto de hambre ▪ comer como un cerdo ▪ comer como una lima ▪ ponerse el quico ▪ ponerse las botas ▪ hartarse de comer ▪ hartarse con la comida ➤ He eats like a horse. Come como una lima. ▪ Se pone el quico. ▪ Se pone las botas. ▪ Se harta de comer.

to **eat out** *(breakfast, lunch, or supper)* ▪ to go out to eat comer fuera ▪ salir a comer

to **eat sloppily** ▪ to be a sloppy eater comer como un cerdo ▪ comer como un bestia ▪ comer como un chancho

to **eat someone out of house and home** comer lo que hay en casa de alguien

to **eat something (all) up** comerse algo (todo) ➤ The dogs ate it (all) up. Los perros se lo comieron (todo).

to **eat something up** comérselo ➤ The pigs will eat it up. Los cerdos se lo comen. ▪ Los cerdos se lo comerán.

to **eat away at one** ▪ to get in one's craw carcomer a uno

to **eat away at something** corroer algo ▪ desgastar algo ▪ carcomer algo

ebb tide marea baja ▪ *la* bajamar

to **echo someone's sentiments** hacerse eco de la opinión de alguien

to **echo someone's words** hacerse eco de las palabras de alguien

ecological balance equilibrio ecológico

economic position posición económica

economic recovery *la* recuperación de la economía

economic report informe económico ▪ reporte económico

economic situation situación económica

economic slowdown ▪ slowing of the economy ▪ slowdown of the economy ▪ cooling off of the economy enfriamiento de la economía ▪ baja de la economía ▪ merma de la economía ▪ *la* disminución de la economía

economic status estado económico

Ecumenical Council *(of Pope John XXIII)* ▪ Vatican Two Concilio universal ▪ Concilio Ecuménico ▪ Vaticano Dos

edge of a coin ▪ rim of a coin *el* borde de una moneda ▪ *(Sp.)* canto de una moneda

edge of the forest ▪ edge of the woods *el* borde del bosque ▪ *el, la* linde del bosque ▪ *(literary)* lindero del bosque

edge of the knife ▪ knife edge ▪ knife's edge filo del cuchillo

edge of the razor ▪ razor's edge filo de la navaja

edge of town: at the ~ en la orilla del pueblo ▪ al extremo del pueblo ▪ en el extremo del pueblo

edition of a newspaper ▪ issue of a newspaper *la* edición de un periódico ▪ número de un periódico

editor in chief redactor(-a) principal

editorial war guerra editorial ▪ guerra de editoriales ➤ Mark Twain's *Journalism in Tennessee* is about an editorial war between two rural newspapers-two at first, that is. *El periodismo en Tennessee* de Mark Twain se trata de una guerra editoral entre dos periódicos rurales-es decir, al principio dos.

educated society sociedad bien instruida ▪ sociedad bien educada

eenie, meenie, miney, mo, catch a tiger by his toe; if he hollers, let him go; eenie, meenie, miney, mo *(Mex.)* de tín marín de don pingüe, cúcara mácara títere fue, yo no fui, fue te te, pégale pégale que ella fue ▪ de tín marín de don pingüe, cúcara mácara títere fue, yo no fui, fue te te, zúmbale zúmbale que ella fue ▪ *(Sp.)* pito, pito, colorito, ¿donde vas tan bonito?, uno, dos, tres, cuatro ▪ en un café rifaron un gato, al que le toque el número cuatro: uno, dos, tres, cuatro *(On "cuatro" the selection is made.)*

effect on people efecto sobre la gente ▪ *(literary)* acción sobre la gente ➤ *(from Unamuno's* San Manuel Bueno*)* His effect on people was such that no one dared lie to him. Su acción sobre la gente era tal que nadie se atrevía a mentir ante él.

to be **effective against** ser eficaz contra

to be **effective April first** ▪ to go into effect April first ▪ to take effect April first ser efectivo a partir del primero de abril ▪ entrar en vigencia a partir del primero de abril ▪ entrar en vigor a partir del primero de abril ▪ ser efectivo el primero de abril ▪ entrar en vigor el primero de abril

efforts are under way to... ▪ there are efforts under way to... hay esfuerzos encaminados para...

efforts to do something esfuerzos para hacer algo ➤ Efforts to normalize relations between the two countries are under way. Esfuerzos para normalizar las relaciones entre los dos países están en marcha.

egg white clara (de huevo) ➤ Beat the egg whites until the peaks are stiff. Bate las claras a punto de nieve.

eggnog: spiked ~ *(Mex.) el* rompope ▪ *(Sp.) el* ponche de huevo con alcohol

either by... or by... bien por... o bien por... ▪ o... o... ➤ Either by diplomacy or by force Bien por el esfuerzo diplomático o bien por la fuerza ▪ O por el esfuerzo diplomático o por la fuerza

either from... or from... o... o... ▪ bien por... o bien por... ➤ The victim could have died either from the blows suffered or from heart failure. La víctima podría haber muerto o por los golpes sufridos o por parada cardiorespiratoria.

either one 1. either of the two cualquiera de los dos **2.** whichever you prefer da igual

either one of them ▪ either one ▪ either of them **1.** o el uno o el otro **2.** either of the two cualquiera (de los dos)

either one of them: not ~ ▪ neither one of them ninguno de los dos ➤ We can't afford either one of them. No tenemos suficiente dinero para ninguno de los dos.

Either/Or *(Kierkegaard's magnum opus) O lo uno o lo otro*

either... or... o... bien... ▪ o... o... ➤ Relationships can be problematic: either she likes him and he doesn't like her, or vice versa. Las relaciones pueden ser problemáticas: o bien a ella le gusta él y ella no le gusta a él, o viceversa. ➤ Relationships can be problematic: either he likes her and she doesn't like him, or vice versa. Las relaciones pueden ser problemáticas: o bien a él le gusta ella y él no le gusta a ella, o viceversa.

either time: not ~ ▪ neither time ninguna de las dos veces ➤ She didn't vote for the incumbent either time. No votó por el titular ninguna de las dos veces.

either way cualquier de las dos formas ▪ de cualquier modo ▪ de todos modos

either we'll all play, or no one is going to play! ¡o jugamos todos o nadie juega! ▪ ¡o jugamos todos, o se rompe la baraja!

to **eke out a living** buscárselas a duras penas ▪ ganarse la vida a duras penas ▪ buscarse la vida a duras penas

elaborate ceremony ceremonia elaborada ▪ ceremonia suntuosa

elaborately decorated ▪ richly decorated ▪ luxuriously decorated ▪ finely decorated decorado(-a) a todo lujo ▪ decorado(-a) de forma muy elaborada

elapsed time tiempo transcurrido

the **elderly** las personas mayores ▪ las personas de la tercera edad ▪ los ancianos ▪ los viejos

elderly friend ▪ aging friend ▪ friend who's up in years amigo(-a) de la tercera edad

to **elect someone by secret ballot** elegir a alguien con voto secreto

to **elect someone president** elegir presidente a alguien

election campaign campaña electoral

election day *el* día de las elecciones ▪ día de los comicios electorales ▪ jornada de voto

election returns resultados del escrutinio

electoral upset *(victory or defeat)* vuelco electoral

electrical charge carga eléctrica

electrical engineer ingeniero electricista ➤ He graduated in electrical engineering. ▪ He got his degree in electrical engineering. Se licenció como ingeniero electricista.

electrical outlet toma eléctrica ▪ enchufe eléctrico ➤ I need an extension cord with three outlets and a ground. Necesito un alargador con seis tomas y una toma de tierra. ▪ Necesito un alargador con seis enchufes y una toma de tierra.

electrical plug enchufe eléctrico *("Clavijas" are the prongs of the plug.)*

electrical supplies suministros eléctricos

electricity supply ▪ supply of electricity suministro eléctrico ▪ suministro de la electricidad ➤ *(headline)* State of emergency in California over the disruption of the electrical power supply Estado de emergencia en California por el colapso del suministro eléctrico

electricity went off ▪ power went off se cortó la luz ▪ se apagó la electricidad ▪ se fue la electricidad ▪ se fue la luz

electrolyte balance equilibrio electrolítico

electromagnetic spectrum espectro electromagnético

electronic mail ▪ E-mail correo electrónico ▪ el mail ▪ *(colorful)* emilio

elementary school ▪ primary school ▪ grade school (escuela) primaria ▪ *(Sp.)* colegio

to **elevate the blood pressure** ▪ to raise the blood pressure subir la tensión (arterial) ▪ subir la presión (arterial)

elevation above sea level altura sobre el nivel del mar ▪ *la* altitud sobre el nivel del mar

elevator car cabina del ascensor ▪ caja del ascensor

elevator shaft hueco del ascensor

the **elevator stops** el ascensor para ➤ The elevator doesn't stop until it reaches the twentieth floor. El ascensor no para hasta el piso veinte.

to **eliminate the default settings** *(computers)* ▪ to eliminate the defaults ▪ to turn off the defaults ▪ to remove the defaults ▪ to delete the defaults suprimir las configuraciones por defecto ▪ anular las configuraciones por defecto

elimination of jobs ▪ axing of jobs *la* eliminación de puestos de trabajo ▪ *la* supresión de puestos de trabajo

to **embarrass someone** abochornar a alguien ▪ avergonzar a alguien ▪ dar vergüenza a alguien ➤ It embarrasses me when you kiss me in public. Me avergüenza que me beses en público. ➤ I'm a little embarrassed. Estoy un poco abochornado(-a). ➤ It embarrassed me. Me dio verguënza.

to be **embarrassed at something** estar abochornado de algo ▪ estar avergonzado de algo ▪ abochornarse de algo ▪ ser abochornado por algo

to be **embarrassed by something** estar abochornado de algo ▪ estar avergonzado de algo ▪ abochornarse de algo ▪ ser abochornado por algo ➤ I was embarrassed by what he said. Me abochorné de lo que dijo.

to be **embarrassed to admit it** tener vergüenza de admitirlo ▪ tener vergüenza de confesarlo

to be **embarrassed to be...** pasar vergüenza al... ▪ pasar vergüenza cuando... ▪ sentir bochorno al... ▪ sentir bochorno cuando... ➤ I was embarrassed to be seen there. Pasé vergüenza al ser visto allí. ▪ Pasé vergüenza cuando fui visto allí. ▪ Sentí tanto bochorno al ser visto allí. ▪ Sentí tanto bochorno cuando fui visto allí.

to be **embarrassed when...** pasar vergüenza al... ▪ pasar vergüenza cuando... ▪ sentir bochorno al... ▪ sentir bochorno cuando... ➤ I was so embarrassed when... ¡Qué bochorno pasé al...!

embarrassing explanation explicación vergonzosa ▪ incómoda explicación

embarrassing moment momento bochornoso ▪ momento vergonzoso ▪ momento violento ▪ momento embarazoso

embarrassing situation situación embarazosa ▪ situación bochornosa ▪ situación avergonzante ▪ situación violenta

to be an **embarrassment to one** ser una vergüenza para uno

to **embed the sword** *(bullfighting)* empotrar el estoque ▪ dar la estocada

to **embezzle money** ▪ to embezzle funds desfalcar dinero ▪ desfalcar fondos

to **embody an ideal** encarnar un ideal

to be **embroiled in an argument** estar enfrascado en una riña

embroiled in an argument: to become ~ ▪ to get into an argument enfrascarse en una riña

embryonic cells células embrionarias

to **emerge from a survey** ▪ to come out of a survey desprenderse de una encuesta

to **emerge from a study** ▪ to come out of a study desprenderse de un estudio ➤ It's now a fact: Hispanics equal blacks in number in the United States-and might even already outnumber them, according to early data emerging from last year's census. Ya es un hecho: los Hispanos igualan en número a los negros en EE UU-incluso puede que los superan ya; así se desprende de los primeros datos del censo efectuado el pasado año.

emergency exit salida de emergencia ▪ salida de socorro
emergency meeting *la* reunión de urgencia
emergency room las urgencias ➤ They ended up in the emergency room. Acabaron en urgencias.
emotional support apoyo sentimental
to **emphasize that...** recalcar que... ▪ enfatizar que... ▪ hacer resaltar que... ▪ hacer hincapié en que...
empty-handed: to come away ~ marcharse con las manos vacías
to **empty one's pockets** vaciar los bolsillos
empty promise promesa vana ▪ promesa en vano
empty words: to be (just) ~ no ser más que palabras vanas ▪ ser nada más que palabras vanas ➤ They are just empty words. No son más que palabras vanas. ▪ Son nada más que palabras vanas.
to **enable a computer program** activar un programa informático ➤ You must enable Javascript before using this browser. Hay que activar Javascript para utilizar este navegador.
to **enact a law** ▪ to pass a law aprobar una ley ▪ promulgar una ley
to **encompass many things** abarcar muchas cosas
encore! ¡otra, otra! ▪ ¡más! ▪ ¡bis!
to **encourage someone to do something** animar a alguien para que haga algo
to **end at a street** ▪ to tee into a street terminar en una calle ▪ morir en una calle ➤ La Avenida de los Shiris ends at Avenida Seis de Diciembre. La Avenida de los Shiris termina en la Avenida Seis de Diciembre. ▪ La Avenida de los Shiris muere en la Avenida Seis de Diciembre.
end cap *(in a store with aisles)* cabecera
to **end in** ▪ to end up in acabar en ▪ terminar en ➤ The debate ended (up) in a shouting match. El debate terminó a gritos. ▪ El debate acabó a gritos.
to **end in (a) stalemate** ▪ to stalemate acabar en tablas ▪ quedar en tablas ▪ hacer tablas ➤ The negotiations ended in a stalemate. Las negociaciones acabaron en tablas.
the **end is in sight** se ve el final ▪ el final está a la vista
the **end is near** *el* final está próximo ▪ se acerca el final
end of a book *el* fin de un libro
end of a movie *el* fin de una película
end of a nightmare *el* fin de una pesadilla
end of a play *el* fin de una obra (teatral)
end of one's days término de los días de uno ▪ *el* fin de los días de uno ▪ *el* final de los días de uno
end of one's life *el* final de la vida de uno ▪ *el* fin de la vida de uno ➤ He did not suffer at the end of his life. Al final de su vida no sufrió.
end of the line 1. *(metro line) el* final del trayecto (del metro) ▪ final de (la) línea **2.** *(telephone line)* lado de la línea (telefónica) ➤ Tacuba and Tasqueña are the ends of the (metro) line. Tacuba y Tasqueña son los finales del trayecto. ▪ Tacuba y Tasqueña son los finales de la línea uno. ➤ I think the problem is on this end of the line. Creo que el problema es de este lado de la línea. ▪ Creo que el problema es de este teléfono. ▪ Creo que el problema es de allí.
end of the month: at the ~ a fin de mes
end of the month: toward the ~ a fines de mes ▪ hacia finales del mes ▪ a finales de mes
to be the **end of the road for someone** ser el final del camino para alguien ▪ ser el fin del camino para alguien ▪ ser el final del trayecto para alguien ▪ ser el fin del trayecto para alguien ▪ ser el final del viaje para alguien ▪ ser el fin del viaje para alguien
end of the runway final de la pista ➤ The airplane ran off the end of the runway. El avión se salió del final de la pista. ▪ El avión se salió de la pista. ➤ The airplane slid off the end of the runway. El avión patinó del final de la pista.
end of the street: to be at the ~ estar en el fondo de la calle ▪ estar en el final de la calle ▪ estar en el extremo de la calle
end of the street: to go to the ~ ir al fondo de la calle ▪ ir al final de la calle ➤ Go to the end of the street and you'll see it (just off) to the right. *(tú)* Ve al fondo de la calle y lo verás justo a la derecha. ▪ Ve al final de la calle y lo verás (justo) a la derecha. ▪ *(usted)* Vaya (usted) al fondo de la calle y lo verá justo a la derecha. ▪ Vaya (usted) al final de la calle y lo verá justo a la derecha.
the **end of the year 1.** the final days of the year el final del año **2.** the last day of the year el fin de año ➤ The end of the year is almost here. El final del año casi está aquí. ▪ El final del año ya está aquí. ▪ El fin del año ya casi está aquí.
end of the year: at the ~ **1.** in the final days of the year al final del año **2.** on the last day of the year a fin de año
end of the year: toward the ~ hacia finales del año ▪ a finales del año ▪ hacia el fin del ano
to **end on a sour note** acabar con un sabor agrio (en la boca)
end run: to do an ~ **1.** *(American football)* correr una larga distancia hacia el gol con el balón de fútbol en vez de pasarlo a otro jugador **2.** *(figurative)* to go around your boss ▪ to go to your boss' boss saltarse al jefe ▪ saltarse a la jefa
to **end the discrimination** terminar (con) la discriminación
to **end the year with a (budget) surplus** cerrar el año con un superávit ▪ cerrar el año con un excedente
to **end up doing something** acabar haciendo algo ▪ acabar por hacer algo ▪ concluir haciendo algo ▪ concluir por hacer haciendo algo ➤ We ended up going out to eat. Acabamos saliendo a comer. ➤ The neighbors ended up in court. Los vecinos acabaron ante el tribunal.
to **end up (back) where one started** revertir al punto de partida ▪ regresar al punto de partida ▪ volver al punto de partida ▪ acabar donde uno empezó
to **end up having to do something (oneself)** acabar por tener que hacer algo ▪ acabar teniendo que hacer algo ➤ I ended up having to do it myself. Acabé por tener que hacerlo. ▪ Acabé teniéndolo que hacer yo mismo. ▪ Acabé teniendo que hacerlo yo mismo.
to **end up in a shouting match** terminar a gritos ▪ acabar a gritos ➤ The debate ended (up) in a shouting match. El debate terminó a gritos. ▪ El debate acabó a gritos.
to **end up in jail** ▪ to land in jail acabar en la cárcel ▪ dar con los huesos en la cárcel ▪ dar con los huesos en el bote
to **end up in the middle of nowhere** ir a parar en medio de la nada ▪ ir a parar al quinto pino ▪ ir a parar en el quinto pino ▪ *(Sp., off-color)* ir a parar en el quinto coño ➤ We took a wrong turn and ended up in the middle of nowhere. Tomamos un giro equivocado y fuimos a parar al quinto pino.
to **end up on bad terms** acabar mal ▪ acabar como el rosario de la aurora
to **end up with** acabar con ➤ I ate so many hot peppers that I ended up with a stomachache. Comí tantos pimientos que acabé con un dolor de estómago.
the **end was near** el final estaba cerca ▪ el final estaba próximo
ending of a book, movie, play *el* final de un libro, una película, una obra (teatral)
endless curiosity *la* curiosidad sin fin
an **endless number of** una infinidad de ▪ un sin fin de
ends of a cord extremos de un cable
to **endure criticism** soportar críticas ▪ aguantar críticas
to **endure hardship** soportar dificultades ▪ aguantar dificultades
to **endure the pain** ▪ stand the pain ▪ withstand the pain soportar el dolor ▪ aguantar el dolor ▪ tolerar el dolor
to **endure to the end** ▪ to persevere to the end perseverar hasta el fin
enemy combatant combatiente enemigo
energy consumption ▪ consumption of energy consumo energético
to **enforce the law** aplicar la ley ▪ llevar a cabo la ley ➤ The law is not enforced. No se lleva a cabo la ley.
to **enforce the no smoking rule** aplicar la normativa en contra de fumar ▪ hacer cumplir la normativa en contra de fumar
to **engage in a conversation** meterse en una conversación ▪ involucarse en una conversación
to **engage in an uphill battle** enzarzarse en una lucha contracorriente ▪ enzarzarse en una lucha contra la corriente ▪ meterse en una lucha contracorriente ▪ meterse en una lucha contra la corriente ▪ liarse en una lucha contracorriente ▪ liarse en una lucha contra la corriente
to **engage in light conversation** ▪ to engage in small talk ▪ to chat ▪ to chitchat hablar de trivialidades

to **engage in small talk** ▪ to engage in light conversation ▪ to chat ▪ to chitchat hablar de trivialidades

to **engage in wishful thinking** ▪ to build castles in the air hacerse ilusiones ▪ hacer castillos en el aire ▪ construir castillos en el aire ▪ soñar

to **engage (on a personal level)** establecer una relación ▪ entablar una conversación ➤ He doesn't want to engage. No quiere establecer una relación. ▪ No quiere entablar una conversación.

to **engage the clutch** 1. *(driver's action)* soltar el embrague 2. *(mechanism's action)* sujetar el embrague

engaged couple prometidos ▪ comprometidos ▪ novios

to be **engaged in a conversation** ▪ to be having a conversation estar (metido) en una conversación ▪ estar (involucrado) en una conversación

to be **engaged in an activity** estar metido(-a) en una actividad ▪ estar enzarzado(-a) en una actividad ➤ The elephants are engaged in a mating battle. Los elefantes están enzarzados en una lucha de apareamiento.

to be **engaged in combat** estar metido en el combate ▪ estar entablado en combate

to be **engaged to someone (to be married)** estar comprometido(-a) con alguien ➤ They're engaged (to be married). Están comprometidos.

engine backfired ▪ motor backfired *el* motor hizo explosiones (por el caño de escape) ▪ motor petardeó

engine failure paro de motor(es) ▪ fallo del motor ▪ falla del motor

engine is flooded motor está ahogado ▪ motor se ahogó

engine is stalled ▪ motor is stalled se quedó el motor ▪ se apagó el motor ▪ se ha apagado el motor ➤ Try not to let it stall (on you). Intenta de que no se te quede. ▪ Intenta de que no se te apague. ➤ The motor stalled because I didn't depress the clutch in time. El motor se quedó porque no pisé el embrague a tiempo.

English as a second language el inglés como segundo idioma

English common law derecho consuetudinario inglés

English speaker *el, la* angloparlante ▪ *el, la* anglohablante

English-speaking de habla inglesa ▪ angloparlante ▪ anglohablante

English-speaking country *el* país de habla inglesa ▪ país angloparlante ▪ país anglohablante

English-speaking peoples pueblos angloparlantes ▪ pueblos de habla inglesa ➤ Winston Churchill wrote *History of the English-Speaking Peoples.* Winston Churchill escribió *La historia de los pueblos de angloparlantes.*

English-speaking world mundo de habla inglesa

to be **engrossed in a conversation** ▪ to be absorbed in a conversation estar enfrascado en una conversación ▪ estar absorto en una conversación

engrossed in a conversation: to become ~ enfrascarse en una conversación

to **enhance one's image** realzar la imagen ▪ dar realce a la imagen

to **enhance the figure** realzar la figura

to **enhance the flavor** realzar el sabor

to **enjoy doing something** disfrutar haciendo algo ▪ disfrutar hacer algo ➤ I enjoy skiing. Disfruto esquiando. ▪ Disfruto esquiar... *(In English, you cannot say "I enjoy to ski," and in Spanish, you can say "disfruto esquiar" only if the infinitive is followed by a prepositional or adverbial phrase, e.g., "Disfruto esquiar sólo cuando hay nieve fresca.")*

to **enjoy someone's company** congeniar con alguien

to **enjoy the view** recrear la vista ▪ disfrutar la vista

enjoy your dinner! ▪ bon appétit! ▪ enjoy your meal! ¡buen provecho! ▪ ¡qué aproveche!

enjoyable chat ▪ pleasant chat amena charla ▪ charla amena ➤ We had an enjoyable chat. Tuvimos una amena charla. ➤ I had an enjoyable chat with him. Tuve una charla amena con él.

enjoyable evening velada amena ▪ velada agradable

enlargement of the heart agrandamiento del corazón

to **enlighten someone on a subject** ilustrar a alguien sobre un tema

to **enlist in the army** ▪ to join the army ▪ to enlist in military service alistarse en el ejército ▪ enrolarse en el ejército ▪ reclutarse en el ejército ▪ hacerse a las armas *(Hispanic countries differentiate less between the branches of the military than the United States does. The Spanish refers to any and all branches of military service.)*

to be **enough for** ser lo suficiente para

enough is enough! ¡ya está bien!

enough of that! ¡ya está bien! ▪ ¡ya basta eso!

to be **enough to** ser suficiente para

to be **enough to go around** ▪ to be enough for everyone ser suficiente(s) para todos

to be **enough to live on** alcanzar para vivir ▪ ser suficiente para vivir ➤ It's not a big salary, but it's enough to live on. No es un gran salario pero alcanza para vivir. ▪ No es un gran salario pero es suficiente para vivir.

to be **enough to make you...** ser para como... ➤ It's enough to make you want to cry. Es para como hacerte llorar.

to **enrich uranium** enriquecer uranio

to **enroll in an academy** darse de alta en una academia ▪ apuntarse en una academia

to **enroll in the university** ▪ to register at the university matricularse en la universidad ▪ inscribirse en la universidad

to **enter a country legally** entrar al país legalmente ▪ llegar a un país por vía legal

to **enter by force** ▪ to break into entrar por la fuerza ▪ asaltar

to **enter data in a computer** ingresar datos en una computadora ▪ meter datos en una computadora ▪ *(Sp.)* meter datos en un ordenador ➤ Enter your name in the dialogue box. Mete tu nombre en el cuadro de diálogo.

to **enter into a contract with someone for something** ▪ to contract with someone for something ▪ to hire someone to do something contratar con algo para algo

to **enter politics** ▪ to go into politics ▪ to get into politics adentrarse en la política ▪ meterse en la política ▪ dedicarse a la política

to **enter the bloodstream** ▪ to get into the bloodstream pasar al torrente sanguíneo

to **enter the fray** saltar a la palestra

to **enter the limelight** ▪ to step into the limelight salir a la palestra

entertainment section *(of a newspaper)* la sección de amenidades ▪ cartelera ▪ guía de entretenimiento ▪ guía del ocio

to **entice someone to do something** ▪ to entice someone into doing something inducir a alguien a hacer algo

enticing apple manzana tentadora

enticing dessert ▪ tempting dessert postre tentador

entire expanse toda la extensión ➤ If it were possible to look down on our solar system from the Pole Star, the entire expanse across Pluto's orbit would appear to be a mere speck. Si fuera posible mirar hacia abajo a nuestro sistema solar desde la estrella polar, toda la extensión a través de la órbita de Plutón parecería un mero punto.

the **entire morning** ▪ the whole morning ▪ all morning toda la mañana ▪ la mañana entera ➤ We waited the entire morning. ▪ We waited all morning. ▪ We waited the whole morning. Esperábamos toda la mañana.

the **entire time** ▪ the whole time todo el rato ▪ todo el tiempo

to be **entitled to** tener el derecho a esperar ➤ You were entitled to an answer. Tenía derecho a esperar una respuesta.

entrance hall ▪ entry hall ▪ foyer recibidor ▪ vestíbulo

entry in a dictionary ▪ dictionary entry entrada en un diccionario

entry-level position *la* posición inicial

entry phone teleportero ▪ conserje automático

envelope marked... ▪ envelope labeled... sobre rotulado...

envelope containing *el* sobre con ➤ An envelope containing white powder Un sobre con polvos blancos

to be **enveloped in flames** estar envuelto en llamas ▪ quedar envuelto en llamas ➤ *(newspaper picture caption)* The airplane falls onto a parallel runway, breaks into three pieces, and is enveloped in flames. El avión se desploma sobre una pista lateral, queda partido en tres trozos y envuelto en llamas.

environmental problems los problemas ambientales

Environmental Protection Agency (EPA) Oficina de protección ambiental

to be the **epitome of something** ser la representación de algo ▪ ser el paradigmo de algo ▪ ser la estampa de algo ➤ Scott Joplin, the creator of ragtime, is the epitome of American musical originality. Scott Joplin, el creador de ragtime, es la representación de la originalidad musical norteamericana.

equal partners socios de plenos derechos

to be **equally divided** estar dividido en partes iguales ➤ When the Senate is equally divided, the vice president breaks the tie. Cuando el Senado está dividido en partes iguales, el vicepresidente deshace el empate. ➤ The estate was equally divided among the children of the deceased. La propiedad se dividió en partes iguales entre los hijos del difunto.

to be **equally full of** estar igual de lleno de

equals sign signo de igual

to be **equipped with** estar provisto(-a) de ▪ estar dotado(-a) de ▪ estar dotado(-a) con ➤ *(bank sign)* Office equipped with security measures Oficina dotada de medidas de seguridad

to **erase the (black)board** borrar la pizarra ▪ borrar el pizarrón

errand boy mozo de carga ▪ botón ▪ *(Mex.)* chacho

to **escape from someone's clutches** ▪ to escape (from) the clutches of someone huir de las garras de alguien ▪ escapar de las garras de alguien

to **escape injury** ▪ to come away uninjured ▪ to come away unharmed ▪ to come away unhurt ▪ to come away unscathed ▪ to escape uninjured ▪ to escape unharmed ▪ to escape unscathed ▪ to escape without injury salir ileso ▪ salir indemne

to **escape one's notice** ▪ to escape one's attention escapársele la atención de uno

to be an **escape valve** ▪ to serve as an escape valve servir de válvula de escape

escape velocity velocidad de escape ➤ Escape velocity is the minimum velocity a body must attain to escape a gravitational field. La velocidad de escape es la velocidad mínima que un cuerpo debe alcanzar para escaparse de un campo gravitacional.

escaped convict ▪ prison escapee ▪ escaped prisoner preso huido ▪ prófugo

especially: and ~ y especialmente

to be **especially pretty** ser particularmente bonito

essential ingredient *el* ingrediente esencial

essential ingredient: to have as its ~ estar hecho a base de ▪ tener como su ingrediente esencial

to be an **established fact** ▪ to be a proven fact ser un hecho cierto ▪ ser un hecho probado

to **estimate conservatively** calcular por lo bajo

to **estimate on the high side** ▪ to estimate on the high end calcular por lo alto

to **estimate the damages (to be) in the millions** calcular que los daños se encuentran en los millones

estimated time of arrival ▪ E.T.A. tiempo aproximado de llegada

estranged couple pareja distanciada ▪ *(literary)* pareja enajenada

estrogen patch *el* parche de estrógeno

et cetera ▪ and other things ▪ and so on et cetera ▪ y así sucesivamente

ethnic cleansing limpieza étnica

to **euthanize an animal** ▪ to put an animal to sleep sacrificar a un animal (para que no sufra)

to **evacuate a building** desalojar un edificio ▪ evacuar un edificio

to be **evacuated to** evacuarle a ➤ The wounded were evacuated to a field hospital. Evacuaron a los heridos a un hospital de campaña.

evacuation of a building desalojo de un edificio ▪ la evacuación de un edificio

to **evade a question** ▪ to dodge a question esquivar una pregunta ▪ contestar con una evasiva ➤ He evaded the question. ▪ He dodged the question. Esquivó la pregunta. ▪ Contestó con una evasiva.

to **evade responsibility** eludir la responsabilidad ▪ esquivar la responsabilidad

to **evade the censor** ▪ to get around the censor burlar el censor ▪ burlar la censura

to **evade the draft** ▪ to dodge the draft evitar ser llamado a filas ▪ evitar ser llamado a quintas ▪ evitar el reclutamiento militar

to **evade the issue** ▪ to dodge the issue esquivar el tema ▪ eludir el asunto ▪ evadir el asunto ▪ echar balones fuera

evasion of responsibility ▪ shirking of responsibility *la* evasión de responsabilidad ▪ *la* dejación de responsabilidad

evasive answer respuesta evasiva

even among incluso entre

even farther aún más lejos

even further ▪ even more ▪ further still ▪ further yet aún más

even I hasta yo ▪ incluso yo

even if así ▪ incluso si ➤ Even if it takes all summer Así lleve todo el verano ▪ Incluso si lleve todo el verano

even if by doing so incluso si de esa manera ▪ incluso si de esa forma ▪ incluso si haciendo eso

even if I incluso si yo

even if it is only siquiera sea ▪ si solamente sea

even if it were only si solamente fuera ▪ si solamente fuese

even less menos aún

even more ▪ even further ▪ further still ▪ further yet aún más ➤ To complicate matters even more... Para enturbiar aún más las cosas...

even now aún ahora ▪ aún en la actualidad ▪ incluso ahora ▪ incluso en la actualidad

even number número par

even-numbered day un día par

even so aun así ▪ así y todo ▪ incluso así

to be **even (steven)** ▪ to be even ▪ to be square estar en paz ▪ estar a mano ▪ estar al par ➤ We're even (steven). ▪ We're square. ▪ You don't owe me anything. We're even (steven). ▪ You don't owe me anything. We're square. Estamos en paz. ▪ Estamos a mano. ▪ No me debes nada. Estamos en paz. ▪ No me debes nada. Estamos a mano.

even than aún que ▪ incluso que ➤ It is more powerful even than... Es más poderoso aún que... ▪ Es más poderoso incluso que...

even when incluso cuando

even without incluso sin

to be **even worse than** ser aún peor que

evening traffic tráfico vespertino

to be **evenly balanced** estar igualmente balanceado ▪ estar equilibrado

to be **evenly distributed** estar distribuido uniformemente ▪ estar distribuido por partes iguales ▪ estar distribuido en partes iguales

to be **evenly divided** estar dividido en partes iguales ➤ Public opinion is about evenly divided on the issue. La opinión pública está dividida más o menos en partes iguales.

to be **evenly matched** estar bien equiparados

ever again: not ~ ▪ never again nunca más ➤ I don't ever want to have her for a teacher again. No quiero volver a tenerla como profesora nunca más.

ever been to: to have ~ estar alguna vez en ▪ conocer ➤ Have you ever been to Montevideo? ¿Has estado alguna vez en la Montevideo? ▪ ¿Conoces la Montevideo? ➤ It's doubtful that the president has ever read the document. Es dudoso que el presidente haya leído alguna vez el documento.

ever discovered jamás descubierto ➤ TrES-4 is the largest planet ever discovered. TrES-4 es el planeta más grande jamás descubierto.

ever heard: to have ~ jamás haber oído ➤ That's the most absurd thing I've ever heard. Es lo más absurdo que jamás he oído.

ever more ▪ more and more cada vez más

ever since ▪ since then siempre desde que ▪ desde que

evergreen tree ▪ perennial tree el árbol de hoja perenne

every cloud has a silver lining no hay mal que por bien no venga ▪ cada martes tiene su domingo
every day todos los días
every few a cada pocos ➤ Every few minutes A cada pocos minutos ➤ Every few lines A cada pocas líneas
every Friday todos los viernes
every last one of them todos hasta el último
every little bit helps todo granito de arena cuenta
every living soul todo bicho viviente
every man for himself: (it's) ~ sálvese quien pueda ▪ sálvese el que pueda ▪ sálvate tu mismo
every Monday cada lunes ▪ todos los lunes
every move I make cada cosa que hago ➤ He criticizes every move I make. Critica cada cosa que hago.
every once in a while ▪ every now and then ▪ from time to time de vez en cuando ▪ a cada rato
every other day ▪ on alternating days un día sí y otro no ▪ en días alternos ▪ *(Mex.)* cada tercer día ➤ During the oil crisis, we could only buy gasoline every other day. ▪ During the oil crisis, we could buy gasoline only on alternating days. Durante la crisis petrolera, pudimos comprar gasolina sólo un día sí y otro no. ▪ Durante la crisis petrolera, pudimos comprar gasolina en días alternos.
every other weekend cada fin de semana por medio ▪ un fin de semana sí y otro no ➤ We go to Bariloche every other weekend. Vamos a Bariloche cada fin de semana por medio.
every other year ▪ every two years ▪ once every two years ▪ once each two years cada dos años ▪ un año sí y otro no ▪ cada tercer año
every second counts cada segundo cuenta
every so often a cada tanto
every time he opens his mouth cada vez que abre la boca
every Tom, Dick, and Harry cualquier hijo de vecino ▪ cada hijo de vecino ▪ todo hijo de vecino
every trick in the book: to know ~ conocerse todos los trucos habidos y por haber
every two years ▪ every other year ▪ once every two years ▪ once each two years cada dos años ▪ un año sí y otro no ▪ *(Mex.)* cada tercer año
every weekend cada fin de semana ▪ todos los fines de semana
every which way ▪ any old way así como así
every word 1. toda palabra ▪ cada palabra **2.** palabra por palabra ➤ Are you listening?-To every word! ¿Me estás escuchando?-¡Palabra por palabra!
every year todos los años
everybody and his brother ▪ everybody under the sun ▪ every Tom, Dick, and Harry todo bicho viviente
everybody I know ▪ everyone I know todos mis conocidos
everybody under the sun ▪ everybody and his brother todo bicho viviente
everyday life ▪ daily life vida cotidiana ▪ vida rutinaria
everyday shoes zapatos de batalla
everyone I know ▪ everybody I know todos mis conocidos
everyone is invited todos quedan invitados
everyone who ▪ all (those) who ▪ whoever todo el que ▪ todos los que ▪ cuantos ▪ cuantas personas ▪ quienquiera que ➤ Almost everyone who reads *Don Quijote* is struck by how entertaining it is to read. Todo el que lee *Don Quijote* queda impresionado por lo entretenido que resulta.
everything about her todo en ella
everything about him todo en él
everything about it todo acerca de ello ➤ I want to know everything about it. Quiero saber todo acerca de ello.
everything else todo lo demás
everything from cualquier cosa entre ➤ Oh, your name is Helle. I was calling you everything from Helen to Ellen to Elena. O, te llamas Helle. Te he llamado cualquier cosa entre Elena y Helen.
everything in the store todo lo que hay en la tienda
everything is all set ▪ everything's all set todo está listo
everything is in order ▪ everything's in order todo está en orden
everything made with todo lo hecho con
everything one stands for todo lo que representa uno ➤ The former prime minister still leaves no one undecided: the conservatives still adore her, and the liberals continue to hate everything she stands for. La ex primera ministra sigue sin dejar a nadie indiferente: los conservadores aún la adoran y los liberales siguen odiando todo lo que representa.
everything you can *(tú)* todo lo que puedas ▪ *(usted)* todo lo que pueda (usted)
everything someone said todo lo que alguien dijo
everything under the sun todo lo habido y por haber ▪ lo humano y lo divino ▪ de todo como en botica
everything's all set todo listo ▪ todo está listo
everything's going to be okay ▪ everything's going to be all right todo va a salir bien
everything's okay 1. todo está bien **2.** *(after a mishap)* ya pasó todo
everything's under control todo está controlado
everywhere at once en todas partes a la vez ➤ I just want to start everywhere at once. Sencillamente quiero empezar en todas partes a la vez.
everywhere I go ▪ wherever I go dondequiera que voy
everywhere one looked ▪ wherever one looked mirase a donde mirase
everywhere you look ▪ wherever you look por donde se mire
eviction notice aviso de embargo ▪ aviso de desalojo ▪ apercibimiento de desahucio
evil eye: to give someone the ~ echarle el mal de ojo a alguien
evil intentions malas intenciones ▪ *(Sp.)* intenciones aviesas
ex officio ▪ by virtue of one's office ▪ by virtue of one's position ▪ automatically nato
ex officio member miembro nato ▪ miembro ex officio ▪ miembro en virtud del cargo
exact change dinero justo
to be the **exact moment the train is supposed to depart** ser la hora justa en la que el tren debe partir
to be the **exact opposite (of)** ▪ to be completely different (from) ser el polo opuesto (a) ➤ Marco is the exact opposite of Paco. ▪ Marco is completely different from Paco. ▪ Marco and Paco are completely different. Marco es el polo opuesto a Paco.
exact words palabras textuales
exact words were: one's ~ dijo textualmente
exactly as ▪ exactly the way tal y como
exactly one year ago ▪ a year ago today ▪ one year ago today al año exactamente ▪ hace exactamente un año ▪ hace un año hoy mismo
to be **exactly the right person for the job** ▪ to be exactly the right person for the post ▪ to be exactly the right person for the position ▪ to be the ideal person for the job ser la persona idónea para el cargo ▪ ser la persona idónea para el trabajo ▪ ser la persona idónea para el puesto
exactly the way ▪ exactly as tal y como
to **exaggerate the facts** exagerar los hechos ▪ abultar los hechos
to **exalt someone** ▪ to extol someone ▪ to revere someone sublimar a alguien ▪ ensalzar a alguien ▪ enaltecer a alguien
to **exasperate someone** exasperar a alguien ▪ sacarle de quicio a alguien ▪ sacarle de tino a alguien
to **exceed one's expectations** ▪ to surpass one's expectations rebasar la expectativas de uno
to **exceed the limit** ▪ to be over the limit exceder el límite de velocidad ▪ superar el límite de velocidad
to **exceed the speed limit** ▪ to break the speed limit exceder el límite de velocidad
to **excel at** ▪ to excel in sobresalir en
except for 1. apart from a excepción de **2.** with the exception of excepto para ▪ *(literary)* fuera de ➤ Except for an occasional letter... Excepto para una carta ocasional... ▪ Fuera de alguna carta...
except that excepto que ▪ lo único que
except to excepto para

except with excepto con ■ si no es con ➤ He never goes bowling except with his students. Nunca va a jugar a los bolos excepto con sus estudiantes. ■ Nunca va a jugar al boliche si no es con sus estudiantes.

exception of: to make an ~ dejar a salvo

to **exercise the mind** ■ to be good mental exercise hacer trabajar el cerebro

to **exchange a few words with someone** cambiar unas palabras con alguien

to **exchange dollars for pesos** ■ to change dollars into pesos cambiar dólares por pesos

to **exchange glances** ■ to glance at each other intercambiar miradas ➤ We exchanged glances. Intercambiamos miradas.

exchange of insults *el* cruce de insultos

exchange of prisoners ■ prisoner exchange *el* canje de prisioneros ■ intercambio de prisioneros

to **exchange one's favors for money** ■ to trade one's favors for money cambiar sus favores por dinero

exchange rate ■ rate of exchange tipo de cambio ■ tasa de cambio ■ el valor del cambio ➤ What is the euro-to-dollar exchange rate today? ¿Cuál es el (tipo de) cambio del euro a dólar hoy?

to **exchange vows** ■ to exchange marriage vows intercambiar votos (matrimoniales) ■ hacer promesas solemnes de matrimonio

excitement of the moment: in the ~ en la excitación del momento

exciting life: to live an ■ to lead an exciting life llevar una vida muy emocionante ■ vivir una vida muy emocionante ➤ I live a very exciting life: twelve hours a day at the computer. Llevo una vida muy emocionante: doce horas al día (metido) en la computadora.

to **exclaim something without thinking** escapársele

exclamation mark signo de admiración

excuse doesn't cut it ■ excuse doesn't fly ■ excuse isn't good enough excusas no corran ➤ That excuse doesn't cut it. ■ That excuse isn't good enough. ■ That excuse doesn't fly. Esas excusas no corren.

excuse me *(tú)* perdona ■ discúlpame ■ *(usted)* perdone ■ disculpe ■ *(L. Am.)* dispénseme ■ *(when trying to get by, on the metro, etc.)* con permiso

executive branch poder ejecutivo

executor of an estate testamentario ■ encargado del patrimonio

exemplary citizen cuidadano(-a) consecuente ■ cuidadano(-a) ejemplar

to be **exempt from military service** estar exento del servicio militar

to be **exempt from something** estar exento de algo

to be **exempt from taxes** ■ to be tax-exempt estar exento de impuestos

to **exercise one's right** usar de su derecho

to **exert oneself (in, to)** esforzarse (en, para) ■ afanarse (en, para)

to **exert pressure on 1.** *(physical pressure, as on a wound)* ejercer presión sobre **2.** *(psychological pressure)* ejercer presión en

to **exhaust the possibilities (for)** agotar las posibilidades (para) ■ exhaustar las posibilidades (para)

to **exhaust natural resources** ■ to use up natural resources agotar los recursos naturales ■ exhaustar los recursos naturales

exhibition of paintings *(by a single artist) la* exhibición de pinturas

exposition of paintings *(by multiple artists) la* exposición de pinturas

to **exit from the program** *(computers)* cerrar el programa ➤ When you exit from the program correctly... Cuando cierras adecuadamente el programa...

exit poll sondeo a pie de urna ■ encuesta a pie de urna ■ sondeo a boca de urna ■ encuesta a boca de urna ➤ Exit polls taken in Peru indicated a virtual tie between Alberto Fujimori and Alejandro Toledo. Sondeos a pie de urna realizados en Perú indicaban un virtual empate entre Alberto Fujimori y Alejandro Toledo.

to **exonerate someone of something** exculpar a alguien de algo

exorbitant rent *el* impresionante alquiler

expandable memory *(computers)* memoria ampliable ➤ Is the memory expandable? ¿Está ampliable la memoria?

to **expect nothing less of someone** ■ not to expect anything less of someone no esperar menos de alguien ➤ I expect nothing less of you. No espero menos de ti.

to **expect that...** anticipar que... ➤ We expect that the weather will change by tomorrow. Anticipamos que el tiempo cambie para mañana.

to **expect that someone will do something** ■ to expect someone to do something anticipar que alguien haga algo ■ esperar que alguien haga algo ➤ I was expecting that twenty people would attend the party, and fifty showed up. ■ I was expecting twenty people to attend the party, and fifty showed up. Anticipaba que veinte personas asistieran a la fiesta, y aparecieron cincuenta.

to **expect to be** ■ to anticipate being esperar estar ➤ We expect to be there by nine tomorrow. ■ We anticipate being there by nine tomorrow. Esperamos estar allí para las nueve (Dios mediante).

to **expect to have something finished** ■ to expect to finish something ■ to expect to have something done ■ to anticipate having something finished esperar terminar algo ■ calcular haber hecho algo para ➤ I expect to have this finished by the eighteenth. ■ I expect to finish this by the eighteenth. ■ I anticipate having this finished by the eighteenth. Espero terminar esto para el dieciocho.

to be **expected that 1.** ser de suponerse que **2.** tenerse previsto que ➤ It's to be expected that... Es de suponer que... ➤ It was to be expected that... Era de suponerse que... ➤ When is it expected to arrive? ¿Cuándo se tiene previsto que llegue?

to be **expected to** pretenderse que ■ esperarse que ➤ In some countries, you're expected to be on time. In others, you're not. En algunos países, se pretende que llegues puntualmente, y en otros no. ■ En algunos países, se espera que llegues a tiempo, y en otros no.

to be **expecting a baby** estar esperando un niño

to **expel a diplomat** expulsar a un diplomático ■ *(informal)* echar a un diplomático

to **expel a student** expulsar a un(-a) estudiante ■ echar a un(-a) estudiante

to **experience great hardship(s)** ■ to undergo great hardship(s) ■ to suffer great hardship(s) pasar grandes penas ■ pasar por muchas dificultades ■ pasar por grandes penurias

experience it! ¡vívelo!

experience shows that... la experiencia muestra que...

experimental stage: to be in the ~ ■ to be at the experimental stage estar en la etapa experimental

expert marksman ■ crack shot tirador(-a) experto(-a)

to **experience a drop in blood pressure** ■ to suffer a drop in blood pressure ■ to have a drop in blood pressure tener una bajada de tensión ■ sufrir una bajada de tensión

expiration date fecha de caducidad ■ fecha de vencimiento

to **expire on a certain date** vencer en una determinada fecha ■ vencerse en una determinada fecha ■ caducar en una determinada fecha ➤ My visa extension expires (on) July 26. ■ My visa extension expires on the 26th of July. Mi prórroga de estancia de mi visa se vence el 26 de julio.

to **explain one's position** ■ to explain one's point of view exponer su postura ■ explicar su postura

to **explain something in minute detail** ■ to explain something in great detail explicar algo (muy) detalladamente ■ explicar algo con pelos y señales

explanatory note aclaración ■ nota aclaratoria ■ nota explicativa

to **explode a bomb** ■ to set off a bomb ■ to detonate a bomb hacer estallar una bomba ■ hacer detonar una bomba

to **explore every avenue to** ■ to go to great lengths to examinar todos los medios (habidos y por haber) para ■ remover Roma con Santiago para

explosive device: to set off an ~ ▪ to detonate an explosive device hacer estallar un artefacto explosivo ▪ hacer detonar un artefacto explosivo

explosives expert ▪ bomb disposal expert artificiero

to be an **exponent of...** ▪ to be a representative of... ser un exponente de... ▪ ser un representante de... ➤ Benito Jerónimo de Feijóo is the principal exponent of the Enlightenment in Spain. Benito Jerónimo de Feijóo es el principal exponente de la Ilustración en España.

to **expose an error** ▪ to point out an error hacer ver un error ▪ señalar un error

to **expose someone for what one is** hacer ver a alguien que es ➤ *(eulogy to* Chicago Tribune *columnist Mike Royko)* Now there won't be anybody to expose the idiots for what they are. Ya no habrá quien haga ver a los idiotas que son idiotas.

express checkout caja rápida ▪ caja especial para minus válidos ➤ Express checkout: maximum fifteen items Caja rápida: máximo quince artículos

to **express on paper** expresar sobre papel ▪ plasmar sobre papel

to **express one's appreciation for** ▪ to express one's gratitude for expresar su agradecimiento por

to **express one's concern about** ▪ to express one's concern over mostrar su preocupación por

to **express one's displeasure at** expresar su malestar por ▪ expresar su descontento por

to **express one's gratitude for** ▪ to express one's thanks for expresar su agradecimiento por

to **express one's satisfaction at** expresar su satisfacción a ▪ manifestar su satisfacción a

to **express one's surprise** expresar su sorpresa ▪ manifestar su sorpresa

to **express oneself** expresarse

to **express the intention to** mostrar la intención de ▪ manifestar la intención de

to **express the vision of** expresar la visión de ▪ plasmar la visión de ➤ The works of Miguel Delibes express the vision of a liberal Catholic. Las obras de Miguel Delibes plasman la visión de un católico liberal.

expression of friendship gesto de amistad ▪ la expresión de amistad

expression on one's face *la* expresión de su cara ▪ expresión que uno pone ➤ You should have seen the expression on his face. Deberías haber visto la expresión de su cara. ▪ Deberías haber visto la cara que puso.

to **extend an invitation** hacer extensiva una invitación ➤ They extended the invitation to the fiancee's parents. Hicieron extensiva la invitación a los padres de la novia.

to **extend from... to** extenderse desde... hasta ➤ The Pan-American Highway extends from Canada to Patagonia. La Carretera Panamericana se extiende desde Canadá hasta Patagonia.

to **extend one's hand** ▪ to outstretch one's hand tender la mano

to **extend the ceasefire** prolongar el alto el fuego

extended forecast pronóstico a largo plazo ▪ pronóstico ampliado

extension cord extensión eléctrica ▪ *la* extensión ▪ *el* alargador ▪ *el* prolongador ▪ *(Sp.)* el ladrón ➤ I need an extension cord with six outlets and a ground. Necesito una extensión con seis tomas y una toma de tierra. ➤ Extension cord with multiple outlets Alargador de enchufes multiples ▪ Prolongador con tomas multiples ▪ Ladrón con tomas multiples

extension of tourist visa prórroga de estancia

extensive coverage ▪ wide coverage ▪ broad coverage cobertura amplia ▪ amplísima cobertura

extent of the crisis ▪ depth of the crisis *el* alcance de la crisis

extent of the damage *la* extensión de los daños ▪ *el* alcance de las daños

extent of the danger *el* alcance del peligro

extent to which hasta qué punto

extinct animal animal extinto

extinct volcano volcán extinto

extinction of a species *la* extinción de una especie ▪ *la* desaparición de una especie

to **extinguish a fire** ▪ to put out a fire extinguir un incendio ▪ apagar un incendio ▪ sofocar un incendio

to **extol the virtues of someone** ▪ to extol someone's virtues ▪ to sing someone's praises cantar las alabanzas de alguien ▪ ensalzar a alguien

extra, extra! read all about it! ¡extra! ¡extra! ¡descúbralo todo! ▪ ¡extra! ¡extra! ¡entérense de todo!

extreme left *(politically)* ▪ far left extrema izquierda ▪ izquierda más dura

extreme right *(politically)* ▪ far right extrema derecha ▪ derecha más dura ➤ *(headline)* Extreme right holds the key to the governability of Portugal Derecha más dura tiene la llave de la gobernabilidad de Portugal

extremely dangerous situation situación extremamente peligrosa ▪ situación límite

to be **extremely disappointed** ▪ to be terribly disappointed ▪ to be really disappointed ▪ to be really let down ▪ to feel really let down estar sumamente decepcionado(-a) ▪ estar sumamente desilusionado(-a)

extremely slowly sumamente lento ▪ con excesiva lentitud

to be **extremely tired** estar sumamente cansado ▪ estar sumamente fatigado ▪ estar fatigado en extremo

extremes meet each other los extremos se tocan

extremist groups grupos extremistas ▪ grupos ultras

to **exude sensuality** rebosar sensualidad ▪ derrochar sensualidad ▪ exultar sensualidad

eye examination ▪ eye exam *la* revisión ocular ▪ *el* examen de la vista ▪ *(Mex.)* chequeo de los ojos ▪ chequeo ocular ▪ chequeo de la vista

eye for an eye and a tooth for a tooth ojo por ojo, y diente por diente ▪ *la* ley de talión

eye of a hurricane ojo de un huracán ▪ *el* vórtice de un ciclón

eye shadow *(makeup)* sombra de ojos

to **eye someone distrustfully** ▪ to eye someone with suspicion mirar a alguien con recelo

to **eye someone with suspicion** ▪ to eye someone distrustfully mirar a alguien con recelo ▪ mirar a alguien receloso

eyes are stinging: my ~ *(from soap, etc.)* ▪ my eyes are smarting ▪ my eyes are burning me arden los ojos ▪ me escuecen los ojos

eyes as big as saucers ojos como platos ➤ My eyes were as big as saucers. Me quedé con los ojos como platos. ▪ Se me pusieron los ojos como platos.

eyes checked: to get one's ~ ▪ to have one's eyes checked ▪ to have one's eyes examined hacerse un chequeo ocular ▪ hacerse un chequeo de la vista ▪ *(Sp., for glasses)* graduarse los ojos ➤ I have to get my eyes checked. Tengo que graduarme los ojos.

eyes examined: to have one's ~ ▪ to get one's eyes examined ▪ to get one's eyes checked hacerse un chequeo ocular ▪ hacerse un chequeo de la vista ▪ *(Sp.)* graduarse los ojos ➤ I have to get my eyes checked. Tengo que graduarme los ojos.

eyes fixed on something: to have one's ~ tener los ojos fijos en algo ▪ los ojos puestos en algo

eyes flashed (in anger): one's ~ sus ojos chispearon

eyes half closed ▪ half-closed eyes ▪ eyes half shut ▪ half-shut eyes ojos entornados ▪ ojos medio cerrados ▪ ojos entreabiertos

eyes met se cruzaron los ojos ▪ se cruzaron las miradas ➤ At that moment, our eyes met. En ese momento nuestros ojos se cruzaron.

eyewitness testigo visual ▪ testigo presencial

fabric softener *el* suavizante para ropa

to **face a choice** encarar una decisión

to **face a dilemma** ▪ to be faced with a dilemma ▪ to be on the horns of a dilemma afrontar un dilema ▪ verse ante un dilema

to **face a problem** ▪ to address a problem ▪ to deal with a problem enfrentarse a un problema ▪ enfrentarse con un problema ▪ sortear un problema

to **face a situation** estar frente a ➤ Are we facing an ecological crisis? ¿Estamos frente a una crisis ecológica?

to **face adversity** afrontar la adversidad

face down: to put something ~ ▪ to place something face down poner algo boca abajo ▪ poner algo cara abajo ➤ Put the paper in the copier face down. Pon el papel cara abajo en la copiadora. ➤ Put the (computer) monitor in the box face down. Mete el monitor de la computadora en la caja boca abajo.

face down: to lie ~ ▪ to lie prone yacer boca abajo ▪ tenderse boca abajo ➤ The victim was lying face down on the pavement. La víctima estaba tendida boca abajo en el pavimento.

to **face down an opponent** ▪ to face an opponent down amilanar a un(-a) oponente ▪ doblegar a un(-a) oponente

face down on the ground: to fall ~ caer de bruces ➤ The victim was lying face down on the ground. La víctima cayó de bruces al suelo.

to **face each other 1.** verse las caras ▪ estar enfrente uno del otro **2.** *(in a fight or debate)* enfrentarse ➤ In the Mexican dance, the shuffle, the man and woman face each other and hold hands. En el baile mexicano, la raspa, el hombre y la mujer están enfrente uno del otro y se agarran (de) las manos.

to **face east** dar al este ▪ estar orientado al este ▪ tener orientación este ➤ The overlook faces east toward the Atlantic Ocean. El mirador da al este hacia el (océano) Atlántico. ➤ The building faces east. El edificio da al este. ➤ (In) which direction does the house face? It faces east. ¿Qué orientación tiene la casa? Está orientada al este. ▪ ¿Qué orientación tiene la casa? Tiene orientación este.

face is familiar (to me) cara me es conocida ▪ cara me resulta familiar ▪ cara me suena ➤ Her face is familiar. Su cara me es conocida. ▪ Su cara me resulta familiar. ▪ Su cara me suena.

to **face life without someone** darse a la vida sin alguien

face-lift: to get a ~ 1. *(person)* to have aesthetic surgery hacerse la (cirugía) estética **2.** *(building)* to refurbish the façade reformarse la fachada ▪ renovarse la fachada **3.** *(buildings with historical or aesthetic value)* estar restaurando la fachada ▪ *(coll.)* estar dando un lavado de cara ➤ The famous comedienne got a face-lift. La famosa comediante se hizo la (cirugía) estética. ➤ The inner city is getting a face-lift thanks to the association of small businesses. Al interior de la ciudad le están dando un lavado de cara, gracias a la asociación de pequeños comercios.

face of fear rostro de miedo

face of the earth *la* faz de la tierra

to **face off** encararse uno al otro ▪ confrontarse uno al otro ▪ enfrentarse uno al otro ➤ The Democratic and Republican presidential candidates faced off in a debate. Los candidatos presidenciales demócrata y republicano se encararon uno al otro en un debate.

to **face reality** ▪ to face up to reality afrontar la realidad ▪ asumir la realidad ▪ enfrentarse a la realidad ➤ We have to face (up to) reality. Tenemos que afrontar la realidad. ▪ Tenemos que asumir la realidad. ▪ Debemos enfrentarnos a la realidad.

to **face someone 1.** to face up to someone encarar a alguien **2.** to turn and face someone darse la vuelta y enfrentar a alguien **3.** *(in sports)* enfrentar a alguien

to **face the consequences** afrontar las consecuencias ▪ encarar las consecuencias ▪ apechar con las consecuencias ▪ apechugar con las consecuencias ▪ apencar con las consecuencias ▪ pechar con las consecuencias

to **face the death penalty** enfrentarse a la pena de muerte ▪ afrontar la pena de muerte ➤ *(news item)* The Washington sniper faces the death penalty. El francotirador de Washington se enfrenta a la pena de muerte.

to **face the facts** afrontar los hechos ▪ asumir los hechos

to **face the music** dar la cara ▪ aguantar la vela ▪ rendir cuentas ▪ asumir mis responsabilidades ➤ I have to face the music. Tengo que dar la cara. ▪ Tengo que aguantar mi vela. ▪ Tengo que rendir cuentas. ▪ Tengo que asumir mis responsabilidades.

to **face the opposition** encarar la oposición ▪ encararse a la oposición ▪ encararse con la oposición

to **face the other way 1.** dar al otro lado ▪ dar en la otra dirección **2.** mirar para el otro lado ➤ The ski slope faces the other way. La pista de esquí da al otro lado. ▪ La pista de esquí da en la otra dirección. ➤ Face the other way for a second. Mira para el otro lado un segundo.

to **face the reality of something** enfrentarse a la realidad de algo

face to face: to mate ~ aparearse cara a cara ➤ Orangutan(g)s mate face to face. Los orangutáns se aparean cara a cara.

face to face: to stand ~ estar de pie cara a cara ▪ estar parados cara a cara

face to face: to talk ~ hablar frente a frente ▪ hablar cara a cara

to **face (toward) something** dar a algo ▪ lindar con algo ➤ The apartment faces Sor Ángela de la Cruz. El piso da a Sor Ángela de la Cruz. ➤ The university store faces the rectory. La fachada de la tienda universitaria da al rectorado. ➤ The building faces north toward a vacant field. El edificio linda al norte con un descampado. ▪ El edificio da al norte hacia un descampado.

to **face up** quedar boca arriba ▪ estar mirando hacia arriba ➤ Turn the box so that it faces up before you open it. Dale la vuelta a la caja de modo que quede boca arriba antes de abrirla. ▪ Dale la vuelta a la caja de modo que mire hacia arriba antes de abrirla. ➤ Make sure the box is facing up before you open it. Asegúrate de que la caja esté mirando boca arriba antes de que la abras.

face up: to lie ~ ▪ to lie supine ▪ to lie on one's back yacer boca arriba ➤ The victim was lying face up. ▪ The victim was lying supine. La víctima estaba tendida boca arriba. ➤ You accidentally put the paper in the copier face up. Accidentalmente pusiste el papel boca arriba en la copiadora. ➤ Put the monitor in the box face up. Mete el monitor en la caja boca arriba.

to **face up to a crisis** afrontar una crisis ▪ encarar una crisis ▪ hacer frente a una crisis

to **face (up to) reality** enfrentarse a la realidad

to **face up to the fact that...** enfrentarse a que...

face value *el* valor nominal ➤ It's sold at face value and bought for (its) face value. Se vende al valor nominal y se compra por el valor nominal.

face value: to take something at ~ tomar algo en sentido literal ■ tomar algo tal cual ■ tomar algo tal cual viene ■ tomar algo a secas ■ tomar algo en bruto ➤ If you took the TV images at face value, you'd think the bulls were running loose all over Spain. Si tomaras las imágenes de la tele tal cual están, pensarías que los toros están corriendo sueltos alrededor de toda España.

faced with the prospect of... ante la perspectiva de...

faced with... ante... ➤ Faced with the risk of... Ante el riesgo de...

to be **faced with** ■ to be facing enfrentarse a ■ hacer frente a ➤ The country is faced with a growing budget deficit. ■ The country is facing a growing budget deficit. El país se enfrenta a un creciente déficit presupuestario. ■ El país hace frente a un creciente déficit presupuestario.

to be **faced with a dilemma** ■ to face a dilemma ■ to be on the horns of a dilemma afrontar un dilema ■ verse ante un dilema

facial scar ■ scar on the face *la* cicatriz en la cara ■ *(from street violence)* chirlo

facing each other: to sit ~ ■ to sit face to face sentarse frente a frente ■ sentarse cara a cara

facing each other: to stand ~ ■ to stand face to face estar (de pie) frente a frente ■ estar (de pie) cara a cara

to be **facing in the opposite direction** estar de cara al lado contrario ■ estar mirando al lado contrario ■ estar de cara al otro lado ■ estar mirando al otro lado

to be **facing the front** estar dando al frente

to be **facing the other way** estar dando en otra dirección ■ estar dando al otro lado

to be **facing towards** estar dando hacia ■ estar dando a

fact-finding commission comisión de investigación (de hechos) ➤ The president appointed a fact-finding commission. El presidente nombró una comisión de investigación de hechos.

fact-finding tour *el* viaje de investigación (de hechos) ➤ The senators went on a fact-finding tour. Los senadores fueron de viaje de investigación de hechos. ■ Los senadores fueron en viaje de investigación de hechos.

the **fact is that** el hecho es que ■ el caso es que ■ es el caso que ■ es que

fact of life ■ harsh reality cruda realidad ■ triste realidad (de la vida) ■ dura realidad (de la vida) ■ el pan de cada día ➤ Traffic jams are a fact of life in big cities. Los atascos son la cruda realidad de las grandes ciudades. ■ Los atascos son nuestro pan de cada día en las ciudades grandes.

the **fact remains that** la realidad sigue siendo que...

the **fact that...** **1.** el hecho de que... **2.** el que... ➤ The fact that he has been a good worker should guarantee him a good retirement. El hecho de que haya sido un buen trabajador debería garantizarle una buena jubilación. ➤ The fact that we've gotten this far proves that we're the fastest. El que hayamos llegado hasta aquí prueba que somos los más rápidos.

to the **fact that...** a que... ■ al hecho que...

to be a **fact that...** ser un hecho que...

factor analysis *el* análisis de factores

to **factor analyze** analizar los factores ➤ The psychologists factor analyzed the results of the personality test. Los psicólogos analizaron los factores del resultado de test de personalidad.

to be a **factor in one's decision to...** ser un factor en la decisión de uno de... ■ ser un hecho a tomar en cuenta en la decisión de uno de... ➤ His health was a factor in his decision to move to a warmer climate. Su salud fue un factor en su decisión de mudarse a climas más cálidos.

to **factor in the cost** tomar en cuenta el costo ➤ Food processing companies must factor in the cost of packaging. Las compañías que elaboran la comida deben tomar en cuenta el costo adicional del empaquetado.

to be a **factor in the cost** ser un aspecto en el costo de ■ ser un factor en el costo de ■ ser una consideración en el costo de ➤ Packaging is a factor in the cost of food. El empaquetado es un elemento que influye en el costo de la comida.

to be **factored into** ser tenido en cuenta en ➤ The cost of the can must be factored into the cost of the frijoles. El costo de la lata debe ser tenido en cuenta en el costo total de los frijoles.

facts and figures datos y cifras ■ *(Sp.)* hechos y cifras

facts of life: to learn the ~ ■ to learn where babies come from saber como se hacen los niños ■ saber los detalles de la reproducción ➤ How old were you when you learned the facts of life? ¿Cuántos años tenías cuando supiste cómo se hacen los niños?

factual basis *la* base factible

factual error *el* error de hecho

factual evidence evidencia del hecho ➤ There is no factual evidence to support the claim that... No hay evidencia del hecho para apoyar el reclamo que...

factual information ■ the facts información basada en hechos reales ➤ They did not have the factual information on which to base such a conclusion. No tenían información basada en hechos puntuales sobre la que basar tal conclusión.

to be **factually correct** estar basado en hechos totalmente correctos ■ estar basado en hechos totalmente reales

to be **factually in error** ■ to be factually incorrect ■ to be factually mistaken ■ to be factually inaccurate ser un error ■ estar equivocado ➤ This article is factually in error. Este artículo tiene errores de hechos.

faculty (of a school) cuerpo docente ■ profesorado

to **fade into the darkness** desvanecerse en la oscuridad ■ difuminarse en la oscuridad

to **fade out** *(light or sound)* desvanecerse

to **fail a course** ■ to fail a subject reprobar una materia ■ *(Sp.)* suspender una asignatura ■ *(Sp., slang)* cargarle una asignatura

to **fail a grade** *(elementary school)* reprobar el año escolar ■ reprobar el curso ■ suspender el curso ➤ He almost failed fourth grade. Casi suspendió el cuarto (de primaria). ➤ He failed the grade. Suspendió el curso.

to **fail a student in a subject** suspender a un estudiante en una asignatura ■ cargar a un estudiante en una asignatura ■ *(Sp., coll.)* tirar a un estudiante ➤ The professor failed the student in calculus. El catedrático suspendió al estudiante en cálculo.

to **fail in one's attempt to** fracasar en el intento de

to **fail out of a university** ■ to flunk out of a university reprobar la universidad ➤ He's on probation (at the university), if he hasn't failed out, that is. Está a prueba (en la universidad), eso si no le han reprobado.

to be **fail-safe** estar a prueba de fallos

to **fail someone as a friend** fallarle a alguien como amigo ➤ I feel that I have failed you as a friend. Siento que te he fallado como amigo. ➤ I feel as if I have failed you as a friend. ■ I feel as though I have failed you as a friend. Siento como si (yo) te hubiera fallado como amigo.

to **fail to do something** fracasar en hacer algo ■ fallar en hacer algo ➤ I failed to write down the book's call number. Fracasé en apuntar la cota del libro.

to **fail to meet someone's expectations** no satisfacer (las) expectativas (puestas en uno) ■ fallar en alcanzar las expectativas de alguien

to **fail to understand** no poder comprender ■ no poder entender ➤ I fail to understand how you could win the lottery and a month later be broke. No puedo entender cómo pudiste ganar la lotería y estar quebrado un mes después.

failed attempt ■ unsuccessful attempt intento fallido ■ intento fracasado ➤ After nine years of failed attempts, a functioning transatlantic telegraph cable between the United States and Great Britain was laid in 1866. Después de nueve años de intentos fallidos, un cable transatlántico funcional entre los Estados Unidos y Gran Bretaña fue tendido en 1866. ■ Después de nueve años de intentos fracasados, un cable transatlántico funcional entre los Estados Unidos y Gran Bretaña fue tendido en 1866.

failed coup intento fallido de golpe de estado ■ *(Sp.)* intentona fallida de golpe de estado

failed transmission transmisión fallida

failing that en su defecto ➤ I plan to have the project ready by the end of the year, or failing that, by February. Pienso tener el proyecto listo para el fin del año, o en su defecto, para febrero.

failing this ▪ short of this en su defecto

failure to communicate falla de comunicación ➤ What we have here is a failure to communicate. Lo que tenemos aquí es una falla de comunicación.

failure to do something *la* omisión de hacer algo

faintest idea: not to have the ~ ▪ not to have the foggiest idea no tener la más mínima idea

fair and square: to beat someone ~ ganar a alguien con todas las de la ley ▪ *(archaic)* ganar a alguien en buena lid ➤ They beat us fair and square. Nos ganaron con todas las de la ley.

fair and square: to win ~ ganar con todas las de la ley ➤ He won the race fair and square. Ganó la carrera con todas las de la ley.

fair complexion tez (muy) blanca

fair-haired boy 1. *(literal)* blond-haired boy niño rubio **2.** *(figurative)* potential heir apparent apadrinado

to be **fair-minded** ser imparcial

fair play juego limpio ➤ It violated the rules of fair play. Violó las reglas de juego limpio.

the **fair sex** ▪ the female sex el sexo bello

fair shake: to get a ~ *(coll.)* ▪ to be treated fairly and equally ▪ to receive fair and equal treatment recibir un trato justo

fair shake: to give someone ~ *(coll.)* ▪ to treat someone fairly and equally dar a alguien un trato justo

to be **fair to warn you** ▪ to be only fair to warn you ser justo avisarle ➤ I think it's only fair to warn you that... ▪ I think it only fair to warn you... Pienso que sólo es justo avisarle que...

to be a **fair-weather friend** ser un(-a) amigo(-a) convenenciero(-a) ▪ ser un(-a) interesado(-a) ▪ ser un(-a) convenido(-a) ▪ ser un(-a) amigo(-a) cuando a uno le conviene ▪ por el interés, te quiero Andrés ▪ *(coll.)* ser un arrimao

fairgrounds recinto ferial

fairly: to act ~ ▪ to act justly actuar con justicia ▪ actuar con equidad

fairy dust polvos mágicos

fairy godmother hada madrina

fairy tale ▪ fairy story cuento de hadas

to be **faithful to someone** ser fiel a alguien ➤ He is faithful to his wife. Es fiel a su esposa.

to be **faithful to something** ▪ to reflect accurately ▪ to be true to ser fiel a algo ➤ The movie version of *Legend of Sleepy Hollow* is not faithful to Washington Irving's story. La versión cinematográfica de la *Leyenda de la Hondonada Soñolienta* no es fiel al cuento de Washington Irving.

to **fake being** ▪ to feign being ▪ to pretend to be hacer de ▪ simular estar ▪ simular ser ➤ The reporter had to fake being a waitress at the wedding of a mafioso in order to get material for an article. La reportera tuvo que hacer de camarera en la boda de un mafioso a fin de conseguir datos para un artículo. ➤ *(headline)* A youth fakes being kidnapped Un joven simula estar secuestrado

to **fall apart** caerse a pedazos ▪ hacerse trizas ▪ desarmarse ▪ *(coll., esp. old books)* descuajaringarse ▪ *(Arg.)* descuajeringarse ➤ I hate hamburgers that fall apart. No soporto las hamburguesas que se deshacen. ▪ No soporto las hamburguesas que se desarman.

to **fall asleep** dormirse ▪ quedarse dormido ▪ caer dormido ▪ conciliar el sueño ▪ venirle el sueño ▪ quedarse cuajado

to **fall away** perder la fe ▪ apostatar ➤ He was a terrorist, and he fell away and became a peace advocate. El terrorista perdió la fe en el terrorismo y llegó a ser un defensor de la paz.

to **fall back on** ▪ to have as backup ▪ to be able to use in an emergency recurrir a

to **fall backwards onto** caer de espaldas sobre

to **fall behind** ▪ to get behind quedarse atrás ▪ rezagarse ▪ retrasarse

to **fall below** caer por debajo de ➤ The Dow Jones fell below 10,000 for the first time since March. El Dow Jones cayó por debajo del 10.000 por primera vez desde marzo.

to **fall by the wayside** ▪ to fall into disuse caer en desuso

to **fall due** ▪ to come due ▪ to be due llegar al vencimiento ▪ llegar a su vencimiento ➤ The note fell due in November. El pagaré llegó a su vencimiento en noviembre.

to **fall fast asleep** caer rendido de sueño

to **fall flat 1.** *(plans)* irse al traste **2.** *(joke)* no hacer ni pizca de gracia ➤ My plans to go Montevideo have fallen flat. Mis planes para ir a Montevideo se han ido al traste. ➤ His jokes fell flat. Sus chistes no hicieron ni pizca de gracia.

to **fall flat on one's face** caerse de bruces ▪ caerse de boca

to **fall for (a deception)** ▪ to be duped ▪ to be taken in (by) creérselo ➤ *(Wile E. Coyote, plotting against Road Runner)* My trick is working. He's falling for it. Mi truco sirve. ¡Se lo está creyendo! ➤ I'm not going to fall for that. No me la creo.

to **fall for someone** ▪ to flip over someone ▪ to fall head over heels in love with someone volverse loco(-a) por alguien

fall from grace *(noun phrase)* pérdida de la gracia ▪ caída en desgracia

to **fall from grace 1.** caer de la gracia (de alguien) ▪ caer en desgracia **2.** *(theologically)* perder la gracia (divina)

to be the **fall guy** pagar el pato ▪ pagar los platos rotos ▪ ser el chivo expiatorio

to **fall hard** caer de plomo

to **fall headfirst** caer de cabeza

to **fall in** *(military)* ▪ to get into formation ponerse en la formación ▪ formarse

fall in! ¡a la formación! ▪ ¡fórmense!

to **fall in love with someone** enamorarse de alguien ▪ prendarse de alguien

to **fall in the middle of** caer en medio de ➤ The tax deadline falls right in the middle of exams. El fecha límite de pago de impuestos cae justo en medio de los exámenes.

to **fall into a swoon** ▪ to swoon caer desvanecido(-a) ▪ desvanecerse ▪ desmayarse

to **fall into a trap** caer en una trampa

to **fall into bad ways** caer en el mal ▪ irse por el mal camino

to **fall into bed** caer en cama

to **fall into disgrace** caer en desgracia

to **fall into disrepair** deteriorarse ➤ The cabin has fallen into disrepair. La cabaña se ha deteriorado.

to **fall into disuse** ▪ to fall by the wayside caer en desuso

to **fall into line** entrar por el aro ▪ pasar por el aro

to **fall into one's hands** venir a las manos ▪ llegar a las manos

to **fall into one's lap** venirle rodado algo a alguien ▪ caerle como anillo al dedo ➤ The opportunity fell into his lap. La oportunidad le vino rodada (a él). ➤ The opportunity fell into her lap. La oportunidad le vino rodada (a ella).

to **fall into place** caer en su lugar ▪ salir a pedir de boca ➤ First choose a realistic goal, pursue it singlemindedly, and your life will fall into place. Primero fija una meta posible, persíguela con toda tu mente, y tu vida caerá en su lugar. ➤ Everything just (sort of) fell into place. Todo salió a pedir de boca.

to **fall into someone's clutches** caer en sus garras

to **fall into temptation** caer en la tentación

to **fall into the water** caerse al agua

to **fall into the wrong hands** ir a parar a malas manos

to **fall mortally wounded** caer herido mortalmente

fall of man caída del hombre

to **fall off (of) 1.** caerse de **2.** to come off desprenderse de ➤ He fell off (of) the horse. Se cayó del caballo. ➤ The plastic window falls off (of) the microwave oven. La ventana plástica se desprende del horno microondas.

to **fall on a certain date** ▪ to occur on caer en determinada fecha ➤ The Day of the Innocents, the Spanish equivalent of April Fools Day, falls on December 28. El Día de los Inocentes, equivalente español al Día de los tontos de abril, cae en el veintiocho de diciembre.

to **fall on deaf ears** ▪ to go in one ear and out the other caer en saco roto ▪ entrar por una oreja y salir por la otra

to **fall on hard times** caer en tiempos difíciles

to **fall on one's knees** caerse de rodillas ▪ caerse de hinojos

to **fall out 1.** *(of a military formation)* to break ranks romper filas ▪ romper formación **2.** *(bottom of a box)* to give way desfondarse **3.** *(tooth filling)* to come loose ▪ to come out desprenderse ➤

The bottom of the box fell out under the weight of the books. La caja se desfondó bajo el peso de los libros. ➤ My filling fell out. Mi empaste se desprendió.

to **fall out of** salirse de ➤ The plug falls out of the socket. El enchufe se sale del toma (corrientes).

to **fall out of bed** caerse de la cama ➤ Did you fall out of bed? ¿Te caíste de la cama?

to **fall out of favor with someone** ▪ to lose favor with someone perder el favor de alguien

to **fall peacefully asleep** ▪ to fall peacefully to sleep quedarse apaciblemente dormido(-a)

to **fall prey to** caer víctima de

to **fall short** quedarse corto ➤ *(news item)* The American administrator in Iraq acknowledges that the first calculations fell short. El administrador norteamericano en Irak reconoce que los primeros cálculos se quedaron cortos.

to **fall short of one's expectations** quedarse corto en las expectativas de alguien

to **fall short of one's goals** **1.** quedarse corto en los objetivos de uno **2.** *(personal goals)* quedarse corto en las metas de uno

to **fall short of something** quedarse corto de algo ➤ The movie falls short of the (quality of the) book. La película se queda corta (de la calidad) del libro.

to **fall through** haber un cambio de planes ➤ I was going to go skiing this weekend, but my plans fell through. Iba a ir a esquiar este fin de semana, pero hubo un cambio de planes.

falling apart: the building is ~ el edificio está cayéndose a pedazos

falling apart: I'm ~ **1.** *(in body)* me estoy poniendo achacoso(-a) **2.** *(in spirit)* me estoy derrumbando

falling apart: my hamburger is ~ ▪ my hamburger is coming apart mi hamburguesa se está desarmando

falling apart: the car is ~ el coche está destartalado ▪ el coche se está cayéndo a pedazos ▪ *(Mex.)* el carro está destartalado ▪ el carro se está cayendo a pedazos

falling in love **1.** *(noun phrase)* enamoramiento **2.** *(verb phrase)* enamorándose

false alarm falso aviso ➤ *(news item)* Two more minors arrested for a false bomb alarm. Detenidos otros dos menores por falso aviso de bomba.

false lead pista falsa

false modesty modestia fingida

false positive: to give a ~ dar un falso positivo ➤ Some drug detection tests can give a false positive. Algunas pruebas de detección de drogas pueden dar un falso positivo.

false premise: to start with a ~ ▪ to start from a false premise empezar con una premisa falsa

false pretenses: under ~ bajo falsos pretextos ➤ He entered the base under false pretenses. Entró a la base bajo falsos pretextos.

falling out (with someone): to have a ~ ya no tratarse más ➤ They had a falling out. Ya no se tratan más.

false start **1.** intento fallido **2.** *(sports, especially swimming and track)* to begin before the signal is given comienzo en falso ▪ arranque fallido ➤ After several false starts, I finally have E-mail. Después de varios intentos fallidos, finalmente tengo correo electrónico. ➤ After two false starts, the runner was disqualified. Después de dos arranques fallidos, el atleta fue descualificado.

false statement declaración falsa

false teeth ▪ dentures dentaduras postizas

faltering voice *la* voz titubeante

familiar face cara conocida ➤ His face is familiar. Su cara es conocida.

to be **familiar with** ▪ to be knowledgeable about estar familiarizado ▪ conocer ▪ haber probado ➤ *(to grocery clerk)* Are you familiar with the coffee? ¿Estás familiarizado con estos cafés? ▪ ¿Conoces los cafés? ▪ ¿Has probado estos cafés?

family affair asunto de familia

the **family comes first** la familia es lo primero

family doctor ▪ general practitioner médico de cabecera

family get-together *la* reunión familiar

family heirloom reliquia de familia

to be a **family matter** ser un asunto que concierne a la familia ▪ ser un tema familiar ▪ ser un asunto familiar

family member *el, la* miembro de la familia ▪ *el, la* integrante de la familia

family of *x* familia de *x* miembros ➤ A family of five Una familia de cinco miembros

family oriented para toda la familia ➤ It's a family-oriented movie. Es una película para toda la familia.

family reunion *la* reunión familiar

family resemblance *el* aire de familia ➤ You can see the family resemblance in the photo. Se puede ver el aire de familia en la foto.

family secrets secretos de la familia ▪ secretos familiares

family ties lazos de familia ▪ lazos familiares

family tree árbol de familia ▪ árbol geneológico ▪ tronco familiar

to be **famous for being...** tener fama de ser...

to be **famous for something** ser famoso por algo ➤ Margarita Island is famous for its beautiful white beaches. La Isla Margarita es famosa por sus hermosas playas de blanca arena.

famous last words! ¡famosas últimas palabras!

fan club **1.** *(of a show business personality)* *el* club de admiradores **2.** *(of an athletic team)* club de aficionados

fan deck ▪ color chart escalera de color

to **fan resentment(s)** incitar resentimientos

to **fan the flames** **1.** *(literal, as when making a fire)* avivar las llamas **2.** *(figurative, as to incite unrest)* poner leña al fuego

to **fancy something** ▪ to desire something apetecerle a uno *(always third-person in Spanish)* ➤ She fancies that dress. A ella le apetece ese vestido. ➤ I fancy that Corvette. Me apetece ese Corvette.

fancy clothes ropa elegante ▪ ropa chic

to **fancy oneself to be...** creerse uno mismo... ▪ dárselas de...

fancy sports car coche deportivo lujoso ▪ coche deportivo opulento ▪ *(Mex.)* carro deportivo lujoso ▪ carro deportivo opulento

fancy that! ▪ imagine that! ¡vaya por donde! ▪ ¡imagínate! ▪ ¡mira por donde!

far and away *(coll.)* ▪ by far con diferencia ▪ con mucho ▪ de lejos ➤ It's far and away the best Mexican restaurant in Madrid. ▪ It's by far the best Mexican restaurant in Madrid. Es con mucho el mejor restaurante mexicano en Madrid. ▪ Es de lejos el mejor restaurante mexicano en Madrid.

far and wide: to look ~ ▪ to look everywhere buscar a lo largo y a lo ancho ▪ buscar por todas partes ➤ We've looked far and wide for a Spanish lace tablecloth that would fit this table. Hemos buscado a lo largo y a lo ancho un mantel de encaje español que le quede bien a esta mesa.

to be **far apart** estar muy alejados (uno del otro) ➤ Helsinki and St. Petersburg are not very far apart. Helsinki y San Petersburgo no están muy alejados. ➤ The candidates are far apart on the basic issues. Los candidatos están muy alejados en los temas básicos.

far be it from me nada más lejos de mi intención ▪ no lo pretendo

far be it from me to... nada más lejos de mi intención que...

far better than ▪ far superior to mucho mejor del que ▪ mucho mejor de la que ▪ muy superior a ➤ In my teacher's opinion, Gottschalk is a far better composer than I am. En la opinión de mi profesor, Gottschalk es un compositor mucho mejor del que soy yo. ▪ En la opinión de mi profesor, Gottschalk es un compositor muy superior a mí.

far beyond: to go ~ ir mucho más lejos que ➤ Magellan's voyages went far beyond those of Columbus. Los viajes de Magallanes fueron mucho más lejos que los de Colón.

Far East lejano oriente ▪ extremo oriente

far end: at the ~ en el (otro) extremo

far-fetched story **1.** *(fiction)* cuento poco probable ▪ cuento inverosímil **2.** *(non-fiction)* historia poco probable ▪ historia inverosímil ➤ The story of Joan of Arc seems far-fetched, yet Mark Twain notes that the facts of her life are beyond the inventive reach of fiction. La historia de Juana de Arco parece poco probable, sin embargo Mark Twain nota que los hechos de su vida están más allá del alcance inventivo de la ficción.

to be **far from** estar lejos de

to be **far from being** **1.** *(permanent quality)* estar lejos de ser **2.** *(transitory condition)* ser lejos de estar ➤ Far from being arrogant, he's a very humble person. Lejos de ser arrogante, es una persona muy humilde. ➤ The ex-football player finds himself today far from being in condition to participate on the playing field. El ex-futbolista se encuentra hoy en día lejos de estar en condiciones de participar en el campo de juego.

far from it! ¡ni mucho menos! ▪ en absoluto

to be **far from over** estar lejos de terminar

to be **far from perfect** ser ni mucho menos perfecto ▪ distar bastante de ser perfecto

to be **far from the truth** estar alejado de la verdad

far left *(politically)* ▪ extreme left izquierda extrema

far less than mucho menos de lo que

far more than mucho más de lo que

far-off lands ▪ faraway lands ▪ distant lands tierras lejanas

far out! ¡cojonudo! ▪ ¡macanudo!

Far Side *(Larson cartoon)* El lado opuesto

far side of a hill ▪ other side of a hill ▪ opposite side of a hill lado opuesto de una colina ➤ Ships as they reach the horizon disappear as if they were descending the far side of a hill, long before they reach the vanishing point of distant objects. Los barcos al alcanzar el horizonte desaparecen como si estuviesen descendiendo el lado opuesto de una colina, mucho antes de alcanzar el punto de fuga de los objetos distantes.

to be **far superior to** ser muy superior a

far-reaching agreement acuerdo de gran alcance

far-reaching consequences consecuencias de gran alcance

far right *(politically)* ▪ extreme right extrema derecha ▪ derecha más dura ➤ *(headline)* Far right holds the key to the governability of Portugal Derecha más dura tiene la llave de la gobernabilidad de Portugal

to be **far worse than** ▪ to be much worse than ser mucho peor de lo que

faraway lands ▪ far-off lands ▪ distant lands tierras lejanas

faraway place *el* lugar muy distante

farewell address discurso de despedida ▪ discurso de adiós

to be **farther along than...** estar más lejos de lo que... ➤ Columbus led his sailors to believe they were farther along than they really were. Colón hizo creer a sus marineros que ellos estaban más lejos de lo que en realidad estaban.

farther back más atrás ➤ Let's sit farther back. Vamos a sentarnos más atrás.

to be **farther down** **1.** to be farther along estar más para abajo **2.** to be lower down estar más abajo ➤ The bus stop is farther down. La parada de autobúses está más para abajo.

farther on más allá ▪ más adelante

farther than más lejos de lo que ➤ Columbus told his sailors they had advanced farther than they really had. A sus marineros Colón les dijo que habían avanzado más de lo que realmente habían.

farther than you think más lejos de lo que imaginas

to be **farther up the road** ▪ to be farther down the road ▪ farther along the road estar más adelante (en el camino)

farthest reaches puntos más distantes ▪ alcances más distantes ➤ Today's space telescopes penetrate the farthest reaches of the universe. Los telescopios espaciales de hoy en día penetran los puntos más distantes del universo.

to be the **farthest thing from one's mind** ser la cosa más lejana de la mente de uno ▪ ser la cosa más distante de la mente de uno ➤ That was the farthest thing from my mind. Era la cosa más lejana de mi mente. ▪ Era la cosa más distante de mi mente.

fashion designer diseñador(-a) de moda

fashion show *la* exhibición de moda ▪ *el* desfile de moda

fast-acting barbiturate barbitúrico de acción rápida ➤ Mortally injured animals are usually given a fast-acting barbiturate. Animales heridos mortalmente se les suelen dar barbitúrico de acción rápida.

to be **fast approaching** aproximarse rápidamente ➤ The holiday season is fast approaching. La temporada navideña se aproxima rapidamente.

fast as you can ▪ as fast as you can tan rápido como puedas ▪ tan rápido como pueda (usted)

fast cars carros veloces ▪ *(Sp.)* los coches veloces

to be **fast enough** ser (lo) suficientemente rápido(-a)

fast enough: to go ~ ir lo suficientemente rápido

to **fast forward** adelantar

fast lane: to be in the ~ **1.** *(literal)* estar en la vía rápida ▪ estar en el carril de alta velocidad **2.** *(figurative)* to live life in the fast lane vivir quemando etapas

fast rate ▪ rapid rate tarifa expresa ➤ Is the postage for a fast rate? ¿Es éste el franqueo para la tarifa expresa?

to **fasten a necklace** abrochar un collar ▪ engarzar un collar

to **fasten one's seat belt** abrocharse el cinturón de seguridad ▪ abrochar el cinturón de seguridad ▪ ajustar el cinturón de seguridad ➤ Please fasten your seat belts. Por favor, abróchense los cinturones de seguridad.

fastest-growing economy economía de crecimiento rápido

fastest way forma más rápida ▪ vía más rápida ▪ manera más rápida ➤ What's the fastest way to send this to England? ¿Cuál es la vía más rápida de enviar esto a Inglaterra?

fat cat *(self-interested rich person) el* pez gordo

fat chance! ▪ dream on! ¡ni lo sueñes! ▪ ¡ni lo pienses! ▪ ¡ni creas!

fat chance of that (happening) no caerá esa breva

Fatal Attraction *(film title) Relación mortal*

fatal illness ▪ terminal illness *la* enfermedad mortal ▪ enfermedad terminal

fate decreed that... el destino decretó que... ▪ el azar quiso que...

fate of the pilot and crew destino del piloto y tripulado ▪ *la* suerte del piloto y tripulado

fateful day día aciago ▪ día fatídico ▪ aciago día

father figure figura paterna

father-in-law suegro ▪ padre político

Father of Waters *(Native American name of the Mississippi River)* el río Misisipi ➤ *(Abraham Lincoln)* The Father of Waters again goes unvexed to the sea. El padre de las aguas de nuevo va tranquilamente al mar. *(Spoken after the fall of Vicksburg, which gave Union forces control of the Mississippi.)*

to **fatten (up) an animal** cebar un animal ▪ (hacer) engordar un animal

fattening food comida que hace engordar

fatty tissue tejido adiposo

to **fault someone for something** ▪ to blame someone for something culpar a alguien por algo ➤ I don't fault you for not tipping that waiter. No te culpo por no dar propina a ese camarero.

faultfinding: to engage in ~ ▪ to find fault ver la paja en el ojo ajeno

faulty reasoning razonamiento erróneo

faulty wiring cableado dañado ▪ cableado estropeado ➤ The short circuit was caused by faulty wiring. El cortocircuito fue causado por un cableado dañado.

the **favor of a reply is requested** R.S.V.P. se ruega contestación ▪ SRC

to **favor one's leg** ▪ to limp slightly cojear ▪ renguear ➤ You're favoring your right leg. Did you hurt it? Estás cojeando de la pierna derecha. ¿Te hiciste daño (en la pierna)?

to **favor someone** **1.** estar a favor de alguien ▪ simpatizar con alguien **2.** to resemble someone tener un parecido ➤ I don't want to say who I favor for president. No quiero decir a favor de quien estoy para presidente. ➤ The new baby favors the mother's side of the family. El nuevo bebé tiene más parecido al lado materno. *("Bebé" is masculine even when it refers to a female.)*

favorable circumstances: under ~ bajo circunstancias favorables

to be **favored (to win)** ser favorito a ▪ llevar las de ganar ➤ Raúl is expected to win the Golden Football Award. Raúl es favorito al "Balón de Oro". ➤ Who's favored (to win)? ¿Quién es el favorito?

favorite dish plato favorito ▪ plato preferido

favorite subject asignatura favorita ▪ materia favorita

 favorite thing to do cosa favorita para hacer ▪ actividad favorita

to **fear for one's life** temer por su vida

fear of failure miedo al fracaso

fear of recession miedo de la recesión ➤ Fear of recession is stronger than the fear of war. El miedo de la recesión puede más que el miedo de la guerra.

fear of the dark miedo de la oscuridad

to **fear the worst** temerse lo peor

to be **fearful that...** estar temeroso de que...

fearing that... ▪ afraid that... ▪ for fear that... ▪ out of fear that... por temor a que...

feast or famine: to be either ~ ser todo o nada

to **feather a propeller** colocar (las cuerdas de) las palas de una hélice paralelas a la línea de vuelo

to be a **feather in one's cap** ser un tanto para apuntarse

to **feather one's nest (by)** lucrarse (de)

feature-length film película de largo metraje

to **feature someone on the cover (of a magazine)** destacar a alguien en la portada (de una revista) ➤ The cover features Ricky Martin. ▪ Ricky Martin is featured on the cover. La portada destaca a Ricky Martin. ➤ A program featuring the royal family Un programa destacando a la familia real

features of a computer características de una computadora ▪ *(Sp.)* características de un ordenador ➤ This computer has some features that the old one didn't. Esta computadora tiene algunas características que la vieja no tenía.

to be **fed up with having to do something** estar harto de tener que hacer algo ▪ estar hasta la coronilla de tener que hacer algo ▪ *(Sp.)* estar hasta las narices de tener que hacer algo

to be **fed up with someone (or something)** estar harto de alguien (o algo) ▪ estar hasta el gorro de alguien (o algo) ▪ estar hasta la coronilla de alguien (o algo) ▪ *(Sp.)* estar hasta las narices de alguien (o algo)

fed up with someone (or something): to get ~ quedar harto de alguien (o algo) ▪ quedar hasta el gorro de alguien (o algo) ▪ quedar hasta la coronilla de alguien (o algo) ▪ quedar hasta las narices de alguien (o algo)

Federal Reserve Board Reserva Federal

to **feed a hundred people** dar de comer a cien personas ▪ alimentar a cien personas

to **feed on** alimentarse de

to **feed someone a line** venirle con historias a alguien ▪ venirle con cuentos (chinos) a alguien ➤ He's feeding you a line. Don't buy it. Te viene con historias. No se lo creas. ➤ You've been fed a line. Don't buy it. Te han venido con historias. No se lo creas.

to **feed the dog** dar de comer al perro ▪ alimentar al perro ➤ The dogs are fed twice a day. Se les da de comer a los perros dos veces al día.

to **feed the baby** dar de comer al bebé ▪ alimentar al bebé

to **feel a draft** sentir una corriente de aire

to **feel an earthquake** sentir un terremoto ▪ sentir un seísmo ▪ notar un seísmo ➤ *(news item)* An earthquake felt in Spain leaves 564 dead in Morocco. Un seísmo que se notó en España deja 564 muertos en Marruecos.

to **feel an undercurrent of** ▪ to sense an undercurrent of ▪ to detect an undercurrent of sentir un trasfondo de ▪ sentir una contracorriente de

to **feel animosity toward someone** ▪ to feel antipathy for someone sentir antipatía por alguien

to **feel attracted to someone** sentirse atraído(-a) por alguien

to **feel apprehensive that...** sentirse inquieto de que... ▪ sentir aprensión que... ▪ temer que...

to **feel at home** sentirse como en casa

to **feel awful** sentirse fatal ▪ estar fatal ➤ I feel awful. Me siento fatal. ▪ Estoy fatal.

to **feel bad about something** 1. sentirse mal por algo 2. *(for which one feels responsible)* tener cargo de conciencia por algo ➤ I don't want you to feel bad about it. No quiero que te sientas mal por eso.

to **feel bad that...** 1. sentirse mal de que... 2. *(for which one feels responsible)* darle cargo de conciencia que...

to **feel certain** sentir con certeza ➤ I feel certain that he will agree. Siento con certeza que él estará de acuerdo.

to **feel compassion for someone** sentir compasión por alguien ▪ sentir compasión para con alguien

to **feel confident about it** sentirse con confianza al respecto ➤ Do you feel confident about it? *(tú)* ¿Te sientes con confianza al respecto? ▪ *(usted)* ¿Se siente (usted) con confianza al respecto?

to **feel deeply** sentir a lo más vivo ➤ She felt it deeply. Ella lo sintió a lo más vivo.

to **feel dispirited** sentirse desasosegado

to **feel dizzy** sentirse mareado

to **feel drawn to someone** sentirse simpatía por alguien ▪ sentirse atraído por alguien

to **feel drowsy** sentirse somnoliento(-a)

to **feel embarrassed for someone** ▪ to feel ashamed for someone sentir vergüenza ajena ➤ The talk show guests came out with so many personal revelations that I felt embarrassed for them. Los invitados del programa televisivo soltaban tantas intimidades que (yo) sentía vergüenza ajena.

to **feel exhausted** sentirse exhausto ▪ sentirse agotado

to **feel free to** sentirse con libertad de

to **feel good about something** ▪ to have a good feeling about something sentirse bien por algo ➤ I feel good about his decision to go into business for himself. Me siento bien por su decisión de montar un negocio por cuenta propia.

to **feel faint** ▪ to feel like one is going to faint sentir que uno está por desmayarse ➤ I feel faint. ▪ I feel like I'm going to faint. Siento que me voy a desmayar. ▪ Siento que estoy por desmayarme.

to **feel great** ▪ to feel wonderful sentirse de maravilla

to **feel guilty (for...)** ▪ to feel guilty (about...) sentirse culpable (por...)

to **feel happy (about something)** sentirse feliz

to **feel happy for someone** ▪ to be happy for someone alegrarse por alguien ➤ I feel happy for you. ▪ I'm happy for you. Me alegro por ti.

to **feel homesick** ▪ to be homesick extrañar el hogar ▪ extrañar la casa ▪ *(Sp.)* sentir morriña ▪ tener morriña ▪ echar de menos la familia ▪ *(Ven.)* tener casitis aguda

to **feel hurt** sentirse herido(-a) ▪ sentirse lastimado(-a)

to **feel ill will toward someone** ▪ to have ill will for someone tener mala voluntad hacia alguien ▪ tener mala voluntad con alguien ▪ tener mala voluntad para con alguien

to **feel intense dislike for someone** ▪ to intensely dislike someone ▪ not to be able to stomach someone atragantársele ▪ no pasarse a alguien ➤ He felt intense dislike for someone. Se le atraganta. ▪ No se lo(-a) pasa.

to **feel it beneath one to do something** ▪ to feel that it's beneath one to do something caérsele los anillos ▪ menospreciar algo ➤ Though a former president, Jimmy Carter does not feel that it's beneath him to work as a carpenter. Aún siendo el antiguo presidente, a Jimmy Carter no se le caen los anillos por trabajar como carpintero.

to **feel it in one's bones** tener una corazonada sobre algo ▪ tener un presentimiento de algo

to **feel left out** sentirse excluido ▪ sentirse marginado

to **feel like** ▪ to feel as if ▪ to seem like sentirse como ➤ What does it feel like? ¿Cómo se siente?

to **feel like a fool** sentirse como un tonto. ➤ I feel like a fool. Me siento como un tonto. ➤ I felt like a fool when I ripped the back of my pants. Me sentí como un tonto cuando se me rasgó la parte de atrás de mi pantalón.

to **feel like a new person** sentirse como nuevo(-a)

to **feel like death warmed over** ▪ to feel terrible ▪ to feel really sick encontrarse fatal

to **feel like doing something** tener ganas de hacer algo ▪ *(Sp.)* apetecerle a alguien hacer algo ➤ I feel like going for a walk. Tengo ganas de dar un paseo. ▪ Me apetece dar un paseo.

to **feel lonesome** sentirse solo(-a)

to **feel modest** ▪ to feel modesty tener pudor

feel of the controls *la* sensación de los mandos (de control) ▪ sensación que dan los mandos (de control) ➤ The feel of the controls changes just before the airplane stalls. La sensación

de los mandos cambia justo antes de que el avión pierda velocidad de vuelo.
feel of the weave ▪ feel of the cloth ▪ feel of the fabric *el* roce del tejido ▪ *la* sensación del tejido
to **feel one's forehead** *(to check for a fever)* tocar la frente
to **feel one's oats** sentirse vigoroso ➤ Feeling your oats today, huh? Sintiéndote vigoroso hoy, ¿no?
to **feel one's way along** ▪ to grope one's way along ▪ to grope along tantear ▪ andar a tientas ➤ The blind man felt his way along with his cane. El ciego tanteaba el suelo con el bastón.
to **feel oppressed** sentirse oprimido
to **feel optimistic about something** sentirse optimista acerca de algo
to **feel out of place** sentirse fuera de lugar ▪ sentirse fuera del tiesto
to **feel pity for someone** sentir pena por alguien
to **feel reluctant to do something** sentirse renuente a hacer algo ▪ sentirse reacio a hacer algo
to **feel sheepish** sentirse vergonzoso ▪ sentirse abochornado
to **feel sick** encontrarse mal ➤ I feel sick. Me encuentro mal.
to **feel sick to one's stomach** ▪ to feel sick at one's stomach sentirse mal del estómago ▪ estar nauseabundo ▪ tener nauseas
to **feel sleepy** tener sueño ▪ estar soñoliento ▪ estar somnoliento ▪ sentirse adormecido
to **feel slighted** sentirse desairado(-a)
to **feel sorry for oneself** sentir lástima por uno(-a) mismo(-a)
to **feel sorry for someone** sentirlo por alguien ▪ compadecer a alguien ▪ tener compasión de alguien ▪ inspirar lástima a alguien ▪ darle pena a alguien ➤ I feel sorry for that beggar. Lo siento por ese vagabundo. ▪ Me da pena ese vagabundo. ➤ I feel sorry for him. Lo compadezco. ▪ *(Sp., leísmo)* Le compadezco. ➤ I feel sorry for her. La compadezco.
to **feel strongly about something** tener una profunda opinión sobre algo ▪ tener una profunda opinión acerca de algo ➤ I feel very strongly that tacos should not fall apart when you eat them. Tengo una profunda opinión de que los tacos no se desarmen cuando uno los come.
to **feel sympathetic to** ▪ to be sympathetic to tener simpatía por
to **feel sympathy for someone** ▪ to have sympathy for someone tener simpatía por alguien
to **feel taken advantage of** sentir que se han aprovechado de uno ▪ *(Arg.)* sentirse currado
to **feel ten years younger** sentirse diez años más joven ➤ After I lost twenty pounds, I felt ten years younger. Después de perder veinte libras, me sentí diez años más joven.
to **feel terrible** ▪ to feel really sick sentirse mal ▪ *(Sp.)* encontrarse fatal
to **feel that...** sentir que... ➤ I feel that standing people up is bad form. Siento que dejar a alguien plantado es de mal educados.
feel that cool air! ¡siente esa corriente de aire fresco!
to **feel the effects of** sentir los efectos de ➤ Did you feel the effects of the hurricane in Cuba? ¿Sentiste los efectos del huracán en Cuba?
to **feel the heat** **1.** *(literal)* sentir el calor **2.** *(figurative)* to feel the pressure sentir la presión
to **feel the pressure** *(physical or emotional)* sentir la presión
to **feel the same way** sentirse igual ➤ In your place, I would have felt the same way. Yo en tu lugar me habría sentido igual.
to **feel uncomfortable** sentirse incómodo(-a) ▪ sentirse a disgusto
to **feel uneasy** ▪ to feel restless ▪ to feel on edge sentirse inquieto(-a) ▪ sentirse desasosegado(-a)
to **feel up someone** ▪ to feel someone up meter mano a alguien ▪ *(Mex.)* manosear a alguien ▪ *(Sp.)* magrear a alguien
to **feel violated** ▪ to feel treated unjustly sentirse invadido(-a)
to **feel welcome** sentirse bienvenido(-a) ➤ They made me feel welcome in their home. Me hicieron sentir bienvenida en su hogar.
to **feel well** ▪ to feel okay sentirse bien ▪ encontrarse bien ▪ *(Sp., always negative and accompanied by "muy")* estar católico ➤ Are you feeling well? ▪ Are you feeling okay? ¿Te encuentras bien? ▪ ¿Te sientes bien? ➤ I don't feel well. No me siento bien. ▪ No estoy muy católico.
to **feel wonderful** ▪ to feel great sentirse de maravilla
feelers of a crayfish ▪ antennae of a crayfish los bigotes de una langosta
the **feeling is mutual** el sentimiento es mutuo
feeling of being...: to have the ~ **1.** to have the feeling that one was being... tener la impresión de ser... ▪ tener la impresión de estar... **2.** tener la sensación de ser... ▪ tener la sensación de estar... ➤ Dealing with him, I had the feeling of being conned. Negociando con él, tuve la impresión de estar siendo estafado. ▪ Negociando con él, tuve la sensación de ser estafado.
feeling of belonging ▪ sense of belonging sentido de pertenecer
to be **feeling no pain** ▪ to be slightly high (on alcohol) estar alegre ▪ coger el puntillo
to be **feeling rambunctious** sentirse bullicioso(-a)
feeling that...: to have the ~ ▪ to have the sense that... tener la impresión (de) que... ▪ tener la sensación (de) que...
to be **feeling the heat** estar sintiendo la presión
to be **feeling the pressure to** ▪ to be pressured to recibir fuertes presiones para ➤ The Bank of Europe is feeling the pressure today to lower rates. El Banco Europeo recibe fuertes presiones para bajar hoy los tipos.
feelings are running high los ánimos están subidos
to be ***x* feet high** **1.** to be *x* feet in height tener *x* pies de alto ▪ tener *x* pies de altura **2.** to be *x* feet above the ground tener *x* pies de altitud ➤ The stones at Stonehenge are more than fifteen feet high. ▪ The stones at Stonehenge are more than fifteen feet in height. Las piedras de Stonehenge tienen más de quince pies de alto. ▪ Las piedras de Stonehenge tienen más de quince pies de altura.
to be ***x* feet in height** ▪ to be *x* feet high tener *x* pies de alto ▪ tener *x* pies de altura ▪ tener *x* pies de altitud
to be ***x* feet in length** ▪ to be *x* feet long tener *x* pies de longitud ▪ tener *x* pies de largo
to be ***x* feet in width** ▪ to be *x* feet wide tener *x* pies de anchura ▪ *x* pies de ancho
to be ***x* feet long** ▪ to be *x* feet in length tener *x* pies de largo ▪ tener *x* pies de longitud
feet wet: to get one's ~ *(literal and figurative)* mojarse los pies
feet wide ▪ in width los pies de ancho ▪ pies de anchura
feet stink: one's ~ apestarle los pies a uno ▪ *(Sp., colorful)* cantarle los pinreles a uno
to **feign a smile** sonreír sin la mayor gana ▪ sonreír sin la menor gana ▪ fingir una sonrisa
to **feign affection** fingir cariño ▪ fingir afecto
to **feign being a hick** hacerse el paleto
to **feign disappointment** fingir decepción
to **feign ignorance of** desentenderse de ▪ fingir ignorancia
feigned sleep ▪ pretended sleep sueño de la liebre
feisty little dog perrito lanzado ▪ perrito zarpado
felicitous idea *(literary)* idea oportuna
to **fell a tree** ▪ to cut down a tree talar un árbol
to **fell an opponent** *(with a blow)* derribar a un oponente
to be **felled by** ▪ to be stricken by desplomarse por ▪ to be brought down by ser derribado por ➤ The athlete is attended after being felled by a stomach cramp. El deportista es atendido tras desplomarse por un corte de digestión.
fellow in a guild socio de un gremio ➤ Fellow in the American Guild of Organists Socio del Gremio de Organistas Estadounidenses
fellow actor también actor
fellow actress también actriz
fellow citizen *el, la* compatriota ▪ conciudadano(-a)
fellow countryman paisano(-a)
fellow man: one's ~ su prójimo
fellow singer un(-a) también cantante
fellow student condiscípulo(-a) ▪ compañero(-a) de clase
fellow traveler ▪ communist sympathizer ▪ political ally *el, la* simpatizante comunista *("Fellow traveler" originally meant "com-*

munist sympathizer." Today, it can refer humorously to any like-minded colleague.)*

female boss jefa

female lead ▪ female star ▪ leading lady ▪ heroine protagonista feminina

to **fence in someone** ▪ to fence someone in acorralar a alguien ➤ Don't fence me in. No me acorrales. ➤ The farmer built a pen to fence in the chickens and turkeys. El granjero construyó un corral para encerrar a los pollos y los pavos.

fenced (in) yard jardín vallado ▪ *(implies a grass lawn)* césped vallado

to **fence off a plot (of ground)** ▪ to fence a plot (of ground) off cercar una parcela ▪ cercar un terreno ▪ cercar una zona ➤ We fenced off the vegetable garden. ▪ We fenced the vegetable garden off. Cercamos la huerta. ➤ We fenced it off. La cercamos.

to be a **fence straddler** ser jugador(-a) a dos bandas ▪ ser jugador(-a) a dos puntas ▪ querer quedar bien con Dios y con el diablo

fence straddling doesn't cut it jugar a dos bandas no vuela

to **fend for oneself** valerse por sí mismo

to **fend off someone** ▪ to fend someone off mantener alejados ▪ mantener distanciados ➤ The government troops fended off the insurgents. Las tropas del gobierno mantuvieron alejados a los insurgentes. ➤ The government troops fended them off. Las tropas del gobierno los mantuvieron alejados.

ferial and ember days *(Catholic feast days and fasting days)* días feriados y témporas

ferry between ▪ ferry from *el* transbordador entre ▪ transbordador que cubre el recorrido entre ➤ Ferry between Santander and Plymouth ▪ Ferry from Santander to Plymouth (and back) El transbordador (que cubre el recorrido) entre Santander y Plymouth

fertile field campo fértil ▪ vega

to be **fertile ground for** ser suelo fértil para

to **fertilize an egg** fertilizar un huevo

to **fertilize the soil** fertilizar el suelo

festering sore **1.** llaga ulcerada ▪ llaga ulcerosa **2.** *(emotional injury)* herida que el tiempo no cura

to **festoon with balloons and crepe paper streamers** decorar con globos y serpentinas

to **fetch a high price** *(coll.)* ▪ to bring a high price ▪ to garner a high price obtener un alto precio

to **fetch something** ir a buscar y traer algo ➤ Our dog will fetch the newspaper off the porch and bring it into the house. Nuestro perro irá a buscar el periódico afuera en el porche y lo traerá dentro la casa.

feudal contract contrato feudal

to be **few and far between** ser pocos y escasos

few books pocos libros ▪ unos libros ➤ *(Spanish proverb)* Books and friends, few and good. Libros y amigos, pocos y buenos.

few clues pocas pistas ▪ escasas pistas

few hundred votes unos centenares de votos

few inches away a una cuarta *("Una cuarta" is the distance from thumb tip to little-finger tip when the hand is stretched open.)*

to be a **few kilograms overweight** tener algunos kilos de más ▪ tener unos kilitos de más

to be a **few pounds overweight** tener algunas libras de más

fewer than usual menos de lo normal ➤ Because of the strike, there are fewer taxis than usual this morning. Por la huelga esta mañana, hay menos taxis de lo normal.

fiberglass fibra de vidrio

fiction or non-fiction? ¿ficción o realidad?

to **fiddle while Rome burns** ▪ to stand there and do nothing ▪ to stand by and do nothing quedarse de brazos cruzados

fictitious name: to register under a ~ inscribirse bajo un nombre supuesto

field day: to have a ~ darse un festín ➤ The students were having a field day with the substitute. Los alumnos se daban un festín con el suplente.

field trip: to go on a ~ **1.** *(primary, secondary school)* salir de excursión escolar **2.** *(university)* salir de excursión universitaria

field of expertise campo de pericia

field of research campo de investigación ▪ área de investigación

field of vision ▪ visual field campo visual

fierce determination ▪ iron determination firme determinación ▪ determinación de hierro ▪ férrea determinación

fierceness of the combat ▪ intensity of the combat *la* ferocidad del combate

fiery red color (rojo) fuego

Fifth of May *(Mexican holiday commemorating the defeat of the French in the Battle of Puebla, 1862)* Cinco de mayo

fifty-fifty chance *la* posibilidad cincuenta cincuenta

fight back (to counter something) retomar (algo) ➤ Crime has dropped because people in the inner cities are fighting back. El crimen ha bajado porque la gente en el centro de las ciudades están retomando vecindades.

to **fight for one's life** debatirse entre la vida y la muerte ➤ The attack victim was fighting for his life. El agredido se debatía entre la vida y la muerte.

to **fight for something one believes in** luchar por algo en lo que un cree ▪ luchar por las creencias de uno

to **fight in a war** pelear en una guerra ▪ luchar en una guerra ➤ His grandfather fought in the Second World War. Su abuelo peleó en la Segunda Guerra Mundial.

to **fight it out** pelearlo ➤ *(Ulysses S. Grant)* I intend to fight it out on this line if it takes all summer. Pienso pelearlo en esta línea así lleve todo el verano.

to **fight like cats and dogs** pelear como perros y gatos ➤ They fight like cats and dogs. Pelean como perros y gatos.

to **fight over something** **1.** *(literal)* pelear por algo **2.** *(figurative)* to argue over something discutir sobre algo ➤ The children were fighting over the toys. Los niños estaban peleando por los juguetes. ➤ The members of the European Union were fighting over the text of the new constitution. Los miembros de la Unión Europea discutían sobre el texto de la nueva constitución.

to be a **fight to the death** *(noun phrase)* **1.** *(between two or more people)* lucha a muerte **2.** *(between two people)* duelo a muerte

to **fight to the death** pelear hasta la muerte

to be a **fight to the finish** *(noun phrase)* ser una lucha hasta el final ▪ ser una lucha hasta sus consecuencias ▪ ser una pelea hasta el final ▪ ser una pelea hasta sus consecuencias

to **fight to the finish** *(verb phrase)* luchar hasta el final

to **fight tooth and nail** pelear con uñas y dientes ▪ luchar con uñas y dientes

fighter (airplane) ▪ fighter aircraft caza

fighter jet ▪ jet fighter caza a reacción ▪ caza de reacción

fightin' words ▪ fighting words palabras provocadoras ➤ Those are fightin' words. Son palabras provocadoras.

fighting chance: to give someone a ~ darle a alguien al menos una posibilidad

fighting chance: to have a ~ tener (al menos) una posibilidad ➤ The tiger, once facing extinction, now has a fighting chance (to survive). El tigre, una vez enfrentado con la extinción, ahora tiene una posibilidad (de sobrevivir).

figurative sense sentido figurativo

to **figure it out** encontrarle la vuelta ➤ I've figured it out. There's a way. Le he encontrado la vuelta. Hay una forma. ➤ I couldn't work the Rubik's Cube, but if you could take it apart, you could figure it out. No pude resolver el Cubo Rúbico, pero si se pudiera desarmar, podría encontrársele la vuelta.

figure of speech figura retórica

to **figure on** ▪ to count on ▪ to anticipate contar con ➤ I hadn't figured on that. (Yo) no contaba con eso.

to **figure out a math problem** ▪ to solve a math problem encontrarle la vuelta a un problema de matemática ▪ resolver un problema de matemática ➤ Can you figure out this math problem? ▪ Can you solve this math problem? ¿Puedes resolver este problema de matemática?

to **figure out a way to do something** ingeniárselas para hacer algo ▪ encontrarle la vuelta para hacer algo ➤ We need to figure out a way to keep the kids from finding their Christmas presents. Debemos ingeniárnoslas para evitar que los niños encuentren sus regalos de Navidad. ▪ Debemos encontrarle la vuelta para evitar que los niños encuentran sus regalos de Navidad.

to **figure out how to do something** encontrarle la vuelta de algo ■ saber como hacer algo ■ descubrir la manera de hacer algo ➤ I need to figure out how to work this TV remote. Necesito encontrarle la vuelta de este control remoto. ➤ I couldn't work the Rubik's Cube, but if you could take it apart, you could figure it out. No pude resolver el Cubo Rúbico, pero si se pudiera desarmar, podría encontrársele la vuelta.

to **figure out what...** descubrir lo que... ➤ I've figured what causes the computer to start scrolling. He descubierto lo que causa que la computadora empiece a desplazarse.

to **figure out what to do** descubrir lo que se debe hacer

to **figure out what to fix for supper** decidir qué preparar para la cena ➤ Claudia's a vegetarian, so I'm trying to figure out what to fix for supper. Claudia es vegetariana, así que estoy decidiendo qué preparar para la cena.

to **figure out whether... or** llegar a entender si... o ➤ *(interviewer to a famous writer)* I haven't figured out whether you believe in God or God believes in you. No he llegado a entender si usted cree en Dios o es Dios quien cree en usted.

to **figure out who...** to determine who determinar quien... ➤ It may take DNA testing to figure out who they were. ■ It may take DNA testing to determine who they were. Tal vez necesite una prueba de ADN para determinar quienes eran.

to **figure right** ■ to figure correctly calcular correctamente

figure skating patinaje artístico

to **figure that...** ■ to assume that... ■ *(más culto)* to surmise that... suponerse que... ➤ I figured that you had been delayed. Me supuse que algo te demoró.

to **figure wrong** ■ to figure incorrectly ■ to calculate incorrectly calcular incorrectamente ■ *(Arg.)* pifiarle

to **file a claim** presentar un reclamo

to **file a flight plan** presentar un plan de vuelo

to **file a land claim** presentar un reclamo de tierras

to **file a lawsuit against someone** ■ to file suit against someone presentar una demanda judicial contra alguien ■ presentar un juicio contra alguien ■ admitir un juicio a trámite contra alguien ➤ Once filed, the lawsuit must be heard unless the plaintiff drops it. Una vez admitida a trámite, el juicio debe ser celebrado a menos que el demandante desista.

to **file a report** presentar un informe

to **file a story** ■ to turn in a story entregar un informe

to **file an application** ■ to submit an application **1.** *(on one's own initiative)* presentar una solicitud **2.** *(in response to an ad, etc.)* entregar una solicitud ➤ The patent and trademark applications were filed last August. Los formatos de patente y registro de marcas fueron hechos el agosto pasado.

file cabinet *el* archivador ■ *(made to fit the decor) el* mueble archivador

to **file charges against someone** presentar cargos contra alguien

file folder carpeta ➤ I need some tabs for file folders. Necesito pestañas para las carpetas. ➤ I need to create some new file folders on the computer. Necesito crear unas nuevas carpetas en el ordenador.

to **file one's income tax return** presentar la declaración de rentas

to **file suit (in court) against someone for something** ■ to file a court suit against someone for something ■ to bring an action (in court) against someone for something querellarse contra alguien por algo ■ presentar un querella contra alguien por algo ➤ The machinists union filed suit against the company. El sindicato de maquinistas se querelló contra la compañía. ➤ Once the suit was filed, there was no choice but to let the legal process take its course. Una vez que la demanda fue presentada, no había opción, sólo dejar que el proceso legal siguiera su curso.

to **file suit (in court) to...** presentar una demanda (ante la corte) para... ■ hacer una demanda (ante la corte) para...

to be **filed by** ser entregado por ■ ser presentado por ➤ Taxes must be filed by the fifteenth. La declaración debe ser presentada para el quince. ➤ The return was filed by our accountant. La declaración fue entregada por nuestro contador.

to **fill a position** ■ to fill a post cubrir un puesto

to **fill a prescription** surtir una receta ■ llenar una receta ➤ I need to get this prescription filled. Necesito que me surtan esta receta. ■ Necesito que me llenen esta receta.

to **fill a vacancy** llenar una vacante ■ cubrir una vacante

to **fill an order** llenar un pedido ■ surtir un pedido ■ dar abasto a un pedido

to **fill in the blanks** llenar los espacios en blanco ■ *(Sp.)* rellenar los espacios en blanco

to **fill (in) the cracks** rellenar las ranuras ■ llenar las ranuras

to **fill in the gaps 1.** *(in one's knowledge, for example)* llenar las lagunas **2.** *(in one's insurance, for example)* cubrir las lagunas ➤ I still have gaps in my knowledge of Spanish, but I'm closing in on them. Aún tengo lagunas en mis conocimientos de español, pero ando llenándolas.

to **fill out a form** rellenar un formulario ■ rellenar un impreso ■ *(L. Am.)* llenar una planilla

to **fill out an application (form)** llenar una solicitud ■ rellenar un formulario de solicitud

fill the time: (in order) to ~ ■ (in order) to kill the time para hacer tiempo ■ para rellenar el tiempo

to **fill to the brim** llenar hasta el tope ■ llenar hasta el borde ➤ He filled the cup to the brim. Llenó la taza hasta el tope.

to **fill the (gas) tank** llenar el depósito ■ llenar el tanque

to **fill with** llenarse de ■ cargarse de

to **fill up with fuel** ■ to fuel up cargar con combustible

to be **filled to capacity** estar al completo

to be **filled to the brim** estar lleno hasta el tope

to be **filled with air** estar inflado de aire

to be **filled with doubt(s) about something** ■ to be wracked with doubt(s) about ■ to be wracked by doubt(s) about something ■ to be filled with doubt(s) about something ■ to be consumed with doubt(s) about something ■ to be plagued by doubt(s) about something tener muchas dudas sobre algo ■ acometerle (las) dudas sobre algo ■ asaltarle (las) dudas sobre algo ■ tormentarle (las) dudas sobre algo

to be **filled with pride** estar henchido de orgullo

to be **filled with rage** llenarse de furia

to be **filled with surprises** estar lleno de sorpresas ■ estar cargado de sorpresas ➤ *(news item)* The days immediately following the arrest were also filled with surprises. Los días inmediatos a la detención también estaban cargados de sorpresas.

filling came out: my ~ ■ I lost a filling se me cayó el empaste ■ se me desprendió el empaste

filling is loose está suelto el empaste ■ el empaste está suelto ➤ My filling is loose. Mi empaste está suelto. ■ Está suelto mi empaste.

film footage *el* metraje ■ secuencias filmadas

to **filter through** filtrarse por

filthy lucre ■ dirty money dinero sucio

to be **filthy rich** ser asquerosamente rico ■ estar podrido en plata ■ *(Sp.)* estar podrido de dinero

final approach *(aviation)* (maniobra de) aproximación final

final call última llamada

final date ■ deadline (date) fecha límite ■ fecha tope

final days: one's ~ ■ one's last days los últimos días de uno

final disposition of the case últimas disposiciones del caso

final draft *el* borrador final

final say: to have the ~ ■ to be the one who decides tener la última palabra ■ tener la última decisión ➤ The boss has the final say. El jefe tiene la última palabra.

final score 1. tanteo final ■ resultado final ■ marcador final **2.** *(when the scoring is by a panel of judges) la* puntuación final ➤ What was the final score? ¿Cuál ha sido el tanteo final? ■ ¿Cuál fue el resultado final? ■ *(most common, refers only to team sports)* ¿Cómo han quedado (al final)? ➤ What was the final score? ¿Cuál fue la puntuación final?

final stages of: to be in the ~ estar en la fase final de ■ estar en la última fase de

financial independence independencia económica ■ independencia financiera

financial institution entidad financiera

financial statement extracto financiero

financial straits estrecheces económicas ▪ estrecheces financieras ▪ apuro

to be **financially independent** ser independente económicamente ▪ ser independiente financieramente

to be **financially viable** ▪ to be economically viable ser viable financieramente ▪ ser viable económicamente

to **find a good use for something** encontrar un buen uso para algo ▪ dar destino a algo

to **find a job** ▪ to find work encontrar trabajo ▪ encontrar un puesto de trabajo

to **find a parking place** encontrar un hueco ▪ encontrar un estacionamiento

to **find a reason to do something** encontrar una razón para hacer algo ▪ buscar una razón para hacer algo

to **find a way out of doing something** ▪ to find a way to get out of doing something ▪ to weasel out of doing something encontrar una salida de hacer algo ▪ encontrar una triquiñuela para no hacer algo

to **find a way to do something** encontrar una manera de hacer algo ▪ encontrar una manera de poder hacer algo

to **find a way (to get) out of doing something** encontrar una manera para zafarse de hacer algo

to **find fault with someone** buscarle los fallos a alguien ▪ ponerle peros a alguien

to **find fault with something** buscarle fallos ▪ poner los peros

to **find information on someone** encontrar información acerca de alguien

to **find it difficult** resultarle difícil

to **find it difficult to do something** hacérsele difícil hacer algo ▪ resultarle difícil hacer algo ▪ encontrarlo difícil hacer algo

to **find it hard to believe** ▪ to find it difficult to believe hacérsele difícil de creerlo ▪ resultarle difícil de creer ▪ encontrarlo difícil de creer ▪ costarle a uno creer algo

not to faze someone ▪ not to have the slightest effect on someone ▪ to have no effect on someone no hacer mella a alguien

to **find no trace of** ▪ not to find any trace of no encontrar rastro de

to **find one's mind wandering** ▪ to find one's mind drifting encontrarse divagando ▪ encontrarse en la luna

to **find one's way around a place** orientarse en un lugar

to **find out 1.** *(by asking)* to inquire enterarse de **2.** *(by hearing)* to learn saber **3.** *(by investigating)* to look into averiguar ▪ descubrir ➤ How did you find out about it? ¿Cómo te enteraste de ello? ▪ ¿Cómo supiste de ello? ➤ How can I find out about it? ¿Cómo puedo enterarme de ello? ▪ ¿Cómo puedo saber de ello? ➤ Here's what I found out. ▪ This is what I found out. Esto es lo que descubrí. ▪ Esto es de lo que me enteré. ▪ Esto es de lo que me he enterado. ➤ Were you able to find out anything yesterday? ¿Pudiste enterarte de algo ayer? ➤ Would you find out about it for me? ▪ Would you look into it for me? ¿Lo averiguarías por mí?

to **find out all about it** enterarse de todo acerca de ello ▪ averiguar todo acerca de ello

to **find out for oneself what...** ▪ to see for oneself what... ▪ to see firsthand what... saber desde dentro qué...

to **find out from someone that...** ▪ to learn from someone that... enterarse por alguien de que... ▪ saber algo por alguien que...

to **find out how to do something** informarse de como hacer algo

to **find out otherwise** enterarse de que no es así

to **find out something from someone** saber algo por alguien ➤ I found out the news from my neighbor. Supe la noticia por mi vecina.

to **find out that...** enterarse de que... ▪ comprobar que... ▪ *(esp. in the preterite)* saber que... ➤ I found out that you had a party. Supe que hiciste una fiesta.

to **find out what...** enterarse de lo que... ▪ enterarse de qué... ▪ *(esp. in the preterite)* saber lo que... ▪ saber qué...

to **find reasons** encontrar argumentos ➤ One always finds reasons... Siempre se encuentran argumentos...

to **find someone** ▪ to locate someone encontrar a alguien ▪ localizar a alguien

to **find someone a house** buscar a alguien una casa

to **find someone difficult to get to know** encontrar a alguien difícil de llegar a conocer ➤ I find them very difficult to get to know. Los encontré muy difíciles de llegar a conocer.

to **find someone guilty** declararle a alguien culpable

to **find someone to do something** encontrar a alguien para hacer algo ➤ I've already found somebody to do it, but thanks anyway. Ya he encontrado a alguien para hacerlo, pero gracias de todos modos.

to **find that... 1.** comprobar que... **2.** hacérsele... **3.** encontrar(se)... ▪ hallar(se)... ➤ The colonel found that the canister was empty. El coronel comprobó que el tarro estaba vacío. ➤ I find that hard to believe. Se me hace difícil de creer. ➤ I'm trying to diet, but I find that I'm hiding food from my husband. Trato de hacer dietas, pero me encuentro escondiendo comida de mi marido. ▪ Trato de hacer dietas, pero me hallo escondiendo comida de mi marido.

to **find the middle ground** encontrar el punto medio

to **find the right one** encontrar el correcto ▪ encontrar la correcta ▪ encontrar el adecuado ▪ encontrar la adecuada

to **find the subject interesting** encontrar el tema interesante

to **find (the) time to** encontrar (el) tiempo para

to **find the (value of the) unknown factor** *(mathematics)* despejar la incógnita

to **find the words to...** encontrar las palabras para... ➤ He couldn't find the words to express his feelings. No pudo encontrar las palabras para expresar sus sentimientos.

to **find time to** encontrar (el) tiempo para ▪ encontrar un hueco para

to **find to be** encontrar (ser)

to **find work** ▪ to find a job encontrar trabajo

finding that... 1. *(verb phrase)* al darse cuenta de... **2.** *(noun phrase) la* conclusión de que... ▪ resultado de que... ➤ Finding that he had been betrayed... Al darse cuenta de que le habían traicionado... ➤ I disagree with the finding of the committee that light rail is unaffordable. No estoy de acuerdo con la conclusión del comité de que el sistema de tranvías no se pueda afrontar.

the **finding that...** *(noun phrase)* el hallazgo de que... ➤ Even more surprising was the finding that... Aún más sorprendente resulta su hallazgo de que...

finding(s) of the court *la* resolución de la corte ▪ *la* conclusión de la corte

fine arts bellas artes

fine as frog's hair! ▪ just super! ¡guay de Paraguay!

fine line between ▪ thin line between delgada línea entre ▪ fina línea entre

fine point punta fina ▪ *(illogical, but common)* trazo fino ➤ I need a pen with a fine point and blue ink. Necesito un bolígrafo con trazo fino y tinto azul.

fine print letra pequeña ➤ Be sure and read the fine print. Asegúrate y lee las letras pequeñas.

fine sand arena menuda

fine tuning fino ajuste

to be **fine with me** ▪ to be okay with me no hay problema conmigo ▪ estar bien conmigo ▪ venirme bien ➤ It's fine with me. Me viene bien.

(finely) chiseled features rasgos muy marcados ▪ rasgos muy bien formados

(finely) chiseled profile perfil muy marcado

to be **finely diced** estar cortado en taquitos

finer points 1. los puntos más sofisticados **2.** los matices más sútiles ➤ My friend is a black belt who has been teaching me some of the finer points of karate. Mi amigo es un cinturón negro que ha estado enseñándome los puntos más sofisticados del karate.

finer virtues *las* virtudes superiores

finger food comida que se come sin cubiertos

to be **finger-licking good** ▪ to be scrumptuous estar de chuparse los dedos

finger pointing señalar ➤ Enough of finger pointing! Who's responsible for this? ¡Basta con señalar! ¿Quién es responsable de esto?

(finger)nail is snagging ■ (finger)nail is catching uña está arañando ➤ My fingernail is snagging my shirt. Mi uña está arañándome la camisa.

fingerprints huellas dactilares ■ huellas digitales

to **finish doing something** terminar de hacer algo ■ acabar de hacer algo

finish line línea de llegada ■ meta

finish line: to make it to the ~ llegar a la línea final ■ llegar a la meta

to **finish off a bottle of wine** ■ to polish off a bottle of wine despachar una botella de vino ■ rematar una botella de vino

to **finish off food** ■ to finish food off terminar la comida

to **finish off someone** ■ to finish someone off apuntillar a alguien ➤ *The London Times* finished off the Conservative leader, supporting the Labor vote for the first time in its history. *El Times de Londres* apuntilló al líder conservador al apoyar el voto laborista por primera vez en su historia.

to **finish off a bottle of wine** ■ to drink what's left of a bottle of wine acabar una botella de vino ■ agotar una botella de vino ■ terminar una botella de vino ■ rematar una botella de vino

to **finish off the bull (in a bullfight)** apuntillar al toro

to **finish one's degree** ■ to complete one's degree terminar el título ■ completar la titulación

to **finish one's sentence** ■ to complete one's sentence **1.** terminar su oración ■ terminar su frase **2.** *(prison sentence)* cumplir su condena ■ terminar su condena ➤ Let me finish my sentence. Déjame terminar mi oración. ➤ The robber finished his sentence a new man and became a model citizen. El atracador cumplió su condena hecho un nuevo hombre y llegó a ser un ciudadano modelo.

to **finish one's term** terminar su mandato ■ acabar su mandato ➤ *(1998 headline)* Most Americans want Clinton to finish his term La mayoría de estadounidenses apoyan que Clinton acabe su mandato

to **finish reading** terminar de leer

to **finish something in no time** *(coll.)* ■ to finish something in no time flat no demorarse nada en terminar algo ■ terminar algo en un tris ■ terminar algo en un periquete

to **finish someone off** acabar con alguien ■ terminar con alguien ■ *(Sp.)* rematar a alguien

to **finish something off** ■ to finish off something barrer con algo

to **finish up** acabar ■ terminar

finished product: to look over the ~ ■ to check (over) the finished product revisar el acabado

finishing carpenter ■ finish carpenter *el, la* ebanista

finishing touches toques finales ■ últimos toques ■ los remates ➤ Miguel is putting the finishing touches on his airplane model. Miguel da los últimos toques a su modelo de avión.

to **finish up something** ■ to finish something up rematar algo ➤ We'll finish up the book on Thursday. ■ We'll finish the book up on Thursday. Remataremos el libro el jueves. ➤ We'll finish it up on Thursday. Lo remataremos el jueves.

fire! ¡fuego! ■ ¡descargue(n)!

to **fire a twenty-one gun salute in honor of** disparar veinte y unas salvas en honor a ➤ A twenty-one gun salute was fired in honor of Ronald Reagan. Dispararon veinte y unas salvas en honor a Ronald Reagan.

to **fire a shot** disparar un tiro ■ hacer un disparo ■ pegar un tiro ■ disparar ➤ How many shots were fired? ¿Cuántos disparos se hicieron? ■ ¿Cuántos tiros dispararon? ■ ¿Cuántos tiros pegaron? ■ ¿Cuántas veces dispararon?

to **fire across the bow of a ship** ■ to shoot over the bow of a ship disparar por encima de la proa de un barco

to **fire an employee** ■ to let an employee go ■ to dismiss an employee ■ to terminate an employee ■ to sack an employee despedir a un empleado ■ echar a un empleado

to **fire at someone at pointblank range** pegar un tiro a alguien a quemarropa ■ disparar a alguien a quemarropa

fire away! *(with questions)* ¡adelante!

fire crackles fuego cruje ➤ The fire crackles especially when the logs have a lot of moisture in them. El fuego cruje especialmente cuando los troncos tienen mucha humedad dentro.

fire drill simulacro de fuego

fire extinguisher *el* extintor de incendios

fire hazard riesgo de incendio ■ peligro de incendio ■ riesgo de fuego ■ peligro de fuego

to **fire off a letter** ■ to fire a letter off ■ to dash off a letter escribir una carta volando ■ escribir una carta a toda prisa ➤ The editorial made me so mad that I fired off a letter to the publisher. ■ The editorial made me so mad that I fired a letter off to the publisher. El editorial me enfadó tanto que escribí apurado una carta al editor. ➤ I fired it off to the publisher. La escribí apurado al editor.

to **fire (off) questions at someone** soltarle preguntas a alguien

to **fire up someone** ■ to fire someone up ■ to make someone enthusiastic about something encender el entusiasmo de alguien ■ despertar el entusiasmo de alguien

to **fire up the engine** *(coll.)* ■ to fire the engine up ■ to start the engine ■ to turn on the engine encender el motor ■ arrancar el motor ■ prender el motor

to **fire up the computer** *(coll.)* ■ to fire the computer up ■ to turn on the computer ■ to turn the computer on encender la computadora ■ prender la computadora ■ *(Sp.)* encender el ordenador

to **fire up the imagination** encender la imaginación ■ hacer volar la imaginación ■ exaltar la imaginación

to **fire warning shots** hacer disparos de advertencia

firefight ■ skirmish escaramuza

fireside chat *(Franklin Roosevelt's radio program)* charla al calor de la lumbre

fireworks display ■ pyrotechnic display ■ display of fireworks ■ display of pyrotechnics *el* despliegue de fuegos artificiales

firm commitment sólido compromiso ➤ I need a firm commitment for the sixteenth. Necesito un sólido compromiso para el dieciséis.

firm decision *la* decisión firme

firm handshake *el* apretón de manos firme

to be **firm in one's insistence** ■ to be firm in insisting estar firme en la insistencia ➤ The teacher was firm in the insistence that students write for each class. La profesora estaba firme en la insistencia de que los estudiantes escriban para cada clase.

to be **firm in one's resolve** ■ to be firm in one's determination estar firme en su determinación ➤ The country needs to be firm in its resolve. El país necesita estar firme en su determinación

firm offer: to make a ~ ■ to present a firm offer hacer una oferta en firme

to **firm up** *(intransitive verb)* consolidarse ■ concretarse ➤ My schedule has firmed up. Mi horario se ha consolidado. ■ Mi horario se ha concretado.

to **firm up muscles** ■ to firm muscles up definir los músculos ■ reafirmar los músculos

to **firm up the plans** ■ to firm the plans up concretar los planes ➤ We need to firm up our plans. ■ We need to firm our plans up. Necesitamos concretar nuestros planes. ➤ We need to firm them up. Necesitamos concretarlos.

to be **firm with someone** ser firme con alguien ■ ser recto con alguien ➤ We need to be firm with the children on the no-sweets-before-supper rule. Necesitamos ser firmes con los niños en la regla de los "no dulces" antes de la cena.

to be **firmly entrenched** estar firmemente arraigado ■ estar firmemente atrincherado ➤ After the American Civil War, the Republicans became firmly entrenched, and only one Democratic president, Grover Cleveland, was elected during the next fifty-two years. Después de la Guerra Civil estadounidense, los Republicanos llegaron a estar firmemente arraigados, y sólo un presidente Demócrata, Grover Cleveland, fue elegido durante los siguientes cincuenta y dos años.

firmly packed *(cigarettes, soil, etc.)* bien tensado

first-aid kit *el* botiquín de primeros auxilios ■ botiquín de urgencias

first and foremost ante todo ■ ante todas cosas ■ en primer lugar y ante todo

to **first appear** aparecer por primera vez ➤ The legend of the Holy Grail first appeared in 1180. La leyenda del Santo Grial apareció por primera vez en mil ciento ochenta.

first ballot: to win on the ~ ganar en la primera votación

first choice primera elección ➤ My first choice of a place to have dinner is... Mi primera elección para ir a comer es...

first choice: to have ~ eligir primero ➤ They had first choice. Eligieron primero.

first-class (railroad) car *el* vagón de primera

first-class restaurant *el* restaurante de primera (clase)

first come, first served primero en llegar, primero en servirse ▪ el primero que llega, el primero que se sirve

first come, first served basis: on a ~ bajo el principio del que llega primero, se sirve primero ▪ bajo el criterio del que llega primero, se sirve primero ➤ Students will be admitted to the class on a first come, first served, basis. Los estudiantes serán admitidos a la clase bajo el principio del que llega primero, se sirve primero.

first cousin primo(-a) hermano(-a)

first cousin once removed 1. *(son or daughter of one's first cousin)* sobrino(-a) segundo(-a) ▪ hijo(-a) del primo hermano o de la prima hermana de uno 2. *(first cousin of one's mother or father)* tío(-a) hermano(-a) de parte del padre o de la madre ▪ primo(-a) hermano(-a) del padre o de la madre

to be the **first (ever) to do something** ser el primero en hacer algo ➤ Charles Lindbergh was the first person (ever) to fly solo and nonstop across the Atlantic Ocean. Charles Lindbergh fue la primera persona en volar solo y sin escalas a través del océano Atlántico.

first got here: when I ~ cuando (yo) acababa de llegar ▪ cuando (yo) había acabado de llegar

first grade teacher profesor(-a) de primero

first hint of ▪ first sign of ▪ first indication of primer atisbo de

first impulse primer impulso ➤ When taking a foreign language test, your first impulse is usually the right one. Cuando estás tomando un examen de una lengua extranjera, el primer impulso suele ser el que vale.

to be **first in line** ▪ to be at the front of the line ▪ to be at the beginning of the line ▪ to be at the head of the line ser el primero de la cola ▪ estar a la cabeza de la cola ➤ I was first in line. (Yo) era el primero en la cola. ▪ (Yo) era la primera en la cola.

to be **first in line for the presidency** ▪ to be the immediate successor to the presidency ser el sucesor inmediato a la presidencia ▪ estar el primero en línea para la presidencia

to be first in one's class ser el primero de su clase ➤ She was first in her class. Era la primera de su clase.

first indication of ▪ first sign of ▪ first hint of primera señal de ▪ primer atisbo de

first indication that... ▪ first sign that... primera señal de que... ➤ The first indication that something was wrong was... La primera señal de que algo iba mal fue...

first mortgage primera hipoteca

first name ▪ given name *el* nombre (de pila)

first of all antes que nada ▪ en primer lugar ➤ First of all, I want to call the roll. ▪ Antes que nada, quiero pasar lista. ➤ First of all, I couldn't understand him. En primer lugar, no lo podía entender. ▪ *(Sp., leísmo)* En primer lugar, no le podía entender.

first off *(coll.)* ▪ first of all lo primero de todo ▪ antes que nada ➤ First off, I want to call the roll. Antes que nada, quiero pasar lista.

first one and then the other ▪ in order primero el uno y después el otro ▪ por orden

to be the **first one to do something** *(he)* ser el primero en hacer una cosa ▪ *(she)* ser la primera en hacer una cosa

first order of business *el* tema principal a tratar ▪ *(coll.)* plato fuerte

to be the **first person to do something** ser la primera persona en hacer algo ➤ The first man to set foot on the moon was Neil Armstrong. El primer hombre en pisar la luna fue Neil Armstrong.

to be **first published in** ser publicado por primera vez en ➤ The book was first published in Mexico. El libro fue publicado por primera vez en México.

first quarter 1. *(of the year)* primer trimestre 2. *(of the lunar month)* cuarto creciente

first-rate ▪ top notch de primera línea ▪ de la crema y nata ➤ The professors are first-rate scholars. Los catedráticos son eruditos de primera línea. ➤ Her acting is first-rate. Su actuar es de primera línea.

first responders primeros en actuar ➤ The police, fire department, and ambulance are the first responders at any catastrophe. La policía, el cuerpo de bomberos y la ambulancia son los primeros en actuar en cualquier catástrofe.

first sign of ▪ first hint of ▪ first indication of primer signo de ▪ primer atisbo de ➤ *(news item)* The Hubble Telescope has found the first sign of water on a planet outside the solar system. El telescopio Hubble ha encontrado el primer signo de agua en un planeta fuera del sistema solar.

first step toward: to take the ~ dar el primer paso hacia ▪ dar el primer paso para ➤ The government has taken the first step toward implementation of the new policy. El gobierno ha dado el primer paso hacia implementación de la nueva política.

first steps: to take one's ~ dar sus primeros pasos ➤ Our little girl took her first steps today. Nuestra pequeña dio sus primeros pasos hoy.

first stop 1. *(bus)* primera parada 2. *(airplane, ship)* primera escala

first-strike capability *la* capacidad para dar el primer golpe

first taste of primer sabor a ➤ The refugee's first taste of freedom El primer sabor a libertad del refugiado

first thing I did was lo primero que hice fue

first thing I noticed was lo primero que noté fue ➤ The first thing I noticed was the smell of dampness. Lo primero que noté fue el olor de la humedad.

first thing I thought of was lo primero que se me ocurrió fue

first thing in the morning 1. first thing every morning a primera hora de la mañana 2. first thing tomorrow morning mañana a primera hora

first thing that struck me was... lo primero que me impresionó fue...

first thing tomorrow ▪ first thing in the morning ▪ first thing tomorrow morning a primera hora de la mañana

first things first lo primero es lo primero

the **first three chapters** los tres primeros capítulos ➤ We have to read the first three chapters for Monday. Tenemos que leer los tres primeros capítulos para el lunes.

to be a **first-time offender** 1. *(minor infractions)* ser infractor(-a) por primera vez 2. *(serious infractions)* ser delincuente por primera vez

to be the **first time one had done something** *(imperfect, implying that the action was repeated)* ser la primera vez que uno hacía una cosa ▪ *(preterite, implying that we do not know if the action was repeated)* ser la primera vez que uno hizo una cosa ➤ It was the first time Pablo had gone out with Lola. Era la primera vez que Pablo salía con Lola. ▪ Fue la primera vez que Pablo salió con Lola. ➤ We were the first Westerners who had gone to that untamable land in years. Eramos los primeros occidentales que iban a esa tierra indómita en años.

to be the **first time one has done something** ser la primera vez que uno ha hecho algo ➤ This is the first time we have been to Nicaragua. Es la primera vez que hemos estado en Nicaragua.

first-time parents padres primerizos

first-time user usuario por primera vez

to be the **first to do something** ser el primero en hacer algo ▪ ser la primera en hacer algo ➤ I'd be the first to suggest that... (Yo) sería el primero en sugerir que... ➤ I'd be the first to admit that... (Yo) sería la primera en admitir que...

first try primer intento

first work *(of an artist)* primera obra ▪ ópera prima

firsthand: to know something ~ saber algo de primera mano ▪ saber algo de primeras ➤ I know (it) firsthand. Lo sé de primera mano. ▪ Lo sé de primeras.

firsthand account relato de primera mano

fiscal year año fiscal ▪ año económico

fish and chips *(L. Am.)* pescado rebozado servido con papas fritas ▪ *(Sp.)* pescado rebozado servido con patatas bravas

fish are biting peces están picando ▪ *(Sp.)* peces están mordiendo ➤ The fish are not biting (for us) today for some reason. Los peces no están picando (para nosotros) hoy por alguna razón. ▪ Los peces no están mordiendo (para nosotros) hoy por alguna razón.

to **fish for a compliment** estar buscando un cumplido ▪ buscar un cumplido

to **fish in troubled waters** nadar en aguas turbulentas

fish out of water gallina en corral ajeno

to **fish something out of something** pescar algo dentro de algo ➤ The new bride fished her wedding ring out of the disposal. La recién casada pescó su anillo de boda dentro del triturador.

to **fish through one's pockets** ▪ to rummage through one's pockets ▪ to go through one's pockets registrarse los bolsillos

Fisher King *(in grail legendry)* Rey Pescador

fishing boat barco pesquero

fishing expedition: to go on a ~ **1.** ir en una expedición de pesca **2.** *(figurative)* to look for information to justify a criticism buscar pretextos de críticas

fishing line *el* sedal

fishing rod caña (de pescar)

fistful of puñado de

to **fit a description** responder a una descripción ▪ encajar a una descripción

to **fit a profile** responder a un perfil

to **fit a small suitcase** ▪ to accommodate a small suitcase caber una maleta ➤ Will the overhead compartment fit a small suitcase? ▪ Will a small suitcase fit in the overhead bin? ¿Cabrá una maleta pequeña en el compartimento superior?

to **fit a stereotype** responder a un estereotipo

to **fit exactly** caber justo ➤ Is there an envelope that will fit this card exactly? ¿Hay un sobre en el que esta tarjeta quepa exactamente?

to be **fit for** ▪ to be suited for ser idóneo para ➤ The candidate is not fit for the office, in my opinion. El candidato no es idóneo para el cargo, en mi opinión.

to be **fit for a king** ▪ to be good enough for a king ser adecuado para un rey

to **fit in something** ▪ to fit into something ▪ to go into something caber en algo ▪ *(esp. in the sense of "to lock into place")* calzar en algo ▪ *(Sp.)* entrar en algo ➤ I need an index card that fits in my shirt pocket. ▪ I need an index card that fits into my shirt pocket. Necesito un fichero que quepa en el bolsillo de mi camisa. ➤ Let's see if the CD will fit into this slot. ▪ Let's see if the CD will go into this slot. Vamos a ver si este CD entrará en esta celda.

to **fit in(to a group)** encajar en el grupo ▪ encajar al grupo ➤ Sometimes it's better to fit out than to fit in. A veces es mejor no encajar que encajar.

to **fit into the picture** ▪ to fit in encajar en la historia ➤ Speaking of Mexican history, where do the heroic children fit in(to the picture)? Hablando de la historia de México, ¿dónde encajan los niños héroes?

to **fit just right** ▪ to fit perfectly ▪ to be just the right size ▪ to be exactly the right size quedar bien ▪ quedarle perfecto ▪ ajustarse perfectamente a ▪ quedarle como anillo al dedo ▪ venirle a alguien que ni pintado ➤ This suit fits (me) perfectly. ▪ This suit is just the right size. Este traje me queda perfecto. ➤ These shoes fit perfectly. Estos zapatos me quedan perfectos. ▪ Estos zapatos se ajustan perfectamente a mis pies.

to **fit like a glove** calzar como un guante

fit of anger ▪ purple fit *el* ataque de ira ▪ arrebato de ira ▪ *el* arranque de ira ▪ *(in psychology)* acceso de ira ▪ *(rare)* corajina

fit of jealousy ▪ jealous rage *el* ataque de celos

fit of laughter *el* ataque de risa

fit of rage ▪ purple fit *el* ataque de rabia ▪ arrebato de rabia ▪ acceso de rabia

to **fit one** *(clothes, shoes)* ▪ to be the right size quedarle bien ➤ These shoes fit (me). Estos zapatos me quedan bien. ➤ These shoes don't fit (me). Estos zapatos no me quedan bien.

to **fit out something with** *(informal)* ▪ to equip something with equipar algo con ▪ proveer algo de ➤ This laboratory is fitted out with the most advanced technology. Este laboratorio está equipado con la tecnología más avanzada. ▪ Este laboratorio está provisto de la tecnología más avanzada.

to **fit right in** estar en su ambiente ▪ caer muy bien ➤ You'd fit right in. Estarías en tu ambiente. ▪ Caerías muy bien.

to **fit something** caberle exactamente a algo ▪ quedar ajustado a algo ➤ Do you have a box that will fit this exactly? ¿Tiene usted una caja que le quepa exactamente? ▪ ¿Tiene usted una caja que le quede ajustada a esto?

to **fit the mold** estar al estilo (de)

to **fit the stereotype of** responder al estereotipo de ▪ corresponder al estereotipo de

to **fit through** caber por ▪ caber a través ➤ Will the large bottles fit through the hole? ¿Caben las botellas grandes por el agujero? ▪ ¿Cabrán por el agujero?

to be **fit to** estar en condiciones para ➤ This computer may not be fit to give away. Puede que esta computadora no esté en condiciones para regalarse.

to be **fit to be tied** estar loco(-a) de atar

to be **fit to serve** ser idóneo(-a) para servir

to **fit together perfectly** encajar perfectamente ➤ Some DNA segments can't be fitted together perfectly. Algunos segmentos del ADN no se pueden encajar (unos con otros) perfectamente. ➤ It all fits together. Todo encaja.

to **fit well** quedarse bien ➤ These pants fit (me) well. Estos pantalones me quedan bien. ▪ *(Sp.)* Este pantalón me queda bien.

fits and starts: by ~ ▪ in fits and starts a trompicones ▪ a tontas y locas ▪ a empujones

fitted sheet sábana de contour ▪ *(Sp.)* sábana ajustable ▪ sábana bajera

five-car accident ▪ five-vehicle accident *el* accidente de cinco carros ▪ accidente quíntuple

five-course guitar ▪ five-string guitar guitarra de cinco cuerdas

five o'clock shadow ▪ two days' growth barba de dos días

the **five senses** los cinco sentidos ➤ The five senses are sight, hearing, smell, taste, and touch. Los cinco sentidos son vista, oído, olfato, gusto y tacto.

five years ▪ half a decade cinco años ▪ lustro

fives for a ten: to have two ~ tener dos de a cinco por un diez ▪ *(Sp.)* tener dos de cinco por un diez ➤ Do you have two fives for a ten? ¿Tiene usted dos de cinco por un diez? ▪ ¿Tiene usted dos de a cinco por un diez?

to **fix dinner** ▪ to make dinner ▪ to get dinner ready **1.** *(afternoon meal)* preparar la comida **2.** *(evening meal)* to fix supper preparar la cena

to **fix something to eat** preparar algo para comer ➤ Go fix yourself something to eat. Ve y prepárate algo para comer.

to **fix supper** ▪ to make supper ▪ to get supper ready ▪ to prepare supper preparar la cena

fixed income: to live on a ~ vivir con ingresos fijos

fixed-rate mortgage hipoteca de tasa fija

to be **fixing to do something** *(Southern U.S., coll.)* ▪ to be preparing to do something ▪ to be getting ready to do something ▪ to be about to do something estar preparándose para hacer algo ➤ We're fixing to go eat lunch. Do want to go with us? Estamos preparándonos para ir a almorzar. ¿Quieres ir con nosotros?

to **fizzle (out)** esfumarse ▪ quedarse en nada ▪ esparcirse ➤ The demonstration fizzled out in half an hour. La manifestación se esfumó en media hora. ▪ La manifestación se quedó en nada en media hora. ▪ La manifestación se esparció en media hora.

to be **flabbergasted (at something)** quedarse atónito(-a) ▪ quedarse pasmado(-a) ➤ I was flabbergasted at the news. Me quedé boquiabierto ante la noticia. ▪ Me quedé boquierto con la noticia.

to **flag a taxi** parar un taxi ▪ llamar un taxi

to **flag down a car** *(L. Am.)* parar un carro ▪ *(Sp.)* parar un coche to **flag the waiter** ▪ to get the waiter's attention llamar al camarero ▪ llamar al mesero ➤ Flag that waiter; I want to go over the bill with him. Llama al camarero. Quiero revisar la cuenta con él.

flagging interest *el* interés decreciente

flagging spirits ánimos caídos ▪ ánimos decaídos

flagship newspaper, store, etc. ▪ the largest newspaper, store, etc. in a chain periódico principal, tienda, etc., de una cadena

flagship work ▪ principal work *el* buque insignia ▪ obra principal

to **flake (off)** ▪ to peel *(paint)* pelarse ▪ desconcharse ▪ *(skin)* escamarse ▪ pelarse ➤ The paint is flaking off. La pintura se está pelando. ▪ La pintura se está desconchando. ➤ The sunburned skin is flaking off. La piel quemada por el sol está escamándose. ➤ My sunburn is peeling. Mi piel achicharrada se está escamando.

to **flap in the breeze** ondear en la brisa ▪ agitarse en la brisa ➤ The flag was flapping in the breeze. La bandera se ondeaba en la brisa. ➤ The barn door was flapping in the breeze. ▪ The barn door was flapping in the wind. La puerta del granero estaba agitándose de la brisa.

to **flap their wings** ▪ to beat their wings aletear ▪ batir las alas ➤ Leonardo da Vinci recognized that, except during takeoff, birds flap their wings for propulsion, not lift. Leonardo da Vinci se dio cuenta de que, excepto durante el despegue, las aves aletean para propulsarse, no para mantenerse en el aire.

flare-up 1. *(pain, infection, etc.)* recaída **2.** *(violence)* estallido ➤ He had another flare-up of back pain. Tuvo una recaída del dolor de espalda. ➤ There was a flare-up of violence in the war-torn region. Hubo un estallido de violencia en la región devastada por la guerra.

to **flare up 1.** *(pain, infection, etc.)* recrudecer **2.** *(violence)* estallar ➤ Old injuries can flare up without warning. Lesiones anteriores pueden recrudecer sin aviso.

flash flooding ▪ flash flood(s) pronta inundación ▪ riada ➤ The torrential rains caused flash flooding in some areas. Las lluvias torrenciales causaron la pronta inundación en algunas areas.

to be a **flash in the pan 1.** ser (una) flor de un día **2.** ser un mero susto ➤ His candidacy was a flash in the pan. Su candidatura fue sólo una flor de un día. ➤ The hurricane, despite the dire warnings, turned out to be a flash in the pan. El huracán, a pesar de las serias advertencias resultó ser un mero susto.

flash (of a flashbulb) fogonazo (de una cámara) ▪ el flash

flash of light centelleo

flash of lightning 1. bolt of lightning relámpago ▪ rayo **2.** sheet lightning fucilazo

to **flash one's headlights** ▪ to flash one's lights dar ráfagas ▪ dar las largas ▪ dar luces largas ➤ The car behind me flashed its lights (at me) so that I would let it pass me. El coche que iba detrás me dio las largas para que le dejara pasar. ▪ El coche que iba detrás, me dio ráfagas para que le dejara pasar. ➤ The driver behind me flashed his lights (at me) so that I would let him pass me. El conductor que iba detrás me dio ráfagas para que le dejara pasar. ▪ El conductor que iba detrás me dio las largas para que le dejara pasar.

flashbulbs are popping ▪ flashbulbs are going off los flash están titilando ▪ las bombillas de flash están titilando ➤ The flashbulbs were popping when Mr. Bean knocked down the queen. Las bombillias de flash estaban titilando cuando Mr. Bean tumbó a la reina.

flashing light *la* luz intermitente ▪ luz parpadeante

flashlight battery pila para linterna de mano

flashover fire ▪ sudden, intensely hot consuming fire fuego abrasador

to be **flat-chested** ser plana de pecho ▪ ser de Castellón de la Plana

flat denial *la* negación contundente ▪ negación de plano

flat fee precio fijo ▪ costo fijo ➤ The club negotiates a flat fee per member for the lunch. El club negocia un precio fijo por cada miembro para la comida.

flat feet pies planos

flat finish *(paint, varnish, etc.)* acabado mate

flat major bemol mayor ➤ Schubert's piano trio in E-flat major El trio para piano en mi bemol mayor de Schubert

flat minor bemol menor ➤ Chopin's Sonata in B-flat minor La sonata para piano en si bemol menor de Chopin

a **flat "no"** un "no" tajante ▪ un "no" contundente ▪ un "no" de plano

flat note ▪ off-key note nota discordante ▪ *(when sung)* gallo ➤ That was a flat note! Qué gallo le ha salido. ➤ He sang a flat note. Soltó un gallo.

flat out: to tell someone ~ 1. *(insensitively)* decirle a alguien por todo el morro ▪ decirle a alguien tieso y parejo **2.** *(directly)* decirle a alguien de plano ▪ decirle a alguien sin más ➤ She told me flat out that the other students speak better than I do. Ella me dijo por todo el morro que los otros estudiantes hablan mejor que yo.

flat paint pintura mate

flat rate tarifa fija ▪ tarifa plana ➤ I have a flat-rate Internet connection. Tengo (una) tarifa plana en Internet.

flat roof tejado plano

flat, semigloss, and gloss *(paints and finishes)* mate, satinado y esmalte

flat soft drink refresco que se queda sin gas ▪ gaseosa que se queda sin gas

flat surface superficie plana

flat terrain terreno llano ▪ terreno plano

flat tire llanta desinflada ▪ neumático desinflado

to **flatly deny** ▪ to deny flatly **1.** *(allegation)* negar de plano ▪ negar contundentemente ▪ negar tajantemente ▪ negar rotundamente **2.** *(rumor)* desmentir tajantemente ▪ desmentir rotundamente

to **flatly refuse to do something** negarse tajantemente a hacer algo ▪ negarse de plano a hacer algo

to **flatly reject something** rechazar algo tajantemente ▪ rechazar algo de plano

flatness to the personality personalidad unidimensional ➤ There's a flatness to his personality. Tiene una personalidad unidimensional.

to **flatten out** aplanar(se) ▪ allanar(se) ➤ Over time this pillow has flattened out. Con el paso del tiempo esta almohada se ha aplanado.

to **flatter oneself on...** enorgullecerse de...

to **flatter someone 1.** halagar a alguien ▪ regalar los oídos a alguien **2.** to fawn on someone dar coba a alguien ▪ adular a alguien

to **flaunt something** hacer alarde de algo

flavors mingle los sabores se mezclan ➤ If you let the chimichurri stand for a day, the flavors mingle. Si dejas reposar el chimichurri durante un día, los sabores se mezclan.

flawed argument argumento erróneo ▪ razonamiento defectuoso

flawless performance ▪ perfect performance *la* actuación sin falla (alguna) ▪ actuación inmaculada ▪ actuación perfecta ▪ actuación sin defectos

fleabag hotel hotelucho ▪ el hotel de mala muerte ▪ hotel de tres al cuarto

to **fleece someone** ▪ to take all of someone's money ▪ to gouge someone desplumar a alguien ▪ *(Sp.)* dejar a alguien en bragas

fledgling democracy democracia incipiente

to **flee for cover** ▪ to run for cover huir a refugiarse ▪ huir en busca de refugio ▪ huir a buscar refugio ▪ correr a refugiarse ▪ correr en busca de refugio ▪ correr a buscar refugio

to **flee on foot** darse a la fuga a pie ➤ The assailants fled on foot. Los atracadores se dieron a la fuga a pie.

to **flee the country** ▪ to escape from the country huir del país

fleet of buses flota de autobuses

fleet of cars flota de coches

to be **fleet of foot** *(literary)* ▪ to be a fast runner ser de pies ligeros

fleet of ships flota de barcos

fleet of trains *el* parque motor

fleet of trucks flota de camiones

fleeting glance mirada fugaz

fleeting memory recuerdo fugaz
fleeting moment momento huidizo
Flemish bond *(system of brick patterns found especially in early American houses) el* enlace de ladrillo flamenco ➤ The house has Flemish bond every fourth course, that is, a brick is laid sideways at regular intervals. La casa tiene el enlace de ladrillo flamenco en cada cuarta camada, es decir, un ladrillo se coloca de lado a intervalos regulares.
flesh crawl: to make one's ~ estremecerle a alguien la carne ➤ That movie made my flesh crawl. Esa película me estremeció la carne.
to **flex a muscle** tensar un músculo
flicker of hope ▪ ray of hope rayo de esperanza
flicker of interest atisbo de interés ➤ I detect a slight flicker of interest. Detecto un ligero atisbo de interés.
flicker of light parpadeo de luz
flickering light *la* luz parpadeante
flight attendant *el, la* asistente de vuelo ▪ *el, la* auxiliar de vuelo ▪ azafata ▪ comisario de vuelo ▪ *(Mex.)* aeromozo(-a)
flight deck *(airliner)* cabina (del avión)
flight instructor instructor(-a) de vuelo
flight of stairs ▪ flight of steps tramo de escalera ➤ It's three flights up from here. Está a tres tramos más arriba.
flights of fancy: to have ~ ▪ to have flights of the imagination remontarse en alas de la imaginación
flights of the imagination: to have ~ ▪ to have flights of fancy remontarse en alas de la imaginación
to **flinch at a remark** sobresaltarse ante un comentario ▪ recular ante un comentario ▪ dar una reculada ante un comentario
to **flip a coin** echar una moneda a cara o cruz ▪ echarlo a cara o cruz ▪ lanzar una moneda al aire ▪ echar una moneda al aire ▪ *(Mex.)* echar un volado
to **flip a pancake** darle la vuelta a una tortita
to **flip channels** ▪ to channel surf ▪ to flip through (the) channels ▪ to change channels in rapid succession cambiar de canal a cada rato ▪ *(Sp., coll.)* hacer "zapping" ▪ zapear
to **flip over** dar una vuelta de campana ➤ The airplane ran off the end of the runway, hit a fence, and flipped over. El avión se salió del extremo de la pista, chocó con una valla y dio una vuelta de campana.
floaters (in the eyes) moscas volantes
flock of birds bandada de aves
flood of calls ▪ flood of phone calls ▪ avalanche of calls ▪ barrage of calls *el* alud de llamadas ▪ avalancha de llamadas
flood of humanity riada de gente ▪ riada de personas
flood of refugees oleada de refugiados ▪ riada de refugios
to **flood the carburetor** to flood the engine ahogar el carburador ▪ calar el carburador ▪ calar el motor
to **flood the engine** ▪ to flood the motor calar el motor ▪ ahogar el motor
flood plain llanura de inundación
flooding of a stream desbordamiento de un arroyo
flooding of the Nile desbordamiento del Nilo
floods ravage the region ▪ floods devastate the region las inundaciones asolan la región ➤ *(headline)* Heavy flooding ravages China Fuertes inundaciones asolan China
floor it! *(the accelerator)* ▪ step on it! ¡písale!
floor of a building ▪ story of a building planta de un edificio ▪ piso de un edificio ➤ *(news item)* The child fell from the fourth floor. El niño se cayó de la cuarta planta.
floor plan 1. *(of a dwelling) la* distribución ▪ plano de casa **2.** *(of a building)* planta ▪ plano del piso ➤ The apartment has a bad floor plan. El piso tiene una mala distribución.
to **floor the accelerator** pisar el acelerador a fondo ▪ pegar el acelerador a fondo
floor under wages suelo por debajo de los salarios ➤ Speaking of globalization, what is needed is an international floor under wages. Hablando de la globalización, lo que se necesita es un suelo internacional por debajo de los salarios.
to **flop down in an easy chair** desplomarse en un sillón
to **flop down on the couch** ▪ to flop down on the sofa desplomarse en el sofá
to **flounder in life** estar a la deriva en la vida ➤ I floundered during that period of my life. Yo estaba a la deriva durante ese época de mi vida.
to **flow into** ▪ to be a tributary of fluir a ▪ ser un afluente de ➤ The Cifuentes River flows into the Tagus. ▪ The Cifuentes River is a tributary of the Tagus. El río Cifuentes fluye al Tajo. ▪ El río Cifuentes es un afluente del Tajo.
flow of immigrants flujo migratorio
flower garden *el* jardín
fluctuations in a fever altibajos de una fiebre ▪ fluctuaciones de una fiebre
fluctuations in the stock market ▪ stock-market fluctuations altibajos de la bolsa ▪ altibajos en la bolsa ▪ *las* fluctuaciones en la bolsa
fluent speaker hablante desenvuelto(-a) ▪ hablante fluido(-a)
to **fluff a pillow** ▪ to fluff up a pillow mullir una almohada
to **fluff the rice with a fork** separar el arroz con un tenedor
fluke: legal ~ ▪ legal loophole ▪ legal technicality chiripa legal ▪ chiripazo legal ▪ carambola legal ➤ As a result of legal flukes, the rapist went free. Como resultado de carambolas legales, el violador salió en libertad.
to **flunk a test** tirarse un examen ➤ He flunked the test. Se tiró el examen.
flurry of activity ráfaga de actividad
to **flush a covey of birds** hacer salir volando una nidada ▪ levantar una nidada
to **flush the toilet** apretar el botón del inodoro ▪ tirar la cadena del inodoro ▪ *(Mex.)* jalar la bomba del inodoro
to be **flushed with anger** estar colorado de ira ▪ estar colorado de enfado
to **fly across the Atlantic Ocean** cruzar el océano Atlántico en avión ▪ *(coll.)* cruzar el charco ▪ brincar el charco
to **fly across the country** cruzar el país en avión
to **fly an airplane** ▪ to pilot an airplane **1.** *(light airplane)* guiar una avioneta ▪ pilotar una avioneta **2.** *(large airplane)* guiar un avión ▪ pilotar un avión **3.** *(aircraft in general)* guiar una aeronave ▪ pilotar una aeronave
to **fly away** irse volando ▪ marchar(se) volando ▪ escapar volando ▪ emprender vuelo
to **fly blind** *(aviation)* volar a ciegas
fly in the ointment pelo en la sopa ➤ He's the fly in the ointment. Es el pelo en la sopa.
to **fly into a rage** ▪ to have a purple fit enfurecerse ▪ llenarse de ira ▪ perder los estribos ▪ darle un arrebato ➤ He flew into a rage. ▪ He had a purple fit. Le dio un arrebato.
to **fly into a storm** meterse en una tormenta ➤ The airplane flew into a storm and crashed. El avión se metió en una tormenta y cayó.
fly is open: your ~ tu bragueta está desabrochada ▪ tienes la bragueta abierta ▪ *(colorful)* se te va a escapar el pájarito
to **fly off** ▪ to break away by centrifugal force salir volando ➤ Oops, it flew off! ¡Ay, salió volando! ➤ He slid down the bannister and flew off the end. Resbaló por la barandilla y salió volando.
to **fly off the handle** perder los estribos ▪ *(Sp.)* agarrar un cabreo ▪ coger un cabreo ▪ pillar un cabreo
to **fly over the ocean** sobrevolar el océano ▪ volar sobre el océano
to **fly the coop** ▪ to quit without giving notice irse a la francesa ▪ pirarse ➤ The maid flew the coop today. La criada se fue a la francesa hoy. ▪ La criada se piró hoy.
to **fly the flag** volar la bandera
to **fly the flag at half mast** ▪ to fly the flag at half staff volar la bandera a media asta
to **fly to** ir en avión a ➤ We flew to Concepción. Fuimos a Concepción en avión.
flying buttress *el* arbotante *("El contrafuerte" is the vertical member in the wall that the buttress connects to.)*
flying colors: to pass (an examination) with ~ irle estupendamente en el examen ▪ *(coll.)* irle de lujo en el examen ▪ salir requetebién en el examen ➤ She passed the examination with flying colors. Le fue estupendamente en el examen. ▪ Le fue de lujo en el examen. ▪ Salió requetebién en el examen.

flying lessons: to take ~ tomar clases de vuelo ▪ recibir clases de vuelo
to **foam at the mouth** echar espuma por la boca ▪ *(Sp.)* echar espumarajos por la boca
to **focus on one thing** ▪ to limit oneself to one main focus ▪ to concentrate on one thing enfocarse en una sola cosa
to be **focused on** enfocarse en ▪ estar enfocado en ➤ In 1865, as a result of the assassination of President Abraham Lincoln, conspiracy theories were focused on the Confederate leaders. En 1865, como consecuencia del asesinato del presidente Abraham Lincoln, las teorías de la conspiración se enfocaron en los líderes de la Confederación surista.
fog bank velo de niebla ▪ cortina de niebla
to **fog up** ▪ to steam up empañarse
to be **fogged up** estar empañado ➤ The car windows are fogged up. Los vidrios del carro están empañados. ▪ Las lunas están empañadas.
foggy morning mañana con (mucha) neblina ▪ mañana brumosa
to **foil a plot** hacer fracasar un plan ▪ abortar un plan ▪ *(often plural in Spanish)* hacer fracasar los planes ▪ abortar los planes
to **foil an attempt** desbaratar un intento ▪ hacer fracasar un intento ▪ abortar un intento ➤ I foiled the pickpocket attempt. Hice fracasar el intento del carterista.
foiled attempt intento desbaratado ▪ intento frustrado
foiled robbery attempt intento desbaratado de robo ▪ intento frustrado de robo
to **fold a piece of paper** plegar una hoja de papel ▪ doblar una hoja de papel ▪ plegar un folio ▪ doblar un folio
to **fold along the dotted line** doblar por la línea de puntos
to **fold clothes** doblar las ropas ➤ Would you like me to fold these for you? *(tú)* ¿Te las doblo? ▪ *(usted)* ¿Se las doblo? *("Las" refers to "camisas.")*
to **fold in the flaps** *(assembling a box)* doblar las solapas
folding bed cama plegable
folding chair silla plegable
folk song *la* canción tradicional
to **follow closely** seguir de cerca
to **follow in someone's footsteps** ▪ to follow in the footsteps of someone seguir las huellas de alguien
follow me! *(waiter to customer)* ▪ come with me! *(tú)* ¡acompãna! ▪ *(usted)* ¡acompañe!
to **follow one's instinct** guiarse por su instinto ➤ I followed my instincts. Me guié por mi instinto.
to **follow one's suggestion to...** seguir su sugerencia de...
to **follow someone** seguir a alguien ➤ He followed his companions into the church. Siguió a sus compañeros hasta el interior de la iglesia.
to **follow suit** ▪ to do as another has done ▪ to follow someone's example hacer lo mismo (que alguien) ▪ seguir el ejemplo (de otra persona) ➤ He joined in the dancing and called to María to follow suit. Se unió al baile y llamó a María para que hiciera lo mismo. ➤ Wall Street nosedived, and the Asian markets followed suit. Wall Street cayó en picado, y las bolsas de Asia hicieron lo mismo.
to **follow the crowd** ▪ to follow the herd hacer lo que todos (hacen) ▪ hacer siempre lo que hacen los demás
to **follow the directions** ▪ to follow the instructions seguir las instrucciones
to **follow the herd** ▪ to follow the crowd hacer lo que todos (hacen) ▪ hacer siempre lo que hacen los demás
to **follow the instructions** ▪ to follow the directions seguir las instrucciones
to **follow the money** *(esp. in criminal investigations)* seguir la ruta del dinero
to **follow the promptings of one's heart** seguir el dictado del corazón
to **follow the story** ▪ to follow the developments of a story as they occur seguir los acontecimientos de lo ocurrido
follow-up complementario ➤ The reporter asked a follow-up question. El periodista hizo una pregunta complementaria.
to **follow with interest** seguir con atención ▪ seguir atento ➤ I have followed the presidential campaign with interest. ▪ I have followed with interest the presidential campaign. He seguido con atención la campaña presidencial.
followed by 1. estar seguido de 2. ser perseguido por ▪ ser seguido por ➤ The meeting was followed by a luncheon. La reunión estuvo seguida de una comida. ➤ The fugitive was followed by the police. El fugitivo fue perseguido por la policía. ▪ El fugitivo fue seguido por la policía.
following: loyal ~ séquito leal
following day: (on) the ~ ▪ the next day al día siguiente
following morning: (on) the ~ ▪ the next morning a la mañana siguiente
the **following year** al año siguiente
fondest dream sueño más anhelado ▪ *(poetic)* más anhelado sueño
Food and Drug Administration *(USA)* Dirección de Alimentos y Medicinas
food cart *(on an airliner)* carrito de catering ▪ carrito de comida
food coloring colorante alimenticio
to be **food for thought** ▪ to be something to think about ser algo para pensarlo ▪ *(literary)* ser algo para reflexionar
food poisoning intoxicación alimenticia
food supplements ▪ vitamin supplements complementos alimenticios ▪ complementos vitamínicos
food value ▪ nutritional value valor alimenticio
to **fool someone into believing that...** ▪ to trick someone into believing that... engañar a alguien a creer que...
fools rush in where angels fear to tread necio es atrevido y el sabio comedido
foot-and-mouth disease *(contagious viral disease which can afflict pigs and cattle)* ▪ hoof-and-mouth disease fiebre aftosa
foot of the bed ▪ end of the bed *el* pie de la cama ➤ The dog sleeps at the foot of the bed. ▪ The dog sleeps at the end of the bed. El perro duerme al pie de la cama.
foot of the page ▪ bottom of the page *el* pie de la página ▪ *la* parte inferior de la página
football fan aficionado(-a) al fútbol americano ▪ fanático(-a) del fútbol americano) ▪ *el, la* fan del fútbol americano ▪ *(Sp.)* forofo(-a) del fútbol americano *(Outside the United States, "fútbol" means "soccer.")*
foothills of a mountain range estribaciones de una cordillera
to be **footloose and fancy free** ser libre como el viento
for a change para variar
(for) a crowd to gather around... producirse una aglomeración en torno a...
(for) a dream to come true cumplirse un sueño ➤ Our dream has come true. Se nos ha cumplido un sueño.
for a long time 1. in a long time por mucho tiempo 2. for an extended period ▪ long mucho tiempo ▪ durante mucho tiempo ▪ *(especially L. Am.)* por largo tiempo ➤ I haven't seen her for a long time. ▪ I haven't seen her in a long time. Hace mucho tiempo que no la veo. ➤ Will he have to stay in bed (for) a long time? ▪ Will he have to stay in bed long? ¿Tendrá que guardar cama por mucho tiempo? ➤ He stayed (for) a long time. Se quedó por largo tiempo.
for a minute por un minuto ▪ durante un minuto
for a moment por un instante ▪ *(Sp.)* durante un instante ➤ Imagine for a moment that... Imagina durante un instante que...
to be **for a reason (that)...** ▪ to be for good reason (that)... ▪ not to be for nothing (that)... ser por algo que... ➤ It's for a reason that they say (that)... ▪ It's for good reason that they say (that)... ▪ It's not for nothing that they say (that)... Es por algo que dicen que...
to be **for a team** ser de un equipo ▪ estar con un equipo ➤ We're for Alianza Lima. Somos de la Alianza Lima. ▪ Estamos con la Alianza Lima.
for a time ▪ for a while 1. *(minutes or hours)* durante un rato 2. *(weeks or months)* durante un tiempo ➤ I read for a time and then went to bed. ▪ I read for a while and then went to bed. Leí durante un rato y luego me fui a la cama. ➤ She attended the university for a time. ▪ She attended the university for a while. Asistía a la universidad durante un tiempo.

for a while ■ for a time *(minutes or hours)* durante un rato ■ *(weeks or months)* durante un tiempo ➤ I read for a while and then went to bed. ■ I read for a time and then went to bed. Leí durante un rato y luego me fui a la cama. ➤ They lived in San Lorenzo, Paraguay, for a while. ■ They lived in San Lorenzo, Paraguay, for a time. Vivían en San Lorenzo, Paraguay, durante un tiempo.

for a while now ■ for some time now de un tiempo a esta parte

for ages desde hace mucho tiempo ■ desde siempre ➤ Why, we've known each other for ages. Si nos hemos conocido hace mucho. ■ Si nos conocemos desde hace mucho tiempo. ■ Si nos conocemos desde siempre.

for all audiences para todo público

for all I know que sé yo ■ por lo que sé

for all intents and purposes a toda razón y efecto ➤ If the Spanish Supreme Court rejects the Ibarretxe Plan, it is, for all intents and purposes, dead. Si la Corte Suprema española rechaza el Plan Ibarretxe, éste será a toda razón y efecto muerto.

for all that 1. because of all that ■ in exchange for all that por todo eso **2.** in spite of all that a pesar de todo eso

for all the time a pesar de todo el tiempo ■ con todo el tiempo ➤ For all the time she's spent in Spain, she has yet to see a bullfight. Con todo el tiempo que ha pasado en España, todavía no ha visto una corrida de toros.

for all the wrong reasons por todas las razones equivocadas

for all the wrong things por todas las cosas equivocadas

for all we know que sabemos nosotros ■ por lo que sabemos

for all you know *(tú)* por lo que sabes ■ *(usted)* por lo que sabe (usted)

for an instant por un instante ■ durante un instante

for another por otro ➤ Why don't you want to go?-Well, for one thing, I've got too much homework, and for another, I don't have the money. ¿Por qué no quieres ir?-Bueno, por un lado, tengo demasiadas tareas, y por otro, no tengo (el) dinero. ■ ¿Por qué no quieres ir?-Bueno, por una parte, tengo demasiadas tareas, y por otra, no tengo (el) dinero.

for another year 1. *(present and future)* hasta que pase otro año ■ (durante) otro año más **2.** *(past)* hasta que pasara otro año ■ hasta que pasase otro año ■ (durante) otro año más ➤ We won't be able to return to Montevideo for another year. No podremos volver a Montevideo hasta que pase otro año. ■ No podremos regresar a Montevideo hasta que pase otro año. ➤ We couldn't return to Montevideo for another year. No podríamos volver a Montevideo hasta que pasara otro año. ➤ She'll be in school there for another year. Estará en la facultad (durante) otro año más.

for anyone who para quien ➤ For anyone who has been lucky enough to... Para quien ha tenido la suerte de...

for as long as I can remember ■ for as long as I can recall desde que tengo memoria

for as long as I could remember ■ for as long as I could recall desde que tenía memoria ➤ I had been a bird watcher for as long as I could remember. Observaba aves desde que tenía memoria.

for as long as it takes por el tiempo que tome ■ por el tiempo que tarde ■ por el tiempo que lleve

for being 1. because of something's being por ser **2.** in spite of being con ser ➤ For being poor, they manage to make ends meet. Con ser pobres, logran llegar a fin de mes. ■ Siendo pobres aún logran llegar a fin de mes.

for better or for worse para bien o para mal

for clarity para mayor claridad

for crying out loud! ¡qué caramba! ■ ¡qué caray! ■ *(Sp.)* ¡caramba! ■ ¡caray!

for daily use ■ for everyday use ■ for day-to-day use para uso diario ■ para usarse a diario

for day-to-day use ■ for everyday use ■ for daily use para diario ■ para usarse a diario

for days on end durante días enteros ■ por días enteros ■ por días y días

for doing something ■ for having done something por hacer algo ■ por haber hecho algo

for double that amount ■ for twice that amount por el doble de esa cantidad

for every action there is an equal and opposite reaction *(Newton's Third Law of Motion)* por cada acción hay una reacción de igual magnitud y sentido opuesto

for everyday use ■ for day-to-day use ■ for daily use de uso diario ■ para diario ■ de uso cotidiano

for example ■ e.g. ■ for instance ■ to give you an example por ejemplo ■ p.ej. ■ verbigracia

for fear of ■ out of fear of ■ fearing por temor a ■ por el miedo de ➤ Spain closed its borders to French and Irish beef for fear of "mad cow" (disease). España cerró sus fronteras a reses de Francia e Irlanda por temor a las "vacas locas". ■ España cerró sus fronteras a la carne de res de Francia e Irlanda por temor a las "vacas locas".

for fear that por temor a que ■ por el miedo de que

for future reference por si hace falta consultarlo en el futuro ■ para una futura referencia ■ para futuras referencias

for future reference: to save the instructions ~ ■ to keep the instructions for future reference guardar las instrucciones para una eventual consulta posterior

for generations a lo largo de generaciones ■ durante generaciones

for God's sake por amor de Dios ■ por el amor de Dios

for good definitivamente ■ para siempre ➤ I hope you've quit smoking for good. Espero que hayas dejado de fumar definitivamente. ■ Espero que hayas dejado de fumar para siempre.

for good measure de propina

for good or ill para bien o para mal

for good reason: and ~ y por una buena razón

for heaven's sake! ■ good heavens! ¡Dios mío! ■ por Dios ■ ¡Ave María Purísima!

for he's a jolly good fellow porque él es un buen compañero *(sung on birthdays and other special occasions)*

for hours on end ■ for hours ■ hour after hour durante horas ■ hora tras hora ➤ Santiago, when he was seven, would look at the illustrated map of Disneyland for hours on end. Santiago, cuando tenía siete años, contemplaba el plano ilustrado de Disneylandia durante horas. ■ Santiago, cuando tenía siete años, contemplaba el plano ilustrado de Disneylandia hora tras hora.

for instance ■ for example por ejemplo ■ es decir

to be **for it** ■ to be in favor of it ■ to favor it estar a favor (de ello) ➤ I'm for it. Estoy a favor.

for it to que ➤ I like for the gelatine to cool down before I add the chopped vegetables. Me gusta que la gelatina se enfríe antes de añadir las verduras picadas.

for it to work ■ in order for it to work para que funcione ■ para que sirva ■ para que resulte

for its own sake ■ for itself por sí mismo(-a) ■ por su propio valor ➤ Literature is writing that should be read for its own sake. ■ Literature is writing that should be read for itself. La literatura es algo que debería leerse por sí misma.

for itself ■ for its own sake por sí mismo(-a) ■ por su propio valor ➤ Literature is writing that should be read for itself. La literatura es algo que debería leerse por sí mismo.

for lack of a falta de ➤ For lack of a better word... A falta de una palabra mejor...

for less than por menos de ➤ You can get them for less than ten dollars. Se consiguen por menos de diez dólares.

for life ■ for the rest of one's life de por vida ➤ He's a friend for life. Es amigo de por vida.

for love of ■ out of love for por amor al ■ por amor a la

for love nor money: one would not do something ~ no haría algo ni por amor ni por dinero ■ no haría algo ni para remedio

for (many) kilometers around ■ for (many) kilometers in all directions ■ for (many) kilometers in every direction en muchos kilómetros en torno ■ en muchos kilómetros a la redonda

for (many) miles around ■ for (many) miles in all directions ■ for (many) miles in every direction en muchas millas en torno ■ en muchas millas a la redonda

for many years 1. desde hace muchos años **2.** por muchos años ■ durante muchos años

for me **1.** para mí **2.** por mí **3.** de mi parte ▪ por mi parte ➤ Say hello to them for me. Salúdalos de mi parte. ▪ *(Sp., leísmo)* Salúdales de mi parte.

for medical purposes con fines médicos ▪ para fines médicos

for miles around ▪ for miles in every direction en muchas millas a la redonda ▪ en muchos kilómetros a la redonda ➤ The national park stretches for miles around the town. ▪ The national park extends for miles around the town. El parque se extiende en muchas millas a la redonda del pueblo.

for military affairs: national security adviser ~ asesor de seguridad nacional en materia militar

for months **1.** desde hace meses **2.** por meses ▪ durante meses

for months at a time durante meses enteros ➤ Ships' crews in the old days remained at sea for months at a time. En los tiempos antiguos, los tripulados de los barcos se quedaron en altamar durante meses enteros.

for more than por más que ▪ por más de ▪ en más de

for more than *x* years desde hace más de *x* años ▪ durante más de *x* años

for most of ▪ during the greater part of durante la mayor parte de ➤ For most of the fall... ▪ For the greater part of the fall... Durante la mayor parte del otoño...

for most of one's life por la mayor parte de la vida de uno ▪ durante la mayor parte de la vida de uno

for most of the way durante la mayor parte del trayecto ▪ durante la mayor parte del camino

for my part por mi parte

for no good reason sin (ninguna) razón ▪ sin causa

(for) no stone to be left unturned no quedar piedra por mover ▪ no quedar piedra sobre piedra ➤ No stone was left unturned. No quedó piedra por mover. ▪ No quedó piedra sobre piedra.

for nothing **1.** in vain para nada ▪ a lo tonto **2.** for free gratis ➤ I made the trip for nothing. Hice el viaje para nada. ▪ Hice el viaje a lo tonto. ➤ We got this lamp for nothing. Conseguimos la lámpara gratis.

for now ▪ for the time being ▪ for the present por ahora

for obvious reasons por razones más que obvias ▪ evidentemente ➤ For obvious reasons, I can't go into details. Evidentemente no puedo revelar detalles.

for once por una vez

for one thing por un lado ▪ por una parte ➤ Why don't you want to go?-Well, for one thing, I've got too much homework. ¿Por qué no quieres ir?-Bueno, por un lado, tengo demasiadas tareas. ▪ ¿Por qué no quieres ir?-Bueno, por una parte, tengo demasiadas tareas.

for one to que

(for) one's eyes to get as big as saucers ▪ to be wide-eyed (with amazement) ponérsele los ojos como platos ➤ When I met Martha Anne, my eyes got as big as saucers. Cuando conocí a Martha Anne, se me pusieron los ojos como platos.

(for) one's health to improve mejorarse la salud ▪ mejorar ▪ ganar mucho en salud ➤ My health has improved. Mi salud se ha mejorado. ▪ He mejorado. ▪ He ganado mucho en salud.

(for) one's life to be hanging in the balance ▪ to fight for one's life debatirse entre la vida y la muerte ➤ The attack victim's life was hanging in the balance. El agredido se debatía entre la vida y la muerte.

(for) one's nose to be running ▪ to have a runny nose gotearle la nariz ➤ My nose is running. Me gotea la nariz.

to be **for one's own good** ser por su propio bien ➤ It's for your own good. *(tú)* Es por tu propio bien. ▪ *(usted)* Es por su propio bien.

for oneself: to see ~ comprobar uno mismo ▪ constatar el hecho por sí mismo ➤ See for yourself! ¡Comprueba tú mismo! ▪ ¡Compruébalo tú mismo! ▪ ¡Constata el hecho por ti mismo!

for others **1.** para otros **2.** por otros

to **do something for pleasure** hacer algo por placer ▪ hacer algo por el gusto ➤ We listen to classical music for pleasure. Escuchamos música clásica por placer. ▪ Escuchamos música clásica por el gusto.

for profit: to run a business ~ ▪ to operate a business for profit gestionar un negocio con fin de lucro

for purposes of a efectos de ▪ para el propósito de ➤ For the purposes of the study, all the populations were given the same weight. A efectos de la investigación se les dio a todos las poblaciones el mismo peso.

for quite some time durante bastante tiempo ▪ por bastante tiempo

for rent se alquila ▪ de alquiler ▪ se renta

to be **for rent** estar de alquiler

for sale *(on a sign)* se vende

to be **for sale** estar en venta

(for) several years: to have been there ~ haber estado allí (por) varios años

for some reason por alguna razón ▪ por algún motivo

for some reason or other por una razón u otra ▪ por alguna que otra razón ▪ por un motivo u otro ▪ *(colorful)* por pitos o por flautas

for some time hace (ya) tiempo ▪ hace algún tiempo ▪ durante algún tiempo ▪ dentro de mucho tiempo ➤ I haven't seen her for some time (now). Hace tiempo que no la veo. ▪ No la he visto hace ya tiempo. ▪ Hace bastante (tiempo) que no la veo. ➤ I won't be returning to the United States for some time. *(L. Am.)* No regresaré a los Estados Unidos durante algún tiempo. ▪ No regresaré a los Estados Unidos dentro de mucho tiempo. ▪ *(Sp.)* No volveré a los Estados Unidos durante algún tiempo. ▪ No volveré a los Estados Unidos dentro de mucho tiempo.

for some time now ▪ for a while now de algún tiempo a esta parte ▪ de un tiempo a esta parte

for something to happen como para que algo ocurra ➤ Big stars burn out too quickly for advanced life to evolve on the planets around them. La grandes estrellas se consumen demasiado rápido como para que la vida avanzada evolucione en los planetas alrededor.

to be **for supper** ▪ to have for supper tener de cena ▪ haber para la cena ➤ What's for supper? ▪ What are we having for supper? ¿Qué hay de cena? ▪ ¿Qué hay para la cena?

for sure **1.** for certain seguro ▪ seguramente ▪ seguro ▪ con seguridad ▪ *(coll.)* bien bien **2.** *(in response to a question)* seguro que sí ➤ I don't know for sure. No lo sé seguro. ▪ No estoy seguro. ➤ For sure there are other civilizations like our own in the Milky Way. Seguro que hay otras civilizaciones como la nuestra la Vía Láctea. ➤ I thought for sure (that)... Pensé que seguramente... ▪ Pensé que seguro... ➤ Nobody knows for sure. Nadie sabe con seguridad. ➤ I don't remember for sure. No me acuerdo bien (bien).

for that matter llegado al caso ➤ I wouldn't trust the owner of the shop or any of his mechanics, for that matter. Llegado al caso, no confiaría en el dueño del taller, ni en sus mecánicos.

for that reason ▪ that's why por eso ▪ por esa razón ▪ por eso motivo

for that very reason ▪ that's the very reason why por esa misma razón ▪ por lo mismo ▪ por eso mismo ▪ precisamente por eso

for the asking con sólo pedirlo ➤ It's yours for the asking. Es tuyo con sólo pedirlo.

to be **for the best** ▪ to be the best thing ser lo mejor ➤ He felt bad when he broke up with his girlfriend, but now he believes it was for the best. Se sentía infeliz al romper con su novia, pero ahora cree que fue lo mejor.

to be **for the birds** ser de los tontos ▪ ser para los bobos ▪ ser de bobos ➤ It's for the birds. Es de los tontos.

for the fact is that... pues el caso es que...

for the first time por primera vez

for the fun of it: to do something ~ hacer algo por diversión ▪ hacer algo por divertirse

for the good of en beneficio de ▪ en provecho de ▪ para beneficio de ▪ para provecho de

for the immediate future para un futuro inmediato

for the impression (that it makes) ▪ in order to make a good impression para dar una buena impresión ➤ It's important for the impression. Es importante para dar una buena impresión.

for the last time por última vez

for the life of me que me aspen si

for the most part por la mayor parte ▪ mayormente

for the next several years 1. *(past)* por los años siguientes ■ durante los años siguientes 2. *(future)* por los próximos años ■ durante los próximos años
for the next *x* years 1. *(past)* por los *x* años siguientes ■ durante los *x* años siguientes 2. *(future)* por los *x* próximos años ■ durante los *x* próximos años
for the present *(literary, journalistic)* ■ for now ■ for the time being por ahora
for the purpose of ■ with the intention of ■ intending to con el propósito de
for the rest of one's life por el resto de la vida de uno ■ de por vida
for the rest of the time durante el resto del tiempo
for the sake of por ➤ Some editorial writers howl for the sake of howling. Algunos editorialistas claman por clamar. ■ Algunos editorialistas gruñen por gruñir.
for the sole purpose of con el único propósito de ■ para el único próposito de
for the time being ■ for now ■ for the present ■ temporarily ■ for the moment por ahora ■ temporariamente ■ *(Sp.)* temporalmente ➤ For the time being, we don't have a cat. ■ For the time being, we have no cat. Por ahora no tenemos gato.
for the umpteenth time por inésima vez
for there to be ■ in order for there to be para que haya ➤ For there to be peace in the Middle East, people must be taught peace. Para que haya paz en el Medio Oriente, la paz se debe enseñar a la gente.
for this time of year para esta época del año ➤ It's mild for this time of year. Normally it's colder. Hace una temperatura suave para esta época del año. Normalmente hace más frío.
for those of us who are... para los que somos... ■ para nosotros que somos... ■ para aquellos que somos...
for those of us who want (to)... para los que queremos... ■ para nosotros que queremos... ■ para aquellos que queremos...
for twice that amount ■ for double that amount por el doble de esa cantidad ■ por dos veces esa cantidad
for wearing around the house ■ to wear around the house para andar por casa ■ de andar por casa
for what it's worth por lo que valga ■ por lo que pueda valer
for whatever reason por cualquier razón
for which por lo que ■ por lo cual ■ por la que ■ por la cual
for whoever *(informal)* ■ for whomever para quien
For Whom the Bell Tolls *(Hemingway novel)* *Por quién doblan las campanas*
(for) *x* cases of the illness to be reported registrarse *x* casos de la enfermedad ➤ Nearly a thousand cases of the illness have been reported. Se han registrado casi mil casos de la enfermedad.
for *x* hours desde hace *x* horas ➤ Marta has been playing the piano for two hours. Marta toca el piano desde hace dos horas.
for *x* months desde hace *x* meses ➤ I've been married for two months. Estoy casado(-a) desde hace dos meses.
for *x* years ■ over a period of *x* years 1. *(present perfect)* desde hace *x* años 2. *(past)* durante *x* años ➤ I have known him for seven years. Le conozco desde hace siete años. ➤ The Normans ruled England for seven hundred years. Los Normandos mandaron Inglaterra durante setecientos años.
for years durante años ■ por años
for years: to have done something ~ hacer algo desde hace años ➤ For years I have taken a walk every morning. Desde hace años doy un paseo todas las mañanas.
for your information ■ FYI *(tú)* para que te enteres ■ para tu información ■ *(usted)* para que se entere ■ para su información
to **force a smile** forzar una sonrisa
to **force evacuation of** obligar al desalojo de ■ forzar la evacuación de ➤ *(headline)* Bed bug infestation forces evacuation of train Una plaga de chinches obliga al desalojo de un tren
force of gravity fuerza de gravedad
to **force one's way in** entrar a la fuerza ■ entrar por la fuerza ➤ We had to force our way in. Tuvimos que entrar a la fuerza. ➤ We had to force our way into the house. Tuvimos que entrar a la casa a la fuerza.
to **force one's way through** abrirse paso a la fuerza ■ abrirse paso por la fuerza
to **force oneself to do something** obligarse a hacer algo ➤ I would force myself to get up early. Me obligaba a levantarme temprano.
to **force someone back** hacerle retroceder a alguien ➤ The waves forced him back. Las olas le hacían retroceder.
to **force someone to do something** ■ to make someone do something forzar a alguien a hacer algo ■ forzar a alguien que haga algo ■ obligar a alguien a hacer algo ■ obligar a alguien que haga algo
forced landing: to make a ~ aterrizaje forzoso
to be **forced out of one's home** ser desplazado de su hogar
forced smile sonrisa forzada ■ sonrisa sujeta
forced sterilization ■ compulsory sterilization esterilización forzosa
to be **forced to do something** 1. ser obligado a hacer algo 2. obligarse a hacer algo
forced withdrawal retiro forzoso
to **ford a river** vadear un río a pie ■ cruzar un río vadeando ■ apear un río ■ franquear un río
foreign affairs asuntos internacionales
foreign aid ayuda foránea
foreign country país extranjero
foreign policy política exterior
foreign relations relaciones extranjeras ■ relaciones internacionales
foreign suppliers proveedores extranjeros
foremost expert on máximo experto en
forest fire incendio forestal
forest landscape ■ forest terrain ■ wooded landscape ■ wooded terrain paisaje boscoso
forever and ever para siempre jamás
to be **forever complaining** pasar todo el día quejándose ■ no hacer más que quejarse ■ pasarse quejándose siempre ➤ He is forever complaining. Se pasa el día quejándose. ■ No hace más que quejarse. ■ Siempre se pasa quejándose.
to **forge a check** falsificar un cheque
to **forge an alliance** fraguar una alianza
to **forge one's character** forjar el carácter de uno
to **forget all about something** ■ to completely forget something olvidársele por completo ■ olvidársele de plano ■ pasársele completamente ➤ I forgot all about it. ■ I completely forgot (about it). Se me olvidó por completo. ■ Se me pasó completamente. ■ Se me olvidó de plano. ■ Me olvidé de plano.
forget it! ■ just forget it! ¡olvídalo! ■ ¡deja eso! ■ ya puedes olvidarte ■ nada ➤ Well then, forget it. Pues entonces nada. ■ ¡Ya puedes olvidarte!
to **forget to do something** olvidarse de hacer algo ■ olvidársele de hacer algo
to **forget (to take) something** ■ to leave something (behind) dejar olvidado algo en un lugar ■ dejar algo atrás ➤ She left her strawberries in the produce department. Dejó olvidadas sus fresas en la frutería. ■ Dejó sus fresas atrás en la frutería. ➤ She forgot them. Las dejó olvidadas.
to **forgive a debt** ■ to cancel a debt condonar una deuda ■ cancelar una deuda ■ anular una deuda
to **forgive and forget** perdonar y olvidarse
forgiveness of sins *el* perdón de los pecados
forgiving of a debt ■ cancellation of a debt condonación de una deuda ■ *la* cancelación de una deuda ■ *la* anulación de una deuda
fork in the river *la* bifurcación en el río ■ delta fluvial
fork in the road *la* bifurcación en la carretera ■ *la* ramificación en la carretera ■ horquilla en la carretera
fork it over! ■ pay up! *(tú)* ¡apoquina! ■ *(usted)* ¡apoquine!
to **fork over the dough** ■ to fork it over soltar la tela
forked tongue lengua bífida
forklift carretilla elevadora ■ toro
to **form a circle** formar un círculo ■ formar un corro
to **form a coalition government** formar un gobierno de coalición ■ pactar un gobierno de coalición

to **form a political faction** formar una facción política ▪ *(colorful)* hacer corro aparte

to **form a protective barrier against** ▪ to provide protection from ▪ to shield from ▪ to protect from abrigar de

to **form an impression** sacar una impresión

to **form holes 1.** *(transitive verb)* to make holes formar agujeros ▪ hacer agujeros **2.** *(intransitive verb)* to develop holes formarse agujeros ▪ hacerse agujeros ➤ Fry the pancake until it forms little holes in the batter, and then flip it. Freír la tortita hasta que forme agujeritos en la masa, y darle la vuelta. ➤ Fry the pancake until little holes form in the batter, and then flip it. Freír la tortita hasta que se formen agujeritos en la masa, y darle la vuelta.

to **form the border between** ▪ to delineate the border between delimitar ➤ The Mason-Dixon line forms the border between Pennsylvania and Maryland. La línea Mason-Dixon delimite Pensilvania y Maryland.

to **format a (blank) disk** formatear un disco (en blanco)

to **format a document** formatear un documento

formative years años formativos

former president ▪ ex-president ex-presidente ▪ antiguo presidente *("Ex-president" is a less dignified term than "former president.")*

former Soviet bloc countries ▪ countries of the former Soviet bloc los países del bloque de la antigua unión soviética

former student *el, la* ex-estudiante ▪ antiguo(-a) estudiante

formidable rival ▪ formidable opponent *el, la* rival de cuidado ➤ He has to face a formidable rival. Tiene que enfrentar a un rival de cuidado.

to **forswear (the use of) something** abjurar de ▪ renegar a

forte: to be one's ~ ▪ to be one's strong suit ser el punto fuerte de uno

fortunately for por suerte para

forty something cuarenta y tantos ➤ She's forty something. Ella tiene cuarenta y tantos años.

forward slash barra para adelante

to be **foul-mouthed** tener mala boca

to **found a company** fundar una compañía

to be **found alive** aparecer con vida ▪ hallarlo con vida ▪ *(Sp.)* hallarle con vida

to be **found dead** aparecer muerto ▪ hallarlo muerto ▪ encontrarlo muerto ▪ *(Sp.)* encontrarle muerto ▪ hallarle muerto

to be **found guilty of a crime** ▪ to be convicted of a crime ser declarado culpable de un crimen ▪ ser condenado por un crimen

to be **found hanged** aparecer ahorcado(-a) ▪ encontrar a alguien ahorcado(-a) ▪ hallar a alguien ahorcado(-a) ➤ The prisoner was found hanged in his cell. El prisionero ha aparecido ahorcado en su celda. ▪ Encontraron al prisionero ahorcado en su celda. ▪ Hallaron al prisionero ahorcado en su celda.

to be **founded by** ser fundado por ➤ The English College in Valladolid was founded by Philip the Second. El colegio inglés en Valladolid fue fundado por Felipe Segundo.

fountain of youth *la* fuente de la juventud

four-car accident *el* accidente cuádruple

four fifths cuatro quintos

four-vehicle accident *el* accidente cuádruple

fourth power: to raise to the ~ elevar al cuarto poder

frame: door ~ marco de la puerta

frame: kite ~ el armazón de un papalote ▪ armazón de una cometa

frame: picture ~ marco de un cuadro

to **frame a picture** enmarcar un cuadro ▪ *(photograph)* enmarcar una foto

frame of mind estado de ánimo ▪ el humor

frame of reference marco de referencia

framers of the constitution *los, las* artífices de la constitución

frames and lenses *(of a pair of glasses)* monturas y cristales ➤ Do you want metal or plastic frames? ¿Quieres monturas metálicas o de plástico? ▪ ¿Quieres monturas metálicas o de pasta?

framework of a building esqueleto de un edificio

framing shop tienda que enmarca cuadros

fraternal twins gemelos fraternos ▪ gemelos fraternales

frayed garment ▪ frayed article of clothing prenda raída

freak: Christmas tree ~ maniático de los árboles de navidad ▪ fanático de los arboles de navidad ➤ I'm a Christmas tree freak, you know, great big with lots of lights. Soy un maniático de los árboles de navidad sabes, grandísimos con muchas luces.

freak: pizza ~ maniático de las pizzas ➤ I'm a pizza freak. Soy maniático de las pizzas.

freak accident accidente insólito

freak show espectáculo estrambótico

free: to do something (for) ~ hacer algo gratis ▪ hacer algo por la gorra ▪ hacer algo de gorra ▪ hacer algo por la cara

free admission entrada gratis ▪ entrada libre

to be **free as a bird** ser más libre que el aire

free association *(in psychoanalysis) la* libre asociación

free estimates! ¡presupuestos gratis!

free-for-all barullo ▪ follón ▪ despendole ➤ The traffic in Mexico City is a free-for-all at times. El tráfico en la Ciudad de México es un follón a ratos.

free kick *(soccer) el* friqui

to be **free of blame** estar limpio de culpa

free of charge ▪ for nothing gratis ▪ gratuito ▪ de balde

free on board ▪ F.O.B. franco a bordo ▪ F.A.B.

to be **free on bond** ▪ to be free on bail estar libre bajo fianza

free rein to...: to give ~ dar vía libre a... ▪ dar rienda suelta a... ▪ dar carta blanca a...

free sample muestra gratuita

free time ▪ spare time ratos libres ▪ tiempo libre

free will: of one's own ~ a libre albedrío

freedom of choice *la* libertad de escoger

freedom to move about *la* libertad de moverse ▪ libertad de desplazarse

freehand drawing dibujo a pulso

to **freeze funds** ▪ to freeze bank accounts congelar cuentas bancarias

to **freeze to death** fallecer congelado ▪ morir congelado ▪ morir de frío

to be **freezing cold 1.** hacer un frío que pela **2.** pelarse de frío ➤ It is freezing cold today. Hoy hace un frío que pela. ➤ I'm freezing cold. Me pelo de frío.

freight elevator ▪ service elevator *el* montacargas

freight train *el* (tren de) mercancías

French bread *el* baguette

French kiss beso de tornillo

French roast *(coffee)* tostado a la francesa

frequency modulation ▪ FM **1.** *(noun) la* modulación de frecuencia **2.** *(adjective)* frecuencia modulada ➤ An FM radio Una radio de frecuencia modulada

fresh air aire fresco ➤ Open the window to let some fresh air into the room. Abre la ventana para que entre un poco de aire fresco en la habitación.

to **freshen up** arreglarse ▪ refrescarse ➤ After supper, the ladies went to the powder room to freshen up. Después de la cena, las damas fueron al baño de señoras para arreglarse.

freshly baked bread pan recién hecho

to be **freshly made** estar recién hecho ▪ estar acabado de hacer

freshly squeezed orange juice jugo de naranja recién exprimido ▪ *(Sp.)* zumo de naranja recién exprimido

freshman in college ▪ college freshman ▪ university freshman estudiante de primer año

freshman in high school ▪ high school freshman estudiante del noveno curso

freshman senator flamante senador(-a)

Freudian slip desliz Freudiano ▪ *el* lapsus

friction between people *la* fricción entre personas ➤ There's friction between them. Hay fricción entre ellos.

friction of the air *la* fricción del aire

Friday night and early Saturday en la noche del viernes al sábado

Friday the thirteenth *el* viernes trece *(In Hispanic countries, it is Tuesday the thirteenth, "martes trece," which is feared by the superstitious.)*

fried egg huevo frito ▪ huevo estrellado

friend from work amigo(-a) del trabajo
friend (of mine) amigo(-a) mío(-a)
friend of ours amigo(-a) nuestro(-a) ➤ She's a good friend of ours. Es muy amiga nuestra.
friend or foe ▪ friend or enemy amigo o enemigo
friendly fire *(in battle)* fuego amigo
friends from home amigos del pueblo de uno ➤ Some friends from home are visiting. Unos amigos de mi pueblo están de visita.
from a certain angle desde determinado ángulo ▪ desde cierto ángulo ▪ desde cierta posición ➤ There is a boulder that, seen from a certain angle, gives the appearance of being a songbird. Hay un peñasco que, visto desde determinada posición, guarda una cierta semejanza con la figura de un pájaro.
to be **from a place 1.** ser de un lugar **2.** to represent a place ser por un lugar ➤ The family is from Managua. La familia es de Managua. ➤ Republican from Long Island republicano por Long Island ➤ Democrat from Los Angeles demócrata por Los Angeles
from a place: to be (a certain distance) ~ distar a cierta distancia de un lugar ▪ quedar a cierta distancia de un lugar ▪ estar a cierta distancia de un lugar ➤ Paysandú is about a hundred kilometers from Salto. Paysandú dista cien kilómetros de Salto. ▪ Paysandú queda a cien kilómetros de Salto. ▪ Paysandú está a cien kilómetros de Salto.
from a previous marriage: to have children ~ tener hijos de un matrimonio anterior ➤ He has two other children from a previous marriage. Tiene otros dos hijos de un matrimonio anterior.
from about como entre ➤ From about 1856 to 1858, several unsuccessful attempts were made to lay the trans-Atlantic cable. Entre 1856 y 1858, se hicieron varios intentos fallidos de colocar el cable trans-Atlántico.
from an early age desde temprana edad
from an old and distinguished family de una familia distinguida y de abolengo ▪ de una familia de distinguido abolengo ▪ de un familia de rancio abolengo
from around the world de todo el mundo ➤ (Speaking) to more than a hundred and fifty world leaders, the president... Ante más de ciento cincuenta dirigentes de todo el mundo, el presidente...
from back to front de atrás para adelante
from bad to worse de mal en peor ▪ *(colorful)* de Guatemala a guatepeor
from beginning to end desde el principio hasta el final
from behind: to come ~ venir desde atrás ➤ Boca Juniors came from behind to beat Arsenal. Boca Juniors vino desde atrás para ganar a Arsenal.
from cover to cover: to read a book ~ ▪ to read a book all the way through ▪ to read a book from beginning to end leer un libro de tapa a tapa ▪ tragarse un libro entero ▪ leer hasta la dedicatoria de un libro ➤ I read that book (from) cover to cover. Leí ese libro de tapa a tapa. ▪ Me tragué ese libro entero.
from dawn to dusk de sol a sol
from day to day día a día ▪ de día en día
from different points of view ▪ from differing points of view desde diferentes puntos de vista ▪ desde distintos puntos de vista
from each other: to be very different ~ ser muy diferentes uno del otro ➤ The twins are very different from each other. Las gemelas son muy diferentes una de la otra.
from end to end de un extremo al otro ▪ de cabo a rabo
from experience that...: to know ~ saber por experiencia que... ➤ I know from experience that... Yo sé por experiencia que...
from force of habit ▪ out of force of habit ▪ by force of habit por la fuerza de la costumbre
from head to foot ▪ from head to toe de la cabeza a los pies ▪ de pies a cabeza
from head to tail de pies a cabeza ▪ de arriba a abajo
from here on out ▪ from now on de ahora en adelante
from house to house: to go ~ ir de casa en casa
from infancy desde pequeño ➤ She is bilingual from infancy. (Ella) es bilingüe desde pequeña.
from inside de dentro ▪ desde dentro
from me de mi parte ➤ It's a present from me to all your family. Es un regalo de mi parte para toda tu familia. ▪ Es un detalle de mi parte para toda tu familia. ▪ Es un presente de mi parte para toda tu familia.
from my point of view desde mi punto de vista ▪ bajo mi punto de vista
from now en ▪ de aquí en ➤ What do you want to be doing five years from now? ¿Qué te gustaría estar haciendo (de aquí) en cinco años? ➤ We'll be in San Salvador an hour from now. Estaremos en San Salvador en una hora.
from now on ▪ from this point on de ahora en adelante ▪ en lo sucesivo ▪ desde ahora ▪ a partir de ahora
from nowhere ▪ out of nowhere de la nada ➤ He came from nowhere to win the election. Salió de la nada y ganó la elección.
from one another *(implies several people)* unos de los otros ➤ They're very different from one another. Son muy diferentes unos de los otros.
from one end to the other 1. de un extremo a otro **2.** de cabo a rabo ➤ The Phoenicians sailed the Mediterranean from one end to the other. Los fenicios cruzaron el Mediterráneo de un extremo a otro.
from one to ten: to count ~ contar del uno al diez
from pillar to post: to run ~ ▪ to run hither and thither ir de la Ceca a Meca ▪ ir de Herodes a Pilato ➤ I've spent the day running from pillar to post. He pasado el día yendo de la Ceca a la Meca. ➤ They have me running from pillar to post. Me tienen corriendo de la Ceca a la Meca.
from place to place: to go ~ ir de lugar en lugar
from scratch: to make something ~ **1.** *(cake, etc.)* to make something without a mix hacer algo sin usar un preparado **2.** *(airplane model, etc.)* to make something without a kit ▪ to scratch build something construir algo sin modelo (previo)
from scratch: to start ~ empezar desde cero
from side to side de extremo a extremo ▪ de lado a lado ▪ a los lados
from start to finish desde el principio hasta el fin
from that day on desde aquel día en adelante
from that day to this desde entonces acá
from that time on a partir de allí ▪ de aquel momento en adelante
from the age of *x* to *y* desde los *x* hasta los *y* ➤ I lived in that house from the age of five to eighteen. Viví en esa casa desde los cinco hasta los dieciocho años.
from the bottom of my heart ▪ with all my heart de todo corazón
from the frying pan to the fire: to go ~ saltar de la sartén y dar en las brasas
from the get-go *(coll.)* ▪ from the (very) beginning desde el principio
from the left in the photo por la izquierda en la foto ➤ Quiroga is the third from the left. Quiroga es el tercero por la izquierda.
from the moment that desde el instante en que
from the outset ▪ from the start ▪ right off desde el comienzo ▪ desde el primer momento ▪ de primeras ➤ From the outset, I knew he was lying. Desde el comienzo, sabía que estaba mintiendo. ▪ Desde el primer momento, sabía que estaba mintiendo.
from the outside desde fuera
from the point of view of desde el punto de vista de ▪ bajo el punto de vista de
from the right in the photo por la derecha en la foto ➤ Einstein is the third from the right. Einstein es el tercero por la derecha.
to be **from the same generation** ▪ to be of the same generation ser de la misma generación ▪ *(Sp.)* ser de la misma quinta
from the start desde el principio
from the time of de la época de
from the very start desde un principio
from then on desde entonces en adelante ▪ a partir de entonces

from time to time de vez en cuando ▪ de cuando en cuando ▪ de vez en vez ▪ de tiempo en tiempo

from this point on 1. *(in time)* from now on ▪ from here on out a partir de ahora 2. *(in space)* from here on ▪ from this point on desde aquí en adelante

from time to time ▪ (every) now and then de vez en cuando ▪ de tarde en tarde

from... to 1. *(one person to another)* de... para 2. *(one place to another)* de... a ▪ desde... hasta ➤ Happy Birthday from Susana to Marta Feliz cumpleaños de Susana para Marta ➤ The flight from Atlanta to Madrid El vuelo de Atlanta a Madrid ▪ El vuelo desde Atlanta hasta Madrid

from today: a month ~ de hoy en un mes ▪ de aquí a un mes ▪ desde hoy en un mes

from today: a week ~ de hoy en una semana ▪ de aquí a una semana ▪ desde hoy en una semana

from today: *x* weeks ~ de aquí a *x* semanas ▪ de hoy en *x* semanas ➤ Two weeks from today De aquí a dos semanas

from top to bottom de arriba a abajo ➤ The porter's wife cleaned this kitchen from top to bottom. La esposa del portero limpió esta cocina de arriba abajo.

(from) week to week (de) semana a semana ▪ de semana en semana

from which del que ▪ de la que ▪ de lo que ▪ de los que ▪ de las que ➤ The same launchpad from which the first astronaut, Yuri Gagarin, took off in 1961 ▪ The same launch pad that the first astronaut, Yuri Gagarin, took off from in 1961 La misma plataforma de la que despegó en 1961 el primer astronauta, Yuri Gagarin

from year to year de año en año

front and back *el* frontal y el dorso ▪ la cara y el dorso

front and back (sides) ▪ both sides ambas caras ➤ Would you Xerox this for me, front and back? ¿Me copiará esta hoja, ambas caras?

front business empresa tapadera

(front) cover portada

front door puerta principal ▪ puerta de la calle

front gate *(made of wrought iron)* cancela

front for illegal activities: to serve as a ~ ▪ to serve as a front for illicit activities servir como pantalla para actividades ilegales ▪ servir como pantalla para actividades ilícitas ▪ funcionar como pantalla para actividades ilegales ▪ funcionar como pantalla para actividades ilícitas ▪ hacer de pantalla para actividades ilegales ▪ hacer de pantalla para actividades ilícitas

front of the envelope: on the ~ en el anverso del sobre ▪ en la parte de delante del sobre ▪ por delante del sobre

to be **front-page news** ser noticia de portada

front pocket bolsillo de delante ▪ bolsillo delantero

front-row seats: to have ~ tener plazas en primera fila ▪ tener asientos en primera fila

front-runner ▪ the one in the lead 1. *(in a race)* corredor(-a) que va a la cabeza ▪ corredor(-a) que va primero 2. *(in an election campaign)* favorito(-a)

to be the **front-running candidate for the presidency** ser el candidato favorito para la presidencia ▪ ser la candidata favorita para la presidencia

front steps escalinata

front-wheel drive tracción delantera

front wheels ruedas delanteras

front windshield *el* parabrisas delantera ▪ *(Sp.)* luna delantera

front yard jardín principal ▪ jardín delantero

frosted glass vidrio opaco

to be **frowned on** ▪ to be frowned upon no estar bien mirado ➤ Getting married during Lent is frowned on in the Catholic Church. Casarse durante la cuaresma no está bien mirado en la iglesia católica.

frozen pond estanque congelado

to be **frozen stiff** *(coll.)* ▪ to be chilled to the bone ▪ to be chilled to the quick estar duro de frío ▪ estar yerto de frío ▪ quedarse como un témpano

fruit cocktail ▪ fruit cup macedonia de frutas

frustrated attempt intento frustrado

frustrated longing anhelo frustrado

frustrated urge impulso frustrado ▪ *(sexual)* deseo frustrado

¡fucking A, man! *(off-color)* ¡que te cagas!

fuel consumption consumo de combustibles ▪ consumo de carburantes

to be **fuel efficient** obtener un buen rendimiento del combustible ➤ The new cars are more fuel efficient. Los nuevos coches obtienen un mayor rendimiento del combustible.

to be **fuel for** ser carne de ➤ It's fuel for a second book. Es carne de un segundo libro.

fuel prices ▪ price of fuel precio de los carburantes ➤ Fuel prices rose again yesterday for the fifth time in fourteen days. ▪ The price of fuel rose again yesterday for the fifth time in fourteen days. El precio de los carburantes volvió a subir ayer por quinta vez en catorce días.

fuel supply ▪ supply of fuel *(all countries)* suministro de combustible ▪ *(Sp.)* suministro de carburantes

to **fuel up** ▪ to fill up with fuel cargar con combustible

to **fulfill one's obligations** cumplir con sus obligaciones

full blast: to go ~ ir a toda pastilla ▪ ir a todo gas

full blast: to turn up the sound ~ ▪ to turn up the volume full blast poner el sonido a todo volumen ▪ subir el volumen a toda pastilla ➤ My mother, who does not hear well, turns the TV up full blast. Mi madre, que no oye bien, pone la tele a toda pastilla.

full-bodied wine vino fuerte

full circle círculo completo

full employment pleno empleo

full extent of ▪ magnitude of *la* magnitud de ▪ el alcance de

full-fledged de hecho y de derecho

full-length mirror espejo de cuerpo entero

full moon luna llena

full nelson *(wrestling)* llave completa ➤ My opponent pinned me with a full nelson. Mi oponente me sujetó con una llave completa.

to be **full of** estar lleno de ▪ estar cuajado de

to be **full of nonsense** decir chorradas

to be **full of one's usual nonsense** hablar el buey y decir mu ➤ He was full of his usual nonsense. Habló el buey y dijo mu.

to be **full of oneself** ir de divo(-a)

to be **full of poison** destilar veneno

to be **full of shit** *(off-color)* ▪ not to know what one is talking about estar lleno de mierda ▪ *(benign alternatives)* estar lleno de aire ▪ hablar el buey y decir mu

full tank tanque lleno ▪ depósito lleno

full throttle: to go (at) ~ ir a todo motor ▪ ir a todo gas

full-time: to work ~ trabajar tiempo completo ▪ trabajar jornada completa ▪ trabajar a tiempo completo

to be **full (to capacity)** estar lleno ▪ estar completo ▪ estar hasta la bandera ➤ The class is full. La clase está completa. ➤ The bus is full. El autobús está completo. ➤ The restaurant was packed. El restaurante estaba hasta la bandera.

full-time job jornada completa ▪ tiempo completo

to be **fully aware of** tener plena conciencia de ▪ darse cuenta totalmente de ▪ tener conciencia cabal de

to be **fully informed** estar completamente enterado ▪ estar al corriente ➤ Only a handful of people in the defense ministry are fully informed. Sólo un puñado de personas en el ministerio de defensa están completamente enterado. ▪ Sólo un puñado de personas en el ministerio de defensa están al corriente.

to **fume (with anger)** bufar (de ira) ▪ estar que bufa ▪ echar humo

to **function optimally** funcionar a pleno rendimiento

functional illiterate analfabeto funcional

fundamentalist preacher predicador(-a) fundamentalista

fundamentals of geometry fundamentos de geometría

funeral arrangements circunstancias del funeral

funny bone hueso de la risa

funny how that works! ¡qué irónico! ▪ *(Arg.)* ¡qué changa!

funny lines *(e.g., Bob Hope)* frases cómicas

funny papers ▪ funnies ▪ (newspaper) comic strips historietas cómicas

funny person ▪ comical person persona graciosa ▪ persona divertida

funny story cuento divertido ▪ chascarillo ▪ cuento gracioso

the **funny thing about it is (that)...** 1. the curious thing about it is... lo curioso (del caso) es que... ▪ lo raro (del caso) es que... ▪ lo extraño (del caso) es que... 2. the comical thing about it is... lo gracioso es que...

funny you should ask! ¡qué justo que preguntas! ▪ ¡qué puntería que preguntas!

to **furnish power to** proporcionar potencia para ➤ Igor Sikorsky developed the first helicopter with a single rotor that furnished enough power to lift off. Igor Sikorsky desarrolló el primer helicóptero que, con un único rotor, proporcionaba suficiente potencia para elevarse.

to **furnish the materials** proporcionar los materiales

furnished or unfurnished? ¿amueblado o sin muebles?

further word: to await ~ esperar nuevas comunicaciones ➤ We're awaiting further word from (military) headquarters. Esperamos nuevas comunicaciónes del cuartel general.

further word: to receive ~ recibir nuevas comunicaciones

to be **fussy about something** ser remilgado con algo ➤ She's fussy about food. Es remilgada con la comida.

future attack 1. *(indefinite)* futuros ataques 2. *(definite)* ataque eventual ➤ The government has given the okay for military aircraft to launch a future attack. El gobierno ha dado el visto bueno para que la aeronave militar lanzara un ataque eventual.

gable roof *la* techumbre a dos aguas ▪ tejado a dos aguas
to **gain access to** ▪ to get access to lograr acceso a ▪ conseguir acceso a
to **gain altitude** ganar altura ▪ tomar altura ▪ *(Sp.)* coger altura ➤ The airplane regained altitude. El avión volvió a tomar altura.
to **gain control of** ganar control de ▪ apoderarse de
to **gain entry (in)to** conseguir entrar en
to **gain momentum** cobrar momento ▪ ganar empuje
to **gain someone's confidence** ganarse la confianza de alguien ▪ adquirir confianza de alguien ▪ arrancarle la confidencia a alguien
to **gain speed** tomar velocidad ▪ ganar velocidad
to **gain weight** ▪ to put on weight ganar peso ▪ engordar ▪ *(Sp.)* coger peso
galley proofs pruebas de galera ▪ galeradas
gambling chips fichas
gambling joint ▪ gambling den garito
game preserve reserva de animales ▪ *(where controlled hunting is permitted)* coto de caza
games online juegos en red
gang of thieves ▪ band of thieves banda de ladrones
to **gang up on someone** conchabarse contra alguien ▪ aliarse contra alguien ▪ unirse contra alguien
gap between intention and action *el* lapsus entre conducta e intención
gaps in one's knowledge lagunas (en los conocimientos) ➤ I still have gaps in my knowledge of Spanish, but I'm closing in on them. Todavía tengo lagunas en mis conocimientos de español, pero ando llenándolas.
garbage can ▪ trash can cubo de basura
garbage dump vertedero de basura
to **garner someone the prize** ▪ to earn someone the prize ▪ to get someone the prize valerle a alguien el premio
to **garner support against** ▪ to win support against ▪ to gather support against recabar apoyo contra
to **garner support for** ▪ to win support for ▪ to gather support for recabar apoyo para
to **garner the prize** ▪ to win the prize ▪ to get the prize ▪ to take the prize ganar el premio ▪ recibir el premio ▪ obtener el premio
gas chromatograph cromatógrafo gaseoso
gas chromatography cromatografía gaseosa
gas pump *(at a filling station) el* surtidor de gasolina
gas stove cocinilla a gas ▪ estufa a gas
to **gather around...** agruparse en torno a... ▪ juntarse en torno a... ▪ juntarse alrededor...
to **gather by hand** ▪ to pick by hand ▪ to be hand-gathered recolectar a mano ➤ *(on a wine label)* Made from select Tempranillo grapes gathered by hand in our vineyards. Elaborado con la mejor selección de uva Tempranillo recolectada a mano en nuestros viñedos.
to **gather evidence (of a crime)** recoger pruebas de un crimen ▪ juntar pruebas de un crimen ▪ recolectar pruebas de un crimen *(The verbs "juntar" and "recolectar" can also be used.)*
to **gather force** cobrar fuerza ➤ The hurricane gathered force with the warm air coming from the east. El huracán cobró fuerza con el cálido aire proveniente del este.
to **gather (in) the harvest 1.** cosechar ▪ recoger la cosecha ▪ recoletar la cosecha **2.** *(grapes)* vendimiar
to **gather information about something** reunir datos sobre algo ▪ reunir información sobre algo ▪ recopilar datos sobre algo
to **gather support against** ▪ to garner support against ▪ to win support against recabar apoyo contra
to **gather support for** ▪ to garner support for ▪ to win support for recabar apoyo para
to **gather that...** tener entendido que... ▪ sacar la consecuencia de que...
to **gather together** reunirse ▪ agruparse en ▪ juntarse ▪ amontarse ▪ apiñarse
to **gather up one's belongings** ▪ to gather up (all) one's things ▪ to gather up (all) one's stuff ▪ to gather one's things (together) recoger las pertenencias de uno ▪ *(coll.)* recoger los bártulos de uno
to **gather up one's things** ▪ to gather up one's stuff ▪ to gather up one's belongings recoger los bártulos ▪ recoger las pertenencias de uno
to **gauge something** tomarle el pulso a algo
gay lover compañero(-a) sentimental
Gaza Strip Franja de Gaza
gear shift lever 1. *(straight or automatic shift)* palanca de cambio **2.** *(straight shift)* palanca de cambio manual
gene therapy terapia genética
general elections *las* elecciones generales ▪ comicios generales
general feeling ▪ common feeling ▪ general view ▪ common view *el* sentir general ▪ *la* opinión general
general practitioner médico de medicina general
the **general public** el gran público ▪ el público en general
general relativity *(Einstein) la* relatividad general
general strike huelga general
to **generally do something** ▪ to usually do something soler hacer una cosa
generally speaking en términos generales
generation after generation ▪ down through the generations generación tras generación ▪ a lo largo de las generaciones
a **generation ago** una generación atrás ➤ Medical technology is light-years ahead of where it was a generation ago. La tecnología médica está a años luz de lo que estaba una generación atrás.
generation gap brecha de generaciones ▪ brecha generacional
Generation of 1898 ▪ Generation of '98 La generación de noventa y ocho ▪ La generación de 98 *(The group of distinguished Spanish-language writers concerned about Spain's decline as a world power, as symbolized by its defeat in the Spanish-American War of 1898. The group includes Azorín (José Martinez Ruiz), Miguel de Unamuno, Menéndez Pidal, Antonio and Manuel Machado, Ramón Pérez de Ayala, Juan Ramón Jiménez, Ruben Darío, Ramón del Valle-Inclán, Pío Baroja, Ramiro de Maeztu, Vicente Blasco Ibáñez, Jacinto Benavente, José María Linares Rivas, los hermanos Quintero, Francisco Villaespesa, and José Ortega y Gassett.)*
genetic fingerprint ▪ genetic blueprint huella genética
Geneva Convention *la* Convención de Ginebra
to be a **genius at** ▪ to be a genius in ser un genio en ▪ ser un genio para ▪ *(coll.)* ser una bestia en ➤ She's a genius at math. Ella es un bestia en las matemáticas.
genius disdains a beaten path el genio desdeña el camino trillado
to be **gentle as a lamb** ser más manso que un cordero
gentle breeze brisa suave ▪ brisa mansa ▪ vientecillo

German chocolate cake tarta de chocolate al estilo alemán
to be **germane to the discussion** atañer a la discusión
to be **germane to the issue** atañer al asunto
to be **germane to the situation** atañer a la situación
to be **germane to the subject** atañer al tema
Germanic language idioma germánico ▪ lengua germánica
to **get a babysitter** conseguir un(-a) cuidador(-a) de niños ▪ *(Sp.)* conseguir un canguro ➤ Were you able to get a babysitter for tomorrow night? ¿Pudiste conseguir canguro para mañana por la noche?
to **get a better angle on something** obtener un mejor ángulo para algo ➤ Stand over there. That way I can get a better angle (for the picture). Ponte allí. Así puedo obtener un mejor ángulo para la foto.
to **get a bill** ▪ to receive a bill venirle una factura ▪ llegarle una factura ▪ recibir una factura ▪ venirle una cuenta ▪ llegarle una cuenta ▪ recibir una cuenta ➤ I haven't gotten the phone bill. No me ha venido la factura de teléfono.
to **get a bill changed** ▪ to get change for a bill cambiar un billete ➤ I need to get this twenty changed. ▪ I need to get change for this twenty. Necesito cambiar este (billete de) veinte.
to **get a bill passed by Congress** *(U.S.)* hacer aprobar un proyecto de ley por el congreso
to **get a bill through Congress** *(U.S.)* hacer pasar un proyecto de ley por el congreso
to **get a black eye** amoratarse el ojo ➤ I got a black eye (when I was) playing baseball. Me amoraté el ojo jugando al béisbol.
to **get a breath of fresh air** ▪ to get some fresh air tomar una bocanada de aire fresco ▪ tomar el fresco ▪ oxigenarse ▪ airearse
to **get a chance to** ▪ to have a chance to tener la oportunidad de ▪ tener ocasión de ➤ I never got a chance to call you. No tuve la oportunidad de llamarte. ▪ No tuve ocasión de llamarte.
to **get a check off to someone** ▪ to send a check to someone ▪ to send someone a check girarle un cheque a alguien ➤ Let me know how much it is, and I'll get a check off to you. Dime a cuánto va a ascender, y te giraré un cheque.
to **get a commission** recibir una comisión ▪ llevar comisión
to **get a commitment from someone** conseguir un compromiso de alguien ▪ conseguir que alguien se comprometa
to **get a conversation going** ▪ to start a conversation trabar una conversación ▪ entablar una conversación
to **get a criminal record** ficharle ➤ You don't get a criminal record until you're sixteen. No te fichan hasta los dieciséis tacos.
to **get a degree in...** obtener un título (universitario) en...
to **get a divorce (from someone)** divorciarse (de alguien) ➤ They're going to get a divorce. Ellos se van a divorciar. ➤ She got a divorce. Ella se divorció.
to **get a doctor** conseguir a un médico
to **get a drink of water** ir a beber agua ▪ ponerse un vaso de agua ▪ *(Sp.)* cogerse un vaso de agua ➤ I'm going to get a drink of water. Voy a beber agua.
get a drink of water?: may I ~ *(tú)* ¿me das agua? ▪ *(usted)* ¿me da agua?
to **get a foot in the door** abrirse paso ▪ meter la cabeza ▪ meterse en ese mundillo ➤ I had to struggle to get a foot in the door. Tuve que esforzarme para abrirme paso.
to **get a good deal on something** salirle algo a alguien muy bien de precio ➤ I got a good deal on my car because it had been used as a demonstrator (by the dealership). El coche me salió muy bien de precio porque había sido utilizado para pruebas por el concesionario.
to **get a good look at something** llegar a ver bien algo ➤ We had only three hours in Seville, so I didn't get a very good look at it. Sólo tuvimos tres horas en Sevilla, así que no llegué a verla bien.
to **get a good look at someone** llegar a ver a alguien con claridad ➤ Did you get a good look at him? ¿Llegaste a verle con claridad?
to **get a good night's sleep** dormir bien por la noche ▪ descansar bien por la noche ➤ Get a good night's sleep before your trip to Spain, because you're going to have to stay up all day that first day. Descansa bien (por la noche) antes de ir a España porque el primer día lo tendrás que pasar despierto.
to **get a good seat** conseguir un buen asiento ▪ *(Sp.)* coger un buen asiento
to **get a grade** sacar una nota ➤ I got an A on the test. Saqué un sobresaliente en el examen. ▪ Saqué una A en el examen.
to **get a grasp of a subject** dominar un tema ▪ entender un tema
to **get a great deal on** hacer un pan como una hostia en
to **get a grip on oneself** ▪ to pull oneself together ▪ to control oneself sobreponerse
to **get a haircut** cortarse el pelo ➤ I have to get a haircut today. ▪ I've got to get a haircut today. Tengo que cortarme el pelo hoy.
to **get a hard on** *(graphic)* ▪ to get an erection ponérsele dura a uno ▪ ponérsele tiesa a uno ▪ empinársele ▪ *(L. Am.)* ponérsele parado ▪ *(Sp.)* empalmarse ▪ *(slang)* ponérsele morcillona
to **get a head start** salir con ventaja (en una carrera) ▪ tener un comienzo avanzado ▪ comenzar avanzado
to **get a (jail) sentence** ▪ to be sentenced to jail ser condenado a pena de prisión ➤ The robber got ten years. El ladrón fue condenado a diez años. ➤ The terrorist got thirty years without parole. ▪ The terrorist was sentenced to thirty years without parole. El terrorista fue condenado a treinta años sin derecho a libertad condicional.
to **get a job** conseguir trabajo ▪ conseguir un puesto (de trabajo)
to **get a kick out of something** ▪ to get a charge out of something hacerle gozar mucho algo ▪ emocionarse mucho con algo ▪ gozar mucho con algo ➤ I got a kick out of your electronic Thanksgiving card that played "Turkey in the Straw." Me hizo gozar mucho tu tarjeta electrónica de Acción de Gracias que tocó "Turkey in the Straw".
to **get a late start** salir con retraso ▪ partir con retraso
to **get a laugh out of** reírse mucho de ➤ We got a laugh out of the computer translation of "Dodger fan," which came out "ventilador del trampista." Nos reímos mucho de la traducción computarizada de la expresión "hincha de los Dodgers" que resultó siendo "ventilador del trampista".
to **get a letter from someone** ▪ to receive a letter from someone ▪ to have a letter from someone recibir una carta de alguien ▪ llegarle una carta de alguien ▪ *(especially in the past tense)* tener una carta de alguien ➤ I got a letter from Javier yesterday. Ayer recibí una carta de Javier. ▪ Ayer me llegó una carta de Javier. ▪ Ayer tuve una carta de Javier. ➤ I got a letter from him yesterday. Ayer recibí una carta de él. ▪ Ayer me llegó una carta de él. ▪ Ayer tuve una carta de él.
get a life! ¡búscate la vida! ▪ ¡que te busques la vida!
to **get a little older** hacerse un poco más mayor ➤ We want to go to Spain when our daughter gets a little older. Queremos ir a España cuando nuestra hija se haga un poco más mayor.
get a load of...! *(coll.)* ¡pesca...! ▪ ¡mira...! ▪ ¡fíjate...! ➤ Get a load of that rhythm section! ¡Pesca esa sección rítmica!
to **get a loan** ▪ to take out a loan ▪ to secure a loan conseguir un préstamo ▪ concederle a alguien un préstamo ➤ We got a loan to buy a house. ▪ We took out a loan to buy a house. Conseguimos un préstamo para comprar una casa. ▪ Nos concedieron un préstamo para comprar una casa.
to **get a look at** llegar a ver ➤ I didn't get a look at his face. No llegué a verle la cara (de él).
to **get a lot done** aprovechar el tiempo para trabajar mucho
to **get a lot of enjoyment from** ▪ to get a lot of enjoyment out of disfrutar mucho con
to **get a lot of light** recibir mucha luz ▪ darle a algo mucho la luz ▪ darle a algo mucha luz ➤ This apartment gets a lot of light. Este piso recibe mucha luz. ▪ A este piso le da mucho la luz. ▪ A este piso le da mucha luz.
to **get a lot of pleasure from** ▪ to get a lot of enjoyment from disfrutar mucho con ▪ disfrutar mucho de ➤ We get a lot of pleasure from our new sound system. Disfrutamos mucho de nuestro nuevo sistema de sonido.
to **get a lot of rain** abundar la lluvia ▪ menudear la lluvia ➤ Galicia and Asturias both get a lot of rain. Tanto en Galicia

como en Asturias abunda la lluvia. ▪ Tanto en Galicia como en Asturias menudea la lluvia.

to **get a lot out of something** sacar (mucho) provecho de algo ▪ sacar (mucho) partido de algo ➤ I got a lot out of the Latin American short story course. Saqué mucho provecho de la clase en el cuento latinoamericano. ▪ Saqué mucho partido de la clase en el cuento latinoamericano.

to **get a lump in one's throat** anudarse la voz ▪ hacérsele a uno un nudo en la garganta

to **get a manicure** hacerse la manicura ➤ I got a manicure yesterday. Me hice la manicura ayer.

to **get a message 1.** recibir un mensaje **2.** *(on a computer screen)* salir un mensaje ▪ aparecer un mensaje **3.** to transport a message hacer llegar un mensaje ➤ I got twenty-two messages on my answering machine yesterday. Recibí veintidós mensajes en mi contestador automático ayer. ➤ I turned on the computer and got an error message. Encendí el ordenador y me salió un mensaje de error en el sistema. ➤ In the 19th century, Pony Express could get a message from Kansas City to Denver in three days. En el siglo XIX, el Pony Express hacía llegar un mensaje desde Kansas City a Denver en tres días.

to **get a message across** hacer entender un mensaje

to **get a new car** comprar un carro nuevo ▪ *(Sp., Arg.,)* comprar un coche nuevo *(If you won or were given a new car, you must say that specifically.)*

to **get a nibble 1.** *(while fishing)* picar ▪ dar tirones (al anzuelo) ▪ tirar (del anzuelo) **2.** *(in response to ad, resume, etc.)* recibir poquísimo interés ➤ This is not a good fishing spot. I'm not getting any nibbles. No es un buen sitio para pescar. Los peces no están picando. ➤ She's answered about two dozen job ads, but so far she's only gotten a few nibbles. Respondió a unas dos docenas de anuncios de trabajo y hasta ahora sólo ha recibido poquísimo interés.

to **get a picture of 1.** to take a picture of sacar una foto(grafía) de **2.** to form a concept of formar un dibujo mental de

to **get a present for someone** ▪ to buy a present for someone comprar un regalo para alguien ▪ comprar un obsequio para alguien ▪ hacerle un regalo a alguien ▪ hacerle un obsequio a alguien ▪ adquirir un regalo para alguien

to **get a present from someone** recibir un regalo de alguien

to **get a raise** ▪ to be given a raise concederle a alguien un aumento (salarial) ➤ I got a raise. ▪ They gave me a raise. Me concedieron un aumento salarial.

to **get a ride with someone** llevarle a alguien ▪ acercar a alguien ▪ *(L. Am.)* darle a alguien un aventón ➤ Could we get a ride downtown with you? ¿Nos acercas al centro? ▪ ¿Nos llevas al centro? ➤ She had gotten a ride with some friends. Unos amigos la habían llevado. ▪ Unos amigos le dieron un aventón.

to **get a salary** ▪ to make a salary ▪ to earn a salary ganar un sueldo ▪ ganar un salario ➤ He gets a salary plus commission. Gana un sueldo más comisión. ▪ Gana un salario más comisión. ➤ He gets a good salary. ▪ He makes a good salary. Gana un buen sueldo. ▪ Gana un buen salario.

to **get a shock from** *(electric shock)* ▪ to get shocked by ▪ to be shocked by recibir un choque eléctrico ▪ darle un choque eléctrico a alguien ➤ I got a shock from the light switch. ▪ I got shocked by the light switch. ▪ I was shocked by the light switch. ▪ The light switch shocked me. El interruptor de la luz me dio un choque. ▪ Recibí un choque del interruptor de la luz.

to **get a surprise** llevarle una sorpresa

to **get a tan** broncearse ▪ dorarse ▪ *(coll.)* tostarse ▪ ligar bronce

to **get a ticket 1.** *(traffic ticket)* to be cited ponerle una multa **2.** *(admission ticket)* to buy a ticket comprar una entrada **3.** *(airline, train, bus)* comprar un billete ➤ I got a ticket for speeding. ▪ I got a speeding ticket. Me pusieron una multa por velocidad. ➤ She got a ticket for speeding. ▪ She got a speeding ticket. Le pusieron una multa por velocidad. ➤ I got us tickets to the concert. ▪ I got us tickets for the concert. He comprado entradas para el concierto. ➤ I couldn't get a train ticket for the early train. They were sold out. No pude comprar un billete para el tren de primera hora. Estaban todos vendidos.

get a word in edgewise: not to be able to ~ no poder abrir la boca ▪ no poder meter la cuchara ▪ *(Sp.)* no poder meter baza ▪ *(L. Am.)* no poder decir ni chis ni mus ➤ I couldn't get a word in edgewise. No pude meter la cuchara. ▪ No pude meter baza.

to **get about** ▪ to get around desplazarse ➤ It's hard to get about in the snow. Es difícil desplazarse por la nieve.

to **get access to** ▪ to gain access to conseguir acceso a ▪ lograr acceso a ➤ Is there any indication (as to) how they got access to all that ammunition? ▪ Is there any indication (as to) how they gained access to all that ammunition? ¿Hay alguna pista sobre cómo consiguieron acceso a toda esa munición? ▪ ¿Hay alguna pista sobre cómo lograron acceso a toda esa munición?

to **get acclimated to** ▪ to adjust to ▪ to adapt to adaptarse a ▪ acostumbrarse a ▪ aclimatarse a ➤ You eventually get acclimated to the Spanish schedule. Acabarás acostumbrándote al horario español. ▪ Acabarás aclimatándote al horario español.

to **get accomplished** sacar trabajo adelante ➤ I didn't get accomplished all I had hoped to accomplish. No saqué adelante todo el trabajo que esperaba.

to **get acquainted** conocer a alguien con mayor profundidad ▪ trabar conversación ➤ We got acquainted at a cocktail party. Nos conocimos (con mayor profundidad) en un cóctel. ▪ Trabamos conversación en un cóctel.

to **get across a bridge** ▪ to cross a bridge cruzar un puente

to **get across a concept** ▪ to get a concept across hacer entender un concepto ▪ lograr comunicar un concepto ▪ transmitir un concepto ➤ The singularity is a difficult concept to get across. ▪ The singularity is a concept that's difficult to get across. La singularidad es un concepto difícil de transmitir. ▪ Es un concepto difícil de hacer entender. ▪ Es un concepto difícil de lograr comunicar.

to **get across one's point** ▪ to convey one's point successfully lograr que uno entienda el punto (de discusión) ➤ In the *Meno*, Plato gets the point across that a prior knowledge is recalled, not learned. En el *Menón*, Platón logra que entendamos el punto que el conocimiento a priorí no es aprendido, sino recordado.

to **get ahead** progresar ▪ prosperar ▪ ponerse en cabeza ▪ ir adelante ➤ She is eager to get ahead. Ella tiene ganas de progresar.

to **get ahead in life** hacer progresos en la vida ▪ ir adelante ➤ A good education can help you get ahead in life. Una buena educación puede ayudar a hacer progresos en la vida.

to **get ahead of a car** ▪ to get around a car ▪ to pass a car adelantar a un coche ▪ ponerse por delante de un coche ▪ rebasar un carro

to **get ahead of oneself** adelantarse ➤ But I'm getting ahead of myself. First, I want to say that... Pero me estoy adelantando. Primero, quiero decir que...

to **get all balled up** hacerse bolas ▪ *(Sp.)* estar hecho un lío ➤ I got all balled up trying to explain the word "could" without translating it. Me hice bolas tratando de explicar la palabra "could" sin traducirla.

to **get all bent out of shape over something** ponerse fuera de sí por algo

to **get all dressed up** ponerse de punta en blanco ▪ ponerse todo elegante ▪ ponerse hecho un pincel

to **get all mixed up** hacerse un taco ▪ armarse un taco ▪ trastocarse ▪ hacerse un lío ▪ liarse

to **get all the blanks filled in** ▪ to fill in all the blanks ▪ to fill all the blanks in rellenar todos los huecos ▪ rellenar todos los espacios en blanco

to **get all wet** mojarse entero ▪ mojarse del todo ▪ mojarse completamente ▪ mojarse por completo ➤ I dropped the homework assignment in a puddle and got it all wet. Se me cayeron los deberes en un charco y se mojaron enteros.

to **get (all) worked up** ▪ to get upset ▪ to get all bent out of shape excitarse ▪ acalorarse ▪ exaltarse ▪ desmadejarse ▪ molestarse ➤ Don't get so worked up. No te excites. ▪ No te acalores. ▪ No te exaltes. ▪ No te desmadejes. ▪ No te molestes.

to **get along 1.** to like each other llevarse bien **2.** to fare llevarlo ➤ They get along very well. Se llevan muy bien. ➤ *(doctor to patient at post-surgery checkup)* How are you getting along? ¿Qué tal lo llevas? ▪ ¿Cómo lo llevas?

to **get along by oneself** ▪ to manage by oneself ▪ to fend for oneself valerse por sí mismo ▪ valerse por uno mismo ▪ valerse sólo to **get along famously (together)** *(colorful)* llevarse magníficamente bien ■ llevarse de maravilla ➤ We get along famously. Nos llevamos magníficamente bien. ■ Nos llevamos de maravilla.

to **get along in a foreign language** defenderse en un idioma extranjero

to **get along like dogs and cats** llevarse como el perro y el gato

to **get along (together)** ■ to get along entenderse bien ■ llevarse bien ➤ They get along great together. ■ They get along great. Se entienden muy bien. ■ Se llevan muy bien.

to **get along well (together)** llevarse bien (uno con el otro) ■ llevarse bien (juntos)

to **get along (well) with someone** llevarse bien con alguien ■ estar a bien con alguien ■ estar a buenas con alguien

to **get along without something** ■ to do without something arreglárselas sin algo ■ apañárselas sin algo ➤ We can get along without a car for the time being. Podemos arreglárnosla sin coche por el momento. ■ Podemos apañárnosla sin coche por el momento.

to **get an A** sacar un sobresaliente ■ sacar un diez ■ sacar la nota máxima ■ ponerle un sobresaliente ➤ I got an A on the test. Saqué un sobresaliente en el examen. ■ Me han puesto un sobresaliente en el examen. ➤ I got an A on my paper. Saqué un sobresaliente en mi trabajo.

to **get an answer** recibir (una) respuesta ■ contestarle ➤ I haven't gotten an answer. ■ They haven't answered me. No he recibido respuesta. ■ No me han contestado. ➤ I haven't been able to get an answer. No he podido recibir respuesta.

to **get an argument (from someone)** ponerse alguien a discutir con uno ■ montarle un pollo a alguien ■ salir con su cantaleta ➤ I know from experience, if you tell him you can't lend him any money, you'll get an argument. Sé por experiencia que si le dices que no puedes prestarle dinero, se pondrá a discutir contigo.

to **get an early start** **1.** *(on a trip)* salir pronto **2.** *(on a project)* empezar pronto

to **get an erection** ponerse (el pene) erecto

to **get an idea into one's head** ■ to get it into one's head that ponérsele entre ceja y ceja ■ metérsele entre ceja y ceja ➤ When you get an idea into your head, you're impossible. Cuando algo se te pone entre ceja y ceja, ¡no hay manera!

to **get an idea of** hacerse una idea de ■ hacerse una composición de lugar de ➤ Just so you can get an idea of... *(tú)* Para que te hagas una composición de lugar de... ■ *(usted)* Para que se haga una composición de lugar de...

to **get an impression** llevarse una impresión ■ sacar una impresión ➤ How did you get that impression? ¿Cómo te llevaste esa impresión? ■ ¿Cómo sacaste esa impresión? ➤ Where did you get that impression? ¿Dónde te llevaste esa impresión? ■ ¿De dónde sacaste esa impresión?

to **get angry with someone** ■ to get angry at someone ■ to get mad at someone enojarse de alguien ■ *(Sp.)* enfadarse con alguien ■ cabrearse con alguien

to **get anywhere with** ■ to make any headway with conseguir hacer carrera con ➤ Did you get anywhere with the boss today? ¿Conseguiste hacer carrera con el jefe hoy?

to **get around** **1.** to make the scene saber (como) moverse ■ estar por todas partes ■ no caérsele la casa por encima **2.** to move around desplazarse ■ moverse **3.** *(rumor)* to circulate correr ➤ That guy really gets around. Este tipo sabe (como) moverse. ■ Ese tipo está por todas partes. ■ A ese tipo no se le cae la casa por encima. ➤ His arthritis makes it difficult (for him) to get around. Su artritis le hace muy difícil desplazarse. ■ Su artritis le hace muy difícil moverse. ➤ The rumor is getting around that... Corre el rumor de que...

to **get around a vehicle** **1.** to pass a vehicle pasar un vehículo ■ rebasar un vehículo ■ *(Sp.)* adelantar un vehículo **2.** to get around a vehicle that's blocking you in esquivar un vehículo ➤ See if you can get around that car. ■ See if you can pass that car. Mira si puedes rebasar ese carro. ■ Mira si puedes adelantar ese coche. ➤ Can you get around the car that's blocking you in? ¿Puedes esquivar ese coche que te bloquea el paso?

to **get around doing something** ■ to avoid doing something ■ to get out of doing something escaquearse de hacer algo

to **get around in the snow** ■ to get about in the snow desplazarse en la nieve ➤ It's hard to get around in the snow. Es difícil desplazarse por la nieve.

to **get around the censor** ■ to evade the censor burlar la censura

to **get around the rules** saltarse las reglas ➤ We'll have to figure out some way to get around the rules. ■ We'll have to figure out some way of getting around the rules. Tendremos que imaginar algún modo de saltarnos las reglas.

to **get around to (doing) something** sacar tiempo para hacer algo ■ llegarle el momento ■ ponerse a algo ■ ponerse con algo ➤ I (just) haven't gotten around to it. No he sacado tiempo para hacerlo. ■ Aún no me he puesto con ello. ➤ I'll get around to it one of these days. Sacaré tiempo para eso un día de estos. ■ Me pondré con ello un día de estos. ➤ I hadn't gotten around to it. No había sacado tiempo para hacerlo. ■ No me había puesto a ello.

to **get around without a car** desplazarse sin coche ■ moverse sin coche

to **get arrested** ■ to be arrested ■ to be placed under arrest ser arrestado

to **get at something** ■ to drive at something llegar a algo ➤ What are you getting at? ■ What are you driving at? ¿A dónde quieres llegar? ➤ We're trying to get at the truth. Intentamos llegar a la verdad. ➤ We're trying to get to the root of the problem. Intentamos llegar a la raíz del problema.

to **get attached to someone** *(people, pets)* ■ to become attached to someone ■ to grow fond of someone encariñarse con alguien ■ *(Sp.)* cogerle cariño a alguien ➤ Children get very attached to their pets. Los niños se encariñan con sus mascotas. ■ Los niños cogen cariño a sus mascotas.

to **get attacked by an animal** ser atacado por un animal

to **get away** **1.** to escape lograr huir ■ conseguir huir **2.** to have a change of scene escaparse ■ hacer una escapada ➤ The bank robbers got away. Los atracadores del banco consiguieron huir. ➤ We need to get away for the weekend. Necesitamos (hacer) una escapada este fin de semana.

to **get away from something** **1.** to move away alejarse de algo **2.** to stop doing something dejar de hacer algo ➤ Get away from the wall. It could collapse. Aléjate de la pared. Podría derrumbarse. ➤ People have gotten away from saying "sir." La gente ha dejado de decir "señor".

to **get away with murder** salirse uno con la suya ■ hacer lo que le da a uno la gana ➤ He gets away with murder. Se sale con la suya. ■ Hace lo que le da la gana.

to **get away with something** hacer conseguir algo ■ salir impune de algo ■ *(in the negative)* no lograrlo ➤ You'll never get away with it! ¡No te saldrás con la tuya! ➤ He gets away with a lot more than I do. Se sale con la suya muchas más veces que yo. ■ Le consienten mucho más que a mí.

get back! ¡atrás! ■ ¡retrocedan! ■ ¡retírese! ■ ¡retírense! ■ ¡retírate! ■ ¡retiraos!

to **get back** *(intransitive verb)* **1.** to step back ■ to move back retroceder ■ situarse para atrás **2.** to return (from somewhere) volver ■ regresar ➤ The police ordered the crowd to get back. La policía dio ordenes a la multitud de que retrocediera. ➤ When did you get back from Barcelona? ¿Cuándo has vuelto de Barcelona?

to **get back at someone for something** ■ to get revenge against someone for something ■ to take revenge on someone for something vengarse de alguien ■ pagarle a alguien con la misma moneda ■ devolverle la jugada

to **get back in touch with someone** ■ to reestablish contact with someone recuperar contacto con alguien ■ volver a contactarse con alguien ➤ I hope you've gotten back in touch with your friends. ■ I hope you've reestablished contact with your friends. Espero que hayas recuperado contacto con tus amigos.

to **get back in(to) circulation** ■ to go back in circulation volver a estar en circulación ■ volver a ponerse en circulación

to **get back into the car** ■ to get back in the car volver a meterse en el carro ■ volver a subir al carro ➤ You all get back in the car! Vuelvan a meterse en el carro. ▪ *(Sp., vosotros)* Volved a meteros en el coche.

to **get back on one's feet 1.** to get back up on one's feet volver en pie **2.** to be up and about (after an illness) ▪ to land on one's feet after a personal failure salir a flote ➤ The boxer got back (up) on his feet before the count of ten. El boxeador volvió en pie antes de que el arbitro contara (hasta) diez.

to **get back on track** (volver a) coger el hilo

to **get back to normal** volver a la normalidad ▪ *(after political or social unrest)* volver las aguas a su cauce ➤ Life is getting back to normal after the devastating floods. La vida vuelve a la normalidad tras las devastadoras inundaciones. ➤ Things are hopefully getting back to normal in Haiti. Esperemos que las aguas vuelvan a su cauce en Haiti.

to **get back to someone 1.** to report back to someone ▪ to call someone back volver a ponerse en contacto con alguien **2.** llegar a oídos de alguien ➤ He said he'd get back to me, but I never heard from him. Dijo que se volvería a poner en contacto conmigo, pero no volví a tener noticias suyas. ➤ I wouldn't mention it to anyone, because it might get back to her. (Yo) no se lo diría a nadie porque podría llegar a sus oídos.

to **get back to the subject** ▪ to return to the subject ▪ to come back to the subject volver al tema ▪ volver al asunto

to **get back to work** volver a la tarea ▪ volver a las labores ▪ volver a trabajar ➤ Get back to work! ¡Vuelve a trabajar!

to **get beat up 1.** to get a lot of wear and tear recibir una tunda **2.** to be beaten recibir una paliza ▪ darle una paliza ➤ The sofa got pretty beat(en) up. El sofá recibía buenas tundas. ➤ He got beat up. Recibió una paliza. ▪ Le dieron una paliza.

to **get behind 1.** to fall behind ▪ to lag behind quedarse rezagado ▪ atrasarse **2.** to situate oneself behind ponerse detrás de ➤ *(reporter to interview subject)* I'm sorry, I got behind you a little bit. Lo siento me he quedado un poquito rezagado(-a). ▪ Lo siento me he atrasado un poco.

to **get behind in one's work** retrasarse en el trabajo

to **get behind the wheel** ponerse al volante

to **get benefit from something** sacar beneficio de algo ▪ *(coll.)* sacar tajada de algo

to **get better** mejorarse

to **get better and better** ponerse cada vez mejor ▪ mejorar cada vez más ▪ ponerse mejor (por momentos)

to **get better at (doing) something** mejorar en (hacer) algo

to **get better with age** mejorar con el tiempo ➤ Wines get better with age. Los vinos mejoran con el tiempo.

to **get beyond** pasar de ▪ ir más allá de ➤ When I try to see my E-mail, it doesn't get beyond "authorizing." Cuando intento ver mi correo electrónico no pasa de "autorizando".

to **get bigger and bigger** volverse cada vez más grande

to **get bitten by a dog** ▪ to be bitten by a dog ser mordido por un perro

to **get bitten by a snake** ▪ to be bitten by a snake ser mordido por una serpiente

to **get blamed for** ▪ to be blamed for ser culpado(-a) de

to **get bogged down in** empantanarse en ▪ andar empantanado con ▪ atascarse en ▪ estar liado con ➤ We get bogged down in details, and we don't move fast enough. Andamos empantanados con los detalles y no avanzamos lo suficientemente rápido.

to **get bogged down in traffic** empantanarse en el tráfico

to **get bored** aburrirse

to **get boring** volverse aburrido ▪ ponerse aburrido

to **get burned 1.** to suffer a burn quemarse **2.** to suffer adverse consequences pillarse los dedos

to **get busted** *(coll.)* ser pillado por la policía ▪ ser cogido por la policía

get busy! ▪ get cracking! *(tú)* ¡ponte a trabajar! ▪ *(vosotros)* ¡poneos a trabajar!

to **get busy 1.** to start working ▪ to apply oneself ponerse manos a la obra **2.** to experience an increase in the work pace empezar a estar ocupado ▪ empezar a estar liado ▪ empezar a tener jaleo **3.** to get to cracking entrarle la prisa ➤ We got busy, and in six months we had finished the house. ▪ We got to work, and in six months we had finished the house. Nos pusimos manos a la obra, y en seis meses habíamos terminado la casa. ➤ The restaurant starts getting busy around 10 p.m. El restaurante empieza a estar muy ocupado sobre las diez. ▪ El restaurante empieza a estar muy liado sobre las diez. ▪ El restaurante empieza a tener jaleo sobre las diez. ➤ When the boss came in, he got busy all of a sudden. ▪ When the boss came in, he got cracking. Cuando llegó el jefe, le entró la prisa de repente.

to **get butterflies (in one's stomach)** darle a uno mariposas en el estómago ➤ I got butterflies before giving my speech. Antes de dar el discurso, me dieron mariposas en el estómago.

to **get by (in a course)** pasar con las justas ▪ pasar raspando

to **get by in a foreign language** hablar un idioma medianamente bien ▪ defenderse en un idioma

to **get by (just barely)** ▪ to hang in there ir tirando ▪ estar pasándolo ➤ I'm getting by. ▪ I'm hanging in there. Voy tirando.

to **get by on** ▪ to manage on apañarse con ▪ subsistir con ▪ arreglárselas con ➤ He gets by on 1,000 euros a month. Subsiste con 1.000 euros por mes.

to **get by one 1.** to escape one's notice ▪ to escape one pasársele **2.** to pass one on the highway pasar ➤ The news got by me. Se me pasaron las noticias. ➤ Pull over and give the bus room to get by. Apártate y dejar sitio al autobús para que pase.

to **get by someone** ▪ to get past (someone) in a crowd pasar a alguien ➤ Excuse me, may I get by? Disculpe, ¿me permite pasar?

to **get by to see someone** ▪ to go by to see someone ▪ to go by and see someone pasar a ver a alguien ➤ I'm going to try to get by and see my aunt in the hospital. Voy a intentar pasar a ver a mi tía en el hospital.

to **get by (without help)** arreglarse sólo ▪ *(Sp.)* apañarse sólo ➤ Can you get by okay (without my help)? ¿Te las puedes arreglar tú sólo? ▪ ¿Te apañas bien (sin mi ayuda)?

to **get carried away** dejarse llevar ▪ dejarse llevar por la corriente ➤ I got carried away. Me dejé llevar.

to **get caught in a blizzard** alcanzarle una tormenta de nieve a alguien ▪ *(Sp.)* cogerle una tormenta de nieve a alguien ▪ ➤ We got caught in a blizzard in Wyoming. Nos cogió una tormenta de nieve en Wyoming. ▪ Nos alcanzó una tormenta de nieve en Wyoming.

to **get caught in a machine** ▪ to get jammed in a machine atascarse en una máquina ▪ pillarse con ▪ engancharse con ➤ The paper gets caught in the printer. El papel se atasca en la impresora.

to **get caught in the act** ▪ to be caught in the act ser pillado en el acto ▪ ser pillado infraganti ▪ ser agarrado en el acto ▪ ser agarrado infraganti ▪ *(Sp.)* ser cogido en el acto ▪ ser cogido infraganti

to **get caught in the rain** alcanzar la lluvia a alguien ▪ *(L. Am., Sp.)* coger la lluvia a alguien ➤ I don't want to get caught in the rain. No quiero que me coja la lluvia. ▪ No quiero que me alcance la lluvia. ➤ I got caught in the rain. Me cogió la lluvia. ▪ Me alcanzó la lluvia.

to **get caught up in the excitement** quedarse sumido en la conmoción ▪ hallarse sumido en la conmoción

to **get caught up on** ▪ to bring oneself up-to-date on ▪ to get current on ponerse al día en

to **get caught up on one's sleep** ▪ to catch up on one's sleep recuperar el sueño perdido

to **get caught with** ser pillado con

to **get caught with one's pants down** ser pillado con los pantalones bajados ▪ ser pillado con el culo al aire ▪ ser pillado en bragas ▪ ser cogido con los pantalones bajados

to **get change** conseguir cambio ▪ cambiar ➤ Where can I get change? ¿Dónde puedo conseguir cambio? ➤ I need to get change for a fifty-dollar bill. Necesito conseguir cambio de un billete de cincuenta dólares. ▪ Necesito cambiar un billete de cincuenta dólares.

to **get clear of the debris** zafarse de los escombros ▪ librarse de los escombros ▪ escaparse de los escombros

to **get cold feet 1.** *(literal)* (for) one's feet to get cold enfriársele los pies **2.** to chicken out rajarse

to **get compensated for by** quedar compensado por ➤ Gaps in biblical accounts get compensated for by apocryphal literature. The legend of the Holy Grail is a perfect example. Las lagunas en los relatos bíblicos quedan compensados por la literatura apócrifa. La leyenda el Santo Grial es un ejemplo perfecto.

to **get confused** ■ to get mixed up ■ to get one's wires crossed cruzársele a uno los cables

to **get control of one's time** hacerse control de su tiempo ■ controlar su tiempo ➤ You need to get control of your time. Necesitas controlar tu tiempo.

to **get control of something** hacerse el control de algo

to **get cracking** *(coll.)* ■ to get to work ■ to get busy ponerse a la faena ➤ If you plan to finish that by tomorrow, you'd better get cracking. Si tienes intención de acabar eso para mañana, más vale que te pongas a la faena. ■ Si piensas acabar eso para mañana, más vale que te pongas a la faena.

to **get crazy** volverse loco(-a) ■ ponerse loco(-a) ■ ponerse como un(-a) loco(-a) ■ enloquecer ➤ Things are getting crazy around here. Las cosas se están poniendo locas por aquí.

to **get creative on** ■ to get creative with ser creativo(-a) con ■ resultar creativo(-a) con ➤ I got creative on the colors. ■ I got creative with the colors. Fui muy creativo con los colores. ■ Resulté muy creativo con los colores.

to **get current** ■ to get caught up ■ to bring oneself up-to-date ponerse al día

to **get cut off** ■ to get disconnected cortarse (la línea) ➤ I got cut off. Se cortó la línea. ➤ Somehow we got cut off. Se nos cortó la línea.

to **get dark** atardecer ■ anochecer ■ hacerse de noche ■ oscurecer ■ ir anocheciendo ➤ In Spain in the summer, it gets dark between 10 and 11 p.m. En verano en España anochece entre las 22:00 y las 23:00. ➤ It's getting dark. Va anocheciendo.

to **get deep into a conversation about something** enrollarse hablando de algo

to **get depressed over something** ■ to get depressed about something deprimirse por algo ■ atribularse por algo

to **get dirty** ensuciarse

to **get disconnected** to get cut off cortarse la línea ➤ I got disconnected. Se ha cortado la línea. ➤ Somehow we got disconnected. Se nos ha cortado la línea.

to **get down 1.** to duck agacharse **2.** to climb down bajar ➤ Get down! ■ Duck! *(tú)* ¡Agáchate! ■ *(usted)* ¡Agáchese! ➤ *(to a dog)* (Get) down! ¡Abajo! ■ ¡Quita! ➤ Get down from there! ¡Bájate de allí!

to **get down from a ladder** ■ to get (down) off a ladder bajarse de una escalera

to **get down to brass tacks** ir a lo concreto ■ ir al grano

to **get down to business** entrar en funciones ■ ponerse a la obra

to **get down to the nitty-gritty** ponerse con lo más duro (de la tarea)

to **get dragged into an argument** verse arrastrado a la discusión ■ verse arrastrado al debate

to **get dragged into something** ■ to be dragged into something verse arrastrado a algo ➤ Some of the neighboring countries got dragged into the conflict. ■ Some of the neighboring countries were dragged into the conflict. Algunos países vecinos se vieron arrastrados al conflicto.

to **get drawn into the conversation** verse absorbido por la conversación

to **get drawn into the debate** verse absorbido por el debate

to **get drawn into the discussion** verse absorbido por la tertulia

to **get drenched in the rain** ■ to get drenched by the rain ■ to get soaked in the rain empaparse en la lluvia ■ calarse en la lluvia ■ estar hecho una sopa en la lluvia

to **get dressed** ■ to put on one's clothes ■ to put one's clothes on vestirse ■ ponerse la ropa ➤ Are you getting dressed? ¿Te vistes?

get dressed! *(tú)* ¡vístete! ■ *(vosotros)* vestíos! ■ *(usted)* ¡vístase! ■ *(ustedes)* ¡vístanse!

to **get eaten (up)** comérselo todo ➤ It was such a good cake I knew it would get eaten (up). Era un pastel tan bueno que sabía que se lo comerían todo.

to **get embarrassed** avergonzarse ■ abochornarse ➤ I was getting more and more embarrassed, instead of less and less. Me estaba avergonzando cada vez más en vez de menos. ■ Me estaba avergonzando más y más en vez de menos. ■ Me estaba abochornando cada vez más en vez de menos. ■ Me abochornaba más y más en vez de menos.

to **get embroiled in a fight** enzarzarse en una pelea

to **get embroiled in an argument** enzarzarse en una discusión

to **get engaged (to be married)** prometerse (en matrimonio) ➤ Guess what! Marisol got engaged this weekend. ¡Adivina qué! Marisol se prometió este fin de semana.

to **get even with someone** saldar cuentas con alguien ■ ajustar cuentas con alguien

to **get even with someone for something** ■ to get revenge on someone for something ■ to take revenge on someone for something vengarse de alguien por algo ■ coger a alguien por banda

to **get excited 1.** *(with anticipation)* entusiasmarse ■ hacerle a uno mucha ilusión **2.** *(said especially of children)* alborotarse **3.** *(sexually)* excitarse **4.** *(atomic particles)* excitarse **5.** *(agitated or nervously excited)* agitarse

to **get exercised about something** ■ to get exercised over something ■ to get bent out of shape over something ■ to get worked up about something ■ to get one's nose out of joint ■ to get one's shirt in a knot ponerse fuera de sí...

to **get fresh with someone** ponerse de listo con alguien ■ ser atrevido con alguien

to **get frustrated** sentirse frustrado ➤ I used to get really frustrated trying to explain it in Spanish. Me sentía muy frustrado al intentar explicarlo en español.

to **get further and further away (from)** irse alejando (de)

to **get gas** poner gasolina (al carro) ■ echar gasolina (al carro) ➤ We have to stop and get gas. Tenemos que parar y poner gasolina. ■ Tenemos que parar y echar gasolina.

get going! ■ get moving! ¡andando, que es un gerundio!

to **get going** ponerse en marcha ➤ Get going! ¡En marcha! ■ ¡Marchando! ■ *(tú)* ¡Camina! ■ *(usted)* ¡Camine! ➤ Let's get going! ¡(Pongámonos) en marcha! ➤ We'd better get going! ¡Más vale que nos pongamos en marcha!

to **get good mileage** ■ to have good fuel efficiency tener bajo consumo de combustible

to **get goose bumps** ■ to get goose pimples ■ to get goose flesh ponérsele la carne de gallina ■ enchinársele la piel ■ *(Mex.)* enchinársele el cuero

to **get gored by a bull** ■ to get gored sufrir una cornada

to **get here early** ■ to be early ■ to arrive early llegar pronto ■ llegar temprano

to **get here okay** ■ to get here without any problems acertar a llegar ➤ Did you get here okay? ¿Acertaste a llegar?

to **get here first** ■ to be here first llegar antes ■ llegar primero

get him out of here! ¡sácale (a él) de aquí!

to **get hit by something** ■ to be hit by something ■ to be struck by something ■ to get struck by something ser alcanzado por algo ➤ *(headline)* Boy dies after getting hit by a fireworks shell Fallece un niño tras ser alcanzado por la carcasa de unos fuegos artificiales

to **get hit with** ■ to get hit by recibir el impacto de ➤ Arnold Schwarzenegger got hit with an egg during his election campaign. Arnold Schwarzenegger recibió el impacto de un huevo durante su campaña electoral.

to **get hitched** *(coll.)* ■ to tie the knot dar el sí

to **get hold of someone** ■ to reach someone hacerse con alguien ■ ponerse en contacto con alguien ➤ Things were at a standstill until we got hold of the technician. Las cosas estuvieron parados hasta que nos hicimos con el técnico. ■ Las cosas estuvieron parados hasta que nos pusimos en contacto con el técnico.

to **get hold of something** hacerse con algo ■ conseguir algo ➤ I'm trying to get hold of a copy. Estoy tratando de hacerme con una copia.

to **get home** ■ to arrive home ■ to arrive at the house ■ to arrive at the apartment llegar a casa *("Casa" can refer to either a house* or an apartment and is usually the latter.) ➤ I got home around 10 p.m. Llegué a casa a eso de las diez de la noche.

to **get horny** ponerse caliente ▪ ponerse cachondo ▪ arrecharse

to **get hot 1.** to get hot outside ponerse calor ▪ subir la temperatura **2.** to feel hot acalorarse ➤ The weather in Madrid gets hot in July and August. En julio y agosto el tiempo en Madrid se pone caliente. ➤ It's going to get hot today. Va a subir la temperatura hoy. ➤ It's getting hot in here. Va subiendo la temperatura aquí dentro. ▪ Me estoy acalorando.

to **get hot under the collar** ▪ to get steamed sulfurarse ▪ *(L. Am.)* enojarse ▪ *(Sp.)* enfadarse

to **get hung up** ▪ to hang something up quedarse colgado ➤ The computer has gotten hung up. We might have to restart it. ▪ Something has hung the computer up. We might have to restart it. El ordenador se quedó colgado. Tal vez tengamos que reiniciarlo.

to **get hung up on 1.** to become entangled in enredarse en **2.** *(telephone)* colgarle a uno ➤ We got hung up on the details of the plan. Nos enredamos en los detalles del plan. ➤ I just got hung up on. ▪ The person hung up on me. Me colgó.

to **get hungry** entrarle a uno el hambre ▪ abrirse el apetito ▪ abrírsele un apetito

to **get hurt** lesionarse

to **get hysterical** ponerse histérico(-a)

to **get in 1.** *(a car)* subir ▪ montarse en ▪ meterse en ▪ entrar **2.** to arrive llegar ▪ llegarle **3.** *(to come into office)* ganar en las elecciones ➤ Get in! ▪ Hop in! *(tú)* ¡Sube! ▪ *(usted)* ¡Suba! ➤ What time does the plane get in? ▪ What time does the plane arrive? ¿A qué hora llega el avión? ➤ *(to store clerk)* Did you get in the CD jewel cases? ¿Te llegaron las cajas para CDs? ➤ The Republicans got in last time. ▪ Los republicanos han ganado la última vez.

to **get in a car** ▪ to get into a car subir a un carro ▪ meterse en un carro ▪ *(Sp.)* subir al coche ▪ meterse en el coche ▪ entrar en el coche ▪ ➤ She got in her car. (Ella) subió a su carro. ▪ (Ella) entró en su carro. ▪ (Ella) se metió en su carro. ➤ Get in the car! ¡Sube al carro!

to **get in a few (good) licks** *(coll.)* **1.** to get in some hits meterle a alguien unos cuantos golpes **2.** to get some work done meterle (buena) mano a algo ▪ darle un buen repaso a algo ➤ The victim grabbed the pickpocket's hand and managed not only to hang onto his wallet but get in a few good licks before the guy got away. La víctima agarró la mano del carterista y consiguió no sólo retener su cartera sino también meterle algunos golpes. ➤ We got in a few good licks on the translation today. Le hemos metido (buena) mano a la traducción hoy.

to **get in a fight** *(coll.)* ▪ to get into a fight meterse en una pelea

to **get in bed** ▪ to get into bed meterse en la cama

to **get in line** ▪ to line up ▪ to form a line ponerse en la cola ▪ ponerse a la cola ▪ ponerse en fila ▪ *(Mex.)* formarse ▪ alinearse ➤ You have to get in line. Hay que ponerse a la cola. ▪ Hay que formarse.

to **get in on the action** ser parte de la acción ▪ involucrarse en la acción

to **get in on the deal** entrar a formar parte de un trato ▪ entrar a former parte de un negocio

to **get in on the secret** hacerse partícipe del secreto

to **get in one's two cents' worth** apostar uno su granito de arena ▪ poner su granito de arena

to **get in shape** ponerse en forma

to **get in the way** entorpecer el paso ▪ estorbar el paso

to **get in to see someone 1.** lograr ver a alguien **2.** dejarse ver por alguien ➤ Did you get in to see the doctor? ¿Lograste ver al médico? ➤ Lincoln fired a general one time because nobody could get in to see him. Lincoln despidió a un general cierta vez porque éste no se dejaba ver por nadie.

to **get in touch with someone** ponerse en contacto con alguien ▪ entrar en contacto con alguien ➤ Is there any way to get in touch with him? ¿Hay forma de ponerse en contacto con él?

to **get in trouble** ▪ to be in for it meterse en problemas ▪ acarrearse en problemas ▪ tener problemas ▪ cargársela ➤ He got in trouble for doing it. Se metió en problemas por hacerlo. ▪ Se metió en problemas por hacer eso. ➤ You're going to get in trouble. ▪ You're going to get in(to) trouble. Te la vas a cargar.

to **get infected** ▪ to become infected infectarse ▪ ponérsele infectado ▪ enconarse

to **get information on something** ▪ to get information about something conseguir información sobre ▪ obtener información sobre

to **get information out of someone** sacar información de alguien ▪ tirar a alguien de la lengua

to **get interested in** ▪ to become interested in interesarse

to **get into a conversation with someone** trabar conversación con alguien ➤ I got into a conversation with Marta about life in present-day Chile. Trabé una conversación con Marta sobre Chile de hoy en día. ➤ She spoke, and he spoke back, and they got into a conversation. Ella habló, él respondió, y trabaron una conversación.

to **get into a discussion about** meterse en una conversación sobre ▪ entrar en una conversación sobre

to **get into a fight** ▪ to get in a fight meterse en una pelea

to **get into a jam** ▪ to get into a tight spot ▪ to get into a mess meterse en un lío ▪ meterse en un embolado ▪ meterse en un jaleo ▪ meterse en un mogollón

to **get into a lot of trouble** meterse en muchos problemas

to **get into a mess** ▪ to get into a difficult situation ▪ to get into a tight spot ▪ to get into a jam meterse en un embolado ▪ meterse en un jaleo ▪ meterse en un lío ▪ meterse en un mogollón

to **get into a profession** empezar en una profesión ▪ adentrarse en una profesión ➤ How did you get into journalism? ¿Cómo empezaste en el periodismo?

to **get into a routine** ▪ to adopt a routine adquirir un hábito ▪ adquirir una costumbre

to **get into a rut** hacerse esclavo de una rutina anodina ▪ estarse anquilosando ▪ estarse estancando

to **get into a song** entregarse a una canción ➤ "Cielito Lindo" is a song you can really get into. "Cielito Lindo" es una canción a la que puedes entregarte. ▪ "Cielito Lindo" es una canción a la que se puede entregar.

to **get into a spin** *(aviation)* ▪ to go into a spin entrar en barrena

to **get into a subject** entrar en un tema ▪ meterse en un tema ➤ I'm not going to get into that. No voy a entrar en eso. ▪ No voy a meterme en eso. ▪ No me voy a meter en eso.

to **get into a tight spot** ▪ to get into a jam meterse en un apuro

to **get into an argument** meterse en una discusión

to **get into boots** ▪ to fit entrar en las botas ▪ quedarle bien las botas ➤ I can't get into these boots. They're too small. No entro en estas botas. Son pequeñas. ➤ These boots don't fit (me). Estas botas no me quedan bien.

to **get into clothes 1.** to put on clothes ponerse ropas **2.** to fit into clothes quedarle bien ropas ▪ caber en ropas ➤ I want to get into something more comfortable. Quiero ponerme algo más cómodo. ➤ This jacket doesn't fit (me). Esta chaqueta no me queda bien. ▪ No quepo en esta chaqueta.

to **get into debt** contraer una deuda ▪ contraer dudas

to **get into drugs** ▪ to get involved in drugs meterse en las drogas ▪ verse involucrado en las drogas ➤ How did he get into drugs? ¿Cómo se metió en las drogas? ▪ ¿Cómo se vio involucrado en las drogas?

to **get into formation** *(military)* ▪ to fall in ponerse en formación

to **get into politics** ▪ to get involved in politics ▪ to enter politics ▪ to go into politics meterse en política ▪ entrar en política ▪ adentrarse en la política

to **get into the bloodstream** ▪ to enter the bloodstream pasar a la corriente sanguínea ▪ pasar al flujo sanguíneo ▪ pasar al torrente sanguíneo ▪ pasar a la sangre

to **get into the business of** entrar en el negocio de ▪ entrar en el mundo de ▪ entrar en el mundillo de

to **get into the fuel** mezclarse con el combustible ➤ The fuel-water separator extracts any condensed moisture in the fuel tank that has gotten into the fuel. El separador de agua y combustible extrae cualquier elemento de agua procedente de condensación que se haya mezclado con el combustible del depósito.

to **get into the future** remontarse al futuro

to **get into the groove** agarrar el ritmo ■ coger el ritmo ■ coger el ritmillo

to **get into the habit of doing something** ■ to get in the habit of doing something tomar el hábito de hacer algo ■ acostumbarse a hacer algo ■ habituarse a hacer algo ■ *(Sp.)* coger el hábito de hacer una cosa ■ coger la costumbre de hacer una cosa

to **get into the swing of things** agarrar el ritmo ■ *(Sp.)* coger el ritmo ■ coger el ritmillo

to **get into this business of...** meterse en este rollo de... ■ meterse en lo de...

to **get into trouble** ■ to get in trouble meterse en problemas ■ tener problemas ■ acarrearle un problema

to **get involved in politics** ■ to go into politics ■ to get into politics ■ to enter politics adentrarse en la política

to **get involved in something** involucrarse en algo ■ verse involucrado en algo ■ verse envuelto en algo

to **get it 1.** *(joke)* to catch onto it entenderlo ■ cogerlo ■ saber de qué va **2.** *(math problem)* to figure it out ■ to solve it resolverlo ■ solucionarlo **3.** to get the big picture saber qué se cuece ■ saber de qué va la vaina ■ saber por dónde van los tiros ■ saber de qué va el tema **4.** *(retaliation, reprisal)* to get in trouble ganársela ➤ Did you get it? ■ Did you catch on? ¿Lo entendiste? ■ ¿Lo has cogido? ➤ Did you get it? ¿Lo resolviste? ■ ¿Lo solucionaste? ➤ He just doesn't get it. ■ He just doesn't see the big picture. No sabe qué se cuece. ■ No sabe de qué va la vaina. ■ No sabe por dónde van los tiros. ➤ You're gonna get it if you don't straighten up. Te la vas a ganar si no te corriges.

to **get it all wrong** ■ to have (got) it all wrong no entender nada ■ *(coll.)* no dar ni una ➤ He's got it all wrong. No ha entendido nada. ➤ They've got my order all wrong. No han dado ni una con mi pedido.

to **get it down (in writing)** ■ to get it written down tener algo anotado ■ tener algo apuntado ➤ The speaker was talking so fast that I didn't get it down. El conferenciante hablaba tan rápido que no pude anotarlo. ■ El conferenciante hablaba tan rápido que no pude apuntarlo.

to **get it going** mantenerlo en marcha

get it in writing! ■ get it in black and white! *(tú)* que te lo den por escrito ■ que te lo pongan por escrito ■ *(usted)* que se lo den por escrito ■ que se lo pongan por escrito

to **get it into one's head that** ■ to get an idea into one's head ponérsele algo entre ceja y ceja ■ metérsele algo entre ceja y ceja ■ ponérsele algo en la cabeza ■ metérsele algo en la cabeza

to **get (it) off with someone** *(sexually graphic)* ■ to get it on with someone montárselo con alguien ■ hacérselo con alguien ➤ You're never going to get it off with her. Nunca te lo montarás con ella. ■ Nunca te lo harás con ella.

to **get it on with someone** *(graphic)* ■ to get (it) off with someone montárselo con alguien ■ hacérselo con alguien

to **get it the worst** ■ to get the worst of it llevar la peor parte

get it over with, quick! *(tú)* ¡acaba con esto rápido! ■ *(usted)* ¡acabe con esto rápido!

to **get it to work** conseguir que haga algo ➤ I can't get it to work. ■ I can't get this thing to work. No consigo que (esto) funcione.

to **get it out of one's head that...** ■ to get the idea out of one's head that... quitarse de la cabeza la idea de que...

to **get it wrong** errar el tiro

to **get jammed** ■ to get caught atascarse ➤ The paper gets jammed in the printer. El papel se atasca en la impresora.

to **get kicked out of a bar** ■ to be bodily removed from a bar echarle a alguien a patadas del bar ■ ser echado a patadas ■ ser echado con cajas destempladas ➤ The drunk got kicked out of the bar. Al borracho le echaron a patadas del bar.

to **get kicked out of school** ■ to get expelled from school ■ to be expelled from school *(high school)* ser expulsado del secundaria ■ *(Sp.)* ser expulsado del instituto ■ *(university)* ser expulsado de la universidad ➤ Edgar Allan Poe got kicked out of the University of Virginia. Edgar Allan Poe fue expulsado de la Universidad de Virginia.

to **get left behind** ■ to be left behind ser dejado atrás ■ quedarse rezagado ➤ I got left behind. Fui dejado atrás. ■ Me quedé rezagado.

to **get left out of...** quedarse fuera de... ➤ Last time, I got left out of the office football pool. La última vez, me quedé fuera de la porra de la oficina.

to **get lost** perderse ➤ If you get lost, call us. Si te pierdes, llámanos. ➤ Let me give you my phone number in case you get lost. Déjame darte mi número telefónico en caso de que te pierdas. ■ Déjame darte mi número telefónico por si te pierdas.

get lost! ¡vete a hacer puñetas! ■ ¡vete a hacer gárgaras! ■ ¡vete al carajo! ■ *(L. Am.)* ¡vete al guano!

to **get lost in the shuffle** ■ to get put in the wrong place ■ to be put in the wrong place ■ to be mislaid ■ to get mislaid traspapelarse ➤ My message (to you) must have gotten lost in the shuffle. ■ My message must have gotten put in the wrong place. ■ My message must have been mislaid. Me parece que se ha traspapelado el mensaje mío.

to **get lower in the sky** ■ to get closer to the horizon acercarse al horizonte bajarse ■ cada vez más en el cielo ➤ As a ship travels south, the (northern) pole star gets lower in the sky. Conforme un barco viaja al sur, la estrella polar se acerca más al horizonte.

to **get lucky 1.** to have a stroke of (good) luck tener un golpe de suerte **2.** to have a streak of luck tener una racha de buena suerte ➤ He had a stroke of (good) luck. ■ He got lucky. Tuvo un golpe de suerte.

to **get mad at someone** *(coll.)* ■ to get angry at someone ■ to get angry with someone cabrearse con alguien ■ *(Mex.)* enojarse con alguien ■ *(Sp.)* enfadarse con alguien ➤ Don't get mad! ¡No te cabrees! ■ ¡No te enojes! ■ ¡No te enfades!

to **get married** casarse ■ contraer matrimonio ➤ Gonzalo and María Jesus got married on April fifteenth. Gonzalo y María Jesús se casaron el quince de abril. ➤ They finally got married. Por fin se casaron. ➤ *(attributed to Quevedo)* Juan Silla and Pura Mier got married in Sevilla. And today the lady's name is Doña Pura Mier de Silla. En Sevilla se casaron Juan Silla con Pura Mier y es hoy de Juan su mujer Doña Pura Mier de Silla.

to **get medicine down** ■ to get down medicine tragar el medicamento ■ bajar la medicina

to **get mixed up 1.** to get confused confundirse ■ hacerse un lío **2.** to get mixed together mezclarse ➤ I got mixed up and brought the wrong book. ■ I got confused and brought the wrong book. Me confundí y traje el libro equivocado. ■ Me hice un lío y traje el libro equivocado. ➤ The papers got mixed up. ■ The papers got mixed together. Los papeles se mezclaron (entre ellos).

to **get mixed up in** enredarse en ■ embrollarse en

to **get money out of someone** sacarle dinero a alguien ➤ You won't get any money out of her. No vas a sacarle dinero a ella. ➤ It seems like a ruse to get money out of him. ■ It seems like a trick to get money out of him. Parece una estratagema para sacarle dinero.

to **get more and more interesting** ponerse cada vez más interesante ■ ponerse más interesante (por momentos)

to **get more comfortable** ponerse más cómodo

to **get more for one's money** conseguir más por su dinero

to **get more out of something** sacar más provecho de algo ➤ You'll get more out of this textbook than the others. Sacarás más provecho de este texto que los otros.

to **get more than one bargained for** recibir lo que uno nunca imaginó

get moving! ■ get going! ¡andando, que es un gerundio!

to **get muddled** ■ to get in a muddle ■ to get (all) mixed up hacerse un taco ■ armarse un taco ■ trastocarse ■ embrollarse

to **get my homework done** ■ to do my homework hacer los deberes ➤ Mom said I have to get my homework done before I can go skiing. Mamá me ha dicho que tengo que hacer los deberes antes de poder ir a esquiar.

to **get nervous** ponerse nervioso

to **get news of someone** ▪ to receive news of someone recibir noticias de alguien

to **get next to the counter** ▪ to get up next to the counter acercarse al mostrador ➤ Excuse me, please, I'm trying to get next to the counter. Disculpe, quiero acercarme al mostrador.

to **get no further than that** de ahí no salir ➤ I got no further than that. De ahí no salí.

to **get nowhere** ▪ not to get anywhere no conseguir nada ▪ no vender una escoba ▪ no comerse una rosca

to **get (nowhere) near** (ni) acercarse a ➤ Some people can't get anywhere near peanuts or perfume. Hay gente que no puede (ni) acercarse a los cacahuetes ni al perfume. ➤ I don't want to get anywhere near that place. No quiero ni acercarme a ese lugar.

to **get nowhere with** ▪ not to get anywhere with no conseguir nada con ▪ no lograr nada con ▪ no comerse una rosca con ➤ He went to the dean, but he got nowhere. ▪ He went to the dean, but he didn't get anywhere. Fue al decano, pero no consiguió nada.

to **get off a bus** bajar(se) de un autobús ➤ What stop do get off at? ▪ Where do you get off? ¿En qué parada te bajas? ▪ ¿Dónde te bajas? ➤ I'd like to get off at the next stop. Quiero bajarme en la próxima parada. ➤ I get off at Moncloa. Me bajo en Moncloa.

to **get off a plane** ▪ to get off an airplane bajarse de un avión

to **get off a train** bajarse de un tren

to **get off a subject** dejar un tema

to **get off course** desviarse del rumbo ➤ Lindbergh got only sixty miles off course on his transatlantic flight. Lindbergh se desvió sólo sesenta millas de su rumbo durante su vuelo transatlántico.

get off my property! ▪ get off my land! ¡fuera de mi propiedad! ▪ ¡fuera de mis tierras!

to **get off on a subject** terminar en un tema ➤ How did I get off on that subject? ¿Cómo terminé en ese tema?

to **get off on the right foot** ▪ to get off to a good start empezar con el pie derecho ▪ empezar con buen pie

to **get off on the wrong foot** ▪ to get off to a bad start empezar con mal pie ▪ empezar con el pie izquierdo

to **get off one's high horse** ▪ to come down from one's high horse bajar los humos ▪ apearse del burro ▪ bajarse del burro ▪ caerse del burro

to **get off probation 1.** *(academic probation)* terminar el período de prueba ▪ acabar el período de prueba **2.** *(legal probation, parole)* acabar el período de libertad condicional ▪ terminar el período de libertad condicional

to **get off scot-free** irse de rositas

to **get off someone's back** dejar a alguien en paz ▪ dejar de fastidiar a alguien

to **get off someone's case** dejar a alguien tranquilo ▪ dejar a alguien en paz

to **get off the airplane** ▪ to get off the plane bajar(se) del avión

to **get off the bus** bajar(se) del autobús ▪ apearse del autobús

to **get off the elevator** salir del ascensor ➤ Turn left as you get off the elevator. ▪ Turn left when you get off the elevator. Gira a la izquierda cuando salgas del ascensor.

to **get off the metro** ▪ to get off the subway bajar(se) del metro

to **get off the subject 1.** to go off on a tangent apartarse del tema ▪ desviarse del tema ▪ salirse por la tangente **2.** to drop the subject dejar el tema ➤ I'm getting off the subject. Me estoy apartando del tema. ➤ Not to get off the subject, but... No es por desviarme del tema, pero... ➤ I don't want to get too far off the subject. No quiero desviarme mucho del tema. ➤ What do you say we get off that subject? ▪ What do you say we drop the subject? ¿Qué te parece si dejamos el tema?

to **get off the subway** ▪ to get off the metro bajar(se) del metro ➤ We get off the metro at División del Norte. ▪ We get off the subway at División del Norte. (Nos) bajamos del metro en División del Norte.

to **get off the telephone** dejar el teléfono ▪ colgar ➤ Fernando, would you get off the telephone? I need to make an urgent call. Fernando, ¿podrías dejar el telefóno? Tengo que hacer una llamada urgente. ▪ Fernando, ¿podrías colgar? Tengo que hacer una llamada urgente.

to **get off the train** bajar(se) del tren ▪ apearse del tren

to **get off to a bad start** ▪ to get off on the wrong foot empezar con el pie izquierdo

to **get off to a good start** ▪ to get off on the right foot empezar con el pie derecho

to **get off to a late start** ▪ to start (off) late empezar tarde

to **get off to an early start** ▪ to start (off) early empezar temprano

to **get off (work)** salir de trabajar ▪ acabar de trabajar ➤ What time do you get off (work)? ¿A qué hora sales de trabajar? ➤ I get off (work) at five o'clock. Acabo de trabajar a las cinco.

get off your duff! ▪ get the lead out of your butt! ¡espabila! ▪ ¡sacúdete la pereza de los huesos!

to **get old 1.** to grow old envejecer ▪ (ya) ir para viejo **2.** to become boring volverse aburrido

to **get older 1.** *(any age)* hacerse más mayor **2.** to grow old envejecer ➤ We want to go to Argentina when our daughter gets a little older. Queremos ir a la Argentina cuando nuestra hija se haga un poco más mayor.

to **get on a bus** subirse a un autobús

to **get on a freeway** meterse por una autopista

to **get on a horse** montarse en un caballo

to **get on a plane** montar en avión ▪ subir a un avión

to **get on a test** sacar (nota) en un examen ➤ What (grade) did you get on the test? ¿Qué (nota) sacaste en el examen?

to **get on a train** subir(se) a un tren ▪ montarse en un tren

to **get on an elevator** subir(se) a un ascensor ▪ montarse en un ascensor

to **get on someone's nerves** poner a alguien a cien ▪ dar cien patadas en la barriga a alguien ➤ He gets on my nerves. Me pone a cien. ➤ He gets on her nerves. Él la pone a cien. ➤ One student gets on the teacher's nerves pretty bad. Hay un alumno que pone a la profesora a cien.

to **get on the bandwagon** ▪ to jump on the bandwagon unirse a la mayoría

to **get on the freeway** meterse por la autopista ➤ We got on the M-30 in Madrid. Nos metimos por la M-30 en Madrid.

to **get on the metro** ▪ to get on the subway subir(se) al metro ▪ montarse en el metro

to **get on the stick** espabilarse ➤ You'd better get on the stick. ▪ You better get on the stick. Más vale que espabiles.

to **get on the subway** ▪ to get on the metro subir(se) al metro ▪ montarse en el metro

to **get on the train** subirse al tren

get on with...! ¡que siga...!

get on with it! ¡a ello! ▪ ¡sigue! ▪ ¡adelante! ▪ *(Sp.)* ¡a por ello!

to **get on with it** seguir adelante ➤ Let's get on with it. Sigamos adelante. ➤ Let him get on with it. Déjale que siga adelante ➤ In Biblical times, Jewish males were commanded to marry by age eighteen and to have a child within a year. You were dead by forty, so you had to get on with it. En los tiempos de la Biblia, los varones judíos estaban obligados a casarse para los dieciocho años y a tener un hijo al año (de la boda). Uno se moría a los cuarenta, así que había que seguir adelante.

to **get on with one's work 1.** to continue with one's work ▪ not to interrupt one's work seguir uno con su trabajo **2.** to resume one's work reanudar uno su trabajo

to **get on with something** ▪ to continue with something ▪ not to interrupt something seguir con algo ➤ I need to get on with my homework. I'll call you later. Necesito seguir con mi tarea. Te llamo luego.

to **get on with the show!** ¡que siga el espectáculo!

to **get one free** dos por uno ➤ Buy one, get one free! ¡Dos por uno!

to **get one's act together** apurarse ▪ *(Sp.)* espabilarse

to **get one's attention** llamarle la atención

to **get one's bearings** ▪ to have one's bearings orientarse ➤ Could you help me get my bearings? ¿Me podrías ayudar que me oriente? ➤ I looked at the street map to try to get my bearings. Miré el plano para intentar orientarme.

to **get one's breath** recuperar el aliento ■ *(Sp.)* coger aire ➤ He began coughing so hard he couldn't get his breath. Empezó a toser tan fuerte que no podía recuperar el aliento.

to **get one's choice of** elegir lo que uno quiera de ➤ The owner of the stud gets his choice of the puppies in the litter. El propietario del semental puede elegir el cachorro que él quiera de la camada.

to **get one's clock cleaned** ■ to get the tar beat out of one ■ to get beat up darle una tunda de palos ■ *(old-fashioned)* zurrarle la badana ■ curtir el lomo

to **get one's comeuppance** recibir lo que uno se merece ■ recibir uno su merecido ■ estarle a uno bien empleado

to **get one's ears pierced** ■ to have one's ears pierced hacerse agujeros en las orejas ■ hacerse los agujeros de los pendientes ➤ She got her ears pierced. ■ She had her ears pierced. Ella se hizo agujeros en las orejas.

to **get one's feet on the ground** establecerse bien ■ asentarse bien ➤ They want to get their feet on the ground financially before starting a family. Quieren establecerse bien económicamente antes de comenzar una familia.

to **get one's feet wet** mojarse los pies ■ *(Sp., coll.)* mojarse el culo

to **get one's fill of something** ■ to have one's fill of something tener más que suficiente de algo

to **get one's finger caught in** atascársele el dedo en ➤ Marcus got his finger caught in the basket crank on the basketball court. El dedo de Marcus se atascó en la manivela de la canasta de la concha de baloncesto.

to **get one's foot in the door** abrirse camino ■ entrar en el mundillo

to **get one's hackles up** ■ to get irritated encresparse ➤ Don't get your hackles up! ¡No te encrespes!

to **get one's hands dirty** ensuciarse las manos *(The Spanish is both literal and figurative, meaning "to soil one's hands" by gritty work and "to dirty one's hands" by unethical conduct.)*

to **get one's hands on someone** ponerle las manos a alguien ➤ If I get my hands on that guy, I'll wring his neck. Si le pongo las manos al tío ese, le retuerzo el pescuezo. ➤ Wait til I get my hands on that guy. Espera a que le ponga las manos al tío ese.

to **get one's hands on something** ■ to get (hold of) something ■ to obtain something hacerse con algo ➤ I wish I could get my hands on a copy. ■ I wish I could get (hold of) a copy. ■ I wish I could obtain a copy. Ojalá pudiera hacerme con una copia.

to **get one's hopes up** hacerse ilusiones ➤ I tried not to get my hopes up too much. Intenté no hacerme demasiadas ilusiones.

to **get one's just desserts** ■ to get what one deserves llevarse su merecido

to **get one's money back** recuperar su dinero ■ conseguir un reembolso

to **get one's money's worth** recibir el valor de su dinero

to **get one's nose out of joint** *(colorful)* ■ to get one's shirt in a knot ■ to get exercised ponerse fuera de sí ■ salirle humo por las orejas ■ sulfurarse ➤ When I would get upset, my father would say, "Don't get your nose out of joint" or "don't get your shirt in a knot." Cuando me disgustaba, mi padre solía decirme, "No te pongas fuera de ti" o "que no te salga humo por las orejas" o "no te sulfures".

to **get one's (own) way** ■ to get one's way ■ to have one's (own) way salirse uno con la suya *("La suya" refers to "intención.")*

to **get one's phone cut off** ■ (for) one's telephone to get turned off ■ (for) one's telephone to be turned off cortarle la línea a alguien ➤ My telephone got cut off. ■ My telephone was cut off. ■ They cut off my telephone. Me han cortado la línea.

to **get one's pick** *(coll.)* ■ to get one's choice elegir el que uno quiera ■ elegir la que uno quiera ■ elegir lo que uno quiera

to **get one's point across** ■ to get across one's point hacerse entender ➤ I'm having a hard time getting my point across. Me cuesta mucho hacerme entender.

to **get one's share** recibir su parte

to **get one's shirt in a knot** ■ to get one's nose out of joint ■ to get exercised salirle humo por las orejas ➤ Now, don't get your shirt in a knot. ■ Now, don't get your nose out of joint. Que no te pongas fuera de ti. ■ Que no te salga humo por las orejas.

to **get one's way** ■ to get one's own way ■ to have one's (own) way salirse uno con la suya *("La suya" refers to "intención.")*

to **get one's way with someone** salirse con la suya con alguien

to **get one's wires crossed** ■ to get mixed up ■ to get confused hacerse un lío ■ *(off-color)* hacerse la picha un lío

to **get oneself into a pickle** ■ to get oneself into a (real) pickle ■ to get oneself into a (real) mess ■ to get oneself into a (big) mess meterse en un berenjenal

to **get organized** organizarse

to **get out** *(intransitive)* **1.** to become known trascenderse algo ■ saberse algo ■ salir algo a la luz **2.** to leave marcharse ■ largarse **3.** to get out and about salir **3.** to let out desocuparse un recinto ➤ We can't let this get out. No podemos dejar que esto trascienda. ■ No podemos dejar que esto se sepa. ■ No podemos dejar que esto salga a la luz. ➤ We told him to get out. Le dijimos que se fuera. ■ Le dijimos que se marchara. ➤ At 93, he doesn't get out (and about) much anymore. Con noventa y tres años ya no sale mucho. ➤ As the concert was getting out, we ran into some friends. Mientras se desocupaba el recinto del concierto nos encontramos con unos amigos. ■ Conforme se desocupaba el recinto del concierto nos encontramos con unos amigos.

to **get out something** *(transitive)* **1.** to get something out ■ to take out something ■ to take something out sacar algo ➤ Students, please get out a pencil and paper. Alumnos, por favor, saquen lápiz y papel. ➤ I got out the phone book and went through all the Garcías until I found it. Saqué la guía de teléfonos y miré en todos los "García" hasta que dí con él. ➤ We've got to get this edition out. Tenemos que sacar esta edición.

get out! ■ leave! ¡fuera! ■ ¡márchate! ■ ¡vete! ■ ¡lárgate!

to **get out of a fix** ■ to get out of a jam salir de un apuro ■ salir de un atolladero

to **get out of a jam** ■ to get out of a fix salir de un apuro ■ salir del atolladero

to **get out of bed** levantarse de la cama ➤ He can barely get out of bed in the morning. Se levanta a duras penas de la cama por la mañana.

to **get out of breath** quedarse sin respiración

to **get out of class** salir de clase ➤ What time do you get out of class? ¿A qué hora sales de clase?

to **get out of debt** saldar todas las deudas de uno ■ saldar todas las cuentas de uno

to **get out of (doing) something** zafarse de (hacer) algo ■ *(Sp.)* escaquearse de (hacer) algo ■ evitar (hacer) algo

to **get out of hand** desmadrarse ■ desmelenarse ■ salirse de sus casillas ➤ The kindergarten children are getting out of hand. Los niños de la guardería se están desmadrando.

get out of here! ¡largo de aquí! ■ ¡fuera! ■ *(tú)* ¡sal de aquí! ■ *(ustedes)* ¡salga(n) de aquí! ■ *(Sp., vosotros)* ¡salid de aquí!

to **get out of here** ■ to get the hell out of here volar de aquí ➤ Let's get out of here. Volemos de aquí.

to **get out of it 1.** to avoid it salir del bulto ■ evadir algo ■ *(Mex.)* rajarse ■ *(Sp.)* escaquearse de algo **2.** to obtain from it obtener algo ■ sacar provecho de algo ■ ganar algo ➤ I'm going to try to get out of it. Voy a intentar salir del bulto. ■ Voy a intentar escaquearme. ➤ What do you hope to get out of it? ¿Qué esperas obtener (de eso)? ■ ¿Qué provecho esperas sacar de ello? ■ ¿Qué esperas ganar con ello?

to **get out of jail** salir de la cárcel

to **get out of last place** zafarse del último lugar ➤ It's going to be difficult to get out of last place. Va a ser difícil zafarse del último lugar.

to **get out of school (for the day)** acabar las clases ■ salir de clase ➤ What time does school get out? ■ What time do you get out of school? ¿A qué hora acabas las clases? ■ ¿A qué hora sales de las clases?

to **get out of school (for the summer)** ■ to let out for the summer salir de la escuela (para el verano) ■ acabar el colegio ■ terminar las clases ➤ When do you get out of school for the summer? ¿Qué día salen de la escuela para las vacaciones de verano?

to **get out of someone's way** quitarse de en medio de alguien ▪ apartarse del camino de alguien ➤ The only way I can get out of your way, so that you can get on, is to get off. So *you* get out of my way, so (that) I can get off! La única forma de que me quite de en medio, para que tú puedas entrar, es que yo pueda salir. Así que, quítate de en medio para que yo pueda salir.

to **get out of step 1.** *(in a marching formation)* perder el paso **2.** *(when dancing)* perder el ritmo ▪ perder el compás

to **get out of the car** bajar(se) del coche ▪ salir del coche ▪ *(Mex.)* bajar(se) del carro ▪ salir del carro

to **get out of the habit of doing something** perder la costumbre de hacer algo ▪ quitarse la costumbre de hacer una cosa ▪ dejar la costumbre de hacer una cosa ▪ desacostumbrarse de hacer una cosa ▪ quitarse el hábito de hacer una cosa ▪ dejar el hábito de hacer una cosa

to **get out of the sun** ▪ to get in the shade quitarse del sol ▪ ponerse a la sombra

to **get out of the way** quitarse de en medio ▪ quitarse del camino ▪ apartarse del camino ➤ Get out of the way! *(tú)* ¡Quítate de en medio! ▪ *(usted)* ¡Quítese de en medio! ▪ *(ustedes)* ¡Quítense de en medio! ▪ *(vosotros)* ¡Quitaos de en medio!

to **get out of the wrong side of the bed** ▪ to get up on the wrong side of the bed levantarse con el pie izquierdo

to **get out of there** ▪ to get the hell out of there salir por piernas

to **get out of this mess** salir de este lío ▪ salir de este embrollo ▪ salir de este jaleo ➤ How are we going to get out of this mess? ¿Cómo vamos a salir de este lío? ▪ ¿Cómo vamos a salir de este embrollo? ▪ ¿Cómo vamos a salir de este jaleo?

to **get out something** ▪ to get something out sacar algo ➤ Let's get out the electric train and set it up. Vamos a sacar y montar el tren eléctrico.

to **get over a cold** recuperarse de un resfriado ▪ pasársele a uno un resfriado

to **get over a trauma** ▪ to get over a shock (to the system) superar un trauma ▪ recuperarse de un (estado de) shock

to **get over an attitude** pasársele a alguien un estado de ánimo ➤ I got over my bad mood. Se me pasó el mal humor.

to **get over something** superar algo ▪ rehacerse de algo ▪ pasársele a uno algo ➤ It took him a long time to get over his grief. Tardó mucho en superar su pena. ▪ Tardó mucho en rehacerse de su pena. ▪ Tardó mucho en pasársele la pena.

get over it! ¡supéralo! ▪ ¡tienes que superarlo!

to **get over one's culture shock** ▪ to recover from one's culture shock reponerse uno del choque cultural

to **get over one's point** ▪ to get across one's point hacer uno entender su postura

to **get over one's surprise** reponerse uno de la sorpresa ➤ I can't get over your winning the lottery. No puedo reponerme de (la sorpresa de) que te halla tocado la lotería.

to **get over the loss of a loved one** ▪ to recover from the loss of a loved one rehacerse de la pérdida de un ser querido ➤ He had a hard time getting over the loss of his wife. ▪ He had a hard time recovering from his wife's death. Le costó rehacerse de la pérdida de su esposa.

to **get over to the left** ▪ to move over to the left ponerse a la izquierda ▪ moverse a la izquierda ▪ echarse a la izquierda ▪ desplazarse a la izquierda

to **get over to the right** ▪ to move over to the right ponerse a la derecha ▪ moverse a la derecha ▪ echarse a la derecha ▪ desplazarse a la derecha

to **get paint on oneself 1.** *(general)* mancharse de pintura **2.** *(by smearing or rubbing against wet paint)* embarrarse de pintura **3.** *(by spattering or splattering)* salpicarse de pintura

to **get paint on something** manchar algo de pintura ▪ mancharse de pintura algo ➤ I accidentally got paint on it. Lo manché de pintura sin querer. ▪ La manché sin querer. ➤ I don't want to get paint on my new clothes. No quiero mancharme de pintura la ropa nueva. ➤ I got paint all over everything. Manché todo de pintura.

to **get past a problem** ▪ to get around a problem eludir un problema ➤ I need to know how to get past the locking problem when it occurs. Necesito saber cómo eludir el problema de "locked for editing" cada vez que ocurra.

to **get past someone** *(sports)* ▪ to get around someone ▪ to outmaneuver someone regatear a alguien ➤ Number seven got past the player blocking him. ▪ Number seven got around the player blocking him. ▪ Number seven outmaneuvered the player blocking him. El número siete regateó a su marcador.

to **get permission** conseguir permiso

to **get permission from someone to do something** conseguir el permiso de alguien para hacer algo

to **get physical** *(relationship)* ▪ to become physical pasar a mayores

to **get pissed off** *(off-color)* ▪ to get ticked off ponerse de mala hostia

to **get played up** ▪ to be played up renombrar ➤ Did it get played up in the U.S. news as much as it did over here? ¿Fue tan renombrado en las noticias estadounidenses como aquí?

to **get possession of something** hacerse con algo ➤ The wife got possession of the house in the divorce. La esposa se hizo con la casa en el divorcio.

to **get pregnant** ▪ to become pregnant quedarse embarazada ▪ quedarse preñada

to **get rain 1.** to get some rain llover **2.** to get a lot of rain ser lluvioso ➤ It looks like we're going to get some rain today. ▪ It looks like it's going to rain today. Parece que va a llover hoy. ➤ This area used to get a lot of rain, but it doesn't anymore. Esta zona solía ser muy lluviosa, pero ahora ya no. ▪ En esta zona solía llover mucho, pero ahora ya no.

to **get rained on** lloverle encima ➤ We got rained on during our chalupa ride at Xochimilco. Nos llovió encima durante nuestro paseo en chalupa en Xochimilco. ➤ I don't want to get rained on. No quiero que me llueva encima.

to **get rattled** ▪ to get flustered ▪ to get upset alterarse ➤ When I get rattled, my Spanish gets tangled. Cuando me altero, mi español se me enreda.

get ready! *(tú)* ¡apréstate! ▪ *(usted)* ¡apréstese! ▪ *(ustedes)* ¡apréstense! ▪ *(Sp., vosotros)* ¡aprestaos! ▪ *(tú)* ¡ve preparándote! ▪ ¡prepárate! ▪ *(usted)* ¡vaya preparándose! ▪ ¡prepárese! ▪ *(ustedes)* ¡vayan preparándose! ▪ ¡prepárense! ▪ *(Sp., vosotros)* ¡id preparándoos! ▪ ¡preparaos!

to **get ready for** prepararse para ▪ aprestarse para

to **get ready for bed** ▪ to get ready to go to bed disponerse a acostarse

to **get ready to do something** disponerse a hacer algo ▪ aprestarse a hacer algo ▪ prepararse para hacer algo ▪ alistarse para hacer algo ➤ We need to get ready to leave. Necesitamos prepararnos para salir.

to **get ready to go to bed** ▪ to get ready for bed prepararse para acostarse

get real! ▪ you're pulling my leg! ▪ noooo! ▪ come on! ¡eso sí que no! ▪ ¡venga ya! ▪ ¡ven ya! ▪ ¡no me tomes el pelo! ▪ ¡bájate de la moto! ▪ ¡anda ya! ▪ ¡menos lobos, Caperucita! ▪ ¡a mí con otros cuentos!

to **get red as a beet** *(from sunburn or blushing)* ▪ to turn red as a beet ponerse como un tomate

to **get results** conseguir resultados ➤ Get results fast with our miracle potion. Consiga resultados rápidamente con nuestra poción milagrosa.

to **get revenge (on someone for something)** ▪ to take revenge (on someone for something) vengarse (de alguien por algo) ▪ tomar venganza (de alguien por algo)

to **get rid of a headache** quitarse de encima un dolor de cabeza

to **get rid of someone** quitarse a alguien de encima ▪ deshacerse de alguien ▪ zafarse de alguien ▪ librarse de alguien ➤ He latched onto her at a cocktail party, and she couldn't get rid of him. Se le pegó como una lapa en un cóctel y no pudo deshacerse de él. ▪ Se le pegó como una lapa en un cóctel y no pudo zafarse de él. ▪ Se le pegó como una lapa en un cóctel y no pudo librarse de él.

to **get rid of something** deshacerse de algo ▪ desprenderse de algo ▪ librarse de algo ▪ quitarse algo de encima ▪ arrojar de sí algo ▪ acabar con algo ➤ The insurgency got rid of the corrupt regime, but failed to replace it with a prosperous one. Los insurgentes se deshicieron del régimen corrupto pero no lograron reemplazarlo por uno más próspero.

to **get right to the point** ■ to go right to the point ir directo al grano

to **get royalties** ■ to be paid royalties cobrar derechos de autor

to **get run over** ■ to be run over ser atropellado

to **get said** ■ to finish saying acabar de decir ➤ I cut you off, and you didn't get said what you were trying to say. Te corté y no acabaste de decir lo que intentabas decir.

to **get scared** darse miedo

get screwed! *(off-color)* ■ up yours! ¡qué te den por el culo!

get screwed!: they can ~ *(L. Am., Sp.)* ¡que los jodan! ■ *(Mex.)* ¡que los chinguen! ■ ¡que los jodan! ■ *(Sp.)* ¡que los follen! ➤ If they don't like it, they can get screwed! Si no les gusta, ¡que los jodan! ■ Si no les gusta, ¡que los chinguen! ■ Si no les gusta, ¡que los follen!

get serious! ¡ponte serio!

(get) set! ¡listos! ➤ On your mark, get set, go! ■ Ready, set, go! ¡Preparados, listos, ya!

to **get shafted** ■ to get the shaft ■ to give someone the shaft hacerle la pascua a alguien ■ hacerle la puñeta a alguien ➤ I got shafted at work today. ■ I got the shaft at work today. ■ They gave me the shaft at work today. Me han hecho la pascua hoy en el trabajo. ■ Me han hecho la puñeta hoy en el trabajo.

to **get shocked by** ■ to get a shock from ■ to be shocked by recibir un calambre de ■ darle un calambre a alguien ➤ I got shocked by the light switch. ■ I got a shock from the light switch. ■ I was shocked by the light switch. ■ The light switch shocked me. El interruptor de la luz me dio un calambre. ■ Recibí un calambre del interruptor de la luz.

to **get short of breath** cortársele el aliento ■ darle un ahogo ➤ *(Unanamo)* He got short of breath and, once recovered, went on... Le dio un ahogo y, repuesto de él, prosiguió...

to **get shot down** **1.** *(aircraft)* ser abatido **2.** *(figurative)* ser dejado en ridículo

to **get sick** enfermarse ■ ponerse enfermo(-a)

to **get sidetracked** despistarse ■ desviarse del tema ■ hacerse desviar del tema ■ distraerse haciendo otra cosa

to **get sleepy** ■ to become sleepy entrarle a uno sueño

to **get smashed** **1.** to get broken into pieces hacerse trizas **2.** to get drunk (as a skunk) ■ to get looped ■ to get soused ■ to get plastered pillar una tajada ■ *(Mex.)* agarrar una cogorza ■ *(Sp.)* coger una (buena) cogorza

to **get soaked by the rain** ■ to get drenched by the rain ponerse como una sopa en la lluvia ■ empaparse en la lluvia ■ calarse en la lluvia

to **get soggy** ponerse blando ■ *(colorful)* ponerse blandengue ➤ I hate it when tacos get soggy and fall apart. Odio cuando los tacos se ponen blandos y se deshacen. ■ Odio cuando los tacos se ponen blandengues y se deshacen.

to **get some fresh air** ■ to get a breath of fresh air tomar el fresco ■ tomar el aire fresco ■ oxigenarse

to **get (some) gas** *(coll.)* ■ to get gasoline poner gasolina ■ echar gasolina ➤ We have to stop and get (some) gas. ■ We have to stop for gas. Tenemos que parar a echar gasolina. ■ Tenemos que parar a poner gasolina.

to **get some perspective** tomar perspectiva ■ coger perspectiva ➤ *(news commentator)* Let's get some perspective here. Tomemos algo de perspectiva aquí. ■ Cojamos algo de perspectiva aquí.

to **get some shut-eye** *(coll.)* ■ to get some sleep darse un sueñecito ■ echar(se) un sueñecito ■ echar(se) un sueñito

to **get some sleep** dormir ➤ You need to get some sleep. Necesitas dormir.

to **get some sun** ■ to sunbathe ■ *(coll.)* to soak up some rays tomar el sol

to **get someone** **1.** to strike someone ■ to hit someone darle a alguien ■ alcanzarle a alguien **2.** to cause the death of someone acabar con alguien **3.** to hit someone funny hacerle gracia a alguien ■ tener gracia **4.** to get someone down echar para atrás ■ echar hacia trás ■ derrumbarse ■ arredrarse ➤ A bullet got him in the shoulder. Una bala le dio en el hombro. ■ Una bala le alcanzo en el hombro. ➤ A heart attack finally got him. Un ataque al corazón acabó con él. ➤ Her jokes get me. Sus chistes me hacen gracia. ■ Sus chistes tienen gracia. ➤ She is amazing. Nothing gets her (down). Es asombrosa. Nada la echa para atrás. ■ Es asombrosa. No se arredra (ante nada). ■ Es asombrosa. No se derrumba por nada.

to **get someone going** **1.** to energize someone despabilar a alguien **2.** to wind someone up ■ to get someone started on (a subject) darle cuerda a alguien ■ darle coba a alguien ■ lograr que alguien hable de ■ darle pie para que se ponga a hablar de **3.** to spur someone on espolear a alguien **4.** to pester someone chinchar a alguien **5.** to throw barbs at someone ■ to get a rise out of someone enchinchar a alguien ■ picarle a alguien ■ provocar a alguien ➤ He needs a caffeine blast in the morning to get (himself) going. Necesita un chute de cafeína por la mañana para despabilarse. ➤ The cat bites the other cat's tail just to get him going. La gata le muerde la cola al otro (tan) sólo para provocarlo. ■ La gata le muerde la cola al otro (tan) sólo chincharle. ➤ Hume and Rousseau got Kant going. Hume y Rousseau espolearon a Kant. ➤ Don't get me going on that. ■ Don't get me started on that. No me des cuerda. ■ No me des coba.

to **get someone good** pillar a alguien a base de bien ➤ That damned bird got us good. Ese maldito ave nos pilló a base de bien.

to **get someone in on something** ■ to include someone in something incluir a alguien en algo ➤ I told him I'd like to get you all in on it. ■ I told him I'd like to include you in it. Le dije que me gustaría que estuvieses todos incluidos.

to **get someone interested in** hacer que alguien se interese en ■ interesar a alguien en ■ *(Sp.)* hacer que alguien se interese por ■ interesar a alguien por ➤ John Kennedy got many young people interested in politics. John Kennedy hizo que muchos jóvenes se interesaran por la política. ■ John Kennedy interesó a muchos jóvenes en la política.

to **get someone in(to a place)** pasar a alguien a un sitio ➤ *(thirteen-year-old)* My friend got us into the discotheque. Mi amigo nos pasó a la discoteca.

to **get someone off one's back** ■ to get someone off one's case hacer que alguien lo deje en paz a uno ■ hacer que alguien lo deje tranquilo a uno ➤ Why don't you get a job and move out of the house? That'll get the old man off your back. ¿Por qué no te buscas un trabajo y te vas de casa? Eso haría que tu viejo te dejara en paz. ■ ¿Por qué no te buscas un trabajo y te vas de casa? Eso haría que tu viejo te dejara tranquilo.

to **get someone on the telephone** ■ to reach someone on the telephone ponerse a alguien por teléfono ■ hablar con alguien ➤ I tried to call her last night, but I couldn't get her. La intenté llamar anoche, pero no pude hablar con ella.

to **get someone somewhere** ■ to take someone somewhere llevar a alguien a algun lugar ➤ I have to get the children to school. ■ I have to take the children to school. Tengo que llevar a los niños al cole. ➤ Now we're getting somewhere. Ahora estamos en camino.

to **get somewhere** **1.** *(literal)* to be somewhere llegar a alguna parte ■ llegar a algún lugar **2.** *(figurative)* to begin to make progress estar en camino ■ empezar a hacer progresos ■ llevarle a buen camino a alguien ■ *(in the negative)* no llevar a alguien a ninguna parte ➤ Now we're getting somewhere. Ahora estamos en camino. ➤ Having two part-time jobs isn't getting me anywhere. I need *one* good job. Tener dos trabajos de media jornada no me lleva a ninguna parte. Necesito uno solo bueno. ➤ After hitting numerous dead ends, the scientists have hit on a line of investigation that is finally getting them somewhere. Después de muchos intentos fallidos, los científicos han dado con una línea de investigación que finalmente los está llevando por buen camino.

to **get someone started** darle a alguien para empezar ➤ Did the leads I gave you get you started, or do you need more? Las pistas que te mandé, ¿te dieron para empezar o necesitas más?

to **get someone the prize** ■ to earn someone the prize ■ to garner someone the prize ■ to win someone the prize valerle a alguien el premio

to **get someone to do something** hacer que alguien haga algo ■ conseguir que alguien haga algo ➤ I can't get my students to write voluntarily. I have to make them (do it). No puedo hacer que mis estudiantes escriban voluntariamente. Tengo que obligarlos.

to **get someone to obey** ▪ to get someone to mind conseguir que le obedezca a uno ➤ The substitute can't get the second-graders to obey him. El sustituto no consigue que los de segundo le obedezcan.

to **get someone to go along** conseguir que alguien acceda ▪ conseguir que alguien consienta ➤ The company resorted to palm greasing to get the zoning commission to go along. La compañía recurrió a untar la mano para conseguir que la comisión urbanística accediera. ▪ La compañía recurrió a untar la mano para conseguir que la comisión urbanística consienta.

to **get someone to mind** *(coll.)* ▪ to get someone to obey hacer que alguien le obedezca a uno ▪ conseguir que alguien le obedezca a uno ➤ I can't get the children to mind me. No puedo hacer que me obedezcan los niños.

to **get someone's attention** ▪ to catch someone's attention llamar la atención de alguien ➤ A TV news item got my attention. Una noticia de la tele me llamó la atención. ➤ See if you can get the waiter's attention. A ver si puedes llamar la atención del camarero. ➤ The cat walked in front of the computer screen to get my attention. El gato se paseó por delante de la pantalla de la computadora para llamarme la atención.

to **get someone's name 1.** to obtain someone's name obtener el nombre de alguien **2.** to hear (clearly) someone's name oír el nombre de alguien ▪ *(Sp.)* coger el nombre de ➤ I got the doctor's name off the insurance provider's website. Obtuve el nombre del médico del sito web de la compañía de seguros. ➤ I'm sorry, I didn't get your name. *(tú)* Lo siento. No oí tu nombre. ▪ *(usted)* Lo siento. No oí su nombre.

to **get something across** ▪ to make oneself understood hacerse entender

to **get something back from someone** tener algo de vuelta ▪ ser algo devuelto ➤ I'd like to get it back from you next week. Me gustaría tenerlo de vuelta la semana que viene. ▪ Me gustaría que me lo devolvieras la semana que viene.

to **get something done** terminar algo ▪ poder hacer algo ➤ Most bosses don't care what your problems with the task are. They just want you to get it done. A la mayoría de los jefes no les importa los problemas que tengas con tu tarea. Sencillamente quieren que la termines. ➤ I didn't get it done. No lo terminé. ▪ No lo pude hacer.

to **get something going** montar algo ▪ preparar algo ➤ We need to get a party going. Tenemos que montar una fiesta. ▪ Tenemos que preparar una fiesta.

to **get something home 1.** to take something home llevar algo a casa **2.** to bring something home traer algo a casa ➤ How are we going to get this Christmas tree home? ¿Cómo vamos a llevar este árbol de Navidad a casa? ➤ How are you all going to bring the Christmas tree home? ¿Cómo vais a traer el árbol de Navidad a casa?

to **get something in one's eye** metérsele algo en el ojo a uno ▪ entrarle algo en el ojo a uno ➤ I got something in my eye. Se me ha metido algo en el ojo. ▪ Me entró algo en el ojo.

to **get something off (of) something** ▪ to remove something from something quitar algo de algo ➤ I couldn't get the label glue off the bottom of the new dishes. No pude quitar el pegamento de la etiqueta del reverso de los platos nuevos. ➤ Please get your stuff off the dining room table. Por favor quita tus cosas de la mesa de comedor.

to **get something off the ground** conseguir que algo salga adelante ➤ We couldn't get the project off the ground. No conseguimos que el proyecto saliera adelante.

to **get something on something 1.** to soil something with something mancharse algo con algo **2.** to get information about something conseguir información sobre algo ▪ buscar información sobre algo ➤ The painter got paint on the piano. El pintor se manchó el piano con pintura. ➤ When I was eating french fries, I got ketchup on my shirt. Cuando comía patatas fritas, me manché la camisa con ketchup. ➤ The editor said to the reporter, see if you can get something on the new high school principal. El editor le dijo al reportero, ve a ver si puedes conseguir algo sobre el nuevo director de la secundaria.

to **get something open 1.** abrir algo **2.** *(lid, cap)* destapar algo ➤ I can't get this bottle of ketchup open. ▪ I can't get the top off this bottle of ketchup. No puedo abrir la botella de ketchup. ▪ No puedo destapar la botella de ketchup.

to **get something out of one's mind** ▪ to put something out of one's mind apartar algo de la mente ➤ I can't get it out of my mind. ▪ I can't put it out of my mind. No puedo apartarlo de la mente.

to **get something out of one's system** ▪ to let off steam ▪ to vent (one's feelings) ▪ to blow off steam sacarse la tensión ▪ desfogarse ▪ desahogarse

to **get something out of someone** ▪ to elicit information from someone tirar a alguien de la lengua ▪ sacar algo de alguien

to **get something out of the way 1.** to remove something blocking quitar algo de en medio **2.** to get something done quitarse algo de en medio ▪ quitarse algo de encima ➤ I'm going to do my grocery shopping this morning and get it out of the way. Voy a hacer la compra esta mañana y quitármelo de en medio. ▪ Voy a hacer la compra esta mañana y quitármelo de encima. ➤ That way, I'll get it out of the way. De ese modo, me lo quito de en medio. ▪ De ese modo, me lo quito de encima.

to **get something over with (once and for all)** hacer algo de una vez (por todas) ▪ concluir algo de una vez ▪ acabar con algo ➤ The dentist said I had to have my wisdom teeth out at some point, so I might as well get it over with. El dentista me dijo que me tienen que sacar las muelas del juicio en algún momento, así que más vale hacerlo de una vez. ➤ Let's get it over with once and for all. Concluyamos esto de una vez (por todas). ▪ Quitémonos esto de encima de una vez por todas. ➤ Get it over with quick. *(tú)* Acaba con esto rápido. ▪ *(usted)* Acabe con esto rápido. ▪ *(ustedes)* Acaben con esto rápido. ▪ *(Sp., vosotros)* Acabad con esto rápido.

to **get something read** lograr leer algo ➤ I didn't get the assignment read. *(L. Am.)* No logré leer la tarea. ▪ *(Sp.)* No logré leer los deberes.

to **get something ready for** dejar algo listo para ▪ preparar algo para ▪ disponer algo para

to **get something right** ▪ to do something right **1.** hacer algo bien ▪ hacer algo correctamente **2.** *(answer)* salirle algo bien ▪ hacer algo bien **3.** *(overall result)* quedar algo bien ➤ I'll get it right this time. ▪ I'll do it right this time. Lo haré bien esta vez. ➤ Did you get it right (on the test)? ¿Te salió bien (en el examen)? ➤ The important thing is to get it right. Lo importante es que salga bien. ▪ Lo importante es que quede bien. ➤ The waiter didn't get the change right. El camarero no me dio el cambio bien. ➤ I can't get the light right. No puedo ajustar la luz bien. ➤ When color TV first came out, it was hard to get the color right. Cuando apareció la televisión en color por primera vez, era difícil ajustar el color. ➤ I can't get the heat right in here. It's either too much or too little. No puedo ajustar la calefacción aquí. O me paso o no llego.

to **get something through devious means** conseguir algo con malas artes ▪ conseguir algo con patrañas ▪ conseguir algo con embustes

to **get something through the door** pasar algo a través de la puerta

to **get something to do something** conseguir hacer algo ▪ conseguir que algo haga algo ➤ John Logie Baird carried out the first trials of television in 1928 and eight years later got it to broadcast in color and with higher definition. John Logie Baird realizó las primeras pruebas de televisión en 1928 y ocho años después consigió emitir en color y con una definición más alta.

to **get something to eat 1.** comer algo ▪ picar algo **2.** *(late morning)* almorzar **3.** *(late afternoon)* merendar ➤ Do you want to stop and get something to eat? ¿Quieres parar y comer algo? ➤ We were waiting for our train to leave, and since it was going to be a while, we decided to get something to eat at the station. Estabamos esperando a que saliera nuestro tren, y como iba para largo, decidimos almorzar en la estación.

to **get something to work** hacer que funcione ➤ I couldn't get it to work. No pude hacer que funcionara. ➤ Did you get it to work? ¿Hiciste que funcionara? ▪ ¿Lo hiciste funcionar? ➤ Were you able to get it to work? ¿Pudiste hacer que funcionara? ▪ ¿Pudiste hacerlo funcionar?

to **get stranded in a blizzard** quedar atrapado en una tormenta de nieve ▪ quedar tirado en una tormenta de nieve to **get struck by a car** ▪ to be hit by a car ser atropellado por un carro ▪ *(Sp.)* ser atropellado por un coche ▪ ser cogido por un coche *("Ser atropellado" means both "to get hit" and "to get run over.")*

to **get struck by lightning** ser alcanzado por un rayo

to **get stuck** *(gadget, device)* ▪ to be stuck ▪ to be jammed quedar encallado ▪ quedar atascado

to **get stuck between** atascarse entre ▪ trabarse entre ➤ The comedienne Joan Rivers said a certain actress got stuck between the arches as she was leaving McDonalds. La humorista Joan Rivers dijo que cierta actriz se atascó entre los arcos cuando salía de McDonalds. ▪ La humorista Joan Rivers dijo que cierta actriz se trabó entre los arcos cuando salía de McDonalds.

to **get stuck in** quedar atascado(-a) en ▪ atascarse en ➤ Don't get stuck in the snow! ¡Qué no se atasquen en la nieve! ▪ *(Sp., vosotros)* ¡Qué no os atasquéis en la nieve!

to **get stuck in a (traffic) bottleneck** quedarse en un embotellamiento ▪ quedarse atascado en un embotellamiento

to **get stuck in an elevator** ▪ to be trapped in an elevator quedarse encerrado en un ascensor ▪ quedarse atrapado en un ascensor ▪ quedarse colgado en un ascensor

to **get stuck with having to do something** ▪ to get stuck doing something ▪ to get stuck holding the bag tocarle a uno hacer algo cargar con el mochuelo ➤ I always get stuck with having to do the dishes. Siempre me toca (tener que) lavar los platos. ▪ Siempre nos toca el mochuelo de lavar los platos.

to **get stuck with the job** ▪ to get the job dumped on one tocarle a uno el trabajo ▪ endilgarle el trabajo a uno ➤ I got stuck with the job. Me endilgaron el trabajo.

to **get stuck with the kids** tocarle quedarse con los niños

to **get sunburned** achicharrarse ▪ quemarse con el sol ▪ quemarse ▪ *(Sp., coll.)* pegársele el sol ➤ I got sunburned. Me achicharré. ➤ My head got sunburned. Se me achicharró la cabeza.

to **get taken for a ride** ▪ to be taken for a ride hacerse el primo

to **get the baby to go to sleep** dormir al bebé ▪ adormecer al bebé ➤ We couldn't get the baby to go to sleep. No pudimos dormir al bebé.

to **get the best of one** poder más que uno ▪ sobrepasarle a uno ▪ superarle a alguien ➤ My curiosity got the best of me. Mi curiosidad pudo más que yo. ➤ My temper got the best of me. Mi mal genio me sobrepasó.

to **get the best out of someone** sacar lo mejor de alguien

to **get the better of one** ▪ to get the best of one poder más que...

to **get the big picture (on the question of...)** ▪ to get the big picture (when it comes to...) ▪ to see the big picture (on...) ver las cosas de forma global ▪ ver las cosas en perspectiva (sobre...) ▪ tener perspectiva (sobre...) ▪ tener perspectiva (de...)

to **get the car running** conseguir hacer funcionar el carro ▪ *(Sp.)* conseguir hacer funcionar el coche

to **get the connection** ▪ to see the connection ver la relación ➤ I still don't get the connection. Sigo sin ver la relación.

to **get the country back on its feet** conseguir levantar el país ▪ conseguir que el país se levante

to **get the feel of something** *(Sp.)* cogerle el tranquillo a algo ▪ acostumbrarse a algo ➤ Once I got the feel of front-wheel drive, I preferred it. Una vez que le cogí el tranquillo al coche de tracción delantera, lo prefería a cualquier otro. ➤ I think if you worked with me for a couple of days, you'd get the feel of how this goes. Creo que si trabajases conmigo durante un par de días, le cogerías el tranquillo a esto.

to **get the feel of the (light) airplane** cogerle el tranquillo a la avioneta ▪ pillarle el truco a la avioneta

to **get the feel of the language** cogerle el tranquillo al idioma ▪ pillarle el tranquillo al idioma

to **get the feel of the situation** tenerlo claro ▪ verlo claro ▪ saber por dónde van los tiros ➤ Clark Clifford, President Johnson's second defense secretary, said it took (him) some months to get the feel of the Vietnam situation. Clark Clifford, segundo secretario de defensa del Presidente Johnson, dijo que le llevó algunos meses tener clara la situación en Vietnam. ▪ Clark Clifford, segundo secretario de defensa del Presidente Johnson, dijo que le llevó algunos meses ver clara la situación en Vietnam. ▪ Clark Clifford, segundo secretario de defensa del Presidente Johnson, dijo que le llevó algunos meses saber por dónde iban los tiros en Vietnam.

to **get the gist of something** ▪ to get the central idea of something captar lo esencial de algo

to **get the go-ahead to** ▪ to get the green light to ▪ to get the authorization to obtener la luz verde para ▪ recibir el pistoletazo de salida para ▪ obtener la autorización para

to **get the green light to** ▪ to get the go-ahead to obtener la luz verde para ▪ recibir el pistoletazo de salida para

to **get the hang of something** ▪ to get the knack of something pillar el tranquillo de algo ▪ pillarlo ▪ *(Sp.)* coger el tranquillo de algo ▪ cogerlo ➤ I'm getting the hang of it. Lo estoy cogiendo.

to **get the hell out of there** ▪ to get the hell out of Dodge poner los pies en polvorosa ▪ esfumarse de allí ▪ pirarse de allí enseguida ▪ largarse de allí enseguida ▪ tomar las de Villa Diego ➤ We got the hell out of there. Pusimos los pies en polvorosa. ▪ Tomamos las de Villa Diego. ▪ Nos esfumamos de allí.

to **get the highest score 1.** to get a higher score than anyone else conseguir la máxima puntuación de todos **2.** to get the highest possible score conseguir la máxima puntuación posible

to **get the hint** ▪ to catch the hint captar la indirecta ▪ *(Sp.)* coger la indirecta

to **get the idea** ▪ to begin to understand ▪ to catch on entender

to **get the idea for...** darle la idea para...

to **get the idea that...** darle la idea de que...

to **get the idea to do something** darle a uno la idea de hacer algo ▪ sacar la idea de hacer algo

to **get the idea out of one's head that...** ▪ to get it out of one's head that... quitarse de la cabeza la idea de que...

to **get the kids** ▪ to pick up the kids recoger a los peques

to **get the knack of something** ▪ to get the hang of something pescar el truco de algo ▪ cogerle el truco ▪ cogerle la maña de algo ▪ cogerle tranquillo de algo

get the lead out of your butt! ¡sacúdete la pereza de los huesos!

to **get the license number** coger la matrícula ▪ anotar la matrícula ▪ memorizar la matrícula ▪ ver (el número de) la matrícula ➤ Did you get the license number? ¿Anotaste la matrícula?

to **get the lion's share** llevarse la parte del león ▪ llevarse la mejor parte ▪ llevarse la mejor tajada

to **get the most out of something** sacar lo máximo de algo ▪ conseguir lo máximo en algo

to **get the most votes** *(either a relative or absolute majority)* ▪ to receive the largest number of votes ▪ to receive the greatest number of votes ▪ to receive the highest number of votes recibir el más alto número de votos

to **get the motor running** lograr mantener el motor en marcha

to **get the motor started** ▪ to get the motor to start hacer que arranque el motor

to **get the news from someone** llegarle a alguien las noticias por alguien ▪ llegarle a alguien las noticias vía alguien ▪ recibir las noticias por alguien ▪ recibir las noticias vía alguien ▪ tener noticias por alguien ▪ tener noticias vía alguien ➤ I got the news from Juana. ▪ I heard the news from Juana. Me llegaron las noticias por Juana. ▪ Me llegaron las noticias vía Juana. ▪ Recibí las noticias por Juana. ▪ Recibí las noticias vía Juana. ▪ Tuve noticias por Juana. ▪ Tuve noticias vía Juana.

get the phone! ▪ get the telephone! ¡al aparato! ▪ ¡al teléfono!

to **get the phone** ▪ to get the telephone ponerse (al teléfono) ▪ coger el teléfono ➤ Tell Javier to get the phone. Dile a Javier que se ponga. ➤ He'll get it in a second. Ahora mismo se pone.

to **get the short end of the stick** bailar con la más fea

to **get something for less than** conseguir algo por menos de ➤ You can get them for less than ten dollars. Se consiguen por menos de diez dólares.

to **get the surprise of one's life** llevarse la mayor sorpresa de su vida ➤ He's going to get the surprise of his life. Va a llevarse la mayor sorpresa de su vida.

to **get the stain out** ■ to remove the stain ■ to get rid of the stain quitar la mancha ■ limpiar la mancha

to **get the top off of something** destapar algo ➤ I can't get the top off (of it). No puedo destaparlo. ➤ See if you can get the top off (of) this bottle of ketchup. Mira a ver si puedes destapar el bote de ketchup.

to **get the word out** dar a conocer ■ comentarlo ■ hablarlo ■ comunicarlo ■ transmitirlo ➤ We need to get the word out. Hay que darlo a conocer. ■ Hay que comentarlo. ■ Hay que comunicarlo. ■ Hay que transmitirlo.

to **get the worst of it** llevar la peor parte

to **get the wrong end of the stick** tomar el rábano por las hojas

to **get the wrong impression** llevarse la impresión equivocada

to **get there early** ■ to be early ■ to arrive early llegar pronto ■ llegar con antelación ■ llegar con anticipación ■ llegar antes ■ irse pronto ■ irse con antelación ■ irse con anticipación ■ irse antes ➤ Get to the airport two hours early. Vete al aeropuerto con dos horas de antelación. ■ Vete al aeropuerto con dos horas de anticipación. ■ Vete al aeropuerto dos horas antes. ■ Llega al aeropuerto con dos horas de antelación. ■ Llega al aeropuerto dos horas antes.

to **get things done** conseguir que se hagan las cosas ➤ President Polk, said the historian Bernard DeVoto, knew how to get things done. El Presidente Polk, dijo el historiador Bernard DeVoto, supo cómo conseguir que se hicieran las cosas.

get this! ¡fíjate! ■ ¡mira por dónde!

to **get through the day** sortear el día

to **get ticked off** ■ to get mad ■ to get angry ponerse borde ■ enojarse ■ cabrearse ■ *(Sp.)* enfadarse

to **get tied down with something** ■ to tie oneself down with something atarse a algo ➤ I don't want to get tied down with a debt. ■ I don't want to tie myself down with a debt. No quiero atarme a una deuda. ■ No me quiero atar a una deuda.

to **get tired of something** ■ to grow tired of something cansarse de algo

to **get to a place 1.** to arrive in a place ■ to arrive at a place llegar a un lugar **2.** *(during a walk, or when doing things in a sequence)* dar con un lugar ➤ When we got to Atlanta... ■ When we arrived in Atlanta... Cuando llegamos a Atlanta... ➤ When we got to the airport... ■ When we arrived at the airport... Cuando llegamos al aeropuerto... ➤ We were sightseeing in Segovia, and when we got to the Alcázar... Estábamos haciendo turismo en Segovia, y cuando dimos con el Alcázar...

to **get to a point where** ■ to get to the point that llegar a un punto que

to **get to do something** poder hacer algo ➤ *(child's complaint)* Why does she get to go and not me? ¿Por qué ella puede ir y yo no? *(More correct but less common: "Why does she get to go and not I?")*

to **get to doing something** ponerse a hacer algo ➤ I'll start reading on my thesis this summer, but I won't get to writing it until early next year. ■ I won't get to the writing of it until early next year. Empezaré a consultar bibliografía para mi tesis este verano, pero no me pondré a redactar hasta principios del año que viene.

to **get to know someone** llegar a conocer a alguien ■ establecer una relación con alguien ➤ She's impossible to get to know. Es imposible llegar a conocerla. ■ Es imposible establecer una relación con ella. ■ *(Sp., leísmo)* Es imposible llegar a conocerle (a ella).

to **get to know a place** ■ to learn one's way around llegar a conocer un lugar

to **get to know someone 1.** llegar a conocer a alguien **2.** *(gradually)* over time ir conociendo a alguien ➤ We got to know each other at the university. Llegamos a conocernos en la universidad. ➤ I had gradually gotten to know him. Lo había ido conociendo. ■ *(Sp., leísmo)* Le había ido conociendo. ➤ I had gradually gotten to know her. La había ido conociendo. ➤ Once you get to know him Una vez que lo conozcas ■ *(Sp., leísmo)* Una vez que le conozcas ➤ Once you get to know her Una vez que la conozcas

to **get to sleep** quedarse dormido ■ dormirse ■ *(literary)* conciliar el sueño ■ *(Sp.)* coger el sueño

to **get to someone 1.** to shake someone up llegar profundamente a alguien ■ realmente llegar a alguien **2.** to touch someone ■ to evoke tenderness conmover a alguien ➤ Elie Wiesel's book *Night* really got to the class. El libro *Noche* de Elie Wiesel llegó profundamente a la clase. ➤ That music really got to me. Esa música realmente me llegó. ■ Esa música me llegó profundamente. ■ Esa música me conmovió.

to **get to the bottom** ■ to reach the bottom llegar al fondo ➤ A one-pound steel ball, dropped into the ocean above the Marianas Trench, takes sixty-three minutes to get to the bottom. Una bola de acero de una libra, dejada caer al océano sobre las Fosas Marianas, tarda sesenta y tres minutos en llegar al fondo.

to **get to the bottom of the matter** llegar al fondo del asunto

to **get to the bottom of the mystery** llegar al fondo del misterio

to **get to the heart of a person** llegar al corazón de una persona

to **get to the heart of the matter** llegar al meollo de la cuestión ■ dar con el quid de la cuestión

to **get to the point** ■ to get straight to the point ir a lo concreto ■ ir al grano ■ hablar sin ambages ➤ Get to the point! ¡A lo concreto! ■ *(tú)* ¡Ve al grano! ■ ¡Habla sin ambages! ■ *(usted)* ¡Vaya al grano! ■ ¡Hable sin ambages!

to **get to the point that...** llegar al punto que...

to **get to (the point) where...** llegar al punto en que... ➤ It had gotten to (the point) where it was taking about fifty tries to log onto the server. Había llegado al punto en que había que hacer cincuenta intentos para conectarse al servidor.

get to work! ¡manos a la obra! ■ ¡a trabajar! ■ *(tú)* ¡ponte a trabajar! ■ *(usted)* ¡póngase a trabajar! ■ *(ustedes)* ¡pónganse a trabajar! ■ *(Sp., vosotros)* ¡poneos a trabajar!

to **get to work 1.** to begin to work ponerse a trabajar ■ marchar a trabajar **2.** to travel to work llegar a su trabajo ■ ir a trabajar ■ marchar a trabajar ➤ Let's get to work! ¡Pongámonos a trabajar! ■ ¡Marchemos al trabajo! ➤ How do you get to work in the mornings? Do you drive or take the commuter train? ¿Cómo llegas al trabajo por las mañanas? ¿Conduces o tomas el tren de cercanías? ■ ¿Cómo vas al trabajo por las mañanas? ¿Conduces o tomas el tren de cercanías?

to **get to work on** ponerse a trabajar en ■ poner por obra ■ poner en obra

to **get together** juntarse ■ reunirse ➤ Last Saturday, we all got together for lunch. El sábado pasado nos juntamos para comer. ■ El sábado pasado no reunimos para comer.

to **get together some volunteers** ■ to round up some volunteers reunir a unos voluntarios

to **get tongue-tied** trabársele la lengua ➤ I got tongue-tied. Se me trabó la lengua.

to **get too late to do something** hacérsele tarde para hacer algo ➤ It got too late to take the bus, so we took a taxi. Se nos hizo tarde para tomar el áutobus así que tomamos un taxi.

to **get under cover** ■ to take cover ponerse a cubierto

to **get under one's skin** irritar a alguien

to **get under way** empezar a moverse ■ ir cobrando forma ■ ya ir adelantando

get up! *(tú)* levántate ■ *(usted)* levántese

to **get up 1.** to stand up levantarse ■ ponerse de pie **2.** to get out of bed ■ to arise levantarse (de la cama)

to **get up from the table** levantarse de la mesa

to **get up on one's feet** apoyarse en los pies ➤ He got up on his feet. Se apoyó en los pies.

to **get up the courage (to)** ■ to get up the nerve (to) armarse de valor (para) ■ echarle valor (para) ■ hacerse de valor (para)

to **get up the nerve (to)** ■ to get up one's nerve to llenarse de valor para ■ armarse de valor (para) ■ echarle valor (para)

to **get up out of a chair** levantarse de una silla ■ alzarse de una silla

to **get up speed** ■ to gain speed ■ to increase in velocity cobrar velocidad ■ ganar velocidad ■ aumentar de velocidad to **get up steam** 1. *(steam engine, turbine, etc.)* acumular vapor ▪ dar presión 2. *(figurative)* to get up the energy, motivation cobar fuerzas (para)

to **get up the nerve to do something** armarse de valor para hacer algo

to **get uptight** ponerse tenso(-a) ▪ ponerse nervioso(-a) ➤ Don't get uptight. No te pongas tenso(-a). ▪ No te pongas nervioso(-a).

to **get up to speed** ponerse al punto ▪ familiarse con la mecánica de... ▪ familiarse con la dinámica de... ➤ Carlos got up to speed in his new job very quickly. Carlos se familiarizó con la mecánica de su nuevo trabajo muy rápido. ▪ Carlos se familiarizó con la dinámica de su nuevo trabajo muy rápido.

to **get upset** disgustarse ▪ alterarse ➤ Don't get upset. *(tú)* No te disgustes. ▪ No te alteres. ▪ *(usted)* No se disguste (usted). ▪ No se altere (usted).

to **get used up** ir a acabarse ➤ I didn't think it would get used up. ▪ I didn't think we'd run out. ▪ No pensé que se fuera a acabar.

to **get warm** *(by the fire)* 1. entrar en calor 2. *(in a guessing game)* ¡caliente! ➤ Let's build a fire and get warm. Vamos a hacer un fuego para entrar en calor. ▪ Vamos a encender la chimenea para entrar en calor. ➤ You're getting warm! ▪ You're getting close! ▪ You're about to guess it! ¡Caliente, caliente! ▪ ¡Quemando, quemando!

to **get way over to the left** ponerse muy a la izquierda

to **get way over to the right** ponerse muy a la derecha ➤ Get way over to the right. Ponte muy a la derecha.

to **get well** aliviarse ▪ recuperarse ▪ mejorarse ▪ reponerse

get well soon! ¡que te mejores pronto! ▪ ¡que te alivies pronto!

to **get what one deserves** ▪ to get one's just desserts llevarse su merecido ▪ recibir su merecido ▪ recibir lo que merece uno

get with it! ¡espabílate!

to **get worked up about something** ▪ to get all worked up about something ▪ to get exercised about something ▪ to fly into a rage exaltarse por algo ▪ encorajinarse de algo ▪ calentársele la boca a alguien ➤ He got all worked up when I told him what she said. Se exaltó cuando le dije lo que ella dijo. ➤ Don't get so worked up. No te exaltes.

to **get worse** empeorar ▪ recrudecer ➤ His condition is getting worse. Su condición está empeorando. ▪ Su condición está recrudeciendo.

getaway car coche (preparado) para la huida ▪ medio de escape ▪ auto de escape

getting back to what I was telling you *(a ti)* volviendo a lo que te estaba diciendo ▪ *(a usted)* volviendo a lo que le estaba diciendo ▪ *(a vosotros)* volviendo a lo que os estaba diciendo ▪ *(a ustedes)* volviendo a lo que les estaba diciendo *(In Spain, "iba diciendo" is also common.)*

to be **getting better** ▪ to be on the road to recovery estar mejorando ▪ ir mejor ➤ The patient is getting better. El paciente va mejor. ➤ Your Spanish is getting better all the time. Tu español está mejorando constantemente.

getting by: to be (just) ~ estar tirando ➤ I'm (just) getting by. Estoy tirando.

to be **getting dark** ir anocheciendo ➤ It's getting dark. Va anocheciendo.

getting down to brass tacks ▪ getting to the point (vamos) a lo concreto ▪ vamos al punto

to be **getting on in years** ▪ to be getting up in years ▪ to be getting up there estar entrado(-a) en años ▪ ser entrado(-a) en años ▪ entrar en años

to be **getting old** estar envejeciendo ▪ ya ir para viejo ▪ estar entrando en años ▪ ir envejeciendo ➤ He's getting old. Ya va para viejo. ▪ Está entrando en años. ▪ Va envejeciendo.

to be **getting pretty good (at something)** írsele dando bien algo ▪ estar saliendo bien en algo ▪ estar haciéndose bastante bien en ➤ He's getting pretty good at basketball. Se le va dando bien el baloncesto. ▪ Está saliendo bastante bien en el baloncesto.

to be **getting up in years** ▪ to be getting on in years ▪ to be getting up there estar entrado(-a) en años ▪ estar pasado(-a) de años

gift horse caballo regalado ➤ Don't look a gift horse in the mouth. A caballo regalado no se le miran los dientes.

gift wrapping paper papel de regalo

gift of gab: to have the ~ tener (mucha) labia ▪ tener un pico de oro ▪ tener un piquito de oro ➤ To be a salesman, you have to have the gift of gab. Para ser vendedor, hay que tener mucha labia.

gift of understanding el don de la comprensión

to **gild the lily** rizar el rizo

gilded cage jaula de oro

to **give a blast on one's trumpet** ▪ to give a blast of one's trumpet ▪ to sound one's trumpet soltar un trompetazo

to **give a description** hacer una descripción

to **give a lecture** dar una conferencia ▪ pronunciar una conferencia

to **give a little** ▪ to give slightly ceder un poco ▪ ceder ligeramente ➤ The suspension bridge gave a little under the weight of the crowd. El puente colgante cedió un poco bajo el peso de la muchedumbre. ▪ El puente colgante cedió ligeramente bajo el peso de la muchedumbre.

to **give a nod** acertar la cabeza ➤ He gave a nod and went straight to his work. Acertó la cabeza y fue directamente a su trabajo.

to **give a reason for** alegar una razón para

to **give a rehash** ▪ to do a rehash hacer un refrito ➤ He gave us a rehash of the day's news. Nos hizo un refrito de las noticias del día.

to **give a seminar** impartir un seminario

to **give a speech** ▪ to make a speech ▪ to deliver a speech dar un discurso ▪ pronunciar un discurso

to **give a start** pegar un brinco ▪ dar un brinco ▪ dar un sobresalto

to **give a talk** dar una charla

to **give a thumbnail sketch (of)** esbozar ▪ hacer un esbozo (de) ▪ contárselo en dos palabras

to **give a thumbs up** hacer un signo aprobatorio

to **give advice on** ▪ to advise on dar consejos sobre ▪ dar un consejo sobre ▪ aconsejar sobre

to **give an example** ▪ to cite an example dar un ejemplo ▪ citar un ejemplo ▪ *(Sp.)* poner un ejemplo ➤ I'll give you an example. Te pongo un ejemplo. ➤ Could you cite an example? ¿Podrías citarme un ejemplo? ➤ Let me give you an example. Déjame darte un ejemplo. ▪ Déjame ponerte un ejemplo.

to **give an ultimatum** dar un ultimatum ➤ She gave her fiancé an ultimatum: either the tarantula goes or I go. Le dio a su novio un ultimatum. O la tarántula sale o salgo yo.

give and take: to engage in ~ andar en dares y tomares ▪ estar que tira y afloja

give and you shall receive ▪ give and thou shalt receive dad y recibiréis

to **give as an example** ▪ to cite as an example poner como ejemplo

to **give away a secret** ▪ to give a secret away ▪ to spill the beans revelarle un secreto a alguien ▪ descubrir el pastel

to **give away something (as a gift)** ▪ to give something away as a gift regalar algo ➤ They're giving away free tickets to the concert. ▪ They're giving free tickets to the concert away. Están regalando entradas gratis para el concierto. ➤ They're giving them away. Las están regalando. ▪ Están regalándolas.

to **give away a secret** revelar un secreto ▪ delatar un secreto

to **give away the bride** entregar a la novia ▪ llevar a la novia al altar

to **give away the ending of the story** destripar el cuento

to **give away the punch line of the joke** destripar el chiste

to **give back something** ▪ to give something back devolver algo ▪ retornar algo ➤ She gave it back (to me). (Me) lo devolvió. ▪ (Me) lo retornó.

to **give birth (to)** dar a luz (a)

to **give blood** ▪ to donate blood donar sangre

to **give change** devolver cambio ➤ This machine gives change. Esta máquina devuelve cambio.

to **give credit where credit is due** dar a cada uno su merecido ▪ dar a alguien su merecido to **give differing accounts of** discrepar sobre

to **give for someone's birthday** regalar por el cumpleaños alguien ➤ What did you give him for his birthday? ¿Qué le regalaste por el cumpleaños?

to **give free rein to** dar rienda suelta a

to **give ground** *(in a debate, argument, battle)* ceder terreno

to **give hardly any...** dar apenas ▪ casi no dar...

give her my best *(tú)* dale (a ella) mis mejores recuerdos ▪ *(usted)* déle (a ella) mis mejores recuerdos

give him an inch and he'll take a mile déle el pie y se tomará la mano

give him my best *(tú)* dale mis mejores recuerdos ▪ *(usted)* déle mis mejores recuerdos

to **give in (to)** ceder (a) ▪ ceder (ante)

to **give in to pressure** ▪ to buckle under pressure ▪ to cave in to pressure ▪ to yield under pressure claudicar ante la presión ▪ ceder ante la presión

to **give in to temptation** ceder a la tentación

to **give information** dar información ▪ dar razón

to **give instructions to** dar instrucciones a

to **give it a coat of paint** darle una mano de pintura ▪ darle una pasada de pintura ▪ darle una capa de pintura

to **give it a shot** ▪ to give it a go ▪ to give it a try ▪ to give it a whirl intentarlo

to **give it all you've got** ▪ to give it your all dar el todo por el todo ▪ darle todo lo que uno tiene ▪ darle el do de pecho ▪ echar los pulmones ➤ Give it all you've got! Dale todo lo que tengas. ▪ Dale el do de pecho.

to **give it another try** intentar otra vez

to **give it one's all** ▪ to give one's all darle el do de pecho ▪ dar todo lo que uno tenga

to **give it time** darle tiempo al tiempo ➤ Give it time. *(tú, vos)* Dale tiempo al tiempo. ▪ *(usted)* Dele tiempo al tiempo. ▪ *(ustedes)* Denle tiempo al tiempo. ▪ *(vosotros)* Dadle tiempo al tiempo.

to **give it to someone** dárselo a alguien ▪ regalárselo a alguien

give it up ▪ not a chance ▪ no way aquí no hay tu tía

to **give leeway to someone** ▪ to give someone leeway ▪ to take the pressure off someone dar cuartel a alguien ▪ dar cuartelillo a alguien

give me a break! ¡ya déjame, por favor!

give me a hand, will ya? ▪ help me out, will ya? ¿me echas una mano? ▪ *(Mex.)* ¿me das una manita?

give me a high five! *(refers to the fingers)* ¡chócalos cinco! ▪ *(refers to the hand)* ¡chócala!

give me a ring ▪ call me dame un timbrazo ▪ llámame (por teléfono)

give me... *(tú)* dame... ▪ ponme... ▪ *(usted)* deme... ▪ póngame... ➤ *(customer to produce clerk)* Give me five tomatoes. Deme cinco tomates. ▪ Póngame cinco tomates.

give my regards to... saluda a... ▪ da recuerdos a...

to **give notice (that...)** *(one is quitting a job or moving)* ▪ to turn in one's notice (that...) informar que uno se va ▪ dar el preaviso (de que...)

to **give off a foul odor** ▪ to give off a repulsive odor despedir un olor hediondo

to **give off a scent of** exhalar un olor a

to **give off fumes** soltar vapores

to **give off light** despedir luz

to **give one goose bumps** ponerle piel de gallina a uno

to **give one's approval** dar su aprobación

to **give one's all** ▪ to give it one's all dar el do de pecho *(literally, "to give the high C" on the musical scale)*

to **give one's best** ▪ to give the best of oneself dar lo mejor de sí mismo ▪ dar lo mejor de uno mismo ➤ The candidates gave their best during the debate. ▪ The candidates gave the best of themselves during the debate. Los candidatos dieron lo mejor de sí mismos durante el debate.

to **give one's consent** dar su conformidad

to **give one's eye teeth for** dar un ojo de la cara por

to **give oneself airs** ▪ to put on airs darse importancia ▪ darse tono ▪ darse ínfulas

to **give reasons for 1.** *(a past action)* dar razones por ▪ alegar razones por **2.** *(a future action)* dar razones para ▪ alegar razones para ▪ *(always followed by a noun or noun phrase)* dar razones de

to **give rise to** ▪ to generate dar lugar a ▪ dar origen a

to **give safe haven to** dar refugio a ▪ dar abrigo a ▪ dar cobijo a ▪ albergar a

to **give shelter to an orphan** ▪ to take in an orphan ▪ to shelter an orphan albergar a un niño huérfano ▪ acoger a niño huérfano ▪ recoger a un niño huérfano

to **give someone a back scratch** ▪ to scratch someone's back rascarle la espalda a alguien ➤ Would you give me a back scratch? ▪ Would you scratch my back? ¿Me rascas la espalda? ➤ I like to get my back scratched. Me gusta que me rasquen la espalda.

to **give someone a beating** ▪ to trounce someone vapulear a alguien ▪ dar a alguien una paliza

to **give someone a black eye** ponerle un ojo morado a alguien

to **give someone a bloody nose** ▪ to bloody someone's nose hacerle a alguien sangrar por la nariz

to **give someone a blow-by-blow account of something** contarle algo a alguien con pelos y señales

to **give someone a break 1.** dar a alguien un descanso ▪ dar a alguien un recreo ▪ dar a alguien un receso ▪ dar a alguien un respiro ▪ conceder a alguien un descanso ▪ conceder a alguien un recreo ▪ conceder a alguien un receso ▪ conceder a alguien un respiro **2.** dar a alguien su primera gran oportunidad ▪ conceder a alguien su primera gran oportunidad ➤ The professor gave the students a ten-minute break. El catedrático dio un descanso de diez minutos a los estudiantes. ▪ El catedrático concedió un descanso de diez minutos a los estudiantes. ➤ Ed Sullivan gave the Beatles their first big break in the United States. Ed Sullivan le dio a los Beatles su primera gran oportunidad en los Estados Unidos.

to **give someone a chance (to...)** darle a alguien una oportunidad (de...)

to **give someone a cold** contagiarle a alguien un resfriado ▪ darle a alguien un resfriado ▪ pasarle a alguien un resfriado ▪ pegarle a alguien un resfriado ➤ I don't want to give you my cold. ▪ I don't want you to catch my cold. No quiero pegarte mi resfriado. ▪ No quiero contagiarte mi resfriado.

to **give someone a compliment** ▪ to pay someone a compliment hacerle a alguien un cumplido

to **give someone a dirty look** mirarle feo a alguien ▪ ponerle a alguien mala cara ▪ ponerle a alguien cara de pocos amigos

to **give someone a discount** hacerle a alguien un descuento

to **give someone a dose of his own medicine** pagar a alguien con la misma moneda ▪ pagar a alguien en la misma moneda

to **give someone a dressing down** ▪ to chew someone out echar una bronca a alguien ▪ echar un rapapolvo a alguien ➤ The drill sergeant gave the new recruit a dressing down. El sargento instructor echó un rapapolvo al cadete nuevo. ▪ El sargento instructor echó una bronca al cadete nuevo.

to **give someone a fit** poner a alguien con los nervios de punta ➤ The pupil gives his teachers a fit. El alumno pone a sus profesores con los nervios de punta.

to **give someone a gift** ▪ to give someone a present hacerle un regalo a alguien ▪ tener un detalle con alguien ➤ My family wants to give you a gift. Mi familia quiere tener un detalle contigo.

to **give someone a hand 1.** to lend someone a hand echarle una mano a alguien ▪ echarle un cable a alguien **2.** to give someone a round of applause dar un aplauso a alguien ▪ darle una ovación a alguien ➤ Can you give me a hand for a minute? ▪ Can you help me for a minute? ¿Puedes echarme una mano un minuto? ▪ ¿Puedes echarme un cable? ➤ Let's give them a hand. ▪ Let's give them a round of applause. Démosles un aplauso. ▪ Démosles una ovación.

to **give someone a hard time** ▪ to give someone a bad time ▪ to hassle someone fastidiar a alguien ▪ molestar a alguien ▪ *(literary)* darle a alguien a beber hieles

to **give someone a hint 1.** *(suggestion)* darle una pauta ▪ darle a alguien una indirecta **2.** *(clue)* darle a alguien una pista

to **give someone a lecture** sermonear a alguien ▪ venirle uno con sermones ▪ salirle a alguien con sermones ▪ venirle a uno con monsergas ▪ salirle a uno con monsergas ➤ My mother-in-law gives us a lecture when we let the children stay up late. Mi suegra nos viene con monsergas cuando dejamos que los niños estén despiertos hasta tarde.

to **give someone a lift** ▪ to give someone a ride llevar a alguien ▪ acercar a alguien a un sitio ▪ *(L. Am.)* dar a alguien un aventón ▪ *(Sp.)* acercarle a alguien ➤ They gave me a lift to work. Me llevaron a mi trabajo. ➤ Can you give me a ride downtown? ¿Me acercas al centro?

to **give someone a light** darle lumbre a alguien ▪ darle fuego a alguien

to **give someone a line of credit** ▪ to grant someone (a line of) credit ▪ to extend someone (a line of) credit darle a alguien una línea de crédito ▪ otorgarle a alguien una línea de crédito ▪ extenderle a alguien una línea de crédito

to **give someone a lot of crap** *(coarse)* ▪ to give someone a bad time darle a alguien mucha lucha ▪ darle a alguien mucha guerra ▪ darle a alguien muchos pesares

to **give someone a lot of trouble** darle a alguien muchos problemas ▪ darle guerra a alguien ➤ This car has given me a lot of trouble. Este coche me ha dado muchos problemas. ▪ Este coche me ha dado guerra. ➤ One of the students causes a lot of trouble in class. Uno de los estudiantes me da muchos problemas en la clase. ▪ Uno de los estudiantes me da mucha guerra en la clase.

to **give someone a lot to think about** ▪ to give someone much to think about darle a alguien mucho en que pensar ▪ darle a alguien mucho en que cavilar

to **give someone a manicure** hacerle a alguien la manicura ▪ cuidar las manos y las uñas

to **give someone a pat on the back** ▪ to pat someone on the back darle a alguien una palmadita en la espalda

to **give someone a physical (examination)** practicarle a alguien un examen

to **give someone a place to live** poner casa a alguien

to **give someone a present** ▪ to give someone a gift darle un regalo a alguien ▪ regalar algo a alguien ▪ *(Sp.)* tener un detalle con alguien ➤ My family wants to give you a present. Mi familia quiere regalarte algo. ▪ Mi familia quiere tener un detalle contigo.

to **give someone a punch in the nose** ▪ to punch someone in the nose pegarle a alguien un puñetazo en la nariz

to **give someone a raise** subir el sueldo a alguien ▪ subir el salario a alguien

to **give someone a ride somewhere** ▪ to give someone a lift somewhere llevar a alguien a algún sitio ▪ llevar a alguien a algún lugar ▪ acercar a alguien a un sitio ▪ acercar a alguien a un lugar ➤ Could you give me a ride to the airport? ¿Me podrías llevar al aeropuerto? ▪ ¿Me podrías acercar al aeropuerto? ▪ ¿Me acercas al aeropuerto?

to **give someone a ring 1.** *(telephone call)* dar un telefonazo a alguien **2.** *(engagement ring)* darle a alguien un anillo de compromiso

to **give someone a shot** ▪ to give someone an injection aplicarle a alguien una inyección ▪ ponerle a alguien una inyección

to **give someone a shot at it** ▪ to give someone a try hacer la prueba con alguien ➤ Give Mauricio a shot at it. ▪ Give Mauricio a try. Haz la prueba con Mauricio.

to **give someone a spanking** ▪ to tan someone's hide dar a alguien un azote ▪ darle a alguien de azotes ▪ darle a alguien una zurra ▪ darle una azotaina a alguien ▪ darle a alguien de palos ▪ darle a alguien una tunda ➤ I'm going to give you a spanking for... Te voy a dar un palo por...

to **give someone a taste of his own medicine** darle a alguien de su propia medicina

to **give someone a taste of something** darle a alguien a probar algo ➤ I gave her a taste of the cake. Le di a probar el pastel.

to **give someone a ticket (for a violation)** ponerle una multa a alguien

to **give someone a try** ▪ to give someone a shot at it hacer la prueba con alguien ➤ Give Mauricio a try. ▪ Give Mauricio a shot at it. Haz la prueba con Mauricio.

to **give someone (academic) credit for** darle crédito (académico) por

to **give someone an inch and he'll take a mile** darle la mano a alguien y se toma el codo ▪ dar a alguien el pie y se toma la mano

to **give someone an order to do something** darle una orden a alguien para hacer algo ▪ darle una orden a alguien para que haga algo

to **give someone an ultimatum** ▪ to deliver (someone) an ultimatum dar a alguien un ultimátum ▪ plantear a alguien un ultimátum

to **give someone an update** ▪ to bring someone up-to-date poner al corriente a alguien ▪ poner al día a alguien ➤ I just wanted to give you an update. Sólo quería ponerte al corriente. ▪ Sólo quería ponerte al día.

to **give someone away 1.** to reveal someone's secret delatar a alguien **2.** to give away the bride entregar a la novia ▪ llevar a la novia al altar ➤ His accent gives him away. Su acento lo delata. ▪ *(Sp., leísmo)* Su acento le delata. ➤ Her accent gives her away. Su acento la delata. ➤ Your accent gives you away. *(a ti)* Tu acento te delata. ▪ *(a usted)* Su acento lo delata. ▪ *(a usted, Sp., leísmo)* Su acento le delata. ➤ The bride's father gave her away. El padre de la novia la entregó.

to **give someone cardiopulmonary resuscitation** ▪ to give someone CPR ▪ to administer CPR darle a alguien la resucitación cardiopulmonar ▪ darle a alguien la reanimación cardiopulmonar ▪ aplicarle a alguien la resucitación cardiopulmonar

to **give someone confidence** ▪ to instill confidence in someone infundir confianza a alguien

to **give someone credit for a course** darle a alguien crédito por una asignatura ➤ They gave me graduate credit for the course. Me dieron crédito posgrado por el asignatura.

to **give someone credit (where credit is due)** reconocer a alguien (por lo que ha hecho) ➤ I have to give him credit (where credit is due). Tengo que reconocerlo por lo que ha hecho. ▪ *(Sp., leísmo)* Tengo que reconocerle por lo que ha hecho. ➤ I have to give her credit where credit is due. Tengo que reconocerla por lo que ha hecho.

to **give someone free rein to...** dar rienda suelta a alguien para...

to **give someone his due** darle a alguien lo que le corresponde ▪ darle a alguien lo que es de justicia

to **give someone permission to do something** ▪ to grant someone permission to do something darle permiso a alguien para hacer algo ▪ darle permiso a alguien para que haga algo ▪ darle consentimiento a alguien para hacer algo

to **give someone some advice** darle un consejo a alguien

to **give someone something for Christmas** darle a alguien algo por (la) Navidad ▪ regalarle a alguien algo por (la) Navidad

to **give someone something for one's birthday** darle a alguien algo por su cumpleaños ▪ regalarle a alguien algo por su cumpleaños

to **give someone the go-ahead (to do something)** ▪ to give someone the green light (to do something) darle a alguien luz verde (para hacer algo)

to **give someone the benefit of the doubt** conceder a alguien el beneficio de la duda ▪ darle a alguien el beneficio de la duda

to **give someone the boot** ▪ to fire someone ▪ to send someone packing dar puerta a alguien ▪ despedir a alguien ▪ echar a alguien con cajas destempladas ▪ despedir a alguien con cajas destempladas

to **give someone the cold shoulder** hacer el vacío a ▪ darle calabazas a alguien ▪ darle rejalgares

to **give someone the creeps** darle espeluznos a alguien ➤ That guy gives me the creeps. Ese tipo me da espeluznos.

to **give someone the nickname (of)** ponerle a alguien el mote de ▪ imponérsele el mote de ➤ They gave Cervantes the nickname (of) "the one-handed man of Lepanto." Se le impusieron a Cervantes el nombre de "el manco de Lepanto". ➤ They gave him that nickname. Le pusieron ese mote.

to **give someone the runaround** darle largas a alguien ▪ darle evasivas a alguien ▪ darle esquinazo ➤ She keeps giving me the runaround. No deja de darme largas. ▪ No deja de darme evasivas. ▪ Me está dando esquinazo constantemente.

to **give someone the silent treatment** darle a alguien la ley de hielo ▪ dar a alguien la callada por respuesta ▪ darle a alguien la espalda

to **give someone time off** concederle tiempo libre ▪ darle tiempo libre a alguien ➤ They gave me (some) time off at work. Me han concedido tiempo libre en el trabajo. ▪ Me han dado permiso en el trabajo.

to **give someone time off for** concederle tiempo libre para ➤ They gave me time off to go to the wedding. Me concedieron tiempo para ir a la boda.

to **give someone until a certain date to do something** darle a alguien hasta cierta fecha para hacer algo ➤ She gave me until Monday to finish the paper. Me dio hasta el lunes para terminar mi ensayo. ▪ *(Sp.)* Me dio hasta el lunes para terminar mi trabajo.

to **give someone up for dead** dar a alguien por muerto

to **give something a thorough cleaning** ▪ to clean something thoroughly limpiar algo a conciencia

to **give something back to someone** ▪ to return something to someone devolver algo a alguien

to **give testimony** dar testimonio ▪ prestar declaración

to **give the class a new teacher** ▪ to assign the class a new teacher poner un nuevo profesor ➤ They gave us a new teacher. ▪ They assigned us a new teacher. Nos pusieron un professor nuevo.

to **give the class a quiz** poner un examen a la clase ▪ hacer un examen a la clase ➤ The teacher gave us a pop quiz. El profesor nos puso un examen sorpresa.

to **give the impression that...** **1.** to lead one to believe that... ▪ to make one think that... hacer pensar que... ▪ dar que pensar que... **2.** to say in so many words that... ▪ to insinuate that... ▪ to imply that... dar a entender que... ▪ insinuar que...

to **give up** dar por vencido ▪ rendirse ➤ (Do you) give up? *(tú)* ¿Te das por vencido? ▪ ¿Te retiras? ▪ ¿Te rindes? ▪ *(usted)* ¿Se da por vencido? ▪ ¿Se retira? ▪ ¿Se rinde?

to **give up an apartment** *(Mex.)* dejar un departamento ▪ dejar un apartamento ▪ *(L. Am.)* dejar un apartamento ▪ *(Sp.)* dejar un piso ▪ *(large apartment)* dejar un apartamento

to **give up hope (of)** ▪ to lose hope (of) perder las esperanzas (de) ▪ renunciar la esperanza (de)

to **give up power** ▪ to relinquish power ▪ to step aside abandonar el poder ▪ *(colorful)* apearse del burro ➤ He doesn't want to give up power. No quiere abandonar el poder. ▪ No quiere apearse del burro.

to **give up someone for lost** ▪ to give someone up for lost dar a alguien por perdido

to **give up the ghost** entregar el alma

to **give up the idea of** abandonar la idea de

to **give way under the weight of** **1.** *(from the top)* to collapse under the weight of derrumbarse bajo el peso de **2.** *(from the bottom)* to fall out desfondarse bajo el peso de ➤ The suspension bridge gave way under the weight of the pedestrians. El puente colgante se derrumbó bajo el peso de los peatones. ➤ The bottom of the box gave way under the weight of the books. La caja se desfondó bajo el peso de los libros.

to **give way to** dar paso a ▪ ceder el paso a ➤ In 1854 the Missouri Compromise gave way to the new doctrine of popular sovereignty, which made slavery a local option. En 1854 el Compromiso de Misuri dio paso a la nueva doctrina de soberanía popular, la cual hizo la esclavitud una opción local.

to **give way under the weight of** ▪ to collapse under the weight of derrumbarse bajo el peso de ▪ desfondarse bajo el peso de ➤ The suspension bridge gave way under the weight of the pedestrians. El puente colgante se derrumbó bajo el peso de los peatones. ➤ The bottom of the box gave way under the weight of the books. La caja se desfondó bajo el peso de los libros.

to **give weight to someone's opinion** ▪ to lend weight to someone's opinion conceder valor a la opinión de alguien

to **give you an idea of how...** ▪ to give you some idea of how... dejarte ver cómo... ▪ dejarle ver cómo... ➤ This gives you an idea of how... ▪ This gives you some idea of how... Esto te deja ver cómo... ▪ Esto le deja ver cómo...

given situation: in a ~ en una situación determinada

given the chance dado(-a) la oportunidad ▪ si le dan a uno la ocasión

given (the fact) that... ▪ considering... siendo que... ▪ dado que...

given the situation ▪ given the circumstances dadas las circunstancias ▪ así las cosas

to be **given to histrionics** ▪ always to be on stage tener mucho teatro

to be **given to doing something** ser dado a hacer algo ➤ "In Mexico we are very given to making (up) new phrases," said Arturo. "En México somos muy dados a hacer frases nuevas", dijo Arturo.

to be **given to something** ser dado a algo

to be **glad about** alegrarse de

to be **glad (that)...** alegrarse de que... ▪ alegrarle a uno que... ▪ estar contento que... ➤ I'm glad you came. Me alegro de que hayas venido. ▪ Me alegra que hayas venido. ▪ Estoy muy contento(-a) que hayas venido. ➤ We're glad you came. ▪ We're glad you've come. Estamos contentos que hayas venido. ▪ Estamos contentos que (usted) haya venido.

to be **glad to** alegrarle ▪ encantarle ▪ ser un placer ➤ I'd be glad to help you. ▪ I'll be glad to help you. Me encantaría ayudarte. ▪ Será un placer ayudarte. ➤ Would you feed the cat for me while I'm away?-I'd be glad to. ¿Darías de comer al gato mientras estoy ausente?-Me encantaría. ➤ I'm glad to hear it. Me alegra oírlo. ▪ Me alegra oír decirlo.

to be **glad to see someone** alegrarse de ver a alguien

to **glance through it** echarle un vistazo

glaring mistake ▪ glaring error *el* error garrafal

glass sculpture escultura de cristal ▪ talla de cristal

to be **glassed in** estar encerrado en vidrio ▪ estar encerrado en cristal

glazed tile azulejo

glide path *(aviation)* ▪ path followed by an aircraft during final approach to landing senda de planeo

to **glide through the air** planear por el aire

glimmer of hope ▪ ray of hope rayo de esperanza ▪ resquicio de esperanza

to **glisten with tears** brillar de lágrimas ➤ Her eyes were glistening with tears. Sus ojos brillaban de lágrimas.

to **gloat over something** regodearse en algo ▪ regodearse con algo

global warming calentamiento global

globe of the moon ▪ lunar globe globo lunar

globe of the world ▪ terrestrial globe globo terráqueo

glorified version of *la* versión con pretensiones de

Glorious Mysteries *(Catholicism)* Misterios Gloriosos

to **glower at someone** mirar sombríamente a alguien

glue stick pegamento en barra

to be **glued to one's seat** quedarse pegado a la butaca

to be **glued to the TV** estar pegado a la tele

go! *(to the driver of a car)* ¡tira! ▪ ¡vamos!

to **go a step further** ▪ to go one step further dar un paso más

to **go about doing something** ser los pasos para hacer algo ▪ hacer para ➤ I don't know how to go about turning off the software defaults. No sé los pasos para suprimir las configuraciones de serie del ordenador. ▪ No sé la forma de anular las configuraciones de serie. ▪ No sé qué hacer para suprimir las configuraciones de serie del ordenador. ➤ How do you go about renewing a passport? ¿Cuáles son los pasos para renovar un pasaporte? ▪ ¿Qué se hace para renovar un pasaporte? ➤ How do you go about ordering by the case? ¿Cómo se hace para comprar por cajas?

to **go about in search of** ▪ to wander about in search of vagar en busca de ➤ The knights went about in search of the grail. Los caballeros vagaban en busca del grial.

to **go about one's business** ir a lo suyo ▪ estar a lo suyo ➤ The shoppers were just going about their business when all of a sudden there was a lot of commotion. Los clientes iban a lo suyo cuando de repente hubo este gran tumulto. ➤ Go on about your business. *(tú)* Sigue a lo tuyo. ▪ *(usted)* Siga a lo suyo.

■ *(ustedes)* Sigan a lo suyo. ■ *(vosotros)* Seguid a lo vuestro. ➤ I was just going about my business when I heard the sirens. Yo estaba a lo mío cuando oí unas sirenas. ■ Yo iba a lo mío cuando oí unas sirenas.

to **go about something** proceder con algo ➤ I don't know how to go about it. No sé cómo proceder.

to **go abroad** ■ to travel abroad salir al extranjero ■ irse al extranjero ■ viajar al extranjero ➤ We're going abroad this summer. Este verano salimos al extranjero. ➤ Have you ever been abroad? ■ Have you ever traveled abroad? ¿Has salido alguna vez al extranjero?

to **go according to plan** ir (tal y) como estaba planeado ■ ir (tal y) como estaba previsto ➤ If everything goes according to plan, we should finish by April first. Si todo va tal y como estaba planeado, deberíamos acabar para el primero de abril. ■ Si todo va tal y como estaba previsto, deberíamos acabar para el primero de abril.

to **go after 1.** to follow in a sequence seguir **2.** to pursue ■ to chase perseguir ■ ir tras ■ correr tras ■ salir en la persecución de ■ *(Sp.)* ir a por ➤ The cops went after the bank robbers. La poli persiguió a los atracadores del banco. ■ La poli fue tras los atracadores del banco. ■ La poli corrió tras los atracadores del banco.

to **go against** ir en contra de

to **go against the grain** ir contra la corriente ■ ir contra corriente ■ ir a contra corriente

to **go ahead and cry** ándale, llora ■ *(Peru, coll.)* dále, llora no más ■ dále no más, llora si quieres

to **go ahead and do something** meterse a fondo con ➤ I'd like to go ahead and pay for this. Me gustaría meterme a fondo con el pago de esto.

(go ahead), make my day! *(Clint Eastwood in movie role as Harry Callahan)* ¡alégrame el día!

to **go ahead with** seguir adelante con

to **go all out** ■ to shoot the moon ■ to put the big pot in the little one echar la casa por la ventana ■ tirar la casa por la ventana

to **go all out for something** ir a por todas por algo ■ batirse el cobre por algo ■ batirse en duelo por algo

to **go alone** ■ to go by oneself ir solo ■ asistir solo ➤ I went to the movies by myself. ■ I went to the movies alone. Fui yo solo a la cine.

to **go along with anything** conformarse con cualquier cosa

to **go along with something** conformarse con algo ➤ We have to go along with it. No hay más que conformarnos.

to **go along with what someone is saying** *(with feigned interest or agreement)* seguirle a la corriente de alguien

to **go along with someone's doing** seguirle haciendo algo

to **go (and) get something** ir a buscar algo

go and see if *(tú)* ve(te) a ver si ■ *(usted)* váyase a ver si

to **go around** dar la vuelta ■ dar una vuelta ➤ We went around the traffic circle and exited onto Rhode Island Avenue. Dimos la vuelta a la rotonda y salimos a la Avenida Rhode Island.

go around: to be enough to ~ haber suficiente para todos ➤ Is there enough champagne to go around? ¿Hay suficiente cava para todos? ➤ Are there enough mashed potatoes to go around? ¿Hay suficiente puré de papas para todos? ■ *(Sp.)* ¿Hay suficiente puré de patatas para todos?

to **go around in a circle** to revolve dar vueltas ➤ The merry-go-round goes around in a circle. El tiovivo da vueltas.

to **go around someone 1.** to walk around someone rodear a alguien **2.** to go around someone who is blocking your intention saltarse a alguien

to **go around the block** dar la vuelta a la manzana

to **go around the world** dar la vuelta al mundo ■ ir alrededor del mundo

to **go as a guest** ir de invitado(-a) ■ asistir (en carácter) de invitado(-a)

to **go as far as** llegar hasta ■ ir hasta

to **go ashore** desembarcar

to **go astray 1.** *(animal)* to stray perderse ■ descarriarse **2.** *(person)* to get lost extraviarse ■ perderse **3.** *(morally)* to go bad ir por mal camino

to **go at a gallop** ir galopando

to **go at high speed** ■ to travel at high speed circular a alta velocidad ➤ The car was going over 160 kph. El coche circulaba a más de 160 kph. ➤ Spain has eighteen Ave trains designed to go at 300 kph. España cuenta con dieciocho trenes Ave diseñados para circular a 300 kph.

to **go at it** ya estar (con) ■ ya estar en ello ➤ The dog and the cat are going at it again. Ya están otra vez el perro y el gato. ➤ The kids with the new video game are really going at it. Ya están los niños con el nuevo videojuego. ➤ My neighbors were really going at it last night. Anoche ya estaban mis vecinos en ello.

go away! ■ beat it! ■ scram! ■ get lost! ¡lárgate! ■ ¡vete! ■ ¡vade retro! ■ ¡multiplícate por cero!

to **go away 1.** to leave salir **2.** *(headache, etc.)* to subside irse ➤ We're going away for the weekend. Vamos a salir durante el fin de semana. ➤ I wish my headache would go away. Ojalá se fuera el dolor de cabeza.

to **go away empty-handed** retirarse con las manos vacías ■ marcharse con las manos vacías

to **go away sulking** alejarse enfurruñado(-a)

to **go awry** desquiciarse ➤ Children love for everything to go awry. A los niños les encanta que todo se desquicie.

to **go back a long time** ■ to go back a long way venir de largo

to **go back and forth** ir y venir ■ pasarse yendo y viniendo ➤ Henry goes back and forth from his room to the bathroom for an hour. Henry se pasa una hora yendo y viniendo de su habitación al baño. ■ Henry va y viene durante una hora de su habitación al baño.

to **go back in time** ■ to turn back the clock volver el tiempo atrás

to **go back on one's word** ■ to break one's promise faltar a su palabra ■ faltar a su promesa ■ incumplir un compromiso ■ incumplir con su promesa

to **go back over one's steps** ■ to retrace one's steps desandar el camino ■ deshacer el camino

to **go back to** ■ to date from ■ to date back to remontarse a ➤ The present conflict goes back to January of last year. El conflicto actual se remonta a enero del año pasado.

to **go back to one's old tricks** volver a hacer las suyas

to **go back to one's old ways** volver a las andadas

to **go back to square one** ■ to start over from the (very) beginning revertir al punto de partida ■ volver a empezar desde el principio

to **go back to the beginning** ■ to return to the beginning volver al comienzo

to **go back to the time when...** remontar a los tiempos en que...

to **go bad 1.** to spoil echar a perder ■ ponerse malo **2.** *(milk)* to (go) sour cortarse la leche **3.** to go kaput ■ to fail descomponerse **4.** to turn corrupt volverse corrupto ■ ir por mal camino ➤ The turkey will keep for two or three days in the refrigerator before it goes bad. ■ The turkey will keep for two or three days before it turns bad. El pavo aguantará dos o tres días en el frigorífico hasta que se eche a perder. ➤ The milk's gone bad. ■ The milk's gone sour. Se ha cortado la leche. ➤ The brakes went bad on the truck. Los frenos de la camión se descompusieron. ➤ He was a good cop gone bad. Fue un buen policía que se volvió corrupto.

to **go badly** andar mal

to **go bald** quedarse calvo

to **go bar hopping** ir de bareo ■ ir de tascas ■ tasquear ■ *(Sp., colorful)* hacer el viacrucis

to **go barreling down the street** ir embalado por la calle ➤ The cars go barreling down Don Sancho Ave. at eighty kilometers per hour. Los coches van embalados por Avda. Don Sancho a ochenta kilómetros por hora.

to **go before the judge** presentarse ante el juez

to **go berserk 1.** *(humans)* cruzársele los cables **2.** *(cats, especially)* pasárselo pipa ➤ The guy went berserk and started shooting at people. Al tío se le cruzaron los cables y empezó a disparar a la gente. ➤ The cats are going berserk. Los gatos se lo están pasando pipa.

to **go beyond** ir más allá de ■ pasar los límites de

to **go bicycle riding** ■ to go bike riding andar en bicicleta

to **go boating** ir a dar un paseo en bote
to **go both ways** ■ to be AC-DC ■ to be bisexual hacer a todo ■ ser bisexual
to **go bowling** ■ to bowl jugar al boliche ■ *(Sp.)* jugar a los bolos
to **go blind** ■ to lose one's eyesight quedarse ciego ■ perder la vista
to **go by** ■ to be called llamarse ■ le dicen a uno ➤ My name is Maxwell but I go by Max. Me llamo Maxwell pero me llaman Max. ■ Me llamo Maxwell pero me dicen Max.
to **go by bus** ir en autobús
to **go by car** ir en coche
to **go by in the car** ■ to drive by *(L. Am.)* pasar con el carro ■ *(Sp.)* pasar con el coche
to **go by sea** ir por mar
to **go by someone** ■ to walk past someone ■ to pass by someone pasar por el lado de alguien ➤ She went by me without speaking. Pasó por mi lado sin saludarme.
to **go by taxi** ■ to take a taxi ir en taxi
to **go by the board** ■ to go by the wayside ir al trasto
to **go by the book** ■ to adhere to the letter ■ to play (strictly) by the rules ceñirse a la letra ■ actuar según las reglas ■ proceder según el reglamento ➤ You won't be able to convince the judge. He always goes by the book. No podrás convencer al juez. Siempre se ciñe a la letra.
to **go by the wayside** ■ to go by the board ir al trasto
to **go by train** ir en tren
to **go by way of** ir por
to **go crazy** ■ to become crazy volverse loco ■ chiflarse ➤ I'm going crazy. Me vuelvo loco. ■ Me chiflo.
to **go dancing** ir a bailar ■ *(colorful)* mover el esqueleto
to **go deaf** ■ to lose one's hearing quedarse sordo
to **go deep into debt** ■ to saddle oneself with debt cargarse de deudas
to **go directly to...** ■ to go straight to... ir derecho a...
to **go do something** ir a hacer algo
to **go down a street** **1.** to take a street tirar una calle **2.** to go along a street enfilar una calle ➤ Go down that street! ■ Take that street! *(tú)* ¡Tira esa calle! ■ *(usted)* ¡Tire esa calle! ➤ The procession is going down Toledo Street. ■ The procession is going along Toledo Street. La procesión está enfilando la Calle Toledo.
to **go down in history as** pasar a la historia como ■ pasar a la posteridad como
to **go downhill** ■ to decline ir cuesta abajo
to **go down(stairs) to do something** bajar a hacer algo ■ bajar para hacer algo ➤ She went down(stairs) to get the mail. Ella bajó a buscar el correo. ■ Ella bajó para buscar el correo. ■ *(Sp.)* Ella bajó a coger el correo. ■ Ella bajó para coger el correo.
to **go downtown** ir al centro
to **go Dutch** ■ to each pay one's own tab pagar cada uno lo suyo ■ pagar cada quien lo suyo ■ *(Sp.)* ir a la americana ➤ Let's go Dutch. Que cada uno paga lo suyo.
to **go even further** ir todavía más allá ➤ *(news item)* The ambassador went even further and confirmed that the existence of weapons of mass destruction was the principal reason Spain supported the war. El embajador fue todavía más allá y confirmó que la existencia de armas de destrucción masiva fue la razón principal que indujo a España a apoyar la guerra.
to **go further** llegar más lejos ➤ *(ad)* Make your money go further. Haga que su dinero llegue más lejos.
to **go fifty-fifty** ■ to go halves ir a medias
go fly a kite! ■ go jump in a lake! ■ (go) take a flying leap! ■ go take a hike! *(tú)* ¡vete a paseo! ■ ¡vete a freír espárragos! ■ *(usted)* ¡váyase usted a paseo! ■ ¡vayase a freír espárragos!
to **go flying by** pasar embalado ■ pasar volando
to **go flying through the air** salir despedido por los aires
to **go for a cup of coffee** ■ to go have a cup of coffee ir por un café ■ ir a tomar un café ■ *(Sp.)* ir a por un café ➤ Do you want to go for a cup of coffee? ¿Quieres ir a tomar un café? ■ ¿Quieres ir a por un café? ➤ Do we have time to go for a cup of coffee? ¿Tenemos tiempo de ir a tomar un café? ■ ¿Tenemos tiempo para ir a tomar un café? ■ ¿Nos da tiempo ir a tomar un café?
to **go for a drive** dar un paseo en coche
to **go for a ride** dar un paseo en coche
to **go for a second helping** ■ to go for seconds repetir ➤ I'd like to go for a second helping. Me gustaría repetir. ➤ Don't hesitate to go for seconds. No dudes en repetir.
to **go for a swim** ■ to go swimming ir a nadar ➤ Let's go for a swim. Vamos a nadar.
to **go for a walk** ■ to take a walk (ir a) dar un paseo ■ ir de paseo ■ ir a dar una vuelta
to **go for broke** ■ to use all of one's available resources jugarse el todo por el todo
to **go for days on** estarse días con ■ tirarse días con ■ pasarse días con ➤ I could go for days on this subject. Yo podría estarme días con este tema.
go for it! *(L. Am.)* ¡ve por ello! ■ *(Sp.)* ¡a por ello! ■ ¡échale el lazo! ■ ¡lánzate a por ello(-a)!
to **go for months on** estar meses con ■ pasar meses con ➤ Mark Twain said he could go for months on a good compliment. Mark Twain dijo que podía estar meses con un buen cumplido. ■ Mark Twain dijo que podía pasar meses con un buen cumplido.
to **go for one's gun** echar la mano a la pistola
to **go for the first time** ■ to visit for the first time ir por primera vez ■ ir a conocer ➤ When we went for the first time to the Smithsonian Air and Space Museum... Cuando fuimos por primera vez al Museo del Aire y el Espacio Smithsonian... ■ Cuando fuimos a conocer el Museo del Aire y el Espacio Smithsonian...
to **go for weeks on** estarse semanas con ■ tirarse semanas con ■ pasarse semanas con
to **go free** salir en libertad ■ quedar libre
to **go from bad to worse** ir de mal en peor
to **go from the frying pan to the fire** saltar de la sartén y dar en las brasas *("Sartén" is masculine in some parts of South America.)*
to **go from one end to the other** ir de un extremo a otro
to **go from one extreme to the other** ir de un extremo a otro ■ pasar de un extremo a otro
to **go from tree to tree** ir de árbol en árbol ■ *(literary)* recorrer los árboles uno por uno ➤ Horacio Quiroga's lazy bee went from tree to tree to drink the nectar of the blossoms. La abeja haragana de Horacio Quiroga recorría los árboles uno por uno para tomar el jugo de las flores.
to **go from *x* to *y*** ir de *x* a *y* ■ pasar de *x* a *y* ➤ Thanks to a repair, the tilt of the Leaning Tower of Pisa has gone from 6 to 5.5 degrees. Gracias a una reforma, el desnivel de la torre inclinada de Pisa ha pasado de 6 a 5,5 grados.
to **go full speed** ir a toda velocidad ■ ir a toda pastilla ■ dar caña ■ meter caña
to **go further** **1.** to add something to what someone has said ir más lejos **2.** to top something someone has said superar algo que ha dicho alquien ➤ The president went further: "This kind of incident is not a positive step in relations between our countries." El presidente fue más allá: "Este tipo de incidentes no supone un avance constructivo en las relaciones entre nuestros paises".
to **go get something** ir a buscar algo ■ *(Sp.)* ir a por algo ➤ I've got to go get my shirts from the cleaners. Voy a buscar mis camisas en la tintorería. ■ Voy a la lavandería a por mis camisas.
go-getter *el, la* buscavidas
go! go! go! go! ¡venga! ¡venga! ¡venga! ¡venga!
to **go great guns** ir que arde ■ *(off-color, but very common)* ir de puta madre
to **go grocery shopping** ■ to go to the grocery store ir a hacer la compra ➤ I'm going grocery shopping. Voy a hacer la compra.
to **go guy hunting** *(Sp.)* ■ to cat around irse de picos pardos
to **go halves** ■ to go fifty-fifty ■ to split the bill ir mitad y mitad ■ ir a medias ■ *(Sp.)* ir a pachas ■ *(Mex., coll.)* irse a michas ➤ Javier and Daniel went halves to buy a present for their parents. ■ Javier and Daniel went halves to buy their parents a present. Javier y Daniel fueron a medias para comprarle un regalo a sus padres.
to **go hand in glove** venir como anillo al dedo
to **go hand in hand (with)** **1.** *(literal)* ir mano a mano (con) **2.** *(figurative)* ir acompañado (de) ➤ Democratic reform must

go hand in hand with economic reform. La reforma democrática debe ir acompañado de la reforma económica.

to **go have a cup of coffee** ■ to go for a cup of coffee ir a tomar un café ■ *(Sp.)* ir a por un café ➤ Do you want to go have a cup of coffee? ■ Do you want to go for a cup of coffee? ¿Quieres ir a tomar un café? ■ ¿Tomamos un café? ■ ¿Tomamos un cafetito?

to **go hiking** ■ to go on a hike ■ to hike hacer senderismo ■ ir de excursión ➤ We went hiking in the Pyrenees. Fuimos de excursión a Pirineos.

to **go home** ir a casa ➤ I'm going home. Voy a casa. ➤ I'm going home at six o'clock. (Me) voy a casa a las seis. ■ Me vuelvo a casa a las seis. ➤ I'm going home for Christmas, with my suitcase full of turron(es). Vuelvo a casa por Navidad, con la maleta llena de turrón.

to **go hungry** ■ to suffer (from) hunger ■ to starve pasar hambre ■ padecer hambre

to **go hunting** ir de caza ■ salir a cazar

to **go in on** ■ to go in together on ■ to chip in on ■ to share the cost of ir a pachas ■ ir a medias ■ pagar a partes iguales

to **go in one ear and out the other** entrar por un oído y salir por el otro

to **go in pairs** ir en parejas

to **go in the direction of** ■ to go toward(s) ir hacia ■ ir de rumbo a ■ ir en la dirección de

to **go into 1.** to enter meterse en ■ entrar en **2.** to get involved in dedicarse a ■ adentrarse en ➤ He went into the kitchen. Se metió en la cocina. ➤ Have you thought of going into politics? ¿Se te ha ocurrido dedicarse a la política?

to **go into a spin** *(aviation)* ■ to get into a spin entrar en barrena ■ caer en barrena

to **go into a subject** ■ to get into a subject meterse en un tema ➤ In class today, we got into the polemic between Domingo Faustino Sarmiento and Andrés Bello. En la clase hoy, nos metimos en el tema de la polémica entre Domingo Faustino Sarmiento y Andrés Bello. ➤ Let's not go into that subject. ■ Let's not get into that subject. No nos metamos en esa tema. ➤ I don't want to go into it. ■ I don't want to go into that. No quiero entrar en detalles.

to **go into battle** partir a la batalla

to **go into business for oneself** montar un negocio por cuenta propia ■ montar un negocio por su propia cuenta

to **go into detail** ■ to go into the details ■ to get into details ■ to go into the particulars entrar en (los) detalles pormenorizar ■ entrar en pormenores ■ extenderse ➤ You don't need to go into detail. No hay que pormenorizar. ■ No hace falta que pormenorices.

to **go into effect** *(law)* ■ to take effect entrar en vigor

to **go into exile** marcharse al exilio

to **go into politics** ■ to enter politics ■ to get into politics adentrarse en la política ■ entrar en política ■ meterse en pólitica

to **go into the kitchen** ■ to go in the kitchen meterse en la cocina ■ entrar en la cocina

to **go it alone** montárselo por su cuenta

go jump in a lake! ■ go fly a kite! ■ go take a flying leap! ■ go take a hike! *(tú)* vete a paseo ■ vete a freír espárragos ■ *(usted)* váyase usted a paseo ■ váyase a freír espárragos

to **go like a bat outta hell** ir a toda hostia ■ ir como alma que lleva el diablo

to **go like a lamb to the slaughter** ir como oveja al matadero

to **go looking for a good time** irse de picos pardos

go, man, go! ¡dale, macho!

to **go mountain climbing** ir a hacer alpinismo

to **go meet someone** ir a esperar a alguien ■ ir al encuentro de alguien

to **go nuts** volverse loco ■ volverse chiflado ■ estar como una cabra

to **go off 1.** *(electricity, telephone)* cortarse **2.** *(alarm)* sonar **3.** *(gun)* dispararse **4.** *(bomb)* explotar ■ detonar **5.** to wander off marcharse ➤ The phone went off today. Hoy se cortó el teléfono. ➤ The alarm went off at 7 a.m. La alarma sonó a las siete de la mañana. ➤ The gun went off accidentally. La pistola se disparó accidentalmente. ➤ A bomb just went off. Una bomba acaba de explotar. ➤ The dog went off this morning and hasn't come home. El perro se marchó esta mañana y no ha regresado. ■ El perro se marchó esta mañana y no ha vuelto.

to **go off on a tangent** salirse por una tangente ■ irse por una tangente ■ salir por peteneras ■ irse por las ramas ■ *(L. Am.)* irse por los imbornales

to **go off on one's own** ir a su aire

to **go on 1.** to take place ■ to happen haber ■ suceder **2.** to act on ■ to follow actuar ■ empezar a trabajar **3.** to continue ■ to keep on ■ to carry on seguir ■ continuar ➤ As we walked through Salamanca on Saturday, there was a wedding going on in almost every church. Según paseábamos el sábado por Salamanca, había una boda prácticamente en cada iglesia. ➤ Does that go on in Spain? ¿Hay de eso en España? ➤ This has been going on ever since I've lived here. Esto lleva sucediendo desde que vivo aquí. ➤ The police don't have any leads to go on. ■ The police have no leads to go on. La policía no tiene pistas con las que actuar. ➤ Her support gave me the courage to go on. ■ Her support gave me the courage to continue. ■ Her support gave me the courage to keep on. ■ Her support gave me the courage to carry on. Su apoyo me dio el coraje para seguir.

to **go on a diet** ponerse a régimen ■ ponerse a dieta ■ hacer dietas

to **go on a hike** ■ to go hiking ir de caminata ■ ir de senderismo ■ hacer senderismo

to **go on a pilgrimage** ir de peregrinación ■ ir en romería

to **go on a tour of** ■ to take a tour of hacer un recorrido de

to **go on about one's business** seguir con lo suyo

to **go on and on** hablar sin parar ■ seguir dale que dale ■ seguir dale que te pego ■ comer lengua ■ *(archaic)* dar al manubrio

to **go on and on about something** hablar sin parar sobre algo ■ seguir dale que dale (hablando) sobre algo ■ seguir dale que te pego (hablando) sobre algo ■ soltar una parrafada sobre algo

to **go on doing something** seguir haciendo algo

to **go on foot** ■ to walk ir de pie ■ ir a pie ■ ir andando ■ ir caminando ➤ We're going to walk (the distance). ■ We're going to go on Shank's pony. Vamos de pie. ■ Vamos a ir en el coche de San Fernando.

to **go on for a long time** ir para largo ➤ Her treatments for rheumatoid arthritis will go on for a long time. Sus tratamientos para el reumo van para largo.

to **go on for a while** seguir durante un tiempo ➤ The insurgency could go on for a while. La insurgencia podría seguir durante un tiempo. ➤ It looks like Fidel could go on for a while. Me parece que Fidel tiene cuerda para rato.

go on, I'm listening *(tú)* adelante, te escucho ■ *(usted)* adelante, le escucho

to **go on like this** seguir así ➤ We can't go on like this anymore. Ya no podemos seguir así. ➤ I can't go on like this. No puedo seguir así.

to **go on living** seguir viviendo

to **go on Shank's pony** *(humorous)* to walk (as opposed to riding) ■ to go on foot ir en el coche de San Fernando ➤ I went on Shank's pony. ■ I walked. Fui en el coche de San Fernando (un rato a pie y otro rato caminando).

to **go on sick leave** ■ to be out on sick leave darse de baja

to **go on (stage)** subir al escenario ■ *(colorful)* pisar las tablas ➤ Tell Miss Cruz she goes on in five minutes. Dígale a la Srta. Cruz que sube al escenario en cinco minutos.

to **go on the air** entrar en antena

to **go on to become** llegar a ser

to **go on to do something** pasar a hacer algo ➤ Many employees go on to occupy higher positions in the company. Muchos empleado pasan a ocupar más altos en la compañía.

to **go on to something else** pasar a otra cosa

to **go on to talk about** pasar a hablar de

to **go on to the next thing** pasar a lo siguiente

to **go on with** ■ to continue with proseguir con

to **go one step at a time** ir por partes ➤ Let's go one step at a time. Vamos por partes.

to **go one step further** ■ to go a step further dar un paso más

to **go one's own way** seguir de largo ■ ir por su camino ■ hacer rancho aparte ➤ Let them go their own way, and we'll go ours. Deje que vayan por su camino y nosotros iremos por el nuestro.

to **go one's separate ways** irse cada uno por su lado ➤ They went their separate ways. Se fueron cada uno por su lado. ➤ We went our separate ways. Nos fuimos cada uno por su lado.

go open the door (for someone) vete a abrir

to **go out 1.** to leave salir **2.** to go off apagarse ➤ They went out for supper. Salieron a cenar. ➤ The lights just went out. ■ The lights just went off. Se apagaron las luces.

to **go out for a walk** salir a dar un paseo ■ salir de paseo ■ salir de vuelta ■ *(L. Am.)* salir a caminar

to **go out for breakfast** salir a desayunar ■ desayunar fuera

to **go out for dinner** *(afternoon)* salir a comer (fuera) ■ comer fuera ■ ir a comer fuera ■ *(evening)* salir a cenar (fuera) ■ cenar fuera ■ salir a cenar ■ ir a cenar fuera ➤ We're going out for dinner. Vamos a comer fuera.

to **go out for lunch** salir a comer

to **go out for some fresh air** salir a tomar aire fresco ■ salir a tomar el aire ■ salir a tomar el fresco

to **go out for something** ■ to go out to get something salir a la calle para algo ➤ Alberto went out for some bread. ■ Alberto went out to get some bread. Alberto salió a la calle para comprar el pan.

to **go out for supper** salir a cenar (fuera) ■ cenar fuera ■ ir a cenar fuera

to **go out in the sun** ponerse al sol ➤ I should know better than to go out in the sun without sunscreen. Cómo se me ocurre ponerme al sol sin protector solar. ■ Vaya idea la mía de ponerme al sol sin protector solar.

to **go out into the street** salir a la calle

to **go out of business** ■ to fold ■ to go under ■ *(factory)* to shut down quebrar ■ cerrar

to **go out of control** perder control ➤ The car went out of control on the ice. El carro perdió el control en el hielo. ■ *(Sp.)* El coche perdió control en el hielo.

to **go out of one's way to 1.** salir de su camino para **2.** to upset one's routine volcarse para

to **go out of style** ■ to be going out of style ■ to be on the way out pasar de moda

to **go out of turn** saltarse el turno ■ arrancar ante del tiempo

to **go out on the town** salir a la calle ■ ir de juerga

to **go out for something** salir a la calle para algo ➤ Cesar went out to get some bread. Cesar salió a la calle para comprar el pan.

to **go out without a coat** ■ to go outside without a coat salir a cuerpo gentil

to **go outside** salir al exterior

to **go outside without a coat** ■ to go out without a coat salir sin abrigo ■ salir a cuerpo gentil

to **go over** ■ to review recorrer ■ repasar ■ revisar

to **go over a fence** *(like a baseball or Frisbee)* colarse al otro lado de una varra ➤ The baseball went over the fence. El béisbol se coló al otro lado de la varra.

to **go over someone's head 1.** ir por sobre la autoridad de alguien **2.** ir más allá de la comprensión de alguien

to **go over something with a fine-tooth comb** mirar algo con lupa

to **go over to the enemy** pasarse al enemigo

to **go overboard 1.** *(literal)* to fall into the water caerse al agua **2.** *(figurative)* to do more than required pasarse

to **go partying** ir de pachanga

go prepared vete preparado

to **go right by someone (without acknowledging)** pasar a alguien de largo ➤ She went right by me. Me pasó de largo.

to **go right to the point** ■ to get right to the point ir directo al grano

to **go running around** ir y venir de un lado para otro

to **go sailing** hacer regata ■ hacer vela

(go) see who's at the door mira quién ha llamado

to **go shopping** ir de compras ■ *(Sp., for groceries)* to go grocery shopping ir a hacer la compra

to **go sightseeing** hacer turismo

to **go sleigh riding** ir a tirarse en trineo ■ ir a pasear en trineo ➤ We're going sleigh riding. Vamos a tirarnos en trineo.

to **go slowly** ■ to go slow ir despacio

to **go smoothly (for one)** ■ to go without a hitch desenvolverse sin incidente ■ desenvolverse con normalidad ■ desenvolverse sin contratiempos ■ venirle rodado algo a alguien

to **go so far as to mention** llegar a mencionar

to **go so far as to say that...** llegar hasta el extremo de decir que... ■ llegar a decir que... ➤ I'd go so far as to say that... Llegaría a decir que...

to **go so far as to tell someone that...** llegar a decirle a alguien que... ➤ She went so far as to tell me that... Ella llegó a decirme que...

to **go so long without...** aguantar tanto tiempo sin... ➤ The trapped miners can only go so long without food. Los mineros atrapados sólo pueden aguantar tanto tiempo sin comida.

to **go sour** *(milk, cream, etc.)* ■ to turn sour ■ to curdle ■ to go off cortarse ➤ The milk has gone sour. Se ha cortado la leche.

go stand in the hall! ¡vete al pasillo!

to **go steady** andar de novios ➤ José and Carol are going steady. José y Carol andan de novios.

to **go straight (ahead)** ■ to keep going straight ahead tirar adelante ■ seguir todo derecho ■ seguir todo recto ➤ Go straight ahead. ■ Keep going straight (ahead). Tira adelante.

to **go straight to...** ■ to go directly to... ir derecho a...

to **go straight to bed** irse directamente a la cama

to **go straight towards** dirigirse directamente hacia ➤ We went straight towards them. Nos dirigimos directamente hacia ellos. ➤ She went straight towards them. Ella se dirigió directamente hacia ellos.

go tell it to the marines! ¡cuéntaselo a tu abuelita! ■ ¡a otro perro con ese hueso!

to **go that way** ir por allí ■ ir por ese camino ■ ir por ese lado

to **go the extra mile** hacer la segunda milla

to **go the other way** ■ to go in the opposite direction ■ to travel in the opposite direction ■ to move in the opposite direction ir por el sentido contrario ■ circular por el sentido contrario ➤ *(news item about an accident)* At that moment, the concrete mixer was going the other way. En ese momento, la hormigonera iba por el sentido contrario.

to **go the same route** ir por el mismo camino

to **go the wrong way 1.** to take the wrong route equivocarse de camino **2.** to go the wrong way on a one-way street equivocarse de sentido

to **go this way** ir por aquí ■ ir por este camino ■ por este lado ➤ Let's go this way. Vamos por este lado.

to **go through 1.** *(phone call)* comunicar **2.** *(electronic transaction)* hacerse efectivo ➤ The call didn't go through. La llamada no comunicó. ➤ The funds transfer didn't go through. La transferencia de fondos no se hizo efectiva.

to **go through a phase in which...** *(coll.)* ■ to go through a phase where... pasar por una etapa en la que...

to **go through a process** pasar por un proceso

to **go through an experience** vivir una experience ➤ *(bride's father, referring to the wedding)* I've just been through one. Acabo de vivir una.

to **go through an ordeal** pasar por una dura prueba

to **go through customs** pasar la aduana ■ cruzar la aduana

to **go through hardship(s)** ■ to undergo hardship(s) ■ to suffer hardship(s) ■ to experience hardship(s) pasar por grandes penas ■ pasar por momentos muy duros

to **go through hell** *(coarse)* pasarlas más putas que Caín ■ pasarlas putas

to **go through it** *(a document)* darle la vuelta ➤ We just need to go through it and fill it in. Sólo hay que darle la vuelta para rellenarlo.

to **go through one's mind** pasar por su mente ➤ What went through your mind when...? ¿Qué pasó por tu mente cuándo...?

to **go through (proper) channels** seguir los cauces reglamentarios

to **go through the roof 1.** *(prices, blood pressure, etc.)* to go sky high ponerse por las nubes **2.** *(person)* to lose one's temper perder los estribos ➤ At Christmas, the price of seafood goes through the roof. En la navidad el marisco se pone por las nubes. ➤ The boss went through the roof today. El jefe perdió sus estribos hoy. ▪ El jefe estaba que trinaba hoy.

to **go to a lot of trouble to do something** tomarse muchas molestias para hacer algo ➤ He went to a lot of trouble to persuade him. Se tomó muchas molestias para persuadirlo. ▪ *(Sp., leísmo)* Se tomó muchas molestias para persuadirle. ➤ He went to a lot of trouble to persuade her. Se tomó muchas molestias para persuadirla. ▪ *(Sp., leísmo)* Se tomó muchas molestias para persuadirle.

to **go to a play** ir a ver una obra de teatro ▪ ir a ver una obra teatral ▪ ir al teatro

to **go to bed hungry** acostarse con hambre ➤ *(headline)* A billion people go to bed hungry every night Mil millones de personas se acuestan todas las noches con hambre

to **go to bed with the chickens** ▪ to go to bed early acostarse con las gallinas

to **go to confession** ir a confesar

to **go to court 1.** acudir a los tribunales **2.** ir a juicio ➤ *(headline)* Bush goes to court to prevent another recount by hand Bush acude a los tribunales para impedir un nuevo recuento a mano

to **go to any lengths to** ▪ to do anything to ▪ to do anything in order to estar dispuesto a todo con tal de ➤ She'll go to any lengths to save her father. Está dispuesta a todo con tal de salvar a su padre.

to **go to bat for someone** ▪ to intercede on behalf of someone ▪ to intercede on someone's behalf dar la cara por alguien ▪ interceder por alguien

go to bed! ¡vete a la cama!

to **go to bed** ▪ to turn in ir a la cama ▪ acostarse ➤ It's midnight; I'm going to bed. Es medianoche, voy a la cama. ▪ Es medianoche, voy a acostarme.

to **go to bed with the chickens** ▪ to go to bed early acostarse con las gallinas ▪ acostarse a la hora de las gallinas

to **go to great lengths to do something** tomarse mucha molestia para hacer algo ▪ tocar muchas teclas para hacer algo ▪ tocar muchas teclas para lograr algo

to **go to great pains to do something** ▪ to take great pains to do something esmerarse en hacer algo ➤ The boy went to great pains to make the airplane model look completely authentic. El chico se esmeró en hacer que la maqueta de la avioneta pareciera auténtica.

to **go to heaven** ganarse la gloria ▪ ganarse el cielo

go to hell! ¡vete al diablo! ▪ *(benign alternative)* ¡vete a freír espárragos!

to **go to one's head** írsele a subir a la cabeza ▪ subírsele a la cabeza ➤ Success isn't going to go to our heads. El éxito no nos va a subir a la cabeza. ➤ The wine goes to her head. El vino se le sube a la cabeza.

to **go to pieces** quedar deshecho(-a)

to **go to press** ir a la imprenta

to **go to sea** hacerse a la mar

to **go to sleep 1.** to fall asleep irse a dormir **2.** *(arm, leg)* to get numb from reduced circulation dormírsele ➤ My arm has gone to sleep. Se me ha dormido el brazo.

to **go to seed** *(old neighborhood)* ▪ to go down ▪ to decline venir a menos

to **go to someone** ir con alguien ➤ You must go to him. Debes ir con él.

to **go to someone for something** ▪ to turn to someone for something recurrir a alguien para algo ▪ acudir a alguien para algo ➤ I went to my friend to ask him to fill in for me. Recurrí a mi amigo para pedirle que me supliera.

to **go to someone's house** ir a casa de alguien *("Casa" refers to living quarters, usually an apartment. A freestanding house is "un chalet.")*

to **go to such lengths to** llegar a tanto para

to **go to the boss** ▪ to take one's case to the boss ▪ to appeal to the boss escalar al jefe

to **go to the dogs** venirse abajo ▪ echarse a los perros

to **go to the grocery store** ▪ to go grocery shopping ir a hacer la compra ➤ I'm going to the grocery store. Voy a hacer la compra.

to **go to the movies** ir al cine

to **go to the polls** acudir a las urnas

to **go to town 1.** to go downtown ir al centro **2.** to go great guns ir a lo grande ➤ I'm going to town this afternoon. ▪ I'm going downtown this afternoon. Voy al centro esta tarde. ➤ The kids are really going to town on the ice cream. ▪ The kids are going great guns on the ice cream. Los peques van a lo grande con el helado.

to **go to the trouble to...** ▪ to take the trouble to... tomarse el trabajo de... ➤ I went to the trouble to fix them lunch, and then they didn't want to stay. Me tomé el trabajo de preparar su almuerzo, y luego no quisieron quedarse.

to **go to waste** ▪ to be thrown away unused desperdiciarse ➤ Don't let food go to waste. No permitas que la comida se desperdicie.

to **go together 1.** to accompany each other ir juntos ▪ acompañarse **2.** to go steady andar de novios **3.** to complement each other combinar bien ▪ hacer conjunto ➤ We went to the movies together. Fuimos juntos al cine. ➤ Frank and Elizabeth are going together. Paco e Isabel andan de novios. ➤ The tie goes with the shirt. ▪ The tie and the shirt go together. La corbata y la chaqueta combinan bien. ▪ La corbata hace conjunto con la camisa.

to **go too far 1.** to miss *(the turn, house, etc.)* pasarse **2.** to be out of bounds pasarse de la raya ▪ ir un por de más ▪ excederse **3.** to take liberties ▪ to get fresh propasarse ➤ That's going too far. Es uno por de más. ➤ We've gone too far. ▪ We've missed the turn. Nos hemos pasado de la salida.

to **go too far or not far enough** ▪ to go either too far or not far enough pasarse o no llegar ➤ With teenagers, it's hard to know how much discipline is too much or to little, and you end up going too far or not far enough. Con los adolescentes es difícil saber si la disciplina es mucha o poca, y uno acaba pasándose o no llegando.

to **go towards 1.** to go in the direction of ir hacia **2.** to incline towards tirar hacia

to **go unclothed** *(because of poverty)* padecer desnudez

to **go underground** pasar a la clandestinidad

to **go unnoticed** pasar desapercibido ▪ pasar inadvertido

to **go unnoticed by someone** pasar desapercibido para alguien

to **go unpunished (for)** quedar sin castigo (por) ▪ quedar impune (de) ➤ Many crimes go unpunished. Muchos delitos quedan sin castigo. ➤ The perpetrators of terrorism will not go unpunished. Los autores del terrorismo no quedarán impunes.

to **go up a street 1.** to take a street meterse por una calle ▪ tirar una calle **2.** to go along a street enfilar una calle ➤ Go up that street! *(tú)* ¡Tira esa calle! ▪ *(usted)* ¡Tire esa calle! ➤ The procession is going up the Gran Vía. La procesión está enfilando la Gran Vía.

to **go up and get someone** subir por alguien ➤ Go up and get him. Sube por él.

to **go up in an airplane** ▪ to go up in a plane subir en avión ▪ *(light airplane)* subir en avioneta

to **go up (in price)** subir (de precio) ➤ Food prices have gone up. ▪ Food has gone up in price. Los precios de la comida han subido.

to **go up in smoke** ▪ to fizzle chafársele ▪ quedar reducido a cenizas ▪ caérsele ▪ saltar por los aires ➤ All his plans have gone up in smoke. Se le han chafado todos sus planes. ▪ Todos sus planes han quedado reducido a cenizas. ➤ His weekend plans have gone up in smoke. Se le ha caído su fin de semana. ➤ *(headline)* The truce between the U.S. and Shiite leader Al Sadr goes up in smoke La tregua de EE UU y el líder chíe Al Sader salta por los aires

to **go up the stairs** ▪ to go up the steps ▪ to ascend the stairs subir las escaleras

to **go up to someone** acercársele a alguien

to **go up *x* floor** subir *x* plantas ➤ You have to go up one more (floor). Hay que subir otra (planta) más.

to **go well together** ▪ to complement each other ▪ to match hacer juego ▪ combinarse bien

to **go well with** casarse bien con

to **go white** ▪ to turn white as a sheet quedarse pálido ▪ quedarse blanco como la cal ▪ quedarse blanco como la cera ▪ empalidecer ▪ palidecer ➤ When she heard the news, her face went white. ▪ When she heard the news, she turned white as a sheet. Cuando supo la noticia, se quedó pálido. ▪ Cuando supo la noticia, se quedó blanco como la cal. ▪ Cuando supo la noticia, palideció.

to **go wild** volverse loco ▪ desmelenarse ▪ desmadrarse ▪ despendolarse ➤ The fans of River Plate went wild. Los fans de River Plate se volvieron locos. ▪ Los fans de River Plate se desmadraron. ▪ Los fans de River Plate se desmelenaron. ▪ Los fans de River Plate se despendolaron. ➤ The rock concert fans are going wild. Los fans del concierto de rock se están desmelenando. ➤ The lovers were going wild. Los amantes se volvían locos.

to **go window shopping** ir a mirar escaparates

to **go with a political faction** ▪ to side with a political faction ponerse de parte de una facción política ▪ ponerse de lado de una facción política ▪ tomar partido a favor de ▪ ir a favor de una facción política ➤ I'm going (to go) with the moderates. ▪ I side with the moderates. Voy a favor de los políticos moderados.

to **go with someone 1.** to accompany someone acompañar a alguien ▪ ir con alguien **2.** to go steady with someone andar de novios (con alguien) ➤ I want to go with him. Quiero ir con él. ▪ Quiero acompañarlo. ▪ Lo quiero acompañar. ▪ *(Sp., leísmo)* Quiero acompañarle. ▪ Le quiero acompañar. ➤ María is going (steady) with Francisco. María y Francisco andan de novios.

to **go with something** ▪ to complement something ir con algo ▪ combinar con algo ▪ entonar con algo ➤ These pillowcases go with the sheets. Estas fundas van con las sábanas. ➤ What colors go with red hair? ¿Qué colores van con el pelo rojo? ▪ ¿Qué colores combinan con el pelo rojo?

to **go with the flow** ir con la corriente ▪ adaptarse a las circunstancias ▪ bailar al son que le tocan ▪ ir normalito y bien ▪ andar al uso ➤ Why can't you just go with the flow? ¿Por qué no puedes ir normalito y bien? ➤ You have to go with the flow. Hay que ir con la corriente. ▪ Hay que adaptarse a las circunstancias.

to **go without a fixed plan** *(esp. when traveling)* ▪ to rough it irse a la ventura

to **go without a hitch** ▪ to go smoothly desenvolverse sin incidente ▪ desenvolverse sin contratiempos ▪ desenvolverse con normalidad

to **go without food** ▪ to be without food estar sin comer ▪ perecer sin comida ➤ The shipwrecked sailor went (for) ten days in a raft without food. El náufrago estuvo diez días en una balsa sin comer.

to **go wrong** salir mal ▪ ir mal ▪ *(plan)* marrar ➤ What went wrong? ¿Qué salió mal?

to **go *x* miles per hour** ▪ to travel at *x* miles per hour ir a *x* millas por hora ▪ circular a *x* millas por hora ▪ correr a *x* millas por hora

goal in life: to have a ~ tener una meta en la vida

goal kick *(soccer) el* saque de puerta ▪ saque de portería ▪ saque de meta

God-fearing temeroso de Dios

God forbid! no lo quiera Dios ▪ Dios me libre

God helps those who help themselves a quien se ayuda, Dios le ayuda

God knows Dios sabe

God only knows (what...) sólo Dios sabe (que...)

God willing si Dios quiere ▪ si quisiera Dios ▪ *(Mex.)* primero Dios

to be a **godsend** llegar como bajado del cielo ▪ aparecer como bajado del cielo ▪ venirle como agua de mayo ▪ venirle como caído del cielo ▪ ser agua de mayo

gofer: office ~ *(Sp.) el, la* IBM ▪ y ve me

to be **going at it** estar dale que dale ➤ My neighbors are going at it. Mis vecinos están dale que dale.

going-away present regalo de despedida

to be **going deaf** ▪ to be losing one's hearing estar quedándose sordo(-a) ➤ She's going deaf. ▪ She's losing her hearing. Se está quedando sorda.

going down? *(elevator)* ¿para abajo? ▪ ¿baja?

going, going, going... gone! *(at an auction)* ¡se va, se va, se va... adjudicado! ➤ Going, going, going, gone! Sold to the gentleman in the green necktie! ¡Se va, se va, se va, a la una, a las dos, a las tres, adjudicado al señor de la corbata verde!

to be **going great (for one)** irle de maravilla ➤ Things are going great (for us). Nos va de maravilla.

to be **going on *x* o'clock** ir a ser la(s) *x* ➤ It's going on five o'clock. Van a ser las cinco. ➤ It was going on one o'clock when... Iba a ser la una cuando...

to be **going on *x* (years old)** ir para los *x* (años) ➤ She's going on thirty. (Ella) va para los treinta.

to be **going on *x* years since...** *(coll.)* ▪ to have been nearly *x* years since... ▪ nearly *x* years have gone by since... ▪ nearly *x* years have passed since... ir para *x* años que... ➤ It's going on ten years since we came to Spain. ▪ It's been nearly ten years since we came to Spain. Va para diez años que venimos a España.

to be **going the other way** *(traffic)* ▪ to be going in the opposite direction ▪ to be going the opposite way ir por el sentido contrario ▪ circular por el sentido contrario ➤ At that moment, the concrete mixer was going in the opposite direction. En ese momento, la hormigonera circulaba por el sentido contrario.

to be **going through a difficult time** pasar por una mala racha

to be **going through withdrawal** *(from drug addiction)* ▪ to be in withdrawal padecer el síndrome de abstinencia ▪ estar con el mono

to be **going to do something** ir a hacer algo ➤ I'm going to do my homework this afternoon. Voy a hacer mis deberes esta tarde.

going up? *(elevator)* ¿para arriba? ▪ ¿sube?

gold fever *la* fiebre de oro

gold, frankincense, and myrrh oro, incienso y mirra

gold inlay ▪ gold marquetry *la* incrustación de oro ▪ marquetería de oro

gold mine of information venero de información ▪ venero de datos ▪ *la* gran fuente de información ▪ abundante fuente de información

to be **gold-plated** estar chapado en oro ▪ tener un plaqué de oro

golden age *la* edad de oro ▪ época dorada ▪ Siglo de Oro ➤ World War I was the golden age of military aviation. La Primera Guerra Mundial fue la época dorada de la aviación militar.

Golden Rule: do unto others as you would have them do unto you regla de oro: no hagas a los demás lo que no quieres que te hagan a ti

golf course campo de golf

to be **gone by then** ▪ to have left by then haber salido para entonces ➤ They'll be gone by then. ▪ They will have left by then. Habrán salido para entonces.

gone out: to have ~ ▪ to be away from the house estar fuera de casa ➤ They've gone out. Están fuera de casa.

Gone with the Wind *(Margaret Mitchell novel) Lo que el viento se llevó*

good afternoon! ¡buenas tardes! *(In Spain, this greeting is used between dinner and supper, even after dark.)*

to be **good and cold** ▪ to be nice and cold estar bien frío ➤ This beer is good and cold. ▪ This beer is nice and cold. Esta cerveza está bien fría.

good and evil el bien y el mal ▪ lo bueno y lo malo

good appetite: to have a ~ tener un buen apetito ▪ tener buen saque

to be **good at something** ser bueno(-a) en algo ▪ ser bueno(-a) haciendo algo ▪ hacer algo bien ▪ dársele bien algo ▪ tener buena mano para hacer algo ▪ tener mano en una cosa ▪ ser bueno para ▪ ser hábil en ➤ He's good at (playing) basketball. Es muy bueno en baloncesto. ▪ Es muy jugando al baloncesto. ▪ Se le da muy bien el baloncesto. ▪ Juega al baloncesto muy bien.

good block! *(football, soccer, etc.)* ¡buena parada!

good-bye and good riddance! ▪ (and) good riddance! ¡adiós muy buenas! ▪ a enemigo que huye, puente de plata

good catch! **1.** *(baseball, Frisbee, etc.)* ¡bien agarrada! ▪ *(Sp.)* ¡bien cogida! **2.** *(error)* ¡qué bien visto! ▪ ¡qué bien detectado!

to be a **good catch** ser un buen partido ➤ The women all think he's a good catch. Todas las mujeres piensan que él es un buen partido. ▪ Todas las mujeres creen que él es un buen partido.

good cholesterol ▪ high-density lipoproteins ▪ HDL colesterol bueno ▪ lipoproteínas de alta densidad ▪ LAD

to be a **good comparison** ser una buena comparación ➤ That's not a good comparison. No es una buena comparación.

to be a **good conversationalist** ser un(-a) buen(-a) conversador(-a) ▪ hablar de perlas ▪ hablar de maravilla ▪ *(Mex.)* ser un(-a) buen(-a) platicador(-a)

to be a **good cook** ser un(-a) buen(-a) cocinero(-a) ▪ guisar muy bien ▪ ser un(-a) artista de la cocina

to be a **good decision** ser una buena decisión ▪ ser un acierto

to be **good enough** ser lo suficientemente bueno(-a)

to be **good enough for** **1.** ser lo suficientemente bueno(-a) para **2.** *(esp. in the negative)* no ser lo bastante bueno para ▪ no satisfacerle ▪ no llenarle ▪ no molarle ➤ My doctor said if chamomile tea is good enough for Peter Rabbit, it's good enough for me. Mi médico dijo que si el té de manzanilla es lo suficientemente buena para el Conejo Pedrito, lo será también para mí. ➤ That's not good enough for him. No le satisface. ▪ No le llena. ▪ No le mola.

good evening! **1.** *(until supper time)* ¡buenas tardes! **2.** *(after supper)* ¡buenas noches!

to be a **good explainer** explicar bien ▪ darle el tema mascado

good figure: to have a ~ tener una buena silueta ▪ tener cintura de avispa ▪ tener un talle de avispa

to be **good for a medical condition** valer para una condición médica ➤ Ibuprofen is good for sore muscles. Ibuprofena vale para los músculos adoloridos.

to be **good for (curing)** ▪ to be good for alleviating ▪ to be a good cure for **1.** ser bueno para curar ▪ ser un buen lenitivo para **2.** valer para ➤ Two aspirins dissolved in a hot lemonade is good for curing colds and bronchitis. Dos aspirinas disueltas en una limonada caliente son un buen lenitivo para los catarros y la bronquitis. ➤ Ibuprofen is good for sore muscles. Ibuprofena vale para los músculos adoloridos.

to be **good for nothing** ▪ not to be good for anything no servir para nada

to be a **good-for-nothing bum** ser un bueno para nada ▪ ser un vago de siete suelas

to be **good for you** ▪ to be healthy (for you) ser saludable ➤ Too much saturated fat is not good for you. Demasiada grasa saturada es poco saludable.

good for *you*! ¡enhorabuena! ▪ ¡bien hecho!

Good Friday Viernes Santo

good fuel efficiency: to have ~ ▪ to get good mileage ser un vehículo con bajo consumo de combustible

good God! ¡santo Dios! ▪ ¡válgame Dios!

good guy buen tipo

good heavens! ▪ for heaven's sake! ¡Ave María Purísima! ▪ ¡válgame el cielo! ▪ ¡válgame Dios!

good job! ¡buen trabajo!

to be **good-natured** tener buen fondo

good heavens! ¡canastos! ▪ ¡Dios mío! ▪ ¡cielos!

to be **good looking** estar bien parecido(-a) ▪ ser guapo(-a) ▪ ser bien plantado(-a) ▪ tener buena planta

Good Lord! ¡Dios mío!

good luck! ¡buena suerte! ▪ ¡que te vaya bien! ▪ ¡que te vaya bonito!

good-luck charm amuleto de suerte

good manners buenos modales

good mileage: to get ~ ▪ to have good fuel efficiency ser un vehículo de bajo consumo de combustible ▪ *(coll.)* consumir combustible como un mechero *(In Spanish it is more usual to say "a car with low fuel consumption": "un carro con bajo consumo de combustible.")*

good morning! ¡buenos días! *(In Spain this greeting is used until the afternoon meal served between 2 and 3 p.m.)*

good-natured bonachón(-a) ▪ de naturaleza buena

good night **1.** *(farewell)* buenas noches **2.** *(as an expression of surprise)* ¡qué cosa!

the **good outweighs the bad** lo bueno pesa más que lo malo

to be **good politics** hacer política sabia ➤ That's just good politics. Eso es hacer política sabia.

good question! ¡buena pregunta!

good rates buenas tarifas

good riddance! ▪ good-bye and good riddance! a enemigo que huye, puente de plata ▪ ¡enhoramala!

to be a **good shot** ser un(-a) buen(-a) tirador(-a) ▪ ser un(-a) tirador(-a) certero(-a) ▪ ser un(-a) tirador(-a) de mucha calidad

to be a **good sign** ser una buena señal ▪ ser un buen presagio

to be a **good sport** ▪ to be a good loser tener buen perder

to be a **good student** ▪ to be a fast learner ▪ to be a quick study tener cabeza para los estudios

the **good thing about** lo bueno de

the **good thing about it** lo bueno que tiene ➤ The good thing about this one is that... Lo bueno que tiene esto es que...

good things come in small packages la esencia viene en frascos pequeños

good thinking! ¡bien pensado!

good timing: that was ~ ¡justo a tiempo! ▪ ¡vaya cálculo! ▪ ¡en el momento exacto!

to be **good to someone** ▪ to be nice to someone portarse bien con alguien

to be **good with** **1.** to taste good with estar bueno con ▪ saber bien con **2.** to be adept with dársele muy bien con ➤ Applesauce is good with pork chops. ▪ Applesauce tastes good with pork chops. El puré de manzana está bueno con chuletas de puerco. ▪ El puré de manzana sabe bien con chuletas de puerco. ➤ He is good with a balero. ▪ He is adept with a balero. Se le da muy bien con un balero.

goodwill gesture gesto de buena voluntad ▪ gesto de manos tendidas

to **goof off** hacer el vago ▪ gandulear

the **goose that laid the golden egg** la gallina de los huevos de oro

to **gore a bullfighter** pegarle una cornada a un torero ➤ The fifth bull gored the bullfighter in the back (side) of the right thigh. El quinto toro le pegó al torero una cornada en la cara posterior del muslo derecho.

to be **gored by a bull** ▪ to get gored by a bull recibir una cornada de un toro ▪ pillarle un toro ➤ The bullfighter was gored in the leg. El torero recibió una cornada en la pierna. ➤ Don't get gored by a bull! ¡Que no te pille un toro!

gorgeous: drop-dead ~ guapa de cojones ▪ guapa de narices

gosh! ¡caramba!

Gospel according to... evangelio según...

gotcha! ▪ (I) got you! ¡te pesqué! ▪ ¡te cogí!

to **gouge someone** **1.** to overcharge someone clavar a alguien **2.** to jab someone darse un tajo ➤ They gouged us at the flamenco bar. ▪ They overcharged us at the flamenco bar. Nos clavaron en el bar de flamenco. ➤ I gouged myself trying to open an oyster. Me di un tajo intentando abrir una ostra.

gourmet cook *el, la* artista de la cocina

to **grab a chair** *(informal)* ▪ to pull up a chair arrimar una silla ▪ acercar una silla ▪ *(Sp.)* cogerse una silla ➤ Grab a chair! ▪ Pull up a chair! ¡Arrima una silla! ▪ ¡Cógete una silla!

to **grab at straws** agarrarse a un clavo ardiendo

to **grab someone by the arm** ▪ to seize someone by the arm agarrar a alguien por el brazo ➤ The officer grabbed him by the arm. ▪ The officer seized him by the arm. El agente lo agarró por el brazo. ▪ *(Sp., leísmo)* El agente le agarró por el brazo.

to **grab someone by the hair** asirlo a alguien de los pelos ▪ *(Sp., leísmo)* asirle a alguien de los pelos ➤ He grabbed her by the hair. La asió de los pelos.

to **grab the basketball** agarrar el balón ▪ arrebatar el balón ▪ *(Sp.)* coger el balón ➤ He grabbed the basketball and made his way down the court. Agarró el balón y corrió regateándolo por la concha. ▪ Arrebató el balón y corrió regateándolo por la concha. ▪ *(Sp.)* Cogió el balón y corrió regateándolo por la concha.

to **grade on a curve** ▪ to curve the grades dar puntuación

grade school ▪ elementary school ▪ primary school (escuela) primaria ▪ *(Sp.)* colegio

gradual deterioration deterioro gradual ▪ deterioro paulatino

gradual recovery recuperación gradual ▪ recuperación paulatina

to **gradually do something** ir haciendo algo ➤ She had gradually gotten to know him. Ella había ido conociéndolo. ▪ Ella lo había ido conociendo. ▪ *(Sp., leísmo)* Ella había ido conociéndole. ▪ Ella le había ido conociendo.

graduate credit 1. *(general)* crédito posgrado **2.** *(master's credit)* crédito para el master **3.** *(doctoral credit)* crédito para el doctorado

graduate degree título posgrado

to **graduate from high school** *(Mex.)* graduarse del secundario ▪ graduarse de la preparatoria ▪ *(Sp.)* graduarse del instituto

to **graduate from the university** licenciarse en la universidad ▪ terminar la carrera ▪ obtener el título ▪ graduarse de la universidad

graduate school escuela graduada

graduate studies estudios posgraduados ▪ estudios posgrados

graham cracker crust base de galleta integral ➤ *(menu item)* Cheesecake on a graham cracker crust Cheesecake sobre una base de galleta integral

grain of the wood veta de la madera ➤ Don't sand across the grain of the wood. Sand with the grain. No se lija en contra de la veta de la madera. Se lija hacia la veta.

Grand Central Station: to be like ~ parecer un cine ➤ It's like Grand Central Station in here! ¡Esto parece un cine (aquí dentro)!

(grand) opening of a store *la* inauguración de una tienda

grandfather clock *el* reloj de pie ▪ reloj de caja

grandma and grandpa yaya y yayo ▪ abuela y abuelo

granola bar barra de cereal

to **grant a favor** conceder un favor

to **grant a pardon** ▪ to pardon conceder un indulto

to **grant a request** conceder una petición

to **grant a stay of execution** conceder una suspensión de la ejecución

to **grant a time-out** *(sports)* conceder un tiempo muerto

to **grant a wish** ▪ to grant someone's wish concederle un deseo a alguien ▪ satisfacer un deseo ➤ When he was granted all his wishes... Al concedérsele a él todos sus deseos...

to **grant an interview to someone** ▪ to grant someone an interview conceder una entrevista a alguien

to **grant for the sake of argument that...** ▪ to concede for the sake of argument that... dar de barato que...

to **grant forgiveness** otorgar el perdón ➤ If he asks you to forgive him, what's to be gained by not granting it? Si él te pide perdón, ¿qué ganas con no otorgárselo?

to be **granted a wish** ▪ to get one's wish concedérsele un deseo ➤ He was granted his wish. ▪ He got his wish. Se le concedío su deseo.

granted that... sentada la base de que... ▪ suponiendo que (es cierto que)...

grapevine: to hear something through the ~ enterarse de algo por radio macuto ▪ oír algo por ahí ➤ I heard it through the grapevine. Me enteré por radio macuto. ▪ Lo oí por ahí.

graph paper papel milimetrado *(Small light squares within larger, darker squares; compare with "cuadrille paper.")*

to **grapple with** asirse con ▪ confrontar

to **grasp at straws** agarrarse a un clavo ardiendo

to **grasp that...** ▪ to realize that... captar que...

grass widow *(coll.)* ▪ divorcée divorciada

gravelly voice *(like Louis Armstrong's)* voz rugosa

to **gravitate toward someone** decantarse por alguien ▪ decantarse hacia alguien

to **gravitate toward something** decantarse por algo ▪ decantarse hacia algo

gravitational constant *(physics) la* constante de la gravitación

gravitational field campo gravitatorio

gravy boat salsera

gray area zona mal delimitada ▪ zona de límites confusos ▪ zona permitida

gray hair pelo cano

gray-haired de pelo canoso

gray-haired man canoso

gray-haired woman canosa

gray matter *(brain)* materia gris

graying hair ▪ salt-and-pepper hair pelo entrecano

to **grease someone's palm** ▪ to bribe someone untar la mano a alguien ▪ untar el bolsillo a alguien ▪ sobornar a alguien ▪ *(Mex.)* darle una mordida a alguien

great! ▪ that's great! ¡genial! ▪ ¡estupendo!

great artist *el, la* gran artista

great atmosphere: what a ~ ▪ what a perfect atmosphere qué ambientazo ➤ Jolín, ¡qué ambientazo! Wow, what a great atmosphere!

great-aunt tía segunda ▪ tía abuela

a **great deal of** ▪ a lot of mucho ➤ It costs a great deal of money. Cuesta mucho dinero. ➤ It cost a great deal of money. Costó mucho inero.

great deal on something from someone: to get a ~ ▪ to get a great deal from someone on something hacer un buen negocio con algo ➤ I got a great deal on my new computer. *(L. Am.)* Hice un buen negocio con mi nueva computadora. ▪ *(Sp.)* Hice un buen negocio con mi nuevo ordenador. ➤ I got a great deal from them on my new computer. *(L. Am.)* Hice un buen negocio con ellos al comprar mi nueva computadora. ▪ *(Sp.)* Hice un buen negocio con ellos al comprar mi nuevo ordenador.

to be **great for** ▪ to be ideal for ser estupendo para ▪ ser ideal para ➤ Ballpoint pen tops are great for cleaning ears and digging under toenails. Las tapas de los bolígrafos son estupendos para limpiarse los oídos y las uñas del pie.

great-grandparent bisabuelo(-a)

great-great-grandparent tatarabuelo(-a)

great-great-great grandparent bistatarabuelo(-a)

great guy *(L. Am., Sp.)* tipo formidable ▪ *(Sp.)* tío formidable

great, I hope espero que la respuesta sea fenomenal ➤ How's everything going? Great, I hope. ¿Qué tal te va todo? Espero que la respuesta sea fenomenal.

great man gran hombre ▪ gran prócer ▪ prócer máximo ▪ *(archaic)* varón esclarecido

great moments in history grandes momentos de la historia ▪ momentos estelares de la historia

great-nephew hijo de sobrino(-a) ▪ sobrino en segundo grado ▪ resobrino

great-niece hija de sobrino(-a) ▪ sobrina en segundo grado ▪ resobrina

the **Great Plains** *(USA)* las extensas praderas ▪ las grandes llanuras

great president *el* gran presidente ▪ *la* gran presidenta ➤ Lincoln was a great president, and Taft was a big president. Lincoln fue un gran presidente, y Taft fue un presidente grande.

the **great thing about** lo grande de ▪ la gran ventaja de

great-uncle tío abuelo ▪ tío segundo

to be the **greatest challenge of my life** ser mi mayor reto de la vida

the **greatest concentration of** ▪ the largest concentration of la concentración más grande de ▪ el mayor colectivo de ➤ The greatest concentration of northwest Africans in Madrid lives in Lavapiés. ▪ The largest concentration of northwest Africans lives in Lavapiés. El mayor colectivo de magrebíes en Madrid vive en Lavapiés.

greatest dream sueño dorado

the **greatest show on earth** el mayor espectáculo del mundo

greatest work obra cumbre

Greek city-state ciudad-estado griega

to be **green behind the ears** ▪ to be inexperienced tener pocas barbas

Green Berets *(elite U.S. military force)* los Boinas Verdes

green vegetables los vegetales verdes *("Verduras" is deceptive because it refers to vegetables of all colors.)* ➤ Does the plate include a green vegetable? ¿Hay un vegetal verde con este plato?

to be **green with envy** ▪ to be very envious tener mucha envidia

greenhouse effect efecto invernadero

greenhouse gases los gases que producen el efecto invernadero

to **greet someone with open arms** saludar a alguien con los brazos abiertos

to **greet with skepticism** recibir con escepticismo ▪ acoger con escepticismo

to be **greeted by** **1.** ser acogido por **2.** ser acogido con ➤ The president was greeted by the mayor on his arrival in the city. Al llegar a la ciudad, el presidente fue acogido por el alcalde. ➤ His words were greeted by an outburst of laughter. ▪ His words were greeted by peals of laughter. Sus palabras fueron acogidas con una gran carcajada.

to be **greeted with skepticism** ser acogido con escepticismo ▪ ser recibido con escepticismo

Gregorian correction *(of the calendar)* corrección gregoriana ➤ On September 2, 1751, the Gregorian correction advanced the calendar date to September 14, and New Year's Day was moved from March 25 to January 1. El 2 de septiembre de 1751, la corrección gregoriana adelantó la fecha del calendario al día 14 de septiembre, y el día del año nuevo fue cambiado del 25 de marzo al primero de enero.

grid paper ▪ cuadrille paper papel cuadriculado *(whose grids are all the same shade, as opposed to "graph paper" consisting of lighter grids within dark ones)*

to **grill meat** cocinar carne a la parrilla ▪ freír carne a la parrilla

to **grill with questions** freír a preguntas

grilled chicken pollo a la parrilla

grilled steak *el* bisté a la parrilla ▪ *el* bistec a la parrilla ▪ *el* filete a la parrilla

to **grin and bear it** aguantar mecha ▪ tomarse con soda ▪ tragar bilis ▪ tragar quina ▪ *(as a command)* ¡a lo hecho, pecho! ➤ Grin and bear it! ¡a lo hecho, pecho! ▪ Tómate con soda. *(Arg., vosotros)* Tomáte con soda.

grin and bear it: to have to ~ tener que aguantar mecha ▪ tener que tragar bilis ▪ tener que tragar quina

to **grin at each other** dirigirse una amplia sonrisa ➤ They grinned at each other. Se dirigieron una amplia sonrisa (uno al otro).

to **grin from ear to ear** tener una sonrisa de oreja en oreja

grit sandpaper lija de grano ➤ Eighty-grit sandpaper ▪ 80-grit sandpaper Lija de grano ochenta ▪ Lija de grano 80

grocery business negocio de los comestibles

grocery cart carro de compra

grocery store tienda de ultramarinos ▪ tienda de comestibles ▪ tienda de abarrotes

to **grope for answers** dar palos de ciego para las respuestas

to **grope for solutions** dar palos de ciego para las soluciones

to **grope one's way along** ▪ to feel one's way along tantear el camino

gross national product (GNP) producto interior bruto (PIB)

to **gross out** repugnar ➤ That magazine grosses me out. Esa revista me repugna.

gross! ¡asqueroso! ▪ ¡repulsivo! ▪ ¡repugnante!

ground beef carne molida ▪ carne picada

ground-breaking work ▪ seminal work una obra rompedora ▪ una obra innovadora

ground cinnamon ▪ powdered cinnamon canela en polvo ➤ Sprinkle ground cinnamon on top. Espolvorear canela en polvo por encima.

ground corn maíz molido ▪ maíz pisado

ground floor planta baja ▪ piso bajo

ground pepper pimienta molida

ground speed velocidad absoluta

ground transportation *el* transporte terrestre

ground troops tropas terrestres

ground zero punto muerto ▪ zona cero ▪ nivel cero *("Zona cero" and "nivel cero" are newer phrases, taken into Spanish from English since 9-11.)*

grounds for divorce motivos de divorcio

grounds for impeachment motivos de destitución

grounds of the university *(University of Virginia)* predios de la universidad

group portrait retrato de grupo

to **grow a beard** dejarse crecer la barba ▪ dejarse la barba

to **grow a mustache** dejarse crecer el bigote ▪ dejarse el bigote ➤ He grew a mustache. Se dejó crecer el bigote. ▪ Se dejó el bigote.

to **grow an average of** ▪ to grow at an average rate of crecer una media de

to **grow at the rate of** ▪ to increase at the rate of crecer al ritmo de ▪ aumentar al ritmo de

to **grow back** *(hair, weeds, etc.)* volver a crecer ➤ It'll grow back. Volverá a crecer.

to **grow dim** ▪ to get dim ▪ to dim desvanecerse ➤ The light is growing dim. La luz se desvanece.

to **grow fond of someone** encariñarse con alguien

to **grow in importance** ▪ to take on importance adquirir importancia

to **grow in leaps and bounds** **1.** *(of adolescents)* to shoot up like a weed pegar un estirón ▪ dar un estirón **2.** *(of a business or a city)* crecer a pasos agigantados

to **grow like weeds** crecer como la espuma ▪ crecer como la mala hierba

to **grow on someone** gustarle más cada vez ▪ irle gustando ➤ I didn't like living in a small town at first, but it's growing on me. Al principio no me gustaba vivir en un pueblo, pero ahora me gusta cada vez más. ➤ He's growing on me. I like him better than I did at first. Me va gustando. Me cae mejor que al principio.

to **grow out of something** **1.** to arise from something proceder de algo ▪ venir de algo ▪ provenir de algo **2.** to outgrow something no entrar en algo ▪ no caber en algo ▪ no entrarle algo ▪ no caberle algo ➤ The political crisis has grown out of frustration with the dictatorial regime. La crisis política procede de la frustración del régimen dictorial. ➤ When my big brother grows out of his clothes, my parents hand them down to me. Cuando mi hermano mayor no entra en su ropa, mi padres me la pasan.

to **grow stupid** embrutecerse

to **grow tired** ▪ to get tired cansarse

to **grow tired of something** ▪ to grow weary of something ▪ to get tired of something cansarse de algo ▪ hastiarse de algo

to **grow up** **1.** to reach adulthood crecer ▪ criarse **2.** to act like an adult ser mayor ▪ criarse ➤ Iván grew up in Necochea. Iván creció en Necochea. ➤ The house we grew up in remains a part of us. La casa donde nos criamos sigue siendo una parte de nosotros. ➤ Peter Pan didn't want to grow up. Peter Pan no quería ser mayor. ➤ Why don't you grow up?! ¡¿Por qué no creces?!

to **grow up in a place** crecer en un sitio ➤ That's the house I grew up in. ▪ That's the house where I grew up. Es la casa donde crecí.

to **grow weary of something** ▪ to grow tired of something ▪ to get tired of something hastiarse de algo ▪ cansarse de algo

to **grow wider** ampliarse ▪ hacerse más amplio ▪ volverse más amplio ➤ We must prevent the disparity between rich and poor from growing wider. Debemos evitar que la disparidad entre los ricos y los pobres se amplíe. ▪ Debemos evitar que la disparidad entre los ricos y los pobres se haga más amplia. ▪ Debemos evitar que la disparidad entre los ricos y los pobres se vuelva más amplia.

to be a **growing boy** ser un niño en la edad de crecer ▪ ser un niño en la edad de crecimiento

growing concern una preocupación creciente

growing importance: to take on (a) ~ adquirir creciente importancia

growing number of número creciente de

growing trend pauta ascendente ▪ tendencia ascendente

to **growl at someone** gruñirle a alguien ➤ That dog growls at me. Ese perro me gruñe.

to be **grown (up)** ya estar criado ➤ Their children are grown. Sus hijos ya están criados.

grown-ups gente talluda ▪ los grandes

grueling schedule horario de castigo ➤ The president's schedule is grueling. ■ The president has a grueling schedule. El horario del presidente es de castigo.

to **guarantee a loan** ■ to be the guarantor of a loan avalar un préstamo

guarantee payment ■ payment to guarantee something *la* señal

to **guarantee someone a seat** garantizar a alguien un asiento ■ asegurar a alguien un asiento

to **guard against** precaver de ■ precaver contra ■ guardarse de

to **guard jealously** guardar con solicitud ■ guardar con vigilancia

to **guard one's health** ■ to be careful about one's health ■ to look after one's health velar por la salud

to be **guardedly optimistic** ■ to be cautiously optimistic ■ to feel guardedly optimistic ■ to feel cautiously optimistic ser moderadamente optimista ■ ser optimista de forma moderada ■ ser comedidamente optimista ■ sentirse moderadamente optimista ■ sentirse optimista de forma moderada ■ sentirse comedidamente optimista

guardian angel ángel de la guarda ■ ángel guardián ■ ángel custodio(-a)

guardrail *(beside a road)* valla de protección

to **guess correctly** suponer correctamente ➤ The psychiatrist guessed correctly that the child was acting out something she had seen on TV. El psiquiatra supuso correctamente que la niña estaba imitando algo que había visto en la tele.

guess what! ¡adivina qué! ■ ¡agárrate!

guessing game juego de ingenio

guest star estrella invitada

guide dog perro guía ■ perro lázaro

to be **guilty of a crime** ser culpable de un delito ■ ser culpable de un crimen

guilty or innocent culpable o inocente

to be the **guinea pig** ser el conejillo de Indias

guitar factory fábrica de guitarras

to **gun the engine** ■ to rev (up) the engine ■ to gun the accelerator darle más gas al motor ■ dar una aceleración al motor ➤ Gun the engine and then ease off on the accelerator. Dale más gas al motor y luego disminuye gradualmente. ■ Da una aceleración al motor y luego disminuye gradualmente.

gunked up: to get (all) ~ llenarse de porquería ➤ The inside of the trackball mouse is all gunked up. ■ This ball mouse is all gunked up inside. Este ratón de bola se llena de porquería.

gurgling of the water gorgoteo del agua

gurgling sound sonido de gorgoteo ■ sonido de gárgaras

to **gush out** salir a borbotones ■ salir a chorros

gust of wind racha de viento ■ ráfaga de viento

gusty winds vientos racheados

guts: he's got ~ esos son pantalones

to be a **guy thing** ser cosa de hombres ➤ It's a guy thing. Es cosa de hombres.

ha, ha, ha! ¡ja, ja, ja!

had better be...: something ~ más vale que algo sea... ➤ Your excuse (had) better be good. Más vale que tu excusa sea buena.

had grown tired of: one ~ uno se había cansado de

had I done it... ▪ if I had I done it... de haberlo hecho... ▪ si lo hubiera hecho...

had I had time ▪ if I had had time si (yo) hubiera tenido tiempo ▪ de haber tenido tiempo ▪ de haberme dado tiempo ▪ si me hubiera dado tiempo

had it coming: one ~ lo tenía bien merecido(-a) ▪ se lo estaba buscando ➤ You had it coming. Lo tenías bien merecido(-a). ▪ Te lo estabas buscando.

had it not been for ▪ if it had not been for ▪ if it hadn't been for de no haber sido por ▪ si no hubiera sido por ▪ si no llega a ser por ➤ The victim of the collapse would have died had it not been for the paramedics. La víctima del derrumbe habría muerto de no haber sido por los servicios de emergencia.

had it not been for you ▪ if it hadn't been for you *(tú)* de no haber sido por ti ▪ si no hubiera sido por ti ▪ *(usted)* de no haber sido por usted ▪ si no hubiera sido por usted

had it up to here with: to have ~ estar hasta la coronilla de ➤ I've had it up to here with... Estoy hasta la coronilla de...

had just...: one ~ uno acababa de... ➤ I was showing off an expression I had just learned. Estaba alardeando de una expresión que acababa de aprender. ➤ I had just walked in the door when the telephone rang. (Yo) acababa de entrar cuando sonó el teléfono.

had known all along that...: one ~ uno sabía desde un principio que... ➤ I had known all along that... (Yo) sabía desde un principio que...

had known it all along: one ~ uno lo sabía desde un principio ➤ I had known it all along. (Yo) lo sabía de un principio.

had previously known: one ~ **1.** *(a fact)* uno sabía de antemano **2.** *(a person)* uno tenía conocimiento previo ▪ uno conocía anteriormente a

had not done something since: one ~ uno no hacía algo desde ➤ California had not suffered blackouts since World War Two. California no sufría cortes de luz desde la Segunda Guerra Mundial.

had to be *(with "it" or singular noun)* **1.** *(simple past)* tuvo que ser ▪ debió ser ▪ hubo de ser ▪ hubo que ser ▪ tuvo que estar ▪ debió estar ▪ hubo de estar ▪ hubo que estar **2.** *(past continuous)* tenía que ser ▪ debía ser ▪ tenía que estar ▪ debía estar ▪ había de ser ▪ había de estar ▪ había que ser ▪ había que estar **3.** *(conjecture, also equating to "must have been")* debió de ser ▪ debía de ser ▪ debió de estar ▪ debía de estar ➤ It had to be that way. Tuvo que ser así. ➤ The summit (conference) had to be adjourned because of the protests. La cumbre tuvo que ser suspendida por las protestas. ➤ The athlete had to be disqualified. El atleta debió ser descalificado. ➤ *(song title)* "It Had to Be Love" "Debió ser el amor" ➤ He had to be removed from his post. *(Mex.)* Hubo de ser quitado de su puesto. ▪ *(Arg.)* Hubo de ser sacado de su puesto. ➤ You had to be a real simpleton to believe anything like that. Bastante papanatas hubo que ser para creer semejante cosa. ➤ The doctor had to be in his office the entire day. El médico tuvo que estar todo el día en el consultorio. ➤ It had to be in June of last year. Debió estar en junio del año pasado. ➤ A country powered by wind and sun is something that had to be. Un país impulsado por el viento y el sol es algo que hubo de estar. ➤ Each city had to be ready to defend itself. Cada ciudad hubo de estar preparada para defenderse. ➤ You just had to be there at the time (in order to appreciate it). Solo hubo que estar allí en ese momento (para comprenderlo). ➤ For the wedding, the tablecloth had to be pure linen. Para la boda, el mantel tenía que ser de lino puro. ➤ Life didn't have to be that way. La vida no debía ser así. ➤ Ptolemy was convinced, wrongly as it turned out, that the Earth had to be at the center of the planetary system. Erróneamente, Tolomeo estaba convencido de que la Tierra tenía que estar en el centro del sistema planetario. ▪ Erróneamente, Tolomeo estaba convencido de que la Tierra debía estar en el centro del sistema planetario. ▪ Erróneamente, Tolomeo estaba convencido de que la Tierra debía de estar en el centro del sistema planetario. ➤ Because of his contract, the pharmacist had to be on duty until midnight during the week. Debido a su contrato, el fármaco debía estar de guardia entresemana hasta la medianoche. ➤ *(from* Don Quixote*)* That place, seeming to him to be sacred, had to be held in respect. Pareciéndole aquel lugar como sagrado, había que ser tenido en respeto. ➤ You had to be blind not to see it. Había que estar ciego para no verlo.

had you noticed? ¿habías caído en la cuenta? ▪ ¿te habías dado cuenta?

to **haggle over the price of something** regatear ▪ discutir sobre el precio de algo

Hail Mary, full of grace *(Catholicism)* Ave María Purísima

hail of bullets lluvia de balas

hair loss caída del cabello ▪ caída del cabello

hairline crack *(in china, glass, etc.)* grieta fina ▪ pelo

hairpin turn ▪ hairpin curve curva cerrada (en la carretera)

hairy chest: to have a ~ tener un pecho de lobo ▪ *(Sp.)* tener un pecho lobo

to be **half a bubble off plumb** ▪ to be a couple bricks shy of a load ▪ to be a couple (of) quarts low ▪ to be not quite with it faltarle un hervor

half an hour ago ▪ a half hour ago hace media hora

half an hour into the flight ▪ a half hour into the flight a media hora de vuelo

half an hour later ▪ a half hour later media hora después ▪ pasada media hora

to be **half asleep** estar medio dormido ▪ estar entre sueños ▪ estar adormecido

to be **half awake** estar medio dormido

half brother medio hermano

half-closed eyes ▪ eyes half closed ojos entornados ▪ ojos medio cerrados

to be **half done** estar hecho a medias

half-life of radioactive materials vida media de material radiactivo

half mast: to be (flying) at ~ estar (ondeando) a media asta ➤ The flags were (flying) at half mast. Las banderas estaban (ondeando) a media asta.

half measures: to take ~ ▪ to apply half measures poner paños calientes ▪ aplicar paños calientes

half nelson *(wrestling)* media llave ➤ My opponent pinned me with a half nelson. Mi oponente me sujetó con una media llave.

to be **half open** estar entreabierto

to be **half over** estar a mitad ➤ This month is already half over. Ya estamos a mitad de mes. ➤ The class is not even half over. La clase no está ni medio acabada. ▪ La clase no está ni medio terminada.

half serious ▪ half seriously mitad en serio

half seriously, half in jest entre burlas y veras ■ mitad en serio mitad en broma ➤ He said it half seriously, half in jest. Lo dijo entre burlas y veras. ■ Lo dijo mitad en serio, mitad en broma.

half sister media hermana

half-truth una verdad a medias

to be **halfway** estar a mitad de camino ■ estar a medio camino

to be **halfway between** estar a medio camino entre

to be **halfway decent** 1. to be presentable estar presentable 2. to be pretty good ser decente ■ parecer decente ➤ Are you halfway decent? ■ Are you presentable? ¿Estás presentable? ➤ My salary is halfway decent. Mi sueldo es decente. ➤ This place looks halfway decent. El lugar parece decente.

to be **halfway home** estar a medio camino a casa ■ estar a mitad del camino a casa ➤ We're almost halfway home. Estamos casi a medio camino a casa. ■ Estamos casi a mitad de camino a casa.

halfway through ■ midway through a mitad de ➤ Normally, there is a midterm exam halfway through the course. ■ Normally, there is a midterm exam midway through the course. Normalmente, hay una examen parcial a mitad del curso.

to be **halfway through** estar a mitad del camino ■ estar a medio camino

halfway through: to go ~ ir a la mitad del camino ■ ir a medio camino

hallowed be thy name santificado sea tu nombre

to **halt the advance of an illness** ■ to stop the advance of an illness detener el avance de una enfermedad

to **halt traffic** ■ to snarl traffic ■ to bring (the) traffic to a halt colapsar el tráfico ■ parar el tráfico

ham biscuit *(Sp.)* montado *(In Spain, ham biscuits typically consist of a hard roll, serrano ham, cheese, and tomato.)*

ham bits trocitos de jamón

hamburger with nothing on it ■ hamburger without anything on it hamburguesa tal cual ■ hamburguesa sin nada

to **hammer out an agreement** ■ to hammer an agreement out arrancar un acuerdo

to be **hand delivered** estar entregado en mano ■ ser entregado en mano

hand grenade granada de mano

to **hand in a paper** entregar un trabajo ■ entregar un ensayo ■ entregar un papel ➤ Were we supposed to hand in our papers yesterday? ¿Deberíamos haber entregado nuestros trabajos ayer?

hand-me-downs ropa usada ➤ I always wore my brother's hand-me-downs. A mi siempre me tocaba la ropa de mi hermano. ➤ My brother always wore my hand-me-downs. A mi hermano siempre le tocaba mi ropa.

to **hand out newpapers** repartir periódicos

hand over fist: to make money ~ ganar dinero a puñados ■ ganar dinero a espuertas ➤ He makes money hand over fist. Gana dinero a puñados. ■ Gana dinero a espuertas.

hand over the dough! ¡suelta la lana!

to **hand someone something** ■ to hand something to someone pasarle algo a alguien ➤ He handed me the phone. Me pasó el teléfono.

to **hand someone something on a silver platter** ■ to serve someone something on a silver platter dárselo a alguien en una charola de plata ■ entregárselo a alguien en una charola de plata

hand-to-hand combat *el* combate a brazo partido ■ combate cuerpo a cuerpo

to **handcuff someone** colocar las esposas a alguien

handful of people puñado de gente ■ puñado de personas

a **handful of shrimp, please** un puñado de gambas, por favor

to **handle a situation** bastarse uno mismo ■ controlar ➤ We can handle it, thanks. Gracias, nos bastamos. ➤ I'll handle it. ■ I'll take care of it. Voy a controlar eso.

to **handle a situation with kid gloves** tratar una situación con guante blanco

to **handle someone with kid gloves** ■ to treat someone with kid gloves tratar a alguien con guantes de seda ■ tratar a alguien a mano blanda

handle with care! manejar con cuidado ■ manéjese con cuidado

handling characteristics *(car, airplane, etc.)* características de manejo ■ características de conducción ■ características propias

handouts (that the teacher gives the class) unidades didácticas

to **handpick grapes** ■ to pick by hand ■ to gather by hand recolectar la uvas a mano

to **handpick one's successor** elegir a alguien a dedo como el sucesor de uno ■ elegir uno mismo el sucesor de uno ■ elegir personalmente al sucesor de uno ➤ Theodore Roosevelt handpicked William Howard Taft as his successor. Theodore Roosevelt eligió a dedo a William Howard Taft como su sucesor.

to be **handpicked** ■ to be picked by hand ■ to be gathered by hand ser recolectado a mano ➤ *(on a wine label)* Made from the best selection of handpicked Tempranillo grapes from our own vineyards. Elaborado con la mejor selección de uva Tempranillo, recolectada a mano en nuestros propio viñedos.

hands of a clock manecillos de un reloj ■ saetas de un reloj ■ minute hand minutero

hands off! 1. don't touch it! ■ leave it alone! ■ ¡manos fuera! 2. *(especially to children)* keep your hands to yourself! ¡manos quietas!

hands up ■ with one's hands up manos en alto ➤ They came out with their hands up. Salieron manos en alto.

hands up! ¡manos arriba!

handshake *el* apretón de manos

to **hang around for a while** *(coll.)* ■ to stay for a while quedarse un rato

to **hang around with a bad crowd** ■ to hang out with a bad crowd ■ to run around with a bad crowd rondar con mala gente ■ merodear con mala gente ■ holgazanear con mala gente ■ haraganear con mala gente ■ andar con mala gente ■ reunirse con mala gente

to **hang by a thread** pender de un hilo ■ colgar de un hilo

hang glider ala delta

hang gliding vuelo con ala delta

hang gliding: to go ~ (ir a) volar con ala delta

to **hang in the air** flotar en el aire

to **hang in the balance** debatirse entre ■ pender de un hilo ➤ His life was hanging in the balance. Él se debatía entre la vida y la muerte.

hang in there! ¡ánimo! ■ ¡aguanta!

to **hang in there** ir tirando ➤ I'm hanging in there. Voy tirando.

hang on! 1. hold on (tight)! ¡agárrate! ■ ¡no te sueltes! 2. wait a second! espera un momentito ■ *(telephone)* no cuelgues

hang on a second espera un momentito ■ *(telephone)* don't hang up no cuelgues

to **hang onto someone** seguir pegado a alguien ■ mantenerse cerca de alguien

to **hang onto every word someone says** estar pendiente de los labios de alguien ■ estar colgado de los labios de alguien

to **hang out** pasar el rato ■ pasarlo ➤ This is my home in Spain. It's where I hang out. Es mi hogar en España. Es donde lo paso. ➤ Last night I hung out with my friends. Anoche lo pasé con mis amigos.

to **hang out clothes to dry** tender la ropa a secar ■ tender la ropa para que se seque

to **hang over** cernerse sobre ➤ The threat of winter hangs over the Afghan refugees. La amenaza del invierno se cierne sobre los refugiados afganos.

to **hang up and redial** colgar y volver a marcar ➤ Hang up and redial. Cuelgue y vuelva a marcar.

to **hang up one's coat** colgar el abrigo ■ dejar el abrigo (en la percha)

to **hang up the computer** ■ to hang the computer up *(L. Am.)* hacerle colgar a la computadora ■ quedarse colgada la computadora ■ hacer colgar a la computadora ■ *(Sp.)* colgarse el ordenador ■ quedarse colgado el ordenador ➤ Something has hung up the computer. We might have to restart it. *(L. Am.)* Algo ha hecho que se quede colgada la computadora. Tal vez tengamos que reiniciarla. ➤ Something has hung it up. Algo la ha colgado.

to **hang up the (tele)phone** ■ to hang up the receiver colgar el teléfono ➤ Hang up the phone downstairs. ■ Hang the phone up downstairs. Cuelga el teléfono abajo. ➤ Hang it up. Cuélgalo.

to be **hanging by a thread** estar colgado de un hilo ■ estar pendiente de un hilo ■ estar pendiente de un cabello

to **happen to do something** hacer algo casualmente ➤ I happened to see her on the street. Casualmente me la encontré en la calle. ➤ I happened to see it in the newspaper. Lo vi en el periódico por casualidad.

to **happen unexpectedly** ocurrir inesperadamente ■ sobrevenir

it happens to the best of us eso le pasa hasta al más pintado

happily single woman compuesta y sin novio ■ soltera y entera

to be **happy as a lark** ■ to be happy as can be estar como unas pascuas ■ estar como unas castañuelas

happy childhood infancia feliz

happy ending: to have a ~ acabar bien ■ tener un feliz desenlace ■ tener un final feliz

happy face: to have a ~ tener un rostro feliz ■ tener una cara feliz

happy medium: to find a ~ encontrar un término medio

happy medium: to hit a ~ alcanzar un término medio ■ llegar a un término medio

Happy Thanksgiving Feliz Día de Acción de Gracias

to **harbor a feeling** guardar un sentimiento

to **harbor a grudge against someone for something** ■ to nurse a grude against someone for something ■ to have a grudge against someone for something ■ to bear a grudge against someone for something guardarle rencor a alguien por algo ■ tenerle inquina a alguien por algo ■ tenerle tirria a alguien por algo ■ tenerle manía a alguien por algo

to **harbor resentment (toward)** guardar resentimientos (hacia) ■ abrigar resentimientos (hacia)

to **harbor terrorists** ■ to give safe haven to terrorists dar cobijo a los terroristas

to be a **hard act to follow** ser difícil llenar el vacío que alguien dejó ■ ser difícil de continuar la trayectoria de alguien

to be **hard as a rock** quedarse duro como una piedra

to be **hard at it** ■ to be hard at work estar dale que dale ■ estar dale que te pego ■ estar en plena faena

to be **hard at work** ■ to be hard at it estar en plena faena ■ trabajar sin pausa

to **hard-boil an egg** cocer un huevo

hard-boiled egg huevo duro ■ huevo cocido

hard cash ■ cold cash dinero contante y sonante ■ efectivo

hard copy copia impresa

hard drive disco rígido ■ *(Sp.)* disco duro

hard drugs drogas duras

hard-fought competition competición (muy) reñida

hard landing *el* aterrizaje impactante

hard line against...: to take a ~ tomar una postura dura en contra de...

hard liquor bebida fuerte

to be **hard of hearing** ■ to be deaf ser duro de oído ■ estar sordo ■ *(coll.)* estar teniente

hard-on: to get a ~ *(L. Am.)* ponerse la verga tiesa ■ *(Sp.)* empalmarse

hard-on: to have a ~ tener la verga tiesa ■ *(Sp.)* estar empalmado

to be **hard on one** ser duro para uno ■ resultarle duro a uno ➤ His mother's death when he was ten was very hard on him. La muerte de su madre cuando tenía diez años fue muy duro para él. ➤ Leaving so many family (members) behind was really hard on me. ■ To leave so many family (members) behind was really hard on me. Dejar a tanta familia me resultó especialmente duro.

to be a **hard one to pull off** ser difícil de realizar

to be the **hard part** ser la parte difícil ■ ser lo difícil

to be **hard-pressed for cash** estar necesitado de dinero contante y sonante

to be **hard to come by** ser difícil de conseguir ➤ The old one-peso bills are hard to come by these days. Los viejos billetes de un peso son difíciles de conseguir hoy en día.

to be **hard to decipher** ser difícil de descifrar

to be **hard to get to** ser de difícil acceso

to be **hard to get to know** ser difícil de conocer

to be **hard to please** ■ to be difficult to please ser difícil de complacer ■ ser difícil de contentar

hard-to-reach areas zonas de difícil acceso

to be **hard to swallow** ser difícil de tragar

to be **hard to understand** ■ to be difficult to understand ser difícil de entender

to be **hard up for money** ■ to be hard up financially ■ to be hard up estar apurado de dinero

the **hard way** de la manera más difícil

hard way: to do something the ~ hacer algo por la manera más difícil

hard way: to learn something the ~ aprender algo por el camino difícil ■ aprender algo de la manera difícil

to be **hard work** ser (un) trabajo difícil ■ ser trabajo duro

hard work: to take ~ llevar (un) trabajo difícil ■ costar (un) trabajo difícil ■ costar mucho trabajo

harder, harder! ¡tira, tira!

the **harder I look** por más que miro ■ por más que busco

the **hardest hit** *el, la* más castigado(-a) ➤ The area hardest hit by the hurricane El área más castigado por el huracán ➤ The areas hardest hit Las áreas más castigadas

the **hardest part is still to come** ■ the worst (part) is yet to come ■ the worst (part) is still to come la peor parte está por llegar ■ la peor parte está por verse ■ (aún) le falta a uno lo peor ■ *(colorful)* queda el rabo por desollar

to be **hardheaded** ser cabeza dura ■ ser cabezón ■ ser cabezota

hardly any left: there's ~ queda muy poco ■ apenas queda un poquito ■ queda muy poco ■ queda casi nada ➤ There is hardly any wine left. Queda muy poco (de) vino. ■ No queda casi nada de vino. ■ Apenas queda vino.

hardly anyone ■ almost no one casi nadie ■ apenas unos cuantos

hardly ever (do something) ■ almost never (do something) casi no (hacer algo) ■ casi nunca (hacer algo) ■ apenas ■ rara vez (hacer algo) ➤ He was hardly ever home. ■ He was almost never home. Apenas estaba en casa. ■ Casi nunca estaba en casa. ➤ Never?-Well, hardly ever. ¿Nunca?-Pues, casi nunca.

to **hardly know someone** ■ to barely know someone apenas conocer a alguien ➤ She hardly knew her father. ■ She barely knew her father. Apenas conoció a su padre. ➤ She hardly knew him. Ella apenas lo conoció. ■ *(Sp., leísmo)* Apenas le conoció a su padre.

to **hardly know something** ■ to barely know something apenas saber algo

hardly suppose: one would ~ ni siquiera se imaginaría ■ apenas se imaginaría ■ ni siquiera se supondría ■ casi no se supondría

hardly tell the difference between: one can ~ apenas notar la diferencia entre ■ apenas ver la diferencia entre ■ apenas distinguir entre ➤ I can hardly tell the difference between rib steak and sirloin. Apenas noto la diferencia entre entrecote y solomillo.

hardwood floors pisos de madera dura ■ piso de madera noble ■ *(Sp.)* entarimado ■ tarima flotante

hardworking: to be (very) ~ ser muy aplicado ➤ The pupils are very hardworking. Los alumnos son muy aplicados.

hare-brained idea idea de bombero ■ idea peregrina

harsh reality dura realidad ■ cruda realidad

harsh treatment tratamiento brutal

harsh winter ■ bitter winter ■ hard winter invierno crudo ■ invierno duro

harshness of his tone dureza de su tono

harshness of the climate la dureza del clima ■ *la* rigidez del clima

harvest time ▪ time of the harvest época de la cosecha ▪ *(grape harvest)* época de la vendimia

has anyone ever told you that...? *(tú)* ¿te han dicho alguna vez que...? ▪ *(usted)* ¿le han dicho alguna vez que...? ➤ Has anyone ever told you that you look like someone famous? *(tú)* ¿Te han dicho alguna vez que te pareces a un famoso? ▪ *(usted)* ¿Le han dicho a usted alguna vez que se parece a un famoso?

has-been un(a) acabado(-a) ▪ una persona acabada

has it ever occurred to you that...? ¿se te ha ocurrido alguna vez que...?

has the plane come in? ¿ha llegado el avión?

has my order come in? ¿ha llegado mi pedido?

has seen its better days: it ~ ha visto tiempos mejores

hasn't got a clue: he ~ no tiene zorra idea

to be a **hassle** ser un rollo ➤ It's a hassle. Es un rollo.

to **hassle someone** fastidiar a alguien ➤ He wants to hassle you. Quiere fastidiarte.

haste makes waste las prisas son malas consejeras ▪ *(colorful)* vístame despacio que tengo prisa

to **hasten one's demise** apurar la caída de alguien

to **hasten to add that...** apresurarse a añadir que...

to **hatch a scheme to** tramar una estratagema ➤ Mr. Martin hatches a scheme to get Mrs. Barrows fired. Sr. Martin trama una estratagema para que despidan a la Sra. Barrows.

hatched: the egg ~ **1.** *(chicken)* el pollo salió del huevo ▪ el pollo salió del cascarón ▪ el pollo rompió el huevo y salió **2.** *(insect, literally "it emerged")* eclosionó

to **hate a food** no poder ver una comida ▪ detestar una comida ➤ I hate beets. No puedo ver las remolachas.

to **hate it when** no soportarlo que ➤ I hate it when they turn off the water while I'm taking a shower. No lo soporto que cierran el agua mientras me estoy duchando.

to **hate someone's guts** querer beber la sangre a alguien

to **hate to (have to) tell you this** lamentar decirle esto

to **haul ass** *(slang)* ▪ to go as fast as one can ir cagando leches ▪ ir a toda hostia ▪ ir en un pispás ▪ ir en un flis

to **haul off and belt him one** arremeter contra él y embestirlo

to **have a baby on the way** ▪ to have a child on the way tener un niño en camino

to **have a bachelor's degree in Spanish from a university** ser licenciado en filología hispánica por una universidad

to **have a bad back** tener la espalda mal ➤ She has a bad back. Tiene la espalda mal.

to **have a bad day** tener un mal día ▪ tener un pésimo día

to **have a bad disposition** tener mal genio ▪ *(coll.)* tener mala uva ▪ tener malas pulgas ➤ He has a bad disposition. Tiene mala uva. ▪ Tiene mal genio. ▪ Tiene mala uva. ▪ Tiene malas pulgas.

to **have a bad habit of...** tener la fea costumbre de...

to **have a bad temper** ▪ to be bad tempered tener malas pulgas ▪ tener mala baba

to **have a bad time** pasar un mal rato ▪ pasar las de Caín ➤ He had a bad time after his accident. Pasó un mal rato después de su accidente.

to **have a ball** ▪ to have a blast ▪ to have a great time pasarlo grande

to **have a bearing on what...** redundar en lo que... ▪ influir lo que...

to **have a big breakfast** desayunar fuerte

to **have a bite to eat** tomar un bocado

to **have a blast** ▪ to have a great time pasarlo bomba ▪ pasarlo de cañones ➤ We had a blast at the beach party. Lo pasamos bomba en la fiesta de la playa. ▪ Lo pasamos bomba en la fiesta playera.

to **have a bloody nose** ▪ to have a nosebleed ▪ (for one's) nose to be bleeding sangrar por la nariz ➤ I have a bloody nose. ▪ I have a nosebleed. ▪ My nose is bleeding. Sangro por la nariz. ▪ Estoy sangrando por la nariz.

to **have a blowout** ▪ (for) a tire to blow out pinchársele una rueda ➤ On the trip to Valencia, I had a blowout. ▪ On the trip to Valencia, the tire blew out (on me). En el viaje a Valencia se me pinchó una rueda.

to **have a case** tener caso ➤ The police didn't have (much of) a case. La policía no tenía caso.

to **have a cast-iron stomach** poder comerse un estribo de cobre ▪ *(Sp.)* tener un estómago a prueba de bombas

to **have a certain... quality** tener un no sé qué de... ➤ She has a certain mysterious quality. Tiene un no sé que de misterio.

to **have a certain something** ▪ to have that certain something tener su aquél

to **have a child on the way** ▪ to have a baby on the way tener un niño en camino

to **have a clear conscience** ▪ to have a clean conscience tener la conciencia tranquila ▪ tener la conciencia limpia

to **have a close call** salvarse por los pelos

to **have a conniption (fit)** ▪ to have a conniption ▪ to go through the roof ▪ to hit the ceiling ponerse por las nubes ▪ perder los estribos

to **have a conversation about...** mantener una conversación sobre...

to **have a crew cut** ▪ to wear one's hair in a crew cut llevar el pelo cortado al cepillo

to **have a crush on someone** estar por alguien ➤ Sally Brown has a crush on Linus. Sally Brown está por Linus.

to **have a cure for everything** tener un remedio para todo ▪ tener remedios a manta

to **have a date** tener una cita ▪ salir con alguien ➤ I have a date tonight. Tengo una cita esta noche. ▪ Voy a salir con alguien esta noche.

to **have a degree in a subject** ser licenciado en una disciplina académica ▪ tener una carrera ➤ He has a degree in English. Es licenciado en filología inglesa. ▪ Tiene la carrera de filología inglesa.

to **have a dickens of a time doing something** ▪ to have a terrible time doing something ▪ to have an awful time doing something pasarlas canutas para hacer algo

to **have a disconcerted look** ▪ to look disconcerted tener un aire de desconcierto

to **have a dream about someone** ▪ to dream about someone soñar con alguien

to **have a falling out with someone** ▪ to fall out with someone disgustarse con alguien ▪ reñir con alguien

to **have a feeling (that)...** darle la impresión de que... ▪ tener el presentimiento que... ➤ *(Dorothy in* The Wizard of Oz*)* Toto, I've a feeling we're not in Kansas anymore. Toto, tengo el presentimiento que ya no estamos en Kansas.

to **have a fever** ▪ to have a temperature tener fiebre ▪ tener calentura

to **have a few drinks** tomar unas copas

to **have a fit** tener un ataque de rabia

to **have a foul mouth** tener mala boca

to **have a get-together** hacer una fiesta

to **have a good appetite** tener buen apetito ▪ *(Sp., coll.)* tener buen saque

to **have a good clientele** tener una buena clientela

to **have a good ear for...** tener (un) buen oído para... ➤ She has a good ear for music. (Ella) tiene (un) buen oído para la música. ➤ He has a good ear for languages. (Él) tiene (un) buen oído para los idiomas.

have a good evening *(tú)* que pases una feliz noche ▪ que tengas una buena noche ▪ *(usted)* que pase una feliz noche ▪ que tengas una buena noche

to **have a good figure** tener buen tipo ▪ tener una buena figura

to **have a (good) head for business** tener una aptitud para los negocios ▪ tener (una buena) cabeza para los negocios

to **have a good look at something** ▪ to take a good look at something mirar algo detenidamente

to **have a good rapport with someone** entenderse (muy) bien con alguien ▪ tener (muy) buena relación con alguien ▪ *(coll.)* haber buen rollo entre dos personas

to **have a good time** divertirse ▪ pasarlo bien ▪ pasar el grande ▪ pasar un rato divertido ➤ Have a good time! *(tú)* ¡Que te diviertas! ▪ ¡Pásalo bien! ▪ *(usted)* ¡Que se divierta (usted)! ▪ ¡Páselo bien! ▪ *(ustedes)* ¡Que se diviertan (ustedes)! ▪ *(Sp., vosotros)* ¡Que os divertáis! ▪ ¡Pasadlo bien!

have a good weekend! ■ have a nice weekend! ¡que tengas un buen fin de semana! ■ ¡que tengas un bonito fin de semana!

to **have a great influence on someone** tener gran influencia sobre alguien

to **have a great time** pasarlo grande ■ pasarlo divino ■ pasarlo lindo ■ pasarlo pipa

to **have a grudge against someone for something** ■ to nurse a grude against someone for something ■ to harbor a grudge against someone for something ■ to bear a grudge against someone for something guardarle rencor a alguien por algo ■ tenerle inquina a alguien por algo ■ tenerle tirria a alguien por algo

to **have a guilty conscience** remordarle a uno la conciencia

to **have a gut feeling that...** tener un pálpito de que... ■ tener una corazonada de que...

to **have a happy ending** acabar bien ■ tener un feliz desenlace ■ tener un final feliz

to **have a hard time doing something** ■ to have difficulty doing something costarle (trabajo) hacer una cosa ■ tener dificultades para hacer algo ➤ I had a hard time finding a place to park. Me costó mucho (trabajo) encontrar un sitio para aparcar.

to **have a hard time understanding** tener problemas para entender ■ tener dificultades para entender

to **have a hard time with something** costarle trabajo a uno hacer algo ➤ I'm having a hard time with this jar top. Can you get it off? Me cuesta trabajo abrir la tapa de este jarro. ¿Puedes destaparlo? ➤ I'm having a hard time with that politician's speech. El discurso de ese político me está indignando.

to **have a head for business** tener cabeza para los negocios

to **have a head for dates** tener buena cabeza para las fechas

to **have a head on one's shoulders** tener la cabeza sobre los hombros

to **have a headache** dolerle la cabeza ■ tener (un) dolor de cabeza ➤ I have a headache. Me duele la cabeza.

to **have a heart of stone** tener corazón de piedra ■ no tener alma

to **have a hell of a time 1.** to have a great time pasarlo grande **2.** to have a difficult time sudar la gota gorda ■ ver la suya ➤ We had a hell of a time at the party. ■ We had a great time at the party. Nos la pasamos de película en la fiesta. ➤ We had a hell of time getting the car unstuck in the snow. Sudamos la gota gorda desatascando el carro de la nieve.

to **have a hidden agenda** ■ to have an ulterior motive tener segundas intenciones ■ tener un motivo ulterior ■ tener otras intenciones

to **have a history of** tener antecedentes de ➤ His family has a history of heart problems. Su familia tiene antecedentes de problemas cardiacos.

to **have a key made** hacer que le hagan una llave ➤ I need to have a key made. Necesito que me hagan una llave.

to **have a knack for doing something** tener el truco de hacer algo ■ tener la maña de hacer algo ■ tener la facilidad para hacer algo

to **have a knowledge of** tener un saber de

to **have a lasting impact on someone** dejar en alguien una impronta indelible

to **have a lasting influence on someone** tener una influencia impercedera sobre alguien ■ tener una influencia indelible sobre alguien

to **have a leisurely conversation with someone** hablar largo y tendido con alguien

to **have a life of its own** tener vida propia ➤ Great music has a life of its own. Gran música tiene vida propia.

to **have a long way to go** quedarle a uno mucho camino ■ faltar mucho camino ➤ We (still) have a long way to go. Nos queda mucho camino. ■ Nos falta mucho camino.

to **have a look** echar una ojeada ➤ The doctor said, "Let's have a look." El médico dijo, "Vamos a echar una ojeada".

to **have a look around** ■ to take a look around echar un vistazo más ➤ *(sales clerk to customer)* Have a look around. ■ Take a look around. Eche un vistazo más.

to **have a look at something** ■ to take a look at something echar un vistazo a algo ■ echar un ojo a algo ■ echarle un vistazo a algo ■ darle una ojeada a algo ➤ Let's have a look at the house. Echémosle un vistazo a la casa.

to **have a lot of ability** tener mucho talento

to **have a lot of explaining to do** tener mucho que explicar

to **have a lot of fight (in one)** ir a dar mucha guerra ➤ I still have a lot of fight in me. Aún voy a dar mucha guerra.

to **have a lot of fun** ■ to have a great time divertirse mucho ■ pasarlo pipa ➤ The kids had a lot of fun at Disneyland. ■ The kids had a great time at Disneyland. Los retoños lo pasaron pipa en Disneyland.

to **have a lot of ins and outs** ■ to have a lot of complexity tener tela (marinera) ■ tener tela que cortar ■ ser complejo

to **have a lot of nerve** ■ to have got a lot of nerve ■ to have a lot of gall ■ to have a lot of cheek tener (mucho) morro

to **have a lot of problems** tener muchos problemas ■ *(coll.)* tener muchos marrones

to **have a lot of something** tener mucho de una cosa ■ tener bien de algo

to **have a lot of studying to do** tener mucho que estudiar

to **have a lot of talent** tener mucho talento

to **have a lot of things to tell someone** ■ to have a whole bunch of things to tell someone tener muchas cosas que decir a alguien ■ tener un montón de cosas que decirle a alguien

to **have a lot (of work) to do** ■ to have plenty (of work) to do ■ to have a lot of work on one's hands ■ to have plenty of work on one's hands tener mucho que hacer ■ tener tela para rato

to **have a lot on one's mind** tener la mente ocupada en muchas cosas

to **have a lot on the ball** ■ to be really sharp estar con la onda ■ ser muy listo(-a)

to **have a lot to be thankful for** tener mucho por dar gracias

to **have a lot to do** ■ to have a lot of things to do ■ to have much to do ■ to have many things to do tener mucho que hacer

to **have a lot to lose** tener mucho que perder

to **have a lot to say** tener algo que decir ➤ She is very thoughtful and has a lot to say. Ella es muy pensativa y tiene algo que decir.

to **have a lot to talk about regarding** ■ to have a lot to talk about concerning tener mucho que comentar sobre ■ tener tema para rato sobre ➤ We have a lot to talk about regarding your recent trip to Guatemala and El Salvador. Tenemos mucho que comentar sobre tu viaje reciente a Guatemala y El Salvador.

to **have a lover** tener un amante ■ tener un compañero sentimental ■ tener una compañera sentimental ➤ The gossips say your wife has a lover. Las malas lenguas dicen que tu mujer tiene un amante.

to **have a lovesick look** tener ojos de carnero degollado

to **have a low opinion of** ■ to have a poor opinion of tener una mala opinión de ■ tener un muy mal concepto de

to **have a lot on one's mind** ■ to have a lot of worries or concerns tener mucho en la mente ■ tener mucho en la cabeza ■ dar vuelta a asuntos que se tienen pendientes ■ dar vuelta a asuntos que hay pendiente(s)

to **have a master's degree in something from** tener una maestría en algo de ■ *(Sp.)* tener un master en algo por ➤ She has a master's in Spanish from the University of Salamanca. Tiene un master en la filología hispánica por la Universidad de Salamanca.

to **have a medical procedure** ■ to undergo a medical procedure hacerse un procedimiento médico ➤ I had a CAT scan for my headaches. Me hice un TAC por mis dolores de cabeza. ■ Me hice un scanner por mis dolores de cabeza. ➤ Have you had an EKG? ¿Te has hecho un electrocardiograma? ➤ Daniel had his tongue pierced. Daniel se hizo un agujero en la lengua.

to **have a mind of one's own** tener mente propia ■ tener sus propias ideas ■ tener sus propias opiniones

to **have a mistress** tener una amante ➤ The gossips say her husband has a mistress. Las malas lenguas dicen que su marido tiene una amante.

to **have a nap** ■ to take a nap dormir la siesta ■ tomar una siesta ■ echarse una siesta

to **have a narrow escape** volver a nacer ▪ escapar por los pelos ▪ volver a nacer

have a nice weekend! ▪ have a good weekend! *(tú)* ¡que tengas un bonito fin de semana! ▪ ¡que tengas un buen fin de semana! ▪ *(usted)* ¡que tenga (usted) un bonito fin de semana! ▪ ¡que tenga (usted) un buen fin de semana!

have a nice life! *(sarcastic)* ¡que te vaya bonito! ▪ ¡que te vaya de lujo!

to **have a nose for a bargain** tener olfato para una ganga

to **have a nosebleed** ▪ to have a bloody nose ▪ (for) one's nose to be bleeding sangrar por la nariz ➤ I have a nosebleed. ▪ I have a bloody nose. ▪ My nose is bleeding. Sangro por la nariz. ▪ Estoy sangrando por la nariz.

to **have a pair of shoes stretched** ▪ to get a pair of shoes stretched hacer que metan los zapatos en la horma ▪ hacer que den los zapatos de sí ➤ I have to take these shoes to have them stretched. ▪ I have to get these shoes stretched. Tengo que llevar los zapatos para que los metan en la horma. ▪ Tengo que llevar los zapatos para que me los dé de sí.

to **have a paper to hand in** tener un trabajo que entregar ▪ tener una tesina que entregar

to **have a party** hacer una fiesta

to **have a prescription filled** ▪ to get a prescription filled (hacer) surtir una receta ▪ hacer que surtan una receta

to **have a purple fit** ▪ to fly into a rage ponerse rojo de ira ▪ darle un arrebato ▪ enfurecerse ▪ perder los estribos ➤ He had a purple fit. ▪ He flew into a rage. Le dio un arrebato. ▪ Se enfureció. ▪ Perdió los estribos.

to **have a quick temper** ▪ to be quick-tempered ▪ to be hot-tempered ▪ to have a short fuse tener sus prontos de enojo ▪ tener sus prontos ▪ tener pulgas

to **have a race** hacer una carrera

to **have a rash** tener picores ▪ salirle erupciones en la piel ▪ salirle un salpullido en la piel ▪ tener un salpullido ▪ salirle ronchas en la piel ▪ *(Sp.)* salirle un sarpullido en la piel ▪ tener un sarpullido

to **have a relapse** ▪ to suffer a relapse sufrir una recaída

to **have respect for someone** tener respeto por alguien ➤ The young people in the town have no respect for the colonel. Los jóvenes del pueblo no tienen ningún respeto por el coronel.

to **have a rough time (of it)** pasar un trago amargo ▪ pasar un mal rato

to **have a rude awakening** darse de bruces con la realidad

to **have a runny nose** ▪ (for) one's nose to be running gotearle la nariz ➤ I have a runny nose. ▪ My nose is running. Me gotea la nariz.

to **have a roll in the hay with someone** pegarse un revolcón con alguien ▪ darse un revolcón con alguien

to **have a scar 1.** *(anywhere on the body)* tener una cicatriz **2.** *(facial scar)* tener un chirlo

to **have a screw loose** ▪ to have bats in one's belfry faltarle un tornillo

to **have a seat** ▪ to take a seat ▪ to sit down tomar asiento ▪ sentarse ➤ Have a seat! *(tú)* Siéntate. ▪ *(usted)* Siéntese. ▪ *(ustedes)* Siéntense. ▪ *(Sp., vosotros)* Sentaos.

to **have a seating capacity of *x* people** ▪ to seat *x* people tener un aforo de *x* personas

to **have a second helping** ▪ to have some more repetir ➤ I'd like to have a second helping. Me gustaría repetir. ➤ Please, have some more. Por favor, repite. ▪ Por favor, repita usted. ➤ I've had a second helping of mashed potatoes. He repetido de puré de patatas.

to **have a seizure** sufrir un ataque (cerebral)

to **have a sharp eye** tener ojo clínico ▪ tener ojos de lince

to **have a short fuse** ▪ to have a quick temper ▪ to be quick-tempered tener poca correa ▪ tener sus prontos (de enojo) ▪ tener sus prontos (de enfado)

to **have a sick child** ▪ (for) one's child to be sick tener un(-a) hijo(-a) enfermo(-a) ➤ My daughter's sick. Tengo la hija enferma.

to **have a snack** tener una botana ▪ *(Sp., around 11 a.m.)* almorzar ▪ *(around 6:30 p.m.)* merendar ▪ *(anytime)* comer algo ➤ Do you want to have a little snack? ¿Quieres comer algo?

to **have a slow reaction time** ser lento al reaccionar ▪ tardar en reaccionar

to **have a solid foundation 1.** *(building)* tener buenos cimientos **2.** *(in a subject)* tener una base sólida

to **have a sore throat** tener dolor de garganta

to **have a smooth ride** tener una rodada suave

to **have a steady hand** tener buen pulso ▪ tener buen tino

to **have a streak of bad luck** tener una racha de mala suerte ▪ tener la negra

to **have a strong character** ▪ to have (good) character tener temperamento ▪ tener buen carácter

to **have a stroke of luck** ▪ to get lucky tener un golpe de suerte ➤ He had a stroke of luck. ▪ He got lucky. Tuvo un golpe de suerte.

to **have a superiority complex** creerse más que nadie

to **have a tantrum** ▪ to throw a tantrum tener una rabieta ▪ agarrarse un berrinche ▪ *(Sp.)* coger un berrinche

to **have a temperature** ▪ to have a fever tener fiebre ▪ tener calentura

to **have a tendency to** tener tendencia a ▪ tener propensión a ▪ tener inclinación para

to **have a terrible time doing something** ▪ to have a dickens of a time doing something ▪ to have an awful time doing something pasarlas canutas para hacer algo

to **have a third helping** ▪ to have three helpings ir a repetir ▪ volver a repetir ➤ I've had three helpings of mashed potatoes. Me he repetido el puré de papas por segunda vez. ▪ He vuelto a repetir el puré de patatas.

to **have a tooth extracted** ▪ to have a tooth pulled ▪ to have a tooth (taken) out tener una extracción dental ▪ sacarse un diente ▪ sacarse una muela

to **have a tooth out** ▪ to have a tooth pulled ▪ to have a tooth extracted sacarse un diente ▪ sacarse una muela ▪ tener una extracción dental ➤ I have to have my wisdom teeth out. Me tienen que sacar las muelas de juicio. ▪ Tienen que sacarme las muelas de juicio.

to **have a tooth pulled** ▪ to have a tooth extracted ▪ to have a tooth taken out sacarse un diente ▪ sacarse una muela ▪ tener una extracción dental

to **have a way with animals** tener una habilidad con los animales ▪ tener una actitud con los animales

to **have a way with people** tener don de gentes

to **have a way with words** tener (una) facilidad de palabra ▪ tener don de palabra

to **have a ways to go** faltarle un buen trecho

to **have a whole bunch of things to tell someone** ▪ to have a lot of things to tell someone tener un montón de cosas que decirle a alguien

to **have a wonderful time** ▪ to have a great time divertirse muchísimo ▪ pasarlo grande

to **have a word with someone** hablar con alguien de algo ▪ hablar con alguien sobre algo ➤ May I have a word with you? ¿Puedo hablar contigo?

to **have access to** tener acceso a

to **have all one can handle** ▪ to have one's hands full emplearse al fondo ➤ I'm taking care of two grandkids and the neighbor's dog, and I have to make potato salad for twenty people, so I've got all I can handle. Cuido dos nietos y el perro del vecino, y tengo que preparar ensalada de papas para veinte personas, así que me empleo al fondo.

to **have an accident** sufrir un accidente ▪ ocurrirle un accidente ➤ Look after Mr. Bond. He might have an accident. Encárgate del Sr. Bond. Podría ocurrirle un accidente.

to **have an ace up one's sleeve** tener un as en la manga

to **have an advantage over someone** llevarle una ventaja a alguien

to **have an affair (with someone)** tener una aventura (con alguien) ➤ The boss is having an affair with his secretary. El jefe tiene una aventura con su secretaria. ➤ They're having an affair. Tienen una aventura.

to **have an affair in one's mature years** echar una cana al aire ▪ echar una canita al aire

to **have an announcement to make** tener algo que anunciar

to **have an appointment** haber quedado ▪ tener (una) cita ▪ tener hora ➤ I have a doctor's appointment. He quedado con el médico. ▪ Tengo una cita con el médico. ➤ I have an appointment at noon. Tengo una cita a las doce (del mediodía). ➤ I have an appointment at the university. ➤ Tengo una cita en la universidad.

to **have an appointment with** quedar con ▪ tener una cita con ▪ tener cita con ➤ He had an appointment with the owner, but he didn't show up. Él quedó con la dueña pero no llegó él. ➤ I have an appointment at five. He quedado a las cinco. ➤ I had a doctor's appointment yesterday. ▪ I had an appointment with the doctor yesterday. Tuve cita con el médico ayer.

to **have an attachment to** tener apego a ➤ St. Francis had no attachment to material things. San Francisco no tuvo ningún apego a las cosas materiales.

to **have an awful time doing something** ▪ to have a dickens of a time doing something ▪ to have a terrible time doing something pasarlas canutas para hacer algo ▪ pasarlas canutas haciendo algo

to **have an ax to grind** ▪ to have an ulterior motive ▪ to have a selfish interest tener un interés personal ▪ actuar de manera interesada ➤ The author had a ax to grind when he wrote the article. El autor tenía un interés personal cuando escribió el artículo. ▪ El autor actuaba de manera interesada cuando escribió el artículo.

to **have an ear for music** tener oído para la música

to **have an easy-payment plan** dar facilidades de pago

to **have an idea** ocurrírsele una idea ➤ I have an idea! ▪ I've got an idea! ¡Se me ocurre una idea!

to **have an impact on** surtir efecto en

to **have an innocent look** tener cara inocente ▪ tener cara de inocencia

to **have an ulterior motive** ▪ to have a hidden agenda ▪ to have an ax to grind tener segundas intenciones

to **have an upset stomach** ▪ to be sick to one's stomach ▪ to be sick on one's stomach ▪ to be nauseated ▪ to feel nauseated estar mal del estómago ▪ andar mal del estómago ▪ tener náuseas ▪ estar descompuesto

to **have another commitment** tener otro compromiso ➤ I can't go because I have another commitment. No puedo ir porque tengo otro compromiso.

to **have another thought coming** ▪ to have got another thought coming estar arreglado ▪ llevarse un chasco ➤ If he thinks I'm going to call him, he's got another thought coming. Está arreglado si cree que le voy a llamar. *(It is also possible to say, "lo voy a llamar." However, this leísmo is common in Latin America as well as Spain.)*

to **have any...** tener... ➤ Do you have any stamps? ¿Tienes sellos? ➤ No, I don't have any. No, no tengo.

to **have any change (on one)** llevar cambio (encima) ➤ Do you have any change (on you)? ▪ Have you any change? ¿Llevas cambio?

to **have as one's objective** ▪ to have as one's goal tener por objetivo

to **have bad luck** ▪ to be unlucky tener mala suerte ▪ tener mal fario

to **have balls** *(off-color)* ▪ to have guts tener un par de huevos ▪ tener un par de cojones ▪ tenerlos bien puestos ▪ tenerlos en su sitio ▪ tener pelotas

to **have barely scratched the surface** ▪ to barely scratch the surface no haber hecho más que empezar

to **have bats in one's belfry** ▪ to have a few bats in one's belfry tener pájaros en la cabeza

to **have become of** ▪ to become of haber sido de ▪ haberse hecho ➤ Whatever has become of your Mexican friend? ¿Qué ha sido de tu amiga méxicana? ▪ ¿Qué se ha hecho tu amiga méxicana?

to **have been** haber sido ▪ ser ➤ His father has been a professor for a long time. Su padre es catedrático desde hace mucho tiempo.

to **have been at something for a long time** ▪ to have been doing something for a long time llevar mucho tiempo haciendo algo ➤ I've been at this for a long time. ▪ I've been doing this for a long time. Llevo mucho tiempo haciendo esto.

to **have been gone** haberse ausentado ▪ llevar fuera ➤ After I had been gone a month... Tras haberme ausentado un mes... ➤ He's been gone (for) three weeks. Lleva tres semanas fuera.

to **have been married before** ▪ to have been previously married ya haber estado casado(-a) ▪ ya haber sido casado(-a)

to **have been up since...** estar levantado desde... ➤ I've been up since six forty-five this morning. Estoy levantado desde las seis y cuarenta y cinco esta mañana.

to **have before one** ▪ to have in front of one tener ante sí ➤ I have before me... Tengo ante mí...

to **have big boobs** *(coarse)* ▪ to be stacked tener buenas domingas ▪ estar que se sale

to **have breakfast** ▪ to eat breakfast tomar el desayuno ▪ desayunar

to **have breathing problems** ▪ to have trouble breathing sufrir dificultad respiratoria

to **have calluses** tener callos

to **have cause** ▪ to have reason tener razón para ▪ haber antecedentes para ▪ tener antecedentes para

to **have changed a lot** estar muy cambiado(-a) ➤ She's changed a lot. Está muy cambiada.

to **have Christmas dinner** *(afternoon)* celebrar la comida navideña ▪ *(evening)* celebrar la cena navideña

to **have come a long way** haber recorrido un largo camino ➤ He's come a long way since... Ha recorrido un largo camino desde que...

to **have confidence in** tener confianza en

to **have confidence in someone** tener confianza en alguien

to **have connections** ▪ to have well-connected friends tener enchufe ▪ tener influencias ▪ tener padrinos

to **have control over...** tener control sobre...

to **have dealings with someone** tratar con alguien

to **have designs on** tramar en contra de ▪ tener la mira puesta en ➤ *(Biblical dream)* Those who had designs on the life of the child are dead. Los que tramaban en contra de la vida del niño están muertos.

to **have differing accounts of something** tener discrepancias sobre algo ▪ discrepar sobre algo

to **have difficulty understanding** ▪ to have a hard time understanding ▪ to have problems understanding tener problemas para entender ▪ costarle a uno entender

to **have dinner with** comer con ▪ estar comiendo con ➤ I had dinner with my family. Comí con mi familia. ▪ Estuve comiendo con mi familia.

to **have doubts about...** tener dudas sobre... ▪ tener dudas con lo de...

to **have earned the right** haberse ganado el derecho ➤ You've earned the right. Te has ganado el derecho.

to **have enough guts to** ▪ to have the guts to... tener suficientes narices para... ▪ tener agallas para... ▪ tener suficientes cojones para...

to **have enough to eat** ▪ to have enough food tener para comer

to **have enough to worry about** ya tener bastantes preocupaciones ▪ ya tener suficientes preocupaciones ➤ Don't tell him. He has enough to worry about right now. Que no se lo digas. Ya tiene bastantes preocupaciones en este momento.

to **have every intention of** tener toda la intención de ➤ Ceci said that during her vacation she has every intention of staying as far from a computer as possible. Ceci dijo que durante las vacaciones tiene toda la intención de estar lo más alejada de la computadora que pueda.

to **have every reason to** ▪ to have good reason(s) to tener todas las razones para ➤ He has every reason to seek a new trial. Tiene todas las razones para solicitar un nuevo juicio.

to **have everything** tener de todo ➤ That store has everything. Esa tienda tiene de todo.

to **have extensive knowledge of something** tener conocimientos amplios de algo ▪ estar muy versado en algo ▪ estar muy bien documentado sobre algo ▪ ➤ He has extensive knowledge of Spanish literature. Está muy versado en la literatura española. ➤ When it comes to Spanish literature, he really knows his stuff. En cuanto a literatura española, él sabe latín. ➤ He really knows his stuff. Este sabe latín.

to **have gas** ▪ to pass gas tener gases ▪ ventosear ➤ *(doctor's question)* Do you have gas? ▪ Are you passing gas? *(tú)* ¿Tienes gases? ▪ ¿Ventoseas? ▪ *(usted)* ¿Tiene gases? ▪ ¿Ventosea?

to **have good qualities** **1.** *(people)* tener cualidades buenas **2.** *(things)* tener calidades buenas ➤ She has many good qualities. Ella tiene muchas cualidades buenas.

to **have good reason to** ▪ to have every reason to tener toda razón a ➤ He has good reason to seek a new trial. Tiene toda razón al solicitar un nuevo juicio.

to **have (good) reason to believe** ▪ to have sufficient reason to believe tener razón de sobra para creer ▪ tener razones para creer ▪ tener motivos para creer

to **have (good) reason to do something** tener (buena) razón para hacer una cosa ➤ He has good reason to seek a new trial. Tiene buena razón para solicitar un nuevo juicio.

to **have good taste in** tener buen gusto al ➤ She has good taste in clothes. Tiene buen gusto al vestirse.

to **have (got) paint all over one** ▪ to be covered with paint estar cubierto de pintura ▪ estar perdido de pintura ➤ He's got paint all over him. ▪ He has paint all over him. Está cubierto de pintura. ▪ Está perdido de pintura.

to **have (got) someone by the balls** *(graphic)* ▪ to have someone over a barrel tenerle agarrado por los cojones

to **have got someone wrapped around one's little finger** ▪ to have someone wrapped around one's little finger tener a alguien metido en el puño ▪ tener a alguien en el puño

to **have (got) someone's number** **1.** *(literal)* to have (got) someone's phone number tener el número telefónico de alguien **2.** *(figurative)* to have (got) someone pegged tener fichado a alguien

to **have (got) guts** ▪ to have a lot of guts tener agallas ▪ tener muchas agallas ➤ That guy's got guts. ▪ That guy's got a lot of guts. ▪ That guy has (a lot of) guts. Ese tipo tiene (muchas) agallas.

to **have gradually gotten to know someone** haber ido conociendo a alguien ▪ haber ido conociendo a alguien gradualmente ▪ haber ido conociendo a alguien poco a poco

to **have group sex** ▪ to have an orgy hacer una cama redonda ▪ hacer una orgía

to **have had a falling out with someone** ▪ to be on the outs with someone estar de morros con alguien

to **have had all one can take** estar hasta la coronilla ▪ estar harto ▪ haber llegado al colmo ➤ I've had all I can take. He llegado al colmo.

to **have had enough of** ▪ to be fed up with estar harto de

to **have had it** **1.** *(worn-out thing)* estar para la basura ▪ no aguantar más **2.** *(worn-out person)* ya no aguantar más ➤ This pair of socks has had it. Este par de calcetines está para la basura. ➤ I've had it! ¡Ya no aguanto más!

to **have had more than enough** ▪ to have had more than one's share ya tener lo suficiente ▪ tener bastante y de sobra

to **have had one too many** haber tomado una copa de más

to **have had one's fill of...** darse un empacho de... ▪ darse un hartazgo de...

to **have had someone do something** haber gente que hacía algo ➤ My grandfather, who looked like Eisenhower, had people come up to him and ask for his autograph. Debido a que mi abuelo se parecía a Eisenhower, había gente que se le acercaba para pedirle su autógrafo.

to **have had time to do something** haber dispuesto de tiempo... ➤ He's had eleven years to... Ha dispuesto de once años...

have her call me ▪ have her give me a call *(tú)* dile que (ella) me llame ▪ *(usted)* dígale que (ella) me llame

have her come in ▪ tell her to come in que entre (ella) ▪ hágala pasar

have her give me a call ▪ have her call me *(tú)* dile que (ella) me llame ▪ *(usted)* dígale que (ella) me llame

have her take a seat hága que tome un asiento ▪ *(patronizing)* que espere sentado(-a)

have him call me ▪ have him give me a call *(tú)* dile que (él) me llame ▪ *(usted)* dígale que (él) me llame

have him come in ▪ tell him to come in que entre (él) ▪ que pase

have him give me a call ▪ have him call me *(tú)* haz que (él) me llame ▪ *(usted)* haga que (él) me llame

have him take a seat que espere sentado

to **have homework (to do)** tener tarea(s) ▪ *(Sp.)* tener deberes (para casa)

have I forgotten anyone? ▪ have I overlooked anyone? ¿he olvidado a alguien? ▪ ¿me he olvidado de alguien? ▪ ¿he pasado a alguien por alto?

have I got news for you! ¡te tengo un notición! ▪ ¡qué novedad te tengo!

to **have important matters to attend to** tener asuntos importantes que atender

to **have in store for** depararle el futuro ▪ aguardarle el futuro ➤ I don't know what the future has in store for me. No sé lo que me depare el futuro. ▪ No sé lo que me deparará el futuro. ➤ I don't know the future that awaits me. No sé el futuro que me aguarda.

to **have influence with someone** ▪ to have pull with someone tener influencia con alguien ▪ tener mucha vara con alguien

to **have it all to oneself** quedarse con todo ▪ poder estar solo con

to **have it both ways** mamar y beber leche ➤ The only way to have it both ways is to hedge. Put half your funds in dollars and half in euros. When one falls, the other rises, and you maintain the value of your savings. La única manera de mamar y beber leche es salvaguardarse. Ponga la mitad de sus fondos en dólares y la otra en euros. Cuando caigan unos, subirán los otros, y usted mantendrá el valor de sus ahorros.

to **have it coming** tenerlo merecido

to **have it in for someone** tenerle ojeriza a alguien ▪ tenerle tirria a alguien

to **have it made** ▪ to have got it made montárselo bien ➤ My friend's got it made. He's found a job that covers his expenses and leaves him enough time to attend the university. ▪ My friend has it made. He's found a job that covers his expenses and leaves him enough time to attend the university. Mi amigo se lo monta bien: ha encontrado un trabajo que le deja tiempo libre para ir a la universidad y cubrir sus gastos. ➤ You've got it made. Te lo has montado bien.

to **have it on good authority that...** ▪ to know from a reliable source that... saberlo de buena tinta que... ▪ saberlo a través de una fuente fidedigna que... ▪ beber en buenas fuentes que... ▪ tener noticias fiables que... ▪ tener noticias certeras que... ▪ saber de buena fuente que...

to **have it out with someone** habérselas con alguien

to **have it right** ▪ to get it right tenerlo claro ➤ Victor Borge said, "Santa Claus has it right. Visit just once a year." Victor Borge dijo, "Santa Claus lo tiene claro. Visitar sólo una vez al año".

to **have it sewn up** ▪ to have got it sewn up ▪ to have it in the bag tenerlo en el bote ➤ He's got it sewn up. ▪ He's got it all sewn up. Lo tiene en el bote.

to **have it soundproofed** hacerlo a prueba de sonido ▪ ponerlo a prueba de sonido ➤ You should close off the classical music area and have it soundproofed. Debería encerrar el área de la música clásica y ponerla a prueba de sonido.

have it your way! *(tú)* salte con la tuya ▪ puedes salirte con la tuya ▪ *(usted)* sálgase (usted) con la suya ▪ puede (usted) salirse con la suya

to **have itchy feet** **1.** *(literal)* (for) one's feet to itch picarle los pies **2.** *(figurative)* to love to travel encantarle estar de aquí para allá ▪ to be restless estar inquieto(-a) ▪ ser muy movido(-a)

to **have its drawbacks** ▪ to have some drawbacks tener sus desventajas ▪ tener sus inconvenientes ▪ tener sus bemoles

to **have (its) good and bad points** ▪ to have its good points and its bad ▪ to have its pros and cons tener sus puntos buenos y malos

to **have just done something** acabar de hacer algo ➤ We have just finished dinner. Acabamos de comer. ➤ We had just finished dinner when the phone rang. Acabábamos de comer cuando sonó el teléfono. ➤ We were just finishing dinner when the phone rang. Estábamos acabando de comer cuando sonó el teléfono.

to **have just enough time for something** tener el tiempo justo para algo

to **have just enough time to do something** tener el tiempo justo para hacer algo

to **have known someone for** conocerle a alguien desde hace ➤ We have known him for ten years. Lo conocemos desde hace diez años. ▪ *(Sp., leísmo)* Le conocemos desde hace diez años.

to **have learned one's lesson** haber escarmentado ▪ haberse curado ▪ haber aprendido uno su lección

to **have left** ▪ to remain quedarle ▪ restarle ➤ He has fifteen years left before he retires. Le quedan quince años antes de que se jubile. ➤ She has five days of vacation left. Le restan cinco días de vacaciones. ➤ After we all put our addresses in your little address book, you won't have any pages left. Después de escribir todas nuestras direcciones en tu librito de direcciones, no te quedará ninguna página.

to **have links to** tener lazos con ▪ tener nexos con ▪ estar conectado con

to **have links to organized crime** ▪ to have ties to organized crime tener nexos con el crimen organizado ▪ tener lazos con el crimen organizado ▪ tener vinculación con el crimen organizado

to **have little to lose** ▪ not to have much to lose tener poco que perder ▪ no tener mucho que perder

to **have long hair** ▪ to wear one's hair long tener el pelo largo ▪ llevar el pelo largo

to **have many years left** quedarle muchos años ➤ *(doctor to patient)* You have many years left if you stop smoking. Le quedan muchos años si usted deja de fumar.

to **have mixed feelings about something** ▪ to have conflicting feelings about something tener sentimientos contradictorios sobre algo ▪ tener sentimientos contradictorios acerca de algo ▪ tener sentimientos contradictorios (con) respecto a algo ▪ tener sentimientos encontrados sobre algo ▪ tener sentimientos contrapuestos ▪ tener sentimientos enfrentados sobre algo

to **have more important things to do** tener cosas más importantes que hacer

to **have more than enough food** tener más de lo suficiente de comida ▪ tener comida de sobra

to **have more than enough of something** tener más de lo suficiente de algo ▪ tener algo de sobra ➤ I have more than enough socks. Tengo calcetines de sobra.

to **have more than enough reason to** ▪ to have more than sufficient to sobrarle motivos para

to **have nerves of steel** tener nervios de acero

to **have never had it so good** ▪ never to have had it so good nunca haberle ido mejor a alguien ➤ We've never had it so good. Nunca nos ha ido mejor.

to **have never seen anything like it** nunca haber visto algo así ➤ *(news item)* Never before had astronomers seen anything like it in the universe: a water bubble one and a half times as large as the solar system, surrounding a star in formation. Nunca hasta ahora habían visto los astrónomos algo así en el universo: una burbuja de agua, de un tamaño igual a una vez y media el Sistema Solar, envolviendo una estrella en formación.

to **have no alternative** ▪ to have no choice ▪ not to have any alternative ▪ not to have any choice no tener (otra) alternativa ▪ no tener otra opción ▪ no tener otra salida ➤ I have no alternative. ▪ I don't have any alternative. ▪ I've got no alternative. ▪ I haven't got any alternative. No tengo otra alternativa. ▪ No me queda otra.

to **have no alternative but to...** ▪ to have no choice but to... ▪ not to have any alternative but to... ▪ not to have any choice but to... ▪ not to have any alternative other than to... ▪ not to have any choice other than to... no tener más alternativa que... ▪ no tener más opción que... ▪ no tener otra opción que... ▪ no tener otra salida que...

to **have no alternative left** ▪ not to have any alternative left no quedarle (otra) alternativa ▪ no quedarle más remedio ▪ no quedarle otra ▪ no quedarle otro recurso

to **have no appetite** ▪ not to have any appetite ▪ not to have an appetite estar sin apetito ▪ estar desganado

to **have no bounds** ▪ to know no bounds ▪ to have no limits ▪ to know no limits no tener límites ▪ no conocer límites ▪ no saber de límites ➤ Her generosity has no bounds. ▪ Her generosity knows no bounds. Su generosidad no conoce límites.

to **have no business doing something** no tener derecho a hacer algo ▪ no tener derecho de hacer algo ▪ no tener porque hacer algo ➤ You have no business going into your sister's room without her permission. No tienes derecho a entrar en la habitación de tu hermana sin (su) permiso.

to **have no choice** ▪ to have no alternative ▪ not to have any choice ▪ not to have any alternative no tener elección ▪ no tener alternativa ➤ I have no choice. ▪ I don't have any choice. ▪ I've got no choice. ▪ I haven't got any choice. No tengo elección.

to **have no choice but to** ▪ to have no choice other than to no tener más remedio que ▪ no tener otra opción que ➤ U.S. Attorney General Janet Reno explained that she had no choice but to order the intervention. La fiscal general de EE UU, Janet Reno, explicó que no tuvo más remedio que ordenar la intervención.

to **have no effect on** ▪ not to have any effect on ▪ to fail to sway no surtir efecto en ➤ Beijing's threats to resort to force to prevent the formal secession of Taiwan had no effect on yesterday's presidential elections. Las amenazas de Pekín de recurrir a las armas para evitar la secesión formal de Taiwan no surtieron efecto en las elecciones presidenciales celebradas ayer.

to **have no ethics** ▪ not to have any ethics no tener la ética

to **have no guile** ▪ to be guileless no tener astucia ▪ no tener malicia ▪ *(literary)* no tener hiel

to **have no idea** ▪ not to have any idea no tener idea

to **have no idea of what is coming** ▪ to have no idea of what one is in for ▪ not to have any idea of what is coming ▪ not to have any idea of what one is in for no tener ni idea de lo vendrá ▪ no tener ni un barrunto de lo que se viene ▪ no tener ni un indicio de lo que se viene ▪ no tener ni una sospecha de lo que se viene

to **have no intention of** ▪ not to have any intention of no tener ninguna intención de

to **have no limits** ▪ to know no limits ▪ to have no bounds ▪ to know no bounds no tener límites ▪ no conocer límites

to **have no one to turn to** ▪ not to have anyone to turn to no tener a quien acudir

to **have no part in** no tener parte en ➤ She was an innocent bystander. She had no part in the robbery. Ella era una inocente espectadora. No tuvo parte en el robo.

to **have no place in** no tener ningún lugar en

to **have no proof of that** no tener ninguna prueba de eso

to **have no proof that...** ▪ not to have any proof that... no tener ninguna prueba de que...

to **have no qualms about doing something 1.** *(doubts, misgivings, reservations)* no tener reparo en hacer algo ▪ no tener ninguna duda para hacer algo **2.** *(scruples, pangs of conscience)* no tener ningún escrúpulo para hacer algo

to **have no replacement for someone** ▪ not to have any replacement for someone ▪ to have no one to replace someone ▪ not to have anyone to replace someone no tener quien reemplace a alguien ▪ no tener relevo para alguien ▪ no tener substituto para alguien ➤ *(news item)* The team has no replacement as yet for Del Bosque, who yesterday was offered a coaching position which he declined. El equipo no tiene relevo aún para Del Bosque al que se le ofreció ayer una dirección deportiva que el técnico declinó.

to **have no say in the matter** ▪ not to have any say in the matter no tener ni voz ni voto en el asunto ▪ ni quitar ni poner rey

to **have no use for someone** ▪ not to have any use for someone ▪ not to like someone no caerle bien a uno ➤ I don't have any use for him. No me cae bien.

to **have no way of knowing** no tener manera de saberlo ➤ We have no way of knowing. No tenemos manera de saberlo.

to **have nothing better to do** ▪ not to have anything better to do ▪ not to have got anything better to do no tener nada mejor que hacer to **have nothing good to say about...** no tener nada bueno que decir de...

to **have nothing to be ashamed of** ▪ not to have anything to be ashamed of no tener nada por qué avergonzarse ▪ no tener por qué bajar la cabeza delante nadie ▪ no tener por qué agachar la cabeza delante nadie ➤ You have nothing to be ashamed of. No tienes por qué bajar la cabeza delante nadie.

to **have nothing to lose** ▪ not to have anything to lose no tener nada que perder

to **have nothing to say about a matter** ▪ not to have anything to say about a matter no tener nada que decir sobre un asunto

to **have nothing to worry about** ▪ not to have anything to worry about no tener de qué preocuparse

to **have nowhere to turn** ▪ not to have anywhere to turn no tener adonde acudir

to **have on** ▪ to be wearing llevar puesto ▪ tener puesto ➤ The bullfighter has on a suit of lights. El torero lleva puesta un traje de luces.

to **have one** tener ▪ tenerlo ▪ tener uno ➤ Do you have a bulletin board here?-No, we don't have one. ¿Tiene un tablón de anuncios aquí?-No, no (lo) tenemos.

to **have one too many** beber más de la cuenta ▪ pasarse de copas ➤ It looks like that guy has had one too many. Parece que ese tipo ha bebido más de la cuenta. ▪ Parece que ese tipo se pasó de copa.

to **have one's arms crossed** estar de brazos cruzados

to **have one's back to the wall** ▪ to be (caught) between a rock and a hard place encontrarse entre la espada y la pared ▪ dar la espalda a al pared ▪ estar entre la espada y la pared ▪ estar acorralado

to **have one's back turned to someone** estar de espaldas a uno ➤ He had his back turned to me. Él estaba de espaldas a mí.

to **have one's blood drawn** sacarle sangre a uno ➤ I'm here to have my blood drawn. Estoy aquí para que me saquen sangre. ▪ Vine para que me saquen sangre.

to **have one's cholesterol checked** hacerse una prueba de colesterol ➤ You should have your cholesterol checked. Deberías hacerte una prueba de colesterol.

to **have one's coffee** tomar su café ➤ I've already had my coffee. Ya he tomado mi café.

to **have one's ears pierced** ▪ to get one's ears pierced hacerse agujeros en las orejas ➤ She had her ears pierced. Se hizo agujeros en las orejas.

to **have one's eye on someone** tener el ojo echado a alguien ▪ echar el ojo a alguien ▪ echar la vista encima

to **have one's eye on something** tener el ojo echado a algo ▪ tener los ojos en algo

to **have one's feet on the ground** tener los pies sobre el suelo

to **have one's fill of something** tener un empacho de algo ▪ darse un empacho de algo ▪ atiborrarse de algo ▪ darse un hartazgo de algo

to **have one's hands full** ▪ to have all one can handle emplearse al fondo

to **have one's hands tied** tener atadas las manos

to **have one's head in the clouds** estar en las nubes

to **have one's head in the sand** jugar al avestruz

to **have one's head on straight** tener la cabeza en su sitio

to **have one's heart set on** tener tanta ilusión de algo ▪ tener tanta ilusión para algo ▪ estar tan puesto para algo

to **have one's heart set on something** ▪ to set one's heart on something tener el corazón puesto en algo ▪ poner el corazón en algo

to **have one's (menstrual) period** tener la regla ▪ *(Sp., colorful)* venirle el primo de América

to **have one's mind made up** ▪ to have decided tenerlo decidido ➤ I still haven't made up my mind. Todavía no lo tengo decidido.

to **have one's mind on other things** tener la mente puesta en otras cosas

to **have one's nap** ▪ to take a nap dormir la siesta

to **have one's own way of looking at things** ▪ to think for oneself tener su propio criterio ▪ pensar por sí mismo

to **have one's picture taken** ▪ to get one's picture taken hacer sacar la foto ▪ hacer que le saquen la foto ▪ ser fotografiado

to **have one's sights set on** ▪ to set one's sights on tener la mira puesta en

to **have one's tonsils out** quitarle a uno las amígdalas ▪ *(Mex., Ven.)* quitarle a uno las anginas ➤ I had my tonsils out. Me quitaron las amígdalas. ▪ Me quitaron las anginas.

to **have one's tubes tied** *(female birth control method)* ▪ to have one's Fallopian tubes tied ligarle las trompas (de Falopio) ➤ She had her tubes tied. Le ligaron las trompas.

to **have only one chance to** ▪ to have only one opportunity to tener una sola oportunidad para

to **have plenty of food** ▪ to have more than enough food tener comida de sobra

to **have plenty of money** tener dinero de sobra ➤ Don't worry, I have plenty of money. No te preocupes, tengo dinero de sobra.

to **have plenty of time** ▪ to have more than enough time tener mucho tiempo por delante ▪ tener tiempo de sobra

to **have plenty to spare** tener para dar y tomar

to **have promise** ▪ to have a lot of promise prometer ser ➤ The child has (a lot of) promise. *(he)* El niño promete ser. ▪ *(she)* La niña promete ser.

to **have priority over someone** ▪ to be ahead of someone tener prioridad sobre alguien

to **have pull** ▪ to have connections tener palanca

to **have reached the limits of one's endurance** ▪ to be complete exhausted haber llegado al límite de sus esfuerzas ▪ estar al límite de sus esfuerzas

to **have reason to believe** tener razones para creer ▪ tener motivos para creer

to **have regular habits** ser metódico(-a) ▪ ser ordenado(-a) (en sus costumbres)

to **have room for** tener cabida para ▪ tener espacio para ▪ *(Sp., in an elevator)* entrar ➤ Is there room for one more (person)? ¿Entra uno(-a) más?

to **have scars** ▪ to show scars tener cicatrices ▪ ostentar cicatrices ➤ He fought in the battle and has the scars to show for it. Peleó en la batalla y tiene las cicatrices para probarlo.

to **have seen its better days** haber visto tiempos mejores

to **have seen one's better days** haber visto días mejores ▪ haber visto tiempos mejores

to **have seen something happen** haber visto suceder algo

to **have (serious) consequences** tener (serias) consecuencias ▪ traer cola

to **have sex** practicar el sexo

to **have short hair** ▪ to wear one's hair short llevar el pelo corto

to **have some errands to run** ▪ to have some errands to do **1.** *(for oneself)* tener unas tareas domésticas **2.** *(for someone else)* tener que hacer unos recados ▪ tener unos quehaceres

to **have some good news and some bad news** traer una buena y una mala noticia

to **have some money** tener (algún) dinero ▪ tener (algo de) dinero

to **have some more** ▪ to have another helping repetirse ➤ I'm going to have some more potatoes a la huancaína. Voy a repetirme la papa a la huancaína.

to **have some news** ▪ to have a piece of news traerle noticias ➤ I have some news (for you). *(tú)* Te traigo noticias. ▪ *(usted)* Le traigo noticias (a usted).

to **have someone arrested** hacer prender a alguien ▪ hacer arrestar a alguien ▪ hacer detener a alguien ➤ *(Ricardo Palma)* He had Don Alonso Yánez arrested and executed. Hizo prender y dar muerte a Don Alonso Yánez.

to **have someone by the balls** *(off-color)* ▪ to have someone over a barrel tener agarrado a alguien por los cojones ▪ tener cogido a alguien de los huevos

to **have someone for a class** darle a uno clase ➤ I don't have him for a class this quarter. No me da clase este trimestre. ▪ No llevo una clase con él este trimestre. ▪ No estoy en su curso este trimestre. ➤ I have him for a class this semester. Me da un clase este trimestre. ▪ Llevo una clase con él. ▪ Estoy en su curso.

to **have someone in one's pocket** tener a alguien en el bolsillo ➤ I've got him in my pocket. Lo tengo en el bolsillo. ▪ Le tengo en el bolsillo.

to **have someone in stitches** tener a alguien muriéndose de risa (con...)

to **have someone on a pedestal** tener a alguien en un pedestal

to **have someone over a barrel** ▪ to put someone in an untenable position ▪ to be at the mercy of one's enemies tener a alguien al merced de uno ▪ tener a alguien con el agua al cuello ➤ The general contractors had the construction lender over a barrel. Los contratistas generales tenían al prestamista con el agua al cuello.

to **have someone pegged** ▪ to have someone's number ▪ to have got someone's number ▪ to have got someone pegged tener a alguien fichado ▪ tener a alguien calado ▪ *(Sp.)* cogerle la medida a alguien

to **have someone to take care of** tener alguien que cuidar ➤ She had three children to take care of. Tenía tres hijos que cuidar. ▪ Tenía tres niños que cuidar.

to **have someone to talk to** tener a alguien con quien hablar

to **have someone to thank for** tener a alguien agradecer por

to **have someone trained** ▪ to have got someone trained tener a alguien bien entrenado ➤ I've got that waiter trained. Tengo a ese camarero muy bien entrenado.

to **have someone under one's spell** tener hechizado a alguien

to **have someone under one's thumb** tener a alguien en un puño

to **have someone wait** hacer esperar a alguien ▪ hacer que alguien espere ➤ Have her wait outside. *(tú)* Hazla esperar afuera. ▪ Que espere afuera. ▪ *(usted)* Hágala esperar afuera. ▪ Que espere afuera.

to **have someone worried** tenerle a alguien preocupado ➤ Her silence has me worried. Su silencio (de ella) me tiene preocupado.

to **have someone wrapped around one's little finger** ▪ to have got someone wrapped around one's little finger tener a alguien metido en el puño ▪ tener a alguien en el puño ▪ tener mano con alguien

to **have someone's number 1.** *(telephone)* tener el número (telefónico) de alguien **2.** *(figurative)* to have someone pegged ▪ to have got someone's number ▪ to have got someone pegged tener fichado(-a) a alguien

to **have something 1.** to possess, own something tener algo **2.** *(esp. with the verb "poder")* to keep something quedarse con algo ➤ You can have the newspaper. ▪ You can keep the newspaper. Puedes quedarte con el periódico.

to **have something against someone** tener algo en contra de alguien ▪ tener algo en contra suya ▪ tener algo contra alguien ➤ What do you have against *me*? ¿Qué tienes en contra de mí? ▪ ¿Qué tienes en contra mía? ▪ Qué tienes contra mí?

to **have something built** hacer construir algo ➤ We had a house built. Hicimos construir una casa.

to **have something caught in one's throat** tener algo atorado en la garganta

to **have something crated and shipped** hacer empaquetear algo en un cajón de embalaje y enviarlo

to **have something done** hacer que haga algo ▪ mandar hacer algo ▪ dar algo a hacer ➤ I'd like to have some copies made. *(tú)* Me gustaría que me hagas unas copias. ▪ *(usted)* Me gustaría que me haga (usted) unas copias.

to **have something for breakfast** desayunar con algo ➤ We're having eggs for breakfast. Vamos a desayunar con huevos.

to **have something in a mess** tener algo hecho un lío

to **have something installed** mandar algo instalar

to **have something made 1.** *(literal)* to have something built mandar hacer algo ▪ mandar que le hagan a uno ▪ mandar hacer algo ▪ mandar que le hagan a uno **2.** *(figurative)* (for) something to be a fait accompli tener hecho algo ➤ I had this shelf made at a shop that builds unfinished furniture. Mandé hacer esta estantería en una tienda de bricolaje. ▪ Mandé que me hicieran una estantería en la tienda de bricolaje. ➤ *(editorial)* Between the oil slick and the war, the socialists had it made. Entre el asunto de la marea negra y la guerra, los socialistas lo tuvieron hecho.

to **have something on one's mind** tener algo en la mente

to **have something ready for someone** tener algo preparado para alguien ➤ We'll have it ready for you by Friday. Lo tendremos preparado para usted para el viernes.

to **have something sent out to be done** ▪ to send something out to be done enviar algo para que hagan algo ▪ mandar algo para que hagan algo ➤ I had the rug sent out to be cleaned. Envié la alfombra para que la limpien.

to **have something to one's credit** tener algo a su haber ➤ The fledgling actress now has two hit movies to her credit. La actriz novata ahora tiene dos películas éxitos a su haber.

to **have something under control** tener algo bajo control

to **have something under way** tener algo en marcha ➤ I've got dinner under way. Tengo la comida en marcha.

to **have something with one** ▪ to have something on one's person tener algo consigo ➤ I don't have my passport with me. ▪ I don't have my passport on me. No tengo mi pasaporte conmigo. ➤ He doesn't have his passport with him. No tiene su pasaporte consigo.

to **have spring fever** la primavera la sangre altera

to **have stage presence** tener tablas

to **have taken its toll on** deteriorar ➤ Time has taken its toll on the ancient ruins. El tiempo ha deteriorado las ruinas antiguas. ➤ Health problems have taken a toll on his looks. Sus problemas de salud han deteriorado su físico.

to **have that certain something** ▪ to have a certain something tener un no sé qué ▪ tener su aquél

to **have the ability to do something** tener la habilidad de hacer algo ▪ tener la capacidad de hacer algo ▪ ser capaz de hacer algo

to **have the appointment down for...** tener la cita apuntada a las... ▪ constar la cita a las... ➤ I have your appointment down for 6 p.m. Please verify. Tengo su cita apuntada a las seis (de la tarde). Por favor confírmemela. ▪ Su cita consta a las seis (de la tarde). Por favor confírmemela.

to **have the audacity to...** tener la osadía de...

to **have the blues** estar con la depre ▪ estar bajeras

to **have the courage to** tener el valor de

to **have the doctor check you over** ▪ to have the doctor examine you hacerse ver del médico ➤ Have the doctor check you over. Hazte ver del médico.

to **have the dubious honor of being...** caberle el dudoso honor de ser...

to **have the gift of gab** tener un pico de oro ▪ tener un piquito de oro ▪ tener labia

to **have the guts to...** ▪ to have enough guts to... tener suficientes narices para... ▪ tener suficientes cojones para...

to **have the feeling that...** tener el presentimiento que... ▪ tener la sensación de que... ▪ tener la impresión de que... ▪ darle la impresión de que... ▪ darle la sensación de que... ▪ tener una corazonada de que... ▪ latirle que... ➤ I have the feeling that someone is looking at me. Tengo la impresión de que alguien me está mirando. ▪ Me da la impresión de que alguien me esté mirando. ▪ Me da la sensación de que alguien me esté mirando. ▪ Tengo una corazonada de que Marta va a llegar temprano. ▪ Me late que Marta va a llegar temprano.

to **have the gall to do something** ▪ to have the nerve to do something tener el descaro de hacer algo ▪ tener el morro de hacer algo

to **have the good fortune to** tener la suerte de ▪ tener la buena fortuna de

to **have the guts to do something** tener agallas para hacer algo ▪ tener arrestos para hacer algo ▪ *(off-color)* tener los huevos para hacer algo

to **have the hiccups** ▪ to have the hiccoughs tener hipo

to **have the knack of it** ▪ to have the hang of it tener la maña para hacerlo ▪ tener el tranquillo para hacerlo to **have the laundry done** ▪ to send out the laundry ▪ to send the laundry out dar a lavar y planchar las ropas ▪ poner la ropa a hacer ▪ *(Sp.)* dar a hacer la colada

to **have the makings of an actor** tener madera de actor

to **have the memory of an elephant** tener memoria de elefante

to **have the nerve to do something** tener (la) cara de hacer algo

to **have the patience of Job** tener más paciencia que el santo Job

to **have the patience to do something 1.** *(as a character trait)* tener la paciencia de hacer algo **2.** *(in situations)* tener la paciencia para hacer algo

to **have the power to decide** tener el poder de decidir

to **have the power to do something 1.** *(magical or miraculous power)* tener la virtud de **2.** *(political authority)* tener el poder de ➤ Superman has the power to see through walls. Superman tiene la virtud de ver a través de las paredes.

to **have the right number** tener el número correcto ▪ tener el número que es

to **have the right of way** tener el derecho de paso ▪ (for) the right of way to favor ser la preferencia de paso de alguien ➤ *(news item)* The traffic light was green in both directions, but the right of way favored the concrete truck. Los semáforos de ambos sentidos estaban en verde, pero la preferencia de paso era de la hormigonera.

to **have the right to do something** tener derecho a hacer algo

to **have the same point of view** tener el mismo punto de vista ▪ tener la misma tesis

to **have the say** ▪ to call the shots ▪ to be the boss llevar la voz cantante ▪ ser el que decide ▪ ser la que decide

to **have the situation under control** tener la situación bajo control

to **have the strength of one's convictions** tener la fuerza de sus convicciones

to **have the urge to do something** ▪ to get the urge to do something entrarle a uno ganas de hacer algo

to **have tickets (to)** tener entradas (para)

to **have time** darle tiempo ▪ tener tiempo ➤ I'll go if I have time. Iré si me da tiempo. ▪ Iré si tengo tiempo. ➤ I'd go if I had time. Iría si me diera tiempo. ▪ Iría si tuviera tiempo. ➤ I would have gone if I had had time. Habría ido si me hubiera dado tiempo. ▪ Habría ido si hubiera tenido tiempo. ➤ I would have had time to go to the movies if I had finished my homework. Me habría dado tiempo ir al cine si hubiera terminado mis deberes. ▪ Habría tenido tiempo ir al cine si hubiera terminado mis deberes. *(A corruption of English grammar is to say, "if I would have had time" (si yo habría tenido tiempo) instead of "if I had had time" (si yo hubiera tenido tiempo)." Students of English need to recognize this mistake but avoid imitating it.)*

to **have time to do something** tener tiempo para hacer algo ▪ darle tiempo para ▪ tener tiempo de ▪ darle tiempo de ➤ I had more time to get caught up in the other class. Tuve más tiempo para ponerme al día en la otra clase.

to **have to be coaxed** ▪ to have to coax someone hacerse de rogar ▪ engatusar a alguien para que haga algo ➤ We invited him to the party, but he had to be coaxed into accepting. ▪ We invited him to the party, but we had to coax him into accepting. Le invitamos a la fiesta, pero se hizo de rogar hasta que aceptó. ▪ Le invitamos a la fiesta pero tuvimos que engatusarlo para que acepte.

to **have to be eligible for** tener que ser (declarado) eligible para ➤ Do you have to be sixty-five to be eligible for the senior discount? ¿Hay que tener cumplidos sesenta y cinco años para ser eligible para el descuento para mayores?

to **have to be pleaded with (to...)** tener que ser suplicado (para...)

to **have to be somewhere** tener que estar en algún lugar ▪ tener que estar en algún sitio ➤ I have to be somewhere by nine o'clock. Tengo que estar en un sitio para las nueve.

to **have to (do something)** tener que hacerlo ➤ I have no choice. I have to. No tengo otra opción. Tengo que hacerlo.

to **have to do with** tener que ver con ▪ atañer a ▪ referirse a ➤ Many of the questions had to do with... Muchas preguntas se referían a... ➤ It has nothing to do with you. No tiene nada que ver contigo. ▪ Eso no te atañe.

to **have to get married** ▪ to have a shotgun wedding casarse por el sindicato

to **have to have an operation** ▪ to have to have surgery ▪ to have to undergo surgery ▪ to have to be operated on **1.** *(a uno)* to have to be operated on tener que operarse ▪ tener que someterse a una operación **2.** *(a alguien)* to have to operate on someone else tener que operarle ▪ tener que someterle a una operación ➤ I have to have an operation on my knee. Tengo que tener una operación en la rodilla. ▪ Tienen que operarme en la rodilla.

to **have to undergo surgery** ▪ to have to have an operation ▪ to have to have surgery ▪ to have to be operated on tener que someterse a una operación ▪ tener que operarse (de) ➤ Our son had to undergo surgery. Nuestro hijo se tuvo que someter a una operación.

to **have trouble breathing** ▪ to have difficulty breathing ▪ to have a problem breathing ▪ to have breathing problems sufrir dificultad respiratoria

to **have trouble doing something** tener dificultad en hacer algo ▪ tener problemas para hacer algo ➤ You won't have any trouble finding it. No tendrás ninguna dificultad en localizarlo.

to **have waited long enough** ya haber cumplido con esperar ➤ I've waited long enough. Ya he cumplido con esperar.

to **have well-connected friends** ▪ to have connections tener padrinos ▪ tener amigos bien enchufados

to **have what it takes (to succeed)** ▪ to have got what it takes (to succeed) tener lo que se requiere (para triunfar) ▪ tener lo que se necesita (para triunfar) ▪ poseer lo que se requiere (para triunfar) ➤ You have what it takes (to succeed). ▪ You've got what it takes (to succeed). Tienes lo que se requiere para triunfar. ▪ Tienes lo que se necesita para triunfar. ▪ Posees lo que se requiere para triunfar. ▪ Posees lo que se necesita para triunfar.

to **have work to do** tener trabajo que hacer

to **have *x* gears** tener *x* velocidades ➤ The car has five gears. El carro tiene cinco velocidades. ▪ *(Sp.)* El coche tiene cinco velocidades.

to **have *x* years left until...** quedarle *x* años hasta que...

have you been working there long? ▪ have you been working there for a long time? ▪ have you worked there long? ¿trabajas mucho tiempo allí? ▪ ¿llevas mucho tiempo trabajando allí?

have you ever been there (before)? ¿has estado allí alguna vez?

have you ever been to...? ¿has estado alguna vez en...? ▪ ¿conoces...?

have you ever heard about...? ¿has oído alguna vez sobre...?

have you ever heard of...? ¿has oído alguna vez de...?

have you ever seen...? ¿has visto alguna vez...? ▪ ¿no has visto nunca...?

have you ever seen it? ▪ have you seen it before? ¿lo has visto alguna vez?

have you ever seen anything like it? ¿has visto alguna vez una cosa igual? ▪ ¿has visto alguna vez algo igual?

have you ever noticed that...? *(tú)* ¿te has fijado alguna vez en que...? ▪ ¿te has fijado alguna vez de que...? ▪ ¿te has fijado alguna vez que...? ▪ *(usted)* ¿se ha fijado (usted) alguna vez en que...? ▪ ¿se ha fijado (usted) alguna vez de que...? ▪ ¿se ha fijado (usted) alguna vez que...?

have you ever noticed how...? ¿te has fijado alguna vez en cómo...? ▪ ¿te ha llamado la atención que...?

have you ever thought about how...? ¿has pensado alguna vez (en) cómo...?

have you ever thought about what...? ¿has pensado alguna en vez lo que...? ▪ ¿has pensado alguna vez en qué...?

have you ever thought that...? ¿has pensado alguna vez que...?

have you ever wondered how...? *(tú)* ¿alguna vez te has preguntado cómo...? ▪ ¿te has preguntado alguna vez cómo...?

■ *(usted)* ¿alguna vez se ha preguntado cómo...? ■ ¿se ha preguntado alguna vez cómo...?

have you ever wondered what...? *(tú)* ¿alguna vez te has preguntado lo que...? ■ ¿alguna vez te has preguntado qué...? ■ *(usted)* ¿alguna vez se ha preguntado (usted) lo que...? ■ ¿alguna vez se ha preguntado (usted) qué...?

have you got a light? ■ do you have a light? ¿tienes fuego? ■ ¿me das fuego?

have you got (any) plans this weekend? ■ do you have (any) plans this weekend? *(tú)* ¿tienes planes este fin de semana? ■ *(usted)* ¿tiene usted planes este fin de semana?

have you got the time? ■ do you have the time? *(tú)* ¿tienes la hora? ■ *(usted)* ¿tiene usted la hora? ■ *(Arg.)* ¿me tirás las agujas?

have you heard anything from...? *(tú)* ¿sabes algo de...? ■ *(usted)* ¿sabe (usted) algo de...? ➤ Have you heard anything from your cousins? ¿Sabes algo de tus primos?

have you heard the latest? ¿has oído lo último? ■ ¿sabes lo último?

have you heard the news? ¿has oído la noticia?

have you lost your senses? *(tú)* ¿has perdido el juicio? ■ *(usted)* ¿ha perdido (usted) el juicio?

have you seen it before? ■ have you ever seen it? *(movie)* ¿la has visto alguna vez? ■ *(show)* ¿lo has visto ya?

have you seen it yet? *(show)* ¿lo has visto ya? ■ *(movie)* ¿la has visto ya?

have you thought of...? *(tú)* ¿se te ha ocurrido...? ■ *(usted)* ¿se le ha ocurrido...? ➤ Have you thought of going into politics? ¿Se te ha ocurrido dedicarte a la política?

haven for wildlife ■ refuge for wildlife remanso para fauna ■ refugio para fauna

having been raised in... habiéndome criado en...

having come this far ■ at this point ■ at this stage (of the game) llegado este punto ➤ I can't quit school, having come this far. ■ I can't quit school at this point. ■ I can't quit school at this stage (of the game). No puedo dejar mis estudios llegado este punto.

having come to that (habiendo) llegado al caso

having said (all) this habiendo dicho todo esto

having said as much habiendo dicho tanto

having said it dicho eso

having said that dicho eso ■ dicho lo cual

having said that... habiendo dicho que...

having said this dicho esto ■ dicho lo cual

having stated that... declarado eso... ■ declarado lo cual... ■ habiendo declarado que...

having to do with referente a ■ que tiene que ver con ■ relacionado con ■ propio de

having to do something eso de tener que ■ tener que ➤ Having to get up so early every day is a grind. Eso de tener que levantarme temprano es una pelma. ➤ Having to keep quiet about it made him feel guilty. ■ To have to keep quiet about it made him feel guilty. Tener que callarse le hizo sentirse culpable.

to **hazard a guess** ■ to venture a guess ■ to make a guess aventurar una respuesta

hazard lights *(of a car)* balizas

he and my father mi padre y él ➤ He and my father used to be business partners. Mi padre y él eran socios en un negocio.

he can't be no puede serlo

he can't be... no puede ser... ■ no debe ser... ➤ He can't be very bad. No debe ser muy malo.

he doesn't even know I exist (él) ni siquiera sabe que existo ■ (él) ni siquiera me da bola ■ *(Mex.)* (él) ni siquiera me pela

he doesn't know which end is up no sabe por donde se anda

he doesn't look like one no tiene aspecto de serlo

he even incluso ■ y todavía ➤ He even mentioned it once. Incluso él lo mencionó una vez. ➤ He even went so far as to... Y todavía tuvo el cuajo de...

he goes and goes ■ he's always on the go ■ he keeps on the go ■ he stays on the go (él) va y va

he goes by (the name) ■ they call him (a él) le dicen ➤ His name is Franklin but he goes by Frank. Se llama Francisco pero le dicen Paco.

he had his way with her ■ he seduced her hizo lo que quiso con ella ■ hizo con ella lo que quiso

he is what he is ■ he is who he is es quien es

he made his bed, and now he can sleep in it él se lo guisa y él se lo come ■ que le aproveche

he might know (él) puede que sepa

he must not... debe de ser que no... ➤ He must not wash his hair. Debe de ser que no se lava el pelo. ➤ He must not give up. No debe darse por vencido.

he only wanted to... ■ all he wanted to do was... no quería hacer nada más que... ■ no quería sino... ➤ The young Schubert only wanted to sing and write music. El joven Schubert no quería sino cantar y componer música.

he thinks he's God se cree Dios

he told me what to do me dijo lo que tenía que hacer yo ■ me dijo qué tenía que hacer yo

he was right 1. *(over time)* (él) tenía razón **2.** *(in a specific instance)* (él) acertó ■ (él) tuvo razón

he was still very young era aún muy niño ■ era aún muy joven

he was the one who ■ it was he who **1.** *(simple past)* él fue quien ■ él fue el que **2.** *(past continuous)* él era quien ■ él era el que ➤ He was the one who wrote the article. ■ Él fue el que escribió el artículo. ■ Él fue quien escribió el artículo. ➤ He was the one who was playing the piano. Él era el que tocaba el piano. ■ Él era quien tocaba el piano. ➤ He was the technician who was here yesterday. (Él) era el técnico que estuvo ayer aquí. ■ (Él) era el técnico el cual estuvo ayer aquí.

he went on to say that... (él) añadió que...

he who quien ■ el que ■ *(Biblical)* aquel que ➤ He who seeks, finds. El que busca encuentra.

he who bites the hand that feeds him does himself in él que muerde la mano del que le da de comer se arruina ■ él que le pega a su familia se arruina

he who laughs last, laughs best él que ríe último, ríe mejor ■ quien ríe último, ríe mejor

he who lives by the sword dies by the sword él que a hierro mata, a hierro muere

he who sings scares his woes away quien canta sus males espanta

to **head (for) home** ir para casa ■ dirigirse para casa

head in the sand: to have one's ~ tener los ojos tapados ■ ser como el avestruz ■ jugar al avestruz

head of hair mata de pelo

head of state ■ chief of state jefe(-a) de estado

head of the family cabeza de la familia ■ jefe(-a) de la familia

head on de frente

head-on collision *el* choque de frente ■ choque frontal

to be **head over heals in love with someone** estar locamente enamorado de alguien ■ estar enamorado hasta los tuétanos de alguien

to **head straight for** ir directamente a ■ ir de cabeza a ■ *(coll.)* ir directo a ➤ When the kids get home from school, they head straight for the refrigerator. Cuando los niños llegan de la escuela, van directo al refrigerador. ■ *(Sp.)* Cuando los peques llegan a casa del cole, van de cabeza al frigo.

to **head the list** ■ to be at the top of the list encabezar la lista

to be **headed for disaster** ■ to be headed for (a) catastrophe irse directamente al desastre ■ ir a dar un vuelco

heading of the document encabezado del documento

headline news noticia de portada

headline (over an article) ■ headline over the article *el* titular (sobre un artículo)

headline of the newspaper ■ newspaper headline *el* titular de un periódico

headlong into: to run ~ ir de bruces a

headquartered in con sede en

to be **headquartered in** ■ to have its headquarters in ■ to be based in tener su cede en

headquarters: military ~ *el* cuartel general

headquarters of a company *la* cede de una empresa
headwaters (of a river) ▪ source of a river *la* fuente de un río ▪ cabecera de un río
heads are going to roll van a rodar cabezas
heads or tails? *(Mex.)* ¿águila o sol? ▪ *(Sp.)* ¿cara o cruz?
headset: (telephone) ~ conjunto de auricular y micrófono *("Micrófono" is often shortened to "micro" in Spanish and to "mike" in English.)*
headwind: to have a ~ tener un viento de frente
to **heal old wounds** cerrar viejas heridas
health insurance ▪ medical insurance seguro médico
to **heap abuse on someone** echar pestes sobre alguien
heaping tablespoon cucharada bien colmada
heaping teaspoon cuchara bien colmada
to **hear a cat meowing** oír (a) un gato maullando ▪ oír (a) un gato haciendo miau ▪ oír (a) un gato que maúlla ▪ oír a un gato que hace miau ➤ Do you hear that cat meowing? ¿Oyes (a) ese gato maullando? ▪ ¿Oyes (a) ese gato haciendo miau?
to **hear a dog barking** oír (a) un perro ladrando ▪ oír (a) un perro que ladra
to **hear a lawsuit** celebrar un juicio ➤ Once filed, the lawsuit must be heard unless the plaintiff drops it. Una vez admitida a trámite, el juicio debe ser celebrado a menos que el demandante desista.
to **hear a pin drop** oír un alfiler cayendo(se) ▪ oír el ruido de un alfiler cayéndose ➤ When Mel Blanc told the kids, in Bugs Bunny's voice, "be ve-wee, ve-wee qui-et," you could have heard a pin drop. Cuando Mel Blanc dijo a los niños en la voz de Bugs Bunny, "Be ve-wee, ve-wee qui-et" (estense muy, muy callados), se podrá haber oído caer un alfiler.
to **hear a sound** ▪ to hear a noise ▪ to hear something oír un sonido ▪ oír un ruido ▪ oír algo ➤ I heard the sound of a whippoorwill. Oí el sonido de un chotacabras.
hear a sound: not to ~ ▪ not to hear a thing no oír ni un sonido ▪ no oír ni un ruido ▪ no oír nada (de nada) ➤ I didn't hear a sound. No oí nada. ▪ No oí nada de nada.
to **hear about...** oír lo que... ➤ Did you hear (about) what happened? ¿Oíste lo que pasó?
to **hear (back)** ▪ to receive a reply ▪ to get a reply recibir una respuesta ▪ contestarle ▪ tener (una) respuesta ➤ I haven't heard back from them yet. No me han contestado todavía. ▪ No he tenido (una) respuesta todavía.
to **hear footsteps** oír el ruido de pisadas
to **hear from someone** saber de alguien ➤ It's good to hear from you. Es bueno saber de ti. ▪ ¡Qué bien saber de ti! ▪ ¡Qué bueno es saber de ti! ➤ It was good to hear from you. Era bueno saber de ti. ▪ ¡Qué bueno fue saber de ti! ➤ What do you hear from Miguel? ¿Qué sabes de Miguel? ▪ ¿Qué has oído de Miguel? ➤ You'll hear from me next week. Sabrás de mí la semana que viene.
to **hear it from someone** saberlo por alguien ▪ saberlo por boca de alguien
to **hear on** saber de ▪ oír sobre ➤ I still haven't heard anything on my residency application. Todavía no sé nada de mi solicitud de residencia. ▪ Todavía no he oído nada sobre mi solicitud de residencia.
to **hear someone calling** oír que alguien llama ➤ When I heard him calling me... Cuando oí que me llamaba...
to **hear someone coming** oír (a) alguien acercándose ▪ oír (a) alguien que se acerca ▪ oír (a) alguien viniendo ▪ oír (a) alguien que viene ▪ oír (a) alguien llegando ▪ oír a alguien que llega
to **hear someone crying** oír (a) alguien llorando ▪ oír (a) alguien que llora
to **hear someone doing something** oír (a) alguien haciendo algo ▪ oír (a) alguien que hace algo
to **hear someone say...** escuchar (a) alguien decir... ▪ oír (a) alguien que dice... ▪ oír (a) alguien diciendo... ➤ I heard someone say... Escuché a alguien decir... ▪ Oí a alguien decir... ➤ I heard the president say it, and then I saw how the newspaper quoted it. Oí decir eso al presidente, y luego vi cómo lo citó el periódico.
to **hear someone saying...** oír (a) alguien diciendo...
to **hear someone's footsteps** oír los pasos de alguien
to **hear something through the grapevine** oír algo de terceras personas ▪ decirle un pajarito algo a alguien ▪ *(Sp.)* oír algo por radio macuto
to **hear that...** oír decir que... ➤ I hear that Cuban jazz is really good. He oído (decir) que el jazz cubano es realmente bueno. ➤ I have heard that. He oído (decir) eso.
to **hear the latest** oír lo último ▪ saber lo último ➤ Have you heard the latest? ¿Has oído lo último? ▪ ¿Sabes lo último?
to **hear the music in one's head** oír la música por dentro
heart leaped: my ~ el corazón me dio un brinco
heart of stone: to have a ~ no tener alma ▪ tener corazón de piedra
heart of the matter meollo de la cuestión ▪ cogollo del asunto ▪ fondo del asunto
heart patient enfermo(-a) del corazón ▪ paciente cardiaco(-a)
heart problems ▪ heart trouble problemas cardiacos ▪ dolencias cardiacas ▪ afección cardiaca
heart skipped a beat: one's ~ le dio un vuelco el corazón a uno ➤ My heart skipped a beat. Me dio un vuelco el corazón.
heart trouble: to have ~ ▪ to have heart problems tener problemas cardiacos ▪ estar mal del corazón
heart was pounding le daba golpes el corazón ▪ corazón golpeaba ➤ His heart was pounding, and so was hers. A él le daba golpes el corazón, y también a ella. ➤ Her heart was pounding, and so was his. A ella le daba golpes el corazón, y también a él.
to **heartily congratulate someone** felicitarle a alguien de corazón
to **heartily recommend that...** recomendar encarecidamente que...
heat wave ola de calor
heated argument: to be having a ~ ▪ to be engaged in a heated argument tener una discusión acalorada
heated argument: to provoke a ~ provocar una discusión acalorada ▪ suscitar un acalorado argumento ➤ It provoked a heated argument. Ha suscitado un acalorado argumento.
heated debate: to spark a ~ desatar una gran polémica ▪ desatar una fuerte polémica ▪ desencadenar un acalorado debate
heated discussion discusión acalorada
to **heave a sigh** ▪ to sigh deeply soltar un suspiro ▪ dar un suspiro ➤ She heaved a sigh. ▪ She sighed deeply. ▪ She sighed heavily. Ella soltó un profundo suspiro.
heavenly body 1. astronomical body cuerpo celeste **2.** gorgeous (human) body cuerpo celestial ➤ A syzygy is the alignment of three heavenly bodies, such as the Earth, moon, and sun. Solar and lunar eclipses are syzygies. Un "syzygy" es la alineación de tres cuerpos celestiales, tal como la Tierra, la luna y el sol. Los eclipses solares y lunares son "syzygies".
heavier-than-air aircraft: flight by means of a ~ vuelo con una máquina más pesada que el aire
to be **heavily involved in** estar metido de lleno ▪ estar de lleno metido ▪ estar completamente involucrado ➤ She is heavily involved in cancer research. Está metida de lleno en las investigaciones de cancer.
heavy drinker bebedor(-a) empedernido(-a)
to be **heavy enough to** ser lo suficientemente pesado para
to be **heavy going** hacérsele pesado ▪ hacérsele cuesta arriba ▪ ser tedioso ➤ Kant's "Critique of Pure Reason" is pretty heavy going. "La crítica de la razón pura" de Kant se me hace muy pesada.
heavy heart: with a ~ con un corazón apesadumbrado ▪ con un corazón acongojado
heavy losses pérdida cuantiosa ▪ cuantiosas pérdidas
heavy metal metal pesado
heavy rains fuertes lluvias
heavy smoker ▪ chain smoker fumador(-a) empedernido(-a)
heavy snow fuerte nevada
heavy traffic tráfico pesado
to be **heavyset** estar muy fuerte ▪ fornido
heck, no! ¡qué va!
hectic day día ajetreado
hectic pace: to maintain a ~ mantener un ritmo ajetreado
heel and sole of a shoe el tacón y la suela de un zapato

height above sea level ▪ elevation (above sea level) altura sobre el nivel de mar *(On a relief map, the number indicating the height above sea level is called "la cota.")*

height above the water altura sobre el nivel del agua

to be the **height of the absurd** ser el colmo de lo absurdo

to be the **height of the ridiculous** ser el colmo de lo ridículo

to **heighten one's suspicion** ▪ to intensify one's suspicion aguijonearle en la sospecha

to **heighten one's sense of** realizar el sentido de ▪ aumentar el sentido de ➤ Quitting smoking heightens the senses of taste and smell. Dejar de fumar realza los sentidos del gusto y del olfato.

heir apparent *el* delfín

to be **held at** darse en ➤ The reception will be held at the home of the bride's grandparents. ▪ The reception will be held at the bride's grandparents' house. La recepción se dará en casa de los abuelos de la novia.

to be **held in** darse en ▪ celebrarse en ▪ tener lugar en ➤ The wedding reception was held in the Shenandoah Room. La recepción de boda se dio en el Salón Shenandoah.

he'll be here any minute (now) (él) ya mero llega ▪ llegará en cualquier momento

to be **hell bent on doing something** ▪ to be bound and determined to do something vaya perro con hacer algo ➤ He's hell bent on seeing the countries of South America. Vaya perro con ver los países de la América del Sur.

hello! ¡hola!

help! ¡socorro!

to **help (out) someone** ▪ to help someone out echar una mano a alguien ▪ ayudarle a alguien ➤ Help me out (here) for a second. Échame una mano un momento. ➤ Can you help me out? ¿Puedes echarme una mano? ▪ ¿Puedes ayudarme un momento?

to **help (out) with the chores** ayudar con los labores

to **help someone by doing something** ayudar a alguien con hacer algo ➤ She helped me just by listening. Ella me ayudó con sólo escucharme.

to **help someone (to) be more...** ayudar a alguien a ser más...

to **help someone to his feet** ayudar a alguien a ponerse en pie

to **help someone up** ayudar a alguien a levantarse

help wanted se necesita personal ▪ se busca personal ▪ se precisa personal

help yourself! *(tú)* ¡sírvete (tú mismo)! ▪ *(usted)* ¡sírvase (usted mismo)!

helpful person persona servicial ➤ José Manuel, the computer lab supervisor, is very helpful. José Manuel, el encargado del laboratorio de ordenadores, es muy servicial.

to be **helpful to someone** ▪ to help someone serle de ayuda a alguien ➤ I'm delighted that it's helpful to you. ▪ I'm delighted that it helps you. Celebro que te sea de ayuda.

helping hand: to give someone a ~ ▪ to lend someone a helping hand echar una mano a alguien ▪ prestar (una) ayuda a alguien

helpless person persona desvalida ➤ Babies are helpless. Los bebes son desvalidos.

to **hem and haw** ▪ to beat around the bush ▪ to avoid giving a direct answer andar con medias tintas ▪ andarse con rodeos

hem of a garment 1. *(on any part of the garment)* costura de una prenda de vestir **2.** *(at the bottom of the garment)* bajo ▪ dobladillo **3.** *(at the waist)* cintura ▪ cinturilla

hem of a pair of pants 1. *(at the cuff)* bajo del pantalón ▪ dobladillo del pantalón **2.** *(at the waist)* cintura del pantalón ▪ cinturilla del pantalón

hence the name: (and) ~ de ahí el nombre ➤ Nat's tail is "not all there," (and) hence the name. A Nat le falta parte de su cola, de ahí el nombre.

henpecked husband calzonazos ➤ He's henpecked. Es un calzonazos.

Herculian task tarea hercúlea ▪ tarea ímproba

herd instinct instinto de la manada

here! *(handing someone something) (tú)* ¡toma! ▪ ¡aquí tienes! ▪ *(usted)* ¡tome! ▪ ¡aquí tiene!

here comes trouble ahora vienen los problemas ▪ aquí llega el problema ▪ aquí llegan los problemas ▪ *(colorful)* aquí viene Paco con las rebajas

here goes! ¡ahí va!

here I come! ¡allá voy!

here I go! ¡allá voy!

here is he aquí

here it is ▪ here you go *(tú)* aquí lo tienes ▪ *(usted)* aquí lo tiene usted ▪ ya está

here lies aquí yacen los restos de

to be **here to stay** estar aquí para quedarse ➤ Mediocre though they are, TV sitcoms are here to stay. Por mediocres que sean, los comedias de la televisión están aquí para quedarse.

here's how... mira cómo... ➤ Here's how you make the tilde on this computer. Mira cómo se pone la tilde en esta computadora.

here's the whole thing 1. *(literal)* aquí está la cosa entera **2.** *(figurative)* this is the heart of the matter este es el meollo del asunto ▪ este es el guid de la cuestión

here's to us! *(a toast)* ¡por nosotros!

here we go! ¡allá vamos! ▪ ¡vamos allá!

here's what to do ▪ here's what you need to do esto es lo que hay que hacer

herniated disk hernia discal

heroic deeds heroicas proezas

he's going to be okay ▪ he's going to recover ▪ he'll recover (él) va a ponerse bien

he's harmless es (totalmente) inofensivo

he's in a meeting está en una reunión ▪ está reunido

he's late (él) está tardando

he's nuts! ▪ he's cracked está chiflado ▪ está reloco ▪ está requeteloco

he's out of the office está fuera de la oficina ▪ ha salido (de la oficina)

he's out of the office today ▪ he's away today hoy está fuera de la oficina ▪ hoy no está en la oficina ▪ hoy no ha venido a la oficina

he's stepped away from his desk ▪ he's away from his desk no está en su escritorio

to **hesitate between** vacilar entre

to **hesitate to...** dudar en...

hey, you! ¡chis!

heyday of silent movies ▪ golden age of silent movies apogeo del cine mudo ▪ la edad de oro del cine mudo

hidden agenda in doing something: to have a ~ tener razones subrepticias para hacer algo ▪ tener motivos ocultos para hacer algo ▪ tener segundas intenciones para hacer algo ▪ tener segundos motivos para hacer algo

hidden clue pista desapercibida

to be **hidden from each other** estar ocultos uno del otro ▪ estar ocultos uno de los otros ▪ estar ocultos unos de los otros

hidden meaning significado escondido ▪ significado oculto

hidden money 1. *(under the mattress)* dinero escondido **2.** *(under the table)* dinero negro **3.** *(financial term)* dinero B

hidden talents: to have ~ tener talentos escondidos

hidden treasure tesoro escondido ▪ tesoro oculto

to **hide behind something** ocultarse detrás de algo ▪ esconderse detrás de algo

hiding place *el* escondite ▪ escondrijo

high: to be *x* feet ~ ▪ to be *x* feet above the floor ▪ to be *x* feet from the floor ▪ to be *x* feet off the floor tener *x* pies de altura

high: to be *x* revolutions ~ tener *x* revoluciones por encima ▪ tener *x* revoluciones de más

high altitude *la* gran altitud ➤ At high altitudes, longer cooking times may be necessary. A gran altitud quizá sea necesario prolongar el tiempo de cocimiento.

high blood pressure: to have ~ tener la tensión alta

high C do de pecho

high-density lipoproteins ▪ HDL ▪ good cholesterol lipoproteínas de alta densidad ▪ LAD ▪ colesterol bueno

High German *(spoken in the mountainous regions of central and southern Germany, Switzerland, and Austria)* alto alemán *("High" refers to elevation above sea level.)*

high goals: to set ~ ▪ to set lofty goals fijar metas altas

high government official ▪ high-ranking official ▪ senior official funcionario(-a) de algo rango ▪ alto(-a) cargo(-a) del gobierno ▪ alto(-a) funcionario(-a) del gobierno

high heat *(cooking)* fuego fuerte ▪ llama alta

high heels ▪ high-heeled shoes tacones altos ➤ She was wearing high heels. Llevaba tacones altos.

high hopes: to have ~ tener esperanzas altas ▪ tener ambiciones celestiales

to be **high in the sky** estar en lo alto del cielo

high-level talks *las* conversaciones de alto nivel

high levels of ozone ▪ high ozone levels rebasados los niveles de ozono ➤ *(headline)* High levels of ozone in Aranjuez, Alcobendas, and Fuenlabrada Rebasados los niveles de ozono en Aranjuez, Alcobendas y Fuenlabrada

High Mass misa mayor ▪ misa solemne ▪ misa cantada

high notes notas altas

high official alto cargo ▪ alto funcionario

to be **high on drugs** ▪ to be under the influence of a drug ▪ to be on a drug ir puesto de drogas ▪ estar a tope con drogas ➤ He's high on drugs. Está bajo los efectos de drogas. ➤ High without drugs A tope sin drogas ➤ They were on something. Iban puestos de algo.

high point of one's career cúspide de su carrera ➤ He's at the high point of his career. Está en la cúspide de su carrera. ▪ Se encuentra en la cúspide de su carrera.

high-pressure area *(weather)* ▪ area of high pressure *el* anticiclón *(implies good weather)*

high-pressure system *(weather) el* sistema de altas presiones ▪ sistema de alta presión *(implies good weather)*

high-ranking official funcionario(-a) de alto rango

high school *(Mex.)* preparatoria ▪ secundaria ▪ escuela superior ▪ *(Sp.)* instituto

high school diploma título de bachillerato

high society alta sociedad

high-sounding words palabras altisonantes

high tension lines los cables de alta tensión

high tide *la* pleamar ▪ marea alta

high time: it's ~ ▪ it's about time ya es hora

high (voter) turnout alta participación (de votantes)

high waves *el* fuerte oleaje ➤ *(news item)* Radars did not detect the dinghy because of the high waves. Los radares no detectaron la patera por el fuerte oleaje.

high winds ▪ strong winds fuertes vientos

high without drugs a tope sin drogas

higher and higher cada vez más arriba ▪ cada vez más alto

higher education *la* educación superior

to be **higher than average** ser superior a lo normal

to be **higher than usual** ▪ to be more expensive than usual ser más caro de lo normal

to be **higher up** estar más arriba

highest number of votes: to receive the ~ ▪ to receive the greatest number of votes ▪ to get the most votes ser el más votado ▪ recibir una mayoría relativa

highest rate of ▪ highest incidence of tasa más alta de ➤ *(headline)* Madrid has the highest rate of AIDS in Europe. Madrid tiene la tasa de SIDA más alta de Europa.

to **highlight something** ▪ to emphasize something ▪ to put something into relief destacar algo ▪ poner algo de relieve ▪ poner algo en relieve

highlight text *(computers)* marcar el texto

to **highlight the message** *(computers)* marcar el mensaje ▪ señalar el mensaje

highlighted text *(computers)* texto en negrita

highlighter pen *el* resaltador ▪ *el* rotulador

highly paid muy bien pagado ▪ muy bien remunerado ▪ de alto caché ➤ Highly paid actress Actriz de alto caché ➤ Highly paid bullfighter Torero de alto caché

to be **highly regarded** tener buena fama

highway robbery 1. *(literal, especially in earlier centuries when people traveled by animal)* robo en las carreteras **2.** grossly overpriced atraco a mano armada ▪ robo a mano armada

highway safety seguridad vial

to **hijack an airplane** secuestrar un avión

himself: the king ~ el propio rey ▪ el mismo rey ➤ In the Middle Ages nobles sometimes had more power than the king himself. En la Edad Media algunos nobles tuvieron más poder que el propio rey.

hint of a smile ▪ faint smile amago de sonrisa ▪ atisbo de una sonrisa

to **hire someone to do something** ▪ to contract with someone for something ▪ to enter into contract with someone for something contratar algo a alguien

hired killer ▪ hit man asesino a sueldo

historic struggle contienda histórica ▪ lucha histórica

historical events aconteceres históricos ▪ acontecimientos históricos

history of philosophy *(from the ancient Greeks to the 21st century)* historia universal de la filosofía

history of the universe *(from the Big Bang to now)* historia universal

history repeats itself la historia se repite

to **hit a note** ▪ to give a note darle una nota ➤ Hit a C. ▪ Give me a C. Dame un do.

to **hit a snag** dar con un escollo ➤ The negotiations have hit a snag. Las negociaciones han dado con un escollo.

to **hit a sore spot** ▪ to touch a nerve ▪ to strike a nerve ▪ to touch on something unpleasant poner el dedo en la llaga

to **hit a target** dar en el blanco ▪ dar en el objetivo ▪ dar en la diana

to **hit a tree** chocar con un árbol

hit and miss ▪ haphazard de todo un poco ▪ al azar

to be **hit by something** ▪ to get hit by something ▪ to be struck by something ser alcanzado por algo ➤ *(headline)* Nine U.S. soldiers die when two helicopters are hit in Afghanistan Nueve soldados de EE UU mueren al ser alcanzados dos helicópteros en Afganistán ➤ *(headline)* Boy dies after being hit by a fireworks shell ▪ Boy dies after being struck by a fireworks shell Fallece un niño tras ser alcanzado por la carcasa de unos fuegos artificiales

to **hit (close to) home** tocar de cerca a uno

to **hit it off with someone** ▪ to really hit it off with someone hacer buenas migas con alguien

hit man ▪ hired killer asesino a sueldo

hit of cocaine raya de cocaína ▪ tiro de cocaína ▪ *el* rayote

to **hit on an idea** dar con una idea ▪ atinar con una idea

to **hit on someone** ▪ to come on to someone sexually ▪ to put the make on someone ▪ to make a pass at someone tirar los tejos a alguien ▪ tirarse un lance con alguien

to **hit on the solution** atinar con la solución ▪ dar con la solución

to **hit one's head** darse (un golpe) en la cabeza ▪ golpearse en la cabeza ▪ darse un coscorrón ▪ darse una testarada ▪ darse un testarazo ➤ He hit his head. Se dio en la cabeza. ▪ Se dio un golpe en la cabeza. ▪ Se golpeó en la cabeza. ▪ Se dio un coscorrón. ▪ Se dio un testarazo. ➤ I hit my head on the door frame. ▪ I bumped my head on the door frame. Me he dado un coscorrón en el marco de la puerta.

hit ratio *el* porcentaje de acierto(s)

to **hit rock bottom** ▪ to reach the lowest level possible tocar fondo

to **hit someone** ▪ to punch someone dar de bofetadas a alguien

to **hit someone between the eyes 1.** *(literal and figurative)* to strike someone between the eyes dar a alguien entre ceja y ceja ▪ alcanzar a alguien entre ceja y ceja

to **hit someone hard** ▪ to strike someone hard pegar fuerte a alguien

to **hit someone in the head** ▪ to strike someone in the head darle a alguien en la cabeza ▪ alcanzarle a alguien en la cabeza ▪ golpearle a alguien en la cabeza ➤ The bullet hit him in the head. ▪ The bullet struck him in the head. La bala le dio en la cabeza. ▪ La bala le alcanzó en la cabeza.

to **hit someone on the head** darle a alguien en la cabeza ➤ The apple didn't really hit Newton on the head. La manzana realmente no le dio a Newton en la cabeza.

to **hit someone right in the face** darle a alguien en plena cara

to **hit someone right smack in...** ▪ to hit someone square in... ▪ to strike someone right smack in... ▪ to strike someone square in... alcanzarle a alguien de lleno en... ➤ The pie hit him right smack in the face. ▪ The pie hit him square in the face. ▪ The pie struck him right smack in the face. ▪ The pie struck him square in the face. ▪ El pastel lo alcanzó de lleno en la cara. ▪ El pastel lo dio de lleno en la cara. ▪ *(Sp., leísmo)* El pastel le alcanzó de lleno en la cara. El pastel le dio de lleno en la cara.

to **hit something** ▪ to strike something golpear algo ▪ golpear un objeto ➤ The pilot reported that the airplane had hit something. El piloto comunicó que el avión había golpeado un objeto.

to **hit the ball with one's head** *(soccer)* dar de cabeza la pelota

to **hit the books** *(coll.)* ▪ to study poner los codos (en la mesa) ▪ estudiar

to **hit the bull's-eye** dar en el blanco

to **hit the ceiling** ▪ to go through the roof ▪ to have a conniption ponerse por las nubes ▪ ponerse hecho un basilisco ▪ ponerse como un basilisco

to **hit the floor** dar con el suelo

to **hit the mark** acertar

to **hit the sack** ▪ to hit the hay ▪ to go to bed irse al sobre ▪ ir a la cama ➤ I'm going to hit the hay. ▪ I'm going to hit the sack. ▪ I'm going to bed. Me voy al sobre. ▪ Me voy a la cama.

to **hit the spot** dar en el blanco ➤ A good cold beer on a hot day really hits the spot. En un día caluroso, una cerveza bien fría da en el blanco.

to **hit upon an idea** *(literary)* ▪ to hit on an idea dar con una idea ▪ atinar con una idea

to **hitchhike to a place** ▪ to thumb one's way to a place ir a un lugar a dedo ▪ hacer autostop ▪ hacer dedo ➤ He hitchhiked to San Sebastian. ▪ He thumbed his way to San Sebastian. ▪ He thumbed a ride to San Sebastian. Fue a San Sebastian a dedo.

hog jowl jeta de cerdo

to **hog the camera** ▪ to be a camera hog chupar cámara

to **hoist the flag** ▪ to raise the flag izar la bandera

to **hold a job** mantener un trabajo

to **hold a meeting** ▪ to have a meeting celebrar una reunión ▪ tener una reunión ➤ The meeting will be held (this) Thursday. La reunión se celebrará el jueves.

to **hold a political office** desempeñar un cargo político ▪ ocupar un cargo político

to **hold a position in the company** desempeñar un cargo en la compañía ▪ ocupar un cargo en la compañía

to **hold a press conference** celebrar una rueda de prensa ▪ celebrar una rueda de periodista ▪ dar una conferencia de prensa ▪ dar una rueda de prensa

to **hold a title** **1.** *(in a competition)* ostentar un título **2.** *(to property)* tener el título de la propiedad

to **hold a trial** ▪ to conduct a trial celebrar un juicio

to **hold at bay** tener a raya

to **hold back (from)** contenerse (de) ➤ I held back from telling her off. Me contuve de decirle sus cuatro verdades.

to **hold back something from someone** ocultar algo a alguien

to **hold down food** ▪ to hold food down ▪ to keep down food ▪ to keep food down retener (la) comida ▪ retener los alimentos ➤ She can't hold down food. ▪ She can't hold food down. (Ella) no puede retener (la) comida. ▪ (Ella) no puede retener los alimentos. ➤ She can't hold it down. ▪ She can't keep it down. No puede retenerla. ▪ No puede retenerlos.

to **hold down the fort** ▪ to hold the fort down estar al pie del cañón ▪ hacerse cargo (temporariamente)

to **hold elections** celebrar elecciones

to **hold fast in the face of** mantenerse firme frente a

to **hold hands** cogerse de la mano

to **hold in awe** ▪ to be in awe of tener respeto reverencial por ▪ sentir respeto reverencial por

hold it tight ▪ hold onto it tight *(tú)* sujétalo bien ▪ *(usted)* sujételo bien

hold me tight abrázame fuerte ▪ estréchame fuerte

to **hold off (on)** ▪ to wait (for) esperarse ➤ Hold off until we've gotten a confirmation of the payment. ▪ Wait until we've gotten the confirmation of payment. Espérese hasta que hayamos recibido la confirmación de pago.

to **hold off someone** ▪ to hold someone off ▪ to hold someone at bay mantener a raya a alguien ▪ mantener a distancia a alguien ➤ The battalion is trying to hold off the attackers until reinforcements arrive. ▪ The battalion is trying to hold the attackers off until reinforcements arrive. El batallón intenta mantener a raya a los atacantes hasta que lleguen los refuerzos.

hold on! **1.** hold (on) tight! ▪ don't let go! ¡agárrate! ▪ ¡afírmate bien! ▪ ¡no te sueltes! **2.** hold on just a minute! ▪ wait a second! ¡espera un momentito! ▪ ¡aguanta un pelo! ▪ ¡aguanta un pelín! ▪ ¡(espera) un momento! ▪ ¡sooooo! **3.** *(telephone)* hold the phone ▪ don't hang up *(tú)* no cuelgues ▪ no te retires ▪ *(usted)* no cuelgue ▪ no se retire

to **hold one's breath** contener la respiración ▪ contener el aliento

to **hold one's ears** ▪ to cover one's ears taparse los oídos ▪ taparse las orejas

to **hold one's head** cogerse la cabeza

to **hold one's head high** erguir la cabeza ▪ levantar la frente en alto

to **hold one's own** defenderse bien ▪ arreglárselas muy bien ➤ In a rapid conversation in Spanish, she can hold her own. En una conversación rápida en español, se las arregla muy bien. ▪ En una conversación rápida en español, se defiende muy bien.

to **hold oneself up as** erigirse en ➤ *(news item)* The opposition leader criticizes the president for holding himself up as the only one capable of unifying the country. El dirigente de la oposición censura al presidente por erigirse en el único capaz de cohesionar el país.

hold onto: to need something to ~ necesitar algo en lo que apoyarse ▪ necesitar algo a lo que aferrarse ▪ necesitar algo a lo que asirse ▪ *(coll.)* necesitar algo de lo que echar mano ➤ Young people, even though they rebel, need an anchor to hold onto. Los jóvenes, aunque se rebelan, necesitan un pilar en el que apoyarse. ▪ Los jóvenes, aunque se rebelan, necesitan un asidero al que aferrarse. ▪ *(coll.)* Los jóvenes, aunque se rebelan, necesitan un asidero al que echar mano. ▪ Los jóvenes, aunque se rebelan, necesitan un asidero (al que asirse).

hold (onto) it tight *(tú)* sujétalo bien ▪ *(usted)* sujételo bien

to **hold onto someone's friendship** conservar la amistad de alguien

to **hold onto the banister** mantenerse sujeto al barandilla

to **hold onto the railing** ▪ to hold onto the handrail mantenerse sujeto al pasamanos ➤ *(metro station sign)* Hold onto the railing. ▪ Hold onto the handrail. Manténgase sujeto al pasamanos.

to **hold out one's hand** tenderse la mano

to **hold promise** ▪ to hold a lot of promise prometer mucho

to **hold public office** ocupar un cargo público ▪ desempeñar un cargo (público)

to **hold someone at bay** ▪ to keep someone at bay mantener a alguien a raya ▪ tener a alguien a raya ▪ poner a alguien a raya

to **hold someone hostage** tener a alguien como rehén ▪ retener a alguien como rehén

to **hold someone in high esteem** ▪ to hold someone in high regard ▪ to esteem someone highly ▪ to regard someone highly ▪ to esteem someone greatly tener a alguien en alta estima ▪ tener a alguien en aprecio ▪ estimarle a alguien grandemente ▪ apreciar a alguien

to **hold someone in high regard** ▪ to hold someone in high esteem ▪ to regard someone highly ▪ to esteem someone highly ▪ to esteem someone greatly tener a alguien en alta estima ▪ tener a alguien en aprecio ▪ estimarle a alguien grandemente ▪ apreciar a alguien

to **hold someone responsible for** hacer a alguien responsable por ■ responsabilizar a alguien de

to **hold someone to something** obligar a alguien a cumplir ➤ I'm going to hold you to it. Te voy a obligar a cumplir.

to **hold someone's place** ■ to save someone's place ■ to keep someone's place guardar el sitio de alguien ■ *(Sp.)* guardar la vez a alguien

to **hold something for someone** sujetárselo ➤ Hold this for me for a minute. *(tú)* Sujétame esto un momento. ■ *(usted)* Sujéteme esto un momento.

to **hold something in place** ■ to hold something steady sujetar algo

hold still! ■ be still! ¡estate quieto! ■ ¡no te muevas!

hold that thought! ¡aguanta esa idea! ■ ¡manten esa idea!

to **hold the key to** tener la llave de ➤ *(headline)* Far right holds the key to the governability of Portugal La derecha más dura tiene la llave de la gobernabilidad de Portugal

to **hold the opinion** ■ to be of the opinion ■ to subscribe to the opinion adherirse a la opinión

hold the phone! *(tú)* ¡no cuelgues! ■ ¡no te retires! ■ *(usted)* ¡no cuelgue! ■ ¡no se retire!

to **hold the presidency** ostentar la presidencia

to **hold the promise of** encerrar la promesa de

to **hold the record as** mantener el récord como

to **hold the record for** ■ to hold the title for mantener un récord por ■ ostentar un récord por ■ ostentar un título por ■ mantener un récord de ■ ostentar un récord de ■ ostentar un título de

to **hold the title 1.** *(in a competition)* mantener el título ■ ostentar el título **2.** *(to property)* tener el título ■ tener la escritura (de propiedad)

hold this for me for a minute *(tú)* sujétame esto un momento ■ *(usted)* sujéteme esto un momento

to **hold up a bank** ■ to hold a bank up ■ to rob a bank atracar un banco ➤ A trio of robbers held up the bank. ■ A trio of robbers held the bank up. Un trío de atracadores robaron el banco. ■ Un trío de ladrones atracaron el banco. ➤ A trio of robbers held it up. Un trío de atracadores lo robaron. ■ Un trío de ladrones lo atracaron.

to **hold up someone** ■ to hold someone up ■ to delay someone ■ to keep someone ■ to detain someone retrasar a alguien ■ detener a alguien ■ parar a alguien

to **hold up someone as an example to someone** ■ to hold someone up as an example to someone poner a alguien como ejemplo a alguien ➤ The teacher held the diligent student up as an example to the class. La profesora puso al alumno diligente como un ejemplo a la clase. ➤ The teacher held him up as an example to the class. La profesor le puso como un ejemplo a la clase.

to **hold up something to the light** ■ to hold something up to the light mirar algo a contraluz

to **hold up the works** paralizar todo ➤ *(in a slow grocery store line)* Something's holding up the works. Algo paraliza todo.

hold your horses! ■ be patient! ¡arrepa! ■ ¡para el carro! ■ ¡ten paciencia!

to **hold *x* people** ■ to have room for *x* people tener cupo para *x* personas ➤ Each train holds a thousand people. Cada tren tiene cupo para mil personas.

to be **holding hands with his wife** estar de la mano de su esposa

holding one's head high ■ with one's head held high con la frente muy alta ■ con la frente en alto

holding pattern: to enter the ~*(aviation)* entrar al circuito de espera ■ incorporarse al circuito de espera

to be a **holdover from** ser un vestigio de ➤ My love of electric trains is a holdover from (my) childhood. Mi pasión por los trenes eléctricos es un vestigio de mi niñez.

hole in one *(golf)* un hoyo en uno

hole in one's pants agujero en el pantálon ■ agujero en los pantalones

hole in one's pants' pocket: to get a ~ hacérsele un agujero en el bolsillo del pantalón ■ hacérsele un roto en el bolsillo del pantalón ➤ I got a hole in my (pants') pocket. Se me hizo un agujero en el bolsillo del pantalón.

hole in one's pants' pocket: to have a ~ ■ to have got a hole in one's pants' pocket tener un agujero en el bolsillo del pantalón ■ tener un roto en el bolsillo del pantalón ➤ I have a hole in my (pants') pocket. ■ I've got a hole in my (pants') pocket. Tengo un agujero en el bolsillo del pantalón. ■ Se me ha hecho un agujero en el bolsillo del pantalón.

hole in one's sock: to have a ~ tener un agujero en el calcetín ■ *(Sp., in the toe of the sock)* tener un tomate

to be **holed up in** estar atrincherado en

Holy Bible Santa Biblia ■ Sagrada Biblia

holy cow! ■ holy smokes! ¡san cristo! ■ ¡anda mi madre!

holy day of obligation *(Catholicism)* ■ obligatory feast un día de precepto ■ fiesta de guardar ■ fiesta de precepto

Holy Roman Empire Imperio sacroromano

holy shroud of Turin la sábana santa de Turín

the **holy water** *el* agua bendita *("Agua" is feminine, and only the singular article is masculine. The plural is "las aguas.")*

Holy Week Semana Santa ■ Semana de Pasión

home address *la* dirección particular

home cooking cocina casera

home front: on the ~ ■ on the domestic front en el frente interno

home remedy remedio casero

home run! ¡carrera!

home run: to hit a ~ *(baseball)* ■ to run the full quadrangle with a single hit cuadrangular ■ hacer jonrón

home stretch recta final

home turf: to be on one's ~ ■ to be on one's own turf estar en su propio terreno

homemade bomb artefacto (explosivo) de fabricación casera

homemade device artefacto de fabricación casera

hometown *la* ciudad natal ■ pueblo natal ■ ciudad de origen

homework assignment ■ homework *(L. Am.)* tarea ■ *(Sp.)* deberes

homicide attempt ■ attempted homicide ■ attempted murder intento de asesinato ■ tentativa de asesinato

hominy grits sémola de maíz

honest! ¡palabra! ➤ Honest! I don't know her. ¡Palabra! No la conozco.

to **honk the horn** ■ to sound the horn tocar el claxon ■ tocar la bocina

to **honor a person** honrar a una persona

to **honor a request** cumplir con una petición

to **honor academic credits** homologar créditos académicos

to **honor an academic degree** ■ to certify an academic degree homologar un título ➤ The Spanish education ministry honored my American university degree. El ministerio de educación español ha homologado mi título de la universidad estadounidense.

to **honor an agreement** cumplirse un acuerdo ➤ The prime minister reminded the king that the agreement is clear and must simply be honored. El primer ministro recordó al rey que el acuerdo es "nítido" y sólo debe cumplirse.

to be **honored to** ■ to have the honor to tener una honra en

hood ornament (of a vehicle) *el* embellecedor

to **hoodwink someone** mistificar a alguien

hook, line, and sinker: to swallow it ~ creérselo ■ tragar el anzuelo

hooray! ¡olé!

hooray, hooray! ¡tachín, tachán!

to **hop a train** *(implies a short trip)* tomar un tren ■ *(Sp.)* coger un tren

to **hop along** ■ to hop dar saltos ■ brincar

hop in! ■ *(taxi driver)* get in! *(tú)* ¡sube! ■ *(usted)* ¡suba!

to **hop into the car** ■ to jump into the car ■ to get into the car subir de un salto al carro ■ *(Sp.)* subir de un salto al coche

to **hop on one foot** ir a pata coja ■ saltar a pata coja

to **hop on two feet** ■ to jump dar saltos ■ brincar

to **hope against hope** esperar desesperando

the **hope that...** la esperanza de que... ■ la ilusión de que...

to **hope that...** desear que... ➤ They hope that the weather will change by tomorrow. Desean que el tiempo cambie para mañana.

to be a **hopeless case 1.** to be hopeless ■ to be beyond hope ■ to be a lost cause no tener remedio ■ no tener arreglo ■ ser un caso sin salvación ■ ser un caso perdido **2.** *(figurative)* ser un negado(-a) ➤ He's a hopeless case when it comes to calculus. Es un negado para el cálculo.

to be **hopelessly in love with someone** estar perdidamente enamorado de alguien

hopes are fading for... se desvanecen las esperanzas de... ■ se esfuman las esperanzas de... ■ se agotan las esperanzas de... ■ se acaban las esperanzas de... ➤ Hopes are fading for a peace agreement by Christmas. ■ Hopes for a peace agreement by Christmas are fading. Se esfuman las esperanzas para un acuerdo de paz para la navidad.

hopes are fading that... las esperanzas se desvanecen de que... ■ se esfuman las esperanzas de que... ■ se agotan las esperanzas de que... ■ se acaban las esperanzas de que... ➤ Hopes are fading that a peace agreement can be reached by Christmas. ■ Hopes that a peace agreement can be reached by Christmas are fading. Se desvanecen las esperanzas de que se pueda acordar la paz para la navidad.

to be **hopping mad** estar que brinca ➤ The boss is hopping mad that you didn't call to say you'd be late. El jefe está que brinca que no llamaste para decir que llegarías tarde.

horizontal stabilizer *(aerodynamics) el* timón de profundidad

hors d'oeuvres los entremeses ■ cosas que picar

to **horse around** hacer el tonto ■ hacer el jaimito ■ hacer el indio

horse-drawn carriage carroza de caballos ■ carroza tirada por caballos

horse-drawn coach ■ stagecoach diligencia ■ coche de caballos ■ coche tirado por caballos

horse-drawn wagon carro de caballos ■ carro tirado por caballos

horse with blinders: to be like a ~ ser como un caballo con orejeras

horseback riding *la* equitación ➤ She was injured in a horseback riding accident. Fue lesionado en un accidente de equitación.

hot-air balloon globo aerostático

hot air rises *el* aire caliente sube para arriba

to be **hot and sweaty** tener bochorno ➤ I'm hot and sweaty. Tengo bochorno. *("Hace bochorno" for "it's muggy," although common, is illogical, and in prescriptive grammar, incorrect.)*

to be **hot as the hinges of hell** ■ to be blazing hot hacer un calor de todos los demonios ■ hacer un calor de mil demonios

to be a **hot-blooded person** ser una persona de sangre caliente

hot day día caluroso ■ día de mucho calor

hot flashes *(in menopause)* sofocos

to be **hot on someone's heels** ■ to be hot on someone's tracks ■ to be hot on someone's footsteps pisar los talones de alguien ■ estar pisando los talones de alguien ■ estar sobre los talones de alguien ■ estar tras (de) las pistas de alguien ■ estar tras (de) la pista de alguien ■ estar tras (de) las pisadas de alguien ■ es estar tras (de) las huellas de alguien ➤ In the dream, I could feel the bear hot on my heels. En mi sueño sentía al oso pisándome los talones. ➤ We're hot on their heels. Estamos pisándoles los talones.

hot pants paños calientes

hot plate plancha caliente

hot salsa picante salsa picante fuerte

hot spot punto caliente

hot spring *la* fuente termal

hot topic *el* tema en candelero

hotbed of rumors hervidero de rumores

hotbed of terrorism semillero de terrorismo ■ caldo de cultivo de terrorismo ■ hervidero de terrorismo

hotline teléfono rojo

hottest part of the summer pleno verano ■ *el* rigor del verano ■ la parte más caliente del verano

to **hotwire a car** ■ to hotwire the ignition ■ to start a car without the ignition key hacerle el puente a un carro ➤ The thief hotwired the car. El ladrón le hizo el puente al carro.

to be **hounded by** ser acosado(-a) de

an **hour early** una hora antes ➤ We arrived an hour early. Llegamos una hora antes.

hourglass *el* reloj de arena

hourglass figure: to have an ~ tener un talle de avispa

to be **hours ahead of** ■ to be hours later than llevar horas de adelanto sobre ➤ Madrid is six hours ahead of New York. ■ It is six hours later in Madrid than (it is) in New York. Madrid lleva seis horas de adelanto sobre Nueva York.

hours' difference horas de diferencia ➤ There are six hours' difference between New York and Madrid. Hay seis horas de diferencia entre Nueva York y Madrid.

to **house a collection** albergar una colección ■ acoger una colección ➤ The Prado houses the works of Velázquez, Goya, and El Greco, as well as a great collection of Italian and Dutch paintings. El Prado alberga así las obras de Velázquez, Goya y El Greco, como una gran colección de pintura italiana y holandesa.

house arrest: to be placed under ~ ■ to be put under house arrest quedarse en (situación de) arresto domiciliario ■ ser puesto en arresto domiciliario ➤ Galileo was placed under house arrest by the Inquisition. Galileo fue puesto en arresto domiciliario por la Inquisición. ➤ Ex-president Slobodan Milosevic of Yugoslavia was placed under house arrest at 1:30 a.m. today. El ex-presidente de Yugoslavia, Slobodan Milosevic, quedó a la 1:30 hoy en situación de arresto domiciliario.

house I grew up in casa donde me crié ■ casa donde crecí

house in casa en ■ casa de ➤ They all claim to have visited your house in Santiago de Chile. Todos dicen haber visitado su casa de Santiago de Chile.

house of ill repute ■ red-light house ■ whorehouse ■ house of prostitution ■ brothel casa de citas ■ casa de putas ■ prostíbulo

House of Lords *(British parliament)* Cámara de los Lores

house of prostitution ■ house of ill repute ■ red-light house ■ whorehouse ■ brothel prostíbulo ■ casa de citas ■ casa de putas

House of Representatives *(U.S.)* Cámara de Representantes

house painter pintor(-a) de brocha gorda

house plan ■ floor plan of a house *la* distribución ■ plano de casa

household chores ■ housework tareas domésticas ■ quehaceres domésticos ■ tareas del hogar

housewares department departamento de enseres domésticos

housewarming (party) fiesta de inauguración de casa

how about...? ■ what do you think of...? *(tú)* ¿qué te parece...? ■ *(usted)* ¿qué le parece...? ➤ How about going out for supper? ¿Qué te parece salir a cenar?

how about in there? ¿qué tal ahí?

how about it? ■ what do you think? ¿qué te parece?

how am I doing? ¿qué tal voy? ■ ¿cómo voy?

how am I doing on the time? ¿cómo voy de tiempo? ■ ¿qué tal voy de tiempo?

how am I supposed to know? ■ how would I know? ¿cómo lo voy a saber?

how are things (going) at work? ■ how is work? ¿cómo te va en tu trabajo? ■ ¿qué tal te va en tu trabajo?

how are we doing on the time? ¿cómo vamos de tiempo? ■ ¿qué tal vamos de tiempo?

how are you? *(tú)* ¿cómo estás? ■ ¿qué tal estás? ■ *(usted)* ¿cómo está usted? ■ ¿qué tal está usted?

how are you coming (along) on your work? ■ how's the work coming (along)? ¿cómo va el trabajo? ■ ¿qué tal va el trabajo?

how are you doing? 1. how are you? ¿cómo estás ■ ¿qué tal estás? ■ ¿qué tal andas? **2.** how are you feeling? ¿cómo vas? ■ ¿qué tal vas?

how are you getting along? *(tú)* ¿cómo lo llevas? ■ ¿qué tal lo llevas? ■ *(usted)* ¿cómo lo lleva (usted)? ■ ¿qué tal lo lleva (usted)?

how awful! ¡qué barbaridad!

how beautiful you look lo guapa que estás

how big around is it? 1. *(circle)* what's the circumference? ¿cuál es la circunferencia? ■ ¿cuánto tiene de circunferencia? **2.**

(polygon) what's the perimeter? ▪ what's the distance around it? ¿qué perímetro tiene?

how big around it is 1. *(circle)* la circunferencia que tiene ▪ la circunferencia que tenga **2.** *(polygon)* el perímetro que tiene ▪ el perímetro que tenga ➤ I don't know how big around the tree is, but for sure it's big enough for a tree house. No sé la circunferencia que tiene el árbol, pero seguro que es suficiente para construir una casita. ▪ No sé el perímetro que tiene el árbol, pero seguro que es suficiente para construir una casita. ➤ I don't know if we can get a Christmas tree in the trunk. It depends on how big around it is. No sé si podemos meter un árbol de navidad en el baúl. Depende de la circunferencia que tenga. ▪ No sé si podemos meter un árbol de Navidad en el baúl. Depende del perímetro que tenga.

how can anyone ice-skate like that? ¿quién pudiera patinar sobre hielo así?

how can anyone play the piano like that? ¿quién pudiera tocar el piano así?

how can I forget? ▪ there's no way I could forget ¿cómo no voy a recordarlo?

how can I help you? ▪ what can I do for you? ¿qué es lo que se le ofrece?

how can you tell? ¿cómo se deja notar? ▪ ¿cómo se nota?

how clever! ¡qué listo!

how clever you are! ▪ you're very clever! ¡qué mañoso(-a) eres!

how close is it to...? ¿cuánto está de...? ➤ How close is it to the metro station? ¿Cuánto está de la estación de metro?

how close it is to que tan cerca está

how close to... cuánto se parece a... ➤ How close to a real piano do the electronic keyboards sound? ¿Cuánto se parece a un piano real es el sonido de un teclado electrónico?

how come? *(coll.)* ¿por qué? ▪ ¿y eso?

how could it be? ¿cómo podría serlo?

how could it not be? 1. ¿cómo no lo ha de estar? **2.** ¿cómo no lo ha de ser?

how could there be? ¿cómo podría haber?

how *could* you?! ¿cómo tendría valor de? ➤ *Lady to steakhouse waiter:* How could you kill those poor animals?-*Waiter:* How could you eat them alive? *Una señora al camarero en un asador:* ¡No sé cómo tienes valor de matar a esos pobres animales!-*Camarero:* ¿Cómo tendría usted valor de comérselos vivo?

how could you lie to me? ¿cómo has podido mentirme?

how could you miss the target? 1. how would it be possible to miss the target? ¿cómo podrías fallar...? **2.** ▪ how did you manage to miss the target? ¿cómo has podido fallar...?

how dare you! *(tú)* ¿cómo te atreves? ▪ *(usted)* ¿cómo se atreve (usted)? ▪ ¡no me falte usted! ➤ How dare you (all) ask our help to attack an allied country? ¿Cómo se atreven a pedir nuestra ayuda para atacar a un país aliado?

how did he do it? ¿cómo lo hizo (él)?

how did he get it? *(disease)* ¿cómo lo contrajo?

how did it go? 1. *(a task)* ¿cómo te fue? ▪ ¿cómo le fue (a usted)? **2.** *(a song)* ¿cómo era?

how did that get there? ¿cómo entró eso?

how did you arrive at that conclusion? ▪ how did you come to that conclusion? *(tú)* ¿cómo sacaste esa conclusión? ▪ ¿cómo llegaste a esa conclusión? ▪ *(usted)* ¿cómo sacó (usted) esa conclusión? ▪ ¿cómo llegó a esa conclusión?

how did you come to have...? ¿cómo llegaste a tener...?

how did you come to that conclusion? ▪ how did you arrive at that conclusion? *(tú)* ¿cómo sacaste esa conclusión? ▪ ¿cómo llegaste a esa conclusión? ▪ *(usted)* ¿cómo sacó (usted) esa conclusión? ▪ ¿cómo llegó (usted) a esa conclusión?

how did you come up with the idea? ▪ how did you get that idea? ▪ where did you get that idea? ¿de dónde sacaste esa idea? ▪ ¿cómo se te ocurrió eso?

how did you get along? *(doctor to patient at post-surgery checkup)* ▪ how'd you get along? ¿cómo lo pasaste? ▪ ¿qué tal saliste? ▪ ¿cómo te fue? ▪ ¿cómo lo pasó usted? ▪ ¿qué tal salió? ▪ ¿cómo le fue (a usted)?

how did you get along in...? ¿cómo te fue en...? ➤ How did you get along in the calculus class? ¿Cómo te fue en la clase de cálculo?

how did you get that idea? ▪ how did you come up with that idea? ▪ where did you get that idea? *(tú)* ¿de dónde sacaste esa idea? ▪ ¿de dónde sacaste eso? ▪ ¿cómo se te ocurrió? ▪ *(usted)* ¿de dónde sacó esa idea? ▪ ¿de dónde sacó eso? ▪ ¿cómo se le ocurrió eso?

how difficult it is ▪ how hard it is cómo es de difícil

how do I look? 1. *(general appearance)* ¿qué tal estoy? ▪ ¿cómo estoy? ▪ ¿qué aspecto tengo? **2.** *(clothes specifically)* how does it look on me? ¿qué tal me queda?

how do you make...? ¿cómo se hace...? ▪ ¿cómo se prepara...? ➤ How do you make chimichurri sauce? ¿Cómo se hace el chimichurri? ▪ ¿Cómo se prepara el chimichurri?

how do you feel about...? ▪ what do you think about...? *(tú)* ¿qué te parece...? ▪ ¿qué piensas de... ▪ ¿qué opinas de...? ▪ *(usted)* ¿qué le parece...? ▪ ¿qué piensa (usted) de...? ▪ ¿qué opina (usted) de...?

how do you get to...? ¿por dónde se va a...? ➤ How do you get to the main square? ¿Por dónde se va a la plaza mayor?

how do you know? ¿cómo lo sabes?

how do you like it? ▪ what do you think of it? ▪ how does it taste? ▪ how do you like it prepared? *(a ti)* ¿cómo te gusta? ▪ *(a usted)* ¿cómo le gusta?

how do you like *that*? *(tú)* ¡te parece bonito! ▪ *(usted)* ¡le parece bonito!

how do you like your new job? *(tú)* ¿qué te parece tu nuevo trabajo? ▪ ¿cómo te gusta tu nuevo trabajo? ▪ *(usted)* ¿qué le parece su nuevo trabajo? ▪ ¿cómo le gusta su nuevo trabajo?

how does it look (on me)? ¿qué tal me queda? ▪ ¿qúe tal me sienta?

how does that sound? ¿qué te parece?

how easy it is cómo es de fácil

how embarrassing! ¡qué vergüenza! ▪ ¡qué bochorno! ▪ ¡qué metida de pata! ▪ ¡qué tal vergüenza!

how exciting! ¡qué emocionante! ▪ ¡qué emoción! ➤ Wow! How exciting! ¡Vaya! ¡Qué emocionante!

how far along I am: it depends on ~ depende de hasta donde (yo) haya llegado

how far apart...? ¿cómo de lejos...? ➤ How far apart are the stops? ¿Cómo de lejos quedan las paradas?

how far are we going? ¿hasta dónde vamos?

how far are you going? *(tú)* ¿hasta dónde vas? ▪ *(usted)* ¿hasta dónde va (usted)?

how far (away) is it? ¿qué tan lejos está? ▪ ¿a qué distancia está? ▪ ¿a cuánto está? ➤ How far (away) is the horizon? ¿A qué distancia está el horizonte?

how far (away) is the horizon? ¿a qué distancia está el horizonte? ➤ From an airliner flying at 35,000 feet, how far (away) is the horizon?-It is two hundred twenty-nine miles away. ¿Desde una aerolínea volando a los 35.000 pies, a qué distancia está el horizonte?-Está a doscientos veintinueve millas.

how far down (the street) is it from the corner? ¿cómo de lejos está desde la esquina? ▪ ¿cómo de lejos está yendo desde la esquina?

how far is it (from here) to...? ▪ how far is... from here? ¿a qué distancia está...? ▪ ¿cuánto hay de aquí a...? ▪ ¿cuánto camino hay de aquí a...?

how far it had gone cuánto había avanzado

how fast 1. at what speed a qué velocidad **2.** how quickly ¿qúe tan rápido...? ➤ How fast are we going? ¿A qué velocidad vamos? ➤ How fast will this get there? ¿Qué tan rápido llegará?

how funny! ¡qué gracia!

how good qué tan bueno(s)

how handsome you look! ▪ you look so handsome! ¡lo guapo que estás! ▪ ¡qué guapo tú estás!

how hard is it to...? ¿qué tan difícil es...? ➤ How hard is it to learn Chinese? ¿Qué tan difícil es aprender chino?

how hard it can be ▪ how difficult it can be lo difícil que puede ser

how hard it is (for me) to have to... ▪ how much it hurts (me) to have to... la pena que me da tener que...

how hard it must be ■ how difficult it must be lo difícil que debe (de) ser ■ lo duro que debe (de) ser ■ qué difícil debe (de) ser ■ qué duro debe (de) ser ➤ I can't imagine how hard it must be to do some Hollywood stunts. No puedo ni imaginar lo difícil que debe ser doblar algunas escenas de acción en Hollywood. ■ No puedo ni imaginar lo duro que debe ser doblar algunas escenas de acción en Hollywood. ➤ How hard it must be to endure her as a mother-in-law! ¡Lo difícil que debe ser soportarla de suegra! ■ ¡Lo duro que debe ser soportarla de suegra! ■ ¡Qué difícil debe ser soportarla de suegra! ■ ¡Qué duro debe ser soportarla de suegra! *(It is more common to omit "de" in this expression. Adding it makes the sentence more speculative or conjectural.)*

how hard it must have been ■ how difficult it must have been lo difícil que debe haber sido ■ lo duro que debe haber sido ■ qué difícil debe haber sido ■ qué duro debe haber sido ➤ I can't imagine how hard it must have been to build the aqueduct in Segovia. No puedo ni imaginar lo difícil que debe haber sido construir el acueducto de Segovia. ■ No puedo ni imaginar lo duro que debe haber sido construir el acueducto de Segovia.

how hard would it be to...? ¿costaría mucho trabajo...? ■ ¿sería muy difícil...? ➤ How hard would it be to glue this pitcher back together so that the cracks are invisible? ¿Costaría mucho trabajo pegar esta jarra para que las grietas no se vean? ■ ¿Sería muy difícil pegar esta jarra para que las grietas no se vean?

how have you been? *(L. Am.)* ¿cómo has estado? ■ *(Sp.)* ¿qué tal lo has pasado? ■ ¿cómo te ha ido?

how high is...? ■ ¿qué altura tiene...? ■ ¿cuánto mide...? ➤ How high is the ceiling in here? ¿Qué altura tiene el techo aquí? ➤ How high are Popo and Ixta? ¿Qué altura tienen el Popo y el Ixta? ➤ How high is that tree? ■ How tall is that tree? ¿Qué altura tiene ese árbol? ■ ¿Cuánto mide ese árbol?

how I envy you! ¡cuánto te envidio! ■ ¡cómo te envidio!

how I like my hair cut: to tell the barber ~ decirle al peluquero cómo me gusta mi corte de pelo

how I wish... ■ I sure wish... cuánto me gustaría... ■ cómo me gustaría... ■ cuánto desearía... ■ cómo desearía...

how in love are you? ¿cuán enamorado(-a) estás tú?

how in the dickens...? ¿cómo demonios...? ➤ How in the dickens am I going to manage that? ¿Cómo demonios voy a lograr eso?

how in the world...? ¿cómo narices...?

how incredible! ¡qué bárbaro!

how is...? ¿qué tal es...?

how is ice cream made? ■ how do you make ice cream? ¿cómo se hace el helado?

how is it possible that...? ¿cómo es posible que...?

how is school? **1.** ¿qué tal la escuela? ■ ¿qué tal te va la escuela? **2.** *(referring to a university)* ¿cómo te van las clases? ■ ¿qué tal te van las clases?

how is that possible? ■ how is it possible? ¿cómo es (eso) posible?

how is work? ■ how are things (going) at work? ¿cómo te va en tu trabajo?

how it looks from the outside cómo se ve desde el exterior

how it was **1.** what it was (like) lo que era **2.** the way it was así era ➤ He remembered how it was to be penniless. ■ He remembered what it was like to be penniless. ■ He remembered what it was to be penniless. Recordaba lo que era estar sin un céntimo. ➤ That's how it was back in those days. ■ That's what it was like back in those days. Así era en aquella época. ■ Eso era así en aquella época.

how late? ¿hasta qué hora? ➤ How late can I call you? ¿Hasta qué hora puedo llamarte?

how late did you stay up? ¿hasta qué hora te quedaste levantado?

how little... **1.** *(quantity)* lo poco que... **2.** *(size)* how small...? ¿cómo de pequeño...? ➤ How little one has changed Lo poco que uno ha cambiado ➤ How little is an atom? ¿Cómo es de pequeño un átomo?

how long ago? ¿hace cuánto tiempo?

how long are you going to be? ¿cuánto vas a tardar? ■ ¿cuánto vas a demorar?

how long did you...? ¿durante cúanto tiempo...?

how long does it take to...? ¿cuánto se tarda en...? ➤ How long does it take to get there? ¿Cuánto se tarda en llegar?

how long has it been since...? **1.** *(followed by a noun clause)* ¿cuánto (tiempo) hace de...? ■ ¿cuánto (tiempo) hace desde...? **2.** *(followed by a verb phrase)* ¿cuánto (tiempo) hace desde que...? ■ ¿cuánto (tiempo) hace que...? ➤ How long has it been since your last vacation? ¿Cuánto (tiempo) hace de tus últimas vacaciones? ■ ¿Cuánto (tiempo) hace desde tus últimas vacaciones? ➤ How long has it been since you saw a doctor? ¿Cuánto (tiempo) hace que viste a un médico? ■ ¿Cuánto (tiempo) hace desde que viste a un médico?

how long has it been snowing? ¿cuánto tiempo hace que nieva?

how long have you been taking English? ¿cuánto tiempo llevas estudiando inglés? ■ ¿cuánto tiempo que estudias inglés? ■ ¿desde cuándo recibes clases de inglés?

how long have you been waiting? *(tú)* ¿cuánto tiempo llevas esperando? ■ ¿cuánto tiempo has estado esperando? ■ *(usted)* ¿cuánto tiempo lleva (usted) esperando? ■ ¿cuánto tiempo ha estado (usted) esperando? ➤ How long have you been waiting?-Not long. ¿Cuánto tiempo llevas esperando? No mucho. ■ ¿Cuánto tiempo has estado esperando?-No mucho.

how long has it been raining? ¿cuánto tiempo hace que llueve?

how long have you...? ¿desde cuánto tiempo...?

how long have you had that car? ¿cuánto tiempo (hace que) tienes ese coche?

how long have you been...? ¿cuánto tiempo llevas...? ➤ How long have you been working here? ¿Cuánto tiempo llevas trabajando aquí?

how long have you been taking Spanish? ¿cuánto tiempo hace que estudias español? ■ ¿cuánto tiempo llevas estudiando español?

how long have you lived here? *(tú)* ¿desde cuándo vives aquí? ■ *(usted)* ¿desde cuándo vive (usted) aquí?

how long it will take to... cuánto tiempo se tardará en... ■ cuánto tiempo se demorará...

how long it would take (one) to do something cuánto tiempo iba a tardar en hacer algo ➤ I left early because I didn't know how long it would take to get here. Salí pronto porque no sabía cuánto tiempo iba a tardar en llegar. ➤ We left early because we didn't know how long it would take to get (us) here. Salimos pronto porque no sabíamos cuánto tiempo íbamos a tardar en llegar.

how low qué bajo ■ qué tan bajo ➤ *(ad)* Have you seen how low our prices are? ¿Has visto qué bajos son nuestros precios? ➤ How low is the oil? ¿Qué tan bajo está el aceite?

how many? ¿cuántos?

how many are left? ¿cuántos quedan?

how many are there? **1.** ¿cuántos hay? **2.** how many of you are there? *(ustedes)* ¿cuántos son (ustedes)? ■ *(Sp., vosotros)* ¿cuántos sois?

how many exposures? *(buying film)* ■ how many frames? ¿cuántas fotos?

how many hours' difference are there between here and there? ■ how many hours apart are we? ¿a cuántas horas estamos de diferencia? ■ ¿cuántas horas de diferencia hay?

how many months pregnant is she? ■ how far along is she? ¿de cuántos meses está embarazada? ■ ¿de cuánto está (ella)?

how many of you are there? *(ustedes)* ¿cuántos son (ustedes)? ■ *(Sp., vosotros)* ¿cuántos sois?

how many times do I have to tell you...? ¿cuántas veces tengo que decirte? ■ te lo tengo dicho...

how much? ¿cuánto?

how much...: to think about ~ pensar en lo mucho que...

how much are...? ¿cuánto cuestan? ■ ¿a cuánto están...?

how much are you asking for...? ■ what are you asking for... ¿cuánto pides por...? ■ ¿qué pides por...?

how much are you asking for it? ■ how much do you want for it? ■ what are you asking for it? ■ what do you want for it? ¿cuánto pides? ■ ¿qué pides?

how much did you get for...? ¿por cuánto vendiste...? ■ ¿cuánto te pagaron por...? ➤ How much did you get for your car? ■ How much did you sell your car for? ¿Por cuánto vendiste tu carro? ■ ¿Cuánto te pagaron por tu carro?

how much did you pay for it? ¿cúanto pagaste? ■ ¿a cómo lo compraste? ■ ¿a cómo lo has comprado?

how much do I owe you? *(tú)* ¿cuánto te debo? ■ *(usted)* ¿cuánto le debo?

how much do you charge for...? ■ what do you charge for...? ¿cuánto cobra usted por...? ➤ How much do you charge for a haircut? ¿Cuánto cobra usted por un corte de pelo?

how much do you want for...? ■ how much are you asking for...? ■ what do you want for...? ■ what are you asking for...? ¿cuánto pides por...? ■ ¿qué pides por...?

how much do you want for it? ■ how much are you asking for it? ■ what do you want for it? ■ what are you asking for it? ¿cuánto pides? ■ ¿qué pides?

how much does it cost? ¿cuánto cuesta?

how much does it come (out) to? ■ what does it come to? ¿a qué asciende? ■ ¿a cuánto asciende? ■ ¿a cuánto sale? ■ ¿a cuánto está(n)? ■ *(Sp., coll.)* ¿a cómo está(n)?

how much does it cost to get in? ¿cuánto cuesta entrar?

how much farther is it to...? ¿cuánto falta para (llegar a)? ■ ¿cuánto más falta para...? ➤ How much farther is it to Bariloche? ¿Cuánto falta para (llegar a) Bariloche?

how much is...? ¿cuánto es...? ■ ¿a cuánto está...?

how much is it? ¿cuánto es? ■ ¿qué precio tiene?

how much is left? ¿cuánto queda?

how much is your profit? ■ what's your profit? *(tú)* ¿cuál es tu beneficio? ■ *(usted)* ¿cuál es su beneficio?

how much it hurts (me) to have to... ■ how hard it is (for me) to have to... la pena que me da tener que...

how much do I owe you? ■ what do I owe you? *(tú)* ¿cuánto te debo? ■ ¿qué te debo? ■ *(usted)* ¿cuánto le debo? ■ ¿qué le debo?

how much the tree has grown lo mucho que ha crecido el árbol ■ cuánto ha crecido el árbol

how much will it be? ■ how much will it come to? ■ how much is it going to come to? ¿cuánto será eso? ■ ¿a cuánto estará? ■ ¿cuánto saldrá?

how near are we to...? ■ how close are we to...? ■ how much farther is it to...? ¿cómo estamos de cerca a...? ■ ¿cuánto nos queda para llegar a...?

how nice! ¡qué simpático! ■ ¡qué detalle! ■ ¡qué gesto tan simpático!

how often con qué frecuencia ■ con cuánta frecuencia ■ cada cuánto (tiempo) ■ cómo de a menudo

how old? ¿de qué edad?

how old could he have been...? ■ how old do you think he was...? ¿cuántos años podría haber tenido (él)...?

how old do you think he is? ■ how old do you reckon he is? ■ how old would you guess he is? ¿cuántos años le das (a él)? ■ ¿cuántos años le pones? ■ ¿cuántos años le echas?

how old do you think it is? 1. *(tree, etc.)* ¿cuántos años tendrá? 2. *(building, structure)* ¿cuántos años de antigüedad tendrá?

how old do you think she is? ■ how old do you reckon she is? ■ how old would you guess she is? ¿cuántos años le das (a ella)?

how old is he? ¿cuántos años tiene (él)? ■ ¿qué edad tiene (él)? ■ *(for an infant less than a year old)* ¿cuánto tiempo tiene (él)? ■ ¿qué tiempo tiene (él)? ■ ¿cuántos meses tiene (él)?

how old would you guess he is? ■ how old do you think he is? ■ how old would you say he is? ■ how old do you reckon he is? ¿cuántos años le das? ■ ¿cuántos años le pones? ■ ¿cuántos años le echas?

how quickly time passes! ■ how quickly time goes (by)! ■ how time flies! ¡qué de prisa pasa el tiempo! ■ ¡qué rápido pasa el tiempo!

how rich I am lo rico que soy ➤ I checked my balance to see how rich I am. Verifiqué mi saldo para ver lo rico que soy.

how serious is the problem? ¿hasta dónde llega el problema? ■ ¿qué tan serio es el problema? ■ ¿cómo es de serio el problema?

how simple it is cómo es de sencillo ■ lo sencillo que es

how so? ■ in what way? ¿de qué manera?

how soon...? 1. ¿qué tan pronto...? 2. ¿cuándo...? ➤ How soon can you get here? ¿Cuándo puedes llegar?

how tall are you? *(tú)* ¿cuánto mides? ■ ¿de qué altura eres? ■ *(usted)* ¿cuánto mide usted? ■ ¿de qué altura es usted?

how thick is...? ¿qué grosor tiene...?

how thick is it? ¿qué grosor tiene?

how to get around in Madrid *(travel guide heading)* cómo moverse en Madrid

how to use modo de empleo

how was I supposed to know? ■ how was I to know? ¿y cómo (yo) iba a saberlo?

how was I to know? ■ I was I supposed to know? ¿cómo iba a saberlo? ■ ¿y cómo iba a saberlo?

how was your trip? *(tú)* ¿cómo (te) fue tu viaje? ■ *(usted)* ¿cómo (le) fue su viaje?

how well one does something lo bien que uno hace algo

how weird! ■ that's weird! ■ how strange! ■ how odd! ¡qué cosa tan rara!

how would I know? ■ how should I know? ■ how am I supposed to know? ¿cómo lo voy a saber? ■ ¿yo qué sé? ■ ¡qué sé yo!

how would you like your steak? ■ how do want your steak? ¿cómo quiere usted la carne? ■ ¿cómo le gustaría la carne? ➤ How would you like your steak-rare, medium, or well done? ¿Cómo le gustaría la carne-poco hecha, en el punto, o muy hecha?

how wrong he was! ¡qué equivocado estaba!

how wrong she was! ¡qué equivocada estaba!

how you've changed! ■ my, you've changed! ¡qúe cambiado(-a) estás! ■ ¡pero qué cambiazo has dado!

how'd you get along? *(doctor to patient after surgery)* ■ how did you get along? ¿cómo lo llevas?

how'd you like...? ■ how did you like...? *(tú)* ¿qué te ha parecido...? ■ *(usted)* ¿qué le ha parecido...?

however great por grande que sea ■ lo grande que sea ➤ *(William Whewell)* And so no force, however great, can stretch a cord, however fine, into a horizontal line which shall be absolutely straight. Así que ninguna fuerza, por grande que sea, puede estirar una cuerda, por fino que sea, en una línea horizontal que sea absolutamente recta.

however it turns out ■ whatever the outcome ■ whatever the result sea cual sea el resultado

however long it takes to... el tiempo que haga falta para... ■ el tiempo que sea necesario para... ■ por el tiempo que tome ■ por el tiempo que lleve ■ por el tiempo que se tarde

however much you like ■ as much as you like lo mucho que te guste

however remote lo remoto que sea ■ lo remoto que fuera ■ aunque fuera leve

however you look at it ■ whichever way you look at it por donde se mire ■ se mire por donde se mire ■ por cualquier lado que se mire

howling of the wind rugido del viento ■ *el* ulular del viento

how's it going? ■ how's everything going? ¿qué tal? ■ ¿qué tal va? ■ ¿qué tal andas?

how's life treating you? ■ how's it going? ¿cómo te trata la vida? ■ ¿cómo te va?

how's that (again)? ■ come again? *(tú)* ¿cómo? ■ ¿qué? ■ ¿puedes repetirme eso? ■ *(usted)* ¿cómo dice? ■ ¿disculpe? ■ ¿me lo repite?

how's the work going *(tú)* ¿cómo te va el trabajo? ■ *(usted)* ¿cómo le va el trabajo?

how's your arm? *(tú)* ¿cómo está tu brazo? ■ *(usted)* ¿cómo está su brazo?

hubbub: a lot of ~ mucho jaleo ■ mucho bullicio ■ mucho griterío ■ mucha confusión

hue of a color ■ shade of a color *la* tonalidad de un color

to **huff and puff** soplar y resoplar

huge city ciudad grandísima

huge disappointment chasco enorme ■ *la* decepción enorme

human error fallo humano

human race ■ humankind ■ mankind raza humana ■ género humano

human rights advocate ▪ civil rights advocate ▪ civil liberties advocate defensor(-a) de las libertades civiles
humdrum existence vida anodina
humid climate clima húmedo
humidity in the air ▪ water vapor in the air *la* humedad en el aire
humiliating defeat derrota humillante
humiliating treatment: to subject someone to ~ ▪ to subject someone to degrading treatment someter a alguien al trato vejatorio
to **humor someone** complacer a alguien ▪ seguirle el humor a alguien ▪ seguirle la corriente a alguien
hunch: to have a ~ tener una corazonada ▪ tener un presentimiento ▪ *(Mex.)* latirle que ➤ I've got a hunch... Tengo una corazonada... ▪ Tengo un presentimiento que... ▪ Me late que...
hundred people: about a ~ around a hundred people alrededor de un centenar de personas
hundred percent 1. completely cien por ciento **2.** *(percentage)* al ciento por ciento ➤ The concert hall was completely full. El salón de concierto estuvo repleto cien por ciento. ➤ We need to increase our intake one hundred percent. Necesitamos multiplicar nuestros ingresos al ciento por ciento.
hundred yard dash cien metros lisos
hundred yard hurdles cien metros vallas
hundreds and hundreds tropecientos
hundredth anniversary: the (one) ~ efímero centenario
hundreds of calls cientos de llamadas
hundreds of friends cientos de amigos ➤ He has hundreds of friends. Tiene cientos de amigos.
hundreds of soldiers centenares de soldados
hundreds of years centenares de años
hunger is the best sauce a buena hambre no hay mal pan ▪ a falta de pan buenas son tortas
to be **hungry as a bear** ▪ to be starving ▪ to be famished tener más hambre que un maestro de escuela ▪ tener más hambre que vista un galgo ▪ tener un hambre canina
to **hunt and peck** escribir a máquina con dos dedos
to **hunt animals** cazar animales
to **hunt for something** ▪ to look for something ▪ to search for something buscar algo
hurry! ▪ quick! ¡corre!
hurry or we'll be late *(tú)* date prisa, que llegamos tarde ▪ *(usted)* dese prisa, que llegamos tarde ▪ *(ustedes)* dense prisa, que llegamos tarde ▪ *(Sp., vosotros)* daos prisa, que llegamos tarde
to **hurry over to...** acudir presuroso a... ➤ The boss hurried over to her desk. El jefe acudió presuroso a su escritorio.
to **hurry (up)** darse prisa
hurry (up)! ¡date prisa! ▪ ¡apresúrate! ▪ *(Sp.)* ¡apúrate! ▪ ¡ándale! ▪ ¡venga! ▪ ¡date prisa!
to **hurt one's arm** hacerse daño en el brazo ➤ He hurt his arm playing soccer. Se hizo daño en el brazo jugando al fútbol.
to **hurt one's knee** lastimarse la rodilla ▪ hacerse daño en la rodilla ▪ dañarse la rodilla
to **hurt oneself** lastimarse ▪ hacerse daño ▪ dañarse ➤ Don't hurt yourself! ¡No te lastimes! ▪ ¡No te hagas daño! ➤ I hurt my foot. Me hice daño en el pie.
to **hurt sales** dañar las ventas
to **hurt someone's feelings** herir los sentimientos a alguien
to **hurt someone's reputation** ▪ to damage someone's reputation ▪ to hurt someone's good name ▪ to stain someone's reputation tiznar la reputación de alguien
hurtful words palabras hirientes
to **hush it up** silenciarlo ▪ echar tierra encima de ello
hustle and bustle mucho ajetreo
hydraulic jack gato hidráulico ▪ *(S.Am.)* gata hidráulica

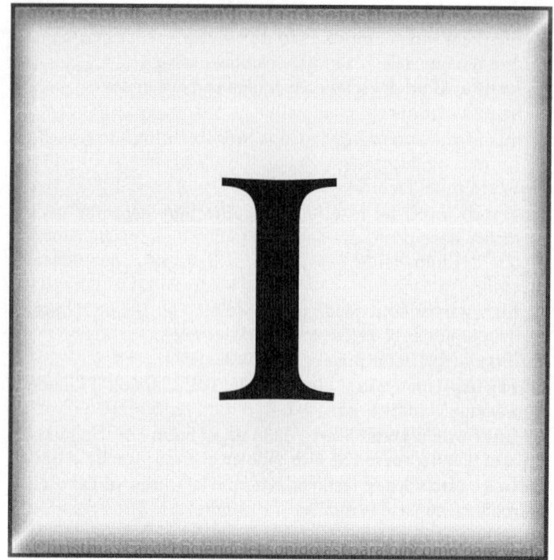

I accept your invitation *(de ti)* acepto tu invitación ▪ *(de usted)* acepto su invitación

I accept your offer *(de ti)* acepto tu propuesta ▪ *(de usted)* acepto su propuesta

I actually prefer it en realidad lo prefiero ▪ realmente lo prefiero

I agree estoy de acuerdo

I agree on that estoy de acuerdo con eso ▪ coincido en eso ▪ en eso coincido

I agree with you completely ▪ I completely agree with you ▪ I totally agree with you estoy completamente de acuerdo contigo ▪ estoy totalmente de acuerdo contigo ▪ coincido totalmente contigo ▪ en eso coincidimos

I agree with you on that estoy de acuerdo contigo en eso ▪ coincido contigo en eso

I agree with you wholeheartedly ▪ I agree with you completely ▪ I completely agree with you ▪ I totally agree with you estoy completamente de acuerdo contigo (sin reservaciones) ▪ estoy totalmente de acuerdo contigo (sin reservaciones) ▪ coincido sin reservaciones contigo

I almost forgot casi lo olvidé ▪ casi se me olvidó ➤ I almost forgot to tell you to leave the key with the concierge. Casi me olvidé de decirte que dejes la llave con el portero. ➤ I almost forgot to tell you what happened. Casi me olvidé de contarte lo que pasó.

I almost had a heart attack ▪ I practically had a heart attack ▪ I nearly had a heart attack casi me dio un ataque al corazón ▪ casi me dio un infarto ▪ casi me da un ataque al corazón ▪ casi me da un infarto *(Spanish speakers often use the present tense where an English speaker would use the past.)*

I almost missed the bus ▪ I just barely made it to the bus casi perdí el autobús ▪ estuve a punto de perder el autobús ▪ *(colorful, implying the feet are dragging the pavement)* agarré el autobús barriéndome ▪ *(Arg.)* a gatas agarré el colectivo ▪ *(Sp.)* cogí el bus por los pelos ▪ casi se me va el bus ▪ cogí el autobús por los pelos

I almost missed the plane ▪ I barely made (it to) the plane casi perdí el avión ▪ por poco perdí el avión ▪ *(Sp.)* apenas cogí el avión

I alone... ▪ I was the only one who... sólo yo... ➤ I alone went to class. ▪ I was the only one who went to class. Sólo yo fui a la clase. ▪ Fui el único que asistió a la clase. ▪ No fue nadie más que yo a la clase.

I already know what I want *(to a waiter or waitress)* ya sé que es lo que quiero ▪ ya sé lo que quiero

I always... yo habitualmente... ▪ yo siempre... ▪ siempre me toca...

I am confident that... confío (en) que... ▪ tengo plena confianza de que... ▪ tengo plena confianza en que...

I am glad of that ▪ I'm glad of that me alegro de eso ▪ eso me alegra ➤ I *am* glad of that. Sí que me alegro de eso.

I am looking forward to... ▪ I'm looking forward to... tengo ganas de... ▪ estoy deseando... ▪ me ilusiona... ▪ espero con (mucha) anticipación...

I appreciate it *(of you)* te lo agradezco ▪ se lo agradezco (a usted) ▪ *(of him)* se lo agradezco (a él) ▪ *(of her)* se lo agradezco (a ella)

I appreciate it so much! ▪ thank you so much! ¡cómo te lo agradezco!

I appreciate your call *(tú)* agradezco tu llamada ▪ te agradezco tu llamada ▪ *(usted)* agradezco su llamada ▪ le agradezco su llamada

I appreciate your help *(tú)* te agradezco la ayuda ▪ agradezco tu ayuda ▪ *(usted)* le agradezco la ayuda ▪ agradezco su ayuda

I ask that... ▪ I request that... ruego que... ▪ pido que... ▪ *(in a business letter)* le solicito que...

I asked you to be quiet te pedí que te quedases callado(-a) ▪ te pedí que te quedaras callado(-a)

I asked you to be still te pedí que te quedases quieto(-a) ▪ te pedí que te quedaras quieto(-a)

I asked you not to ▪ I asked you not to do it *(a ti)* te pedí que no lo hicieras ▪ te pedí que no lo hicieses ▪ *(a usted)* le pedí que no lo hiciera ▪ le pedí que no lo hiciese ▪ *(ustedes)* les pedí que no lo hicieran ▪ les pedí que no lo hiciesen ▪ *(Sp., vosotros)* os pedí que no lo hicierais ▪ os pedí que no lo hicieseis

I asked you not to... ▪ I asked that you not... *(a ti)* te pedí que no... *(a usted)* le pedí que no... ➤ I asked you not to make so much noise. ▪ I asked that you not make so much noise. Te pedí que no hicieses tanto ruido. ▪ Te pedí que no hicieras tanto ruido. ▪ *(more adamant)* Te pedí no hacer tanto ruido.

I assumed as much ▪ I guessed as much ▪ I figured as much lo suponía ▪ me lo imaginaba ▪ me lo figuraba

I barely got... apenas pude... ➤ I barely got the assignment finished before I handed it in. Apenas pude terminar la tarea antes de entregarla.

I beg your pardon ¿perdón? ▪ *(tú)* ¿perdona? ▪ *(usted)* ¿perdone? ➤ I beg your pardon. Could you repeat that? ¿Perdón? ¿Podrías repetir eso?

I bet (you) *(coll.)* ▪ I'll bet (you)... te apuesto que... ▪ a que... ▪ van... ➤ I bet you anything that... ▪ I'll bet you anything that... ▪ I'd bet you anything that... Apostaría la cabeza que... ➤ I bet you fifty euros (that) they're going to lose two to one. Van cincuenta euros que van a perder dos a uno.

I bet you can't guess who *I* am! *(child with mask)* ¡a que no adivinas quién soy! ▪ te apuesto que no adivinas quién soy ▪ ¡¿quién soy?!

I bet you can't guess who this is *(on the phone)* a que no sabes quién soy ▪ a que no adivinas quién soy

I bet you, if I put my mind to it, I could (do it) te apuesto que, si me lo propongo, lo logro

I bet (you) *x* dollars that... te apuesto *x* dólares a que... ▪ van *x* dólares a que...

I bet you're glad (that...) seguro que estás contento(-a) (que...)

I better go 1. *(coll.)* I'd better go ▪ I'd better leave mejor me voy ▪ será mejor que me vaya **2.** I'd better attend mejor voy ▪ será mejor que vaya

I blushed me sonrojé ▪ me puse colorado(-a) ▪ me puse como un tomate (de oferta)

I botched it la fastidié ▪ la jorobé ▪ *(Mex.)* la regué

I can almost see it 1. *(focusing problem)* casi puedo verlo **2.** *(interference from an obstacle)* casi alcanzo a verlo **3.** it's as if I were seeing it como si lo viera

I can appreciate how... ▪ I can see how... ▪ I can understand how... puedo comprender cómo... ▪ puedo apreciar cómo...

I can barely hear you ▪ I can hardly hear you *(a ti)* casi no te escucho ▪ te escucho a duras penas ▪ *(a usted)* casi no le escucho ▪ casi no le oigo

I can barely make it out ▪ I can hardly make it out casi no puedo distinguirlo ▪ apenas puedo distinguirlo

I can do it myself puedo hacerlo yo mismo(-a)

I can feel it in my bones puedo sentirlo en mis adentros ▪ puedo sentirlo dentro de mí

I can handle it ▪ I can deal with it (yo) puedo manejarlo ▪ (yo) puedo con ello ▪ (yo) puedo solo ▪ (yo) me encargo solo ▪ *(Sp.)* (yo) me apaño solo ▪ (yo) solo me apaño ➤ I can handle it, thanks. Ya me encargo yo, gracias. ▪ (Yo) puedo con ello, gracias. ▪ (Yo) puedo solo, gracias.

I can hardly hear you ▪ I can barely hear you *(a ti)* casi no te oigo ▪ te oigo a duras penas ▪ *(a usted)* casi no le oigo ▪ le oigo a duras penas

I can hardly make it out ▪ I can barely make it out apenas lo puedo divisar ▪ casi no lo puedo divisar

I can hardly see it ▪ I can (just) barely see it apenas puedo verlo ▪ casi no puedo verlo ▪ casi no lo veo

I can hardly stand the wait ▪ I can hardly wait casi no puedo esperar ▪ apenas (si) puedo esperar ▪ casi no aguanto la espera

I can hardly wait ▪ I can hardly stand the wait casi no puedo esperar ▪ apenas si puedo esperar ▪ apenas puedo esperar

I can imagine! ¡ya me imagino! ▪ ¡me lo imagino! ▪ ¡me lo figuro! ▪ ¡ya me lo figuro!

I can (just) barely hear you *(a ti)* casi no te oigo ▪ casi no puedo ni oírte ▪ apenas te oigo ▪ apenas puedo oírte ▪ *(a usted)* casi no le oigo ▪ casi no puedo ni oírle ▪ apenas le oigo ▪ apenas puedo oírle

I can just picture it now ▪ I just see it now es como si lo estuviera viendo ▪ es como si estuviera viéndolo ▪ es como si lo viera

I can just see her now 1. *(literal)* la estoy viendo **2.** *(figurative)* ya me la puedo imaginar ➤ I can just see her now laughing over my letter. Me la puedo imaginar riéndose al leer mi carta.

I can just see him now 1. *(literal)* lo estoy viendo **2.** *(figurative)* me lo puedo imaginar

I can just see it! 1. *(literal)* ¡lo(-a) estoy viendo! **2.** *(figurative)* ya me lo(-a) puedo imaginar

I can (just) see it now 1. I can just imagine it lo estoy viendo **2.** it's just coming into view ahora estoy empezando a verlo

I can manage by myself ▪ I can manage on my own ▪ I'll manage puedo manejarme solo(-a) ▪ me las puedo arreglar solo(-a) ▪ me las arreglo solo(-a) ▪ puedo valerme por mí mismo

I can manage on my own ▪ I can manage by myself ▪ I'll manage puedo manejarme solo(-a) ▪ me las puedo arreglar solo(-a) ▪ me las arreglo solo(-a) ▪ puedo valerme por mí mismo

I can see her now 1. I can just imagine her now me la puedo imaginar ▪ me la imagino **2.** she's just come into view ahora la veo

I can see him now 1. I can just imagine him now me lo puedo imaginar ▪ me lo imagino **2.** he's just come into view ahora lo veo ▪ *(Sp., leísmo)* ahora le veo

I can see how... ▪ I can appreciate how... ▪ I can understand how... puedo comprender cómo...

I can see it coming 1. *(literal)* lo veo venir **2.** *(figurative)* ya lo veo venir ➤ The bus just turned the corner. I can see it coming. El autobús acaba de dar la vuelta a la esquina. Lo veo venir. ➤ He's going to get in trouble. I can see it coming. Él va a meterse en problemas. Ya lo veo venir.

I can see it now! 1. it has come into view! ¡ahora lo veo! **2.** I can just imagine it me lo puedo imaginar

I can see liking... ▪ I can imagine liking... ▪ I can understand liking... puedo entender que a alguien le guste... ▪ me puedo imaginar que a alguien le guste... ▪ puedo comprender que a alguien le guste...

I can see myself doing that 1. puedo verme haciendo eso ▪ me veo haciendo eso **2.** *(fanciful)* I can just see myself doing that! ¡figúrate! ¡yo haciendo eso!

I can see that 1. it's visible to me puedo ver eso **2.** I can understand that puedo entender eso **3.** I have noticed that lo noto ▪ se nota ▪ lo he notado

I can see that... puedo ver que...

I can still taste todavía tengo en la boca el sabor de ▪ todavía me sabe la boca a ▪ *(when burping)* me está repitiendo ➤ I can still taste the coffee I drank this morning. Todavía tengo en la boca el sabor del café de esta mañana. ➤ I can still taste the vitamin pill I took two hours ago. Todavía me sabe la boca a las vitaminas que tomé hace dos horas. ➤ I can still taste the tamale (that) I ate a while ago. Me está repitiendo el tamal que comí hace un rato.

I can tell ▪ I can tell it ya me doy cuenta ▪ ya lo veo ▪ lo noto ▪ se nota ➤ She's mad at her boyfriend.-Yes, I can tell. Está enojada con su novio.-Sí, lo noto.

I can tell (it to) you *(a ti)* puedo decírtelo ▪ *(a usted)* puedo decírselo ➤ I can tell it to you now because it's already come out. Puedo decírtelo ahora porque ya se ha dado a conocer. ▪ Puedo decírtelo ahora porque ya es del dominio público.

I can tell (that) ▪ I can tell it ya me he dado cuenta ▪ ya lo veo ▪ lo noto

I can tell that... me doy cuenta que...

I can tell you that... (yo) te puedo decir que... ▪ (yo) puedo decirte que...

I can, too yo también (puedo)

I can understand how... ▪ I can see how... ▪ I can appreciate how... puedo comprender cómo...

I can understand that puedo comprender esto ▪ lo puedo comprender ▪ puedo comprenderlo ▪ puedo entender esto ▪ te entiendo ▪ te comprendo

I can understand that... puedo entender que...

I can't afford it no puedo afrontarlo ▪ no me sale a cuenta ▪ no puedo darme el lujo ▪ *(Sp.)* no puedo permitírmelo ▪ se me sale de cuenta

I can't afford to no me alcanza el dinero para ▪ no tengo plata suficiente para ▪ *(colorful)* no me da el cuero para ➤ I can't afford to buy a house right now. No me alcanza el dinero para comprar una casa ahora. ▪ No me da el cuero para comprar una casa ahora.

I can't believe... no puedo creer que... ▪ me cuesta creer que... ▪ vaya con... ➤ I can't believe the rise in the price of milk! ▪ I can't believe the increase in the price of milk! No puedo creer la subida del precio de la leche. ▪ Vaya con la subida del precio de la leche.

I can't believe it! ¡no me lo puedo creer! ▪ ¡no puedo creérmelo! ▪ ¡no puedo creerlo! ▪ parece mentira

I can't believe my eyes no doy crédito a mis ojos ▪ no puedo creer lo que ven mis ojos

I can't believe (that)... parece mentira que... ▪ no puedo creer que...

I can't believe what... no me creo lo que...

I can't bring myself to... ▪ I cannot bring myself to... no me siento con el valor suficiente para... ▪ *(everywhere but Mexico)* no tengo coraje para... *(In Mexico, "coraje" means a frustrated, powerless anger.)*

I can't come no puedo venir

I can't complain ▪ I can find nothing to complain of no me puedo quejar

I can't conceive of... no puedo concebir la idea de...

I can't conceive of it no puedo concebirlo

I can't concentrate no me puedo concentrar

I can't decide no me puedo decidir ▪ no puedo decidirme

I can't decide whether no puedo decidir si

I can't do it no puedo hacerlo ▪ soy incapaz de hacerlo

I can't do it by myself ▪ I can't do it alone no puedo hacerlo (yo) solo ▪ yo solo no puedo hacerlo

I can't explain it 1. *(to another)* no puedo explicarlo **2.** *(to myself)* no puedo explicármelo

I can't face her no puedo enfrentarla ▪ no puedo enfrentarme a ella ▪ no puedo hacerle frente (a ella) ▪ *(Sp., leísmo)* no puedo enfrentarle (a ella)

I can't face him no puedo enfrentarlo ▪ no puedo enfrentarme a él ▪ no puedo hacerle frente (a él) ▪ *(Sp., leísmo)* no puedo enfrentarle

I can't face it no puedo hacerlo frente ▪ no puedo afrontarlo

I can't find it no puedo encontrarlo ▪ no lo encuentro ▪ no puedo hallarlo

I can't find it anywhere no lo encuentro por ninguna parte

I can't find one no puedo encontrar uno

I can't get it out of my head no puedo quitármelo de la cabeza ■ no me lo puedo quitar de la cabeza ■ no puedo apartarlo de mi mente

I can't get it out of my mind no puedo apartarlo de mi mente ■ no me lo puedo quitar de la mente ■ no puedo quitármelo de la mente ■ no puedo apartarlo de mis pensamientos

I can't get it to work no puedo hacerlo funcionar ■ no puedo ponerlo en marcha ■ no consigo que funcione ■ no puedo conseguir que funcione ■ no puedo hacer que ande

I can't get the hang of it no le puedo agarrar la mano ■ no le puedo encontrar la vuelta ■ *(Sp.)* se me resiste ■ no le puedo pillar el tranquillo ■ no le puedo coger el tranquillo

I can't go on like this no puedo seguir así ■ no puedo más

I can't hear a word you're saying ■ I can't hear a thing you're saying no puedo oír (ni) una palabra de lo que dices ■ no puedo oír ni una palabra de lo que (me) estás diciendo

I can't help but... no puedo dejar de... ■ no puedo evitar que... ■ no puedo más que... ■ no resisto la tendencia de...

I can't help but think that... ■ I can't help thinking that... no puedo dejar de pensar que... ■ no puedo dejar de creer que...

I can't help it no lo puedo remediar ■ no puedo remediarlo

I can't help smoking no puedo más que fumar

I can't help thinking about... no puedo más que pensar en... ■ no puedo evitar pensar en...

I can't help thinking that... no puedo más que pensar que... ■ no puedo evitar pensar que...

I can't imagine! ■ I have no idea! ■ I can't fathom it ■ I haven't got a clue ini idea! ■ no tengo la más mínima idea ■ no tengo la más remota idea

I can't imagine (doing something) no me imagino (haciendo algo) ■ no puedo imaginarme (haciendo algo)

I can't imagine it no me lo puedo imaginar ■ no puedo imaginármelo ■ no puedo imaginarlo

I can't imagine what... no (me) puedo imaginar lo que... ■ no (me) puedo imaginar qué... ➤ I can't imagine what the miners went through. No (me) puedo imaginar lo que sufrieron los mineros. ■ No (me) puedo imaginar qué sufrieron los mineros.

I can't make any sense out of this explanation no saco nada en claro de esta explicación

I can't make heads or tails out of... no puedo sacar nada de...

I can't make heads or tails out of it esto no tiene ni pies ni cabeza (para mí) ■ esto no tiene sentido para mí

I can't make up my mind no puedo decidir ■ no puedo decidirme

I can't pass up pointing out that... ■ I can't not point out that... no puedo dejar de señalar que... ■ no puedo dejar pasar esta oportunidad sin señalar que... ■ no puedo dejar pasar la oportunidad de señalar que...

I can't pass up the chance to... ■ I can't pass up the opportunity to... no puedo dejar pasar la oportunidad de... ■ no puedo dejar pasar esta oportunidad sin...

I can't pass up the opportunity to... no puedo dejar pasar la oportunidad de... ■ no puedo dejar pasar esta oportunidad sin...

I can't place her no la ubico ■ no la sitúo

I can't place him no lo ubico ■ no lo sitúo ■ *(Sp., leísmo)* no le ubico ■ no le sitúo

I can't put it into words no puedo explicarlo con palabras

I can't put my finger on... no logro captar... ➤ I can't (quite) put my finger on what the spice is in this bread. No logro captar cuál es la especia en este pan.

I can't put my finger on it no logro captarlo ■ no puedo dar con ello ■ no consigo dar con ello

I can't quite understand it no puedo entenderlo completamente ■ no puedo comprenderlo completamente ■ (yo) no acierto a explicármelo

I can't remember a time when no recuerdo la época cuando ■ no recuerdo el tiempo cuando ➤ I can't remember a time when we didn't have a dog. No recuerdo una época cuando no tuviéramos un perro.

I can't remember your name *(tú)* no me acuerdo de tu nombre ■ no recuerdo tu nombre ■ *(usted)* no me acuerdo de su nombre ■ no recuerdo su nombre

I can't say 1. I don't know no sé decirte ■ no sé decirle 2. I'm not at liberty to say no puedo decirlo ■ no puedo decirte ■ no puedo decirle

I can't say much for no puedo decir mucho a favor de... ➤ I can't say much for her disposition. No puedo decir mucho a favor de su temperamento.

I can't stand... no soporto... ■ no aguanto... ■ no tolero...

I can't stand any more (of) ■ I can't take any more (of) no soporto más (de) ■ no aguanto más (de) ■ no tolero más (de)

I can't stand her no la soporto ■ no la aguanto ■ no puedo soportarla ■ no puedo aguantarla ■ le tengo manía (a ella)

I can't stand him no lo soporto ■ no lo aguanto ■ no puedo soportarlo ■ no puedo aguantarlo ■ le tengo manía (a él)

I can't stand it no lo puedo soportar ■ no puedo soportarlo

I can't stand it any longer no lo resisto más ■ no lo aguanto más ■ no lo aguanto ni un minuto más ■ no lo resisto ni un minuto más

I can't stand the idea of doing that no puedo soportar la idea de hacer eso

I can't stand the sight of her no puedo verla ■ no puedo ni verla ■ no puedo verla ni en pintura

I can't stand the sight of him no puedo verlo ■ no puedo ni verlo ■ no puedo verlo ni en pintura ■ *(Sp., leísmo)* no puedo verle

I can't stand the thought of it no quiero ni pensarlo ■ no quiero ni imaginármelo

I can't stand the way... no soporto la manera en la que...

I can't stand up no puedo ponerme de pie ■ no puedo pararme

I can't stand up straight no me tengo derecho ■ no puedo ponerme derecho ■ no me puedo poner derecho ■ no puedo enderezarme ■ no me puedo enderezar

I can't stay long no puedo quedarme mucho tiempo ■ *(colorful)* ésta es una visita relámpago

I can't stop thinking about it ■ I can't get it out of my head no me lo puedo quitar de la cabeza ■ no puedo quitármelo de la cabeza ■ no puedo apartarlo de mis pensamientos

I can't take any more ■ I can't stand any more no soporto más ■ no aguanto más ■ no me resisto más

I can't take it any longer no lo resisto más ■ no aguanto más ■ no soporto más ■ ya no lo soporto ■ se acabó ■ no doy más

I can't take long no puedo tardarme ■ no puedo tomarme mucho tiempo

I can't take my eyes off of you no puedo dejar de mirarte ■ no puedo apartar mis ojos de ti ■ no puedo dejarte de mirar

I can't tell no puedo distinguir ■ no puedo saber

I can't tell them apart no los puedo distinguir ■ no los distingo ■ *(when all direct objects are feminine)* no las puedo distinguir ■ no las distingo

I can't tell what... no puedo distinguir qué... ■ no puedo distinguir lo que...

I can't tell you 1. *(because I don't know)* I couldn't tell you no sé decirte ■ no puedo decirte 2. *(because it's a secret)* I'm sworn to secrecy no puedo contarte ■ no te lo puedo decir ■ no te lo puedo contar ■ no se me permite decírtelo

I can tell you for a fact that... *(tú)* por seguro te digo que... ■ *(usted)* por seguro le digo que...

I can't tell you how glad I am that... no sabes qué alegría me da que... ■ no sabes cuánto me alegra que...

I can't tell you how glad I am to... no sabes qué alegría me da que... ■ cuánto me alegro de...

I can't tell you how much... no sabes cuánto... ■ no sabes cómo... ➤ I can't tell you how much our family enjoyed the black paw ham you gave us. ■ I can't tell you how much our family liked the black paw ham you gave us. No sabes cuánto le gustó a nuestra familia el jamón (de) pata negra que nos diste. ■ No sabes cómo le gustó a nuestra familia el jamón (de) pata negra que nos diste.

I can't tell you whether... *(tú)* no sé decirte si... ■ *(usted)* no sé decirle si...

I can't think of it ■ it's not coming to me no se me ocurre ■ no me sale

I can't understand... no puedo entender... ■ no puedo comprender... ■ no me explico...

I can't wait to... no puedo esperar para... ➤ I can't wait to see your new apartment. No puedo esperar para ver tu nuevo apartamento.

I caught the bus by the skin of my teeth tomé el autobús por los pelos ▪ pesqué el autobús por los pelos ▪ *(Sp., colorful, implying that your feet were dragging)* cogí el autobús barriéndome

I caused this problem causé este problema

I challenge you to 1. te desafío a ▪ le desafío (a usted) a **2.** *(to a duel)* le reto (a usted) a ➤ On the first day of class, I challenge all of my students to make an A in the course. El primer día de clase, desafío a todos mis alumnos a lograr un sobresaliente en el curso. ➤ For insulting my honor, I challenge you to a duel. Por insultar mi honor, le reto a un duelo.

I changed my mind ▪ I've changed my mind cambié de opinión ▪ cambié de parecer ▪ *(Sp.)* he cambiado de opinión ▪ he cambiado de parecer ▪ ➤ I changed my mind. I'll have sparkling water instead. Cambié de opinión. Prefiero agua con gas. ▪ Cambié de parecer. Prefiero agua con gas.

I chose it for a reason lo elegí por una razón ▪ lo escogí por una razón ▪ lo elegí por un motivo ▪ lo escogí por un motivo

I completely agree with you ▪ I agree with you completely ▪ I totally agree with you ▪ I agree with you wholeheartedly estoy completamente de acuerdo contigo ▪ estoy totalmente de acuerdo contigo ▪ estoy absolutamente de acuerdo contigo ▪ coincido completamente contigo

I completely forgot me olvidé completamente ▪ se me olvidó de plano

I concur ▪ I'm of the same opinion ▪ I agree ▪ we agree on that en eso coincido ▪ estoy de acuerdo ▪ en eso coincidimos

I could barely... apenas podía... ▪ a duras penas (yo) podía... ▪ a duras penas (yo) pude... ➤ In the dark, I could barely see the name on the mailbox. En la oscuridad, apenas podía ver el nombre en el buzón.

I could be persuaded 1. I am persuadable me podrían persuadir **2.** you could persuade me me podrías persuadir ➤ With a little cajoling, I could be persuaded. Con un poco de labia, me podrían persuadir. ➤ With a little cajoling, you could persuade me. Con un poco de labia, me podrías persuadir.

I could do with... no me vendría mal... ➤ I could do with a good cold beer right now. No me venía mal una cerveza bien fría ahora.

I could give a damn! ▪ I could care less! ▪ I couldn't care less! ¡me importa un cuerno! ▪ ¡me importa un pito! ▪ ¡me importa un pepino! ▪ me importa un bledo ▪ me vale

I could give a shit *(off-color)* ▪ I couldn't give a shit ▪ I could care less ▪ I couldn't care less me importa una mierda ▪ me la trae floja ▪ ¡me la suda! ▪ me importa un carajo ▪ *(benign alternative)* no me importa un bledo ▪ me importa un carancho

I could go after all ▪ I would be able to go after all finalmente yo podría ir ➤ I called her back and told her I could go after all. ▪ I called her back and told her I'd be able to go after all. Volví a llamarla para decir que finalmente sí (yo) podría ir.

I could go for a drink right now ▪ I could really go for a drink right now se me antoja una bebida ahora mismo

I could go if ▪ I would be able to go (yo) podría ir si ➤ I could go if we went on Friday night instead of Saturday. ▪ I'd be able to go if we went on Friday night instead of Saturday. Podría ir si fuéramos el viernes por la noche en vez del sábado.

I could hardly... ▪ I could barely... (yo) apenas podía... ▪ *(Sp.)* a duras penas (yo) podía... ▪ (yo) casi no podía... ➤ I could hardly keep up with him. Apenas podía mantener su ritmo. ▪ Apenas podía mantener su paso.

I could hardly believe it casi no podía creerlo

I could hardly believe my eyes casi no podía creer lo que veían mis ojos ▪ casi no daba crédito a mis ojos ▪ apenas di crédito a mis ojos

I could hardly keep my eyes open casi no podía mantener los ojos abiertos ▪ apenas podía mantener los ojos abiertos

I could have danced all night podría haber bailado toda la noche

I could have done it better myself pude haberlo hecho mejor yo mismo ▪ (yo) podría haberlo hecho mejor ▪ podría haberlo hecho mejor (yo mismo)

I could have (done something) (yo) podría haber (hecho algo) ▪ pude haber (hecho algo) ➤ I could have gone, but I didn't feel like it. Podría haber ido, pero no me apetecía. ➤ He could have done much more than he did. Pudo haber hecho mucho más de lo que hizo.

I could have sworn... (yo) hubiera jurado que... ▪ (yo) hubiese jurado que... ▪ (yo) podría haber jurado que...

I could really go for a drink right now me vendría bien una bebida ahora mismo ▪ se me antoja una bebida en este momento

I could see at a glance that... me bastó una mirada para comprobar que... ▪ pude ver de una mirada que...

I could see how... pude ver cómo... ▪ pude contemplar cómo...

I could see it coming lo vi venir

I could see myself pude verme ➤ I could see myself in the reflection of the water. Pude verme en el reflejo del agua.

I could see myself that... ▪ I could see for myself that... yo mismo pude ver que...

I could swear... podría jurar... ▪ juraría... ▪ puedo asegurarte... ▪ te aseguro que... ➤ I could swear the expression on that pig's face changed when they carved it. Podría jurar que cambió la expresión del cerdo cuando lo trincharon.

I could tell lo notaba

I could tell that... notaba que... ▪ percibía que... ▪ me daba cuenta de que... ▪ podía percibir que...

I could use your help me vendría bien tu ayuda ▪ me vendría bien trabajar contigo

I couldn't add anything more no pude añadir una cosa más ▪ no hay más que decir

I couldn't agree with you more *(tú)* no podría estar más de acuerdo contigo ▪ *(usted)* no podría estar más de acuerdo con usted

I couldn't ask for anything more no podría pedir más ▪ no hay más que pedir

I couldn't avoid it no pude evitarlo

I couldn't believe it no podía creerlo ▪ no pude creerlo

I couldn't believe my eyes no daba crédito a mis ojos ▪ no di crédito a mis ojos

I couldn't bring myself to do something no pude forzarme a mí mismo a hacer algo ▪ no me pude obligar a mí mismo a hacer algo

I couldn't care less no me importa un bledo ▪ (a mí) me la refanfinflas

I couldn't (do it) even if I tried yo no podría (ni) aunque lo intentara ▪ yo no podría por más que lo intentara ▪ yo no podría (ni) aunque lo intentase ▪ yo no podría por más que lo intentase

I couldn't even do it 1. I wasn't even given the opportunity to do it ni siquiera pude hacerlo **2.** I was given the opportunity but was unable to do it ni siquiera podía hacerlo

I couldn't figure it out (yo) no pude encontrarle la vuelta ▪ *(followed by a dependent clause)* (yo) no podía encontrarle la vuelta

I couldn't get a word in edgewise no pude meter baza

I couldn't get it to work no pude hacerlo funcionar ▪ no pude ponerlo en marcha ▪ no pude conseguir que funcionara

I couldn't get to sleep ▪ I couldn't sleep no me pude dormir ▪ no pude conciliar el sueño ▪ no pude dormir

I couldn't get up 1. *(tried once but failed)* no pude levantarme **2.** *(made repeated unsuccessful attempts or no attempt at all)* no podía levantarme

I couldn't have said it better myself! ¡no lo podría haber dicho mejor (yo)!

I couldn't help... no pude evitar... ➤ I couldn't help eating all the pistachios. No pude evitar comer todos los pistachos.

I couldn't help it no pude evitarlo ▪ no lo pude evitar ▪ no lo pude remediar ▪ no pude remediarlo

I couldn't help noticing that... ▪ I couldn't but notice that... no he podido evitar notar que...

I couldn't help seeing... (yo) no había podido dejar de ver...

I couldn't prevent it no pude prevenirlo

I couldn't put it down *(a good book)* no pude dejarlo

I couldn't quite understand it no pude entenderlo completamente ▪ no pude comprenderlo completamente ▪ (yo) no acertaba a explicármelo ▪ no podía explicármelo

I couldn't say ▪ I couldn't tell you ▪ I can't say no sé decirte ▪ no sé decirle

I couldn't stand it any longer ▪ I just couldn't stand it any longer no pude más ▪ no aguanté más ▪ no pude soportarlo más ▪ no pude aguantarlo más ▪ no soporté más

I couldn't swear by it, but... no lo sé a ciencia cierta, pero...

I couldn't tell no me di cuenta ➤ Had he been drinking?-I couldn't tell. ¿Estuvo él bebiendo?-No me di cuenta.

I couldn't tell what... no me daba cuenta de lo que... ▪ *(further in the past)* no me di cuenta de lo que...

I couldn't tell you 1. *(because I don't know)* no sé decirte **2.** *(because it was a secret)* no podía contarte ▪ no te lo podía decir ▪ no te lo podía contar

I couldn't turn it down no pude rechazarlo

I couldn't wish for anything more no podría desear nada más ▪ no podría pedir nada más

I couldn't work the Rubik's Cube, but if you could take it apart, you could figure it out no pude resolver el cubo Rúbico, pero si se pudiera desarmar, podría encontrársele la vuelta.

I dare you! 1. *(as a challenge)* ¡a que no te atreves! **2.** *(as a warning)* ¡atrévete y verás! ▪ ¡atrévete!

I dare you to... a que no te atreves a... ➤ I dare you to try to jump across the creek. A que no te atreves a saltar por encima del arroyo.

I *did* sí lo hice

***I* did** lo hice yo

I did indeed ▪ yes, I did sí efectivamente ➤ I did indeed receive the CD. ▪ Yes, I did receive the CD. Sí efectivamente recibí el CD.

I did it myself lo hice yo mismo(-a)

I did not! ¡no he sido yo! ➤ You brought it up!-I did not! ¡Tú lo has sacado!-¡No he sido yo!

I did that once before ▪ I already did that once ya lo hice una vez ▪ ya lo he hecho una vez

I did the best I could hice lo mejor que pude

I did what I could to... hice lo que pude para...

I did, too ▪ so did I **1.** yo también **2.** *(with "gustar")* a mí también ➤ I went to Midnight Mass this year.-I did, too. Fui a la misa de gallo este año.-Yo también. ➤ I liked the music at Midnight Mass.-I did, too. Me gustó la música en la misa del gallo.-A mí, también.

I didn't bargain on... no contaba con que... ➤ I didn't bargain on their returning a day early. No contaba con su regreso un día antes.

I didn't catch that ▪ I didn't catch what you were saying no lo he cogido ▪ no he cogido eso ▪ no he cogido lo que decías

I didn't even notice (it) ni siquiera lo noté ▪ ni siquiera me di cuenta ▪ ni cuenta me di

I didn't even think of that ni siquiera se me ocurrió ▪ ni siquiera lo pensé

I didn't get it ▪ I didn't catch on no he caído ▪ no entendí

I didn't get much (work) done no alcancé a hacer mucho trabajo ▪ *(Sp.)* no me ha cundido el trabajo

I didn't get to go no tuve la oportunidad de ir

I didn't get to it no alcancé a hacerlo ➤ I didn't get to it today, but I will tomorrow for sure. Hoy no alcancé a hacerlo, pero mañana seguro que lo haré.

I didn't get to see her no llegué a verla ▪ no alcancé a verla

I didn't get to see him no llegué a verlo ▪ no lo llegué a ver ▪ *(Sp., leísmo)* no llegué a verle ▪ no le llegué a ver

I didn't get to see it 1. *(a show)* no llegué a verlo ▪ no lo llegué a ver **2.** *(a movie)* no llegué a verla ▪ no la llegué a ver

I didn't get to take the courses I wanted no conseguí tomar los cursos que quería ▪ *(Sp.)* no conseguí tomar las asignaturas que quería

I didn't have any choice ▪ I had no (other) choice no tenía elección ▪ no podía hacer otra cosa ▪ no tenía otra opción ▪ no tuve más remedio ▪ no tuve manera de elegir

I didn't have any choice but to... ▪ I had no (other) choice but to... (yo) no tenía otra elección que... ▪ no podía hacer otra cosa que... ▪ (yo) no tenía otra opción que...

I didn't know a soul when I got here no conocía un alma cuando llegué aquí

I didn't know anybody when I got here no conocía a nadie cuando llegué aquí

I didn't know (that) you were... (yo) no sabía que estuviera(s)... ➤ I didn't know you were working in Madrid. No sabía que estuvieras trabajando en Madrid. ▪ No sabía que (usted) estuviera trabajando en Madrid.

I didn't know what time the plane was going to arrive ▪ I didn't know what time the plane would arrive no sabía a qué hora iba a llegar el avión ▪ no sabía a qué hora llegaría el avión

I didn't know what time the plane would arrive ▪ I didn't know what time the plane was going to arrive no sabía a qué hora llegaría el avión ▪ no sabía a qué hora iba a llegar el avión

I didn't know what to expect no sabía qué esperar

I didn't like it at all no me gustó nada ▪ no me agradó en lo más mínimo

I didn't look at it that way no lo vi de esa manera

I didn't make it 1. *(I couldn't get there)* no pude llegar **2.** *(I didn't achieve it)* no logré hacerlo ▪ no pude hacerlo **3.** *(colorful, for either context)* me ha pillado el toro

I didn't mean it ▪ I was just kidding ▪ I was just joking ▪ I was only joking fue de mentira ▪ era de mentiritas ▪ (yo) estaba bromeando ▪ te estaba vacilando

I didn't mean it that way no quise decir eso ▪ no intenté decir eso ▪ no quería decir eso

I didn't mean to no quería ▪ lo hice sin querer ▪ no lo pretendía

I didn't mean to scare you no era mi intención asustarte ▪ no pretendía asustarte ▪ no quería asustarte

I didn't notice no me fijé ▪ no me di cuenta ▪ no lo noté ▪ *(literary, journalistic)* no me percaté

I didn't notice anything ▪ I wasn't aware of anything no noté nada ▪ no me di cuenta de nada ▪ no me percaté de nada ▪ no observé nada ➤ *(newspaper quote)* I got pickpocketed on the metro. At the time, I didn't notice anything. ▪ I got pickpocketed on the metro. At the time, I wasn't aware of anything. Me sustrajeron la cartera en el metro. En ese momento, no me percaté de nada.

I didn't notice it no me di cuenta de eso ▪ no lo noté ➤ When you were in Yonkers, what did you think of the accent?-I don't know. I didn't notice it. Cuándo estuviste en Yonkers, ¿qué pensabas del acento?-No sé. No lo noté.

I didn't pay much attention to... no me fijé mucho en... ▪ no presté mucha atención a...

I didn't say that no dije eso

I didn't sleep a wink last night no pegué ojo anoche

I didn't think anything of it at the time no le di ninguna importancia en ese momento

I didn't think to ask no pensé en preguntar ▪ no se me ocurrió preguntar ➤ I didn't think to ask her. No pensé en preguntarle (a ella). ▪ No se me ocurrió preguntarle (a ella).

I didn't think you would mind ▪ I didn't think you'd mind no creí que te importara ▪ no pensé que te importara ▪ no creí que te fuera a importar ▪ no pensé que te fuera a importar

I didn't use to like... antes no me gustaba... ➤ I didn't use to like classical music, but I do now. Antes no me gustaba la música clásica, pero ahora sí.

I didn't want anyone to find out no quería que supiera nadie ▪ no quería que supiese nadie ▪ no quería que se enterara nadie ▪ no quería que se enterase nadie

I didn't want anyone to know no quería que supiera nadie ▪ no quería que supiese nadie

I didn't want the same thing to happen to me no quería que me pasara lo mismo

I disagree no estoy de acuerdo ▪ estoy en desacuerdo

I do? ¿sí? ▪ ¿de veras?

I do have sí que tengo

I do know (that...) sí sé (que...)

I *do* remember sí que me acuerdo ▪ sí (lo) recuerdo

I don't? ¿no?

I don't appreciate it ▪ I just don't appreciate it no lo aprecio ▪ no me hace gracia

I don't believe it ▪ I don't believe that no lo creo ▪ *(more emphatic, as if to say, "I don't buy it")* no me lo creo

I don't believe so ▪ I don't think so creo que no ▪ no creo

I don't believe you *(tú)* no te creo ▪ *(usted)* no le creo

I don't blame you (for it) no te culpo (por eso) ▪ no te echo la culpa (por eso)

I don't buy it! ¡(eso) no me convence! ▪ ¡no cuela! ▪ ¡no me lo creo!

I don't care 1. it's not important to me no me importa **2.** I have no preference me da igual ▪ me es igual

I don't care at all no me importa nada

I don't care about all that no me importa nada de eso ▪ paso de esas historias

I don't care for any, thanks no me apetece, gracias

I don't care for any more, thank you ▪ I don't care for any more, thanks ya no me apetece más, gracias ▪ no quiero nada más, gracias

I don't care for her no me preocupa nada su vida ▪ (ella) no me afecta para nada ▪ no me afecta para nada lo que haga ella ▪ (ella) no me cae bien

I don't care for him no me preocupa nada su vida ▪ (él) no me afecta para nada ▪ no me afecta para nada lo que haga él ▪ (él) no me cae bien

I don't care if ▪ it doesn't matter if me da igual si ▪ me da igual que ▪ no me importa si

I don't care one way or the other ▪ it makes no difference to me no tengo (ninguna) preferencia ▪ ni me va ni me viene

I don't care what people think ▪ I don't care what other people think ▪ I don't care what anyone thinks ande yo caliente y ríase la gente

I don't care whether... no me importa si... ▪ *(milder)* me es indiferente que... ➤ I don't care whether they like it or not. Que les guste o no me es indiferente.

I don't catch on ▪ I don't get it no caigo ▪ no entiendo ▪ no me cosco

I don't either ▪ neither do I (ni yo) tampoco

I don't even have to... no tengo ni que... ▪ ni siquiera tengo que... ➤ The envelopes come in lots of twenty-five. I don't even have to count them. Los sobres vienen por lotes de veinticinco. No tengo ni que contarlos. ▪ Los sobres vienen por lotes de veinticinco. Ni siquiera tengo contarlos. ➤ I don't even have to go to the store. I just give them a call. Ni siquiera tengo que ir a la tienda. Con llamar por teléfono basta.

I don't even know ni lo sé ▪ ni siquiera lo sé

I don't even know your name ni siquiera sé tu nombre

I don't ever want to have her for a teacher again no quiero volver a tenerla como profesora nunca más

I don't feel any different (from anyone else) (yo) no me siento diferente

I don't feel good about it no me da buena espina

I don't feel guilty at all no me siento culpable para nada

I don't feel like it no tengo ganas

I don't feel like going no me apetece ir ▪ no tengo ganas de ir

I don't follow you I'm not following you no te sigo ▪ no te entiendo

I don't get it ▪ I don't catch on no caigo ▪ no entiendo ▪ no me cosco

I don't get to see them very often no puedo verles mucho ▪ no les veo demasiado

I don't get what you mean no chanelo ▪ no lo cojo ▪ no te capto ▪ no le agarro

I don't give a damn *(coarse)* ni hostias ▪ ni huevos

I don't have any change ▪ I haven't got any change no tengo cambio ▪ no tengo nada suelto ▪ *(Chi.)* no tengo sencillo ▪ *(Mex., slang, especially to a beggar)* no tengo feria

I don't have any idea ▪ I have no idea no tengo la menor idea ▪ no tengo la más mínima idea

I don't have any place to put it ▪ I don't have anywhere to put it no tengo sitio donde ponerlo ▪ no tengo lugar donde ponerlo

I don't have anywhere to put it ▪ I don't have any place to put it no tengo sitio donde ponerlo ▪ no tengo lugar donde ponerlo

I don't have change (for) ▪ I haven't got change (for) no tengo cambio (para)... ➤ I don't have change for a twenty. No tengo cambio para uno de veinte. ▪ No tengo cambio de veinte.

I don't have the slightest idea no tengo la menor idea ▪ no tengo la más mínima idea

I don't have much time no tengo mucho tiempo ▪ tengo poco tiempo ▪ voy fatal de tiempo

I don't have much time left ▪ I'm running out of time me queda poco tiempo ▪ se me acaba el tiempo

I don't have one no tengo ▪ no lo tengo

I don't have the slightest idea ▪ I haven't the slightest (idea) no tengo ni la más mínima idea ▪ no tengo ni la más ligera idea

I don't just think so, I know so no es que lo crea, es que estoy absolutamente seguro

I don't know no lo sé ▪ no sé

I don't know a soul here no conozco ni un alma aquí ▪ no conozco a nadie aquí

I don't know about it no estoy enterado de eso ▪ no estoy enterado de ello

I don't know about that ▪ I don't know anything about that ▪ I'm not informed about that no sé nada de eso

I don't *know* about that 1. I don't know if I believe it no sé si creérmelo ▪ no me convence **2.** I don't know if I believe you no sé si creerte

I don't know about you, but I... *(tú)* no sé tú, pero yo... ▪ *(usted)* no sé usted, pero yo...

I don't know any no conozco ninguno

I don't know anyone here no conozco a nadie aquí

I don't know anyone who... no conozco a nadie que...

I don't know anything about that no sé nada de eso

I don't know either (yo) tampoco lo sé

I don't know her by sight ▪ I wouldn't recognize her if I saw her no la conozco de vista ▪ (yo) ni la reconocería si la viera

I don't know him by sight ▪ I wouldn't recognize him if I saw him no lo conozco de vista ▪ ni lo reconocería si lo viera ▪ *(Sp., leísmo)* no le conozco de vista ▪ ni le reconocería si le viera

I don't know of any no sé de ninguno

I don't know of anyone no sé de nadie

I don't know of anyone who... no sé de nadie que... ➤ I don't know of anyone who can translate like Cecilia and Iván. No sé de nadie que sepa traducir como Cecilia e Iván. ➤ I don't know of anyone who can outdo her. No sé de nadie que le pueda ganar. ▪ No sé de nadie que lo haga mejor que ella. ➤ I don't know of anyone who can outdo him. No sé de nadie que le pueda ganar. ▪ No sé de nadie que lo haga mejor que él.

I don't know of anything no sé de nada ▪ no tengo idea de nada

I don't know of anything that would stop me no sé de nada que me detenga ▪ no sé de nada que me pueda parar

I don't know what became of it ▪ I don't know what(ever) happened to it no sé qué pasó con eso ▪ no sé qué fue de eso

I don't know what came over me no sé lo que me ha pasado ▪ no sé qué me ha pasado

I don't know what got into me no sé lo que me ha dado ▪ no sé qué me ha dado

I don't know what he looks like ▪ I don't know him by sight ▪ I wouldn't recognize him if I saw him no sé que aspecto tiene (él) ▪ no lo conozco de vista ▪ ni lo reconocería si lo viera ▪ ni lo reconocería si lo viese ▪ *(Sp., leísmo)* no le conozco de vista ▪ ni le reconocería si le viera ▪ ni le reconocería si le viese

I don't know what she looks like ▪ I don't know her by sight ▪ I wouldn't recognize her no sé que aspecto tiene (ella) ▪ no la conozco de vista ▪ ni la reconocería si la viera ▪ ni la reconocería si la viese

I don't know what to do about it no sé qué hacer con eso ▪ no sé qué hacer al respecto ▪ no sé qué es lo que debo hacer ▪ no sé lo que hacer con eso ▪ no sé lo que hacer al respecto

I don't know what to make of it no sé cómo explicármelo ▪ no sé qué pensar de esto

I don't know what to think no sé qué pensar

I don't know what to think about it no sé qué pensar de eso ▪ no sé qué pensar sobre eso

I don't know what's come over me no sé qué me ha pasado ▪ no sé qué me ha podido pasar ▪ no sé lo que se me viene encima

I don't know who to turn to no sé a quién recurrir ▪ no se a quién acudir

I don't know yet ▪ I still don't know todavía no lo sé ▪ aún no lo sé ▪ no lo sé aún ▪ no lo sé todavía

I don't know you at all ▪ I hardly know you ▪ I don't even know who you are ▪ I don't even know you *(tú)* no sé ni quién eres ▪ ni siquiera te conozco ▪ no te conozco en absoluto ▪ no te conozco para nada ▪ *(usted)* no sé ni quién es (usted) ▪ *(to a man)* ni siquiera lo conozco (a usted) ▪ no lo conozco en absoluto ▪ *(to a woman)* ▪ ni siquiera la conozco (a usted) ▪ no la conozco en absoluto ▪ *(primarily Sp., leísmo, to a man or woman)* ni siquiera le conozco ▪ no le conozco en absoluto ▪ no le conozco para nada

I don't like... no me gusta ▪ *(Sp.)* no me va ➤ I don't like heavy metal. No me gusta el rock pesado. ▪ No me va el rock pesado.

I don't like being told what to do no me gusta que me digan lo que tengo que hacer

I don't like (for) no me gusta que ➤ I don't like (for) the computer to make any assumptions about what I'm doing. No me gusta que la computadora haga suposiciones sobre lo que estoy haciendo. ➤ I don't like (for) the computer defaults to change the text. No me gusta que las configuraciones predeterminadas del ordenador cambien el texto.

I don't like it no me gusta ▪ no me agrada

I don't like it at all no me gusta nada ▪ no me agrada en lo más mínimo

I don't like it, either tampoco me gusta ▪ a mí tampoco me gusta ▪ no me gusta tampoco ▪ tampoco me agrada ▪ a mí tampoco me agrada ▪ no me agrada tampoco

I don't like the look of it no me gusta su aspecto ▪ no me gusta la pinta que tiene

I don't like to think about it no me gusta pensar en ello ▪ no me gusta pensar en eso

I don't live here no vivo aquí ▪ no soy de la casa

I don't look at it that way ▪ I don't see it that way no lo veo así

I don't mean to be rude, but... no quiero ser impertinente, pero... ▪ no quiero parecer mal educado, pero...

I don't mean to pry, but... no tengo intención de inmiscuirme, pero... ▪ no pretendo inmiscuirme, pero...

I don't mind no me importa

I don't need a ride ▪ you don't need to give me a ride no hace falta que me lleves ▪ no necesito que me lleves

I don't need it no me hace falta ▪ no lo necesito ➤ You take it. I don't need it. Tómalo, no me hace falta. ▪ Tómalo. No lo necesito.

I don't need to no me hace falta ▪ no necesito

I don't put any stock in it no le doy ningún crédito a eso

I don't put any stock in what he says no le doy ningún crédito a lo que dice

I don't quite no del todo ➤ I thought I had enough money, but I don't quite. Creía que tenía suficiente dinero, pero no del todo. ▪ Creía que tenía suficiente dinero, pero no me llega.

I don't see any no veo ninguno

I don't see any way out of it no veo ninguna salida ▪ no veo escapatoria posible ▪ no veo ninguna escapatoria

I don't see it anywhere no lo veo por ninguna parte

I don't see it that way ▪ I don't look at it that way no lo veo así

I don't see one no veo ninguno

I don't see the connection no veo la relación

I don't see why... no entiendo por qué...

I don't smell anything no huelo a nada ▪ no me huele nada

I don't stand a chance (of) ▪ I don't have any chance (of) no tengo la más mínima oportunidad (de)

I don't think he'll do it no creo que lo haga ▪ creo que no lo haga ▪ creo que no lo hará

I don't think it matters no creo que importe ▪ creo que no importa

I don't think it's right (to...) no me parece bien... ▪ no creo que sea justo...

I don't think it's *that* no creo que sea eso ▪ no me parece que sea eso

I don't think so no lo creo ▪ creo que no ▪ pienso que no

I don't think so, either (yo) tampoco lo creo

I don't think that's a good idea no creo que sea una buena idea

I don't think that's it ▪ I don't think that's the reason no creo que sea por eso ▪ no creo que ése sea el motivo

I don't think that's such a good idea no creo que sea una idea tan buena

I don't think there's any doubt about it ▪ I don't think there's any question about it no creo que haya ninguna duda al respecto ▪ no creo que haya ninguna duda sobre eso ▪ no creo que quepa la menor duda al respecto

I don't think there's any doubt that... ▪ I don't think there's any question that... no creo que haya la menor duda de que...

I don't think there's any question about it ▪ I don't think there's any doubt about it no creo que haya ninguna duda al respecto ▪ no creo que haya ninguna duda sobre eso ▪ no creo que quepa la menor duda al respecto

I don't think there's any question that... ▪ I don't think there's any doubt that... no creo que haya la menor duda de que...

I don't think you can beat it 1. it can't be surpassed creo que no se puede superar ▪ no creo que se pueda mejorar ▪ creo que es insuperable **2.** it's the best one no creo que haya nada mejor ▪ creo que no hay nada mejor ▪ creo que es lo mejor que hay ➤ For Mexican food in Madrid, I don't think you can beat it. Con respecto a la comida mexicana en Madrid, creo que no hay ninguna mejor que ésta. ➤ For Mozart recordings, I don't think you can beat it. En cuanto a grabaciones de Mozart, creo que ésta es insuperable.

I don't think you can improve on it 1. *(impersonal "you")* creo que no se puede mejorar **2.** *(personal "you")* creo que no puedes mejorarlo ▪ creo que usted no puede mejorarlo

I don't trust him no confío en él ▪ no me fío de él ▪ no le tengo confianza (a él)

I don't want anything to do with it ▪ I want nothing to do with it no quiero tener nada que ver con eso ▪ de esta agua no beberé

I don't want to no quiero hacerlo ▪ no me apetece ▪ no tengo ganas

I don't want to be told what to do no quiero que me digan lo que tengo que hacer

I don't want to get into it 1. I don't want to talk about it ▪ I don't want to go into it no quiero entrar en ello ▪ no quiero hablar de eso **2.** I don't want to get involved in it no quiero meterme en eso

I don't want to get involved (in it) no quiero mezclarme con eso ▪ no quiero verme en esas ▪ no quiero involucrarme en eso

I don't want to go down that road 1. *(literal)* I don't want to take that road no quiero meterme en esa calle **2.** *(figurative)* I don't want to get into that no quiero meterme en ese tema ▪ no quiero entrar en ello **3.** *(figurative)* I don't want to take that course of action no quiero seguir ese camino

I don't want to go into it ▪ I don't want to get into it ▪ I don't want to talk about it no quiero entrar en eso ▪ no quiero meterme en eso ▪ no quiero hablar de eso ▪ no quiero hablar del tema

I don't want to go into that ▪ I don't want to get into that ▪ I don't want to talk about that no quiero hablar de eso ▪ no quiero entrar en eso ▪ no quiero hablar de ese tema

I don't want to keep you ■ I don't want to detain you no quiero retenerte ■ no quiero entretenerte ➤ I don't want to keep you any longer. No quiero retenerte más.

I don't want to pry, but... no quiero inmiscuirme, pero...

I don't want to push no quiero presionar

I don't want to take any chances no quiero correr ningún riesgo

I don't want to take the chance no quiero correr el riesgo

I doubt it lo dudo ■ lo estoy dudando

I dreamed I was... 1. soñé estar... ■ soñé que estaba... 2. soñé ser... ■ soñé que era... ➤ I dreamed I was in Bariloche. Soñé estar en Bariloche. ➤ I dreamed I was a first-rate chef. Soñé ser un cocinero de primera.

I drove (here) vine en auto ■ vine manejando ■ vine en carro ■ *(Sp.)* vine conduciendo ■ vine en coche

I drove (there) fui manejando ■ *(Sp.)* fui conduciendo ➤ We took turns. I drove while my wife slept, and then vice versa. Alternamos. Conducí cuando mi esposa estaba durmiendo, y al revés.

I ended up having to do it acabé teniéndolo que hacer ■ acabé por tener que hacerlo ■ terminé haciéndolo

I ended up in the middle of nowhere fui a parar al quinto pino

I enjoy it lo disfruto ■ me entretiene

I enjoyed it a lot 1. lo disfruté mucho ■ me gustó mucho 2. *(party)* me lo pasé estupendamente ■ me lo pasé genial

I enjoyed meeting you (estoy) encantado de haberte conocido ■ ha sido un gusto conocerte

I enjoyed seeing you me encantó verte ■ me alegra que nos hayamos visto

I feel at home here aquí me siento como en casa

I feel bad about what happened me siento mal por lo que pasó

I feel bad that... me da pena que... ➤ I feel bad that you haven't linked up with my friends in Guatemala. Me da pena que no te hayas podido encontrar con mis amigos en Guatemala.

I feel funny ■ I feel strange ■ I feel unwell me siento raro ■ no me siento bien ■ me encuentro mal

I feel it in my bones (that...) tengo la corazonada (de que...) ■ me da el pálpito (de que...) ■ tengo la impresión (de que...) ■ tengo la idea (de que...) ■ me da la sensación (de que...) ■ me da en la punta de la nariz (que...)

I feel like... tengo ganas de... ■ me da por...

I feel like a fool me siento como un tonto

I feel like I belong here *(coll.)* ■ I feel that I belong here me siento bien aquí ■ éste es mi lugar

I feel like I'm... *(coll.)* ■ I feel as though I'm siento como si fuera

I feel nauseated tengo náuseas ■ sentirse descompuesto(-a)

I feel privileged to... me siento privilegiado(-a)... ➤ I feel privileged to be invited to speak to you today. Me siento privilegiada de ser invitada a hablarles a ustedes hoy.

I feel really bad about it me siento muy mal por eso ■ me siento muy mal con eso ■ me siento muy mal en cuanto a eso

I feel sick about it ■ I'm sad about it eso me enferma

I feel so embarrassed me siento muy avergonzado(-a)

I feel so embarrassed (that) I just want to run and hide trágame tierra ■ tierra, trágame

I feel sorry for her (ella) me da lástima ■ lo siento por ella ■ lo lamento por ella

I feel sorry for him (él) me da lástima ■ lo siento por él ■ lo lamento por él

I feel sorry for you me das lástima ■ lo siento por ti ■ lo lamento por ti

I feel terrible 1. I feel ill me siento terrible ■ me encuentro fatal 2. I feel sorry me siento fatal

I feel terrible about what happened me siento fatal por lo que pasó

I feel that... tengo la sensación de que... ■ tengo la impresión de que... ■ me da la impresión de que...

I fell in love at first sight me enamoré a primera vista ■ me dio un flechazo ■ *(literary)* me quedé prendado

I figured as much ■ that's what I figured es lo que suponía ■ ya lo suponía ■ es lo que supuse

I figured that 1. *(main clause)* that's what I figured ■ I surmised that ■ I assumed that me lo imaginé 2. *(dependent clause)* I figured that... (me) supuse que... ■ (me) imaginé que... ■ me figuré que... ➤ I figured you'd been delayed. Supuse que algo os había retrasado. ➤ When I didn't hear from you, I figured you weren't coming. Cuando no tuve noticias tuyas, (me) imaginé que no venías. ■ Cuando no tuve noticias tuyas, (me) supuse que no venías.

I find it entertaining me parece muy entretenido ■ lo encuentro muy entretenido ■ lo veo muy entretenido

I find it hard to believe lo encuentro difícil de creer ■ lo veo difícil de creer ■ me parece difícil de creer ■ me cuesta creerlo

I find it hard to believe that... lo encuentro difícil de creer que... ■ lo veo difícil de creer que... ■ me parece difícil de creer que... ■ me cuesta creer que...

I find it interesting that... me resulta interesante que... ■ me parece interesante que...

I find it very interesting ■ I find that very interesting lo encuentro muy interesante ■ me resulta muy interesante

I find that... considero que... ■ encuentro que...

I forget se me olvida ■ se me pasa

I forgot se me olvidó ■ se me pasó

I forgot all about it se me olvidó por completo ■ se me pasó por completo ■ se me olvidó de plano ■ se me olvidó del todo

I forgot to ask se me olvidó preguntar ➤ I forgot to ask her. Se me olvidó preguntarle (a ella).

I forgot to bring something he olvidado traer algo ■ se me ha olvidado traer algo

I forgot to get something ■ I forgot to bring something me he dejado algo ■ *(in the grocery store)* se me olvidó buscar algo ■ *(Sp.)* se me olvidó coger algo

I forgot something se me olvidó algo ■ olvidé algo ■ me dejé algo (olvidado) ■ se me quedó algo

I forgot what I was saying ■ I lost my train of thought se me ha olvidado lo que estaba diciendo ■ se me fue la pinza ■ se me fue el santo (al cielo) ■ *(Mex., coll.)* se me fue la onda ■ *(Sp., coll.)* se me fue la olla

I forgot your name se me olvidó tu nombre ➤ I'm sorry, I forgot your name. Lo siento, se me olvidó tu nombre. ■ Disculpa, no recuerdo tu nombre.

I found it very interesting me ha resultado muy interesante ■ me pareció muy interesante

I found myself... 1. *(literal)* me encontré... 2. I realized that I... me di cuenta de que... ➤ Suddenly I found myself telling her all my deepest feelings. De repente me encontré contándole a ella mis sentimientos más profundos. ➤ As I stood in line to buy the ticket, I found myself not wanting to see the movie. Mientras hacía cola para comprar la entrada, me di cuenta de que no quería ver la película.

I found out about it through a friend ■ I found out about it from a friend me enteré por un amigo

I found out later that... ■ I later found out that... más tarde supe que... ■ más adelante supe que... ■ después supe que... ■ con el tiempo supe que... ■ luego supe que... ■ pasado el tiempo supe que... ➤ I found out later that my friend had lied to me. ■ I later found out that my friend had lied to me. Más tarde supe que mi amigo me había mentido.

I fully expected it yo lo esperaba totalmente

I fully understand the consequences entiendo perfectamente las consecuencias ■ tengo claras las consecuencias

I gather that... por lo visto ■ parece que... ➤ I gather that building a house takes less time than it used to. Por lo visto construir una casa lleva menos tiempo que antes.

I gathered that lo suponía ■ me lo imaginaba

I gathered that... suponía que... ■ me imaginaba que...

I get a kick out of it ■ I get a charge out of it eso me entusiasma

I get carried away me dejo llevar

I get frustrated when... me frustra cuando... ■ me siento frustrado cuando... ➤ I get really frustrated when... Me frustra mucho cuando... ■ Me frustra un montón cuando... ■ Me siento muy frustrado cuando...

I get it! ■ Oh, I get it! ¡ahora (lo) entiendo! ■ ¡ya entiendo! ■ *(Sp.)* ¡ya lo cojo! ■ ¡ah, ya lo cojo!

I get my share consigo mi parte ■ recibo mi parte ■ obtengo mi parte

I get so carried away (by) me dejo llevar (por) ■ me entusiasma tanto (por)

I get so sick of it... quedo tan harto...

I get the feeling that... me da la corazonada de que... ■ me da la sensación de que... ■ me da la impresión de que... ■ me da en el corazón que... ■ me da en la espina que... ■ *(L. Am.)* me late que...

I get to thinking sometimes (that)... a veces me pongo a pensar que... ■ a veces me da por pensar que...

I give up 1. I surrender me rindo **2.** *(in guessing)* me doy por vencido ■ me doy

I go there sometimes voy allí de vez en cuando

I got a kick out of it eso me entusiasmó

I got a lot going (on) *(coll.)* ■ I've got a lot going on ■ I have a lot going on estoy metido(-a) en muchas cosas ■ estoy metido(-a) en muchos proyectos

I got carried away me dejé llevar

I got cut off ■ we got cut off se cortó (la comunicación) ■ perdí la comunicación

I got here first ■ I was here first yo llegué primero ■ llegué antes ■ he llegado antes

I got it for free lo conseguí gratis ■ me lo llevé por la cara ■ me la llevé por la cara

I got really frustrated me frustré mucho

I got something in my eye tengo algo en el ojo ■ me cayó algo en el ojo ■ *(Sp.)* me entró algo en el ojo

I got sunburned me quemé con el sol ■ *(coll.)* me achicharré con el sol

I got the impression from him that... él me dio la impresión de que... ■ me dio a entender que...

I got to see all my family ■ I got to see my whole family pude ver a toda mi familia

I got to thinking me puse a pensar

I got to thinking about this me puse a pensar en esto

I guarantee you... *(tú)* te lo aseguro ■ *(usted)* se lo aseguro

I guess not supongo que no

I guess so supongo que sí

I guess the thing that... supongo que lo que...

I guess we better creo que deberíamos ■ supongo que deberíamos

I guessed as much ■ I figured as much ■ I assumed as much me lo suponía ■ me lo imaginaba ■ me lo figuraba

I had a lot of explaining to do tuve que dar muchas explicaciones

I had a lot of growing up to do tuve que madurar mucho

I had been walking for four hours when... (yo) había caminado (por) cuatro horas cuando... ■ caminaba desde hace cuatro horas cuando... ■ llevaba cuatro horas caminando cuando... ■ *(Sp.)* (yo) andaba desde hace cuatro horas cuando... j llevaba cuatro horas andando cuando...

I had better ■ I'd better más (me) vale que ➤ I had better hurry. ■ I'd better hurry. Más vale que me dé prisa.

I had dinner at my in-laws' (house) comí en la casa de mi familia política ■ *(Sp.)* estuve comiendo en la casa de mi familia política

I had dinner with my in-laws comí con mi familia política ■ *(Sp.)* estuve comiendo con mi familia política

I had done nothing but wait no había hecho nada más que esperar

I had expected to hear from you by now (yo) esperaba haber sabido de ti a estas alturas ■ (yo) había esperado saber de ti para estas alturas

I had forgotten all about it se me había olvidado por completo

I had forgotten that me había olvidado de eso

I had forgotten that... se me había olvidado que...

I had hoped to hear from you by now tenía la esperanza de haber sabido de ti a estas alturas ■ tenía la esperanza de haber sabido de ti para estas alturas

I had my reasons for... tenía mis razones para... ■ tenía mis motivos para... ➤ I had my reasons for choosing it. Tenía mis razones para escogerlo. ■ Tenía mis razones para elegirlo. ■ Tenía mis motivos para escogerlo. ■ Tenía mis motivos para elegirlo.

I had no idea how... no tenía ni idea de cómo...

I had no (other) choice ■ I didn't have any choice (yo) no tenía otra elección ■ (yo) no podía hacer otra cosa

I had no (other) choice but to... ■ I didn't have any choice but to... (yo) no tenía otra elección que... ■ (yo) no podía hacer otra cosa que...

I had only been working there a week when... sólo llevaba una semana trabajando allí cuando...

I had to have stitches me tuvieron que dar puntos

I had wanted to... (yo) había querido... ➤ I had wanted to paint my own apartment, and when I saw the job the painters did, I wished I had. (Yo) había querido pintar mi apartamento, y cuando vi el trabajo que hicieron los pintores, deseé que lo hubiese hecho.

I hadn't bargained on... no había previsto...

I hadn't even thought of that ni siquiera lo había pensado ■ ni siquiera se me había ocurrido

I hadn't figured on that ■ I didn't figure on that ■ I hadn't taken that into account no contaba con eso ■ no había contado con eso

I hadn't noticed no me había fijado ■ no me había dado cuenta ■ no lo había notado ➤ Oh really? I hadn't noticed. ¿De verdad? No me había fijado. ■ ¿De verdad? No me había dado cuenta. ■ ¿De verdad? No lo había notado.

I hadn't thought of it that way no lo había visto desde esa perspectiva ■ no lo había visto así

I hardly ever buy it apenas lo compro ■ apenas la compro

I hardly have time to... apenas tengo tiempo de... ➤ I hardly have time to have dinner. ■ I hardly have time to eat. Apenas tengo tiempo de comer.

I hate to admit it, but... odio admitirlo, pero...

I have a car ■ I own a car tengo carro ■ tengo auto ■ *(Sp.)* tengo coche

I have a concern tengo una inquietud ■ tengo una preocupación

I have a date tonight voy a salir con alguien esta noche ■ tengo una cita esta noche

I have a feeling that... ■ I've a feeling that... tengo el presentimiento de que ■ presiento que... ■ barrunto que... ■ *(L. Am.)* se me pone que... ➤ Toto, I've a feeling (that) we're not in Kansas anymore. Toto, tengo el presentimiento de que ya no estamos en Kansas.

I have a friend who... tengo un amigo que... ■ tengo una amiga que... ➤ I have a friend who helps me with my Spanish. ■ I have a friend who helps me with Spanish. Tengo un amigo que me ayuda con el español.

I have a friend to whom... *(literary)* ■ I have a friend that... tengo un(a) amigo(-a) a quien... ➤ I have a friend to whom I am indebted for helping me with my Spanish. ■ I have a friend that I am indebted to for helping me with my Spanish. Tengo un amigo a quien estoy muy agradecido por ayudarme con el español.

I have a headache me duele la cabeza ■ tengo dolor de cabeza

I have a meeting tengo una reunión ■ me reúno... ➤ I have a meeting at five o'clock. Tengo una reunión a las cinco. ■ Me reúno a las cinco.

I have a runny nose ■ my nose is running me gotea la nariz ■ me moquea la nariz ■ *(Sp.)* se me caen las velas

I have an idea ■ I've got an idea tengo una idea ■ se me ha ocurrido una idea

I have been... ■ I've been hace (un tiempo) que... ■ he estado... ■ he sido... ■ soy... ➤ I have been in this country for two weeks. Hace dos semanas que estoy en este país. ■ Llevo dos semanas en este país. ■ He estado en este país por dos semanas. ➤ I have been an avid hiker all my life. He sido una excursionista entusiasta toda mi vida. ➤ I have been a reader of your magazine for years. Soy un lector de su revista desde hace años.

I have been doing something for... ■ I've been doing something for... **1.** *(short duration)* estar haciendo algo desde **2.** *(long*

duration) hacer algo desde ➤ I have been playing the piano for two hours. Estoy tocando el piano desde hace dos horas. ➤ Stephen has been playing the piano since he was six. Stephen toca el piano desde los seis años.

I have been married since June ▪ I've been married since June estoy casado(-a) desde junio

I have been thinking about what you said ▪ I've been thinking about what you said he estado pensando en lo que dijiste

I have found out that... ▪ I have learned that... me he enterado de que...

I have gone ahead and... ▪ I've gone ahead and... al fin de cuentas... ➤ I've gone ahead and bought a new computer. Al fin de cuentas, me compré una nueva computadora.

I have had a beard for five years ▪ I've had a beard for five years tengo barba desde hace cinco años

I have known him (for) a long time ▪ I've known him (for) a long time lo conozco (desde hace) mucho tiempo ▪ *(Sp., leísmo)* le conozco (desde hace) mucho tiempo

I have learned that... ▪ I have found out that... ▪ it has come to my attention that... ▪ it has been brought to my attention that... me he enterado de que...

I have lived here all my life ▪ I've lived here all my life ▪ I've always lived here vivo aquí de toda la vida ▪ vivo aquí desde siempre

I have lived here since... ▪ I've lived here since... vivo aquí desde... ➤ I've lived here since 1998. Vivo aquí desde 1998.

I have long anticipated the day when... ▪ I've long anticipated the day when... he esperado mucho tiempo el día en el que... ▪ me he estado anticipando este día mucho tiempo

I have mixed feelings about it tengo sentimientos contradictorios sobre eso ▪ tengo sentimientos encontrados sobre eso ▪ tengo sentimientos contrapuestos sobre eso

I have my reasons tengo mis razones

I have my suspicions tengo mis sospechas ➤ I don't know who's stopping up the sink all the time, but I have my suspicions. No sé quién atasca el fregadero, pero tengo mis sospechas.

I have never seen her ▪ I've never seen her nunca la he visto ➤ I have never seen her cry. Nunca la he visto llorar.

I have never seen him ▪ I've never seen him nunca lo he visto ▪ *(Sp.,leísmo)* nunca le he visto

I have never seen it 1. *(a show)* nunca lo he visto **2.** *(a movie)* nunca la he visto

I have no alternative no tengo alternativa ▪ ¡qué remedio!

I have no complaints no me quejo de nada

I have no doubt in my mind no me cabe la menor duda

I have no say in these matters no tengo ni voz ni voto ▪ ni quito ni pongo rey

I have one (ya) tengo uno ▪ (ya) lo tengo ▪ (ya) tengo una ▪ (ya) la tengo

I have one left me queda uno

I have played the piano for *x* years toco el piano desde hace *x* años ▪ he tocado el piano por *x* años

I have some good news and some bad news tengo dos noticias, una buena y una mala

I have some money ▪ I've got some money tengo dinero ▪ tengo algo de dinero

I have some thoughts about... tengo algunas ideas sobre...

I have some thoughts about how... tengo algunas ideas sobre cómo... ▪ se me ocurren algunas ideas sobre cómo...

I have some thoughts about that tengo algunas opiniones sobre eso ▪ tengo algunas otras opiniones sobre eso

I have the feeling (that) I'm forgetting something tengo la impresión de que se me olvida algo ▪ tengo la impresión de que se me pasa algo

I have the opposite impression tengo la impresión contraria

I have to... tengo que... ▪ he de... ▪ debo... ➤ I have to go to the grocery store. Tengo que ir al mercado. ▪ He de ir al mercado. ▪ Debo ir al mercado. ➤ I *must* emphasize that... He de recalcar que... ➤ I have to be a witness at a trial. He de ser testigo en un juicio. ➤ I have to go back there. Tengo que volver allí. ▪ Tengo que volver allá. ▪ Tengo que volver ahí.

I have to admit... ▪ I must admit... tengo que admitir... ▪ debo admitir... ▪ he de admitir... ➤ I have to admit (my) defeat. ▪ I have to concede (my) defeat. Tengo que admitir mi derrota. ▪ Debo admitir mi derrota. ▪ He de admitir mi derrota.

I have to admit that... tengo que admitir que... ▪ tengo que aceptar que... ➤ I have to admit that you're right. Tengo que admitir que tienes razón. ▪ Tengo que aceptar que tienes razón.

I have to go 1. I have to leave me tengo que ir ▪ tengo que irme ▪ tengo que salir (de aquí) **2.** I have to attend tengo que ir ▪ tengo que asistir

I have to go to court tengo un juicio

I have to hurry ▪ I've got to hurry tengo que darme prisa ▪ *(L. Am., especially)* tengo que apurarme

I have wanted for a long time to... hace mucho tiempo que tengo ganas de... ▪ hace mucho tiempo que quiero...

I have *x* left me quedan *x* ➤ I have ten left. Me quedan diez.

I haven't been back since ▪ I haven't gone back since no he vuelto desde entonces ▪ desde entonces no he vuelto ➤ We were so poorly treated at that restaurant that we haven't been back since. Nos trataron tan mal en ese restaurante que desde entonces no hemos vuelto. ▪ Nos atendieron tan mal en ese restaurante que no hemos vuelto desde entonces.

I haven't been there for... ▪ I haven't been there in... no he estado allí desde hace... ▪ no estuve allí desde hace... ➤ I haven't been there for a year. Hace un año que no estoy allí. ▪ No estuve allí desde hace un año. ▪ Desde hace un año no estoy allí. ▪ En un año, no estuve por allí. ➤ I haven't been there for ages. Hace siglos que no estoy allí. ▪ Hace cientos de años que no estoy allí.

I haven't been there in *x* months no he ido allí en (los últimos) *x* meses ▪ no he estado allí en (los últimos) *x* meses ▪ no he ido allí desde hace *x* meses ▪ no he estado allí desde hace *x* meses ➤ I haven't been in Tegucigalpa in eighteen months. No he estado en Tegucigalpa desde hace dieciocho meses. ▪ No he ido a Tegucigalpa desde hace dieciocho meses. ▪ No he estado en Tegucigalpa en los últimos dieciocho meses. ▪ No he ido a Tegucigalpa en los últimos dieciocho meses.

I haven't been there in years ▪ I haven't been there for years hace años que no voy por allí

I haven't been there since... no estoy allí desde que... ▪ no he estado allí desde que...

I haven't decided no lo he decidido

I haven't done it yet todavía no lo he hecho ▪ aún no lo he hecho ▪ sigo sin hacerlo ▪ todavía sigo sin hacerlo ▪ aún sigo sin hacerlo ▪ estoy por hacerlo ▪ me queda por hacer

I haven't finished ▪ I'm not finished ▪ I'm not through ▪ I'm not done no he terminado

I haven't gone anywhere! ▪ I've been here the whole time! ¡no he ido a ninguna parte!

I haven't gone back since ▪ I haven't been back since no he vuelto desde entonces ➤ I was so shabbily treated at that store that I haven't gone back since. Me trataron tan penosamente en esa tienda que no he vuelto desde entonces.

I haven't got a cent ▪ I don't have a cent no tengo ni un centavo ▪ estoy sin un cuarto

I haven't got a clue no tengo zorra idea

I haven't got any change ▪ I don't have any change no tengo cambio ▪ no tengo suelto ▪ no tengo calderilla ▪ no tengo chatarra ▪ *(Chi.)* no tengo sencillo ▪ *(Mex., especially to a beggar)* no tengo feria

I haven't gotten to it no me he puesto a hacerlo

I haven't heard from her for a while ▪ I haven't heard from her in a while no he oído nada de ella durante un tiempo ▪ no he oído nada de ella desde hace tiempo ▪ no tengo entendido nada de ella desde hace tiempo

I haven't heard from you in a long time cuánto tiempo sin saber de ti

I haven't heard the last of it el asunto aún colea

I haven't heard yet ▪ I still haven't heard sigo sin oír(lo) ▪ todavía sigo sin oír(lo) ▪ aún sigo sin oír(lo) ▪ estoy por oír(lo) ▪ estoy esperando a oír(lo)

I haven't made up my mind no me he decidido

I haven't seen her again no la he vuelto a ver

I haven't seen her in years ▪ I haven't seen her for years hace años que no la veo

I haven't seen him again no lo he vuelto a ver ▪ *(Sp., leísmo)* no le he vuelto a ver

I haven't seen him in years ▪ I haven't seen him for years hace años que no lo veo ▪ *(Sp., leísmo)* hace años que no le veo

I haven't seen it again no lo(-a) he vuelto a ver ▪ no volví a verlo(-a)

I haven't seen it yet ▪ I have yet to see it me queda por ver ▪ no lo he visto todavía ▪ no la he visto todavía ▪ no lo tengo visto ▪ no la tengo vista ▪ todavía estoy por verlo(-a)

I haven't seen you in ages! ▪ I haven't seen you for ages! ▪ I haven't seen you forever! ▪ long time, no see! ¡cuánto tiempo sin verte! ▪ ¡tanto tiempo! ▪ ¡hace la tira que no te veo! ➤ I haven't seen you in ages. Catch me up on yourself. Hace la tira que no te veo. Ponme al corriente de tu vida.

I haven't the foggiest idea ▪ I haven't the foggiest notion ▪ I haven't got the slightest idea no tengo la más mínima idea ▪ ni idea

I haven't thought that far ahead no he llegado tan lejos ▪ no lo he pensado hasta ese punto

I haven't thought that far back no llegué tan lejos ▪ no (me) lo pensé hasta ese punto

I hear you loud and clear! ¡te oigo alto y claro! ▪ *(colorful)* ¡más claro no canta un gallo!

I heard her say it se lo oí decir (a ella) ▪ le oí decirlo

I heard him say it se lo oí decir (a él) ▪ le oí decirlo

I heard it from a friend me enteré por un amigo

I heard the news before anyone else me enteré de las noticias antes que nadie

I hereby invite you por la presente te invito

I hit the "send" key by accident di con la tecla "enviar" por casualidad

I hope everything's going okay (for you) espero que todo te vaya bien ▪ espero que lo estés pasando bien

I hope I don't have to... espero no tener que... ▪ ojalá no tenga que... ➤ I hope I don't have to get up early tomorrow. Espero no tener que levantarme temprano mañana. ▪ Ojalá no tenga que levantarme temprano mañana.

I hope it stays that way espero que eso siga así

I hope I've... espero haber... ➤ I hope I've been helpful. Espero haber sido de utilidad.

I hope not espero que no

I hope (that) it won't be espero que no lo sea

I hope (that) it won't be... espero que no sea...

I hope (that) there won't be espero que no lo haya

I hope (that) there won't be... espero que no haya... ➤ I hope there won't be another war. Espero que por eso no haya de empezar otra guerra.

I hope so espero que sí ▪ eso espero

I hope things are going well for you espero que te vayan bien las cosas ▪ espero que lo estés pasando bien

I hope this helps espero que esto ayude ▪ espero que esto sirva ▪ espero que esto valga

I hope you don't already have it *(tú)* espero que todavía no lo(-a) tengas ▪ espero que no lo(-a) tengas todavía ▪ *(usted)* espero que todavía no lo(-a) tenga ▪ espero que no lo(-a) tenga todavía

I hope you don't already have one *(tú)* espero que no tengas ya uno(-a) ▪ *(usted)* espero que no tenga ya uno(-a)

I hope you make a killing ▪ I hope you make a bundle ▪ I hope you clean up ¡que te cunda! ▪ ¡que te rinda!

I hurt my arm me lastimé el brazo ▪ me he lastimado el brazo ▪ me he hecho daño en el brazo

I insist! ¡insisto!

I just assumed (that)... di por supuesto que...

I just arrived ▪ I just got here acabo de llegar

I just barely made it to the bus agarré el autobús por los pelos ▪ *(colorful, meaning one caught hold of the bus with one's feet dragging the ground)* agarré el autobús barriéndome ▪ *(Sp.)* cogí el (auto)bús por los pelos

I just barely missed it acabo de perderlo en este instante ▪ acabo de perderlo en este momento ▪ lo perdí por los pelos

I just came in (from outside) vengo de afuera ▪ acabo de entrar (desde afuera)

I just can't simplemente no puedo

I just can't cope es que no doy abasto

I just can't understand it simplemente no puedo entenderlo ▪ justamente no puedo entenderlo ▪ me cuesta poder entenderlo

I just do ▪ just because (I do) porque sí

I just don't ▪ just because (I don't) porque no

I just don't get it ▪ I just don't catch on simplemente no entiendo ▪ simplemente no capto (la) onda ▪ simplemente no lo agarro ▪ *(Sp.)* simplemente no lo cojo

I just found out that... me acabo de enterar de que... ▪ acabo de enterarme de que... ▪ acabo de saber que...

I just found (that) out acabo de enterarme (de eso)

I just got here ▪ I just arrived acabo de llegar

I just missed it acabo de perderlo

I just missed the bus acabo de perder el autobús

I just remembered... acabo de acordarme... ▪ me acaba de venir a la mente... ▪ acabo de recordarlo...

I just stood there (while being ignored) estuve ahí de pie ignorado ▪ me ignoraron mientras estuve allí

I just (this second) walked in the door acabo de llegar en este momento ▪ acabo de llegar ahora mismo ▪ *(Mex.)* apenas voy llegando

I just want to go run and hide, I feel so embarrassed! ¡tierra, trágame!

I just wanted to bring you up-to-date ▪ I just wanted to give you an update sólo quería ponerte al corriente ▪ sólo quería ponerte al día ▪ sólo quería ponerte al tanto

I just wanted to remind you that... *(tú)* sólo quería recordarte que... ▪ *(usted)* sólo quería recordarle que...

I just wanted you to be aware of... sólo quería que estuvieras enterado de...

I just wanted you to be aware that... sólo quería que estuvieras enterado de que...

I just woke up acabo de despertarme ▪ me despierto en este momento

I keep forgetting se me sigue olvidando

I kid you not ▪ I'm serious ▪ I'm not kidding te (lo) digo en serio ▪ no bromeo ▪ no estoy bromeando

I knew you would come ▪ I knew you'd come (yo) sabía que vendrías

I know lo sé

***I* know!** ▪ I've got it! ¡ya sé! ▪ ¡ya lo tengo!

I know all too well lo sé de sobra

I know all too well that... ▪ I know only too well that... sé de sobra que... ▪ sé demasiado que... ▪ demasiado sé que...

I know damned well that... *(mildly profane)* ▪ I know perfectly well that... (yo) sé muy bien que...

I know exactly what you mean te entiendo perfectamente

I know exactly where it is sé exactamente dónde está

I know full well that... ▪ I know all too well... lo sé de sobra que...

I know it lo sé

I know of no one else who... ▪ I don't know of anyone else who... no conozco a nadie más que... ➤ I know of no one else who can do it. ▪ I don't know of anyone else who can do it. No conozco a nadie más que pueda hacerlo.

I know only too well that... ▪ I know all too well that... demasiado sé que...

I know the song by heart me sé la canción de memoria

I know the telephone number (by heart) ▪ I've memorized the phone number me sé el telefóno (de memoria)

I know very well that... (yo) sé efectivamente que... ▪ (yo) sé muy bien que...

I know what I'm doing sé lo que hago

I know what you mean lo comprendo

I know what you mean about... sé lo que quieres decir sobre... ▪ entiendo lo que quieres decir ▪ me hago cargo de lo que dices ▪ sé qué quieres decir sobre...

I know what you're going through sé por lo que estás pasando

I know what you're thinking sé lo que estás pensando

I know you from somewhere te conozco de algo ▪ de algo te conozco

I know you will sé que lo hará

I later found out that... ▪ I found out later that... más tarde supe que... ▪ supe más tarde que...

I like... 1. *(singular)* me gusta... **2.** *(plural)* me gustan... ➤ I like Mexican music. Me gusta la música mexicana. ➤ I like the traditional songs of Mexico. Me gustan las canciones tradicionales de México.

I like her (ella) me cae bien ▪ la aprecio *("Me gusta ella" can have a sexual overtone.)*

I like him (él) me cae bien ▪ lo aprecio (a él) ▪ *(Sp., leísmo)* le aprecio *("Me gusta él" can have a sexual overtone.)*

I like it me gusta

I like nothing better (than) ▪ there's nothing I like better (than) no hay nada que me guste más (que) ▪ a mí no hay nada que me guste más (que)

I like the fact that... me gusta el hecho de que...

I like the way you handled it ▪ I like the way you handled that *(tú)* me gusta cómo lo manejaste ▪ *(usted)* me gusta cómo lo manejó (usted)

I like the way you handled the situation me gusta cómo manejaste la situación

I like them 1. *(people)* me caen bien **2.** *(things)* me gustan

I like this one better (than that one) ▪ I like this one more (than that one) prefiero éste (a ése) ▪ prefiero éste (sobre ése)

I like this one more (than that one) ▪ I like this one better (than that one) prefiero éste (a ése) ▪ prefiero éste (sobre ése)

I like this one the best ▪ I like this one the most éste es el que más me gusta ▪ ésta es la que más me gusta

I like this one the most ▪ I like this one the best éste es el que más me gusta

I like you me caes bien ▪ te aprecio ▪ *(with sexual overtones)* me gustas

I like your hair ▪ I like the way you've fixed your hair ▪ I like the way you've done your hair me gusta tu peinado

I like your haircut me gusta tu corte de pelo

I lived there until I was *x* years old viví allí hasta que tuve *x* años ▪ viví allí hasta que cumplí los *x* años ▪ estuve viviendo allí hasta que tuve *x* años ▪ estuve viviendo allí hasta que cumplí los *x* años

I locked myself out of the car me he dejado las llaves dentro del coche

I locked myself out of the house me he dejado las llaves dentro de la casa ▪ me he quedado afuera ▪ *(Mex.)* me quedé afuera

I look forward to hearing from you *(business letter closing)* esperando recibir noticias suyas ▪ quedo a la espera de noticias suyas

I lost my train of thought perdí el hilo de las ideas ▪ perdí el hilo ▪ se me ha ido de la cabeza ▪ se me ha ido ▪ se me ha ido el santo al cielo

I lost you ▪ I got to a point where I no longer followed you dejo de comprenderte ▪ dejé de comprenderte

I love it me gusta cantidad ▪ me encanta ▪ *(coll.)* me pone ▪ me mola

I love this part (of the song) este trocito me encanta ▪ me encanta este trocito

I love you 1. *(platonic)* te amo **2.** *(romantic)* te quiero ➤ I love you.-I love you, too Te amo.-Y yo a ti. ▪ Te quiero.-Y yo a ti.

I made a mistake cometí un error ▪ me equivoqué

I made *x* dollars today me gané *x* dólares hoy ➤ I made a hundred dollars today. Me gané cien dólares hoy.

I may have to... ▪ I might have to... puedo tener que... ▪ tal vez yo tenga que... ➤ I may have to leave early. Puedo tener que salir temprano.

I may never... puede que nunca...

I mean digo ▪ quiero decir ▪ más bien ➤ Really pile it on.-The peanut butter, I mean. Úntame mucha.-La crema de cacahuete, digo.

I mean it lo digo en serio

I mean (that)... ▪ what I mean is (that)... ▪ what I'm trying to say is (that)... quiero decir que...

I mean that seriously lo digo en serio

I meant it lo dije en serio

I meant to ask you tenía la intención de preguntarte ▪ quería preguntarte

I meant to say tenía la intención de decir ▪ quería decir

I meant to tell you tenía la intención de decirte ▪ quería decirte

I meant to, though sin embargo, tenía la intención

I meant to, too tenía la intención (de hacerlo), también

I might add podría añadir ▪ podría agregar ➤ She always ordered the most expensive thing on the menu, and, I might add, she never returned the favor. Ella siempre pedía lo más caro que había en la carta, y podría añadir, ¡nunca devolvió el favor! ▪ Ella siempre pedía lo más caro que había en la carta, y podría agregar, ¡nunca devolvió el favor!

I might already have it tal vez ya lo tenga ▪ puede que ya lo tenga ▪ quizá(s) ya lo tenga

I might as well 1. I won't be any worse off if ▪ there's nothing to gain by not igual le valdría a uno **2.** what the heck! ¡(es) una raya más para el tigre! ▪ *(Sp.)* ¡de perdidos al río! ➤ As long as we're here, we might as well look around. Ya que estamos aquí, igual nos valdría echar una mirada alrededor. ➤ Everyone knows you did it, so you might as well confess. Todo el mundo sabe que lo hiciste, así que igual te valdría confesarlo. ➤ The dentist said I had to have my wisdom teeth out at some point, so I might as well get it over with. El dentista me dijo que tenía que sacarme las muelas del juicio en algún momento, así que igual me valdría hacerlo ahora para salir de eso. ➤ I might as well have. Más me valdría haberlo hecho.

I might as well get it over with más vale hacerlo de una vez ▪ al mal paso, dale prisa ➤ I might as well get it over with. Al mal paso, dale prisa.

I might as well smoke it igual me valdría fumármelo ➤ I had one cigarette left, so I said to myself, "I might as well go on and smoke it." Me quedaba un cigarrillo, así que me dije a mí mismo, igual me valdría fumármelo. ▪ Me quedaba un cigarrillo, así que me dije a mí mismo, "¡qué es una raya más para el tigre!" ▪ *(Sp.)* Me quedaba un cigarrillo, así que me dije a mí mismo, "¡de perdidos al río!"

I might have known! me podría haber imaginado ▪ me podía haber imaginado ▪ ¡tendría que haberlo sabido!

I might have liked... puede que me hubiera gustado... ➤ I might have liked the pumpkin pie if they had put a little whipped cream on it. Puede que me hubiera gustado la tarta de calabaza si hubiera habido un poco de nata.

I might have to... ▪ I may have to... tal vez yo tenga que... ▪ puede (ser) que tenga que... ▪ a lo mejor tengo que... ➤ I might have to eat my words. Tal vez yo tenga que tragarme las palabras.

I might like for... ▪ I might want... puede que yo quiera... ➤ I might like for you to go with me to be my interpreter if I have problems. ▪ I might want you to go with me to be my interpreter if I have problems. Puede que yo quiera que me acompañes para ser mi intérprete por si acaso tengo problemas.

I might like it puede que me guste ▪ tal vez me guste ▪ a lo mejor me gustaría ▪ *(coll.)* tal vez me ponga ▪ tal vez me mole

I might like to puede que me guste (hacerlo) ▪ tal vez me guste (hacerlo) ▪ a lo mejor me gustaría (hacerlo)

I might not have 1. *(as a complete sentence)* podría no haberlo hecho **2.** *(as a dependent clause)* podría no haber... ➤ I might not have met her if I hadn't gone to the party. Podría no haberla conocido si no hubiera ido a la fiesta.

I must admit ▪ I have to admit debo admitir ▪ he de admitir

I must be doing *something* right algo debo de estar haciendo bien

I must be hearing things debo de estar oyendo cosas

I must be losing it ▪ I must be losing my marbles no sé que me pasa ▪ estaré perdiendo las canicas ➤ I must be losing it:

I left my glasses on the train and my book at the restaurant. No sé que me pasa porque dejé los anteojos en el tren y el libro en el restaurante. ▪ Estaré perdiendo las canicas porque dejé los anteojos en el tren y el libro en el restaurante.

I must be seeing things debo de estar viendo cosas

I must find out debo averiguarlo

I must have been about *x* years old when... ▪ I must have been around *x* years old when... tendría (unos) *x* años cuando... ▪ debía de tener (unos) *x* años cuando... ▪ debía de rondar los *x* años cuando... ➤ I must have been (about) ten years old when... Tendría (unos) diez años cuando... ▪ Debía de tener diez años cuando... ▪ Debía de rondar los diez años cuando... ▪ Debía de rondar unos diez años cuando...

I must have been hearing things debo de haber estado oyendo cosas ▪ estaría oyendo cosas

I must have been seeing things debo de haber estado viendo cosas ▪ estaría viendo cosas

I must have (done something) me debo de haber (hecho algo) ▪ debo de haberme (hecho algo) ➤ I must have swallowed one of those hot peppers. Me debo de haber tragado uno de esos chiles picantes. ▪ Debo de haberme tragado uno de esos chiles picantes. ➤ I must have eaten something that didn't agree with me. Debo de haber comido algo que no me cayó bien.

I must have had... debo de haber tenido... ➤ I must have had my headphones on when you called. Debo de haber tenido los auriculares puestos cuando me llamaste. ▪ Debía de tener puestos los auriculares cuando me llamaste.

I must say (that)... ▪ I have to say (that)... debo decir (que...) ▪ tengo que decir (que...)

I myself yo mismo(-a) ▪ yo en persona ▪ yo personalmente

I nearly died of embarrassment casi me muero de (la) vergüenza

I nearly had a heart attack ▪ I almost had a heart attack ▪ I practically had a heart attack casi me da un ataque al corazón

I need all the help I can get necesito toda la ayuda posible

I need an envelope that will fit this necesito un sobre en el que quepa esto

I need it badly lo necesito desesperadamente

I need some glasses ▪ I need a pair of glasses necesito lentes ▪ necesito anteojos ▪ *(Sp.)* necesito gafas ▪ *(Sp., to an optometrist)* vengo a graduarme

I need some help necesito ayuda ▪ necesito algo de ayuda ▪ necesito un poco de ayuda

I need you to help me with this necesito que me ayudes con esto

I never... nunca... ➤ I never charge anything. ▪ I never buy anything on credit. Nunca compro nada a plazos. ▪ Nunca pido crédito.

I never did find out nunca me enteré

I never did get to 1. to have the opportunity to tener la oportunidad de **2.** to manage to llegar a hacer algo ▪ conseguir hacer algo ➤ I never did get to go with them. Nunca tuve la oportunidad de ir con ellos. ➤ I never did get to the Palencia cathedral. ▪ I never did make it to the Palencia cathedral. Nunca llegué a la catedral de Palencia. ▪ Nunca conseguí llegar a la catedral de Palencia.

I never did hear nunca oí ➤ I never did hear what happened. Nunca oí lo que sucedió. ➤ I never did hear the outcome. Nunca oí en qué dio todo aquello.

I never did make it to ▪ I never did get to nunca llegué a ▪ nunca he llegado a ➤ I never did make it to Palencia to see the cathedral, but I hear it's beautiful. ▪ I never did get to Palencia to see the cathedral, but I hear it's beautiful. Nunca he llegado hasta Palencia a ver la catedral, pero he oído que es preciosa.

I never dreamed (that)... nunca (me) imaginé que...

I never explain anything *(Mary Poppins)* nunca doy explicaciones

I never gave any thought to... nunca pensé en...

I never got to see her ▪ I didn't get to see her nunca la llegué a ver ▪ nunca llegué a verla

I never got to see him ▪ I didn't get to see him nunca lo llegué a ver ▪ nunca llegué a verlo ▪ *(Sp., leísmo)* nunca le llegué a ver ▪ nunca llegué a verle

I never got to see it ▪ I didn't get to see it **1.** *(a show)* nunca lo llegué a ver **2.** *(a movie)* nunca la llegué a ver

I never had a chance (to...) nunca tuve una oportunidad (de...) ▪ nunca tuve una oportunidad (para...)

I never had the chance (to...) nunca tuve la oportunidad (de...) ▪ nunca tuve la oportunidad (para...)

I never have heard from... ▪ I have never heard from... nunca he oído de...

I never heard anything (back) from... ▪ I never got any response from... nunca escuché nada de regreso de... ▪ nunca he oído nada de regreso de... ▪ nunca he oído nada de respuesto de... ▪ nunca supe nada de regreso de...

I never heard anything from... nunca oí nada de...

I never heard from... nunca oí de...

I never know when to call you nunca sé cuando llamarte

I never looked at it that way nunca lo vi de esa manera

I never saw her 1. nunca la vi ▪ nunca llegué a verla ▪ nunca la llegué a ver **2.** we didn't cross paths no coincidimos ▪ nunca nos encontramos

I never saw her again nunca la volví a ver ▪ nunca volví a verla

I never saw him 1. nunca lo vi ▪ nunca llegué a verlo ▪ nunca lo llegué a ver ▪ *(Sp., leísmo)* nunca le vi ▪ nunca llegué a verle ▪ nunca le llegué a ver **2.** we didn't cross paths no coincidimos ▪ nunca nos encontramos

I never saw him again nunca lo volví a ver ▪ nunca volví a verlo ▪ *(Sp., leísmo)* nunca le volví a ver ▪ nunca volví a verle

I never saw it 1. *(a show)* no lo vi nunca ▪ nunca lo vi ▪ no lo llegué a ver nunca **2.** *(a movie)* no la llegué a ver nunca ▪ no la vi nunca

I never saw you *(tú)* no te vi ▪ no llegué a verte ▪ *(usted)* no lo vi (a usted) ▪ no llegué a verlo (a usted) ▪ *(Sp., leísmo)* no le vi (a usted) ▪ no llegué a verle (a usted) ➤ Were you at the dance? I never saw you. ¿Estuviste en el baile? No te vi. ▪ ¿Estuviste en el baile? No llegué a verte.

I never see you anymore *(tú)* ya no te veo nunca ▪ *(usted, to a male)* ya no lo veo nunca ▪ *(usted, to a female)* ya no la veo nunca ▪ *(Sp., leísmo, to a male)* ya no le veo nunca *(The Royal Spanish Academy accepts leísmos only in the masculine.)*

I never should have gone nunca debí ir

I never thought it could happen to me nunca creí que me pudiera pasar a mí

I never thought it would come to that nunca pensaba que iba a llegar a eso

I never went back to see her nunca volví a verla

I never went back to see him nunca volví a verlo ▪ *(Sp., leísmo)* nunca volví a verle

I never would give in (to someone's demands) no quise ceder... ▪ no quise rendirme... ▪ no quise consentir... ➤ They pleaded and pleaded, but I never would give in. Por más que suplicaron no cedí.

I notice it me di cuenta ▪ lo noté

I notice that... observo que... ▪ me fijo (en) que... ▪ me doy cuenta de que... ▪ noto que...

I noticed ▪ so I noticed me di cuenta ▪ lo noté ▪ me percaté ▪ lo vi

I noticed that me di cuenta de eso ▪ lo noté

I noticed that... noté que... ▪ me di cuenta de que...

I object protesto

I object, your honor protesto, (su) señoría ➤ I object, your honor.-(Objection) sustained. Protesto, (su) señoría.-Se acepta (la protesta). ➤ I object, your honor.-(Objection) overruled. Protesto, (su) señoría.-Protesta denegada. ▪ Queda denegada.

I once had... una vez tuve...

I overslept me quedé dormido ▪ dormí de más ▪ se me pegaron las sábanas

I owe you an apology te debo una disculpa

I personally... yo personalmente... ▪ yo en mi caso... ➤ I personally am going to work that day. Yo en mi caso voy a trabajar ese día.

I pledge allegiance to the flag of the United States of America, and to the Republic for which it stands, one

nation under God, indivisible with liberty and justice for all. Juro fidelidad a la bandera de los Estados Unidos de América, y a la república que simboliza, una nación Dios mediante, indivisible con libertad y justicia para todos. *(In the analogous Spanish ceremony, soldiers, government officials, and others kiss the flag and say "Todo por la patria.")*

I practically had a heart attack ▪ I nearly had a heart attack ▪ I almost had a heart attack casi me da un ataque cardiaco

I promise yo prometo ▪ *(a ti)* te lo prometo ▪ *(a usted)* se lo prometo

I ran out of time se me agotó el tiempo ▪ se me acabó el tiempo ▪ *(coll.)* me ha pillado el toro

I read it somewhere lo leí en alguna parte ▪ lo he leído en alguna parte

I read somewhere that... leí en alguna parte que...

I read your book 1. *(literal)* leí tu libro ▪ leí su libro **2.** *(figurative)* I learned the tactic from you ▪ I turned the tables on you *(tú)* ¡aprendí de ti! ▪ *(usted)* ¡aprendí de usted! ▪ *(vosotros)* ¡aprendí de vos!

I realize that ▪ I realize it ya me he dado cuenta

I really appreciate it (te) estoy muy agradecido ▪ (te) lo agradezco mucho ▪ (te) estoy enormemente agradecido ▪ (te) estoy infinitamente agradecido

I recognize her la reconozco

I recognize him lo reconozco ▪ *(Sp., leísmo)* le reconozco

I recognize it lo reconozco ▪ la reconozco

I recognize you from somewhere tu cara me suena ▪ me suenas de algo ▪ te recuerdo de algo

I remember lo recuerdo ▪ yo recuerdo

I remember asking you 1. *(the question)* me acuerdo de habértelo preguntado ▪ recuerdo preguntarte ▪ recuerdo haberte preguntado **2.** *(the favor)* me acuerdo de haberte pedido ▪ recuerdo haberte pedido

I remember asking you to (do it) recuerdo haberte pedido que lo hagas ▪ me acuerdo de pedirte que lo haga

I remember it to this day lo recuerdo hasta hoy mismo ▪ lo recuerdo hasta el día de hoy

I remember seeing it me acuerdo de haberlo visto ▪ recuerdo haberlo visto

I remember telling you recuerdo que te dije ▪ recuerdo haberte dicho

I remember that, too también me acuerdo

I remember thinking... recuerdo haber pensado...

I repeat: vuelvo a señalar: ▪ repito:

I rest my case a las pruebas me remito ▪ concluyo mi alegato ▪ he dicho

I said to myself me dije a mí mismo(-a)

I saw her earlier la vi antes

I saw him earlier lo vi antes ▪ *(Sp., leísmo)* le vi antes

I saw it 1. *(a show)* lo vi **2.** *(a movie)* la vi

I saw it coming 1. *(the ending)* lo vi venir **2.** *(the reaction)* la vi venir

I saw it earlier 1. *(the show)* lo vi antes **2.** *(the movie)* la vi antes

I saw that 1. I observed that lo vi ▪ vi eso **2.** I realized that (ya) me di cuenta ▪ ya me di cuenta (de eso)

I saw that... vi que... ▪ me di cuenta de que...

I saw you talking to someone te vi hablando con alguien ➤ I saw you talking to Mayte the other day. Te vi hablando con Mayte el otro día.

I see ▪ I understand ▪ I get it ya veo ▪ ya, ya ▪ (ya) entiendo

I see it 1. *(literal)* lo veo ▪ la veo **2.** I understand it ahora lo veo ▪ ahora me doy cuenta ➤ I didn't understand your argument at first, but now I see it. Al principio no entendía tu argumento, pero ahora lo veo.

I see that 1. *(main clause)* ya lo veo **2.** *(dependent clause)* I see that... veo que... ▪ por lo que veo... ▪ por lo que yo veo... ➤ I see (that) you like blue. Por lo que veo, te gusta el (color) azul. ➤ I see (that) you like the blue one. Por lo que veo, te gusta el azul. ➤ I see you haven't left yet Veo que todavía no te has ido. ▪ Veo que aún no te has ido.

I see what you mean (ya) comprendo ▪ (ya) entiendo

I seem to recall that 1. *(main clause)* creo recordarlo ▪ eso me suena **2.** *(dependent clause)* I seem to recall that... creo recordar que... ▪ me suena que...

I should be able to get it done ▪ I should be able to finish it debería poder terminarlo ➤ I should be able to get it done over the weekend. Debería poder terminarlo durante el fin de semana. ➤ I should be able to get it done by Friday. Debería poder terminarlo para el viernes.

I should have begun sooner ▪ I should have started sooner debí haber empezado antes

I should have gotten a flu shot debería haberme vacunado contra la gripe

I should have it done by... debería tenerlo acabado para... ➤ I should have it done by Friday. Debería tenerlo acabado para el viernes. ➤ I should have it done by the weekend. Debería tenerlo acabado para el fin de semana.

I should have it ready by... debería tenerlo listo para...

I should have known debería habérmelo imaginado ▪ debería haberlo sabido

I should have known better vaya una idea la mía

I should have known that debería haberlo sabido ▪ debería habérmelo imaginado

I should have known that... debería haber sabido que... ▪ debería haberme imaginado que...

I should have started sooner ▪ I should have begun sooner debí haber empezado antes

I should have worn my coat debería haber llevado puesto mi abrigo ▪ tenía que haber usado mi abrigo

I should know better vaya idea la mía ▪ vaya una idea la mía ▪ cómo se me ocurre

I should know better than to... vaya idea la mía de... ▪ cómo se me ocurre... ➤ I should know better than to go out in the sun without sunscreen. Cómo se me ocurre ponerme al sol sin protector solar. ▪ Vaya idea la mía de ponerme al sol sin protector solar.

I should like to *(archaic)* **1.** I would like to ▪ I'd like to me gustaría **2.** *(implying that you can't)* I wish I could ojalá pudiera ▪ quisiera poder

I should say mejor dicho ▪ debería decir

I shouldn't have to ask no debería tener que preguntárte(lo) ▪ no tendría que preguntártelo

I smell a rat aquí hay gato encerrado

I spaced it 1. I forgot (to do it) ▪ I completely forgot se me olvidó de plano ▪ me olvidé (de hacerlo) ▪ se me fue el santo al cielo **2.** my mind wandered ▪ I spaced out me distraje

I spent... ▪ it took me... estuve... ▪ tardé... ▪ me llevó... ➤ I spent four hours changing the battery. ▪ It took me four hours to change the battery. Estuve cuatro horas cambiando la batería. ▪ Tardé cuatro horas cambiando la batería. ▪ Me llevó cuatro horas cambiando la batería.

I spoke too soon hablé antes de tiempo

I stand by what I said me atengo a lo que dije

I started to like... me empezó a gustar... ➤ I started to like the city after I had lived there a few months. Me empezó a gustar la ciudad cuando había vivido allí unos meses. ➤ I started to like it. Me empezó a gustar.

I stepped in it metí el pie

I stepped on it lo pisé ▪ la pisé

I still am 1. sigo siéndolo ▪ todavía lo soy ▪ aún lo soy **2.** sigo estándolo ▪ todavía lo estoy ▪ aún lo estoy ➤ I still am (a romantic). Sigo siéndolo (un romántico). ➤ I still am (single). Sigo estándolo (soltero).

I still do sigo haciéndolo ▪ lo sigo haciendo

I still don't get it todavía no lo entiendo ▪ todavía no lo cojo ▪ no lo entiendo todavía ▪ no lo cojo todavía ▪ todavía no lo capto ▪ no lo capto todavía *("Aún" can be substituted for "todavía" in all cases.)*

I still don't know ▪ I don't know yet aún no lo sé ▪ todavía no lo sé ▪ sigo sin saber ➤ I still don't know why I did that. Sigo sin saber por qué hice eso.

I still don't see the connection sigo sin ver la relación

I still have... todavía tengo... ▪ aún tengo...

I still have a ways to go ▪ I have a ways to go yet me queda un buen trecho ▪ todavía me queda trayecto por recorrer ▪ todavía me queda camino por andar

I still haven't decided ▪ I still haven't made up my mind todavía no lo he decidido ▪ todavía no lo tengo decidido

I still haven't done it ▪ I haven't done it yet todavía no lo he hecho ▪ no lo he hecho todavía ▪ todavía me queda por hacer *("Aún" can replace "todavía" in all cases.)*

I still haven't finished it ▪ I haven't finished it yet todavía no lo he terminado ▪ aún no lo he terminado ▪ no lo he terminado aún ▪ no lo he terminado todavía

I still haven't heard ▪ I haven't heard yet ▪ I still haven't received an answer ▪ I haven't heard back todavía no sé nada ▪ todavía no me han contestado ▪ todavía no he recibido contestación ▪ todavía no he recibido respuesta ▪ sigo sin saberlo

I still haven't made up my mind ▪ I still haven't decided todavía no lo he decidido ▪ todavía no lo tengo decidido

I still haven't tried... ▪ I haven't yet tried... ▪ I have yet to try... **1.** I still haven't tasted... ▪ I still haven't sampled... todavía no he probado... ▪ aún no he probado... ▪ sigo sin probar... **2.** I still haven't attempted to... todavía no he intentado... ▪ todavía no he tratado de... ▪ aún no he intentado... ▪ aún no he tratado de... ▪ sigo sin intentar... ▪ sigo sin tratar de...

I still say (that)... sigo diciendo que...

I still think (that)... sigo pensando que... ▪ sigo creyendo que... ▪ sigo opinando que...

I sure hope so sinceramente lo espero

I sure need to claro que necesito hacerlo ▪ por cierto necesito hacerlo ▪ ciertamente necesito hacerlo

I sure wish I could claro que quisiera poder ▪ ojalá pudiera ▪ claro que querría (poder) ▪ sí que me gustaría (poder) ➤ Are you coming for Christmas?-I sure wish I could. ¿Puedes venir para la Navidad?-Ojalá pudiera.

I sure wish I had ojalá ➤ I didn't go to the beach with my friends, but I sure wish I had. No fui a la playa con mis amigos pero ojalá lo hubiera hecho.

I sure wish I had been ojalá hubiera sido ▪ ojalá hubiera estado

I sure wish I were ojalá fuera ▪ ojalá estuviera

I swear I could have juro que hubiera podido

I swear (it) lo juro

I swear to God! ¡(te) lo juro por Dios!

I take it según lo entiendo ▪ por lo que me parece entender ➤ The letter implies, I take it, that the trademark has been granted. La carta implica, según la entiendo, que se ha concedido la marca registrada.

I take it back ▪ I take that back ▪ I take back what I said retiro lo dicho ▪ me retracto ▪ miento

I take your word for it *(tú)* te tomo la palabra ▪ *(usted)* le tomo la palabra

I tell you te digo ▪ te aseguro

I tell you one thing *(coll.)* ▪ I'll tell you one thing una cosa te digo

(I) tell you what mira ▪ *(vosotros)* mirá

I tend to... en general ▪ por lo general ▪ tiendo ▪ tengo la tendencia a ▪ tengo la tendencia de ➤ I tend not to like country music. Por lo general no me gusta la música country.

I tend to be... tiendo a ser ➤ I tend to be a perfectionist. Tiendo a ser perfeccionista. ➤ I tend to be on time. Tiendo a ser puntual.

I tend to doubt it tiendo a dudarlo ▪ me inclino a dudarlo

I think I better... será mejor que...

I think I have it ▪ I think I've got it creo que lo tengo

I think I told you that... creo haberte dicho que ...

I think I'll pass creo que paso

I think I'm... **1.** *(permanent state)* creo que soy... ▪ me parece que soy... **2.** *(temporary state)* creo que estoy... ▪ me parece que estoy... ➤ I think I'm the perfect candidate. Creo que soy la candidata perfecta. ➤ I think I'm the ideal person for the job. Me parece que soy la persona ideal para el trabajo. ➤ I think I'm falling in love. Creo que estoy enamorado. ▪ Me parece que estoy enamorado. ➤ I think I'm seeing things. Creo que estoy viendo cosas.

I think it really *is*... me parece que más bien *es*...

I think it's a good idea me parece muy bien ▪ me parece una buena idea

I think I've got it ▪ I think I have it creo que lo tengo

I think so creo que sí ▪ pienso que sí

I think (that)... pienso que... ▪ creo que... ▪ me parece que...

I think the same (thing) opino lo mismo ▪ pienso lo mismo

I think the thing that... creo que lo que...

I think the world of you te tengo en gran estima ▪ te tengo en gran consideración ▪ *(Mex.)* te estimo grandemente ▪ te estimo mucho

I think, therefore I am *(Descartes)* ▪ cogito ergo sum pienso, luego existo

I think you're right creo que tienes razón ▪ pienso que tienes razón

I thought as much ya me lo figuraba ▪ ya me parecía ▪ me lo estaba imaginando ▪ me lo estaba figurando ▪ lo pensaba yo

I thought it was never going to end pensé que nunca se iba a acabar

I thought for sure (that)... pensé que seguramente... ▪ di por supuesto que... ▪ bien creí que... ➤ I thought for sure I wasn't going to like it. Pensé que seguramente no me iba a gustar.

I thought of you when... pensé en ti cuando... ▪ me acordé de ti cuando...

I thought so lo pensé

I thought to myself pensé para mí mismo

I thought you... ▪ I thought that you... creía que tú... ▪ creía que usted... ➤ I thought you hated sweets. Creía que odiabas los dulces.

I thought you meant me ▪ I thought you were referring to me pensé que te referías a mí ▪ pensé que se refería (usted) a mí

I thought you were... ▪ I took you to be... te suponía...

I thought you'd forgotten (about it) ya pensaba que te habías olvidado

I threw it away lo tiré a la basura ▪ lo deseché ▪ lo eché a la basura

I timed that really well hice eso en el momento exacto ▪ hice eso muy oportunamente

I *told* you! ▪ I *told* you so! (ya) te lo dije ▪ te lo advertí ▪ ya te lo había dicho

I told you about it *(tú)* te lo comenté ▪ *(usted)* se lo comenté (a usted)

I told you, I don't know te he dicho que no lo sé

I told you so ▪ I mentioned it to you before ▪ I had mentioned it to you te lo había dicho (ya) ▪ te lo había comentado

I took it easy me lo tomé con calma ▪ lo cogí suave ➤ I took it easy during my vacation. Me lo tomé con calma durante las vacaciones.

I took you to be someone else ▪ I thought you were someone else le confundí con otra persona ▪ le confundí con otro ▪ creí que era otra persona ▪ pensé que era otra persona

I tore this place apart looking for it lo puse todo patas arriba buscándolo

I totally agree with you ▪ I completely agree with you ▪ I agree with you wholeheartedly estoy totalmente de acuerdo contigo ▪ estoy completamente de acuerdo contigo

I tried it, but it didn't work lo intenté, pero no funcionó ▪ quise hacerlo, pero no funcionó

I tried it, but it wouldn't work lo intenté, pero no funcionaba

I understand (lo) entiendo ▪ (lo) comprendo ▪ me hago cargo

I understand that lo entiendo

I understand that... tengo entendido que...

I understand what you're saying entiendo lo que dices ▪ entiendo lo que estás diciendo

I understand you te entiendo ▪ te comprendo

I used to be able to... solía poder... ➤ They took down the time-and-temperature sign that I used to be able to see from my window. Quitaron el panel de la temperatura y la hora que solía poder ver desde mi ventana.

I used to know it by heart (yo) me lo sabía de memoria

I used to like rock 'n' roll me gustaba el rock and roll ▪ solía gustarme el rock and roll

I used to smoke antes (yo) fumaba ▪ (yo) solía fumar ▪ (yo) fumaba

I usually... suelo... ▪ usualmente yo

I walked into that one! ▪ I provoked that response ¡me la busqué! ▪ ¡se las he puesto en bandeja!

I want it in black and white ▪ I want it in writing lo quiero por escrito

I want it in writing ▪ I want it in black and white lo quiero por escrito

I want to call your attention to... *(tú)* quiero llamar tu atención sobre... ▪ quiero llamar tu atención a... ▪ *(usted)* quiero llamar su atención sobre... ▪ quiero llamar su atención a... ▪ *(ustedes)* quiero llamar su atención sobre... ▪ quiero llamar su atención a... ▪ *(Sp., vosotros)* quiero llamar vuestra atención sobre... ▪ quiero llamar vuestra atención a...

I want to emphasize that... quiero recalcar que... ▪ quiero hacer hincapié en que... ▪ quiero enfatizar que...

I want to emphasize this point quiero recalcar este punto ▪ quiero hacer hincapié en este punto ▪ quiero enfatizar este punto

I want to encourage you to... quiero animarte a...

I want to give it a shot ▪ I want to give it a go ▪ I want to give it a try ▪ I want to give it a whirl ▪ I want to have a shot at it quiero ponerme a prueba ▪ quiero intentarlo ▪ *(often said in this context)* lo voy a intentar

I want to go first! *(especially said by children)* ▪ I want to be first! ¡me pido primer!

I want to speak to you alone ▪ I want to speak with you alone *(tú)* quiero hablar contigo a solas ▪ *(usted)* quiero hablar con usted a solas

I want to surprise her quiero sorprenderla ▪ quiero darle una sorpresa (a ella)

I want to surprise him quiero sorprenderlo ▪ quiero darle una sorpresa ▪ *(L. Am., Sp., leísmo)* quiero sorprenderle

I want to talk to you alone ▪ I want to talk with you alone *(tú)* quiero charlar contigo a solas ▪ *(usted)* quiero charlar con usted a solas

I want to thank you for... te quiero dar las gracias por... ▪ quiero darte las gracias por... ▪ quiero agradecerte por... ➤ I want to thank you for helping me today. Quiero agradecerte el ayudarme hoy. ▪ Quiero agradecerte que me hayas ayudado hoy.

I want to think it over quiero pensarlo ▪ quiero pensármelo ▪ me lo quiero pensar

I wanted to do it **1.** (yo) quería hacerlo **2.** *(further back in time)* (yo) quise hacerlo

I wanted to let you know that... quería hacerte saber que... ▪ quería dejarte saber que... ▪ quería avisarte que...

I wanted to remind you that... *(tú)* quería recordarte que... ▪ te quería recordar que... ▪ *(usted)* quería recordarle que... ▪ le quería recordar que...

I wanted to tell you that... quería decirte que... ▪ quería comentarte que...

I warned you *(a ti)* ¡te lo advertí! ▪ *(a usted)* ¡se lo advertí!

I was a little concerned by... (yo) estaba un poco preocupado por...

I was a little concerned that... (yo) estaba un poco preocupado de que...

I was about to... (yo) estaba a punto de... ▪ iba ya a... ▪ ya me... ➤ I was about to leave when the phone rang. Estaba a punto de salir cuando sonó el teléfono. ▪ Iba ya a irme cuando sonó el teléfono. ▪ Ya me iba cuando sonó el teléfono.

I was afraid of that ▪ that's what I was afraid of temía eso ▪ me temía eso ▪ es lo que temía

I was asked to... se me pidió que... ▪ me pidieron que...

I was beginning to feel better ▪ I was starting to feel better me estaba empezando a sentir mejor ▪ estaba empezando a sentirme mejor

I was beginning to think that... (yo) estaba empezando a pensar que... ▪ (yo) estaba empezando a creer que... ➤ I was beginning to think you weren't coming. Estaba empezando a pensar que no venías.

I was fascinated (by) me quedé fascinado(-a) (con) ▪ *(singular)* me fascinó ▪ me fascinaba ▪ *(plural)* me fascinaron ▪ me fascinaban

I was first (in line) yo estaba primero (en la cola) ▪ yo estaba antes

I was glad to hear from you me alegré de recibir noticias tuyas ▪ me alegró recibir noticias tuyas

I was going to say that... (yo) iba a decir que...

I was gonna say! *(coll.)* ▪ I was going to say! ¡lo iba a decir!

I was here first ▪ I'm next in line yo estaba antes ▪ estaba yo antes ▪ yo estaba primero ▪ yo soy el siguiente

I was hoping that... (yo) esperaba que... ➤ I was hoping the university would revise the curriculum. Esperaba que la universidad revisara el curriculum.

I was just getting home when... (yo) estaba llegando a casa cuando...

I was just guessing sólo estaba adivinando ▪ sólo era una suposición

I was just kidding ▪ I didn't mean it ▪ I was just joking ▪ I was only joking era broma ▪ (yo) iba de broma ▪ sólo estaba bromeando

I was just noticing something in your letter justo estaba dándome cuenta de algo en tu carta

I was just saying that justo estaba diciendo eso

I was just saying that... **1.** I was only saying that... sólo decía que... **2.** I was just now saying that... justo estaba diciendo que...

I was just sitting there when... estaba ahí sentado cuando...

I was just standing there me tenían ahí, esperando ▪ estaba ahí parado(-a) ▪ me estaba(n) ignorando completamente

I was just trying to help sólo pretendía ayudar

I was just trying to remember... estaba intendando acordarme de... ▪ estaba intentando recordar...

I was just wondering sólo me preguntaba ▪ simple curiosidad

I was just wondering if... sólo me preguntaba si... ▪ era una simple curiosidad... ▪ por simple curiosidad... ▪ no sé si...

I was just wondering whether or not... sólo me preguntaba si... o no ▪ no sé si... o no ➤ I was just wondering whether or not to take an umbrella. ▪ I was just wondering whether to take an umbrella or not. Sólo me preguntaba si llevaba un paraguas o no.

I was just wondering whether to... sólo me preguntaba si debería... ➤ I was just wondering whether to take an umbrella. Me preguntaba si debería llevar un paraguas.

I was led to believe that... me hicieron creer que...

I was left just standing there me dejaron ahí parado

I was minding my own business when... estaba en lo mío cuando... ▪ estaba a lo mío cuando... ▪ *(coll.)* iba a mi bola cuando...

I was next (in line) **1.** yo estaba primero en la cola **2.** *(implying that you were skipped over)* (yo) era el próximo ▪ (yo) estaba antes

I was referred to you by... me envía... ▪ ...me habló de usted ➤ I was referred to you by my family doctor. Me envía mi médico de cabecera. *(Spanish prefers present tense.)*

I was sorry to hear about... lamenté enterarme de... ▪ lamenté saber de... ▪ me supo mal enterarme de...

I was sorry to hear that lo lamenté ▪ lamenté saberlo ▪ lamenté enterarme de eso ▪ me supo mal

I was sorry to hear (that)... sentí mucho saber que... ▪ lamenté mucho saber que... ▪ *(Sp.)* me supo mal saber que... ➤ I was sorry to hear that you can't come to our class reunion. Me supo mal saber que no vendrás a la reunión de antiguos compañeros.

I was starting to feel better ▪ I was beginning to feel better estaba empezando a sentirme mejor

I was surprised to see... me sorprendió ver...

I was the first one here ▪ I got here first ▪ I was first fui el primero en llegar

I was thinking about what you said estaba pensando en lo que dijiste

I was to learn that... habría de saber que... ➤ Later I was to learn that he was right. Más tarde (yo) habría de saber que tenía razón.

I was told that... me dijeron que...

I was under the impression that... ■ I had the impression that... tenía la impresión de que... ➤ I was under the impression that you were going to be here at eight o'clock. Tenía la impresión de que ibas a estar aquí a las ocho.

I was very impressed estuve muy impresionado ■ me quedé muy impresionado ■ ¡vaya impresión que me lleve!

I was wondering if you could tell me...? ¿sería tan amable de decirme...? ■ *(tú)* perdona... ■ *(usted)* perdone... ➤ I was wondering if you could tell me how to get to the Plaza Mayor? Perdone, ¿por dónde se va a la Plaza Mayor? ■ ¿Sería tan amable de decirme por dónde se va a la Plaza Mayor?

I was wondering if you would like to...? me pregunto si te gustaría... ■ me preguntaba si querrías... ➤ I was wondering if you would like to go to the dance with me? Me preguntaba si te gustaría ir al baile conmigo. ■ Me preguntaba si querrías ir al baile conmigo.

I was wrong 1. *(incorrect idea)* me equivoqué ■ estaba equivocado **2.** *(incorrect choice)* me confundí

I was wrong about you me equivoqué contigo

I wasn't aware of anything ■ I didn't notice anything no me percaté de nada ➤ *(newspaper quote)* I got pickpocketed on the metro, between (the stops of) Plaza Elíptica and Manuel Becerra. I wasn't aware of anything. Me sustrajeron la cartera en el metro, en el trayecto entre Plaza Elípitica y Manuel Becerra. No me percaté de nada.

I wasn't born yesterday no nací ayer ■ *(L. Am., coll.)* no soy caído del catre

I wasn't just doing that for my health ■ I wasn't doing that just for my benefit no lo hice por puro capricho ■ no lo hice por mi propio beneficio

I wasn't thinking no estaba pensando

I wasn't very hungry no tenía mucha hambre ■ tenía poca hambre

I waved to the waiter to come over le hice señas al camarero para que viniera

I went ahead and... fui y... ➤ I went ahead and called the repairman to come fix the air conditioner. Fui y llamé al técnico para que (me) viniera a reparar el aire acondicionado. ■ Fui y llamé al técnico para que (me) viniese a reparar el aire (acondicionado).

I will 1. (así) lo haré **2.** contradicting ¡que sí! ➤ Okay, I will. *(agreeing)* Está bien, (así) lo haré. ➤ You will *not*.-I *will*. ¡Que no!-¡Que sí! ➤ Do you think in Spanish? In another year, I will. ¿Piensas en español? Pasado un año, lo haré. ➤ I will (do it) in a minute. Lo haré en un minuto. ➤ I will, sir, I will. Así lo haré, señor, así lo haré.

I will never forget... 1. *(memory)* nunca olvidaré... ■ jamás olvidaré... **2.** *(future promise)* jamás me olvidaré de... ■ nunca me olvidaré de... ➤ I'll never forget the day we met. Nunca olvidaré el día (en) que nos conocimos. ➤ I'll never forget your birthday. Nunca me olvidaré de tu cumpleaños.

I will never forget it nunca lo olvidaré ■ *(emphatic)* jamás lo olvidaré

I will never forget the time that... nunca olvidaré aquella vez que...

I will never forget you nunca te olvidaré ■ no te olvidaré nunca ■ *(with more feeling)* jamás te olvidaré ■ no te olvidaré jamás

I wish! ¡ojalá!

I wish I could ojalá pudiera ■ quisiera poder

I wish I could go 1. *(main clause)* quisiera poder ir ■ ojalá pudiera ir **2.** *(dependent clause, which must be followed by "pero")* me gustaría poder ir

I wish I could have quisiera haber podido ■ me gustaría haber podido ■ me habría gustado poder ■ me hubiera gustado haber podido

I wish I could have done something ojalá hubiera podido hacer algo ■ desearía haber podido hacer algo

I wish I could have gone quisiera haber podido ir ■ ojalá hubiera podido ir ■ me gustaría haber podido ir ■ me habría gustado poder ir ■ me hubiera gustado poder ir ■ me hubiese gustado poder ir

I wish I could say the same (thing) ojalá pudiera decir lo mismo ■ *(wistfully, with a sigh)* si yo pudiera decir lo mismo

I wish I could say the same for ■ I wish I could say the same of si (yo) pudiera decir lo mismo para ■ si (yo) pudiera decir lo mismo de

I wish I didn't ojalá que (yo) no

I wish I didn't have to (do it) ojalá (yo) no tuviera que (hacerlo)

I wish I didn't have to (go) ojalá (yo) no tuviera que (ir)

I wish I didn't know ojalá (yo) no lo supiera

I wish I had desearía haberlo hecho ■ ojala que sí

I wish I had done something ojalá hubiera hecho algo ■ desearía haber hecho algo

I wish I had gone with them ojalá hubiera ido con ellos ■ ojalá los hubiera acompañado ■ *(Sp., leísmo)* ojalá les hubiera acompañado

I wish I had never met her ojalá nunca la hubiera conocido

I wish I had never met him ojalá nunca lo hubiera conocido ■ *(Sp., leísmo)* ojalá nunca le hubiera conocido

I wish I had said something ojalá hubiera dicho algo

I wish I had seen her ojalá la hubiera visto

I wish I had seen him ojalá lo hubiera visto ■ *(Sp., leísmo)* ojalá le hubiera visto

I wish I had seen it 1. *(a show)* ojalá lo hubiera visto **2.** *(a movie)* ojalá la hubiera visto

I wish I hadn't ojalá que no

I wish I hadn't gone ojalá no hubiera ido

I wish I hadn't known ojalá no (lo) hubiera sabido

I wish I hadn't said that ■ I wish I hadn't said it ojalá (yo) no lo hubiera dicho ■ ojalá (yo) no lo hubiese dicho

I wish I knew ojalá supiese ■ ojalá supiera ■ ojalá me supiese ➤ I wish I knew his telephone number. Ojalá (me) supiese su número de teléfono. ■ Ojalá (me) supiera su número de teléfono. ➤ I wish I knew the address. Ojalá me supiese la dirección. ■ Ojalá me supiera la dirección.

I wish I remembered ojalá me acordase ■ ojalá me acordara ■ ojalá recordase ■ ojalá que recordara ➤ I wish I remembered the address. Ojalá me acordase de la dirección. ■ Ojalá me acordara de la dirección. ➤ I wish I remembered it. Ojalá me acordase (de ello). ■ Ojalá (y) que lo recordara. ➤ I wish I remembered that... Ojalá recordase que...

I wish I were (yo) quisiera ser ■ ojalá (yo) fuera

I wish it did... ojalá lo hiciera... ➤ Does it snow often in Madrid?-No, but I wish it did. It snows perhaps once a year. ¿Nieva mucho en Madrid? No, pero ojalá lo hiciera. A lo mejor nieva una vez al año.

I wish it had... ojalá hubiera... ■ ojalá hubiese... ➤ Did this calculator come with batteries?-No, but I wish it had, because now I don't have any batteries for it. ¿Esta calculadora venía con las pilas?-No, pero ojalá las hubiera traído, porque en este momento no tengo pilas.

I wish it would... deseo que... ■ que se quede... ➤ I wish it would cool off. Deseo que se enfríe. ■ Que se quede fresco. ➤ I wish the anti-virus software would screen out popups. ■ I wish the anti-virus software screened out popups. Deseo que el software anti-virus bloqueara los popups.

I wish it would stop ojalá parara ■ ojalá parase

I wish the weather were like this all year ■ I wish the weather would stay like this all year ojalá el tiempo se quedase así todo el año

I wish there were some way (that)... ojalá hubiera alguna manera de... ■ desearía que hubiera alguna manera de... ➤ I wish there were some way that I could go to the party. Ojalá hubiera alguna manera de que pudiera ir a la fiesta. ➤ I wish there were some way that I could get in touch with you. Ojalá hubiera alguna manera de que me pusiera en contacto contigo. ■ Ojalá hubiera alguna manera de contactarme contigo. ■ Ojalá hubiera alguna manera de ponerme en contacto contigo.

I wish there were some way to... ojalá hubiera alguna manera de... ■ ojalá hubiese alguna manera de... *(See previous entry examples.)*

I wish you were here ojalá estuvieras aquí ■ ojalá estuvieses aquí ■ me gustaría que estuvieras aquí ■ me gustaría que estuvieses aquí ■ desearía que estuvieras aquí ■ desearía que estuvieses aquí

I wish you would ojalá que puedas ■ espero que sí ➤ I'd like to come see you while I'm in Madrid.-I wish you would. Me gustaría ir a verte mientras estoy en Madrid.-Ojalá que puedas. ■ Espero que sí.

I wish you wouldn't ojalá no lo hicieras ■ ojalá no lo hicieses

I wish you'd reconsider *(tú)* me gustaría que lo reconsideraras ■ me gustaría que lo reconsiderases ■ quisiera que lo reconsideraras ■ quisiera que lo reconsiderases ■ *(usted)* me gustaría que (usted) lo reconsiderara ■ me gustaría que (usted) lo reconsiderase ■ quisiera que (usted) lo reconsiderara ■ quisiera que (usted) lo reconsiderase

I wished I could have done something ■ I wished that I could have done something deseé poder hacer algo

I wished I had (yo) deseé haberlo hecho ➤ I had wanted to paint my own apartment, and when I saw the job the painters did, I wished I had. Hubiera querido pintar mi apartamento yo mismo, y cuando vi el trabajo que hicieron los pintores, deseé haberlo hecho.

I wished I had gone with them deseé haber ido con ellos ■ deseé haberlos acompañado ■ *(Sp., leísmo)* deseé haberles acompañado

I wished I had said something deseé haber dicho algo

I won *x* dollars me tocaron *x* dólares ■ gané *x* dólares

I wonder if... me pregunto si... ■ a saber si...

I wonder if it still works that way no sé si aún funciona así

I wonder if you'd mind? *(tú)* ¿te importaría? ■ *(usted)* ¿le importaría?

I wonder what it would be like? ¿me pregunto cómo sería? ■ ¿cómo será?

I wonder what it would be like to...? ¿me pregunto cómo sería...? ➤ I wonder what it would be like to be a dog or a cat? Me pregunto cómo sería ser un perro o un gato.

I wonder whether... me pregunto si... ■ a saber si...

I wonder why *(curiosity)* me pregunto por qué ■ ¿por qué será? ■ ¿y por qué? ■ *(sarcasm)* ¡me imagino!

I won't be back ■ I'm never going back nunca voy a regresar ■ nunca voy a volver ■ no pienso volver ■ *(tú)* me puedes esperar sentado ■ *(usted)* me puede (usted) esperar sentado ■ *(ustedes, ellos)* me pueden esperar sentados

I won't go! ■ I'm not going! ¡no iré! ■ ¡no me iré!

I won't have anything to do with it no tendré nada que ver con eso ■ *(colorful)* de esta agua no beberé

I won't hear of it no lo consideraré

I won't leave ■ I refuse to leave no voy a salir

I won't put up with your speaking to me that way ■ I won't tolerate your speaking to me that way no tolero que me hables así ■ no te consiento que me hables así

I won't stand for it ■ I won't put up with it ■ I won't tolerate it no lo tolero ■ no lo consiento

I won't take any more of your time *(tú)* no te quito más tiempo ■ *(usted)* no le quito más tiempo

I won't tolerate your judging me no tolero tus juicios sobre mí ■ no te consiento juicios sobre mí

I won't tolerate your speaking to me that way ■ I won't put up with your speaking to me that way no tolero que me hables así ■ no te consiento que me hables así

I would appreciate it if... ■ I'd appreciate it if... agradecería que... ■ *(impatience)* si me permites... ➤ I would appreciate it if you'd let me explain... Si me permites explicar...

I would be grateful if... *(tú)* te agradecería que... ■ *(usted)* le agradecería (a usted) que... ➤ I'd be grateful if you'd go with me. Le agradecería que me acompañaras.

I would have been surprised if... me hubiera sorprendido si... ■ me habría sorprendido si...

I would have liked to go ■ I would like to have gone me habría gustado ir ■ me gustaría haber ido ■ me hubiera gustado ir ■ me hubiese gustado ir

I would have loved to have... 1. me habría encantado tener... 2. *(when "have" is an auxiliary verb)* me habría encantado haber...

I would have to... 1. tendría que... 2. había que... 3. debía... ➤ I would have to know more about it. Tendría que saber más acerca de ello. ■ Tendría que saber más al respecto. ➤ The doctor told me I would have to put drops in my eyes. El doctor me dijo que habría de ponerme gotas en los ojos. ■ El doctor me dijo que tenía que ponerme gotas en los ojos. ➤ They told me I would have to change my schedule. ■ They told me I was going to have to change my schedule. (Ellos) me dijeron que yo tendría que cambiar mi horario. ■ Me dijeron que yo debía cambiar mi horario.

I would have to say in all honesty ■ I'd have to say in all honesty debería decir con total honestidad

I would just as soon... ■ I would sooner... (yo) preferiría

I would like to have gone ■ I would have liked to go me gustaría haber ido ■ me habría gustado ir ■ me hubiera gustado ir ■ me hubiese gustado ir

I would love to have gone ■ I would have loved to go me habría encantado ir ■ me hubiera encantado ir ■ me hubiese encantado ir

I would love to have had... ■ I would have loved to have... me hubiera encantado tener... ■ me hubiera encantado haber tenido... ■ me hubiese encantado tener... ■ me hubiese encantado haber tenido... ➤ I would love to have had the opportunity to take flying lessons. Me hubiera encantado tener la oportunidad de tomar lecciones de vuelo. ■ Me hubiese encantado haber tenido la oportunidad de tomar lecciones de vuelo.

I would love to, thank you ■ I'd love to, thank you me encantaría, gracias

I would much rather... ■ I'd much rather... preferiría mucho más...

I would never do that (yo) nunca haría eso

I would never give it to them nunca se lo daría a ellos ➤ I would never give it to them under any circumstances. Nunca se lo daría a ellos bajo ninguna circunstancia.

I would rather do one thing than do another ■ I would prefer doing one thing over doing another ■ I would prefer to do one thing rather than another preferiría hacer una cosa que otra ➤ I'd rather eat out tonight than cook. (Yo) preferiría cenar fuera esta noche que cocinar.

I would really enjoy... realmente disfrutaría de...

I wouldn't be caught dead at... ni muerto ni vivo me verán en...

I wouldn't be caught dead in... ni muerto ni vivo me verán en...

I wouldn't be caught dead with you contigo ni a misa

I wouldn't go so far as to predict... no iría tan lejos como para predecir...

I wouldn't go so far as to say... no iría tan lejos como para decir...

I wouldn't have believed it if I had not seen it no lo hubiera creído si no lo hubiera visto

I wouldn't have it even if they gave it to me no lo quiero ni regalado

I wouldn't hear of it no lo iba a oír

I wouldn't know! ¡no lo sabría!

I wouldn't mind no me importaría

I wouldn't mind... ■ I could do with... no me vendría mal... ➤ I wouldn't mind a good cold beer right now. ■ I could do with a good cold beer right now. No me vendría mal una cerveza bien fría ahora mismo.

I wouldn't mind if you did ■ it wouldn't matter to me if you did no me importaría si tú lo hicieras

I wouldn't miss it for anything ■ I wouldn't miss it for the world no me lo perdería por nada (del mundo)

I wouldn't put it past him no lo descartaría ■ no lo sacaría de la lista ■ lo creo capaz de hacerlo ➤ Do you think the treasurer absconded with the money?-From my impression of his character, I wouldn't put it past him. ¿Crees que el tesorero haya huido con el dinero?-Desde mi impresión de su carácter, no lo sacaría de la lista.

I wouldn't swear to it no lo afirmaría

I wouldn't trade it for anything esto no lo cambio por nada ■ no lo cambiaría por nada

I wouldn't wish it on anyone no se lo desearía ni a mi peor enemigo

I wouldn't worry about it ■ I wouldn't worry about it if I were you no me preocuparía al respecto ■ no me preocuparía acerca de ello

ice cold ■ good and cold ■ nice and cold bien frío

ice cream cone barquillo (de helado) ▪ cono de helado

ice cream sundae sandy

ice cube cubito de hielo

to **ice up 1.** *(refrigerator)* formarse hielo **2.** *(wings of an airplane)* formarse hielo sobre las alas

to **ice-skate** patinar sobre hielo

ice skating *el* patinaje sobre el hielo

ice skating rink pista de hielo

ice tray (of a refrigerator) cubitera

to **ice up 1.** *(refrigerator)* hacer escarcha **2.** *(car windshield, airplane wings, etc.)* congelarse ➤ I tell you one thing I don't like about this new refrigerator. It's already starting to ice up. Te digo una cosa que no me gusta acerca de este nuevo frigorífico. Ya está haciendo escarcha.

ice water *el* agua helada

icon of the culture ▪ cultural icon ícono de la cultura ▪ símbolo de la cultura ➤ Adelita, Pancho Villa's sidekick in the Mexican Revolution, who is always portrayed with pigtails and a bullet belt draped over her shoulder, is an icon of Mexican culture. Adelita, la compañera de Pancho Villa en la Revolución Mexicana, que sale siempre retratada con coletas y un cinturón de balas caído sobre el hombro, es un ícono de la cultura mejicana.

icy wind viento helado ▪ viento siberiano

ID card ▪ identification (card) carnet de identidad ▪ carné de identidad ➤ Could I see your ID? ▪ Could I see your identification? ¿Podría ver su carnet de identidad?

I'd be careful if I were you yo que tú tendría ojo ▪ tendría cuidado si fuera tú ▪ yo que tú tendría cuidado ▪ *(Sp.)* yo que tú me andaría con ojo ▪ yo que tú me andaría con cuidado

I'd be delighted con mucho gusto

I'd be delighted if... me encantaría si... ➤ I'd be delighted if you could go with us. Me encantaría si pudieras acompañarnos.

I'd be glad if... me alegraría si...

I'd be glad to ▪ I'll be glad to lo haré con gusto ▪ lo haré encantado

I'd be interested in finding out... ▪ I'd be interested to find out... me gustaría averiguar... ▪ me gustaría enterarme de... ▪ me gustaría descubrir...

I'd be interested in hearing... ▪ I'd be interested to hear... ▪ I'd be interested in knowing... ▪ I'd be interested to know... me interesaría oír... ▪ me interesaría saber... ➤ I'd be interested in hearing what happened at the party last night. Me interesaría oír lo que pasó en la fiesta anoche. ▪ Me interesaría saber lo que pasó en la fiesta anoche.

I'd be interested in knowing me interesaría saber ▪ estaría interesado en saber ➤ I'd be interested in knowing what happened at the meeting last night. Me interesaría saber lo que pasó en la reunión anoche.

I'd be the first to admit that... (yo) sería el primero en admitir que... ▪ (yo) sería la primera en admitir que...

I'd be willing to... ▪ I would be willing to... (yo) estaría dispuesto(-a) a...

I'd better... ▪ I had better... mejor será ▪ más me vale... ▪ más me valdría... ▪ por la cuenta que me trae ➤ I'd better be there. Mejor será que esté allí.

I'd better be going más vale que me vaya ▪ más vale que me marche

I'd better get busy ▪ I'd better get to work más vale que me ponga a trabajar

I'd better get going 1. I'd better be going ▪ I'd better be on my way más vale que me marche **2.** I'd better get busy (doing my work) más vale que me ponga a trabajar ▪ más vale que me ocupe de...

I'd better get to work 1. más vale que me ponga a trabajar **2.** I'd better be on my way to work más me vale ir a trabajar

I'd better go 1. I'd better leave mejor me voy ▪ será mejor que me vaya **2.** I'd better attend mejor voy ▪ será mejor que vaya

I'd better not ▪ *(coll.)* I better not mejor que no

I'd even go so far as to say that... *(tú)* hasta te diría que... ▪ *(usted)* hasta le diría (a usted) que...

I'd forget my head if it weren't attached se me olvidaría la cabeza si no la tuviese pegada a los hombros

I'd give anything to... (yo) daría cualquier cosa por...

I'd give my eye teeth to... (yo) daría un ojo de la cara por...

I'd given you up! ¡ya no contaba contigo! ➤ I'd given you up. I didn't think you were going to come. Ya no contaba contigo. Creí que no ibas a venir. ➤ I'd given you up. I didn't think you were going to call me. Ya no contaba contigo. Creí que no ibas a llamar.

I'd guess he's about *x* (years old) ▪ I'd say he's about *x* (years old) le doy unos *x* años ▪ le echo unos *x* años ▪ le supongo unos *x* años

I'd guess you for twenty-five ▪ I'd guess you're about twenty-five te echo unos veinticinco

I'd have to say... tengo que reconocer... ▪ tengo que decir... ▪ debo decir...

I'd like nothing better (than...) nada me gustaría más (que...) ▪ nada me agradaría más (que...)

I'd like to get this framed ▪ I'd like to have this framed me gustaría enmarcar esto

I'd like to go me gustaría ir

I'd like to have this framed ▪ I'd like to get this framed me gustaría enmarcar esto

I'd like to hear what you have to say about that me gustaría saber qué tienes que decir sobre eso ▪ me gustaría saber qué tienes que decir respecto a eso

I'd like to introduce you to... me gustaría presentarte a... ➤ I'd like to introduce you to my date. Me gustaría presentarte a mi cita.

I'd like to think that... quiero pensar que...

I'd like to, though ▪ however, I'd like to no obstante, me gustaría

I'd like you to come over for supper *(tú)* quiero que te vengas a cenar ▪ *(usted)* quiero que se venga a cenar ▪ *(ustedes)* quiero que se vengan a cenar ▪ *(Sp., vosotros)* quiero que os vengáis a cenar

I'd like you to meet... *(a ti)* me gustaría presentarte a... ▪ *(a usted)* me gustaría presentarle (a usted)... ➤ I'd like you to meet my cousins, Emily, Alice, and Andy. Me gustaría presentarte a mis primos, Emily, Alice y Andy.

I'd love to ▪ I'd be delighted to me encantaría ▪ (yo) encantado ▪ lo haré encantado

I'd love to do it me encantaría hacerlo ▪ yo lo hago encantado ▪ lo haré encantado

I'd love to know me encantaría saberlo

I'd love to know... me encantaría saber...

I'd love to, thank you ▪ I would love to, thank you ▪ *(archaic)* I should love to, thank you me encantaría, gracias

I'd really like to, but bien yo querría, pero

I'd say (that)... (yo) diría que... ➤ I'd say (that) some updated pictures of the grandchildren are in order. Diría que algunas fotos recientes de los nietos son de lo más pertinente. ▪ Diría que algunas fotos recientes de los nietos son de lo más adecuado. ▪ Diría que algunas fotos recientes de los nietos vendrían muy bien.

I'd sure like to ya lo creo que sí ▪ desde luego que sí ▪ por supuesto que sí ▪ ya lo creo que me gustaría ▪ desde luego que me gustaría ▪ por supuesto que me gustaría ➤ Do you want to come with us?-I'd sure like to! ¿Te gustaría venir con nosotros?-¡Ya lo creo que sí!

I'd sure like to... seguro que me gustaría... ➤ I'd sure like to have my own house. Seguro que me gustaría tener mi propia casa.

I'd sure like to know... sí que me gustaría saber...

I'd swear I could have... juraría haber... ▪ hubiera jurado...

idea that... idea de que... ➤ Schopenhauer shares with Freud the idea that human behavior can be reduced to a few basic drives. Schopenhauer comparte con Freud la idea de que el comportamiento de los seres humanos se reduce a unas pocas instintos básicos.

the **ideal and the actual** lo ideal y lo real

ideal situation situación ideal ▪ situación óptima

identical to the way it was ▪ identical to how it was tal y como estaba ▪ exactamente en las mismas condiciones en que estaba ➤ Please return the processor identical to the way it was, without doing any repairs. Por favor devuelva el procesador exactamente en las mismas condiciones en que estaba sin hacer reparación alguna.

identical twins mellizos ▪ gemelos univitelinos

identification tag ▪ identification label etiqueta de identificación ▪ marchamo de identidad

to **identify the culprit** esclarecer la autoría

idiot box ▪ boob tube caja tonta ▪ caja idiota

idle hands are the devil's workshop las manos ociosas son el juguete del demonio

idle question pregunta ociosa

if all else fails... si todo lo demás falla...

if and only if *(symbolic logic)* si y sólo si ▪ *(coll.)* siempre y cuando

if any si es que tiene alguno ➤ It is of minor, if any, importance. Es de poca importancia, si es que tiene alguna.

if any conclusion can be drawn from what happened, it is that... si podemos extraer una conclusión de lo ocurrido, es que... ▪ si podemos sacar una conclusión de lo ocurrido, es que... ▪ si podemos sacar una conclusión de lo que ocurrió, es que... ▪ si podemos extraer una conclusión de lo que ocurrió, es que...

if anyone wants to... si alguien quiere... ▪ quien quiera... ➤ If anyone wants to ask a question, this is the time to ask it because no questions are permitted during the exam. Si alguien quiere hacer una pregunta, que la haga ahora, porque no se permiten preguntas durante el examen. ▪ Quien quiera hacer una pregunta, que la haga ahora, porque no se permiten preguntas durante el examen.

if anything comes up *(tú)* si te surge algo ▪ *(usted)* si le surge algo ▪ si sale algún tema ➤ If anything comes up, call me. Si te surge algo, llámame.

if anything like that happened... si algo así sucediera... ▪ si sucediera algo así... ▪ si sucediera semejante cosa... ▪ si semejante cosa sucediera...

if anything like that happens... si algo así sucede... ▪ si sucede algo así... ▪ si sucede semejante cosa... ▪ si semejante cosa sucede...

if anything like that should happen si algo así sucediera ▪ si sucediera algo así ▪ de suceder algo así

if at all eso si... ➤ I would request time off only for a very good reason, if at all. Sólo pediría días libres por una buena razón, eso si los pido. ➤ *(From Reader's Digest)* If my husband took a parachute jump at all, it would be because the airplane was going to crash! Si mi marido saltara en paracaídas, eso si llegara a saltar, sería porque el avión estaría a punto de estrellarse.

if at all possible si existe alguna (remota) posibilidad ▪ si existe alguna posibilidad (por remota que sea)

if by (any) chance si por casualidad (alguna) ▪ por si acaso

if envy were dirt, the whole world would be dirty *(Spanish proverb)* si la envidia fuera tiña, cuántos tiñosos habría

if everything goes as planned si todo marcha según lo planeado

if for any reason si por cualquier razón ▪ si por cualquier motivo

if for no other reason than aunque sólo sea por

if for some reason si por alguna razón ▪ si por algún motivo

if he had (done it) si lo hubiera hecho ➤ I would have been surprised if he had (done it). Yo me habría sorprendido si él lo hubiera hecho.

if he's not there, leave a message on his answering machine si no está, déjale un mensaje en su contestadora

if, however... ▪ if, on the other hand... ▪ but if... si, por otra parte... ▪ sin embargo, si... ▪ si, en cambio... ▪ mas si...

if I *am* de estarlo ▪ de serlo ➤ I don't know at this point if I'll be here that weekend, but if I am, count me in. No sé decirte desde ahora si estaré ese fin de semana, pero de estarlo cuenta conmigo.

if I can ever help you, let me know si alguna vez necesitas ayuda, dímelo *("If you ever need help" is more natural in Spanish.)*

if I (can) get through today si paso de hoy

if I can help you with anything si puedo ayudarte en algo ➤ If I can help you with anything, let me know and I'll do what I can to help you. Si puedo ayudarte en algo, házmelo saber y haré lo posible por ayudarte.

if I can make it happen ▪ if I can pull it off si lo consigo ▪ si lo logro

if I can manage it ▪ if I can swing it si lo consigo ▪ si lo logro

if I can pull it off *(coll.)* ▪ if I can make it happen si lo consigo ▪ si lo logro

if I can swing it *(coll.)* ▪ if I can manage it si lo consigo ▪ si lo logro

if I catch you doing that again... si te vuelvo a pillar haciendo eso ▪ *(Sp.)* si te vuelvo a coger haciendo eso

if I could have done it, I would have si (yo) hubiera podido hacerlo, lo hubiera hecho

if I could just think of something (to...) si se me ocurriera algo (para...) ▪ si pudiera pensar en algo (para...)

if I could only... ▪ if only I could... si tan sólo (yo) pudiera... ▪ si al menos pudiera...

if I do say so myself ▪ modesty aside modestia aparte

if I don't de no ser así ▪ si no (lo hago) ➤ I need to apologize to her. If I don't, she'll never speak to me again. Necesito pedirle disculpas a ella. De no ser así, nunca me volverá a hablar. ▪ Necesito pedirle disculpas a ella. Si no, nunca me volverá a hablar.

if I ever catch you doing that again... si alguna vez te vuelvo a pillar haciendo eso... ▪ *(Sp.)* si alguna vez te vuelvo a coger haciendo eso...

if I ever find out si alguna vez me entero ▪ si alguna vez descubro

if I get any mail si viene alguna carta para mí

if I had been... si me hubiera... ▪ si hubiera... ▪ de haberme... ▪ de haber... ▪ si hubiera estado... ▪ si hubiera sido... ▪ si hubiese estado... ▪ si hubiese sido...

if I had had... ▪ had I had... si (yo) hubiera... ▪ si (yo) hubiese... ▪ de haber tenido... ➤ If I had had time, I would have gone with you. ▪ Had I had time, I would have gone with you. Si (yo) hubiera tenido tiempo, te habría acompañado. ▪ Si (yo) hubiese tenido tiempo, te habría acompañado. *(American English speakers, often say incorrectly "if I would have had..." ("si yo habría tenido") instead of "if I had had" ("si yo hubiera/hubiese tenido"). It is important to avoid this error because it blurs an essential logical distinction between different meanings.)*

if I had done it... ▪ had I done it... si lo hubiera hecho ▪ de haberlo hecho ▪ a haberlo hecho

if I had had my wits about me si hubiera estado en mis cabales ▪ si hubiese estado en mis cabales

if I had had time ▪ had I had time si (yo) hubiera tenido tiempo ▪ si (yo) hubiese tenido tiempo ▪ si me hubiera dado tiempo ▪ si me hubiese dado tiempo ▪ de haber tenido tiempo ▪ de haberme dado tiempo

if I had (it) my way si se hiciera a mi manera ▪ si se hiciese a mi manera ▪ si se hiciera como yo digo ▪ si se hiciese como yo digo

if I had it to do over again ▪ if I could do it all over again si (yo) tuviera la oportunidad de volver a hacerlo ▪ si (yo) pudiera volver a hacerlo

if I had known how long it would take (me)... ▪ had I known how long it would take (me)... si (yo) hubiera sabido cuánto tiempo (me) iba a llevar... ▪ de haber sabido cuánto tiempo (me) iba a llevar...

if I had known how much it would cost (me)... ▪ had I known how much it would cost (me)... si yo hubiera sabido cuánto (me) iba a costar... ▪ si yo hubiese sabido cuánto me iba a costar(me)... ▪ de haber sabido cuánto iba a costar(me)...

if I had known how to... ▪ had I known how to... si (yo) hubiera sabido cómo... ▪ si (yo) hubiese sabido cómo... ▪ de habido sabido cómo... ➤ If I had known how to foresee the changes in the market, I would have developed a different sales strategy. Si hubiera sabido cómo anticipar los cambios del mercado, habría desarrollado una estrategia de ventas distinta.

if I had known (it) ▪ if I had known (that) si lo hubiera sabido ➤ If I had known (it) ahead of time, I would have warned you. Si lo hubiera sabido con tiempo suficiente, te habría avisado.

if I had known that ▪ had I known that si (yo) lo hubiera sabido ▪ si (yo) lo hubiese sabido ▪ de haberlo sabido

if I had known that... ▪ had I known that... si (yo) hubiera sabido que... ▪ si (yo) hubiese sabido que... ▪ de haber sabido que...

if I had known what... ▪ had I known what... si (yo) hubiera sabido lo que... ▪ si (yo) hubiera sabido qué... ▪ si (yo) hubiese sabido lo que... ▪ si (yo) hubiese sabido qué...

if I had known what I was getting myself into... si (yo) hubiera sabido dónde me metía... ▪ si (yo) hubiera sabido en qué me metía... ▪ si (yo) hubiera sabido en lo que me metía *("Hubiese" can replace "hubiera" in all examples.)*

if I had known what to expect... ▪ had I known what to expect... si (yo) hubiera sabido qué esperar... ▪ si (yo) hubiese sabido qué esperar...

if I had known what would happen... ▪ had I known what would happen... ▪ if I had known what was going to happen... ▪ had I known what was going to happen... si (yo) hubiera sabido lo que iba a pasar... ▪ si (yo) hubiese sabido lo que iba a pasar... ▪ de haber sabido lo que iba a pasar...

if I had my choice ▪ if I could choose si pudiera elegir ▪ si pudiera escoger ▪ si me dieran a elegir ▪ de poder elegir ▪ de poder escoger ➤ If I had my choice, I'd rather... Si (yo) pudiera elegir, preferiría... ▪ Si (yo) pudiera escoger, preferiría... ▪ Si me dan a elegir, preferiría... Si me dan a escoger, preferiría... ▪ De poder elegir, (yo) preferiría... ▪ De poder escoger, (yo) preferiría...

if I had my druthers *(slang, from "would rather")* ▪ if I had my choice si (yo) pudiera elegir ▪ si (yo) pudiera escoger ▪ si me dan a elegir ▪ si me dan a escoger ▪ de poder elegir ▪ de poder escoger

if I had my pick (of something) si me dan a elegir (algo)

if I had my way ▪ if I could do what I wanted (to) ▪ if I could do what I felt like si pudiera hacer lo que (yo) quisiera ▪ si pudiera hacer lo que (a mí) me diera la gana ▪ si pudiera salirme con la mía

if I had not succeeded... si no lo conseguía... ▪ si no hubiera logrado... ▪ de no haber(lo) logrado... ➤ If I had not succeeded by the time... Si (yo) no lo conseguía cuando...

if I had time si me diera tiempo ▪ si tuviera tiempo

if I had to do it all over again... si tuviera que volver a hacerlo... ▪ si tuviera que hacerlo otra vez...

if I hadn't been... ▪ had I not been... si no me hubiera... ▪ si no hubiera... ▪ de no haberme... ▪ de no haber... ➤ If I hadn't been delayed by the train, I would have gone to your recital. Si no me hubiera retrasado por el tren, habría ido a tu recital. ▪ De no haberme retrasado por el tren, habría ido a tu recital.

if I have any si lo tengo

if I have any say in the matter si se me permite opinar en este asunto ▪ si se me permite opinar sobre este asunto

if I have one si lo tengo

if I have time si me da tiempo

if I may say so si puedo decir así ▪ si me permites decirlo

if I might ask ▪ if you don't mind my asking si se me permite la pregunta

if I put... *(present)* si pongo... ▪ *(preterite)* si puse... ▪ *(subjunctive)* if I were to put... si pusiera...

if I put my mind to it si me lo propongo ➤ If I put my mind to it, I could. Si me lo propongo, lo logro.

if I remember right ▪ if I remember correctly ▪ if my memory serves me (correctly) si mal no recuerdo ▪ *(Sp.)* si mal no me acuerdo

if I should... si acaso... ➤ If I should see her... Si acaso (yo) la viera...

if I were in your place ▪ if I were you *(tú)* yo en tu lugar ▪ si yo fuera tú ▪ *(usted)* yo en su lugar ▪ si yo fuera usted

if I were in your shoes ▪ if I were in your place si yo estuviera en tu pellejo ▪ si yo fuera tú

if I were to put ▪ if I put si pusiera

if I were you yo que tú ▪ si yo fuera tú ▪ yo en tu lugar

if I weren't what I am si no fuera lo que soy ▪ de no ser lo que soy ➤ If I weren't what I am, I'd be a journalist. Si no fuera lo que soy, sería (un) periodista. ▪ De no ser lo que soy, sería periodista.

if I would say si yo decía ➤ If I would say anything, the teacher would tell me to see her after class. Si yo decía algo, la profesora me decía que la viera después de la clase.

if I'm not here... si yo no estoy... ➤ If I'm not here when you come, the neighbor has a key. Si no estoy cuando llegues, el vecino tiene llave.

if I'm not mistaken si no me equivoco ▪ si no me engaño

if it came to that si llegara a eso ▪ si llegase a eso ▪ llegado al caso

if it comes to that ▪ if that happens si llega a eso ▪ llegado al caso

if it doesn't work out, don't worry about it si fracaso, ni caso

if it had not been for ▪ if it hadn't been for ▪ had it not been for si no hubiera sido por ▪ de no haber sido por ▪ si no fuese por ▪ si no fuera por ➤ The victim of the collapse would have died if it had not been for the paramedics. ▪ The victim of the collapse would have died had it not been for the paramedics. La víctima del derrumbe habría muerto si no hubiera sido por los servicios de emergencia. ▪ La víctima del derrumbe habría muerto si no fuese por los servicios de emergencia.

if it had not been for you ▪ if it hadn't been for you ▪ had it not been for you *(tú)* de no haber sido por ti ▪ si no hubiera sido por ti ▪ *(usted)* de no haber sido por usted ▪ si no hubiera sido por usted

if it is... **1.** if it be si sea así **2.** if it were si fuera así **3.** if that's the case ▪ that being the case de ser así **4.** then entonces

if it isn't... ▪ if it's not... de no ser así

if it was si fue así

if it was really a dream: to know ~ **1.** saber cuánto de real había en el sueño **2.** (in order) to know if it was really a dream para saber cuánto de real había en el sueño

if it was really true si de hecho era cierto

if it was you si fuiste tú ➤ I don't know if it was you, but somebody left dirty dishes in the sink. No sé si fuiste tú pero alguien dejó los platos sucios en el fregadero.

if it were si fuera así

if it were not for ▪ if it weren't for ▪ were it not for si no fuera por ▪ de no ser por ▪ a no ser por ▪ si no llega a ser por

if it were not for the fact that ▪ if it weren't for the fact that si no fuera porque

if it were up to me si de mí dependiera

if it weren't for the fact that... de no ser porque...

if it weren't for you ▪ were it not for you *(tú)* de no ser por ti ▪ si no fuera por ti ▪ *(usted)* de no ser por usted ▪ si no fuera por usted

if it's any consolation to you ▪ if it's any consolation *(tú)* si te sirve de consuelo ▪ *(usted)* si le sirve de consuelo

if it's asking too much ▪ if that's asking too much ▪ if it's too much to ask si es demasiado pedir ▪ si es mucho pedir

if it's not too much trouble si no es demasiado problema

if it's really true ▪ if that's really true si de hecho es cierto ▪ si bien es verdad ▪ si bien es cierto

if it's too much to ask ▪ if it's asking too much ▪ if that's asking too much si es demasiado pedir ▪ si es mucho pedir

if it's too much trouble si es demasiado problema

if looks could kill... si las miradas matasen...

if my memory serves me (correctly) ▪ if I remember correctly ▪ if I remember right si mal no recuerdo ▪ si no me falla la memoria ▪ si la memoria no me engaña ▪ *(Sp.)* si mal no me acuerdo

if not **1.** si es que si no **2.** if one cannot ▪ if one does not si no **3.** unless ▪ if (it were) not for a no ser que ➤ If the will is not notarized, it is not valid. Si es que si no tiene sello notarial, el testamento no es válido. ➤ Call me if you can't come. ▪ Call me if you can't make it. Llámame si no puedes venir. ➤ I won't finish if I don't get to work. No terminaré si no me pongo a trabajar. ➤ We'll be late if we don't leave on time. ▪ We'll be late unless we leave on time. Llegaremos tarde a no ser que salgamos a tiempo.

if one could do something **1.** if one were able to do something si uno pudiera hacer algo ▪ si se pudiera hacer algo **2.** if one would be able to do something si uno podría hacer algo ▪ si se podría hacer algo ➤ If you could go, I could give you a ride. ▪ If you could go, I could take you. Si pudieras ir, yo podría llevarte.

if one had to choose ▪ if you had to choose si se tuviera que elegir ▪ si uno tuviera que elegir ➤ If one had to choose the most important scientist in history, the choice would probably be Isaac Newton. Si se tuviera que elegir el científico más importante de la historia, la elección probablemente recaería en Isaac Newton.

if one should die ▪ if one were to die ▪ if one dies si uno se muriera

if one were to choose ▪ if you were to choose si se hubiera de elegir ▪ si uno hubiera de elegir ▪ si se fuera de elegir ▪ si uno fuera de elegir

if one's year were up si el año de uno se terminara ▪ si el año de uno se terminase

if only 1. si tan sólo **2.** I wish! ¡házmela buena! ▪ ¡ojalá!

if only by aunque sea (sólo) por ➤ James Bond always beats the clock, if only by a second. James Bond siempre le gana al tiempo, aunque sea (sólo) por un segundo.

if only for a moment aunque sea sólo un momento

if only I could... si tan sólo (yo) pudiera... ▪ ojalá (yo) pudiera ➤ If only I could fly like a bird... Ojalá pudiera volar como un pájaro...

if only I could (do it) si tan sólo (yo) pudiera hacerlo

if only I had known! ▪ if only I'd known! si tan sólo (yo) hubiera sabido ▪ si tan sólo (yo) hubiese sabido ▪ ¡de haberlo sabido!

if only they knew ▪ if they only knew si sólo supieran ▪ si tan sólo supieran

if possible si fuera posible ▪ de ser posible ▪ a ser posible

if so si es así ▪ si fuera así ▪ de ser así

if the occasion should arise ▪ should the occasion arise ▪ if the occasion arises si se presenta la ocasión ▪ si se tercia

if that happens ▪ if it comes to that llegado el caso

if that's asking too much ▪ if it's asking too much ▪ if it's too much to ask si es demasiado pedir ▪ si es mucho pedir

if that's really true ▪ if it's really true si bien es verdad ▪ si bien es cierto

if that's the case si es así

if the shoe fits, wear it al que le caiga el sayo que se lo ponga ▪ al que le venga el sayo que se lo ponga

if there are any si los hay ▪ si las hay

if there ever was one si alguna vez lo hubiera

if there had been ▪ had there been si lo hubiera habido ▪ de haberlo habido

if there had been... ▪ had there been... si hubiera habido... ▪ de haber habido...

if there is a question about si hay una duda sobre ▪ si hay una pregunta sobre ▪ *(coll.)* si cabe (una duda, es) que

if there is one si lo hay ▪ si la hay ➤ The branch of the bank would be on this street if there is one. La sucursal del banco estaría en esta calle, si la hay.

if there were going to be si fuera a haber ▪ si fuese a haber

if there were to be si fuera a haber

if that doesn't work si (eso) no da resultado ▪ si esto no da resultado

if this doesn't work si esto no da resultado

if worst comes to worst en el peor de los casos

if you ask me para mí que

if you can't beat 'em, join 'em si no puedes con ellos, úneteles

if you consider that... ▪ if you take into consideration that... si se considera que...

if you could call it that si se le puede llamar así

if you could get it to (do something) si se pudiera conseguir que (hiciera algo) ➤ Leonardo da Vinci's helicopter would work if you could get the rotor to spin fast enough. El helicóptero de Leonardo da Vinci funcionaría si se pudiera conseguir que la hélice girara lo suficientemente rápido.

if you don't (do it) si no lo haces

if you don't hurry up si no te das prisa ▪ si no aceleras ▪ como no te menees

if you don't like it, you can lump it si no te gusta, te chinchas

if you don't mind *(tú)* si no te importa ▪ *(usted)* si no le importa

if you don't mind my asking si se me permite la pregunta

if you get disconnected si se corta la línea ▪ si se corta la comunicación

if you got it to do something si se consiguiese que hiciera algo ▪ si se consiguiera que hiciese algo *(Spanish speakers instinctively dislike repetition of sound and would vary the subjunctive forms even though all are correct.)*

if you have any problems... *(tú)* si tienes algún problema... ▪ *(usted)* si tiene algún problema...

if you have any questions 1. *(in a classroom)* si tienes preguntas **2.** *(sales pitch, tour, or requesting information)* para cualquier información

if you insist 1. si insistes ▪ si usted insiste **2.** if you're going to press the issue si me apuras ▪ si te empeñas

if you know the extension, dial it now si conoce la extensión, márquela ahora ▪ si sabe la extensión, márquela ahora

if you like si te parece bien

if you look at... si te fijas en... ➤ If you look at the bottom of the page... Si te fijas al pie de la página...

if you look really hard... si te fijas muy bien...

if you raise up a child in the way he should go, he will not depart from it *(Biblical proverb)* si instruyes al niño en su camino, aún cuando sea viejo no se apartará de él

if you say so *(tú)* si tú lo dices ▪ *(usted)* si usted lo dice

if you see her si la ves ▪ de verla

if you see him si lo ves ▪ de verlo ▪ *(Sp., leísmo)* si le ves ▪ de verle

if you should see her *(tú)* si (acaso) la vieras ▪ si llegas a verla ▪ *(usted)* si (acaso) la viera usted ▪ si usted llega a verla ▪ de verla ▪ *(vosotros)* si llegás a verla

if you should see him *(tú)* si (acaso) lo vieras ▪ *(usted)* si (acaso) lo viera usted ▪ de verlo ▪ *(Sp., leísmo, tú)* si (acaso) le vieras ▪ *(usted)* si (acaso) le viera usted ▪ de verle

if you still have doubts si persisten las dudas ▪ *(tú)* si todavía tienes dudas ▪ si aún tienes dudas ▪ *(usted)* si (usted) todavía tiene dudas ▪ si (usted) aún tiene dudas

if you still have questions si persisten las preguntas ▪ si persisten las dudas ➤ If you still have questions, send them to me. Si persisten las dudas, házmelas llegar.

if you stop to think about it si se detiene a pensarlo bien

if you take into consideration (that...) ▪ if you consider that... si se toma en consideración (que...) ▪ si se considera (que...)

if you think you can handle it... *(tú)* si crees que puedes con ello... ▪ si crees que puedes manejarlo... ▪ *(usted)* si cree que puede con ello... ▪ si cree que puede manejarlo...

if you want it done right, (it's better to) do it yourself vale más hacer que mandar

if you want to si quieres (hacerlo) ▪ si así lo quieres ▪ si así lo deseas

if you want to know the truth... 1. *(literal)* si quieres saber la verdad... **2.** to tell you the truth para decirte la verdad ▪ para serte honesto(-a)

if you would be so kind as to... si fuera tan amable de...

if you'd be interested ▪ if you'd like to *(tú)* si te interesara ▪ si te interesase ▪ si es de tu interés ▪ *(usted)* si le interesara ▪ si le interesase ▪ si es de su interés

if you'll excuse me... *(tú)* si me disculpas ▪ *(usted)* si me disculpa usted ▪ *(ustedes)* si me disculpan ▪ *(Sp., vosotros)* si me disculpáis

if you'll pardon the expression si se me permite la expresión ▪ hablando en plata

if you're really interested *(tú)* si de verdad estás interesado(-a) ▪ si de verdad te interesa ▪ *(usted)* si de verdad está (usted) interesado(-a) ▪ si de verdad le interesa (a usted)

if you've seen one, you've seen them all si has visto uno, los has visto todos ▪ si has visto una, las has visto todas ▪ *(Sp.)* da lo mismo ocho que ochenta ▪ *(S. Am.)* para muestra basta un botón

if walls could talk... si las paredes hablaran...

to **ignite something** ■ to set fire to something ■ to set something on fire ■ to set something afire ■ to light something prender fuego a algo ■ encender algo ➤ When you make Irish coffee, you ignite the whiskey. ■ When you make Irish coffee, you light the whiskey. ■ When you make Irish coffee, you set fire to the whiskey. Al prepararse el café irlandés se prende el whiskey.

to **ignore someone's advice** hacer caso omiso de los consejos de alguien ■ desoír los consejos de alguien

to **ignore the facts** no tener en cuenta los hechos

I'll be back at *x* o'clock estaré de vuelta a la(s) *x* ➤ I'll be back at one (o'clock). Estaré de vuelta a la una.

I'll be damned! ¡que me ahorquen! ■ ¡que me aspen!

(I'll be) damned if I can understand it que me aspen si lo entiendo ■ que me ahorquen si lo entiendo

(I'll be) damned if I can't que me aspen si no ■ que me ahorquen si no

(I'll be) damned if I know! ¡que me parta un rayo si lo sé! ■ ¡que me muera si lo sé! ■ *(Sp.)* ¡que me aspen si lo sé! ■ ¡que me ahorquen si lo sé!

I'll be glad to ■ I'd be glad to lo haré con gusto ■ lo haré encantado ■ tengo mucho gusto en ello

I'll be home at *x* o'clock estaré en casa a la(s) *x* ➤ I'll be home at one (o'clock). Estaré en casa a la una.

I'll be in touch soon te contactaré pronto

I'll be right back ya vuelvo ■ ya vengo ■ ahora vuelvo ■ espera que ahora vengo

I'll be right down enseguida bajo ■ ya bajo

I'll be right out enseguida salgo ■ ya salgo ■ ahora mismo salgo ■ *(Mex.)* ahorita salgo

I'll be right over ahora voy ■ estoy allí enseguida

I'll be right there ahora voy ■ estaré allí enseguida

I'll be right with you *(tú)* estaré contigo enseguida ■ en un momento estaré contigo ■ *(usted)* estaré con usted enseguida ■ en un momento estaré con usted

I'll be sending you (some) more te iré mandando más ■ te voy a ir mandando ➤ I'll be sending you (some) more photos in the coming days. Te iré mandando más fotos con los días. ■ Te voy a ir mandando más fotos en el correr de los próximos días.

I'll *be* there! ¡allí estaré!

I'll be there in *x* minutes llego en *x* minutos ■ estoy allí en *x* minutos ■ llegaré en *x* minutos ■ estaré allí en *x* minutos

I'll believe it when I see it lo creeré cuando lo vea ■ ¡qué largo me lo fiáis! ■ ¡cuán largo me lo fiáis! ■ ¡tan largo me lo fiáis!

I'll bet you anything (that)... apostaría la cabeza que... ■ te apuesto lo que quieras que... ➤ I'll bet you anything that... ■ I bet you anything that... ■ I'd bet you anything that... Apostaría la cabeza que...

I'll bet you *do*! ¡apuesto a que sí!

I'll *bet* you do! ¡no lo dudo! ■ ¡sin duda!

I'll bet you're glad ■ you must be glad estarás contento

I'll bet you *x* dollars that... te apuesto *x* dólares a que... ■ van *x* dólares a que...

to be **ill bred** ■ to be poorly brought up ser malcriado(-a) ■ ser mal educado(-a)

I'll bring it right back (to you) (te) lo devuelvo enseguida ■ (se) lo devuelvo enseguida

I'll buy you a cup of coffee te invito a tomar un café

I'll call you later *(tú)* te llamo luego ■ te llamo después *(usted, to a man)* lo llamo luego ■ lo llamo después ■ *(usted, leísmo, to a man or woman)* le llamo luego ■ le llamo después ■ *(usted, to a woman)* la llamo luego ■ la llamo después

I'll catch up with her later la alcanzo más tarde ■ la alcanzo después ■ la alcanzo luego

I'll catch up with him later lo alcanzo más tarde ■ lo alcanzo después ■ *(Sp., leísmo)* le alcanzo más tarde ■ le alcanzo después

I'll catch up with you later *(tú)* te alcanzo más tarde ■ te alcanzo después ■ *(usted, to a man)* lo alcanzo (a usted) más tarde ■ lo alcanzo (a usted) después ■ *(usted, to a woman)* la alcanzo (a usted) más tarde ■ la alcanzo después ■ *(Sp., leísmo, to a man or woman)* le alcanzo más tarde

I'll come up with the money somehow conseguiré el dinero de alguna forma

I'll connect you ■ I'll put you through *(tú)* te paso ■ *(usted)* le paso

I'll deal with him later ya hablaré con él ■ hablaré con él más tarde

I'll definitely... ■ for sure con toda seguridad... ➤ Unless something unavoidable comes up, I'll definitely go. ■ Unless something comes up, I'll go for sure. A no ser que me surja algo ineludible en el congreso, iré con toda seguridad.

I'll do it myself lo hago yo mismo(-a) ■ lo haré yo mismo(-a)

I'll do that así lo haré

I'll do the rest haré lo demás ■ hago lo demás

I'll do what I can haré lo que pueda

I'll do what I can to help you haré lo posible por ayudarte ➤ If I can help you with anything, let me know and I'll do what I can to help you. Si puedo ayudarte en algo déjamelo saber y haré lo posible por ayudarte.

I'll drink to that brindo por eso

ill-fated malhadado ■ desafortunado ■ desaventurado

I'll find out (for you) *(tú)* te lo averiguo ■ te lo averiguaré ■ *(usted)* se lo averiguo ■ se lo averiguaré

I'll fix *her*! ¡ya le arreglaré (a ella)! ■ ¡ya le arreglaré las cuentas (a ella)!

I'll fix *him*! ¡ya le arreglaré (a él)! ■ ¡ya le arreglaré las cuentas (a él)!

I'll fix it 1. I'll repair it ya se lo arreglo ■ ya se lo arreglaré 2. I'll prepare it. ya lo preparo ■ lo prepararé ■ la prepararé

I'll fix *you*! *(tú)* ¡ya te arreglaré (las cuentas)! ■ *(usted)* ¡ya le arreglaré (las cuentas)!

I'll fix you some supper que te hago de cenar

I'll get back to you *(tú)* volveré a llamarte ■ *(usted, speaking to a man)* volveré a llamarlo (a usted) ■ *(usted, speaking to a woman)* volveré a llamarla (a usted) ■ *(leísmo, to a man or woman)* volveré a llamarle

I'll get it! *(door or telephone)* ¡voy! ■ ¡yo lo cojo! ■ ¡yo contesto!

I'll get over it se me pasará ■ me recuperaré

I'll get used to it me acostumbraré (a ello)

I'll give it some thought lo voy a pensar ■ *(Mex., colorful)* le echo una pensada

I'll give you an example *(tú)* te pongo un ejemplo ■ *(usted)* le pongo un ejemplo

I'll give you another try *(tú)* te daré otra oportunidad ■ *(usted)* le daré otra oportunidad

I'll give you *one more* try te voy a dar una última oportunidad

I'll give you three guesses te daré tres oportunidades de adivinar

I'll give you three tries te doy tres oportunidades ■ te dejo probar tres veces ■ te dejo que pruebes tres veces

I'll go ahead and... voy a meterme para adelante y... ■ *(with "decirle")* igual ➤ I'll go ahead and tell her. Igual voy a decirle (a ella).

I'll go down and get it bajaré y lo buscaré

I'll go look for him voy a buscarlo ■ *(Sp., leísmo)* voy a buscarle

I'll go see ■ I'll see ■ I'll look (and see) voy a ver

I'll go up and get it subiré y lo buscaré ■ subiré y la buscaré

ill-gotten gain(s) ■ filthy lucre ganancias ilícitas ■ ganancias de dudosa procedencia

I'll handle it (yo) me encargo de esto

I'll have... 1. *(in a bar)* me pones... ■ me pone usted... 2. *(in a restaurant)* quiero... ➤ I'll have a plate of anchovies and a draft beer. Me pones una ración de anchoas y una caña.

I'll have it (ready) for you by Friday *(tú)* te lo tengo preparado para el viernes ■ te la tengo preparado para el viernes *(usted)* se lo tengo preparado para el viernes ■ te la tengo preparado para el viernes

I'll have to admit... ■ I have to admit... ■ *(coll.)* I gotta admit... tengo que admitir... ➤ I'll have to admit that weather-wise, we've got you beat. ■ I gotta admit that weather-wise, we got you beat. Tengo que admitir que en lo que se refiere al tiempo os ganamos.

I'll have to charge you (extra) for it ■ it's extra ■ it's not included in the price *(tú)* te lo tengo que cobrar (aparte) ■ te lo cobro (aparte) ▪ *(usted)* se lo tengo que cobrar (aparte) ▪ se lo cobro (aparte) ▪ no está incluido (en el precio)

I'll have to do it myself tendré que hacerlo yo mismo

I'll have to say... ▪ I'll have to admit... tendré que decir... ▪ tendré que admitir...

I'll have to wait and see habrá que ver

I'll have you know... para tu información... ▪ para que sepas...

I'll keep an eye out (for) ▪ I'll keep my eyes open (for) mantendré los ojos abiertos (por) ▪ *("alerta" is both masculine and feminine)* estaré alerta (por) ▪ estaré al pendiente (de) ▪ *(Sp., coll.)* estaré al loro (por)

I'll keep it in mind ▪ I'll keep that in mind lo tendré presente ▪ lo tendré en mente

I'll keep my eyes open ▪ I'll keep an eye out mantendré los ojos abiertos ▪ *(Sp., coll.)* estaré al loro

I'll keep you posted *(a ti)* te mantendré al tanto ▪ *(a usted, to a man)* lo mantendré al tanto ▪ *(a usted, to a woman)* la mantendré al tanto ▪ *(a usted, leísmo)* le mantendré al tanto

I'll know ▪ I will know ▪ I shall know sabré ➤ I'll know in five minutes if this macro is going to work. Sabré en cinco minutos si va a funcionar este macro.

I'll leave it for you in... *(tú)* te lo dejo en... ▪ *(usted)* se lo dejo en...

I'll leave it for you with... te lo dejo con... ➤ I'll leave it for you with the concierge. Te lo dejo con el conserje. ▪ Te lo dejo con el portero.

I'll leave it to you ▪ it's up to you ▪ I'll let you decide *(tú)* te lo dejo a ti ▪ te lo dejaré a ti ▪ tú estás encargado ▪ *(usted)* se lo dejo a usted ▪ se lo dejaré a usted ▪ usted está encargado

I'll leave it to *you* ▪ you're in charge te dejo al cargo ▪ te quedas al cargo ▪ te quedas encargado

I'll leave it (up) to you to decide ▪ I'll let you decide lo dejo a tu criterio ▪ te dejo decidir

I'll leave you to it *(a ti)* te dejo con lo que estabas ▪ *(a usted)* le dejo con lo que estaba

I'll let it go this time (por) esta vez lo perdono ▪ lo dejaré pasar (por) esta vez ▪ lo dejo pasar (por) esta vez ▪ dejaré la cosa así (por) esta vez ▪ *(L. Am.)* déjalo, así no más

I'll let you go *(as a closing)* te dejo ▪ le dejo (a usted)

I'll let you in te abro

I'll let you know *(tú)* te avisaré ▪ te dejo saber ▪ te hago saber ▪ ya te diré ▪ *(usted)* le avisaré ▪ le dejo saber ▪ le hago saber ▪ ya le diré

I'll let you know ahead of time *(tú)* te aviso con tiempo ▪ te lo haré saber con tiempo ▪ *(usted)* le aviso con tiempo ▪ se lo haré saber con tiempo

I'll let you know if... te avisaré si...

I'll let you know, though pero te lo cuento (en cuanto lo sepa)

I'll look into it voy a ver que encuentro ➤ *Bill Clinton:* It's the first I've heard of it. I'll look into it. Es la primera vez que oigo eso. Voy a ver que encuentro.

I'll make you a deal te propongo un trato

I'll manage somehow ▪ I'll get along somehow ▪ I'll survive somehow me las arreglaré yo sólo

ill-mannered descortés

I'll never do that again no lo volveré a hacer nunca ▪ no lo volveré a hacer en mi vida ▪ nunca volveré a hacer eso ▪ nunca volveré a hacerlo

I'll never (ever) forget that day jamás me olvidaré de aquel día ▪ jamás se me olvidará aquel día ▪ jamás me olvidaré de ese día ▪ jamás se me olvidará ese día

I'll never forget the day (that)... nunca olvidaré el día en que... ▪ nunca se me olvidará el día en que...

I'll never forget the time that... nunca olvidaré aquella vez que... ▪ nunca olvidaré esa vez que...

I'll pass paso ▪ voy a pasar ➤ I think I'll pass, thanks. Creo que voy a pasar, gracias.

I'll pay you back tomorrow te lo devuelvo mañana ▪ te lo devolveré mañana

I'll put you through ▪ I'll connect you *(tú)* te paso ▪ *(usted)* le paso ➤ I'll put you through to their room. *(a ti)* Te paso a su habitación. ▪ *(a usted)* Le paso a su habitación.

I'll ring it up for you *(store clerk)* ▪ I'll ring you up *(tú)* te (lo) cobro ▪ *(usted)* se (lo) cobro

I'll see what I can do ya veré qué puedo hacer

I'll see you nos vemos ▪ nos veremos

I'll see you home *(archaic)* ▪ I'll take you home ▪ I'll walk you home te acompaño a casa

(I'll) see you later hasta luego

(I'll) see you when I get back hasta la vuelta

I'll show you te lo mostraré ➤ Here, I'll show you. Aquí, te lo mostraré.

I'll stick with you through thick and thin ▪ I'll stick by you through thick and thin contigo, pan y cebolla

I'll suggest it to her se lo sugeriré (a ella)

I'll suggest it to him se lo sugeriré (a él)

I'll take care of it (yo) me ocuparé de ello ▪ yo me ocupo

I'll take it 1. *(an apartment)* me lo quedo **2.** *(merchandise from a store)* me lo llevo

I'll take this one me llevo esto ▪ me quedo con esto *(or "éste, ésta")*

I'll take you home *(tú)* te llevo a casa ▪ *(usted, to a man)* lo llevo a usted a casa ▪ *(usted, to a man or woman)* le llevo a casa ▪ *(usted, to a woman)* la llevo a usted a casa

I'll take your word for it *(tú)* te tomo la palabra ▪ *(usted)* le tomo la palabra

I'll tell her you called *(tú)* le diré que has llamado ▪ *(usted)* le diré que usted ha llamado

I'll tell him you called *(tú)* le diré que has llamado ▪ *(usted)* le diré que usted ha llamado

I'll tell you a secret te confiaré un secreto

I'll tell you one thing ▪ I'll say one thing *(tú)* una cosa sí te diré ▪ una cosa sí te digo ▪ *(usted)* una cosa sí le diré ▪ una cosa sí le digo ➤ I'll tell you one thing I don't like about this new refrigerator, it's already starting to ice up. Una cosa sí te diré que no me gusta de la nevera, que ya está empezando a hacer escarcha.

(I'll) tell you what... *(tú)* te diré lo que haremos ▪ *(usted)* le diré lo que haremos

I'll think it over ▪ I'm going to think about it lo pensaré (bien) ▪ lo voy a pensar (bien)

I'll trade you te lo cambio

ill-trained ▪ poorly trained ▪ inadequately trained mal entrenado ▪ vagamente entrenado ▪ inadecuadamente entrenado

I'll try again later, thanks llamaré más tarde, gracias ▪ luego llamo, gracias

I'll wait outside espero fuera

illegal possession of weapons ▪ illegal weapons possession tenencia ilícita de armas

illustrated text texto con ilustraciones ➤ In the art course, we need an illustrated text. En la asignatura de arte, necesitamos un libro de texto con ilustraciones.

illustrious group of ▪ illustrious collection of ▪ star-studded group of ▪ star-studded collection of *la* pléyade de

I'm a fan of yours *(tú)* soy un(-a) admirador(-a) tuyo(-a) ▪ *(usted)* soy un(-a) admirador(-a) suyo(-a)

I'm a little concerned estoy algo preocupado(-a)

I'm a little concerned about... estoy algo preocupado(-a) por...

I'm a little concerned about it estoy un poco preocupado(-a) al respecto

I'm a little concerned that... estoy algo preocupado(-a) de que... ▪ me preocupa algo que...

I'm a stranger here myself 1. *(literal)* yo mismo soy extranjero aquí ▪ yo tampoco soy de aquí **2.** *(figurative)* I don't know myself yo también soy sapo de otro pozo

I'm afraid me temo ➤ It's just the TV repairman, I'm afraid. Es sólo el técnico de la tele, me temo.

I'm afraid not me temo que no

I'm afraid so me temo que sí

I'm after her ▪ I'm behind her ▪ I'm next (after her) soy el (*o* la) siguiente después de ella ▪ estoy detrás de ella ▪ estoy atrás de ella ▪ soy el (*o* la) siguiente a ella

I'm all for it estoy completamente a favor

I'm almost done (with it) ▪ I'm almost finished (with it) ▪ I'm almost through (with it) estoy a punto de terminar ▪ estoy a punto de acabar ▪ estoy por terminar ▪ estoy por acabar ▪ ya casi termino

I'm almost finished ▪ I'm almost done ▪ I'm almost through ya casi termino ▪ estoy a tiro de acabar ▪ ya casi he acabado con ello

I'm almost through (with it) ▪ I'm almost finished (with it) ▪ I'm almost done with it estoy a tiro de acabar ▪ *(with a masculine antecedent)* ya casi he acabado con eso ▪ *(with a feminine antecedent)* ya casi he acabado con esa ➤ Are you through with the newspaper?-Well, I'm almost through with it. ¿Has acabado ya con el periódico?-Sí, casi he acabado de leerlo. ➤ Are you through with the entertainment section?-Well, I'm almost through with it. ¿Has acabado ya con la cartelera?-¿Sí, casi he acabado de revisarla.

I'm always amazed at how... siempre me asombra cómo...

I'm always amazed at the way... siempre me asombra la forma en que...

I'm always amazed that... siempre me asombro de que...

I'm always ready to... estoy siempre listo para... ▪ estoy siempre dispuesto para... ▪ estoy siempre dispuesto a...

I'm always vigilant about estoy siempre atento(-a) de ➤ I'm always vigilant about my wallet in crowded places. Estoy siempre atento de mi cartera en los sitios muy concurridos.

I'm anxious to see you tengo ansias de verte ▪ estoy ansioso por verte

I'm as well as I can be (under the circumstances) estoy todo lo bien que puedo estar (teniendo en cuenta las circunstancias)

I'm asking you please to... ▪ I'm asking you to please... te estoy pidiendo por favor que... ▪ te estoy pidiendo que por favor...

I'm awfully sorry cuánto lo siento ▪ lo lamento

I'm bad at remembering names soy muy malo(-a) para recordar nombres

I'm baffled by it ▪ it baffles me no lo logro entender ▪ no me lo explico ▪ me desconcierta

I'm beat ▪ I'm pooped ▪ I'm whipped ▪ I'm bushed ▪ I'm knackered estoy hecho migas ▪ estoy hecho polvo ▪ estoy agotado ▪ estoy que no puedo con mi alma ▪ estoy para el arrastre

I'm beginning not to like está empezando a no gustarme ➤ I'm beginning not to like the way he relies on me instead of fending for himself. Está empezando a no gustarme la forma en que él se apoya en mí en vez de defenderse por sí mismo.

I'm beginning to believe you ▪ I'm starting to believe you te empiezo a creer

I'm beginning to feel better ▪ I'm starting to feel better voy sintiéndome mejor ▪ estoy empezando a sentirme mejor

I'm behind her (in line) ▪ I'm right behind her in line estoy detrás de ella (en la cola) ▪ estoy después de ella (en la cola) ▪ estoy justo detrás de ella (en la cola)

I'm being helped, thank you me atiende, gracias ▪ me atienden, gracias

I'm betting on you apuesto por ti

I'm burning up me aso ▪ me ardo

I'm bushed ▪ I'm pooped ▪ I'm whipped ▪ I'm beat ▪ I'm knackered estoy hecho migas ▪ estoy hecho polvo ▪ estoy agotado ▪ estoy que no puedo con mi alma ▪ estoy para el arrastre

I'm positive ▪ I'm certain (of it) ▪ I'm sure (of it) estoy bien seguro

I'm bound to say *(rare)* ▪ I must say he de decir ▪ debo decir ▪ me siento obligado a decir

I'm calling about the ad llamo por el anuncio ➤ I'm calling about the ad in the paper for an apartment. ▪ I'm calling in response to the ad in the paper for an apartment. Llamo por el anuncio del piso en el periódico. *("Departamento" and "apartamento" also mean apartment.)*

I'm cold tengo frío

I'm coming down with a cold ▪ I'm getting a cold ▪ I'm catching a cold ▪ I'm starting to get a cold me estoy resfriando ▪ me está rondando un resfriado

I'm coming to that ▪ I'm getting to that a eso voy

I'm confused about... estoy confundido por... ▪ estoy confuso por... ▪ me he hecho un lío con... ▪ estoy liado con...

I'm confused by... estoy confundido por... ➤ I'm confused by the maze of road signs just before that interchange. Estoy confundido por esa multitud de señales de tráfico justo antes del paso a desnivel.

I'm counting on you cuento contigo

I'm delighted that... celebro que... ➤ I'm delighted that it helps you. ▪ I'm delighted that it's helpful to you. Celebro que te sea de ayuda.

I'm delighted to meet you ▪ (I'm) pleased to meet you ▪ it's good to meet you ▪ it's nice to meet you **1.** *(tú)* encantado(-a) de conocerte **2.** *(usted, to a man)* encantado de conocerlo ▪ *(usted, to a woman)* encantado de conocerla ▪ *(Sp., usted, to a man, leísmo)* encantado de conocerle

I'm done for ▪ I've had it estoy apañado

I'm down to the wire se me viene el tiempo encima ▪ tengo el tiempo pegado (al culo)

I'm early he llegado pronto ▪ he llegado temprano

I'm expecting a call estoy pendiende de una llamada

I'm fading fast me estoy cayendo de sueño

I'm finished **1.** I'm done ▪ I'm through he terminado ▪ he acabado **2.** I'm done for ▪ I've had it ▪ I'm through estoy acabado

I'm for... estoy a favor de... ➤ I'm for the moderates. Estoy a favor de los moderados.

I'm for it estoy a favor

I'm full estoy satisfecho ▪ estoy lleno ▪ me he puesto las botas *(In some social settings in both English- and Spanish-speaking countries, it is impolite to say "I'm full" or "estoy lleno(-a)." It is better to say, "No thank you, I don't care for any more": "No gracias, estoy satisfecho(-a)" or "No me apetece más, gracias.")*

I'm getting ahead of myself me estoy adelantando ▪ me estoy adelantando a los acontecimientos

I'm getting ahead of you me estoy adelantando a ti

I'm getting the hang of it voy cogiendo el truco ▪ voy cogiendo el truquillo ▪ voy agarrando el tino

I'm getting the picture! ¡ya lo estoy visualizando!

I'm getting to that ▪ I'm coming to that a eso voy

I'm glad... ▪ I'm glad that... me alegro de que... ▪ me alegra que... ➤ I'm glad you've come. Me alegro de que hayas venido. ▪ Me alegra que hayas venido.

I'm glad I waited me alegra haber esperado

I'm glad of that me alegro de ello

I'm glad (that)... ▪ I'm happy that... me alegro de que... ▪ me alegra que...

I'm glad you asked me alegro de que me preguntaras ▪ me alegra que me preguntaras

I'm glad you asked me that question me alegro de que me hicieras esa pregunta ▪ me alegra que me hicieras esa pregunta

I'm glad you called me alegro de que me llamaras ▪ me alegra que me llamaras

I'm going for the holidays voy para las fiestas

I'm going for Christmas voy en Navidad ▪ voy para las Navidades

I'm going home **1.** *(volunteering the information)* me voy a casa **2.** *(answering the question "where are you going?")* voy a casa **3.** *(implying that the questioner is unfamiliar with your house)* voy a mi casa

I'm going out voy a salir

I'm going to bed (ya) me voy a la cama ▪ me voy a dormir ▪ me voy a acostar

I'm going to give him a piece of my mind ¡me va a oír!

I'm going to miss you voy a echarte de menos ▪ voy a extrañarte

I'm going to pass **1.** I'm going to decline voy a pasar ▪ paso **2.** I'm going to make a passing grade voy a aprobar

I'm going to think about it ▪ I'm going to give it some thought ▪ I'm going to think it over ▪ I'll think it over ▪ I'll think about it ▪ I'll give it some thought me lo voy a pensar

I'm hanging in there voy tirando

I'm happy for you me alegro por ti

I'm happy to be here me alegro de estar aquí ▪ me alegra estar aquí ➤ *(Comedienne Minnie Pearl)* I'm just so happy to be here. Me alegro tanto de estar aquí. ▪ Me alegra tanto estar aquí.
I'm having a party doy una fiesta
I'm having my students for a buffet supper doy un "bufet" (por la noche) para mis estudiantes
I'm having quite a day (of it)! ¡qué día tengo!
I'm having second thoughts me lo estoy pensando dos veces ▪ me lo estoy pensando más detenidamente
I'm here to get my vision checked ▪ I'm here to get (some) glasses he venido a que me revisen la vista ▪ *(Sp.)* vengo a graduarme (la vista)
I'm here to tell you te lo digo yo que lo conozco ▪ te lo digo de primerísima mano ▪ te lo digo porque lo sé ➤ I'm here to tell you that those traffic circles in Washington really throw you for a loop! Te lo digo yo que lo conozco, las rotondas de Washington te dejan de lo más anonadado.
I'm here when you need me estoy aquí cuándo me necesites
I'm home! ¡ya estoy aquí! ▪ ¡estoy en casa!
I'm hungry as a bear tengo más hambre que el perro de un ciego ▪ estoy tan hambriento(-a) que devoraría un elefante
I'm in charge of... me encargo de...
I'm in no mood for... no estoy de humor para... ▪ no estoy de ánimo para...
I'm in the process ▪ I'm working on it estoy en ello
I'm just a... ▪ I'm only a... no soy más que...
I'm just doing what I was told to do ▪ I'm just doing what I was told sólo soy un mandado
I'm just giving you a bad time sólo te estoy dando malos tiempos ▪ sólo te hago pasar un mal rato
I'm just kidding te bromeo
I'm just looking, thanks sólo estoy mirando, gracias ▪ sólo estaba mirando, gracias
I'm just not ready for that yet aún no estoy preparado para eso
I'm just pulling your leg ▪ I'm just teasing (you) te estoy vacilando
I'm just teasing (you) ▪ I'm just kidding ▪ I'm just pulling your leg te estoy vacilando
I'm just waiting to see if sólo estoy esperando a ver si
I'm late ▪ I'm running behind schedule voy tarde ▪ voy con retraso
I'm late (arriving) llego tarde
I'm learning as I go estoy aprendiendo sobre la marcha
I'm like everyone else soy como todo el mundo
I'm listening! *(tú)* te escucho ▪ ¡dime! ▪ *(usted)* le escucho ▪ ¡dígame!
I'm looking forward to it me hace (mucha) ilusión
I'm looking forward to seeing you (again) estoy deseando verte (de nuevo) ▪ tengo ganas de verte (de nuevo) ▪ estoy deseando verte (otra vez) ▪ tengo ganas de verte (otra vez) ▪ deseo verte otra vez
I'm losing patience ▪ I'm running out of patience estoy perdiendo la paciencia
I'm majoring in me estoy especializando en ▪ me especializo en
I'm missing the match to this sock me falta el par de este calcetín ▪ no encuentro la pareja de este calcetín
I'm next (in line) soy el próximo (en la fila) ▪ soy el próximo (en la cola)
I'm not afraid no me doy miedo ▪ no tengo miedo ▪ no (lo) temo
I'm not ashamed to admit it no me avergüenzo de admitirlo ▪ no me avergüenza admitirlo
I'm not ashamed to admit that... no me avergüenzo de admitir que... ▪ no me avergüenza admitir que... ▪ no me siento avergonzado de admitir que... ▪ *(C.J. Cela)* no se me rasgan las vestiduras al reconocer que...
I'm not at liberty no estoy autorizado ➤ I'm not at liberty to tell you. No estoy autorizado a decirte.
I'm not bad at it no se me da mal
I'm not done ▪ I'm not through ▪ I'm not finished ▪ I haven't finished no he terminado
I'm not dressed no estoy vestido
I'm not finished ▪ I'm not through ▪ I haven't finished ▪ I'm not done no he terminado
I'm not getting anywhere (with this) así no voy a llegar a ninguna parte
I'm not going! ▪ I won't go! ¡no iré!
I'm not going anywhere no voy a ningún lado
I'm not going to lose any sleep over it no me quita el sueño
I'm not going to worry about it, then ▪ then I'm not going to worry about it no me voy a preocupar por eso entonces ▪ entonces no me voy a preocupar por eso
I'm not hungry no tengo hambre
I'm not in any hurry ▪ there's no hurry no tengo prisa ▪ no hay prisa
I'm not into that no me va eso ▪ paso de eso
I'm not just saying that no lo digo por decir(lo) ▪ lo digo sinceramente ▪ no lo digo sólo para echarte flores
I'm not keeping score 1. no llevo el tanteo ▪ no llevo el marcador **2.** *(figurative)* no llevo la cuenta ➤ Frank is keeping score. Paco lleva el tanteo. ➤ I don't know whose turn it is to treat. I'm not keeping score. No sé a quien le toca pagar. No llevo la cuenta.
I'm not offended no me ofendo
I'm not one of those (people) who... no soy de los que...
I'm one of those (people) who... soy de los que...
I'm not positive ▪ I'm not absolutely sure no estoy seguro ▪ no podría decirlo con total seguridad
I'm not ready for that yet no estoy listo para eso aún
I'm not real sure no lo tengo muy claro
I'm not saying it's no estoy diciendo que no (lo) es
I'm not so sure no estoy tan seguro(-a)
I'm not sure no estoy seguro(-a) ▪ lo estoy dudando ▪ me he quedado dudando
I'm not sure if no estoy seguro(-a) si
I'm not sure what I think about it ▪ I'm not sure what to think about it no estoy seguro(-a) de lo que pienso al respecto
I'm not sure what to make of it ▪ I'm not sure quite what to make of it no sé cómo explicármelo ▪ no sé cómo tomármelo
I'm not sure whether... (or not) no sé si... ➤ I'm not sure whether to take the umbrella (or not). No sé si coger el paraguas (o no).
I'm not sure whether or not no sé si... o no... ➤ I'm not sure whether or not to take an umbrella. No sé si coger el paraguas o no (cogerlo). ▪ No sé si coger o no el paraguas.
I'm not talking about anyone specifically ▪ I'm not talking about any one person no hablo de nadie en concreto
I'm not the one to judge no soy quien para juzgar(lo) ▪ no me cabe a mí juzgar
I'm not up to it no doy de sí ▪ no tengo fuerzas
I'm not very hungry no tengo mucha hambre ▪ tengo poca hambre
I'm not wild about... no me entusiasma... ▪ no me apasiona mucho... ▪ no me enloquece mucho... ▪ no me vuelve loco(-a)... ➤ I'm not wild about Italian food. I prefer Spanish, Mexican... and Peruvian cuisine. No me entusiasma la comida italiana. Prefiero la cocina española, mexicana y peruana. ➤ What do you think of the color?-I'm not wild about it. ¿Qué te parece el color?-No me apasiona mucho.
I'm of two minds about that tengo ideas contrarias al respecto
I'm off! ▪ I'm on my way! ¡me voy! ▪ ¡me marcho! ▪ ¡estoy saliendo! ▪ *(L. Am.)* ¡voy de salida!
I'm okay with it me parece bien ▪ no me parece mal
I'm old enough to be your father (yo) podría ser tu padre
I'm on my way! ▪ I'm off! ¡me voy!
I'm on my way home voy para casa
I'm on my way to... voy para... ▪ estoy en camino a...
I'm on the phone ▪ I'm on the telephone ▪ *(rare)* I'm on the horn hablo por teléfono
I'm on your side estoy de tu parte
I'm one of those (people) who... soy de los que...
I'm out of time se me agota el tiempo ▪ se me acaba el tiempo

(I'm) pleased to meet you ▪ (I'm) delighted to meet you ▪ it's good to meet you ▪ it's nice to meet you **1.** *(tú)* encantado(-a) de conocerte **2.** *(usted, to a man)* encantado de conocerlo ▪ *(usted, to a woman)* encantado de conocerla ▪ *(Sp., usted, to a man, leísmo)* encantado de conocerle

I'm pooped ▪ I'm beat ▪ I'm whipped ▪ I'm bushed estoy hecho migas ▪ estoy hecho polvo ▪ estoy agotado ▪ estoy que no puedo con mi alma ▪ estoy para el arrastre

I'm positive ▪ I'm absolutely certain ▪ I'm absolutely sure estoy completamente seguro

I'm prejudiced soy parcial ▪ soy juez y parte ▪ no puedo ser objetivo(-a) ▪ no puedo tener objetividad ▪ no tengo objetividad ➤ She's the most beautiful baby I've ever seen, but I'm prejudiced because she's my granddaughter. Es la bebé más guapa que jamás he visto, pero soy parcial porque es mi nieta.

I'm puzzled by... me desconcierta... ▪ estoy desconcertado(-a)...

I'm rarin' to go estoy pletórico(-a)

I'm really excited about... me da mucha ilusión... ▪ me hace mucha ilusión... ▪ estoy muy ilusionado(-a) por... ➤ I'm really excited about it. Estoy muy ilusionado(-a).

I'm really getting to like you me estás gustando

I'm really impressed by ▪ I'm really impressed at realmente me impresiona ➤ I'm really impressed by how good your Spanish is. ▪ I'm really impressed at how good your Spanish is. Realmente me impresiona lo bueno que es tu español.

I'm really looking forward to... esperar... con ansiedad ▪ estoy ansioso(-a) por... ▪ me da mucha ilusión... ▪ me hace mucha ilusión... ➤ I'm really looking forward to your party. Espero tu fiesta con ansiedad. ➤ I'm really looking forward to it. La espero con ansiedad.

I'm running around in circles llevo todo el día de arriba abajo ▪ llevo todo el día de acá para allá ▪ llevo todo el día de un sitio para otro

I'm running behind schedule ▪ I'm running late voy retrasado ▪ voy atrasado

I'm running late ▪ I'm running behind schedule voy retrasado ▪ voy atrasado

I'm running out of patience ▪ I'm losing patience estoy perdiendo la paciencia

I'm running out of time se me agota el tiempo ▪ me queda poco tiempo

I'm sick about it estoy disgustado por eso ▪ estoy dolido por eso ▪ estoy hundido por eso

I'm so glad... cuánto me alegro de...

I'm so glad to see you! ¡cuánto me alegro de verte! ▪ ¡cómo me alegro de verte!

I'm so glad you asked me alegro tanto de que preguntaras ▪ me alegra tanto que preguntaras

I'm so glad you asked me that question me alegro tanto de que me hicieras esa pregunta ▪ me alegra tanto que me hicieras esa pregunta

I'm sorry 1. *(apology)* lo siento (mucho) **2.** *(expression of sympathy)* I'm awfully sorry lo lamento

I'm sorry about... 1. *(apology)* siento mucho lo de... **2.** *(expression of sympathy)* siento lo de... ▪ lamento lo de... ➤ I'm sorry about yesterday. Siento mucho lo de ayer. ➤ I'm sorry about your father. Siento mucho lo de tu padre.

I'm sorry I can't help you *(tú)* siento no poder ayudarte ▪ *(usted, to a man)* siento no poder ayudarlo ▪ *(usted, to a woman)* siento no poder ayudarla (a usted) ▪ *(Sp., leísmo, to a man or woman)* siento no poder ayudarle

I'm sorry I missed you siento que no coincidiéramos ▪ siento que no nos viéramos

I'm sorry I'm late siento llegar tarde ▪ siento haber llegado tarde

I'm sorry to hear that siento oír eso ▪ lamento saberlo

I'm sorry to keep you waiting siento haberte hecho esperar

I'm starting to believe you ▪ I'm beginning to believe you te empiezo a creer

I'm starting to feel better ▪ I'm beginning to feel better voy sintiéndome mejor ▪ voy aliviándome

I'm starting to feel like a new person empiezo a ser persona ➤ Now that I've had my morning coffee, I'm starting to feel like a new person. Ahora que me he tomado mi primer café, empiezo a ser persona.

I'm still hungry aún tengo hambre ▪ todavía tengo hambre ▪ me quedo con hambre

I'm still in... Todavía estoy en... ➤ I'm still in Texas for one more week. Todavía estoy en Texas por una semana más.

I'm supposed to meet someone estoy supuesto a reunirme con alguien ➤ I'm supposed to meet someone here at nine o'clock. Estoy supuesto a reunirme aquí con alguien a las nueve de la mañana.

I'm sure it can be arranged estoy seguro(-a) de que se puede arreglar ▪ estoy seguro(-a) de que puede arreglarse

I'm sure (that)... estoy seguro(-a) de que... ▪ me consta que...

I'm surprised at me sorprende que ▪ me sorprende de ➤ I'm surprised at you for not showing up when you were supposed to. Me sorprende que no te hayas presentado cuando debías hacerlo.

I'm surprised at you *(mainly negative)* ▪ you surprise me *(tú)* me disilusionas ▪ me sorprendes ▪ *(usted)* (usted) me disilusiona ▪ me sorprende usted

I'm surprised by... me sorprende... ➤ I'm surprised by how fast the surface mail packages came. Me sorprende lo rápido que llegaron los paquetes enviados vía marítima.

I'm surprised that... me sorprende que... ▪ me quedo sorprendido que...

I'm surprised to... estoy sorprendido de... ➤ I'm surprised to see him here, especially since he wasn't invited. ▪ *(more colorful)* I'm surprised to see him here, being as he wasn't invited. ▪ I'm surprised to see him here, seeing as how he wasn't invited. Estoy sorprendido de verlo aquí, ya que no fue invitado.

I'm swamped (with work) estoy completamente saturado(-a) (de trabajo)

I'm telling you! ¡te lo digo yo!

I'm telling you, it's true! ¡como lo oyes!

I'm telling you wrong ▪ that's not right miento

I'm the only one who likes it sólo me gusta a mí ➤ I almost never make kidney stew because I'm the only one who likes it. Yo no hago casi nunca estofado de riñones porque sólo me gusta a mí.

I'm through 1. I'm finished ▪ I've finished ▪ I'm done terminé ▪ acabé **2.** I've had it ▪ I'm done for ▪ I'm finished estoy apañado

I'm through! ▪ I've had it! ¡ya vale! ▪ ¡basta! ▪ ¡se acabó!

I'm tied up estoy liado

I'm to be he de ser ➤ I'm to be the master of ceremonies tomorrow. He de ser el maestro de ceremonia(s) mañana.

I'm too busy to think about it estoy demasiado ocupado para pensarlo

I'm too old for that ya soy mayorcito para eso

I'm trusting you *(tú)* confío en ti ▪ *(usted)* confío en usted

I'm waiting for a call estoy esperando una llamada

I'm whipped ▪ I'm pooped ▪ I'm bushed ▪ I'm beat estoy hecho migas ▪ estoy hecho polvo ▪ estoy agotado ▪ estoy que no puedo con mi alma ▪ estoy para el arrastre

I'm willing to give it a try estoy dispuesto a intentarlo ▪ estoy dispuesto a probar

I'm working on it ▪ I'm in the process estoy en ello

I'm worried about... estoy preocupado(-a) por... ▪ me preocupa...

imaginary number *(mathematics)* número imaginario

imagine that! *(tú)* ¡date cuenta! ▪ ¡imagínate! ▪ *(usted)* ¡dése cuenta! ▪ ¡imagínese!

to **imagine that...** imaginarse que... ▪ figurarse que... ➤ Imagine that you're walking along... *(tú)* Figúrate que caminas por... ▪ *(usted)* Figúrese que camina por... ▪ *(ustedes)* Figúrense que caminan por... ▪ *(Sp., vosotros)* Figuráos que camináis por...

to **imagine what something is like** hacerse una idea de algo

Immaculate Conception Inmaculada Concepción

immaculate suit traje inmaculado ▪ traje intachable

immediate family familia más cercana ▪ los familiares más cercanos

immediate future futuro inmediato

immediate objective ▪ immediate goal objetivo inmediato

immediately afterwards inmediatamente después ▪ acto seguido ▪ acto continuo
immediately following inmediatos a ➤ *(news item)* The days immediately following the arrest were also filled with surprises. Los días inmediatos a la detención también están llenos de sorpresas. *(Spanish sometimes employs the present tense in past narrative.)*
to **immerse oneself in a pursuit** meterse de lleno en una actividad ▪ sumergirse en una actividad
imminent decision decisión inminente ▪ decisión que está al llegar ▪ decisión que está al caer ➤ The decision is imminent. La decisión está al llegar.
impact on impacto en
to **impart a flavor to** ▪ to give a flavor to dar un sabor a ➤ The oak barrel imparts a flavor to the wine. La barrica de roble da un sabor al vino.
to be **impatient for something** estar impaciente por algo
to be **impatient to do something** estar impaciente por hacer algo
impeachment procedure against procedimiento de destitución de
impediment to impedimento para
impenetrable barrier barrera impenetrable ▪ barrera infranqueable
to **implicate oneself in a crime** implicarse en un crimen ▪ autoinculparse en un crimen ▪ imputarse en un crimen
to be **implicated in a crime** estar implicado en un crimen ▪ estar implicado en un delito
important decision *la* decisión importante ▪ decisión transcendental
to be an **important figure** ser una figura importante ▪ ser una gran figura
important study ▪ major study estudio importante ▪ estudio de gran repercusión
the **important thing** lo importante ▪ el caso ➤ The important thing is that he not delay. Lo importante es que no demore. ▪ El caso es que no demore.
to **impose a curfew** **1.** *(parental restriction)* dar permiso hasta (cierta hora) ▪ **2.** *(imposed by civil or military authority)* imponer un estado de excepción ▪ imponer un toque de queda ▪ imponer un estado extraordinario
to **impose a sentence** dictar una sentencia ▪ imponer una sentencia ▪ emitir una sentencia
to **impose limits on** ▪ to impose restrictions on ▪ to curtail cercenar
to **impose restrictions on** ▪ to impose limits on ▪ to curtail imponer restricciones a ▪ cercenar
to **impose sanctions** aplicar sanciones
to be **impossible (to deal with)** ser intratable ➤ You're impossible! ¡Eres intratable!
to be **impossible to please** ser imposible de complacer ▪ ser imposible de contentar ▪ ser de mal contento
the **impression it made (on me)** la impresión que (me) produjo
to **improve one's Spanish** perfeccionar su español
improvement mejora ▪ perfeccionamiento
improvement over last year's profits ▪ increase over last year's profits incremento sobre los beneficios del año pasado ▪ mejora sobre los beneficios del año pasado
to be **improving something** ir mejorando algo
to be **in a bad mood** ▪ to be in a bad humor estar de mal humor ▪ estar de malas ▪ tener un humor de perros
in a better position than en mejor situación que
to be **in a bind** estar en un apuro
in a bind: to get ~ meterse en un apuro
in a broader sense ▪ in a larger sense en un sentido más amplio
to be **in a class** estar en una clase ▪ ir a una clase ➤ Are you in that class? ¿Estás en esa clase? ▪ ¿Vas a esa clase?
to be **in a class by itself** ▪ to be in a class all by itself ser una clase aparte
to be **in a coma** estar en coma
to be **in a daze** ▪ to be dazed quedar atontolinado
in a desperate attempt to en un intento desesperado por
in a difficult position en un compromiso ➤ You've put me in a difficult position. Me has puesto en un compromiso.
to be **in a family way** *(coll.)* ▪ to be pregnant ▪ to be expecting estar encinta ▪ estar embarazada ▪ *(much less common)* estar grávida
in a few cases en unos pocos casos
in a few minutes en (unos) pocos minutos
to be **in a fix** ▪ to be in a jam ▪ to be in a pickle estar en un atolladero ▪ estar en un aprieto
in a flash en menos que canta un gallo
in a gesture of goodwill ▪ in a goodwill gesture en un gesto de buena voluntad ▪ en un gesto de mano tendida ➤ *(news item)* In a goodwill gesture, the king of Morocco announced yesterday that... En un gesto de mano tendida, el rey de Marruecos anunció ayer que...
in a given situation en una situación determinada
to be **in a good humor** ▪ to be in a good mood estar de buen humor
in a good light: to be seen ~ **1.** *(literal)* to be seen with good light ser visto con buena luz **2.** *(figurative)* to be seen in a favorable light ser bien visto ▪ bajo un prisma favorable
to be **in a good mood** estar de buen humor ▪ estar de buen talante ▪ tener buen humor
to be **in a good position to do something** estar en una buena posición para hacer algo ▪ estar en una posición privilegiada para hacer algo
to be **in a holding pattern** **1.** *(aviation)* estar a la espera de pista para poder aterrizar **2.** *(figurative)* estar en compás de espera
to be **in a hopeless situation** estar en una situación desesperada ▪ no tener para remedio
in a humorous vein en sentido humorístico
to be **in a hurry** tener prisa ▪ estar con prisa ▪ andar con prisa
in a hurry: to leave ~ marcharse con prisas ▪ marcharse corriendo ➤ He left in a hurry. Se marchó con prisas. ▪ Se marchó corriendo.
to be **in a hurry to do something** tener prisa por hacer algo ▪ tener apuro por hacer algo
to be **in a jam** ▪ to be in a fix ▪ to be in a pickle estar en un aprieto ▪ estar en un atolladero
in a jam: to get ~ ▪ to get (oneself) into a jam ▪ to get (oneself) into a pickle meterse en un aprieto ▪ meterse en un lío ▪ meterse en un berenjenal ➤ Newspapers can get in a pickle by offending an important advertiser. Los periódicos se pueden meter en un prieto si ofenden a un anunciante importante. ▪ Los periódicos se pueden meter en un lío si ofenden a un anunciante importante.
in a jiffy ▪ in no time en menos que canta un gallo ▪ en un santiamén ▪ en un periquete ▪ en un pispás ▪ volando ▪ en dos patadas ▪ en dos zancadas ▪ en un quitarme las pajas ➤ The secretary processed all the mail in a jiffy. La secretaria acabó con la correspondencia en menos que canta un gallo. ▪ La secretaria acabó con la correspondencia en un santiamén. ▪ La secretaria acabó con la correspondencia en un periquete.
in a larger sense ▪ in a broader sense en un sentido más amplio
in a light vein en un tono ligero
in a long time en mucho tiempo
in a low voice ▪ in a subdued voice ▪ in a soft voice ▪ softly por lo bajo ▪ a media voz
in a lump sum en un solo pago
in a matter of days en cuestión de días
in a matter of hours en cuestión de horas
in a matter of minutes en cuestión de minutos
to be **in a meeting** estar en una reunión ▪ estar reunido ➤ She's in a meeting. (Ella) está en una reunión. ▪ Está reunida.
to be **in a mess** tener algo desordenado ▪ tener algo liado ▪ *(papers)* tener todo traspapelado ➤ All my papers are in a mess. Tengo todo traspapelado.
in a month **1.** within a month ▪ in the next thirty days dentro de un mes **2.** a month from now en un mes ➤ We can finish it in a month. Podemos terminarlo dentro de un mes. ➤ We can start it in a month. Podemos empezarlo en un mes.
in a month's time *(redundant)* ▪ in a month en un mes

to be **in a movie** estar en una película ➤ Tom Hanks and Meg Ryan are in the movie. Tom Hanks y Meg Ryan están en la película.

in a nutshell muy resumido ▪ en pocas palabras ➤ Here's what it is in a nutshell... Por ponerlo en pocas palabras...

to be **in a pickle** ▪ to be in a jam estar (metido) en un berenjenal ▪ estar (metido) en un lío ▪ estar (metido) en un aprieto ▪ estar (metido) en aprietos ▪ estar (metido) en un embrollo

in a pickle: to get oneself ~ ▪ to get oneself into a (real) pickle ▪ to get oneself into a (real) mess ▪ to get oneself into a (big) mess meterse en un berenjenal ▪ meterse en un lío ▪ meterse en un aprieto ▪ meterse en aprietos ▪ meterse en un embrollo

in a pinch: it will do ~ en un apuro servirá

to be **in a position to...** estar en posición de... ➤ I'm not in a position to comment. No estoy en posición de comentar. ▪ No estoy en una posición de hacer comentarios.

to be **in a position to do something about it** estar en posición de hacer algo al respecto

to be **in a position to know** estar en posición de saber ➤ How is he in a position to know? ¿Cómo es que está en posición de saber(lo)? ➤ By virtue of his being a pharmacist, he's in a position to know the rules of shipping medicines. En virtud de ser farmacéutico, está en posición de saber la legislación para embarcar medicinas.

in a precarious position en una situación precaria

to be **in a quandary over whether to...** ▪ to be in a quandary about whether to... estar sin saber qué hacer con respecto a... ▪ estar en un dilema sobre si...

in a remarkably short time en un tiempo notablemente corto

in a roundabout way dando rodeos ▪ con rodeos ▪ de una manera (muy) indirecta

in a row: to plant seeds ~ plantar semillas en una fila ➤ Lucy planted her brussels sprouts in a neatly marked row. Lucy plantó sus coles de bruselas en una fila marcada con precisión.

in a row: to win *x* games ~ ganar *x* partidos seguidos ▪ ganar *x* partidos al hilo ➤ The Argentine team River Plate won three games in row. El River Plate argentino ganó tres partidos seguidos. ▪ El River Plate argentino ganó tres partidos al hilo.

to be **in a rut** estar metido en una rutina ▪ estar en una dinámica

in a sense en cierto sentido

in a serious vein en un tono serio ▪ de forma seria ▪ de manera seria ➤ But in a (more) serious vein... Pero en un tono (más) serio... ▪ Pero de forma (más) seria... ▪ Pero de manera (más) seria... ▪ Pero de modo (más) serio...

in a single day en un solo día

in a situation in which ▪ in a situation where en una situación en la que

in a soft voice ▪ in a low voice ▪ softly por lo bajo ▪ a media voz

to be **in a state of chaos** ▪ to be in a chaotic state ▪ to be topsy-turvy estar en un estado de caos ▪ estar manga por hombro ▪ andar manga por hombro

to be **in a state of shock over...** ▪ to be in a state of shock from... estar en estado de conmoción por...

to be **in a stew** sudar la gota gorda

in a straight line en línea recta ▪ a cordel

in a subdued voice ▪ in a low voice ▪ in a soft voice ▪ softly a media voz ▪ por lo bajo

in a tight place en una situación difícil

in a tight spot estar en un apuro ▪ *(colorful)* estar con la soga al cuello ▪ estar con el agua al cuello

in a twinkling en un santiamén ▪ en un abrir y cerrar de los ojos

in a vacuum en el vacío ➤ In a vacuum the feather falls just as fast as the rock. En el vacío una pluma cae igual de rápido que una piedra.

in a way en cierto modo ▪ de una manera ▪ en cierta forma ➤ In a way, yes, and in a way, no. En cierto modo sí y en cierto modo no.

in a way (that was) not intended by the manufacturer: to use something ~ usar algo de manera no provista por el fabricante

in a way that was not stipulated de forma no estipulada

in a way that you approve of *(tú)* en una manera que tú consientas ▪ *(usted)* en una manera que usted consienta

in a week *(means both "within a week" and "a week from now")* en una semana ➤ We can finish in a week. Podemos terminar(lo) en una semana. ➤ We can start in a week. Podemos empezar(lo) en una semana.

in a week's time *(redundant)* ▪ in a week en una semana

in a year 1. *(within a year)* dentro de año ▪ en un año 2. *(a year from now)* en un año

in a year's time *(redundant)* ▪ in a year en un año

in about a month ▪ in approximately a month en más o menos un mes ▪ en aproximadamente un mes ▪ en torno a un mes

in accordance with de conformidad con ▪ en conformidad con

in accordance with the law conforme a la ley ▪ de acuerdo con la ley

in accordance with the rules de acuerdo con las reglas ▪ según las reglas

in (actual) practice en la práctica

in addition además ▪ en adición ▪ por añadidura

in addition to además de

in advance: to call ~ ▪ to call ahead of time ▪ to call beforehand llamar con antelación ▪ llamar con anticipación ▪ llamar de antemano ➤ Call in advance. ▪ Call ahead of time. *(tú)* Llámame con antelación. ▪ *(usted)* Llámeme con antelación.

in advance: to make a reservation ~ ▪ to make reservations in advance ▪ to make advance reservations ▪ to make a reservation ahead of time hacer una reserva con antelación ▪ hacer una reserva por adelantado

in advance: to make reservations ~ ▪ to make a reservation ahead of time hacer reservas con antelación

in advance: to make reservations *x* days ~ reservar con *x* días de antelación ▪ hacer una reserva con *x* días de antelación

in advance: to pay ~ pagar por anticipado ▪ pagar por adelantado

to be **in agreement** estar de acuerdo ▪ estar conforme

to be **in agreement that...** estar de acuerdo en que...

in all ▪ all told en total ▪ todo dicho ➤ There are three in all, right? ¿Hay tres en total, sí?

in all honesty con toda sinceridad ➤ I would have to say in all honesty... Tendría que decir con toda sinceridad...

in all its splendor en todo su esplendor ▪ con todo su esplendor

in all my born days *(colorful)* ▪ in all my life ▪ in my whole life en mi vida ▪ en toda mi vida

in all my life ▪ in my whole life ▪ *(colorful)* in all my born days en mi vida ▪ en toda mi vida

in all the time (that) I've known you... *(a ti)* en todo el tiempo que te he conocido ▪ en todo el tiempo que te conozco ▪ *(a usted)* en todo el tiempo que lo he conocido ▪ en todo el tiempo que lo conozco ▪ *(Sp., leísmo)* en todo el tiempo que le he conocido ▪ en todo el tiempo que le conozco

in almost every instance ▪ in almost every case prácticamente en todos los casos

in an apparent ▪ in what appears to be en lo que parece ➤ In an apparent coup attempt... En lo que parece un intento de golpe de estado...

in an attempt to en un intento por

in an awkward position: to be put ~ ser puesto en una situación incómoda

in an awkward position: to sleep ~ dormir en mala postura

in an effort to...: to do something ~ hacer algo en un esfuerzo por... ▪ hacer algo por hacer... ➤ Alexander Pope wrote *The Rape of the Lock* in an effort to bring two alienated families back together. Alexander Pope escribió *El rapto del rizo* en un esfuerzo por reconciliar a dos familias enemistadas. ▪ Alexander Pope escribió *El rapto del rizo* para reconciliar a dos familias enemistadas.

in an emergency en una emergencia ▪ en una urgencia

in an expeditious manner ▪ expeditiously de manera expedita

in an hour ▪ in an hour's time en una hora ▪ dentro de una hora

in ancient times en tiempos antiguos

in and around en y/o cerca de ➤ One of our apartment mates spends half the day in and around the kitchen. Uno de nuestros compañeros de piso se pasa la mitad del día en y/o cerca de la cocina.

in and of itself de por sí ➤ Bringing up children is in and of itself a real challenge. La tarea de educar a los hijos es de por sí todo un desafío.

in and out entrando y saliendo ➤ I'll be in and out most of the day. Voy a estar todo el día entrando y saliendo.

in another year en otro año ▪ en un año ▪ de aquí a un año

in answer to your question en respuesta a tu pregunta

in any case en cualquier caso ▪ de todas maneras ▪ de todos modos ▪ de todas formas

in any event de cualquier forma ▪ de cualquier modo

in Argentina alone 1. just in Argentina sólo en Argentina ▪ solamente en Argentina **2.** by oneself in Argentina solo(-a) en Argentina

in arrears: payments ~ pagos atrasados

to be **in arrears 1.** *(account)* estar morosa **2.** *(customer)* ser moroso(-a) ➤ The account is ninety days in arrears. La cuenta está morosa noventa días. ➤ The client is in arrears. La abonada es morosa. ➤ The customer is ninety days in arrears. El abonado lleva noventa días de moroso.

in as many days *(in the same number of days)* en sendos días ▪ en otros tantos días ➤ It was the third suicide bombing in as many days. ▪ It was the third suicide bombing in three days. Fue la tercera bomba suicida en sendos días. ▪ Fue la tercera bomba suicida en otros tantos días.

to be **in bad shape** ▪ to be in a sad state estar que da pena ▪ estar en malas condiciones ▪ estar de mala forma

in bad taste ▪ in poor taste de mal gusto ▪ de mal efecto

in back of detrás de

in batches por tandas

to be **in big trouble** estar metido en un gran lío

in bits and pieces ▪ piecemeal por adarmes ▪ a remiendos

in black and white ▪ in writing en negro y blanco ▪ por escrito ➤ I want it in black and white. Lo quiero en negro y blanco. ▪ Lo quiero por escrito.

in bloc en bloque

in bold letters ▪ in bold type en negrita ▪ en negrilla ➤ I want it in bold red letters. Lo quiero en letra negrita roja. ▪ Lo quiero en letra negrilla roja.

in broad daylight a pleno sol ▪ a pleno día ▪ en pleno día ▪ a plena luz del sol ▪ a las claras

in bulk: to buy ~ comprar a granel

in bulk: to sell ~ vender a granel ➤ Do you sell nuts in bulk? ¿Se venden frutos secos a granel?

(in) care of John Doe atención Fulano de tal

in case por si ▪ en caso de que ▪ por si acaso ➤ Take another credit card in case they don't accept this one. Lleva otra tarjeta de crédito por si no acepten ésta. ➤ In case I don't see you again Por si no te vuelvo a ver

in case one does something... ▪ in case one should do something... ▪ in case one might do something... ▪ *(literary)* lest one do something... por si... ▪ no vaya a ser que... ▪ no sea que... ➤ They monitored the parolee in case he tried to escape. Mantuvieron un ojo en el prisionero en libertad condicional por si trata de escapar. ▪ Mantuvieron un ojo en el prisionero en libertad condicional no vaya a ser que trate de escapar. ▪ Mantuvieron un ojo en el prisionero en libertad condicional no sea que trate de escapar.

in case you're interested *(tú)* por si te interesa ▪ *(usted)* por si le interesa

in cash en efectivo ▪ en metálico

in certain respects en ciertos aspectos

in charge: to be (the one) ~ ▪ to be the person in charge ser el encargado ▪ ser la encargada ➤ Are you (the one) in charge here? ¿Es usted el encargado aquí? ▪ ¿Es usted la encargada aquí? ➤ Is anyone in charge here? ¿Hay algún encargado? ▪ ¿Está el encargado?

to be **in charge of** estar a cargo de ▪ estar encargado(-a) de

to be **in close proximity (to)** estar muy próximo (el uno del otro) ➤ Small cities in close proximity to larger ones will increase in population. Las ciudades pequeñas que están próximas a ciudades grandes aumentarán en habitantes.

to be **in close pursuit of the (retreating) enemy** picar la retaguardia del enemigo ▪ picar la retaguardia al enemigo

in cold blood a sangre fría

in collaboration (with) ▪ jointly ▪ together (with) en colaboración (con) ▪ conjuntamente (con)

in color de color ▪ en color ➤ Is the movie in color or in black and white? ¿La película es en color o en blanco y negro? ➤ The beak of the bird is red (in color). El pico del ave es (de color) rojo.

in common: to have something ~ tener algo en común ▪ parecerse en algo

to be **in complete agreement with...** estar al cien por cien de acuerdo con...

in complete detail ▪ down to the last detail con todo lujo de detalles

in compliance with conforme a

in conclusion ▪ to conclude en conclusión

in confidence: to tell someone something ~ ▪ to tell something to someone in confidence decirle a alguien algo en confianza ▪ decirle a alguien algo en confidencia

to be **in conflict with someone** estar en conflicto con alguien ▪ no verse cara a cara ➤ The government has sometimes been in conflict with the church. El gobierno ha estado a veces en conflicto con la iglesia.

in consultation with en consultación con ▪ con consejo de ▪ en consejo de ➤ The Spanish government made the decision in consultation with other European governments. El gobierno español tomó la decisión en consultación con otros gobiernos europeos.

to be **in consultation with someone** ▪ to be consulting with someone estar consultando con alguien ▪ estarse asesorando con alguien ▪ estar siendo asesorado por alguien ➤ The Spanish government is in consultation with other European governments. ▪ The Spanish government is consulting with other European governments. El gobierno español está consultando con otros gobiernos europeos. ▪ El gobierno español se está asesorando.

in contrast to en contraste con

in custody ▪ in police custody en detención policial ▪ en dependencias policiales

to be **in danger** estar en peligro ▪ correr peligro ▪ *(esp. in the negative)* peligrar ➤ The head of the government says the revolution is in no danger. El jefe del gobierno dice que la revolución no peligra.

to be **in deep shit** *(off-color)* ▪ to be in big trouble estar con la mierda hasta el cuello

to be **in delapidated condition** ▪ to be delapidated ▪ to be falling apart **1.** *(car)* estar destartalado **2.** *(building)* estar en penosas condiciones

to be **in demand** estar muy solicitado ▪ estar en demanda ▪ estar muy demandado ▪ haber mucha demanda ➤ Santiago, the concierge of our building, is very much in demand around the neighborhood as a window washer, consultant, and handyman. Santiago, el conserje de nuestro edificio, está muy solicitado en el vecindario como limpiador de ventanas, consultor y manitas.

to be **in denial about something** estar en un estado de abulia sobre algo ▪ tener los ojos cerrados a algo

in depth ▪ thoroughly en profundidad

in-depth analysis *el* análisis en profundidad

in-depth discussion discusión profunda ➤ *(news item)* The summit was an in-depth discussion of common challenges facing Europe. La cumbre fue una discusión profunda sobre los desafíos comunes que encara (toda) Europa.

in desperation en desesperación ▪ con desesperación

in detail detalladamente ▪ en detalle ▪ largo y tendido ▪ pormenorizadamente

in detail: to analyze ~ analizar detalladamente ▪ analizar en detalle ▪ analizar pormenorizadamente

to be **in disarray** estar desordenado ▪ estar desarreglado ▪ estar desaliñado ▪ estar en desbandada

to be **in disrepair** estar deteriorado(-a)

to be **in doubt** ▪ to be uncertain ser incierto ➤ The outcome is in doubt. El resultado es incierto.

to be **in doubt about** ▪ to have doubts about tener dudas sobre

in droves a montones ➤ People came in droves to the close-out sale. La gente vino a montones a la liquidación.

in droves: to stay away ~ venir cuatro gatos (locos) ▪ venir cuatro pelagatos (locos) ➤ People stayed away in droves. Vinieron cuatro gatos (locos). ▪ Vinieron cuatro pelagatos (locos).

in due course a su debido tiempo ▪ a su tiempo ▪ a su debido momento

in duplicate por duplicado

in early... a principios de... ➤ They are getting married in early June. Se casan a principios de junio.

in early fall ▪ in early autumn ▪ early in the fall ▪ early in the autumn al comienzo del otoño ▪ a principios de otoño

in equal measure ▪ at the same pace a la par

in every particular ▪ to the last particular ▪ to the letter ▪ strictly al pie de la letra ▪ a rajatabla ▪ a pies juntillas ➤ Few people today accept in every particular the theories of Freud. Pocas personas hoy en día aceptan a pies juntillas las teorías de Freud.

in every sense of the word en el sentido más amplio de la palabra ▪ en toda extensión de la palabra

in every way en todos los sentidos ➤ Mary Poppins is practically perfect in every way. Mary Poppins es prácticamente perfecta en todos los sentidos.

in excess ▪ to excess en exceso ▪ en demasía ▪ con demasía

in exchange for ▪ in return for a cambio de ▪ a trueque de

in fact ▪ as a matter of fact de hecho ▪ en efecto ▪ en rigor ▪ en realidad

in fact, it is you who... es más, eres tú él que... ▪ es más, eres tú la que... ▪ precisamente es usted él que... ▪ precisamente es usted la que...

in fact, it was you who... es más, fuiste tú él que... ▪ es más, fuiste tú la que... ▪ precisamente fue usted él que... ▪ precisamente fue usted la que...

to be **in favor of** estar a favor de ▪ estar en pro de

to be **in financial straits** ▪ to have financial problems ▪ to be going through hard times (financially) estar en apuros ▪ estar ajustado(-a) de dinero ▪ estar apretado(-a) de dinero

in fits and starts ▪ by fits and starts a trompicones ▪ a empujones ▪ a tontas y locas ▪ a saltos y corvos

to be **in for** venírsele encima ➤ He has no idea what he's in for. No tiene ni idea de lo que se le viene encima.

to be **in for a big surprise** esperarle una gran sorpresa ➤ She was in for a big surprise. (A ella) le esperaba una gran sorpresa.

to be **in for a rude awakening (when)** ir a caerse de narices (al)

to be **in for a shock** ir a llevarse un chasco

to be **in for a surprise** ir a llevarse una sorpresa

in for it now: you're ~ te la has buscado

in front of: to get ~ ponerse delante de ➤ That red car passed me and (then) got right in front of me. Ese carro rojo me arrebasó y se puso delante de mí. ➤ You can get in front of me in line. Puedes ponerte delante de mí en la cola.

in front of: to park ~ estacionarse frente al ➤ You can usually find a parking spot (right) in front of the building. Por lo general se puede encontrar un lugar para estacionarse frente al edificio.

in front of: to stand ~ estar frente a ▪ estar delante de ➤ I'll be standing right in front of the building. Estaré frente al edificio. ▪ Voy a estar frente al edificio.

to be **in front of someone (in line)** estar delante de alguien ➤ He's in front of me. Está delante de mí.

to be **in full swing** estar en pleno desarrollo ▪ estar en pleno apogeo ▪ estar en plena época ➤ The U.S. election campaign gets into full swing after the political conventions in August. La campaña electoral estadounidense entra en pleno desarrollo tras las convenciones políticas en agosto.

in garlic sauce al ajillo ➤ Shrimp in garlic sauce is a popular dish in Spain. Gambas al ajillo es un plato popular en España.

to be **in gear** estar en marcha ➤ Is it in gear? ¿Está en marcha? ➤ What gear is it in? ¿En qué marcha está? ➤ My brain isn't in gear. Mi cerebro no está en marcha.

in gear: to leave it ~ *(transmission)* dejar (el auto) con una marcha metida

in gear: to put it ~ *(transmission)* meter una marcha ▪ meter un cambio

in general por lo general

in God we trust en Dios confiamos

in good conscience de buena fe ➤ I can't in good conscience vote for him. No puedo votar por él de buena fe.

to be **in good health** estar bien de salud

to be **in good shape** *(physically)* estar en forma ▪ estar en buena forma física ▪ *(financially, etc.)* estar en buen estado

in good taste: to be done ~ ▪ to be tastefully done estar hecho con buen gusto

in great detail: to describe something ~ ▪ to describe something in rich detail ▪ to describe something in complete detail describir algo con (todo) lujo de detalles ▪ *(Sp.)* describir algo ce por ce ▪ describir algo ce por be

to be **in heat** ▪ to be in estrus estar en celo

to be **in here** estar aquí dentro ➤ It's in here. Está aquí dentro.

in hindsight ▪ with the benefit of hindsight en retrospectiva ▪ al mirar atrás

to be **in hot pursuit of** estar pisándole los talones de

to be **in hot water 1.** *(literal and figurative)* estar metido en agua caliente **2.** *(figurative)* to be in trouble estar metido en aguas turbias

in hot water: to get ~ *(figurative)* ▪ to get in(to) trouble meterse en aguas calientes ▪ meterse en aguas turbias

in house: to work ~ ▪ *(meaning that you cannot take the work home)* to work on site trabajar en el sitio

in it en ello ▪ le ➤ Could you put a good shot of whiskey in it? ¿Podrías echarle un buen chorro de whiskey?

in italics ▪ italicized en cursiva

in its day en su día

in its entirety en su totalidad

to be **in its infancy** estar en ciernes ▪ estar en su infancia ▪ estar en sus principios

in itself en sí (mismo) ▪ de por sí ▪ per se ▪ de suyo ➤ This salad is a meal in itself. Esta ensalada es una comida en sí (misma). ➤ Technology in itself is neither good nor bad. It all depends on how we use it. La tecnología, en sí, no es buena ni mala: todo depende de cómo la apliquemos.

to be **in jail** ▪ to be behind bars estar en la cárcel ▪ estar encarcelado(-a) ▪ estar preso(-a) ▪ estar entre rejas ▪ estar tras las rejas

in jest de chacota ▪ en broma ▪ en plan de broma

in just a few minutes sólo a unos minutos

in just under en poco menos de ➤ Lincoln delivered the Gettysburg Address in just under three minutes. Lincoln pronunció el discurso de Gettysburg en poco menos de tres minutos.

to be **in keeping with** estar a tono con ▪ estar en conformidad con ▪ estar de conformidad con

in large measure en gran medida

in large part en gran parte

to be **in last place** ocupar el último lugar ▪ quedar último(-a)

in late April a finales de abril

in-laws parientes políticos

in length ▪ long de largo

in line for en línea de ➤ He's second in line for the throne. Es el segundo en la línea del trono. ➤ He's next in line for the presidency. Es el siguiente en la línea de la presidencia.

in lots of por lotes de ➤ The envelopes come in lots of fifty. I don't even have to count (them). Los sobres vienen por lotes de cincuenta. No tengo ni que contarlos.

to be **in love with someone** estar enamorado(-a) de alguien ▪ andar enamorado(-a) de alguien ➤ I was in love with his sister. Estuve enamorado de su hermana. ▪ Anduve enamorado de su hermana.

in love with someone: to fall ~ enamorarse de alguien ▪ prendarse de alguien

in many ways de muchas maneras ▪ de muchas formas

in memory of en memoria de ▪ en memoria a
in mid afternoon a media tarde
in mid air en el aire ▪ en pleno vuelo
in mid morning a media mañana
to be **in military service** ▪ to be in the service hacer el servicio militar ▪ *(Sp., coll.)* hacer la mili ▪ *(Arg., coll.)* hacer la colimba
in mind: to keep ~ ▪ to bear in mind tener en cuenta ▪ tener presente ▪ tener en mente
in mint condition *(old books, coins, antique cars, etc.)* en condiciones perfectas
in moderation con moderación ▪ con prudencia ▪ con parquedad ▪ con mesura ▪ con medida ➤ Eat healthy fats in moderation. Come grasas sanas con moderación.
in more ways than one en más de un sentido
in most cases en la mayoría de los casos
to be **in motion** estar en movimiento
in motion: to set ~ poner en movimiento ▪ poner en marcha
to be **in mourning** estar de luto ▪ estar de rigoroso luto
in my day en mis días ▪ en mis tiempos ▪ en mi época
in my dreams en mis sueños ➤ At night, in my dreams, I call your name. De noche en mis sueños pronuncio tu nombre.
in my experience ▪ in my personal experience ▪ in my own experience en mis vivencias ▪ en mi experiencia ▪ en mis experiencias personales ▪ en experiencia propia
in my hurry to con las prisas de ▪ con las prisas por
in my judgment en mis juicios
in my opinion ▪ to me ▪ to my way of thinking en mi opinión ▪ a mi juicio ▪ a mi ver ▪ para mí ▪ a mi manera de ver ▪ opino ▪ creo ▪ pienso que ▪ me parece que ▪ considero que ▪ desde mi punto de vista ▪ por mi parte ▪ yo personalmente ▪ según mi parecer ▪ según mi opinión
in my own life en mi propia vida
in my own way a mi manera
in my years as ▪ during my time as en mis tiempos de ➤ In my years as a journalist ▪ During my time as a journalist En mis tiempos de periodista
in my younger days ▪ in my youth en mis años mozos ▪ en mi juventud
in my youth ▪ in my younger days en mi juventud ▪ *(Sp.)* en mis años mozos
to be **in need of tuning** ▪ to need a tune-up necesitar una puesta a punto
in neighboring Argentina en la vecina Argentina
in neighboring Mexico en el vecino México
to be **in no hurry to...** *(implies dawdling)* ▪ not to be in any hurry to... tomarse todo el tiempo en el mundo para...
to be **in no mood for fun and games** ▪ not to be in the mood for fun and games no estar (de humor) para fiestas
to be **in no mood for jokes** no estar (de humor) para bromas
to be **in no mood to do something** no estar de humor para hacer algo
in no time (at all) en nada ▪ en un periquete ▪ en un abrir y cerrar de ojos ▪ en un santiamén ▪ en una patada
in no uncertain terms: to tell someone something ~ decirle algo a alguien sin pelos en la lengua ▪ decirle algo a alguien de una manera tajante ▪ decirle algo a alguien de una manera inequivocable
in number... del... ➤ The fellow in number eight El chaval del ocho
in number: to be *x* ~ ser *x*
in office de mandato ▪ en el cargo ➤ On his last day in office, the president... En su último día de mandato, el presidente... ➤ As the president nears completion of his fifth month in office Cuando el presidente está a punto de cumplir cinco meses en el cargo
in old age ▪ in one's old age en la vejez
to be **in on a secret** ser partícipe de un secreto
in on a secret: to get ~ hacerse partícipe en un secreto
in one fell swoop de una sentada ▪ de un solo golpe
in one go de una tirada ▪ en una tirada ▪ de un tirón
in one sitting de un tirón ▪ *(Sp.)* de una tacada ➤ She read the book in one sitting. Ella leyó el libro de un tirón. ▪ Ella leyó el libro de una tacada.
in one's backyard 1. *(literal)* en el patio de atrás de uno **2.** *(figurative)* too close for comfort ▪ in one's own backyard estar a la vuelta de la esquina ➤ For people in the Middle East, the Iraq war was in their own backyard. Para la gente de Oriente Medio, la guerra de Irak estaba a la vuelta de la esquina.
in one's behalf ▪ on one's behalf en nombre de alguien ▪ de parte de uno ▪ en nombre de uno ▪ para uno ▪ a favor de uno ➤ A Miami judge rejects the asylum petition in Elián González' behalf and says he must return to Cuba. Un juez de Miami desestima la petición de asilo para Elián González y dice que debe volver a Cuba.
to be **in one's birthday suit** ▪ to be wearing one's birthday suit ▪ to be naked estar como Dios lo(-a) trajo al mundo ▪ estar desnudo(-a)
to be **in one's blood** llevar algo en la sangre ▪ venirle de casta a uno
in one's book en lo que a mí concierne ➤ He's a genius in my book. En lo que a mí concierne, es un genio.
in one's capacity as en calidad de
in one's day ▪ in one's time en su día ▪ en sus tiempos
to be **in one's dotage** estar en la senectitud de la vida ▪ estar en la chochera ▪ estar en la chochez
in one's eagerness to... en su afán por...
to be **in one's element** ▪ to feel at home ▪ to feel at ease estar en su elemento ▪ estar en su (propia) salsa ▪ estar a sus anchas ▪ estar como pez en el agua
to be **in one's face 1.** *(literal)* en la cara de uno **2.** *(figurative)* encontrárselo(-a) en todos lados ▪ encontrárselo(-a) hasta en la sopa ➤ He's always in my face. ▪ Me lo encuentro en todos lados. ▪ Me lo encuentro hasta en la sopa.
to be **in one's fifties** andar por los cincuenta
to be **in one's forties** andar por los cuarentena
in one's heart ▪ deep down en el fondo (de mi corazón) ▪ en el fuero interno de uno ▪ para los adentros de uno ➤ I know in my heart that... ▪ I know deep down that... Sé en el fondo (de mi corazón) que...
in one's judgment a juicio de uno ➤ In my judgment A mi juicio
to be **in one's old age** estar en la vejez
in one's opinion en (la) opinión de uno ▪ para uno ➤ In my opinion... En mi opinión... ▪ Para mí... ➤ In my father's opinion... En (la) opinión de mi padre... ▪ Para mi padre...
in one's own handwriting de su puño y letra
in one's own right por mérito propio ▪ por derecho propio
(in) one's own way: to do things ~ hacer las cosas a su modo ▪ hacer las cosas a su manera ▪ ser maestrillo que tiene su librillo ➤ He likes to do things (in) his own way. Le gusta hacer las cosas a su modo. ▪ Es maestrillo que tiene su librillo.
in one's own words en las propias palabras de uno ➤ Tell us in your own words *(tú)* Dinos en tus propias palabras ▪ *(usted)* Díganos en su propias palabras
to be **in one's price range** estar dentro del presupuesto de uno
to be **in one's prime** ▪ to be in one's heyday ▪ to be in one's peak years ▪ to be in the flower of youth estar en el albor de la vida ▪ estar en la flor de la vida ▪ estar en plena juventud ➤ He's in his prime. Está en el albor de la vida. ▪ Está en la flor de la vida.
to be **in one's right mind** ▪ to be in possession of one's faculties estar en sus cabales ▪ estar en su juicio
in one's sights: to have someone ~ tener a alguien en el punto de mira
in one's spare time a ratos perdidos
to be **in one's thirties** estar en la treintena
to be **in one's twenties** estar en la veintena
to be **in order** estar en regla
in order for there not to be ▪ in order that there not be ▪ for there not to be para que no haya
in order for there to be ▪ for there to be para que haya
in order not to ▪ so as not to para no
in order that para que ▪ a medida que
in order that there not be ▪ in order for there not to be ▪ for there not to be para que no haya
in order to para ▪ a fin de que ▪ con el fin de que

(in order) to better understand something ▪ (in order) to understand something better para comprender algo mejor ▪ con tal de comprender algo mejor ➤ In order to understand flames better, the investigators filmed them in slow motion. Con tal de comprender mejor las llamas, los investigadores las filmaron a cámara lenta.

(in order) to fill the time para hacer tiempo

(in order) to find out para averiguarlo

(in order) to keep from freezing **1.** *(present and future)* para evitar que se hiele **2.** *(past)* para evitar que se helara ▪ para evitar que se helase

(in order) to let in some fresh air para que entre un poco de aire fresco ➤ Open the window (in order) to let some fresh air into the room. Abre la ventana para que un poco de aire fresco entre en la habitación.

(in order) to save time para ahorrar tiempo

(in order) to hear as well as see ▪ so that one can hear as well as see ▪ (in order) to both hear and see así para oír como para ver ➤ Turn on the sound in order to hear as well as see the electronic Christmas card. ▪ Turn on the sound so that you can hear as well as see the electronic Christmas card. ▪ Turn on the sound in order to both hear and see the electronic Christmas card. Enciende el sonido así para oír como para ver la tarjeta navideña electrónica.

in other parts of the world en otras partes del mundo ▪ en distintos lugares del mundo

in other words en otros términos ▪ es decir

in our midst entre nosotros

in our own day ▪ in our own time en nuestra propia época ▪ en nuestro día

to be **in no hurry** ▪ not to be in any hurry no correr prisa ▪ no tener prisa

to be **in pain** sentir dolor ▪ sufrir dolor ▪ sentir dolores ▪ sufrir dolores ➤ He was in severe pain. Sentía fuerte dolor. ▪ Sufría fuertes dolores.

in pairs ▪ two by two ▪ two at time ▪ by two's a pares

in parentheses entre paréntesis

in particular de particular ▪ en especial

in passing: to hear ~ oír de refilón ▪ oír de pasada ▪ oír de paso

to be **in perfect health** estar en perfecto estado de salud

in perpetuity a perpetuidad

in place of en lugar de

in places de a trechos ▪ (en) algunas partes ➤ The manuscript is a little rough in places. El manuscrito está un poco imperfecto de a trechos. ▪ Al manuscrito le falta pulir en algunas partes.

in plain language en términos cotidianos

in plenty of time to con tiempo sobrado para ▪ con tiempo sobrado a

to be **in poor physical shape** ▪ to be out of shape estar en pésima forma física

to be **in poor taste** ▪ in bad taste ser de mal gusto

in popular speech en el habla popular

to be **in possession of one's faculties** ▪ to be in one's right mind estar en sus cabales

to be **in power** estar en el poder

in practice ▪ in actual practice en la práctica

in private en privado ▪ a solas ➤ I want to talk to you in private. ▪ I want to speak to you in private. *(tú)* Quiero hablarte en privado. ▪ *(usted)* Quiero hablarle en privado.

in process ▪ in progress en curso ▪ en progreso

in progress ▪ in process en curso ▪ en progreso

in proportion to en proporción a ▪ al paso de

in protective custody en detención preventiva

in public ▪ publicly en público ▪ públicamente ▪ de puertas afuera ➤ In public the dictator maintains an invariable coldness as if nothing had happened. De puertas afuera, el dictador exhibe una frialdad inmutable como si nada ocurriera.

to be **in radio contact with someone** ▪ to be in radio communication with someone estar en contacto por radio con alguien ▪ estar en comunicación por radio con alguien ➤ Are you in radio contact with your delivery trucks? ¿Está usted en contacto por radio con sus camiones de reparto? ▪ ¿Está usted en comunicación por radio con sus camiones de reparto?

to be **in rags** **1.** *(clothes)* estar en harapos ▪ estar hecho jirones **2.** *(paper)* estar gastadito ➤ My Bach is just in *rags*. Mi Bach está gastadito.

in rapid succession muchas veces seguidas ▪ uno tras otro

in real life en la vida real

in recent years ▪ in the last few years en los últimos años

to be **in recess** ▪ to be recessed estar en receso

in record time en tiempo récord ▪ en un tiempo récord

in reference to ▪ with reference to ▪ apropos (of) en lo que se refiere a ▪ a propósito de ➤ In reference to your other question... ▪ With reference to your other question... En lo que se refiere a su otra pregunta... ▪ A propósito de su otra pregunta...

in relation to con relación a ▪ en relación con

in relation to its size con relación a su tamaño ▪ en relación con su tamaño

in reply to en respuesta a

in residence residente

in response to **1.** as a reaction to como respuesta a **2.** in answer to ▪ about por lo de ➤ The government bombed the targets in response to the lynching of three soldiers. El gobierno bombardeó los objetivos como respuesta al ahorcamiento de tres soldados. ➤ I am calling in response to the ad in the paper for an apartment. Llamo por el anuncio en el periódico para un piso.

in retrospect en retrospectiva

in return a cambio ▪ como compensación

in return for en recompensa de

in search of en busca de ▪ a la búsqueda de

to be **in shape** ▪ to be in good physical condition ▪ to be physically fit ▪ *(said especially of older people)* to be fit as a fiddle estar en (buena) forma

in short en suma ▪ en fin ▪ en definitiva

in slices ▪ sliced en lonchas

to be **in slow motion** estar a cámara lenta ▪ estar en cámara lenta ▪ estar al ralentí

in some respects en algunos aspectos

in some way ▪ somehow de alguna manera ▪ de alguna forma ▪ de algún modo

in some ways en ciertos aspectos ▪ en cierta forma

to be **in someone else's shoes** estar en el pellejo de alguien

to be **in someone's face** encontrárselo hasta en la sopa ➤ He's always in my face. ▪ It's almost like he follows me around. Me lo encuentro hasta en la sopa.

to be **in someone's name** estar a nombre de alguien ➤ The house is in my mother's name. La casa está a nombre de mi madre

in someone's name: to do something ~ hacer algo en nombre de alguien

to be **in someone's sights** estar en el punto de mira de alguien

in someone's time en tiempos de alguien ➤ In my grandparents' time... En tiempos de mis abuelos...

in speaking ▪ when I'm speaking al hablar

in spite of pese a ▪ a pesar de

in spite of everything ▪ even so a pesar de todo ▪ pese a todo ▪ así y todo

in spite of it all a pesar de todo ▪ pese a todo

in spite of oneself a pesar de sí mismo(-a) ▪ a pesar de uno mismo ➤ I laughed when I saw him in spite of myself. Me reí cuando lo vi a pesar de mí mismo. ▪ *(Sp., leísmo)* Me reí cuando le vi a pesar de mí mismo.

in spite of that a pesar de eso ▪ pese a ello

in spite of the fact that ▪ even though ▪ in spite of having y eso que

in spots a trechos

in-state tuition matrícula preferencial ➤ Medical students from Wyoming and Idaho who attend the University of Utah medical school pay in-state tuition. Estudiantes de medicina de Wyoming y Idaho que asisten a la facultad de medicina en la Universidad de Utah pagan matrícula preferencial.

in step ▪ in agreement de acuerdo con ▪ conforme

in stock: to have merchandise ~ tener mercancías en existencia ▪ tener mercancías en depósito

in store for one: to have ~ deparar para uno ➤ What does the future have in store for us? ¿Qué nos depara el futuro? ▪ ¿Qué nos deparará el futuro?

to be **in style** estar de moda

to be **in such a hurry** ir con tanta prisa ▪ tener tanta prisa ➤ Why are you in such a hurry? ¿Por qué vas con tanta prisa? ▪ ¿Por qué tienes tanta prisa?

in such a way (that) de tal manera para (que...) ➤ It's best to live in such a way that your conscience is clear. Es mejor vivir de tal manera para que tu conciencia esté limpia.

in such circumstances en tales circunstancias

in sum ▪ to sum up después de todo ➤ In sum, I can say that my stay in Chile was unforgettable. Después de todo puedo decir que mi estancia en Chile fue inolvidable.

to be **in suspense** sentirse en tensión ➤ It's a great movie. You're in suspense the whole time. Es una película estupenda. Te sientes en tensión todo el rato.

in terms of en términos de ▪ en concepto de

in that en el aspecto que ▪ en el aspecto de que ▪ en cuanto que ▪ en la medida que ➤ The design is defective in that it does not permit the replacement of worn parts. El diseño es defectuoso en el aspecto que no permite cambiar las piezas deterioradas.

in that respect en ese aspecto ▪ al respecto

in that situation en esa situación

in that tone of voice en este tono de voz

to be **in the audience** estar en el público ▪ estar entre el público

in the back of en el fondo de

in the background en segundo plano ▪ de fondo ➤ You could hear in the background... De fondo se escuchaba...

in the bag: to have it ~ ▪ to have it (all) sewn up tenerlo en el bote

in the ballpark 1. approximately accurate grosso modo ▪ a grosso modo **2.** within the limits of what one wants to spend a grosso modo ➤ Cassini's calculation of the size of the solar system was in the ballpark. El cálculo de Cassini del tamaño del sistema solar fue a grosso modo. ➤ Twenty thousand dollars is in the ballpark of what I want to spend on a car. Veinte mil dólares es grosso modo lo que quiero gastar en un auto.

in the black ▪ with a surplus con superávit

to be **in the buff** ▪ to be naked estar en cueros ▪ estar en pelotas ▪ estar en bolas

in the buff: to parade around ~ andar en cueros ▪ andar en pelotas ▪ andar en bolas

in the capacity of en calidad de

to be **in the cards** estar en las cartas

in the course of the year ▪ during the year en el curso del año ▪ en el trayecto del año ▪ a lo largo del año

in the course of time ▪ with the passage of time ▪ over time ▪ with time a lo largo del tiempo

to be **in the dark 1.** *(literal)* without light estar a oscuras ▪ estar en la oscuridad **2.** *(figurative)* to be out of the loop estar desenchufado(-a) ➤ You can't read in the dark. No se puede leer a oscuras. ➤ I'm completely in the dark. Tell me what's going on. Estoy completamente desenchufado. Dime lo que está pasando.

in the dark: to be left ~ quedarse a oscuras ➤ The lights went off at home, and we were left in the dark. Se fue la luz de mi casa, y nos quedamos a oscuras.

in the days following ▪ in the days that followed en los días siguientes ▪ en los días posteriores

in the distance a lo lejos ▪ en lontananza

in the early evening ▪ early in the evening ▪ in the early hours of the evening a prima noche ▪ en las primeras horas de la noche

in the early stages incipiente ➤ The doctor said she had cataracts in the early stages. El médico dijo que tenía cataratas incipientes.

in the east en el este

in the emergency room en urgencias ➤ They ended up in the emergency room. Acabaron en urgencias.

in the end a fin de cuentas ▪ al final ▪ al cabo ▪ finalmente

in the eyes of a los ojos de ➤ In the eyes of the state... A los ojos del estado...

in the face of frente a ▪ ante

in the final analysis en el último análisis ▪ en último término ▪ a fin de cuentas

to be **in the first grade** cursar primero ▪ estar en el primer grado ➤ When I was in the first grade... Cuando cursaba primer grado... ➤ Our daughter is in the first grade. Nuestra hija está en el primer grado. ▪ Nuestra hija está en el primer curso.

in the first place en primer lugar

in the first year of life ▪ during the first year of life en el primer año de vida ▪ durante el primer año de vida

in the flower of youth ▪ in the prime of life en plena juventud

in the form of a en forma de

in the future 1. en el futuro ▪ en adelante **2.** from now on ▪ henceforth ▪ thenceforth ▪ thenceforward en el futuro ▪ en lo sucesivo

in the good old days en los buenos tiempos

in the heart of Madrid en pleno corazón de Madrid

in the heat of battle en lo más reñido de la batalla ▪ en el calor de la batalla

in the heat of the moment en el calor del momento

in the home environment ▪ in the family environment ▪ within the home ▪ within the family en el entorno familiar

to be **in the hospital** estar en el hospital ▪ estar ingresado(-a)

in the immediate future en un futuro inmediato

in the interest of ▪ in pursuit of en aras de

in the intervening week ▪ during the week ▪ during the next week entresemana

in the intervening years ▪ in the years in between en los años intermedios

to be **in the know** estar al tanto ▪ estar enterado(-a) ▪ estar en el ajo ▪ andar en el ajo ▪ estar en la pega

to be **in the land of nod** *(poetic)* ▪ to be in a sound sleep estar en el octavo sueño ▪ estar dormido(-a) profundamente

in the last few days en los últimos días

in the last few minutes en los últimos minutos

in the last few years ▪ in recent years en los últimos años

to be **in the lead** ▪ to be first ▪ to be ahead ir en cabeza ▪ ir por delante ▪ ir en primer lugar

in the legislative mill *(coll.)* ▪ in the legislative process en trámite legislativo ▪ en trámite parlamentario

in the legislative process en trámite legislativo ▪ en trámite parlamentario

to be **in the limelight** estar en el candelero

in the long run a la larga ▪ a largo plazo

in the long run: to be cheaper ~ ▪ to come out cheaper salir más barato ➤ It's cheaper in the long run to buy a bus pass. Sale más barato comprar un pase de autobús. ▪ *(Sp.)* Sale más barato comprar un bónobus.

in the making ▪ developing ▪ budding en proceso ▪ en ciernes ▪ en (proceso de) la formación ▪ en potencia

in the manner to which one has become accustomed de la forma en la que uno se ha acostumbrado

in the meantime ▪ in the interim mientras tanto ▪ entretanto

in the mid... a mediados de... ➤ In the mid 19th (nineteenth) century... A mediados del siglo XIX (diecinueve)...

to be **in the middle of (doing) something** estar en medio de (hacer) algo

in the middle of everything en medio de todo

to be **in the middle of exams** estar de exámenes

in the middle of nowhere en el medio de la nada ▪ en medio de no sé donde ▪ en el quinto pino ▪ donde el diablo dio las tres voces ▪ *(off-color)* en el quinto carajo ▪ en el quinto coño

in the middle of the book en la mitad del libro

in the middle of the night en el medio de la noche ▪ en plena noche

to be **in the middle of the street** ▪ to be right in the middle of the street estar en medio de la calle ▪ estar en la mitad de la calle ▪ estar en plena calle

in the middle of the week ▪ at midweek a mediados de la semana

in the middle of the winter ▪ in midwinter en mitad del invierno ▪ en pleno invierno

in the midst of en medio de

to be **in the military** ▪ to be in the service hacer el servicio militar ▪ estar en el servicio militar ▪ hacer la mili ▪ prestar el servicio militar ➤ When I was in the service... Cuando estaba haciendo la mili...

to be **in the mood (to do something)** estar de humor (para hacer algo) ▪ estar en vena (para hacer algo)

to be **in the mood (for something)** estar de humor (para algo) ▪ estar en vena (para algo) ▪ estar en disposición (de algo) ➤ I'm not in the mood. No estoy de humor.

to be **in the mood to do something** estar de humor para hacer algo

in the morning 1. during the morning por la mañana **2.** *(referring to the hour)* de la mañana ➤ We're going Christmas shopping tomorrow morning. Vamos a comprar los regalos para Navidad mañana por la mañana. ➤ We're leaving to go Christmas shopping at ten in the morning. Saldremos a comprar los regalos para Navidad mañana a las diez de la mañana.

in the name of ▪ under the name of en el nombre de ➤ You're holding a book for me in the name of... ▪ You're holding a book for me under the name of... Tiene un libro que está reservado en el nombre de...

in the near future para un futuro próximo ▪ en un futuro próximo ▪ para un futuro cercano ▪ en un futuro cercano ▪ próximamente ➤ We anticipate a trip to San Salvador in the near future. Tenemos previsto un viaje a San Salvador próximamente. ➤ The new book foresees better times in the near future. El libro nuevo augura mejores tiempos para un futuro próximo.

in the next few days en los próximos días ▪ en fecha próxima

in the next few hours ▪ in the next several hours en las próximas horas

in the next few weeks ▪ over the next few weeks ▪ during the next few weeks en pocas semanas ▪ *(past)* en las siguientes semanas ▪ *(future)* en las próximas semanas

in the north en el norte

in the not-too-distant future en un futuro no muy lejano

to be **in the offing** estar a la vista ▪ estar cerca

in the old days antaño ▪ en los viejos tiempos

to be **in the open** ▪ to be out in the open ▪ to be exposed estar al descubierto

to be **in the open air** estar al aire libre ▪ estar a la intemperie ▪ estar al raso

in the opposite direction: to go ~ ▪ to go the opposite way ▪ to go the other way ir por el sentido contrario

in the opposite direction: to travel ~ ▪ to move in the opposite direction circular en sentido contrario ▪ circular en dirección contraria

to be **in the ozone** ▪ to be off in the ozone ▪ to be spaced out estar en la luna ▪ estar en el guindo ▪ estar en la higuera

to be **in the pipeline** ▪ to be in process estar en trámite

in the prime of life ▪ in the flower of youth en plena juventud

to be **in the process of moving** estar de mudanza

in the pouring rain en medio de una lluvia torrencial ▪ en medio de una lluvia copiosa

to be **in the public domain** ser del dominio público

to be **in the public eye** estar en el punto de mira del público

to be **in the public spotlight** encontrarse bajo la mirada del público

in the raw: to have sex ~ *(coll.)* ▪ to have sex without a condom ▪ to have unprotected sex hacerlo a pelo ▪ practicar el sexo sin preservativo ▪ practicar el sexo sin protección

in the rear ▪ in the back (part) en la parte de atrás ▪ detrás de ▪ *(in a military maneuver)* a retaguardia ▪ *(off-color)* in the ass en el culo ➤ The parking lot is in the rear of the building. ▪ The parking lot is behind the building. El estacionamiento está ubicado en la parte de atrás del edificio. ▪ El estacionamiento está detrás del edificio.

to be **in the red** ▪ to be operating at a loss ▪ not to be covering expenses ▪ not to be breaking even estar en los números rojos

to be **in the right** estar en lo correcto ▪ estar en lo justo

to be **in the right place at the right time** estar en el sitio oportuno en el momento oportuno ▪ estar en el sitio adecuado en el momento justo ▪ estar en el lugar adecuado en el momento oportuno

to be **in the same boat** *(coll.)* ▪ to be in the same situation estar en mi misma situación

to be **in the same place at the same time** coincidir en un lugar ➤ *(news item)* Woody Allen and Bruce Springsteen were both in Madrid yesterday. Woody Allen y Bruce Springsteen coincidieron en Madrid ayer.

in the same vein a este tono ▪ a este tenor ▪ de esta guisa

in the same way del mismo modo ▪ de la misma manera

in the sense that... en el sentido de que...

in the shade a la sombra

in the shadow of a la sombra de ➤ He lives in the shadow of his famous brother-in-law. Vive a la sombra de su cuñado famoso.

in the short term ▪ in the short run a corto plazo ▪ en corto plazo

in the sixth grade en sexto curso ▪ en el sexto grado

in the south en el sur

in the spotlight: to put somone ~ poner a alguien en el candelero

in the spotlight: to put something ~ poner algo en el candelero

in the summertime en verano

in the sun al sol

in the sunshine of success al sol del éxito

in the true sense of the word en el verdadero sentido de la palabra

to be **in the way** estar (por) en medio ▪ estar en el paso ▪ estar ahí en medio ➤ The boxes are in the way. Las cajas están por en medio. ▪ Las cajas están en el paso. ➤ Are the boxes in the way? ¿Le estorban las cajas? ➤ He wanted to talk to you, and I was just in the way. Él quería hablar contigo, y yo estaba ahí en medio.

in the way: things ~ cosas por medio ▪ cosas estorbando el paso

in the west en el oeste ▪ *(sun, moon, etc.)* por el oeste ➤ We are in the west of Spain. Estamos en el oeste de España. ➤ The sun sets in the west. El sol se pone por el oeste.

in what is surely... ▪ in what surely is... en lo que seguramente es... ▪ en lo que se da por seguro es...

in the wild a lo salvaje

in the workplace en el lugar de trabajo ▪ en el centro de trabajo

in the year of our Lord... en el año de Nuestro Señor...

in the years to come en los años venideros ▪ en los años que vienen

in theory ▪ on paper en teoría ▪ teóricamente ▪ sobre el papel

in there 1. allí (dentro) **2.** allí ➤ "Don't go in there," the monks told Marcelino. "No entrés allí," dijeron los monjes a Marcelino. ➤ *(dictionary)* Don't look it up in there. You won't find it. No lo busques allí, no lo encontrarás.

in this respect en este aspecto

in this way de esta forma ▪ de este modo

in this weather con este tiempo ▪ con este clima ▪ en este clima ➤ I don't want to go out in this weather. No quiero salir con este tiempo. ▪ No quiero salir con este clima.

in those circumstances en esas circunstancias ▪ bajo esas circunstancias

in those days por aquellos días ▪ en aquellos días ▪ en aquella época ▪ en esa época ▪ en aquel entonces

in time: to call ~ llamar con tiempo

in time (for one) to do something a tiempo para hacer algo ▪ a tiempo que uno haga algo ➤ We didn't finish in time to go out for coffee. No terminamos a tiempo para salir a tomar un café.

in time for something a tiempo para algo ➤ I didn't get back in time for the party. No llegué a tiempo para la fiesta. ▪ No regresé a tiempo para la fiesta. ▪ No volví a tiempo para la fiesta.

in time to do something a tiempo de hacer algo ➤ The general arrived in time to reform the forces. El general llegó a tiempo de recomponer las fuerzas.

in time with the music ▪ to the beat of the music ▪ in time to the music al compás de la música

to be **in top form** estar en plena forma

in town 1. downtown ▪ in the city center en el centro **2.** in the whole city en toda la ciudad ➤ We had supper in town last night. ▪ We had supper downtown last night. Cenamos en el centro anoche. ➤ It's the best restaurant in town. Es el mejor restaurante en toda la ciudad.

to be **in trouble** estar metido en problemas

in trouble: to get in(to) ~ meterse en problemas

to be **in trouble with the law** tener problemas con la justicia

in trouble with the law: to get ~ meterse en problemas con la justicia ▪ meterse en problemas con la ley

in turn 1. in the proper order a su vez ▪ por turno **2.** by turns sucesivamente ▪ por turnos

in unison: to answer ~ responder a coro ▪ responder al unísono ➤ "Yes," we answered in unison. "Sí," respondimos al unísono. ▪ "Sí," respondimos a coro.

in unison: to clap ~ ▪ to clap to a beat aplaudir al unísono ▪ aplaudir al compás

in unison: to sing ~ cantar al unísono ➤ All of you sing it in unison. Todos vosotros cantadlo al unísono.

to be **in use** estar ocupado ▪ estar en uso

to be **in vain** resultar inútil ➤ All our efforts were in vain. Todos nuestros esfuerzos resultaron inútiles.

in vain: to do something ~ hacer algo en vano ▪ *(coll.)* hacer algo en balde ➤ We made the trip in vain. Hicimos el viaje en vano. ▪ Hicimos el viaje en balde.

in varying degrees of de diversa consideración ➤ A forty-year-old man lost his life and eleven others were injured in varying degrees of seriousness. Perdió la vida un hombre de cuarenta años y otras once personas resultaron heridas de diversa consideración.

in various locations en varias ubicaciones ▪ en puntos dispersos

in various places en distintos lugares ▪ en distintos sitios

in very few cases ▪ in very few instances en poquísimos casos

in view of ▪ taking into account ▪ considering en atención a ▪ a la vista de

in view of: to decide ~ decidir a la vista de

in view of: to do ~ hacer a la vista de

in view of: to take an action ~ tomar una acción a la vista de

in view of the possibility that... ante la posibilidad de que...

in vogue: to be ~ estar en boga

in weeks 1. *(viewed as a short time)* en semanas ▪ *(viewed as a long time)* en muchas semanas

in what appears to be ▪ in an apparent en lo que parece ➤ In what appears to be an attempted coup d'état... ▪ In an apparent coup d'état... En lo que parece un intento de golpe de estado...

in which en el que ▪ en los que ▪ en la que ▪ en las que ▪ en el cual ▪ en la cual ▪ en los cuales ▪ en las cuales

in which case en cuyo caso

in which to live ▪ to live in **1.** en el que vivir **2.** en la que vivir

in width ▪ wide de ancho

to be **in with someone** estar a bien con alguien

to be **in withdrawal** *(from drug addiction)* ▪ to be going through withdrawal tener síndrome de abstinencia ▪ *(informal)* estar con el mono

to be **in working order** ▪ to be working correctly ▪ to be working right funcionar correctamente

in writing por escrito

in *x* alone ▪ in the year *x* alone sólo en (el año) *x* ➤ In (the year) 2004 alone... Sólo en el año 2004...

in *x* years dentro de *x* años ➤ What will people say about you in twenty years? ¿Qué dirá la gente de ti dentro de veinte años?

inasmuch as ▪ seeing that ▪ since como que

to be **inaugurated president** ser investido como presidente ➤ James K. Polk was inaugurated president of the United States on March 4, 1845. James K. Polk fue investido como presidente de los Estados Unidos el día 4 de marzo de 1845.

incentive to *el* aliciente para

inch by inch palmo a palmo ▪ centímetro a centímetro ➤ They searched the terrain inch by inch. Registraron el terreno palmo a palmo. ▪ Registraron el terreno centímetro a centímetro.

the **incident occurred** el incidente se produjo ▪ el hecho ocurrió ➤ The place where the incidents occurred. El lugar donde se produjeron los incidentes. ➤ The incidents occurred on the morning of October twelfth last year. Los hechos ocurrieron en la mañana del doce de octubre del año pasado.

to **incinerate oneself** ▪ to set oneself on fire prenderse fuego a lo bonzo ▪ quemarse a lo bonzo

incipient cataracts ▪ cataracts in the early stages (of development) cataratas incipientes ▪ cataratas nacientes

incipient cold ▪ the beginnings of a cold resfriado incipiente

to **incline towards** ▪ to lean towards **1.** to prefer inclinarse hacia algo ▪ inclinarse a favor de algo ▪ decantarse hacia ▪ tender hacia **2.** to slope towards inclinarse hacia ➤ I'm inclining towards the opposition candidate in this election. ▪ I'm leaning towards the opposition candidate in this election. Me inclino más hacia el candidato de la oposición en estas elecciones. ▪ Me decanto hacia el candidato de la oposición en estas elecciones. ➤ I'm inclining towards the yellows ones. ▪ I'm leaning towards the yellow ones. Me inclino hacia los amarillos. ➤ The roof inclines toward the south, making it the ideal place to put the solar panel. El tejado se inclina hacia el sur, lo cual lo hace el lugar ideal para poner el panel solar.

to be **inclined to do something** decantarse por hacer algo ➤ I'm inclined to waive the course requirement and let her graduate. Me decanto por no exigir la asignatura y dejarla graduarse.

to be **inclined toward(s)** ▪ to incline toward(s) estar inclinado(-a) hacia ➤ The roof is inclined toward the south in order for the solar cells to receive maximum exposure to the sun. ▪ The roof inclines towards the south in order for the solar cells to receive maximum exposure to the sun. El tejado está inclinado hacia el sur para que las células solares reciban la máxima exposición al sol.

including me incluso yo ▪ incluyéndome (a mí)

including mine ▪ mine included incluyendo el mío ▪ incluido el mío ▪ incluyendo la mía ▪ incluido la mía

including *x* Argentinians ▪ among them *x* Argentinians incluyendo *x* argentinos ▪ entre ellos *x* argentinos

including yours ▪ yours (being) one of them incluyendo el tuyo ▪ entre ellos el tuyo ➤ I've graded twenty examinations so far, including yours. He calificado veinte exámenes hasta el momento, incluyendo el tuyo. ▪ He calificado veinte exámenes hasta el momento, entre ellos el tuyo.

income tax impuesto sobre la renta ▪ *(U.S. Latinos)* impuesto en la ganancia

income tax return *la* declaración del impuesto sobre la renta

incoming calls 1. *(present)* las llamadas que entran ▪ llamadas entrantes **2.** *(imperfect)* las llamadas que entraban ▪ llamadas entrantes

incontrovertible fact ▪ indisputable fact hecho indiscutible

to **incorporate the recommendations** recoger las recomendaciones ➤ *(headline)* Annan criticizes Bush's proposed resolution on Iraq for not incorporating his recommendations. Annan critica la propuesta de resolución de Bush sobre Irak por no recoger sus recomendaciones.

incorrect call *(sports)* ▪ incorrect ruling fallo de arbitro

to **increase blood flow** ▪ to increase the flow of blood aumentar el flujo sanguíneo

to **increase from *x* to *y*** aumentar de *x* a *y* ▪ incrementar de *x* a *y* ▪ subir de *x* a *y* ▪ pasar de *x* a *y*

to **increase in size** aumentar de tamaño

increase in pay ▪ pay increase ▪ raise aumento de sueldo

increase in population ▪ population increase aumento de la población

increase in speed aumento de velocidad

increase in the population ▪ growth of the population aumento de la población ▪ crecimiento de la población

increase in unemployment ▪ rise in unemployment subida del desempleo ▪ *(Sp.)* subida del paro

to **increase in value** incrementar su valor ▪ aumentar en valor ➤ Real estate is a good investment because it increases in value. Bienes raíces son una buena inversión porque incrementa su valor. ▪ Bienes raíces son una buena inversión porque aumenta en valor.

increase over last year's profits ▪ improvement over last year's profits incremento sobre los beneficios del año pasado ▪ mejora sobre los beneficios del año pasado

to **increase the number of** incrementar el número de ➤ *(metro station sign)* Because of the bicycle marathon on Sunday, the number of trains will be increased. Con motivo de la vuelta ciclista el domingo, se incrementará el número de trenes.

to **increase the pressure on someone to do something** aumentar la presión sobre alguien para que haga algo

Indecent Proposal *(film title) Poco decoroso* ▪ *(literal)* propuesta indecente

indefinable quality: to have an ~ tener un no sé qué

indelible impression ▪ lasting impression ▪ permanent impression impresión indeleble ▪ impresión duradera ▪ impresión permanente

indelible ink tinta indeleble

indelible memory recuerdo imborrable

to **indent a paragraph** ▪ to make an indentation sangrar un párrafo ▪ hacer una sangría al párrafo

independently of each other de forma independiente ▪ independientemente uno del otro ▪ cada uno por su cuenta ➤ Newton and Leibniz developed calculus at about the same time and independently of each other. Newton y Leibniz desarrollaron el cálculo casi a la vez y de forma independiente. ▪ Newton y Leibniz desarrollaron el cálculo casi a la vez e independientemente uno del otro. ▪ Newton y Leibniz desarrollaron el cálculo casi a la vez y cada uno por su cuenta.

index card ficha

index finger índice ➤ *(Gabriel García Márquez)* The colonel's wife pointed toward the door with an emaciated index finger. La esposa del coronel dirigió hacia la puerta un índice escuálido.

Indian summer veranillo de San Miguel ▪ veranillo de San Martín

to **indicate that...** ▪ to lead one to believe that... señalar que... ▪ permitir anticipar que... ➤ The medical tests indicate that the patient ingested something toxic. Las pruebas médicas señalan que el paciente ingirió algo tóxico. ➤ *(news item)* Several experts believe that the behavior pattern exhibited in the five crimes indicates that the killer will act again. Varios expertos creen que el patrón de comportamiento en los cinco crímenes permite anticipar que el asesino volverá a actuar.

indication that... ▪ sign that... *la* indicación de que... ▪ muestra de que... ▪ *la* señal de que...

indifference to indiferencia para con ➤ He resented their indifference to his criticism. Él se resintió por la indiferencia de los otros para con sus críticas.

to be **indifferent to** ser indiferente acerca de

to be **indignant at** estar indignado(-a) ante

to be **indiscriminate in one's criticism** ▪ to criticize someone no matter what he does criticar a alguien por lo que haga o deje de hacer ▪ criticar a alguien de todas maneras ▪ dar un palo por bogar o no bogar

indispensable man hombre imprescindible ▪ hombre indispensable

individual income tax impuesto de la renta al individuo ▪ impuesto de la renta sobre el individuo

individual tastes ▪ personal tastes gustos personales ▪ gustos de cada uno ▪ gustos de cada cual ➤ It's a matter of individual tastes. Es una cuestión de gustos personales.

indoor football fútbol sala ▪ fútbol de sala

indoor plumbing fontanería interna

indoor pool piscina cubierta

induction coil ▪ inductor bobina de inducción

to **indulge oneself** darse un gusto ▪ darse un capricho

to **indulge in something** permitirse algo ▪ darse a algo ▪ entregarse a algo

to **indulge someone** consentirle a alguien algo

Industrial Revolution Revolución Industrial ➤ Historian Bruce Catton said the American Civil War came about because the Industrial Revolution reached the North before the South, creating conflicting demands on the federal government. El historiador Bruce Catton dijo que la Guerra Civil norteamericana se produjo porque la Revolución Industrial llegó al norte antes que al sur, creando al gobierno federal demandas en conflicto.

industrious person persona trabajadora

inexhaustible mine *el* filón inagotable ▪ mina inagotable

inferior wine ▪ rotgut wine ▪ ripple vino peleón

infestation of plaga de ▪ *la* infestación de ➤ *(headline)* Infestation of bedbugs forces evacuation of a train Plaga de chinches obliga evacuación de un tren

to be **infested with something** estar infestado(-a) de algo ▪ estar plagado(-a) de algo ➤ The apartment building is infested with roaches. El edificio de apartamentos está infestado de cucarachas.

to **incite the mob** excitar a la chusma

to **inflame the masses** enardecer a las masas

inflatable toy *el* juguete hinchable ▪ juguete inflable

to **inflate the mileage** inflar el kilometraje ▪ abultar el kilometraje

to **inflate the trip** ▪ to make unnecessary turns ▪ to take a longer route than necessary dar vueltas a lo tonto

influence peddling tráfico de influencias

influence with influencia ante

influential friends amigos influyentes ▪ *las* amistades de peso

to **inform you that...** informarle de que...

information available at the front desk razón portería ▪ información portería

information booth cabina de información

to **infringe on a patent** infringir una patente ▪ saltarse un patente

to **infringe on one's rights** infringir los derechos de uno

ingrained habit hábito arraigado

to **ingratiate oneself to someone** congraciarse con alguien ▪ hacerse el simpático a alguien

ingrown nail uña encarnada

to **inherit something from someone** heredar algo de alguien

initial debate on incoado debate sobre ▪ primer debate sobre ▪ debate inicial sobre

initial step primer paso

to **injure one's back** ▪ to hurt one's back herirse la espalda ▪ hacerse daño en la espalda ➤ I injured my back. Me hice daño en la espalda. ▪ Me herí la espalda.

to be **injured in an accident** ▪ to be hurt in an accident resultar herido en un accidente

inner calling llamada interior

the **inner child** ▪ the child within (each of) us el niño que llevamos dentro

inner circle círculo más allegado

inner city zonas céntricas de la ciudad

inner direction dirección interna

inner ear oído interno

inner peace *la* paz interior

inner planets *los* planetas interiores

inner self fuero interno

inner thoughts pensamientos íntimos ▪ pensamientos secretos

inner tube cámara (de neumático) ➤ The inner tube is ballooning through the outer layer of the tire. La cámara se está saliendo a través de la llanta formando un globo. ▪ La cámara se está saliendo a través de la llanta formando un huevo.

innermost self: one's ~ los adentros de uno

inopportune moment momento inoportuno ▪ momento inadecuado ➤ At the most inopportune moment En el momento más inoportuno ▪ En el momento más inadecuado

input-output *(computers)* ▪ I.O. entrada y salida ▪ input-output

to **inquire about someone's health** ▪ to ask after someone's health preguntar por la salud de alguien to **inquire about something** ▪ to ask about something preguntar sobre algo ▪ preguntar por algo

ins and outs of ▪ the intricacies of vericuetos de ▪ recovecos de ▪ *los* pormenores de

to **insert a coin in (to)** ▪ to put in a coin ▪ to put a coin in(to) meter una moneda a ▪ introducir una moneda en

to **insert a word** insertar una palabra ▪ intercalar una palabra

to **insert (the) punctuation** insertar la puntuación

inside enemy lines ▪ behind enemy lines ▪ within enemy lines tras las líneas enemigas

inside information *la* información desde dentro

inside out: to know something ~ ▪ to know something forwards and backwards ▪ to know something in depth ▪ to know thoroughly saber algo a fondo ▪ conocer algo a fondo ➤ He knows the subject inside out. Sabe el tema a fondo. ▪ Conoce el tema a fondo.

inside out: to turn something ~ ▪ to turn something wrong side out poner algo al revés ▪ poner algo de dentro hacia fuera

inside pocket bolsillo interior

to **insist on** empeñarse en ▪ insistir en ▪ obstinarse en ▪ erre que erre que ➤ He insisted on going with us. Se empeñaba en acompañarnos.

to **install a pacemaker in someone** colocarle un marcapasos a alguien ➤ Doctors installed a pacemaker in the vice president. Los médicos colocaron un marcapasas al vicepresidente.

installment sale venta a plazos

to be an **instance of** ser un caso de ➤ The Pythagorean theorem is an instance of the binomial theorem. El teorema de Pitágoras es un caso del teorema binomial.

to be **instantly likeable** ▪ to be someone you like right away enseguida caer bien ➤ He's instantly likeable. ▪ He's someone you like right away. Es una persona que enseguida cae bien.

to **instill confidence in someone** ▪ to give someone confidence infundir confianza a alguien

to **instill in someone** inculcarle a alguien ➤ The teacher instilled in him a love of reading. La profesora le inculcó el amor por la lectura.

instinct for survival ▪ survival instinct instinto de supervivencia ▪ instinto para sobrevivir

instrument panel tablero de instrumentos

insulated handle asa aislada ➤ I want a frying pan with an insulated handle. Quiero una sarten con una asa aislada. ➤ I want a double boiler with insulated handles. Quiero un baño de María con asas aisladas.

insurance claim reclamo al seguro ▪ *la* reclamación de seguro

insurance claim: to make an ~ dar parte al seguro

to **insure accuracy** garantizar precisión

integral calculus cálculo integral

intellectual tendencies tendencias intelectuales ▪ *(journalistic, literary)* usos intelectuales

intelligence agency servicio de espionaje ▪ agencia de espionaje

intelligence quotient ▪ I.Q. *el* coeficiente intelectual ➤ Higher than average I.Q. Coeficiente intelectual superior a lo normal

to be **intelligent enough to know that...** ▪ to be smart enough to know that... ser (lo) suficientemente inteligente para saber que...

to be **intended for** estar pensado para ▪ estar dirigido a ▪ estar indicado para ➤ *(news item)* ETA kills two workers with a car bomb intended for a socialist councilman ETA asesina a dos obreros con un coche bomba dirigido a un edil socialista

intended use uso previsto ▪ uso intencionado

intense debate debate intenso ▪ denso debate

intensity of the combat ▪ fierceness of the combat *la* intensidad del combate

intensive care unit ▪ ICU *la* unidad de cuidados intensivos ▪ UCI

interest compounded quarterly interés acumulado en pagos trimestrales ➤ The trust pays five percent interest compounded quarterly. El fondo devenga un interés de cinco por ciento acumulado en pagos trimestrales.

interest from a trust renta de un fondo ➤ He lives on the interest from a trust. Vive de la renta de un fondo.

interest in gusto por ▪ *el* interés en ▪ interés por

interest rate cut ▪ cut in interest rates recorte de los tipos de interés

to be **interested in** interesarse por ▪ estar interesado por ▪ interesarle a alguien ➤ She's interested in renting the parish hall for a birthday party. Le interesa alquilar el salón parroquial para su fiesta de cumpleaños.

to be **interesting to someone** ser materia interesante para ➤ I am healthy, so not very interesting to a doctor. Estoy sano así que no soy materia interesante para un médico.

internal affairs asuntos interiores

internal combustion engine motor de combustión interna

internal dialogue ▪ inner dialogue ▪ inner conversation ▪ conversation with oneself diálogo interno ▪ diálogo consigo

Internal Revenue Service Servicio de Impuestos Interior

interpreter for someone: to act as an ~ ▪ to be an interpreter for someone ▪ to interpret for someone ser intérprete ▪ hacer de intérprete

to be **interrupted by** ▪ to be broken by ser interrumpido por ▪ ser cuarteado por ➤ In darkness interrupted by flashes of lightning En una oscuridad cuarteada por relámpagos

to **intervene in a matter** tomar cartas en un asunto ➤ *(news item)* The Civil Guard has decided to intervene in the matter. La Guardia Civil ha decidido tomar cartas en el asunto.

intervening week semana entre medias ➤ In the intervening week, we're going to paint the house. Durante la semana entre medias vamos a pintar la casa.

intervening years ▪ years in between años intermedios ➤ In the intervening years En los años intermedios

interview with entrevista con ▪ entrevista a

intestinal flu: to have ~ ▪ to have diarrhea estar descompuesto ▪ tener diarrea

to be **into something** estar en la onda de algo ➤ I have a friend who's really into jazz. Tengo un amigo que realmente está en la onda del jazz.

intractable bureaucracy ▪ unmanageable bureaucracy burocracia intratable

to **introduce a bill (into)** presentar un proyecto de ley (a)

to **introduce someone to someone** presentar alguien a alguien ➤ "I'd like to introduce you to my fiancée," said Juan to his friend. Then he turned to his fiancée and said, "Cristina, this is Miguel." Me gustaría presentarte a mi prometida. Entonces se dirigió a su prometida y dijo, "Cristina, te presento a Miguel".

to **introduce someone to something** dar a conocer algo a alguien ▪ conocer algo por alguien ➤ Eduardo and Lola introduced me to flamenco music, and I introduced them to Dixieland jazz. Eduardo and Lola me dieron a conocer la música folk y yo a ellos les di a conocer jazz Dixieland. ➤ A Danish friend introduced me to Havarti cheese. Por una amiga danesa conozco el queso Havarti.

introduction of a plan ▪ establishment of a plan implantación de un plan ▪ introducción de un plan ➤ *(news item)* The bloodshed continues despite the introduction of successive plans against domestic violence. La sangría no cesa pese a la implantación de sucesivos planes contra la violencia doméstica.

introductory offer oferta de estreno ▪ oferta de lanzamiento ▪ oferta por inauguración

to **intrude on someone's solitude** invadir la soledad de alguien

to be **inundated with** ▪ to be deluged with lloverle un aluvión de

to **invade someone's privacy** invadir la privacidad de alguien ▪ invadir la intimidad de alguien

to **invent an excuse** ▪ to make up an excuse ▪ to concoct an excuse inventar una excusa ▪ inventar un pretexto

to be **inversely proportional to** ser inversamente proporcional a ➤ The force of gravitational attraction is inversely proportional to the square of the distance between the two bodies that are attracted to each other and directly proportional to the product of their masses. La fuerza de atracción gravitatoria es inversamente proporcional al cuadrado de la distancia entre los dos cuerpos que se atraen entre sí; y es directamente proporcional al producto de sus masas.

to **invest money** invertir dinero

to **investigate something or someone** investigar algo o a alguien ▪ hacer indagaciones sobre algo o alguien ▪ indagar algo o a alguien

investment portfolio ▪ holdings *los* valores en cartera

to be an **inveterate liar** ▪ to be a compulsory liar ser un mentiroso empedernido ▪ mentir más que hablar ▪ tener más cuento que Calleja ➤ He's an inveterate liar. Es un mentiroso empedernido. ▪ Miente más que habla. ▪ Tiene más cuento que Calleja.

inviolable secrecy of the confessional *(Catholicism)* secreto de la confesión ▪ sigilo sacramental

to **invite someone** invitarlo a ▪ convidarlo

to **invite someone back** ▪ to ask someone back volver a invitar a alguien

to **invite someone over** invitar a alguien a casa ➤ We'd like to invite you over to make tamales with us on Christmas Eve. Quisiéramos invitarlos a preparar tamales en casa en la Nochebuena.

to **invite someone up** invitarlo(-a) alguien a subir ▪ *(Sp., leísmo)* invitarle a alguien a subir

to **involve a lot of thought and planning** involucrar mucha reflexión ➤ It involves a lot of thought and planning. Involucra mucha reflexión.

to **involve expense** implicar un gasto ▪ suponer un gasto

to **involve many things** comprender muchas cosas ▪ abarcar muchas cosas ▪ abarcar muchos aspectos ➤ Love involves many things. El amor comprende muchas cosas. ▪ El amor abarca muchos aspectos.

to **involve risk** implicar riesgo ▪ conllevar riesgo ▪ entrañar riesgo

to **involve someone in something** involucrar a alguien en algo

to **involve (the practice of)** suponer la práctica de

to **involve work** implicar trabajo ▪ conllevar trabajo ▪ importar trabajo

to be **involved in a relationship** estar comprometido en una relación ➤ She's involved in a relationship right now. Ella está comprometida en una relación ahora.

to be **involved in the case** estar implicado en el caso ➤ The three judges involved in the case... Los tres jueces implicados en el caso...

to be **involved with someone** estar involucrado con alguien

involvement in implicación en ➤ Italy asks greater UN involvement in the postwar period. Italia pide una implicación de la ONU en la posguerra.

ipso facto ▪ by definition ipso facto ▪ por definición ➤ A blind person, ipso facto, is not eligible for a driver's license. ▪ A blind person, by definition, is not eligible for a driver's license. Una persona ciega es, ipso facto, inelegible para una licencia de conducir. ▪ Una persona ciega es, por definición, inelegible para una licencia de conducir.

iron curtain cortina de hierro

iron determination ▪ fierce determination férrea determinación

iron discipline disciplina férrea

iron fist: to rule with an ~ regir con mano de hierro

irreconcilable differences diferencias irreconciliables ▪ diferencias insalvables

irrefutable documents *(deeds, contracts, birth certificate, passport, etc.)* documentos fehacientes

irresistible urge to: to have an ~ tener un irresistible deseo de

is anything wrong? ¿algo va mal? ▪ ¿ocurrió algo? ▪ *(tú)* ¿te ocurre algo? ▪ *(usted)* ¿le ocurre algo?

is at (a certain time) es a ➤ Class is at 8:50. La clase es a las 8:50.

is everything: education ~ *la* educación lo es todo ▪ *la* educación es todo

is he there? ¿está? ▪ ¿está ahí él?

is it? ¿de verdad?

is it a deal? it's a deal! ▪ done? done! ¿trato hecho?-¡trato hecho!

is it close enough to walk to? ▪ is it close enough to go on foot? ¿es bastante cerca para ir a pie?

is it long? ▪ does it last long? ¿dura mucho?

is it my fault if...? can I help it if...? ¿tengo (yo) la culpa si...?

is it not true? ▪ isn't it true? ¿no es verdad?

is it perhaps...? ¿es a lo mejor...? ▪ ¿es tal vez...? ▪ ¿es quizá(s)...?

is it serious? ¿es serio? ▪ ¿es grave?

is it that bad? ¿es para tanto?

is needed to hace falta para

is recommended es recomendable ➤ A grounded outlet is recommended. Es recomendable un enchufe con toma de tierra.

is said to have ▪ reportedly has dijo tener ➤ Police are searching for the hijacker, who is said to have family problems... La policía busca al pirata aéreo que dijo tener problemas familiares...

is she there? ¿está (ella)?

is still in one piece sigue entero ➤ I want to turn on the TV for a second to see if the world is still in one piece. Quiero prender la tele un rato para ver si el mundo sigue entero.

is that all? ▪ is that everything? ▪ will that be all? ¿es todo?

is that *all*?! ▪ that's *it*?! ¡¿eso es todo?! ▪ ¡¿nada más?!

is that clear? ¿queda claro?

is that it? **1.** is that all? ¿es todo? **2.** is that the one? ¿es ése? ▪ ¿es ésa? **3.** is that what you mean? ¿es (eso) lo que quieres decir?

is that okay with you? ¿te parece bien? ▪ ¿te viene bien?

is that really the case? ▪ is it? ¿será así?

is that right? **1.** really? ¿es verdad? ▪ ¿de veras? **2.** is it correct? ¿es correcto?

is that so? ¿de verdad? ▪ ¿en serio?

is that true of you? ▪ is that true in your case? ¿es tu caso?

is that where...? ¿es allí donde...? ➤ Is that where he lives? ¿Es allí donde vive?

is that you in the picture? *(to a male)* ¿eres tú el de la foto? ▪ *(to a female)* ¿eres tú la de la foto?

is there an envelope that fits it exactly? ¿hay un sobre en el que quepa exactamente?

is there any mail for me? ▪ did I get any mail? ¿hay carta para mí? ▪ ¿hay correspondencia para mí?

is there any way to...? ▪ is there a way to...? ¿hay alguna forma de...? ➤ Is there any way to get in touch with him? ¿Hay alguna forma de ponerse en contacto con él?

is there room for one more? *(Mex.)* ¿cabe uno más? ▪ *(Sp.)* ¿entra uno más?

is there still...? ¿sigue habiendo...? ➤ Is there still an open-air market on Sundays near the Tetuán metro? ¿Sigue habiendo un mercado al aire libre los domingos cerca del metro Tetuán?

is this it? ▪ is this the one? ¿es éste? ▪ ¿es ésta?

is this one okay? ¿está bien éste? ▪ ¿por ejemplo? ➤ *(produce seller, holding up a tomato, to customer)* Is this one okay? ¿Por ejemplo? ▪ ¿Está bien éste?

is this the García Pérez residence? *(on the telephone)* ¿es la residencia García Pérez?

is this yours? ▪ does this belong to you? *(tú)* ¿es tuyo? ▪ ¿te pertenece? ▪ *(usted)* ¿es suyo? ▪ ¿le pertenece?

is usually called se le suele llamar

island kingdom reino insular

isn't it? ▪ is it not? ¿(es) verdad? ▪ ¿no es cierto? ▪ ¿no es así?

isn't it true? ▪ is it not true? ¿no es verdad?

isn't it wonderful? ▪ isn't that wonderful? ▪ isn't it marvelous? ▪ isn't that marvelous? ¿acaso no es maravilloso?

isn't that lovely! ¡qué bonito!

isn't that right? ¿no es así?

isolated incidents from his past retazos de su pasado

to **issue a passport to someone** ▪ to issue someone a passport expedirle un pasaporte a alguien

to **issue a student ID** expedir un carnet estudiantil ➤ They issue you an ID card when you register. Te expeden un carnet al matricularte.
to **issue a credit card to someone** ▪ to issue someone a credit card emitirle una tarjeta de crédito a alguien
to **issue a decree** pasar un decreto
to **issue a warning** emitir una advertencia
to **issue an indictment against** ▪ to indict ▪ to issue an indictment of ▪ to file legal proceedings against abrir un sumario contra ▪ instruir un sumario contra ▪ formular cargos sobre ▪ formular cargos en contra de
to **issue an invitation** proponer una invitación
to **issue an order for** dictar una orden de ▪ dictar una orden para...
to **issue an order that...** dictar una orden que... ▪ dictar una orden para que...
to **issue an order to** dictar una orden para
to **issue bonds** emitir bonos
to **issue from** proceder de ▪ provenir de
the **issue is that...** el punto en cuestión es... ▪ el tema es que...
issue of a magazine edición de una revista ➤ When will the April issue be on the stand? ¿Cuándo estará la edición de abril en el quiosco?
issue of a newspaper ▪ edition of a newspaper número de un periódico ▪ edición de un periódico
issues with: to have ~ diferir en ciertos puntos ▪ no estar de acuerdo con ▪ cuestionar
it all began with ▪ it all started with todo empezó con
it all boils down to... todo se reduce a...
it all depends (on) todo depende (de)
it all fits together todo encaja
it all goes back to todo se remonta a
it amounts to the same thing ▪ it comes to the same thing viene a ser lo mismo
it appears that... ▪ it seems that... ▪ it seems to be that... aparenta que... ▪ parece que... ▪ parece ser que...
it backfired *(internal combustion engine)* petardeó
it backfired (on him) ▪ it had an effect contrary to what he intended le salió el tiro por la culata
it baffles me ▪ I'm baffled (by it) me perpleja ▪ me desconcierta
(it) beats me! no tengo (ni) idea ▪ ni idea
it blew me away ▪ it blew my mind me dejó alucinado
it blows me away ▪ it blows my mind me deja alucinado
it burns me up me saca de quicio
it came loose se desprendió
it came over the news on TV that... ▪ it came on the TV news that... en la tele dieron la noticia de que...
it came to be believed that... ▪ people came to believe that... se llegó a creer que... ▪ llegó a creerse que...
it can be done ▪ yes, we can se puede conseguir ▪ se puede lograr ▪ *(United Farm Workers slogan)* ¡sí se puede!
it can be fatal puede ser fatal ▪ puede ser mortal
it can be said that... ▪ you could say that... ▪ it could be said that... ▪ one can say that... se diría que...
it can be served with ▪ you can serve it with puede servirse con ➤ It can be served with rice or potatoes. ▪ You can serve it with rice or potatoes. Puede servirse con arroz o patatas.
it can be told puede contarse ▪ puede ser contado
it can hardly be expected that... apenas cabe esperar que...
it can't be... 1. no puede ser... 2. *(when surmising)* no debe ser... ➤ How big is Antigua? I don't know, but it can't be very big. ¿Cómo es de grande Antigua? No sé, pero no debe ser muy grande.
it can't be done ▪ it cannot be done ▪ it's impossible ▪ there's no way no se puede hacer ▪ no hay manera ▪ *(coll.)* ni en pedo se puede hacer
it can't be very... no debe de ser muy... ▪ no debe de estar muy... ▪ *(weather)* no debe de hacer mucho... ➤ It can't be very cold. No debe de hacer mucho frío.
it caught me by surprise me agarró de sorpresa ▪ me pilló de sorpresa ▪ *(Sp.)* me cogió de sorpresa
it caught on se hizo costumbre ▪ se quedó (con...)
it certainly does ▪ it sure does claro que sí ➤ Does it rain a lot in Costa Rica?-It certainly does. ¿Llueve mucho en Costa Rica?-Claro que sí.
it certainly isn't claro que no ▪ ya lo creo que no
it comes as no surprise that... no ha sorprendido a nadie que... ▪ no ha extrañado a nadie que...
it comes down to money ▪ the bottom line is money ▪ what it boils down to is money se reduce al dinero
it comes with va incluido ▪ van incluidos ➤ It comes with a belt. ▪ The belt is included with the set. El cinturón va incluido con el conjunto. ➤ The salad bowl comes with a wooden spoon and fork. Con la ensaladera van incluidos una cuchara y un tenedor de madera.
it cost me a pretty penny me costó un ojo de la cara
it could almost be casi podría ser ▪ podría ser casi ➤ If the situation weren't so serious, it could almost be funny. Si la situación no fuera tan seria, casi podría ser graciosa.
it could be argued that... se podría argüir que... ▪ podría argüirse que...
it could be weeks or months podrían pasar semanas o meses
it could have been prevented pudo haberse prevenido ▪ podría haber sido prevenido
it could have been worse pudo ser peor ▪ podría haber sido peor
it could have caused pudo causar ▪ podría haber causado
it could take ▪ that could take podría llevar ▪ podría tardar ▪ se podría tardar ➤ It could take weeks or months to finish this project. Podría llevar semanas o meses para terminar este proyecto.
it could well be that... 1. bien podría ser que... 2. *(less certain)* bien pudiera ser que...
it could well have been bien pudo ser ▪ bien pudo ser así ▪ bien podría haber sido
it depends (on) depende (de) ➤ It depends on how much I get done. Depende de cuánto pueda hacer. ▪ Depende de hasta donde llegue. ➤ It depends a lot on... Depende mucho de...
it depends on how you look at it depende de cómo se mire
it depends on what happens depende de lo que pase
it didn't come off 1. it didn't happen ▪ it didn't take place ▪ it didn't come together no cuajó 2. it didn't wash off no salió 3. it didn't detach no se desprendió ▪ no se cayó
it didn't help (matters) that... no ayudó la situación que... ▪ no le valió que...
it didn't occur to me to ask no se me ocurrió preguntar ➤ It didn't occur to me to ask her. No se me ocurrió preguntarle (a ella).
it didn't register ▪ it went in one ear and out the other no se me quedó ▪ no lo registré ▪ entró en una oreja y salió por la otra ➤ I think you did tell me that, but it didn't register. Creo que me lo dijiste, pero simplemente no lo registré.
it didn't take long to... no tardó en... ▪ no se tardó mucho en...
it didn't used to be that way antes no era así ▪ no solía ser así
it didn't work no funcionó ➤ I tried it, but it didn't work. Lo probé, pero no funcionó.
it didn't work out no dio resultado
it does not lend itself to no se presta a
it doesn't come up (on the screen) no sale (en la pantalla) ▪ no me consta (en la pantalla)
it doesn't come with one no lleva ▪ no lleva uno(-a) ▪ no lo(-a) lleva
it doesn't count no vale nada ➤ *(Bill Clinton)* No American can ever again say: my vote doesn't count. Ningún americano podrá decir jamás: mi voto no vale nada.
it doesn't do any good de nada sirve
it doesn't do any good to complain ▪ it doesn't do a bit of good to complain de nada sirve quejarse
it doesn't do anything for me ▪ it leaves me cold a mí me deja frío
it doesn't do much good no sirve de mucho
it doesn't even ni siquiera

it doesn't fit 1. it's not the right size (for one) no le queda bien a uno ▪ no es el talle correcto **2.** it won't go in no entra **3.** it's too big no cabe ➤ This jacket doesn't fit (me) anymore. Esta chaqueta ya no me queda bien. ➤ This key doesn't fit. Esta llave no entra. ➤ This box doesn't fit in the suitcase. ▪ This box won't fit in the suitcase. Esta caja no cabe en la maleta.

it doesn't fit (me) no me va bien ▪ no me queda bien

it doesn't get any better than this no hay nada mejor que esto

it doesn't give the time *(of something scheduled)* ▪ it doesn't say what time ▪ it doesn't state the time no dice la hora

it doesn't look like (it's going to) rain ▪ there's no rain in sight no tiene trazas de llover

it doesn't look like he's here ▪ it looks like he's not here no parece que esté (él) ▪ parece que no está

it doesn't look like he's going to show up ▪ it looks like he's not going to show up ▪ there's no sign of him no parece que vaya a venir ▪ no tiene trazas de venir ▪ parece que no viene ▪ parece que no va a venir

it doesn't look like one no tiene aspecto de serlo ▪ no tiene aspecto de serla

it doesn't look like she's here no parece que esté (ella)

it doesn't make any difference ▪ it makes no difference no importa ▪ es lo mismo ▪ lo mismo da ▪ es igual

it doesn't make any difference to me ▪ it makes no difference to me me da lo mismo

it doesn't matter no importa ▪ me da igual ▪ *(L. Am.)* no le hace

it doesn't offend me at all no me ofende nada ➤ Please correct my Spanish; it doesn't offend me at all. Por favor, corrige mi español; no me ofende nada.

it doesn't register (with me) ▪ it doesn't ring a bell ▪ it doesn't sound familiar no me suena

it doesn't say much for... esto no dice mucho a favor de...

it doesn't say what time ▪ it doesn't give the time no dice la hora

it doesn't show ▪ you can't see it no se ve ▪ no se nota ▪ no se muestra ▪ no es obvio

it doesn't sting no escuece ▪ no arde

it doesn't work ▪ it isn't working ▪ it's not working no va ▪ no funciona

it doesn't write no pinta ➤ This ballpoint pen doesn't write. Este bolígrafo no pinta.

it drives me crazy 1. *(all senses of the term)* me vuelve loco(-a) ▪ me enloquece **2.** *(evoking anger or frustration)* me saca de quicio ▪ me saca de tino

it embarrassed me me dio vergüenza ▪ me avergonzó ▪ me abochornó ▪ pasé papelón

it embarrasses me me da vergüenza ▪ me avergüenza

it embarrasses me to admit it me da vergüenza admitirlo ▪ me avergüenza admitirlo

it embarrasses me to say so ▪ it embarrasses me to say it me da vergüenza decirlo

it feels like... da una sensación de...

it fits (you) *(clothing, nickname, etc.) (a ti)* te queda (bien) ▪ te sienta bien ▪ *(a usted)* le queda (bien) a usted ▪ le sienta bien

it fits in your hand ▪ it fits in the hand cabe en la mano

it frustrates me that... me frustra que...

it frustrates me when... me frustra cuando...

it gives me great pleasure to announce me complace anunciar

it gets in your blood se hace parte de quien uno es ➤ Flying (light airplanes) gets in your blood. Pilotear avionetas se hace parte de quien uno es.

it goes a long way cunde mucho ▪ da para mucho

it goes back to the time when se remonta al tiempo en que ▪ se remonta al tiempo cuando

it goes on to say that... sigue para decir que... ▪ continúa para decir que...

it goes to show you (that...) ▪ it just goes to show you (that...) sirve para demostrar (que...) ▪ sirve para ver (que...)

it goes with the territory ▪ it's all in a day's work es un gaje del oficio

it goes without saying that... huelga decir que... ▪ sobra decir que... ▪ se sobrentiende que... ▪ ni que decir tiene que..

it got her the prize ▪ it won her the prize le valió el premio (a ella)

it got him the prize ▪ it won him the prize le valió el premio (a él)

it got me (to) thinking that... me dio a pensar que... ▪ me dio por pensar que...

it got so bad that... llegó al punto tal que... ▪ llegó a tal punto que...

it grieves me that... me da pena que...

it had been a long time since... hacía mucho tiempo que no... ▪ hacía mucho que no... ➤ It had been a long time since I had seen him. ▪ It had been a long time since I'd seen him. Hacía mucho (tiempo) que no lo veía. ▪ *(Sp., leísmo)* Hacía mucho (tiempo) que no le veía. ➤ It had been a long time since I had seen her. ▪ It had been a long time since I'd seen her. Hacía mucho (tiempo) que no la veía.

it had better be good más (le) vale que sea bueno

it had better not... ▪ *(coll.)* it better not... más (le) vale que no... ➤ After waiting 10 days for that blasted avocado to ripen, it (had) better not spoil by tomorrow. Después de esperar diez días a que el puñetero aguacate madure, más (le) vale que no se eche a perder para mañana.

it happened in Bogotá sucedió en Bogotá ▪ ocurrió en Bogotá ▪ tomó lugar en Bogotá ▪ aconteció en Bogotá ▪ pasó en Bogotá

it happened just like that 1. it happened in a flash ocurrió en un santiamén **2.** that's exactly how it happened ocurrió así sin más

it happened suddenly ocurrió de golpe ▪ ocurrió de repente

it happened that... sucedió que... ▪ dio la casualidad de que...

it happens that... ▪ it (just) so happens that... sucede que... ▪ da la casualidad de que...

it happens to the best of us eso le pasa hasta al más pintado

it has a ring to it tiene cierta musicalidad

it has been brought to my attention that... ▪ it has been called to my attention that.. se me ha dado a conocer que... ▪ se me ha hecho saber que... ▪ *(takes a noun phrase)* me han llamado la atención a...

it has been raining for a week ▪ it's been raining for a week está lloviendo desde hace una semana

it has been scientifically proved that... ▪ it has been scientifically proven that... ha sido científicamente comprobado que...

it has been shown that... se ha demostrado que...

it has come to my attention that... ▪ it has been brought to my attention that ha llegado a mi atención que...

(it) has it that... quiere que... ➤ His versión has it that... ▪ His version maintains that... ▪ His version claims that... Su versión quiere que...

it has proved (to be)... ha resultado ser... ▪ se ha demostrado ser... ➤ In all political systems, it has proved (to be) difficult to eradicate poverty. En todos sistemas políticos, se ha demostrado ser difícil eradicar la pobreza.

it hasn't always been that way no es así desde siempre

it hit me funny 1. *(L. Am.)* se me hizo chistoso ▪ me hizo gracia ▪ *(Sp.)* me pareció divertido ▪ me pareció gracioso ▪ me pareció chistoso **2.** it struck me as odd that... me pareció un poco raro que... ▪ me pareció un poco fuera de lugar que...

it hurt her feelings hirió sus sentimientos ▪ hirió los sentimientos de ella

it hurt his feelings hirió sus sentimientos ▪ hirió los sentimientos de él

it hurt my feelings hirió mis sentimientos ▪ hirió los sentimientos míos

it is a commonplace that... es común y corriente que... ▪ es de cajón que... ▪ cae de cajón que...

it is as if ▪ it's as if es como si ➤ When the light passes through a slit, it is as if the electrons are waves, not particles. Cuando la luz pasa a través de una ranura, es como si los electrones fueran ondas, no partículas.

it is believed to be ▪ it is thought to be... se cree que es... ▪ se le supone...

it is better vale más ▪ más vale ▪ es mejor ➤ It is better to be alone than in bad company. Más vale estar solo que mal acompañado.
it is better (to do something) vale más (hacer algo)
it *is* contagious ▪ you *can* catch it sí da *(pun found on an AIDS-prevention poster, SIDA being the Spanish acronym for AIDS, "el SIDA sí da.")*
it is difficult es difícil ▪ cuesta ➤ It is difficult to tell them apart. Es difícil distinguirlos. ▪ Cuesta distinguirlos.
it is doing well ▪ it's doing well va bien
it is entitled ▪ the title is lleva por título ➤ It is entitled "Gone with the Wind." Lleva por título "Lo qué el viento se llevó".
it is essential, then, for you... *(tú)* debes pues... ▪ es esencial que tú... ▪ es fundamental que tú... ▪ *(usted)* debe pues... ▪ es esencial que usted... ▪ es fundamental que usted...
it is estimated that... se estima que... ▪ se calcula que...
it is extremely cold hace un frío intenso
it is finished! *(the last words of Jesus of Nazareth)* ¡queda cumplido!
it is forgiven por perdonado
it is going well ▪ it's going well va bien
it is he who has to... ▪ it is he who must... ▪ he's the one who has to... a él le corresponde...
it is hoped that... se espera que...
it is I ▪ *(coll.)* it's me soy yo
it is I who... ▪ I'm the one who... **1.** I am he who... soy yo él que... **2.** I am she who... soy yo ella que... **3.** a mí me corresponde...
it is impossible for... ▪ it's impossible for... es imposible que... ➤ It is impossible for me to meet you at the airport. Es imposible que te encuentre en el aeropuerto. ➤ It is impossible for a rocket to reach the speed of light, much less exceed it. Es imposible que un cohete alcance la velocidad de la luz, y mucho menos sobrepasarla.
it is impossible ▪ it's impossible es imposible... ➤ It is impossible to reach the velocity of light. Es imposible alcanzar la velocidad de la luz.
it is included ▪ it comes with it está incluido ▪ *(Sp.)* va incluido ➤ The battery is included. ▪ It comes with the battery. La pila está incluida. ▪ La pila va incluida.
it is intolerable (that...) ▪ it's intolerable (that...) es intolerable (que...)
it is, isn't it? verdad ¿que sí?
it is likely that... ▪ it is probable that... es probable que...
it is missing ha desaparecido ▪ *(colorful)* salió sin decir adiós ▪ me falta *(The subject in the latter can vary depending who the observer is.)*
it is necessary to do something es necesario hacer algo ▪ hay que hacer algo ▪ es menester hacer algo
it is no accident that... no es casualidad que... ▪ no es accidente que...
it is not known whether ▪ it is unknown whether se ignora si ▪ no se sabe si
it is probable that... ▪ it is likely that... es probable que...
it is recommended es recomendable ➤ A grounded outlet is recommended. Es recomendable un enchufe con toma de tierra.
it is not right for one not to ▪ it isn't right for one not to... ▪ it's not right for one not to... no está bien que uno no...
it is not right for one to ▪ it isn't right for one to... ▪ it's not right for one to... no está bien que uno...
it is right for one not to... ▪ it's right for one not to... está bien que uno no...
it is right for one to... ▪ it's right for one to... está bien que uno...
it is safe to say that... cabe decir que... ▪ podría decirse que...
it is said that... se dice que...
it is still... ▪ it continues to be... sigue siendo...
it is thought to be... ▪ it is believed to be... se le supone... ▪ está pensado ser...
it is to be expected that... ▪ it's to be expected that... es de suponer que...
(it) is, too 1. it is also también lo es **2.** oh, yes it is que sí (lo es)
it is unacceptable no es de recibo
it is usually fatal suele ser mortal
it is well known that... es bien sabido que... ▪ es bien conocido que...
it is well to remember that... ▪ it should be remembered that... conviene recordar que...
it isn't ▪ it's not **1.** *(main clause)* no lo es **2.** *(dependent clause)* no es ➤ No, it isn't. ▪ No, it's not. No, no lo es. ➤ It isn't possible. ▪ It's not possible. No es posible.
it isn't a matter of ▪ it's not a matter of no es cosa de
it isn't working ▪ it's not working no funciona ▪ no va
it just... ▪ it only... no sirve más que para... ➤ It just wastes time. ▪ It only wastes time. No sirve más que para perder el tiempo.
it just came to me me vino a la mente
it just clicked *(esp. in a relationship)* ▪ something just clicked algo sucedió ▪ algo brotó
it (just) goes to show you hay que ver
it (just) goes to show you that... sirve para ver que... ▪ sirve para demostrar que...
it (just) makes me sick that... me da (tanto) asco que... ▪ me da (tanto) asco lo que... ▪ ➤ It makes me sick that... Me da tanto asco que... ➤ What she did makes me sick. Me da (tanto) asco lo que hizo ella.
it just occurred to me (that...) se me acaba de ocurrir (que...)
it (just) so happened that... dio la casualidad de que...
it (just) so happens that... da la casualidad que...
it just won't... (que) no quiere... ➤ It just won't get cold this winter. (Que) no quiere enfriarse este invierno. ➤ It just won't quit. (Que) no quiere parar. ▪ No quiere dejar.
it keeps me out of trouble me mantiene alejado de los problemas
it leads me to believe that... me lleva a creer que...
it leaves a lot to be desired ▪ it leaves much to be desired deja mucho que desear
it leaves me cold ▪ it doesn't do anything for me a mí me deja frío
it leaves nothing to be desired no deja nada que desear
it looks as if ▪ it looks as though parece que ▪ tiene pinta de ➤ It looks as if it might rain. ▪ It looks as though it might rain. Parece que va a llover. ▪ Tiene pinta de llover.
it looks funny 1. it looks strange se ve extraño(-a) ▪ se ve raro(-a) **2.** it looks comical se ve gracioso(-a)
it looks like... parece (ser)... ▪ parece que... ➤ It looks like a wedding. Parece (ser) una boda. ▪ Parece que es una boda.
it looks like rain *(informal)* ▪ it looks as if it might rain ▪ it looks as though it might rain parece que va a llover ▪ tiene pinta de llover
it looks like you've had quite a night of it parece que te ha dado la noche
it looks really good on you te pega mucho ▪ te pega tanto
it made an impression on me me impresionó
it made me not like it hizo que no me gustara ▪ hizo que no me gustase
it made me sad me puso triste ▪ me produjo tristeza
it made me stop liking it hizo que dejara de gustarme ▪ hizo que me dejara de gustar ▪ hizo que dejase de gustarme ▪ hizo que me dejase de gustar
it makes for sirve para ▪ es para ➤ It makes for a very enjoyable evening. Sirve para pasar una velada muy amena. ▪ Es para pasar una velada muy amena.
it makes me furious when... me reviente que... ▪ me saca de quicio cuando...
it makes me mad ▪ *(Mex.)* me enoja ▪ me molesta ▪ me fastidia ▪ *(Sp.)* me enfada ▪ me cabrea
it makes me sad ▪ it makes me feel sad ▪ it saddens me me pone triste ▪ me produce tristeza
it makes me sick (that...) me enferma (que...) ▪ me da asco (que...) ➤ It makes me sick that... Me da tanto asco que... ➤ What she did makes me sick. Me da (tanto) asco lo que hizo ella.
it makes me sick when... me enferma cuando... ▪ me da asco cuando...

it makes me think that... me hace pensar que...

it makes more sense to... ▪ it's better to tiene más sentido (para) que... ▪ es más sensato...

it makes my blood boil hace que me hierva la sangre ▪ me revuelve la bilis

it makes my mouth water se me hace agua la boca ▪ *(Sp.)* se me hace la boca agua

it makes no difference ▪ it doesn't make any difference ▪ it doesn't matter no importa ▪ da igual ▪ da lo mismo ▪ es lo mismo ▪ lo mismo da ▪ es igual ▪ tanto monta

it makes no sense to do something... ▪ it doesn't make any sense to do something... ▪ there's no sense in doing something... no tiene sentido hacer una cosa...

it makes perfect sense tiene sentido perfecto ▪ es absolutamente lógico

it makes the point convence ▪ da la pauta

it makes the point that... hace ver que... ▪ hace entender que... ▪ hace comprender que... ▪ da la pauta que...

it makes you want to get the hell out of there es para salir más que a prisa ▪ es para salir pitando

it makes you want to run the other way es para salir corriendo

it matches 1. *(clothing)* hace juego (con) ▪ queda bien (con) **2.** *(description)* coincide

it matters little if poco importa si ▪ importa poco si

it matters little whether ▪ it doesn't make much difference whether poco importa si ➤ It matters little whether we go by train or bus. Poco importa si vamos en tren o en autobús.

it may never be known ▪ we may never know puede que nunca se sepa ▪ puede que nunca (lo) sepamos ▪ puede que nunca llegaremos a saber(lo) ➤ Pluto could at one time have been a satellite of Neptune, but whether it (ever) was may never be known. ▪ Pluto might at one time have been a satellite of Neptune, but we may never know whether it (ever) was. Plutón pudiera haber sido en algún tiempo un satélite de Neptuno, per si (alguna vez) lo fue, puede que nunca se sepa. ▪ Plutón pudiera haber sido en algún tiempo dado un satélite de Neptuno, per si (alguna vez) lo fue, puede que nunca lo sepamos.

it means a lot to me para mí significa mucho ▪ me significa algo ▪ para mí me representa mucho ▪ me representa mucho

it meant that... 1. significaba que... **2.** significó que... ▪ ➤ The arranged marriages meant that monarchs married people they barely knew. Las bodas arregladas significaban que los monarcas se casaban con alguien a quien apenas conocían. ➤ The curved shadow across the moon's surface during eclipses meant that the Earth couldn't possibly be flat. La sombra curvilínea de la Tierra sobre la superficie de la luna durante una eclipse significó que la Tierra no podía ser plana.

it might be 1. *(as a main clause)* puede ser **2.** *(as a dependent clause)* puede que sea... ▪ tal vez sea... ▪ quizás sea...

it might not be 1. *(as a main clause)* puede que no lo sea **2.** *(as a dependent clause)* puede (que) no sea... ▪ tal vez no sea... ▪ quizás no sea...

it might not seem like much, but... puede no parecer mucho, pero... ▪ podría no parecer mucho, pero...

it must be 1. tiene que serlo ▪ debe serlo **2.** *(conjectural)* debe de serlo

it must be... ha de ser... ▪ debe de ser...

it must be a mistake debe ser un error ▪ tiene que ser un error

it must be done right away hay que hacerlo inmediatamente

it must be getting late debe de ser ya tarde ▪ se estará haciendo tarde ▪ estará haciéndose tarde ▪ ya debe estarse haciendo tarde

it must be kept in mind that... ▪ you have to keep in mind that debe tenerse en cuenta que... ▪ se tiene que tener en cuenta que... ▪ tiene que tenerse en cuenta que... ▪ ha de tenerse en cuenta que...

it must be said that... debe decirse que... ▪ se tiene que decir que... ▪ tiene que decirse que... ▪ *(more formal)* se impone decir que...

(it) must have been... *(with "it" or a noun subject)* **1.** *(permanent state)* debe haber sido... ▪ debió ser... ▪ tiene que haber sido... ▪ seguramente fue... ▪ *(more conjectural)* debe de haber sido... **2.** *(temporary state)* debe haber estado... ▪ *(more conjectural)* debe de haber estado... ➤ He must have been kidnapped. Debe haber sido secuestrado. ➤ The lava flow must have been very rapid. El flujo de lava debe haber estado muy rápido. ▪ *(more conjectural)* El flujo de lava debe de haber estado muy rápido.

it must have been about one o'clock sería como la una ▪ debe de haber sido como la una

it must have been about *x* o'clock sería(n) como la(s) *x* ▪ había(n) de ser como la(s) *x* ▪ debe (de) haber sido como la(s) *x* ➤ It must have been about one o'clock when... Sería como la una cuando... ▪ Había de ser como la una cuando... ➤ It must have been about two o'clock when ... Serían como las dos cuando... ▪ Habían de ser como las dos cuando... ▪ Debe de haber sido como las dos cuando... *("Más o menos," "cerca de," and "aproximadamente" are possible alternatives to "como.")*

it must have been like that así habrá sido

it must have been planned 1. *(conjecture)* debe de haber sido planeado ▪ habrá sido planeado **2.** *(certainty)* it had to have been planned tuvo que ser planeado

it must have cost a fortune ha debido de costar una fortuna

it must seem strange that... parecerá extraño que...

it must still be there debe existir allí todavía ▪ todavía debe estar allí ▪ todavía debe quedar allí ▪ *(S. Am., literary)* debe haberlo(la) todavía *("Aún" can replace "todavía" in all examples.)*

it needs no explanation va sin explicación

it needs salt falta sal

it never ceases to amaze me nunca deja de sorprenderme ▪ jamás deja de asombrarme ▪ es una sorpresa permanente

it never crossed my mind jamás se me pasó por cabeza

it no longer exists ▪ it has ceased to exist ya no existe ▪ deja de existir ▪ ha dejado de existir

it now has... 1. ya tiene... ▪ tiene ya... ▪ ahora tiene... ▪ tiene ahora... **2.** *(as an auxiliary verb)* ya ha... ➤ The company now has two hundred branches. La compañía ya tiene doscientos sucursales.

it occurred to me that... se me ocurrió que...

it occurs to me that... se me ocurre que...

it only... ▪ it just... sólo... ➤ It only goes to show you... ▪ It just goes to show you... Sólo sirve para que veas que...

it only makes matters worse sólo empeora las cosas

it ought to be debería serlo

it ought to be... debería ser...

it puzzles me no lo logro entender ▪ me hace rascar la cabeza

it remains to be seen queda por verse ▪ está por verse

it reminds me of me recuerda a ▪ me hace recordar

it rings a bell ▪ it sounds familiar me suena

it ruins the moment te corta el rollo

it runs in the family es cosa de esta familia

it seems as if parece como si

it seems impossible parece imposible ▪ parece mentira

it seems like it's getting hotter la sensación de calor aumenta

it seems like just the other day parece como si hubiese sido el otro día (que...) ▪ parece (que fue) el otro día

it seems like yesterday (that...) parece como si hubiese sido ayer (que...) ▪ parece (que fue) ayer

it seems that... ▪ it appears that... ▪ it looks as if... parece que...

it seems to be that... parece ser que...

it seems to me that... me parece que... ▪ se me figura que... ▪ se me antoja que...

it serves my purposes ▪ it serves my purpose me apaño con esto ▪ me sirve

it serves you right! te lo mereces ▪ te está bien empleado ▪ bien merecido lo tienes

it should be made clear that... es de dejar en claro que...

it should be noted that... ▪ it should be pointed out that... cabe señalar que... ▪ habría que señalar que...

it should be pointed out that... ▪ it should be noted that... cabe señalar que... ▪ habría que señalar que...

it should be remembered that... conviene recordar que... ▪ convendría recordar que...

it should have arrived by now ya debería de haber llegado ▪ debe (de) haber llegado ya
it should not be forgotten that... no cabe olvidar que... ▪ no debería olvidarse que... ▪ no se debería olvidar que...
it shouldn't be long (now) no debe faltar mucho
it shows! ¡se muestra! ▪ ¡se nota! ▪ lo exterioriza ▪ se exterioriza
it shows that... se ve que...
it slipped my mind ▪ I forgot about it me olvidé ▪ se me olvidó por completo ➤ It slipped my mind completely. ▪ It completely slipped my mind. ▪ I forgot all about it. Se me olvidó por completo. ▪ Se me pasó por completo.
it smells good huele bien ➤ The air freshener smells good. Huele bien el ambientador.
it smells good in here! ¡qué bien huele aquí!
it smells bad huele mal
it so happens that... da la casualidad de que...
it sounds crazy (to me) me suena loco
it sounds delicious suena delicioso ▪ suena riquísimo
it sounds familiar ▪ it rings a bell me suena ▪ suena famililar
it sounds ridiculous me suena ridículo
it sounds urgent me parece urgente ▪ *(more detached)* parece ser urgente
it sounds weird (to me) me suena raro
it still... no deja de... ▪ sigue siendo ▪ sigue estando ▪ todavía es ▪ todavía está
it still exists aún existe
it sure does ▪ it certainly does claro que sí ➤ Does it snow a lot in the Andes?-It sure does! ¿Nieva mucho en los Andes?-¡Claro que sí!
it sure is! ¡lo es! ▪ ¡claro que sí! ▪ ¡sí que lo es!
it takes a long time se tarda mucho
it takes a lot of guts to... hace falta mucho arrojo para...
it takes all kinds (to make a world) se necesita de todo para hacer un mundo ▪ de todo hay en la viña de Señor ▪ tiene que haber de todo
it takes longer to do something than to do something else se tarda más en hacer una cosa que en hacer otra
it takes several attempts lleva various intentos ➤ During peak hours, it takes several attempts to log on. Durante las horas punta, lleva varios intentos conectarse. ▪ Durante las horas punta, lleva varios intentos entrar.
it takes the subjunctive lleva el subjuntivo
it takes two to tango dos no riñen si uno no quiere
it took me... me llevó ▪ tardé ➤ It took me four hours to change the battery. Me llevó cuatro horas cambiar la batería. ▪ Tardé cuatro horas cambiando la batería.
it turned out that... resultó que...
it turns out that... resulta que...
it upsets me me da pena ▪ me desconcierta ▪ me disgusta
it used to be that... solía ser que...
it was a bluff era un farol
it was a fluke se aventó un churro
it was a sight to see ▪ that was something to see era una cosa digna de verse
it was after *x* in the afternoon eran más de *x* de la tarde ➤ It was after five in the afternoon. Eran más de las cinco de la tarde.
it was almost dark when... ya casi era de noche cuando...
it was and still is ▪ it was and continues to be fue y sigue siendo
it was as if... ▪ it was as though... parecía que...
it was at that moment that... fue en ese momento cuando...
it was decided that... se decidió que...
it was believed to be... se creyó que era...
it was discussed se habló de ello ➤ It was discussed at some length. Se habló de ello en detalle.
it was first... se comenzó a... ➤ *(news item)* The water contamination was first detected in the summer of 2000. La contaminación del agua se comenzó a detectar en el verano de 2000.
it was for the best ▪ it was the best thing fue lo mejor ➤ He felt bad when he broke up with his girlfriend, but now he believes it was for the best. Se sentía infeliz al romper con su novia, pero ahora cree que fue lo mejor.
it was going on iba(n) a ser ➤ It was going on one o'clock (in the afternoon). Iba a ser la una (de la tarde). ➤ It was going on eight o'clock. Iban a ser las ocho. ➤ It was going on (twelve) noon. Iban a ser las doce del mediodía. ➤ It was going on midnight. Iba a ser la medianoche.
it was good to meet you ▪ it was nice to meet you ▪ it was great to meet you **1.** *(tú)* encantado(-a) de haberte conocido **2.** *(usted, speaking to a man)* encantado(-a) de haberlo conocido **3.** *(usted, speaking to a woman)* encantado(-a) de haberla conocido **4.** *(Sp., leísmo, speaking to a man or woman)* encantado(-a) de haberle conocido
it was hard to see apenas se veía ➤ It was hard to see Gibraltar from Marbella because of the haze. Por la bruma apenas se veía Gibraltar desde Marbella.
it was her opinion that... (ella) opinó que...
it was his opinion that... (él) opinó que...
it was impossible for era imposible para
it was impossible to era imposible para que
it was in the year 1492 that... corría en el año 1492 cuando...
it was just my imagination eran sólo figuraciones mías
it was late era tarde
it was like *(coll.)* ▪ it was as if ▪ it was as though fue como ▪ parecía que
it was like that when I bought it estaba así cuando lo compré ▪ ya era así cuando lo compré ▪ es así desde el principio
it was love at first sight fue amor a primera vista ▪ fue un flechazo
it was lucky for her that... fue una suerte para ella que...
it was lucky for him that... fue una suerte para él que...
it was meant to be ocurrió porque tenía que pasar
it was my duty era mi deber
it was my duty to (yo) tenía el deber de
it was my fault (yo) tenía la culpa ▪ era culpa mía ▪ fue culpa mía ➤ It was all my fault. (Yo) tenía toda la culpa. ▪ Todo era culpa mía. ▪ Todo fue culpa mía.
it was my last chance era mi última oportunidad
it was not just my imagination no era una simple imaginación
it was not what I expected ▪ it's not what I expected ▪ it's not what I was expecting no fue lo que (yo) esperaba ▪ no era lo que esperaba
it was nothing but no era más que ▪ no era sino ▪ no era nada más que
it was official era oficial
it was pouring rain se vino el cielo abajo ▪ llovía en baldes
it was really frustrating era de lo más frustrante
it was recommended to me me lo recomendaron ▪ se me recomendó
it was recommended to me that... me lo recomendaron que... ▪ se me recomendó que...
it was he who ▪ he was the one who fue él que
it was she who ▪ she was the one who fue ella que
it was so-and-so's idea esta idea salió de fulano ➤ It was Frank's idea. Esta idea salió de Paco.
it was something to see ▪ it was quite a sight ▪ it was a great sight to see fue digno de verlo
it was the first time era la primera vez ▪ fue la primera vez ➤ It was the first time Jim had seen Hanna. Era la primera vez que Jim veía a Hanna. ▪ Fue la primera vez que Jim vio a Hanna.
it was the first time in his life that... era la primera vez en su vida que...
it was the making of her fue lo que le consagró (a ella)
it was the making of him fue lo que le consagró (a él)
it was then that... ▪ that was when... fue entonces cuando...
it was thought that... se creía que... ▪ se pensaba que... ▪ se pensó que...
it was (to be) expected era esperable
it was to be expected that... era de suponer que...
it was too late to ya era tarde para ▪ ya era demasiado tarde para

it was torture 1. *(literal)* fue tortura 2. it was extremely difficult fue un tormento ▪ fue un martirio
it was, wasn't it? verdad ¿que sí?
it was worth a try valió la pena intentarlo ▪ *(in storytelling)* valía la pena intentarlo
it was worth it valió la pena ▪ *(in storytelling)* valía la pena
it wasn't all my fault no fue del todo culpa mía
it wasn't long before... no pasó mucho tiempo antes de que...
it wasn't profitable no era rentable
it weighs a lot ▪ it's heavy pesa mucho ▪ pesa un montón ▪ *(colorful)* pesa un huevo
it will come out all right in the end al final todo saldrá bien
it will change your life *(tú)* te cambiará la vida ▪ *(usted)* le cambiará la vida
it will come out all right in the end todo se andará
it will do you good ▪ it will do you a lot of good *(tú)* te vendrá muy bien ▪ *(usted)* le vendrá muy bien a usted
it won her the prize ▪ it got her the prize le valió el premio (a ella)
it won him the prize ▪ it got him the prize le valió el premio (a él)
it won't be long before... no va a pasar mucho tiempo antes de que... ➤ It won't be long before there is... No va a pasar mucho tiempo antes de que haya...
it won't be long now no falta mucho (tiempo) ahora
it won't fit no entra
it won't go back any farther *(car seat)* ▪ that's as far back as it'll go no va más para atrás
it works! ¡sí funciona! ▪ ¡sí sirve! ▪ ¡da resultado! ➤ (You) see? It works! ¿Lo ves? ¡Da resultado!
it would be a good idea (to do something) ▪ it would be good (to do something) sería conveniente (hacer algo) ▪ harías bien (haciendo una cosa) ➤ It would be a good idea to arrive early. Sería conveniente llegar pronto. ▪ Harías bien llegando pronto.
it would be a good idea if you... ▪ it would be well for you to... *(tú)* a ti te convendría si... ▪ *(usted)* a usted le convendría si...
it would be a pleasure *(accepting an invitation)* sería un placer
it would be better for one to do something sería mejor que uno hiciera algo ▪ sería mejor si uno hiciese algo
it would be better if one did something sería mejor que uno hiciera algo ▪ sería mejor si uno hiciera algo
it would be better to do something sería mejor hacer algo ▪ más valdría hacer algo ➤ It would be better to come to Madrid when it's not so hot. Sería mejor venir a Madrid cuando no haga tanto calor. ▪ Más valdría venir a Madrid cuando no haga tanto calor.
it would be good if... haría falta que...
it would be hard to find sería difícil encontrar ▪ difícilmente encontraríamos ▪ difícilmente podríamos encontrar
it would be nice sería bonito ➤ It would be nice to stop and have a drink after the concert. Sería bonito tomar una copa después del concierto.
it would be perfect if... 1. *(idealized circumstance)* sería perfecto si... 2. *(something achievable with minor adjustment)* estaría perfecto si...
it would be well for you to ▪ it would be a good idea if you *(tú)* a ti te conviene ▪ *(usted)* a usted le conviene
it would be you! *(tú)* ¡tendría que ser tú! ▪ *(usted)* ¡tendría que ser usted!
it would change his life forever iba a transformar su vida para siempre
it would have been better (for her) to... más le habría valido...
it would have been better (for you) to... más te habría valido...
it would mean 1. *(literal)* significaría 2. it would involve implicaría ▪ sería ➤ *(news item)* Giscard affirms that the entrance of Turkey would mean the end of the European Union. Giscard afirma que la entrada de Turquía sería el fin de la Unión Europea.
it wouldn't be a bad thing if no estaría nada mal si ▪ no sería nada malo si ➤ It wouldn't be a bad thing if Spain won the EuroCup. No estaría nada mal si España ganase la Eurocopa. ▪ No sería nada malo si España ganase la Eurocopa.
it wouldn't break my heart if... no se me partiría el corazón si...
it wouldn't break my heart to... no se me partiría el corazón al...
it wouldn't do any good sería inútil
it wouldn't work no funcionaba ➤ I tried it, but it wouldn't work. Lo intenté, pero no funcionaba.
it yields five cups ▪ yields five cups rinde cinco tazas ▪ cunde cinco tazas
to **itemize a bill** detallar una cuenta
itemized bill factura detallada
itemized billing facturación detallada
itemized statement extracto detallado
it'll be a year... hará un año... ➤ It'll be a year since I arrived in Madrid. Hará un año que llegué a Madrid. ▪ Hará un año que arribé a Madrid.
it'll change your life ▪ it will change your life *(a ti)* te cambiará la vida ▪ *(usted)* le cambiará la vida
it'll come to me ya se me va a ocurrir ▪ ya se me ocurrirá
it'll get the prize que tiene premio
it'll go away *(headache, etc.)* 1. I'll get over it se me pasará 2. you'll get over it se te pasará ▪ se le pasará (a usted)
it's a bit premature ▪ it's a little premature es un tanto prematuro
it's a cinch ▪ it's a piece of cake es coser y cantar ▪ es facilísimo
it's a compliment es un cumplido ▪ es un halago
it's a deal! ¡trato hecho!
it's a different story now ▪ it's another story now se han vuelto las tornas
it's a drag ▪ it's a pain es un tostón ▪ es un fastidio ▪ es un bodrio
it's a fine time to tell me that! ¡menudo momento para decirme eso!
it's a good thing that... menos mal que... ▪ *(L. Am.)* qué bueno que... ▪ *(Sp.)* qué bien que... ➤ It's a good thing they got there when they did. Qué bien que llegaran en ese momento. ▪ Qué bueno que llegaran en ese momento.
it's a good time to... es propicio para... ➤ This month is a good time to start preparing for winter. Este mes es propicio para preparar para el invierno.
it's a hassle es una faena
it's a joke 1. es una broma ▪ es un chiste 2. it's laughable es una risa ➤ The emergency room of a certain hospital whose name I'd rather not recall is a joke: they keep you waiting until midnight. Ir a urgencias en cierto hospital cuyo nombre no quiero acordarme, es una risa: te tienen esperando hasta la medianoche.
it's a known fact that... es un hecho conocido que...
it's a lie! ¡mentira!
it's a little bit complicated está medio complicado
it's a little premature ▪ it's a bit premature ▪ it's a little early es un tanto prematuro
it's a little tricky es un poco tramposo
it's a long story es (muy) largo de contar
it's a long way es mucho camino ▪ queda muy lejos
it's a matter of es cosa de ▪ es cuestión de
it's a matter of individual tastes es cuestión de gustos ▪ depende de los gustos de cada cual
it's a matter of principle es una cuestión de principios
it's a packed house está colmado (de gente) ▪ hay un lleno absoluto ▪ está hasta las topes ▪ *(gesturing with the hands)* está así de gente
it's a pain ▪ it's a drag es un tostón
it's a pain in the ass es una espina en el culo
it's a pattern of hers ▪ it's a pattern in her es un patrón que (ella) tiene
it's a pattern of his ▪ it's a pattern in him es un patrón que (él) tiene
it's a pittance menos es nada ▪ es una miseria
it's a privilege es un (verdadero) privilegio
it's a question of es cuestión de

it's a road we've been down before *(literal and figurative)* ▪ we've been down this road before es un camino que hemos recorrido antes ▪ es un camino que ya hemos recorrido
it's a small world el mundo es un pañuelo
it's a true story es una historia verídica
it's a whole new ball game se han vuelto las tornas
It's a Wonderful Life *(film title) ¡Qué bello es vivir!*
it's about time! ▪ it's high time! ▪ at last! ¡ya es hora! ▪ ¡ya va siendo hora! ▪ ¡acabáramos!
it's about time you got here ▪ it's high time you got here ya es hora que llegaras
it's after one es más de la una
it's after *x* son más de las *x* ➤ It's after five. Son más de las cinco.
it's against the rules va en contra de las reglas
it's all gone ▪ there isn't any more no queda más
it's all Greek to me a mí todo me suena a chino
it's all in a day's work ▪ it goes with the territory es un gaje del oficio
it's all in your mind es pura sugestión
it's all I've got on me es todo lo que llevo encima
it's all my fault yo tengo la culpa de todo ▪ es todo culpa mía
it's all over se acabó
it's all over town está por todo el pueblo
it's all right now ya se ha arreglado
it's all the same to me me es completamente igual
it's all there in the history books viene en la historia
it's almost all gone queda poco
it's already been taken care of ya está resuelto
it's anyone's guess ▪ it's anybody's guess ▪ your guess is as good as mine ▪ who knows? ¿quién sabe? ▪ vete a saber ▪ cualquiera dice
it's always been that way es así desde siempre
it's an outrage es un ultraje
it's another story now ▪ it's a different story now se han vuelto las tornas
it's anyone's guess ▪ it's anybody's guess ▪ your guess is as good as mine ▪ who knows? vete tú a saber ▪ ¿quién sabe? ▪ cualquier dice
it's as good as it gets ▪ that's as good as it gets va que arde
it's as simple as that es tan sencillo como eso ▪ es así de fácil
it's based on a true story está basado en una historia verídica ▪ está basado en hechos reales
it's bedtime toca irse a la cama ▪ a dormir
it's been a month since hace un mes que ➤ It's been a month since I visited Montevideo. Hace un mes que no voy a Montevideo.
it's been in the refrigerator (for)... ha estado en la nevera... ▪ lleva *x* en la nevera... ➤ It should be cold. It's been in the refrigerator for four hours. Debería estar frío. Ha estado en la nevera cuatro horas.
it's been raining for a week ▪ it has been raining for a week está lloviendo desde hace una semana
it's been so long that I've forgotten hace mucho tiempo que lo tengo olvidado
it's been through the mill ya duró bastante
it's *been x* minutes ya han pasado *x* minutos
it's been years since... hace años que... ▪ años ha que...
it's best to... ▪ it is best to... lo mejor es... ➤ To plan a trip it's best to consult the tourism site on the Internet. Para planear un viaje, lo mejor es consultar el sitio de turismo en el Internet.
it's better for you *(food)* es más sano(-a)
it's better than nothing (eso) es mejor que nada ▪ más vale algo que nada ▪ poco es algo, menos es nada ▪ *(Sp.)* menos da una piedra
it's beyond *me* está más allá de mí ▪ no tengo idea ▪ me supera
it's beyond me! me supera ▪ es superior a mis fuerzas ▪ me sobrepasa ▪ me desborda
it's bound to happen ▪ it has to happen ▪ it's going to happen ▪ *(coll.)* it's gonna happen tiene que ocurrir
it's breakeven (only) ▪ there's no money in it ▪ it's not profitable **1.** sale lo comido por lo servido **2.** *(established by actual experience)* ha sido lo comido por lo servido
it's busy *(telephone)* comunica ▪ está comunicando ▪ la línea está ocupada ➤ Is it ringing or is it busy?-It's busy. ¿Está sonando o está comunicando?-Está comunicando. ▪ ¿Está sonando o está ocupada?-Está ocupada.
it's cheaper in the long run sale más barato
it's cloudy está nublado
it's coming back to me ▪ I'm beginning to recall it ya me empiezo a acordar
it's cool! *(Mex.)* ¡es (muy) padre! ▪ *(Sp.)* ¡es (muy) guay! ▪ ¡es muy chuli! *(Arg.)* ¡es muy copado! ▪ ¡es (muy) bárbaro! ▪ ¡es muy jolla! ▪ ¡es una masa! ▪ ¡está mortal! *(Chi.)* es muy bacán
it's dangerous puede ser peligroso
it's dark in here qué oscuro está aquí dentro
it's definitely... decididamente, es...
it's doable *(coll.)* ▪ it can be done es factible ▪ es realizable
it's doubtful that es dudoso que ➤ It's doubtful that the president has ever read the document. Es dudoso que el presidente haya leído alguna vez el documento.
it's due (on)... tiene que estar para... ▪ debe estar para... ➤ The library book is due (on) May third. El libro de la biblioteca tiene que estar para el tres de mayo.
it's earlier in the United States than in Spain es más temprano en los Estados Unidos que en España
it's early es temprano
it's easy to see why y se explica
it's embarrassing es vergonzoso ▪ es bochornoso ▪ *(esp. humiliation to another)* es lastimoso
it's enough for es suficiente para ▪ basta para
it's enough to live on alcanza para vivir ▪ es suficiente para vivir
it's enough to make you cry es para llorar
it's enough to make you leave in tears es para salir llorando
it's enough to make you scream es para gritar
it's essential that... es esencial que... ▪ es fundamental que...
(it's) every man for himself sálvate tú mismo ▪ sálvese quien pueda ▪ sálvese el que pueda
it's fair to say that... es justo decir que...
it's foggy hay niebla
it's for... sirve para...
it's for good reason that they say (that)... ▪ not for nothing do they say (that)... no se dice por nada que... ▪ bien se dice que...
it's for the birds es de tontos
it's for your own good *(tú)* es por tu propio bien ▪ *(usted)* es por su propio bien
it's getting late (on me) se (me) está haciendo tarde ▪ se (me) hace tarde
it's getting to be time ya va siendo hora ➤ It's getting to be time to leave. Ya va siendo hora de salir.
it's going on *x* years since... ▪ it's been nearly *x* years since... ▪ nearly *x* years have gone by since... va para *x* años que... ➤ It's going on six years since I came to Spain. Va para cinco años que vine a España.
it's going to be a while va para largo ➤ We were waiting for our train to leave, and since it was going to be a while, we decided to get something to eat at the station. Estábamos esperando a que saliera nuestro tren, y como iba para largo, decidimos picar algo en la estación.
it's good *(food)* está bueno ▪ *(book)* es bueno ▪ *(movie)* es buena
it's good to be back es bueno volver ▪ es bueno estar de vuelta
it's good to meet you ▪ it's nice to meet you ▪ (I'm) delighted to meet you ▪ (I'm) pleased to meet you **1.** *(tú)* encantado(-a) de conocerte **2.** *(L. Am., speaking to a man)* encantado(-a) de conocerlo **3.** *(usted, speaking to a woman)* encantado(-a) de conocerla **4.** *(Sp., usted, speaking to a man, leísmo)* encantado(-a) de conocerle
it's good to see you again ▪ it's nice to see you again me alegro de volverte a ver

it's gotten late on me ▪ I'm running late se me ha hecho tarde

it's great to be home, isn't it? qué rico es estar en casa, ¿verdad?

it's great to see you! ▪ (it's) so good to see you! ¡tanto bueno por aquí!

it's growing on me me va entrando

it's guaranteed se garantiza ▪ *(expressing irony)* es matemático ➤ It's guaranteed. If you wash the car, it'll rain. Es matemático. Si lavas el carro seguro que llueve.

it's hard to believe ▪ that's hard to believe cuesta creerlo

it's hard to believe that it could have been es difícil creer que pudiera haber sido

it's hard to know es difícil saberlo

it's hard to put my finger on it me cuesta bastante dar con ello

it's hard to say ▪ it's hard to know es difícil saberlo

it's heavy ▪ it weighs a lot pesa mucho ▪ pesa un montón ▪ *(colorful)* pesa un huevo

it's high time! ▪ it's about time! ▪ at last! ¡ya es hora! ▪ ¡acabáramos! ▪ ¡por fin!

it's high time you got here ▪ it's about time you got here ya es hora que llegaras

it's hopeless no hay ninguna esperanza

it's impossible to know ▪ there's no way to know no se puede saber

it's impossible to say no se puede saber

it's in the way está estorbando ▪ está entorpeciendo el camino

it's intolerable no se puede tolerar ▪ es intolerable ▪ no es de recibo

it's just a matter of getting used to it es sólo cuestión de acostumbrarse ▪ es todo acostumbrarse

it's just a matter of time es sólo cuestión de tiempo

it's just like someone (to) ser muy propio de uno ➤ It's just like him. Es muy propio de él.

it's just that... es sólo que...

it's just that you don't know him ▪ you just don't know him lo que pasa es que no lo conoces ▪ *(Sp., leísmo)* lo que pasa es que no le conoces

it's just the opposite ▪ it's (just) the other way around es todo lo contrario ▪ es justo lo contrario

it's just typical! ▪ that's just typical! ▪ typical! ¡lo típico!

it's later in Spain than in the United States es más tarde en España que en los Estados Unidos

it's later than you think la hora es más avanzada de lo que piensas

it's light outside es de día

it's likely that... es probable que...

it's lost its charm se ha perdido el encanto

it's lucky for me that... es una suerte para mí que...

it's me *(coll.)* ▪ it is I soy yo

it's missing ha desaparecido

it's more than I can eat es más que (yo) pueda comer

it's more than just a... es algo más que un(-a) mero(-a)...

it's mutual es mutuo ▪ y yo a... ▪ y él a... ▪ y ella a... ▪ y tú a... ▪ y usted a... ▪ y nosotros a... ▪ y ustedes a... ▪ *(Sp., vosotros)* y vosotros a... ➤ Your students like you a lot.-It's mutual. Sus estudiantes le quieren mucho.-Y yo a ellos.

it's my business ▪ that's my business es asunto mío ▪ es cuenta mía

it's my duty es mi deber

it's my duty to tengo el deber de

it's my fault es culpa mía ▪ tengo la culpa

(it's) my pleasure el gusto es mío ▪ el placer es mío

it's my time ▪ my time has come es mi hora

it's my treat *(tú)* te invito ▪ *(vosotros)* os invito

it's my turn 1. *(when playing a game)* me toca a mí ▪ es mi turno ▪ ahora voy yo **2.** *(to be waited on)* yo soy el siguiente ▪ me toca a mí ▪ es mi turno

it's never crossed my mind jamás se me ha pasado por la cabeza

it's nice outside hace buen tiempo

it's nice to meet you ▪ it's good to meet you ▪ (I'm) delighted to meet you ▪ (I'm) pleased to meet you **1.** *(tú)* encantado(-a) de conocerte **2.** *(usted, speaking to a man)* encantado(-a) de conocerlo **3.** *(usted, speaking to a woman)* encantado(-a) de conocerla **4.** *(Sp., usted, leísmo)* encantado(-a) de conocerle

it's nice to see you again ▪ it's good to see you again me alegro de volverte a ver

it's no big thing 1. it's nothing to get upset about no es gran cosa ▪ no es para tanto **2.** it's nothing to write home about no es nada del otro jueves

it's no contest no hay color

it's no coincidence that... no en vano... ▪ no es una una casualidad que...

it's no good no sirve para nada ▪ no vale para nada ▪ es inútil

it's no laughing matter no es como para reírse ▪ no es nada como para reírse ▪ no es un asunto del que uno se pueda reír

it's no telling what they're up to ▪ there's no telling what they're up to a saber lo que estarán tramando

it's no use no hay nada que hacer

it's no use crying over spilled milk ▪ there's no use crying over spilled milk a lo hecho, pecho ▪ agua pasada no mueve molino

it's no use denying it ▪ there's no use denying it no vale la pena negarlo ▪ no merece la pena negarlo

it's no wonder that... ▪ it's little wonder that... no es de extrañar que... ▪ es lógico que... ▪ no me extraña que... ▪ con razón...

it's none of your business ▪ it is no concern of yours ▪ it's no concern of yours *(tú)* no es asunto tuyo ▪ no es de tu incumbencia ▪ no pintas nada en esto ▪ *(usted)* no es asunto suyo ▪ no es de su incumbencia ▪ usted no pinta nada en esto

it's not ▪ it isn't no es ▪ no lo es

it's not a big deal ▪ it isn't a big deal no es gran cosa ▪ no tiene importancia

it's not a matter of ▪ it isn't a matter of no es cosa de ▪ no es cuestión de

it's not a question of ▪ it isn't a question of no es cuestión de

it's not all that interesting no es que sea muy interesante

it's not always easy ▪ it isn't always easy no siempre es fácil

it's not anywhere near that hot no hace tanto calor ▪ *(looking at an outdoor thermometer)* no hace tanto calor como pone

it's not as if ni que fuera ▪ tampoco es como para ➤ I don't know why she's so stuck up, it's not as if she were Miss Universe. No sé porque es tan engreída, ni que fuera Miss Universo.

it's not because I don't want to ▪ it's not that I don't want to no es por falta de ganas

it's not beneath one to ▪ not to be above no caérsele los anillos ➤ Though he is a former president, it is not beneath Jimmy Carter to work as a carpenter. ▪ Though he is a former president, Jimmy Carter is not above working as a carpenter. Aunque haya sido presidente de los Estados Unidos, a Jimmy Carter no se le caen los anillos por trabajar de carpintero.

it's not coming to me ▪ I can't think of it no me sale ▪ no se me ocurre

it's not coming up on the screen ▪ it's not coming up no me sale en la pantalla

it's not critical no es esencial ▪ no es fundamental ▪ no es crítico

it's not deserved no está merecido ➤ The criticism is not deserved. La crítica no está merecida.

it's not difficult to imagine ▪ it's not hard to imagine no es difícil de imaginar

it's not exactly... no es exactamente... ▪ no es que digamos... ➤ *(Fiddler on the Roof)* Well, Anatevka isn't exactly the garden of Eden. Pues, Anatevka no es exactamente el jardín de Edén. ▪ Pues, Anatevka no es que digamos el jardín de Edén.

it's not fair no es justo ▪ no hay derecho

it's not for me 1. it's not my place ▪ it's not intended for me no es para mí **2.** for my sake ▪ for my benefit no es por mí ➤ It's not for me to agree or disagree. No es para mí coincidir o discrepar.

it's not for me to judge no me cabe juzgar(lo) ▪ no es para mí juzgar(lo)

it's not for me to say no es para mí decir(lo) ▪ no me cabe decirlo
it's not for my sake that... no es para mí (beneficio) que...
it's not for nothing that they say that... ▪ not for nothing do they say that... ▪ it's for good reason that they say that... no se dice por nada que... ▪ bien se dice que...
it's not hard to imagine ▪ it's not difficult to imagine no es difícil de imaginar
it's not here yet *(next month's issue)* sigue sin venir
it's not in the cards no está en su destino
it's not just any... no se trata de... cualquiera ➤ My dog's not just any old dog! ¡Mi perro no se trata de un perro cualquiera!
it's not just my imagination no es una simple imaginación
it's not like her no es propio de ella
it's not like him no es propio de él
it's not like you *(tú)* no es propio de ti ▪ *(usted)* no es propio de usted
it's not my concern no me atañe
it's not my cup of tea no es lo mío ▪ no es santo de mi devoción
it's not my fault no es mi culpa
it's not necessary ▪ you don't need to no hace falta ▪ no es necesario
it's not over no ha terminado
it's not possible no es posible ▪ no puede ser
it's not profitable ▪ there's no money in it ▪ it's breakeven (only) no es rentable ▪ sale lo comido por lo servido ▪ ha sido lo comido por lo servido
it's not right ▪ it's wrong **1.** it's not correct no es correcto ▪ está equivocado **2.** it's not fair ▪ it's not just ▪ it's unjust no es justo ▪ no hay derecho
it's not so easy ▪ it's not that easy no es tan fácil
it's not that ▪ that's not it no es eso
it's not that bad no es para tanto ▪ no hay para tanto ▪ ni tanto, ni tan poco
it's not that easy ▪ it's not so easy no es tan fácil
it's not that I don't want to ▪ it's not because I don't want to no es por falta de ganas
it's not that simple no es así de sencillo
it's not the right time ▪ this is not the right time no está el patio para bollos ▪ no está el horno para bollos
it's not what I expected no es lo que (yo) esperaba
it's not what it used to be ▪ it's not what it once was ya no es lo que era
it's not working ▪ it isn't working ▪ it doesn't work no funciona ▪ no va
it's nothing! 1. not to worry! ¡qué hay! **2.** don't think anything of it! ¡no es nada! ▪ ¡poca cosa!
it's nothing new no es ninguna novedad ▪ no es nada nuevo
it's nothing personal no es nada personal
it's nothing to be ashamed of no es ninguna vergüenza
it's nothing to get alarmed about ▪ don't be alarmed no se alarme
it's nothing to worry about no es preocupante
it's nothing to write home about no es la cosa del otro jueves
it's now a fact ya es un hecho
it's official es oficial
it's okay by me *(coll., but incorrect)* ▪ it's okay with me ▪ it's fine with me me parece bien ▪ me parece muy bien
it's okay with me ▪ it's fine with me me parece bien ▪ me parece muy bien
it's on its way out está en camino de desaparecer
it's on me ▪ I'm buying **1.** *(tú)* te invito **2.** *(usted)* le invito **3.** *(ustedes)* les invito **4.** *(Sp., vosotros)* os invito
it's on the tip of my tongue ▪ it's right on the tip of my tongue lo tengo en la punta de la lengua
it's on your way te queda de paso ▪ te pilla de paso ▪ te pilla de camino ➤ Could you put this in the mailbox for me? It's on your way. ¿Podrías poner esto en el buzón por mí? Te pilla de paso. ▪ Te pilla de camino.
it's one of the reasons why... es una de las razones por las que...
it's one reason why... es una razón por la que...
it's one thing for una cosa es que ➤ It's one thing for someone to be important to us, but it's another to take over their freedom. Una cosa es que nos importe el otro, pero otra es adueñarse de su libertad.
it's only to be expected that... sólo se pretende que... ▪ sólo se aguarda que...
it's our own little secret ▪ it's just between you and me queda entre nosotros
it's our treat ▪ we're treating you te invitamos
it's out of date 1. it's not up to date ▪ it's not current está obsoleto ▪ no está al día **2.** it's out of style ▪ it's behind the times está pasado de moda ▪ está desfasado **3.** it's expired está caducado ▪ está vencido
it's out of the question ni soñarlo ▪ *(tú)* ni lo pienses ▪ *(usted)* ni lo piense (usted)
it's over se acabó
it's possible that I won't go es posible que no vaya
it's raining está lloviendo
it's really busy right now *(to phone customer)* hay mucho jaleo aquí
it's really easy en realidad es muy fácil
it's really frustrating es de lo más frustrante
it's right here está justo aquí
it's right in front of you está justo enfrente tuyo
it's right on the corner está justo en la esquina ▪ está en la mera esquina
it's (right) on the tip of my tongue lo tengo en la punta de la lengua
it's ringing *(telephone)* **1.** *(on your end)* está sonando **2.** *(on the other end)* está sonando ▪ está llamando ➤ Is it ringing or is it busy?-It's ringing. ¿Está sonando o está comunicando?-Está sonando. ▪ ¿Está llamando o está comunicando?-Está llamando.
it's rumored that... se rumorea que... ▪ se dice que...
it's scary te da miedo
it's silly es una bobada ▪ es una tontería
it's still busy sigue ocupado ▪ continúa ocupado
it's still too early to tell ▪ it's too early to tell es aún pronto para saber ▪ es pronto para saber
it's still too soon to aún es pronto para
it's stuck *(videocassette, etc.)* está atascado ▪ se ha atascado
it's stuffy in here el ambiente está repleto ▪ el ambiente está cargado ▪ está cargado aquí
it's that simple es así de fácil
it's the first time I've ever seen that es la primera vez que veo eso ▪ es la primera vez que lo veo ➤ It's the first time in my life I've ever seen that. Es la primera vez en mi vida que veo eso.
it's the least I can do ▪ that's the least I can do es lo menos que puedo hacer
it's the least I could do ▪ that's the least I could do es lo menos que podía hacer
it's threatening to rain amenaza lluvia
it's time to es hora de ▪ ha llegado el momento de
it's time to go es (la) hora de irse ▪ es la hora de marcharse ▪ es la hora
it's time to go to work es hora de ir a trabajar
it's time we got back to work ya es hora de volver al trabajo
it's time we got down to work ya es hora de empezar a trabajar
it's time we went home ya es hora de que nos vayamos a casa
it's to be expected that... ▪ it is to be expected that... es de suponer que...
it's to die for da ganas de morir ▪ dan ganas de morir
it's too early to... es aún pronto para... ➤ The authorities indicated it was too early to determine the causes of the (airplane) crash. Las autoridades indicaron que era aún pronto para averiguar las causas del siniestro.
it's too early to tell ▪ it's too soon to tell es (demasiado) pronto para saber ▪ es aún pronto para saber ▪ aún no se puede saber
it's too late for that es demasiado tarde para eso

it's too noisy ▪ there's too much noise se oye demasiado ▪ *(coll.)* hay mucha bulla
it's too soon to es pronto para
it's too soon to tell ▪ it's too early to tell es pronto para saber ▪ es aún pronto para saber ▪ aún no se puede saber
it's torture 1. *(literal)* es tortura **2.** *(figurative)* es un tormento ▪ es un martirio ➤ It's torture to lug these heavy suitcases all over Europe. Es un martirio llevar estas maletas por toda Europa.
it's understandable se entiende
it's understandable that... se entiende que
it's unheard of es inaúdito
it's up to you *(tú)* a ti te toca ▪ te toca a ti ▪ de ti depende ▪ depende de ti ▪ es de tu incumbencia ▪ te encumbe ▪ *(usted)* depende de usted ▪ le encumbe (a usted) ▪ es de su incumbencia
it's urgent es urgente
it's useless to es por demás que
it's very foggy está muy espesa
it's very kind of you ▪ that's very kind of you es muy amable (por su parte) ▪ muy amable
it's water under the bridge es agua pasada
it's well worth the money bien vale el dinero ▪ bien vale ese dinero
it's well worth the trouble bien vale la pena
it's working! *(idea, invention, trick, etc.)* ¡sirve! ▪ ¡ha funcionado! ➤ My idea is working! ¡Mi idea sirve!
it's worth a try vale la pena intentarlo
it's worth it 1. it's worth the trouble vale la pena **2.** it's worth the cost vale el coste ▪ compensa comprarlo ➤ If you ride the metro more than four times a day, it's worth it to buy a pass. Si tomas el metro más de cuatro veces al día, compensa comprar un abono transporte. ➤ It's worth it to buy one. Compensa comprarlo.
it's worth the effort vale la pena el esfuerzo ▪ merece la pena el esfuerzo ▪ París bien vale una misa
it's worth the trouble ▪ it's worth it vale la pena ▪ merece la pena
it's *x* degrees hace *x* grados ➤ It's sixty-eight degrees Fahrenheit outside. Hace sesenta y ocho grados Fahrenheit afuera. *(68°F equals 20°C.)*
it's yours! ▪ take it! *(tú)* ¡llévatelo! ▪ ¡quédatelo! ▪ *(usted)* ¡lléveselo! ▪ ¡quédeselo! ➤ It's yours for just ten dollars! ¡Llévatelo por sólo diez dolares!
I've almost finished estoy a lo último
I've already done that eso ya lo hice ➤ I've already done that once and don't want to do it again. Eso ya lo hice antes y no quiero volverlo a hacer.
I've always known that lo he sabido desde siempre
I've always known that... he sabido desde siempre que...
I've been asked if se me ha preguntado si
I've been asked whether se me ha preguntado si
I've been here for... estoy aquí desde hace... ➤ I've been here for seven and a half years. Estoy aquí desde hace siete años y medio.
I've been here the whole time! ▪ I haven't gone anywhere! ▪ the ball's in your court! ¡tú mismo (y tu mecanismo)! ▪ ¡allá tú!
I've been hit! ¡me han dado! ▪ ¡me han alcanzado!
I've been to the beach he ido a la playa
I've been wearing ▪ I've worn llevo usando ▪ llevo gastando ➤ I've been wearing these shoes for five years. Llevo cinco años usando estos zapatos. ▪ Llevo cinco años gastando estos zapatos.
I've changed my mind he cambiado de opinión ➤ I've changed my mind; I'll have a soft drink instead. He cambiado de opinión; prefiero un refresco.
I've done it now! ▪ look what I've done! ¡la he hecho buena!
I've done that once ya lo he hecho una vez
I've got an idea! ▪ I have an idea! tengo una idea! ▪ ¡se me ocurre una idea! ▪ ¡se me ha ocurrido una idea!
I've got him trained *(the waiter)* le tengo bien enseñado ▪ le tengo bien amaestrado
I've got it! 1. *I* know! ¡ya lo tengo ▪ ¡ya sé! **2.** I've figured it out! ▪ I've solved it! ¡ya lo tengo! ▪ ¡ya lo domino! ▪ ¡ya está!
I've got my hands full ▪ I've got all I can deal with ▪ I've got a full plate estoy muy ocupado ▪ estoy completamente ocupado
I've got some money ▪ I have some money tengo dinero ▪ tengo algo de dinero
I've got to hurry ▪ I have to hurry tengo que darme prisa
I've got you ya te tengo
I've got you cornered! ¡ya te tengo acorralado!
I've got you pegged ▪ I've got your number ▪ I know what you're up to te tengo calado ▪ veo por dónde vienes
I've gotten into the habit of ▪ I've acquired the habit of he cogido el hábito de ▪ he cogido la costumbre de ▪ me he habituado a ▪ me he acostumbrado a ▪ he adquirido el hábito de ▪ he adquirido la costumbre de
I've gotten to (the point) where he llegado al punto donde ▪ he llegado al punto en que
I've had a beard for five years tengo barba desde hace cinco años
I've had it! 1. I'm fed up ¡ya he tenido bastante! ▪ ¡estoy harto! ▪ ¡se acabó! **2.** I'm done for ¡estoy apañado!
I've just been through one *(an earthquake)* acabo de vivirlo ▪ *(a wedding)* acabo de vivirla
I've missed hearing from you hace tiempo que no oigo de ti
I've never seen anything like it no he visto nada igual ▪ nunca he visto algo semejante ▪ nunca he visto algo así ➤ *(Colin Powell on the tsunami)* I've never seen anything like it in my life. No he visto nada igual en mi vida.
I've noticed lo he notado
I've noticed that lo he notado
I've noticed that... he notado que...
I've only got half an hour sólo dispongo de media hora
I've reconsidered lo he pensado mejor
I've told you a hundred times te he dicho cientos de veces
I've worn ▪ I've been wearing llevo usando ▪ llevo gastando ➤ I've worn these shoes for five years. Llevo cinco años usando estos zapatos. ▪ Llevo cinco años gastando estos zapatos.
ivory tower *la* torre de marfil

to **jab at somone** 1. *(with a knife)* intentar acuchillar a alguien ▪ tratar de acuchillar a alguien 2. *(verbally)* to take jabs at someone tirar dardos a alguien

to **jab someone with a pencil** clavarle un lápiz a alguien

to **jab someone with one's elbow** ▪ to give someone a jab with one's elbow darle un codazo a alguien

to be a **jack of all trades** valer lo mismo para un fregado que para un barrido ▪ valer igual para un fregado que para un barrido ▪ servir lo mismo para un fregado que para un barrido ▪ igual valer para un roto que para un descosido

to be a **jack of all trades and a master of none** ser aprendiz de mucho, maestro de nada ▪ ser oficial de mucho, maestro de nada ▪ ser maestro de todo, experto de nada

Jack Robinson: before you can say ~ en un abrir y cerrar de los ojos

Jack the Ripper *(infamous London murderer)* Jack el estripador

jail sentence: to get a ▪ to receive a jail sentence condenársele a la cárcel

Jalisco, Mexico native *(coll.)* tapatío(-a)

to be **(jam) packed** ▪ to be packed like sardines estar de bote en bote ▪ estar hacinado(s) ▪ no caber ni un alfiler

to be **jammed into a small space** estar apiñado en un espacio pequeño ▪ estar atestado en un espacio pequeño

to **jangle one's nerves** jugar los nervios

jaundiced view of something: to have a ~ tener una opinión negativa de algo

to be **jealous of someone** tener celos de alguien ▪ celarse de alguien

jet (airplane) *el* avión de reacción ▪ avión de chorro

jet-black más negro que el azabache ▪ negro como el azabache

jet engine *el* reactor ▪ *el* motor de reacción ▪ motor a reacción ▪ motor de chorro

jet lag: to have ~ estar desfasado ▪ no estar con el cambio de horario ➤ I have jet lag. Estoy desfasado. ▪ No estoy con el cambio de horario.

to **jettison fuel** ▪ to dump fuel arrojar combustible ▪ evacuar combustible ➤ The airplane was jettisoning kerosene before the crash. El avión arrojaba queroseno antes del siniestro.

to be a **jewel** ser una perla ➤ She's a jewel. Es una perla.

jingle bells cascabeles

job involves puesto conlleva

job is on the line because of this: one's ~ le va el trabajo en esto

job market mercado de trabajo

job shortage *la* escasez de puestos de trabajo

to **jockey for position** manipular para neutralizar

to **join a choir** unirse a un coro

to **join a class** unirse a una clase ➤ Do you want to join our class? ¿Quieres unirte a nuestra clase?

to **join a club** ▪ to sign up as a member of a club darse de alta en un club ▪ apuntarse en un club

to **join a company** ▪ to join a firm darse de alta en una empresa ▪ entrar en una compañía ▪ entrar en una empresa

to **join a firm** ▪ to join a company darse de alta en una empresa ▪ entrar en una compañía ▪ entrar en una empresa

to **join a political party** unirse con un partido político ▪ sumarse a un partido político ▪ adherirse a un partido político

to **join an association** adherirse a una asociación ▪ incorporarse a una asociación

to **join forces against** unir fuerzas contra ➤ *(headline)* Conservatives and socialists join forces against the rule of fear in País Vasco Conservadores y socialistas unen fuerzas contra el voto de miedo en Euskadi

to **join forces to do something** unirse para hacer algo ▪ aunar esfuerzos para hacer algo ▪ combinarse para hacer algo

to **join forces with someone** unir (sus) fuerzas con alguien

to **join in** participar en ▪ sumarse a

to **join in the singing** unirse al canto

to **join someone** unírsele a alguien ➤ He joined them in Guatemala City. Se les unió en la Ciudad de Guatemala.

to **join the army** ▪ to enlist in the army unirse al ejército ▪ enlistarse en el ejército ▪ alistarse en el ejército ▪ enrolarse en el ejército

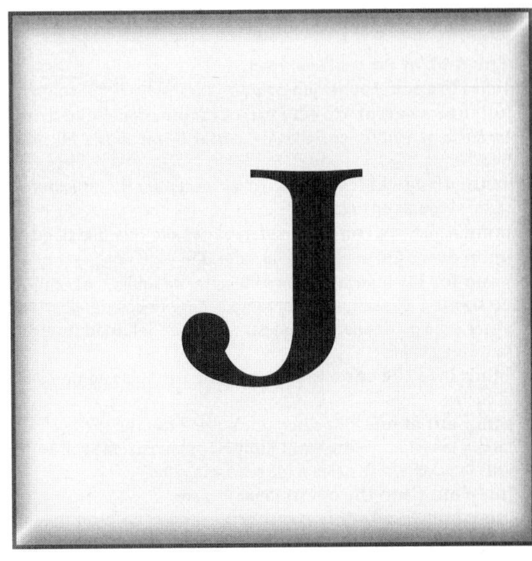

to **join the circus** unirse al circo ➤ He ran away from home to join the circus. ▪ He ran away from home and joined the circus. Huyó de su casa para unirse al circo.

to **join the department** unirse al departamento ➤ When he joined the department, he was its youngest member. Cuando se unió al departamento, era el miembro más joven.

to **join the ranks of** incorporarse a filas de

to be **joined at...** *(Siamese twins)* estar unidos por... ➤ The Siamese twins were joined at the head. Las hermanas siameses estaban unidas por la cabeza.

joining me now is... junto a mí ahora es...

joint bank account cuenta bancaria conjunta

Joint Chiefs Of Staff junta de jefes ▪ cúpula militar estadounidense

joint session: to call a ~ convocar un pleno

to be a **joke** ser puro chiste ➤ That literary theory course is a joke. Ese curso en la teoría literaria es puro chiste.

to **joke about it** bromear al respecto

jolly good fellow: for he's a ~ porque él es un buen compañero *(It is also common on birthdays, etc., to say "for you're a jolly good fellow": "porque eres un buen compañero.")*

to **jot down** tomar nota ▪ apuntar

journalist's ear for the language manejo del lenguaje de un periodista

Joyful Mysteries *(Catholicism)* Misterios Gozosos

to **judge by appearances** ▪ to go by appearances fiarse de las aparencias ➤ Don't judge by appearances. No te fíes de las aparencias.

judge for yourself *(tú)* juzga tú mismo ▪ *(usted)* juzgue usted mismo

judge not that you be not judged *(Matthew 7:1)* 1. *(Reina-Valera)* no juzguéis para que no seáis juzgados 2. *(Nueva Versión Internacional)* no juzguen a nadie, para que nadie los juzgue a ustedes ▪ *(Sociedad Bíblica Americana)* no juzguen a otros, para que Dios no les juzgue a ustedes

to **judge something by eye** ▪ (to judge) by looking at something ▪ to estimate by eye calcular algo a ojo ▪ calcular algo a simple vista ▪ (calcular) a ojo de buen cubero ➤ Judging (him) by eye, I'd say he's about two meters tall. ▪ (Judging) by looking at him, I'd say he's about two meters tall. ▪ Estimating by eye, I'd say he's about two meters tall. (Calculando) a ojo, diría que mide unos dos metros.

to be **judged on the basis of** ser juzgado sobre la base de

judging by appearances por las trazas ▪ según las trazas

judging from ▪ judging by a juzgar por ➤ There had to have been a storm here, judging from the fallen branches. ▪ There must have been a storm here, judging by the fallen branches.

Tuvo que haber una tormenta aquí, a jugar por todas las ramas caídas.

Judgment Day Día del Juicio Final

judicial branch *el* poder judicial

to **julienne a carrot** ▪ to cut a carrot in thin, matchlike strips cortar la zanahoria en juliana ▪ cortar la zanahoria en tiras finas

julienned vegetables *(carrots, celery, peppers, etc., cut into thin strips)* verduras en juliana

to **jump as high as one can** saltar lo más alto que uno puede

to **jump down from** bajar de un salto de

to **jump for joy** brincar de alegría ▪ saltar de júbilo ▪ dar saltos de alegría ▪ dar saltos de contento ▪ dar brincos de alegría ▪ pegar brincos de alegría ▪ pegar saltos de felicidad ▪ pegar saltos de alegría

to **jump into the car** ▪ to hop into the car subir de un salto al coche

to **jump out at one** ▪ to catch one's eye ▪ to take the eye saltarle a la vista ➤ The word jumped out at me. Me saltó a la vista la palabra. ▪ La palabra me saltó a la vista.

to **jump out (into the open)** saltar al claro

to **jump out the window** saltar por la ventana ➤ Peter Rabbit escaped by jumping out the window. Pedrito Conejo se escapó saltando por la ventana.

to **jump over something** saltar por encima de algo ➤ *(nursery rhyme line)* The cow jumped over the moon. La vaca saltó por encima de la luna.

to **jump rope** ▪ to skip rope saltar a la comba ▪ saltar a cordel

to **jump-start a car by coasting it and popping the clutch** arrancar un carro de tirón dejándolo deslizarse y soltando el embrague de golpe ➤ To jump-start the car by coasting it, turn on the ignition, put it in second, coast it downhill a few yards, and pop the clutch. ▪ To jump-start the car by coasting it, turn on the ignition, put it in second, let it coast downhill a few yards, and pop the clutch. Para arrancar el carro dejándolo deslizarse, gira la llave, mete segunda, déjalo deslizarse unos metros por la pendiente, y suelta el embrague de golpe.

to **jump-start a car by pushing it and popping the clutch** arrancar un carro de tirón empujándolo y soltando el embrague de golpe ➤ To jump-start the car by pushing it, turn on the ignition, put it in second, push it for a few yards, and then pop the clutch. Para arrancar el carro de tirón empujándolo, gira la llave, mete segunda, empújalo unos metros y suelta el embrague de golpe.

to **jump-start a car with jumper cables** ▪ to jump-start a car by using jumper cables arrancar un carro con pinzas ▪ arrancar el carro con cocodrilos

to **jump through a few hoops** ▪ to go through a few hoops hacer malabarismos ➤ To get a student visa you have to jump through a few hoops. Para conseguir un visado estudiantil, hay que hacer malabarismos.

to **jump to conclusions** precipitarse a una conclusión ▪ concluir precipitadamente

to **jump to one's feet** levantarse de un salto ▪ levantarse de un brinco

to **jump up and down** saltar arriba y abajo ▪ pegar saltos

jumper cables ▪ booster cables cables para pasar corriente ▪ pinzas ▪ cocodrilos

junior high school ▪ middle school escuela de enseñanza media

junk food comida basura ▪ *(Mex.)* comida chatarra

to be **just a front** ▪ to be just a mask (that the real person hides behind) no ser más que una coraza

to be **just a mask (that the real person hides behind)** ▪ to be just a front no ser más que una coraza

just a minute! ¡un momento! ➤ Just a minute! What's going on here? ¡Un momento! ¿Qué pasa aquí?

just a second! ¡un segundín!

just a short note sólo cuatro líneas

just a touch sólo una pizca ▪ sólo un toque

just about ▪ practically prácticamente

to be **just around the corner** estar justo a la vuelta de la esquina ➤ There's an off-hours store just around the corner. Hay una tienda que está abierta fuera de hora justo a la vuelta de la esquina. ➤ September is just around the corner. Septiembre está al caer.

just as 1. just when justo cuando **2.** true to what tal como ▪ tal y como ▪ así como ▪ al igual que ▪ lo mismo que ➤ The phone rang just as I was leaving. Justo cuando salía, sonó el teléfono. ➤ Just as I told you... Tal como te dije...

just as easily as con la misma facilidad que ➤ From the Plaza de Castilla, you can get to Tribunal just as easily on line ten as on line one. Desde la Plaza de Castilla se puede llegar hasta Tribunal por la línea diez con la misma facilidad que por la uno.

just as fast igual de rápido ➤ In a vacuum, the feather falls just as fast as the rock. Una pluma cae al vacío igual de rápido que una piedra. ▪ En el vacío una pluma cae igual de rápido que una piedra.

to be **just as good** estar igual de bueno

just as I had said tal como (yo) había dicho

just as I had said it would (be) y tal y como (yo) había dicho que sería

just as I had said it would (turn out) y tal y como (yo) había dicho que resultaría

just as I thought tal y como me lo imaginaba ▪ así como me lo imaginaba

just as I told you tal y como te dije

just as it is ▪ just the way it is ▪ as is tal cual

(just) as it should be tal y como debería ser

just as much ▪ equally igual ▪ igualmente ➤ When I was growing up I liked dogs (the) best, but as an adult I have come to like cats just as much. Cuando crecía me gustaban más los perros, pero de adulto, me han llegado a gustar los gatos igual.

just as one never knows... como tampoco uno sabe...

just as quickly igual de rápido ➤ From the Plaza de Castilla, you can get to Tribunal just as quickly on line ten as on line one. Desde la Plaza de Castilla, se puede llegar a Tribunal igual de rápido en la línea diez que en la uno.

just as one... 1. in the same way that one... así como uno... **2.** at the moment (that) one... justo cuando uno...

(just) as soon as I can en cuanto (yo) pueda ▪ lo antes que pueda ▪ tan pronto como (yo) pueda

just as you proposed tal y como (lo) planteaste

just as you said tal y como (lo) dijiste

just as you suggested tal y como (lo) sugeriste

to be **just average** ▪ to be only average no exceder de lo corriente

to be **just awful** ser una paliza ▪ to taste awful saber a rayos (y centellas)

just barely por los pelos ➤ I just barely made it to the bus. ▪ I almost missed the bus. Cogí el autobús por los pelos.

to **just barely get by (in a course)** aprobar por los pelos ▪ llevarla con alfileres ▪ llevarla cogido con pinzas

to **just barely touch the floor** llegar al ras del suelo

just be aware of that *(tú)* que te des cuenta de eso ▪ date cuenta de eso ▪ *(usted)* que se dé cuenta de eso ▪ dese cuenta de eso

(just) be aware that... *(tú)* que te des cuenta (de) que... ▪ date cuenta (de) que... ▪ *(usted)* que se dé cuenta (de) que... ▪ dese cuenta (de) que...

just because *(indefinite reply)* **1.** just because I do porque sí **2.** just because I don't porque no **3.** simply because sólo porque ▪ sólo que ▪ por el solo hecho de ➤ Just because you have... Sólo porque tienes... ➤ Just because something is impossible doesn't mean that somebody won't try to do it. Sólo que algo sea imposible no quiere decir que nadie intente hacerlo.

just because of nada más que por ▪ sólo por

just before... ▪ right before... justo antes de (que)... ▪ un momento antes de (que)... ➤ Antonio called (me) just before dinner. Justo antes de comer, me llamó Antonio. ➤ Antonio called me just before you got here. Un momento antes de que vinieses, Antonio me llamó.

just before dark ▪ right before dark justamente antes del anochecer

just before that ▪ right before that justo antes de eso ➤ Just before that, I heard the screeching of the brakes. Justo antes de eso, oí el chirrido de los frenos.

to be **just begging for it** estar pidiéndolo a gritos ➤ You're just begging for it. Estás pidiéndolo a gritos.
just beginning en bozo
just between us girls *(coll.)* ▪ just 'tween us girls en petit comité
just between you and me entre nosotros
to be **just big enough to** ser ya lo suficiente grande para
just by ▪ simply by con sólo
just by listening: to help someone ~ ayudar a alguien con sólo escucharlo(-a)
just call me Frank llámame simplemente Paco
just cause 1. righteous cause causa justificada **2.** sufficient reason motivo suficiente ▪ *la* razón suficiente ➤ Your cause is just, but I can't help you. Tu causa está justificada, pero no puedo ayudarte. ➤ You have just cause to complain. Tienes motivo suficiente para quejarte. ▪ Tienes razón suficiente para quejarte.
just checking sólo comprobando ▪ probando
just cool it! ▪ cool it! ¡tranquilízate! ▪ ¡cálmate!
to be **just delighted that...** ▪ to be tickled pink that... estar chocho de que...
just desserts: one's ~ su merecido
just do it! ¡hazlo y punto!
just for fun por diversión ▪ para divertirse ▪ por deporte
just for the fun of it por amor al arte
just get here acabar de llegar ➤ I just got here. Acabo de llegar. ➤ Did you just get here? ¿Acabas de llegar?
(just) get up your nerve and... échate valor y...
just imagine that... figúrate que...
just in case por si acaso ▪ por las dudas ▪ *(coll.)* por si las moscas
to be **just in the beginning of...** estar justo en el principio de...
just in time justo a tiempo
just in time for... justo a tiempo para... ▪ justo para...
just in time to... justo para... ▪ justo a tiempo de... ➤ I arrived in Madrid just in time to catch the train for Salamanca. Llegé a Madrid justo para coger el tren para Salamanca.
to be **just jealous** estar celoso ▪ darle a uno envidia ➤ You're just jealous. Estás celoso. ▪ Te da envidia.
to be **just joking** ▪ to be just kidding ▪ to be only joking ▪ to be only kidding sólo bromearle ▪ sólo vacilarle ▪ sólo tomarle el pelo ▪ sólo ser de mentira ➤ I was just joking. ▪ I was just kidding. Sólo te bromeaba. ▪ Sólo te estaba vacilando. ▪ Sólo te estaba tomando el pelo.
just kidding! 1. *(present)* ¡es broma! ▪ estoy bromeando ▪ te estoy vacilando **2.** *(past)* ¡era broma! ▪ estaba bromeando ▪ te estaba vacilando
just let him try! ¡que lo intente!
just like ▪ the same as igual que ➤ Plants breathe just like we do. Las plantas respiran igual que nosotros.
just like one never knows... *(coll.)* ▪ just as one never knows... como tampoco uno sabe...
to be **just like someone** ser muy propio de alguien ➤ It's just like him. Es muy propio de él.
just like that 1. just like you have it ▪ just the way it is así tal cual **2.** immediately sin más (ni más)
just like *that* 1. as if it were nothing como si nada **2.** instantly, suddenly así sin más ▪ así de golpe ▪ de repente ➤ It happened just like that. Ocurrió de repente.
just like you ▪ in the same way you did ▪ just as you did de manera parecida a la suya ➤ I began my vocation many years ago just like (all of) you. Empecé mi vocación hace muchos años de manera parecida a la vuestra.
just like you heard it ▪ it's true así como lo oyes
just long enough to apenas lo justo para ➤ He lived just long enough to know that his daughter had won the Nobel Prize. Apenas vivió lo justo para saber que su hija había ganado el Premio Nobel.
(just) look at you! ¡mírate!
just married! ¡recién casados!
just now ▪ a moment ago ahora mismo ➤ I heard it, just now. Lo acabo de oír, ahora mismo.
just one sólo uno(-a)
just one out of every... ▪ only one out of every... ▪ only one in every... tan sólo uno(-a) de cada... ▪ solamente uno de cada... ➤ Just one out of every fifteen hundred people exposed to the bacteria will develop symptoms of the disease. Tan sólo una de cada mil quinientas personas expuestas a la bacteria, desarrollará síntomas de la enfermedad.
just opposite (from) where ▪ right across from where justo frente a donde
just over the top of justo por encima de ➤ From about a hundred meters down the street, you can see the heads of the baby storks just over the top of the nest. Desde más o menos cien metros de distancia se alcanzan a ver las cabezas de las cigüeñitas justo por encima del nido.
to be **just passing through** ▪ to be just visiting estar de paso ➤ We're not from here, we're just passing through. No somos de aquí, estamos de paso.
just plain a secas ➤ They called Lincoln "Old Abe" or just plain "Abe." A Lincoln lo llamaban "Old Abe" o "Abe" a secas.
just plug it in basta enchufarlo ➤ This shaver is easy to use. Just plug it in. Esta rasuradora es fácil de usar, basta enchufarla.
just remember (that)... conste que... ➤ Just remember, I told you. ▪ Just remember, I warned you. Conste que te lo dije.
to be **just right** estar en su punto ▪ ni falta más ni falta menos ➤ Does it need salt? No, it's just right. ¿Le falta sal? No, está en su punto.
to **just say it** ▪ to come right out and say it hablar mal y pronto
to **just sit there (and do nothing)** estar de brazos cruzados
to be **just so** ser así ➤ Her coffee has to be just so. Su café tiene que ser así.
just so you can get an idea of *(tú)* sólo para que te hagas una idea de ▪ *(usted)* sólo para que se haga una idea de
just so you know para que lo sepas ▪ para que conste
just so you know that... para que lo sepas que... ▪ para que conste que...
just that: to remain ~ quedarse sólo en eso
to be **just the beginning** ser sólo el principio
just the idea of sólo la idea de ▪ sólo pensar en
to be **just the opposite** ▪ to be just the other way around ▪ to be quite the opposite ser (justo) todo lo contrario ➤ It's just the opposite. ▪ It's just the other way around. Es (justo) todo lo contrario.
just the other day sólo hace unos días ➤ I saw her just the other day. La vi sólo hace unos días. ➤ Just the other day I was saying that... Sólo hace unos días yo decía que...
to be **just the same** seguir tal cual
just the thought of... ▪ the mere thought of... ▪ just thinking of... ▪ merely the thought of... sólo de pensar en... ▪ sólo pensar en... ▪ sólo la idea de... ➤ At the thought of having to go to the doctor, children are fearful. Sólo de pensar que tienen que ir al médico, los niños pasan miedo.
just the thought of it... ▪ just thinking about it... ▪ the very thought of it... ▪ merely thinking of it... sólo de pensarlo...
just then ▪ at that moment justo entonces ▪ en ese momento ▪ al momento
just think! ¡piénsalo! ▪ ¡imagínate! ▪ ¡figúrate! ➤ *Lincoln:* Just think of a sucker like me as president! ¡Imagínate un pardillo como yo de presidente!
just think what it means! ¡considere usted el caso!
just thinking about it... ▪ just the thought of it... ▪ the very thought of it... ▪ merely thinking of it... sólo de pensarlo...
just this morning esta misma mañana
just this once sólo por esta vez
just to be following orders ▪ simply to be following orders limitarse a cumplir órdenes
just to be polite por ser cortés ▪ por cumplir
just to give you an example ▪ to give you an example ▪ as an example ▪ by way of example a guisa de ejemplo
just to give you an idea of *(a ti)* sólo para darte una idea de ▪ *(a usted)* sólo para darle una idea de ➤ Just to give you an idea of the size of the solar system, if the sun were the size of a grapefruit, the Earth would be the size of a pinhead 10.7 meters away. Sólo para darte una idea del tamaño del sistema

solar, si el sol fuera el tamaño de un pomelo, la Tierra sería el tamaño de una cabeza de alfiler a una distancia de 10.7 metros.

just to let someone be ▪ to simply let someone be simplemente dejar ser a alguien ▪ simplemente dejar a alguien en paz

just to prove it ▪ to prove it sólo para comprobarlo ▪ sólo para probarlo

just to remind you... ▪ I just wanted to remind you that... sólo quería recordarte que... ▪ sólo para recordarte...

just today ▪ this very day sólo hoy ▪ hoy mismo

just turned *x* con *x* años recién cumplidos ➤ *(newspaper article)* Camilo José Cela, just turned eighty-five... Camilo José Cela, con ochenta y cinco años recién cumplidos...

just turned a certain age: to have ~ acabar de cumplir cierta edad ➤ Her grandfather just turned sixty-five. Su abuelo acaba de cumplir sesenta y cinco.

just 'tween us girls en petit comité

to **just up and do something** darle la venada y hacer algo ➤ Sr. Stewart just upped and dyed his hair green. Sr. Stewart le dio la venada y se tiñó el pelo de verde.

to be **just visiting** ▪ to be just passing through sólo estar de visita ▪ sólo estar de paso

to be **just weeks away** estar a tan sólo semanas ➤ Christmas is just two weeks away. La Navidad está a tan sólo dos semanas.

just what I need justo lo que necesito

just what the doctor ordered 1. *(for me)* justo lo que me ha recetado el médico 2. *(for him or her)* justo lo que le ha recetado el médico

just wait! 1. *(tú)* ¡espera! ▪ *(usted)* ¡espere! 2. you'll see! ¡ya verás! ▪ ¡ya verá usted!

(just) who does he think he is? pero, ¿qué se ha creído? ▪ ¿quién se ha creído que es? ▪ ¿de qué va?

just yesterday ▪ only yesterday ayer mismo ▪ mismamente ayer

justice of the peace juez(a) de paz

to **justify something by saying that...** ▪ to justify something by maintaining that... justificar algo amparándose en que...

keen sense of humor: to have a ~ ▪ to have a good sense of humor tener sentido del humor muy agudo ▪ tener un buen sentido del humor

to **keep a close eye on** ▪ to monitor closely ▪ to watch closely vigilar estrechamente

to **keep a cool head** mantener la cabeza fría

to **keep a count of** *(coll.)* ▪ to keep track of llevar la cuenta de

to **keep a low profile** ▪ to stay in the backgound mantenerse en segundo plano ▪ proceder de matute

to **keep a promise** cumplir una promesa

to **keep a record of** mantener un registro de ▪ llevar un registro de

to **keep a record of one's expenses** llevar cuentas ➤ Do you keep a record of your expenses? ¿Llevas cuentas?

to **keep a secret** guardar un secreto ➤ Can you keep a secret? ¿Puedes guardar un secreto?

to **keep a tight rein on someone** ▪ to keep someone on a short leash atar corto a alguien ▪ llevar a alguien corto de rienda

to **keep abreast of one's studies** ▪ to keep on top of one's studies ▪ to stay current in one's studies ▪ to stay on top of one's studies mantenerse al día en sus estudios

to **keep abreast of the latest developments** ▪ to stay abreast of the latest developments mantenerse al tanto de los últimos acontecimientos

to **keep abreast of the times** ▪ to stay abreast of the times ▪ to keep up with the times evolucionar con su tiempo ➤ *(news item)* The president of China emphasizes the necessary "transformation of Marxism" (in order) to keep abreast of the times. El presidente de China hace hincapié en la necesaria "transformación del marxismo" a fin de que China evolucione con su tiempo.

to **keep alive one's hopes** ▪ to keep one's hopes alive mantener viva la esperanza

to **keep an appointment** cumplir una cita

to **keep an eye on** echarle un ojo a ▪ echarle un vistazo a ➤ Will you keep an eye on my things while I make a phone call? ¿Les echas un ojo a mis cosas mientras hago una llamada? ▪ ¿Les echas un vistazo a mis cosas mientras hago una llamada?

to **keep an eye out for someone** ▪ to watch for someone mantenerse alerta por alguien ➤ Keep an eye out for Marta. She should be here any minute. Mantente alerta por Marta. Ella estará aquí en cualquier momento.

to **keep at it** seguir en la brecha

keep away! ▪ stay back! *(tú)* mantente alejado ▪ *(usted)* manténgase alejado

to **keep away someone** ▪ to keep someone away mantener a alguien alejado ➤ At first Scrooge wanted to keep away the ghosts. ▪ At first Scrooge wanted to keep the ghosts away. Al principio, Scrooge quería mantener a los fantasmas alejados. ➤ At first Scrooge wanted to keep them away. Al principio, Scrooge quería mantenerlos alejados.

to **keep books** llevar libros ▪ llevar cuentas

keep clear! manténgase este espacio libre ▪ *(Sp.)* ivado permanente!

to **keep coming** ▪ to keep on coming no dejar de venir ▪ seguir viniendo ▪ seguir acercándose

to **keep doing something** ▪ to continue doing something ▪ to continue to do something seguir haciendo algo ▪ no dejar de hacer algo ➤ I kept asking him... Seguí preguntándole ... ▪ No dejé de preguntarle...

to **keep down costs** ▪ to keep costs down mantener los costos bajos

to **keep down food** ▪ to keep food down ▪ to hold down food ▪ to hold food down retener (la) comida ▪ retener los alimentos ➤ She can't keep down food. ▪ She can't keep food down. ▪ She can't hold down food. ▪ She can't hold food down. (Ella) no puede retener (la) comida. ▪ (Ella) no puede retener los alimentos. ➤ She can't keep it down. ▪ She can't hold it down. No puede retenerla. ▪ No puede retenerlos.

to **keep forgetting** seguir olvidándosele a uno ➤ I keep forgetting. Se me sigue olvidando.

to **keep from** hacer que no ▪ lograr que algo no ➤ How are you going to keep the candles from blowing out outside? ¿Cómo vas a hacer que no se apaguen la velas afuera? ▪ ¿Cómo vas a lograr que no se apaguen las velas afuera?

to **keep from doing something** ▪ to avoid doing something para no hacer algo ▪ *(present and future)* para evitar que haga algo ▪ *(past)* para evitar que hiciera algo ▪ para evitar que hiciese algo ➤ You're so tall that you'll have to lower your head to keep from bumping the top of the door frame. ▪ You're so tall that you'll have to duck (down) to keep from bumping the top of the door frame. Eres tan alto que tienes que bajar la cabeza para no darte un golpe contra el marco de la puerta.

to **keep going** seguir en marcha ▪ seguir adelante ▪ seguir funcionando ▪ seguir circulando ▪ continuar en marcha ▪ continuar adelante ▪ continuar funcionando ▪ continuar circulando ➤ *(news item)* After the fire broke out, the train kept going. Después de que el fuego empezara el tren siguió circulando.

to **keep going straight (ahead)** ▪ to continue straight ahead seguir derecho ▪ seguir todo recto ▪ meterle para adelante ▪ *(Sp., coll.)* tirar adelante ➤ Keep going straight (ahead). *(tú)* Sigue derecho. ▪ *(usted)* Siga derecho.

to **keep good time** *(watch, clock)* andar bien

to **keep in mind** ▪ to bear in mind tener en mente ▪ tener presente ➤ Keep in mind that you have to get up early tomorrow. Ten en mente que tienes que madrugar mañana.

to **keep in shape** ▪ to stay in shape mantenerse en forma ▪ mantenerse a punto ➤ I like to keep in shape. Me gusta mantenerme en forma.

to **keep in step** ▪ to stay in step llevar el paso ▪ llevar el compás

to **keep in touch with someone** seguir en contacto con alguien ➤ (Let's) keep in touch! ¡Seguimos en contacto! ▪ ¡Sigamos en contacto!

to **keep insisting that...** porfiar que...

keep it up! ¡sigue así! ▪ ¡consérvalo así! ▪ ¡consérvate así!

to **keep looking at something** seguir mirando algo

to **keep looking for something** seguir buscando algo

to **keep moving** seguir en movimiento

to **keep (on) coming** no dejar de venir ▪ seguir viniendo ▪ seguir acercándose

to **keep (on) doing something** seguir haciendo algo ▪ no parar de hacer algo

to **keep on (going)** seguir adelante

to **keep (on) saying something** no dejar de decir algo

to **keep on top of one's studies** ▪ to keep up-to-date in one's studies mantenerse al día en sus estudios

to **keep one out of trouble** mantenerle a uno alejado de los problemas ➤ Working after school keeps me out of trouble. Trabajar después de la escuela me mantiene alejado de los problemas.

to **keep one's cool** ▪ to keep one's temper ▪ to put on a brave face aguantar el tipo ▪ mantener el tipo

to **keep one's distance from** guardar las distancias ante ▪ guardar distancia...

to **keep one's eyes open for** estar pendiente de ▪ estar en alerta por ➤ Keep your eyes open for a new apartment. Mantente pendiente de un nuevo apartamento. ▪ Estate en alerta por un nuevo apartamento.

to **keep one's fingers crossed** tener los dedos cruzados ▪ mantener los dedos cruzados ➤ Keep your fingers crossed! Ten los dedos cruzados. ▪ Mantén los dedos cruzados. ▪ ¡Cruza los dedos!

to **keep one's guard up** ▪ to keep up one's guard ▪ to maintain one's guard llevar la guardia alta

to **keep one's hands steady** mantener firmes las manos ➤ Keep your hands steady. ▪ Hold your hands steady. Mantén firmes las manos.

to **keep one's hands to oneself** no poner las manos encima de los demás ▪ no ponerle las manos ➤ *(teacher to hyper kids)* Keep your hands to yourself! ¡Manos quietas!

to **keep one's lips zipped** coserse la boca

to **keep one's mouth shut** guardar la lengua ▪ mantenerse callado(-a)

to **keep one's opinions to oneself** callar su opinión

to **keep one's wits about one** tener cabeza ➤ When you're in Tepito, you've got to keep your wits about you. Cuando estás en Tepito, tienes que tener cabeza.

to **keep one's word** cumplir (su) palabra ▪ mantener su palabra

keep out! ▪ no trespassing prohibido el paso

to **keep out of trouble** mantenerse alejado(-a) de los problemas

keep quiet! ¡calla!

to **keep quiet about something** callarse sobre algo ➤ Having to keep quiet about it made us feel quilty. Tener que callarnos sobre ello nos hizo sentirnos culpable.

keep refrigerated conservar en el frigorífico

to **keep score** llevar la cuenta (del marcador) ▪ llevar el marcador ▪ llevar el tanteo ➤ Will you keep score at the match this afternoon? ¿Llevarás la cuenta del partido esta tarde? ➤ We need someone to keep score at the game this afternoon. Necesitamos que alguien se lleve la cuenta del partido esta tarde.

to **keep someone alive** mantener vivo a alguien ➤ The victim was kept alive through artificial respiration. La víctima fue mantenida viva gracias a la respiración artificial. ▪ La víctima fue mantenida viva a través de respiración articificial.

to **keep someone at a distance** ▪ to keep someone at bay mantener a alguien a distancia

to **keep someone at bay** ▪ to hold someone at bay mantener a alguien a distancia ▪ mantener a alguien apartado

to **keep someone away** ▪ to keep away someone mantener a alguien alejado ➤ At first Scrooge wanted to keep the ghosts away. ▪ At first Scrooge wanted to keep away the ghosts. Al principio, Scrooge quería mantener a las fantasmas alejadas. ➤ At first Scrooge wanted to keep them away. Al principio, Scrooge quería mantenerlas alejadas.

to **keep someone back** ▪ to keep back someone mantener a alguien apartado ➤ (The) police kept the crowds back as the motorcade passed. La policía mantuvo a la multitud apartada mientras pasaba la caravana.

to **keep someone company** hacerle compañía a alguien

to **keep someone distracted** mantener distraído a alguien ▪ mantener entretenido a alguien ➤ The police kept the man distracted while they surrounded him. La policía mantuvo al hombre distraído mientras lo rodeaban. ▪ La policía mantuvo al hombre entretenido mientras lo rodeaban. ▪ *(Sp., leísmo)* La policía mantuvo al hombre distraído mientras le rodeaban. ▪ La policía mantuvo al hombre entretenido mientras le rodeaban.

to **keep someone entertained** mantener entretenido a alguien ➤ The children kept us entertained. Los niños nos mantuvieron entretenidos.

to **keep someone from doing something** ▪ to prevent someone from doing something evitar que alguien haga algo ▪ impedir que alguien haga algo ▪ impedir que alguien hiciera algo ▪ impedir hacer algo

to **keep someone from going** ▪ to prevent someone from going impedir que alguien vaya ▪ impedir a alguien que acuda

to **keep someone in jail** mantener a alguien encarcelado

to **keep someone in line** mantener a alguien a raya ➤ It's good she's overbearing because she keeps me in line. Es bueno que ella sea pesada porque me mantiene a raya. ➤ She keeps them in line. Ella los mantiene a raya.

to **keep someone in suspense** dar carrete a alguien ▪ mantener a alguien en vilo ▪ tener a alguien en vilo ➤ *Around the World in Eighty Days* has a surprise ending that keeps the reader in suspense until the very end. *La vuelta al mundo en ochenta días* tiene un final sorprendente que mantiene al lector en vilo hasta el último instante.

to **keep someone informed** ▪ to keep someone posted mantenerle informado ▪ tenerle informado ➤ Keep me informed. ▪ Keep me posted. *(tú)* Mantenme informado. ▪ Tenme informado. ▪ *(usted)* Manténgame informado. ▪ Téngame informado.

to **keep someone on a short leash** ▪ to keep a tight rein on someone atar corto a alguien ▪ mantener a alguien con una correa corta

to **keep someone up all night** dar la noche a alguien ➤ The baby came down with something and kept us up all night. El bebé se puso malo y nos dio la noche.

to **keep someone waiting** dejar a alguien esperando ▪ tener a alguien esperando ▪ hacer esperar a alguien ➤ Sorry to keep you waiting. *(tú)* Perdona por dejarte esperando. ▪ Perdona por tenerte esperando. ▪ *(usted)* Perdone por dejarlo esperando. ▪ Perdone por tenerlo esperando.

to **keep something (a) secret** mantener algo en secreto

to **keep something clean** mantener algo limpio ▪ tener algo limpio

to **keep something (for oneself)** ▪ to have something quedárselo para sí ➤ *(referring to a newspaper)* You can keep it. ▪ You can have it. Puedes quedarte con ello. ▪ Puedes quedártelo. ▪ Quédatelo. ➤ *(referring to a magazine)* You can keep it. ▪ You can have it. Puedes quedarte con ella. ▪ Puedes quedártela. ▪ Quédatela.

to **keep something from being...** ▪ to keep something from getting... evitar que... ➤ The steering wheel bar keeps the car from being stolen. La barra en el volante evita que se robe el coche.

to **keep something from getting in the way** procurar que no se lo interponga en su camino

to **keep something simple** dejarlo lo más sencillo posible ▪ dejarlo lo más simple posible ▪ simplificarlo lo más que se pueda ▪ simplificarlo al máximo

to **keep something to oneself** ▪ not to tell anyone something quedarse algo para sí (mismo) ▪ guardarse algo para sí (mismo) ▪ quedarse algo para sus adentros ➤ Just keep it to yourself. ▪ Don't tell anyone. ¡Guárdatelo para tí! ➤ I'm going to keep it to myself. ▪ I'm going to keep that to myself. ▪ I prefer to keep that to myself. Me lo guardo para mí.

to **keep something with one** llevar algo consigo ➤ I always keep a three-by-five card with me, in my shirt pocket. Siempre llevo una ficha de setenta y cinco por ciento veinte y cinco milímetros conmigo, en el bolsillo de mi camisa.

to **keep staring at someone** quedársele mirando a alguien ➤ Then he keeps staring at me and says something. Luego se me queda mirando y dice algo.

to **keep tabs on** ▪ not to lose track of seguirle la pista ▪ no perderle la pista ▪ vigilar ▪ controlar

to **keep the books** ▪ to do the bookkeeping llevar la contabilidad ▪ llevar los libros

keep the change! *(tú)* ¡quédate con el cambio! ▪ ¡quédate con la vuelta! ▪ *(usted)* ¡quédese con el cambio ▪ ¡quédese con la vuelta!

to **keep the line clear** mantener la línea (telefónica) desocupada

to **keep the rest** quedarse con lo que sobra ▪ quedarse con el resto ▪ quedarse con todos los demás

to **keep the traditions alive** mantener vivas las tradiciones

to **keep to the point** atenerse al tema

to **keep track of** controlar ▪ seguir de cerca ▪ tener en cuenta ▪ llevar la cuenta de ➤ Keep track of your hours. Ten en cuenta tus horas.

to **keep track of one's time** mantener los tiempos que uno gasta ➤ Keep track of your time. Mantén los tiempos que gastas.

keep trying! *(tú)* ¡sigue intentando! ▪ *(usted)* ¡siga intentando!

to **keep under lock and key** guardar bajo llave ▪ guardar a cal y canto

to **keep up appearances** ▪ to maintain appearances guardar las formas

keep up the good work! ¡sigue con el buen trabajo!

to **keep up-to-date in one's studies** ▪ to keep on top of one's studies mantenerse al día en sus estudios

to **keep up with someone** mantenerse al ritmo de alguien ▪ ir al paso con alguien

to **keep up with the Joneses** no poder ser menos que fulano ▪ no poder ser menos que mengano

to **keep walking** ▪ to continue walking ▪ to walk on seguir caminando ▪ *(Sp.)* seguir andando

to **keep warm** mantenerse en calor

to **keep you** *(tú)* detenerte ▪ *(usted, to a man)* detenerlo (a usted) ▪ *(usted, to a woman)* detenerla (a usted) ▪ *(Sp., leísmo, to a man)* detenerle (a usted) ➤ If you have to go, I don't want to keep you. *(tú)* Si tienes que irte, no quiero detenerte. ▪ *(usted)* Si tiene que irse, no quiero detenerlo. ▪ Si tiene que irse, no quiero detenerle.

keep your fingers crossed! ¡mantén cruzados los dedos! ▪ ¡mantén cruzados tus dedos! ▪ ¡cruza los dedos!

keep your hands to yourself! ¡(las) manos quietas!

keep your seat! sigue sentado ▪ no se levante ▪ no te levantes

keg of beer *el* tonel de cerveza

to be **kept alive** estar mantenido vivo

kernel of truth ▪ grain of truth un atisbo de la verdad ▪ una pizca de verdad ▪ un grano de verdad

to **key in data** teclear datos

the **key is in the lock** la llave está puesta en la cerradura

key issues asuntos claves ▪ las cuestiones más importantes

key signature *(music)* armadura de clave ➤ The key of F major has the same signature as the key of D minor: all B's are played as flats. La clave de fa mayor tiene la misma armadura que la tonalidad de re menor: hay que bemolar todo B.

key to the house ▪ house key *la* llave de casa

key to the mystery *la* llave del misterio

key to something: to hold the ~ tener la llave de

to be the **key to success** ser la llave del éxito

keyboard instrument instrumento de teclado

keypad almohadilla

keys to the house ▪ house keys las llaves de (la) casa

to **kick off the presidential campaign** ▪ to kick off the campaign for the presidency ▪ to open the presidential campaign dar el pistoletazo de salida a la campaña presidencial ▪ abrir la carrera por la presidencia

to **kick somebody around** tratar a alguien a puntapiés

to **kick someone out of the house** echarle a alguien de la casa

to **kick someone out on his ass** ▪ to throw someone out on his ass dar de culo a alguien

to **kick the ball** 1. *(soccer and American football)* patear el balón ▪ patear la pelota ▪ chutar (el balón) 2. *(soccer)* patear el esférico 3. *(general)* darle al balón ▪ darle a la pelota

to **kick the bucket** ▪ to croak palmarla ▪ estirar la pata

to **kick up a little dust** ▪ to dance mover el esqueleto ▪ echar un pasillo ▪ bailar

kickoff: opening ~ *(soccer) el* saque inicial ▪ saque del centro

kid gloves los guantes de cabritilla

kid gloves: to handle someone with ~ ▪ to treat someone with kid gloves tratar a alguien con guantes de seda ▪ tratar a alguien a mano blanda

to **kidnap someone** secuestrar a alguien

kidding aside ▪ all kidding aside ▪ seriously, though bromas aparte ▪ fuera de broma

kidney failure fallo renal ➤ Experts linked the deaths caused by kidney failure to a new anti-cholesterol drug. Los expertos relacionaron las muertes por fallo renal con un nuevo fármaco contra el colesterol.

to **kill off someone as a customer** ▪ to kill someone off as a customer ▪ to lose someone as a customer perder a alguien como cliente

to **kill someone** 1. asesinar a alguien ▪ matar a alguien 2. *(journalistic)* darle muerte a alguien ➤ The tank fired, killing the photographer. El tanque disparó dándole muerte al fotógrafo.

to **kill someone dead in his tracks** dejar a alguien en su sitio

to **kill the goose that lays the golden egg** matar la gallina de los huevos de oro

kill them! ¡muerte! ▪ *(tú)* ¡mátalos! ▪ *(usted)* ¡mátelos! ▪ *(ustedes)* ¡mátenlos! ▪ *(Sp., vosotros)* ¡matadlos!

to **kill time** hacer tiempo ▪ matar el tiempo ▪ rellenar tiempo

to **kill two birds with one stone** matar dos pájaros de un tiro ▪ matar dos pájaros en un tiro

to be **killed in action** *(in written reports)* ▪ to be KIA ser muerto en acción ➤ He was killed in action. ▪ He was KIA. Fue muerto en acción.

to be **killing me** estar matándome ▪ tener algo que me muero ➤ My feet are killing me. Mis pies me están matando. ➤ My headache is killing me. Tengo un dolor de cabeza que me muero.

kilometers squared kilómetros al cuadrado ➤ This town is four kilometers squared, that is, four kilometers by four kilometers, or sixteen square kilometers in area. El área de este pueblo es de cuatro kilómetros al cuadrado, es decir, cuatro kilómetros por cuatro kilómetros, o dieciséis kilómetros cuadrados.

to be **kind-hearted** ▪ to be good-hearted tener buen fondo

kind of ▪ variety of un cierto ▪ tipo ▪ más o menos ▪ un especie de ➤ Fuchsia is a kind of bluish red. Fucsia es una especie de rojo azulado.

to be **kind of complicated** ser un poco complicado

to be the **kind of guy who...** ser uno de esos tíos que...

to be **kind to someone** ser bondadoso con alguien ▪ ser amable con alguien ▪ *(literary)* ser gentil con alguien

to **kindly refrain from doing something** se ruega que no hacer eso ▪ se ruega que no haga eso

kindness to *la* amabilidad con ▪ amabilidad para con

kinetic energy energía cinética

king and queen los reyes

Kingdom of Spain *(official name)* Reino de España

kings and queens of Spain los reyes de España

to **kiss each other on the cheek** darse besos en las mejillas ▪ darse un beso en la mejilla

to **kiss the money good-bye** decirle adiós al dinero

kitchen cabinets armarios de cocina

kitchen counter encimera

kitchen crew ▪ kitchen help los de la cocina ▪ *el* personal de la cocina ➤ Let's give the kitchen crew a round of applause. Démosle un aplauso a los de la cocina. ▪ Un aplauso a los de la cocina. ▪ Un aplauso para los de la cocina.

kitchen help ▪ kitchen crew plantilla de la cocina

kitchen privileges derecho a cocina

kitchen towel paño de cocina

kitty litter arena absorbente (para gatos) ▪ arena para gatos

knack of it ▪ hang of it truco ➤ Once you get the knack of it, it's a piece of cake. Una vez que descubras el truco, es pan comido.

to be **knee deep** ▪ to come up to the knees estar a la altura de la rodilla ▪ llegar hasta la altura de la rodilla ➤ The water was knee deep. El agua estaba a la altura de las rodillas.

knee-length hasta la rodilla ➤ Knee-length argyle socks ▪ Knee-length argyles Calcetines de rombos hasta la rodilla

to **kneel before the altar** arrodillarse frente al altar ▪ arrodillarse delante del altar ▪ ponerse de rodillas frente al altar ▪ ponerse de rodillas delante del altar

to **kneel (down)** ▪ to get down on one's knees ponerse de rodillas ▪ arrodillarse

knife edge ▪ edge of the knife ▪ knife's edge filo del cuchillo

knight of the woeful countenance *(Don Quixote)* caballero de la triste figura
to **knight someone** ▪ to dub someone a knight armar caballero a alguien
to **knit (a sweater)** tejer (un suéter) ▪ hacer punto a
knit shirt ▪ polo shirt polo ▪ *el* niqui
to **knock at the door** llamar a la puerta
to **knock down something** ▪ to knock something down tumbar algo ▪ derrumbar algo ▪ derribar algo ▪ abatir algo ▪ hacer que caiga algo
knock it off! ¡ya está bien! ▪ ¡ya vale! ▪ ¡deja eso!
to **knock it off** 1. to cease and desist parar de una (buena) vez 2. to call it a day dejarlo aquí ➤ Tell the kids to knock it off. It's time to go to bed. Diles a los niños que paren de una vez. Es hora de irse a la cama. ➤ It's five o'clock. Let's knock it off. ▪ It's five o'clock. Let's call it a day. Son las cinco. Dejémoslo aquí.
to **knock on the door** llamar a la puerta
knock on wood! ¡toca madera!
to **knock oneself out doing something** ▪ to work oneself to the bone doing something darse la paliza haciendo algo ▪ matarse haciendo algo ➤ María knocked herself out cleaning the house. ▪ María worked herself to the bone cleaning the house. María se dio una paliza limpiando la casa.
to **knock oneself out trying to do something** matarse a hacer algo ▪ matarse por intentar hacer algo ▪ matarse intentando hacer algo
to **knock over a glass of wine** tirar una copa de vino
to **knock over a piece of furniture** volcar un mueble
to **knock someone's block off** romperle la crisma ▪ romperle la cabeza
to be a **knockout** ▪ to be really good-looking estar como un tren ▪ estar como un camión ▪ ser guapo(a) de narices
knot on one's head ▪ bump on one's head el chichón en la cabeza
to **know all about it** conocérselo todo ➤ I know all about it. Yo me lo conozco todo.
to **know all the good places to eat** controlar los sitios de comer ▪ conocer los sitios de comer
to **know beforehand** saber de antemano ▪ saber con antelación ▪ saber a priori
to **know better than to do something** saber (bien) que no hay que hacer algo ➤ Doctors, of all people, should know better than to smoke. Los médicos, más que nadie, deberían saber (bien) que no hay que fumar. ➤ Young man, you're old enough to know better than to microwave an egg. Jovencito, ya tienes edad suficientemente para saber que no hay que meter un huevo en el microondas.
to **know by heart** saber de memoria
to **know by name** conocer por el nombre ▪ conocer de nombre ➤ I know everybody who works there by name, even the cooks. Conozco por el nombre a todo el que trabaja ahí, cocineros incluidos.
to **know damn well (that)...** saber perfectamente (bien) que...
to **know every trick in the book** sabérselas todas
to **know exactly what one is doing** saber muy bien lo que (se) hace (uno) ➤ The saboteurs knew exactly what they were doing. Los saboteadores sabían muy bien lo que (se) hacían.
to **know for a fact that...** saber de hecho que... ▪ saber a ciencia cierta que... ➤ I know it for a fact. Lo sé de hecho. ➤ I know for a fact that... Sé de hecho que...
to **know for sure** ▪ to be positive saber con seguridad ▪ estar seguro ➤ I don't know for sure. ▪ I'm not positive. No sé con seguridad. ▪ No estoy seguro.
to **know for sure that...** ▪ to know it to be true that... ▪ to be sure that... ▪ to be certain that... saber de seguro ▪ saber con seguridad ▪ tener por cierto ▪ tener por seguro
to **know from a reliable source that...** ▪ to have it on good authority that... saberlo a través de una fuente fidedigna que... ▪ saberlo de buena tinta que...
to **know from personal experience** saber por (la) vivencia ▪ saber por la experiencia (personal) ▪ saber por experiencia propia ▪ saber de (la) vivencia ▪ saber de la experiencia (personal) ▪ saber de experiencia propia ➤ I know from (personal) experience that... Sé de la vivencia que... ▪ Sé de experiencia que... ▪ Sé de la experiencia (personal) que...
to **know full well (that)...** saber perfectamente que...
to **know how someone feels** saber cómo alguien se siente ➤ I know how you feel. Sé cómo te sientes. ➤ Now I know how you feel. Ahora sé cómo te sientes.
to **know how to get one's way with someone** saber cómo salirse con la suya con alguien
to **know how to get things done** saber cómo conseguir que se hagan las cosas ➤ President Polk, said historian Bernard DeVoto, knew how to get things done. El Presidente Polk, dijo el historiador Bernard DeVoto, supo cómo conseguir que se hicieran las cosas.
to **know how to get to a place** ▪ to know the way to a place saber ir a un sitio ➤ Do you know how to get there? ▪ Do you know the way? ¿Sabes ir?
to **know how to use something** saber usar algo
to **know in depth** conocer a fondo
know-it-all sabelotodo ▪ enterado
to **know it for a fact** saberlo de hecho ▪ saberlo a ciencia cierta
to **know no bounds** ▪ to have no bounds ▪ to know no limits ▪ to have no limits no conocer límites ▪ no tener límites
to **know no limits** ▪ to know no bounds ▪ to have no limits ▪ to have no bounds no conocer límites ▪ no tener límites
to **know nothing about** ▪ not to know anything about no saber nada de ▪ no saber nada sobre
to **know of something** saber de algo ➤ Do you know of any toy stores in this area? ¿Sabes de alguna juguetería en esta zona? ➤ There aren't any that I know of. No hay ninguna que yo sepa. ➤ Not that I know of. No que yo sepa.
to **know one's ground on an issue** saber el terreno que pisa ▪ pisar terreno firme
to **know one's lines in a script** saberse las frases de un guión
to **know one's stuff** saber de su materia ➤ When it comes to Spanish literature, our professor really knows his stuff. Cuando se trata de la literatura española, nuestro profesor sí que sabe de su materia.
to **know one's way around** saber (cómo) moverse ➤ Esteban really knows his way around Montevideo. Esteban sí que sabe moverse en Montevideo.
to **know one's way around a place** saber andar por un sitio
to **know perfectly well that...** ▪ to know full well that... ▪ to know very well that... saber perfectamente que... ▪ bien saber que... ➤ *(editorial)* He knows perfectly well that he would lose an open election by secret ballot. Sabe perfectamente que perdería unas elecciones abiertas, con voto secreto.
to **know some Spanish** saber algo de español
to **know someone by sight** conocer a alguien de vista
to **know someone like a book** conocer a alguien a fondo ▪ conocer a alguien como la madre que lo parió
to **know someone to speak to** conocer a alguien de charlar ▪ conocer a alguien superficialmente ➤ I know him to speak to, but that's about it. Lo conozco de charlar con él, pero eso es todo.
to **know something firsthand** saber algo de primera mano ▪ saber algo de primeras ➤ I know (it) firsthand. Lo sé de primera mano. ▪ Lo sé de primeras.
to **know something is wrong** saber que algo anda mal ➤ His father knew something was wrong when he found his son lying on the bed crying. Su padre supo que algo andaba mal al encontrar a su hijo recostado en la cama llorando.
to **know something like the back of one's hand** conocer algo como la palma de la mano ▪ saber algo como la palma de la mano
to **know something upside down and backwards** conocer algo como el abecé ▪ saberse algo al dedillo
to **know the difference** notar la diferencia ▪ darse cuenta ➤ Nobody will know the difference. Nadie notará la diferencia. ▪ Nadie se dará cuenta.
to **know the difference between** saber la diferencia entre ▪ saber cuál es la diferencia entre ➤ Do you know the difference between "prone" and "supine"? To lie prone is to lie face down. To lie supine is face up. ¿Sabes (cuál es) la diferencia

entre "decúbito prono" y "decúbito supino"? Estar en decúbito prono es estar boca abajo. Estar en decúbito supino es estar boca arriba.

to **know the ins and outs** saberse los entresijos

to **know the score** saber el percal ▪ conocer el percal ▪ saber latín ▪ tener ojos en la espalda ▪ estar al cabo de la calle

to **know the way** saber el camino ▪ conocer el camino

to **know the way to a place** ▪ to know how to get to a place saber ir a un sitio ➤ Do you know the way? ▪ Do you know how to get there? ¿Sabes ir?

know thyself *(Socrates)* conócete a ti mismo ▪ sé tú mismo

to **know what...** saber lo que...

know what I mean? ▪ see what I mean? ▪ you know what I mean? ¿entiendes lo que quiero decir? ▪ ¿comprendes? ▪ ¿sabes lo que quiero decir?

to **know what is really going on** ▪ to know what is really happening ▪ to know all about it estar en antecedentes ➤ But I, who knew what was really going on... ▪ But I, who knew what was really happening... ▪ But I, who knew all about it... Pero yo, que estaba en antecedentes...

to **know what it involves** saber lo que conlleva ▪ saber lo que implica

to **know what one is capable of** saber de lo que uno es capaz

to **know what one is doing** saber lo que está haciendo uno ➤ You have to know what you're doing when you're dealing with him. Tienes que saber lo que estás haciendo cuando haces negocios con él.

to **know what one is getting into** saber dónde se mete ▪ saber en qué se mete ➤ I knew what I was getting into. Yo sabía dónde me metía.

to **know what one is talking about** saber de lo que habla ▪ saber de lo que está hablando ➤ He really knows what he's talking about. Realmente sabe de lo que habla. ▪ Realmente sabe de lo que está hablando. ➤ He doesn't know what he's talking about. No sabe de lo que habla. ▪ No sabe de lo que está hablando.

to **know what time it is** saber la hora ➤ I knew what time it was by what was on TV. Sabía la hora por lo que estaba pasando en la tele.

to **know what to do with oneself** ▪ to know what to do with one's life saber qué hacer con su vida ➤ There are people in this world who wouldn't know what to do with themselves if they didn't get up and go to war every morning. Hay gente en este mundo que no sabría qué hacer con su vida si no se levantara y fuera a la guerra todas las mañanas.

to **know what's going on** conocerse el percal ➤ I know what's going on. Me conozco el percal.

to **know what's what** estar al tanto ▪ estar al cabo de la calle

to **know when to keep quiet** ▪ knowing when to keep quiet saber (cuándo) callarse ➤ To know when to keep quiet is necessary for a happy marriage. ▪ Knowing when to keep quiet is necessary for a happy marriage. Saber (cuándo) callarse es necesario para la felicidad conyugal.

to **know which side one's bread is buttered on** ▪ to know where one's bread is buttered saber dónde le aprieta el zapato

to **know who it is right off** conocer a alguien a simple vista

to **know who one's friends are** saber con qué buey ara ▪ saber con qúe bueyes ara ▪ saber con los bueyes que ara

to **know with absolute certainty** saber a ciencia cierta

to **know with certainty** ▪ to know for sure conocer con certeza ➤ The information is too fragmented to know with certainty. La información es muy fragmentada para conocer con certeza.

knowing full well that... sabiendo perfectamente que...

knowing that... a sabiendas de que...

knowing *you* conociéndote ▪ sabiendo cómo eres ▪ conociéndote como te conozco ➤ Knowing you, you won't drink the whole thing. Conociéndote, no te lo vas a beber todo. ▪ Conociéndote, no te vas a beber todo eso.

to be **known as** ser conocido como ➤ It used to be known as... Solía ser conocido como...

to be a **known fact that...** ser un hecho conocido que... ➤ It was a known fact that... Era un hecho conocido que...

known reserves of oil ▪ known oil reserves reservas comprobadas petroleras

known someone all his life: to have ~ haber conocido a alguien desde la cuna

known the world over ▪ world-renowned mundialmente conocido

to be **knowledgeable about** ser docto en

known to have: to be ~ ser conocido por tener

known to man ▪ known to mankind que ha parido madre ➤ He's the meanest person known to man. Es la persona más antipática que ha parido madre.

to **knuckle under** ▪ to fall into line pasar por el aro ▪ entrar por el aro

to **kowtow to someone** ▪ to bow down to someone bajar la cabeza ante alguien ▪ agachar la cabeza ante alguien ▪ *(Arg., Uru.)* agachar las guampas ante alguien ▪ doblar la rodilla a alguien

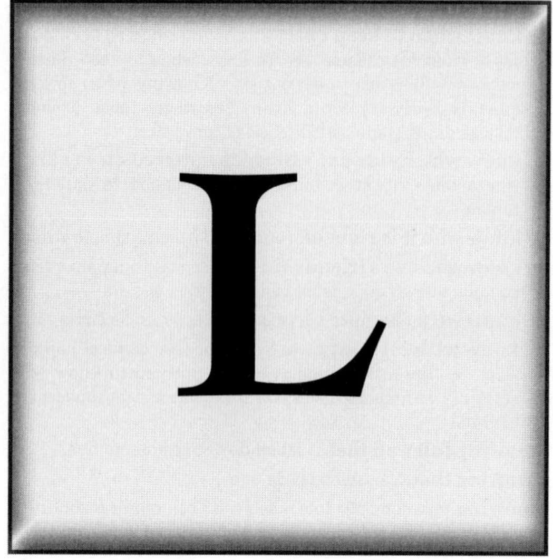

to **label someone as something** ■ to hang the label of something on someone calificar a alguien de ■ tildarle a alguien de ■ tacharle a alguien de ■ colgarle a alguien la etiqueta de ■ colgar el sambenito de algo a alguien ➤ Elvis sighters risk being labeled insane. Los videntes de Elvis se exponen a ser tildados de demente.
to **label something as** calificar algo de ■ tildar algo de ■ tachar algo de
to **lace up a pair of athletic shoes** poner las trencillas de las zapatillas de deporte
to **lace up a pair of shoes** poner los cordones de los zapatos
laced coffee *(containing a shot of whiskey or brandy)* café con gotas ■ café con piquete ■ café con pintadito
lack of a convincing motive ■ absence of a convincing motive falta de un motivo convincente ■ ausencia de un motivo convincente
lack of cooperation ■ absence of cooperation ausencia de cooperación
lack of foresight falta de previsión ■ imprevisión
lack of respect falta de respeto
lack of sleep falta de sueño ➤ My lack of sleep is catching up with me. Me está llegando la falta de sueño.
lackadaisical attitude ■ lazy attitude ■ indolent attitude actitud informal ■ actitud floja ■ actitud perezosa
ladies first las damas por delante
lady at the cash register *la* chica de la caja (registradora)
lady at the ticket counter *la* chica de la taquilla
to **lag behind** estar por detrás de
lagging in the polls ■ with the pollings running against one con las encuestas en su contra
to be **laid low** *(coll.)* reducirlo a uno a cama ■ ser reducido(-a) a cama ➤ He was laid low by the flu. La gripe lo redujo a cama. ■ Fue reducido a cama por la gripe.
laminar flow flujo laminar
to **land at Normandy** desembarcar en Normandía
land grabber *el* roba parcela
to **land in jail** ■ to end up in jail dar con los huesos en la cárcel
land of make-believe ■ world of make-believe mundo de ensueño ■ reino de la fantasía
to **land on one's feet** salir a flote
landing at Normandy *(World War II)* desembarco de Normandía
landing gear *el* tren de aterrizaje ➤ The landing gear is down. El tren de aterrizaje está fuera.
lands across the sea ■ lands over the sea tierras de ultramar
landslide (of soil, mud, etc.) corrimiento de tierras ■ derrumbamiento de tierras ■ derrumbe de tierras ■ desprendimiento de tierras
landslide victory over: to win a ~ conseguir una victoria arrolladora sobre ■ conseguir una victoria arrasadora sobre ■ conseguir una victoria aplastante sobre ■ obtener una victoria arrolladora sobre ■ obtener una victoria arrasadora sobre ■ obtener una victoria aplastante sobre ■ conseguir una victoria arrolladora frente a ■ conseguir una victoria arrasadora frente a ■ conseguir una victoria aplastante frente a ■ obtener una victoria arrolladora frente a ■ obtener una victoria arrasadora frente a ■ obtener una victoria aplastante frente a
language of dreams ■ dream language *el* lenguaje onírico
lapdog perro faldero
lapse of memory lapsus de memoria
lapse of time lapso de tiempo
to be **large enough to hold something** ser lo suficientemente grande como para contener algo ■ ser lo sufiicientemente grande como para que algo quepa dentro
large family familia numerosa ■ familia grande
large intestine intestino grueso
large scale a gran escala ■ en gran escala
the **largest concentration of** ■ the greatest concentration of el mayor colectivo de ➤ The largest concentration of northwest Africans in Madrid lives in Lavapiés. ■ The greatest concentration of northwest Africans lives in Lavapiés. El mayor colectivo de magrebíes en Madrid vive en Lavapiés.
largest minority minoría más grande
laser-guided missile misil teledirigido con laser
to **lash out at** dar palos a ciego
to **last a short time** ■ not to last (very) long durar poco
last April en abril pasado ■ el pasado mes de Abril
last bank statement 1. most recent bank statement último extracto de cuenta bancaria **2.** previous bank statement último extracto de cuenta bancaria ■ anterior extracto de cuenta bancaria ■ último anterior extracto de cuenta bancaria
last but not least el último pero no en importancia ■ el último pero no por ello el menos importante
last car *(in a race) el* coche escoba
last class 1. *(the class that meets right before this one)* la clase anterior **2.** *(the last meeting of this class)* la última clase
last-ditch effort: to make a ~ hacer un último intento (antes de darse por vencido)
to **last do something** ■ to be the last time one did something hacer algo por última vez ➤ When did you last see her? ■ When was the last time you saw her? ¿Cuándo la viste por última vez?
to **last forever** durar para siempre ■ durar eternamente
last Friday el viernes pasado
last holdout ■ last stronghold ■ last redoubt último reducto
last hope última esperanza ■ tabla de salvación
last I heard lo último que oí
to **last in the refrigerator** resistir en el frigorífico
to **last long** durar mucho
last-minute appeal último recurso
last month el mes pasado
last months as president: one's ~ los meses que le quedan de presidente
last name ■ surname apellido *(In Hispanic cultures a person has two last names, "el primer apellido" being the father's surname, and "el segundo apellido" being the mother's; note that in Asian cultures the surname is the first name.)*
last night anoche ■ ayer por la noche
Last of the Mohicans *(James Fenimore Cooper novel)* ***El último mohicano***
the **last one 1.** the final one ■ the only one left el último ■ la última **2.** the previous one el anterior ■ la anterior
last one is a rotten egg el último es cola de perro ■ la última es cola de perro
last place último lugar ■ última posición ■ última plaza ➤ It's going to be difficult to get out of last place. Va a ser difícil salir del último lugar.
last resort último recurso
last rites *(Catholicism)* últimos sacramentos
to be the **last straw** ser el colmo ■ no faltar más ■ ser la última gota ■ ser la gota que colma el vaso ■ colmar la medida ■ llenar

la medida ➤ That's the last straw! ¡Es el colmo! ▪ ¡No faltaba más!

last stronghold ▪ last holdout ▪ last redoubt último reducto

to be the **last time one did something** ▪ to last do something hacer algo por última vez ➤ When was the last time you saw her? ▪ When did you last see her? ▪ When did you see her last? ¿Cuándo la viste por última vez?

last thing lo último ➤ That's the last thing I expected. Eso es lo último que me esperaba.

to be the **last thing I wanted** ser lo último que hubiese deseado ▪ ser lo último que hubiera deseado

to be the **last thing one needs** ser lo último que uno necesita ➤ That's the last thing I need. ▪ It's the last thing I need. Es lo último que necesito. ➤ That was the last thing I needed. ▪ It was the last thing I needed. Era lo último que (yo) necesitaba.

last turnaround next 20 kilometers ▪ there won't be another turnaround for twenty more kilometers último cambio de sentido en los próximos 20 kilómetros

to **last up to...** durar hasta... ➤ The effect can last up to half an hour. El efecto puede durar hasta media hora.

last year el año pasado

lasting impact on someone: to have a ~ dejar en alguien una impresión indeleble ▪ dejar en alguien una huella indeleble ▪ dejar en alguien una impronta indeleble

lasting impression (on someone): to make a ~ ▪ to make an indelible impression on someone ▪ to make a permanent impression on someone causar una impresión duradera (en alguien) ▪ causar una impresión indeleble (en alguien) ▪ causar una impresión permanente (en alguien)

late fee sobrecargo por pago fuera de fecha

to be **late for an appointment** llegar tarde a una cita

to be **late for dinner** llegar tarde a comer

to be **late for school** llegar tarde a la escuela

to be **late for supper** llegar tarde a cenar

late in the day a finales del día

late in the month ▪ toward the end of the month ▪ near the end of the month a finales de mes

late in the summer of a finales del verano de

late in the year at the end of the year ▪ towards the end of the year para finales de(l) año ➤ Late in the year, the sun is near the solstice. ▪ At the end of the year, the sun is near the solstice. ▪ Towards the end of the year, the sun is near the solstice. Para finales de(l) año, el sol se encuentra próximo al solsticio.

late Middle Ages baja Edad Media

late pregnancy: in ~ ▪ late in the pregnancy en los meses mayores

late twenties: to be in one's ~ tener veintimuchos ➤ She looks like she's in her late twenties or early thirties. Parece tener veintimuchos o treinta y pocos.

late twentieth-century Spanish cinema cine español del final del siglo XX

late yesterday a última hora de ayer

later on ▪ sometime after that más adelante

later work obra tardía

latest film última película

latest movie ▪ most recent movie ▪ newest movie última película

latest release último lanzamiento

latest technology ▪ state-of-the-art technology ▪ cutting-edge technology tecnología punta ▪ último grito de la tecnología ▪ tecnología vanguardista

latex enamel esmalte sintético

Latin America la América Latina ▪ Latinoamérica ▪ Hispanoamérica ▪ Iberoamérica

to **laugh at oneself** reírse de sí mismo

to **laugh one's head off** reír a mandíbula batiente

to **laugh till one is blue in the face** ▪ to split one's sides laughing desternillarse de risa ▪ retorcerse de risa ▪ reírse a más no poder

to **laugh with, not at** reírse con, no reírse de ➤ I'm laughing with you, not at you. Me río contigo, no me río de ti.

to be the **laughingstock** ser el hazmereír

to **launch a boat** echar un barco al agua

to **launch an attack on** desplegar un ataque a

launchpad ▪ launching pad plataforma de lanzamiento ▪ rampa de lanzamiento ▪ plataforma de despegue ▪ rampa de despegue

to **lavish praise on someone** ▪ to lavish someone with praise ▪ to sing someone's praises echar flores a alguien

law firm agencia de abogados

law of averages *la* ley de probabilidades

law of parsimony *(philosophy of science)* ▪ Ockham's razor principio de economía ▪ la navaja de Occam ➤ The law of parsimony, or Ockham's razor, says that the simplest complete explanation is the true one. El principio de economía, o la navaja de Occam, afirma que la explicación completa más sencilla es la verdadera.

law of physics ▪ physical law ▪ natural law *la* ley de física ➤ Pascal's law of pressure states that the pressure within a fluid (liquid or gas) expands in all directions, as a balloon expands uniformly when inflated with air. La ley Pascal de presiones enuncia que la presión se transmite en el seno de los fluidos (un líquido o gas) en todas direcciones, como se expande un globo uniformemente cuando se infla con aire.

law of sanctuary *(Catholicism)* derecho de asilo ➤ The rectory of the University of Valladolid is protected by the law of sanctuary. El rectorado de la Universidad de Valladolid se protege por el derecho de asilo.

law practice abogacía

to be a **law unto oneself** hacer lo que le da gana

laws of planetary motion *(Johannes Kepler)* las leyes del movimiento de los planetas

to **lay a trap for someone** tenderle una trampa a alguien

to **lay an egg 1.** *(literal)* poner un huevo **2.** *(figurative)* to get upset sulfurarse ▪ cabrearse ➤ When I told her, she practically laid an egg. Cuando se lo dije ella prácticamente se sulfuró. ➤ Well, don't lay an egg. Pues, no te sulfures.

to **lay bricks** colocar ladrillos

to **lay down the law** dictar la ley ▪ dar la ley

to **lay eyes on** poner los ojos en

lay of the land ▪ geographic features of the land rasgos geográficos de la tierra ▪ rasgos geográficos del territorio ▪ características geográficas

lay one low ▪ to be laid low reducirlo(la) a cama ➤ The flu laid her low. ▪ She was laid low by the flu. La gripe la redujo a cama.

to **lay one's cards on the table** ▪ to lay all one's cards on the table poner las cartas sobre las mesa ▪ poner las cartas boca arriba ▪ jugar a cartas vistas

to **lay out a newspaper** ▪ to do the layout of a newspaper maquetar el periódico

to **lay rubber** ▪ to spin one's wheels salir haciendo ruedas ▪ hacer ruedas ➤ The car laid rubber as it started off from the traffic light. El coche salió haciendo ruedas del semáforo.

to **lay sideways** colocar de lado

to **lay siege to a city** sitiar una ciudad ▪ poner cerco a una ciudad

to **lay someone** *(off-color)* tirarse a alguien

to **lay the blame on someone for something** ▪ to put the blame for something on someone cargar a alguien la culpa de algo ▪ echar la culpa a alguien por algo ▪ colgar a alguien el sambenito

to **lay the blame on someone for what happened** ▪ to put the blame for what happened on someone echarle la culpa a alguien por lo que pasó ▪ cargar a alguien (con) la culpa de lo que pasó ▪ achacarle (la culpa) a alguien de lo que pasó

to **lay the foundation (of a structure)** poner los cimientos (de una construcción)

to **lay the groundwork for** ▪ to prepare the way for ▪ to make the preparations for sentar las bases de ▪ realizar los preparativos para

layer of bricks ▪ course of bricks camada de ladrillos ▪ tanda de ladrillos ▪ estrato de ladrillos

laying off of employees *la* supresión de empleados ▪ suspensión temporal (por falta de trabajo)

laying on of hands *la* imposición de manos

layout of a house ■ floor plan of a house *la* distribución de una casa ■ plano de una casa ■ *el* plan de una casa

to **lead a dog's life** llevar una vida de perros

to **lead a normal life** llevar una vida normal

to **lead an active life** llevar una vida activa

to **lead by *x* points** ■ to be ahead by *x* points imponerse a *x* puntos por ■ mantener una ventaja de *x* puntos sobre ➤ Bush leads Gore by 537 votes at the close of the Florida recount. Bush se impone a Gore por 537 votos al cierre del recuento en Florida.

to **lead one to believe** llevar a uno a pensar ■ llevarle a uno a creer ■ conducirle a uno a creer ■ *(journalistic, literary)* permitir anticipar que ➤ It leads me to believe that... Me lleva a pensar que... ■ Me lleva a creer que... ➤ *(news item)* Several experts believe that the behavior pattern (exhibited) in the five crimes indicates that the killer will act again. Varios expertos creen que el patrón de comportamiento en los cinco crímenes permite anticipar que el asesino volverá a actuar.

to **lead one to suspect that...** hacer a alguien sospechar que...

to **lead someone around by the nose** llevar a alguien de la barba

to **lead someone astray** llevar a alguien por el mal camino

to **lead someone to a place** llevar a alguien a un lugar ■ dirigir a alguien a un lugar ➤ The psychic led the police to the scene of the crime. La vidente llevó a la policía hasta la escena del crimen. ■ La vidente dirigió a la policía hasta la escena del crimen. *("Vidente" can be masculine or feminine.)*

to **lead someone to believe** llevarle a alguien a creer ■ conducirle a alguien a creer

to **lead someone to do something** determinar a alguien a hacer algo

to **lead the army into battle** llevar el ejército a la batalla

to **lead the parade** ■ to head the parade abrir el desfile

to **lead the way** marcar el camino ➤ Since you have the flashlight, you lead the way. Ya que tienes la linterna, marca tú el camino.

to **lead to a friendship** desembocar en una amistad ➤ The interview led to a friendship. ■ The interview resulted in a friendship. La entrevista desembocó (en) una amistad.

to **lead to a place** ■ to go to a place ■ to take one to a place llevar a un lugar ■ dirigirse a un lugar ■ salir a un lugar ■ conducir a un lugar ➤ This road leads to Toluca. ■ This road goes to Toluca. ■ This road takes you to Toluca. Esta carretera lleva hasta Toluca. ■ Esta carretera se dirige a Toluca.

to **lead to a result** desembocar en un resultado ■ llevar a un resultado ➤ Decisions made by Presidents Fillmore, Pierce, and Buchanan led to the American Civil War. Decisiones tomadas por los presidentes Fillmore, Pierce y Buchanan desembocaron en la Guerra Civil Estadounidense. ■ Decisiones tomadas por los presidentes Fillmore, Pierce y Buchanan llevaron a la Guerra Civil Estadounidense.

to **lead to someone** conducir hasta alguien ➤ *(news report)* The investigation led to the suspect. Las investigaciones condujeron hasta el sospechoso.

lead us not into temptation no nos dejes caer en la tentación

leader of men *el, la* líder de hombres

leaders of the insurgency cabecillas de la insurgencia

leadership qualities las dotes de mando

leading edge of a wing *el* borde de ataque de un ala ■ borde anterior de un ala ■ borde delantero de un ala

leading the search for... a la cabeza de la búsqueda de...

to **leaf through a magazine** hojear una revista

to **leak classified information** filtrar información clasificada

to **leak in your pocket** gotear en el bolsillo ■ chorrear en el bolsillo ➤ This ballpoint pen won't leak in your pocket. Este bolígrafo no gotea en el bolsillo. ■ Este bolígrafo no chorrea en el bolsillo.

to **leak information to the press** filtrar datos a la prensa ■ filtrar información a la prensa

leak of information ■ information leak *la* filtración de información

to **leak through** filtrarse por ➤ The water damage from the neighbor's apartment leaked through the walls and baseboards. El agua procedente del apartamento de los vecinos causó daños al filtrarse por las paredes y los rodapiés.

leaked information: to receive ~ recoger filtraciones

to **lean against something** apoyar la espalda contra algo

to **lean away from someone** echarse para atrás de alguien ■ alejarse de alguien

to **lean back** echarse atrás

to **lean down** inclinarse hacia abajo

lean meat carne magra ■ carne sin grasa

to **lean on** recostarse en ■ recostarse sobre

to **lean on the horn** ■ to ride the horn ■ to honk like crazy pegarse al claxon ■ quedarse pegado al claxon ■ pitar como (un) loco

to **lean over** inclinarse sobre ➤ Galileo leaned over the railing of the Leaning Tower of Pisa and dropped cannonballs of different weights and sizes. Galileo se inclinó sobre la barandilla de la torre inclinada de Pisa y dejó caer balas de cañón de distintos pesos y tamaños.

lean years ■ years of financial hardship años de las vacas flacas

leaning against the door frame apoyado en el marco de la puerta

to be **leaning on** estar arrimado a

Leaning Tower of Pisa la torre inclinada de Pisa

leap year año bisiestro

to **learn a lesson** quedarse resabiado ■ salir resabiado

to **learn about... 1.** to acquire knowledge of aprender sobre... ■ informarse sobre... **2.** to find out about... ■ to hear about... ■ to learn of... enterarse de... ■ *(in past tense only)* saber de... ■ oír sobre...

to **learn as one goes (along)** aprender sobre la marcha ➤ I learn as I go (along). Aprendo sobre la marcha.

to **learn by heart** ■ to memorize aprender de memoria

to **learn from experience** aprender de las experiencias

to **learn from other people's mistakes** ■ to learn from the mistakes of others aprender de los errores de los demás ■ escarmentar en cabeza ajena

to **learn from someone that...** ■ to find out from someone that... enterarse por alguien de que...

to **learn of** ■ to find out about ■ to hear about ■ to learn about enterarse de ■ *(in past tense only)* saber de ■ oír sobre

to **learn one's lesson** quedar resabiado ■ salir resabiado ➤ I learned my lesson. Quedé resabiado. ■ Salí resabiado.

to **learn one's way around** *(city, university campus, large building, etc.)* hacerse composición del lugar

to **learn one's way around (an interior)** ■ to familiarize oneself with a floor plan hacerse composición de un lugar

to **learn that...** ■ to find out enterarse de que... ■ saber que... ➤ When he learned that... Al enterarse de que... ■ Cuando se enteró de que... ■ Al saber que... ■ Cuando supo que...

to **learn the hard way 1.** *(general)* aprender por las malas ■ aprender por los golpes **2.** to make beginner's mistakes pagar la novatada

learning disorder trastorno de aprendizaje

least little thing mínima ➤ The least little thing gets that dog going. A la mínima salta ese perro.

to be the **least of it** ser lo de menos

to be the **least of one's problems** ser lo de menos

least of one's worries la más mínima de todas mis preocupaciones ■ lo de menos ➤ That's the least of my worries. Es la más mínima de todas mis preocupaciones.

to be the **least one can do** ser lo menos que uno puede hacer ➤ It's the least I can do. Es lo menos que puedo hacer.

least one could ■ as little as one could lo menos que podía

leather goods *los* bienes de cuero ■ calzados

leave! ■ just leave! *(tú)* ¡sal! ■ *(usted)* ¡salga (usted)! ■ *(ustedes)* ¡salgan (ustedes)! ■ *(Sp., vosotros)* ¡salid!

to **leave a lot to be desired** dejar bastante que desear ■ dejar mucho que desear

to **leave a message** dejar un mensaje ■ dejar un recado

to **leave a ring on a piece of furniture** *(from a wet drinking glass)* dejar un cerco en un mueble to **leave a total of** dejar un total de ▪ dar un total de ▪ arrojar un balance de ➤ I've formatted four hundred and fifty pages, and that leaves a total of nine hundred to go. ▪ I've formatted four hundred and fifty pages, which leaves a total of nine hundred to go. He dado formato a cuatro cientas cincuenta páginas, lo que deja un total de novecientas para terminar. ➤ The collision left a total of eight people injured. La colisión ha arrojado un balance de ocho personas heridas.

to **leave behind something** ▪ to leave something behind **1.** *(on purpose, deliberately, intentionally)* to abandon ▪ not to take dejar algo tirado ▪ quedar algo ▪ abandonar algo ▪ irse sin algo ▪ partir sin algo **2.** *(accidentally, unintentionally)* to forget to take ▪ to accidentally leave something dejar olvidado algo **3.** to leave as a legacy dejar para la posteridad ▪ dejar tras de sí ➤ I left the book on the table (on purpose). Me quedé el libro encima de la mesa. ➤ I left it on the table (accidentally). Me lo quedé encima de la mesa. ➤ He left it (behind) on the table. Se lo quedó en la mesa. ▪ Lo dejó en la mesa.

to **leave early** salir pronto ▪ irse pronto ▪ marcharse pronto ▪ salir antes ➤ I left home early. ▪ I left the house early. Salí pronto de casa. ➤ They came back from their trip a day early and caught me red-handed. Volvieron de su viaje un día antes, y me pillaron con las manos en la masa.

to **leave for** salir para ▪ salir con destino a ▪ partir con dirección a ➤ They left for Buenos Aires on the twenty-third. Salieron para Buenos Aires el veintitrés. ▪ Salieron con destino a Buenos Aires el veintitrés.

to **leave home** salir de casa

to **leave in a huff** ▪ to storm out ▪ to stalk out coger la puerta ▪ azotar la puerta ▪ detener la puerta

to **leave it as it is** ▪ to leave it the way it is ▪ *(coll.)* to leave it like it is dejarlo tal cual

to **leave it on** **1.** *(coat)* dejárselo puesto **2.** *(light)* dejarla encendida

to **leave it the way it is** ▪ to leave it as it is ▪ *(coll.)* to leave it like it is dejarlo tal cual

to **leave it to chance** dejarlo al azar

leave it to me *(tú)* déjalo a mí ▪ déjalo de mi cuenta ▪ déjalo a mi cuenta ▪ *(usted)* déjelo a mí ▪ déjelo de mi cuenta ▪ déjelo a mi cuenta ▪ *(ustedes)* déjenlo a mí ▪ déjenlo de mi cuenta ▪ déjenlo a mi cuenta ▪ *(Sp., vosotros)* déjadlo a mí ▪ déjadlo de mi cuenta ▪ déjadlo a mi cuenta

to **leave it up to someone to do something** dejar en manos de alguien el hacer algo ▪ dejar a alguien el hacer algo ➤ Let's leave it up to the tour guide to choose the restaurant. ▪ Let's leave it up to the tour guide to pick the restaurant. ▪ Let's leave the choice of the restaurant up to the tour guide. Dejemos en manos del guía el elegir el restaurante. ▪ Dejemos al guía el elegir el restaurante.

leave me alone *(tú)* déjame en paz ▪ *(usted)* déjeme (usted) en paz

to **leave no stone unturned** no dejar piedra por mover

to **leave nothing to chance** no dejar nada a la suerte

to **leave nothing to the imagination** no dejar nada a la imaginación

to **leave now** salir ahora ▪ salir ya ▪ ya salir ➤ Are you leaving right now? ¿Ya sales?

to **leave off** **1.** to stop dejarlo **2.** to omit omitir ➤ Where did we leave off? ¿Dónde lo dejamos? ➤ You left off the period at the end of the sentence. Omitiste el punto al final de la oración.

to **leave office** dejar el cargo ➤ After leaving office... Tras dejar el cargo... ➤ On leaving office... Al dejar el cargo...

to **leave one's job** abandonar su puesto de trabajo

to **leave one's post** ▪ to step down darse de baja

to **leave one's shirttails out** ▪ to wear one's shirttails out llevar la camisa por fuera del pantalón ➤ Of all my shirts that can be worn with the tails out, this (one) is the only one that has a collar. De todas las camisas que puedo llevar por fuera, ésta es la única que tiene cuello.

to **leave oneself time for** darse tiempo para

to **leave oneself time to...** darse tiempo para que...

to **leave port** dejar puerto

to **leave room for dessert** dejar un hueco para el postre

to **leave someone** dejar a alguien ➤ His wife left him. Su esposa lo ha dejado. ➤ Her husand left her. Su marido la ha dejado.

to **leave someone a message** dejarle a alguien un mensaje ▪ dejarle a alguien un recado ▪ dejarle a alguien algo dicho

to **leave someone a note saying...** dejarle a alguien una nota diciendo...

to **leave someone all alone** dejar a alguien a solas

to **leave someone alone** dejarlo en paz ➤ Leave me alone. Déjame en paz.

to **leave someone behind** dejar a alguien atrás ▪ irse sin alguien ▪ partir sin alguien ▪ dejar a alguien olvidado ▪ quedársele

to **leave someone for dead** dejar a alguien por muerto ➤ The robbers beat the victim and left him for dead. Los atracadores golpearon a la víctima, y se marcharon dejándola por muerta.

to **leave someone high and dry** dejar a alguien en la estacada

to **leave someone holding the bag** dejarlo con la carga en las costillas

to **leave someone in a predicament** ▪ to leave someone in a fix dejar a alguien en apuros ▪ dejar a alguien en bragas

to **leave someone in the dust** dejar a alguien por los suelos

to **leave someone out of something** **1.** *(unintentionally, accidentally)* dejar a alguien fuera de algo **2.** *(intentionally, deliberately)* dar a alguien de lado ➤ Last time, they (accidentally) left me out of the office football pool. La última vez, me dejaron fuera de la porra de la oficina. ➤ Last time, they (deliberately) left me out of the office football pool. La última vez, me dieron de lado en la porra de la oficina.

to **leave someone something** ▪ to leave something to someone ▪ to bequeath something to someone dejar algo (en herencia) a alguien ➤ She left her entire fortune to her dog. Dejó toda su fortuna a su perro.

to **leave someone speechless** quitar el habla a alguien ▪ dejarle sin habla a alguien

to **leave someone to his fate** ▪ to abandon someone to his fate abandonar a alguien a su suerte ▪ dejar a alguien de la mano de Dios

to **leave something (behind)** dejar algo atrás

to **leave something exactly as one found it** ▪ to return something to its original condition dejar algo tal como lo había encontrado

to **leave something for tomorrow** dejar algo para mañana

to **leave something in someone's hands** ▪ to leave something in the hands of someone dejar algo en manos de alguien

to **leave something intact** dejar algo intacto

to **leave something the way it is** dejar algo tal cual está ▪ dejar algo como está ▪ dejar algo igual que está ➤ Do you want the sideburns left the way they are? ¿Quieres que te deje las patillas tal cual están? ▪ ¿Las patillas tal cual?

to **leave something till last** *(coll.)* ▪ to leave something until last dejar algo al último ▪ dejar algo para lo último

to **leave something to be desired** dejar algo que desear ▪ dejar un poco que desear

to **leave something to chance** dejar algo a la suerte

to **leave something until last** ▪ to leave something till last dejar algo al último ▪ dejar algo para lo último

to **leave something up in the air** ▪ to leave something unresolved dejar algo en el aire

to **leave something up to someone** dejar algo en manos de alguien ▪ dejar algo a alguien ➤ Let's leave the choice of the restaurant up to the tour guide. ▪ Let's leave it up to the tour guide to choose the restaurant. ▪ Let's leave it up to the tour guide to pick the restaurant. Dejemos al guía la elección del restaurante. ▪ Dejemos en manos del guía la elección del restaurante.

to **leave something with someone** dejar algo con alguien

to **leave the children on their own** dejar a los niños solos

to **leave the premises** *(office, commercial, or government building)* abandonar el local ➤ He left the office an hour ago. Abandonó la oficina hace una hora.

to **leave the priesthood** dejar el sacerdocio ▪ *(most common)* colgar el hábito ▪ *(colorful)* ahorcar los hábitos to **leave the telephone on** ▪ to leave the cell phone on dejar el teléfono abierto

to **leave things the way they are** ▪ to leave things as they are dejar así las cosas

to **leave without someone** marcharse sin alguien ➤ They left without me. Se han marchado sin mí.

to **leave word** ▪ to leave a message dejar recado ➤ I left word for you to call. ▪ I left a message for you to call. Dejé recado que me llamaras.

lecture tour gira de conferencias

to be **led off to** ser conducido a

to be **led to** ser conducido a

to be **left all alone** ▪ to be left alone quedarse a solas

to be **(left) at home alone while the rest of the family is away** *(Mex.)* estar de solano(-a) casa ▪ estar solano(-a) ▪ *(Sp., coll.)* estar de Rodríquez

to **left click on** pulsar con el botón izquierdo en ▪ presionar con el botón izquierdo en ▪ hacer clic con el botón izquierdo ▪ *(coll.)* cliquear con el botón izquierdo en

left field: to come out of ~ salir de nada ➤ His insult came out of left field. Su insulto salió de nada.

to be **left-handed** ser zurdo(-a)

left-handed person zurdo(-a)

left-handed thread ▪ reverse thread rosca al revés ➤ You tighten a left-handed thread counterclockwise. ▪ You tighten a reverse thread counterclockwise. La rosca al revés se aprieta hacia la izquierda. ▪ Se aprieta la rosca al revés hacia la izquierda.

to be **left holding the bag** ▪ to get left holding the bag ▪ to catch the blame for something (unfairly) ▪ to get blamed for something cargarle con el muerto a alguien ▪ dejar a alguien colgado de la responsabilidad de algo

left hook *(boxing)* gancho de izquierdo

to be **left in the dark** quedarse en la luna de Valencia

to be **left of center politically** ser de izquierdas ➤ She's a little left of center. Es un poco de izquierdas.

to be **left out on the street** quedarse en la puerta de la calle ➤ He was left out on the street. Se quedó en la puerta de la calle.

to be **left speechless** quedarse con la boca abierta

to be **left to one's own devices** estar abandonado a su suerte ▪ ser abandonado a su suerte

leg of a race manga de una carrera

leg of a spider pata de una araña ➤ Spiders have eight legs. ▪ A spider has eight legs. Las arañas tienen ocho patas.

leg of a table ▪ table leg pata de una mesa

leg of a trip trayecto de un viaje ➤ On the train trip from Valladolid to Toledo, there is a short leg in Madrid where you must change trains. En el viaje en tren de Valladolid a Toledo, hay un trayecto corto en Madrid que te obliga a cambiar de tren.

leg of lamb pierna de cordero

legal loophole ▪ loophole in the law agujero legal ▪ laguna legal ▪ *(colorful)* carambola legal ➤ The law has a loophole (in it). La ley tiene un agujero. ▪ La ley tiene una laguna.

legal owner propietario en derecho

legendary film leyenda de celuloide ➤ The legendary film *Midnight Express* pales in comparison to the reality of the Turkish jails. La leyenda de celuloide del *Expreso de Medianoche* palidece ante la realidad de las cárceles turcas.

legislative branch poder legislativo

legislative session pleno de la cámara

leisure time tiempo de ocio

lemon-flavored tea té al limón

lemon rind ▪ lemon peel cáscara de limón ▪ corteza de limón

to **lend a hand** tender una mano

to **lend a helping hand** hacer el quite

to **lend an atmosphere** proporcionar un ambiente

to **lend money to someone** ▪ to lend someone money prestarle dinero a alguien *("To loan" is common but incorrect.)*

to **lend weight to someone's opinion** ▪ to give weight to someone's opinion conceder valor a la opinión de alguien

length of one's life ▪ (personal) longevity *la* longevitud (de la vida de uno) ▪ longevitud del individuo ➤ The length of one's life depends both on genetics and (personal) habits. ▪ Personal longevity depends both on genetics and habits. La longevitud de la vida de uno depende tanto de la genética como de los hábitos personales. ▪ La longevitud del individuo depende tanto de la genética como de sus hábitos personales.

length of time ▪ how long *la* extensión de tiempo

lengthy stay prolongada estancia

lenient father padre indulgente ▪ padre benévolo

lenient judge juez(-a) indulgente ▪ juez(-a) benévolo(-a)

lenient sentence sentencia benévola ▪ sentencia suave

a **leopard cannot change its spots** la cabra siempre tira al monte ▪ genio y figura hasta la sepultura

to be **less desirable** ser menos deseable

the **less said, the better** a menos palabras, menos pleitos

less than one should have: to provide someone ~ ▪ to short someone proporcionar (de) menos ▪ dar (de) menos ➤ They gave me one less than they should have. ▪ They shorted me one. Me dieron uno (de) menos. ➤ I put a little less Worcestershire sauce than I should have. Puse un poco menos de salsa Perrins de la que debía.

less than usual menos de lo normal

lesser evil *el* mal menor

to **let air out of a tire** desinflar un neumático ➤ Let some air out of the tire. Desinfla un poco el neumático.

to **let bygones be bygones** ➤ Let bygones be bygones Lo pasado, pasado

to **(let) cook** dejar cocer ➤ Bring it to a boil, stirring occasionally. Cover partially and (let it) cook on low heat. Llevarlo a ebullición removiendo de vez en cuando. Tapar parcialmente y dejar cocer a fuego lento.

let down: to feel (really) ~ ▪ to be really let down llevarse un buen chasco ▪ pegarse un buen chasco

to **let down one's guard** ▪ to let one's guard down bajar la guardia ▪ abandonar la vigilancia

to **let down the hem** ▪ to let out the hem bajar el dobladillo

to **let everyone know** comunicar a todo el mundo ➤ I want to send an E-mail to everyone letting them know my new address. Quiero enviar una nota por mail a todo el mundo comunicando mi nueva dirección.

let go of her! ▪ let her go! ¡suéltala!

let go of him! ▪ let him go! ¡suéltalo! ▪ *(Sp., leísmo)* ¡suéltale!

let go of it! ▪ let it go! ¡suéltalo!

to **let go of something** soltar algo ▪ abandonar algo

to **let in some fresh air** ▪ to let some fresh air in dejar entrar un poco de aire fresco ➤ Open the window to let some fresh air into the room. Abre la ventana para que entre un poco de aire fresco en la habitación.

let it be entered in the minutes (that...) ▪ let it be stated in the minutes (that...) ▪ include it in the minutes (that...) que conste en acta (que...)

let it be noted that... ▪ make sure you record that... ▪ make note of the fact that... que conste que... ➤ Make note of the fact that we have paid him. Que conste que le hemos pagado.

let it be noted in the record (that...) ▪ let it be stated in the record (that...) que conste en acta (que...)

to **let it cool (down)** ▪ to let it cool off dejar que se enfríe ▪ dejarlo enfriar ▪ esperar a que se enfríe ➤ Remove from heat and let it cool (down). Retirar del fuego y esperar a que se enfríe.

to **let it dry** dejarlo secar ▪ dejar que se seque ➤ You have to let it dry before you can tell if it needs a second coat. Hay que dejarlo secar antes de ver si necesita una segunda mano. ▪ Hay que dejar que se seque antes de ver si necesita una segunda mano.

to **(let it) ring once and hang up** hacer una llamada perdida

to **let (it) slip that...** dejarse decir que... ▪ irse de la lengua que...

let me begin by saying... *(ustedes)* permítanme comenzar diciendo... ▪ *(Sp., vosotros)* permitidme comenzar diciendo...

let me (do it)! ¡déjame a mí!

let me do it deja que lo haga yo

let me do the talking tú déjame hablar a mí

let me down! ¡déjame al suelo!

let me explain voy a explicarme ▪ te doy una explicación

let me explain something to you déjame que te explique una cosa

let me finish deja que siga

let me give you a hand *(a ti)* deja que te eche una mano ▪ *(a usted)* deje que le eche una mano

let me go! ¡suéltame!

let me guess *(tú)* déjame adivinar ▪ *(usted)* déjeme adivinar

let me have that for a second permítemelo un segundo ▪ permítemelo un momento ▪ déjamelo un segundo ▪ déjamelo un momento

let me help you with your coat ▪ let me take your coat *(a ti)* deja que te ayude con el abrigo ▪ permíteme el abrigo ▪ *(a usted)* deje que le ayude con el abrigo ▪ permítame el abrigo

let me in! ¡déjame entrar!

let me just say one thing deja que sólo diga una cosa

let me just say (that...) *(tú)* déjame sólo decir que... ▪ *(usted)* déjeme sólo decir que...

let me know *(tú)* avísame ▪ hazme saber ▪ déjame saber ▪ déjamelo saber ▪ *(usted)* avíseme ▪ hagame saber ▪ déjeme saber ▪ déjemelo saber ➤ If I can help you with anything, let me know, and I'll do whatever I can to help you. Si puedo ayudarte en algo, déjamelo saber y haré lo posible por ayudarte.

let me off at... *(tú)* déjame en... ▪ *(usted)* déjeme en... ▪ *(Mex., coll.)* me deja en... ➤ Let us off at Sanborns. Nos deja en Sanborns.

let me put it this way ▪ let me say it this way *(a ti)* deja que te lo ponga de esta manera ▪ *(a usted)* deje que se lo ponga de esta manera

let me rephrase that *(tú)* deja que lo diga de otra manera ▪ *(usted)* deje que lo diga de otra manera

let me say at the outset ▪ let me begin by saying *(tú)* deja que empiece diciendo ▪ *(usted)* deje que empiece diciendo

let me show you *(tú)* deja que te lo muestre ▪ *(usted)* deje que se lo muestre

let me take your coat ▪ let me help you with your coat *(tú)* permíteme el abrigo ▪ deja que te ayude con el abrigo ▪ *(usted)* permítame el abrigo ▪ deje que le ayude con el abrigo

let me tell you *(tú)* déjame que te cuente ▪ deja que te cuente ▪ *(usted)* dejéme que le cuente ▪ deje que le cuente

let me tell *you*! conste que ▪ *(tú)* sepas tú ▪ *(usted)* sepa usted

let me tell you something *(tú)* déjame que te diga una cosa ▪ *(usted)* déjeme que le diga una cosa

to **let nothing stand in one's way** ▪ not to let anything stand in one's way ▪ to let nothing get in one's way no dejar que nada se meta en el camino de uno ▪ *(Sp.)* no reparar en pelillos ▪ no pararse en pelillos

to **let off** *(referring to a taxi)* dejar ➤ Let me off on San Borja. Me deja en San Borja.

to **let off steam** ▪ to blow off steam ▪ to vent (one's feelings) ▪ to get something out of one's system desfogarse ▪ desahogarse

to **let one's arm be twisted** ▪ to let your arm be twisted ▪ to let someone twist your arm dar el brazo a torcer

to **let one's hair down** ▪ to relax expansionarse ▪ soltarse el pelo ▪ soltarse la melena ▪ soltarse la rienda

to **let one's hair grow** dejarse crecer el pelo ▪ dejarse el pelo largo ➤ She should let her hair grow longer. (Ella) debería dejarse crecer el pelo. ▪ (Ella) debería dejarse el pelo largo.

to **let oneself be used by...** prestarse a ser usado por...

to **let out** ▪ to get out vaciarse el recinto ➤ As the concert was letting out, we ran into some friends. ▪ As the concert was getting out, we ran into some friends. Según se vaciaba el recinto del concierto nos encontramos con unos amigos. ▪ Conforme se vaciaba el recinto del concierto nos encontramos con unos amigos.

to **let out a howl** lanzar un aullido

to **let out a roar** lanzar un rugido ▪ dar un rugido ▪ proferir un rugido

to **let out the dog** ▪ to let the dog out dejar salir al perro ➤ Please let out the dog. ▪ Please let the dog out. Deja salir al perro, por favor.

let sleeping dogs lie mejor no menearlo

to **let someone by** ▪ to let someone get by dejar a alguien pasar ➤ I let her by. La dejé pasar. *("La dejé pasar" can also mean "I let her in.")*

to **let someone do something** ▪ to permit someone to do something dejar a alguien hacer algo ➤ I don't know if my parents will let me go. No sé si mis padres me dejarán ir.

to **let someone down** ▪ to disappoint someone fallar a alguien ▪ defraudar a alguien ▪ defraudar la confianza de alguien

to **let someone get by** ▪ to let someone by dejar a alguien pasar

to **let someone go 1.** to fire someone despedirle a alguien **2.** to release someone ▪ to let go of someone soltarlo ▪ dejar que se vaya ➤ Let him go! ▪ Let go of him! ¡Suéltalo! ▪ ¡Deja que se vaya!

to **let someone go through** ▪ to let someone pass dejarle pasar a alguien

to **let someone have it 1.** *(verbally)* to bawl someone out regañar a alguien ▪ atacar a alguien **2.** *(physically)* to assault someone agredir a alguien ▪ atacar a alguien

to **let someone have something** permitir a alguien algo ▪ dejar algo a alguien ▪ dejar a alguien quedarse (con) algo ➤ Let me have that for a second. ▪ Give me that for a second. ▪ Hand me that for a second. Permítemelo un segundo. ▪ Permítemelo un momento. ▪ Déjamelo un segundo. ▪ Déjamelo un momento. ➤ I let him have the newspaper. ▪ I let him keep the newspaper. Le dejé quedarse (con) el periódico.

to **let someone in 1.** *(when it's up to you)* dejar entrar a alguien ▪ dejar pasar a alguien **2.** *(when it's up to someone else)* dejarle pasar a alguien ➤ The manager told the bouncer not to let the DJ admit any more of his friends unless they pay. El gerente dijo al patovica que no le dejase pasar al DJ más de sus amigos sin pagar.

to **let someone in on a secret** compartir el secreto con alguien

to **let someone off** ▪ to drop someone off dejar ▪ to lift someone's punishment levantarle el castigo a alguien ➤ Let us off at Sanborns, please. Nos deja en Sanborns, por favor.

to **let someone push one around** ▪ to let oneself be pushed around by someone dejarse avasallar por alguien ➤ Don't let him push you around. ▪ Don't let yourself be pushed around by him. ▪ Don't allow yourself to be pushed around by him. No te dejes avasallar por él.

to **let someone twist your arm** ▪ to let your arm be twisted dar el brazo a torcer

to **let someone up** ▪ to let someone break the line dejar que se cuele ▪ dejarse colar ▪ dejar colarse ➤ I'll let you up. Voy a dejar que te cueles. ▪ Voy a dejarte colar. ▪ Voy a dejar colarte.

to **let something cook** dejar algo cocinar ▪ proseguir la cocción ➤ Let it cook until the chicken is tender. Dejar cocinar hasta que el pollo esté tierno. ▪ Proseguir la cocción hasta que el pollo esté tierno.

to **let something cool down** *(cooking)* ▪ to let something cool off dejar que algo se enfríe

to **let something go to waste** dejar que algo se pierda ▪ echar algo en saco roto

to **let something take its course** dejar algo tomar un curso ▪ dejar que algo tome su curso ➤ There's no cure for the common cold. You have to let it take its course. No hay cura para el resfriado. Hay que dejarlo tomar su curso.

to **let the beans soak overnight** ▪ to soak the beans overnight dejar los frijoles en remojo durante toda la noche ▪ remojar los frijoles durante toda la noche *(Spanish has many words for beans depending on the type, including "habas, frijoles, judías, alubias, garbanzos," etc.)*

to **let the cat out of the bag** levantar el liebre ▪ descubrir el pastel ▪ tirar el diablo de la manta ▪ tirar de la manta ▪ irse de la boca ▪ *(Mex.)* írsele a alguien la lengua ➤ She let the cat out of the bag. Ella se fue de la boca. ▪ Se le fue la lengua.

to **let the chips fall where they may** caiga quien caiga

to **let the dog out** ▪ to let out the dog dejar salir al perro ➤ Please let the dog out. ▪ Please let out the dog. Por favor, deja salir al perro.

to **let the engine run** ▪ to let the motor run dejar el motor funcionando

let the good times roll! ¡a divertirnos! ▪ ¡vamos a divertirnos!
to **let the motor run** ▪ to let the engine run dejar el motor en marcha
let them come! ¡que vengan!
let them have it 1. let 'em have it ▪ give it to 'em good and hard! ¡dadles fuerte! 2. let them keep it deja que se lo queden
let there be light! ¡hágase la luz!
to **let up** ▪ to subside ▪ to lose its punch remitir ➤ The storm is letting up. Remite la tormenta. ▪ Remite el temporal.
let us pray oremos
to **let your arm be twisted** ▪ to let someone twist your arm dar el brazo a torcer
let's assume that... ▪ let's suppose that... ▪ let's say that... supongamos que... ▪ hemos de suponer que... ▪ digamos que...
let's assume (that) there is... ▪ let's suppose (that) there is... supongamos que haya...
let's assume (that) there were... ▪ let's suppose (that) there were... supongamos que hubiera... ▪ supongamos que hubiese...
(let's) dig in! ¡hinquémosle el diente!
let's drop the subject ▪ let's (just) drop it no se hable más de ello ▪ despachemos
let's face it! ¡desengáñate!
let's flip over it ▪ let's flip a coin to decide nos lo jugamos a cara o cruz
let's get going! ¡vamos! ▪ ¡vámonos! ▪ ¡andando!
let's get on with it! let's get to work! ▪ ¡vamos al tajo!
let's get one thing straight! ▪ let's get this straight! ¡vamos a aclarar una cosa! ▪ ¡entérate de una vez!
let's get out of here! ¡larguémonos!
let's get started empecemos ▪ al avío
let's get to the point vamos al grano ▪ vamos al caso
let's get to work! ¡manos a la obra!
let's go Dutch que cada uno pague lo suyo
let's go halves ▪ let's split the bill vamos a medias ▪ vamos a pachas
let's go have a cup of coffee ▪ let's go get a cup of coffee ▪ let's go (out) for a cup of coffee vamos a tomar un café ▪ *(Sp.)* vamos a por un café
let's go in here vamos a meternos aquí
let's go one step at a time ▪ let's take one step at a time vamos por partes
let's go there! vamos para allí ▪ vamos pá allá
let's have a beer *(slang)* pillamos una cerveza ➤ Let's have a beer and some fried potatoes. Pillamos un mini y unas bravas.
let's have a good time ▪ let's have fun a divertirnos ▪ vamos a pachas
let's have some music! ¡venga la música!
let's hope esperemos ▪ con tal que ➤ Let's hope it doesn't happen again. Esperemos que no pase otra vez. ▪ Con tal que no pase otra vez.
let's just drop it apaga y vámonos ▪ ignóralo ▪ pasa de eso
let's keep in touch seguimos en contacto ▪ sigamos en contacto ▪ seguiremos en contacto
let's leave it at that! ▪ that settles it! ¡lo dicho!
let's make a deal hágamos un trato
let's not waste (any) time no perdamos el tiempo
let's put it that way ▪ shall we say digámoslo así
let's roll! ▪ go for it! ¡a por ello!
let's say (that)... 1. vamos a decir (que) ... ▪ digamos (que)... 2. let's suppose (that)... pongamos que...
let's see a ver ▪ vamos a ver
let's see if they'll fall for it ▪ let's see if we can get away with it a ver si cuela
let's see what happens a ver qué pasa ▪ a ver qué tal
(let's) shake on it! idémonos la mano! ▪ vamos a estrechar la mano
let's stay in touch ▪ let's keep in touch seguiremos en contacto ▪ seguimos en contacto
let's suppose (that) there is... ▪ let's assume (that) there is... supongamos que haya...
let's suppose (that) there is one ▪ let's assume (that) there is one supongamos que lo haya ▪ supongamos que la haya
(let's) suppose (that) there are *(all countries)* supongamos que haya ▪ *(L. Am.)* hagamos cuenta de que haya
(let's) suppose (that) there had been 1. *(singular)* supongamos que hubiera habido ▪ supongamos que hubiese habido 2. *(plural)* supongamos que hubieran habido ▪ supongamos que hubiesen habido
(let's) suppose (that) there has been supongamos que haya habido
(let's) suppose (that) there have been supongamos que haya habido
(let's) suppose (that) there is supongamos que hay ▪ *(L. Am.)* hagamos cuenta de que hay
(let's) suppose (that) there was supongamos que hubiera ▪ supongamos que hubiese ▪ *(L. Am.)* hagamos cuenta de que hubiera ▪ hagamos cuenta de que hubiese
(let's) suppose (that) there were ▪ let's assume that there were 1. *(main clause)* supongamos que lo hubiera ▪ supongamos que lo hubiese 2. *(dependent clause)* supongamos que hubiera... ▪ supongamos que hubiese...
let's take a break vamos a descansar ▪ vamos a tomar un recreo
let's take one step at a time ▪ let's go one step at a time vamos por partes
let's talk vamos a hablar ▪ hablemos ▪ hablamos ➤ Let's talk during the break. Hablamos durante el descanso. ▪ Hablamos al descansar.
let's try for a boy vamos a por el niño
let's try for a girl vamos a por la niña
let's welcome...! ¡démosle la bienvenida a...!
letters to the editor cartas al director
to be **level** estar a nivel ▪ estar horizontal ➤ The table is not level. La mesa no está a nivel. ▪ La mesa no está horizontal.
to **level criticism at someone (for)** hacer críticas sobre a alguien (por)
level edge *(as opposed to a beveled edge)* ▪ flat edge borde plano
level flight vuelo nivelado
level of stress ▪ stress level ▪ degree of stress grado de estrés
to be **level with** ▪ to be even with estar al nivel de ▪ estar a la altura de
to be **leveled at** caer sobre ➤ A barrage of criticism is being leveled at the government for... Una avalancha de críticas está cayendo sobre el gobierno por...
to **levy a tax** aplicar un impuesto
liar! ¡mentiroso! ▪ ¡falsario!
lick of work pizca de trabajo ▪ cacho de trabajo ➤ I'd better get going. I haven't done a lick of work today. Más vale que me marche. No he hecho ni una pizca de trabajo hoy. ▪ Más vale que me marche. No he hecho ni un cacho de trabajo hoy.
to **lie about something** mentir sobre algo
to **lie ahead** ▪ (for) the future to have in store estar por venir ▪ deparar el futuro ➤ We don't know what lies ahead, but we're optimistic. ▪ We don't know what the future has in store, but we're optimistic. No sabemos lo que está por venir, pero somos optimistas. ▪ No sabemos lo que depara el futuro, pero somos optimistas.
to **lie down** recostarse ▪ echarse
to **lie down on a sled** tumbarse en un trineo
to **lie down on one's back** ▪ to lie down face up ▪ to lie supine tumbarse boca arriba ▪ echarse boca arriba ▪ tumbarse en decúbito supino
to **lie down on one's stomach** ▪ to lie down facedown ▪ to lie prone tumbarse boca abajo ▪ echarse boca abajo ▪ tumbarse en decúbito prono
to **lie face up** ▪ to lie on one's back ▪ to lie supine yacer boca arriba ▪ estar tumbado boca arriba ▪ estar tumbado en decúbito supino
to **lie facedown** ▪ to lie on one's stomach ▪ to lie prone yacer boca abajo ▪ estar tumbado boca abajo ▪ estar tumbado en decúbito prono
to **lie in state** estar de cuerpo presente
to **lie in wait for someone** ▪ to wait in ambush for someone acechar a alguien ▪ estar al acecho de alguien

to **lie on the floor** yacer en el suelo

to **lie prone** *(medical)* ▪ to lie facedown ▪ to lie in a prone position estar (en) decúbito prono ▪ estar (en) decúbito dorsal ▪ estar boca abajo ▪ yacer (en) decúbito prono ▪ yacer (en) decúbito dorsal ▪ yacer boca abajo

to **lie supine** *(medical)* to lie face up ▪ to lie in a supine position estar (en) decúbito supino ▪ estar boca arriba ▪ yacer (en) decúbito supino ▪ yacer boca abajo

to **lie to a grand jury** mentirle al gran jurado ▪ mentir ante un gran jurado

to **lie unconscious** yacer inconsciente ▪ *(from fainting)* yacer desmayado(-a)

to **lie under oath** ▪ to commit perjury ▪ to perjure oneself mentir bajo juramento ▪ cometer perjurio ▪ jurar en falso ▪ perjurar(se)

lies the town of... ▪ se sitúa el pueblo de... ▪ se levanta el pueblo de...

life after death ▪ the hereafter la vida después de la muerte ▪ el más allá ▪ el otro mundo

life everlasting ▪ everlasting life ▪ eternal life vida eterna

life expectancy 1. *(of a person)* expectativa de vida ▪ esperanza de vida **2.** *(of a population)* promedio de vida

life goes (by) so quickly la vida se pasa tan rápido ▪ la vida se pasa volando ▪ la vida se pasa tan deprisa

life goes on sigue la vida ▪ la vida continúa

life imprisonment cadena perpetua

life imprisonment without parole cadena perpetua sin la posibilidad de salir en libertad condicional

life insurance seguro de vida

life is full of surprises la vida está llena de sorpresas ▪ la vida siempre da sorpresas ▪ la vida es una caja de sorpresas

life of a battery *la* duración de una pila

life savings ahorros de toda una vida

to be **life-threatening** significar amenaza para la vida ▪ implicar amenaza para la vida

life-threatening illness enfermedad que pone en riesgo la vida

life-threatening situation *la* situación límite

to be the **lifeblood of** ser el sustento de ▪ ser la savia de

life's little pleasures pequeños placeres de la vida

life's ups and downs ▪ ups and downs of life ▪ ups and downs in life altibajos de la vida ▪ los azares de la vida

to be a **lifesaver** ser un balón de oxígeno

lifetime job trabajo para toda la vida

to **lift an embargo on** ▪ to raise an embargo quitar un embargo ▪ levantar un embargo

lift and drag coefficients *(aerodynamics) los* coeficientes de sustentación y arrastre

to **lift one's immunity** levantar la inmunidad a alguien

to **lift the ban on** ▪ to raise the ban on levantar el embargo contra

to **lift the ban on travel** ▪ to lift the travel ban ▪ to raise the ban on travel ▪ to raise the travel ban levantar la prohibición de viajar

to **lift the sanctions on a country for** ▪ to lift the sanctions against a country for ▪ to raise the sanctions on a country for ▪ to raise the sanctions against a country for levantar las sanciones impuestas a un país por

to **lift the siege** ▪ to raise the siege levantar el asedio

lift up! *(dental technician putting on patient's bib)* ▪ lift your head up levante un poco la cabeza ▪ separe un poco ▪ ➤ Lift up a little. Levante un poco la cabeza. ▪ Separe un poco.

lifting of the embargo ▪ raising of the embargo levantamiento del embargo

to **light a candle to a saint** encender una vela a un(-a) santo(-a) ▪ *(L. Am.)* prender una vela a un(-a) santo(-a)

to **light a cigarette** encender un cigarrillo ▪ *(L. Am.)* prender un cigarrillo

to **light a fire** prender un fuego ▪ encender un fuego ➤ Open the front door before you light the fire in the fireplace so the draft will draw the smoke upwards. Abre la puerta delantera antes de prender el fuego en la chimenea para que la corriente haga subir al humo por el tiro.

to **light a match** encender una cerilla ▪ encender un fósforo ▪ encender un mixto

to be **light as a feather** ▪ to be as light as a feather ser tan ligero como una pluma ▪ pesar menos que una pluma

light beer cerveza rubia

light breakfast pequeño desayuno ▪ *(Sp., coll.)* desayuno flojo

light cover of fog ▪ thin layer of fog ▪ light layer of fog ▪ thin cover of fog velo de niebla

to be **light enough to carry** ser lo suficientemente ligero para llevar a mano

light fixtures artefactos de iluminación

light (for a cigarette): to have a ~ tener fuego ➤ Do you have a light? ¿Tienes fuego?

light (in color) claro

light (in weight) liviano ▪ ligero

the **light is bright** *la* luz da fuerte ▪ *la* luz es intensa ➤ The light on the picture is too bright. Move the lamp back a little. La luz da muy fuerte en el cuadro. Retira la lámpara un poco.

the **light is dim** la luz está tenue

light is green: the (traffic) ~ el semáforo está en verde ➤ *(accident notice)* The traffic light was green in both directions, but the concrete truck had the right of way. Los semáforos de ambos sentidos estaban en verde, pero la preferencia de paso era de la hormigonera.

the **light is soft** la luz está suave

light jacket ▪ windbreaker cazadora ▪ chaqueta ligera

light layer of fog ▪ thin layer of fog ▪ light cover of fog ▪ thin cover of fog velo de niebla

light of Velázquez *(for which his paintings are noted) la* luz de Velázquez ▪ luz velazqueña ▪ *el* juego de luces que utiliza Velázquez

light opera ▪ operetta opereta

light rain ▪ drizzle llovizna ▪ *(Sp., coll.)* calabobos ▪ *el* chirimiri

light sleeper: to be a (very) ~ tener un sueño muy ligero

light supper cena ligera ▪ cena menuda

light switch *el* interruptor ▪ *el* apagador

to **light the way** alumbrar el camino ▪ iluminar el camino

light winds vientos suaves

light-year año luz

to be **light-years across** estar a años luz de un extremo al otro ➤ The Milky Way is 300,000 light-years across. La Vía Láctea está a 300.000 años luz de un extremo al otro.

to be **light-years ahead of where...** estar a muchos años luz de lo que... ➤ Medical technology is light-years ahead of where it was a generation ago. La tecnología médica está a muchos años luz de lo que estaba una generación atrás.

to be **light-years apart** estar a años luz aparte ➤ The sun and Alpha Centauri are four light-years apart. El sol y Alfa Centauri están a cuatro años luz aparte.

to be **light-years apart on an issue** ▪ to be diametrically opposed on a issue estar a años luz en un asunto ▪ estar separados años luz en un asunto ▪ ser diametralmente opuestos en un asunto ▪ estar diametralmente opuestos en un asunto ➤ The political right and left are light-years apart. La izquierda y la derecha estan a años luz. ▪ La izquierda y la derecha están separados años luz. ▪ La izquierda y la derecha son diametralmente opuestos.

to be **light-years away** ▪ to be light-years distant estar a años luz ▪ quedar a años luz ➤ The closest star to the sun is four light-years away. La estrella más cercana al sol está a cuatro años luz. ▪ La estrella más cercana al sol queda a cuatro años luz. ➤ The Pole Star is 430 light years away, plus or minus a hundred light years. La Estrella Polar está a 430 años luz, con una incertidumbre de más o menos cien años luz. ▪ La Estrella Polar queda a 430 años luz, con una incertidumbre de más o menos cien años luz.

to be **light-years in diameter** ▪ to be light-years across ser el diámetro de años luz ▪ tener años luz de un extremo al otro ➤ The Milky Way is 300,000 light-years in diameter. ▪ The Milky Way is 300,000 light-years across. El diámetro de la Vía Láctea es de 300.000 años luz. ▪ La Vía Láctea tiene 300.000 años luz de un extremo al otro.

lighted sign letrero luminoso

lighthouse beacon faro

lighthouse icon *(computers)* icono del faro
lightning bolt ▪ bolt of lightning relámpago ▪ rayo
lightning rod pararayos ➤ The president is a lightning rod for the critics. El presidente es un pararayos para los críticos.
lightning strikes something algo es alcanzado por un rayo
lightweight wood *(balsa, alder)* madera liviana
like a bat outta hell *(coll.)* como alma que lleva el diablo
like a charm como por arte de magia
like a chicken with its head cut off: to run around ~ correr como un pollo sin cabeza
like a duck takes to water: to take to something ~ *(coll.)* como un pez en el agua
to be **like a fish out of water** estar como gallina en corral ajeno ▪ estar como gallo en corral ajeno
like a flash ▪ in a flash como un bólido
like a lot of other people al igual que muchas otras personas
like a madman como un enajenado
like a madwoman como una enajenada
to be **like a member of the family** ▪ to be like one of the family ser muy de adentro ▪ ser como (uno más) de la familia
like a shot: to be off ~ salir disparado ▪ salir como una flecha
like carrying coals to Newcastle como llevar leña al monte ▪ como llevar agua al mar
like clockwork como el reloj
like everyone else como todos los demás ▪ como cada quisque ▪ como todo quisque
like father, like son de tal palo, tal astilla
to be **like it** ▪ to be similar to it **1.** ser parecido ▪ ser semejante **2.** to be just like it ▪ to be exactly like it ▪ to be identical to it ser idéntico
like it or not lo quiera o no
like me igual que yo ▪ como yo ➤ ... who, like me... ... que, como yo...
like new! ¡bien conservado!
like old times como en los viejos tiempos
to be **like one of the family** ▪ to be like a member of the family ser muy de adentro ▪ ser como (uno más) de la familia
to **like opera** gustarle las óperas ➤ The Italians like opera. A los italianos les gustan las óperas.
to **like someone** caerle bien alguien ▪ apreciarle a alguien *("Gustarle" has a sexual connotation.)* ➤ I like him a lot. Me cae muy bien.
to be **like talking to a brick wall** como si se hablara con la pared
like that: a friend ~ un amigo así ▪ una amiga así
like the back of one's hand: to know ~ conocer como la palma de la mano ➤ He knows Madrid like the back of his hand. Conoce Madrid como la palma de la mano.
like the one ▪ similar to the one similar a la de ▪ similar al de
like the plague como de la peste ➤ She avoids him like the plague. Le huye como de la peste.
to be **like trying to find a needle in a haystack** ser más difícil que encontrar una aguja en un pajar
to **likely do something** ser probable que haga algo ▪ ser fácil que haga algo ➤ They'll likely do it. Es fácil que lo hagan. ➤ The most likely (thing) Lo más fácil ▪ Lo más probable
to **liken something to something** comparar algo con algo ▪ equiparar algo con algo
lime tree tilo ▪ limero
to be the **limit 1.** ser el límite **2.** to be the last straw ser el colmo ▪ ser la gota que colma el vaso ▪ pasar de castaño oscuro **3.** *(of people)* ser de lo que no hay
to **limit oneself to one main focus** ▪ to focus on one thing ▪ to concentrate on one thing ceñirse a un tema
linseed oil *el* aceite de las semillas de lino
line: ancestral ~ ▪ ancestral lineage ▪ stock *la* estirpe ▪ casta ▪ *el* linaje ▪ *(metaphorical)* cepa
line is busy comunica ▪ está comunicando ▪ la línea está ocupada
line of cars 1. *(moving, funeral procession, or motorcade)* hilera de coches **2.** *(stopped or moving slowly)* fila de coches ➤ There was a long line of cars in the funeral procession. Había una larga hilera de coches en el funeral. ➤ There was a long line of cars backed up at the toll booths. Había una fila de coches retenidos en los puestos de peaje.
line of sight línea de mira ▪ línea de visión
line of thinking ▪ line of thought corriente de pensamiento
line of work medio de trabajo ▪ ámbito profesional ▪ ámbito laboral
line one *(telephone, metro, etc.)* la línea uno ➤ You have a call on line one. Tiene una llama en la línea uno. ▪ Le llaman en la línea uno. ➤ Which metro line is the public library on?-One. The stop is Iglesia. ¿En qué línea del metro queda la biblioteca pública?-La uno, la parada es Iglesia.
to **line up** to get in line ▪ to form a line hacer cola ▪ ponerse en fila ▪ *(Mex.)* formarse ▪ alinearse ➤ You have to line up. ▪ You have to get in line. Hay que hacer cola. ▪ *(Mex.)* Hay que formarse. ➤ Okay students, line up single file. ▪ Get in line single file. Poneos en una sola fila.
to **line up by twos** formarse en fila de a dos ➤ Okay, students, line up by twos. Bueno, alumnos, fórmense en fila de a dos.
to **line up correctly** ▪ to align correctly coincidir ➤ This zipper's teeth don't line up correctly, and it catches. Los dientes de esta cremallera no coinciden, y se atasca. ▪ Los dientes de esta cremallera no coinciden, y se detiene. ▪ Los dientes de esta cremallera no coinciden, y no puede seguir.
to be **lined with** estar forrado de
lines on the highway rayas en la carretera
lines were down las líneas estaban caídas
link of a chain ▪ link in a chain *el* eslabón de una cadena
to **link something and something** ▪ to link something with something ▪ to link something to something conectar algo con algo ➤ In the nineteenth century, the trans-Atlantic cable linked the United States and Europe. En el siglo diecinueve, el cable transatlántico conectó a los Estados Unidos y Europa.
to **link someone to something** implicar a alguien en algo ▪ conectar a alguien a algo ➤ The suspect was linked to the crime. El sospechoso fue implicado en el crimen. ➤ DNA evidence has linked the suspect to the crime scene. Las pruebas de ADN han conectado al sospechoso con la escena del crimen. ▪ Las pruebas de ADN han vinculado al sospechoso con la escena del crimen. ➤ Experts linked the deaths caused by kidney failure to a new anti-cholesterol drug. Expertos relacionaron las muertes por fallo renal con un nuevo fármaco contra el colesterol.
to **link (up) computers** *(L. Am.)* conectar las computadoras ▪ *(Sp.)* conectar los ordenadores ➤ I linked (up) my office computer to my home computer. ▪ I linked up my office and home computers. Conecté mi computadora en la oficina con mi computadora en casa.
to **link up (with someone)** ▪ to get together with someone juntarse con alguien ▪ conectarse con alguien
to be **linked to 1.** to be associated with ▪ to have ties to estar asociado con **2.** to be connected to estar conectado con
lingering doubt ▪ persistent doubt reparo ▪ duda persistente
lion's share bocado del león
list of expressions listado de expresiones ▪ lista de expresiones ➤ This is my list of expressions. Éste es mi listado de expresiones.
list of names lista de nombres ▪ *la* relación de nombres
list of people in arrears ▪ list of payment delinquencies lista de morosos
list of registered voters ▪ voter list registro electoral
to be **listed in the census** ▪ to appear in the census figurar en el censo
to be **listed in the dictionary** estar listado en el diccionario ➤ It's not listed. No está listado.
to be **listed in the telephone directory** ▪ to be listed in the phone book ▪ to appear in the telephone directory figurar en la guía telefónica ▪ aparecer en la guía telefónica
to be **listed under** ▪ to be in the dictionary under estar listado bajo ➤ It's listed under "make" in the dictionary. Está listado bajo "make" en el diccionario.
to **listen out for** estar a la escucha de
to **listen to someone else's conversation** poner la oreja
listen, you! ¡oye, tú!

listings for listados de ▪ altas de ➤ I found you in the listings for August. ▪ I found you in the August listings. Te encontré en los listados de agosto. ▪ Te encontré en las altas de agosto.

to be **literal-minded** seguir algo a pies juntillas

literary word palabra culta ➤ That word is literary; the man on the street wouldn't understand it. Es una palabra culta. El hombre en la calle no lo entendería.

literary debut lanzamiento literario

litter box *(for cats)* caja de arena

little bird told me me lo ha contado un pajarito ▪ un pájaro me lo ha dicho

to be a **little (bit) down** quedarse un poco triste ➤ I've been a little bit down. Me he quedado un poco triste.

little (bit) late: to be going to be a ~ ▪ to be a little (bit) late tardar un poco ▪ tardar un poquito ➤ She's going to be a little bit late. Ella tarda un poquito.

little by little ▪ gradually poco a poco ▪ paulatinamente ▪ gradualmente ➤ The company decided to gradually dismantle the plant. La compañía decidió desmantelar la planta poco a poco. ▪ La compañía decidió desmantelar la planta paulatinamente. ▪ La compañía decidió desmantelar la planta gradualmente.

little did he know poco sabía ▪ no tenía idea de lo que ▪ cuán lejos estaba de saber que

little did he think that cuán lejos estaba de pensar que

little dish of salsa ▪ ramekin of salsa *el* ramiquín de salsa

little ditty tonadilla

little does he know (that)... poca idea tiene que...

little finger dedo meñique

to be a **little fish in a big pond** estar como garbanzo en olla grande

"Little House on the Prairie" *(TV series)* "Casa de la pradera"

little light went on in my head: this ~ ▪ a little light went on in my head se inciende esta lucecita

little match girl pequeña vendedora de cerillas

little more coffee? *(Mex.)* ¿un poco más de café? ▪ *(Sp.)* ¿un poco más café?

little princess: my ~ mi reina ➤ How's my little princess? ¿Cómo está mi reina?

Little Red Riding Hood Caperucita Roja

the **little that's left of** ▪ what little remains of ▪ what little is left of lo poco que queda de

to **live a lie** vivir en la mentira

to **live a long way from someone** ▪ to live far from someone vivir muy separado de alguien

to **live a normal life** llevar un tren de vida normal ▪ hacer la vida normal

to **live a middle-class life** llevar una vida de clase media ➤ The double agent lived a middle-class life in a Washington suburb. El agente doble llevaba una vida de clase media en uno de los suburbios de Washington.

to **live alone** ▪ to live by oneself vivir solo ➤ She lives alone. ▪ She lives by herself. Vive sola.

to **live an ascetic life** llevar una vida ascética

live and learn vivir para ver

to **live beyond one's means** vivir por encima de sus posibilidades (económicas) ▪ gastar más de lo que uno gana

to **live by oneself** ▪ to live alone vivir solo ➤ She lives by herself. ▪ She lives alone. Vive sola.

live concert concierto en directo ▪ concierto en vivo

to **live conservatively** vivir de una forma modesta

to **live down something** ▪ to live something down lograr que se olvide ➤ He'll never live it down. Jamás logrará que se lo olviden. ➤ He'll never live that down. Jamás logrará que se olvide eso.

to **live each day to the fullest** vivir al máximo cada día

to **live far from someone** ▪ to live a long way from someone vivir muy separado de alguien

to **live from hand to mouth** vivir al día

to **live in a house with maid service** ▪ to have maid service ir a mesa puesta y cama hecha

to **live it up** darse la gran vida ▪ vivir a lo grande ➤ They're living it up. Se están dando la gran vida. ▪ Viven a lo grande.

to **live life to the fullest** ▪ to live life to the full vivir la vida al límite ➤ Life must be lived to the full(est). ▪ Must live life to the full(est). La vida hay que vivirla al límite.

to **live like a king** vivir a cuerpo de rey ▪ vivir como un rajá ▪ estar en grande

to **live longer** vivir más

live music música en vivo ➤ Is the music live, or is that a recording? ¿Es la música en vivo, o es una grabación?

to **live next door to each other** vivir al lado el uno del otro ▪ vivir puerta con puerta ➤ Falstaff, in the *Merry Wives of Windsor*, sends love letters to two women who live next door to each other. Falstaff en *Las alegres comadres de Windsor* envía cartas de amor a dos mujeres que viven puerta con puerta.

to **live next door to someone** vivir al lado de alguien

to **live off the backs of someone** gorronear a alguien ▪ vivir a expensas de alguien

to **live on** seguir viviendo ➤ His legacy lives on. Su legado sigue viviendo.

to **live on very little** arreglárselas para vivir con muy pocos recursos ➤ The family managed to live on very little. La familia se las arreglaba para vivir con muy pocos recursos.

to **live part of the year in a place** residir por temporadas en un lugar

live performance actuación en directo ▪ actuación en vivo

to **live through someone else** ▪ to live through the experiences of someone else vivir otra vida a través de alguien

to **live through something** 1. to experience something vivir algo 2. to survive something ▪ to come out of something alive sobrevivir a algo

to **live to see** vivir para ver ➤ He lived to see his first great grandchild. Vivió para ver a su primera bisnieta. ➤ I never thought I'd live to see the day when... Nunca pensé que iba a vivir para ver el día en que...

to **live to tell about it** vivir para contarla

to **live together** ▪ to cohabit arrejuntarse ▪ amancebarse

to **live up to one's reputation** estar a la altura de su reputación

to **live up to someone's expectations** estar a la altura de las expectativas de alguien

to **live up to the agreement** ▪ to honor the agreement cumplir con el acuerdo ▪ cumplir el trato ▪ respetar el acuerdo

to **live up to the claim (made in the ad)** estar a la altura del anuncio ▪ cumplir las expectativas del anuncio ➤ Their ad said that it was stainless steel, but the flatware did not live up to the claim. El anuncio afirmaba que se trataba de acero inoxidable, pero la cubertería no estuvo a la altura del anuncio. ▪ El anuncio afirmaba que se trataba de acero inoxidable, pero la cubertería no cumplió las expectativas del anuncio.

to be a **live wire** 1. *(electrical)* dar corriente ▪ ser un cable con tensión pelado ▪ ser cable electrificado pelado ▪ ser un cable con corriente pelado ▪ ser un cable que da calambre 2. *(especially young children)* to be a bundle of energy ser puro nervio ➤ That wire is live. Ese cable da corriente. ➤ That little girl is a live wire. Esa niña es puro nervio.

to **live with something** vivir con algo ➤ The doctor said he would have to live with his condition for the rest of his life. El médico dijo que tendría que vivir con su condición durante el resto de su vida.

to **live with the consequences of** apencar con las consequencias de

to **live within one's income** ▪ to live within one's means vivir de acuerdo con los propios medios económicos ▪ vivir de acuerdo con sus ingresos ▪ vivir sólo de sus ingresos

to **liven up the party** amenizar la fiesta

living will testamento vital

lo and behold mira por donde ▪ zas ▪ he aquí ➤ And lo and behold... Y mira por donde... ▪ Y zas... ▪ Y he aquí...

to **load a camera** cargar una cámara

to **load a dishwasher** cargar un lavavajillas ▪ cargar un lavaplatos

to **load a gun** cargar un arma de fuego ▪ cargar una pistola *(Although "gun" can refer to all types of firearms, it usually refers to pistols.)*

to **load a program onto the computer** cargar un programa al ordenador

to **load a truck with** cargar un camión con

load-bearing wall muro de carga ▪ pared de carga ▪ pared maestra

load of laundry carga de ropa ➤ If I bring you a load of laundry by noon, can I pick it up this evening? Si les traigo una carga de ropa para las doce, ¿puedo recogerla esta tarde? ➤ If I brought you a load of laundry by noon, could I pick it up this evening? ¿Si les trajera una carga de ropa para las doce, podría recogerla esta tarde?

to **load someone down with responsibilities** ▪ to give someone a lot of responsibilities cargar a alguien con responsabilidades

to **load something onto a truck** cargar algo en un camión

loaded camera cámara cargada

loaded gun pistola cargada

loaded question pregunta doble intencionada

to be **loaded with** estar cargado de

loads of food ▪ tons of food comida a patadas

loaf of bread *el* pan de molde ▪ barra de pan ▪ hogaza de pan

local time at destination hora local en la ciudad del destino

locate someone ▪ to find someone localizar a alguien ▪ encontrar a alguien

to **locate something** localizar algo

to **lock horns (with someone)** enzarzarse en una disputa (con alguien)

to **lock it (up)** echarle la llave ▪ cerrarlo con llave

lock of hair *el* mechón de pelo

to **lock oneself out** quedarse afuera ▪ olvidar las llaves dentro ▪ dejar la llave dentro ➤ I locked myself out. Me quedé afuera. ▪ Olvidé las llaves dentro. ▪ He dejado la llave dentro.

to **lock onto a transmitter** ▪ to beam into a transmitter fijarse en la señal de un transmisor

to **lock someone out** dejarlo sin llave ➤ Why are you locking us out? ¿Por qué nos deja sin llave?

to be **locked for editing** *(computers)* estar protegido contra escritura ▪ edición bloqueada

to **lodge a complaint about** ▪ to file a complaint about ▪ to make a (formal) complaint about presentar una reclamación sobre ▪ presentar una denuncia sobre ▪ presentar una queja sobre

lofty goals: to set ~ ▪ to set high goals fijar metas altas

to **log off** salir del sistema

to **log on** ▪ to log in entrar (al sistema)

logical basis for base lógica para ▪ fundamento lógico para

lonely feeling *la* sensación de soledad

to **long for** suspirar por ▪ anhelar por

long-awaited tan esperado

long-distance relationship *la* relación a larga distancia

long hours largas horas

long line ▪ long ancestral line una antigua estirpe

long, long ago in the time of ▪ long, long ago in the days of allá en tiempo de

a **long, long time ago** hace muchísimo tiempo ▪ en épocas muy remotas ▪ en épocas pretéritas

long-playing record ▪ long-play record ▪ LP disco de larga duración

long-range missile *el* misil de alcance largo ▪ misil de largo alcance

long-range plan *el* plan a largo plazo

long road to recovery largo camino hacia la recuperación ▪ *(literary)* larga singladura hacia la recuperación

long since hace mucho

long-sleeve shirt camisa de manga larga

long-standing disagreement ▪ disagreement of long standing desacuerdo que viene de largo

long-standing friendship antigua amistad

to be a **long story** ser largo de contar ➤ It's a long story. Es largo de contar.

long-term de larga duración

long-term relationship relación de larga duración

a **long time ago** hace mucho tiempo ▪ *(literary)* mucho tiempo ha ➤ It happened a long time ago. Sucedió hace mucho tiempo. ▪ Sucedió mucho tiempo ha.

a **long time before** mucho antes

long wait larga espera ▪ espera prolongada

to be a **long way away** ▪ to be a long way off estar muy lejos ▪ estar lejísimos ▪ estar allá a lo lejos ▪ estar muy allá ▪ *(Sp., coll.)* estar a tomar por saco

long way from here: to live a ~ ▪ to live far from here vivir lejos de aquí ➤ I live a long way from here. ▪ I live far from here. Vivo lejos de aquí.

to be a **long way from perfection** faltar mucho para la perfección ▪ recorrer un largo camino hasta la perfección

to be a **long way off** **1.** to be a long way away estar muy lejos ▪ estar lejísimos ▪ estar allá a lo lejos ▪ estar muy allá **2.** to be far in the future estar muy lejos (en el futuro) **3.** to be highly inaccurate estar muy equivocado ▪ ser muy impreciso ➤ I've never seen anyone fly a kite such a long way off before. Nunca había visto antes a nadie volar una cometa tan lejos. ➤ Cassini's 1677 estimate of the sun's distance from the Earth was a long way off. La estimación de Cassini de la distancia entre el sol y la Tierra en 1677 fue muy imprecisa.

long-winded sentence ▪ mouthful un parrafón

longest run *(play)* estreno más largo ▪ *(movie)* longest showing puesta más larga

longest-running de mayor duración ▪ de más duración ➤ *The Fantasticks* was the longest-running play in the history of Broadway. *The Fantasticks* era la obra teatral de más duración de la historia de Broadway.

longing for justice *la* sed de justicia

look! ¡mira! ▪ ¡fíjate!

to **look a certain age** aparentar cierta edad ➤ Alberto looks twenty-five, but he has an eighteen-year-old son. Alberto aparenta veinticinco, pero tiene un hijo de dieciséis años. ➤ Even though he looks twenty-one, they won't let him in. Aunque aparenta tener veintiuno, no lo van a dejar entrar.

to **look a lot older** ▪ to look much older ▪ to look years older parecer mucho mayor

to **look a lot younger** ▪ to look much younger ▪ to look years younger parecer mucho menor

to **look after one's health** ▪ to guard one's health ▪ to be careful about one's health velar por la salud

to **look after someone** ▪ to take care of someone mirar por alguien ▪ cuidar de alguien

to **look alike** parecerse ➤ They look alike. Se parecen. ➤ The sisters look alike. Las hermanas se parecen.

look and see if mira a ver si

to **look angry** ▪ to look mad tener cara de pocos amigos

to **look around (one)** mirar a su alrededor ▪ girar la vista ➤ Look around (you). Mira a tu alrededor.

to **look as if one is about to** hacer ademán de

to **look askance at someone** ▪ to look at someone askance ▪ to eye someone distrustfully mirar a alguien con recelo

to **look at a book** ▪ to look through a book ojear un libro

to **look at both sides of an issue** ▪ to consider both sides of an issue considerar ambos aspectos de un asunto

to **look at each other** mirarse el uno al otro ▪ mirarse entre ellos ➤ They looked at each other. Se miraron el uno al otro. ▪ Se miraron entre ellos. ▪ *(two females)* Se miraron la una a la otra. ▪ Se miraron entre ellas.

to **look at each other in the mirror** mirarse uno al otro en el espejo

to **look at it** **1.** *(a book)* mirarlo **2.** *(a photo)* mirarla

to **look at it cold** mirarlo en frío

to **look at one another** *(three or more people)* mirarse entre ellos ➤ They looked at one another. Se miraron entre ellos. ▪ *(all females)* Se miraron entre ellas.

to **look at oneself in the mirror** mirarse en el espejo ▪ mirarse al espejo

to **look at someone** mirar a alguien ➤ I looked at her. La miré. ➤ I looked at him. Lo miré. ▪ *(Sp., leísmo)* Le miré.

to **look at someone out of the corner of one's eye** mirar a alguien de reojo ▪ mirar a alguien por el rabillo del ojo to **look at someone suspiciously** mirarle a alguien con recelo

to **look at someone with mistrust** ▪ to look at someone with suspicion ▪ to regard someone with mistrust ▪ to regard someone with suspicion ▪ to eye someone with mistrust ▪ to eye someone with suspicion ▪ to look upon someone with mistrust ▪ to look upon someone with suspicion mirar a alguien con recelo ▪ mirar a alguien receloso

to **look at someone's side of an issue** considerar la opinión de alguien en un asunto ▪ considerar la postura de alguien en un asunto

to **look at something** mirar algo ▪ contemplar algo ➤ Santiago would look at the map of Disneyland for hours on end. Santiago contemplaba el plano de Disneyland horas enteras.

look at you! ▪ just look at you! ¡mírate!

to **look away** apartar la mirada ▪ apartar la vista ▪ mirar hacia el otro lado

to **look away from** apartar la mirada de ▪ apartar la vista de

to **look away from someone** desviar su mirada de alguien

to **look awful on someone** ▪ to look terrible on someone ▪ to look dreadful on someone quedarle de pena ➤ That hat looks awful on her. ▪ That hat looks terrible on her. ▪ That hat looks dreadful on her. Ese sombrero le queda de pena.

to **look back** mirar detrás

to **look bad if...** quedar mal si...

to **look bitter** tener cara de vinagre

to **look directly at someone** ▪ to look someone in the eye mirarle a alguien a la cara ▪ mirarle a alguien a los ojos

to **look disconcerted** ▪ to have a disconcerted look tener un aire de desconcierto

to **look down** bajar la vista

to **look down on 1.** to observe from a height mirar hacia abajo a **2.** to disdain menospreciar ➤ If it were possible to look down on our solar system from the Pole Star, the entire expanse of Pluto's orbit would appear to be a mere speck. Si fuera posible mirar hacia abajo a nuestro sistema solar desde la estrella polar, toda la extensión a través de la órbita de Plutón parecería un mero punto en el cielo. ➤ I think the teacher looks down on her students. Creo que la profesora menosprecia a sus estudiantes.

to **look dreadful on someone** ▪ to look terrible on someone ▪ to look awful on someone quedarle de pena ➤ That hat looks dreadful on her. ▪ That hat looks terrible on her. Ese sombrero le queda de pena.

to **look familiar** ▪ to be familiar ▪ to ring a bell serle familiar ▪ resultarle familiar ➤ It looks familiar. Me es familiar. ▪ Me resulta familiar. ➤ His face looks familiar. ▪ His face is familiar. ▪ His face rings a bell. Me suena su cara.

to **look for a place to live** buscar casa

to **look for something** *(lost, or to give as a gift, etc.)* buscar algo

to **look for trouble** ▪ to go looking for trouble andar buscando camorra ➤ Don't go looking for trouble, dude. No andes buscando camorra, tío.

to **look forward to doing something** tener ganas de hacer algo ➤ I'm looking forward to seeing you. Tengo ganas de verte. ➤ *(business letter closing)* I look forward to hearing from you. Esperando recibir noticias suyas.

to **look forward to something** hacerle ilusión algo ▪ estar deseando algo ➤ I'm really looking forward to it. ▪ I'm looking forward to it a lot. Me hace mucha ilusión. ➤ I'm looking forward to my vacation. Estoy deseando mis vacaciones.

to **look good on someone** ▪ to be becoming to someone quedarle bien ▪ resultarle ▪ sentarle bien ▪ irle bien ➤ That dress looks really good on you. Ese vestido te queda muy bien. ▪ Ese vestido le queda muy bien. ➤ That tie doesn't look good on you. Esa corbata no te resulta. ▪ Esa corbata no le resulta. ➤ That sweater looks good on you. Ese suéter te sienta bien. ▪ Ese suéter le sienta bien. ➤ That hat does not look good on her. Ese sombrero no le va bien.

to **look ill-kept** ▪ to look ill-kempt ▪ to look sloppy estar descuidado ▪ parecer descuidado ▪ verse descuidado

to **look in the rearview mirror** ▪ to look through the rearview mirror mirar por el espejo retrovisor ➤ I looked in the rearview mirror and saw that the car behind me was tailgating (me). Miré por el espejo retrovisor y vi que el carro de detrás me venía pegado. ▪ Miré por el espejo retrovisor y vi que el carro de detrás venía besándome el culo.

to **look interested 1.** *(real interest)* parecer interesado(-a) **2.** *(feigned interest)* poner cara de interés ➤ She looked interested in what you were saying. Parecía interesada en lo que estabas diciendo. ➤ I try to look interested. Pongo cara de interés.

to **look into a matter** investigar un asunto ▪ indagar un asunto ▪ averiguar un asunto ➤ Would you look into it for me? ▪ Would you find out about it for me? ¿Lo averiguarías por mí?

to **look into the possibility of** indagar la posibilidad de ▪ estudiar la posibilidad de

to **look like 1.** to resemble parecerse **2.** to show signs of parecer ➤ He looks like his father. Se parece a su padre. ➤ She and her sister look a lot alike. Ella y su hermana se parecen un montón. ➤ It looks like it might snow tonight. ▪ It shows signs of snowing tonight. Parece que va a nevar esta noche.

to **look like a madman** tener cara de loco

to **look like one is going to do something** parecer que uno va a hacer algo ➤ They look like they are going to kiss each other. Parece que van a besarse.

to **look like rain** tener pinta de llover ▪ tener aspecto de llover

to **look like someone** ▪ to resemble someone parecerse a alguien ▪ parecérsele a alguien ▪ darse un aire a alguien ➤ I look like my father. Me parezco a mi padre. ▪ Me doy un aire a mi padre. ➤ He looks like you. *(a ti)* (Él) se parece a ti. ▪ (Él) se te parece. ▪ *(a usted)* (Él) se parece a usted ▪ (Él) se le parece. ➤ She looks like you. *(a ti)* (Ella) se parece a ti. ▪ (Ella) se te parece. ▪ *(a usted)* (Ella) se parece a usted. ▪ (Ella) se le parece.

to **look like (something)** tener aspecto de (algo) ▪ ir hecho un

look of: to have a ~ tener cara de ▪ tener mirada de ➤ She had a look of astonishment on her face. ▪ She had a look of amazement on her face. Tuvo la cara de asombro. ▪ Tuvo mirada de asombro.

to **look off into the distance (from)** ver a lo lejos (desde) ➤ When you look off into the distance from the tower of the Alcázar of Segovia, you can almost see Don Quijote on his steed, Rocinante, and Sancho beside him, coming over the hill. Cuando ves a lo lejos desde la torre del Alcázar de Segovia, casi puedes ver a Don Quijote en su corcel, Rocinante, y a Sancho a su lado, viniendo de la colina.

to **look older than...** parecer mayor que... ➤ She looks a lot older than her sister. Parece mucho mayor que su hermana. ➤ He looks older than he did the last time I saw him. Parece más avejentado que la última vez que lo vi. ▪ *(Sp., leísmo)* Parece más avejentado que la última vez que le vi.

look on one's face ▪ expression on one's face expresión de su cara ▪ expresión en su cara ➤ You should have seen the look on his face. Deberías haber visto la expresión en su cara.

to **look on someone's book** mirar su libro ➤ May I look on your book? ▪ Can I look on your book? ¿Me dejas mirar tu libro?

to **look on the bright side** mirar el lado bueno

to **look one's age** aparentar su edad ▪ representar su edad ➤ She doesn't look thirty-eight. No aparenta sus treinta y ocho años.

to **look one's best** tener el mejor aspecto posible ➤ I want to look my best. Quiero tener el mejor aspecto posible.

look out! ¡cuidado! ▪ ¡ojo! ▪ ¡con ojo!

to **look out for number one** ▪ to look out for oneself ▪ to put oneself first ir a lo suyo ▪ barrer para casa ▪ barrer hacia dentro ▪ barrer para dentro

to **look out for one's safety** velar por la seguridad (de uno)

to **look out from** mirar desde

to **look out the window** ▪ to look out of the window mirar por la ventana ▪ *(L. Am.)* aguaitar por la ventana

to **look over one's shoulder** mirar por encima del hombro

to **look (really) great on someone** quedarle algo a alguien pero que muy bien ➤ That dress looks (really) great on you. Ese vestido te queda pero muy bien.

to **look really hard** fijarse muy bien

to **look serious** 1. parecer serio 2. to adopt a serious demeanor ponerse serio

to **look sick** ▪ to look ill ▪ not to look well tener mal aspecto

to **look sloppy** ▪ to look ill-kempt ▪ to look ill-kept tener mal aspecto

to **look so pretty** hacer tan bonito

to **look someone in the eye** mirarle a los ojos a alguien ➤ He looked her in the eye and winked. Le miró a los ojos y guiñó.

to look someone in the face mirar a los ojos de alguien ▪ mirarle de frente a alguien ➤ He looked (at) her intently in the face. Le miró intentamente de frente. ▪ Le miró fijadamente de frente.

to **look someone straight in the eye** mirar a alguien a los ojos de frente ▪ mirar a alguien derechamente a los ojos ➤ I looked him straight in the eye. Lo miré a los ojos de frente. ▪ *(Sp., leísmo)* Le miré a los ojos de frente. ➤ I looked her straight in the eye. La miré a los ojos de frente.

to **look someone up and down** mirar de arriba a abajo a alguien ▪ mirar de hito en hito

to **look straight at something** mirar algo de frente

to **look terrible on someone** ▪ to look awful on someone ▪ to look dreadful on someone quedarle de pena ➤ That hat looks terrible on her. ▪ That hat looks awful on her. ▪ That hat looks dreadful on her. Ese sombrero le queda de pena.

to **look terrific in** estar estupendo con ▪ verse estupendo

to **look the other way** 1. to turn a blind eye hacer la vista gorda 2. to turn one's head mirar hacia el otro lado

to **look the problem in the face** mirar de cara al problema

to **look through a telescope at something** ▪ to look at something through a telescope mirar algo por un telescopio

to **look through a window** mirar por una ventana

to **look through one's pockets** ▪ to search one's pockets registrarse los bolsillos

to **look through the rearview mirror** ▪ to look in the rearview mirror mirar por el espejo retrovisor ➤ I looked through the rearview mirror and saw that the car behind me was tailgating (me). Miré por el espejo retrovisor y vi que el coche de detrás venía besándome el culo.

to **look unfriendly** tener cara de perros

to **look up** levantar la vista ▪ levantar la mirada

to **look up a word in the dictionary** buscar una palabra en el diccionario

to **look up at the stars** alzar la mirada a las estrellas

to **look up to someone** ▪ to admire someone ▪ to respect someone ▪ to esteem someone ▪ to hold someone in high esteem respetar a alguien ▪ admirar a alguien ▪ estimar a alguien

to **look very carefully** mirar con detenimiento ▪ mirar con mucho cuidado

to **look well** tener buen aspecto

look what I did! ¡mira lo que he hecho!

look what I've done! ▪ I've done it now! ¡la he hecho buena!

look what you've done! ¡mira lo que has hecho!

look who's talking mira quién habla ▪ mira quién fue a hablar

to **look younger than...** tener un aspecto menor que... ➤ She looks a lot younger than her sister. Tiene un aspecto bastante menor que tiene su hermana. ▪ Tiene un aspecto bastante más joven que el de su hermana.

to **loop the loop** *(aerobatic flying)* rizar el rizo

to **loose an arrow** *(literary)* ▪ to shoot an arrow disparar una flecha

to be a **loose cannon** ser una caja de bombas

loose change ▪ small change ▪ pocket change moneda suelta ▪ calderilla ▪ dinero del bolsillo ▪ *(Chi.)* sencillo

loose ends: to tie up ~ atar los cabos sueltos

to be **loose-tongued** no moderarse la lengua ▪ soltarse la lengua

to **loosen a screw** aflojar un tornillo

to **loosen one's belt a notch** aflojar la cintura un agujero

to **loosen the phlegm** ▪ to cough up phlegm ▪ to bring up the plegm arrancar la flema ▪ despedir la flema arrancándola ▪ hacer salir la flema arrancándola ➤ The doctor prescribed him an expectorant to loosen the phlegm. El médico le prescribió un expectorante para arrancar la flema.

lopsided contest ▪ uneven match competencia desigual ▪ competencia desventajada ▪ competición desigual

to **lose a limb** volarle un miembro ➤ He lost his right hand in the Second World War. Le volaron la mano derecha en la Segunda Guerra Mundial.

to **lose a tooth** ▪ (for) a tooth to fall out ▪ (for) a tooth to come out caérsele un diente

to **lose all sense of time** perder toda noción de tiempo

to **lose altitude** perder altura ▪ ir perdiendo altura ➤ The airplane was losing altitude. El avión perdía altura. ▪ El avión iba perdiendo altura.

to **lose consciousness** perder el conocimiento ▪ perder el sentido ▪ perder la consciencia

to **lose control of something** perder el control de algo ➤ The driver lost control of the car on the ice. *(L. Am.)* El conductor perdió el control del carro en el hielo. ▪ *(Sp.)* El conductor perdió el control del coche en el hielo. ➤ He lost control of his right arm after his stroke. Perdió el control del brazo derecho después del derrame cerebral.

to **lose count (of)** perder la cuenta (de)

to **lose everything** quedarse sin nada ➤ The family lost everything in the fire. En el incendio la familia se ha quedado sin nada.

to **lose ground** perder terreno

to **lose heart** desanimarse ▪ abatirse ▪ desfallecer de ánimo

to **lose hope (of)** ▪ to give up hope (of) perder las esperanzas (de) ▪ renunciar la esperanza (de)

to **lose its punch** ▪ to subside ▪ to let up remitir ▪ írsele ➤ The storm has lost its punch. ▪ The storm has subsided. ▪ The storm has let up. Ha remitido la tormenta. ▪ Ha remitido el temporal.

to **lose no time in** no perder tiempo para

to **lose one's accent** perder el acento

to **lose one's ass** *(off-color)* ▪ to lose one's shirt ▪ to lose everything perder hasta el culo ▪ *(benign alternatives)* perder todo ▪ perder hasta el alma

to **lose one's balance** perder el equilibrio

to **lose one's bearings** perder la brújula

to **lose one's composure** perder el aplomo ▪ perder los nervios ▪ perder la compostura

to **lose one's cool** perder la calma

to **lose one's cultural identity** perder uno su identidad cultural

to **lose one's eyesight** ▪ to lose one's sight ▪ to go blind perder la vista ▪ quedarse ciego

to **lose one's figure** perder la línea

to **lose one's footing** perder pie

to **lose one's grip on power** ▪ to lose one's hold on power perder el control del poder

to **lose one's job** perder el trabajo

to **lose one's marbles** perder la chaveta

to **lose one's momentum** perder comba ▪ perder ritmo

to **lose one's moorings** perder las ataduras morales

to **lose one's nerve** perder el valor

to **lose one's patience** perder la paciencia

to **lose one's place in line** perder el sitio en una cola

to **lose one's sanity** perder la razón

to **lose one's senses** perder el sentido común ▪ volverse loco ➤ Have you lost your senses? ¿Te has vuelto loco?

to **lose one's shirt** ▪ to lose everything perder hasta la camisa

to **lose one's sight** ▪ to lose one's eyesight perder la vista ▪ perder la visión

to **lose one's temper** perder el control ▪ perder la compostura

to **lose one's temper with someone** ▪ to lose one's temper at someone perder la compostura con alguien ▪ perder los nervios con alguien ▪ perder los estribos con alguien ▪ encolerizarse

to **lose one's train of thought** perder el hilo ▪ perder el hilo de las ideas ▪ haberse ido el santo al cielo ▪ írsele ➤ I lost my train of thought. Perdí el hilo. ▪ Perdí el hilo de las ideas. ▪ Se me ha ido el santo al cielo. ▪ Se me ha ido.

to **lose one's virginity** perder la virginidad

to **lose one's voice** ■ to get hoarse ■ to become hoarse quedarse afónico ■ quedarse sin voz ■ tener la voz tomada

to **lose overwhelmingly** perder estrepitosamente ➤ The president went to Miami to lend the candidate a hand, but in the end it didn't do any good because he lost overwhelmingly. El presidente se acercó a Miami para echar una mano al candidato, pero al final no le sirvió de nada porque perdió estrepitosamente.

to **lose popular esteem** ■ to lose popularity perder el calor popular ➤ *(titular)* The prime minister loses popular esteem. ■ The prime minister loses popularity. El primer ministro pierde el calor popular.

to **lose radio contact with** perder contacto por radio con alguien

to **lose sight of someone** perder de la vista a alguien ➤ I've lost sight of him. Lo he perdido de vista. ■ *(Sp., leísmo)* Le he perdido de vista. ➤ I've lost sight of her. La he perdido de vista.

to **lose sight of something** perder de vista de algo ■ perder la visión de algo ■ perder algo de vista ➤ At the water level, I lost sight of the coast. Desde el nivel del mar, perdí la visión de la costa. ■ Desde el nivel del mar, perdí de vista la costa. ➤ Don't lose sight of your goal. No pierdas de vista tus objetivos.

to **lose sleep** perder sueño ➤ You lose a night's sleep flying from the United States to Spain. Se pierde una noche de sueño volando de los Estados Unidos a España.

to **lose sleep over something** perder el sueño por algo ■ quitarle el sueño ➤ I wouldn't lose any sleep over it if I were you. Yo no perdería el sueño por eso si fuera tú. ■ Yo no dejaría que eso me quitara el sueño.

to **lose something** perder algo ➤ I've lost your address. He perdido tu dirección.

to **lose to** perder frente a

to **lose track of someone** perder la pista de alguien

to **lose track of the time** perder la noción del tiempo

to **lose touch with reality** perder contacto con la realidad

to **lose weight** ■ to slim down bajar de peso ■ perder peso ■ adelgazar ■ *(jargon)* bajar la tripa

to **lose *x* kilos** adelgazar *x* kilos

to **lose *x* pounds** adelgazar *x* libras

losing hand (of cards): to have a ~ llevar una mala mano (de cartas)

loss of bearings pérdida de orientación ➤ European art of the post–World War I period reflects the culture's loss of bearings. El arte Europeo posterior a la Primera Guerra Mundial refleja la pérdida de orientación de la cultura.

loss of consciousness pérdida de la conciencia

lost and found objetos perdidos ➤ Where is lost and found? ¿Dónde está objetos perdidos? ➤ Is there a lost and found here? ¿Hay un objetos perdidos aquí?

to be a **lost cause** ■ to be beyond hope ■ to be hopeless **1.** ser causa perdida ■ ser cosa perdida ■ ser una batalla perdida ■ no tener remedio **2.** *(humorously, non-seriously)* no tener arreglo ■ no tener remedio ➤ Young lady, you're a lost cause. ■ Young lady, you're hopeless. ■ Young lady, you're beyond hope. Hija mía, es que no tienes arreglo.

lost cause: to give something up as a ~ abandonar algo por ser una causa perdida

to be **lost in thought** estar absorto en los pensamientos ■ estar absorto en sus pensamientos

to be **lost on someone** no decirle nada a alguien ➤ Their assurances are lost on me. I don't trust them. Sus garantías no me dicen nada. No me fío de ellos.

lost soul *el* alma perdida

lot (in life): one's ~ lo que le ha tocado a uno en la vida ➤ The fate of humans is to have to work; it's our lot in life. El destino de los humanos es tener que trabajar. Es lo que nos ha tocado en la vida. ➤ They seem satisfied with their lot in life. Parecen satisfechos con lo que les ha tocado en la vida.

lot of little things ■ lots of little things muchas menudencias ➤ A lot of little things caused the rift in their friendship. Muchas menudencias causaron las desavenencias en su amistad.

to be a **lot of trouble** ser un jaleo muy grande ➤ It's a lot of trouble to get it out and set it up. Sacarlo y montarlo es un jaleo muy grande.

lot of trouble: to go to a ~ costarle mucho trabajo a alguien ➤ I went to a lot of trouble to pack the box and send it to you. Me costó mucho trabajo empaquetar la caja y mandártela.

lot on the line: to have a ~ ■ (for there) to be a lot on the line tener mucho en juego ■ haber mucho en juego

a **lot remains to be done** queda mucho por hacer

lot to do: there's a ~ falta mucho por hacer ■ hay mucho que hacer

lot to think about: to give one a ~ darle mucho en qué pensar ➤ You've given me a lot to think about. Me has dado mucho en qué pensar.

lots of ■ a lot of *(singular)* mucho ■ *(plural)* muchos ➤ Children need lots of praise. ■ Children need a lot of praise. Los niños necesitan muchos elogios. ■ Los niños necesitan muchas alabanzas. ➤ There are lots of ways to skin a cat. ■ There are a lot of ways to skin a cat. Hay muchas formas de pelar el pavo. ■ Hay muchas maneras de pelar el pavo.

lots of ways to ■ all sorts of ways to toda clase de formas de

lottery ticket *el* cupón de la lotería

loud and clear: I hear you ~ más claro no canta un gallo

to be a **lousy driver** ser muy torpe conduciendo

lousy horse mal caballo

lousy roommate 1. pésimo compañero de habitación **2.** sharer of the same apartment pésimo compañero de piso ➤ I was a lousy roommate. Fui un pésimo compañero de habitación. ■ Fui un pésimo compañero de piso.

lousy weather *(coll.)* tiempo de perros ■ tiempo pésimo ■ día de perros

to **love a food** encantarle un alimento ➤ Horses love apples. A los caballos les encantan las manzanas.

love affair relación amorosa ■ *(illicit)* amorío

to be **love at first sight** ser amor a primera vista ■ ser un flechazo ➤ It was love at first sight. Fue amor a primera vista. ■ Fue un flechazo.

to **love baseball** amar el béisbol ■ gustarle mucho el béisbol ■ adorar el béisbol ■ encantarle el béisbol

to **love books** amar los libros ■ gustarle mucho los libros ■ adorar los libros ■ encantarle los libros ➤ She loved books and spent her free time reading. Amaba los libros y dedicaba el tiempo libre a leer. ■ Le gustaban mucho los libros y dedicaba el tiempo libre a leer.

love for amor por ➤ *(Prokofiev melody)* The Love for Three Oranges El amor por tres naranjas

love-hate relationship *la* relación amor-odio

love is blind al amor lo pintan ciego

love is eternal el amor es eterno ■ el amor nunca deja de ser

love letter carta de amor ■ esquela amatoria

love life vida amorosa

love one another as I have loved you amaos los unos a los otros como yo os he amado

to **love one's work** ■ to love what one does (for a living) encantarle su trabajo ➤ He loves his work. Le encanta su trabajo. ➤ I love my work. ■ I love what I do. Me encanta mi trabajo.

love poem *el* poema de amor ➤ Quevedo wrote the most beautiful love poem in the Spanish language. Quevedo escribió el poema de amor más hermoso de la lengua española.

love potion filtro de amor

to **love someone** amar a alguien ■ querer a alguien

love thy neighbor as thyself: thou shalt ~ ■ *(Leviticus 19:18)* you shall love your neighbor as yourself ■ *(Reina-Valera)* amarás a tu prójimo como a ti mismo ■ *(Nueva Versión Internacional)* ama a tu prójimo como a ti mismo

to **love to read** encantarle la lectura *(The infinitive "encantar" must take a noun.)* ➤ She loves to read. Le encanta leer. ➤ She loves reading. Le encanta la lectura.

loved ones seres queridos ■ seres más queridos

low: to be *x* revolutions ~ tener *x* revoluciones por debajo ■ tener *x* revoluciones de menos ➤ The engine's thirty revolutions low. What do you make of it? Damp air? El motor está treinta revoluciones por debajo. ¿Cómo te lo explicas? ¿Aire húmedo?

low-budget de bajo presupuesto ▪ a baja inversión ➤ Low-budget film ▪ Low-budget movie Película de bajo presupuesto

Low Countries *(Belgium, Luxembourg, and Holland)* Países Bajos

low-cut dress vestido (muy) escotado

low-density lipoproteins ▪ LDL ▪ bad cholesterol lipoproteínas de baja densidad ▪ LBD ▪ colesterol malo

low frequency baja frecuencia

low-frequency de baja frecuencia

Low German *(spoken in the northern lowlands of Germany)* alemán bajo

low-income family familia de bajos recursos ▪ familia de bajos ingresos

low-level flight vuelo rasante

to be the **low man on the totem pole** ser el último mono

low pay poco sueldo

low-paying job without medical or retirement benefits trabajo chapuza

low-pressure area *(weather)* ▪ area of low pressure borrasca

low-pressure system *(weather)* *el* sistema de bajas presiones ▪ sistema de baja presión

low tide *la* bajamar ▪ marea baja

low to the ground *(cars, etc.)* bajo

low (voter) turnout baja participación (de votantes) ▪ menguada asistencia (de votantes) ▪ alta abstención (de votantes)

low water level *el* estiaje

low white cell count *la* escasez de glóbulos blancos

to be a **lowbrow** no tener dos dedos de frente

to **lower a flag** arriar una bandera ➤ They lowered the flag to half mast. Arriaron la bandera a media asta.

lower-class people ▪ people of the lower social classes gente de clase baja ▪ gente de clase pobre

lower end of the scale *el* límite inferior de la escala ▪ extremo inferior de la escala

to **lower expectations** ▪ to reduce expectations rebasar las expectativas

lower lip labio inferior

to **lower one's glasses over one's nose** bajarse las gafas ➤ He lowered his glasses and peered out over his nose. Se bajó las gafas y miró por encima de su nariz.

to **lower one's head 1.** to duck agacharse (la cabeza) ▪ bajar la cabeza **2.** to bow one's head bajar la cabeza ➤ He lowered his head to avoid hitting the door frame. Se agachó la cabeza para no dar con el marco de la puerta. ➤ She lowered her head in prayer. ▪ She bowed her head in prayer. Bajó la cabeza cuando oraba.

to **lower one's voice** ▪ to speak more quietly bajar la voz

to **lower taxes on** bajar los impuestos a

lower than normal inferior a lo normal

to **lower the landing gear** ▪ to put down the landing gear ▪ to put the landing gear down ▪ to extend the landing gear bajar el tren de aterrizaje ▪ extender el tren de aterrizaje ▪ abrir el tren de aterrizaje

to **lower the price** rebajar el precio

to **lower the risk** ▪ to reduce the risk ▪ to mitigate the risk mitigar el riesgo ▪ reducir el riesgo

lowering of interest rates bajada de los tipos de interés

lowest common multiple mínimo común multiple

loyal following séquito leal

to be **loyal to someone** ▪ to stand by someone ▪ to stick by someone ser fiel a alguien

LSD: tab of ~ piedra de tripi ▪ *el* tripi

luck held out *la* suerte se mantuvo ▪ *la* suerte perduró ▪ *la* suerte duró

lucky day *el* día de suerte

lucky number número de la suerte

lucky one *la* afortunada ➤ Who's the lucky one? ¿Quién es la afortunada?

luggage rack baca de vehículo

to be **lukewarm toward religion** ser tibio en materia de la religión

lukewarm water *el* agua tibia ▪ agua templada

lukewarm welcome acogida con indiferencia ➤ *(news item)* EU gives Haider a lukewarm welcome. UE acoge con indiferencia a Haider.

lumber company centro maderero ▪ tienda de maderas ▪ tienda de bricolaje

lump in one's throat nudo en la garganta

lump of sugar ▪ sugar lump *el* terrón (de azúcar)

lunatic fringe franja lunática

lush vegetation ▪ luxuriant vegetation vegetación exuberante

lust for money *el* ansia de dinero

lust for power *el* ansia de poder

luxury cruise crucero de lujo ➤ A luxury Mediterranean cruise Un crucero de lujo por el Mediterráneo

luxury item artículo de lujo

to be **lying facedown** estar tumbado boca abajo

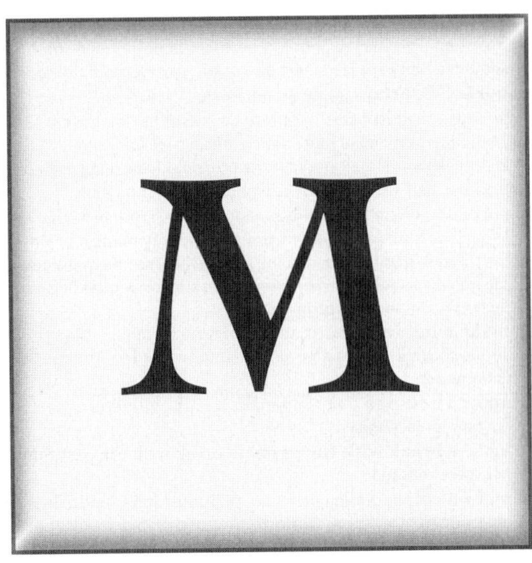

machine code código máquina

to be **mad as a hatter** ▪ to be crazy as a bedbug ▪ to be nutty as a fruitcake ▪ to be cracked estar chiflado ▪ ser una regadera ▪ estar como una regadera

to be **mad as a hornet** estar que muerde

mad cow disease *el* mal de las vacas locas ▪ encefalopatía esponjiforme bovina

to be **made by hand** ▪ to be handmade estar hecho a mano ➤ This scarf was made by hand. ▪ This scarf is handmade. La bufanda está hecha a mano.

to be **made by machine** ▪ to be machine-made estar hecho a máquina ➤ This oriental rug was made by machine. ▪ This oriental rug is machine-made. Esta alfombra oriental está hecha a máquina.

to be **made by someone** **1.** to be created by someone ser hecho por alguien **2.** to be effected by someone ser hecho por alguien ▪ ser realizado por alguien ➤ The scarf was made by my grandmother. La bufanda fue hecha por mi abuela. ➤ The deposit was made by the store clerk. El depósito fue hecho por el dependiente de la tienda.

to be **made for each other** estar hecho el uno para el otro

to be **made from scratch** ser hecho del comienzo ▪ comenzarse con nada ➤ It was made from scratch. Fue hecho del comienzo. ▪ Se comenzó con nada.

made in USA hecho en EE UU ▪ hecho en EUA ▪ fabricado en EE UU ▪ fabricado en EUA ▪ hecho en USA ▪ fabricado en USA

to be **made into** ▪ to be converted into **1.** *(building)* transformar algo en algo ▪ convertir algo en algo **2.** *(movie)* hacer algo de algo ➤ They made my old dormitory into administrative offices of the university. Transformaron mi antigua residencia universitaria en oficinas administrativas. ▪ Convirtieron mi antigua residencia en oficinas administrativas de la universidad. ➤ The book was made into a movie. ▪ They made the book into a movie. Convirtieron el libro en una película.

to be **made of...** ▪ to be made out of... ser de... ▪ estar construido con...

to be **made of wood** ser de madera

to be **made public** hacerse público ▪ ser hecho público ➤ Before it was made public... ▪ Before being made public... Antes de hacerse público...

to be **made to do something** ▪ to be required to do something ▪ to be ordered to do something ▪ to be forced to do something hacer que uno haga algo ▪ obligarle a alguien hacer algo ➤ They made us get off the metro. Hicieron que bajáramos del metro. ▪ Nos obligaron a bajar del metro.

to be **made to order** **1.** to be custom built estar hecho a medida **2.** to suit one exactly venirle a uno pintiparado ▪ venirle a uno al pelo

to be **made up of** **1.** to be composed of componerse de **2.** to be staffed by ser formado por ➤ This packet is made up of the following ingredients. ▪ This packet contains the following ingredients. Este sobre se compone de los siguientes ingredientes. ➤ The surgical team, made up of fifty people... El equipo quirúrgico, formado por cincuenta personas...

to be **made with...** estar construido con... ▪ ser construido con... ▪ estar elaborado con...

mag wheels llantas de aleación

magic show espectáculo de magia

the **magic spell was broken** la magia se deshizo ▪ el encanto se deshizo

magic trick truco de magia

magic wand vara mágica ▪ varita mágica

magnetic compass brújula magnética

magnetic field campo magnético

to be a **magnetic person** ▪ to have personal magnetism ser como un imán

magnetic strip tira magnética

magnum opus obra maestra

maid of honor ▪ matron of honor dama de honor

maiden name apellido de soltera

to **mail a letter** echar al correo una carta ▪ franquear una carta ▪ meter una carta al buzón ➤ I have to mail the payment today. Tengo que echar al correo el pago hoy. ➤ How much does it cost to mail a letter to the United States? ¿Cuánto cuesta franquear una carta a los Estados Unidos? ➤ I mailed it this morning. La metí al buzón esta mañana. ▪ La eché al correo esta mañana.

mailing labels ▪ address labels etiquetas de correo ▪ etiquetas para sobres

main attraction plato principal ▪ atractivo principal

main cause of ▪ principal cause of ▪ primary cause of causa principal de ▪ principal responsible de

main character *el, la* protagonista

main course plato fuerte ➤ Nacho ordered gazpacho as an appetizer, and paella as his main course. Nacho pidió gazpacho para empezar, y de plato fuerte, paella.

main gate puerta principal

the **main ones** los principales ▪ los más significantes ➤ I have a lot of hobbies but my main ones are sports. Tengo muchos pasatiempos pero los más significantes son los deportes.

main point clavo ➤ To drive home the main point... Remachar el clavo... ▪ Para remachar el clavo...

main reason for *la* razón principal de ▪ razón principal por la que

main sequence *(in the evolution of a star)* secuencia principal

main source of income ▪ principal source of income *la* principal fuente de ingresos

main thing lo primero ➤ That's the main thing. Es lo primero. ➤ The main thing is... Lo primer es...

to **maintain (an opinion)** sostener (una opinión) ➤ The author maintains that... El autor sostiene que... ▪ El autor sostiene la opinión de que...

to **maintain close relations with** mantener estrechas relaciones con

to **maintain close ties with** mantener estrechos lazos con

to **maintain control of** conservar el control de

to **maintain that...** sostener que...

major artists *los, las* grandes artistas

major crisis grave crisis ▪ crisis seria

major damage: to cause ~ producir daños de importancia

major events of the 20th century sucesos de altura del siglo XX ▪ sucesos claves del siglo XX ▪ sucesos más relevantes del siglo XX ▪ sucesos más importantes del siglo XX

to **major in a subject** especializarse en una materia ➤ Jaime majored in English. Jaime se especializó en (el) inglés. ➤ María was a physics major. María se especializó en (la) física.

major key *el* clave mayor

major offensive: to launch a ~ lanzar una mayor ofensiva ▪ desplegar una mayor ofensiva

major street calle principal

major study ▪ important study estudio de gran repercusión

major surgery on: to perform ~ realizarle una operación mayor en ➤ They're going to perform major surgery on his shoulder. Van a realizarle una operación mayor en el hombro.

major traffic artery vía de gran tránsito

to be **majoring in** hacer la carrera de ▪ estudiar (la carrera de) ➤ Alicia is majoring in English. Alicia hace la carrera de filología inglesa. ▪ Alicia estudia (la carrera de) fílología inglesa.

to **make a bad impression** causar una mala impresión

to **make a beeline for** salir disparado hacia ▪ lanzarse hacia ➤ When the kids came home from school, they made a beeline for the refrigerator. Cuando los peques llegaron de la escuela, salieron disparados para la nevera. ▪ Cuando los peques llegaron de la escuela, se lanzaron hacia la nevera.

to **make a big fuss about something** ▪ to raise a big stink about something dar algo por la tremenda ▪ tomar algo por la tremenda

to **make a boo-boo** *(coll.)* ▪ to make a faux pas meter la pata ▪ *(Sp.)* meter la gamba

to **make a break with the past** ▪ to break with the past romper con el pasado

to **make a call** hacer una llamada ➤ I must have made thirty long-distance calls to Chile in August. Habré hecho unas treinta llamadas de larga distancia a Chile en agosto. ▪ *(Sp.)* Yo haría unas treinta llamadas de larga distancia a Chile en agosto.

to **make a check out to someone** escribir un cheque a alguien

to **make a choice** hacer una elección ▪ elegir ➤ You made a good choice. Hiciste una buena elección. ▪ Elegiste bien. ➤ I made an incorrect career choice early in life and had a hard time getting out of it. Hice una elección incorrecta de carrera cuando era joven, y me costó salir de ello.

to **make a choice between** ▪ to choose between elegir entre

to **make a claim** **1.** *(insurance claim)* reclamar al seguro **2.** *(for damaged goods)* hacer una reclamación ▪ presentar una reclamación

to **make a colossal mess** ▪ to make a terrible mess ▪ to turn (the place) into a pigpen ▪ to turn (the place) into a pigsty dejar un sitio hecho una leonera ➤ The kindergarten children made a colossal mess but pointed the finger at the other class. ▪ The kindergarden children turned the place into a pigpen but pointed the finger at the other class. Los niños de la guardería dejaron la clase hecha una leonera pero le cargaron el mochuelo a la otra clase.

to **make a comeback** protagonizar un regreso

to **make a comment** hacer un comentario ➤ I'd like to make a comment. Me gustaría hacer un comentario. ▪ *(more polite)* Quisiera hacer un comentario.

to **make a commitment** comprometerse ➤ And even when he makes a commitment he cancels at the last minute. Incluso cuando se compromete anula la cita en el último minuto.

to **make a complaint** ▪ to lodge a complaint presentar una denuncia

to **make a complete fool of oneself** hacer el idiota completamente ▪ hacer un completo ridículo

to **make a concession** hacer una concesión ▪ efectuar una concesión

to **make a connection** *(bus, train, or plane)* ▪ to change hacer transbordo ➤ We made a connection in Asunción, Paraguay. ▪ We changed planes in Asunción, Paraguay. Hicimos transbordo en Asunción, Paraguay.

to **make a connection between two things** relacionar dos cosas ▪ hacer una conexión entre dos cosas ➤ At first I made no connection between the sound of sirens and the smoke. ▪ At first I did not make any connection between the sound of the sirens and the smoke. Al principios no relacioné el sonido de las sirenas con el humo.

to **make a copy** sacar una copia

to **make a critical difference** suponer una diferencia radical ➤ Reducing the tilt of the Leaning Tower of Pisa from 6 to 5.5 degrees has made a critical difference in its stability. El reducir la inclinación de la Torre Inclinada de Pisa de 6 a 5,5 grados supone una diferencia radical en su estabilidad.

to **make a date with someone** quedar con alguien ▪ hacer una cita con alguien ▪ concretar una cita con alguien

to **make a deal** hacer un trato

to **make a decision** tomar una decisión ▪ tomar una determinación

to **make a deposit** ingresar dinero

to **make a difference** importar

to **make a dress** hacer un vestido ▪ confeccionar un vestido

to **make a good impression (on someone)** darle una buena impresión a alguien ▪ causarle una buena impresión a alguien

to **make a good salary** ganar un buen salario

to **make a face** **1.** hacer una mueca ▪ poner una mueca **2.** to make an angry face torcer el gesto ▪ arrugar el gesto ▪ *(comical)* torcer el morro ▪ torcer el hocico

to **make a faux pas** ▪ to make a boo-boo meter la pata

to **make a fist** ▪ to clench one's fist cerrar el puño ▪ apretar el puño

to **make a fool of oneself** hacer el ridículo ➤ I made a perfect fool of myself for all the world to see. Hice el ridículo ante todo el mundo.

to **make a fool of someone** hacer el ridículo a alguien

to **make a fuss** hacer aspavientos

to **make a fuss over someone** hacer mimos a alguien

to **make a good impression (on someone)** causar una buena impresión (en alguien)

to **make a lasting impression on someone** dejar una huella duradera en alguien

to **make a list** ▪ to make up a list hacer una lista ▪ confeccionar una lista ➤ I need to make (up) a grocery list. Necesito hacer una lista para la compra. ▪ Necesito confeccionar una lista para la compra.

to **make a lot of noise** ▪ to raise a ruckus armar un escándolo

to **make a lot of sacrifices** sacrificar muchas cosas

to **make a lot of sense** tener mucho sentido

to **make a lucky guess** acertar por chambra ▪ sonar la flauta por casualidad

to **make a mess** armar un lío ➤ I'm making a mess. Estoy armando un lío.

to **make a mistake** **1.** cometer un error **2.** equivocarse

to **make a mockery of something** poner algo en ridículo ▪ hacer el ridículo sobre algo ▪ dejar algo en ridículo ▪ dejar algo por ridículo

to **make a mountain out of a molehill** hacer una montaña de un granito ▪ hacer una montaña de un grano de arena ▪ hacer de una pulga un elefante

to **make a name for oneself** hacerse un nombre

to **make a New Year's resolution** hacer un propósito para el Año Nuevo

to **make a note of** tomar nota de ➤ I've made a note of your address. He tomado nota de tu dirección. ➤ Make a note of it. Toma nota. ▪ Apúntalo. ▪ Tome (usted) nota. ▪ Apúntelo (usted).

to **make a parachute jump** ▪ to parachute out of an airplane ▪ to parachute (down) lanzarse en paracaídas

to **make a pass at someone** ▪ to come on to someone sexually arrastrarle el ala ▪ menearle el ala ▪ tirale los tejos a alguien

to **make a point of** hacer hincapié en ▪ insistir en

to **make a practice of** tener como norma

to **make a profit from** ▪ to make a profit off of lucrarse de

to **make a profit on** conseguir beneficios de

to **make a racket** armar barullo ▪ hacer barullo ▪ armar un escándolo

to **make a refueling stop** ▪ to stop for refueling hacer una escala técnica

to **make a reservation** hacer una reserva

to **make a rough guess** echarlo a bulto

to **make a salary** ▪ to get a salary ganar un sueldo ▪ ganar un salario ➤ She makes a good salary. Ella gana un buen sueldo. ▪ Ella se defiende muy bien. ➤ He makes a salary plus commission. ▪ He gets (a) salary plus commission. Gana un sueldo más una comisión.

to **make a scene** ▪ to carry on ▪ to pitch a fit montar una escena ▪ montar un número ▪ montar un numerito ▪ dar un escándolo ▪ *(L. Am.)* montar un berrinche ▪ montar un pataleta ▪ *(Sp.)* montar la de Dios ➤ I'll make a scene! ¡Daré un escándolo!

to **make a sharp turn (to)** ejecutar un brusco virage (a)

to **make a speech** ▪ to give a speech ▪ to deliver a speech echar un discurso ▪ pronunciar un discurso

to **make a statement** prestar declaración ▪ hacer una declaración ▪ afirmar

to **make a stop in a place** ▪ to stop (over) in a place ▪ to stop in a place hacer escala en un lugar ▪ hacer una parada en un lugar ▪ parar en un lugar ➤ The plane makes a stop in Asunción, Paraguay. ▪ The plane stops over in Asunción, Paraguay. ▪ The plane stops in Asunción, Paraguay. El avión hace escala en Asunción, Paraguay. ▪ El avión hace una parada en Asunción, Paraguay. ▪ El avión para en Asunción, Paraguay.

to **make a visor with one's hands** ▪ to cup one's fingers over one's eyes hacerse visera con los dedos

to **make a will** ▪ to make out a will ▪ to write a will otorgar testamento

to **make a wish** pedir un deseo ▪ formular un deseo ▪ pensar en un deseo ➤ *(to a child in front of a birthday cake)* Make a wish! ¡Pide un deseo! ▪ ¡Piensa en un deseo! ➤ *(genie in Aladdin's lamp)* Make three wishes! ¡Formula tres deseos!

to **make an adjustment** hacer un ajuste ▪ hacer ajustes

to **make an angry face** torcer el gesto ▪ arrugar el gesto ▪ *(comical)* torcer el morro ▪ torcer el hocico

to **make an announcement** hacer un anuncio

to **make an appearance** hacer una aparición

to **make an appointment** citarse ▪ quedar

to **make an appointment with someone** citarse con alguien ▪ quedar con alguien ▪ concretar una cita con alguien ▪ hacer una cita con alguien

to **make an arrest** practicar una detención ➤ The police made more than a hundred arrests. La policía practicó más de cien detenciones.

to **make an attempt** hacer un intento

to **make an effort to** hacer un esfuerzo para ▪ esforzarse para ▪ hacer un poder para

to **make an enemy** buscarse un enemigo ▪ ganarse un enemigo

to **make an impression on someone** impresionar a alguien ▪ dejar una impresión en alguien ▪ hacer mella en alguien ▪ hacer una brecha en alguien ▪ abrir una brecha en alguien

to **make an issue of something** hacer un caso sobre algo ▪ crear un caso sobre algo ➤ I don't want to make an issue of it. No quiero hacer un caso sobre ese punto.

to **make an observation** hacer una observación ➤ I'd like to make an observation. Quisiera hacer una observación. ▪ Me gustaría hacer una observación.

to **make an offer** hacerle a alguien una oferta ▪ hacerle a alguien un ofrecimiento ➤ Did you make him an offer? ¿Le hiciste una oferta?

to **make arrangements ahead of time** hacer preparativos por adelantado

to **make arrangements beforehand** hacer preparativos de antemano

to **make arrangements for something** hacer preparaciones para algo ➤ We're making arrangements for our trip. Estamos haciendo preparaciones para nuestro viaje. ▪ Estamos haciendo preparaciones para viajar.

to **make arrangements in advance** hacer preparativos con antelación

to **make arrangements to do something** hacer los arreglos para hacer algo ➤ We need to make (the) arrangements to have all this stuff shipped. Tenemos que hacer los arreglos para mandar las cosas.

to **make beer** elaborar cerveza

to **make believe** ▪ to pretend hacer creer ➤ Let's make believe that we're soldiers. Hagamos creer que somos soldados.

to **make clear that...** ▪ to make it clear that... dejar (en) claro que... ▪ aclarar que... ▪ dejar bien patente que... ➤ Let me make this perfectly clear. Déjame aclarar esto perfectamente. ➤ I thought I had made that clear. Creí que ya lo había dejado (en) claro.

to **make concessions** efectuar concesiones

to **make demands on someone** venirle a alguien con exigencias

to **make do with** ▪ to get by on ▪ to survive on ▪ to manage on ▪ to manage with arreglárselas con ▪ apañarse con

to **make ends meet** llegar a fin de mes ➤ For being poor, they manage to make ends meet. Con ser pobres, logran llegar a fin de mes.

to **make faces at someone** hacer morisquetas a alguien ▪ hacer muecas a alguien

to **make for 1.** to create hacer **2.** to (make a) run for correr hacia ➤ Laurie Lee's trek across Spain in the 1930s makes for a great story. La caminata de Laurie Lee que atravesó España a pie en los años mil novecientos treinta hace una gran historia. ➤ We made for the barn when the thunderstorm broke. Corrimos así al granero cuando empezaron los truenos y relámpagos. ▪ Corrimos así al granero cuando empezó a tronar y a relampaguear.

to **make friends** hacerse amigos ▪ *(literary, journalistic)* entablar una amistad

to **make from scratch** hacer (algo) sin usar un preparado o una maqueta

to **make fun of someone** ▪ to tease someone burlarse de alguien ▪ embromar a alguien ▪ dar vaya a alguien

to **make good progress** ▪ to progress well evolucionar bien ➤ *(news item)* The Pope will remain hospitalized for several days, even though he is making good progress. ▪ The Pope will remain hospitalized for several days, even though he is progressing well. El Papa seguirá hospitalizado varios días, aunque evoluciona bien.

to **make good time** ir bien de tiempo ▪ hacer buen tiempo

to **make good use of one's time** usar tiempo de manera eficiente ➤ Connie makes good use of her time. Connie usa su tiempo de manera eficiente.

to **make hay while the sun shines** ▪ to strike while the iron is hot ▪ to take advantage of an opportune moment a la ocasión la pintan calva ▪ aprovecharse la ocasión

to **make headlines** saltar a los titulares

to **make headway on** ▪ to make progress on avanzar en

to **make headway with** ▪ to make progress with hacer avance con ➤ Did you make any headway with the boss today? ¿Has hecho algún avance con el jefe hoy?

make her stop! *(tú)* ¡haz que pare! ▪ *(usted)* ¡haga que pare!

make him do it *(tú)* haz que lo haga él ▪ *(usted)* haga que lo haga (él)

make him stop! *(tú)* ¡haz que pare! ▪ *(usted)* ¡haga que pare!

to **make history** hacer historia ▪ llegar a la historia

to **make huge strides** avanzar a pasos agigantados ➤ Technology is making huge strides. La tecnología avanza a pasos agigantados.

to **make into a movie** hacer una película de un libro ▪ sacar una película de un libro

to **make it clear that** ▪ to make clear that dejar en claro que

to **make it difficult (for one) to do something** ▪ to make it hard for one to do something hacérsele difícil a uno hacer algo ➤ The cast on my leg makes it difficult (for me) to run. ▪ The cast on my leg makes it hard (for me) to run. Se me hace difícil correr con el yeso en la pierna.

to **make it difficult for someone to do something** ponérsele difícil para que alguien haga algo ▪ dificultársele a alguien hacer algo

to **make it easy for someone** ponérsele fácil a alguien ➤ We make it easy for you. Te lo ponemos fácil.

make it four! *(to a waiter, bartender, etc.)* ▪ make that four! ¡pon cuatro! ▪ ¡que sean cuatro!

to **make it happen** conseguirlo ➤ *(Beauty and the Beast)* If he didn't make it happen by the time the last petal fell... Si no lo conseguía para cuando cayera el último pétalo...

to **make it necessary** hacer que sea necesario ➤ The problems with the Internet provider have made it necessary to change to a new one. Los problemas con el proveedor de Internet han hecho que sea necesario cambiar a uno nuevo.

to **make it possible for someone to do something** ▪ to enable someone to do something hacer posible que alguien haga algo ▪ hacer posible algo para alguien ➤ He made it possible for me to start in professional sports. Hizo posible que yo empezara en los deportes profesionales.

to **make it possible to...** hacer(lo) posible que...

to **make it sound like** ■ to make it sound as if hacer que suene como si ➤ You make it sound like something you do every day. ■ You make it sound like something one does every day. Haces que suene como si fuera algo que se haga todos los días.

to **make it through the month** ■ to make it to the end of the month llegar a fin de mes ➤ We have a hard time making it through the month. Llegamos con dificultad a fin de mes.

to **make it with someone** ■ to get it on with someone ■ to get (it) off with someone enrollarse con alguien ■ comerse una rosca con alguien ■ *(Sp., slang)* papeársela ➤ *(from José Ángel Mañas:* Historías del Kronen*)* You're never going to make it with her. A ésa no te la papeas ni de coña.

to **make its departure** efectuar su salida

to **make its entrance into** efectuar su entrada en ➤ The train is going to make its entrance into the station. El tren va a efectuar su entrada en la estación.

to **make jokes about something** hacer bromas sobre algo

to **make known** revelar ■ hacer saber ➤ The candidate made it known that he was not conceding defeat. El candidato hizo saber que no se daba por derrotado.

to **make life difficult for someone** dar mal rato a alguien

to **make light of** ■ to play down the importance of ■ to play down sacar a plomo

to **make love with someone** hacer el amor con alguien ■ hacerle el amor a alguien

to **make matters worse** empeorar las cosas

to **make mincemeat of a team** hacer papilla a un equipo ■ *(Sp., coll.)* dar traste con un equipo

to **make mincemeat of an argument** ■ to demolish an argument ■ to tear an argument to pieces hacer picadillo un argumento

to **make no bones about it** ■ not to make any bones about it ■ to be up front about it no andar con rodeos (en decirlo) ■ ir con la verdad por delante

to **make no difference** ■ not to make any difference ser lo mismo ■ dar lo mismo ➤ It makes no difference. ■ It doesn't make any difference. Es lo mismo. ■ Da lo mismo. ➤ It makes no difference to me. ■ It doesn't make any difference to me. Me da lo mismo. ■ Para mí es lo mismo.

to **make no sense** ■ not to make any sense no tener sentido

to **make noise** armar ruido ■ producir ruido

make of it: not to know what to ~ no saber cómo explicárselo

to **make off with** ■ to escape with ■ to get away with llevarse un botín de ■ escaparse con ➤ The assailants, who managed to flee, made off with eleven million pesetas. Los atracadores, que consiguieron huir, se llevaron un botín de once millones de pesetas.

to **make one blush** sacarle los colores ■ salirle los colores

to **make one curious** resultarle curioso a alguien

to **make one drowsy** darle la modorra a uno ➤ Dinner always makes me drowsy. La comida siempre me da la modorra.

to **make one feel ashamed** darle vergüenza a uno

to **make one feel sick** producirle náuseas a uno ■ sentarle algo mal a alguien ➤ The smell of strong cheeses makes me feel sick. El olor de los quesos fuertes me produce náuseas. ■ El olor de los quesos fuertes me sienta mal.

to **make one hungry** ■ to get hungry when dar hambre a uno ■ entrarle a uno hambre ➤ The smell of the bakery makes me hungry. La aroma de la panadería me da hambre. ➤ The smell of barbecue makes me hungry. Me entra hambre cuando me huele barbacoa.

to **make one shudder** hacer que uno se estremezca ■ hacer estremecerse ➤ It makes me shudder. Hace que me estremezca. ■ Me hace estremecer.

to **make one sit through** tenerle sentado a uno ➤ They made us sit through a five-hour session. Nos tuvieron cinco horas sentados.

to **make one sleepy** darle sueño a uno ■ darle modorra ■ entrarle sueño cuando ➤ The dinner has made me sleepy. La comida me ha dado sueño. ■ La comida me ha dado modorra.

to **make one suspicious that...** ■ to make one suspect that... hacer a alguien sospechar que... ■ hacer a alguien barruntar que... ■ hacer a alguien pensar que...

to **make one tired** dejar a uno cansado ■ hacer que alguien se canse ■ hacer a alguien que se canse ➤ The cough has made him tired. La tos le ha dejado cansado. ■ La tos (le) ha hecho que se canse.

to **make one's blood boil** hervirle la sangre a alguien ■ bullirle la sangre a alguien ■ revolverle la bilis a alguien

to **make one's day** alegrarle el día ➤ It made my day. Me alegró el día.

to **make one's dream come true** ■ to make one's dream a reality hacer realidad un sueño

to **make one's ears ring** hacerle zumbar los oídos ■ hacer que le zumben los oídos ➤ The discotheques make your ears ring. Las discotecas le hacen zumbar los oídos. ■ Las discotecas hacen que le zumben los oídos.

to **make one's first appearance before the camera** debutar ante las cámaras ➤ Actor Javier Bardem made his first appearance before the camera at age four. El actor Javier Bardem debutó ante las cámaras a los cuatro años.

to **make one's first appearance in the play** salir a escena por primera vez ➤ Falstaff makes his first appearance in the second act. Falstaff sale a escena en el segundo acto.

to **make one's hair stand on end** ■ to make one's hair stand up (straight) ponérsele a alguien los cabellos de punta ■ erizársele los pelos ■ ponerle los pelos de punta a alguien

to **make one's head spin** levantarle a uno los cascos

to **make one's heart ache** darle un vuelco al corazón ➤ The trip made my heart ache, because leaving behind so many family, my son, daughter-in-law, and granddaughter in Ecuador was especially hard on me, and I couldn't hold back the tears. El viaje me ha dado un vuelco al corazón, pues dejar a tanta familia, mi hijo, nuera, y nieta en Ecuador me resultó especialmente duro y no pude evitar que se me cayeron lágrimas.

to **make one's mouth water** hacérsele la boca agua ➤ The paella made our mouths water. La paella se nos hizo la boca agua.

to **make one's peace with God** encomendarse a Dios

to **make one's presence felt** hacerse presente ➤ He wanted to make his presence felt. Ha querido hacerse presente.

to **make one's rounds** hacer la ronda ➤ The doctor is making his rounds. El médico hace la ronda.

to **make one's way in the world** abrirse camino en el mundo

to **make one's way through the crowd** abrirse camino a través de la multitud ■ abrirse paso a través de la multitud

to **make one's will** hacer el testamento

to **make oneself clear** haber sabido explicarse ➤ Perhaps I haven't made myself clear. No habré sabido explicarme.

to **make oneself comfortable** ponerse cómodo(-a) ➤ Make yourself comfortable! ¡Ponte cómodo(-a)!

to **make oneself heard** hacerse escuchar ■ hacerse oír ■ dejarse escuchar ■ dejarse oír

to **make oneself understood** hacerse entender ■ darse a entender ➤ He speaks Spanish well enough to make himself understood. Habla español lo suficientemente bien para hacerse entender.

to **make out a will** ■ to make a will ■ to write a will otorgar testamento

to **make out an object in the distance** divisar un objeto en la lejanía

to **make out in the distance** ■ to discern in the distance divisar a lo lejos ■ vislumbrar a lo lejos ■ atisbar a lo lejos

to **make people laugh at...** conseguir que la gente se ría de... ■ conseguir que se ría la gente de... ➤ You would only make people laugh at you. Tan sólo conseguirías que la gente se riera de ti.

to **make plans** hacer planes

to **make possible** hacer posible

to **make public** hacer público ➤ Before being made public Antes de hacerse público

to **make public appearances** ■ to appear in public presentarse en público ➤ The young musician began to make public appearances at the age of eight. El músico joven empezó a presentarse en público cuando tenía ocho años.

to **make reservations in advance** ▪ to make a reservation in advance ▪ to make advance reservations ▪ to make reservations ahead of time hacer una reserva con antelación ▪ hacer una reserva por adelantado

to **make room for** ▪ to make a place for dar cabida a ▪ hacer sitio para ▪ hacer lugar para ▪ hacer corro para ▪ hacer espacio para ▪ hacer rancho para

to **make rounds** ▪ to make one's rounds hacer la ronda ➤ The doctor is making his rounds. El médico está haciendo la ronda.

to **make sense** tener sentido

to **make short work of something** barrer con algo

to **make smart remarks** ▪ to make wisecracks ▪ to wisecrack echar pullas

to **make someone a grandparent** hacer abuelo a alguien ➤ *(headline)* Chabela makes Julio Iglesias a grandfather. Chabela hace abuelo a Julio Iglesias.

to **make someone angry** ▪ to make someone mad *(Mex.)* enojar a alguien ▪ *(Sp.)* enfadar a alguien

to **make someone aware of it** poner al tanto a alguien ➤ The landlord is coming to inspect tomorrow. I just wanted to make you aware of it. Llega el dueño mañana para hacer una inspección, y te quería poner al tanto.

to **make someone aware of something** *(Mex.)* concientizar a alguien de algo

to **make someone blush** sacarle los colores ▪ salirle los colores

to **make someone cringe** dar dentera a alguien ▪ dar grima a alguien ▪ dar repeluzno a alguien ▪ dar repelús a alguien ➤ When he runs his fingernails down the blackboard, it makes me cringe. Cuando araña la pizarra, me da dentera.

to **make someone do something 1.** to require someone to do something ▪ to require that someone do something hacer que alguien haga algo ▪ hacer hacer algo **2.** to incite someone to do something incitarle a alguien hacer algo **3.** to compel someone to do something comprometer a alguien a hacer algo ➤ The teacher makes us work hard. La profesora nos hace trabajar mucho. ➤ The dog makes her sit down when she is about to faint. El perro la hace sentar cuando está a punto de desmayarse. ➤ What made her do it? ¿Qué la hizo hacer eso? ▪ ¿Qué la incitó a hacerlo? ➤ I made him get here on time. Lo hice venir a tiempo.

to **make someone do the dirty work** ▪ to make someone do one's dirty work hacer que alguien haga el trabajo sucio

to **make someone feel better** hacerlo a alguien sentir mejor ▪ reconfortar a alguien ➤ A cup of tea will make you feel better. Una taza de té te hará sentir mejor. ▪ Una taza de té te reconfortará.

to **make someone furious** darle mucho coraje a alguien ➤ It made me furious. Me dio mucho coraje. ➤ It makes me furious when... Me da mucho coraje que...

to **make someone happy** hacer feliz a alguien ➤ *(newspaper quote)* My dream is to be happy and to make the people around me happy. Mi sueño es ser feliz y hacer felices a quienes me rodean.

to **make someone horny** ponerle cachondo a alguien

to **make someone jealous** dar celos a alguien ▪ dar achares a alguien ▪ poner celoso a alguien

to **make someone late** hacer que alguien llegue tarde por culpa de uno ➤ I hope I didn't make you late. Espero que no hayas llegado tarde por mi culpa.

to **make someone laugh at...** conseguir que la gente se ría de... ▪ conseguir que se ría la gente de... ➤ You'll only make him laugh at you. Tan sólo conseguirás que él se ría de ti.

to **make someone mad** *(coll.)* ▪ to make someone angry *(Mex.)* enojar a alguien ▪ *(Sp.)* enfadar a alguien

to **make someone out to be something** ▪ to make someone sound like something hacerle a alguien parecer algo ➤ He made me out to be a liar. ▪ He made me sound like a liar. Me hizo parecer un mentiroso.

to **make someone sound like** ▪ to make someone out to be hacerle parecer ➤ He made me sound like a liar. ▪ He made me out to be a liar. Me hizo parecer un mentiroso.

to **make someone talk** meter el dedo a alguien

to **make someone the scapegoat for...** hacerlo a alguien pagar el pato... ▪ hacer que alguien pague el pato... ▪ hacer de alguien el chivo expiatorio de...

to **make someone uncomfortable** hacer a alguien sentirse incómodo

to **make someone understand** darle a alguien a entender

to **make someone's life miserable** darle mala vida a alguien

to **make something clear** poner algo (en) claro

to **make something do something** hacer que algo haga algo

to **make something from scratch** hacer algo del comienzo

to **make something like new** poner algo como nuevo

to **make stops in** efectuar parada en ➤ This train makes stops in Valdelasfuentes and Alcobendas. Este tren efectúa parada en Valdelasfuentes y Alcobendas.

to **make straight A's** *(all countries)* sacar solamente sobresalientes ▪ *(EEUU)* sacar solamente A's ▪ *(Arg.)* sacar puros dieces ▪ *(Uru.)* sacar puros doces ▪ *(Chi.)* sacar puros sietes

to **make supper** ▪ to fix supper ▪ to get supper ready preparar la cena

to **make sure** ▪ to be sure asegurarse ▪ cerciorarse ➤ Make sure your computer is secure. Asegúrate de que tu computadora esté segura. ▪ Cerciórate de que tu computadora esté segura.

to **make sure one has** procurar tener ➤ The bookseller always made sure he had new books for her. El librero siempre procuraba tener libros nuevos para ella.

to **make sure that** asegurarse de que ▪ *(literary)* mirar bien si ➤ *(from Miguel de Unamuno:* San Manuel Bueno, mártir*)* Make sure God has forgiven you. Mira bien si Dios te ha perdonado. ▪ Asegúrate de que Dios te haya perdonado.

make sure you... asegúrate de...

make sure you don't... asegúrate de que no... ▪ no vayas a...

to **make taut** ▪ to draw taut tensar

make that two! ¡qué sean dos! ▪ ¡pon dos! ➤ I'll have an Irish coffee. Make that two! Tendré un café irlandés. ¡Pon dos! ▪ Tendré un café irlandés. ¡Qué sean dos!

to **make the arrangements to do something** hacer los arreglos para hacer algo ➤ We have to make the necessary arrangements to hold the auction. Tenemos que hacer los arreglos necesarios para hacer la subasta. ▪ Tenemos que hacer los arreglos necesarios para (tener) la subasta.

to **make the bed** hacer la cama ▪ arreglar la cama

to **make the best of a situation** sacar el mejor partido posible de la situación

to **make the best-seller list** llegar a la lista best-seller

to **make the cover of a magazine** lograr salir en la portada de una revista

to **make the exam** poner el examen ➤ No matter how easy I make the exam, somebody will flunk. Por más fácil que ponga el examen, alguien suspenderá.

to **make the front page** ▪ to make page one ▪ to make front page news salir en la primera plana ▪ salir en la primera página

to **make the most of** sacar partido de ▪ sacar partido a

make the most of it! *(tú)* ¡sácate partido! ▪ *(usted)* ¡sáquese partido! ▪ *(ustedes)* ¡sáquense partido! ▪ *(vosotros)* ¡sácaos partido!

to **make the necessary changes to...** poner en práctica los cambios necesarios para...

to **make the news** saltar a las noticias

to **make the pain go away** hacer que se vaya el dolor ➤ I used to stretch, and it would make the pain go away. Solía estirarme y hacía que se fuera el dolor.

to **make the point that...** hacer ver que... ▪ hacer entender que... ▪ hacer comprender que... ➤ Kant's treatise makes the point that any dispute can be resolved if both parties have the will to resolve it. El tratado de Kant hace ver que cualquier desacuerdo puede resolverse si ambas partes tienen la voluntad de resolverlo.

to **make (the) reservations in advance** ▪ to make advance reservations hacer las reservas con antelación ▪ hacer las reservas con anticipación

to **make the sign of the cross 1.** hacer la seña de la cruz **2.** to cross oneself asignarse ▪ santiguarse

to **make things easier** facilitar las cosas

to **make things with one's hands** hacer manualidades ➤ My son likes to make things with his hands. A mi hijo le gusta hacer manualidades.

to **make time for something** hacer tiempo para algo

to **make trouble for someone** fastidiar a alguien ▪ crear un lío para alguien

to **make up a story 1.** to create a story ▪ to invent a story ▪ to think up a story inventar un cuento **2.** to fabricate a story ▪ to lie hacer inventos ▪ inventar(se) cuentos

to **make up a list** ▪ to make a list confeccionar una lista ➤ Make up a list of things we need to get at the store. Confecciona una lista de las cosas que tenemos que comprar en el mercado.

to **make up a test** ▪ to take a makeup test recuperar un examen ▪ tomar un examen a que uno no pudo asistir

to **make up an excuse** ▪ to invent an excuse forjar una excusa

to **make up for** ▪ to compensate for resarcirse de ➤ Real Madrid's victory makes up for the defeat suffered last year. La victoria de Real Madrid se resarce de la derrota sufrida el año pasado.

to **make up for lost time** recuperar el tiempo perdido

to **make up one's mind** ▪ to decide determinarse ▪ tomar una decisión ➤ Do you have trouble making up your mind? -Well, yes and no. ¿Tienes algún problema para tomar una decisión?-Bueno, sí y no. ➤ I haven't made up my mind. ▪ I haven't decided. No me he deteminado.

to **make up one's mind that...** ▪ to resolve that... mentalizarse de que... ▪ concienciarse de que... ▪ asumir que... ➤ You have to make up your mind that you won't see him again. ▪ You have to make up your mind not to see him again. Debes mentalizarte de que no lo verás más. ▪ Debes concienciarte de que no lo verás más. ▪ Debes asumir que no lo verás más.

to **make up one's mind to do something** animarse a hacer algo ▪ resolverse a hacer algo

to **make up something** ▪ to make something up ▪ to think up something ▪ to think something up ▪ to invent something inventar algo

to **make use of something for something** ▪ to use something for something servirse de algo para algo ▪ echar mano de algo para algo ▪ valerse de algo para algo

to **make waves** ▪ to rock the boat hacer olas

make way! ▪ stand back! ¡a un lado! ▪ ¡atrás!

to **make way** abrirse paso ▪ hacerse camino

to **make wisecracks** ▪ to wisecrack ▪ to make smart remarks echar pullas

make yourself at home! *(tú)* ¡estás en tu casa! ▪ *(usted)* ¡está en su casa!

make yourself comfortable *(tú)* ponte cómodo(-a) ▪ *(usted)* póngase cómodo(-a)

makeshift repair: to do a ~ hacer una reparación provisional ▪ hacer una reparación provisoria ▪ hacer una ñapa

makeup of the court ▪ composition of the court *la* constitución del tribunal

makings for a recipe ▪ ingredients for a recipe ▪ ingredients of a recipe *los* ingredientes para una receta

male boss jefe hombre

male-female relationships relaciones entre hombres y mujeres

male lead ▪ male star ▪ leading man ▪ hero protagonista masculino

man alive! ¡hombre de Dios!

man, I tell you hombre, ya te digo

man is a creature of habit el hombre es un animal de costumbres

man is known by the company he keeps dime con quién andas y te diré quien eres ▪ dime con quién vas y te diré quien eres

man-made hecho por el hombre

to be a **man of few words** ser hombre de pocas palabras

man of principle hombre de principios

to be a **man of regular habits** ▪ to have regular habits ser de costumbres fijas ➤ The philosopher Immanuel Kant was a man of regular habits. El filósofo Immanuel Kant era un hombre de costumbres fijas.

man of stature hombre de estatura

man of the hour hombre de la hora

man overboard! ¡hombre al agua!

man with a double life ▪ man (who is) living a double life ▪ man who has a double life hombre de doble vida

man you can trust ▪ man who can be trusted hombre de confianza

to **manage a business** manejar un negocio ▪ gestionar un negocio ▪ regentar un negocio

to **manage an organization** manejar una organización ▪ gestionar una organización

to **manage money** administrar dinero

to **manage on** ▪ to get along on arreglarse con

to **manage on one's own** apañárselas solo ▪ arreglárselas solo

to **manage somehow** ▪ to get by somehow ▪ to manage as best one can estar pasándola ➤ We're managing somehow. ▪ We're getting by somehow. La estamos pasando. ▪ Estamos pasándola.

to **manage time** administrar tiempo

to **manage to avoid someone** conseguir eludirle a alguien

to **manage to do something** arreglárselas para hacer algo ▪ poder hacer algo ▪ conseguir hacer algo ▪ lograr hacer algo ▪ agenciárselas (para) ➤ The family managed to live on very little. La familia se las arreglaba para vivir con muy pocos recursos. ➤ We've managed to survive. Hemos podido sobrevivir. ➤ I'll manage to (do it) somehow. Me la(s) arreglaré de alguna manera. ➤ I'll manage somehow to turn it in on time. Me las voy a arreglar de alguna forma para entregarlo a tiempo.

to **manage to do two things at once** ▪ to manage to combine two activities arreglarse para compaginar dos actividades

to **manage to escape** ▪ to manage to get away lograr darse a la fuga ➤ The attackers managed to escape. Los atacantes lograron darse a la fuga.

to **manage to find out** hacer para saber ▪ lograr averiguar

to **manage to get into the house** lograr introducirse en la casa ➤ The images of the rescue, taken by a photographer who managed to get into the house with the federal agents. Las imágenes del rescate, tomadas por un fotógrafo que logró introducirse en la casa con los agentes federales.

to **manage to get through** conseguir abrirse camino

management of high-speed trains *la* gestión del sistema de los trenes de alta velocidad

management versus labor gerencia versus el sindicato ▪ *la* administración versus la labor

manila paper *el* papel café

manna from heaven maná del cielo

manner to which one has become accustomed: in the ~ de la forma a la que uno(-a) esté acostumbrado(-a) ▪ de la manera a la que uno(-a) esté acostumbrado(-a) ▪ del modo al que uno(-a) esté acostumbrado(-a)

manpower shortage ▪ personnel shortage insuficiencia de personal

many are called, but few are chosen muchos son los llamados y pocos los elegidos

many happy returns: and may you have ~ y que cumplas muchos más

many, many years ago hace muchos, muchos años

many of which muchos de los cuales ▪ muchas de las cuales

many of whom muchos de los cuales ▪ muchas de las cuales

many other things otras muchas cosas ▪ muchas otras cosas

many years ago ya hace años ▪ hace muchos años ▪ muchos años ha

map of the city ▪ city map ▪ street map plano callejero (de la ciudad)

map of the world ▪ world map planisferio ▪ mapamundi

to map out an itinerary ▪ to plan an itinerary planear un itinerario ➤ Let's map out our itinerary. ▪ Let's plan our itinerary. Vamos a planear nuestro itinerario.
to map out legislative initiatives ▪ to sketch out legislative initiatives esbozar iniciativas legislativas
to map out one's plans ▪ to make one's plans hacer sus planes ➤ Let's map out our plans. ▪ Let's make our plans. Vamos a hacer nuestros planes.
to **map the human genome** secuenciar el genoma humano ▪ secuenciar el genomio humano
maple sugar candy caramelo de azúcar del arce
maple syrup *el* jarabe de arce ▪ *el* sirope de arce
mapping of the human genome secuenciación del genoma humano
March on Washington *(led by Martin Luther King, Jr., August 28, 1963)* marcha sobre Washington
margin of victory *el* margen de la victoria ▪ amplitud de la victoria ➤ The margin of Blair's victory will be a barometer of the extent to which the conservative ploy of scaring the British with the specter of Europe and its currency has failed. La amplitud de la victoria de Blair será un termómetro de hasta que punto ha fracasado la apuesta conservadora de espantar a los británicos con el fantasma de Europa y su moneda.
Mariana Trench *(in the Pacific Ocean)* fosas Marianas
mark my word! ¡fíjate en lo que digo! ▪ ¡que conste en acta!
to **mark someone absent** ponerle falta a alguien
marked increase in subida acusada de
to be **market driven** estar controlado por el mercado
market economy economía de mercado
market share reparto de mercado ▪ cuota de mercado
married before: to have been ~ ▪ to have been previously married ▪ to have been married previously ya haber estado casado(-a)
married couple pareja casada ▪ matrimonio
married life vida conyugal ▪ vida de casados
married name nombre de casada ▪ apellido de casada
to **marry into a family** emparentar con una familia
to **marry someone for money** dar el braguetazo ➤ He married her for her money. Ha dado un braguetazo. ➤ She married him for his money. Se casó por su dinero.
marrying age: she has passed the ~ se le ha pasado el arroz ▪ se le pasó el arroz
martial law: to be under ~ 1. *(what the military calls it)* estar bajo la ley marcial **2.** *(what ordinary people call it)* estar en estado de sitio
to **mash the avocados** hacer un puré de los aguacates ▪ *(S.Am.)* hacer un puré de las paltas
to **mash the potatoes** hacer un puré de las papas ▪ *(Sp.)* hacer un puré de las patatas
mason's trowel paleta de albañil
mass exodus éxodo masivo
mass mailing envío masivo de cartas
to **massage in a lotion** ▪ to massage a lotion in ▪ to rub in a lotion ▪ to rub a lotion in aplicar una loción frotando
massive dose *la* dosis de caballo
master key llave maestra
to be the **master of one's fate** ser el dueño de su destino ▪ ser la dueña de su destino
to be the **mastermind of** ▪ to be the mastermind behind ▪ to mastermind ser el autor intelectual de
master's degree *el* master ▪ maestría
master's in business administration ▪ MBA master en administración de empresas
mat for a picture ▪ matting for a picture paspartú ▪ paspartout ▪ passe-partout *(The "backing" is "fondo" or "respaldo.")*
mat to sleep on *(in the tropics and subtropics)* ▪ sleeping mat *el* petate
to **match a color** hacer un color ➤ Please match this color. Por favor haga este color.
to **match an offer to** igualar una oferta para ➤ *(headline)* Putin matches Bush's offer to reduce his nuclear arsenal Putin iguala la oferta de Bush para reducir su arsenal nuclear
to **match column A to column B** conectar la columna A con la B ▪ correlacionar las columnas A y B
to **match one's input** pegar con su entrada ▪ ser igual ➤ *(New York Times automated switchboard)* There are four names to match your input. Hay cuatro nombres que pegan con su entrada. ▪ Hay cuatro nombres que son iguales.
to **match up** coincidir
matches to a name coincidencias con un nombre ➤ There are hundreds of matches to the name Juan García. Hay cientos de coincidencias con el nombre Juan García.
material breach ruptura material
material witness testigo material
maternity hospital hospital materno-infantil
mathematical proof demostración matemática ▪ prueba matemática
mating battle: to be engaged in a ~ estar enzarzado en una lucha de apareamiento ➤ The elephants are engaged in a mating battle. Los elefantes están enzarzados en una lucha de apareamiento.
mating dance *(observed in penguins, elephants, etc.)* *el* baile de cortejo
matriculated or non-matriculated matriculado o sin matricular ➤ Are you matriculated or non-matriculated? ¿Estás matriculado o sin matricular?
the **matter of ~** el asunto de ▪ la cuestión de ▪ lo de ▪ la cosa de
matter of course: as a ~ ▪ as a general rule por norma ▪ como regla general
matter-of-fact ▪ deadpan prosáico ▪ despasionado ▪ práctico
matter of opinion *la* cuestión de opiniones ➤ That's a matter of opinion. Es una cuestión de opiniones.
matter of principle asunto de principios
to be a **matter of taste** depender de los gustos de cada cual ➤ It's a matter of taste. ▪ It's a matter of individual taste(s). Depende de los gustos de cada cual.
matters of the heart ▪ affairs of the heart las lides del amor
to be **mature for one's age** ser muy maduro(-a) para la edad de uno ➤ She's very mature for her age. Es muy madura para su edad.
Maundy Thursday *(Thursday of Holy Week)* jueves santo
maximum salary salario máximo ▪ sueldo máximo ▪ *el* tope de salario
maximum ten items máximo diez artículos ➤ Express checkout: maximum ten items Caja rápida: máximo diez artículos
may be necessary sea necesario ▪ se requiera
may God protect him que Dios le acoja en su seno ▪ que Dios lo ampare ▪ *(Sp., leísmo)* que Dios le ampare
may have died: one ~ ▪ one might have died ▪ one could have died uno pudo morir ➤ *(news item)* The victim may have died the day of his disappearance eleven months ago. La víctima pudo haber muerto el mismo día de la desaparición, hace once meses.
may he rest in peace que en paz descanse ▪ que en gloria esté ▪ que Dios lo tenga en la gloria
may I? ▪ can I? ¿me permites?
may I ask why? ¿se puede saber por qué?
may I be excused? ¿puedo ir (al baño)? ▪ ¿me disculpan? ▪ ¿me permiten salir?
may I borrow a dollar? ▪ can I borrow a dollar? ▪ would you lend me a dollar? ¿me dejas un dólar? ▪ ¿me prestas un dólar?
may I call you again? ¿puedo volverte a llamar?
may I come in? ¿se puede? ▪ ¿puedo pasar?
may I come with you? ▪ can I come with you? ▪ may I go with you? ▪ can I go with you? *(tú)* ¿puedo acompañarte? ▪ ¿puedo ir contigo? ▪ *(usted, to a man or woman)* ¿puedo acompañarle? ▪ ¿puedo ir con usted?
may I get a drink of water? ¿puedo tener un vaso de agua? ▪ ¿puedo beber agua?
may I get by? ▪ may I get past? ▪ could I get by? con permiso ▪ *(tú)* ¿me dejas pasar? ▪ ¿me permites pasar? ▪ *(usted)* ¿me deja pasar? ▪ ¿me permite pasar? ➤ Excuse me. May I get by? ▪ Excuse me. May I get past? ▪ Excuse me. Could I get by? Perdone, ¿me deja pasar?

may I go with you? ▪ can I go with you? *(tú)* ¿puedo acompañarte? ▪ ¿puedo ir contigo? ▪ *(usted, to a man or woman)* ¿puedo acompañarle? ▪ ¿puedo ir con usted?

may I have this dance? ¿me concedes este baile? ▪ ¿por favor concederme este baile?

may I join you? 1. *(to one person)* ¿puedo unirme a ti? ▪ ¿puedo unirme a usted? **2.** *(to two or more people)* ¿puedo unirme a ustedes? ▪ *(Sp., vosotros)* ¿puedo unirme a vosotros?

may I look on your book? ▪ can I look on your book? ¿podemos compartir tu libro? ▪ ¿puedo mirar el libro contigo?

may I make a suggestion? ¿podría hacer una sugerencia? ▪ *(a ti)* ¿puedo hacerte una propuesta? ▪ *(a usted)* ¿puedo hacerle una propuesta?

may I offer you a drink? ▪ can I offer you a drink? ¿te convido una copa?

may I speak with Juan? ▪ may I please speak with Juan? *(L. Am., Sp.)* ¿puedo hablar con Juan? ▪ ¿se puede hablar con Juan? ▪ ¿me puede poner con Juan? ▪ ¿me puede pasar a Juan? ▪ *(L. Am.)* ¿me podría comunicar con Juan?

may I use the bathroom? ▪ may I use your bathroom? ¿puedo pasar al baño? ▪ *(tú)* ¿me permites el baño? ▪ *(usted)* ¿me permite (usted) el baño?

may it come to pass (that...) que así sea (que...)

may or may not have done haya o no hecho

may she rest in peace que en gloria esté ella

may the force be with you! *(Star Wars)* ¡que la fuerza te acompañe!

may the Lord bless you and keep you que el Señor te bendiga y te guarde

maybe I could have said that... quizás (yo) hubiera podido decir que...

maybe I could have told them that... quizás (yo) hubiera podido decirles que...

maybe it isn't such a good idea puede que no sea tan buena idea

maybe it wasn't such a good idea puede que no fuera tan buena idea

maybe, maybe not puede que sí, puede que no ▪ igual sí, igual no ▪ tal vez sí, tal vez no

maybe next time otra vez será

maybe not ▪ perhaps not tal vez no ▪ puede que no

maybe so ▪ perhaps tal vez sí ▪ puede ser

maybe some other time ▪ perhaps some other time tal vez en otra ocasión ▪ otra ocasión será ▪ otra vez será

maybe *x* people there: there were ~ habría unas *x* personas allí

me either *(coll.)* ▪ I don't either ▪ neither do I ▪ nor I tampoco ▪ (ni) yo tampoco

to **mean a lot to one** significar algo para uno ➤ It means a lot to me. Significa algo para mí.

to be **mean as a snake** ser una víbora

to **mean by that (that...)** querer decir con eso (que...) ➤ What do you mean by that? ¿Qué quieres decir con eso? ➤ By that I mean that... Quiero decir con eso que...

mean distance distancia media ➤ In round figures, the mean distance from the Earth to the sun is 150 million kilometers. En números redondos la distancia media entre la Tierra y el sol es de 150 millones de kilómetros.

to **mean doing something** ▪ to involve doing something significar ▪ comprender ▪ incluir ➤ It means a great deal to me. Representa mucho para mí. ➤ It means a lot to me. Representa mucho para mí.

to **mean it** hablar en serio

mean, median, and mode *(statistics)* media, mediana y moda

to **mean no harm** ▪ not to mean any harm no tener malas intenciones

mean people gente mala ▪ gente antipática ▪ gente desagradable ▪ gente desalmada ▪ gente mezquina

mean people never die el bicho malo nunca muere ▪ mala yerba nunca muere ▪ mala hierba nunca muere

mean people suck *la* gente mala apesta

to **mean someone** ▪ to refer to someone referirse a alguien ➤ I thought you meant me. ▪ I thought you were referring to me. Pensé que te referías a mí.

to **mean something 1.** to refer to something referirse a algo **2.** to be defined as something significar algo **3.** to involve something suponer ▪ implicar ▪ involucar

to be **mean-spirited** faltarle de piedad ▪ tener saña ➤ I thought his criticism was mean-spirited. Pensé que a sus críticas les faltaba piedad.

mean streak: to have a ~ ▪ to have a streak of meanness (in one) tener un rasgo cruel

to **mean to do something** ▪ to intend to do something tener la intención de hacer algo ➤ I meant to tell you about it. ▪ I intended to tell you about it. Yo tenía la intención de decirte acerca de ello.

to **mean well** tener buenas intenciones

meaning of life sentido de la vida ▪ significado de la vida

meaning of the joke ▪ point of the joke gracia del chiste

meaningful look mirada significativa

means of transportation medios de transporte

means to an end medio para lograr un fin ▪ medio para conseguir un fin

to be **meant to be** corresponder al destino de uno ➤ This was not meant to be. No corresponde a su destino.

measly helping trozo raquítico

to **measure up** dar la talla

measuring tape ▪ tape measure cinta métrica ▪ metro ➤ Whenever you shop for furniture, always take a measuring tape. Siempre que vayas de compras para muebles, lleva contigo un metro. ▪ Siempre que vayas de compras para muebles, lleva contigo una cinta métrica.

mechanical pencil *(L. Am.)* lapicero ▪ *(Sp.) el* portaminas

to be **mechanically adept** ▪ to be (very) mechanical ser manitas ➤ My brother is more mechanically adept than I am. Mi hermano es más manitas que yo.

media attention: to receive ~ ▪ to receive media coverage recibir la atención de los medios de comunicación

media circus circo mediático

media empire imperio mediático

medical checkup revisión médica

medical history historial médico

medical insurance ▪ health insurance seguro médico

medical problems ▪ health problems problemas médicos ▪ problemas de salud

medical reasons razones médicas ➤ He was exempted from military service for medical reasons. Estuvo exento del servicio militar por razones médicas.

medical report *el* parte facultativo

medical school *la* facultad de medicina

medical supplies suministros médicos

medicine cabinet *el* botiquín ▪ armario de las medicinas

medium-range missiles *los* misiles de alcance medio

medium rare steak medio crudo

medium steak *(between rare and well-done) el* filete en su punto ▪ filete al punto ▪ filete medio hecho

to **meet an ill fate** ▪ to come to a bad end parar en mal ▪ acabar en mal

meet me... ▪ let's meet encontrémonos ▪ nos vemos ▪ quedamos de vernos ▪ quedamos de encontrarnos ➤ *(New York)* Meet me under the clock at the Biltmore. Encontrémos debajo del reloj del Biltmore. ➤ *(Madrid)* Meet me at the bear in the arbutus. Quedamos de vernos en el oso del madroño.

to **meet one's death in** encontrar la muerte en ▪ encontrar su muerte en

to **meet one's expenses** ▪ to cover one's expenses cubrir sus gastos

to **meet one's match** dar con la horma de su zapato ▪ ver la suya

to **meet someone 1.** *(for the first time)* conocer a alguien **2.** *(business)* reunirse con alguien **3.** *(social)* encontrarse con alguien ▪ *(Sp.)* quedar con alguien **4.** *(literary, chance encounter)* salir al paso de alguien ➤ Have you met him? ¿Lo has conocido? ▪ *(Sp., leísmo)* ¿Le has conocido? ➤ Have you met her? ¿La has conocido? ➤ The couple had met four years earlier. La pareja se había conocido cuatro años atrás. ▪ La pareja se había conocido hacía cuatro años. ➤ Juan Bobo was on his way to the market when he met a lot of people coming from a wedding. Juan Bobo iba al mercado cuando salió a su paso mucha gente que venía de una boda. ■ Juan Bobo iba al mercado cuando se encontró con mucha gente que venía de una boda. ➤ Meet me under the clock at the Biltmore. Vamos a encontrarnos debajo del reloj en el Biltmore. ■ Quedamos debajo del reloj en el Biltmore. ➤ The class meets three times a week. La clase se reúne tres veces por semana. ➤ The committee meets every Monday. El comité se reúne todos los lunes.

to **meet someone at the airport** recibir a alguien en el aeropuerto ■ buscar a alguien en el aeropuerto ■ encontrarse con alguien en el aeropuerto ■ ir al encuentro de alguien en el aeropuerto ➤ I'm going to meet them at the airport. Voy a recibirlos en el aeropuerto. ■ *(Sp., leísmo)* Voy a recibirles en el aeropuerto.

to **meet someone for** reunirse con alguien para ➤ We're going to meet for supper. Vamos a reunirnos para la cena.

to **meet someone halfway** partir el camino con alguien

to **meet someone who** encontrar a un ser que

to **meet someone's expectations** satisfacer las expectativas de alguien

to **meet someone's needs** ■ to meet the needs of someone cubrir las necesidades de alguien ➤ This software doesn't meet the user's needs. ■ This software doesn't meet the needs of the user. Este software no cubre las necesidades del usuario.

to **meet something head-on** abordar algo de lleno ➤ The European summit in Lisbon yesterday approved a series of reforms to meet head-on the challenge presented by the Internet to develop the economy and create employment. La cumbre europea de Lisboa aprobó ayer un programa de reformas para abordar de lleno el desafío presentado por el Internet para desarrollar la economía y crear empleo.

to **meet the challenge** afrontar el reto

to **meet the demand** cubrir la demanda ■ responder a la demanda ➤ There is not enough petroleum in the world to meet the demand. No hay suficiente petróleo en el mundo para cubrir la demanda. ■ No hay suficiente petróleo en el mundo para responder a la demanda.

to **meet the needs of someone** ■ to meet someone's needs cubrir las necesidades de alguien ➤ This software doesn't meet the needs of the user. ■ This software doesn't meet the user's needs. Este software no cubre las necesidades del usuario.

to **meet the requirements** cumplir los requisitos ■ reunir los requisitos

to **meet with someone** unirse con alguien ■ entrevistarse con alguien ➤ The foreign minister met with the secretary general. El ministerio de exteriores se entrevistó con el secretario general.

to **meet *x* times a week** reunirse *x* veces a la semana ■ *(Sp.)* haber *x* clases a la semana ➤ The class meets three times a weeks. La clase se reúne tres veces a la semana. ■ Hay tres clases a la semana.

the **meeting is adjourned** se levanta la sesión

meeting of two people encuentro de dos personas

meeting place ■ place to meet punto de encuentro ■ lugar de encuentro ■ sitio de encuentro

melting pot ■ mix of cultures *el* crisol ■ mezcla de culturas

member of a club socio de un club ■ miembro de un club

member of a parish church feligrés de una parroquia ■ miembro de una parroquia ■ integrante de una parroquia

member of a team integrante de un equipo

member of Congress 1. *(U.S., refers to both houses)* Representative, Congressman congresista ■ Senator Senador **2.** *(Sp., refers only to the lower house)* diputado

member of one's generation *el, la* integrante de su generación

member of the family *el, la* familiar ■ *el, la* integrante

member of the public ■ citizen ciudadano

members of the public público ➤ The concert was private; there were not many members of the public there. El concierto fue particular; no había mucho público allí.

memorable feat hazaña memorable

memories of recuerdos de

memory is stored... se almacenan los recuerdos...

men and women alike ■ both men and women ■ men as well as women tanto hombres como mujeres ■ lo mismo hombres que mujeres

menial task tarea de baja categoría ■ *(coll.)* tarea a pico y palo

menial work trabajo de baja categoría ■ *(coll.)* trabajo a pico y palo

mental arithmetic cálculo mental

mental exercise: to be good ~ ■ to exercise the mind ser buen ejercicio mental ■ hacer trabajar el cerebro

mental picture cuadro mental ■ dibujo mental

mental telepathy telepatía mental ■ *la* transmisión de entendimiento

to be **mentally ill** ser un enfermo mental ■ ser una enferma mental

to **mention in passing** mencionar de paso

Mercury Rising *(film title) Al rojo vivo*

the **mere fact of** ■ just solo hecho de

the **mere fact that...** ■ just solo hecho de que...

the **mere sight of** ■ just the sight of la mera visión de ■ la simple visión de

Merry Christmas! ¡Feliz Navidad!

Merry Widow *(Franz Lehár work) Viuda alegre*

Merry Wives of Windsor *(Shakespeare) Las comadres alegres de Windsor*

mess of: a whole ~ un enredo de ➤ There was a whole mess of letters on the table. Había un enredo de cartas en la mesa.

to be **messed up** ■ to be screwed up ■ to be awry ■ to have gone awry estar desquiciado ➤ The vehicular traffic in Madrid this summer is all messed up because of the construction everywhere. El tráfico vehicular en Madrid está desquiciado este verano por todas las obras.

messy person persona desordenada ■ persona guarra

metal detector detector de metales ➤ A security guard checks the customers over with a metal detector before entering the café. Un guardia de seguridad revisa a los clientes con un detector de metales antes de entrar en el café.

meteor shower lluvia de estrellas ■ lluvia de meteoritos

meter(s) long: to be *x* ~ ■ to be *x* meter(s) in length tener *x* metros de longitud

method of preparation *(recipe)* método de preparación ■ así se hace

Mexico City la Cuidad de México ■ México, D.F. ■ *(coll.)* el D.F.

Mexico City native *(coll.)* chilango(-a)

microwave oven (horno de) microondas

Mid-Atlantic Ridge *la* Dorsal Media del Atlántico

mid month a mediados del mes ➤ She's leaving in mid December. Sale a mediados de diciembre.

middle-age spread curva de felicidad

middle-aged de mediana edad ➤ She is middle-aged. Ella es de mediana edad. ➤ *(James Thurber novel) The Middle-Aged Man on the Flying Trapeze El hombre de mediana edad en el trapecio*

Middle East El Oriente Medio

middle finger dedo corazón ■ dedo de corazón

middle ground término medio ➤ You either love or hate that director's movies. There's no middle ground. Las películas de ese director se aman o se odian. No hay término medio. ➤ The negotiators are trying to find some middle ground. Los negociadores intentan encontrar un término medio.

middle initial inicial del segundo nombre

middle management mando medio ■ cargos medios

middle name segundo nombre ➤ What does the C in your middle name stand for? ¿Qué representa la C en su segundo nombre?

middle school ■ junior high school escuela de enseñanza media

Midnight Mass *(on Christmas Eve)* misa de gallo

midriff bulge ■ spare tire *el* michelín

midsummer pleno verano

midterm exam examen parcial

midtown Manhattan el pleno (corazón de) Manhattan ■ el centro de Manhattan

midway through ■ halfway through a mitad de ➤ Normally, there is a midterm exam midway through the course. ■ Normally, there is a midterm exam halfway through the course. Normalmente, hay una examen parcial a mitad de la asignatura.

might as well: (one) ~ **1.** it hardly makes any difference igual le valdría a uno **2.** what the heck! ¿qué le hace una raya más al tigre? ■ *(Sp.)* ¡de perdidos al río! **3.** it's tantamount to eso equivale a ➤ As long as we're here, we might as well look around. Y ya que estamos aquí, igual nos valdría pasear. ➤ Everyone knows you did it, so you might as well confess. Y ya que todo el mundo sabe que lo hiciste, igual te valdría confesarlo. ➤ The dentist said I had to have my wisdom teeth out at some point, so I might as well get it over with. Y ya que el dentista me dijo que tenía que sacarme las muelas del juicio en algún momento, igual me valdría hacerlo ahora para salir de esto. ➤ I might as well get it over with. Igual me valdría hacerlo de una vez. ■ Igual me valdría salir de esto (de una vez). ➤ I might as well have. Igual me valdría haberlo hecho. ➤ I might as well have... Igual me valdría haber... ■ Igual me hubiese valido haber... ➤ I was going to quit smoking at midnight New Year's Eve, but at 12:01 I noticed that I had one cigarette in the pack, and I said, "What the heck, I might as well smoke it!" Iba a dejar de fumar a la medianoche del Año Viejo, pero a las doce y un minuto, me di cuenta que me quedaba un cigarrillo en el paquete, y dije, "¡Qué cuernos!, ¡Qué le hace una raya más para el tigre!, voy a fumármelo". *(A Spaniard would say "De perdidos al río, a fumármelo.")* ➤ They might as well take all our money. Eso equivale a que se queden con todo nuestro dinero. ➤ We might as well be strangers. Es como si no nos conociésemos. ■ Es como si no nos conociéramos.

might be: it ~ podría ser ■ tal vez sea ■ puede que sea ■ quizás sea ➤ It might be difficult to get that many volunteers. ■ It could be difficult to get that many volunteers. Podría ser difícil reunir tantos voluntarios. ■ Tal vez sea difícil reunir tantos voluntarios. ■ Puede que sea difícil reunir tantos voluntarios. ■ Quizás sea difícil reunir tantos voluntarios.

might be willing to do something: one ~ uno tal vez esté dispuesto a hacer algo ➤ He might be willing to help you. Tal vez él esté dispuesto a ayudarte.

might have... *(Spanish varies with person and number)* **1.** tal vez tenga... ■ quizás tenga... **2.** *(as an auxiliary verb)* tal vez haya... ■ quizás haya... ➤ *(news item)* Police said the youth might have drug problems. La policía dijo que el joven tal vez tenga problemas con las drogas. ➤ Police said the youth might have had drug problems. La policía dijo que el joven tal vez haya tenido problemas con las drogas.

might have been *(with "it," "you," or singular noun)* ■ may have been **1.** *(permanent state)* (tal vez) haya sido ■ (quizás) haya sido ■ puede haber sido **2.** *(temporary state)* (tal) vez haya estado ■ (quizás) haya estado ■ puede haber estado **3.** *(more doubtful)* might conceivably have been ■ could conceivably have been pudiera haber sido ■ pudiese haber sido ■ podría haber sido ■ podría haber estado ■ pudiera haber estado ■ pudiese haber estado ➤ The fire might have been caused by a short circuit. El incendio quizás haya sido provocado por un corto circuito. ■ El incendio tal vez haya sido provocado por un corto circuito. ■ El fuego podría haber sido provocado por un corto circuito. ➤ Whatever might have been the reason for the error... Cualquiera haya sido la razón por el error... ➤ Someone might have been here during our absence. Alguien tal vez haya estado aquí durante nuestra ausencia. ➤ The needle might have been infected. La aguja haya estado infectada. ➤ The missing man might have been kidnapped. El desaparecido puede haber sido secuestrado. ➤ He might have been exposed to the virus. Puede haber estado expuesto al virus. ➤ A blemish that might (conceivably) have been generated by the photocopier Una imperfección que pudiera haber sido generada por la fotocopiadora ■ Una imperfección que pudiese haber sido generada por la fotocopiadora ■ Una imperfección que podría haber sido generada por la fotocopiadora. ➤ Who might have been here? ¿Quién pudiera haber estado?

might have been: there ~ **1.** there may have been (tal vez) haya habido ■ (quizás) haya habido ■ pudo haber habido **2.** *(more doubtful)* there might (conceivably) have been podría haber habido ■ pudiera haber habido ■ pudiese haber habido

might have considered podía haber tenido en cuenta ■ podría haber considerado

might have had *(with "it," "one," or a noun subject)* **1.** tal vez haya tenido ■ pudo haber tenido **2.** *(more doubtful)* podría haber tenido ■ pudiera haber tenido ➤ Police said the youth might have had drug problems. La policía dijo que el joven tal vez haya tenido problemas con las drogas. ■ La policía dijo que el joven podría haber tenido problemas con las drogas.

might have to do something: one ~ **1.** uno tal vez tenga que hacer algo **2.** *(in past tense phrases)* tenía que ➤ A century ago, people couldn't listen to a Beethoven concerto at will, but might have to wait years to hear it. Hace un siglo atrás, la gente no podía escuchar un concierto de Beethoven a su voluntad, sino que tenían que esperar años hasta que se presentara. ■ Hace un siglo, la gente no podía escuchar un concierto de Beethoven a su voluntad, sino que tenían que esperar años hasta que se presentara la ocasión.

might I ask? *(accusatory)* ¿me permites la pregunta? ■ ¿te puedo preguntar?

migrant worker jornalero ■ itinerante ■ *(in Cataluña, Sp.)* charnego *(who usually comes from Murcia)*

migratory birds aves peregrinos

mild heart attack: to have a ~ tener amago de infarto ■ tener un infarto leve

mild salsa picante salsa picante suave

mild temperature: to have a ~ ■ to have a slight temperature ■ to have a low fever tener unas décimas ➤ She has a slight temperature. ■ She has a mild temperature. ■ She has a low fever. Tiene unas décimas.

miles square ■ miles squared millas al cuadrado ➤ This town is four miles square, that is, four miles by four miles, or sixteen square miles in area. El área de este pueblo es de cuatro millas al cuadrado, es decir, cuatro millas por cuatro millas, o dieciséis millas cuadradas.

to be a **milestone in** marcar un jalón en ■ marcar un hito en

military commander *el, la* comandante militar

military-industrial complex complejo industrial-militar

military tribunal ■ military court *el* tribunal militar ■ consejo de guerra

milk run ■ the bus that makes all the stops, not the express lechero

to **mill around** arremolinarse

minced almonds almendras machacadas

minced onions cebollas secas picadas ■ cebollas secas troceadas

to be **mind-blowing** ser alucinante

to be **mind-boggling** ser de locos

to **mind one's manners** cuidar sus modales

to **mind one's own business** estar a lo suyo ■ estar centrado en lo suyo ➤ I was minding my own business when he interrupted me. Yo estaba a lo mío cuando él me interrumpió.

mind wandered la mente divagó ■ la mente divagaba ■ se distrajo ■ se distraía ➤ My mind wanders during the lecture. Mi mente divaga durante la conferencia.

mind you! ten en cuenta que... ■ te advierto que... ■ toma en cuenta que... ■ considera que... ➤ Mind you! We have to be at the airport in two hours. Ten en cuenta que tenemos que estar en el aeropuerto en un par de horas.

mind your manners cuida tus modales

mind your own business! ¡zapatero a tus zapatos! ■ no te apartes de tu carril ■ tú a lo tuyo

mine clearance limpiado de minas

mine field campo minado

mine included ■ including mine incluido el mío ■ incluida la mía ■ incluyendo el mío ■ incluyendo la mía

mine of information ■ gold mine of information venero de información ■ *la* gran fuente de información

to **mingle with a crowd** mezclarse con la multitud ■ mezclarse con la gente ➤ President Obama left his limousine and mingled with the crowd. El presidente Obama bajó de su limusina y se mezcló con la multitud. ➤ If you let the chimichurri stand for a day, the flavors mingle, and it tastes better. Si dejas reposar el chimichurri durante un día, los sabores se mezclan y sabe mejor.

to **mingle with people** mezclarse con la gente ▪ alternar con la gente ▪ asociarse con la gente

to **minimize the importance of something** ▪ to downplay the importance of something ▪ to play down the importance of something restar importancia a algo ▪ quitar importancia a algo

mining town pueblo minero

mink coat abrigo de lomos de visón

minor cuts and bruises los cortes y moratones de poca importancia ➤ The victim suffered minor cuts and bruises in the accident. La víctima sufrió cortes y moratones de poca importancia.

minor details los detalles sin importancia

minor key tono menor

minor scandal pequeño escándalo

minority opinion *(U.S. Supreme Court)* ▪ dissenting opinion escrito de discrepancia ▪ *la* opinión discrepante de la minoría ➤ In the minority opinion signed by the three justices... ▪ In the dissenting opinion signed by the three justices... En el escrito de discrepancia firmado por los tres magistrados...

to **mint money** acuñar dinero

minute hand *(of a watch)* minutero

the **minute I saw you** ▪ the moment I saw you en el momento que te vi ▪ en cuanto te vi ➤ The minute I saw you, I was in love. En el momento que te vi, me enamoré.

the **minute I see you...** en el momento que te vea ▪ en cuanto te vea

minutes into the flight a minutos del vuelo ➤ Four minutes into the flight A cuatro minutos del vuelo

minutes of a meeting *las* actas de una reunión

mirror image reflejo del espejo

mirror images of each other imágenes simétricas ▪ imágenes de espejo ➤ The floor plans of the two apartments are mirror images of each other. Los planes de los dos pisos son simétricos. ➤ The famous San Francisco twins are mirror images of each other. Las famosas gemelas de San Francisco son como imágenes de espejo.

mirror of his thoughts: a man's conversation is a ~ cada uno habla quien es ▪ por las palabras se conoce la intención

miscarriage of justice injusticia judicial

to **misdeal cards** dar mal los naipes

misdeeds finally catch up with you: your ~ ▪ the chickens finally come home to roost tanto va el cántaro a la fuente (que se rompe)

miserable weather ▪ lousy weather tiempo de perros ➤ The weather is miserable. Hace un tiempo de perros.

to **miss a chance to do something** ▪ to miss an opportunity to do something perder una oportunidad de hacer algo

to **miss a target** errar un blanco ▪ fallar en un tiro blanco ▪ marrar un blanco

to **miss class** faltar a clase ▪ ausentarse de la clase ▪ dejar de asistir a la clase ➤ He rarely misses class. Casi nunca falta a clase. ➤ I had to miss class yesterday. Tuve que dejar de asistir a la clase ayer.

to **miss one's connection 1.** *(plane)* perder la conexión de vuelo ▪ perder el vuelo de conexión **2.** *(train, bus)* perder el trasbordo ▪ perder la conexión ➤ I don't want to miss my (plane) connection. No quiero perder mi conexión de vuelo. *("Perder la conexión" can also mean to lose one's electrical, telephone, or Internet connection. The ambiguity can be avoided by adding "de vuelo, de tren, del autobús.")*

to **miss out (on something)** perdérsele la oportunidad (de algo) ➤ She's missing out on the chance of a lifetime. A ella se le pierde la oportunidad de una vida.

to **miss someone 1.** to be lonesome for echar de menos a alguien ▪ extrañar a alguien **2.** to fail to coincide no encontrarse con alguien ➤ I really miss you. Realmente te echo de menos. ▪ Realmente te extraño. ➤ I'm sorry I missed you today. Siento que no pudiéramos encontrarnos hoy. ▪ Siento que no pudiésemos encontarnos hoy.

to **miss something** ▪ to notice something is missing echar de menos algo ➤ I missed it when I came home from work. ▪ I noticed it was missing when I came home from work. Lo eché de menos al volver de mi trabajo.

to **miss the beat** perder el compás ▪ perder el ritmo ▪ discrepar el compás

to **miss the point** pasársele lo crucial ▪ no darse cuenta ▪ no entender ▪ no comprender ▪ pasársele el punto ▪ *(colorful)* pasársele la Misa de una ➤ You're missing the whole point. Se te pasa lo crucial.

to **miss the target** errar al blanco ▪ fallar en el tiro al blanco ▪ marrar el blanco

to **miss what someone said** pasársele lo que alguien dijo ▪ escapársele lo que alguien dijo

to **miss work** faltar al trabajo ▪ ausentarse del trabajo ➤ He rarely misses work. Casi nunca falta a su trabajo.

to be **missing from** haber desaparecido de ▪ haberse extraviado de

missing link eslabón perdido

mission accomplished! ¡trabajo hecho! ▪ ¡listo el pollo!

mission of something ▪ purpose of something cometido de algo ➤ The high-speed train unit has eleven locomotives whose mission is to pull the Talgo trains. La unidad de trenes de alta velocidad cuenta con once locomotoras cuyo cometido es remolcar los trenes Talgo.

missionary position *(sexual intercourse)* postura del misionero

mistakenly called ▪ incorrectly called ▪ wrongly called mal llamado

miter joint *el* inglete

mitigating circumstances ▪ attenuating circumstances circunstancias atenuantes

to **mix and match** hacer combinaciones

to **mix apples and oranges** mezclar churras con merinas

to **mix up something** ▪ to mix something up ▪ to get something mixed up ▪ to have something mixed up confundir algo ➤ I mixed up the days. ▪ I mixed the days up. ▪ I got the days mixed up. ▪ I had the days mixed up. Confundí los días.

to be a **mixed blessing** ser una bendición diluida

mixed feelings (about something): to have ~ ▪ to have conflicting feelings about something ▪ to have contradictory feelings about something ▪ to have ambivalent feelings about something tener sentimientos enfrentados ▪ tener sentimientos contrapuestos ➤ I have mixed feelings (about it). Tengo sentimientos enfrentados (al respecto). ▪ Tengo sentimientos contrapuestos (al respecto).

mixed results resultados dispares

mixed reviews reseñas dispares

mixed success éxito parcial ➤ The success of the Mars exploration missions to date can best be described as mixed. Como mejor se puede describir el éxito de las misiones de exploración de Marte es como parcial.

to be **mixed up** hacerse un lío ▪ armarse un lío ➤ I'm really mixed up. Me hago un lío. ▪ Me armo un lío.

mixed up: to get something ~ ▪ to have something mixed up ▪ to mix up something ▪ to mix something up confundir algo ➤ I got the days mixed up. ▪ I had the days mixed up. ▪ I mixed up the days. ▪ I mixed the days up. Confundí los días.

to be **mixed with** estar revuelto con ➤ Residues of coffee grounds mixed with the rust from the can. Raspaduras del polvo de café revueltas con óxido de lata.

mock exam simulacro de examen

to **mock someone** hacer quedar a alguien en ridículo ▪ poner a alguien en ridículo ▪ dejar a alguien en ridículo ▪ dejar a alguien por ridículo

model citizen ▪ upstanding citizen ciudadano ejemplar ▪ ciudadano modelo

to be a **model of** ser un paradigma de

modest price módico precio ▪ precio modesto

modest sum módica suma ▪ modesta suma

modus operandi ▪ MO ▪ way of doing things ▪ way of going about things manera de obrar

moisture (contained) in something *(sponge, bale of hay, etc.)* amount of water in something *la* humedad en algo

moment I saw you momento en que te vi ➤ The moment I saw you, I was in love. El momento en que te vi, estuve enamorado. ➤ From the moment I saw you, I was in love. Desde el momento en que te vi, estuve enamorado.

moment of truth hora de la verdad ➤ It's the moment of truth. Ha llegado la hora de la verdad.

momentary loss of consciousness ▪ temporary loss of consciousness pérdida temporal de la conciencia

moments later pasados unos momentos

monastic life vida cenobítica

Monday night and early Tuesday en la noche del lunes al martes

Monday through Friday ▪ on weekdays de lunes a viernes ▪ los días laborales

money doesn't grow on trees el dinero no crece en las plantas

money laundering blanqueo de dinero ▪ lavado de dinero

money order: bank ~ giro bancario

money order: postal ~ giro postal

money talks poderoso caballero es don dinero

money to burn: to have ~ ▪ to have more money than one knows what to do with tener dinero para tirar a la chuña

money trail pista al dinero ➤ *(headline)* Obstacles to following the money trail. Barricadas para seguir la pista al dinero.

money's not everything ▪ money is not everything el dinero no es todo ▪ dinero no es lo todo

to **monitor closely** ▪ to watch closely ▪ to keep a close eye on vigilar estrechamente

monkey see, money do lo que ven, lo copian

monkey suit *(slang)* ▪ tails *el* traje de pengüino

the **month before** el mes anterior ▪ el mes antes

to be a **month premature** nacer con un mes de antelación ▪ ser un ochomesino ➤ The baby was a month premature. El bebé nació con un mes de antelación. ▪ El bebé fue "ochomesino".

monthly rate taza mensual

monthly statement extracto mensual

month's salary mesada

month's wages mesada

mood swings cambios anímicos ▪ cambios de humor

to **moonlight as** ▪ to work a second job as tener un pluriempleo

Moonlight Sonata *(Beethoven)* Sonata claro de luna

to **mop the floor** *(L. Am.)* pasar el coleto ▪ pasar el trapeador ▪ *(Sp.)* pasar la fregona

to **mop up** enjugar

moral compass brújula ética

moral high ground fundamento moral

moral laxity flaqueza moral

moral of the story moraleja de la historia ▪ moraleja del cuento

moral stature talla moral

more and more ▪ increasingly cada vez más

more and more likely ▪ increasingly likely ▪ more and more probable ▪ increasingly real cada vez más probable ▪ cada vez más real

to be **more convinced than ever that...** estar más convencido que nunca de que... ▪ creer aún más que...

to be **more expensive than usual** ▪ to be higher than usual ser más caro de lo normal

more money than one knows what to do with ▪ money to burn dinero para tirar a la chuña

more of the same más de lo mismo

more often más a menudo ➤ You should write your parents more often. Deberías escribirles a sus padres más a menudo.

to be **more like** parecerse más a ▪ ser más bien ➤ An ultralight airplane is more like a big kite. Una avioneta ultraligera se parece más a una cometa grande. ▪ Una avioneta ultraligera es más bien una cometa grande.

more or less más o menos ▪ poco más o menos

more than 1. *(counting)* más de **2.** *(comparing)* más de lo que ▪ por encima de **3.** *(over and above)* por encima de ➤ He likes music more than (he does) the visual arts. Le gusta la música más que los artes visuales. ➤ I have been in Washington more than 20 times. He estado en Washington más de 20 veces. ➤ The senator was more ethical than the press gave him credit for being. El senador era más ético de lo que la prensa le daba crédito.

more than amply ▪ and then some con creces

more than anything else por encima de todo ▪ más que nada

more than anything else for ▪ primarily for ▪ mostly for más que nada por ➤ I did it more than anything else for the money. ▪ I did it for the money more than anything else. ▪ I did it primarily for the money. ▪ I did it mostly for the money. Lo hice más que nada por el dinero.

to be **more than capable of** ▪ to be perfectly capable of bastarse y sobrarse para

more than enough más que suficiente ▪ de sobra ➤ More than enough watering (of the plants) Agua de sobra (para las plantas)

more than ever más que nunca

more than ever before ▪ as never before como nunca

more than half más de la mitad ➤ Can you believe (that) the year is already more than half over? ¿Te puedes creer que ha pasado ya más de la mitad del año?

more than I can eat: it's ~ es más de lo que (yo) pueda comer

more than I do más que yo ▪ *(to emphasize the "yo")* más de lo que yo hago ➤ She goes to the movies more than I do. Ella va al cine más que yo. ➤ He likes spicy food more than I do. A él le gusta la comida picante más que a mí.

to be **more than justified in doing something** ▪ to have more than sufficient reason for doing something tener motivos de sobra por hacer algo

more than once más de una vez

more than one should have más de lo que uno debiera

more than usual más de lo normal

more than you think *(tú)* más de lo que tú piensas ▪ *(usted)* más de lo que usted piensa ▪ más de lo que piensa usted

more to the point sin ir tan lejos

morning after mañana posterior (a)

morning-after pill *(emergency contraception)* píldora del día siguiente

morning coffee café mañanero ▪ café matutino ▪ café matinal

morning fog niebla matinal ➤ The morning fog burns off the San Francisco Bay by 11 a.m. ▪ The morning fog on the San Francisco Bay dissipates by 11 a.m. La niebla matinal se retira de la Bahía de San Francisco para las once de la mañana.

morning person persona matutina

morning sun *el* sol matinal

morning twilight crepúsculo del alba ▪ crepúsculo matutino ▪ crepúsculo matinal

to **mortgage a house** ▪ to take out a mortgage on a house hacer una hipoteca sobre una casa

to **most admire about someone** ▪ to most admire in someone más admirar de alguien ➤ That's what I most admire about her. Es lo que más admiro de ella.

most certainly! ▪ for sure! ▪ of course! ¡qué digamos! ▪ ¡por supuesto!

to be the **most convenient time for me** ▪ to be the best time for me ▪ to be the time that suits (me) best ser la hora que me viene mejor ▪ ser cuando me viene mejor

most likely explanation ▪ the most probable explanation ▪ the best explanation *la* explicación más probable

most likely thing lo más probable ▪ lo más fácil

most of la mayoría de ▪ la mayor parte de ▪ el grueso de ➤ Most of these books are overdue. La mayoría de estos libros están vencidos. ➤ The government withdrew most of its troops. El gobierno retiró el grueso de sus tropas.

most of all ▪ more than anything else ▪ more than anything más que nada

most of the time la mayor parte del tiempo

most of the times la mayoría de las ocasiones ▪ las más veces

most of those who la mayoría de quienes

most of which la mayoría de los cuales ▪ la mayoría de las cuales

most of whom la mayoría de los cuales ▪ la mayoría de las cuales

most people ▪ the majority (of the people) la mayor parte de la gente ▪ la mayoría (de la gente) ➤ Contrary to what most

people think... Al contrario de lo que piensa la mayoría ■ Al contrario de lo que piensa la mayor parte de la gente...
the **most probable explanation** ■ the most likely explanation ■ the best explanation la explicación más probable ■ la explicación más posible
most recent bank statement último extracto de cuenta ■ último resúmen de cuenta
the **most sensible thing to do is** la cosa más sensata que hacer es
most unusual ■ highly unusual ■ very unusual insólito
moth-eaten apolillado
mother cells células madres
mother-in-law suegra ■ madre política
motion detector detector de presencias
motion picture set ■ movie set ■ filming set plató de rodaje
to **motion to someone to come over** llamar a alguien por señas para que venga ■ llamar a alguien por señas para que se acerque
motive for the crime *el* móvil del crimen ■ *el* motivo del crimen
motor backfired ■ engine backfired el motor hizo explosiones ■ motor petardeó
motor stalled ■ engine stalled se ha calado el motor ■ se ha apagado el motor ➤ Try not to let it stall (on you). Intenta que no se te cale. ■ Intenta que no se te apague.
motorized rubber raft lancha neumático a motor
motorless airplane ■ glider ■ sailplane planeador
mountain climbing alpinismo ■ *(S. Am.)* andinismo
mountain goat cabra montesa
mountain lion ■ wildcat gato montés ■ puma
mountain pass puerto de montaña
mountain sickness ■ altitude sickness *el* mal de montaña ■ mal de altura
to **mourn the death of someone** ■ to mourn someone's death llorar la muerte de alguien
to **mourn the loss of someone** ■ to mourn someone's loss llorar la pérdida de alguien
to **mourn their dead** llorar sus muertos
mouse pad *(computers)* alfombrilla del ratón
mouthful of: to take a ~ tomar un buche de
to **move about** ■ to move around ■ to get around desplazarse
to **move about the Internet** moverse por el Internet ➤ A Canadian who moved about the Internet under the nickname of Mafiaboy... Un adolescente canadiense que se movía por Internet bajo el apodo de Mafiaboy...
to **move about with complete freedom** moverse con entera libertad
to **move against the background of the stars** moverse respecto al fondo de estrellas ➤ The Babylonian astronomers had noticed that the sun moves against the background of the stars. ■ The Babylonian astronomers had noticed that the sun changes its position against the background of the stars. Los astrónomos de Babilonia habían notado que el sol se mueve respecto al fondo de estrellas.
to **move aside** apartarse
to **move away 1.** alejarse **2.** to move to another locale mudarse lejos
to **move backwards** echarse para atrás ■ retroceder
to **move closer** ■ to move up closer irse acercando ■ estar acercándose ➤ I can't see. Let's move (up) closer. No veo nada. Vamos acercándonos. ■ No veo nada. Vamos a irnos acercando. ➤ The enemy troops are moving closer to us. Las tropas del enemigo se están acercando.
to **move forward** avanzar
to **move here** *(L. Am.)* mudarse acá ■ *(Sp.)* mudarse aquí ➤ When we moved here... Cuando nos mudamos acá... ➤ When we moved into the house we live in now... Cuando fuimos a vivir en la casa donde vivimos... ■ Cuando fuimos a vivir a la casa donde vivimos...
to **move into an apartment** *(Mex., S. Am.)* entrar (a vivir) en un departamento ■ mudarse a un departamento ■ trasladarse a un departamento ■ *(L. Am.)* entrar (a vivir) en un apartamento ■ mudarse a un apartamento ■ trasladarse a un apartamento ■ *(Sp.)* entrar (a vivir) en un piso ■ mudarse a un piso ■ trasladarse a un piso ■ *(large apartment)* entrar (a vivir) en un apartamento ■ mudarse a un apartamento ■ trasladarse a un apartamento
to **move on** ■ to move along circular ■ no pararse
to **move out of an apartment** *(Mex.)* dejar un departamento ■ *(L. Am.)* dejar un apartamento ■ *(Sp.)* dejar un piso ■ *(large apartment)* dejar un apartamento
to **move over 1.** *(farther away)* ponerse más allá ■ alejarse **2.** *(closer)* arrimarse ■ acercarse ■ aproximarse **3.** *(either direction)* moverse ■ echarse a un lado ■ hacerse a un lado ■ ponerse a un lado ■ *(S. Am. only)* correrse ➤ Move over. ■ Make more room. *(tú)* ¡Ponte más allá. ■ *(usted)* Póngase más allá. ■ *(ustedes)* Pónganse más allá. ■ *(Sp., vosotros)* Poneos más allá. ➤ Move over. ■ Move closer. ■ Move this way. ■ *(tú)* Arrímate. ■ *(usted)* Arrímese. ■ *(ustedes)* Arrímense. ■ *(vosotros)* Arrimaos. ➤ Move over. *(either direction) (tú)* Muévete. ■ *(usted)* Muévase. ■ *(ustedes)* Muévanse. ■ *(Sp., vosotros)* Moveos. ■ *(S. Am. only)* Córrete. ■ Córrase.
move over a couple (of) seats! *(tú)* muévete un par de asientos más allá ■ ponte un par de asientos más allá ■ *(usted)* muévase un par de asientos más allá ■ póngase un par de asientos más allá ■ *(ustedes)* muévanse un par de asientos más allá ■ pónganse un par de asientos más allá ■ *(vosotros)* moveos un par de asientos más allá ■ poneos un par de asientos más allá ■ *(coll., but incorrect)* poneros un par de asientos más allá ■ moveros un par de asientos más allá
to **move over to the left** ■ to get over to the left ponerse a la izquierda ■ moverse a la izquierda ■ echarse a la izquierda ■ desplazarse a la izquierda
to **move over to the right** ■ to get over to the right ponerse a la derecha ■ moverse a la derecha ■ echarse a la derecha ■ desplazarse a la derecha
to **move someone deeply** ■ to touch someone deeply emocionar a alguien vivamente ■ conmoverle a alguien profundamente
to **move something away from something** ■ to separate something from something alejar algo de algo
to **move something (somewhere else)** ■ to put something somewhere else cambiar algo a otro sitio
to **move the car (out of the way)** retirar el coche
to **move to a new house** cambiar a una nueva casa
to **move to the left** *(politically)* pasarse a la izquierda
to **move toward something 1.** to approach something acercarse a algo **2.** to lean toward something ■ to tend toward something ■ to incline toward something decantarse hacia algo
to be **moved by** ■ to be touched by emocionarse por ■ conmoverse por
to be **moved with compassion** conmoverse
movie camera cámara de cine
movie set ■ motion picture set ■ filming set plató de rodaje
movie that's on ■ movie that's showing película que ponen
movie was over... ■ movie got out... ■ movie ended... película terminó... ➤ The movie was over at ten o'clock. ■ The movie got out at ten o'clock. ■ The movie ended at ten o'clock. La película terminó a las diez.
moving parts partes mecanizadas
moving right along *(gently changing the subject)* corramos un tupido velo
to **mow the lawn** ■ to cut the grass cortar el césped
Mr. Right media naranja *("Media naranja" also means "one's other half.")*
Mr. Scrooge Señor Cascarrabias
Mrs. John Doe Señora Fulano de tal ■ la de Fulano de tal
much ado about nothing mucho ruido y pocas nueces ■ más es el ruido
much less 1. *(referring to quantity)* mucho menos **2.** not to mention y mucho menos ➤ He earns much less now than he did a year ago. Gana mucho menos dinero que hace un año. ➤ It is impossible for a rocket to reach the speed of light, much less exceed it. Es imposible que un cohete alcance la velocidad de la luz, y mucho menos sobrepasarla.
much talked about muy mentado ■ muy sonado
much to one's chagrin para el gran disgusto de uno

much to one's liking muy del gusto de uno

much to one's surprise para la gran sorpresa de uno

to **muddy the water** enturbiar la situación

muggy weather tiempo bochornoso ▪ tiempo caluroso y humedo

mule-drawn wagon carro tirado por mula ▪ carro de mula

multimillion dollar contract contrato millonario

multiplication tables tablas de multiplicar

mum's the word de esto no se habla ▪ esto se calla

murder weapon ▪ weapon used in the murder ▪ weapon used to commit the murder arma empleada en el asesinato

Murphy's Law: if anything can go wrong, it will la ley de Murphy: si algo puede salir mal, saldrá mal

muscle cramp ▪ *(coll.)* charley horse *el* calambre ▪ espasmo

music box caja de música

music lover melómano

to be **music to one's ears** sonar a música celestial

musical scale escala musical ➤ C D E F G A B C ▪ do re mi fa so (*or* sol) la ti do do re mi fa sol la si do ➤ Concerto in B-flat Concierto en si bemol

musical score partitura musical

must be *(Spanish varies with person and number)* **1.** *(permanent state and to form passive voice)* debe ser **2.** *(temporary state and preceding predicate adjectives)* debe estar **3.** *(conjecture)* debe de ser ▪ ha de ser ▪ será ▪ debe de estar ▪ ha de estar ▪ estará ➤ *(headline)* Fujimori must be tried for violating the Constitution. Fujimori debe ser juzgado por violar la Constitución. ➤ The country must be prepared for the consequences of its inaction. El país debe estar preparado para las consecuencias de su inacción. ➤ *(Ogden Nash poem)* It must be the milk! ¡Debe de ser la leche! ▪ ¡Será la leche! ➤ She must be tired. Debe de estar cansada. ▪ Estará cansada. ▪ Ha de estar cansada. ➤ You must be dumbfounded at what I did. Debes de estar estupefacto ante lo que hice. ▪ Has de estar estupefacto ante lo que hice. ▪ Estarás estupefacto ante lo que hice.

must be tired: one ~ uno estará cansado(-a) ▪ uno ha de estar cansado(-a) ➤ She must be tired. Estará cansada.

must have been... *(with any subject)* ▪ had to have been... **1.** *(permanent state)* debe haber sido... ▪ ha de haber sido... ▪ tiene que haber sido... **2.** *(temporary state)* tiene que haber estado... ▪ debe haber estado... ▪ ha de haber estado... **3.** *(more conjectural)* debe de haber sido... ▪ seguramente fue...

must have been told: one ~ deben de haberle dicho a uno ➤ He must have been told. Deben de haberle dicho.

must have done something: one ~ uno debe de haber hecho algo ▪ habrá hecho algo ➤ I must have seen a hundred movies this year. Debo de haber visto cien películas este año. ▪ Habré visto cien películas en este año.

to be a **must-read** ser una lectura obligada

to be a **must-see** **1.** *(movie)* ser un película obligada ▪ ser una película para no perdérsela ▪ ser una película que hay que ver **2.** *(play)* ser un obra obligada ▪ ser una obra para no perdérsela ▪ ser una obra que hay que ver **3.** *(show)* ser un espectáculo obligado ▪ ser un espectáculo para no perdérselo ▪ ser un espectáculo que hay que ver **4.** *(museum)* ser un museo obligado ▪ ser un museo para no perdérselo ▪ ser un museo que hay que ver ▪ ser una visita obligada

to **muster all of one's inner strength** valerse de toda su fuerza interior

to **muster up one's courage** armarse de valor

to **mutter words** ▪ to mutter things ▪ to mutter something mascullar palabras

mutual acquaintance conocido mutuo

mutual agreement acuerdo mutuo

mutual friend amigo común

mutual fund fondo de inversión

mutual trust confianza mutua

to **muzzle a dog** poner bozal al perro

to **muzzle the press** amordazar la prensa

my age: people ~ la gente de mi edad

my aunt and uncle mis tíos

my (best) guess is that... calculo que...

my curiosity got the best of me no aguanté más la curiosidad

my darling mi cielo ▪ hija mía

my dear amor mío

My Dear Sir *(formal letter greeting)* Muy señor mío

my dream came true se me cumplió el sueño ▪ se me ha cumplido el sueño

my eyes are blurry veo borroso

my eyes were as big as saucers me quedé los ojos como platos

my grandfathers ▪ my mother's father and my father's father el padre de mi madre y el padre de mi padre

my grandparents mis abuelos

my guess is that... calculo que... ▪ a mí me parece que... ▪ creo yo que...

my head got sunburned se me achicharró la cabeza

my heart leaped el corazón me dio la vuelta

my heart melted mi corazón se derritió

my heart sank mi corazón se hundió ▪ se me cayó el alma a los pies

my heart shrank when... se me encogió el corazón cuando...

my heart skipped a beat me dio un vuelco el corazón

my heart was pounding mi corazón palpitaba ▪ mi corazón latía fuertemente

my hometown mi cuidad natal ▪ mi patria chica

my, how you've grown! ¡pero cómo has crecido!

my life's work trabajo de mi vida

my little princess mi princesita

my love! ¡vida mía!

my mouth is on fire *(from eating hot peppers)* mi boca está que arde

my name is... **1.** me llamo... ▪ mi nombre es **2.** *(referring to one's last name)* mi apellido es ▪ mis apellidos son

my nose is running ▪ I have a runny nose me gotea la nariz ▪ me moquea la nariz ▪ *(Sp.)* se me caen las velas

my objective is... tengo por objetivo...

my only alternative is to... lo único que me resta es...

my only alternative was to... lo único que me restaba era...

my only concern mi única preocupación

my own favorite ▪ my personal favorite mi favorito(-a) personal ▪ personalmente, mi favorito(-a)

my point is that... a lo que quiero llegar es que...

my question today mi pregunta de hoy ➤ My question today concerns... Mi pregunta de hoy concierne a...

my recollection is that mi memoria me dice que ▪ mi recuerdo me dice que ▪ mi recuerdo es que

my time has come ▪ it's my time es mi hora

my treat: it's ~ *(a ti)* te invito ▪ *(a usted)* le invito ▪ *(a ustedes)* les invito ▪ *(Sp., a vosotros)* os invito

my uncle and aunt mis tíos

my uncles ▪ the brothers of my mother and/or father los hermanos (varones) de mi madre y/o mi padre

my watch is *x* minutes fast mi reloj está *x* minutos adelantado ▪ mi reloj lleva *x* minutos adelantado ➤ My watch is three minutes fast. Mi reloj está tres minutos adelantado. ▪ Mi reloj está adelantado tres minutos.

my watch is *x* minutes slow mi reloj está *x* minutos atrasado ▪ mi reloj lleva *x* atrasado ➤ My watch is three minutes slow. Mi reloj está tres minutos atrasado. ▪ Mi reloj está atrasado tres minutos.

my way ▪ in my own way a mi manera

my, you've changed! ▪ how you've changed! ¡pero qué cambiazo has dado! ▪ ¡qué cambiado(-a) estás!

Mysteries of Light *(Catholicism)* Misterios Luminosos

na, na, na, na *na, na* *(taunt)* chincha rabiña, que tengo una piña con muchos piñones y tú no los comes

to **nab someone** trincar a alguien ▪ agarrar a alguien

to be **nabbed by the police** ▪ to be picked up by the police ser trincado por la policía ▪ ser agarrado por la policía

to be a **nag** ser un(a) pesado(-a) ➤ You're a terrible nag. Eres más pesado(-a) que una vaca en brazos.

nail is snagging ▪ fingernail is snagging ▪ fingernail is catching uña está arañando

nail set *(carpentry tool)* botador cilíndrico

to **nail something into the wall** clavar algo en la pared ➤ When I try to nail this doodad into the wall, it flips up. Cuando trato de clavar esta chuchería en la pared, se me sube.

to be **naked as a jaybird** estar en cueros ▪ estar en pelotas

name fits nombre le queda ▪ nombre le pega ▪ el nombre le calza ➤ The name Boudreaux fits the dog perfectly. El nombre Boudreaux le queda al perro perfectamente. ▪ El nombre Boudreaux le pega al perro a la medida. ▪ El nombre Boudreaux le calza al perro a la perfección.

the **name doesn't ring a bell** el nombre no me suena (nada)

to **name names** dar nombres ▪ decir nombres ➤ I'm not going to name names. No voy a dar nombres. ▪ No voy a decir nombres.

name of the course nombre de la asignatura ➤ What's the name of the course? ¿Qué es el nombre del curso?

to **name someone for someone** *(USA)* ▪ to name someone after someone ponerle el nombre por alguien ▪ llamársele por alguien ➤ They named him Thomas for his great-grandfather. ▪ They named him Thomas after his great-grandfather. Le pusieron Tomás por su bisabuelo. ▪ Se le llamó Thomas por su bisabuelo. *(In Great Britain, only "after" is used in this context.)*

name (was) not given nombre no se cita ➤ Whose name was not given... Cuyo nombre no se cita...

to **name *x* people** citar *x* personas ➤ Name ten outstanding figures of the last thousand years. Cita diez personajes sobresalientes de los mil últimos años.

to be **named after someone** ▪ to be named for someone ponérsele el nombre por alguien ▪ llamársele por alguien ➤ He was named Thomas after his great-grandfather. ▪ He was named Thomas for his great-grandfather. Se le puso Thomas por su bisabuelo. ▪ Se le llamó Thomas por su bisabuelo. ➤ Virginia was named Virginia for Queen Elizabeth the First of England. ▪ Virginia was named after Queen Elizabeth the First of England. Se le llama Virginia (el estado norteamericano) por la Reina Elizabeth Primera de Inglaterra.

napkin ring servilletero

to **narrow down the search** estrechar la búsqueda

narrow escape: to have a ~ ▪ to be lucky to be alive casi no escapar ▪ volver a nacer

to be **narrow-minded** tener la cabeza cuadrada ▪ ser de mentalidad cerrada ▪ tener una mentalidad cerrada

narrow stairway ▪ narrow stairs ▪ narrow stair angosta escalera ▪ escalera estrecha

narrow victory ajustado triunfo ➤ Portuguese voters have ended a socialist period with the narrow victory of the social democrats. Los votantes portugueses han dado por concluido un ciclo socialista con el ajustado triunfo de los socialdemócratas.

nasal passages fosas nasales

nascent science of ▪ young science of incipiente ciencia de

national anthem himno nacional ➤ Juan León Mera wrote the lyrics of Ecuador's national anthem. Juan León Mera escribió la letra del himno nacional del Ecuador.

national hero héroe de la patria

National Security Council *(USA)* Consejo de Seguridad Nacional

nationwide: to be distributed ~ distribuirse en todo el país

nationwide address discurso a todo el país

nationwide appeal llamamiento a todo el país

nationwide broadcast transmisión a todo el país

nationwide search búsqueda por todo el país

native country ▪ native land ▪ homeland tierra natal ▪ *el* país de origen

N

native language ▪ first language ▪ mother tongue lengua materna ▪ idioma materno ▪ lengua nativa ▪ idioma nativo ▪ lengua propia

native of Texas ▪ Texas native ▪ Texan procedente de Tejas ▪ originario de Tejas ▪ tejano

natural affinity ▪ natural sympathy afinidad natural ▪ simpatía natural ➤ Terrorist groups have a natural affinity for each other. Grupos terroristas tienen una afinidad natural unos para los otros.

natural disposition to disposición natural a

natural gas powered propulsión a gas natural

natural leader ▪ born leader líder nato

natural sciences ciencias de la naturaleza

natural wonder prodigio de la naturaleza

naturally carbonated con gas del mismo manantial ➤ Naturally carbonated mineral water Agua mineral reforzada con gas del mismo manantial

nature abhors a vacuum la naturaleza aborrece el vacío ▪ la naturaleza tiene el horror al vacío

neap tide *(lowest tide, midway between spring tides)* marea muerte

to be **near completion** ▪ to be close to completion estar cerca de la completación ▪ estar cerca de la terminación

to **near completion of something** estar a punto de cumplir algo ➤ As the president nears completion of his fifth month in office... A medida que el presidente está a punto de cumplir cinco meses en el cargo...

Near East Oriente Próximo

to be **near the end of something** ▪ to have almost finished estar a lo último

near the end of the month ▪ late in the month ▪ toward the end of the month a finales de mes

nearby: to be sitting ~ estar sentado cerca

nearby: to be standing ~ estar de pie cerca

nearby city ▪ neighboring city cercana ciudad

nearby house casa cercana

nearby star estrella cercana

the **nearest cross street** calle más cercana que cruza ésta ▪ calle más cercana que atraviesa ésta ➤ The nearest cross street is Orense. La calle más cercana que cruza ésta es Orense.

nearest exit salida más próxima ▪ salida más cercana

nearest metro (station) ▪ closest metro station la estación de metro más cerca ▪ estación de metro más cercana ▪ metro más cerca ▪ metro más cercano ➤ The nearest metro (station) is División del Norte. ▪ The closest metro (station) is División del Norte. La estación de metro que está más cerca es División del Norte. ▪ La estación de metro más cercana es División del Norte.

nearest town pueblo más próximo ▪ pueblo más cercano

nearly half of all... ▪ close to half of all... cerca de la mitad de los...

to **need a breather** ▪ to need a breathing spell necesitar un respiro

to **need advice on** ▪ to need advice about necesitar consejo sobre ▪ *(professional advice)* necesitar asesoramiento sobre ➤ I need some advice on how to proceed. Necesito consejo sobre cómo proceder. ▪ Necesito asesoramiento sobre cómo proceder

need for necesidad de ▪ necesidad de que

to **need something** necesitar algo ▪ hacer falta

to **need the money** hacerle falta el dinero ➤ We needed the money. El dinero nos hacía falta.

to **need to get here (where I'm standing)** necesitar un poco de sitio ➤ Do you need to get here? ¿Necesitas un poco de sitio?

to be **needed to** hacer falta para ▪ necesitarse para ➤ They are needed to... Hacen falta para... ▪ Se necesitan para...

the **neediest in our society** los más necesitados de nuestra sociedad

needle-nose pliers alicates de punta

needless to say huelga decir

needlework shop tienda de confección de punto ➤ My sister had a needlework shop. Mi hermana tenía una tienda de confección de punto.

neglected streets calles descuidadas

to **negotiate a turn** tomar la curva ➤ The driver failed to negotiate the turn. El conductor falló al tomar la curva.

to **negotiate something** negociar que... ➤ The union leaders want to negotiate two breaks a day for the plant workers. Los líderes del sindicato quieren negociar que los trabajadores de planta tengan dos descansos diarios.

negotiating table mesa de negociación ▪ mesa de diálogo

negotiating team equipo negociador

the **negotiations are deadlocked** las negociaciones están en un punto muerto

neighborhood school colegio del barrio

neighboring region ▪ adjacent region región vecina ▪ región colindante

neighboring star estrella vecina

neighboring town pueblo vecino

neither can I ▪ I can't either ▪ nor can I ni yo tampoco ▪ tampoco ➤ My wife can't stand traffic jams, and neither can I. Mi esposa no puede soportar los atascos, y yo tampoco (puedo).

neither do I ▪ I don't either ▪ nor I ni yo tampoco ▪ (yo) tampoco

neither do I: and ~ ▪ and I don't either y yo tampoco ▪ y a mí tampoco ➤ Andrés doesn't like heavy metal music, and neither do I. A Andrés no le gusta el heavy metal, y a mí tampoco.

neither have I ▪ I haven't either yo tampoco

to **neither like nor dislike something** no gustarle ni disgustarle una cosa ➤ He neither liked nor disliked it. No le gustaba ni le disgustaba.

neither... nor ni... ni

neither of the two ninguno de los dos

neither of them ninguno de ellos

neither of us ninguno de nosotros

neither thing ninguna de las dos cosas ▪ ni una cosa ni la otra ➤ Neither thing will be published in that newspaper, because it only publishes what supports its line. Ninguna de las dos cosas saldrá publicada en ese periódico porque sólo publica aquello que apoya su línea. ▪ Ni una cosa ni la otra saldrá publicada en ese periódico porque sólo publica aquello que apoya su línea.

neither to affirm nor deny ▪ not to affirm or deny ▪ neither to confirm nor deny ▪ not to confirm or deny ni afirmar ni negar ▪ no afirmar o negar

neither to confirm nor deny ▪ not to confirm or deny ▪ neither to affirm nor deny ▪ not to affirm or deny ni afirmar ni negar ▪ no afirmar o negar

neon sign letrero de neón

nerves of steel nervios bien templados

to be **nervous about** estar nervioso por

nervous breakdown: to have a ~ ▪ to suffer a nervous breakdown tener un ataque de nervios ▪ tener una crisis nerviosa ▪ sufrir un ataque de nervios ▪ sufrir una crisis nerviosa

nervous tick tic nervioso

to be a **nervous wreck** estar hecho un manojo de nervios ▪ ser un manojo de nervios

to **net a good profit** ▪ to bring in a good profit dejar buena ventaja

net income ingreso(s) neto(s)

net profit beneficio(s) neto(s)

net result resultado(s) neto(s)

net weight peso neto

network layer device dispositivo de la capa de red

neural networks *las* redes neuronales

neutron star estrella de neutrones

never a dull moment: there's ~ no paramos quietos ▪ no nos aburrimos ➤ Around here there's never a dull moment. ▪ There's never a dull moment around here. Aquí no paramos quietos. ▪ Aquí no nos aburrimos.

never again! ¡nunca más!

never before ▪ never until now nunca hasta ahora ➤ Never before had astronomers seen anything like it: a bubble of water one and a half times the size of the solar system surrounding a star in formation. Nunca hasta ahora habían visto los astrónomos algo así en el universo: una burbuja de agua, de un tamaño igual a una vez y media el sistema solar, envolviendo una estrella en formación.

never before known jamás conocido antes

never before seen ▪ previously unknown ▪ unlike anything seen before jamás conocido

to **never do anything right** nunca hacer nada bien ➤ Never say to yourself, "I never do anything right." Nunca te digas a ti mismo, "Nunca hago nada bien".

never-ending process proceso sin fin ▪ proceso interminable

never-ending story ▪ cuento de nunca acabar

never ever ▪ not in a million years jamás de los jamases

never fail to do something no olvidarse nunca de hacer algo

to **never get anywhere with someone** no ir a ninguna parte con alguien ▪ no llegar a ninguna parte con alguien ➤ You're never going to get anywhere with her. Forget it! No vas a ninguna parte con ella. ¡Olvídate! ▪ No llegarás a ninguna parte con ella. ¡Olvídate!

to **never get away with it** nunca salirse alguien con la suya ➤ You'll never get away with it! ¡Nunca te saldrás con la tuya!

never give up! *(tú)* nunca te rindas ▪ *(usted)* nunca se rinda usted

to **never lose an opportunity to** no perder ocasión de

never mind! ¡déjalo! ➤ Do you know where the scissors are? Never mind, I found them. ¿Sabes dónde están las tijeras? Déjalo, las encontré.

to **never miss a thing** no pasársele nada ➤ She never misses a thing. No se le pasa nada a ella.

never say never nuncas digas de este agua no beberé

never should have done something: one ~ ▪ one should never have done something uno nunca debió hacer algo ➤ He should never have come here. Nunca debió venir aquí.

never to be heard from again no volver a oírse nada más ➤ They were never heard from again. No volvieron a oírse nada más.

never to have had it so good ▪ to have never had it so good nunca haberle ido mejor a alguien ➤ We've never had it so good. Nunca nos ha ido mejor.

never to have hurt a fly no haber matado una mosca en su vida

never to have seen anything like it nunca haber visto algo así ▪ nunca haber visto algo semejante ➤ Never before had astronomers seen anything like it in the universe: a water bubble one and a half times as large as the solar system, surrounding a star in formation. Nunca hasta ahora habían visto los astrónomos algo así en el universo: una burbuja de agua, de un tamaño igual a una vez y media el sistema solar, envolviendo una estrella en formación.

never to miss a chance to no desaprovechar ocasión para

never to miss a thing no pasársele nada ➤ She never misses a thing. No se le pasa nada a ella.
never would do something: one ~ uno nunca quiso hacer algo ➤ I never would give it to them. Nunca quise dárselo.
new artists *los, las* artistas noveles
to be **new at this game** ser novato(-a) en estos lides ➤ She's new at this game. Es novata en estos lides.
new car: (brand) ~ carro de paquete ▪ carro flamante
new development 1. recent change ▪ recent unfolding novedad ▪ cambio ▪ acontecimiento **2.** housing development nueva urbanización ➤ There's a new development in the Irish bank robbery investigation. Hay una novedad en la investigación del atraco del banco irlandés. ➤ There's a new development in cancer treatment. Hay una novedad en el tratamiento de cáncer. ➤ A new development is going up on what used to be the old fairgrounds. Hay una nueva urbanización en lo que era el viejo recinto ferial.
new issue *(of a stamp)* última emisión
new moon luna nueva
to be a **new person** ▪ to be a different person ser una persona nueva ▪ ser otra persona ➤ I'll be a new person. ▪ I'll be a different person. Seré una persona nueva. ▪ Seré otra persona.
new release nueva entrega ▪ último lanzamiento
new twist nuevo envoltorio
new wave of nueva oleada de
new ways of thinking nuevas formas de pensar
new wine vino de quema
New Year's Eve noche vieja
New Year's resolution: to make a ~ hacerse el propósito de año nuevo
the **newest of the new** ▪ the very latest lo último de lo último ▪ el último de lo último ▪ lo ultísimo
newest son-in-law: my ~ el más nuevo de mis yernos ▪ el más reciente de mis yernos
newly elected Senator senador recien elegido ▪ flamante senador(a)
news coverage ▪ coverage of the news cobertura informativa ▪ cobertura de una información
news got by me ▪ the news escaped me ▪ I didn't hear the news no me enteré de la noticia
news photographer ▪ photojournalist fotógrafo periodístico
newspaper story ▪ newspaper article artículo en el periódico
next April ▪ this April el próximo mes de abril
to be the **next best thing** ser la mejor cosa próxima
next day ▪ the next day ▪ the following day ▪ on the following day al día siguiente ▪ al otro día ▪ el otro día
next door ▪ next door to it ▪ next to it de al lado ▪ al lado ▪ pegadito
next-door neighor vecino(-a) de al lado
next floor down ▪ floor below planta inferior
next floor up ▪ floor above planta superior
to be **next (in line)** seguir ▪ tocarle ▪ *(Sp., coll.)* dar la vez ➤ Who's next? ¿Quién sigue? ▪ ¿A quién le toca? ▪ ¿Quién va? ▪ ¿Quién da la vez?
to be the **next in line 1.** *(grocery store, bank, etc.)* ser el siguiente en la fila ▪ ser el siguiente en la cola ▪ ser el siguiente en la línea ▪ ser la siguiente en la fila ▪ ser la siguiente en la cola ▪ ser la siguiente en la línea **2.** *(succession to the throne, presidency, etc.)* ser el siguiente en la línea ▪ ser la siguiente en la línea
the **next morning** ▪ the following morning a la mañana siguiente
next move: one's ~ ▪ what one will do next siguiente movimiento
the **next phase** la siguiente fase ➤ To begin the next phase... Iniciar la siguiente fase...
next question siguiente pregunta
next room ▪ adjoining room *la* habitación de al lado ▪ pieza de al lado ▪ *(in a museum)* pieza inmediata
next showing (of a movie) próximo pase (de película) ➤ Next showing 7:15 p.m. El próximo pase de película 7:15 p.m.
next step siguiente paso
the **next stop** la próxima parada ▪ *(Mex.)* la otra parada
the **next thing I knew** lo siguiente que supe
next thing you know lo siguiente que sabes
next time 1. *(past)* la siguiente vez **2.** *(future)* la próxima vez ➤ The next time I saw her La siguiente vez que la vi ➤ The next time I see her La próxima vez que yo la vea
the **next time I see you** en nuestro próximo encuentro ➤ I'll give it to you the next time I see you. Te lo doy en nuestro próximo encuentro.
the **next time one does something** la próxima vez que uno haga algo ➤ The next time you call me La próxima vez que me llames ▪ El siguiente día que me llames
next to ▪ beside junto a ▪ al lado de ▪ a continuación a ➤ The assassins drove up next to him. Los asesinos conducieron a continuación a él. ➤ The empty seat next to me El asiento vacío que hay junto a mí
next to each other: to be (right) ~ estar juntos (el uno con el otro) ▪ estar siguientes (el uno con el otro) ▪ estar pegaditos ➤ Our apartments are right next to each other. Nuestros apartamentos están juntos el uno con el otro. ▪ Nuestros apartamentos están seguidos el uno con el otro. ▪ Nuestros apartamentos están pegaditos.
to be **next to impossible** ▪ to be almost impossible ▪ to be nearly impossible ▪ to verge on the impossible estar al filo de lo imposible
next to the bottom shelf ▪ second shelf (up) from the bottom ▪ second-from-the-bottom shelf segunda repisa desde abajo ▪ segundo estante desde abajo ➤ It's on the second-from-the-bottom shelf. ▪ It's on the second shelf (up) from the bottom. Está en la segunda repisa desde abajo. ▪ Está en el segundo estante desde abajo.
next to the top shelf ▪ second shelf (down) from the top ▪ the second-from-the-top shelf segunda repisa desde arriba ▪ segundo estante desde arriba ➤ It's on the second-from-the-top shelf. ▪ It's on the second shelf (down) from the top. Está en la segunda repisa desde arriba. ▪ Está en el segundo estante desde arriba.
the **next train** el próximo tren ➤ When does the next train leave? ¿Cuándo sale el próximo tren?
next weekend ▪ this (coming) weekend el próximo fin de semana
next year el año que viene ▪ el año próximo ▪ el próximo año
nice and... ▪ good and... bien... ➤ The beer is nice and cold. ▪ The beer is good and cold. La cerveza está bien fría. ▪ La cerveza está (bien) fresquita. ➤ The coffee is nice and hot. ▪ The coffee is good and hot. El café está bien caliente. ▪ El café está (bien) calentito. *("Nice and..." and "good and..." can also be expressed by adding the diminutive "-ito" to the adjective.)*
nice and easy 1. at a relaxed pace despacito ▪ con calma **2.** carefully con cuidado ▪ *(esp. something breakable)* con cariño ➤ Play ragtime nice and easy, never fast. Toca ragtime despacito, nunca rápido. ▪ Toca ragtime con calma, nunca rápido. ➤ Open the oven door nice and easy so the cake won't fall. Abre la puerta del horno con cuidado para que el bizcocho cuaje.
to be **nice and hot** *(food)* ▪ to be good and hot estar bien caliente ▪ estar calentito
nice and smooth ▪ smooth as silk **1.** *(batter)* bien cremoso ▪ suave como la seda **2.** *(surface)* liso ▪ suave como la seda **3.** *(engine)* suave como la seda ➤ Whip the batter until it's nice and smooth. Bate bien la masa líquida hasta que quede cremosa. ➤ After applying the sealer, sand the wood until it's nice and smooth. Después de aplicar el tapaporos, lija la madera hasta que quede lisa. ▪ Después de aplicar el tapaporos, lija la madera hasta que esté suave como la seda. ➤ Now that the timing is adjusted, the engine is running nice and smooth. Ahora que hemos ajustado la sincronización, el motor va suave como la seda.
to be **nice and warm** estarse calentito ▪ estar agradable ➤ It's nice and warm in here. Se está calentito aquí. ▪ Está agradable aquí.
nice chat with someone: to have a ~ ▪ to have a pleasant chat with someone ▪ to have an enjoyable chat with someone tener una amena charla con alguien
nice city ciudad bonita ▪ ciudad acogedora
nice guy buen tipo ▪ tío majo
to be a **nice house** ser una casa bonita

to be **nice to someone** portarse bien con alguien ▪ estar simpático con alguien ➤ *(Bill Gates, to an audience of high school students)* Be nice to nerds. You'll probably end up working for one. Pórtense bien con los nerds. Probablemente acabarán trabajando para uno de ellos. ▪ *(Sp.)* Portáos bien con los empollones. Probablemente acabaréis trabajando para uno.
nice try! ¡buen intento!
nieces and nephews sobrinos
night and day: to be as different as ~ ser tan diferentes como el día y la noche ➤ They're identical twins, but they're as different as night and day. Son gemelas idénticas pero son diferentes como el día y la noche.
night before last anteanoche ▪ ante ayer por la noche ▪ antes de anoche
night is falling la noche va declinando
night of it: to have a ~ darle a uno la noche ➤ It looks like you've had quite a night of it. Parece que te ha dado la noche.
night on the town noche de juerga
night person persona vespertina
night shift turno de la noche ▪ tanda de noche
night watchman vigilante nocturno
nightclub club nocturno
nightlife ambiente nocturno ▪ marcha nocturna ▪ movida nocturna
nine times out of ten nueve veces sobre diez
to **nip it in the bud** cortarlo antes de tiempo ▪ cortarlo de raíz ➤ My headache is just starting, so I want to nip it in the bud with an aspirin. Mi dolor de cabeza está comenzando apenas, así que quiero cortarlo de raíz con una aspirina.
no buts about it ▪ no ifs, ands, or buts about it no hay pero que valga
no choice but to: to have ~ ▪ not to have any choice but to no tener más opción que
no comment sin comentarios
no doubt ▪ without a doubt sin duda (alguna) ▪ a no dudar
no doubt about it sin lugar a dudas ▪ sin ninguna duda ▪ no cabe duda
no dumping prohibido verter escombros
no easy way to: there's ~ no hay una vía fácil para ➤ There's no easy way to finish this book. No hay una vía fácil para acabar este libro.
no end por lo suyo ➤ It worried him no end. Se preocupaba por lo suyo. ➤ It bugs me no end. Me irrita lo suyo.
no hope of: to have ~ ▪ not to have any hope of ▪ to be with no hope of ▪ to be without any hope of sin esperanza alguna ➤ They were trapped in the submarine with no hope of (ever) getting out. Estuvieron atrapados en el submarino sin esperanza alguna de poder salir.
no ice, please ▪ without ice, please sin hielo, por favor
no ifs, ands, or buts ▪ no ifs, ands, or buts about it ▪ no buts about it no hay pero que valga
no, it isn't ▪ no, it's not no, no es así ▪ no, no lo es ➤ Is it true that boys don't cry?-No, it isn't. ¿Es verdad que los muchachos no lloran?-No, no lo es. ▪ ¿Es verdad que los muchachos no lloran?-No, no es así.
no kidding? ¿no fastidies? ▪ ¿en serio? ▪ ¿de veras?
no kidding! ¡no es broma! ➤ I got a little wet in the rain.-¡No kidding! Me mojé un poco en la lluvia.-¡No es broma!
no later than tomorrow mañana mismo
no less ni más ni menos ➤ *The Harvard Dictionary of Music*, and in Spanish, no less. *El diccionario de la música Harvard*, y en español, ni más ni menos.
no less so (than...) no menos (que...)
to **no longer do something** dejar de hacer algo ➤ *(news item)* Foreigners no longer head the list of people arrested for drug trafficking at Barajas. Los extranjeros dejan de encabezar la lista de detenidos por tráfico de drogas en Barajas.
no-man's-land tierra de nadie
no matter how bad por mal que ➤ No matter how bad the photos turn out... Por mal que salgan las fotos...
no matter how easy por más fácil que ➤ No matter how easy I make the exam, somebody will flunk. Por más fácil que haga el examen, alguien perderá.
no matter how hard por mucho que
no matter how hard I try por mucho que intente ▪ por más que intente ▪ por mucho que me empeñe ▪ por más que me empeñe ▪ por mucho que trate ▪ por más que trate
no matter how long it takes: to do something ~ ▪ to do something however long it takes hacer algo se tarde lo que se tarde
no matter how much ▪ however much por mucho que ▪ por más que
no matter how threatening por más amenazador que ➤ The flight instructor said that high clouds won't rain, no matter how threatening they look. El instructor de vuelo dijo que las nubes altas no dan lluvia, por más amenazadoras que parezcan.
no matter what 1. *(present)* pase lo que pase ▪ *(past)* pasara lo que pasara ▪ pasase lo que pasase **2.** *(followed by a verb phrase)* sea cuál sea... ▪ fuera cuál fuera... ▪ fuese cuál fuese...
no matter what anybody thinks ▪ no matter who doesn't like it ▪ no matter who it offends a pesar de lo que piensen los demás
no matter what happened ▪ no matter what pasara lo que pasara ▪ pasase lo que pasase ▪ a toda costa ➤ The helicopter pilot was determined to save the mountain climbers, no matter what. El piloto del helicóptero estaba decidido a salvar a los alpinistas, pasara lo que pasara.
no matter what happens ▪ no matter what pase lo que pase ▪ suceda lo que suceda
no matter what it takes: to do something ~ ▪ to do something whatever it takes ▪ to do something come hell or high water hacer algo cueste lo que cueste ▪ hacer algo contra viento y marea ▪ hacer algo por narices
no matter what the weather is haga el tiempo que haga
no matter what you buy *(tú)* compres lo que compres ▪ *(usted)* compre lo que compre
no matter where you're from *(tú)* sea de donde seas ▪ *(usted)* sea de donde sea ➤ *(telephone ad)* No matter where you're from, we speak your language. Sea de donde sea, hablamos su idioma.
no matter which one ▪ regardless of which one sea cuál sea ➤ The new Greek government, no matter which one emerges victorious from the polls El nuevo gobierno griego que surja de las urnas, sea cuál sea el ganador final
no matter who doesn't like it ▪ no matter who I offend ▪ no matter what anybody thinks pese a quien pese
no mean... no... cualquiera
to be **no mean feat** ser una gran proeza
no more than no más que ▪ *(when counting)* no más de
no new messages ningún mensaje nuevo
no one but ▪ no one except nadie salvo
no one can ▪ it is impossible no hay quien pueda
no one can beat her ▪ there's no one who can beat her ▪ nobody can beat her ▪ there's nobody who can beat her no hay quien le gane (a ella)
no one can beat him ▪ there's no one who can beat him ▪ nobody can beat him ▪ there's nobody who can beat him no hay quien le gane (a él)
no one can stop him no hay quien le pare
no one dared to... nadie se atrevía a...
no one else, not even ▪ nobody else, not even nadie más, menos aún
no one except ▪ no one but nadie salvo
no one has been more surprised at something than... nadie se sorprende tanto de algo como...
no one in his right mind ▪ nobody in his right mind nadie en su sano juicio
no one is more surprised at something than... nadie se sorprende tanto de algo como...
no one knows ▪ nobody knows nadie sabe ▪ no se sabe
no one knows what tomorrow will bring ▪ nobody knows what tomorrow will bring ▪ you never know what tomorrow will bring nadie sabe qué traerá el nuevo día ▪ nunca se sabe qué traerá el nuevo día
no one learns from others' mistakes *(Spanish saying)* nadie escarmienta en cabeza ajena

no one thought it was possible 1. no one thought it would be possible nadie pensaba que fuera posible **2.** nobody thought it was possible nadie pensó que fuera posible

no one to be found: there was ~ no había ni un alma ➤ I looked around to see who was speaking, and there was no one to be found. Miré a mi alrededor para ver quién estaba hablando, y no había ni un alma.

no one was more surprised at something than... nadie se sorprendía tanto de algo como... ➤ No one was more surprised at the outcome of the election than the candidate himself. Nadie se sorprendía tanto del resultado de las elecciones como el propio candidato.

no one with any sense ▪ nobody with any sense nadie que tenga dos dedos de frente

No One Writes to the Colonel *(Gabriel García Márquez novel)* *El coronel no tiene quien le escriba* ▪ Nadie escribe al coronel

no problem! ¡no hay ningún problema!

no question about it ▪ no question ▪ there's no question about it sin duda ▪ no hay duda

no shoes (permitted) *(swimming pool area sign)* ▪ no shoes allowed pies descalzos

no sign of ni sombra de ➤ There's no sign of him. No hay ni sombra de él.

no-smoking area ▪ non-smoking area zona no fumadores

no sooner apenas ▪ ni bien ➤ No sooner was I alone than I began to hear strange noises coming from the apartment next door. Apenas me encontré solo empecé a oír ruidos extraños que venían del piso de al lado. ▪ Ni bien me quedé solo empecé a oír ruidos extraños que venían del piso de al lado.

no sooner had I ni bien ▪ nada más ▪ ni bien hube ▪ apenas hube ▪ apenas me había ▪ en cuanto ▪ tan pronto como ➤ No sooner had I gotten off the plane than I heard my name over the P.A. Ni bien me bajé del avión, oí mi nombre por el altavoz. ▪ Nada más al bajarme del avión, oí mi nombre por el altavoz.

no sooner said than done dicho y hecho

no sooner than no antes de ➤ The shuttle has been scheduled for launch from the Kennedy Spaceport no sooner than Friday. El transbordador ha sido programado para lanzarse no antes del viernes.

no-stick ▪ non-stick anti-adherente ➤ A no-stick frying pan ▪ A non-stick frying pan Una sartén anti-adherente

no stone was left unturned no quedó piedra por mover

to be **no stranger to** no serle ajeno (algo a alguien) ➤ The guest artist is no stranger to the concert stage. Al artista invitado no le es ajeno el escenario de concierto.

no strings attached sin ataduras ▪ sin compromisos

no such luck! ni de coña ▪ ¡no caerá esa breva! ▪ no hay tanta suerte ▪ no tengo *(etc.)* tanta suerte

no talking! ¡sin hablar! ▪ *(followed by a temporal clause)* ¡no se habla...! ➤ No talking during the quiz! ¡No se habla durante la prueba!

no, there weren't *(both as the answer to a question and as a contradiction)* no, no había

no trespassing prohibido el paso

no way! ¡de ninguna manera!

no wonder! no es de extrañar (que...) ▪ es lógico (que...) ▪ no me extraña (que...) ▪ con razón...

noble savage *(in Rousseau's philosophy)* *el* buen salvaje ▪ noble salvaje

nobody can beat her ▪ no one can beat her no hay quien le gane (a ella)

nobody can beat him ▪ no one can beat him no hay quien le gane (a él)

nobody can stand to live here ▪ nobody can suffer this place nadie puede soportar vivir aquí ▪ aquí no hay quien viva

nobody does anything about it nadie hace nada al respecto ▪ al respecto nadie hace nada ▪ al respecto no hace nadie nada

nobody else, not even ▪ no one else, not even nadie más, menos aún

nobody gets hurt no les pasa nada

nobody in his right mind ▪ no one in his right mind nadie en su sano juicio ▪ ninguno en su sano juicio ➤ Nobody in his right mind takes thirteen hours of graduate courses at once. Nadie en su sano juicio cursaría trece horas de cursos de posgrado de golpe.

nobody is safe nadie está a salvo ▪ ni la reina se salva ▪ no se salva ni la reina

nobody knows ▪ no one knows no se sabe ▪ nadie sabe ▪ ninguno sabe

nobody thought (that)... nadie pensaba que... ▪ ninguno pensaba que... ▪ no se pensaba que...

nobody was around ▪ there was nobody around no había nadie

nobody was home nadie estaba en casa ➤ I went to the house, but nobody was home. Fui a la casa, pero nadie estaba. ▪ Fui a la casa, pero no estaba nadie. ➤ I called, but nobody was home. Llamé, pero nadie estaba en casa.

nobody was there ▪ there was nobody there no había nadie allí ▪ no estaba nadie

nobody with a grain of sense nadie que tenga dos dedos de frente

nobody's perfect nadie es perfecto ▪ el mejor escribano echa un borrón

to **nod to someone** ▪ to nod at someone **1.** *(to give the go-ahead)* hacerle una seña a alguien con la cabeza **2.** *(in agreement)* asentir a alguien con la cabeza **3.** *(formally, in homage)* hacerle una venia a alguien ➤ The conductor nodded to the trombonist. El director (de la orquesta) le hizo una seña con la cabeza al trombonista. ➤ I nodded at her. Le hice una seña con la cabeza.

to **nod (one's head) in agreement** asentir con la cabeza

noise pollution contaminación acústica

noisy street calle ruidosa ▪ calle bulliciosa ▪ calle bullanguera

nomadic hunters ▪ wandering hunters ▪ itinerant hunters cazadores errantes

non-profit organization ▪ non-profit association asociación no lucrativa ▪ asociación sin ánimo de lucro

non-reflecting glass *(used in picture frames, etc.)* vidrio antireflejo

non-refundable ticket *el* billete no reembolsable

non sequitur ▪ conclusion that does not follow from the premises conclusión ilógica ▪ incongruencia

non-stick coating capa anti-adherente

non-stick frying pan *la* sartén anti-adherente ▪ *(Ven., Chi., Nic.)* *el* sartén anti-adherente

non-stop argument *la* discusión sin descanso

none of that nada de eso

to be **none other than...** no ser otro que...

none that I liked ▪ not any that I liked nada que me gustara ▪ nada que me gustase ➤ I shopped for a sofa today, but I saw none that I like. ▪ I shopped for a sofa today, but I didn't see any that I liked. ▪ I shopped for a sofa today, but I didn't see one that I liked. Fui a comprar un sofá hoy, pero no vi ninguno que me gustara. ▪ Fui a comprar un sofá hoy, pero no vi ninguno que me gustase.

none too soon ▪ not any too soon ▪ in the nick of time justo a tiempo ▪ por los pelos ▪ en buena hora ➤ I took the soft drinks out of the freezer none too soon. Saqué las bebidas con gas del congelador justo a tiempo. ▪ Saqué las bebidas con gas del congelador por los pelos.

nonsense! ¡tonterías!

nonsense: to be full of (one's usual) ~ estar lleno de tonterías ▪ hablar el buey y decir mu ➤ He was full of (his usual) nonsense. Estaba lleno de sus tonterías. ▪ Habló el buey y dijo mu.

nonviolence la no violencia

nooks and crannies: to have a lot of ~ tener muchos recovecos

noon: (twelve) ~ ▪ midday mediodía ▪ *(Sp.)* las doce del mediodía

noooo! ▪ come on! ▪ get real! ▪ you're pulling my leg! ¡venga ya! ▪ ¡no me vaciles!

nor do I intend to ni tengo la intención ▪ y no tengo tampoco la intención

nor do I want to ni quiero hacerlo

nor do I want to hear it ni quiero oírlo

nor do I want to see her ni la quiero ver ▪ ni quiero verla

nor do I want to see him ni lo quiero ver ▪ ni quiero verlo ▪ *(Sp., leísmo)* ni le quiero ver ▪ ni quiero verle

nor do I want to see it ni lo quiero ver ▪ ni quiero verlo ▪ ni la quiero ver ▪ ni quiero verla

nor even sino tampoco

to be **normal for one's age** ser propio de la edad de uno ➤ The doctor said (his) thumbsucking was normal for his age. El médico dijo que su costumbre de chuparse el dedo era propio de su edad.

normal range: to be in the ~ estar en el rango normal ➤ The doctor said his blood pressure is in the normal range. El médico dijo que su presión sanguínea estaba en el rango normal.

normal self: to be one's ~ ser su ser normal

north pole polo norte

north side of the building cara norte del edificio

north side of the street lado norte de la calle

North Star ▪ Polaris ▪ pole star estrella polar

north wind *el* alquilón ▪ *(in Aragón and Navarra, Spain)* cierzo

northern Europe Europa del Norte ▪ Europa septentrional

northern exposure cara norte ➤ I want an apartment with a northern exposure so that it won't get direct sunlight. Deseo un apartamento en la cara norte para no recibir la luz del sol directamente.

northern hemisphere hemisferio norte ▪ hemisferio septentrional

northern lights ▪ aurora borealis ▪ aurora polaris aurora boreal

nose of an airplane morro de un avión

nose out of joint: to get one's ~ ▪ to get mad subírsele un tufo a las narices

nose wheel (of an airplane) rueda delantera *("Rueda delantera" can also refer to the front wheel of a tricycle.)*

not a bit ▪ not at all ▪ not in the least nada ▪ para nada ▪ ni un pelo ▪ ni un ápice ▪ ni pizca ▪ ni por sombra ➤ I'm not a bit interested. ➤ You haven't changed a bit. ▪ You haven't changed at all. No has cambiado (en) nada. ▪ No has cambiado ni un pelo.

not a day goes by that... ▪ not a day passes that... no pasa un día en que...

not a day goes by without... ▪ not a day passes without... no pasa un día sin...

not a few no pocos ➤ *(news item)* The United States yesterday observed Halloween, the day children and not a few adults dress up as monsters, clowns, witches, and scarecrows. Ayer los Estados Unidos observó Halloween, el día en el que los niños, y no pocos adultos, se visten como monstruos, payosos, brujas y espantapájaros.

not a peep out of ni pío ➤ There wasn't a peep out of him. No dijo ni pío. ➤ We didn't hear a peep out of him. No oímos ni pío de él.

not a single one ni uno(-a)

not a very good idea idea no muy acertada ➤ It was not a very good idea. No fue una idea muy acertada.

not a week goes by that... no pasa una semana en que...

not a week goes by that I don't (do something) no pasa una semana sin que yo no (haga algo)

to be **not above doing something** ▪ not to be beneath one to do something no caérsele a uno los anillos ➤ Jimmy Carter, though a former president, is not above working as a carpenter. ▪ Although he is a former president, it is not beneath Jimmy Carter to work as a carpenter. A Jimmy Carter, a pesar de ser un ex-presidente, no se le cae los anillos trabajando de carpintero.

not anymore ya no

not as... ▪ not so... no tan... ➤ Weather forecasting is not as inaccurate as it used to be. ▪ Weather forecasting is not so inaccurate as it used to be. Pronosticar el tiempo no es tan impreciso como solía ser. *("Not as" was once considered ungrammatical, the correct form being "not so," which is still preferable in formal writing.)*

not as bad as it appears to be: it's ~ ▪ it's not so bad as it appears to be no es tan malo de lo que parece ▪ es mejor de lo que parece

not at all ▪ not in the least en absoluto ▪ no, en absoluto ▪ nada ▪ ¡qué va!

to be **not at all fond of** ▪ not to be at all fond of ser poco amigo de ▪ ser poco fanático de ➤ He's not at all fond of cooking. Es poco amigo de cocinar. ▪ Es poco fanático de cocinar.

to be **not at all well** no encontrarse nada bien ➤ She's not at all well. No se encuentra nada bien.

not bad! ¡no está mal!

not by a long shot ni con mucho

not completely no del todo

not counting ▪ excluding sin contar

not either one ▪ neither one ninguno de los dos ▪ ni el uno ni el otro ▪ ni cualquiera de los dos ➤ We can't afford either condominium. No podemos afrontar ninguno de los dos apartamentos. ▪ No podemos afrontar ni el uno ni el otro.

not even ni siquiera ▪ ni aun ➤ Nothing else, not even... Nada más, ni siquiera... ▪ Nada más, ni aun... ➤ Nobody else, not even... ▪ No one else, not even... Nadie más, ni siquiera... ▪ Nadie más, ni aun...

not even...? ¿ni siquiera...?

not even if I wanted to ni aunque quisiera ▪ ni siquiera lo piense

not even remotely ni remotamente

not even to have time to ni siquiera tener tiempo para ▪ *(Sp.)* ni siquiera darle a uno tiempo para

not far away ▪ a short distance away no muy lejos de aquí

not for nothing no por nada ▪ por algo

not for nothing do they say (that)... ▪ it's not for nothing that they say that... ▪ it's for good reason that they say (that)... no se dice por nada que... ▪ bien se dice que...

not good enough for: that's ~ no es (lo) suficientemente bueno para ▪ no le satisface ▪ no le llega ▪ no le llena ▪ *(Sp., slang)* no le mola

to be **not here** no estar ▪ *(in an office)* no encontrarse ➤ She isn't here. ▪ She's not here. (Ella) no está. ▪ (Ella) no se encuentra.

not here! ▪ this is not the right place ¡aquí, no!

not I yo no

not in a million years ▪ never ever jamás de los jamases

not in one's wildest dreams ni en sueños

not in the least 1. not in the slightest ▪ not at all no en lo más mínimo ▪ *(Sp.)* ni por el forro ▪ ni por el toro **2.** heck, no! ¡qué va!

not in the slightest 1. not in the least ▪ not at all ni por el forro ▪ ni por el toro **2.** heck, no! ¡qué va!

not long no mucho (tiempo) ➤ How long have you been waiting?-Not long. ¿Cuánto tiempo has estado esperando?-No mucho.

not long afterwards no mucho después

not long ago no hace mucho

not me a mí no ▪ *(coll.)* yo no

not meant to...: it's ~ no es para...

not much poca cosa ➤ What's going on?-Not much. ¿Qué pasa?-Poca cosa. ➤ What's new?-Not much. ¿Qué hay de nuevo?-Poca cosa.

not much choice but to...: there's ~ ▪ there's not much choice other than to... no haber más opción (que...) ▪ no haber más alternativa (que...) ➤ There's not much choice but to finish what we have started. No hay más alternativa que terminar lo que hemos empezado. ▪ No hay más opción que terminar lo que hemos empezado.

not necessarily no necesariamente ▪ no forzosamente ▪ no tiene por qué (ser así)

not on your life! ¡cualquier día! ▪ ¡ni por ensueño! ▪ ¡jamás de los jamases!

not only have I not... no sólo no he... ➤ Not only have I not heard the expression, (but) it is not found in any of my dictionaries. ▪ Not only have I not heard the expression, but neither is it found in any of my dictionaries. No sólo no he oído la expresión, sino que no viene en ninguno de mis diccionarios.

to be **not quite as far as** estar un poco menos lejos de ▪ quedar un poco menos lejos de ➤ By applying the law of sines to his visual observations, Copernicus determined that Venus is not quite three-fourths as far from the sun as the Earth is. Al aplicar la ley de senos a sus observaciones visuales, Copérnico determinó que Venus queda a un poco menos de tres cuartos de la distancia que hay entre el sol y la Tierra.

to be **not quite as long as** *("not quite" is untranslatable)* ▪ to be not quite so long as ser un poquito más corto que ➤ This route is not quite as long as the other. Esta ruta es un poquito más corta que la otra. ➤ The Beethoven fourth piano concerto is not quite as long as the fifth. El cuarto concierto de Beethoven es un poquito más corto que el quinto.

not quite as many people ▪ not quite so many people un poco menos de gente ➤ There were not quite as many people at the party this year as last. No había tanta gente en la fiesta este año como el año pasado. ▪ Había un poco menos de gente en la fiesta este año que el año pasado.

not since nunca desde

not so fast! ¡no tan deprisa!

not that! ¡eso no!

not that I know of no que yo sepa ▪ que yo sepa, no

not that it makes any difference ▪ not that it changes anything no es que importe ▪ no es que cambie las cosas

not that much no tanto ➤ I didn't want that much. No quería tanto.

not this one, but that one no éste, sino ése ▪ no ésta, sino ésa

not this time esta vez, no

not to agree with someone **1.** no estar de acuerdo con alguien **2.** no ir con alguien ➤ Strong cheeses don't agree with me. Los quesos fuertes no van conmigo.

not to amount to a hill of beans ser de poca valía ▪ ser de poca monta ➤ That's doesn't amount to a hill of beans. Eso es de poca monta.

not to appreciate how... no valorar lo... ➤ She doesn't appreciate how hard he works. No valora lo duro que trabaja.

not to bat an eye no mover (ni una) pestaña ▪ quedarse tan pimpante ▪ quedarse tan ancho ▪ estar tan ancho ▪ quedarse tan campante ▪ estar tan campante ▪ quedarse tan tranquilo ▪ estar tan tranquilo ▪ quedarse tan pancho ▪ estar tan pancho ▪ estar tan pimpante ▪ no movérsele (ni) un músculo de la cara ▪ no movérsele (ni) un pelo ▪ *(Madrid)* quedarse tan pichi ▪ estar tan pichi ➤ He didn't bat an eye. Ni se inmutó. ▪ Se quedó tan pimpante. ▪ Se quedó tan ancho. ▪ Estaba tan ancho. ▪ No se le movió (ni) un músculo de la cara.

not to be able to do more than ▪ to be able to only no poder hacer más que ▪ no poder más que

not to be able to get (anywhere) near no poder (ni) acercarse a ➤ Some people can't get anywhere near peanuts or perfume. Hay gente que no puede (ni) acercarse a los cacahuetes ni al perfume.

not to be able to help **1.** *(literal)* to be unable to give assistance no poder ayudar **2.** *(figurative)* not to be able to avoid... no poder evitar... ▪ no poder menos que... ➤ I can't help thinking that he was hiding something. No pude evitar pensar que él ocultaba algo. ▪ No pude menos que pensar que él ocultaba algo.

not to be able to cope no dar abasto ➤ We (just) can't cope. Es que no damos abasto.

not to be able to cope with a situation no dar abasto con algo ▪ no poder con algo ▪ no poder más ➤ The hospitals couldn't cope with so many injured people. Los hospitales no daban abasto con tantos heridos. ➤ I can't cope (anymore). No puedo más.

not to be able to deal with something **1.** *(practical situation)* no dar abasto con algo ▪ no poder con algo **2.** *(emotional crisis)* no poder superar algo ➤ I can't deal with all this paperwork. No doy abasto con todo este papeleo. ▪ No puedo con todo este papeleo. ➤ We can't deal with all these orders. No damos abasto con tantos pedidos. ➤ He can't deal with his wife's death. No puede superar la muerte de su esposa.

not to be able to decide whether to dudar si

not to be able to figure out something ▪ not to be able to figure something out ▪ not to be able to solve something no poder con algo (complicado) ▪ no poder resolver algo (complicado) ➤ I can't figure out these equations. ▪ I can't figure these equations out. ▪ I can't solve these equations. No puedo con estas ecuaciones. ▪ No puedo resolver estas ecuaciones. ➤ I can't figure them out. ▪ I can't solve them. No puedo con ellas.

not to (be able to) fit in a space with someone no caber con alguien en un espacio

not to be able to get a word in edgewise no poder meter baza ➤ I couldn't get a word in edgewise. No pude meter baza.

not to be able to go on no poder más ➤ I can't go on. No puedo más.

not to be able to hear someone at all no oírle a alguien de pijo ➤ We can't hear you at all. No le oímos a usted de pijo.

not to be able to help no poder menos de

not to be able to hold a candle to someone ▪ not be nearly as good at something as someone else ▪ not to be able to compare with someone no llegarle ni a los talones de alguien ▪ *(Peru, slang)* no llegarle ni al ombligo do alguien ➤ As a pianist, he can't hold a candle to Claudio Arrau. Como pianista no le llega ni a los talones a Claudio Arrau.

not to be able to hold one's liquor tener mal vino

not to be able to hurt a flea no ser capaz de matar una mosca ➤ He couldn't hurt a flea. No es capaz de matar una mosca.

not to be able to make up one's mind no poder decidir ▪ no saber qué decisión tomar ▪ no saber qué decidir

not to be able to see no poder ver ➤ After his bicycle accident, José Manuel couldn't see for several hours. Después de su accidente de bicicleta, José Manuel no pudo ver durante varias horas.

not to be able to stand someone no poder ver a alguien ▪ no aguantar a alguien ▪ no soportar a alguien ▪ no tolerar a alguien ➤ I couldn't stand him. No podía verlo. ▪ *(Sp., leísmo)* No podía verle. ➤ I couldn't stand her. No podía verla. ➤ We couldn't stand each other. No podíamos vernos. ➤ They couldn't stand each other. No podían verse.

not to be able to stand something ▪ not to be able to tolerate something ▪ not to be able to endure something no poder con algo (insoportable) ➤ I can't stand trash TV. No puedo con la telebasura. ▪ No tolero la telebasura. ▪ No aguanto la telebasura. ▪ No soporto la telebasura.

not to be able to stand something boring ▪ not to be able to endure something boring no soportar algo ▪ no poder con algo (aburrido) ➤ I can't stand boring staff meetings. No soporto las reuniones de personal aburridas.

not to be able to stand the curiosity any longer no aguantar más la curiosidad ➤ She couldn't stand the curiosity any longer. ▪ Her curiosity got the best of her. Ella no aguantó más la curiosidad.

not to be able to stand the sight of someone no poder verlo(-a) a alguien ni en pintura ➤ I couldn't stand him. No podía verlo ni en pintura. ▪ No podía verla ni en pintura. ▪ *(Sp., leísmo)* No podía verle ni en pintura.

not to be able to stomach someone ▪ not to be able to stand someone atragantársele a alguien ➤ I can't stomach him. Se me atraganta (él).

not to be able to stomach... ▪ not to be able to stand... no tragar... ▪ no pasar... ➤ I can't stomach it. No lo trago. ▪ No lo paso.

not to be able to stop someone from it no poder impedírselo a alguien

not to be able to tell the difference no apreciarse la diferencia

not to be able to understand anything someone says no entender nada de lo que dice alguien ▪ no entendérsele nada a alguien ➤ I can't understand anything she says. No entiendo nada de lo que (ella) dice. ➤ You can't understand anything she says. No se le entiende nada de lo que dice (ella).

not to be afraid of anybody no ahorrárselas con nadie ▪ no ahorrar con nadie

not to be alone ▪ not to be the only one ▪ not to be unique no encontrarse solo ▪ no estar solo ▪ no ser el único ➤ *(news item)* The black hole in the center of the Milky Way is not alone. ▪ The black hole in the center of the Milky Way is not the only one. ▪ The black hole in the center of the Milky Way is not unique. El agujero negro en la Vía Láctea no se encuentra solo.

not to be all it's cracked up to be *(coll.)* ▪ not to be all that it's claimed to be ▪ not to be all that it's reputed to be no ser todo lo que se dice que es

not to be anything alike ▪ to be nothing alike ▪ to be as different as night and day no parecerse en nada ▪ ser totalmente diferentes ▪ ser totalmente distintos ▪ parecerse en el blanco de los ojos y en el blanco de los dientes

not to be anything special ▪ to be nothing special ▪ not to be anything to write home about no ser nada especial ▪ no ser nada del otro mundo ▪ no ser nada del otro jueves

not to be anything to write home about ▪ to be nothing to write home about ▪ not to be anything special ▪ to be nothing special no ser nada del otro jueves ▪ no ser nada del otro mundo ▪ no ser nada especial

not to be at all fond of ser poco amigo de ➤ He's not at all fond of cooking. Es poco amigo de cocinar.

not to be at liberty to do something no estar autorizado a hacer algo ▪ no tener autorización para hacer algo ➤ I'm not at liberty to tell you. No estoy autorizado a decirte. ▪ No tengo autorización para decirte.

not to be bad at something no ser malo en algo ▪ no ser malo para algo ▪ *(Sp.)* no dársele mal ➤ He's not bad at it. No es malo en eso. ▪ No se le da mal. ➤ He's not bad at math. No es malo en (las) matemáticas. ▪ No es malo para las matemáticas. ▪ No se le da mal la matemática.

not to be beneath someone to do something ▪ not to be above doing something no caérsele los anillos haciendo algo ➤ It is not beneath Jimmy Carter, though a former president, to work as a carpenter. ▪ Though a former president, Jimmy Carter is not above working as a carpenter. A Jimmy Carter, a pesar de ser un ex-presidente, no se le cae los anillos trabajando de carpintero.

not to be big enough for quedarse pequeño en ➤ *(headline)* The Almudena Cathedral was not big enough for the funeral. La catedral de la Almudena se quedó pequeña en el funeral.

not to be born yesterday no nacer ayer ▪ no caerse de un guindo ➤ I wasn't born yesterday. No nací ayer. ▪ No me he caído de un guindo.

not to be doing very well no andar muy bien ➤ My grandmother is not (doing) very well. Mi abuela no anda muy bien.

not to be hard to figure out that... ▪ not to be difficult to figure out that... no resultarle difícil colegir que... ➤ It wasn't hard (for me) to figure out that... No me resultó difícil colegir que... ➤ It wasn't hard (for her) to figure out that... No le resultó difícil (a ella) colegir que... ➤ It wasn't hard (for him) to figure out that... No le resultó difícil (a él) colegir que...

not to be here yet aún no haber llegado ▪ no haber llegado todavía ▪ todavía no haber llegado ➤ He's not here yet. (Él) aún no ha llegado. ▪ No ha llegado todavía. ▪ Todavía no ha llegado.

not to be hungry no tener hambre ▪ tener poca hambre ➤ I wasn't very hungry. No tenía mucha hambre. ▪ Tenía poca hambre.

not to be in any hurry ▪ to be in no hurry no tener prisa

not to be in one's right mind no estar en sus cabales

not to be in the mood for fun and games ▪ to be in no mood for fun and games no estar para fiestas

not to be in the mood to... no tener humor para...

not to be introduced to someone quedarse en la luna de Valencia ➤ My friend talked to her friend for 10 minutes and didn't introduce me. Mi amiga habló con su amiga durante diez minutos, y me quedé en la luna de Valencia.

not to be one of one's virtues entre sus virtudes no contarse

not to be one's cup of tea 1. *(person)* no ser santo(-a) de la devoción de uno ▪ no irle **2.** *(things)* no ser lo suyo ▪ no cuadrarle a uno ▪ *(Sp.)* no irle a uno ➤ She's not my cup of tea. No es santa de mi devoción. ➤ Heavy metal music is not my cup of tea. El heavy metal no es lo mío. ▪ El heavy metal no me cuadra. ▪ El heavy metal no me va.

not to be one's fault no ser la culpa de uno

not to be outdone para no ser menos

not to be self-conscious no tener pelos en la lengua

not to be sneezed at ▪ not to be taken lightly no tomarse a la ligera

not to be so lucky tener menos suerte ➤ He wasn't so lucky. Tuvo menos suerte.

not to be suitable for no ser apto para ▪ no ser apropiado para ➤ *(toy label)* Not suitable for children under thirty-six months No aptos para menores de treinta y seis meses

not to be sure what is happening ▪ not to be sure what is going on no saber muy bien lo que pasa ➤ The commuters are not sure what is happening. Los viajeros no saben muy bien lo que pasa. ➤ The commuters were not sure what was happening. Los viajeros no sabían muy bien lo que pasaba.

not to be taken lightly ▪ not to be sneezed at no tomarse a la ligera

not to be the brightest person in the world no haber inventado la pólvora

not to be the only one 1. *(who has done something)* no sólo uno lo hace **2.** *(that something has happened to)* no pasarle sólo a uno ➤ He's not the only one. No sólo él lo hace. ▪ No sólo a él le pasa.

not to be to one's liking no ser del agrado de uno

not to be too bright ▪ not to be very bright ser poco brillante

not to be very bright ▪ not to be too bright ser poco brillante

not to be what one had in mind no ser lo que uno buscaba ▪ no ser lo que uno esperaba

not to be worth anything ▪ to be worthless ▪ to be worth nothing no valer nada ▪ *(slang)* ser de pacotilla

not to be worth the paper it's written on ser papel mojado

not to belong there ▪ not to go there no ir ahí

not to bother about something no preocuparse por algo ▪ no molestarse con algo ▪ no tomarse molestias con algo ➤ Don't bother about it at all, I'll take care of it. No te preocupes por eso. Ya cuidaré yo de ello. ▪ No te molestes con eso. Ya cuidaré yo de ello. ▪ No te tomes la molestia con eso. Ya cuidaré yo de ello.

not to brag, but... ▪ not to blow my own horn, but... no es por tirarme flores, pero...

not to budge ▪ not to move no alterarse ➤ The children didn't budge. Los niños no se alteraron.

not to budge an inch 1. *(figurative)* ni inmutarse ▪ no alterarse **2.** *(literal)* no ceder un ápice ➤ The boy didn't budge an inch. El muchacho ni se inmutó. ▪ El muchacho no se alteró. ➤ The government didn't budge an inch. El gobierno no cedió un ápice.

not to care for someone *(euphemism)* ▪ not to like someone no caerle bien a uno ➤ I don't care for him. No me cae bien.

not to change a bit no cambiar nada ➤ When I went back to Guatemala City, all my friends said I hadn't changed a bit. Cuando volví a la Ciudad de Guatemala, todos mis amigos decían que yo no había cambiado nada.

not to count no valer nada ▪ no valer (para nada) ▪ no contar nada ▪ no contar (para nada) ➤ *(Bill Clinton)* No American can ever again say: my vote doesn't count. Ningún americano podrá decir jamás: mi voto no vale nada. ➤ They treat me as if I don't count. Me tratan como si yo no contara (para nada).

not to count for much no suponer mucho

not to cut it no correr ▪ no colar ➤ That exuse doesn't cut it. Esa excusa no corre. ▪ *(Sp.)* Esa excusa no cuela.

not to deny one's origins ▪ not to forget where one came from no negar la cruz de su parroquia

not to do a lick of work ▪ not to lift a finger no dar ni clavo ▪ no dar ni chapa ▪ no dar ni golpe

not to do any good ▪ to be useless no servir de nada ▪ no ser útil ▪ ser inútil ➤ The president campaigned for the senator, but it didn't do any good because the candidate lost overwhelmingly. El presidente hizo campaña a favor del senador, pero no le sirvió de nada porque el candidato perdió estrepitosamente. ➤ I reminded him, but it didn't do any good. Se lo recordé, pero fue inútil.

not to do anything at all no hacer nada en absoluto ➤ I couldn't do anything at all. No pude hacer nada en absoluto.

not to do anything but work ▪ to do nothing but work no hacer nada más que trabajar ➤ I don't do anything but work. ▪ I do nothing but work. No hago nada más que trabajar.

not to do anything right no hacer nada bien ▪ no dar pie con bola

not to do anything to deserve it no hacer nada para merecerlo

not to do justice to someone ▪ not to do someone justice no hacer justicia a alguien ➤ The driver's license photo doesn't do her justice. La foto de la carnet de conducir no le hace justicia a ella.

not to do justice to something ▪ not to do something justice no hacer justicia a algo ➤ The movie doesn't do the book justice. ▪ The movie doesn't do justice to the book. La película no hace justicia al libro. ➤ The movie doesn't do it justice. La película no le hace justicia.

not to do something: one is ~ no haber de hacer una cosa

not to dredge up the past dejar que el pasado permanezca enterrado

not to eat a bite all day no probar bocado durante todo el día

not to even... ni siquiera... ➤ I don't even think they'll ask that. Ni siquiera creo que pregunten eso.

not to even bat an eye ▪ not to so much as bat an eye ni inmutarse

not to expect anything less of someone ▪ to expect nothing less of someone no esperar menos de alguien

not to faze someone ▪ not to have the slightest effect on someone ▪ to have no effect on someone no hacer mella a alguien

not to find any trace of ▪ to find no trace of no encontrar rasgo de

not to fit 1. not to be the right size for one no quedarle bien a alguien ▪ no valerle bien a alguien **2.** not to go in no entrar **3.** to be too big for the space no caber en el espacio ➤ This jacket doesn't fit (me) anymore. Esta chaqueta ya no me queda bien. ▪ Esta chaqueta ya no me vale bien. ➤ This key doesn't fit. Esta llave no entra. ➤ This box doesn't fit in the suitcase. ▪ This box won't fit in the suitcase. Esta caja no cabe en la maleta. ➤ These shoes don't fit (me). Estos zapatos no me quedan.

not to forget where one came from ▪ not to deny one's origins no negar la cruz de su parroquia

not to gain anything by doing something ▪ not to get anywhere by doing something no ganar nada con hacer algo

not to get a moment's rest no tener (ni) un momento de respiro ▪ no tener (ni) un momento de descanso ▪ no darle cuartel ▪ no darle tregua ➤ The terrorists are not going to get a moment's rest. Los terroristas no tendrán (ni) un momento de respiro. ▪ Los terroristas no tendrán (ni) un momento de descanso. ▪ No vamos a darle cuartel a los terroristas. ▪ No vamos a darle tregua a los terroristas.

not to get along no llevarse bien ▪ llevarse mal ➤ They don't get along. No se llevan bien. ▪ Se llevan mal.

not to get anywhere ▪ to get nowhere no conseguir nada de ▪ no comerse una rosca con ➤ He went to the dean, but he didn't get anywhere. Fue al decano, pero no consiguió nada.

not to get anywhere by doing something ▪ not to gain anything by doing something no ganar nada con hacer algo

not to get enough sleep dormir menos de lo necesario ▪ no dormir suficiente ➤ *(news item)* Young people don't get enough sleep. Los jóvenes duermen menos de lo necesario. ▪ Los jóvenes no duermen suficiente.

not to "get it" ▪ not to see the big picture no saber qué se cuece ▪ no saber de qué va la vaina ▪ no saber por dónde van los tiros

not to get to do what one wanted no llegar a hacer lo que uno quería

not to get very far no llegar muy lejos ▪ no avanzar mucho

not to give a damn about *(coarse)* no importarle a alguien un bledo de

not to give a (flying) fuck *(off-color)* no importarle un carajo a uno ▪ pasarse por el forro ▪ pasarse por el arco de triunfo ▪ pasarse por el coño (de la tía Bernarda) ➤ I don't give a (flying) fuck what he thinks. Su opinión me la paso por el forro. ▪ Su opinión me la paso por el arco de triunfo. ▪ Me paso lo que él dice por el arco del triunfo. ▪ Me paso lo que él dice por el forro.

not to give a shit *(off-color)* no importarle una mierda a uno ➤ They don't give a shit. No les importa una mierda.

not to give someone the time of day no sacarle ni la hora a alguien ➤ That guy won't give you the time of day. A ése no le sacas ni la hora.

not to give way to no dejarse ganar por

not to go along with something no irla con algo

not to go anywhere without someone no dar un paso sin alguien

not to go back very far *(a history)* ▪ to be short durar (muy) poco

not to go far enough no abarcar lo suficiente ▪ no cubrir lo necesario ➤ Some people think the health care reform bill does not go far enough, and others think it goes too far. Algunas personas piensan que el nuevo proyecto de ley de salubridad no abarca lo suficiente, y otras piensan que abarca demasiado.

not to go there ▪ not to belong there no ir ahí

not to go together (at all) *(clothes, colors)* ▪ not to match ▪ to clash hacer mal juego ▪ no hacer juego ▪ no pegar ni con cola

not to go (well) with ▪ not to look good with no pegar con ▪ no combinar con ▪ no quedar bien con ➤ The tie doesn't go with the shirt. ▪ The tie doesn't look good with the shirt. La corbata no queda bien con la camisa.

not to have a cent to one's name ▪ not to have two pennies to rub together no tener un céntimo

not to have a chance no tener la más mínima posibilidad ➤ He doesn't have a chance. No tiene la más mínima posibilidad.

not to have a clue no tener la menor idea ▪ no tener la más mínima idea ▪ no tener la más remota idea ▪ no saber por dónde se anda

not to have a moment's rest no tener ni un minuto de respiro

not to have a pot to piss in *(coarse)* ▪ to be dirt poor no tener donde caerse muerto ▪ no tener ni para pipas ▪ no tener ni para tirar petardos ▪ ser paupérrimo

not to have any alternative ▪ to have no alternative no tener alternativa

not to have any appetite ▪ to have no appetite ▪ not to have an appetite estar sin apetito ▪ estar desganado

not to have any broken bones no tener hueso roto

not to have any choice ▪ to have no choice ▪ not to have much choice no tener elección ▪ no tener alternativa

not to have any choice but to ▪ to have no alternative but to no tener más remedio que

not to have any ethics ▪ to have no ethics no tener la ética

not to have any idea of what is coming ▪ not to have any idea of what one is in for ▪ to have no idea of what is coming ▪ to have no idea of what one is in for no tener ni barrunto de lo que se le viene encima

not to have any intention of ▪ to have no intention of no tener ninguna intención de

not to have any place to stay quedarse a la luna de Valencia

not to have any proof that... ▪ to have no proof that... no tener ninguna prueba de que...

not to have any say in the matter ▪ to have no say in the matter no tener ni voz ni voto en el asunto

not to have anyone to turn to ▪ to have no one to turn to ▪ not to have anyone else to turn to no tener a quien acudir ➤ I didn't have anyone to turn to. No tenía a quien acudir.

not to have anything better to do ▪ to have nothing better to do ▪ not to have got anything better to do no tener nada mejor que hacer

not to have anything planned no haber hecho ningún tipo de plan ➤ I don't have anything planned that day. No he hecho ningún tipo de plan ese día.

not to have anything to be ashamed of ▪ to have nothing to be ashamed of no tener por qué bajar la cabeza delante nadie ▪ no tener por qué agachar la cabeza delante nadie ➤ You don't have anything to be ashamed of. No tienes por qué bajar la cabeza delante de nadie.

not to have anything to do with something ▪ to have nothing to do with something no tener nada que ver con algo ▪ no atañerle a alguien ▪ pasar de

not to have anything to lose ▪ to have nothing to lose no tener nada que perder

not to have anything to say about a matter ▪ to have nothing to say about a matter no tener nada que decir sobre un asunto ▪ no tener nada que opinar sobre un asunto

not to have anything to worry about ▪ to have nothing to worry about no tener de qué preocuparse ▪ no tener nada de qué preocuparse

not to have anywhere to turn ▪ to have nowhere to turn no tener a donde acudir

not to have been to a place (before) no conocer un lugar ➤ We hadn't been to either place (before). No conocíamos ninguno de los dos lugares.

not to have changed a bit ▪ not to have changed at all no haber cambiado nada ▪ no haber cambiado ni un pelo ▪ no haber cambiado ni un poquito

not to have done a lick of work no haber dado golpe

not to have done something since no hacer una cosa desde ▪ no hacer una cosa desde hace ➤ California had not suffered blackouts since the Second World War. California no sufría cortes de luz desde la Segunda Guerra Mundial.

not to have even 1. not to possess even... no tener siquiera... **2.** *(as the auxiliary)* no haber ni siquiera...

not to have had a bite to eat all day no haber pasado bocado en todo el día ▪ no haber probado bocado en todo el día

not to have much choice (but to...) no tener más alternativa (que...) ▪ no tener más opción (que...) ➤ He doesn't have much choice but to... No tiene más alternativa que...

not to have much time ▪ to be short of time ▪ to be short on time no andar bien de tiempo

not to have much to lose ▪ to have little to lose tener poco que perder

not to have ruled out seguir sin descartar

not to have seen anything like it no haber visto nada igual ➤ The doctors have not seen anything like it. Los médicos no han visto nada igual.

not to have shit for sense *(off-color)* ▪ not to have shit for brains ▪ not to have a grain of sense tener mierda en la cabeza ▪ pensar con el culo ▪ *(benign alternative)* pensar con los pies ➤ That guy doesn't have shit for sense. Este tío piensa con el culo.

not to have the balls to do something *(off-color)* no tener los huevos para hacer algo ▪ no tener los cojones para hacer algo ▪ no darle las pelotas a uno para hacer algo

not to have the faintest idea ▪ not to have the slightest idea no tener la idea más remota

not to have the guts to *(coll.)* no tener agallas de hacer algo ▪ no tener agallas para hacer algo ▪ no tener arrestos para hacer algo

not to have the nerve ▪ to be too shy ▪ to be too embarrassed darle vergüenza a alguien ▪ darle corte a alguien ➤ I'd like to ask her to go to the dance with me, but I don't have the nerve. ▪ I'd like to ask her to the dance, but I don't have the nerve. Me gustaría pedirle que venga al baile conmigo, pero me da corte.

not to have the slightest idea ▪ not to have the faintest idea no tener la idea más remota

not to have words to express no tener palabras para expresar ➤ I don't have words to express to him my appreciation. No tengo palabras para expresarle mi agradecimiento.

not to hesitate to do something no vacilar en hacer algo ▪ no dudar en hacer algo

not to involve doing something at all no suponer hacer algo en absoluto

not to keep one's promise faltar a su promesa

not to keep one's word faltar a su palabra

not to know no saber ▪ desconocer ➤ *(news item in November 2000)* The United States did not know yesterday who its future president would be. Los Estados Unidos desconocía ayer el nombre de su futuro presidente.

not to know a lot about something no saber gran cosa de algo

not to know beans about no tener ni idea de

not to know definitively ▪ not to know definitely no saber de fijo ➤ I don't know definitively whether they are coming (or not). No sé de fijo si vienen o no.

not to know for sure no saber con seguridad ▪ no saber de fijo ➤ Nobody knows for sure. Nadie lo sabe con certeza. ▪ Nadie lo sabe con seguridad.

not to know of anyone who can... no saber de nadie que pueda... ➤ I didn't know of anyone who could help me. No sabía de nadie que pudiera ayudarme.

not to know one's ass from a hole in the ground *(off-color)* ▪ not to know shit from shinola confundir la velocidad con el tocino

not to know that 1. *(main clause)* no saber eso **2.** *(dependent clause)* to be unaware that... no saber que... ▪ desconocer que... ▪ ignorar que... ➤ Many who are afflicted with cancer do not know that they have it at first. Muchas personas que están aquejadas de cáncer desconocen que lo padecen al principio.

not to know the first thing about something no saber ni la A sobre algo ▪ no saber ni papa

not to know the score 1. *(literal)* no saber el tanteo **2.** *(figurative)* ser un poco corto ▪ ser un poco duro de mollera

not to know what one has been missing no saber lo que se ha perdido ➤ You don't know what you've been missing. No sabes lo que te has perdido.

not to know what one is missing no saber lo que se pierde ➤ He doesn't know what he's missing. No sabe lo que se pierde.

not to know what to do quedarse sin saber qué hacer ➤ I didn't know what to do. Me quedé sin saber qué hacer.

not to know what to do with oneself no saber dónde meterse ▪ no saber qué hacer con la vida

not to know what to say no saber qué decir

not to know what to think no saber qué pensar ➤ I don't know what to think. No sé qué pensar.

not to know what's what no saber qué es qué

not to know where one stands on a question no saber a qué atenerse

not to know where one stands with someone no saber en qué punto está la relación con alguien ➤ I don't know where I stand with the boss. No sé en qué punto está mi relación con el jefe.

not to know whether one is coming or going tener un quilombo en la cabeza

not to know whether to... dudar entre... ▪ no saber si... ➤ They didn't know whether to stay or go. No sabían si quedarse o irse. ➤ We didn't know whether to stay or go. No sabíamos si quedarnos o irnos.

not to know which end is up confundir la velocidad con el tocino ▪ no saber por donde se anda

not to know who to believe *(coll.)* ▪ not to know whom to believe no saber a quién creer

not to know why or how no saber por qué ni cómo

not to lack for anything ▪ not to need anything no faltarle nada ▪ no necesitar nada

not to leave any loose ends no dejar ni un sólo cabo suelto

not to let any grass grow under one's feet no írsele a caer la casa encima ➤ He doesn't let any grass grow under his feet. No se le va a caer la casa encima.

not to let anybody else get a word in edgewise ▪ to monopolize the conversation no dejar hablar a nadie ▪ no dejar meter baza a nadie

not to let anything stand in one's way ▪ to let nothing stand in one's way ▪ not to let anything get in one's way no reparar en pelillos ▪ no pararse en pelillos

not to lift a finger no mover un dedo ▪ no bullir pie ni mano ▪ no dar ni clavo ▪ no dar ni chapa ▪ no dar ni golpe

not to like no gustarle ▪ no irle ▪ no molarle ➤ I don't like it. No me gusta. ▪ No me va. ▪ No me mola.

not to like someone at all no caerle nada bien ▪ no gustarle nada alguien ➤ I didn't like him at all. No me cayó nada bien. ▪ No me gustó nada. ➤ She didn't like him at all. Él no le cayó nada bien a ella. ▪ (A ella) no le gustó nada. ▪ No le gustó nada (a ella).

not to live a good life ▪ not to live prudently ▪ to live imprudently llevar mala vida

not to look anything alike ▪ to look nothing alike no parecerse en nada ▪ no parecerse en absoluto ▪ parecerse en el blanco de los ojos y en el blanco de los dientes

not to look good with ▪ not to go (well) with no hacer juego con ▪ no combinar con ➤ The tie doesn't look good with the shirt. ▪ The tie doesn't go with the shirt. La corbata no hace juego con la camisa. ▪ La corbata no combina con la camisa.

not to look it no aparentarlo

not to look one's age no aparentar su edad ▪ no representar su edad ➤ She doesn't look thirty-eight. No aparenta sus treinta y ocho años.

not to look well ▪ to look sick tener mal aspecto

not to make any difference ▪ to make no difference dar lo mismo

not to make any sense ▪ to make no sense no tener sentido

not to mean any harm ▪ to mean no harm no tener malas intenciones ➤ I didn't mean to. No tenía malas intenciones. ▪ No fue mi intención. ▪ Si no quería.

not to mention por no hablar de ▪ sin mencionar

not to mince words no tener pelos en la lengua

not to mind no importarle a uno ➤ I don't mind. No me importa.

not to miss a trick no perder comba ▪ no perder ripio

not to miss much ▪ not to be missing anything no perderse mucho ➤ You're not missing anything. No te pierdes nada. ▪ No te estás perdiendo nada. ➤ You didn't miss much. No te perdiste mucho.

not to move a muscle 1. not to do a lick of work no hacer absolutamente nada ▪ no hacer nada en absoluto **2.** not to budge ▪ not to react at all ni inmutarse ▪ ni alterarse

not to need anything ▪ not to lack for anything no faltarle nada ▪ no necesitar nada

not to need something no hacerle falta algo ▪ no necesitar algo ➤ You take it. I don't need it. Tómalo, no me hace falta.

not to open one's mouth no decir esta boca es mía

not to put up with any nonsense no aguantar pulgas ➤ She doesn't put up with any nonsense. Ella no aguanta pulgas.

not to register (with one) no caer en la cuenta ➤ At first it didn't register. Al principio no caí en la cuenta.

not to remember doing something no recordar haber hecho algo ➤ I don't remember hearing the Strauss piece. No recuerdo haber escuchado la pieza de Strauss.

not to remember having done something no recordar haber hecho algo ▪ no acordarse de haber hecho algo

not to say a word no decir palabra ▪ no decir ni jota ▪ no decir (ni) esta boca es mía ▪ no decir ni mu

not to see each other again for... no volver a verse en... ➤ They didn't see each other again for seven years. No volvieron a verse en siete años.

not to see the big picture ▪ not to "get it" no saber qué se cuece ▪ no saber de qué va la vaina ▪ no saber por dónde van los tiros

not to see the connection no ver la relación ➤ I see no connection. ▪ I don't see any connection. No veo ninguna relación.

not to seem to be no tener aire de

not to seem to mind no parecer que le importe a alguien ➤ They don't seem to mind. No parece que les importe.

not to so much as bat an eye ▪ not to even bat an eye ni inmutarse

not to stand a chance no tener la más mínima oportunidad

not to stop someone from doing something no obstar que alguien haga algo

not to take any more of someone's time no quitarle más tiempo a alguien ➤ I won't take any more of your time. No te quito más tiempo.

not to take it in ▪ not to register no enterarse ➤ At first I didn't take it in. Al principio no me enteré.

not to take kindly to something no tomárselo bien ➤ The mother cow didn't take too kindly to my approaching the calf when she was not right there to protect him. La vaca madre no se lo tomó muy bien que me acercara al ternero cuando ella no estaba allí mismo para protegerlo.

not to take long no hacerse esperar ▪ no tardar mucho ▪ no tardarse mucho ➤ The response to the terrorist attack didn't take long. La respuesta al ataque terrorista no se ha hecho esperar. ➤ The test didn't take long. El examen no se tardó mucho. ➤ It didn't take me long. ▪ I didn't take long. No tardé mucho.

not to talk of anything else ▪ to talk of nothing else ▪ to be all one talks about no hablar de otra cosa

not to tell the whole truth ▪ to tell only part of the story ▪ to hem and haw ▪ to beat around the bush ▪ to avoid giving a direct answer hablar a medias

not to test routinely for ▪ not to routinely do a test no soler hacer pruebas para ➤ When someone comes in for bronchitis, we do not routinely test for tuberculosis. Cuando alguien viene por el bronquitis, no solemos hacerle una prueba de tuberculosis.

not to touch one's food no probar bocado

not to understand a thing no entender ni jota ➤ Reading Alfred North Whitehead's book, I didn't understand a thing. Al leer el libro de Alfred North Whitehead, no entendí ni jota.

not to wait another minute no esperar ni un minuto más ➤ I'm not going to wait another minute. No voy a esperar ni un minuto más.

not to want anything to do with something ▪ to want nothing to do with something no querer tener nada que ver con algo ▪ querer desentenderse de algo

not to work out no dar resultado ➤ It didn't work out. No dio resultado.

not to work properly ▪ not to work right no funcionar bien

not to worry ▪ it's nothing ¡qué hay!

not to worry someone in the least no preocuparle a alguien en lo más mínimo ➤ It doesn't worry me in the least. No me preocupa en lo más mínimo.

not today hoy no

to be **not unexpected** no resultar (precisamente) inesperado ▪ no ser (precisamente) inesperado ➤ The minister's resignation was not unexpected. La dimisión del ministro no resultó (precisamente) inesperada.

not very ▪ not particularly poco ➤ Are you hungry?-Not very. ¿Tienes hambre?-Poca. ➤ Are you interested in going?-Not very. ¿Te interesa ir?-No mucho.

not welcome here: one is ~ aquí uno no es bien recibido ➤ You are not welcome here. Aquí no eres bien recibido.

not what one expected no ser lo que uno (se) había esperado ➤ This is not quite what I expected. Esto no es precisamente lo que (yo me) había esperado.

not what one was expecting no ser lo que uno (se) esperaba ➤ That's not exactly what I was expecting. No es exactamente lo que (yo me) esperaba.

not what one would expect no lo que uno esperaría ▪ no lo que cabría esperar ➤ It's not exactly what you would expect (of...) No es exactamente lo que se esperaría (de...) ▪ No es exactamente lo que cabría esperar (de...)

not without good reason ▪ not without reason no es para menos ▪ no era para menos

not without regrets no sin cierta pena

not *x* (y) no *x* ➤ We ordered three bottles of wine, not two. Pedimos tres botellas de vino, (y) no dos. ➤ I thought eight people were coming to the party, not sixteen! Pensé que vendrían ocho invitados, (y) no dieciséis.

not yet aún no ▪ todavía no

to **notarize a signature** legitimar una firma ▪ dar fe a una firma ▪ legitimizar una firma

notary's signature firma notorial

to **note down for posterity** ▪ to record for posterity consignar

note of impatience in one's voice: to detect a ~ percibir un atisbo de impaciencia en su voz

note of sarcasm in one's voice: to detect a ~ percibir un atisbo de sarcasmo en su voz

to **note that...** hacer notar que...

nothing at all nada en absoluto

to be **nothing but skin and bone** estar en carne y hueso ▪ estar en los huesos ▪ estar en el hueso pelado to be **nothing but trouble** ▪ to cause nothing but trouble no darle más que penas a alguien ▪ no darle más que disgustos a alguien ▪ no hacer nada sino darle problemas a alguien ▪ no reportar nada sino que disgustos

nothing came of it **1.** it fizzled terminó en agua de borrajas ▪ quedó en agua de borrajas **2.** it ended peacefully no llegó la sangre al río

nothing could be further from the truth ▪ nothing could be farther from the truth nada más lejos de la realidad ▪ nada podría estar más alejado de la verdad ▪ no hay nada más lejos de la verdad

nothing doin'! ¡ni hablar! ▪ ¡nada! ▪ nanai de nanai

nothing else nada más

nothing else to do but...: there's ~ no hay más remedio que... ▪ no ninguna otra ocupación que... ➤ There's nothing else to do but wait. No hay ninguna otra ocupación que esperar. ▪ No hay más remedio que esperar.

nothing has changed no ha cambiado nada ▪ nada ha cambiado

nothing in particular ▪ nothing specifically nada de particular

nothing like this nada similar a esto

nothing more ▪ nothing else ▪ that's all nada más ➤ Just coffee. Nothing more. Solo café. Nada más. ➤ That's all I meant. Nothing more. Es lo único que quería decir. Nada más.

nothing of the kind ▪ nothing of the sort nada por el estilo ▪ nada parecido ➤ I said nothing of the kind. No dije nada por el estilo.

nothing of the sort ▪ nothing of the kind nada por el estilo

nothing shocks me anymore estoy curado de espanto

to be **nothing special** ▪ not to be anything special ▪ to be nothing to write home about ▪ not to be anything to write home about no ser nada especial ▪ no ser nada del otro mundo ▪ no ser nada del otro jueves

nothing that I can't solve nada que (yo) no pueda solucionar

to be **nothing to sneeze at** *(coll.)* no ser poco ➤ That's nothing to sneeze at. Eso no es poco.

nothing to wear nada que ponerse ➤ *(magazine cover)* Jackie Kennedy also suffered from nothing to wear. Jackie Kennedy también sufría de nada que ponerse.

to be **nothing to write home about** ▪ not to be anything to write home about ▪ to be nothing special ▪ not to be anything special no ser nada del otro mundo ▪ no ser nada del otro jueves ▪ no ser nada especial

nothing ventured, nothing gained quien no se arriesga, no pasa la mar ▪ quien nada arriesga, nada gana

nothing's coming up *(on the computer screen)* no me sale nada

nothing's stopping you *(tú)* nada te lo impide ▪ *(usted)* nada se lo impide

to **notice it** darse cuenta ➤ I'm starting to notice it. ▪ I'm starting to notice that. Estoy empezando a darme cuenta.

to **notice something** reparar en algo

to **notice something is missing** ▪ to miss something echar de menos algo ➤ I noticed it was missing when I came home from work. Lo eché de menos al volver de mi trabajo.

to **notice that** fijarse en eso ▪ darse cuenta (de eso)

to **notice that...** fijarse en que... ▪ darse cuenta de que... ▪ notar que... ▪ apercibirse de que...

to **notice the slightest change in** advertir el cambio más imperceptible en

to **notice the way** ▪ to see the way fijarse en cómo ➤ Did you notice the way she looked at you? *(tú)* ¿Te fijaste en cómo ella te miró? ▪ *(usted)* ¿Se fijó usted en cómo ella lo miró? ▪ *(usted)* ¿Se fijó usted en cómo ella le miró?

nouveau riche ▪ new rich nuevo rico

the **novelty has worn off** *la* novedad se ha desvanecido

now comes the hard part ahora viene lo difícil

now I get it! ▪ now I know! ¡ya caigo!

now I'm getting the idea ▪ now I'm starting to get the idea ahora lo voy empezando a entender

now I'm not sure ahora me he quedado dudando

now in DVD ya en DVD

now is the time to... ahora es el momento en el que...

now, is there anything about me that you *do* like? y bien, ¿hay algo de mí que sí te gusta?

now I've heard everything lo que me faltaba por oír

now more than ever ahora más que nunca

now, now! ¡no y no!

now on sale ya a la venta

now that... ahora que... ▪ ya que...

now that I think about it mirándolo bien

now that you mention it ahora que lo dices ▪ *(Mex.)* ahorita que lo dices

now that's what I call... eso sí que se llama...

now that's what you call... eso sí que se llama...

now we're cooking with gas **1.** *(literally)* ahora estamos cocinando con butano ▪ ahora estamos cocinando a butano ▪ ahora estamos cocinando por butano **2.** now we're getting somewhere ▪ now we're in business ¡andando! ▪ vamos por buen camino

now we're getting somewhere ▪ now we're cooking with gas ▪ now we're in business ¡andando! ▪ vamos por buen camino

now what do we do? ¿y ahora qué hacemos?

now, where was I? bien, ¿dónde estaba? ▪ bien, ¿en qué iba?

***now* you show up!** ¡a buenas horas (mangas verdes)! ▪ ¡muerto el burro, la cebada al rabo!

***now* you tell me!** ¡a buenas horas (mangas verdes)! ▪ ¡muerto el burro, la cebada al rabo!

***now* you're talking!** ¡eso sí que se llama hablar!

to be **nowhere in sight** ▪ not to be anywhere in sight no estar a la vista

to be **nowhere near** ▪ not to be anywhere near... no quedar nada cerca de...

to be **nowhere to be found** no estar en ningún lado ➤ She looked everywhere for her necklace, but it was nowhere to be found. Buscó su collar por todas partes, pero no estaba en ningún lado.

nth degree enésimo grado

nuclear fission ▪ splitting of the atom *la* fisión nuclear ▪ fisión atómica ▪ escisión nuclear

nuclear power plant *la* central nuclear ▪ planta nuclear

nuclear warhead ojiva nuclear ▪ *(informal)* cabeza nuclear

nude beach playa nudista

number is *x* times that ese número se multiplica por *x* ➤ The army insists that the number is ten times that. El ejército insiste en que ese número se multiplica por diez.

the **number of...** la cantidad de...

number of different... diversos...

to be **number one** ser el número uno ▪ ser la número uno

to **nurse a grudge against someone for something** ▪ to hold a grudge against someone ▪ to have a grudge against someone for something ▪ to harbor a grudge against someone for something ▪ to bear a grudge against someone for something guardarle rencor a alguien por algo ▪ tenerle inquina a alguien por algo ▪ tenerle tirria a alguien por algo ▪ tenerle manía a alguien por algo

nutritional value ▪ food value valor alimenticio

to be **nutty as a fruitcake** ▪ to be crazy as a bedbug ▪ to be mad as a hatter ser una regadera ▪ estar como una regadera ▪ estar loco de remate to **obey an order** obedecer una orden

to **obey the law** acatar la ley ■ respetar la norma

to **object that...** objetar que... ■ poner la objeción de que...

object the size of Mars objeto del tamaño de Marte

to **object to** oponerse a ■ tener inconveniente en que

object to: not to ~ no oponerse a ■ no decir que no a ■ no tener inconveniente

objection overruled! ¡protesta rechazada! ■ ¡protesta denegada! ■ ¡queda denegada! ■ no ha lugar la protesta ➤ I object, your honor.-(Objection) overruled. Protesta, (su) señoría.-Protesta rechazada. ■ Protesta denegada. ■ Queda denegada.

objection sustained! ¡protesta aceptada!

objection, your honor! protesta, (su) señoría

obligatory de precepto ■ preceptivo ■ obligatorio

to be **oblivious to one's surroundings** ser ajeno a lo que pasa alrededor ■ ser ajeno a lo que te rodea ■ estar ajeno a lo que pasa alrededor ■ estar ajeno a lo que te rodea

to be **oblivious to the fact that...** ser ajeno al hecho de que...

to be **oblivious to the situation** ser ajeno a la situación ■ hacer caso omiso de la situación

obstacle course carrera de obstáculos

to be **obvious that...** ser obvio que... ■ ser patente que...

occasional letter carta ocasional ■ alguna carta ➤ Except for an occasional letter Con la excepción de una carta ocasional ■ Fuera de alguna carta

to be **occasioned by** ser ocasionado por ➤ The toast was occasioned by the announcement of the couple's engagement. El brindis fue ocasionado por el anuncio del compromiso de la pareja.

occupant of the building *el, la* ocupante del edificio ■ *el, la* residente del edificio ■ vecino(-a) del edificio

occupant of the White House *el, la* titular de la Casa Blanca

to be an **occupational hazard** ser un gaje del oficio

to **occur to one** ocurrírsele ■ venirle a la boca a alguien ➤ It didn't occur to me. No se me ocurría. ➤ It just occurred to me. Acaba de venirme a la boca.

occurred: the incident ~ el incidente se produjo ➤ The incident occurred as he was leaving his office. El incidente se produjo mientras abandonaba su oficina. ➤ The accident occurred near Salamanca. El accidente se produjo cerca de Salamanca.

ocean floor ■ ocean bottom fondo del océano

Ockham's Razor *(philosophy of science)* ■ law of parsimony navaja de Occam ■ principio de economía ➤ Ockham's Razor, or the law of parsimony, says that the simplest complete explanation is the true one. La navaja de Occam, o el principio de economía, reza que la explicación completa más sencilla es la verdadera.

octave range extensión de octavas ➤ The organ has the widest octave range of any instrument. El órgano tiene la extensión de octavas más amplia de cualquier instrumento.

to be an **odd duck** ser un bicho raro

to be the **odd man out** ser el tercero en discordia

odd number número impar ■ *(plural)* números impares

odd number of times número impar de veces

odd-numbered day el día impar

odd word palabreja

odds and ends: to do ~ hacer minucias

odor of sanctity olor de santo

of about como de ➤ The rubble reached a height of about six or seven floors. Los escombros alcanzaban una altura como de seis o siete pisos.

to be **of age** ■ to be of legal age ser mayor de edad

of all kinds de toda laya

of all people de entre todas las personas...menos que nadie ➤ Doctors, of all people, should know better than to smoke. De entre todas las personas, los médicos deberían saber mejor que nadie que no hay que fumar. ■ De entre todas las personas, los médicos deberían saber mejor que nadie que no se debe fumar. ■ De entre todas las personas, los médicos deberían saber bien que no hay que fumar. ■ De entre todas las personas, los médicos deberían saber bien que no se debe fumar.

of all time de todos los tiempos ➤ Virgil Fox was one of the great(est) organists of all time. Virgil Fox fue uno de los organistas más grandes de todos los tiempos.

of biblical proportions de proporciones cataclísmicas ■ *(less common)* de proporciones bíbilicas ➤ It was a flood of biblical proportions. Fue una inundación de proporciones cataclísmicas. ■ Fue una inundación de proporciones bíblicas. ➤ My kitchen is a mess of biblical proportions. Mi cocina es un desbarajuste de proporciones cataclísmicas.

of color ■ black de color ■ negro ➤ Thurgood Marshall was the first black member of the U.S. Supreme Court. Thurgood Marshall es el primer miembro de color en el Tribunal Supremo.

to be **of consequence** importar

of considerable importance de bastante importancia ■ de alguna importancia

of course! ¡como no! ■ ¡por supuesto! ■ desde luego ■ ¡no faltaba más! ■ claro ■ claro está ■ vaya sí ■ naturalmente

of course I can claro que puedo ■ por supuesto que puedo

of course I did por supuesto que sí (que lo hice)

of course I do por supuesto que sí (que lo hago)

of course I remember sí que me acuerdo ■ por supuesto me acuerdo ■ ¿cómo no voy a acordarme?

of course I will (do it) claro que lo haré ■ por supuesto que lo haré

of every kind de toda clase

of great stature de gran tallarín

of its own sus propios ➤ The new government is making a lot of mistakes of its own. El nuevo gobierno está cometiendo sus propios errores.

of last month del mes pasado

to be **of legal age** ■ to be of age ser mayor de edad

of little value de poco valor ■ *(coll.)* de poca monta

to be **of no account** no tener importancia ■ *(coll.)* ser de poca monta

to be **of no avail** ■ to be useless ser inútil ■ dar en vano ➤ In a Chinese restaurant, giving me chopsticks is of no avail. I have to have a fork. En un restaurante chino, darme los palillos es inútil. Tengo que tener un tenedor. ■ En un restaurante chino, darme los palillos es dar en vano. Tengo que tener un tenedor.

to be **of no interest** interesarle a uno

to be **of no use (at all)** ■ to be useless no servir para nada

of one: to be true ~ ■ to be true in one's case ■ to be true for one ser el caso de uno ➤ Is that true of you? ■ Is that true in your case? ¿Es tu caso?

of one who ■ of someone who de quien ➤ He spoke with the authority of one who knows. Habló con la autoridad de quien sabe.

of one's own para uno solo ➤ My sister wanted a dog of her very own. Mi hermana quería tener un perro para ella sola.

of one's own accord por propia voluntad ▪ por su propia cuenta ▪ espontáneamente

of one's own free will a libre albedrío ▪ motu proprio

to be **of one's stripe** ▪ to be of the same stripe ▪ to be of the same ilk *(derogatory)* calaña de uno ➤ People of his stripe La gente de su calaña

of ours: a friend ~ un amigo nuestro ▪ una amiga nuestra

of people who ▪ of those who ▪ of all those who ▪ of everyone who de quienes

of proven loyalty de probada lealtad ▪ *(literary)* de alquilatada lealtad

of recent vintage: wine ~ vino joven

of someone to por su parte ▪ de su parte

of someone who ▪ of one who de quien ➤ He spoke with the authority of someone who knows. Habló con la autoridad de quien sabe.

of that kind semejante

of that magnitude de esa envergadura

of that name del mismo nombre

of that nature ▪ like those de esa índole

of the kind ▪ of the sort por el estilo

to be **of the same generation** ▪ to be from the same generation ser de la misma generación ▪ *(Sp.)* ser de la misma quinta

to be **of the same ilk** *(humorous, derogatory)* ▪ to be of the same stripe ser de la misma calaña ➤ *(Ogden Nash)* The cow is of the bovine ilk. One end is moo, the other, milk! La vaca es de la calaña bovina, un extremo es mu, el otro, leche.

to be **of the same opinion as someone** ▪ to be in agreement with someone ▪ to agree with someone coincidir con alguien ▪ estar de acuerdo con alguien ➤ I'm of the same opinion as you. ▪ I'm in agreement with you. *(tú)* Coincido contigo. ▪ Estoy de acuerdo contigo. ▪ *(usted)* Coincido con usted. ▪ Estoy de acuerdo con usted.

to be **of the same stripe** *(derogatory)* ▪ to be of the same ilk ser de la misma calaña

of the worst stripe de la peor especie ➤ He's a politican of the worst stripe. Es un político de la peor especie.

of this month del actual ▪ del corriente ➤ The 15th (fifteenth) of this month. El quince del actual. ▪ El quince del corriente.

of those consulted de los consultados ▪ de las personas consultadas

of those surveyed de los encuestados ▪ de las personas encuestadas ➤ Sixty percent of those surveyed... ▪ Sixty percent of those surveyed... El sesenta por ciento de los encuestados...

of those who ▪ of people who ▪ of all who ▪ of whoever ▪ of everyone who de quienes

to be **of two minds about something** no saber en qué carta quedarse

of unknown causes por causas que se desconocen ▪ por causas desconocidas

of what is coming de lo que va a llegar ➤ He seems to have resigned himself to the idea of what is coming. Parece haberse resignado a la idea de lo que va a llegar.

of you to: to be generous ~ por su parte ▪ de su parte

of yours: a friend ~ *(de ti)* un(a) amigo(-a) tuyo(-a) ▪ *(de usted)* un(a) amigo(-a) suyo(-a)

of yours: this obsession ~ esta obsesión tuya ▪ esta obsesión suya

to be **off 1.** to be on one's way marcharse ▪ en marcha ▪ irse **2.** to be turned off estar apagado ▪ estar cerrado **3.** to be cancelled estar anulado **4.** to be inaccurate ser impreciso ▪ ser erróneo ▪ estar equivocado ➤ We're off! ¡En marcha! ▪ ¡Nos vamos! ➤ She's off! ¡Se va! ▪ ¡Ya se fue ella! ➤ Be off! *(poetic)* ¡Vete! ▪ ¡Márchate! ➤ The party's off. ▪ The party's been cancelled. La fiesta está anulada. ➤ The calculation is off. ▪ The calculation is inaccurate. El cálculo es erróneo. ▪ El cálculo está equivocado. ▪ El cálculo es equívoco. ➤ The measurement is a little bit off. ▪ The measurement is slightly inaccurate. La medida es ligeramente errónea. ▪ La medida está ligeramente equivocada. ▪ La medida es ligeramente equívoca.

to be **off again, on again** ▪ to be on and off ir a intervalos ▪ ir y venir ▪ estar a veces sí, a veces no ➤ Their relationship is on again, off again at this point. ▪ Their relationship is on and off at this point. En estos momentos su relación va a intervalos. ▪ En estos momentos su relación va y viene. ▪ En estos momentos, en su relación a veces sí están, y a veces no.

off and on 1. *(adjective)* intermitente **2.** *(adverb)* intermitentemente

to be **off and running** salir disparado ▪ salir volando ➤ The president of the New York Stock Exchange paid the young Thomas Edison forty thousand dollars for the stock ticker, and from that moment Edison was off and running. El presidente de la Bolsa de Nueva York le pagó al joven Thomas Edison cuarenta mil dólares por el teletipo, y desde ese momento Edison salió disparado. ▪ El presidente de la Bolsa de Nueva York le pagó al joven Thomas Edison cuarenta mil dólares por el teletipo, y desde ese momento Edison salió volando.

to be **off by** *(calculation, estimate)* tener un error de ➤ Cassini's 1677 estimate of the distance from the Earth to the sun was off by about six million miles. El cálculo de Cassini de la distancia desde la Tierra hasta el sol tuvo un error de aproximadamente seis millones de millas.

to be **off center** estar descentrado ➤ That picture is a little off center. Ese cuadro está un poco descentrado.

off-color fuera de tono ▪ subido de tono ▪ verde

off-color joke un chiste verde ▪ un chiste subido de tono ▪ un chiste impropio ▪ un chiste fuera de lugar ➤ He told an off-color joke. Contó un chiste verde. ▪ Contó un chiste subido de tono. ▪ Contó un chiste impropio. ▪ Contó un chiste fuera de lugar.

to be **off course** estar fuera de rumbo ▪ estar fuera de ruta ▪ estar fuera de trayecto ▪ desviar su trayecto

off course: to get ~ desviarse de su rumbo ▪ desviarse (de) su trayecto ▪ desviarse (de) su ruta ▪ salirse de ruta ▪ salirse de trayecto

off he goes sale disparado ➤ The bugle sounds, and off he goes. Suena la corneta y sale disparado.

off hours horas bajas ➤ During the off hours, we went sight seeing. Durante las horas bajas hicimos turismo.

off-hours fuera de horario ➤ Is there an off-hours store nearby? ¿Hay una tienda abierta fuera de horario cerca de aquí?

off in the distance allí a lo lejos

to be **off in the ozone** estar en la higuera ▪ estar en el guindo ▪ estar en la luna ▪ estar en los celajes ▪ estar en alfa

to be **off like a shot** partir como una bala

off-season fare tarifa de temporada baja

to be **off the beaten path** ▪ to be off the beaten track estar en un lugar bastante apartado ▪ estar alejado del camino

off the coast of frente a la costa de

to be **off the ground** haber despegado ➤ The airplane is off the ground. El avión ha despegado.

to be **off the hook** salir de rositas

off the record en primicio ▪ en secreto

off the set fuera de plató

off the top of one's head ▪ right off the top of one's head a bote pronto ▪ a vuela pluma

to be **off the track** estar despistado

to be **off to a good start** tener una gran salida ➤ He's off to a good start. Ha tenido una gran salida.

to **offend someone's sensibilities** molestar la sensibilidad de alguien

to be **offended by something** ▪ to take something badly llevar mal una cosa

offensive question pregunta que ofende ▪ pregunta ofensiva

offensive remark comentario ofensivo

to **offer a reward** ofrecerle una recompensa ➤ The police have offered a five-million-dollar reward to whoever... La policía ha ofrecido una recompensa de cinco millones a quien(quiera)...

to **offer an easy-payment plan** ▪ to have an easy-payment plan dar facilidades de pago

to **offer one's hand** ▪ to extend one's hand ▪ to outstretch one's hand tender la mano to **offer someone a drink** convidarle una copa ➤ May I offer you a drink? *(a ti)* ¿Te convido una copa? ▪ *(a usted)* ¿Le convido una copa?

to **offer someone a job** ofrecerle a uno un puesto de trabajo

to **offer to do something** ▪ to volunteer to do something brindarse a hacer algo ➤ She volunteered to go with me. ▪ She offered to go with me. Ella se brindó a ir conmigo.

to **offer to help** ofrecer una ayuda

offhand de improviso

office staff *el* personal ▪ *(Sp.)* plantilla

office supplies store tienda de material de oficina

officer! ¡oficial!

official tally el balance oficial ➤ The first official tally El primer balance oficial

oh, and what would that be? ¿o, y qué sería eso? ▪ ¿el qué?

oh, my God! ¡vaya por Dios!

oh, no! ¡o, no!

oh, no you haven't! ¡no, te equivocas!

oh, no you're not! ¡no, te equivocas!

oh, really? ¿en serio?

oh, well, that's good ah, bueno, menos mal

oh, yeah? *(expressing surprise)* ¿ah, sí?

oil field campo petrolífero ▪ yacimiento petrolífero

oil, lube, and filter cambio de aceite, engrase y filtro

oil painting pintura al oleo

oil pipeline oleoducto

oil slick marea negra

okay! **1.** agreed! de acuerdo ▪ *(Mex.)* ¡órale! ▪ *(Sp.)* ¡vale! **2.** now! ▪ now then! ¡ahora bien!

okay? ¿ya? ▪ ¿está bien? ▪ ¿conforme? ▪ ¿vale?

okay, fine! ¡muy bien! ▪ *(S. Am.)* ¡bueno! ▪ ¡regio!

okay, I guess supongo que bien

okay, José! ▪ okay, McKay! ¡vale, tío!

okay, then ándale pues

to be **old as the hills** tener más espolones que un gallo

old ballad antigua balada

to be **old enough to be someone's father** tener edad para ser el padre de alguien

to be **old enough to be someone's mother** tener edad para ser la madre de alguien

to be **old enough to do something** tener edad suficiente para hacer algo

to be **old enough to know better than to do something** ser lo suficientemente mayor para saber que no le conviene hacer algo ▪ ser lo suficientemente mayor para saber que le conviene no hacer algo

to be **old enough to shave** haberle salido la barba

to be **old enough to vote** tener la edad para votar ▪ ser lo suficientemente mayor para votar ➤ In 1960 my grandfather was for Kennedy, but he wasn't old enough to vote. En 1960, mi abuelo estaba a favor de Kennedy, pero no tenía la edad para votar. ▪ En 1960, mi abuelo estaba a favor de Kennedy, pero no era lo suficientemente mayor para votar.

old-fashioned anticuado

to be **old-fashioned** estar anticuado ▪ estar pasado de moda ▪ estar chapado a la antigua

old fogey vejestorio

old friend viejo amigo ▪ viega amiga

to be **old hat** estar más visto que un tebeo

to be an **old wives' tale** ser cuento de viejas

older gentleman señor mayor

to be **older than** ser mayor que

Olympic torch antorcha olímpica ▪ llama olímpica

ominous-looking clouds nubes nefastas

to **omit something** ▪ to skip over something ▪ to pass over something pasar algo por alto

to be **on** ▪ to be turned on estar encendido ▪ estar abierto ➤ Somebody left the light on. Alguien (se) dejó la luz encendida. ➤ You left your headlights on. *(tú)* (Te) dejaste los faros encendidos. ▪ *(usted)* (Se) dejó los faros encendidos. ➤ The light was on in the window when I drove by. ▪ The light in the window was on when I drove by. Había luz en la ventana cuando pasé con el coche. ➤ Is the water (turned) on? ¿Está el grifo abierto? ▪ *(from a central source)* ¿Está el agua dada?

on a certain avenue: to be (located) ~ estar en la avenida... ▪ quedar en la avenida... ➤ Are you (located) on Constitution? ¿Queda su tienda en la Avenida Constitución?

on a dare: to do something ~ hacer algo porque a uno le dicen que no se atreve ➤ I did it on a dare. Lo hice porque me dijeron que no me atrevía.

to be **on a diet** estar en un régimen ▪ estar a dieta ▪ seguir un régimen ▪ estar siguiendo un régimen

on a diet: to be put ~ ponerle en un régimen ➤ He was put on a 1,400-calorie-per-day diet. ▪ They put him on a 1,400-calorie-per-day diet. Le pusieron en un régimen de mil cuatrocientas calorías diarias. ➤ The doctor put him on a 1,400-calorie-per-day diet. El médico le puso en un régimen de mil cuatrocientas calorías diarias.

on a diet: to go ~ ponerse a régimen

on a few occasions ▪ on a limited number of occasions ▪ a few times ▪ a limited number of times en contadas ocasiones

to be **on a first-name basis** tratar a alguien de tú a tú ➤ The president and I are on a first-name basis. El presidente y yo nos tratamos de tú a tú.

on a fluke: to do something ~ hacer algo en un impulso ▪ hacer algo en un ataque ▪ hacer algo en un rapto

on a Friday night una noche de viernes

on a given day ▪ on a certain day en un día determinado

on a happy note: to end ~ acabar con un final feliz

on a humorous note en clave de humor

on a limited number of occasions ▪ on a few occasions ▪ a few times ▪ a limited number of times en contadas ocasiones

to be **on a medication** estar bajo medicación

on a number of occasions ▪ on quite a few occasions ▪ on various occasions bastantes veces ▪ en diversas ocasiones

on a regular basis de manera regular

on a sad note: to end ~ acabar con un final triste

on a salary a sueldo

on a shoestring budget al alpargata

on a tour of de gira por

to be **on a trip** ▪ to be away estar de viaje ▪ estar fuera

on a typical day ▪ on an ordinary day en un día cualquiera

to be **on a war footing** estar en pie de guerra

on a yearly basis ▪ on an annual basis ▪ annually cada año ▪ anualmente

on account of ▪ because of por motivo de ▪ a causa de ▪ por causa de ➤ The plane detoured on account of the thunderhead in its path. El avión se desvió a causa del cúmulo en su trayectoria. ➤ It's better to sleep on it than (to) lose sleep on account of it. Es mejor consultar las cosas con la almohada a tiempo que perder el sueño por su causa después.

on-again, off-again relationship relaciones de ahora sí, ahora no ➤ Aristotle Onassis and Maria Callas, Elizabeth Taylor and Richard Burton had on-again, off-again relationships. Aristóteles Onassis y María Callas, Elizabeth Taylor y Richard Burton tuvieron relaciones de ahora sí, ahora no.

on all fours a gatas ▪ a rastras ▪ en cuatro patas

on all fronts en todos los frentes ➤ The administration is playing its cards right on all fronts. La administración está jugando sus cartas en todos los frentes.

on all points: to agree ~ estar de acuerdo en todos los puntos ▪ estar de acuerdo en todos los aspectos

on alternating days ▪ every other day en días alternos ▪ un día sí y otro no ➤ During the oil crisis, we could buy gasoline only on alternating days. ▪ During the oil crisis, we could only buy gasoline every other day. Durante la crisis petrolera, pudimos comprar gasolina en días alternos. ▪ Durante la crisis petrolera, pudimos comprar gasolina sólo un día sí y otro no.

on American soil en territorio estadounidense ➤ After a brief stop in Guam, the crew (members) landed on American soil. Tras una breve escala en Guam, los tripulantes aterrizaron en territorio estadounidense.

on an empty stomach con el estómago vacío ➤ I shouldn't have eaten all that hot salsa on an empty stomach. No debería haberme comido toda esa salsa picante con el estómago vacío.

to be **on an equal footing** estar a la misma altura que ➤ Bilingual education should be on an equal footing with literature in university Spanish programs. La educación bilingüe debería estar a la misma altura que la literatura en los programas universitarios de filología hispánica.

on an equal footing: to put something ~ ▪ to put something on an even footing poner algo a la misma altura que ➤ Bilingual education should be put on an equal footing with literature in graduate programs in Spanish. ▪ Bilingual education should be put on an even footing with literature in graduate programs in Spanish. La educación bilingüe debería ponerse a la misma altura que la literatura en los programas de postgrado de filología hispánica.

to be **on an even keel** estar en equilibrio ▪ estar equilibrado

on an ordinary day ▪ on a typical day en un día cualquiera

to be **on and off 1.** to be intermittent ser intermitente **2.** to be occasional ser por temporadas **3.** to be tempestuous estar juntos en ratos ▪ estar a veces sí, a veces no ▪ estar por épocas ➤ Their relationship was on and off. Están juntos en ratos. ▪ Están juntos por épocas.

on and off: to go ~ irse y venirse ➤ The thread of the light fixture is rough, and the light keeps going on and off. La rosca de la lámpara adosada está dura, la luz se va y viene.

on and on: to go ~ seguir y seguir ▪ seguir sin parar ▪ seguir dale que dale ▪ seguir dale que te pego ➤ He went on and on for twenty minutes. ▪ He rambled on and on for twenty minutes. Él siguió y siguió durante veinte minutos. ▪ Él siguió sin parar durante veinte minutos. ▪ Él siguió dale que dale durante veinte minutos. ▪ Él siguió dale que te pego durante veinte minutos.

on and on: to ramble ~ ponerse a hablar a la buena de Dios ➤ He rambles on and no, and nobody can follow what he's talking about. Se pone a hablar a la buena de Dios, y nadie puede seguir lo que está diciendo.

on average ▪ on the average de media ▪ por término medio

to be **on bad terms** andar a malas

to be **on bad terms with someone** andar a malas con alguien

on balance ▪ considering all aspects valorando todos los aspectos ▪ teniendo en cuenta todos los aspectos

on behalf of en nombre de ▪ de parte de

on being ingested ▪ when it is ingested ▪ when you ingest it al ingerirlo ➤ Beta carotine turns into vitamin A when it is ingested. Beta caroteno se convierte en vitamina A al ingerirlo.

on bended knee ▪ abjectly ▪ pleadingly de rodillas

to be **on call** estar de retén

to be **on chapter two** ir por el capítulo dos ➤ We're on chapter two. Vamos por el capítulo dos.

on consignment: to sell goods ~ ▪ to sell merchandise on consignment vender mercancías en consignación

on credit al fiado

to be **on crutches** ir con muletas

to be **on display** estar expuesto

on doctor's orders ▪ on the doctor's orders por prescripción médica

to be **on duty** estar de guardia ▪ estar de turno ▪ tener guardia ▪ *(police, military, security guards)* estar de servicio ➤ Who's on duty? ¿Quién está de guardia? ➤ There's an on-duty pharmacy list in the window of every pharmacy. Hay una lista de farmacias de turno en la ventana de cada farmacia. *(In Hispanic countries, pharmacies which stay open 24 hours are called "farmacias de turno," literally, the pharmacy whose turn it is to stay open late.)*

on each visit 1. each time he visits cada vez que visita **2.** each time he visited ▪ each time he would visit cada vez que visitaba

to be **on edge** ▪ to be edgy ▪ to feel edgy estar a flor de piel ▪ tener los nervios de punta ▪ tener los nervios crispados ➤ My nerves are on edge. ▪ I'm edgy. ▪ I feel edgy. Mis nervios están a flor de piel. ▪ Tengo los nervios de punta. ▪ Tengo los nervios crispados.

on edge: to feel ~ sentir crispación de los nervios

on either side of 1. on one side or the other en cualquier lado de **2.** on both sides of a ambos lados de ➤ *(news item)* Two vans parked on either side of the car contained the shock wave, preventing it from inflicting serious injuries. La presencia de dos furgonetas a ambos lados del coche retuvieron la onda expansiva impidiendo que se produjeran heridos de gravedad.

to be **on empty** *(fuel tank)* estar a cero

to be **on fire** ▪ to be in flames estar en llamas ▪ estar ardiendo ▪ *(from eating hot peppers)* estar la boca que arde

on foot: to go ~ ▪ to walk ▪ *(coll., humorous)* to go on Shank's pony ir a pie ▪ *(L. Am.)* caminar ▪ *(Sp.)* andar ▪ *(coll., humorous)* ir en el coche de San Fernando ➤ We went on foot. Fuimos a pie. ▪ Anduvimos.

on good authority that...: to have it ~ saber de buena fuente que...

to be **on good terms with someone** estar a bien con alguien ▪ estar a buenas con alguien ▪ estar en términos amistosos con alguien

to be **on guard against** estar en guardia contra

to be **on guard duty** estar a punto fijo

on hand: to have ~ ▪ to have available tener disponible ▪ tener a la disposición de uno

on hearing something like that ▪ when one hears something like that ante algo así

on hearing the news al oír la noticia

to be **on hold** estar en espera

on horseback a lomos de un caballo

on horseback: to go ~ ▪ to ride horseback ir a caballo ▪ montar a caballo

on in years: to be getting ~ ▪ to be getting up in years ▪ to be getting up there estar entrado en años ▪ ser entrado en años

on it sobre ello ▪ en ello ➤ It has something written on it. Hay algo escrito sobre ello. ▪ Hay algo escrito en ello.

to be **on its last legs** estar en sus últimas

to be **on key** estar a tono

to be **on leave** estar de permiso

on me ▪ with me conmigo

to be **on medication** estar medicado

on medication: to put one back ~ volver a medicarle a alguien ▪ volver a ponerle la medicación a alguien ➤ The doctor put me back on (my) medication. ▪ The doctor put me back on (the) medication. El médico ha vuelto a medicarme. ▪ El médico ha vuelto a ponerme la medicación.

on my account por mí

on my part de mi parte

on numerous occasions en repetidas ocasiones ➤ As I have said on numerous occasions Como he dicho en reiteradas ocasiones

on-off switch *el* interruptor ▪ *el* botón de encendido

on one condition con una condición ➤ I'll do it on one condition, namely, that... Lo haré con una condición, a saber, que...

on one's back a cuestas

on one's back: to lie ~ recostarse boca arriba ▪ recostarse supino ▪ echarse boca arriba ▪ echarse supino ▪ tenderse boca arriba ▪ tenderse supino

on one's behalf ▪ in one's behalf para uno ▪ a favor de uno ▪ de parte de uno ▪ en nombre de uno ➤ A Miami judge has rejected the asylum petition on Elián's behalf and says he must return to Cuba. Un juez de Miami ha desestimado la petición de asilo para Elián y dice que debe volver a Cuba. ➤ I'm calling you on Marta's bahalf. Lo llamo a usted de parte de Marta. ▪ Lo llamo en nombre de Marta.

on one's death a su muerte

on one's father's side (of the family) de parte de padre ▪ por parte de padre

to be **on one's guard (against something)** estar en guardia (contra algo) ▪ estar sobre aviso (contra algo) ▪ escamarse

on one's hands: to have a problem ~ tener un problema entre manos ➤ We have a real problem on our hands. ▪ We've got a real problem on our hands. Tenemos un auténtico problema entre manos. ➤ He has a huge undertaking on his hands. ▪ He's got a huge undertaking on his hands. Tiene una empresa enorme entre manos. ▪ Tiene una tarea enorme entre manos.

on one's hands: to have time ~ tener todo el tiempo del mundo ➤ I've got time on my hands, and I'm looking for something to do. Tengo todo el tiempo del mundo, y busco algo que hacer.

to be **on one's knees** ▪ to be kneeling estar de rodillas

to be **on one's last legs** estar en sus últimas ▪ *(Sp., colorful)* quedarle dos telediarios ➤ He's on his last legs. Le quedan dos telediarios.

on one's mother's side (of the family) de parte de madre ▪ por parte de madre

to be **on one's own** andar por su cuenta

on one's own: to do something ~ **1.** alone, by oneself hacer algo solo **2.** on one's own initiative hacer algo por cuenta propia ➤ I decided to investigate on my own. Decidí investigar por cuenta propia.

on one's own (authority): to act ~ actuar por su cuenta ▪ actuar por su propia cuenta ➤ He agreed to it on his own. Accedió a ello por su propia cuenta.

on one's own initiative por iniciativa propia ▪ de motu proprio ▪ por su propia cuenta

on one's part por parte de uno

to be **on one's side** estar de su lado

to be **on one's time** estar en el tiempo de uno ➤ We're on my time right now. Let's worry about that when we're on company time. Ahora estamos en mi tiempo. Ya nos preocuparemos de eso en el tiempo de trabajo.

to be **on one's toes** estar alerta ▪ mantenerse en alerta

to be **on one's way 1.** to leave ya ir para allá **2.** to be situated along the way pillarle de paso ➤ I'm on my way. Ya voy para allá. ➤ It's on your way. Te pilla de paso.

to be **on one's way over** ▪ to be on one's way ya ir para allá ➤ I'm on my way over. Ya voy para allá.

to be **on one's way (to a place)** ir de camino a un lugar ▪ ir en camino a un lugar ▪ estar en camino a un lugar ➤ We were on our way to Marta's. Íbamos de camino a la casa de Marta. ▪ Íbamos en camino a la casa de Marta. ▪ Estabamos en camino a la casa de Marta.

on other occasions ▪ at other times en otras ocasiones

to be **on our side** ser de los nuestros ▪ estar de nuestra parte

to be **on page one (of the newspaper)** estar en primera plana

on paper ▪ in theory sobre el papel ▪ en teoría

to be **on part two** ir por la parte dos ➤ We're on part two. Vamos por la parte dos.

to be **on pins and needles** estar en ascuas ▪ estar en vilo

on principle por principio

on purpose: to do something ~ ▪ to do something deliberately ▪ to do something intentionally hacer algo aposta ▪ hacer algo adrede ▪ hacer algo intencionadamente ▪ hacer algo a propósito ▪ hacer algo con mala intención ▪ *(off-color)* hacer algo con mala hostia

on quite a few occasions ▪ on a number of occasions ▪ a number of times ▪ quite a few times en bastantes ocasiones

to be **on sale 1.** to be on special ▪ to be reduced in price estar rebajado de precio ▪ estar en oferta **2.** to be for sale de venta ▪ se vende *("On sale" means "reduced in price" except when followed by the words "here" or "now." The phrase "now on sale" is ambiguous.)*

on sale here de venta aquí

on sale now ▪ now on sale ya de venta ▪ ya se vende

to be **on schedule** ir según lo previsto ▪ ir según lo programado ▪ salir según lo previsto ▪ ir como estaba previsto ▪ salir como estaba planeado ➤ Construction on the house is on schedule and should be complete by mid February. ▪ Construction of the house is on schedule and should be complete by mid February. La construcción de la casa va según lo previsto y debería estar terminada para mediados de febrero.

on schedule: to arrive ~ llegar a la hora prevista ➤ *(pilot to passengers)* We expect to arrive on schedule. Esperamos llegar a la hora prevista.

on second thought pensándolo bien

on seeing it al verlo ▪ al verla

on seeing something like that ▪ when one sees something like that ante algo así

on seeing that... ▪ when one sees that... ▪ when one saw that... al comprobar que... ▪ al ver que...

on several occasions en varias ocasiones

on short notice en poco tiempo ▪ con poco tiempo ▪ a corto plazo ▪ al último momento ▪ con poca antelación ▪ con tan poca antelación

to be **on sick leave** estar de baja

on so many other occasions en otras tantas ocasiones

on someone's advice ▪ on the advice of someone por consejo de alguien

on someone's part por parte de alguien

to be **on someone's side** estar del lado de alguien

to be **on someone's turf** estar en terreno de alguien

to be **on special** ▪ to be on sale ▪ to be reduced in price estar en oferta ▪ estar rebajado de precio

on stage: to always be ~ ▪ to be given to histrionics tener mucho teatro

on stage: to go ~ pisar las tablas

on such and such a date en tal fecha

on tap: to have beer and ale ~ tener cerveza de barril ➤ The pub has beer and ale on tap. El pub tiene cerveza de barril.

on tap: to have something ~ *(informal)* ▪ to have something available tener algo disponible

to be **on target** quedar en el objetivo

on that we agree ▪ we agree on that en eso coincidimos ▪ estamos de acuerdo en eso

on the advice of someone ▪ on someone's advice por consejo de alguien

on the assumption that... sobre la base de que... ▪ suponiendo que...

on (the) average de media ▪ en promedio ▪ por término medio ▪ como término medio ▪ como promedio

on the back of the envelope ▪ on the reverse side of the envelope en el reverso del sobre ▪ en la parte de atrás del sobre ▪ por detrás del sobre ▪ en el dorso del sobre ▪ en la parte trasera del sobre

to be **on the ball** ser despabilado ▪ estar al tanto ▪ ser listo

on the banks of a orillas de ➤ Ciudad Bolivar, founded in 1595, lies on the banks of Venezuela's Orinoco River. Ciudad Bolivar, fundada en 1595, está situada a orillas del Río Orinoco en Venezuela.

on the basis of ▪ based on en base a

on the chance that suponiendo que ▪ en caso de que

on the cheap al alpargata

to be **on the clock** cobrar el tiempo ➤ Let's stop ten minutes early, but you'll still be on the clock. Paremos diez minutos antes, pero cobrarás el tiempo completo.

on the condition that... con la condición de que... ▪ a condición de que...

on the contrary al contrario ▪ todo lo contrario ▪ antes bien ▪ por el contrario ▪ antes al contrario ▪ de lo contrario

to be **on the corner** estar en la equina ▪ hacer esquina ➤ The restaurant is on the corner. El restaurante está en la esquina. ▪ El restaurante hace esquina.

on the count of ten a la cuenta de diez ▪ a las diez

on the count of three a la cuenta de tres

to be **on the cover of** ser portada de ➤ His picture was on the cover of *Time.* Su cuadro fue portada de *Time.*

to be **on the cutting edge** estar en la vanguardia ➤ Contemporary Cuban jazz is on the cutting edge. El jazz cubano contemporáneo está en la vanguardia. ▪ El jazz cubano actual está en la vanguardia.

to be **on the decline** andar de caída ▪ estar en declive

to be **on the decrease** ir diminuyendo

to be **on the defensive** estar a la defensiva ▪ estar receloso(-a)

on the defensive: to go ~ ponerse a la defensiva

on the doctor's orders por recomendación médica

on the domestic front ▪ on the home front en el frente interno ▪ en el frente doméstico

on the dot en punto ➤ At six o'clock on the dot. A las seis en punto.

on the double! ▪ quick! ¡deprisa!

on the eve of en vísperas de

to be **on the exam** salir en el examen ▪ poner en el examen ➤ It's going to be on the exam. Va a salir en el examen. ▪ Lo van a poner en el examen.

on the face of it ▪ when first considered en apariencia ▪ a primera vista

on the following day ▪ the following day ▪ (the) next day al día siguiente ▪ al otro día

to be **on the fringes of society** estar al márgen de la sociedad ▪ ser marginado(-a)

on the front of the envelope en el anverso del sobre ▪ en la parte de delante del sobre ▪ por delante del sobre

to be **on the go** andar la carrera ➤ He's really on the go. Siempre anda la carrera.

on the high seas en alta mar

on the home front ▪ on the domestic front en el frente doméstico ▪ en el frente interno

to be **on the horns of a dilemma** ▪ to face a dilemma ▪ to be faced with a dilemma afrontar un dilema ▪ verse ante un dilema ▪ estar entre la espada y la pared

to be **on the house** ser a cuenta de la casa ▪ correr a cuenta de la casa ➤ Drinks are on the house. Las bebidas son a cuenta de la casa. ▪ La bebidas corren a cuenta de la casa.

on the ice con el hielo ➤ Be careful on the ice. Ten cuidado con el hielo. ➤ It's difficult to turn on the ice. Es difícil dar la vuelta con el hielo.

to be **on the increase** ▪ to be increasing ▪ to be rising ir en aumento ▪ ir en ascenso ➤ The number of complaints is constantly on the increase. ▪ The number of complaints is constantly increasing. ▪ The number of complaints is rising constantly. La cantidad de quejas va en aumento constante.

on the inside por dentro

on-the-job accident ▪ accident at work ▪ accident on the job ▪ accident while at work accidente laboral

on the left ▪ to the left a la izquierda ▪ de la izquierda ➤ The illustration on the left La ilustración de la izquierda

to be **on the lookout for** ▪ to be on the watch for estar a la mirada de ▪ estar a la expectativa de

to be **on the loose** ▪ to be loose andar suelto

to be **on the make** echar el agua a su molino ▪ llevar el agua a su molino

to be **on the market** estar puesto en el mercado

on the morning of por la mañana de ▪ en la mañana de ➤ The incidents occurred on the morning of October twelfth last year. Los hechos ocurrieron en la mañana del doce de octubre del año pasado.

on the move andando de acá para allá

on the next line en la próxima línea

on the night of *x* el *x* por la noche ➤ On the night of December eighteenth El dieciocho de diciembre por la noche

on the other end of the (telephone) line al otro lado de la línea (telefónica)

on the other hand en cambio ▪ por otra parte ▪ por otro lado

on the other side al otro lado

to be **on the other side of** ▪ to be behind estar detrás de ➤ The metro station is on the other side of this building. La estación del metro está detrás de este edificio.

on the other side of town from here ▪ on the other side of town ▪ on the other end of the city ▪ across town en la otra punta de la ciudad

to be **on the outs with someone** ▪ to have had a falling out with someone estar de morros con alguien ▪ estar reñido con alguien ▪ haber regañado con alguien

on the outside por fuera

to be **on the outside looking in** ver algo desde fuera ▪ estar desde fuera mirando a dentro ▪ estar desde fuera mirando hacia dentro ▪ estar viendo los toros desde la barrera ➤ I'm on the outside looking in. Lo veo desde fuera.

to be **on the payroll** estar de plantilla ▪ estar en (la) plantilla

to be **on the phone** estar al teléfono ▪ estar hablando por teléfono ➤ I'm on the phone. Estoy hablando por teléfono. ▪ Estoy al teléfono. ➤ Who's on the phone? ¿Quién está llamando? ▪ ¿Quién está utilizando el teléfono? ➤ He's been on the phone for an hour. Hace una hora que habla por teléfono.

on the pretext of ▪ under the pretext of con el pretexto de ▪ en achaque de ▪ *(law)* so pretexto de

to be **on the rag** *(off-color)* ▪ to be having one's menstrual period estar con el semáforo rojo

on the right ▪ to the right a la derecha ▪ de la derecha ➤ The illustration on the right La ilustración de la derecha

to be **on the right track** ir por (el) buen camino ▪ estar en el buen camino ▪ estar bien encaminado ➤ You're on the right track. Vas por buen camino. ▪ Estás en el buen camino.

to be **on the rise** estar en alza

to be **on the road to recovery** ▪ to be getting better estar mejorando ▪ ir mejorando

to be **on the ropes** estar contra las cuerdas

on the ropes: to put someone ~ empujar a alguien contra las cuerdas ▪ *(Sp.)* colocar a alguien contra las cuerdas

to be **on the run** estar huyendo ➤ The fugitives are on the run. Los fugitivos están huyendo.

on the run: to do something ~ hacer algo de prisa y corriendo ➤ We ate on the run. Comimos de prisa y corriendo.

on the run: to have (got) someone ~ hacer andar a alguien a salto de mata ➤ We've got him on the run. Le hacemos andar a salto de mata.

to be **on the safe side** ▪ to play it safe curarse en salud ➤ I'll buy some extra bulbs (just) to be on the safe side. Compraré alguna bombillas adicionales para curarme en salud. ▪ Compraré alguna bombillas extras y me curaré en salud.

on the shores of ▪ by the shores of a orillas de ➤ On the shores of the gulf ▪ On the gulf shores A orillas del golfo

on the sly a solapo ▪ de ocultis

on the spot ▪ then and there ▪ while one waits en el acto ▪ allí mismo ➤ I signed the document on the spot and gave it back to the courier to return to the sender. Firmé el documento en el acto y se lo volví a entregar al mensajero para que lo devolviera al remitente. ➤ The victim's leg was so badly injured that the rescuers had to amputate it on the spot. La víctima acabó con la pierna derecha tan dañada que los socorristas tuvieron que amputársela allí mismo.

on the spur of the moment: to do something ~ ▪ to do something without having planned it ahead of time hacer algo sin pensar(lo) ▪ hacer algo sin pararse a pensar ▪ hacer algo sin reflexión ▪ en un arranque ▪ hacer algo sobre la marcha ▪ hacer algo de improviso

to be **on the table** 1. estar en la mesa ▪ estar sobre la mesa 2. to be under consideration estar sobre el tapete ➤ The book is on the table where I left it. El libro está en la mesa donde lo dejé. ➤ There are several proposals on the table. ▪ There are several proposals under consideration. Hay varias propuestas sobre el tapete.

to be **on the threshold of** estar en el umbral de ➤ We're on the threshold of a new change. Estamos en el umbral de un nuevo cambio.

on the tip of one's tongue: to be (right) ~ ▪ to have something on the tip of one's tongue tener algo en la punta de la lengua ➤ It's (right) on the tip of my tongue. Lo tengo en la punta de la lengua.

on the top of the box en la parte superior de la caja ▪ en lo alto ▪ en la cima

on the trail of the horses siguiendo las huellas de los caballos

on the underside of en los bajos de

to be **on the verge of** estar al borde ▪ estar cerca de ➤ *(film title) Women on the Verge of a Nervous Breakdown Mujeres al borde de un ataque de nervios* ➤ *(news item)* The capital of the country is on the verge of chaos. La capital del país está cerca del caos.

on the verge of collapse al borde del colapso ➤ A new strike in the transportation sector has placed automobile plants on the verge of collapse. Una nueva huelga en el sector del transporte ha colocado a las plantas automovilísticas al borde del colapso.

to be **on the verge of war** estar al borde de la guerra

on the way ▪ along the way sobre la marcha ▪ en tránsito ➤ We'll stop for lunch on the way. ▪ We'll stop for lunch along the way. Paramos para comer sobre la marcha.

on the way back a la vuelta ▪ al regreso

on the way back from ▪ coming back from ▪ on returning from al volver de ▪ a la vuelta de ▪ al regreso de ➤ On the way back from the airport... Al volver del aeropuerto...

to be **on the way back from a place** ir de vuelta de un lugar ▪ venir de vuelta de un lugar

on the way to camino de ▪ con rumbo a

to be **on the wrong track** ir por el mal camino ▪ ir por mal camino

on thin ice: to tread ~ danzar sobre un volcán

to be **on to someone** conocerle el juego a alguien ▪ verle el juego a alguien

to be **on top** estar encima

to be **on top of** estar encima de

on top of that encima de eso

to be **on tour** estar de gira

on tour: to go ~ ir de gira

to be **on TV** dar en la tele ▪ poner en la tele ▪ *(referring to a movie)* pasar en la tele ➤ What's on TV? ¿Qué dan en la tele? ▪ ¿Qué están dando en la tele? ▪ ¿Qué están pasando en la tele?

on weekdays ▪ Monday through Friday los días laborables ▪ de lunes a viernes

on weekends los fines de semana ▪ de sábado a domingo

on which en los que ▪ en las que ➤ *(news item)* In Spain, Fridays and Sundays are the days on which most computer attacks occur. En España, los viernes y los domingos son los días en los que se producen más ataques informáticos.

on you go to... se va luego a...

on your mark, get set, go! ¡preparados, listos, ya!

to be **on vacation** estar de vacaciones

on vacation: to go ~ irse de vacaciones

once a humble immigrant antes inmigrante humilde

once a month una vez al mes

once a week una vez a la semana

once a year una vez al año ▪ una vez por año

once again 1. as I say ▪ to repeat como he dicho ▪ lo dicho **2.** an additional time otra vez

once and for all de una vez por todas ▪ de una vez para siempre ▪ una vez por todas ▪ de una vez ▪ definitivamente

once every two years ▪ every other year ▪ once each two years ▪ every two years ▪ every second year cada dos años ▪ un año sí y otro no

once I had (done something)... ▪ when I had (done something)... una vez que hube (hecho algo)... ➤ Once I had written the letter, I went for a walk. ▪ When I had written the letter, I went for a walk. Una vez que hube escrito la carta, fui de paseo.

once I read the article ▪ after I read the article ▪ when I read the article **1.** *(past, pronounced "red")* una vez que leí el artículo ▪ al leer el artículo **2.** *(future, pronounced "reed")* una vez que (yo) lea el artículo ▪ al leer el artículo

once in ya en ➤ Once in Madrid, he went straight to his hotel. Ya en Madrid fue directamente a su hotel.

once in a blue moon cada muerte de obispo ▪ de uvas a peras ▪ de higos a brevas ▪ de pascuas a ramos

once in a great while muy de vez en cuando ▪ de tarde en tarde ▪ poco frecuentemente

once in a lifetime una vez en la vida

once-in-a-lifetime de una vez en la vida

once in a while de vez en cuando

once too often una vez en demás ➤ She was insubordinate once too often, and it cost her her job. Ella se insubordinó una vez en demás, y ello le costó su trabajo.

once upon a time érase una vez ▪ érase que se era

once upon a time there was érase una vez ▪ érase que era ▪ había una vez

once upon a time there were éranse una vez

once when ▪ one time when en una ocasión en que

once you get to know her *(tú)* una vez que la conozcas ▪ *(usted)* una vez que (usted) la conozca

once you get to know him *(tú)* una vez que lo conozcas ▪ *(usted)* una vez que (usted) lo conozca ▪ *(Sp., leísmo)* una vez que le conozcas ▪ una vez que (usted) le conozca

oncoming vehicle vehículo contrario

one after another uno detrás de otro ▪ catarata ➤ She ate one chocolate after another. ▪ She ate chocolate after chocolate. Comía un bombón detrás del otro. ➤ One scandal after another ▪ Scandal after scandal Una catarata de escándalos

one after the other ▪ in a continuous stream en fila india ▪ uno detrás de otro ▪ uno tras otro ▪ uno después de otro ➤ The cars in the funeral procession came one after the other for miles. Los coches en el funeral recorrieron millas en fila india.

one always finds reasons... siempre se encuentra argumentos...

one and a half times as large as ▪ one and a half times the size of de un tamaño igual a una vez y media ➤ *(news item)* Never before had astronomers seen anything like it in the universe: a bubble of water one and a half times as large as the solar system. Nunca hasta ahora habían visto los astrónomos algo así en el universo: una burbuja de agua, de un tamaño igual a una vez y media el sistema solar.

one and a half times the size of ▪ one and a half times as large as de un tamaño igual a una vez y media ➤ Never before had astronomers seen anything like it in the universe: a bubble of water one and a half times the size of the solar system. Nunca hasta ahora habían visto los astrónomos algo así en el universo: una burbuja de agua, de un tamaño igual a una vez y media el sistema solar.

one and the same uno mismo

one at a time ▪ one by one uno por uno ▪ uno detrás de otro ▪ uno después de otro ▪ uno por vez ▪ uno cada vez ▪ de uno en uno ▪ de a uno ➤ Let's do them one at a time. Hágamoslos uno por uno. ➤ One at time, please! ¡De uno en uno, por favor! ▪ ¡De a uno, por favor!

to be **one block over** *(implying a street parallel to the one you are on)* ▪ to be one street over quedar a una calle ▪ estar a una calle

one by one uno a uno ▪ uno por uno ▪ uno en uno ▪ de uno en uno

one can see that... ▪ you can see that... se echa de ver que...

one can see why ▪ you can see why se ve por qué

one could see why ▪ you could see why se veía por qué

one day ▪ on a certain day cierto día ▪ un buen día ➤ One day, Schubert's father went to his son's school to look at his school record. It was terrible. Cierto día, el padre de Schubert fue a la escuela de su hijo para ver su historial académico. Fue malísimo.

one day at a time: to take life ~ ▪ to take life a day at a time ▪ to live life one day at a time vivir la vida al día ▪ vivir cada día ➤ Right now, after the death of my friend, I'm just taking life one day at a time. Estos días, después de la muerte de mi amiga, vivo la vida al día. ▪ Estos días, después de la muerte de mi amiga, vivo cada día.

one eighteenth un dieciochavo ▪ un dieciochoavo

one eighth un octavo

one eleventh un onceavo

one fifteenth un quinceavo

one fifth un quinto

one fiftieth un cincuentavo

one fifty-first un cincuentiunavo

one fine day un buen día

one for the money, two for the show, three to get ready, and four to go! *(children's version of "on your mark, get set, go!")* ▪ one for the money, two for the show, three to make ready, and four to go! ¡preparados, listos, ya! ▪ ¡a la de una, a la de dos, a la de tres!

one fortieth un cuarentavo

one forty-first un cuarentiunavo

one fourteenth un catorceavo

one fourth un cuarto

one good turn deserves another amor con amor se paga

one had obviously gotten ▪ one obviously got habría conseguido

one half un medio ▪ la mitad ➤ Five tenths of something represents (one) half of it. Cinco partido por diez representa la mitad de una cosa. ▪ Cinco décimos representan la mitad de una cosa. ▪ Cinco décimas partes representan la mitad de una cosa.

one has ever: that ~ que uno ha pasado en su vida ▪ de la vida de uno ➤ *(Mark Twain)* The coldest winter I've ever spent was a summer in San Francisco. El invierno más frío de mi vida fue un verano (que pasé) en San Francisco.

one hell of a party *(L. Am.)* pachanga sideral ▪ *(Sp.)* fiesta de puta madre ▪ juerga monumental ▪ fiesta de más ➤ It was one hell of a party! ¡La fiesta estuvo de más! ▪ ¡Armaron una pachanga sideral!

the **(one) hundredth anniversary** el efímero centenario

the **one I really like** el que de verdad me gusta ▪ la que de verdad me gusta

to be **one in a million** ser uno entre un millón

one last chance ▪ one more chance una oportunidad más ▪ una última oportunidad ➤ I'll give you one last chance. ▪ I'll give you one more chance. Le daré la última oportunidad.

one like it uno igual ▪ una igual

one man, one vote un hombre, un voto

one-man show (of paintings) *la* exhibición (de pinturas)

one might not have done something puede que uno no hubiera hecho algo ▪ puede que uno no hubiese hecho algo ▪ uno podría no haber hecho algo ▪ uno pudo no haber hecho algo ➤ I might not have done this book if I had known how long it was going to take. Puede que no hubiera hecho este libro si hubiera sabido cuánto tiempo me iba a llevar. ▪ Podría no haber hecho este libro si hubiera sabido cuánto tiempo me iba a llevar. ➤ *(news items)* The pilot of the ill-fated airplane might not have understood the control tower's instructions. El piloto del avión siniestrado pudo no haber entendido las instrucciones de la torre de control. ➤ Without your help I might not have undertaken the project. Sin tu ayuda puede que no hubiera emprendido este proyecto.

one month before ▪ one month earlier un mes antes

one month before something happened un mes antes de que ocurriera algo ▪ un mes antes de que pasara algo ▪ un mes antes de que aconteciera algo

one more thing! ¡una cosa más! ▪ ¡hay otra cosa!

one mustn't... ▪ one must not... no se debiera...

one never knows uno nunca sabe

one-night stand una actuación de una sola noche

one nineteenth un diecinueveavo

one ninth un noveno

to be **one of a kind** ▪ to be unique **1.** *(thing)* ser único en su tipo ▪ ser único en su género **2.** *(person)* ser un fuera de serie ▪ ser una persona fuera de serie ▪ ser una persona excepcional

one of her *(general)* uno(-a) de sus ▪ *(unique to the person)* de los suyos **2.** uno de sus ➤ The opera singer threw one of her tantrums. La cantante de ópera lanzó un berrinche de los suyos. ▪ La cantante de ópera lanzó uno de sus berrinches.

one of his *(general)* uno(-a) de sus ▪ *(unique to the person)* de los suyos ➤ *(news item)* John McEnroe feigned one of his tantrums. John McEnroe fingió una rabieta de las suyas. ▪ John McEnroe fingió una de sus rabietas.

one of the few uno de los pocos

to be **one of the few that...** *(referring to things)* ser (uno) de los pocos que... ▪ ser (una) de las pocas que...

to be **one of the few who...** *(referring to people)* ser (uno) de los pocos que... ▪ ser (una) de las pocas que...

to be **one of the first (people) to do something** ▪ to be among the first people to do something ser de las primeras personas en hacer algo ➤ I was one of the first people to sign up. Fui una de las primeras personas en inscribirme.

one of the regulars uno de los parroquianos

one of these days un día de estos

to be **one of these people who** ▪ to be one of those (people) who ser de los que... ➤ I'm one of these people who... Soy de los que...

one of those uno de esos ➤ I must have swallowed one of those hot peppers. Me he debido de tragar uno de esos chiles picantes. ▪ Me he debido haber tragado uno de esos chiles picantes. ➤ He's one of those adventurous types. Es uno de esos tipos aventureros.

to be **one of today's...** ser uno de... de la actualidad ➤ He is one of today's most prolific authors, with more than three hundred books to his credit. Es uno de los autores más prolíficos de la actualidad con más de trescientos libros en su haber.

to be **one of us** ser uno de los nuestros ➤ He's one of us. Es uno de los nuestros. ➤ She's one of us. Es una de las nuestras.

one one-hundredth ▪ a hundredth un centésimo

the **one one really likes** el que de verdad le gusta ▪ la que de verdad le gusta ▪ lo que verdad le gusta ➤ The one she really likes is... El que de verdad le gusta es...

one other otro ➤ I've lived in only one other place longer than I have lived in this apartment, and that's the house I grew up in. He vivido sólo en otro lugar durante más tiempo de lo que he vivido en este piso, y es la casa donde me crié. ➤ I've only been there one other time. Sólo he estado allí en otra ocasión.

one-party system sistema de partido único

one right after the other uno detrás del otro ➤ You should have two copies on the hard disk and save one right after the other. Deberías tener dos copias en el disco duro y guardar una detrás de la otra.

one seventeenth un diecisieteavo

one seventh un séptimo

one seventieth un sesentavo

one seventy-first un sesentaiunavo

to be **one short** ▪ to be shorted one faltar uno ▪ tener uno de menos ▪ darle uno de menos ➤ I'm one short. Me falta uno. ▪ Tengo uno de menos. ➤ They shorted me one. Me dieron uno de menos.

one-sided view *la* opinión parcial

one sixteenth un dieciséisavo

one sixth un sexto

one sixtieth un sesentavo

one sixty-first un sesentiunavo

to be **one step ahead of someone** ▪ to be a step ahead of someone estar un paso más por adelante de alguien

one tenth un décimo

one thing after another de susto en susto

one thing at a time! ¡cada cosa a su vez! ▪ ¡sólo una cosa por vez! ▪ ¡no todo a la vez! ▪ ¡no tantas cosas a la vez!

one thing led to another una cosa llevó a la otra

one third un tercio

one thirteenth un treceano

one thirtieth un treintavo

one thirty-first un treintaiunavo

one time ▪ once alguna vez ▪ cierta vez ➤ *(Unamuno)* One time a mother asked don Manuel to heal her son. ▪ Once a mother asked don Manuel to heal her son. Alguna vez una madre le pidió a don Manuel que le curara a su hijo.

one time when ▪ once when en una ocasión en que

one too many (drinks): to have had ~ tener unas copas de más ▪ tomar unas copas de más ➤ Somebody else should drive. He's had one too many. Otra persona debería conducir. Tiene unas copas de más. ▪ Ha tomado unas copas de más.

one-track mind: to have a ~ tener una mente de una línea

one twelfth un doceavo

one twentieth un veinteavo ▪ un veintavo ▪ un vigésimo

one twenty-first un veinteunavo ▪ uno sobre veintiuno

one twenty-second un veintedosavo ▪ uno sobre veintidós

one way de un trayecto ➤ The fare is ninety-four euros one way and one hundred twenty-two round trip. El pasaje de un trayecto es noventa y cuatro euros y ciento veinte y dos de ida y vuelta.

one way or another de una forma o de otra ▪ de una forma u otra

one-way street *la* calle de un (solo) sentido ▪ calle de un sentido ▪ calle de sentido único ▪ calle de dirección única

one-way ticket billete de ida (solamente) ▪ billete sencillo

one way to prevent... una manera de evitar...

to be the **one who** ser el que ▪ ser la que ➤ His mother was the one who took it the worst. Su madre era la que lo llevaba peor. ➤ His father was the one who took it the worst. Su padre era el que lo llevaba peor.

the **one who caused...** el que causó... ▪ la que causó... ▪ el causante de... ▪ la causante de...

to be the **one who does it best** ▪ to be the best there is ser el que mejor lo hace

to be the **one who said...** ser quien dijo... ▪ ser aquél que dijo... ▪ ser el que dijo... ➤ It was Mark Twain who said... Fue Mark Twain quien dijo... ▪ Fue Mark Twain aquél que dijo... ▪ Fue Mark Twain el que dijo... ➤ It was Joan of Arc who said... Fue Juana de Arco quien dijo... ▪ Fue Juana de Arco aquella que dijo... ▪ Fue Juana de Arco la que dijo...

one would be better off... ▪ it would be better to... le convendría más a uno... ▪ le quedaría mejor a uno... ➤ You'd be better off waiting. ▪ It would be better to wait. Te convendría más esperar. ▪ Te quedaría más esperar.

one would be willing to do something uno estaría dispuesto a hacer algo ▪ uno querría hacer algo ➤ I was wondering if you would be willing to help me. Me preguntaba si querrías ayudarme.

one would do well to... uno haría bien en... ▪ se haría bien en...

one would hardly suppose ni siquiera se supondría ▪ casi no se supondría ▪ ni siquiera se imaginaría ▪ apenas se imaginaría

one would think that... ▪ you would think that... uno podría pensar que... ▪ se podría pensar que... ▪ cabe pensar que... ▪ cabría pensar que...

one's age: people ~ la gente de la edad de uno

one's age group: people in ~ la gente del mismo grupo etario ▪ la gente en el mismo grupo etario ▪ la gente del segmento de edad de uno

one's better half su media naranja ▪ su cara mitad

to be **one's business** ▪ to be one's own business corresponderle a uno

to be **one's concern** ▪ to concern one atañerle a uno ➤ That's not my concern. ▪ That doesn't concern me. Eso no me atañe. ➤ It's not my concern. No me atañe.

to be **one's cost** estar a la cuenta de uno ➤ It shouldn't be my cost. The landlord should pay for it. No debería estar a mi cuenta. El casero debería pagarlo.

one's doing something que uno haga algo ▪ que uno haya hecho algo ➤ We really appreciate your staying in touch. Realmente apreciamos que te hayas mantenido en contacto con nosotros. ➤ Your dropping out of the class surprised me. El que hayas abandonado la clase me sorprendió. ▪ El que te hayas retirado de la clase me sorprendió.

one's having done something el que uno haya hecho algo

one's life's work trabajo de la vida de uno

to be **one's normal self** ser su ser normal

one's not doing something el que uno no haga algo

one's not having (done something) el que uno no haya (hecho algo) ➤ We really don't understand your not having written. De veras no entendemos el que no hayas escrito.

one's only concern su único preocupación

one's own ▪ belonging to oneself propio(o) ▪ mismo(o) ▪ el suyo ➤ The robber's own brother turned him in. El propio hermano del atracador lo denunció. ➤ She has a mind of her own. Ella piensa por sí misma. ➤ Not my own (wedding), my daughter's. No la (boda) mía, la de mi hija.

to be **one's own doing** ser obra suya

one's people ▪ one's family los suyos

one's things: to gather up ~ recoger los bártulos

one's things: to put ~ poner los bártulos de uno ➤ I'll show you where to put your things. Te enseño dónde poner tus bártulos. ▪ Te digo dónde poner tus bártulos.

one's things: to put away ~ colocar los bártulos de uno

one's time su época (de uno)

to be **one's turn** tocarle a uno ➤ So Friday it was my turn. Así que el viernes me tocó a mí.

to be **oneself** ser uno mismo ➤ Be yourself. *(tú)* Sé tú mismo. ▪ *(usted)* Sea usted mismo. ➤ I'm myself in spite of myself, but I'd like to be myself on purpose. Soy yo mismo a pesar de mí mismo, pero me gustaría ser yo mismo adrede.

to be an **ongoing battle** ser una batalla abierta ➤ The relationship between José and Marta is an ongoing battle. La relación entre José y Marta es una batalla abierta.

ongoing problems problemas continuos ➤ There are serious ongoing problems with their equipment. Hay problemas serios y continuos con su equipo.

onion rings aros de cebolla

online en línea con ➤ Sky High Airlines online En línea con Sky High Airlines

to be **only a matter of time before...** ser sólo cuestión de tiempo hasta que...

to be **only a month until** quedar sólo un mes para

only a week before... a sólo una semana de...

to be **only a week until** quedar sólo una semana para

the **only alternative is (to...)** la única alternativa es (que...)

to be **only average** ▪ to be just average no exceder de lo corriente

only child: to be an ~ ser hijo único ➤ She's an only child. Ella es hija única.

to **only go as far as** ▪ to go only to sólo llegar hasta ▪ sólo llegar a ➤ This street only goes as far as the Plaza de Castilla. ▪ This street only goes to the Plaza de Castilla. Esta calle sólo llega a la Plaza de Castilla. ▪ Esta calle sólo llega hasta la Plaza de Castilla. ➤ This train only goes as far as Chamartín. You have to take the commuter train or metro to Atocha. Este tren sólo llega hasta Chamartín. Hay que coger el tren de cercanías o el metro a Atocha. ▪ Este tren sólo llega hasta Chamartín. Hay que tomar el tren de cercanías o el metro a Atocha.

only hours later tan sólo horas después

to be **only joking** ▪ to be just joking ser de mentira

only now 1. at this moment sólo hasta ahora **2.** just recently recién ahora **3.** in our time sólo hoy en día **4.** only *now* apenas ahora pero ➤ Only now there are medications to treat the disease. Sólo hasta ahora existen medicinas para tratar la enfermedad. ➤ Only now are there medications to treat the disease. Sólo hoy en día hay medicamentos para tratar la enfermedad. ➤ Only *now*, she's saying just the opposite. Apenas ahora, dice justo lo contrario.

the **only one** el único ▪ la única ▪ sólo ▪ solamente ➤ I was the only one who attended class. Fui la única que asistió a la clase. ▪ Sólo yo asistí a la clase. ▪ Solamente yo asistí a la clase. ➤ I'm the only one left. Soy el único que queda.

only surviving ▪ only one left único(-a) que queda ➤ My grandmother is my only surviving grandparent. Mi abuela es la única que (me) queda.

only then sólo entonces

only then did I realize it sólo entonces caí en la cuenta ▪ sólo entonces me di cuenta

only then did I realize that... sólo entonces caí en la cuenta de que... ▪ sólo entonces me di cuenta de que...

the **only thing I care about is...** ▪ all I care about is... lo único que me interesa es...

the **only thing I thought about was...** lo único en que (yo) pensaba era en...

the **only thing it's good for is...** sólo sirve para...

the **only thing it's good for is to...** ▪ all it's good for is to... sólo sirve para...

the **only thing that even comes close to something** lo único que siquiera está a la altura de algo ▪ lo único que siquiera se aproxima a algo ▪ lo único que siquiera se parece a algo

only to be expected that...: it's ~ sólo se pretende que... ▪ sólo se aguarda que...

the **only way to 1.** *(all contexts)* la única manera de ▪ la única vía para **2.** the only route to el único camino a ▪ el único camino hacia ➤ The only way to get to the ranch is via Highway 36. La única vía para llegar al rancho es la Carretera 36.

only *x* (out) of *y* tan sólo *x* de *y* ➤ *(news item)* Only 29 (out) of 350 legislators belong to groups that have expressed their support for considering the bill. Tan sólo 29 de 350 diputados pertenecen a formaciones que han manifestado su apoyo a la toma en consideración del proyecto.

only yesterday ▪ just yesterday mismamente ayer

onset of puberty comienzo de la pubertad

onset of symptoms *la* aparición de los síntomas

to be **onto someone** conocerle el juego

to **open a (big) can of worms** destapar la olla

to **open a law practice** ▪ to establish a law practice ▪ to begin practicing law abrir (un) bufete

open-air cafe ▪ outdoor cafe *el* café al aire libre

open-air market mercado al aire libre ▪ mercadillo

to **open an account 1.** *(bank)* abrir una cuenta **2.** *(medical insurance, etc.)* darse de alta

to **open an investigation** abrir expediente

to be an **open book** ser (como) un libro abierto

open country campo raso ▪ lo raso

to **open fire** abrir fuego ▪ comenzar a disparar

open-heart surgery operación a corazón abierto

to **open into** ▪ to lead to conducir a

to **open inwards** abrirse hacia dentro ▪ abrirse para dentro ➤ The door opens inwards. La puerta se abre hacia dentro.

open mind: to have an ~ ▪ to be open-minded tener una mentalidad abierta

open mind: to keep an ~ mantener una mentalidad abierta

to be **open-minded** ▪ to have an open mind tener una mentalidad abierta

to **open oneself to** abrirse a

to **open onto** ▪ to open out onto abrirse a ▪ dar a ▪ acceder ➤ This door opens onto the patio. Esta puerta se abre al patio. ▪ Esta puerta da al patio.

to **open outwards** ▪ to open out ▪ to open away from you abrirse hacia fuera ▪ abrirse para fuera ➤ The door opens outwards. La puerta se abre hacia fuera. ▪ La puerta se abre para fuera.

open stretch trecho abierto ▪ tramo despejado

to **open the curtains** ▪ to draw back the curtains abrir las cortinas

to **open the season** iniciar la temporada ➤ The game between Tennessee and Auburn opens the season. El partido entre Tennessee y Auburn inicia la temporada.

open ticket *(usable any time, usually referring to a return trip)* billete abierto ➤ Is it an open ticket? ¿Es un billete abierto?

to be **open to suggestions** estar abierto(-a) a sugerencias

to **open towards you** abrirse hacia ti ▪ abrirse hacia usted ➤ The door opens towards you. La puerta se abre hacia ti. ▪ La puerta se abre hacia usted.

open university universidad a distancia

to **open up** **1.** *(store, restaurant)* abrir (las puertas) **2.** to let down one's guard and disclose one's thoughts to someone abrirse a alguien ▪ abrirse con alguien **3.** to become visible abrirse ante uno ➤ What time do you open (up)? ¿A qué hora abre (las puertas)? ➤ A spectacular view opened up in front of us. ▪ A spectacular view opened up before us. Una vista espectacular se abrió ante nosotros.

opening act acto de apertura

opening night noche del estreno ➤ The dress rehearsal was rocky, but the opening night came off without a hitch. El ensayo general resultó flojo, pero la noche del estreno salió sin ningún contratiempo.

opening of a store ▪ grand opening *la* inauguración de una tienda

opening of bidding ▪ taking of bids apertura pública de concurso de obras

opening of bids apertura de las pujas

opening prayer ▪ invocation *la* oración de apertura ▪ oración inicial ▪ *la* invocación

opening soon! ¡abrimos proximamente!

opening today! ¡abrimos hoy!

to **operate a business** ▪ to run a business regentar un negocio ▪ llevar un negocio

to **operate a machine** ▪ to run a machine manejar una máquina

to **operate a private taxi service with one's own car** botear (con su propio coche)

to **operate at a loss** ▪ to run at a loss trabajar a pérdida

to **operate at full capacity** ▪ to run at full capacity funcionar a tope ▪ correr a todo dar

to **operate for profit** ▪ to run for profit gestionar con ánimo de lucro ▪ gestionar a fin de lucro ▪ gestionar a fin de lucrar

to **operate on a patient** operar a un(-a) paciente ➤ I know a surgeon who operated on his dog. Conozco un cirujano que operó a su perro.

operated on: to have one's knee ~ operarse de la rodilla ▪ operarle de la rodilla a alguien ➤ I had my knee operated on. Me he operado de la rodilla. ▪ Me han operado de la rodilla. ➤ He had his knee operated on. Se ha operado de la rodilla.

to be **operating in the red** estar en números rojos

operating system *(computer)* sistema operativo

opinion poll sondeo (de opinión) ▪ encuesta ➤ Opinion polls capture a cross section of society. Los sondeos captan una muestra representativa de la sociedad.

opposite direction sentido contrario

to be the **opposite of** ser el contrario de ▪ ser lo contrario de ▪ ser el opuesto de ➤ South is the opposite of north. Sur es el contrario de norte. ▪ Sur es lo contrario de norte. ➤ What's the opposite of red?-Green! ¿Cual es el contrario de rojo?-¡Verde! ➤ The opposite of heavy is light. El contrario de pesado es ligero. ▪ Lo contrario de pesado es ligero.

opposite sex sexo opuesto

opposite side of ▪ other side of cara opuesta de ▪ antípodas de ➤ *(news item)* The NASA robot lands successfully on the opposite side of Mars from its twin "Spirit." ▪ The NASA robot lands successfully on the other side of Mars from its twin "Spirit." El robot de NASA aterriza con éxito en la cara opuesta de Marte donde está su gemelo "Spirit". ▪ El robot de NASA aterriza con éxito en las antípodas de Marte donde está su gemelo "Spirit".

opposite something: to be (directly) ~ estar opuesto a algo ➤ It is on the wall opposite the clock. Está en la pared opuesta a la del reloj.

opposites attract los polos opuestos se atraen

optical illusion ilusión óptica ▪ trampantojo ▪ ilusión de óptica

or am I? ¿o sí? ➤ I'm not needed anymore, or am I? ¿Ya no me necesitan, o sí?

or are we? ¿o sí? ➤ We're not needed anymore, are we? ¿Ya no nos necesitan, o sí?

or better yet ▪ or even better o mejor aún ▪ o mejor todavía

or both o ambas cosas

or does it? ¿o sí?

or (else) ▪ or otherwise ▪ because otherwise ▪ because if you don't si no ▪ de lo contrario ▪ o si no ➤ I need to close my storage locker by the ninth, or (else) I'll have to pay another month's rent. Necesito cerrar mi trastero para el día nueve, si no tendré que pagar otro mes de alquiler.

or even... e incluso... ▪ *(following a negative verb)* ni tampoco ➤ I couldn't find the house or even the street. No pude encontrar la casa ni tampoco la calle.

or even better ▪ or better yet o mejor aún

or even worse ▪ or worse yet o peor aún

or is it? ¿o sí?

or otherwise ▪ or else o de otra manera ▪ de otra manera

or rather (o) mejor dicho o bien ▪ más bien ▪ o más bien

or so ▪ in about ▪ or thereabouts o así ▪ o por ahí ▪ más o menos ➤ In an hour or so ▪ In about an hour En una hora más o menos

or so he says o por lo menos eso dice él ▪ o según dice él ▪ o así lo dice él ▪ o según (él) dice ▪ o según (el) lo dice

or so it seemed o eso parecía

or so it seems o eso parece

or so they say o eso dicen ▪ o al menos eso dicen ▪ o según dicen ▪ o así lo dicen

... or something? pero ¿es que...?

or something like that o algo así

or something to that effect o algo por el estilo

or vice versa o viceversa ▪ o al revés

or we'll be late que llegamos tarde ➤ Come on, or we'll be late. Venga, venga que llegamos tarde.

or words to that effect o palabras por el estilo

or worse yet ▪ or even worse o peor aún

orchestra conductor ▪ symphony conductor director de la orquesta

to **order a part** encargar una pieza

to **order a pizza** encargar una pizza

to **order merchandize** encargar mercancías

order of business: the first ~ el primer asunto (de negocios)

order of the court ▪ court order sentencia del tribunal

to be the **order of the day** estar a la orden del día

to **order merchandise** **1.** encargar mercancías ▪ pedir mercancías ▪ encargar mercadería ▪ pedir mercadería **2.** to special order merchandise pedir mercancías de encargo ▪ pedir mercancías por encargo ▪ dejar encargadas mercancías ▪ pedir mercadería de encargo ▪ pedir mercadería por encargo ▪ dejar encargada mercadería ➤ Could you (special) order them for me? ¿Me los puede pedir? ▪ ¿Los puedo dejar encargados?

to **order someone to do something** ordenar a alguien que haga algo

to **order something from a store** pedir algo a una tienda ▪ encargar algo a una tienda

to **order something from a supplier** encargar algo a un suministrador

to **order that** ordenar que ▪ mandar que ➤ Lincoln ordered that Fort Sumter be provisioned. Lincoln ordenó que Fort Sumter fuera abastecido. ▪ Lincoln ordenó que Fort Sumter fuera provisto.

ordinary citizens ciudadanos corrientes

an **ordinary day** un día cualquiera

ordinary objects objetos ordinarios ▪ objetos corrientes

ordinary people *la* gente corriente

Ordinary Sunday *(film title) Un domingo cualquiera*

organ donor *el, la* donante de órganos

organic waste desechos orgánicos

to **organize one's notes** ▪ to make a clean copy of one's notes ▪ to put one's notes in order pasar a limpio sus apuntes ▪ pasar sus apuntes a limpio

to be **orphaned** quedar huérfano

orthopedic mattress colchón anatómico ▪ colchón ortopédico

the **other day** ▪ several days ago ▪ a few days ago el otro día

other half: my ~ ▪ my better half mi media naranja

other side of ▪ opposite side of cara opuesta de ▪ antípodas de ➤ *(news item)* The NASA robot lands successfully on the other side of Mars from its twin "Spirit." ▪ The NASA robot lands successfully on the opposite side of Mars from its twin "Spirit." El robot de NASA aterriza con éxito en la cara opuesta de Marte donde está su gemelo "Spirit". ▪ El robot de NASA aterriza con éxito en las antípodas de Marte donde está su gemelo "Spirit".

other side of a person otra mitad de una persona

Other Side of Midnight *(Sidney Sheldon novel) Más allá de la medianoche*

the **other team** el equipo contrario

other than alguno que no sea ▪ otro... que no sea ➤ The country's bureaucracy is for the inhabitants of some planet other than Earth. La burocracia del país es para los habitantes de otro planeta que no sea la Tierra.

other than that ▪ apart from that ▪ otherwise fuera de eso ▪ aparte de eso ▪ sin incluir eso ▪ por lo démas ➤ I'm getting married in two weeks, but other than that, my life is not too exciting. Me caso en dos semanas, pero aparte de eso mi vida no es demasiado emocionante.

the **other two** los dos otros ▪ las dos otras

to be the **other way around** ser al revés ▪ estar al revés ➤ I thought it was the other way around. Pensaba que era al revés. ➤ Bert was catching more fish than Ernie, or was it the other way around? Bert estaba pescando más que Ernie, ¿o estuvo al revés?

otherwise: (because) ~ que si no ➤ Tell him to call me by nine, (because) otherwise I won't get the message. Dile que me llame antes de las nueve, que, si no, no me pasan el mensaje.

an **ounce of prevention is worth a pound of cure** vale más prevenir que curar

our ancestors nuestros antepasados ▪ nuestros predecesores

our daily bread el pan nuestro de cada día ▪ nuestro pan de cada día

to **oust someone from a position** desbancar a alguien de un puesto ▪ hacerle a alguien abandonar un puesto

to be (an) **out-and-out liar** ser mentiroso de tomo y lomo ▪ ser embustero de tomo y lomo ▪ mentiroso acérrimo

out-and-out lie ▪ whopper mentira mentira descarada ▪ mentira grande como una casa

to be **out cold** ▪ to be out like a light estar roque ▪ estar sin conocimiento

to be **out in force** hacer una gran presencia

to be **(out) in the open 1.** to be in the open air estar al aire libre **2.** to be made public ▪ to be exposed estar al descubierto ▪ estar expuesto al público ▪ ser hecho público

to be **out like a light** ▪ to be out cold estar roque ▪ estar sin conocimiento ➤ He just went to bed and he's already out like a light. Se acaba de acostar y ya está roque.

out loud: to say something ~ ▪ to say something aloud decir algo en voz alta

out of action fuera de combate

to be **out of adjustment** estar fuera de ajuste ▪ estar mal arreglado

to be **out of air** quedarse sin aire ➤ The scuba diver surfaced because he was almost out of air. El buceador fue al superficie porque casi se quedaba sin aire.

to be **out of alignment** *(wheels)* ▪ to wobble no estar alineado ▪ *(coll.)* ir mal ➤ Look at that car in front of us. The wheels are way out of alignment. Mira el carro delante de nosotros. Las ruedas van muy mal.

to be **out of breath** ▪ to be breathless estar sin aliento ▪ estar sin resuello

to be **out of commission 1.** to be out of action estar fuera de servicio ▪ estar fuera de acción **2.** *(ship)* to have been decommissioned estar retirado del servicio **3.** to be convulsed with laughter morirse de risa ➤ I told my class in Mexico City, "Today is my dog's birthday," and, hell, they were out of commission for about five minutes. Le dije a mi clase en la Ciudad de México, "Hoy es el cumpleaños de mi perro," y, hostias, se murieron de risa como por cinco minutos.

out of commission: to put someone ~ dejarle fuera de combate a alguien

out of compassion: to do something ~ hacer algo por compasión

to be **out of control** estar fuera de control ➤ The situation is out of control. La situación está fuera de control.

out of control: to go ~ quedar fuera de control ➤ The car went out of control on the ice. El carro quedó fuera de control con el hielo.

out of context: to take something ~ sacar algo fuera de contexto

to be **out of danger** ▪ to be safe estar a salvo

to be **out of date 1.** to have expired estar pasado(-a) de fecha ▪ estar caducado(-a) **2.** to be old-fashioned estar pasado(-a) de moda ▪ estar pasado(-a)

out of (every) *x* sobre de cada *x* ➤ Nine out of (every) ten Nueve de (cada) diez ▪ Nueve sobre (cada) diez

to be **out of favor** no tener aceptación ▪ estar mal visto

out of favor: to fall ~ ▪ to fall in(to) disfavor caer en desgracia

out of fear for one's life: to act ~ actuar por temor a su vida

out of fear of: to act ~ ▪ to act for fear of ▪ to act from fear of actuar por temor a ➤ *(news item)* Spain closes its borders to French and Irish beef out of fear of mad cow disease. España cierra sus fronteras a reses de Francia e Irlanda por temor a las "vacas locas".

to be **out of focus** estar fuera de foco

out of force of habit ▪ from force of habit ▪ through force of habit por la fuerza de la costumbre

out of love for ▪ for love of por amor a

out of nowhere de la nada ➤ He appeared out of nowhere. Salió de la nada.

to be **out of one's control** ▪ to be beyond one's control escapárse al control de uno ➤ It's out of my control. ▪ It's beyond my control. Se escapa a mi control.

to be **out of one's depths** ▪ to be in over one's head ▪ not to be up to the task meterse en camisa de once varas ➤ The president was out of his depths. El president se metió en camisa de once varas.

to be **out of one's mind** ▪ to be deranged estar enajenado ▪ estar perturbado

out of one's own imagination de su propia cosecha ▪ de su propia imaginación ➤ Out of his own imagination De su propia cosecha ▪ De su propia imaginación

to be **out of order 1.** to be broken estar descompuesto ▪ estar estropeado ▪ estar fuera de servicio ▪ no funcionar **2.** to be out of numerical sequence estar fuera de orden numérico ▪ estar fuera de secuencia numérica **3.** to be chaotic estar en desorden ▪ estar fuera orden ▪ estar desordenado **4.** to be inappropriate estar inoportuno ➤ The elevator is out of order. El ascensor está descompuesto. ▪ El ascensor está fuera de servicio. ▪ El ascensor no funciona. ➤ The unruly witness was completely out of order. El testigo rebelde declaró inoportúnamente.

to be **out of place** estar desplazado ▪ estar fuera de lugar ▪ estar fuera de tono

to be **out of practice** ▪ to need to practice faltarle práctica ➤ I'm out of practice. Me falta práctica.

to be **out of print** estar fuera de prensa ▪ estar fuera de catálogo ➤ He deals in out-of-print books. Comercia con libros fuera de prensa. ▪ Comercia con libros fuera de catálogo.

out of print: to go ~ terminarse de imprimir ➤ The book went out of print. El libro se terminó de imprimir.

out-of-print book libro fuera de prensa ▪ libro fuera de imprenta ▪ libro fuera de catálogo ➤ The book is out of print. El libro está fuera de prensa. ▪ El libro está fuera de catálogo.

to be **out of proportion to** estar desproporcionado a

to be **out of range** *(mobile telephone)* estar fuera de cobertura

to be **out of reach** estar fuera del alcance ▪ estar fuera de alcance

to be **out of seats** *(airplane, train, bus, boat)* ▪ to run out of seats quedarse sin plazas ▪ agotarse las plazas

to be **out of service** estar fuera de servicio

out of sheer gall de puro descaro

out of sheer stupidity de puro tonto

out of sight, out of mind ojos que no ven, corazón que no siente ▪ la distancia es el olvido

to be **out of something** no tener por haberse agotado ▪ no tener algo ▪ estar sin algo ➤ The store is out of bottled water. La tienda está sin agua embotellada.

out of something: to run ~ ▪ to be out of something **1.** *(until restocked)* quedarse sin algo ▪ habérsele acabado algo **2.** *(permanently)* quedarse sin algo ▪ haberse agotado algo ➤ They were out of caffeine-free soft drinks at the store. Se quedaron sin refrescos sin cafeína en la tienda. ▪ Se habían quedado sin refrescos descafeinados en la tienda. ➤ They're (all) out of tickets. ▪ The tickets are all gone. ▪ They've run out of tickets. Se han agotado las entradas. ➤ We're out of gas. ▪ We've run out of gas. Nos hemos quedado sin gasolina. ▪ Se ha agotado la gasolina.

to be **out of sorts 1.** to be cranky estar un poco gruñón ▪ estar un poco irritable **2.** to be feeling unwell no encontrarse bien ▪ *(Sp., coll.)* no estar muy católico ➤ The child is a little out of sorts because his mother would not buy him candy at the grocery store. El niño está un poco gruñón porque su madre no le ha comprado caramelos en la tienda. ➤ I'm (feeling) a little out of sorts today so I'm going to skip the gym. Hoy no me encuentro muy bien, así que me voy a saltar el gimnasio.

out of spite: to do something ~ hacer algo por despecho

out-of-state tuition matrícula sin subsidio

to be **out of step 1.** perder el paso ▪ perder el ritmo **2.** *(figurative)* vivir en otra época ▪ estar fuera de onda ➤ When marching, it's easy to get out of step. En las marchas es facíl perder el paso.

to be **out of stock** estar agotado

out of the blue de la nada ▪ caído del cielo ▪ caído de las nubes ▪ llovido del cielo ▪ cuando menos se lo esperaba ▪ de repente

out of the corner of one's eye con el rabillo del ojo

to be **out of the ordinary** ser fuera de lo común ▪ ser fuera de lo normal ▪ ser inusual ▪ ser insólito ➤ We didn't see anything out of the ordinary. ▪ We saw nothing out of the ordinary. No vimos nada fuera de lo común. ➤ I didn't see anything out of the ordinary when I was there. No vi nada fuera de lo común cuando estaba allí.

to be **out of the picture** estar fuera de la escena ▪ estar fuera de escena

out of the way: to get ~ quitar de en medio ▪ quitarse de en medio

to be **out of tickets** ▪ to run out of tickets quedarse sin entradas ▪ agotarse las entradas ➤ They've run out of concert tickets. ▪ They're out of concert tickets. Las entradas se han agotado. ▪ Nos hemos quedado sin entradas.

to be **out of time** agotársele el tiempo ▪ acabársele el tiempo ➤ We're out of time. Se nos agota el tiempo. ▪ Se nos acaba el tiempo.

to be **out of tune 1.** *(engine)* estar mal de punto **2.** *(musical instrument)* estar desafinado

out of wedlock: to be born ~ nacer fuera del matrimonio

out of wedlock: to have a child ~ tener un hijo fuera del matrimonio

to be **out of work** estar en paro ▪ estar sin trabajo ▪ estar sin oficio ni beneficio ▪ no tener ni oficio ni beneficio ▪ quedarse sin trabajo

to be **out on the street** quedarse en la calle

out on the street: to be left ~ quedarse en la puerta de la calle ➤ He was left out on the street. Se quedó en la puerta de la calle.

to be **out to get someone** ir a por alguien

outbreak of the plague *el* brote de la peste

outbreak of violence estallido de violencia

outdoor café ▪ open-air café *el* café al aire libre

outcome (of something) will be revealed algo se librará ➤ *(news item)* The outcome of the battle for the White House will be revealed in the Florida Supreme Court. La batalla por la Casa Blanca se librará mañana en el Tribunal Supremo de Florida.

the **outcome of which** ▪ whose outcome el resultado del cual ▪ cuyo resultado

outcry over an injustice ▪ outcry against an injustice protesta en contra de una injusticia

outcry over an injustice: to raise an ~ protestar en contra de una injusticia

to **outdo oneself** ▪ to surpass oneself pasarse ▪ superarse ➤ You outdid yourself with the paella! ¡Te pasaste con la paella! ▪ ¡Te superaste con la paella!

to **outdo someone** ▪ to surpass someone ▪ to top someone superar a alguien ▪ ganar a alguien ▪ hacer algo mejor que alguien ➤ I don't know of anyone who can outdo her as a cook. No sé de nadie que la pueda superar como cocinera. ▪ No sé de nadie que la pueda ganar como cocinera. ▪ No sé de nadie que cocine mejor que ella. ➤ I don't know of anyone who can outdo him at computer games. No se de nadie que lo pueda superar en los juegos de computadora. ▪ No sé de nadie que lo pueda ganar en los juegos de computadora. ▪ No sé de nadie que juegue los juegos de computadora mejor que él. ▪ *(Sp., leísmo)* No sé de nadie que le pueda superar en los juegos de ordenador. ▪ No sé de nadie que le pueda ganar en los juegos de ordenador. ▪ No sé de nadie que juegue los juegos de ordenador mejor que él.

outer ear oído externo

outer planet *el* planeta exterior

outer space ▪ deep space espacio sideral ▪ espacio profundo

outgoing president presidente saliente ▪ presidenta saliente

to **outgrow clothes** quedarle pequeña la ropa ➤ I've outgrown this coat. Este abrigo me ha quedado pequeño.

outlandish hat sombrero estrambótico ▪ sombrero estrafalario

outlying areas of a city ▪ area surrounding a city extrarradio de una ciudad

to **outnumber the enemy** superar en número al enemigo

to **outnumber them two to one** ser dos veces más que ellos

outpatient clinic ambulatorio

outside air temperature temperatura exterior

outside world mundo exterior

outskirts of a city afueras de una ciudad ▪ faldas de una ciudad

outskirts of the town afueras del pueblo

outstanding student *el, la* estudiante sobresaliente

to **outstretch one's hand** ▪ to extend one's hand tender la mano

outward appearance apariencia externa

Oval Office *(of the president of the United States)* despacho oval

over! *(in radio communication)* ¡cambio y corto!

to be **over** ya estar terminado

to be **over a barrel** ▪ to be in an untenable position ▪ to be at the mercy of one's opponents ▪ to be without alternatives estar con el agua al cuello

over an *x*-year period en plazo de *x* años ➤ Political leaders are advancing their vision of achieving Middle East peace over a three-year period. Los líderes políticos están avanzando su visión de lograr la paz en Oriente Medio en un plazo de tres años.

over and above ▪ beyond más allá de ▪ sobre

over and out! *(in radio communication)* ¡corto y cierro! ▪ ¡cambio y fuera!

over and over again una y otra vez ▪ repetidas veces ▪ dale que dale

over any little thing ▪ over the least little thing a la mínima ▪ con cualquier motivo

over Christmas durante las Navidades

over my dead body! ¡por encima de mi cadáver! ▪ ¡sobre mi cadáver!

over nothing ▪ over any little thing ▪ over any little picayune thing a la mínima ▪ por cualquier quítame allá esas pajas ▪ por una simpleza ➤ Why do you get so worked up over nothing? ¿Por qué te pones así por una simpleza?

over one's objection(s) contra la voluntad de uno

to be **over one's shoulders** estar por encima de los hombros ➤ The water is over his shoulders. El agua está por encima de sus hombros.

to be **over someone** ▪ to be superior in rank to someone estar por encima de alguien ➤ There's no one over her in the department. No hay nadie por encima de ella en el departamento.

over the centuries ▪ throughout the centuries a lo largo de los siglos

over the counter ▪ without a prescription sin receta ▪ de mostrador

over the hill ▪ past one's prime pasado la flor de la vida

over the least little thing ▪ over any little thing con cualquier motivo

over the long term a largo plazo

over the next few weeks ▪ during the next few weeks ▪ in the next few weeks en pocas semanas ▪ en las próximas semanas ▪ *(past)* en las siguientes semanas ➤ Over the next few weeks, their relationship completely changed. En pocas semanas, su relación cambió por completo. ▪ En las siguientes semanas su relación cambió por completo.

over the short term a corto plazo

over the weekend ▪ during the weekend durante el fin de semana

over the years ▪ with the passing of the years con el correr de los años

over there por allí ▪ por allá

over time ▪ in time ▪ eventually ▪ in the course of time ▪ with the passage of time a lo largo del tiempo ▪ con el tiempo ▪ de forma progresiva ➤ The flavor of the wine improves over time. El sabor del vino mejora con el tiempo. ➤ Over time this mattress has flattened out. A lo largo del tiempo mi colchón se ha hundido. ➤ The property tax appraisal must allow for the depreciation of the vehicle over time. El impuesto de propiedad debe considerar la progresiva devaluación del vehículo.

over time: depreciation ~ devaluación progresiva ▪ progresiva devaluación ➤ The property tax appraisal must allow for the depreciation of the vehicle over time. El impuesto de propiedad debe considerar la progresiva devaluación del vehículo.

over whether ▪ about whether acerca de si ▪ en relación a si

to be **over *x* (years of age)** ▪ to be over *x* years old ser mayor de *x* ➤ He's over forty. Es mayor de cuarenta.

overall appearance vitola

overall rate tasa bruta

to **overbook a flight** vender más billetes que hay asientos

overbooked flight vuelo donde hay pasajeros con billetes pero sin asientos

overcast sky cielo encapotado

to **overcharge a battery** sobrecargar una batería ▪ sobrecargar una pila

to **overcharge someone** ▪ to gouge someone clavar a alguien

to **overcharge someone (by) *x* dollars for something** cobrar *x* dólares de más a alguien por algo

to **overcome an attitude** sobreponerse a un estado de ánimo

to be **overcome by sleepiness** ▪ to be overcome by drowsiness acometerle el sueño ➤ He was overcome by sleepiness. Le acometió el sueño.

to **overcome one's fears** ▪ to conquer one's fears vencer sus miedos

to **overcome shyness** ▪ to conquer shyness vencer la timidez

to **overcook food** cocinar comida demasiado

overdose: to take an ~ *(medication, drugs)* tomar una sobredosis

to **overdose on something** *(coll.)* ▪ to have one's fill of something darse un empacho de

overdrawn: (for) one's account to be ~ estar en los números rojos

to be **overdue** estar vencido ▪ haber vencido la fecha de entrega ▪ haber vencido el plazo ➤ The book is overdue at the library. El libro de la biblioteca está vencido. ▪ La fecha de entrega del libro ha vencido. ➤ It's overdue. El plazo ha vencido.

to **overflow its banks** desbordarse ➤ The creek overflowed its banks. El arroyo se desbordó.

to be **overgrown with** estar cubierto de ➤ The ruins were overgrown with weeds. Las ruinas estaban cubiertas de mala hierba.

overhasty precipitado

overhead compartment *(on an airplane)* ▪ overhead bin compartimiento superior ▪ compartimento superior

overhead light ▪ ceiling light *la* luz de arriba ▪ luz del techo

overhead projector *el* retroproyector

to be **overindulgent** ▪ to be overly indulgent tener la manga ancha

to be **overjoyed to hear that...** ▪ to be overjoyed when one hears that... ▪ to be overjoyed on hearing that... llenarse de júbilo al oír que... ▪ llenarse de júbilo al saber que...

to be **overjoyed to learn that...** ▪ to be overjoyed to find out that... llenarse de júbilo al enterarse de que...

to be **overjoyed to think that...** ▪ to be overjoyed at the thought that... llenarse de júbilo al pensar que...

overleaf of a book jacket dorso de la sobrecubierta de un libro

to **overlook from a height** mirar desde lo alto

to **overlook (someone's faults)** disimular ▪ hacer caso omiso

to be **overlooked by someone** ser pasado por alto por alguien

overnight: to change ~ cambiar de la noche a la mañana ➤ She changed overnight. Ella cambió de la noche a la mañana.

to **overplay the importance of** ▪ to give too much importance to dar excesiva importancia a ▪ dar excesiva relevancia a

overriding concern ▪ primary concern ▪ greatest concern interés primordial ▪ preocupación primordial ▪ motivo de preocupación primordial ▪ interés preponderante ▪ preocupación preponderante ▪ motivo de preocupación preponderante

overriding importance: of ~ ▪ of primary importance ▪ of greatest importance de importancia primordial ▪ de importancia imperiosa

to **overrule a decision** derogar una decisión ▪ anular una decisión ▪ invalidar una decisión ➤ The Supreme Court overruled the lower court's decision. ▪ The Supreme Court overruled the decision of the lower court. El Tribunal Supremo ha derogado la decisión del tribunal inferior.

to **overrule someone** desautorizar a alguien ➤ The dean gave me permission to do a special study for graduate credit, and the graduate school overruled him. El decano me dio permiso para tomar un curso de estudio especial por crédito posgrado, y el departamento de estudios posgrados lo desautorizó.

to **oversee the federal territories** supervisar los territorios federales

to **overshadow someone** hacer sombra a alguien

to **overshadow something** hacer sombra a algo

to **overstep the bounds** ▪ to go too far sobrepasar los límites ▪ ser una pasada

to **overtake a car** ▪ to pass a car adelantar un carro ▪ *(Mex.)* rebasar un carro ▪ *(Sp.)* adelantar un coche

to **overtake a horse** rebasar un caballo

to **overthrow the government** derrocar el gobierno

overtime pay pago por (las) horas extras

to **overturn a court decision** ■ to reverse a court decision ■ to strike down a court decision ■ to overrule a court decision derogar una decisión ■ anular una decisión ■ invalidar una decisión ➤ The Supreme Court overruled the lower court's decision. ■ The Supreme Court overruled the decision of the lower court. El Tribunal Supremo ha derogado la decisión del tribunal inferior.

overview of the situation visión somera de la situación

overwhelming majority mayoría abrumadora

overwhelming victory victoria demoledora

overwhelmingly positive abrumadoramente positivo(-a)

to **owe someone an apology** deberle disculpas a alguien

to **owe someone money** deberle dinero a alguien ➤ How much do I owe you? ¿Cuánto le debo? ➤ I owe her fifty euros. Le debo (a ella) cincuenta euros.

to **owe someone something** deber algo a alguien

to **own property** ■ to own real estate tener bienes raíces ■ tener inmobiliario ■ pertenecer a ■ ser de ➤ Marta owns a lot of property. ■ Marta owns a lot of real estate. Marta tiene muchos terrenos. ■ Marta tiene muchos bienes. ➤ Who owns this building? ¿Quién es el dueño de este edificio? ■ ¿A quién pertenece este edificio? ■ ¿De quién es este edificio? ➤ He sold the condominium that he owned in Miami Beach. Vendió el apartamento que tenía en Miami Beach.

own up! ■ make yourself known! ■ show yourself! ■ (whoever did it) come forward! ■ (whoever did it) admit it! ¡que dé la cara!

own water heater *(real estate ad)* caldera individual

to be **owned by** ■ to be the property of ser propiedad de

to be the **owner of property** ■ to own property ■ to be the property owner ■ to be the proprietor ser el dueño de propiedad ➤ Who is the owner of the building? ■ Who owns this building? ■ Who is the proprietor of this building? Quién es el propietario de este edificio? ■ ¿Quién es el dueño de este edificio? ■ ¿De quién es este edificio?

owning of slaves *la* posesión de esclavos

ozone decay descomposición del ozono

ozone layer ■ ozonosphere capa de ozono ■ ozonosfera

P.A. system ▪ public announcement system megafonía ▪ *el* sistema de anuncios públicos ▪ *el* altoparlante

to **pace back and forth** ▪ to pace up and down ir de un lado para otro ▪ andar de un lado a otro ▪ dar vueltas de aquí para allí ➤ He paces back and forth like a caged lion. Anda de un lado a otro como un león enjaulado. ➤ The groom was pacing back and forth waiting on the bride. El novio andaba de adelante a atrás esperando a la novia.

pace of life ritmo de la vida ➤ People say the pace of life is slower in Madrid than in Barcelona. Dicen que el ritmo de la vida es más lento en Madrid que en Barcelona.

to **pace off the distance** medirlo a pasos ➤ I paced it off. Lo medí a pasos. ➤ I measured the living room by pacing it off. Medí la sala a pasos.

to **pace the floor** caminar de un lado a otro ▪ recorrer la habitación ▪ pasearse ▪ dar zancadas ➤ Would you quit pacing the floor like a caged lion? ¿Quieres dejar de ir de un lado a otro como león enjaulado?

to **pace up and down** ▪ to pace back and forth pasear de arriba a abajo ▪ ir y venir

to **pack a suitcase** hacer la maleta ▪ hacer las maletas

pack of envelopes *el* lote de sobres ➤ A pack of five envelopes Un lote de cinco sobres

pack of lies sarta de mentiras

to **pack something in something** empaquetar algo en algo ➤ I'm going to pack the computer and printer in boxes for shipping. Voy a empaquetar la computadora y la impresora en cajas para el envío.

to **pack something with something** ▪ to pack something in something embalar algo con algo ▪ embalar algo en algo ➤ I'm going to pack the computer and printer with bubble pack. Voy a embalar la computadora en papel de burbujas. ▪ Voy a embalar la computadora con papel de burbujas.

to **pack up one's belongings** ▪ to pack up one's things empacar sus cosas ▪ embalar sus cosas ▪ embalar sus bienes ▪ empaquetar sus cosas ▪ empaquetar sus bienes ▪ *(informal)* liar los bártulos ▪ preparar los bártulos

to be **packed like sardines** ▪ to be (jam) packed ir como sardinas en lata ▪ estar como piojos en costura ▪ estar de bote en bote ▪ estar hasta los topes ▪ no caber ni un alfiler

to be **packed with people** estar abarrotado de gente ▪ estar lleno de gente ▪ estar hasta la bandera ▪ estar a tope de gente ▪ estar ciento y la madre ➤ Spain is one big bar, and the bars are just packed. España es un gran bar, y los bares siempre están hasta la bandera.

to **pad a theme** meterle paja a un trabajo

pad of paper *el* bloc de papel

padded envelope sobre acolchado ▪ sobre guateado

page break: to insert a ~ ▪ to put in a page break insertar un salto de página

to **page someone** localizar con el busca ➤ Can you page her? ¿Puede localizarla con el busca?

to be **paid by the day** ▪ to be paid daily ▪ to get paid on a daily basis trabajar al jornal

to be **paid royalties** ▪ to get royalties cobrar derechos de autor

to be a **pain in the ass** *(off-color)* ser un torcijón en el culo ▪ ser un coñazo ➤ The instruction manual for the TV remote is a real pain in the ass. El manual de instrucciones para el control remoto de la tele es un torcijón en el culo. ▪ El manual de instrucciones para el control remoto de la tele es un coñazo.

to be a **pain in the neck** dar jaqueca a alguien ▪ ser un pelma ▪ dar la tabarra ▪ ser más pesado que una vaca en brazos

the **pain will go away** pasará el dolor ▪ *el* dolor remitirá

the **pain wouldn't go away** el dolor no remitía

paint has deteriorated pintura ha empeorado

to **paint in miniature** miniar

to **paint the town red** *(coll.)* correrse una juerga

paintbrush 1. *(artist's)* un pincel **2.** *(house painter's)* brocha

pair of binoculars *el* par de catalejos ▪ par de prismáticos ▪ par de anteojos de larga vista

pair of jeans unos jeans ▪ unos vaqueros

pair of pants pantalón ➤ I bought two pairs of pants today. Hoy me compré dos pantalones.

pair of shoes (par de) zapatos ➤ I had this pair of shoes stretched. Me dieron de sí estos zapatos. ▪ Me dieron de sí este par de zapatos. ➤ I have to take these shoes to have them stretched. ▪ I have to get these shoes stretched. Tengo que llevar los zapatos para que los metan en la horma. ▪ Tengo que llevar los zapatos para que me los dé de sí.

pair of shorts unos shorts

pair of socks par de calcetines ▪ *(L. Am.)* par de medias

to **pale in comparison to** empalidecerse en comparación a ▪ palidecer ante ➤ The legendary film *Midnight Express* pales in comparison to the reality of the Turkish jails. La película legendaria *Expreso de Medianoche* palidece ante la realidad de las cárceles turcas.

palindromatic phrase ▪ palindrome frase capicúa ▪ palindromo

palliative care cuidados paliativos

Palm Sunday domingo de ramos

to be a **panacea for all our problems** ser un bálsamo para todos nuestros problemas

Pandora's box caja de Pandora

to **panel a wall** revestir una pared ▪ forrar una pared

paneling: wood ~ forro de madero ▪ revestimiento de madera

pang of jealousy *el* aguijón de los celos

panic spread through the village ▪ panic engulfed the village cundió el pánico en la aldea

to be **panned by the critics** ser dejado por los suelos por los críticos ▪ ser dejado por el piso por los críticos ➤ The movie was panned by the critics. La película fue puesta por los suelos por los críticos. ▪ La película fue dejada por los suelos por los críticos.

paper pusher ▪ petty bureaucrat chupatintas

paperback book libro de tapa rústica ▪ libro de bolsillo

paperback edition edición rústica ▪ edición en cuadernación rústica ▪ edición de bolsillo

papers to correct: to have ~ tener papeles que corregir ➤ The teacher has a lot of papers to grade. La profesora tiene muchas papeles que corregir.

papers to grade: to have ~ tener papeles que calificar

par excellence por excelencia ▪ por antonomasia

to be **par for the course** ser el pan de cada día ▪ ser lo más normal ▪ ser siempre la misma cosa

parachute jump: to make a ~ lanzarse en paracaídas ▪ hacer un descenso en paracaídas

to **parachute (out of an airplane)** ▪ to make a parachute jump ▪ to parachute (down) lanzarse en paracaídas ➤ The crew parachuted to safety after the plane's engine failed. La tripulación se lanzó en paracaídas hasta un lugar seguro después de que el motor del avión fallara.

to **parade around in one's undies** *(coll.)* ▪ to go parading around in one's underpants andar en calzonetas ▪ andar en paños menores

to **parade around in the nude** ▪ to parade around in the buff andar desnudo ▪ andar en cueros ▪ andar en pelota ▪ andar encuerado

to **parade as** ▪ to pass itself off as hacerse pasar por ➤ It's a daily work of fiction parading as a newspaper. ▪ It's a daily work of fiction passing itself off as a newspaper. El diario es una obra de ficción que se hace pasar por un periódico.

parade ground plaza de armas

paradigm shift cambio de paradigma

paranoid break ataque paranoide ▪ ataque de paranoia ▪ ataque paranoico

paranoid delusions delirios paranoicos

parcel of land parcela *("Parcela" can also mean "lot.")*

parcel post *el* paquete postal

pardon! *(tú)* ¡perdona! ▪ *(usted)* ¡perdone! ▪ ¡perdón!

parent who has lost a child padre al que se le muere un hijo

parental acceptance aceptación paterna

parental permission permiso paterno

parental rejection rechazo paterno

to **park at a ninety-degree angle to the curb** ▪ to park perpendicular to the curb ▪ to pull straight in aparcar en batería

to **park at an angle to the curb** *(L. Am.)* estacionar en batería ▪ *(Sp.)* aparcar en batería

to **park "by ear"** aparcar de oído

to **park the car** *(L. Am.)* estacionar el carro ▪ *(Sp.)* aparcar el coche

parking lot *(L. Am.)* estacionamiento ▪ *(Sp.)* aparcadero ▪ *el* parking

parking lot attendant *el* aparcacoches

parking place ▪ parking space ▪ parking spot sitio para aparcar ▪ hueco

parking space ▪ parking place ▪ parking spot sitio para aparcar ▪ hueco

parole violation *la* violación de la libertad condicional

parsley sprig ▪ sprig of parsley ramita de perejil

to **part company with someone** separarse de alguien ▪ romper vínculos con alguien

to **part the sea** hendir el mar ▪ hender el mar

part-time: to work ~ trabajar media jornada

to **participate in** participar en

participatory singing canto participativo

particle physicist *el, la* físico de partículas ➤ She's a particle physicist. Ella es físico de partículas.

a **particular person** una persona en particular ▪ una persona concreta

particular person: to be a (very) ~ ▪ to be a person who likes things just so ser muy suyo ➤ My boss is very particular. Mi jefe es muy suyo.

particular problem *el* problema particular

particulars: to know the ~ ▪ to know the details saber las señas particulares ▪ saber los detalles

parties involved *las* partes

partisan politics pólitica partidista

partition(ing) wall ▪ non-loadbearing wall *el* tabique ▪ *la* pared

to be **partly cloudy** haber nubes y claros

to be **partly correct** ▪ to be partially correct ser parcialmente correcto

to be **partly responsible** ▪ to be partially responsible ser en parte responsable ▪ ser parcialmente responsable

to be **partly responsible for** ser parcialmente responsible de ▪ tener responsabilidad en parte de

to be **partly to blame for** ser parcialmente culpable de ▪ ser en parte culpable de ➤ I'm partly to blame for what happened. En parte lo que pasó fue culpa mía.

to be **partners in crime 1.** *(said seriously)* compañeros de crimen **2.** *(said in jest)* compañeros de fechorías

party: to have a ~ ▪ to give a party ▪ to have a get-together hacer una fiesta ▪ dar una fiesta

party animal *el, la* juerguista ▪ fiestero(-a)

party leaders *los* dirigentes del partido

to be a **party pooper** ▪ to be a wet blanket aguar la fiesta

to be **party to** prestarse a

to be **party to an agreement** ▪ to be a party in an agreement ▪ to be one of the parties in an agreement ser parte en un acuerdo

party's over for someone la fiesta se ha acabado para alguien ▪ es el fin de fiesta para alguien ➤ The party's over for the conservatives. La fiesta se ha acabado para los conservadores.

paschal candle *(Catholicism)* cirio pascual

paschal lamb *(Judaism and Catholicism)* cordero pascual

to **pass a bill** aprobar un proyecto de ley

to **pass a car on the highway** *(Mex.)* rebasar un carro en la carretera ▪ *(Sp.)* adelantar a un coche en la carretera

to **pass a law** ▪ to enact a law aprobar una ley ▪ promulgar una ley

to **pass a place** *(without stopping)* pasar de largo por ➤ He passed the post office on the way. Pasó de largo por la casa de correos en camino.

to **pass a test** aprobar un examen

to **pass alongside** pasar por el costado

to **pass an exam** aprobar un examen

to **pass around the roll sheet** ▪ to pass the roll sheet around pasar la lista

to **pass away** ▪ to pass on ▪ to die írsele ▪ morirse ➤ She passed away last year. Ella se nos fue el año pasado.

to **pass counterfeit money** ▪ to spend counterfeit money colocar dinero falso ➤ *(news item)* The first counterfeit euros have been detected in Burriana (Castellón), Spain. A Polish man tried to pass them in several stores. Los primeros euros falsos se han detectado en Burriana (Castellón); los intentó colocar un polaco en varias tiendas.

to **pass each other** pasarse uno a otro ▪ pasarse al lado ➤ We passed each other on the street the other day. Nos pasamos al lado en la calle el otro día. ➤ Normally people pass each other on the right. Normalmente la gente se pasa uno a otro por la derecha.

to **pass gas** *(doctor's phrasing)* ▪ to have gas ventosear ▪ tener gases ➤ Are you passing gas? ▪ Do you have gas? *(tú)* ¿Ventoseas? ▪ ¿Tienes gases? ▪ *(usted)* ¿Ventosea? ▪ ¿Tiene gases?

to **pass in front of** pasar al frente de

to **pass in front of it** pasar al frente

to **pass inspection** pasar inspección

to **pass it on** *(tú)* hazla circular ▪ *(usted)* hágala circular

to **pass judgment on someone** ▪ to judge someone superficially juzgar a alguien a la ligera

pass me that ▪ pass that to me pásame eso ▪ *(Sp.)* cógeme eso

to **pass out** ▪ to faint ▪ to lose consciousness desmayarse ▪ perder la conciencia ▪ sufrir un desmayo

to **pass out the papers** repartir las hojas ▪ repartir los papeles

to **pass over something** ▪ to skip over something ▪ to omit something pasar algo por alto

to **pass responsibility back and forth between them** pasar la pelota entre ellos ➤ The general contractor and the developer passed the painter back and forth between them to avoid paying him. El contratista y el promotor se pasaban la pelota entre ellos para no pagar al pintor.

to **pass someone on the highway** ▪ to go around someone on the highway pasar en frente a alguien en la autopista

to **pass the ball between the legs of the opposition player** *(soccer)* hacer un caño

to **pass the buck** pasarse el muerto ▪ echarse el muerto unos a otros ▪ pasar la bola unos a otros

pass the butter, please ▪ would you pass (me) the butter? pásame la mantequilla, por favor ▪ ¿podrías pasarme la mantequilla? ▪ *(Sp.)* cógeme la mantequilla, por favor

to **pass the hat** pasar la gorra

to **pass the marrying age** *(coll.)* **1.** *(L. Am.)* quemársele el arroz ▪ *(Sp.)* pasársele el arroz ➤ She has passed the marrying age. Se le quemó el arroz. ▪ Se le pasó el arroz.

to **pass the test 1.** to pass the exam aprobar el examen **2.** to meet the challenge pasar la prueba ▪ superar la prueba to **pass through a stage in which** ▪ to go through a phase in which pasar por una etapa en la que

to **pass unanimously** ▪ to be passed unanimously aprobar por unanimidad ▪ ser aprobado por unanimidad ▪ aprobarse por unanimidad ▪ aprobar por unanimidad ➤ The Senate passed the bill unanimously. ▪ The bill (was) passed by the Senate unanimously. El Senado aprobó el proyecto de ley por unanimidad. ▪ El proyecto de ley se aprobó por unanimidad. ▪ Aprobaron el proyecto de ley por unanimidad.

to **pass up something** ▪ to pass something up ▪ to miss something dejar pasar algo ▪ perderse algo ➤ How can I pass up a bargain like that? ¿Cómo puedo dejar pasar una ganga así? ▪ ¿Cómo puedo dejar pasar una ganga como esa? ▪ ¿Cómo puedo perderme una ganga así? ▪ ¿Cómo me puedo perder una ganga así? ➤ *That* you can't pass up. Eso *no* lo puede dejar pasar eso. ➤ You can't pass that up. ▪ You can't miss that. ▪ You mustn't miss that. *(tú)* Que no puedes perderte. ▪ Que no te puedes perder. ▪ No puedes dejar pasar eso. ▪ *(usted)* Que no puede perderse. ▪ Que no se puede perder. ▪ No puede dejar pasar eso. ➤ I can't pass it up. No puedo dejarlo pasar. ➤ I couldn't pass it up. No pude dejarlo pasar.

passage of time paso del tiempo

to be **passed down from father to son** ser pasado de padres a hijos ▪ pasarse de padres a hijos ➤ Grape growers from father to son since 1889 Viticultores de padres a hijos desde 1889 ➤ The winery has been passed down from father to son for four generations. La bodega ha sido pasada de padres a hijos por cuatro generaciones.

to be **passed unanimously** ▪ to pass unanimously ser aprobado por unanimidad ➤ The bill was passed unanimously. El proyecto de ley fue aprobado por unanimidad.

passing clouds nubes pasajeras ➤ Is it going to rain? No, they're just passing clouds. ¿Va a llover? No, son nubes pasajeras.

passing electricity through water ▪ the passing of electricity through water ▪ hydrolysis pasar la electricidad a través del agua ▪ el paso de la electricidad a través del agua ▪ hidrólisis

passing the buck juego de pasabola

passion for sports *la* pasión hacia los deportes

passerby ▪ *(plur.)* passersby transeunte ▪ yentes y vinientes

password: to change the ~ cambiar la contraseña ▪ cambiar la clave

to be **past one's prime** ▪ to be over the hill haber pasado la flor de la vida ▪ haber pasado los años mozos ▪ *(Sp., humorous)* ser carroza

past perfect tense ▪ pluperfect tense tiempo pasado perfecto ▪ tiempo pluscuamperfecto

pat on the back: to give someone a ~ ▪ to pat someone on the back darle a alguien una palmada en la espalda ▪ darle a alguien (una palmadita) en la espalda

to **pat someone on the shoulder** dar a alguien en el hombro

patch of ice placa de hielo ➤ The car hit a patch of ice and slid off the road. El coche dió con una placa de hielo y derrapó fuera de la carretera.

to **patch the nail holes** resanar los agujeros de los clavos ▪ parchar los agujeros (de los clavos)

to **patch up ones' differences** *(coll.)* hacer las paces

patent leather *el* charol ➤ Patent leather shoes Zapatos de charol

patent pending *el* patente en trámite

path of a bullet trayectoria de una bala

path of a tornado paso de un tornado ➤ The tornado annihilated everything in its path. El tornado aniquiló cuanto encontraba a su paso.

path of least resistance camino de menos resistencia ▪ sendero de menos resistencia ▪ camino más fácil

patience of Job: to have the ~ tener más paciencia que el santo Job

patrol car carro patrullero ▪ coche patrullero

patronizing attitude ▪ condescending attitude *la* actitud condescendiente

patter of footsteps golpeteo de pasos ▪ tamborileo de pasos

patter of little feet ▪ pattering of little feet golpeteo de pies pequeños ▪ tamborileo de pies pequeños

patter of (the) rain on the roof ▪ pattering of (the) rain on the roof ▪ drumming of the rain on the roof ▪ beating of the rain on the roof ▪ rain beating on the roof repiqueteo de la lluvia sobre el tejado ▪ repiqueteo de la lluvia en el tejado

pattern emerges verse un patrón ▪ notarse un patrón ▪ verse una pauta ▪ notarse una pauta ➤ A pattern is beginning to emerge. Empieza a verse un patrón. ▪ Empieza a notarse un patrón.

pattern of behavior ▪ behavior pattern *el* patrón de comportamiento ▪ modelo de comportamiento ➤ *(news item)* Several experts believe that the pattern of behavior (exhibited) in the five crimes indicates that the killer will act again. Varios expertos creen que el patrón de comportamiento en los cinco crímenes permite anticipar que el asesino volverá a actuar.

to **patronize a business** ▪ to be a patron of a business ser cliente de un negocio ▪ utilizar los servicios de un negocio

to **patronize someone 1.** to treat someone condescendingly tratar a alguien con condescendencia **2.** to do business with someone servirse de alguien ➤ *(headline)* What makes Madrid men patronize prostitutes? ¿Qué mueve a los madrileños a servirse de las prostitutas?

paws of an animal patas de un animal ▪ *(of a clawed animal)* zarpas de un animal

to **pave the way for** allanar el camino para

to **pay a compliment** hacer un cumplido

to **pay a premium** pagar un premio

to **pay a surprise visit to** visitar por sorpresa a

to **pay an insurance premium** pagar un premio de seguros

to **pay as much as** ▪ to pay up to llegar a pagar ▪ pagar hasta ➤ We've paid as much as a hundred euros for a seat at a bullfight. ▪ We've paid up to a hundred euros for a seat at a bullfight. Hemos llegado a pagar hasta cien euros por un asiento en una corrida de toros. ▪ Hemos pagado hasta cien euros por un asiento en una corrida de toros.

to **pay attention** prestar atención

to **pay attention to someone** prestarle a alguien atención ▪ hacerle caso a alguien ▪ hacer caso de alguien ▪ ponerle atención ➤ She paid no attention to him. ▪ She didn't pay any attention to him. No le hizo caso.

to **pay back money with interest** ▪ to pay money back with interest pagar con creces

to **pay back someone** ▪ to pay someone back **1.** to return money borrowed devolver a alguien dinero préstado **2.** to get revenge against someone pagar con creces a alguien

to **pay cash in advance for something** pagar dinero por adelantado por algo

to **pay cash on the line for something** ▪ to pay cold cash for something ▪ to pay hard cash for something pagar sonante y contante por algo ▪ *(Sp.)* pagar a tocateja por algo

to **pay cold cash for something** ▪ to pay hard cash for something ▪ to pay cash on the line for something pagar sonante y contante por algo ▪ *(Sp.)* pagar a tocateja por algo

to **pay hard cash for something** ▪ to pay cold cash for something ▪ to pay cash on the line for something pagar sonante y contante por algo ▪ *(Sp.)* pagar a tocateja por algo

to **pay homage to someone** ▪ to pay tribute to someone rendir homenaje a alguien ▪ rendir pleitesía a alguien ▪ tributar homenaje a alguien

to **pay in advance** pagar por adelantado

to **pay (in) cash** pagar en efectivo

to **pay in installments** pagar a plazos ▪ pagar en abonos

to **pay interest of *x* percent compounded quarterly** ▪ to pay *x* percent interest dar interés del *x* por ciento acumulados en pagos trimestrales ▪ devengar interés del *x* por ciento acumulados en pagos trimestrales

to **pay lip service to something** apoyar algo de labios para fuera

pay no attention to her ▪ don't pay any attention to her no le hagas caso (a ella) ▪ no le pongas atención (a ella)

pay no attention to him ▪ don't pay any attention to him no le hagas caso (a él) ▪ no le pongas atención (a él)

pay no attention to it ▪ don't pay any attention to it no le hagas caso a eso ▪ no le des atención alguna a eso

to **pay no attention to someone** no hacerle caso a alguien

to **pay off a debt** ▪ to pay a debt off saldar una deuda

to **pay off a mortgage** redimir una hipoteca ▪ cumplir una hipoteca

to **pay off someone** ▪ to pay someone off **1.** to close out a debt ▪ to retire a debt terminar de pagar a alguien ▪ salir de una deuda con alguien **2.** to bribe someone untarle la mano a alguien

to **pay one's own way** mantenerse a sí mismo ▪ apoquinar lo suyo ▪ pagar lo suyo ▪ *(through school)* pagarse los estudios ➤ Each (person) pays his own way. Cada uno apoquina lo suyo.

to **pay ransom (money) for** pagar un rescate por

pay scale escala salarial

to **pay someone a compliment** ▪ to give someone a compliment hacerle a alguien un cumplido

to **pay someone a visit** hacer una visita a alguien

to **pay someone back 1.** to repay someone devolverle el dinero a alguien ▪ devolvérselo **2.** to get revenge pagar con creces a alguien ➤ I'll pay you back tomorrow. Te lo devuelvo mañana. ▪ Te lo devolveré mañana. ➤ I'm going to pay you back for that. ▪ I'm going to get even with you for that. Te voy a pagar con creces por eso.

to **pay taxes** contribuir los impuestos ▪ pagar los impuestos

to **pay the tab** *(at a restaurant)* pagar lo consumido ▪ pagar la consumición

to **pay the difference** pagar lo que hace falta

to **pay the expenses of** correr con los gastos de ▪ pagar los gastos de

to **pay through the nose for** ▪ to pay far too much for pagar hasta la camisa por

pay to the order of... páguese a orden de...

pay to the order of cash páguese al portador

to **pay tribute to someone** ▪ to pay homage to someone rendir homenaje a alguien ▪ rendir pleitesía a alguien ▪ tributar homenaje a alguien

pay up! ▪ fork it over! *(tú)* ¡apoquina! ▪ *(usted)* ¡apoquine!

to **pay up to a certain amount** ▪ to pay as much as a certain amount llegar a pagar hasta... ➤ We've paid up to a hundred euros for a seat at a bullfight. ▪ We've paid as much as a hundred euros for a seat at a bullfight. Hemos llegado a pagar hasta cien euros por un asiento en una corrida de toros.

to **pay with interest** pagar con creces

to be **pea-brained** tener menos seso que un mosquito

peace of mind ▪ inner peace *la* paz mental ▪ paz interior

peak hours horas puntas

peak season temporada alta

peak-season fare tarifa de temporada alta

pearl necklace *el* collar de perlas ▪ gargantilla de perlas

pedestrian crossing ▪ crosswalk paso de cebra ▪ paso de peatones

to **peel off 1.** *(paint)* pelar la pintura ▪ pelarse la pintura **2.** *(aerobatic or formation flying)* separarse escorando

to **peel off a label** despegarse ▪ estirar ➤ Peel carefully. Despéguese con cuidado.

to **peel off a sticker** despegar una pegatina

to **peel off one's clothes** quitarse la ropa sensualmente

peeling of (the) drums llanto de tambores

peep out of: for there not to be a ~ no decir ni un pío ➤ There wasn't a peep out of him. No dijo ni un pío.

to **peepee** *(said by childen)* hacer pipí ▪ hacer pichí

Pelican Brief *(film title)* *El informe pelícano*

pen pal amigo(-a) de correspondencia

pencil: lead ~ *el* lápiz

pencil: mechanical ~ *(L. Am.)* lapicero ▪ *(Sp.)* *el* portaminas

pencil lead 1. *(for a wooden pencil)* lámina de lápiz **2.** *(mechanical pencil)* lámina del lapicero

peninsular Spanish *(Iberian peninsular Spanish)* español peninsular ▪ español de la Península Ibérica ➤ Your Spanish has become very peninsular. Tu español se ha vuelto muy peninsular. ▪ Tu castellano se ha vuelto muy como de España.

to be **penniless** estar sincero ▪ estar sin blanca ▪ estar sin un duro ➤ They're penniless. Están sinceros.

people always assume the worst la gente piensa siempre lo peor

people are just people la gente es simplemente la gente

the **people around one** quienes le rodean a alguien ▪ el mundo de alguien ➤ *(Madrid newspaper quote)* My dream is to be happy and to make the people around me happy. Mi sueño es ser felíz y hacer felices a quienes me rodean.

people I didn't even know... gente que ni siquiera conocía...

people over *x* (years old) mayores de *x* ➤ People over sixty-five should be vaccinated. Mayores de sesenta y cinco deben vacunarse.

(the) **people who live** la gente que vive

people who live in glass houses shouldn't throw stones quien tiene el tejado de vidrio no tire piedras al de su vecino

(the) **people (who were) surveyed** la gente encuestada

people with money ▪ rich people gente de dinero ▪ gente rica

per capita income renta per cápita

per household por vivienda

per month por mes

per se ▪ in and of itself ▪ in itself de suyo ▪ en sí

per week ▪ a week a la semana ▪ por semana ➤ The class meets three times per week. ▪ The class meets three times a week. La clase se reúne tres veces a la semana. ▪ La clase se reúne tres veces por semana.

to **perch on** posarse en ▪ posar sobre ➤ The parrot was perched on the pirate's shoulder. El loro se posaba sobre el hombro del pirata.

to be **perched above** estar encaramado sobre

to **percolate coffee** colar el café ▪ filtrar el café

percolated coffee ▪ brewed coffee *el* café de máquina ▪ café de filtro ➤ Is your decaf percolated? ▪ Is your decaf brewed? ¿Es su descafeinado de máquina?

perfect match pareja perfecta ➤ She's a perfect match for me. Ella es una pareja perfecta para mí.

perfect set of instructions *la* serie de instrucciones infalibles

perfect tense tiempo (verbal) perfecto

to be **perfectly capable of** ▪ to be more than capable of bastarse y sobrarse para

to be **perfectly suited to one** estar hecho a la medida de uno ➤ This task is perfectly suited to me. Esta tarea está hecha a mi medida.

to **perforate with a fork** perforar con un tenedor ▪ pinchar con un tenedor

to **perform a coup de grâce** ▪ to do a coup de grâce dar el golpe de gracia ▪ dar la puntilla

to **perform an abortion** practicar un aborto

to **perform an autopsy** practicar una autopsia

to **perform an experiment** ▪ to conduct an experiment ▪ to do an experiment realizar un experimento

to **perform music** interpretar la música ➤ We're going to perform some pieces by Bach. Vamos a interpretar unas piezas de Bach.

to **perform one's role perfectly** bordar su papel ➤ The actress performed her role perfectly. La actriz bordó su papel.

to **perform surgery on someone** ▪ to operate on someone operar a alguien ▪ realizarle una operación a alguien ➤ They're going to perform major surgery on his shoulder. Le van a operar el hombro de importancia. ▪ Van a realizarle una operación mayor en el hombro.

to **perform well** hacer buen papel ➤ The player performed well in the tournament. El jugador hizo buen papel en el torneo.

to **perform well academically** rendir bien ▪ ser aplicado en sus estudios

to **perform well under pressure** rendir bajo presión ➤ I don't perform well under pressure. No rindo muy bien si estoy bajo presión.

performance of an opera *la* actuación de una ópera ▪ *la* interpretación de una ópera ▪ *la* representación de una ópera

performance of flamenco ▪ flamenco performance *la* actuación de flamenco ➤ There is a flamenco performance tonight. Hay una actuación de flamenco esta noche.

performance statistics estadísticas de funcionamiento ▪ estadísticas de rendimiento

perhaps I haven't made myself clear tal vez no me haya explicado bien ▪ no habré sabido explicarme

perhaps it would be advantageous to... ▪ perhaps it might be advantageous to... quizá fuese provechoso que... ▪ quizá fuera provechoso que...

perimeter of the plaza orilla de la plaza

period, end of dictation punto y final

period, next sentence *(dictation)* punto y seguido

period, paragraph *(dictation)* punto y aparte ▪ punto y párrafo

perish the thought! ¡no lo permita Dios! ▪ no llames a esa puerta tan negra

perishable food alimento perecedero

to **perjure oneself** ▪ to commit perjury ▪ to lie under oath perjurarse ▪ cometer perjurio ▪ mentir bajo juramento ▪ jurar en falso

perpetrator of a crime autor de un delito

perpetrator of an injustice autor de una injusticia

persecution complex manía persecutoria

to **persist at doing something** insistir en hacer algo ➤ If I persist, the system eventually lets me log on. Si insisto, el sistema eventualmente me deja entrar.

to **persist doggedly in doing something** ▪ to be dogged in one's pursuit of something emperrarse en hacer algo

persistence pays off la perseverencia da sus frutos ▪ la constancia da sus frutos ▪ quien la sigue, la consigue

persistent cough *el* tos pertinaz

persistent rain(s) pertinaz lluvia

person in charge el encargado ▪ el responsable ▪ la encargada ▪ la responsable

person of few words persona de pocas palabras

person of singular attainments persona de logros excepcionales

person who speaks English ▪ someone who speaks English *(anybody)* persona que hable inglés ▪ *(specific person)* persona que habla inglés ➤ I am looking for a teller who speaks English. Busco a un cajero que hable inglés. ➤ I am looking for the teller who speaks English. Busco al cajero que habla inglés.

the **person you least expect** ▪ the person of whom you least expect it la persona de quien menos te lo esperas

persona non grata ▪ unwanted person persona non grata ▪ persona no grata

personal items aseos personales

personal journey trayectoría personal

personal magnetism: to have ~ ▪ to be a magnetic person ser como un imán

personal physician médico de confianza

personal property *la* propiedad personal ▪ *el* capital mueble

personal question: to ask someone a ~ preguntar a alguien algo personal ▪ hacerle a alguien una pregunta personal

personality trait rasgo de la personalidad

personally, my opinion is that... ▪ personally, I'm of the opinion that... personalmente, considero que... ▪ considero que, por mi parte...

personnel file *el* expediente personal

personnel shortage ▪ manpower shortage insuficiencia de personal

to **persuade someone to do something** convencer a alguien que haga algo ➤ They persuaded us to stay for supper. Nos convencieron que nos quedáramos a cenar. ▪ Nos convencieron que nos quedáramos para la cena.

pertaining to relacionado a ▪ relacionado con

to **pervade the atmosphere** campear en el ambiente ▪ impregnar el ambiente

to **pet an animal** acariciar a un animal ▪ hacerle una caricia a un animal

petri dish caja de Petri

petty bureaucrat ▪ paper pusher chupatintas

petty details detalles insignificantes ▪ detalles nimios

phase of an operation *el* escalón de una operación

philosopher's stone piedra filosofal

photographic memory memoria fotográfica

phrasal verb: separable ~ verbo frasal separable *(Verbs of Germanic origin consisting of two or more words, such as "to pick up something / to pick something up" ("recoger algo"), in which the noun object can separate the elements of the verb or come at the end. The pronoun object, however, must separate the elements: "to pick it up" ("recogerlo").)*

to **phrase the question** estructurar la pregunta

physical disability menusvalía física

to be **physically fit** ▪ to be in good physical shape ▪ to be in good shape estar en forma

to **pick a fight with someone** buscar pelea con alguien ▪ buscar líos con alguien ▪ *(coll.)* buscar bronca con alguien ▪ *(literary)* buscar pleito

to **pick a flower** recoger una flor

to **pick a number** escoger un número ➤ Pick a number from one to ten. Escoge un número del uno al diez.

to **pick apart something** ▪ to pick something apart **1.** *(argument)* desmontar punto por punto **2.** *(flesh, etc.)* desmenuzar ➤ The teacher picked my argument apart (point by point). ▪ The teacher picked apart my argument (point by point). El profesor desmontó mi argumentación punto por punto. ➤ He picked it apart. Lo desmontó punto por punto. ➤ The chef picked the chicken apart. El cocinero desmenuzó el pollo. ➤ The vulture picked the carcass apart. ▪ The vulture picked apart the carcass. El buitre desmenuzó el cadáver del animal. ➤ The vulture picked it apart. El buitre lo desmenuzó.

to **pick berries** recoger bayas

to **pick by hand** ▪ to gather by hand recolectar a mano

to **pick flowers** recoger flores

pick of the litter ▪ choice of the litter primera elección de la camada

pick on somebody your own size métete con alguien de tu tamaño ▪ métete con alguien del mismo tamaño ▪ prueba con alguien de tu tamaño ▪ prueba con alguien del mismo tamaño

to **pick one's nose** hurgarse las narices

to **pick out a tie** ▪ to pick a tie out ▪ to select a tie ▪ to choose a tie **1.** *(necktie)* elegir una corbata **2.** *(bow tie)* elegir un corbatín ▪ elegir una pajarita ➤ Have you picked out a tie? ▪ Have you picked a tie out? ¿Has elegido una corbata? ➤ Have you picked one out? ▪ Have you selected one? ▪ Have you chosen one? ¿La has elegido?

to **pick someone's brain** exprimirle el cerebro a alguien ▪ exprimirle el coco a alguien ▪ exprimirle el seso a alguien

to **pick someone's pocket** robarle la cartera a alguien

to **pick up** *(intransitive)* to increase **1.** *(business)* ir mejor ▪ moverse **2.** *(wind)* levantarse ➤ Business is picking up. Business is starting to pick up. Los negocios empiezan a moverse. ➤ The wind is picking up. Se está levantando viento.

to **pick up a hitchhiker** ▪ to pick a hitchhiker up recoger un autoestopista

to **pick up a special order** recoger un pedido ▪ recoger un encargo ➤ I'm here to pick up my (special) order. Vengo a recoger un pedido. ▪ Vengo a recoger un pedido que hice. ▪ Vengo a recoger un encargo que hice. ➤ I'm here to pick up the book I (special) ordered. Vengo a recoger el libro que dejé pedido. ▪ Vengo a recoger el libro que dejé encargado.

to **pick up a station** *(radio, television)* ▪ to pick a station up captar una emisora ▪ agarrar una emisora ▪ *(Sp.)* coger una emisora

to **pick up a subject (quickly)** ▪ to pick a subject up (quickly) ▪ to learn a subject quickly aprender algo (con rapidez) ▪ captar una materia rápidamente ➤ She picked up the rudiments of Spanish in six months. Aprendió los rudimentos de español en seis meses. ➤ She picked it up (quickly). ▪ She picked it right up. Lo aprendió con rapidez.

to **pick up a suspect** ▪ to pick a suspect up ▪ to nab a suspect pillar a un sospechoso ▪ trincar a un sospechoso

to **pick up on something** darse cuenta de algo

to **pick up someone at the airport** ▪ to pick someone up at the airport recoger a alguien en el aeropuerto ➤ I'm on my way to the airport to pick up my girlfriend. ▪ I'm on my way to the airport to pick my girlfriend up. Voy en camino al aeropuerto para recoger a mi novia. ▪ Voy en camino al aeropuerto a buscar a mi novia. ➤ I'm on my way to the airport to pick her up. Voy en camino al aeropuerto para recogerla (a ella).

to **pick up someone in a bar** ▪ to pick someone up in a bar enrollarse con alguien en un bar ▪ *(female)* ligársela en un bar ▪ *(male)* ligárselo en un bar ➤ She picked him up in a bar. Se lo ligó en un bar. ➤ He picked her up in a bar. Se la ligó en un bar.

to **pick up something at the store** ▪ to pick something up at the store ▪ to get something at the store comprar algo en la tienda ➤ I have to stop and pick up a few things at the store. ▪ I have to stop and get a few things at the store. Tengo que pasar por la tienda a comprar unas cosas. ➤ I'm on my way to pick it up. Voy en camino a recogerlo. ➤ Will you pick up some things for me at the store? ¿Me traes unas cosas de la tienda?

to **pick up something off the floor** ▪ to pick something up off the floor recoger algo del suelo ▪ recoger algo del piso ➤ Pick up your socks and put them in the (clothes) hamper. ▪ Pick your socks up and put them in the (clothes) hamper. Recoge tus calcetines y ponlos en el canasto (de ropa).

to **pick up speed** acelerar ▪ cobrar velocidad ▪ *(wind)* levantar velocidad

to **pick up the kids** ▪ to pick the kids up ▪ to get the kids recoger a los peques

to **pick up the receiver** ▪ to pick the receiver up levantar el auricular ▪ tomar la bocina ▪ *(Sp.)* coger el auricular

to **pick up the tab** ▪ to pay the tab pagar la cuenta

to **pick up where someone leaves off** retomar algo donde alguien lo dejó

to be **picked by hand** ▪ to be hand-picked ▪ to be gathered by hand ser recolectado a mano ➤ *(on a wine label)* Made from the best selection of Tempranillo grapes, hand-picked in our own vineyards Elaborado con la mejor selección de uva Tempranillo, recolectada a mano en nuestros propio viñedos

to be **picked up by the police** ▪ to be nabbed by the police ser trincado por la policía

to be a **picky eater** ser contumerioso para la comida ➤ I'm not a picky eater, but some strong cheeses don't agree with me. No soy muy contumerioso (para la comida), pero no puedo con algunos quesos fuertes.

picky, picky! ▪ don't be so picky! ¡te estás pasando! ▪ ¡no seas tan picajoso! ▪ ¡no seas melindroso! ▪ ¡no seas melindres!

picture caption ▪ caption under a picture *el* pie de foto ▪ pie de la fotografía

a **picture is worth a thousand words** una imagen vale más de mil palabras

picture-taking session sesión fotográfica

Pictures at an Exhibition *(orchestral suite by Mussorgsky)* Pinturas en una exposición

piddling wars guerras de poca monta ➤ The feudal barons were always engaging in little piddling wars. Los barones feudales siempre se metían en guerras insignificantes. ▪ Los barones feudales siempre se metían en guerras de poca monta.

piece by piece trozo a trozo ▪ por piezas ➤ They are going to dismantle the Windsor Tower piece by piece. Van a desarmar la Torre Windsor por piezas.

piece of advice ▪ some advice consejo

to be a **piece of cake** ▪ to be duck soup ▪ to be easy to do ser pan comido ▪ ser pan

piece of ham taco de jamón

piece of paper ▪ sheet of paper **1.** *(with holes to go in a loose-leaf notebook)* hoja **2.** *(without lines or holes)* folio

piece of Scotch® tape ▪ piece of cellophane tape pieza de cinta adhesiva

piece of scratch paper ▪ scratch paper papel en sucio ➤ Do you have a piece of scratch paper? ¿Tienes un papel en sucio?

Pied Piper (of Hamelin) el flautista de Hamelin

to **pierce one's tongue** ▪ to have one's tongue pierced perforarse la lengua

to **pierce something with a fork** pinchar algo con un tenedor ➤ Pierce the potato with a fork to make sure it's done. Pincha la patata con un tenedor para asegurar que esté hecha.

pierced ears orejas agujereadas

piercing wind viento cortante

to be **pig-headed about** ▪ to be stubborn when it comes to estar empecinado en

to **pig out on ice cream** darse un atracón de helado

pile it on! ¡échale un montón! ➤ Really pile on the peanut butter. Really pile the peanut butter on. Échale un montón de crema de cacahuete. ➤ Really pile it on. Échale un montón.

pile of junk montón de basura ➤ How can you find anything with that pile of junk on your desk? ¿Cómo puedes encontrar cualquier cosa con ese montón de basura en ese escritorio?

to be a **pile of junk** ▪ to be a piece of junk ser un cachivache ▪ no valer para nada ▪ *(colorful)* no valer madre ➤ That car is a pile of junk. Ese carro es un cachivache. ▪ Ese carro no vale para nada. ▪ Ese carro no vale madre.

to **pile something on something** amontonar algo sobre algo

to **pile up** amontonarse ▪ acumularse ➤ The work really piled up while I was on vacation. El trabajo de veras que sí se amontonó cuando estuve de vacaciones. ▪ El trabajo de veras se acumuló cuando estuve de vacaciones.

to **pile up on one's desk** amontonarse en el escritorio ▪ acumularse en el escritorio.

pin a wrestler sujetar a un luchador ➤ He pinned me with a half nelson. Me sujetó con una media llave de cuello. ➤ He pinned me with a full nelson. Me sujetó con una llave de cuello.

pin drop: to hear a ~ oír caer un alfiler al suelo ➤ You could have heard a pin drop. Se podía haber oído caer un alfiler al suelo.

PIN (number) ▪ personal identification number *la* clave ▪ número de identificación personal

to **pinch someone on the chin** pellizcar a alguien en la barbilla ➤ He pinched her affectionately on the chin. La pellizcó cariñosamente en la barbilla.

to **pinpoint a location** señalar con precisión un sitio

to **pinpoint the date** precisar la fecha ➤ References to solar and lunar eclipses in ancient manuscripts can sometimes pinpoint the date of their origin. Referencias a los eclipses solares y lunares en los manuscritos antiguos pueden a veces precisar la fecha de su origen.

pinstriped suit *el* traje con raya diplomática

pipefuls of tobacco: to smoke ~ fumar pipas de tabaco ➤ He would smoke a couple pipefuls of tobacco after supper. Solía fumar un par de pipas de tabaco después de cenar.

pipes: water ~ **1.** *(for clean water)* tubería **2.** *(for dirty water)* cañería

piping hot ▪ steaming hot humeante

piping (on a pillow, bedspread, mattress, etc.) *el* reborde (de una almohada, colcha, colchón, etc.)

to **pique one's curiosity** ▪ to arouse one's curiosity ▪ to get one's curiosity up ▪ to awaken one's curiosity picarle la curiosidad a uno ▪ despertarle la curiosidad a uno ▪ *(coll.)* ya picarle el gusanillo a uno ➤ You've piqued my curiosity. ▪ You've aroused my curiosity. ▪ You've got my curiosity up. ▪ You've awakened my curiosity. Me has picado la curiosidad. ▪ Ya me has picado el gusanillo.

to **pique one's interest** despertarle el interés a uno

to **pirate compact discs** ▪ to pirate CDs piratear discos compactos

piston rod vástago de émbolo

pit of one's stomach boca del estómago

to **pitch a tent** ▪ to put up a tent **1.** *(camping tent)* armar una carpa **2.** *(military, circus, or nomadic tent)* armar una tienda de campaña ▪ montar una tienda de campaña

to be **pitch-dark** ▪ to be pitch-black dark ▪ to be pitch-black estar oscuro como boca de lobo ▪ estar como boca de lobo

pitch of a propeller ▪ angle of incidence of a propeller ángulo de una hélice ▪ ángulo de incidencia de las palas de una hélice ➤ The airplane has a variable-pitch propeller. El aeroplano tiene una hélice de ángulo variable. ▪ La avioneta tiene una hélice de ángulo variable. ▪ El avión tiene una hélice de ángulo variable.

pitch of a roof *el* pendiente del tejado

to **pitch to the left** *(airplane, ship)* ladearse a babor ▪ cabecear a babor

to **pitch to the right** *(airplane, ship)* ladearse a estribor ▪ cabecear a estribor

pitched battle: to erupt into a ~ ▪ to break out into pitched battle estallar en una batalla campal ➤ The street demonstration erupted into a pitched battle. ▪ The street demonstration broke out into a pitched battle. La manifestación en la calle estalló en una batalla campal.

place: in *x*th ~ puesto número *x* ➤ *(news item)* Among nations with the highest per capita income, Spain is in thirteenth place. Entre las naciones con los ingresos personales más altos, España está en puesto número trece.

to **place a restraining order on someone** arraigar a alguien

to **place an ad** colocar un anuncio

to **place an order** hacer un pedido

to **place an order with someone for** hacer un pedido a alguien por ➤ We placed an order with the supermarket for two hundred rolls. *(Mex.)* Hicimos un pedido al supermercado por doscientos bolillos. ▪ *(Sp.)* Hicimos un pedido al hipermercado por doscientos panecillos.

to **place one's confidence in** depositar la confianza en

to **place one's hopes in** depositar las ilusiones en

to **place responsibility on someone** darle la responsabilidad a alguien

to **place restrictions on** ▪ to curtail cercenar de ➤ The new military government placed restrictions on the citizens' freedom. ▪ The new military government curtailed the citizens' freedom. El nuevo gobierno militar cercenó de las libertades de los ciudadanos.

place setting *(includes dishes but may or may not include flatware)* vajilla ▪ juego individual de la vajilla

place setting of flatware *(silverware, stainless steel, etc.)* cubertería ▪ cubiertos

to **place someone on alert** ▪ to put someone on alert poner a alguien en alerta

to **place something within one's reach** poner algo al alcance de uno

place to meet sitio de encuentro ➤ We need to decide on a place to meet. Necesitamos concretar un sitio de encuentro.

place to park hueco libre para aparcar

place to stay *el* lugar para quedarme ▪ lugar para estar ➤ I need a place to stay. Necesito un lugar para quedarme. ▪ Necesito un lugar para estar.

place your bets! ¡hagan juego!

to be **placed in the hands of someone** ponerse en manos de alguien

to be **placed under house arrest** ▪ to be put under house arrest quedar en (situación de) arresto domiciliario ▪ ser puesto en arresto domiciliario ➤ Galileo was placed under house arrest. Galileo fue puesto en arresto domiciliario. ➤ Ex-president Slobodan Milosevic of Yugoslavia has been placed under house arrest. El ex-presidente de Yugoslavia, Slobodan Milosevic, ha quedado en situación de arresto domiciliario.

places to find... ▪ places where you can find... sitios donde encuentras...

plaid shirt ▪ checked shirt camisa cuadrada

to be **plain as day** ▪ to be obvious ▪ to be crystal clear estar más claro que el agua

plain-looking de aspecto sencillo

plain water *el* agua sin gas

plainclothes policeman policía encubierto ▪ agente encubierto

to **plan a crime** planear un crimen

to **plan a vacation** planificar unas vacaciones

to **plan for something to** planear que ➤ I had planned for this to take a year. Había planeado que tardaría un año.

plan of a building ▪ floor plan of a building ~ plano de un edificio ▪ *la* distribución de un edificio

to **plan to do something** pensar hacer algo ➤ If you're planning to buy a house... Si piensas comprar una casa...

to **plan to meet with someone** tener previsto reunirse con alguien ➤ Clinton plans to meets with party leaders today. Clinton tiene previsto reunirse con líderes del partido hoy.

to **plan to take (time)** planear tomar (tiempo) ▪ planear dedicarle (tiempo) ➤ I had planned to take a year with this project. Había planeado tomar un año para este proyecto. ▪ Había planeado dedicarle un año a este proyecto.

plane crash ▪ airplane crash *(Sp.) el* accidente de avión ▪ *(Mex.)* siniestro de avión

plane ticket ▪ airplane ticket boleto de avión ▪ *(Sp.) el* billete de avión ▪ billete de vuelo

to **plane wood** acuchillar madera

plank paneling placas de madera ▪ paneles de madera

plans and elevations *(of a building)* plantas y alzados ▪ planos y alzados

to **plant a flag** *(like the Iwo Jima soldiers)* enarbolar una bandera

to **plant a mine** plantar una mina

to **plant a tree** sembrar un árbol

to **plant explosives** colocar explosivos

plant world mundo vegetal

plantar fascitis *(foot inflammation)* fascitis ▪ inflamación de la fascia plantar

plastic frames *(of a pair of glasses)* monturas de pasta ➤ Do you want metal or plastic frames? ¿Quieres monturas metálicas o de pasta?

plate of anchovies, please ▪ a serving of anchovies, please una ración de anchoas, por favor

to **play a card** echar un naipe ▪ tirar un naipe ➤ He played his ace. Echó el as. ▪ Tiró el as.

to **play a dirty trick on someone** hacerle una mala jugada a alguien ▪ hacer una jugada sucia a alguien ▪ hacerle una mala faena a alguien

to **play a joke on someone** gastar una broma a alguien ▪ hacer una burla a alguien

to **play a more active role in** desempeñar un papel más activo en

to **play a prank on someone** gastarle una broma a alguien

to **play a role in** jugar un papel en ▪ desempeñar un papel en

to **play a team** jugar contra un equipo ➤ Real Madrid plays Barcelona this weekend. Real Madrid juega contra Barcelona este fin de semana.

to **play a trick on someone** hacerle una broma a alguien ▪ jugarle un truco a alguien ▪ *(Sp.)* gastarle una broma a alguien ▪ dar un chasco a alguien

to **play as a stand-alone** tocarse solo ▪ tocarse sin el resto

to **play at home** *(sports)* ▪ to play a home game jugar en casa

to **play badly** **1.** *(musical instrument)* tocar mal **2.** *(sport)* jugar mal

to **play by ear** tocar de oído

play by play *(sports)* jugada a jugada

to **play cops and robbers** jugar a policías y ladrones

to **play dead** hacerse el muerto ▪ hacerse la muerta

to **play doubles** jugar por pareja

to **play down the importance of something** ▪ to downplay the importance of something ▪ to minimize the importance of something restar importancia de algo ▪ quitar importancia de algo

to **play drums** ▪ to play (the) drums tocar la batería ▪ tocar los tambores

to **play dumb** hacerse el sueco ▪ hacerse el tonto ▪ hacer como que no comprende ▪ hacerse el despistado ▪ simular no comprender

to **play fair** jugar limpio

to **play for high stakes** jugar fuerte

to **play games** jugar juegos

to **play havoc with** ▪ to wreak havoc with crear un caos en ▪ causar estragos con

to **play hide-and-seek** jugar a escondite

to **play hooky** ▪ to feign illness (as a pretext for not going to school) hacer novillos ▪ hacer pirola ▪ fingir una indisposición para no asistir al colegio

to **play into someone's hands** ▪ to play into the hands of someone redundar en el beneficio de alguien to **play it safe** ▪ to be on the safe side curarse en salud ▪ ir a lo seguro ▪ cuidarse

to **play no part in** ▪ to play no role in ▪ not to play any part in ▪ not to play any role in no tomar parte en ▪ no entrar ni salir en

to **play on one's home court** ▪ to play at home jugar en casa

play on words juego de palabras ▪ juego de voces ▪ *(literary term)* retruécano

to **play one's cards right** jugar bien sus cartas ▪ jugar bien su baza ▪ jugar bien las cartas ▪ *(Sp.)* jugar bien la baza

to **play peekaboo** *(L. Am.)* jugar al escondite ▪ jugar al cucú

to **play phone tag** ▪ to play telephone tag jugar a la pega por teléfono ▪ jugar al te busco y no te encuentro ▪ jugar al desencuentro

to **play pool** ▪ to shoot pool jugar al billar ▪ billar

to **play someone** ▪ to play the part of someone ▪ to play the role of someone encarnar a alguien ▪ interpretar a alguien ▪ representar a alguien ▪ hacer el papel de alguien

to **play sports** practicar los deportes

play station *la* estación de juego

to **play tag** jugar a pillar

to **play the field** picar de flor en flor ▪ ser un picaflor

to **play the fool** hacer el ganso ▪ hacerse el tonto ▪ hacerse el idiota

to **play the piano beautifully** tocar el piano magníficamente ▪ tocar el piano que da gusto

to **play the radio** tocar la radio

to **play (the role of) someone** ▪ to play (the part of) someone ▪ to play someone hacer el papel de alguien en una obra teatral ▪ interpretar el papel de alguien en una obra teatral ▪ representar a alguien en una obra teatral ▪ encarnar a alguien ➤ In *Catch Me If You Can*, Leo DiCaprio plays an infamous con man. En *Atrápame si puedes*, Leo DiCaprio encarna a un estafador famoso.

to **play the stereo** sonar el estereo

to **play the stock market** jugar a la bolsa

to **play to the grandstand** ▪ to play to the gallery expresarse con doble fin

to **play tricks on someone** jugarle trucos a alguien

to **play well 1.** *(musical instrument)* tocar bien **2.** *(sport)* jugar bien

to **play-act** jugar al teatro ▪ hacer teatro

to be **played as a stand-alone** tocarse independientemente ➤ Saint Saëns' *The Swan*, which is part of "The Carnival of the Animals," is often played as a stand-alone. *El Cisne de Saint Saëns*, que es parte del "Carnaval de los Animales", a menudo se toca independientemente.

to be **playing** estarse estrenando ▪ poner ➤ Is *Titanic* playing anywhere? ¿Ponen *Titanic* en alguna parte? ▪ ¿Se está estrenando *Titanic* en alguna parte?

playing field terreno de juego

to **plead guilty** declararse culpable ▪ confesarse culpable ➤ The suspect pleaded guilty to the charges. ▪ The suspect pled guilty to the charges. El sospechoso se declaró culpable de los cargos. ▪ El sospechoso se confesó culpable de los cargos.

pleasant chat with someone: to have a ~ ▪ to have an enjoyable chat with someone ▪ to have a nice chat with someone tener una amena charla con alguien

pleasant evening velada amena

please bear with me les ruego paciencia ➤ It takes a minute to explain this, so please bear with me. Lleva un minuto explicarlo, por eso les ruego paciencia.

please continue to hold por favor, siga la espera ▪ por favor, permanezca la escucha

please do! ¡pero por Dios!

please don't! *(a ti)* ¡te pido que no lo hagas! ▪ *(a usted)* ¡le pido que no lo haga!

please ring the bell *(at a business entrance)* por favor llamar al timbre

please wait 1. *(all contexts)* por favor, manténgase en espera **2.** *(on the phone)* por favor no se retire

please wait to be seated por favor, espere a recibir asiento ▪ por favor, espere para recibir asiento

pleased to meet you! encantado(-a) ▪ *(tú)* encantado(-a) de conocerte ▪ *(usted)* encantado(-a) de conocerlo(-a) ▪ *(leísmo)* encantado(-a) de conocerle a usted ▪ *(casual to the point of impoliteness in formal settings)* ¡tanto gusto!

to be **pleased with** estar contento(-a) con ▪ estar satisfecho(-a) con ▪ estar complacido(-a) por

to be **pleased with oneself for...** estar pagado(-a) de sí mismo(-a) por... ▪ ser pagado(-a) de sí mismo(-a) por... ➤ He was very pleased with himself. Estaba muy pagado de sí mismo. ▪ Era muy pagado de sí mismo.

to be **pleasing to the eye** dar gusto de verlo ▪ dar gozo de verlo

to **pledge allegiance to the flag** hacer el juramento a la bandera ▪ jurar fidelidad a la bandera

pledge of allegiance to the flag *(U.S.A.)* juramento (de fidelidad) a la bandera ▪ jura (de fidelidad) a la bandera ➤ I pledge allegiance to the flag of the United States of America, and to the Republic for which it stands, one nation under God, indivisible, with liberty and justice for all. Juro fidelidad a la bandera de los Estados Unidos de América, y a la república que simboliza, una nación Dios mediante, indivisible, con libertad y justicia para todos.

plenty of room: to have ~ tener suficiente espacio ➤ I have plenty of room. Tengo suficiente espacio.

plenty to spare: to have ~ tener más de lo suficiente para dar y tomar

to **plot a crime** tramar un crimen ▪ tramar un delito ▪ urdir un crimen ▪ urdir un delito ➤ They plotted to rob the bank. Tramaron atracar el banco. ▪ Urdieron atracar el banco.

the **plot thickens** se va enredando la madeja ▪ se está enredando la madeja

to **pluck a chicken** desplumar un pollo

to **pluck a grape** tomar una uva ▪ *(Sp.)* coger una uva

to **pluck grapes** ▪ to pick grapes ▪ to gather grapes recolectar uvas

to **pluck one's eyebrows** depilarse las cejas

to **pluck up one's courage** ▪ to get up one's courage ▪ to get up one's nerve ▪ to pluck up one's nerve echarle valor

to **plug in something** ▪ to plug something in enchufar algo

to **plug into** ▪ to connect to enchufar a ▪ conectar sobre ➤ *(extension cord instructions)* Plug your extension cord into an outlet with ground. Conecte su prolongador sobre un enchufe con toma de tierra.

plug of (chewing) tobacco *(Cuba, Mex.)* andullo

to be **plumb out of something** *(Southern U.S., coll.)* ▪ to be completely out of quedarse completamente sin algo

to be **plumb tuckered (out)** *(Southern U.S., coll.)* ▪ to be pooped (out) ▪ to be worn to a frazzle ▪ to be beat ▪ to be completely exhausted estar derrengado ▪ estar hecho polvo ▪ estar para el arrastre ▪ estar agotado

plummeted to the ground: the airplane ~ se desplomó el avión ▪ *(light airplane)* se desplomó la avioneta

to **plunge into (a) recession** precipitarse hacia la recesión ➤ *(headline)* The world plunges into (a) recession El mundo se precipita hacia la recesión

to be **plunged into** quedar sumido en

to be **plunged into total chaos** sumirse en el caos más absoluto

plus or minus de más o menos ➤ The Pole Star is 430 light years away, plus or minus a hundred light years. La Estrella Polar está aproximadamente a 430 años luz, con un posible error de más o menos cien años luz. ➤ The poll has a possible error of plus or minus three percent. La encuesta tiene un posible error de más o menos el tres por ciento.

to **ply the seas** surcar los mares

to **poach an egg** escalfar un huevo

to **poach animals** cazar (furtivamente) animales vedados ▪ atrapar animales en veda

pocket change ▪ small change ▪ loose change dinero del bolsillo ▪ calderilla ▪ *(Chi.)* sencillo

pocket of resistance bolsa de resistencia ▪ foco de resistencia ➤ *(news item)* The troops are trying to eliminate a pocket of resistance dug in in hard-to-reach snow-covered mountains. Las tropas tratan de eliminar una bolsa de resistencia atrincherada en unas montañas nevadas de difícil acceso.

poetic license licencia poética

poignant letter carta conmovedora

poignant reminder recordatorio conmovedor

point at issue punto conflictivo ➤ The point at issue is... El punto conflictivo es...

to **point at someone** señalar a alguien con el dedo ➤ Don't point at people. Que no señales a las personas con el dedo.

point-blank range: to shoot at ~ ■ to fire at point-blank range disparar a quemarropa ■ pegar un tiro a quemarropa ■ tirar a quemarropa

point by point punto por punto ■ *a* por *a* y *b* por *b*

to **point in a direction** señalar a una dirección ■ apuntar a una dirección ➤ The compasses used on Columbus' ships still point north. Las brújulas utilizadas en los barcos de Colón aún señalan al norte. ■ Las brújulas utilizadas en los barcos de Colón aún apuntan al norte.

the **point is that...** el caso es que...

point is that...: my ~ lo que quiero señalar es que... ■ lo que quiero dejar claro es que... ■ lo que quiero plantear es que... ■ lo que quiero decir es que... ■ lo que quiero probar es que...

point of departure punto de partida ➤ It serves as a point of departure for the discussion. Serve del punto de partida para la discusión.

point of reference punto de referencia

point of sale punto de venta

point of the joke ■ meaning of the joke gracia del chiste

to **point out something to someone** ■ to point something out to someone **1.** *(literally, to point with one's finger)* señalar algo a alguien ■ indicarle algo a alguien (con el dedo) ■ mostrarle algo a alguien **2.** *(figuratively, to call attention)* señalarle algo a alguien ➤ Would you point out my mistakes? ¿Me señalas mis errores? ■ ¿Quisieras señalarme mis errores? ➤ Would you point them out for me? ¿Me los señalas? ■ ¿Quisieras señalármelos?

to **point out that...** señalar que... ■ hacer notar que... ➤ Gabi pointed out that the castle is the symbol of Castilla and the lion the symbol of León. Gabi señaló que el castillo es el símbolo de Castilla y el león de León.

to **point the finger at someone else** ■ to put the blame on someone else cargarle el mochuelo a alguien ■ señalar a alguien (con el dedo) ■ echarle la culpa a otra persona ➤ The kindergarten children made a colossal mess but pointed the finger at the other class. Los niños de la guardería dejaron la clase hecha una leonera pero le cargaron el mochuelo a la otra clase.

pointed end: to have a ~ acabar en punta

pointed window ventana ojival

to be ***x* points ahead** ■ to lead by *x* points llevar puntos de ventaja ➤ Our team is ten points ahead (of the other team). Nuestro equipo le lleva diez puntos de ventaja al otro.

to be ***x* points behind** estar *x* puntos detrás ■ tener *x* puntos menos ➤ Our team is ten points behind (the other team). Nuestro equipo está diez puntos detrás del otro. ■ Nuestro equipo tiene diez puntos menos que el otro.

poisonous snake víbora venenosa ■ serpiente venenosa

to **poke a hole through** perforar un agujero de lado a lado ■ punzar un agujero de lado a lado

to **poke along** ■ to go poking along ■ to go way below the speed limit ■ to drive way below the speed limit andar como una tortuga ■ ir a medio gas

to **poke someone in the eye (with something)** darle a alguien en el ojo (con algo) ■ clavarle a alguien (con algo) en el ojo

to **poke something in someone's eye** darle a alguien con algo en el ojo ■ clavarle a alguien con algo en el ojo

poker chips fichas

poker face cara de póquer ■ rostro hermético

to be **poker-faced** ■ to have a poker face ■ not to change one's expression ■ to have a deadpan expression tener cara de póquer ■ tener cara de impávido ■ tener una cara sin inmutarse ■ ni inmutarse ➤ The accused was poker-faced. El presunto culpable ni se inmutó.

polar ice caps capas de hielo polar

Pole Star ■ North Star ■ Polaris estrella polar ■ estrella del norte

to be **poles apart** ser polos opuestos ➤ The candidates are poles apart on the issues. Los candidatos son polos opuestos en los asuntos.

police account relato de la policía

police artist's sketch retrato robot ■ retrato reconstruido

police dragnet cerco policial

police force cuerpo de policía

police lineup rueda de reconocimiento

police officer *el, la* agente de policía ■ *el, la* policía

police raid ■ raid by the police batida de la policía ■ redada policial

police record ficha policial

police roundup redada policial

policy of appeasement ■ appeasement policy política de apaciguamiento ■ política de confraternización

to **polish off** *(food, wine, beer, etc.)* **1.** to consume quickly despachar **2.** to finish (what's left) liquidar ■ rematar ■ apurar

to **polish shoes, boots** ■ to shine shoes, boots lustrar zapatos, botas ■ sacar brillo a zapatos, botas ■ *(Sp.)* limpiar zapatos, botas

to **polish silver** lustrar plata ■ sacar brillo a plata

to **polish up the rough parts** *(essay, manuscript, etc.)* ■ to clean up the rough parts retocar las partes que lo necesitan ■ depurar las partes a las que les hace falta un retoque ■ depurar las partes a las que les hace falta ser retocadas

polished style ■ refined style estilo depurado ■ estilo refinado

politeness itself la educación en persona

political arena palestra política ■ ruedo político

political capital ganancia política

political cartoon caricatura política

political contest lid política

political correctness tacto político ■ corrección política

political environment ámbito político

political finesse delicadeza política ■ destreza política

political give-and-take toma y daca política

political infighting luchas internas de un partido

political leanings tendencias políticas

political rival *el, la* contrincante político(-a)

political rumpus polvareda política

political splintering escisión política

political unrest crispación política

to be **politically motivated** tener motivación política ■ estar políticamente motivado ■ ser de tipo político ■ realizarse en el ámbito político ➤ The accusations were politically motivated. Las acusaciones fueron de tipo político. ■ Las acusaciones fueron realizados en el ámbito político. ➤ Some newspapers treat politically motivated accusations as if they were accomplished fact. Algunos periódicos tratan las acusaciones de tipo político como si fueran un hecho dado. ■ Algunos periódicos tratan las acusaciones en el ámbito político como si fueran hechos dados.

politics of intimidation política de acoso

to **pollute the air** enrarecer el aire ■ contaminar el aire

pool of players cantera de jugadores

pool of talent ■ talent pool cantera de talento

pool table ■ billiard table mesa de billar

to be **pooped out** ■ to be pooped ■ to be beat ■ to be whipped ■ to be dead tired ■ to be dog tired ■ to be knackered estar agotado(-a) ■ estar muerto(-a) de cansancio ■ quedarse sin gas ■ estar cansado(-a) como un perro ■ *(Arg., Uru.)* estar recansado(-a) ■ estar fundido(-a) ■ estar refundido(-a) ■ estar molido(-a)

poor as a church mouse: to be (as) ~ ser tan pobre como ratón de iglesia ■ ser tan pelado como una rata ■ ser tan pobre como ratón de sacristía

to be a **poor choice of words** ser un uso poco afortunado de las palabras ➤ It was a poor choice of words. Fue un uso poco afortunado de las palabras.

to be **poor in spirit** ser pobre de espíritu

to be a **poor loser** ■ to be a sore loser tener mal perder

poor management ■ bad management mala gestión

poor memory: to have a tener mala memoria

poor opinion of: to have a ■ to have a low opinion of tener un muy mal concepto de

poor shot tirador de poca calidad ➤ He's a poor shot. Es un tirador de poca calidad.

poor visibility escasa visibilidad

to **pop a balloon** ■ to burst a balloon explotar un globo

pop-eyed con los ojos desorbitados ■ de ojos saltones

to **pop the clutch** ■ to release the clutch instantly soltar el embrague de golpe ■ soltar rápido el embrague ➤ To jump-start the car by coasting it, turn on the ignition, put it in second, let it coast downhill for a few feet, and then pop the clutch. Para arrancar el coche de tirón dejándolo caer, gira la llave, mete segunda, déjalo caer unos metros por la pendiente y suelta el embrague de golpe.

popular: to be very ~ ser muy popular ■ *(coll.)* tener más visitas que un ministro

popular demand: by ~ a petición del público

popular song *la* canción popular ■ canción de moda

Port-au-Prince, Haiti Puerto Príncipe, Haití

port authority autoridad portuaria

to **pose a problem** ■ to present a problem plantear un problema ■ plantear una dificultad

to **pose a question** formular una pregunta

to **pose a threat** suponer una amenaza

to **pose for a photograph** posar para una foto(grafía)

to **pose for a portrait** ■ to sit for a portrait posar para un retrato

to **position oneself** 1. to take up a position apostarse 2. to stand between ■ to sit between situarse entre ■ ubicarse entre

to be **positioned on** 1. estar colocado en ■ colocarse en 2. *(military)* apostado en ■ apostarse en

possession of weapons ■ weapons possession tenencia de armas

possessor of a secret dueño de un secreto

possibility that... la posibilidad de que...

to **post a letter** ■ to pay the postage on a letter franquear una carta

Post-it® notes hojitas autoadhesivas

post office casa de correos ■ oficina de correos

to **post something on the bulletin board** poner algo en el tablón de anuncios

to **post something on the web** colgar algo en la red ■ publicar algo en Internet

post-war de posguerra ➤ Post-war England Inglaterra de posguerra

postage stamp sello de correos ■ estampilla ■ *(Mex.) el* timbre

postal code ■ zip code código postal

to be **posted on the web** estar colgado en la red

poster board cartulina

to **postpone a meeting because of** posponer una reunión debido a... ■ postergar una reunión debido a... ■ aplazar una reunión debido a... ■ diferir una reunión debido a...

to **postpone the debate** aplazar el debate

the **pot is calling the kettle black** ■ the pot's calling the kettle black la olla llama negra a la sartén

potato chips *(Sp.)* patatas fritas

pots and pans batería de cocina ■ cacharros de cocina

to **pound a target** *(in warfare)* abatir un objetivo ■ abatir un blanco

pound cake *el* pastel de bizcocho denso y amarillo, parecido a una magdalena ■ *(Cuba)* pon que ➤ The unique thing about a pound cake is its density. Lo que distingue un pon que es su densidad.

pound key *(key pad, keyboard)* cuadrado ■ almohadilla

to **pound on the wall** golpear la pared ➤ The neighbor pounded on the (common) wall between the houses. La vecina golpeó la pared divisoria.

pound sign *(key pad, keyboard)* cuadrado

to **pound the pavement** ■ to beat the pavement ■ to look for a job ■ to job hunt patear el asfalto ■ patear la calle

to **pour down rain** venirse el cielo abajo ■ caer la lluvia a torrentes ➤ The rain was pouring down. ■ It was pouring down rain. El cielo se venía abajo. ■ La lluvia caía a torrentes.

to **pour drop by drop** ■ to pour a drop at a time verter a cuentagotas ■ verter con cuentagotas

pour me some... échame...

to **pour the contents of the envelope** ■ to pour the contents of the packet verter el contenido del sobre ➤ Pour the contents of the envelope into one liter of lukewarm water. ■ Pour the contents of the packet into a liter of tepid water. Verter el contenido del sobre en un litro de agua templada. ■ Verter el contenido del sobre en un litro de agua tibia.

powder keg *el* barril de pólvora

to be a **powder keg** ■ to be a dangerous person ser un barril de pólvora ■ ser una caja de bombas ■ ser una bomba a punto de estallar

power failure ■ power outage *el* apagón ■ el corte de luz

power of reason fuerza de la razón

power outage ■ power failure *el* apagón ■ *el* corte de luz ➤ I need a battery-powered clock for traveling and power outages. Necesito un reloj a pilas para los viajes y para los cortes de luz.

power steering dirección asistida

power supply ■ power source ■ source of electricity ■ feed *la* fuente de energía ■ fuente de alimentación

power surge subida de tensión

power vacuum vacío de poder

power went off ■ electricity went off electricidad se apagó

power windows elevalunas eléctricas

to be **powered by** 1. to run on funcionar con 2. to be propelled by moverse con ➤ The toy is powered by batteries. ■ The toy runs on batteries. El juguete funciona con pilas. ➤ This bus is powered by natural gas. ■ This bus is propelled by natural gas. Este autobús se mueve con gas natural.

powerful argument argumento poderoso

powerful blast ■ powerful explosion *la* fuerte explosión

powerful computer *el* ordenador potente ■ *el* ordenador de mucha capacidad

powerful current *el* corriente fuerte

powerful engine *el* motor potente

powerful explosion ■ powerful blast la potente explosión ■ fuerte explosión

powerful explosive el potente explosivo

powerful movie película muy fuerte

powerful poison veneno potente

powerful politician político poderoso

powerful storm tormenta fuerte ■ *(literary, poetic) la* tempestad fuerte ■ *(wind and rain lasting a short time) el* fuerte temporal

to be **powerless to do something** verse impotente para hacer algo

the **power's gone off** se ha ido la luz

the **powers that be** los poderes fácticos ■ los poderes existentes

to **practice basketball** entrenar al baloncesto

to **practice law** ejercer de abogado ■ ejercer como abogado ■ ejercer la abogacía

practice makes perfect la práctica hace al maestro

to **practice medicine** ejercer medicina

to **practice singing** ensayar cantos ➤ We practiced the Verdi today. Ensayamos el Verdi hoy. ■ Repasamos el Verdi hoy. ■ *(Sp.)* Hemos ensayado el Verdi hoy. ■ Hemos estado repasando el Verdi hoy. ➤ We practiced the Verdi yesterday. Ayer ensayamos el Verdi. ■ Ayer repasamos el Verdi. ■ *(Sp.)* Ayer estuvimos repasando el Verdi.

to **practice soccer** entrenar al fútbol

to **practice the piano** ensayar el piano ■ practicar el piano

to **practice what one preaches** ■ to preach by example practicar lo que uno predica ■ hacer lo que uno dice ■ predicar con el ejemplo

practiced non-payer moroso ■ manguta

practicing Catholic católico practicante

praise God! ■ God be praised! ¡alabado sea Dios!

to **praise someone to the skies** ▪ to sing someone's praises hablar maravillas de alguien
praiseworthy person persona encomiable
pre-arranged visit ▪ pre-arranged tour visita concertada
pre-recorded grabado en diferido
pre-stamped envelope sobre prefranqueado
precautionary measures medidas cautelares
to be **preceded by 1.** *(in a sequence)* estar precedido(-a) de **2.** *(in death)* ser precedido(-a) por
precision instrument instrumento de regulación preciso
to **predict the election results** vaticinar los resultados de las elecciones
to **prefer to do one thing rather than another** ▪ to prefer doing one thing over another preferir hacer una cosa más bien que otra
pregnancy test prueba de embarazo
to **preheat the oven** poner a precalentar el horno
preliminary search búsqueda preliminar
premature birth parto prematuro
preoccupation with preocupación por
preparations for war preparativos bélicos
to **prepare for the worst** prepararse para lo peor
to **prepare to do something** prepararse a hacer algo
to **prescribe medication** recetar medicamento ➤ The doctor prescribed me antibiotics. El médico me ha recetado antibióticos.
prescription glasses ▪ prescription lenses gafas graduadas ▪ lentes graduados ➤ Are those prescription lenses? ¿Están graduados los lentes?
prescription lenses lentes graduados
prescription sunglasses gafas de sol graduadas
presence of mind presteza mental ▪ presencia de ánimo
to **present a problem** ▪ to pose a problem ▪ to create a problem plantear un problema ▪ plantear una dificultad
present and future habido y por haber ▪ presente y futuro
present balance saldo actual
present company excepted excluyendo lo presente ▪ no agravando los presentes ▪ mejorando lo presente
present-day actual ▪ de hoy (en día)
present-day knowledge: according to ~ según los conocimientos actuales
preside over presidar por ➤ Presided over by Chief Justice Earl Warren, the Warren Commission... Presidada por el presidente del Tribunal Supremo, Earl Warren, la Comisión Warren...
president of the United States presidente de los Estados Unidos ▪ presidente norteamericano ▪ presidente estadounidense
Presidents' Day *(February holiday commemorating the birthdays of Washington and Lincoln)* el día de los presidentes
president's pardon of someone indulto del presidente a alguien
to **press a button** ▪ to push a button pulsar un botón ▪ presionar un botón ▪ empujar un botón ▪ marcar un botón ➤ To save the message, press two. Para conservar el mensaje, pulse dos.
press any key to continue presione cualquier tecla para continuar
to **press charges against someone for** presentar cargos contra alguien por
press conference: to hold a ~ celebrar una rueda de prensa ▪ celebrar una rueda de periodista ▪ celebrar una conferencia de prensa
to **press on regardless** ponérsele nada por delante ▪ romper por todo ▪ liarse la manta a la cabeza
to **press one's face against the window** pegar la frente a la ventana
to **press one's luck** ▪ to tempt fate tentar a la suerte ➤ Don't press your luck! ¡No tientes a la suerte!
to **press the pound key** ▪ to press pound pulsar la tecla cuadrada
to **press the star key** ▪ to press star pulsar la tecla estrella
to be **pressed for time** ▪ to be pushed for time ir fatal de tiempo ▪ ir justo de tiempo ▪ estar apurado de tiempo ▪ andar escaso de tiempo ➤ I'm (really) pressed for time. Voy fatal de tiempo. ▪ Voy justo de tiempo.
pressing issue *la* cuestión candente
pressure cooker olla a presión
pressure on: to put ~ poner presión contra
to **pressure someone to do something** presionar a alguien para que haga algo ▪ hacer caña a alguien para que haga algo
to **presume (to be) dead** ▪ to give up for dead dar por muerto ➤ Russia presumes the one hundred and eighteen submarine crew members are dead. Rusia da por muertos los ciento dieciocho tripulantes del submarino.
to **pretend like** ▪ to pretend that ▪ to play like hacer para si
to **pretend not to know about something** desentenderse de algo
to **pretend that one is doing something** hacerse pasar por ▪ fingir que
to **pretend that one is something** ▪ to pretend to be something ▪ to feign being something fingir ser algo ▪ fingir que uno es algo
to be **pretty average** ser bastante normalito ▪ ser bastante corriente ▪ ser de medio nivel ▪ ser del montón
to be **pretty cold** ▪ to be fairly cold ▪ to be somewhat cold hacer algo de frío ➤ It's still pretty cold here. Hace algo de frío aquí todavía.
pretty good: to be doing ~ *(coll.)* ▪ to be doing pretty well estar tirando ➤ How are you doing?-Pretty good! ¿Qué tal?-¡Tirando!
to be **pretty late to do something** ser más bien tarde para hacer algo ➤ It's pretty late in the day to start cutting the grass. Es más bien tarde para empezar a cortar el cesped.
pretty much ▪ for the most part prácticamente ➤ We've pretty much exhausted the subject. Hemos prácticamente agotado el tema.
pretty penny: to cost one a ~ costarle una pasta gansa ➤ It cost me a pretty penny. Me costó una pasta gansa.
pretty soon bien pronto ▪ pasado un poco más tiempo
pretty well ▪ fairly well ▪ just about ▪ almost más o menos bien
prevailing situation *la* situación reinante
to **prevent someone from doing something** ▪ to keep someone from doing something impedir que alguien haga algo ▪ *(past tense)* impedir que alguien hiciera algo
to **prevent someone from falling** ▪ to break someone's fall impedir que se caiga ▪ *(past tense)* impedir que se cayera
to **prevent someone from going** ▪ to keep someone from going impedir a alguien acudir ➤ *(headline)* Elections in Egypt prevent Mubarak from going to the UN Las elecciones en Egipto impiden a Mubarak acudir a la ONU
to **prevent something from happening** impedir que ocurra algo ▪ prevenir que ocurra algo ▪ evitar que ocurra algo ▪ *(past tense)* impedir que ocurriera algo ▪ prevenir que ocurriera algo ▪ evitar que ocurriera algo ➤ The bar on the steering wheel is to prevent the car from being stolen. La barra en el volante evita que se robe el coche. ➤ The bar on the steering wheel prevented the car from being stolen. La barra en el volante evitó que se robara el coche. ▪ La barra en el volante evitó que se robase el coche.
preventive measures medidas preventivas
previous attempts intentos anteriores
previous edition *(book)* ▪ earlier edition edición anterior ➤ A previous edition ▪ An earlier edition Una edición anterior ➤ The previous edition La edición anterior
previous issue *(magazine)* ▪ earlier issue edición anterior ➤ A previous issue ▪ An earlier issue Una edición anterior ➤ The previous issue La edición anterior
previous marriage matrimonio anterior ➤ She has two other children from a previous marriage. Ella tiene otros dos hijos de un matrimonio anterior.
previous night *la* noche anterior
the **previous one** ▪ the last one el anterior ▪ la anterior
previously married: to have been ~ ▪ to have been married previously ▪ to have been married before ya haber estado casado(-a)

previously owned ▪ secondhand de segunda mano

previously unknown 1. until now unknown hasta ahora desconocido 2. until then unknown hasta entonces desconocido

the **price has doubled** el precio se ha duplicado

price of something precio de algo ▪ *el* coste de algo

price on someone's head precio por la cabeza de alguien ➤ There's a price on his head. Hay un precio por su cabeza.

price range: to be in a ~ situarse en una gama de precios ➤ The marketing studies indicate the items will sell best in the twenty- to twenty-five dollar price range. Los estudios de mercadería indican que los artículos se venderán mejor entre la gama de veinte a veinticinco dólares. ➤ He'd like to find a studio in the 60,000-peseta price range. Quiere encontrar un estudio alrededor de las 60.000 pesetas.

price range: to be out of one's ~ ▪ to be beyond one's price range ser más allá de las posibilidades de uno ▪ ser más allá del alcance de uno

price skyrockets precio dispara ➤ *(headline)* Price of housing skyrockets in Madrid El precio de viviendas dispara en Madrid

price to pay precio a pagar

to be **priced within the market** estar en el mercado

to **prick one's finger** pincharse en el dedo

to **prick up one's ears** poner las orejas tiesas ▪ echar las orejas ▪ parar la oreja

to **pride oneself on** preciarse de ▪ hacer algo a gala ▪ hacer gala de

priest's collar *el* collarín

primary school ▪ elementary school ▪ grade school (escuela) primaria ▪ *(Sp.)* colegio

prime of life *la* plenitud de la vida ▪ *la* flor de la vida

prime suspect primer sospechoso ▪ máximo sospechoso ➤ Prime suspect in the case Máximo sospechoso del caso

prime time franja de máxima audiencia

Prince Charming príncipe azul

prince of darkness príncipe de las tinieblas

prince of peace príncipe de la paz

principal rival ▪ principal opponent máximo rival ➤ New York mayor Rudolph Giuliani, the principal rival of Hillary Clinton as senator from New York El alcalde de Nueva York, Rudolph Giuliani, máximo rival de Hillary Clinton como senador de Nueva York

print of a painting estampa de una pintura ▪ lámina de una pintura

printing of a book tirada de un libro ➤ The first printing was 10,000 copies. La primera tirada fue diez mil ejemplares.

prior history (of) 1. *(medical)* historial médico de... 2. *(criminal)* rap sheet *los* antecedentes penales ➤ He has a history of heart problems. Tiene un historial médico de problemas cardiacos. ➤ He has a prior history of violent crime. Tiene antecedentes penales de crímenes violentos.

prior to previo a ▪ antes de ▪ anterior a

prison sentence pena de prisión

prisoner exchange ▪ exchange of prisoners *el* canje de prisioneros

private matter asunto privado ➤ It's a private matter. Es un asunto privado.

private parts partes pudendas ▪ *(coll.)* las vergüenzas

private practice *(law)* bufete privado

privy council consejo del reino

prize for: to win the ~ ganar el premio de ➤ John F. Kennedy won the Pulitzer Prize for literature. John F. Kennedy ganó el Premio Pulitzer de literatura.

prized possession bien preciada ➤ The rooster is his most prized possession. El gallo es su bien más preciado.

pro-democracy movement movimiento en pro de la democracia ▪ movimiento favorable a la democracia

pro-life groups grupos que están a favor de la vida

the **probability that...** las probabilidades de que...

probably will: one ~ es fácil que lo haga uno ▪ es probable que lo haga uno

probationary status ▪ probation situación de prueba

to **probe into** escarbar en ▪ sonsacar de ▪ sonsacar en

a **problem has come up** ▪ a problem has arisen un problema ha surgido

the **problem is that...** el problema es que... ▪ lo malo es que... ▪ *(colorful, Quechuan)* lo chungo es que...

problem underlying: to be the (basic) ~ ser el problema básico que sustenta ▪ ser problema de fondo en ▪ ser el problema básico que subyace ➤ What is the basic problem underlying terrorism? ¿Cuál es el problema básico que sustenta el terrorismo? ▪ ¿Cuál es el problema de fondo en el origen del terrorismo? ▪ ¿Cuál es el problema básico que subyace el terrorismo?

procedural flaw defecto de procedimiento

to **proceed at a good pace** avanzar a buen paso ➤ The construction is proceeding at a good pace. La construcción avanza a buen paso.

to **proceed normally** desenvolverse con normalidad ▪ desenvolverse sin incidente

proceeds from the sale beneficios de la venta ▪ producto de la venta ➤ Proceeds from the sale were not sufficient to pay off my debts. El producto de la venta no me llegaba para liquidar mis deudas.

processed foods alimentos elaborados ➤ *(headline)* Unhealthy fats in three out of four processed foods Grasas insalubres en tres de cada cuatro alimentos elaborados

to **proclaim oneself** proclamarse

to **proctor an examination** vigilar un examen

prodigal son hijo pródigo

to **produce an effect** ▪ to cause an effect provocar un efecto

produce department frutería

to **produce the same effect** ▪ to cause the same effect provocar el mismo efecto

to be the **product of** ser producto de ➤ We humans are the product of both heredity and environment. Nosotros los seres humanos somos el producto de la herencia y el medio ambiente.

production cost(s) costo(s) de producción

to **profit from** ▪ to benefit from beneficiarse de ▪ beneficiarse con ▪ sacar provecho de ▪ *(coll.)* sacar tajada de

to **profit from one's experience** ▪ to learn from experience ▪ to learn by experience beneficiarse de la experiencia de uno ▪ beneficiarse con la experiencia de uno ▪ sacar provecho de la experiencia de uno ▪ *(coll.)* sacar tajada de la experiencia de uno

profitable business negocio rentable

program of university courses curso universitario

to **progress steadily** progresar a un ritmo constante

progressively better: to get ~ volverse (ya) cada vez mejor ▪ ir mejorando poco a poco ➤ It gets progressively better. Se vuelve (ya) cada vez mejor. ▪ Va mejorando poco a poco.

progressively less ya cada vez menos

progressively more ya cada vez más

progressively worse: to get ~ volverse ya cada vez peor

Prohibition era *(U.S.A., 1920-33)* época de la ley seca

prolonged drought sequía pertinaz

prominent businessman destacado empresario ▪ destacado hombre de negocio

promiscuous woman mujer promiscua ▪ *(slang)* gallina muy ponedora

a **promise is a promise** lo prometido es deuda

to **promise to call someone** comprometerse a llamarle a alguien (por teléfono)

to **promote a cause** ▪ to advance a cause promover una causa ➤ Susan B. Anthony promoted the rights of women in the United States. Susan B. Anthony promovió los derechos a la mujer en los Estados Unidos.

to **promote growth** potenciar el crecimiento

to **promote tolerance** ▪ to increase tolerance promover la tolerancia

to **prompt someone to do something** llevar a alguien a hacer algo ▪ mover a alguien a hacer algo ➤ The Battle of Antietam was the turning point in the American Civil War, prompting Lincoln to announce the Emancipation Proclamation. La Batalla de Antietam fue el punto determinante en la Guerra

Civil Americana, llevando a Lincoln a anunciar la Proclamación de Emancipación.

to be **prone to** ser propenso a

pronounced accent ▪ strong accent acento acusado

proof (in mathematics) ▪ mathematical proof demostración matemática

to **proofread a manuscript** revisar un manuscrito (por si hay errores)

prop wash *(coll.)* ▪ wake of a propeller ▪ wind blast from a propeller estela de hélice ▪ estela de viento generada por una hélice

propane tank *(for gas stoves)* bombona

to be **propelled by** ▪ to be powered by moverse con

propeller blades ▪ blades of a propeller palas de una hélice ▪ aspas de una hélice

propensity to propensión a ➤ Human beings have an innate propensity to reject the unfamiliar. Los seres humanos tienen una propensión innata a rechazar lo extraño.

proper functioning ▪ correct functioning buen funcionamiento

proper motion *(actual movement not caused by the observer's shifting position)* movimiento propio ➤ The British astronomer Edmond Halley discovered the proper motion of the stars. El astrónomo británico Edmond Halley descubrió el movimiento propio de las estrellas.

to be **properly adjusted** *(machinery)* ▪ to be correctly adjusted ▪ to be in proper adjustment estar bien ajustado ▪ estar bien regulado

properly so-called propiamente llamado ➤ The conflict between Catholics and Protestants in Northern Ireland has nothing to do with religion, properly so-called. El conflicto entre los católicos y los protestantes en Irlanda del Norte no tiene nada que ver con la religión, propiamente llamada.

properly understood bien entendido

property boundaries ▪ boundaries of the property los límites de la propiedad

property line *el* límite de la propiedad

prophecy that profecía según la cual

prophetic dream sueño premonitorio

to **propose a toast** proponer un brindis

to **propose an amendment** plantear una enmienda

proposed resolution propuesta de resolución

pros and cons pros y contras

prosecution witness ▪ witness for the prosecution testigo de cargo

the **prospect of having to...** la perspectiva de tener que...

prospective guest invitado(-a) posible

prostitution ring *la* red de prostitución

to be **protected by** ser protegido con ▪ estar protegido por ▪ ser protegido por ➤ They were protected by fireproof suits. Fueron protegido con trajes ignífugos. ➤ Endangered species are protected by law. Las especies en peligro de extinción están protegidas por ley. ➤ The president is protected by the secret service. El presidente es protegido por el servicio secreto.

protected from all anxiety *(Catholic Mass)* protegido de toda perturbación

protective clothing ropa protectora

protective custody: in ~ en prisión preventiva

to **protest (against) something** protestar en contra de algo

to **protest an action** protestar una acción

to **protest because of something** protestar por (causa de) algo

protruding eyes ▪ *(coll.)* bug eyes ▪ pop eyes ojos saltones ▪ ojos reventones ▪ ojos de sapo

to be **proud to announce that...** enorgullecerse de anunciar...

to be **proud to name someone** enorgullecerse de nombrar a alguien

to **prove conclusively** ▪ to prove beyond a shadow of a doubt probar de manera determinante ▪ probar determinantemente

to **prove the relevance of something** demostrar la relevancia de algo

to be a **proven fact** ▪ to be an established fact ▪ to be an accomplished fact ser un hecho probado ▪ ser un hecho cierto

proven loyalty: of ~ de aquilatada lealtad ▪ de lealtad probada

to **provide an avenue for the expression of something** dar cauce a algo

to **provide an escort for someone** poner escolta a alguien

to **provide electrity to** ▪ to furnish electricity to proporcionar electricidad para

to **provide housing for** proporcionar casa a ▪ proporcionar viviendas a

to **provide more warmth than** ▪ to be warmer than abrigar más que ➤ The new plastic windbreakers provide more warmth than the older canvas ones. ▪ The new plastic windbreakers are warmer than the older canvas ones. Las cazadoras nuevas de plástico abrigan más que las viejas de lona.

to **provide proof** aportar pruebas

to **provide protection from** ▪ to shield from ▪ to protect from ▪ to form a protective barrier against abrigar a uno de ▪ proteger a uno contra

to **provide support for software** proporcionar asistencia técnica de(l) software

provided that ▪ so long as con tal de que ➤ You can fold the curtains provided that they don't get wrinkled. ▪ You can fold the curtains so long as they don't get wrinkled. Puedes doblar las cortinas con tal de que no se arruguen.

to **provision a fort** abastecer un fuerte ▪ enviar provisiones a un fuerte ▪ proveer un fuerte ▪ aprovisionar un fuerte

provisioning of a fort *el* abastecimiento de un fuerte

provisions for *x* months ▪ *x* months' provisions los víveres para *x* meses

to **provoke aggression** provocar agresión ▪ provocar ataque

to **pry into someone's business** ▪ to pry into someone's affairs ▪ to stick one's nose into someone else's business (entro)meterse en los asuntos de alguien ▪ meterse ▪ curiosear ➤ I don't mean to pry, but... No quiero meterme, pero... ▪ No es que quiera meterme, pero...

to **pry open something** ▪ to pry something open abrir algo usando palanca

public appearance aparición en público

public domain: to be in the ~ ser del dominio público

public figure figura pública ▪ hombre público ▪ mujer pública

public knowledge conocimiento público ➤ It should be public knowledge that... Debería ser conocimiento público que...

public official funcionario público

public opinion opinión pública ▪ *el* qué dirán ➤ Public opinion at the moment La opinión pública del momento ▪ *(Sp.)* El qué dirán de turno

public reaction reacción pública

public statement declaración ▪ comparecencia pública

public works: department of ~ ministerio de fomento

public works: director of ~ ministro de fomento

public works project obra civil

publicity stunt aritmaña publicitaria ▪ ardid publicitario ▪ truco publicitario ▪ teatrada publicitaria

to be **publicly financed** tener financiación pública

publicly held company compañía que se cotiza en bolsa ▪ sociedad anónima

to **puff (on) a cigarette** dar una calada a un cigarrillo

to **puff one's pipe** dar una calada a una pipa

to **puke one's guts out** echar la pota

pull: to have ~ ▪ to have influence tener enchufe ▪ estar enchufado ➤ His father has a lot of pull at the university. Su padre tiene enchufe en la universidad. ➤ His father has a lot of pull with the boss. Su padre tiene enchufe con el jefe.

to **pull a fast one** hacer la pirula ➤ When nobody was looking, he pulled a fast one and did an illegal U-turn. Cuando nadie le miraba hizo la pirula y dio la vuelta donde estaba prohibido.

to **pull a plow** tirar un arado

to **pull a tooth** ▪ to extract a tooth sacar un diente ▪ sacar una muela ▪ extraer un diente ▪ extraer una muela

to **pull in closer to the curb** acercarse más al bordillo

to **pull information out of someone** sacar información de alguien to **pull off something** 1. *(literal)* to remove something quitar(se) algo ▪ sacar(se) algo 2. *(figurative)* to achieve something salirse con la suya ▪ llevarse el gato al agua ➤ Oscar pulled it off. Oscar se llevó el gato al agua. ➤ He pulled off his boots. Se quitó las botas. ▪ Se sacó las botas.

to **pull oneself together** componerse ▪ acapacitarse ▪ calmarse ▪ tranquilizarse

to **pull out all the stops** ▪ to throw all the stops echar la casa por la ventana ▪ *(Sp.)* tirar la casa por la ventana ▪ tocar todos los resortes

to **pull out one's shirttail(s)** ▪ to pull one's shirttail(s) out sacar la camisa (fuera)

to **pull over a car for speeding** ▪ to pull a car over for speeding parar un carro por sobrepasar el límite de velocidad

to **pull someone toward oneself** jalar a alguien hacía sí mismo ▪ tirar a alguien hacia sí mismo

to **pull someone's leg** ▪ to be kidding tomarle el pelo a alguien ▪ estarle vacilando a alguien ➤ I'm just pulling your leg. Te estoy tomando el pelo. ▪ Te estoy vacilando.

to **pull straight in** *(parking)* entrar derechito

to **pull the rug out from under someone** dejar a alguien chiflando en la loma ▪ dejar a alguien sin Juanis y sin las gallinas ➤ They pulled the rug out from under me. Me dejaron chiflando en la loma. ▪ Me dejaron sin Juanis y sin las gallinas.

to **pull the trigger** apretar el gatillo

to **pull the wool over one's eyes** dar gato por liebre ▪ poner una venda en los ojos a alguien ➤ They pulled the wool over my eyes when I bought this car. Me han dado gato por liebre al comprar este coche.

to **pull together** unirse ▪ juntarse ▪ jalar juntos ➤ Democracies need to pull together. Las democracias necesitan unirse. ▪ Las democracias necesitan juntarse. ▪ Las democracias necesitan jalar juntas.

to **pull up a chair** arrimar una silla ▪ rodar una silla ▪ cogerse una silla ▪ arrastrar una silla ➤ Pull up a chair! ¡Arrima una silla! ▪ ¡Cógete una silla!

to **pull up a plant by the roots** arrancar una planta de cuajo ▪ arrancar una planta de raíz ▪ extirpar una planta ➤ He pulled up the sprout by the roots. ▪ He pulled the sprout up by the roots. Arrancó de cuajo el retoño. ➤ He pulled it up by the roots. Lo arrancó de cuajo.

to **pull weeds** arrancar las malas hierbas

pull yourself together! ▪ collect yourself! *(tú)* ¡recapacítate! ▪ *(usted)* ¡recapacítese!

to **pump money into** inyectar dinero en

to **pump someone for information** sonsacar a alguien

to **pump the brakes** bombear los frenos

to **pump up an air mattress** ▪ to inflate an air matress inflar un colchón de aire (con una bomba de aire)

pumpkin pie tarta de calabaza

to **punch in** ▪ to clock in fichar (la entrada) ▪ marcar tarjeta ▪ checar tarjeta

punch line of the joke desenlace del chiste ▪ gracia del chiste

to **punch out** ▪ to clock out fichar (la salida) ▪ marcar tarjeta ▪ checar tarjeta

to **punch someone** ▪ to hit someone dar de bofetadas a alguien ▪ pegarle un puñetazo a alguien

to **punch someone in the nose** ▪ to give someone a punch in the nose pegarle a alguien un puñetazo en la nariz

to **punch tickets** picar billetes ➤ The conductor came through the train car punching the passengers' tickets. El revisor pasó por el coche del tren picando los billetes de los pasajeros.

to be **punishable by death** castigarse con la muerte ➤ The crime is punishable by death in some countries. El delito se castiga con la muerte en algunos países.

punished by someone for something ser castigado por alguien por algo

purchasing power ▪ buying power poder adquisitivo

pure gold oro puro

to be **pure in heart** ser limpio de corazón

pure unadulterated bullshit *(off-color)* mierda pura y dura ➤ All of this "metrosexual" hype is pure unadulterated bullshit. Todo este bombo publicitario del "metrosexual" es mierda pura y dura.

purpose in life: to have a ~ tener un propósito en la vida

purpose of something *el* propósito de algo ➤ The purpose of the "u" in "build" is just to confuse the Spanish speakers learning English. El propósito de la "u" en "build" es sólo para confundir a los hispanohablantes.

to **push as hard as one can** ▪ to push with all one's might empujar tan fuerte como uno puede ▪ empujar con todas las fuerzas

push-button phone teléfono de teclas ➤ Even though it's a push-button phone, in its internal electronics it is a dial telephone. Aunque es un teléfono de teclas, en su electrónica interna es un teléfono de disco.

to **push one's luck** ▪ to press one's luck tentar la suerte

to **push one's way in** entrar a empujones

to **push someone around** tratar a zapatazos ▪ amedrentar

to **push someone aside** apartar a alguien a empujones

to **push someone out of the way** apartar a alguien a empujones

to **push something in** meter algo para dentro

to **push the envelope too much** ▪ to stretch the limits too much tensar los límites ▪ forzar los límites ▪ *(coll.)* tirar de la cuerda

to **push with all one's might** ▪ to push as hard as one can empujar con todas sus fuerzas ▪ empujar tan fuerte como uno puede

to be **pushed for time** ▪ to be pressed for time estar apurado de tiempo ▪ andar escaso de tiempo ▪ ir fatal de tiempo ➤ I'm really pushed for time. ▪ I'm really pressed for time. Voy fatal de tiempo. ▪ Voy corto de tiempo. ▪ Estoy corto de tiempo.

to be **pushing a certain age** estar pisando cierta edad ▪ rondar cierta edad ▪ estar llegando a cierta edad ▪ *(Don Quijote)* frisar cierta edad ➤ He's pushing forty. Ronda los cuarenta. ▪ Colea los cuarenta. ▪ Frisa los cuarenta.

to be **pushing up daisies** ▪ to be six feet under estar criando malvas ▪ estar a dos metros bajo tierra ▪ estar bajo tierra

to be a **pushover** *(easy to persuade, seduce, deceive, etc.)* ser incauto(-a) ▪ *(said of males only)* ser un pelele

to **put a bug in someone's ear** ▪ to tell someone a secret dejarle a alguien con la mosca detrás de la oreja ▪ contarle a alguien un secreto

to **put a coin in(to) (the slot)** ▪ to insert a coin in(to) the slot ▪ to put in a coin insertar una moneda (en la ranura) ▪ meter una moneda en la ranura ▪ introducir una moneda en la ranura

to **put a curse on someone** maldecir a alguien ▪ ponerle una maldición a alguien ▪ lanzar una maldición a alguien

to **put a high price on** 1. *(as a demand, followed by a verb)* poner un alto precio para 2. *(asking price, followed by a noun)* poner un alto precio por ➤ *(headline)* Hezbollah puts a high price on handing over its three Israeli hostages. Hezbolá pone un alto precio para entregar a sus tres rehenes israelíes. ▪ Hezbolá pone un alto precio por la entrega de sus tres rehenes israelíes.

to **put a lot of effort into** poner mucho empeño en

to **put a positive spin on** darle una vuelta positiva a ➤ The Presidential Palace hoped it could put a positive spin on the defeat. La Casa de Gobierno esperaba que pudiera darle una vuelta positiva a la derrota.

to **put a stop to something** ▪ to put an end to something ▪ to stop something ponerle coto a algo ▪ ponerle fin a algo ▪ ponerle término a algo ▪ ponerle punto y final a algo

to **put all one's eggs in one basket** ▪ to pin all one's hopes on one thing poner todos los huevos en una sola canasta ▪ poner todas las esperanzas en una sola cosa

to **put an ad in the (news)paper** ▪ to place an ad in the paper ▪ to run an ad in the paper poner un anuncio en el periódico ➤ If you want to put an ad in the paper, call us at... Si quiere poner un anuncio en el periódico llámenos al...

to **put an animal to sleep** ▪ to euthanize an animal ▪ to put an animal down sacrificar un animal ➤ After the animal was injured, the veterinarian put it to sleep with a fast-acting barbiturate. Después de que el animal fuera herido, el veterinario lo sacrificó con un barbitúrico de acción rápida.

to **put an end to it** ponerle fin

to **put an end to something** ponerle fin a algo ▪ terminar con algo ▪ poner punto final a algo

put and call options *(stocks)* ▪ puts and calls *las* opciones a vender y a comprar

to **put aside something** ▪ to put something aside dejar algo a un lado ➤ To concentrate on school, I need to clear the deck (by putting aside all the extraneous activities of daily life). Para concentrarme en mis estudios, necesito eliminar las distracciones (dejando de lado todo lo que no tenga que ver con mi carrera). ➤ I need to put it aside. Necesito dejarlo a un lado.

to **put away one's things** ▪ to put up one's things colocar las pertenencias de uno ▪ *(coll.)* colocar los bártulos de uno

to **put away the dishes** ▪ to put the dishes away guardar los platos

to **put away the groceries** ▪ to put the groceries away ▪ to put up the groceries guardar las compras ▪ *(Arg.)* guardar los mandados ▪ *(Sp.)* guardar la compra ➤ I have to put away the groceries. ▪ I have to put the groceries away. Tengo que guardar las compras. ➤ I have to put them away. Tengo que guardarlas.

to **put back something the way it was** ▪ to put something back the way it was poner algo como estaba ➤ Please put the CDs back the way they were. ▪ Please put back the CDs the way they were. Por favor pon los CDs como estaban. ➤ Please put them back the way they were. Por favor ponlos como estaban.

to **put down a rebellion** ▪ to suppress a rebellion sofocar una revuelta ▪ reprimir una revuelta

to **put down roots** echar raíces

to **put down something** ▪ to put something down ▪ to set down something ▪ to set something down dejar algo ➤ Put the broom down and go answer the door. ▪ Put down the broom and go answer the door. Deja la escoba y vete a abrir la puerta. ➤ Put it down and go answer the door. Déjala y mira quién ha llamado.

to **put down the landing gear** ▪ to put the landing gear down ▪ to lower the landing gear ▪ to extend the landing gear bajar el tren de aterrizaje ▪ extender el tren de aterrizaje ▪ poner el tren de aterrizaje

to **put dressing on a salad** ▪ to dress a salad poner la salsa en la ensalada ▪ aderezar la ensalada ▪ poner el aderezo en la ensalada ▪ poner el aliño en la ensalada ▪ *(Sp.)* aliñar una ensalada ▪ arreglar una ensalada

to **put everything to one side 1.** to place everything to one side dejar todo a un lado **2.** to clear the deck ▪ to eliminate distractions dejar toda distracción de lado

to **put forward** *(proposal, reason, argument, etc.)* plantear ▪ esgrimir

to **put Humpty Dumpty back together** recomponer a Humpty Dumpty ▪ reconstruir a Humpty Dumpty

to **put in a cassette** poner un casete ▪ meter un casete

to **put in a comment** ▪ to interject a comment ▪ to inject a comment poner un comentario ▪ introducir un comentario ▪ dar un comentario

to **put in a long day** ▪ to work a lot of hours trabajar un día larguísimo

to **put in an appearance** hacer acto de presencia ▪ hacer voto de presencia

to **put in for overtime (pay)** ▪ to submit a request for overtime pay someter la lista de horas extras ▪ pedir pago por trabajar horas extras ▪ solicitar pago por trabajar horas extras

to **put in one's two cents' worth** meter su granito de arena ▪ aportar su granito de arena

to **put in overtime** ▪ to work overtime trabajar horas extras ▪ hacer horas extras

to **put in time** ▪ to put time in dedicar tiempo ➤ Cecilia has put in about four hundred hours on the project. ▪ Cecilia has put about four hundred hours in on the project. Cecilia ha dedicado como cuatrocientas horas al proyecto.

to **put into port** entrar al puerto ▪ tomar el puerto

to **put it in first (gear)** ▪ to put it in low ▪ to shift into first ▪ to shift into low meter en primera ▪ cambiar a primera ▪ *(Sp.)* meter la primera

to **put it in gear** *(car transmission)* **1.** *(low gear)* poner primera **2.** *(reverse)* ponerlo en marcha atrás ▪ ponerlo en reversa

to **put it in neutral** ponerlo en punto muerto ▪ meterlo en punto muerto

to **put it in second (gear)** poner segunda ▪ *(Sp.)* meter segunda ➤ To jump-start the car, turn on the ignition, put it in second, push it or let it coast downhill a few yards, and pop the clutch. Para hacer arrancar el coche sin batería, gira la llave, mete segunda, empújalo o déjalo tomar velocidad cuesta abajo por unos metros y soltar el embrague de golpe.

to **put it in writing** ponerlo por escrito

put it on! *(article of clothing) (tú)* ¡póntelo! ▪ ¡póntela! ▪ *(usted)* ¡póngaselo! ▪ ¡póngasela!

put it on my account, please *(tú)* por favor, ponlo en mi cuenta ▪ *(usted)* por favor, póngalo en mi cuenta

put it on pause *(video, etc.)* pon pausa ▪ ponle pausa ▪ *(Arg., vosotros)* poné pausa

put it on the bill, please ▪ (just) put it on the bill, please *(tú)* ponlo en la cuenta, por favor ▪ *(usted)* póngalo en la cuenta, por favor

to be **put off 1.** to be postponed posponerse ▪ *(formal or business occasions)* aplazarse ▪ quedar aplazado **2.** to be offended ofenderse ➤ The party's been put off. La fiesta se ha pospuesto. ➤ The host was put off when the dinner guests arrived two and a half hours late. El anfitrión se ofendió cuando los invitados a la cena llegaron con dos horas y media de retraso.

to **put off something** ▪ to put something off ▪ to postpone something ▪ to delay something **1.** retrasar algo ▪ posponer algo ▪ aplazar algo **2.** to put off doing something dejar algo (para más tarde)

to **put on a brave face** poner al mal tiempo buena cara ▪ mantener el tipo ▪ aguantar el tipo

to **put on a CD** ▪ to play a CD poner un CD

to **put on a display** to make a scene hacer un berrinche ▪ montar una escena ▪ hacer una escena ▪ hacer un mitote

to **put on a DVD** poner un DVD ▪ meter un DVD

to **put on a long face** poner (la) cara larga ▪ hacer mohínes ▪ poner cara de amargado

to **put on airs** ▪ to give oneself airs ▪ to have an exaggerated opinion of oneself darse aires (de grandeza) ▪ darse tono ▪ darse ínfulas

to **put on an act** hacer teatro ▪ fingir ▪ simular ➤ She's always putting on an act. Siempre está haciendo teatro. ▪ Siempre está fingiendo. ▪ Siempre está simulando.

to **put on boots** ▪ to put boots on ponerse las botas ▪ calzarse las botas ➤ I put on my boots. Me puse las botas. ▪ Me calcé las botas.

to **put on one's clothes** ▪ to put one's clothes on ▪ to get dressed ponerse la ropa ▪ vestirse

to **put on one's makeup** ▪ to put one's makeup on pintarse ▪ maquillarse

to **put on one's shoes** ponerse los zapatos ▪ calzarse

to **put on the brakes** ▪ to apply the brakes frenar ▪ dar un frenazo

to **put one to sleep** dormir a uno ➤ The patter of the rain put me to sleep. Me durmió el rumor de la lluvia en el tejado. ➤ My sister says my historical monologues put people to sleep. Mi hermana dice que mis monólogos históricos duermen a la gente.

to **put one's best foot forward** mostrar lo mejor de sí mismo

to **put one's cards on the table** poner las cartas sobre la mesa

to **put one's elbows on the table** poner los codos en la mesa ▪ acodarse en la mesa ➤ He put his elbows on the table. Se acodó en la mesa.

to **put one's faith in someone** ▪ to put one's trust in someone poner la fe en alguien ▪ poner la confianza en alguien

to **put one's feet up** poner los pies en alto ▪ colocar los pies en alto

to **put one's hands in one's pockets** meterse las manos en los bolsillos

to **put one's hopes in someone** ▪ to place one's hopes in someone poner toda la esperanza en alguien ▪ esperanzarse en alguien to **put one's mind to it** proponérselo ▪ decidirse a hacerlo ▪ concentrarse en ello ▪ ponerle empeño a algo ➤ I'll bet you if I put my mind to it, I could do it. Te apuesto si me decido a hacerlo, lo logro.

to **put one's own interests before the interests of the group** poner los propios intereses antes de los del grupo

to **put one's shoulder to the wheel** arrimar el hombro

to **put one's trust in someone** ▪ to put one's faith in someone confiar en alguien

to **put out a cigarette** ▪ to put a cigarette out ▪ to extinguish a cigarette apagar un cigarrillo ▪ extinguir un cigarrillo

to **put out a fire** ▪ to put a fire out ▪ to extinguish a fire apagar un incendio ▪ apagar un fuego ▪ extinguir un incendio ▪ extinguir un fuego

to **put out a publication** ▪ to put a publication out sacar una publicación ➤ The association puts out a weekly newsletter. La asociación saca un noticiero semanal. ➤ The association puts one out. La asociación saca uno.

to **put out feelers** ▪ to put feelers out hacer gestiones discretamente

to **put out the dog** ▪ to put the dog out poner al perro afuera

to **put out the lights** ▪ to turn out the lights ▪ to turn off the lights apagar las luces

to **put pressure on someone to do something** ▪ to pressure someone to do something ▪ to apply pressure on someone to do something presionar a alguien para hacer algo ▪ presionar a alguien para que haga algo

to **put pressure on something** *(physical pressure)* ▪ to apply pressure to something ponerle presión a algo

to **put someone down** **1.** to demean someone menospreciar a alguien **2.** to set someone down dejar a alguien ➤ She puts her husband down in front of other people. Menosprecia a su marido delante de otra gente. ➤ Honey, would you put the baby down for a minute and come help me? Cariño, ¿puedes dejar al bebé por un minuto y venir a ayudarme?

to **put someone down for something** **1.** *(to note)* apuntar a alguien para hacer algo **2.** *(to disparage)* despreciar a alguien por algo ➤ Put us down for four seats. Apúntenos para cuatro asientos. ➤ You shouldn't put him down just because he isn't athletic. No deberías despreciarlo sólo porque no es atlético. ▪ *(Sp., leísmo)* No deberías despreciarle sólo porque no es atlético.

to **put someone in control** ▪ to give someone control darle a alguien el control ➤ It puts me in control. Me da el control.

to **put someone in his place** ▪ to take someone down a peg poner a alguien en su sitio ▪ bajarle los humos a alguien ▪ bajarle el copete a alguien ▪ poner a alguien en su lugar

to **put someone off** dar largas a alguien

to **put someone on a diet** poner a alguien en un régimen (alimenticio)

to **put someone on a pedestal** poner a alguien en un pedestal ▪ poner a alguien en un altar

to **put someone on hold** poner a alguien en espera ➤ They put me on hold for fifteen minutes. Me pusieron en espera por quince minutos. ▪ *(Sp.)* Me pusieron en espera durante quince minutos.

to **put someone on the spot** poner a alguien en un brete ▪ mandar a alguien al frente ▪ meter a alguien en la boca del lobo

to **put someone out of commission** dejarle fuera de combate a alguien

to **put someone to the test** poner a alguien a prueba

to **put someone to work** poner a trabajar a alguien

to **put someone's eye out** ▪ to blind someone in an eye cegar a alguien de un ojo ▪ sacarle el ojo a alguien

to **put something back (where it was)** poner algo donde estaba ▪ reponer algo

to **put something back together** **1.** *(something broken)* recomponer algo **2.** *(something taken apart)* volver a armar algo

to **put something down** ▪ to put down something ▪ to set something down dejar algo ▪ depositar algo ➤ He walked in, put his books down on the desk, and called the dog. Entró en la casa, dejó sus libros en la mesa y llamó al perro.

to **put something in jeopardy** ▪ to place in jeopardy poner algo en peligro ➤ The leaking of the criminal evidence to the press has put the prosecution's case in jeopardy. La filtración de las pruebas a la prensa ha puesto en peligro las alegaciones de la acusación. ➤ Smoking puts one's health in jeopardy. Fumar pone en peligro la salud.

to **put something in one's pocket** ▪ to pocket something meterse algo en el bolsillo ➤ Tom Sawyer put the coin in his pocket. ▪ Tom Sawyer pocketed the coin. Tom Sawyer se metió la moneda en el bolsillo.

to **put something in perspective** ▪ to put something into perspective poner algo en perspectiva

to **put something in the dirty clothes (hamper)** ▪ throw something in the dirty clothes (hamper) echar algo a la ropa sucia ▪ echar algo en la canasta de la ropia sucia ▪ *(Sp.)* echar algo en el cesto de ropa sucia

to **put something in the mailbox** ▪ to mail something echar algo en el buzón ▪ meter algo en el buzón ▪ tirar algo en el buzón

to **put something in the permanent record** ▪ to put something into the permanent record poner algo en expediente permanente ▪ quedar algo asentado en el expediente permanente

to **put something in the wrong place** **1.** poner algo en el lugar equivocado **2.** *(papers, usually on a desk)* to mislay something ▪ to misplace something ▪ to lose something traspapelar algo ➤ I lost your message. ▪ I mislaid your message. ▪ I misplaced your message. ▪ I lost your message. Traspapelé tu mensaje.

to **put something into practice** ▪ to put something in practice llevar algo a la práctica ▪ poner algo en práctica

to **put something on a wound** ▪ to apply something to a wound aplicar algo en una lesión ▪ poner algo en una lesión ➤ Put a little salve on the burn. ▪ Apply a little salve to the burn. Ponte un poco de pomada en la quemadura. ➤ I put some salve on it. Me puse algo de pomada en la quemadura.

to **put something on hold** suspender algo ▪ dejar aparcado algo ➤ The project has been put on hold. El proyecto ha sido suspendido. ▪ El proyecto se ha dejado aparcado.

to **put something on one's account** ▪ to put something on one's bill poner algo en la cuenta de uno ➤ Put it on my bill, please. *(tú)* Ponlo en mi cuenta, por favor. ▪ *(usted)* Póngalo en mi cuenta, por favor.

to **put something on sale** **1.** to put something on special ▪ to reduce the price of something poner algo en oferta ▪ rebajar (el precio de) algo **2.** to put something on the market poner algo a la venta

to **put something on the list** poner algo en la lista ▪ apuntar algo en la lista

to **put something somewhere else** ▪ to move something (somewhere else) poner algo en otro lugar

to **put something to good use** ▪ to make good use of something hacer buen uso de algo

to **put something to music** ▪ to set something to music ponerle música a algo ➤ Paco Ibáñez has put the great Spanish lyric poems to music. ▪ Paco Ibáñez has put to music the great Spanish lyric poems. Paco Ibáñez les ha puesto música a los grandes poemas de la lírica española.

to **put something to the test** ▪ to try out something ▪ to try something out ▪ to test something poner algo a prueba ▪ poner a prueba algo ➤ For 117 days, the astronauts will put to the test the largest orbiting device in history. En una estancia de 117 días, los astronautas pondrán a prueba el mayor ingenio orbital de la historia.

to **put something where someone can see it** poner algo a la vista de alguien

put that in your pipe and smoke it! ¡chúpate esa!

to **put the beans in water to soak** poner los frijoles en remojo

to **put the big pot in the little one** ▪ to go all out ▪ to shoot the moon tirar la casa por la ventana ▪ echar la casa por la ventana

to **put the car in reverse** *(gear)* poner el coche en marcha atrás to **put the cart before the horse** empezar la casa por el tejado

to **put the dog out** poner al perro afuera ▪ poner el perro afuera

to **put the finishing touches on something** dar los últimos toques a algo

to **put the groceries away** ▪ to put away the groceries poner las compras (en su sitio) ▪ colocar las compras (en su sitio) ▪ *(Sp.)* poner la compra (en su sitio) ▪ colocar la compra (en su sitio)

to **put the screws to someone** apretarle las tuercas a alguien ▪ apretarle las clavijas a alguien ▪ *(Sp., Cuba)* darle caña a alguien

to **put the stamp(s) on an envelope** ▪ to stamp an envelope poner estampillas en un sobre ▪ poner sellos en un sobre ▪ franquear un sobre

to **put through a caller** ▪ to put a caller through pasar a alguien ➤ *(hotel switchboard operator)* I'll put you through to their room. *(a ti)* Te paso a su habitación. ▪ *(a usted, to a man)* Lo paso a usted a su habitación. ▪ *(a usted, to a woman)* La paso a su habitación. ▪ *(a usted, Sp., leismo, to a man or woman)* Le paso a usted a su habitación.

to be **put to the test** ser puesto a prueba ➤ They've put me to the test. Me han puesto a prueba. ➤ They've put her to the test. La han puesto a ella a prueba.

to **put together a kit** ▪ to assemble a kit armar una maqueta

to **put together the parts** ▪ to put the parts together ▪ to assemble the parts **1.** *(of a kit)* montar las piezas **2.** *(industrial process, furniture)* ensamblar la piezas

to **put together the pieces of a puzzle** ensamblar la piezas de un rompecabezas

to **put two and two together** atar cabos ➤ You don't have to be around those two for long (in order) to put two and two together. No hay que pasar mucho tiempo con ellos para atar cabos.

to **put up a fight** dar batalla ▪ montar las de San Quintín

to **put up a smoke screen** ▪ to throw up a smoke screen echar una cortina de humo

to **put up a tent 1.** *(camping tent)* to pitch a tent montar una tienda (de campaña) ▪ armar una tienda (de campaña) ▪ ensamblar una tienda (de campaña) **2.** *(beach tent)* armar una carpa ▪ montar una carpa ▪ ensamblar una carpa **3.** *(circus tent)* armar una carpa de circo ▪ montar una carpa de circo ▪ ensamblar una carpa de circo **4.** *(dwelling tent, tribal tent)* montar una tienda ▪ ensamblar una tienda

to **put up one's things** ▪ to put away one's things poner las pertenencias de uno en su sitio ▪ colocar las pertenencias de uno ▪ *(coll.)* colocar los bártulos de uno

to **put up shelves** ▪ to put shelves up montar estantes ▪ ensamblar estantes

to **put up signs** poner carteles ▪ colocar carteles ▪ *(Sp.)* fijar carteles ➤ Putting up signs is prohibited in the tunnel. Prohibido fijar carteles en el túnel.

to **put up the capital** ▪ to put up the money ▪ to put up the cash aportar el capital ▪ poner el capital

to **put up the collar** subirse el cuello ▪ levantarse el cuello

to **put up the landing gear** ▪ to retract the landing gear ▪ to raise the landing gear subir el tren de aterrizaje ▪ plegar el tren de aterrizaje ▪ elevar el tren de aterrizaje

to **put up the money** poner el dinero

to **put up with a lot** aguantar mucho ➤ He puts up with a lot. El aguanta mucho.

put up with a lot: to be able to ~ tener mucho aguante ➤ He can put up with a lot. Tiene mucho aguante.

to **put up with murder** soportarlo todo ▪ tragar carros y carretas ▪ aguantar carros y carretas ▪ tragárselo todo

to **put up with someone** aguantar a alguien ▪ soportar a alguien

to **put up with something** aguantar algo ▪ soportar algo ▪ apechar con algo ▪ apechugar con algo ▪ apencar con algo

put us down for four people apúntenos para cuatro personas

to **put wood on the fire** echar leña al fuego

to **put words in one's mouth** ponerle a alguien palabras en la boca ▪ decir cosas que uno no ha dicho ➤ Don't put words in my mouth. No me pongas palabras en la boca. ▪ No digas cosas que yo no he dicho.

put your arms around me abrázame ➤ *(Julio Iglesias song)* Put your arms around me. Don't say anything. Just put your arms around me. Abrázame, y no me digas nada, sólo abrázame.

put yourself in my place *(tú)* ponte en mi lugar ▪ *(usted)* póngase en mi lugar

puts and calls *(stocks)* ▪ put and call options *las* opciones a vender y a comprar ▪ opciones de compra y venta

Pyrex® dish *la* fuente de Pyrex

Pyrrhic victory victoria pírrica

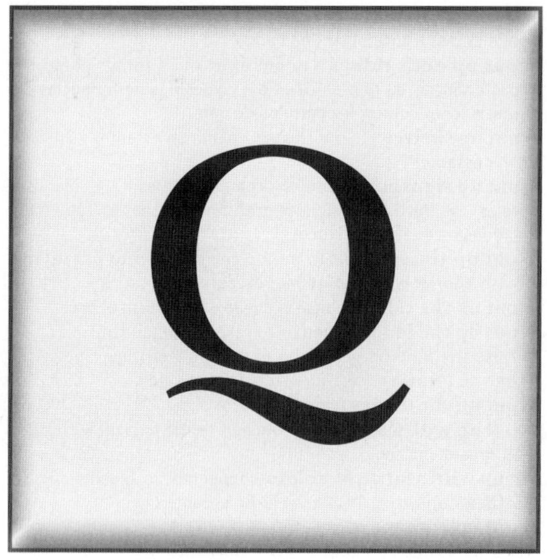

Q-tip® bastoncillo (de algodón)
Q&A ■ question and answer P&R ■ pregunta y respuesta
Q.E.D. *(in mathematics proofs)* ■ quod erat demonstrandum entonces queda demostrado ■ Q.E.D.
quadratic equation ecuación cuadrática ■ ecuación de segundo grado
to **qualify a remark** matizar un comentario
to **qualify a statement** matizar una declaración
to **qualify what one said earlier** matizar lo que uno dijo antes
quality control gestión de calidad ■ control de calidad
quantum leap salto cuántico
to **quarrel over a matter** ■ to quarrel about a matter discutir un asunto ■ discutir por un asunto
quarter after y cuarto ➤ It's quarter after five. Son las cinco y cuarto.
quarter till: at ~ a menos cuarto ➤ *(bus driver)* We arrive at Plaza de Castilla at quarter till. Llegamos a la Plaza de Castilla a menos cuarto.
to **quash a proposal** ■ to reject a proposal ■ to throw out a proposal echar abajo una propuesta
to **quash rumors about** ■ to dispel rumors about zanjar los rumores sobre
quest for the holy grail búsqueda del santo grial
question and answer ■ Q&A pregunta y respuesta ■ P&R
question-and-answer period ■ question-and-answer session turno de preguntas
to **question authority** cuestionar la autoridad
to be a **question I don't know the answer to** ser una pregunta de la que no sé la respuesta ■ ser una pregunta a que no sé responder ➤ That's a question I don't know the answer to. Es una pregunta de la que no sé la respuesta. ■ Es una pregunta a que no sé responder.
question mark signo de interrogación ■ interrogativo
to be a **question mark** ser una incertidumbre ➤ The future of the Middle East peace process is a question mark. ■ The future of the Middle East peace process is unknown. El futuro del proceso de paz en el Medio Oriente es una incertidumbre.
to **question someone's intentions** preguntar las intenciones de alguien
to **question something** ■ to bring something into question cuestionar algo ■ poner algo en tela de juicio
question whether cuestión de si ➤ Leaving aside the question whether... Leaving to one side the question whether... ■ Setting aside the question whether... Dejando de lado la cuestión de si... ■ Dejando a un lado la cuestión de si... ■ Haciendo a un lado la cuestión de si...
to **question whether** preguntar si
questionable past pasado turbio
questioning look una mirada interrogante
quick! ¡deprisa!
the **quick and the dead** ■ the living and the dead los vivos y los muertos ■ vivos y muertos
quick sketch *(pen, pencil, charcoal)* boceto
to be **quick-tempered** ■ to have a quick temper ■ to have a short fuse tener sus prontos de enojo ■ tener sus prontos
to **quicken one's pace** ■ to quicken one's step apresurar el paso
to **quicken one's step** ■ to quicken one's pace ■ to speed up the pace apresurar el paso
the **quickest way to** la manera más rápida para ■ forma más rápida para *("De" can be substituted for "para.")* ➤ What's the quickest way back to town from here? ¿Cuál es la manera más rápida de volver al pueblo desde aquí?
to **quickly disappear** pronto desaparecer
to **quit beating around the bush!** ■ stop beating around the bush! ¡no andes con rodeos! ■ ¡no te andes por las ramas! ■ ¡no te andes con rodeos! ■ ¡al grano! ■ ¡a lo concreto!
to **quit smoking** ■ to stop smoking dejar de fumar ■ cesar de fumar ➤ The best way to quit smoking is to quit cold turkey. La mejor forma de dejar de fumar es dejar de golpe. ➤ I've quit smoking for good. He dejado de fumar definitivamente.
to **quit without giving notice** ■ to walk off the job largarse sin avisar ■ salir a la francesa
quite a... todo un... ■ un señor... ➤ That's quite a car. Es todo un coche. ■ Es un señor coche.
quite a beating: to give someone ~ darle cada golpe ■ darle una buena paliza ➤ They gave him quite a beating. Le dieron cada golpe. ■ Le dieron una buena paliza.
quite a bit bastante
to be **quite a challenge** ser todo un reto
to be **quite a character** ser todo un personaje ➤ She's quite a character. Ella es todo un personaje.
quite a few bastantes ■ unos cuantos ■ unas cuantas ■ unos pocos ■ unas pocas
quite a lot bastante
quite a place menudo sitio
quite a trick todo un milagro ➤ It was quite a trick getting that chaise lounge through the front door. Fue todo un milagro conseguir que la tumbona pasara por la puerta principal.
quite a ways un buen trecho
quite a while un buen rato ■ cantidad de tiempo ➤ It's been quite a while since we've come to Madrid. Hace cantidad de tiempo que no venimos a Madrid.
quite often bastante a menudo ■ bastante frecuentemente
quite satisfied más que satisfecho ■ bastante satisfecho
quite the opposite ■ just the opposite todo lo contrario
to be **quite the thing** estar muy de moda
quiz show concurso de preguntas y respuestas
to **quote someone word for word** citar a alguien palabra por palabra ■ citar a alguien textualmente
quote unquote entre comillas *(Spanish speakers nearly always use fingers to mimic quotation marks.)*

rabid feminist feminista rabiosa
race against the clock ■ race against time carrera contra reloj
to **race against the clock** ■ to race against time correr contra (el) reloj
race against time ■ race with time carrera contra el tiempo
to **race against time** ■ to race against the clock correr contra (el) reloj
race car *el* coche de carreras *(In this expression, the word "coche," normally used in only Spain, is used throughout Latin America as well.)*
race for the White House carrera hacia la Casa Blanca
to **race with somone** correr con alguien ➤ I think that guy is racing with you. Creo que ese tío está corriendo contigo.
racehorse caballo de carreras
racist tinge: to have a ~ ■ to be tinged with racism tener un tinte racista
to **rack one's brains** comerse el coco ■ devanarse los sesos ■ cargarse la cabeza ■ exprimirse el cerebro ■ calentarse la cabeza ■ atropellarse a pensar
to **rack up points** ya tener puntos en su haber ■ saldarse con puntos
radar installation plataforma de radar
radial or transversal ■ widthwise or lengthwise radial o transversal
radially or transversally ■ widthwise or lengthwise radialmente o transversalmente ■ a lo ancho o a lo largo
radio beacon *(aviation)* radiofaro
radio communications *la* comunicación por radio
radio contact contacto por radio ■ la comunicación por radio ➤ The tower lost radio contact with the plane. La torre perdió el contacto por radio con el avión. ➤ Are you in radio contact with your delivery trucks? ¿Está usted en contacto por radio con sus camiones de reparto? ■ ¿Está usted en comunicación por radio con sus camiones de reparto?
to be **radio controlled** estar teledirigido
radio station emisora de radio
radio waves ondas de radio
radioactive waste detrito radioactivo ■ basura radioactiva
ragged clothes ropa harapienta ■ ropa andrajosa ■ ropa deshilachada
ragged edge 1. *(knife, cutting edge)* filo mellado **2.** *(table edge, etc.)* borde mellado
ragged haircut *el* corte de pelo irregular
raid by the police ■ police raid batida de la policía
rail against something ■ to rail at something cargar contra algo ■ despotricar contra algo
to **rail at someone about something** ■ to rail at someone for something cargar contra alguien por algo ■ recriminar a alguien por algo ■ despotricar contra alguien por algo
to **rail at something** ■ to rail against something cargar contra algo ■ despotricar contra algo
rain: to (give) ~ *(when the subject is "clouds")* dar lluvia ■ traer lluvia ➤ Our flight instructor said that high clouds won't rain, no matter how threatening they look. Nuestro instructor de vuelo dijo que las nubes altas no dan lluvia, por más amenazadoras que parezcan.
to **rain a lot** llover mucho ➤ It rains here a lot. Llueve mucho aquí.
rain beating against the window la lluvia golpeando contra la ventana
to **rain cats and dogs** llover a cántaros
to **rain (down) hard** llover muy duro ➤ It's raining (down) hard. Está lloviendo muy duro.
to **rain down on** llover sobre ➤ Confetti rained down on the parade. El confeti llovió sobre el desfile. ■ Los papelillos llovieron sobre el desfile.
rain forests bosques lluviosos ■ *(tropical)* selvas lluviosas
to **rain hard** llover con fuerza ■ llover mucho
the **rain has subsided** la lluvia ha remitido
to **rain in buckets** ■ to come down in buckets llover a raudales
to **rain on someone** ■ to get rained on lloverle encima ➤ I don't want to get rained on. No quiero que me llueva encima.

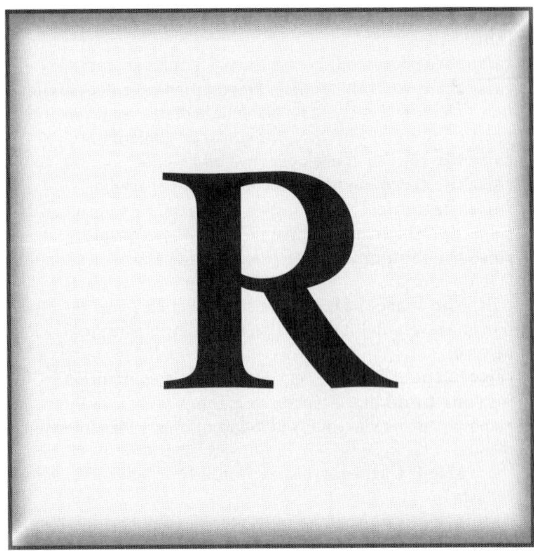

to **rain on someone's parade** ■ to throw cold water on someone's hopes echar un jarro de agua fría a alguien
rain or shine ■ come rain or (come) shine llueva o truene
to be **raining** estar lloviendo ■ llover ➤ It's raining. Está lloviendo. ■ Llueve.
rainstorm ■ heavy rain ■ downpour *el* temporal de lluvia ■ aguacero
rainy day *el* día de lluvia ■ día lluvioso
rainy spell tiempo lluvioso
to **raise a big stink about something** ■ to make a big fuss about something dar algo por la tremenda ■ tomar algo por la tremenda
to **raise a ruckus** ■ to make a lot of noise armar un escándalo
to **raise children** criar a los hijos ■ educar a los hijos
to **raise difficulties** plantear dificultades
to **raise doubts about something** ■ to raise questions about something plantear dudas sobre algo ■ poner reparos a algo
to **raise false expectations** crear falsas expectativas
to **raise false hopes** crear falsas esperanzas
to **raise fears that...** hacer temer que...
to **raise funds for** recaudar fondos para ■ recabar fondos para ■ juntar fondos para
to **raise money for** recaudar dinero para ■ recabar dinero para ■ juntar dinero para
to **raise one's eyebrows** enarcar las cejas ■ arquear las cejas
to **raise one's eyes** ■ to look up levantar la vista
to **raise one's hand 1.** alzar la mano **2.** *(threatening violence)* levantar la mano
to **raise one's voice** alzar la voz ■ alzar su voz ➤ Don't raise your voice. No alces tu voz.
to **raise questions** plantear dudas ■ plantear preguntas ■ plantear cuestiones ➤ We were baffled by the specifications, which raised more questions than they answered. Estábamos desconcertados por las especificaciones, que plantearon más preguntas que las que respondieron.
to **raise someone's salary** *(to give someone a pay raise)* subirle el sueldo a alguien
to **raise suspicions that...** levantar sospechas de que...
to **raise the ban on** ■ to lift the ban on levantar la prohibición de
to **raise the ban on travel** ■ to raise the travel ban ■ to lift the travel ban ■ to lift the ban on travel levantar la prohibición de viajar
to **raise the blood pressure** ■ to elevate the blood pressure subir la tensión ■ subir la presión arterial
to **raise the embargo on** levantar el embargo contra

to **raise the flag** ▪ to hoist the flag izar la bandera ▪ enarbolar la bandera
to **raise the price** ▪ to increase the price subir el precio
to **raise the question** llevarlo a preguntarse ▪ plantear la cuestión ▪ plantear la pregunta ▪ plantear la duda ➤ It raises the question (for me) whether... Me lleva a preguntarme si...
to **raise the rent** subir el alquiler ▪ subir la renta
to **raise the siege** ▪ to lift the siege levantar el asedio
to **raise the subject** ▪ to bring up the subject ▪ to broach the subject sacar a colación el asunto ▪ abordar el asunto
to **raise the temperature** ▪ to increase the temperature subir la temperatura
to **raise the travel ban** ▪ to lift the travel ban ▪ to raise the ban on travel ▪ to lift the ban on travel levantar la prohibición de viajar
to **raise to the *n*th power** elevar a la enésima potencia
raise your hand *(tú)* levántate la mano ▪ *(usted)* levántese la mano ▪ *(vosotros)* levantaos la mano ▪ *(ustedes)* levántense la mano
to be **raised Catholic** criarse católico ▪ educarse como católico
to be **raised from the dead** resuscitar de entre los muertos
to be **raised on** criarse con ➤ Marcelino was raised on goat's milk. Marcelino se crió con la leche de la cabra.
to **rake someone over the coals** zurrar la badana a alguien ▪ calentar la badana a alguien ▪ sobar la badana a alguien ▪ no dejar a alguien hueso sano
to be **ramrod straight** estar más derecho que una vela
to **range from *x* to *y*** ir de *x* a *y* ▪ oscilar de *x* a *y* ▪ ir desde *x* a *y* ➤ The figure ranges from 25 to 40 percent. La cifra va del 25 al 40 por ciento. ➤ Ranging from *x* to *y* Oscilando de *x* a *y*
to **range in age from *x* to *y*** oscilar entre *x* y *y* años (de edad) ➤ Three hundred teenagers ranging in age from thirteen to nineteen Trescientos adolescentes cuyas edades oscilaban entre trece y diecinueve años
range of options abanico de opciones ▪ gama de opciones
ranging in age from *x* to *y* con edades comprendidas entre *x* y *y* años ➤ *(news item)* Two spectacular automobile accidents within twenty minutes of each other took the lives of four youths ranging in age from nineteen to twenty-two. Dos espectaculares accidentes automovilísticos ocurridos en un intervalo de apenas veinte minutos acabaron con la vida de cuatro jóvenes con edades comprendidas entre diecinueve y veintidós años.
to **rank among** ▪ to rank in figurarse entre ➤ Gabriel García Márquez ranks among the greatest writers of our time. Gabriel García Márquez se figura entre los escritores más grandes de nuestra época.
rank and file *(members of an organization other than the leadership)* plebeos ▪ miembros de fila
to **rank in the top ten** ▪ to rate in the top ten figurar en los diez mejores ▪ *(Sp.)* situar en el "top ten" ▪ situar entre los diez mejores
to **rant and rave about something** despotricar por algo
to **rant and rave against something** despotricar contra algo
to **rant on (and on)** desbarrar
rap sheet *(coll.)* ▪ criminal record *los* antecedentes penales ▪ antecedentes criminales
to **rappel down** *(mountain climbing, spelunking)* ▪ to rappel off (of) ▪ to descend on a rope off (of) descender haciendo rappel ▪ hacer rappel
rare bird bicho raro ▪ rara especie ➤ He's a rare bird. Es un bicho raro. ▪ Es una rara especie.
to be a **rare find** ser un hallazgo raro
rare finds: (for) there to be ~ ▪ to make some rare finds hacer unos hallazgos raros ➤ There were some rare finds at the art exhibit. ▪ We made some rare finds at the art exhibit. Hicimos unos hallazgos raros en la exposición de arte.
rare, medium, or well done poco hecho, en el punto o muy hecho ➤ How would you like your steak-rare, medium, or well done? ¿Cómo le gustaría la carne-poca hecha, en su punto o muy hecha?
rare opportunity oportunidad excepcional ▪ oportunidad única
rare steak filete poco hecho
rarely if ever rara vez o nunca ▪ contadas ➤ She rarely if ever misses a chance. Ella rara vez o nunca pierde una oportunidad. ▪ Son contadas las oportunidades que pierde.
to **rate high in someone's book** *(coll.)* tenerle a alguien en alta estima ▪ dejarle bien (parado) en su libro ➤ He doesn't rate very high in her book. Ella no le tiene en alta estima. ▪ Ella no le deja bien (parado) en su libro.
rate of climb *(aviation)* ▪ climb rate **1.** *el* ritmo de ascenso **2.** *(maximum rate)* ritmo máximo de ascenso
rate of descent ritmo de descenso ➤ We are descending at a rate of... Llevamos un ritmo de descenso de... ▪ Descendemos al ritmo de...
rate of exchange ▪ exchange rate tipo de cambio ➤ What is the euro-to-dollar rate of exchange today? ¿Cuál es el tipo de cambio del euro a dólar hoy?
rate of growth (in) ▪ growth rate (in) ritmo de crecimiento (de)
to **rate something in the top ten** ▪ to rank something in the top ten situar algo en el "top ten" ▪ situar algo entre los diez mejores (del ranking)
to be **rather difficult** ser un tanto difícil ▪ ser bastante difícil
rather than antes de ▪ mejor que
to **ratify a contract** ratificar un contrato
to **ratify a treaty** ratificar un tratado
ratio of *x* to *y* relación de *x* a *y* ▪ proporción de *x* a *y*
to **rattle one's nerves** jugar con los nervios de uno
rattletrap (of a car) ▪ beat-up car ▪ bucket of bolts ▪ rolling ghetto tartana
to be **ravaged by floods** ser asolado por las inundaciones
to **rave about something** hacerse lengua de algo ▪ pirrarse por algo ▪ poner algo por las nubes
rave review reseña entusiasta
ravenous hunger ▪ ravenous appetite *el* hambre atroz
raw data datos "en crudo"
raw materials materias primas
ray of hope rayo de esperanza ▪ resquicio de esperanza
to **raze a building** ▪ to tear down a building derrumbar un edificio ▪ tirar un edificio
Razor's Edge: The ~ *(Somerset Maugham novel) El filo de la navaja*
to **reach a certain age** ▪ to turn a certain age cumplir tantos años ▪ llegar a (una) cierta edad ▪ alcanzar (una) cierta edad ➤ She's reached forty. Ha cumplido los cuarenta. ▪ Ha llegado a los cuarenta. ▪ Ha alcanzado los cuarenta.
to **reach a milestone** ▪ to cross a milestone marcar un hito
to **reach a point where** llegar a un punto que ▪ llegar a un punto en que
to **reach a settlement** llegar a un acuerdo
to **reach a turning point** marcar un punto de partida
to **reach a verdict** alcanzar un veredicto ➤ The jury has reached a verdict. El jurado ha alcanzado un veredicto.
to **reach age *x*** cumplir los *x* años
to **reach agreement on** llegar a un concierto sobre ▪ llegar a un acuerdo sobre ▪ ponerse de acuerdo sobre ▪ alcanzar un acuerdo sobre
to **reach an agreement to...** alcanzar un acuerdo para... ▪ llegar a un acuerdo para... ▪ ponerse de acuerdo para... ▪ llegar a un concierto para...
to **reach and get** alcanzar ➤ Reach and get me the salt, would you? Alcánzame la sal, ¿quieres?
to **reach out and touch someone** llegar y tocar a alguien
to **reach out (of) the door** sacar la mano por la puerta
to **reach out (of) the window** sacar la mano por la ventana
to **reach out to someone** **1.** *(literal)* to outstretch one's hand to someone extenderle la mano a alguien **2.** *(figurative)* to extend oneself to someone tender puentes a alguien ▪ acercarse a alguien ➤ *(headline)* The Shiites reach out to the Sunni minority after the elections in Iraq Los chiítas tienden la mano a la minoría suní tras las elecciones en Irak
to **reach someone by phone** localizar a alguien por teléfono ▪ contactar con alguien por teléfono ➤ He can be reached at this number. Lo puedes localizar en este número. ▪ *(Sp., leísmo)*

Le puedes localizar en este número. ➤ She can be reached at this number. Puede ser localizada en este número. ▪ La puedes localizar en este número. ▪ *(Sp., leísmo)* Le puedes localizar en este número.

to **reach someone on the phone** ▪ to get (hold of) someone on the telephone lograr contactarse con alguien por teléfono ▪ lograr comunicarse con alguien por teléfono

to **reach the crest of a hill** alcanzar la cima de una colina ▪ *(L. Am.)* rematar la cuesta de una loma

to **reach the limits of one's endurance** llegar al límite de sus fuerzas

to **reach the point where** ▪ to reach the point that llegar al punto que ▪ llegar al punto en el que

to **reach the surface** llegar a la superficie

to **reach through the window** sacar la mano por la ventana

to **react under stress** reaccionar ante el estrés

to **read a book from cover to cover** ▪ to read a book all the way through leer un libro de tapa a tapa ▪ leer un libro de cubierta a cubierta ▪ tragarse el libro entero ▪ leer hasta la dedicatoria de un libro ➤ He read the book from cover to cover. Leyó el libro de tapa a tapa. ▪ Se tragó el libro entero.

to **read between the lines** leer entre líneas

to **read (from) cover to cover** ▪ to read all the way through leer de tapa a tapa ▪ tragarse ➤ He read it cover to cover. Lo leyó hasta las tapas.

to **read like** leerse como ▪ parecerle a uno ➤ Your letter reads like a Jules Verne novel. Tu carta se lee como una novela de Julio Verne.

to **read one's mind** leerle el pensamiento a uno ▪ leerle la mente a uno ➤ He was reading my mind when he turned down the stereo. Me estaba leyendo el pensamiento cuando bajó el estereo.

to **read someone the riot act** cantarle a alguien la cartilla ▪ leerle a alguien la cartilla

to **read someone's writing** ▪ to read someone's handwriting entenderle la letra a alguien ▪ decifrar su escritura ➤ I can't read her writing. No le entiendo la letra.

to **read someone's writings** ▪ to read someone's works leer los escritos de alguien

to **read something carefully** leer algo detenidamente

to **read the directions** ▪ to read the instructions leer las instrucciones ▪ *(in the expression "when all else fails...")* seguir las instrucciones ➤ When all else fails, read the directions. Cuando todo lo demás falla, sigue las instrucciones.

to **read to page *x*** ▪ to read as far as page *x* leer hasta la página *x*

to **read up on something** informarse de algo ▪ leer sobre algo

readership of a newspaper audiencia de un periódico

reading glasses gafas de miope

reading speed *la* rapidez de lectura ➤ Your reading speed in Spanish has improved. Tu rapidez de lectura en español ha mejorado.

ready, aim, fire! ¡preparados, listos, ya!

to be **ready for action** ▪ to be ready to go venir con las pilas puestas ▪ tener las pilas puestas

to be **ready for takeoff** estar preparado para el despegue

ready for whatever comes one's way preparado para lo que venga

to be **ready to do something** estar listo para hacer algo ▪ estar preparado para hacer algo ➤ *(to a waiter)* We're ready to order. Estamos listos para pedir.

to be **ready to go 1.** to be ready to leave estar listo para marcharse ▪ estar listo para irse **2.** to be ready for action venir con las pilas puestas ▪ tener las pilas puestas

ready to serve *(food label)* ▪ ready to eat listo para servir ▪ listo para comer ▪ *(Sp.)* listo para tomar

to be **ready to strike** estar preparado para atentar

to be **ready to throw out** ▪ to be ready to throw away estar de botar

real analysis *(in math)* análisis matemático

to be a **real drag** ser un pelma ▪ ser una gaita ➤ It's a real drag. Es una pelma.

real estate *(L. Am.)* los bienes raíces ▪ *(Sp.)* inmobiliario ▪ los bienes inmuebles ▪ los valores inmuebles

real estate appraiser tasador(a) de inmobiliario

to be a **real-life history about...** ▪ to be a true story about... ser una historia de la vida real sobre...

the **real McCoy** ▪ the genuine article el mero mero ▪ el auténtico ▪ el genuino

real number número real

to be a **real project** ser toda una empresa ▪ ser toda una aventura

the **real reason** ▪ the true reason ▪ the actual reason *la* razón de verdad ▪ la razón verdadera ▪ la razón real

realistic goal ▪ achievable goal meta realista ▪ meta alcanzable ➤ First set a realistic goal, pursue it singlemindedly, and your life will fall into place. Primero fija una meta realista, resueltamente, y realizarás tus sueños.

to **realize a dream** realizar un sueño

to **realize how...** darse cuenta de lo... ▪ enterarse de lo... ➤ I hadn't realized how badly I wrap packages. No me había dado cuenta de lo mal que envuelvo paquetes. ▪ No me había enterado (de) lo mal que envuelvo paquetes. *(In casual speech, "de" is often omitted.)*

to **realize one's mistake** darse cuenta de su error ▪ caerse del burro ▪ caer del burro

to **realize that...** darse cuenta de que... ▪ percatarse de... ▪ constatar que... ➤ I was beginning to realize that... Yo empezaba a darme cuenta de que... ➤ I didn't realize that you had left. No me di cuenta de que te habías ido.

to **realize that something is wrong** verle las orejas al lobo

to be **really cold 1.** estar muy frío ▪ estar bien frío **2.** to feel cold tener mucho frío ➤ I don't like milk unless it's really cold. No me gusta la leche a menos que esté muy fría. ▪ No me gusta la leche a menos que esté bien fría. ➤ I'm really cold. ▪ I'm very cold. ▪ I feel really cold. Tengo mucho frío.

to be **really dangerous** ser verdaderamente peligroso

to be **really embarrassing** pasarle mucha vergüenza ▪ darle vergüenza ▪ darle corte ▪ resultarle embarazoso ▪ sentirse violento ▪ *(Sp.)* quedar a la altura del betún

to **really get to someone** realmente llegar a alguien ➤ That play really got to me. Esa obra teatral realmente me llegó.

to be **really good at something** dársele muy bien ▪ ser realmente bueno en algo ➤ He's really good at it. Se le da muy bien. ▪ Es realmente bueno en eso.

to be **really great** estar pero que muy bien ➤ The movie is really great. La película está pero que muy bien.

to **really know how...** realmente saber cómo...

to be **really nice** ser bastante simpático(-a)

to be **really pretty** ser bonito de verdad ▪ ser realmente bonito

to be **really surprised** quedarse de sorpresa ▪ quedarse de piedra ➤ I was really surprised. Me quedé de sorpresa.

to **reap success** cosechar éxitos ➤ *(*Chicago Tribune *columnist)* Mike Royko reaped one success after another. Mike Royko cosechó un éxito tras otro.

to **reap the benefits of one's labors** ▪ to reap the benefits of one's efforts recoger los beneficios de su trabajo ▪ obtener los frutos de su trabajo ▪ cosechar los beneficios de su trabajo ▪ recoger la aceituna

to **reap what one sows** recoger lo que uno siembra ▪ recogerse lo que se siembra ➤ We reap what we sow. Recogemos lo que sembramos. ➤ You reap what you sow. Se recoge lo que se siembra.

to **rear-end a vehicle** recular con un vehículo

rear-end collision *la* colisión por alcance

to **rear up** *(horse)* empinarse ▪ encabritarse

rear wheels ruedas traseras

rear windshield luna trasera

rearview mirror: to look in the ~ mirar por espejo retrovisor ➤ I looked in the rearview mirror and saw that the car behind me was tailgating (me). Miré por el espejo retrovisor y vi que el coche de detrás venía besándome el culo.

to be **reason enough to** ▪ to be sufficient reason to ▪ to be good reason to ser motivo suficiente para ▪ ser razón de sobra para

the **reason for** la razón para

the **reason for it is that...** la razón de ello es que...

the **reason I asked is...** te pregunto porque...

the **reason I'm telling you is...** *(a ti)* te lo digo porque... ▪ te lo menciono porque... ▪ *(a usted)* se lo digo porque...

the **reason one does something** la razón por la que uno hace una cosa ➤ The reason I bought it... La razón por la que lo compré...

reason to believe: to have ~ tener motivos para creer ▪ tener razones para creer

the **reason why** la razón por la que ▪ motivo por el cual ➤ This is one reason why... Es una razón por la que... ➤ This is one of the reasons why... Es una de las razones por las que...

reasonable price ▪ moderate price precio moderado ▪ precio razonable

to **reboot the computer** ▪ to restart the computer reinicializar la computadora ▪ reiniciar la computadora ▪ *(Sp.)* reinicializar el ordenador ▪ reiniciar el ordenador

to **rebroadcast a program** retransmitir un programa ▪ volver a transmitir un programa

to **receive a bill** ▪ to get a bill recibir una cuenta ▪ llegarle una cuenta a alguien ▪ llegarle una factura a alguien ▪ venirle una factura ▪ venirle una cuenta ➤ I haven't received the phone bill. No he recibido la cuenta del teléfono.

to **receive communion** ▪ to take communion comulgar ➤ *(photo caption)* Vicente Fox receives communion before assuming the presidency of Mexico. ▪ Vicente Fox takes communion before assuming the presidency of Mexico. Vicente Fox comulga antes de asumir la presidencia de México.

to **receive someone with open arms** recibir a alguien con los brazos abiertos

to **receive the ashes (on Ash Wednesday)** *(Catholicism)* tomar la ceniza (el miércoles de ceniza)

to **receive the highest number of votes** recibir la mayor cantidad de votos ▪ ser el más votado

receiver of a telephone ▪ telephone receiver *(Mex.)* bocina ▪ *(Sp.)* auricular

recent engagement (to marry) reciente compromiso ▪ incipiente noviazgo

recent past pasado cercano ▪ pasado reciente

recent vintage *(wine)* vino joven

recently released ▪ newly released ▪ just released **1.** *(motion picture)* recientemente estrenada **2.** *(publication)* recién salido de la imprenta

reception: to have a good ~ tener una buena acogida ➤ Mike Royko's column in the *Chicago Tribune* had such a good reception that he was given carte blanche. La columna de Mike Royko en el *Chicago Tribune* tuvo tan buena acogida que le dieron carta blanca.

to be **receptive to** ser receptivo a

to **recharge one's batteries 1.** to rest up ▪ to recover one's energy cargar (las) pilas ▪ recuperar las fuerzas ▪ cobrar fuerzas **2.** to allow one to recharge one's batteries permitirle cargar las pilas a uno ▪ permitirle recuperar las fuerzas a uno ▪ permitirle cobrar fuerzas a uno ▪ servirle para cargar las pilas a uno ▪ servirle para recuperar las fuerzas a uno ▪ servirle para cobrar fuerzas a uno ➤ I need to recharge my cell phone batteries. Necesito cargar las pilas de mi móvil. ➤ I need to recharge my batteries. ▪ I need to rest and regain my energy. Necesito cobrar fuerzas. ▪ Necesito cargar pilas. ➤ The two weeks in Acapulco recharged my batteries. Las dos semanas en Acapulco me permitieron cargar las pilas. ▪ Las dos semanas en Acapulco me servieron para cobrar fuerzas. ▪ Las dos semanas en Acapulco me servieron para recuperar fuerzas.

to **recharge the battery 1.** *(large battery: car, etc.)* cargar la batería ▪ cargar el acumulador **2.** *(small battery: cell phone, etc.)* cargar la pila **3.** *(when "battery" is the subject)* cargarse la batería ▪ cargarse la pila ➤ I need to recharge my cell phone batteries. Necesito cargar las pilas de mi móvil. ➤ The cell phone battery is recharging. Se carga la pila del móvil. ▪ Se está cargando la pila del móvil.

to **reciprocate an invitation** ▪ to return an invitation reciprocar una invitación ▪ corresponder a una invitación ➤ They accepted the dinner invitation but never reciprocated it. Aceptaron la invitación a cenar pero no la reciprocaron. ▪ Aceptaron la invitación a cenar pero no la correspondieron. ➤ The dinner invitation was accepted but not reciprocated. La invitación a cenar fue aceptada pero no fue reciprocada. ▪ La invitación a cenar fue aceptada pero no fue correspondida.

reckless driver conductor(-a) temerario(-a)

reckless driving conducción temeraria ➤ The policeman stopped the car and ticketed the driver for reckless driving. El policía paró al coche y multó al conductor por conducción temeraria.

to **recognize someone by sight** reconocer a alguien a simple vista

to **recognize something by name** ▪ to recognize something by its name reconocer algo por su nombre ➤ I didn't recognize "el pudín español" by its name. No reconocí el pudín español por su nombre. *("Pudding" is "flan" in Spanish.)*

to **recognize that...** ▪ to realize that... darse cuenta de que... ➤ Leonardo da Vinci recognized that, except during takeoff, birds flap their wings for propulsion, not lift. Leonardo da Vinci se dio cuenta de que, excepto durante el despegue, las aves aletean para propulsarse, no para mantenerse en el aire.

to be **recognized as** reconocérsele como

to **recommend someone for a job** recomendar a alguien para un trabajo ▪ recomendar a alguien para un puesto de trabajo ➤ I'm going to recommend Marta for the job. Voy a recomendar a Marta para el trabajo.

to **reconcile conflicting points of view** reconciliar puntos de vista en conflicto

reconciliation issue *(Catholicism) el* tema de la reconciliación

reconnaissance aircraft ▪ reconnaissance plane *el* avión de reconocimiento

to **record for posterity** ▪ to set down for posterity ▪ to write down for posterity escribir para la posteridad

record of a transaction ▪ transaction record registro de una transacción ▪ recibo de una transacción ➤ Do you save the records of your ATM transactions? ¿Guardas los recibos de la transacción del cajero automático?

record of long standing *(sports, etc.)* ▪ long-standing record *el* récord de larga duración ▪ récord imbatible

record of the payments registro de los pagos

the **record player skips** el tocadiscos funciona a saltos

the **record skips** el disco salta

to **record sound** grabar (el) sonido

the **records show that...** los registros muestran que...

to **recover bodies** rescatar cadáveres ▪ recuperar cuerpos ➤ Authorities last night had recovered forty-seven bodies. Las autoridades habían rescatado anoche cuarenta y siete cadáveres.

to **recover from an illness** ▪ to get over an illness recuperarse de una enfermedad ▪ restablecerse de una enfermedad ▪ reponerse de una enfermedad ▪ recobrarse de una enfermedad

to **recover from an injury** recuperarse de una herida ▪ recuperarse de una lesión

to **recover from the loss of a loved one** ▪ to get over the loss of a loved one rehacerse de la pérdida de un ser querido ➤ He had a hard time recovering from the death of his wife. ▪ He had a hard time getting over the death of his wife. Le costó rehacerse de la muerte de su esposa.

to **recover lost ground** recuperar el terreno perdido

to **recover one's composure** ▪ to regain one's composure recobrar la compostura ▪ recuperar el aplomo ▪ reponerse

to **recover one's sanity** ▪ to regain one's sanity recuperar la cordura ▪ recobrar el sentido común

to **recover the document** ▪ to retrieve the document recuperar el documento ➤ Do you think you can recover the document? ¿Crees que puedes recuperar el documento?

to **recover the feeling in** ▪ to recover the sensation in recobrar la sensación de ➤ After the accident, he gradually recovered the feeling in his arm. Después del accidente, recobró gradualmente la sensación de su brazo.

to **recover the sensation in** ▪ to recover the feeling in recobrar la sensación en ➤ After the accident, he gradually recovered the sensation in his arm. Después del accidente, recobró gradualmente la sensación en el brazo.

to **recover (well)** ▪ to make (good) progress ▪ to progress well evolucionar bien ➤ *(news item)* The Pope will remain hospitalized for several days, even though he is recovering well.

■ The Pope will remain hospitalized for several days, even though he is progressing well. ■ The Pope will remain hospitalized for several days, even though he is making (good) progress. El Papa seguirá hospitalizado varios días, aunque evoluciona bien.

recovered from: to have ~ haberse recuperado de ■ estar ya mejor de ■ haberse repuesto de

to be **recovering from** estar en proceso de recuperación de

recruiting arm ■ recruiting aparatus aparato de captación

recurrent theme tema reiterativo ■ tema recurrente

recycle bin *(computers)* papelera de reciclaje

to be **red as a lobster** ■ to be badly sunburned ■ to be severely sunburned estar como un cangrejo

red giant (star) *(astronomy)* (estrella) gigante roja

red-haired pelirrojo ■ cabellos color rojo

red-handed: to catch someone ~ ■ to catch someone in the act pillar a alguien con las manos en la masa ■ agarrar a alguien con las manos en la masa ■ pillar a alguien in fraganti ■ agarrar a alguien in fraganti ■ *(Sp.)* coger a alguien con las manos en la masa ■ coger a alguien in fraganti ➤ They caught him red-handed. Le pillaron con las manos en la masa. ■ Le agarraron con las manos en la masa. ■ Le cogieron con las manos en la masa.

to be **red hot** estar al rojo vivo

red-letter day día feriado ■ día que se imprime en rojo en el calendario ➤ Christmas and Columbus Day are red-letter days on the calendar. En el calendario la Navidad y el Día de la Raza se imprimen en color rojo.

red light ■ traffic light on red semáforo en rojo

red-light house ■ whorehouse ■ house of ill repute ■ house of prostitution prostíbulo ■ casa de citas ■ casa de putas ■ *(Sp.)* mancebía ■ *el* club alterne

red meat carne roja

red shift *(astrophysics)* desplazamiento hacia el rojo

red wine vino tinto

red wine spritzer tinto de verano ■ vino tinto con gaseosa

to **reduce a fraction to its lowest common denominator** *(mathematics)* reducir una fracción al mínimo denominador ■ reducir una fracción a su mínimo denominador

to **reduce an equation to its simplest form** *(mathematics)* reducir una ecuación a la mínima expresión ■ reducir una ecuación a su mínima expresión

to **reduce costs** reducir (los) costos ■ *(Sp., and less common)* reducir (los) costes

to **reduce expectations** ■ to lower expectations reducir las expectativas ■ aminorar las expectativas

to **reduce expenditures** reducir (los) gastos

to **reduce expenses** reducir (los) gastos

to **reduce the price of an item** abaratar un artículo ■ rebajar el precio de un artículo

to **reduce the rate of** reducir la tasa de

to **reduce the risk of** ■ to lower the risk of ■ to mitigate the risk of reducir el riesgo de ■ mitigar el riesgo de

to be **reduced in price from *x* to *y*** estar rebajado de precio de *x* a *y* ➤ The price was reduced from 50,000 to 40,000 pesos. El precio estuvo rebajado de 50.000 a 40.000 pesos.

reduction in personnel ■ personnel layoffs ■ reduction in the work force *el* recorte de plantilla

reduction in the work force ■ reduction in personnel ■ personnel layoffs *el* recorte de plantilla

reduction of force ■ downsizing reducción de personal ■ *el* expediente de crisis

to **reek of alcohol** heder a alcohol ■ apestar a alcohol ■ despedir un tufo de alcohol

reel back in awe: to make one ~ ■ to be stunning ser como para caerse de espaldas ■ estar como para caerse de espaldas ➤ The Escorial makes you reel back in awe. ■ The Escorial is stunning. El Escorial es como para caerse de espaldas.

to **reel off facts and figures** ■ to spiel off facts and figures ■ to recite facts and figures soltar una retahíla de hechos y cifras ■ recitar hechos y cifras ■ decir hecho y cifras de carrerilla

to **reel off statistics** ■ to reel statistics off ■ to spiel off statistics ■ to recite statistics soltar (un montón de) estadísticas ■ soltar (una retahíla de) estadísticas ■ decir las estadísticas de carrerilla ➤ He reeled off a bunch of statistics. Soltó un montón de estadísticas.

to be **reelected to another term (as)** ser reelegido(-a) para otro mandato (como) ■ ser reelegido para otro período (como) ➤ The president was reelected to a second term (in office). El presidente fue reelegido para un segundo mandato.

to **reenact a historical event** reproducir un evento histórico ➤ They reenacted the Wright Brothers flight on its centennial, December 17, 2003. Reprodujeron el vuelo de los Hermanos Wright en su centenario, el 17 de diciembre de 2003.

to **refer to someone** ■ to mean someone referirse a alguien ■ ir por alguien ➤ I thought you were referring to me. ■ I thought you meant me. Pensé que te referías a mí. ➤ I'm not referring to him. No me refiero a él. ■ Eso no va por él. ■ Eso no va para él. ➤ I wasn't referring to him. No me refería a él. ■ Eso no iba por él. ■ Eso no iba para el.

to be **referred by another doctor** ser enviado por otro médico

refined tastes gustos depurados ■ gustos refinados

to **refinish a piece of furniture** darle a un mueble un nuevo acabado ➤ I refinished this table. Le di a esta mesa un nuevo acabado.

to **reflect an image** reflejar una imagen ■ devolver una imagen

refractive index *(ratio of light's speed in a vacuum to its speed through gases, liquids, solids)* índice de refracción ➤ The refractive index of water is 1.333. El índice de refracción del agua es 1,333.

to **refresh one's memory** refrescar la memoria ■ reivindicar la memoria

refreshing break descanso refrescante

refreshing candor *el* candor refrescante

to **refuel** repostar combustible ■ rellenar de combustible ■ reabastecer de combustible

refusal to negativa de

to **refuse an offer** ■ to decline an offer rechazar una oferta ■ rehusar una oferta ■ declinar una oferta

to **refuse to believe it** resistirse a creerlo

to **refuse to cooperate with someone** negarse a colaborar con alguien ➤ The suspects have so far refused to cooperate with the police. Hasta el momento los sospechosos se han negado a colaborar con la policía.

to **refuse to do something** negarse a hacer algo ➤ After the technician installed the parts wrong, the store refused to send him back. Al instalar mal las partes el técnico, la tienda se negó a volver a enviarle. ➤ *(sports car ad)* Refuse to grow up! ¡Niégate a ser mayor!

to **refuse to go away** negarse a desaparecer ➤ My cold refuses to go away. Mi resfriado se niega a desaparecer.

to **refuse to yield** ■ to resist stubbornly ■ to be unyielding mantenerse en sus trece ■ permanecer en sus trece ■ seguir en sus trece ■ estar en sus trece ■ afirmarse en los estribos

to **regain consciousness** recuperar la consciencia ■ volver en sí

to **regain control of** recuperar el control de ➤ The moderates regained control of the legislature. Los moderados recuperaron el control de la asamblea legislativa.

to **regain one's composure** ■ to recover one's composure recobrar la compostura ■ recuperar el aplomo ■ reponerse

to **regain one's sanity** ■ to recover one's sanity recuperar la cordura ■ *(coll.)* recobrar el sentido común

to **regard someone as** considerar a alguien como ➤ Virtually all U.S. historians regard Lincoln as the greatest American president. Casi todos los historiadores estadounidenses consideran a Lincoln como el más grande de los presidentes de los Estados Unidos.

to **regard someone with contempt** ■ to be contemptuous of someone tener en poco a alguien

Regarding Henry *(film title) A propósito de Enrique* ■ *(also possible)* en cuanto a Enrique ■ en lo que respecta a Enrique ■ en lo tocante a Enrique ■ sobre Enrique

regardless of the cost ■ no matter how much it costs sin reparar en gastos ■ cueste lo cueste ■ sin importar los gastos

regardless of the outcome ■ no matter what the outcome salga lo que salga ■ a lo que salga

regardless of which one (it is) ■ no matter which one it is ■ whichever one it is sea cual sea ■ sin importar cual sea

regional differences diferencias regionales ■ diferencias geográficas ➤ Regional differences in health care availability Diferencias regionales en la disponibilidad de atención médica ■ Diferencias geográficas en la disponibilidad de atención médica

to **register for class(es)** inscribirse en las clases ■ apuntarse a las clases ➤ Have you registered for classes yet? ¿Te has inscrito en las clases ya? ■ ¿Te has apuntado a las clases ya?

to **register *x* on the Richter scale** ■ to measure *x* on the Richter scale registrar *x* puntos en la escala Richter ■ ser de *x* en la escala Richter puntos en la escala Richter ➤ The quake registered 6.8 on the Richter scale. El terremoto fue de 6.8 en la escala Richter.

registration fee(s) matrícula (de inscripción)

to **regret doing something** ■ to regret having done something ■ to be sorry one did something arrepentirse de haber hecho algo ■ pesarle a uno haber hecho algo ➤ I regret doing it. ■ I regret having done it. ■ I'm sorry I did it. Me arrepiento de haberlo hecho. ■ Me pesa haberlo hecho.

to **regret having to do something** ■ to regret to have to do something lamentar tener que hacer algo ■ sentir tener que hacer algo

to **regret that...** sentir que... ■ lamentar que... ■ arrepentirse de que...

to **regret to inform someone that...** lamentar tener que informarle a alguien que... ■ sentir tener que informarle a alguien que... ➤ We regret to inform you that... Lamentamos tener que informarle a usted que...

to be a **regular customer** ser cliente habitual ■ ser habitual del local ■ ser parroquiano(-a) ■ ser parroquiano(-a) asiduo(-a)

regular habits: to be a person of ~ ser una persona de costumbres persistentes ■ tener costumbres persistentes ➤ The philosopher Immanuel Kant was a man of regular habits. El filósofo Immanuel Kant era (un hombre) de costumbres fijas.

regular price precio fijo

regular reader lector(-a) asiduo(-a) ➤ I am a regular reader of your newspaper. Soy lector asiduo de su periódico. ■ Soy asiduo lector de su periódico.

regular teacher profesor habitual ■ profesor titular ■ profesor fijo ➤ Our regular teacher is in the hospital. Nuestra profesora habitual está en el hospital.

regulation triangles *(reflective triangles required by law in Hispanic countries to be carried in vehicles)* triángulos (homologados) ■ balizas

reign of a monarch ■ rule of a monarch reinado de un(-a) monarca

reigning champion vigente campeón(a)

to **rein in someone** ■ to check someone ponerle freno a alguien

to **reinstall the software** recargar el programa ■ reinstalar el programa

to **reinstate the draft** reinstaurar el servicio militar obligatorio

to **reject a proposal** ■ to quash a proposal ■ to throw out a proposal rechazar una propuesta ■ echar abajo una propuesta

to **reject something categorically** ■ to reject something emphatically ■ to reject something flatly rechazar algo tajantemente

to **reject something flatly** rechazar algo de plano

to **relate something to something else** relacionar algo con otra cosa ■ establecer una relación entre dos cosas

to be **related to 1.** *(genetically)* ser pariente de ■ ser familia de **2.** *(causally)* estar relacionado con

relating to ■ concerning concerniente a

relations between them are strained las relaciones entre ellos están tirantes

relations between us are strained nuestras relaciones están tirantes

relative humidity humedad relativa ➤ Relative humidity is the amount of water vapor in the air divided by the amount of water vapor the air can hold. La humedad relativa es la cantidad de vapor en el aire dividido por la cantidad del agua que el aire puede contener.

relatively few relativamente pocos(-as)

relatively little 1. *(quantity)* relativamente poco(-a) **2.** *(size)* relativamente pequeño(-a)

to **relax a requirement** relajar un requisito ■ rebajar un requisito

to **relay a message to someone** ■ to give a message to someone ■ to convey a message to someone pasarle un mensaje a alguien ➤ Would you relay the message to her? ¿Le pasarías el mensaje a ella?

relay race carrera de relevos

to **release a prisoner** soltar a un presionero ■ excarcelar a un preso ■ liberar a un preso ■ poner en libertad a un preso ➤ The prisoner could be released shortly. El preso podría ser excarcelado en breve. ■ El preso podría ser excarcelado dentro de poco.

release (from detention) puesta en libertad

to **release one from one's promise** absolver a uno de su promesa

to **release someone from detention** ■ to free someone ■ to set someone free poner a alguien en libertad ■ excarcelar a alguien

to **release someone from prison** ■ to release someone from jail excarcelar a alguien

to **release someone from the hospital** darle a uno de alta del hospital ➤ She was released from the hospital yesterday. A ella le dieron de alta ayer. ■ Recibió el alta hospitalaria ayer.

to **release the brake** soltar el freno

to **release the clutch pedal** ■ to let out the clutch ■ to take one's foot off the clutch pedal soltar el embrague

to **release the funds** liberar los fundos

to be **released from prison** ■ to be released from jail ser excarcelado(-a) ■ ser liberado(-a) de la prisión ➤ The prisoner could be released shortly. El preso podría ser excarcelado en breve.

to be **released from the hospital** ser dado de alta del hospital ■ darle de alta del hospital ■ dejarle salir del hospital ➤ The athlete was released from the hospital a week after being injured. El atleta fue dado de alta del hospital a la semana de ser lesionado. ■ Al atleta le dieron de alta a la semana de ser lesionado. ■ Al atleta le dejaron salir del hospital a la semana de ser lesionado.

relentless pursuit acoso sin tregua

to **relentlessly attack** ■ to attack relentlessly atacar sin tregua

to be **relentlessly attacked** ser atacado sin tregua

relevant authorities ■ appropriate authorities *las* autoridades pertinentes

reliability of a report *la* fiabilidad de un informe ■ solvencia de un informe

to be a **reliable car** *(L. Am.)* ser un carro muy fiable ■ *(Sp.)* ser un coche fiable

reliable map mapa fiable ■ *(street map)* plano fiable ➤ The maps in Columbus' day were not very reliable. Los mapas en época de Colón no eran muy fiables.

reliable person persona de confianza ■ persona responsable ■ persona fiable ■ persona formal

reliable source ■ trustworthy source fuente fiable ■ fuente fidedigna ■ fuente de confianza

relic of the past reliquia del pasado

relief: to put something in(to) ~ 1. to bring something into focus ■ to make something "come alive" poner algo de relieve **2.** *(map)* to show the elevations in relation to sea level mostrar las elevaciones del terreno en relación al nivel del mar

relief map *(shows the elevations in relation to sea level)* mapa de relieve ■ mapa físico

relief painting *(such as Japanase wood sculptured paintings)* pintura en relieve

religious fundamentalism integrismo religioso ■ fundamentalismo religioso

religious fundamentalist integrista religioso(-a) ■ fundamentalista religioso(-a)

to **relinquish power** ■ to give up power ■ to step down ■ to step aside ceder el poder ■ *(colorful)* apearse del burro

to be **reluctant to do something** estar reacio a hacer algo ■ mostrarse reacio a hacer algo ■ estar poco dispuesto a hacer algo ▪ estar renuente a hacer algo ▪ estar reticente a hacer algo

to **rely on someone** ▪ to count on someone confiar en alguien ▪ depender de alguien ▪ contar con alguien

to **rely on something** ▪ to count on something contar con algo ▪ depender de algo

to **remain at large** seguir en libertad ▪ andar suelto(-a)

to **remain closed** ▪ to stay closed seguir cerrado ➤ *(news item)* Argentine banks will remain closed until Friday. Los bancos argentinos seguirán cerrados hasta el viernes.

to **remain faithful to someone** mantenerse fiel a alguien ▪ permanecer fiel a alguien

to **remain impassive** quedarse hierático(-a)

to **remain in bed** ▪ to stay in bed guardar cama ▪ permanecer en la cama

to **remain intact** ▪ to be left intact quedar intacto

to **remain loyal to someone** seguir siendo leal a alguien

to **remain seated** permanecer sentado(-a) ▪ estarse sentado(-a) ▪ quedarse sentado(-a)

to **remain silent** permanecer en silencio ▪ permanecer callado(-a) ➤ You have the right to remain silent. *(usted)* Tiene el derecho de permanecer callado.

to **remain standing** mantenerse en pie ▪ permanecer en pie

to **remain to be done** quedar por hacer

to **remain to be seen** quedar por verse ▪ aún estar por verse ➤ That remains to be seen. Eso queda por verse. ➤ It remains to be seen whether... Aún queda por verse si... ▪ Aún está por verse si...

to **remain unconvinced** quedarse sin convencer

remaining questions preguntas restantes ▪ preguntas que quedan ▪ preguntas que faltan ➤ To clear up the remaining questions Aclarar las preguntas restantes ▪ Aclarar las preguntas que quedan ▪ Aclarar las preguntas que faltan

Remains of the Day *(film title) Lo que queda del día*

remarkable achievement logro a destacar ▪ logro a remarcar ▪ logro destacable

remarkably accurate extraordinariamente exacto

remarkably short time: in a ~ en un tiempo notablemente corto

remember? ▪ do you remember? *(tú)* ¿te acuerdas? ▪ *(usted)* ¿se acuerda (usted)?

to **remember someone fondly** acordarse de alguien con cariño ▪ recordar a alguien con cariño

remember that... ▪ keep in mind that... ▪ bear in mind that... *(tú)* ten en cuenta que... ▪ piensa que... ▪ *(usted)* tenga en cuenta que... ▪ piense que... ➤ Remember that it is very difficult for a child to accept a flat "no," so if you deny him something, talk over your refusal. Piensa que para un niño es muy difícil aceptar un "no" tajante, así que si le niegas algo, razona tu negativa.

to **remember to do something** ▪ to remember that acordarse de hacer algo ▪ recordar que ➤ Remember to take the garbage out! ¡Acuérdate de sacar la basura! ▪ ¡Recuerda que tienes que sacar la basura!

to be **remembered as** ser recordado como

to **remind someone of someone** recordarle a alguien ▪ *(L. Am.)* hacerle recordar a alguien ➤ She reminds me of my sister. Me recuerda a mi hermana. ➤ Do you know who you remind me of? ¿Sabes a quién me recuerdas? ▪ ¿Sabes a quién me haces recordar?

to **remind someone of something** recordarle a alguien algo ▪ hacer recordar algo a alguien ➤ Thank you for reminding me of it. Gracias por recordármelo. ➤ You'd better remind him of his doctor's appointment; he's gotten pretty forgetful in his old age. Será mejor que le recuerdes su cita con el médico; se está haciendo muy olvidadizo con la edad. ➤ What reminded me of it was your saying that you always pay people back. Lo que me lo recordó (que me debes dinero) fue cuando dijiste que siempre devuelves a la gente lo que te prestan.

to **remind someone of what...** recordarle a alguien lo que... ▪ *(L. Am.)* hacerle a alguien recordar lo que...

to **remind someone that...** recordarle a alguien que...

to **remind someone to do something** recordarle a alguien que haga algo ➤ Remind me to pick up the dry cleaning. ▪ Remind me to pick the dry cleaning up. Recuérdame que recoja la ropa de la tintorería. ➤ Remind me to pick it up. Recuérdame que la recoja.

reminder! ¡recuerde! ▪ ¡recordatorio!

reminder of recordatorio de

reminder of what... recordatorio de lo que...

reminder that... recordatorio de que...

to **reminisce about** rememorar sobre

remission of sins *la* remisión de los pecados

remnants of a supernova *(astronomy)* vestigios de una explosión supernova ▪ restos de una explosión supernova

to **remodel a building** ▪ to renovate a building reformar un edificio ▪ remodelar un edificio

remote (control device) *(TV, VCR, stereo)* control remoto ▪ mando a distancia

remote location lugar remoto ▪ lugar lejano ➤ You should be able to check your university E-mail account from remote locations. Deberías poder mirar tu cuenta de correo de la universidad desde lugares remotos.

remote possibility posibilidad lejana ▪ posibilidad remota ➤ How remote a possibility is that? ▪ How remote is that possibility? ¿Qué tan remota es la posibilidad?

removal of debris ▪ clearing of debris retirada de escombros

to **remove a name from a list** ▪ to take a name off a list ▪ to drop a name from a list tachar un nombre de una lista ▪ borrar un nombre de una lista ▪ eliminar un nombre de una lista

to **remove a tumor** ▪ to extract a tumor ▪ to take out a tumor extirpar un tumor ▪ extraer un tumor ▪ quitar un tumor ▪ sacar un tumor

to **remove macros from the computer** ▪ to delete the macros ▪ to erase the macros ▪ to eliminate the macros suprimir los macros de la computadora ▪ borrar los macros ▪ eliminar los macros *(In Spain, "computer" is "ordenador.")*

to **remove the default settings** *(computers)* ▪ to turn off the defaults ▪ to eliminate the defaults ▪ to delete the defaults suprimir las configuraciones por defecto ▪ anular las configuraciones por defecto

to **remove the shells** *(seafood, paella, etc.)* ▪ to peel off the shells pelar las cáscaras ▪ quitar las cáscaras

render unto Caesar that which is Caesar's, and unto God that which is God's *(synoptic gospels)* dad al César lo que es de César, y a Dios lo que es de Dios

to **renew a subscription** renovar una suscripción

to **renew an acquaintance with someone** ▪ to renew one's acquaintance with someone reanudar relaciones con un conocido

to **renew an insurance policy** renovar una poliza de seguro

to **renew one's membership in an organization** renovar la membresía de uno en una organización ➤ I need to renew my membership. Necesito renovar mi membresía.

to **renew one's passport** renovar el pasaporte (de uno)

rent increase ▪ increase in the rent subida del alquiler ▪ aumento del alquiler ➤ I got a huge rent increase in September. Me dieron un aumento enorme en el alquiler en septiembre. ▪ Me dieron un aumentazo de la renta en septiembre.

rental agreement ▪ rental contract contrato de arrendimiento ▪ contrato de alquiler

rental car ▪ rented car *el* automóvil de alquiler

rental car agency ▪ car rental agency agencia de alquiler de coches *(In this expression, the word "coche" is used in Latin America as well as Spain.)*

rented car ▪ rental car *el* coche de alquiler

to **reopen the case** reabrir el caso ▪ retomar el caso

to **repay someone's favor (generously)** ▪ to repay someone's favor (many times over) pagarle a alguien un favor (con creces)

to **repay someone's kindness generously** ▪ to repay someone's kindness many times over pagar a alguien con creces

to **repeal a law** ▪ to abolish a law derogar una ley ▪ revocar una ley ▪ abrogar una ley

repeat after me *(ustedes)* repitan (ustedes) después de mí ▪ *(Sp., vosotros)* repetid después de mí

repeated failures fallas reiteradas ■ repetidas fallas ■ reiterados fracasos ■ fracasos repetidos

to **rephrase something** expresar algo de otra manera

to **rephrase the question** expresar la pregunta de otra manera

to **replace personnel** reemplazar al personal ■ sustituir al personal

to **replace something (that has been) broken** ■ to replace something which has been broken reemplazar algo (que se ha) roto

replacement parts ■ spare parts piezas de repuesto

replay of an earlier program ■ repeat of an earlier program *la* repetición de un programa anterior

to **reply that...** ■ to respond that... ■ to answer that... reponer que... ■ responder que... ■ contestar que...

to **report cases of an illness** registrar casos de una enfermedad ➤ Nearly a thousand cases of the illness have been reported. Se han registrado casi mil casos de la enfermedad.

to **report findings** informar de las conclusiones ■ informar de los hallazgos ■ informar de los descubrimientos

to **report on** informar sobre

to **report someone to the police** denunciar a alguien a la policía

to **report something to someone** dar cuenta de algo a alguien ■ *(to the police, insurance company, etc.)* dar parte a alguien de algo

to **report that...** informar que... ■ *(by radio)* comunicar que... ➤ Diplomatic sources reported that... Fuentes diplomáticas han informado que... ➤ The pilot reported that the airplane had struck something on the takeoff roll. ■ The pilot reported that the airplane had struck something during the takeoff roll. El piloto comunicó que el avión ha golpeado un objeto durante el recorrido de despegue.

to **report the facts** difundir los hechos ■ informar los hechos ■ reportar los hechos

to **reportedly have** ■ to be said to have decir tener ➤ Police are searching for the hijacker, who reportedly has family problems. ■ Police are searching for the hijacker, who is said to have family problems. La policía busca al pirata aéreo que dijo tener problemas familiares.

reporter (out) on his beat ■ reporter (out) covering his beat reportero a pie de calle

reprehensible act *la* acción reprehensible ■ acción censurable ■ acción reprobable

representative sample muestra representativa

reproachful look ■ look of reproach mirada de reproche

reputation as fama de

to **request a meeting with someone** ■ to request to meet with someone pedir una reunión con alguien ■ solicitar una reunión con alguien

request for *la* petición por

request for information *la* petición de información ■ *la* solicitud de información

to **reschedule an appointment** ■ to reset an appointment **1.** to change the date cambiar la fecha de una cita **2.** to change the time (hour) cambiar la hora de una cita ➤ I rescheduled the appointment for the sixteenth. Cambié la fecha de la cita para el dieciséis.

rescue team equipo de rescate ■ equipo de salvamento

to be **rescued alive** ser rescatado(-a) con vida ■ ser rescatado(-a) vivo(-a)

research and development ■ R and D ■ R&D investigación y desarrollo ■ I plus D ■ I+D

research grant beca de investigación

resemble someone ■ to look like someone parecerse a alguien ■ parecérsele a alguien ➤ He looks like his father. Se parece a su padre. ➤ He looks a lot like him. Se le parece mucho. *("Se le parece" can also mean "he takes after him.")*

reservations for two (people): to make ~ hacer reservaciones para dos (personas)

to **reserve a seat** reservar un asiento ■ reservar un sitio ➤ I'd like to reserve two seats for the concert this Friday. Me gustaría reservar dos asientos para el concierto de este viernes.

to **reserve a table** reservar (una) mesa ➤ We'd like to reserve a table for six this Saturday for supper. Nos gustaría reservar (una) mesa para seis este sábado para cenar.

to **reserve the date** reservar el día ■ reservar la fecha

to **reserve the right to** dejar a salvo su derecho de

residence permit permiso de residencia

residual knowledge conocimientos residuales

to **resign from a job** ■ to resign from a position ■ to resign from a post renunciar a un puesto de trabajo ■ dimitir de un puesto de trabajo

to **resign (from) one's post as** renunciar a su cargo de ➤ *(headline)* Pinochet resigns from his senate post Pinochet renuncia a su cargo de senador

to **resign from public office** dimitir de un cargo público ■ presentar la dimisión en un cargo público ■ renunciar a un cargo público

to be **resigned to one's fate** ■ to be resigned to one's plight estar resignado a su destino ■ resignarse a su suerte

to **resist temptation** ■ to withstand temptation resistir la tentación

resistance of the air ■ friction of the air rozamiento del aire

to **resolve to do something** resolverse a hacer algo ■ hacer propósito de hacer algo ■ hacerse (el) propósito de hacer algo ➤ I resolve to turn over a new leaf. Hago propósito de enmienda.

to **resonate with the public** tener eco (en la sociedad)

to **resort to extreme measures** ■ to resort to radical measures recurrir a medidas extremas ■ recurrir a medidas radicales

to **resort to force** recurrir a (la) fuerza ■ recurrir a las armas

resounding "no" ■ a flat "no" ■ a categorical "no" un "no" rotundo ■ un "no" contundente ■ un "no" apabullante

resounding "yes" un "sí" contundente ■ un "sí" categórico

to **respect one's elders** respetar a los mayores de uno

to be **respectful of** estar respetuoso(-a) con ■ mostrarle respeto a

respiratory arrest parada respiratoria ■ arresto respiratorio

response time tiempo de respuesta ➤ Why is the response time of the computer so slow? ¿Por qué es el tiempo de respuesta de la computadora tan lento?

response was... respuesta fue... ■ reacción fue... ➤ Your response was to blame him. Tu respuesta fue culparle. ■ Tu reacción fue culparle.

to be **responsible for something** tener la responsabilidad de (hacer) algo ■ ser responsable de (hacer) aglo

responsible position puesto de responsabilidad

to be **responsible to someone for something** ser responsable ante alguien por algo

responsibility for doing something: to take ~ ■ to be responsible for doing something asumir la responsabilidad de hacer algo ➤ Will you take responsibility for locking the CD player in the closet after class? ■ Will you be responsible for locking the CD player in the closet after class? ¿Asumes la responsabilidad de encerrar el lector de CD en el armario después de la clase?

responsibility to do something: to be one's ~ ■ to have the responsibility to do something tener la responsabilidad de hacer algo ➤ It was my responsibility to see that the animals were fed. Yo tenía la responsabilidad de ver que se les diera de comer a los animales.

to be **responsive to the needs of others** ■ to be responsive to other people's needs ser atento a las necesidades de otros

responsiveness to the needs of others ■ responsiveness to other people's needs atención a las necesidades de los demás

to **rest against** ■ to lean against apoyar(se) contra ■ inclinarse contra ■ recostarse contra

the **rest of the time** el resto del tiempo

the **rest of us are...** el resto somos... ■ los demás somos... ■ el resto estamos... ■ los demás estamos...

to **rest on 1.** *(weight)* descansar en ■ descansar sobre **2.** *(decision)* depender de ➤ The main beam rests on the cross beam. La viga maestra descansa en la viga transversal. ➤ The decision rests entirely on the economic situation. La decisión depende enteramente en la situación económica.

to **rest on one's laurels** dormirse en sus laureles ▪ dormirse sobre sus laureles

to **rest on the assumption that...** quedarse con la suposición de que... ▪ basarse en la suposición de que...

to **rest on the theory that...** basarse en la teoría de que...

to **rest with one** corresponderle a uno ▪ tener que tomar uno ➤ You realize, of course, that the final decision must rest with me. Por supuesto, usted se da cuenta de que la decisión final debe corresponderme a mí. ▪ Por supuesto, usted se da cuenta de que la decisión final tengo que tomarla yo.

to **restart the computer** ▪ to reboot the computer reinicializar la computadora ▪ reiniciar la computadora ▪ *(Sp.)* reinicializar el ordenador ▪ reiniciar el ordenador

to **restart the software** reinicializar el programa ▪ reiniciar el programa

to **restore a building** restaurar un edificio ➤ *(plaque on a building)* Restored and renovated in 1982 Restaurado y reformado en el año 1982

to **restore power** ▪ to restore the flow of electricity restaurar el fluido eléctrico

to **restore something to its original condition** ▪ to make something the way it was ▪ to make something as it was restaurar algo a su estado original ▪ volver algo a su estado original

to **result from something** ▪ to be the result of something ser resultado de algo

to **result in something** tener como resultado algo ▪ *(journalistic)* valerle algo ➤ The gaffe resulted in his electoral defeat. La metida de pata resultó en su derrota en las elecciones. ▪ La metida de pata le valió su derrota en las elecciones.

to be the **result of...** ser el resultado de... ▪ ser la secuela de... ➤ His thinness is the result of his illness. Su delgadez es la secuela de su enfermedad.

to **resume one's studies** ▪ to take up one's studies again retomar los estudios ▪ reanudar los estudios

retail price ▪ store price precio al por menor ▪ precio de venta al pública ▪ PVP

retail sales venta al por menor

to **retake an exam** volver a hacer un examen ▪ hacer un examen una segunda vez

retirement income renta vitalicia ▪ (renta de) jubilación

retirement pension ▪ pension ▪ annuity *la* pensión de jubilación

to **retrace one's steps** ▪ to go back over one's steps desandar el camino ▪ deshacer el camino ▪ desandar sus pasos ▪ volver sobre sus pasos ➤ By looking at this map, we can retrace our steps today. Mirando este mapa, podemos desandar nuestros pasos hoy.

to **retract a concession** ▪ to withdraw a concession retractarse de una concesión

to **retract a confession** ▪ to take back a confession ▪ to withdraw a confession retractarse de una confesión

to **retract a statement** ▪ to retract an affirmation retractarse de una afirmación

to **retract an allegation** ▪ to withdraw an allegation retractarse de una acusación

to **retract claws** retraerse las garras

to **retract the landing gear** ▪ to put up the landing gear ▪ to raise the landing gear subir el tren de aterrizaje ▪ levantar el tren de aterrizaje

retractable landing gear *(aviación) el* tren de aterrizaje plegable ▪ tren de aterrizaje replegable ▪ tren de aterrizaje retractil

to **retrieve a document** *(computers)* ▪ to recover a document recuperar un documento ➤ Do you think you can retrieve the document? ¿Crees que puedes recuperar el documento?

to **return a book to the library** devolver un libro a la biblioteca

to **return a compliment** devolver un cumplido ➤ When I paid him the compliment, he returned it. Cuando le hice el cumplido, me lo devolvió.

to **return a favor** ▪ to repay a favor devolver un favor

to **return a greeting** ▪ to speak back corresponder a un saludo

to **return a telephone call** regresar una llamada ▪ devolver una llamada de teléfono ▪ retornar una llamada ➤ She didn't return my call. No regresó mi llamada.

to **return an invitation** ▪ to reciprocate an invitation devolver una invitación ➤ The dinner invitation was accepted but not returned. La invitación a cenar fue aceptada pero no devuelta.

to **return money 1.** to pay back money devolver dinero **2.** to refund money reembolsar dinero

return of inflation retorno de la inflación

return of the prodigal son retorno del hijo pródigo

return policy *(at a retail store)* política de devolución

to **return someone's call** ▪ to call someone back *(L. Am.)* regresar la llamada de alguien ▪ *(Sp.)* devolver la llamada de alguien

to **return something to someone** devolverle algo a alguien

to **return the favor** ▪ to return someone's favor devolverle el favor a alguien

to **return the serve** *(sports)* devolver el servicio

to **return to a place 1.** to come back to it volver a un lugar **2.** to go back to it volver a un lugar ➤ I want to keep this apartment and return to it in the summers. Quiero quedarme con este piso y volver a él en los veranos.

to **return to normal** ▪ to get back to normal volver a la normalidad ▪ normalizarse ▪ volver a su orden ▪ volver a su cauce ➤ Things gradually returned to normal. Gradualmente las cosas volvieron a la normalidad. ▪ Gradualmente las cosas se normalizaron. ▪ Gradualmente las cosas volvieron a su cauce. ▪ Gradualmente las cosas volvieron a su orden.

to **return to reality** volver a la realidad

to **return to the beginning** ▪ to go back to the beginning volver al comienzo ▪ volver al principio

to **return to the fold** volver al redil

to **return to the subject** ▪ to come back to the subject ▪ to get back to the subject volver al tema ▪ volver al asunto

return trip ▪ trip back viaje de vuelta ➤ The return trip was faster than the trip out. El viaje de vuelta fue más rápido que el de ida.

to **reveal one's age** ▪ to disclose one's age ▪ to show one's age revelar la (verdadera) edad de uno

to **reveal one's true nature** revelar la verdadera naturaleza de uno

to **revel in something** ▪ to delight in something ▪ to make merry (by doing something) deleitarse en algo ▪ regocijarse en algo ▪ gozar de algo

to **reverse a decision** *(law)* ▪ to overrule a decision ▪ to strike down a decision derogar una decisión ➤ The Supreme Court reversed the decision of the lower court. La Corte Suprema derogó la decisión de la corte baja.

reverse psychology psicología inversa ▪ psicología revertida ➤ Mary Poppins used reverse psychology to get the kids to go to sleep. Mary Poppins usó psicología inversa para conseguir que los niños se fueran a dormir.

to **reverse the damage resulting from...** ▪ to reverse the damage caused by... revertir el daño resultante de...

to **reverse the negative** darle la vuelta al negativo ➤ This picture is printed backwards. They reversed the negative. La foto está impresa al revés. Le han dado la vuelta al negativo.

to **reverse the order 1.** *(command)* to rescind the order rescindir la orden **2.** *(sequence)* to reverse the sequence cambiar el orden en sentido contrario

reverse thread ▪ left-handed thread rosca al revés ▪ rosca a izquierdas ➤ You tighten a reverse thread counterclockwise. La rosca al revés se aprieta a la izquierda. ➤ Careful, that screw has a left-handed thread! ▪ Careful, that screw has a reverse thread. ¡Cuidado!, ese tornillo va a izquierdas.

to **review the lesson** repasar la lección

to **review the troops** pasar revista a las tropas ▪ revistar a las tropas

to **revise a contract** ▪ to modify a contract ▪ to change a contract modificar un contrato ▪ revisar un contrato ▪ alterar un contrato ▪ remodelar un contrato

revival of interest in... recuperación de interés en... ▪ renovado interés por ▪ renacimiento de

to **revive someone** reanimar a alguien ▪ resucitar a alguien

revolutions per minute ▪ RPM revoluciones por minuto ▪ RPM ▪ vueltas por minuto

to **revolve around 1.** to orbit darle la vuelta a ▪ girar alrededor de ▪ girar en torno a **2.** to be centered around girar en torno a ▪ girar alrededor de ➤ The Earth rotates on its axis and revolves around the sun. La Tierra rota en su eje y le da vuelta al sol. ▪ La Tierra rota en su eje y gira alrededor del sol. ▪ La tierra rota en su eje y gira en torno al sol. ➤ García Márquez' story revolves around Florentino Ariza. El cuento de García Márquez gira en torno a Florentino Ariza. ▪ El cuento de García Márquez gira alrededor de Florentino Ariza.

to **reward someone handsomely** recompensar a alguien con generosidad ▪ recompensar a alguien generosamente

to **rewind a tape** rebobinar una cinta ➤ You forgot to rewind the video. Te olvidaste de rebobinar el video.

rhetorical question pregunta retórica

rhyme scheme esquema métrico ➤ The rhyme scheme is ABBA. El esquema métrico es ABBA.

rib cage caja torácica

rib steak *el* entrecot

rich food ▪ food high in fat and sugar comida fuerte ➤ These desserts are too rich for my diet. Estos postres son muy fuertes para mi régimen.

to be **rich in content** ser rico en contenido

to be **rich in meaning** ser rico en significado ➤ Shakespeare's plays are rich in meaning. Las obras de Shakespeare son ricas en significado.

rich neighborhood ▪ well-to-do neighborhood barrio rico ▪ barrio de bien ▪ barrio pudiente

rich people ▪ wealthy people ▪ the rich gente rica ▪ gente pudiente ▪ gente de bien ▪ los ricos

richly decorated ▪ luxuriously decorated ▪ elaborately decorated ▪ finely decorated decorado a todo lujo ▪ decorado ricamente

to be **richly rewarded** ser generosamente recompensado

to be **riddled with** *(problems, flaws, corruption, etc.)* ▪ to be fraught with estar atestado de ▪ estar lleno de

to be **riddled with bullets** estar acribillado a balazos ▪ estar cosido a balazos

to **ride a bicycle** montar en bicicleta ➤ Our little girl is learning (how) to ride a bicycle. Nuestra niña está aprendiendo a montar en bicicleta.

to **ride a horse** ▪ to ride horseback montar a caballo ▪ cabalgar

to **ride backwards** *(on a train or bus)* ir de espaldas ▪ sentarse de espaldas ➤ I don't like to ride backwards on a train. On a long trip it sometimes makes me nauseated. No me gusta ir de espaldas en el tren. En los viajes largos a veces me marea.

to **ride hard** cabalgar contra viento y marea

to **ride herd on someone** dar caña a alguien ➤ The new department head is really riding herd on the teaching assistants. El nuevo jefe del departamento está dando caña a los asistentes de profesores.

to **ride horseback** ▪ to ride a horse montar a caballo ▪ cabalgar

to **ride in a car** montar en coche ➤ Have you ever ridden in a Rolls-Royce? ¿Has montado alguna vez en un Rolls-Royce?

to **ride in a helicopter** montar en un helicóptero

to **ride in an airplane** ▪ to fly in an airplane montar en avioneta ➤ That airplane is not the one I rode in. ▪ That airplane is not the one I flew in. Ésa no es la avioneta en la que yo monté.

Ride of the Valkyries *(Wagner composition)* La cabalgata de las Walkyrias

to **ride off into the sunset** perderse en el horizonte ➤ At the end of the Western (movie), the hero rides off into the sunset. Al final de la película de vaqueros, el héroe se pierde en el horizonte.

to **ride on a camel, donkey, elephant, etc.** ir montado en camello, burro, elefante, etc.

to **ride on a sled** ▪ to sleigh ride ▪ to go sleigh riding ▪ to go sledding montar en trineo ➤ I like to ride on a sled. ▪ I like to sleigh ride. ▪ I like to go sleigh riding. ▪ I like to go sledding. Me gusta montar en trineo. ➤ Our dog likes to ride on the sled. A nuestro perro le gusta que le montemos en el trineo.

to **ride out the storm** ▪ to weather the storm capear la tormenta ▪ capear el temporal ▪ aguantar el temporal ▪ aguantar el chubasco

to **ride shotgun** *(coll.)* ir en el asiento del copiloto

to **ride sidesaddle** cabalgar a mujeriegas

to **ride the clutch** conducir con el pie en el embrague ▪ dejar medio pisado el embrague

to **ride the horn** to lean on the horn pegarse al claxon ▪ quedarse pegado al claxon ▪ pitar como (un) loco

to **ride the waves** surcar las olas

ridiculous idea ▪ harebrained idea ▪ absurd idea idea ridícula ▪ idea peregrina ▪ idea más peregrina ▪ idea absurda ➤ What a ridiculous idea! ¡Qué idea (más) peregrina!

ridiculous situation situación ridícula ▪ situación absurda ▪ situación muy caricaturesca

riding boots: to wear ~ ▪ to have on riding boots ▪ to have riding boots on llevar botas de montar

to be **riding high** ser la bomba ▪ estar en la onda ➤ We're riding high! ¡Somos la bomba! ▪ Estamos en la onda.

to be **riding on** ▪ to depend on irle mucho en ▪ depender mucho en ➤ A lot is riding on this project. Nos va mucho en este proyecto. ▪ Mucho depende de este proyecto.

rifle range ▪ firing range campo de tiro

to **rig the election** apañar la elección ▪ amañar la elección ▪ falsificar la elección *("General election" is expressed in Spanish by making the noun plural: "las elecciones.")*

right! ¡efectivamente! ▪ ¡claro que sí! ▪ ¡eso es!

to **right a wrong** enmendar una injusticia ▪ hacer justicia de un injusticia

right about now ▪ around this time alrededor de esta hora ▪ sobre esta hora ▪ en cualquier momento

right across from where... ▪ just opposite where... justo frente a donde... ▪ justo enfrente a donde...

to be **right across the street** estar justo enfrente ▪ estar justo al otro lado de la calle

right across the street: to live ~ vivir justo al otro lado de la calle ▪ vivir justo enfrente ➤ I live right across the street. Vivo justo al otro lado de la calle.

to be **right across the street from...** estar justo enfrente de... ▪ estar justo al otro lado de la calle ➤ *(cell phone caller)* I'm right across the street from your place. Estoy justo enfrente de tu casa.

right across the street from...: to live ~ ▪ to live directly across the street from... vivir justo enfrente de... ➤ I live right across the street (from the university hospital). Vivo justo enfrente del hospital universitario.

right after ▪ shortly after justo después de ▪ a raíz de ▪ a partir de ▪ luego de ▪ a renglón seguido ▪ nada más ▪ inmediatamente después de ➤ The European stock markets benefitted by this rebound, which began right after the session opened. Las bolsas europeas se vieron beneficiadas por este rebote, iniciado nada más abrir la sesión. ➤ Right after takeoff, the airplane went down after losing an engine. Nada más despegar, el avión se desplomó tras perder un motor.

right after that ▪ right afterwards ▪ immediately afterwards justo después de eso ▪ a renglón seguido ➤ He had an argument with his wife and, right after that, left the house. Discutió con su mujer y, a renglón seguido, se marchó de casa.

right afterwards ▪ immediately afterwards ▪ right after that justo después ▪ inmediatamente después ▪ a renglón seguido

right amount of cantidad correcta de ▪ cantidad adecuada de

right and wrong: to know the difference between ~ ▪ to know right from wrong saber la diferencia entre el bien y el mal ▪ ser capaz de distinguir el bien del mal ➤ To stand trial, he must be judged to know the difference between right and wrong. Para poder ser juzgado, se debe comprobar que él es capaz de distinguir el bien del mal.

to be the **right approach (to)...** ▪ to be the right way to go about doing something ser el método apropiado para... ▪ ser el enfoque correcto (para...) ▪ ser la politica correcta (para...)

right arm: to be someone's ~ ▪ to be someone's right-hand man ser el brazo derecho de alguien

right ascension *(astronomy)* ascensión recta

right at the end ▪ at the very end justo al final ➤ Add the chopped green pepper right at the end. ▪ Add the chopped green pepper at the very end. Añade el pimiento verde picado justo al final.

right away enseguida ▪ ahora mismo ▪ a toda prisa ▪ *(Chi.)* al tiro

to be **right back** ▪ to be back in a second ▪ to be back in a minute ▪ to be back in a jiffy volver en seguida ▪ regresar en seguida ▪ volver en un periquete

right before... ▪ just before... **1.** *(preceding a noun)* justo antes de... ▪ *(preceding a verb)* justo antes de que... ➤ Right before that, I heard the screeching of the brakes. Justo antes de eso, oí el chirrido de los frenos.

right by ▪ right next to justo al lado de ▪ justo a la altura de ▪ justo con ▪ a dos pasos de ▪ a cuatro pasos de ➤ I live right by the grocery store. Vivo justo a la altura de la tienda de comestibles. ➤ The store is right by the Estrecho metro entrance. La tienda está justo a la altura de la boca de metro Estrecho. ➤ It's on the corner right by the Plaza San Miguel. Queda justo en la esquina con la Plaza San Miguel. ➤ It's right by where I live. ▪ It's just steps away from where I live. ▪ It's just out the door from where I live. Está justo al lado de donde vivo. ▪ Está a dos pasos de donde vivo. ▪ Está muy cerca de donde vivo.

to **right click on** picar con el botón derecho en ▪ cliquear con el botón derecho en ▪ hacer un clic con el botón derecho en

right decision ▪ correct decision decisión acertada ▪ decisión correcta

to be **right down the street from** ▪ to be just down the street from estar justo calle abajo de aquí ▪ estar situado muy cerca calle abajo de aquí ▪ estar a dos pasos de ▪ estar muy cerca de ➤ It's right down the street from where I live. Está a dos pasos de donde vivo. ▪ Está muy cerca de donde vivo.

right down to the last detail hasta el último detalle

to be **right for** ser adecuado(-a) para ▪ darse para ➤ *(news item)* Sharon says conditions are right for coming to a historic agreement with the Palestinians. Sharon dice que se dan las condiciones para llegar a su "acuerdo histórico" con los palestinos.

right from the start justo desde el principio

right-hand man: to be someone's ~ ▪ to be someone's right arm ser la mano derecha de alguien ▪ ser el brazo derecho de alguien

to be **right-handed** ser diestro(-a)

right-handed person diestro(-a)

to be **right here** estar justo aquí ▪ estar aquí mismo ➤ On the map, we're right here. En el plano estamos justo aquí. ▪ En el plano estamos aquí mismo.

right hook *(boxing)* gancho de derecho

right in the face justo en la cara ▪ de lleno en la cara

right in the middle justo en medio

right in the middle of the performance 1. *(theatrical)* en plena obra ▪ (justo) en el medio de la obra **2.** *(musical)* en plena función ▪ (justo) en el medio de la función

right in the middle of the street (justo) en el medio de la calle ▪ en plena calle

right near ▪ very near ▪ very close to muy cerca de ➤ I live right near San Pablo's (Church). Vivo muy cerca de la iglesia de San Pablo.

to be **right nearby** estar a dos pasos ▪ estar muy cerca ➤ The hardware store is right nearby. La ferretería está muy cerca. ▪ La ferretería está a dos pasos.

right now 1. immediately ahora mismo ▪ *(Mex.)* ahorita **2.** at this time en estos momentos ▪ ahora **3.** *(emphatic)* this minute! ¡ya mismo! ▪ ¡en este instante! ▪ ¡ya pronto! **4.** at this moment ahora ➤ I'll do it right now. Lo haré ahora mismo. ➤ Anything can happen in my life right now. Cualquier cosa puede suceder en mi vida en estos momentos. ➤ I'm in Stockholm on vacation right now. Ahora estoy en Estocolmo de vacaciones. ➤ Come here right now! ▪ Come here this minute! ¡Ven ya mismo! ▪ ¡Ven en este instante! ▪ ¡Ven ahora mismo! ➤ I don't have time right now. Ahora no tengo tiempo. ▪ Ahora no me da tiempo.

to be **right of center (politically)** ser de derechas ➤ He's a little right of center. Es un poco de derechas.

right of way derecho de paso ▪ derecho de tránsito ▪ preferencia de paso

right of way: to have the ~ ▪ (for) the right of way to favor someone tener el derecho de paso ▪ ser la preferencia de paso de alguien ➤ *(news item)* The traffic light was green in both directions, but the right of way favored the concrete truck. Los semáforos de ambos sentidos estaban en verde, pero la preferencia de paso era de la hormigonera.

right off ▪ at once al primer envite ▪ en seguida

right off: to cut something ~ cortar algo de un tajo ➤ The swordsman cut the dragon's head right off. El espadachín cortó la cabeza del dragón de un tajo.

right off the bat de buenas a primeras ▪ de entrada

right on! 1. well said! ¡y tú que lo digas! ▪ ¡muy bien dicho! ▪ ¡así se habla! **2.** well done! ¡bien hecho!

to be **right on the corner** estar en la mera esquina ▪ quedar en la mera esquina ➤ The bank is right on the corner. El banco está en la mera esquina. ▪ El banco queda en la mera esquina.

to be **right on time 1.** *(person)* ser puntual **2.** *(trains, etc.)* pasar a su hora ▪ ser puntual ➤ She's always on time. Ella siempre es puntual. ➤ The Spanish trains are right on time. Los trenes españoles siempre pasan a su hora. ▪ Los trenes españoles son puntuales.

the **right one** *(to marry, etc.)* el adecuado ▪ la adecuada

right or wrong con razón o sin ella

right person 1. person best suited persona adecuada ▪ persona ad hoc **2.** person sought persona que se busca

right person for the job persona idónea para el cargo ▪ persona idónea para el trabajo ▪ persona idónea para el puesto

right place 1. correct place lugar correcto **2.** suitable place lugar adecuado ➤ You've come to the right place. Has venido al lugar correcto. ➤ We've found the right place to open our restaurant. Hemos encontrado el lugar adecuado para abrir nuestro restaurante.

right side out: to turn a garment ~ poner una prenda del derecho ▪ poner una prenda bien ➤ Turn it right side out. *(sock)* Pónlo del derecho. ▪ *(T-shirt)* Pónla del derecho.

right side up del derecho ➤ Turn the box right side up before you open it. Pon la caja del derecho.

right smack in...: to hit someone ~ ▪ to hit someone square in... ▪ to strike someone right smack in... ▪ to strike someone square in... alcanzar a alguien de lleno en... ▪ dar a alguien de lleno en... ➤ The pie hit him right smack in the face. ▪ The pie hit him square in the face. ▪ The pie struck him right smack in the face. ▪ The pie struck him square in the face. El pastel lo alcanzó de lleno en la cara. ▪ El pastel lo dio de lleno en la cara. ▪ *(Sp., leísmo)* El pastel le alcanzó de lleno en la cara. El pastel le dio de lleno en la cara.

to **right the aircraft** enderezar la aeronave

right there allí mismo ▪ ahí ▪ justo ahí ➤ Sit right there! ¡Siéntate ahí! ▪ Siéntate ahí mismo. ▪ Siéntate allí mismo.

right thing: to do the ~ hacer lo correcto ▪ hacer lo que uno debe

right thing to do lo correcto ➤ It's the right thing to do. Es lo correcto.

right through someone: to look a hole ~ echarle a alguien una mirada penetrante ➤ The principal looked a hole right through the pupil. El director le echó al alumno una mirada penetrante.

right time: at the ~ en el momento preciso ▪ el momento adecuado ▪ en el momento justo

right time: it's not the ~ ▪ this is not the right time no es el momento para tratar de eso ▪ *(Sp., coll.)* no está el patio para bollos ▪ no está el horno para bollos

to be **right to do something** hacer bien haciéndo algo ➤ You were right to leave. Hiciste bien marchándote.

right to know derecho a saber

right to one's face derecho a la cara de uno

right track: to be on the ~ estar bien encaminado ▪ ir por buen camino ➤ You're on the right track. *(tú)* Vas por el buen camino. ▪ *(usted)* Va por el buen camino.

right under ▪ right underneath justo debajo ▪ justo debajo de

right under one's nose: to do something ~ hacer algo en las propias barbas de alguien

right up to the end ▪ up to the very end ▪ until the very end hasta el fin del final ➤ He died at (age) ninety-five and was lucid and not deaf right up to the end. Se murió con noventa y cinco años y estuvo lúcido y de buen oído hasta el fin (del final).

right you are! ▪ you're exactly right! ¡estás en lo cierto! ▪ ¡tienes razón! ▪ ¡tienes toda la razón!

rightly so con razón ▪ con toda razón

rigor mortis *el* rigor mortis

rim of a coin ▪ edge of a coin canto de una moneda

to **ring a bell 1.** to sound a bell sonar un timbre **2.** *(figurative)* to sound familiar sonarle ➤ It rings a bell. ▪ It sounds familiar. Me suena. ➤ It does ring a bell. Sí me suena. ➤ Has the bell rung? ¿Ha sonado el timbre? ➤ What time does the bell ring? ¿A qué hora suena el timbre?

ring finger ▪ fourth finger dedo anular

to **ring once and hang up** ▪ to let it ring once and hang up hacer una llamada perdida

to **ring the doorbell and run** tocar el timbre y echarse a correr ▪ *(Arg.)* jugar al rin-raje

to **ring true to one** sonar cierto a uno ▪ sonar verdadero a uno

to **ring up a sale** cobrar ➤ Can you ring me up at this register? ¿Me cobra en esta caja registradora? ▪ ¿Me cobra en esta caja? ➤ Can you ring it up for me? ¿Me puede cobrar esto? ➤ Have you already rung it up? ¿Ya me lo ha cobrado?

ringing voice voz estentórea

rings of Saturn anillos de Saturno

riot police policía antidisturbia ▪ policía antimotines

rip cord *(of a parachute)* cuerda de apertura

rip-off timo

to **rip off someone** ▪ to rip someone off ▪ to con someone timar a alguien ▪ vender un buzón a alguien ▪ embromar a alguien

to **rip one's clothing** ▪ to tear one's clothing rompérsele la ropa ▪ rasgársele la ropa ➤ Oops, I ripped my shirt. ▪ Oops, I tore my shirt. ¡Anda! ¡Se me ha roto la camisa! ▪ ¡Anda! ¡Se me rasgó la camisa!

to **rip something to shreds** ▪ to tear something to shreds ▪ to tear something to pieces hacer trizas de algo ▪ descuartizar algo

ripple effect: to have a ~ ▪ to produce a ripple effect ▪ to cause a ripple effect tener un efecto mimético ▪ provocar un efecto mimético ▪ causar un efecto mimético ➤ The civil unrest in Haiti is having a ripple effect in Venezuela. La crispación civil en Haiti está teniendo un efecto mimético en Venezuela.

to **rise above a certain level** crecer por encima... ▪ situarse por encima de...

to **rise and set** salir y ponerse ➤ The sun rises today (August seventh) at 6:30 a.m. and sets at 8:37 p.m. Hoy (el siete de agosto) el sol sale a las 6:30 y se pone a las 20:37.

to **rise from the ashes** levantarse de su cenizas

to **rise from the dead** levantarse de entre los muertos

to **rise higher and higher** subir cada vez más alto

rise in inflation el alza de la inflación ▪ subida de la inflación

rise in unemployment ▪ increase in unemployment incremento del desempleo ▪ subida del desempleo ▪ *(Spain)* subida del paro

to **rise like a phoenix from the ashes** emerger como el ave fénix de las cenizas

rise of Lincoln subida de Lincoln

rise of totalitarianism *el* auge de totalitarismo

to **rise through the ranks to become something 1.** ascender de algo a algo **2.** *(in the military)* ascender de rango ▪ subir de categoría ➤ He rose through the ranks from errand boy to president of the company. Ascendió de mozo de carga a presidente de la compañía ➤ He rose through the ranks from private to general. Ascendió de rango de soldado raso a general. ▪ Subió de categoría de soldado raso a general.

rise to stardom escalada al estrellato

to **rise to stardom** alcanzar el estrellato

to **rise to the occasion** crecerse con las circunstancias ▪ estar a la altura de las circunstancias ▪ estar al nivel de las circunstancias

to **rise to the presidency** subir a la presidencia ▪ alcanzar la presidencia ➤ Lincoln rose from relative obscurity to the presidency in two years. Lincoln subió de una relativa osuridad a la presidencia en dos años.

to **rise to the status of...** erigirse en... ➤ In the nineteenth century, the United States rose to the status of a world power. En el siglo diecinueve, los Estados Unidos se erigió en una potencia mundial.

to **rise up against...** alzarse contra... ➤ *(headline)* The Pashtun tribes rise up against the Taliban Los tribus pastunes se alzan contra los talibanes

to **rise up in arms** alzarse en armas

to **rise up into the air** elevarse por los aires

rising cost of costo creciente de

rising costs costos crecientes ▪ *(Sp., referring to public expenditures) los* costes crecientes

rising expectations expectativas crecientes ▪ crecientes expectativas

rising of a river ▪ swelling of a river crecida de un río

rising of a stream crecida de un arroyo

rising sun *el* sol naciente

to **risk being...** exponerse a ser... ➤ Elvis sighters risk being labeled insane. Los que dicen ver a Elvis vivo se exponen a ser tildados de dementes.

to **risk everything** jugárselo todo ▪ jugarse hasta la camisa ▪ jugarse el tipo

to **risk having to do something** arriesgarse a tener que hacer algo ▪ exponerse a tener que hacer algo ➤ *(news item)* At present, U.S. citizens who travel to Cuba without permission risk having to pay a fine (of) between $7,500 and $8,000. En estos momentos, los ciudadanos estadounidenses que viajen a Cuba sin permiso se exponen a tener que pagar entre 7.500 y 8.000 dólares de multa.

to **risk it** arriesgarse ➤ Let's risk it. Vamos a arriesgarnos.

to **risk one's life** jugarse la vida ▪ *(coll.)* jugarse el pellejo

to **risk one's neck** ▪ to risk one's life jugarse el pellejo ▪ jugarse la vida

risks associated with riesgos asociados con ▪ riesgos derivados de

river forks 1. *(noun phrase) las* bifurcaciones del río **2.** *(verb phrase)* río se bifurca

river overflowed its banks río se desbordó

river rafting: to go ~ hacer canotaje ▪ hacer rafting

riverbank orilla del río

the **road forks** la calle se bifurca ▪ el camino se bifurca ▪ se bifurca la calle ▪ se bifurca el camino ➤ Where the road forks, one fork leads to Salamanca, and the other (fork leads) to Valladolid. Donde la calle se bifurca, una ramificación lleva a Salamanca, y la otra a Valladolid.

Roadmap to Peace *(Middle East peace process)* Hoja de ruta hacia la paz

roar of the crowd *el* clamor de la multitud

to **rob a bank** ▪ to commit a bank robbery atracar un banco ▪ robar un banco

to **rob Peter to pay Paul** desnudar a un santo para vestir a otro

rock band banda de rock ➤ In Valladolid, there's a rock band called "Platero y Tú." En Valladolid hay una banda de rock llamada "Platero y Tú".

rock climbing escalada en rocas ▪ alpinismo ▪ andinismo

rock climbing: to go ~ escalar rocas ▪ hacer alpinismo ▪ *(in the Andes)* hacer andinismo

to **rock the boat** ▪ to make waves hacer olas

rocking horse caballito (de madera)

Rocky Mountains Montañas Rocosas

rocky ravine ▪ rocky gorge desfiladero rocoso

to **roll heads** rodar cabezas ▪ cortar cabezas ➤ Heads are going to roll. Van a rodar cabezas.

roll of film *el* carrete ▪ rollo de película

roll of stamps tira de timbres ▪ tira de estampillas ▪ tira de sellos *(literally a "strip" of stamps)*

to **roll one's eyes** virar los ojos ▪ poner los ojos en blanco

to **roll out the red carpet for someone** extender la alfombra roja para alguien

to **roll over and over** *(vehicle)* ▪ to roll over repeatedly dar vueltas de campana ▪ volcar de campana ▪ dar vuelcos de campana

to **roll over and play dead** darse la media vuelta y hacerse el muerto

to **roll over repeatedly** *(vehicle)* ▪ to roll over and over volcar de campana ▪ dar vuelcos de campana

to **roll over something** rodar sobre algo

to **roll up one's sleeves 1.** remangarse la camisa ▪ subirse las mangas ▪ arremangarse la camisa **2.** *(figurative, with "and get to work")* ponerse las pilas (y darle duro al trabajo) ➤ *(doctor to patient)* Roll up your sleeve. Remángate la camisa. ▪ Súbete la manga. ➤ Let's roll up our sleeves and get to work. Vamos a ponernos las pilas y darle duro al trabajo.

rolled map *(geographic or political map)* mapa enrollado (mural) ▪ *(street map)* plano enrollado

rolled, not folded enrollado, no doblado ▪ enrollado, no plegado ➤ I want a map that is rolled, not folded, suitable for mounting or framing. Quiero un mapa enrollado, no doblado, apto para montar o encuadrar. ▪ Quiero un mapa enrollado, no plegado, apto para montar o encuadrar. ▪ Quiero un mapa en la forma de un poster, apto para montar o encuadrar.

roller coaster montaña rusa

rolling blackouts apagones programados

rolling ghetto ▪ beat-up car ▪ rattletrap (of a car) ▪ bucket of bolts tartana ▪ cascajo ▪ tartajo

to be **rolling in dough** rebosar en dinero ▪ nadar en dinero ▪ nadar en abundancia

rolling pin rodillo

a **rolling stone gathers no moss** piedra movediza nunca moho cobija

Rome wasn't built in a day Zamora no se ganó en una hora

roof over one's head cubierta... ▪ tejado...

room and board pensión completa

room enough for both of us sitio suficiente para nosotros dos ▪ sitio suficiente para ambos de nosotros

room for: to leave ~ dejar espacio para ▪ dejar hueco para

room for rent se alquila habitación ▪ se arrienda habitación

room temperature: at ~ a temperatura ambiente ▪ *(unheated)* al tiempo ▪ *(Sp.)* del tiempo ➤ The medicine should be stored at room temperature. La medicina debería guardarse a temperatura ambiente. ➤ Would you like the taco riojano heated or at room temperature. ¿Quieres el taco riojano caliente o del tiempo?

room to criticize: not to have ~ no tener lugar para criticar ➤ I don't think they have much room to criticize. ▪ I don't think they have any room to criticize. No tienen porque criticar. ▪ No tienen el derecho de criticar.

to **root out corruption** cortar de raíz la corrupción ▪ sacar de raíz la corrupción

to **rope someone into doing something** ponérselo a huevo ➤ She roped him into it. Ella se lo puso a huevo. ➤ They roped me into it. Me lo pusieron a huevo.

rosy-cheeked rubicundo

to **rotate crops** cultivar (cosechas) en rotación ▪ alternar cultivos

to **rotate on its axis** rotar en su eje ▪ rotar sobre su eje ▪ girar sobre su eje ▪ girar en torno a su eje ➤ The Earth rotates on its axis and revolves around the sun. La Tierra rota en su eje y da vueltas alrededor del sol. ▪ La Tierra gira sobre su eje y da vueltas alrededor del sol.

rotgut wine ▪ ripple vinazo ▪ vino peleón

to be **rotten to the core** estar podrido hasta la médula

rough air aire revuelto ▪ viento racheado ➤ The air's a little rough today. El aire está un poco revuelto hoy.

rough cloth ▪ coarse cloth tela burda ▪ paño burdo

rough crowd ▪ tough crowd chusma ➤ He hangs out with a rough crowd. Él se junta con la chusma. ▪ Él se mete con la chusma.

rough draft borrador

rough idea idea tosca ▪ idea más o menos ▪ *(literary)* tosca idea

to be **rough on the hands** ▪ to be rough on one's hands ajar las manos ▪ estropear las manos ➤ Repeated exposure to solvents is rough on your hands. Una exposición repetida a disolventes aja las manos. ▪ Una exposición repetida a disolventes estropea las manos.

rough road ahead 1. bumpy road ahead ▪ rocky road ahead carretera llena de baches ▪ camino pedregoso **2.** *(figurative)* difficult time ahead camino difícil ➤ There's a rough road (up) ahead, so drive more slowly. Hay una carretera llena de baches al frente, así que conduce más lento. ➤ The western democracies have a rough road ahead in the struggle against terrorism. ▪ The western democracies have a rocky road ahead in the struggle against terrorism. Las democracias occidentales tienen un difícil camino por delante en la lucha contra el terrorismo.

rough sea mar embravecido ▪ mar agitado ▪ mar revuelto

rough surface superficie áspera

rough voice voz áspera

to **round a curve** tomar una curva ➤ The metro drivers take a certain pleasure in rounding the curve north of Cuatro Caminos at high speed. Los conductores del metro sienten cierto placer al tomar la curva norte de Cuatro Caminos a alta velocidad.

round and round: to go ~ girar y girar ▪ dar vueltas y vueltas ➤ The merry-go-round goes round and round. El tiovivo gira y gira. ▪ La calecita gira y gira. ▪ El tiovivo da vueltas y vueltas. ▪ La calecita da vueltas y vueltas.

round and round: to turn (oneself) ~ ▪ to spin (oneself) round and round darse vueltas y vueltas (uno mismo)

round and round: to turn someone ~ ▪ to spin someone round and round darle vueltas y vueltas a alguien ▪ girar y girar a alguien ➤ Before you swing at the piñata, they blindfold you and turn you round and round. Antes de darle a la piñata, te vendan los ojos y te dan vueltas y vueltas.

round of applause: to give someone a ~ un aplauso para alguien ▪ darle un aplauso a alguien ➤ Let's give the kitchen crew a round of applause. Un aplauso para el personal de cocina. ➤ Let's give them a round of applause. Démosles un aplauso.

to **round off a number** redondear un número ➤ Pi rounded off to the nearest hundredth is 3.14, and to the nearest ten thousandth, 3.1416. ▪ Pi rounded off to two decimal places is 3.14, and to four decimal places, 3.1416. Pi redondeado al segundo decimal es 3,14, y al cuarto decimal, 3,1416. *(Spanish speakers rarely say, "a la centena más cercana" or "al ciento más cercano," to the nearest hundredth, or "a la milena más cercana" or "al mil más cercano," to the nearest thousandth, preferring "al segundo decimal," to two decimal places, or "al tercer decimal," to three decimal places, and so on.)*

round-trip de ida y vuelta ➤ The ticket was about four hundred dollars round-trip. ▪ The round-trip ticket was about four hundred dollars. El billete fue más o menos cuatrocientos dólares de ida y vuelta.

round-trip fare *el* pasaje de ida y vuelta

round-trip ticket el billete de ida y vuelta

to **round up some volunteers** ▪ to get together some volunteers reunir a unos voluntarios

rounded tablespoon cucharada colmada

rounded teaspoon cuchara colmada

routine checkup revisión rutinaria

row houses ▪ townhouses casas adosadas ▪ chalets adosados

royal pain rollo ➤ The professor's tests are a royal pain. Los exámenes del profesor son un rollo.

royal "we" plural mayestático ➤ So this is Kate! I've heard a lot about you! ¡La famosa Kate! Hemos oído hablar mucho de ti! *(Spanish prefers the royal "we.")*

R.S.V.P. ▪ Respondez s'il vous plaît ▪ the favor of a reply is requested SRC ▪ se ruega contestación

to **rub in an ointment** ▪ to rub an ointment in ▪ to massage in an ointment ▪ to massage an ointment in aplicar un ungüento frotando ▪ aplicar una pomada frotando to **rub it in** 1. to massage it in aplicarlo(-a) frotando 2. to reiterate something hurtful refregárselo por la nariz ▪ refregárselo por las narices

to **rub off on someone** contagiársele a alguien ▪ pegársele a alguien ➤ My mother's Christmas spirit rubbed off on me. El espíritu navideño de mi madre se me pegó. ▪ El espíritu navideño de mi madre se me contagió. ▪ Mi madre me contagió su espíritu navideño. ➤ It might rub off on you. A ver si se te pega. ➤ Be careful with the newspaper because the ink might rub off on you. Ten cuidado con el periódico porque la tinta se te pega. ▪ Ten cuidado con el periódico porque la tinta te mancha.

to **rub one's eyes** frotarse lo ojos

to **rub one's hands** frotarse las manos

to **rub salt into a wound** poner el dedo en la llaga ▪ ponerle sal a la herida

to **rub shoulders with the rich and famous** codearse con gente rica y famosa *(literally "to rub elbows with")*

to **rub someone the wrong way** venirle a contrapelo a alguien ➤ Whining politicians rub me the wrong way. Los políticos quejicas me vienen a contrapelo.

rubber check *el* talón sin fondos

to **rubber-stamp** firmar en blanco

rubber strip 1. *(soft rubber)* banda de goma ▪ franja de goma 2. *(hard rubber)* banda de caucho ▪ franja de caucho *("Caucho" is also the rubber in a tire.)*

ruckus: there was a ~ *(Mex.)* hubo un mitote ▪ *(Sp.)* hubo un tomate ▪ *(Arg.)* hubo un quilombo

ruddy cheeks mejillas rubicundas

ruddy complexion complexión rubicunda

ruddy sky ▪ red sky cielo rojizo

to be a **rude awakening** ser un despertar duro ▪ ser un despertar de gran sobresalto ➤ It was a rude awakening. Fue un despertar duro. ▪ Fue un despertar de gran sobresalto.

rude awakening: to have a ~ darse de bruces con la realidad

ruff: lace ~ gorguera de encaje *(The ruff is the round linen collar worn by Renaissance gentlemen and ladies; its style can be used to date some oil portraits.)*

rugged terrain terreno abrupto ▪ terreno quebrado ▪ terreno escabroso

to **ruin one's day** ▪ to cast a cloud on one's day arruinar el día de alguien ▪ dar a alguien el día

to **ruin someone's evening** darle la velada a alguien ▪ arruinar la velada a alguien

to **rule in a (court) case** declarar una decisión ▪ dictaminar en un caso ➤ *(news item)* The Canadian supreme court ruled yesterday that neither national nor international law permits Quebec to secede. El tribunal supremo de Canadá declaro ayer que ni el derecho nacional ni internacional permite la secesión de Quebec. ▪ El tribunal supremo de Canadá dictaminó ayer que ni el derecho nacional ni internacional permite la secesión de Quebec.

to **rule in favor of** dictaminar a favor de ▪ dar razón a

rule of a monarch ▪ reign of a monarch reinado de un(a) monarca

rule of fear voto del miedo ➤ *(titular)* Conservatives and socialists join forces against the rule of fear in País Vasco. Conservadores y socialistas unen fuerzas contra el voto del miedo en Euskadi.

to **rule out** descartar la posibilidad de ▪ excluir la posibilidad de ▪ rechazar ➤ *(headline)* British government rules out building more nuclear plants El gobierno británico rechaza construir más centros nucleares

to **rule out a hypothesis** descartar una hipótesis

to **rule out an idea** ▪ to rule an idea out ▪ to abandon an idea ▪ to reject an idea descartar una idea

to **rule out something** ▪ to rule something out descartar algo ➤ I ruled it out. Lo descarté.

to **rule out the possibility that...** descartar la posibilidad de que...

rule specifies that... reglamento determina que...

to **rule that a law is unconstitutional** ▪ to declare a law unconstitutional derogar por inconstitucional una ley ▪ derogar una ley por inconstitucional

to **rule the roost** dirigir el cotarro ▪ manejar el tinglado ▪ llevar la voz cantante ▪ llevar la batuta

to **rule with an iron fist** regir con mano dura

rules of engagement *(military)* reglas de compromiso

the **rules of the game** las reglas del juego

ruling class *la* clase reinante ▪ clase dirigente ▪ clase dominante

rum and Coke® *(with a squeeze of lime) el* Cuba libre ▪ *(Sp.) el* cubata

to **rummage through** hurgar en ▪ hurgar entre ▪ rebuscar en algo ▪ rebuscar entre ▪ registrar en ▪ registrar entre ➤ The thief rummaged through the drawers. El ladrón rebuscó en los cajones. ▪ El ladrón hurgó en los cajones. ▪ El ladrón registró en los cajones.

rumor has it that... ▪ the rumor is (going around) that... ▪ it's been going around that... ▪ the scuttlebutt is that... está circulando el rumor de que... ▪ corre el rumor de que... ▪ hay el rumor de que... ▪ corre la voz de que... ▪ circula el rumor de que... ▪ por lo que se rumorea

to **run a blockade** *(naval blockade)* violar un bloqueo

to **run a business** ▪ to operate a business llevar un negocio ▪ regentar un negocio ➤ The company that runs the airport... ▪ The company that operates the airport... La compañía que lleva el aeropuerto... ▪ La compañía que regenta el aeropuerto...

to **run a risk** correr un riesgo ▪ correr un peligro

to **run a risk of** correr un riesgo de

to **run after someone** correr detrás de alguien ▪ salir en persecución de alguien ▪ correr en pos de alguien

to **run after something** correr detrás de algo ▪ salir en persecución de algo ▪ correr en pos de algo

to **run aground** *(ship)* vararse ▪ quedar encallado

to **run all over town** ▪ to go all over town recorrerse la ciudad de punta en punta ▪ recorrerse la ciudad de cabo a rabo ▪ recorrerse la ciudad de un lado a otro

to **run an ad in the (news)paper** ▪ to put an ad in the newspaper anunciar en el periódico

to **run an article** publicar un artículo

to **run an errand** 1. hacer un mandado ▪ hacer una diligencia 2. *(for another person)* hacer un mandado ▪ hacer un recado

to **run around like a chicken with its head cut off** correr como un pollo sin cabeza ▪ *(off-color)* andar como calzón de puta (para arriba y abajo)

to **run (as a candidate) for** presentarse como candidato a ▪ postular(se) como candidato a

to **run as fast as one can** correr lo más rápido que uno puede ▪ correr lo más de prisa que uno pueda *(The first gives the sense of knowing one's limits, the second has the sense of trying to exceed one's limits.)*

to **run away and get married** ▪ to run off and get married ▪ to elope escaparse de casa para casarse ▪ fugarse de casa para casarse ➤ She ran away and got married when she was sixteen. Se escapó de casa para casarse cuando tenía dieciséis años. ▪ Se fugó de casa para casarse cuando tenía dieciséis años.

to **run away from home** escaparse de casa ▪ fugarse de casa ▪ huir de su casa ➤ He ran away from home when he was sixteen. Se escapó de casa cuando tenía dieciséis años. ▪ Se fugó de casa cuando tenía dieciséis años. ➤ He ran away from home to join the circus. Huyó de su casa para unirse al circo.

to be **run by** estar dirigido por ▪ lo dirige ➤ This foundation is run by a chairman and board of directors. La fundación está dirigida por un presidente y una junta directiva.

to be **run down** ▪ to be in run-down condition estar (muy) dejado ▪ estar bien dejado ▪ estar en la última lona ➤ This restaurant is run down. Este restaurante está dejado.

to **run down to a place** ▪ to run over to a place correr a un lugar ➤ I have to run down to the grocery store. Tengo que correr a la tienda (de abarrotes).

to **run downstairs** bajar corriendo ▪ bajar deprisa

to **run for cover** correr a refugiarse ▪ correr en busca de refugio

to **run for office** ▪ to run for public office postular para un cargo público ▪ presentarse para un cargo público ➤ When he ran for senator Cuando postuló para senador ➤ Do you think you'll run again for president? ¿Volverá a presentarse para la presidencia?

to **run for one's life** correr para salvar la vida ▪ correr para ponerse a salvo ▪ *(coll.)* correr para salvar el pellejo

to **run for profit** ▪ to operate for profit gestionar con ánimo de lucro

to **run from one place to another** **1.** to extend from one place to another correr de un lugar a otro **2.** to go back and forth hacer el recorrido entre dos lugares **2.** to run from pillar to post ir de la Ceca a la Meca (y a la Tortoleca) ▪ ir de Herodes a Pilato ➤ The Alaska pipeline runs from Alaska to the continental United States. El oleoducto de Alaska corre de Alaska a los Estados Unidos continentales. ➤ The bullet train runs from Madrid to Seville. ▪ El tren de alta velocidad hace el recorrido de Madrid a Sevilla.

to **run headlong into** darse de narices con ▪ chocarse de narices con ▪ darse precipitadamente con ➤ I ran headlong into a nest of bees. Me di de narices con una colmena de abejas. ▪ Me choqué de narices con una colmena de abejas.

run in one's stocking: to have a ~ tener una carrera en la media ▪ *(L. Am.)* corrérsele la media

to **run in the family** venir de familia ▪ venir en la familia ▪ ser de familia ➤ Blood disorders run in her family. Los trastornos de sangre vienen de familia.

to **run into opposition** to encounter opposition tropezar con una oposición ➤ Clinton's bill to detect money laundering ran into strong opposition in the Senate Banking Committee. El proyecto de ley de Clinton para detectar el lavado de dinero tropezó con una fuerte oposición en el Comité Bancario del Senado.

to **run into problems** tropezar con problemas

to **run into someone** **1.** to cross paths with someone encontrarse con alguien ▪ cruzarse con alguien **2.** to collide with someone chocar con alguien

to **run into something** ▪ to collide with something darse con algo ▪ darse contra algo ▪ chocar con algo ▪ estrellarse contra algo ▪ colisionar con algo ➤ He ran into a post and got a black eye. Se dio con un poste y se amoratό el ojo.

to **run its course** *(illness, etc.)* llevar su curso

to **run laps** correr vueltas ➤ We have to run two laps around the track. Tenemos que correr dos vueltas alrededor de la pista.

run-of-the-mill corriente y moliente

to **run off the road** salirse de la carretera ➤ The car ran off the road. El coche se salió de la carretera.

to **run off the runway** salirse de la pista ➤ The airplane ran off the end of the runway, hit a fence, and flipped over. El avión se salió del extremo de la pista, chocó con una valla y dio una vuelta de campana.

to **run off with someone** escaparse con alguien ▪ fugarse con alguien ➤ The boss ran off with his secretary. El jefe se escapó con su secretaria. ▪ El jefe se fugó con su secretaria.

run on a bank pánico bancario ▪ pánico bursátil ➤ In *Mary Poppins*, Jane and Michael caused a run on the bank. En *Mary Poppins*, Jane y Michael causaron un pánico bancario.

to **run on batteries** funcionar con pilas ➤ It runs on double-A batteries. Funciona con pilas doble A.

to **run on fuel** funcionar con combustible ▪ funcionar con carburante ➤ Jet engines run on kerosene. Motores de reacción funcionan con keroseno. ➤ The buses run on natural gas. Los autobuses funcionan con gas.

to **run out** **1.** to use up ▪ to exhaust a supply quedar sin ▪ agotársele ▪ acabar **2.** to leave running salir corriendo ➤ I didn't think we'd run out. ▪ I didn't think we'd use it up. No pensé que se fuera a acabar. ➤ Where is he, anyway?-He ran out. A propósito, ¿dónde está?-Salió corriendo.

to **run out of ink** agotarse la tinta ▪ estar agotado la tinta ▪ estar por terminarse la tinta ▪ terminársele la tinta ➤ The printer cartridge is running out of ink. El cartucho de tinta de la impresora se está agotando. ▪ El cartucho de tinta de la impresora está por agotarse.

to **run out of patience** agotársele la paciencia ➤ I'm running out of patience. Se me agota la paciencia. ▪ Se me está agotando la paciencia.

to **run out of steam** ▪ to poop out acabársele la pilas ▪ írsele las pilas ▪ quedarse sin gas ➤ I've run out of steam. ▪ I'm pooped out. Se me acabaron las pilas. ▪ Se me fueron las pilas. ▪ Me quedé sin gas.

to **run out of supplies** quedarse sin provisiones ▪ acabarse las provisiones

to **run out of time** ▪ *(poetic)* (for) one's time to grow short acabársele el tiempo ▪ quedarse sin tiempo ▪ agotársele el tiempo ▪ hacerse corto el tiempo ➤ He was running out of the time allotted to finish the project. Se le acababa el tiempo fijado para terminar el proyecto. ➤ *(poetic)* My time grows short. Mi tiempo se hace corto.

to **run out of time to do something** acabársele el tiempo para hacer algo ▪ quedarse sin tiempo para hacer algo

to be **run over** ▪ to get run over ser atropellado ▪ morir atropellado ➤ The dog was run over by a car (and killed). ▪ The dog got run over by a car. El perro fue atropellado por un coche. ▪ El perro murió atropellado por un coche.

to **run over someone** arrollar a alguien ➤ *(headline)* Bus runs over three pedestrians Un autobús arrolla a tres peatones

to **run over something** atropellar algo ▪ arrollar algo

to **run over to** ▪ to run down to ir corriendo a ▪ correr a ➤ I'm going to run over to the store and get some sugar. ▪ I'm going to run down to the store and get some sugar. Voy a correr a la tienda para comprar azúcar.

to **run overtime** ▪ to extend past the allotted time pasarse (de tiempo) ▪ *(Sp., coll.)* darle la uvas ➤ We've run overtime. Nos hemos pasado (de tiempo). ➤ I ran (way) overtime. ▪ It got really late on me. Me dieron las uvas. ➤ We ran (way) overtime. ▪ It got really late on us. Nos dieron las uvas.

to **run right into something** **1.** *(literal)* to hit something darse de narices con algo **2.** *(figurative)* to lead to desembocar en ➤ I ran right into a spiderweb. Me di de narices con una telaraña. ➤ Just take this street. It runs right into it. Toma esta calle. Desemboca justo allí.

to **run rings around someone** ▪ to be far superior to someone dar muchas vueltas a alguien ▪ dar mil vueltas a alguien ▪ pasar a alguien con los ojos cerrados ➤ She runs rings around the other technician. Ella le da muchas vueltas al otro técnico.

to **run roughshod over someone** hacer tabla rasa de alguien ▪ dar un empellón a alguien

to **run slow** *(computer, clock, etc.)* andar lento ➤ *(L. Am.)* The computer runs slow. ▪ The computer is running slow. La computadora anda lento. ▪ *(Sp.)* El ordenador anda lento.

to **run someone down** **1.** to track someone down ▪ to find someone rastrear a alguien ▪ ubicar a alguien **2.** to disparage someone despreciar a alguien **3.** to run over someone (with a car) atropellar a alguien

to **run someone off the sidewalk** forzar a alguien a salirse de la acera

to **run the antivirus** *(computers)* ▪ to run a virus scan ejecutar el anti-virus ▪ pasar el anti-virus

to **run the gamut** pasar por toda la gama de

to **run the length of** ir a lo largo de ➤ At the Autonoma there's a sidewalk that runs the length of the campus. En la Autónoma hay una acera que va a lo largo de campus.

to **run the show** ▪ to call the shots llevar las riendas ▪ cortar el bacalao

to **run through** **1.** *(literal)* to run on foot through cruzar corriendo ▪ atravesar corriendo ▪ correr a través de **2.** to permeate penetrar por todo **3.** to pass through pasar por ➤ I run through the park every day on my morning jog. Atravieso el parque corriendo todas las mañanas. ▪ Corro a través del parque todas las mañanas. ➤ Humor runs (all) through Jules Verne's *From the Earth to the Moon*. El humor penetra por toda la obra *De la tierra a la luna* de Julio Verne. ➤ A river runs through it. Un río pasa por allí.

to **run upstairs** subir corriendo ▪ subir deprisa

to **run wild** destramparse ▪ desmelenarse ➤ They proceeded to run wild. Empezaron a destramparse. ▪ Empezaron a desmelenarse.

runaway best seller best-seller arrollador

runaway horse caballo desbocado

runaway slave esclavo fugitivo

runaway truck ■ truck with failed brakes *el* camión sin frenos ■ camión sin control

runaway truck lane pista de frenado

to be a **running fool** *(Forrest Gump)* tener manía de correr ➤ That's kid's a running fool. Qué manía de correr tiene ese niño.

running of the bulls *(Pamplona)* encierro de los toros ■ *el* encerrón de los toros ■ encerrona de los toros

to be **running out of patience** ■ to be at the end of one's patience estársele agotando la paciencia ■ estársele acabando la paciencia ■ estar al borde de la paciencia

running water *el* agua corriente *("Agua" is feminine. Only the masculine singular article is irregular. The plural is "las aguas.")*

runny nose: to have a ■ for one's nose to be running gotearle la nariz ➤ I have a runny nose. Me gotea la nariz.

runoff election segunda vuelta (electoral)

to **rush around** ■ to rush about ajetrearse

rush hour hora punta ■ hora pico ➤ *(headline)* Power outage at rush hour causes chaos in London ■ Rush-hour power outage causes chaos in London Un apagón en hora punta provoca el caos en Londres

rush hour: at the height of the ~ en plena hora punta ■ en plena hora pico *("Hora pico" is also the Mexican name for "Saturday Night Live.")*

to **rush in** entrar apresurado(-a) ■ entrar presuroso(-a)

rush of adrenalin ■ burst of adrenalin descarga de adrenalina ■ *el* subidón de adrenalina

to **rush someone 1.** to hurry someone up apresurar a alguien ■ meterle prisa a alguien **2.** to run toward and subdue someone correr hacia alguien y subyegarlo(-a) ■ *(Sp., leísmo)* correr hacia alguien y subyegarle

Russian roulette ruleta rusa

to **saber rattle** hacer ruido de sables ▪ tocar tambores de guerra
to be **saber rattling** ser ruido de sables ▪ ser tambores de guerra
sacred hymn himno sagrado ▪ alabado
sad ending: to have a ~ tener un triste final
sad fate destino triste
to be **saddened by...** estar entristecido(-a) por... ▪ entristecerse por... ▪ estar apesadumbrado(-a) por...
to **saddle a horse** ensillar un caballo
to **saddle oneself with work** cargarse con trabajo
saddle soap crema para acondicionar el cuero ▪ *(Sp.)* crema para acondicionar piel
to be **saddled with work** ▪ to be loaded down with work estar cargado(-a) de trabajo
to be **sadly mistaken** estar miserablemente equivocado ▪ *(Sp.)* ir fresco ▪ estar fresco
to be **safe and sound** estar sano(-a) y salvo(-a)
safe-deposit box caja de seguridad
to be **safe from** estar a salvo de ▪ estar al resguardo de
safe haven (in): to seek ~ buscar refugio seguro (en)
safe sex: to practice ~ practicar el sexo seguro
to be **safe to do something** ser seguro hacer una cosa ➤ Is it safe to walk in this neighborhood at night? ¿Es seguro andar por la noche en este barrio?
safety lock *(on a firearm)* seguro
said of dícese de ▪ dicho de
to be **said to have** ▪ to reportedly have decirse tener ➤ Police are searching for the hijacker, who is said to have family problems. La policía busca al secuestrador aéreo de quien se dice tener problemas familiares.
sale price precio venta
sales force *la* personal de venta ▪ *la* red de venta
sales tax ▪ value-added tax ▪ VAT *(Mex., S. Am.)* impuesto al valor agregado ▪ IVA ▪ *(Sp.)* impuesto al valor añadido ▪ IVA
sallow complexion: having a ~ ▪ with a sickly complexion de color amarillento ▪ de color cetrino
salsa and chips salsa y totopos ▪ salsa y tostaditas y ▪ salsa y tostitos ▪ *(Sp.)* salsa y Doritos®
salt and pepper *la* sal y pimienta
salt-and-pepper hair ▪ graying hair pelo entrecano
salt and pepper shakers salera y pimentera
salt of the earth ▪ person with the best human qualities *la* sal de la tierra
saltwater *el* agua salada *("Agua" is feminine. Only the singular article is irregular.)*
to **salve one's conscience** descargar la conciencia ▪ tranquilizar la conciencia
the **same as** ▪ just as ▪ just like igual que ➤ Plants breathe the same as we do. Las plantas respiran igual que nosotros.
to be the **same as** ser el mismo como ▪ corresponder con ➤ Before connecting the appliance, check to see that the voltage is the same as that indicated on the identification plate. Antes de conectar el electrodoméstico, compruebe que el voltaje corresponde al que se indica en la placa de caracteristicas.
same-day delivery: to have ~ ▪ to deliver (on) the same day entregar el mismo día
same here ▪ likewise lo mismo digo ▪ igualmente
same last name as el mismo apellido que ➤ In our neighborhood, the dogs had the same last names as their owners. En nuestra vecindad, los perros tenían el mismo apellido que los dueños.
to be the **same old story** ▪ to be the same old thing ▪ to be the same song, fiftieth verse ▪ to be the same old same old ser la misma cantinela de siempre ▪ ser la misma canción de siempre ▪ ser la misma historia de siempre ▪ llover sobre mojado
to be the **same old thing** ser lo mismo de siempre ▪ (ser) otra vez sopa ▪ *(and everyone is familiar with it)* ser lo consabido
the **same place as before** el mismo lugar de antes ▪ el mismo sitio de antes
same side of the street (as...): to be on the ~ estar en el mismo lado de la calle (donde está...) ▪ estar en la misma acera (donde está...) ➤ Is it on the same side of the street as the train station? ¿Está en el mismo lado de calle donde está la estación de trenes? ▪ ¿Está en misma acera donde está la estación de trenes?

to be the **same size (as)** ser del mismo tamaño que ▪ *(clothes)* ser de la misma talla que
to be the **same song, fiftieth verse** ▪ to be the same old story ▪ to be the same old line ser la misma cantaleta de siempre ▪ ser la misma canción (de siempre) ▪ ser la misma cantinela (de siempre) ▪ ser la misma historia de siempre
the **same thing (as)** lo mismo (de) ▪ igual (que)
the **same thing happened to me** (a mí) me pasó lo mismo ▪ me pasó igualito ▪ igual me pasó
same to you! ¡igualmente! ▪ *(a ti)* ¡lo mismo te digo! ▪ *(a usted)* ¡lo mismo le digo (a usted)! ▪ *(teenage slang)* ¡dito!
to **sand a wall** **1.** *(general)* lijar una pared **2.** *(heavy sanding)* raspar una pared *("Raspar" usually means "to scrape" but can refer to machine sanding with coarse sandpaper.)*
to **sand a (wood) floor** lijar un piso (de madera)
to **sand with the grain of the wood** lijar con la veta de la madera ➤ Don't sand across the grain of the wood. Sand with the grain. No se lija en contra de la veta. Se lija con la veta.
sandbag saco de arena
Santa Claus ▪ Father Christmas Papá Noel *(In Hispanic countries, "Los Reyes Magos," the three kings, Gaspar, Melchior, and Balthasar, bring the gifts while the children are sleeping on the eve of "Reyes," or Epiphany, January 6.)*
to **sap one's strength** agotar las fuerzas de uno ▪ minar las fuerzas de uno
sardonic humor ▪ derisive humor humor sardónico ▪ humor burlón ▪ humor desdeñoso
sardonic laughter ▪ derisive laughter risa sardónica
to **sashay around** petardear
satchel bag *el* neceser ▪ *el* maletín
satellite dish ▪ parabolic antenna antena parabólica
to **satirize something** satirizar algo ▪ ironizar sobre algo
to be **satisfied with** estar satisfecho con ▪ darse por satisfecho con ➤ The senator was not satisfied with the president's reassurances. El senador no estuvo satisfecho con las aseguranzas del presidente. ▪ El senador no se dio por satisfecho las aseguranzas del presidente.
Saturday night and early Sunday en la noche del sábado al domingo
saucepan cazo ▪ cacerola *(Although these two words can be exact synonyms meaning a saucepan with a bar handle, "cacerola" also can refer to a larger vessel with handles on each side.)*
to **save a lot of time** ahorrar mucho tiempo ▪ suponer un gran ahorro de tiempo

to **save a message** conservar un mensaje

to **save one's receipt** ▪ to save the receipt guardar tu recibo

to **save one's skin** salvar el pellejo

to **save oneself a lot of trouble by doing something** ahorrarse problemas haciendo algo

to **save oneself a lot of trouble if** ahorrarse problemas si ▪ ahorrarse mucha molestia si

to **save oneself a trip** ahorrarse un viaje

to **save someone's place in line** ▪ to hold someone's place in line guardarle el sitio a alguien ▪ cuidarle el lugar a alguien ▪ *(also said in this context, "to save someone's turn")* guardarle el turno a alguien

to **save something for a special occasion** reservar algo para una ocasión especial ➤ I'm saving this wine for Christmas Eve dinner. Estoy reservando este vino para la cena navideña.

to **save something for later** dejar algo para más tarde ▪ guardar algo para más tarde ➤ Don't eat it all at once. Save half for later. No lo comas de una vez. Deja la mitad para más tarde. ▪ No lo comas de una vez. Guarda la mitad para más tarde.

to **save something for someone** guardar algo para alguien ➤ She saves the entertainment section for me. ▪ She saves me the entertainment section. Ella me guarda la cartelera. ➤ She saves it for me. Ella me la guarda.

to **save the day (for someone)** sacarlo a alguien del apuro ▪ *(Sp., leísmo)* sacarle a alguien del apuro

to **save time** ahorrar tiempo ▪ ganar tiempo ▪ suponer un ahorro de tiempo ➤ You'll save time by taking the metro to the airport. Ganarás tiempo si coges el metro al aeropuerto. ➤ (In order) to save time... Para ahorrar tiempo...

to be **saved by the bell** salvarle la campana ➤ I was saved by the bell. Me salvó la campana.

say: (let's) ~ supongamos

say ahhhh! *(said by the doctor) (tú)* ¡di treinta y tres! ▪ *(usted)* ¡diga treinta y tres!

say cheese! ▪ smile for the camera! ¡una sonrisita! ▪ ¡di patatas!

to **say coolly** decir con suficiencia

to **say for sure** decir con toda seguridad

to **say good morning to someone** darle los buenas días a alguien

to **say good-bye to each other** 1. *(you and I, you all and I)* despedirnos 2. *(they)* despedirse ➤ We said good-bye to each other. Nos despedimos. ➤ They said good-bye to each other. Se despidieron.

to **say good-bye to someone** despedirse de alguien

to **say hello to someone for me** saludar a alguien de mi parte ➤ Say hello to Esperanza for me. Saluda a Esperanza de mi parte.

to **say (it) in so many words** ▪ to insinuate ▪ to imply dar a entender ▪ insinuar ▪ sugerir ➤ She didn't come right out and say it, but she said it in so many words. No fue directamente al grano, pero lo dio a entender.

to **say Mass** ▪ to celebrate Mass decir misa ▪ oficiar misa ▪ celebrar misa

to **say no** 1. decir que no 2. to refuse rehusar ▪ negarse 3. to decline rechazar

to **say no such thing** no decir tal cosa ➤ You're twisting my words. I said no such thing. Estás torciendo mis palabras. No dije tal cosa.

to **say simply that...** ▪ simply to say that... limitarse a decir que... ➤ He said simply that... ▪ He simply said that... Se limitó a decir que...

to **say something about...** decir algo relacionado con...

to **say something half seriously, half in jest** decir algo entre burlas y veras ▪ decir algo mitad en serio mitad en broma

to **say something in jest** decir algo de mentira

to **say something in passing** decir algo de pasada

to **say something in response** responder algo ➤ The Indian, in awe, tried to say something in response, but he couldn't. El indio, maravillado, quiso responder algo, pero no pudo.

to **say something to someone** ▪ to tell someone something decirle algo a alguien

to **say something with complete sincerity (holding back nothing)** decir algo con el corazón en la mano ▪ decir algo francamente ▪ decir algo sin pelos en la lengua

to **say something without really meaning it** decir algo sin sentirlo ▪ *(Sp.)* decir algo con la boca pequeña ▪ decir algo con la boca chica

to **say that one is...** ▪ to claim to be... decir ser...

to **say the first thing that comes to mind** decir lo primero que a alguien le viene a la mente ➤ I said the first thing that came to my mind. Dije lo primero que me vino a la mente.

to **say the wrong thing** mentar la soga en casa del ahorcado

to **say to do something** decir que uno haga algo ➤ They said for us to wait for them. ▪ They told us to wait for them. Nos dijeron que los esperaramos.

say what you will ▪ regardless of what you say ▪ no matter what you say ▪ whatever you say *(tú)* digas lo que digas ▪ *(usted)* diga lo que diga

to **say yes** decir que sí

to **say yes to everything** ▪ to say yes to anything comprometerse a todo

scale model modelo a escala ▪ *(from a kit)* maqueta

(scale) model of a building maqueta de un edificio

to **scalp someone** 1. arrancar la cabellera a alguien 2. to cut someone's hair very short cortar el pelo al cero ➤ They really scalped you at the barbershop! ¡Vaya, que pelada te han hecho en esa peluquería! ▪ ¡Vaya pelada te han hecho en esa peluquería! ➤ He's going to scalp you if he finds out. Te va a arrancar la cabellera si se entera.

to be the **scapegoat** ser la cabeza de turco ▪ ser el pagapato

scapegoat: to make someone the ~ hacerlo a alguien pagar el pato ▪ hacer que alguien pague el pato ➤ They made him the scapegoat. Lo hicieron pagar el pato. ▪ Hicieron que él pagara el pato.

scar on the face ▪ facial scar *la* cicatriz en la cara ▪ *(from a knife wound)* chirlo

scar tissue tejido cicatrizado

scarce commodity el bien escaso

scarcity of ▪ shortage of *la* escasez de ▪ carestía de

to **scare someone** darle un susto a alguien ▪ asustar a alguien ➤ It scared me a lot. ▪ It scared the wits out of me. Me dio un susto bastante grande.

to **scare someone away** ▪ to scare someone off ahuyentar a alguien

to **scare someone off** ▪ to scare someone away ahuyentar a alguien

to **scare someone to death** darle un susto de muerte a alguien ▪ darle un susto padre a alguien

scare tactics tácticas para amedrentar

to **scare the crap out of someone** *(coarse)* pegarle un susto de aquellos a alguien ➤ The explosion scared the crap out of me. La explosión me pegó un susto de aquellos.

to **scare the wits out of someone** darle un susto de película

to be **scared shitless** *(off-color)* estar cagado(-a) de miedo ▪ *(benign alternative)* estar muerto(-a) de miedo

the **scarier the better** *(horror movies, thrillers)* cuanto más miedo, mejor

to **scatter someone's ashes** esparcir las cenizas de alguien ➤ The playwright's ashes will be scattered in the Mediterranean. Las cenizas del dramaturgo serán esparcidas en el Mediterráneo.

to be **scatterbrained** ser alegre de cascos ▪ tener cabeza de chorlito

to be **scattered (all) over something** quedar esparcido por algo ➤ The truck's freight was scattered all over the highway. La carga de la camión quedó esparcida por toda la carretera.

scattered clouds nubes dispersas

scene of a battle escenario de una batalla ➤ The Shenandoah Valley was the scene of many American Civil War battles. El Valle Shenandoah fue el escenario de muchas batallas de la guerra civil norteamericana.

scene takes place in... escena ocurre en... ▪ estampa ocurre en... ▪ escena está ambientada en... ➤ The scene takes place in Buenos Aires. La escena ocurre en Buenos Aires. ▪ La estampa ocurre en Buenos Aires. ▪ La escena está ambientada en Buenos Aires.

scenes from the life of *las* representaciones de la vida de

to **schedule a delivery** ▪ to arrange (for) a delivery acordar una entrega ▪ citar una entrega ▪ citar un reparto

to **schedule a meeting** ▪ to set the time of the meeting fijar una reunión ▪ programar una reunión

to **schedule a pickup** citar una recogida

schedule of classes ▪ class schedule horario de clases

schedule of events horario de actividades ▪ horario de eventos

to **schedule one for...** ▪ to schedule one's appointment for... ▪ to set one's appointment for... darle hora para... ➤ He scheduled me for Monday. ▪ He scheduled my appointment for Monday. ▪ He set my appointment for Monday. Me ha dado hora para lunes.

scheduled flight: (regularly) ~ vuelo programado ➤ It was a (regularly) scheduled flight. Fue un vuelo programado.

to be **scheduled for a certain time** estar programado para un tiempo determinado ➤ The meeting is scheduled for the twenty-third at 3 o'clock. La reunión está programada para el veinte y tres a las tres.

schematic diagram diagrama esquemático

scheme of things el esquema de las cosas ➤ It has little importance in the eternal scheme of things. Tiene poca importancia en el esquema eterno de las cosas.

scholarly paper ensayo erudito ▪ ponencia

school board consejo escolar

school bus *el* autobús escolar

school night noche antes del colegio ➤ Sunday through Thursday nights are school nights. Las noches del domingo al jueves son noches antes del colegio.

school of fish banco de peces

school of thought escuela de pensamiento

school supplies *el* material escolar

school years años de formación académica

schoolboy *el* escolar

schoolchildren *los* escolares ▪ alumnos escolares

schoolgirl *la* escolar

scientific advances adelantos de la ciencia

to **scold someone** ▪ to call down someone ▪ to call someone down regañar a alguien

scoop of ice cream bola de helado

to **score a goal** marcar un gol ▪ *(basketball)* to score a basket anotar un tanto

to **score a point** anotar un punto ▪ *(basketball)* to score a basket anotar un tanto

to **score five hundred on the TOEFL test** marcar quinientos en el examen TOEFL ▪ tener una puntuación de quinientos en el examen TOEFL ▪ sacar un quinientos en el examen TOEFL

score one for...! ¡un tanto para...! ▪ ¡premio para...!

to be **scored against (by the opposing team)** encajar un gol ➤ Barcelona was scored against two points by Madrid. El Barcelona encajó dos goles del Madrid.

Scotch Tape® dispenser ▪ cellophane tape dispenser portarollo de cinta Scotch ▪ portarollo de cinta celo

to **scramble a message** *(coll.)* ▪ to encode a message codificar un mensaje

to **scramble eggs** revolver los huevos

to **scramble fighters** hacer despegar los cazas (con urgencia)

scrambled eggs huevos revueltos

to **scrap one's plans** echar tierra a sus plans ▪ abandonar sus planes

scrapbook libro de memorias

to **scrape off something** ▪ to scrape something off quitar algo raspando ➤ You use a solvent to loosen the paint before you scrape it off. Se utiliza un disolvente para ablandar la pintura antes de quitarla raspando. ➤ Use this solvent to scrape it off. Se utiliza un disolvente para quitarla raspando.

to **scrape one's elbow, knee** ▪ to skin one's elbow, knee rasparse el codo, la rodilla ▪ despellejarse el codo, la rodilla

to **scratch an itch** rascarse una comezón ▪ *(from a rash, etc.)* rascarse una picazón

to **scratch at the door** arañar la puerta ➤ The dog is scratching at the door. El perro está arañando la puerta.

scratch paper: (piece of) ~ *el* papel en sucio

to **scratch someone** arañarle a alguien

to **scratch someone's back** ▪ to give someone a back scratch rascarle la espalda a alguien ➤ Would you scratch my back? ▪ Would you give me a back scratch? ¿Me rascas la espalda? ➤ I like to get my back scratched. Me gusta que me rasquen la espalda.

to **scratch something** ▪ to mar something rayar algo ▪ arañar algo ➤ Would you help me move the bookcase? I don't want to scratch the floor. ¿Me ayudarías a mover la estantería? No quiero rayar el piso.

to **scream bloody murder over** ▪ to scream bloody murder because of ▪ to scream bloody murder for poner el grito en el cielo por

screeching of brakes ▪ squealing of brakes chirrido de frenos

screw loose: to have a ~ tener tuerca floja ▪ tener un tornillo suelto ➤ He has a screw loose. Tiene una tuerca floja. ▪ Tiene un tornillo suelto.

to **screw someone 1.** to put the screws to someone apretar las clavijas a alguien **2.** *(off-color)* to fuck someone ▪ to lay someone follar a alguien ▪ joder a alguien ▪ tirarse a alguien ▪ echar un polvo a alguien ▪ *(Mex.)* chingar a alguien

scroll bar barra de desplazamiento

to **scroll down** mover la pantalla hacia abajo ▪ mover la barra de desplazamiento hacia abajo

to **scroll up** mover la pantalla hacia arriba ▪ mover la barra de desplazamiento hacia arriba

scruffy person ▪ slovenly person persona desaliñada

scuff mark ▪ scratch arañazo

to **scuttle a ship** ▪ to sink a ship (as a way of discarding it) dar barreno a un barco ▪ echar un barco al fondo

the **scuttlebutt is that...** ▪ the inside talk is that... ▪ the rumor has it that... ▪ the rumor is that... ▪ it's been going around that... por lo que se dice...

sea breeze brisa marina

sea change ▪ radical change cambiazo ▪ cambio contundente ▪ *el* viraje

sea lion lobo marino ▪ león marino *(Sea lions differ from seals in having external ears. In Spanish sea lions are more frequently called "sea wolves," "lobos marinos.")*

seafloor spreading *(geology) la* expansión del lecho marino ▪ el derrame del lecho marino

to **seal a crack** ▪ to fill a crack tapar una grieta ▪ llenar una ranura

to **seal a plastic bag** precintar una bolsa de plástico ➤ Please don't seal the bag. I'm going to eat them right now. Por favor, no precintes la bolsa; voy a comerlos ahora mismo.

to **seal an envelope** cerrar un sobre

to **seal off something** ▪ to seal something off precintar algo

to **seal (up)** ▪ to seal sellar ➤ That hole is an entry point for roaches and rodents, and it needs to be sealed up. Ese agujero es un foco de entrada para cucarachas y roedores y se necesita sellar.

sealed bid: to submit a ~ mandar un presupuesto bajo (sistema de) plica

sealed entry (to a literary competition): to submit a ~ mandar un manuscrito bajo (sistema de) plica ➤ Nicanor Parra, the self-styled Chilean "antipoet," on submitting three manuscripts anonymously to a literary competition, won first, second, and third prize. Nicanor Parra, el autodenominado "antipoeta" chileno, al mandar tres manuscritos bajo (sistema de) plica, ganó el primero, segundo y tercer puesto de un concurso literario.

to **search a building** registrar un edificio

search-and-destroy mission ▪ search-and-destroy operation *la* operación de acoso y derribo

search-and-rescue operations tareas de rescate y recuperación

search engine *el* buscador ▪ *el* motor de búsqueda

search for someone búsqueda de alguien

to **search for someone** buscar a alguien ➤ Search for the missing reporters Búsqueda de los reporteros desaparecidos

search for something búsqueda de algo
to **search from top to bottom** registrar de arriba abajo
to **search inch by inch** registrar palmo a palmo
search me! ¡a mí que me registren! ▪ ni idea
search of telephone records registro de llamadas realizadas ▪ batida de llamadas ▪ redada de las llamadas
to **search one's pockets** ▪ to look through one's pockets registrarse los bolsillos
to **search telephone records** batir llamada ▪ registrar las llamadas
to **search the area** batir la zona
to **search the sky for the satellite** escrutinar el cielo por el satélite
search warrant *la* orden de registro ▪ orden de cateo
season of the year 1. *(calendar)* estación del año **2.** *(holiday and sports)* temporada del año
seat of a diocese *la* cede de una diócesis
seat of a monarchy *la* cede de una monarquía
to **seat *x* people** ▪ to have a seating capacity of *x* people tener capacidad para *x* personas ▪ tener un aforo de *x* personas
to **secede from the union** segregarse de la unión
second-class citizen ciudadano de segunda
second-class (railroad) car el vagón de segunda
second favorite segundo favorito ➤ Woody Allen said the brain was his second favorite organ. Woody Allen dijo que el cerebro era su segundo órgano favorito.
second helping: to have a ~ ▪ to have some more ▪ to go for seconds repetir ➤ I'd like (to have) a second helping. Me gustaría repetir. ➤ I'm going for seconds. ▪ I'm going to have a second helping. Voy a repetir.
second mortgage hipoteca subsidiaria
the **second most powerful man** el segundo hombre más poderoso ➤ *(headline)* The second most powerful man in America is Alan Greenspan. El segundo hombre más poderoso en los Estados Unidos es Alan Greenspan.
second of an arc *(geometry)* ▪ arc second segundo de arco
second-rate de segunda
second wind: to get a ~ conseguir recobrar fuerzas
Second World War ▪ World War II Segunda Guerra Mundial ▪ II Guerra Mundial ➤ California had not suffered blackouts since World War II. California no sufría cortes de luz desde la II Guerra Mundial.
secondhand de segunda mano
secondhand: to hear something ~ oír algo por referencia ➤ I heard it secondhand. Lo oí por referencia.
secondhand bookstore librería de lance
secrecy of the confessional *(Catholicism)* secreto de la confesión ▪ sigilo sacramental
the **secret is to...** el secreto está en...
section of road, highway, track, etc. tramo ➤ *(metro station sign)* Section closed for repairs Tramo suspendido por obras
to **secure a loan** ▪ to get a loan ▪ to take out a loan concederle a alguien un préstamo
to **secure one's retirement** asegurar su jubilación
Securities and Exchange Commission *(USA) la* Comisión del Mercado de Valores
security expert autoridad en materia de seguridad
security guard vigilante de seguridad
security loophole salida en el control de seguridad
security measures medidas de seguridad ➤ Tight security (measures) have been put into place. Extremas medidas de seguridad han sido implementadas.
to **seduce someone** seducir a alguien ▪ *(Sp.)* llevar a alguien al huerto
to **see a change** ▪ to witness a change observarse un cambio ➤ Now we are seeing a change. ▪ Now we are witnessing a change. Ahora se está observando un cambio.
see back mira en el dorso
to **see before one** ver ante sí ▪ *(poetic or mysterious)* aparecer ante sí
to **see beyond the end of one's nose** ver más allá de su nariz ➤ He rarely sees beyond the end of his nose. Raramente ve más allá de su nariz.
to **see close up** ver de cerca
to **see firsthand what...** ▪ to see for oneself what... ▪ to find out for oneself what... saber desde dentro qué...
to **see fit to do something** tener a bien hacer algo
to **see for oneself** comprobar por uno mismo ▪ constatar el hecho por sí mismo ➤ See for yourself! ¡Comprueba tu mismo! ➤ You can see for yourself that... Puedes constatar el hecho por ti mismo de que...
to **see for oneself what...** ▪ to see firsthand what... ▪ to find out for oneself what... saber desde dentro qué...
to **see how...** comprobar cómo...
see how easy it is? ¿ves qué fácil?
to **see how it fits one** ver cómo le sienta a uno ▪ ver cómo le queda a uno ➤ Let's see how it fits (me). A ver cómo me sienta. ➤ Let's see how it fits (you). A ver cómo te sienta. ▪ A ver cómo le sienta.
to **see how the land lies** tantear el terreno
to **see if...** probar a ver si... ▪ probar para ver si... ➤ See if it works now. Prueba a ver si funciona ahora.
to **see if I can make something do something** para ver si hace algo ➤ I'm going to water this plant to see if I can make it grow. Voy a regar esta planta para ver si crece.
to **see if it fits (me)** ver si es mi talla ▪ ver si me queda
to **see if it fits (you)** ver si es tu talla ▪ ver si te queda ▪ ver si es su talla (de usted) ▪ ver si le queda (a usted)
to **see if the coast is clear** tantear el terreno ▪ ver si hay moros en la costa
to **see it coming** verlo venir ➤ I can see it coming. Lo veo venir. ➤ I could see it coming. Lo veía venir. ➤ I saw it coming. Lo vi venir.
to **see it differently** tener formas distintas de apreciar la situación
to **see right off that...** ▪ to see straightaway that... enseguida darse cuenta de...
to **see someone as being like everyone else** verle a alguien como a uno más
to **see someone do something** ▪ to see someone doing something ver a alguien hacer algo ▪ ver a alguien haciendo algo ➤ I saw him leave. ▪ I saw him leaving. Le vi salir. ▪ Le vi saliendo. ➤ I saw her leave. ▪ I saw her leaving. La vi salir. ▪ La vi saliendo.
to **see someone off** despedirse de alguien (en un viaje) ➤ We went to the airport to see our son and daughter-in-law off on their honeymoon. Fuimos al aeropuerto para despedirnos de nuestro hijo y nuera en su viaje de luna de miel.
to **see someone through** bastarle a uno para ▪ tener lo suficiente para ➤ Do you have enough money to see you through? ¿Te basta el dinero? ▪ ¿Tienes suficiente dinero para...?
to **see someone to the door** ▪ to show someone to the door acompañar a alguien a la puerta ➤ I'll see you to the door. ▪ I'll show you to the door. Te acompaño a la puerta.
to **see someone's point** ver su punto de vista ▪ ver lo que uno quiere decir ➤ I see your point. Veo tu punto de vista. ▪ Veo lo que quieres decir. ➤ You see my point. Ves mi punto de vista. ▪ Ves lo que quiero decir.
to **see something coming** ver algo llegar ➤ He didn't see the train coming. No vio llegar el tren.
to **see something through** llevar algo a cabo
to **see stars** *(from pain, a blow to the head, etc.)* ver las estrellas
to **see straightaway that...** ▪ to see right off that... en seguida echarse de ver que... ➤ I could see straightaway that... ▪ I could see right off that... En seguida me echaba de ver que... ▪ En seguida pude ver que... ▪ Inmediatamente pude ver que...
to **see that...** comprobar que... ▪ ver que... ➤ The colonel saw that the canister was empty. El coronel comprobó que el tarro estaba vacío.
to **see the big picture** saber por dónde van los tiros ▪ saber de qué va la vaina ▪ saber qué se cuece
to **see the connection** ▪ to get the connection ver la relación ➤ I still don't see the connection. ▪ I still don't get the connection. Sigo sin ver la relación.
to **see the handwriting on the wall** ver las barbas al lobo ➤ I can see the handwriting on the wall. Puedo ver las barbas al lobo.

to **see the light** ▪ to become enlightened caérsele a uno la venda de los ojos
to **see the light at the end of the tunnel** ▪ to see the end of a long ordeal ver la luz al final del túnel
to **see the overall picture** ▪ to see the big picture ▪ to connect the dots concatenar los hechos ▪ atar los cabos
to **see the world through rose-colored glasses** ver el mundo de color de rosa
to **see the world through the eyes of a child** ver el mundo a través de los ojos de un niño ➤ Winnie the Pooh enables us to see the world through the eyes of a child. Winnie the Pooh nos permite ver el mundo a través de los ojos de un niño.
to **see things differently** ver las cosas de otro modo
see what I mean? ▪ do you see what I mean? ¿ves lo que (te) quiero decir?
to **see what is coming** ▪ to see what the future has in store ver lo que va a venir ▪ ver lo que el futuro depara ➤ He didn't see what was coming. No vio lo que iba a venir. ▪ No vio lo que el futuro deparaba.
see who's at the door ▪ go see who's at the door mira a ver quién toca ▪ mira quién ha llamado
see you in a week! ¡hasta dentro de una semana!
see you later: (I'll) ~ hasta luego
see you next time! ¡hasta el próximo día!
see you soon: (I'll) ~ ¡hasta muy pronto!
to **see you to the door** ▪ to show you to the door *(tú)* acompañarte a la puerta ▪ *(usted, female)* acompañarla (a usted) a la puerta ▪ *(usted, male)* acompañarlo (a usted) a la puerta ▪ *(Sp., leísmo)* acompañarle (a usted) a la puerta
to **see you to your room** ▪ to show you to your room *(tú)* pasarte a tu habitación ▪ *(usted, female)* pasarla (a usted) a su habitación ▪ *(usted, male)* pasarlo (a usted) a su habitación ▪ *(Sp., leísmo)* pasarle (a usted) a su habitación
see you tomorrow hasta mañana
see you when I get back: (I'll) ~ hasta la vuelta
seeds sprout ▪ seeds germinate ▪ seeds are sprouting ▪ seeds are germinating semillas germinan ▪ semillas están germinando
seeing is believing ver para creer
to **seek a new trial** solicitar un nuevo juicio ➤ He has good reason to seek a new trial. Tiene toda razón al solicitar un nuevo juicio.
seek and ye shall find ▪ seek and you will find quien busca halla ▪ quien busca encuentra
seek and ye shall find, ask and it shall be given to you, knock and it shall be opened to you buscad y hallaréis, pedid y se os dará, llamad y se os abrirá
to **seek common ground** buscar un punto en común
to **seek refuge in** buscar refugio en
to **seek safe haven** buscar refugio seguro
to **seek sanctuary 1.** *(in a church)* acogerse a sagrado **2.** *(to seek safe haven)* buscar asilo ▪ buscar refugio seguro
to **seem not to notice** parecer no fijarse en
to **seem okay** parecer que uno está bien ➤ He seems okay. Parece que está bien. ➤ He seemed okay this morning. Parecía que estaba bien esta mañana.
to **seem to be** parecer ser ▪ tener aire de
to **seem to someone** parecerle a alguien ▪ antojársele a alguien
to **seethe with desire for revenge** hervir en deseos de venganza
to **seethe with hatred** hervir de odio
to **seize on an excuse** encontrar una excusa rápidamente ➤ She seized on the excuse hastily, as if she were looking for one. Encontró la excusa rápidamente, como si la estuviera buscando.
to **seize (on) an opportunity** valerse de una oportunidad
to **seize power** ▪ to take power tomar el poder ▪ adueñarse del poder
to **seize someone by the arm** ▪ to grab someone by the arm agarrar a alguien por el brazo ➤ The officer seized him by the arm. ▪ The officer grabbed him by the arm. *(Mex.)* El agente lo agarró por el brazo. ▪ *(Sp.)* El agente le agarró por el brazo.
seize the day ▪ carpe diem vive en el momento
to **select at random** ▪ to choose at random ▪ *(informal)* to pick (out) at random escoger al azar
to be **selected at random** ▪ to be randomly selected ser seleccionado aleatoriamente ▪ ser seleccionado al azar
selected works obras elegidas ▪ obras seleccionadas
self-confidence ▪ confidence in oneself confianza en uno mismo ▪ confianza en sí mismo ▪ seguridad en sí mismo ➤ He has a lot of self-confidence. ▪ He has a lot of confidence in himself. Tiene mucha confianza en sí mismo. ➤ She has a lot of self-confidence. ▪ She has a lot of confidence in herself. Tiene mucha confianza en sí misma. ➤ You have a lot of self-confidence. *(a él)* Tienes mucha confianza en ti mismo. ▪ *(a ella)* Tienes mucha confianza en ti misma.
to be **self-employed** trabajar a cuenta propia ▪ trabajar por su cuenta
self-esteem autoestima
self-fulfilling attitude *la* actitud autorealizable ➤ Optimism is a self-fulfilling attitude. El optimismo es una actitud autorealizable. ➤ Hatred begets hatred. It's a self-fulfilling attitude. El odio genera más odio. Es una actitud autorealizable.
self-fulfilling prophecy profecía autorealizable
self-image *la* imagen de sí mismo
self-made man hombre hecho a sí mismo ▪ hombre que se ha hecho a sí mismo
self-mortification *(religious practice) la* mortificación personal
self-pity *la* autocompasión
self-portrait autorretrato
self-preservation conservación
to be **self-prompting** *(computers)* ser auto-indicativo ▪ ser auto-instructivo
sell-by date *(on grocery store items)* ▪ expiration date fecha de caducidad ▪ fecha de vencimiento
to **sell like hotcakes** venderse como churros ▪ venderse como pan caliente ➤ The book is selling like hotcakes. El libro se vende como churros.
to **sell oneself** *(to a prospective employer)* ▪ to tout one's strengths ▪ to tout one's virtues venderse caro
to **sell something at a good price** ▪ to sell something for a good price vender algo bien
to **sell something for a song** ▪ to sell something for peanuts vender algo por una tontería
to **sell something for peanuts** ▪ to sell something for a song vender algo por una tontería
to **sell something for whatever you can get (for it)** *(tú)* vender algo por lo que te den ▪ *(usted)* vender algo por lo que le den
to **sell something on credit** vender algo a crédito ▪ vender algo a plazos ▪ dar algo fiado
to **sell something retail** vender algo al por menor
to **sell something wholesale** vender algo al por mayor
to **sell the shirt off one's back** ▪ to sell everything one owns vender hasta la camisa ➤ He's so bad off financially that he's (practically) had to sell the shirt off his back. Está tan mal que ha tenido que vender hasta la camisa.
sellers' market mercado al alza
senate races las elecciones al senado ➤ The TV news so far has not broken down the senate races. Los noticieros de televisión hasta este momento no nos han dado los detalles de las elecciones al senado.
to **send a telegram** mandar un telegrama
to **send for someone** mandar buscar a alguien ▪ mandar llamar a alguien ➤ I sent for you. *(a ti)* Te mandé a buscar. ▪ *(a usted)* Le mandé a buscar.
to **send out the laundry** ▪ to send the laundry out ▪ to have the laundry done dar a lavar y planchar las ropas ▪ poner la ropa a hacer ▪ dar a hacer la colada
to **send someone back** volver a mandar ➤ The technician installed the modem wrong, and the store refused to send him back. El técnico instaló mal el módem y la tienda se negó a volver a mandarlo.
to **send someone packing** ▪ to give someone the boot echar a alguien con cajas destempladas ▪ despedir a alguien con cajas destempladas ▪ despachar a alguien

to **send someone to school** mandarlo a la escuela ➤ His parents worked hard to send him to school. Sus padres trabajaron mucho para mandarlo a la escuela.

to **send something as an attachment** enviar algo como un adjunto ▪ enviar algo como datos adjuntos ▪ enviar algo como archivos adjuntos

to **send stocks soaring** disparar la bolsa

to **send up a trial balloon** ▪ to send a trial balloon up lanzarse un globo sonda ▪ *(plural)* lanzarse globos sonda

sender (of a letter) *el, la* remitente (de una carta)

senior citizen ciudadano de la tercera edad ▪ persona de la tercera edad

to **sense an undercurrent of** ▪ to detect an undercurrent of ▪ to feel an undercurrent of sentir un trasfondo de

Sense and Sensibility *(novel title) Sentido y sensibilidad*

to **sense danger** percibir peligro

sense of belonging ▪ feeling of belonging sentido de pertenencia

sense of direction sentido de orientación ➤ I have a poor sense of direction. Tengo un mal sentido de orientación.

sense of duty sentido del deber

sense of guilt sentimiento de culpa ▪ sentimiento de culpabilidad

sense of modesty sentimiento de pudor

sense of propriety sentimiento de decoro ▪ el pudor ➤ Out of a sense of propriety Por pudor

sense of time: to lose all ~ perder la noción del tiempo

to **sense that...** ▪ to intuit that sentir que... ▪ darse cuenta de que...

the **sensible thing to do is** la cosa sensata que hacer es ➤ The most sensible thing to do is... La cosa más sensata que hacer es...

sensory overload: to suffer from ~ sufrir sobrecarga sensorial

sent items elementos enviados

to **sentence to death** condenar a muerte

to **sentence to life imprisonment** condenar a cadena perpetua

to **sentence to prison** condenar a la prisión

separate dining room *(real estate ad)* salón comedor independiente

separate kitchen with utility porch *(real estate ad)* cocina independiente con tendedero *(From "tender ropa," which means to "hang out clothes to dry")*

to **separate the men from the boys** distinguir a los hombres de los chicos

to **separate the trash in order to recycle** separar los residuos para reciclar

to **separate the wheat from the chaff** separar el grano de la paja

serial killer ▪ serial murderer asesino en serio

series of cadena de ➤ *(headline)* Series of terrorist attacks claim fifteen lives Cadena de atentados se cobran la vida de quince personas

series of reforms *el* programa de reformas

serious crisis *la* crisis profunda

serious illness enfermedad grave

serious injury herida grave ▪ herida de gravedad ▪ gravísima lesión ➤ Two vans parked on either side of the car contained the shock wave, preventing it from inflicting serious injuries. La presencia de dos furgonetas a ambos lados del coche retuvieron la onda expansiva impidiendo que se produzcan heridas de gravedad.

serious person persona seria

to be **seriously injured** ▪ to be badly injured ser herido gravemente

seriously, though ▪ (all) kidding aside bromas aparte ▪ fuera de broma

Sermon on the Mount *el* Sermón del Monte ▪ Sermón de la Montaña

to **serve an apprenticeship** ▪ to do an apprenticeship hacer un aprendizaje

to **serve as** 1. to constitute servir como 2. to act as funcionar como ▪ actuar como ▪ *(Mex.)* fungir como ➤ The hors d'ouevres serve as the first course. Los entremeses sirven como el primer plato. ➤ Who's serving as chairman of the committee? ¿Quién funge como presidente del comité?

to **serve as a buffer against** hacer de amortiguador... ▪ servir de colchón para...

to **serve as a front for illegal activities** ▪ to serve as a front for illicit activities hacer de pantalla para actividades ilegales ▪ hacer de pantalla para actividades ilícitas ▪ servir como pantalla para actividades ilegales ▪ servir como pantalla para actividades ilícitas ▪ funcionar como pantalla para actividades ilegales ▪ funcionar como pantalla para actividades ilícitas

to **serve as a guide for...** 1. *(literal)* servir de guía para... 2. to serve as an example for... servir de pauta para...

to **serve as proof of** servir de prueba de

to **serve as proof that...** servir de prueba de que...

to **serve in the military** ▪ to serve in the armed forces servir en las fuerzas armadas ▪ servir a la patria ▪ *(Sp.)* servir al rey

to **serve no useful purpose** ▪ not to serve any useful purpose no servir para nada

to **serve one's own interests** convenirle a sus intereses

to **serve one's purpose** serle adecuado ➤ That map didn't serve my purposes, so I threw it away. Ese plano no me fue adecuado, así que lo tiré.

to **serve someone right (for doing something)** merecérselo (por hacer algo) ▪ estarle bien empleado a alguien (por hacer algo)

to **serve someone well** ▪ to work well for someone servirle mucho a alguien

to **serve time in jail** cumplir tiempo de cárcel ➤ One of the captured had served eighteen years in jail. Uno de los capturados había cumplido dieciocho años de cárcel.

to **serve up** ▪ to present ▪ to offer presentar ▪ ofrecer ➤ The committee served up its findings. El comité ofreció sus hallazgos.

to be **served as** servirse como ➤ The hors d'ouvres are served as the first course. Los entremeses se sirven como el primer plato.

to be **served with** ser acompañado de ▪ ser servido con ➤ *(menu item)* Creamy cheese sauce with spinach and sausage bits served with crunchy tortilla chips. Cremosa salsa de queso con espinacas y picadillo de chorizo acompañada de totopos crujientes.

service call: to make a ~ hacer una visita a domicilio *(The Spanish term can apply either to a home or to a business.)*

service charges cargos a cuenta

service elevator ▪ freight elevator *el* montacargas

service road vía del servicio

serving (of food) ▪ plate of food *la* ración (de comida) ➤ A serving of anchovies, please. ▪ A plate of anchovies, please. Una ración de anchoas, por favor.

the **session is adjourned** ▪ the meeting is adjourned se levanta la sesión

session of the court sesión del tribunal (en pleno) ▪ pleno del tribunal

session of the legislature ▪ legislative session pleno de la cámara ▪ sesión de la cámara

to **set a broken bone** asentar un hueso roto ▪ colocar un hueso roto

to **set a clock** poner en hora un reloj

to **set a date for** fijar una fecha para ▪ concretar una fecha para ▪ poner fecha para ▪ acordar un día para

to **set a fire** causar un incendio ▪ provocar un incendio

to **set a goal** ▪ to establish a goal fijar una meta ▪ establecer una meta ▪ fijar un objetivo ▪ establecer un objetivo

to **set a precedent** ▪ establish a precedent sentar un precedente ▪ establecer un precedente ▪ dejar un precedente

to **set a time for something** concretar una hora para algo ▪ fijar una hora para algo ▪ establecer una hora para algo ▪ poner una hora para algo

to **set a time to do something** concretar una hora para hacer algo ▪ fijar una hora para hacer algo ▪ establecer una hora para hacer algo ▪ poner una hora para hacer algo ➤ I need to set a regular time to exercise. Necesito concretar una hora fija para hacer ejercicio. ▪ Necesito fijar una hora ejercicio. ▪ Necesito establecer una hora para hacer ejercicio. ▪ Necesito poner una hora para hacer ejercicio.

to **set a timetable for** fijar las fechas para ▪ fijar el calendario de

to **set a trap for an animal** poner una trampa para un animal ▪ preparar una trampa para un animal

to **set a trap for someone** ▪ to lay a trap for someone ▪ to prepare a trap for someone ponerle una trampa a alguien ▪ prepararle una encerrona a alguien

to **set a trap to...** prepararle una trampa para...

to **set a watch** poner en hora un reloj (de pulsera)

to **set about the task of doing something** disponerse a abordar la tarea de hacer algo

to **set an alarm** poner una alarma

to **set an animal free** dejar en libertad a un animal ▪ soltar a un animal

to **set an example** dar ejemplo ▪ dar un buen ejemplo

to **set apart someone** ▪ to set someone apart **1.** to make someone distinguishable from others distinguir a alguien **2.** to give someone a special calling apartar a alguien

to **set aside** dejar a salvo ▪ apartar

to **set aside time for** reservar tiempo para

to **set aside time to do something** ▪ to make time to do something dedicar tiempo a hacer algo

to **set back the clock** ▪ to set the clock back ▪ to turn back the clock ▪ to turn the clock back atrasar el reloj

to **set fire to something** ▪ to set something on fire prender fuego a algo ▪ pegar fuego a algo

to **set foot in** poner (un) pie en ➤ As long as they live in that house, I'll never set foot in it. Mientras vivan en esa casa, jamás pondré un pie en ella.

to **set foot on** poner (un) pie en

to be **set free** ▪ to be freed ▪ to be released ser liberado ▪ ser puesto en libertad

to **set goals** fijar metas ▪ establecer metas

to **set in** empezar ▪ instalarse ➤ A spell of bad weather has set in. Un período de mal tiempo ha empezado.

to be **set in a place** estar ambientado en un lugar ▪ tener como marco un lugar ➤ The story is set in Rota. El cuento está ambientado en Rota.

to **set in motion** poner en movimiento

to be **set in one's ways** tener manías muy arraigadas

to **set in type** poner en letras para la imprenta ▪ poner letras para ser impresa

to **set limits on something** ▪ to place limits on something ▪ to put limits on something ▪ to impose limits on something fijar límites a algo ▪ establecer límites a algo ▪ poner límites a algo ➤ *(headline)* Germany sets strict entry limits on citizens from twenty-two countries Alemania fija fuertes límites a la entrada de ciudadanos de veintidós países

set lofty goals fijar metas altas

set of books juego de libros ➤ I have a complete leatherbound set of Emerson's essays. Tengo un juego encuadernado en piel de los ensayos de Emerson.

set of CDs juego de discos compactos ▪ juego de CDs ➤ He has a complete set of Mozart's piano concertos on CD. Tiene un juego completo de los conciertos de piano de Mozart en discos compactos.

set of china vajilla de porcelana ▪ vajilla china ➤ This set of china comes in a variety of colors. Esta vajilla de porcelana viene en varios colores. ▪ Esta vajilla china viene en un amplio surtido de colores.

set of glasses juego de vasos

set of instructions la serie de instrucciones ➤ We need a perfect set of instructions, step by step, for checking our E-mail. Necesitamos una serie de instrucciones, paso a paso, para ver nuestro correo electrónico.

set of keys juego de llaves

set of symptoms cuadro de síntomas

set of teeth dentura (completa) ▪ sistema dental

to **set off a bomb** ▪ to detonate a bomb ▪ to explode a bomb hacer estallar una bomba ▪ detonar una bomba

to **set off a firecracker** hacer estallar un petardo

to **set off a trap** hacer saltar una trampa ➤ The mouse set off the trap and got away with the cheese. El ratón hizo saltar la trampa y se quedó con el queso.

to **set off along the path** ▪ to set off down the path ▪ to start down the path adentrarse en el sendero ▪ encaminarse por el sendero

to **set off an alarm** ▪ to set an alarm off ▪ to trip an alarm hacer sonar una alarma ▪ hacer saltar una alarma ▪ hacer disparar una alarma

to **set off an explosion** hacer estallar una explosión ▪ provocar una explosión

to **set off an explosive** hacer estallar un artefacto explosivo ➤ On the sixteenth of September, which is Mexican Independence Day, we set off firecrackers and fireworks. En el dieciséis de septiembre, que es el día de la Independencia mexicana, hicimos estallar cuetes y fuegos artificiales.

to **set off for a place** marcharse a un lugar ▪ marcharse a un sitio ➤ After the children set off for school, I took a deep breath, sat down, and read the paper. Después de que los niños se marcharon a la escuela, respiré hondo, me senté y leí el periódico.

to **set one's sights on** ▪ to have one's sights set on marcarse como objetivo ▪ tener la mira puesta en ➤ *(headline)* Aznar sets his sights on counteracting the nationalists in this legislature. Aznar se marca como objetivo neutralizar a los nacionalistas en esta legislatura.

to **set one's watch back** retrasar el reloj ➤ Don't forget to set your watch back an hour tonight. No te olvides de retrasar el reloj esta noche.

to **set one's watch by...** poner el reloj con el tiempo de... ➤ I set my watch by the clock in the newsroom, which is synchronized with the U.S. Naval Observatory clock. Puse mi reloj de pulsera con el tiempo del reloj en la sala de redacción, el cual está sincronizado con el del observatorio de la marina estadounidense.

to **set oneself on fire** ▪ to burn oneself alive ▪ to incinerate oneself quemarse a lo bonzo ▪ prenderse fuego a lo bonzo ▪ quemarse vivo ▪ incinerarse

to **set out by car** partir en coche ➤ We set out by car toward the northeast. Partimos en coche en dirección noroeste.

to **set out for** emprender marcha a ▪ ponerse en camino a ▪ ponerse en camino hacia ▪ ponerse en camino para

to **set out for home** ▪ to set off for home ▪ to head (for) home ▪ to set off on one's way home emprender el camino de su casa

to **set out on one's way back home** to set off on one's way back home ▪ to head back home emprender el camino de regreso a casa ▪ emprender el camino de vuelta a su casa

set phrase ▪ expression ▪ idiom frase hecha

to **set sail** ▪ to go to sea hacerse a la mar ▪ hacerse a la vela ▪ darse a la vela

to **set sail for** hacerse a la vela con rumbo a ▪ hacerse a la mar con rumbo a ▪ zarpar con rumbo a

to **set someone apart** ▪ to set apart someone **1.** to make someone distinguishable from others distinguir a alguien **2.** to give someone a special calling apartar a alguien

to **set someone free** ▪ to free someone ▪ to release someone liberar a alguien ▪ dejar a alguien en libertad

to **set someone straight** sacar a alguien de su error ▪ sacar a alguien del error

to **set someone up** **1.** *(negative)* tenderle una trampa a alguien **2.** *(positive)* equipar a alguien ➤ Gore Vidal's novel *Lincoln* raises the question whether Lincoln set himself up on the night of his assassination. La novela *Lincoln* de Gore Vidal plantea la cuestion si Lincoln se tendió su propia trampa la noche de su asesinato. ➤ The groom's parents set the newlyweds up with a new house and car. Los padres del novio equiparon a los recién casados con una casa y coche nuevo.

to **set someone's appointment for...** ▪ to schedule one's appointment for... ▪ to schedule one for... darle hora para... ➤ He set my appointment for Monday. ▪ He scheduled my appointment for Monday. ■ He scheduled me for Monday. Me ha dado hora para lunes.

to **set something down** ■ to put something down posar algo ■ dejar algo

to **set something down in writing** ■ to set down something on paper poner algo por escrito ➤ I've set a few ideas down in writing that I'd like to go over with you sometime. He puesto unas ideas por escrito que me gustaría comentar contigo en algún momento.

to **set something in type** ■ to typeset something componer algo ➤ The computer sets the document in type. ■ The computer typesets the document. La computadora compone el documento. ■ *(Sp.)* El ordenador compone el documento.

to **set something on fire** ■ to set fire to something prender fuego a algo

to **set something on something** ■ to put something on something ■ to place something on something **1.** *(object)* poner algo en algo ■ dejar algo en algo **2.** *(dial, indicator, etc.)* poner algo en algo ■ programar algo en algo ➤ Set it on the table. Ponlo en la mesa. ■ Ponla en la mesa. ■ Déjalo en la mesa. ■ Déjala en la mesa. ➤ Set it on high for thirty seconds. Ponlo en alto durante treinta segundos. ■ Prográmalo en alto durante treinta segundos.

to **set something to music** ponerle música a algo

to **set the alarm 1.** *(clock)* poner el despertador **2.** *(burglar alarm)* poner la alarma ➤ Six forty-five a.m. is the time I always set the alarm for. Las seis y cuarenta y cinco es la hora a que siempre pongo el despertador.

to **set the clock** fijar el reloj ■ poner en hora el reloj

to **set the clock an hour ahead** ■ to set the clock ahead an hour adelantar el reloj una hora ➤ To change to Daylight Savings Time in early spring, you set the clock one hour ahead. ■ To change to Daylight Savings Time in early spring, you set the clock forward one hour. Para cambiar al horario de verano a principios de la primavera, se adelanta el reloj una hora.

to **set the clock back an hour** atrasar el reloj una hora

to **set the cycle on...** *(washing machine, dryer, etc.)* poner el ciclo en... ■ programar el ciclo en... ➤ Set the cycle on permanent press. Pon el ciclo en planchado permanente. ■ Programar el ciclo en planchado permanente.

to **set the date of something** ■ to set the date for something ■ to schedule something for a certain date fijar la fecha de algo ■ programar la fecha de algo

to **set the date of the meeting** ■ to schedule the meeting programar la fecha de la reunión ■ fijar la fecha de la reunión

to **set the delivery for a certain day** ■ to arrange the delivery for a certain day programar la entrega para cierto día

to **set the dial** regular el botón ■ poner el botón ➤ Set the dial in the desired position. Regular el botón en la posición deseada. ■ Poner el botón en la posición deseada.

to **set the dog on someone** ■ to sick the dog on someone ■ to sic the dog on someone echarle el perro a alguien

to **set the equation equal to zero** igualar la equación a cero

to **set the example** marcar las pautas ■ dar el ejemplo

to **set the goal of** ■ to set as a goal ponerse la meta de ■ ponerse como objetivo

to **set the margins** fijar los margenes ➤ Would you show me how to set the margins? ¿Me enseñarías cómo fijar los margenes?

to **set the price** fijar el precio

to **set the propeller at *x* revolutions per minute of a propeller** ■ to set the RPM (of a propeller) at *x* fijar la hélice a *x* revoluciones por minuto ■ poner la hélice a *x* revoluciones por minuto ➤ Set the propeller at twenty-seven hundred revolutions per minute for takeoff, then at an altitude of five hundred feet reduce the RPM to twenty-five hundred, and then again at cruise altitude to twenty-four hundred. Fija la hélice a dos mil setecientas revoluciones por minuto para el depegue, luego a la altitud de quinientos pies reduce las RPM a dos mil quinientas, y al alcanzar la altitude de crucero, a dos mil cuatrocientas. ■ Pon la hélice a dos mil setecientas revoluciones por minuto para el depegue, luego a la altitud de quinientos pies reduce las RPM a dos mil quinientas, y al alcanzar la altitude de crucero, a dos mil cuatrocientas.

to **set the record for** establecer el récord por

to **set the record straight** desmentir una información ■ aclarar los tantos

to **set the standard** dar la talla

to **set the standard for** dar la talla para

to **set the table** poner la mesa

to **set the temperature** programar la temperatura ■ seleccionar la temperatura

to **set the time of something** concretar la hora de algo ■ fijar la hora de algo ■ establecer la hora de algo ■ poner la hora de algo ➤ We need to set a time for the meeting. Tenemos que concretar la hora de la reunión. ■ Tenemos que fijar la hora de la reunión.

to **set the timer** programar el temporizador ■ programar el contador ■ fijar el temporizador ■ fijar el contador ■ fijar el timer

to **set the tone for** dar el tono para ■ establecer el tono para

to **set the tone of** establecer el tono de

set theory *(mathematics, logic)* la teoría de conjuntos

to **set things right** arreglar las cosas

to **set things straight** desmentir una información ■ aclarar las cosas

to be **set to music** ponerle música ➤ The poem has been set to music. Se le ha puesto música al poema.

to **set up** *(intransitive verb)* **1.** *(glue)* to harden ■ to dry secar ■ pegarse ■ solidificarse **2.** *(gelatin)* to jell ■ to congeal cuajarse **3.** *(water)* to solidify ■ to freeze ■ to turn to ice hacerse hielo ➤ It takes epoxy only a matter of seconds to set up. Resina epoxídica se seca en cuestión de segundos. ➤ How long does it take this glue to set up? ■ How long does it take this glue to dry? ¿Cuánto (tiempo) tarda este pegamento en secar? ➤ It takes four to five hours for the gelatin to set (up). La gelatina tarda en cuajarse entre cuatro y cinco horas. ➤ It takes several hours for the ice cubes to set up. ■ It takes several hours for the water to solidify into ice. El hielo tarda algunas horas en hacerse.

to be **set up 1.** to be established estar establecido **2.** to be framed hacerle la cama a alguien ➤ I´d like to stay here in Spain; I'm set up here. Me gustaría quedarme en España. Estoy establecido aquí. ➤ He was set up by the mafia. ■ He was framed by the mafia. La mafia le hizo la cama.

to **set up a display** ■ to set a display up montar una exposición

to **set up an appointment** arreglar una cita

to **set up something** *(transitive verb)* ■ to set something up ■ to connect all the pieces of something montar algo ➤ Have you set up the computer and printer? ¿Has montado ya el ordenador y la impresora? ➤ We set up an electric train around the Christmas tree. Montamos un tren eléctrico alrededor del árbol de Navidad.

setting for salida para

the **setting of the story is** ■ the story takes place in ■ the story is set in el cuento está ambientado en ➤ The setting of Alarcón's story *The Stub Book* is Rota. ■ Rota is the setting of Alarcón's story *The Stub Book*. El cuento de Alarcón *El libro talonario* está ambientado en Rota.

setting sun *el* sol poniente

to **settle a debt** ■ to pay off a debt saldar una deuda

to **settle accounts 1.** to settle up ■ to get square ■ to square things up arreglar cuentas ■ ajustar cuentas **2.** to get even ajustar cuentas ■ saldar cuentas

to **settle an account** saldar una cuenta

to **settle down 1.** to get quiet calmarse ■ tranquilizarse **2.** to get established echar raíces ➤ The substitute teacher couldn't get the seventh graders to settle down. El substituto no pudo hacer que los chicos del séptimo curso no se calmaran. ■ El substituto no pudo hacer que los chicos del séptimo curso no se tranquilizaran. ■ El substituto no pudo hacer que los chicos del séptimo curso no se calmasen. ■ El substituto no pudo hacer que los chicos del séptimo curso se tranquilizasen. ➤ Now settle down and get to work! ¡Cálmense y pónganse a trabajar! ■ *(Sp.)* ¡Disponeos a trabajar! ➤ I've decided to settle (down) in my hometown after having lived away for many years. He decidido echar raíces en mi ciudad natal después de haber vivido fuera durante muchos años. ▪ He decidido establecerme en mi ciudad natal después de haber vivido fuera durante muchos años.

to **settle for** ▪ to be content with conformarse con ➤ I'd settle for that. Me conformaría con eso.

to **settle in** instalarse ➤ The cold weather has settled in. El tiempo frío se ha instalado.

to **settle in a place** instalarse en un lugar ▪ asentarse en un lugar ▪ radicarse ➤ After the war the family settled in the United States. Después de la guerra la familia se instalaron en los Estados Unidos. ➤ The Gauls settled in Galicia and in other parts of Europe. Los galos se asentaron en Galicia y en otras partes de Europa.

to **settle in one's lungs** situarse en los pulmones ▪ asentarse en los pulmones ➤ The infection has settled in his lungs. La infección se ha situado en los pulmones. ▪ La infección se ha asentado en los pulmones.

to **settle into an armchair** ▪ to sink into an armchair apalancarse en un sillón

to **settle the question** zanjar el tema

to **settle up** ▪ to settle accounts ajustar cuentas ▪ arreglar cuentas

settling of accounts el ajuste de cuentas

seven deadly sins siete pecados capitales

several years varios años ➤ The remains had been there for several years. Los restos llevaban allí varios años.

severance package: to receive a ~ recibir una liquidación ▪ recibir una indemnización por despido

Severe Acute Respiratory Syndrome ▪ SARS neumonía atípica

to **sew on a button** coser un botón ▪ *(coll.)* pegar un botón ➤ Would you sew on this collar button for me? ¿Me coserías el bóton del cuello (de la camisa)?

to be **sewn onto the sleeve** ▪ to be worn on the sleeve llevar bordado en la manga

sex appeal atractivo sexual

sex education *la* educación sexual

sex life vida sexual

sexist joke *el* chiste machista

sexual harassment acoso sexual

sexual pleasure gozo sexual ▪ *el* goce sexual

sexually transmitted disease ▪ STD *la* enfermedad de transmisión sexual

shade of a color ▪ hue of a color *el* matiz de un color ▪ *la* tonalidad de un color

Shadow Lands *(film title) Tierras de penumbra*

shady past pasado sombrío

shady side ▪ side in the shade lado de la sombra ➤ Let's walk on the shady side of the street. ▪ Let's walk on the side of the street that's in the shade. Vamos a caminar en el lado sombrío de la calle. ▪ *(Sp.)* Vamos a andar en el lado sombrío de la calle.

shady spot *el* paraje sombreado ▪ paraje con sombra

to **shake hands with someone** darse la mano con alguien ▪ *(formal)* estrechar la mano de alguien ➤ We shook hands. Nos dimos la mano. ➤ We shook hands firmly. Nos dimos la mano con firmeza. ▪ Estrechamos nuestras manos con firmeza. ➤ I shook hands with President Obama. Di la mano al presidente Obama.

to **shake like a leaf** estar como un flan

to **shake off** sacudirse ➤ Two birds, shaking off the fuel... Dos aves, sacudiéndose el combustible...

to **shake off one's fears** deshacerse de sus miedos

to **shake off the effects of the drug** sacudirse los efectos de la droga

to **shake off the tyranny of** sacudirse la tiranía de

shake on it! ▪ let's shake on it démonos la mano ▪ estrechemos la mano

to **shake on the deal** darse la mano para cerrar el trato ➤ We shook on the deal. Nos dimos la mano para cerrar el trato. ➤ (Let's) shake on it. Vamos a darnos la mano para cerrar el trato.

to **shake one's head** menear la cabeza ▪ mover la cabeza

to **shake the dew off the rose** *(colorful)* ▪ to take a leak sacar el canario a pacer

to **shake up someone** ▪ to shake someone up quedar (muy) dolido ▪ quedar (muy) sentido ▪ inquietar a alguien

to be **shaken to its foundations** quedar sacudido hasta los cimientos

to be **shaken to one's foundations** quedar sacudido hasta los cimientos ▪ quedar sacudido hasta las entrañas

to be **shaken up** ▪ to be badly shaken ser (muy) conmocionado ➤ The stagecoach passengers were shaken up when the horses bolted in fright because of a thunderclap. ▪ The stagecoach passengers were badly shaken when the horses bolted in fright from a thunderclap. Los pasajeros de la diligencia fueron muy conmocionados cuando los caballos se echaron a correr por el asusto de un trueno.

shall I fold these for you? *(shirts) (tú)* ¿te las doblo? ▪ *(usted)* ¿se las doblo?

shall I slice it for you? ▪ would you like me to slice it for you? *(tú)* ¿te lo rebano? ▪ ¿te lo troceo? ▪ *(usted)* ¿se lo rebano? ▪ ¿se lo troceo?

shall I spell out the number or write it (as numerals)? ¿lo pongo en número o en letra?

shall we be on our way? ▪ shall we go? ¿nos vamos?

shall we say 1. let's say digamos **2.** let's put it that way digámoslo así

shall we talk? ¿hablamos?

shame on you! ¡qué vergüenza!

Shank's pony: to go on ~ *(humorous)* ▪ to go on foot ▪ to walk ir en el coche de San Fernando ▪ ir a pie ➤ I went on Shank's pony. ▪ I went on foot. ▪ I walked. Fui en el coche de San Fernando. ▪ Fui a pie.

shape of an object forma de un objeto ➤ I don't like the shape of the jar. It can turn over in the refrigerator. No me gusta la forma de la jarra. Se puede voltear en el frigorífico.

to **shape something with the hands** dar forma a algo con las manos ▪ formar algo con las manos ▪ plasmar algo con las manos

shapely legs piernas bien torneadas ▪ piernas bien esculpidas

to **share an apartment with someone** ▪ to share a flat with someone compartir un piso con alguien

share of the blame *la* porción de culpa

share of the pie: to get a ~ *(literal and figurative)* conseguir una porción de la tarta

to **share something with someone 1.** to have in common compartir algo con alguien **2.** to use in common compartir algo con alguien **3.** to divide between ▪ to split between ▪ to distribute between repartir algo con alguien ➤ Schopenhauer shares with Freud the idea that human behavior can be reduced to a few basic drives. Schopenhauer comparte con Freud la idea de que el comportamiento de los seres humanos se reduce a unos pocos instintos básicos. ➤ We shared an apartment when we were students. Compartimos un piso cuando eramos estudiantes. ➤ Do you want to share the rest of the ice cream with me? ¿Quieres repartir el resto del helado? ➤ Do you want to share what's left of the ice cream? ¿Quieres repartir lo que queda del helado?

sharp curve in the road recodo del camino ▪ recodo en el camino ▪ curva cerrada en el camino

sharp drop fuerte caída ▪ fuertes caídas ➤ Sharp drop in stock prices Fuertes caídas en los precios de las acciones

sharp increase in costs fuerte subida de costos

sharp increase in prices fuerte subida de precios

sharp knife cuchillo afilado

sharp major sostenido mayor ➤ Chopin's "Barcarolle in F-sharp major" "El Barcarolle en Fa sostenido" de Chopin

sharp minor sostenido menor ➤ Rachmaninoff's "Prelude in C-sharp minor" "El preludio en Do menor" de Rachmaninoff

sharp pain dolor acerbo ▪ dolor punzante

sharp point punta afilada ➤ I like to draw with this (mechanical) pencil because it has a sharper point than the other one. Me gusta dibujar con este portaminas porque tiene la punta más afilada que el otro.

sharp-pointed puntiagudo

sharp teeth dientes afilados

sharp wit ▪ keen wit ingenio agudo

to **sharpen one's wits** aguzar el ingenio ▪ alfilar el ingenio

sharps and flats sostenidos y bemoles
to **shave one's beard** afeitarse la barba
to **shave one's head** cortarse el pelo al cero ▪ raparse
to **shave someone's beard** hacer la barba a alguien
shavings of a carrot ▪ carrot shavings pestañas de zanahoria *(cut in spiral or swirls)*
she and my mother mi madre y ella ➤ She and my mother are friends. Mi madre y ella son amigas.
she doesn't even know I exist ella ni siquiera sabe que existo ▪ ella ni siquiera me da bola
she doesn't look like one ella no tiene aspecto de serla
she even y aún ▪ y todavía ▪ incluso
she goes and goes ▪ she's always on the go ▪ she keeps on the go ▪ she stays on the go (ella) va y va
she goes by... ▪ they call her... (a ella) le dicen...
she has passed the marrying age *(coll.)* se le ha pasado el arroz ▪ se le pasó el arroz
she is what she is ▪ she is who she is es quien es
she might know puede que sepa (ella) ▪ tal vez ella sepa
she must not... debe de ser que no... ➤ She must not wash her hair. Debe de ser que no se lava el pelo.
she only wants to... ▪ all she wants is to... no quiere sino...
she was right (ella) tuvo razón ▪ (ella) tenía razón ▪ (ella) acertó
she was still very young era aún muy niña
she was the one who... ▪ it was she who... fue ella que...
she who... ella que...
to **shear sheep** trasquilar ovejas ▪ esquilar ovejas
shearing season: (sheep) ~ temporada de esquileo
to **shed crocodile tears** derramar lágrimas de cocodrilo
to **shed light on something** arrojar luz sobre algo
to **shed tears** verter lágrimas ▪ derramar lágrimas
to be a **sheer coincidence** ▪ to be a mere coincidence ▪ to be just a coincidence ▪ to be purely coincidental ser una mera casualidad
to be **sheer luck (that...)** ▪ to be pure luck (that...) ser de pura suerte (que...) ▪ *(Mex., coll.)* salirle de pura chapupa
sheet of paper ▪ piece of paper **1.** *(without lines or holes)* folio ▪ pliego **2.** *(with holes)* hoja
she'll be furious se pondrá furiosa
she'll be here any minute (now) (ella) llega en cualquier momento ▪ *(Mex.)*(ella) ya mero llega
shelled nuts frutos secos pelados
shelled pecans *(Mex.)* nueces peladas ▪ nueces sin cáscara
shelled seafood mariscos sin su concha ▪ mariscos ya pelados
shelled walnuts *(Sp.)* nueces peladas ▪ nueces sin cáscara
to **shelve a bill** aparcar un proyecto de ley
to **shelve a matter** ▪ to postpone a matter ▪ *(informal)* ▪ to put a matter on the back burner aparcar un asunto ▪ aplazar un asunto
to **shelve a motion** dar carpetazo a una moción
to **shelve books** colocar libros en los estantes ➤ I shelved books at the university library when I was a student. Colocaba libros en los estantes en la biblioteca universitaria cuando yo fui estudiante.
she's a ten es una mujer diez
she's going on *x* (years of age) (ella) va para *x* (años)
she's going to be okay ▪ she's going to recover ▪ she'll recover ella va a estar bien ▪ ella va a salir adelante ▪ ella va a ponerse bien
she's growing on me ▪ I like her better than I did at first me va entrando
she's interesting to talk to es interesante hablar con ella
she's late (ella) está tarde ▪ ella está tardando
she's not here yet (ella) aún no ha llegado
she's not the only one no sólo ella lo hace ▪ no sólo a ella le pasa
she's not the only one who... (ella) no es la única que...
she's nuts ▪ she's cracked ▪ she's crazy está chiflada ▪ está loca
to **shield oneself against** abroquelarse contra ▪ protegerse de
to **shield someone from something** ▪ to form a protective barrier against something abrigar a alguien de algo ▪ proteger a alguien de algo
to **shift during flight** moverse durante el vuelo ➤ Items tend to shift during flight. Los artículos tienden a moverse durante el vuelo.
to **shift for oneself** arreglárselas
to **shift gears** ▪ to change gears cambiar de marcha ▪ pasar cambios
shift in the wind ▪ shifting of the wind ▪ change in the wind salto de viento ▪ cambio en la dirección del viento
to **shift into first gear** ▪ to shift into low gear ▪ to put it into low meter (la) primera
to **shift into low gear** ▪ to shift into first gear ▪ to put it into low gear meter (la) primera
to **shift into reverse** ▪ to put it in reverse meter marcha atrás ▪ poner marcha atrás
to **shift one's attention to** desplazarse la atención hacia
shifting of the wind ▪ shift in the wind ▪ change in the wind salto de viento ▪ cambio en la dirección del viento
to **shine one's shoes** lustrar los zapatos ▪ limpiar los zapatos
shipment of goods: to send a ~ **1.** hacer un envío de bienes **2.** *(large and crated)* enviar una partida de bienes
to **shirk responsibility** esquivar la responsabilidad ▪ zafarse de la responsabilidad
shirking of responsibility ▪ evasion of responsibility *la* evasión de la responsabilidad ▪ *la* dejación de responsabilidad
shirttails: to pull out one's ~ ▪ to pull one's shirttails out sacarse la camisa (por fuera) *("Shirttail" is "bajo de camisa" or "los bordes de la camisa.")*
shirttails: to tuck in one's ~ ▪ to tuck one's shirttails in meterse la camisa (por dentro)
shirttails out: to leave one's ~ ▪ to wear one's shirttails out llevar la camisa por fuera del pantalón ➤ Of all my shirts that can be worn with the tails out, this (one) is the only one that has a collar. De todas las camisas que puedo llevar por fuera, ésta es la única que tiene cuello.
shish kebab brocheta
the **shit's gonna hit the fan** *(off-color)* ▪ *(benign alternative)* The Moregrow's gonna hit the Mixmaster la mierda va a salpicar mucho ▪ se va a armar la podrida
shiver ran up my spine un escalofrío recorrió todo mi cuerpo ▪ un temblor recorrió todo mi cuerpo
shock absorber el amortiguador
shock (of an impact) el choque (de un impacto)
shock wave **1.** *(of an earthquake)* resonancia **2.** *(of a bomb)* onda expansiva
to be **shocked by the news** ▪ to be stunned by the news quedarse impactado por la noticia ▪ chocarle la noticia ▪ *(journalistic, literary)* quedarse conmocionado
shoe leather: to be like ~ *(steak)* ▪ to be tough as shoe leather estar como la suela de un zapato
the **shoe's on the other foot** ▪ se han vuelto las tornas
to **shoo the flies** espantar las moscas
to **shoot a movie** rodar una película ▪ grabar una película
to **shoot an arrow** disparar una flecha
to **shoot at a goal** *(sports)* ▪ to shoot for the goal tirar al gol ▪ tirar al arco
to **shoot at someone** dispararle a alguien
to **shoot at something** dispararle a algo
to **shoot down an airplane** derribar un avión ▪ abatir (a tiros) un avión ➤ They shot down a civilian airplane. Se bajaron un avión civil. ▪ Derribaron un avión civil.
to **shoot for a goal** **1.** *(sports)* tirar al gol **2.** *(figurative)* intentar alcanzar un objetivo (antes de un tiempo determinado) ➤ Let's shoot for sometime next week. Vamos a buscar un hueco algún día de la semana que viene.
to **shoot from the hip** **1.** *(literal)* to shoot with the pistol at hip level disparar a la altura de la cadera **2.** *(figurative)* to give an opinion off the top of one's head expresar una opinión espontánea sin estudiar una materia detenidamente
to **shoot off** *(graphic)* ▪ to come ▪ to ejaculate correrse ▪ venirse

to **shoot off fireworks** 1. *(backyard fireworks)* tirar cohetes 2. *(aerial fireworks)* tirar fuegos artificiales

to **shoot off one's (big) mouth** ■ to shoot off at the mouth ■ to run off at the mouth írse(le) la boca a alguien ■ *(colorful)* soltar la sin hueso

to **shoot oneself** pegarse un tiro

to **shoot over the bow of a ship** ■ to fire across the bow of a ship disparar por encima de la proa de un barco

to **shoot pool** ■ to shoot some pool ■ to play pool jugar al billar ■ billar

to **shoot someone** dispararle a alguien ➤ He shot him in the back. Le disparó en la espalda.

to **shoot someone dead** ■ to shoot someone to death fulminar a alguien de un tiro ■ matar a alguien de un tiro ■ asesinar a alguien a tiros

to **shoot the bull** ■ to shoot the breeze ■ to engage in small talk *(Mex.)* platicar ■ *(Sp.)* charlar

to **shoot the moon** ■ to go all out 1. to put the big pot in the little one ■ to spare no expense tirar la casa por la ventana ■ echar la casa por la ventana 2. to buy the most expensive one comprar el más caro

to **shoot to kill** disparar a matar

to **shoot up like a weed** ■ to grow like a weed ■ to have a growth spurt pegar un estirón ■ crecer como la mala hierba

shooting star estrella fugaz ■ *la* exhalación

shopping cart carro de compras

shopping center centro comercial

short circuit *la* derivación ■ cortocircuito ➤ A short circuit in the hot water heater tripped the circuit breaker. Saltó el automático general por una derivación en el termo de agua caliente. ■ Un cortocircuito en el calentador del agua caliente hizo saltar el cortacircuitos.

short distance away ■ not far away al alcance de la vista

to be a **short distance to** faltar poco para llegar a

to be **short for** 1. to be an abbreviation of ser una abreviatura de 2. to be a shortened form of ser el diminutivo de ■ ser apócope de ➤ CentCom is short for Central Command. CentCom es una abreviatura de Central Command. ➤ Mayte is short for María Teresa. Mayte es el diminutivo de María Teresa. ➤ Prop is short for propeller. Prop es apócope de propeller.

short notice: to do something on ~ hacer algo en poco tiempo ■ hacer algo con poco tiempo ➤ He left on short notice. Salió en poco tiempo.

to be **short of** andar escaso de

to be **short of breath** estar corto(-a) de respiración ■ estar corto(-a) de aliento

short of that ■ failing that en su defecto

short of this ■ failing this en su defecto

to be **short of time** ■ not to have much time ■ to be short on time andar escaso de tiempo ■ no andar bien de tiempo ■ ir fatal de tiempo

to be **short on money** ■ to be short on cash estar corto de dinero

to **short-sheet the bed** hacer la petaca

short sketch ■ brief sketch crónica

short-sleeve shirt camisa de mangas cortas

to **short someone** ■ to give one less than one should have darle de menos ➤ They shorted me one. ■ I was shorted one. Me dieron uno de menos.

short-term memory loss ■ loss of short-term memory pérdida de la memoria de corto plazo

short time ago hace poco tiempo

shortage of ■ scarcity of la escasez de ■ carestía de

to **shortchange someone** darle de menos en el cambio

to **shorten one's stride** ■ to take smaller steps acortar el paso

to **shorten the trip by *x* minutes** ■ to take *x* minutes off the trip ■ to cut *x* minutes off the trip acortar el viaje *x* minutes

shortest possible time el menos tiempo posible

to be the **shortest way** ■ to be the most direct route ser la ruta más corta ■ ser la ruta más directa

shortly: to be along ~ ■ to arrive shortly ■ to be here shortly ■ to get here shortly ■ to be along soon ■ to arrive soon ■ to be here soon ■ to get here soon llegar dentro de poco ■ llegar en breve ➤ Another bus will be along shortly. ■ Another bus will arrive shortly. ■ Another bus will be here shortly. ■ Another bus will get here shortly. Dentro de poco llegará otro autobús.

shortly after poco después de ■ nada más ➤ The airplane crashed shortly after takeoff. El avión se estrelló poco después de despegar. ➤ Shortly after takeoff, the airplane went down after losing an engine. Nada más despegar, el avión se desplomó tras perder un motor.

shortly before... (muy) poco antes de que...

shortly into a los pocos minutos ➤ Shortly into the debate the atmosphere became heated. El ambiente se caldeó a los pocos minutos del debate.

shortsighted corto de miras

to be **shot in the arm** ■ to get shot in the arm ■ to get hit in the arm by a bullet herirle una bala en el brazo ■ alcanzarle una bala en el brazo

to be a **shot in the arm** ■ to be a boost ■ to be a lifesaver ser un balón de oxígeno ■ suponer un balón de oxígeno

shot in the arm: to get ~ ■ to be shot in the arm ■ to get hit in the arm by a bullet herirle una bala en el brazo ■ alcanzarle una bala en el brazo ■ pegarle una bala en el brazo

shot in the arm: to get a ~ ponerle una inyección en el brazo ➤ I got a shot in the arm. ■ They gave me a shot in the arm. Me pusieron una inyección en el brazo.

shot of whiskey 1. *(taken straight)* chupito ■ pelotazo 2. *(poured into another beverage)* chorro ■ pelotazo ➤ Give a me shot of bourbon. Dame un chupito de bourbon. ■ Dame un pelotazo de bourbon. ➤ Could you put a shot of whiskey in it? ¿Podrías echarle un chorro de whiskey? ■ ¿Podrías echarle un pelotazo de whiskey?

to be **shot through the chest** ■ to get shot through the chest atravesarle una bala el pecho ➤ He was shot through the chest. ■ He got shot through the chest. Una bala le atravesó el pecho.

shotgun wedding boda de penalty

should be...: one ~ uno debería ser... ■ uno debería estar... ■ que lo... ➤ He should be punished if he did it. Que lo castiguen si lo hizo.

should have done something: one ~ uno debería haber hecho algo ➤ I should have had him send me a test message. Yo debería haberle hecho enviarme un mensaje de prueba.

should have known: one ~ debería haberlo adivinado ■ debería haberlo sabido ➤ I should have known. (Yo) debería haberlo adivinado.

should I assume command ■ if I should assume command ■ if I were to assume command si yo asumiese el mando ➤ And should I assume command... ■ And if I were to assume the command... Y si yo asumiese el mando...

should never have done something: one ~ ■ one never should have done something uno nunca debió de hacer algo ➤ He should never have come here. Nunca debió de haber venido.

should the occasion arise ■ if the occasion should arise ■ if the occasion arises si se tercia ■ si se encarta

to **shoulder a responsibility** ■ to bear the responsibility llevar una responsabilidad

shoulder arms! ¡armas al hombro!

shoulder to cry on: to be someone's ~ ser el paño de lágrimas de alguien

shoulder to cry on: to need a ~ necesitar un hombro sobre el cual llorar ■ necesitar desahogarse

shoulder to the wheel: to put one's ~ arrimar el hombro ■ poner el hombro a la lid

to **shout as loud as one can** gritar lo más fuerte que uno puede

to **shout at each other** gritarse el uno al otro ■ gritarse entre ellos ➤ They ended up shouting at each other. Acabaron gritándose el uno al otro. ■ Acabaron gritándose entre ellos. ■ *(all females)* Acabaron gritándose la una a la otra. ■ Acabaron gritándose entre ellas.

to **shout at one another** gritarse entre ellos ➤ They ended up shouting at one another. Acabaron gritándose entre ellos. ■ *(all females)* Acabaron gritándose entre ellas.

to **shout at the top of one's lungs** gritar a pleno pulmón

to **shout for joy** gritar de alegría ▪ gritar de júbilo

to **shout it from the rooftops** pregonarlo a los cuatro vientos

to **shout oneself hoarse** desgañitarse ▪ gritar hasta roncarse ▪ gritar hasta quedar afónico(-a)

to **show a balance** arrojar un saldo ➤ The account shows a current balance of eight hundred dollars. La cuenta arroja un saldo actual de ochocientos dólares.

to **show a movie** echar una película ▪ poner una película ▪ pasar una película ➤ They're going to show *Catch Me If You Can* on TV this Friday. ▪ The movie *Catch Me If You Can* is going to be on TV this Friday. Van a echar *Atrápame* si puedes en la tele este viernes. ➤ Is *Titanic* showing anywhere? ¿Ponen *Titanic* en algún sitio?

to **show a payment** mostrar un pago ▪ mostrar algún pago ➤ Do you show a payment in February? ¿Se muestra un pago en febrero? ▪ ¿Se muestra algún pago en febrero?

to **show a result** dar un resultado ▪ arrojar un resultado

to **show affection for someone** ▪ to show someone affection manifestarle afecto a alguien ▪ mostrarle afecto a alguien

to **show an interest in someone** ▪ to take an interest in someone interesarse en alguien ▪ interesarse por alguien

to **show an interest in something** ▪ to take an interest in something interesarse en algo ▪ interesarse por algo

show business negocio del espectáculo ▪ mundo del espectáculo

to **show clearly that...** indicar claramente que... ▪ demostrar claramente que...

to **show her to her room** ▪ to see her to her room pasarla a su habitación ▪ acompañarla a su habitación

to **show her to the door** ▪ to see her to the door acompañarla a la puerta

to **show him to his room** ▪ to see him to his room pasarlo a su habitación ▪ *(Sp., leísmo)* pasarle a su habitación

to **show him to the door** ▪ to see him to the door acompañarlo a la puerta ▪ *(Sp., leísmo)* acompañarle a la puerta

to **show it** ▪ to betray it ▪ to reveal it ▪ to give it away ▪ to let on demostrar ▪ exteriorizarlo ➤ I always feel apprehensive before going on stage, even though I don't show it. Siempre me siento inquieto antes de subir al escenario aunque no lo demuestro. ▪ Siempre me siento inquieto antes de subir al escenario aunque no lo exteriorizo.

to **show itself to be** revelarse como

to **show movies** poner películas ▪ pasar películas ▪ dar ➤ They were showing *Gone with the Wind*. Daban *Lo que el viento se llevó*.

to **show no mercy** no mostrar misericordia

to **show no sign(s) of** ▪ not to show any signs of no dar ninguna seña de ▪ no tener trazas de

to **show no signs of life** ▪ not to show any signs of life no dar señales de vida

show of affection ▪ expression of affection *la* demostración de afecto

show of force ▪ deployment of force *el* despliegue de fuerza

show of wealth *el* despliegue de riquezas

to **show off** lucirse ▪ *(Arg.)* hacerse el canchero ▪ *(Sp.)* postinear

to **show off a new car** lucirse con un coche nuevo

to **show one's face** darse ver

to **show one's feelings** mostrar sus sentimientos ▪ revelar sus sentimientos

to **show one's hand** ▪ to reveal one's hand mostrar sus cartas ▪ descubrir las cartas

to **show one's true self** ▪ to show one's true colors mostrar el verdadero yo ▪ *(coll.)* enseñar el cobre ▪ pelar el cobre

to **show oneself to be** revelarse como

to **show respect for someone** mostrar respeto hacia alguien

to **show scars** ▪ to have scars ostentar cicatrices

to **show signs of** presentar signos de ➤ The body showed no signs of violence. El cuerpo no presentaba signos de violencia.

to **show signs of life** dar señales de vida

to **show someone how to do something** enseñar a alguien (como) hacer algo

to **show someone into** indicarlo a ▪ hacerle pasar a ➤ The butler showed him into the garden. El mayordomo lo indicó al jardín.

to **show someone to one's room** mostrar a alguien a su habitación ▪ llevar a alguien a su habitación ▪ acompañar a alguien a su habitación ▪ indicarle a alguien a su habitación ➤ The butler showed him to his room. El mayordomo le mostró a su habitación.

to **show someone to the door** ▪ to see someone to the door ▪ to accompany someone to the door acompañar a alguien a la puerta ▪ llevar a alguien a la puerta ➤ Would you show him to the door? ¿Lo acompañarías a la puerta? ▪ *(Sp., leísmo)* ¿Le acompañarías a la puerta?

to **show up** aparecer ▪ acudir ▪ presentarse ➤ He didn't show up. No se presentó. ➤ *Now* you show up! ¡Ahora apareces! ▪ ¡A buenas horas, mangas verdes! ➤ I was expecting twenty people at the party and fifty showed up. Esperaba que vinieran veinte personas a la fiesta y se presentaron cincuenta. ➤ The electrician hasn't shown up. El electricista no se ha presentado. ▪ El electricista no ha venido. ➤ Often nothing much is expected of you, just that you show up. A menudo no se espera mucho de ti, salvo que te presentes.

to **show up at the wrong time** aparecer en un mal momento ➤ He showed up at the wrong time. Apareció en un mal momento.

to **show up for work** presentarse a trabajar ➤ He didn't show up for work yesterday. No se presentó a trabajar ayer.

show window *el* escaparate ▪ vidriera

show yourself! ▪ own up! ▪ (whoever did it) come forward! ¡que dé la cara!

shower stall el pie de ducha

showing (of a movie) el pase (de película) ➤ Next showing 7:15 p.m. El próximo pase de película 7:15 p.m.

shred of evidence: not to have a ~ no tener ni una sola prueba ▪ no tener ni la más mínima prueba ➤ The police don't have a shred of evidence. La policía no tiene ni una sola prueba. ▪ La policía no tiene ni la más mínima prueba.

to **shred paper** triturar papel

shredded beef carne ripiada ▪ carne deshebrada

shredded documents documentos triturados

to **shrug one's shoulders** encoger los hombros ▪ alzarse los hombros

a **shudder convulsed me** un temblor recorrió todo mi cuerpo

a **shudder ran (up and) down my spine** un temblor me recorrió todo el cuerpo

to be a **shut-in** ▪ to be lonely estar entre cuatro paredes

to **shut one's eyes** ▪ to close one's eyes cerrar los ojos

to **shut someone up** taparle el gallo

to **shut the door** to close the door cerrar la puerta

shut up! *(impolite)* ¡cállete! ▪ ¡cállate la boca! ▪ *(Sp., vosotros)* ¡cállaos! ▪ ¡a callar!

to **shy away from doing something** recatarse de hacer algo

to **shy away from something** recatarse de algo

Siamese twins hermanos(as) siameses(as) ▪ siameses(as) ➤ The Siamese twins were joined at the head. Las (hermanas) siamesas estaban unidas por la cabeza.

to be **sick and tired of something** estar empachado con algo ➤ I'm sick and tired of being a football widow! Estoy empachada con ser la esposa de un teleadicto al fútbol.

to be **sick of someone** ▪ to be fed up with someone estar empachado de alguien ▪ estar harto de alguien

to be **sick of something** ▪ to be fed up with something estar empachado de algo ▪ estar harto de algo

to **sick the dog on someone** ▪ to sic the dog on someone ▪ to set the dog on someone echarle el perro a alguien

to be **sick to death of** estar hasta los moños de

to be **sick to one's stomach** ▪ to be sick on one's stomach estar descompuesto

side dish ▪ side order *el* acompañante

side effect efecto secundario

side of a building cara de un edificio

side of a CD lado de un CD

side of a hill ▪ hillside ▪ slope of a hill falda de una colina

side of a mountain ▪ mountainside ▪ slope of a mountain ▪ mountain slope lado de una montaña ▪ cara de una montaña
side of a street lado de una calle
side of an argument la parte ➤ I listened to both sides of the argument. Escuché a las dos partes del argumento.
side of the body hemisferio del cuerpo ▪ la parte del cuerpo
side of the mountain ▪ mountainside ladera de la montaña
side of the road ▪ roadside orilla del camino
side order ▪ order of something on the side acompañamiento ▪ guarnición ▪ pequeño plato
side salad ensalada acompañante
side-splitting laughter risa desternillante
side view vista de perfil
to **side with someone** estar del lado de alguien
to **side with someone in a dispute** **1.** to take sides with someone in a dispute ponerse de parte de alguien en una disputa ▪ ponerse a favor de alguien en una disputa **2.** to be on someone's side estar de parte de alguien en una disputa ▪ estar del lado de alguien en una disputa ➤ President Hayes sided with Paraguay in the dispute over the Chaco. ▪ President Hayes took Paraguay's side in the dispute over the Chaco. ▪ El presidente Hayes se puso de parte de Paraguay en la disputa fronteriza sobre el Chaco. ➤ President Hayes sided with Paraguay in the dispute over the Chaco. ▪ President Hayes was on Paraguay's side in the dispute over the Chaco. El presidente Hayes estuvo de lado de Paraguay en la disputa sobre el Chaco. ▪ El presidente Hayes estuvo de parte de Paraguay en la disputa sobre el Chaco.
sidearms armas cortas
sideline: to do something as a ~ hacer algo como empleo suplimentario
sides of a pan *las* paredes de una cacerola ▪ *(Sp.)* paredes de un cazo
sides of a pot *las* paredes de una olla
sides of an issue ▪ sides of a question aspectos de una cuestión ➤ There are two sides to this issue. Esta cuestión presenta dos aspectos.
sidesaddle: to ride ~ montar a caballo a mujeriegas ▪ montar a caballo a la mujeriega
to **sideswipe something** golpear algo de refilón ➤ *(news item)* An Airbus A380 swipeswiped a building as it was taxi-ing at the Bangkok Airport. Un Airbus A380 golpeó de refilón un edificio cuando transitaba en el aeropuerto do Bangkok. ▪ Un Airbus A380 raspó contra un edificio cuando transitaba en el aeropuerto de Bangkok. ➤ Our car was sideswiped in the parking lot. Otro vehículo raspó contra nuestro carro en el estacionamiento.
sideways: to place something ~ colocar algo de lado ▪ colocar algo de soslayo ▪ colocar algo al soslayo ▪ colocar algo de refilón ➤ Every tenth brick was laid sideways. Cada décimo ladrillo fue colocado de lado.
to **sift flour** pasar harina por el tamiz
sigh of relief suspiro de alivio
to be a **sight for sore eyes** dichosos los ojos ➤ You're a sight for sore eyes! ¡Dichosos los ojos!
to **sight land** ▪ to spot land avistar la tierra ▪ divisar la tierra ➤ From the crow's nest of the Pinta, Rodrigo de Triana sighted land. Desde la vigía de la Pinta, Rodrigo de Triana avistó la tierra.
sight of blood: not to be able to stand the ~ no poder ver (la) sangre ➤ She can't stand the sight of blood. (Ella) no puede ver la sangre.
sight to see: it was a ~ ▪ that was something to see era una cosa digna de verse
to **sign a bill into law** ▪ to sign a bill refrendar una ley ▪ firmar una ley
to **sign a document** firmar un documento
to **sign for a letter** firmar el recibo de una carta
to **sign for a package** firmar el recibo de un paquete
to **sign one's name to a document** firmar un documento
sign saying **1.** sign that says letrero que pone **2.** sign that said letrero que ponía
the **sign says...** el letrero dice... ▪ el letrero pone... ▪ la señal dice... ▪ la señal pone... ▪ el cartel dice... ▪ el cartel pone... ➤ Look, the sign says: (this way) up to the castle. Mira, el letrero pone: subida al castillo.
to be a **sign that...** ▪ to be an indication that... indicar que... ▪ señalar que... ➤ The increasing loudness of the thunder is a sign that the storm is moving this way. ▪ The increasing loudness of the thunder is a sign that the storm is moving this way. El progresivo aumento en el sonido del trueno indica que la tormenta se está moviendo en esta dirección.
to **sign up for a class** ▪ to register for a class apuntarse a una clase *("To sign up" usually refers to a class and "to register" usually refers to the university.)*
to **sign up for a course** apuntarse a una clase ▪ anotarse en una clase
to **sign up with a server** darse de alta en un servidor
to **signal (to) someone to pull over** **1.** *(present)* hacerle señas para que se detenga **2.** *(past)* hacerle señas para que se detuviera ➤ He's signaling (to) you to pull over. Te hace señas para que te detengas. ➤ The traffic policeman signaled (to) me to pull over. El policía de tráfico me hizo señas para que me detuviera.
to **signal with one's hands** *(military)* ▪ to communicate with hand signals ▪ to communicate using hand signals hablar por señas
the **signing of the accord** la firma del acuerdo
silence implies consent callar es otorgar ▪ quien calla otorga ▪ él que calla, otorga
silence is golden el silencio vale oro ▪ al buen callar llaman Sancho
silent letter letra muda ➤ The "h" in "hour" is silent. La "h" en "hour" es muda.
silent movies ▪ silent film(s) el cine mudo
silent treatment: to give someone the ~ negarle la palabra ▪ no dirigirle la palabra a alguien ▪ darle a alguien la ley de hielo ▪ darle a alguien la espalda
silicon chip lasca de silicio ▪ el chip de silicio
silly!: don't be ~ ¡no seas tonto!
to be **silver-plated** estar chapado en plata ▪ tener un plaqué de plata
similar to the one ▪ like the one similar a la de ▪ similar al de
simple affair asunto sencillo
simple as pie: to be (as) ~ ▪ to be easy as pie ▪ to be a piece of cake ser pan comido ▪ ser más sencillo que el mecanismo de un chupete
simple explanation explicación sencilla
the **simple fact that...** ▪ the mere fact that... el simple hecho de que... ▪ el mero hecho de que...
simple procedure procedimiento sencillo ➤ Using a simple procedure ▪ Through a simple procedure Mediante un procedimiento sencillo
simplistic idea idea simplista
to be **simply irresistible** ser simplemente irresistible ▪ sencillamente irresistible
to **simply tell someone that...** limitarse a decirle a alguien que... ➤ I simply told him that... Me limité a decirle (a él) que... ➤ I simply told her that... Me limité a decirle (a ella) que...
simply to be following orders ▪ just to be following orders limitarse a cumplir órdenes
simply to say that... ▪ to say simply that... limitarse a decir que...
since Friday desde el viernes
since getting back from my trip a la vuelta de mi viaje
since man as such has existed on Earth desde que el hombre como tal existe en la Tierra
since one was *x* years old desde tenía *x* años
since (that time) desde entonces ➤ I haven't seen her since (that time). No la he visto desde entonces.
since that's the way I am como yo soy así
since the dawn of civilization desde los albores de la civilización
since the day I was born desde el día en que nací
since the days of desde los tiempos de ➤ Since the days of the telegraph. Desde los tiempos del telégrafo.
since the night before ▪ since the previous night desde la noche anterior

since the previous night ▪ since the night before desde la noche anterior
since the world began desde que hay mundo
since then ▪ ever since desde entonces ▪ de entonces acá
to **sing a flat note** soltar un gallo
to **sing bass** cantar de bajo
to **sing by ear** cantar de oído
to **sing off beat** cantar fuera de tiempo ▪ cantar a descompás ▪ cantar a destiempo
to **sing off-key** cantar desafinado ▪ cantar a destiempo
to **sing someone's praises** ▪ to extol someone's virtues ▪ to extol the virtues of someone ▪ to praise someone to the skies cantar las alabanzas de alguien ▪ ensalzar a alguien ▪ hablar maravillas de alguien
to **sing through the nose** ganguear (canciones)
single-course meal *(Spanish restaurants, where dinner and supper typically consist of two courses)* plato combinado
single-family dwelling vivienda unifamiliar
single file en fila de uno ▪ en reata
single-spaced and without paragraph indentations a renglón seguido
singular attainments: person of ~ ▪ person of singular achievements ser una persona de logros especiales
to **sink to a five-year low** hundirse en una sima no vista en un lustro ▪ hundirse en una sima no vista en cinco años
to **sip one's coffee** sorber el café
sirloin steak solomillo ➤ For Susana's birthday, we're all going to Don Enrique's Restaurant for sirloin steak. Para el cumpleaños de Susana, todos vamos a ir al Mesón Don Enrique para comer solomillo.
to **sit across from someone** 1. to sit facing someone sentarse de frente a alguien 2. to sit across the aisle from someone sentarse en el otro lado ➤ She sat across from me at the dinner table. Ella se sentó enfrente de mí en la mesa. ➤ She sat across from me on the airplane. Ella se sentó en el otro lado del avión.
to **sit around the fire** sentarse alrededor del fuego ▪ sentarse en torno al fuego
to **sit at an angle to the corner** 1. *(a building)* estar (ubicado) en diagonal con respecto a la esquina 2. *(entry to a building)* quedar justo en la esquina ▪ hacer esquina ➤ The building sits at an angle to the corner. El edificio está en diagonal con respecto a la esquina. ➤ The store entrance sits at an angle to the corner. La entrada queda justo en la esquina. ▪ La entrada a la tienda hace esquina.
to **sit at opposite ends of the table (from each other)** sentarse al otro extremo de la mesa (del uno al otro)
to **sit back and enjoy...** recostarse y disfrutar (de)... ▪ reclinarse y disfrutar (de)... ➤ Sit back and enjoy the show. *(tú)* Recuéstate y disfruta el espectáculo. ▪ *(usted)* Recuéstese y disfrute el espectáculo.
to **sit by the fire** sentarse al amor de la lumbre ▪ sentarse junto al fuego
to **sit down and negotiate** ▪ to sit down to negotiate sentarse a negociar
to **sit down at the table** sentarse a la mesa
to **sit down to negotiate** ▪ to sit down and negotiate sentarse a negociar
to **sit face to face** sentarse frente a frente ➤ They were sitting face to face. Estaban sentados frente a frente.
to **sit facing each other** sentarse cara a cara
to **sit for a portrait** posar para un retrato
to **sit in back** ▪ to sit in the back sentarse atrás ➤ I'll sit in back. Me siento atrás. ▪ Me sentaré atrás.
to **sit in front** ▪ to sit up front ▪ to sit in the front seat sentarse adelante
to **sit on one's ass** *(off-color)* ▪ to sit on one's butt estar de brazos cruzados ▪ rascarse la barriga ▪ tocarse la barriga ▪ cruzarse de brazos
to **sit there doing nothing** quedarse sin hacer nada
to **sit tight** mantenerse a la espera ▪ mantenerse a la expectativa ▪ quedarse a la espera
to **sit up** incorporarse ➤ He sat up in the bed. Se incorporó en la cama.
to **sit up straight** sentarse erguido(-a) ▪ sentarse derecho(-a)
sit-ups: to do ~ hacer sentadillas ▪ hacer abdominales
to be **sitting against** estar recostado en ➤ I was sitting against the tree trunk. Estaba recostado en el tronco.
Sitting Bull *(Native American chief)* Toro Sentado
to be a **sitting duck** ▪ to be an easy target ser un blanco fácil
to be **sitting face to face** estar sentados frente a frente
to be **sitting in the catbird seat** *(James Thurber)* ▪ to be sitting pretty ▪ to be in an advantageous position estar en una posición ventajosa
to be **sitting on the edge of one's chair** ▪ to be (sitting) on the edge of one's seat estar al borde del asiento
to be **sitting pretty** estar en una posición ventajosa
the **situation I find myself in** ▪ the situation in which I find myself la situación en que quedo ▪ la situación en la que me encuentro
six of one and half a dozen of the other tres cuartos de lo mismo
six-pack *(beer, soft drinks)* *el* pack de seis (cervezas) ▪ *el* paquete de seis (cervezas) ➤ Pick up a couple six-packs (of beer) while you're at the store. Compra un par de packs de seis (cervezas).
sixth sense sexto sentido
size *(of a calibrated object)* medida ➤ This screw is a different size. Este tornillo es de otra medida.
size of a tax cut cuantía de una rebaja fiscal
size of an object tamaño de un objeto
size of clothes talla de ropa ➤ I don't know my shirt size in metrics. No sé mi talla de camisa en el sistema métrico.
to **size up a situation** tantear una situación
to **skate on (the) ice** ▪ to ice skate patinar sobre hielo
skating rink pista de patinaje
skeet shooting ▪ clay pigeon shooting tiro al plato ▪ tiro al pinchón
to **skew the results** ▪ to bias the results ▪ to distort the results ▪ to doctor the results mediatizar los resultados ▪ distorcionar los resultados
ski lift remonte mecánico ▪ telesillas
to **skid on a curve** derrapar en una curva ➤ At the auto rallies, the drivers skid on practically all the curves. En los rallies los conductores derrapan en casi todas las curvas.
to **skid on the ice** pegar un patinazo ▪ dar un patinazo ▪ derrapar sobre el hielo ▪ patinar sobre el hielo
skim milk ▪ fat-free milk leche descremada ▪ *(Sp.)* leche desnatada
skin and bone: to be nothing but ~ quedarse en los huesos
to **skin one's elbow** ▪ to scrape one's elbow rasparse el codo ▪ despellejarse el codo
to **skin one's knee** ▪ to scrape one's knee rasparse la rodilla ▪ despellejarse la rodilla ➤ I skinned my knee raw when I fell off my bicycle. Tenía la rodilla en carne viva cuando me caí de la bicicleta.
skinhead cabeza rapada ▪ *el* eskín
to be **skinny as a rail** ser flaco como un palillo ▪ estar como un fideo ▪ estar como el canto de un duro ▪ estar como un silbido ▪ estar flaquísimo
to be **skinny as a reed** estar hecho una flauta
to **skip a beat** *(heart)* darle un vuelco (el corazón) ▪ saltearle un latido (el corazón)
to **skip one's nap** saltarse la siesta ▪ no echarse la siesta
to **skip over something** ▪ to omit something ▪ to pass over something pasar algo por alto
to **skip rope** ▪ to jump rope saltar la soga ▪ saltar a la cuerda ▪ *(Sp.)* saltar al cordel ▪ saltar a la comba
to **skip school** *(Mex.)* irse de pinta ▪ *(Arg.)* hacerse la rata ▪ *(Sp.)* hacer novillos ▪ *(all countries)* hacerse la rabona ▪ *(archaic)* hacer cimarra
to be a **skirt chaser** ▪ to be a womanizer gustarle las faldas ▪ ser un faldero ▪ ser un mujeriego
to be **skittish about** ▪ to be reluctant to mostrarse reacio(-a) a ▪ ser reacio(-a) a
skittish horse caballo asustadizo
to **slack off** flojear

to **slam on the brakes** dar un frenazo brusco

to **slam the door** dar un portazo ▪ *(Mex.)* azotar la puerta

to **slam the door in someone's face** darle a alguien con la puerta en las narices ▪ *(Mex.)* azotarle la puerta a alguien en las narices

slamming on of the brakes ▪ slamming of the brakes frenazo

to **slap someone** darle una bofetada ▪ abofetear ▪ cruzarle la cara alguien ▪ darle un manotazo a alguien ➤ She slapped him. Le cruzó la cara.

to **slap someone on the back** darle a alguien una palmada en la espalda

to **slaughter an animal (for human consumption)** sacrificar un animal (para el consumo humano)

to **slave away** ▪ to work like a dog ▪ to be hard at it trabajar como un condenado ▪ trabajar como un burro ▪ currar (de sol a sol) ➤ I'm slaving away at the computer. ▪ I'm working like a dog at the computer. Estoy trabajando como un condenado en la computadora. ▪ Estoy trabajando como un burro en la computadora.

to **sleep in** ▪ to sleep until one wakes up naturally despertarse por uno mismo ▪ dormir hasta tarde ➤ I like to sleep in on Sunday morning. Me gusta despertarme por mí mismo los domingos por la mañana.

to **sleep like a log** dormir como un tronco ▪ quedarse como un tronco

to **sleep on it** consultar con la almohada ▪ consultarlo con la almohada ▪ consultar la almohada ➤ It's better to sleep on it than (to) lose sleep because of it. Es mejor consultar las cosas con la almohada a tiempo que perder el sueño por su causa después.

to **sleep through 1.** to remain asleep during quedarse dormido durante **2.** to miss because of oversleeping perderse algo por quedarse dormido ➤ I was so tired this morning that I slept through class. Estaba tan cansado esta mañana que me quedé dormido durante la clase. ➤ I almost slept through my first class today. ▪ I almost overslept my first class today. Casi me perdí la primera clase de hoy por quedarme dormido.

to **sleep with someone** ▪ to go to bed with someone acostarse con alguien

sleeper cells células durmientes

sleeping bag bolsa de dormir ▪ saco de dormir

Sleepless in Seattle *(film title) Desvelado en Seattle*

sleepless night: to have a ~ pasar la noche en vela

sleigh pulled by a horse ▪ horse-drawn sleigh trineo de caballo ▪ trineo tirado por un caballo

slice: thick ~ *(cheese, ham, beef, etc.)* trozo

slice: thin ~ *(cheese, ham, beef, bacon, etc.)* feta finita ▪ *(Sp.)* loncha

slice: radial ~ *(cucumber, carrot, salami, etc.)* rodaja

to **slice a banana** cortar una banana ▪ trocear un plátano

to **slice bacon 1.** *(Mex., Arg., thin)* cortar el tocino en tiras ▪ *(thick)* trocear el tocino ▪ cortar el tocino en trozos **2.** *(Col., thin)* cortar el tocineta en tiras **3.** *(Sp., thin)* cortar el beicon en lonchas ▪ *(thick)* trocear el beicon ▪ cortar el beicon en trozos

slice of bacon *(Mex.)* tira de tocino ▪ *(S. Am.)* tira de tocineta ▪ *(Sp.)* tira de beicon

slice of bread rebanada de pan

slice of cake tajada de pastel ▪ tajada de tarta

slice of pizza ▪ piece of pizza trozo de pizza ▪ *la* porción de pizza ▪ cacho de pizza ▪ *la* ración de pizza

slice of tomato rodaja de tomate

to **slice radially** *(carrot, cucumber, long sausage, etc.)* ▪ to slice crosswise rebanar en rodajas

to **slice the bread** cortar el pan

to **slice the (loaf of) bread thick** cortar el pan en rebanadas gruesas

to **slice the (loaf of) bread thin** cortar el pan en rebanadas finas

slick road ▪ slippery road camino resbaladizo ▪ carretera resbaladiza

Slick Willy *(Bill Clinton, to his enemies)* Escurridizo Willy

slide: microscope ~ lámina ▪ *el* portaobjetos

to **slide down the banister** deslizarse por el pasamanos ▪ deslizarse por la barandilla ➤ He slid down the banister and flew off the end. Se deslizó por la barandilla y salió volando.

to **slide on the ice** resbalarse

slide projector el proyector de diapositivas

slide rule regla de cálculo

slight accent acento leve

slight advantage ligera ventaja ▪ leve ventaja

slight slope ligera pendiente

slight temperature: to have a ~ ▪ to have a low fever tener unas décimas ➤ She has a slight temperature. ▪ She has a low fever. Tiene unas décimas.

slightest idea: not to have the ~ no tener la más mínima idea

slightly! ¡ligeramente! ➤ Are you ticked at me? Slightly! ¿Estás mosqueado conmigo? ¡Ligeramente!

slightly different ligeramente diferente ▪ ligeramente distinto

to **slim down** ▪ to lose weight adelgazar ▪ perder peso ▪ bajar la tripa

to **sling something on one's back** echárse algo a la espalda

to **slip away from one** ▪ to slip through one's fingers ▪ to get away from one írsele de las manos ▪ escapársele de las manos ➤ It slipped away from us. Se nos ha ido de las manos. ▪ Se nos ha escapado de las manos

to **slip away (unnoticed)** ▪ to slip out salir sin que nadie se dé cuenta

to **slip by** *(coll.)* **1.** to slip past pasar de lado sin ser visto **2.** to forget pasársele de lado ➤ He slipped by me without my seeing him. Me pasó de lado sin que lo haya visto. ▪ *(Sp., leísmo)* Me pasó de lado sin que le haya visto. ➤ She slipped by me without my seeing her. Me pasó de lado sin que la haya visto. ➤ It slipped by me. ▪ It got by me. ▪ I forgot it. Se (me) pasó de lado. ▪ Se me olvidó.

to **slip into the house** deslizarse hacia el interior de la casa

slip of the hearing ▪ Freudian slip ▪ parapraxis *el* despiste (al oír)

slip of the pen ▪ Freudian slip ▪ parapraxis *el* despiste (al escribir)

slip of the tongue ▪ Freudian slip ▪ parapraxis escapársele la lengua ▪ *el* despiste (al hablar) ▪ lapsus linguae

to **slip on the ice** resbalarse en el hielo ▪ patinarse en el hielo

to **slip through one's fingers** ▪ to slip away from one escurrírsele entre los dedos ➤ The time slipped through my fingers. ▪ The time slipped away from me. El tiempo se me escurrió entre los dedos.

to **slip through the crowd** escabullirse entre la multitud

slovenly person ▪ scruffy person persona desaliñada

to be **slow: to be *x* minutes ~** llevar *x* minutos de retraso ➤ My watch is five minutes slow. Mi reloj lleva cinco minutos de retraso.

slow but steady despacio pero constante ▪ lento pero constante ▪ sin prisa, pero sin pausa ➤ The work is going slow but steady. El trabajo me va despacio pero constante.

slow down! *(tú)* ¡reduce! ▪ ¡frena, frena! ▪ *(usted)* ¡reduzca! ▪ ¡frene! ➤ Slow down! You're going too fast. ¡Reduce! Vas muy rápido.

to **slow down 1.** *(on foot)* reducir el paso ▪ aminorar el paso **2.** *(driving)* reducir la velocidad ▪ disminuir la velocidad ▪ aminorar la velocidad **3.** *(sportscaster, describing a race)* aminorar la marcha **4.** *(computer, etc.)* enlentecer **5.** *(as a command)* slow down! ¡más despacio! ➤ When the processor is thinking, the cursor slows down. Cuando el procesador está pensando, el cursor se enlentece. ➤ Slow down. You're getting ahead of me. Reduce el paso. Te me estás adelantando. ➤ Slow down. I can't keep up with you. Reduce el paso. No puedo mantenerme a tu ritmo. ▪ Reduce el paso. No puedo mantenerme el ritmo. ➤ The new antivirus slows down the computer. ▪ The new antivirus slows the computer down. El nuevo antivirus ralentiza la computadora. ▪ El nuevo antivirus enlentece la computadora. ▪ *(Sp.)* El nuevo antivirus ralentiza el ordenador. ▪ El nuevo antivirus enlentece el ordenador.

slow motion: to be in ~ estar a cámara lenta ▪ estar al ralentí

to be **slow to anger** ser difícil de enfadar

to be **slow to react** ser lento en reaccionar ▪ tardar en reaccionar

to be **slow to respond** ser lento en responder ➤ The alliance has been slow to respond militarily to the attacks. La alianza ha sido lenta al responder militarmente a los ataques.

slowdown in the economy ▪ slowing (down) of the economy ▪ economic slowdown ▪ cooling off of the economy ▪ cooling down of the economy *la* ralentización de la economía ▪ enfriamiento de la economía

slowing down of the economy ▪ slowing of the economy ▪ economic slowdown ▪ slowdown in the economy ▪ cooling off of the economy ▪ cooling down of the economy *la* ralentización de la economía ▪ enfriamiento de la economía

slowly and clearly: to speak ~ hablar despacio y claro ▪ hablar despacio y que se le entienda (a alguien) ➤ Please speak slowly and clearly. Por favor habla despacio y claro. ▪ Por favor habla despacio y que se te entienda.

slowly but steadily ▪ *(coll.)* slow but steady lento pero constante

slowly but surely lento pero seguro

slowness of the process *la* lentitud del proceso

smack one's lips *(from enjoyment of the food)* relamerse de gusto

small change ▪ loose change ▪ pocket change calderilla ▪ dinero de bolsillo ▪ moneda suelta ▪ sencillo

to be **small comfort** ser pobre consuelo

to be **small enough to fit in something** ser lo suficientemente pequeño para caber en algo ➤ This suitcase is small enough to fit in the overhead bin of the airplane. Esta maleta es lo suficientemente pequeña para caber en el compartimiento superior del avión.

small family familia pequeña ▪ familia chica ▪ familia corta

small intestine intestino delgado

to be **smart as hell** ▪ to be very smart ▪ to be extremely smart ser más listo(-a) que el diablo

to be **smart enough to know that...** ▪ to be intelligent enough to know that... ser lo suficientemente inteligente como para saber que... ▪ ser inteligente para saber que...

to be a **smart move** ser un acierto

to **smash a criminal ring** ▪ to dismantle a criminal ring desarticular una red criminal

to **smash somebody's face** partirle la cara a alguien

smattering of vocabulary: to have a ~ tener una noción del vocabulario ➤ I have just a smattering of Arabic vocabulary. Tengo sólo una noción del vocabulario árabe.

to **smear a candidate** difamar a un candidato

smear campaign campaña de difamación

to **smear (the) ink** emborronar la tinta

to **smear (the) lipstick** correrse el lápiz labial ▪ *(Sp.)* embadurnar el pincel de labios

to **smear (the) makeup** correrse el maquillaje ▪ *(Sp.)* embadurnar el maquillaje

to **smear (the) paint** correrse la pintura

to **smell a rat** olerle a gato encerrado ▪ olerle mal el asunto ➤ I smell a rat. Esto me huele a gato encerrado.

to **smell good** oler bien

to **smell like something** oler a algo ▪ oler como algo ➤ It smells like licorice. Huele a regaliz. ➤ He smells like the bottom of a birdcage. Huele como el fondo de una jaula de pájaros.

to **smell of something** *(esp. alcohol and tobacco)* ▪ to give off the odor of something ▪ to smell like something oler a algo ➤ He smells of alcohol. (Él) huele a alcohol. ➤ He smells of tobacco. (Él) huele a tabaco. ➤ I've been around smokers, and now my clothes smell of tobacco. He estado cerca de fumadores, y ahora mi ropa huele a tabaco.

to **smell something** olerle a algo ➤ I smell smoke. Me huele a humo. ▪ Huelo humo. ➤ She smelled smoke. Le olió a humo. ▪ Olió humo. ➤ We smell the skunk, all right. Let's just hope the skunk doesn't smell us. Olemos el zorrillo, sin lugar a dudas. Esperemos que el zorrillo no nos huela a nosotros.

to **smell something burning** oler algo quemándose ▪ oler algo que se está quemando ▪ detectar un olor a quemado ➤ I smell something burning. Huelo a algo que se quema. ▪ Me huele a algo que se quema. ➤ I smell wood burning. (Me) huele a madera quemada. ➤ I noticed the smell of something burning and went to investigate. Sentí el olor de algo quemándose, y fui a investigar.

to **smell strongly of something** ▪ to reek of something despedir un fuerte olor a algo ▪ despedir un fuerte tufo a algo ▪ emitir un fuerte olor a algo

to **smile an empty smile** dar una sonrisa vacía ▪ dar una sonrisa sosa ▪ *(L. Am.)* dar una sonrisa desabrida

to **smile dryly** sonreír con desgano

to **smile faintly** esbozar una sonrisa

the **smile on one's face** la sonrisa en la cara ▪ la sonrisa que se dibuja en el rostro

to **smile to oneself** sonreírse

to **smoke a pipe** fumar en pipa

smoke screen: to put up a ~ echar una cortina de humo ▪ echar una pantalla de humo ▪ echar una bomba de humo

smoke screen: to serve as a ~ servir de cortina de humo ▪ servir de pantalla de humo ▪ servir de bomba de humo ➤ It serves as a smoke screen. Sirve de pantalla de humo. ▪ Sirve de cortina de humo.

smoke signals *las* señales de humo

to be **smooth as glass** estar liso como la mar serena

to be **smooth as silk** *(temporarily)* estar (suave) como la seda ▪ *(permanently)* ser (suave) como la seda ➤ Her skin is smooth as silk. Su piel está suave como la seda. ▪ Su piel es suave como la seda.

smooth as silk: to run ~ ir como la seda ➤ The engine is running smooth as silk. El motor va como la seda. ➤ The business is running smooth as silk. El negocio va como la seda. ▪ La empresa va como la seda.

smooth flight: to have a ~ tener un vuelo plácido

smooth ride: to have a ~ tener un andar suave

smooth sailing: to find ~ ir viento en popa

to **smother someone with kisses** comerse a besos a alguien ▪ colmarle de besos a alguien

to **smuggle contraband** contrabandear ▪ pasar contrabando ▪ matutear *("Pasar de contrabando" means to get a single contraband item into the country, usually through customs.)*

smuggled goods contrabando ▪ *los* matutes

snack: to have a ~ picar algo ▪ *(Mex.)* tener una botana ▪ *(Sp.)* tomar un tentempié ▪ tener un piscolabis ➤ Do want to have a (little) snack to tide you over? ▪ Do you want to eat (a little) something to tide you over? ¿Quieres tener una botana para matar el gusanillo? ▪ ¿Quieres tomar un tentempié para matar el gusanillo? ▪ ¿Quieres picar algo para matar el gusanillo?

snack bar *(Mex.)* merendero ▪ *(Sp.) el* mesón ▪ *el* bar de tapas

snake coils víbora se enrosca

to **snap at someone 1.** *(literal, as a dog)* tirarle un mordisco a alguien **2.** *(figurative)* to speak sharply hablar en mal tono a alguien

to **snap one's fingers** chasquear los dedos ➤ He's popular with kids because he can snap two fingers at a time. Es popular con los peques porque puede chasquear dos dedos a la vez.

to **snap when it breaks** ▪ to snap as it breaks ▪ to break with a snap partirse con un chasquido ➤ I stepped on a twig, which snapped when it broke. ▪ I stepped on a twig, which snapped as it broke. ▪ I stepped on a twig, which broke with a snap. Pisé una ramita que se partió con un chasquido.

to **snarl traffic** ▪ to halt traffic ▪ to bring (the) traffic to a halt colapsar el tráfico ▪ provocar un entorpecimiento del tráfico

to **snatch something (away) from someone** ▪ to grab something (away) from someone arrebatarle algo a alguien ➤ He snatched it from her. Se lo arrebató a ella.

to **sneak in without paying** ▪ to sneak in entrar colándose

to **sneak into a place** colarse en un lugar ➤ The thief snuck into the victim's room. El ladrón se coló en la habitación de la víctima.

to **sneak out** salir a hurtadillas ▪ salir sin que se den cuenta

to **sneak up on someone 1.** *(on him, her, it)* ir por detrás cautelosamente **2.** *(on me)* venir por detrás cautelosamente

sneeze at: to be nothing to ~ ▪ to be nothing to make light of no ser moco de pavo ▪ no ser de despreciar

snippet of DNA segmento de ADN
snooze: to have a ~ echar una cabezada ▪ echarse una cabeza
snow-covered peak cima nevada
the **snow didn't stick** la nieve no se quedó ▪ la nieve no cuajó
the **snow is sticking** la nieve se está quedando ▪ la nieve se está acumulando ▪ la nieve está cuajando
snow, snow, and more snow nieve, renieve, requetenieve
snow-white blanco como *el* algodón
Snow White and the Seven Dwarfs Blanca Nieves y los siete enanos
snowball effect efecto de bola nieve
to be **snowed in** quedar aislado por la nieve
to be **snowed under (with work)** estar agobiado de trabajo
snowstorm tormenta de nieve ▪ el temporal de nieve
so? ¿y qué?
so act that you could will the maxim of your action to be a universal law *(Kant's categorical imperative)* obra de modo que tu acción pueda servir de norma a todos los hombres ▪ obra de tal manera que tus máximas pueden constituirse por ellas mismas en leyes universales naturales
so are you going? ¿entonces vas?
so as not to ▪ in order not to para no
so as to be 1. *(present)* como para que sea **2.** *(past)* como para que fuera ➤ With the last name of Schlabotnik, we must be cousins, and hopefully not so far back as to be academic. Con el apellido de Schlabotnik le dije que debíamos ser primos, y esperaba no tan lejanos como para que fuera sólo en teoría.
so as to facilitate ▪ in order to facilitate para facilitar
so big that... ▪ so large that... tan grande que... ▪ así de grande que...
so-called llamado
so-called because llamado así porque
to be **so courageous that...** ser tal su valor que...
so did I ▪ I did, too **1.** yo también **2.** *(after "gustarle," "encantarle," etc.)* a mí también ➤ I went to Midnight Mass this year.-So did I. Fui a la misa de gallo este año.-Yo también. ➤ I liked the music at Midnight Mass.-So did I. Me gustó la música en la misa de gallo.-A mí, también.
so do I ▪ I do, too **1.** yo también **2.** *(after "gustarle," "encantarle," etc.)* a mí también ➤ I want to go to the library.-So do I. Quiero ir a la biblioteca.-Yo también. ▪ I like to go to the library.-So do I. Me gusta ir a la biblioteca.-A mí también.
to be **so easy** ser de puro fácil ▪ ser tan fácil ▪ ser facilísimo
so far hasta ahora ▪ hasta aquí ▪ hasta la fecha ▪ hasta el momento ➤ So far I've received two offers of a place to stay. Hasta ahora me han ofrecido dos sitios donde quedarme. ➤ Yours is the second offer I've gotten so far. La tuya es la segunda oferta que he recibido hasta ahora. ➤ The suspects have so far refused to cooperate with the police. Hasta el momento los sospechosos se han negado a colaborar con la policía.
so far as I know ▪ as far as I know que yo sepa ▪ hasta donde yo sé
so far as I'm concerned ▪ as far as I'm concerned en lo que a mí me concierne ▪ por lo que a mí respecta
so far as is possible ▪ to the extent possible en la medida en que sea posible
to be **so far away** estar tan allá ▪ estar tan lejos ➤ The speakers are so far away I can't hear them. Los bafles están tan allá que no puedo oírlos.
so far back in time ▪ so far back tan atrás ▪ tan lejanos ➤ With the same last name, I said we had to be cousins, and hopefully not so far back as to be academic. Con ese apellido yo le dije que debíamos de ser primos, con suerte no tan lejanos como para que fuera irrelevante.
to be **so far behind** estar tan atrasado
to be **so far gone** estar tan deteriorado
so far, so good hasta ahora (todo) bien
so far this week en lo que va de semana ▪ en lo que va de la semana
so far this year en lo que va de año ▪ en lo que llevamos de año ▪ en lo que va del año ▪ en lo que llevamos del año
so fast ▪ so quickly tan rápido ▪ tan deprisa ▪ en un momento ➤ I'm glad you caught the error so fast. ▪ I'm glad you caught the error so quickly. Me alegro que hayas detectado el error en un momento. ▪ Me alegro que hayas pillado el error tan rápido.
so fierce was his hatred toward... tal era su odio hacia...
so good to see you! ▪ it's great to see you! ¡qué bueno verte! ▪ ¡tanto bueno por aquí!
so I did! ¡así que lo hice!
so I noticed! así me di cuenta ▪ así me enteré ▪ así lo noté ▪ así me percaté
so I want... quiero por tanto... ➤ So I want to send everyone an E-mail with my new address. Quiero, por tanto, enviar una nota por mail a todo el mundo comunicando mi nueva dirección.
so it seems: (or) ~ eso parece
so little that... ▪ so small that... tan pequeño que... ▪ así de pequeño que...
to be **so little that... 1.** so small that... ser tan pequeño que... ▪ *(gesturing with the hand)* ser así de pequeño que... **2.** such a small quantity that... ser tan pequeña cantidad que... ▪ ser tan poco que...
so long as 1. provided that con tal de que ▪ en tanto que **2.** while mientras ➤ You can fold the curtains so long as they don't get wrinkled. ▪ You can fold the curtains provided that they don't get wrinkled. Puedes doblar las cortinas con tal de que no se arruguen. ➤ In Cuba, authorities warned that the "open courts" and mobilizations would continue so long as Elián and his father could not return to the island. En Cuba, las autoridades han advertido de que los "tribunales abiertos" y las movilizaciones continuarán mientras Elián y su padre no puedan regresar a la isla.
so many tantos
so many different ways of doing something tantas formas distintas de hacer una cosa
so many other occasions otras tantas ocasiones
so much tanto
so much for... allá...
so much for his loyalty! ¡allá él y su lealtad!
so much for that! 1. *(resignation, as when breaking something one has just bought)* ¡adiós, muy buenas! **2.** *(dismissing something as of no value)* ¡allá penas!
so much so that ▪ to such an extent that a tal punto que ▪ a tal grado que
so much the better ▪ all the better tanto mejor ▪ mejor que mejor
so named for llamado así por
so now its *my* fault! ¡a que ahora resulta que la culpa la tengo yo! ▪ ¡ahora resulta que yo tengo la culpa! ▪ ¡o sea que ahora yo tengo la culpa!
so quickly ▪ so fast tan rápido ▪ tan deprisa ▪ en un momento ➤ I'm glad you caught the error so quickly. ▪ I'm glad you caught the error so fast. Me alegro que hayas detectado el error en un momento. ▪ Me alegro que hayas pillado el error tan rápido.
so small that... ▪ so little that... tan pequeño que...
so that... ▪ in order that... para que... ▪ así es que... ▪ por lo que... ▪ de modo que... ▪ de forma que... ▪ de manera que... ➤ What can we do so that I can meet her? ¿Qué podemos hacer para que (yo) la conozca?
so that I can para que (yo) pueda
so that I could para que (yo) pudiera ▪ para que (yo) pudiese
so that I would have to... para que tuviera que... ➤ The consulate granted the student visa for less than the duration of the course so that I would have to pay another tuition to extend it. El consulado otorgó el visado estudiantil con menos fecha que el de la duración del curso para que tuviera que pagar otra matrícula para extenderlo.
so the story goes así va el cuento
so there! 1. take that! ¡así que te chinchas! ▪ ¡así que te jorobas! ▪ ¡chínchate! **2.** and that's it! ¡pues, eso! ➤ Sally Brown said to Linus, "I suppose you thought I'd think you were calling to ask me to go to the movies. Well, I didn't, and I wouldn't go with you now even if you asked me, so there!" Sally Brown le dijo a Linus, "Supongo que pensabas que me iba a creer que me estabas llamando para invitarme a ir al cine. Bueno, no lo pensé, y no iría contigo ahora aunque me invitaras, ¡así que te chinchas!" ▪ Sally Brown le dijo a Linus, "Supongo que pensabas

que me iba a creer que me estabas llamando para invitarme a ir al cine. Bueno, no lo pensé, y no iría contigo ahora aunque me invitaras, ¡así que te jorobas!"

so this conque ▪ así que

so this...! ¡es el famoso...! ▪ ¡es la famosa...! ➤ So this is Rosa! I've heard so much about you! ¡Es la famosa Rosa! ¡Hemos oído hablar mucho de ti! *(Spanish prefers the royal "we" in this situation.)*

so this is where you live así que es aquí donde vives ▪ conque vives aquí

so this is where you work así que es aquí donde trabajas ▪ con que trabajas aquí

so to speak ▪ as it were digamos ▪ por así decir ▪ por decir así ▪ por así decirlo ▪ por decirlo así ▪ a lo que se dice ▪ podríamos decir ▪ como si dijeramos

so what? ▪ what of it? ¿y qué? ▪ ¿qué hay?

so what am I supposed to do now? ¿y entonces qué se supone que haga (yo) ahora?

so what else is new?! ¡qué más hay de nuevo! ▪ ¡vaya novedad!

to **soak in lavender** impregnar de lavanda ➤ A handkerchief soaked in lavender Un pañuelo impregnado de lavanda

to **soak in water** dejar a remojar en agua ▪ dejar remojando en agua ▪ dejar en remojo

to **soak something overnight** ▪ to let something soak overnight dejar algo en remojo durante la noche ▪ remojar algo durante toda la noche ➤ Soak the beans overnight. Deje las habas en remojo durante la noche. *(Spanish has many words for beans, "habas" being the most generic, but when referring to frijoles, judías, alubias, garbanzos, etc., these words are used specifically.)*

to **soak up the atmosphere** absorber el ambiente

to be **soaked to the bone** estar hecho una sopa ▪ estar empapado hasta los huesos ▪ estar calado hasta los huesos ➤ I got caught in the rain, and I'm soaked. Me agarró la lluvia y estoy hecho una sopa.

to be **soaking wet** estar empapado

soap opera telenovela ▪ *(Sp.) el* culebrón

to **sober up** quitarse la borrachera ▪ sacarse la borrachera

soccer fan aficionado(-a) al fútbol ▪ *el, la* fan del fútbol ▪ forofo(-a) del fútbol *("Fútbol" to a Hispanic always means"soccer." To refer to American football you must specify "fútbol americano.")*

social and environmental studies conocimiento del medio ▪ *(student jargon)* "el cono"

social blight lacra social

(social) circles planos sociales ➤ We don't run in the same (social) circles. ▪ We don't move in the same social circles. No nos movemos en los mismos planos sociales.

social climber trepador(-a) ▪ *el, la* trepa ▪ *el, la* arribista

social events actos sociales

social fabric entramado social ▪ ámbito social ➤ Deep political differences strain the social fabric. Las diferencias políticas profundas enrarecen el ámbito social.

social standing rango ▪ *la* posición social

social status *la* posición social

social unrest *la* crispación social ▪ descontento social

to **sock it to someone on the bill** ▪ to sock it to someone with the bill dar un palazo a alguien con la factura ➤ The car repair shop socked it to me on the bill. El taller mecánico me dio un palazo con la factura.

sockets: diagonal ~ *(used in Sp.)* alveolos en diagonal

to **soft boil an egg** pasar un huevo por agua

soft-boiled egg huevo pasado por agua

soft butter ▪ softened butter mantequilla blanda

soft drugs drogas blandas

soft money dinero blando ▪ contribuciones anónimas que no están reguladas por la ley

to be **soft on crime** ser (muy) benévolo(-a) para con el crimen

to be **soft-spoken** ser de voz suave ▪ ser tranquilo(-a) al hablar

soft spot for: to have a ~ tener una debilidad por

to be **softhearted** ▪ to be tenderhearted ser blando de corazón ▪ tener un corazón blando

solar battery batería solar

solar cell célula solar

solar flare llamarada solar

sold! *(at an auction)* ¡adjudicado! ▪ ¡vendido! ➤ Sold! To the lady in the outlandish hat! ¡Adjudicado, a la señora en el sombrero estrambótico!

sold out! 1. ¡todo está vendido! ▪ no quedan existencias **2.** *(seats)* ¡no hay localidades!

to be **sold out** *(concert, etc.)* agotarse las entradas ▪ estar todas vendidas *(The adjectives are feminine because the two most common words for admission tickets are "entradas" and "localidades.")*

sole of a shoe suela de un zapato

solid stream of cars ▪ unbroken stream of cars ▪ continuous stream of cars *(Mex.)* flujo continuo de carros ▪ tránsito ininterrumpido de carros ▪ *(Sp., Arg.)* flujo continuo de coches ▪ tránsito ininterrumpido de coches ➤ The solid stream of cars is making it impossible to cross the street. El flujo continuo de carros hace imposible cruzar la calle.

solitary confinement: to be in ~ estar incomunicado(-a) ▪ estar en celda de castigo

to **solve a case** ▪ to crack a case resolver un caso ▪ esclarecer un caso

to **solve a crime** ▪ to identify the culprit resolver un crimen ▪ esclarecer un crimen ▪ esclarecer la autoría de un crimen

to **solve a math(ematics) problem** ▪ to work a math(ematics) problem resolver un problema de matemáticas ▪ solucionar un problema de matemáticas

to **solve a problem** resolver un problema ▪ solucionar un problema

some air: to get ~ ▪ to get some fresh air tomar un poco de aire ▪ respirar aire fresco

some doubt about cierta duda sobre ➤ There was some doubt about... Existía cierta duda sobre...

some friend he is! ¡valiente amigo! ▪ ¡vaya amigo! ▪ ¡menudo amigo!

some friend she is! ¡valiente amiga! ▪ ¡vaya amiga! ▪ ¡menuda amiga!

some friend you are! ¡valiente amigo(-a)! ▪ ¡vaya amigo(-a)! ▪ ¡menudo(-a) amigo(-a)!

some good can come out of it ▪ some good can come from it ▪ something good can come out of it ▪ something good can come from it algo (de) bueno puede salir de ello ▪ algo (de) bueno puede resultar de ello ▪ no hay mal que por bien no venga

Some Like It Hot *(Billy Wilder film) Con faldas y a lo loco*

some more 1. *(singular)* más **2.** *(plural)* algunos más ▪ otros tantos ▪ otro tanto ➤ I want some more ice cream. Quiero más helado. ➤ I've corrected twenty pages, and this afternoon I'll do some more. He revisado veinte páginas, y esta tarde revisaré algunas más. ▪ He revisado veinte páginas, y esta tarde revisaré otras tantas.

some more than others algunos más que otros ▪ unos más que otros

some of you algunos de ustedes ▪ *(Sp., vosotros)* algunos de vosotros ➤ As some of you already know Como algunos de ustedes ya saben ▪ Como algunos de vosotros ya sabéis

some other time ▪ another time en otro momento ➤ We'll talk some other time. (Ya) hablarémos en otro momento.

some people algunas personas ▪ algunos

some pig! *(E.B. White's "Wilbur")* ¡menudo cerdo!

some semblance of una cierta apariencia de

some time ago ▪ *(coll.)* some time back hace tiempo ▪ hace un tiempo atrás ▪ tiempo atrás

some *x* people una *x* de personas ➤ Some twenty people Unas veinte de personas ▪ Una veintena de personas

some *x* percent alrededor de un *x* por ciento ➤ Some twenty percent Alrededor de un veinte por ciento

someday algún día ▪ el día de mañana

someone besides me somebody besides me alguien aparte de mí ▪ otra persona aparte de mí

someone else's ▪ somebody else's de otro ▪ ajeno ➤ That's someone else's problem. Es problema de otro. ▪ Es problema ajeno.

someone I can trust alguien de quien me puedo fiar ▪ alguien de fiar ▪ alguien de confianza ▪ *(Sp., coll.)* alguien legal

someone I know ▪ somebody I know alguien que conozco ▪ alguien a quien conozco ▪ un(-a) conocido(-a)

someone, somewhere alguien en algún lugar ➤ H.L. Mencken said (that) puritanism was the haunting fear that someone, somewhere, may be happy. H.L. Mencken dijo que el puritanismo es el miedo angustioso de que alguien en algún lugar pueda ser feliz.

to be **someone to be reckoned with** ser alguien a quien hay que rendirle cuentas

to be **someone to be wary of** ser de cuidado

someone will be with you shortly en breve le atenderemos ▪ en breves momentos le atenderemos

someone with a cold alguien resfriado(-a)

someone you don't trust alguien en quien no se confía ▪ alguien en quien no se tiene confianza

someone's at the door alguien llama a la puerta ▪ llaman a la puerta

someone's replacement 1. *(temporary)* relevo de alguien ▪ *el, la* suplente de alguien 2. *(permanent)* reemplazo de alguien ▪ substituto de alguien *("Substituto" when referring to a substitute teacher is Spanglish. The correct term is "suplente.")*

to be **someone's shadow** ser la sombra de alguien

somersault dive 1. *(forward)* salto mortal 2. *(backward)* salto mortal de espaldas

something else (alguna) otra cosa

something is better than nothing ▪ a little is better than none at all algo es mejor que nada ▪ peor es nada

something is missing ▪ something's missing falta algo ▪ hay algo que falta

something is up ▪ something's up algo está maquinando ▪ algo está tramando ▪ algo se está maquinando ▪ algo se está tramando ▪ se trae algo entre manos

something is wrong ▪ something's wrong algo va mal ▪ algo anda mal

something just clicked (between us) ▪ it just clicked ▪ we immediately hit it off congeniamos en el acto ▪ algo brotó ▪ algo sucedió

something like that ▪ something of the sort algo así ▪ algo parecido ▪ algo por el estilo ▪ algo semejante

something of the sort ▪ something like that algo por el estilo ▪ algo semejante ▪ algo parecido ▪ algo así

something or other no sé cuantito ➤ Alfonso something or other... ▪ Alfonso somebody... Alfonso no sé cuantito...

something or other (about) no sé qué (de)

something to drink algo de tomar ▪ algo para tomar ▪ *(Sp.)* algo de beber ▪ algo para beber

something to eat algo de comer ▪ algo para comer

something to tide you over algo para aguantar ▪ *(Sp.)* algo para matar el gusanillo ➤ Do you want to eat something to tide you over until supper? ¿Quieres una botana para aguantar hasta cena? ▪ ¿Quieres picar algo para matar el gusanillo hasta la cena?

something's missing ▪ something is missing hay algo que falta

something's not right ▪ something is not right 1. *(in a situation)* algo no va bien 2. *(factually)* algo no es correcto

something's up ▪ something is up algo está maquinando ▪ algo está tramando ▪ algo se está maquinando ▪ algo se está tramando ▪ algo se trae entre manos

something's wrong ▪ something is wrong ▪ something's not right algo va mal ▪ algo anda mal

sometime after that ▪ later on más adelante

sometime in April algún día de abril

sometime in the future ▪ at some time in the future ▪ at some future time en un futuro

sometime soon antes de que pase mucho tiempo ▪ dentro de poco

sometime today en algún momento del día de hoy ➤ What time's the bigwig from St. Louis going to get here?-Sometime today. ¿A qué hora llega el pez gordo de St. Louis?-En algún momento del día de hoy.

sometime when... en algún momento que... ➤ Sometime when you're on the Internet, look up... En algún momento que estés en Internet, busca...

someway or other de alguna manera u otra ▪ de alguna u otra manera

to be **somewhere around here** ▪ to be around here somewhere andar por ahí ➤ There must be an ATM machine somewhere around here. Debe de haber un cajero automático por aquí.

to be **somewhere between** estar entre ▪ oscilar entre

to be **somewhere else** ▪ to be elsewhere estar en otra parte

somewhere in en un lugar de ▪ en algún lugar de ➤ Somewhere in the Pacific En un lugar del Pacífico

somewhere in the house en algún lugar de la casa ▪ en la casa por alguna parte

to be **somewhere near...** ▪ to be around here somewhere... estar por aquí (en alguna parte) ➤ The post office is somewhere near here. ▪ The post office is around here somewhere. El correo está por aquí (en alguna parte).

somewhere on the island en algún lugar de la isla ▪ en la isla por alguna parte

to be **somewhere or other** estar en alguna parte

son-in-law yerno

son of a bitch *(off-color)* hijo de puta

songwriter compositor(-a) de canciones ▪ tonadillero(-a)

sonic boom estampido sónico ▪ explosión sónica ▪ estruendo sónico

soon after poco después de ▪ al poco tiempo de ➤ Soon after arriving in... Poco después de llegar a... ▪ Al poco tiempo de llegar a...

soon afterwards poco después ▪ al poco tiempo

soon enough lo suficientemente pronto ➤ That's not soon enough. I need it before then. No es lo suficientemente pronto. Lo necesito antes.

soon enough: you'll find out ~ ya lo sabrás ▪ pronto lo sabrás ▪ ya te enterarás ▪ pronto te enterarás ▪ ya te darás cuenta (de que...) ▪ pronto te darás cuenta (de que...)

soon find out: we'll ~ ya lo sabremos ▪ pronto lo sabremos ▪ pronto nos enteraremos ▪ pronto descubriremos ▪ ya nos daremos cuenta (de que...) ▪ pronto nos daremos cuenta (de que...)

the **sooner it is forgotten the better** cuanto antes se olvide, mejor

the **sooner it was forgotten the better** cuanto antes se olvidara, mejor ▪ cuanto antes se olvidase, mejor

sooner or later tarde o temprano ▪ a la larga o a la corta ▪ a la corta o a la larga ▪ antes o después

sooner than expected antes de lo que se esperaba ▪ antes de lo esperado ➤ U.S. Hispanics have equaled the black population much sooner than expected. Los hispanos de EE UU han igualado a la población negra mucho antes de lo esperado.

sooner than I expected ▪ sooner than I had expected antes de lo que (yo) esperaba

sooner than I had expected (it to) antes de lo que yo esperaba

sooner (than that) ▪ before that antes (de eso) ▪ más pronto ➤ We can meet sooner (than that) if you need to. Podemos reunirnos antes si lo necesitas.

the **sooner the better** cuanto antes mejor ▪ antes hoy que mañana

sore back: to have a ~ *(L. Am.)* tener la espalda adolorida ▪ *(Sp.)* tener la espalda dolorida ➤ I have a sore back. ▪ My back is sore. Tengo la espalda dolorida. ▪ Tengo la espalda adolorida.

to be a **sore loser** ▪ to be a poor loser ser un(-a) mal(-a) perdidor(-a) ▪ tener mal perder

sore muscles músculos doloridos ➤ My muscles were sore after the hike. ▪ I had sore muscles after the hike. Tuve los músculos doloridos después de la caminata. ▪ Mis músculos se quedaron doloridos después de la caminata.

sore throat: to have a ~ tener la garganta irritada ▪ tener la garganta dolorida ▪ tener dolor de garganta ▪ dolerle a uno la garganta

Sorrowful Mysteries *(Catholicism)* Misterios Dolorosos

sorry I haven't written sooner ▪ sorry not to have written sooner siento no haberte escrito antes

sorry I'm late: (I'm) ~ siento llegar tarde

to be **sorry to hear about** sentir mucha pena cuando uno se entera de ➤ I was sorry to hear about your grandfather. Sentí mucha pena cuando me enteré de lo de tu abuelo.
to be **sorry to hear that** lamentar saberlo
sorry to keep you waiting *(tú)* perdona por dejarte esperando ▪ perdona por tenerte esperando ▪ perdona por haberte hecho esperar *(usted)* perdone por dejarlo esperando ▪ perdone por tenerlo esperando ▪ perdone por haberle hecho esperar
to be **sorry to see that...** sentir ver que... ➤ He was sorry to see that... Sentía ver que... ▪ Sintió ver que...
sort of más o menos ▪ algo así ▪ algo parecido
sort of a ▪ kind of a una especie de ▪ algo como un(-a) ➤ The sermon was sort of a harangue. ▪ The sermon was a sort of harangue. El sermón fue una especie de arenga. ▪ El sermón fue algo como una arenga.
sort of like algo así como
to **sort out something** ▪ to sort something out ordenar algo
to **sort through papers** separar papeles importantes del montón ▪ *(Sp.)* hacer una criba
soul mate *el* alma gemela
to **sound a trumpet** ▪ to give a blast on a trumpet hacer sonar una trompeta ▪ soltar un trompetazo
sound barrier barrera del sonido
sound carries el sonido se transmite ➤ Sound carries especially well across water. El sonido se transmite especialmente bien sobre el agua.
sound effects efectos de sonido
to **sound familiar** ▪ to ring a bell sonarle ➤ The (last) name sounds familiar. ▪ The (last) name rings a bell. El apellido me suena. ➤ It sounds familiar. ▪ It rings a bell. Me suena.
to **sound flat** **1.** to sound off-key sonar desafinado **2.** to sound insipid sonar insípido
to **sound funny** **1.** to sound strange sonar raro **2.** not to sound right no sonar bien **3.** to sound comical sonar cómico ▪ sonar gracioso ▪ *(L. Am.)* sonar chistoso
to **sound good** sonar bien
to **sound someone out** tantear a alguien ▪ tomar el pulso a alguien
sound system el sistema de sonido ▪ equipo de sonido
sound track banda sonora
sound wave onda sónica
to **sound worse than it is** sonar peor de lo que es
to **sound worse than one is** sonar peor de lo que uno está ➤ Because I'm hoarse, I sound worse than I am. Por estar ronco, sueno peor de lo que estoy. ▪ Por estar ronco, parece que estoy peor de lo que en realidad estoy.
sounds good! ¡suena bien!
sounds good to me me parece bien
sour cream *(L. Am.)* crema agria ▪ *(Sp.)* nata agria
sour note: to end on a ~ terminar en una nota amarga ▪ terminar en una nota mala ➤ Our date ended on a sour note. Nuestra cita terminó en una nota mala. ▪ Nuestra cita terminó en una nota amarga.
sour note: to have a ~ ▪ to have an off-key note tener una nota desafinada ➤ This piano has a sour note. Este piano tiene una nota desafinada.
to **sour relations between** ▪ to strain relations between amargar las relaciones entre
source code *(computers)* código fuente
source of fiber *la* fuente de fibra ➤ Whole wheat bread is a great source of fiber. El pan integral es una gran fuente de fibra.
source of financing *la* fuente de financiación
source of income: main ~ ▪ principal source of income *la* principal fuente de ingresos
to be a **source of pride to one** ser motivo de orgullo para uno
sourpuss rancio(-a)
southern hemisphere hemisferio sur
to **sow discord (among people)** ▪ to create rifts between people sembrar cizaña (entre) ▪ meter cizaña (entre) ▪ meter cisco entre
space bar *(on a keyboard)* barra espaciadora
space between the lines ▪ space between two lines espaciado entre líneas ▪ regleta
space cadet despistado(-a)
space probe sonda espacial
space shuttle transbordador espacial ▪ shuttle ▪ lanzadera espacial
space-time *(physics)* espacio-tiempo
to be **spaced out** ▪ to be (off) in the ozone estar en el guindo ▪ estar en la luna
spaceship ▪ spacecraft *la* nave espacial ▪ *la* astronave
Spain peninsular time hora peninsular española ➤ Spain peninsular time is one hour later than Greenwich Mean Time. La hora peninsular española es una hora más tarde que la hora de Greenwich.
Spanish Armada: defeat of the ~ *(1588)* la derrota de la Armada Española
Spanish Main *(coastal region from the Isthmus of Panama to the mouth of Venezuela's Orinoco River, crossed by Spanish ships in the 16th and 17th centuries)* cuenca del Caribe ➤ The legendary pirates of the Spanish Main inspired the Disney movie and Disneyland ride, "Pirates of the Caribbean." Los legendarios piratas de la cuenca del Caribe inspiraron la película de Disney y la atracción de Disneylandia "Los piratas del Caribe".
Spanish speaker *el, la* hispanohablante ▪ hispanoparlante
Spanish-speaking de habla española ▪ de habla hispana ▪ hispanohablante
Spanish-speaking country *el* país de habla española ▪ país de habla hispana ▪ país hispanohablante
Spanish-speaking peoples pueblos hispanohablantes ▪ pueblos de habla española ▪ pueblos hispanoparlantes ▪ pueblos de habla hispana ▪ *las* gentes hispanohablantes ▪ gentes de habla española ▪ gentes hispanoparlantes ▪ gentes de habla hispana ▪ gentes hispanoparlantes
Spanish-speaking world mundo hispanohablante ▪ mundo de habla española ▪ mundo de habla hispana ▪ mundo hispanoparlante
to **spank someone** ▪ to give someone a spanking darle unas palmadas a alguien ▪ darle una azotaína a alguien
spanking: to get a ~ ganarse una azotaína ▪ ganarse unas palmadas ➤ Young man, if you give your kidney stew to the dog one more time, you're going to get a spanking. Jovencito, si le vuelves a dar tu estofado de riñones al perro una vez más, vas a ganarte una azotaína.
to **spar with someone** ▪ to engage in polemics andar en dimes y diretes ▪ andar en dares y tomares con alguien
spare key *la* llave de repuesto
to **spare no effort to** ▪ not to spare any effort to no escatimar esfuerzos para
to **spare no expense** ▪ not to spare any expense ▪ to spare no cost ▪ not to spare any cost no escatimar gastos ▪ no reparar en gastos
spare parts ▪ replacement parts piezas de repuesto
to **spare someone the details** ahorrarle los detalles a alguien
spare time ▪ free time tiempo libre ▪ ratos libres ▪ ratos de ocio
spare tire **1.** rueda de repuesto **2.** midriff bulge *el* michelín
to **spark a debate** ▪ to touch off a debate ▪ to cause a debate provocar un debate ▪ propiciar un debate ▪ desencadenar un debate
to **spark a stock market rally** ▪ to spark a rally in the stock market disparar la bolsa ▪ hacer saltar la bolsa
sparkling personality *la* personalidad efervescente ▪ personalidad chispeante ▪ personalidad coruscante
sparkling stars ▪ *(more common)* twinkling stars estrellas centellantes
sparkling water ▪ carbonated water *el* agua con gas ▪ agua mineral con gas
sparkling wine vino espumoso ▪ vino espumante
spate of ties *(sports)* racha de empates
speak! *(tú)* ¡habla! ▪ ¡que hables! ▪ *(usted)* ¡hable (usted)! ▪ ¡que hable (usted)!
to **speak a language fluently** hablar un idioma con fluidez ▪ hablar un idioma con soltura
to **speak badly of someone** ▪ to speak ill of someone hablar mal de alguien ▪ decir mal de alguien

to **speak beautifully** ▪ to speak very well hablar de perlas ▪ hablar divinamente

to **speak directly** ▪ to speak plainly ▪ to be direct no andarse con rodeos ▪ ir al grano ▪ hablar en derecho ▪ hablar en derechura

to **speak for everyone** hablar en nombre de todos ➤ I think I speak for everyone when I say you are the best English teacher we have ever had. Creo que hablo en nombre de todos cuando digo que eres el mejor profesor de inglés que jamás hemos tenido.

to **speak for oneself only** decir a título personal ➤ I'm speaking for myself only. Esto lo digo a título personal.

to **speak for someone** ▪ to speak in someone's behalf hablar en nombre de alguien ▪ hablar por alguien

to **speak for the others** hablar por los demás

to **speak highly of someone** hablarle a alguien bien de alguien ➤ She speaks very highly of you. (Ella) habla muy bien de ti. ➤ She spoke very highly of you. (Ella) habló muy bien de ti.

to **speak ill of someone** ▪ to speak badly of someone decir mal de alguien ▪ hablar mal de alguien

to **speak (in) a language** hablar (en) un idioma ➤ The first man, who warned that one of the trains was going in the wrong direction, was speaking (in) French, but the other responded in Flemish. El primero, que avisó de que uno de los trenes marchaba en dirección errónea, hablaba en francés, pero el otro le respondió en flamenco.

to **speak in non-technical language** hablar en lenguaje no técnico ▪ hablar en lenguaje poco técnico

to **speak in plain language** hablar en lenguaje sencillo ▪ hablar claro y raspado ▪ hablar en cristiano ▪ hablar en lenguaje directo ➤ The authors of this linguistics text are supposedly language experts, but they can't write in plain language. Los autores de este texto de lingüística son supuestamente expertos del idioma, pero no pueden hablar claro y raspado. ▪ Los autores de este texto de lingüística son supuestamente expertos del idioma, pero no pueden hablar en lenguaje sencillo.

to **speak in Spanish** hablar en español

to **speak knowledgeably about a subject** ▪ to talk knowledgeably about a subject hablar con propiedad sobre un tema ▪ hablar con conocimiento de causa

to **speak like a native** hablar igual que un nativo ▪ hablar como un nativo

to **speak one's mind** despacharse a gusto

to **speak personally** expresar sus sentimientos más íntimos ▪ hablar de corazón ➤ If I may speak personally. Si me permiten expresar mis sentimientos más íntimos.

to **speak plainly** **1.** to speak clearly hablar claramente **2.** to speak frankly hablar con franqueza ▪ hablar sin tapujos ▪ hablar sin ambages ▪ hablar sin vueltas

to **speak separately to two (or more) people** ▪ to talk separately with two or more people hablar por separado con dos (o más) personas

to **speak slowly** hablar despacio ▪ hablar lentamente ▪ hablar con voz pausada

to **speak softly** hablar quedo ▪ hablar en voz baja

to **speak Spanish** hablar español

to **speak to an issue** ▪ to address an issue ▪ to deal with an issue tratar un tema

to **speak unambiguously** ▪ to speak without equivocation hablar sin ambigüedades ▪ hablar sin subterfugios

to **speak very properly** hablar muy finamente

to **speak very well** hablar muy bien ▪ *(Sp., informal)* hablar de vicio ▪ hablar de miedo ▪ tener buena labia

to **speak with authority about a subject** hablar con autoridad sobre un tema ▪ hablar ex cátedra sobre un tema

to **speak without equivocation** ▪ to speak unambiguously hablar sin vaguedades ▪ hablar sin ambigüedades ▪ hablar sin equívocos

speaker: loud ~ *(L. Am.)el* altoparlante ▪ *(Sp.) el* altavoz

speaker: stereo ~ pantalla acústica ▪ *el* bafle ▪ *(L. Am.)* bocina ▪ *(Sp.) la* altavoz ▪ *(plural)* altavoces

speaker alluded to the fact that... *el, la* hablante aludió al hecho de que... ▪ *el, la* discursante aludió al hecho de que... ▪ *(Sp.) el, la* conferenciante aludió al hecho de que... ▪ *el, la* ponente aludió al hecho de que...

speaking of... ▪ apropos of... ▪ with reference to... hablando de... ▪ a propósito de... ➤ Speaking of globalization, what is needed is an international floor under wages. Hablando de la globalización, lo que se necesita es un suelo internacional por debajo de los salarios. ▪ A propósito de la globalización, lo que se necesita es un suelo internacional por debajo de los salarios.

speaking part *(in a play)* parte hablada

speaking to... hablando a... ▪ ante... ➤ Speaking to more than a hundred and fifty world leaders, the president... Hablando a más de ciento cincuenta dirigentes de todo el mundo, el presidente... ▪ Ante más de ciento cincuenta dirigentes de todo el mundo, el presidente...

special forces comandos especiales

special interests intereses particulares ▪ intereses privados

to **special order merchandise** encargar mercancías ▪ hacer un pedido especial de mercancías ▪ pedir mercancías (de encargo) ▪ encargar mercancías a la fábrica ➤ Can you special order a book for me? ¿Me puede hacer un pedido especial por un libro? ▪ ¿Me puede pedir un libro de encargo?

special relativity *(Einsteinian physics)* relatividad restringida

special session pleno extraordinario

specific gravity *(physics)* gravedad específica ➤ Ebony has a specific gravity of 1.1, which means that a block of it placed in water will sink. El ébano tiene una gravedad específica de 1.1, lo cual quiere decir que un bloque de ello, colocado en agua, se hundirá.

specific target objetivo concreto ➤ The investigators are working with the certain knowledge that the perpetrators had specific objectives. Los investigadores trabajan con la certeza de que los autores tenían objetivos concretos.

speck of dust mota de polvo

spectacular accident accidente aparatoso

spectacular goring cornada aparatosa

to **speculate about** ▪ to speculate on ▪ to conjecture about hacer cábalas sobre ▪ especular sobre

speed checked by radar velocidad controlada por radar

speed limit *el* límite de velocidad

speed of sound ▪ velocity of sound *la* velocidad del sonido ➤ The airliners of the future will reach speeds several times that of sound. Los aviones de pasajeros del futuro alcanzarán velocidades varias veces superiores a la del sonido.

to **speed up** ▪ to go faster embalarse ▪ acelerarse

to **speed up the learning process** ▪ to facilitate learning acelerar el (proceso de) aprendizaje ▪ agilizar el (proceso de) aprendizaje ▪ agilitar el (proceso de) aprendizaje

speeding: to stop someone for ~ parar a alguien por conducir a exceso de velocidad ▪ detener a alguien por conducir a exceso de velocidad ▪ parar a alguien por ir a exceso de velocidad ▪ detener a alguien por ir a exceso de velocidad ➤ The policeman stopped him for speeding. El policía lo hizo parar por conducir a exceso de velocidad. ▪ El policía lo paró por conducir con exceso de velocidad. ▪ *(Sp., leísmo)* El policía le hizo parar por conducir a exceso de velocidad. ▪ El policía le paró por conducir a exceso de velocidad. ➤ The policeman stopped her for speeding. El policía la hizo parar por conducir a exceso de velocidad. ▪ El policía la paró por conducir con exceso de velocidad. ▪ *(Sp., leísmo)* The policeman stopped her for speeding. El policia le hizo parar por conducir a exceso de velocidad. ▪ El policía le paró por conducir con exceso de velocidad.

to **spell it out** **1.** to write it out escribirlo ▪ ponerlo en letra **2.** to explain it point by point explicarlo punto por punto

spell of bad weather racha de mal tiempo ▪ temporadita de mal tiempo ▪ temporada de mal tiempo

to **spell out the number (in letters)** deletrear el número ▪ poner el número en letra ➤ Shall I write the number as numerals or spell it out in letters? ▪ Shall I write the number in numerals or in letters? ¿Pongo el número en cifras o lo deletreo? ▪ ¿Pongo el número en cifras o en letra?

to be **spelled with** escribirse con ➤ It's spelled with a *y*. Se escribe con *y*.

spelling mistakes faltas de ortografía ▪ errores ortográficos to **spend beyond one's means** gastar por encima de las posibilidades de uno(-a) ▪ gastar más de lo que uno(-a) gana ▪ irse más allá de sus posibilidades ▪ gastar más allá de sus posibilidades

to **spend money on something** gastar(se) dinero en algo ▪ gastar en algo ➤ If you won the lottery, what would you spend the money on? ¿Si te tocara la lotería, en qué (te) gastarías el dinero? ➤ What would you spend it on? ¿En qué (te) lo gastarías?

to **spend one's whole life doing something** pasarse la vida entera haciendo una cosa ➤ There are people who spend their whole lives... Hay quien se pasa la vida entera...

to **spend the night** ▪ to stay the night pasar la noche ▪ pernoctar

to **spend the weekend** pasar el fin de semana ➤ I spent the weekend with my parents. Pasé el fin de semana con mis padres. ▪ Estuve pasando el fin de semana con mis padres.

to **spend time** pasar tiempo ▪ dedicar tiempo ▪ estar ➤ She loved books and spent her free time reading. Le gustaban mucho los libros y dedicaba el tiempo libre a leer. ➤ We spent a lot of time this weekend at home. Hemos estado en casa mucho tiempo este fin de semana.

to **spend time alone with someone** pasar tiempo a solas con alguien

to **spend time together** pasar tiempo juntos

spent bullet bala gastada

spent comet ▪ dead comet cometa extinguido

spiked eggnog *(Mex., C.A.) el* rompope ▪ *(Sp.) el* ponche de huevo con alcohol ▪ *(general)* licor de huevo

to **spill something on oneself** echárselo encima ➤ Oops, I spilled it on me! ▪ Oops, I spilled it on myself! ¡Ay, me lo eché encima!

to **spill something on someone** tirarle algo encima a alguien ➤ He bumped into me and spilled his coffee on me. Me tiró encima el café cuando chocó conmigo.

to **spill something on something 1.** *(liquid)* derramar algo sobre algo **2.** *(solid)* desparramar algo sobre algo **3.** *(liquid or solid)* echár algo encima de algo ➤ The waitress spilled the coffee all over the newspaper the customer was reading. La camarera derramó el café por todo el periódico que el cliente estaba leyendo. ➤ I spilled the sugar. Desparramé el azúcar.

to **spill the beans** descubrir el pastel ▪ irse de la lengua

to **spill over** desbordarse ▪ derramarse ➤ If you pour any more, it's going to spill over. Si echas más, se va a desbordar. ▪ Si echas más, se va a derramar.

spilled milk: there's no use crying over ~ a lo hecho, pecho ▪ de nada sirve llorar sobre leche derramada

to **spin a web** tejer una telaraña

to **spin around 1.** *(vehicle)* hacer trompos ▪ dar vueltas **2.** *(swivel chair)* girar ▪ dar vueltas

spin doctor asesor de imagen ➤ The president's spin doctors went to work to control the political damage. Los asesores de imagen del presidente se pusieron a trabajar para controlar el daño político (sufrido).

to **spin one's wheels** ▪ to expend effort fruitlessly estar estancado ▪ patinar en seco ➤ We keep going over the same twenty-five pages. We're just spinning our wheels. Seguimos trabajando en las mismas veinticinco páginas. Estamos estancados.

to **spin someone around blindfolded** darle vueltas a alguien con los ojos vendados

to **spin yarns** ▪ to tell colorful stories hilar historias pintorescas ➤ Lincoln spun colorful yarns. ▪ Lincoln told colorful stories. Lincoln hilaba historias pintorescas.

spine of a book canto de un libro ▪ lomo de un libro

spiral staircase escalera de caracol

spirit of helpfulness *el* espíritu de ayuda

Spirit of St. Louis* 1.** *(airplane piloted by Charles Lindbergh, which in May 1927 made the first nonstop solo transatlantic flight)* ***El espíritu de San Luis **2.** *(Spanish title of the Billy Wilder film* Spirit of St. Louis, *which chronicles Lindbergh's flight)* ***El héroe solitario***

spirited discussion 1. conversación animada ▪ conversación enérgica **2.** *(euphemism for an argument) la* discusión acalorada ▪ fuerte discusión

spirited horse caballo fogoso ▪ caballo con nervio ▪ caballo de mucho nervio

spiritual sustenance ▪ spiritual food manjar espiritual

to be the **spitting image of someone** ▪ to look just like someone ▪ to look exactly like someone ser clavado a alguien ▪ ser clavadito(-a) a alguien ▪ ser la viva imagen de alguien ▪ ser la viva estampa de alguien ▪ ser el mismísimo doble de alguien ▪ ser pintado a alguien

splash of liquid chorrito de líquido ➤ Add six tablespoons of flour and, last, a splash of milk. Se añade seis cucharadas de harina y por último un chorrito de leche.

splatter guard *(for a frying pan)* tapadera antiproyección

splinter: to get a ~ clavársele una astilla ➤ I got a splinter. Se me clavó una astilla.

to **splinter a conversation** iniciar una conversación aparte de la del grupo ➤ I don't want to invite him because he always splinters the conversation at the dinner table. No quiero invitarlo porque siempre inicia una conversación aparte de la del grupo en la mesa de comedor.

splinter group grupo escindido del principal ▪ grupo escindido

to **split a log with an ax(e)** partir un tronco con un hacha

to **split firewood** partir leña ▪ requebrar leña

to **split hairs** buscarle la quinta pata al gato ▪ buscarle tres pies al gato

to **split into factions** dividirse en facciones ▪ escindirse en facciones

to **split into groups** ▪ to split up into groups ▪ to divide up into groups dividirse en grupos ➤ I don't like it when the teacher makes us split (up) into groups. ▪ I don't like it when the teacher makes us divide up into groups. No me gusta cuando la profesora nos hace dividirnos en grupos.

to **split off** separarse

to **split off politically** ▪ to splinter escindirse

to **split one's sides laughing** ▪ to laugh till one is blue in the face desternillarse de risa ▪ retorcerse de risa

to **split open something** ▪ to split something open abrirle algo ➤ The impact of the rock split his head open. ▪ The impact of the rock split open his head. El impacto de la roca le abrió la cabeza. ➤ The impact of the rock split it open. El impacto de la roca se la abrió.

to **split rails** partir rieles

split shift jornada partida

to **split something** tomar algo a medias ▪ *(Sp.)* tomar algo a pachas ➤ Do you want to split a dessert? ¿Quieres tomar un postre a medias? ▪ ¿Quieres tomar un postre a pachas?

to **split something down the middle (lengthwise)** ▪ to divide something down the middle partir algo por el medio ➤ We split the watermelon down the middle and each ate half. Partimos la sandía por el medio y cada uno de nosotros se comió una mitad.

to **split the bill evenly among everybody** ▪ to divide the bill (up) evenly among everybody pagar entre todos ▪ dividir la cuenta entre todos

to **split the coalition** escindir la coalición ▪ dividir la coalición

to **split up 1.** to get a divorce divorciarse **2.** *(boyfriend, girlfriend)* to break up cortar con alguien ▪ romper con alguien ▪ terminar con alguien **3.** *(posse, for example)* dividirse en grupos ➤ The posse split up, one group searching down by the river, the other taking the mountain road. El pelotón se dividió, un grupo buscando por el río y el otro tomando el camino de la montaña.

splitting headache *el* dolor de cabeza atroz

to **spoil a child** mimar a un niño ▪ malcriar a un niño

to **spoil everything** echar(lo) todo a perder

to **spoil for a fight** ▪ to look for a fight buscar pelea ➤ The school bully was spoiling for a fight. El matón de la escuela buscaba pelea. ▪ El matón de la escuela estaba buscando pelea.

to **spoil the ending of the story** ▪ to give away the ending of the story arruinar el final del cuento ▪ estropear el final del cuento ▪ destripar el cuento ▪ echar a perder el final del cuento ▪ ➤ I don't want to spoil the ending (for you). *(a ti)* No quiero estropear(te) el final. ▪ *(a usted)* No quiero estropear(le) el final.

to **spoil the punch line of the joke** ▪ to give away the punch line of the joke destripar el chiste ▪ fastidiar el chiste ▪ estropear el chiste

to **spoil the surprise** estropear la sorpresa
to **spoil your appetite** quitarte el apetito
spoiled ballot papeleta estropeada
spoiled brat malcriado(-a) ■ niñato(-a) ■ niño(-a) consentido(-a) ■ *(Mex., coll.)* niño(-a) chiple
spoiled child niño(-a) mimado(-a)
to be **spoiled (rotten)** ■ to be overindulged estar malcriado(-a) ■ estar consentido(-a)
the **spoils of war** el botín de (la) guerra
to be **spoken for** ■ to be claimed estar apalabrado ■ haber sido comprometido ➤ The first ten copies are already spoken for. Los diez primeros ejemplares ya están apalabrados. ■ Los diez primeros ejemplares ya han sido comprometidos.
to **sponsor a bill** patrocinar un proyecto de ley
sponsor of a bill patrocinador de un proyecto de ley *(Usually plural, since there are typically two sponsors, one from each house of the legislature.)*
sponsor of an amendment patrocinador de la enmienda
spoof of: to do a ~ to do a spoof on ■ to spoof ■ to do a take-off on hacer una parodia de ■ parodiar *(Although "spoof of" and "spoof on" may refer to people or things, "spoof of" is more common; "spoof on" is more likely to refer to people.)*
sport shirt camisa de sport
sporting goods artículos deportivos
sports car coche deportivo
to **spot something at a glance** divisar algo de un vistazo ■ ver algo a simple vista ➤ You could spot it at a glance. Se podía divisar de un vistazo. ■ Se divisaba de un vistazo. ■ Se veía a simple vista.
to **spot something in the distance** divisar algo en la distancia ■ divisar algo a lo lejos ➤ Rodrigo de Triana, from the crow's nest of the Pinta, spotted the bonfires of the native Americans at a distance of about nine miles. Rodrigo de Triana, desde su puesto de vigía en la Pinta, divisó las fogatas de los nativos americanos a una distancia de unas nueve millas.
spotless record ■ unblemished record *el* expediente sin tacha ■ expediente sin mancha
spots of an animal manchas de un animal
to **spout off propaganda** arrojar un chorro de propaganda ■ arrojar chorros de propaganda ■ arrojar nubes de propaganda
to **spout off statistics** ■ to reel off statistics recitar una retahíla de estadísticas ■ arrojar estadísticas ■ soltar estadísticas
to **sprain one's ankle** hacerse un esguince en el tobillo
to **sprawl out** *(on the floor, sofa, chair, etc.)* repanchigarse ■ repantigarse
to **spray one's enemies** rociar a sus enemigos ➤ Skunks spray their enemies. Las mofetas rocían a sus enemigos.
to **spray gunfire** ■ to spray with gunfire ■ to spray bullets ■ to spray with bullets disparar a mansalva ■ tirar ráfagas de disparos
to **spread a tablecloth** ■ to spread out a tablecloth poner un mantel ■ extender un mantel ■ *(L. Am.)* tender un mantel
to **spread by word of mouth** transmitirse de boca a boca
to **spread its wings** desplegar sus alas ■ extenderse sus alas ■ expandirse sus alas
to **spread like wildfire** correr como la pólvora ■ propagarse como la pólvora ➤ The news spread like wildfire. La noticia corrió como la pólvora.
to **spread one's legs** despatarrarse ■ abrirse de piernas
to **spread one's wings** *(figurative)* desplegar las alas ➤ *(song lyric)* I could have spread my wings and done a thousand things I've never done before. Pude haber desplegado mis alas y haber hecho mil cosas que jamás he hecho.
to **spread oneself too thin** dispersar sus fuerzas (demasiado)
to **spread out a blanket** tender una manta
to **spread someone's legs** despatarrar a alguien
to **spread something on something** ■ to spread something over something ■ to spread something with something untar algo con algo ■ extender algo sobre algo ➤ Spread the crushed garlic on the fillet and let it rest for an hour with a marinade of Worcestershire, soy sauce, and spices. Untar el filete con los ajos machacados y dejarlo una hora con un adobo de salsa Perrins®, salsa de soja y especias.
to **spread the word** (hacer) correr la voz
sprig of parsley ■ parsley sprig ramita de perejil
to **spring a leak** **1.** *(pressure leak)* hacerse una fuga **2.** *(dripping leak)* hacerse una gotera **3.** *(fissure)* hacerse una fisura **4.** *(in a boat)* abrirse una vía de agua
spring chicken yogurín ■ yogurina ■ crío(-a)
spring fever: to have ~ *(L. Am.)* tener fiebre de primavera ■ *(Sp.)* la primavera la sangre altera
spring is in the air la primavera se siente en el aire ■ la primavera está en el ambiente ■ la primavera está en la atmósfera
spring runoff *(caused by snow melting in higher elevations)* deshielo
to **spring something on someone** espetarle a alguien una cosa
springlike day *el* día primaveral
to **spur a horse** espolear a un caballo ■ clavarle espuelas al caballo ■ picar a un caballo
spur of the moment: on the ~ sin pensarlo ■ sin pensarlo dos veces
spur-of-the-moment decision decisión tomada al instante
to **spur someone on** espolear a alguien ■ aguijonear a alguien
to be **spurred on by someone** ser espoleado por alguien ➤ *(news item)* Mobs spurred on by Mugabe kill another white farmer in Zimbabwe. Turbas espoleadas por Mugabe matan a otro granjero blanco en Zimbabue.
to **squander money** derrochar dinero ■ dispilferrar dinero
to **squander one's inheritance** dilapidar la herencia (de uno)
to **squander something** desperdiciar algo
square in...: to hit someone ~ ■ to hit someone right smack in... ■ to strike someone square in... ■ to strike someone right smack in... alcanzar a alguien de lleno en ■ darle a alguien de lleno en ➤ The pie hit him square in the face. ■ The pie hit him right smack in the face. El pastel lo alcanzó de lleno en la cara. ■ El pastel le dio de lleno en la cara. ■ *(Sp., leísmo)* El pastel le alcanzó de lleno en la cara.
square kilometers kilómetros cuadrados ➤ The town covers four square kilometers. El pueblo cubre cuatro kilómetros cuadrados.
square miles millas cuadradas ➤ The town covers four square miles. El pueblo cubre cuatro millas cuadradas.
square root raíz cuadrada
to **square something with something else** compaginar algo con algo ■ arreglar algo con alguien ➤ Let me square it with the boss before we proceed any further. Déjame compaginarlo con el jefe antes de que seguir adelante.
to be **squared** ■ to be multiplied by itself estar elevado al cuadrado
to **squash a mosquito** aplastar un mosquito ■ *(L. Am.)* destripar un zancudo
the **squeaky wheel gets the grease** el que no llora no mama
squealing of brakes ■ screeching of brakes chirrido de frenos
to **squeeze blood out of a turnip** sacar agua de las piedras ■ dar lo que no tiene ➤ You can't squeeze blood out of a turnip. Nadie puede dar lo que no tiene.
to **squeeze in (together)** ■ to double up ■ *(coll.)* to squinch up apretujarse ➤ If we squeeze in together, we can all fit. ■ If we double up, we can all fit. ■ If we squinch up, we can all fit. Si nos apretujamos (un poco), cabremos todos.
to **squeeze someone's hand** apretarle la mano a alguien
to **squelch questions** apabullar preguntas ■ callar pregunta ➤ I don't like the teacher because he squelches questions. No me cae bien el profesor porque apabulla las preguntas.
squiggle over the *n* tilde sobre la *n* (ñ) ■ *(coll.)* rabillo sobre la *n* (ñ)
to **squinch up** *(coll.)* ■ to double up ■ to squeeze in (together) apretujarse ➤ If we squinch up, we can all fit. ■ If we squeeze in together, we can all fit. ■ If we double up, we can all fit. Si nos apretujamos (un poco), cabremos todos.
to **squint from the sun** ■ to squint in the sun entrecerrar los ojos por el sol ■ entornar los ojos por el sol
St. John's wort hierba de San Juan
St. Martin of the Fields San Martín de la Vega
to **stab someone to death** matar a alguien a puñaladas ■ matar a alguien de una puñalada

to be **stabbed to death** morir apuñalado ▪ ser apuñalado hasta la muerte ▪ ser acuchillado hasta la muerte

stacks in a library *los* anaqueles de una biblioteca

stage fright: to get ~ entrarle a uno miedo escénico ▪ darle a uno miedo escénico ▪ agarrarle a uno miedo escénico ▪ entrarle a uno pánico escénico ▪ darle a uno pánico escénico ▪ agarrarle a uno pánico escénico

stage fright: to have ~ tener miedo escénico ▪ tener pánico escénico

stage left lateral izquierdo (del escenario)

stage of treatment fase de un tratamiento ▪ línea de tratamiento ➤ Oncologists have tested the use of methadone in the early stages of cancer treatment. Oncólogos han probado el uso de la metodona en fases tempranas del tratamiento del cáncer.

stage presence: to have ~ tener tablas

stage right lateral derecho (del escenario)

to **stagger around** ▪ to stagger ir tambaleándose ▪ ir dando tumbos ▪ hacer eses ▪ dar trompicones

to **stain a fabric** manchar un tejido ➤ The grape juice stained the tablecloth. El zumo de uva manchó el mantel.

to **stain the reputation of someone** ▪ to stain someone's reputation ▪ to damage someone's reputation manchar la reputación de alguien ▪ tiznar la reputación de alguien

to **stain wood** darle un tono de fondo a madera ➤ I'm going to stain and varnish this table. Voy a darle un tono de fondo y barnizar esta mesa.

stained glass vidrio de colores

stained-glass window *el* vitral ▪ *(Sp.)* vidriera (de colores)

stainless steel flatware cubertería de acero inoxidable

to **stake out an area** jalonar una área ▪ jalonar un terreno

stalk of celery ▪ celery stalk rama de apio

to **stalk out** ▪ to storm out ▪ to leave in a huff coger la puerta ▪ azotar la puerta ▪ detener la puerta

to **stall (on landing)** *(aeronautics)* estar en pérdida

to **stall the motor** **1.** to kill the motor calar el motor **2.** *(by flooding the carburetor)* ahogar el motor ➤ I stalled the motor by releasing the clutch too quickly. ▪ I killed the motor by releasing the clutch (pedal) too quickly. Calé el motor al soltar la maneta del embrague demasiado de prisa.

to **stall (the) negotiations** llevar a punto muerto las negociaciones ▪ estancar las negociaciones

stall warning *(of an airplane)* alarma de velocidad insuficiente ➤ The stall warning sounds just before the airplane stalls. La alarma de velocidad insuficiente suena justo antes de que el avión pierda velocidad de vuelo.

stalled negotiations negociación estancada ➤ Negotiations to reach an agreement were stalled last night. La negociación en busca de un pacto quedó estancada anoche.

stalled: the car ~ *(L. Am.)* se le caló el carro a uno ▪ *(Sp.)* se le caló el coche a uno ➤ The car stalled (on me). ▪ My car stalled. Se me caló el carro. ▪ Se me caló el coche.

to **stamp a passport** refrendar un pasaporte ▪ sellar un pasaporte

to **stamp an envelope** **1.** *(to put the postage on an envelope)* franquear un sobre ▪ poner el sello a un sobre **2.** *(to rubber-stamp something on an envelope)* sellar un sobre

to **stand a good chance of** ▪ to have a good chance of tener buenas posibilidades de

stand-alone: to be played as a ~ tocarse solo ▪ tocarse sin el resto ▪ tocarse de modo independiente ➤ "The Swan" from Saint-Saëns' "Carnival of the Animals" is often played as a stand-alone. "El cisne" del "Carnaval de los animales" de Saint-Saëns a menudo se toca solo.

to **stand aside** ▪ to stand to the side ▪ to stand to one side situarse a un lado ▪ hacerse a un lado ➤ Please stand aside. ▪ Please stand to the side. ▪ Please stand to one side. Por favor sitúense a un lado. ▪ Por favor háganse a un lado.

to **stand back** ▪ to get back mantenerse atrás ▪ situarse atrás ➤ Stand back! ¡Atrás!

to **stand behind someone** **1.** *(literal)* to stand in back of someone ponerse detrás de alguien **2.** *(figurative)* to support someone ▪ to back someone (up) respaldar a alguien ▪ apoyar a alguien

to **stand beside** estar parado junto a

to **stand by and do nothing** ▪ to stand there and do nothing ▪ to fiddle while Rome burns quedarse de brazos cruzados

to **stand by someone** **1.** *(literal)* to stand next to someone estar de pie al lado de alguien **2.** *(figurative)* to be loyal to someone ser(le) fiel a alguien ➤ She was standing by him in the reception line. Estaba de pie a su lado en la fila de la recepción.

to **stand down** ▪ to concede ▪ to resign retirarse ▪ renunciar ▪ dimitir

to **stand firm** mantenerse firme ▪ mantenerse en sus trece ▪ estar en sus trece ▪ no dar su brazo a torcer

to **stand for** **1.** to represent representar ▪ corresponder **2.** to tolerate tolerar ➤ What does the C in your middle name stand for? ¿Qué representa la C de tu segundo nombre? ▪ ¿A qué (nombre) corresponde la C de tu segundo nombre? ➤ The former prime minister still leaves no one undecided: the conservatives still adore her, and the liberals continue to hate everything she stands for. La ex-primera ministra sigue sin dejar a nadie indiferente: los conservadores aún la adoran y los liberales siguen odiando todo lo que ella representa.

to **stand for reelection** presentarse a la reelección

to **stand guard** montar guardia ➤ *(picture caption)* A soldier stands guard at the official presidential residence. Un soldado monta guardia en la residencia oficial del presidente.

to **stand here** ▪ to stand right here ponerse aquí ➤ Stand (right) here. Ponte aquí.

to **stand in front of** ponerse delante de

to **stand in front of the mirror** ▪ to stand before the mirror ponerse ante el espejo ▪ pararse delante del espejo

to **stand in line** hacer cola ▪ estar en la cola ➤ We were standing in line at the movies when... Estabamos haciendo cola en el cine cuando... ▪ Estabamos en la cola en el cine cuando... ▪ Estabamos en la cola del cine cuando...

stand in the hall: to go ~ irse al pasillo ➤ Go stand in the hall. Vete al pasillo. ➤ The teacher made him stand in the hall. El profesor lo mandó al pasillo.

to **stand next to someone** ponerse junto a alguien

to **stand on one's hands** pararse de manos ▪ hacer el pino ➤ The diver stands on his hands at the end of the diving board before diving into the water. El saltador se para de manos al final del trampolín antes de lanzarse al agua. ▪ El saltador hace el pino al final extremo del trampolín antes de lanzarse al agua.

to **stand on tiptoes** ▪ to stand on one's toes ponerse de puntillas ▪ alzarse sobre puntos de los pies ▪ *(S. Am.)* empinarse

to **stand one's ground** **1.** to remain firm in one's convictions ▪ to stick to one's guns seguir en la brecha ▪ permanecer en sus trece ▪ seguir en sus trece ▪ mantenerse en sus trece ▪ estar en sus trece ▪ mantenerse firme en sus principios **2.** to hold one's territory in battle ▪ to maintain the integrity of one's position in debate mantener su terreno

to **stand out** destacarse ▪ llamar la atención

to **stand out like a sore thumb** verse a la legua

to **stand right behind someone** estar de pie justamente detrás de alguien ▪ plantarse justamente detrás de alguien

to **stand something upright** ▪ to stand something on end ▪ to stand something vertically poner algo vertical ▪ poner algo derecho ▪ colocar algo en vertical

to **stand the pain** ▪ to endure the pain ▪ to withstand the pain tolerar el dolor ▪ aguantar el dolor

to **stand there and do nothing** ▪ to stand by and do nothing ▪ to fiddle while Rome burns quedarse de brazos cruzados

to **stand there doing nothing** ▪ to sit there doing nothing quedarse sin hacer nada

to **stand there like an idiot** quedarse (ahí) como un pasmarote

to **stand to the left** situarse a la izquierda ▪ ponerse a la izquierda

to **stand to the right** situarse a la derecha ▪ ponerse a la derecha ➤ Please stand to the right. Por favor sitúense a la derecha. ▪ Por favor pónganse a la derecha.

to **stand under a tree** estar de pie debajo de un árbol ▪ *(L. Am.)* estar parado debajo de un árbol

to **stand up** ponerse de pie ▪ ponerse en pie

to **stand up by themselves** *(dirty socks and pants)* andar solos to **stand up someone** ▪ to stand someone up dejar plantado(-a) a alguien ▪ dar (un) plantón a alguien ▪ plantar a alguien ➤ He stood up his date for the dance. ▪ He stood his date up for the dance. Él dejó plantada a la chica para el baile. ➤ He stood her up for the dance. La dejó plantada para el baile. ▪ Le dio un plantón para el baile. ▪ *(Sp., leísmo)* La dio plantón para el baile. ➤ He stood me up! ¡Me dejó plantado(-a)! ▪ ¡Me dio plantón! ➤ She stood him up. *(L. Am.)* Ella lo dejó plantado. ▪ *(Sp., leísmo)* Ella le dejó plantado. ➤ He stood her up. Él la dejó plantada.

to **stand up straight** ponerse derecho ➤ The mother said to her son, "Stand up straight." La madre le dijo a su hijo, "Ponte derecho".

to **stand up to someone** hacerle frente a alguien

to **stand with one's hands on one's hips** estar en jarras ▪ estar de pie con los brazos en jarras

to **stand with one's legs apart** estar de pie con las piernas abiertas ▪ situarse con las piernas abiertas ▪ estar de pie con las piernas separadas ▪ situarse con las piernas separadas

standard English inglés normativo ▪ inglés estándar

to be **standard equipment** ser equipamiento de serie ▪ tener algo (como equipamiento) de serie ➤ It's standard equipment. Es equipamiento de serie.

standard equipment: to have something as ~ tener algo (como equipamiento) de serie ➤ The car has air conditioning as standard equipment. El carro tiene aire condicionado de serie.

standard of living *el* nivel de vida

standard Spanish español normativo ▪ español estándar

Standard Time horario de invierno ➤ To change to Standard Time in the fall, you set the clock back one hour. Para cambiar al horario de invierno en (el) otoño, se atrasa el reloj una hora.

standardized test *(TOEFL, GRE, SAT, etc.)* ▪ standardized examination examen estandardizado ▪ examen tipo test

standing before her de pie ante ella ▪ de pie delante de ella

standing before him de pie ante él ▪ de pie delante de él

standing idle sin trabajar ▪ desocupado

standing in the community: one's ~ *la* reputación de uno en la comunidad

standing invitation invitación fija ▪ invitación constante

standing order pedido fijo

standing room only solamente caber de pie ➤ There is standing room only (for us). Solamente cabemos de pie.

staph infection *la* infección por estafilococo

staple of the diet comida básica

star cluster cúmulo estelar ▪ cúmulo de estrellas

star pupil alumno estrella

star-studded group of ▪ star-studded collection of ▪ illustrious group of ▪ illustrious collection of *la* pléyade de

Star Wars *(film title) Guerra de las galaxias*

to **star with someone** ▪ to co-star with someone compartir el papel protagonista con alguien ▪ compartir el papel estelar con alguien

star witness ▪ principal witness testigo principal

to **stare at someone** clavar la mirada en alguien ▪ mirar fijadamente a alguien ▪ mirar con fijeza a alguien ➤ She stared at me. Ella me clavó la mirada.

stark atmosphere ambiente austero

to be **stark naked** estar en porretas ▪ estar en cueros vivos ▪ estar en pelotas ▪ estar en pelota picada

to be **stark raving mad** ▪ to be stark raving nuts ▪ to be crazy as a loon ▪ to be a nut case estar loco(-a) de remate ▪ estar completamente chiflado(-a)

the **stars and stripes** *(American flag)* ▪ Old Glory las barras y estrellas ▪ la bandera norteamericana ▪ la bandera estadounidense

to **start a car without the ignition key** ▪ to hotwire a car hacer el puente a un coche

to **start afresh** ▪ to wipe the slate clean ▪ to begin a new page hacer borrón y cuenta nueva ▪ zanjar algo ▪ empezar de cero

to **start an engine** arrancar un motor

to **start at square one** ▪ to start at the very beginning ▪ to start from scratch empezar desde cero

to **start at the very beginning** ▪ to start at square one empezar desde cero ▪ empezar desde el principio

to **start crying** ▪ to start to cry ponerse a llorar ▪ echarse a llorar

to **start doing something** ponerse a hacer algo ▪ *(for the first time)* empezar a hacer algo ▪ comenzar a hacer algo ➤ She started riding (horses) when she was six. Empezó a montar (a caballo) a los seis años.

to **start from scratch** partir de cero

to **start going steady with someone** ennoviarse con alguien ➤ They started going together last year. Se ennoviaron el año pasado. ➤ Stan started going with Barb last year. Stan se ennovió con Barb el año pasado.

to **start laughing** echarse a reír

to **start moving** ponerse en movimiento

start of the meter *(in a taxi)* bajada de bandera

to **start off on the right foot** ▪ to get off to a good start empezar con el pie derecho ▪ empezar con buen pie

to **start off on the wrong foot** ▪ to get off to a bad start empezar con el pie izquierdo

to **start on something** empezar con algo ➤ I still haven't started on the translation. Todavía no he empezado con la traducción.

to **start out for** ponerse en camino para

to **start over (again)** volver a empezar

to **start over from the very beginning** ▪ to go back to square one volver a empezar desde el principio ▪ volver a empezar de cero

to **start something back up** volver a poner en marcha algo

to **start the engine** ▪ to start the motor arrancar el motor ▪ poner en marcha el motor ▪ encender el motor

to **start the engine back up** volver a arrancar el motor

to **start the meter** *(in a taxi)* ▪ to turn on the meter bajar la bandera

to **start to boil** ▪ to begin to boil ▪ to commence boiling ▪ to break into a boil romper a hervir

to **start to get difficult** ▪ to start to get hard ▪ to begin to get difficult ▪ to begin to get hard empezar a ponerse difícil ▪ empezar a hacerse difícil ▪ empezar a hacérsele cuesta arriba ➤ This course is starting to get difficult. Esta asignatura se me está haciendo difícil.

to **start to like** ▪ to begin to like empezar(le) a gustar a ▪ empezarle a caer bien a ▪ empezar a valorar a ➤ This dog is starting to like me. ▪ This dog is beginning to like me. (Le) empiezo a gustar a este perro. ▪ (Le) empiezo a caer bien a este perro.

to **start walking** ▪ to start out (on a hike) echar a andar

to **start with** ▪ to begin with empezar por ➤ The phone number starts with nine. El número de teléfono empieza por nueve.

to **start work** 1. *(new job)* empezar a trabajar 2. *(regular job)* entrar a trabajar ➤ I start work (on) April 1. Empiezo a trabajar el primero de abril. ➤ I start work at nine a.m. ▪ I start work at nine each morning. Entro a trabajar a las nueve de la mañana.

starting at *x* dollars a partir de *x* dólares ▪ desde *x* dólares ➤ Starting at forty-nine dollars A partir de cuarenta y nueve dólares ▪ Desde cuarenta y nueve dólares ➤ *(ad)* Paella delivered to your house, starting at 700 pesetas per person Paellas a domicilio a partir de 700 pts. por persona

starts April first *(movie, show, etc.)* estreno el uno de abril ▪ estreno el primero de abril

starts today el estreno es hoy ▪ se estrena hoy

starvation wages: to pay ~ pagar sueldos miserables ▪ pagar sueldos de hambre y miseria

state-of-the-art de última generación ▪ de punta ▪ de vanguardia ▪ puntera ➤ State-of-the-art radar Radar de última generación

state-of-the-art technology ▪ cutting-edge technology ▪ latest technology tecnología punta ▪ tecnología vanguardista ▪ tecnología puntera ▪ tecnología de punta ▪ lo último en tecnología ▪ último grito de la tecnología

to **state that...** hacer constar que...

statement to the press la declaración a la prensa

to be **stationed in** estar destinado en

Stations of the Cross *(Catholicism) las* Estaciones de la Cruz ▪ *el* Vía Crucis

to **stay afloat** mantenerse aflote

to **stay after school** quedarse después de clase ➤ I had to stay after school. Tuve que quedarme después de clase.

to **stay as far away from something as possible** estar lo más alejado posible de algo ➤ Ceci said that during her vacation she has every intention of staying as far from a computer as possible. Ceci dijo que durante sus vacaciones tiene toda la intención de estar lo más alejada posible de la computadora.

to **stay at a hotel** alojarse en un hotel ▪ hospedarse en un hotel

to **stay at someone's house** quedarse en la casa de alguien ▪ alojarse en la casa de alguien ▪ hospedarse en la casa de alguien

to **stay away (from)** mantenerse alejado (de)

to **stay away in droves** venir cuatro gatos ➤ People stayed away in droves. Vinieron cuatro gatos.

to **stay behind** echarse para atrás

to **stay in** ▪ to stay indoors quedarse dentro (de casa)

to **stay in a hotel** alojarse en un hotel ▪ hospedarse en un hotel

to **stay in bed** ▪ to remain in bed quedarse en cama ▪ guardar cama ▪ permanecer en la cama

to **stay in shape** ▪ to keep in shape mantenerse en forma ▪ mantenerse a punto ➤ I like to stay in shape. Me gusta mantenerme en forma. ▪ Me gusta mantenerme a punto.

to **stay in step** ▪ to keep in step llevar el paso

to **stay indoors** ▪ to stay in quedarse dentro (de casa)

stay of execution suspensión de la ejecución

stay or to go?: is this to ~ ▪ for here or to go? ¿para tomar o para llevar?

to **stay out late** permanecer fuera (de casa)

to **stay out of trouble** mantenerse alejado(-a) de los problemas

to **stay out until *x* in the morning** quedarse hasta las *x* de la mañana ▪ salir hasta las *x* de la mañana

to **stay overnight** ▪ to stay over ▪ to stop over hacer noche ▪ trasnochar

stay right here! estate aquí ▪ no te muevas de aquí

stay right there! estate ahí ▪ no te muevas de ahí

to **stay that way** durar ▪ seguir así ▪ seguir igual ➤ It's nice and cool outside. I hope it stays that way. Está bien fresco afuera. Espero que dure. ▪ Está bien fresco afuera. Espero que siga así. ▪ Está bien fresco afuera. Espero que siga igual.

to **stay up 1.** not to go to bed quedarse (levantado) **2.** to stay upright mantenerse derecho **3.** *(pants)* sujetársele ➤ We stayed up until two a.m. Nos quedamos hasta las dos de la mañana. ➤ I can't get the thing to stay up. It keeps falling over. No puedo hacer que se mantenga derecho. Se sigue cayendo. ➤ I want a pair of pants that will stay up without a belt. Quiero un pantalón que se me sujete sin cinturón.

to **stay up all night** pasar la noche en blanco ▪ estar en velo ▪ desvelarse ▪ trasnochar

to **stay up late** trasnochar

stay where you are! ¡estate ahí!

steady hand ▪ firm hand pulso firme

steady job: to have a ~ tener un trabajo estable

steady stream of cars flujo continuo de carros ▪ *(Sp.)* flujo continuo de coches

steady stream of visitors flujo continuo de visitantes

to **steal something** robar algo ▪ *(with stealth or cunning)* sustraer algo ➤ *(news item)* A shipment of Viagra was stolen at the harbor. Un cargamento de Viagra fue sustraído en el puerto.

to **steal the show** quedarse con el espectáculo ▪ meterse el espectáculo en el bolsillo ➤ By the luck of the draw, the little-known candidate got the first question, and she basically stole the show. Gracias al sorteo, el concursante menos conocido consiguió la primera pregunta, y básicamente se quedó con el espectáculo.

steaming hot *(food)* ▪ piping hot humeante

steel mill acería ▪ acerería

steep (in price) excesivo ▪ exagerado ▪ elevado ▪ demasiado ➤ Condos in the tourist sections of the old city are steep. Los precios de apartamentos en los sectores turísticos del casco antiguo de la ciudad son excesivos. ➤ Five dollars for a cup of coffee is a bit steep, don't you think? Let's go somewhere else. Cinco dólares por una taza de café es exagerado, ¿no lo crees? Vamas a otro lugar.

steep slope pendiente pronunciada

to **steep the tea** dejar reposar el té ▪ dejar en reposo el té ➤ Let it steep for a minute. Déjalo reposar un momento. ▪ Déjalo en reposo un momento.

to **steer clear of** alejarse de ▪ huir de

to **stem from** resultar de ▪ provenir de ▪ proceder de

stem of a wine glass el talle de una copa

to **stem the flow of blood** ▪ to stop the flow of blood ▪ to halt the flow of blood restañar la sangre

to **stem the tide** frenar la desbandada

to be a **step ahead of someone** ▪ to be one step ahead of someone estar un paso más por adelante de alguien

to **step aside** hacerse a un lado ▪ echarse a un lado ▪ apearse del burro ➤ He doesn't want to step aside. ▪ He doesn't want to give up power. No quiere apearse del burro.

to **step aside for someone** ▪ to let someone go in front of one ▪ to give someone the right of way cederle paso a alguien ➤ *(Reader's Digest)* I don't step aside for imbeciles.-Well I do, go ahead. No le cedo el paso a ningún imbécil.-Pues yo sí, ¡pase!

a **step away from** a paso de ➤ A step away from agreement on... A un paso del acuerdo sobre...

to **step back** dar pasos hacia atrás

step by step paso a paso

to **step down** ▪ to leave one's post darse de baja

to **step forward 1.** *(literal)* dar un paso (hacia) adelante **2.** *(figurative)* ofrecerse (a)

to be a **step in the right direction** ser un paso por el camino correcto

step in the right direction: to take a ~ dar un paso hacia el camino correcto ▪ tomar un paso hacia el camino derecho

to **step into the limelight** ▪ to enter the limelight salir a la palestra

to **step on it** ▪ to speed up ▪ to go faster meter caña

step on it! ¡písale! ▪ ¡caña! ▪ ¡mete caña!

step over here, please pasa por aquí, por favor

to **step up the attacks on** acentuar los ataques contra

to **step up the pressure for** ▪ to step up the pressure to get acentuar la presión para que

to **step up the pressure on someone** ▪ to increase the pressure on someone aumentar la presión a alguien

to **step up the pressure to get** acentuar la presión para que ➤ *(headline)* U.S. steps up the pressure to get NATO to support its war plans EE UU acentúa la presión para que la OTAN apoye sus planes de guerra

stepping-stone 1. piedra que permite cruzar un arroyo **2.** *(figurative)* peldaño hacia el éxito

stereo speakers pantallas acústicas ▪ *los* bafles ▪ *(L. Am.)* bocinas ▪ *(Sp.) las* altavoces

stick cinnamon canela en rama

to **stick it to somebody** darle caña a alguien ▪ meterle caña a alguien

stick of cinnamon ▪ cinnamon stick rama de canela

to **stick one's head out (of) the window 1.** *(of a car, bus, train)* sacar la cabeza por la ventanilla **2.** *(of a house)* sacar la cabeza de la ventana ➤ Don't stick your head out (of) the window. No saques la cabeza por la ventana. ▪ No saques la cabeza por la ventanilla.

to **stick one's nose into other people's business** meter el hocico...

to **stick one's tongue out at someone** ▪ to stick out one's tongue at someone sacar la lengua a alguien

to **stick out** dar el cante

to **stick out like a sore thumb** resaltar como una mosca en la leche

to **stick out one's tongue at someone** ▪ to stick one's tongue out at someone sacar la lengua a alguien

stick shift *(coll.)* ▪ straight shift cambio manual

to **stick to one's guns** ▪ to stand one's ground ▪ not to let one's arm be twisted mantenerse firme en sus principios ▪ afirmarse en los estribos ▪ permanecer en sus trece ▪ seguir en sus trece ▪ mantenerse en sus trece ▪ estar en sus trece ▪ no dar el brazo a torcer

to **stick to the surface** quedarse pegado a la superficie

to **stick to the text** ceñirse al texto

to **stick up for somebody** luchar a brazo partido por alguien ➤ He stuck up for me. Él luchó a brazo partido por mí.

to **stick with something** perseverar con algo ➤ Stick with it, and don't give up! Persevera y no te rindas. ➤ If he sticks with it, he'll be a good student. Si persevera, será un buen estudiante.

to be a **stickler for accuracy** ser un rigorista de la exactitud ▪ ser meticuloso en la precisión

sticky hands *(especially of children)* manos golosas ▪ manos pringadas

to be **stiff after nine hours on the airplane** estar estragado(-a) después de nueve horas en el avión

to be **stiff as a board** estar tieso como un palo ▪ estar más tieso que un ajo

stiff back espalda tensa ▪ espalda en tensión ▪ espalda rígida ➤ My back is stiff. Mi espalda está tensa. ▪ Mi espalda está en tensión. ▪ Mi espalda está rígida.

stiff muscles: to have ~ tener agujetas

stiff reprisals duras represalias

still ahead 1. coming up todavía por delante ▪ aún por delante **2.** still to be done ▪ yet ahead ▪ yet to be done por hacer

to be **still alive** aún seguir vivo ▪ estar sobreviviendo ▪ seguir con vida ➤ He's still alive. Aún sigue vivo. ▪ Está sobreviviendo. ▪ Sigue con vida.

to **still be available** todavía quedar ➤ A few seats are still available. Todavía quedan unas butacas.

to **still be in one piece** seguir de una pieza

to be **still doing something** seguir haciendo algo ➤ They were still waiting for her. Seguían esperándola.

still fresh in my memory todavía fresco(-a) en mi memoria

to **still have...** no dejar de tener... ➤ She still has her charms. No deja de tener sus encantos.

to **still have to** quedarle por ➤ We still have to buy the wine for the party. Nos queda por comprar el vino para la fiesta.

to **still have tough times ahead** quedar momentos duros

still life *(art)* naturaleza muerte ▪ el bodegón

to be **still living** vivir aún ▪ vivir todavía ➤ Is he still living? ¿Vive aún? ▪ ¿Vive todavía?

to **still not get it** seguir sin ➤ I still don't get it. Sigo sin entenderlo.

to **still not see** seguir sin ver ➤ I still don't see the connection. Sigo sin ver la relación.

to be **still on for** mantenerse ▪ seguir en pie ▪ seguir en pie lo de ➤ Is your trip to Madrid still on for January? ▪ Is your trip to Madrid in January still on? ¿Se mantiene tu viaje a Madrid para enero? ▪ ¿Sigue en pie lo de ir a Madrid para enero?

to be **still planning to** estar aún planeando ▪ tener aún en mente

to be **still to be determined** ▪ to be yet to be determined ▪ to be as yet undetermined ser aún por evaluar

to be **still waiting** seguir esperando

stillbirth parto muerto

to be **stillborn** nacer muerto(-a) ▪ *(in past tenses)* haber nacido muerto(-a) ➤ The infant was stillborn. El infante nació muerto.

to **stimulate the economy** estimular la economía ▪ activar la economía

stimulating drink bebida excitante

sting of a wound picadura de una herida

to **sting the eyes** ▪ to sting one's eyes escocer los ojos ➤ This shampoo doesn't sting the eyes. ▪ This shampoo doesn't sting your eyes. ▪ This shampoo won't sting the eyes. ▪ This shampoo won't sting your eyes. Este champú no escuece los ojos.

to stir a liquid remover un líquido ➤ Bring the milk to a boil, stirring constantly. Deje que hierva la leche mientras que la remueve continuamente.

stir-fry sofrito

to **stir-fry food** ▪ to sauté food saltear alimentos ▪ sofreír alimentos

to **stir occasionally** remover de vez en cuando ➤ Bring it to a boil, stirring occasionally. Llevarlo a ebullición removiendo de vez en cuando.

to **stir things up** ▪ to provoke controversy provocar las cosas

to **stir up a hornets' nest** revolver un avispero ▪ alborotar un avispero ▪ desatar una tormenta

to **stir up controversy over** atizar la polémica de

to **stir up rumors** suscitar rumores ▪ provocar rumores

to **stir up trouble** armar... ▪ incitar... ▪ echar leña al fuego ▪ meter cizaña

to **stir vigorously** remover enérgicamente ➤ Add the eggs whole, stirring vigorously until blended into the dough. Incorporar los huevos enteros, removiendo enérgicamente hasta integrarlos en la pasta.

stirring constantly ▪ stirring continuously sin dejar de remover ➤ Cook over low heat for several minutes, stirring constantly. Cocerlo a fuego lento unos minutos sin dejar de remover.

stock clerk ▪ stocker reponedor

stock exchange mercado bursátil

stock market mercado de valores ▪ bolsa ▪ mercado bursátil

stock market crash caída de la bolsa ▪ *(the great crash of 1929)* el crack

stock portfolio el paquete de acciones

to **stock up on** abastecerse de ▪ abastecerse con

to **stoke the fire** atizar el fuego ▪ avivar el fuego

stomach cramp el corte de digestión ▪ el torcijón del estómago ▪ torcijón en el estómago ➤ *(news photo caption)* The athlete is attended to after being felled by a stomach cramp El deportista es atendido tras desplomarse por un corte de digestión

stomach growl rugido del estómago

stomach is growling: my ~ mi estómago está rugiendo ▪ se queja mi estómago

stomachache el retortijón de tripas ▪ el dolor de estómago

stone age la edad de piedra

to be **stone cold 1.** to be uncomfortably cold estar tan frío como la muerte **2.** to be unreceptive estar como piedra ➤ The basement is stone cold. We can't sleep down here. El sótano está tan frió como la muerte. No podemos dormir aquí. ➤ When I was a teenager, my father was stone cold to the idea of buying me a car. Cuando era adolescente, mi padre estaba como piedra en la idea de comprarme un carro.

to **stone someone (to death) for** lapidar a alguien por ▪ matar a alguien a pedradas

to be **stoned to death for** lapidarse a alguien por

to be a **stone's throw away** ▪ to be a stone's throw from a place estar a un tiro de piedra ➤ It's a stone's throw from here. Es un tiro de piedra de aquí. ➤ St. Jerome's Church is a stone's throw from the Museo del Prado. La Iglesia de San Jerónimo está a un tiro de piedra del Museo del Prado.

to be **stoop shouldered** estar caído de hombros

to be **stooped over one's cane** estar encorvado sobre su bastón

to **stop along the way** ▪ to stop on the way detenerse en el camino

to **stop and listen** pararse y escuchar

to **stop at nothing** no pararse en barras

to **stop by** pasar por ▪ asomarse por ➤ Would you stop by the store on the way home? ¿Puedes pasar por la tienda en camino a casa? ➤ I was in the neighborhood, and I thought I'd stop by. Andaba por la vecindad y se me ocurrió asomarme por aquí.

stop crying! ¡déjate de llantos! ▪ ¡deja ya d llanto! ▪ ¡deja de llorar! ▪

to **stop crying** dejar el llanto

to **stop dead in one's tracks** quedarse parado sobre sus huellas ▪ quedarse parado en sus huellas ▪ quedarse quieto sobre sus huellas ▪ quedarse quieto en sus huellas

to **stop doing something** desistir de hacer algo ▪ dejar de hacer algo

stop fidgeting! ▪ be still! ▪ hold still! ¡estate quieto(-a)!

to **stop for refueling** ▪ to make a refueling stop hacer una escala técnica to **stop here for today** dejar aquí por hoy ➤ Let's stop here for today. Vamos a dejar aquí por hoy. ➤ We'll stop here for today. Dejemos aquí por hoy.

stop it! ¡basta!

to **stop making noise** parar de hacer ruido

to **stop over in a place** **1.** to go through a place estar de paso en un lugar **2.** to spend the night in a place trasnochar en un lugar ➤ We stopped over at the Atlanta airport. Estuvimos de paso en Atlanta. ➤ We stopped over in Córdova. Trasnochamos en Córdova.

to **stop raining** dejar de llover ▪ escampar

stop sign panel de stop

to **stop smoking** ▪ to quit smoking dejar de fumar ▪ cesar de fumar

to **stop someone dead in his tracks** pararle en seco a alguien ▪ pararle los pies a alguien ▪ pararle a mitad de trayecto a alguien

to **stop someone for speeding** pararlo a alguien por ir con exceso de velocidad ➤ The policeman stopped me for speeding. El policía me paró por ir con exceso de velocidad.

to **stop someone from doing something** reprimir a alguien de hacer algo ▪ privar a alguien de hacer algo

to **stop subscribing** ▪ to terminate a subscription darse de baja

to **stop talking** dejar de hablar ▪ parar de hablar

stop that man! ¡a por ése!

to **stop the bleeding** atajar la hemorragia

to **stop the recount** parar el recuento

to **stop to consider** pararse a considerar

to **stop to smoke** ▪ to stop to have a smoke pararse a fumar ▪ pararse para fumar ➤ I stopped to (have a) smoke. Me he parado a fumar.

to **stop to think about** detenerse a reflexionar en ➤ We rarely stop to think about... Pocas veces se detiene a reflexionar en...

stop what you're doing! ¡deja que estás haciendo!

stopping at nothing ▪ not letting anything get in the way sin pararse en barras

storage battery batería de reserva

storage bin *(in an apartment building)* trastero

storage facility el guardamuebles

storage locker ▪ storage unit el guardamuebles ▪ *(in an apartment building)* (cuarto) trastero

storage room trastero

storage space **1.** espacio de almacenamiento **2.** storage bin trastero

storage unit ▪ storage locker cuarto trastero ▪ el guardamuebles

to **store at room temperature** almacenar a temperatura ambiente

store-bought de la tienda ▪ comprada en tienda ➤ Store-bought pizza is not as good as homemade. La pizza de la tienda no es tan buena como hecha en casa. ▪ La pizza comprada en tienda no es tan buena como hecha en casa.

to **store food** guardar comida ▪ conservar comida ▪ abastecer comida

to **store in the memory** *(computers)* almacenar en la memoria ▪ salvar en la memoria

to **store memory** almacenar los recuerdos ➤ Where in the brain is memory stored? ¿Dónde en el cerebro se almacenan los recuerdos?

store of knowledge acervo de conocimientos

to **store something in a locker** almacenar algo en un guardamuebles

to **store supplies** almacenar suministros

to **store up** hacer acopio de

to be **stored under pressure** estar almacenado a presión ➤ The gas is stored under pressure in cylindrical tanks. El gas está almacenado a presión en tanques cilíndricos.

storm broke tormenta irrumpió

storm drain el colector

to **storm in** ▪ to come storming in entrar a degüello a ▪ *(Sp.)* entrar a degüello en

storm lets up ▪ storm subsides ▪ storm loses its punch remite el temporal

to **storm out** ▪ to stalk out ▪ to leave in a huff salir como un huracán ▪ azotar la puerta al salir ▪ largarse de casa

stormy day día tormentoso ▪ día de tormenta ▪ día de temporal

stormy sea mar borrascoso ▪ mar tormentoso

stormy weather tiempo tormentoso

story **1.** *(fictional story)* tale cuento **2.** *(newspaper story)* account relato ▪ el informe

the **story goes that...** ▪ the story is that... va de cuenta que...

the **story is about...** el cuenta va de... ▪ el cuenta trata de...

the **story is that...** ▪ the story goes that... va de cuento que...

story takes place in Rota ▪ setting of the story is Rota el cuento está ambientado en Rota ▪ la acción pasa en Rota

stove hood campana extractora de humos ▪ campana extractora

to **stow away (on a ship)** ir de polizón

to **straddle the fence** estar entre Pinto y Valdemoro ▪ nadar entre dos aguas ▪ estar entre dos aguas ▪ no querer mojarse ▪ jugar a dos bandas

straight ahead *(Mex.)* todo derecho ▪ *(Sp.)* todo recto

straight A's: to make ~ ▪ to get straight A's sacar solamente sobresalientes ▪ sacar solamente dieces

straight down: to go ~ ▪ to descend vertically bajar en vertical ▪ descender en vertical

straight face: to put on a ~ poner cara de palo

straight from the horse's mouth: to have it ~ saber algo de buena tinta

straight line línea recta ➤ A straight line is the shortest distance between two points. La línea recta es la más corta entre dos puntos.

to be **straight overhead** ▪ to be directly overhead justo encima de la cabeza

straight shift ▪ stick shift cambio manual

straight stretch trayecto recto

straight up: to go ~ ▪ to rise straight up ▪ to rise vertically subir en vertical ▪ ascender en vertical

to **straighten out something** ▪ to straighten something out poner algo en orden **1.** *(rigid, like wire)* enderezar algo **2.** *(flexible, like rope)* estirar algo **3.** to put something in order **4.** to rectify something rectificar algo ➤ I need to straighten out the kitchen cabinets. Necesito poner en orden los armarios de la cocina.

to **straighten (up) one's room** ordenar su habitación ▪ arreglar su habitación ▪ recoger su habitación

to **straighten (up) the house** ▪ to straighten the house up ordenar la casa ▪ arreglar la casa ▪ recoger la casa ➤ We have got to straighten it up. Tenemos que ordenar la casa. ▪ Tenemos que arreglar la casa. ▪ Tenemos que recoger la casa.

straightforward manner ▪ straightforwardness llaneza en el trato

straightforward person una persona sin doblez

to **strain one's eyes** castigar la vista

to **strain one's voice** esforzar la voz

Strait of Dover Paso de Calais

straitjacket: to be in a ~ ▪ to be in a straightjacket llevar una camisa de fuerza ▪ llevar chaleco de fuerza

to be **stranded by the storm** estar aislado a consecuencias del temporal ➤ Hundreds of people were stranded by the storm. Cientas de personas estaban aisladas a consecuencias del temporal.

strange as it may seem por extraño que parezca

strange that... curioso que... ➤ Strange that he should think of it just then. Curioso que lo pensara entonces.

strapless evening gown *(L. Am., Sp.)* vestido de noche sin tirantes ▪ *(Sp.)* vestido (con un cuello de) palabra de honor

to be **strapped for cash** andar escaso de dinero ▪ andar corto de dinero ▪ andar mal de dinero

to be the **straw that breaks the camel's back** ser la gota que colma el vaso ➤ It was the straw that broke the camel's back. Fue la gota que colmó el vaso.

stray bomb bomba perdida

stray bullet bala perdida
stray dog perro extraviado ▪ perro perdido
streak of bad luck temporada de mala suerte
streak of (good) luck: to have a ~ tener buena racha
streak of meanness ▪ mean streak veta mezquina
stream of consciousness *(James Joyce)* fluir de ideas ▪ fluir de pensamientos ▪ monólogo interior ▪ corriente de pensamiento
stream of insults ▪ barrage of insults flujo de insultos ▪ retahíla de insultos ▪ la cantidad de improperios ▪ rosario de insultos ▪ avalancha de insultos ▪ plétora de insultos
stream of particles *(physics)* el haz de partículos
streams of light chorros de luz
street map ▪ city map **1.** plano **2.** *(book of maps used by taxi drivers, tourists)* callejero
street musician músico callejero
street sign el cartel de la calle ➤ Bill Clinton waves in front of the street sign of a street in Little Rock that has been named for him. Bill Clinton saluda ante el cartel de la calle de Little Rock que ha sido bautizada con su nombre.
street slang lenguaje callejero ▪ (lenguaje) macarra
strength fuerza ▪ vigor ▪ pujanza
strength of one's convictions fuerza de sus convicciones
to **strengthen the family** fortalecer la familia
to **strengthen the foundation** realzar la base enterrada *(e.g., of the Leaning Tower of Pisa)*
to **strengthen ties between** estrechar relaciones entre
strengthening of fortalezamiento de
strengths and weaknesses: to have ~ tener limitaciones y fortalezas
strengths and weaknesses: to know one's ~ conocer sus limitaciones y fortalezas
to **stress a point** hacer hincapié en un punto ▪ insistir en un punto ▪ subrayar un punto
to **stress the importance of** resaltar la importancia de
stressful job (puesto de) trabajo estresante
stressful situation la situación estresante
to **stretch one's legs** estirar las piernas
to **stretch out toward** extenderse hacia
to **stretch shoes** meter zapatos en la horma ▪ dar de sí los zapatos
to be **stretched out** estar tendido a lo largo
stretching exercises: to do ~ hacer ejercicios de estiramiento ▪ hacer estiramientos
to be **stricken by** ▪ to be felled by desplomarse por ➤ The athlete is attended after being stricken by a stomach cramp. El deportista es atendido tras desplomarse por un corte de digestión.
to be **strictly prohibited** quedar prohibido terminantemente ▪ quedar rigurosamente prohibido ▪ estar prohibido terminantemente ▪ estar rigurosamente prohibido ➤ It is strictly prohibited to stand at the edge of the platform. Queda prohibido terminantemente permanecer al borde del andén.
to **strike a balance** mantener un balance
to **strike a bargain** llegar a un acuerdo ▪ cerrar un trato
to **strike a nerve** ▪ to touch a sensitive spot tocar en lo vivo
to **strike again 1.** to attack again golpear otra vez **2.** to hit the nail on the head again darle en el clavo otra vez ➤ *(headline)* Bin Laden strikes again in the heart of Arabia. Bin Laden golpea otra vez el corazón de Arabia. ➤ Wile E. Coyote strikes again! ¡Wile E. Coyote le da en el clavo otra vez!
to **strike an object** ▪ to smash into an object ▪ to crash into an object chocar contra un objeto ▪ chocar un objeto ➤ The car struck a wall. El carro chocó contra una pared. ▪ El carro chocó contra una barda.
to **strike and abate** sobrevenir y ceder ➤ The illness can strike, and abate, unexpectedly. La enfermedad puede sobrevenir y ceder inesperadamente.
to **strike down a law** derogar una ley
to **strike gold** encontrar oro
strike one! *(baseball)* estraik uno ▪ primer fallo
to **strike one as...** parecerle a uno... ➤ He strikes me as (being) a bit of a cad. Me parece algo canalla.
to **strike out** *(baseball)* poncharse
to **strike (out) at someone** arremeterse contra alguien
to **strike out for a place** echar camino adelante hacia un lugar ▪ emprender el camino hacia un lugar ▪ emprender la marcha hacia un lugar
to **strike someone a fatal blow** ▪ to deal someone a fatal blow asestarle un golpe mortal
to **strike someone a mortal blow** ▪ to deal someone a mortal blow asestarle un golpe mortal
to **strike something** ▪ to hit something golpear un objeto ➤ The pilot reported that the airplane had struck something. El piloto comunicó que el avión había golpeado un objeto.
to **strike the hour** dar la hora ➤ The clock struck midnight. El reloj dio la medianoche.
to **strike up a conversation with someone** ▪ to get into a conversation with someone pegar la hebra con alguien ▪ entablar una conversación con alguien ▪ trabar conversación con alguien
to **strike up a friendship** trabar amistad ▪ entablar una amistad ▪ iniciar una amistad
strike while the iron is hot a la ocasión la pintan calva ▪ la ocasión la pintan calva
string of lies ▪ pack of lies sarta de mentiras
string of lights la serie de luces ➤ We want a string of Christmas lights that don't blink. Queremos un hilo de luces navideñas que no parpadean. ▪ Queremos un hilo de luces navideñas que son fijas, no intermitentes.
to **string someone along** embaucar a alguien
stringed instruments instrumentos de cuerda
strings attached ▪ hidden strings ▪ hidden conditions algo por debajo de la cuerda ➤ There are some strings on this deal. Hay algo aquí por debajo de la cuerda.
to **strip a bed** quitar la ropa de una cama
strip cartoon ▪ comic strip tira cómica
to **strip from the waist down** desnudarse de cintura para abajo
to **strip from the waist up** desnudarse de cintura para arriba
strip of bacon ▪ slice of bacon *(Mex.)* tira de tocino ▪ *(Sp.)* tira de beicon
strip of land banda de tierra
to **strip off one's clothes** ▪ to strip one's clothes off ▪ to strip nude empelotarse ▪ desprenderse de la ropa ▪ quitarse la ropa ▪ desvestirse
to **strip off paint** ▪ to strip paint off quitar (la) pintura ➤ We stripped the paint off the table, then stained and varnished it. ▪ We stripped off the paint from the table, then stained and varnished it. Quitamos la pintura de la mesa, y luego la dimos un tono de fondo y la barnizamos.
to **strip someone of something** despojar a alguien de algo ➤ The committee stripped the athlete of his title when it was discovered that he had taken performance-enhancing drugs. El comité despojó al atleto de su título cuando fue descubierto que había tomado drogas para realzar su rendimiento.
to **strip the gears** estropear las velocidades
to **strip the threads of the screw** barrerse la rosca del tornillo ▪ estropear la rosca del tornillo ▪ pasar de vueltas ▪ pasar de rosca ➤ The threads of the screw are stripped. La rosca del tornillo está barrida. ▪ La rosca del tornillo está estropeada. ➤ If you screw it in too tight, you will strip the threads. Si lo aprietas demasiado, lo vas a pasar de vueltas. ▪ Si lo aprietas mucho, lo vas a pasar de rosca.
stripe: of one's ~ *(derogatory)* de la calaña de uno ➤ People of his stripe La gente de su calaña
striped shirt camisa a rayas
stroke: to suffer a ~ ▪ to suffer a cerebral hemorrhage sufrir un derrame cerebral ▪ sufrir una congestión cerebral ▪ sufrir un infarto cerebral
stroke of luck el golpe de suerte ▪ braguetazo
stroke of the pen trazo de pluma
to **stroll through the park** pasearse por el parque
strong accent ▪ pronounced accent acento acusado
to be **strong as an ox** ser fuerte como un león ▪ ser más duro que un roble ▪ ser fuerte como un roble
strong character: to have a ~ tener carácter

strong coffee café fuerte ■ café muy cargado

strong drink *(brandy, etc.)* vino vigoroso

strong odors olores agresivos

strong suit ■ forte punto fuerte

strong winds ■ high winds fuertes vientos

strongbox ■ safe caja fuerte

to be a **stronghold of** ■ to be a bastion of ser un reducto de ■ ser un bastión de ➤ During the U.S. Civil War, East Tennessee was a stronghold of Unionist sentiment within the Confederacy. ■ During the U.S. Civil War, East Tennessee was a bastion of Unionist sentiment within the Confederacy. Durante la Guerra Civil Americana, la parte este de Tennessee fue un reducto de sentimiento unionista dentro de la Confederación. ■ Durante la Guerra Civil Americana, la parte este de Tennessee fue un bastión de sentimiento unionista dentro de la Confederación.

strongly worded letter carta bastante dura ■ carta muy dura

to be **struck by a bullet** ■ to be hit by a bullet ser alcanzado por una bala ➤ The victim was struck in the chest as he was parking his vehicle. La víctima ha sido alcanzado en el pecho cuando estacionaba el vehículo.

to be **struck by a vehicle** ■ to be hit by a vehicle ser embestido por un vehículo ➤ *(news item)* Three men died yesterday after the sedan in which they were riding was struck by a concrete-mixing truck. Tres hombres murieron ayer después de que el turismo en el que viajaban fuera embestido por un camión hormigonera.

to be **struck by an idea** impactarle una idea ■ asaltarle una idea

to be **struck by lightning** ■ to get struck by lightning caerle un rayo ➤ One of the hikers was struck by lightning. ■ One of the hikers got struck by lightning. A uno de los senderistas le cayó un rayo.

struggle against something ■ struggle with something lucha contra algo ■ lucha en contra de algo.

to **struggle against something** luchar contra algo ■ luchar en contra de algo

to **struggle financially** pasar (por) dificultades económicas ■ tener dificultades económicas ■ pasar por dificultades económicas ■ estar falto(-a) de dinero ■ estar en la última lona

struggle for survival lucha por la supervivencia

to **struggle to keep up with others** luchar por mantenerse al mismo nivel que otros

to **struggle to survive** luchar por sobrevivir

to **struggle with a subject** resistírsele una asignatura ➤ I'm struggling with calculus. Se me resiste el cálculo.

to **strut around in** andar echando tiros con

to **stub one's (big) toe on something** darse con el dedo (gordo) del pie contra algo

to **stub one's little toe on something** darse con el dedo meñique del pie contra algo ■ darse con el dedo pequeño del pie

to be **stubborn as a mule** ser terco(-a) como una mula

to **stubbornly insist on (doing) something** insistir tercamente en (hacer) algo ■ insistir testarudamente en (hacer) algo

to be **stuck in the snow** estar atascado(-a) en la nieve

stuck in the snow: to get ~ atascarse en la nieve ➤ Don't get stuck in the snow. *(tú)* (Que) no te atasques en la nieve. ■ *(usted)* (Que) no se atasque en la nieve. ■ *(ustedes)* (Que) no se atasquen en la nieve. ■ *(Sp., vosotros)* (Que) no os atasquéis en la nieve.

to be **stuck in traffic** estar atrapado en el tráfico

to be **stuck on oneself** ■ to be conceited ■ *(coll.)* to be stuck up tenérselo creído ■ ser vanidoso(-a)

to be **stuck on someone** estar colgado por alguien ➤ Are you stuck on her? ¿Estás colgado por ella?

to be **stuck up** *(coll.)* ■ to be stuck on oneself ■ to be conceited tenérselo creído ■ ser vanidoso(-a) ➤ He's very conceited. ■ He's stuck up. Se lo tiene creído.

student days época de estudiante

student riot revuelta estudiantil

studio apartment piso de un solo ambiente

to **study for a test** estudiar para un examen

the **study found that...** el estudio encontró que...

study guide guía didáctica

study of a certain number of people ■ study involving a certain number of people estudio en el que participaron ➤ In a recent study of three hundred heart patients... En un reciente estudio en el que participaron trescientos pacientes cardiacos...

to **study someone** contemplar a alguien ➤ Felipe studied him with an inquisitive look. Felipe lo contempló con una mirada inquisitiva.

to **study Spanish** estudiar español

to **stuff ballot boxes** inflar las urnas

to **stuff oneself (to the gills) with...** empacharse de... ■ empacharse con... ➤ At the birthday party, the children stuffed themselves (to the gills) with cake and ice cream. En la fiesta de cumpleaños los niños se empacharon de pasteles y helado. ■ En la fiesta de cumpleaños los niños se empacharon con pasteles y helado.

to **stuff oneself (with food)** atiborrarse de comida

to be **stuffed in a drawer** estar embutido en un cajón

stuffed shirt *el, la* pedante ■ estirado ■ *(off-color)* pedorro

stumbling block in the negotiations escollo de las negociaciones ■ escollo para las negociaciones

to be **stunned by** quedarse anonadado por

stunt man el especialista (de cine) ■ el doble

stunt woman la especialista (de cine) ■ la doble

a **subhead (saying...)** *(journalism)* un apartado (que ponía...)

subject: academic ~ asignatura ➤ What subjects are you taking? ¿Qué asignaturas haces?

subject line *(E-mail)* campo asunto

to be the **subject of a book** ser el tema de un libro ■ ser el argumento de un libro

to be **subject to** ■ to be contingent on ■ to be contingent upon ■ to be dependent on ■ to be dependent upon ■ to depend on ■ to be subordinate to estar supeditado a ■ depender de ➤ It's subject to what they decide. ■ It's contingent on what they decide. ■ It's contingent upon what they decide. ■ It's dependent on what they decide. ■ It's dependent upon what they decide. ■ It depends on what they decide. ■ It's subordinate to their decision. Está supeditado a lo que deciden. ■ Depende de lo que deciden.

subliminal advertising la publicidad subliminal

submarine sandwich *(Sp.)* montado

to **submit a manuscript anonymously (as in a literary competition)** mandar un manuscrito bajo (sistema de) plica ➤ Nicanor Parra, the self-styled Chilean "antipoet," on submitting three manuscripts anonymously to a literary competition, won first, second, and third prize. Nicanor Parra, el autodenominado "antipoeta" chileno, al mandar tres manuscritos bajo (sistema de) plica, ganó el primero, segundo y tercer puesto de un concurso literario.

to **submit a request** presentar una petición

to **submit an application** presentar una solicitud

to **submit an entry to the book** enviar una sugerencia para ser incluida en el diccionario entrada

to **submit that...** ■ to suggest that... ■ to propose that... sugerir que... ■ proponer que...

to **submit to authority** someterse a una autoridad

to **subscribe to the idea that...** adherirse a la idea...

substantial reinforcement refuerzo de firme

to **substitute for someone** hacer una suplencia por alguien

to **substitute for something** ■ to replace something ■ to be substituted for something substituir a algo ➤ "Más tarde" can substitute for "después" in all contexts. ■ "Más tarde" can replace "después" in all contexts. ■ "Más tarde" can be substituted for "después" in all contexts. "Más tarde" puede substituir a "después" en todos los contextos.

to **substitute teach** hacer una suplencia por un profesor

to **subtract a number from a number** ■ to take away a number from a number restar un número de un número

subway entrance ■ metro entrance boca de metro

to **succeed at something** ■ to be successful at something tener éxito en algo

to **succeed in a field of endeavor** ■ to be successful in a field of endeavor tener éxito ➤ *(play and film title) How to Suc-*

ceed in Business Without Really Trying Cómo tener éxito en los negocios sin realmente tratar

to **succeed in doing something** ▪ to manage to do something lograr hacer algo ▪ atinar a hacer algo ➤ After numerous failed attempts, they finally succeeded in laying a transatlantic cable that worked. Después de numerosos intentos fallidos, por fin lograron instalar el cable trasatlántico que funcionó. ➤ I succeeded in finding him. ▪ I managed to find him. Logré encontrarlo.

to **successfully complete...** ▪ to complete successfully... cumplir con éxito...

succinct exposition of an idea *(oral or written)* ▪ clear and concise exposition of an idea exposición clara y concisa de una idea ▪ exposición sucinta de una idea

such a... semejante ▪ un... tan ➤ Such a small animal Un animal tan pequeño

such a long time tanto tiempo

such a thing tal cosa

such and such a day: on ~ en tal día

such hatred tal odio ▪ tan negra entraña

such things tales cosas

to **suck up to someone** adular a alguien ▪ *(Sp.)* bailarle el agua a alguien

suckling lamb *(culinary)* cordero lechal ▪ *(Sp.)* cordero recental

suckling pig *(culinary)* cochinillo ▪ *el* lechón ▪ lechoncito

suction cup ventosa

sudden death muerte súbita

sudden drop in temperature repentina bajada en temperatura

sudden increase in temperature repentina subida en temperatura

sudden reversal cambio imprevisto de rumbo ➤ His sudden reversal surprised me. Me sorprendió su cambio imprevisto (de rumbo).

suddenly: to happen ~ suceder de repente ▪ suceder de pronto ▪ suceder de improvisto ▪ suceder repentinamente ➤ It happened suddenly. Sucedió de repente. ▪ Sucedió de pronto. ▪ Sucedió de improvisto. ▪ Sucedió repentinamente.

to **sue someone for something** demandar a alguien por algo ▪ poner en pleito a alguien por algo

to **suffer a disappointment** ▪ to be disappointed ▪ to be chagrined sufrir una desilusión

to **suffer a drop in blood pressure** ▪ to experience a drop in blood pressure ▪ to have a drop in blood pressure sufrir una bajada de tensión ▪ tener una bajada de tensión

to **suffer a relapse of** ▪ to have a relapse of sufrir una recaída de

to **suffer a scratch** sufrir un rasguño ➤ The president suffered a scratch on the cheek. El presidente sufrió un rasguño en el pómulo.

to **suffer from** adolecer de

to **suffer great hardship(s)** ▪ to undergo great hardship(s) ▪ to experience great hardship(s) pasar grandes penas

to **suffer the consequences** cargar con las consecuencias

to **suffer the embarrassment of...** sufrir la vergüenza de... ▪ sufrir la pena de... ➤ After suffering the embarrassment of... Tras sufrir la vergüenza de...

to be **suffering from** estar aquejado de ➤ She was suffering from cancer. Estaba aquejada de cancer.

suffice it to say that... basta decir que...

to be **sufficient reason to** ▪ to be reason enough to ser motivo suficiente para

sugar bowl azucarero

sugar lump ▪ lump of sugar el terrón (de azúcar)

sugar wafers barquillos

suggest it to her! *(tú)* ¡sugiéreselo (a ella)! ▪ *(usted)* ¡sugiéraselo (a ella)!

suggest it to him! *(tú)* ¡sugiéreselo (a él)! ▪ *(usted)* ¡sugiéraselo (a él)!

suicidal depression depresión suicida

suicide attempt ▪ attempted suicide tentativa de suicidio

suicide bomber terrorista suicida

to **suit one to a T** venirle al pelo ▪ irle que ni pintado ▪ venir de perlas ▪ venir de perilla ➤ It suits me to a T. Me viene al pelo. ▪ Me va que ni pintado.

to be **suitable for** ser apto para ▪ servir para ▪ valer para ➤ Beaches are not suitable for bathing. ▪ Beaches are unsuitable for bathing. Las playas no son aptas para el baño. ➤ The movie is suitable for children. La película es apta para los niños. ➤ This pan is suitable for meat, fish, and vegetables. Esta cacerola sirve para carne, pescado y verduras. ▪ Esta cacerola vale para carne, pescado y verduras.

to **sum up the bill** ▪ to sum the bill up ▪ to add up the bill ▪ to total the bill sumar la cuenta

to **sum up the main points** ▪ to sum the main points up en resumen ▪ resumir los puntos principales

summer camp campamento de verano

summer day *el* día de verano

summer schedule jornada de verano ▪ horario de verano

summer vacation ▪ summer holidays vacaciones estivales

summery day ▪ summerlike day día caluroso ▪ día veraniego

the **summing up** *la* síntesis

to be **summoned to testify** ser citado(-a) a declarar

the **sun came up** salió el sol ➤ The sun came up just as we were approaching the coast of Galicia. Salió el sol justo cuando nos acercábamos a la costa de Galicia.

sun glare *el* resol

the **sun is out** ▪ it's sunny out(side) hay sol

the **sun is shining** el sol está brillando ▪ el sol brilla ▪ brilla el sol ▪ *(literary)* el sol está luciendo ▪ luce el sol ▪ el sol luce

the **sun rose at 7:03 a.m.** salió el sol a las 7:03

sunburn is peeling: my ~ mi piel achicharrada se pela ▪ mi piel achicharrada se está pelando

Sunday best: to dress in one's ~ prepararse de domingo

Sunday night and early Monday en la noche del domingo al lunes

Sunday supplement *(of a newspaper)* suplemento dominical

sunken eyes ▪ deep-set eyes ojos hundidos

to be a **sunny day** ser un día de sol ▪ ser un día asoleado ➤ It was a sunny day. Era un día de sol. ▪ Era un día asoleado.

sunny side of the street acera del sol

sunny spot paraje asoleado

superconducting battery *(battery made of superconducting materials)* batería superconductora ➤ Superconducting batteries store electricity... Las baterías superconductoras almacenan la electricidad...

superiority complex: to have a ~ creerse más que nadie

supply and demand: law of ~ la ley de la oferta y la demanda

to **supply electricity to** suministrar la electricidad a

supply of electricity ▪ electricity supply suministro de la electricidad ▪ suministro eléctrico ➤ State of emergency in California over the disruption of the electrical power supply. Estado de emergencia en California por el colapso del suministro eléctrico.

to **supply someone with something** surtirle de algo a alguien ▪ suministrarle algo a alguien ▪ abastecerle de algo a alguien

to **supply the context of** ▪ to give the context of ▪ to provide the context of dar el contexto de

to **supply the market with something** ▪ to supply something to the market suministrar de algo al mercado ▪ abastecer de algo al mercado ▪ surtir el mercado con algo

support for someone apoyo a alguien

to **support life** albergar la vida

to **support one's family** mantener a la familia de uno

to **support someone's candidacy for a position** apoyar a una candidatura para un puesto de trabajo

to **support the weight** ▪ to bear the weight soportar el peso

suppose it rains ▪ what if it rains? ¿qué tal si llueve? ▪ *(tú)* supón que llueva ▪ *(usted)* suponga que llueva

suppose you won the lottery *(tú)* supón que te tocase la lotería ▪ supón que te tocara la lotería ▪ *(usted)* suponga que le tocase la lotería ▪ suponga que le tocara la lotería ▪ *(Mex., tú)* haz de cuenta que te tocara la lotería ▪ *(usted)* haga de cuenta que le tocara la lotería

supposed to be...: is ~ se supone que... ▪ debería ser ▪ *(referring to age)* debería tener ➤ This job was supposed to be part-time. Se suponía que este trabajo iba a ser de medio tiempo. ➤ To buy beer, you're supposed to be twenty-one. Para comprar cerveza se supone que tienes que tener veintiún años.

supposed to be here: one was ~ supuestamente uno debiera estar aquí ▪ uno tenía que haber estado ▪ uno tenía que haber venido ▪ uno tenía que haber llegado ▪ *(farther back in time)* uno tendría que haber venido ➤ You were supposed to be here four hours ago! ¡Supuestamente debieras estar aquí hace cuatro horas! ▪ ¡Tenías que haber venido hace cuatro horas!

to be **supposed to come by** debería pasar ▪ suponerse que habrá de pasar ➤ What time is the bus supposed to come by? ¿A qué hora debería pasar el autobús? ➤ What time was the bus supposed to come (by here)? ¿A qué hora se supone que debiese pasar el autobús? ➤ When is this damned bus supposed to come by here, anyway? ¿A qué hora se supone que habrá de pasar el maldito autobús?

to be **supposed to cost** debiera costar ▪ *(implies more culpability)* debería costar ➤ Lending you the money wasn't supposed to cost me anything. Remember? Prestarte el dinero no debería haberme costado nada, ¿te acuerdas?

to be **supposed to do something** suponerse que uno tiene que hacer algo ▪ suponerse que uno debe hacer algo ▪ quedar en hacer algo ▪ deber hacer algo ➤ What am I supposed to do? ¿Qué se supone que deba hacer yo? ➤ I didn't know what the damned electrician was supposed to do! ¿Cómo iba a saber yo lo que el maldito electricista se suponía que tenía que hacer. ➤ *(Don Quijote)* We're not supposed to capitulate to the world as it is, we're supposed to make it the way it ought to be. No se supone que tengamos que capitular ante el mundo como es, sino que se supone que lo tenemos que transformar en lo que debería ser. ➤ Was I supposed to call you? ¿Quedé en llamarte? ▪ ¿Habíamos quedado (en) que yo te llamara? ➤ To fast properly, you're supposed to go an entire day, from getting up to going to bed, without food. Para ayunar correctamente se supone que tienes que pasar un día completo sin comida desde que te levantas hasta que te acuestas. ➤ Were we supposed to hand in our papers yesterday? ¿Se supone que ayer había que entregar los trabajos? ▪ ¿Deberíamos haber entregado nuestros trabajos ayer? ➤ I'm supposed to pick her up at the airport in an hour. Se supone que voy a buscarla al aeropuerto dentro de una hora. ▪ Se supone que me encuentro con ella en el aeropuerto dentro de una hora. ➤ We're supposed to meet (up) at the bar at eleven. Se supone que nos encontraremos en el bar a las once.

to be **supposed to happen** haber de pasar ▪ haber de suceder ▪ tener que pasar ▪ tener que suceder ➤ If it's supposed to happen, it will. Si ha de pasar, pasará. ▪ Si ha de suceder, sucederá. ▪ Si tiene que pasar, pasará. ▪ Si tiene que suceder, sucederá.

supposed to know?: how am I ~ ▪ how should I know? ▪ how would I know? ¿cómo voy a saberlo (yo)? ▪ ¿cómo debería saberlo (yo)?

supposed to know?: how was I ~ ▪ how would I have known? ¿cómo iba a saberlo (yo)? ▪ ¿cómo habría (yo) de saberlo?

supposed to rain: it's ~ se espere lluvias ▪ se supone que lloverá ➤ It's supposed to rain tomorrow. Se espera lluvia para mañana. ▪ Se supone que mañana va a llover. ▪ Se supone que va a llover mañana. ▪ Se supone que lloverá mañana.

supposing that... ▪ let's suppose that... suponiendo que... ▪ admitiendo que... ▪ supongamos que... ▪ admitamos que...

to **suppress a rebellion** ▪ to put down a rebellion reprimir una revuelta ▪ sofocar una revuelta

Supreme Court: United States ~ ▪ U.S. Supreme Court Tribunal Supremo de los Estados Unidos ▪ Tribunal Supremo de EE UU

sure as my name's... ¡cómo me llamo..., que...!

sure enough efectivamente ➤ And sure enough, it was. Y efectivamente, fue así.

sure, go ahead! ¡claro, adelante!

to be **sure of oneself** ir seguro de sí ➤ He was very sure of himself. Iba muy seguro de sí.

to be **sure that...** estar seguro de que...

to be a **sure thing** ser una cosa cierta

sure thing! ▪ you got it! ¡claro que sí!

surefire remedy *la* mano de santo

to **surf the net** ▪ to surf the web navegar el Internet

surface mail: by ~ ▪ by ship por vía marítima

surface noise chirrido ▪ ruido de la superficie ▪ ruido exterior

surface of a planet *la* superficie de un planeta ▪ suelo de un planeta ➤ *(headline)* The European (space) probe "Beagle 2" begins the home stretch toward the surface of Mars. ▪ The European (space) probe "Beagle 2" begins its final descent toward the surface of Mars. La sonda europea "Beagle 2" inicia la recta final hacia el suelo de Marte.

surface-to-air missile *el* misil tierra-aire

surge protector ▪ power surge protector *la* base con protección ▪ *el* ladrón con protección ➤ I need a surge protector with six outlets. Necesito una base con seis tomas y protección. ▪ Necesito un ladrón con seis tomas y protección.

to **surpass one's expectations** ▪ to exceed one's expectations rebasar las expectativas

surprise ending final inesperado ➤ Jules Verne's *Around the World in Eighty Days* has a surprise ending on the last page. *La vuelta al mundo en ochenta días* de Julio Verne tiene un final inesperado en la última página.

to **surprise one that...** sorprender a uno que... ➤ It surprised me that so few people showed up. Me sorprendió que tan poca gente acudiese. ▪ Me sorprendió que tan poca gente acudiera.

surprise party fiesta sorpresa ➤ Surprise birthday party Fiesta sorpresa de cumpleaños

to **surprise someone in the act** coger en el acto

to be **surprised at** estar extrañado ante

to be **surprised by something** ser sorprendido por algo ▪ *(literary)* quedar admirado por algo ▪ admirarse de ➤ His sudden reversal surprised me. Me quedé admirado por su cambio imprevisto. ▪ Me admiré de su cambio imprevisto.

to **surrender unconditionally** rendirse sin condiciones

to **surround oneself with** rodearse de ➤ The president has surrounded himself with top-notch people. El presidente se ha rodeado de primeras figuras.

to be **surrounded by** estar rodeado de

surrounding area zona circundante ▪ *los* alrededores

surrounding region *la* región en su conjunto ▪ región circundante

surrounding the matter que rodea el asunto ▪ que envuelve el asunto

surroundings contorno ▪ afueras ▪ alrededores

to **survey a situation** estudiar la situacion ▪ analizar la situación

survey course recorrido

the **survey shows that...** la encuesta demuestra que...

survival of the fittest ▪ social Darwinism la ley del más fuerte

to **survive something** ▪ to live through something sobrevivir a algo

to be **susceptible to an illness** estar susceptible a una enfermedad

suspended sentence *la* prisión eludible ➤ The judge imposed a suspended sentence. El juez impuso prisión eludible.

suspension bridge *el* puente colgante ➤ The suspension bridge gave a little under the weight of the crowd. ▪ The suspension bridge gave slightly under the weight of the crowd. El puente colgante cedió un poco bajo el peso de la muchedumbre. ▪ El puente colgante cedió ligeramente bajo el peso de la muchedumbre.

suspicious character tipo sospechoso ▪ sujeto sospechoso

sustainable growth crecimiento sostenible

sustained growth crecimiento sostenido

to **swallow one's anger** tragar bilis

to **swallow one's pride** comerse el orgullo

to **swallow the bait (hook, line, and sinker)** ▪ to take the bait tragar el anzuelo ▪ caer en el anzuelo ▪ picar en el anzuelo

to **swallow the story (hook, line, and sinker)** ▪ to believe the story tragar(se) la historia to be **swamped with work** estar completamente saturado de trabajo ▪ estar agobiado de trabajo ▪ estar desbordado de trabajo

swan song ▪ farewell appearance ▪ farewell performance ▪ final performance ▪ final work canto de cisne ➤ *Tales from Hoffman* was Offenbach's swan song. *Cuentos de Hoffman* fue el canto de cisne de Offenbach.

to be **swarming with 1.** *(people)* bullir de gente ▪ ser un hormiguero de ▪ haber una multitud de personas **2.** *(bees)* enjambrar ▪ estar enjambrando **3.** *(flies, mosquitos)* pulular ▪ estar pululando ▪ revoltear ▪ estar revolteando ▪ estar lleno de

to **swear someone in(to office)** ▪ to administer the oath (of office) to someone administrarle a alguien juramento del cargo ▪ tomarle juramento del cargo a alguien

to **swear to something** jurarlo ▪ meter la mano al fuego ▪ poner la mano en el fuego ➤ I wouldn't swear to it. No lo juraría. ▪ (Yo) no pondría la mano en el fuego.

swear word ▪ *(coll.)* cuss word taco ▪ palabrota

swearing in toma de posesión

to **sweat blood** sudar tinta ▪ sudar la gota gorda ▪ sudar petróleo

sweat glands glándulas sudoríparas

to **sweep something under the rug** *(literal and figurative)* meter algo bajo la alfombra

sweeping generalizations: to make ~ hacer generalizaciones dramáticas ▪ hacer generalizaciones demasiado amplias

sweeping reforms: to make ~ llevar a cabo amplias reformas

to be **sweet as pie** ▪ to be a peach ▪ to be a sweetheart estar hecho un almíbar

sweet deal negocio redondo

sweet dreams! ¡felices sueños!

sweet sixteen *(singular)* feliz dieciséis ▪ los quince años ▪ los felices quince años ▪ *(plural)* felices dieciséis

to **sweet-talk someone** engatusar a alguien ▪ acaramelar a alguien ▪ hacerle juego a alguien

sweet tooth: to have a ~ ser goloso(-a)

to **sweeten a deal, offer** endulzar un trato, oferta

to **sweeten coffee** endulzar el café

to **swell up** hincharse ➤ His ankle swelled up like a balloon. Su tobillo se hinchó como un globo.

to **swell with pride** hincharse de orgullo

swelled head: to have a ~ ▪ to have an exaggerated opinion of oneself ▪ to be conceited tener la cabeza grande

the **swelling has gone down** la hinchazón (se) ha bajado

the **swelling is going down** la hinchazón (se) está bajando

swelling of a river ▪ rising of a river crecida de un río

swelling of the joints la hinchazón de las articulaciones

to be **sweltering** abrasarse de calor

Swept Away *(film title)* *Barridos por la marea*

to be **swept away** ser arrastrado ▪ ser arrebatado ▪ ser barrido ➤ The man was swept away by the current. El hombre fue arrastrado por la corriente.

to be **swept off one's feet (by infatuation)** dejarse llevar por el enamoramiento ▪ dejarse llevar por el encaprichamiento

to **swerve all over the road** dar bandazos

to **swerve sharply** ▪ to swerve abruptly ▪ to lurch dar un giro brusco ▪ dar un bandazo

to **swerve to miss an oncoming vehicle** esquivar para no chocar con un vehículo que viene en el sentido opuesto

to **swim across** atravesar a nado ▪ atravesar nadando ▪ cruzar a nado ▪ cruzar nadando ➤ He swam across the lake. Atravesó el lago a nado. ➤ He swam across the river. ▪ He swam the river. Cruzo el río a nado.

to **swim laps** nadar largos

to **swim the river** ▪ to swim across the river cruzar el río a nado ▪ cruzar el río nadando

swine fever fiebre porcina

swine flu gripe porcina

to **swing on (the) swings** columpiar en los columpios

to **swing the oars** revolear los remos ▪ rebolear los remos

to **swing to and fro** ▪ to swing back and forth balancearse

swing vote voto bisagra

to **swipe something from someone** robarle algo a alguien ▪ sustraerle algo a alguien ▪ birlarle algo a alguien ▪ raparle algo a alguien

Swiss roll *(rolled layer cake)* brazo de gitano ▪ brazo gitano

switch engine locomotora de maniobras

to **switch exams** dar el cambiazo *(a form of cheating on an exam in which the original is exchanged for one prepared in advance)*

to **switch on** ▪ to turn on poner en funcionamiento

to **switch sides** ▪ to change sides ▪ to change allegiances cambiar de chaqueta ▪ cambiar de parecer ▪ cambiar de camisa

swollen river río henchido

to be **swollen shut** hincharse hasta al grado de no poder abrir(se) ▪ hincharse hasta el punto de no poder abrir(se) ➤ My nasal passages are swollen shut. Mis fosas nasales están hinchadas al punto de no poder abrirse. ➤ The boy's eyes were swollen shut from poison ivy. Los ojos del niño estaban hinchados al grado de no poder abrirlos debido a la hiedra venenosa.

to **swoop down on** abatirse sobre

sworn statement declaración jurada

symbol of wealth signo de riqueza ➤ The Rolls-Royce is a symbol of wealth. El Rolls-Royce es un signo de la riqueza.

symbolic logic ▪ mathematical logic lógica simbólica

to be **sympathetic to** ser simpatizante de

sympathy for someone: to have ~ tener simpatía por alguien

symphony conductor ▪ orchestra conductor director(a) de la orquesta

symptoms disappeared: one's ~ ▪ one's symptoms went away se le pasaron los síntomas a alguien ➤ When I took the medicine, my symptoms disappeared. ▪ When I took the medicine, my symptoms went away. Después de tomarme el medicamento, se me pasaron los síntomas.

to **synchronize the calendar with the movement of the sun** sincronizar el calendario con el movimiento del sol ▪ acompasar el calendario con el movimiento del sol

to be **synonymous with** ser sinónimo de

system of coordinates *el* sistema de coordinadas

tab (of a file folder) pestaña (de una carpeta)
tab of LSD piedra de tripi
table leg pata de la mesa
table of contents tabla de materias
table rocks ▪ table wobbles mesa cojea ▪ mesa se bambolea ▪ mesa se mueve
table wine vino de mesa
table wobbles ▪ table rocks mesa cojea ▪ mesa se bambolea ▪ mesa se mueve
tacit agreement ▪ unspoken agreement acuerdo tácito
tacit approval aprobación tácita
to **tag along (with someone)** pegarse (a alguien)
to **tag an item** ▪ to mark an item ▪ to block an item marcar un artículo
to **tail a car** ▪ to follow a car controlar los movimientos de un carro ▪ *(Sp.)* controlar los movimientos de un coche ➤ We think the car behind us is tailing us. Creemos que el carro detrás de nostros está controlando nuestros movimientos.
tail is wagging the dog él que debería obedecer, dirige
to **tailgate (a car)** *(L. Am.)* ir pegado a un carro ▪ venir pegado a un carro *(informal)* ir besando el culo de otro carro ▪ venir besando el culo del carro ▪ *(Sp.)* ir pegado a un coche ▪ venir pegado a un coche ➤ I looked in the rearview mirror and saw that the car behind me was tailgating (me). Miré por el espejo retrovisor y vi que el carro detrás venía pegado. ▪ Miré por el espejo retrovisor y vi que el coche de detrás venía besándome el culo.
tailored shirt camisa entallada
tailwind: to have a ~ tener un viento de cola
to be **tainted by association with someone** verse empañado(-a) por la asociación con alguien
to **take a bath** bañarse
to **take a beating** ser vapuleado ➤ The conservatives took a beating in the polls. Los conservadores fueron vapuleados en las encuestas.
to **take a bill** ▪ to accept a bill tragarse un billete ➤ Will the machine take a five-dollar bill? ¿Se traga la máquina un billete de cinco dolares?
to **take a bite of food** dar un mordisco de comida
to **take a bizarre twist** tomar un cariz dantesco ▪ tomar un cariz grotesco ▪ tomar un cariz esperpéntico ▪ tomar un giro dantesco ▪ tomar un giro grotesco ▪ tomar un giro esperpéntico
to **take a break** tomarse un recreo ▪ tomarse un descanso ▪ hacer un paréntesis ▪ hacer una pausa ➤ Let's take a break. Hagamos un paréntesis.
to **take a breather** tomarse un respiro
to **take a certain route** tomar cierta ruta ▪ ir por cierto camino ➤ We took the scenic route. Tomamos la ruta pintoresca. ➤ We took the mountain route. Fuimos por el camino de las montañas.
to **take a chance** arriesgarse
to **take a chance on something** arriesgarse con algo
to **take a class** tomar una clase ➤ I'm taking a programming class. Tomo una clase de programmación.
to **take a coin** ▪ to accept a coin tragarse una moneda ➤ Will the machine take a two-euro coin? ¿Se traga la máquina una moneda de dos euros?
to **take a course** hacer un curso ➤ Alberto Jr. is taking a course in graphic design. Alberto hijo está haciendo un curso de diseño gráfico.
to **take a deep breath** **1.** respirar profundamente **2.** *(figurative)* to screw up one's courage ▪ to get up one's nerve hacer (de) tripas corazón
to **take a different tack** ▪ to change one's strategy or course of action cambiar de estrategia ▪ abordar un problema desde otro punto de partida ▪ cambiar de táctica
to **take a firm stand on** ponerse firme sobre
to **take a good long time to** ▪ to take one's time to tomarse todo el tiempo para
to **take a good look at something** ▪ to have a good look at something mirar algo con detenimiento ▪ mirar algo bien mirado
to **take a guided tour** hacer una excursión guiada
to **take a hard line** tomar una posición dura
to **take a joke** aceptar una broma ➤ Can't you take a joke? ¿No puedes aceptar una broma?
to **take a keen interest in something** interesarse mucho en algo
to **take a leak** ▪ *(coarse)* to take a piss ▪ to take a pee echar una meada ▪ cambiar el agua a los garbanzos ▪ cambiar el agua a las aceitunas ▪ hacer pis ▪ *(esp. said by children)* hacer pichí ➤ I have to take a leak. ▪ I've got to take a leak. Tengo que cambiar el agua a los garbanzos.
to **take a left** ▪ to turn (to the) left ▪ *(coll.)* to hang a left girar a la izquierda ▪ virar a la izquierda ▪ doblarse a la izquierda ➤ Take a left at the next corner. Gira a la izquierda en la próxima esquina.
to **take a liking to someone** tomarle simpatía a alguien ▪ cogerle simpatía a alguien
to **take a long time** tardar mucho (tiempo) ▪ tardarse mucho (tiempo) ➤ Codifying the document takes a long time. Codificar el documento tarda mucho tiempo. ➤ It takes a long time. Se tarda mucho (tiempo).
to **take a longer route than necessary** ▪ to make unnecessary turns dar vueltas a lo tonto ➤ The taxi driver took a longer route than necessary. El taxista dio vueltas a lo tonto.
to **take a look at something** **1.** *(literal)* echar un vistazo a algo **2.** *(figurative)* to examine something dar un repaso a algo ➤ Let's take a look. Vamos a echar un vistazo. ➤ The book takes a look at Catholicism in contemporary Spain. El libro da un repaso al catolicismo en la España contemporánea.
to **take a lot of flack** ▪ to catch a lot of flack ▪ to take a lot of criticism ▪ to take a lot of abuse aguantar muchas críticas
to **take a makeup test** ▪ to make up a test hacer un examen de recuperación ▪ hacer un examen que no se puede asistir
to **take a message from someone for someone** tomar un recado de alguien para alguien ▪ tomar un mensaje de alguien para alguien ▪ tomar nota de alguien para alguien ➤ I took a message from Aurora for Susana. Tomé un mensaje de Aurora para Susana. ▪ Tomé un recado de Aurora para Susana.
to **take a mouthful (of water)** tomar un buche (de agua)
to **take a nap** tomar una siesta ▪ echar una siesta
to **take a pee** ▪ to pee hacer pis ▪ cambiar el agua a los garbanzos ▪ cambiar el agua a las aceitunas ▪ cambiar las aguas ▪ *(old-fashioned)* desaguarse ▪ *(esp. said by children)* to wee-wee hacer pipí ▪ hacer pichí ➤ I have to take a leak. ▪ I've got to take a leak. Tengo que cambiar el agua a los garbanzos.
to **take a pill** tomarse una pastilla ▪ tomarse una píldora ▪ tomarse una gragea ▪ tomarse una tableta
to **take a piss** *(coarse)* ▪ to take a leak ▪ to take a pee echar una meada

to **take a plane to** ▪ to fly to ir en avión a ▪ *(Sp.)* coger un avión a ➤ We took a plane from La Paz to Cuzco. Fuimos en avión de La Paz a Cuzco. ▪ Cogimos un avión de La Paz a Cuzco.

to **take a poll** hacer un sondeo ▪ hacer una encuesta ▪ realizar un sondeo ▪ realizar una encuesta

to **take a position on an issue** adoptar una postura sobre un tema

to **take a right** ▪ to turn right ▪ to turn to the right ▪ *(coll.)* to hang a right virar a la izquierda ▪ doblarse a la izquierda

to **take a seat** ▪ to have a seat tomar asiento

to **take a shit** *(off-color)* ▪ to shit cagar ▪ *(benign alternative)* to use the bathroom ir al baño

to **take a shortcut** tomar un atajo ▪ atajar por ▪ atajar a través de ▪ cortar el camino ➤ To get here in twenty minutes, I had to take a shortcut. Para llegar aquí en veinte minutos, tuve que tomar un atajo. ➤ We took a shortcut through Central Park. Tomamos un atajo a través del Parque Central. ▪ Atajamos a través del Parque Central. ➤ I took a shortcut: instead of crushing the peanuts for the soup, I used peanut butter. Tomé un atajo. En vez de moler los cacahuetes para la sopa, usé crema de cacahuete.

to **take a shower** darse una ducha ▪ echarse una ducha ▪ *(Mex.)* darse un regaderazo ▪ *(Sp.)* ducharse ▪ *(informal)* pegarse una ducha

to **take a sip** tomar un sorbo ▪ beber un sorbo ➤ I took a sip of wine. Tomé un sorbo de vino.

to **take a stand against** oponerse a ▪ adoptar una postura en contra de

to **take a step** dar un paso

to **take a step backward** dar un paso atrás

to **take a step forward** dar un paso adelante ▪ dar un paso al frente ▪ *(Sp.)* echar el pie adelante

to **take a step in that direction** dar un paso en ese sentido ➤ *(news item)* Al Gore's team emphasized that it has taken no step in that direction. El equipo de Al Gore subrayó que no ha dado ningún paso en ese sentido

to **take a street** ▪ to go down a street ▪ to go up a street tomar una calle ▪ meterse en una calle ▪ meterse por una calle ▪ *(Sp.)* tirar (por) una calle ➤ Take that street! *(tú)* ¡Tira por esa calle! ▪ *(usted)* ¡Tire por esa calle!

to **take a subject** cursar una materia ▪ estudiar una materia ▪ tomar una materia ➤ I took three years of high school Spanish. Estudié español por tres años en el instituto. ▪ Cursé tres años de español en el instituto.

to **take a suspect into custody** ▪ to apprehend a suspect ▪ to detain a suspect poner a un sospechoso bajo custodia judicial ▪ detener a un sospechoso ➤ Some potential suspects were taken into custody for questioning. ▪ Some potential suspects were detained for questioning. ▪ Some potential suspects were apprehended for questioning. Algunos potenciales sospechosos fueron detenidos para ser interrogados. ▪ Algunos potenciales sospechosos fueron puestos bajo custodia judicial para ser interrogados.

to **take a taxi** ▪ to go in a taxi ▪ to go by taxi tomar un taxi ▪ ir en taxi

to **take a test** hacer un examen ▪ presentar un examen ▪ sufrir un examen

to **take a trip** hacer un viaje

to **take a turn for the better** tomar un giro favorable ▪ mejorarse

to **take a turn for the worse** ▪ to get worse desmejorarse

to **take a vacation** tomarse unas vacaciones

to **take a vow** hacer un voto

to **take a walk** ▪ to go for a walk dar un paseo

to **take a while to get used to** tardar en acostumbrarse a ▪ costarle acostumbrarse ➤ It took me a while to get used to... Tardé en acostumbrarme a... ▪ Me costó acostumbrarme...

to **take a wrong turn** ▪ to take the wrong street ▪ to make a wrong turn dar un giro equivocado ▪ tomar una calle equivocada ▪ meterse por una calle equivocada ▪ *(Sp.)* tirar por una calle equivocada

to **take a year off** tomarse un año de descanso ▪ tomarse un año sabático

to **take action against** tomar medidas en contra de ▪ actuar en contra de ▪ proceder en contra de

to **take action (to)** ▪ to take measures (to) actuar (para) ▪ tomar medidas (para)

to **take advantage of an opportunity** aprovecharse de una oportunidad ▪ prevalecerse de una oportunidad

to **take advantage of someone** ▪ to take unfair advantage of someone tomar ventaja de alguien ▪ aprovecharse de alguien ▪ propasarse con alguien ▪ abusar de alguien

to **take advice** seguir el consejo de alguien ▪ llevarse por el consejo de alguien ▪ llevarse por los consejos de alguien ➤ Take my advice. Sigue mi consejo. ➤ If he takes our advice. Si se lleva de nuestro consejo.

to **take after someone** ▪ to resemble someone parecerse a alguien ▪ salir a alguien

to **take all day** ▪ to take the whole day llevarle todo el día a alguien ▪ tardarse todo el día ➤ It took me all day to write ten pages. Me llevó todo el día escribir diez páginas. ▪ Tardé todo el día escribiendo diez páginas. ➤ It took all day to get the stage ready for the play. Se tardó todo el día preparando el escenario para la obra.

to **take all year** llevar todo el año ▪ tomar todo el año ▪ tardar todo el año

to **take along something** ▪ to take something along llevarse algo

to **take an examination** dar un examen ▪ tomar un examen ▪ presentar un examen

to **take an hour (for)** llevar una hora ▪ tardarse una hora ➤ It takes an hour for the paint to dry. ▪ It takes the paint an hour to dry. Lleva una hora en secar(se) la pintura. ▪ Lleva una hora para que (se) seque la pintura.▪ Se tarda una hora para que (se) seque la pintura.

to **take an interest in** interesarse por ▪ interesarse en

to **take an unexpected turn** tomar un giro inesperado ▪ dar un giro inesperado

to **take attendance** ▪ to take the attendance ▪ to call (the) roll pasar lista ▪ pasar la lista

to **take away all hope from someone** ▪ to leave someone destitute sacarle las esperanzas a alguien ▪ quitarle las esperanzas a alguien ▪ desahuciar a alguien

to **take away something from someone** ▪ to take something away from someone quitar algo a alguien

to **take back a remark** ▪ to take back what one said retirar lo dicho ➤ I take it back. Lo retiro.

to **take back merchandise** **1.** to return merchandise devolver mercancías ▪ devolver mercadería **2.** to accept returned merchandise aceptar la devolución de mercancías ▪ aceptar (la devolución de) mercaderías ➤ I am going to take these gloves back. They're the wrong size. Voy a devolver estos guantes, son de la talla equivocada. ➤ They won't take them back. No me los aceptarán.

to **take care of a matter** encargarse de un asunto ▪ ocuparse de un asunto ➤ I'll take care of it. Yo me ocuparé de ello.

to **take care of a problem** resolver un problema

to **take care of business** resolver asuntos

to **take care of everything** cuidarse de todo ▪ preocuparse de todo ➤ I'll take care of everything. Me cuido de todo. ▪ Me preocupo de todo.

to **take care of itself** resolverse solo

to **take care of oneself** cuidarse ▪ cuidar de uno mismo

to **take care of some business** resolver unos asuntos

to **take care of someone** ▪ to look after someone cuidar de alguien ▪ cuidar a alguien ▪ ocuparse de alguien ➤ She takes care of her invalid husband. Ella se ocupa de su marido inválido.

to **take care that...** ▪ to make sure that... ▪ to be sure that... cuidarse de que... ▪ asegurarse de que...

to **take chances** arriesgarse ▪ correr riesgos ➤ Don't take any chances. No te arriesgues. ▪ No corras riesgos.

to **take charge of something** hacerse cargo de algo ▪ encargarse de algo ▪ enfrentar la situación ➤ The FBI has taken charge of the case. El Federal Bureau of Investigation (FBI) se ha hecho cargo del caso. ➤ You need to take charge of the situation. *(tú)* Necesitas hacerte cargo de la situación. ▪ *(usted)* (Usted) necesita hacerse cargo de la situación.

to **take classes** tomar clases ▪ darle clases a alguien ▪ *(Sp.)* recibir clases ➤ I'm taking three Spanish classes. Tomo tres clases de español. ▪ Me dan tres clases de español.

to **take coins** aceptar monedas ▪ tragar monedas ➤ This phone doesn't take coins. Este teléfono no traga monedas.

to **take comfort in...** encontrar consuelo en... ▪ hallar consuelo en...

to **take command** tomar el mando

to **take communion** ▪ to receive communion comulgar ➤ *(photo caption)* Fox takes communion before assuming the presidency of Mexico. ▪ Fox receives communion before assuming the presidency of Mexico. Fox comulga antes de asumir la presidencia de México.

to **take control of one's life** tomar las riendas de la vida de uno ➤ Take control of your life! ¡Toma las riendas de tu vida!

to **take control of one's senses** ▪ to come to one's senses hacerse del control de sus sentidos ▪ entrar en sus cabales ▪ entrar en razón

to **take control of something** tomar el control de algo ▪ hacerse del control de algo ▪ apoderarse de algo

to **take control of the situation** tomar el control de la situación ▪ hacerse dueño de la situación ▪ adueñarse de la situación

to **take courses** tomar cursos ▪ *(Sp.)* tomar asignaturas *(In Spain "curso" means "program of courses.")*

to **take cover** ▪ to get under cover ponerse a cubierto

to **take down a picture** descolgar un cuadro

to **take down the Christmas tree** ▪ to take the Christmas tree down desmontar el árbol de Navidad ▪ quitar el árbol de Navidad ➤ We take down the Christmas tree after January sixth. Desmontamos el árbol de Navidad después del seis de enero. ▪ Quitamos el árbol de Navidad después del seis de enero. ➤ We take it down after January sixth. Lo desmontamos después del seis de enero. ▪ Lo quitamos después del seis de enero.

to **take down the curtains** ▪ to take the curtains down quitar las cortinas

to **take drastic action** tomar medidas drásticas ▪ cortar por lo sano

to **take effect 1.** *(medicine)* surtir efecto ▪ hacer efecto **2.** *(new law, policy)* to go into effect entrar en vigor

to **take exception to something** ▪ to take offense at something ofenderse por algo

to **take first prize** llevarse el primer premio

to **take flight** ▪ to fly away ▪ to fly off batir vuelo ▪ emprender vuelo

to **take flying lessons** tomar clases de vuelo

to **take for example** ▪ to take as an example tomar por ejemplo ▪ tomar como ejemplo ➤ Take Spain, for example... Toma España, por ejemplo...

to **take for granted that...** dar por sentado que... ▪ dar por sabido que... ▪ dar por hecho que... ▪ dar por supuesto que...

to **take French leave** ▪ to fly the coop salir a la francesa ▪ despedirse a la francesa

to **take great pains to do something** ▪ to go to great pains to do something esmerarse en (hacer) algo ▪ tomarse trabajo en (hacer) algo ▪ llevar algo a cabo con gran esfuerzo

to **take great pride in** sentirse gran orgullo en

to **take heart** tomar aliento ▪ animarse ▪ cobrar valentía

take him away! *(tú)* ¡llévatelo! ▪ *(usted)* ¡lléveselo!

to **take hold** ▪ to gel ▪ to catch on cuajar

to **take hold of one** ▪ to seize one *(strong emotion)* hacer presa en uno

take-home pay ▪ net pay salario neto ▪ sueldo neto

to **take in a movie** incluir una película

to **take in a pair of pants 1.** *(waist)* achicar la cintura del pantalón ▪ tomarle la cintura al pantalón **2.** *(inseam)* meterle a los pantalones ▪ tomarle de los lados a los pantalones *(In Spain, "pantalón" means "pair of pants" and "pantalones" means "pairs of pants." Latin-American Spanish is parallel to English: "pantalones" means "pair of pants.")*

to **take in a stray dog** adoptar a un perro callejero ▪ acoger a un perro callejero

to **take in an orphan** ▪ to give shelter to an orphan ▪ to shelter an orphan acoger a un niño huérfano

to **take in food** ▪ to ingest food tomar comida ▪ ingerir comida

to **take in someone** ▪ to take someone in ▪ to give shelter to someone acoger a alguien en su seno

to **take in the groceries** llevar las compras del coche a la casa ▪ entrar las bolsas de los mandados

to **take into account something** ▪ to take something into account tener en cuenta ▪ tomar en cuenta ▪ hacer de cuenta ➤ Taking into account the fact that... Tomando en cuenta (el hecho de) que... ➤ Taking that fact into account... Teniendo ese hecho en cuenta...

to **take into consideration** ▪ to count (when grading) tomar en consideración

to **take inventory** cuadrar el inventario ▪ hacer inventario

to **take issue with** discrepar de ▪ discrepar con ▪ disentir de ▪ disentir con ▪ disentir en ▪ contradecir a ▪ mostrar desacuerdo con

take it! ▪ it's yours! *(tú)* ¡llévatelo! ▪ ¡quédate con ello! ▪ *(usted)* ¡lléveselo! ▪ ¡quédese con ello!

to **take it as a compliment** tomarlo como un cumplido

to **take it as a reflection on oneself** tomarlo como reflexión de uno mismo ▪ tomarlo como reflexión de sí mismo

to **take it as an insult** tomarlo como un insulto

to **take it back 1.** *(a remark)* retirarlo **2.** *(store merchandise)* devolverlo ➤ I take it back. Lo retiro.

to **take it badly** tomárselo mal

take it easy! 1. calm down ¡tranquilízate! ▪ ¡cálmate! **2.** don't work too hard *(L. Am.)* tómalo con calma ▪ *(Sp.)* que te sea leve ▪ *(off-color)* ¡no te acojones! ▪ *(Arg.)* tomátelo con calma

to **take it easy** tumbarse a la bartola ▪ echarse a la bartola ▪ tenderse a la bartola

to **take it from here** ▪ to do the rest oneself desde aquí encargarse uno ▪ ya hacerlo ▪ a partir de aquí hacerlo ▪ a partir de aquí encargarse uno ▪ desde aquí hacerlo ▪ desde aquí encargarse ➤ We'll take it from here, thanks. A partir de aquí lo hacemos nosotros, gracias. ▪ A partir de aquí nos encargamos (nosotros), gracias. ▪ Desde aquí lo hacemos nosotros. ▪ Desde aquí nos encargamos (nosotros).

to **take it home with one** llevárselo consigo a casa ➤ He took it home with him. (Él) se lo llevó consigo a casa. ➤ She took it home with her. (Ella) se lo llevó consigo a casa.

to **take it the worst** tocárle a alguien lo peor ➤ His mother was the one who took it the worst. Fue a su madre a quien le tocó lo peor. ▪ Fue a su madre a quien le tocó la peor parte.

to **take it upon oneself to** encargarse de ▪ echarse encima ▪ darse el trabajo de ▪ asumir

to **take its course** ▪ to run its course llevar su curso

to **take its toll on** ajar ▪ causar pérdidas en ▪ mermar ➤ Time had taken its toll on the ancient ruins. El tiempo había ajado las ruinas antiguas. ➤ The drought has taken its toll on the crops. La sequía ha causado pérdidas en la cosecha. ➤ His health problems have taken their toll on his once youthful energy and vigor. Su problemas de salud han mermado su energía y vigor juvenil de un tiempo anterior.

to **take leave of someone** *(literary)* ▪ to say good-bye to someone despedirse de alguien

to **take legal action against someone** ▪ to file suit against someone querellarse contra alguien ▪ entablar acción contra alguien ▪ entablar demanda contra alguien

to **take lessons** tomar lecciones

to **take liberties** propasarse ▪ tomarse muchas licencias ▪ tomarse muchas libertades ▪ tomarse confianzas ▪ ser atrevido(-a) ➤ He takes a lot of liberties in my house, getting soft drinks, answering the phone, and coming in without ringing the doorbell. Se toma muchas licencias en mi casa, cogiéndose refrescos, contestando el teléfono y entrando sin llamar. ➤ *(Ricardo Palma)* If he doesn't take any more liberties... Si es que a más no se propasa... ▪ Si es que no se propasa más...

to **take lightly something** ▪ to take something lightly tomarse algo a la ligera ➤ He took his obligations very lightly. Se tomó sus obligaciones a la ligera.

to **take longer than it should** tardar más de lo debido ▪ llevar más (tiempo) de lo debido

to **take longer than one thinks (it will)** ▪ to take longer than one thinks (it is going to) tardar más de lo que uno piensa

to **take longer to do something than to do something else** tardarse más en hacer una cosa que en hacer otra ➤ It takes longer to fix dinner than (it does) to clean the kitchen. Se tarda más en preparar la comida que en limpiar la cocina.

to **take matters into one's own hands** tomar cartas en un asunto

take me to him *(tú)* llévame donde está él ▪ *(usted)* lléveme donde está él

to **take money out of an account** ▪ to take out money from an account ▪ to withdraw money from an account sacar dinero de una cuenta

take my advice *(tú)* sigue mi consejo ▪ *(usted)* siga mi consejo

take my hand toma mi mano ▪ agarra mi mano ▪ *(Sp.)* coge mi mano

take my word for it *(tú)* tómame la palabra ▪ *(usted)* tómeme la palabra ▪ *(Arg., vos)* tomame la palabra

to **take notes** *(L. Am.)* tomar apuntes ▪ *(Sp.)* coger apuntes

to **take off 1.** *(aircraft)* to become airborne despegar **2.** *(bird)* to take flight echarse al aire **3.** *(coll.)* to leave marcharse ▪ abrirse ▪ irse ▪ *(Mex.)* ir de salida ➤ I'm gonna take off. ▪ I'm off. Me voy. ▪ Me voy a ir. ▪ Voy a irme. ▪ Voy a marcharme. ▪ Voy de salida.

to **take off like a shot** salir disparado ▪ lanzarse en carrera

to **take off one's clothes** ▪ to take one's clothes off quitarse la ropa ▪ desnudarse ▪ desvestirse

to **take off one's glasses** ▪ to take one's glasses off quitarse los lentes ▪ *(Sp.)* quitárselas gafas ➤ He took off his glasses. ▪ He took his glasses off. Se quitó los lentes. ▪ Se quitó las gafas. ➤ He took them off. Los quitó. ▪ Las quitó.

to **take off one's hat** ▪ to take one's hat off descubrirse

to **take off running** ▪ to start running ▪ to break into a run echarse a correr

to **take office** asumir el cargo

to **take on a life of one's own** cobrar su vida propia ➤ The leftovers in the refrigerator have taken on a life of their own. Las sobras en el refrigerador han cobrado su vida propia.

to **take on a new dimension** adquirir una nueva dimensión

to **take on a project** ▪ to undertake a project emprender un proyecto ➤ When I undertook the project, I didn't realize what I was getting (myself) into. ▪ When I took on the project, I didn't realize what I was getting (myself) into. Cuando emprendí el proyecto no me di cuenta en lo que me estaba metiendo.

to **take on importance** ▪ to grow in importance cobrar importancia ▪ adquirir importancia

to **take on meaning** cobrar sentido ▪ adquirir sentido ▪ cobrar significado ▪ adquirir significado ➤ Since his death, his words have taken on special meaning. Desde su muerte sus palabras han cobrado un sentido especial.

to **take on more than one can handle** ▪ to overextend oneself comprometerse a (hacer) más de lo que uno puede

to **take on new meaning** cobrar un sentido nuevo ▪ cobrar un significado nuevo ▪ adquirir un sentido nuevo ▪ adquirir un significado nuevo

to **take on responsibility** asumir responsabilidad(es)

to **take on someone** ▪ to take someone on enfrentarse a alguien ▪ enfrentarse con alguien

to **take on the job of** asumir el trabajo de ▪ encargarse del trabajo de

to **take on the task of** asumir la tarea de ▪ encargarse de la tarea de

take one! ¡toma! ▪ *(Sp.)* ¡coge!

to **take one an hour (to)** llevarle una hora ▪ tomarle una hora ➤ It took me an hour to download this blasted E-mail. Me llevó una hora bajar este puñetero correo electrónico. ▪ Me tomó una hora bajar este puñetero correo electrónico.

to **take one back in time to** llevarle a uno (hacia) atrás en el tiempo ▪ hacerle volver atrás en el tiempo ▪ transportarlo a uno atrás en el tiempo ➤ This movie takes you back in time. Esta película te lleva atrás en el tiempo. ▪ Esta película te transporta atrás en el tiempo. ➤ Looking through a telescope takes you back in time. Mirar por un telescopio te lleva (hacia) atrás en el tiempo.

to **take one back to the beginning** devolverle a uno al principio ➤ If you press "control" and "home," it takes you back to the beginning. Si pulsas "control" e "inicio" te devuelve al principio.

to **take one by surprise 1.** *(L. Am.)* tomarlo a uno de sorpresa ▪ agarrar a uno de sorpresa ▪ pillarlo a uno de sorpresa ▪ *(Sp.)* coger a uno de sorpresa **2.** *(off guard, unprepared)* tomarlo a uno desprevenido ▪ agarrarlo a uno desprevenido(-a) ▪ *(Sp.)* coger a uno de sorpresa ▪ coger a uno desprevenido(-a)

to **take one day at a time** tomar el tiempo como viene ▪ tomar el tiempo conforme viene

to **take one last look around** echar un último vistazo ▪ echar una última ojeada

to **take one to the top** llevarle a uno a la cima

to **take one's advice** seguir el consejo de uno ▪ llevarse de consejo ▪ hacerle caso ▪ conseguir el consejo de uno ➤ Take my advice. Sigue mi consejo. ➤ If he takes our advice... Si se lleva de nuestro consejo... ➤ I took your advice. Te hice caso. ➤ Take my advice. *(tú)* Consigue mi consejo. ▪ *(usted)* Consiga mi consejo.

to **take one's afternoon nap** ▪ to have one's afternoon nap dormir la siesta ▪ tomar una siesta ▪ echarse una siesta

to **take one's blood pressure** tomarle la tensión (arterial)

to **take one's breath away** dejarlo a uno sin aliento ▪ dejarlo a uno boquiabierto ▪ asombrarlo ▪ ser para caerse atrás ▪ *(Sp., leísmo)* dejarle a uno sin aliento ▪ dejarle a uno boquiabierto ▪ asombrarle ➤ The interior of the cathedral took our breath away. El interior de la catedral nos dejó sin aliento.

to **take one's clothes off** quitarse la ropa ▪ desnudarse ▪ desvestirse

to **take one's lunch to work** llevarse el almuerzo al trabajo

to **take one's medication** ▪ to take one's medicine tomar la medicina ▪ tomar el medicamento ▪ *(old-fashioned, quaint)* tomar el remedio

to **take one's order** *(in a restaurant)* tomarle nota ▪ apuntar la orden ▪ tomar la orden ▪ *(Sp.)* cogerle nota de lo que uno quiere ➤ Has your order been taken? ▪ Has anyone taken your order? *(tú)* ¿Te han tomado nota? ▪ *(usted)* ¿Le han tomado nota? ➤ Would you take our order, please? ¿Nos toma(s) nota? ▪ ¿Nos coge(s) (la) nota?

to **take one's own life** ▪ to commit suicide poner fin a su vida ▪ suicidarse ➤ Suffering from cancer, she took her own life. Aquejada de cáncer, ella puso fin a su vida.

to **take one's responsibility seriously** tomarse su responsabilidad en serio

to **take one's time** tomar su tiempo ▪ *(Sp.)* coger su tiempo ➤ Take your time. Toma tu tiempo. ▪ Coge tu tiempo.

to **take one's time doing something** ▪ to take plenty of time doing something ▪ to take a good long time doing something tomar su tiempo haciendo algo ▪ tomar su tiempo para hacer algo ▪ *(Sp.)* coger su tiempo

to **take out a loan** ▪ to get a loan ▪ to secure a loan pedir un préstamo ▪ concederle a alguien un préstamo ➤ He took out a loan. Pidió un préstamo. ▪ Le concedieron un préstamo. ➤ I took out a loan. Pedí un préstamo. ▪ Me concedieron un préstamo.

to **take out a military target** dejar fuera de fuego un objetivo militar ▪ *(coll.)* cepillárselo ➤ When they detect a radar turned on, they go and take it out. Cuando detectan un radar encendido, van y se lo cepillan.

to **take out a mortgage on a house** ▪ to mortgage a house hacer una hipoteca sobre una casa

to **take out for something** ▪ to draft the bank account for something ▪ to withhold something from the bank account descontar algo de la cuenta bancaria ➤ Every October they take out for the insurance. ▪ Every October they draft the account for the insurance. Cada octubre descuentan el seguro de la cuenta corriente.

to **take out money from an account** ▪ to take money out of an account ▪ to withdraw money from an account sacar dinero de una cuenta ▪ retirar dinero de una cuenta

to **take out the dog for a walk** ▪ to take the dog out for a walk sacar al perro a pasear ▪ sacar a la perra a pasear

to **take out the garbage** ▪ to take the garbage out sacar la basura ▪ retirar la basura ➤ Would you take out the garbage? ▪ Would you take the garbage out? ¿Sacarías la basura?

to **take over** ▪ to take charge of asumir control de ▪ hacerse cargo de

to **take over from someone** tomar el relevo de alguien ▪ recoger el relevo a alguien

to **take over the house** tomar posesión de la casa ▪ adueñarse de la casa ➤ The cat just walked in one day and took over. La gata entró en la casa cierto día y tomó posesión de la casa. ▪ La gata entró en la casa cierto día y se adueñó de la casa.

to **take over the world** adueñarse del mundo

to **take pains to do something** tomar empeño en hacer algo ▪ poner esmero en (hacer) algo

to **take part in something** tomar parte en algo ▪ intervenir en algo

to **take pictures** ▪ to take photographs ▪ to take photos sacar fotografías ▪ sacar fotos

to **take pity on someone** compaderse de alguien

to **take place in** ▪ to be held in **1.** *(meeting)* tener lugar en **2.** *(wedding, etc.)* llevarse a cabo en ▪ celebrarse en **3.** *(unexpected event)* to occur producirse en ▪ tener lugar en ▪ transcurrir en **4.** *(fictional or historical narrative)* to be set in estar ambientado en ▪ desarrollarse en ▪ tener lugar en ▪ pasar en **5.** *(a period of time)* pasar ➤ The conference will take place in Asunción. ▪ The conference will be held in Asunción. La reunión se llevará a cabo en Asunción. ➤ The meeting will take place at the Meliá Castilla Hotel. La reunión tendrá lugar en el Hotel Meliá Castilla. ➤ The accident took place near Salamanca. ▪ The accident occurred near Salamanca. El accidente se produjo cerca de Salamanca. ➤ The story takes place in Rota. El cuento se desarrolla en Rota. ▪ El cuento está ambientado en Rota. ➤ The action takes place in Vera Cruz. La acción pasa en Vera Cruz. ➤ Mark Twain notes that Joan of Arc's career took place in a mere breath of time. Mark Twain señala que la historia de Juana de Arco pasó en un suspiro.

to **take pleasure in** *(often negative)* ▪ to enjoy disfrutar de

to **take possession of something** ▪ to get possession of something hacerse con algo ▪ tomar posesión de algo ▪ apoderarse de algo ➤ Ferdinand and Isabella took possession of a good part of Latin America through a series of conquests. ▪ Ferdinand and Isabella took possession of a good part of Latin America through a series of conquests. Los Reyes Católicos se hicieron con una buena parte de Latinoamérica a través de sucesivas conquistas. ▪ Los Reyes Católicos tomaron posesión de una buena parte de Latinoamérica a través de sucesivas conquistas.

to **take power** asumir el poder

to **take pride in** sentirse orgulloso en

to **take pride in one's accomplishments** enorgullecerse de sus logros

to **take refuge in** refugiarse en ▪ guarecerse en

to **take responsibility for something 1.** *(that has to be done)* asumir la responsabilidad de algo ▪ responsabilizarse de algo ▪ hacerse responsable de algo **2.** *(to take the blame for something)* aceptar ser responsable de algo

to **take risks** tomar riesgos

to **take root (in)** arraigarse (en)

to **take seriously** tomar en serio

to **take shape** ir tomando forma ➤ The project is taking shape. El proyecto va tomando forma.

to **take shelter at** refugiarse en ▪ acogerse en

to **take shelter from** refugiarse de ▪ resguardarse de ▪ guarecerse de

to **take shelter in** refugiarse en ▪ acogerse en

to **take sides in a dispute** tomar partida en una disputa

to **take sides in an argument** tomar partido en una discusión

to **take smaller steps** ▪ to shorten one's stride acortar el paso

to **take so long to do something** tardar tanto en hacer algo ▪ llevar tanto tiempo para hacer algo ➤ Why is it taking so long for the file to open? ¿Por qué tarda tanto en abrirse el archivo? ▪ ¿Por qué lleva tanto tiempo para abrirse el archivo? ➤ Sorry it's taken (me) so long to get back to you. Siento haber tardado tanto en responder.

to **take some time off** tomarse unos días (libres)

to **take someone alive** capturar vivo(-a) a alguien ▪ *(Sp., leísmo)* capturarle vivo

to **take someone aside** llevar aparte a alguien ▪ llevar a un lado a alguien

to **take someone by surprise** ▪ to surprise someone sorprender a alguien ▪ agarrar a alguien desprevenido(-a) ▪ pillar a alguien desprevenido(-a)

to **take someone for a fool** tomar a alguien por tonto

to **take someone for a ride 1.** *(literal)* llevar a alguien de paseo **2.** to mislead someone ▪ to trick someone darle gato por liebre a alguien **3.** *(esp. among gangsters)* to kill someone mandar a alguien al otro lado

to **take someone for a walk** llevar a alguien a pasear ➤ My cat loves to be taken for a walk, just like a dog. A mi gata le encanta que le llevemos a pasear, igual que a un perro.

to **take someone for an airplane ride** llevar a dar una vuelta en un avioneta ➤ Martha Anne took us for an airplane ride. Martha Anne nos llevó a dar una vuelta en avioneta.

to **take someone for granted** no saber valorar a alguien ▪ no saber apreciar a alguien

to **take someone for someone else** ▪ to think someone is someone else ▪ to confuse someone with someone else tomar a alguien por otra persona ▪ confundir a alguien por otra persona ▪ pensar que alguien es otra persona ▪ creer que alguien es otra persona ➤ Pardon me. I took you for someone else. ▪ Pardon me. I thought you were someone else. ▪ Pardon me. I confused you with someone else. ▪ Pardon me. I confused you for someone else. *(to a man)* Perdone. Lo tomé por otra persona. ▪ Perdone. Lo confundí por otra persona. ▪ *(Sp.), leísmo* Perdone, le tomé por otra persona. ▪ Le confundí por otra persona. ▪ *(to a woman)* Perdone. La tomé por otra persona. ▪ La confundí por otra persona. ▪ *(to a man or woman)* Perdone. Pensé que era otra persona. ▪ Perdone. Creí que era otra persona.

to **take someone hostage** tomar a alguien como rehén ▪ agarrar a alguien como rehén

to **take someone in** ▪ to take in someone **1.** to give someone shelter ▪ to give someone a home acoger a alguien **2.** to hoodwink someone engañar a alguien

to **take someone into one's confidence** confiarse a alguien

to **take someone off a list 1.** to take someone's name off a list ▪ to take off a name from a list quitar a alguien de una lista ▪ borrar a alguien de una lista **2.** to cross someone off a list tachar a alguien de una lista

to **take someone on a tour** ▪ to give someone a tour llevar a alguien en una excursión

to **take someone out on a date** tener una cita amorosa

to **take someone prisoner** hacer prisionero a alguien

to **take someone to a place** llevarle a alguien a un lugar ➤ *(to a taxi driver)* Take us to the Olid Melia Hotel, please. Nos lleva al Hotel Olid Melia, por favor.

to **take someone to court** llevar a juicio a alguien ▪ llevar a alguien a la corte ▪ llevar a alguien al tribunal ▪ llevar a alguien ante el tribunal

to **take someone to someone** llevar a alguien con alguien ➤ Take me to him! ¡Llévame con él!

to **take someone to task for...** llevar la contraria a alguien por...

to **take someone to the altar** ▪ to marry someone llevar a alguien al altar ▪ llevar a alguien a la vicaria ▪ casarse con alguien

to **take someone to the cleaners** arrancarle la cabeza a alguien ▪ limpiar bien a alguien ▪ meter el clavo a alguien ▪ pelar a alguien ➤ The hotel really took us to the cleaners. El hotel nos limpió bien. ▪ El hotel nos metió un buen clavo. ▪ El hotel nos metió una buena clavada. ▪ El hotel nos peló.

to **take someone under one's wing** poner a alguien bajo el ala

to **take someone way too long to do something** llevarle a alguien muchísimo tiempo hacer algo ■ *(Sp., colorful)* darle las uvas (a alguien) *(The Spanish eat twelve grapes in the last twelve seconds of the year, hence the metaphor.)* ➤ You're taking way too long. Te van a dar las uvas.

to **take someone's blood pressure** tomarle la presión a alguien ■ tomarle la tensión a alguien

to **take someone's breath away** ■ to leave someone in awe dejar a alguien boquiabierto

to **take someone's order in a restaurant** tomarle nota a alguien en un restaurante ➤ Has someone (already) taken your order? ■ Has your order been taken? ¿Le han tomado nota?

to **take someone's place** ocupar el lugar de alguien

to **take someone's pulse** tomarle el pulso a alguien

to **take someone's temperature** medir la temperatura a alguien ■ tomar la temperatura a alguien

to **take someone's time** quitarle el tiempo a alguien ➤ I don't want to take any more of your time. No quiero quitarle más tiempo.

to **take someone's word (for it)** contar con la palabra de alguien (de que...) ■ fiarse de la palabra de alguien

to **take something as a joke** tomárselo como chiste ■ tomárselo como broma

to **take something as gospel** tomar algo como doctrina ➤ Despite its unenforceability in the South, the Emancipation Proclamation was taken as gospel by the slaves themselves, who began deserting their masters in ever-increasing numbers. A pesar de su inejecutibilidad en el Sur, la Proclamación de Emancipación fue tomada como doctrina por los propios esclavos, quienes empezaron a dejar a sus amos en números cada vez más grandes.

to **take something (away)** llevarse algo ➤ That waiter took (away) the salt. Ese camarero se llevó la sal.

to **take something away from someone** quitarle algo a alguien

to **take something badly** tomar algo a mal

to **take something by force** tomar algo por la fuerza ■ llevarse algo a la fuerza

to **take something downstairs** bajar algo ➤ Would you take this downstairs for me? ¿Me bajas esto? ■ ¿Me bajarías esto?

to **take something for granted** dar algo por sentado ■ dar algo por supuesto ➤ To take it for granted that... Darlo por sentado que... ■ Darlo por supuesto que...

to **take something from something** tomar algo de algo

to **take something home with one** llevarse algo a casa ➤ I'll take it home with me and read it over the weekend. Me lo llevo a casa y lo leeré durante el fin de semana.

to **take something in stride** tomarse algo con soda ■ tomarse algo con calma

to **take something into account** ■ to take into account something tomar algo en cuenta ■ tener algo en cuenta

to **take something literally** tomar(se) algo literalmente ■ tomar(se) algo al dedillo ➤ Don't take it literally. No (te) lo tomes literalmente.

to **take something out on someone** agarrársela con alguien ■ ensañarse con alguien ➤ Don't take it out on me! ¡No te las agarres conmigo! ■ ¡No te ensañes conmigo!

to **take something personally** tomarse algo como algo personal ➤ Don't take what she said personally. No (te) tomes lo que ella dijo como algo personal. ➤ Don't take it personally. No (te) lo tomes como algo personal.

to **take something philosophically** tomar algo con filosofía

to **take something right** ■ to take something the right way tomar(se) algo por el lado positivo ■ tomar(se) algo por las buenas ■ tomar(se) algo de buena manera

to **take something seriously** tomarse algo en serio

to **take something somewhere** llevar algo a alguna parte ➤ Will you take this letter to the mailbox for me? ¿Me llevas esta carta al buzón?

to **take something the right way** ■ to take something right tomar(se) algo por el lado positivo ■ tomar(se) algo por las buenas ■ tomar(se) algo de buena manera

to **take something the wrong way** tomar(se) algo a mal ■ tomar(se) algo por el lado negativo ■ tomar(se) algo por las malas ■ tomar(se) algo de mala manera ■ tomar(se) algo de manera equivocada ➤ She took it the wrong way. Se lo tomó a mal. ■ Lo tomó a mal.

to **take something to heart** tomar algo a pecho

to **take something upstairs** subir algo ➤ Would you take this upstairs for me? ¿Me subes esto? ■ ¿Me subirías esto?

to **take something well** llevar algo bien

to **take something with a grain of salt** no creerse algo al pie de la letra ■ no tomarse algo al pie de la letra ■ *(Arg., Chile)* tomar algo con pinzas ➤ I took what he said with a grain of salt. Tomé lo que dijo con un poco de sal. ➤ I took it with a grain of salt. Lo tomé con un poco de sal.

to **take something with one** llevárselo consigo ➤ He took it with him. (Él) se lo llevó consigo. ➤ She took it with her. (Ella) se lo llevó consigo. ➤ Why don't you take it with you? *(tú)* ¿Por qué no te lo llevas contigo? ■ *(usted)* ¿Por qué no se lo lleva consigo?

to **take Spanish** ■ to take a Spanish course ■ to take a course in Spanish estudiar español ■ cursar español ■ recibir una clase de español ■ hacer un curso de español ➤ I took three years of high school Spanish. Estudié el español tres años en el instituto.

to **take steps to** tomar medidas para ■ adoptar medidas para

to **take stock of the situation** ■ to take stock of one's situation hacerse una composición de lugar ➤ I need to take stock of the situation. ■ I need to take stock of my situation. Necesito hacerme una composición de lugar.

to **take subjects** hacer asignaturas

take that! ■ put that in your pipe and smoke it! ¡chúpate esa mandarina! ■ ¡chúpate ésa! ■ *(Sp.)* ¡chínchate! ■ *(vos)* ¡tomá! ■ ¡fagocitate esa! ■ ¡fumate esa! ■ ¡chupate esa mandarina!

take that! and that! and that! ¡pim! ¡pam! ¡pum!

to **take the advice of** seguir el consejo de ■ conseguir el consejo de ■ llevarse de consejo ■ hacerle caso ➤ Take my advice. *(tú)* Sigue mi consejo. ■ Consigue mi consejo. ■ *(usted)* Siga mi consejo. ■ Consiga usted mi consejo. ➤ If he takes our advice Si se lleva de nuestro consejo ➤ I took your advice. Te hice caso.

to **take the attendance** ■ to take attendance ■ to call the roll pasar lista ■ pasar la lista

to **take the baton 1.** *(in a relay race)* tomar el testigo ■ recoger el testigo ■ *(Sp.)* coger el testigo **2.** *(figurative)* to take over from someone recoger el relevo ■ tomar el testigo

to **take the bull by the horns** agarrar el toro por los cuernos ■ coger al toro por los cuernos

to **take the bus** *(Mex., C.A.)* tomar el camión ■ *(Sp.)* coger el autobús ■ *(Uru.)* tomar el ómnibus ■ *(Arg.)* tomar el colectivo ■ *(Cuba, Puerto Rico, Dominican Republic, Canary Islands)* tomar la guagua

to **take the case to court** llevar el caso a juicio ■ llevar el caso a la corte ■ llevar el caso ante el juez

to **take the census** hacer el censo

to **take the chance (that...)** correr el riesgo (de que...) ➤ I don't want to take the chance. No quiero correr el riesgo.

to **take the day off** tomarse el día libre ➤ Take the day off! ¡Tómate el día libre! ➤ Do you have Friday off during the long weekend? ¿Haces fiesta el viernes del puente?

to **take the dog (out) for a walk** ■ to walk the dog sacar al perro a pasear ■ pasear al perro

to **take the easy way out** tomar la salida fácil ■ echar por el atajo

to **take the floor** *(in parliamentary procedure)* hacer uso de la palabra ■ tomar la palabra ■ *(Sp.)* coger la palabra ■ coger las palabras

to **take the helm** tomar el timón ■ llevar el timón

to **take the initiative** tomar la iniciativa

to **take the lead** tomarle la delantera ■ ganar de mano ■ tomar ventaja ■ *(Sp.)* cogerle la delantera

to **take the left fork** ■ to bear left at the fork tomar la bifurcación a la izquierda ■ quedarse a la izquierda en la bifurcación ■ hacerse a la izquierda en la bifurcación ■ *(Sp.)* coger la bifurcación a la izquierda to **take the liberty of** tomarse la libertad de ➤ I took the liberty of showing her your letter. Me tomé la libertad de enseñarle tu carta.

to **take the measurements of something** tomar las medidas de algo

to **take the news calmly** ▪ to receive the news calmly tomar la noticia con calma ▪ recibir la noticia con calma

to **take the next left** tomar la próxima calle a la izquierda ▪ *(Sp.)* meterse en la próxima calle a la izquierda

to **take the next right** tomar la próxima calle a la derecha ▪ *(Sp.)* meterse en la próxima calle a la derecha

to **take the oath of office** jurar el cargo ▪ *(Uru.)* hacer el juramento de asunción del mando ▪ prestar el juramento de asunción del mando

to **take the opposite view** ▪ to take the opposing view ▪ to take the other side of the argument llevar la contraria

to **take the other side of the argument** ▪ to take the opposing view llevar la postura contraria ▪ llevar la contraria

to **take the path of least resistance** tomar el camino más fácil ▪ seguir el camino más fácil ▪ seguir la ley del mínimo esfuerzo

to **take the phone off the hook** ▪ to take the telephone off the hook descolgar el teléfono

to **take the place of someone** ▪ to change places with someone ocupar el lugar de otra persona ▪ ocupar el lugar de alguien ➤ Would you like to take the place of a person you know? ▪ Would you like to change places with someone you know? ¿Te gustaría ocupar el lugar de otra persona a la que conoces? ▪ ¿Te gustaría ocupar el lugar de alguien al que conoces?

to **take the place of something** ▪ to replace something ▪ to substitute for something sustituir a algo ➤ *(editorial)* The television networks have taken the place of the written dailies as the authors of monumental blunders. Las cadenas de televisión han sustituido a los diarios escritos en el protagonismo de pifias monumentales.

to **take the plunge** tirarse a la piscina ▪ echarse al agua ▪ dar el salto ▪ liarse la manta a la cabeza

to **take the plural** llevar el plural

to **take the pressure off someone** ▪ to give someone (a little) leeway ▪ to give (a little) leeway to someone dar cuartel a alguien ▪ dar cuartelillo a alguien

to **take the rap (for someone)** ▪ to take the blame for another's crime **1.** *(intentionally)* cargar con la culpa ▪ *(coll.)* cargar con el mochuelo **2.** *(unintentionally)* ▪ to be the scapegoat ▪ to be the fall guy pagar el pato ▪ pagar los platos rotos ▪ ser el chivo expiatorio ▪ *(Sp.)* ser la cabeza de turco

to **take the reins** tomar las riendas ▪ *(Sp.)* coger las riendas

to **take the right fork** ▪ to bear right at the fork tomar la bifurcación a la derecha ▪ quedarse a la derecha en la bifurcación ▪ hacerse a la derecha en la bifurcación ▪ *(Sp.)* coger la bifurcación a la derecha

to **take the subjunctive** llevar el subjuntivo

take the time that you need *(tú)* tómate el tiempo que te haga falta ▪ tómate el tiempo que necesites ▪ *(usted)* tómese el tiempo que le haga falta (a usted) ▪ tómese el tiempo que necesite (usted)

to **take the time to do something** dedicar el tiempo para hacer algo

to **take the top off (of) the can** destapar el tarro ▪ destapar el pote

to **take the train to** tomar el tren a ▪ tomar el tren hacia ▪ *(Sp.)* coger el tren a ▪ coger el tren hacia ➤ I took the train to Valladolid. Tomé el tren a Valladolid. ▪ Tomé el tren hacia Valladolid.

to **take the trouble to...** ▪ to go to the trouble to... molestarse en... ▪ tomarse la molestia de...

to **take the wind out of someone's sails** cortarle las alas a alguien ▪ bajarle los humos a alguien ▪ dejar a alguien con los palmos de narices

to **take the words right out of one's mouth** quitar a alguien de la boca una cosa ➤ You took the words right out of my mouth. Me lo quitaste de la boca.

to **take time off** tomarse tiempo ▪ concederse tiempo ➤ I took time off to go out to dinner with Susana. Me tomé tiempo para salir a comer con Susana. ▪ Me concedí tiempo para salir a comer con Susana.

to **take time to do something** tomarse tiempo (para) hacer algo ▪ tardar(se) tiempo para hacer algo ▪ tardarse tiempo en hacer algo ➤ It took me two years to learn English. Me tomó dos años (para) aprender inglés. ➤ It took a week to get the smoke out of the curtains. Tardó una semana para quitar el olor a humo de las cortinas. ➤ After the shooting, it took him three days to die. Después del disparo, tardó tres días en morir. ➤ It takes an hour to get there. Se tarda una hora en llegar.

to **take to one's heels** ▪ to flee apretar los talones ▪ salir corriendo ▪ salir disparando ▪ salir pitando ▪ poner los pies en polvorosa

to **take to something naturally** tomar a algo por naturaleza ▪ hacer algo por naturaleza ➤ Daniel Pedroza took to motorcycles naturally when he was only thirteen. Daniel Pedroza tomó a las motocicletas por naturaleza desde los trece años. ➤ Poodles take naturally to swimming. Los perros de lana nadan por naturaleza. ▪ Los perros de lana son nadadores por naturaleza.

to **take to the streets** salir a la calle ▪ tomar a la calle ▪ echarse a la calle ➤ *(headline)* Unemployed Argentinians take to the streets Los parados argentinos toman a la calle ▪ Los parados argentinos salen a la calle

to **take too long** **1.** *(with a personal pronoun object)* tardar demasiado (tiempo) ▪ llevarle a uno demasiado tiempo **2.** *(with "it" as the subject and no personal pronoun object)* tardarse demasiado (tiempo) ➤ It was taking me too long. (Yo) tardaba demasiado. ▪ Me llevaba demasiado tiempo. ▪ Me estaba llevando demasiado tiempo. ➤ It was taking too long. Se tardaba demasiado. ▪ Se estaba tardando demasiado. ▪ Estaba llevando demasiado tiempo.

to **take turns doing something** ▪ to alternate doing something turnarse para hacer algo ▪ hacer algo por turnos ▪ alternarse en hacer algo ➤ We took turns doing the dishes. Nos turnamos para lavar los platos.

to **take turns with someone doing something** turnarse con alguien para hacer algo ➤ I take turns with my brother and sister doing the dishes. Me turno con mi hermano y hermana para fregar los platos.

to **take twice as long** tardar en doble

to **take twice as long as expected** ▪ to take twice as long as anticipated tardar el doble de lo previsto

to **take unfair advantage of a situation** aprovecharse injustamente de una situación

to **take (unfair) advantage of someone** aprovecharse de alguien

to **take up a hobby** empezar un pasatiempo nuevo ▪ empezar un hobby nuevo

to **take up a pair of pants** ▪ to take a pair of pants up **1.** to raise the cuff of a pair of pants meter las bastas del pantalón ▪ *(Sp.)* coger el bajo del pantalón **2.** to take in the waist of a pair of pants meter la cintura del pantalón

to **take up arms** tomar armas

to **take up space** ocupar espacio

to **take up the hem *x* centimeters** subirle *x* centímetros al dobladillo ▪ entrar el dobladillo *x* centímetros ▪ *(Sp.)* coger el dobladillo *x* centímetros al dobladillo

to **take upon oneself the task of** asumir la tarea de ▪ asumir el cargo de ▪ encargarse de ▪ echarse encima la tarea de

to **take with it** arrastrar a ➤ The company's fall has taken with it most technology stocks. La empresa ha arrastrado en su caída a la mayoría de valores tecnológicos.

to **take work** costar trabajo

to **take *x* people to do something** hacer falta *x* personas para hacer algo ➤ It took twenty years and twenty thousand slaves to build the pyramid at Giza. Hicieron falta veinte años y veinte mil esclavos para construir el pirámide de Giza.

to **take *x* years to do something** ▪ (for) *x* years to be needed to do something tardarse *x* años en hacer algo ▪ hacer falta *x* tiempo para hacer algo

to **take years off (of) one** quitarle años (de encima)

take your pick! ▪ take your choice! *(tú)* ¡elige! ▪ ¡escoge! ▪ *(usted)* ¡elija (usted)! ▪ ¡escoja (usted)!

take your time *(tú)* toma tu tiempo ▪ *(Sp.)* coge tu tiempo ▪ *(usted)* tome su tiempo ▪ coja su tiempo

to be **taken aback** quedarse desconcertado(-a) ▪ dejarle a uno desconcertado(-a) ▪ quedarse sorprendido(-a) ▪ dejarle a uno sorprendido(-a)

taken as a whole ▪ taken in its entirety tomado en su conjunto ▪ tomado en su totalidad

to be **taken for a ride** ▪ to get taken for a ride hacerse el primo

to be **taken for a walk** ser llevado de paseo

to be **taken for what it is** ser tomado como lo que es ▪ tomarse como lo que es

to be **taken from the reading** estar sacado de la lectura ▪ ser sacado de la lectura

to be **taken in 1.** to be fooled ▪ to be deceived ser engañado **2.** to be cheated ▪ to be hoodwinked ser estafado ▪ ser timado **3.** to be given shelter ser acogido **4.** to be adopted ser adoptado **5.** *(hem of a garment)* to be taken up ser cogido ➤ I had the hem taken in. ▪ I had the hem taken up. Me cogieron el dobladillo.

taken in its entirety ▪ taken as a whole tomado en su conjunto ▪ tomado en su totalidad

takeoff roll: on the ~ *(airplane)* ▪ during the takeoff roll en el recorrido de despegue ▪ en la carrera de despegue

taking all into account ▪ without exception ▪ bar none contándolos todos

to be **taking exams** ▪ to be in the middle of exams estar de exámenes

taking into account ▪ in view of ▪ considering en atención a

to be **taking it all in** estar con cien ojos

to be **taking shape** estar tomando forma ▪ ir tomando forma

talcum powder polvos de talco

Tale of Two Cities: A ~ *(Dickens novel) La historia de dos ciudades*

talent scout *el, la* cazatalentos

talent show espectáculo de talentos

to **talk a blue streak** hablar a borbotones ▪ hablar por los codos ▪ hablar a destajo ▪ hablar como un descosido

to **talk a lot** hablar mucho

talk about crazy! ¡vaya locura!

to **talk about everything** hablar de lo mucho y de lo poco

to **talk among oneselves** hablar entre sí ➤ They were talking among themselves. Hablaban entre sí. ➤ We were talking among ourselves. Hablabamos entre nosotros.

to **talk and talk** hablar sin parar ▪ hablar sin cesar ▪ estar de palique ➤ They talked and talked. Estaban de palique. ➤ We talked till 5 in the morning. Estabamos de palique hasta las cinco de la mañana.

to **talk as equals** ▪ to talk without social barriers hablar de igual a igual ▪ hablar de tú a tú

to **talk back to someone** replicar a alguien (de forma insolente) ▪ responder a alguien (de forma insolente) ▪ contestarle a alguien ➤ Don't (you) talk back to me! ¡No me repliques! ▪ ¡No me respondas! ▪ ¡No me contestes!

to **talk behind someone's back** hablar a (las) espaldas de alguien ▪ hablar por detrás de alguien

to **talk in one's sleep** hablar en sueños ▪ hablar dormido

to **talk just to talk** hablar por hablar

to **talk knowledgeably about a subject** ▪ to speak knowledgeably about a subject hablar con propiedad sobre un tema ▪ hablar con conocimiento sobre un tema

to **talk loud** hablar fuerte ▪ hablar recio

to **talk nonstop** hablar sin parar ▪ hablar una carraca ▪ hablar como un loro

talk of: there is ~ hay rumores de ▪ hay rumores sobre

to **talk of nothing else (but...)** ▪ not to talk of anything else ▪ to be all one talks about no hablar de otra cosa (que...) ▪ no hablar de otra cosa (más que...)

to be the **talk of the town** andar en boca de todos ▪ andar de boca en boca

to **talk on and on** ▪ to talk and talk hablar y hablar ▪ no parar de hablar

to **talk on and on (without getting to the point)** hablar y hablar sin llegar a concretar

to **talk on the telephone** hablar por teléfono ➤ Have you all talked on the telephone at least? ¿Han hablado ustedes por teléfono al menos? ▪ *(Sp.)* ¿Os habéis hablado por teléfono al menos?

to **talk out of both sides of one's mouth** tener doble discurso ➤ I'm not just talking out of both sides of my mouth. No es que tenga doble discurso.

to **talk out of order** hablar fuera de turno

to **talk out of school** hablar de lo que no te incumbe ▪ hablar de lo que no te corresponde

to **talk really loud** hablar muy fuerte ▪ hablar muy alto ▪ hablar gritando ▪ *(Sp.)* hablar a voz en grito

to **talk separately with two (or more) people** ▪ to speak separately with two or more people hablar por separado a dos (o más) personas

to **talk some sense into someone** hacerle entrar en razón a alguien

to **talk someone down** ▪ to haggle over the price regatear ▪ acordar a la baja

to **talk someone into doing something** ▪ to talk someone into something convencer a alguien para hacer algo ▪ convencer a alguien para que haga algo ▪ persuadir a alguien para que haga algo ▪ *(coll.)* vender la burra a alguien ▪ vender la moto a alguien ➤ We talked her into going to the bullfight this Saturday. Le convencimos para ir a los toros el próximo sábado. ▪ Le convencimos para que fuera a los toros el próximo sábado. ➤ You talked me into it. Me has convencido.

to **talk someone out of doing something** ▪ to dissuade someone from doing something disuadir a alguien de que haga algo ▪ persuadir a alguien para que no haga algo

to **talk through the nose** ▪ to have a twang ganguear

to **talk to a brick wall** hablar con las paredes

to **talk to each other** hablarse uno al otro

to **talk to oneself** hablar para sí ▪ hablarse a sí mismo ▪ hablar consigo mismo

to **talk to the man upstairs** ▪ to pray hablar con el Jefe ▪ orar

to **talk to the wind** hablar al aire

to **talk turkey** no tener pelos en la lengua

to **talk very loud** ▪ to talk really loud hablar muy alto

to **talk with one's hands** gesticular

to be **talking** estar hablando en ➤ We go back about fifty years. I'm talking geological time here. Volvimos cincuenta años atrás. (Estoy) hablando en años solares.

talking now: this is the expert ~ habló el experto ▪ habla el experto

tall building edificio alto

tall man hombre alto ▪ tipo alto ▪ hombre de gran estatura

to be a **tall order** ▪ to be a lot to ask ser mucho pedir ➤ That's a tall order. Es mucho pedir.

tall tale cuento chino

to **tally votes** ▪ to count votes ▪ to tally the vote escrutar votos

to **tamper with something** manipular algo

to be **tampered with** estar manipulado ➤ *(news item)* The Civil Aviation Agency had affirmed that the helicopter had not been tampered with but now has left open that possibility. La Agencia de Aviación Civil había asegurado que el helicóptero no había sido manipulado, pero ahora ha dejado abierta esta posibilidad.

to **tan someone's hide** ▪ to give someone a spanking ▪ to spank someone zurrar a alguien ▪ calentar el culo a alguien ▪ poner el culo como un tomate a alguien ▪ dar unos azotes a alguien ▪ dar unos azotes en el culo a alguien ▪ dar a alguien en el culo ▪ azotar a alguien (en el trasero)

to be **tangent to** ser tangente a ➤ When Venus is at its maximum angular distance from the sun, our line of sight to Venus is tangent to its orbit. Cuando Venus está a su máxima distancia angular del sol, nuestra línea de visión a Venus es tangente a su órbita.

tangible evidence pruebas tangibles ▪ evidencia tangible

tangible reasons *las* razones tangibles

tangible results resultados tangibles ➤ The leaders tried to put a positive spin on the talks, which produced few tangible results. Los líderes intentaron dar una vuelta positiva a sus conversaciones, las cuales produjeron pocos resultados tangibles.

tangle of wires enredo de cables ▪ *(Sp.)* maraña de cables

to be **tangled up** estar liado ➤ The wires are all tangled up. Los cables están liados.

tanned hide piel curtida

to be **tantamount to** ser equivalente a ▪ equivaler a

to **tap a (tele)phone line** ▪ to tap a phone ▪ to wiretap ▪ to bug a telephone pinchar un teléfono ▪ pinchar una línea telefónica

to **tap one's fingers** ▪ to strum one's fingers toquetear

to **tap someone on the shoulder** llamar a alguien en el hombro

tap water *el* agua del grifo

tape dispenser 1. *(small for wrapping gifts, etc.)* portarollo de cinta **2.** *(large, with handle, for taping cardboard boxes)* precintadora

tape measure ▪ measuring tape metro ▪ cinta métrica

tape recorder *el* reproductor de cintas ▪ grabadora

to **target civilians** hacer el blanco en los civiles ▪ hacer que los civiles son el blanco

target of terrorist attacks blanco de ataques terroristas

tart apple manzana ácida ➤ The recipe calls for cored tart apples. ▪ The recipe calls for tart apples with the core removed. La receta exige manzanas ácidas, sin corazón.

task force grupo de trabajo

to **taste awful** ▪ to taste terrible saber horrible ▪ saber a rayos (y centellas) ▪ saber terriblemente mal ▪ *(L. Am.)* saber a huácala

to **taste good** saber bien ▪ estar bueno ▪ *(wine)* tener buena boca ➤ This wine tastes good. ▪ This is good wine. Este vino tiene buena boca.

to **taste like** saber a ➤ What does milk from a box taste like? ¿A qué sabe la leche en una caja? ➤ It tastes like milk to me. A mí me sabe a leche.

to be a **taste of what was coming** ser un adelanto de lo que se avecinaba ▪ ser un adelanto de lo que pasaría ▪ ser un adelanto de lo que se venía encima

to **taste terrible** ▪ to taste awful saber terroríficamente mal ▪ saber terriblemente mal ▪ saber penoso ▪ saber a rayos (y centellas)

to be **tastefully done** ▪ to be done in good taste estar hecho con buen gusto

tax assessor tasador(-a) de hacienda

tax audit *la* intervención fiscal

tax base *la* base imponible

tax cut rebaja fiscal ➤ *(news item)* German government delays tax cut (in order) to rebuild areas devastated by floods. El gobierno alemán aplaza la rebaja fiscal para reconstruir las zonas arrasadas por las riadas.

tax deduction *la* desgravación

tax deduction: to be able to be declared as a ~ desgravar ➤ *(news item)* Children under three can be declared as a deduction of a hundred euros. Los hijos de menores de tres años desgravarán cien euros.

tax haven paraíso fiscal

taxi stand parada de taxi

to **teach English** dar clases de inglés

to **teach first grade** ▪ to be a first grade teacher ser profesor(a) de primero

to **teach philosophy** profesar filosofía *("Profesar" always implies "filosofía.")* ➤ Immanuel Kant taught philosophy at the University of Koenigsberg. Immanuel Kant profesó filosofía en la Universidad de Koenigsberg.

teacher's pet preferido(-a) del profesor ▪ preferido(-a) de la profesora

team sport juego de equipo

to **tear down a building** ▪ to tear a building down ▪ to raze a building derrumbar un edificio ▪ arrasar un edificio ▪ tirar un edificio ➤ They tore down the building. ▪ They tore the building down. Derrumbaron el edificio. ▪ Tiraron el edificio. ➤ They tore it down. Lo derrumbaron. ▪ Lo tiraron.

tear in one's clothing: to have a ~ ▪ to get a tear in one's clothing tener una rotura en la ropa ▪ tener un rasgón en la ropa ▪ *(Sp.)* tener un siete (en la ropa) ▪ hacérsele un siete (en la ropa) ➤ I have a tear in my T-shirt pocket. Tengo una rotura en el bolsillo de mi camiseta. ▪ Tengo un rasgón en el bolsillo de mi camiseta.

to **tear one's clothing** ▪ to rip one's clothing rompérsele la ropa ▪ rasgársele la ropa ➤ Oops, I tore my shirt. ▪ Oops, I ripped my shirt. ¡Anda! ¡Se me ha roto la camisa! ▪ ¡Anda! ¡Se me rasgó la camisa!

to **tear (out) a page from** ▪ to tear a page out of arrancar una página de ➤ Some of the pages have been torn out of the book. Algunas páginas han sido arrancadas del libro. ▪ Algunas páginas se han arrancado del libro. ➤ She tore the flyleaf out of her missal and wrote a note on it. Ella arrancó la hoja de guarda de su misal y escribió una nota en ella.

to **tear something to pieces** ▪ to tear up something ▪ to tear something up ▪ to tear something to shreds ▪ to rip something to shreds hacer algo trizas ▪ descuartizar algo

to **tear something to shreds** ▪ to tear something all to pieces ▪ to rip something to shreds hacer trizas

to **tear up something** ▪ to tear something up ▪ to tear something to pieces hacer trizas algo ▪ hacer pedazos algo ▪ hacer pedacitos algo ▪ despedazar algo ➤ The puppy tore up the newspaper. ▪ The puppy tore the newspaper up. El perrito hizo trizas el periódico.

technological marvel prodigio de la técnica

teddy bear *el* peluche

to **tee into a street** ▪ to end at a street morir en una calle ▪ desembocar en una calle ➤ Avenida de los Shiris tees into Avenida Seis de Diciembre. ▪ Avenida de los Shiris ends at Avenida Seis de Diciembre. La Avenida de los Shiris muere en la Avenida Seis de Diciembre. ▪ La Avenida de los Shiris termina en la Avenida Seis de Diciembre.

teenage slang *el* argot juvenil

to **teeter on the brink** tambalearse ➤ The government is teetering on the brink. El gobierno se tambalea.

telephone book ▪ telephone directory *(Sp.)* guía telefónica

telephone jack clavija telefónica

telephone pole poste telefónico

telephone tap escucha telefónica

the **telephone went dead** ▪ the phone went dead se cortó la línea ▪ se cortó el teléfono

television commentator ▪ TV commentator *el, la* comentarista de televisión

television crew ▪ TV crew equipo de televisión

television program ▪ television show ▪ TV show *el* programa de televisión ▪ programa televisivo

television series ▪ TV series *la* serie de televisión

television set ▪ TV set *el* televisor

television show ▪ TV show ▪ television program *el* programa de televisión ▪ programa televisivo ➤ My favorite show comes on at eight. Pasan mi programa favorito a las ocho.

to **tell a joke** contar un chiste

to **tell a lie** contar una mentira ▪ decir una mentira

to **tell a story 1.** contar una historia **2.** *(children's story)* contar un cuento ➤ Mark Twain, like all great writers, told the stories that only he could tell. Mark Twain, como todos los grandes escritores, contó historias como sólo él podía contarlas. ➤ Momma, tell us a story! ¡Mamá, cuéntanos un cuento!

to **tell apart** distinguir ➤ My sister has twin daughters who are difficult to tell apart. Mi hermana tiene hijas gemelas, a quienes cuesta mucho distinguir. ➤ It is difficult to tell them apart. Cuesta mucho distinguirlas.

to **tell by (means of)** ▪ to be able to tell by saberse por ➤ You can tell the age of an animal by examining its teeth. Se sabe la edad de un animal por sus dientes.

to **tell everything** hablarlo todo

to **tell everything to someone** hablárselo todo a alguien

tell her! *(tú)* ¡díselo (a ella)! ▪ *(usted)* ¡dígaselo (a ella)!

tell her to come in! ▪ have her come in invítale a pasar ▪ (dígale) que entre

tell him! *(tú)* ¡díselo (a él)! ▪ *(usted)* ¡dígaselo (a él)!

tell him for me that... dile de mi parte que... ▪ dígale de mi parte... ▪ *(coll.)* le dice de mi parte

to **tell him the score 1.** *(literal)* decirle el resultado (final) **2.** *(figurative)* dictarle la ley

to **tell someone to do something** decirle a alguien que haga algo ➤ Tell her to do it. *(tú)* Dile (a ella) que lo haga. ▪ *(usted)*

Dígale (a ella) que lo haga. ➤ I told her to (do it). Le dije (a ella) que lo hiciera.

tell him to come in! ▪ have him come in invítale a pasar ▪ (dígale) que entre

tell it to the Marines! ▪ go tell it to the Marines! cuéntaselo a tu abuelita ▪ ¡a otro perro con ese hueso!

to **tell jokes** contar chistes ▪ gastar bromas

tell me! *(tú)* ¡dime! ▪ *(usted)* ¡dígame!

tell me about... háblame de...

tell me about it *(tú)* cuéntamelo ▪ *(usted)* cuéntemelo

tell me all about it cuéntamelo todo ▪ cuéntame todo (de esto) ▪ cuéntame todo (sobre esto) ▪ cuéntame la jugada

tell me what you boast about, and I'll tell you what you lack *(saying)* dime de qué presumes y te diré de qué careces

tell me what you mean *(tú)* dime lo que quieres decir ▪ explícate ▪ *(usted)* dígame lo que (usted) quiere decir ▪ explíquese

to **tell on someone** chivar a alguien ➤ Don't tell my mom. Que no chives a mi madre.

to **tell one about it** contárselo a uno ➤ Tell me about it. Cuéntamelo.

to **tell one's fortune** decirle a alguien la buenaventura ▪ echarle a alguien la buenaventura

to **tell someone about something** contarle algo a alguien

to **tell someone everything** ▪ to unburden oneself to someone decírselo todo a alguien ▪ contárselo todo a alguien ▪ vaciar el costal a alguien ▪ vaciar el saco a alguien

to **tell someone flat out (that...)** decirle a alguien lisa y llanamente (que...) ▪ decirle a alguien de plano ▪ decirle a alguien sin tapujos (que...)

to **tell someone flat out what...** decirle a alguien lisa y llanamente lo que... ▪ decirle a alguien de plano lo que... ▪ decirle a alguien sin tapujos lo que...

to **tell someone off** cantarle las cuarenta a alguien

to **tell someone something** decir algo a alguien ➤ I want to tell you something. Quiero decirte una cosa. ▪ Te quiero decir una cosa. ➤ Did you tell her?-No, I didn't say anything to her. ¿Le dijiste (a ella)?-No, no le dije nada.

to **tell someone something in confidence** ▪ to tell something to someone in confidence hacerle confidencias a alguien ▪ decirle a alguien algo en confidencia ▪ decirle a alguien algo en confianza ➤ I've told her some very personal things in confidence. Le he hecho confidencias muy delicadas.

to **tell someone something straight out** ▪ to tell someone flat out hablarle claro a alguien

to **tell someone something to his face** decirle a alguien algo a la cara

to **tell someone to do something** decirle a alguien que haga algo ➤ My professor told me to read *Cuentos de la Selva* by Quiroga. Mi profesora (de la universidad) me dijo que leyera *Cuentos de la Selva* de Quiroga.

to **tell someone what time it is** decir la hora ▪ *(Arg., Uru., coll.)* tirarle las agujas ➤ Could you tell me what time it is? ▪ Do you know what time it is? ¿Podría decirme qué hora es? ▪ ¿Podrías decirme la hora? ▪ ¿Me tirás las agujas?

to **tell someone what to do 1.** to give someone instructions decir a alguien lo que tiene que hacer ▪ decir a alguien qué tiene que hacer **2.** *(imperiously)* to boss someone around mangonear a alguien ▪ mandonear a alguien ➤ *(1950s song)* And then the witch doctor, he told me what to do. Y entonces el curandero, me dijo lo que tenía que hacer. ▪ Y entonces el curandero me dijo qué tenía que hacer.

to **tell someone where to get off** *(euphemism)* ▪ to tell someone to go to hell ▪ to tell someone to go take a walk decirle a alguien que se vaya a pasear ▪ mandar a alguien a pasear

to **tell someone's fortune** decirle a alguien la buenaventura ▪ echarle a alguien la buenaventura

to **tell that...** ▪ to detect that... ▪ to notice that... darse cuenta de que... ▪ notarse que... ➤ I can't tell that English is not your native language. No puedo darme cuenta de que inglés no es tu lengua materna. ➤ You can't tell. No se nota.

to **tell the difference** apreciar la diferencia ➤ You can't tell the difference. No se aprecia la diferencia. ▪ No se nota.

to **tell the difference between** distinguir entre ➤ Can you tell the difference between canola oil and olive oil? ¿Puedes distinguir entre el aceite de canola y el aceite de oliva?

to **tell them apart** distinguirlos

to **tell time** leer el reloj ▪ leer la hora ➤ I learned to tell time when I was seven. Aprendí a leer el reloj cuando tenía siete años. ▪ Aprendí a leer la hora cuando tenía siete años.

tell you what ▪ I'll tell you what ¿qué tal si...? ▪ ¿qué te parece si...?

temperate climate clima templado ▪ clima cálido

tempers flared los ánimos se caldearon

tempest in a teapot *la* tempestad en un vaso de agua ▪ tormenta en un vaso de agua

temple pieces *(of a pair of glasses)* varillas

temples dripping with perspiration ▪ temples dripping with sweat *las* sienes chorreantes

temporary address *la* dirección temporal

temporary loss of consciousness ▪ momentary loss of consciousness pérdida temporal de la conciencia

temporary loss of memory pérdida temporal de la memoria

temporary permit permiso temporal

temporary status estado temporal

to **tempt fate** tentar a la suerte ➤ Let's wait for the light. I don't want to tempt fate with my knee. Vamos a esperar el semáforo. No quiero tentar a la suerte con mi rodilla.

to **tend to** tender a ▪ inclinarse a

to **tend to be** tender a ser ▪ soler ser ➤ It tends to be slow. Suele ser lento.

to **tend to do something** tender a hacer algo ▪ ser propenso a hacer algo ▪ tener propensión a hacer una cosa ▪ propender a hacer algo ➤ The candidates tend to exaggerate. Los candidatos son propensos a exagerar. ▪ Los candidatos tienden a exagerar. ➤ *(Unamuno of Renan)* He tends not to see beyond the humanity of Jesus. Propende a no ver más que la humanidad de Jesús.

tender loving care: to need a lot of ~ ▪ to need a lot of TLC necesitar muchos mimos y besos ▪ necesitar muchos besos y mimos ▪ necesitar unos mimitos y besitos ▪ necesitar algunos mimitos y besitos

to be **tenderhearted** ▪ to be softhearted ser blando de corazón ▪ tener un corazón blando

tennis court campo de tenis ▪ pista de tenis

tens of thousands of people decenas de miles de personas

tense moments momentos de tensión ▪ momentos de nervios ➤ There were some tense moments in the negotiations. Hubo momentos de tensión en las negociaciones.

tension-filled atmosphere *el* ambiente lleno de tensión

tensions have lessened ▪ tensions have been reduced ▪ tensions have been eased *la* tensión se ha reducido

term of office mandato ➤ Clinton is the first Democrat since Roosevelt to win a second term. Clinton es el primer demócrata que gana un segundo mandato desde Roosevelt.

terminal cancer *el* cáncer terminal

terminal illness: to have a ~ tener una enfermedad terminal ▪ tener una enfermedad mortal

terminally ill: to become ~ ▪ to fall terminally ill enfermarse de muerte

to **terminate a subscription** ▪ to stop subscribing darse de baja

to **terminate one's membership in an organization** ▪ to quit an organization ▪ to drop out of an organization ▪ to sever one's membership in an organization darse de baja en una organización ▪ *(Mex.)* renunciar a su membresía en una organización ▪ dejar su membresía en una organización

terra firma ▪ dry land tierra firme

terraced roof *(common in Latin America and used as porches)* ▪ flat roof azotea

to be **terribly disappointed (by...)** ▪ to be terribly disappointed with ▪ to be really disappointed ▪ to be really let down ▪ to feel really let down estar muy decepcionado de... ▪ estar muy decepcionado con... ▪ estar muy disgustado con... ▪ estar muy disgustado de... ▪ estar muy descontento con... ▪ llevarse un buen chasco ▪ pegarse un buen chasco

territorial waters *las* aguas jurisdiccionales
terrorist act ▪ act of terrorism hecho terrorista
terrorist group banda terrorista
test of one's leadership prueba de la gestión de uno
test pattern carta de ajuste
test pilot piloto de prueba
to **test routinely for** soler hacer pruebas para
test tube probeta
test-tube baby *el* bebé de probeta
to **test with a fork** ▪ to perforate with a fork pinchar con un tenedor
to be **tested on** ser probado en ▪ probarse en ➤ *(news item)* Europe prohibits cosmetics tested on animals. Europa prohíbe los cosméticos probados en los animales. ➤ Later this year the procedure will be tested on humans. Más tarde este año el procedimiento será probado en humanos. ➤ When the procedure is tested on humans... Cuando el procedimiento se pruebe en humanos...
to **testify against** declarar contra ➤ *(news item)* Sub-Saharan prostitutes in Casa de Campo refuse to testify against the mafias. Las subsaharianas que se prostituían en la Casa de Campo se niegan a declarar contra las mafias.
to **testify before a grand jury** declarar ante un gran jurado ▪ rendir cuentas ante un gran jurado
than all get-out: to be busier ~ *(coll.)* estar más ocupado que una colmena ➤ I'm busier than all get-out. Estoy más ocupado que las abejas de una colmena.
than I (am) que yo ➤ He's taller than I am. Es más alto que yo. *("Than me" is extremely common but incorrect. "Than" is a conjunction, not a preposition, and cannot take an object.)*
than I had planned to de lo que había pensado ▪ de lo que había planeado
than I used to de lo que solía ▪ de lo que acostumbraba
than I was at that age ▪ than I was at the same age de lo que era a la misma edad
than I was led to believe de lo que me hizo creer ▪ de lo que me hicieron creer
than it usually is de lo que suele ser ➤ This November, it's been rainier than it usually is. Este noviembre ha sido más lluvioso de lo que suele ser.
than meets the eye: there is more (to something) ~ hay más en algo de lo que se ve ➤ There is more to it than meets the eye. Hay más en esto de lo que se ve.
than one knows what to do with para tirar para arriba ▪ para tirar a la chuña ➤ He has more money than he knows what to do with. Tiene dinero para tirar para arriba. ▪ Tiene dinero para tirar a la chuña.
than one usually is de lo que acostumbra a ser ➤ That morning the bus driver was nicer than he usually is. Aquella mañana el chofer del autobús era más amable de lo que acostumbra (a ser).
than one would think ▪ than you would think de lo que se pensaría
than previously believed de lo que se creía
than previously thought de lo que se pensaba
than we were led to believe de lo que nos hizo creer ▪ de lo que no hicieron creer
than you think *(tú)* de lo que piensas ▪ *(usted)* de lo que piensa (usted) ▪ de lo que (usted) piensa
than you would think 1. *(than you personally would think)* de lo que pensarías ▪ de lo que (usted) pensaría **2.** than one would think ▪ than would generally be thought de lo que se pensaría
thank God for that gracias a Dios por ser así
thank goodness! ¡menos mal! ▪ ¡bendito sea Dios!
to **thank someone for something** agradecerle a uno por algo
to **thank someone profusely** agradecerle a alguien vivamente
thank you anyway ▪ thanks anyway ▪ thanks just the same gracias por todos modos ▪ gracias por todas formas
thank you for all you have done for me gracias por todo lo que has hecho por mí
thank you for all your help gracias por lo que me has ayudado
thank you for offering ▪ thanks for offering *(tú)* gracias por ofrecerte ▪ *(usted)* gracias por ofrecerse
thank you for the compliment gracias por el cumplido
thank you for your cooperation gracias por su colaboración
thank you just the same *(in response to a sincere offer)* gracias de todos modos ▪ gracias de todas formas
thanks a bunch ▪ thanks a million ▪ a thousand thanks gracias un montón ▪ te lo agradezco un montón ▪ mil gracias
thanks anyway ▪ thank you anyway ▪ thanks just the same gracias de todos modos ▪ gracias de todas formas
thanks for the lift ▪ thanks for the ride gracias por llevarme ▪ gracias por traerme ▪ *(Mex.)* gracias por el aventón
thanks for the offer ▪ thanks for your offer gracias por tu ofrecimiento
thanks to gracias a
Thanksgiving Day *(USA, fourth Thursday in November) el* Día de Acción de Gracias
that and other things eso y otras cosas más ▪ eso y más cosas ▪ eso y más ▪ eso y aún más ▪ eso y más aún
that are said to be... que dicen ser...
that being the case eso sí
that blasted... ▪ that damned... ese maldito ▪ de puñetero ▪ puñetero(-a) de marras ➤ That blasted skunk ruined our camping trip. Ese maldito zorrillo arruinó nuestro viaje de campamento.
that business about eso de
that could be ▪ that's possible ▪ maybe so puede que así sea ▪ será eso
that could be... podría ser... ➤ That could be difficult. Eso podría ser difícil.
that could be found que se pudo encontrar ▪ que pudiera hallarse ➤ It was the best gift that could be found. Fue el mejor regalo que se pudo encontrar. ▪ Fue el mejor regalo que pudiera hallarse.
that could be the one ▪ that might be the one puede que sea ese
that could take months podrían pasar meses
that could take weeks podrían pasar semanas
that depends eso depende
that did it! ▪ now it's war! ▪ the war is on! ¡ya estaba armada!
that did the trick eso hizo el truco
that different (from): it's not ~ no hay gran diferencia ➤ *(White House correspondent)* Covering the White House is not that different from covering city hall. No hay gran diferencia entre ser corresponsal en la Casa Blanca y en el ayuntamiento.
that does it! ▪ now it's war! ▪ the war is on! ¡ya está armada!
that doesn't count eso no cuenta
that doesn't say much for... eso no dice mucho a favor de...
that doesn't surprise me at all ▪ that doesn't surprise me a bit no me sorprende nada ▪ no me extraña nada
that explains everything eso lo explica todo
that explains it eso lo explica
that feels so good! ¡qué bien se siente!
that figures (me) lo suponía ▪ (me) lo imagino ▪ (me) lo imaginaba ▪ no me extraña
that goes for you, too ▪ that means you, too (eso) va por ti también ▪ eso también va por ti
...that I can't put my finger on ...con lo que no puedo dar ▪ ...con lo que no consigo dar ➤ She has a certain something that I can't (quite) put my finger on. Ella tiene algo con lo que no puedo dar. ▪ Ella tiene algo con lo que no consigo dar.
***that* I couldn't tell you** yo, de eso, no sé decirte
***that* I don't know** yo, de eso, no sé
that I might have said que yo haya dicho
that is... ▪ I mean ▪ at least por lo menos ▪ al menos ▪ es decir... ➤ I guess it's not so strange to eat flies, for a lizard, that is. Supongo que comer moscas no es tan extraño para una lagartija, por lo menos.
that is one of the reasons why... es una de las razones por las que...
that is one reason why... es una razón por la que...

that is said to be ▪ which is said to be que dice ser
that is when... es entonces cuando
that is where ahí es donde ▪ allí es donde ▪ en eso ➤ That is where I used to live. Ahí es donde solía vivir. ➤ That is where we disagree. En eso es donde no estamos de acuerdo. ▪ Ahí es donde no estamos de acuerdo.
that is why ▪ that's why es por eso que ▪ por eso es que ▪ es por ello que ▪ he aquí por qué ➤ *(Ogden Nash: "The Termite")* Some primeval termite knocked on wood, and tasted it and found it good. And that is why your cousin Mae fell through the parlor floor today. Una termita primigenia tocó madera, y la probó y la encontró buena, y es por eso que tu prima Mae se cayó por el piso de la sala hoy.
that isn't to say that... no es decir que... ▪ *(literary)* no obsta para decir que...
that it is 1. *(main clause)* it certainly is! ¡seguro que sí! ▪ ¡segurísimo! **2.** *(dependent clause)* so as to be... como para que sea... ➤ She lives far enough away that it's a problem to take her home. Su casa queda lo suficientemente lejos como para que sea un problema llevarle a casa.
that it was 1. *(main clause)* it certainly was! seguro que sí ▪ ¡segurísimo! **2.** *(dependent clause)* como para que fuera... ➤ She lived far enough away that it was a problem to take her home. Su casa quedaba lo suficientemente lejos como para que fuera un problema llevarla a su casa.
that kind of thing cosas por el estilo
that looks delicious! ¡qúe buena pinta! ▪ ¡qué pinta tiene!
that makes two of us ¡vaya dos! ▪ ya somos dos ▪ *(more emphatic)* ¡vaya par de dos!
that many... tantos... ➤ It could be difficult to get that many volunteers. Podría ser difícil reunir a tantos voluntarios.
that means you, too ▪ that goes for you, too eso va por ti también ▪ eso también va por ti
that might be expected ▪ that one might expect ▪ that you might expect ▪ which might be expected ▪ which one might expect ▪ which you might expect **1.** *(with a singular antecedent)* que es de suponer **2.** *(with a plural antecedent)* que son de suponer
that might be the one ▪ that could be the one puede que sea ese
that night esa noche ▪ aquella noche ▪ a la noche
that of... el de... ▪ la de...
that one might expect ▪ that you might expect ▪ that might be expected ▪ which one might expect ▪ which you might expect ▪ which might be expected **1.** *(all contexts)* que uno podría esperar **2.** *(with a singular antecedent)* ...que es de suponer **3.** *(with a plural antecedent)* ...que son de suponer
that one might have said ▪ that one may have said que uno haya dicho
that one refers to a lo que se refiere ▪ a los que se refiere ➤ The errors that you refer to Los errores a los que te refieres
that remains to be seen (eso) está por ver
that reminds me! ¡eso me recuerda!
that same day 1. ese mismo día **2.** *(further in the past)* aquel mismo día
that says it all eso lo dice todo
that settles it 1. it's settled ▪ it's decided ya queda decidido ▪ ya queda resuelto ▪ eso lo resuelve ▪ eso lo decide **2.** *(with impatience)* we're not going to talk about it anymore no hay más que hablar ▪ entonces ya está ▪ pues ya está ▪ lo dicho
that should do it 1. that should accomplish it eso debería lograrlo ▪ con eso se debería conseguir ▪ con eso se debería lograr **2.** that should cover it ▪ that should be more than enough ▪ that should be plenty va que chuta ▪ va que se mata
that something ese algo
that sort of thing cosas por el estilo
that still exists que aún existe ▪ que todavía existe
that stuff eso (que hay...) ➤ What is that stuff? ¿Qué es eso?
that sums it up eso lo resume todo
that very day ese mismo día ▪ *(further in the past)* aquel mismo día
that was a long time ago ▪ it was a long time ago eso fue hace mucho tiempo
that was delicious estaba buenísimo ▪ estaba riquísimo ▪ estaba delicioso ▪ me supo a gloria
that was good timing! ▪ that was perfect timing! ¡justo a tiempo! ▪ ¡qué oportuno! ▪ ¡qué sincronización! ▪ ¡vaya cálculo!
that was something to see ▪ it was a sight to see ▪ that was quite a sight ▪ that was a great sight to see fue digno de verlo ▪ era una cosa digna de verse
that was to be expected era de esperarse
that was when... ▪ it was then that... fue entonces cuando...
that wasn't it no era eso
that wasn't the deal ▪ that wasn't what we agreed on (ése) no era el trato
that wasn't what we agreed to ▪ that's not what we agreed to ▪ that wasn't the deal (ése) no era el trato
that way 1. in that way ▪ by doing that de ese modo ▪ de esa manera ▪ de esa forma ▪ así ▪ así pues ▪ entonces **2.** in that direction *(L. Am.)* para allá ▪ por allá ▪ *(Sp.)* por ahí ➤ That way, you'll have some money left over. De ese modo, te quedará algo de dinero. ➤ Because that way, there wouldn't be anyone who could... Porque, de esa manera, no habría nadie que pudiera... ➤ It's that way. Está para allá. ▪ Está para allí. ▪ Queda por allí. ▪ Queda por ahí.
that which ▪ what lo que
that will be difficult if not impossible va a ser difícil, por no decir imposible ▪ va a resultar difícil, por no decir imposible ▪ va a ser complicado, por no decir imposible ▪ va a resultar complicado, por no decir imposible
that will fit this donde quepa esto ➤ Do you have an envelope that will fit this? ¿Tiene un sobre donde quepa esto?
that works for me that suits me me viene bien
that would be different (eso) sería diferente ▪ *(coll.)* otro gallo cantaría
that would be great sería genial ▪ sería estupendo
that would not take long to... *(after a singular antecedent)* que no tardaría en... ▪ *(after a plural antecedent)* que no tardarían en...
that you might expect ▪ that one might expect ▪ that might be expected ▪ which one might expect ▪ which you might expect ▪ which might be expected que es de suponer ▪ que son de suponer
that you refer to *(tú)* a lo(s) que te refieres ▪ a la(s) que te refieres ▪ *(usted)* a lo(s) que usted se refiere ▪ a la(s) que usted se refiere ➤ The errors that you refer to... Los errores a los que te refieres...
that you told me about *(tú)* que me dijiste ▪ *(usted)* que me dijo ➤ I went to the store (that) you told me about. Fui a la tienda que me dijiste.
that'll be all ▪ that's all eso es todo
that'll teach him a lesson eso le enseñará ▪ lo tiene bien empleado ▪ bien empleado le está
that'll teach him who's boss eso le enseñará quien manda
that'll teach you a lesson eso te enseñará ▪ lo tienes bien empleado ▪ bien empleado te está
that's a different kettle of fish eso es harina de otra costal
that's a different story es una historia distinta ▪ es harina de otro costal ▪ es otro cantar
that's a good one es uno de los buenos ▪ es una de las buenas
that's a good question es una buena pregunta
that's a good sign es buena señal ▪ es una buena señal ➤ They called me for an interview, so that's a good sign. Me han llamado para una entrevista, así que eso es buena señal.
that's a lie! ¡eso es mentira!
that's a mouthful ▪ that's pretty long-winded es un parrafón
that's a tough one ▪ that's a tough question está difícil ▪ se las trae
that's about it! ▪ that (about) sums it up no hay más que decir
that's about right ▪ you're not too far off por ahí va la cosa
that's absurd es absurdo ▪ no tiene ni pies ni cabeza ▪ eso no tiene sentido
that's all 1. that's all it is eso es ▪ nada más ▪ es nada más que eso **2.** that'll be all eso es todo ➤ *(Lindbergh)* The engine's thirty revolutions low. What do you make of it? Damp air?-That's all. Nothing mechanical. El motor está treinta

revoluciones por debajo. ¿Cómo te lo explicas? ¿Aire húmedo? Eso es. Nada mecánico.

that's all? ¿nada más?

that's all, folks *(Porky Pig)* eso es todo, amigos

that's all I needed! ¡(justo) lo que me faltaba! ■ ¡(justo) lo que necesitaba! ■ ¡éramos pocos y parió mi abuela!

that's all the more reason to... es razón de más para (que...) ➤ That's all the more reason (for me) to change telephone companies. Es razón de más para cambiar de compañías de teléfono. ➤ That's all the more reason (for you) to change telephone companies. Es razón de más para que cambies de compañías de teléfono. ■ Es razón de más para cambiar de compañías de teléfono.

that's all there is to it! 1. it's that easy! ■ it's as easy as that! así de fácil ■ ¡y punto! ■ y eso es todo ■ y ya está ■ y sanseacabó **2.** and that's all there is to say about it no hay más que decir ■ y no hay más que hablar ■ se acabó ➤ You boil the tomato juice, add the lemon Jell-O® and some spices, and that's all there is to it. Se hierve el zumo de tomate, se añade la gelatina de limón y unas especias, y sanseacabó.

that's all there is to say about it ■ there's nothing else to say about it ■ there's nothing more to say about it no hay más que hablar ■ no hay más que decir

that's all we needed ■ as if we didn't have enough problems (already) ■ as if we didn't have enough problems as it is no cabíamos en casa, y parió la abuela

that's amazing! ¡es asombroso!

that's an understatement ■ that's putting it mildly es un eufemismo

that's another story es otra historia ■ eso es otro canto

that's another thing altogether ■ that's something else again es un capítulo aparte

that's as far as I'm going hasta ahí voy

that's as far back as it'll go *(a car seat)* ■ it won't go back any farther no va más para atrás

that's beautiful! ¡qué hermoso!

that's beside the point no viene al caso ■ está fuera de la cuestión ■ no tiene nada que ver ■ *(coll.)* no viene a cuento

that's bullshit! *(off-color)* ■ that's a crock! ■ horsefeathers! ¡es pura mierda! ■ ¡es puro pedo! ■ *(benign alternative)* es pura mentira ■ *(Arg.)* es un bolazo

that's conjecture es un suponer

that's cool ¡bárbaro! ■ *(Sp.)* ¡es guay!

that's debatable es discutible ■ eso es muy opinable

that's delicious está buenísimo ■ está riquísimo ■ está rico ■ está delicioso ■ está sabroso ■ me sabe a gloria

that's different eso es otra cosa ■ esto es otra cosa

that's easy for *you* to say! ¡tan fácil decirlo!

that's for others to say qué lo digan los demás

that's for sure! ¡qué va a ser cierto!

that's funny! ■ that's strange! ¡qué curioso! ➤ That's funny; I could swear I left my keys here. ¡Qué curioso! Podría jurar que dejé las llaves aquí.

that's going too far se pasa de la raya ■ es un abuso ■ es un por de más ■ se pasa de castaño a oscuro

that's good ■ it's a good thing ¡menos mal! ➤ Oh, well, that's good. Ah, bueno, menos mal.

that's good news about... ■ that's great news about... ¡qué buenas noticias lo de...! ➤ That's good news about (your scholarship)! ■ That's great news about your scholarship! ¡Qué buenas noticias lo de la beca!

that's gratitude for you! ■ what an ingrate! ¡qué agradecimiento!

that's great! ¡qué bien! ■ ¡estupendo! ■ *(Sp.)* ¡qué chachi! ■ *(Mex.)* ¡qué bueno!

that's great news about...! ■ that's good news about...! ¡qué buenas noticias lo de...! ■ ¡qué gran notición lo de...!

that's gross! ¡qué asco!

that's hard to believe ■ it's hard to believe cuesta creerlo ■ no paso a creerlo

that's her problem ese es su problema (de ella) ■ allá se las componga (ella)

that's his problem ese es su problema (de él) ■ allá se las componga (él)

that's how... ■ that's the way... así es como... ■ eso es como... ➤ That's how I would translate it. Así es como yo la traduciría. *("La" refers to "la frase.")* ➤ That's how you have to do it. Eso es como hay que hacerlo.

that's how I like it ■ that's the way I like it así me gusta ■ así me gusta a mí

that's how it is ■ that's the way it is así están las cosas ■ es así

that's how it is, and if you don't like it, tough! así son las cosas y si no te gusta, mala suerte ■ estas son lentejas (si las quieres las comes, y si no, las dejas)

that's how it is, and there's nothing more to say about it ■ that's the way it is, and there's nothing more to say about it así son las cosas, y no hay más que decir (sobre el tema) ■ esto es así y no hay más cáscaras ■ eso es así y no hay más cáscaras

that's how it ought to be así debería ser

that's how it used to be done ■ that's the way it used to be done ■ that's how it was formerly done ■ that's the way it was formerly done así se hacía antes

that's how it used to be made ■ that's the way it used to be made así se hacía antes

that's how it was formerly made ■ that's the way it was formerly made así se hacía antes

that's how they used to do it ■ that's the way they used to do it así se hacía antes

that's how they used to make it ■ that's the way they used to make it así se hacía antes ■ *(something manufactured)* así se fabricaba antes ■ *(commerically processed food)* así se elaboraba antes ■ *(esp. food)* así se preparaba antes

that's it 1. that's right así es **2.** that's all there is to say about it no hay más que decir **3.** it's over se acabó **4.** that's all eso es todo

that's it for today ■ that's all for today por hoy nada más ■ aquí vamos a quedar hoy ■ aquí quedamos ■ lo dejamos aquí ■ se acaba por hoy

that's just all there is to it! 1. and that's all there is to say about it ■ and that's that ¡y no hay más que hablar! ■ y punto final **2.** and that's all ¡y sanseacabó! ■ y punto final ➤ We have to add that expression to the dictionary this minute. That's just all there is to it! Tenemos que añadir esa expresión al diccionario ahora mismo. ¡Y no hay más que hablar!

that's just it ahí está el meollo del asunto ■ ahí está la madre del cordero

that's just the tip of the iceberg es sólo la punta del iceberg

that's (just) the way I am ■ that's just how I am así soy ■ yo soy así

that's just what I was thinking eso es justo lo que pensaba

that's life ■ c'est la vie ■ that's the way the cookie crumbles así es la vida

that's like... eso es lo mismo que... ■ eso es como... ■ eso es igual que...

that's mean! ¡qué malo! ■ ¡qué cruel! ■ ¡es una maldad! ■ ¡es una crueldad!

that's more like it! ■ now that's more like it! ■ now you're talking! eso sí que se llama hablar ■ eso está mejor ■ ahora sí me gusta (más)

that's my business ■ it's my business es asunto mío ■ es cuenta mía

that's neither here nor there ni me va ni me viene *(In Spanish the pronoun can vary.)*

that's not a bad idea no me parece mala idea

that's not a bad thing no está nada mal

that's not good enough for her ■ that doesn't satisfy her a ella no le basta ■ no le satisface ■ no le llega ■ no le llena ■ no le mola

that's not good enough for him ■ that doesn't satisfy him a él no le basta ■ no le satisface ■ no le llega ■ no le llena ■ no le mola

that's not how it's done no se hace así

that's not it ■ it's not that no es eso

that's not my concern eso no me atañe

that's not saying a whole lot ■ that's not saying much (eso) no es decir gran cosa ■ (eso) no es decir mucho

that's not saying much ■ that's not saying a whole lot (eso) no es decir gran cosa ■ (eso) no es decir mucho
that's not to say that... no quiere decir que... ■ *(journalistic)* no obsta para que...
that's not what I had in mind no es lo que tenía en mente ■ no es la cosa que tenía en mente
that's not what we agreed to ■ that wasn't what we agreed to ■ that wasn't the deal (ése) no era el trato
that's okay **1.** that's good está bien **2.** no problem ■ no harm done no pasa nada ■ no hay (ningún) problema ■ no importa
that's okay, don't worry about it no pasa nada, no te preocupes
that's one of the reasons why... es una de las razones por las que...
that's one reason why... es una razón por la que...
that's out of the question está fuera de discusión ■ ni hablar
that's really something eso ya es algo
that's right eso es ■ efectivamente ■ así es ■ es correcto
that's scary vaya susto ■ qué susto
that's something else again ■ that's another thing altogether ■ that's something else again es un capítulo aparte
that's something else altogether ■ that's another thing altogether ■ that's something else again ■ that's a different thing altogether es un tema totalmente diferente ■ es un capítulo aparte
that's the kind of thing I'm talking about es de lo que estoy hablando
that's the last thing I expected eso es lo último que (me) esperaba
that's the least I can do ■ it's the least I can do es lo menos que puedo hacer
that's the least I could do ■ it's the least I could do es lo menos que podía hacer ■ es lo menos que pude hacer
that's the least of it (eso) es lo de menos
that's the limit! ■ that's the last straw! ¡esto es el colmo! ■ ¡esto es la gota que colma el vaso! ■ ¡esto pasa de castaño oscuro! ■ ¡hasta aquí hemos llegado! ■ ¡no faltaba más! ■ ¡faltaría más!
that's the main thing es lo primero
that's the price you have to pay eso te lo tienes que pagar tú
that's the reason why... es la razón por la que... ■ es el motivo por el que...
that's the rumor eso se comenta ■ eso se cuenta ■ eso se dice
that's the understatement of the year has descubierto la pólvora con eso ■ has descubierto el motor de agua ■ es el eufemismo del año
that's the very reason why ■ for that very reason por eso mismo ■ precisamente por eso
that's the way I am ■ that's just the way I am ■ that's just how I am yo soy así ■ así soy
that's the way it is ■ that's how it is así están las cosas ■ es así
that's the way it is, and there's nothing more to say about it ■ that's how it is, and there's nothing more to say about it es así y no hay más que hablar al respecto ■ esto es así y no hay más cáscaras ■ eso es así y no hay más cáscaras
that's the way it used to be done ■ that's how it used to be done ■ that's the way it was formerly done ■ that's how it was formerly done así se hacía antes
that's the way it was formerly made ■ that's how it used to be made ■ that's how it was formerly made **1.** *(food)* así se preparaba antes ■ así se elaboraba antes ■ así se hacía antes **2.** *(manufactured good)* así se fabricaba antes ■ así se hacía antes
that's the way the ball bounces ■ that's the way the cookie crumbles así es la vida
that's the way the cookie crumbles ■ that's the way the ball bounces ■ that's life así es la vida
that's the way they used to do it ■ that's how they used to do it así se hacía antes
that's the way they used to make it ■ that's how they used to make it así se hacía antes **1.** *(food)* así se preparaba antes ■ así se elaboraba antes ■ así se hacía antes **2.** *(manufactured good)* así se fabricaba antes ■ así se hacía antes
that's the whole problem (ése) es todo el problema
that's their problem ése es su problema ■ que se las arreglen como puedan ■ *(Sp.)* allá se las compongan
that's to be expected es de esperarse
that's too bad es una pena ■ ¡qué pena! ■ ¡qué mala suerte!
that's very kind of you ■ it's very kind of you es muy amable por su parte ■ qué amable de tu parte
that's water under the bridge ya ha pasado a la historia
that's weird! ■ (how) weird! ■ how strange! ■ how odd! ¡qué raro! ■ ¡qué cosa tan rara!
that's what burns me up (esto) es lo que me quema ■ (esto) es lo que me revienta ■ (esto) es lo que me saca de mis casillas ■ (esto) es lo que me saca de quicio ■ (esto) es lo que me hace perder los estribos ■ esto es lo que me cabrea ■ *(off-color)* (esto) es lo que me pone de mala hostia
that's what everyone calls me ■ that's what they call me así me llaman
that's what friends are for para eso son los amigos
that's what happened así se hizo
that's what I did es lo que hice ■ eso hice
that's what I figured lo suponía (yo)
that's what I get for... esto es lo que me pasa por... ■ esto me pasa por... ➤ That's what I get for sleeping in and missing class. Esto es lo que me pasa por quedarme a dormir y perder la clase.
that's what *I* say ¡eso digo yo!
that's what I thought (eso) es lo que pensé
that's what I thought, anyway ■ that's what I thought, at any rate eso creía, por lo menos
that's what I wanted to tell you *(a ti)* eso fue lo que quise decirte ■ *(a usted)* eso fue lo que quise decirle
that's what I was afraid of (eso) es lo que me temía
that's what I was doing es lo que (yo) estaba haciendo
that's what I was thinking es lo que (yo) estaba pensando ■ es lo que (yo) pensaba
that's what I'm afraid of eso es lo que me temo
that's what I'm here for para eso estoy
that's what it's all about es de lo que se trata ■ es todo de lo que se trata
that's what they call me ■ that's what I go by así me llaman ■ así me dicen
that's what they say así dicen ■ eso se cuenta
that's what you have to do eso es lo que hay que hacer ➤ That's what you have to do, you write to them saying... Eso es lo que hay que hacer, escribirles una carta diciendo...
that's what you've been saying for... ■ you've been saying that for... estás diciendo lo mismo desde hace ■ hace (*x tiempo*) que estás diciendo lo mismo ➤ That's what you've been saying for twenty years. ■ You've been saying that for twenty years. Hace veinte años que dices lo mismo. ■ Hace veinte años que estás diciendo lo mismo.
that's why ■ that is why por eso es que ■ es por eso que ■ es por lo que ■ por eso
that's *you* ése eres tú ■ así eres tú ■ ése es usted ■ así es usted
that's your problem *(tú)* (eso) es tu problema ■ es cosa tuya ■ *(Sp.)* allá te las compongas ■ arréglatelas como puedas ■ allá tú ■ *(usted)* (eso) es su problema ■ es cosa suya ■ arrégleselas como pueda ■ allá usted ■ *(Sp.)* allá se las componga
the accused ■ the alleged el presunto ■ el acusado ➤ The accused killer El presunto asesino
the best by far el mejor con diferencia ■ el mejor con mucho
the best known el más conocido ■ la más conocida
to be **the best (one) there is** **1.** ser el mejor que hay ■ ser la mejor que hay **2.** to be the one who does something best ser él que mejor lo hace ■ ser la que mejor lo hace
the bigger, the better cuanto más grande, mejor ■ *(coll.)* caballo grande, ande o no ande
the bill, please la nota, por favor ■ la cuenta, por favor ■ *(tú)* me cobras, por favor ■ *(usted)* me cobra, por favor *("Tú" is acceptable if the waiter is young.)*
the day before el día antes
the closer one gets to something ■ the closer to something one gets... cuanto más uno se acerca a... ■ mientras más uno se

acerca a... ➤ The closer you get to sixty, the younger it seems. Cuanto más se acerca uno a los sesenta, más joven parece.

the closest one to 1. *(in distance)* el más cercano a ▪ la más cercana a 2. *(in resemblance)* el más parecido a ▪ la más parecida a

the closest thing (there is) to lo más parecido a ▪ lo que más se aproxima a ▪ como ➤ Exercise is the closest thing there is to a medical panacea. El ejercicio es lo más parecido a una panacea médica. ▪ El ejercicio es lo que más se aproxima a una panacea médica. ➤ *(ad for cheap flights)* The closest thing to having wings Los más parecido a tener alas ▪ (Es) como tener alas

the dead los difuntos ▪ los muertos ▪ los fallecidos

the deceased *(Sp.)* el fallecido ▪ la fallecida ▪ *(L. Am.)* el finado ▪ la finada

the eighteenth ▪ 18th 1. el decimoctavo (18°) ▪ la decimoctava (18ª) 2. *(of the month)* el dieciocho

the eighth ▪ 8th 1. el octavo (8°) ▪ la octava (8ª) 2. *(of the month)* el ocho

the elderly los ancianos

the eleventh ▪ 11th 1. el décimoprimero ▪ el undécimo (11°) ▪ la décimoprimera ▪ la undécima (11ª) 2. *(of the month)* el once

the fact that... que...

the fifteenth ▪ 15th 1. el decimoquinto (15°) ▪ la decimoquinta (15ª) 2. *(of the month)* el quince

the fifth ▪ 5th 1. el quinto (5°) ▪ la quinta (5ª) 2. *(of the month)* el cinco

the fiftieth ▪ 50th el quincuagésimo (50°) ▪ la quincuagésima (50ª)

the first ▪ 1st el primero (1°) ▪ la primera (1ª) 2. *(of the month)* el primero ▪ el uno

the following *(noun)* lo siguiente ▪ *(adjective) el, la* siguiente

the former ése(a) ▪ el antiguo ▪ la antigua

the fortieth ▪ 40th el cuadragésimo (40°) ▪ la cuadragésima (40ª)

the fourteenth ▪ 14th 1. el decimocuarto (14°) ▪ la decimocuarta (14ª) 2. *(of the month)* el catorce

the fourth ▪ 4th 1. el cuarto (4°) ▪ la cuarta (4ª) 2. *(of the month)* el cuatro

the good life la vida en rosa

the half of it: you don't know ~ *(tú)* no sabes ni la media ▪ *(usted)* (usted) no sabe ni la media

the hard way: to do something ~ hacer algo de la forma más difícil

the hard way: to learn something ~ aprender por las malas ▪ aprender algo a los golpes

the hots: to have the ~ ▪ to be turned on sexually tener un calentón ▪ estar caliente

the impossible lo imposible

the Joneses 1. *(Mr. and Mrs. Jones)* el matrimonio Jones 2. *(the Jones family)* los Jones

the Joneses: to keep up with ~ no ser menos que los demás

the late el fallecido ▪ el finado ▪ la fallecida ▪ la finada ➤ The late John F. Kennedy El fallecido John F. Kennedy ▪ El finado John F. Kennedy

the last thing I (had) wanted lo último que hubiese deseado ▪ lo último que hubiera deseado ➤ That's the last thing I wanted. Es lo último que (yo) hubiese deseado. ▪ Es lo último que (yo) hubiera deseado.

the later it gets cuanto más tarde es ➤ The later it gets, the more people there are. Cuanto más tarde es, más gente hay.

the latter éste ▪ ésta

the least you could have done is lo mínimo que podrías haber hecho es

the less cuanto menos

the less said, the better cuanto menos se diga, mejor ▪ a menos palabras, menos pleitos

the longer mientras más ▪ cuanto más (tiempo) ➤ The longer we wait, the more impatient we get. Cuanto más esperamos, más impacientes nos ponemos. ▪ Cuanto más esperamos, más impacientes nos volvemos.

the middle one ▪ the one in the middle el del medio ▪ la del medio

the more 1. *(singular)* cuanto más 2. *(plural)* cuantos más ➤ *(Victor Hugo)* The more I know about people, the more I love my animals. Cuánto más conozco a las personas, más quiero a mis animales.

the more I try, the more... cuanto más trato, más... ▪ cuanto más (lo) intento, más...

the more people, the more... cuanto más gente, más...

the more, the better cuanto más, mejor ▪ mientras más mejor

the more, the merrier cuanto más, mejor

the most 1. the best el más ▪ la más 2. the majority más ➤ I like this one the most. ▪ I like this one the best. Éste me gusta más. ▪ El que más me gusta es éste. ➤ In our house, my wife writes the most checks. En nuestra casa mi esposa extiende más cheques.

the most apt to ▪ the most likely to ▪ the most prone to el más propenso a ▪ la más propensa a

the most likely to ▪ the most apt to ▪ the most prone to el más propenso a ▪ la más propenso a

the new... el último... ➤ *(headline)* The new Clinton El último Clinton

the next day ▪ (on) the following day al día siguiente ▪ al otro día

the next morning ▪ (on) the following morning a la mañana siguiente

the nineteenth ▪ 19th 1. el decimonoveno (19°) ▪ la decimonovena (19ª) 2. *(of the month)* el diecinueve

the ninth ▪ 9th 1. el noveno (9°) ▪ la novena (9ª) 2. *(of the month)* el nueve

the one ▪ the only el único ➤ The one pickpocketing I have witnessed happened on the crowded platform of a train station. El único robo de cartera del que he sido testigo tuvo lugar en un andén atestado (de gente) de la estación de tren.

the one in the middle ▪ the middle one el del medio ▪ la del medio

the one of el de ▪ la de ➤ Of all these photos, the one of you is the best. De todas estas fotos, la de ti es la mejor. ➤ Of all these photos, yours (the one you took) is the best. De todas estas fotos, la tuya (la que sacaste) es la mejor.

the one someone likes el que le gusta ▪ la que le gusta ➤ The one he really likes is... El que de veras le gusta (a él) es... ▪ La que de veras le gusta (a él) es... ➤ The one she really likes is... El que de veras le gusta (a ella) es... ▪ La que de veras le gusta (a ella) es...

to be **the one who** 1. *(he)* ser el que ▪ ser quien 2. *(she)* ser la que ▪ ser quien ➤ His mother was the one who took it the worst. Su madre era la que lo llevaba peor. ▪ Su madre era quien lo llevaba peor.

the one who caused... el que causó... ▪ el que provocó... ▪ el causante de... ▪ la que causó... ▪ la que provocó... ▪ la causante de...

the one with el de ▪ la de ➤ The one with the pipe ▪ The one who's smoking the pipe El de la pipa ➤ The one with the red blouse ▪ The one who's wearing the red blouse La de la blusa roja

the one you told me about él del que me hablaste ▪ ella de la que me hablaste ➤ Is he the one you told me about? ¿Es él del que me hablaste? ➤ Is she the one you told me about? ¿Es ella de la que me hablaste?

the one you want *(tú)* el que quieras ▪ la que quieras ▪ *(usted)* el que quiera (usted) ▪ la que quiera (usted)

the ones you want *(tú)* los que quieras ▪ las que quieras ▪ *(usted)* los que quiera (usted) ▪ las que quiera (usted) ➤ *(digital camera photos)* Keep the ones you want, and erase the others. Guarda las que quieras, y borra las demás.

the only other thing lo único más

the only thing lo único

the other day ▪ several days ago ▪ a few days ago el otro día

the other thing lo otro ➤ The other thing I wanted to tell you is that... Lo otro que quería decirte es que...

the others 1. the other ones los otros 2. the rest los demás

the past 1. *(literal)* el pasado 2. what's done ▪ what's been done lo hecho

the person who la persona que ➤ I'm looking for the teller who speaks English. Busco al cajero que habla inglés.

to be **the pits** dar lástima ▪ *(Sp.)* ser la leche *("Ser la leche" can be positive or negative, depending on the tone of voice.)*

the poor los pobres
the rest el resto ▪ los demás ➤ We've only had two sunny days, the rest have been cloudy and rainy. Sólo hemos tenido dos días de sol, los demás nublados y lloviendo.
the said ▪ the aforesaid el tal ▪ susodicho
the same one el mismo ▪ la misma ➤ This is the same VIPS where we had supper that night. Este es el mismo VIPS donde cenamos esa noche. ➤ This is the same one where we had supper that night. Éste es el mismo donde cenamos esa noche.
the same thing lo mismo ▪ la misma cosa ➤ I was thinking the same thing. (Yo) pensaba lo mismo. ▪ (Yo) pensaba la misma cosa.
the scarier, the better *(horror movies, thrillers)* cuanto más miedo, mejor
the second ▪ 2nd **1.** el segundo (2°) ▪ la segunda (2ª) **2.** *(of the month)* el dos
the seventeenth ▪ 17th **1.** el decimoséptimo (17°) ▪ la decimoséptima (17ª) **2.** *(of the month)* el diecisiete
the seventh ▪ 7th **1.** el séptimo (7°) ▪ la séptima (7ª) **2.** *(of the month)* el siete
the sick los enfermos
the sixteenth ▪ 16th **1.** el decimosexto (16°) ▪ la decimosexta (16ª) **2.** *(of the month)* el dieciséis
the sixth ▪ 6th **1.** el sexto (6°) ▪ la sexta (6ª) **2.** *(of the month)* el seis
the sooner cuanto antes ➤ The sooner you buy airplane tickets, the cheaper they'll be. Cuanto antes compres los billetes aéreos, más baratos serán.
the sooner, the better cuánto antes, mejor
the soonest lo más pronto (posible) ➤ Friday would be the soonest. El viernes sería lo más pronto (posible). ➤ The soonest I can go is Monday. Lo más pronto que puedo ir es el lunes. ➤ The soonest I could go would be Monday. Lo más pronto que podría ir sería el lunes.
The Sound and the Fury *(William Faulkner novel)* *El ruido y la furia*
the Spanish (people) los españoles
the tenth ▪ 10th **1.** el décimo (10°) ▪ la décima (10ª) **2.** *(of the month)* el diez
the then el entonces ▪ la entonces ▪ el que fuera ▪ la que fuera ▪ el antaño ▪ la antaña ➤ The then national security advisor Condoleeza Rice... La entonces consejera de seguridad nacional Condoleeza Rice... ▪ La que fuera consejera de seguridad nacional Condoleeza Rice... ▪ La antaña consejera de seguridad nacional Condoleeza Rice... ➤ The then child actor Elijah Wood... El entonces niño actor Elijah Wood...
the thing of it is that... la cosa es que...
the thing that gets me is... 1. what bothers me is lo que me fastidia es que... **2.** the thing that amazes me is lo que me asombra es
the things you come up with! ¡las cosas tuyas!
the third ▪ 3rd **1.** el tercero (3°) ▪ la tercera (3ª) **2.** *(of the month)* el tres
the thirteenth ▪ 13th **1.** el decimotercero (13°) ▪ la decimatercera (13ª) **2.** *(of the month)* el trece
the thirtieth ▪ 30th **1.** el trigésimo (30°) ▪ la trigésima (30ª) **2.** *(of the month)* el treinta
the twelfth ▪ 12th **1.** el décimosegundo ▪ el duodécimo (12°) ▪ la décimosegunda ▪ la duodécima (12ª) **2.** *(of the month)* el doce
the twentieth ▪ 20th **1.** el vigésimo (20°) ▪ la vigésima (20ª) **2.** *(of the month)* el veinte
the twenty-first ▪ 21st **1.** el vigésimo primero (21°) ▪ la vigésimo primera (21ª) **2.** *(of the month)* el veintiuno
the twenty-second ▪ 22nd **1.** el vigésimo segundo (22°) ▪ la vigésimo segunda (22ª) **2.** *(of the month)* el veintidós
the two los dos ▪ las dos ➤ The two sisters did not get along well at all. Las dos hermanas no se llevaban nada bien.
the unconscious (mind) *el* inconsciente
the undersigned los abajo firmantes
the usual lo de siempre ▪ lo mismo de siempre ▪ lo consabido ➤ (Just) the usual, coffee and toast. Lo de siempre, un café y pan tostado.
The Way We Were *(movie title)* *Tal como éramos*
the whole time ▪ the entire time ▪ continuously el tiempo entero ▪ todo el tiempo ▪ continuamente
the whole trip todo el viaje
the whole truth toda la verdad
the worst by far ▪ by far the worst **1.** *(modifying a masculine noun)* el peor con diferencia ▪ con diferencia el peor ▪ el peor con mucho ▪ con mucho el peor **2.** *(modifying a feminine noun)* la peor con diferencia ▪ con diferencia la peor ▪ la peor con mucho ▪ con mucho la peor
the worst (thing) that can happen ▪ the most that can happen lo peor que puede pasar ▪ lo peor que puede ocurrir ▪ lo más que puede pasar
their son 1. su hijo **2.** *(in cases where there are also children by a previous marriage)* hijo de ambos
theme song *el* tema musical
themes and variations *(music)* variaciones sobre el mismo tema
then and there ▪ on the spot en el acto
then how do you explain it? *(tú)* ¿cómo lo explicas entonces? ▪ *(usted)* ¿cómo lo explica (usted) entonces?
then I found out that... entonces me enteré de que... ▪ luego me enteré de que...
then off he goes with se va luego con
then one must have... *(as conjecture)* pues será que... ➤ *(Valle-Inclán)* Then they must have killed him in reprisal. Pues será que le mataron por (una) venganza.
then suddenly ▪ and suddenly y de repente ▪ y de pronto ▪ y de improviso
there are hay ▪ existen
there are a lot of them hay muchos ▪ hay muchos de ellos ▪ son muchos
there are a lot of us somos muchos ▪ hay muchos de nosotros
there are a lot of ways to interpret it 1. *(song)* tiene muchas maneras de entenderla **2.** *(poem)* tiene muchas maneras de entenderlo
there are cases when ▪ there are cases where hay casos en los que
there are cases where ▪ there are cases when hay casos en los que
there are going to be ▪ there will be **1.** *(singular)* va a haber ▪ habrá **2.** *(plural)* van a haber ▪ habrá
there are lots of ways to... hay muchas maneras de... ▪ existen muchas maneras de...
there are many things I don't understand hay muchas cosas que no entiendo
there are no traces of no hay rasgos de
there are none so deaf as those who will not hear no hay peor sordo que el que no quiere oír
there are once again vuelve a haber ➤ *(headline)* There are once again political exiles Vuelve a haber exiliados políticos
there are people who ▪ there are those who hay personas que ▪ hay gente que ▪ hay quienes
there are people who say that... ▪ there are those who say that... ▪ some people say that... hay algunos que dicen que... ▪ hay quienes dicen que... ▪ los hay que dicen que... ▪ hay quien dice que...
there are so many people who son tantas las personas que ▪ son muchas las personas que ▪ hay tantas personas que
there are some who say that... los hay que dicen que... ▪ hay algunos que dicen que...
there are still a lot of things to see ▪ there are a lot of things still to see ▪ there are a lot of things left to see ▪ we still have a lot to see ▪ we have a lot still to see queda mucho por ver ▪ quedan muchas cosas por ver
there are those who say that... ▪ there are some who say that... ▪ there are people who say that... hay quienes dicen que... ▪ los hay que dicen que... ▪ hay algunos que dicen que...
there are those who think that... ▪ there are people who think that... ▪ some people think that... hay quienes piensan que... ▪ los hay que piensan que... ▪ hay algunos que piensan que...
there are times when... hay veces que... ▪ hay veces cuando... ➤ There are times when I don't use the metro at all. Hay veces que no uso el metro nada.

there are two sides to this issue hay dos lados de esta cuestión ■ *(journalistic)* esta cuestión presenta dos aspectos

there are *x* of them son *x* ➤ There are six of them. Son seis.

there are *x* of us somos *x* ➤ There are six of us. Somos seis.

there aren't any left ■ there aren't any more ya no hay ■ no hay más ■ no quedan más

there aren't any more ■ there aren't any left ya no hay ■ no hay más ■ no quedan más

there aren't enough seats faltan asientos ■ no hay suficientes asientos ■ *(concert, bus, and other sold seats)* faltan plazas ■ no hay suficientes plazas

there can be puede haber

there could be podría haber

there could have been podría haber habido ■ pudo haber habido

there could only be one explanation solamente podría haber una sola explicación

there do not appear to be any parece que no hay (ninguno)

there does not appear to be one... parece que no hay (ninguno)

there followed... a esto siguió...

there had been... había habido...

there had to be **1.** *(main clause)* tuvo que haberlo(-a) ■ tenía que haberlo(-a) **2.** *(dependent clause)* tuvo que haber... ■ tenía que haber...

there had to have been ■ there must have been tuvo que haber ■ tiene que haber habido ➤ There had to have been a storm last night, judging from the fallen branches. ■ There must have been a storm last night, judging from the fallen branches. Tuvo que haber una tormenta anoche, a juzgar por las ramas caídas.

there has been ha habido ➤ There has been a misunderstanding. Ha habido un mal entendido. ➤ There has been a change of plans. Ha habido un cambio de planes

there has to be **1.** *(preceding a complement)* tiene que haber... **2.** *(as a complete sentence)* tiene que haberlo(-a)

there has to have been **1.** *(main clause)* tiene que haberlo(-a) habido **2.** *(dependent clause)* tiene que haber habido...

there have been **1.** *(main clause sentence)* lo ha habido **2.** *(preceding a complement)* ha habido...

there have been times when ha habido ocasiones en las que

there have to be **1.** *(main clause)* tiene que haberlos ■ tiene que haberlas **2.** *(dependent clause)* tiene que haber...

there he goes again! **1.** *(literal)*y ahí va otra vez **2.** oh, no! not again! ¡y dale!

there I go again! *(Ronald Reagan)* ¡ahí voy otra vez!

there is **1.** *(main clause)* lo hay ■ la hay **2.** *(dependent clause)* hay...

there is another person going with us ■ someone else is going with us otra persona nos acompaña ■ otra persona va con nosotros

there is going to be ■ there's going to be ■ there will be **1.** *(main clause)* va a haberlo ■ va a haberla ■ lo habrá ■ la habrá ■ va a haber ■ habrá **2.** *(dependent clause)* va a haber... ■ habrá...

there is no alternative (but to...) ■ there is no alternative (other than to...) no hay otra alternativa más que... ■ no hay otra posibilidad más que...

there is no doubt that... no hay duda de que... no cabe duda de que...

there is no longer any doubt that... ya no cabe duda de que...

there is no one who... no hay nadie que... ■ no hay quien... ■ no haya nadie que... ➤ There is no one who can cook like my wife. No hay quien pueda cocinar como mi mujer. ➤ I think (that) there is no one who can cook like my wife. Creo que no haya nadie que pueda cocinar como mi mujer.

there is no reason to... ■ no hay razón para... ■ no tiene por qué...

there is no such... ■ there's no such... no existe dicho... ■ no hay tal...

there is no such thing (as) ■ there's no such thing as no hay tal cosa (como)

there is no time to lose ■ there's no time to lose no hay tiempo que perder

there is no trace of no hay rasgos de

there is nothing anyone can do no se puede hacer nada

there is once again... vuelve a haber... ■ una vez más hay... ■ hay una vez más...

there is reason to believe that... hay razones para creer que... ■ hay motivos para creer que...

there is room for hay cabido para ■ cabe(n) ➤ There is room for one more. Cabe uno más. ➤ There is room for a hundred people. Caben cien personas.

there is to be hay de haber

there isn't any more ■ it's all gone no queda más ■ no queda nada más ■ no hay más

there it goes ahí va

there it is ahí está

there lived **1.** *(singular)* vivía **2.** *(plural)* vivían ➤ Once upon a time there lived... Érase una vez vivía...

there may be ■ there might be ■ it is possible that there is tal vez haya ■ tal vez lo haya ■ tal vez la haya ■ puede que haya ■ puede que lo haya

there may have been tal vez haya habido

there might be ■ there may be ■ there could be tal vez haya ➤ There might be a meeting tomorrow morning. Tal vez haya una reunión mañana por la mañana.

there might have been **1.** there may have been (tal vez) haya habido ■ (quizás) haya habido ■ pudo haber habido **2.** *(more doubtful)* there might (conceivably) have been podría haber habido ■ pudiera haber habido ■ pudiese haber habido

there must be **1.** there has to be debe haber ■ tiene que haber **2.** *(conjecture)* debe de haber ➤ There must be a spare tire in the trunk. ■ There has to be a spare tire in the trunk. Debe haber una rueda de repuesto en el baúl. ■ Tiene que haber una rueda de repuesto en el baúl. ➤ There must be an ATM machine around here somewhere. Tiene que haber una cajera automática por ahí.

there must be about... habrá unos...

there must be some mistake debe haber algún error

there must have been ■ there had to have been **1.** *(certainty)* debe haber habido **2.** *(conjecture)* debe de haber habido ➤ There must have been a mistake. ■ There had to have been a mistake. Debe haber habido un error. ➤ There must have been some mistake. Debe de haber habido algún error.

there need(s) to be necesita haber ■ *(Sp.)* se necesita (que...) ➤ There needs to be a traffic light at that intersection. Necesita haber un semáforo en ese cruce. ■ Se necesita un semáforo en ese cruce.

there ought to be debería haber

there ought to have been debería haber habido

there, see?! ¡ahí está!, ¿ves?

there shall be *(literary)* ■ there will be habrá

there she goes again! ¡y dale!

there should be **1.** *(with a complement)* debería haber **2.** *(as complete sentence)* debería haberlo ■ debería haberla

there should have been **1.** *(main clause)* debería haberlo(-a) habido ■ debía haberlo(-a) habido ■ tendría que haberlo(-a) **2.** *(dependent clause)* debería haber habido... ■ debía haber habido... ■ tendría que haber...

there stands se alza ➤ A short distance from the tree there stands a large rock. A poca distancia del árbol se alza una gran roca.

there stood ■ there was se alzaba ■ había ➤ A short distance from the fountain there stood a kiosk. A poca distancia de la fuente se alzaba un quiosco.

there was a long silence se hizo un largo silencio ■ hubo un silencio largo

there was a time when... hubo un tiempo en (el) que...

there was an explosion in the engine hubo una explosión en el motor ■ se produjo una explosión del motor

there was going to be **1.** *(main clause)* iba a haberlo(-a) **2.** *(dependent clause)* iba a haber...

there was indeed **1.** *(main clause)* lo había por cierto ■ la había por cierto ■ desde luego lo había ■ desde luego la había **2.** *(dependent clause)* por cierto había... ■ desde luego había...

there was no answer **1.** *(telephone)* no había nadie ■ no contestaron **2.** *(door)* no hubo respuesta ■ nadie contestó

there was no longer any doubt that... ya no cabía duda de que...
there was no one who... 1. no había nadie que... 2. *(in subjunctive clauses)* no hubiera nadie que... ▪ no hubiese nadie que... ➤ I thought that there was no one who... No creí que hubiera alguien que... ▪ No creí que hubiese alguien que... *("No creía" is also possible.)*
there was no (other) alternative no había otra alternativa ▪ no había otra posibilidad
there was no reaction no hubo reacción
there was no sound ▪ you couldn't hear anything no se oía nada
there was no time to lose no había tiempo que perder
there was no way to 1. *(main clause)* no hubo modo de hacerlo ▪ no había modo de hacerlo 2. *(dependent clause)* no hubo modo de (que...) ▪ no había modo de (que...)
there was nothing anyone could do no hubo nada que alguien pudiera hacer ▪ no hubo nada que alguien pudiese hacer ▪ no había nada que alguien pudiera hacer ▪ no había nada que alguien pudiese hacer ▪ no se pudo hacer nada ▪ no se podía hacer nada ▪ así que nada
there was once ▪ there once was ▪ once upon a time había una vez ▪ érase una vez ▪ érase que se era
there was supposed to be se suponía que había ➤ There was supposed to be some tiramisu ice cream in the refrigerator. Se suponía que había helado de tiramisú en la nevera.
there was to be... iba a haber ▪ había de haber
there were a lot of things I didn't get to see hubo muchas cosas que no llegué a ver
there were going to be 1. *(main clause)* iba a haberlo(-a) ▪ iba a haberlos(-as) 2. *(dependent clause)* iba a haber...
there were just myself and my brother *(coll.)* ▪ there were (just) my brother and me éramos sólo mi hermano y yo
there were many different kinds of había muchas clases de ▪ había muchos tipos de
there were no arrests ▪ nobody got arrested no hubo ningún arresto ▪ no hubo ningún detenido
there were times when... 1. *(instances)* había veces que... 2. *(extended periods)* temporadas hubo en que...
there were to be había de haber
there were *x* of them eran *x* ➤ There were six of them. Eran seis.
there were *x* of us éramos *x* ➤ There were six of us. Éramos seis.
there weren't enough seats no había suficientes asientos ▪ faltaban asientos
there will be 1. *(main clause)* lo habrá ▪ la habrá ▪ los habrá ▪ las habrá 2. *(dependent clause)* habrá... ➤ There will be another bus along shortly. Habrá otro bus dentro de poco.
there will be a lot of us ▪ there will be a big group of us seremos muchos ▪ *(colorful)* vamos a ir a barullo
there will be (one) soon (lo) va a haber pronto ▪ (la) va a haber pronto
there will have been habrá habido
there will have to be 1. *(main clause)* tendrá que haberlo(-a) ▪ tendrá que haberlos(-as) 2. *(dependent clause)* tendrá que haber...
there will soon be... pronto habrá...
there would be 1. *(conditional)* habría 2. *(imperfect, singular)* there was going to be iba a haber ▪ habría 3. *(imperfect, plural)* there were going to be iban a haber ▪ habría
there would have been 1. *(main clause)* lo(-a) habría habido ▪ los(-as) habría habido 2. *(dependent clause)* habría habido...
there would have to be 1. *(as a dependent clause)* tendría que haber... ▪ habría que... 2. *(as a complete sentence)* tendría que haberlo(-a) ▪ habría que haberlo(-a) ➤ There would have to be more students in the class to justify the cost. Tendría que haber más estudiantes en la clase para justificar el coste. ➤ Would there be transparency in the use of bailout funds? There would have to be. ¿Habría transparencia en el uso de los fondos de rescate? Tendría que haberla.
there would have to have been 1. *(main clause)* habría tenido que haberlo(-a) ▪ tendría que haberlo(-a) habido 2. *(dependent clause)* habría tenido que haber... ▪ tendría que haber habido...
there's a limit to one's patience la paciencia tiene un límite
there's a (little) trick to it hay un truquito ▪ hay un truquillo ▪ hay un tranquillo
there's a lot of commotion hay mucho alboroto ▪ hay mucho jaleo
there's a lot of difference between... ▪ there's a big difference between... hay mucha diferencia entre... ▪ hay una gran diferencia entre... ▪ va mucho de... a
there's a lot still to see ▪ there's still a lot to see ▪ there's a lot left to see ▪ we have a lot still to see ▪ we still have a lot to see queda mucho por ver
there's a pattern of hay un patrón de ▪ hay una pauta de ➤ There's a pattern of indifference. Hay un patrón de indiferencia. ▪ Hay una pauta de indiferencia.
there's a ring to it tiene cierta musicalidad
there's a rumor going around that corre la voz de que
there's a sucker born every minute *(P.T. Barnum)* nace un pardillo cada minuto ▪ cada minuto nace un ingenuo
there's a way hay un modo
there's always room for improvement siempre se puede mejorar
there's always room for one more donde caben dos, caben tres ▪ en la mesa de San Francisco, donde comen cuatro comen cinco
there's another bus every ten minutes 1. *(literal)* the bus comes every ten minutes hay un autobús cada diez minutos 2. *(figurative)* easy come, easy go a rey muerto, rey puesto
there's been a change of plans ▪ there has been a change of plans ha habido un cambio de planes
there's chemistry between them hay química entre ellos ▪ *(coll.)* hay onda entre ellos
there's going to be 1. *(with a complement)* va a haber... 2. *(as a complete sentence)* va a haberlo(-a)
there's going to be a lot of talking ▪ it's going to provoke a lot of comment va a dar mucho que hablar
there's going to be trouble ▪ *(colorful)* there's gonna be trouble va a haber problemas ▪ va a haber lío ▪ *(Sp.)* va a haber hule ▪ habrá hule
there's hardly any left no queda casi nada ▪ queda muy poco
there's more to it than meets the eye ▪ there's more here than meets the eye esto tiene su miga
there's no answer 1. *(telephone)* no contestan ▪ no hay nadie 2. there's no solution no hay solución
there's no backing out ▪ there's no turning back no hay marcha atrás ▪ no hay vuelta atrás
there's no chance of no hay ninguna posibilidad de ▪ no existe posibilidad alguna de
there's no chance that... no hay ninguna posibilidad de que... ▪ no existe posibilidad alguna de que...
there's no comparison no hay comparación ▪ no hay punto de comparación ▪ no hay color
there's no comparison between... no hay comparación entre... ▪ no hay punto de comparación entre... ▪ no se puede comparar (algo con algo)
there's no contest no hay color ▪ no hay punto de comparación ▪ no hay competencia
there's no doubt about it no cabe duda ▪ no cabe la menor duda ▪ sin duda
there's no doubt that... ▪ undoubtedly... no hay duda de que es... ▪ es indudable que es...
there's no easy way to no hay una manera fácil de ▪ no hay buena combinación para
there's no end in sight (to) no se ve el final (de) ▪ no hay fin a la vista ▪ no vislumbrarse ➤ There's no end in sight to the violence in the Middle East. No se ve el final de la violencia en el Medio Oriente. ▪ No se vislumbra el fin de la violencia en Medio Oriente.
there's no getting around it 1. there's no denying it no hay forma de negarlo 2. there's no escaping it no hay manera de evitarlo ▪ no hay vuelta ▪ no tiene vuelta
there's no harm in asking por preguntar nada se pierde ▪ con preguntar no se pierde nada
there's no hurry ▪ there's no rush no hay prisa ▪ no nos corre prisa ▪ no hay apuro

there's no letup in ha continuado sin descanso ▪ ha continuado sin tregua ➤ There's no letup in the violence. Ha continuado sin descanso la violencia. ▪ Ha continuado sin tregua la violencia.

there's no longer any doubt ya no hay ninguna duda ▪ ya no existe ninguna duda ▪ ya está fuera de duda

there's no middle ground no hay término medio ▪ no hay puntos intermedios

there's no money in it 1. *(business venture)* it's not profitable ▪ it's break even (only) no es rentable ▪ no da ganancias ▪ sale lo comido por lo servido ▪ ha sido lo comido por lo servido 2. *(bank account)* it's empty está a cero

there's no need ▪ you don't need to no hace falta

there's no need to... no hace falta que... ▪ no hay que...

there's no need to apologize for... no hay que disculparse por... ▪ no tienes que disculparte por...

there's no need to explain no hay necesidad de explicar ▪ no hay necesidad de explicación

there's no other choice no hay otra opción ▪ no hay otra alternativa

there's no other way to do it ▪ there is no other way to do it no tiene otra solución ▪ no hay otra forma de hacerlo ▪ no hay otra manera de hacerlo

there's no place like home se está mejor en casa que en ningún otro sitio ▪ no hay ningún sitio como la propia casa ▪ no hay mejor sitio que la casa de uno

there's no question that... no cabe la menor duda de que... ▪ no cabe pensar que...

there's no room (for) no hay sitio (para) ▪ no hay lugar (para) ▪ no cabe ▪ *(L. Am.)* no hay campo (para)

there's no rush ▪ there's no hurry no hay prisa ▪ no nos corre prisa ▪ no hay apuro

there's no such person living here no existe dicha persona aquí ▪ esa persona no vive aquí

there's no such thing (as)... no existe tal cosa (como) ▪ no hay tal cosa (como)

there's no telling vete a saber ▪ vaya uno a saber

there's no telling what they're up to ▪ it's no telling what they're up to ¡a saber lo que estarán tramando! ▪ ¡vaya a saber en qué andan! ▪ ¡quién sabe en qué andan!

there's no time to lose no hay tiempo que perder

there's no trace of no hay ni rastro de ▪ no queda ni rastro de ▪ no hay pista de ➤ There's no trace of him. No hay ni rastro de él. ▪ No queda ni rastro de él. ▪ No hay pista de él.

there's no turning back no hay marcha atrás ▪ no hay vuelta atrás

there's no use crying over spilled milk ▪ what's done is done a lo hecho, pecho ▪ lo hecho, hecho está

there's no way (to) no hay manera (de)

there's no way to know ▪ it's impossible to know no hay manera de saber ▪ no se puede saber

there's not enough to go around ▪ there isn't enough to go around ▪ there's not enough for everyone ▪ it won't go around no hay para todos ▪ no da abasto

there's nothing else to say about it ▪ that's all there is to say about it ▪ there's nothing more to say about it no hay más que hablar ▪ no hay más que decir

there's nothing I don't like about... ▪ there's nothing I dislike about... no hay nada que no me guste de... ▪ no me disgusta nada sobre...

there's nothing I like better ▪ I like nothing better (a mí) no hay nada que me guste más

there's nothing like... no hay como... ➤ There's nothing like a good cold beer on a hot day. No hay nada como una cerveza bien fría en un día caluroso.

there's nothing more to say no hay más que decir ▪ no hay nada más que decir

there's nothing to discuss ▪ there's nothing to talk about no hay nada de qué hablar

there's nothing to fear no hay nada que temer

there's nothing to it 1. it's easy es cosa fácil ▪ es facilísimo ▪ no tiene ciencia 2. it's not true es falso ▪ no es cierto ➤ You can make this omelet in five minutes. There's nothing to it. *(Mex.)* Se puede preparar esta torta de huevos en cinco minutos. Es facilísimo. ▪ *(Sp.)* Se puede preparar esta tortilla francesa en cinco minutos. Es cosa fácil. ➤ Don't believe the rumor. There's nothing to it. No te creas el rumor. Es falso.

there's nothing to lose in... no hay nada que perder en...

there's nothing to talk about ▪ there's nothing to discuss no hay nada de que hablar

there's nothing to worry about no hay de que preocuparse ▪ no hay cuidado (alguno)

there's nothing whatever to fear no hay cuidado alguno ▪ no hay nada que temer en absoluto

there's nothing wrong with no hay nada malo con ▪ no hay nada de malo con

there's nothing wrong with it 1. *(mechanically)* no hay nada estropeado ▪ todo está bien 2. *(ethically)* no hay nada malo en eso ▪ no tiene nada de malo ▪ no hay nada malo en ello

there's nothing wrong with that no hay nada malo en eso ➤ Oh, well, that's good. There's nothing wrong with that. Ah, bueno, menos mal. No hay nada malo en eso.

there's nothing you can do about it no hay nada que se pueda hacer al respecto ▪ ya no tiene remedio ▪ ¡qué le vamos hacer!

there's room for *x* people caben *x* personas ▪ hay espacio para *x* personas

there's someone here to see you *(a ti)* hay alguien aquí que quiere verte ▪ *(a usted)* hay alguien aquí que quiere verlo(-a) (a usted) ▪ *(Sp., leísmo)* hay alguien aquí que quiere verle

there's something fishy about this ▪ there's something fishy about it (me) huele a chamusquina

there's something fishy going on here (me) huele a chamusquina

there's something that's been bothering me hay algo que me ha estado molestando

there's still a lot of... sigue habiendo mucho... ▪ aún hay mucho... ▪ aún queda mucho...

there's still a lot to do ▪ a lot remains to be done queda mucho por hacer

there's still a lot to see ▪ there's a lot still to see ▪ there's a lot left to see ▪ we still have a lot to see ▪ we have a lot still to see queda mucho por ver ▪ todavía hay mucho por ver ▪ aún hay mucho por ver ▪ falta mucho por ver

there's strength in numbers la unión hace la fuerza

there's too much noise ▪ it's too noisy hay demasiado ruido

there's work to be done hay trabajo por hacer

these shoes are too small estos zapatos no me caben ▪ estos zapatos no me entran

these things take time estas cosas llevan tiempo ▪ *(colorful)* las cosas de palacio van despacio

these will do éstos me valdrán ▪ éstos estarán bien ➤ These will do. I'll take them. Éstos me valdrán. Me los llevo. ▪ Éstos estarán bien. Me los llevo.

they both ▪ both (of them) ellos dos ▪ los dos ▪ ambos ➤ They both attend the university. ▪ Both (of them) attend the university. Ellos dos asisten a la universidad. ▪ Los dos asisten a la universidad. ▪ Ambos asisten a la universidad.

they call her that because... la llaman así porque...

they call him that because... lo llaman así porque... ▪ *(Sp., leísmo)* le llaman así porque...

they call them... los llaman ▪ las llaman ▪ les dicen ▪ se les dice... ▪ *(Sp., leísmo)* les llaman

they carry them *(merchandise)* you can get them there ▪ they have them allí hay

they cleaned us out ▪ they robbed us blind nos dejaron en pelotas ▪ nos dejaron en la calle

they didn't have what I needed no tenían lo que necesitaba (yo) ▪ no tenían lo que (me) faltaba ▪ no tenían lo que me hacía falta ▪ no tenían lo que (yo) precisaba

they don't fit (me) 1. *(shoes, either too big or too little)* no me van bien 2. *(shoes, too little)* no me entran 3. *(clothes, either too big or too little)* no me quedan bien 4. *(clothes, too little)* no me entran

they don't show no se notan ▪ no se ven ▪ no son obvios

they had to... ▪ it was necessary to... 1. *(main clause)* tuvieron que hacerlo ▪ tenían que hacerlo ▪ había que hacerlo ▪ hubo que hacerlo 2. *(dependent clause)* tuvieron que... ▪ tenían que... ▪ había que... ▪ hubo que...

they have them *(merchandise)* they carry them allí hay ▪ ahí tienen ▪ ellos tienen

they may be... puede que sean... ➤ They may be identical twins, but their personalities are as different as night and day. Puede que sean gemelos idénticos, pero sus personalidades son tan diferentes como de la noche al día.

they might know puede que sepan

they only come to here *(socks)* sólo (me) llegan hasta aquí

they robbed us blind ▪ they cleaned us out nos han dejado sin pestañas

they say that... ▪ people say that... ▪ it is said that... se dice que... ▪ dicen que... ▪ se habla de que...

they should have had deberían haber tenido

they were and still are ▪ they were and continue to be **1.** *(main clause)* lo fueron y siguen siéndolo ▪ lo eran y siguen siéndolo **2.** *(dependent clause)* fueron y siguen siendo... ▪ eran y siguen siendo...

they were out of... se quedaron sin... ➤ They were out of mineral water at the store. Se quedaron sin agua mineral en la tienda.

they'll do it every time lo harán siempre ▪ siempre lo van a hacer

they'll get you ▪ they'll catch you ▪ you'll get caught te van a agarrar ▪ te van a pescar ▪ te ficharán

they're even *(sports)* ▪ they're tied ▪ it's a draw están empatados ▪ van empatados ▪ van iguales

they're made for each other están hechos el uno para el otro

they're not that different no son tan diferentes

they're tied *(sports)* ▪ they're even ▪ it's a draw van iguales ▪ van empatados

to be **thick as thieves** ser uña y carne ▪ ser culo y calzón

thick ice hielo grueso ▪ hielo gordo

thick layer capa gruesa ▪ estrato grueso ▪ estrato gordo

to be **thick-skinned** ▪ to withstand slings and arrows no entrarle ni las balas ▪ ser de caparazón dura

thick-sliced bread *el* pan en rodajas gruesas

thick smoke humo denso ▪ humo espeso

to be **thickheaded** ser cabezón(-a) ▪ ser cabeza dura ▪ ser porfiado(-a)

to **thin a liquid** diluir un líquido ▪ aclarar un líquido ▪ hacer un líquido menos espeso

thin air 1. *(literal)* aire escaso **2.** *(figurative, with "to disappear, vanish into")* aire ➤ The air above 12,000 feet is very thin. El aire arriba de 12.000 pies es muy escaso. ➤ Police said the suspect seemed to have disappeared into thin air. La policía dijo que el sospechoso parecía haberse desaparecido en el aire.

to **thin blood** diluir la sangre ▪ hacer la sangre menos espesa

thin coat *(paint, lacquer, etc.)* ▪ light coat capa fina ➤ The best way to apply the lacquer is to thin it and spray several thin coats. La mejor manera de aplicar la laca es diluirla y aplicar varias capas finas.

thin layer 1. capa delgada ▪ capa fina **2.** *(in scientific contexts)* estrato fino ➤ There's a thin layer of ice on the road. Hay una capa fina de hielo en la carretera. ➤ There's a thin layer of ice on the pond. Hay una capa fina de hielo en el charco. ➤ They isolated the protein by means of fine-layer chromatography. Aislaron la proteina por cromatografía de estrato fino.

thin layer of fog velo de niebla

to **thin (out) 1.** *(hair)* ralear ▪ ir raleando **2.** *(crowd)* mermar

to **thin paint** diluir (la) pintura

to be **thin-sliced** ▪ to be sliced thin ▪ to be thinly sliced estar loncheado ▪ *(radially, like French bread)* estar cortado en rodajas finas ▪ *(Sp.)* estar cortado en lonchas

thin-sliced bread 1. *el* pan en rebanadas finas **2.** *(baguette, like French bread)* pan en rodajas finas

thin wing *el* ala fina ▪ *(plural) las* alas finas

the **thing I liked about it** ▪ what I liked about it **1.** *(recent)* lo que me ha gustado **2.** *(less recent)* lo que me gustó ➤ The thing I liked about it was the ending. ▪ What I liked about it was the ending. Lo que me ha gustado fue el final. ▪ Lo que me gustó fue el final.

the **thing in itself** *(philosophy)* ▪ das Ding an sich ▪ noumenon la cosa en sí misma

thing I've ever done que jamás he hecho ▪ que nunca he hecho ▪ que jamás he podido hacer ▪ que nunca he podido hacer

thing like that cosa así ▪ semejante cosa ➤ Who would do a thing like that? ¿Quién haría una cosa así? ▪ ¿Quién haría semejante cosa?

thing of it: a little ~ una poca cantidad ➤ A little thing of it costs two hundred and forty-five euros. Una poca cantidad cuesta doscientos cuarenta y cinco euros.

the **thing of it is** la cosa es que ▪ la cosa con esto es ▪ lo que pasa con esto es

to be a **thing of the past** ser una cosa del pasado ▪ ser ya cosa pasada ▪ ser algo del pasado ➤ Cheap surface mail rates are a thing of the past. Tarifas baratas de correo por vía marítima son una cosa del pasado.

the **thing that gets me is 1.** the thing that bothers me is la cosa que me molesta es ▪ lo que me molesta es **2.** the thing that impresses me la cosa que me impresiona es ▪ lo que me impresiona es ▪ lo que me impacta es

the **thing that's bad about it is** ▪ the bad thing about it is lo malo con esto es que ▪ lo chungo es que ▪ la cosa mala de eso es que ▪ lo malo es que

the **thing to do is** la cosa más sensata de hacer es ▪ lo más sensato de hacer es ▪ lo que se debería hacer es ➤ That's the thing to do. Es lo que se debería hacer. ➤ The thing to do is... Lo que se debería hacer es... ➤ The most sensible thing to do is... La cosa más sensata que hacer es...

thing to see cosa que ver ▪ algo que ver ➤ The Nutcracker ballet is a beautiful thing to see. El ballet Cascanueces es una cosa bella que ver. ▪ El ballet Cascanueces es algo muy lindo para ver. ▪ El ballet Cascanueces es algo muy lindo de ver.

things (always) come in three's ▪ things happen in three's no hay dos sin tres

things are getting out of hand las cosas se nos están yendo de las manos ▪ *(Sp.)* pintan bastos

things are going great (for me) las cosas (me) van estupendamente ▪ las cosas (me) van divinas de la muerte ▪ todo va viento en popa ▪ todo va a pedir de boca

things are going smoothly ▪ things are running smoothly ▪ things are rolling las cosas marchan sobre ruedas

things are going well las cosas marchan bien ▪ las cosas van bien

things couldn't be better las cosas no podrían estar mejor ▪ las cosas no podrían ir mejor ▪ mejor imposible

things couldn't be worse las cosas no podrían estar peor ▪ las cosas no podrían ir peor ▪ peor imposible

things couldn't get any worse las cosas no podrían ir peor ▪ las cosas no podrían empeorar

things happen in threes ▪ things (always) come in threes no hay dos sin tres

things in the way cosas por medio ▪ cosas estorbando el paso ▪ obstáculos en el camino ▪ piedras en el camino

things like that cosas así ▪ cosas de esas ▪ cosas por el estilo

things of that sort cosas por el estilo ▪ cosas tales ▪ cosas de ese tipo

things to do cosas que hacer ➤ There are so many things to do in Buenos Aires. Hay tantas cosas que hacer en Buenos Aires.

things to read cosas que leer

things to study cosas que estudiar

the **things you come up with!** ▪ the things you think of! ▪ ¡las cosas que se te ocurren! ▪ ¡se te ocurre cada cosa! ▪ ¡tus ocurrencias! ▪ ¡tú y tus ocurrencias! ▪ ¡tú y tus cosas!

think about: to give someone a lot to ~ darle a alguien mucho que pensar ➤ That teacher gave me a lot to think about. Ese profesor me dio mucho (en) que pensar.

to **think about doing something** ▪ to consider doing something pensar en hacer algo ➤ I have thought about buying a microwave for this apartment. He pensado en comprar un microondas para este piso.

to **think about how** pensar en cómo

to **think about how much...** pensar en lo mucho que... ▪ pensar en cuánto...

think about it! ▪ give it some thought ▪ think it over **1.** *(tú)* piénsalo ▪ medítalo **2.** *(usted)* piénselo ▪ medítelo to **think about it for a moment** ▪ to think about it for a second pensarlo un momento ▪ quedarse pensativo un momento ➤ He thought about it for a moment and then said... Se quedó pensativo un momento y luego dijo... ▪ Lo pensó un momento y dijo...

think again! *(tú)* ¡piénsalo otra vez! ▪ *(usted)* ¡piénselo otra vez!

to **think ahead** pensar a la fecha ➤ I haven't thought that far ahead. No lo he pensado a la fecha.

to **think alike** pensar igual ▪ pensar igualmente ▪ pensar de la misma manera ➤ We think alike. Pensamos igual. ▪ Pensamos igualmente. ▪ Pensamos de la misma manera.

to **think back over** hacer un repaso de

to **think badly of** tener mala opinión de ▪ *(literary)* conocer mal a ➤ A judge who thought badly of don Manuel... Un juez que conocía mal a don Manuel...

to **think for a moment** ▪ to reflect for a moment reflexionar un momento ➤ She thought for a moment and then said... ▪ She reflected for a moment and then said... Ella reflexionó un momento y luego dijo...

to **think for oneself** ▪ to have one's own way of looking at things pensar por sí mismo ▪ tener su propio criterio ▪ tener su propia opinión ▪ tener su propio juicio

to **think it over** ▪ to think about it ▪ to give it some thought pensarlo ▪ pensárselo ▪ meditarlo ▪ pensar en ello ▪ pensar en eso ▪ recapacitar ➤ I want to think it over. Quiero pensarlo. ▪ Quiero pensármelo. ▪ Quiero meditarlo. ▪ Quiero pensar en ello. ▪ Quiero pensar en eso. ➤ Think it over! ¡Piénsalo!

to **think of** 1. to remember ▪ to call to mind recordar ▪ pensar 2. to occur to one venirle a uno ▪ venirle a la cabeza ▪ venirle a la mente ▪ venirle en mente ▪ salirle a uno ➤ The word I couldn't think of was... La palabra que no podía recordar era... ➤ That was the only thing I could think of. Eso era lo único en lo que podía pensar. ▪ Eso fue lo único en lo que pude pensar.

to **think of everything** pensársela bien ▪ pensar en todo ➤ They've thought of everything. Se la pensaron bien.

to **think of it** ocurrírsele a uno ▪ venirle a uno ▪ acordarse ➤ Give me a minute; I'll think of it. ▪ Give me a minute; it'll come to me. Déjame pensar un minuto, que se me ocurrirá. ▪ Déjame un minuto que ya me va a venir. ▪ Déjame pensar un minuto que ya me acordaré.

to **think of it as (being)** considerarlo como ▪ pensarlo como si fuera ➤ The Spanish surname *Pérez* is not pronounced *Perezz.* Think of it as (being) *Perris.* El apellido español *Pérez* no se pronuncia *Perézz.* Considéralo como *Perris.* ▪ El apellido español *Pérez* no se pronuncia *Perézz.* Piensalo como si fuera *Perris.* *(In Spain, pronounced "Perreth.")*

to **think of oneself as** verse como ▪ darse aires de ➤ I like to think of myself as... Me gusta darme aires de...

to **think of someone** 1. to come up with the name of someone pensar en alguien ▪ ocurrírsele alguien 2. to have an opinion of someone pensar de alguien ▪ tener una opinión de alguien ➤ If I could just think of someone to ask. Si (tan) sólo pudiera pensar en alguien a quien preguntar(le). ▪ Si se sólo me ocurriera alguien a quien preguntar(le). ➤ What do you think of the new president? ¿Qué piensas del nuevo presidente? ▪ ¿Qué opinión tienes del nuevo presidente?

think of something! *(tú)* ¡piensa en algo! ▪ *(usted)* ¡piense en algo!

to **think of something** 1. to remember something acordarse de algo ▪ recordar algo 2. (for) something to occur to one ocurrírsele algo 2. to have an opinion about something pensar de algo ➤ I'm trying to think of his name. Estoy intentando acordarme de su nombre. ▪ Estoy intentando recordar su nombre. ➤ Give me a minute; I'll think of something. Déjame pensar un minuto, que se me ocurrirá algo. ▪ Déjame pensar un minuto, que algo se me ocurrirá. ➤ What do the Spanish think of Valladolid? ¿Qué piensan los españoles de la ciudad de Valladolid? *(The question "¿Qué piensan los españoles de Valladolid?" is ambiguous, meaning both "What do the Spanish think of Valladolid?" and "What do the Spanish from Valladolid think?" Inserting "la cuidad" does not resolve the ambiguity technically, but the question will be understood.)*

to **think out loud** pensar en voz baja

to **think over something** ▪ to think something over ▪ to reflect on something recapacitar sobre algo

to **think someone is someone else** ▪ to confuse someone with someone else ▪ to confuse someone for someone else ▪ to take someone for someone else pensar que alguien es otra persona ▪ creer que alguien es otra persona ▪ confundir a alguien por otra persona ▪ tomar a alguien por otra persona ➤ Pardon me. I thought you were someone else. ▪ Pardon me. I confused you with someone else. ▪ Pardon me. I confused you for someone else. ▪ Pardon me. I took you for someone else. *(to a man or woman)* Perdone, pensé que era otra persona. ▪ Perdone, creí que era otra persona. ▪ *(to a man)* Perdone, lo confundí por otra persona. ▪ Perdone, lo tomé por otra persona. ▪ *(Sp., leísmo)* Perdone, le confundí por otra persona. ▪ Perdone, le tomé por otra persona. ▪ *(to a woman)* Perdone, la confundí por otra persona. ▪ Perdone, la tomé por otra persona.

to **think something through** pensar algo detenidamente

to **think (that) someone is...** parecerle a uno ▪ tenerlo por ➤ Her neighbors thought (that) she was a bit odd. ▪ Her neighbors thought her (to be) a bit odd. A sus vecinos les parecía un poco rara. ➤ They think you're a tourist. Lo tienen por turista. ▪ *(Sp., leísmo)* Le tienen por turista.

to **think (that) something is funny** pensar que algo es gracioso ▪ pensar que algo tiene gracia ▪ pensar que algo es divertido

to **think the world revolves around oneself** creerse el centro del mundo ▪ creerse que es el ombligo del mundo ▪ mirarse el ombligo

to **think things over** reflexionar sobre...

to **think twice** pensarlo dos veces

to **think up an excuse** ▪ to think an excuse up ▪ to come up with an excuse ▪ to make up an excuse inventar un pretexto ▪ inventar una excusa

to **think up an idea** ▪ to come up with an idea inventar una idea ▪ imaginar una idea ▪ ocurrírsele una idea ➤ The ability to think up these situations is a kind of genius. La capacidad de imaginar estas situaciones es un tipo de genio. ▪ La capacidad para imaginar estas situaciones es un tipo de genio.

think up something! ▪ make up something! ¡inventa algo!

to be **thinking about something** estar pensando en algo ➤ (Are you) thinking about buying a house? ¿(Estás) pensando en comprar una casa?

to be **thinking of doing something** pensar en hacer algo

to be **thinly disguised (as)** ser apenas disimulado como ▪ ser sutilmente disfrazada de ➤ It was a criticism thinly disguised as a compliment. Fue una crítica apenas disimulado como un cumplido. ▪ Fue una crítica sutilmente disfrazada de un cumplido.

to be **thinly sliced** ▪ to be sliced thin(ly) 1. *(radial slices, French bread, tomatoes, cucumbers, etc.)* estar cortado en rodajas finas 2. *(transversal slices, sandwich bread, etc.)* estar cortado en rebanadas 3. *(cheese, meat)* estar cortado en fetas finas ▪ *(Sp., cheese, meat)* estar loncheado

to be **thinly veiled as** estar apenas velado como

third grade: to be in the ~ estar en el tercer curso ▪ estar en (el) tercer grado

third party tercera parte

third quarter 1. *(lunar phase) la* fase de luna llena 2. *(fiscal quarter, usually July through September)* tercer trimestre 3. *(academic quarter, usually mid March to early June)* tercer trimestre

third-rate de tercera

third world tercer mundo

third-world country *el* país del tercer mundo ▪ país tercermundista

thirst for adventure *el* afán de aventuras

thirst for learning *la* sed de aprender ▪ sed por aprender ▪ ansias de aprender

thirtysomething treinta y tantos ▪ treinta y algo ▪ treinta y pico

this August ▪ this coming August ▪ next August el próximo mes de agosto

to be **this big** *(indicating with the hands)* ser así de grande

this blasted ▪ this lousy este maldito ➤ This blasted zipper always gets stuck. Esta maldita cremallera siempre se atasca.

this business of esto de ▪ eso de
this can't go on ▪ this can't continue ▪ this can't keep happening esto no puede seguir (así) ▪ esto no puede continuar (así) ▪ esto no puede continuar sucediendo
this (coming) weekend ▪ the weekend coming up ▪ next weekend el próximo fin de semana ▪ el fin de semana que viene
this coming year el año que viene ▪ este otro año
this doesn't do it for me esto no me vale ▪ esto no me sirve
this end up *(on a cardboard box)* ▪ this side up este lado para arriba
this is a test estamos en (una) prueba
this is because... esto es porque... ▪ esto se debe a que...
this is he! ▪ speaking! soy yo ▪ él habla
this is it llegó la hora
this is just between you and me te lo digo entre nosotros ▪ esto es entre nosotros ▪ entre nos
this is my last one *(drink, cigarette, joke, etc.)* me voy con esto ▪ el del estribo ▪ la del estribo
this is not the right time ▪ it's not the right time no es el momento apropiado ▪ no es el momento adecuado ▪ *(Sp., coll.)* no está el horno para bollos ▪ no está el patio para bollos
this is one of the reasons why... ésta es una de las razones por las que...
this is one reason why... ésta es una razón por la que...
this is serious esto es serio ▪ la cosa va en serio
this is she! ▪ speaking! soy yo ▪ ella habla
this is the end esto es el acabose ▪ éste es el fin ▪ esto es el fin
this is the way to... por aquí se va a...
this is where I belong es donde me encuentro a mí mismo ▪ es donde me siento mejor ▪ es donde me siento bien
to be **this little** *(indicating with the hands)* ser así de pequeño
this little light went on in my head se enciendió esta lucecita ▪ se me prendió la lamparita
this minute! ▪ immediately! de una vez (por todas) ▪ inmediatamente ▪ en seguida ▪ al punto ➤ Come home this minute! ¡Vuelve a casa de una vez! ➤ Straighten up your room this minute! ¡Ordena tu cuarto de una vez (por todas)!
this mustn't go any further ▪ this is strictly between you and me esto no debe salir de aquí ▪ éste no debe salir de estas cuatro paredes
this one, but not that one éste, pero no ése ▪ ésta, pero no ésa ▪ éste, pero no aquel ▪ ésta, pero no aquella
this or that esto o lo otro ▪ esto o aquello
this (past) weekend este fin de semana (pasado)
this side up ▪ this end up este lado para arriba
this street turns into ▪ this street becomes ▪ the name of this street changes to esta calle se convierte en ▪ la continuación de esta calle es ▪ la prolongación de esta calle es ▪ esta calle se prolonga en ▪ esta calle se continúa en ➤ This street, Sor Ángela de la Cruz, turns into Alberto Alcocer when you cross the Castellana. La prolongación de esta calle, Sor Ángela de la Cruz, es Alberto Alcocer cuando cruzas la Castellana. ▪ Esta calle se prolonga en Alberto Alcocer.
this time esta vez ▪ en esta ocasión ➤ We're going to take another trip, this time to Uruguay. Vamos a hacer otro viaje, en esta ocasión a Uruguay.
this time last year 1. *(exactly)* el año pasado en esta fecha **2.** *(approximately)* el año pasado por estas fechas
this vale of tears *el* valle de lágrimas
this very day este mismo día ▪ hoy mismo
this way por aquí ▪ hacia aquí
this way up to the castle *(directional sign)* subida al castillo
this weekend 1. this past weekend este fin de semana (pasado) **2.** this coming weekend este fin de semana ▪ el próximo fin de semana ▪ el fin de semana que viene
this weekend is out ▪ this weekend I can't este fin de semana, no puedo
to be a **thorn in one's side** ▪ to be a bother ▪ to be an irritation ser una espina en el costado ▪ ser una molestia
thorny issue asunto espinoso ▪ tema espinoso ▪ tema escabroso
thorough cleaning: to give something a ~ ▪ to clean something thoroughly limpiar algo a fondo ▪ limpiar algo a conciencia
to be **those of** ▪ to belong to pertenecer a ➤ Most of the bones are those of youths who died of massive head injuries caused by shots fired at close range. La mayoría de los huesos pertenecen a personas jóvenes que murieron por la destrucción de masa encefálica a causa de disparos de armas de fuego hechos desde muy cerca.
those opposed ▪ all opposed (todos) los que se oponen ➤ Those opposed please indicate by a show of hands. ▪ All opposed please indicate by a show of hands. (Todos) los que se oponen, por favor manifiéstenlo levantando la mano.
those things 1. *(close by)* esas cosas **2.** *(farther away)* aquellas cosas ➤ I asked you not to move those things. Te pedí que no movieras esas cosas. ▪ Te pedí que no movieses esas cosas. ▪ Te pedí que no movieras aquellas cosas. ▪ Te pedí que no movieses aquellas cosas.
though: I'd like to, ~ ▪ however, I'd like to ▪ I'd like to, however no obstante, me gustaría ▪ sin embargo, me gustaría
though that may be ▪ however that may be comoquiera que sea eso ▪ comoquiera que eso sea
thought and planning planificación ➤ The relief efforts for the tsunami victims require a lot of thought and planning. Los esfuerzos para auxiliar a las víctimas del maremoto exigen mucha planificación. *(In Spanish, planning implies thought.)*
to be **thought-provoking** hacer reflexionar ➤ The book is very thought-provoking. El libro hace reflexionar. ▪ Es un libro que hace reflexionar.
thousands of 1. miles de **2.** *(coll.)* lots of ▪ tons of ▪ scads of la tira de ▪ un montón de ▪ un millón de ➤ He has thousands of friends. Tiene la tira de amigos. ▪ Tiene un montón de amigos. ▪ Tiene un millón de amigos.
thousandths of a second milésimas de segundo
to **threaten to do something** amenazar con hacer algo ➤ The government threatens to resort to force. El gobierno amenaza con recurrir a la fuerza.
three-by-five card ▪ index card ficha de 75 por 125 (milímetros) ▪ tarjeta de 75 por 125 (milímetros)
three-car accident *el* accidente de tres coches ▪ accidente triple (de coches)
three-fourths of the total tres cuartos del total ▪ tres cuartas partes del total
three guesses tres adivinanzas
the **three o'clock news** *(Sp.)* el telediario ▪ el noticiero de las tres ▪ las noticias de las tres
three-vehicle accident accidente triple
three-way ▪ menage à trois triángulo amoroso
three-way contest competencia entre tres ➤ The presidential race could be a three-way contest. La carrera para la presidencia podría ser entre tres personas.
three-way tie *el* empate a tres ▪ empate triple ▪ triple empate
three's a crowd tercero en discordia ▪ tres es multitud
throbbing headache el dolor de cabeza palpitante
through and through ▪ to the core todo un(-a) ▪ por los cuatro costados ▪ auténtico(-a) ▪ por donde se mire ▪ hasta los tuétanos ▪ completamente ➤ You're a gentleman through and through. Es usted todo un caballero. ▪ Es un auténtico caballero.
through channels ▪ through proper channels por conductos oficiales ▪ por conducto regular ▪ por conducto oficial ▪ por los medios correspondientes ▪ por medios oficiales
through force of habit ▪ from force of habit ▪ out of force of habit por la fuerza de la costumbre ▪ por hábito
through Friday hasta el viernes inclusive
through no fault of one's own sin haber hecho nada ▪ sin comerla ni beberla
through one's employer por medio de ▪ a través de ➤ He has his E-mail account through his employer. Tiene su cuenta de correo electrónico a través de su empleador.
through (proper) channels por conductos oficiales ▪ por conducto regular ▪ por conducto oficial
through sheer luck por pura suerte ▪ por puro golpe de suerte ▪ por chiripa ▪ de chiripa ▪ a puros golpes de suerte

through the grapevine: to hear something ~ enterarse de algo por terceros ▪ oír algo por boca de terceros ▪ *(Sp.)* enterarse de algo por radio macuto ➤ I heard it through the grapevine. Me enteré por radio macuto. ➤ I heard through the grapevine that... Me enteré por radio macuto de que...

through the nose: to talk ~ ganguear *("To sing through the nose is "cantar gangueando.")*

throughout history a lo largo de la historia ▪ a través de la historia

throughout the centuries ▪ over the centuries a lo largo de los siglos

throughout the country ▪ all over the country ▪ nationwide ▪ far and wide a lo largo y ancho del país ▪ en todo el territorio nacional

to **thresh wheat** trillar trigo

to **throw a tantrum** ▪ to have a tantrum tener una rabieta ▪ agarrarse un berrinche ▪ *(Sp.)* coger un berrinche

to **throw cold water on someone's ideas** tirar a alguien un jarro de agua fría (encima) ▪ tirar a alguien un balde de agua fría (encima) ▪ echar a alguien un jarro de agua fría (encima)

to **throw cold water on someone's plans** aguar los planes ▪ echar un jarro de agua fría sobre los planes de alguien ▪ tirarle un jarro de agua fría sobre los planes de alguien ▪ tirar(le) un balde de agua fría sobre los planes de alguien

to **throw down the gauntlet** ▪ to challenge someone to fight arrojar el guante

to **throw from** arrojar desde ➤ The child was thrown from the fourth floor. La niña fue arrojada desde el cuarto piso.

throw-in *(soccer) el* saque de banda ▪ saque de mano ▪ *el* lateral

to **throw in the towel** arrojar la toalla ▪ tirar la toalla ▪ arrojar la esponja

to **throw light on a subject** arrojar luz sobre un tema

to **throw money around** despilfarrar

to **throw one's arms around someone** echarle los brazos a alguien

to **throw one's head back** echar la cabeza hacia atrás ▪ echar la cabeza para atrás ▪ tirar la cabeza hacia atrás ▪ tirar la cabeza para atrás

to **throw oneself at men** lanzarse a los hombres

to **throw oneself at women** lanzarse a las mujeres

to **throw rocks at something** tirar piedras contra algo ▪ arrojar piedras contra algo ▪ lanzar piedras contra algo

throw rug el alfombrín

to **throw someone a life preserver** tirarle un salvavidas a alguien ▪ echarle un salvavidas a alguien ▪ arrojarle un salvavidas a alguien

to **throw someone for a loop** dejar a alguien anonadado ▪ dejar a alguien desconcertado ▪ dejar a alguien de una pieza ➤ Did the traffic circles in Washington throw you for a loop? Las glorietas en Washington, ¿te dejaron anonadado?

to **throw someone to the wolves** arrojar a alguien a los lobos ▪ tirar a alguien a los lobos

to **throw something against something** arrojar algo contra algo ▪ tirar algo contra algo ▪ lanzar algo contra algo

to **throw something at someone** tirar algo a alguien ➤ She threw it at him. Ella se lo tiró.

to **throw something at something** arrojarle algo a algo ▪ tirarle algo a algo ▪ lanzar algo a algo ➤ The farmer threw a rock at the fleeing rabbit. El granjero tiró una piedra al conejo en su huida.

to **throw something away** ▪ to throw away something echar algo a la basura ▪ tirar algo a la basura ➤ I threw it away. Lo eché a la basura. ▪ Lo tiré a la basura.

to **throw something in someone's face** echar algo en cara a alguien

to **throw something in the dirty clothes** ▪ to put something in the dirty clothes echar algo a la ropa sucia ▪ poner algo en la ropa sucia ▪ poner algo con la ropa sucia

to **throw something into the bargain** *(coll.)* ▪ to include something additional for the same price incluir(le) algo por el mismo precio ➤ He not only sold us the stereo system, he threw a set of Beethoven discs into the bargain. No sólo nos vendió el equipo de música, nos incluyó una conjunto de discos de Beethoven por el mismo precio.

to **throw something overboard** tirar algo por la borda ▪ echar algo por la borda ▪ tirar algo a la borda ▪ echar algo a la borda

to **throw stones (at)** **1.** *(literal)* tirar piedras (contra) ▪ tirar piedras (a) **2.** *(figurative, in one expression)* to criticize criticar ➤ People who live in glass houses shouldn't throw stones. El muerto se queja del degollado.

to **throw the book at someone** castigar a alguien con todo el peso de la ley ▪ castigar a alguien con todo el rigor de la ley ➤ A Barcelona judge threw the book at the kids who were caught defacing the metro windows. Un juez en Barcelona castigó con todo el peso de la ley a los jóvenes a quienes pillaron estropeando las ventanas del metro. ▪ Un juez en Barcelona castigó con todo el rigor de la ley a los jóvenes a quienes pillaron estropeando las ventanas del metro.

to be **thrown for a loop** dejar anonadado(-a) a alguien

to **thumb a ride** ▪ to hitchhike ▪ to hitch a ride hacer dedo ▪ hacer auto stop

to **thumb one's way (to a place)** ▪ to hitchhike to a place ▪ to hitch rides to a place ir a un lugar a dedo ➤ We thumbed our way to Sevilla. ▪ We hitchhiked to Sevilla. Fuimos a Sevilla a dedo.

thumbnail sketch: to give (someone) a ~ darle a alguien una pequeña reseña ▪ contárselo en dos palabras ▪ decírselo en dos palabras

thunder of applause el clamor de los aplausos ➤ The thunder of applause could be heard on the sidewalk outside the concert hall. El clamor de los aplausos podía oírse en la acera afuera de la sala de concierto.

thunderclap ▪ clap of thunder trueno

thunderous applause aplauso estruendoso ▪ aplauso atronador

thunderous ovation aplauso estruendoso ▪ aplauso atronador ▪ ovación cerrada ➤ The pianist received a thunderous ovation for his performance of Beethoven's Fourth. El pianista recibió una ovación cerrada por su interpretación del cuarto concierto de Beethoven.

Thursday night and early Friday en la noche del jueves al viernes ▪ en la noche del jueves para viernes

thus far hasta ahora ▪ hasta aquí

thy kingdom come venga a nosotros tu reino ▪ vénganos tu reino

thy will be done hágase tu voluntad

tic-tac-toe tres en raya ▪ ta-te-ti

ticket: admission ~ entrada

ticket: airplane ~ *el* billete de avión ▪ boleto de pasaje

ticket: cash register ~ ▪ (cash register) receipt *el* ticket (de compra) ▪ *el* comprobante ▪ recibo

ticket sales **1.** *(concert, museum, etc.)* venta de entradas **2.** *(airplane, train, etc.)* venta de billetes ▪ venta de boletos ▪ venta de tickets **3.** *(all contexts)* venta de boletos ▪ *(Sp., all contexts)* venta de tickets

to be a **ticket to nowhere** llevar a alguien a ninguna parte ▪ ser un billete a ninguna parte ➤ His attitude is a ticket to nowhere. Su actitud no lo lleva a ninguna parte. ▪ *(Sp., leísmo)* Su actitud no le lleva a ninguna parte. ▪ Su actitud es un billete a ninguna parte.

to **tickle someone** hacerle cosquillas a alguien ▪ *(Sp., coll.)* hacer el quiliquili a alguien

to be **tickled pink that...** ▪ to be just delighted that... estar chocho(-a) de que... ▪ estoy encantado(-a) de que...

to be **ticklish** tener cosquillas ➤ Are you ticklish? ¿Tienes cosquillas? ▪ ¿Eres cosquilloso?

to **tide one over** **1.** *(food)* aguantar hasta comer algo ▪ ir haciendo boca ▪ *(Sp.)* matar el gusanillo ▪ *(Arg.)* entretener el estómago hasta la próxima comida **2.** *(money)* aguantar ➤ Do you want to have a little snack to tide you over until supper? ¿Quieres una botana para aguantar hasta la cena? ▪ ¿Quieres picar algo para matar el gusanillo hasta la cena? ▪ ¿Quieres comer algo para ir haciendo boca hasta la cena? ➤ Could you lend me twenty dollars to tide me over until payday? ¿Podrías prestarme veinte dólares para aguantar hasta el día de pago?

to **tidy up the house** ordenar la casa ▪ poner la casa en orden ▪ poner la casa en condiciones

to **tie a bow** atar un lazo ▪ hacer un lazo ▪ hacer una moña

to **tie a bow (around)** atar un lazo alrededor de ▪ poner un lazo alrededor de

to **tie a knot** atar un nudo ▪ hacer un nudo ▪ amarrar un nudo

to **tie a little bow around one's finger (as a reminder)** ponerse un lacito en el dedo

to **tie a necktie** hacer el nudo de la corbata ▪ hacerse la corbata

to **tie down something** ▪ to tie something down sujetar algo ▪ amarrar algo ▪ atracar algo ➤ We tied down the boat. ▪ We tied the boat down. Amarramos el barco. ▪ Sujetamos el barco. ▪ Atracamos el barco. ➤ We tied it down. Lo amarramos. ▪ Lo atracamos. ➤ We tied down the airplanes before the winds hit. ▪ We tied the airplanes down before the winds hit. Amarramos las avionetas antes de que llegaran los vientos.

to **tie nothing to nothing** *(sports)* empatar a cero ➤ Madrid and Manchester tied nothing to nothing. Madrid y Manchester empataron a cero.

to **tie one's shoes** atarse los zapatos

to **tie oneself down with something** ▪ to get tied down with atarse a algo ➤ I don't want to tie myself down with a debt. ▪ I don't want to get tied down with a debt. No me quiero atar a una deuda. ▪ No quiero atarme a una deuda.

to **tie securely** amarrar fuertemente ▪ atar fuerte ▪ atar con fuerza

to **tie someone's hands** *(with rope or cord)* ▪ to bind someone's hands atarle las manos a alguien ▪ maniatar a alguien

to **tie someone's hands behind his back** atarle las manos a la espalda

to **tie something to something 1.** atar algo a algo ▪ amarrar algo a algo ▪ anudar algo a algo **2.** to link something to something anexar algo a algo ➤ They tie the student visa to advance tuition payment. Anexan el visado estudiantil al pago de la matricula.

to **tie the rope around something** atar la cuerda alrededor de algo ➤ He tied the rope around the tree. Ató la cuerda alrededor del árbol.

to **tie the rope to something** atar la cuerda a algo

to **tie up an animal** atar (a) un animal ▪ amarrar (a) un animal ▪ sujetar (a) un animal

to **tie up loose ends** ▪ to tie up the loose ends ▪ to tie up some loose ends atar los cabos sueltos

to **tie up someone** ▪ to tie someone up **1.** to bind someone with rope atar a alguien ▪ *(L. Am.)* ligar a alguien **2.** to occupy all of someone's time tener a alguien ocupado(-a) ▪ estar ocupado(-a) ➤ The robbers tied up the victim. ▪ The robbers tied the victim up. ▪ The robbers bound the victim. Los ladrones ataron a la víctima. ▪ Los ladrones ligaron a la víctima. ➤ The robbers tied him up. ▪ The robbers bound him. Los ladrones lo ataron. ▪ Los ladrones lo ligaron. ▪ *(Sp., leísmo)* Los ladrones le ataron. ➤ A series of meetings has tied up the boss all this week. Una serie de reuniones ha tenido al jefe ocupado toda la semana. ▪ Una serie de reuniones ha tenido ligado al jefe toda la semana. ➤ The boss is tied up in a meeting all day. El jefe estará ocupado todo el día en una reunión.

to **tie (up) someone's hands and feet** ▪ to bind someone's hands and feet atar de pies y manos a alguien ▪ *(L. Am.)* ligar las manos y los pies a alguien ➤ The robbers tied up the victim and gagged him. ▪ The robbers tied the victim up and gagged him. ▪ The robbers bound and gagged the victim. Los ladrones ataron y amordazaron a la víctima. ➤ They tied him up and gagged him. ▪ They bound and gagged him. Lo ataron y lo amordazaron. ▪ *(Sp., leísmo)* Le ataron y le amordazaron.

to **tie up the loose ends** atar los cabos sueltos

to be **tied (nothing to nothing)** estar empatados (a cero) ▪ estar empatados (cero a cero) ▪ ir iguales (cero a cero) ➤ At halftime, Madrid and Manchester were tied nothing to nothing. Al medio tiempo, Madrid y Manchester estaban empatados a cero.

to be **tied to one's mother's apron strings** estar pegado a las faldas de su madre ▪ estar en las faldas de su madre ▪ estar enmadrado ▪ estar bajo las faldas de su madre ▪ estar bajo la pollera de la madre

to be **tied up** estar liado ▪ estar ocupado

to be a **tiger in bed** ser una fiera en la cama

to be **tight as a tick** ▪ to be tighter than a tick ▪ to be a tightwad ser muy codo ▪ ser muy tacaño ▪ ser amarrete ▪ *(Sp.)* ser más agarrado(-a) que un chotis ▪ ser de la virgen del puño ▪ ser devoto(-a) de la virgen del codo

tight budget: to be on a ~ tener un presupuesto ajustado ➤ I'm on a really tight budget this year. Este año tengo un presupuesto muy ajustado.

tight buns *(graphic)* ▪ firm buns ▪ tight ass culo prieto ▪ culo duro ▪ trasero duro ▪ cola dura ▪ nalgas duras

to be **tight-fitting** ▪ to be body-tight estar ceñido ▪ estar ajustado ▪ estar apretado

tight pants pantalón ajustado ▪ pantalón justo ▪ pantalón ceñido *("Un pantalón" is "a pair of pants." "Pairs of pants" is "pantalones.")*

tight security fuerte control de seguridad ▪ extremas medidas de seguridad ▪ extremas medidas de seguridad

tight shoes zapatos apretados ▪ zapatos estrechos

tight spot: to get into a ~ ▪ to get into a jam ▪ to get into a mess meterse en un lío ▪ meterse en líos ▪ meterse en un embolado

to **tighten a screw** apretar un tornillo ▪ ajustar un tornillo

to **tighten one's belt 1.** apretarse el cinturón ▪ ajustarse el cinturón **2.** to reduce expenditures reducir los gastos

to **tighten one's belt a notch** apretar la cintura un agujero ▪ ajustarse el cinturón un agujero

to **tighten the noose (around) 1.** *(someone's neck)* apretar el nudo corredizo **2.** *(figurative)* to close in on someone achicar el cerco a alguien ▪ achicar el perímetro en torno a alguien

to **till the soil 1.** to cultivate the land ▪ to work the land cultivar la tierra ▪ labrar la tierra **2.** to turn over the soil using a tiller dar vuelta a la tierra

tilt of the Leaning Tower of Pisa el desnivel de la torre inclinada de Pisa ▪ la inclinación de la torre de Pisa ➤ Thanks to a repair, the tilt of the Leaning Tower of Pisa has gone from 6 to 5.5 degrees. Gracias a una reforma, el desnivel de la torre inclinada de Pisa ha pasado de 6 a 5,5 grados.

timber! ¡tronco va! ▪ ¡árbol va! ▪ ¡árbol abajo!

time allotted tiempo establecido ▪ tiempo asignado ➤ The time allotted for the test is two hours. El tiempo establecido para el examen es dos horas.

time and again una y otra vez

time and time again una y otra vez

time bomb bomba de relojería ▪ bomba de tiempo ➤ Global warming is a ticking time bomb. El calentamiento global es una bomba de tiempo activada.

time card ficha ▪ tarjeta horaria

time difference (between) diferencia horaria (entre)

time enough: to have ~ ▪ to have enough time tener suficiente tiempo ▪ disponer del tiempo suficiente

time factor *el* factor (de) tiempo

time flies el tiempo vuela ▪ ¡cómo corre el tiempo!

the **time has come to** ha llegado el momento de ▪ ha llegado la ocasión de

time has taken its toll on... el tiempo ha deteriorado... ▪ el tiempo ha ajado... ➤ Time has taken its toll on the ancient ruins. El tiempo ha deteriorado la ruinas antiguas. ▪ El tiempo ha ajado las ruinas antiguas.

time heals all wounds el tiempo todo lo cura ▪ el tiempo lo cura todo ▪ el tiempo cura todas las heridas ▪ el tiempo sana todas las heridas

to **time how long it takes to do something** ▪ to measure the time it takes to do something medir el tiempo que uno tarda en hacer algo ▪ contar el tiempo que se tarda en hacer algo ➤ He timed how long it took him to get to the university. Él contó el tiempo que tardó en ir a la universidad.

time involved el tiempo implicado

time is money el tiempo es oro

time is running out el tiempo se acaba ▪ se acaba el tiempo

time is running out for someone ▪ someone's time is running out se le acaba el tiempo a alguien

time is up ▪ time's up ha terminado el tiempo

the **time it takes** 1. el tiempo que lleva ▪ el tiempo que tarda ▪ el tiempo que demora ▪ el tiempo que emplea 2. *(when there is a reference to a person)* el tiempo que se tarda ➤ A year is the time it takes (for) the Earth to go around the sun. El año es el tiempo que tarda la tierra en dar una vuelta alrededor del sol. ➤ The time it takes (one) to drive from Montevideo to Salto El tiempo que se tarda en conducir de Montevideo a Salto

time limit *el* límite de tiempo

time management *la* gestión de tiempo ▪ manejo del tiempo ▪ *la* administración del tiempo

time of one's death fecha de la muerte de uno

time of one's death: (up) until the ~ ▪ up to the time of one's death hasta la fecha de la muerte de uno

time-out *(sports)* tiempo muerto

time-out! ¡tiempo!

time-release capsule gragea de liberación repetida ▪ gragea de liberación lenta ▪ píldora de liberación lenta

the **time remaining** ▪ the time left el tiempo restante ▪ el tiempo que queda

the **time remaining until arrival** *(esp. on airline flights)* tiempo para el destino

time service servicio de hora ➤ Does Spain have a time service?-Yes, dial 093. ¿Tiene España un servicio de hora?-Sí, se marca 093.

to **time something** cronometrar ▪ medir el tiempo ▪ contar el tiempo ▪ calcular el tiempo ➤ We need someone to time the talks. Necesitamos que alguien mida el tiempo de los discursos. ➤ I timed my trip so as not to miss class. Calculé el tiempo de mi viaje para no perder clases.

to be the **time that suits one best** ▪ to be the best time for one ▪ to be the time that is most convenient for one ser la hora que le viene mejor a uno ▪ ser cuando le viene mejor a uno ▪ ser la hora que más le conviene a uno

to be **time to do something** ser tiempo de ▪ ser tiempo para ▪ ser la hora de

time to do something: (for) there to be ~ haber tiempo para hacer una cosa ▪ haber tiempo para que haga una cosa

time to do something: to have ~ tener tiempo para hacer algo ▪ tener tiempo de hacer algo ▪ darle tiempo a uno para hacer algo ▪ darle tiempo a uno de hacer algo ➤ Do we have time to go for a beer? ¿Tenemos tiempo para ir por una cerveza? ▪ ¿Nos da tiempo para ir por una cerveza?

time to go ▪ time to leave hora de irse ▪ hora de marchar(se) ➤ It's time (for me) to leave. Es hora de irme. ➤ It's time (for us) to leave. Es hora de irnos. ▪ Es hora de marcharnos.

time to go to work 1. time to leave for work hora de ir a trabajar ▪ hora de salir a trabajar 2. time to get busy hora de ponerse a trabajar ➤ It's time to go to work. Es hora de ir a trabajar. ▪ Es hora de salir a trabajar. ➤ It's time (for us) to go to work. ▪ It's time (for us) to get busy. Es hora de ponernos a trabajar.

time to leave: it's ~ ▪ it's time to go es hora de marchar(se) ▪ es hora de irse ▪ es hora de salir

time trial *la* contrarreloj

time warp salto de tiempo ▪ salto en el tiempo

time was *(coll.)* ▪ there was a time when hubo un tiempo en que

the **time will come when** ha de llegar el momento en que... ▪ vendrá el tiempo en que...

time will tell el tiempo (lo) dirá

time zone huso horario ▪ franja horaria

to be **timed to go off** ▪ to be set to go off 1. *(explosion)* estar sincronizado para explotar ▪ estar sincronizado para estallar 2. *(timer)* estar sincronizado para dispararse

timeless gift regalo para toda la vida ▪ regalo intemporal

timeless story cuento de siempre ▪ cuento intemporal ▪ cuento clásico

times a week veces a la semana ▪ veces por semana ➤ He lifts weights three times a week. Levanta pesos tres veces a la semana. ▪ Levanta pesos tres veces por semana.

times as veces más ➤ A dog's sense of smell is at least three hundred times as sharp as a human's. El olfato canino es al menos trescientas veces más agudo que el humano.

times as large as ▪ times the size of de un tamaño igual a una vez y media ➤ Never before had astronomers seen anything like it in the universe: a bubble of water one and a half times as large as the solar system. Nunca hasta ahora habían visto los astrónomos algo así en el universo: una burbuja de agua, de un tamaño igual a una vez y media el sistema solar.

times the size of ▪ times as large as de un tamaño igual a una vez y media ➤ Never before had astronomers seen anything like it in the universe: a bubble of water one and a half times the size of the solar system. Nunca hasta ahora habían visto los astrónomos algo así en el universo: una burbuja de agua, de un tamaño igual a una vez y media el sistema solar.

time's up ▪ time is up se acabó el tiempo ▪ ha terminado el tiempo

the **timing is not right** 1. the timing is off la sincronización está desajustada 2. it's not the right time ▪ it's not the right moment no es el momento ▪ no es el momento adecuado ▪ no es un buen momento ▪ no es el mejor momento

tin foil *el* papel de estaño

tin soldier soldadito de plomo

to be **tinged with racism** ▪ to have a racist tinge tener un tinte racista

to **tinker with an idea** ▪ to turn an idea over in one's mind darle vueltas a una idea (en la cabeza)

tiny little minúsculo ▪ chiquitito

tiny minority pequeña minoría

to be the **tip of the iceberg** ▪ to be just the tip of the iceberg ser la cima del iceberg ▪ ser la punta del iceberg ➤ That's just the tip of the iceberg. Sólo es la cima del iceberg. ▪ Sólo es la punta del iceberg.

to **tip one's hat** tocar el ala del sombrero ➤ In the old days, men tipped their hats at the ladies. Antiguamente los hombres tocaban el ala de su sombrero al paso de una dama.

to **tip the scales in favor of** inclinar la balanza a favor de

tips on how to... consejos de cómo...

tiptoe: to walk on ~ ▪ to go on tiptoe *(L. Am.)* caminar de puntillas ▪ caminar en puntas de pie ▪ empinarse ▪ *(Sp.)* andar de puntas

tire blew out (on me) ▪ I had a blowout se me pinchó una rueda ➤ On the trip to Valencia, the tire blew out (on me). ▪ On the trip to Valencia, I had a blowout. En el viaje a Valencia se me pinchó una rueda.

tireless efforts incansables esfuerzos ▪ denodados esfuerzos

to be **tit for tat** ▪ to be retaliation in kind ser tal para cual ▪ ser el uno para el otro

title deed título de propiedad

the **title is** ▪ it is entitled lleva por título

to a certain extent en cierta medida ▪ hasta cierto punto

to a considerable extent en buena medida

to a lesser extent en menor medida ▪ en menor grado

to add insult to injury para más inri ▪ para mayor inri ▪ (y) encima con recochineo ▪ por si fuera poco ➤ *("INRI" was inscribed on the cross, meaning "Iesus Nazarenus Rex Iudaeorum" ("Jesus of Nazareth, King of the Jews").)* And, to add insult to injury... Y para más inri... ▪ Y para mayor inri... ▪ Encima con recochineo... ➤ That just adds insult to the injury. Sólo pone vinagre en la herida. ▪ Sólo echa vinagre a la herida. ▪ Echa leña al fuego.

to all ▪ to everybody ▪ to everyone para todos ▪ a todos ▪ a todo el mundo ➤ *(C.C. Moore's "A Visit from St. Nicholas")* Merry Christmas to all and to all a good night! ¡Feliz Navidad a todos y a todos buenas noches!

to and fro de acá para allá

to and fro: to swing ~ *(literary)* ▪ to swing back and forth hamacarse ▪ balancearse ▪ columpiarse

to answer your question ▪ in answer to your question para responder a su pregunta ▪ para contestar su pregunta ➤ To answer your question, we need to get into some higher math. Para contestar tu pregunta, necesitamos meternos con matemática avanzada.

to be announced ▪ TBA a ser anunciado

to be exact ▪ to be precise para ser exacto ▪ para ser preciso ▪ para más señas ▪ por más señas ▪ concretamente

to be frank ▪ to be honest (with you) para ser(te) sincero

to be honest (with you) ▪ to be frank para ser(te) sincero

to be more precise: (or) ~ bueno, para ser más exactos

to be or not to be, that is the question *(Shakespeare's* Hamlet*)* ser o no ser, ésa es la cuestión ■ ser o no ser, he aquí la cuestión

to be sure *(appositional phrase)* ciertamente ■ bien cierto es ■ por cierto ➤ He's incompetent, to be sure. Bien cierto es que es incompetente.

to begin this year que debe comenzar este mismo año ➤ The European summit in Lisbon yesterday approved a series of reforms to begin this year. La cumbre europea de Lisboa aprobó ayer un programa de reformas, que debe comenzar este mismo año.

to begin with para empezar ➤ *(opening sentence of "A Christmas Carol" by Dickens)* Marley was dead, to begin with. Digamos que, para empezar, Marley ya estaba muerto. *("To begin with" and "para empezar" are puns in English and Spanish, meaning both "to begin the narrative" and "at first, but only at first.")*

to be **to blame for** tener la culpa de ■ ser el culpable de ■ ser la culpable de

to boot 1. *(in a positive sense)* de paso **2.** *(in a negative sense)* por si fuera poco ■ para rematarla ■ y hasta ➤ I fixed the leak in the sink and repaired the light switch to boot. Arreglé la gotera en la pileta y reparé el interruptor de la luz de paso. ➤ The thieves took all the silver and the mantel clock to boot. Los ladrones se llevaron toda la platería y hasta el reloj del manto.

to choose between a elegir entre ➤ *(breakfast menu)* Cereals to choose between Cereales a elegir entre

to choose from para escoger ■ a elegir ➤ There are (a variety of) lodgings to choose from. Hay alojamientos para escoger.

to cite an obvious example ■ to give you an obvious example para no ir más lejos ■ sin ir más lejos

to coin a phrase para acuñar una frase

to complicate matters para complicar las cosas ■ para enturbiar las cosas ■ para enredar la madeja

to cover up one's action ■ in order to cover up one's action para disimular su acción ➤ *(news item)* To cover up his action, the youth went to the window and asked what happened. Para disimular su acción, el joven se asomó a la ventana y preguntó que sucedía.

to date ■ up to today ■ up to now ■ so far hasta la fecha ■ hasta el momento ■ a la fecha

to each his own a cada uno lo suyo ■ a cada cual lo suyo ■ cada cual a su aire ■ cada uno a su antojo ■ cada uno con lo suyo ■ cada cual con lo suyo ■ cada maestro con su librito

to each other uno al otro ■ entre ➤ They spoke to each other. ■ They greeted each other. ■ They said hello to each other. Se saludaron uno al otro. ■ Se saludaron entre ellos.

to everybody ■ to everyone ■ to all a todos ■ a todo el mundo ■ para todos ■ para todo el mundo

to everyone ■ to everybody ■ to all a todos ■ a todo el mundo

to everything a todo ➤ He's the type of person who says no to everything. Es la clase de persona que dice que no a todo.

to find out ■ in order to find out para averiguarlo ■ para saberlo ■ para enterarse

to find out what... ■ in order to find out what... para averiguar lo que... ■ para averiguar qué... ■ para enterarse de que...

to get on with the story para seguir con la historia ■ para proseguir con la historia

to give you an example ■ just to give you an example ■ as an example ■ by way of example por ejemplo ■ a guisa de ejemplo ■ a modo de ejemplo

to give you an idea of how... ■ in order to give you some idea of how... para darte una idea de cómo... ■ (usted) para darle una idea de cómo...

to give you an obvious example ■ to cite an obvious example para darte un ejemplo obvio ■ para no ir más lejos ■ sin ir más lejos

to go 1. to take out para llevar **2.** remaining por delante ➤ Is this to stay or to go? ■ For here, or to go? ¿Es para consumir aquí o para llevar? ■ ¿Para aquí o para llevar? ■ *(Sp.)* ¿Para tomar (aquí) o para llevar? ➤ We have a month to go until Christmas vacation. Tenemos un mes por delante hasta las vacaciones navideñas.

to go on ■ to act on con las que actuar ■ para empezar a trabajar ➤ The police don't have any leads to go on. ■ The police don't have any leads to act on. La policía no tiene pistas con las que actuar. ➤ I hope they caught him; they had a license number to go on. Espero que le cojan. Tienen su matrícula para empezar a trabajar.

to his men a los suyos

to hold onto de que asirse ■ de donde agarrarse ➤ There's no railing to hold onto. No hay pasamano de que asirse. ■ No hay pasamanos de donde agarrarse.

to keep it from freezing ■ in order to keep it from freezing **1.** *(present and future)* para evitar que se hiele ■ para evitar que se congele **2.** *(past)* para evitar que se helara ■ para evitar que se congelara ■ para evitar que se helase ■ para evitar que se congelase

to make a long story short y para abreviar ■ en resumen ■ en resumidas cuentas

to make up for it ■ in order to make up for it para compensar ■ como contrapartida

to me ■ in my opinion para mí ➤ To me most TV is boring. Para mí, la mayoría de la televisión es aburrida.

to mention a few por mencionar algunos

to my knowledge ■ so far as I know ■ as far as I know que yo sepa ■ hasta donde yo sé

to my sorrow para mi desdicha ■ para mi desgracia

to my surprise para mi sorpresa

to my way of thinking ■ the way I see it a mi modo de ver ■ a mi entender

to name a few para mencionar sólo unos cuantos ■ por mencionar sólo unos cuantos

to be **to one's advantage** convenirle a uno ■ redundar en beneficio suyo ➤ It's to your advantage to... Redunda en beneficio tuyo...

to one's credit 1. in one's favor a su favor **2.** to one's name en su haber ➤ To her credit, she didn't reveal the secret. A su favor, no reveló el secreto. ➤ Isaac Asimov is one of the world's most prolific authors, with more than four hundred books to his credit. Isaac Asimov es uno de los autores más prolíficos del mundo con más de cuatrocientos libros en su haber.

to one's face directamente a la cara ■ de frente

to one's heart's content a pedir de boca

to be **to one's liking** ser del agrado de uno ■ ser a gusto de uno

to one's satisfaction a salvo de uno ■ a satisfacción de uno ■ ser a gusto de uno

to one's sorrow a desdicha de uno ■ para la desdicha de uno ■ para la desgracia de uno

to oneself para uno mismo ■ para sus adentros

to perfection a la perfección ➤ This steak is cooked to perfection. Este filete está cocido a la perfección.

to prevent accidents en evitación de accidentes ■ para evitar accidentes ➤ *(swimming pool sign)* To prevent accidents bathers must know how to swim. En evitación de accidentes los bañistas deben saber nadar. ■ Para evitar accidentes los bañistas deben saber nadar.

to prove it ■ (and) just to prove it ■ (and) to prove it (y) para probarlo

to prove my point... para que veas que tengo razón... ■ para mostrarte que tengo razón...

to save time ■ in order to save time para ahorrar tiempo

to say nothing of por no hablar de

to scale: to draw something ~ dibujar algo a escala ■ dibujar algo a la medida ➤ I want to draw this floor plan to scale on my computer. Quiero dibujar este plano a escala en mi ordenador.

to set the record straight para que quede claro ➤ To set the record straight, I never said that! ¡Para que quede claro nunca dije eso!

to some (people) para algunos ■ para unos

to speak with an operator, press zero para hablar con un(-a) operador(-a), pulse cero ■ para hablar con un(-a) operador(-a) presione cero ■ para hablar con un(-a) operador(-a) marque cero ■ para hablar con un(-a) operador(-a) teclee cero

to such an extent that ■ so much so that a tal grado que ■ a tal punto que

to sum up (the main points) ▪ in order to sum up the main points ▪ summing up the main points ▪ by way of summing up para resumir los puntos principales ▪ a modo de resumen

to tell you the truth a decir verdad ▪ a la verdad ▪ para ser sincero ▪ en honor a la verdad ▪ para decir la verdad

to that end para ese fin ▪ con ese fin ▪ para ese propósito ▪ para ello

to the best of my ability **1.** *(present and future)* lo mejor que pueda ▪ lo mejor que me sea posible **2.** *(past)* lo mejor que pude

to the best of my knowledge según mi saber y entender ▪ hasta donde yo sé

to the best of my recollection ▪ as best I can recall ▪ as far as I can remember hasta donde puedo recordar ▪ hasta donde puedo acordarme ▪ hasta donde (yo) me acuerdo

to the death hasta la muerte ▪ a muerte ▪ a vida o muerte

to the death: a fight ~ duelo a muerte

to the death: to fight ~ pelear a muerte ▪ luchar a muerte

to the detriment of en detrimento de

to the disappointment of para decepción de

to the end of the aisle al fin del pasillo ▪ al fondo del pasillo ▪ al extremo del pasillo ➤ Continue down to the end of the aisle and turn left. Sigue al fin del pasillo y gira a la izquierda. ▪ Sigue al fondo del pasillo y gira a la izquierda. ▪ Sigue al extremo del pasillo y gira a la izquierda. ▪ Sigue hasta el final del pasillo y dobla a la izquierda.

to the ends of the Earth hasta los confines del mundo ▪ hasta los confines de la Tierra

to the exclusion of all else ▪ to the exclusion of everything else excluyendo todo lo demás

to the extent possible ▪ so far as (is) possible ▪ as far as possible en la medida de lo posible ▪ en la medida en que sea posible

to the extent that one can en lo que uno pueda ▪ hasta donde uno pueda

to the fact that a que ➤ The speaker alluded to the fact that... El orador aludió a que...

to the greatest extent possible ▪ to the maximum extent possible ▪ to the extent possible en la medida de lo posible ▪ hasta donde sea posible ▪ tanto como sea posible

to the highest level in history ▪ to its highest level in history ▪ to historic highs al máximo histórico ➤ *(headline)* The heat wave in Spain rockets electricity consumption to its highest level in history. La ola de calor dispara en España el consumo de la energía eléctrica al máximo histórico.

to the letter ▪ strictly ▪ in every particular ▪ to the last particular al pie de la letra ▪ a rajatabla ▪ a pies juntillas ▪ sin cuestionamiento ➤ Few people today accept to the letter the theories of Freud. Pocas personas hoy en día aceptan a pies juntillas las teorías de Freud.

to the rescue al rescate

to the top *(literal and figurative)* a la cima ▪ a la cumbre ➤ This road takes you to the top of the mountain. Este camino te lleva a la cima de la montaña. ➤ His newest CD took him to the top of the charts. Su último CD lo llevó a la cima del ranking.

to the utmost a más no poder ▪ hasta más no poder

to the verge of a paso de ➤ Poor management has taken the company to the verge of bankruptcy. ▪ Poor management has brought the company to the verge of bankruptcy. ▪ Poor management has taken the company to the point of bankruptcy. ▪ Poor management has brought the company to the point of bankruptcy. ▪ Poor management has put the company on the verge of bankruptcy. La pésima gestión ha puesto a la compañía a un paso de la bancarrota.

to think that... ¡pensar que...!

to this day hasta el día de hoy ▪ hasta hoy en día ▪ aún hoy en día ▪ hasta hoy ▪ hasta este momento ▪ hasta la fecha

to top it all off **1.** and as if that weren't enough para colmo ▪ para postre ▪ y de postre ▪ y para rematarla ▪ y por si fuera poco **2.** to add insult to injury para más inri

to varying degrees en distinta medida ➤ Almost a hundred cars were damaged to varying degrees. Casi cien coches resultaron dañados en distinta medida.

to visit friends ▪ for the purpose of visiting friends ▪ in order to visit friends para visitar a amigos ➤ Saturday I'm going to Coslada to visit some friends from home. El sábado voy a Coslada para visitar a amigos de mi pueblo.

to wear around the house ▪ for (wearing) around the house para andar por casa ▪ de andar por casa ▪ de entre casa

to what extent hasta qué punto ▪ hasta dónde

to what he called... a lo que llamaba...

to which a lo que ▪ a la que

to whoever answers *(coll.)* ▪ to whomever answers a quien conteste ➤ Just give the message to whoever answers. Sólo da el mensaje a quien conteste.

to whom a que ▪ a quien

to whom? ¿a quién?

to wit *(literary)* ▪ namely a saber

to you **1.** a ti ▪ a usted **2.** in your case para ti ▪ para usted ➤ I'm Mrs. McDougall, Margie to you. Soy la Señora McDougall, Margie para ti.

today more than ever hoy más que nunca

today's lesson **1.** *(present or future)* the lesson for today la lección de hoy ▪ la lección para hoy **2.** *(past)* the lesson which was presented today la lección por hoy

today's special *(L. Am.)* el especial del día ▪ el plato del día ▪ el platillo del día ▪ *(Sp.)* el menú del día *(The complete menu is "la carta.")*

today's world: in ~ en el mundo de hoy (en día)

together at last finalmente juntos ▪ ¡al fin juntos!

together or separate? *(check)* ¿juntos o separados?

together with ▪ along with ▪ combined with junto con ▪ en compañía de ▪ en unión con ▪ unido a ▪ así como ▪ en combinación con ➤ *(news item)* Fog, together with excessive speed and lack of safe distances between cars, caused fourteen deaths. La niebla, unida al exceso de velocidad y a la falta de distancias de seguridad, causó catorce muertos.

the **toilet overflowed** el water se desbordó ▪ el retrete se desbordó

toilet water *(archaic)* ▪ (eau de) cologne (el agua de) colonia

to be **told what to do** ...que le digan lo que tiene que hacer ➤ He doesn't like to be told what to do. ▪ He doesn't like being told what to do. ▪ He doesn't like anyone to tell him what to do. No le gusta que le digan lo que tiene que hacer.

toll an illness has taken estragos de la enfermedad

tollbooth caseta de peaje

tomorrow morning mañana por la mañana ▪ mañana de mañana ▪ mañana en la mañana

to **tone something down** ▪ to tone down something rebajar el tono de ▪ moderar el tono de

tongue-in-cheek con la boca pequeña ▪ en broma ▪ en chiste

to be **tongue-tied** tener lengua de trapo

tonic water ▪ quinine water *el* agua tónica

tons of food ▪ loads of food una bestialidad de comida ▪ comida a patadas

too bad! ¡mala suerte! ▪ ¡ajo y agua!

to be **too big for** ser grande para ▪ ser demasiado grande para ▪ ser muy grande para

to be **too busy to do something** estar demasiado ocupado para hacer algo ➤ I've been too busy to clean the apartment. He estado demasiado ocupado para limpiar el piso.

to be **too deep to touch bottom** haber suficiente profundidad ➤ I tried to touch bottom, but it was still too deep. Traté de tocar fondo, pero todavía estaba demasiado profundo. ▪ Traté de tocar fondo, pero todavía estaba muy profundo.

to be **too early to** ser aún pronto para ➤ The authorities indicated it was too early to determine the causes of the (airplane) crash. Las autoridades indicaron que aún era pronto para determinar las causas del siniestro.

to be **too embarrassed** ▪ to be too shy ▪ not to have the nerve darle vergüenza a alguien ▪ darle corte a alguien ➤ I'd like to ask her to go to the dance with me, but I'm too embarrassed. ▪ I'd like to ask her to the dance, but I don't have the nerve. ▪ I'd like to ask her to go to the dance with me, but I'm too shy. Me gustaría pedirle que venga al baile conmigo, pero me da corte. ▪ Me gustaría pedirle que venga al baile conmigo, pero me da vergüenza.

to be **too far away from** estar demasiado lejos de ➤ I was too far away from the podium to hear well. Estaba demasiado lejos del podio para oír bien.

to be **too fragmented** ser muy fragmentado(-a) ➤ The information is too fragmented to know with certainty. La información está muy fragmentada para saber con certeza.

to be **too good to be true** ser muy bueno para ser cierto ▪ *(Sp.)* ser de película ➤ It's too good to be true. No puede ser. ▪ Es de película.

to be **too late** ya ser demasiado tarde ➤ When the doctor arrived, it was already too late. Cuando llegó el médico, ya era demasiado tarde.

too little time demasiado poco tiempo ▪ muy poco tiempo ▪ poquísimo tiempo

to be **too loud** estar muy alto ▪ estar muy fuerte ➤ The stereo is too loud. El estéreo está muy fuerte. ▪ El estéreo está demasiado fuerte. ▪ El estéreo suena muy alto. ▪ El estéreo está muy alto.

too many cooks spoil the broth ▪ there are too many chiefs and not enough Indians muchos cocineros dañan el puchero ▪ muchos jefes y pocos indios

to be **too much 1.** to cost too much ser demasiado ▪ cuesta demasiado **2.** to be the limit ▪ to be over the top ser el colmo **3.** *(person)* ser la repanocha ▪ pasarse ➤ You're too much! ¡Eres la repanocha! ▪ ¡Tú te pasas! ▪ *(vos)* ¡Vos te pasás!

to be **too much for someone (to handle)** venirle ancho a alguien ▪ quedarle grande a alguien

to be **too narrow** ser muy angosto ▪ ser demasiado angosto ➤ This parking space is too narrow for the van. Este aparcamiento es demasiado angosto para la furgoneta.

to be **too shy** ▪ to be too embarrassed ▪ not to have the nerve darle vergüenza a alguien ▪ darle corte a alguien ➤ I'd like to ask her to go to the dance with me, but I'm too shy. ▪ I'd like to ask her to the dance, but I don't have the nerve. ▪ I'd like to ask her to go to the dance with me, but I'm too embarrassed. Me gustaría pedirle que venga al baile conmigo, pero me da corte.

to be **too tight** *(clothes, shoes)* estar muy ajustado ▪ estar muy apretado ▪ estar muy justo ▪ estar demasiado ajustado ▪ estar demasiado apretado ▪ estar demasiado justo ▪ quedarle muy ajustado ▪ quedarle muy apretado ▪ quedarle muy justo ▪ apretarle ➤ It's too tight (on me). ▪ It fits me too tight. ▪ It's too tight a fit. Me aprieta. ▪ Me queda muy ajustado. ▪ Me queda muy justo. ▪ Me queda muy apretado. ➤ These shoes are too tight. Estos zapatos me aprietan. ▪ Estos zapatos me quedan muy ajustados. ▪ Estos zapatos me quedan muy apretados.

too tight: to screw something in ~ apretar algo demasiado ▪ apretar algo mucho ➤ Don't screw it in too tight, or you'll strip the threads. No lo aprietes mucho, o lo pasarás de rosca.

tooth and nail: to defend someone ~ defender a alguien con uñas y dientes ▪ defender a alguien con capa y espada ▪ defender a ultranza

toothless gums encías sin dientes ▪ encías desnudas

top brass *(military)* cúpula (militar)

top fee honorario máximo ▪ *(people with agents)* máximo caché

top floor último piso

top hat sombrero de copa alta

top-heavy ▪ having too high a center of gravity inestable

top-level talks conversaciones al más alto nivel

top-notch ▪ first-rate de primera fuerza ▪ de primera línea

top of a hill ▪ crest of a hill cima de una colina ▪ cresta de una colina

to be the **top of the line** ser el más alto de la gama ▪ ser el más alto de la fila

top of the mountain cima de la montaña ▪ cuerda de la montaña

top of the world techo del mundo ▪ cima del mundo

top of the world: to be on ~ estar en el séptimo cielo ▪ estar en la cima del mundo

the **top one** el superior ▪ la superior

to be **top priority** ser primordial ▪ ser de prioridad máxima ▪ ser de máxima prioridad

top secret top secret ▪ secreto de estado

to be **topsy-turvy** ▪ to be in a state of chaos estar manga por hombro ▪ andar manga por hombro ▪ estar en estado caótico

to be **torn between (two alternatives)** debatirse entre (dos alternativas) ▪ estar en la disyuntiva

torn cartilage cartílago roto

torrential rain(s) lluvia torrencial

torrents of water *los* torrentes de agua ▪ *el* agua a raudales ▪ agua a caudales

to **toss a coin** ▪ to flip a coin echar una moneda al aire ▪ tirar una moneda al aire ▪ *(Mex.)* echar volado

to **toss and turn** dar vueltas (y vueltas) ▪ pasarse dando vueltas ➤ I tossed and turned all night. Di vueltas (y vueltas) toda la noche. ▪ Me pasé dando vueltas toda la noche.

to **toss one's cookies** *(slang)* ▪ to throw up ▪ to vomit echar las tripas ▪ echar los hígados

to **toss the salad** remover la ensalada ▪ revolver la ensalada ▪ mezclar la ensalada

to **total a car 1.** dejar el coche un siniestro total ▪ dejar el coche para la historia ▪ dejar el auto hecho trizas **2.** *(claims adjuster's call)* to declare a car totalled declarar un coche un siniestro total ➤ The insurance agent totalled out the car. El agente de seguros ha declarado el coche un siniestro total.

total chaos: to be plunged into ~ estar sumido en el caos más absoluto ▪ sumirse en el caos más absoluto

total eclipse *el* eclipse total ▪ eclipse anular

a **total of** un total de ▪ un balance de ➤ A total of ninety people died in the crash. Un total de noventa personas murieron en el accidente aéreo. ▪ Un balance de noventa personas murieron en el accidente aéreo.

to be **totally useless** ser un cero a la izquierda ▪ ser totalmente inútil

to **touch a sore spot** ▪ to strike a nerve tocar en lo vivo ▪ meter el dedo en la llaga ▪ tocar un punto sensible ▪ tocar un punto neurálgico

touch and go's: to do ~ *(flying lessons)* ▪ to land and take off again repeatedly tocar (tierra) y despegar

to **touch bottom** tocar (el) fondo ▪ hacer pie

touch of one's hand *el* roce de la mano de uno ▪ contacto con la mano de uno

to **touch off a crisis** provocar una crisis ▪ propiciar una crisis

to **touch off a debate** ▪ to spark a debate ▪ to cause a debate provocar un debate ▪ propiciar un debate ▪ incitar a un debate

to **touch on the subject of** tocar el tema de ▪ abordar el tema de ➤ The script touches on some interesting subjects. El guión toca unos temas interesantes. ▪ El guión aborda unos temas interesantes.

to **touch someone deeply** ▪ to move someone deeply conmover a alguien profundamente ▪ emocionar a alguien vivamente

to **touch the floor** *(bedspread, comforter)* arrastrar el suelo

to be **touched by** ▪ to be moved by emocionarse por

to be **touched in the head** ▪ to be cracked estar loco(-a) de remate ▪ estar chiflado(-a)

to be **tough as nails** no entrarle ni las balas

to be **tough as shoe leather** *(steak)* ▪ to be like shoe leather estar (duro) como la suela de un zapato

tough guy tipo duro ▪ tipo recio

tough luck! ▪ too bad! ¡chínchate! ▪ ¡lástima! ▪ ¡ajo y agua! ▪ ¡mala suerte! ▪ ¡te fastidias! ▪ ¡a aguantarse! ▪ ¡a jorobarse! ▪ *(off-color)* ¡a joderse!

to be a **tough nut to crack** ▪ to be a hard person to persuade ▪ to be a difficult person to persuade *(L. Am.)* un clavo duro de morder ▪ *(Sp.)* un hueso duro de roer

tour bus autobús turístico

tour guide guía turístico ▪ guía turística

tour of Europe ▪ European tour gira de Europa ▪ gira europea

tour of the White House recorrido de la Casa Blanca ▪ recorrido por la Casa Blanca

to **tow a vehicle** remolcar un vehículo

to **tow away a vehicle** ▪ to tow a vehicle away remolcar un vehículo ➤ They towed away the car. ▪ They towed the car away. Remolcaron el carro. ➤ They towed it away. Lo remolcaron.

tow truck *el* camión (de) remolque

toward the end of the month ▪ near the end of the month ▪ late in the month ▪ as the end of the month approaches ▪ as we approach the end of the month a finales de mes

toward the end of the week hacia el fin de semana ▪ al final de la semana ▪ a fines de (la) semana

toward the end of the year ▪ as the end of the year approaches ▪ as we approach the end of the year hacia el final del año ▪ a finales del año

toward you hacia atrás ➤ Open the door toward you. Abra la puerta hacia atrás.

tower of Babel ▪ chaotic scene *la* torre de Babel

town councilman ▪ city councilman *el, la* edil

town hall *(all countries)* ayuntamiento ▪ *(L. Am.) la* municipalidad ▪ *(Arg., Uru.)* intendencia municipal

toy soldier soldado de juguete ▪ soldadito de juguete

to **toy with the idea (of)** ▪ to consider the idea (of) darle vueltas a la idea (de) ▪ considerar la idea (de)

trace of rastro de

trace of: to find no ~ no encontrar rastro de

a **trace of snow** un poquito de nieve ▪ algo de nieve ▪ *(Sp., coll.)* un pelín de nieve ➤ There is a trace of snow on the grass today, but none on the pavement. Hoy hay un pelín de nieve sobre la hierba, pero no sobre el pavimento.

to **track a package** hacer un seguimiento de un paquete ▪ rastrear un paquete

to **track a shipment** hacer un seguimiento de un envío ▪ rastrear un envío

track-and-field events *(sports)* atletismo

to **track down someone** ▪ to track someone down rastrear a alguien ▪ localizar a alguien ▪ averiguar el paradero de alguien ➤ When I go to Spain, I'm going to try to track down my old Spanish professor. Cuando vaya a España, quiero rastrear a mi antiguo catedrático de lengua española. ▪ Cuando vaya a España, voy a intentar localizar a mi antiguo catedrático de lengua española.

track record el historial ▪ los antecedentes

track *x* *(on a CD)* ▪ band *x* pista *x* ➤ The song is on track six. ▪ The song is on band six. La canción está en la pista seis.

tracker organ órgano mecánico

tracking number(s) número de seguimiento

traction: good ~ buena tracción ▪ *el* buen agarre ➤ I need a heel and sole with good traction. Necesito un tacón y una suela con buen agarre.

trade agreement acuerdo comercial con otro país ➤ *(headline)* President gets special powers to negotiate trade agreements El presidente consigue poderes especiales para negociar acuerdos comerciales con otros países

to be a **trade-off** ser una elección entre ➤ It's a trade-off between speed and accuracy. Es una elección entre velocidad y precisión.

to **trade off with someone** *(coll.)* ▪ to alternate with someone ▪ to trade places with someone cambiar de turno con alguien ▪ cambiarle el turno a alguien ▪ sustituir a alguien ▪ reemplazar a alguien

to **trade places with someone 1.** to trade shifts with someone cambiar el turno con alguien ▪ cambiarle el turno a alguien **2.** to trade seats with someone cambiar de sitio con alguien **3.** to put oneself in another's shoes ponerse en el lugar de otra persona ▪ ocupar el lugar de otra persona

trade school escuela de oficios

trade secret secreto del oficio

trade winds vientos alisios

traditionalist that he was ▪ being the traditionalist that he was con lo tradicional que era ▪ con lo clásico que era

traffic circle *(Mex.)* glorieta ▪ *(Sp.)* rotunda ▪ glorieta ▪ rotonda

traffic jam atasco (de tráfico) ▪ embotellamiento (de tráfico) ▪ *la* retención (de tráfico)

traffic officer *el, la* agente de circulación ▪ agente de tránsito

trail of blood: to leave a ~ dejar un reguero de sangre

trail of oil: to leave a ~ ▪ to spill a trail of oil dejar un reguero de gasóleo ▪ verter un reguero de gasóleo ➤ *(news item)* The Portuguese tanker which sank on the seventeenth of this month off the Biscayan coast has begun to spill a trail of gas oil. El carguero portugués que se hundió el pasado día 17 frente a la costa vizcaína ha empezado a dejar un reguero de gasóleo. *("Gasóleo" is both "heating oil" and "diesel fuel oil.")*

to **trail off** *(voice)* irse apagando ➤ He said he'd help me, but when I tried to pin him down on a time, his voice trailed off and he changed the subject. Dijo que me ayudaría, pero cuando intenté concretar una hora para quedar, su voz se fue apagando y cambió de tema.

to **train a priest** formar a un sacerdote ➤ The English College in Valladolid, founded by Felipe II, trains English Catholic priests to this day. El Colegio Inglés en Valladolid, fundado por Felipe Segundo, forma sacerdotes ingleses católicos aún hoy en día.

to **train an animal** amaestrar a un animal ▪ adiestrar a un animal

train for ▪ train to ▪ train bound for *el* tren con destino a

train hub ▪ connecting point of the trains *el* enlace de (los) trenes ▪ *el* intercambiador de los trenes

the **train is at the platorm** el tren ya está puesto (en el andén) ▪ el tren ya está en la plataforma

the **train is coming** ▪ the train is approaching **1.** *(when the train is in sight)* se acerca el tren ▪ el tren se acerca **2.** *(but I can't see it yet)* el tren está al caer ▪ el tren está por caer

train of thought: to lose one's ~ perder el hilo (de lo que uno estaba diciendo) ▪ írsele el santo al cielo ➤ I lost my train of thought. Perdí el hilo. ▪ Se me fue el santo al cielo.

train station ▪ railroad station estación de ferrocarril ▪ estación ferroviaria

trained dog 1. perro amaestrado **2.** *(especially trained, such as a guide dog, police or sniffer dog, etc.)* perro adiestrado

training camp campo de entrenamiento

training course: to take a ~ hacer un curso de formación ▪ hacer un curso de capacitación

transcript: academic ~ certificado de notas ▪ certificado de escolaridad ▪ historial escolaridad ▪ historial académico

to **transfer an employee** trasladar a un empleado ▪ transferir a un empleado

transfer of power traspaso de poder

transitory effect 1. *(lasting hours or days)* efecto transitorio **2.** *(lasting only moments)* momentary effect ▪ fleeting effect efecto fugaz ▪ efecto pasajero ▪ efecto momentáneo ➤ The medication has a transitory effect. La medicina tiene un efecto fugaz. ➤ Its effect is transitory. El efecto es fugaz.

to be **translated as** traducirse como ➤ The phrase "Dodger fan" (fan de los Dodgers) was translated on the Internet as "el ventilador del trampista" (the trickster's electric fan). La frase "Dodger fan" (fan de los Dodgers) se tradujo en Internet como "el ventilador del trampista" (the trickster's electric fan).

to be **trapped in an elevator** estar encerrado en un ascensor ▪ quedarse encerrado en un ascensor ▪ estar atrapado en un ascensor ▪ quedarse atrapado en un ascensor

trash can ▪ garbage can cubo de basura ▪ lata de (la) basura

to **travel abroad** ▪ to go abroad viajar al extranjero ▪ irse al extranjero ▪ viajar al exterior ▪ irse al exterior

to **travel all over the country** viajar por todo el país

to **travel at high speed** circular a alta velocidad ▪ ir a alta velocidad ▪ desplazarse a alta velocidad ➤ The car was traveling at 90 miles per hour. El coche circulaba a 90 millas por hora. ▪ El coche iba a 90 millas por hora. El coche se desplazaba a 90 millas por hora.

to **travel at *x* miles per hour** ▪ to go *x* miles per hour circular a *x* millas por hora ▪ ir a *x* millas por hora

to **travel by train** viajar en tren

traveling companion compañero(-a) de viaje

traveling salesman vendedor ambulante

to **tread lightly** ir con pies de plomo ▪ pisar de puntillas ➤ Tread lightly! *(tú)* ¡Ve con pies de plomo! ▪ *(usted)* Vaya con pies de plomo!

to **tread on thin ice** ▪ to be on slippery ground danzar sobre un volcán ▪ estar en arenas movedizas ▪ estar parado(-a) en arenas movedizas ▪ estar pisando terreno resbaladizo

to **treat a subject** tratar un tema

to **treat it as such** tratarlo(-a) como tal

to **treat oneself to something** regalarse algo ▪ obsequiarse algo ➤ Treat yourself to an ice cream! ¡Regálate un helado! ▪ ¡Obséquiate un helado!

to **treat someone right** tratar bien a alguien ▪ tratar a alguien correctamente ▪ hacerle bien a alguien

to **treat someone to something** regalarle algo a alguien ▪ obsequiarle algo a alguien

to **treat something lightly** dar poca importancia a algo

to **treat them as such** tratarlos(-as) como tales

to be **treated as such** tratársele como tal ▪ ser tratado como tal

tree house casa en el árbol ▪ casa del árbol ▪ cabaña en el árbol

to **tremble with fear** ▪ to tremble with fright ▪ to tremble from fright temblar de miedo

trial and error: by ~ por tanteos ▪ por tanteo ▪ al tanteo ➤ We found the solution by trial and error. Encontramos la solución por tanteos.

trial balloon: to send up a ~ lanzar un globo sonda ▪ enviar un globo sonda ▪ *(plural)* lanzar globos sonda

to be a **tributary of** ▪ to flow into ser un afluente de ▪ fluir a ▪ desembocar en ➤ The Cifuentes River is a tributary of the Tagus. ▪ The Cifuentes River flows into the Tagus. El río Cifuentes es un afluente de Tajo. ▪ El río Cifuentes fluye al Tajo. ▪ El río Cifuentes desemboca en el Tajo.

trick question pregunta tramposa ▪ pregunta capciosa

to **trick someone into believing (that...)** ▪ to fool someone into believing (that...) engañar a alguien para que crea (que...)

trickle of *(water, blood, etc.)* reguero de

tricks of the trade mañas del oficio

to **trigger a chemical reaction** desencadenar una reacción química

to **trigger a debate** ▪ to cause a debate ▪ to provoke a debate provocar un debate ▪ incitar (a) un debate ▪ fomentar un debate

trim (on a house) adornos ➤ It's a brick house with white trim. Es una casa de ladrillos con adornos blancos.

trim tab *(of an airplane)* el compensador (dinámico) ▪ aleta de compensación

trip abroad *el* viaje al extranjero ▪ viaje al exterior

to **trip someone** ▪ to put one's foot in front of someone hacer una zancadilla a alguien ▪ echar una zancadilla a alguien

to **trip the circuit breaker** ▪ to throw the circuit breaker ▪ to flip the circuit breaker hacer saltar el (automático) central ▪ hacer saltar el (automático) general ▪ hacer saltar la llave central ▪ hacer saltar la llave general ➤ A short circuit in the water heater tripped the circuit breaker. Un cortocircuito en el calentador del agua hizo saltar la llave general. ➤ An electrical overload tripped the circuit breaker. Una sobrecarga eléctrica hizo saltar la llave general.

trip to the doctor visita al médico

trip to the grocery store: to make a ~ ▪ to go to the grocery store hacer un viaje al mercado ▪ hacer un viaje a la tienda de abarrotes ▪ ir al almacén ▪ *(Sp.)* hacer un viaje al ultramarino ➤ I've made three trips to the grocery store today. He hecho tres viajes al mercado hoy. ▪ He ido tres veces al almacén hoy.

trip up someone: to try to ~ 1. *(literal)* intentar que alguien tropiece **2.** *(figurative)* to try to make someone make a mistake intentar que alguien se equivoque ▪ intentar que alguien se confunda ▪ tratar de que alguien cometa un error

trivial pursuit: to play ~ jugar al trivial

trivialization of *la* trivialización de

troop deployment ▪ deployment of troops *el* despliegue de tropas

tropical storm tormenta tropical ▪ la sudestada

the **trouble began...** el problema empezó... ➤ The trouble began with... El problema empezó con... ➤ The trouble began when... El problema empezó cuando...

the **trouble is that...** la pena es que... ▪ lo malo es que... ▪ el problema es que...

troubled life vida atribulada ▪ vida aquejada de problemas

to **trounce someone** *(sports, debate, election, etc.)* ganar sobradamente a alguien ▪ vapulear a alguien ▪ ganar por amplia ventaja ▪ ganar por amplia diferencia

true, but... ▪ that's true, but... ▪ it's true, but... muy cierto, pero... ▪ es cierto, pero...

true extent of the damage *el* alcance real del daño ▪ alcance real de la avería

true friend amigo(-a) auténtico(-a) ▪ amigo(-a) verdadero(-a) ▪ *(Mex., in the masculine only)* amigo del bueno

true love amor verdadero ▪ *(L. Am.)* amor del bueno

the **true meaning of...** el verdadero significado de...

true self: one's ~ el verdadero yo de uno ▪ el verdadero yo interior *("El yo" refers to both male and female.)*

to be a **true story (about...)** ▪ to be a real life story (about...) ser una historia verdadera (sobre...) ▪ ser una historia de la vida real (sobre...) ➤ The movie is based on a true story. La película está basada en una historia verdadera.

to be **true to one's promise** ser fiel uno a su promesa ▪ cumplir uno con su promesa

to be **true to one's word** ser fiel uno a su palabra ▪ cumplir uno con su palabra

true vegetable vegetal propiamente dicho ➤ The tomato is not a true vegetable, but a fruit. El tomate no es un vegetal propiamente dicho, sino una fruta.

trust in appearances: not to ~ ▪ not to be deceived by appearances no fiarse de las apariencias ▪ no dejarse engañar por las apariencias ▪ no dejarse llevar por las apariencias ➤ Don't trust in appearances. ▪ Don't be deceived by appearances. No te fíes de las apariencias. ▪ No te dejes engañar por las apariencias. ▪ No te dejes llevar por las apariencias.

to **trust in God** fiar en Dios ▪ confiar en Dios

to **trust in love** confiar en el amor

trust me *(tú)* confíame ▪ confía en mí ▪ *(usted)* confíeme ▪ confíe en mí

to **trust someone** fiarse de alguien ▪ confiar en alguien ➤ I trust you. Me fío de ti. ▪ Confío en ti.

trustworthy person persona fiable ▪ persona confiable

the **truth is that...** la verdad es que... ▪ lo cierto es que... ▪ en realidad...

the **truth was that...** la verdad era que... ▪ lo cierto era que... ▪ en realidad...

the **truth will come out** ▪ the truth will come to light la verdad saldrá a la luz ▪ la verdad se descubrirá ▪ las mentiras tienen patas cortas

to **try again** ▪ to give it another try ▪ to have another try (at it) intentar otra vez ▪ intentar nuevamente ▪ probar otra vez ▪ probar de nuevo ▪ probar nuevamente

to **try an experiment** *(cooking, etc.)* ▪ to improvise hacer un experimento ▪ experimentar ▪ hacer un experimento ▪ improvisar ▪ probar algo

to **try doing something (a certain way)** probar hacer algo ➤ Try doing it this way. *(tú)* Prueba hacerlo así. ▪ *(usted)* Pruebe hacerlo así.

to **try everything to** probar de todo para que ▪ tratar por todos los medios que ▪ tratar por activa y por pasiva de

to **try it 1.** to sample it probarlo **2.** to attempt it intentarlo

to **try it again** ▪ to give it another try volver a intentarlo ➤ Try it again. ▪ Give it another try. *(tú)* Vuelve a intentarlo. ▪ *(usted)* Vuelva a intentarlo.

to **try not to let something...** tratar de que algo no... ▪ intentar que algo no... ▪ procurar que algo no... ➤ Try not to let the car stall (on you). Trata de que el carro no se te cale. ▪ Intenta que el carro no se te apague. ➤ Try not to let it bother you. Trata de que no te moleste.

to **try not to miss** tratar de no perderse ➤ I'll try not to miss Friday's performance. Trataré de no perderme la actuación del viernes.

to **try not to think about something** intentar no pensar en algo ▪ tratar de no pensar en algo ➤ Try not to think about it. *(tú)* Intenta no pensar en ello. ▪ Trata de no pensar en ello. ▪ *(usted)* Intente no pensar en ello. ▪ Trate de no pensar en ello.

to **try on clothes** probarse ropas

to **try one's luck** probar fortuna ▪ probar suerte

to **try one's luck at something** probar (la) suerte en algo

to **try one's luck with something** probar (la) suerte con algo ▪ probar suerte en algo ▪ probar fortuna con algo to **try one's patience** poner a prueba la paciencia de uno ▪ probar la paciencia

to **try out for a play** ▪ to try out for a part in a play presentarse a una prueba para una obra teatral ▪ intentar pasar las pruebas de una obra teatral ▪ competir para una obra teatral

to **try out something** probar algo ➤ I'm trying out a new monitor. Estoy probando un monitor nuevo.

to **try someone's patience** acabarle la paciencia a alguien ▪ colmarle la paciencia a alguien ▪ gastarle la paciencia a alguien ▪ fregarle la paciencia a alguien

to **try to do something** tratar de hacer algo ▪ intentar hacer algo ▪ pretender hacer algo ▪ procurar hacer algo ➤ The government tried to maintain order. El gobierno pretendió mantener el orden. ▪ El gobierno trató de mantener el orden. ▪ El gobierno intentó mantener el orden. ▪ El gobierno procuró mantener el orden. ➤ We're going to try to go to the movies tonight. Vamos a intentar ir al cine esta noche.

to **try to do too many things at once** intentar hacer demasiadas cosas al mismo tiempo ▪ intentar hacer demasiadas cosas a la vez ▪ tratar de hacer demasiadas cosas a la vez ▪ abarcar muchas cosas a la vez ▪ abarcar demasiadas cosas a la vez

to **try to draw out someone** ▪ to try to draw someone out **1.** *(because someone is shy)* animar a alguien a que hable **2.** *(because someone is holding something back)* buscar la boca a alguien

to **try to find time to do something** ▪ to try to make time to do something buscar tiempo para hacer algo ▪ intentar encontrar tiempo para hacer algo ▪ tratar de hacer tiempo para hacer algo

to **try to get someone to do something** tratar de que alguien haga algo ➤ They're trying to get me to enroll in the graduate program. Están tratando de que me matricule en el programa posgrado.

try to go to sleep ▪ try and go to sleep procura dormir ▪ procura dormirte ▪ procura adormecerte

to **try to keep something from happening** ▪ to try to prevent something from happening tratar de impedir que algo ocurra ▪ pretender que algo no ocurra ➤ The president is trying to keep his leaving office from weakening his political leadership. El presidente pretende que su salida del gobierno no merme su liderazgo político.

to **try to prevent something from happening** ▪ to try to keep something from happening pretender que algo no ocurra

to **try to remember something** ▪ to try to recall something tratar de recordar algo ▪ tratar de acordarse de algo ▪ tratar de hacer memoria de algo

to **try to talk someone into doing something** hacer el artículo a alguien para que haga algo

try to understand! ¡trata de entender! ▪ ¡trata de comprender! ▪ ¡no te ofusques!

to **try unsuccessfully to do something** intentar hacer algo sin conseguirlo ▪ intentar hacer algo sin resultado ▪ intentar hacer algo sin éxito

to **tuck in one's shirttails** ▪ to tuck one's shirttail(s) in meterse la camisa ➤ Tuck in your shirttails! *(tú)* ¡Métete la camisa! ▪ *(usted)* ¡Métase la camisa! ➤ I want a shirt that you don't have to tuck in. ▪ I want a shirt that can be worn with the tails out. Quiero una camisa que se puede llevar por fuera (del pantalón).

to be **tucked away (in a safe place)** estar guardado a buen recaudo

tucked in 1. *(shirt)* metida **2.** *(children, in bed)* arropado ➤ I don't like to wear my shirts tucked in, but rather with the tails out. No me gusta llevar mis camisas metidas, sino sueltas. ➤ The children are tucked in. Los niños están arropados (en la cama).

Tuesday night and early Wednesday en la noche del martes al miércoles ▪ en la noche del martes para el miércoles

to **tug at someone's sleeve** tirarle a alguien de la manga ▪ jalonear la manga de alguien ▪ cincharle a alguien de la manga

tuition (fees) matrícula ➤ How much was your tuition? ▪ How much were your tuition fees? ¿Cuánto fue tu matrícula? ¿Cuánto pagaste de matrícula?

to **tune into a radio station** sintonizar una emisora de radio ➤ If you just tuned in... Si acaban de sintonizar...

to **tune out something** ▪ to tune something out desconectarse de algo

to **tune (up) an engine** poner a punto un motor ▪ ajustar un motor

tune-up of an engine puesta a punto de un motor ▪ *el* ajuste de un motor

tunnel vision ▪ reduced peripheral vision *la* visión túnel ▪ visión periférica restringida

turn: to be one's ~ tocarle a uno ➤ So Friday it was my turn. Así que el viernes me tocó a mí.

to **turn a blind eye to** hacer la vista gorda a ▪ dejar pasar

to **turn a certain age** cumplir tantos años ▪ llegar a cierta edad ➤ He just turned forty. Acaba de cumplir los cuarenta años. ▪ Acaba de llegar a los cuarenta.

to **turn a color** volverse un color ▪ ponerse un color

to **turn a deaf ear to someone** hacer oídos sordos a alguien ▪ no darse por entendido

to **turn against someone** voltearse en contra de alguien ▪ volverse en contra de alguien ▪ ponerse contra alguien

to **turn aggressive** ▪ to become aggressive ponerse agresivo

to **turn all the way around** ▪ to turn completely around ▪ to do a loop ▪ to turn around three hundred and sixty degrees girar completamente ▪ virar completamente ▪ girar en redondo ▪ virar en redondo

to **turn and look** darse vuelta y mirar ▪ voltear y mirar ➤ She turned and looked in the direction of the noise. Se dio vuelta y miró en la dirección del ruido. ▪ Volteó y miró en la dirección del ruido.

to **turn around 1.** *(person, 180°)* to turn halfway around darse media vuelta ▪ dar un giro (de ciento ochenta grados) **2.** *(person, 360°)* to turn all the way around dar una vuelta entera ▪ virar en redondo ▪ darse (la) vuelta ▪ dar un giro (de tres cientos sesenta grados) **3.** *(car, 180°)* dar vuelta **4.** to turn back and retrace one's steps devolverse ➤ Turn around! *(tú)* ¡Date vuelta! *(usted)* ¡Dese vuelta! ➤ Turn around! I want to see your new dress. Date vuelta. Quiero ver tu vestido nuevo. ➤ That car's in the way. There's not enough room to turn around. Ese coche está estorbando el paso, no hay sitio para dar vuelta.

to **turn around and go back the other way** dar una vuelta completa

to **turn around completely** ▪ to turn completely around ▪ to turn all the way around ▪ to turn around three hundred and sixty degrees virar en redondo

to **turn away from someone 1.** to face away from someone apartar la cara ▪ volver la espalda **2.** *(figurative)* to reject someone voltear la espalda a alguien ▪ volver la espalda a alguien ▪ rechazar a alguien ▪ darle la espalda a alguien

to **turn away someone** ▪ to turn someone away negarle la entrada a alguien ▪ no dejar entrar a alguien ▪ no admitir a alguien ➤ When he tried to get into the theater, they turned him away. Cuando quiso entrar al teatro, le negaron la entrada. ▪ No lo dejaron entrar. ▪ No lo admitieron.

to **turn back** volver hacia atrás

to **turn back the clock 1.** to turn the clock back ▪ to set back the clock ▪ to set the clock back atrasar el reloj **2.** to go back in time volver el tiempo atrás

to **turn bad** ▪ to go bad ponerse malo ➤ The turkey will keep for two or three days before it turns bad. ▪ The turkey will keep for two or three days before it goes bad. El pavo aguantará dos o tres días hasta que se ponga malo.

to **turn down a request** ▪ to turn a request down ▪ to deny a request ▪ to refuse a request rechazar una petición ▪ denegar una petición a alguien

to **turn down an invitation** ▪ to turn an invitation down ▪ to decline an invitation rechazar una invitación

to **turn down someone** ▪ to turn someone down rechazar a alguien ▪ decirle a alguien que no ➤ He asked her for a date, but she turned him down. La invitó a salir, pero ella lo rechazó.

to **turn down the heat** ▪ to turn the heat down bajar la calefacción ➤ We turn down the heat at bedtime. ▪ We turn the heat down at bedtime. Bajamos la calefacción a la hora de acostarse. ➤ We turn it down at bedtime. La bajamos a la hora de acostarse.

to **turn down the heat on the stove** ■ to turn the heat down on the stove ■ to reduce the heat on the stove ■ to lower the heat on the stove bajar el fuego

to **turn down the volume** ■ to turn the volume down bajar el volumen

to **turn gray** volverse gris ■ ponerse gris

to **turn green 1.** *(traffic light)* abrir ■ ponerse verde ■ cambiar a verde ■ *(in the subjunctive only)* estar en verde **2.** *(grass, chameleon, etc.)* ponerse verde ➤ The light just turned green. El semáforo se puso verde. ■ La luz se puso verde. ■ Abrió la luz. ■ Abrió el semáforo. ➤ When the light turns green... Cuando el semáforo se ponga verde... ■ Cuando el semáforo esté en verde...

to **turn green with envy** ponerse verde de envidia

to **turn in** entrar ■ girar ■ meterse ➤ Turn in right here. This is the entrance to the parking lot. Entra por aquí, es la entrada del estacionamiento. ■ Gira por aquí. ■ Métete por aquí.

to **turn in (for the night) 1.** to go to bed ir a la cama ■ irse a la cama ■ irse a dormir ■ acostarse **2.** *(colorful)* to hit the sack irse al sobre ➤ It's midnight. I'm going to turn in. Es medianoche, voy a la cama.

to **turn in one's notice to someone** darle el aviso a alguien ■ darle el preaviso a alguien

to **turn in one's resignation** ■ to tender one's resignation presentar uno su dimisión ■ presentar uno su renuncia

to **turn in someone to the police** ■ to turn someone in to the police entregar a alguien a la policía ■ denunciar a alguien a la policía ➤ The robber's own brother turned him in. El propio hermano del ladrón le entregó. ■ El propio hermano del ladrón lo denunció.

to **turn into...** ■ to become volverse... ■ ponerse... ➤ It was cloudy this morning, but it's turning into a beautiful day. Estaba nublado esta mañana, pero se está volviendo un día hermoso. ■ Estaba nublado esta mañana, pero se está poniendo (un día) precioso.

to **turn it off** *(electricity)* apagarla ■ *(water)* cerrarlo (el grifo) ■ cerrarla (la canilla)

to **turn it on** *(electricity)* encenderla ■ prenderla ■ *(water)* abrirlo (el grifo) ■ abrirla (la canilla)

turn it right side out ponlo bien

turn it right side up ponlo bien

to **turn left** ■ to turn to the left ■ *(coll.)* to hang a left tirar a la izquierda ■ girar a la izquierda ■ virar a la izquierda ■ doblar a la izquierda

turn of events cauce que los acontecimientos han tomado ■ rumbo que han tomado las cosas ■ curso de los acontecimientos ➤ The turn of events in the last few days... ■ The turn events have taken in the last few days... El cauce que los acontecimientos han tomado en los últimos días...

Turn of the Screw *(Henry James novel)* *Otra vuelta de tuerca*

to **turn off the default settings** *(computers)* ■ to turn the default settings off ■ to turn off the defaults ■ to remove the defaults ■ to eliminate the defaults ■ to delete the defaults suprimir las configuraciones por defecto ■ anular las configuraciones por defecto ➤ Turn off the default settings. ■ Turn the default settings off. *(tú)* Suprime las configuraciones por defecto. ■ Anula las configuraciones por defecto. ■ *(usted)* Suprima las configuraciones por defecto. ■ Anule las configuraciones por defecto. ➤ Turn them off. *(tú)* Suprímelas. ■ Anúlalas. ■ *(usted)* Suprímalas. ■ Anúlelas. ➤ Don't turn them off. *(tú)* No las suprimas. ■ No las anules. ■ *(usted)* No las suprima. ■ No las anule.

to **turn off the gas** ■ to turn the gas off cortar el gas ■ cerrar el gas ➤ Turn off the gas off. ■ Turn the gas off. Corta el gas. ■ Cierra el gas. ➤ Turn it off. Córtalo. ■ Ciérralo.

to **turn off the light** ■ to turn the light off ■ to turn out the light ■ to turn the light out apagar la luz ➤ Turn off the light. ■ Turn the light off. Apaga la luz. ➤ Turn it off. Apágala.

to **turn off the main road** salir de la calle principal ■ abandonar la calle principal

to **turn off the tap** ■ to turn off the faucet cerrar el grifo ➤ Turn off the tap. ■ Turn the tap off. *(tú)* Cierra el grifo. ■ *(usted)* Cierre el grifo. ➤ Don't turn off the tap. ■ Don't turn the tap off. *(tú)* No cierres el grifo. ■ *(usted)* No cierre el grifo. ➤ Turn it off. *(tú)* Ciérralo. ■ *(usted)* Ciérrelo. ➤ Don't turn it off. *(tú)* No lo cierres. ■ *(usted)* No lo cierre.

to **turn off the water** ■ to turn the water off cerrar el agua ➤ Turn off the water. ■ Turn the water off. *(tú)* Cierra el agua. ■ *(usted)* Cierre el agua. ➤ Don't turn off the water. ■ Don't turn the water off. *(tú)* No cierres el agua. ■ *(usted)* No cierre el agua. ➤ Turn it off. *(tú)* Ciérralo. ■ *(usted)* Ciérrelo. ➤ Don't turn it off. *(tú)* No lo cierres. ■ *(usted)* No lo cierre.

to **turn on the charm** ■ to turn the charm on mostar sus mejores encantos

to **turn on the computer** ■ to turn the computer on *(L. Am.)* prender la computadora ■ *(Sp.)* encender el ordenador

to **turn on the light** ■ to turn the light on *(L. Am.)* prender la luz ■ *(Sp.)* encender la luz ➤ Turn on the light. ■ Turn the light on. Prende la luz. ■ Enciende la luz. ➤ Turn it on. Préndela. ■ Enciéndela.

to **turn on the meter** *(in a taxi)* ■ to turn the meter on ■ to start the meter bajar la bandera

to **turn one's back on someone** ■ to reject someone darle la espalda a alguien

to **turn one's back to someone** ■ to face away from someone darle la espalda a alguien ➤ The minute Grandma turned her back, we made a beeline for the cookie jar. En cuanto abuelita nos dio la espalda, salimos disparados para el tarro de galletas.

to **turn one's head** volver la cabeza ➤ "Did you say something?," said Alberto, turning his head. ¿Decías algo?, preguntó Alberto, volviendo la cabeza.

to **turn one's stomach** revolverle el estómago a uno ➤ It turns my stomach. Me revuelve el estómago.

to **turn out badly** salir mal ■ resultar mal

to **turn out for the best** ser para mejor ➤ It turned out for the best. Ha sido para mejor.

to **turn out great** *(food)* salir de lujo ■ resultar bárbaro

to **turn out perfectly** salir a pedir de boca ■ salir a la perfección

to **turn out really well** salir muy bien ■ quedarle algo a alguien pero que muy bien ■ quedarle de maravilla ■ *(Sp., off-color but universal)* quedarle de puta madre ➤ Your pie turned out really well. *(Mex.)* El pay les quedó pero que muy bien. ■ *(Sp., vosotros)* La tarta os ha quedado pero que muy bien.

to **turn out that...** resultar que... ➤ It turns out that... Resulta que... ➤ It turned out that... Resultó que...

to **turn out the lights** ■ to turn the lights out ■ to turn off the lights ■ to turn the lights off apagar las luces ➤ Don't forget to turn out the lights when you leave. ■ Don't forget to turn the lights out when you leave. No te olvides de apagar las luces cuando salgas.

to **turn out to be** resultar ser ■ resultar ➤ *(news item)* Police detained the suspect on finding stolen jewels in his knapsack that later turned out to be the victim's. La policía detuvo al presunto autor del homicidio al encontrarle en su mochila joyas sustraídas que después resultaron ser de la víctima. ➤ His predictions have turned out to be remarkably accurate. Sus predicciones han resultado extraordinariamente exactas. ➤ It turned out to be true. Resultó ser cierto. ➤ It turned out to be the truth. Resultó ser la verdad.

to **turn out well (for one)** salirle bien a uno ■ resultar bien para uno ➤ It turned out well for her. Le salió bien (a ella).

to **turn over 1.** *(vehicle)* volcar **2.** *(motor)* girar ■ hacer girar **3.** *(person)* darse la vuelta ➤ *(headline)* Nineteen deaths when a bus of retirees turns over in Huelva (Andalucía) Diecinueve muertos al volcar en Huelva un autobús de jubilados ➤ When I tried to start the car, the motor wouldn't turn over, so the battery must be dead. Cuando intenté arrancar el motor, no giró, así que la batería debe estar muerta. ➤ Turn over and I'll give you a back scratch. Date (la) vuelta y te rascaré la espalda.

to **turn over a new leaf** enmendarse ■ empezar de nuevo ■ hacer borrón y cuenta nueva

to **turn over an idea in one's mind** ■ to turn over an idea in one's mind ■ to tinker with an idea darle vueltas a una idea (en la cabeza) to **turn over authority** ▪ to hand over authority entregar la autoridad ▪ entregar las riendas del poder ▪ entregar el mando ▪ traspasar el poder ▪ traspasar el mando ➤ The interim government will turn over authority to the new government in January. ▪ The interim government will hand over authority to the new government in January. El gobierno interino entregará la autoridad al nuevo gobierno en enero. ▪ El gobierno provisional entregará la autoridad al nuevo gobierno en enero.

to **turn over in one's grave** revolverse en su tumba ▪ retorcerse en la tumba ➤ *(commentary)* Bismarck would turn over in his grave if a Bavarian became chancellor. Bismarck se retorcerá en la tumba si un bávaro llega a canciller.

to **turn over something 1.** to knock something over tirar algo ▪ volcar algo **2.** to flip something over dar vuelta algo ▪ voltear algo ➤ The painter turned over a can of paint. El pintor tiró un bote de pintura. ➤ The supper guest turned the china plate over to see the brand name. El invitado a cenar giró el plato de porcelana para ver el nombre de la marca. ➤ He turned it over to see the brand name. Lo dio vuelta para ver el nombre de la marca.

to **turn over the soil** ▪ to turn the soil over ▪ to till the soil remover la tierra ▪ dar vuelta (la) tierra

to **turn pale** ▪ to become pale ▪ to get pale ponerse pálido

turn radius ▪ turning radius radio de giro

to **turn red** *(traffic light)* ponerse rojo ▪ cerrar el semáforo ▪ prenderse la roja ▪ cerrar la luz ➤ The light just turned red. Acaba de cerrar la luz. ▪ Cerró el semáforo. ➤ What the heck are you doing? The light's turned red! ¿Qué diablos haces? ¡Se puso rojo!

to **turn red as a beet 1.** *(in the face, from embarrassment)* to blush ponerse como un tomate ▪ ponerse como la grana ▪ ponerse colorado ▪ quedarse colorado **2.** *(from sunburn)* ponerse rojo (de la pena) ▪ ponerse colorado ▪ ruborizarse

to **turn red in the face** ▪ to blush ponerse colorado ▪ ponerse rojo

to **turn right** ▪ to turn to the right ▪ to take a right ▪ *(coll.)* to hang a right girar a la derecha ▪ doblar a la derecha ▪ virar a la derecha ▪ *(Sp.)* tirar a la derecha ➤ Turn (to the) right. ▪ Take a right. ▪ Make a right. ▪ Hang a right. Dobla a la derecha. ▪ Gira a la derecha. ▪ Vira a la derecha. ▪ Tira a la derecha.

to **turn round and round** ▪ to turn around and around girar y girar

to **turn someone against oneself** ▪ to alienate someone ponerse a alguien en contra de uno ➤ By not inviting my mother-in-law to go to the beach with us, I've turned her against me. Al no invitar a mi suegra a ir a la playa con nosotros, me la he puesto en contra. ➤ By not inviting his mother-in-law to go to the beach with them, he's turned her against him. Al no invitar a su suegra a ir a la playa con ellos, se la ha puesto en contra.

to **turn someone against someone** poner a alguien en contra de alguien ▪ echar a alguien contra alguien

to **turn someone off** repugnarle a alguien ➤ His condescending attitude turns me off. Su actitud condescendiente me repugna.

to **turn someone on** ▪ to arouse someone sexually calentar a alguien ▪ encender a alguien ▪ *(Mex.)* prender a alguien ▪ *(Sp.)* hacerle tilín a alguien ▪ poner a alguien a cien ➤ She turns me on. Ella me hace tilín. ▪ Ella me calienta.

to **turn someone over to someone** entregar a alguien a alguien

to **turn something a color** ponérsele algo un color ➤ The candy turned our mouths green. Los dulces se nos pusieron la boca verde. ▪ Los dulces nos dejaron la boca verde.

to **turn something back in** ▪ to return something devolver algo ▪ regresar algo ➤ I've already turned the book back in. ▪ I've already returned the book. Ya he devuelto el libro. ▪ Ya he regresado el libro.

to **turn something into something** convertir algo en algo ➤ They've turned the search for a new pope into a media circus. Han convertido la búsqueda de un nuevo papa en un circo mediático.

to **turn something to one's advantage** convertir algo en algo ventajoso para uno mismo ▪ transformar algo en algo beneficioso para uno (mismo) ▪ convertir algo en algo ventajoso para uno (mismo) ▪ hacer algo jugar a favor de uno ➤ In the Emancipation Proclamation, Lincoln turned to his advantage the Supreme Court's decision in the Dred Scott case. En la Proclamación de Emancipación, Lincoln volvió a su ventaja la decisión del Tribunal Supremo en el caso de Dred Scott. ▪ En la Proclamación de Emancipación, Lincoln hizo jugar a su favor la decisión del Tribunal Supremo en el caso de Dred Scott.

to **turn something upside down** dar la vuelta ▪ poner patas arriba ▪ revolver

to **turn sour** ▪ to go sour **1.** *(milk)* cortarse la leche **2.** *(disposition, atmosphere)* volverse rancio ▪ deteriorarse

to **turn the corner 1.** *(literal)* doblar la esquina ▪ dar la vuelta a la esquina **2.** *(figurative)* to begin to improve empezar a mejorar ➤ With the Palestinian and Iraqi elections, everyone hopes the Middle East situation has turned the corner. Con las elecciones palestinas e iraquíes, todo el mundo espera que la situación del Medio Oriente haya empezado a mejorar.

to **turn the house upside down** poner la casa patas arriba ▪ voltear la casa al revés ▪ revolver la casa ➤ We turned the house upside down until we found the receipt. Pusimos la casa patas arriba hasta que dimos con el comprobante.

to **turn the job over to someone** ▪ to turn over the job to someone pasar el cargo a alguien ▪ pasarle el trabajo a alguien ▪ traspasar el cargo a alguien

to **turn the matter over in one's mind** darle vueltas al asunto

to **turn the other cheek** poner la otra mejilla

to **turn the page** pasar la página ▪ pasar de página ▪ pasar la hoja ▪ dar vuelta la página ▪ dar vuelta la hoja

to **turn the tables** ▪ to change the status quo dar la vuelta a la tortilla

to **turn to someone 1.** *(literal)* to turn toward someone volverse hacia alguien ▪ volverse a alguien ▪ dirigirse a alguien **2.** *(figurative)* to turn to someone for help, support acudir a alguien ▪ recurrir a alguien ➤ She turned to her mother and said... Se dirigió a su madre y le dijo... ▪ Se volvió hacia su madre y le dijo... ➤ I don't know who to turn to. No sé a quién recurrir. ▪ No sé a quién acudir.

to **turn to the left** ▪ to turn left doblar a la izquierda ▪ girar a la izquierda ▪ virar a la izquierda ▪ tirar a la izquierda

to **turn to the right** ▪ to turn right doblar a la derecha ▪ girar a la derecha ▪ virar a la derecha ▪ tirar a la derecha

to **turn up** ▪ to show up ▪ to be found ▪ to appear aparecer ➤ There's no telling where the fugitives will turn up. ▪ It's no telling where the fugitives will turn up. ¡Quién sabe dónde aparecerán los fugitivos! ▪ A saber dónde aparecerán los fugitivos. ▪ Vete a saber dónde aparecerán los fugitivos. ➤ They're liable to turn up anywhere. Pueden aparecer en cualquier sitio.

to **turn up one's nose at something** ▪ to turn one's nose up at something hacer ascos de algo ▪ hacer ascos a algo

to **turn up the heat** ▪ to turn the heat up subir la calefacción

to **turn up the volume full blast** ▪ to turn the volume up full blast poner el volumen a toda pastilla ▪ poner el volumen a todo trapo ▪ poner el sonido a toda pastilla ▪ poner el sonido a todo volumen

to **turn white as a sheet** ponerse blanco como una sábana ▪ ponerse blanco como la cera ▪ ponerse más blanco que la cera ▪ ponerse pálido ▪ empalidecérsele a uno la cara ➤ When he heard the news, he turned white as a sheet. Al oír la noticia, se puso blanco como la cera.

turnabout is fair play donde las dan, las toman ➤ Sharks eat people, so turnabout is fair play. Los tiburones comen a los seres humanos, así que donde las dan, las toman.

turnaround: last ~ último cambio de sentido ➤ *(highway sign)* Last turnaround next 20 kilometers Último cambio de sentido en los próximos 20 kilómetros

turned away from someone: to sit with one's face ~ ▪ to sit facing away from someone sentarse de perfil a alguien

turned away from someone: to stand with one's face ~ estar de perfil a alguien

turned crooked hecho un truhán

turned soil suelo removido

turning point momento crucial ▪ punto decisivo ▪ momento decisivo
turning radius ▪ turn radius radio de giro
turnstile: entrance ~ torno de entrada
turnstile: exit ~ torno de salida
turnstile: to go through the ~ pasar por el torno ➤ I went through the exit turnstile by accident. Pasé por el torno de salida sin darme cuenta.
turtleneck sweater suéter de cuello alto ▪ *(Sp.)* jersey de cuello vuelto ▪ *(Uru.)* buzo de cuello alto
tutoring session una clase particular
TV commentator ▪ television commentator *el, la* comentarista de televisión
TV news anchorperson 1. anchorman presentador ▪ informativista **2.** anchorwoman presentadora ▪ informativista
TV remote mando de la tele ▪ *el* control (remoto) de la tele
to **tweak someone's ears** darle a alguien un tirón de orjeas ▪ tirarle a alguien (de) las orejas ▪ jalarle las orejas a alguien ▪ darle a alguien un jalón de orejas
tweet, tweet! ¡pío, pío!
Tweety and Sylvester Piolín y Silvestre
Twelfth Night *(Shakespeare play)* Epifanía
twelve noon las doce del mediodía
twice a day dos veces al día ▪ dos veces por día ➤ The dogs are fed twice a day. Se les da de comer a los perros dos veces al día.
twice as fast el doble de rápido
twice as many (as) *(plural)* dos veces más (que) ▪ el doble (que) ➤ The blast injured twice as many people as first thought. La explosión hirió a dos veces más el número de personas de lo que se pensó originalmente. ▪ La explosión hirió al doble de personas de lo que se pensó originalmente.
twice as much (as) *(singular)* dos veces más (que) ▪ el doble (que) ➤ Lettuce costs almost twice as much as it did last year. La lechuga cuesta casi dos veces más de lo que costaba el año pasado.
twice as often (as) dos veces más (que)
to be **twice someone's age** doblarle la edad ▪ doblarlo a alguien en edad ➤ He's twice her age. Le dobla la edad. ▪ La dobla en edad.
to **twiddle one's thumbs 1.** *(literal)* hacer juegos con los dedos pulgares **2.** *(figurative)* to fail to act hacer bola ▪ hacer bolillos ▪ rascarse (la barriga) ▪ *(coarse)* hacer huevo *(Spanish has no literal term for "to twiddle one's thumbs.")*
twin-engine airplane *el* avión bimotor ▪ avioneta bimotor
Twin Towers of the World Trade Center *las* Torres gemelas del Centro mundial de comercio
twin victory victoria doble
twinkle toes! ¡rey de mambo!
twinkling stars estrellas centelleantes
to **twirl a baton** girar un bastón ▪ revolear un bastón ▪ hacer girar un bastón con los dedos
to **twirl something on one's fingers** hacer girar algo con los dedos
to **twist one's ankle** torcerse el tobillo
to **twist someone's words** ▪ to twist what someone says distorcionar las palabras de alguien ▪ distorcionar lo que alguien dice
twists and turns: to have a lot of ~ tener muchos recovecos
two and two are four ▪ two and two make four ▪ two and two equals four dos y dos son cuatro ▪ dos y dos suman cuatro
two at a time ▪ two by two ▪ by two's ▪ in pairs **1.** en pares ▪ a pares **2.** two at once de dos en dos ▪ de a dos ➤ He runs up the steps two at a time. Sube corriendo los escalones de dos en dos. ▪ Sube corriendo los escalones de a dos.
two-bit de poco valor ▪ de poca monta
two by two ▪ two at a time ▪ by two's ▪ in pairs a pares ▪ de dos en dos
two can play that game donde las dan, las toman
two days' growth *(like Brad Pitt)* barba de dos días
to be **two-faced** tener dos caras (como el queso) ▪ ser de dos haces ▪ hacer doble juego ▪ *(Arg., Uru., coll.)* ser falluto(-a)
two front teeth paletas
two heads are better than one dos cabezas piensan mejor que una ▪ cuatro ojos ven más que dos
two more dos más ▪ otros dos
two of a kind tal para cual ▪ el uno para el otro ➤ They're two of a kind. Son tal para cual.
two-percent milk *(containing two-percent milk fat)* leche semidesnatada ▪ leche semidescremada
to be **two sides of the same coin** ser caras de la misma moneda
two-thirds dos tercios ▪ dos terceras partes
two-thirds of the total dos tercios del total ▪ dos terceras partes del total
two-way radio transmisor-receptor
two-way street 1. *(literal)* la calle de doble sentido ▪ calle de ida y vuelta ➤ Orense becomes a two-way street when you reach Gen. Perón Ave. La calle Orense se hace de doble sentido cuando llegas a la Avenida del Gen. Perón. **2.** *(figurative)* tener ambas partes el mismo voto ▪ tener ambas partes los mismos derechos ▪ tener ambas partes voz y voto ➤ Marriage is a two-way street. En el matrimonio los dos tienen el mismo voto. ▪ En el matrimonio los dos tienen los mismos derechos. ▪ En el matrimonio los dos tienen voz y voto.
two weeks' notice: to give an employee ~ despedir al empleado con dos semanas de preaviso
two weeks' notice: to give an employer ~ dejar el trabajo con dos semanas de preaviso ▪ dar el preaviso
Two Years Before the Mast *(Richard Henry Dana novel)* ▪ two years as a seagoing sailor *Dos años al pie del mástil* *(as translated by Francisco Torres Oliver)*
type size tamaño de la letra ▪ tamaño de fuente
typestyle la fuente de la letra
typical of típico de ▪ propio de ➤ My cat has two traits that are more typical of a dog: she'll come when you call her, and she likes to go for a walk. Mi gata tiene dos rasgos que son más típicos de un perro: viene cuando la llamas y le gusta ir de paseo.
typing skills *(mentioned on a résumé)* habilidades mecanográficas ▪ *(coll.)* habilidad de escribir a máquina

ulterior motive ▪ hidden agenda motivo ulterior ▪ razón oculta ▪ motivo oculto ▪ segunda intención

to be the **ultimate** ser lo último ▪ ser el no va más

umpteenth time: for the ~ por enésima vez

UN Security Council Consejo de Seguridad de la ONU

to be **unable to get over a trauma** ▪ to be unable to get over a shock no poder superar un trauma ▪ no poder recuperarse de un shock ▪ no poder sobreponerse a un trauma ▪ no poder sobreponerse a un shock

to be **unable to get over an illness** ▪ to be unable to recover from an illness no poderse recuperar de una enfermedad

unaided eye: to be visible to the ~ ▪ to be visible to the naked eye ▪ to be visible without a telescope ser visible a simple vista ▪ saltar a la vista

unanimously: to pass ~ ser aprobado por unanimidad

unanswerable question pregunta sin respuesta

unanswered question pregunta aún sin resolver

unappealing image imagen poco atractiva ➤ To see people sitting around talking is an unappealing image on a TV screen, which is why they jazz up the sets. Ver a gente sentada charlando es una imagen poco atractiva para la tele, y es por eso que alegran los platós.

to be **unaware of something 1.** not to know something ignorar algo ▪ desconocer algo ▪ no saber algo **2.** not to have heard about something no enterarse ▪ no estar al tanto de algo ▪ no estar al corriente de algo **3.** no ser consciente de algo ➤ I was unaware that it is possible to lose color vision in a single band of the spectrum. ▪ I didn't know that it was possible to lose color vision in a single band of the spectrum. Yo ignoraba que fuera posible perder la visión de color en una sola franja del espectro. ▪ Yo desconocía que fuera posible perder la visión de color en una sola franja del espectro. ➤ I was not aware of the situation. Yo no estaba al tanto de la situación. ➤ The patient was unaware of his surroundings. El paciente no era consciente de su paradero.

to be **unaware that...** ▪ not to know that... ignorar que... ▪ no saber que... ▪ desconocer que... ➤ Many who are afflicted with cancer are unaware that they have it. ▪ Many who are afflicted with cancer don't know that they have it. Muchas personas aquejadas de cáncer ignoran que lo padecen. ▪ Muchos que tienen cáncer no lo saben.

to be **unbearable** ▪ to be unendurable ser insoportable ▪ no poder soportar ➤ The pain in his leg was unbearable. El dolor de la pierna era insoportable. ▪ No podía soportar el dolor de la pierna.

to be an **unbeatable combination** ser una combinación invencible ▪ ser una combinación imbatible

unbeknownst to one ▪ without one's being aware of it ▪ without one's realizing it **1.** *(present, future)* sin que uno se dé cuenta **2.** *(past)* sin que uno se diera cuenta

unbiased account of the events ▪ balanced account of the events valoración objetiva de los hechos

unblemished record ▪ spotless record *el* expediente sin tacha ▪ expediente sin mancha

unbridled tongue lengua desenfrenada ▪ lengua sin freno

unbroken record *(sports, etc.)* récord invicto

unbroken stream of cars ▪ solid stream of cars ▪ continuous stream of cars *(L. Am.)* flujo constante de carros ▪ flujo ininterrumpido de carros ▪ *el* desfile constante de carros ➤ The unbroken stream of cars makes it impossible to get across the street. ▪ The solid stream of cars makes it impossible to cross the street. ▪ The solid stream of cars prevents us from crossing the street. ▪ The solid stream of cars keeps us from crossing the street. El flujo ininterrumpido de carros lo hace imposible cruzar la calle.

to **unburden oneself to someone** ▪ to tell someone everything desahogarse con alguien ▪ vaciar el costal a alguien ▪ vaciar el saco a alguien

to **unbutton one's shirt** desabrocharse la camisa

uncanny ability to...: to have an ~ tener la extraña habilidad de... ▪ tener una extraña habilidad para...

uncanny accuracy asombrosa exactitud

uncanny knack for...: to have an ~ tener un don misterioso para (hacer algo) ▪ tener un don misterioso de (algo)

uncanny resemblance parecido asombroso

uncertain future futuro incierto

uncharted territory territorio inexplorado

uncle and aunt: my ~ mis tíos

to be **uncomfortable with the situation** sentirse incómodo con la situación

unconditional surrender *la* rendición incondicional ▪ rendición sin condiciones

unconscious (mind) ▪ the unconscious el inconsciente

uncooperative witness *el, la* testigo nada cooperador(-a) ▪ testigo que no coopera

uncouth person persona zafia ▪ persona inculta ▪ persona torpe ▪ persona bruta

uncultivated land *(untilled)* tierra sin cultivar ▪ el erial ▪ eriazo ➤ The lands were uncultivated. Los terrenos estaban sin cultivar.

undeniable fact hecho innegable

to be **under arrest** quedar detenido ▪ quedar arrestado ▪ estar bajo arresto ➤ You're under arrest. Queda (usted) detenido. ▪ Queda (usted) arrestado. ▪ Está (usted) bajo arresto.

to be **under attack** estar siendo atacado

to be **under construction** estar en construcción ▪ *(public works)* estar en obras

to be **under control** estar bajo control ➤ Is everything under control? ¿Está todo bajo control?

under control: to have something ~ tener algo bajo control

under cover of darkness: to flee ~ huir al amparo de la noche ▪ huir al amparo de la oscuridad ▪ *(literary)* huir bajo el manto de la oscuridad

under cover of darkness: to operate ~ obrar con nocturnidad

to be **under discussion** estar en discusión ▪ estar siendo discutido ▪ estar estudiando el asunto ▪ estar estudiando el tema ➤ The matter is under discussion. El asunto está siendo discutido. ➤ It's under discussion. Están discutiéndolo.

under false pretenses con falsas pretensiones ▪ bajo falsas pretensiones

under fire: to come ~ ponerse a disparar sobre ▪ ser objeto de un tiroteo ▪ ser tiroteado ➤ The president's limousine came under fire. Se pusieron a disparar sobre la limusina del presidente. ▪ La limusina del presidente fue objeto de un tiroteo. ▪ La limusina del presidente fue tiroteada.

to be **under house arrest** estar bajo arresto domiciliario ▪ estar en (situación de) arresto domiciliario

under house arrest: to be placed ~ ser puesto en arresto domiciliario ▪ quedar en (situación de) arresto domiciliario ➤ Galileo was placed under house arrest by the Inquisition.

Galileo fue puesto en arresto domiciliario por la Inquisición. ▪ Galileo quedó en situación de arresto domiciliario por la Inquisición.

to be **under lock and key** estar bajo llave

under lock and key: to put someone ~ encerrar a alguien bajo siete llaves

under lock and key: to put something ~ poner algo bajo siete llaves

under new management bajo nueva administración

under no circumstances bajo ningún concepto ▪ bajo ninguna circunstancia ▪ en ningún caso

under oath: testify ~ declarar bajo juramento ▪ prestar declaración bajo juramento

under one's breath: to say something to someone ~ decir algo a alguien en un susurro ▪ *(coll.)* decir algo a alguien por lo bajinis

under one's nose ante las (mismas) narices de uno ➤ Could the terrorists have regrouped under our noses? ¿Pueden los terroristas haberse reagrupado ante nuestras (mismas) narices?

under one's purview dentro del ámbito de uno

under one's skin: to get ~ irritarle a uno

under one's thumb: to have someone ~ tener a alguien en un puño ➤ The boss has me constantly under his thumb. El jefe me tiene constantemente en un puño. ➤ I hate being under his thumb. Odio que me tenga así, en un puño.

under one's wing: to take someone ~ poner a alguien bajo el ala

under police protection: to be placed ~ ser puesto bajo (la) protección policial

to be **under pressure 1.** *(person)* estar bajo presión ▪ bajo presiones **2.** *(gas)* estar a presión ➤ The prime minister is under great pressure from the opposition party. El primer ministro está bajo mucha presión del partido de la oposición.

under pressure: to be stored ~ estar almacenado a presión ➤ The gas is stored under pressure in cylindrical tanks. El gas está almacenado a presión en tanques cilíndricos.

to be **under scrutiny** estar bajo escrutinio ▪ estar siendo analizado minuciosamente

to be **under siege** estar en estado de sitio ▪ estar sitiado

under someone's command bajo el mando de alguien ▪ del comando de alguien

under the aegis of bajo la tutela de

under the auspices of ▪ under the aegis of bajo los auspicios de ▪ bajo el auspicio de ▪ bajo el patrocinio de

under the circumstances ▪ given the circumstances bajo las circunstancias ▪ ante las circunstancias ▪ dadas las circunstancias

to be **under the command of** estar al mando de

under the flag of ▪ under the banner of bajo la bandera de ▪ bajo el pabellón de

under the guise of ▪ on the pretext of ▪ under the (false) pretense of con el pretexto de ▪ so capa de ▪ bajo capa de

to be **under the gun** ▪ to be under great pressure estar con la soga al cuello ▪ estar bajo mucha presión

to be **under the impression that...** ▪ to have the impression that... tener la impresión de que...

under the name (of) ▪ in the name of a nombre de

under the president bajo el presidente ▪ bajo el mandato del presidente

under the pretense of ▪ on the pretext of ▪ under the guise of con el pretexto de ▪ so capa de ▪ bajo capa de

under the pretext of ▪ on the pretext of con el pretexto de ▪ en achaque de ▪ *(law)* so pretexto de

under the protection of bajo la protección de ▪ al amparo de ▪ al arrimo de

under the table bajo cuerda ▪ en negro ▪ bajo la mesa

under the table: to pay someone ~ pagarle a alguien bajo la mesa ▪ pagarle a alguien bajo cuerda ▪ pagarle a alguien en negro ▪ pagarle a alguien con dinero B

under-the-table money ▪ hidden money dinero negro ▪ dinero B

to be **under the tutelage of 1.** to be tutored by estar bajo la enseñanza de **2.** to be under the protection of ▪ to be a ward of estar bajo la tutela de

to be **under the weather** estar malito(-a) ▪ estar enfermito(-a) ▪ estar un poco pocho(-a) ▪ *(Sp.)* estar pachucho(-a)

to be **under tight security** estar bajo altas medidas de seguridad ▪ estar entre fuertes medidas de seguridad

to be **under warranty** estar en garantía ➤ Is it under warranty? ¿Está en garantía?

under which ▪ under whose provisions ▪ under the provisions of which ▪ whereby por el cual ▪ por la cual ▪ por lo cual ➤ A treaty under which fishing in these waters is prohibited Un tratado por el cual queda prohibida la pesca en estas aguas

to be **underage** ser menor de edad

undercover agent *el, la* agente encubierto(-a) ▪ agente de incógnito ➤ European airlines introduce undercover agents on some flights. Aerolíneas europeas introducen agentes encubiertos en algunos vuelos. ▪ Aerolíneas europeas introducen agentes de incógnito en algunos vuelos.

to **underestimate how long something will take** quedarse corto al calcular cuánto tiempo se tardará en hacer algo ▪ quedarse corto al calcular cuánto tiempo se demorará en hacer algo

to **underestimate how much something will cost** quedarse corto al calcular el costo de algo

to **underestimate someone** subestimar a alguien ▪ infravalorar a alguien

to **underestimate the effect of** subestimar el efecto de ▪ infravalorar el efecto de

to **underestimate the time it takes** subestimar el tiempo que lleva ▪ subestimar el tiempo que requiere ➤ I underestimated the time it would take (me) to get here. Subestimé el tiempo que me llevaría llegar aquí.

to be **underfoot** tener (alguien) pegado ▪ estar por en medio ➤ It's hard to do housework with children and dogs underfoot. Es difícil hacer las tareas (del hogar) con los niños y perros pegados. ▪ Es difícil hacer las tareas (del hogar) con niños y perros por en medio.

to **undergo a process** ▪ to go through a process pasar por un proceso

to **undergo a transformation** sufrir una transformación

to **undergo great hardship(s)** ▪ to experience great hardship(s) ▪ to suffer great hardship(s) pasar (por) grandes penas ▪ pasar por momentos muy duros

to **undergo medical tests** ▪ to have medical tests ser sometido a exámenes médicos ➤ *(news item)* Pinochet will undergo medical tests. Pinochet será sometido a exámenes médicos.

to **undergo surgery** ▪ to have surgery ▪ to have an operation someterse a cirugía

to **undergo surgery for** ▪ to be operated on for ▪ to have an operation for ser operado de ▪ operararse de ▪ ser operado por ▪ operarse por ➤ I have to undergo surgery... Tengo que someterme a cirugía... ▪ He de someterme a cirugía... ➤ The child is undergoing surgery for appendicitis. ▪ The child is being operated on for appendicitis. ▪ The child is having an operation for appendicitis. El niño está siendo operado de apendicitis. ➤ The victim is undergoing surgery for abdominal injuries. La víctima está siendo operada por heridas abdominales.

to **undergo treatments for an illness** estar sometido a tratamientos para una enfermedad ▪ ser sometido a tratamientos para una enfermedad ▪ someterse a tratamientos para una enfermedad ➤ He underwent a series of treatments for leukemia. Estuvo sometido a una serie de tratamientos por la leucemia. ▪ Fue sometido a una serie de tratamientos por la leucemia. ▪ Se sometió a una serie de tratamientos por la leucemia. *("Por leucemia" is also possible but means "because of" or "as a result of.")*

to be **undergoing repairs** ▪ to be being repaired estar en reparación ▪ estar en revisión ➤ It's undergoing repairs. ▪ It's being repaired. Está en reparación. ▪ Lo están reparando.

underground movement movimiento sumergido ▪ movimiento underground ➤ The Catholic youth movement was underground in Communist Poland. El movimiento de los jóvenes católicos era sumergido en la Polonia comunista. ▪ El movimiento de los jóvenes católicos estaba sumergido en la Polonia comunista.

underhandedly: to do something ~ hacer algo solapadamente

to **underlie the problem** haber de fondo en el problema ▪ sustentar el problema ➤ What underlies the problem of terrorism? ¿Qué hay de fondo en el problema del terrorismo? ▪ ¿Qué sustenta el problema del terrorismo?

underlying cause causa subyacente

underlying motive motivo subyacente

underlying problem problema subyacente

to **undermine confidence in someone** minar la confianza en alguien ▪ socavar la confianza en alguien ▪ menoscabar la confianza en alguien ▪ deteriorar la confianza en alguien ➤ *(headline)* Accusations of corruption undermine confidence in the prime minister Las acusaciones de corrupción minan la confianza en el primer ministro

to **undermine one's health** minar la salud ▪ carcomer la salud ▪ deteriorar la salud

to **undermine self-trust** minar la confianza en uno mismo ▪ menoscabar la confianza en uno mismo ▪ deteriorar la confianza en uno mismo ➤ Fundamentalist sects take psychological control of people by undermining self-trust. Las sectas fundamentalistas toman control psicológico de la gente minando la confianza en sí mismos.

underneath this one ▪ below this one ▪ under this one ▪ beneath this one debajo de éste ➤ The apartment underneath this one El piso debajo de éste

to **understand a situation** entender una situación ▪ comprender una situación

to **understand each other 1.** *(on an intellectual level)* entenderse mutuamente ▪ entenderse el uno al otro **2.** *(on an emotional level)* comprenderse mutuamente ▪ comprenderse el uno al otro

to **understand that...** tener entendido que... ➤ I understand that you like cats. Tengo entendido que te gustan los gatos.

understanding with our neighbors ▪ agreement with our neighbors acuerdo con nuestros vecinos ▪ trato con nuestros vecinos

to be **understood that...** estar dado por sentado que... ▪ sobrentenderse que...

to **undertake a project** ▪ to take on a project emprender un proyecto ➤ When I undertook the project, I didn't realize what I was getting (myself) into. ▪ When I took on the project, I didn't realize what I was getting (myself) into. Cuando emprendí el proyecto no me di cuenta en lo que me estaba metiendo.

undeveloped country país sin desarrollo ▪ país no desarrollado ▪ país sin desarrollarse ➤ The country remains undeveloped. El país queda sin desarrollo. ▪ El país permanece sin desarrollo. ▪ El país sigue sin desarrollo. ▪ El país permanece sin desarrollo.

undocumented worker trabajador indocumentado

uneasiness about... ▪ uneasiness over *la* inquietud de... ▪ *el* desazón de... ▪ desazón por... ▪ desazón sobre... ▪ *la* incomodidad de...

uneasy feeling about something: to have an ~ tener un sentimiento inquietante acerca de algo ▪ darle mala espina ➤ I have an uneasy feeling about him. Tengo un sentimiento inquietante acerca de él. ➤ I have an uneasy feeling about it. Me da mala espina.

uneasy feeling that...: to have an ~ inquietarle que...

unemployment rate tasa de paro ▪ tasa de desempleo ▪ *el* índice de desempleo ▪ tasa de desocupación ▪ índice de desocupación

unequal treatment tratamiento desigual ▪ trato desigual ▪ agravio comparativo

uneven terrain ▪ rough terrain ▪ broken terrain ▪ rugged terrain terreno desnivelado ▪ terreno desigual ▪ terreno abrupto ▪ terreno quebrado ▪ terreno fragoso

unexpected consequences: to have ~ ▪ to have unforeseen consequences tener consecuencias imprevistas ▪ tener otras consecuencias

unexpected turn giro inesperado

unexpectedly: to do something ~ hacer algo de improviso ▪ hacer algo sin previo aviso ▪ hacer algo de repente ▪ hacer algo sin mediar palabra

unexpectedly: to happen ~ ocurrir inesperadamente

unfair competition competencia injusta

to be **unfaithful to someone** ▪ to cheat on someone ▪ to stray ser infiel a alguien ▪ ponerle (los) cuernos a alguien ▪ ponerle (las) guampas a alguien ▪ dársela (con queso) a alguien

unfathomable depths abismos insondables

unfettered access acceso libre ▪ acceso libre de las restricciones ▪ acceso sin límites

unfinished business asunto inconcluso ▪ tema inconcluso ▪ negocio inconcluso

unfinished furniture muebles en estado natural (sin tinte o barniz)

Unfinished Symphony *(Schubert)* Sinfonía inconclusa ▪ Sinfonía inacabada

unfinished task tarea inacabada

to be **unfit for human consumption** no ser apto para (el) consumo humano

unfolding of the case la evolución del caso ▪ el desarrollo del caso

unforeseeable consequences: to have ~ tener consecuencias imprevisibles ▪ tener consecuencias impredecibles ▪ tener otras consecuencias

unforgettable experience experiencia inolvidable ▪ experiencia que no se puede olivdar ▪ experiencia que no se puede olvidar

unhappy childhood infancia infeliz ▪ infancia desdichada

unheard of insólito ▪ desusado ▪ nunca visto ▪ fuera de lo común ▪ raro

the **unique thing about** ▪ what is unique about ▪ what distinguishes something from something else lo que distingue ▪ lo que diferencia ▪ lo que es único de ➤ The unique thing about a pound cake is its density. ▪ What is unique about a pound cake is its density. ▪ What distinguishes a pound cake (from other cakes) is its density. Lo que distingue un pound cake es su densidad.

to be **united in holy matrimony** unirse en santo matrimonio ▪ unirse en sagrado matrimonio

university campus campus de una universidad ▪ recinto universitario

university fees tasas universitarias ➤ *(news item)* Blair will raise university fees despite opposition from his (own) party. Blair subirá las tasas universitarias pese a la oposición de su (propio) partido.

university grounds *(University of Virginia)* predio de la universidad ▪ predio universitario

university tuition matrícula universitaria

to **unleash a wave of attacks** desatar una ola de ataques

unless I'm mistaken ▪ if I'm not mistaken si no me equivoco ▪ a menos que (yo) esté equivocado

unless it is... a menos que esté... ▪ a menos que sea... ▪ a no ser que... ➤ I don't like milk unless it's really cold. No me gusta la leche a menos que esté bien fría.

unless something comes up a no ser que (me) surja algo *(The indirect object pronoun can vary.)*

unless you just want an interchange of ideas a no ser que lo que quieras sea simplemente un intercambio de ideas ▪ a menos que lo único que quieras sea un intercambio de ideas

to be **unlike anything (ever) seen before** ▪ to be never before seen ser jamás visto antes ▪ ser nunca visto antes

unlike in a diferencia de ▪ al revés que ➤ *(news item)* The elections there were clean and transparent, unlike in the majority of countries in the region. Las elecciones allí han sido limpias y transparentes a diferencia de la mayoría de los países de la región.

unlike someone a diferencia de ➤ My mother, unlike my father... Mi madre, a diferencia de mi padre...

to be **unlikely that...** ser poco probable que... ▪ ser difícil que...

unlimited possibilities ilimitadas posibilidades ▪ posibilidades ilimitadas

unlimited quantities cantidades ilimitadas ➤ Seawater and silicon, the two natural resources needed to harness solar energy, are available in unlimited quantities. El agua del mar y la arena, los dos recursos naturales que se necesitan para aprovechar la energía solar, están disponibles en cantidades ilimitadas.

unlined index cards fichas sin rayas ▪ fichas lisas

unlisted number número que no figura en la guía ▪ número secreto ▪ número privado ▪ número excluido de guía

unmade bed cama deshecha ▪ cama no hecha

unmanned airplane aeroplano no tripulado ▪ aeroplano sin tripulación

unmanned flight vuelo no tripulado ▪ vuelo sin tripulación

unmistakable flavor el sabor inconfundible ➤ *(fast-food sign)* Unmistakeable flavor of the American plains El sabor inconfundible de las praderas americanas

to **unpack a box** desembalar una caja ➤ Next, I have to unpack my boxes of books. Ahora me toca desembalar mis cajas de libros.

to **unpack (one's suitcase)** desempacar (la maleta) ▪ desempacar (la valija) ▪ deshacer (la maleta)

unpaid overtime horas extras sin pagar ▪ horas extras no pagadas

to **unravel the structure of DNA** ▪ to piece together the structure of DNA desentrañar la estructura de ADN

unread messages *(E-mail)* mensajes sin leer ▪ mensajes no leídos

unrefined sugar *el* azúcar sin refinar ▪ azúcar no refinada *("Azúcar" is feminine, despite the article.)*

unrelenting criticism ▪ relentless criticism ▪ constant criticism crítica constante ▪ crítica inexorable ▪ crítica implacable

unreliable car carro poco fiable ▪ auto poco fiable ▪ *(Sp.) el* coche poco fiable

unreliable person persona no confiable ▪ persona informal

unreliable source *la* fuente no fiable ▪ fuente que no es de fiar

unreliable witness *el, la* testigo no confiable ▪ testigo que no es de fiar

unrestricted access acceso sin restricción ▪ acceso no restringido

unscathed: to escape ~ escaparse indemne ▪ escaparse ileso(-a) ▪ escaparse incólume ▪ salir ileso(-a)

unshakeable faith *la* fe inquebrantable

unsolved mystery misterio sin resolver ▪ misterio irresuelto ▪ misterio irresoluto

unspeakable atrocity *la* atrocidad indecible ▪ atrocidad inconfesable

unsportsmanlike conduct conducta antideportiva

to be **unsteady on one's feet** ser de paso vacilante ▪ ser de paso tambaleante ➤ The old man was very unsteady on his feet. El viejo fue de paso muy vacilante. ▪ El viejo fue de paso muy tambaleante.

to be **unstinting in one's praise of someone** no escatimar uno en alabanzas a alguien

to be **unsuccessful in business** no tener éxito en el negocio ▪ no ser próspero en el negocio

unsung hero héroe olvidado

untenable situation *la* situación insostenible

until all hours hasta las altas horas de la madrugada ▪ hasta las mil y quinientas ▪ hasta las tantas

until all the liquid is absorbed ▪ until all the liquid has been absorbed hasta que todo el líquido se absorba ▪ hasta que todo el líquido se haya absorbido ▪ hasta que todo el líquido haya sido absorbido

until finally hasta que al final

until Friday hasta el viernes

until further notice hasta nuevo aviso

until hell freezes over hasta que los pericos mamen ▪ hasta que las ranas críen pelo

until I tell you: not to do something ~ no hacer algo sin antes decirte

until instructed to do so ▪ until told to do so hasta nueva orden

until it runs out ▪ until it's used up hasta que se agote ▪ hasta que se acabe

until it's used up ▪ until it runs out hasta que se agote ▪ hasta que se acabe

until now ▪ up to now hasta ahora ▪ hasta el momento

until recently hasta hace poco

until the very end ▪ up to the very end hasta el fin del final ▪ hasta el mismo final

until told to do so ▪ until instructed to do so hasta nueva orden

until very recently hasta hace bien poco

until well into next year hasta bien entrado (en) el próximo año ▪ hasta bien entrado (en) el año que viene

unto us a child is born *(Handel's "Messiah")* nos ha nacido un niño

untrimmed airplane avión desnivelado

unvarnished truth *la* verdad lisa y llana ▪ verdad monda y lironda ▪ verdad sin adornos

to **unveil a plan** destapar un plan ▪ revelar un plan

to **unveil a statue** descubrir una estatua

unwanted pregnancy embarazo indeseado ▪ embarazo no deseado

unwaxed dental floss seda dental sin cera ▪ hilo dental sin cera

unwillingly: to do something ~ ▪ to do something reluctantly hacer algo de mala gana ▪ hacer algo a regañadientes

to **unwind after a hard day's work** desconectarse después de un día de duro trabajo ▪ desconectarse después de una ardua jornada de trabajo

unwritten rule regla no escrita

to **up and do something** ▪ to just up and do something darle la vena y hacer algo ▪ darle un arranque y hacer algo ▪ darle la loca y hacer algo ➤ Patrick upped and dyed his hair green. A Patrick le dio la vena y se tiñó el pelo de verde.

up and down de arriba para abajo ▪ de acá para allá

to be **up and running** estar en funcionamiento ➤ My E-mail is finally up and running. Por fin, mi correo electrónico está en funcionamiento.

up and running: to get something ~ ▪ to have something up and running poner algo en funcionamiento

up awful early, aren't you?! ¡qué madrugador!, ¿verdad? ▪ ¡qué madrugador!

up close de cerca

to be **up front about it** ir con la verdad por delante ▪ ir de frente

to be **up here** estar aquí arriba ➤ I'm up here. Estoy aquí arriba.

up high en lo alto

to be **up in the air** estar en el aire

up in years: to be getting ~ ▪ to be getting on in years ▪ to be getting up there estar entrado en años ▪ ser alguien entrado en años

up the street calle arriba

to be **up there** estar allí arriba

to be **up to a certain length** ▪ to reach a certain length alcanzar cierta longitud ▪ llegar a cierta longitud ➤ By April 5, 1998, the file was up to two thousand lines. Para el 5 de abril de 1998 el archivo había alcanzado dos mil líneas.

up to a point hasta cierto punto ▪ en cierta manera ▪ en cierta medida

to be **up-to-date** estar al día

to be **up to here** estar hasta la coronilla ▪ estar hasta las cachas

to be **up to it** tener fuerzas ▪ estar en condiciones ▪ estar dispuesto(-a) ➤ Are you up to it? ¿Tienes fuerzas?

up to now hasta el momento

to be **up to one's neck** estar hasta las cachas ▪ estar hasta el cuello

to be **up to one to decide** corresponderle a uno decidir ▪ ser quien tiene que decidir ▪ incumbirle decidir ➤ It's up to you to decide. A ti corresponde decidir.

to be **up to one's old tricks** hacer de las suyas

to be **up to something** estar tramando algo ▪ andar en algo ➤ There's no telling what they're up to. ▪ It's no telling what they're up to. ¡A saber lo que estarán tramando! ▪ ¡Quién sabe en qué andan! ▪ ¡Vaya a saber en qué andan!

up to speed: to bring someone ~ ▪ to get someone up to speed poner a alguien al día ▪ poner a alguien al tanto

up to that time hasta entonces

up to the very end ▪ until the very end hasta el fin del final ▪ hasta el mismo final

up to this point hasta aquí

up to *x* percent of... hasta el *x* por ciento de...

to be **up until all hours (of the night)** ▪ to be up until the wee hours (of the night) ▪ to be up until the middle of the night quedarse levantado hasta las tantas ▪ estar levantado hasta las tantas ▪ estar levantado hasta altas horas ➤ I was up until all hours last night trying to get my paper finished in time to turn it in today. Anoche me quedé hasta las tantas intentando terminar un trabajo a tiempo para entregarlo hoy.

up until all hours (of the night): to stay ~ estar levantado(-a) hasta altas horas de la noche ▪ estar levantado(-a) hasta las tantas ▪ estar levantado(-a) hasta las mil y quinientas

up yours! *(off-color)* ¡que te den por el culo! ▪ ¡métete por el culo!

the **upcoming episode** ▪ the next episode el episodio siguiente

to **update someone on the situation** *(coll.)* ponerlo al día a alguien sobre la situación ▪ poner a alguien al tanto sobre la situación

to **update the file 1.** *(computer, card, or folder)* actualizar el archivo **2.** *(card or folder)* actualizar el fichero

to **update the settings** ▪ to update the configurations actualizar las configuraciones

to be an **uphill battle** ser una lucha contracorriente ▪ ser una lucha contra la corriente

uphill battle: to engage in an ~ enzarzarse en una lucha contracorriente ▪ enzarzarse en una lucha contra la corriente ▪ meterse en una lucha contracorriente ▪ meterse en una lucha contra la corriente ▪ liarse en una lucha contracorriente ▪ liarse en una lucha contra la corriente

upper crust 1. *(of the earth)* corteza terrestre alta **2.** cream of society la flor y nata ▪ cogollo de la sociedad

upper echelons 1. *(business)* top management cuadros directivos ▪ altas esferas **2.** *(military)* top brass cúpula **3.** *(government or party leadership)* cúpula

upper joint *(chicken, turkey)* ▪ thigh contramuslo

upper left corner ▪ upper lefthand corner margen superior izquierdo

upper lip labio superior

upper middle class alta burguesía

upper right corner ▪ upper righthand corner margen superior derecho

upright piano piano vertical

upright position la posición vertical

upriver río arriba

ups and downs: (for) there to be ~ haber sus más y sus menos

ups and downs of life ▪ life's ups and downs altibajos de la vida ▪ altibajos en la vida

to be **upset** estar alterado ➤ He was very upset. Estaba muy alterado.

to be **upset because** estar molesto porque

to **upset one's plans** trastornar los planes de uno ▪ frustrar los planes de uno

to **upset one's stomach** ▪ to make one nauseated sentar mal a uno ▪ producirle náuseas a uno ➤ Certain things will upset the baby's stomach. Ciertas cosas le sientan mal al bebé.

to be **upset with someone** estar molesto(-a) con alguien

to be **upside down** estar patas arriba ▪ estar invertido ▪ estar cabeza abajo ▪ estar boca abajo ➤ With the letters upside down Con las letras invertidas ▪ Con las letras patas arriba. ➤ Put the wine glasses upside down on the shelf. Pon las copas boca abajo en el estante.

upside-down question mark *la* interrogación inicial ▪ interrogación de inicio

upstanding citizen ▪ model citizen ciudadano(-a) de a pie

upwards of ▪ more than más de

urban renewal renovación urbana ▪ reforma del barrio

to **urge someone to do something** instar a alguien a hacer algo ▪ instar a alguien que haga algo ➤ *(headline)* Bush urges Zapatero not to withdraw troops from Iraq yet Bush insta a Zapatero que no retire todavía las tropas de Irak

to **use one's charms to...** valerse de sus encantos para... ➤ She used her charms to sweet-talk the guard. Se valió de sus encantos para engatusar al guarda.

to **use one's imagination** utilizar la imaginación

to **use someone as a tool** tomarle a alguien de instrumento

to **use up natural resources** ▪ to exhaust natural resources esquilmar (los) recursos naturales

used bookstore ▪ secondhand bookstore librería de ocasión

to be **used to** estar acostumbrado(-a) a ▪ soler

used to: one ~ antes sí ▪ solía hacerlo ➤ I used to. Antes sí. ▪ (Yo) solía hacerlo.

used to: to get ~ acostumbrarse ▪ llegar a acostumbrarse

used to say: one ~ solía decir ➤ My father used to say... Mi padre solía decir...

using a simple procedure... ▪ through a simple procedure... mediante un procedimiento sencillo...

to **utter a roar** ▪ to let out a roar proferir un rugido ▪ proferir un gruñido ➤ The man's scent made the tiger let out a warning growl. El olor del hombre hizo que el tigre profiera un gruñido de advertencia.

to **vacate a post** dejar un puesto
to **vacate an apartment** ▪ to move out of an apartment dejar un piso
to be **vacuum-packed** ser envasado al vacío
vagaries of fortune altibajos de la fortuna
vague idea idea nebulosa
vague impression impresión nebulosa
to be **vain and poor at the same time** tener vanidad y pobreza, en una pieza
vale of tears: this ~ este valle de lágrimas
Valladolid, Spain, native Vallisoletano(-a) ▪ Pucelano(-a) *(Valladolid is also called "Pucela.")*
to **value a person** apreciar a una persona
to be **valued by someone as** ser apreciado por alguien como
valued friend amigo apreciado
vanishing point punto de fuga
vantage point atalaya ▪ punto panorámico ▪ punto de vista
vapor trail *(jet aircraft)* estela
variable-pitch propeller *(aeronautics)* hélice de ángulo variable ▪ hélice de palas orientables ➤ The airplane has a variable-pitch propeller. El aeroplano tiene una hélice de ángulo variable. ▪ El aeroplano tiene una hélice de palas orientables.
variety is the spice of life en la variedad está el gusto ▪ pan con pan, comida de tontos ▪ entre col y col, lechuga
to **varnish a piece of furniture** ▪ to apply (the) varnish to a piece of furniture ▪ to put varnish on a piece of furniture dar barniz a un mueble
to **vary the pitch of the propeller (blades)** ▪ to change the pitch of the propeller (blades) cambiar el ángulo (de incidencia) de las palas de la hélice
the **vast majority** la inmensa mayoría
Vatican City la Ciudad del Vaticano
vegetable garden huerta
to be **vehemently opposed to something** oponerse tajantemente a algo ▪ estar tajantemente en contra de algo ▪ ser tajante contra algo
to be a **veiled reference to** ser una alusión apenas disimulada a ▪ ser una referencia apenas disimulada a
veiled reference to: to make a ~ hacer alusión disimulada a ▪ hacer una referencia disimulada a
to **vent one's anger at someone** ensañarse con alguien
to **vent one's feelings** desahogarse
Vera Cruz, Mexico, native *(informal)* jarocho(-a)
to **verge on** ▪ to border on estar al borde de ▪ estar en los umbrales de ▪ *(literary)* frisar en lo ridículo ➤ That verges on the ridiculous. Eso está al borde de lo ridículo. ▪ Eso está en los umbrales de lo ridículo. ▪ Frisa en lo ridículo.
verily I say unto you *(Biblical)* en verdad os digo
vernal equinox *(the moment spring begins)* ▪ spring equinox equinoccio vernal ▪ equinoccio de primavera
to be **very careful** **1.** tener mucho cuidado **2.** to tread lightly andar con pies de plomo
very carefully con mucho cuidado
very center of the city mismo centro de la ciudad
very close friends amigos muy unidos
to be **very compatible** estar bien avenidos ▪ ser una pareja bien avenida
very day of: (on) the ~ (en) el mismo día de
to be a **very different person** ▪ to be a completely different person ▪ to have changed a lot ▪ to have changed a great deal ya ser muy otro
the **very end** el fin del final ▪ el último instante ➤ He died at ninety-five, and was lucid and not deaf right up to the very end. Se murió con noventa y cinco años y fue lúcido y no sordo hasta el fin del final. ➤ The book has a surprise ending that keeps the reader in suspense until the very end. El libro tiene un final sorprendente que mantiene al lector en vilo hasta el último instante.
to be **very flexible** tener manga ancha
to be **very glad to** tener mucho gusto en
very good **1.** muy bueno **2.** very well done muy bien hecho
very good! *(L. Am.)* ¡qué bueno! ▪ *(Sp.)* ¡qué bien!

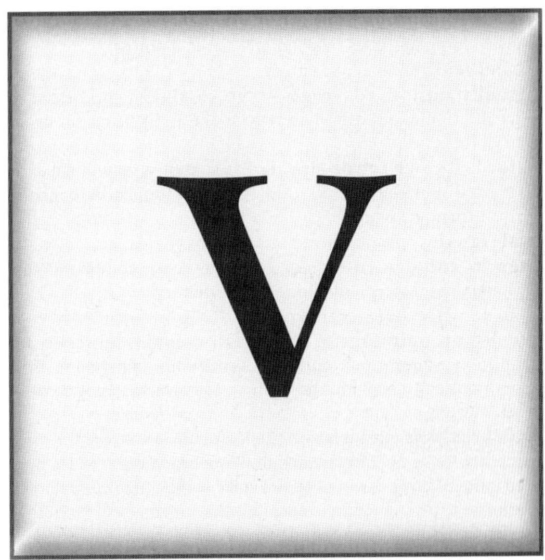

to be **very important** ser muy importante ▪ significar mucho ➤ Football is very important. El fútbol es muy importante. ▪ El fútbol significa mucho.
the **very latest** ▪ the newest of the new lo ultísimo ▪ el último de lo último
to be the **very latest** ser el último grito
to be **very much alone** estar muy solo
very much so muchísimo
very much to one's taste(s) muy de su gusto
very one justo lo que ➤ That's the very one I was looking for. Es justo lo que estaba buscando.
very own: one's ~ su propio
very pretty muy bonito ▪ bonitísimo
very rarely muy de vez en cuando ▪ raras veces
the **very same** ▪ the exact same ▪ exactly the same justo el mismo ▪ justo la misma ▪ *(Mex.)* mismísimo ➤ John Adams and Thomas Jefferson died on the very same day, July 4, 1826. John Adams and Thomas Jefferson se murieron justo en el mismo día, el 4 de julio de 1826. ▪ John Adams and Thomas Jefferson se murieron en el mismísimo día, el 4 de julio de 1826.
very tall man hombre de gran estatura
very thought of it sólo de pensarlo
very well! ¡entendido!
very well done muy bien hecho
vested interest interés creado
veto power ▪ power to veto *el* poder de veto
vice mayor *el, la* teniente de alcalde
vicious circle: to become a ~ formarse círculo vicioso ➤ It becomes a vicious circle. Se forma un círculo vicioso.
victim of a physical assault ▪ assault victim ▪ mugging victim agredido
victim of an illness víctima ▪ fatality víctima mortal ➤ The outbreak of legionella has claimed its fifth victim. ▪ The outbreak of legionella has claimed its fifth fatality. El brote de legionella se cobra su quinta víctima mortal.
to be the **victim of one's own success** morir de éxito
victims of a flood damnificados por una inundación
video game videojuego
video (rental) store el videoclub
video store *(where VCR and DVD machines are sold)* tienda de video
videocassette el videocasete ▪ cinta ▪ película
videocassette recorder (and player) ▪ VCR el videocasetera ▪ video
village idiot tonto del pueblo
vintage wine vino añejo ▪ vino de solera

to **violate the law** ▪ to break the law infringir la ley ▪ quebrantar la ley ▪ vulnerar la ley ▪ delinquir ▪ saltar la norma

virtual reality *la* realidad virtual

virtually unnoticed: to go ~ ▪ to go almost unnoticed ▪ hardly to make a stir ▪ barely to make a stir pasar sin pena ni gloria

virtue is its own reward la virtud es su propia recompensa

vise (on a workbench) ▪ workbench vise tornillo de banco ▪ *(coll.)* torno de banco

vital signs los constantes vitales ▪ indicios vitales

vitamin supplements ▪ food supplements complementos vitamínicos ▪ complementos alimenticios

vivid recollection recuerdo nítido

to **voice an opinion** ▪ to express an opinion ▪ to state an opinion expresar una opinión ▪ verter una opinión ➤ The opinions expressed for and against. Las opiniones que se vierten a favor y en contra.

voice breaks se quebra la voz ▪ se le quebra la voz

voice broke se quebró la voz ▪ se le quebró la voz ➤ He had to quit the boy's choir when his voice broke. Tuvo que salir del coro de niños cuando se le quebró la voz.

a **voice in the wilderness** una voz en el desierto

voice mail ▪ voice messaging ▪ answering machine contestador automático

voice of caution *la* voz de cautela

voice of conscience *la* voz de la conciencia

voice recognition software *el* programa de reconocimiento de voz ▪ software de reconocimiento de voz

voiced consonant consonante sonora ➤ The letter *D* is a voiced *T*, and *B* is a voiced *P*, and *G* as in *gate* is a voiced *K* as in *kilo*. La letra *D* es una *T* sonora, y la *B* es una *P* sonora, y la *G* de *gate* es el sonido sonoro *K* de *kilo*.

voiced fricative fricativa sonora ➤ The English *V* is voiced *F*. La *V* inglesa es una *F* sonora.

voiced stop (consonante) oclusiva sonora ➤ The consonants *B*, *D*, and *G* as in *go* are voiced stops. Las consonantes *B*, *D* y *G* de *go* son consonantes oclusivas sonoras.

voiceless consonant ▪ unvoiced consonant consonante sorda ➤ The letter *T* is a voiceless *D*, and *P* is a voiceless *B*, while *K* is a voiceless *G*. ▪ The letter *T* is an unvoiced *D*, and *P* is an unvoiced *B*, while *K* is an unvoiced *G*. La letra *T* es una *D* sorda, y la *P* es una *B* sorda, a la par que el sonido *K* es una *G* sorda.

voiceless fricative ▪ unvoiced fricative fricativa sorda ➤ The *F* is a voiceless English *V*. ▪ The *F* is an unvoiced English *V*. La *F* es una *V* inglesa sorda.

voiceless stop ▪ unvoiced stop oclusiva sorda ➤ The consonants *T*, *P*, and *K* are voiceless stops. ▪ The consonants *T*, *P*, and *K* are unvoiced stops. Las consonantes *T*, *P* y *K* son consonantes oclusivas sordas.

the **volcano is erupting** el volcán está en erupción

volley of protests lluvia de protestas

volley of shots ráfaga de tiros ▪ descarga de balas

volley of shots: to fire a ~ tirar una salva ▪ lanzar una ráfaga

voluntarily: to do something ~ hacer algo por voluntad propia ▪ hacer algo voluntariamente ▪ hacer algo mutuo propio

to **volunteer for military service** ir voluntario al servicio militar ▪ *(coll.)* ir voluntario a la mili

to **volunteer information** brindarse a dar información

to **volunteer to do something** brindarse a hacer algo

to **vote (according to) one's conscience** votar en conciencia

to **vote against someone** votar contra alguien

to **vote against something** votar en contra de algo

to **vote by absentee ballot** votar por correo

to **vote down something** ▪ to vote something down ▪ to defeat something in a vote ▪ to reject something in a vote votar contra algo ▪ votar en contra de algo ➤ *(news item)* Denmark yesterday voted down the euro. ▪ Denmark yesterday voted the euro down. Dinamarca votó ayer contra el euro. ➤ They voted it down. (Ellos) votaron en contra.

to **vote for a measure** ▪ to vote in favor of a measure votar a favor de una medida

to **vote for someone** votar a alguien ▪ votar por alguien ➤ Who are you going to vote for? ▪ Who are you voting for? ¿A quién vas a votar? ➤ I'm going to vote for the opposition candidate. ▪ I'm voting for the opposition candidate. Voy a votar al candidato de la oposición. ▪ Voy a votar por el candidato de la oposición. ➤ I'm going to vote for the incumbent. Voy a votar al que está en el cargo.

vote getter máquina de conseguir votos

vote of censure *la* moción de censura

vote of confidence *la* moción de confianza

the **vote on the nomination** la votación del nombramiento

to **vote on the nomination** someter el nombramiento a votación

to **vote one's conscience** ▪ to vote according to one's conscience votar a conciencia

to **vote one's pocketbook** votar con la billetera ▪ votar con el bolsillo ➤ People vote their pocketbooks, generally. La gente vota con su billetera, generalmente. ▪ La gente vota con su bolsillo, generalmente.

to **vote someone out of office** ser expulsado por votación ➤ The corrupt government was voted out of office. El gobierno corrupto fue expulsado por votación.

voter list ▪ list of registered voters registro electoral ▪ censo

voter preference poll ▪ voter preference survey ▪ poll of voter preference ▪ survey of voter preference encuesta de intención de voto

voter turnout *la* concurrencia de votantes ▪ *la* participación de votantes

voter turnout: heavy ~ ▪ large voter turnout ▪ high voter turnout elevada concurrencia de votantes ▪ gran número de votantes ▪ alto porcentaje de electores

voter turnout: high ~ ▪ heavy voter turnout ▪ large voter turnout elevada concurrencia de votantes ▪ gran número de votantes ▪ alto porcentaje de electores

voter turnout: low ~ ▪ light voter turnout ▪ small voter turnout baja concurrencia de votantes ▪ escasa participación de electores ▪ elevada abstención (de votantes)

votes cast against something sufragios emitidos en contra de algo

votes cast in favor of something ▪ votes cast for something sufragios emitidos a favor de algo

voting bloc fuerza votada ➤ The Democratic party is the largest voting bloc in Hong Kong. El partido democrático es la fuerza más votada de Hong Kong.

voting booth cabina de votación

to **vouch for someone** responder por alguien

vow of chastity voto de castidad

wad of bills fajo de billetes ■ taco de billetes

wad of chewing gum bola de goma de mascar

wad of dough *(coll.)* **1.** lump of dough bola de masa **2.** wad of bills fajo de billetes

to **wade across a river** ■ to ford a river vadear un río (a pie) ■ cruzar un río vadeando ■ apear un río ■ franquear un río

to **wade into the water** entrar en el agua caminando ■ entrar en el agua andando

wafer-thin majority ■ razor-thin majority muy estrecha mayoría ■ muy delgada mayoría

to **waffle on an issue** ■ to go back and forth on an issue cambiar de camisa repetidas veces ■ cambiar de chaqueta repetidas veces

wage and price controls el control de precios y salarios

wage and price freeze congelamiento de precios y salarios

wage earner trabajador a sueldo ■ asalariado ■ trabajador por cuenta ajena

to **wage war** ■ to make war hacer guerra

wail of a siren aullido de una sirena

wail of an infant vagido de un bebé ■ vagido de un niño

waist of a pair of pants cintura de un pantalón

waist size talla de cintura ■ medida de cintura

wait! ¡espera!

wait a second ■ hold on a second aguanta un pelo ■ aguanta un pelín ■ (espera) un momento

wait and see! ¡espera y verás!

to **wait and see** esperar y luego ver ■ estar a la expectativa ➤ Let's just wait and see. Vamos a esperar y luego vemos.

to **wait because of someone** esperar por alguien

to **wait because of something** esperar por algo

to **wait for hours** esperar horas

to **wait for it to...** esperar (a) que... ➤ The skiers are waiting impatiently for it to snow. Los esquiadores esperan con impaciencia a que nieve. ■ Los esquiadores están esperando con impaciencia a que nieve.

to **wait for someone** esperar a alguien ➤ I'm waiting for the concierge. Espero al portero. ■ Estoy esperando al portero. ➤ Does the concierge know you're waiting for him? ■ Does the concierge know you're waiting on him? ¿Sabe el portero que le esperas?

to **wait for someone to do something** ■ to wait on someone to do something esperar a que alguien haga algo ■ esperar hasta que alguien haga algo ➤ I'm waiting for my friend (to come). ■ I'm waiting on my friend. Espero a que venga mi amigo. ➤ I'm waiting for Susana to call. ■ I'm waiting on Susana to call. Estoy esperando a que Susana llame. ➤ I was waiting for you to call. ■ I was waiting for your call. ■ I was waiting on your call. Estaba esperando a que llamaras. ■ Estaba esperando a que llamases.

to **wait for something to happen** esperar a que ocurra algo ■ esperar a que suceda algo ■ esperar a que pase algo ➤ We're waiting for the elevator to go up. Esperamos a que el ascensor suba. ➤ The pilots are waiting for the weather to change. Los pilotos esperan a que cambie el tiempo. ➤ The skiers are waiting for it to snow. Los esquiadores esperan a que nieva.

to **wait for the bus** ■ to wait on the bus esperar el autobús ➤ I'm waiting for the bus. ■ I'm waiting on the bus. Estoy esperando el autobús.

to **wait for the cows to come home** ■ to wait for the crows to come home ■ to wait till hell freezes over esperar a que las ranas crién pelo ■ esperar a que los pericos mamen ■ esperar hasta que las ranas crién pelo ■ esperar hasta que los pericos mamen

to **wait for the crows to come home** ■ to wait for the cows to come home esperar a que las ranas crién pelo ■ esperar a que los pericos mamen ■ esperar hasta que las ranas crién pelo ■ esperar hasta que los pericos mamen

to **wait for the results of the medical tests** ■ to await the results of the medical tests esperar los resultados de las pruebas médicas

to **wait forever for** ■ to wait interminably for esperar interminablemente ■ esperar horas

to **wait in ambush for someone** ■ to lie in wait for someone acechar a alguien

to **wait on someone 1.** to attend someone (in a restaurant, etc.) atender a alguien **2.** to wait for someone esperar a alguien ➤ I've already been waited on, thank you. Ya me atienden, gracias. ➤ I'm waiting on my friend. Espero a mi amigo. ■ Estoy esperando a mi amigo.

to **wait on someone hand and foot** traerle a alguien en palmitas ■ tener a alguien en palmitas ■ traerle a alguien entre algodones ■ tener a alguien entre algodones ➤ She waits on him hand and foot. Ella le trae en palmitas. ■ Ella le tiene en palmitas. ■ Ella le trae entre algodones. ■ Ella le tiene entre algodones.

to **wait one's turn** esperar uno su turno ➤ Please wait your turn. Por favor, espere su turno.

to **wait outside** esperar fuera

to **wait tables** ■ to work as a waitress servir mesas ➤ She earns her tuition by waiting tables in a restaurant. Se paga los estudios sirviendo mesas en un restaurante.

to **wait till** *(coll.)* ■ to wait until esperar hasta ■ esperar a ➤ We'll have to wait till next Monday to buy our texts. Tendremos que esperar hasta el lunes próximo para comprar nuestros textos. ■ Tendremos que esperar al lunes próximo para comprar nuestros textos. ➤ "Wait'll I tell you what the boss did in the meeting!" "Espera a que te cuente lo que hizo el jefe en la reunión".

wait till you see what... *(tú)* espera a ver lo que... ■ espérate a ver lo que... ■ *(usted)* espere a ver lo que... ■ espérese a ver lo que...

to **wait to be seated** esperar a que le asignen asiento a uno ■ esperar a recibir asiento ■ esperar para recibir asiento ■ esperar para recibir puesto ➤ Please wait to be seated. Por favor espere a que le asignen asiento. ➤ Do we have to wait to be seated, or can we go on in? ¿Tenemos que esperar a que nos asignen asiento, o entramos directamente? ■ ¿Tenemos que esperar para que nos asignen asiento, o entramos directamente?

to **wait until** ■ *(coll.)* to wait till esperar hasta ■ esperar a

to **wait *x* minutes for...** esperar *x* minutos para que... ■ esperar *x* minutos por

waiting for...: to have been ~ estar esperando desde hace... ➤ I've been waiting for an hour. Estoy esperando desde hace una hora.

to be **waiting for a call** estar esperando una llamada ■ esperar una llamada

waiting for Godot: to be like ~ esperar a que las ranas crién pelos ➤ It's like waiting for Godot. Es como esperar a que las ranas crién pelos.

to be **waiting for one's ride** estar esperando a que le vengan a buscar a uno ➤ I'm just waiting for my ride. Sólo estoy esperando a que me vengan a buscar.

to be **waiting for someone to do something** estar esperando a que alguien haga algo ▪ estar pendiente de que alguien haga algo

to be **waiting for word from someone** ▪ to be awaiting word from someone esperar noticias de alguien

to be **waiting in the wings** estar esperando entre bastidores

waiting since...: to have been ~ estar esperando desde... ➤ I've been waiting since noon. Estoy esperando desde las doce del mediodía.

to be **waiting to** estar pendiente de

to be **waiting to hear (from someone)** esperar noticias de alguien ▪ estar en compás de espera *(The latter expression implies that you cannot make your next move until you hear.)*

to **waive an option** renunciar a una opción ▪ dejar una opción ▪ abandonar una opción

to **waive the right to** renunciar al derecho de

wake of a boat: to travel in the ~ ir a la estela de un barco ▪ ir a rebufo de un barco

wake of a race car: to travel in the ~ ▪ to slipstream ir a rebufo (de una carrera de autos)

wake of an airplane: to travel in the ~ ir a rebufo de un avión ▪ ir en la estela de un avión

to **wake up** ▪ to awaken despertarse ➤ I woke up at 6 a.m. ▪ I awoke at 6 a.m. Me desperté a las seis de la mañana. ➤ The neighbor's TV woke me up. ▪ The neighbor's TV awakened me. La tele de la vecina me despertó.

to **wake up someone** ▪ to wake someone up ▪ to awaken someone despertar a alguien ➤ Go wake up your father and tell him it's time to get ready for work. ▪ Go wake your father up and tell him it's time to get ready for work. ▪ Go awaken your father and tell him it's time to get ready for work. Ve a despertar a tu padre y dile que es hora de prepararse para ir a trabajar. ➤ Go wake him up. ▪ Go awaken him. Ve a despertarlo. ▪ *(Sp., leísmo)* Ve a despertarle. ➤ The alarm clock awakens me at six forty-five each morning. ▪ The alarm clock wakes me up at quarter to seven each morning. El reloj despertador me despierta cada mañana a las siete menos cuarto.

to **wake up to reality** ▪ to come down out of the clouds despertar a la realidad ▪ bajar a la realidad ▪ bajar de las nubes

to **walk a mile in someone's shoes** ▪ to put oneself in someone else's shoes ponerse en el lugar de alguien

to **walk a tightrope** *(literal and figurative)* andar en la cuerda floja ▪ caminar sobre la cuerda floja

to **walk all over someone** tratar a alguien a las patatas ▪ pisotear a alguien

to **walk all over the place** caminar por todas partes ▪ andar por todas partes

to **walk along** ir caminando ▪ venir caminando ▪ *(Sp.)* ir andando ▪ venir andando

to **walk along the sidewalk** ▪ to walk down the sidewalk *(L. Am.)* ir caminando por la banqueta ▪ *(Sp.)* ir andando por la acera

to **walk along the street** ▪ to walk down the street ir caminando por la calle ▪ ir andando por la calle

to **walk around something** rodear ▪ girar alrededor de ➤ He walked around the horse. Giró alrededor del caballo.

to **walk away without a scratch** ▪ to come away without a scratch ▪ to escape unharmed salir ileso

to **walk back** regresarse caminando ▪ volverse andando ➤ I walked back home. Me regresé a casa caminando.

walk-in closet *el* vestidor ▪ armario en el que se puede andar dentro

to **walk in front of someone 1.** to walk ahead of someone ir por delante de alguien **2.** to walk across someone's path (in close proximity) cruzarse con alguien (muy de cerca)

to **walk in one's sleep** ▪ to sleepwalk ▪ to somnambulate caminar en sueños

walk light semáforo peatonal

to **walk off without something** salir sin algo ▪ dejarse algo ➤ I walked off without my glasses. He salido sin gafas. ▪ Me he dejado las gafas.

to **walk on** ▪ to keep walking *(L. Am., Sp.)* seguir caminando ▪ *(Sp.)* seguir andando

to **walk on all fours 1.** caminar a gatas ▪ andar a cuatro patas **2.** *(children)* to crawl gatear

to **walk on crutches** ▪ to walk with crutches ▪ to use crutches llevar muletas

to **walk on eggs** pisar de puntillas

to **walk someone through something** ▪ to explain something to someone step by step guiarlo a alguien paso a paso por algo ▪ *(Sp., leísmo)* guiarle a alguien paso a paso por algo ▪ explicar algo a alguien paso a paso ➤ I need (for) someone to walk me through the installation. Necesito que alguien me guie paso a paso por la instalación. ▪ Necesito que alguien me explique paso a paso por la instalación.

to **walk straight into someone** ir de bruces hacia alguien ▪ venir de bruces hacia uno ➤ He walked straight into me. Vino de bruces hacia mí.

to **walk the dog** ▪ to take the dog for a walk pasear al perro ▪ sacar a pasear al perro

to **walk through** cruzar a pie ➤ He walked through the Campo Grande to the train station. Cruzó el Campo Grande a pie a la estación de trenes.

to **walk through the mud** caminar entre el barro

to **walk up and down the ramp** *(like models)* ▪ to parade up and down the ramp desfilar en la pasarela

to **walk with crutches** ▪ to walk on crutches ▪ to use crutches llevar muletas

to be a **walking encyclopedia** hablar como un libro abierto ▪ hablar como un libro ▪ ser un enciclopedia viviente

wall: load-bearing ~ *la* pared de carga ▪ pared maestra ▪ muro de carga

wall: partition(ing) ~ ▪ non-load-bearing wall *el* tabique ▪ la pared

wall of an artery *la* pared de una arteria

wall of silence muro de silencio

wall of the intestines ▪ intestinal wall *la* pared del intestino

wall of the stomach *la* pared del estómago

wall-to-wall carpeting moqueta

wall-to-wall sunshine *(coll.)* sol de punta a punta

walls have ears ▪ walls can hear las paredes oyen

to **wander aimlessly** errar sin rumbo fijo

to **wander around** vagar ▪ andar de ronda

to **wander around a place** vagar por un lugar

waning moon luna menguante

wanna bet? *(coll.)* ▪ do you want to bet? ¿te juegas algo?

want a bite? ¿quieres un poco? ▪ ¿quieres probarlo? ▪ ¿te apetece un trozo?

to **want for breakfast** apetecerle (para) desayunar ▪ querer (para) desayunar ▪ apetecerle para el desayuno ▪ querer para el desayuno ➤ What do you want for breakfast? ▪ What would you like for breakfast? *(a ti)* ¿Qué te apetece para desayunar? ▪ ¿Qué quieres para desayunar? ▪ *(a usted)* ¿Qué le apetece para desayunar? ▪ ¿Qué quiere (usted) para desayunar? ▪ ¿Qué desea (usted) para desayunar?

to **want (for) there to be** querer que haya ➤ I don't want (for) there to be any surprises. No quiero que haya sorpresas. ▪ No quiero que haya ninguna sorpresa.

to **want it back** quererlo de regreso

to **want nothing to do with something** ▪ not to want anything to do with something no querer tener nada que ver con algo

to **want something back** querer algo de vuelta ➤ *(Mark Twain)* A banker is a fellow who lends you his umbrella when the sun is shining and wants it back again the minute it starts to rain. Un banquero es un tipo que te presta su paraguas cuando el sol brilla, y lo quiere de vuelta en cuanto empieza a llover.

to **want there to be** ▪ to want for there to be querer que haya ➤ I don't want (for) there to be any surprises. No quiero que haya sorpresas.

want to come? ▪ do you want to come with me? ¿me acompañas?

want to hear a joke? ¿te cuento un chiste?

to **want to run the other way** querer salir corriendo ➤ When I saw the kitchen after the party, I (just) wanted to run the other way. Cuando vi la cocina después de la fiesta, quise salir corriendo.

wanted dead or alive se busca vivo o muerto
war effort esfuerzo bélico
war on terrorism guerra contra el terrorismo
war-torn machacado por guerra
to **ward off an animal** ahuyentar (a golpes) un animal
to **ward off the blow** ▪ to deflect the blow ▪ to avert the blow parar el golpe ▪ detener el golpe ➤ He warded off the blow. Paró el golpe. ➤ He warded it off. Él lo detuvo.
to **ward off the threat** parar la amenaza ▪ conjurar la amenaza
to be **warm** ▪ to hold heat dar calor ➤ Which comforter is warmer, the down or the dacron? ▪ Which of the comforters is warmer, the down or the dacron? ¿Cuál de los edredones da más calor, el de plumas o de dacrón?
warm atmosphere ▪ inviting atmosphere ambiente cálido ▪ ambiente acogedor ➤ Your apartment has a warm atmosphere. Tu piso tiene un ambiente cálido. ▪ Tu piso tiene un ambiente muy acogedor.
to be **warm-blooded** ser de sangre caliente
warm-blooded animal animal de sangre caliente
warm climate clima templado ➤ The climate of Mexico City is not very warm because of its elevation above sea level. El clima de la Ciudad de México no es muy templado por su altitud sobre el nivel del mar.
warm clothes ropa de abrigo ➤ Do you have warm clothes to wear in the Sierra? ¿Tienes ropa de abrigo para llevar en la Sierra?
warm clothing ropa de abrigo
warm coat abrigo caliente
warm front *(weather)* frente cálido
to be **warm in the winter** **1.** *(house)* estar calentita **2.** *(coat)* abrigar mucho ▪ dar mucho calor
warm months meses cálidos
to **warm up** **1.** *(body)* entrar en calor **2.** *(weather, etc.)* empezar a hacer calor ➤ In spite of the cold air, my body warmed up quickly as I hiked. *(L. Am.)* A pesar del aire frío, mi cuerpo entró en calor rápido conforme caminaba. ▪ *(Sp.)* A pesar del aire frío, mi cuerpo entró en calor rápido conforme andaba. ➤ When is the weather going to warm up? ¿Cuándo va a empezar a hacer calor?
to **warm up before exercising** ▪ to do warm-up exercises hacer ejercicios de calentamiento
warm-ups ▪ warm-up exercises ejercicios de calentamiento
warm weather tiempo cálido ▪ tiempo caluroso
warm welcome cálida bienvenida ▪ calurosa bienvenida ▪ cálida acogida ▪ calurosa acogida
to be **warmer than...** ▪ to provide more warmth than... abrigar más que... ▪ ser más cálido que... ▪ ser más abrigado que... ▪ calentar más que... ➤ The new "moon boots" are warmer than the old leather ones. Las nuevas botas espaciales abrigan más que las antiguas (botas) de cuero. ▪ Las nuevas botas espaciales son más cálidas que las antiguas (botas) de cuero. ▪ Las nuevas botas espaciales son más abrigadas que las antiguas (botas) de cuero. ▪ Las nuevas botas espaciales calientan más que las antiguas (botas) de cuero.
warmth: to have a lot of ~ *(human quality)* tener calor humano ▪ tener calidez humana
to **warn of** alertar sobre ➤ The Red Cross warns of a humanitarian catastrophe. La Cruz Roja alerta sobre una catástrofe humanitaria.
to **warn someone of something** advertir a alguien de algo ▪ advertir a alguien sobre algo ➤ I'm warning you! ¡Te lo advierto! ➤ The doctor warned the patient of the risks of smoking heavily. El médico advirtió al paciente sobre los riesgos de fumar mucho.
to **warn (someone) that...** advertir (a alguien) de que...
warning lights las luces de emergencia
wartime budget presupuesto de tiempos de guerra
was being estaba siendo ➤ The boat was being towed to a French port. El barco estaba siendo remolcado hacia un puerto francés.
was completed se terminó ▪ fue terminado ▪ se acabó ▪ fue acabado ➤ Construction of the Prado Museum was completed in 1819. En 1819 se terminó de construir el Museo del Prado. ▪ En 1819 se acabó de construir el Museo del Prado.
was experiencing vivía ➤ *(news item)* The Rota naval base was experiencing its longest strike in history. La base naval de Rota vivía la huelga más larga de su historia.
was going to arrive ▪ would arrive iba a llegar ▪ llegaría ➤ They didn't know what time the plane was going to arrive. ▪ They didn't know what time the plane would arrive. No sabían a qué hora iba a llegar el avión. ▪ No sabían a qué hora llegaría el avión.
was gone había desaparecido ➤ I dreamed I ate a huge marshmallow, and when I woke up, my pillow was gone. Soñé con comer una nube grandísima, y cuando me desperté, mi almohada había desaparecido.
was I long? ¿he tardado mucho? ▪ ¿tardé mucho? ▪ ¿demoré mucho?
was I supposed to call you? ¿quedé en llamarte? ▪ ¿habíamos quedado que yo te llamara?
was it that bad? ¿era tan mal?
was killed murió ▪ resultó muerto ➤ Manolete was killed fighting a bull. Manolete murió toreando. ➤ The driver was killed. El conductor resultó muerto. ▪ *(race car)* El piloto resultó muerto.
was still doing something: one ~ uno seguía haciendo algo ➤ He was still waiting for her. (Él) seguía esperándola.
was that the bus for...? ¿era ése el autobús que va a...? ▪ ¿era ése el autobús para...? ➤ Was that the bus for Toluca? ▪ Was that the Toluca bus? ¿Era ése el autobús que va a Toluca? ▪ ¿Era ése el autobús para Toluca?
was that you? ¿has sido tú? ▪ ¿fuiste tú? ▪ ¿ha sido usted? ▪ ¿fue usted?
to **wash down food** pasar las migas ▪ regar comida ➤ Do you want a little glass of wine to wash it down? ¿Quieres una copa de vino para pasar las migas?
to **wash one's hands of something** desentenderse de algo
to **wash the dishes** fregar los cacharros ▪ fregar los platos ▪ fregar la loza ▪ fregar la vajilla
to be **washed up** ▪ to be all washed up ▪ to have had it ▪ to be done for estar para el arrastre ▪ estar apañado ➤ He's all washed up. ▪ He's had it. Está para el arrastre.
wasn't there a...? ¿qué no hubo un...?
to **waste away** marchitarse
to **waste energy** derrochar energía ▪ desperdiciar energía ▪ malgastar energía ▪ dilapidar energía
to **waste money** despilfarrar dinero ▪ derrochar dinero
to **waste natural resources** despilfarrar recursos naturales
to be a **waste of effort** ser un esfuerzo inútil
to be a **waste of money** ser un despilfarro de dinero ▪ ser un gasto (de dinero) inútil
to be a **waste of time** ser tiempo perdido ▪ ser una pérdida de tiempo
to **waste one's life** malgastar la vida
to **waste someone's time** malgastar el tiempo de alguien ▪ perder el tiempo de alguien ▪ desaprovechar el tiempo de alguien ▪ desperdiciar el tiempo de alguien ▪ despilfarrar el tiempo de alguien
to **waste time** perder (el) tiempo ▪ malgastar el tiempo ▪ desaprovechar el tiempo ▪ desperdiciar el tiempo ▪ despilfarrar el tiempo
to **waste time and energy** gastar la pólvora en salvas
wastebasket ▪ trash basket **1.** *(for paper)* papelera **2.** *(for organic trash, as in a kitchen)* cubo de la basura
wasting one's time: to be (just) ~ estar escribiendo en la arena ▪ escribir en la arena ▪ estar perdiendo el tiempo ➤ You're (just) wasting your time. *(tú)* Estás escribiendo en la arena ▪ *(usted)* (Usted) está escribiendo en la arena.
to **watch a parade** ver un desfile ▪ *(with horses and riders)* ver una cabalgata
to **watch carefully** mirar atentamente ➤ Watch carefully! *(tú)* Mira atentamente. ▪ *(usted)* Mire atentamente. ▪ *(ustedes)* Miren (ustedes) atentamente. ▪ *(Sp., vosotros)* Mirad atentamente.
to **watch cartoons** ver dibujos animados ➤ We were watching cartoons. Veíamos dibujos animados.
to **watch closely** ▪ to monitor closely ▪ to keep a close eye on vigilar estrechamente ➤ The enemy must understand that

we are watching him closely. El enemigo tiene que entender que le vigilamos estrechamente.

watch for her! ▪ keep an eye out for her! *(tú)* ¡estate atento(-a) a ella! ▪ ¡estate atento(-a)! ▪ *(usted)* ¡estese atento(-a) a ella! ▪ ¡estese atento(-a)!

watch for him! ▪ keep an eye out for him! *(tú)* ¡estate atento(-a) a él! ▪ ¡estate atento(-a)! ▪ *(usted)* ¡estese atento(-a) a él! ▪ ¡estese atento(-a)!

watch for it! *(upcoming TV program, etc.)* ▪ keep an eye out for it! *(tú)* ¡estate atento (a ello)! ▪ *(usted)* ¡estese atento (a ello)!

watch is fast: my ~ mi reloj está adelantado

watch is slow: my ~ mi reloj está atrasado

watch it! 1. look out! ¡ojo! ▪ ¡cuidado! **2.** watch what you're doing! ¡cuida lo que hagas!

watch my things for a minute atiende mis cosas por un momento ▪ cuida de mis cosas un momento

to **watch one's alcohol consumption** controlarse con la bebida

to **watch out** ▪ to be careful andarse con ojo ▪ tener cuidado

to **watch over something** celar por algo ▪ celar sobre algo ▪ velar por algo ➤ The shepherds watched over their flocks. Los pastores celaban por sus rebaños. ▪ Los pastores celaban sobre sus rebaños. ▪ Los pastores velaban por sus rebaños.

watch runs fast ▪ watch gains time reloj se adelanta

watch runs slow ▪ watch loses time reloj se retrasa

to **watch someone like a hawk** ▪ not to take one's eyes off (of) someone no quitar los ojos de encima a alguien ▪ no quitarle los ojos de encima (a alguien) ▪ seguir a alguien con lupa

to **watch something like a hawk** ▪ not to take one's eyes off (of) something no quitar los ojos de encima a algo ▪ no quitarle los ojos de encima (a algo) ▪ seguir algo con lupa

watch what he does! ¡mira lo que hace! ▪ ¡ve lo que hace!

watch what you're doing! ¡presta atención a lo que haces! ▪ ¡cuidado con lo que haces! ▪ ¡ojo con lo que haces!

watch where you're going! *(tú)* ¡fíjate por donde vas! ▪ ¡mira por donde andas! ▪ ¡mira por donde vas! *(usted)* ¡fíjese por donde va (usted)! ▪ ¡mire por donde anda! ▪ ¡mire por donde va!

watch your backside cuidarse las espaldas

watch your head! ¡cuidado con la cabeza!

to **water down a statement** ▪ to water a statement down ▪ to qualify a statement ▪ to soften a statement suavizar una declaración

water fountain ▪ drinking fountain la fuente de beber ▪ fuentecilla

the **water has come to boil** el agua ha roto a hervir

the **water is boiling** ▪ the water's boiling el agua está hirviendo

water shortage *la* escazez de agua ▪ falta de agua

to **water-ski** hacer esquí acuático

water spigot boca de riego

water table capa freática ➤ At water-table level... ▪ At the level of the water table... A nivel freático...

to be **water under the bridge** ser agua pasada

watercolor artist pintor de acuarelas

to be **waterproof 1.** water cannot damage it ser a prueba de agua ▪ estar a prueba de agua **2.** water cannot penetrate it ser impermeable

waterproof watch *el* reloj resistente al agua

watershed event ▪ decisive event acontecimiento bisagra

to **wave at one's fans 1.** *(all contexts)* saludar (de lejos) a sus admiradores ▪ saludar a sus aficionados **2.** *(sports figure)* saludar (de lejos) a sus hinchas

to **wave at someone 1.** *(as a greeting)* saludar (de lejos) a alguien **2.** *(to attract someone's attention)* hacerle señas a alguien

wave band ▪ frequency banda de frecuencia ▪ faja de frecuencia

wave crest ▪ crest of a wave cresta de una ola

to **wave good-bye** dar la señal de partido ▪ hacer un ademán de despedida

wave mechanics *(physics)* mecánica ondulatoria

wave of oleada de ▪ marejada de ▪ marea de

wave of acts of violence oleada de actos de violencia

wave of protests marea de protestas

to **wave to** ▪ to wave at saludar a ▪ agitar la mano a ➤ The president-elect waves to his fans in Austin. El presidente electo saluda a sus seguidores en Austin.

wavelength *(physics)* la longitud de onda

the **waves broke on the boulders** ▪ the waves crashed against the boulders las olas rompían contra los peñascos ▪ las olas se estrellaban contra los peñascos

to **wax the floor** encerar el suelo ▪ encerar el piso ▪ darle cera al suelo ▪ darle cera al piso ➤ We need to mop and wax the floor. Hay que pasar la fregona y darle cera al suelo. ▪ Hay que pasar la fregona y encerar al suelo.

waxed dental floss hilo dental con cera ▪ seda dental con cera

waxing moon luna creciente

way below the speed limit: to go ~ ▪ to go far below the speed limit ▪ to poke along ir muy por debajo del límite de velocidad

the **way I look at it** ▪ the way I see it ▪ to my way of thinking a mi modo de ver ▪ a mi manera de ver ▪ a mi entender

the **way I see it** ▪ the way I look at it ▪ to my way of thinking a mi modo de ver ▪ a mi manera de ver ▪ a mi entender

the **way in which...** ▪ the way that... la forma en la que...

the **way it has to be** ▪ the way it's got to be ▪ as it has to be (tal y) como debe ser

the **way it should be** ▪ as it should be como debería ser

way of doing something ▪ way to do something manera de hacer algo

way of doing things ▪ way of going about things ▪ modus operandi ▪ method of operating manera de obrar

way of life modo de vida ▪ postura de vida ▪ medio de vida

to be **way off** ser de lo más impreciso ▪ no tener nada que ver ➤ Cassini's measurement of the sun's distance from the Earth in 1677 was way off, although his method was correct. La medición de Cassini de la distancia entre el sol y la Tierra en 1677 fue de lo más impreciso, aunque su método era correcto. ➤ That's way off. No tiene nada que ver.

way out 1. exit salida **2.** escape route escapatoria ▪ **3.** far away muy lejos ▪ muy alejado ➤ There is no way out. No hay escapatoria. ▪ No hay salida. ➤ There is no way out of the situation. No hay ninguna escapatoria de la situación. ➤ There is no way out of this. No hay modo de salir de esto. ➤ They live way out from the city center. ▪ They live a long way from the city center. Viven muy lejos del centro de la ciudad. ▪ Viven muy alejados del centro de la ciudad. ➤ It's not convenient to give him a ride. He lives way out of the way. ▪ He lives way off the beaten track. No es conveniente llevarlo. Vive muy lejos del camino.

to be **way over to the left** estar muy a la izquierda ➤ Get way over to the left. Ponte muy a la izquierda.

to be **way over to the right** estar muy a la derecha ➤ Get way over to the right. Ponte muy a la derecha.

the **way things are** según están las cosas

the **way things are going...** tal y como están yendo las cosas... ▪ tal y como están marchando las cosas... ▪ tal y como están...

way to método para ▪ manera de ➤ That's a better way to do it Es un mejor método para hacerlo. ▪ Es una mejor manera de hacerlo. ➤ That's the best way to do it. Es el mejor método para hacerlo. ▪ Es la mejor manera de hacerlo.

the **way to a man's heart is through his stomach** con la menta, el amor entra

way to approach the problem manera de tratar el problema ➤ The way I'd approach the problem is this... La manera en que yo trataría el problema es ésta...

way to go! ¡así se hace! ▪ ¡torero!

to be **way too big** ser demasiado grande ▪ ser enorme ▪ nadar en ➤ These shoes are way too big. Estos zapatos son demasiado grandes. ▪ Estos zapatos son enormes. ▪ Me nadan los pies en estos zapatos.

to be **way up there** estar muy alto

way up to the castle *(on a directional sign)* subida al castillo

The ***Way We Were*** *(movie title)* *Tal como éramos*

we all have our problems ▪ everyone has a cross to bear cada cual tiene sus problemas ▪ cada cual lleva su cruz

we all make mistakes ▪ nobody's perfect quien tiene boca, se equivoca

we are of the same opinion ▪ we're of the same opinion somos de la misma opinión

we are pleased to... nos es grato...

we ask that... ▪ we request that... rogamos que... ▪ se ruega que... ➤ We ask that you hold your applause until the end of the concert. Rogamos que no aplaudan hasta el final del concierto. ▪ Se ruega que esperen a aplaudir hasta el final del concierto.

we both ▪ both of us nosotros dos ▪ ambos ▪ los dos ➤ We both make the same mistakes. Nosotros dos cometemos los mismos errores. ▪ Ambos cometemos los mismos errores. ▪ Los dos cometemos los mismos errores.

we can all todos nosotros podemos

we do have class today ▪ the class does meet today ▪ there *is* a class today sí se da la clase hoy

we each ▪ each one of us cada uno de nosotros

we got cut off *(telephone)* ▪ I got cut off se cortó (la comunicación) ▪ perdí la comunicación

we have to go along with it no hay más que conformarse

we have to take what comes our way que cada palo aguante su vela

we hear you loud and clear más claro no canta un gallo

we hope you have a pleasant trip esperamos que su viaje sea agrado

we may never know ▪ it may never be known puede que nunca lo sepamos ▪ puede que nunca sepamos ▪ puede que nunca lleguemos a saberlo ▪ puede que nunca se sepa ➤ Pluto might at one time have been a satellite of Neptune, but we may never know whether it (ever) was. ▪ Pluto could at one time have been a satellite of Neptune, but whether it (ever) was may never be known. Plutón pudiera haber sido en un momento dado un satélite de Neptuno, pero si (alguna vez) lo fue, puede que nunca lo sepamos. ▪ Plutón pudiera haber sido en un momento dado un satélite de Neptuno, pero si (alguna vez) lo fue, puede que nunca se sepa.

we open at *x* a las *x* abrimos ➤ We open at ten. A las diez abrimos.

we request that... ▪ we ask that... se solicita que...

we shall see ▪ we will see ▪ we'll see ya veremos

we should like to *(archaic)* ▪ we would like to ▪ we'd like to nos gustaría

we still have a ways to go todavía nos queda trayecto por recorrer

we were asked if se nos preguntó si ▪ nos preguntaron si

we were asked to se nos pidió que ▪ nos pidieron que

we were asked whether... or not se nos preguntó si... o no ▪ nos preguntaron si... o no

we were *just* talking about you en nombrando al ruin de Roma, por la puerta asoma

weak pulse: to have a ~ tener el pulso bajo

weak-willed sin fuerza de voluntad

weaker sex *(politically incorrect)* ▪ women sexo débil

wealthy client ▪ well-to-do client acaudalado(-a) cliente

weapons of mass destruction armas de destrucción masiva

to **wear a hat** llevar un sombrero ▪ usar un sombrero

to **wear a mask** llevar disfraz ▪ llevar antifaz ➤ They were wearing masks. Llevaban disfraces. ▪ Llevaban antifaz.

to **wear a ring** llevar un anillo (por costumbre) ▪ usar un anillo ➤ She wears a ring. (Ella) lleva un anillo. *("Lleva un anillo" means both "she wears a ring" and "she is wearing a ring." "Usar un anillo" means "she wears a ring all the time.")*

to **wear a shirt with the tails out** llevarse una camisa suelta ▪ llevarse una camisa por fuera (del pantalón) ➤ The guayabera, a shirt common in tropical climates, is worn with the tails out. La guayabera, una camisa común en climas tropicales, se lleva suelta.

to **wear away** desgastar ➤ The mountains wore away as the result of millions of years of rain and wind. El desgaste de las montañas es el resultado de millones de años de lluvia y viento.

to **wear civilian clothes** vestir de civil ▪ llevar ropa de civil

to **wear clothes** vestir ropa ▪ tener puesto ▪ vestirse de ▪ llevar ▪ traer ➤ He's wearing a pair of gray pants. Viste un pantalón gris. ➤ The player will not wear the Madrid jersey again. El jugador no volverá a vestir la camisa de Madrid.

to **wear contact lenses** ▪ to wear contacts llevar lentillas

to **wear glasses** llevar lentes ▪ llevar anteojos ▪ llevar gafas ▪ llevar puestas gafas

to **wear good shoes** irse bien calzado

to **wear off** **1.** *(paint, lipstick, etc.)* desgastarse **2.** *(effects, physical or psychological)* pasarse ➤ My nail polish and lipstick have worn off. Mi esmalte de uñas y lápiz labial se han desgastado. ➤ At least the initial shock of the news has worn off. Por lo menos (se) pasó el susto inicial de la noticia. ➤ The effects of the medication have worn off. Los efectos de la medicación se han pasado.

wear one down: to start to ~ hacerse cuesta arriba ➤ This moving is starting to wear me down. La mudanza se me está haciendo cuesta arriba.

to **wear one's hair long** ▪ to have long hair llevar el pelo largo

to **wear one's hair short** ▪ to have short hair llevar el pelo corto

to **wear one's shirttail(s) out** ▪ to leave one's shirttail(s) out llevar la camisa por fuera (del pantalón) ➤ Of all my shirts that can be worn with the tails out, this (one) is the only one that has a collar. De todas las camisas que puedo llevar por fuera, ésta es la única que tiene cuello.

to **wear out one's welcome (with someone)** abusar de la hospitalidad de alguien ▪ quedarse demasiado tiempo

to **wear someone out** agotar a alguien ➤ A pair of four-year-old twins can wear a mother out in about two hours. Un par de gemelos de cuatro años pueden agotar a una madre en unas dos horas.

to **wear something across one's chest** llevar algo en bandolera

to **wear a uniform** llevar puesto un uniforme

to be **wearing** ▪ to have on ▪ to be dressed in llevar (puesto algo) ▪ ir en ▪ ir de ▪ ponerse ➤ She was wearing a bathing suit. (Ella) llevaba un traje de baño. ▪ (Ella) iba en traje de baño. ➤ She was wearing leather. (Ella) llevaba cuero. ▪ (Ella) iba de cuero. ➤ He was wearing a ring. Llevaba un anillo. ▪ Tenía puesto un anillo. ▪ Usaba un anillo.

to be **wearing glasses** llevar puestas lentes ▪ llevar puestas anteojos ▪ llevar puestas gafas

to be **wearing (on someone)** ser muy pesado con alguien ▪ ser muy cansino con alguien ▪ ser muy plasta con alguien ➤ The relentless attacks of the press have been very wearing on the prime minister. Los ataques incesantes de la prensa han sido muy pesados con el primer ministro.

to **weasel out of doing something** escurrir el bulto ▪ encontrar una triquiñuela para no hacer algo

weather forecast pronóstico del tiempo ▪ pronóstico meteorológico ➤ What's the weather forecast for tomorrow? ¿Cuál es el pronóstico del tiempo para mañana? ➤ The weather forecast for tomorrow is partly cloudly. ▪ Tomorrow (it) will be partly cloudy. El pronóstico para mañana es de tiempo parcialmente nuboso. ▪ Para mañana se espera tiempo parcialmente nuboso. ▪ Mañana estará parcialmente nuboso. *("Nubloso" is also possible.)*

the **weather is miserable** hace un tiempo de perros

to **weather the storm** ▪ to ride out the storm capear la tormenta ▪ capear el temporal ▪ aguantar el temporal ▪ aguantar el chubasco ▪ campear el temporal

weather-wise en cuanto al clima ▪ (con) respecto al clima ▪ a nivel del clima ➤ Weather-wise we've got you beat. En cuanto al clima, ganamos. ▪ A efectos del clima, ganamos. ▪ En lo que al clima respecta, ganamos. ▪ A nivel de clima, ganamos.

to **weave (all over the road)** ▪ to zigzag all over the road hacer zigzag (por toda la carretera) ▪ hacer eses (por toda la carretera)

we'd like you to come over for supper queremos que (te) vengas a cenar

we'd love to, thank you ▪ we would love to, thank you ▪ *(archaic)* we should love to, thank you nos encantaría, gracias

wedding anniversary ▪ anniversary aniversario de su matrimonio ➤ They were celebrating their fiftieth wedding anniversary. Estaban celebrando el cincuagésimo aniversario de su matrimonio.

wedding band ▪ wedding ring alianza ▪ anillo de boda ▪ anillo nupcial ▪ anillo de matrimonio

wedding party comitiva de boda ▪ comitiva nupcial ➤ The bride, the groom, the matron of honor, and the ringbearer are all members of the wedding party. La novia, el novio, la madrina y el portaanillos, todos son miembros de la comitiva de boda.

wedding ring ▪ wedding band alianza ▪ anillo de boda ▪ anillo nupcial ▪ anillo de matrimonio

Wednesday night and early Thursday en la noche del miércoles al jueves

wee hours las tantas ▪ las mil ➤ The children stayed up until the wee hours hoping to see the comet. Los niños se quedaron despiertos hasta las tantas esperando ver el cometa. ▪ Los niños se quedaron despiertos hasta las mil esperando ver el cometa.

wee hours: in the ~ en las horas intempestivas

the **week before** ▪ the previous week ▪ the preceding week ▪ the week prior la semana anterior

week by week ▪ (from) week to week semana a semana ▪ de semana en semana

to be a **week from today** ser de hoy en una semana ➤ Exams are a week from today. Los exámenes son de hoy en una semana.

weekend before last hace dos fines de semana

to **weigh a ton** 1. *(literal)* pesar una tonelada 2. *(figurative)* pesar lo suyo

to **weigh anchor** levar anclas

to **weigh on one's conscience** remorderse la consciencia ➤ It weighs on my conscience. Me remuerde la conciencia.

to **weigh on one's mind** ▪ to weigh on one pesarle a uno ▪ preocuparle a uno ➤ The decision whether to go fishing or build a tree house weighed heavily on the boy's mind. La decisión de ir de pesca o construir una casa en el árbol le pesaba al chico.

to **weigh the options** sopesar las opciones

to **weigh the pros and cons** sopesar los pros y contras

to be **weird** ser raro de narices ▪ *(off-color)* ser raro de cojones

welcome back bienvenido de nuevo ▪ bienvenido de nuevo a casa

welcome to the United States bienvenidos a los Estados Unidos

welding torch el soplete soldador

well! 1. *(emphasis)* ¡hombre! ▪ ¡vaya! 2. *(expressing indignation)* ¡acabáramos! ▪ ¡vaya!

well, actually pues, realmente

well ahead of time con suficiente antelación

well, and I did... ▪ and, well, I did... y, bueno, sí (lo hice)

to be **well-adjusted** *(person)* ▪ to be well-balanced estar bien equilibrado ▪ estar bien centrado ▪ estar bien adaptado

well and good, but... ***that's all*** ~ todo eso está muy bien, pero...

well, anyway... entonces... ▪ aparte... ▪ por otra parte...

we'll be in touch seguiremos en contacto

we'll be right back *(said by TV show host)* ahora nos vemos

we'll be (right) over vamos para allá (en seguida)

to be **well behaved** 1. *(in general)* estar (bien) educado 2. *(on a specific occasion)* portarse bien

to be **well bred** estar bien emparentado ▪ ser de buen tono

to be **well built** ▪ to have a good physique estar macizo ▪ estar fornido

well-built body ▪ well-built frame cuerpo fornido

we'll call it even lo dejaremos así ▪ estaremos en paz ➤ Give me a thousand pesetas, and we'll call it even. Dame mil pesetas, y lo dejaremos así. ▪ Dame mil pesetas, y estaremos en paz.

to be **well connected** ser un enchufado

well-done steak filete bien hecho ▪ filete muy hecho ▪ bistec bien hecho ▪ bistec muy hecho

to be **well dressed** ir bien vestido

to be **well educated** ser muy culto ▪ tener una buena educación ▪ haber estudiado mucho

to be **well endowed** estar bien dotado

well enough to lo suficientemente bien para

well-founded bien fundado

well-founded suspicion sospecho bien fundado

we'll have to make do with what we have tenemos que conformarnos con lo que tenemos ▪ a falta de pan buenas son tortas

we'll have to wait and see ▪ we'll just have to wait and see habrá que ver

to be **well heeled** ▪ to be well off financially tener bien cubiertos los riñones

well, I'll be damned! ▪ I'll be damned ¡que me ahorquen! ▪ ¡que me aspen!

well, I'll be damned if... ▪ I'll be damned if... ▪ damned if I... que me ahorquen si... ▪ que me aspen si... ➤ (Well, I'll be) damned if I can understand it... Que me aspen si lo entiendo...

to be **well informed on** ▪ to be well informed about estar bien enterado(-a) en ▪ estar bien documentado(-a) en ▪ estar bien enterado(-a) sobre ▪ estar bien documentado(-a) sobre ▪ estar al tanto de

to be **well intentioned** tener buenos deseos ▪ estar de buenos deseos ▪ tenerle a alguien de buena gana

to be **well into** 1. *(years)* estar bien adentrado en 2. *(book, etc.)* haber cubierto una buena parte ➤ He's well into his sixties. Está bien adentrado en los sesenta. ➤ The class is well into the book. ▪ The class has covered a good part of the book. La clase ha cubierto buena parte del libro.

well into next year bien entrado en el próximo año ▪ bien entrado en el año que viene

well-known ▪ noted (bien) conocido ▪ de nota ➤ Well-known neurologist Neurólogo conocido

well-known case ▪ notable case ▪ famous case sonado caso

we'll leave it at that quedamos en eso

we'll leave it the way it is lo dejaremos así ▪ dejaremos la cosa así

to be **well made** ser de buena factura ▪ ser de buena hechura

well-made boots botas de buena factura *(Clearer than "bien hecho," which also means "well done.")*

well-made suit el traje de buena hechura

well, no pues, no

to be **well preserved** ▪ to be young for one's age estar hecho un mozo

well put! ▪ I couldn't have said it better myself! ¡nunca mejor dicho!

to be **well read** ser bastante leído

to be **well received by someone** ser bien recibido por alguien ▪ ser bien acogido por alguien ▪ tener buena acogida por alguien

to be **well respected by someone** ser muy respetado por alguien

to be **well rounded** ser muy completo ➤ She's well rounded: good student, athletic, likes all kinds of music. Es muy completa: buena estudiante, atleta, le gusta todo tipo de música.

we'll see ▪ we shall see ya veremos

we'll see about that! ¡ya lo veremos!

we'll see what happens a ver qué pasa

to be **well seen** ▪ to be approved of estar bien visto ▪ estar bien considerado

well, senator así bien, senador

well-spoken bien hablado

well, then y bien ▪ ahora bien ▪ pues bueno ▪ pues bien

well then, forget it! ¡pues entonces nada!

to be **well thought of** ▪ to be thought well of ▪ to be favorably viewed ▪ to be favorably perceived ser bien pensado(-a) ▪ ser bien percibido(-a) ▪ estar bien conceptuado(-a) ➤ Her fiancé was not thought well of by the family at first. Su novio no fue bien percibido por la familia al principio. ▪ No estaba bien conceptuado por la familia al principio.

well-to-do family ▪ wealthy family ▪ affluent family ▪ family with money ▪ rich family familia acomodada ▪ familia pudiente ▪ familia acaudalada ▪ familia adinerada ▪ familia rica

well, well vaya, vaya

well, what do you know?! ¡no me digas! ▪ ¡quién iba a decirlo!
were being estaban siendo ▪ eran ➤ The boats were being towed to a French port. Los barcos estaban siendo remolcados hacia un puerto francés.
we're both... los dos somos... ▪ *(both females)* las dos somos ➤ We're both optimists. Los dos somos optimistas.
we're cooking with gas! ¡vamos viento en popa!
we're engaged! ▪ we're going to get married! ¡vamos a casarnos!
we're getting by vamos tirando ▪ estamos sobreviviendo
we're going to get married! ▪ we're getting married ▪ we're engaged! ¡vamos a casarnos!
we're going to try for a boy vamos a por el niño
we're going to try for a girl vamos a por la niña
we're hanging in there vamos tirando
we're in luck! hemos tenido suerte ▪ ¡qué suerte! ▪ *(slang)* ¡qué coña!
were it not for you ▪ if it weren't for you *(tú)* de no ser por ti ▪ si no fuera por ti ▪ *(usted)* de no ser por usted ▪ si no fuera por usted
we're off! ¡vamos! ▪ ¡nos las piramos!
we're ready to order estamos listos para pedir
we're screwed! ¡estamos jodidos! ▪ ¡hay que joderse! ▪ *(Mex.)* ¡estamos chingados!
we've known each other for... nos conocemos desde hace... ➤ We've known each other for twenty years. Nos conocemos desde hace veinte años.
we've known each other since... nos conocemos desde... ➤ We've known each other since 1990. Nos conocemos desde 1990. ➤ We've known each other since we were ten years old. Nos conocemos desde que teníamos diez años.
West Side *(of Manhattan)* zona oeste
West Virginia Virginia Occidental
west wind ▪ wind from the west ▪ wind out of the west viento de poniente
to be a **wet blanket** ▪ to be a party pooper ser un aguafiestas ▪ aguar la fiesta
wet nurse ama de cría
to **wet one's whistle** ▪ to have something to drink mojar el gaznate ▪ refrescar(se) el gaznate ▪ humedecerse los labios
wet paint pintura mojada ▪ recién pintado
to **wet the bed** orinarse en la cama
we've already met ya nos hemos conocido ▪ ya nos conocemos
we've been down this road before *(literal and figurative)* ▪ it's a road we've been down before es un camino que hemos recorrido antes ▪ es un camino que ya hemos recorrido
we've been had ▪ *(off-color)* ▪ we've been screwed nos han jodido
whaling industry industria ballenera
what a bargain! ▪ what a deal! ¡vaya chollo! ▪ ¡vaya ganga!
what a beehive of activity! ¡vaya ritmo de trabajo que se lleva! ➤ What a beehive of activity this office is! ¡Vaya ritmo de trabajo que se lleva en esta oficina!
what a bomb! ▪ what a flop! ¡vaya fracaso!
what a brat! ¡vaya niñato(-a)! ▪ ¡menudo bicho! ▪ ¡vaya bicho! ▪ ¡menudo trasto! ¡vaya trasto!
what a bummer! ▪ what a downer! ▪ what a letdown! ¡vaya chasco! ▪ ¡qué bajón! ▪ ¡qué mal rollo!
what a bummer that's going to be for her ▪ that's going to be a bummer for her ▪ what a bummer qué chasco se va a llevar (ella)
what a bummer that's going to be for him ▪ that's going to be a bummer for him ▪ what a bummer qué chasco se va a llevar (él)
what a bunch of nonsense (you're feeding me)! ▪ you're feeding me a bunch of nonsense! ▪ you're feeding me a line! ¡qué chorradas dices!
what a bunch of partiers (your friends are)! ¡vaya ritmo llevan (tus amigos)!
what a character! ¡menudo personaje!
what a cheapskate! ▪ what a tightwad! ¡qué tacaño! ▪ ¡qué agarrado! ▪ ¡qué pesetero!
what a coincidence! ¡qué casualidad!
what a comedown! ¡qué bajón! ▪ ¡qué mal rollo!
what a couple! ▪ what a duo! ▪ what a pair! ▪ what a twosome! ¡vaya dos! ▪ *(more emphatic)* ¡vaya par de dos!
what a crashing bore! ▪ what a dreary character! ▪ that guy is a crashing bore ¡qué coñazo de tío! ▪ ¡vaya coñazo!
what a crock! ▪ that's nonsense! ▪ that's a lie! ¡qué cuento! ▪ ¡qué rollo! ▪ ¡qué trola! ▪ ¡qué mentira!
what a crock of shit! *(off-color)* ▪ that's bullshit! ¡vaya mierda! ▪ ¡esto es una mierda! ▪ *(even stronger)* ¡(esto) es una puta mierda! ▪ ¡es una putísima mierda!
what a day! ¡vaya día! ▪ I'm having quite a day (of it) ¡qué día tengo! ▪ you're having quite a day (of it) ¡qué día tienes!
what a bargain! ¡vaya chollo! ▪ ¡qué chollo! ▪ ¡menudo chollo! ▪ ¡vaya ganga! ▪ ¡menuda ganga!
what a deal! ¡menudo negocio! ▪ ¡menudo trato! ▪ ¡vaya negocio! ▪ ¡vaya trato! ▪ ¡qué negocio! ▪ ¡qué trato!
what a difference between...! ¡lo que va de...! ▪ ¡qué diferencia de...! ➤ What a difference (there is) between those two! ¡Lo que va de uno a otro! ▪ ¡Qué diferencia de uno a otro!
what a disaster! ¡qué desastre!
what a dive! ▪ what a dump! ¡vaya sitio! ▪ ¡qué sitio más cutre! ▪ ¡qué cutre! ▪ ¡qué cutrez!
what a dreary character! ▪ what a crashing bore! ¡qué coñazo de tío!
what a dump! ▪ what a dive! ¡vaya sitio! ▪ ¡qué sitio más cutre! ▪ ¡vaya bodrio!
what a duo! ▪ what a pair! ▪ what a couple! ▪ what a twosome! ¡vaya dos! ▪ *(more emphatic)* ¡vaya par de dos!
what a flop! ▪ what a bomb! ¡vaya fracaso!
what a fright! ▪ that's scary! ¡vaya susto! ▪ ¡qué susto!
what a great atmosphere! ▪ what a perfect atmosphere! ¡qué ambientazo!
what a great place! ¡vaya sitio!
what a guy! ¡qué tío!
what a hot day! ¡qué día de calor! ▪ ¡qué calor hace!
what a letdown! ▪ what a bummer! ¡vaya chasco!
what a lot of nerve! ¡qué confianzas son esas!
what a lousy... ¡qué puñetero...! ▪ *(off-color)* vaya coñazo de...
what a mess! 1. *(clutter)* ¡vaya desbarajuste! ▪ ¡vaya desorden! **2.** *(foul-up)* ¡vaya confusión! ▪ ¡qué confusión! **3.** *(confusing situation)* ¡menudo lío! ▪ ¡qué lío! ▪ ¡vaya lío! ▪ ¡qué embrollo! ➤ What a mess! It's going to take all day to clean this apartment up. ¡Vaya desbarajuste! Vamos a tardar todo el día en limpiar el apartamento. ➤ What a mess! They've changed all the train schedules. ¡Vaya confusión! Han cambiado todos los horarios de los trenes. ➤ What a mess! After the facelifts, they couldn't tell Saddam Hussein from bin Laden. ¡Vaya lío! Después de la cirugía estética, no podían distinguir a Saddam Hussein de bin Laden.
what a mob scene! ¡qué de gente!
what a name! ¡vaya nombre!
what a pain! 1. *(person)* ¡qué pesado! **2.** *(situation)* ¡qué faena! ▪ ¡qué lata!
what a pain in the ass! *(off-color)* ¡vaya coñazo! ▪ *(benign alternative)* ¡vaya incordio!
what a pair! ▪ what a couple! ▪ what a duo! ▪ what a twosome! ¡vaya par! ▪ ¡vaya dos!
what a party animal! ¡qué juerguista! ▪ ¡qué marchoso!
what a piece of work! ¡vaya cosa!
what a pity! ¡qué lástima!
what a predicament! ▪ what a situation! ¡vaya papeleta!
what a racket! 1. what a lot of noise! ¡qué jaleo! **2.** what a scam! ¡qué estafa! ▪ ¡qué timo!
what a rogue! ¡qué pícaro! ▪ ¡menudo canalla! ▪ ¡menudo pájaro está hecho!
what a scare! ¡vaya susto!
what a scorcher! *(hot day)* ¡menudo calor! ▪ ¡menuda calorina!
what a sight! ¡vaya facha! ▪ ¡qué facha! ▪ ¡qué pintas!
what a situation! ▪ what a predicament! ¡vaya papeleta!
what a soap opera! ¡vaya folletín!

what a stench! ▪ it stinks to high heaven! ¡vaya cante! ▪ ¡qué peste!
what a strange bird! ▪ what a weirdo! ¡qué tío más raro!
what a stuffed shirt! ¡qué tío más rancio! ▪ ¡qué tío más estirado!
what a stupid thing to do! ¡qué estupidez! ▪ ¡qué burrada! ▪ *(off-color)* ¡qué gilipollez!
what a tiger (you are)! ▪ you're a tiger! ¡qué animal eres! ▪ ¡eres una bestia! ▪ ¡qué bruto eres!
what a tightwad! ▪ what a cheapskate! ¡qué tacaño!
what a trip! 1. ¡qué viaje! **2.** what a mind-blowing experience! ¡vaya flipe! ▪ ¡vaya alucine! ▪ ¡menudo flipe! **3.** *(referring to drugs)* ¡vaya colocón!
what a turkey! ¡vaya cuervo! ▪ ¡vaya mamón! ▪ ¡vaya cretino! ▪ ¡vaya capullo! ▪ ¡vaya pringao!
what a twosome! ▪ what a pair! ▪ what a duo! ▪ what a couple! vaya dos! ▪ *(more emphatic)* ¡vaya par de dos!
what a waste! ¡qué desperdicio!
what a waste of time! ¡qué pérdida de tiempo! ▪ ¡qué manera de perder el tiempo!
what a way to...! ¡qué forma de...!
what a world (we live in)! ¡en qué mundo vivimos! ▪ ¡qué mundo este! ➤ Look (at) what a world we live in! ¡Hay que ver, en qué mundo vivimos!
what about...? ¿y si...?
what about it? 1. so what? ¿y qué? ▪ ¿y qué tal entonces? ▪ ¿qué tiene? ▪ ¿entonces qué? **2.** what do you think? ¿qué te parece?
what about you? ¿y tú (qué)? ▪ ¿y a ti (qué)? ➤ I went to the bullfight Saturday; what about you? Fui a la corrida de toros el sábado. ¿Y tú (qué)? ➤ I like jazz. What about you? Me gusta jazz. ¿Y a ti (qué)?
what accounts for...? ▪ what explains...? ▪ what causes...? ¿qué causa...? ▪ ¿cuál es la causa de...? ➤ What accounts for the bluish color? ¿Qué causa el color azulón? ▪ ¿Cuál es la causa del color azulón?
what accounts for the fact that...? ▪ why is it that...? ¿a qué se debe que...?
what am I going to do with you? *(feigned desperation)* **1.** no sé qué voy a hacer contigo ▪ ¿qué voy a hacer contigo? **2.** *(royal "we")* no sé qué vamos a hacer contigo ▪ ¿qué vamos a hacer contigo?
what am I supposed to do? ¿qué se supone que deba hacer? ▪ ¿qué se supone que tenga que hacer?
what am *I* supposed to do? ¿qué se supone que deba hacer yo?
what am I to do? ▪ what do I do? ¿qué tengo que hacer?
what an animal! ¡qué pedazo de animal! ▪ ¡qué bestia! ▪ ¡so bestia!
what an early riser you are! ¡qué mañanero eres! ▪ ¡qué madrugador eres!
what an experience! 1. what a trip! ¡qué experiencia! ▪ ¡qué alucinante! **2.** *(teenage slang)* ¡vaya flipe! ▪ ¡qué alucine! ▪ ¡menudo flipe! **3.** what a bummer! ¡qué horror! ▪ ¡qué rollo! ▪ ¡qué fastidio!
what anyone says ▪ what other people say el qué dirán
what appears to be... lo que parece (ser)... ➤ In what appears to be an attempted coup d'état. En lo que parece (ser) un intento de golpe de estado.
what are the prospects? ¿qué posibilidades hay?
what are these things? ¿qué son estas cosas?
what are we supposed to wear to the party? ▪ what's the dress for the party? ¿qué tipo de ropa hay que llevar a la fiesta? ▪ ¿qué tipo de ropa hay que llevar para la fiesta?
what are we waiting for? ¿qué estamos esperando?
what are you afraid of? ¿a qué le temes? ▪ ¿a qué le tienes miedo?
what are you doing *(tú)* ¿qué estás haciendo? ▪ ¿qué haces? ▪ *(usted)* ¿qué hace usted?
what *are* you doing? ▪ what in the world are you doing? ¿qué es lo que haces?
what are *you* doing here?! ¿a qué has venido? ▪ ¡tú por aquí!
what are you driving at? ▪ what are you getting at? ¿dónde quieres ir a parar? ▪ ¿a dónde quieres llegar?
what are you getting at? ▪ what are you driving at? ¿dónde quieres ir a parar? ▪ ¿a dónde quieres llegar?
what are you going to do about it? ¿qué vas a hacer (al respecto)?
what are you good at? ▪ what do you do well? *(a ti)* ¿qué se te da bien? ▪ *(a usted)* ¿qué se le da bien?
what are you laughing at? *(tú)* ¿de qué te ríes? ▪ *(usted)* ¿de qué se ríe (usted)?
what are you majoring in? ▪ what's your major? ¿qué carrera estudias? ▪ ¿qué es lo que estudias? ▪ ¿cuál es tu especialización (académica)?
what are you planning to do? ▪ what do you plan to do? ¿qué piensas hacer?
what are you planning to do about it? ▪ what do you plan to do about it? ¿qué piensas hacer al respecto? ▪ ¿qué piensas hacer sobre ello?
what are you referring to? *(tú)* ¿a qué te refieres? ▪ *(usted)* ¿a qué se refiere (usted)?
what are you smiling about? *(tú)* ¿qué hay de tu sonrisa? ▪ *(usted)* ¿qué hay de su sonrisa?
what are you so angry about? ▪ what are you so mad about? ▪ why are you so angry? ▪ why are you so mad? ▪ *(off-color)* what are you so pissed off about? ▪ *(L. Am.)* ¿por qué estás tan enojado? ▪ *(coll.)* ¿por qué estás tan mosqueado? ▪ *(Sp.)* ¿por qué estás tan enfadado?
what are you so sad about? ▪ why are you so sad? ¿por qué estás tan triste?
what are you so worried about? ▪ why are you so worried? ¿por qué estás tan preocupado? ▪ ¿qué te preocupa tanto? ▪ ¿qué te tiene tan preocupado?
what are you taking? ▪ what classes are you taking? ▪ what subjects are you taking? ¿qué clases tienes? ▪ ¿qué asignaturas tienes? ▪ ¿qué materias tienes? ▪ ¿qué estás cursando?
what are you talking about? 1. ¿de qué estás hablando? ▪ ¿de qué hablas? **2.** *(doubtful, skeptical)* ¿qué dices?
what are you waiting for? ¿qué esperas? ▪ ¿qué estás esperando?
what assurance do you have that...? ¿cómo puedes estar seguro de que...?
what became of...? ¿qué pasó con...? ▪ ¿qué ha sido de...? ▪ ¿qué fue de...?
what better... qué mejor... ➤ What better knot to bind our hearts? ¿Qué mejor manera de enlazar nuestros corazones?
what brings one to do something? ▪ what leads one to do something? ▪ what causes one to do something? ¿qué lleva uno a hacer algo?
what brought it on? ▪ what precipitated it? ¿qué lo ha acarreado? ▪ ¿qué lo ha precipitado? ▪ ¿qué lo ha causado? ▪ ¿qué lo ha provocado?
what burns me up is... lo que me quema es... ▪ lo que me saca de mis casillas es... ▪ lo que me saca de quicio es... ▪ lo que me hace perder los estribos es... ▪ lo que me cabrea es... ▪ *(off-color)* lo que me pone de mala hostia es...
what bus was that (that just left)? ▪ which bus was that (that just left)? ¿qué autobús era ese? ▪ ¿cuál autobús era ese? ▪ ¿qué autobús era el que acaba de pasar?
what business did...? ¿qué interés...? ➤ What business did you have telling her that? ▪ What business was it of yours to tell her that? ¿Qué interés tenías en decirle eso?
what business is it of *yours*? ▪ who asked *you*? ¿a ti qué te importa? ▪ ¿(a ti) quién te ha dado vela en este entierro?
what business was...? ¿qué interés...? ➤ What business was it of yours to tell her that? ¿Qué interés tenías en decirle eso?
what can be done about...? ¿qué se puede hacer con...? ▪ ¿qué podemos hacer con...?
what can be done about it? ▪ what's to be done? ▪ what can we do about it? ▪ what shall we do about it? ¿qué se ha de hacer? ▪ ¿qué se le ha de hacer? ▪ ¿qué se puede hacer al respecto?
what can I do for you? ▪ how can I help you? ¿qué puedo hacer por usted? ▪ ¿qué es lo que se le ofrece? ▪ ¿en qué le puedo servir?
what can you tell me about it? ¿qué me puedes decir sobre ello?

what color...? ¿de qué color...? ➤ What color is it? ¿De qué color es? ➤ What color is this? ¿Qué color es este? ➤ What color would you have painted them? ¿De qué color los habrías pintado? ■ ¿De qué color los hubieras pintado?

what computer to buy *(L. Am.)* qué computadora comprar ■ *(Sp.)* qué ordenador comprar

what could it be? ¿qué será? ■ ¿qué puede ser?

what day is (it) today? ¿a qué día estamos? ■ ¿qué día es hoy?

what days ■ on what days ■ on which days en qué días ➤ I don't know yet (on) what days I have class. ■ I don't know yet (on) which days I have class. Aún no sé en qué días tengo clases. ■ Aún no sé los días en que voy a tener clase.

what did he allow? *(Southern USA, coll.)* ■ what'd he 'low? ■ what did he have to say? ¿qué tenía que decir?

what did he look like? ¿qué aspecto tenía (él)?

what did I tell you? ■ what'd I tell you? ¿qué te dije?

what did she look like? ¿qué aspecto tenía (ella)?

what did you accomplish? 1. what did you get done? ¿qué has conseguido? ■ ¿qué has logrado? 2. what impact did you have? ¿qué resultado obtuviste?

what did you do that for? ¿por qué has hecho eso?

what did you do to your hair? ¿qué te has hecho en el pelo? ■ ¿qué te has hecho al pelo?

what did you do to your knee? ¿qué te has hecho en la rodilla?

what did you expect? 1. *(tú)* ¿qué pretendías? 2. *(usted)* ¿qué (usted) pretendía?

what did you find out? *(tú)* ¿de qué te enteraste? ■ ¿de qué te has enterado? ■ ¿qué averiguaste? ■ ¿qué has averiguado? ■ *(usted)* ¿de qué se enteró (usted)? ■ ¿de qué se ha enterado (usted)? ■ ¿qué averiguó (usted)? ■ ¿qué ha averiguado (usted)?

what did you get on the exam? ¿qué te han puesto en el examen? ■ ¿qué has sacado en el examen? ■ ¿qué nota te ha puesto en el examen? ■ ¿qué nota le ha puesto a tu examen? ■ ¿qué nota has sacado en el examen? ■ ¿qué nota tienes en el examen?

what did you go shopping for? ■ what were you shopping for? ¿qué fuiste a comprar? ■ ¿qué comprabas?

what did you have for breakfast? ¿qué has desayunado?

what did you have for dinner? ¿qué has comido?

what did you have for lunch? ¿qué has almorzado?

what did you have for supper? ¿qué has cenado?

what did you have in mind? *(tú)* ¿qué tenías en mente? ■ ¿qué tenías pensado? ■ *(usted)* ¿qué tenía (usted) en mente? ■ ¿qué tenía (usted) pensado?

what did you put in it? *(recipe)* ¿qué le has puesto? ■ ¿qué le has echado?

what did you say? ■ pardon? ■ I beg your pardon? ■ what? ■ *(coll.)* huh? ¿qué has dicho? ■ ¿cómo? ■ *(Mex.)* ¿mande?

what did you think of...? 1. *(people and things)* ¿qué te ha parecido...? 2. *(especially of people)* ¿qué piensas de...? ➤ What did you think of that jewelry collection? ¿Qué te ha parecido la colección de joyas? ➤ What did you think of the new mayor? ¿Qué piensas del nuevo alcalde?

what difference does it make? ¿qué más da?

what difference does it make to you? ■ what does it matter to you? ¿a ti qué más te da? ■ ¿qué te va en ello?

what difference does that make to you? ■ what does that matter to you? ¿a ti qué más te da? ■ ¿qué te va en eso?

what difference would it make? ¿qué más daría?

what difference would that make? ¿qué más daría eso?

what distinguishes ■ the unique thing about lo que distingue ➤ What distinguishes a pound cake (from other cakes) is its density. ■ The unique thing about a pound cake is its density. Lo que distingue un pound cake es su densidad.

what do I care? ¿y a mí qué más me da? ■ ¿y a mí qué? ■ ¿a mí qué me importa? ■ *(slang)* y a mí, plin

what do I do? ■ what must I do? ¿qué debo hacer?

what do I have to do? ■ what things do I have to do? ■ what things do I need to do? ¿qué tengo que hacer?

what do I have to lose? ■ what have I got to lose? ¿qué puedo perder? ■ ¿qué tengo que perder?

what do I have to show for it? ¿qué (poco) me ha cundido? ■ ¿cómo me ha servido? ➤ I've spent six years at this blasted university, and what do I have to show for it? He gastado seis años en esta puñetera universidad, y ¿qué me ha cundido? ■ He gastado seis años en esta puñetera universidad, y ¿cómo me ha servido?

what do I owe you? ■ how much do I owe you? *(tú)* ¿cuánto te debo? ■ ¿qué te debo? ■ *(usted)* ¿cuánto le debo? ■ ¿qué le debo?

what do we do now? ■ now what do we do? y ahora, ¿qué hacemos?

what do you bet...? ¿qué te apuestas a que...? ■ ¿qué te va a que...?

what do *you* care? *(a ti)* ¿a ti qué (te importa)? ■ ¿qué te importa? ■ *(usted)* ¿a usted qué le importa? ■ ¿qué le importa?

what do you charge for...? ■ how much do you charge for...? ¿cuánto cuesta...? ■ ¿cuánto vale...? ■ ¿cuánto cobras por...?

what do you do for a living? *(tú)* ¿en qué trabajas? ■ ¿cómo te ganas la vida? ■ *(usted)* ¿en qué trabaja (usted)? ■ ¿cómo se gana (usted) la vida? ■ ¿cuál es tu oficio? ■ ¿a qué te dedicas? ■ ¿en qué te ocupas?

what do you do well? ■ what are you good at? *(a ti)* ¿qué se te da bien? ■ *(a usted)* ¿qué se le da bien?

what do you expect? ¿qué pretendes? ■ ¿qué esperas?

what do you expect *me* to do? *(tú)* ¿qué pretendes que haga (yo)? ■ *(usted)* ¿qué pretende (usted) que haga (yo)?

what do you have in mind? *(tú)* ¿qué tienes en mente? ■ ¿qué tienes pensado? ■ *(usted)* ¿qué tiene (usted) en mente? ■ ¿qué tiene (usted) pensado? ■ *(law, literary)* ¿qué tiene en mientes?

what do you have in your hand? ¿qué es lo que tienes en la mano?

what do you have (to choose from)? *(to a waiter)* ■ what are the choices? ¿qué hay? ■ ¿qué tenéis? ■ *(especially a flavor of a drink, ice cream, etc.)* ¿de qué puede ser? ➤ What do you have to drink? *(L. Am.)* ¿Qué tienes para tomar? ■ ¿Qué hay para tomar? ■ *(Sp.)* ¿Qué tienes para beber? ■ ¿Qué hay para beber?

what do you have to lose? ■ what have you got to lose? ¿qué puedes perder? ■ ¿qué tienes que perder?

what do you have to say about that? ¿qué tienes que decir sobre eso? ■ ¿cómo me vas a explicar eso? ■ ¿cómo me puedes explicar eso?

what do you have to show for it? ¿qué tienes para demostrarlo?

what do you hear from Ed? *(Mex.)* ¿qué noticias tienes de Lalo? ■ ¿qué sabes de Lalo? ■ *(Sp.)* ¿qué noticias tienes de Edu? ■ ¿qué sabes de Edu?

what do you hope to get out of it? ¿qué esperas sacar (de esto)? ■ ¿qué esperas obtener (de esto)?

what do you know about it? ¿qué sabes tú de eso? ■ ¿qué sabe usted de eso?

what do you like about it? ¿en qué te ha gustado? ■ ¿qué es lo que te ha gustado de...?

what do you make of it? ¿cómo te explicas esto? ■ ¿cómo te lo explicas? ■ ¿qué te parece esto? ■ *(coll.)* ¿y eso cómo se come? ➤ *(Lindbergh)* The engine's thirty revolutions low. What do you make of it? Damp air? El motor está a treinta revoluciones por debajo. ¿Cómo te lo explicas? ¿Aire húmedo? ■ El motor está a treinta revoluciones por debajo. ¿Cómo te explicas esto? ¿Aire húmedo?

what do you mean? 1. what are you saying? ¿qué quieres decir? ■ ¿qué pretendes decir? 2. what are you referring to? ¿a qué te refieres? ➤ What do you mean by "otro día"? ¿Qué quieres decir con "otro día"?

what do you mean by that? *(tú)* ¿qué quieres decir con eso? ■ *(usted)* ¿qué quiere (usted) decir con eso?

what do you mean, interesting? ¡qué interesante ni qué interesante si...? ➤ What do mean, interesting? I almost fell asleep. ¡Qué interesante ni qué interesante si me duermo!

what do you mean, no? ¿cómo que no?

what do you mean, what for? ¿cómo que para qué?

what do you mean, why? ¿cómo que por qué?

what do you mean, yes? ¿cómo que sí?

what do you mean, you can't? ¿cómo que no puedes?

what do you not like about it? ▪ what about it do you not like? ▪ why don't you like it? ¿en qué no te ha gustado? ▪ ¿qué es lo que no te ha gustado de...? ▪ ¿por qué no te ha gustado?

what do you plan to do? ¿qué piensas hacer? ▪ ¿qué tienes intención de hacer (con...)?

what do you plan to do about it? ¿qué piensas hacer sobre eso? ▪ ¿qué piensas hacer al respecto?

what do you say? *(prompting a child to say, "thank you")* ¿qué se dice? ▪ la palabrita mágica

what do you say we...? ¿qué tal si...? ▪ ¿y si...? ➤ What do you say we go shoot some pool? ¿Qué tal si vamos a jugar al billar? ▪ ¿Y si vamos a jugar al billar?

what do you teach? *(tú)* ¿de qué das clases? ▪ *(usted)* ¿de qué da (usted) clases? ▪ *(less common)* ¿qué enseñas?

what do you think? **1.** what's your opinion? *(tú)* ¿qué opinas? ▪ *(usted)* ¿qué opina (usted)? **2.** how about it, yes or no? *(tú)* ¿qué te parece? ▪ *(usted)* ¿qué le parece?

what do *you* think? *(tú)* ¿y qué opinas? ▪ *(usted)* ¿y qué opina?

what *do you* think? ¿y tú de verdad qué piensas? ▪ ¿y tú de verdad qué opinas?

what do you think about it? ¿qué piensas al respecto? ▪ ¿qué piensas sobre eso?

what do you think of...? ▪ how about...? *(tú)* ¿qué te parece...? ▪ *(usted)* ¿qué le parece...? ➤ What do you think of this suit? ¿Qué te parece este traje?

what do you think of it? ¿qué te parece?

what do you think of *that*? *(tú)* ¿qué te parece? ▪ ¿qué me dices? ▪ *(usted)* ¿qué le parece? ▪ ¿qué me dice?

what do you think you're doing!? ¡¿qué crees que estás haciendo?!

what do you want for...? ▪ how much do you want for? ▪ what are you asking for...? ¿qué pides por...? ▪ ¿cuánto pides por...?

what do you want for it? ▪ how much do you want for it? ▪ what are you asking for it? ¿qué pides? ▪ ¿cuánto pides?

what do you want to be when you grow up? ¿qué quieres ser de mayor?

what do you want to get out of it? ¿qué se quiere obtener?

what does he have to show for it? ¿en qué le ha cundido?

what does he look like? ¿qué aspecto tiene él?

what does he see in her? ¿qué ve en ella? ▪ ¿qué es lo que ve en ella?

what does it accomplish? ▪ what good does it do? ¿y de qué sirve?

what does it come to? ▪ how much does it come out to? ¿a qué asciende? ▪ *(Sp., coll.)* ¿a cómo está?

what does it do? ▪ what's it do? ▪ what is its function? ▪ what's its function? ¿para qué sirve? ▪ ¿qué hace? ▪ ¿qué función tiene?

what does it look like? ¿qué aspecto tiene? ▪ ¿cómo es?

what does it matter? ▪ what difference does it make? ¿qué importancia tiene?

what does it matter to you? ▪ what difference does it make to you? ¿qué te va en ello?

what does it say? ¿qué dice? ▪ ¿qué parte ha dado?

what does it take to...? ¿qué se necesita para...?

what does she look like? ¿qué aspecto tiene ella?

what does she see in him? ¿qué ve en él? ▪ ¿qué es lo que ve en él?

what does that matter to you? ▪ what difference does that make to you? ¿qué te va en eso?

what does the course consist of? ¿en qué consiste el curso?

what does the police report say? ¿qué parte han dado los guardias?

what else? ¿qué otra cosa?

what else can I do? ¿qué otra cosa puedo hacer? ▪ ¿qué remedio me queda?

what else is new? ¿qué más hay de nuevo?

what flavors do you have? ¿qué sabores hay? ▪ ¿qué sabores tienen? ▪ *(vosotros)* ¿qué sabores tenéis?

what for? ¿para qué? ▪ ¿a qué?

what gets me is 1. what bothers me is lo que me molesta es ▪ lo que me fastidia es ▪ me repatea que... **2.** what impresses me is lo que me impresiona es ▪ lo que me llama la atención es

what goes around comes around ▪ you reap what you sow *(both positive and negative)* lo que haces a ti te pasará ▪ lo que haces se te revierte ▪ *(positive)* favor con favor se paga ▪ *(negative)* quien hace mal espere otro tal

what good does it do? ▪ what's the use? ¿de qué sirve?

what good is it? ¿de qué sirve? ▪ ¿qué más da?

what good is that? ¿y eso de qué sirve?

what good will that do? ¿y eso de qué va a servir? ▪ ¿qué va a conseguir con eso?

what good will that do me? ▪ where will that get me? ¿de qué me sirve eso?

what good would that do? ¿de qué serviría? ▪ ¿qué conseguirías con eso?

what got me was... 1. *(positive)* lo que me impresionó fue... **2.** *(negative)* lo que a mí me molestó fue... ▪ lo que a mí me dio rabia fue... ▪ lo que a mí me cabreó fue... ▪ lo que a mí me indignó fue...

what great news! ¡qué notición! ▪ ¡qué grandes noticias!

what had become of... lo que le pasó a... ▪ lo que había sido de...

what has become of...? ▪ whatever became of...? ▪ whatever happened to...? ¿qué ha sido de...? ▪ ¿qué fue de...?

what have I got to lose? ¿qué puedo perder? ▪ ¿qué tengo que perder?

what have I got to show for it? ¿en qué me ha cundido?

what have I gotten myself into? ¿en qué me habré metido?

what have we here? ¿qué tenemos aquí?

what have you been doing? ¿qué habéis hecho? ▪ ¿qué has estado haciendo?

what have you been up to? ¿qué has estado haciendo?

what have you got to lose? ¿qué puedes perder?

what he says, goes lo que dice va a misa

what I get: that's ~ me está bien empleado ▪ es lo que me merezco ➤ That's what I get for not doing my homework. Me está bien empleado por no hacer los deberes. ▪ Es lo que me merezco por no hacer la tarea.

what I like about it is... ▪ the thing I like about it is... lo que me gusta de esto es...

what I like best of all is that... lo que más me gusta de todo es que...

what I liked about it ▪ the thing I liked about it **1.** *(recent)* lo que me ha gustado **2.** *(less recent)* lo que me gustó ➤ What I liked about it was the ending. ▪ The thing I liked about it was the ending. Lo que me ha gustado fue el final. ▪ Lo que me gustó fue el final.

what I mean is (that)... ▪ what I'm trying to say is (that)... ▪ I mean (that)... quiero decir que...

what I realize is that... de lo que me doy cuenta es que...

what I realized was that... de lo que me he dado cuenta es que... ▪ de lo que me di cuenta es que...

what I said was... lo que dije fue...

what I said was that... lo que dije fue que...

what I said was this... lo que dije fue lo siguiente...

what I suggest is that... lo que sugiero es que...

what I was going to say... ▪ what I was going to tell you... a lo que te iba...

what I was going to tell you... ▪ what I was going to say... a lo que te iba...

what I would like to do is this... lo que me gustaría hacer es lo siguiente...

what if...? ¿qué tal si...? ▪ ¿y si...?

what if he didn't do it? ▪ what if he wasn't the one who did it? ¿y si él no lo hizo? ▪ ¿y si él no fue quien lo hizo?

what if he hadn't done it? ¿y si no llega a hacerlo? ➤ What if Polk hadn't prepared the presidency for Lincoln? ¿Y si Polk no le hubiera preparado la presidencia a Lincoln?

what if I call you about nine o'clock your time? ¿y si te llamo sobre las nueve de allí?

what if I called you about nine o'clock your time? ¿y si te llamase sobre las nueve de allí? ■ ¿y si te llamara sobre las nueve de allí? ■ ¿Y si te llamo sobre las nueve de allí?
what if I were to? ¿y si yo fuera a...?
what if it isn't? ¿y si no lo es?
what if it's true? ¿y si es verdad?
what I'm getting at is... a lo que voy es...
what I'm getting to is... a donde voy es...
what I'm not sure about is whether... de lo que no estoy seguro(-a) es de si
what I'm not sure of is that... de lo que no estoy seguro es de que...
what I'm sure about is that... ■ what I'm sure of is that... de lo que estoy seguro es que...
what I'm sure of is that... de lo que estoy seguro es que...
what I'm trying to say is (that)... ■ what I mean is (that)... ■ I mean (that)... lo que quiero decir es que... ■ a lo que me refiero es que...
what (in) the hell is that? ¿qué diablos es eso?
what in the world are you doing? ■ what *are* you doing? ¿qué es lo que haces?
what in the world is that? ¿qué porras es eso? ■ ¿qué narices es eso?
what is being called en lo que se ha dado en llamar
what is good lo bueno
what is his profit? ¿cuál es su beneficio?
what is it? 1. what are you holding back? ¿qué cosa es? 2. what's going on? ¿qué pasa?
what is needed is... lo que hace falta es... ➤ Capitalism creates wealth, socialism distributes it, and what is needed is a balance between them. El capitalismo genera riqueza, el socialismo la distribuye, y lo que hace falta es un equilibrio entre ambos.
what is the date today? ■ what's today's date? ■ what's the date today? ■ what is today's date? ■ what day is today? ¿cuál es la fecha de hoy? ■ ¿qué fecha es hoy? ■ ¿a cuántos estamos hoy?
what is the meaning of... ¿cuál es el significado de...?
what is the score? ■ what's the score? ¿cómo va el marcador? ■ ¿cómo van? ■ ¿cuál es la puntuación?
what is the weather forecast? ¿cuál es el pronóstico del tiempo? ➤ What's the weather forecast for tomorrow? ¿Cuál es el pronóstico del tiempo para mañana?
what is the world coming to? ■ what's the world coming to? ¿hacia dónde va este mundo?
what is there to do? ■ what's there to do? ¿qué tiene de interés? ■ ¿qué se puede hacer? ➤ What is there to do in Monaco? ¿Qué tiene Monaco de interés? ■ ¿Qué se puede hacer en Monaco?
what is this? ■ what's this? ¿qué es esto?
what is today's date? ■ what's today's date? ■ what day is it today? ■ what's the date today? ¿qué fecha es hoy? ■ ¿a cuántos estamos? ■ ¿cuál es la fecha de hoy?
what is your attitude toward...? ¿qué te parece...?
what it boils down to is that... ■ it boils down to this... ■ it boils down to the fact that... se reduce al hecho de que...
what it involves lo que conlleva ■ el trabajo que se supone
what it was like ■ how it was ■ what it was lo que era ➤ He remembered what it was like to be penniless. ■ He remembered how it was to be penniless. ■ He remembered what it was to be penniless. Recordaba lo que era estar sin un céntimo.
what it was like when... cómo eran las cosas cuando...
what it would be like a qué sentiría
what it's about lo que se hace
what it's all about: not to know ~ 1. not to be informed about it no saber de lo que se trata 2. to be out of it ■ to be clueless no tener ni idea ➤ He doesn't know what it's all about. No sabe de lo que se trata. ■ Él no tiene ni idea.
what it's like a qué siente ■ como es
what I've found is that... ■ my experience has been that... en mi experiencia
what I've said all along ■ what I've said from the beginning lo que he dicho siempre ■ lo que he dicho desde el principio ➤ This just confirms what I've said all along. ■ This just confirms what I've said since the beginning. Esto sólo confirma lo que he dicho siempre. ■ Esto no hace más que confirmar lo que he dicho desde el principio.
what kind of...? 1. what type of...? ¿qué clase de...? ■ ¿qué tipo de...? 2. what brand of...? ■ what make of...? ¿qué marca de...? ➤ What kind of jets were those (that) we saw at the air show? ¿Qué clase de reactores fueron los que vimos en la exhibición aérea? ➤ What kind of wine do you want, red or rosé? ¿Qué tipo de vino quieres, tinto o rosado? ➤ What kind of car do you have? ¿Qué marca de coche tienes?
what kind of an answer is *that*? ¿qué clase de respuesta es esa?
what kind of car is it? ■ what make of car is it? *(L. Am.)* ¿qué marca de carro es? ■ *(Sp.)* ¿qué marca de coche es?
what kind of clothes do you like to wear? ¿qué estilo de ropa te gusta (llevar)?
what kind of money are we talking about (here)? ¿de cuánto dinero estamos hablando?
what kinds of dressing do you have? ¿qué tipos de aliño (para ensaladas) tiene usted?
what kinds of things...? ¿qué tipo de cosas...? ➤ What kinds of things were they saying to you? ¿Qué tipo de cosas te decían? ➤ What kinds of things were they selling at the flea market? ¿Qué tipo de cosas vendían en el rastro?
what leads someone to do something? ■ what causes someone to do something? ■ what makes someone do something? ¿qué lleva alguien a hacer algo?
what little... lo poco que...
what little French I know lo poco francés que sé
what little is left of ■ what little remains of ■ the little that's left of lo poco que queda de
what little news I have las pocas noticias que tengo ➤ What little news I have is confined to three things. Las pocas noticias que tengo se limitan a tres cosas.
what little remains of ■ what little is left of ■ the little that's left of lo poco que queda de
what looks like lo que parece ser
what luck! ¡qué suerte! ■ *(slang)* ¡qué chorra! ■ ¡qué coña!
what made you think of that? *(tú)* ¿qué te hizo pensar en eso? ■ *(usted)* ¿qué le hizo (a usted) pensar en eso?
what makes it do that? ¿qué lo hace hacer eso?
what makes it so funny is... ■ what makes it so comical is... ■ the comical thing about it is... lo gracioso es que...
what memories! ¡qué recuerdos!
what metro stop is it? ¿qué parada de metro es?
what more could you ask? *(tú)* ¿qué más podrías pedir? ■ *(usted)* ¿qué más podría (usted) pedir? ■ *(uno)* ¿qué más se podría pedir?
what must I do? ■ what do I do? ¿qué debo hacer?
what occurred to me is that lo que se me ha ocurrido es que
what one gets for lo que le pasa a uno por ➤ That's what you get for being late. Eso es lo que te pasa por llegar tarde.
what one is going through lo que uno está pasando ➤ People have no idea what we're going through. Nadie se imagina lo que estamos pasando.
what one may or may not have done lo que uno haya o no hecho
what one thinks of 1. *(impression)* lo que a uno le parece 2. *(opinion)* lo que uno piensa de ➤ You'll have to tell us what you thought of your trip to Scandinavia. Tendrás que contarnos qué te pareció tu viaje a Escandinavia. ➤ Tell us what you thought of the president's speech. Dinos lo que pensaste del discurso del presidente.
what other people say ■ what anyone says el qué dirán ■ lo que dice la gente
what prompted me to call you was that... *(tú)* lo que me ha llevado a llamarte es que... ■ *(usted, to a man)* lo que me ha llevado a llamarlo (a usted) es que... ■ *(usted, to a woman)* lo que me ha llevado a llamarla (a usted) es que... *(usted, leísmo, to man or woman)* lo que me ha llevado a llamarle es que...
what prompted you to...? *(tú)* ¿qué te impulsó a...? ■ ¿qué te llevó a...? *(usted)* ¿qué le impulsó a...? ■ ¿qué le llevó a...?

what prompts me to call you is that... *(a ti)* lo que me impulsa a llamarte es que... ■ lo que me lleva a llamarte es que... *(a usted, man or woman)* lo que me impulsa a llamarle es que... ■ lo que me lleva a llamarle es que...

what really... lo que en realidad...

what reminded me of it lo que me hizo recordarlo ■ lo que me lo recordó ■ lo que me hizo pensar en ello ➤ What reminded me of it was your saying you always pay people back. Lo que me hizo recordarlo fue lo que decías de que siempre devuelves el dinero (prestado).

what rotten...! ¡vaya coñazo de...!

what rotten luck! ¡vaya una sombra negra! ■ ¡vaya coñazo de...!

what seems to be lo que parece ser

what shall I do? ¿qué hago?

what shall I do with that? qué hago con eso?

what shall I wear? ¿qué me pongo?

what shall we do? ¿qué hacemos?

what she says goes lo que dice va a misa

what should I wear? ¿qué debo ponerme? ■ ¿cómo debo ir vestido?

what size do you wear? **1.** *(clothes, tú)* ¿cuál es tu talla? ■ ¿qué talla llevas? ■ ¿qué talla usas? ■ *(usted)* ¿cuál es su talla? ■ ¿qué talla lleva (usted)? ■ ¿qué talla usa (usted)? **2.** *(shoes, tú)* ¿qué número de zapato calzas? ■ *(usted)* ¿qué número de zapato calza (usted)?

what smells so good? ¿qué es lo que huele tan bien? ■ ¿qué es ese olor tan bueno?

what some people will do to get attention! ■ what some people won't do to get attention! ¡lo que hacen algunos para llamar la atención!

what some people won't do to get attention! ■ what some people will do to get attention! ¡lo que hacen algunos para llamar la atención!

what someone is like cómo es alguien ➤ Tell me what she's like. Dime cómo es (ella).

what sorts of...? ¿qué tipo de...? ➤ What sorts of activities are planned for the conference? ¿Qué tipo de actividades están programadas para la reunión?

what (subjects) are you taking? ¿qué asignaturas tomas? ■ ¿qué materias tienes? ■ ¿qué estás cursando? ■ ¿qué clases das?

what the fuck! *(off-color)* ¡qué carajo! ■ ¡qué coño!

what the fuck is that? *(off-color)* ¿qué coño es eso? ■ ¿qué cojones es eso? ■ *(benign alternative)* ¿qué cuerno es eso?

what the future holds ■ what the future has in store lo que depara el futuro ■ lo que depare el futuro ■ qué depara el futuro ■ qué depare el futuro

what the heck! ■ oh, well! ■ I might as well! ¡(es) una raya más para el tigre! ■ *(Sp.)* ¡de perdidos al río!

what the hell! *(off-color)* ¡qué diablos! ■ ¡qué demonios! ■ ¡qué carajo! ■ ¡qué cojones! ■ *(benign alternative)* ¡pero qué...!

what the hell is that? ■ what in the hell is that? ¿qué demonios es eso? ■ ¿qué diablos es eso?

what the market will bear lo que aguanta el mercado

what the weather will be like cómo será el tiempo

what then? ■ what happened next? ¿y luego? ■ ¿y qué pasó?

what, then? ■ what's the alternative? ¿pues qué (entonces)?

what time? ■ at what time? ¿a qué hora?

what time do you expect her? ¿a qué hora la esperas?

what time do you expect him? *(L. Am.)* ¿a qué hora lo esperas? ■ *(Sp., leísmo)* ¿a qué hora le esperas?

what time do you get off? ¿a qué hora terminas (de trabajar)? ■ ¿a qué hora sales (del trabajo)?

what time does the news come on? ¿a qué hora ponen las noticias?

what time is it? ¿qué hora es?

what time shall we meet? ¿a qué hora quedamos? ■ ¿a qué hora nos encontramos?

what timing! ¡vaya cálculo! ■ *(humorous)* ¡vaya cálculo en el riñón!

what to do about it: to know ~ saber qué hacer al respecto ➤ I don't know what to do about it. No sé qué hacer al respecto.

what to do next qué hacer ahora ■ qué hacer próximamente ➤ I don't know what to do next. No sé qué hacer ahora. ■ No sé qué hacer próximamente. ➤ What are we going to do next? ¿Qué vamos a hacer ahora? ■ ¿Qué vamos a hacer próximamente?

what to my wondering eyes should appear... *(C.C. Moore)* qué ante mis ojos asombrados aparecieron...

what train just left? ■ what train was that? ■ which train was that? ■ where was that train headed? ¿a dónde iba ese tren? ■ ¿qué tren acaba de salir?

what troubles me about this is... lo que me preocupa de esto es...

what was I supposed to do? ¿qué se suponía que hiciera? ■ ¿qué se suponía que hiciese? ■ ¿qué se suponía que debía hacer?

what was I talking about? ■ what was I saying? ¿de qué estaba hablando? ■ ¿qué estaba diciendo?

what was it like to...? *(tú)* ¿cómo te sentiste al...? ■ *(usted)* ¿cómo se sintió al...?

what was it like when...? ¿cómo eran las cosas cuando...?

what was said lo dicho

what was that? **1.** ¿qué ha sido eso? **2.** would you repeat that? ¿cómo?

what was *that*? ¿qúe ha sido eso?

what was *that* about? ¿a qué ha venido eso? ■ ¿a qué se debe eso?

what was that (noise)? ¿qué ha sido eso? ■ ¿qué ha sido ese ruido? ■ ¿qué ruido ha sido ese?

what was the (final) score? ¿cuál fue la puntuación final? ■ ¿cómo terminó el marcador?

what was the score at halftime? ¿cómo andaba el marcador en el descanso?

what went wrong? ¿qué salió mal? ■ ¿qué ha ido mal?

what were we supposed to do today? **1.** what was it we had to do today? ¿qué se suponía que teníamos que hacer hoy? **2.** what were we going to do today? ¿qué se suponía que íbamos a hacer hoy? ■ ¿qué es lo que teníamos que hacer hoy?

what were you expecting? ¿qué pretendías? ■ ¿qué esperabas?

what were you saying? *(tú)* ¿qué estabas diciendo? ■ ¿qué decías? ■ *(usted)* ¿qué estaba (usted) diciendo? ■ ¿qué decía (usted)?

what were you thinking that I should do? ¿qué suponías que debiera de haber hecho? ■ ¿qué suponías que debiese de haber hecho?

what will you be doing...? ■ what are you going to do...? ¿qué estarás haciendo...? ➤ What will you be doing in Guadalajara? ¿Qué estarás haciendo en Guadalajara?

what with one thing and another entre pitos y flautas

what would become of...? ¿qué sería de...?

what would have become of...? ¿qué habría sido de...? ■ ¿qué hubiera sido de...?

what would it be like...? ¿cómo sería ser...? ■ ¿qué se sentirá...? ➤ What would it be like to be a dog or a cat? ¿Qué se sentirá ser un perro o un gato?

what would that be? ¿qué será eso? ■ ¿el qué?

what would you have wanted to happen? *(tú)* ¿qué habrías querido que pasara? ■ ¿qué habrías querido que sucediera? ■ ¿qué habrías querido que ocurriera? ■ ¿qué habrías querido que pasase? ■ ¿qué habrías querido que sucediese? ■ ¿qué habrías querido que ocurriese? ■ *(usted)* ¿qué habría querido que pasara? ■ ¿qué habría querido que sucediera? ■ ¿qué habría querido que ocurriera? ■ ¿qué habría querido que pasase? ■ ¿qué habría querido que sucediese? ■ ¿qué habría querido que ocurriese?

what would you like? ¿qué se le ofrece? ■ ¿qué manda usted?

what would you want for it? ■ how much would you sell it for? ■ what would you sell it for? ¿cuánto querrías por ello? ■ ¿por cuánto lo venderías?

what year is the car? ■ how old is the car? ¿de qué año es el coche?

what year was the wine bottled? ¿de qué reserva es el vino? ▪ ¿de qué añada es el vino?
what you don't know won't hurt you nada pierde con ignorar
what you have to do is... lo que hay que hacer es...
what you see is what you get ▪ wysiwyg lo que se ve es lo que hay ▪ esto es lo que hay ▪ no hay más cera que la que arde ▪ (y) no hay más cáscaras
whatever! ¡lo que toque! ▪ ¡da igual! ▪ ¡lo que sea!
whatever became of...? ▪ whatever happened to...? ¿qué habrá pasado con...? ▪ ¿qué habrá sido de...? ▪ ¿qué fue de...?
whatever does something ▪ anything that does something todo lo que haga algo ▪ cualquier cosa que haga algo
whatever happened to? ▪ whatever became of? ¿qué habrá pasado con...? ▪ ¿qué habrá sido de...? ▪ ¿qué fue de...? ➤ *(Bette Davis film) Whatever Happened to Baby Jane? ¿Qué fue de Baby Jane?*
whatever it is lo que sea ➤ Whatever it is, tell me quick. Lo que sea, dímelo pronto.
whatever it may be ▪ whatever it might be ▪ whatever it is sea cual sea ▪ lo que fuere
whatever it might be ▪ whatever it may be ▪ whatever it is sea cual sea ▪ lo que fuere
whatever (it was) ▪ no matter what ▪ regardless of what fuera lo que fuera ▪ fuese lo que fuese ➤ Whatever it was, it worked. ▪ Whatever (it was) they would discuss, they always got very heated. Fuera lo que fuera lo que discutían aquellos dos, se veían muy acalorados.
whatever may be lo que fuere
whatever one did hiciera lo que hiciera
whatever one says, goes lo que diga uno, vale ➤ Whatever you say, goes. Lo que digas, vale.
whatever one wants to lo que a uno le dé la gana ➤ Tell them to take it away and do whatever they want to with it. Les dices que se lo lleven y hagan con él lo que les dé la gana.
whatever possessed you to...? ¿qué te ha dado por...? ▪ ¿qué te ha dado con...? ▪ ¿qué locura es esa de...? ▪ ¿qué ventolera te ha entrado de...? ➤ Whatever possessed you to take a balloon trip to northern Alberta? ¿Qué locura es esa de irte en globo al norte de Alberta? ▪ ¿Qué te ha dado por irte en globo al norte de Alberta? ➤ *(Valle-Inclán)* Whatever possessed you to become an organ-grinder? ¿Qué ventolera te ha entrado de ponerte a organillero?
whatever the cost **1.** no matter how much it costs cueste lo que cueste ▪ sin reparar en gastos **2.** regardless of the difficulty ▪ no matter how difficult it is cueste lo que cueste ▪ por difícil que sea ▪ no importa qué tan difícil sea
whatever (the) direction you decide to take in life ▪ whatever path you choose in life sea cual sea el rumbo que decidas tomar en la vida
whatever the outcome ▪ whatever the result sea cual sea el resultado
whatever the result ▪ whatever the outcome sea cual sea el resultado
whatever works best for you *(tú)* lo que a ti te vaya mejor ▪ *(usted)* lo que a usted le vaya mejor
whatever you do, don't... hagas lo que hagas, no...
whatever you say **1.** anything you say lo que tú digas ▪ lo que usted diga **2.** say what you will *(tú)* digas lo que digas ▪ *(usted)* diga (usted) lo que diga ➤ Yes, Mom, whatever you say. ▪ Yes, Mom, anything you say. Sí, mamá, lo que tú digas. ➤ She contradicts whatever you say. ▪ She contradicts you no matter what you say. ▪ Say what you will, she contradicts you. Te contradice digas lo que digas ➤ Whatever you say, don't give away the surprise party. Digas lo que digas, que no se te escape lo de la fiesta sorpresa.
what'll they think of next?! ¿qué se les ocurrirá después? ▪ ¿qué vendrá después? ▪ ¿qué será lo siguiente? ➤ Metrosexuals and technosexuals? Egad! What'll they think of next?! ¿Metrosexuales y tecnosexuales? ¡Dios mío! ¿Qué se les ocurrirá después?
what'll you have? *(tú)* ¿qué te pongo? ▪ ¿qué se te ofrece? ▪ *(usted)* ¿qué le pongo? ▪ ¿qué se le ofrece?
what's all the racket? ¿qué escándalo es ese?
what's all this about walking? ¡qué andar ni qué andar! ➤ What's all this (talk) about walking? I have a car. ¡Qué andar ni qué andar si tengo coche!
what's behind...? ¿qué hay detrás de...?
what's below the belt ▪ the genitals lo de abajo
what's bugging him?: (I wonder) ~ ¿qué mosca le habrá picado?
what's bugging *you*? ¿qué mosca te ha picado? ▪ ¿qué mosca te habrá picado?
what's come over you? ▪ what has come over you? ¿qué te habrá pasado?
what's done is done lo hecho, hecho está
what's expected of you *(tú)* lo que se espera de ti ▪ *(usted)* lo que se espera de usted
what's for dessert? ¿qué hay de postre?
what's for dinner? ¿qué hay de comer? ▪ ¿qué hay de comida?
what's for supper? ¿qué hay de cenar? ▪ ¿qué hay de cena?
what's funny about that? ▪ what's so funny about that? no le veo la gracia
what's going on lo que pasa
what's going on? ¿qué pasa? What's going on?-Not much. ¿Qué pasa?-Poca cosa.
what's happened to you? ¿qué te pasa?
what's happening is that... ▪ what it is, is that... ▪ the thing of it is, (is) that... lo que pasa es que...
what's hard about it? ▪ what's difficult about it? ¿qué tiene de duro? ▪ ¿qué tiene de chungo?
what's he doing up there? ¿por qué está allí?
what's-her-name esa cómo se llame ▪ no sé cuantos ▪ fulana ▪ no sé qué ➤ Did you see what's-her-name at the party? ¿Viste a esa cómo se llame en la fiesta? ➤ Marta what's-her-name Marta no sé qué ▪ Marta no sé cuantos
what's-his-name ese cómo se llame ▪ no sé cuántos ▪ fulano ▪ no sé qué ➤ Did you see what's-his-name at the party? ¿Viste a ese cómo se llame en la fiesta? ➤ Javier what's-his-name Javier no sé qué ▪ Javier no sé cuántos
what's it about? ▪ what is it about? ¿de qué va? ▪ ¿de qué se trata? ➤ What's the movie about? ¿De qué va la película? ▪ ¿De qué se trata la película?
what's it for? ¿para qué sirve? ▪ ¿para qué vale?
what's it like? ¿qué tal es? ▪ ¿cómo es?
what's left of lo que queda de ▪ lo que ha quedado de ➤ Look what's left of... Mira lo que queda de...
what's left of it lo que queda de ello(-a) ➤ *(news item)* The space probe "Contour," or what's left of it, is in its planned orbit around the sun, but broken into at least three pieces. La sonda espacial "Contour," o lo que queda de ella, se encuentra en su órbita prevista alrededor del sol, pero partido en al menos tres trozos.
what's more lo que es más ▪ más todavía ▪ además
what's new? ¿qué hay de nuevo? ▪ ¿qué novedades me traes?
what's new is that... la novedad es que...
what's new with you? ¿qué pasa de nuevo contigo? ▪ ¿qué es de tu vida?
what's on at the movies? ▪ what's playing at the movies? ¿qué películas están dando? ▪ ¿qué hay en la cartelera?
what's on TV lo que están pasando en la tele ▪ lo que están dando en la tele ➤ I knew what time it was by what was on TV. Sabía la hora por lo que estaban pasando en la tele.
what's on TV? ¿qué dan en la tele? ▪ ¿qué están dando en la tele? ▪ ¿qué ponen en la tele? ▪ ¿qué están pasando en la tele? ▪ ¿qué echan (en la tele)? ▪ ¿qué echan?
what's on your mind? *(tú)* ¿qué es lo que te preocupa? ▪ *(usted)* ¿qué es lo que le preocupa?
what's playing at the movies? ▪ what's on at the movies? ¿qué está en la cartelera? ▪ ¿qué echan?
what's really going on lo que está ocurriendo realmente
what's so funny? ¿de qué te ríes? ▪ ¿qué te ha hecho (tanta) gracia?
what's (so) funny about that? ¿qué es tan gracioso de eso? ▪ no le veo la gracia
what's the address? ¿cuál es la dirección?

what's the best way to...? ¿cuál es la mejor forma de...? ➤ What's the best way to send this package to the United Kingdom? ¿Cuál es la mejor forma de mandar este paquete al Reino Unido?

what's the big deal? ▪ why are you making such a fuss? ¿por qué te pones así?

what's the big idea (of...)? ¿qué es esto de...? ▪ ¿qué es eso de...? ➤ What's the big idea of bursting in here without knocking? ¿Qué es esto de irrumpir aquí sin tocar la puerta?

what's the date today? ▪ what's today's date? ▪ what is the date today? ¿cuál es la fecha de hoy? ▪ ¿a cuántos estamos? ▪ ¿qué fecha es hoy?

what's the difference? ¿cuál es la diferencia?

what's the difference between...? ¿qué diferencia hay entre...? ▪ ¿cuál es la diferencia entre...? ▪ ¿en qué se diferencia(n)...? ▪ ¿cómo se diferencian...? ➤ What's the difference between "cara" and "rostro"? ¿Qué diferencia hay entre "cara" y "rostro"? ▪ ¿Cuál es la diferencia entre "cara" y "rostro"? ▪ ¿En qué se diferencian "cara y rostro"? ▪ ¿En qué se diferencia "cara" de "rostro"? ▪ ¿Cómo se diferencian "cara" y "rostro"? ▪ ¿Cómo se diferencia "cara" de "rostro"? *("Rostro" is a poetic and literary equivalent of "cara.")*

what's the dress for the party? ▪ what are we supposed to wear to the party? ¿qué tipo de ropa hay que llevar a la fiesta? ▪ ¿qué tipo de ropa hay que llevar para la fiesta?

what's the earliest I can call you? *(a ti)* ¿cuál es la hora más temprana en que puedo llamarte? ▪ *(a usted)* ¿cuál es la hora más temprana que puedo llamarlo a usted? ▪ ¿cuál es la hora más temprana que puedo llamarla a usted? ▪ *(Sp., Mex., leísmo)* ¿cuál es la hora más temprana que puedo llamarle?

what's the explanation? ¿cuál es la explicación?

what's the latest? ¿cuál es la última?

what's the latest I can call you? *(a ti)* ¿qué es la hora más tarde en que puedo llamarte? ▪ *(a usted)* ¿qué es la hora más tarde que puedo llamarle?

what's the latest on...? ¿qué es lo último sobre...?

what's the matter? **1.** *(tú)* ¿qué tienes? ▪ ¿qué te pasa? ▪ *(usted)* ¿qué tiene usted? ▪ ¿qué le pasa? **2.** *(referring to a situation, not to the person)* ¿qué hay?

what's the matter with you? *(impatience, irritation, etc.)* ¿qué pasa contigo? ▪ ¿qué te pasa?

what's the meaning of this? ¿cómo se entiende?

what's the movie about? ¿(a propósito) de qué va la película?

what's the population of... ? ¿cuántos habitantes tiene...? ➤ What's the population of Santiago de Chile? ¿Cuántos habitantes tiene Santiago de Chile?

what's the price? ¿qué precio tiene?

what's the score? ¿cómo van? ▪ ¿cuál es marcador? ➤ It's three to one. Van tres a uno.

what's the use if...? ¿de qué vale si...?

what's the use of...? ¿para qué sirve...?

what's the weather forecast for tomorrow? ¿cuál es el pronóstico del tiempo para mañana?

what's the world coming to? ¿cómo está el patio?

what's there to do? ▪ what is there to do? ¿qué tiene de interés? ▪ ¿qué se puede hacer? ➤ What's there to do in Monaco? ¿Qué tiene Monaco de interés? ▪ ¿Qué se puede hacer en Monaco?

what's this? ▪ what is this? ¿qué es esto?

what's this all about? ¿de qué va todo esto? ▪ ¿de qué se trata todo esto?

what's this I hear about...? ¿de qué va todo esto que me dicen de...?

what's to be done? ▪ what can be done about it? ▪ what can we do about it? ▪ what shall we do about it? ¿qué se ha de hacer? ▪ ¿qué se le ha de hacer?

what's today's date? ▪ what's the date today? ▪ what is the date today? ▪ what day is today? ¿qué fecha es hoy? ▪ ¿a cuánto estamos? ▪ ¿cuál es la fecha de hoy? ▪ ¿qué día es?

what's unique about ▪ the unique thing about lo que distingue ➤ What's unique about a pound cake is its density. Lo que distingue un pound cake es su densidad.

what's up? ¿qué hay? ▪ ¿qué pasa?

what's up, doc? *(Bugs Bunny)* ¿qué hay de nuevo, viejo?

what's *with* you? ▪ what's with *you?* ¿qué mosca te habrá picado? ▪ ¿qué te pasa?

what's wrong? ▪ what's the matter? ¿qué te pasa? ▪ ¿qué tienes? *(In Spanish, the pronoun can change depending on who the referent is.)*

what's wrong with that? ¿qué tiene de malo? ▪ ¿qué ves de malo?

what's your hurry? ¿cuál es el apuro?

what's your hurry to...? ¿cuál es el apuro de...?

what's your major? ▪ what are you majoring in? ¿qué carrera estudias? ▪ ¿qué es lo que estudias? ▪ ¿cuál es tu especialización (académica)?

what's your name? *(tú)* ¿cómo se llama usted? ▪ *(usted)* ¿cómo te llamas? ▪ *(asking only for the first name)* ¿cuál es tu nombre? ▪ tu nombre, ¿cuál es? ▪ ¿cuál es su nombre? ▪ su nombre, ¿cuál es?

what's your opinion about it? ▪ what do you think about it? *(tú)* ¿qué piensas al respecto? ▪ *(usted)* ¿qué piensa (usted) al respecto?

what's your phone number? ¿cuál es tu número telefónico? ▪ ¿cuál es tu teléfono?

what's your profit? ▪ how much is your profit? *(tú)* ¿cuál es tu beneficio? ▪ *(usted)* ¿cuál es su beneficio?

the **wheel that squeaks (the loudest) is the one that gets the grease** ▪ the squeaky wheel gets the grease él que no llora no mama

to be **wheelchair-bound** ▪ to be confined to a wheelchair encontrarse en silla de rueda

wheeling and dealing tratos, ofertas y picardeo

wheezing (sound) *(when breathing)* la respiración de fuelle

when are you coming to Mexico? *(tú)* ¿cuándo vienes a México? ▪ ¿cuándo vas a venir a México? ▪ ¿cuándo vendrás a México? ▪ *(usted)* ¿cuándo viene (usted) a México? ▪ ¿cuándo va (usted) a venir a México? ▪ ¿cuándo vendrá (usted) a México?

when could I call back? ¿cuándo podría volver a llamar?

when did it get here? ¿cuándo ha llegado?

when did you get back? ¿cuándo has vuelto? ➤ When did you get back from Barcelona? ¿Cuándo has vuelto de Barcelona?

when did you last see a doctor? ▪ when was the last time you saw a doctor? ▪ how long has it been since you've seen a doctor? ▪ how long has it been since you last saw a doctor? *(tú)* ¿cuándo viste un médico por última vez? ▪ ¿cuándo fue la última vez que viste un doctor? *(usted)* ¿cuándo vio (usted) un médico por última vez? ▪ ¿cuándo fue la última vez que vio (usted) un doctor?

when did you see her? ¿cuándo la has visto?

when did you see him? ¿cuándo le has visto?

when did you see it? **1.** *(the show)* ¿cuándo lo has visto? **2.** *(the movie)* ¿cuándo la has visto?

when do classes resume? ¿cuándo se reanudan las clases?

when faced with ante ➤ What to do when faced with an aggressive driver Qué hacer ante un conductor agresivo

when he saw that... cuando vio que... ▪ al ver (él) que... ▪ cuando comprobó que... ▪ al comprobar (él) que...

when he was asked about it al ser preguntado sobre ello

when he was still a baby siendo él aún un bebé

when hell freezes over cuando los pericos mamen ▪ cuando la rana tenga pelos ▪ cuando las ranas críen pelos

when I first got here cuando acababa de llegar ▪ cuando había acabado de llegar

when I first got this en los primeros días que lo tuve

when I get old cuando yo esté entrado en años ▪ cuando me envejezca

when I got home cuando llegué a casa ▪ de vuelta a casa

when I grow up cuando (yo) sea mayor ▪ cuando crezca (yo)

when I had ▪ once I had cuando hube ▪ al ➤ When I had finished the letter, I went for a walk. Cuando hube terminado la carta, fui de paseo. ▪ Al terminar la carta, fui de paseo.

when I have a minute ya ➤ I'll do it when I have a minute. Ya lo haré.

when I heard the news cuando oí la noticia ▪ al oír la noticia

when I leave cuando (yo) salga ▪ cuando (yo) me vaya

when I read it 1. *(present)* cuando lo leo 2. *(future)* cuando lo lea 3. *(past)* cuando lo leí *(The present and future are pronounced "reed." The past is pronounced "red.")*
when I saw that... cuando vi que... ▪ al ver que... ▪ cuando comprobé que... ▪ al comprobar que...
when I told her that... cuando le dije (a ella) que... ▪ con decirle (a ella) que...
when I told him that... cuando le dije (a él) que... ▪ con decirle (a él) que...
when I want: to come and go ▪ to come and go as I please ir y venir cuando yo quiero
when I was a child ▪ as a child cuando era niño(-a) ▪ cuando niño(-a) ▪ de niño(-a)
when I was around *x* years old cuando tenía alrededor de *x* años
when I was growing up... cuando crecía... ▪ cuando estaba creciendo...
when I was on duty estando de servicio
when I was your age cuando (yo) tenía tu edad
when I went to look at it al irlo a mirar
when I'm gone cuando (yo) me haya ido
when in doubt, throw it out ante la duda, es mejor tirar la comida pasada de fecha a la basura
when in Rome, do as the Romans do donde estuvieres, haz lo que vieres ▪ cuando fueres a Roma vive como romano
when is it due? 1. *(baby, library book, etc.)* ¿para cuándo es? 2. *(baby)* ¿cuándo sale? ▪ ¿cuándo saldía? ▪ ¿para cuándo es? 3. when is it due back? ¿hasta cuándo tengo? ▪ ¿hasta cuándo lo puedo tener? ▪ ¿cuánto tengo de plazo? ▪ ¿cuándo hay que traerlo (de vuelta)? ▪ ¿cuándo hay que devolverlo?
when is it over? ¿cuándo se acaba?
when is the weather going to warm up? ▪ when's the weather going to warm up? ¿cuándo va a venir el buen tiempo?
when it became known that al saberse que
when it comes to en cuanto a ▪ *(literary, journalistic)* en lo relacionado a ▪ en materia de ▪ cuando se trata de ▪ cuando hablamos de ▪ a la hora de ➤ When it comes to love affairs... En materia de amoríos... ▪ En lo relacionado a los amoríos... ▪ Cuando se trata de amoríos... ➤ When it comes to putting a lock back together, I'm all thumbs. Soy un manazas cuando se trata de volver a armar el pomo en las puertas. ▪ Soy un manazas a la hora de volver a armar el pomo en las puertas.
when it comes to a boil ▪ when it starts to boil ▪ when it begins to boil cuando vaya a hervir ▪ en cuanto hierva ▪ cuando empiece a hervir
when it is ingested ▪ on being ingested ▪ when you ingest it al ingerirlo ▪ al ingerirse ▪ cuando se ingiere ▪ cuando es ingerido ➤ Beta-carotene turns into vitamin A when it is ingested. Beta caroteno se convierte en vitamina A al ingerirlo.
when it rains, it pours al perro flaco, todo se le vuelven pulgas ▪ al perro flaco, todo son pulgas
when it really mattered cuando importaba de verdad ▪ a la hora de la verdad
when it really matters cuando importa de verdad ▪ a la hora de la verdad
when it was over cuando hubo concluido
when it was time cuando ya era hora
when it's all over cuando todo esto pase
when least expected 1. when it is least expected cuando menos se lo espera ▪ el día menos pensado 2. when it was least expected cuando menos se lo esperaba ▪ el día menos pensado
when one grows up cuando uno sea mayor ▪ de mayor ➤ What do you want to be when you grow up? ¿Qué quieres ser de mayor?
when one had ▪ once one had cuando hubo ➤ When she had finished the letter, she went for a walk. Cuando hubo terminado la carta, ella fue de paseo.
when one hears something like that ▪ on hearing something like that ante algo así
when one sees something like that ▪ on seeing something like that ante algo así
when one's watch says... cuando el reloj marca...
when she saw that... cuando (ella) vio que... ▪ al ver (ella) que... ▪ cuando (ella) comprobó que... ▪ al comprobar (ella) que...
when she was still a baby siendo ella aún bebé
when that day comes cuando llegue ese día
when the chips are down en la hora de la verdad ▪ en el momento de jugarse el todo por el todo
when the clock strikes... cuando el reloj marca...
when the dust settles ▪ when things settle down ▪ when things get back to normal cuando el río vuelva a su cauce ▪ cuando las aguas se decanten ➤ When the dust settles, let's see where things stand. Cuando el río vuelva a su cauce, veremos cómo quedan las cosas. ▪ Cuando las aguas se decanten, veremos cómo quedan las cosas.
when the going gets tough, the tough get going a más mar, más vela
when the meeting was over acabada la reunión
when the mood strikes one cuando le dé la vena
when the news broke cuando se supo la noticia ▪ cuando conoció la noticia ▪ *(literary, journalistic)* conocida la noticia
when the party was over terminada la fiesta
when the time comes cuando llegue el momento
when the time is right a su debido tiempo
when the time is up cumplido el tiempo
when the time was up cumplido el tiempo
when the war was over al acabar la guerra
when things settle down ▪ when things return to normal ▪ when things get back to normal cuando las aguas vuelvan a su cauce
when you can get to it en cuanto usted pueda ▪ en cuanto le sea posible
when you come to ▪ when you get to cuando llegues a ▪ a la altura de
when you get past una vez superado ▪ por encima de la política ➤ When you get past politics and religion, people are just people. Una vez superada la política y la religión, es claro que la gente es simplemente la gente. ▪ Por encima de la política, todos somos seres humanos.
when you get to ▪ when you come to cuando llegues a ▪ a la altura de
when you have a second en cuanto puedas
when you ingest it ▪ when it is ingested ▪ on being ingested al ingerirlo ➤ Beta-carotene turns into vitamin A when it is ingested. Beta caroteno se convierte en vitamina A al ingerirlo.
when you least expect (it) cuando menos te lo esperas ▪ cuando menos se lo espera ▪ el día menos pensado
when you need it most *(tú)* cuando más lo necesitas ▪ *(usted)* cuando más lo necesita
when you put it that way dicho así
when was the last time you saw a doctor? ▪ when did you last see a doctor? ▪ how long has it been since you've seen a doctor? ▪ how long has it been since you last saw a doctor? *(tú)* ¿cuándo viste un médico por última vez? ▪ ¿cuándo fue la última vez que viste un doctor? *(usted)* ¿cuándo vio (usted) un médico por última vez? ▪ ¿cuándo fue la última vez que vio (usted) un doctor?
whenever I can siempre que puedo ▪ siempre que tengo la oportunidad ▪ cuando tenga la oportunidad
whenever I used to come here... siempre que (yo) venía aquí...
whenever I would go... siempre que iba... ➤ Whenever I would go down to the farm in Hardy, Virginia, I would smoke those great home-rolled cigarettes. Siempre que iba a la granja en Hardy, Virginia, solía fumar esos estupendos cigarros caseros.
whenever one does something... cada vez que uno hace algo... ▪ siempre que uno hace algo... ▪ cuandoquiera que uno hace algo... ➤ Whenever I have clothes to wash, I come to this laundromat. Siempre que tengo que lavar ropas, vengo a esta lavandería. ➤ Whenever I have clothes to wash, I'm coming to this laundromat. Siempre que tengo que lavar ropas, voy a venir a esta lavandería.
whenever one feels like it cuando le dé la gana a uno
whenever one jolly well pleases ▪ whenever the hell one feels like it cuando se le canten las reales (ganas)

whenever one wanted (to) ▪ anytime one wanted (to) ▪ at will cuando (uno) quería ▪ *(literary)* cuando le placía a uno ▪ a voluntad

whenever one wants (to) ▪ anytime one wants (to) ▪ at will cuando (uno) quiere ▪ *(literary)* cuando le place a uno ▪ a voluntad

whenever possible siempre que sea posible

whenever you like *(tú)* cuando lo desees ▪ cuando te guste ▪ *(usted)* cuando lo desee ▪ cuando le guste

whenever you want (to) **1.** *(at the moment you want to)* cuando quieras ▪ cuando lo desees **2.** *(on every occasion that you want to)* siempre que quieras

whenever you wish ▪ whenever you want (to) **1.** *(at the moment you wish)* cuando lo desees **2.** *(on every occasion that you wish)* siempre que lo desees

when's the baby due? ¿para cuándo es? ▪ ¿cuándo sale de cuentas? ▪ ¿para cuándo espera?

where are you from? *(tú)* ¿de dónde eres? ▪ *(usted)* ¿de dónde es usted?

where are you going to go from here? ¿desde aquí a dónde vas?

where are you headed? ¿para dónde vas?

where did it come from? ▪ where'd it come from? ¿de dónde salió?

where did we leave off? ▪ where'd we leave off? ¿dónde andábamos?

where did you get it? ▪ where'd you get it? ¿dónde lo conseguiste? ▪ ¿de dónde lo tienes? ▪ ¿dónde lo has comprado?

where did you get that idea? ▪ where'd you get that idea? ¿de dónde sacaste esa idea?

where do you draw the line? ¿dónde se fijan los límites? ▪ ¿dónde se fija el límite?

where do you inquire? ¿dónde tienes que preguntar?

where do you want to meet? ▪ where shall we meet? ¿dónde quieres quedar? ▪ ¿dónde quedamos? ▪ ¿dónde nos vemos?

where do you work? ¿en dónde trabajas?

where have you been? *(tú)* ¿de dónde vienes? ▪ ¿dónde has estado? ▪ *(usted)* ¿de dónde viene (usted)? ▪ ¿dónde ha estado (usted)?

where I can buy one donde puedo comprar uno(-a)

where (in) the hell...? ¿dónde coño...? ➤ Where (in) the hell are the scissors? ¿Dónde coño están las tijeras?

where is this getting us? ¿a dónde nos lleva esto? ▪ ¿a dónde nos conduce esto?

where is this going to end? *(frustration)* ¡adónde va a parar!

where it curves donde sale la curva ➤ Follow the road down to where it curves, and the station is on the right. Sigue la calle a donde sale la curva, y la estación queda en la derecha.

where it says donde pone(n) ▪ donde dice ➤ Continue down this aisle to where it says "canned goods." Sigue por este pasillo a donde ponen "artículos enlatados".

to be **where one belongs** estar donde pertenece ▪ estar donde le llaman ▪ estar donde debe de estar ➤ Having returned to her Vera Cruz apartment, she felt happy. It was where she belonged. Vuelto a su apartamento en Vera Cruz se sentió feliz. Estaba donde debía estar. ➤ I'm moving back to my hometown because that's where I belong. Me mudo de regreso a mi ciudad natal porque es allí donde pertenezco.

where one can discover ▪ where you can discover donde se puede descubrir ▪ donde poder descubrir

where one can enjoy ▪ where you can enjoy donde se puede disfrutar ▪ donde disfrutar

where one's loyalties lie por donde va ➤ I know where his loyalties lie. Yo sé por donde va.

where shall I look for you? ¿dónde te encuentro? ▪ ¿dónde nos encontramos? ▪ *(Sp.)* ¿dónde nos quedamos?

where shall we meet? ▪ where do you want to meet? ¿dónde quedamos? ▪ ¿dónde nos vemos? ▪ ¿dónde quieres quedar?

where the road forks donde la calle se bifurca

where there could have been someone ▪ when there might have been someone cuando podía haber habido alguien

where there's a will, there's a way querer es poder ▪ donde hay la voluntad, hay un camino

where there's smoke, there's fire cuando el río suena, agua lleva ▪ cuando el río suena, piedras lleva

where things stand cómo quedan las cosas ➤ When the dust settles, let's see where things stand. Cuando el río vuelva a su cauce, veremos cómo quedan las cosas. ▪ Cuando las aguas se decanten, veremos cómo quedan las cosas.

where to turn *(for comfort or help)* adónde acudir ▪ ya no saber qué hacer ➤ I don't know where to turn. No sé adónde acudir. ▪ Ya no sé qué hacer.

where was I? ▪ what was I saying? ¿por dónde iba? ▪ ¿de qué estábamos hablando?

where was that train headed? ▪ what train just left? ▪ what train was that? ▪ which train was that? ¿dónde iba ese tren? ▪ ¿qué tren se marcha? ▪ ¿qué tren acaba de marchar? ▪ ¿qué tren acaba de salir?

where was this picture taken? ¿dónde se sacó esta foto?

where were we? ▪ where did we leave off? **1.** *(after telephone interruption)* ¿dónde estábamos? ▪ ¿(por) dónde andábamos? **2.** *(after a longer interruption)* ¿dónde nos habíamos quedado?

where were you? ¿dónde estabas? ➤ Where were you this morning? ¿Dónde estabas esta mañana?

where were you born? *(tú)* ¿dónde naciste? ▪ *(usted)* ¿dónde nació (usted)?

where will that get me? ▪ what good will that do me? ¿de qué me sirve eso?

where you're coming from with that remark a qué viene ese comentario ➤ I don't know where you're coming from with that remark. No sé a qué viene ese comentario.

where'd you get it? ▪ where did you get it? ¿dónde lo conseguiste? ▪ ¿dónde la conseguiste?

where's that going to get us? ¿a dónde nos conduce eso? ▪ ¿a dónde nos lleva eso?

where's the money coming from? ▪ where's the money going to come from? ¿con qué dinero se lo consigue?

where's this going to end? *(frustration)* ▪ where's this going to stop? ¿a dónde va a parar?

wherever he goes vaya donde vaya

wherever I go ▪ everywhere I go dondequiera que voy

wherever I want (to) dónde yo quisiera

wherever it is **1.** *(fixed location)* dondequiera que sea **2.** *(changing location)* dondequiera que esté ➤ Let me off at the next stop, wherever it is. ▪ Let me off at the next stop, whichever one it is. Déjeme en la próxima parada, dondequiera que sea. ➤ We must eliminate hunger, wherever it is. Debemos eliminar el hambre, dondequiera que esté.

wherever it is needed donde se le necesite

wherever one looked ▪ everywhere one looked mírase a donde mírase

wherever possible donde sea posible

wherever she goes vaya donde vaya

wherever you are *(tú)* dondequiera que estés ▪ *(usted)* dondequiera que esté (usted) ➤ Good night, Mrs. Calabash, wherever you are! ¡Buenas noches, Sra. Calabash, dondequiera que estés!

wherever you go *(tú)* vayas donde vayas ▪ *(usted)* vaya donde vaya

wherever you look ▪ everywhere you look ▪ wherever one looks ▪ everywhere one looks se mire donde se mire

whet one's appetite ▪ to give one an appetite abrirle el apetito

whether he likes it or not makes no difference to me ▪ I don't care whether he likes it or not que le guste o no me es indiferente

whether, if si en el caso de que ➤ The interviewer asked the candidate whether, if they offered him the job, he would be willing to relocate. El entrevistador preguntó al candidato si en el caso de que le ofrecieran el trabajo, estaría dispuesto a trasladarse.

whether (it be) ▪ whether it is ya sea ▪ ya bien sea ➤ Children have fears, whether of real or imaginary things. Los niños tienen temores, ya sea a cosas reales o imaginarias.

whether (it is) ▪ whether it be ya sea ▪ ya bien sea ➤ Whether (it is) expressed or implied ▪ Whether explicit or implicit Ya bien sea expresado o implícito

whether one does something or whether one does something else tanto si uno hace una cosa como si hace otra cosa ➤ Whether we go or whether we stay, the result is the same. Tanto si nos vamos como si nos quedamos, el resultado es el mismo. ➤ It matters little whether we go or stay. Importa poco si nos vamos o quedamos.
whether one likes it or not ▪ whether one wants to or not tanto si le gusta a uno como si no ▪ a la brava ▪ por las buenas o por las malas
whether one needs it or not tanto si lo necesita como si no ➤ We give our dog a bath once a year whether he needs it or not. Le damos un baño a nuestro perro una vez al año tanto si lo necesita como si no.
whether one wants to or not ▪ whether one likes it or not tanto si uno quiere como si no ▪ a la brava ▪ por las buenas o por las malas
whether or not sea que ▪ si ➤ Whether I go to Bilbao depends on whether I get my paper done. Sea que yo vaya a Bilbao depende de si termino mi trabajo.
whether you like it or not *(tú)* te guste o no ▪ quieras o no ▪ *(usted)* le guste o no ▪ quiera o no ▪ *(with any pronoun)* a la brava ▪ por las buenas o por las malas
whether you want to or not quieras o no ▪ a la brava ▪ por las buenas o por las malas
whether we like it not nos guste o no ▪ a la brava
whew! ¡vaya!
which are... los que son
which are said to be que dicen ser
which courses...? ▪ what courses...? ¿qué asignaturas...? ▪ ¿qué materias...? ➤ Which courses is she teaching this summer? ¿Qué asignaturas da ella este verano? ▪ ¿Qué materias da ella este verano?
which I have a copy of cuya copia conservo
which I won't go into 1. *(subject)* en el que no voy a entrar 2. *(question)* en la que no voy a entrar
which includes ▪ including que incluye ▪ que comprende
which is (only) natural lo cual es natural
which is said to be que dice ser
which is why que es por lo que ➤ From a distance, the mountains have a bluish cast, which is why they're called the Blue Ridge. En la distancia, las montañas tienen un tono azulado que es por lo que se llaman La Cresta Azul.
which means that... lo que quiere decir que... ➤ I get the keys to the new apartment on Monday, July 30, which means that I will use my vacation to move and settle into the house. Las llaves del nuevo apartamento finalmente me las entregan el lunes 30 de julio, lo que quiere decir que mis vacaciones las emplearé para hacer la mudanza y montar la casa.
which metro stop is it? ¿cuál parada de metro es?
which one do you mean? ¿a cuál te refieres?
which one is this? 1. *(with a masculine antecedent)* ¿cuál es éste? 2. *(with a feminine antecedent)* ¿cuál es ésta?
which ones of you...? ▪ who (among you)...? ¿quienes de ustedes? ▪ *(Sp., familiar)* ¿quienes de vosotros...?
which reads *(with masculine antecedent)* en lo que se lee ▪ *(with feminine antecedent)* en la que se lee ➤ The demonstrator was carrying a placard which read... El manifestante llevaba una pancarta en la que se leía...
which reminds me a propósito recuerda que
which was said to be que dijo ser
which way? ¿por dónde?
which way did he go? *(L. Am., Sp.)* ¿qué camino tomó? ▪ ¿qué dirección tomó? ▪ *(Sp.)* ¿qué camino cogió? ▪ ¿qué dirección cogió?
which way is...? ¿hacia dónde está...? ▪ ¿hacia dónde queda...? ▪ ¿hacia qué dirección está...? ▪ ¿dónde queda desde...? ➤ Which way is north? ¿Hacia dónde queda el norte? ▪ ¿Hacia qué dirección está el norte? ▪ ¿Hacia dónde está el norte? ▪ ¿Dónde queda el norte? ➤ Which way is the metro from here? ¿Hacia qué dirección está el metro? ▪ ¿Hacia dónde queda el metro? ➤ Which way is it from here? ¿Dónde queda desde aquí?
which way the wind is blowing 1. *(literal and figurative)* por donde sopla el viento 2. *(figurative)* por donde van los tiros ➤ Which runway we use depends on which way the wind is blowing. La pista de aterrizaje que usamos depende de por donde sopla el viento. ➤ Some politicians change their opinions according to which way the wind is blowing. Algunos políticos cambian sus opiniones según por donde van los tiros.
which would explain... 1. *(conditional)* lo cual explicaría ▪ lo que explicaría... 2. *(past subjunctive)* que explicara... ➤ A giant meteorite struck the Earth some sixty million years ago, which would explain why the dinosaurs became extinct at that time. Un meteorito gigante chocó con la Tierra hace unos sesenta millones de años lo cual explicaría por qué los dinosaurios se extinguieron en aquel entonces. ➤ Einstein attempted to create a unified field theory which would explain all the known forces in nature. Einstein intentó formular una teoría del campo unificado que explicara todas las fuerzas conocidas de la naturaleza. ➤ In search of a unified field theory that would explain all the known forces in nature, Einstein... En busca de una teoría del campo unificado que explicara todas las fuerzas conocidas en la naturaleza, Einstein...
which would not take long to become 1. *(singular)* que no tardaría en volverse 2. *(plural)* que no tardarían en volverse
whichever comes first lo que ocurra primero ➤ The warranty covers two years or fifty thousand miles, whichever comes first. La garantía cubre dos años o cincuenta mil millas, lo que ocurra primero.
whichever way you look at it ▪ however you look at it por cualquier lado que se mire
while all this was going on a todo esto
while I'm at it ya aprovecho ➤ By the way, while I'm at it, how would you translate...? Por cierto, ya aprovecho, ¿Cómo traducirías...?
while I'm thinking of it... ▪ while it's occurring to me... ▪ while I'm thinking about it... mientras me lo estoy pensando ▪ mientras me lo pienso
while supplies last ▪ as long as supplies last hasta fin de existencias
while the commercials are on ▪ during the commercials ▪ during the commercial break mientras ponen los anuncios
while the commercials were on ▪ during the commercials ▪ during the commercial break mientras ponían los anuncios
while you wait ▪ then and there ▪ on the spot en el acto ➤ Keys made while you wait. Llaves hechas en el acto. ▪ Copiamos sus llaves en el acto.
while you're at it ya que estás en ello
while you're in *(present time)* mientras estás en ▪ *(future time)* mientras estés en ▪ durante tu estancia en
to **whip the butter** ▪ to cream the butter batir la mantequilla
to **whip the cream** batir la crema ▪ batir la nata
whipped cream nata montada ▪ crema batida ➤ I might have liked the pumpkin pie if they had put a little whipped cream on it. Puede que me hubiera gustado la tarta de calabaza si le hubieran echado un poco nata montada.
whippersnapper: little ~ gallito
whirligig *(helicopter-like flying toy)* molinete chino
whirlwind tour fugaz gira ▪ gira intensiva ▪ gira a matacaballo ➤ *(headline)* The American singer winds down his whirlwind tour of Spain El cantante norteamericano pone fin a su fugaz gira de España
whiskers of a cat los bigotes de un gato
to **whisper something in someone's ear** contarle algo a alguien al oído ▪ decirle algo a alguien al oído ▪ hablarle algo a alguien al oído ➤ Whisper it in my ear. Cuéntame al oído. ▪ Dime al oído.
to **whistle at someone** silbar a alguien ➤ As they drove by, the boys whistled at the girls. Conforme pasaron en el carro, los chicos silbaron a las chicas.
to be **white as a sheet** ▪ to be as white as a sheet estar blanco como la cera ▪ estar blanco como una sábana ▪ estar blanco como la nácar ▪ estar blanco como la nieve ▪ estar pálido como un fantasma ▪ *(Ercilla y Zúñiga: "La Auracana")* tener la color mudada ➤ You're white as a sheet. Estás blanco como la cera. ▪ Estás blanco como una sábana. ▪ Estás blanco como la nácar. ▪ Estás pálido como un fastasma.
white as a sheet: to turn ~ ponerse blanco como la cera ▪ ponerse blanco como una sábana ▪ ponerse pálido como un

fantasma ➤ When my husband heard the news, he turned white as a sheet. Al oír la noticia mi marido se puso blanco como la cera.

white-collar crime *el* crimen de alta alcurnia

white-collar criminal *el, la* delincuente de guante blanco

white dwarf *(astronomy)* enana blanca

white flag (of surrender): to raise the ~ ondear la bandera blanca

the **White House** *la* Casa Blanca ➤ The occupant of the White House El titular de la Casa Blanca ▪ La titular de la Casa Blanca

white lie mentira piadosa

to be a **whiz at** ser una hacha para ▪ ser un as para ▪ ser una bestia ▪ ser una lumbrera para ➤ She's a whiz at math. Ella es una lumbrera para la matemática.

who are said to be... que dicen ser...

who are you for? ¿de parte de quién estás? ▪ ¿a quién apoyas?

who asked *you*? ▪ what business is it of *yours*? ¿(a ti) quién te ha dado vela en este entierro? ▪ ¿a ti qué te importa?

who but...? ▪ who except...? ▪ who other than...? ¿quién sino...? ▪ ¿quién salvo...? ▪ ¿quién excepto...? ➤ Who but Shakespeare could have written it? ¿Quién sino Shakespeare pudo haberlo escrito? ▪ ¿Quién salvo Shakespeare pudo haberlo escrito? ▪ ¿Quién excepto Shakespeare pudo haberlo escrito?

who can blame him? ¿quién puede culparle?

who can blame you? *(tú)* ¿quien puede culparte? ▪ *(usted)* ¿quién puede culparle (a usted)?

who cares? ¿qué más da?

who could be calling me? ▪ who could that be? ¿quién me llamará?

who could have written it? ¿quién lo habrá escrito?

who could it be? ¿quién será?

who could possibly understand you? ¿quién iba a comprenderte?

who could that be? 1. *(all contexts)* ¿quién será? ▪ ¿quién puede ser? ▪ ¿quién pudiera ser? **2.** *(telephone)* who could be calling me? ¿quién me llamará?

who died in que murió en ▪ muerto(-a) en ➤ Elián's mother, who died in the crossing... La madre de Elián, muerta en la travesía...

who do I ask for? ▪ who should I ask for? ¿por quién pregunto?

who do I make the check out to? ¿a nombre de quién extiendo el cheque? ➤ Just make it out to cash. *(tú)* Extiéndelo al portador. ▪ *(usted)* Extiéndalo al portador.

who do you have for algebra? ¿quién te da la clase de álgebra? ▪ ¿quién le da la clase de álgebra?

who do you *think*!? ▪ well, who do you *think*!? ¡quién va a ser!

who does he think he is? ▪ just who does he think he is? ¿quién se cree que es? ▪ pero, ¿qué se ha creído? ▪ ¿quién se ha creído que es? ▪ ¿de qué va?

who does this belong to? ▪ whose is this? ¿a quién pertenece esto? ▪ ¿de quién es?

who doesn't? ¿quién no?

who doesn't like... a quien no le gusta(n)... ➤ When the prospective guest asked who was coming, the host withdrew the invitation. Cuando el invitado preguntó quién venía, el anfitrión le retiró la invitación.

who else? ¿qué otras personas?

who gave you permission to...? ¿quién te ha dado permiso para...?

who gets to do something 1. whose turn it is to do something a quien le toca hacer algo **2.** who has the opportunity to do something quien tiene la oportunidad de hacer algo

who goes (there)? ▪ who's there? ▪ who is it? ¿quién va?

who got here first? ¿quién llegó primero? ▪ ¿quién llegó antes?

who had to... que debía... ➤ ... who had to run to keep up with him ...que debían correr para seguirle

who I mean quien te digo ➤ You know who I mean? ¿Sabes quién te digo?

who I'm going to vote for a quien votaré

who is it? ▪ who's there? ▪ who goes (there)? ¿quién va?

who is not yet *x* years old que todavía no ha cumplido *x* años ➤ Our nephew, who is not yet three years old... Nuestro sobrino que todavía no ha cumplido tres años...

who is said to be que dice ser

who is that man? ¿quién es ese hombre? ▪ ¿quién es el hombre ese?

who knows? ¿quién sabe? ▪ ¡vete a saber!

who, like me que, como yo

who loves to have a good time: someone ~ *(he)* alguien al que le encanta divertirse ▪ *(she)* alguien a la que le encanta divertirse

who may I say is calling? ¿de parte de quién?

who scored? ¿quién marcó?

who shall I say is calling? ▪ whom shall I say is calling? ▪ who's calling? ¿de parte de quién?

who should I ask for? ¿por quién pregunto?

who stars in the movie? ¿quién es el protagonista de la película? ▪ ¿quién es la protagonista de la película?

who to? *(coll.)* ▪ to whom? ¿a quién?

who to turn to a quién recurrir ➤ I don't know who to turn to. No sé a quién recurrir. ▪ No sé a quién puedo recurrir.

who told you? *(a ti)* ¿quién te lo ha contado? ▪ ¿quién te dijo? *(a usted)* ¿quién se lo ha contado? ¿quién le dijo?

who was said to be de quien se dijo que ➤ Juana, the daughter of Ferdinand and Isabella who was said to be crazy, was probably not crazy at all. Juana, la hija de Fernando e Isabel de quien se dijo que estaba loca, probablemente no lo estuviera en absoluto.

who was that? ¿quién era?

who was that man? ¿quién fue el hombre ese?

who would believe it! ¡vivir para ver!

who would have thought that...? ¿quien hubiera pensado que...?

who wouldn't? ¿quién no?

whoa! ▪ slow down! ¡soooo!

who'd have thought it? ▪ who would have thought it? ¿quién lo hubiera dicho? ▪ *(coll.)* ¿quién lo diría?

(whoever did it) come forward! ▪ own up! ▪ show yourself! ¡que dé la cara!

whoever did this ▪ whoever has done this quien(quiera) haya hecho esto

whoever goes quienquiera que vaya ▪ cuantas personas van ▪ todos los que vayan

whoever has cuantas personas tienen ▪ todos los que tienen ▪ quienquiera que tenga

whoever he was quienquiera que fuera

whoever is calling quienquiera que llame ➤ Tell whoever is calling that I'll call them back in ten minutes. Dile a quienquiera que llame que le llamo yo en diez minutos. *(The concept of "back" is conveyed in Spanish by the redundant "yo.")*

whoever it could be quienquiera que pueda ser

whoever it is quienquiera que sea

whoever it might be quienquiera que sea

whoever it might have been quienquiera que haya sido

whoever it was quienquiera que fuera ➤ We don't know who composed this piece, but whoever it was was a prodigious talent. No sabemos quién ha compuesto esta pieza, pero quienquiera que fuera tenía un talento prodigioso.

whoever said... quien haya dicho ▪ quienquiera haya dicho

whoever thinks that is kidding himself ▪ anyone who thinks that is kidding himself se engaña quien piense así

whoever was... quienquiera que haya sido... ▪ quienquiera que haya estado... ➤ Whoever was in the bathroom last left the light on. El último que haya estado en el baño ha dejado la luz encendida. ▪ El último en estar en el baño ha dejado la luz encendida.

a **whole bunch of people** una porrada de gente

whole business todo este rollo ▪ todo ello ➤ I'm uncomfortable with the whole business of *tú* and *usted*. Estoy incómodo con todo este rollo de *tú* y *usted*.

the **whole damned day** *(coarse)* ▪ all the livelong day ▪ all day long todo el santo día to be a **whole different kettle of fish** ▪ to be a different kettle of fish ▪ to be a different question altogether ▪ to be another question altogether ser un capítulo aparte

whole 'nother thing: that's a ~ *(corruption of "another whole")* ▪ that's a different thing entirely ▪ that's completely different es completamente diferente ➤ *(coll.)* That's a whole 'nother thing. ▪ *(correct)* That's a different thing entirely. ▪ That's completely different. Es completamente diferente.

whole number número entero

a **whole slew of** ▪ a whole bunch of avalancha de ➤ A whole slew of boats... Una avalancha de pateras...

whole thing todo ➤ I can't believe I ate the whole thing. No puedo creer que lo comiera todo.

the **whole time** ▪ the entire time todo el rato ▪ todo el tiempo ▪ el tiempo entero

whole time one was doing something todo el rato que uno hacía una cosa

the **whole trip** todo el viaje

the **whole truth** toda la verdad ➤ Do you swear to tell the truth, the whole truth, and nothing but the truth, so help you God? ¿Jura usted en frente de Dios decir la verdad, toda la verdad, y nada más que la verdad?

whole wheat trigo integral

whole wheat bread *el* pan integral

whole wheat crackers galletas de pan integral

wholesale price precio al por mayor

to **whoop it up** alborotar ▪ armar una juerga ▪ jaranear

whorehouse ▪ red-light house ▪ house of ill repute ▪ house of prostitution casa de citas ▪ casa de putas ▪ prostíbulo

who's calling? ¿quién llama? ▪ ¿quién está llamando? ▪ ¿quién (me, le, etc.) llama?

who's going to stop you? ▪ *(coll.)* who's gonna stop you? ¿quién te lo prohíbe?

who's in charge here? ¿quién es el encargado aquí? ▪ ¿quién manda aquí?

who's in the movie? ¿quién sale en la película? ▪ ¿quién trabaja en la película?

who's it? ¿quién es? ▪ *(when playing tag)* ¿quién es la mancha?

who's next? ¿quién sigue? ▪ ¿quién es el próximo? ▪ ¿a quién le toca? ▪ ¿quién va ahora? ▪ ¿siguiente?

who's on the phone? **1.** who's using the phone? ¿quién está utilizando el teléfono? ¿quién está usando el telefóno? **2.** who is that (on the other end of the phone)? ¿quién está llamando?

who's that? ¿quíén va? ▪ ¿quién viene?

who's there? ▪ who is it? ▪ who goes (there)? ¿quién va?

whose idea was it? ▪ whose idea was that? ¿a quién se le ocurrió (eso)?

whose is this? ▪ who does this belong to? ¿de quién es? ▪ ¿a quién pertenece esto?

whose name I don't recall cuyo nombre no recuerdo ▪ del cuyo nombre no me acuerdo

whose name is the bill in? ¿a quién corresponde la factura?

whose outcome ▪ the outcome of which cuya salida

whose side are you on? *(tú)* ¿con quién estás? ▪ *(usted)* ¿con quién está (usted)?

whose turn is it? ¿a quién le toca? ▪ ¿quién va?

why bother? ▪ why go to the trouble? ¿y para qué? ▪ ni te molestes

why didn't you say that to begin with? ▪ you could have said that to begin with *(tú)* ya podías haber empezado por ahí ▪ *(usted)* ya podía haber empezado por ahí

why do you ask? ¿por qué me (lo) preguntas?

why don't you...? ¿por qué no...?

why don't you grow up? ¿por qué no creces? ▪ a ver si te haces mayor

why have supper now? ¡qué cenar ni qué cenar si...! ➤ Why have supper now? It's only five o'clock? ¡Qué cenar ni qué cenar si son las cinco!

why in the world...? ▪ why on earth...? ¿a santo de qué...? ▪ ¿por qué regla de tres...?

why is he taking so long? ¿por qué tarda tanto? ▪ ¿por qué está tardando tanto?

why is it taking so long? ¿por qué se tarda tanto? ▪ ¿por qué se tarda tanto? ▪ ¿por qué tanta demora?

why is it that...? ▪ what accounts for the fact that...? ¿a qué se debe que...?

why is that? ▪ what is the reason for that? ▪ what explains that? ¿qué va a explicarlo?

why, it's all gone! ¡pues bueno, no queda nada! ▪ ¡bien, no queda nada!

why me? ¿por qué a mí?

why, no ▪ well, no pues, no

why on earth...? ▪ why in the world...? ¿a santo de qué...? ▪ ¿por qué regla de tres...?

why should I? ¿por qué debería hacerlo?

why take the car...? qué coche ni qué coche si... ➤ Why take the car if we're close by? ¡Qué coche ni qué coche si estamos aquí al lado!

why, we've known each other for ages! ¡si nos conocemos de hace mucho! ▪ ¡si nos conocemos desde hace mucho!

why would I? ¿por qué lo voy a hacer? ▪ ¿por qué voy a hacerlo?

why would that be? ¿por qué sería eso?

why, yes! ¡pues, sí! ▪ ¡sí, pues!

the **whys and wherefores** el cómo y el porqué

wide consensus of ▪ broad consensus of amplio consenso en

wide coverage ▪ extensive coverage amplísima cobertura ➤ The media had given the story wide coverage. Los medios de comunicación habían dedicado amplísima cobertura a la historia.

to be **widely known** ser muy conocida ➤ Nicole Kidman's face is widely known. La cara de Nicole Kidman es muy conocida.

widespread international reaction amplia reacción internacional

widespread opinion ▪ widely held opinion opinión difundida ▪ opinión generalizada ▪ opinión ampliada

to be **wild about something** ▪ to be crazy about something pirrarse por algo

to be a **wild-goose chase** caza de grillos ➤ It was a wild-goose chase. Fue una caza de grillos. ➤ I don't want to go on a wild-goose chase. No quiero estar en una caza de grillos.

wildcat strike huelga salvaje

wildest dreams: not in one's ~ ni en sueños

wildlife vida salvaje

will be held at se va a celebrar en ▪ tomará lugar en ▪ se llevará a cabo en ▪ tendrá lugar en

will be the winner sale premiado

will do ▪ will suffice valdrá ➤ *(Andrew Lloyd Webber song)* Any dream will do. Cualquier sueño valdrá.

will I see you again? ¿volveré a verte?

will it go away? *(medical condition, for example)* ¿se va a ir? ▪ ¿se irá?

will it keep? ¿no se echa a perder?

will-o'-the-wisp fuego fatuo

will of the people la voluntad popular

will there be time? ¿habrá tiempo?

will there be time to...? ¿habrá tiempo para...?

to be **willing to** estar dispuesto a

to **willingly accept** ▪ to accept willingly ▪ willingly to accept aceptar de buen grado ▪ aceptar a buen grado

willingness to do something el talante de hacer algo ▪ la disposición para hacer algo

willingness to talk *la* voluntad de hablar

willpower fuerza de voluntad ▪ el resorte de la voluntad

to **win a case** ganar un pleito

to **win a competition** ganar un concurso ➤ James Hoban's design won the competition. El diseño de James Hoban ganó el concurso.

to **win a contest** ganar un concurso

to **win a game** ganar un juego ▪ ganar un partido

to **win a match** ganar un partido ▪ ganar un juego

to **win a prize** ▪ to be awarded a prize ▪ to receive a prize concederle un premio ▪ galardonar ➤ Gabriel García Márquez won the Nobel Prize. ▪ Gabriel García Márquez was awarded the Nobel Prize. ▪ Gabriel García Márquez received the

Nobel Prize. A Gabriel García Márquez le concedieron el Premio Nobel.

to **win a victory** lograr una victoria

to **win a victory over...** lograr una victoria sobre...

to **win again** repetir mandato

to **win an election** ganar... ▪ obtener...

to **win applause** ganarse la aplausa ➤ He won the applause of the public. Se ganó la aplausa del público.

to **win approval** obtener la aprobación ➤ The president won approval for his health-care reform bill. El presidente obtuvo la aprobación del proyecto de ley para reformar el sistema de salud o sanidad pública.

to **win at cards** ganar a los naipes ➤ I never win at poker, so I never play for money. Jamás gano a póquer, así que nunca juego por dinero.

to **win by a few hundred votes** ganar por unos centenares de votos

to **win by a landslide** arrasar en las urnas

to **win esteem** ganarse el aprecio ➤ He won the esteem of all. Se ganó el aprecio de todo el mundo.

to **win fair and square** ganar con todas las de la ley

to **win fame and fortune** ▪ to achieve fame and fortune hacer el oro y el moro

to **win first place** ganar puesto primero

to **win friends** ▪ to make friends ganar amigos

to **win money from someone** ganar dinero a alguien ➤ I won ten dollars from him playing poker. Le gané diez dólares jugando al póquer.

to **win over someone** **1.** *(friendship, loyalty)* to win someone over congraciar a alguien **2.** *(in a competition)* to defeat someone ▪ to beat someone ganar a alguien ➤ Lincoln said that to win someone over to your cause, you must first convince him that you are his friend. Lincoln dijo que para ganar a alguien a tu causa, primero debes convencerlo que eres su amigo. ➤ *(headline)* Ferrero wins over Agassi ▪ Ferrero defeats Agassi ▪ Ferrero beats Agassi Ferraro gana a Agassi

to **win someone's confidence** ▪ to gain someone's confidence ganarse la confianza de alguien

to **win someone's respect** ganar el respeto de alguien

to **win someone's trust** ▪ to gain someone's trust ganarse la confianza de alguien

to **win support against** ▪ to garner support against ▪ to gather support against recabar apoyo contra

to **win support for** ▪ to garner support for ▪ to gather support for ganar apoyo para ▪ recabar apoyo para

to **win the lottery** tocarle la lotería ➤ He won the lottery. Le tocó la lotería.

to **win the support of** ▪ to gain the support of ganar el apoyo de ▪ lograr el apoyo de

to **win the war** ganar la guerra

win-win situation *la* situación ganar-ganar

to **win *x* dollars from someone** ganar *x* dólares a alguien ➤ I won ten dollars from him. Le gané diez dólares.

to **win *x* games in a row** ganar *x* partidos al hilo

to **wind a clock** dar cuerda a un reloj

to **wind down** **1.** *(clock, watch)* acabársele la cuerda al reloj **2.** *(an activity)* concluir ▪ poner(se) fin ➤ *(headline)* The American singer winds down his whirlwind tour of Spain El cantante norteamericano pone fin a su fugaz gira de España

wind farm parque eólico

the **wind has changed** ha variado el viento

the **wind has picked up** el viento se ha levantado

the **wind is picking up** ▪ the wind is getting up se está levantando el viento

to **wind someone up** ▪ to get someone going darle cuerda a alguien

to **wind through** serpentear por ➤ The country roads wind endlessly through the mountains of that region. Los caminos comarcales serpentean incesantemente por las montañas de esa región. ▪ Las carreteras comarcales serpentean incesantemente por las montañas de esa región.

to **wind up a meeting** ▪ to wind a meeting up ▪ to bring the meeting to a close ▪ to bring the meeting to an end concluir una reunión ▪ finalizar una reunión ➤ We've been here four hours, and we haven't solved a damned thing. We need to wind this up and go home. Llevamos aquí cuatro horas y no hemos resuelto ni una maldita cuestión. Necesitamos concluir esto e irnos a casa.

to **wind up a music box** ▪ to wind a music box up darle cuerda a una caja de música ➤ It takes a crank to wind up those big Swiss music boxes. ▪ It takes a crank to wind those big Swiss music boxes up. Se necesita una manivela para darle cuerda a esas grandes cajas de música suizas. ➤ It takes a crank to wind them up. Se necesita una manivela para darles cuerda.

windchill factor sensación térmica

windfall profits ganancia(s) exagerada(s) ▪ ganancia(s) descabellada(s)

winding narrow streets calles estrechas y tortuosas ▪ calles estrechas y sinuosas ▪ calles estrechas y torcidas

window dressing política para la galería

window-shopping: to go ~ ir a mirar escaparates

windowsill repisa de la ventana ▪ el alfeizar de la ventana ▪ el poyete de la ventana

windy: it's (a little) ~ está (un poco) ventoso ▪ hace (un poco de) viento ▪ hay (un poco de) aire

windy day día ventoso ▪ día de viento

wine store tienda de vinos

winemaking: (the art and science of) ~ enotecnia

to **wink at someone** guiñarle el ojo a alguien

to **wink at something unethical** hacer guiños a algo poco ético

to **wink at violence** hacer la vista gorda a la violencia

to be a **winner** **1.** *(literal)* ser un(-a) ganador(-a) ▪ ser un(-a) acertante ▪ ser un(-a) triunfador(-a) **2.** *(figurative)* to be a very sharp person ser un fenómeno ➤ You're a winner! ¡Eres un fenómeno!

winning streak: to be having a ~ ▪ to be on a winning streak tener una racha de victorias

to **wipe a place off the map** borrar del mapa ➤ The tsunami wiped dozens of towns off the map. El tsunami borró decenas de pueblos del mapa. *(Literally, "decenas" means "tens of.")*

to **wipe away the tears** ▪ to wipe the tears away enjugar las lágrimas

to **wipe off the table** ▪ to wipe the table off enjugar la mesa

to **wipe out a population** aniquilar una población ▪ exterminar una población ▪ diezmar una población ➤ Measles wiped out half the population of Hawaii. El sarampión diezmó la mitad de la población de Hawái.

to **wipe the slate clean** ▪ to start afresh ▪ to begin a new page hacer borrón y cuenta nueva

wire mesh malla de alambre

wire service agencia de noticias

wireless broadband la conexión sin hilo de banda ancha

to be a **wise move** ▪ to be a good decision ser un acierto

the **wish that...** el deseo de que...

to **wish (that) one had done something** querer haber hecho algo ➤ He wished (that) he had done it. Quiso haberlo hecho.

to be **wishful thinking** ser una fantasía de deseo ▪ no ser más que un espejismo

wishful thinking: to engage in ~ construir castillos en el aire ▪ hacerse ilusiones

wishful thought that... espejismo de que...

with a (budget) surplus ▪ in the black con superávit ➤ We finished the year in the black. Terminamos el año con superávit.

with a call for ▪ by calling for con un llamamiento a que ➤ French chief of state Jacques Chirac opened the European Council with a call for maintaining the fundamental agreement between France and Germany. El jefe de estado francés, Jacques Chirac, abrió ayer el Consejo Europeo con un llamamiento a que se mantenga el acuerdo fundamental entre Francia y Alemania.

with a connection in con escala en

with a fine-tooth comb con lupa

with a heavy heart con el pecho oprimido ▪ apesadumbradamente ▪ acongojado

with a little cajoling con un poco de labia ➤ With a little cajoling, I could be persuaded. Con un poco de labia, me podrías persuadir.
with a pencil con lápiz
with a single... ▪ with just one... con un solo... ➤ It's true that one can live with a single kidney. Es cierto que se puede vivir con un solo riñón.
with absolute certainty: to know something ~ saber algo con certeza absoluta ▪ saber algo con certidumbre absoluta ▪ saber algo a tiro fijo
with all due respect con el debido respeto
with all my heart de todo corazón
with all one's heart de corazón ▪ con todo el alma ▪ con todas las entrañas
with all one's might con toda su fuerza e intención
with an angry look con cara de mala leche ▪ con (muy) mala cara
with an expected turnout of *x* visitors con una previsión de *x* visitantes
with close ties to de íntima vinculación a
with difficulty difícilmente
with dismal regularity con harta frecuencia
with each day that passed ▪ with each passing day con cada día que pasaba
with each day that passes ▪ with each passing day con cada día que pasa
with each other el uno al otro ➤ They exchanged Christmas gifts with each other. Intercambiaron regalos de Navidad el uno al otro.
with each passing day 1. with each day that passes con cada día que pasa **2.** with each day that passed con cada día que pasaba
with effort trabajosamente
with enthusiasm con afán
with equal parts of con partes equivalentes de
with flying colors: to come out of something ~ salir airoso de algo
with full authority con plenos poderes
with good intentions con buenas intenciones
with good reason con razón ▪ con toda razón
with great care ▪ with great pains con gran esmero
with great pains ▪ with great care con gran esmero
with hardly any resistance: to fall ~ caer sin apenas resistencia
with heartfelt gratitude agradecido del corazón
with him: to bring ~ traer consigo ➤ He brought a few books with him. Trajo consigo unos cuantos libros.
with him: to go ~ acompañarlo ▪ ir con él ➤ She went with him. Ella lo acompañó. ▪ Ella fue con él.
with it muy metido en lo que está pasando ▪ actualizado
with just one... ▪ with a single... con un solo... ➤ It's true that one can live with just one kidney. Es cierto que se puede vivir con un solo riñón.
with kid gloves a mano blanda
with meals a pasto
with my foot the way it is con el pie que tengo
with no doubt(s) whatever about sin duda alguna sobre
with no embarrassment ▪ without (any) embarrassment sin ningún pudor
with no end in sight sin que parezca que vaya a terminar ➤ The insurgency continues with no end in sight. La insurgencia continua sin que parezca que vaya a terminar.
with no hope of ▪ without any hope of sin esperanza de ➤ They were trapped in the submarine with no hope of ever getting out. Estaban atrapados en el submarino sin esperanza de poder salir nunca.
with no need for sin necesidad de
with no obligation sin compromiso ▪ sin ningún compromiso
with no strings attached ▪ without (any) strings attached sin condiciones ▪ sin compromiso(s) ▪ sin trucos
with nothing but tan sólo con
with nothing else to do but... sin otra ocupación que... ➤ With nothing else to do but wait... Sin otra ocupación que esperar...
with one: to take something ~ llevar algo consigo ➤ He took a few books with him. Llevó consigo unos cuantos libros.
with one's back to de espaldas a
with one's bare hands: to do something ~ hacer algo a mano limpia
with one's doing something con que uno haga algo ➤ There's no problem with your paying me back when you get paid. No hay problema con que me devuelvas el dinero cuando te paguen.
with one's elbows on the windowsill acodado en la ventana
with one's face turned away from someone de perfil a alguien
with one's fist clinched ▪ with one's fist clenched a puño cerrado
to be **with one's friends** estar con los amigos
with one's hands up manos en alto ➤ They came out with their hands up. Salieron manos en alto.
with one's head held high ▪ holding one's head high con la frente muy alta ▪ con la frente en algo
with one's sights set on con la vista puesta en
with one's tail between one's legs ▪ humiliated ▪ cowed con las orejas gachas
with only tan sólo con
with only *x* minutes remaining cuando tan sólo quedaban *x* minutos
with overtones of con tintes de
with prominent features recalcado de facciones
with precision: to do something ~ hacer algo con precisión
with reference to ▪ in reference to ▪ concerning ▪ regarding ▪ apropos of en lo que se refiere a ▪ a propósito de ▪ en cuanto a ➤ With reference to your other question En lo que se refiere a tu otra pregunta
with regard to ▪ concerning en lo concerniente a ▪ con respecto a
with respect to con respecto a ▪ con lo de ▪ con respecto de ▪ respecto a ▪ en torno a ▪ a propósito de ▪ en razón de ▪ en lo tocante a
with room enough for ▪ big enough for ▪ to fit con cabida para
with so much enthusiasm con tanto afán
to be **with someone** ▪ to be in the company of someone ▪ to be accompanied by someone ir con alguien ➤ He was with his wife at the time of the assassination. Iba con su mujer en el momento del atentado.
with something in mind en función de algo
with that in mind pensando en eso
with the best of them como el más pintado
with the bald head: the man ~ el hombre con la cabeza calva
with the consent of con el beneplácito de
with the current 1. *(literal)* aguas abajo **2.** *(literal and figurative)* siguiendo la corriente
with the exception of ▪ except for quitando ▪ aparte de ➤ With the exception of Brazil, Latin America is Spanish-speaking. Quitando Brasil, Latinoamérica es hispanohablante.
with the intention of ▪ intending to con ánimo de
with the money raised ▪ with the proceeds con lo recaudado
with the most votes: the one ~ el más votado ▪ la más votada
with (the passage of) time ▪ with the passing of time ▪ over time ▪ as time goes by a lo largo del tiempo ▪ a medida que pasa el tiempo
with the polling running against one ▪ lagging in the polls con las encuestas en su contra
with the possible exception of con la posible excepción de ▪ exceptuando tal vez a ▪ aparte quizá de
with the proceeds ▪ with the money raised con lo recaudado
with the wind in one's face de cara al viento

with time ▪ over time ▪ with the passage of time ▪ in the course of time ▪ in time ▪ eventually con el tiempo ▪ a lo largo del tiempo ➤ The tumors can become malignant with time. Los tumores pueden volverse malignos con el tiempo.

with which 1. *(singular)* con lo que ▪ con el que ▪ con la que ▪ con el cual ▪ con la cual 2. *(plural)* con los que ▪ con las que ▪ con los cuales ▪ con las cuales

with which to do something ▪ to do something with 1. *(singular)* con que ▪ con el que ▪ con la que ▪ con el cual ▪ con la cual 2. *(plural)* con los que ▪ con las que ▪ con los cuales ▪ con las cuales

with whom 1. *(singular)* con quien ▪ con el cual ▪ con la cual 2. *(plural)* con quienes ▪ con los cuales ▪ con las cuales

with whom do I have the pleasure of speaking? ▪ with whom am I speaking? ¿con quién tengo el gusto de hablar?

with your permission *(de ti)* con tu permiso ▪ *(de usted)* con su permiso

to **withdraw an allegation** retractarse de una acusación

to **withdraw an invitation** retractar una invitación ▪ retirar la invitación ➤ When the invitee asked who was coming, the host withdrew the invitation. Cuando el invitado preguntó quién venía, el anfitrión le retractó la invitación.

to **withdraw from a contest** *(political, etc.)* retirarse de una competencia

to **withdraw from drugs** quitarse de las drogas ▪ desengancharse de las drogas

to **withdraw (into oneself)** ▪ to draw into oneself ▪ to become withdrawn retraerse (en uno mismo) ▪ encerrarse en uno mismo

to **withdraw money** ▪ to take out money retirar dinero ▪ sacar dinero

withdrawal symptoms *los* síntomas de abstinencia ▪ *(coll.)* mono

withdrawal (syndrome) *(from alcohol, drugs) el* síndrome de abstinencia ▪ *(slang)* mono

withered face cara ajada

withered flowers flores marchitas ▪ flores ajadas

to **withhold taxes** retirar los impuestos

within a certain distance of a menos de cierta distancia de

within a few hours (of each other) con pocas horas de diferencia

within a few minutes ▪ within the next few minutes dentro de unos pocos minutos

within a few years dentro de unos años ▪ en (unos) pocos años ➤ Within a few years, viral illnesses will become treatable. Dentro de unos años, las enfermedades retrovirales podrán ser tratadas. ▪ En pocos años, las enfermedades retrovirales podrán ser tratadas.

within a framework of en un marco de

within (a matter of) minutes en cuestión de minutos

within (a period of) *x* days dentro de un plazo de *x* días ▪ en un plazo de *x* días ➤ The fine must be paid within thirty days. La multa deberá ser pagada en un plazo de treinta días.

to be **within a stone's throw of something** ▪ to be a stone's throw from something ▪ to be a stone's throw away (from something) estar a (un) tiro de piedra de algo

within a week antes de una semana ▪ en menos de una semana

within a year en menos de un año ▪ antes de un año

within an hour ▪ in less than an hour antes de una hora ▪ en menos de una hora

to be **within an inch of** ▪ to be at the point of estar a un dedo de

to be **within calling distance of** ▪ *(coll.)* to be a whoop and a holler from estar al alcance de la voz de

within constitutional limits con apego a la constitución

within earshot ▪ within hearing distance al alcance del oído

within enemy lines ▪ behind enemy lines ▪ inside enemy lines en la línea enemiga ▪ tras las líneas enemigas

within minutes 1. *(past or future)* en cuestión de minutos ▪ en pocos minutos ▪ en unos minutos ▪ en cosa de minutos 2. *(past)* a los pocos minutos ➤ The aspirin will take away your headache within minutes. La aspirina te quitará el dolor de cabeza en cuestión de minutos. ➤ The ambulance arrived within minutes. La ambulancia llegó a los pocos minutos.

to be **within one's reach** estar a su alcance

to be **within range (of)** estar a tiro (de)

to be **within reach (of)** estar dentro del alcance (de)

to be **within sight (of)** estar a la vista (de)

within the family ▪ in the home environment dentro de la familia ▪ en el torno familiar

within the past year hace menos de un año ▪ en el último año ➤ He died within the past year. Se murió hace menos de un año. ▪ En el último año.

within the realm of possibility dentro de lo posible

within *x* days ▪ within a period of *x* days en un plazo de *x* días ▪ *(in contractual agreements)* en acuerdos contractuales

within *x* hours ▪ before *x* hours are up 1. *(future)* antes de *x* dentro de un plazo de *x* horas 2. *(past)* a las *x* horas ➤ They'll be here within two hours. ▪ They'll arrive within two hours. Llegarán dentro de dos horas. ➤ The troop reinforcements arrived within hours of the attack. Los refuerzos de las tropas llegaron a las pocas horas del ataque.

within *x* seconds of a *x* segundos de ➤ Airplanes pass within 20 seconds of the White House, Capitol, and Pentagon. Los aviones pasan a 20 segundos de la Casa Blanca, el Capitolio y el Pentágono.

within *x* weeks dentro de *x* semanas

within *x* years dentro de *x* años ▪ antes de *x* años ▪ en el plazo de *x* años ➤ Some experts say the global warming problem must be solved within ten years. Algunos expertos dicen que el problema del calentamiento global deberá resolverse dentro de diez años. ➤ *(news item)* Brussels proposes eliminating the license plate tax within ten years. Bruselas propone suprimir el impuesto de matriculación antes de diez años.

without a doubt ▪ without any doubt ▪ no doubt sin duda ▪ a no dudar

without a hitch sin contratiempos

without a legal basis sin respaldo legal

without a shadow of a doubt ni sombra de duda ▪ de todas todas

without a trace sin dejar rastro ▪ sin rastro

without a trace of sin rastro de

without accusing someone of sin que se le acuse a alguien por

without any advance warning ▪ with no advance warning sin decir agua va

without any doubt ▪ without the slightest doubt ▪ with no doubt(s) whatever sin duda alguna

without (any) embarrassment ▪ with no embarrassment sin ningún pudor ▪ sin vergüenza

without (any) strings attached ▪ with no strings attached sin cortapisas ▪ sin compromisos

without any warning ▪ without any advance warning ▪ with no advance warning sin decir agua va

without anyone's... sin que nadie... ➤ Without anyone's seeing him Sin que nadie lo viera

without anything more sin más

without anything more than sin algo más que

without batting an eye sin pestañear ▪ sin inmutarse

without being aware of it ▪ without realizing it sin darse cuenta ▪ sin enterarse

without delay sin tardanza ▪ sin demora ▪ sin parar ▪ sin dilación

without difficulty sin dificultad ▪ sin reparo

without doing anything to sin hacer nada para ➤ He's always lucky without doing anything to deserve it. Siempre tiene suerte sin hacer nada para merecerla.

without enthusiasm sin entusiasmo ▪ sin la mayor gana ▪ sin la menor gana

without even ▪ without so much as ▪ without even so much as sin siquiera

without even imagining what... sin imaginar siquiera qué...

without ever leaving sin salir siquiera

without exception ▪ bar none ▪ taking all into account contándolos todos

without fail sin falta
without finding a trace of sin encontrar rastro de
without further ado sin más dilación ■ sin más ni más
without further delay sin más demora
without giving it a second thought ■ without giving it another thought sin pensárselo dos veces ■ sin pensárselo más
without giving it another thought ■ without giving it a second thought sin pensárselo más ■ sin pensárselo dos veces
without hang-ups sin complejos
without hesitation sin vacilación ■ sin dudar ■ sin titubear
without hidden strings sin huesos
without hurting oneself at all sin hacerse el menos daño
without interference sin interferencia ■ sinintromisiones
without its being known whether ■ and it remains unknown whether sin que se sepa si
without knowing what to do ■ not knowing what to do sin saber qué hacer
without meaning to ■ by accident sin querer ■ a lo tonto
without my being aware of it ■ unbeknownst to me sin que yo me dé cuenta
without my knowledge sin saberlo yo
without one's realizing it 1. *(with present or future tense)* sin que uno se dé cuenta **2.** *(with past tense)* sin que uno se diera cuenta ■ sin que uno diese cuenta ➤ A pickpocket can steal your wallet without your realizing it. Un carterista puede robar tu cartera sin que te des cuenta. *(British English is "without you realizing it.")*
without pausing from his dinner sin dejar de comer
without protest sin protesta ■ sin poner objecciones
without recourse to sin recurrir a
without reference to sin referirse a
without rhyme or reason sin son ni ton
without saying a word ■ without uttering a word sin decir (una) palabra ■ sin pronunciar una palabra ■ sin hablar nada ■ sin decir nada ■ como el convidado de piedra ■ sin decir esta boca es mía
without saying another word ■ without uttering another word sin decir una palabra más
without so much as ■ without even ■ without even so much as sin siquiera
without taking one's eyes off of sin descuidar los movimientos de
without the slightest doubt ■ without any doubt ■ with no doubt(s) whatever sin duda alguna
without the slightest hint of sin el más mínimo atisbo de ➤ Without the slightest hint of a smile Sin el más mínimo atisbo de una sonrisa
without thinking sin reflexión ■ sin pensarlo
without uttering a word ■ without saying a word sin decir una palabra ■ sin pronunciar una palabra ■ sin hablar nada ■ sin decir nada ■ como el convidado de piedra ■ sin decir esta boca es mía
without uttering another word ■ without saying another word sin decir una palabra más
without waiting any longer sin esperar más
without wanting to sin querer
without warning sin avisar ■ sin previo aviso ■ sin dar aviso
to **withstand temptation** ■ to resist temptation resistir a la tentación
to **withstand the impact** resistir el impacto
to **withstand (the) pain** ■ to endure (the) pain aguantar el dolor
to **witness a change** ■ to see a change observarse un cambio ➤ Now we are witnessing a change. ■ Now we are seeing a change. Ahora se está observando un cambio.
to **witness a historical event** presenciar un acontecimiento histórico
to **witness an accident** presenciar un accidente
witness for the defense ■ defense witness testigo de descargo ■ testigo de defensa
witness for the prosecution ■ prosecution witness testigo de cargo
witness in contempt *el, la* testigo impertinente
witness stand: to be on the ~ estar en el banquillo
to **witness the decline of** estar ante el declinar de
to be **witty** ser salado ■ ser cachondo
wizened face 1. wrinkled face cara arrugada **2.** withered face cara marchita
to **wolf down food** comer a dos carrillos ➤ José wolfed down his lunch. José comió a dos carrillos.
to be a **wolf in sheep's clothes** ■ to be a wolf in sheep's clothing ser un lobo con piel de cordero
wood glue cola
wood paneling forro de madera ■ revestimiento de madera
wood sealer ■ sanding sealer *el* tapaporos
wood stain *el* tinte de madera ■ *el* colorante de madera
wooden fence ■ wood fence valla de madera ■ cerco de madera
wooden shoes zuecos de madera
Worcestershire sauce salsa Perrins®
word for word ■ verbatim ■ to the letter al pie de la letra ■ palabra por palabra ➤ He quoted Lincoln's speech word for word. ■ He quoted Lincoln's speech verbatim. ■ He quoted Lincoln's speech to the letter. Citó el discurso de Lincoln al pie de la letra. ■ Citó el discurso de Lincoln palabra por palabra. ➤ I made a word-for-word transcription of the news program. ■ I made a verbatim transcription of the news program. Hice una transcripción al pie de la letra del informativo. ■ Hice una transcripción palabra por palabra del informativo.
word game *(crossword puzzle, Scrabble, etc.)* juego de palabras
word gets around se corre la voz
the **word is out that...** ■ (the) word has gotten out that... se ha filtrado que... ■ ha salido a la luz que... ➤ Word has gotten out that the troops were planning a surprise attack. Ha salido a la luz que las tropas planeaban un ataque sorpresa.
word (of honor) palabra santa ➤ You have my word (of honor). Tienes mi palabra santa.
word of mouth: to spread by transmitirse de boca en boca ■ propagarse de boca en boca
word processing tratamiento de textos ■ procesamiento de textos
word to the wise is sufficient al buen entendedor, pocas palabras ■ a buen entendedor pocas palabras bastan
words are cheap con buenas palabras nadie come
words failed me las palabras me fallaron
words to that effect algo por el estilo
to **work a problem** ■ to solve a problem hacer un problema ■ resolver un problema ■ solucionar un problema
to **work a puzzle 1.** *(brainteaser puzzle)* to solve a puzzle resolver un rompecabezas **2.** *(picture puzzle)* to put together a puzzle juntar el rompecabezas ➤ I couldn't work the Rubik's Cube, but if you could take it apart, you could figure it out. No pude resolver el Cubo Rúbico, pero si se pudiera desarmar, podría encontrársele la vuelta. ➤ I like to work the puzzles in the newspaper. Me gusta resolver los rompecabezas en el periódico. ➤ Joe and Josh are working a (picture) puzzle. Joe and Josh están juntando un rompecabezas.
to **work a split shift** trabajar jornada partida
to **work against one** actuar en contra de uno ➤ His brashness sometimes works against him. Su impetuosidad a veces actúa en su contra.
to **work against the clock** hacer algo contra reloj
to **work as** trabajar como ■ estar de ➤ Charito works as a nanny. Charito trabaja como una niñera. ■ Charito trabaja como institutriz.
to **work as hard as one can** trabajar lo más que uno pueda
to **work at the computer** *(L. Am.)* trabajar con la computadora ■ *(Sp.)* trabajar con el ordenador
to **work by the job** *(as opposed to earning a fixed salary)* trabajar a destajo ➤ Painters normally work by the job. Los pintores normalmente trabajan a destajo.
to **work by the piece** ■ to do piecework trabajar a destajo ➤ Furniture refinishers work by the piece. ■ Furniture refinishers do piecework. Los restauradores de muebles trabajan a destajo.
work crew ■ staff equipo de trabajo ■ plantilla

work environment ámbito laboral

work experience ▪ work history experiencia laboral

to **work for a cause** trabajar por una causa

to **work for oneself** ▪ to be self-employed trabajar por su cuenta ▪ trabajar a cuenta propia

to **work for peanuts** no ganar ni para pipas

to **work for you** ▪ to serve your purposes ▪ to meet your needs servirle ➤ The university's program will work for you. Creo que el programa de la universidad te servirá.

to **work full-time** trabajar jornada completa

to **work hard** trabajar mucho ▪ trabajar duro

work history ▪ work experience experiencia laboral

to **work in the yard** arreglar el jardín

work is play: my ~ mi trabajo es placer

to **work it out among yourselves** ▪ to resolve it among yourselves aclararos ➤ You all work it out among yourselves! ▪ You all resolve it among yourselves! ¡Aclárense ustedes mismos! ▪ ¡Aclaraos vosotros mismos!

to **work it out so that...** montárselo de tal manera que... ➤ He's worked it out so that he only works four days a week. Se lo ha montado de tal manera que sólo trabaja cuatro días a la semana.

to **work late** trabajar hasta tarde

to **work like a dog** ▪ to slave away trabajar como un buey ▪ trabajar como una fiera ▪ trabajar como un condenado

to **work lovingly on something** trabajar con mimo en algo

work of labores de ➤ *(news item)* The work of cleaning up the World Trade Center site is now complete. Las labores de limpiar el sitio del Centro Mundial de Comercio ya se han completado.

to **work off one's dinner** bajar la comida ➤ Let's go for a walk to work off our dinner. Damos un paseo para bajar la comida.

to **work on** trabajar en ➤ I need to work on it some more. Necesito trabajarlo más.

to **work on something** trabajar en algo

to **work on the computer** ▪ to do things to the computer *(L. Am.)* trabajar en la computadora ▪ manipular la computadora *(Sp.)* trabajar en el ordenador ▪ manipular el ordenador ➤ The technician is working on the computer. ▪ The technician is doing things to the computer. El informático está manipulando la computadora.

to **work one's ass off** *(coarse)* ▪ to bust one's ass ▪ to bust one's butt ▪ to bust one's tail partirse el culo trabajando ▪ partirse el culo de trabajo

to **work one's way through college** costearse sus gastos trabajando durante su etapa estudiantil ➤ He worked his way through college by painting. Él se costeó sus gastos pintando durante su etapa estudiantil.

to **work one's way up (to the top)** labrarse un camino (a la cumbre) ▪ forjarse un camino (a la cumbre) ➤ He began at the bottom and worked his way up. Empezó desde abajo y se labró un camino.

to **work out an agreement** ➤ The environmentalists and the loggers worked out an agreement. Los verdes y los leñadores...

to **work overtime** ▪ to put in overtime trabajar horas extras ▪ hacer horas extras

to **work part-time** trabajar media jornada

work surface *(kitchen, etc.)* ▪ counter(top) encimera

work that involves trabajo que se supone ▪ trabajo que conlleva

the **work that it involves** el trabajo que se supone ▪ el trabajo que conlleva

work to catch up on trabajo retrasado ➤ I have a lot of work to catch up on. ▪ I have a backlog of work. Tengo mucho trabajo retrasado.

to **work up a sweat** trabajar hasta echar la gota

to **work up an appetite** estar abriéndose el apetito ➤ We worked up an appetite going hiking. Estuvimos abriéndonos el apetito haciendo senderismo.

to **work well for someone** ▪ to serve someone well servirle mucho a alguien

to **work well together** trabajar bien juntos ➤ Javier and I work well together. Javier y yo trabajamos bien juntos.

to **work with someone** trabajar al lado de alguien ➤ I've never worked with him. Nunca he trabajado a su lado.

to **work without letup** trabajar a destajo ➤ The flooding caused by the rain caused the firemen to work without letup. Las inundaciones provocadas por la lluvia hicieron trabajar a los bomberos a destajo. *(In Hispanic countries firemen also perform flood-control functions.)*

to be **working as** *(temporarily)* estar de

working lunch almuerzo de trabajo ▪ comida de trabajo

to be **working on something** llevar algo entre manos

World As Will and Representation *(Schopenhauer work)* El mundo como voluntad y representación

world-famous mundialmente famoso

World Health Organization ▪ WHO Organización Mundial de Salud ▪ OMS

world history historia universal

world leaders dirigentes mundiales

world of make-believe ▪ land of make-believe reino de la fantasía ▪ mundo de ensueño

world opinion consenso internacional

world power potencia mundial ➤ In the sixteenth century, Spain became a world power. En el siglo dieciséis, España se erigió en una potencia mundial.

world-renowned ▪ known the world over mundialmente conocido

World Series *(baseball)* la Serie Mundial

a **world to discover** ▪ a whole world to discover un mundo por descubrir

the **world today** ▪ the world at the the present time el mundo en la actualidad ▪ el mundo hoy en día ▪ el mundo hoy día

World War Two ▪ World War II ▪ Second World War 2ª Guerra Mundial ▪ Segunda Guerra Mundial ▪ II Guerra Mundial ➤ California had not suffered blackouts since World War II. California no sufría cortes de luz desde la II Guerra Mundial.

to be **worn down** estar ajado

worn furniture ▪ beat-up furniture muebles ajados ▪ ajado mobiliario

to be **worn out** 1. *(person)* no tenerse en pie ▪ estar hecho polvo ▪ estar exhausto ▪ estar cansadísimo(-a) 2. *(thing)* estar desgastado

to be **worn out with** *(someone or something)* ▪ to be exasperated with ▪ to be sick and tired of estar empachado(-a) de ▪ estar exasperado(-a) de ▪ estar exasperado(-a) con ▪ estar harto(-a) de ▪ empacharse con

to be **worn smooth** estar desgastado ➤ The steps in the castle are worn (smooth). Las escaleras en el castillo están desgastadas.

to be **worn threadbare** estar desgastado ➤ The screw threads were a little bit worn. Las roscas estaban un poco desgastadas.

to be **worn to a frazzle** tener molidos los huesos

to **worry about** preocuparse de ▪ intranquilizarse

to **worry about what people will say** preocuparse por lo que diga la gente ▪ preocuparse por el qué dirán

to **worry about what people will think** preocuparse por lo que piense la gente ▪ preocuparse por el qué pensarán

to **worship the ground she walks on** besar el suelo por donde pisa ella

the **worst has happened** lo peor se ha producido

the **worst is over (now)** (ya) ha pasado lo peor

the **worst is yet to come** ▪ the worst part is yet to come ▪ the worst (part) is still to come ▪ the hardest part is yet to come ▪ the hardest part is still to come (aún) le falta lo peor a uno ▪ queda el rabo por desollar ➤ For me, the worst (part) is yet to come. ▪ The worst (part) is still ahead of me. ▪ The hardest part is still ahead of me. Aún me faltaba lo peor. ➤ For him, the worst (part) is yet to come. ▪ The worst (part) is still ahead of him. ▪ The hardest part is still ahead of him. Aún le falta lo peor (a él). ➤ For her, the worst (part) is yet to come. ▪ The worst (part) is still ahead of her. ▪ The hardest part is still ahead of her. Aún le falta lo peor (a ella).

the **worst (thing) that can happen** ▪ the most that can happen lo peor que puede pasar ▪ lo peor que puede ocurrir ▪ lo más que puede pasar ➤ The worst (thing) that can happen to him is... Lo peor que le puede pasar es... ➤ The worst (thing) that can happen to me is... Lo peor que me puede pasar es...

the **worst was yet to come (for one)** ▪ the worst part was yet to come (aún) le faltaba lo peor (a uno) ➤ The worst (for me) was yet to come. ▪ The worst part (for me) was yet to come. Aún me faltaba lo peor. ➤ The worst (for her) was yet to come. ▪ The worst part (for her) was yet to come. Aún le faltaba lo peor (a ella).

to be **worth a fortune** valer un imperio

to be **worth a lot of money** ▪ to be worth a great deal of money valer un dineral ▪ valer un montón

to be **worth fighting for** ser algo por lo que vale la pena luchar ▪ ser algo por lo que merece la pena luchar ➤ There are ideals worth fighting for. Hay ideales por los que vale la pena luchar.

to be **worth it** valer la pena ▪ merecer la pena

to be **worth one's weight in gold** valer su peso en oro ▪ valer un potosí

to be **worth the effort** resarcirle el esfuerzo ➤ ... but it is worth the effort ...pero le resarce el esfuerzo

to be **worth the trouble** merecer la pena ▪ valer la pena ➤ It isn't worth the trouble. ▪ It's not worth the trouble. No merece la pena. ▪ No vale la pena.

to be **worth *x* points** valer *x* puntos

to be **worthless** ▪ not to be worth anything no valer nada ▪ *(slang)* ser de pacotilla

worthwhile project proyecto que vale la pena ▪ proyecto que merece la pena

to be **worthy of one's position** ser digno de su cargo

to be **worthy of respect** ser digno de respeto ▪ ser acreedor de respeto

would arrive: one ~ 1. *(conditional)* uno llegaría **2.** *(imperfect)* uno llegaría ▪ uno iba a llegar ➤ They said the plane would arrive on time if there was no morning fog. Dijeron que el avión llegaría a tiempo si no había niebla matutina. ➤ They didn't know what time the plane would arrive. ▪ They didn't know what time the plane was going to arrive. No sabían a qué hora llegaría el avión. ▪ No sabían a qué hora iba a llegar el avión.

would come: I knew you ~ (yo) sabía que vendrías

would do something: one ~ 1. *(conditional)* uno haría algo **2.** *(imperfect)* uno hacía algo **3.** *(imperfect subjunctive)* uno hiciera algo ▪ uno hiciese algo ➤ I would go if I had time. (Yo) iría si tuviera tiempo. ▪ (Yo) iría si tuviese tiempo. ▪ (Yo) iría si me diera tiempo. ▪ (Yo) iría si diese tiempo. ➤ I didn't know what time the plane would arrive. ▪ I didn't know what time the plane was going to arrive. No sabía a qué hora llegaría el avión. ▪ No sabía a qué hora iba a llegar el avión. ➤ He was afraid (that) the company would include him in the personnel cutbacks. Temía que la empresa le incluyera en el recorte del personal. ▪ Temía que la empresa le incluyese en el recorte del personal.

would drink it all herself: the lazy bee ~ *(Quiroga: La abeja haragana)* la abeja haragana se lo tomaba del todo

would hardly suppose apenas podría creerse ▪ ni siquiera se le pasaría a uno por la cabeza ▪ ni siquiera se te ocurriría pensar que

would have been: one ~ uno habría estado ▪ uno hubiera estado ▪ uno hubiese estado ▪ uno habría sido ▪ uno hubiera sido ▪ uno hubiese sido

would have to do something: one ~ uno debía hacer algo ➤ The dean told us we would have to change classes. El decano nos dijo que debíamos cambiar de clase.

would it? ¿ah, sí?

would look at: one ~ 1. *(conditional)* uno miraría ▪ uno contemplaría **2.** *(imperfect)* uno miraba ▪ uno contemplaba ➤ Santiago would look at the Disneyland map for hours on end. Santiago contemplaba el plano de Disneylandia horas enteras.

would prefer to do one thing than another: one ~ uno preferiría hacer una cosa más que otra ▪ más le gustaría a uno hacer una cosa que otra ➤ I would prefer to have friends here than go out. ▪ I would rather have friends (come) over than go out. Preferiría invitar a amigos a casa más que salir. ▪ Más me gustaría invitar a amigos a casa que salir.

would rather: one ~ uno prefería ▪ más le gustaría a uno

would you agree with me that...? *(tú)* ¿estarías de acuerdo conmigo en que...? ▪ ¿convendrías conmigo que...? *(usted)* ¿estaría (usted) de acuerdo conmigo en que...? ▪ ¿convendría (usted) conmigo que...?

would you ask her to call me? ¿le pedirías (a ella) que me llame? ▪ ¿le pides (a ella) que me llame?

would you believe?! ¡¿no te lo crees?!

would you check on our order? 1. *(tú)* ¿podrías ver cómo va nuestro pedido? **2.** *(usted)* ¿podría (usted) ver cómo va nuestro pedido?

would you give me your address? *(tú)* ¿me das las señas? ▪ *(usted)* ¿me da (usted) las señas?

would you happen to know if...? ▪ would you by any chance know if...? ¿sabrías por casualidad si...? ▪ ¿sabrías por algún casual si...?

would you happen to know whether (or not)...? ¿sabrías por casualidad si (o no)...? ▪ ¿sabrías por algún casual si (o no)...?

would you have her call me? ¿haría usted que ella me llame?

would you kindly...? ▪ would you please...? ¿quiere tener la bondad de...?

would you like a cup of coffee? ¿te gustaría una taza de café? ▪ ¿te apetece una taza de café? ▪ ¿(te apetece) una tacita de café? ▪ ¿querrías un cafecito?

would you like (for) me to do something for you? ▪ shall I do something for you? *(tú)* ¿te lo hago? ▪ *(usted)* ¿se lo hago? ➤ Would you like me to slice it for you? ▪ Shall I slice it for you? *(tú)* ¿te lo rebano? ▪ ¿te lo troceo? ▪ *(usted)* ¿se lo rebano? ▪ ¿se lo troceo?

would you like me to? ▪ would you like for me to? **1.** *(main clause)* ¿quieres que lo haga? ▪ ¿quiere que lo haga? **2.** *(dependent clause)* ¿quieres que (yo)... ▪ ¿quiere usted que (yo)... ➤ Would you like (for) me to call you? ¿Quieres que (yo) te llame?

would you like some? *(tú)* ¿te gustaría un poco? ▪ ¿quieres? ▪ *(usted)* ¿le gustaría un poco? ▪ ¿quiere?

would you like some more? *(tú)* ¿quieres más? ▪ *(usted)* ¿quiere más?

would you like to? 1. *(main clause)* ¿te gustaría? ▪ ¿le gustaría? **2.** *(dependent clause)* ¿te gustaría...? ▪ ¿te apetece...? ▪ ¿te provoca...? ▪ ¿le gustaría...? ▪ ¿le apetece...? ▪ ¿le provoca...? ➤ Would you like to go to the movies? ¿Te gustaría ir al cine? ▪ ¿Te apetece ir al cine? ▪ ¿Te provoca ir al cine?

would you like to come in? ¿quiere entrar? ▪ ¿quiere pasar?

would you mind...? *(tú)* ¿te importa...? ▪ *(usted)* ¿le importa...? ➤ *(waitress to customer)* Would you mind moving your glasses? ¿Le importa quitar las gafas?

would you pass (me) the salt and pepper, please? ▪ would you please pass me the salt and pepper? ¿me pasas la sal y pimienta, por favor?

would you pass the butter, please? ▪ would you please pass me the butter ¿me pasas la mantequilla, por favor?

would you please...? ▪ would you kindly...? ¿quiere tener la bondad de...?

would you stop that?! ¡¿quieres dejar eso?!

would you take our order? ¿nos toma nota?

would you tell her to call me? ¿le dirías (a ella) que me llame?

would you tell me...? ¿sírvase decirme...?

wouldn't you like to know! ¡a que te gustaría saberlo!

to be **wound around itself** estar enrollado sobre sí mismo

to **wound someone's pride** ajarle a alguien la vanidad ▪ herir su delicadeza

to be **wracked by doubt(s) about something** ▪ to be wracked with doubt(s) about ▪ to be filled with doubt(s) about something ▪ to be consumed with doubt(s) about something ▪ to be plagued by doubt(s) about something estar sumido en dudas sobre algo

wraparound sound sonido envolvente

wrapped around one's little finger: to have (got) someone ~ tener a alguien metido en el puño ▪ tener a alguien en el puño ▪ tener mano con alguien

wrapping paper 1. *(for gifts)* papel de regalo **2.** *(brown paper for mailing)* papel madera

to **wreak havoc** hacer estragos ▪ causar estragos

to **wreak havoc among** ▪ to cause havoc among hacer estragos entre ▪ causar estragos entre

to **wreak havoc in** ▪ to cause havoc in hacer estragos en ▪ causar estragos en

to **wreak havoc with** hacer estragos con ▪ causar estragos con ▪ crear un caos con

to **wrestle with** ▪ to struggle with abrocharse con

to **wring a chicken's neck** retorcer el pescuezo a un pollo

to **wring someone's neck** retorcerle el pescuezo a alguien

to be **wrinkled (from being in water)** ▪ to be shriveled (up) estar como una pasa

wrinkles around the eyes patas de gallo

to **write a check** extender un cheque

to **write a few lines** poner unas líneas

to **write a good, long letter** extenderse en una carta

to **write a paper** hacer una composición ▪ hacer un trabajo

to **write down something** ▪ to write something down ▪ to put down something ▪ to put something down apuntar ▪ imprimir ▪ pasar ➤ I've put it on my list for tomorrow. Lo he imprimido para mañana. ➤ I'll write it down in my notebook. Lo apunto en mi cuaderno de apuntes. ▪ Lo paso a mi cuaderno de apuntes. ➤ Did you write down the license number? ▪ Did you write the license number down? ▪ Did you get the license number? ¿Apuntaste la matrícula? ➤ Did you write it down? ¿La apuntaste?

to **write illegibly** salirle una letra ilegible

to **write itself** escribirse por sí mismo ▪ escribirse por sí solo ➤ *(Richard Rodgers)* When you put a Hammerstein lyric on the piano, the song writes itself. Cuando se pone alguna letra de Hammerstein al piano, la canción se escribe por sí misma. ▪ Cuando se pone alguna letra de Hammerstein al piano, la canción se escribe por si sola.

to **write off something** ▪ to declare something a total loss ▪ to total something out declarar algo un siniestro total ➤ The insurance agent wrote off the car. ▪ The insurance agent declared the car a total loss. ▪ The insurance agent totalled out the car. El agente de seguros declaró el coche un siniestro total.

to **write one's own songs** escribir uno mismo sus canciones ➤ The singer writes her own songs. La cantante escribe ella misma sus canciones.

to **write to each other** ▪ to correspond with someone (regularly) ▪ to correspond with each other ▪ to exchange letters regularly cartearse con alguien ▪ escribirse el uno al otro

writing skills *la* habilidad para escribir

wrong! ¡equivocado! ▪ ¡te equivocaste! ▪ ¡fallaste!

to be **wrong about someone** estar equivocado con alguien ▪ equivocarse con alguien ➤ I see that I was wrong about you. Veo que he estado equivocado contigo. ▪ Veo que me he equivocado contigo.

to be **wrong about something** equivocarse en algo ▪ estar equivocado con algo ▪ equivocarse con algo ➤ I was wrong about the time. Me equivoqué en la hora. ▪ Estaba equivocado con la hora.

wrong answer respuesta equivocada ▪ respuesta incorrecta

wrong crowd malas compañías ▪ gente de mala calaña ➤ As a teenager he ran with the wrong crowd. Cuando era adolescente se rodeaba de malas compañías. ▪ Cuando era adolescente salía con gente de mala calaña.

wrong decision ▪ incorrect decision decisión equivocada

the **wrong one** el equivocado ▪ que no es ▪ que no era ➤ I took the wrong umbrella. Tomé el paraguas equivocado. ▪ Tomé el paraguas que no era. ➤ I took the wrong bus. Tomé el autobús equivocado. ▪ Tomé el autobús que no era.

the **wrong thing** lo que uno no debe ➤ I said the wrong thing. Dije lo que no debía.

wrong turn: to take a ~ ▪ to make a wrong turn dar giro equivocado ➤ What's wrong with saying...? ¿Qué tiene de malo decir...?

wry smile sonrisa irónica

x and up x y más

x-bladed propeller hélice de x palas ➤ A three-bladed propeller Una hélice de tres palas

x columns wide ▪ x columns across a x columnas

x cubed ▪ x al cubo ▪ x elevado al cubo

x days after... x días después de que... ➤ Two days after I left... Dos días después de que (yo) saliera...

x days before ▪ x days earlier x días antes

x days later x días después

x days old con x días de vida

to be **x degrees** hacer x grados ➤ It's 68 degrees Fahrenheit outside. Hace 68 grados Fahrenheit afuera. *(20 degrees centigrade)*

x divided by y 1. x dividido entre y ▪ x entre y ▪ x dividido por y 2. *(fractions)* x partido de y ➤ Thirty divided by six equals five. ▪ Six into thirty goes five times. Treinta (dividido) entre seis da cinco.

x-dollar bill billete de a x dólares ➤ Do you have change for a twenty-dollar bill? ▪ Do you have change for a twenty? ▪ Can you change a twenty? ¿Tienes cambio para uno de veinte? ▪ ¿Tienes cambio para un billete de a veinte?

x down and x to go x hechos y x por hacer ▪ x completados y x por completar ➤ Two down and two to go Dos y dos por hacer ▪ Dos completados y dos por hacer

to be **x feet away** estar a x pies ▪ quedar a x pies

to be **x feet long** ▪ to be x feet in length tener x pies de longitud

to be **x feet up** ▪ to be x feet high ▪ to be x feet off the ground estar x pies para arriba

to be **x feet wide** ▪ to be x feet in width ser de un ancho de x pies ▪ ser de ancho de x pies

(to be) **x floor(s) down** bajando x planta(s) ➤ (It's) one floor down! ¡Bajando una planta! ➤ (It's) two floors down! ¡Bajando dos plantas!

to be **x floor(s) up** subiendo x planta(s) ➤ (It's) one floor up! ¡Subiendo una planta! ➤ (It's) two floors up! ¡Subiendo dos plantas!

x-gauge needle aguja de x-calibre ➤ The twenty-nine-gauge needles are so small in diameter that the cat doesn't even react when we give him his insulin shot. Las agujas de calibre veintineve son tan pequeñas de diámetro que el gato ni siquiera reacciona cuando le damos su inyección de insulina.

to be an **x-grade teacher** ▪ to teach x grade ser profesor de x° ➤ She's a second-grade teacher. ▪ She teaches second grade. Es profesora de segundo.

x-grit sandpaper lija de grano x ➤ Eighty-grit sandpaper Lija de grano ochenta

x hours ago hace x horas ➤ She left two hours ago. Salió hace dos horas. ▪ Se fue hace dos horas.

x hours early con x horas de antelación ▪ con x horas de anticipación ➤ Be at the airport two hours early. Estate en el aeropuerto con dos horas de antelación. ➤ Get to the airport two hours early. Vete al aeropuerto con dos horas de anticipación.

to be **x in number** ser x

x in y ▪ x out of every y x sobre y ➤ One in four Uno sobre cuatro

x into y goes... ▪ y divided by x equals... y dividido por x... ▪ y dividido de x... ▪ y partido de x ... ▪ x entre y

x kilometers away a x kilómetros ➤ Ten kilometers away A diez kilómetros

x kilometers square x kilómetros al cuadrado ▪ cuadrado de x kilómetros de lado

to be **x light-years across** 1. tener x años luz de un extremo al otro 2. to be x light-years in diameter ser el diámetro de x años luz

to be **x light-years away (from)** ▪ to be x light-years distant (from) estar a x años luz (de) ▪ quedar a x años luz (de) ➤ The closest star to the sun is four light-years away. ▪ The closest star to the sun is four light-years distant. La estrella más cercana al sol está a cuatro años luz. ▪ La estrella más cercana al sol queda a cuatro años luz. ➤ Alpha Centauri is four light-years (away) from the sun. ▪ Alpha Centauri is four light-years (distant) from the sun. Alfa Centauri está a cuatro años luz del sol. ▪ Alfa Centauri queda a cuatro años luz del sol.

X mark aspa

to be **x meters long** ▪ to be x meters in length tener x metros de longitud

to be **x meters up** ▪ to be x meters high ▪ to be x meters off the ground estar x metros para arriba

to be **x meters wide** ▪ to be x meters in width ser de un ancho de x metros ▪ ser de ancho de x metros ➤ The bridge is three meters wide. El puente es de un ancho de tres metros.

x miles square cuadrado de x millas de lado

x minus y equals z ▪ x minus y is equal to z x menos y iguala z ▪ x menos y es igual a z

x minutes before a x minutos de ➤ An engine quit three minutes before landing. Falló un motor a tres minutos de aterrizar.

x minutes further along x minutos más de camino

x minutes into the flight a x minutos del vuelo ➤ Thirty minutes into the flight A treinta minutos del vuelo ▪ A media hora de vuelo

to be **x months' pregnant** ...embarazada de x meses ▪ tener x faltas

x more... ▪ another x... otros x ➤ *(news item)* Two more minors arrested for false bomb alarm. Detenidos otros dos menores por falso aviso de bomba.

x-odd ▪ x-some-odd x y tantos ➤ Twenty-odd... ▪ Twenty-some-odd... Veinte y tantos...

x other(s) otros x ➤ I have two other pairs of pants at the cleaners. Tengo otros dos pantalones en la tintorería.

x out of every y ▪ x in y x sobre y ➤ One out of every four Uno sobre cuatro

to **X out something** *(coll.)* ▪ to cross out something ▪ to cross something out ▪ to delete something tachar algo

x percent el x por ciento ➤ Ten percent El diez por ciento

to be **x points ahead** llevar x puntos de ventaja ➤ Two points ahead Lleva dos puntos de ventaja

x-power microscope microscopio de x de aumento ➤ The lab is equipped with a 10,000-power microscope. El laboratorio está equipado con un microscopio de 10,000x de aumento.

x-ray 1. *(beam)* rayo equis 2. *(picture)* radiografía

x square kilometers x kilómetros cuadrados

x square miles x millas cuadradas

x squared x al cuadrado ▪ x elevado al cuadrado

x take away y leaves z ▪ x minus y equals z si le quita y a x, te quedan z

x times a day ▪ x times per day x veces al día

x times as big (as) ▪ x times as large (as) x veces mayor (que)

x times as fast (as) x veces más rápido (que)

x times as sensitive as ▪ x times as sharp as x veces más agudo que ➤ A dog's sense of smell is at least three hundred times as sharp as a human's. ▪ A dog's sense of smell is at least three hundred times as sensitive as a human's. El olfato canino es al menos trescientas veces más agudo que el humano.

***x* times as sharp as** ▪ *x* times as sensitive as *x* veces más agudo que ➤ A dog's sense of smell is at least three hundred times as sharp as a human's. ▪ A dog's sense of smell is at least three hundred times as sensitive as a human's. El olfato canino es al menos trescientas veces más agudo que el humano.

***x* times over** por *x* veces ➤ Three times over Por tres veces

***x* to nothing** *x* a cero ➤ They beat us ten to nothing. Nos ganaron diez a cero.

***x* too many** *x* de más ➤ He tried to get in the express line with fifteen items too many. Él trató de colarse en la caja rápida con quince artículos de más.

to be ***x* weeks away** estar a *x* semanas ➤ Christmas is six weeks away. La Navidad está a seis semanas.

to be ***x* weeks' premature** ser *x* semanas premaduro(-a) ▪ faltarle a alguien *x* semanas de gestación ➤ The baby boy was six weeks' premature. Al bebé le faltaba seis semanas de gestación. ➤ The baby girl was six weeks' premature. Al bebé le faltaba seis semanas de gestación. ➤ The baby girl, who was six weeks' premature... El bebé, a la que le faltaban seis semanas de gestación... ▪ El bebé, a quien le faltaban seis semanas de gestación... ➤ The baby girl, who was six weeks' premature... La bebé que le faltaban seis semanas de gestación...

***x* years ago** hace *x* años ➤ We decided three years ago that... Hace tres años hemos decidido que...

***x* years earlier** *x* años atrás ➤ The couple had met four years earlier. La pareja se había conocido cuatro años atrás.

***x* years from now** de aquí en *x* años ▪ desde hoy en *x* años

***x* years later** ▪ *x* years afterwards *x* años más tarde ▪ *x* años después

to be ***x* years old** tener *x* años ▪ contar *x* años

to be ***x* years older than...** tener *x* años más que... ▪ llevarle *x* años ➤ She's four years older than her sister. Tiene cuatro años más que su hermano. ➤ She is four years older than I am. Me lleva cuatro años. ➤ He's ten years older than she is. Le lleva diez años.

***x* years to go** ▪ *x* years left faltan *x* años ➤ We have two years to go. Nos faltan dos años.

***x* years went by** pasaron *x* años ➤ Two years went by. Pasaron dos años.

yarn spinner ▪ storyteller ▪ political damage controller expert cuentista
yeah! *(enthusiasm, affirmation)* ¡pues sí!
yeah, yeah! *(impatience, incredulity)* ¡que sí, que sí!
year after year año tras año
the **year before** ▪ the previous year ▪ the preceding year el año anterior
year from now desde hoy en un año
year in and year out ▪ year in, year out ▪ year after year año tras año
year round ▪ throughout the year durante todo el año
year to go: to have a ~ quedarle un año a alguien ▪ quedar un año ➤ I have a year to go. Me queda un año.
a **year went by** pasó un año
years ago: (many) ~ ya hace años ▪ años atrás
years before ▪ years prior años atrás
years later años después ➤ Years later, we chanced to run into each other. Años después nos encontramos por casualidad.
years of age: to be *x* ~ ▪ to be *x* years old tener *x* años
years old: to be *x* ~ 1. to be *x* years of age tener *x* años ▪ *(coll.)* tener *x* tacos ▪ tener *x* abriles **2.** *(inanimate objects)* tener *x* años de antigüedad ➤ He's 30 years old. Tiene treinta años. ▪ Tiene treinta tacos. ▪ Tiene treinta abriles. ➤ The new constitution is twenty years old. La nueva constitución tiene 20 años de antigüedad. ➤ The cathedral is eight hundred years old. La catedral tiene ochocientos años de antigüedad.
years older than someone: to be *x* ~ llevar *x* años a alguien ➤ My brother is two and a half years older than I am. Mi hermano me lleva dos años y medio.
years prior ▪ years before años atrás
years to come: in the ~ ▪ in the coming years en los años venideros
years younger than años menos que
yellow journalism ▪ yellow press prensa amarilla
to be a **yes man** ▪ to say yes to everything ser un fantoche ▪ decir a todo amén
yes, I do 1. *(affirming)* claro que sí **2.** *(contradicting)* que sí
yes, indeed! ¡sí, por supuesto! ▪ ¡claro que sí!
yes, it is 1. *(agreeing or answering)* sí lo es ▪ sí que lo es **2.** *(disagreeing or contradicting)* que sí
yes, it was 1. *(agreeing or answering)* sí lo era ▪ sí que lo era **2.** *(disagreeing or contradicting)* que sí
yes, there are sí los hay
yes, there is sí lo hay
yes, there were 1. *(agreeing or answering)* sí que (los) hubo ▪ sí que había **2.** *(disagreeing or contradicting)* que no
yes, there will 1. *(agreeing or answering)* sí que (los) habrá **2.** *(disagreeing or contradicting)* sí que habrá
yes, they do 1. *(affirming)* claro que lo hacen **2.** *(contradicting)* que sí
yes, we can! 1. *(motto of the United Farm Workers and adopted by Obama supporters)* sí se puede ▪ sí, podemos (hacerlo)
yes, we do 1. *(affirming)* claro que lo hacemos **2.** *(contradicting)* que sí
yesterday afternoon ayer por la tarde
yesterday morning ayer por la mañana
yet: not to be able to do something ~ no poder hacer algo todavía ➤ *(bus driver to boarder)* You can't get on yet. ▪ You can't board yet. No puede subir todavía.
to be **yet to be determined** ▪ to be still to be determined ▪ to be as yet undetermined quedar por decidir
to be **yet to be discovered** estar por descubrir
yew bow *(Robin Hood's)* arco de tejo
yield: *x* cups ~ rinde *x* tazas
to **yield the floor to someone** *(parliamentary procedure)* ▪ to give the floor to someone ▪ to give someone the floor dar la palabra a alguien ▪ ceder la palabra a alguien ▪ otorgar la palabra a alguien ▪ ceder el turno de palabra a alguien ➤ I yield the floor to Senator Bedfellow. ▪ I give the floor to Senator Bedfellow. Le doy la palabra al Senador Chaquetero.
to **yield the right of way** ceder el derecho de paso ▪ respetar el ceda de paso ➤ *(accident notice)* The driver of the sedan failed to yield the right of way and began to turn. El conductor del sedán no respetó el ceda de paso y comenzó a girar.
yields *x* servings ~ cunde *x* platos ▪ da para *x* platos
you all look alike *(vosotros)* os parecéis ▪ *(ustedes)* se parecen ustedes
you amaze me me dejas maravillado(-a)
you are *(as an independent clause)* tú lo eres ▪ usted lo es
you are so beautiful eres tan hermosa
you beat me to it! *(tú)* ¡me ganaste! ▪ ¡te me has adelantado! ▪ ¡te me anticipaste! ▪ *(usted)* ¡me ganó (usted)! ▪ ¡se me ha adelantado! ▪ ¡se me anticipó (usted)!
you bet (your life)! ¡ya lo creo! ▪ ¡te apuesto que sí!
you better not *(coll.)* ▪ you'd better not mejor no ▪ será mejor que no ▪ más vale que no
you break it, you've bought it quien rompe, paga
you brought it up! ▪ you're the one who brought it up! ¡tú lo has sacado! ➤ You're the one who brought it up!-No I didn't! ¡Tú lo has sacado!-¡No he sido yo!
you call that art?! ¿¡y a eso lo llamas arte!?
you call that fair?! ¡¿y eso te parece justo?! ▪ ¡¿y eso te parece imparcial?!
you call that writing?! ¿¡y a eso lo llamas escribir!?
you can all... todos ustedes pueden... ▪ *(Sp., vosotros)* todos vosotros podéis...
you can bet on it! ▪ you can be sure of it! ¡puedes estar seguro de eso!
you *can* catch it ▪ it *is* contagious sí da *(pun on an AIDS-prevention poster, SIDA being the Spanish acronym for AIDS)*
you can depend on it puedes estar seguro ▪ puedes depender de ello
you can do as you please ▪ you can do as you like *(tú)* eres muy dueño ▪ *(usted)* usted es muy dueño
you can do it puedes hacerlo
you *can* do it ▪ it can be done puedes conseguirlo ▪ se puede conseguir
you can do the same for me some time hoy por ti y mañana por mí
you can get them there, too ▪ they have them, too ▪ they carry them, too allí también hay
you can guess what happened *(tú)* puedes suponer lo que pasó ▪ *(usted)* puede suponer lo que pasó
you can have it ▪ you can keep it *(tú)* te lo doy ▪ *(usted)* se lo doy a usted
you can imagine how... *(tú)* ya puedes suponer lo que... ▪ *(usted)* ya puede suponer lo que...
you can keep it ▪ you can have it *(tú)* te lo doy ▪ *(usted)* se lo doy a usted

you can say that again! ¡y que lo digas!
you can see that... ▪ one can see that... se echa de ver que...
you can see why ▪ one can see why se ve por qué
you can serve it with ▪ it can be served with puede servirse con ➤ You can serve it with rice or potatoes. ▪ It can be served with rice or potatoes. Puede servirse con arroz o patatas.
you can take it anywhere ▪ you can take it everywhere se puede llevar a todas partes
you can tell ▪ it is noticeable se nota
you *can* tell ▪ it *is* noticeable sí se nota
you can tell by... se reconoce por...
you can't go wrong no cabe equivocarse
you can't resist *(ad for donuts)* no se puede aguantar
you can't teach an old dog new tricks loro viejo no aprende a hablar ▪ a perro viejo no hay tus tus
you can't tell ▪ it isn't noticeable ▪ you don't notice it no se nota ▪ no se distingue
you can't tell the difference no se aprecia la diferencia
you can't win 'em all ▪ you can't win them all no se gana siempre
you catch my drift? *(coll.)* ▪ you know what I'm saying? ¿entiendes lo que te digo? ▪ ¿me dejo entender?
you could have called me bien podías haberme llamado ▪ ya me podías haber llamado
you could have fooled me! ¡pues no se nota!
you could have said that to begin with ▪ why didn't you say that to begin with? ya podías haber empezado por ahí
you could hear se oía
you could say that... ▪ it could be said that... ▪ one can say that... se diría que
you could see ▪ one could see se veía ➤ From Marbella you could see Gibraltar. Desde Marbella se veía Gibraltar.
you could see why ▪ one could see why se veía por qué
you couldn't ask for anything more no podrías pedir nada más ▪ no hay (nada) más que pedir
you couldn't hear anything ▪ there was no sound no se oía nada
you couldn't wish for anything more no podrías desear nada más ▪ no cabe desear nada más
you deserve it *(tú)* te lo mereces ▪ *(usted)* se lo merece
you do? ¿sí?
you *do*? ¿de verdad?
you don't believe it, do you? que no te lo crees, ¿no?
you don't fool me **1.** *(tú)* no me engañas **2.** *(usted)* no me engaña (usted)
you don't know how glad I am to... no sabes cuánto me alegra (que...) ▪ no sabes cuánto me alegro de (que...) ➤ You don't know how glad I am to be back in Guatemala. No sabes cuánto me alegra estar de vuelta en Guatemala. ▪ No sabes cuánto me alegro de haber vuelto a Guatemala.
you don't know how much... no sabes cuánto... ▪ no sabes cómo... ➤ You don't know how much our family enjoyed the black paw ham you gave us. No sabes cuánto le gustó a nuestra familia el jamón (de) pata negra que nos diste. ▪ No sabes cómo le gustó a nuestra familia el jamón (de) pata negra que nos diste.
you don't know the half of it no sabes ni la media
you don't know what you're talking about no sabes lo que dices
you don't look it *(your age, for example)* no lo aparentas ▪ no lo pareces
you don't lose anything by being polite lo cortés no quita lo valiente
you don't need to **1.** *(main clause)* it's not necessary no hace falta **2.** *(dependent clause)* no hace falta que... ▪ no hay que... ➤ You don't need to give me a ride. No hace falta me lleves. ➤ You don't need to go into detail. No hay que pormenorizar. ▪ No hace falta que pormenorices.
you don't notice it ▪ it isn't noticeable ▪ you can't tell no se nota ▪ no se distingue ▪ no se diferencia
you don't say! ¡no me digas! ▪ ¡quia!
you don't think it's a good idea? ▪ you think it's a bad idea? ¿te parece mal?
you dreamer! ¡eres un iluso! ▪ ¡pobre iluso! ▪ ¡pedazo de iluso!
you get the feeling that... ▪ one gets the feeling that... se tiene la sensación de que...
you gotta admit *(coll.)* ▪ you've got to admit ▪ you have to admit es preciso reconocerlo
you gotta be outta your mind! *(coll.)* ▪ you've got to be out of your mind! ¡y un jamón con chorreras!
you had better... ▪ you'd better... más vale que... ▪ harías mejor en...
you had better not... ▪ you'd better not... más vale que (tú) no... ▪ harías mejor en no...
you have a point ▪ you've got a point *(tú)* allí le has dado ▪ *(usted)* allí le ha dado (usted)
you have my word ▪ you have my word of honor tienes me palabra santa
you have to admit hay que reconocerlo
you have to experience it (firsthand) ▪ you have to see it (to understand) es para verlo
you have to, like it or not tienes que hacerlo, te guste o no ▪ *(colorful)* que quiera, que no quiera, el asno ha de ir a la feria
you have to see it (to understand) ▪ you have to experience it (firsthand) es para verlo
you haven't changed a bit no has cambiado un pelo
you haven't seen our new apartment no conoces nuestra nueva casa
you heard me! ¡me has oído!
you keep out of this! ▪ you stay out of this! *(tú)* ¡tú no te metas! ▪ ¡mantente al margen! ▪ ¡tú, aquí, ni entras ni sales! ▪ *(usted)* ¡usted no se meta! ▪ ¡manténgase al margen!
you know ¿viste? ➤ I wasn't born yesterday, you know. No soy caído del catre, ¿viste? ▪ No soy caído del guindo, ¿viste? ▪ No nací ayer, ¿viste?
you know as well as I do tú sabes como yo ▪ usted sabe como yo
you know damned well... sabes efectivamente...
you know I do sabes que sí
you know it wasn't I *(correct but formal)* ▪ you know that I was not the one ▪ *(incorrect but almost universal)* you know it wasn't me sabes que no he sido yo
you know me better than that me conoces bien ➤ You know me better than that. Of course not! Me conoces bien. ¡Por supuesto que no!
you know what I mean? ¿sabes lo que quiero decir? ▪ ¿sabes a qué me refiero?
you know what I'm saying? ¿sabes lo que te digo?
you know what I'm talking about sabes de lo que estoy hablando ▪ sabes de qué estoy hablando
you know what *that's* like ya sabes lo que es eso
you learn something new every day a la cama no te irás sin saber una cosa más ▪ todos los días se aprende una cosa nueva
you left your lights on *(tú)* te dejaste las luces encendidas ▪ *(usted)* se dejó las luces encendidas
you look great today hoy tienes un aspecto fenomenal
you look terrific estás estupendo(-a)
you look tired te veo cansado(-a)
you made me! ¡tú me has hecho a mí!
you made your bed, and now you can sleep in it te lo guisas y te lo comes ▪ tú lo preparas y tú te lo comes ▪ que to aproveche *(This expression can be used with other pronouns.)*
you make me want to cry me das lástima
you may go *(tú)* puedes retirarte ▪ *(usted)* puede retirarse ▪ *(teacher to a class)* pueden irse ▪ podéis iros ▪ pueden salir ▪ podéis salir
you might be! ▪ you could be! ¡podrías! ▪ *(casting more doubt)* ¡pudieras!
you might as well ask **1.** *(request)* te valdría mejor pedir ▪ te conviene pedir ▪ igual te valdría pedir **2.** *(question)* te valdría mejor preguntar ▪ te conviene preguntar ▪ igual te valdría preguntar
you must be dumbfounded at... *(tú)* te habrás quedado estupefacto ante... ▪ debes de estar estupefacto ante... ▪ *(usted)* se habrá quedado estupefacto ante... ▪ debe de estar estupefacto

ante... ▪ *(Mex.)* has de estar estupefacto ante... ▪ ha de estar estupefacto ante... ➤ You must be dumbfounded at what he did. Te habrás quedado estupefacto ante lo que hizo. ▪ *(Mex.)* Has de estar estupefacto ante lo que hizo.

you must be over eighteen ▪ you must be at least eighteen years old ▪ you must be at least eighteen years of age usted debe tener dieciocho años de edad o más

you must have... qué bien debe haber... ➤ You must have had a good breakfast! ¡Qué bien debe haber estado tu desayuno.

you must know has de saber

you must know that... has de saber que...

you mustn't... ▪ one mustn't... no se debiera...

you mustn't do that ▪ don't do that no lo hagas ▪ *(to a child)* no se hace

you mustn't tell them no debes decirles

you mustn't think that no debes pensar eso

you need help, Charlie Brown *(Charles Schulz)* hay que ayudarte, Charlie Brown ▪ necesitas ayuda, Charlie Brown

you need not be afraid ▪ you needn't be afraid no tienes por qué tener miedo

you never can tell nunca se sabe ▪ nunca se puede predecir

you never know ▪ one never knows nunca se sabe ➤ You never know what to expect. ▪ One never knows what to expect. Nunca se sabe lo que puede pasar.

you old fool! ¡tío lila!

you old rascal! ¡mala pieza!

you only ▪ all you do is no hacer más que ➤ You only hurt people. No haces más que hacer daño a la gente.

you only live once ▪ you only go around once sólo se vive una vez ▪ sólo vives una vez

you ought to be ashamed of yourself ▪ you should be ashamed of yourself *(tú)* deberías avergonzarte ▪ *(usted)* debería (usted) avergonzarse

you outdid yourself! *(tú)* ¡te pasaste! ▪ *(usted)* ¡se pasó (usted)!

you overdid it ¡te pasaste! ▪ te has pasado cien pueblos

you owe it to yourself *(tú)* es un deber que tienes contigo mismo ▪ *(usted)* es un deber que tiene consigo mismo

you reap what you sow se recoge lo que se siembra ▪ quien vientos siembra, tempestades recoge

you said it! ¡ya lo has dicho!

you should be ashamed of yourself ▪ you ought to be ashamed of yourself *(tú)* deberías avergonzarte ▪ *(usted)* debería (usted) avergonzarse

you should have 1. *(main clause)* deberías haberlo hecho **2.** *(dependent clause)* deberías haber...

you should have come with us *(tú)* deberías haberte venido con nosotros ▪ *(usted)* debería haberse venido con nosotros

you should have heard... tenías que haber oído...

you should have said so haberlo dicho ▪ lo hubieras dicho

you should have seen it! ¡había que verlo!

you should have seen *that*! ¡tendrías que haberlo visto!

you should have smelled... le hubieras olido... ➤ You should have smelled her perfume! ¡Le hubieras olido su perfume!

you should have told me (about it)! ¡haberlo dicho!

you should know me better than that deberías conocerme mejor

you stay out of this! ▪ you keep out of this! *(tú)* ¡tú no te metas! ▪ ¡mantente al margen! ▪ ¡tú, aquí, ni entras ni sales! ▪ *(usted)* ¡usted no se meta! ▪ ¡manténgase al margen!

you still have a ways to go todavía te queda trayecto por recorrer

you talked me into it! ¡(ya) me has convencido!

you tell me! ▪ I have no idea ▪ you're the one who knows ▪ you decide! dime

you tell them... *(tú)* diles... ▪ *(usted)* dígales... ▪ *(L. Am., coll.)* les dices... ➤ You tell them to take it away and do whatever they want to with it. Les dices que se lo lleven y hagan con él lo que les dé la gana.

you tell them I said to... diles que yo he dicho que... ➤ You tell them I said to take it away. Diles que yo he dicho que se lo lleven.

you took the words right out of my mouth me lo has quitado de la boca

you two look alike se parecen ustedes ▪ *(Sp., vosotros)* os parecéis

you wanna bet?! *(coll.)* ▪ what do you wanna bet? ¿qué apuestas?

you want them to be... quieres que estén ▪ es preferible que estén ➤ Add the chopped green pepper at the very end. You want them to be hot but still crunchy. Añade el pimiento verde picado justo al final. Es preferible que estén calientes pero a la vez crujientes.

you were right to *(tú)* hiciste bien en ▪ *(usted)* hizo bien en

you were supposed to call me *(tú)* tenías que haberme llamado ▪ *(usted)* (usted) tenía que haberme llamado ➤ You were supposed to call me this morning, but if you did, I'm not aware of it. Tenías que haberme llamado esta mañana, pero si lo hiciste, no me enteré. ▪ Tenías que haberme llamado esta mañana, pero si lo hiciste, no me di cuenta.

you won't have any trouble finding it *(tú)* no tendrás ninguna dificultad en localizarlo ▪ *(usted)* no tendrá (usted) ninguna dificultad en localizarlo

you won't regret it *(tú)* no te vas a arrepentir ▪ *(usted)* no se va a arrepentir

you would do better to do something ▪ you'd do better to do something ▪ you would be better off doing something *(tú)* te interesa más hacer algo ▪ *(usted)* le interesa más hacer algo ➤ You would do better to wait. ▪ You'd do better to wait. ▪ You would be better off waiting. ▪ You'd be better off waiting. ▪ It is more in your interest to wait. ▪ It's more in your interest to wait. Te interesa más esperar. ▪ Le interesa (a usted) más esperar.

you would do well to... *(tú)* te harías bien en... ▪ *(usted)* se haría (usted) bien en...

you would expect that... ▪ one would expect that... se supondría que...

you would think that... ▪ one would think that... se podría pensar que... ▪ uno podría pensar que... ▪ cabe pensar que... ▪ cabría pensar que...

you wouldn't know it nadie podría decirlo

you write to them saying... se les escribe diciendo...

you'd be surprised *(tú)* te quedarías sorprendido ▪ *(vosotros)* os quedaríais sorprendidos ▪ *(usted)* se quedaría sorprendido ▪ *(ustedes)* se quedarían sorprendidos

you'd better... mejor que... ▪ más vale que... ➤ You'd better get over here. Mejor que vengas. ▪ Más vale que vengas. ▪ Mejor que llegues. ▪ Más vale que llegues.

you'd better be there conviene que te presentes

you'd better not... ▪ you had better not... más vale que (tú) no... ▪ harías mejor en no...

you'd do better (to...) mejor harías...

you'd have to ask *her* habría que preguntárselo a ella ▪ *(tú)* tendrías que preguntárselo a ella ▪ (usted) tendría que preguntárselo a ella

you'd have to ask *him* habría que preguntárselo a él ▪ *(tú)* tendrías que preguntárselo a él ▪ *(usted)* tendría que preguntárselo a él

you'd have to be crazy to... habría que estar loco para... ▪ tendrías que estar loco para...

you'd think (that)... pensarías que... ▪ se pensaría que... ▪ cualquiera diría que...

you'll be glad you did te lo agradecerás

you'll be sorry! ¡te arrepentirás! ▪ ¡estarás arrepentido!

you'll do fine lo harás bien

you'll find everything hay de todo ▪ encontrarás todo (que buscas) ➤ At that store you'll find everything. En esa tienda hay de todo. ➤ At that store you'll find everything you're looking for. En esa tienda encontrarás todo que buscas.

***you'll* find out!** ¡ya lo sabrás! ▪ ¡te enterarás!

you'll have to wait habrá que esperar ▪ tendrás que esperar

you'll just have to grin and bear it no tienes más remedio que aguantar mecha

you'll never get away with it *(tú)* nunca te saldrás con la tuya ▪ *(usted)* nunca se saldrá con la suya

you'll think of something *(a ti)* se te ocurrirá algo ▪ *(a usted)* se le ocurrirá algo (a usted)

to be **young at heart** ser joven de corazón ➤ She's young at heart. Ella es joven de corazón.

your being here *(tú)* tu estancia aquí ▪ *(usted, ustedes)* su estancia aquí ▪ *(vosotros)* vuestra estancia aquí ➤ We appreciate your being here. Agrademos tu estancia aquí. ▪ Agradecemos su estancia aquí. ▪ Agrademos vuestra estancia aquí.

your choice of a elegir ➤ *(menu item)* Your choice of dressings Aderezos a elegir

your critic is not your enemy él que avisa no es traidor

your fly is open tu bragueta está desabrochada ▪ *(colorful)* se te va a escapar el pájaro *(to which the comical reply is, "Ya volverá porque los huevos están aquí.")*

your friend forever *(letter closing)* para siempre un amigo ▪ amigos para siempre ▪ tu amigo eternamente

your friendly neighborhood supermarket el simpático hipermercado del barrio

your goose is cooked! ▪ you've had it! ¡estás apañado!

your guess is as good as mine *(tú)* tu opinión vale tanto como el mío ▪ sabes tanto como yo ▪ *(usted)* su opinión vale tanto como el mío ▪ (usted) sabe tanto como yo

your having done something *(tú)* que hayas hecho algo ▪ *(usted)* que haya hecho algo ➤ We appreciate your looking after the dog while we were away. Te agradecemos que hayas cuidado al perro mientras estábamos fuera.

your honor su señoría ▪ señor juez

your not having done something *(tú)* el que no hayas hecho algo ▪ *(usted)* el que no haya hecho algo ➤ We really don't understand your not having written. De veras no entendemos (el) que no hayas escrito.

your time allí ➤ What if I called you at one o'clock your time? ¿Qué tal si te llamo a la una allí?

your turn is coming *(a ti)* ya te tocará ▪ *(a usted)* ya le tocará

your wish is my command *(de ti)* tus deseos son órdenes ▪ *(de usted)* sus deseos son órdenes

your word against mine: it's ~ *(tú)* es tu palabra contra la mía ▪ *(usted)* es su palabra contra la mía

you're a dreamer eres un soñador ▪ eres un iluso

you're a romantic ▪ you're an incurable romantic eres un romántico

you're a tiger! ▪ what a tiger (you are)! ¡eres una bestia! ▪ ¡qué animal eres! ▪ ¡qué bruto eres!

you're a winner! ¡eres un fenómeno!

you're an idealist eres idealista *("Idealista" is both masculine and feminine.)*

you're coming with me te vienes conmigo

you're doing it all wrong lo haces todo mal

you're doing it wrong lo haces mal

you're exactly right! ▪ right you are! ¡estás en lo cierto! ▪ ¡tienes razón! ▪ ¡tienes toda la razón!

you're forgetting about... *(tú)* te olvidas de... ▪ *(usted)* se olvida (usted) de...

you're getting ahead of me *(tú)* te estás adelantando a mí ▪ me estás tomando la delantera ▪ *(usted)* (usted) se está adelantando a mí ▪ (usted) me está tomando la delantera

you're going to be okay ▪ you're going to recover vas a ponerte bien

you're going to get it! ▪ *(coll.)* you're gonna get it! vas a ver lo que es bueno ▪ te vas a llevar una buena ▪ te la vas a ganar ➤ You're gonna get it if you don't straighten up. Te la vas a ganar si no te corriges.

you're having quite a day (of it)! ¡qué día tienes!

you're hopeless no tienes remedio

you're impossible! ¡eres intratable!

you're in for it ¡vas a cobrar!

you're invited estás invitado(-a)

you're it! ¡te toca! ▪ te toqué ▪ la traes ▪ *(when playing tag)* ¡eres la mancha!

you're joking! ▪ no kidding? ¿no fastidies?

you're just wasting your time *(tú)* estás escribiendo en la arena ▪ *(usted)* (usted) está escribiendo en la arena

you're lucky that... dichoso tú que... ▪ dichoso usted que...

you're making a big mistake no lleva usted razón

you're misinformed ▪ you've been misinformed *(tú)* estás malinformado ▪ te han informado mal ▪ *(usted)* (usted) está malinformado ▪ le han informado mal (a usted)

you're not bad at it *(tú)* no se te da mal ▪ *(usted)* no se le da mal

you're not going to believe this no te vayas a creer ▪ no te lo vas a creer

you're not making it very easy for me ▪ you aren't making it very easy for me no me lo pones nada fácil

you're not the only one no sólo a ti te pasa

you're not too far off ▪ you've got it about right por ahí va la cosa

you're nuts! estás chiflado(-a) ▪ estás loco(-a)

you're on your own ahora tienes que seguir tú solo ▪ ahora tienes que seguir por tu cuenta ▪ ahora tienes que seguir sin mi ayuda ▪ ahora has dejado el nido

you're pulling my leg! ▪ noooo! ▪ come on! ▪ get real! ¡venga ya! ▪ ¡me estás vacilando! ▪ ¡noooooo! ▪ ¡estás de coña! ▪ ¡te estás quedando conmigo! ▪ estás bromeando conmigo

you're right! *(tú)* ¡tienes razón! ▪ ¡estás en lo cierto! ▪ ¡estás en lo correcto! ▪ *(usted)* ¡(usted) tiene razón! ▪ ¡(usted) está en lo cierto! ▪ ¡(usted) está en lo correcto!

you're right on time! ▪ you're right on the minute! ¡qué puntualidad! ▪ ¡más puntual que un reloj suizo!

you're telling *me*! ▪ yeah, *tell* me about it! ¡a mí me lo vas a contar! ▪ ¡no lo sabes (tú) bien! ▪ ¡a quién se lo cuentas!

you're the boss tú mandas ▪ tú eres él que manda

you're the one eres tú ▪ ése eres tú ➤ *(Sesame Street tune)* Rubber Ducky, you're the one. Rubber Ducky, eres tú. ▪ Rubber Ducky, ése eres tú.

you're to be congratulated *(tú)* deberías ser felicitado(-a) ▪ se te debería felicitar ▪ mereces ser felicitado

you're under arrest! ¡está usted detenido(-a)! ▪ ¡queda usted detenido(-a)! ▪ ¡está usted arrestado(-a)! ▪ ¡queda usted arrestado(-a)!

you're wanted on the phone *(tú)* te llaman por teléfono ▪ *(usted)* le llaman por teléfono

yours truly 1. *(letter closing)* le saluda a usted atentamente ▪ reciba (usted) un cordial saludo ▪ queda de usted atentamente **2.** *(referring to oneself, male or female)* I, me menda lerenda ▪ menda lironda ▪ mendi lerendi ▪ *(male only)* el menda ▪ *(feminine only)* ▪ la menda

youthful indiscretion *el* desliz de la juventud ▪ *(plural)* deslices de la juventud

you've been misinformed ▪ you're misinformed *(tú)* te han informado mal ▪ *(usted)* (a usted) le han informado mal ▪ le han informado mal (a usted)

you've caught me at a bad time estoy en mal momento

you've come a long way, baby! ¡quién te ha visto y quién te ve!

you've got a point (there) ▪ you have a point (there) *(tú)* ahí le has dado ▪ *(usted)* ahí le ha dado (usted)

you've got my curiosity up ▪ you've piqued my curiosity ▪ you've got me curious ▪ you've got my curiosity going me has picado la curiosidad ▪ *(coll.)* ya me has picado el gusanillo

you've got rocks in your head se te sube los ceros a la cabeza

you've had enough time to do it *(rejecting the excuse of lack of time)* ▪ you've had plenty of time to do it has tenido suficiente tiempo para hacerlo ▪ has tenido tiempo suficiente para hacerlo ▪ *(colorful)* veinticuatro horas tiene el día

you've had it ▪ your goose is cooked estás apañado

you've had plenty of time to do it *(rejecting the excuse of lack of time)* ▪ you've had enough time to do it veinticuatro horas tiene el día

you've lost your marbles te has vuelto loco

you've piqued my curiosity ▪ you've got me curious ▪ you've got my curiosity up ▪ you've got my curiosity going me has picado la curiosidad ▪ *(coll.)* ya me has picado el gusanillo

you've taken on too much (te) has cargado con demasiado ▪ usted se ha cargado con demasiado

to **zero in on** centrarse completamente en ▪ apuntar hacia

to **zigzag through the evening air** *(Ogden Nash's bat)* revolotear por el aire de la tarde ▪ hacer eses en el aire de la tarde ▪ serpentear por el aire de la tarde ▪ zigzagear en el aire de la tarde

zip code ▪ postal code código postal

to **zip one's lips** ▪ to button one's lips sellar los labios

zipper catches ▪ zipper sticks ▪ zipper gets stuck cremallera se engancha ▪ cremallera se queda ➤ The zipper's teeth are not lined up correctly, and it catches. Los dientes de la cremallera no coinciden, y se engancha. ▪ Los dientes de la cremallera no coinciden, y se queda.

to be **zonked out** estar roque ➤ He just went to bed and he's already zonked out. Se acaba de acostar y ya está roque.

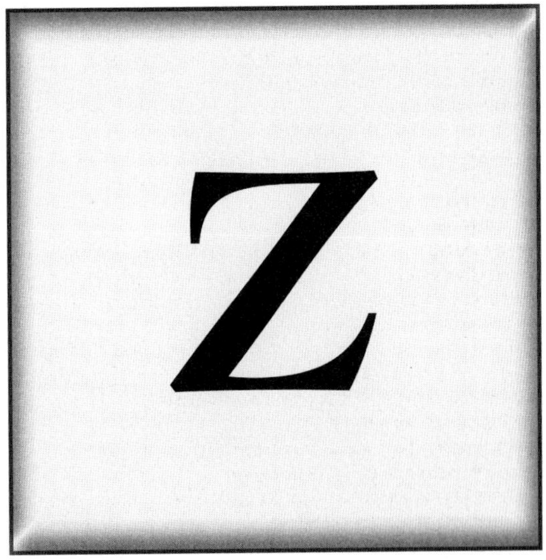